PaineWe

EUROMONEY CAPITAL MARKE'

Editor
Andrew Millard

Senior Researcher
Eddie Kiernan

Researchers
Cindy Chin
Lindsay Fernandes
Gennaro Fiorenzi
Anna di Laurenzio

Advertising Manager Massimo Valeri
mvaleri@euromoneyplc.com

Senior Sales Manager Nicola Gilmour
ngilmour@euromoneyplc.com

Marketing Manager Nick Stainthorpe
nstainthorpe@euromoneyplc.com

Associate Publisher
Christina Vasiliadis
cvasiliadis@euromoneyplc.com

Publisher
Nicholas Ferris
nferris@euromoneyplc.com

Director
Chris Brown

Database & Internet Software Designed by
Ian Stuart, Theseus Innovations Ltd

Data Processing by
Polestar Whitefriars

Printed & Bound by
Polestar Wheatons

Published by
Euromoney Publications PLC
Nestor House, Playhouse Yard, London EC4V 5EX
Tel: +44 (171) 779 8888   Fax: +44 (171) 779 8815
Website: www.euromoneydirectory.com

© Euromoney Publications PLC, London 1999
ISBN 1855645300

FOREWORD FROM THE CHAIRMAN

Dear Colleague,

If you work in the international capital markets, you need this book. For the last 28 years we at Euromoney have tracked the firms and the people who make these markets - banks, underwriters, dealers, traders and brokers. Now, as we present the latest edition, the scale of the changes in international investment banking and trading becomes apparent.

The 1999 directory, as a result, is hugely different from last year. The greatest surge in mergers, takeovers - and bankruptcies - in the recent history of banking and broking is taking place as you read this and the only promise I can make you is that the millennium edition will be very different again because more banks will merge or fail.

Last year we completely redesigned and revised the directory. This year we have built on that to make the directory even more comprehensive. Every entry has been checked with the institution concerned. Where possible, entries contain the same information in the same place for ease of use: for example, all risk management functions now fall under one section. Bond, loan and equity functions are separated. Support services such as repo and securities lending are attached to the appropriate departments - in this case, to bonds and equities respectively. Unverifiable material has been omitted. Entries are more detailed. The layout introduced last year has been extended. For the second year we have also incorporated e-mail addresses and new indexes, including a comprehensive index of bank internet sites.

To keep ahead of the markets, this year we have doubled the number of website addresses; increased the number of total entries by a quarter and the number of individual contacts by more than a third. The new edition has more personal telephone, fax and email addresses than any previous edition.

And the most exciting improvement yet will come soon when we introduce a 24-hour updating service of the directory on the internet. To find this, log on to **www.euromoneydirectory.com**. This new service is available to those who have bought the book and costs an additional £99/$160 a year.

We're here to serve you, the customer, so please write to me at this address, or email me at pfallon@euromoneyplc.com with any suggestions for the directory. Or call our Hotline on 0171 779 8999. In any case we like to hear from you and I hope the directory works well for you.

Padraic Fallon
Chairman and Editor-in-Chief
Euromoney Publications PLC
Nestor House
Playhouse Yard
London EC4V 5EX

CONTENTS

INDEX OF WEBSITES	W1-W16
INDEX OF COMPANIES	A1-A55
LISTING OF COMPANIES BY COUNTRY	1-2047

Key: ⊤ Telephone Number F Fax Number E Email Address 🏛 Central Bank

The greatest care has been taken to ensure accuracy, but the publishers can accept no responsibility for errors or omissions nor any liability occasioned by relying on its content.

Please notify us of any changes as they occur:
Fax: Christina Vasiliadis on +44 (0)171 779 8815
Or send an email to: cvasiliadis@euromoneyplc.com

If you wish to order additional copies of this directory please contact the EUROMONEY HOTLINE on +44 (0)171 779 8999 quoting reference NS10

UK Customers £297 (+ £3 p+p)
Non UK Customers $493 (+ $10 p+p)

All rights reserved. No part of this publication may be reproduced in any material form by any means whether graphic, electronic, mechanical, or other means including photocopying, or information storage and retrieval systems, without the written permission of the publisher, and where necessary any relevant other copyright owner. This publication - in whole or in part - may not be used to prepare or compile other directories or mailing lists, without written permission from the publisher. The use of cuttings taken from this directory in connection with the solicitation of insertions or advertisements, in other publications is expressly prohibited. Measures have been adopted during the preparation of this publication which will assist the publisher to protect its copyright. Any unauthorised use of this data will result in immediate legal proceedings.

INDEX OF WEBSITES

COMPANY	WEBSITE
3i Corporate Finance Limited	www.3icf.co.uk
A/S Haandværkerbanken	www.haandvaerkerbanken.dk
A/S Jyske Bank	www.jyskebank.dk
AB Asesores	www.abasesores.es
AB Bankas Hermis	www.hermis.lt
Abanka dd Ljubljana	www.abanka.si
Abbey National Treasury Services plc	www.ants.co.uk
ABN AMRO Asia Limited	www.hgasia.prx.net
ABN AMRO Bank NV	www.abnamro.be
ABN AMRO Bank NV	www.abnamro.com
ABSA Asia Limited	www.absaasia.com
ABSA Bank Limited	www.absa.co.za
Abu Dhabi Investment Company	www.adic.co.ac
AFC Merchant Bank	www.signet.com.sg/-asean
AIAF Mercado de Renta Fija SA	www.aiaf.es
AIB Group	www.aib.ie
AIB International Financial Services Limited	www.aibifs.ie
AIG Global Investment Corp	www.aiggig.com
AKA Ausfuhrkredit-GmbH	www.akabank.de
AKBANK TAS	www.akbank.com.tr
Al Baraka Turkish Finance House AS	www.albarakaturk.com.tr
Al-Ahli Commercial Bank BSC	www.al-ahlibank.com
Ålandsbanken AB	www.alandsbanken.fi
Al-Bank Al-Saudi Al Fransi	www.saudifransi.com
Alfred Berg Finland Oy Ab	www.alfredberg.fi
Alfred Berg Norway	www.sto.alfredberg.se
Aljba Alliance	www.alal.ru
Allgemeine Deutsche Direktbank AG	www.direktbank.de
Allgemeine Sparkasse Oberösterreich Bankaktien gesellschaft	www.ask.co.at
Alliance Capital Limited	www.alliancecapital.com
Allied Irish Bank Group Treasury	www.aib.ie/capitalmarkets/singapore
Alpha Credit Bank	www.alpha.gr
Alwatany Bank of Egypt	www.alwatany.com.eg
AMMB International Limited	www.ammb.com.my
Anlage-und KreditBank	www.akb.ch
ANZ Bank (Guernsey) Limited	www.pb.grindlays.com
ANZ Investment Bank	www.anz.com
Arab Bank (Switzerland)	www.arabbank.com
Arab Bank AG	www.arabbank.com/branches/europe/germany
Arab Banking Corporation (BSC)	www.arabbanking.com
Arab Banking Corporation (Jordan)	www.abc.com.jo
Arab Jordan Investment Bank	www.ajib.com
Arab National Bank	www.anb.com.sa
Arab-Malaysian Merchant Bank Berhad	www.ambg.com.my
Arbitral International Corp	www.arbitral.com
Arctos Securities Limited	www.arctos.fi
Argenta	www.agt.bvl.com.pe
Argentaria Banco de Negocios	www.argentaria.es
Artesia Bank	www.artesia.be
Artesia Bank Luxembourg SA	www.artesia.lu
AS Eesti Uhispank	www.eyp.ee
AS Era Pank Limited	www.erapank.ee
ASB Bank Limited	www.asbbank.co.nz
Asia Commercial Bank Limited	www.afh.com.hk
Asian Development Bank	www.adberomail.asiandevbank.org
Asian Development Bank	www.asiandevbank.org
ASLK-CGER Bank	www.aslk.be
ASLK-CGER Bank	www.cger.be
Aurel SA	www.aurel.fr
Australia & New Zealand Banking Group Limited	www.anz.co.jp
Australian Guarantee Corporation Limited	www.agc.com.au
Avtobank	Avtobank
BA Australia Limited	www.bofa.com
BACOB Bank	www.bacob.be
Baden-Württembergische Bank AG	www.bw-bank.de

Euromoney Directory 1999 **W-1**

www.euromoneydirectory.com

COMPANY	WEBSITE
Bahrain International Bank EC	www.dilmun.com
Bahrain Monetary Agency	www.bma.gov.bh
Baltic International Bank	www.bib.lv
Ban Hin Lee Bank Berhad	www.bhlbank.com.my
BANAMEX	www.banamex.com
Banca Antoniana-Popolare Veneta	www.antonveneta.it
Banca Carige SpA	www.carige.it
Banca Commerciale Italiana	www.bci.it
Banca CRT SpA	www.bancacrt.it
Banca del Gottardo	www.gottardo.ch
Banca di Roma	www.bancaroma.it
Banca D'Intermediazions Mobiliare IMI SpA	www.bimimin.it
Banca Intesa SpA	www.bancaintesa.it
Banca Monte dei Paschi di Siena SpA	www.mps.it
Banca Monte Paschi (Suisse) SA	www.montepaschi.ch
Banca Nazionale del Lavoro	www.bnl.it
Banca Popolare Asolo e Montebelluna	www.bpam.it
Banca Popolare dell'Alto Adige ScaRL	www.popvoba.it
Banca Popolare di Bergamo-Credito Varesino	www.bpb.it
Banca Popolare di Cividale ScaRL	www.sede.civibank.it
Banca Popolare di Milano SCaRL	www.bpm.it
Banca Popolare di Novara	www.bpn.it
Banca Popolare di Sondrio	www.popso.it
Banca Popolare Udinese ScaRL	www.xnet.it/bpu
Banca Popolare Vicentina scparl	www.popvi.it
Banca Profilo SpA	www.bancaprofilo.it
Banco Ambrosiano Veneto SpA	www.ambro.it
Banco América do Sul SA	www.bas.com.br
Banco Anglo Colombiano	www.bancoanglocolombiano.com
Banco BBA Creditanstalt SA	www.bba.com.br
Banco BICE	www.bice.cl
Banco Bilbao Vizcaya	www.bbv.es
Banco Boavista Interatlântico SA	www.boavista.com.br
Banco Bozano, Simonsen SA	www.bozano.com.br
Banco Central de la República Dominicana	www.bancentral.gov.do
Banco Central de Nicaragua	www.bcn.gob.ni
Banco Central de Reserva de El Salvador	www.bcr.gob.sv
Banco Central del Ecuador	www.bce.fin.ec
Banco Central del Uruguay	www.bcu.gub.uy
Banco Central Hispano	www.bch.es
Banco Cidade S/A	www.bancocidade.com.br
Banco Comercial Português SA	www.bcp.pt
Banco Comercial SA	www.bancocomercial.com.uy
Banco de Chile	www.bancochile.cl
Banco de Crédito e Inversiones	www.bci.cl
Banco de Crédito Nacional SA	www.bcn.com.br
Banco de Investimento Imobiliário	www.embital.pt
Banco de la Nacion Argentina	www.bna.com.ar
Banco de la Provincia de Buenos Aires	www.bpba.com.ar
Banco de Mexico	www.banxico.org.mx
Banco de Occidente	www.bancooccidente.com.co
Banco de Occidente	www.occidente.com
Banco de Portugal	www.bportugal.pt
Banco de Venezuela / Grupo Santander	www.bancodevenezuela.com
Banco del Istmo SA	www.banistmo.com
Banco del Nuevo Mundo S.A.E.M.A.	www.nuevomundo.com.pe
Banco Disa SA	www.bdisa.com
Banco do Brasil SA	www.bancobrasil.com.br
Banco do Brasil SA	www.bancobrasil-nl.com
Banco do Estado de São Paulo SA (BANESPA)	www.banespa.com.br
Banco do Estado do Rio Grande do Sul SA	www.banrisul.com.br
Banco do Nordeste	www.banconordeste.gov.br
Banco Español de Credito SA	www.banesto.es
Banco Espirito Santo	www.bescl.co.uk
Banco Espirito Santo e Comercial de Lisboa SA	www.bes.pt
Banco Europeu para América Latina (BEAL) SA	www.westlb.com

www.euromoneydirectory.com

COMPANY	WEBSITE
Banco Finantia SA	www.finantia.pt
Banco Guipuzcoano SA	www.bancogui.es
Banco Inbursa	www.binbursa.com.mx
Banco Industrial e Comercial SA	www.bicbanco.com.br
Banco Itaú Europa Luxembourg SA	www.itau.com.br
Banco Marka	www.marka.com.br
Banco Mello de Investimento SA	www.bancomello.pt
Banco Mercantil de São Paulo SA FINASA	www.finasa.com.br
Banco Mercantil SA	www.mercantil.com.bo
Banco Nacional de Comercio Exterior SNC	www.mexico.businessline.gob.mx
Banco Nacional Ultramarino SA	www.bnu.pt
Banco Pactual SA	www.pactual.com.br
Banco Popular	www.bancopopular.com.co
Banco Português do Atlântico SA	www.bpatlantico.pt
Banco Real SA	www.real.com.br
Banco Río de la Plata (Grupo Santander)	www.bancorio.com.ar
Banco Sabadell	www.bancsabadell.es
Banco Santander	www.bancosantander.es
Banco Santander de Negocios Portugal SA	www.bnsp.pt
Banco Santander de Negocios Portugal SA	www.sainvest.com
Banco Sud Americano	www.bsa.cl
Banco Sudameris Brasil SA	www.sudameris.com.br
Banco Sul America SA	www.bsa.com.br
Banco Unión CA	www.bancunion.com
Banco Wiese Ltdo	www.wiese.com.pe
Banco Zaragozano SA	www.bancozaragozano.es
Bancomer SA	www.bancomer.com.mx
Bangkok Bank Public Company Limited	www.bbl.co.th
Bank Austria Aktiengesellschaft	www.bankaustria.at
Bank Austria Creditanstalt	www.creditanstalt.co.at
Bank Austria dd Ljubljana	www.bankaustria.si
Bank Brussels Lambert	www.bbl.be
Bank Bumiputra Malaysia Berhad	www.bank.bumiputra.net
Bank Caspiyskiy	www.kcbank.almaty.kz
Bank for Foreign Trade	www.vtb.ru
Bank für Arbeit und Wirtschaft AG	www.bawag.com
Bank für Kärnten und Steiermark AG	www.bks.at
Bank für Tirol und Vorarlberg AG	www.btv.at
Bank Handlowy w Warszawie SA	www.bh.com.pl
Bank Handlowy w Warszawie SA	www.bhw.co.uk
Bank Hapoalim BM	www.bankhapoalim.co.il
Bank Hofmann AG	www.hofmann.ch
Bank Hugo Kahn & Co AG	www.hugokahn.ch
Bank Indonesia	www.bi.go.id
Bank J Vontobel & Co AG	www.vontobel.ch
Bank Julius Baer & Co Limited	www.juliusbaer.com
Bank Leu Limited	www.leu.com
Bank Leumi Le-Israel BM	www.bankleumi.co.il
Bank of America NT & SA	www.bankamerica.com
Bank of Ayudhya Public Company Limited	www.bay.co.th
Bank of Bahrain and Kuwait BSC	www.bbkonline.com
Bank of Canada	www.bank-banque-canada.ca
Bank of Communications	www.bankcomm.com
Bank of Cyprus Limited	www.bankofcyprus.com
Bank of England	www.bankofengland.co.uk
Bank of Hawaii	www.boh.com
Bank of India	www.boiusa.com
Bank of Ireland Asset Management Limited	www.biam.ie
Bank of Ireland Group Treasury Limited	www.treasury.boi.ie
Bank of Israel	www.bankisrael.gov.il
Bank of Jamaica	www.boj.org.jm
Bank of Latvia	www.bank.lv
Bank of Lithuania	www.lbank.lt
Bank of Mauritius	www.bankofmauritius.co.uk
Bank of Montreal	www.bmo.com
Bank of New York - Inter Maritime Bank, Geneva	www.bny-imb.com

www.euromoneydirectory.com

COMPANY	WEBSITE
Bank of New Zealand	www.bnz.co.nz
Bank of Okinawa Limited	www.ryukyu.ne.jp/bank
Bank of Overseas Chinese	www.booc.com.tw
Bank of Taiwan	www.bot.com.tw
Bank of Thailand	www.bot.or.th
Bank of the Ryukyus Limited	www.ryucom.ne.jp/users/ryugin
Bank of Valletta International Limited	www.bov.com
Bank of Western Australia Limited	www.bankwest.com.au
Bank Polska Kasa Opieki - Grupa Pekao SA	www.pekao.com.pl
Bank Rozwoju Eksportu SA	www.bresa.com.pl
Bank Sal Oppenheim jr & Cie (Schweiz) AG	www.oppenheim.ch
Bank Sarasin & Cie	www.sarasin.ch
Bank Universal	www.bankuniversal.astra.co.id
Bank Utama (Malaysia) Berhad	www.cmsb.com.my
Bank van de Nederlandse Antillen	www.centralbank.an
Bank Wegelin (Liechtenstein) AG	www.wegelin.li
Banka Celje dd	www.banka-celje.si
Banka Koper	www.banka-koper.si
Banka Land	www.land.lv
BankAmerica	www.bankamerica.com
BankBoston	www.bankboston.com
Bankers Trust Australia Limited	www.bankerstrust.com.au
Bankers Trust Company	www.btco.com/internet/index.htm
Bankers Trust Corporation	www.bankerstrust.com
Bankgesellschaft Berlin	www.bankgesellschaft.de
Bankhaus Hermann Lampe KG	www.lampebank.de
BANKINTER SA	www.bankinter.es
Banque Banespa International SA	www.uunet.lu\banespa
Banque Cantonale du Valais	www.bcvs.ch
Banque Cantonale du Valais	www.wkb.ch
Banque Cantonale Vaudoise	www.bcv.ch
Banque Commerciale du Maroc	www.attijari.com
Banque CPR	www.cpr.fr
Banque CPR	www.cpr.fr
Banque d'Affaires du Liban et d'Outre-Mer	www.blom.com.lb
Banque Edouard Constant SA	www.bec.ch
Banque et Caisse d'Epargne de l'Etat, Luxembourg	www.bcee.lu
Banque Générale du Luxembourg SA	www.bgl.lu
Banque Internationale à Luxembourg SA	www.bil.lu
Banque Misr	www.banquemisr.com
Banque Misr-Liban SAL	www.blm.com.lb
Banque Nationale de Belgique SA	www.nbb.be
Banque Nationale de Belgique SA	www.bnb.be
Banque Nationale de Belgique SA	www.nationalebank.be
Banque Nationale de Paris	www.bnp.fr
Banque Nationale de Paris	www.calvacom.fr/bnp
Banque Nationale Suisse	www.snb.ch
Banque Saradar SAL	www.saradar.com.lb
Banque Sudameris	www.sudameris.fr
Barclays Bank plc	www.barclays.pt
Barclays Capital Asia Limited	www.barcapint.com
Barclays Capital Securities Limited	www.barclayscapital.com
Barclays Global Investors Limited	www.barclaysglobal.com
Barclays Private Equity Limited	www.bzw.com
Baring Asset Management Limited	www.baring-asset.com
Bayerische Hypo-und Vereinsbank AG	www.vereinsbank.de
Bayerische Landesanstalt für Aufbaufinanzierung	www.lfa.de
Bayerische Landesbank Girozentrale	www.bayernlb.de
Bayerische Landesbank International SA	www.bayernlux.lu
BBV Banco Francés SA	www.bancofrances.com
Bear Stearns International Limited	www.bearstearns.com
Belpromstroibank	www.belpsb.minsk.by
Beogradska Banka AD Beograd	www.beogradskabanka.com
Berkshire Capital Corporation	www.berkcap.com
Berkshire Partners LLC	www.berkshirepartners.com
Bermuda Monetary Authority	www.bma.bm

www.euromoneydirectory.com

COMPANY	WEBSITE
BG BANK A/S	www.bgbank.dk
Board of Governors of Federal Reserve System	www.bog.frb.fed.us
Bondpartners SA	www.bpl-bondpartners.ch
Boram Bank	www.boram.co.kr
Brown Brothers Harriman & Co	www.bbh.com
BSN Commercial Bank (Malaysia) Berhad	www.bsncom.com.my
BULBANK Ltd	www.bulbank.bg
Bunadarbanki Islands	www.bi.is
Burdett Buckeridge & Young	www.bby.com.an
Caboto Holding SIM SpA	www.caboto.it
Caisse Centrale de Réescompte	www.ccpcm.com
Caisse Centrale des Banques Populaires	www.ccbp.fr
Caisse Centrale Desjardins	www.desjardins.com
Caisse Française de Développement	www.cfd.fr
Caixa Cataluña	www.caixacat.es
Caixa Central de Crédito Agrícola Mútuo CRL	www.credito-agricola.pt
Caixa d'Estalvis de Catalunya	www.caixacat.es
Caixa Economica Montepio Geral	www.montepiogeral.com
Caixa Geral de Depositos SA	www.cgd.pt
Caja de Ahorros de Galicia	www.caixagalicia.es
Caja de Ahorros de la Inmaculada de Aragón	www.cai.es
Caja de Ahorros de Manlleu	www.caixamanlleu.es
Caja de Ahorros de Navarra	www.can.es
Caja de Ahorros del Mediterraneo	www.cam.es
Caja de Ahorros y Monte de Piedad de Guipuzkoa y San Sebastián	www.kutxa.es
Caja de Ahorros y Monte de Piedad de Ontinyent	www.caixaontinyen.es
Caja de Ahorros y Monte de Piedad de Segovia	www.cajasagovia.es
Caja de Burgos	www.cajadeburgos.es
Caja General de Ahorros de Canarias	www.cajacanarias.es
Caja Insular de Ahorros de Canarias	www.lacajadecanarias.es
Camara de Liquidacao e Custodia	www.clc.com.br
Canada Trust Company	www.candatrust.com
Canadian Western Bank	www.cwbank.com
Canara Bank	www.canbankindia.com
Canto Consulting	www.canto.ch
Cantonal Bank of Berne	www.bekb.ch
Cantonalbank of Fribourg	www.bcf.ch
Cantor Fitzgerald & Co	www.cantor.com
CARIPLO - Cassa di Risparmio delle Provincie Lombarde SpA	www.cariplo.it
Cariverona Banca SpA	www.cariverona.it
Carnegie Asset Management Finland Limited	www.carnegie.fi
Carnegie Bank A/S	www.carnegie.dk
Carnegie Fondkommission	www.carnegie.se
Cassa di Risparmio di Bolzano SpA	www.spkbz.com
Cassa di Risparmio di Forli	www.carispfo.it
Cassa di Risparmio di Imola SpA	www.crimola.it
Cassa di Risparmio di Padova e Rovigo SpA	www.cariparo.it
Cassa di Risparmio di Pisa SpA	www.caripisa.it
Cassa di Risparmio di Pistoia e Pescia SpA	www.caript.it
Cassa di Risparmio di Reggio Emilia SpA	www.carire.it
Cassa di Risparmio di Venezia SpA	www.carive.it
Cassa di Risparmio in Bologna SpA	www.carisbo.it
Cayman Islands Monetary Authority	www.cimoney.com.ky
Caymanx Trust Co Limited	www.enterprise.net/caymanx
Cazenove & Co	www.cazenove.co.uk
CB Moldova-Agroindbank SA	www.cios.ken.pubs.co.uk
CDI - Corporate Development International	www.cdi-germany.de
CDI-AMandA GmbH	www.cdi-amanda.com
CDM Pekao SA Securities	www.cdmpekao.com.pl
Cedef Capital Services Limited	www.cedef.com
Cedel Bank	www.cedelgroup.com
Cen E Bankiers NV	www.cene.nl
Central Bank of Cyprus	www.centralbank.gov.cy
Central Bank of Kuwait	www.cbk.gov.kw

www.euromoneydirectory.com

COMPANY	WEBSITE
Central Bank of Sri Lanka	www.centralbanklanka.org
Central Bank of the Republic of Turkey	www.tcmb.gov.tr
Central Bank of the Russian Federation	www.cbr.ru
Centro Internationale Handelsbank AG	www.centrobank.com
Ceská Sporitelna as	www.csas.cz
Ceskoslovenská Obchodni Banka as	www.csob.cz
Chiao Tung Bank	www.ctnbank.com.tw
Chicago Board of Trade	www.cbot.com
China Development Corporation	www.cdcdpbnk.com
China Merchants Bank	www.cmbchina.com
Cho Hung Bank	www.chohungbank.co.kr
Chung Shing Bank	www.scbank.com.tw
CIBC Mellon Global Securities Services Co	www.cibcmellon.com
CIBC World Markets	www.cibc.com
CIBC World Markets	www.cibcwm.com
Cit-Group/Commercial Services	www.citgroup.com/cs.htm
Citibank Berhad	www.citibank.com.my
Citibank NA	www.citibank.com
Citibank NA	www.citicorp.com
Citibank NA	www.globalmarkets.citibank.com
Citibank Rt	www.citibank.hu
Citibank SA (Global Consumer)	www.citibank.be
Codan Bank A/S	www.codam.com
Commercial Bank Biochim plc	www.biochim.bg
Commercial Bank of Africa Limited	www.africaonline.co.ke
Commercial Bank of Greece SA	www.combank.gr
Commerzbank AG	www.commerzbank.com
Commerzbank Capital Markets (Eastern Europe) as	www.commerzbank-capital-markets.cz
Commonwealth Bank of Australia	www.commbank.com.au
Commonwealth Bank of Australia	www.fx.sales.btinternet.com
Commonwealth Development Corporation	www.cdc.co.uk
Confederación Española de Cajas de Ahorros	www.ceca.es
Constantia Privatbank AG	www.constantia.co.at
Coop Bank	www.coopbank.ch
Corp Banca	www.corpbanca.cl
Corporación Andina de Fomento - CAF	www.caf.com
Corporacion Financiera Nacional y Suramericana SA	www.corfinsura.com.co
CREDIOP SpA	www.crediop.it
Crédit Commercial de France	www.ccf.fr
Crédit du Maroc	www.creditdumaroc.co.ma
Crédit Industriel d'Alsace et de Lorraine - CIAL	www.cic-banques.fr/cial
Crédit Lyonnais Bank (Austria) AG	www.creditlyonnais.at
Crédit Lyonnais SA	www.creditlyonnais.com
Crédit Lyonnais/PK Airfinance	www.clpk.com
Crédit Populaire du Maroc	www.morocco.web.com/gdp
Credit Suisse Financial Products	www.csfp.co.jp
Credit Suisse First Boston	www.csfb.com
Credit Suisse Group	www.csg.ch
Croatia banka dd	www.open.hr/com/crobanka
Daewoo Securities Co Limited	www.securities.co.kr
Dah An Commercial Bank	www.dab.com.tw
Dah Sing Bank Limited	www.dahsing.com.hk
Dain Rauscher Incorporated	www.dainrauscher.com
Daishin Securities Co Limited	www.daishin.co.kr
Daiwa Europe Limited	www.daiwa.co.jp
Dallah Albaraka (UK) Limited	www.albaraka.co.uk
Danmarks Nationalbank	www.nationalbanken.dk
Dao Heng Bank Limited	www.daoheng.com
Darier Hentsch & Cie	www.darierhentsch.ch
Davy Stockbrokers	www.davy.ie
DBS Bank	www.dbs.com.sg
DBS Finance Limited	www.dbsf.com.sg
De Nationale Investeringsbank NV	www.dnib.com
Den Danske Bank	www.danskebank.dk
Den norske Bank AS	www.dnb.no
Deutsche Ausgleichsbank (DtA)	www.dta.de

www.euromoneydirectory.com

COMPANY	WEBSITE
Deutsche Bank	www.deutsche-bank.de
Deutsche Bank AG	www.deutsche-bank.com
Deutsche Bundesbank	www.bundesbank.de
Deutsche Morgan Grenfell Asset Management (Japan) Limited	www.morgan-grenfell.com
Deutsche Postbank AG	www.postbank.de
DG BANK	www.dgbank.de
Discount Bank & Trust Company	www.dbtc.ch
Diskont Bank AG	www.diskontbank.com
Diskontobanken A/S	www.diskontobank.dk
Doha Bank Limited	www.dohabank.com
Dresdner Bank Brasil	www.brain.dresdnerbank.de
Dresdner Bank Lateinamerika AG	www.dbla.com
Dresdner Kleinwort Benson	www.dresdnerkb.com
DSL Bank	www.dsl.bank.de
Dubrovacka banka dd	www.dubank.hr
Dutch State Treasury Agency	www.dutchstate.nl
E L & C Baillieu Stockbrokering Limited	www.baillieu.com.au.
East-West Investment Bank	www.ewib.com
Ecoban Finance Limited	www.ecoban.com
ED & F Man International Limited	www.edfman.com
Edinburgh Fund Managers plc	www.edfd.com
Eesti Pank/Bank of Estonia	www.ee/epbe
EFG-Hermes	www.efg-hermes.com
Egnatia Securities SA	www.egnatiabank.gr
Egyptian American Bank	www.eab-online.com
Eksportfinans ASA	www.eksportfinans.com
Emirates Bank International PJSC	www.ebil.co.ae
Energobank	www.energobank.ru
ERMGASSEN & Co	www.ermgassen.com
Erste Bank der Österreichischen Sparkassen AG	www.erstebank.at
Estonian Forexbank	www.forex.ee
Euro Brokers Inc	www.ebi.com
Euroclear Operations Centre	www.euroclear.com
EUROHYPO AG Europaische Hypothekenbank der Deutschen Bank	www.eurohypo.com
European Bank for Reconstruction & Development	www.ebrd.com
European Central Bank	www.ecb.int
EVEA Bank Limited	www.evb.ee
Exane	www.exane.com
EXCO AP Singapore Pte Ltd	www.excoap.com.sg
Export Credit Bank of Turkey Inc	www.eximbank.gov.tr
Export Development Corporation	www.edc.ca
F van Lanschot Bankiers NV	www.vanlanschot.nl
Factor banka dd	www.factorb.sl
Faisal Finance (Switzerland) SA	www.ffs.dmitrust.com
Fibi Bank (Switzerland) Limited www.fibi.ch	www.fibi.ch
Filanbanco SA	www.filanbanco.com
FIMAT International Banque	www.fimat.com
FIMATEX SA	www.fimatex.fr
Finacor	www.finacor.co.uk
Financial Security Assurance Inc	www.fsa.com
FINEX Europe	www.nybot.com
Finter Bank Zürich	www.finter.ch
First Bank of Nigeria	www.fbn.com.ng
First Marathon Securities Limited	www.fmarathon.com
First National Bank of Chicago (The)	www.fcnbd.com
First National Bank of Southern Africa Limited	www.fnb.co.za
Fischer Partners Fondkommission AB	www.fip.se
FöreningsSparbanken - SwedBank	www.foreningssparbanken.se
Fortis Bank Luxembourg	www.fortisbank.lu
Fox-Pitt, Kelton Limited	www.fpk.com
Frankfurter Sparkasse	www.fraspa18822.de
Fransabank SAL	www.fransabank.com.lb
Fredericks Michael & Co	www.fm.co.com
Friesland Bank Securities	www.fbs.nl

Euromoney Directory 1999 **W-7**

Get the Latest Information Everyday with the PaineWebber Euromoney Directory ON-LINE

Euromoney Directory On-line is a unique electronic service providing access to the entire directory direct to your computer – continuously updated throughout the year. In addition the site contains:

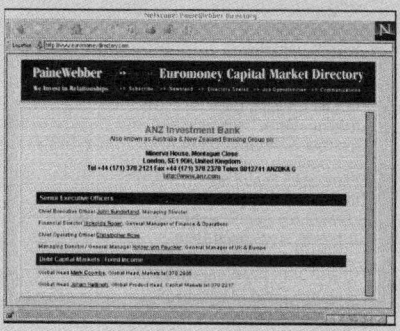

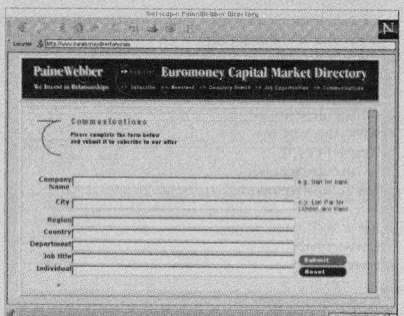

Daily News
New appointments, position/department changes, and the latest market gossip (updated every day).

Recruitment Services
Information and links on the very latest opportunities in the markets direct from the top recruitment consultancies.

PLUS – Sophisticated Search Facilities
Search by one or a combination of categories – including country, region, job title, department, company, name and many more.

Launched in January 1999 this dedicated information service is only available to purchasers of the Directory.

Only £99/$160.

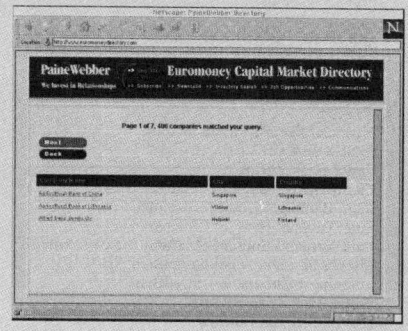

www.euromoneydirectory.com

To gain access to the PaineWebber Directory ON-LINE simply call our hotline on 44 171 779 8999 quoting ref. NSPW1

www.euromoneydirectory.com

COMPANY	WEBSITE
Fubon Commercial Bank	www.fubon.com.tw
Genbel Securities Limited	www.gensec.com
General Banking & Trust Co Limited	www.gtb.hu
Generale Bank	www.gbank.be
Gensec Bank Limited	www.genbel.co.za
Gerrard & King Limited	www.gerrard.com
Gilde Investment Management	www.gilde.nl
GNI Financial Products Limited	www.gni.co.uk
GNI Limited	www.gni.co.uk
Goldman Sachs International	www.gs.com
Gottex Brokers SA	www.gottex.com
Grand Cathay Securities Corporation	www.gcsc.com.tw
Groupo Financiero Serfin	www.serfin.com.mx
Guinness Flight Hambro Asset Management Limited	www.guiness-flight.com
Gulf International Bank BSC	www.gibonline.com
Gulf Investment Corporation (GIC)	www.gic.com.kw
GZB-Bank Genossenschaftliche Zentralbank AG	www.gzb-bank.de
Habib Bank AG Zürich	www.habibbank.com
Hambrecht & Quist LLC	www.hamquist.com
Hamburgische Landesbank - Girozentrale -	www.hamburglb.de
Hang Seng Bank Limited	www.hangseng.com
Hani Securities Limited	www.haninet.com.hk
Hansa Investments	www.hansa.ee/invest
Hansabank	www.hansa.ee
Hansabank-Latvija	www.hbl.lv
Herzog Heine Geduld	www.herzog.com
Hibernia National Bank	www.hiberniabank.com
Hock Hua Bank Berhad	www.hhb.com.my
Hohenzollerische Landesbank-Kreissparkasse	www.ksk-sigmaringen.de
Hong Kong Monetary Authority	www.info.gov.hk/hkma
Hong Leong Bank Berhad	www.hlb.hongleong.com.my
Hongkong Bank of Canada	www.hkbc.com
Hongkong Bank of Canada	www.hkbc.com
HongkongBank Malaysia Berhad	www.hkbank-msia.com
Housing & Commercial Bank	www.hcb.co.kr
Hrvatska narodna banka	www.hnb.hr
HSBC Holdings plc	www.hsbcgroup.com
Hua Chiao Commercial Bank Limited	www.hccb.com
Hungarian Foreign Trade Bank Limited	www.mkb.hu
Hypo Banka Croatia	www.hypo.hr
Hypothekenbank in Essen AG	www.essenhyp.de
HypoVereinsbank Luxembourg Société Anonyme	www.hypovereinsbank.lu
Hyundai International Merchant Bank	www.himb.co.kr
IBJ Schroder Bank & Trust Company	www.ibjs.com
IBJ Securities Co Limited	www.ibjs.co.jp
ICC Bank plc	www.icc.ie
IDB Holding Corporation Ltd	www.idbh.co.il
IFP Intermoney Financial Products Limited	www.ifpmoscow.co.ru
IFP Intermoney Financial Products SA	www.ifp.ch
IKB Deutsche Industriebank AG	www.ikb.de
Index Securities SA	www.index.ch
IndusInd Bank Limited	www.indusind.com
Industrial Bank of Korea	www.ibk.co.kr
Industrial Bank of Latvia	www.lain.bkc.lv
Industrial Development Bank of Turkey	www.tskb.com.tr
ING Bank NV	www.ingbank.com
ING Bank NV	www.ing-barings.com
ING Baring Furman Selz LLC	www.furmanselz.com
ING Barings	www.ing.com.pl
Inkom Capital	www.inkomcap.com.ru
Interacor AG	www.access.ch/interz
Inter-American Development Bank	www.iadb.org
Interbank AS	www.interbank.com.tr/interinvest
Inter-Európa Bank Rt	www.ieb.hu
International Bank of Asia Limited	www.iba.com.hk
International Bank of Taipei	www.ibtpe.com.tw

Euromoney Directory 1999 **W-9**

www.euromoneydirectory.com

COMPANY	WEBSITE
International Company for Finance & Investments	www.icfi.ru
International Finance Corporation	www.ifc.org
INVESTCORP Bank EC	www.investcorp.com
Investec Bank Limited	www.investec.co.za
Investicní a Postovní banka as	www.ipb.cz
Investors Bank & Trust Company	www.ibtco.com
Investors Bank & Trust Company	www.investorsbank.com/biz/ibt
Ionian and Popular Bank of Greece SA	www.kapatel.gr.ionian
Ippa Bank NV	www.ippa.be
Israel Discount Bank Limited	www.discountbank.net
Israel Discount Bank of New York	www.idbny.com
Istituto Bancario San Paolo di Torino SpA	www.sanpaolo.it
Istituto Mobiliare Italiano SpA	www.imispa.it
Istrobanka AS	www.istrobanka.sk
J Henry Schroder & Co Limited	www.schroder.com
Jahangir Siddiqui & Co Limited	www.jahangirsiddiqui.com
Jardine Fleming Limited	www.jfleming.com
JB Were & Son	www.jbwere.com.au
Jefferies & Co Inc	www.jetco.com
JM Finn & Co	www.jmfinn.com
Joint Stock Commercial Bank "Export-Import"	www.eximbank.moldova.net
Jordan National Bank plc	www.ahli.com
Jordan National Bank plcJosé M Cascales & Associates	www.qhli.com www.tradefin.com
JP Bank AB	www.jpbank.se
JP Morgan & Co Incorporated	www.jpmorgan.com
Jyske Bank (Gibraltar) Limited	www.jyske-bank.dk/pbi
Kankaku Securities Co Limited	www.infoweb.or.jp/kankaku
Kärntner Landes-und-Hypothekenbank AG	www.hypo-alpe-adria.com
KAS-Associatie NV	www.kas-associate.com
Kazkommerts Securites	www.kozcombank.almaty.kz
Kazkommertsbank	www.kas-associate.com
KBC Bank	www.kozcombank.almaty.kz
Keppel Bank of Singapore Limited	www.kazcombank.almaty.kz
Keycorp	www.kb.be
Kincheng Banking Corporation	www.keppelbank.com.sg
Klesch & Company Limited	www.key.com
KOÇBANK AS	www.great-china.net/kincheng_bank
Komercijalna Bank AD	www.btinternet.com/-general.klesch
Komercní banka as www.koba.cz	www.kogbank.com.tr
Konsolidacni banka Praha spú	www.kb.com.mk
Kookmin Bank	www.koba.cz
Korea Exchange Bank	www.kobp.cz
Korea International Merchant Bank	www.kookmin-bank.com
Korea Long-Term Credit Bank	www.koexbank.co.kr
Korea Merchant Banking Corporation	www.kimb.co.kr
Kredietbank SA Luxembourg	www.klbank.co.kr
Kreditanstalt für Wiederaufbau	www.kmbe.co.kr
Kredyt Bank PBI SA	www.kbl.lu
Kreissparkasse Köln	www.kfw.de
Kumho Merchant Bank	www.kredytbank.com.pl
Kuwait Finance House KSC	www.ksk-koeln.de
Kuwait Fund for Arab Economic Development	www.kumho.co.kr
Kwangtung Provincial Ban	www.kfh.com
Kwong On Bank Limited	www.kuwait-fund.org
KZI Bank - Kazkommerts-Ziraat International Bank	www.kpb-hk.com
Land Bank of Taiwan	www.kwongonbank.com.hk
Land Bank of the Philippines	www.kzibank.com
Landesbank Hessen-Thüringen	www.landbank.com.tw
Landesbank Rheinland-Pfalz Girozentrale	www.landbank.com
Landesbank Saar Girozentrale	www.helaba.de
Landesbank Sachsen Girozentrale	www.lrp.de
Landesbank Schleswig-Holstein Girozentrale	www.saarlb.de
Landesbank Schleswig-Holstein Girozentrale	www.sachsenlb.de
Landesgirokasse	www.lb-kiel.de
Latvijas Unibanka	www.lbkiel.dk

www.euromoneydirectory.com

COMPANY	WEBSITE
Laurentian Bank of Canada	www.lgbank.de
Lazard Creditcapital Limited	www.unibanka.lv
LBS Bank - New York	www.laurentianbank.com
Lehman Brothers	www.lccindia.com
Lendtech AB	www.lbsbank.com
Leonia plc	www.lehman.com
Lepercq de Neuflize Securities Inc	www.omgroup.com
LG Securities Co Limited	www.leonia.fi
LGT Bank in Liechtenstein AG	www.lepercq.com
Liberty Roussin SA	www.lgsec.co.kr
Liechtensteinische Landesbank AG	www.lgt.com
Lietuvos Taupomasis bankas	www.roussin.com
Lloyds Bank plc	www.llb.li
Lloyds Bank plc	www.ltb.tdd.lt
Lollands Bank	www.lloydsbank.com.br
Ludová banka AS	www.lloydsbank.nl
Luso International Banking Limited	www.lollandsbank.dk
Luzerner Kantonalbank	www.luba.sk
Macquarie Bank Limited	www.lusobank.com.mo
Mandatum Bank Plc	www.lukb.ch
Marusan Securities Co Limited	www.macquarie.com.au
Maybank	www.mandatum.fi
Mediocredito Centrale SpA	www.marusan-sec.co.jp
MeesPierson NV	www.maybank.com.my/maybank
Mellon Bank Corporation	www.mcc.it
Mellon Bank NA	www.meespierson.nl
Mercantile Bancorporation Inc	www.mellon.com
Mercantile Bank Limited	www.mellon.com
Mercantile Safe Deposit & Trust Company	www.mercantile.com
Merchant Bank Ghana Limited	www.mercantile.co.za
Merita Bank Luxembourg SA	www.mercantile.net
Merita Bank Plc	www.ghanaclassifieds.com/merchantbank/index.html
MeritaNordbanken Group	www.merita.fi/luxembourg
Merrill Lynch	www.merita.fi
Merrill Lynch Asset Management Limited	www.meritany.com
MFK Renaissance	www.ml.com
Midland Bank plc	www.merrilllynch.com
Midtbank A/S	www.mfkren.com
Mitsubishi Corporation Finance plc	www.hsbcmarkets.com
MM Warburg & Co Kommanditgesellschaft auf Aktien	www.midtbank.dk
	www.mcf.co.uk
MM Warburg & Co Luxembourg SA	www.mmwarburg.com
Moravia Banka as	www.mmwarburg.Lu
Morgan Stanley	www.moba.cz
Morgan Stanley Dean Witter & Co	www.ms.com
Morsø Bank	www.msdw.com
Moscow Narodny Bank Limited	www.morsbank.dk
Muenchener Hypothekenbank eG	www.moscownarodny.com
Multibanka Joint Stock Company	www.muenchener-hyp.de
Mutuactivos SA SGIIC	www.multibanka.com
Nación Bursátil Sociedad de Bolsa SA	www.mutuactivos.com
Nacional Financiera SNC	www.merval.sba.com.ar/nacion
Nakornthon Bank Public Company Limited	www.nafin.gob.mx
NAL Merchant Bank plc	www.ntb.co.th
Nanyang Commercial Bank Limited	www.nalbank.com.ng
Národná banka Slovenska	www.nanyangbankhk.com
Nassauische Sparkasse	www.nbs.sk
National Australia Bank Limited	www.naspa.de
National Bank of Bahrain	www.national.com.au
National Bank of Egypt	www.nbbonline.com
National Bank of Hungary	www.nbe.com.eg
National Bank of Kuwait SAK	www.mnb.hu
National Development Bank of Sri Lanka	www.nbk.com
National Mutual Funds Management Limited	www.ndb.org
NationsBank	www.nmfm.com.au
Nationwide Building Society	www.nationsbank.com

Euromoney Directory 1999 **W-11**

www.euromoneydirectory.com

COMPANY	WEBSITE
Natwest Global Financial Markets	www.nationwide.co.uk
NatWest Group - North America	www.natwestgfm.com
Nedcor Investment Bank	www.natwestgroup.com
Nederlandse Waterschapsbank	www.nedcor.co.za
New South Wales Treasury Corporation	www.nwb.nl
Nomura Asset Management (UK) Limited	www.tcorp.nsw.gov.au
Nomura International (Hong Kong) Limited	www.nomura-asset.com
Nomura International plc	www.nomura.co.hk
Nomura Securities International	www.nomura.co.uk
Norbank	www.nsiseclend.com
Nordbanken AB (publ)	www.norbank.com.pe
Norddeutsche Landesbank Girozentrale NORD/LB	www.nb.se
Norges Bank	www.nordlb.de
Norinchukin International plc	www.norges-bank.no
Northern Bank Limited	www.noil.co.uk
Nova Kreditna Banka Maribor dd	www.northern-bank.co.uk
Nova Ljubljanska banka dd	www.nkbm.si
Nykredit A/S	www.n-lb.si
Nykredit Bank A/S	www.nykredit.dk
Oberbank	www.nykredit.dk
Oberösterreichische Landesbank AG	www.oberbank.at
Oesterreichische Nationalbank	www.hypo.at
Okobank Ltd	www.oenb.co.at
OLMA Investment Company	www.osuuspankki.fi
OM Gruppen AB	www.olma.co.ru
Omega Securities SA	www.omgroup.com
OMLX - The London Securities & Derivatives Exchange	www.omegasec.gr
	www.omgroup.com
Omni Finance & Investment Group BV	www.omni.nl
Open Joint Stock Company 'TemirBank'	www.temirbank.kz
Open Joint-Stock Company Alfa Bank	www.alfabank.ru
Ord Minnett Securities Group	www.ords.co.nz
ORIX Asia Limited	www.orix.com.hk
Osmanli Bankasi AS	www.ottomanbank.com.tr
Österreichische Investitionskredit AG	www.investkredit.at
Österreichische Postsparkasse Aktiengesellschaft	www.psk.co.at/psk
OTP Securities Limited	www.otpbroker.hu
Oversea-Chinese Banking Corporation Limited	www.ocbc.com.sg
Overseas Union Bank Limited	www.oub.com.sg
Pamukbank TAS	www.pamukbank.com
Pangaea Partners Limited	www.pangaeapartners.com
Paribas	www.paribas.com
Paterson Ord Minnett Limited	www.patersonord.com.au
Patria Finance as	www.patria-finance.com
People's Bank	www.is.lk/ispeoples
Permodalan Nasional Berhad	Pwww.pnb.com.my
Petercam SA	www.petercam.be
PhileoAllied Berhad (PhileoAllied Group)	www.phileo.com.my
Pictet & Cie	www.pictet.com
PIMCO Global Advisors (Europe) Limited	www.pimco.com
PNC Bank Corp	www.pncbank.com
Pol'nobanka AS	www.polnobanka.sk
Postbanken	www.postbanken.no
Postová banka as	www.pabk.sk
Powszechna Kasa Oszczednosci-Bank Panstwowy	www.pkobp.pl
Prebon Yamane	www.prebon.com
Prebon Yamane (UK) Limited	www.prebon.co.uk
Priemyselná banka AS	www.pbko.sk
Probanca Servicios Financieros	www.probanca.com
Probanka dd	www.probanka.si
Prvá komunálna banka AS	www.pkb.sk
Prvá stavebná sporitel'na as	www.pss.sk
První Mestká Banka as	www.pmb.cz
PT (Persero) Danareksa	www.indoexchange.com/dahareksa-holding
PT Bank Bali Tbk	www.bankbali.com
PT Bank Dagang Negara (PERSERO)	www.bdn.co.id

W-12 Euromoney Directory 1999

www.euromoneydirectory.com

COMPANY	WEBSITE
PT Bank Internasional Indonesia Tbk	www.bii.co.id
PT Bank NISP	www.banknisp.com
Publikum dd	www.publikum.si
Pusan Bank	www.pusanbank.co.kr
Qatar National Bank SAQ	www.qatarbank.com
Queensland Treasury Corporation	www.qtc.qld.gov.au
Quelle Bank CA Steinhäusser AG	www.quelle-bank.at
Quelle Bank GmbH & Co	www.quelle-bank.de
Rabobank Group	www.rabobank.nl
Rabobank International	www.rabobank.com
Radanasin Bank Public Company Limited	www.radanasin-bank.co.th
Raiffeisenlandesbank Niederösterreich-Wien GmbH	www.rlbnoew.at
Raiffeisenlandesbank Oberösterreich	www.raiffeisen.at/rbgooe
RealKredit Danmark A/S	www.rd.dk
Republic Bank Limited	www.republictt.com
Republic National Bank of New York	www.rnb.com
Reserve Bank of Australia	www.rba.gov.au
Reserve Bank of India	www.rbi.org.in
Reserve Bank of New Zealand	www.rbnz.govt.nz
Rietumu Banka	www.rietumu.lv
Rigas Komercbanka plc	www.rkb.lv
Rizal Commercial Banking Corporation	www.rcbc.com
Robeco Group	www.robeco.nl
Robert Fleming & Co Limited	www.flemings.lu
Robert Fleming Holdings Limited	www.flemings.com
Rossiyskiy Kredit Bank	www.roscredit.ru
Roussin (Luxembourg) SA	www.roussin.com
Royal Bank of Canada	www.royalbank.com
Royal Bank of Canada (Channel Islands) Limited	www.royalbankci.com
Royal Bank of Trinidad & Tobago Limited	www.rbtt.com
Russian Commercial Bank Limited	www.rkb.ch
Russky Slaviansky Bank	www.russlavbank.com
RW Pressprich & Co Inc	www.pressprich.com
RZB	www.rzb.co.at/rzb
SA Nostra	www.sanostra.es
Sabah Development Bank Berhad	www.borneo-online.com.my/sdb
Sabanci Bank plc	www.sabanci-bank.co.uk
Sakura Dellsher Inc	www.sdinet.com
Salomon Smith Barney Australia Securities Pty Limited	www.ssmb.com.au
Santander Investment	www.bancosantander.com
SBCM Limited	www.sbcm.com
Schroder Investment Management (Luxembourg) SA	www.schroders.lu
Schroder Investment Management Limited	www.schroders.com
Schwäbische Bank AG	www.schwaebische-bank.de
Scotia Capital Markets	www.scotiacapital.com
Scotiabank	www.scotiabank.ca
Sedlabanki Islands	www.sedlabanki.is
Seoulbank	www.seoulbank.co.kr
SG Cowen Securities Corporation	www.socgen.com
SGZ-Bank AG	www.sgz-bank.de
SGZ-Bank International SA	www.sgz-bank.lut
Shinhan Bank	www.shinhanbank.co.kr
Siam Commercial Bank Public Company Limited	www.scb.co.th
Sigma Securities	www.sigma.gr
Skandinaviska Enskilda Banken	www.sebank.se
Skandinaviska Enskilda Banken AB	www.sebweb1.sebank.se
SKB banka dd	www.skb.si
Slovenská Sporitel'na AS	www.slsp.sk
Slovenska Zadruzna	www.szbanka.si
SNS Securities NV	www.snsams.nl
Société Générale	www.socgen.com
Southern Bank Berhad	www.sbbgroup.com.my
SouthTrust Corporation	www.southtrust.com
Spar Nord Bank	www.spanord.dk
Sparebanken Nord Norge	www.snn.no

Euromoney Directory 1999 **W-13**

www.euromoneydirectory.com

COMPANY	WEBSITE
Sparebanken Sør	www.sparesor.no
Sparkasse Bonn	www.sparkasse-bonn.de
Spütz AG	www.sputz.de
SS Kantilal Ishwarlal Securities Limited	www.sski.com
SSB Bank Limited	www.ssb.com.gh
St George Bank Limited	www.stgeorge.com.au
Staal Bank NV	www.staalbankiers.nl
Stadtsparkasse Dortmund	www.sparkasse.dortmund.de
Stadtsparkasse Hannover	www.stadtsparkasse-hannover.de
Stadtsparkasse München	www.sskmde
Stadtsparkasse Nürnberg	www.stadsparkasse-nuernberg.de
Standard Bank London Limited	www.sbl.co.uk
Standard Chartered Bank	www.stanchart.com
Standard Chartered Equitor	www.equitor.com
Staropolski Dom Maklerski Spólka Akeyjna	www.sdm.com.pl
State Bank of Mauritius Limited	www.mauritius-island.com/sbm
State Saving Bank	www.pkobp.pl
State Street Bank & Trust Company	www.statestreet.com
Stuttgarter Bank AG	www.stuttgarter-bank.de
Südwestdeutsche Landesbank	www.suedwestlb.de
Sümerbank	www.turksat.net/sumerbank.rep
Sumisho Lease Co Limited	www.iijnet.or.jp/scl
Sun Hung Kai & Co Limited	www.irasia.com/listco/hk/shkco
SunTrust Banks Atlanta	www.suntrust.com
Suomen Pankki-Finlands Bank	www.bof.fi
Svenska Handelsbanken	www.handelsbanken.se
Sveriges Riksbank	www.riksbank.se
Sydbank A/S	www.sydbank.com
Syndicate Bank	www.syndicatebank.com
Tai Fung Bank Limited	www.taifungbank.com
TAIB Securities Limited	www.taib.com
Taichung Business Bank	www.tcbbank.com.tw
Taishin International Bank	www.taishinbank.com.tw
Taiwan Business Bank	www.tbb.com.tw
Taiwan International Securities Corporation	www.tisc.com.tw
Tatra Banka AS	www.tatrabanka.sk
TC Ziraat Bankasi	www.ziraat.com.tr
Thai Farmers Bank Public Company Limited	www/tfb.co.th
The Asahi Bank Limited	www.asahibank.co.jp
The Bank of Bermuda Limited	www.bankofbermuda.com
The Bank of Ikeda Limited	www.ikedabank.co.jp
The Bank of Japan	www.boj.go.jp/en/index.html
The Bank of Korea	www.bok.or.kr
The Bank of Kuwait & the Middle East, KSC	www.bkme.net
The Bank of New York	www.bankofny.com
The Bank of NT Butterfield & Son Limited	www.bankofbutterfield.com
The Bank of Tokyo-Mitsubishi	www.btm.co.jp
The Bank of Yokohama Limited	www.boy.co.jp
The British Bank of the Middle East	www.britishbank.com
The Chase Manhattan Bank	www.chase.com
The Chiba Bank Limited	www.chibabank.or.jp
The Chinese Bank	www.chinesebank.com.tw
The Chugoku Bank Limited	www.chugin.co.jp
The Chuo Trust & Banking Co Limited	www.chuotrust.co.jp
The Commercial Bank of Korea Limited	www.cbk.co.kr
The Commercial Bank Of Qatar Limited (QSC)	www.cbqbank.com
The Cyprus Popular Bank Limited	www.cypruspopularbank.com
The Dai-Ichi Kangyo Bank Limited	www.dkb.co.jp
The ECU Group plc	www.ecu.co.uk
The Export Import Bank of the Republic of Kazakhstan	www.eximbank.kz
The Export-Import Bank of Japan	www.japanexim.go.jp
The Farmers Bank of China	www.farmerbank.com.tw
The Fuji Bank Limited	www.fujibank.com
The Gunma Bank Limited	www.gunmabank.co.jp
The Hachijuni Bank Limited	www.82bank.co.jp

www.euromoneydirectory.com

COMPANY	WEBSITE
The Hokuriku Bank Limited	www.sphere.ad.jp/hokugin
The Hongkong & Shanghai Banking Corporation Limited	www.hongkongbank.com
The Industrial & Commercial Bank of China	www.icbc.com.ch
The Industrial Bank of Japan Limited	www.ibjbank.co.jp
The International Commercial Bank of China Limited	www.icbc.com.tw
The Iyo Bank Limited	www.iyobank.co.jp
The Joyo Bank Limited	www.joyobank.co.jp
The Long-Term Credit Bank of Japan Limited	www.ltcb.co.jp
The Marine & Fire Insurance Association of Japan Inc	www.sonpo.or.jp
The Mitsui Trust & Banking Co Limited	www.mitsuitrust.co.jp
The Monetary Authority of Singapore	www.mas.gov.sg.
The Mortgage Bank of Denmark	www.hypotekbanken.dk
The Nanto Bank Limited	www.nantobank.co.jp
The National Bank of Dubai PJSC	www.nbd.co.ae
The Nikko Securities Co Limited	www.nikko.co.jp
The Nippon Credit Bank Limited	www.ncb.co.jp
The Nishi-Nippon Bank Limited	www.nishigin.co.jp
The Nomura Securities Co Limited	www.nomura.co.jp
The Northern Trust Company	www.ntrs.com
The Royal Bank of Scotland plc	www.rbos.co.uk
The San-in Godo Bank Limited	www.web-sanin.co.jp/econo/gougin
The Sanwa Bank Limited	www.sanwabank.co.jp
The Shanghai Commercial & Savings Bank Limited	www.scsb.com.tw
The Shiga Bank Limited	www.mediagalaxy.co.jp/shigabank
The Standard Bank of South Africa Limited	www.sbic.co.za/scmb
The State Commercial Bank of Lithuania	www.lvkb.lt
The Tokai Bank Limited	www.csweb.co.jp/tbk
The Toronto-Dominion Bank	www.tdbank.ca
The Toyo Trust & Banking Company Limited	www.toyotrustbank.co.jp
The World Bank	www.worldbank.org
The Yasuda Trust & Banking Company Limited	www.ytb.co.jp
The Zenshinren Bank	www.shinkin.co.jp/scb
Tokai Asia Limited	www.tokaiasia.com.hk
Tokai Bank of California	www.tokai.com
Toprakbank AS	www.toprakbank.com.tr
Traders Royal Bank	www.sequel.net/~trbm
Tradition Financial Services Limited	www.tfsbrokers.com
TSB Bank www.tsbbank.ie	www.tsbbank.ie
Tullett & Tokyo Forex International Limited	www.tullett.co.uk
Türk Ekonomi Bankasi AS	www.teb.com.tr
Türkiye Garanti Bankasi AS	www.garantibank.com.tr
Türkiye Halk Bankåsi AS	www.halkbank.com.tr
Türkiye Is Bankasi AS	www.isbank.com.tr
UBS AG	www.ubs.com
UFB Locabail	www.ufb.locobail.fr
Ukio Bankas	www.ukiobankas.online.lt
Ulster Bank Markets	www.ulsterbank.com
UNIBANCO-União de Bancos Brasileiros SA	www.unibanco.com.br
Unibank A/S	www.unibank.dk
Unicaja	www.unicaja.es
Unico Banking Group	www.unico.nl
UniCredito Italiano SpA	www.credit.it
Union Bank of California	www.uboc.com
Union Bank of Hong Kong Limited	www.unionbank.com.hk
Union Bank of India	www.unionbankofindia.com
Union Bank of Norway	www.internett.nor.no/nvestor/nor-eng
Union Bank of Taiwan	www.ubot.com.tw
Union banka as	www.union.cz
Union Discount Company Limited	www.union_discount.co.uk
United Chinese Bank Limited	www.hkbea.com
United Mizrahi Bank Limited	www.mizrahi.co.il
United Overseas Bank Limited	www.uob.com
Universal Savings Bank Limited	www.usb.com.cy
US Bancorp	www.usbank.com

www.euromoneydirectory.com

COMPANY	WEBSITE
USTrust	www.ustrustboston.com
Valores Mexicanos Casa de Bolsa SA de CV	www.valmex.com.mx
Vanguard Group (The)	www.vanguard.com
Varazdinska banka dd	www.banka.hr
Veronis, Suhler & Associates Incorporated	www.vsacomm.com
Verwaltungs-und Privat-Bank AG	www.vp.bank.li
Vilniaus Bankas AB	www.vb.lt
Vining-Sparks IBG Limited Partnership	www.vsibg.com
Vojvodjanska Banka AD	Vwww.voban.co.yu
Volksbank Hannover eG	www.vbhan.de
Vorarlberger Landes-und Hypothekenbank	www.hypovbg.at
Wachovia Corporation	www.wachovia.com
Warburg Dillon Read	www.wdr.com
Westdeutsche Landesbank Girozentrale	www.westlb.de
Westpac Banking Corporation	www.westpac.com.au
WGZ-Bank Luxemberg SA	www.wgz-bank.lu
WGZ-Bank Westdeutsche Genossenschafts Zentralbank eG	www.wgz-bank.de
Wing Hang Bank Limited	www.whbhk.com
Wing Lung Bank Limited	www.winglungbank.com.hk
Wood & Company	www.wood.com
WorldInvest Limited	www.worldinvest.com
Xiosbank SA	www.netor.gr/xiosbank
Yasar Yatirim AS	www.yasarbank.com.tr
Zivnostenská Banka AS	www.ziba.cz
Zürcher Kantonalbank	www.zkb.ch

Synopsys specialises in developing applications software solutions and providing consultancy services, predominantly for the international financial community. RIMS (Real-time Integrated Multi-product Solution) - Synopsys' flagship product - is the world's leading securities trading and settlement solution for the Global Capital Markets.

RIMS is an integrated front, middle and back office solution providing comprehensive functionality for achieving straight through processing for both local and cross border trading. This enables greater control and efficiency, lower operating costs and improved risk management. RIMS provides integrated support for bonds, equities, warrants and futures together with a full range of multi-legged transactions including repo, stock borrowing/lending, buy/sellback and cash borrowing/lending.

RIMS' unique Fast Track evaluation and implementation programme provides a resource-efficient method of achieving low risk, rapid and successful implementation delivering real business benefits on time and to budget. RIMS supports multi-company, multi-region and multi-timezone business structures allowing the trading of multiple instruments and products on a truly global, multi-currency basis.

Contact: Marketing

Synopsys Ltd
No 27 The Turnmill
63 Clerkenwell Road
London EC1M 5NP
UK

Tel: + 44 (0) 171 250 1990
Fax: + 44 (0) 171 553 4713
E-Mail: marketing@synopsys.ltd.uk
Web: www.synopsys.ltd.uk

W-16   Euromoney Directory 1999

BANK	PAGE NO	BANK	PAGE NO
3i Corporate Finance Limited	1638	ABN AMRO Bank NV, Global Trading Unit (Singapore)	1286
3i Europe plc *(Spain)*	1397	ABN AMRO Bank SA *(Ecuador)*	356
		ABN AMRO Bank (Switzerland) *(Switzerland)*	1467
A & A Actienbank	1466	ABN AMRO Fixed Income France *(France)*	396
AA Nazzaro Associates *(United States)*	1908	ABN AMRO Inc *(United States)*	1908
Aargauische Kantonalbank *(Switzerland)*	1466	ABN AMRO New Zealand Limited *(New Zealand)*	1138
AB Asesores *(Spain)*	1397	ABN AMRO Securities (Japan) Limited *(Japan)*	814
Abanka dd Ljubljana *(Slovenia)*	1370	ABN AMRO Securities (Polska) SA *(Poland)*	1198
Abbey National Financial Products *(United Kingdom)*	1638	ABS Banque *(France)*	396
		ABSA Asia Limited *(Hong Kong, China)*	578
Abbey National Treasury International Limited *(Channel Islands)*	242	ABSA Bank Limited *(South Africa)*	1382
		ABSA Bank Limited *(United Kingdom)*	1642
Abbey National Treasury Services *(France)*	395	Absolutbank *(Belarus)*	126
Abbey National Treasury Services *(Hong Kong, China)*	578	Abu Dhabi Commercial Bank *(United Arab Emirates)*	1631
Abbey National Treasury Services plc *(United Kingdom)*	1638	Abu Dhabi Fund for Development *(United Arab Emirates)*	1631
ABC International Bank plc *(United Kingdom)*	1641	Abu Dhabi Investment Company *(United Arab Emirates)*	1632
ABC Islamic Bank *(Bahrain)*	104	ACCIVAL *(Mexico)*	1076
ABN AMRO *(United Kingdom)*	1641	Adam & Co Investment Management Limited *(United Kingdom)*	1643
ABN AMRO *(United States)*	1908	Adler & Co AG *(Switzerland)*	1467
ABN AMRO Asia Limited *(Hong Kong, China)*	578	AFC Merchant Bank *(Singapore)*	1287
ABN AMRO Asia Merchant Bank (Singapore) Limited *(Singapore)*	1286	Affin Discount Berhad *(Malaysia)*	1035
ABN AMRO Australia Limited *(Australia)*	35	Afghan National Credit & Finance *(United Kingdom)*	1643
ABN AMRO Bank *(Argentina)*	6	AGIFEL International Limited *(Hong Kong, China)*	579
ABN AMRO Bank *(Denmark)*	335	Agora CTVM SA *(Brazil)*	172
ABN AMRO Bank *(Germany)*	454	Agricultural Bank of China *(China)*	269
ABN AMRO Bank *(Monaco)*	1093	Agricultural Bank of China *(Singapore)*	1288
ABN AMRO Bank *(United Kingdom)*	1641	Agricultural Bank of China *(United Kingdom)*	1643
ABN AMRO Bank (België) NV *(Belgium)*	131	Agricultural Bank of Lithuania *(Lithuania)*	965
ABN AMRO Bank (Gibraltar) Limited *(Gibraltar)*	554	Agricultural Cooperative Bank of Armenia - ACBA *(Armenia)*	31
ABN AMRO Bank Kazakhstan *(Kazakhstan)*	892	Agropromstroybank *(Cyprus)*	306
ABN AMRO Bank (Luxembourg) SA *(Luxembourg)*	971	AIAF Mercado de Renta Fija SA *(Spain)*	1398
ABN AMRO Bank NA *(Uruguay)*	2020	AIB Group *(Ireland)*	716
ABN AMRO Bank NV *(Argentina)*	6	AIB Group (UK) PCC *(United Kingdom)*	1643
ABN AMRO Bank NV *(Australia)*	36	AIB International Financial Services Limited *(Ireland)*	717
ABN AMRO Bank NV *(Bahrain)*	104	The Aichi Bank Limited *(Japan)*	814
ABN AMRO Bank NV *(Belgium)*	131	AIG Financial Products Corp *(United States)*	1910
ABN AMRO Bank NV *(Belgium)*	133	AIG Financial Products Hong Kong Limited *(Hong Kong, China)*	579
ABN AMRO Bank NV *(Chile)*	257	AIG Financial Products (Japan) Limited *(Japan)*	814
ABN AMRO Bank NV *(Czech Republic)*	314	AIG Global Investment Corp *(United States)*	1910
ABN AMRO Bank NV *(Ireland)*	715	AIG Global Investment Corp (Europe) *(United Kingdom)*	1643
ABN AMRO Bank NV *(Japan)*	813	AIG Investment Corp (Asia) Limited *(Hong Kong, China)*	579
ABN AMRO Bank NV *(Korea, South)*	903	Aizawa Securities Co Limited *(Japan)*	814
ABN AMRO Bank NV *(Mexico)*	1075	AKA Ausfuhrkredit-GmbH *(Germany)*	455
ABN AMRO Bank NV *(Netherlands)*	1107	AKBANK TAS *(France)*	396
ABN AMRO Bank NV *(Panama)*	1170	AKBANK TAS *(Germany)*	455
ABN AMRO Bank NV *(Spain)*	1398	AKBANK TAS *(Netherlands)*	1108
ABN AMRO Bank NV *(United Kingdom)*	1641	AKBANK TAS *(Turkey)*	1606
ABN AMRO Bank NV *(United States)*	1908		
ABN AMRO Bank NV *(Venezuela)*	2030		
ABN AMRO Bank NV *(Vietnam)*	2033		
ABN AMRO Bank NV Amsterdam *(Switzerland)*	1466		
ABN AMRO Bank NV Asunción *(Paraguay)*	1177		

A-1

BANK	PAGE NO	BANK	PAGE NO
AKBANK TAS *(United Kingdom)*	1643	American Express Bank Limited *(Greece)*	559
Akros Finanziaria *(Italy)*	748	American Express Bank Limited *(Singapore)*	1289
Al Baraka Turkish Finance House AS *(Turkey)*	1607	American Express Bank Limited *(Spain)*	1399
Al Rajhi Banking & Investment Corporation *(Saudi Arabia)*	1276	American Express Bank Limited *(Taiwan, Republic of China)*	1558
Al Rajhi Investment Corporation *(United Kingdom)*	1643	American Express Bank Limited *(United Arab Emirates)*	1632
Alahli Bank of Kuwait *(Kuwait)*	933	
Al-Ahli Commercial Bank BSC *(Bahrain)*	105	American Express Bank Limited *(United Kingdom)*	1647
Ålandsbanken AB *(Finland)*	386	American Express Bank (Luxembourg) SA *(Luxembourg)*	972
Al-Bank Al-Saudi Al Fransi *(Saudi Arabia)*	1277	
Al-Bank Al-Saudi Al-Alami Limited *(United Kingdom)*	1644	American Express Bank (Switzerland) SA *(Switzerland)*	1468
Albertini & C SIM SpA *(Italy)*	749	American Express Bank (Uruguay) SA *(Uruguay)*	2021
Alexandra Investment Management Limited *(United States)*	1910	American Scandinavian Banking Corp *(United States)*	1911
Alfa Bank *(United Kingdom)*	1645	AMMB International Limited *(Malaysia)*	1037
Alfred Berg Bank A/S *(Denmark)*	335	AMP Securities Pty Limited *(Australia)*	36
Alfred Berg Norway *(Norway)*	1147	Amstel Securities NV *(Netherlands)*	1108
Alfred Berg (UK) Limited *(United Kingdom)*	1645	Amstgeld NV *(Netherlands)*	1108
Aljba Alliance *(Russian Federation)*	1250	Amtssparekassen Fyn A/S *(Denmark)*	337
ALKE Stockbrokers SA *(Greece)*	556	Anglo Chinese Securities Limited *(Hong Kong, China)*	581
All Asia Capital & Trust Corporation *(Philippines)*	1185	
All Trading Brokers Europe *(Spain)*	1399	Anglo Irish Bank (Austria) AG *(Austria)*	76
Allami Fejlesztési Intézet Részvénytársaság *(Hungary)*	662	Anglo Irish Bank Corporation plc *(Ireland)*	718
		Anglo-Irish Bank Corporation plc *(United Kingdom)*	1648
Allaria Ledesma y Cia Sociedad de Bolsa SA *(Argentina)*	7	Anglo-Romanian Bank Limited *(United Kingdom)*	1648
		Anker Bank *(Switzerland)*	1468
Allgemeine Deutsche Direktbank AG *(Germany)*	455	Anlage-und KreditBank *(Switzerland)*	1469
Allgemeine HypothekenBank *(Germany)*	455	ANP International Finance Limited *(Ireland)*	718
Allgemeine Sparkasse Oberösterreich Bankaktiengesellschaft *(Austria)*	76	Henry Ansbacher & Co Limited *(United Kingdom)*	1649
		Ansbacher (Guernsey) Limited *(Channel Islands)*	242
Alliance Capital Limited *(United Kingdom)*	1645	Ansbacher (Jersey) Limited *(Channel Islands)*	242
Allied Bank of Pakistan Limited *(United Kingdom)*	1646	Antwerpse Diamantbank NV *(Belgium)*	133
Allied Capital Resources Limited *(Hong Kong, China)*	581	ANZ Bank (Guernsey) Limited *(Channel Islands)*	242
		ANZ Bank (Vanuatu) Limited *(Vanuatu)*	2028
Allied Irish Bank *(United States)*	1910	ANZ Grindlays Bank (Jersey) Limited *(Channel Islands)*	243
Allied Irish Bank Group Treasury *(Singapore)*	1289	
Allied Irish Bank Group Treasury *(United Kingdom)*	1646	ANZ Grindlays Bank Limited *(Qatar)*	1240
Allied Irish Bank Group Treasury *(United States)*	1910	ANZ Grindlays Bank Limited *(Switzerland)*	1470
Allied Irish Bank plc *(Singapore)*	1289	ANZ Grindlays Bank plc *(Bahrain)*	106
Alm Brand Bank *(Denmark)*	336	ANZ Investment Bank *(United Kingdom)*	1650
Alpe Jadran banka dd *(Croatia)*	294	ANZ Investment Bank - Equities Division *(Australia)*	36
Alpha Bank Limited *(Cyprus)*	306	
Alpha Brokerage AE *(Greece)*	557	ANZ Securities (Asia) Limited *(Japan)*	814
Alpha Credit Bank *(Greece)*	557	ANZ Securities Inc *(United States)*	1911
Alpha Credit Bank *(United Kingdom)*	1647	ANZ Securities (USA) Inc *(United States)*	1911
Alpha Securities AG *(Switzerland)*	1467	Apax Partners & Cie Finance SA *(France)*	396
Alpha Trust Investment Services SA *(Greece)*	559	Appenzell-Innerrhodische Kantonalbank *(Switzerland)*	1470
ALUBAF Arab International Bank EC *(Bahrain)*	106	
Alwatany Bank of Egypt *(Egypt)*	359	AR Stavební sporitelna as *(Czech Republic)*	314
Amagerbanken A/S *(Denmark)*	337	Arab African International Bank *(Egypt)*	359
Amanah Finance Malaysia Berhad *(Malaysia)*	1035	Arab African International Bank *(Lebanon)*	953
Amanah Merchant Bank Berhad *(Malaysia)*	1036	Arab African International Bank *(United Arab Emirates)*	1633
AMCM - Autoridade Monetária e Cambial de Macau *(Macau)*	1029	
		Arab African International Bank *(United Kingdom)*	1650
American Bank in Poland Inc *(Poland)*	1199	Arab American Bank *(United States)*	1912
American Express Bank (France) SA *(France)*	396	Arab Bank AG *(Germany)*	456
American Express Bank Limited *(Argentina)*	7	Arab Bank Australia Limited *(Australia)*	36

A-2

BANK	PAGE NO
Arab Bank plc *(Greece)*	560
Arab Bank plc *(Singapore)*	1290
Arab Bank Plc *(United Kingdom)*	1651
Arab Bank (Switzerland) *(Switzerland)*	1470
Arab Banking Corporation (BSC) *(Bahrain)*	106
Arab Banking Corporation (BSC) *(Italy)*	749
Arab Banking Corporation (Jordan) *(Jordan)*	885
Arab Banking Corporation-Daus & Co GmbH *(Germany)*	456
Arab International Bank *(Egypt)*	360
Arab Investment Bank *(Egypt)*	361
The Arab Investment Company *(Bahrain)*	107
Arab Jordan Investment Bank *(Jordan)*	886
Arab Jordan Investment Bank SA *(Cyprus)*	307
Arab National Bank *(Saudi Arabia)*	1277
Arab Petroleum Investments Corporation (APICORP) *(Saudi Arabia)*	1277
Arab Tunisian Bank *(Tunisia)*	1603
Arabian General Investment Corporation *(United Arab Emirates)*	1633
Arabian Gulf Investments (Far East) Limited *(Hong Kong, China)*	581
Arab-Malaysian Bank Berhad *(Malaysia)*	1038
Arab-Malaysian Merchant Bank Berhad *(Malaysia)*	1039
Aragon Fondkommission AB *(Sweden)*	1452
A/S Arbejdernes Landsbank *(Denmark)*	338
Arbitral International Corp *(United States)*	1912
ARCA Merchant SpA *(Italy)*	749
ARCA SIM SpA *(Italy)*	749
Arctos Securities Limited *(Finland)*	387
Argenta *(Peru)*	1178
Argentaria *(Argentina)*	7
Argentaria - Banco Exterior de España *(Portugal)*	1218
Argentaria Banco de Negocios *(Spain)*	1399
Argentaria Caja Postal Banco Hipotecario SA *(Spain)*	1400
Argentaria, Caja Postal y Banco Hipotecario SA (ARGENTARIA) *(United Kingdom)*	1651
Armand von Ernst & Cie AG *(Switzerland)*	1471
Arnhold and S Bleichroeder Inc *(United States)*	1912
J Aron & Co (UK) *(United Kingdom)*	1652
J Aron & Company (Bullion) *(United Kingdom)*	1652
Aros Securities AB *(Sweden)*	1452
Artesia Bank *(Belgium)*	134
Artesia Bank Luxembourg SA *(Luxembourg)*	973
Artesia Bank Nederland NV *(Netherlands)*	1108
Artesia Ireland *(Ireland)*	718
Aruba Bank NV *(Aruba)*	34
Asahi Bank (Deutschland) GmbH *(Germany)*	457
The Asahi Bank Limited *(Australia)*	37
The Asahi Bank Limited *(Brazil)*	173
The Asahi Bank Limited *(China)*	270
The Asahi Bank Limited *(Germany)*	457
The Asahi Bank Limited *(Hong Kong, China)*	581
The Asahi Bank Limited *(Korea, South)*	903
The Asahi Bank Limited *(Malaysia)*	1040
The Asahi Bank Limited *(Singapore)*	1291

BANK	PAGE NO
The Asahi Bank Limited *(Taiwan, Republic of China)*	1558
The Asahi Bank Limited *(Thailand)*	1581
The Asahi Bank Limited *(United Kingdom)*	1652
The Asahi Bank Limited *(United States)*	1913
The Asahi Bank Limited *(Vietnam)*	2033
Asahi Bank (Schweiz) AG *(Switzerland)*	1471
Asahi Finance (Hong Kong) Limited *(Hong Kong, China)*	582
Asahi Finance (UK) Limited *(United Kingdom)*	1652
ASB Bank Limited *(New Zealand)*	1138
ASC Capital Pte Limited *(Singapore)*	1291
AseamBankers Malaysia Berhad *(Malaysia)*	1040
The Ashikaga Bank Limited *(Japan)*	815
Asia Commercial Bank *(Vietnam)*	2033
Asia Commercial Bank Limited *(Hong Kong, China)*	582
Asia Pacific Inc *(Philippines)*	1186
Asian Banking Corporation *(Korea, South)*	903
Asian Development Bank *(Germany)*	457
Asian Development Bank *(Philippines)*	1186
ASLK-CGER *(Luxembourg)*	973
ASLK-CGER Bank *(Belgium)*	135
Associazione Nazionale Banche Private *(Italy)*	750
Astaire & Partners *(Israel)*	741
Astaire & Partners Limited *(United Kingdom)*	1653
Atlantic Rating Limited *(Brazil)*	173
Auctor Securities doo *(Croatia)*	294
Aurea Finance Company *(Luxembourg)*	973
Aurel SA *(France)*	396
Aurora Capital Partners LP *(United States)*	1913
Australia & New Zealand Banking Group Limited *(Australia)*	37
Australia & New Zealand Banking Group Limited *(Brazil)*	173
Australia & New Zealand Banking Group Limited *(France)*	397
Australia & New Zealand Banking Group Limited *(Hong Kong, China)*	583
Australia & New Zealand Banking Group Limited *(Japan)*	815
Australia & New Zealand Banking Group Limited *(Korea, South)*	904
Australia & New Zealand Banking Group Limited *(Malaysia)*	1041
Australia & New Zealand Banking Group Limited *(Singapore)*	1291
Australia & New Zealand Banking Group Limited *(Thailand)*	1581
Australia & New Zealand Banking Group *(United Kingdom)*	1654
Australia & New Zealand Banking Group Limited *(Vietnam)*	2034
Australian Guarantee Corporation Limited *(Australia)*	37
Austrian National Bank *(Belgium)*	137
Austrian National Bank *(France)*	397
Austrian National Bank *(United States)*	1913
Avtobank *(Russian Federation)*	1250

A-3

BANK	PAGE NO
The Awa Bank Limited *(Japan)*...................................	815
AY Bank Limited *(United Kingdom)*...........................	1654
BA Asia Limited..	583
BA Australia Limited *(Australia)*................................	37
BA Futures Incorporated *(United States)*...................	1913
BACOB Bank *(Belgium)*..	137
Baden-Württembergische Bank AG *(Germany)*...........	458
Bahrain International Bank EC *(Bahrain)*...................	108
Bahrain Middle East Bank (EC) *(Bahrain)*.................	109
Bahrain Middle East Bank (EC) *(United Kingdom)*.....	1654
Bahrain Monetary Agency *(Bahrain)*..........................	104
The Bahraini Saudi Bank BSC *(Bahrain)*....................	111
Baltic International Bank *(Latvia)*..............................	942
Baltijas Tranzitu *(Latvia)*...	943
Ban Hin Lee Bank Berhad *(Malaysia)*........................	1041
Ban Hin Lee Bank Berhad *(Singapore)*......................	1291
BANACCI *(Mexico)*...	1076
BANAMEX *(Mexico)*...	1076
Banc Agricol i Comercial d'Andorra SA *(Andorra)*......	2
Banc Internacional d'Andorra SA *(Andorra)*..............	3
Banca Agricola Mantovana SCaRL *(Italy)*.................	750
Banca Agricola Popolare di Ragusa SCaRL *(Italy)*.....	751
Banca Agricola SA *(Romania)*...................................	1243
Banca Akros *(Italy)*...	751
Banca Antoniana-Popolare Veneta *(Italy)*.................	752
Banca Bucuresti SA *(Romania)*.................................	1244
Banca Carige *(United States)*....................................	1914
Banca Carige SpA *(Italy)*...	752
Banca Carige *(United Kingdom)*................................	1654
Banca Cassa di Risparmio di Savigliano SpA *(Italy)*..	753
Banca Cassa di Risparmio di Tortona SpA *(Italy)*......	753
Banca Catalana SA *(Spain)*.......................................	1400
Banca Comerciala Romana *(Romania)*.....................	1244
Banca Commerciale Italiana *(Greece)*.......................	560
Banca Commerciale Italiana *(Italy)*...........................	754
Banca Commerciale Italiana *(Japan)*........................	816
Banca Commerciale Italiana *(Singapore)*..................	1291
Banca Commerciale Italiana *(Spain)*.........................	1401
Banca Commerciale Italiana *(United Kingdom)*.........	1654
Banca Commerciale Italiana *(United States)*............	1914
Banca Commerciale Italiana of Canada *(Canada)*......	212
Banca Commerciale Italiana (Ireland) plc *(Ireland)*.....	719
Banca Commerciale Italiana (Suisse) *(Switzerland)*....	1471
Banca Confia SA *(Mexico)*...	1076
Banca Cooperativa Valsabbina *(Italy)*.......................	755
Banca de Credit si Dezvoltare Romexterra SA *(Romania)*...	1245
Banca di Credito Cooperativo di Carrú e del Monregalese Scrl *(Italy)*..	755
Banca di Credito Popolare Torre del Greco *(Italy)*......	756
Banca CRT *(United States)*.......................................	1914
Banca CRT SpA *(Italy)*..	756
Banca CRT SpA *(United Kingdom)*............................	1655
Banca del Ceresio *(Switzerland)*................................	1471
Banca del Gottardo *(Switzerland)*..............................	1472
Banca del Salento *(United Kingdom)*.........................	1656

BANK	PAGE NO
Banca del Sempione *(Switzerland)*............................	1473
Banca dello Stato del Cantone Ticino *(Switzerland)*..	1473
Banca D'Intermediazions Mobiliare IMI SpA *(Italy)*....	757
Banca d'Italia *(Italy)*...	748
Banca d'Italia *(United Kingdom)*................................	1657
Banca d'Italia *(United States)*...................................	1914
Banca de Export-Import a României *(Romania)*.........	1246
Banca Intermobiliare di Investimenti e Gestioni SpA *(Italy)*...	757
Banca Intesa SpA *(Italy)*...	758
Banca March SA *(Spain)*...	1401
Banca March SA *(United Kingdom)*...........................	1657
Banca delle Marche SpA *(Italy)*.................................	759
Banca Monte dei Paschi di Siena SpA *(Italy)*...........	760
Banca Monte dei Paschi di Siena SpA *(Singapore)*...	1292
Banca Monte dei Paschi di Siena SpA *(United Kingdom)*..	1657
Banca Monte dei Paschi di Siena SpA *(United States)*..	1914
Banca Monte Parma SpA *(Italy)*................................	761
Banca Monte Paschi (Suisse) SA *(Switzerland)*.........	1473
Banca Mora SA *(Andorra)*...	4
Banca Morgan Stanley SpA *(Italy)*............................	761
Banca Nazionale del Lavoro *(Italy)*...........................	761
Banca Nazionale del Lavoro *(United States)*............	1914
Banca Nazionale del Lavoro SpA *(Argentina)*............	7
Banca Nazionale del Lavoro SpA *(Belgium)*..............	138
Banca Nazionale del Lavoro SpA *(China)*..................	270
Banca Nazionale del Lavoro SpA *(Germany)*............	458
Banca Nazionale del Lavoro SpA *(Hong Kong, China)*...	583
Banca Nazionale del Lavoro SpA *(Japan)*.................	816
Banca Nazionale del Lavoro SpA *(Poland)*...............	1199
Banca Nazionale del Lavoro SpA *(Singapore)*...........	1292
Banca Nazionale del Lavoro SpA *(United Kingdom)*..	1658
Banca Nazionale dell'Agricoltura SpA *(Italy)*.............	762
Banca Nazionale dell'Agricoltura SpA *(United Kingdom)*..	1658
Banca Nazionale dell'Agricoltura *(United States)*.......	1915
Banca Popolare di Ancona SpA *(Italy)*......................	764
Banca Popolare di Aprilia SCaRL *(Italy)*...................	764
Banca Popolare Asolo e Montebelluna *(Italy)*...........	764
Banca Popolare di Bergamo-Credito Varesino *(Italy)*..	764
Banca Popolare di Cividale ScaRL *(Italy)*.................	765
Banca Popolare Commercio e Industria *(Italy)*..........	765
Banca Popolare di Crema *(Italy)*...............................	766
Banca Popolare di Cremona *(Italy)*...........................	766
Banca Popolare dell'Adriatico SpA *(Italy)*.................	767
Banca Popolare dell'Alto Adige ScaRL *(Italy)*...........	767
Banca Popolare dell'Emilia Romagna *(Italy)*.............	767
Banca Popolare dell'Etruria e del Lazio *(Italy)*..........	767
Banca Popolare dell'Irpinia *(Italy)*.............................	768
Banca Popolare di Intra ScaRL *(Italy)*......................	768
Banca Popolare di Lodi *(Italy)*...................................	768
Banca Popolare di Luino e di Varese *(Italy)*..............	768
Banca Popolare di Milano *(United Kingdom)*.............	1659
Banca Popolare di Milano SCaRL *(Italy)*..................	768
Banca Popolare di Novara *(France)*..........................	397

A-4

BANK	PAGE NO
Banca Popolare di Novara *(Italy)*	769
Banca Popolare di Novara *(Luxembourg)*	974
Banca Popolare di Novara *(Spain)*	1401
Banca Popolare di Novara *(United Kingdom)*	1659
Banca Popolare di Novara Scrl *(Belgium)*	138
Banca Popolare di Novara Scrl *(Germany)*	459
Banca Popolare di San Felice Sul Panaro SCaRL *(Italy)*	770
Banca Popolare di Sondrio *(Italy)*	770
Banca Popolare Udinese ScaRL *(Italy)*	770
Banca Popolare di Verona San Giminiano e San Prospero *(Italy)*	770
Banca Popolare Vicentina scparl *(Italy)*	771
Banca Privata Solari & Blum SA *(Switzerland)*	1473
Banca Profilo SpA *(Italy)*	771
Banca Regionale Europea SpA *(Italy)*	771
Banca di Roma *(Italy)*	771
Banca di Roma *(United Kingdom)*	1659
Banca di Roma SpA *(Argentina)*	8
Banca di Roma SpA *(France)*	398
Banca di Roma SpA *(Hong Kong, China)*	584
Banca di Roma SpA *(Singapore)*	1292
Banca di Roma SpA *(United States)*	1915
Banca di Romagna Spa *(Italy)*	773
Banca Romana Pentru Dezvoltare *(Romania)*	1246
Banca San Paolo di Brescia *(Hong Kong, China)*	584
Banca San Paolo di Brescia *(United States)*	1915
Banca Sella SpA *(Italy)*	774
Banca Serfin SA *(United Kingdom)*	1660
Banca Toscana SpA *(Italy)*	774
Banca Turco Romana *(Romania)*	1246
Banca Unione di Credito Ginevra *(Switzerland)*	1473
Banca Unione di Credito Lugano *(Switzerland)*	1473
Banca Unione di Credito Zurigo *(Switzerland)*	1474
Banco de A Edwards *(Chile)*	257
Banco ABC Brasil SA *(Brazil)*	173
Banco ABN AMRO *(Brazil)*	174
Banco da Amazônia SA *(Brazil)*	175
Banco Ambrosiano Veneto *(United States)*	1915
Banco Ambrosiano Veneto SpA *(Italy)*	774
Banco América do Sul SA *(Brazil)*	175
Banco Anglo Colombiano *(Colombia)*	284
Banco Argencoop Cooperativo Ltdo *(Argentina)*	8
Banco Atlántico *(Colombia)*	284
Banco Atlántico *(España)* SA *(Mexico)*	1077
Banco Bandeirantes *(United States)*	1915
Banco Bandeirantes SA *(Brazil)*	175
Banco Bansud SA *(Argentina)*	8
Banco BBA Creditanstalt SA *(Brazil)*	175
Banco BI Creditanstalt SA *(Argentina)*	8
Banco BICE *(Chile)*	257
Banco Bilbao Vizcaya *(Argentina)*	9
Banco Bilbao Vizcaya *(France)*	398
Banco Bilbao Vizcaya *(Italy)*	775
Banco Bilbao Vizcaya *(Japan)*	816
Banco Bilbao Vizcaya *(Spain)*	1402
Banco Bilbao Vizcaya (Portugal) SA *(Portugal)*	1218
Banco Bilbao Vizcaya Puerto Rico *(Puerto Rico)*	1239

BANK	PAGE NO
Banco Bilbao Vizcaya SA *(Germany)*	459
Banco Bilbao Vizcaya SA *(United Kingdom)*	1660
Banco BMG SA *(Brazil)*	176
Banco Boavista *(Brazil)*	176
Banco Boavista *(United Kingdom)*	1660
Banco Boavista Interatlântico SA *(Brazil)*	177
Banco Boavista SA *(United States)*	1915
Banco de Bogotá *(Colombia)*	284
Banco Bolivariano CA *(Ecuador)*	357
Banco Boliviano Americano *(United States)*	1916
Banco de Boston *(Chile)*	258
Banco Bozano, Simonsen SA *(Brazil)*	177
Banco BPI SA *(Portugal)*	1218
Banco Bradesco SA *(Brazil)*	179
Banco do Brasil AG *(Austria)*	76
Banco do Brasil (Europe) NV/SA *(Belgium)*	138
Banco do Brasil SA *(Argentina)*	9
Banco do Brasil SA *(Brazil)*	179
Banco do Brasil SA *(Chile)*	259
Banco do Brasil SA *(Germany)*	459
Banco do Brasil SA *(Italy)*	775
Banco do Brasil SA *(Japan)*	816
Banco do Brasil SA *(Netherlands)*	1109
Banco do Brasil SA *(Singapore)*	1293
Banco do Brasil SA *(Spain)*	1402
Banco do Brasil SA *(United Kingdom)*	1661
Banco de Cabo Verde *(Cape Verde Islands)*	240
Banco CCF Brasil SA *(Brazil)*	181
Banco Central de Bolivia *(Bolivia)*	170
Banco Central de Cuba *(Cuba)*	304
Banco Central del Ecuador *(Ecuador)*	356
Banco Central del Paraguay *(Paraguay)*	1176
Banco Central del Uruguay *(Uruguay)*	2020
Banco Central Hispano *(Spain)*	1402
Banco Central Hispano USA *(United States)*	1916
Banco Central Hispanoamericano *(Italy)*	775
Banco Central Hispanoamericano SA *(Japan)*	817
Banco Central Hispanoamericano SA *(Switzerland)*	1474
Banco Central Hispanoamericano SA *(United Kingdom)*	1661
Banco Central de Nicaragua *(Nicaragua)*	1144
Banco Central de la Republica Argentina *(Argentina)*	5
Banco Central de la República Dominicana *(Dominican Republic)*	355
Banco Central de Reserva del Perú *(Peru)*	1178
Banco Central de Reserva de El Salvador *(El Salvador)*	375
Banco Central de São Tomé e Príncipe *(Sao Tomé and Principe)*	1276
Banco Central de Venezuela *(Venezuela)*	2029
Banco di Chiaveri e della Riviera Ligure SpA *(Italy)*	776
Banco de Chile *(Chile)*	259
Banco de Chile *(United States)*	1916
Banco Cidade S/A *(Brazil)*	181
Banco de la Ciudad de Buenos Aires *(Argentina)*	9
Banco de Colombia *(Colombia)*	285
Banco Colpatria *(Colombia)*	285

A-5

BANK	PAGE NO
Banco Colpatria *(United States)*............................	1916
Banco Comafi SA *(Argentina)*...............................	9
Banco Comercial dos Açores *(Portugal)*....................	1219
Banco Comercial Israelita SA *(Argentina)*.................	10
Banco Comercial Português SA *(Portugal)*................	1219
Banco Comercial SA *(Uruguay)*.............................	2021
Banco Comercial Uruguai SA *(Brazil)*......................	182
Banco de Comercio *(Peru)*...................................	1179
Banco de Comercio Exterior de Colombia *(Colombia)*..	286
Banco Confederado de América Latina *(Panama)*......	1170
Banco Continental SA *(Peru)*................................	1179
Banco Cooperativo Español SA *(Spain)*...................	1403
Banco de Crédito *(Colombia)*...............................	286
Banco de Crédito *(Uruguay)*.................................	2021
Banco de Crédito del Perú *(Peru)*..........................	1180
Banco de Crédito e Inversiones *(Chile)*...................	259
Banco de Crédito Nacional SA *(Brazil)*....................	182
Banco Cuscatlan *(El Salvador)*..............................	375
Banco del Desarrollo *(Chile)*................................	260
Banco del Estado de Chile *(Chile)*.........................	261
Banco del Istmo SA *(Panama)*.............................	1171
Banco del Nuevo Mundo SAEMA *(Peru)*.................	1180
Banco del Pacífico *(United Kingdom)*.....................	1661
Banco Desarrollo SA *(El Salvador)*........................	375
Banco Disa SA *(Panama)*...................................	1172
Banco de la Edificadora de Olavarria SA *(Argentina)*..	10
Banco EFISA SA *(Portugal)*.................................	1220
Banco EFISA SA *(United Kingdom)*.......................	1661
Banco de Entre Ríos SA (Bersa) *(Argentina)*............	10
Banco de España *(Spain)*....................................	1397
Banco Español de Crédito *(United Kingdom)*...........	1661
Banco Español de Credito SA *(Spain)*....................	1403
Banco Espirito Santo *(France)*..............................	398
Banco Espirito Santo *(Germany)*...........................	459
Banco Espirito Santo *(Italy)*................................	776
Banco Espirito Santo *(United Kingdom)*..................	1662
Banco Espirito Santo e Comercial de Lisboa SA *(Portugal)*...	1221
Banco Espirito Santo e Comercial de Lisboa *(Spain)*..	1404
Banco ESSI SA *(Portugal)*...................................	1222
Banco do Estado do Rio Grande do Sul SA *(Brazil)*..	182
Banco do Estado de São Paulo *(Spain)*...................	1404
Banco do Estado de São Paulo SA - BANESPA *(Chile)*...	261
Banco do Estado de São Paulo SA (BANESPA) *(Japan)*...	817
Banco do Estado de São Paulo SA *(United Kingdom)*..	1662
Banco do Estado de São Paulo SA - Banespa *(Brazil)*..	182
Banco Europeo para America Latina (BEAL) SA *(Argentina)*...	10
Banco Europeo para America Latina (BEAL) SA *(Chile)*...	261

BANK	PAGE NO
Banco Europeo para America Latina (BEAL) SA *(Venezuela)*..	2030
Banco Europeu para América Latina (BEAL) SA *(Brazil)*..	183
Banco Excel Economico SA *(Brazil)*......................	184
Banco Excel Económico SA *(United Kingdom)*.........	1663
Banco Exterior de América SA *(Argentina)*..............	11
Banco Exterior de España - Argentaria *(Mexico)*......	1077
Banco Exterior de España SA *(China)*...................	270
Banco Exterior de España Sucursal en Bélgica *(Belgium)*..	138
Banco Exterior de los Andes y de España SA *(Colombia)*..	286
Banco Exterior (Suiza) SA *(Switzerland)*.................	1474
Banco de Extremadura SA *(Spain)*........................	1405
Banco Finantia SA *(Portugal)*..............................	1223
Banco de Fomento & Exterior - Portugal *(Spain)*.......	1405
Banco de Galicia y Buenos Aires *(Argentina)*...........	11
Banco de Galicia y Buenos Aires *(United States)*......	1916
Banco de Guatemala *(Guatemala)*........................	573
Banco Guipuzcoano SA *(Spain)*...........................	1405
Banco Herrero SA *(Spain)*..................................	1406
Banco Hipotecario de España *(Spain)*...................	1406
Banco Hipotecario Nacional *(Argentina)*.................	12
Banco de Iberoamérica (Panamá) SA *(Mexico)*.........	1077
Banco Icatu SA *(Brazil)*.....................................	184
Banco Inbursa *(Mexico)*.....................................	1077
Banco Industrial e Comercial SA *(Brazil)*................	184
Banco Inter-Atlantico SA *(Brazil)*..........................	185
Banco Internacional do Funchal *(Portugal)*..............	1224
Banco Inverlat SA *(Mexico)*................................	1077
Banco Inversion SA *(Spain)*................................	1406
Banco de Inversion y Comercio Exterior SA *(Argentina)*...	12
Banco de Investimento Imobiliário *(Portugal)*...........	1224
Banco de Investimentos Garantia SA *(Brazil)*..........	185
Banco Itaú Argentina SA *(Argentina)*.....................	12
Banco Itaú Europa Luxembourg SA *(Luxembourg)*....	974
Banco Itaú Europa SA *(Portugal)*..........................	1224
Banco Itaú SA *(Brazil)*......................................	185
Banco la Caja Obrera *(Uruguay)*...........................	2021
Banco Latinoamericano de Exportaciones SA - BLADEX *(Argentina)*...	12
Banco Latinoamericano de Exportaciones SA - BLADEX *(Panama)*..	1173
Banco de Lima-Sudameris *(Peru)*.........................	1181
Banco Luso Español SA *(Spain)*...........................	1406
Banco Macro Misiones SA *(Argentina)*...................	12
Banco Marka *(Brazil)*..	185
Banco Mello de Investimento SA *(Portugal)*............	1225
Banco Mello (Luxembourg) SA *(Luxembourg)*..........	974
Banco Mercantil - Venezuela *(United Kingdom)*........	1663
Banco Mercantíl Argentina SA *(Argentina)*..............	13
Banco Mercantil SA *(Bolivia)*...............................	171
Banco Mercantil SA *(Honduras)*...........................	577
Banco Mercantil de São Paulo International SA *(Luxembourg)*..	975
Banco Mercantil de São Paulo SA FINASA *(Brazil)*...	186

A-6

BANK	PAGE NO
Banco Mercantil de São Paulo SA FINASA *(United Kingdom)*	1663
Banco Mercurio SA *(Argentina)*	13
Banco Meridional do Brasil SA *(Brazil)*	186
Banco de Mexico *(Mexico)*	1075
Banco de Montevideo SA *(Uruguay)*	2022
Banco de la Nación *(Peru)*	1181
Banco de la Nacion Argentina *(Argentina)*	13
Banco de la Nación Argentina *(Chile)*	261
Banco de la Nación Argentina *(Spain)*	1407
Banco de la Nacion Argentina *(United Kingdom)*	1664
Banco Nacional de Comercio Exterior SNC *(Mexico)*	1078
Banco Nacional de Commerce Exterior *(United Kingdom)*	1664
Banco Nacional del Comercio *(Colombia)*	286
Banco Nacional de Fomento *(Paraguay)*	1177
Banco Nacional de Mexico SA *(United Kingdom)*	1664
Banco Nacional de Panamá *(Panama)*	1170
Banco Nacional Ultramarino SA *(Portugal)*	1226
Banco Nacional Ultramarino SA *(United Kingdom)*	1665
Banco di Napoli *(Italy)*	776
Banco di Napoli *(United Kingdom)*	1665
Banco di Napoli *(United States)*	1917
Banco di Napoli International SA *(Luxembourg)*	975
Banco di Napoli SpA *(Hong Kong, China)*	584
Banco do Nordeste *(Brazil)*	186
Banco de Occidente *(Colombia)*	287
Banco de Occidente *(Guatemala)*	574
Banco de Oriente *(Mexico)*	1079
Banco Pactual SA *(Brazil)*	187
Banco de la Pampa *(Argentina)*	13
Banco Pan de Azúcar *(Uruguay)*	2022
Banco Pastor *(United Kingdom)*	1665
Banco Pastor SA *(Argentina)*	14
Banco Pastor SA *(Spain)*	1407
Banco Pinto & Sotto Mayor *(Portugal)*	1227
Banco Popolare di Verona Luxembourg *(Luxembourg)*	975
Banco Popular *(Colombia)*	287
Banco Popular Español *(Switzerland)*	1474
Banco Popular Español *(United Kingdom)*	1665
Banco Popular Español SA *(Spain)*	1407
Banco de Portugal *(Portugal)*	1217
Banco Português do Atlântico *(Portugal)*	1228
Banco Português do Atlântico *(United Kingdom)*	1665
Banco Português do Atlântico *(United States)*	1917
Banco Português do Atlântico SA *(Portugal)*	1228
Banco Português de Investimento SA *(Portugal)*	1228
Banco Privado para el Desarrollo SA *(Guatemala)*	574
Banco de la Provincia de Buenos Aires *(Argentina)*	14
Banco de la Provincia de Buenos Aires *(Italy)*	776
Banco de la Provincia de Buenos Aires *(Panama)*	1174
Banco de la Provincia de Buenos Aires *(Uruguay)*	2023
Banco de la Provincia de Córdoba *(Argentina)*	14
Banco Quilmes SA *(Argentina)*	14
Banco Real de Argentina SA *(Argentina)*	15
Banco Real de Colombia *(Colombia)*	287

BANK	PAGE NO
Banco Real del Uruguay SA *(Uruguay)*	2023
Banco Real SA *(Brazil)*	187
Banco Real SA *(United Kingdom)*	1666
Banco Republic National Bank of New York (Brasil) SA *(Brazil)*	188
Banco de la Republica Oriental del Uruguay *(Uruguay)*	2023
Banco Río de la Plata (Grupo Santander) *(Argentina)*	15
Banco Roela SA *(Argentina)*	16
Banco Sabadell *(Spain)*	1409
Banco de Sabadell SA *(United Kingdom)*	1666
Banco Safra SA *(Brazil)*	188
Banco de San Juan *(Argentina)*	16
Banco de San Juan SA *(Argentina)*	16
Banco Sanpaolo SA *(Spain)*	1410
Banco Santa Cruz SA *(Bolivia)*	171
Banco de Santa Fe SA *(Argentina)*	16
Banco Santander *(Peru)*	1181
Banco Santander *(Puerto Rico)*	1239
Banco Santander *(Spain)*	1410
Banco Santander *(Spain)*	1411
Banco Santander *(United Kingdom)*	1666
Banco Santander - Chile *(Chile)*	262
Banco Santander Brasil SA *(Brazil)*	189
Banco Santander SA *(El Salvador)*	376
Banco Santander SA *(Japan)*	817
Banco Santander (Suisse) SA *(Switzerland)*	1475
Banco Santiago *(Chile)*	262
Banco Santiago *(United States)*	1917
Banco Santos SA *(Brazil)*	189
Banco Security *(Chile)*	262
Banco di Sicilia *(Italy)*	776
Banco di Sicilia *(United States)*	1917
Banco di Sicilia International SA *(Luxembourg)*	976
Banco di Sicilia SpA *(Italy)*	776
Banco di Sicilia SpA *(United Kingdom)*	1666
Banco Simeon *(Spain)*	1411
Banco Sud Americano *(Chile)*	263
Banco Sudameris *(Chile)*	264
Banco Sudameris *(Uruguay)*	2023
Banco Sudameris Argentina SA *(Argentina)*	17
Banco Sudameris Brasil SA *(Brazil)*	189
Banco Sudameris Colombia *(Colombia)*	288
Banco Sudameris Paraguay SA *(Paraguay)*	1177
Banco Sul America SA *(Brazil)*	190
Banco Sumitomo Brasileiro SA *(Brazil)*	191
Banco Supervielle Société Générale SA *(Argentina)*	17
Banco Tornquist SA *(Argentina)*	17
Banco Totta & Açores SA *(Macau)*	1030
Banco Totta & Açores SA *(Portugal)*	1229
Banco Totta & Açores SA *(United Kingdom)*	1667
Banco Transandino SA *(Argentina)*	18
Banco Unión CA *(Venezuela)*	2030
Banco Union Colombiano *(Colombia)*	288
Banco Urquijo SA *(Spain)*	1412
Banco Urquijo SA *(Switzerland)*	1475
Banco Urquijo SA *(United Kingdom)*	1667

A-7

BANK	PAGE NO
Banco de Valencia SA *(Spain)*	1413
Banco Velox SA *(Argentina)*	18
Banco de Venezuela / Grupo Santander *(Venezuela)*	2030
Banco Votorantim *(Brazil)*	191
Banco Wiese Ltdo *(Peru)*	1182
Banco Zaragozano SA *(Spain)*	1413
Bancomer SA *(Mexico)*	1079
Bancomer SA *(United Kingdom)*	1668
Banedwards SA Corredores de Bolsa *(Chile)*	265
BANEFE *(Chile)*	265
Banexi Italia *(Italy)*	777
Bangko Sentral ng Pilipinas *(Philippines)*	1184
Bangkok Bank Berhad *(Malaysia)*	1042
The Bangkok Bank of Commerce Public Company Limited *(Thailand)*	1581
Bangkok Bank Public Company Limited *(Hong Kong, China)*	584
Bangkok Bank Public Company Limited *(Japan)*	818
Bangkok Bank Public Company Limited *(Singapore)*	1293
Bangkok Bank Public Company Limited *(Thailand)*	1582
Bangkok Bank Public Company Limited *(United Kingdom)*	1668
Bangkok Bank Public Company Limited *(Vietnam)*	2034
Bangkok Metropolitan Bank Public Company Limited *(Thailand)*	1583
Bangladesh Krishi Bank *(Bangladesh)*	123
Bank Adamas AG *(Switzerland)*	1475
Bank of Albania *(Albania)*	1
Bank Al-Jazira *(Saudi Arabia)*	1278
Bank Al-Maghrib *(Morocco)*	1096
Bank of America Canada *(Canada)*	212
Bank of America International Limited *(United Kingdom)*	1668
Bank of America NT & SA *(Argentina)*	19
Bank of America NT & SA *(Belgium)*	138
Bank of America NT & SA *(Belgium)*	139
Bank of America NT & SA *(Chile)*	265
Bank of America NT & SA *(Hong Kong, China)*	585
Bank of America NT & SA *(Ireland)*	719
Bank of America NT & SA *(Japan)*	818
Bank of America NT & SA *(Mexico)*	1081
Bank of America NT & SA *(Netherlands)*	1109
Bank of America NT & SA *(Pakistan)*	1165
Bank of America NT & SA *(Singapore)*	1294
Bank of America NT & SA *(South Africa)*	1382
Bank of America NT & SA *(Switzerland)*	1475
Bank of America NT & SA *(Thailand)*	1584
Bank of America (Polska) SA *(Poland)*	1199
Bank of America SA *(Spain)*	1413
Bank Anhyp Luxembourg *(Luxembourg)*	976
The Bank of Asia *(Thailand)*	1584
Bank Austria *(Italy)*	777
Bank Austria *(United States)*	1918
Bank Austria Aktiengesellschaft *(Austria)*	77
Bank Austria Creditanstalt *(Spain)*	1413
Bank Austria Creditanstalt AG *(Belgium)*	139
Bank Austria Creditanstalt AG *(Japan)*	818

BANK	PAGE NO
Bank Austria Creditanstalt Croatia dd *(Croatia)*	295
Bank Austria Creditanstalt Group *(United Kingdom)*	1668
Bank Austria Creditanstalt Hungary Rt *(Hungary)*	662
Bank Austria Creditanstalt International AG *(Austria)*	78
Bank Austria Creditanstalt International AG *(France)*	399
Bank Austria Creditanstalt International AG *(Germany)*	459
Bank Austria Creditanstalt International AG *(Hong Kong, China)*	585
Bank Austria Creditanstalt International *(Singapore)*	1295
Bank Austria Creditanstalt Poland SA *(Poland)*	1200
Bank Austria Creditanstalt Slovakia as *(Slovak Republic)*	1358
Bank Austria (Moscow) LLC *(Russian Federation)*	1252
Bank of Ayudhya Public Company Limited *(Thailand)*	1585
Bank of Bahrain and Kuwait BSC *(Bahrain)*	111
Bank of Bahrain and Kuwait BSC *(Kuwait)*	934
PT Bank Bali Tbk *(Indonesia)*	690
Bank of Baroda *(India)*	678
Bank of Baroda *(United Kingdom)*	1670
Bank of Beirut & the Arab Countries SAL *(Cyprus)*	307
Bank of Beirut & the Arab Countries SAL *(Lebanon)*	953
Bank of Bermuda (Guernsey) Limited *(Channel Islands)*	243
Bank of Bermuda (Isle of Man) Limited *(United Kingdom)*	1670
Bank of Bermuda Limited *(Bahrain)*	112
Bank of Bermuda Limited *(United Kingdom)*	1670
The Bank of Bermuda Limited *(Bermuda)*	167
The Bank of Bermuda Limited *(Hong Kong, China)*	585
Bank of Bermuda (Luxembourg) SA *(Luxembourg)*	976
Bank of Bermuda (New York) Limited *(United States)*	1918
PT Bank BNP Lippo Indonesia *(Indonesia)*	691
Bank of Boston *(Argentina)*	19
Bank of Botswana *(Botswana)*	172
Bank Brussels Lambert *(Belgium)*	139
Bank Brussels Lambert *(China)*	270
Bank Brussels Lambert *(Germany)*	459
Bank Brussels Lambert *(Italy)*	777
Bank Brussels Lambert *(Japan)*	818
Bank Brussels Lambert *(Korea, South)*	904
Bank Brussels Lambert *(Malaysia)*	1042
Bank Brussels Lambert *(Netherlands)*	1109
Bank Brussels Lambert *(Singapore)*	1295
Bank Brussels Lambert *(Spain)*	1413
Bank Brussels Lambert *(Spain)*	1414
Bank Brussels Lambert *(Thailand)*	1586
Bank Brussels Lambert *(United Arab Emirates)*	1633
Bank Brussels Lambert *(United Kingdom)*	1671
Bank Brussels Lambert *(United States)*	1918
Bank Brussels Lambert (Jersey) Limited *(Channel Islands)*	243

A-8

BANK	PAGE NO
Bank Brussels Lambert SA *(Hong Kong, China)*	586
PT Bank Buana Indonesia *(Indonesia)*	692
Bank Bumiputra Malaysia Berhad *(Malaysia)*	1042
Bank Bumiputra Malaysia Berhad *(United Kingdom)*	1672
The Bank of NT Butterfield & Son Limited *(Hong Kong, China)*	586
Bank of Canada *(Canada)*	211
Bank Caspiyskiy *(Kazakhstan)*	892
Bank Central Asia *(United States)*	1919
Bank of Ceylon *(Sri Lanka)*	1445
Bank of Ceylon *(United Kingdom)*	1672
Bank of China *(China)*	270
Bank of China *(France)*	399
Bank of China *(Germany)*	460
Bank of China *(Hong Kong, China)*	587
Bank of China *(Panama)*	1174
Bank of China *(Singapore)*	1295
Bank of China *(United Kingdom)*	1673
Bank of China *(United States)*	1919
Bank of China (Canada) *(Canada)*	213
Bank of China International (UK) Limited *(United Kingdom)*	1673
Bank of China Luxembourg *(Luxembourg)*	976
Bank Clariden Heusser *(Switzerland)*	1476
Bank of Commerce & Development (Al Tegaryoon) *(Egypt)*	361
Bank of Commerce (L) Berhad *(Malaysia)*	1043
Bank of Commerce (M) Berhad *(Malaysia)*	1043
Bank of Communications *(China)*	271
Bank of Communications *(Singapore)*	1296
Bank of Communications *(United Kingdom)*	1673
Bank of Copenhagen *(Denmark)*	338
Bank Credit Lyonnais Indonesia *(Indonesia)*	692
Bank Creditanstalt SA *(Poland)*	1201
Bank of Crete *(Greece)*	560
Bank of Crete *(United Kingdom)*	1673
Bank of Cyprus Limited *(Cyprus)*	307
PT Bank Dagang Negara (PERSERO) *(Hong Kong, China)*	587
PT Bank Dagang Negara (PERSERO) *(Indonesia)*	693
PT Bank Dai-Ichi Kangyo Indonesia *(Indonesia)*	694
Bank Degroof *(Belgium)*	141
Bank der Österreichischen Postsparkasse AG *(Austria)*	78
Bank Duta *(Indonesia)*	694
The Bank of East Asia Limited *(China)*	271
The Bank of East Asia Limited *(Hong Kong, China)*	587
The Bank of East Asia Limited *(Malaysia)*	1044
The Bank of East Asia Limited *(Singapore)*	1296
The Bank of East Asia Limited *(United Kingdom)*	1673
The Bank of East Asia Limited *(United States)*	1919
The Bank of East Asia Limited *(Vietnam)*	2035
PT Bank Ekspor Impor Indonesia (PERSERO) *(Indonesia)*	695
Bank Ekspor Impor Indonesia (PERSERO) *(United Kingdom)*	1674
Bank of England *(United Kingdom)*	1637

BANK	PAGE NO
Bank for Foreign Economic Affairs (Vnesheconombank) *(Russian Federation)*	1252
Bank for Foreign Trade *(Russian Federation)*	1252
The Bank of Fukuoka Limited *(Japan)*	818
The Bank of Fukuoka Limited *(United Kingdom)*	1674
Bank für Arbeit und Wirtschaft AG *(Austria)*	79
Bank für Handel & Effekten *(Switzerland)*	1476
Bank für Kärnten und Steiermark AG *(Austria)*	79
Bank für Tirol und Vorarlberg AG *(Austria)*	80
Bank of Ghana *(Ghana)*	552
Bank of Greece *(Greece)*	556
Bank Guinness Mahon Flight AG *(Switzerland)*	1476
Bank Gutmann Aktiengesellschaft *(Austria)*	80
Bank of Guyana *(Guyana)*	576
Bank Handlowy w Warszawie SA *(Poland)*	1201
Bank Handlowy w Warszawie SA *(United Kingdom)*	1674
Bank Handlowy w Warszawie SA *(United States)*	1919
Bank Hapoalim BM *(Argentina)*	19
Bank Hapoalim BM *(Canada)*	213
Bank Hapoalim BM *(Israel)*	741
Bank Hapoalim BM *(Mexico)*	1081
Bank Hapoalim BM *(United Kingdom)*	1674
Bank Hapoalim BM *(Venezuela)*	2031
Bank Hapoalim (Switzerland) Limited *(Switzerland)*	1477
Bank of Hawaii *(Singapore)*	1296
Bank of Hawaii *(United States)*	1919
Bank Hofmann AG *(Switzerland)*	1477
Bank Hugo Kahn & Co AG *(Switzerland)*	1478
The Bank of Ikeda Limited *(Japan)*	819
Bank Imperial *(Russian Federation)*	1253
Bank of India *(India)*	678
Bank of India *(Singapore)*	1297
Bank of India *(United Kingdom)*	1675
Bank of India *(United States)*	1920
Bank Indonesia *(Indonesia)*	689
Bank Indonesia *(Japan)*	819
Bank Indonesia *(United Kingdom)*	1675
Bank Indonesia Raya *(Indonesia)*	695
Bank Insinger de Beaufort NV *(Netherlands)*	1109
Bank Internasional Indonesia *(India)*	678
PT Bank Internasional Indonesia Tbk *(Indonesia)*	696
Bank of Ireland *(Japan)*	819
Bank of Ireland Asset Management Limited *(Ireland)*	720
Bank of Ireland Asset Management (UK) Limited *(United Kingdom)*	1675
Bank of Ireland Group *(Ireland)*	720
Bank of Ireland Group Treasury Limited *(Ireland)*	721
Bank of Ireland Securities Services *(Ireland)*	721
Bank of Israel *(Israel)*	740
Bank J Vontobel & Co AG *(Switzerland)*	1478
Bank of Jamaica *(Jamaica)*	812
The Bank of Japan *(Japan)*	813
The Bank of Japan *(United Kingdom)*	1675
Bank of Jordan plc *(Jordan)*	886
Bank Julius Baer & Co Limited *(Switzerland)*	1478
Bank Julius Baer & Co Limited *(United Kingdom)*	1675

A-9

BANK	PAGE NO
Bank Julius Bär (Deutschland) AG *(Germany)*............	460
The Bank of Kansai Limited *(Japan)*........................	819
The Bank of Korea *(Hong Kong, China)*....................	587
The Bank of Korea *(Korea, South)*...........................	902
The Bank of Korea *(Singapore)*................................	1297
The Bank of Korea *(United Kingdom)*.......................	1676
The Bank of Korea *(United States)*..........................	1920
The Bank of Kuwait & the Middle East, KSC *(Kuwait)*..	934
The Bank of Kyoto Limited *(Japan)*..........................	820
The Bank of Kyoto Limited *(United Kingdom)*...........	1676
The Bank of Kyoto Limited *(United States)*..............	1920
Bank Labouchere NV *(Netherlands)*.........................	1110
Bank of Latvia *(Latvia)*..	941
Bank Leu Limited *(Argentina)*..................................	19
Bank Leu Limited *(Singapore)*.................................	1297
Bank Leu Limited *(Switzerland)*...............................	1479
Bank Leu Limited *(Uruguay)*...................................	2023
Bank Leumi *(Luxembourg)*......................................	977
Bank Leumi Le Israel BM *(Australia)*......................	38
Bank Leumi Le-Israel BM *(Israel)*...........................	742
Bank Leumi Le-Israel (Schweiz) *(Switzerland)*.........	1479
Bank Leumi (UK) plc *(United Kingdom)*..................	1676
Bank Leumi USA *(United States)*............................	1920
Bank Lips AG *(Switzerland)*....................................	1480
Bank of Lithuania *(Lithuania)*.................................	964
Bank Markazi Jomhouri Islami Iran *(Iran (Islamic Republic Of))*...	713
PT Bank Mashill Utama Tbk *(Indonesia)*..................	697
Bank of Mauritius *(Mauritius)*.................................	1074
Bank Mellat *(United Kingdom)*................................	1677
Bank Melli Iran *(Bahrain)*.......................................	113
Bank Melli Iran *(France)*..	399
Bank Melli Iran *(Germany)*.....................................	460
Bank Melli Iran *(Hong Kong, China)*.......................	588
Bank Melli Iran *(Iran (Islamic Republic Of))*............	713
Bank Melli Iran *(United Kingdom)*..........................	1677
Bank of Mongolia *(Mongolia)*..................................	1096
Bank of Montreal *(Canada)*.....................................	213
Bank of Montreal *(Japan)*.......................................	820
Bank of Montreal *(United Kingdom)*.......................	1677
Bank of Montreal Asia Limited *(Singapore)*.............	1297
Bank Morgan Stanley AG *(Switzerland)*..................	1481
Bank Muscat Al Ahli Al Omani SAOG *(Oman)*..........	1162
The Bank of Nagoya Limited *(Japan)*......................	821
Bank of Namibia *(Namibia)*....................................	1100
Bank of Nauru *(Nauru)*..	1102
Bank Nederlandse Gemeenten NV *(Netherlands)*.......	1110
PT Bank Negara Indonesia (Persero) Tbk *(Indonesia)*...	698
PT Bank Negara Indonesia (Persero) Tbk *(Singapore)*...	1298
PT Bank Negara Indonesia (Persero) TBK *(United Kingdom)*...	1678
Bank Negara Malaysia *(Malaysia)*............................	1034
Bank Negara Malaysia *(United Kingdom)*................	1678
Bank of New York - Inter Maritime Bank, Geneva *(Australia)*...	38

BANK	PAGE NO
Bank of New York - Inter Maritime Bank, Geneva *(Hong Kong, China)*...	588
Bank of New York - Inter Maritime Bank, Geneva *(Russian Federation)*...	1254
Bank of New York - Inter Maritime Bank, Geneva *(Switzerland)*...	1481
Bank of New York - Inter Maritime Bank, Geneva *(Uruguay)*...	2024
The Bank of New York *(Germany)*............................	460
The Bank of New York *(Japan)*................................	821
The Bank of New York *(Spain)*.................................	1414
The Bank of New York *(United Kingdom)*.................	1679
The Bank of New York *(United States)*....................	1921
Bank of New Zealand *(New Zealand)*.......................	1138
Bank of New Zealand *(Singapore)*...........................	1298
PT Bank NISP *(Indonesia)*......................................	699
The Bank of Nova Scotia *(Taiwan, Republic of China)*...	1558
The Bank of Nova Scotia Asia Limited *(Singapore)*...	1298
The Bank of Nova Scotia Berhad *(Malaysia)*............	1044
The Bank of Nova Scotia *(Argentina)*......................	19
The Bank of Nova Scotia *(Dominican Republic)*........	356
The Bank of Nova Scotia *(Hong Kong, China)*..........	588
The Bank of Nova Scotia *(Korea, South)*..................	904
The Bank of Nova Scotia *(United Kingdom)*.............	1680
The Bank of NT Butterfield & Son Limited *(Bermuda)*..	168
Bank of Okinawa Limited *(Japan)*...........................	821
Bank One Corporation *(United States)*.....................	1921
The Bank of Osaka Limited *(Japan)*........................	822
Bank of Overseas Chinese *(Taiwan, Republic of China)*...	1558
PT Bank Pembangunan Indonesia (PERSERO) *(Indonesia)*...	700
Bank Polska Kasa Opieki - Grupa Pekao SA *(Poland)*..	1202
Bank Polska Kasa Opieki SA *(France)*.....................	399
Bank Polska Kasa Opieki Tel-Aviv (Bank Pekao) Limited *(Israel)*..	743
Bank Prima Express *(Indonesia)*..............................	701
Bank Przemyslowo-Handlowy SA *(Poland)*..............	1203
Bank of Queensland Limited *(Australia)*..................	38
Bank Rozwoju Eksportu SA *(Poland)*.......................	1205
Bank SA *(Australia)*...	39
Bank Saderat Iran *(France)*....................................	399
Bank Saderat Iran *(Iran (Islamic Republic Of))*........	714
Bank Saderat Iran *(United Kingdom)*......................	1680
The Bank of Saga Limited *(Japan)*..........................	822
PT Bank Sakura Swadharma *(Indonesia)*.................	702
Bank Sal Oppenheim jr & Cie (Schweiz) AG *(Switzerland)*...	1482
Bank Sarasin & Cie *(Switzerland)*...........................	1482
Bank of Scotland *(Channel Islands)*.........................	243
Bank of Scotland *(Hong Kong, China)*.....................	588
Bank of Scotland *(United Kingdom)*........................	1681
Bank Sepah *(United Kingdom)*................................	1681
Bank of Singapore Limited *(Singapore)*...................	1299
Bank Slaski SA *(Poland)*..	1206

A-10

BANK	PAGE NO
Bank of Slovenia (Slovenia)	1370
PT Bank Société Générale (Indonesia)	702
PT Bank Sumitomo Niaga (Indonesia)	702
Bank of Taiwan (Hong Kong, China)	588
Bank of Taiwan (Japan)	822
Bank of Taiwan (Taiwan, Republic of China)	1559
Bank of Taiwan (United Kingdom)	1682
Bank of Taiwan (South Africa) Limited (South Africa)	1382
Bank of Tanzania (Tanzania, United Republic Of)	1580
Bank Tejarat (France)	399
Bank Tejarat (United Kingdom)	1682
Bank of Thailand (Thailand)	1580
Bank of Thailand (United Kingdom)	1682
Bank of the Ryukyus Limited (Japan)	822
PT Bank Tiara Asia (Indonesia)	702
Bank of Tokyo-Mitsubishi (Australia) Limited (Australia)	39
Bank of Tokyo-Mitsubishi (Canada) (Canada)	215
The Bank of Tokyo-Mitsubishi (Deutschland) AG (Germany)	460
The Bank of Tokyo-Mitsubishi (France) SA (France)	400
The Bank of Tokyo-Mitsubishi (Holland) NV (Netherlands)	1111
The Bank of Tokyo-Mitsubishi Limited (Argentina)	20
The Bank of Tokyo-Mitsubishi Limited (Austria)	81
The Bank of Tokyo-Mitsubishi Limited (Belgium)	141
The Bank of Tokyo-Mitsubishi Limited (Brazil)	191
The Bank of Tokyo-Mitsubishi Limited (Chile)	265
The Bank of Tokyo-Mitsubishi Limited (Indonesia)	704
The Bank of Tokyo-Mitsubishi Limited (Italy)	777
The Bank of Tokyo-Mitsubishi Limited (Kenya)	900
The Bank of Tokyo-Mitsubishi Limited (Portugal)	1229
The Bank of Tokyo-Mitsubishi Limited (United Arab Emirates)	1633
The Bank of Tokyo-Mitsubishi Limited (United Kingdom)	1682
The Bank of Tokyo-Mitsubishi Limited (United States)	1922
Bank of Tokyo-Mitsubishi (Luxembourg) SA (Luxembourg)	977
Bank of Tokyo-Mitsubishi (Malaysia) Berhad (Malaysia)	1044
Bank of Tokyo-Mitsubishi (Switzerland) Limited (Switzerland)	1483
Bank of Tokyo-Mitsubishi (Switzerland) Limited (Switzerland)	1484
The Bank of Tokyo-Mitsubishi (Japan)	822
Bank Turanalem (Kazakhstan)	893
Bank Universal (Indonesia)	704
Bank Utama (Malaysia) Berhad (Malaysia)	1045
Bank of Valletta International Limited (Malta)	1071
Bank of Valletta plc (Australia)	40
Bank of Valletta plc (Malta)	1072
Bank van de Nederlandse Antillen (Netherlands Antilles)	1136
Bank von Ernst & Cie AG (Switzerland)	1484
Bank von Ernst & Co Limited (Japan)	824

BANK	PAGE NO
Bank von Ernst & Co Limited (United Kingdom)	1682
Bank voor Zeeland NV (Netherlands)	1112
Bank Wegelin (Liechtenstein) AG (Liechtenstein)	962
Bank of Western Australia Limited (Australia)	40
Bank Windhoek Limited (Namibia)	1100
Bank Winter & Co AG (Austria)	81
Bank Wstopracy-Europejskej SA (Poland)	1206
Bank of Yokohama (Europe) SA (Belgium)	142
The Bank of Yokohama Limited (China)	271
The Bank of Yokohama Limited (Hong Kong, China)	589
The Bank of Yokohama Limited (Japan)	824
The Bank of Yokohama Limited (Singapore)	1299
The Bank of Yokohama Limited (Thailand)	1586
The Bank of Yokohama Limited (United Kingdom)	1682
The Bank of Yokohama Limited (United States)	1922
Bank Zachodni SA Wroclaw (Poland)	1206
Bank of Zambia (Zambia)	2042
Banka Celje dd (Slovenia)	1372
Banka Haná as (Czech Republic)	315
Banka Koper (Slovenia)	1373
Banka Land (Latvia)	944
Banka Société Générale dd (Slovenia)	1373
Banka Vipa dd (Slovenia)	1373
BankAmerica (United Kingdom)	1683
AB Bankas Hermis (Lithuania)	966
BankBoston (United Kingdom)	1684
BankBoston Corporation (United States)	1922
BankBoston NA (Hong Kong, China)	589
BankBoston NA (Japan)	826
Bankers Trust AG (Switzerland)	1485
Bankers Trust Australia Limited (Australia)	41
Bankers Trust Company (Bahrain)	113
Bankers Trust Company (Egypt)	361
Bankers Trust Company (Hong Kong, China)	589
Bankers Trust Company (Japan)	826
Bankers Trust Company (Poland)	1206
Bankers Trust Company (Singapore)	1299
Bankers Trust Company (Spain)	1414
Bankers Trust Company (Thailand)	1586
Bankers Trust Corporation (United States)	1923
Bankers Trust Finanziaria SpA (Italy)	777
Bankers Trust International (Asia) Limited (Singapore)	1299
Bankers Trust International plc (Germany)	461
Bankers Trust International plc (Italy)	777
Bankers Trust International plc (United Kingdom)	1684
Bankers Trust Luxembourg SA (Luxembourg)	978
Bankgesellschaft Berlin (United Kingdom)	1686
Bankgesellschaft Berlin AG (Germany)	462
Bankgesellschaft Berlin International SA (Luxembourg)	978
Bankgesellschaft Berlin (Ireland) plc (Ireland)	722
Bankhaus Carl F Plump & Co (Germany)	463
Bankhaus Hermann Lampe KG (Germany)	463
Bankhaus Krentschker & Co (Austria)	81
Bankhaus Reuschel & Co (Germany)	464
BANKINTER SA (Spain)	1414

A-11

BANK	PAGE NO
Banorte *(Mexico)*	1081
Banque AIG *(France)*	400
Banque AIG *(United Kingdom)*	1687
Banque Artesia Nederland NV *(Netherlands)*	1112
Banque Audi (France) SA *(France)*	400
Banque Audi (Luxembourg) SA *(Luxembourg)*	979
Banque Audi SAL *(Lebanon)*	954
Banque Audi (Suisse) SA *(Switzerland)*	1485
Banque Audi (Suisse) SA *(United States)*	1923
Banque Banespa International SA *(Luxembourg)*	979
Banque Banorabe *(United Kingdom)*	1687
Banque Banorabe SA *(France)*	401
Banque Banorient (Suisse) *(Switzerland)*	1486
Banque Baring Brothers (Suisse) SA *(Switzerland)*	1486
Banque Baumann & Cie SA *(Luxembourg)*	979
Banque Belgolaise SA *(Belgium)*	142
Banque Bonhôte & Cie SA *(Switzerland)*	1486
Banque Bruxelles Lambert France *(France)*	401
Banque Bruxelles Lambert (Suisse) SA *(Switzerland)*	1486
Banque Cantonale du Valais *(Switzerland)*	1487
Banque Cantonale de Genève *(Switzerland)*	1487
Banque Cantonale Vaudoise *(Switzerland)*	1488
Banque Carnegie Luxembourg SA *(Luxembourg)*	980
Banque Centrale des Etats de l'Afrique de l'Ouest *(Benin)*	167
Banque Centrale des Etats de l'Afrique de l'Ouest *(Burkina Faso)*	211
Banque Centrale des Etats de l'Afrique de l'Ouest *(Cote D'Ivoire)*	293
Banque Centrale des Etats de l'Afrique de l'Ouest *(Guinea-Bissau)*	575
Banque Centrale des Etats de l'Afrique de l'Ouest *(Mali)*	1071
Banque Centrale des Etats de l'Afrique de l'Ouest *(Niger)*	1144
Banque Centrale des Etats de l'Afrique de l'Ouest *(Senegal)*	1284
Banque Centrale des Etats de l'Afrique de l'Ouest *(Togo)*	1599
Banque Centrale du Luxembourg *(Luxembourg)*	971
Banque Centrale de Madagascar *(Madagascar)*	1033
Banque Centrale de Tunisie *(Tunisia)*	1602
Banque Colbert (Luxembourg) SA *(Luxembourg)*	980
Banque de Commerce et de Placements SA *(Luxembourg)*	981
Banque de Commerce et de Placements SA *(Switzerland)*	1489
Banque de Commerce et de Placements SA *(Turkey)*	1607
Banque Commerciale du Maroc *(Morocco)*	1097
Banque Commerciale pour l'Europe du Nord-Eurobank *(France)*	402
Banque Continentale du Luxembourg SA *(Luxembourg)*	981
Banque Courtois *(France)*	402
Banque CPR *(France)*	402
Banque CPR *(United Kingdom)*	1688

BANK	PAGE NO
Banque d'Affaires du Liban et d'Outre-Mer *(Lebanon)*	954
Banque Degroof Luxembourg SA *(Luxembourg)*	981
Banque Delen & de Schaetzen SA *(Belgium)*	142
Banque de Développement Economique de Tunisie *(Tunisia)*	1603
Banque Dewaay SA *(Belgium)*	143
Banque Dewaay SA Succursale de Luxembourg *(Luxembourg)*	982
Banque d'Hawaii (Vanuatu) Limited *(Vanuatu)*	2028
Banque du Caire *(Egypt)*	362
Banque du Caire Barclays International SAE *(Egypt)*	362
Banque du Caire et de Paris SAE *(Egypt)*	362
Banque du Crédit Agricole (Suisse) *(Switzerland)*	1490
Banque du Liban et d'Outre-Mer SAL *(Cyprus)*	308
Banque du Liban et d'Outre-Mer SAL *(Lebanon)*	954
Banque du Louvre *(France)*	403
Banque Dupuy de Parseval *(France)*	403
Banque Edouard Constant *(Monaco)*	1093
Banque Edouard Constant *(United Kingdom)*	1688
Banque Edouard Constant SA *(Switzerland)*	1490
Banque et Caisse d'Epargne de l'Etat, Luxembourg *(Luxembourg)*	983
Banque et Caisse d'Epargne de l'Etat Luxembourg *(Singapore)*	1299
Banque Européenne pour l'Amérique Latine (BEAL) SA *(Belgium)*	143
Banque Européene d'Investissement *(Luxembourg)*	985
Banque Extérieure d'Algérie *(Algeria)*	1
Banque Fédérative du Crédit Mutuel *(France)*	404
Banque Française de l'Orient *(France)*	404
Banque Française de l'Orient *(Monaco)*	1093
Banque Française de l'Orient *(United Kingdom)*	1688
Banque de France *(France)*	395
Banque Franck SA *(Switzerland)*	1491
Banque Franco Yougoslave *(France)*	405
Banque Générale du Luxembourg *(Hong Kong, China)*	590
Banque Générale du Luxembourg SA *(Germany)*	464
Banque Générale du Luxembourg SA *(Italy)*	778
Banque Générale du Luxembourg SA *(Luxembourg)*	984
Banque Générale du Luxembourg (Suisse) SA *(Switzerland)*	1491
Banque de l'Habitat *(Tunisia)*	1604
Banque Hapoalim (Luxembourg) SA *(Luxembourg)*	987
Banque Hapoalim (Suisse) SA Luxembourg *(Luxembourg)*	987
Banque Hervet *(France)*	405
Banque IBJ (France) SA *(France)*	406
Banque Industrielle et Mobiliere Privée - BIMP *(France)*	406
Banque Internationale à Luxembourg SA *(Luxembourg)*	988
Banque Internationale à Luxembourg BIL (Asia) Limited *(Singapore)*	1300
Banque Internationale à Luxembourg SA *(United Kingdom)*	1689

BANK	PAGE NO
Banque Internationale Arabe de Tunisie *(Tunisia)*	1604
Banque Julius Baer (Geneve) SA *(Switzerland)*	1491
Banque Lehman Brothers SA *(France)*	406
Banque Leu (Luxembourg) SA *(Luxembourg)*	988
Banque Leumi France SA *(France)*	407
Banque de Luxembourg SA *(Luxembourg)*	989
Banque Misr *(Egypt)*	363
Banque Misr *(France)*	407
Banque Misr-Liban SAL *(Lebanon)*	955
Banque Nagelmackers 1747 SA *(Belgium)*	143
Banque Nationale de Belgique *(Luxembourg)*	990
Banque Nationale de Belgique SA *(Belgium)*	131
Banque Nationale d'Algérie *(Algeria)*	2
Banque Nationale de Djibouti *(Djibouti)*	355
Banque Nationale du Rwanda *(Rwanda)*	1274
Banque Nationale de Grèce (France) *(France)*	408
Banque Nationale de Paris *(Argentina)*	20
Banque Nationale de Paris *(France)*	408
Banque Nationale de Paris *(Greece)*	561
Banque Nationale de Paris *(Hong Kong, China)*	590
Banque Nationale de Paris *(Hungary)*	662
Banque Nationale de Paris *(Ireland)*	722
Banque Nationale de Paris *(Israel)*	743
Banque Nationale de Paris *(Italy)*	778
Banque Nationale de Paris *(Malaysia)*	1045
Banque Nationale de Paris *(Mexico)*	1081
Banque Nationale de Paris *(Netherlands)*	1112
Banque Nationale de Paris *(Netherlands)*	1113
Banque Nationale de Paris *(New Zealand)*	1139
Banque Nationale de Paris *(Norway)*	1148
Banque Nationale de Paris *(Philippines)*	1187
Banque Nationale de Paris *(Portugal)*	1229
Banque Nationale de Paris *(Singapore)*	1300
Banque Nationale de Paris *(South Africa)*	1383
Banque Nationale de Paris *(United Arab Emirates)*	1633
Banque Nationale de Paris *(United Kingdom)*	1689
Banque Nationale de Paris *(United States)*	1923
Banque Nationale de Paris *(Uruguay)*	2024
Banque Nationale de Paris *(Vietnam)*	2035
Banque Nationale de Paris - Intercontinentale SA *(Cyprus)*	308
Banque Nationale de Paris (Canada) *(Canada)*	216
Banque Nationale de Paris (Luxembourg) SA *(Luxembourg)*	990
Banque Nationale de Paris Panamá SA *(Panama)*	1174
Banque Nationale de Paris SA *(Belgium)*	144
Banque Nationale de Paris (Switzerland) Limited *(Switzerland)*	1492
Banque Nationale pour le Développement Economique - BNDE *(Morocco)*	1097
Banque Nationale Suisse *(Switzerland)*	1465
Banque de Neuflize, Schlumberger, Mallet *(France)*	410
Banque Nomura France *(France)*	411
Banque OBC Odier Bungener Courvoisier *(France)*	411
Banque Paribas *(Czech Republic)*	315
Banque Paribas *(Italy)*	778
Banque Paribas *(Lebanon)*	955
Banque Paribas Luxembourg *(Luxembourg)*	991

BANK	PAGE NO
Banque Paribas (Suisse) SA *(Switzerland)*	1493
Banque Parisienne de Credit *(France)*	411
Banque Pasche SA *(Switzerland)*	1493
Banque Pictet (Luxembourg) SA *(Luxembourg)*	992
Banque Privée Edmond de Rothschild SA *(Luxembourg)*	992
Banque Privée Edmond de Rothschild *(United Kingdom)*	1689
Banque Regionale du Nord *(France)*	411
Banque de la République d'Haiti *(Haiti)*	576
Banque de la Republique du Burundi *(Burundi)*	211
Banque Saradar France SA *(France)*	411
Banque Saradar SAL *(Lebanon)*	956
Banque SBA *(France)*	412
Banque Société Générale Vostok *(Russian Federation)*	1254
Banque SOFIREC *(France)*	412
Banque Sudameris *(Colombia)*	288
Banque Sudameris *(France)*	412
Banque Sudameris *(Germany)*	464
Banque Sudameris *(Hong Kong, China)*	590
Banque Sudameris *(India)*	679
Banque Sudameris *(Japan)*	826
Banque Sudameris *(Mexico)*	1081
Banque Sudameris *(Monaco)*	1093
Banque Sudameris *(Panama)*	1174
Banque Sudameris *(Peru)*	1182
Banque Sudameris *(Portugal)*	1229
Banque Sudameris *(Spain)*	1415
Banque Sudameris *(United Kingdom)*	1690
Banque Sudameris *(United States)*	1924
Banque Sudameris *(Venezuela)*	2031
Banque Tardy, de Watteville & Cie SA *(Switzerland)*	1493
Banque Trad-Crédit Lyonnais (France) SA *(France)*	413
Banque Transatlantique SA/Banque Transatlantique (Jersey) Limited *(United Kingdom)*	1690
Banque Tuniso-Koweitienne De Developpement *(Tunisia)*	1605
Banque Vernes *(France)*	413
Banque Worms *(Australia)*	41
Banque Worms *(France)*	413
Banque Worms *(Hong Kong, China)*	591
Banque Worms *(Peru)*	1182
Barclays Asset Management France *(France)*	414
Barclays Bank plc *(China)*	272
Barclays Bank plc *(Colombia)*	288
Barclays Bank plc *(Cyprus)*	308
Barclays Bank plc *(Czech Republic)*	315
Barclays Bank plc *(Germany)*	464
Barclays Bank plc *(Greece)*	561
Barclays Bank plc *(Ireland)*	722
Barclays Bank plc *(Portugal)*	1230
Barclays Bank plc *(Singapore)*	1301
Barclays Bank plc *(United Arab Emirates)*	1633
Barclays Bank plc *(United Kingdom)*	1690
Barclays Bank plc *(United States)*	1924
Barclays Bank plc/Barclays Capital Group *(Japan)*	826

A-13

BANK	PAGE NO
Barclays Bank SA *(Spain)*.	1415
Barclays Bank of South Africa Limited *(South Africa)*.	1383
Barclays Bank (Suisse) SA *(Switzerland)*.	1493
Barclays Capital *(France)*.	414
Barclays Capital Asia Limited *(Hong Kong, China)*.	591
Barclays Capital Développement SA *(France)*.	414
Barclays Capital Securities Limited *(United Kingdom)*.	1690
Barclays Global Investors *(Japan)*.	827
Barclays Global Investors *(United States)*.	1925
Barclays Global Investors Limited *(United Kingdom)*.	1692
Barclays International Finanziaria SpA *(Italy)*.	779
Barclays Mercantile Business Finance Limited *(United Kingdom)*.	1693
Barclays Mercantile Highland Finance Limited *(United Kingdom)*.	1694
Barclays Private Equity Limited *(United Kingdom)*.	1694
Barclays Trust & Banking Company (Japan) Limited *(Japan)*.	827
Barex World Trade Corporation *(United States)*.	1925
Baring Asset Management Limited *(United Kingdom)*.	1694
Baring Brothers Burrows & Co Limited *(Australia)*.	41
Baring Brothers (Deutschland) GmbH *(Germany)*.	464
Baring Brothers (España) SA *(Spain)*.	1416
Baring Brothers (Italia) Srl *(Italy)*.	779
Baring Brothers Limited *(Hong Kong, China)*.	591
Baring Brothers Limited *(Japan)*.	827
Barings France SA *(France)*.	415
Barings (Guernsey) Limited *(Channel Islands)*.	243
Barings (Ireland) Limited *(Ireland)*.	723
Basellandschaftliche Kantonalbank *(Switzerland)*.	1493
Bashcreditbank *(Russian Federation)*.	1254
Bashcreditbank *(United Kingdom)*.	1694
Basler Kantonalbank *(Switzerland)*.	1494
Baumann & Cie Banquiers *(Switzerland)*.	1494
Bayerisch-Bulgarische Handelsbank *(Bulgaria)*.	201
Bayerische Handelsbank AG *(Germany)*.	465
Bayerische Hypo-und Vereinsbank AG *(France)*.	415
Bayerische Hypo-und Vereinsbank AG *(Germany)*.	465
Bayerische Hypo-und Vereinsbank AG *(Japan)*.	827
Bayerische Hypo-und Vereinsbank AG *(Singapore)*.	1302
Bayerische Hypo-und Vereinsbank AG *(Spain)*.	1416
Bayerische Hypo-und Vereinsbank AG *(United Kingdom)*.	1695
Bayerische Landesanstalt für Aufbaufinanzierung *(Germany)*.	465
Bayerische Landesbank *(Hong Kong, China)*.	591
Bayerische Landesbank *(Japan)*.	828
Bayerische Landesbank *(Japan)*.	827
Bayerische Landesbank *(Korea, South)*.	905
Bayerische Landesbank *(Singapore)*.	1302
Bayerische Landesbank Girozentrale *(Czech Republic)*.	315
Bayerische Landesbank Girozentrale *(Germany)*.	466
Bayerische Landesbank Girozentrale *(United Kingdom)*.	1695

BANK	PAGE NO
Bayerische Landesbank International SA *(Luxembourg)*.	992
Bayerische Landesbank (Schweiz) AG *(Switzerland)*.	1494
Bayernhypo Finance NV *(Netherlands)*.	1113
BB Securities Limited *(United Kingdom)*.	1696
BBL Australia Limited *(Australia)*.	41
BBL Ireland *(Ireland)*.	723
BBL Lille SA *(France)*.	415
BBL Securities Limited *(United Kingdom)*.	1697
BBV - Banco Ganadero SA *(Colombia)*.	288
BBV Banco Francés SA *(Argentina)*.	20
BBV LatInvest Securities Limited *(United Kingdom)*.	1698
BBV Privanza Bank (Jersey) Limited *(Channel Islands)*.	244
BBV Privanza Bank (Switzerland) Limited *(Switzerland)*.	1494
BBV Securities Inc *(United States)*.	1926
BC Partners Limited *(United Kingdom)*.	1698
BCA Finance Limited *(Hong Kong, China)*.	592
BCEN-EUROBANK *(France)*.	415
BCH Benelux SA *(Belgium)*.	144
BDL Banco di Lugano *(Switzerland)*.	1495
BEAL Venezuela *(Venezuela)*.	2031
Bear Stearns & Co Inc *(United States)*.	1926
Bear Stearns Asia Limited *(Hong Kong, China)*.	592
Bear Stearns Beijing Representative Office *(China)*.	272
Bear Stearns International Limited *(United Kingdom)*.	1698
Bear Stearns (Japan) Limited *(Japan)*.	828
Beeson Gregory Limited *(United Kingdom)*.	1699
Beirut Riyad Bank SAL *(United Kingdom)*.	1699
Belagroprombank *(Belarus)*.	126
Belarussian Bank of Development *(Belarus)*.	126
Belarussian Exchange Bank *(Belarus)*.	127
Belgo-Factors NV *(Belgium)*.	144
BELGOLAISE SA *(United Kingdom)*.	1699
Joint Stock Company 'Belkombank' *(Belarus)*.	127
Belpromstroibank *(Belarus)*.	128
Belvnesheconombank *(Belarus)*.	129
Beogradska Banka AD Beograd *(Yugoslavia)*.	2040
Berenberg Bank *(Germany)*.	469
Berenberg Bank *(Luxembourg)*.	993
Berenberg Finance Limited *(Switzerland)*.	1495
Alfred Berg Finland Oy Ab *(Finland)*.	387
Berkshire Capital Corporation *(United States)*.	1927
Berkshire Partners LLC *(United States)*.	1927
Berliner Bank AG *(Albania)*.	1
Berliner Bank AG *(Argentina)*.	21
Berliner Bank AG *(Chile)*.	265
Berliner Bank AG *(Egypt)*.	363
Berliner Bank AG *(France)*.	416
Berliner Bank AG *(Hong Kong, China)*.	593
Berliner Bank AG *(Hungary)*.	662
Berliner Bank AG *(Poland)*.	1206
Berliner Bank AG *(Russian Federation)*.	1254
Berliner Bank AG *(Ukraine)*.	1628
Berliner Bank AG *(United Kingdom)*.	1700
Berliner Bank AG *(Uzbekistan)*.	2027

A-14

BANK	PAGE NO
Berliner Bank AG *(Vietnam)*	2035
Bermuda Commercial Bank Limited *(Bermuda)*	169
Bermuda International Investment Management Limited (BIIML) *(Bermuda)*	169
Bermuda International Investment Management (Europe) Limited *(United Kingdom)*	1700
Bermuda Monetary Authority *(Bermuda)*	167
Bermuda Trust (Dublin) Limited *(Ireland)*	723
Bermuda Trust (Jersey) Limited *(Channel Islands)*	244
Berner Kantonalbank *(Switzerland)*	1495
Beta Capital SA *(Spain)*	1416
Beta Securities SA *(Greece)*	562
BFC Banque Financière de la Cité *(Switzerland)*	1496
BfG Bank AG *(Germany)*	469
BfG Bank AG *(United Kingdom)*	1700
BfG Bank Luxembourg SA *(Luxembourg)*	993
BFI - Banque de Financement et d'Investissement SA *(Switzerland)*	1496
BG BANK A/S *(Denmark)*	339
BG Bank International SA *(Luxembourg)*	993
BGL Finance (Asia) Limited *(Hong Kong, China)*	593
BHC Securities Inc *(United States)*	1927
BHF Securities Corp *(United States)*	1928
BHF-BANK *(India)*	679
BHF-BANK *(South Africa)*	1383
BHF-BANK *(Spain)*	1416
BHF-BANK *(Vietnam)*	2035
BHF-BANK AG *(Germany)*	471
BHF-BANK AG *(Hong Kong, China)*	593
BHF-BANK AG *(Singapore)*	1303
BHF-BANK AG *(United Kingdom)*	1700
BHF-BANK International SA *(Luxembourg)*	994
BHF-Bank (Jersey) Limited *(Channel Islands)*	244
BHF-BANK (Schweiz) AG *(Switzerland)*	1497
BHF-Finance (Netherlands) BV *(Netherlands)*	1113
BICE Fondos Mutuos SA *(Chile)*	265
BII Finance Company Limited *(Hong Kong, China)*	593
Bikuben Dublin Limited *(Ireland)*	723
Bikuben Girobank A/S *(Denmark)*	339
Bilbao Bizkaia Kutxa *(Spain)*	1416
BlueStone Capital Partners LP *(United States)*	1928
BMO Nesbitt Burns Inc *(Canada)*	216
BMO Nesbitt Burns International Limited *(United Kingdom)*	1701
BMO Nesbitt Burns Securities Inc *(United States)*	1929
BNC - Banco Nacional de Crédito Imobiliário SA *(Portugal)*	1230
BNP Arbitrage *(France)*	416
BNP Bahrain *(Bahrain)*	113
BNP BIBF *(Thailand)*	1586
BNP Finance *(France)*	416
BNP Hong Kong *(Hong Kong, China)*	594
BNP Securities (Japan) Limited *(Japan)*	828
BNP-Dresdner Bank (Bulgaria) AD *(Bulgaria)*	201
BNP-Dresdner Bank (CR) as *(Czech Republic)*	315
BNP-Dresdner Bank (Hungaria) Rt *(Hungary)*	663
BNP-Dresdner Bank (Polska) SA *(Poland)*	1206
BNP-Dresdner Bank (ZAO) *(Russian Federation)*	1254

BANK	PAGE NO
BNP-Dresdner Bank (ZAO) *(Russian Federation)*	1255
BNP-España *(Spain)*	1417
Board of Governors of Federal Reserve System *(United States)*	1908
Bolsa Mexicana de Valores SA de CV *(Mexico)*	1082
Bondpartners SA *(Switzerland)*	1497
Boram Bank *(Hong Kong, China)*	594
Boram Bank *(Korea, South)*	905
Bozano, Simonsen Latin America *(Argentina)*	21
Bozano, Simonsen Securities Inc *(United States)*	1929
Bozano, Simonsen (UK) Limited *(United Kingdom)*	1702
BRED Banque Populaire *(France)*	416
Bremer Landesbank Capital Markets plc *(United Kingdom)*	1703
Bremer Landesbank Kreditanstalt Oldenburg - Girozentrale- *(Germany)*	474
Bridport & Cie SA *(Switzerland)*	1498
Bridport & Co (Jersey) Limited *(Channel Islands)*	245
Brinson Partners Inc *(United States)*	1929
British Arab Commercial Bank Limited *(Lebanon)*	956
British Arab Commercial Bank Limited *(Morocco)*	1098
British Arab Commercial Bank Limited *(United Kingdom)*	1703
The British Bank of the Middle East *(Bahrain)*	113
The British Bank of the Middle East *(Channel Islands)*	245
The British Bank of the Middle East *(Lebanon)*	956
The British Bank of the Middle East *(Qatar)*	1240
The British Bank of the Middle East *(Switzerland)*	1498
The British Bank of the Middle East *(United Arab Emirates)*	1634
British Credit Trust *(United Kingdom)*	1703
The British Linen Bank Limited *(United Kingdom)*	1704
Brockhouse & Cooper Inc *(Canada)*	216
Brown Brothers Harriman & Co *(Japan)*	829
Brown Brothers Harriman & Co *(United States)*	1930
Brown Brothers Harriman Fund Administration Services (Ireland) Limited *(Ireland)*	724
Brown Brothers Harriman Limited *(United Kingdom)*	1704
Brown Brothers Harriman Services AG *(Switzerland)*	1498
Brown Brothers Harriman Trustee Services (Ireland) Limited *(Ireland)*	724
Brown, Shipley & Company Limited *(United Kingdom)*	1704
Brunei Currency Board *(Brunei)*	200
BSI-Banca della Svizzera Italiana *(Argentina)*	21
BSI-Banca della Svizzera Italiana *(Switzerland)*	1498
BSI-Banca della Svizzera Italiana *(United Kingdom)*	1705
BSI-Banca della Svizzera Italiana *(Uruguay)*	2024
BSN - Banco Santander de Negócios Portugal SA *(Portugal)*	1230
BSN Commercial Bank (Malaysia) Berhad *(Malaysia)*	1045
BT Alex.Brown Incorporated *(United States)*	1930
BT Alex.Brown NZ Limited *(New Zealand)*	1139
BT Asia Limited *(Hong Kong, China)*	595
BT Asia Securities Limited *(Japan)*	829

A-15

BANK	PAGE NO
BT Australia (Hong Kong) Limited *(Hong Kong, China)*	595
BT Funds Management Asia Limited *(Hong Kong, China)*	595
BT Trustee Company (Ireland) Limited *(Ireland)*	724
BTM Finanziaria Italia *(Italy)*	779
Buchanan Capital Management Limited *(United Kingdom)*	1705
Budapest Bank Limited *(Hungary)*	663
BULBANK *(Austria)*	81
BULBANK *(Germany)*	475
BULBANK *(United Kingdom)*	1705
BULBANK Ltd *(Bulgaria)*	202
Bulgarian National Bank *(Bulgaria)*	201
Bulgarian Post Bank Limited *(Bulgaria)*	202
Bulgarian Russian Investment Bank plc *(Bulgaria)*	203
Bumi Daya International Finance Limited *(Hong Kong, China)*	595
Bunadarbanki Islands *(Iceland)*	676
Bunting Warburg Inc *(Canada)*	216
Bunting Warburg Inc *(Canada)*	217
Burdett Buckeridge & Young *(United Kingdom)*	1705
Burgan Bank SAK *(Kuwait)*	935
Bursamex, Casa de Bolsa SA de CV *(Mexico)*	1082
Butterfield Trust (Hong Kong) Limited *(Hong Kong, China)*	596
BW Bank (Ireland) plc *(Ireland)*	724
Byblos Bank Belgium SA *(France)*	416
Byblos Bank Belgium SA *(United Kingdom)*	1706
Byblos Bank Europe *(United Kingdom)*	1706
Byblos Bank Europe SA *(Belgium)*	144
BZW Securities Limited *(Channel Islands)*	245
CA IB Financial Advisers SA	1207
CA IB Investmentbank AG *(Austria)*	81
CA IB Securities Limited *(Hungary)*	664
CA IB Securities SA *(Poland)*	1207
CAB SpA *(Italy)*	779
Caboto Holding SIM SpA *(Italy)*	779
Cairo Amman Bank *(Jordan)*	887
Caisse Centrale des Banques Populaires *(France)*	417
Caisse Centrale des Banques Populaires *(Germany)*	475
Caisse Centrale des Banques Populaires *(Hong Kong, China)*	596
Caisse Centrale des Banques Populaires *(Italy)*	781
Caisse Centrale des Banques Populaires *(Poland)*	1207
Caisse Centrale des Banques Populaires *(Spain)*	1417
Caisse Centrale des Banques Populaires *(United Kingdom)*	1706
Caisse Centrale des Banques Populaires *(United States)*	1930
Caisse Centrale Desjardins *(Canada)*	217
Caisse Centrale Raiffeisen *(Luxembourg)*	994
Caisse Centrale de Réescompte *(France)*	417
Caisse des Dépôts et Consignations GmbH *(Germany)*	475

BANK	PAGE NO
Caixa Central de Crédito Agrícola Mútuo CRL *(Portugal)*	1231
Caixa d'Estalvis de Catalunya *(Spain)*	1417
Caixa Economica Montepio Geral *(Portugal)*	1231
Caixa Geral de Depósitos *(France)*	418
Caixa Geral de Depositos *(Portugal)*	1232
Caixa Geral de Depositos SA *(Portugal)*	1232
La Caixa *(Spain)*	1419
Caixa Manresa *(Spain)*	1419
Caja de Ahorros del Mediterraneo *(Spain)*	1420
Caja de Ahorros de Galicia *(Spain)*	1420
Caja de Ahorros de Galicia *(United Kingdom)*	1706
Caja de Ahorros de la Inmaculada de Aragón *(Spain)*	1421
Caja de Ahorros de Manlleu *(Spain)*	1423
Caja de Ahorros Municipal de Vigo - CAIXAVIGO *(Spain)*	1423
Caja de Ahorros de Murcia *(Spain)*	1423
Caja de Ahorros de Navarra *(Spain)*	1424
Caja de Ahorros de Pollença *(Spain)*	1424
Caja de Ahorros Provincial de Guadalajara *(Spain)*	1424
Caja de Ahorros de Santander y Cantabria *(Spain)*	1424
Caja de Ahorros de Valencia, Castellón y Alicante *(Spain)*	1424
Caja de Ahorros de Vitoria y Alava *(Spain)*	1425
Caja de Ahorros y Monte de Piedad del Círculo Católico de Obreros de Burgos *(Spain)*	1425
Caja de Ahorros y Monte de Piedad de Extremadura *(Spain)*	1426
Caja de Ahorros y Monte de Piedad de Guipuzkoa y San Sebastián *(Spain)*	1426
Caja de Ahorros y Monte de Piedad Municipal de Pamplona *(Spain)*	1426
Caja de Ahorros y Monte de Piedad de Ontinyent *(Spain)*	1427
Caja de Ahorros y Monte de Piedad de Segovia *(Spain)*	1428
Caja de Burgos *(Spain)*	1428
Caja General de Ahorros de Canarias *(Spain)*	1429
Caja General de Granada *(Spain)*	1429
Caja Insular de Ahorros de Canarias *(Spain)*	1429
Caja Laboral Popular *(Spain)*	1430
Caja Madrid *(Spain)*	1430
Camara de Liquidacao e Custodia *(Brazil)*	191
Campbell Lutyens & Co Limited *(United Kingdom)*	1706
Canada Trust Company *(Canada)*	218
Canadian Eastern Finance Limited *(Hong Kong, China)*	596
Canadian Imperial Bank of Commerce *(China)*	272
Canadian Imperial Bank of Commerce *(Hong Kong, China)*	596
Canadian Imperial Bank of Commerce *(Japan)*	829
Canadian Imperial Bank of Commerce *(Singapore)*	1303
Canadian Imperial Bank of Commerce *(Switzerland)*	1499
Canadian Imperial Bank of Commerce (Switzerland) SA *(Switzerland)*	1499
Canadian Western Bank *(Canada)*	219
Canara Bank *(India)*	679

A-16

BANK	PAGE NO
Canara Bank *(United Kingdom)*	1706
Canto Consulting *(Switzerland)*	1499
Cantonal Bank of Berne *(Switzerland)*	1500
Cantonal Bank of Saint Gall *(Switzerland)*	1501
Cantonalbank of Fribourg *(Switzerland)*	1501
Cantor Fitzgerald & Co *(United States)*	1930
Cantor Fitzgerald Associates LP *(United States)*	1931
Cantor Fitzgerald International *(United Kingdom)*	1706
Cantor Fitzgerald Partners *(United States)*	1931
Cantor Fitzgerald Securities *(United States)*	1931
Cantor Fitzgerald Shoken Kaisha Limited *(Japan)*	830
Cantrade Private Bank Switzerland (CI) Limited *(Channel Islands)*	245
Cape of Good Hope Bank Limited *(South Africa)*	1383
James Capel SA *(France)*	418
Capital Trust Limited *(India)*	679
Caradas Ireland *(Ireland)*	724
Cargill Financial Markets *(United Kingdom)*	1707
CARIPLO SA - Cassa di Risparmio delle Provincie Lombarde SpA *(Belgium)*	145
CARIPLO - Cassa di Risparmio delle Provincie Lombarde SpA *(China)*	272
CARIPLO - Cassa di Risparmio delle Provincie Lombarde SpA *(Greece)*	563
CARIPLO - Cassa di Risparmio delle Provincie Lombarde SpA *(Hong Kong, China)*	597
CARIPLO - Cassa di Risparmio delle Provincie Lombarde SpA *(Italy)*	781
CARIPLO - Cassa di Risparmio delle Provincie Lombarde SpA *(Japan)*	830
CARIPLO - Cassa di Risparmio delle Provincie Lombarde *(Spain)*	1431
CARIPLO - Cassa di Risparmio delle Provincie Lombarde SpA *(United States)*	1931
Cariplo Bank International SA *(Luxembourg)*	995
Cariplo Banque SA *(France)*	418
CARIPRATO Cassa di Risparmio di Prato SpA *(Italy)*	781
CARIT - Cassa di Risparmio di Terni e Narni SpA *(Italy)*	782
Cariverona Banca SpA *(Italy)*	782
Cariverona Banca SpA *(United Kingdom)*	1707
Carl Kliem & Co *(Germany)*	476
Carnegie Asset Management Finland Limited *(Finland)*	388
Carnegie Bank A/S *(Denmark)*	340
Carnegie Fondkommission *(Sweden)*	1453
WI Carr Indosuez Capital Asia Limited *(Hong Kong, China)*	597
Casa de Bolsa Arka SA de CV *(Mexico)*	1082
Cassa di Risparmio di Alessandria *(Italy)*	783
Cassa di Risparmio di Bolzano SpA *(Italy)*	783
Cassa Risparmio Carpi SpA *(Italy)*	784
Cassa di Risparmio di Cento SpA *(Italy)*	785
Cassa di Risparmio di Cesena SpA *(Italy)*	785
Cassa di Risparmio di Firenze *(United States)*	1931
Cassa di Risparmio di Firenze SpA *(Italy)*	785

BANK	PAGE NO
Cassa di Risparmio di Firenze SpA *(United Kingdom)*	1708
Cassa di Risparmio di Forli *(Italy)*	786
Cassa di Risparmio di Fossano SpA *(Italy)*	786
Cassa di Risparmio di Imola SpA *(Italy)*	786
Cassa di Risparmio in Bologna SpA *(Italy)*	786
Cassa di Risparmio di Padova e Rovigo SpA *(Italy)*	787
Cassa di Risparmio di Parma e Piacenza *(Italy)*	787
Cassa di Risparmio di Pisa SpA *(Italy)*	788
Cassa di Risparmio di Pistoia e Pescia SpA *(Italy)*	788
Cassa di Risparmio di Ravenna SpA *(Italy)*	788
Cassa di Risparmio di Reggio Emilia SpA *(Italy)*	788
Cassa di Risparmio di San Miniato SpA *(Italy)*	789
Cassa di Risparmio di Trieste - Banca SpA *(Czech Republic)*	315
Cassa di Risparmio di Udine e Pordenone SpA *(Italy)*	789
Cassa di Risparmio di Venezia SpA *(Italy)*	790
Casse di Risparmio Joint Representative Office *(Hong Kong, China)*	597
Cater Allen International Limited *(United Kingdom)*	1708
Cater Allen Limited *(United Kingdom)*	1708
Cavell Securities *(Mauritius)*	1074
Cavill White Securities Limited *(New Zealand)*	1140
Cavmont Merchant Bank Limited *(Zambia)*	2043
Cayman Islands Monetary Authority *(Cayman Islands)*	241
Cayman National Bank *(Cayman Islands)*	241
Cayman National Trust Co Limited *(Cayman Islands)*	241
Caymanx Trust Co Limited *(United Kingdom)*	1709
Cazenove & Co *(United Kingdom)*	1709
CB Moldova-Agroindbank SA *(Moldova, Republic Of)*	1090
CBI-TDB Union Bancaire Privée *(Uruguay)*	2024
CBI-UBP International Limited *(United Kingdom)*	1710
CCF Finance M-O SAL *(Lebanon)*	957
CCF (Monaco) SAM *(Monaco)*	1093
CCIC Finance Limited *(Hong Kong, China)*	597
CDC Marchés *(France)*	418
CDI - Corporate Development International *(Germany)*	476
CDI-AMandA GmbH *(Austria)*	82
CDM Pekao SA Securities *(Poland)*	1207
Cedef Assets Limited *(United Kingdom)*	1710
Cedef Assets Management Limited *(Australia)*	41
Cedef Capital Markets (Pty) Limited *(South Africa)*	1384
Cedef Capital Services Limited *(United Kingdom)*	1710
CEDEF SA *(Switzerland)*	1502
Cedel Bank *(Hong Kong, China)*	597
Cedel Bank *(Japan)*	830
Cedel Bank *(Luxembourg)*	995
Cedel Bank *(United Arab Emirates)*	1635
Cedel Bank *(United Kingdom)*	1710
Cedel Bank *(United States)*	1931
The CEF Group *(Hong Kong, China)*	598
CEF (Singapore) Limited *(Singapore)*	1304
Celtic Bank Limited *(United Kingdom)*	1711

A-17

BANK	PAGE NO
Cen E Bankiers NV *(Netherlands)*.................................	1113
Open Joint-Stock Society Bank "Centercredit" *(Kazakhstan)*...	894
Central Banco de Investimento *(Portugal)*.................	1233
Central Bank of Barbados *(Barbados)*.........................	125
Central Bank of Belize *(Belize)*...................................	166
Central Bank of Bosnia & Herzegovina *(Bosnia-Herzegovina)*..	171
The Central Bank of China *(Taiwan, Republic of China)*..	1557
The Central Bank of China *(United Kingdom)*...........	1711
Central Bank of Cyprus *(Cyprus)*................................	305
Central Bank of Ireland *(Ireland)*................................	715
Central Bank of Kenya *(Kenya)*...................................	899
Central Bank of Kuwait *(Kuwait)*................................	932
Central Bank of Kuwait *(United Kingdom)*................	1711
Central Bank of Lesotho *(Lesotho)*.............................	961
Central Bank of Malta *(Malta)*.....................................	1071
Central Bank of Myanmar *(Myanmar)*........................	1100
Central Bank of Oman *(Oman)*.....................................	1161
Central Bank of Samoa *(Samoa (Western))*................	1275
Central Bank of Seychelles *(Seychelles)*....................	1285
Central Bank of Solomon Islands *(Solomon Islands)*..	1381
Central Bank of Sri Lanka *(Sri Lanka)*........................	1445
Central Bank of Swaziland *(Swaziland)*.....................	1451
Central Bank of Syria *(Syrian Arab Republic)*............	1557
The Central Bank of the Bahamas *(Bahamas)*............	101
Central Bank of the Republic of Armenia *(Armenia)*..	31
Central Bank of the Republic of Turkey *(Turkey)*......	1605
Central Bank of the Republic of Turkey *(United Kingdom)*..	1711
Central Bank of the Russian Federation *(Russian Federation)*..	1249
Central Bank of Trinidad and Tobago *(Trinidad and Tobago)*..	1600
Central Bank of Turkey *(United States)*.....................	1932
Central Cooperative Bank *(Bulgaria)*..........................	204
Central European International Bank Limited *(Hungary)*...	665
Central Trust of China *(Taiwan, Republic of China)*...	1559
Centrale Bank van Aruba *(Aruba)*...............................	34
Centro Internationale Handelsbank AG *(Austria)*......	82
Centro Internationale Handelsbank AG *(Poland)*.......	1208
Centrobanca *(Italy)*..	790
Centrum Bank AG *(Liechtenstein)*...............................	962
CERABANK Luxembourg SA *(Luxembourg)*................	996
Česká národní banka *(Czech Republic)*......................	313
Česká Sporitelna as *(Czech Republic)*.......................	315
Ceskomoravská Hypotecni banka as *(Czech Republic)*..	316
Ceskoslovenská Obchodni Banka as *(Czech Republic)*..	317
Ceskoslovenská Obchodni Banka as *(United Kingdom)*..	1711
CFC Securities SA *(Switzerland)*.................................	1502
CFC Securities SA *(United States)*..............................	1932
Chang Hwa Commercial Bank *(United States)*...........	1932

BANK	PAGE NO
Chang Hwa Commercial Bank Limited *(Taiwan, Republic of China)*..	1559
Chang Hwa Commercial Bank Limited *(United Kingdom)*..	1711
Channel Islands Money Brokers Limited *(Channel Islands)*..	245
Chartered Trust plc *(United Kingdom)*.......................	1712
Charterhouse Bank Limited *(United Kingdom)*..........	1712
Charterhouse Development Capital Limited *(United Kingdom)*..	1712
Charterhouse Inc *(United States)*...............................	1932
Charterhouse plc *(United Kingdom)*...........................	1712
Charterhouse Securities Limited *(United Kingdom)*....	1712
Chase Asset Management (London) Limited *(United Kingdom)*..	1712
Chase Bank & Trust Company (CI) Limited *(Channel Islands)*...	246
Chase Manhattan Asia Limited *(Hong Kong, China)*..	599
Chase Manhattan Bank AG *(Germany)*.......................	476
The Chase Manhattan Bank of Canada *(Canada)*......	219
Chase Manhattan Bank International *(Russian Federation)*..	1255
Chase Manhattan Bank (Ireland) plc *(Ireland)*...........	725
Chase Manhattan Bank Luxembourg SA *(Luxembourg)*..	997
The Chase Manhattan Bank (Malaysia) Berhad *(Malaysia)*..	1046
The Chase Manhattan Bank NA *(Argentina)*..............	21
Chase Manhattan Bank New York *(Germany)*............	477
The Chase Manhattan Bank *(Australia)*.....................	41
The Chase Manhattan Bank *(Bahrain)*........................	114
The Chase Manhattan Bank *(Belgium)*.......................	145
The Chase Manhattan Bank *(Channel Islands)*..........	246
The Chase Manhattan Bank *(Chile)*............................	265
The Chase Manhattan Bank *(China)*...........................	272
The Chase Manhattan Bank *(Czech Republic)*...........	318
The Chase Manhattan Bank *(Egypt)*............................	363
The Chase Manhattan Bank *(France)*.........................	420
The Chase Manhattan Bank *(Greece)*..........................	563
The Chase Manhattan Bank *(Hong Kong, China)*.......	599
The Chase Manhattan Bank *(Indonesia)*.....................	704
The Chase Manhattan Bank *(Italy)*.............................	790
The Chase Manhattan Bank *(Japan)*...........................	830
The Chase Manhattan Bank *(Korea, South)*...............	907
The Chase Manhattan Bank *(Lebanon)*.......................	957
The Chase Manhattan Bank *(Mexico)*.........................	1083
The Chase Manhattan Bank *(Netherlands)*.................	1114
The Chase Manhattan Bank *(Poland)*..........................	1209
The Chase Manhattan Bank *(Portugal)*.......................	1233
The Chase Manhattan Bank *(Romania)*......................	1247
The Chase Manhattan Bank *(Singapore)*....................	1305
The Chase Manhattan Bank *(South Africa)*................	1385
The Chase Manhattan Bank *(Spain)*............................	1431
The Chase Manhattan Bank *(Switzerland)*..................	1503
The Chase Manhattan Bank *(Turkey)*.........................	1608
The Chase Manhattan Bank *(United Kingdom)*..........	1713
The Chase Manhattan Bank *(United States)*..............	1932
Chase Manhattan International Limited *(Norway)*.....	1148

A-18

BANK	PAGE NO
Chase Manhattan International Limited *(United Kingdom)*	1714
Chase Manhattan Overseas Corporation *(Pakistan)*	1165
Chase Manhattan plc *(United Kingdom)*	1714
The Chase Manhattan Private Bank (Switzerland) *(Switzerland)*	1503
Chase Securities Inc *(United States)*	1933
Chekiang First Bank Limited *(Hong Kong, China)*	599
Chiao Tung Bank *(Taiwan, Republic of China)*	1560
The Chiba Bank Limited *(Hong Kong, China)*	600
The Chiba Bank Limited *(Japan)*	830
The Chiba Bank Limited *(United Kingdom)*	1715
The Chiba Bank Limited *(United States)*	1934
Chiba International Limited *(United Kingdom)*	1715
The Chiba Kogyo Bank Limited *(Japan)*	831
Chicago Board of Trade *(United States)*	1934
China Banking Corporation *(Philippines)*	1188
China Construction Bank *(United Kingdom)*	1715
China Development Corporation *(Taiwan, Republic of China)*	1561
China Investment Bank *(China)*	272
China Merchants Bank *(China)*	273
China Securities Co Limited *(Taiwan, Republic of China)*	1561
Chinatrust Commercial Bank *(Taiwan, Republic of China)*	1562
Chinatrust Commercial Bank *(United Kingdom)*	1715
Chinese American Bank *(United States)*	1934
The Chinese Bank *(Taiwan, Republic of China)*	1562
Chinfon Commercial Bank *(Taiwan, Republic of China)*	1562
Cho Hung Bank *(China)*	273
Cho Hung Bank *(Korea, South)*	907
Cho Hung Bank *(Singapore)*	1305
Cho Hung Bank *(United Kingdom)*	1715
Cho Hung Securities Co Limited *(Korea, South)*	908
Christiania Bank *(Singapore)*	1306
Christiania Bank *(United States)*	1934
Christiania Bank og Kreditkasse ASA *(Norway)*	1148
Christiania Bank og Kreditkasse ASA *(United Kingdom)*	1715
The Chugoku Bank Limited *(Japan)*	831
The Chugoku Bank Limited *(United Kingdom)*	1716
The Chugoku Bank Limited *(United States)*	1934
Chung Shing Bank *(Taiwan, Republic of China)*	1563
The Chuo Trust & Banking Co Limited *(Hong Kong, China)*	600
The Chuo Trust & Banking Co Limited *(Japan)*	831
The Chuo Trust & Banking Company Limited *(United Kingdom)*	1716
Chuo Trust Asia Limited *(Hong Kong, China)*	600
CIBC Asia Limited *(Singapore)*	1306
CIBC Mellon Global Securities Services Co *(Canada)*	219
CIBC Oppenheimer Corp *(United States)*	1935
CIBC Oppenheimer International Limited *(United Kingdom)*	1716
CIBC Trust Company (Bahamas) Limited *(Bahamas)*	102

BANK	PAGE NO
CIBC Wood Gundy Ireland Limited *(Ireland)*	725
CIBC Wood Gundy Securities Inc *(Canada)*	219
CIBC Wood Gundy Securities (Japan) Limited *(Japan)*	833
CIBC World Markets *(Canada)*	220
CIBC World Markets *(United Kingdom)*	1716
CIC Banques/Caisse Nationale *(Argentina)*	21
CICM Fund Management Limited *(Ireland)*	725
CICM (Ireland) Limited *(Ireland)*	725
Cie Financière Benjamin et Edmond de Rothschild *(United Kingdom)*	1717
Cie Financiere Ottomane *(France)*	420
CIGNA International Investment Advisors Limited *(Chile)*	266
CIM Société de Bourse SA *(Luxembourg)*	997
CISF Dealer SA *(Portugal)*	1233
CITCO Bank Nederland NV *(Netherlands)*	1114
Cit-Group/Commercial Services *(United States)*	1935
Citi Isalmic Investment Bank EC *(Bahrain)*	114
Citibank AG *(Germany)*	478
Citibank as *(Czech Republic)*	318
Citibank Berhad *(Malaysia)*	1047
Citibank (Channel Islands) Limited *(Channel Islands)*	246
Citibank Colombia *(Colombia)*	289
Citibank España SA *(Spain)*	1431
Citibank International plc *(Austria)*	83
Citibank International plc *(Denmark)*	341
Citibank International plc *(Finland)*	388
Citibank International plc *(Norway)*	1151
Citibank International plc *(Sweden)*	1453
Citibank (Luxembourg) *(Luxembourg)*	997
Citibank Maghreb *(Morocco)*	1098
Citibank Mexico SA *(Mexico)*	1083
Citibank NA *(Argentina)*	21
Citibank NA *(Australia)*	42
Citibank NA *(Bahrain)*	114
Citibank NA *(Belgium)*	145
Citibank NA *(Brazil)*	191
Citibank NA *(Canada)*	221
Citibank NA *(Chile)*	266
Citibank NA *(Costa Rica)*	292
Citibank NA *(Cote D'Ivoire)*	293
Citibank NA *(Dominican Republic)*	356
Citibank NA *(Egypt)*	363
Citibank NA *(El Salvador)*	376
Citibank NA *(Gabon)*	452
Citibank NA *(Greece)*	563
Citibank NA *(Guatemala)*	574
Citibank NA *(Haiti)*	577
Citibank NA *(Hong Kong, China)*	600
Citibank NA *(India)*	679
Citibank NA *(India)*	680
Citibank NA *(Ireland)*	726
Citibank NA *(Italy)*	790
Citibank NA *(Jamaica)*	812
Citibank NA *(Japan)*	833
Citibank NA *(Kenya)*	900

A-19

BANK	PAGE NO
Citibank NA *(Korea, South)*	908
Citibank NA *(Lebanon)*	957
Citibank NA *(Monaco)*	1093
Citibank NA *(Netherlands)*	1115
Citibank NA *(New Zealand)*	1140
Citibank NA *(Oman)*	1162
Citibank NA *(Pakistan)*	1166
Citibank NA *(Paraguay)*	1177
Citibank NA *(Peru)*	1182
Citibank NA *(Philippines)*	1188
Citibank NA *(Puerto Rico)*	1239
Citibank NA *(Senegal)*	1284
Citibank NA *(Spain)*	1431
Citibank NA *(Sri Lanka)*	1446
Citibank NA *(Switzerland)*	1503
Citibank NA *(Thailand)*	1586
Citibank NA *(Tunisia)*	1605
Citibank NA *(Turkey)*	1608
Citibank NA *(United Kingdom)*	1718
Citibank NA *(United States)*	1936
Citibank NA *(United States)*	1935
Citibank NA *(Uruguay)*	2024
Citibank (Poland) SA *(Poland)*	1209
Citibank Portugal SA *(Portugal)*	1234
Citibank Romania SA *(Romania)*	1247
Citibank Rt *(Hungary)*	666
Citibank SA *(France)*	420
Citibank SA (Global Consumer) *(Belgium)*	145
Citibank (Slovakia) AS *(Slovak Republic)*	1358
Citibank (Switzerland) *(Switzerland)*	1503
Citibank T/O *(Russian Federation)*	1255
Citibank Trinidad and Tobago Limited *(Trinidad and Tobago)*	1600
Citibank (Zaïre) *(Congo, Democratic Republic)*	291
Citibank (Zambia) Limited *(Zambia)*	2043
CITIC Industrial Bank *(China)*	273
Citic Ka Wah Bank Limited *(United States)*	1936
Citicorp International Limited *(Hong Kong, China)*	601
Citicorp Investment Bank Limited *(Bahrain)*	115
Citicorp Investment Bank (Singapore) Limited *(Singapore)*	1306
Citicorp Investment Company *(Czech Republic)*	319
Citizens Bank Limited *(Hungary)*	667
City National Bank *(United States)*	1936
Clariden Asset Management (Hong Kong) Limited *(Hong Kong, China)*	601
Clariden Asset Management (New York) Inc *(United States)*	1936
Clariden Asset Management (Singapore) Pte Limited *(Singapore)*	1307
Clariden Bank *(Argentina)*	22
Clariden Bank *(Switzerland)*	1504
Clariden Brasil Ltda *(Brazil)*	192
CLF Municipal Bank plc *(United Kingdom)*	1718
CM Capital Markets Brokerage SA AV *(Spain)*	1431
CM Capital Markets Futures SA AV *(Spain)*	1432
Codan Bank A/S *(Denmark)*	341
Cofep SA *(Switzerland)*	1505

BANK	PAGE NO
Cofirene Banco de Inversión SA *(Argentina)*	22
Collins Stewart (CI) Limited *(United Kingdom)*	1718
Commerce International Merchant Bankers Berhad *(Malaysia)*	1047
Commercial & Investment Credit Corp SA *(Switzerland)*	1505
Commercial Bank of Africa Limited *(Kenya)*	900
Commercial Bank Biochim plc *(Bulgaria)*	204
Commercial Bank of Ethiopia *(Ethiopia)*	382
Commercial Bank Expressbank AD *(Bulgaria)*	205
Commercial Bank of Greece *(Cyprus)*	309
Commercial Bank of Greece (Germany) GmbH *(Germany)*	479
Commercial Bank of Greece SA *(Greece)*	563
The Commercial Bank of Korea Limited *(Korea, South)*	909
The Commercial Bank of Korea Limited *(United Kingdom)*	1718
Commercial Bank of Kuwait *(United States)*	1937
The Commercial Bank of Kuwait SAK *(Kuwait)*	935
The Commercial Bank of Namibia Limited *(Namibia)*	1101
Commercial Bank of Oman *(Oman)*	1162
The Commercial Bank Of Qatar Limited (QSC) *(Qatar)*	1241
Commercial International Bank (Egypt) SAE *(Egypt)*	364
Commercial International Investment Company SAE *(Egypt)*	364
Commercial Union Investment Management Limited *(United Kingdom)*	1718
Commerz Securities (Japan) Co Limited *(Japan)*	834
Commerzbank AG *(Argentina)*	22
Commerzbank AG *(Australia)*	43
Commerzbank AG *(Bahrain)*	115
Commerzbank AG *(Belarus)*	130
Commerzbank AG *(Belgium)*	145
Commerzbank AG *(Canada)*	221
Commerzbank AG *(China)*	274
Commerzbank AG *(Czech Republic)*	319
Commerzbank AG *(Denmark)*	343
Commerzbank AG *(Egypt)*	366
Commerzbank AG *(France)*	420
Commerzbank AG *(Germany)*	479
Commerzbank AG *(Hong Kong, China)*	601
Commerzbank AG *(India)*	680
Commerzbank AG *(Indonesia)*	705
Commerzbank AG *(Iran (Islamic Republic Of))*	714
Commerzbank AG *(Italy)*	791
Commerzbank AG *(Japan)*	834
Commerzbank AG *(Kazakhstan)*	895
Commerzbank AG *(Korea, South)*	910
Commerzbank AG *(Lebanon)*	958
Commerzbank AG *(Malaysia)*	1048
Commerzbank AG *(Mexico)*	1083
Commerzbank AG *(Poland)*	1209
Commerzbank AG *(Russian Federation)*	1257
Commerzbank AG *(Slovak Republic)*	1360
Commerzbank AG *(South Africa)*	1385

A-20

BANK	PAGE NO
Commerzbank AG *(Spain)*	1432
Commerzbank AG *(Taiwan, Republic of China)*	1564
Commerzbank AG *(Thailand)*	1587
Commerzbank AG *(Turkey)*	1608
Commerzbank AG *(Ukraine)*	1628
Commerzbank AG *(United Kingdom)*	1719
Commerzbank AG *(United States)*	1937
Commerzbank AG *(Venezuela)*	2032
Commerzbank (Budapest) Rt *(Hungary)*	667
Commerzbank Capital Markets Corporation *(United States)*	1938
Commerzbank Capital Markets (Eastern Europe) as *(Czech Republic)*	320
Commerzbank Europe (Ireland) *(Ireland)*	726
Commerzbank International SA Luxembourg *(Luxembourg)*	997
Commerzbank (Nederland) NV *(Netherlands)*	1115
Commerzbank Rio de Janeiro Serviços Ltda *(Brazil)*	192
Commerzbank São Paulo Serviços Ltda *(Brazil)*	192
Commerzbank (Schweiz) AG *(Switzerland)*	1505
Commerzbank (South East Asia) Limited *(Singapore)*	1307
Commonwealth Bank of Australia *(Australia)*	43
Commonwealth Bank of Australia *(Hong Kong, China)*	601
Commonwealth Bank of Australia *(Japan)*	835
Commonwealth Bank of Australia *(Singapore)*	1308
Commonwealth Bank of Australia *(United Kingdom)*	1721
Commonwealth Development Corporation *(United Kingdom)*	1722
Compagnie d'Investissement et de Financement International *(France)*	421
Compagnie Financière de CIC et de l'Union Européenne *(Singapore)*	1308
Compagnie Financière de CIC et de l'Union Européenne *(United States)*	1938
Compagnie Financière Espirito Santo SA *(Switzerland)*	1506
Compagnie Financière Tradition *(China)*	274
Compagnie Financière Tradition *(Switzerland)*	1506
Compagnie de Gestion et de Banque Gonet SA *(Switzerland)*	1506
Compagnie Monégasque de Banque SAM *(Monaco)*	1094
Confederación Española de Cajas de Ahorros *(Spain)*	1432
Confederación Española de Cajas de Ahorros *(United Kingdom)*	1722
Conseil Alain Aboudaram SA *(Switzerland)*	1506
Constantia Privatbank AG *(Austria)*	83
Coop Bank *(Switzerland)*	1507
Cooperatieve Centrale Raiffeisen-Boerenleenbank BA *(Australia)*	44
Cooperatieve Centrale Raiffeisen-Boerenleenbank BA *(Hong Kong, China)*	602
Co-Operative Central Bank Limited *(Cyprus)*	309

BANK	PAGE NO
Copex International Finance & Trading Limited *(Ireland)*	726
CoreStates Bank NA *(Germany)*	481
Cornèr Bank Limited *(Switzerland)*	1508
Corp Banca *(Argentina)*	22
Corp Banca *(Chile)*	266
Corp Banca CA *(United States)*	1939
Corp Banca CA *(Venezuela)*	2032
Corporación Andina de Fomento - CAF *(Venezuela)*	2032
Corporacion Financiera Nacional y Suramericana SA *(Colombia)*	289
Corporación Metropolitana de Finanzas SA Banco *(Argentina)*	22
Corretora Patente SA CVM *(Brazil)*	192
Cosmo Securities (Europe) Limited *(United Kingdom)*	1722
Cosmorex Zürich AG *(Switzerland)*	1509
Cosmos Bank *(Taiwan, Republic of China)*	1564
Coutts Bank *(Hong Kong, China)*	603
Coutts Bank (Singapore) AG *(Singapore)*	1309
Coutts Bank (Switzerland) Limited *(Switzerland)*	1509
Cowen & Co *(United States)*	1939
Crane Investment Analysis Limited *(United Kingdom)*	1723
Credifinance Securities Limited *(Canada)*	221
CREDIOP SpA *(Italy)*	791
Crédit Agricole Indosuez *(China)*	274
Crédit Agricole Indosuez *(China)*	275
Crédit Agricole Indosuez *(China)*	274
Crédit Agricole Indosuez *(Denmark)*	343
Crédit Agricole Indosuez *(Egypt)*	366
Crédit Agricole Indosuez *(France)*	421
Crédit Agricole Indosuez *(Hong Kong, China)*	603
Crédit Agricole Indosuez *(Italy)*	791
Crédit Agricole Indosuez *(Norway)*	1151
Crédit Agricole Indosuez *(Singapore)*	1309
Crédit Agricole Indosuez *(South Africa)*	1385
Crédit Agricole Indosuez *(Spain)*	1433
Crédit Agricole Indosuez *(Sweden)*	1453
Crédit Agricole Indosuez *(United Kingdom)*	1723
Crédit Agricole Indosuez *(Vietnam)*	2035
Crédit Agricole Indosuez SA *(Luxembourg)*	998
Crédit Agricole Indosuez-Asian Aerospace Group *(Japan)*	835
Credit Andorrà SA *(Andorra)*	4
Credit Bank plc *(Bulgaria)*	206
Crédit Commercial de France *(Belgium)*	146
Crédit Commercial de France *(Chile)*	267
Crédit Commercial de France *(Ecuador)*	357
Crédit Commercial de France *(Egypt)*	366
Crédit Commercial de France *(France)*	423
Crédit Commercial de France *(Hong Kong, China)*	604
Crédit Commercial de France *(India)*	680
Crédit Commercial de France *(Italy)*	792
Crédit Commercial de France *(Portugal)*	1234
Crédit Commercial de France *(United Kingdom)*	1724
Crédit Commercial de France *(United States)*	1940

A-21

BANK	PAGE NO
Crédit Commercial de France (Luxembourg) SA (Luxembourg)	999
Crédit Commercial de France (Suisse) SA (Switzerland)	1510
Crédit Communal de Belgique (Belgium)	146
Credit Communal SA (United States)	1940
Crédit du Maroc (Morocco)	1098
Crédit du Nord (France)	424
Crédit du Nord (Monaco)	1094
Crédit du Nord (Spain)	1433
Crédit Européen SA (Luxembourg)	999
Credit Fiditalia (Italy)	793
Crédit Foncier de France SA (France)	424
Crédit Foncier de Monaco (Monaco)	1094
Crédit Général SA de Banque (Belgium)	147
Crédit Industriel d'Alsace et de Lorraine - CIAL (France)	424
Crédit Local de France Dexia International (France)	425
Crédit Lyonnais (Hong Kong, China)	604
Crédit Lyonnais (Japan)	835
Crédit Lyonnais (Korea, South)	910
Crédit Lyonnais (Mexico)	1083
Crédit Lyonnais (Singapore)	1310
Crédit Lyonnais (Taiwan, Republic of China)	1565
Crédit Lyonnais (United States)	1940
Crédit Lyonnais Bank (Austria) AG (Austria)	84
Crédit Lyonnais Bank Hungary Rt (Hungary)	667
Crédit Lyonnais Bank Polska SA (Poland)	1209
Credit Lyonnais Bank Slovakia AS (Slovak Republic)	1360
Crédit Lyonnais Belgium SA (Belgium)	147
Crédit Lyonnais Brazil (Brazil)	192
Crédit Lyonnais Canada (Canada)	221
Crédit Lyonnais Rouse (France) SNC (France)	426
Crédit Lyonnais Rouse (USA) Limited (United States)	1941
Crédit Lyonnais SA (France)	426
Crédit Lyonnais Securities (United Kingdom)	1724
Crédit Lyonnais Securities (Japan) (Japan)	836
Crédit Lyonnais Securities (Switzerland) AG (Switzerland)	1510
Crédit Lyonnais Securities (USA) Inc (United States)	1941
Crédit Lyonnais (Suisse) SA (Switzerland)	1510
Crédit Lyonnais (Uruguay) SA (Uruguay)	2025
Crédit Lyonnais/PK Airfinance (United States)	1941
Crédit Populaire d'Algérie (Algeria)	2
Crédit Populaire du Maroc (Morocco)	1098
Crédit Professional SA (Belgium)	147
Credit Suisse (Argentina)	23
Credit Suisse (Bahrain)	115
Credit Suisse (Brazil)	193
Credit Suisse (Egypt)	366
Credit Suisse (Mexico)	1083
Credit Suisse (Bahamas) Limited (Bahamas)	102
Credit Suisse Financial Products (Japan)	836
Credit Suisse First Boston (Australia)	45
Credit Suisse First Boston (Egypt)	366

BANK	PAGE NO
Credit Suisse First Boston (Netherlands)	1115
Credit Suisse First Boston (New Zealand)	1140
Credit Suisse First Boston (Switzerland)	1511
Credit Suisse First Boston (United States)	1941
Credit Suisse First Boston Canada (Canada)	222
Credit Suisse First Boston (Europe) Limited (United Kingdom)	1724
Credit Suisse First Boston France SA (France)	428
Credit Suisse First Boston (Hong Kong) Limited (Hong Kong, China)	605
Credit Suisse First Boston (Internationale) AG (Netherlands)	1116
Credit Suisse First Boston (Prague) as (Czech Republic)	321
Credit Suisse First Boston Securities (Japan) Limited (Japan)	837
Credit Suisse (France) SA (Monaco)	1095
Credit Suisse Group (Switzerland)	1511
Credit Suisse (Guernsey) Limited (Channel Islands)	246
Crédit Suisse Hottinguer (France)	428
Credit Suisse Leasing (Switzerland)	1512
Credit Suisse (Luxembourg) SA (Luxembourg)	1000
Credit Suisse Securities Limited (United Kingdom)	1726
Creditanstalt AG (Austria)	85
Creditanstalt AG (Hong Kong, China)	605
Creditanstalt Finanziaria SpA (Italy)	793
Creditanstalt-Bankverein AG (Germany)	481
Credito Bergamasco SpA (Italy)	793
Credito Emiliano SpA (Italy)	795
Credito Predial Português (Portugal)	1234
Croatia banka dd, Zagreb (Croatia)	295
Crowell, Weedon & Co (United States)	1942
Cyclos Securities SA (Greece)	565
The Cyprus Popular Bank Limited (Cyprus)	309
The Cyprus Popular Bank Limited (United Kingdom)	1726
Cyril Finance Gestion (France)	428
Daegu Bank Limited	910
The Daegu Bank Limited (United States)	1942
Daewoo Bank (Hungary) Limited (Hungary)	667
Daewoo Bank (Romania) SA (Romania)	1247
Daewoo Securities (America) Inc (United States)	1942
Daewoo Securities Co Limited (Japan)	837
Daewoo Securities Co Limited (Korea, South)	910
Daewoo Securities (Europe) Limited (United Kingdom)	1726
Dah An Commercial Bank (Taiwan, Republic of China)	1565
Dah Sing Bank Limited (Hong Kong, China)	605
Dai-Ichi Europe Limited (United Kingdom)	1727
Dai-Ichi Kangyo Bank of California (United States)	1942
Dai-Ichi Kangyo Bank (Canada) (Canada)	222
Dai-Ichi Kangyo Bank (Deutschland) AG (Germany)	482
The Dai-Ichi Kangyo Bank Limited (Australia)	45
The Dai-Ichi Kangyo Bank Limited (Bahrain)	115
The Dai-Ichi Kangyo Bank Limited (China)	275
The Dai-Ichi Kangyo Bank Limited (France)	429

BANK	PAGE NO
The Dai-Ichi Kangyo Bank Limited *(Germany)*	482
The Dai-Ichi Kangyo Bank Limited *(Hong Kong, China)*	606
The Dai-Ichi Kangyo Bank Limited *(Italy)*	795
The Dai-Ichi Kangyo Bank Limited *(Japan)*	837
The Dai-Ichi Kangyo Bank Limited *(Korea, South)*	911
The Dai-Ichi Kangyo Bank Limited *(Malaysia)*	1048
The Dai-Ichi Kangyo Bank Limited *(Panama)*	1174
The Dai-Ichi Kangyo Bank Limited *(Singapore)*	1311
The Dai-Ichi Kangyo Bank Limited *(Spain)*	1433
The Dai-Ichi Kangyo Bank Limited *(Taiwan, Republic of China)*	1565
The Dai-Ichi Kangyo Bank Limited *(Thailand)*	1587
The Dai-Ichi Kangyo Bank Limited *(Thailand)*	1588
The Dai-Ichi Kangyo Bank Limited *(Thailand)*	1587
The Dai-Ichi Kangyo Bank Limited *(United Kingdom)*	1727
The Dai-Ichi Kangyo Bank Limited *(United States)*	1942
The Dai-Ichi Kangyo Bank Limited *(United States)*	1943
Dai-Ichi Kangyo Bank (Luxembourg) SA *(Luxembourg)*	1001
Dai-Ichi Kangyo Bank Nederland NV *(Netherlands)*	1116
Dai-Ichi Kangyo Bank (Schweiz) AG *(Switzerland)*	1512
Dai-Ichi Kangyo Trust Company of New York *(United States)*	1943
Dain Rauscher Incorporated *(United States)*	1943
Daishin International (Europe) Limited *(United Kingdom)*	1729
Daishin Securities Co Limited *(Korea, South)*	911
Daiwa Bank (Capital Management) plc *(United Kingdom)*	1729
The Daiwa Bank Limited *(China)*	276
The Daiwa Bank Limited *(China)*	275
The Daiwa Bank Limited *(Hong Kong, China)*	606
The Daiwa Bank *(Hong Kong, China)*	606
The Daiwa Bank Limited *(Japan)*	838
The Daiwa Bank Limited *(Korea, South)*	912
The Daiwa Bank Limited *(Singapore)*	1312
The Daiwa Bank Limited *(Thailand)*	1588
The Daiwa Bank Limited *(United Kingdom)*	1730
The Daiwa Bank Limited *(Vietnam)*	2035
Daiwa Cosmo Bank (Schweiz) AG *(Switzerland)*	1512
Daiwa Europe (Deutschland) GmbH *(Germany)*	482
Daiwa Europe (France) SA *(France)*	429
Daiwa Europe Limited *(United Kingdom)*	1730
PT Daiwa Lippo Finance *(Indonesia)*	705
Daiwa Merchant Bank (Singapore) Limited *(Singapore)*	1312
Daiwa Middle East EC *(Bahrain)*	115
Daiwa Overseas Finance Limited *(Hong Kong, China)*	606
PT Daiwa Perdania Bank *(Indonesia)*	705
Daiwa Securities *(Singapore)*	1312
Daiwa Securities Australia Limited *(Australia)*	46
Daiwa Securities Bank (Switzerland) *(Switzerland)*	1513
Daiwa Securities Co Limited *(Japan)*	838
Daiwa Securities (Hong Kong) Limited *(Hong Kong, China)*	606

BANK	PAGE NO
Daiwa Singapore Limited *(Singapore)*	1312
Dallah Albaraka (UK) Limited *(United Kingdom)*	1731
Dalmatinska Banka dd *(Croatia)*	295
Dalrybbank *(Russian Federation)*	1257
PT (Persero) Danareksa *(Indonesia)*	705
Danish Securities Dealers Association *(Denmark)*	343
Danish Ship Finance *(Denmark)*	343
Danmarks Nationalbank *(Denmark)*	334
Danske Bank Consensus *(Sweden)*	1454
Dao Heng Bank Limited *(Hong Kong, China)*	607
Dao Heng Bank (London) plc *(United Kingdom)*	1732
Darier Hentsch & Cie *(Switzerland)*	1513
Darier Hentsch Canada Inc *(Canada)*	222
Davy Stockbrokers *(Ireland)*	727
DAVY-Protos Stockbrokers Limited *(Finland)*	388
DBS Bank *(Singapore)*	1312
DBS Bank *(United States)*	1944
DBS Finance Limited *(Singapore)*	1314
De Ganay y Quirno SA Sociedad de Bolsa *(Argentina)*	23
Dean Witter Reynolds *(United States)*	1944
Degussa Bank GmbH *(Germany)*	482
Delbrück & Co, Privatbankiers *(Germany)*	483
Delphis Bank *(United Kingdom)*	1732
Delta Finance Berhad *(Malaysia)*	1048
Delta International Bank *(Egypt)*	366
Delta Lloyd Bank NV *(Netherlands)*	1116
Deltec Asset Management Corporation *(United States)*	1945
The Deltec Banking Corporation Limited *(Bahamas)*	102
Deltec Securities (UK) Limited *(United Kingdom)*	1732
Den Danske Bank *(Denmark)*	343
Den Danske Bank *(Poland)*	1209
Den Danske Bank *(United Kingdom)*	1732
Den Danske Bank Aktieselskab *(Finland)*	388
Den Danske Bank Aktieselskab *(Germany)*	483
Den Danske Bank Aktieselskab *(Hong Kong, China)*	608
Den Danske Bank Aktieselskab *(Japan)*	839
Den Danske Bank Aktieselskab *(Norway)*	1151
Den Danske Bank Aktieselskab *(Singapore)*	1314
Den Danske Bank Aktieselskab *(United States)*	1945
Den Danske Bank International SA *(Luxembourg)*	1001
Den Danske Bank International SA *(Spain)*	1433
Den norske Bank *(China)*	276
Den norske Bank AS *(Brazil)*	193
Den norske Bank AS *(Norway)*	1151
Den norske Bank ASA *(Germany)*	484
Den norske Bank ASA *(Singapore)*	1314
Den norske Bank ASA *(Sweden)*	1454
Den norske Bank ASA *(United Kingdom)*	1733
Den norske Bank ASA *(United States)*	1945
DePfa-Bank AG *(United Kingdom)*	1734
DePfa-Bank Europe plc *(Ireland)*	728
Depósito Centralizado de Valores SA *(Ecuador)*	357
Desjardins Trust *(Canada)*	223
Deutsch Türkische Bank AG *(Germany)*	484
Deutsche Apotheker-und Ärztebank eG *(Germany)*	484
Deutsche Ausgleichsbank (DtA) *(Germany)*	484

A-23

BANK	PAGE NO
Deutsche Bank *(Brazil)*	193
Deutsche Bank *(Czech Republic)*	321
Deutsche Bank *(Korea, South)*	912
Deutsche Bank *(Pakistan)*	1166
Deutsche Bank *(Poland)*	1210
Deutsche Bank *(Sri Lanka)*	1446
Deutsche Bank *(Thailand)*	1588
Deutsche Bank *(Vietnam)*	2036
Deutsche Bank AG *(Australia)*	46
Deutsche Bank AG *(Austria)*	85
Deutsche Bank AG *(Bahrain)*	116
Deutsche Bank AG *(Belgium)*	148
Deutsche Bank AG *(Brazil)*	193
Deutsche Bank AG *(Chile)*	267
Deutsche Bank AG *(China)*	276
Deutsche Bank AG *(Colombia)*	290
Deutsche Bank AG *(Croatia)*	296
Deutsche Bank AG *(Egypt)*	367
Deutsche Bank AG *(France)*	429
Deutsche Bank AG *(Georgia)*	453
Deutsche Bank AG *(Germany)*	484
Deutsche Bank AG *(Germany)*	485
Deutsche Bank AG *(Hong Kong, China)*	608
Deutsche Bank AG *(India)*	680
Deutsche Bank AG *(Indonesia)*	706
Deutsche Bank AG *(Iran (Islamic Republic Of))*	714
Deutsche Bank AG *(Japan)*	839
Deutsche Bank AG *(Kazakhstan)*	895
Deutsche Bank AG *(Macau)*	1030
Deutsche Bank AG *(Mexico)*	1083
Deutsche Bank AG *(Netherlands)*	1117
Deutsche Bank AG *(Pakistan)*	1166
Deutsche Bank AG *(Russian Federation)*	1258
Deutsche Bank AG *(Singapore)*	1315
Deutsche Bank AG *(South Africa)*	1385
Deutsche Bank AG *(Turkey)*	1608
Deutsche Bank AG *(Turkmenistan)*	1627
Deutsche Bank AG *(Ukraine)*	1628
Deutsche Bank AG *(United Kingdom)*	1734
Deutsche Bank AG *(United States)*	1946
Deutsche Bank AG *(Uzbekistan)*	2027
Deutsche Bank AG *(Vietnam)*	2036
Deutsche Bank AG - Deutsche Morgan Grenfell *(Germany)*	489
Deutsche Bank AG - NZ *(New Zealand)*	1141
Deutsche Bank AG Tokyo *(Japan)*	839
Deutsche Bank de Bary NV *(Netherlands)*	1117
Deutsche Bank Canada *(Canada)*	223
Deutsche Bank Capital Markets (Asia) Limited *(Hong Kong, China)*	608
Deutsche Bank Finance NV *(Netherlands Antilles)*	1136
Deutsche Bank France SNC *(France)*	429
Deutsche Bank Gilts Limited *(United Kingdom)*	1735
Deutsche Bank de Investimento SA *(Portugal)*	1234
Deutsche Bank Luxembourg SA *(Luxembourg)*	1001
Deutsche Bank (Malaysia) Berhad *(Malaysia)*	1048
Deutsche Bank North America *(United States)*	1947
Deutsche Bank Rt *(Hungary)*	668

BANK	PAGE NO
Deutsche Bank SA *(Argentina)*	23
Deutsche Bank SA *(Brazil)*	193
Deutsche Bank SA *(Spain)*	1433
Deutsche Bank SA Española *(Spain)*	1434
Deutsche Bank Securities *(Peru)*	1182
Deutsche Bank Securities Inc *(Switzerland)*	1513
Deutsche Bank Securities Inc *(United States)*	1947
Deutsche Bank Securities SA *(Spain)*	1434
Deutsche Bank SpA *(Italy)*	795
Deutsche Bank (Suisse) AG *(Switzerland)*	1513
Deutsche Bank Switzerland AG *(Switzerland)*	1514
Deutsche Bank Trust Company *(United States)*	1947
Deutsche Bank/DB Ireland plc *(Ireland)*	728
Deutsche Bau-und Bodenbank AG *(Germany)*	489
Deutsche Börse Clearing AG *(Germany)*	490
Deutsche Bundesbank *(Germany)*	453
Deutsche Bundesbank *(Japan)*	840
Deutsche Capital Hong Kong Limited *(Hong Kong, China)*	608
Deutsche Capital Markets Australia Limited *(Australia)*	46
Deutsche Capital (Singapore) Limited *(Singapore)*	1315
Deutsche Financial Services Corporation *(United States)*	1947
Deutsche Genossenschaftsbank *(Germany)*	490
Deutsche Girozentrale - Deutsche Kommunalbank *(Germany)*	490
Deutsche Girozentrale - Deutsche Kommunalbank *(Luxembourg)*	1001
Deutsche Girozentrale International SA *(Luxembourg)*	1002
Deutsche Handelsbank Aktiengesellschaft *(Germany)*	493
Deutsche Hypothekenbank AG *(Germany)*	493
Deutsche Morgan Grenfell *(Ecuador)*	357
Deutsche Morgan Grenfell *(Poland)*	1210
Deutsche Morgan Grenfell *(Sweden)*	1454
Deutsche Morgan Grenfell *(Venezuela)*	2032
Deutsche Morgan Grenfell & Partners Securities Pte Ltd *(Singapore)*	1316
Deutsche Morgan Grenfell (Andes) Ltda *(Colombia)*	290
Deutsche Morgan Grenfell Asset Management (Japan) Limited *(Japan)*	840
Deutsche Morgan Grenfell Canada Limited *(Canada)*	224
Deutsche Morgan Grenfell Capital Markets Limited *(Hong Kong, China)*	608
Deutsche Morgan Grenfell Capital Markets (Asia) Limited *(Korea, South)*	912
Deutsche Morgan Grenfell Capital Markets Limited *(Korea, South)*	912
Deutsche Morgan Grenfell (CI) Limited *(Channel Islands)*	247
Deutsche Morgan Grenfell (CI) Limited - Guernsey *(Channel Islands)*	247
Deutsche Morgan Grenfell Corporate Services (Ireland) Limited *(Ireland)*	728

BANK	PAGE NO	BANK	PAGE NO
Deutsche Morgan Grenfell (Ireland) Limited (Ireland)	728	DKB Asia Limited *(Hong Kong, China)*	609
		DKB Financial Products Inc *(United States)*	1949
Deutsche Morgan Grenfell Securities Limited *(Hong Kong, China)*	609	The DKB Futures (Singapore) Pte Limited *(Singapore)*	1316
Deutsche Postbank AG *(Germany)*	493	DKB International plc *(United Kingdom)*	1736
Deutsche Postbank International SA *(Luxembourg)*	1002	DKB Investment Management International Limited *(United Kingdom)*	1737
Deutsche Schiffsbank AG *(Germany)*	493		
Deutsche Schiffsbank AG *(United Kingdom)*	1735	DKB Merchant Bank (Singapore) Limited *(Singapore)*	1316
Deutsche Securities Inc *(United States)*	1948		
Deutsche Securities Limited *(Hong Kong, China)*	609	DKB Securities (USA) Corporation *(United States)*	1949
Deutsche Securities Limited *(Japan)*	840	Doha Bank Limited *(Qatar)*	1241
Deutsche Securities Limited *(Singapore)*	1316	Dolenjska Banka dd *(Slovenia)*	1374
Deutsche Securities Sociedad de Bolsa SA *(Argentina)*	23	Donaldson, Lufkin & Jenrette International *(France)*	430
		Donaldson, Lufkin & Jenrette International Limited *(United Kingdom)*	1737
Deutsche Sharps Pixley Metals Limited *(United Kingdom)*	1735		
		Donau-Bank AG *(Austria)*	87
The Development Bank of Singapore Limited *(Japan)*	840	Dresdner Bank AG *(Australia)*	47
		Dresdner Bank AG *(France)*	430
The Development Bank of Singapore Limited *(Korea, South)*	912	Dresdner Bank AG *(Hong Kong, China)*	610
		Dresdner Bank AG *(Italy)*	795
The Development Bank of Singapore Limited *(Taiwan, Republic of China)*	1565	Dresdner Bank AG *(Japan)*	841
		Dresdner Bank AG *(Korea, South)*	912
The Development Bank of Singapore Limited *(United Kingdom)*	1735	Dresdner Bank AG *(Latvia)*	944
		Dresdner Bank AG *(Malaysia)*	1049
Development Bank of Zambia *(Zambia)*	2044	Dresdner Bank AG *(South Africa)*	1385
Development Capital Securities Indonesia *(Indonesia)*	706	Dresdner Bank AG *(United States)*	1949
		Dresdner Bank Brasil *(Brazil)*	194
Devin Banka JSC *(Slovak Republic)*	1360	Dresdner Bank Canada *(Canada)*	224
Dewaay Broking SA *(Belgium)*	148	Dresdner Bank (Ireland) plc *(Ireland)*	728
Dexia Banco Local *(Spain)*	1434	Dresdner Bank Lateinamerika *(Chile)*	267
DG BANK *(Brazil)*	194	Dresdner Bank Lateinamerika AG *(Colombia)*	290
DG BANK *(China)*	276	Dresdner Bank Lateinamerika AG *(Germany)*	496
DG BANK *(France)*	429	Dresdner Bank Lateinamerika AG *(Paraguay)*	1177
DG BANK *(Germany)*	493	Dresdner Bank Lateinamerika AG/Dresdner Bank AG *(Argentina)*	24
DG BANK *(Hong Kong, China)*	609		
DG BANK *(Hungary)*	669	Dresdner Bank Latinoamérica *(Mexico)*	1083
DG BANK *(Italy)*	795	Dresdner Bank Luxembourg SA *(Luxembourg)*	1004
DG BANK *(Japan)*	841	Dresdner Bank (Switzerland) Limited *(Switzerland)*	1516
DG BANK *(Korea, South)*	912	Dresdner Banque Nationale de Paris *(Chile)*	267
DG BANK *(Netherlands)*	1117	Dresdner Kleinwort Benson *(Spain)*	1434
DG BANK *(Poland)*	1210	Dresdner Kleinwort Benson *(United Kingdom)*	1738
DG BANK *(Russian Federation)*	1258	Dresdner Kleinwort Benson (Asia) Limited *(Japan)*	841
DG BANK *(Spain)*	1434	Dresdner Kleinwort Benson Australia *(Australia)*	47
DG BANK *(Thailand)*	1589	Dresdner Kleinwort Benson (Marchés) *(France)*	430
DG Bank *(United States)*	1948	Dresdner Kleinwort Benson North America LLC *(United States)*	1949
DG BANK Deutsche Genossenschaftsbank *(United Kingdom)*	1735		
		Dresdner (South East Asia) Limited *(Singapore)*	1316
DG Bank Luxembourg SA *(Luxembourg)*	1003	Dresdner Suisse *(Switzerland)*	1516
DG Bank (Schweiz) AG *(Switzerland)*	1514	Les Fils Dreyfus & Cie SA, Banquiers *(Switzerland)*	1516
PT Dharmala Securities *(Indonesia)*	707	Drueker & Co GmbH *(Germany)*	497
Dilmun Financial Services *(Ireland)*	728	DSL Bank *(Germany)*	497
Dilmun Investments Limited *(United Kingdom)*	1736	DSL Bank Luxembourg SA *(Luxembourg)*	1004
Discount Bank & Trust Company *(Netherlands)*	1117	DSP Financial Consultants Limited *(India)*	681
Discount Bank & Trust Company *(Switzerland)*	1515	DSP Securities *(India)*	681
Discount Bank (Latin America) *(Uruguay)*	2025	Dubrovacka banka dd *(Croatia)*	296
Diskont Bank AG *(Austria)*	86	Dutch State Treasury Agency *(Netherlands)*	1117
Diskontobanken A/S *(Denmark)*	344		
Djurslands Bank A/S *(Denmark)*	344		

A-25

BANK	PAGE NO
E L & C Baillieu Stockbrokering Limited	49
East Asia Asset Management Company Limited (Hong Kong, China)	610
Eastern Caribbean Central Bank (Saint Kitts and Nevis)	1275
East-West Investment Bank (Russian Federation)	1258
East-West United Bank SA (Luxembourg)	1005
Ecoban Finance (Europe) Limited (United Kingdom)	1738
Ecoban Finance Limited (United States)	1950
Eco-Invest Brd SA (Romania)	1248
The ECU Group plc (United Kingdom)	1739
ED & F Man International Limited (United Kingdom)	1739
Edinburgh Fund Managers plc (United Kingdom)	1740
Eesti Pank/Bank of Estonia (Estonia)	376
AS Eesti Uhispank (Estonia)	377
EFG Bank European Financial Group (Switzerland)	1517
EFG Capital International (United States)	1950
EFG Eurobank SA (Greece)	565
EFG Private Bank (Channel Islands) Limited (Channel Islands)	248
EFG Private Bank Limited (United Kingdom)	1740
EFG Private Bank (Luxembourg) SA (Luxembourg)	1006
EFG Private Bank SA (Switzerland)	1518
EFG-Hermes (Egypt)	367
EFIBANCA SpA (Italy)	795
Egnatia Securities SA (Greece)	566
A/S Egnsbank Nord (Denmark)	344
Egypt Arab African Bank SAE (Egypt)	367
Egyptian American Bank (Egypt)	368
Egyptian British Bank (Egypt)	369
Eksportfinans ASA (Norway)	1153
Elbim Bank (United Kingdom)	1740
Emirates Bank International (United Kingdom)	1740
Emirates Bank International PJSC (United Arab Emirates)	1635
Energobank (Russian Federation)	1258
ENI International Bank Limited (Bahamas)	103
Enskilda Securities (Norway)	1153
Enskilda Securities (Sweden)	1454
Enskilda Securities (United Kingdom)	1741
ENSO Group (Finland)	388
EPS Finance Limited (Switzerland)	1518
Eptasim SpA (Italy)	796
Equator USA Inc (United States)	1950
Equitable Banking Corporation (Hong Kong, China)	610
Equitable Banking Corporation (Philippines)	1188
AS Era Pank Limited (Estonia)	378
Ergo Securities SA (Greece)	566
Ergobank (United Kingdom)	1741
Ergobank SA (Greece)	567
ERMGASSEN & Co (United Kingdom)	1741
Ernesto Allaria Ledesma (Argentina)	24
Erste Bank (Australia)	49
Erste Bank (United States)	1950

BANK	PAGE NO
Erste Bank der Österreichischen Sparkassen AG (Austria)	87
Erste Bank der Österreichischen Sparkassen (Italy)	796
Erste Bank der Österreichischen Sparkassen AG (United Kingdom)	1741
Erste Bank Sparkassen Praha (CR) as (Italy)	796
Erste Finance (Warsaw) Limited (Poland)	1210
Erste Securities Polska SA (Poland)	1210
ES International Holding SA (United Kingdom)	1742
ES-Finance SA/NV (Belgium)	148
Estonian Forexbank (Estonia)	378
Etrufin Reserco Limited (United Kingdom)	1742
EUFINGEST - Compagnia di Gestione e Finanza (Switzerland)	1518
EUFINTRADE SA (Switzerland)	1518
Euro Brokers Canada Limited (Canada)	224
Euro Brokers Inc (United States)	1951
Euro Brokers International Limited (United Kingdom)	1742
Euroclear Clearance System plc (Switzerland)	1519
Euroclear Operations Centre (Belgium)	148
Euroclear Operations Centre (Hong Kong, China)	611
Euroclear Operations Centre (Japan)	841
Euroclear Operations Centre (United Kingdom)	1743
Euroclear Operations Centre (United States)	1951
EUROHYPO AG Europaische Hypothekenbank der Deutschen Bank (Germany)	498
Eurohypo (UK) Limited (United Kingdom)	1743
Eurolease SA/NV (Belgium)	149
Europa Bank AG (Luxembourg)	1007
Europäische HypothekenBank SA (Luxembourg)	1007
European Bank for Reconstruction & Development (Albania)	1
European Bank for Reconstruction & Development (Azerbaijan)	101
European Bank for Reconstruction & Development (Belarus)	130
European Bank for Reconstruction & Development (Bulgaria)	206
European Bank for Reconstruction & Development (Croatia)	296
European Bank for Reconstruction & Development (Czech Republic)	321
European Bank for Reconstruction & Development (Estonia)	378
European Bank for Reconstruction & Development (Hungary)	669
European Bank for Reconstruction & Development (Kazakhstan)	895
European Bank for Reconstruction & Development (Kyrgyz Republic)	941
European Bank for Reconstruction & Development (Latvia)	944
European Bank for Reconstruction & Development (Lithuania)	967
European Bank for Reconstruction & Development (Macedonia)	1032

BANK	PAGE NO
European Bank for Reconstruction & Development (Moldova, Republic Of)	1091
European Bank for Reconstruction & Development (Poland)	1210
European Bank for Reconstruction & Development (Romania)	1248
European Bank for Reconstruction & Development (Russian Federation)	1259
European Bank for Reconstruction & Development (Russian Federation)	1260
European Bank for Reconstruction & Development (Slovak Republic)	1360
European Bank for Reconstruction & Development (Slovenia)	1374
European Bank for Reconstruction & Development (Ukraine)	1629
European Bank for Reconstruction & Development (United Kingdom)	1743
European Bank for Reconstruction & Development (Uzbekistan)	2027
European Bank Limited (Vanuatu)	2029
European Capital (United Kingdom)	1745
European Central Bank (Germany)	453
European Investment Bank (Italy)	796
European Investment Bank (Portugal)	1234
European Investment Bank (United Kingdom)	1745
Euroxx Securities SA (Greece)	567
EVEA Bank Limited (Estonia)	379
Exane (France)	430
Expandia Bank as (Czech Republic)	321
Export Credit Bank of Turkey Inc (Turkey)	1608
Export Development Bank of Egypt (Egypt)	370
Export Development Corporation (Canada)	224
The Export Import Bank of the Republic of Kazakstan (Kazakhstan)	895
The Export-Import Bank of India (Singapore)	1317
The Export-Import Bank of Japan (Australia)	49
The Export-Import Bank of Japan (Colombia)	290
The Export-Import Bank of Japan (France)	431
The Export-Import Bank of Japan (Germany)	499
The Export-Import Bank of Japan (Hong Kong, China)	611
The Export-Import Bank of Japan (India)	681
The Export-Import Bank of Japan (Japan)	841
The Export-Import Bank of Japan (Russian Federation)	1260
The Export-Import Bank of Japan (United Kingdom)	1745
The Export-Import Bank of Japan (United States)	1951
The Export-Import Bank of Japan (United States)	1952
The Export-Import Bank of Korea (Germany)	499
The Export-Import Bank of the Republic of China (Hungary)	669
Joint Stock Commercial Bank "Export-Import" (Moldova, Republic Of)	1091
Exprinter Banco SA (Argentina)	24
Exprinter International Bank NV (Netherlands Antilles)	1136
The Exxel Group SA (Argentina)	25

BANK	PAGE NO
Factor banka dd	1374
Faisal Finance Institution Inc (Turkey)	1609
Faisal Finance (Switzerland) SA (Switzerland)	1519
Faisal Islamic Bank of Egypt (Egypt)	370
The Farmers Bank of China (Taiwan, Republic of China)	1566
Faysal Islamic Bank of Bahrain EC (Bahrain)	116
FBD International Holdings (Ireland)	729
Federal Bank of Lebanon SAL (Lebanon)	958
Federal Bank of the Middle East (Cyprus)	310
Ferrier Lullin & Cie SA (Switzerland)	1519
FH International Financial Services Inc (United States)	1952
Fibi Bank (Switzerland) Limited (Switzerland)	1520
FIBI Bank (UK) plc (United Kingdom)	1745
Fiduciaria Indosuez SIM SpA (Italy)	797
Fiji Development Bank (Fiji)	383
Filanbanco SA (Ecuador)	357
Fimat Futures Asia Pte Limited (Singapore)	1317
FIMAT International Banque (France)	431
Fimat International Banque (Ireland)	729
Fimat International Banque, Sucursal en España (Spain)	1434
Fimat Snc (France)	431
FIMATEX SA (France)	431
Finacor (United Kingdom)	1746
Finacor Deutschland GmbH (Germany)	499
Finacor et Associés SA (Belgium)	149
Finacor Group (France)	431
Finacor-Rabe AG (Germany)	499
Financial Security Assurance Inc (Australia)	49
Financial Security Assurance Inc (Singapore)	1317
Financial Security Assurance Inc (United States)	1952
Financial Security Assurance (UK) Limited (France)	434
Financial Security Assurance (UK) Limited (Spain)	1434
Financial Security Assurance (UK) Limited (United Kingdom)	1746
Finansbank AS (Turkey)	1609
Finansbank (Suisse) SA (Switzerland)	1520
Finansrådet - Danske Pengeinstitutters Forening (Denmark)	344
Finanz AG Zürich (Singapore)	1317
Finanz AG Zürich (Switzerland)	1520
Finanziaria Sumitomo (Italia) SpA (Italy)	797
FINARBIT AG (Switzerland)	1520
FINARBIT SA (Switzerland)	1521
Fincor - Mediação Financiera SA (Portugal)	1235
Fincor Finance Corporation Limited (Zimbabwe)	2045
Fincor Sociedade Corretora SA (Portugal)	1236
Fineurop SpA (Italy)	797
FINEX Europe (Ireland)	729
Finex Swiss Money Broker AG (Switzerland)	1521
JM Finn & Co (United Kingdom)	1746
Finter Bank Zürich (Switzerland)	1521
First Austrian International Limited (United Kingdom)	1747

A-27

BANK	PAGE NO
First Bangkok City Bank Public Limited Company (Thailand)	1589
First Bank of Nigeria (Nigeria)	1144
First Bank of Nigeria plc (United Kingdom)	1747
The First Bank of Toyama Limited (Japan)	841
First Chicago Capital Markets Inc (United States)	1952
First Chicago NBD (United Kingdom)	1747
First Chicago NBD Bank Canada (Canada)	225
First Commercial Bank (Germany)	500
First Commercial Bank (Singapore)	1318
First Commercial Bank (Taiwan, Republic of China)	1566
First Commercial Bank (United States)	1952
First Commercial Bank Limited (United Kingdom)	1748
First East International Bank (Bulgaria)	206
The First International Bank of Israel Limited (Israel)	743
First International Merchant Bank Limited (Malta)	1072
First International Merchant Bank Limited (United Kingdom)	1748
First Investment Bank Limited (Bulgaria)	207
First Marathon Securities Limited (Canada)	225
First National Bank of Chicago (The) (Hong Kong, China)	611
The First National Bank of Chicago (Japan)	842
First National Bank of Maryland (United Kingdom)	1748
First National Bank of Namibia Limited (Namibia)	1101
First National Bank of Southern Africa Limited (South Africa)	1386
First National Bank of Southern Africa Limited (United States)	1953
First Pacific Bank Limited (Hong Kong, China)	611
First Ukranian International Bank (United Kingdom)	1748
First Union National Bank (United States)	1953
Firstar Trust Company (United States)	1953
Firstcorp Merchant Bank Limited (South Africa)	1386
Fischer Partners Fondkommission AB (Sweden)	1455
Five Arrows Leasing Group Limited (United Kingdom)	1748
Robert Fleming & Co Limited (Luxembourg)	1007
Fleming Asset Management (Luxembourg) SA (Luxembourg)	1007
Robert Fleming (Deutschland) GmbH (Germany)	501
Robert Fleming (France) SA (France)	434
Robert Fleming Holdings Limited (United Kingdom)	1749
Robert Fleming Inc (United States)	1953
Fleming Investment Management Limited (Czech Republic)	321
Fleming Latin Pacific Peru SA (Peru)	1183
Fleming Martin Securities Limited (Namibia)	1102
Fleming Martin Securities Limited (South Africa)	1386
Robert Fleming (Polska) SA (Poland)	1211
Robert Fleming Argentina SA (Argentina)	25
Robert Fleming do Brasil Ltdo (Brazil)	194
Robert Fleming Holdings Limited (Lebanon)	958
Robert Fleming Spain AV SA (Spain)	1435
Robert Fleming (Switzerland) AG (Switzerland)	1522
Flemings (Bahrain)	117
Flemings (Jersey) Limited (Channel Islands)	248

BANK	PAGE NO
Fokus Bank ASA (Norway)	1153
Foreign and Colonial Emerging Markets Limited (United Kingdom)	1750
FöreningsSparbanken - SwedBank (Sweden)	1455
Foresbank as (Czech Republic)	321
Fortis Bank Luxembourg (Luxembourg)	1008
Fortis Investments Belgium NV/SA (Belgium)	151
Four Seas Bank Limited (Singapore)	1318
Fox-Pitt, Kelton Limited (United Kingdom)	1750
FR Partners Limited (New Zealand)	1141
Frankfurt Bukarest Bank AG (Germany)	501
Frankfurter Bodenkreditbank AG (Germany)	501
Frankfurter Sparkasse (Germany)	501
Fransabank (France) SA (France)	435
Fransabank SAL (Lebanon)	958
Fredericks Michael & Co (United States)	1954
Friesland Bank Securities (Netherlands)	1117
FRP Securities (New Zealand)	1141
FTI - Banque Fiduciary Trust (Switzerland)	1522
FTI Finance (Ireland)	730
Fubon Commercial Bank (Taiwan, Republic of China)	1566
Fubon Securities Co Limited (Taiwan, Republic of China)	1567
Fuji Bank Canada (Canada)	225
The Fuji Bank Limited (Bahrain)	117
The Fuji Bank Limited (Brazil)	194
The Fuji Bank Limited (France)	435
The Fuji Bank Limited (Hong Kong, China)	612
The Fuji Bank Limited (India)	681
The Fuji Bank Limited (Indonesia)	707
The Fuji Bank Limited (Japan)	842
The Fuji Bank Limited (Korea, South)	912
The Fuji Bank Limited (Malaysia)	1049
The Fuji Bank Limited (Singapore)	1318
The Fuji Bank Limited (Thailand)	1590
The Fuji Bank Limited (United Kingdom)	1751
The Fuji Bank Limited (United States)	1954
The Fuji Bank Limited (United States)	1955
The Fuji Bank Limited (Vietnam)	2036
Fuji Bank (Luxembourg) SA (Luxembourg)	1008
Fuji Bank Nederland NV (Netherlands)	1118
Fuji Bank (Schweiz) AG (Switzerland)	1522
Fuji Capital Markets (HK) Limited (Hong Kong, China)	612
The Fuji Futures (Singapore) Pte Limited (Singapore)	1319
Fuji International Finance (Hong Kong) Limited (Hong Kong, China)	612
Fuji International Finance plc (United Kingdom)	1751
Fujigin Factors Limited (Japan)	842
Fukuoka Finance International Limited (Hong Kong, China)	613
The Fukutoku Bank Limited (Japan)	842
Furman Selz (Japan)	843
Furman Selz (United Kingdom)	1752
Furman Selz Financial Services (Ireland)	730

BANK	PAGE NO	BANK	PAGE NO

Garanti Bank 1118
Garanti Bank *(Switzerland)*.. 1522
Garanti Bank Moscow *(Russian Federation)*............. 1260
Garanti Menkul Klymetler AS *(Turkey)*........................ 1610
Garban Europe Limited *(United Kingdom)*.................. 1752
Garcia Navarro y Cia SA *(Argentina)*.......................... 25
Garlick & Co Limited *(New Zealand)*.......................... 1141
Gartmore Investment Management plc *(United Kingdom)*.. 1752
Garvin GuyButler Corporation *(United States)*........... 1955
Gefina SpA - Generali Group *(Italy)*............................ 797
GeldHandels GmbH HPC *(Germany)*........................... 502
Genbel Securities Limited *(South Africa)*................... 1387
General Banking & Trust Co Limited *(Hungary)*......... 669
General Re Financial Securities Limited *(United Kingdom)*.. 1753
Generale Bank *(Belgium)*... 152
Generale Bank *(China)*.. 276
Generale Bank *(Czech Republic)*................................ 322
Generale Bank *(India)*... 681
Generale Bank *(Indonesia)*... 707
Generale Bank *(Italy)*.. 797
Generale Bank *(Japan)*... 843
Generale Bank *(Mexico)*... 1084
Generale Bank *(Portugal)*... 1236
Generale Bank *(Turkey)*.. 1611
Generale Bank - Banco Belga *(Spain)*........................ 1435
Generale Bank Niederlassung Deutschland *(Germany)*.. 502
Generale Bank SA / NV *(United Kingdom)*.................. 1753
Gensec Bank Limited *(South Africa)*.......................... 1388
Gerrard & King Limited *(United Kingdom)*................. 1754
GFI Group Inc *(United Kingdom)*................................ 1754
Ghana International Bank *(United Kingdom)*............. 1755
The Gibraltar Private Bank Limited *(Gibraltar)*............ 554
Gilde Investment Management *(Netherlands)*............ 1118
Girobank plc *(United Kingdom)*.................................. 1755
Girofin SA *(Switzerland)*... 1523
Giubergia Warburg SIM SpA *(Italy)*............................. 798
Gjensidige Bank AS *(Norway)*..................................... 1155
Glass, Ginsburg Limited *(United States)*.................... 1955
Global Securities *(Turkey)*.. 1611
Glumina Banka dd *(Croatia)*....................................... 297
GNI Financial Products Limited *(United Kingdom)*..... 1755
GNI Limited *(United Kingdom)*................................... 1756
Goldman Sachs & Co *(Switzerland)*........................... 1523
Goldman Sachs & Co *(United States)*........................ 1956
Goldman Sachs & Co oHG / Goldman Sachs & Co Finanz GmbH *(Germany)*.. 503
Goldman Sachs (Asia) LLC *(Hong Kong, China)*......... 613
Goldman Sachs Asset Management International *(United Kingdom)*.. 1757
Goldman Sachs Asset Management Japan Limited *(Japan)*... 843
Goldman Sachs Australia LLC *(Australia)*................... 49
Goldman Sachs Canada *(Canada)*............................. 226

Goldman Sachs Equity Securities (UK) *(United Kingdom)*.. 1757
Goldman Sachs International *(Spain)*........................ 1436
Goldman Sachs International *(United Kingdom)*....... 1757
Goldman Sachs International Bank *(Japan)*.............. 843
Goldman Sachs International Bank *(United Kingdom)*.. 1766
Goldman Sachs International Finance *(United Kingdom)*.. 1766
Goldman Sachs Investment Trust Management Limited *(Japan)*... 843
Goldman Sachs (Japan) Limited *(Japan)*................... 843
Goldman Sachs Paris Inc et Cie *(France)*.................. 435
Goldman Sachs SIM SpA *(Italy)*.................................. 798
Goldman Sachs (Singapore) Pte *(Singapore)*............. 1319
Goodbody Stockbrokers *(Ireland)*............................... 730
Gordon Capital Corporation *(Canada)*...................... 226
Gorenjska banka dd Kranj *(Slovenia)*........................ 1375
Gospodarsko Kreditna banka dd *(Croatia)*................ 297
Gottex Brokers SA *(Switzerland)*................................ 1523
GPA Group plc *(Ireland)*... 730
Eduard de Graaff & Co BV *(Netherlands)*.................. 1119
Grand Cathay Securities Corporation *(Taiwan, Republic of China)*.. 1567
Grand Metroplitan Finance Ireland *(Ireland)*............. 731
Grantchester Securities *(United States)*.................... 1956
Granville Bank Limited *(United Kingdom)*.................. 1767
Granville Holdings plc *(United Kingdom)*................... 1767
Greenwich Capital Markets *(United Kingdom)*........... 1768
Greenwich Capital Markets Inc *(United States)*......... 1956
Greenwich Natwest *(United Kingdom)*....................... 1768
Greig Middleton & Co Limited *(United Kingdom)*....... 1769
Grindlays Private Bank *(United Kingdom)*................. 1770
Groupe BNP Panama *(Panama)*................................ 1175
Groupement des Banquiers Prives Genevois *(Switzerland)*... 1523
Groupo Financiero Serfin *(Mexico)*............................ 1084
Grupo Financiero Banorte *(Mexico)*........................... 1085
Gruppo Arca Nordest *(United Kingdom)*..................... 1770
GTC Globo Trading & Consulting AG *(Switzerland)*... 1523
Guangdong Development Bank *(China)*.................... 277
Guangdong Development Bank *(Hong Kong, China)*... 613
Gudme Raaschou Investment Bankers Limited *(Denmark)*.. 345
Guernsey International Fund Managers Limited *(Channel Islands)*.. 248
Guinness Flight Hambro Asset Management Limited *(United Kingdom)*.. 1770
Guinness Mahon & Co Limited *(United Kingdom)*...... 1771
Guinness Mahon Guernsey Limited *(Channel Islands)*... 248
The Gulf Bank KSC *(Kuwait)*....................................... 936
Gulf International Bank BSC *(Bahrain)*....................... 117
Gulf International Bank BSC *(Lebanon)*..................... 959
Gulf International Bank BSC *(Singapore)*.................. 1319
Gulf International Bank BSC *(United Kingdom)*......... 1771
Gulf International Bank BSC *(United States)*............. 1957
Gulf Investment Corporation (GIC) *(Kuwait)*............... 936

A-29

BANK	PAGE NO
Gulf Monetary Group *(Bahrain)*	119
The Gunma Bank Limited *(Japan)*	844
The Gunma Bank Limited *(United States)*	1957
Guy Butler *(United Kingdom)*	1771
Guyerzeller Bank AG *(Switzerland)*	1524
GZB-Bank Genossenschaftliche Zentralbank AG *(Germany)*	503
H/S Haandværkerbanken	346
Habib Bank AG Zürich *(United Arab Emirates)*	1636
Habib Bank AG Zürich *(United Kingdom)*	1771
Habib Bank Limited *(United Kingdom)*	1772
Habibsons Bank Limited *(United Kingdom)*	1772
Hachijuni Asia Limited *(Hong Kong, China)*	613
The Hachijuni Bank Limited *(Hong Kong, China)*	614
The Hachijuni Bank Limited *(Japan)*	844
The Hachijuni Bank Limited *(Singapore)*	1319
The Hachijuni Bank Limited *(United Kingdom)*	1772
The Hachijuni Bank Limited *(United States)*	1957
Haga Bank *(Indonesia)*	707
Halifax plc *(United Kingdom)*	1772
OJSC Halyk Savings Bank of Kasakstan *(Kazakhstan)*	896
Hambrecht & Quist Euromarkets SA *(France)*	435
Hambrecht & Quist LLC *(United Kingdom)*	1773
Hambrecht & Quist LLC *(United States)*	1957
Hamburger Sparkasse *(Germany)*	504
Hamburgische Landesbank *(United Kingdom)*	1774
Hamburgische Landesbank - Girozentrale *(Germany)*	505
Hamburgische Landesbank - Girozentrale *(Hong Kong, China)*	614
Hana Finance Asia Limited *(Hong Kong, China)*	614
Handelsfinanz-CCF Bank *(Switzerland)*	1525
Handelsfinanz-CCF Bank *(Switzerland)*	1524
Hang Seng Bank Limited *(Hong Kong, China)*	614
Hani Securities Limited *(Hong Kong, China)*	615
Hanil Bank *(Japan)*	845
Hanil Bank *(Singapore)*	1319
Hanil Bank *(United Kingdom)*	1774
Hanil Bank (Deutschland) GmbH *(Germany)*	506
Hansa Financial Services *(Russian Federation)*	1261
Hansa Investments *(Lithuania)*	967
Hansa Investments Group *(Estonia)*	379
Hansa Investments Latvia *(Latvia)*	945
Hansabank *(Estonia)*	380
Hansabank-Latvija *(Latvia)*	945
Harlow Butler Mexico SA de CV *(Mexico)*	1085
Harlow Meyer Savage Canada *(Canada)*	226
Harlow Meyer Savage LLC *(United States)*	1958
Harris Trust & Savings Bank *(United Kingdom)*	1774
Harvard Management Co *(United States)*	1959
Hauck & Aufhäuser Banquiers Luxembourg SA *(Luxembourg)*	1008
Hauck & Aufhäuser Privatbankiers KGaA *(Germany)*	506
Havana International Bank Limited *(United Kingdom)*	1775

BANK	PAGE NO
Hawaii National Bank *(United States)*	1959
TJ Heggeli & Co AS *(Norway)*	1155
Helaba Dublin Landesbank Hessen-Thüringen International *(Ireland)*	731
Helaba Finance BV *(Netherlands)*	1119
Helaba Financial Futures Limited *(United Kingdom)*	1775
Helaba International Finance plc *(Ireland)*	731
Helaba Investment AG *(Switzerland)*	1525
Helaba Luxembourg *(Luxembourg)*	1009
Helaba (Schweiz) Landesbank Hessen Thüringen *(Switzerland)*	1525
Helarb Management SA *(Switzerland)*	1525
Hellenic Bank Limited *(Cyprus)*	310
Henderson Investment Services *(United Kingdom)*	1775
Herzog Heine Geduld *(United States)*	1959
HFC Bank plc *(United Kingdom)*	1775
HG Asia Limited *(Hong Kong, China)*	615
Hibernia National Bank *(United States)*	1960
Hill Samuel Bank (Jersey) Limited *(Channel Islands)*	249
The Hiroshima Bank Limited *(Hong Kong, China)*	615
The Hiroshima Bank Limited *(Japan)*	845
Hispano Commerzbank (Gibraltar) Limited *(Gibraltar)*	554
Hock Hua Bank Berhad *(Malaysia)*	1049
Hoenig & Co Inc *(Japan)*	845
Hoenig & Co Inc *(United States)*	1960
Hoenig & Company Limited *(United Kingdom)*	1776
Hoenig (Far East) Limited *(Hong Kong, China)*	615
Hohenzollerische Landesbank-Kreissparkasse *(Germany)*	506
The Hokkaido Takushoku Bank Limited *(Japan)*	845
The Hokuetsu Bank Limited *(Hong Kong, China)*	616
The Hokuriku Bank Limited *(Japan)*	846
Hokuriku Finance (Hong Kong) Limited *(Hong Kong, China)*	616
Hong Kong Monetary Authority *(Hong Kong, China)*	577
Hong Leong Bank Berhad *(Malaysia)*	1050
Hong Leong Finance Limited *(Singapore)*	1319
The Hongkong & Shanghai Banking Corporation Limited *(Bahrain)*	119
The Hongkong & Shanghai Banking Corporation Limited *(Hong Kong, China)*	616
The Hongkong & Shanghai Banking Corporation Limited *(India)*	681
The Hongkong & Shanghai Banking Corporation Limited *(Indonesia)*	708
The Hongkong & Shanghai Banking Corporation Limited *(Singapore)*	1320
The Hongkong & Shanghai Banking Corporation Limited *(Taiwan, Republic of China)*	1568
The Hongkong & Shanghai Banking Corporation Limited *(Thailand)*	1590
The Hongkong & Shanghai Banking Corporation Limited *(Vietnam)*	2036
Hongkong Bank of Canada *(Canada)*	227
The Hongkong Chinese Bank Limited *(Hong Kong, China)*	618

BANK	PAGE NO
HongkongBank of Australia Limited *(Australia)*	49
HongkongBank Malaysia Berhad *(Malaysia)*	1051
van der Hoop Effektenbank NV *(Netherlands)*	1119
Hottinger & Cie *(Switzerland)*	1526
Housing & Commercial Bank *(Korea, South)*	913
The Housing Bank *(Jordan)*	887
Hrvatska narodna banka *(Croatia)*	293
HSBC Asset Management Australia Limited *(Australia)*	50
HSBC Banco Roberts SA *(Argentina)*	25
HSBC Equator Bank plc *(Kenya)*	901
HSBC Equator Bank plc *(Mozambique)*	1100
HSBC Equator Bank plc *(South Africa)*	1388
HSBC Equator Bank plc *(Uganda)*	1627
HSBC Equator Bank plc *(United Kingdom)*	1776
HSBC Forfaiting Asia Seoul *(Korea, South)*	913
HSBC Forfaiting Limited *(United Kingdom)*	1776
HSBC Holdings plc *(United Kingdom)*	1777
HSBC Investment Bank Asia Limited *(Hong Kong, China)*	618
HSBC Investment Bank Asia Limited *(Japan)*	846
HSBC Investment Bank Cyprus Limited *(Cyprus)*	311
HSBC Investment Bank NV *(Netherlands)*	1119
HSBC Investment Bank plc *(Singapore)*	1320
HSBC Securities *(United Kingdom)*	1777
HSBC Securities Contrepartie SA *(France)*	436
HSBC Securities Inc *(United States)*	1960
HSBC Securities Limited *(Japan)*	846
Hua Chiao Commercial Bank Limited *(Hong Kong, China)*	619
Hua Nan Commercial Bank Limited *(Hong Kong, China)*	620
Hua Nan Commercial Bank Limited *(Taiwan, Republic of China)*	1569
Hua Nan Commercial Bank Limited *(United Kingdom)*	1777
Hua Nan Commercial Bank Limited *(United States)*	1961
Hungarian Foreign Trade Bank Limited *(Hungary)*	670
Hungarian International Finance Limited *(Hungary)*	670
Hungarian International Finance Limited *(United Kingdom)*	1777
The Huntington National Bank *(United States)*	1961
HVB Capital Markets (Asia) Limited *(Japan)*	846
The Hyakugo Bank Limited *(Japan)*	846
The Hyakujushi Bank Limited *(Japan)*	847
The Hyakujushi Bank Limited *(United States)*	1961
HYPO Bank CZ as *(Czech Republic)*	322
Hypo Banka Croatia *(Croatia)*	298
HYPO-Bausparkasse AG *(Austria)*	89
HYPOSWISS *(Switzerland)*	1527
Hypothekenbank in Essen AG *(Germany)*	506
HypoVereinsbank *(Brazil)*	194
HypoVereinsbank *(China)*	277
HypoVereinsbank *(Colombia)*	290
HypoVereinsbank *(Greece)*	567
HypoVereinsbank *(Hong Kong, China)*	620
HypoVereinsbank *(India)*	682
HypoVereinsbank *(Iran (Islamic Republic Of))*	714

BANK	PAGE NO
HypoVereinsbank *(Italy)*	798
HypoVereinsbank *(Korea, South)*	913
HypoVereinsbank *(Mexico)*	1085
HypoVereinsbank *(Russian Federation)*	1261
HypoVereinsbank *(South Africa)*	1388
HypoVereinsbank *(United States)*	1961
HypoVereinsbank *(United States)*	1962
HypoVereinsbank *(Vietnam)*	2036
HypoVereinsbank / Vereins und-Westbank *(Argentina)*	25
A/S HypoVereinsbank *(Latvia)*	946
HypoVereinsbank (Bayerische Hypo und Vereinsbank AG) *(Germany)*	507
HypoVereinsbank Capital Corporation *(United States)*	1962
HypoVereinsbank (CZ) as *(Czech Republic)*	322
HypoVereinsbank Hungaria Rt *(Hungary)*	671
HypoVereinsbank Ireland *(Ireland)*	731
HypoVereinsbank Luxembourg Société Anonyme *(Luxembourg)*	1009
HypoVereinsbank Polska SA *(Poland)*	1211
HypoVereinsbank Slovakia A/S *(Slovak Republic)*	1360
Hythe Securities Limited *(United Kingdom)*	1778
Hyundai International Merchant Bank *(Korea, South)*	913
Hyundai Securities (Europe) Limited *(United Kingdom)*	1778
Ibercaja	1436
Ibero Platina Bank AG *(Argentina)*	26
Ibero Platina Bank AG *(Colombia)*	290
Ibero Platina Bank AG *(Costa Rica)*	292
Ibero Platina Bank AG *(El Salvador)*	376
Ibero Platina Bank AG *(Germany)*	507
Ibero Platina Bank AG *(Guatemala)*	575
Ibero Platina Bank AG *(Peru)*	1183
Ibero Platina Bank AG *(Uruguay)*	2026
IBJ Asia Limited *(Hong Kong, China)*	621
IBJ International plc *(United Kingdom)*	1778
IBJ Merchant Bank (Singapore) Limited *(Singapore)*	1321
IBJ Schroder Bank & Trust Company *(United States)*	1962
IBJ Securities Co Limited *(Japan)*	847
IBJ-Sucursal en España *(Spain)*	1436
IC Banka as *(Czech Republic)*	323
ICC Bank plc *(Ireland)*	731
ICCREA SpA *(Italy)*	798
ICCRI - Istituto di Credito delle Casse di Risparmio Italiane SpA *(Italy)*	799
Ichiyoshi Securities Co Limited *(Japan)*	847
IDB Holding Corporation Limited *(Israel)*	744
Ifabanque SA *(France)*	436
IFDC Limited *(United Kingdom)*	1779
IFP Intermoney Financial Products SIM SpA *(Italy)*	799
IFP Intermoney Financial Products Limited *(Russian Federation)*	1261
IFP Intermoney Financial Products SA *(Switzerland)*	1527

A-31

BANK	PAGE NO	BANK	PAGE NO
Ihag Handelsbank Zürich *(Switzerland)*	1527	Industriebank von Japan (Deutschland) AG	
IKB Deutsche Industriebank AG *(Germany)*	508	*(Germany)*	509
IKB Deutsche Industriebank AG *(Luxembourg)*	1010	Industry & Construction Bank *(Russian Federation)*	1262
IKB International *(Luxembourg)*	1011	ING Bank *(Germany)*	509
Iktisat Bankasi TAS *(Turkey)*	1612	ING Bank *(Greece)*	567
IMI Sigeco (UK) Limited *(United Kingdom)*	1779	ING Bank *(Hungary)*	671
Imperial Bank *(United Kingdom)*	1780	ING Bank *(Italy)*	800
Index Securities SA *(Switzerland)*	1528	ING Bank *(Uruguay)*	2026
Indian Overseas Bank *(Sri Lanka)*	1447	ING Bank of Canada *(Canada)*	228
NV de Indonesische Overzeese Bank *(Indonesia)*	708	ING Bank (Luxembourg) SA *(Luxembourg)*	1011
Indosuez Argentina SA *(Argentina)*	26	ING Bank NV *(Australia)*	50
PT Indosuez Indonesia Bank *(Indonesia)*	708	ING Bank NV *(Japan)*	848
Indosuez Mexico SA de CV *(Mexico)*	1085	ING Bank NV *(Netherlands)*	1121
Indosuez WI Carr Securities Limited *(Hong Kong, China)*	621	ING Bank NV *(Netherlands)*	1120
		ING Bank Rt *(Hungary)*	671
Indover Asia Limited *(Hong Kong, China)*	621	ING Bank Suisse *(Switzerland)*	1529
Indover Bank *(Netherlands)*	1120	ING Bank (Switzerland) *(Switzerland)*	1529
IndusInd Bank Limited *(India)*	682	ING Baring Capital Markets *(Czech Republic)*	323
The Industrial & Commercial Bank of China *(China)*	277	ING Baring Corretora de Valores Mobiliáros	
The Industrial & Commercial Bank of China *(Singapore)*	1322	*(Brazil)*	195
Industrial and Commercial Bank of Vietnam		ING Baring Fiseco *(Chile)*	267
(Vietnam)	2037	ING Baring Furman Selz LLC *(United States)*	1963
The Industrial Bank of Japan (Canada) *(Canada)*	228	ING Baring International *(Thailand)*	1590
The Industrial Bank of Japan Limited *(Bahrain)*	119	ING Baring México SA de CV *(Mexico)*	1086
The Industrial Bank of Japan Limited *(Brazil)*	195	ING Baring Private Bank *(Belgium)*	153
The Industrial Bank of Japan Limited *(China)*	277	ING Baring Private Bank *(Channel Islands)*	249
The Industrial Bank of Japan Limited *(China)*	278	ING Baring Private Bank *(Uruguay)*	2026
The Industrial Bank of Japan Limited *(France)*	436	ING Baring Research (Malaysia) Sendirian Berhad	
The Industrial Bank of Japan Limited *(Hong Kong, China)*	622	*(Malaysia)*	1051
		ING Baring Securities *(Korea, South)*	916
The Industrial Bank of Japan Limited *(Italy)*	800	ING Baring Securities (China) *(China)*	278
The Industrial Bank of Japan Limited *(Japan)*	848	ING Baring Securities (France) *(France)*	436
The Industrial Bank of Japan Limited *(Korea, South)*	915	ING Baring Securities (Hungary) *(Hungary)*	672
		PT ING Baring Securities (Indonesia) *(Indonesia)*	709
The Industrial Bank of Japan Limited *(Malaysia)*	1051	ING Baring Securities (Japan) *(Japan)*	849
The Industrial Bank of Japan Limited *(Mexico)*	1085	ING Baring Securities (Japan) Limited *(Japan)*	849
The Industrial Bank of Japan Limited *(Panama)*	1175	ING Baring Securities (Korea) *(Korea, South)*	917
The Industrial Bank of Japan Limited *(Singapore)*	1322	ING Baring Securities Limited *(Switzerland)*	1529
The Industrial Bank of Japan Limited *(Switzerland)*	1528	ING Baring Securities (London) Limited *(United Kingdom)*	1780
The Industrial Bank of Japan Limited *(Thailand)*	1590	ING Baring Securities (Philippines) *(Philippines)*	1189
The Industrial Bank of Japan Limited *(United States)*	1962	ING Baring Securities (Poland) *(Poland)*	1211
		ING Baring Securities Singapore Pte Limited	
The Industrial Bank of Japan (Luxembourg) SA *(Luxembourg)*	1011	*(Singapore)*	1323
The Industrial Bank of Japan NJ (Switzerland)		ING Baring Securities (Slovakia) *(Slovak Republic)*	1361
Limited *(Switzerland)*	1528	ING Baring Securities (Taiwan) *(Taiwan, Republic of China)*	1570
Industrial Bank of Korea *(Hong Kong, China)*	622	ING Baring Sociedad de Bolsa (Argentina) SA	
Industrial Bank of Korea *(Japan)*	848	*(Argentina)*	26
Industrial Bank of Korea *(Korea, South)*	916	ING Baring (US) Financial Holding Corporation	
Industrial Bank of Korea Europe SA *(United Kingdom)*	1780	*(United States)*	1963
		ING Barings *(Argentina)*	26
Industrial Bank of Kuwait *(Kuwait)*	937	ING Barings *(Austria)*	89
Industrial Bank of Latvia *(Latvia)*	946	ING Barings *(Belgium)*	153
Industrial Development Bank of Turkey *(Turkey)*	1613	ING Barings *(Brazil)*	195
Industrial Development Corporation of Zimbabwe		ING Barings *(Bulgaria)*	208
Limited *(Zimbabwe)*	2045	ING Barings *(Chile)*	268
		ING Barings *(China)*	278

A-32

BANK	PAGE NO
ING Barings *(China)*	279
ING Barings *(China)*	278
ING Barings *(Colombia)*	291
ING Barings *(Cuba)*	305
ING Barings *(Czech Republic)*	324
ING Barings *(Czech Republic)*	323
ING Barings *(Czech Republic)*	324
ING Barings *(Ecuador)*	358
ING Barings *(France)*	437
ING Barings *(Hong Kong, China)*	622
ING Barings *(India)*	682
ING Barings *(Ireland)*	732
ING Barings *(Japan)*	849
ING Barings *(Kazakhstan)*	896
ING Barings *(Korea, South)*	917
ING Barings *(Lebanon)*	959
ING Barings *(Malaysia)*	1051
ING Barings *(Netherlands Antilles)*	1137
ING Barings *(Paraguay)*	1177
ING Barings *(Peru)*	1183
ING Barings *(Philippines)*	1189
ING Barings *(Poland)*	1211
ING Barings *(Romania)*	1248
ING Barings *(Russian Federation)*	1262
ING Barings *(Singapore)*	1323
ING Barings *(Slovak Republic)*	1361
ING Barings *(Spain)*	1436
ING Barings *(Taiwan, Republic of China)*	1570
ING Barings *(Thailand)*	1590
ING Barings *(Turkey)*	1614
ING Barings *(Ukraine)*	1629
ING Barings *(United Kingdom)*	1781
ING Barings *(Venezuela)*	2032
ING Barings *(Vietnam)*	2037
ING Barings *(Zimbabwe)*	2045
ING Barings Asia *(Hong Kong, China)*	622
ING Barings Eurasia ZAO *(Russian Federation)*	1262
ING Barings Futures & Options Clearing Services *(Germany)*	509
ING Barings Futures & Options Clearing Services *(Hong Kong, China)*	622
ING Barings Futures & Options Clearing Services *(Singapore)*	1323
ING Barings Futures & Options Clearing Services *(United Kingdom)*	1782
ING Barings Futures & Options Clearing Services *(United States)*	1963
ING Barings Regional Office-Asia Pacific *(Singapore)*	1323
ING Barings Southern Africa (Pty) Limited *(South Africa)*	1389
ING Belgium *(Belgium)*	153
ING Capital *(United States)*	1963
ING Direct *(Canada)*	228
ING Furman Selz Asset Management *(United States)*	1963
PT ING Indonesia Bank *(Indonesia)*	709
ING Investment Management *(Brazil)*	196

BANK	PAGE NO
ING Investment Management Italia SGR *(Italy)*	801
ING Mercantile Mutual Bank *(Australia)*	51
ING Merchant Bank (Singapore) Limited *(Singapore)*	1324
ING Serviços Ltda *(Brazil)*	196
ING Societe de Gestion *(Monaco)*	1095
ING Trust (Antilles) *(Netherlands Antilles)*	1137
ING Trust (Aruba) NV *(Aruba)*	35
ING Trust (Hong Kong) *(Hong Kong, China)*	623
ING Trust (Jersey) Limited *(Channel Islands)*	249
ING Trust (Luxembourg) *(Luxembourg)*	1011
ING Trust (Suisse) *(Switzerland)*	1529
ING (US) Capital Corporation *(United States)*	1963
ING (US) Financial Holdings *(United States)*	1964
ING-North East Asia Bank *(Korea, Dem. People's Rep Of)*	902
Inkom Capital *(Russian Federation)*	1262
Inkombank *(Cyprus)*	311
Inkombank *(United Kingdom)*	1782
Inserf SA de CV *(Mexico)*	1086
Instinet UK Limited *(United Kingdom)*	1782
Interacor AG *(Switzerland)*	1529
Inter-Alpha Group of Banks - Joint Representative Office *(Iran (Islamic Republic Of))*	714
Inter-American Development Bank *(France)*	437
Inter-American Development Bank *(United States)*	1964
Inter-American Investment Corporation *(United States)*	1964
Inter-Arab Investment Guarantee Corporation (IAIGC) *(Kuwait)*	937
Interbanca SpA *(Italy)*	801
Interbanco SA *(Portugal)*	1236
Interbank AS *(Turkey)*	1614
Interbanka as *(Czech Republic)*	324
Intercapital America Inc *(United States)*	1964
Intercapital plc *(Australia)*	51
Intercapital plc *(Denmark)*	346
Intercapital plc *(Germany)*	509
Intercapital plc *(Switzerland)*	1530
Intercapital plc *(United Kingdom)*	1783
Interchange SA *(Switzerland)*	1530
Inter-Európa Bank Rt *(Hungary)*	672
Interfin SIM SpA *(Italy)*	801
Interfinance Berhad *(Malaysia)*	1051
Interfinance SA *(Belgium)*	154
Intermediate Capital Group *(France)*	437
Intermediate Capital Group plc *(United Kingdom)*	1783
Intermonetary Corp *(United States)*	1965
International Bank of Asia Limited *(Hong Kong, China)*	623
International Bank for Economic Co-operation *(Russian Federation)*	1263
International Bank Services *(United States)*	1965
International Bank of Southern Africa Limited *(South Africa)*	1389
International Bank of Taipei *(Taiwan, Republic of China)*	1570

A-33

BANK	PAGE NO
International Bank of Taipei Macau Branch (Macau)	1030
International Capital Markets SIM SpA (Italy)	801
The International Commercial Bank of China (France)	437
The International Commercial Bank of China Co Limited (Panama)	1175
The International Commercial Bank of China Co Limited (Taiwan, Republic of China)	1570
The International Commercial Bank of China (United States)	1965
International Company for Finance & Investments (Russian Federation)	1263
International Finance Corporation (Argentina)	27
International Finance Corporation (Brazil)	196
International Finance Corporation (China)	279
International Finance Corporation (Czech Republic)	324
International Finance Corporation (France)	437
International Finance Corporation (Hungary)	672
International Finance Corporation (Indonesia)	709
International Finance Corporation (Morocco)	1099
International Finance Corporation (Poland)	1211
International Finance Corporation (Thailand)	1590
International Finance Corporation (Turkey)	1614
International Finance Corporation (United Kingdom)	1783
International Finance Corporation (United States)	1965
International Finance Corporation (Vietnam)	2037
International Finance Corporation (Zimbabwe)	2046
International Moscow Bank (Russian Federation)	1264
International Securities SA (Belgium)	154
INTERSETTLE - Swiss Corporation for International Securities Settlements (Switzerland)	1530
Inversiones Deutsche Morgan Grenfell SA (Chile)	268
Inversiones y Representaciones SA (Argentina)	27
INVESCO Asset Management Deutschland GmbH (Germany)	509
INVESCO Bank Deutschland OHG (Germany)	510
INVESTCORP Bank EC (Bahrain)	120
INVESTCORP International Inc (United Kingdom)	1784
INVESTCORP International Inc (United States)	1968
INVESTCORP Securities Limited (United Kingdom)	1784
INVESTCORP Trading Limited (Bahrain)	120
Investec Bank Limited (South Africa)	1389
Investec Bank (UK) Limited (United Kingdom)	1784
Investicna a Rozvojová banka as (Slovak Republic)	1361
Investiční a Postovní banka as (Czech Republic)	325
Investment Bank of Latvia (Latvia)	946
Investmentbank Austria AG (Austria)	89
Investors Bank & Trust Company (United States)	1968
Ionian and Popular Bank of Greece SA (Greece)	568
Ionian Bank (Bulgaria)	208
Ionian Bank (United Kingdom)	1784
Ippa Bank NV (Belgium)	154
Iran Overseas Investment Bank Limited (United Kingdom)	1785
Irish Intercontinental Bank Limited (Ireland)	732
Islamic International Arab Bank plc (Jordan)	889
Islandsbanki hf (Iceland)	677

BANK	PAGE NO
Israel Continental Bank Limited (Israel)	744
Israel Discount Bank Limited (Argentina)	27
Israel Discount Bank Limited (Israel)	744
Israel Discount Bank Limited (United Kingdom)	1785
Israel Discount Bank of New York (United States)	1968
Istarska Kreditna banka Umag dd (Croatia)	298
Istituto Bancario San Paolo di Torino SpA (Italy)	802
Istituto Bancario San Paolo di Torino SpA (Netherlands)	1122
Istituto Bancario San Paolo di Torino SpA (Singapore)	1324
Istituto Mobiliare Italiano SpA (Italy)	804
Istrobanka AS (Slovak Republic)	1362
Italian International Bank (United Kingdom)	1785
The Iyo Bank Limited (Japan)	849
The Iyo Bank Limited (United Kingdom)	1785
The Iyo Bank Limited (United States)	1969
Jadranska banka dd	299
Jahangir Siddiqui & Co Limited (Pakistan)	1166
Jammal Trust Bank (United Kingdom)	1785
Janata Bank (Bangladesh)	124
The Japan Development Bank (Germany)	510
The Japan Development Bank (United Kingdom)	1786
Japan Leasing Corporation (Japan)	850
Japan Securities Finance Co Limited (Japan)	850
Jardine Fleming Exchange Capital Securities Inc (Philippines)	1189
Jardine Fleming HNB Securities (Pvt) Limited (Sri Lanka)	1447
Jardine Fleming India Broking Limited (India)	682
Jardine Fleming India Securities Limited (India)	683
Jardine Fleming Limited (Hong Kong, China)	623
PT Jardine Fleming Nusantara Investment Management (Indonesia)	709
Jardine Fleming Pakistan (Pvt) Limited (Pakistan)	1168
Jardine Fleming Securities (Asia) Limited (Japan)	850
Jardine Fleming Securities Limited (China)	279
Jardine Fleming Securities Limited (Hong Kong, China)	624
Jardine Fleming Securities Limited (Korea, South)	917
Jardine Fleming Singapore Securities Pte Limited (Singapore)	1324
Jardine Fleming Thanakom Securities Limited (Thailand)	1591
Jefferies & Co Inc (United Kingdom)	1786
Jefferies & Co Inc (United States)	1969
Jian Sing Bank Limited (Hong Kong, China)	624
JM Sassoon & Co Pte Limited (Singapore)	1325
Joint-Stock Commercial Bank for Social Development UKRSOTSBANK (Ukraine)	1629
Jordan International Bank plc (United Kingdom)	1786
Jordan Islamic Bank for Finance & Investment (Jordan)	889
Jordan Kuwait Bank (Jordan)	889
Jordan National Bank plc (Cyprus)	311
Jordan National Bank plc (Jordan)	890

A-34

BANK	PAGE NO
José M Cascales & Associates *(Argentina)*	27
Joyo Bank (Europe) SA *(Belgium)*	155
The Joyo Bank Limited *(China)*	279
The Joyo Bank Limited *(Hong Kong, China)*	625
The Joyo Bank Limited *(Japan)*	850
The Joyo Bank Limited *(United Kingdom)*	1787
The Joyo Bank Limited *(United States)*	1970
JP Bank AB *(Sweden)*	1456
JP Morgan & Cie SA *(France)*	438
JP Morgan & Co Incorporated *(United States)*	1971
JP Morgan GmbH *(Germany)*	510
JP Morgan (Hong Kong) Limited *(Hong Kong, China)*	625
JP Morgan Nederland NV *(Netherlands)*	1122
JP Morgan Securities Asia Limited *(Singapore)*	1325
JP Morgan Securities Inc *(United States)*	1971
JP Morgan Securities Limited *(United Kingdom)*	1788
JP Morgan (Suisse) SA *(Switzerland)*	1531
JTB Forex SpA *(Italy)*	804
JTB Lira Services SIM SpA *(Italy)*	804
Jugobanka AD Beograd *(Yugoslavia)*	2041
Jugobanka DD *(United Kingdom)*	1789
Juroku Bank Limited *(Japan)*	851
Jyske Bank *(United Kingdom)*	1789
A/S Jyske Bank *(Denmark)*	346
Jyske Bank (España) SA *(Spain)*	1437
Jyske Bank (Gibraltar) Limited *(Gibraltar)*	554
Jyske Bank (Schweiz) *(Switzerland)*	1531
KAF-Astley & Pearce Sdn Berhad	1052
The Kagoshima Bank Limited *(Hong Kong, China)*	625
The Kagoshima Bank Limited *(Japan)*	851
The Kangwon Bank Limited *(Korea, South)*	917
Kankaku Securities Co Limited *(Japan)*	852
Kappa Securities SA *(Greece)*	568
Karamanof Securities SA *(Greece)*	568
Karic Banka dd *(Cyprus)*	312
Karlovacka banka *(Croatia)*	299
Kärntner Landes-und-Hypothekenbank AG *(Austria)*	89
KAS-Associatie NV *(Netherlands)*	1122
Kas-Associatie *(United Kingdom)*	1789
Kazkommerts Securites *(Kazakhstan)*	897
Kazkommertsbank *(Kazakhstan)*	897
KB Luxembourg (Monaco) *(Monaco)*	1095
KBC Bank *(Belgium)*	155
KBC Bank *(France)*	438
KBC Bank *(United States)*	1972
KBC Bank NV *(Czech Republic)*	325
KBC Bank NV *(Hong Kong, China)*	625
KBC Bank NV *(Ireland)*	732
KBC Bank NV *(Poland)*	1212
KBC Bank NV *(Spain)*	1437
KBC Bank NV *(United Kingdom)*	1789
KBC NV *(Taiwan, Republic of China)*	1571
KBC NV *(United Kingdom)*	1790
KBC Securities *(Belgium)*	157
KDB Asia Limited *(Hong Kong, China)*	626

BANK	PAGE NO
KDB Bank (UK) Limited *(United Kingdom)*	1790
KEB Australia Limited *(Australia)*	51
KEB International Limited *(United Kingdom)*	1791
Kempen & Co NV *(Netherlands)*	1123
Kempen & Co USA Inc *(United States)*	1972
Keppel Bank of Singapore Limited *(Hong Kong, China)*	626
Keppel Bank of Singapore Limited *(Singapore)*	1325
Kexim Asia Limited *(Hong Kong, China)*	627
Kexim Bank (UK) Limited *(United Kingdom)*	1792
Kexim International (Singapore) Limited *(Singapore)*	1326
Keycorp *(United States)*	1972
Kincheng Banking Corporation *(Hong Kong, China)*	627
The Kiyo Bank Limited *(Japan)*	852
Kleinwort Benson France *(France)*	438
Kleinwort Benson (Jersey) Limited *(Channel Islands)*	249
Kleinwort Benson Limited *(Chile)*	268
Kleinwort Benson Securities Limited *(United Kingdom)*	1792
Klesch & Company Limited *(United Kingdom)*	1792
KOÇBANK AS *(Turkey)*	1615
The Kofuku Bank Limited *(Japan)*	853
Kokusai Europe Limited *(United Kingdom)*	1793
Kokusai Securities Co Limited *(Japan)*	853
Komercijalna Bank AD *(Macedonia)*	1032
Komercni banka *(Germany)*	511
Komercni Banka *(United States)*	1972
Komercni banka as *(Czech Republic)*	325
Komercni Banka as *(United Kingdom)*	1793
Konsolidacni banka Praha spú *(Czech Republic)*	326
Konzumbank Limited *(Hungary)*	673
Kookmin Bank *(Korea, South)*	918
Kookmin Bank *(United Kingdom)*	1793
Kookmin Finance Asia Limited *(Hong Kong, China)*	628
KorAm Bank *(Korea, South)*	919
KorAm Bank *(United Kingdom)*	1793
Korea Commercial Finance Limited *(Hong Kong, China)*	628
Korea Development Bank (Deutschland) GmbH *(Germany)*	511
The Korea Development Bank *(Japan)*	854
The Korea Development Bank *(Korea, South)*	920
The Korea Development Bank *(United Kingdom)*	1793
The Korea Development Bank *(United States)*	1972
Korea Exchange Bank *(France)*	438
Korea Exchange Bank *(Hong Kong, China)*	629
Korea Exchange Bank *(Korea, South)*	920
Korea Exchange Bank *(Singapore)*	1326
Korea Exchange Bank *(United Kingdom)*	1794
Korea First Bank *(Korea, South)*	921
Korea First Bank *(United Kingdom)*	1794
Korea First Bank Securities Co Limited *(Korea, South)*	922
Korea First Finance Limited *(Hong Kong, China)*	629
Korea International Merchant Bank *(Korea, South)*	922
Korea Leasing (Singapore) Pte Limited *(Singapore)*	1327
Korea Long-Term Credit Bank *(Korea, South)*	923

A-35

BANK	PAGE NO
Korea Long-Term Credit Bank *(Singapore)*	1327
Korea Long-Term Credit Bank *(United States)*	1973
Korea Long-Term Credit Bank International Limited *(United Kingdom)*	1795
Korea Merchant Banking Corporation *(Korea, South)*	924
Kredietbank Luxembourg *(Japan)*	854
Kredietbank NV *(United States)*	1973
Kredietbank SA Luxembourg *(Luxembourg)*	1012
Kredietbank SA Luxembourgeoise *(United Kingdom)*	1795
Kredietbank (Suisse) SA *(Switzerland)*	1531
Kredietbank-Bankverein AG *(Germany)*	511
Kredietfinance Corp Limited *(United Kingdom)*	1795
Kreditanstalt für Wiederaufbau *(Germany)*	512
Kredyt Bank PBI SA *(Poland)*	1212
Kreissparkasse Köln *(Germany)*	512
Krungthai Bank Public Company Limited *(Thailand)*	1591
Kumho Merchant Bank *(Korea, South)*	924
Kuwait Finance House KSC *(Kuwait)*	937
Kuwait Fund for Arab Economic Development *(Kuwait)*	938
Kuwait Real Estate Bank *(Kuwait)*	938
The Kwangju Bank Limited *(Korea, South)*	925
Kwangtung Provincial Bank *(Hong Kong, China)*	630
Kwong On Bank Limited *(Hong Kong, China)*	630
Kyongnam Bank *(Korea, South)*	925
KZI Bank - Kazkommerts-Ziraat International Bank *(Kazakhstan)*	898
La Compagnie Financière Edmond de Rothschild	439
Lakshmi Vilas Bank Limited *(India)*	683
Lampebank International SA *(Luxembourg)*	1013
Land Bank of Taiwan *(Taiwan, Republic of China)*	1572
Land Bank of the Philippines *(Philippines)*	1189
Landesbank Hessen-Thüringen *(Germany)*	513
Landesbank Hessen-Thüringen Girozentrale *(Czech Republic)*	326
Landesbank Hessen-Thüringen Girozentrale *(France)*	439
Landesbank Hessen-Thüringen Girozentrale *(Hong Kong, China)*	630
Landesbank Hessen-Thüringen Girozentrale *(Hungary)*	673
Landesbank Hessen-Thüringen Girozentrale *(Poland)*	1213
Landesbank Hessen-Thüringen Girozentrale *(Spain)*	1437
Landesbank Hessen-Thüringen Girozentrale *(United Kingdom)*	1796
Landesbank Hessen-Thüringen Girozentrale *(United States)*	1973
Landesbank Rheinland-Pfalz Girozentrale *(Germany)*	515
Landesbank Rheinland-Pfalz International SA *(Luxembourg)*	1013
Landesbank Saar Girozentrale *(Germany)*	517
Landesbank Sachsen Girozentrale *(Germany)*	517
Landesbank Schleswig-Holstein Girozentrale *(Germany)*	518

BANK	PAGE NO
Landesbank Schleswig-Holstein Girozentrale *(Sweden)*	1457
Landesbank Schleswig-Holstein International SA *(Luxembourg)*	1013
Landesgirokasse *(Germany)*	519
Landes-Hypothekenbank Tirol *(Austria)*	90
Landwirtschaftliche Rentenbank *(Germany)*	520
F van Lanschot Bankiers (Luxembourg) SA *(Luxembourg)*	1013
F van Lanschot Bankiers NV *(Netherlands)*	1123
F van Lanschot Bankiers (Schweiz) AG *(Switzerland)*	1531
Latvijas Krajbanka *(Latvia)*	946
Latvijas Unibanka *(Latvia)*	948
Laurentian Bank of Canada *(Canada)*	229
Lawfin Financial Services (Pty) Limited *(South Africa)*	1390
Lazard Brothers & Co (Jersey) Limited *(Channel Islands)*	250
Lazard Brothers & Co Limited *(United Kingdom)*	1797
Lazard Capital Markets *(United Kingdom)*	1797
Lazard Creditcapital Limited *(India)*	683
Lazard Japan Asset Management KK *(Japan)*	854
LB Kiel *(Denmark)*	347
L-BANK *(Germany)*	520
LBS Bank - New York *(United States)*	1974
Leasing Andino SA *(Chile)*	268
Lehman Brothers *(United Kingdom)*	1798
Lehman Brothers Bankhaus AG *(Germany)*	522
Lehman Brothers Finance SA *(Switzerland)*	1531
Lehman Brothers Inc *(Singapore)*	1327
Lehman Brothers Inc *(United States)*	1974
Lehman Brothers International (Europe) *(Germany)*	522
Lehman Brothers International (Europe) *(United Kingdom)*	1799
Lehman Brothers Japan Inc *(Japan)*	855
Lendtech AB *(Sweden)*	1457
Leonia Bank *(Estonia)*	381
Leonia Bank plc *(Japan)*	855
Leonia Bank plc *(United Kingdom)*	1800
Leonia Bank plc *(United States)*	1975
Leonia Corporate Bank plc *(Finland)*	388
Leonia plc *(Finland)*	389
Leopold Joseph & Sons (Guernsey) Limited *(Channel Islands)*	250
Leopold Joseph & Sons Limited *(United Kingdom)*	1800
Lepercq de Neuflize Securities Inc *(United States)*	1975
Leu Asset Management Services (Asia) Pte Limited *(Singapore)*	1327
Leu Trust & Banking (Bahamas) Limited *(Bahamas)*	103
Leumi Mortgage Bank Limited *(Israel)*	745
Lévesque Beaubien Geoffrion Inc *(Canada)*	230
LG Finance (Hong Kong) *(Hong Kong, China)*	631
LG Merchant Banking Corp *(Korea, South)*	925
LG Petro Bank SA *(Poland)*	1213
LG Securities Co Limited *(Korea, South)*	927
LG Securities (Hong Kong) Limited *(Hong Kong, China)*	631

A-36

BANK	PAGE NO
LG Securities International Limited *(United Kingdom)*	1800
LGT Bank in Liechtenstein AG *(Hong Kong, China)*	631
LGT Bank in Liechtenstein AG *(Switzerland)*	1532
LGT Bank in Liechtenstein AG *(Liechtenstein)*	963
Liberty Eurasia Limited *(United Kingdom)*	1801
Liberty Roussin SA *(France)*	439
Libyan Arab Foreign Bank *(Libya)*	962
Liechtensteinische Landesbank AG *(Liechtenstein)*	963
Liechtensteinische Landesbank AG *(Switzerland)*	1532
Lietuvos Taupomasis bankas *(Lithuania)*	967
Lithuanian Development Bank *(Lithuania)*	968
Liu Chong Hing Bank Limited *(Hong Kong, China)*	631
Lloyds Bank (BLSA) Limited *(Argentina)*	27
Lloyds Bank (BLSA) Limited *(Uruguay)*	2026
Lloyds Bank plc *(Belgium)*	158
Lloyds Bank plc *(Brazil)*	196
Lloyds Bank plc *(Colombia)*	291
Lloyds Bank plc *(Gibraltar)*	555
Lloyds Bank plc *(Guatemala)*	575
Lloyds Bank plc *(Honduras)*	577
Lloyds Bank plc *(Hong Kong, China)*	631
Lloyds Bank plc *(Monaco)*	1095
Lloyds Bank plc *(Netherlands)*	1125
Lloyds Bank plc *(Paraguay)*	1178
Lloyds Bank plc *(Switzerland)*	1532
Lloyds Private Banking (Channel Islands) Limited *(Channel Islands)*	250
Lloyds TSB Bank (Jersey) Limited *(Channel Islands)*	250
Lloyds TSB Group *(United Kingdom)*	1801
Lloyds UDT *(United Kingdom)*	1803
LOCABEL SA *(Belgium)*	158
Lollands Bank *(Denmark)*	347
Lombard Bank Malta plc *(Malta)*	1073
Lombard Odier & Cie *(Switzerland)*	1532
London Financial Group Limited *(United Kingdom)*	1803
London Forfaiting à Paris SA *(France)*	440
London Forfaiting à Paris SA *(Spain)*	1437
London Forfaiting Americas Inc *(United States)*	1975
London Forfaiting Americas Inc *(United States)*	1976
London Forfaiting do Brasil Ltda *(Brazil)*	197
London Forfaiting Company plc *(Finland)*	390
London Forfaiting Company plc *(Romania)*	1249
London Forfaiting Company plc *(Sweden)*	1457
London Forfaiting Company plc *(Turkey)*	1615
London Forfaiting Company PLC *(United Kingdom)*	1803
London Forfaiting Company UK Limited *(United Kingdom)*	1804
London Forfaiting Cyprus Limited *(Cyprus)*	312
London Forfaiting Deutschland GmbH *(Germany)*	523
London Forfaiting Hong Kong Limited *(Hong Kong, China)*	631
London Forfaiting Hong Kong Limited *(Thailand)*	1591
London Forfaiting India Limited *(India)*	684
London Forfaiting Italia SpA *(Italy)*	805
London Forfaiting Polska Sp zoo *(Poland)*	1213
London Forfaiting Praha sro *(Czech Republic)*	327

BANK	PAGE NO
London Forfaiting Syndications Limited *(Russian Federation)*	1264
London Forfaiting Vostok Limited *(Russian Federation)*	1265
London Global Securities *(United Kingdom)*	1804
London Trust Bank Plc *(United Kingdom)*	1805
The Long-Term Credit Bank of Japan Limited *(Canada)*	230
The Long-Term Credit Bank of Japan Limited *(China)*	279
The Long-Term Credit Bank of Japan Limited *(France)*	440
The Long-Term Credit Bank of Japan Limited *(Hong Kong, China)*	632
The Long-Term Credit Bank of Japan Limited *(Indonesia)*	709
The Long-Term Credit Bank of Japan Limited *(Japan)*	855
The Long-Term Credit Bank of Japan Limited *(Korea, South)*	927
The Long-Term Credit Bank of Japan Limited *(Singapore)*	1327
The Long-Term Credit Bank of Japan Limited *(Thailand)*	1591
The Long-Term Credit Bank of Japan Limited *(United States)*	1976
The Long-Term Credit Bank of Japan Limited *(United States)*	1977
The Long-Term Credit Bank of Japan Limited *(United States)*	1976
LTCB Asia Limited *(Hong Kong, China)*	632
LTCB Australia Limited *(Australia)*	51
LTCB Merchant Bank (Singapore) Limited *(Singapore)*	1328
LTCB Trust Company *(United States)*	1977
LTCB UBS Brinson *(Japan)*	856
LTCB Warburg Securities Limited *(Japan)*	856
Ludová banka AS *(Slovak Republic)*	1363
Luen Fat Securities Limited *(Hong Kong, China)*	632
Luso International Banking Limited *(Macau)*	1030
Luzerner Kantonalbank *(Switzerland)*	1534
MacArthur & Co Limited	1805
Macquarie Bank Limited *(Australia)*	52
Maizels, Westerberg & Co AB *(Sweden)*	1457
Maizels, Westerberg & Co Limited *(United Kingdom)*	1806
Malayan Banking Berhad *(Hong Kong, China)*	632
Malayan Banking Berhad *(United Kingdom)*	1806
Malaysian Industrial Development Finance Berhad (MIDF) *(Malaysia)*	1052
Malaysian International Merchant Bankers Berhad *(Malaysia)*	1053
Maldives Monetary Authority *(Maldives)*	1070
Malopolski Bank Regionalam SA *(Poland)*	1214
Management International (Dublin) Limited *(Ireland)*	733

A-37

BANK	PAGE NO

Management International (Guernsey) Limited
(Channel Islands)... 251
Mandatum Bank Plc *(Finland)*.. 390
Mansion House Securities (FE) Limited *(Hong Kong, China)*.. 633
Maple Partners Bankhaus GmbH *(Germany)*................ 523
Marceau Investissement *(France)*.................................. 440
Mariborska Borznoposredniska *(Slovenia)*.................... 1376
The Marine & Fire Insurance Association of Japan Inc *(Japan)*... 857
MW Marshall & Company Limited *(United Kingdom)*.. 1806
MW Marshall (Singapore) Pte Limited *(Singapore)*.... 1328
MW Marshall (UK) Limited *(United Kingdom)*............ 1806
RP Martin (Bahrain) WLL *(Bahrain)*.............................. 120
Martin Brokers (UK) plc *(United Kingdom)*................. 1807
Martorell y Cia SA Sociedad de Bolsa *(Argentina)*.... 28
Marusan Securities Co Limited *(Japan)*...................... 857
MashreqBank psc *(United Kingdom)*............................ 1807
Matheson Bank Limited *(United Kingdom)*................. 1808
Matheson Securities (Channel Islands) Limited *(Channel Islands)*... 251
MATIF SA *(France)*.. 440
Mauritius Commercial Bank Limited *(Mauritius)*........ 1074
Maxcor Financial Inc *(United States)*........................... 1977
Mayban Finance Berhad *(Malaysia)*.............................. 1053
Maybank *(Malaysia)*... 1053
Maybank *(Singapore)*... 1328
MB Finance Limited *(Finland)*....................................... 391
MBf Finance Berhad *(Malaysia)*.................................... 1054
Mecklai & Mecklai *(India)*... 684
Mediobanca - Banca di Credito Finanziario SpA *(Italy)*.. 805
Mediocredito Centrale SpA *(Italy)*............................... 805
Mediocredito Lombardo SpA *(Italy)*............................ 805
Meeschaert - Rousselle *(France)*................................ 440
MeesPierson Asia Limited *(Singapore)*........................ 1328
MeesPierson (CI) Limited *(Channel Islands)*............... 252
MeesPierson Fund Services (Dublin) Limited *(Ireland)*... 733
MeesPierson (Germany) *(Germany)*............................. 523
MeesPierson (Isle of Man) Limited *(United Kingdom)*.. 1808
MeesPierson (Luxembourg) SA *(Luxembourg)*............ 1014
MeesPierson NV *(Netherlands)*..................................... 1126
MeesPierson NV *(United Kingdom)*.............................. 1808
MeesPierson Securities (UK) Limited *(United Kingdom)*.. 1808
Meijiseimei International France SA *(France)*............ 440
Meinl Bank AG *(Austria)*.. 91
Meitan Tradition Co Limited *(Japan)*............................ 857
Mellon Bank Corporation *(United States)*................... 1977
Mellon Bank NA *(United Kingdom)*.............................. 1809
Menatep *(Russian Federation)*..................................... 1265
Merban Limited *(United Kingdom)*............................... 1809
Mercantile Bancorporation Inc *(United States)*.......... 1978
Mercantile Bank Limited *(South Africa)*...................... 1390

Mercantile Safe Deposit & Trust Company *(United States)*.. 1978
Merchant Bank of Central Africa Limited *(Zimbabwe)*... 2046
Merchant Bank Ghana Limited *(Ghana)*...................... 553
Mercury Asset Management Channel Islands Limited *(Channel Islands)*.. 252
Mercury Capital Management *(France)*...................... 441
Mercury Courtage Bancaire *(France)*.......................... 441
Merita Bank Luxembourg SA *(Luxembourg)*............... 1014
Merita Bank Plc *(Estonia)*... 381
Merita Bank Plc *(Finland)*... 391
Merita Bank Plc *(Japan)*.. 858
Merita Bank plc *(Poland)*.. 1214
Merita Bank plc *(Russian Federation)*........................ 1265
Merita Bank plc *(Russian Federation)*........................ 1266
Merita Bank plc *(United Kingdom)*.............................. 1810
Merita Bank Plc/Nordbanken AB (publ) *(Brazil)*......... 197
Merita Bank Plc/Nordbanken AB (publ) *(China)*......... 279
Merita Bank plc/Nordbanken AB (publ) *(Hong Kong, China)*.. 633
MeritaNordbanken Group *(United States)*.................. 1979
MeritaNordbanken Merchant Bank Singapore Limited *(Singapore)*.. 1329
Merrill Lynch *(Brazil)*... 197
Merrill Lynch *(Peru)*... 1183
Merrill Lynch & Co Inc *(Puerto Rico)*........................... 1239
Merrill Lynch & Co Inc *(United States)*....................... 1980
Merrill Lynch (Asia Pacific) Limited *(Hong Kong, China)*.. 633
Merrill Lynch Asset Management Limited *(United Kingdom)*.. 1810
Merrill Lynch Australia PTY Limited *(Australia)*......... 53
Merrill Lynch (Austria) AG *(Austria)*............................ 91
Merrill Lynch Bank & Trust Co Limited *(Cayman Islands)*.. 241
Merrill Lynch Bank & Trust Company (Cayman) Limited *(United Kingdom)*.. 1810
Merrill Lynch Bank (Suisse) SA *(Switzerland)*............ 1535
Merrill Lynch Canada Inc *(Canada)*............................. 230
Merrill Lynch Capital Markets *(France)*...................... 441
Merrill Lynch Capital Markets AG *(Switzerland)*........ 1535
Merrill Lynch Capital Markets Bank Limited *(Germany)*... 523
Merrill Lynch Capital Markets Bank Limited *(Italy)*.... 805
Merrill Lynch Capital Markets Bank Limited *(Japan)*.. 858
Merrill Lynch Capital Markets España *(Spain)*........... 1437
Merrill Lynch Chile SA *(Chile)*...................................... 268
DSP Merrill Lynch *(India)*.. 684
Merrill Lynch Española Agencia de Valores SA *(Spain)*.. 1437
Merrill Lynch Europe Limited *(Turkey)*....................... 1615
Merrill Lynch Financial Services Limited *(Ireland)*...... 733
Merrill Lynch Financial Services KK *(Japan)*.............. 858
Merrill Lynch Futures Japan Inc *(Japan)*..................... 858
PT Merrill Lynch Indonesia *(Indonesia)*...................... 710
Merrill Lynch International *(Panama)*......................... 1175

BANK	PAGE NO
Merrill Lynch International *(Switzerland)*	1535
Merrill Lynch International *(United Kingdom)*	1810
Merrill Lynch International *(United Kingdom)*	1811
Merrill Lynch International & Co *(United Arab Emirates)*	1636
Merrill Lynch International Bank Limited *(Bahrain)*	120
Merrill Lynch International Bank Limited *(Germany)*	523
Merrill Lynch International Bank Limited *(Germany)*	524
Merrill Lynch International Bank Limited *(Italy)*	806
Merrill Lynch International Bank *(Italy)*	806
Merrill Lynch International Bank Limited *(Japan)*	858
Merrill Lynch International Bank Limited *(Singapore)*	1329
Merrill Lynch International Bank *(Thailand)*	1591
Merrill Lynch International Inc *(Korea, South)*	928
Merrill Lynch International Inc *(Switzerland)*	1535
Merrill Lynch International Incorporated *(China)*	279
Merrill Lynch Japan Incorporated *(Japan)*	858
Merrill Lynch Japan Securities Co Limited *(Japan)*	859
Merrill Lynch (Luxembourg) SarL *(Luxembourg)*	1015
Merrill Lynch Mercury Asset Management Japan Limited *(Japan)*	859
Merrill Lynch Mexico *(Mexico)*	1086
Merrill Lynch (New Zealand) Limited *(New Zealand)*	1142
Merrill Lynch NV *(Netherlands)*	1127
Merrill Lynch, Pierce, Fenner & Smith de Argentina SAFM y de M *(Argentina)*	28
Merrill Lynch, Pierce, Fenner & Smith (Hellas) ELDE *(Greece)*	569
Merrill Lynch, Pierce, Fenner & Smith (Middle East) SAL *(Lebanon)*	959
Merrill Lynch, Pierce, Fenner & Smith Venezuela SRA *(Venezuela)*	2033
Merrill Lynch Polska sp zoo *(Poland)*	1214
Merrill Lynch SA Sociedad de Bolsa *(Argentina)*	28
Merrill Lynch SAM *(Monaco)*	1095
Metropolitan Bank & Trust *(United Kingdom)*	1811
Metropolitan Bank SAL *(Lebanon)*	959
B Metzler seel Sohn & Co KGaA *(Germany)*	524
MFC Merchant Bank *(Switzerland)*	1535
MFK Renaissance *(Russian Federation)*	1266
Midas Investimentos *(Portugal)*	1237
Midland Armenia Bank *(Armenia)*	32
Midland Bank AS *(Turkey)*	1615
Midland Bank Offshore Limited *(Channel Islands)*	252
Midland Bank plc *(Argentina)*	28
Midland Bank plc *(Australia)*	53
Midland Bank plc *(Brazil)*	197
Midland Bank plc *(Chile)*	268
Midland Bank plc *(Colombia)*	291
Midland Bank plc *(Greece)*	569
Midland Bank plc *(Italy)*	806
Midland Bank plc *(Malta)*	1073
Midland Bank plc *(Mexico)*	1086
Midland Bank plc *(Panama)*	1175
Midland Bank plc *(Russian Federation)*	1266
Midland Bank plc *(Spain)*	1438

BANK	PAGE NO
Midland Bank plc *(Sweden)*	1458
Midland Bank plc *(United Kingdom)*	1811
Midland Bank plc *(United States)*	1981
Midland Bank plc *(Venezuela)*	2033
Midland Bank plc / Midland International Financial Services (Ireland) Limited *(Ireland)*	734
Midland Bank SA *(France)*	441
Mid-Med Bank Limited *(Malta)*	1073
Midtbank AS *(Denmark)*	347
MIGROSBANK *(Switzerland)*	1535
Mirabaud & Cie *(Switzerland)*	1536
Misr America International Bank *(Egypt)*	370
Misr Exterior Bank *(Egypt)*	371
Misr Iran Development Bank *(Egypt)*	371
Misr Romanian Bank SAE *(Egypt)*	372
Mitsubishi Corporation Finance plc *(United Kingdom)*	1812
Mitsubishi Trust & Banking Corporation (Europe) SA *(Belgium)*	159
The Mitsubishi Trust & Banking Corporation *(Germany)*	525
The Mitsubishi Trust & Banking Corporation *(Hong Kong, China)*	633
The Mitsubishi Trust & Banking Corporation *(Singapore)*	1330
Mitsubishi Trust & Banking Corporation (Switzerland) Limited *(Switzerland)*	1536
The Mitsubishi Trust & Banking Corporation *(Thailand)*	1591
The Mitsubishi Trust & Banking Corporation *(United Kingdom)*	1813
Mitsubishi Trust Australia Limited *(Australia)*	53
Mitsubishi Trust Finance (Ireland) plc *(Ireland)*	734
Mitsubishi Trust International Limited *(United Kingdom)*	1813
Mitsui Leasing & Development (Hong Kong) Co Limited *(Hong Kong, China)*	634
The Mitsui Trust & Banking Co Limited *(Japan)*	859
The Mitsui Trust & Banking Co Limited *(United Kingdom)*	1814
The Mitsui Trust & Banking Company Limited *(United States)*	1981
Mitsui Trust Finance (Hong Kong) Limited *(Hong Kong, China)*	634
Mitsui Trust International Limited *(United Kingdom)*	1814
Mohandes Bank *(Egypt)*	372
Moldindconbank SA *(Moldova, Republic Of)*	1091
The Monetary Authority of Singapore *(Singapore)*	1285
Money Markets International Limited *(Ireland)*	734
Montenegrobanka dd Podgorica *(United Kingdom)*	1814
Montepio Geral *(Portugal)*	1237
Monument Derivatives Limited *(United Kingdom)*	1815
Moravia Banka as *(Czech Republic)*	327
Morgan Grenfell & Co Limited *(Mexico)*	1086
Morgan Grenfell Investment Management (Asia) Limited *(Singapore)*	1330

A-39

BANK	PAGE NO
Morgan Grenfell (Scotland) Limited *(United Kingdom)*	1815
Morgan Guaranty Trust Company of New York *(Argentina)*	28
Morgan Guaranty Trust Company of New York *(France)*	441
Morgan Guaranty Trust Company of New York *(Italy)*	806
Morgan Guaranty Trust Company of New York *(Spain)*	1438
Morgan Stanley & Co International Limited *(United Kingdom)*	1815
Morgan Stanley Asia (Singapore) Pte *(Singapore)*	1331
Morgan Stanley Asset Management Limited *(Netherlands)*	1127
Morgan Stanley Bank AG *(Germany)*	525
Morgan Stanley Dean Witter & Co *(United States)*	1981
Morgan Stanley Dean Witter Asia Limited *(Hong Kong, China)*	634
Morgan Stanley Dean Witter (España) SA *(Spain)*	1438
Morgan Stanley (Europe) Limited *(Russian Federation)*	1266
Morgan Stanley Group (Europe) plc *(United Kingdom)*	1815
Morgan Stanley Japan Limited *(Japan)*	859
Morgan Stanley SA *(France)*	442
Morgan Stanley Trust Company *(India)*	685
Morsø Bank *(Denmark)*	349
The Mortgage Bank of Denmark *(Denmark)*	349
Mosbusinessbank *(Russian Federation)*	1266
Moscow Narodny Bank Limited *(Russian Federation)*	1267
Moscow Narodny Bank Limited *(Singapore)*	1331
Moscow Narodny Bank Limited *(United Kingdom)*	1817
Most-Bank *(United Kingdom)*	1818
Muenchener Hypothekenbank eG *(Germany)*	525
Multi Commercial Bank *(United Kingdom)*	1818
Multi Securities SA *(Switzerland)*	1536
Multibanka Joint Stock Company *(Latvia)*	948
Multi-Purpose Bank Berhad *(Malaysia)*	1054
The Musashino Bank Limited *(Japan)*	860
Muslim Commercial Bank *(United Kingdom)*	1818
Mutuactivos SA SGIIC *(Spain)*	1439
Mutuel Bank Luxembourg *(Luxembourg)*	1015
Nación Bursátil Sociedad de Bolsa SA	28
Nacional Financiera SNC *(Japan)*	860
Nacional Financiera SNC *(Mexico)*	1087
Nacional Financiera SNC *(United Kingdom)*	1819
Nakornthon Bank Public Company Limited *(Thailand)*	1592
NAL Merchant Bank plc *(Nigeria)*	1145
Nam A Commercial Joint Stock Bank *(Vietnam)*	2037
The Nanto Bank Limited *(Hong Kong, China)*	634
The Nanto Bank Limited *(Japan)*	860
Nanyang Commercial Bank Limited *(Hong Kong, China)*	635

BANK	PAGE NO
Národná banka Slovenska *(Slovak Republic)*	1357
Nassauische Sparkasse *(Germany)*	526
Natexis *(France)*	442
Natexis - BFCE *(Indonesia)*	710
Natexis Banque *(United States)*	1982
Natexis Banque - BFCE *(Australia)*	54
Natexis Banque - BFCE *(Singapore)*	1331
Natexis Banque - BFCE *(United Kingdom)*	1819
Natexis Banque - BFCE *(Vietnam)*	2038
Natexis Banque BFCE *(Hong Kong, China)*	635
Natexis Banque (Luxembourg) SA *(Luxembourg)*	1015
National Australia Bank *(Australia)*	54
National Australia Bank Limited *(Australia)*	54
National Australia Bank Limited *(Hong Kong, China)*	635
National Australia Bank Limited *(Indonesia)*	710
National Australia Bank Limited *(Japan)*	861
National Australia Bank Limited *(Singapore)*	1332
National Australia Bank Limited *(Taiwan, Republic of China)*	1572
National Australia Bank Limited *(United Kingdom)*	1820
National Australia Finance (Asia) Limited *(Hong Kong, China)*	635
National Bank of Abu Dhabi *(Egypt)*	373
National Bank of Abu Dhabi *(United Arab Emirates)*	1636
National Bank of Abu Dhabi *(United Kingdom)*	1820
National Bank of Azerbaijan *(Azerbaijan)*	101
National Bank of Bahrain *(Bahrain)*	120
National Bank of Canada *(Canada)*	231
National Bank of Canada *(United Kingdom)*	1820
National Bank of Canada *(United States)*	1983
National Bank of Canada *(United States)*	1982
National Bank of Canada (Asia) Limited *(Singapore)*	1332
National Bank of Dubai *(United Kingdom)*	1820
The National Bank of Dubai PJSC *(United Arab Emirates)*	1636
National Bank of Egypt *(Egypt)*	373
National Bank of Egypt International Limited *(United Kingdom)*	1820
National Bank of Egypt International Limited *(United Kingdom)*	1821
National Bank of Ethiopia *(Ethiopia)*	382
National Bank of Fiji *(Fiji)*	384
National Bank for Development *(Egypt)*	374
National Bank of Georgia *(Georgia)*	452
National Bank of Greece *(Australia)*	55
National Bank of Greece (Canada) *(Canada)*	232
National Bank of Greece (Cyprus) Limited *(Cyprus)*	312
National Bank of Greece SA *(Greece)*	569
National Bank of Greece SA *(United Kingdom)*	1821
National Bank of Hungary *(Hungary)*	661
National Bank of Hungary *(Hungary)*	861
National Bank of Kuwait (International) plc *(France)*	443
National Bank of Kuwait (International) plc *(United Kingdom)*	1822

A-40

BANK	PAGE NO
National Bank of Kuwait (Lebanon) *(Lebanon)*	960
National Bank of Kuwait SAK *(Kuwait)*	939
National Bank of Kuwait SAK *(Singapore)*	1332
National Bank Limited *(Bangladesh)*	124
National Bank of Moldova *(Moldova, Republic Of)*	1089
National Bank of Nigeria Limited *(United Kingdom)*	1822
National Bank of Pakistan *(United Kingdom)*	1822
National Bank of Pakistan *(United States)*	1983
National Bank of Poland *(Poland)*	1198
The National Bank of Romania *(Romania)*	1243
The National Bank of Tajikistan *(Tajikistan)*	1579
The National Bank of the Kyrgyz Republic *(Kyrgyz Republic)*	940
National Bank of the Republic of Belarus *(Belarus)*	125
The National Bank of the Republic of Macedonia *(Macedonia)*	1031
National Bank of Ukraine *(Ukraine)*	1628
National Bank of Yugoslavia *(Yugoslavia)*	2040
National Commercial Bank Jamaica *(United Kingdom)*	1823
The National Commercial Bank Limited *(Hong Kong, China)*	636
The National Commercial Bank *(Germany)*	526
The National Commercial Bank *(Japan)*	861
The National Commercial Bank *(Korea, South)*	928
The National Commercial Bank *(Saudi Arabia)*	1278
The National Commercial Bank *(Singapore)*	1332
The National Commercial Bank *(United Kingdom)*	1823
National Development Bank of Sri Lanka *(Sri Lanka)*	1447
National Financial Services Corp *(United States)*	1983
National Mutual Funds Management Limited *(Australia)*	55
National Reserve Bank of Tonga *(Tonga)*	1599
National Savings & Commercial Bank Limited *(Hungary)*	673
National Securities Co *(Greece)*	570
National Société Générale Bank SAE *(Egypt)*	374
National Westminster Bank *(Hong Kong, China)*	636
National Westminster Bank plc *(Greece)*	570
National Westminster Bank plc *(Japan)*	861
National Westminster Bank plc *(Malaysia)*	1055
National Westminster Bank plc *(Singapore)*	1333
National Westminster Bank plc *(United Kingdom)*	1823
De Nationale Investeringsbank NV *(Netherlands)*	1127
NationsBanc Capital Markets Inc *(United States)*	1984
NationsBank *(United States)*	1984
NationsBank NA *(United Kingdom)*	1823
Nationwide Building Society *(United Kingdom)*	1823
Natwest Global Financial Markets *(United Kingdom)*	1824
NatWest Group - North America *(United States)*	1984
NCL Investments Limited *(United Kingdom)*	1824
NDC Merchant Bank Limited *(Singapore)*	1333
Nedcor Asia Limited *(Hong Kong, China)*	636
Nedcor Bank *(South Africa)*	1391
Nedcor Bank Limited *(United Kingdom)*	1824
Nedcor Bank Limited *(United Kingdom)*	1825

BANK	PAGE NO
Nedcor Investment Bank *(South Africa)*	1391
Nedcor Investment Bank *(South Africa)*	1392
De Nederlandsche Bank NV *(Netherlands)*	1107
Nederlandse Waterschapsbank *(Netherlands)*	1128
Nedship Bank *(Hong Kong, China)*	637
Nedship Bank *(Netherlands)*	1128
Nedship Bank *(United Kingdom)*	1825
Nedship Bank (America) NV *(Netherlands Antilles)*	1137
Nedship Bank (Nordic) *(Norway)*	1155
NedShip Financial Consultants E.P.E *(Greece)*	570
NedShip International Inc *(United States)*	1985
Nedship Merchant Bank (Asia) Limited *(Singapore)*	1334
Nepal Rastra Bank *(Nepal)*	1102
Nesbitt Burns Inc *(Switzerland)*	1537
Nesbitt Burns Inc *(United States)*	1985
Netherlands Caribbean Bank *(Netherlands Antilles)*	1137
The New Japan Securities Co Limited *(Japan)*	862
New Japan Securities Europe Limited *(United Kingdom)*	1825
New South Wales Treasury Corporation *(Australia)*	55
Niaga Finance Company Limited *(Hong Kong, China)*	637
NIB International *(South Africa)*	1392
NIBI Asset Management Limited *(United Kingdom)*	1826
Nikko Bank (Deutschland) GmbH *(Germany)*	526
Nikko Bank (Luxembourg) SA *(Luxembourg)*	1015
Nikko Bank (Switzerland) Limited *(Switzerland)*	1537
The Nikko Bank (UK) plc *(Singapore)*	1334
The Nikko Bank (UK) plc *(United Kingdom)*	1827
Nikko España Sociedad de Valores SA *(Spain)*	1439
Nikko Europe plc *(Netherlands)*	1128
Nikko Europe plc *(United Kingdom)*	1827
Nikko Europe Plc (Middle East Branch) *(Bahrain)*	121
Nikko Italia Societa Di Intermediazione Mobiliare SpA *(Italy)*	806
The Nikko Merchant Bank (Singapore) Limited *(Singapore)*	1334
Nikko Securities Co (Asia) Limited *(Hong Kong, China)*	637
Nikko Securities (Australia) Limited *(Australia)*	56
The Nikko Securities Co International Inc *(United States)*	1985
The Nikko Securities Co Limited *(China)*	280
The Nikko Securities Co Limited *(Japan)*	863
PT Nikko Securities Indonesia *(Indonesia)*	710
Nile Bank Cairo *(Egypt)*	374
The Nippon Credit Bank Limited *(Hong Kong, China)*	638
The Nippon Credit Bank Limited *(Japan)*	864
The Nippon Credit Bank Limited *(Singapore)*	1334
The Nippon Credit Bank Limited *(United Kingdom)*	1828
Nippon Credit International (Hong Kong) Limited *(Hong Kong, China)*	638
Nippon Credit International Limited *(United Kingdom)*	1828
Nippon Trust Bank Limited *(Japan)*	865
The Nishi-Nippon Bank Limited *(Japan)*	865

A-41

BANK	PAGE NO
Nishi-Nippon Finance (Hong Kong) Limited *(Hong Kong, China)*	638
Nittan Exco Limited *(Japan)*	865
Nittan Marshalls (Hong Kong) Limited *(Hong Kong, China)*	638
NM Rothschild & Sons (Australia) Limited *(Australia)*	56
NM Rothschild & Sons (Australia) Limited *(Australia)*	57
NM Rothschild & Sons Canada Limited *(Canada)*	232
NM Rothschild Australia Holdings Pty Limited *(Australia)*	57
NMB - Heller Limited *(United Kingdom)*	1829
NOBIS Société des Banques Privées *(Luxembourg)*	1016
Noble Grossart Limited *(United Kingdom)*	1829
Nomura Asset Management (Singapore) Limited *(Singapore)*	1334
Nomura Asset Management (UK) Limited *(United Kingdom)*	1829
Nomura Australia Limited *(Australia)*	57
Nomura Bank (Deutschland) GmbH *(Germany)*	526
Nomura Bank International plc *(United Kingdom)*	1830
Nomura Bank (Luxembourg) SA *(Luxembourg)*	1016
Nomura Bank Nederland NV *(Netherlands)*	1128
Nomura Bank (Switzerland) Limited *(Switzerland)*	1538
Nomura Canada Inc *(Canada)*	232
Nomura China Investment Co Limited *(Japan)*	865
Nomura España Sociedad de Valores SA *(Spain)*	1439
Nomura Futures (Singapore) PTE Limited *(Singapore)*	1335
Nomura International (Hong Kong) Limited *(Hong Kong, China)*	638
Nomura International plc *(Czech Republic)*	327
Nomura International plc *(United Kingdom)*	1830
Nomura Investment Bank Hungary Limited *(Hungary)*	673
Nomura Investment Banking (Middle East) EC *(Bahrain)*	121
Nomura Italia SIM SpA *(Italy)*	807
The Nomura Securities Co Limited *(Austria)*	91
The Nomura Securities Co Limited *(Italy)*	807
The Nomura Securities Co Limited *(Japan)*	865
Nomura Securities International *(United States)*	1986
Nomura Securities Singapore PTE Limited *(Singapore)*	1335
Nomura Singapore Limited *(Singapore)*	1335
Nomura/JAFCO Investment (Hong Kong) Limited *(Hong Kong, China)*	639
Norbank *(Peru)*	1183
Nordbanken AB (publ) *(Denmark)*	349
Nordbanken AB (publ) *(Egypt)*	374
Nordbanken AB (publ) *(Germany)*	526
Nordbanken AB (publ) *(Iran (Islamic Republic Of))*	715
Nordbanken AB (publ) *(Russian Federation)*	1267
Nordbanken AB (publ) *(Sweden)*	1458
Nordbanken Finans AB (publ) *(Sweden)*	1459
Norddeutsche Hypotheken-und Wechselbank *(Germany)*	526

BANK	PAGE NO
Norddeutsche Landesbank Girozentrale SRN *(Czech Republic)*	327
Norddeutsche Landesbank Girozentrale NORD/LB *(Germany)*	526
Norddeutsche Landesbank Girozentrale *(United Kingdom)*	1831
Norddeutsche Landesbank Girozentrale *(United States)*	1986
Norddeutsche Landesbank Luxembourg SA *(Luxembourg)*	1017
Nordfinanz Bank Zürich *(Switzerland)*	1538
Nordic Investment Bank *(Finland)*	392
Nordlandsbanken ASA *(Norway)*	1156
Nordlandsbanken ASA *(Norway)*	1155
NORD/LB Norddeutsche Landesbank Girozentrale *(Singapore)*	1335
A/S Nordvestbank *(Denmark)*	349
Norfinsud Partners SA *(Switzerland)*	1538
Norges Bank *(Norway)*	1147
Norges Kommunalbank *(Norway)*	1156
The Norinchukin Bank *(Japan)*	866
The Norinchukin Bank *(Singapore)*	1336
Norinchukin International plc *(United Kingdom)*	1832
A/S Nørresundby Bank *(Denmark)*	349
Northern Bank Limited *(United Kingdom)*	1832
The Northern Trust Company *(United Kingdom)*	1833
Norwest Investment Management *(United States)*	1986
SA Nostra *(Spain)*	1439
Nova Kreditna Banka Maribor dd *(Slovenia)*	1377
Nova Ljubljanska banka dd *(Czech Republic)*	327
Nova Ljubljanska banka dd *(France)*	444
Nova Ljubljanska banka dd *(Germany)*	527
Nova Ljubljanska banka dd *(Hungary)*	673
Nova Ljubljanska banka dd *(Italy)*	807
Nova Ljubljanska banka dd *(Russian Federation)*	1267
Nova Ljubljanska banka dd *(Slovenia)*	1378
Nova Ljubljanska banka dd *(United Kingdom)*	1834
Nova Ljubljanska banka dd *(United States)*	1987
Nuevo Banco Idustrial de Azul *(Argentina)*	28
Nuntius Hellenic Securites *(Greece)*	570
Nyenburgh *(Netherlands)*	1128
Nykredit A/S *(Denmark)*	349
Nykredit Bank A/S *(Denmark)*	350

OB Aval ... 328
Oberbank *(Austria)*	91
Oberösterreichische Landesbank AG *(Austria)*	92
Obwaldner Kantonalbank *(Switzerland)*	1539
OCBC Bank (Malaysia) Berhad *(Malaysia)*	1055
OCBC Finance Singapore Limited *(Singapore)*	1336
OCBC Securities (Hong Kong) Limited *(Hong Kong, China)*	639
Oesterreichische Nationalbank *(Austria)*	75
Ogaki Kyoritsu Bank (Europe) *(Belgium)*	159
The Ogaki Kyoritsu Bank Limited *(Japan)*	866
Oita Bank *(Japan)*	866
Okobank Limited *(Finland)*	393

A-42

BANK	PAGE NO
Okobank-Filial *(Sweden)*	1459
OLMA Investment Company *(Russian Federation)*	1267
OM Gruppen AB *(Sweden)*	1459
Oman Development Bank (SAOG) *(Oman)*	1163
Oman International Bank (SAOG) *(Oman)*	1163
Omega Securities SA *(Greece)*	571
OMLX - The London Securities & Derivatives Exchange *(United Kingdom)*	1834
Omni Finance & Investment Group BV *(Netherlands)*	1129
Ong Tradition Singapore (Pte) Limited *(Singapore)*	1336
Open Joint-Stock Company Alfa Bank *(Russian Federation)*	1267
Sal Oppenheim jr & Cie KGaA *(Germany)*	528
Sal Oppenheim jr & Cie KGaA *(Germany)*	529
Sal Oppenheim jr & Cie KGaA *(Germany)*	530
Sal Oppenheim jr & Cie KGaA *(Germany)*	528
Opstock Securities Limited *(Finland)*	394
Ord Minnett *(Australia)*	57
Ord Minnett Securities Group *(New Zealand)*	1142
Oriental Bank Berhad *(Malaysia)*	1056
Oriental Patron Asia Limited *(Hong Kong, China)*	639
ORIX Asia Limited *(Hong Kong, China)*	639
ORIX Ireland *(Ireland)*	734
Oscar Quiroga y Cia *(Argentina)*	29
Oshchadny Bank of Ukraine *(Ukraine)*	1629
Osmanli Bankasi AS *(Turkey)*	1615
Osmanli Bankasi AS *(United Kingdom)*	1834
Österreichische Investitionskredit AG *(Austria)*	93
Österreichische Postsparkasse Aktiengesellschaft *(Austria)*	93
Österreichische Volksbanken AG *(Austria)*	94
OTP Securities Limited *(Hungary)*	673
OTS Limited LLC *(United States)*	1987
Oversea-Chinese Banking Corporation *(Australia)*	58
Oversea-Chinese Banking Corporation Limited *(Japan)*	866
Oversea-Chinese Banking Corporation Limited *(Singapore)*	1337
Oversea-Chinese Banking Corporation Limited *(United Kingdom)*	1834
Oversea-Chinese Banking Corporation Limited *(United States)*	1987
Overseas Trust Bank Limited *(United Kingdom)*	1835
Overseas Union Bank Limited *(Australia)*	58
Overseas Union Bank Limited *(China)*	280
Overseas Union Bank Limited *(Hong Kong, China)*	640
Overseas Union Bank Limited *(Japan)*	866
Overseas Union Bank Limited *(Korea, South)*	928
Overseas Union Bank Limited *(Philippines)*	1190
Overseas Union Bank Limited *(Singapore)*	1338
Overseas Union Bank Limited *(Taiwan, Republic of China)*	1573
Overseas Union Bank Limited *(United Kingdom)*	1835
Overseas Union Bank Limited *(United States)*	1987
Overseas Union Bank Limited *(Vietnam)*	2038
Overseas Union Bank (Malaysia) Berhad *(Malaysia)*	1057

BANK	PAGE NO
Pacific Bank Berhad	1058
Paine Webber Group Inc *(United States)*	1988
Paine Webber Incorporated of Puerto Rico *(Puerto Rico)*	1239
PaineWebber Incorporated *(United States)*	1988
PaineWebber International (Asia) Limited *(Japan)*	867
PaineWebber International Bank Limited *(United Kingdom)*	1835
PaineWebber International Inc *(United States)*	1988
PaineWebber International (Singapore) Pte Limited *(Singapore)*	1339
PaineWebber International (UK) Limited *(Switzerland)*	1539
PaineWebber International (UK) Limited *(United Kingdom)*	1838
Paloma Securities LLC *(United States)*	1988
Pamukbank TAS *(Turkey)*	1617
Pan Asia Bank *(Taiwan, Republic of China)*	1573
P&K Securities SA *(Greece)*	571
Pangaea / EMI Securities Limited *(Zambia)*	2044
Pangaea Partners (Bangladesh) Limited *(Bangladesh)*	124
Pangaea Partners Limited *(South Africa)*	1392
Pangaea Partners Limited *(Turkey)*	1617
Pangaea Partners Limited *(United States)*	1988
Pangaea Partners (UK) Limited *(United Kingdom)*	1835
Parekss-banka *(Latvia)*	949
Parfibank *(Belgium)*	159
Paribas *(China)*	280
Paribas *(France)*	444
Paribas *(Hong Kong, China)*	640
Paribas *(India)*	685
Paribas *(Indonesia)*	710
Paribas *(Japan)*	867
Paribas *(Korea, South)*	928
Paribas *(Malaysia)*	1058
Paribas *(Singapore)*	1339
Paribas *(Taiwan, Republic of China)*	1573
Paribas *(United Kingdom)*	1835
Paribas Asia Equity *(Thailand)*	1593
Paribas Asset Management Japan Limited *(Japan)*	867
Paribas Bank of Canada *(Canada)*	233
Paribas Capital Markets Limited *(Japan)*	867
Paribas Corporation *(United States)*	1989
Paribas Finanziaria SpA *(Italy)*	807
Paribas Frankfurt *(Germany)*	530
Paribas (Japan) Limited *(Japan)*	867
Paribas Limited *(Lebanon)*	960
Paribas SA *(Spain)*	1441
Paterson Ord Minnett Limited *(Australia)*	58
Patria Asset Management as *(Czech Republic)*	328
Patria Finance as *(Czech Republic)*	328
PCI Capital Corporation *(Philippines)*	1190
PCIBank - Philippine Commercial International Bank *(Philippines)*	1191
Peace Bank of Korea *(Korea, South)*	928

A-43

BANK	PAGE NO
Erik Penser Fondkommission AB *(Sweden)*	1460
People's Bank *(Sri Lanka)*	1448
People's Bank of China *(United Kingdom)*	1837
People's Merchant Bank Limited *(Sri Lanka)*	1449
Perdana Merchant Bankers Berhad *(Malaysia)*	1058
Permodalan Nasional Berhad *(Malaysia)*	1059
Pershing Division of Donaldson, Lufkin & Jenrette *(United States)*	1990
Perwira Affin Merchant Bank Berhad *(Malaysia)*	1059
Pesaka Jardine Fleming Sdn Bhd *(Malaysia)*	1060
Petercam Institutional Bonds (PIB) *(Belgium)*	160
Petercam SA *(Belgium)*	160
Pfizer International Bank Europe *(Ireland)*	734
PhileoAllied Berhad (PhileoAllied Group) *(Malaysia)*	1060
Philippine National Bank *(Singapore)*	1340
Philippine National Bank (Europe) plc *(United Kingdom)*	1837
Phillips & Drew *(United Kingdom)*	1837
Pictet & Cie *(Switzerland)*	1539
Pictet Asset Management (Japan) Limited *(Japan)*	867
Pierwszy Polsko-Amerykanski Bank SA *(Poland)*	1214
PIMCO Global Advisors (Europe) Limited *(United Kingdom)*	1837
PKB Privatbank AG *(Switzerland)*	1542
Plus 3 Group *(United States)*	1990
Plzenská banka as *(Czech Republic)*	328
PMD International Inc *(United Kingdom)*	1840
PMD International Inc *(United States)*	1991
PMP GmbH Wertpapiermakler *(Germany)*	532
PNC Bank Corp *(United States)*	1991
Po Sang Bank Limited *(Hong Kong, China)*	641
Polaris Securities (Hong Kong) Limited *(Hong Kong, China)*	641
Pol'nobanka AS *(Slovak Republic)*	1363
Pope & Company *(Canada)*	233
POSBank *(Singapore)*	1341
Post Bank of Slovenia Limited *(Slovenia)*	1378
Postabank és Takarékpénztár Rt *(Hungary)*	674
Postbanken *(Norway)*	1156
Postová banka as *(Slovak Republic)*	1364
Potter Warburg Securities Pty Limited *(Australia)*	59
Power Financial Corporation *(Canada)*	233
Powszechna Kasa Oszczednosci-Bank Panstwowy *(Poland)*	1215
PPM Ventures Limited *(United Kingdom)*	1840
Prager Handelsbank AG *(Germany)*	532
Pragobanka as *(Czech Republic)*	328
Prebon Yamane (Canada) Limited *(Canada)*	233
Prebon Yamane (Hong Kong) Limited *(Hong Kong, China)*	641
Prebon Yamane (Luxembourg) SA *(Luxembourg)*	1017
Prebon Yamane (Nederland) BV *(Netherlands)*	1129
Prebon Yamane (Singapore) Limited *(Singapore)*	1341
Prebon Yamane (UK) Limited *(United Kingdom)*	1840
Premex AG *(Switzerland)*	1543
Priemyselná banka as *(Slovak Republic)*	1365
Primary Industry Bank of Australia Limited *(Australia)*	59

BANK	PAGE NO
Priorbank *(Belarus)*	130
Prisma SAB *(Peru)*	1183
Privatinvest Bank AG *(Austria)*	95
Privredna banka Zagreb dd *(Croatia)*	299
Privredna Banka Zagreb dd *(United Kingdom)*	1841
Privredna banka Zagreb dd / PB Invest u Finanz AG *(Switzerland)*	1543
Probanca Servicios Financieros *(Spain)*	1441
Probanka dd *(Slovenia)*	1379
Prometeus Bank *(Armenia)*	32
Prominvestbank of Ukraine *(Ukraine)*	1630
Promradtekhbank *(Russian Federation)*	1268
Promstroybank of Russia *(Russian Federation)*	1269
Promstroybank of Russia *(United Kingdom)*	1841
Prudential Securities Inc *(United States)*	1992
Prudential-Bache International Limited (Brussels) *(Belgium)*	161
Prudential-Bache Securities AV SA *(Spain)*	1442
Prvá komunálna banka AS *(Slovak Republic)*	1365
Prvà stavebná sporitel'na as *(Slovak Republic)*	1366
První Mestká Banka as *(Czech Republic)*	329
Public Bank Berhad *(Malaysia)*	1062
Publikum dd *(Slovenia)*	1379
Pusan Bank *(Korea, South)*	928

Qatar Central Bank | 1240
Qatar Islamic Bank *(Qatar)*	1242
Qatar National Bank SAQ *(France)*	445
Qatar National Bank SAQ *(Qatar)*	1242
Qatar National Bank SAQ *(United Kingdom)*	1841
Queensland Treasury Corporation *(Australia)*	60
Quelle Bank CA Steinhäusser AG *(Austria)*	95
Quelle Bank GmbH & Co *(Germany)*	533
Quilmes SA *(Argentina)*	29

Rabello y Cia SA | 29
Rabo Australia Limited *(Australia)*	60
Rabo Securities NV *(Netherlands)*	1130
Rabobank *(Singapore)*	1342
Rabobank Deutschland AG *(Germany)*	533
PT Rabobank Duta Indonesia *(Indonesia)*	710
PT Rabobank Finance Indonesia *(Indonesia)*	711
Rabobank Group *(Netherlands)*	1130
Rabobank Guernsey Limited *(Channel Islands)*	253
Rabobank International *(United Kingdom)*	1842
Rabobank Ireland Limited *(Ireland)*	735
Rabobank Luxembourg SA *(Luxembourg)*	1018
Rabobank Nederland *(Mexico)*	1087
Rabobank Nederland *(United States)*	1992
Radanasin Bank Public Company Limited *(Thailand)*	1593
Rahn & Bodmer *(Switzerland)*	1543
Raiffeisen Unicbank Rt *(Hungary)*	674
Raiffeisen ZentralBank Österreich AG - RZB-Austria *(United Kingdom)*	1843
Raiffeisenbank as *(Czech Republic)*	329
Raiffeisenbank (Bulgaria) AD *(Bulgaria)*	208

BANK	PAGE NO
Raiffeisenlandesbank Niederösterreich-Wien GmbH (Austria)	96
Raiffeisenlandesbank Oberösterreich (Austria)	96
Raiffeisenverband Salzburg (Austria)	96
Rand Merchant Bank Limited (South Africa)	1393
Rashid Hussain Securities (Malaysia)	1063
Raymond James & Associates Inc (United States)	1992
RBC Dominion Securities Coporation (United States)	1993
RBC Dominion Securities Inc (Canada)	234
RBC Dominion Securities Inc (France)	445
RBC Dominion Securities Inc (Switzerland)	1543
RBC Dominion Securities Inc (United Kingdom)	1843
RBC DS Inc (United Kingdom)	1844
RBSI Custody Bank Limited (Channel Islands)	253
Rea Brothers (Isle of Man) Limited (United Kingdom)	1845
Rea Brothers Limited (United Kingdom)	1845
RealKredit Danmark A/S (Denmark)	351
Refco Capital Markets Limited (Bermuda)	169
Refco Securities Inc (United States)	1993
Regiobank (Russian Federation)	1269
Renault Finance SA (Switzerland)	1543
Republic Bank Limited (Trinidad and Tobago)	1600
Republic Mase Australia Limited (Australia)	61
Republic National Bank of New York (Argentina)	29
Republic National Bank of New York (Canada) (Canada)	234
Republic National Bank of New York (Guernsey) Limited (Channel Islands)	253
Republic National Bank of New York (Chile)	268
Republic National Bank of New York (France) (France)	445
Republic National Bank of New York (Gibraltar) Limited (Gibraltar)	555
Republic National Bank of New York (Suisse) SA (Hong Kong, China)	642
Republic National Bank of New York (Italy)	808
Republic National Bank of New York (Luxembourg) SA (Luxembourg)	1018
Republic National Bank of New York (Mexico) SA (Mexico)	1087
Republic National Bank of New York (RR) (Russian Federation)	1271
Republic National Bank of New York (Singapore)	1342
Republic National Bank of New York (Suisse) SA (Switzerland)	1543
Republic National Bank of New York (United Kingdom)	1846
Republic National Bank of New York (United States)	1993
Republic National Bank of New York (Uruguay) SA (Uruguay)	2027
Republic New York (UK) Limited (United Kingdom)	1847
Reserve Bank of Australia (Australia)	35
Reserve Bank of Australia (United Kingdom)	1847
Reserve Bank of Australia (United States)	1994
Reserve Bank of Fiji (Fiji)	383

BANK	PAGE NO
Reserve Bank of India (India)	677
Reserve Bank of Malawi (Malawi)	1034
Reserve Bank of New Zealand (New Zealand)	1137
Reserve Bank of Vanuatu (Vanuatu)	2028
Reserve Bank of Zimbabwe (Zimbabwe)	2044
RHB Bank Berhad (Malaysia)	1063
RHB Sakura Merchant Bankers Berhad (Malaysia)	1064
Rheinhyp Rheinische Hypothekenbank AG (United Kingdom)	1847
Riadria Banka dd (Croatia)	301
Rietumu Banka (Latvia)	950
Rigas Komercbanka plc (Latvia)	951
Riggs Bank NA (United Kingdom)	1847
Rigton SA - Financiera Rigton SA - Investor Services SA (Argentina)	29
Rijecka Banka dd (Croatia)	301
Ringkjøbing Landbobank A/S (Denmark)	352
Riyad Bank (Saudi Arabia)	1279
Riyad Bank (United Kingdom)	1847
Riyad Bank Europe Limited (United Kingdom)	1848
Rizal Commercial Banking Corporation (Philippines)	1192
Robeco Group (Netherlands)	1130
Robeco (UK) (United Kingdom)	1848
Rolo Banca 1473 SpA (Hong Kong, China)	642
Rolo Banca 1473 SpA (Italy)	808
Rolo Banca 1473 SpA (Luxembourg)	1018
Rosetbank (United Kingdom)	1848
Rossiyskiy Kredit Bank (Russian Federation)	1271
NM Rothschild & Sons (CI) Limited (Channel Islands)	253
NM Rothschild & Sons (Hong Kong) Limited (Hong Kong, China)	642
NM Rothschild & Sons Limited (Mexico)	1087
NM Rothschild & Sons Limited (United Kingdom)	1848
NM Rothschild & Sons (Singapore) Limited (Singapore)	1343
NM Rothschild & Sons (Wales) Limited (United Kingdom)	1849
Rothschild Asset Management (Isle of Man) Limited (United Kingdom)	1849
Rothschild Asset Management (Japan) Limited (Japan)	868
Rothschild Asset Management Limited (United Kingdom)	1849
Rothschild Australia Asset Management Limited (Australia)	61
Rothschild Bank AG (Hong Kong, China)	643
Rothschild Bank Switzerland (CI) Limited (Channel Islands)	254
Rothschild España SA (Spain)	1442
Rothschild Italia SpA (Italy)	809
Rothschild Japan KK (Japan)	868
Rothschild Trust Guernsey Limited (Channel Islands)	254
Roussin (Luxembourg) SA (Luxembourg)	1019
Royal Bank of Canada (Argentina)	29
Royal Bank of Canada (Brazil)	198
Royal Bank of Canada (Canada)	235

A-45

BANK	PAGE NO	BANK	PAGE NO
Royal Bank of Canada *(China)*	280	The Sakura Bank Limited *(China)*	280
Royal Bank of Canada *(Taiwan, Republic of China)*	1573	The Sakura Bank Limited *(China)*	281
Royal Bank of Canada *(United Kingdom)*	1850	The Sakura Bank Limited *(France)*	445
Royal Bank of Canada *(United States)*	1994	The Sakura Bank Limited *(India)*	686
Royal Bank of Canada (Channel Islands) Limited *(Channel Islands)*	254	The Sakura Bank Limited *(Korea, South)*	929
		The Sakura Bank Limited *(Malaysia)*	1066
Royal Bank of Canada Europe Limited *(Germany)*	533	The Sakura Bank Limited *(Mexico)*	1088
Royal Bank of Canada Investment Management (UK) Limited *(United Kingdom)*	1851	The Sakura Bank Limited *(Singapore)*	1344
		The Sakura Bank Limited *(United Kingdom)*	1854
Royal Bank of Canada (Jersey) Limited *(Channel Islands)*	255	The Sakura Bank Limited *(United States)*	1995
		The Sakura Bank Limited *(United States)*	1994
Royal Bank of Canada (Suisse) *(Switzerland)*	1544	The Sakura Bank Limited *(Vietnam)*	2038
The Royal Bank of Canada *(Canada)*	235	Sakura Bank (Luxembourg) SA *(Luxembourg)*	1019
The Royal Bank of Scotland International Limited *(Bahamas)*	103	Sakura Bank (Schweiz) AG *(Switzerland)*	1545
		Sakura Capital India Limited *(India)*	686
The Royal Bank of Scotland International Limited *(Channel Islands)*	255	Sakura Dellsher Inc *(United States)*	1995
		Sakura Finance Asia Limited *(Hong Kong, China)*	643
The Royal Bank of Scotland International Limited *(Gibraltar)*	555	Sakura Finance International Limited *(United Kingdom)*	1854
The Royal Bank of Scotland International Limited *(United Kingdom)*	1852	Sakura Securities (USA) Inc *(United States)*	1996
		Sal Oppenheim jr & Cie Securities (UK) Limited *(United Kingdom)*	1854
The Royal Bank of Scotland plc *(United Kingdom)*	1852	Salling Bank A/S *(Denmark)*	352
The Royal Bank of Scotland plc *(United States)*	1994	Salomon Brothers Hong Kong Limited *(Hong Kong, China)*	644
The Royal Bank of Scotland *(Greece)*	571		
The Royal Bank of Scotland *(Hong Kong, China)*	643	Salomon Brothers International Limited *(Switzerland)*	1546
The Royal Bank of Scotland *(Singapore)*	1344		
Royal Bank of Trinidad and Tobago Limited *(Trinidad and Tobago)*	1602	Salomon Smith Barney *(Germany)*	534
		Salomon Smith Barney *(United Kingdom)*	1854
Royal Monetary Authority of Bhutan *(Bhutan)*	170	Salomon Smith Barney Australia Securities Pty Limited *(Australia)*	61
Royal Scottish Assurance plc *(United Kingdom)*	1853		
Royal St Georges Banque *(France)*	445	Salomon Smith Barney (Japan) Limited *(Japan)*	868
Royal Trust Asset Management (CI) Limited *(Channel Islands)*	255	Salzburger Kredit-und Wechselbank AG *(Austria)*	98
		Sampath Bank Limited *(Sri Lanka)*	1449
Royal Trust Corporation of Canada *(Canada)*	235	Samuel A Ramirez & Company *(Puerto Rico)*	1240
Rüd, Blass & Cie AG Bankgeschäft *(Switzerland)*	1544	San Paolo Bank *(United Kingdom)*	1858
Rüegg Bank AG *(Switzerland)*	1545	San Paolo Bank *(United States)*	1996
Russian Commercial Bank (Cyprus) Limited *(Cyprus)*	313	Sandown Capital Corporation *(United Kingdom)*	1859
Russian Commercial Bank Limited *(Switzerland)*	1545	The San-in Godo Bank Limited *(Japan)*	868
Russky Slaviansky Bank *(Russian Federation)*	1271	Santander Investment *(Chile)*	269
RW Pressprich & Co Inc *(United States)*	1994	Santander Investment *(Peru)*	1184
RZB *(Austria)*	97	Santander Investment *(Spain)*	1442
RZB-Singapore *(Singapore)*	1344	Sanwa Bank (Deutschland) AG *(Germany)*	535
		The Sanwa Bank Limited *(Australia)*	62
Sabah Development Bank Berhad	1065	The Sanwa Bank Limited *(Belgium)*	161
Sabah Finance Berhad *(Malaysia)*	1065	The Sanwa Bank Limited *(Brazil)*	198
Sabanci Bank plc *(Germany)*	534	The Sanwa Bank Limited *(Hong Kong, China)*	644
Sabanci Bank plc *(United Kingdom)*	1853	The Sanwa Bank Limited *(Indonesia)*	711
Sadela Compañia Financiera *(Argentina)*	30	The Sanwa Bank Limited *(Japan)*	869
Safra Republic Investments Limited *(United Kingdom)*	1854	The Sanwa Bank Limited *(Malaysia)*	1066
		The Sanwa Bank Limited *(Netherlands)*	1131
Saigon Bank for Industry & Trade *(Vietnam)*	2038	The Sanwa Bank Limited *(Singapore)*	1344
Sakura Bank (Canada) *(Canada)*	236	The Sanwa Bank Limited *(United Kingdom)*	1859
Sakura Bank (Deutschland) GmbH *(Germany)*	534	The Sanwa Bank Limited *(United States)*	1996
Sakura Bank Limited *(Hong Kong, China)*	643	Sanwa Bank (Schweiz) AG *(Switzerland)*	1546
The Sakura Bank Limited *(Bahrain)*	122	Sanwa International Finance Limited *(Hong Kong, China)*	645
The Sakura Bank Limited *(Brazil)*	198		
The Sakura Bank Limited *(China)*	281	Saudi American Bank *(Saudi Arabia)*	1280

A-46

BANK	PAGE NO	BANK	PAGE NO
Saudi American Bank *(United Kingdom)*	1860	Seoulbank *(Hong Kong, China)*	646
Saudi British Bank *(United Kingdom)*	1860	Seoulbank *(Korea, South)*	929
The Saudi British Bank *(Saudi Arabia)*	1281	Seoulbank *(United Kingdom)*	1863
Saudi Hollandi Bank *(Saudi Arabia)*	1282	Seoulbank Limited *(Japan)*	870
Saudi International Bank *(United Kingdom)*	1860	Servimédia Sociedade Corretora SA *(Portugal)*	1238
The Saudi Investment Bank *(Saudi Arabia)*	1282	The 77 Bank Limited *(United Kingdom)*	1864
Saudi National Commercial Bank (OBU) *(Bahrain)*	122	SG *(United Kingdom)*	1864
The Saudi National Commercial Bank *(Lebanon)*	961	SG Cowen Securities Corporation *(United States)*	1998
Saules Banka Inc *(Latvia)*	952	SG Hambros Australia Limited *(Australia)*	63
SBC Warburg Premier Securities Co Limited *(Thailand)*	1593	SG Hambros Bank & Trust Company (Guernsey) Limited *(Channel Islands)*	256
SBCM Limited *(United Kingdom)*	1861	SG Securities Asia Limited - Sri Lanka Liaison Office *(Sri Lanka)*	1450
SBI European Bank *(United Kingdom)*	1861	SG Securities (Hong Kong) Limited *(Hong Kong, China)*	646
SBN (Dublin) Limited *(Ireland)*	735		
SBS-Agro *(Spain)*	1442		
Schelcher Prince Finance *(France)*	445	SG Securities (Phils) Inc *(Philippines)*	1195
Schiffshypotekenbank zu Lübeck *(Hong Kong, China)*	645	SG Securities (Singapore) Pte Limited *(Singapore)*	1345
Schiffshypotekenbank zu Lübeck *(Norway)*	1157	SG (Société Générale) - Emerging Markets Repo *(United States)*	1998
Schiffshypothekenbank zu Lübeck AG *(Germany)*	536	SG (Société Générale) Tokyo *(Japan)*	870
SchmidtBank Hof / Saale *(Czech Republic)*	330	SGZ-Bank AG *(Germany)*	537
Schoellerbank Aktiengesellschaft *(Austria)*	98	SGZ-Bank International SA *(Luxembourg)*	1020
Schroder & Co Inc *(United States)*	1997	SGZ-Bank Ireland plc *(Ireland)*	735
J Henry Schroder & Co Limited *(United Kingdom)*	1861	Shah, Munge & Partners Limited *(Kenya)*	901
Schroder Asseily & Co Limited *(United Kingdom)*	1862	The Shanghai Commercial & Savings Bank Limited *(Taiwan, Republic of China)*	1573
Schroder Associati Spa *(Italy)*	809	Shanghai Commercial Bank Limited *(Hong Kong, China)*	647
Schroder International Merchant Bankers Limited *(Singapore)*	1344		
Schroder Investment Management (Luxembourg) SA *(Luxembourg)*	1019	Shanghai Commercial Bank Limited *(United Kingdom)*	1865
Schroder Investment Management Limited *(United Kingdom)*	1862	Shanghai International Finance Company Limited *(China)*	281
Schröder Münchmeyer Hengst AG *(Germany)*	536	Shenyin Wanguo Securities (Hong Kong) Limited *(Hong Kong, China)*	647
Schroder Polska Sp zoo *(Poland)*	1216	The Shiga Bank Limited *(Japan)*	870
Schroders Asia Limited *(Hong Kong, China)*	645	Shinhan Bank *(Japan)*	871
Schroders Australia Limited *(Australia)*	62	Shinhan Bank *(Korea, South)*	929
Schroders (CI) Limited *(Channel Islands)*	256	Shinhan Bank *(Singapore)*	1345
Schroders International Property Fund NV *(Netherlands)*	1131	The Shinwa Bank Limited *(Japan)*	872
Schwäbische Bank AG *(Germany)*	537	Shizuoka Bank (Europe) SA *(Belgium)*	162
Schweizer Verband der RaiffeisenBanken *(Switzerland)*	1546	The Shizuoka Bank Limited *(Japan)*	872
Schwyzer Kantonalbank (SKB) *(Switzerland)*	1547	The Shoko Chukin Bank *(United Kingdom)*	1865
Scotia Capital Markets *(Canada)*	237	Siam City Bank Public Company Limited *(Thailand)*	1594
Scotia Capital Markets *(Japan)*	870	The Siam Commercial Bank Public Company Limited *(Hong Kong, China)*	647
Scotia Capital Markets *(Singapore)*	1344	Siam Commercial Bank Public Company Limited *(Thailand)*	1594
Scotia McLeod Inc *(United Kingdom)*	1863		
Scotiabank *(Canada)*	238	The Siam Commercial Bank Public Company Limited *(United Kingdom)*	1865
Scotiabank de Costa Rica SA *(Costa Rica)*	292		
Scott-Macon Limited *(United States)*	1997	The Siam Sanwa Industrial Credit Public Company Limited *(Thailand)*	1595
Seapower Securities Limited *(Hong Kong, China)*	646		
S-E-Banken BoLån AB *(Sweden)*	1460	SIBEKA - Société d'Entreprise et d'Investissements, SA *(Belgium)*	162
S-E-Banken Luxembourg SA *(Luxembourg)*	1020	Sigma Securities *(Greece)*	571
Securities Investment Bank Limited *(South Africa)*	1393	Sime Bank *(United Kingdom)*	1866
Securities Trading (UK) Limited *(United Kingdom)*	1863	Sime Merchant Merchant Bankers Berhad *(Malaysia)*	1066
Security Bank Corporation *(Philippines)*	1193		
Sedlabanki Islands *(Iceland)*	676		
Sekerbank TAS *(Turkey)*	1617	Sin Hua Bank Limited *(Hong Kong, China)*	647

A-47

BANK	PAGE NO	BANK	PAGE NO
Sinai Yatirim Bankasi AS (Turkey)	1618	Société Générale (Malaysia)	1067
Sindicato de Banqueros de Barcelona SA (Spain)	1443	Société Générale (Netherlands)	1133
Singer & Friedlander Capital Markets Limited (United Kingdom)	1866	Société Générale (Norway)	1157
		Société Générale (Pakistan)	1168
Singer & Friedlander Holdings Limited (United Kingdom)	1866	Société Générale (Panama)	1175
		Société Générale (Poland)	1216
Singer & Friedlander Limited (United Kingdom)	1866	Société Générale (Portugal)	1238
Singer Florencia Capital Markets (Argentina)	30	Société Générale (Romania)	1249
Skandinaviska Enskilda Banken (France)	446	Société Générale (Russian Federation)	1272
Skandinaviska Enskilda Banken (Sweden)	1460	Société Générale (Singapore)	1346
Skandinaviska Enskilda Banken AB (Finland)	394	Société Générale (Slovak Republic)	1367
Skandinaviska Enskilda Banken AB (publ) (Hong Kong, China)	648	Société Générale (South Africa)	1393
		Société Générale (Spain)	1443
Skandinaviska Enskilda Banken AB (publ) (United Kingdom)	1867	Société Générale (Sri Lanka)	1450
		Société Générale (Sweden)	1461
Skandinaviska Enskilda Banken Group (Luxembourg)	1020	Société Générale (Taiwan, Republic of China)	1574
		Société Générale (Turkey)	1619
Skandinaviska Enskilda Banken (South East Asia) Limited (Singapore)	1345	Société Générale (Uzbekistan)	2028
		Société Générale (Vietnam)	2038
SKB banka dd (Slovenia)	1380	Société Générale (Zimbabwe)	2046
SKB Banka dd (United Kingdom)	1868	Société Générale - Bangkok International Banking Facility (Thailand)	1595
SLC Asset Management (United Kingdom)	1868		
Slovenská Kreditná Banka AS (Slovak Republic)	1366	Société Générale Asia Limited (Hong Kong, China)	648
Slovenská Sporitel'na AS (Slovak Republic)	1367	Société Générale Asia (Singapore) Limited (Singapore)	1347
Slovenska Zadruzna (Slovenia)	1381		
Smeets Securities NV (Belgium)	162	Société Générale Asset Management (Asia) Pte Limited (Singapore)	1347
Smith Barney Inc (United States)	1998		
Smith Borkum Hare & Co Inc (South Africa)	1393	Société Générale Australia Limited (Australia)	63
Smurfit Paribas International (Ireland)	735	Société Générale Bank & Trust (Luxembourg)	1021
SNS Bank Nederland NV (Netherlands)	1131	Société Générale Bank & Trust (Monaco) (Monaco)	1096
SNS Securities NV (Netherlands)	1132	Société Générale Bank & Trust (Switzerland)	1548
SocGen-Crosby (China)	281	Société Générale Banka (Czech Republic)	331
SocGen-Crosby Securities India Private Limited (India)	686	Societe Generale de Banques en Cote d'Ivoire (Cote D'Ivoire)	293
Société Bancaire de Paris (France)	446	Société Générale Cyprus Limited (Cyprus)	313
Société de Banque de l'Orleanais (France)	446	Société Générale Equities International (United Kingdom)	1869
Société Européenne de Banque SA (Luxembourg)	1021		
Société Générale (Bangladesh)	124	Société Générale European Emerging Markets Limited (United Kingdom)	1869
Société Générale (Belgium)	162		
Société Générale (Bulgaria)	209	Société Générale Finance (Ireland) Limited (Ireland)	735
Société Générale (Chile)	269	Société Générale Libano Europeene de Banque (Lebanon)	961
Société Générale (China)	281		
Société Générale (Colombia)	291	Société Générale Manila (Philippines)	1195
Société Générale (Croatia)	301	Société Générale Mexico (Mexico)	1088
Société Générale (Czech Republic)	330	Société Générale SA (France)	446
Société Générale (Germany)	538	Société Générale Securities (North Pacific) Limited (Japan)	873
Société Générale (Germany)	539		
Société Générale (Greece)	572	Société Générale Ukraine (Ukraine)	1630
Société Générale (Guatemala)	575	Société Générale Yugoslav Bank AD (Yugoslavia)	2041
Société Générale (Hong Kong, China)	648	Société Générale Zweigniederlassung Wien (Austria)	99
Société Générale (India)	686		
Société Générale (Iran (Islamic Republic Of))	715	Société Marseillaise de Crédit (France)	447
Société Générale (Italy)	809	Société Nationale de Crédit et d'Investissement (Luxembourg)	1023
Société Générale (Japan)	873		
Société Générale (Jordan)	890	Société Tuniso-Séoudienne d'Investissement et de Développement - STUSID (Tunisia)	1605
Société Générale (Kazakhstan)	898		
Société Générale (Korea, South)	930	Soditic Finance Company Limited (United Kingdom)	1869
Société Générale (Latvia)	953	Soditic Finance Limited (Channel Islands)	256

BANK	PAGE NO
Sogecredito *(Venezuela)*	2033
Sonali Bank *(United Kingdom)*	1870
Soneri Bank Limited *(Pakistan)*	1169
SOSERFIN - Serviços Financeiros SA *(Portugal)*	1238
South African Reserve Bank *(South Africa)*	1381
Southern Bank Berhad *(Malaysia)*	1067
SouthTrust Bank NA *(United States)*	1999
SouthTrust Corporation *(United States)*	1999
Spar Nord Bank *(Denmark)*	353
Sparebank 1 Vest *(Norway)*	1157
Sparebanken Mldt-Norge *(Norway)*	1158
Sparebanken Møre *(Norway)*	1158
Sparebanken Nord Norge *(Norway)*	1158
Sparebanken Sør *(Norway)*	1159
Sparkasse Bad Hersfeld-Rotenburg *(Germany)*	540
Sparkasse Bonn *(Germany)*	540
Sparkasse Krefeld *(Germany)*	540
Splitska banka dd *(Croatia)*	302
Springfield Bank & Trust Limited *(Gibraltar)*	555
Spütz AG *(Germany)*	540
SS Kantilal Ishwarlal Securities Limited *(India)*	687
Ssangyong Investment & Securities Co Limited *(Korea, South)*	931
Ssangyong Securities Europe Limited *(United Kingdom)*	1870
SSB Bank Limited *(Ghana)*	554
St George Bank Limited *(Australia)*	64
Staal Bank NV *(Netherlands)*	1133
Stadtsparkasse Dortmund *(Germany)*	541
Stadtsparkasse Duisburg *(Germany)*	541
Stadtsparkasse Hannover *(Germany)*	541
Stadtsparkasse Köln *(Germany)*	541
Stadtsparkasse München *(Germany)*	542
Stadtsparkasse Nürnberg *(Germany)*	542
Stadtsparkasse Wuppertal *(Germany)*	542
Stanbic Bank Botswana Limited *(Botswana)*	172
Stanbic Bank Congo sarl *(Congo, Democratic Republic)*	292
Stanbic Bank Kenya Limited *(Kenya)*	902
Stanbic Bank Swaziland Limited *(Swaziland)*	1452
Stanbic Bank Uganda Limited *(Uganda)*	1627
Stanbic Bank Zimbabwe Limited *(Zimbabwe)*	2046
Stanbic Merchant Bank Nigeria Limited *(Nigeria)*	1146
Standard & Poor's *(United Kingdom)*	1870
Standard Bank Investment Corporation Limited *(South Africa)*	1394
Standard Bank London Limited *(United Kingdom)*	1870
Standard Bank Namibia *(Namibia)*	1102
Standard Bank of South Africa *(United States)*	1999
The Standard Bank of South Africa Limited *(Hong Kong, China)*	649
The Standard Bank of South Africa Limited *(South Africa)*	1394
Standard Chartered Asia Limited *(Hong Kong, China)*	649
Standard Chartered Bank *(Argentina)*	30
Standard Chartered Bank *(Bahrain)*	122
Standard Chartered Bank *(Brazil)*	198

BANK	PAGE NO
Standard Chartered Bank *(China)*	282
Standard Chartered Bank *(Colombia)*	291
Standard Chartered Bank *(Hong Kong, China)*	649
Standard Chartered Bank *(India)*	687
Standard Chartered Bank *(Iran (Islamic Republic Of))*	715
Standard Chartered Bank *(Korea, South)*	931
Standard Chartered Bank *(Macau)*	1031
Standard Chartered Bank *(Oman)*	1164
Standard Chartered Bank *(Peru)*	1184
Standard Chartered Bank *(Philippines)*	1195
Standard Chartered Bank *(Qatar)*	1243
Standard Chartered Bank *(Singapore)*	1347
Standard Chartered Bank *(South Africa)*	1395
Standard Chartered Bank *(Sri Lanka)*	1450
Standard Chartered Bank *(Thailand)*	1595
Standard Chartered Bank *(United Arab Emirates)*	1637
Standard Chartered Bank *(United States)*	1999
Standard Chartered Bank *(Vietnam)*	2038
Standard Chartered Bank *(Vietnam)*	2039
Standard Chartered Bank Australia Limited *(Australia)*	66
Standard Chartered Bank Australia Limited *(Philippines)*	1196
Standard Chartered Bank (CI) Limited *(Channel Islands)*	256
Standard Chartered Bank plc *(United Kingdom)*	1872
Standard Chartered Bank Uganda Limited *(Uganda)*	1627
Standard Chartered Bank Zambia plc *(Zambia)*	2044
Standard Chartered Bank Zimbabwe Limited *(Zimbabwe)*	2047
Standard Chartered Equitor *(Bangladesh)*	125
Standard Chartered Merchant Bank Asia Limited *(Singapore)*	1348
Standard Corporate & Merchant Bank *(South Africa)*	1396
Standard New York Inc *(United States)*	2000
Staropolski Dom Maklerski Spólka Akeyjna *(Poland)*	1216
State Bank of India *(Egypt)*	374
State Bank of India *(France)*	447
State Bank of India *(Japan)*	873
State Bank of India *(Singapore)*	1349
State Bank of India *(United Kingdom)*	1874
State Bank of India (Canada) *(Canada)*	238
State Bank of Mauritius Limited *(Mauritius)*	1075
State Bank of Pakistan *(Pakistan)*	1165
The State Commercial Bank of Lithuania *(Lithuania)*	968
State Export-Import Bank of Ukraine *(Ukraine)*	1630
State Savings Bank *(Bulgaria)*	209
State Street Bank & Trust Company *(Australia)*	67
State Street Bank & Trust Company *(Belgium)*	163
State Street Bank & Trust Company *(Hong Kong, China)*	650
State Street Bank & Trust Company *(Japan)*	874
State Street Bank & Trust Company *(United Arab Emirates)*	1637

A-49

BANK	PAGE NO
State Street Bank & Trust Company Financial Markets Group *(United Kingdom)*	1874
State Street Bank & Trust Company Global Investor Services Group *(United Kingdom)*	1875
State Street Bank Luxembourg SA *(Luxembourg)*	1023
State Street Cayman Trust *(Cayman Islands)*	241
State Street Corporation *(United States)*	2000
State Street Global Advisors Brussels *(Belgium)*	163
Steiermärkische Bank und Sparkassen AG *(Austria)*	99
Sterling Brokers Limited *(United Kingdom)*	1875
Stopanska Banka AD *(Germany)*	542
Stopanska Banka AD *(Macedonia)*	1033
Stopanska Banka AD *(United Kingdom)*	1876
Stuttgarter Bank AG *(Germany)*	542
Sudameris Agencia de Valores Ltda - Santiago *(Chile)*	269
Sudameris Capital Markets SA *(Argentina)*	30
Südwestdeutsche Landesbank *(Germany)*	543
Südwestdeutsche Landesbank (Singapore) *(Singapore)*	1349
SüdwestLB *(Hong Kong, China)*	650
Sümerbank *(United Kingdom)*	1876
Sumisho Lease Co Limited *(Japan)*	874
The Sumitomo Bank Limited *(Bahrain)*	122
The Sumitomo Bank Limited *(Belgium)*	163
The Sumitomo Bank Limited *(Egypt)*	375
The Sumitomo Bank Limited *(France)*	448
The Sumitomo Bank Limited *(Germany)*	544
The Sumitomo Bank Limited *(Iran (Islamic Republic Of))*	715
The Sumitomo Bank Limited *(Japan)*	874
The Sumitomo Bank Limited *(Malaysia)*	1068
The Sumitomo Bank Limited *(Mexico)*	1088
The Sumitomo Bank Limited *(Singapore)*	1350
The Sumitomo Bank Limited *(United Kingdom)*	1876
Sumitomo Bank of New York Trust Company *(United States)*	2002
Sumitomo Bank Securities Inc *(United States)*	2002
Sumitomo Finance (Asia) Limited *(Hong Kong, China)*	650
Sumitomo Finance (Dublin) Limited *(Ireland)*	735
Sumitomo Finance International plc *(United Kingdom)*	1877
Sumitomo International Finance Australia Limited *(Australia)*	67
Sumitomo Trust & Banking Co (USA) *(United States)*	2002
The Sumitomo Trust & Banking Company Limited *(Canada)*	238
The Sumitomo Trust & Banking Company Limited *(Hong Kong, China)*	651
The Sumitomo Trust & Banking Company Limited *(Indonesia)*	711
The Sumitomo Trust & Banking Company Limited *(Singapore)*	1350
The Sumitomo Trust & Banking Company Limited *(United Kingdom)*	1878

BANK	PAGE NO
The Sumitomo Trust & Banking Company Limited *(United States)*	2003
The Sumitomo Trust & Banking Company Limited *(United States)*	2002
Sumitomo Trust & Banking (Luxembourg) SA *(Luxembourg)*	1023
Sumitomo Trust International plc *(United Kingdom)*	1879
Sun Hung Kai & Co Limited *(Hong Kong, China)*	651
Sun Hung Kai Securities Limited *(United Kingdom)*	1879
Sun Trust Bank Tampa Bay *(United States)*	2003
Sundal Collier & Co ASA *(Norway)*	1159
SunTrust Banks Atlanta *(United States)*	2003
Suomen Pankki-Finlands Bank *(Finland)*	384
AB Svensk Exportkredit (publ) *(Sweden)*	1461
Svenska Handelsbanken *(China)*	282
Svenska Handelsbanken *(Finland)*	395
Svenska Handelsbanken *(Japan)*	875
Svenska Handelsbanken *(Russian Federation)*	1272
Svenska Handelsbanken *(Singapore)*	1351
Svenska Handelsbanken *(Sweden)*	1462
Svenska Handelsbanken *(Switzerland)*	1549
Svenska Handelsbanken *(United States)*	2003
Svenska Handelsbanken AB (publ) *(Hong Kong, China)*	652
Svenska Handelsbanken AB (publ) *(Norway)*	1159
Svenska Handelsbanken AB (publ) *(United Kingdom)*	1880
Svenska Handelsbanken Midlands & Northern Corporate Banking *(United Kingdom)*	1880
Svenska Handelsbanken Midlands & Northern Corporate Banking *(United Kingdom)*	1881
Svenska Handelsbanken Niederlassung Frankfurt *(Germany)*	544
Svenska Handelsbanken SA *(Luxembourg)*	1024
Sveriges Riksbank *(Sweden)*	1452
SwedBank *(Japan)*	875
Swedbank *(United States)*	2003
Swedbank (Förenings Sparbanken AB (publ)) *(United Kingdom)*	1881
SwedBank (Luxembourg) SA *(Luxembourg)*	1025
Swissca Securities Limited *(United Kingdom)*	1881
Sydbank A/S *(Denmark)*	353
Syfrets International (UK) Limited *(United Kingdom)*	1882
Syndicate Bank *(India)*	688
Syndicate Bank *(United Kingdom)*	1882

T Garanti Bankasi AS ... 544
T Garanti Bankasi AS *(Russian Federation)* ... 1272
T Garanti Bankasi AS *(United Kingdom)* ... 1882
Tadamon Islamic Bank *(Sudan)* ... 1451
Tai Fung Bank Limited *(Macau)* ... 1031
TAIB Securities Incorporated *(United States)* ... 2003
TAIB Securities Limited *(United Kingdom)* ... 1882
Taichung Business Bank *(Taiwan, Republic of China)* ... 1574
Taiheiyo Securities Co Limited *(Japan)* ... 875
Taipei Business Bank *(Hong Kong, China)* ... 652

BANK	PAGE NO
TAIPEIBANK *(Taiwan, Republic of China)*	1575
Taishin International Bank *(Taiwan, Republic of China)*	1575
Taiwan Business Bank *(Taiwan, Republic of China)*	1575
Taiwan Business Bank *(United States)*	2004
Taiwan Cooperative Bank *(Taiwan, Republic of China)*	1576
Taiwan International Securities Corporation *(Taiwan, Republic of China)*	1576
Talinvest Suprema Securities *(Estonia)*	382
Taris Bank *(Turkey)*	1619
Tatra Banka AS *(Slovak Republic)*	1368
TC Ziraat Bankasi *(Turkey)*	1619
TC Ziraat Bankasi *(United Kingdom)*	1882
TC Ziraat Bankasi *(United States)*	2004
TCW Group *(United States)*	2004
TD Securities *(Canada)*	239
Teachers Insurance *(United States)*	2005
TEC South Africa *(South Africa)*	1396
Tefahot Israel Mortgage Bank Limited *(Israel)*	746
Telenas (Malaysia) Sdn Berhad *(Malaysia)*	1068
Telesis Securities SA *(Greece)*	573
Open Joint Stock Company 'TemirBank' *(Kazakhstan)*	899
TFS Australia PTY Limited *(Australia)*	68
TFS Currencies Pte Limited Singapore *(Singapore)*	1351
TFS Derivatives Corp *(United States)*	2006
TFS Derivatives GmbH *(Germany)*	544
TFS Energy (S) Limited (Singapore) *(Singapore)*	1351
TFS Nordisk Energi AS *(Norway)*	1159
The Thai Bond Dealing Centre *(Thailand)*	1596
The Thai Danu Bank Public Company Limited *(Thailand)*	1596
Thai Farmers Bank Public Company Limited *(Thailand)*	1597
Thai Farmers Bank Public Company Limited *(United Kingdom)*	1883
The Thai Military Bank Public Company Limited *(Thailand)*	1598
Thomas Cook Currency Services Inc *(Canada)*	239
Thurgauer KantonalBank *(Switzerland)*	1549
Tiroler Sparkasse Bank Aktiengesellschaft Innsbruck *(Austria)*	100
The Toho Bank Limited *(Hong Kong, China)*	652
The Toho Bank Limited *(Japan)*	875
Tokai Asia Limited *(Hong Kong, China)*	653
Tokai Australia Finance Corporation Limited *(Australia)*	68
Tokai Bank of California *(United States)*	2006
Tokai Bank Canada *(Canada)*	239
Tokai Bank Europe plc *(United Kingdom)*	1883
The Tokai Bank Limited *(Australia)*	68
The Tokai Bank Limited *(Austria)*	100
The Tokai Bank Limited *(Bahrain)*	122
The Tokai Bank Limited *(Belgium)*	164
The Tokai Bank Limited *(Brazil)*	198
The Tokai Bank Limited *(China)*	282
The Tokai Bank Limited *(France)*	448

BANK	PAGE NO
The Tokai Bank Limited *(Germany)*	545
The Tokai Bank Limited *(Indonesia)*	711
The Tokai Bank Limited *(Iran (Islamic Republic Of))*	715
The Tokai Bank Limited *(Italy)*	809
The Tokai Bank Limited *(Japan)*	875
The Tokai Bank Limited *(Korea, South)*	932
The Tokai Bank Limited *(Malaysia)*	1069
The Tokai Bank Limited *(Malaysia)*	1068
The Tokai Bank Limited *(Malaysia)*	1069
The Tokai Bank Limited *(Mexico)*	1088
The Tokai Bank Limited *(Philippines)*	1196
The Tokai Bank Limited *(Singapore)*	1351
The Tokai Bank Limited *(Taiwan, Republic of China)*	1577
The Tokai Bank Limited *(Thailand)*	1598
The Tokai Bank Limited *(United Kingdom)*	1884
The Tokai Bank Limited *(United States)*	2006
The Tokai Bank Limited *(United States)*	2007
The Tokai Bank Limited *(United States)*	2006
The Tokai Bank Limited *(United States)*	2007
The Tokai Bank Limited *(Vietnam)*	2039
Tokai Bank Nederland NV *(Netherlands)*	1133
Tokai Bank (Schweiz) AG *(Switzerland)*	1550
Tokai Financial Futures (Singapore) Pte Limited *(Singapore)*	1352
PT Tokai Lippo Bank *(Indonesia)*	711
Tokai Maruman Securities (Asia) Limited *(Hong Kong, China)*	653
Tokai Maruman Securities Co Limited *(Japan)*	876
Tokai Maruman Securities (Europe) Limited *(United Kingdom)*	1884
Tokyo Securities Co Limited *(Japan)*	877
The Tokyo Sowa Bank Limited *(France)*	448
Tokyo-Mitsubishi Asset Management (UK) Limited *(United Kingdom)*	1884
Tokyo-Mitsubishi International (Hong Kong) Limited *(Hong Kong, China)*	653
Tokyo-Mitsubishi International plc *(United Kingdom)*	1884
Topdanmark A/S *(Denmark)*	354
Toprakbank AS *(Turkey)*	1620
Tornquist Valores SA Sociedad de Bolsa *(Argentina)*	30
Toronto-Dominion Australia Limited *(Australia)*	68
Toronto-Dominion Bank *(Hong Kong, China)*	654
The Toronto-Dominion Bank *(Canada)*	239
The Toronto-Dominion Bank *(Japan)*	878
The Toronto-Dominion Bank *(United Kingdom)*	1885
Towa International Limited *(United Kingdom)*	1888
Towa Securities Co Limited *(Japan)*	878
Toyo Securities Europe Limited *(United Kingdom)*	1888
Toyo Trust & Banking Co Limited *(Singapore)*	1352
Toyo Trust & Banking Company Limited *(Hong Kong, China)*	655
The Toyo Trust & Banking Company Limited *(Japan)*	879
The Toyo Trust & Banking Company Limited *(United Kingdom)*	1888

A-51

BANK	PAGE NO
Toyo Trust & Banking (Schweiz) AG *(Switzerland)*.....	1550
Toyo Trust Australia Limited *(Australia)*.....................	69
Toyo Trust International Limited *(United Kingdom)*....	1888
Trade Finance Limited *(Ireland)*.................................	736
Traders Royal Bank *(Philippines)*..............................	1196
Tradition Argentina SA *(Argentina)*............................	30
Tradition (Asia) Limited *(Hong Kong, China)*.............	655
Tradition CIS LLC *(Russian Federation)*.....................	1272
Tradition Emerging Markets *(United Kingdom)*...........	1889
Tradition Eurobond SA *(Luxembourg)*........................	1025
Tradition Financial Services (Hong Kong) Limited *(Hong Kong, China)*..	655
Tradition Financial Services Inc *(United States)*........	2007
Tradition Financial Services Japan Limited *(Japan)*...	879
Tradition Financial Services Limited *(United Kingdom)*..	1889
Tradition Government Securities Limited *(United Kingdom)*..	1890
Tradition (Government Securities) Inc *(United States)*..	2007
Tradition Italia SIM SPA *(Italy)*.................................	810
Tradition (North America) Inc *(United States)*...........	2008
Tradition (North America) Inc *(United States)*...........	2007
Tradition SA *(Switzerland)*.......................................	1550
Tradition SA Succursale de Luxembourg *(Luxembourg)*..	1025
Tradition (UK) Limited *(United Kingdom)*...................	1890
Transcambio SA *(Argentina)*....................................	30
Transorient Bank SAL *(Lebanon)*..............................	961
Trgovacka banka dd Zagreb *(Croatia)*.......................	302
Trinkaus & Burkhardt (International) SA *(Luxembourg)*..	1025
Trinkaus & Burkhardt KGaA *(Germany)*....................	545
Trust Bank Limited *(Kenya)*.....................................	902
Trust Bank (Uganda) Limited *(Uganda)*....................	1628
TSB Bank *(Ireland)*..	736
TSB Bank Limited *(New Zealand)*.............................	1142
Tufton Capital Limited *(United Kingdom)*..................	1890
Tufton Oceanic Limited *(United Kingdom)*.................	1891
Tullett & Tokyo Forex (Belgium) SA *(Belgium)*..........	164
Tullett & Tokyo Forex Inc *(United States)*.................	2008
Tullett & Tokyo Forex International Limited *(United Kingdom)*..	1891
Tullett & Tokyo International Securities *(United Kingdom)*..	1892
Turan Corporation *(United States)*............................	2008
Türk Dis Ticaret Bankasi AS *(Turkey)*.......................	1621
Türk Ekonomi Bankasi AS *(Turkey)*..........................	1621
Türk Sakura Bank AS *(Turkey)*.................................	1621
Turkish Bank (UK) Limited *(United Kingdom)*............	1892
Türkiye Garanti Bankasi *(United Kingdom)*...............	1893
Türkiye Garanti Bankasi AS *(Luxembourg)*................	1026
Türkiye Garanti Bankasi AS *(Malta)*..........................	1073
Türkiye Garanti Bankasi AS *(Netherlands)*................	1134
Türkiye Garanti Bankasi AS *(Turkey)*.......................	1622
Türkiye Halk Bankâsi AS *(Turkey)*............................	1623
Türkiye Ihracat Kredi Bankasi AS *(Turkey)*...............	1623
Türkiye Is Bankasi AS *(Turkey)*................................	1624

BANK	PAGE NO
Turkiye Is Bankasi AS *(United Kingdom)*..................	1893
Türkiye Vakiflar Bankasi TAO *(Belgium)*....................	165
UBAF (Hong Kong) Limited......................................	655
UBS AG *(Bahrain)*..	123
UBS AG *(Channel Islands)*.......................................	257
UBS AG *(China)*..	282
UBS AG *(China)*..	283
UBS AG *(Hong Kong, China)*...................................	656
UBS AG *(India)*...	688
UBS AG *(Japan)*...	879
UBS AG *(Japan)*...	880
UBS AG *(Korea, South)*...	932
UBS AG *(Portugal)*..	1238
UBS AG *(Singapore)*..	1352
UBS AG *(Taiwan, Republic of China)*........................	1577
UBS AG *(United Kingdom)*.......................................	1893
UBS AG *(United States)*..	2009
UBS AG *(United States)*..	2010
UBS AG *(United States)*..	2011
UBS AG *(United States)*..	2009
UBS AG *(United States)*..	2010
UBS AG *(United States)*..	2009
UBS AG *(United States)*..	2010
UBS AG *(United States)*..	2011
UBS AG *(United States)*..	2009
UBS AG Osaka *(Japan)*...	880
UBS Bank (Canada) *(Canada)*..................................	240
UBS Beteiligungs-GmbH & Co KG *(Germany)*...........	547
UBS Brinson *(Australia)*...	69
UBS Brinson *(United States)*....................................	2012
UBS Brinson Capital GmbH *(Germany)*.....................	547
UBS Brinson Limited *(United Kingdom)*.....................	1894
UBS Brinson Pte Limited *(Singapore)*.......................	1352
UBS Brinson SA *(France)*..	448
UBS CAPITAL *(Singapore)*.......................................	1352
UBS Fund Management (Japan) Co Limited *(Japan)*..	880
UBS (Luxembourg) SA *(Luxembourg)*.......................	1026
UBS (Nederland) BV *(Netherlands)*...........................	1134
UBS Securities Limited *(Switzerland)*.......................	1550
UBS Securities Limited *(Switzerland)*.......................	1551
UBS Securities Taiwan Limited *(Taiwan, Republic of China)*...	1577
UBS (Trust and Banking) Limited *(Japan)*.................	880
UBS Trust (Canada) *(Canada)*.................................	240
UCO Bank *(Singapore)*..	1352
UFB Locabail *(France)*...	448
UI USA Inc *(United States)*......................................	2012
Ukio Bankas *(Lithuania)*..	969
Ukranian Credit Bank *(Ukraine)*................................	1631
Ulster Bank Commercial Services Limited *(Ireland)*....	737
Ulster Bank Group Treasury (Northern Ireland) *(United Kingdom)*..	1894
Ulster Bank Limited *(Ireland)*...................................	737
Ulster Bank Limited *(United Kingdom)*.....................	1894
Ulster Bank Markets *(Ireland)*..................................	737

BANK	PAGE NO
Ulster Bank Markets - Group Treasury *(Ireland)*........	739
UNIBANCO-União de Bancos Brasileiros SA *(Bahamas)*...	103
UNIBANCO-União de Bancos Brasileiros SA *(Brazil)*..	198
UNIBANCO-União de Bancos Brasileiros SA *(United Kingdom)*...	1895
Unibank A/S *(China)*..	283
Unibank A/S *(Denmark)*...	355
Unibank A/S *(Hong Kong, China)*...............................	656
Unibank A/S *(Japan)*..	880
Unibank A/S *(Norway)*..	1159
Unibank A/S *(United Kingdom)*..................................	1895
Unibank Limited *(South Africa)*.................................	1396
Unibank SA *(Luxembourg)*...	1027
Unicaja *(Spain)*..	1444
Unico Banking Group *(Netherlands)*..........................	1135
Unico Banking Institute *(Netherlands)*......................	1135
UniCredito Italiano SpA *(Hong Kong, China)*.............	656
UniCredito Italiano SpA *(Italy)*...................................	810
UniCredito Italiano SpA *(Singapore)*.........................	1353
UniCredito Italiano SpA *(United Kingdom)*................	1895
UniCredito Italiano SpA *(United States)*...................	2012
Union Bancaire Privée *(Channel Islands)*.................	257
Union Bancaire Privée *(Switzerland)*........................	1551
Union Bancaire Privée *(United Kingdom)*.................	1896
Union Bancaire Privée *(United States)*.....................	2012
Union Bancaire Privée Japan KK *(Japan)*.................	881
The Union Bank of Bangkok Public Company Limited *(Thailand)*...	1598
Union Bank of California *(United States)*.................	2012
Union Bank of California, NA *(Indonesia)*.................	711
Union Bank for Savings & Investment *(Jordan)*........	890
Union Bank of Hong Kong Limited *(Hong Kong, China)*..	656
Union Bank of India *(India)*.......................................	688
Union Bank of Israel Limited *(Israel)*........................	746
Union Bank of Nigeria plc *(United Kingdom)*............	1896
Union Bank of Norway *(Norway)*................................	1160
Union Bank of Norway International SA *(Luxembourg)*..	1027
Union Bank of Taiwan *(Taiwan, Republic of China)*..	1577
Union banka as *(Czech Republic)*..............................	331
Union de Banques à Paris *(France)*...........................	448
Union de Banques Arabes et Françaises - UBAF *(France)*...	449
Union de Banques Arabes et Françaises - UBAF *(Singapore)*..	1353
Union Discount Company Limited *(United Kingdom)*..	1896
Union Européenne de CIC *(Belgium)*.........................	165
Union Européenne de CIC *(Brazil)*.............................	200
Union Européenne de CIC *(Czech Republic)*.............	332
Union Européenne de CIC *(France)*...........................	449
Union Européenne de CIC *(Germany)*........................	547
Union Européenne de CIC *(Hong Kong, China)*.........	656
Union Européenne de CIC *(Russian Federation)*.......	1272
Union Européenne de CIC *(United Kingdom)*............	1897
United Arab Bank *(United Arab Emirates)*................	1637
United Bank *(United Kingdom)*..................................	1897

BANK	PAGE NO
United Bank AG (Zürich) *(Switzerland)*......................	1552
United Bank for Africa plc *(Nigeria)*..........................	1146
United Bank of India *(India)*.....................................	689
The United Bank of Kuwait plc *(United Kingdom)*.....	1898
United Bulgarian Bank AD *(Bulgaria)*........................	210
United Chinese Bank Limited *(Hong Kong, China)*.....	657
United Coconut Planters Bank *(Philippines)*.............	1196
United European Bank *(Switzerland)*........................	1552
United European Bank (Luxembourg) SA *(Luxembourg)*...	1028
United Export Import Bank of Russia *(Russian Federation)*..	1272
United Garanti Bank International NV *(Italy)*............	811
United Garanti Bank International NV *(Netherlands)*...	1135
United Gulf Bank (BSC) EC *(Bahrain)*........................	123
United Gulf Management Limited *(United Kingdom)*	1898
United Mizrahi Bank Limited *(Israel)*........................	747
United Mizrahi Bank Limited *(United Kingdom)*........	1899
United Overseas Bank Limited *(Singapore)*..............	1354
United Overseas Bank Limited *(United Kingdom)*.....	1899
United Overseas Bank Limited *(United States)*.........	2013
United Overseas Bank (Malaysia) Bhd *(Malaysia)*.....	1069
United Saudi Bank *(Saudi Arabia)*.............................	1283
United Securities Hagströmer & Qviberg Fondkommission AB *(Sweden)*...................................	1463
United Taiwan Bank *(Belgium)*..................................	165
United World Chinese Commercial Bank *(Taiwan, Republic of China)*..	1579
Universal banka as *(Czech Republic)*........................	332
Universal Savings Bank Limited *(Cyprus)*.................	313
Universal (UK) Limited *(United Kingdom)*.................	1899
UOB Australia Limited *(Australia)*.............................	69
US Bancorp *(United States)*.......................................	2013
US Bank National Association *(United States)*.........	2014
US Clearing Group *(United States)*............................	2014
USTrust *(United States)*...	2014

Ve Vaderlandsche Spaarbank.................................. 166
Valcourt SA *(Switzerland)*... 1552
Valores Finamex International Inc *(United States)*..... 2014
Valores Mexicanos Casa de Bolsa SA de CV *(Mexico)*... 1088
Vanguard Group (The) *(United States)*...................... 2015
VAR BANK AS *(Norway)*.. 1161
Varazdinska banka dd *(Croatia)*................................ 302
VB International Finance Ireland *(Ireland)*............... 740
Vereins-und Westbank AG *(Germany)*....................... 547
Veronis, Suhler & Associates Incorporated *(United States)*... 2015
Versailles Group Limited *(United States)*.................. 2016
Verwaltungs-und Privat-Bank AG *(Liechtenstein)*...... 963
Via Banque SA *(France)*... 450
PT Vickers Ballas Tamara *(Indonesia)*...................... 712
Victoriabank *(Moldova, Republic Of)*......................... 1092
VID Public Bank *(Vietnam)*.. 2039

A-53

BANK	PAGE NO
Vietnam Export Import Commercial Joint Stock Bank *(Vietnam)*	2039
Vijaya Bank *(India)*	689
Viking Ship Finance Limited *(Switzerland)*	1553
Vilniaus Bankas AB *(Lithuania)*	969
Vining-Sparks IBG *(United States)*	2016
Vining-Sparks IBG Limited Partnership *(United Kingdom)*	1900
Vojvodjanska Banka AD *(United Kingdom)*	1900
Vojvodjanska Banka AD *(Yugoslavia)*	2042
Volksbank as *(Czech Republic)*	332
Volksbank Hannover eG *(Germany)*	547
Vontobel Holding AG *(Switzerland)*	1553
Vorarlberger Landes-und Hypothekenbank *(Austria)*	100
VP Bank (Luxembourg) SA *(Luxembourg)*	1028
Všeobecná úverová banka as *(Czech Republic)*	333
Vseobecná Úverová Banka AS *(Slovak Republic)*	1368
Wachovia Bank NA	1900
Wachovia Corporation *(United States)*	2016
Wafabank *(Morocco)*	1099
Wah Tat Bank Berhad *(Malaysia)*	1070
The Wakashio Bank Limited *(Japan)*	881
Wako Bank (Switzerland) Limited *(Switzerland)*	1553
MM Warburg & Co Kommanditgesellschaft auf Aktien *(Germany)*	548
MM Warburg & Co Luxembourg SA *(Luxembourg)*	1028
MM Warburg Bank *(Indonesia)*	712
Warburg Dillon Read *(Hong Kong, China)*	657
Warburg Dillon Read *(Singapore)*	1355
Warburg Dillon Read *(Sweden)*	1465
Warburg Dillon Read *(Switzerland)*	1553
Warburg Dillon Read *(Switzerland)*	1554
Warburg Dillon Read *(United Kingdom)*	1900
Warburg Dillon Read AG *(Germany)*	548
Warburg Dillon Read (Asia) Limited *(China)*	283
Warburg Dillon Read Australia Limited *(Australia)*	70
Warburg Dillon Read España SA *(Spain)*	1444
Warburg Dillon Read (France) SA *(France)*	451
PT Warburg Dillon Read Indonesia *(Indonesia)*	712
Warburg Dillon Read Italia SIM SpA *(Italy)*	811
Warburg Dillon Read LLC *(United States)*	2017
Warburg Dillon Read LLC *(United States)*	2018
Warburg Dillon Read LLC *(United States)*	2016
Warburg Dillon Read LLC *(United States)*	2017
Warburg Dillon Read (Malaysia) Sdn Berhad *(Malaysia)*	1070
Warburg Dillon Read New Zealand Limited *(New Zealand)*	1142
Warburg Dillon Read New Zealand Limited *(New Zealand)*	1143
Warburg Dillon Read Securities Co Limited *(Taiwan, Republic of China)*	1579
Warburg Dillon Read Securities (Philippines) Inc *(Philippines)*	1198
Warburg Dillon Read (South Africa) (Pty) Limited *(South Africa)*	1397

BANK	PAGE NO
Wasserstein Perella & Co Deutschland GmbH *(Germany)*	549
Wasserstein Perella & Co Inc *(United States)*	2018
Wasserstein Perella & Co Inc *(United States)*	2019
Wasserstein Perella & Co Japan Limited *(Japan)*	881
Wasserstein Perella & Co Limited *(United Kingdom)*	1903
Wasserstein Perella Emerging Markets Asset Management LP *(United States)*	2019
Wasserstein Perella (France) SA *(France)*	451
Wasserstein Perella Group Inc *(United States)*	2019
Wasserstein Perella Securities Inc *(United States)*	2020
Wegelin & Co, General Partners Bruderer, Hummler & Co *(Switzerland)*	1555
Welser Volksbank rGmbH *(Austria)*	100
JB Were & Son *(Australia)*	71
West Merchant Bank Limited *(Germany)*	549
West Merchant Bank Limited *(Indonesia)*	712
West Merchant Bank Limited *(Singapore)*	1355
West Merchant Bank Limited *(Sweden)*	1465
Westbury Capital Markets *(United Kingdom)*	1903
Westdeutsche Landesbank *(Belgium)*	166
Westdeutsche Landesbank *(China)*	283
Westdeutsche Landesbank *(Japan)*	881
Westdeutsche Landesbank (France) SA *(France)*	451
Westdeutsche Landesbank Girozentrale *(Australia)*	72
Westdeutsche Landesbank Girozentrale *(Canada)*	240
Westdeutsche Landesbank Girozentrale *(Czech Republic)*	333
Westdeutsche Landesbank Girozentrale *(Germany)*	549
Westdeutsche Landesbank Girozentrale (WestLB) *(Hong Kong, China)*	658
Westdeutsche Landesbank Girozentrale *(Singapore)*	1356
Westdeutsche Landesbank Girozentrale *(United Kingdom)*	1903
Westdeutsche Landesbank (Hungaria) Rt *(Hungary)*	675
Westdeutsche Landesbank (Ireland) plc *(Ireland)*	740
Westdeutsche Landesbank Madrid *(Spain)*	1444
Westdeutsche Landesbank Polska SA *(Poland)*	1216
Westdeutsche Landesbank (Schweiz) AG *(Switzerland)*	1555
Westfalenbank AG *(Germany)*	549
WestLB International SA *(Luxembourg)*	1029
WestLB Istanbul *(Turkey)*	1626
WestLB (Italia) SpA *(Italy)*	811
WestLB Securities Australia Limited *(Australia)*	72
Westpac Banking Corporation *(Australia)*	72
Westpac Banking Corporation *(China)*	283
Westpac Banking Corporation *(Hong Kong, China)*	659
Westpac Banking Corporation *(Indonesia)*	712
Westpac Banking Corporation *(Japan)*	881
Westpac Banking Corporation *(New Zealand)*	1143
Westpac Banking Corporation *(Singapore)*	1357
Westpac Banking Corporation *(United Kingdom)*	1904
Westpac Banking Corporation *(Vanuatu)*	2029
Westpac Bank-PNG-Limited *(Papua New Guinea)*	1176
Westpac Custodian Nominees Limited *(Australia)*	74
WGZ-Bank Luxemberg SA *(Luxembourg)*	1029

BANK	PAGE NO
WGZ-Bank Westdeutsche Genossenschafts Zentralbank eG *(Germany)*	550
Wielkopolski Bank Kredytowy SA *(Poland)*	1216
Williams de Broë Pankkiiriliike Oy *(Finland)*	395
Williams de Broë plc *(United Kingdom)*	1905
Wing Hang Bank Limited *(Hong Kong, China)*	659
Wing Lung Bank Limited *(Hong Kong, China)*	660
Wood & Company *(Czech Republic)*	333
Woolwich plc *(United Kingdom)*	1905
The World Bank *(Argentina)*	31
The World Bank *(Colombia)*	291
The World Bank *(Ecuador)*	358
The World Bank *(Egypt)*	375
The World Bank *(Ethiopia)*	383
The World Bank *(France)*	451
The World Bank *(Hungary)*	676
The World Bank *(Indonesia)*	713
The World Bank *(Mexico)*	1089
The World Bank *(Pakistan)*	1169
The World Bank *(Poland)*	1217
The World Bank *(Thailand)*	1599
The World Bank *(United Kingdom)*	1905
The World Bank *(Uzbekistan)*	2028
The World Bank *(Vietnam)*	2040
WorldInvest Limited *(United Kingdom)*	1905
Württembergische Hypothekenbank AG *(France)*	452
Württembergische Hypothekenbank AG *(Germany)*	552
Wüstenrot Bank AG *(Germany)*	552
Xiamen International Bank	283
Xiosbank SA *(Greece)*	573
Yagi Euro Corporation	882
Yamagata Bank Limited *(Japan)*	882
The Yamaguchi Bank Limited *(Hong Kong, China)*	660
The Yamaguchi Bank Limited *(Japan)*	882
The Yamanashi Chuo Bank Limited *(Hong Kong, China)*	661

BANK	PAGE NO
Closed Joint Stock Company Yapi Toko Bank *(Russian Federation)*	1273
Yapi ve Kredi Bankasi AS *(Bahrain)*	123
Yapi ve Kredi Bankasi AS *(Turkey)*	1626
Yapi ve Kredi Bankasi AS *(United Kingdom)*	1906
Yasar Yatirim AS *(Turkey)*	1626
Yasuda & Pama Limited *(Japan)*	883
Yasuda Bank & Trust Company (USA) *(United States)*	2020
The Yasuda Trust & Banking Company Limited *(Hong Kong, China)*	661
The Yasuda Trust & Banking Company Limited *(Japan)*	883
The Yasuda Trust & Banking Company Limited *(Singapore)*	1357
The Yasuda Trust & Banking Company Limited *(United Kingdom)*	1906
Yasuda Trust Asia Pacific Limited *(Hong Kong, China)*	661
Yasuda Trust Australia Limited *(Australia)*	74
The Yien Yieh Commercial Bank Limited *(Hong Kong, China)*	661
Yorkshire Bank plc *(United Kingdom)*	1906
Yugbank *(Russian Federation)*	1273
Zagrebacka banka - Pomorska banka dd Split	303
Zagrebacka banka dd *(Croatia)*	303
Zambia Commercial Bank *(United Kingdom)*	1906
The Zenshinren Bank *(Japan)*	884
The Zenshinren Bank *(Singapore)*	1357
The Zenshinren Bank *(United Kingdom)*	1907
Zenshinren International Limited *(United Kingdom)*	1907
Zimbabwe Development Bank *(Zimbabwe)*	2047
Zivnostenská Banka AS *(Czech Republic)*	334
Zivnostenská Banka AS *(United Kingdom)*	1907
Zürcher Kantonalbank *(Singapore)*	1357
Zürcher Kantonalbank *(Switzerland)*	1556

A-55

ALBANIA
(+355)

Bank of Albania

Sheshi Skenderbej 1, Tirana
Tel: (42) 35568; (42) 22752 **Fax:** (42) 23558; (42) 27821 **Telex:** 2153 BANKA AB **Swift:** STAN AL TR
Email: intlrel@boa.tirana.al **Tel:** 22153; 22152

Senior Executive Officers
Governor   Shkëlqim Cani
Deputy Governor   Fatos Ibrahami
Deputy Governor   Dhame Pite

Others (Senior Executives)
Head, Monetary Operations   Fiqiri Baholli Director ☎ **35568 ext 177**
                            Marian Cjermeni Director ☎ **35568 ext 117**
Head, Banking Supervision   Miranda Rama Director ☎ **35568 ext 128**
Head, Payments   Suela Bokshi Director ☎ **35568 ext 152**
Head, Issuing   Palok Kolnikaj Director ☎ **35568 ext 125**
Head, Tirana Stock Exchange Alma Kaso Director ☎ **35568 ext 201**

Other Departments
Economic Research   Teuta Baleta Director, Research & Statistics ☎ **35568 ext 144**

Administration
Head of Administration   Stefan Sevo Acting Director ☎ **35568 ext 118**

Technology & Systems
Head, Information Technology Sokol Qeraxhiu Director ☎ **35568 ext 121**

Legal / In-House Counsel
                            Neritan Kalifa Director ☎ **35568 ext 163**

Accounts / Audit
Head, Accountancy   Ibrahim Buharaja Director ☎ **35568 ext 119**

Other (Administration)
Head, Human Resources Management Sotiraq Findiku Director ☎ **35568 ext 120**

Berliner Bank AG
Representative Office

Rruga Brigada VIII 7, Tirana
Tel: (42) 34516 **Fax:** (42) 34516

Senior Executive Officers
Representative   Lulezim Camishi

European Bank for Reconstruction & Development
Representative Office

Deshmoret e 4 Shkurtit 26, Tirana
Tel: (42) 32898; (42) 32368 **Fax:** (42) 30580

Senior Executive Officers
Resident Representative   Philippe Leclercq

ALGERIA
(+213)

Banque Extérieure d'Algérie
Head Office

Alternative trading name: BEA
11 Boulevard Colonel Amirouche, Algiers
Tel: (2) 711 252 **Fax:** (2) 726 774 **Telex:** 56090 **Swift:** BEXA DZ AL **Telex:** 56091 **Telex:** 56092

Senior Executive Officers
President   Mohamed Benhalima ☎ **239 330**
Chief Executive Officer   Hocine Hannachi Director General ☎ **642 500**

Euromoney Directory 1999   **1**

ALGERIA (+213)

Banque Extérieure d'Algérie (cont)
Senior Executive Officers (cont)
Financial Director — Mohamed Mokhazni Director General ☎ 611 875
Chief Operating Officer — Omar Isaad Director General ☎ 715 655
Treasurer — Ali Mokdad ☎ 612 628

Banque Nationale d'Algérie — Head Office
8 Boulevard Ernesto Che Guevara, Algiers, 16000
Tel: (2) 715 564; (2) 714 719 **Fax:** (2) 714 759 **Telex:** 56005 **Telex:** 50003 **Telex:** 56145
Senior Executive Officers
Chairman & Chief Executive Officer — Slimane Kaci Moussa
Chief Executive Officer — Slimane Kaci Moussa Chairman & Chief Executive Officer
Chief Operating Officer — Saïd Adoul Manager ☎ 901 587
Treasurer — Mohamed Siaci Manager ☎ 657 604
International Division — Farouk Taleb Senior Executive Officer ☎ 732 956
Relationship Manager
International Relations and Foreign Trade — Mahmoud Siouani Manager ☎ 732 956
Money Markets
Head of Money Markets — Mohamed Siaci Manager ☎ 657 604
Foreign Exchange
Head of Foreign Exchange — Mohamed Siaci Manager ☎ 657 604
Corporate Finance / M&A Advisory
Head of Corporate Finance — Holine Bouanani Manager ☎ 713 623
Settlement / Clearing
Head of Settlement / Clearing — Saïd Adoul Manager ☎ 901 587

Crédit Populaire d'Algérie — Head Office
2 Boulevard Colonel Amirouche, Algiers, 16000
Tel: (2) 611 334; (2) 740 528 **Fax:** (2) 644 041 **Telex:** 55147; 67170; 67147 **Swift:** CPAZ AL **Reuters:** CPAA
Senior Executive Officers
President & General Director — El Hachemi Meghaoui
Chief Executive Officer — Mohamed Diabi Chief Executive & Finance Manager
Other Departments
Correspondent Banking — Mr Zabiri Manager, Correspondent Banking

ANDORRA (+376)

Banc Agricol i Comercial d'Andorra SA — Head Office
Avenida Fiter i Rossell 4 bis, Escaldes-Engordany, Andorra la Vella
PO Box 49, Andorra la Vella
Tel: 873 305 **Fax:** 863 905 **Telex:** 201 ANDOBAN **Swift:** BACA AD AD **Email:** banc-agricol@banc-agricol.ad
Reuters: ACAB **Cable:** ANDORRABANK
Senior Executive Officers
Chairman — Manuel Cerqueda Donadeu
General Manager — Jaume Sabater
Secretary General — Josep Sansa
Others (Senior Executives)
— Albert Sanchez-Juarez Deputy General Manager
— Pere Quimesó Business Area Head
Department: General Management Area
Others (Senior Executives)
International Relations Manager — Juan J Cazalla
Building & Security Manager — Xavier Santamaria
Department: Domestic Business Area
Others (Senior Executives)
Central Business Manager — Josep M Cabanes
Domestic Operations Manager — Manel Rodríguez

www.euromoneydirectory.com ANDORRA (+376)

Debt Capital Markets / Fixed Income
Country Head Jordi Bentué *Manager*
Risk Management
Country Head Miquel Noguer *Head of International Risk*
Settlement / Clearing
Operations Alfons Andrès *Operations Manager*
Other Departments
Private Banking Moises Palou *Manager*
 Carles Puig *Manager*
 Joan Junyet *Manager*

Administration
Technology & Systems
Computer, Organization & Means of Payment Carles Ransanz *Manager*
Systems Antoni Armengol *Manager*
Technical Back up Antoni Torres *Manager*
Accounts / Audit
 Santi de Rosselló *Account Manager*

Other (Administration)
Human Management & Development Jordi Checa *Manager*
Market Administration Xavier Cornella *Manager*
Means of Payment Carme Montes *Manager*

Banc Internacional d'Andorra SA   Head Office
Avenida Meritxell 96, Andorra la Vella
Tel: 884 488 **Fax:** 884 499 **Telex:** 222 INTMOARB, 206 INTMOCOM **Swift:** BINA AD AD **Reuters:** BIMA (Dealing)
Senior Executive Officers
Chief Executive Officer Manuel Domingo
Deputy General Manager Santiago Guillén
General Secretary Enrique Recuero
International Division Josep Navas *Assistant General Manager*

General-Investment
Head of Investment Joan Carles Sasplugas *AGM, Merchant Banking*
Relationship Manager
International Relations Enric Juncosa *Manager*

Debt Capital Markets / Fixed Income
Department: Capital Markets
Global Head Josep Navas *Assistant General Manager*
Eurobonds
Head of Trading Agusti Morales *Senior Dealer, Eurobonds*
Syndicated Lending
Other (Syndicated Lending)
Loan Syndication / Asset Sales Josep Navas *Assistant General Manager*
Other (Trade Finance)
Credit & Forfaiting Antoni Sánchez Puerta *Manager*
Foreign Exchange
FX Traders / Sales People
 Olympia Gálvez *Senior Dealer*

Risk Management
Other Currency Swap / FX Options Personnel
Interest & Currency Swaps Lorenzo Mendiguren *Senior Dealer*
Settlement / Clearing
Operations Josep A Palau *Assistant General Manager*
Asset Management
Department: Capital Markets
Head Gilbert Saboya *Manager*
Portfolio Management Josep Navas *Assistant General Manager*
Other Departments
Correspondent Banking Enric Juncosa *Manager*
Economic Research Josep Navas *Assistant General Manager*
Administration
Head of Administration Josep A Palau *Assistant General Manager*
Technology & Systems
 Javier Iriarte *Manager*

ANDORRA (+376)   www.euromoneydirectory.com

Banc Internacional d'Andorra SA (cont)
Legal / In-House Counsel
    Enrique Recuero *General Secretary*
Compliance
    Armando Garcia *General Auditor*

Banca Mora SA — Subsidiary Company
Avenida Meritxell 96, Andorra la Vella
Tel: 884 488 **Fax:** 884 499 **Telex:** 222 INTMOARB, 206 INTMOCOM **Swift:** BINA AD BD **Reuters:** BIMA (Dealing)

Senior Executive Officers
Chief Executive Officer   Manuel Domingo
Deputy General Manager   Santiago Guillén
General Secretary   Enrique Recuero
International Division   Josep Navas *Assistant General Manager*

General-Lending (DCM, SL)
Head of Corporate Banking   Joan Carles Sasplugas *AGM, Commercial Banking*

General-Investment
Head of Investment   Joan Carles Sasplugas *AGM, Merchant Banking*

Relationship Manager
International Relations   Enric Juncosa *Manager*

Debt Capital Markets / Fixed Income
Global Head   Josep Navas *Assistant General Manager*

Eurobonds
Head of Origination   Augusti Morales *Senior Dealer, Eurobonds*

Syndicated Lending
Other (Syndicated Lending)
Loan Syndication / Asset Sales   Josep Navas *Assistant General Manager*

Other (Trade Finance)
Credit & Forfaiting   Antoni Sànchez Puerta *Manager*

Foreign Exchange
FX Traders / Sales People
     Olympia Gálvez *Senior Dealer*

Risk Management
Other Currency Swap / FX Options Personnel
Interest & Currency Swaps   Jordi Coret *Manager*
     Lorenzo Mendiguren *Senior Dealer*

Settlement / Clearing
Operations   Josep Palau *Assistant General Manager*

Asset Management
Head   Gilbert Saboya *Manager*
Portfolio Management   Josep Navas *Assistant General Manager*

Other Departments
Correspondent Banking   Enric Juncosa *Manager*
Economic Research   Josep Navas *Assistant General Manager*

Administration
Head of Administration   Josep Palau *Assistant General Manager*

Technology & Systems
     Javier Iriarte *Manager*

Legal / In-House Counsel
     Enrique Recuero *General Secretary*

Compliance
     Armando García *General Auditor*

Credit Andorrà SA — Head Office
Avenida Meritxell 80, Andorra la Vella
Tel: 888 000 **Fax:** 888 001 **Telex:** 220 CREDIAND **Swift:** CRDA AD AD **Reuters:** CRAN

Senior Executive Officers
Chairman   Jaume Casal
Financial Director   Ramon Buisan
Treasurer   Josep Argelich
Managing Director / General Manager   Josep Peralba

www.euromoneydirectory.com   ARGENTINA (+54)

Debt Capital Markets / Fixed Income
Tel: 888 820 Fax: 888 821
Global Head   Angels Melsio

Equity Capital Markets
Tel: 888 820 Fax: 888 821
Global Head   Emili Ferenczy

Money Markets
Tel: 888 840 Fax: 888 841
Global Head   Josep Argelich

Foreign Exchange
Tel: 888 840 Fax: 888 841
Global Head   Josep Argelich

Other Departments
Private Banking   Xavier Cornella ☎ **888 240**
Correspondent Banking   Antoni Rovira ☎ **888 720**

Administration
Technology & Systems
                                    Antoni Pampliega ☎ **888 710**

Public Relations
                                    Christian Trillas ☎ **888 850**

ARGENTINA
(+54)

Banco Central de la Republica Argentina   🏛 Central Bank

Reconquista 266, Buenos Aires 1003
Tel: (1) 348 3500 **Fax:** (1) 325 4860 **Telex:** 23942 **Cable:** CENTRALBAN
President's Office Fax: 326 3361; Economy & Finance Department Fax: 394 7019; Operations Department
Fax: 348 3934; Administration & Control Fax: 394 7963; International Relations Fax: 348 3931

Senior Executive Officers
President   Pedro Pou
Vice President   Martin Lagos
Vice President   Marcos Rafael Saul
General Manager   Susana Olgiati
Secretary to the Board   Roberto T Miranda

Others (Senior Executives)
                                    Manuel R Domper *Director*
                                    Miguel A Ortiz *Director*
                                    Javier A Bolzico *Director*
                                    Federico Caparros Bosch *Director*
                                    Aldo Pignanelli *Director*
                                    Ricardo Ferreiro *Trustee*
Economy & Finance Department   Andrew Powell *Manager*
Financial Institutions Standards Alfredo Besio *Manager*
Reserves Administration   Alberto R Karlen *Assistant General Manager*
Open Markets   Raul O Planes *Manager*
BCRA Credits   Guillermo Zuccolo *Manager*
Stock Market Control   Victor H Ruiz *Manager*
Banking Supervision   Miguel A Ortiz *Director*
                                    Javier A Bolzico *Director*
                                    Juan C Nougues *Assistant General Manager*
Co-ordination Department   Alejandro G Henke *Assistant General Manager*
Financial Institutions Authorization Daniel Mira Castets *Manager*

General - Treasury
Head of Treasury   Ismael A Salvatore *Manager*

Settlement / Clearing
Settlement (General)   Adolfo C Lavenia *Assistant General Manager*
Operations   Hector Biondo *Assistant General Manager*

Other Departments
Economic Research   Guillermo Escude *Manager*
                                    Daniel F Oks *Manager, Economic Analysis*

ARGENTINA (+54)   www.euromoneydirectory.com

Banco Central de la Republica Argentina (cont)
Administration
Head of Administration   Roberto C Riccardi *Assistant General Manager*
Technology & Systems
IT & Organization   Alejandro Saravia *Assistant General Manager*
Legal / In-House Counsel
Legal Affairs Department   Marcos E Moiseeff *Assistant General Manager*
Legal Research & Reports   Maria Del C Urquiza *Assistant General Manager*
Accounts / Audit
Accounts   Julio C Siri *Manager*
    Jorge H Mazzei *Auditor General*
Other (Administration)
Personnel   Mario E Troiani *Manager*
General Service Department   Julio J J Leguiza *Manager*

ABN AMRO Bank   Representative Office
Florida 361, piso 8°, Buenos Aires 1005
Casilla de Correo 171, Buenos Aires
Tel: (1) 321 2140 **Fax:** (1) 321 2147

Senior Executive Officers
Representative   Patricia Parise ✉ **patricia.parise@abnamro.com**

ABN AMRO Bank NV   Full Branch Office
Florida 361, Buenos Aires 1005
Casilla de Correo 171, Buenos Aires 1005
Tel: (1) 320 0600 **Fax:** (1) 322 0603 **Swift:** ABNA AR BA
Website: www.abnamro.com

Senior Executive Officers
Country Manager   César Deymonnaz ☏ **320 0701**
Chief Executive Officer   André Van Der Meulen *Deputy Country Manager* ☏ **320 0702**
Financial Director   José Fernandez *Senior Vice President* ☏ **320 0680**
Chief Operating Officer   Omar Carballo *Sub-General Manager* ☏ **320 0703**
Treasurer   José Fernandez *Senior Vice President* ☏ **320 0680**
Country Manager   César Deymonnaz ☏ **320 0701**
Company Secretary   Mara Rotman ☏ **320 0903**
General-Lending (DCM, SL)
Head of Corporate Banking   John Smith *Manager* ☏ **320 0640**
Debt Capital Markets / Fixed Income
Head of Fixed Income   Carlos Socas *Vice President* ☏ **320 0698**
Head of Fixed Income Sales   Martin Durruty *Vice President* ☏ **320 0699**
Head of Fixed Income Trading   Carlos Socas *Vice President* ☏ **320 0698**
Domestic Government Bonds
Head of Sales   Martin Durruty *Vice President* ☏ **320 0699**
Head of Trading   Carlos Socas *Vice President* ☏ **320 0698**
Eurobonds
Head of Sales   Martin Durruty *Vice President* ☏ **320 0699**
Head of Trading   Carlos Socas *Vice President* ☏ **320 0698**
Equity Capital Markets
Department: Merchant Banking Unit
Tel: 320 0674 **Fax:** 322 0195
Global Head   Lucrecia Fratini *Head, Merchant Banking* ☏ **320 0674**
Head of Sales   Augusto Darget *Head, Securities* ☏ **320 0716**
Domestic Equities
Head of Sales; Head of Trading   Augusto Darget *Head, Securities* ☏ **320 0716**
Equity Research
Global Head   Christopher de Mattos ☏ **320 0713**
Syndicated Lending
Tel: 320 0674 **Fax:** 322 0195
Head of Origination; Head of Syndication   Lucrecia Fratini *Head, Merchant Banking* ☏ **320 0674**
Loan-Related Activities
Project Finance   Lucrecia Fratini *Head, Merchant Banking* ☏ **320 0674**

www.euromoneydirectory.com ARGENTINA (+54)

Risk Management
Tel: 320 0760 **Fax:** 320 0759
Country Head Andrés de Elizalde *Senior Risk Officer* ☏ **320 0760**

Corporate Finance / M&A Advisory
Department: Structured Finance Unit
Regional Head Ben Rose *Head, Regional SFU* ☏ **+55 (11) 5188 2641**
Country Head Lucrecia Fratini *Head, Merchant Banking* ☏ **320 0674**

Asset Management
Head Patricia Parise *Head, Asset Management* ☏ **321 2140**

Other Departments
Private Banking Patricia Parise *Head, Asset Management* ☏ **321 2140**
Correspondent Banking Dougals Jarvis ☏ **320 0685**

Administration
Head of Marketing Ignacio Latorre *Manager* ☏ **321 2190**
  Victoria Alcayaga *Assistant Marketing Manager* ☏ **321 2195** F **321 2199**

Technology & Systems
  Manuel Alvarez ☏ **320 0880**

Legal / In-House Counsel
  Gustavo Chirio ☏ **321 2149**

Compliance
  Omar Carballo *Sub-General Manager* ☏ **320 0703**

Accounts / Audit
Audit Office Ernesto Campos *Head* ☏ **320 0860**

Allaria Ledesma y Cia Sociedad de Bolsa SA

25 de Mayo 596, piso 15°, Buenos Aires 1002
Tel: (1) 312 8801 **Fax:** (1) 314 4777 **Email:** allaria&cia@allaria.sba.com.ar

Senior Executive Officers
Chairman Ernesto Allaria Ledesma
Chief Executive Officer Ernesto Allaria Ledesma
Financial Director Juan Francisco Politi

Others (Senior Executives)
Commercial Director Enrique Alfredo Marti

Other Departments
Economic Research Nestor De Césare

American Express Bank Limited Representative Office

Marcelo T de Alvear 684, piso 5°, Buenos Aires 1395
Casilla de Correo 3666, Correo Central, Buenos Aires 1000
Tel: (1) 312 9034 **Fax:** (1) 313 0079

Senior Executive Officers
Representative Muriel Zumaran

Argentaria Representative Office

Formerly known as: Banco Exterior De España
Avenida Leandro N Alem 356, piso 11°, Buenos Aires 1003
Tel: (1) 313 0075; (1) 313 0167 **Fax:** (1) 313 0354 **Email:** orba@infovia.com.ar

Senior Executive Officers
Representative Antonio Sacido Martin

Banca Nazionale del Lavoro SpA Full Branch Office

Calle Florida 40, piso 12°, Buenos Aires 1005
Tel: (1) 323 4400 **Fax:** (1) 323 4666/7; (1) 323 4699 **Telex:** 91603

Senior Executive Officers
President Ademaro Lanzara
Managing Director / General Manager Niccólo Pandolfini
International Division Mauro Mazzarelli

Euromoney Directory 1999 7

ARGENTINA (+54) www.euromoneydirectory.com

Banca di Roma SpA
Representative Office

Calle Maipù 267, piso 19°, Buenos Aires 1084
Tel: (1) 326 2145; (1) 326 4626 **Fax:** (1) 326 9506 **Telex:** 9163 ROMAP AR **Cable:** ROMAPLATA

Senior Executive Officers
Representative   Roberto Iannone ℱ **326 9506**

Banco Argencoop Cooperativo Ltdo
Head Office

Primera Junta 2661, Santa Fé 3000
Tel: (42) 552 140 **Fax:** (42) 552 144

Senior Executive Officers
President   Sergio Dannielle Rossini

Banco Bansud SA
Head Office

Formerly known as: Banco del Sud & Banco Shaw

Sarmiento 447, Buenos Aires 1041
PO Box 3697, Buenos Aires 1000
Tel: (1) 348 6500; (1) 329 7800 **Fax:** (1) 325 5641; (1) 325 5642 **Telex:** 18907 BANSU AR **Swift:** BOSU AR BA

Senior Executive Officers
President & Chairman, Board of Directors   Leonardo Anidjar
Financial Director   Jorge Puente *Financial Manager* ☎ **348 6540** ℱ **325 6067**
General Manager   Pablo Peralta ☎ **348 6859** ℱ **329 6959**
International Division   Oscar Bergés *International Division Manager* ☎ **325 6639** ℱ **325 6067**

Others (Senior Executives)
Retail Banking & Special Project   Zulema Ber *Manager* ☎ **348 6809** ℱ **320 8960**
Commercial Manager   Guido Messi
General-Lending (DCM, SL)
Head of Corporate Banking   Jorge Puente *Financial Manager* ☎ **348 6540** ℱ **325 6067**
Debt Capital Markets / Fixed Income
Global Head   Marina Santiago de Albornoz *Manager* ☎ **331 2775**
Risk Management
Global Head   Pablo Chedufau *Manager, Risk Management*
Settlement / Clearing
Operations   Roxana Matias Gago *Manager, Strategic Planning* ☎ **348 6780** ℱ **329 7805**
     Daniel Perrota *DGM, Branches & Operations*

Other Departments
Private Banking   Carlos Medina ☎ **348 6760** ℱ **329 7805**
Correspondent Banking   Horacio Pitrelli *Relations Head* ☎ **348 6621** ℱ **325 6067**
Administration
Technology & Systems
     Eduardo Stanganello *Manager*

Public Relations
Human Resources   Silvana Torres *Manager*

Banco BI Creditanstalt SA
Head Office

Formerly known as: Banco Interfinanzas SA

Bouchard 547, piso 24°, Buenos Aires 1106
Tel: (1) 319 8400; (1) 319 8200 **Fax:** (1) 319 8232; (1) 319 8230 **Telex:** 20192 **Swift:** BIIN AR BA
Email: bl_credit@impsat1.com.ar

Senior Executive Officers
Chairman   Miguel Angel Angelino
Vice Chairman   José Maria Gonzales de la Fuente
Vice Chairman   Alarich Fenyves
Chief Executive Officer   Teddy Plank *Managing Director*
Financial Director   Julio Rovegno *Deputy Chief Executive*
Managing Director   Ricardo Rivero Haedo
International Division   Julio Rovegno *Deputy Chief Executive*

Others (Senior Executives)
     Ottokarl Finsterwalder *Director*
     Mariano Felder *Director*

www.euromoneydirectory.com				ARGENTINA (+54)

General-Investment
Head of Investment				José Irigoyen *Senior Vice President*
Other Departments
Private Banking				Angel Crosignani *Senior Vice President*
Administration
Other (Administration)
Administration & Controlling			Julio Molinari *Executive Vice President*
Commercial Banking				Miguel von Mihaly *Senior Vice President*
Leasing					Andrés Garcia Simón *Manager*

## Banco Bilbao Vizcaya					Representative Office

Avenida Roque Saenz Peôa 832, piso 7°, Buenos Aires 1388
Tel: (1) 328 9313 **Fax:** (1) 11 2446

Senior Executive Officers
Representative				Rafael Belinchón

## Banco do Brasil SA					Full Branch Office

Calle Sarmiento 487, Buenos Aires 1041
Casilla de Correo 2684, Buenos Aires 1041
Tel: (1) 325 6635; (1) 394 9861 **Fax:** (1) 394 9577; (1) 325 6639 **Telex:** 24197 **Swift:** BRASARBRA

Senior Executive Officers
Manager					Helio Testoni

## Banco de la Ciudad de Buenos Aires			Head Office

Florida 302, Buenos Aires 1313
Tel: (1) 329 8600; (1) 329 8700 **Fax:** (1) 11 2098 **Telex:** 22365 banmuar **Swift:** BACI AR BA **Reuters:** ARCU
Telex: 18262 banmuar

Senior Executive Officers
Chairman					Horacio Chighizola 325 2623 325 0046
Financial Director				Jorge Caracoche *Manager* 329 8937 329 8789
General Manager				Hugo Harley Arbarello 325 2591 325 0911
International Division			Vicente R Davenia *Manager* 329 8922 329 8769
Foreign Exchange
Head of Foreign Exchange			Héctor Nicoletti *Manager* 329 8642 329 8866

## Banco Comafi SA					Head Office

Avenida Roque Saenz Peña 660, Buenos Aires 1035
Tel: (1) 328 5000; (1) 328 5555 **Fax:** (1) 328 9068; (1) 328 7036 **Telex:** 20141 COMAFI AR
Email: comafi@comafi.com.ar **Reuters:** Recipient

Senior Executive Officers
President & CEO				Guillermo Cerviño
Chief Executive Officer			Eduardo Maschwitz
Financial Director				Mariano Chouhy
Debt Capital Markets / Fixed Income
Global Head					Guillermo Cerviño *President & CEO*
Domestic Government Bonds
Head of Sales					Emilio Massera
Head of Trading				Estanislao Díaz Saubidet *Director*
Head of Research				Esteban Marx
Eurobonds
Head of Origination				Juan Aldazabal *Director*
Equity Capital Markets
Department: Comafi Bursatil SA
Global Head					Mariano Chouhy
Domestic Equities
Head of Sales					Emilio Massera
Head of Trading				Estanislao Díaz Saubidet *Director*
Head of Research				Esteban Marx

ARGENTINA (+54) www.euromoneydirectory.com

Banco Comafi SA (cont)
Other Departments
Proprietary Trading Estanislao Díaz Saubidet *Director*
Private Banking Juan Aldazabal *Director*

Banco Comercial Israelita SA Head Office

Mitre 702, Provincia Sante Fe, Rosario 2000
Tel: (41) 200 545 **Fax:** (41) 200 500; (41) 201 006

Senior Executive Officers
President David Czarny
General Manager José Eisemberg

Banco de la Edificadora de Olavarria SA Head Office

Rivadavía 3000, Olavarria 7400
Tel: (284) 27646; (284) 42646 **Fax:** (284) 42272
General Tel: 27655; 42655

Senior Executive Officers
President Pablo Erramouspe
General Manager Ricardo Luis Pereyra

Banco de Entre Ríos SA (Bersa) Head Office

Monte Caseros 128, Paraná 3100, Entre Rios
Tel: (43) 201 200; (43) 230 230 **Fax:** (43) 201 221; (43) 213 869

Senior Executive Officers
President Edmundo Muguruza
Financial Director Rubén Kaplán *Financial Manager*
General Manager Erardo Lucas Raspini
International Division Carlos Fernando Colombo *International Manager*

Banco Europeo para America Latina (BEAL) SA Full Branch Office

Alternative trading name: BEAL
Pte Tte Gral Perón 338, Buenos Aires 1038
Tel: (1) 331 6549; (1) 331 6544 **Fax:** (1) 331 2010 **Email:** bealbsas@interprov.com **Tel:** 343 3543; 343 5932;
Fax: 331 8190

Senior Executive Officers
Financial Director Pablo Ladmann ☎ **343 7034** 🖷 **331 8174** ✉ **bealfina@interprov.com**
General Manager Klaus Krüger ☎ **343 3543** 🖷 **331 8190** ✉ **bealbsas@interprov.com**
General Manager Jean-Pierre Smeets ☎ **343 5932** 🖷 **331 8190** ✉ **bealbsas@interprov.com**
General-Lending (DCM, SL)
Head of Corporate Banking Diego Kagel *Senior Manager* ☎ **334 9173**
Antonio Goitisolo *Senior Manager* 🖷 **334 9174** ✉ **bealcorp@interprov.com**
Diego García del Rio *Senior Manager* ☎ **334 9176**

General - Treasury
Head of Treasury Pablo Ladmann *Treasury* ☎ **343 7034** 🖷 **331 8174** ✉ **bealfina@interprov.com**
Corporate Finance / M&A Advisory
Country Head Diego Kagel *Senior Manager* ☎ **334 9173**
Settlement / Clearing
Operations Diana Castro *Head* ☎ **345 5754** 🖷 **345 5756** ✉ **bealdop@interprov.com**
Other Departments
Correspondent Banking Lawrence Daniels *Senior Manager* ☎ **334 9175**
Administration
Accounts / Audit
Accounting Dept. Raúl Fabris *Head* ☎ **343 5887**
Other (Administration)
Risk Analysis Susana Mancini *Head* ☎ **334 9170** 🖷 **345 5755**

www.euromoneydirectory.com ARGENTINA (+54)

Banco Exterior de América SA
Full Branch Office

Leandro N Alem 356, piso 16°, Buenos Aires 1003
Tel: (1) 313 3633; (1) 313 3733 Fax: (1) 313 3223; (1) 11 8169 Telex: 17710 EXTBK AR Swift: EXTE AR BA
Email: extearba@argentaria.arg.com Cable: EXTERIBANK - BAIRES

Senior Executive Officers
General Manager   Guillermo Manuel Rothlisberger
International Division   Marcelo Florena

Syndicated Lending
Loan-Related Activities
Trade Finance   Eduardo Ferrero

Money Markets
Country Head   Luis Spirito

Foreign Exchange
Country Head   Luis Spirito

Risk Management
Country Head   Marcelo Florena

Administration
Head of Administration   Alejandro Vinetz

Banco de Galicia y Buenos Aires
Head Office

Teniente General JD Pérón 407, Buenos Aires 1038
Tel: (1) 329 6000 Fax: (1) 329 6308; (1) 329 6100 Telex: 9012 Swift: GABA AR BA

Senior Executive Officers
Chairman   Eduardo J Escasany ☎ 329 6631 📠 329 6313
Chief Executive Officer   Eduardo J Escasany ☎ 329 6631 📠 329 6313
Financial Director   Sergio Grinenco *Chief Financial Officer* ☎ 329 6253 📠 329 6449
Chief Operating Officer   Daniel Llambias ☎ 329 6250 📠 329 6308
Treasurer   Luis M Ribaya ☎ 329 6153 📠 329 6800
Company Secretary   Eduardo Zimmermann ☎ 329 6634 📠 329 6313
International Division   Héctor Arzeno ☎ 329 6427 📠 329 6486

Debt Capital Markets / Fixed Income
Head of Debt Capital Markets   Sergio Grinenco *Chief Financial Officer* ☎ 329 6253 📠 329 6449
Head of Fixed Income   Horacio Gracia *Head of Bond Trading Desk* ☎ 329 6150 📠 329 6155

Government Bonds
Head of Trading   Horacio Gracia *Head of Bond Trading Desk* ☎ 329 6150 📠 329 6155

Eurobonds
Head of Trading   Horacio Gracia *Head of Bond Trading Desk* ☎ 329 6150 📠 329 6155

Equity Capital Markets
Head of Equity Capital Markets   Diego Giménez *Head of Equity Trading* ☎ 329 6150 📠 329 0155

Domestic Equities
Head of Trading   Diego Giménez *Head of Equity Trading* ☎ 329 6150 📠 329 0155

International Equities
Head of Trading   Diego Giménez *Head of Equity Trading* ☎ 329 6150 📠 329 0155

Asset Management
Head   Carlos Luc *Executive Vice President* ☎ 329 6255 📠 329 6429

Other Departments
Chief Credit Officer   Guillermo Pando *Chief Credit Officer* ☎ 329 6704 📠 329 6704
Private Banking   Pablo Gutierrez *Head of Private Banking* ☎ 329 7605 📠 329 7676

Administration
Head of Administration   Omar H Tioarelli ☎ 329 6263 📠 329 6263
Head of Marketing   Ana Ferrero ☎ 329 6941 📠 329 6475

Technology & Systems
                                   Benito Silva ☎ 329 6335 📠 329 6568

Legal / In-House Counsel
                                   Matilde Hoenig ☎ 329 6252 📠 329 6429

Compliance
                                   Matilde Hoenig ☎ 329 6252 📠 329 6429

Public Relations
                                   Luis Ibarra Garcia ☎ 329 6439 📠 329 2041

Accounts / Audit
                                   Norberto Corizzo ☎ 329 6335 📠 329 6385

Euromoney Directory 1999 **11**

ARGENTINA (+54)   www.euromoneydirectory.com

Banco Hipotecario Nacional
Head Office

Alsina 353, Buenos Aires 1087
Tel: (1) 347 5000 Fax: (1) 347 5583
Accountancy Department Tel: 334 1220

Senior Executive Officers
President — Pablo Rojo ☏ **347 5201**
President — Mr Ocampo
Chief Executive Officer — Mr Garcia Cuerva
Financial Director — Mr Scrivens ☏ **347 5546**

Banco de Inversion y Comercio Exterior SA
Head Office

Formerly known as: BICE

25 de Mayo 526/32, Buenos Aires 1002
Tel: (1) 313 9546; (1) 313 9398 Fax: (1) 313 5596

Senior Executive Officers
Chairman — José Maria Candioti ☏ **313 9508**
Vice President — Ricardo G Sigwald ☏ **313 9531**
Financial Director — Alfredo Ramirez *Finance Manager* ☏ **313 9546**
Chief Operating Officer — Silvia Szalay *Operations Manager* ☏ **313 9546**
General Manager — Rafel Iniesta

Banco Itaú Argentina SA
Subsidiary Company

25 Mayo 476, piso 1°, Buenos Aires 1002
Tel: (1) 315 3348; (1) 315 3375 Fax: (1) 315 3394 Telex: 24020

Senior Executive Officers
Financial Director — Joao de Faria Burnier *Commercial Director*

Others (Senior Executives)
Antonio Carlos Barbosa de Oliveira *General Director*
Máximo Hernández González *Executive Director*

Administration
Head of Administration — José Rodriguez *Director*

Banco Latinoamericano de Exportaciones SA - BLADEX
Representative Office

Reconquista 520, piso 9°, Buenos Aires
Tel: (1) 393 9986 Fax: (1) 325 2206

Senior Executive Officers
Representative — Julio Drot de Gourville

Banco Macro Misiones SA
Head Office

Sarmiento 735, Buenos Aires 1041
Tel: (1) 325 9511; (1) 323 6300 Fax: (1) 325 6935 Telex: 18343 MACRO AR Swift: BANM AR BA

Senior Executive Officers
President & CEO — Jorge Horacio Brito
Chief Executive Officer — Jorge Horacio Brito *President & CEO*
General Manager — Juan Pablo Brito Devoto
General Manager — Claudio Cerezo
International Division — Fernando A Sansuste *International Division Director*

Others (Senior Executives)
Director — Carlos E Videlo

General-Lending (DCM, SL)
Head of Corporate Banking — Santiago M Portais *Commercial & Corporate Banking Vice President*

www.euromoneydirectory.com　　　ARGENTINA (+54)

Banco Mercantíl Argentina SA
Head Office

Avenida Corrientes 629, Capital Federal, Buenos Aires 1324
Tel: (1) 323 5000 **Fax:** (1) 323 5073 **Telex:** 316 9079 **Swift:** BMER AR BA **Cable:** MERBANKAR

Senior Executive Officers
Chairman — Noel Werthein
Vice Chairman — Julio Werthein
Chief Executive Officer — Adrian Werthein *Executive Director*
Financial Director — Heraldo Brado *Deputy General Manager*
General Manager — Guillermo Feldberg
Deputy General Manager — Jorge Mignone
Deputy General Manager — Dario Werthein
International Division — Carlos F Trilnick *Manager*

Others (Senior Executives)
Carlos F Trilnick *Manager*

General-Lending (DCM, SL)
Head of Corporate Banking — Dario Werthein *Deputy General Manager*

Debt Capital Markets / Fixed Income
Head of Fixed Income Trading — Julio Ponieman *Bonds Trading*

Equity Capital Markets
Head of Trading — Felipe Schenone *Equity Trader*

Syndicated Lending

Other (Trade Finance)
Forfaiting — Ricardo Collarini

Banco Mercurio SA
Head Office

Formerly known as: Mercurio

San Martin 233, Buenos Aires 1004
Tel: (1) 320 2600 **Fax:** (1) 320 2693 **Email:** banpriv@ibm.net

Senior Executive Officers
Chairman — Jacques Benadon
Chief Executive Officer — Mauricio Benadon
Financial Director — Claudia Flomembaum

Banco de la Nacion Argentina
Head Office

Bartolomé Mitre 326, Oficina 216, Buenos Aires 1036
Tel: (1) 347 8077; (1) 347 8083 **Fax:** (1) 347 8078; (1) 347 8084 **Telex:** 9190 BNCAM AR **Swift:** NACN AR BA
Website: www.bna.com.ar

Senior Executive Officers
Chairman — Roque Maccarone ☎ **347 6105**
Director — Virgilio Tedin Uriburu ☎ **347 6153**
General Manager — Jesús D'Alessandro ☎ **347 6412**
Secretary of the Board — Luis Duna ☎ **347 6260**
International Division — Luis Garcia *Executive Vice President* ☎ **347 8075**

Others (Senior Executives)
Néstor Sallent *Trustee* ☎ **347 6192**

General-Lending (DCM, SL)
Head of Corporate Banking — Gustavo Gastaud *Senior Vice President* ☎ **347 8081**

Money Markets
Head of Money Markets — Alberto Sgroi *Senior Vice President* ☎ **347 7934**

Risk Management
Head of Risk Management — José Barone *Executive Vice President* ☎ **347 6380**

Banco de la Pampa
Head Office

Formerly known as: Banco de Coronel Dorrego SA

Calle Peligrini 255, Santa Rosa 6300
Tel: (9) 545 1000 **Fax:** (9) 545 1000 **Telex:** DOCEN AR 81925

Senior Executive Officers
Chairman — Nestor Bossio
General Manager — Norberto Cautero

ARGENTINA (+54)   www.euromoneydirectory.com

Banco Pastor SA
Representative Office

Lavalle 643, piso 5° E, Buenos Aires
Correo Postal 1047, Buenos Aires
Tel: (1) 322 7921; (1) 322 5755 Fax: (1) 322 0868

Senior Executive Officers
Representative   Jaime García Marín

Banco de la Provincia de Buenos Aires
Head Office

Alternative trading name: Banco Provincia
San Martin 137, Buenos Aires 1004
Tel: (1) 331 2561; (1) 331 2569 Fax: (1) 331 5154 Telex: 18276 PROBA AR Swift: PRBA AR BA
Email: baprocri@internet.siscotel.com Reuters: ARBP
Website: www.bpba.com.ar

Senior Executive Officers
President	Carlos Sanchez ☎ **331 5111**
Treasurer	Carlos Gabilondo *General Treasurer* ☎ **343 1866**
General Manager	Alberto Canos ☎ **342 7918**
Deputy General Manager	Ernesto Bruggia ☎ **343 7551**
Company Secretary	Hugo Pifarre ☎ **342 0121**
International Division	Mirta Barcus ☎ **342 1270**

General-Lending (DCM, SL)
Head of Corporate Banking   Jorge Maldonado *Manager* ☎ **334 7093**

Debt Capital Markets / Fixed Income
Department: Finance & International Relations Management
Tel: 343 3913 Fax: 331 9401
Country Head   Marcelo Garcia *Manager*

Syndicated Lending
Loan-Related Activities
Trade Finance   Carlos Gonzalez ☎ **343 5488**

Foreign Exchange
Head of Foreign Exchange   Marcelo Caffa ☎ **343 1129**

Other Departments
Correspondent Banking   Pablo Metola ☎ **342 1270**

Administration
Head of Administration   Carlos Novo *Manager* ☎ **342 6859**
Head of Marketing   Juan Carlos De La Vega *Chief* ☎ **331 9707**

Technology & Systems
                             Eduardo González Dalton *Manager* ☎ **343 2317**

Legal / In-House Counsel
                             Miguel Romano *Manager* ☎ **342 3288**

Public Relations
                             Ernesto Rey *Secretary* ☎ **342 7831**

Accounts / Audit
Accounts   Raul Fanelli *General Manager* ☎ **342 0424**

Banco de la Provincia de Córdoba
Head Office

San Jerónimo 166, Córdoba 5000
Tel: (51) 207 200 Fax: (51) 229 718 Telex: 51756 bacor ar Swift: CORD AR BA COR

Senior Executive Officers
Managing Director / General Manager   Cesar Augusto Echavarria
Others (Senior Executives)
                                       Miguel Angel Baggini *First Vice Chairman*

Banco Quilmes SA

Tte General JD Perón 564, Buenos Aires 1038
Tel: (1) 331 8111 Fax: (1) 334 5235 Telex: 18955 BQSA AR

Senior Executive Officers
Chief Executive Officer   Anatol von Hahn *Executive Director*

www.euromoneydirectory.com ARGENTINA (+54)

Debt Capital Markets / Fixed Income
Tel: 331 8111 ext 2518
Head of Debt Capital Markets; Head of Fixed Elena Scolari *Head of Trading*
Income Trading

Equity Capital Markets
Tel: 331 8111 ext 2519
Head of Equity Capital Markets Elena Scolari *Head of Trading*
Head of Trading Patricia Alegre

Money Markets
Tel: 331 8111 ext 2518
Head of Money Markets Elena Scolari *Head of Trading*

Money Markets - General
Trading Jose Luis Fontanela

Foreign Exchange
Tel: 331 8111 ext 2518
Head of Foreign Exchange Elena Scolari *Head of Trading*
Head of Trading Jorge Fowil

Risk Management
Tel: 331 8111 ext 2519
Head of Risk Management Elena Scolari *Head of Trading*

Asset Management
Portfolio Management Gabriel Ruiz
  Andres Ronquieto

Other Departments
Correspondent Banking Armando Feira
  Susana María Romano
  Elvira Aída Cavalieri

Banco Real de Argentina SA Head Office

Calle San Martin 480, Buenos Aires 1004
Tel: (1) 394 1534 **Fax:** (1) 111 608 **Telex:** 24097; 9007 **Email:** realar@ssdnet.com.ar
General Telex: 9007

Senior Executive Officers
Chairman & CEO Lusivander Furlani Leite
Chief Executive Officer Lusivander Furlani Leite *Chairman & CEO*
Financial Director Manuel Meilan *Manager*
General Manager Fernando Bruno Pinto
International Division Julio Luis Belmudes *International Manager*
  Daniel Benitez *Manager*

Others (Senior Executives)
Commercial Banking Pedro Gehrke *Manager*

Administration
Head of Administration Antonio Carlos Vieira *Director*

Accounts / Audit
Controller Mario Iannantuono *Chief Accountant*

Banco Río de la Plata (Grupo Santander) Head Office

Bartolomé Mitre 480, Buenos Aires 1036
Tel: (1) 341 1000 **Fax:** (1) 341 1021 **Telex:** 9117 BADER AR **Swift:** BOER AR BA
Website: www.bancorio.com.ar

Senior Executive Officers
President Ana Patricia Botín
Financial Director Marcelo Castro *Principal Manager*
Chief Operating Officer Angel Agallano
Managing Director & GM Enrique Cristofani
Sub-General Manager Martin Poullier

Global Custody

Other (Global Custody)
Custodial Services Carlos Merino *Assistant Manager*

Administration
Head of Administration Angel Agallano

Euromoney Directory 1999 15

ARGENTINA (+54)   www.euromoneydirectory.com

Banco Roela SA
Head Office

Rosario de Santa Fé 275, piso 1°, Córdoba 5000
Tel: (51) 241 777; (51) 244 022 **Fax:** (51) 230 824 **Telex:** 51791 ROELA AR **Email:** roela@si.cordoba.com.ar

Senior Executive Officers
President
Vice President & General Manager

Victor Mondino
Horacio Parodi

Debt Capital Markets / Fixed Income
Tel: 243 591 **Fax:** AR 27184
Head of Fixed Income
Head of Fixed Income Sales

Andrés Bas *Global Head*
Victor Campana *Global Head*

Banco de San Juan
Head Office

Avenida Jose I de la Roza 85, Oeste, San Juan 5400
Tel: (64) 214 100; (64) 201 114 **Fax:** (64) 214 126 **Telex:** 59152

Senior Executive Officers
President
Chief Executive Officer
Financial Director
Chief Operating Officer

Enrique Eskenazi
Francisco Riobo *General Manager*
Norberto Giudice *Finance Manager*
Leopoldo Malberti *Operations Manager*

Others (Senior Executives)
Commercial Director

Manuel Prieto

Equity Capital Markets
Country Head

Doja Zaldo *Manager*

Money Markets
Global Head

Daniel Idema *Head of Engineering & Financial Planning Dept*

Risk Management
Country Head

Martin Souza *Director*

Settlement / Clearing
Operations

Leopoldo Malberti *Director*

Other Departments
Correspondent Banking
Debt Recovery / Restructuring

Norberto Giudice *Finance Manager*
José Recio *Director*

Administration
Head of Administration
Head of Marketing

Hector Jorge *Resource Director* 🖃 21 4100
Susana Medawar

Technology & Systems
Systems

Eduardo Basombrio *Director*

Legal / In-House Counsel

Ernesto de Leonparga

Accounts / Audit

Arthur Andersen

Banco de San Juan SA
Head Office

Avenida Ignacio de la Roza 85, Oeste, San Juan 5400
Tel: (64) 214 100; (64) 201 114 **Fax:** (64) 214 126 **Telex:** 59152

Senior Executive Officers
President
Chief Executive Officer
Financial Director
Chief Operating Officer

Enrique Eskenazi
Francisco Riobo *General Manager* 🖃 friobo@sanjuan.com.ar
Norberto Giudice *Finance Manager*
Leopoldo Malberti *Operations Manager*

Banco de Santa Fe SA
Head Office

25 de Mayo 2545, Santa Fé 3000
Tel: (42) 553 497; (42) 525 400 **Fax:** (42) 554 543

16   Euromoney Directory 1999

www.euromoneydirectory.com   ARGENTINA (+54)

Banco Sudameris Argentina SA

Tte Gral Juan Domingo Perón 500, Buenos Aires 1038
Casilla de Correo 1849, Correo Central, Buenos Aires 1000
Tel: (1) 329 5200; (1) 329 5300 Fax: (1) 111 525; (1) 334 2398

Senior Executive Officers
Others (Senior Executives)
Carlos Gonzalez Taboada *Executive Director*

Banco Supervielle Société Générale SA   Full Branch Office

Calle Reconquista 320/330, Buenos Aires 1003
PO Box 1193 & 1438, Buenos Aires
Tel: (1) 329 8000 Fax: (1) 329 8080 Telex: 9108/10 BSSG AR Swift: BSSG AR BA

Senior Executive Officers
Chairman & General Manager — Yves Thieffry
Deputy General Manager — Marc-Emmanuel Vives
Deputy General Manager International Division — Hubert Lamy
Oscar Colombo

General-Lending (DCM, SL)
Head of Corporate Banking — Arturo Sappia *Head Corporate Finance*

Other Departments
Private Banking — Carlos Hidalgo

Banco Tornquist SA   Head Office

Bartolomé Mitre 531, Buenos Aires 1036
Tel: (1) 347 1200 Fax: (1) 347 1220 Telex: 20093/4 TQST

Senior Executive Officers
President — Fernando Cañas Berkowitz
Chief Executive Officer — Juan Enrique Vilajuana Rigau *Chief Executive Officer & General Manager*
Financial Director — Marcelo Canabal
Chief Executive Officer & General Manager — Juan Enrique Vilajuana Rigau

General-Investment
Head of Investment — Carlos M Helbling *Director, Investment Banking*

Debt Capital Markets / Fixed Income
Tel: 343 7887/8
Head of Debt Capital Markets — Gustavo Carrusco *Head of Trading*

Domestic Government Bonds
Head of Sales — Marcela Nazer *Sales*
Head of Trading — Martin Rochina

Eurobonds
Head of Sales — Marcela Nazer *Sales*

Fixed-Income Repo
Sales — Marcela Nazer *Sales*

Equity Capital Markets
Tel: 343 7887/8
Head of Equity Capital Markets — Gustavo Carrusco *Head of Trading*

Domestic Equities
Head of Trading — Martin Rochina
Gustavo Carrusco *Head of Trading*

Syndicated Lending
Head of Syndicated Lending; Head of Origination; Head of Syndication — Carlos M Helbling *Director, Investment Banking*

Loan-Related Activities
Trade Finance — Carlos Jürgens
Project Finance — Carlos M Helbling *Director, Investment Banking*

Money Markets
Tel: 343 7887/8
Head of Money Markets — Gustavo Carrusco *Head of Trading*

Domestic Commercial Paper
Head of Sales — Daniel Carreira
Head of Trading — Osvaldo Caresani

ARGENTINA (+54)

www.euromoneydirectory.com

Banco Tornquist SA (cont)
Foreign Exchange
Tel: 343 7887/8
Head of Foreign Exchange — Gustavo Carrusco *Head of Trading*
Head of Trading — Osvaldo Caresani

Risk Management
Tel: 343 7887/8
Head of Risk Management — Gustavo Carrusco *Head of Trading*
Marcela Nazer *Sales*

Corporate Finance / M&A Advisory
Head of Corporate Finance — Carlos M Helbling *Director, Investment Banking*

Other Departments
Private Banking — Daniel Cortina

Banco Transandino SA — Head Office

25 Mayo 294, Buenos Aires 1002
Tel: (1) 320 6200 Fax: (1) 326 4654 Email: bt.mancia@startel.com.ar

Senior Executive Officers
President — Sergio de Castro Spikula
Chief Executive Officer — César Barros Montero
General Manager — Carlos Manciarotti

Other Departments
Private Banking — Jose Luis Sandoval

Banco Velox SA — Head Office

San Martin 298, piso 3°, Buenos Aires 1004
Tel: (1) 320 0200; (1) 320 0320 Fax: (1) 393 7672 Telex: 23882, 24071 VELOX AR Swift: VLOX AR BA Reuters: AR V

Senior Executive Officers
President — Juan Peirano [T] 394 8255
Financial Director — Marcelo Artigala *Finance Manager* [T] 320 0360 [F] 394 1263
Managing Director — Luis Maurette [T] 320 0493
International Division — Alejandro Marfort *Senior Vice President* [T] 320 0320

Debt Capital Markets / Fixed Income
Eurobonds
Head of Sales; Head of Trading — Marcelo Artigala *Manager* [T] 320 0360 [F] 394 1263

Syndicated Lending
Loan-Related Activities
Trade Finance — Laura De Figueroa [T] 320 0351

Money Markets
Tel: (1) 320 0240 Fax: (1) 320 0458
Head of Money Markets — Marcelo Artigala *Manager* [T] 320 0360 [F] 394 1263

Foreign Exchange
Head of Foreign Exchange — Carlos Risso *Manager* [T] 320 0363

Risk Management
Head of Risk Management — Alejandro Borgauer [T] 320 0439

Corporate Finance / M&A Advisory
Global Head — José Peirano *Commercial Manager*

Other Departments
Chief Credit Officer — Juan José Degregorio *Manager* [T] 320 0346
Correspondent Banking — Maria Cristina Contestin *International Banking Officer* [T] 320 0390

Administration
Technology & Systems — Jorge Civano *Systems Manager* [T] 320 0208

Legal / In-House Counsel — Hector De Simone [T] 320 0321

Public Relations — Ricardo Esteves *Director* [T] 320 0261

Accounts / Audit — Ricardo Rocca [T] 320 0333

ARGENTINA (+54)

Bank of America NT & SA
Full Branch Office

25 de Mayo 537, piso 1°, Buenos Aires 1002
Tel: (1) 319 2600 Fax: (1) 311 7294; (1) 313 0476

Senior Executive Officers
Treasurer
Alejandro Ledesma *Treasurer & Head of Dealing*

Debt Capital Markets / Fixed Income
Tel: 313 0496 Fax: 315 6480
Head of Debt Capital Markets
Alejandro Ledesma *Treasurer & Head of Dealing*

Government Bonds
Head of Trading
Fernando Negri

Money Markets
Tel: 313 0496 Fax: 315 6480
Head of Money Markets
Alejandro Ledesma *Treasurer & Head of Dealing*

Domestic Commercial Paper
Head of Trading
Maxmiliano Bloomfill

Foreign Exchange
Tel: 313 0496 Fax: 315 6480
Head of Foreign Exchange
Alejandro Ledesma *Treasurer & Head of Dealing*
Head of Trading; Spot / Forwards Trading
Gonzalo Santillian

Bank of Boston
Full Branch Office

Florida 99, Buenos Aires 1005
Tel: (1) 346 2000 Telex: 21139 BOBSKAR Swift: FNBB AR BAA
Corporate Investors Department Tel: 346 2975; 346 2262; Fax: 346 3080 Fax: 346 3130; Public Relations
Tel: 346 2171; 346 2245

Senior Executive Officers
Chairman
Manuel R Sacerdote

General-Investment
Head of Investment
Marcelo Dupont ☎ 346 2116

Global Custody
Fax: 346 3130
Country Head
Marcelo Dupont ☎ 346 2116

Other (Global Custody)
Relationship Officer
Boris Welyczko ☎ 346 2262
Product Specialist
Victoria Sendrik

Bank Hapoalim BM
Representative Office

Sarmiento 944, piso 13°, Buenos Aires
Tel: (1) 326 2586; (1) 326 8272 Fax: (1) 326 9383; (1) 112 056

Senior Executive Officers
Representative
Efraim Yuhjtman

Bank Leu Limited
Representative Office

Florida 375, piso 4D°, Buenos Aires 1005
Tel: (1) 325 5328 Fax: (1) 327 2257 Email: bankleu@ssdnet.com.ar

Senior Executive Officers
Financial Director
Daniel Sierra *Financial Advisor*
Senior Representative
Marina Cuervo

The Bank of Nova Scotia
Representative Office

Calle Corrientes 456, piso 11°, Suite 111, Buenos Aires 1366
PO Box 3955, Correo Central, Buenos Aires 1000
Tel: (1) 394 0101; (1) 394 0080 Fax: (1) 111 266 Telex: 3324317 Tel: 394 8726

Senior Executive Officers
Vice President & Managing Director
R D Scott

ARGENTINA (+54) www.euromoneydirectory.com

The Bank of Tokyo-Mitsubishi Limited
Full Branch Office

Avenida Corrientes 420, Buenos Aires 1043
Tel: (1) 348 2001; (1) 348 2054 Fax: (1) 322 6607; (1) 320 2000 Telex: 21596 TBKBAAR
Senior Executive Officers
General Manager   Minoru Sekine

Banque Nationale de Paris
Full Branch Office

25 de Mayo 471, Buenos Aires 1002
Casilla de Correo 3498, Correo Central, Buenos Aires 1000
Tel: (1) 318 0318 Fax: (1) 311 1368 Telex: 9225/6 BNPBA AR
Senior Executive Officers
General Manager   Ghislain de Beaucé
General-Lending (DCM, SL)
Head of Corporate Banking   Jorge Toccafondi *Manager*
Risk Management
Country Head   Michel Mur *Manager*

BBV Banco Francés SA
Head Office

Formerly known as: Banco Francés del Río de la Plata SA
Reconquista 199, Buenos Aires 1003
Tel: (1) 346 4000 Fax: (1) 346 4320 Swift: BFRP AR BA
Website: www.bancofrances.com

Senior Executive Officers
Chairman   Gervasio Collar Zabaleta ☏ 346 4370
Chief Executive Officer   Antonio Martinez Jorquera ☏ 346 4343
Financial Director   Jorge Bledel ☏ 346 4340
Chief Operating Officer   Rodorfo Corvi ☏ 346 4310
Treasurer   Carlos Marí ☏ 346 4349
General Manager   Antonio Martínez Jorquera
International Division   Maria Seljak ☏ 346 4326
General-Lending (DCM, SL)
Head of Corporate Banking   Marcelo Canestri *Corporate Banking Director* ☏ 346 4000
General-Investment
Head of Investment   Carlos Villahoz ☏ 346 4311
Debt Capital Markets / Fixed Income
Global Head   Alejandro Etchart ☏ 346 4334
Domestic Government Bonds
Head of Sales   Christian Lascombes ☏ 346 4352
Head of Trading   Ricardo Zuretti ☏ 346 4352
Head of Research   Ernesto Gaba
Eurobonds
Head of Origination; Head of Syndication   Carlos Villahoz ☏ 346 4311
Head of Sales   Christian Lascombes ☏ 346 4352
Head of Trading   Ricardo Zuretti ☏ 346 4352
Head of Research   Ernesto Gaba
Trading - Sovereigns, Corporates, High-yield   Eduardo Gondra ☏ 346 4352
Fixed-Income Repo
Head of Repo   Ricardo Zuretti ☏ 346 4352
Equity Capital Markets
Global Head   Alejandro Etchart ☏ 346 4334
Head of Sales; Head of Trading   Christian Lascombes ☏ 346 4352
Domestic Equities
Head of Origination; Head of Syndication   Carlos Villahoz ☏ 346 4311
Head of Sales; Head of Trading   Christian Lascombes ☏ 346 4352
Head of Research   Ernesto Gaba
Syndicated Lending
Loan-Related Activities
Trade Finance   Juan Lanza ☏ 346 4000
Corporate Finance / M&A Advisory
Global Head   Alejandro Etchart ☏ 346 4334

ARGENTINA (+54)

Asset Management
Head   Tomas Deane ☎ **346 4352**

Other Departments
Private Banking   Gerónimo Escobar ☎ **346 4374**
Correspondent Banking   María Seljak *Managing Director*

Administration
Tel: 346 4000
Head of Administration   Emilio Lanza
Head of Marketing   Gustavo Canil

Technology & Systems
   Alberto Santamaria

Public Relations
   Gonzalo Verdomar Weiss

Other (Administration)
Commercial Banking   Mario Fernández *Commercial Banking Director*

Berliner Bank AG   Representative Office
Sarmiento 930, 6B, Buenos Aires 1386
Tel: (1) 327 2771; (1) 112 258 **Fax:** (1) 111 960

Senior Executive Officers
Representative   Maurici Llado Vila 🖃 **maurici.llado@batlantico.com**

Bozano, Simonsen Latin America   Subsidiary Company
Avenida Alicia Moreau de Justo 1050, piso 4°, Puerto Madero, Buenos Aires 1107
Tel: (1) 345 5355 **Fax:** (1) 345 5358

Senior Executive Officers
Director   Luiz António Pretti 🖃 **pretti@bozano.com.br**

BSI-Banca della Svizzera Italiana   Representative Office
Reconquista 144, piso 16°, Buenos Aires 1003
Tel: (1) 343 5315 **Fax:** (1) 334 6032

Senior Executive Officers
Representative   Alesandro Moreno

The Chase Manhattan Bank NA   Representative Office
Arenales 707, piso 5°, Buenos Aires 1061
Tel: (1) 319 2400 **Fax:** (1) 319 2416 **Telex:** 9138/9 CHASA AR

Senior Executive Officers
Managing Director & General Manager   Marcelo E Podesta

CIC Banques/Caisse Nationale   Representative Office
Alternative trading name: De Credit Agricole
Callao 1870, Buenos Aires 1024
Tel: (1) 806 8877 **Fax:** (1) 806 8383 **Email:** mrp@interactive.com.ar

Senior Executive Officers
Chief Representative   Miguel de Larminat

Citibank NA   Full Branch Office
Bartolomé Mitre 530, Buenos Aires 1036
Tel: (1) 329 1000; (1) 329 1435 **Fax:** (1) 329 1029 **Telex:** 6735457 CITIBUECU **Swift:** CITI US 33 ARR **Reuters:** ARCI
Corporate Dealers **Tel:** 329 1272; 329 1750

Senior Executive Officers
President   Carlos Fedrigotti ☎ **329 1291**
President   Richard Handley ☎ **310 6950**
Treasurer   Jorge Lo Negro *Treasurer*

ARGENTINA (+54)   www.euromoneydirectory.com

Citibank NA (cont)
Debt Capital Markets / Fixed Income
Country Head   Franco Moccia ☏ 329 1438
Equity Capital Markets
Equity Repo / Securities Lending
Head   Marcos Knowles ☏ 329 1845
Settlement / Clearing
Operations   Raúl Grunthal *Transaction Services Head* ☏ 329 1553
Global Custody
Country Head   Hugo Arbat ☏ 329 1640 F 329 1025

Clariden Bank   Representative Office
Avenida Eduardo Madero 900, piso 18°, Buenos Aires 1106
Tel: (1) 315 7900 **Fax:** (1) 315 7901
Senior Executive Officers
Chief Representative   René Imhof

Cofirene Banco de Inversión SA   Head Office
San Lorenzo 778, Corrientes 3400
Tel: (783) 22913; (783) 23376 **Fax:** (783) 24299
Senior Executive Officers
Others (Senior Executives)
    Luciano Rafael Fabris *Vice President*

Commerzbank AG   Representative Office
Avenida Corrientes 456, piso 10°, Oficina 106, Buenos Aires 1360
Tel: (1) 394 9311; (1) 394 0720 **Fax:** (1) 11 1856 **Email:** cbrep@interlink.com.ar
Senior Executive Officers
Representative   Karl-Lutz Ammann
Others (Senior Executives)
    Thomas Krieger *Deputy Representative*

Corp Banca   Head Office
Formerly known as: Banco Unión Comercial e Industrial SA
Avenida España 1342, Mendoza 5500
Tel: (61) 204 000 **Fax:** (61) 380 728 **Telex:** 55240 **Swift:** CNBC AR BM **Email:** fdevoto@corpbanca.com.ar
Senior Executive Officers
Tel: 20 4000
Vice Chairman of the Board   Julio Barriga
Financial Director   Fernando Devoto
Chief Operating Officer   Felipe Lesser
Treasurer   Fernando Devoto
General-Lending (DCM, SL)
Head of Corporate Banking   Claudio Márquez
Risk Management
Head of Risk Management   Roberto Casella
Corporate Finance / M&A Advisory
Head of Corporate Finance   Fernando Devoto

Corporación Metropolitana de Finanzas SA Banco   Head Office
Macacha Guemes 555, Puerto Madero, Buenos Aires 1107
Tel: (1) 318 6800 **Fax:** (1) 318 6844; (1) 318 6859 **Telex:** 27020 CMF **Swift:** CMFB AR BA
Senior Executive Officers
Chairman of the Board & President   José Benegas Lynch ☏ 318 6896
Chief Executive Officer   Ricardo Orgoroso *General Manager* ☏ 318 6831
Financial Director   Fernando Allende *Finance Manager* ☏ 318 6884
Chief Operating Officer   Alberto Llambi Campbell *Director* ☏ 318 6831

22 Euromoney Directory 1999

ARGENTINA (+54)

Senior Executive Officers (cont)
International Division

Roberto Korngolo *Senior Manager, Head of International Division*
T 318 6890

Foreign Exchange
Global Head
Regional Head
Head of Institutional Sales
Corporate Sales
Head of Trading

Fernando Allende *Finance Manager* T 318 6884
Alejandro Crespo *Head Trader*
Mario Cazaux *Manager Investment Division* T 318 6857
Alejandro Ventimiglia *Head Trader*
Alejandro Zuza *Head Trader* T 318 6869

Credit Suisse
Representative Office

Esmeralda 130, piso 11°, Buenos Aires 1035
Tel: (1) 393 3002 **Fax:** (1) 393 9596

Senior Executive Officers
Senior Representative
Representative

Reto Tognola
Kuno Iten

De Ganay y Quirno SA Sociedad de Bolsa
Head Office

25 de Mayo 195, piso 6°, Buenos Aires 1002
Tel: (1) 342 9086 **Fax:** (1) 343 8371 **Email:** degaguir@satlink.com

Senior Executive Officers
Chairman
Chief Executive Officer
MD

Juan de Ganay
Pedro S Quirno Lavallo
Francisco Mühlenkamp

Equity Capital Markets
Head of Equity Capital Markets
Head of Trading

Pedro S Quirno Lavallo
Diego A Lucino

Domestic Equities
Head of Sales
Head of Trading

Pedro S Quirno Lavallo
Diego A Lucino

Equity Research
Head of Equity Research

Francisco Mühlenkamp *MD*

Settlement / Clearing
Head of Settlement / Clearing

José del Prado

Administration
Head of Administration

José del Prado

Deutsche Bank SA
Subsidiary Company

Tucuman 1, Buenos Aires 1049
Casilla de Correo 3466, Buenos Aires 1000
Tel: (1) 590 2800 **Fax:** (1) 590 2921 **Telex:** 23020 DEUTH AR **Swift:** DEUT ARBA

Senior Executive Officers
President & Chief Executive Officer
Relationship Management
Head of Group Services
Relationship Management

Alfred Steffen T 590 2801 F 590 2805 E alfred.steffen@db.com
Juan Guthmann T 590 2842 F 590 2846 E juan.guthmann@db.com
Friedhelm Herb T 590 2802 F 590 2826 E friedhelm.herb@db.com
Alfredo MacLaughlin T 590 2804 F 590 2885
E alfredo.maclaughlin@db.com

Head of Global Markets / Treasury

Ariel Sigal T 590 2803 F 590 2897 E ariel.sigal@db.com

Global Custody
Head of Global Custody

Dirk Reinicke *Head of Custody* T 590 2884 F 590 2990
E dirk.reinicke@db.com

Deutsche Securities Sociedad de Bolsa SA
Subsidiary Company

Tucuman 1, Buenos Aires 1049
Casilla de Correo 3466, Buenos Aires 1000
Tel: (1) 590 2980 **Fax:** (1) 590 2921 **Telex:** 23020 DEUTHAR **Swift:** DEUT AR BA **Cable:** DEUTBANK

Equity Capital Markets
Head of Equity Capital Markets

Daniel Tassan Din *Director* T 590 2970

Euromoney Directory 1999 23

ARGENTINA (+54)   www.euromoneydirectory.com

Dresdner Bank Lateinamerika AG/Dresdner Bank AG
Representative Office
Avenida Corrientes 327, piso 18°, Buenos Aires 1043
Tel: (1) 312 4016/7; (1) 312 8959 Fax: (1) 311 8388

Senior Executive Officers
Representative   Pedro R Nowald

Ernesto Allaria Ledesma
Head Office
25 de Mayo 596, piso 15°, Buenos Aires 1002
Tel: (1) 312 8801 Fax: (1) 314 4677

Senior Executive Officers
Chairman & General Manager   Ernesto Allaria Ledesma
Chief Executive Officer   Enrique Alfredo Martí
Financial Director   Juan F. Politi Chief Financial Officer
Treasurer   Hugo Omar Serra

Exprinter Banco SA
Head Office
San Martin 136, Buenos Aires 1004
Tel: (1) 340 3000 Fax: (1) 334 4402 Telex: 21818 EXPRT AR

Senior Executive Officers
Chairwoman   María del Carmen Algorta de Supervielle
Chief Executive Officer   Crescencio Carlos Lavena Chief Executive Officer
Financial Director   Flavio Simonoto Alternate Director ☏ 340 3025
Chief Operating Officer   Claudio Freijedo
Treasurer   Cristian Pagano
Director   Marcos Ball ☏ 340 3006
Chief Executive Officer   Crescencio Carlos Lavena
Company Secretary   Doraliza Nievas
International Division   Luis A Martín y Herrera International Division Manager ☏ 340 3070

General-Lending (DCM, SL)
Head of Corporate Banking   Marcos Ball Director ☏ 340 3006

Syndicated Lending
Trade Finance   Jorge MacDonald Head of Trade Finance ☏ 340 3202

Foreign Exchange
Global Head   Manuel Baños

Corporate Finance / M&A Advisory
Head of Corporate Finance   Marcos Ball Director ☏ 340 3006

Settlement / Clearing
Regional Head   Silvia Gianetto
Operations   Gabriel Iacobacci

Other Departments
Chief Credit Officer   Alicia Pacheco Chief Credit Officer
Correspondent Banking   Luis A Martín y Herrera International Division Manager ☏ 340 3070

Administration
Head of Administration   Claudio Freijedo
Business Development   Eduardo Astrosa
Head of Marketing   Luis Sanchez Lorca

Technology & Systems
                                        Hector Nocetti

Legal / In-House Counsel
                                        Patricia Giuggiobar

Compliance
                                        Alicia Pacheco Chief Credit Officer

Accounts / Audit
                                        Marta Weiss Audit

www.euromoneydirectory.com ARGENTINA (+54)

The Exxel Group SA
Head Office

Avenida Libertador 602, piso 22°, Buenos Aires 1001
Tel: (1) 815 2001 Fax: (1) 814 3956

Senior Executive Officers
Chairman Juan Navarro

Robert Fleming Argentina SA
Subsidiary Company

Carlos Pellegrini 1149, piso 12°, Buenos Aires 1009
Tel: (1) 328 4300 Fax: (1) 394 4225

Garcia Navarro y Cia SA
Head Office

San Martin 171, Bahia Blanca 8000
Tel: (91) 553 344 Fax: (91) 550 577

Senior Executive Officers
General Manager José Ramón García Navarro

HSBC Banco Roberts SA
Head Office

Formerly known as: Banco Roberts

25 de Mayo 258, Buenos Aires 1002
Tel: (1) 344 3000; (1) 331 1461 Fax: (1) 334 6404 Telex: 9004 Swift: BACO AR BA

Senior Executive Officers
Chairman & Executive Director Jorge A Heinze
Chief Executive Officer Jorge A Heinze *Chairman & Executive Director*
Financial Director Gabriel Castelli *Chief Financial & International Officer*
Chief Operating Officer David Leighton *COO*
General Manager Antonio M Losada
International Division Alberto Saravia *International Division Director*

Others (Senior Executives)
Marcelo E Mut *Deputy General Manager*
Michael Smith *Vice Chairman*

Debt Capital Markets / Fixed Income
Department: HSBC Investment Banking (Capital Markets)
Tel: 344 3333 Fax: 331 5826

Eurobonds
Head of Trading Juan Jorge Racedo Bohtlingk *Trader* ☏ **334 1800**

Equity Capital Markets
Department: HSBC Investment Banking (Capital Markets)
Tel: 344 3333 Fax: 331 5826

International Equities
Head of Origination; Head of Syndication Atilio Serenelli

Corporate Finance / M&A Advisory
Department: HSBC Investment Banking (Capital Markets)
Tel: 344 3333 Fax: 331 5826
Acquistion Finance Malcolm Gibson *Senior Associate*

HypoVereinsbank / Vereins und-Westbank
Representative Office

Formerly known as: Bayerische Vereins Bank & Vereins und-Westbank
San Martin 140, Buenos Aires 1004
Tel: (1) 342 8878 Fax: (1) 331 3711

Senior Executive Officers
Chief Representative Norman Bruce Coates

Euromoney Directory 1999 25

ARGENTINA (+54)   www.euromoneydirectory.com

Ibero Platina Bank AG — Representative Office

Formerly known as: Ibero-Amerika Bank (AG)
Avenida Corrientes 456, Oficina 133, Buenos Aires 1366
Tel: (1) 325 3463 **Fax:** (1) 393 7849 **Email:** platina@overnet.com.ar

Senior Executive Officers
Representative   Bodo von Krosigk

Indosuez Argentina SA — Subsidiary Company

25 de Mayo 555, piso 3°, Buenos Aires 1602
Tel: (1) 313 6111 **Fax:** (1) 313 3222 **Email:** indorep@interprov.com

Senior Executive Officers
Managing Director   Claude Pomper

ING Baring Sociedad de Bolsa (Argentina) SA — Subsidiary Company

Ingeniero Butty 220, piso 22°, Capital Federal, Buenos Aires 1300
Tel: (1) 310 4700; (1) 310 4800 **Fax:** (1) 315 8926; (1) 315 8780 **Telex:** 19056 ING AR **Swift:** ING AR BA

Senior Executive Officers
Country Manager   Steven T Darch ☎ 310 4776 🖷 315 4613
Vice President, Head of Treasury   Martín González Kenny ☎ 310 4741 🖷 315 4662

Debt Capital Markets / Fixed Income
Fixed-Income Research
Analyst   Federico Thomsen ☎ 310 4816

Equity Capital Markets
Country Head   Matias Eickert *Head, Equities* ☎ 310 4875

Domestic Equities
Head of Sales   J Deane *Head of Sales*
Head of Trading   G Rossello *Head Trader*
Head of Research   Hernan Ladeuix *Head of Research* ☎ 310 4848
    ✉ hernan.ladeuix@ing-barings.com

International Equities
Head of Sales   J Deane *Head of Sales*
Head of Trading   G Rossello *Head Trader*

Other (International Equity)
Sales / Trading   Alejandro Fagiani ☎ 310 4810

Equity Research
Global Head   Hernan Ladeuix *Head of Research* ☎ 310 4848
    ✉ hernan.ladeuix@ing-barings.com

Other (Equity Research)
Retail, Tobacco   Tadd Chessen *Analyst* ☎ 310 4884 ✉ tadd.chessen@ing-barings.com

Other Departments
Economic Research   Federico Thomsen *Senior Economist* ☎ 310 4816 🖷 315 4662

ING Barings — Full Branch Office

Ingeniero Butty 220, piso 22°, Capital Federal, Buenos Aires 1300
Tel: (1) 310 4700/5; (1) 310 4800 **Fax:** (1) 314 5210; (1) 315 4613 **Telex:** 19056 INGB AR **Swift:** INGB AR BA

Senior Executive Officers
Country Manager   Steven T Darch ☎ 310 4776 🖷 315 4613

General-Lending (DCM, SL)
Head of Corporate Banking   Fernando Tedín Uriburu ☎ 310 4771 🖷 315 4661

General-Investment
Head of Investment   Mariano Torterola ☎ 310 4725 🖷 315 4661

General - Treasury
Head of Treasury   Martín González Kenny ☎ 310 4741 🖷 315 4662

Risk Management
Head of Risk Management   Pedro Valentine ☎ 310 4710 🖷 315 4661

www.euromoneydirectory.com ARGENTINA (+54)

Other Departments
Department: ING Baring Private Bank
Private Banking Steven T Darch *General Manager* ☎ 310 4700 F 315 4660
 Osvaldo Rodríguez *Manager, Private Banking* ☎ 310 4700 F 315 4660

Administration
Corporate Communications
 Mabel González *Vice President* ☎ 310 4840 F 315 8926

Other (Administration)
Human Resources Adela Abal *Manager* ☎ 310 4715 F 315 8775

International Finance Corporation — Representative Office
Bouchard 547, piso 3°, Buenos Aires 1106
Tel: (1) 315 1666 **Fax:** (1) 312 7184

Senior Executive Officers
Resident Representative Ileana Boza

Inversiones y Representaciones SA — Head Office
Bolivar 108, piso 1°, Buenos Aires 1066
Tel: (1) 342 7555 **Fax:** (1) 323 7597

Senior Executive Officers
Chairman Eduardo Elsztain
Financial Director Ricardo Torres *Chief Financial Officer*

Others (Senior Executives)
 Marcelo Mindlin *Vice President*

Israel Discount Bank Limited — Representative Office
Corrientes 447, Buenos Aires 1043
Tel: (1) 326 3286; (1) 326 3287 **Fax:** (1) 326 3279; (1) 394 0291

Senior Executive Officers
Representative Eorem Graff

José M Cascales & Associates — Head Office
Tucumán 811, piso 3°, Buenos Aires 1049
Tel: (1) 322 2897; (1) 326 1693 **Fax:** (1) 11 2819; (1) 326 9195 **Email:** tradefin@impsatl.com.ar
Website: www.tradefin.com

Senior Executive Officers
Chairman José M Cascales ☎ 322 2897
Chief Executive Officer Pedro Cascales ☎ 322 2897

Lloyds Bank (BLSA) Limited — Full Branch Office
Tronador 4890, Buenos Aires 1430
PO Box 128, Buenos Aires 1000
Tel: (1) 546 9000 **Fax:** (1) 546 9090 **Cable:** COLFORLOYD

Senior Executive Officers
Chief Manager Colin J Mitchell
Assistant Chief Manager David S Smailes

Others (Senior Executives)
Distribution Enrique Garcia Mansilla *Director*

General - Treasury
Head of Treasury Marcelo Scenna *Manager*

Euromoney Directory 1999 **27**

ARGENTINA (+54)   www.euromoneydirectory.com

Martorell y Cia SA Sociedad de Bolsa
Head Office

25 de Mayo 347, piso 4°, Oficina 459, Buenos Aires 1002
Tel: (1) 313 7997 Fax: (1) 313 6939 Telex: 23038 MATEL AR

Senior Executive Officers
Chairman   José Luis Martorell
Chief Operating Officer   Guido R Cytryn *Director Foreign Division*
General Manager   Luciano José Martorell

Merrill Lynch, Pierce, Fenner & Smith de Argentina SAFM y de M
Subsidiary Company

Bouchard 547, piso 21°, Buenos Aires 1106
Tel: (1) 317 7500 Fax: (1) 317 7583

Senior Executive Officers
Others (Senior Executives)
                                      Fernando Erhart *Office Manager*

Merrill Lynch SA Sociedad de Bolsa

Bouchard 547, Torre Bouchard Building, piso 23°, Buenos Aires 1106
Tel: (1) 317 7600 Fax: (1) 314 1739
Website: www.ml.com

Midland Bank plc
Representative Office

701 Avenida de Mayo, piso 25°, Buenos Aires 1084
Tel: (1) 343 8610 Fax: (1) 343 6927

Senior Executive Officers
Group Representative   M Brujis

Morgan Guaranty Trust Company of New York
Representative Office

Avenida Corrientes 411, Buenos Aires 1043
Tel: (1) 325 8046 Fax: (1) 325 1465; (1) 348 7379

Senior Executive Officers
Managing Director & GM   José Alfredo McLoughlin
Managing Director   Pedro Nicolás Carlisle
Managing Director   María Alejandro Trigo de Rosetti

Nación Bursátil Sociedad de Bolsa SA
Head Office

Avenida Corrientes 345, 2° piso, Buenos Aires 1043
Tel: (1) 313 1212; (1) 318 7202 Fax: (1) 313 1572 Email: nacion@overnet.com.ar Bloomberg: fbezic@bloomberg.net
Website: www.merval.sba.com.ar/nacion

Senior Executive Officers
President   Hugo Bruzone
Vice President   Ezequiel Anelli
General Manager   Federico Reese

Nuevo Banco Idustrial de Azul
Head Office

San Martín 549, Azul 7300
Tel: (281) 31779; (281) 31788 Fax: (281) 31789; (281) 31779

Senior Executive Officers
President   Héctor Carlos Gayani
Others (Senior Executives)
                                      Raúl Mauricio Arrastua *Vice President*

www.euromoneydirectory.com   ARGENTINA (+54)

Oscar Quiroga y Cia
Head Office

Pte JD Perón 456, piso 2°, Buenos Aires 1038
Tel: (1) 331 4385 Fax: (1) 331 4385

Senior Executive Officers
Chairman   Oscar V Quiroga

Quilmes SA
Head Office

Formerly known as: Nuevo Banco de Santiago del Estero SA
Avenida del Grano Sur 471, Santiago del Estero 4200
Tel: (85) 224 530 Fax: (85) 219 472

Senior Executive Officers
General Manager   Juan Carlos Juarez

Rabello y Cia SA
Head Office

Avenida Corrientes 345, piso 11°, Buenos Aires 1043
Tel: (1) 313 2209; (1) 313 4609 Fax: (1) 313 3914; (1) 313 2407

Senior Executive Officers
President   J Javier Goñi
International Division   Alejandro P Milito Bianchi *Commercial Manager*

Other Departments
Economic Research   Enrique Cerda Omiste *Research Director*

Administration
Head of Administration   Claudio Fontana *Director of Administration*

Other (Administration)
                                 Alejandro P Milito Bianchi *Commercial Manager*

Republic National Bank of New York
Full Branch Office

Reconquista 100, Buenos Aires 1003
Tel: (1) 349 1600 Fax: (1) 349 1692 Telex: 9237 RNBBA AR Swift: BLIC AR BA
Website: www.rnb.com

Senior Executive Officers
Executive Vice President   Alberto Muchnick
SVP & General Manager   Martin Benegas-Lynch
SVP & Deputy General Manager   Raymond Kassin
SVP & Deputy General Manager   Louis C Marino

Rigton SA - Financiera Rigton SA - Investor Services SA
Head Office

Reconquista 656, piso 2B, Buenos Aires 1003
Tel: (1) 312 7222 Fax: (1) 315 0128; (1) 315 0548

Senior Executive Officers
Chairman & President   Enrique T Onetto
Chief Executive Officer   Enrique T Onetto *Chairman & President*

Royal Bank of Canada
Representative Office

Avenida Libertador 602, piso 18°, Buenos Aires 1001
Tel: (1) 814 5140 Fax: (1) 814 5227

Senior Executive Officers
Representative   Eduardo Pawluszek
Regional Representative   Robert Streeton

Administration
Head of Administration   Patricia Rasmussen *Assistant*

Euromoney Directory 1999   29

ARGENTINA (+54) www.euromoneydirectory.com

Sadela Compañia Financiera
Head Office

Reconquista 555, Buenos Aires 1003
Tel: (1) 314 5500 **Fax:** (1) 314 2553

Senior Executive Officers
General Manager — Jorge Manuel Taboada

Singer Florencia Capital Markets
Head Office

Reconquista 353, piso 5°, Buenos Aires 1003
Tel: (1) 325 5993 **Fax:** (1) 325 5896

Senior Executive Officers
Managing Director — Raúl Palacio

Standard Chartered Bank
Representative Office

Avenida Corrientes 327, piso 9°, Buenos Aires 1042
Tel: (1) 312 3080 **Fax:** (1) 312 3089

Senior Executive Officers
Representative — Steve Grave

Sudameris Capital Markets SA

Tte Gral Juan Domingo Perón 500, Buenos Aires 1038
Tel: (1) 329 5298; (1) 329 5299 **Fax:** (1) 343 7839

Senior Executive Officers
General Manager — Alejandro Schiaffino
Equity Capital Markets
Domestic Equities
Head of Syndication — Nestor Di Biasi *Trade & Distribution*

Tornquist Valores SA Sociedad de Bolsa

Formerly known as: Crédit Lyonnais Securities (Argentina) Sociedad de Bolsa & Lion Bursátil SA Sociedad de Bolsa
Bartolomé Mitre 559, Oficina 432, piso 4°, Buenos Aires 1036
Tel: (1) 342 2873; (1) 342 8461 **Fax:** (1) 347 1200 ext 1089; (1) 342 8461

Senior Executive Officers
Chairman — Juan Carlos Arias

Tradition Argentina SA
Subsidiary Company

Avenida Corrientes 456, Oficina 46, piso 4°, Buenos Aires 1366
Tel: (1) 394 0559; (1) 393 2700 **Fax:** (1) 394 9081 **Email:** aevsasha@impsat1.com.dr

Senior Executive Officers
General Manager — Mariano Millar
Managing Director — Alejandro Andruskiewitsch
Others (Senior Executives)
Head of Emerging Markets — Mariano Millar *General Manager*
Debt Capital Markets / Fixed Income
Emerging Market Bonds
Head — Mariano Millar *General Manager*

Transcambio SA
Head Office

San Martin 140, piso 17°, Buenos Aires 1004
Tel: (1) 331 0854 **Fax:** (1) 343 9077

Senior Executive Officers
General Manager — Jorge Vatuone

www.euromoneydirectory.com ARMENIA (+374)

The World Bank
Representative Office **A**

Bouchard 547, piso 3°, Buenos Aires 1106
Tel: (1) 313 1233; (1) 316 9700 Fax: (1) 313 1233
Website: www.worldbank.org

Senior Executive Officers
Director Myrna Alexander

ARMENIA (+374)

Central Bank of the Republic of Armenia 🏛 Central Bank

6 Nalbandyan Street, 375010 Yerevan
Tel: (2) 580 052 Fax: (2) 580 052 Telex: 243327 SHIS SU Swift: CBRA AM 22 BIC Email: cba@mbox.amilink.net

Senior Executive Officers
Chairman Tigran Sargsyan ☎ 583 882 ✉ 151 107

Others (Senior Executives)
 Rouben Valesyan *Member of the Board* ☎ 564 066
 Ashot Avetisyan *Member of the Board* ☎ 589 266
 Artur Javadyan *Member of the Board* ☎ 589 611
 Nerses Yerisyan *Member of the Board* ☎ 587 306
 Grant Suvaryan *Member of the Board* ☎ 583 533

Head, Monetary Policy Armine Khachatryan ☎ 563 642
Head, Currency Issue & Reserves Gevorg Tumanyan ☎ 589 734
Head, Budget & Capital Investment Aida Hakobyan ☎ 580 634
Head, Banking Supervision Babik Najaryan ☎ 567 972
Head, Regulation & Analysis Hakob Malkbasyan ☎ 589 175
Head, Financial Operations Arman Vardanyan *Head of Department* ☎ 589 569

Settlement / Clearing
Head of Settlement / Clearing Gevorg Machanyon *Head, Settlement & Banking Technology* ☎ 589 655
Settlement (General) Oleg Aghasyan *Head, Development* ☎ 565 041

Administration

Technology & Systems
Head, Automation Samvel Arakelyan ☎ 561 362

Legal / In-House Counsel
Head, Legal Department Kacktsrik Avagyan ☎ 561 771

Public Relations
 Aelita Khachatryan *Head, Public Relations* ☎ 580 052

Accounts / Audit
Internal Audit Andranik Norekyan *Head* ☎ 580 368

Other (Administration)
Head, Personnel Management Emma Yeghiazaryan ☎ 583 882

Agricultural Cooperative Bank of Armenia - ACBA Head Office

One Lord Byron Street, 375001 Yerevan
PO Box 41, 375010 Yerevan
Tel: (2) 565 858; (2) 505 194 Fax: (2) 151 755

Senior Executive Officers
Chairman Stepan Gishyan
President Marat Harutyunyan
Financial Director Vardan Mkrtchyan
Treasurer Sedrak Javadyan
Company Secretary Arsen Petrosyan

Debt Capital Markets / Fixed Income
Domestic Government Bonds
Head of Trading Margarita Zatikyan

Syndicated Lending
Global Head of Credit Committee Hakob Andreasyan

Euromoney Directory 1999 **31**

ARMENIA (+374) www.euromoneydirectory.com

Midland Armenia Bank — Subsidiary Company

Formerly known as: Midland Bank jsc
1 Vramshapouh Arkai Street, Yerevan
Tel: (2) 15 1717 Fax: (2) 15 1858

Senior Executive Officers
Others (Senior Executives)
　　　　　　　　　　J A J Hunt *Senior Officer*

Prometeus Bank — Head Office

19 Hrachia Kochar Street, 375012 Yerevan
Tel: (2) 273 000; (2) 273 110 Fax: (2) 274 818; (2) 273 110 Telex: 243438

Senior Executive Officers
Chairman　　　　　　　　　　　　　　　Emil Soghomonyan
Chief Operating Officer　　　　　　　　Lusik Alekyan *General Accountant* ☎ **273 110**
Treasurer　　　　　　　　　　　　　　　Amalia Sahakyan *Cashier* ☎ **273 090**
Secretary　　　　　　　　　　　　　　　Nune Harutjunyan ☎ **273 000**
International Division　　　　　　　　　Anahit Comtsyan *Head of Department* ☎ **278 821**
Rep. in Moscow　　　　　　　　　　　　Tatos Vardanyan ☎ **273 000**

General-Lending (DCM, SL)
Head of Corporate Banking　　　　　　Harutjun Margaryan *Deputy Chairman* ☎ **273 110**

Debt Capital Markets / Fixed Income
Department: Bank Treasury Department
Tel: 273 110 Fax: 273 110
Head of Fixed Income　　　　　　　　　Lusik Alekyan *General Accountant* ☎ **273 110**
Head of Fixed Income Sales; Head of Fixed　Alvard Mkrtumyan *Accountant* ☎ **277 281**
Income Trading

Government Bonds
Head of Sales; Head of Trading　　　　Anahit Gomtsyan *Head of Department* ☎ **274 821**
Head of Syndication　　　　　　　　　　Ara Nersisyan *Economist* ☎ **274 821**

Eurobonds
Head of Sales　　　　　　　　　　　　　Anahit Gomtsyan *Head of Department* ☎ **274 821**
Head of Trading　　　　　　　　　　　　Anahit Gomtsyan *Head of Department* ☎ **274 821**

Emerging Market Bonds
Head of Emerging Markets　　　　　　Anahit Gomtsyan *Head of Department* ☎ **274 821**
Head of Sales; Head of Trading　　　　Anahit Vanetsyan *Broker* ☎ **274 821**

Fixed-Income Repo
Head of Repo　　　　　　　　　　　　　Anahit Gomtsyan *Head of Department* ☎ **274 821**
Marketing & Product Development　　 Ara Nersisyan *Economist* ☎ **274 821**

Fixed-Income Research
Head of Fixed Income　　　　　　　　　Lusik Alekyan *General Accountant* ☎ **273 110**
Head of Credit Research　　　　　　　Armen Hakobyan *Head of Department* ☎ **276 085**

Equity Capital Markets
Department: Bank Treasury Department
Tel: 273 110 Fax: 273 110
Head of Equity Capital Markets　　　　Lusik Alekyan *General Accountant* ☎ **273 110**
Head of Sales; Head of Trading　　　　Alvard Mkrtumyan *Accountant* ☎ **277 281**

Domestic Equities
Head of Origination　　　　　　　　　　Anahit Gomtsyan *Head of Department* ☎ **274 821**

International Equities
Head of Sales　　　　　　　　　　　　　Anahit Gomtsyan *Head of Department* ☎ **274 821**
Head of Trading　　　　　　　　　　　　Anahit Vanetsyan *Broker* ☎ **274 821**

Equity Research
Global Head　　　　　　　　　　　　　　Anahit Gomtsyan *Head of Department* ☎ **274 821**

Convertibles / Equity-Linked
Head of Sales; Head of Trading　　　　Anahit Gomtsyan *Head of Department* ☎ **274 821**

Equity Repo / Securities Lending
Head　　　　　　　　　　　　　　　　　Armen Hakobyan *Head of Department* ☎ **276 085**
Marketing & Product Development　　 Alaba Petrosyan *Economist* ☎ **276 085**
Head of Prime Brokerage　　　　　　　Arsen Harutjunyan *Economist* ☎ **276 085**
Head of Trading　　　　　　　　　　　　Eduard Pashinyan *Economist* ☎ **276 085**

ARMENIA (+374)

Syndicated Lending
Tel: 276 085 Fax: 276 085
Head of Origination; Head of Syndication   Arsen Harutjunyan *Economist* ☏ 276 085
Head of Trading   Armen Hakobyan *Head of Department* ☏ 276 085

Loan-Related Activities
Trade Finance   Anahit Gomtsyan *Head of Department* ☏ 274 821
Project Finance   Arsen Harutjunyan *Economist* ☏ 276 085

Money Markets
Tel: 274 821 Fax: 274 821 Telex: 273 176
Head of Money Markets   Anahit Gomtsyan *Head of Department* ☏ 274 821

Domestic Commercial Paper
Head of Sales; Head of Trading   Anahit Gomtsyan *Head of Department* ☏ 274 821

Eurocommercial Paper
Head of Sales; Head of Trading   Anahit Gomtsyan *Head of Department* ☏ 274 821

Wholesale Deposits
Marketing   Arman Hakoyan *Head of Department* ☏ 276 085
Head of Sales   Armen Hakobyan *Head of Department* ☏ 276 085

Foreign Exchange
Tel: 244 821 Fax: 244 821 Telex: 243 176
Head of Foreign Exchange   Anahit Gomtsyan *Head of Department* ☏ 274 821
Head of Institutional Sales; Corporate Sales;   Ara Nersisyan *Economist* ☏ 274 821
Head of Trading

Risk Management
Tel: 243 1000
Head of Risk Management   Harutjun Margaryan *Deputy Chairman* ☏ 273 110

Fixed Income Derivatives / Risk Management
Head of Sales; Trading   Armen Hakobyan *Head of Department* ☏ 276 085

Foreign Exchange Derivatives / Risk Management
Spot / Forwards Sales   Anahit Vanetsyan *Broker* ☏ 274 821
Spot / Forwards Trading   Armine Eciazaryan *Economist* ☏ 273 010

OTC Equity Derivatives
Sales; Trading   Anahit Vanetsyan *Broker* ☏ 274 821

Settlement / Clearing
Tel: 273 110 Fax: 273 110
Head of Settlement / Clearing; Equity   Lusik Alekyan *General Accountant* ☏ 273 110
Settlement
Fixed-Income Settlement; Operations   Alvard Mkrtumyan *Accountant* ☏ 277 281

Global Custody
Head of Global Custody   Harutjun Margaryan *Deputy Chairman* ☏ 273 110

Asset Management
Head   Arman Hakoyan *Head of Department* ☏ 276 085

Other Departments
Commodities / Bullion   Amalia Sahakyan *Cashier* ☏ 273 090
Chief Credit Officer   Armen Hakobyan *Head of Department* ☏ 276 085
Correspondent Banking   Anahit Gomtsyan *Head of Department* ☏ 274 821
Cash Management   Amalia Sahakyan *Cashier* ☏ 273 090

Administration
Head of Administration   Susanna Karapetyan *Chief Assistant* ☏ 276 085
Business Development   Harutjun Margaryan *Deputy Chairman* ☏ 273 110
Head of Marketing   Anahit Gomtsyan *Head of Department* ☏ 274 821

Technology & Systems
                                             Nune Musajelyan ☏ 273 110

Legal / In-House Counsel
                                             Susanna Karapetyan *Chief Assistant* ☏ 276 085

Compliance
                                             Aram Asryan *Messenger* ☏ 276 085

Public Relations
                                             Susanna Karapetyan *Chief Assistant* ☏ 276 085

Accounts / Audit
                                             Amalia Loretsyan *Examiner* ☏ 273 085

ARUBA (+297)

Centrale Bank van Aruba
Central Bank

Havenstraat 2, Oranjestad
Tel: (8) 22509 **Fax:** (8) 32251 **Telex:** 5045 **Email:** cbaua@setarnet.aw

Senior Executive Officers
Chairman — C G Maduro
Governor — J H du Marchie Sarvaas
Chief Executive Officer — K A H Polvliet *Executive Director*
A R Caram *Executive Director*
Treasurer — R M Geerman

Others (Senior Executives)
Chief Cashier — H M Dacal
Head, Bank Licensing; Head, Banking Supervision — P Mungra
Head, Economics & Statistics — J R Semeleer
Head, Reserves Management — R M Geerman
Head, Secretariat — O A van der Biezen

Foreign Exchange
Head of Foreign Exchange — R M Geerman

Settlement / Clearing
Head of Settlement / Clearing — R M Geerman

Administration

Technology & Systems
Head, Information Systems — J S Fraser

Legal / In-House Counsel
A D Kensenhuis *Legal Counsel*

Accounts / Audit
Head, Accountancy — R M Geerman
Head, Audit — C A Connor

Other (Administration)
Head, Personnel — F P Meijer

Aruba Bank NV
Head Office

Caya Betico Croes 41, Oranjestad
PO Box 192, Oranjestad
Tel: (8) 21550 **Fax:** (8) 29152 **Telex:** 5040 ABANK **Email:** abank@setarnet.aw

Senior Executive Officers
Chairman of the Board — Klaus Vink
Chief Executive Officer — Irving Durand *Chief Executive & Managing Director*
Financial Director — Sudesh Manichand *Finance Director*
Assistant Managing Director — Glenn Croes

Other Departments
Correspondent Banking — Henk vd Windt *Manager, Financial Reporting*

Administration

Technology & Systems
Edwin Everon *ITS Manager*

Legal / In-House Counsel
Legal Affairs — Helmut Vink *Manager*

Compliance
Pieter De Voogd *Officer*

Public Relations
Liesbeth Manichand *Marketing Manager*

www.euromoneydirectory.com   AUSTRALIA (+61)

ING Trust (Aruba) NV
Subsidiary Company **A**

Lloyd G Smith Boulevard 162, Punto Brabo, Oranjestad
PO Box 4145, Oranjestad
Tel: (8) 27345 **Fax:** (8) 33885

Senior Executive Officers
General Manager   Paul Schuller tot Peursum

AUSTRALIA
(+61)

Reserve Bank of Australia
Central Bank

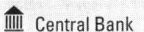

65 Martin Place, Sydney, New South Wales 2000
GPO Box 3947, Sydney, New South Wales 2001
Tel: (2) 9551 8111 **Fax:** (2) 9551 8000 **Telex:** 121636 RSBNK **Swift:** RBSK AU 2S **Email:** rbainfo@rba.gov.au
Reuters: RBA01-RBA35 **Telerate:** 1560-1595 **Bloomberg:** RBA01-RBA35
Website: www.rba.gov.au

Senior Executive Officers
Governor   I J Macfarlane
Chief Executive Officer   S A Grenville *Deputy Governor*
Secretary   D H Emanuel

Others (Senior Executives)
Financial System Group   J F Laker *Assistant Governor*
Economic Group   G R Stevens *Assistant Governor*
Financial Markets Group   Ric Battellino *Assistant Governor*
Business Services Group   G H Board *Assistant Governor*
Corporate Services Group   L J Austin *Assistant Governor*

ABN AMRO Australia Limited

33rd Floor, 101 Collins Street, Melbourne, Victoria 3000
Tel: (3) 9228 7228; (3) 9228 7228 **Fax:** (3) 9228 7200

ABN AMRO Australia Limited
Subsidiary Company

Alternative trading name: ABN AMRO Bank NV (Australian Branch)
Formerly known as: ABN AMRO Australia Hoare Govett; BZW Australia Limited
Level 24, 255 George Street, Sydney, New South Wales 2000
GPO Box 4675, Sydney, New South Wales 1042
Tel: (2) 9259 5711 **Fax:** (2) 9259 5444

Senior Executive Officers
Chief Executive Officer   Steve Crane *Chief Executive*
Chief Operating Officer   Chris Chown

Others (Senior Executives)
    Peter Young *Executive Vice Chairman*
    Olga Zoutendijk *Director, Head of Wholesale Banking*

Debt Capital Markets / Fixed Income
Department: **Debt Capital Markets**
Head of Debt Capital Markets   John McCarthy *Director, Head of Debt Capital Markets*
    Colin McKeith *Director, Head of Treasury & Fixed Income*

Equity Capital Markets
Head of Equity Capital Markets   Simon Perrott *Director, Head of Equity Capital Markets*
    Paul Masi *Director, Head of Equities*
Head of Sales   Grant Patterson *Director, Head of Retail Stockbroking*

Equity Research
Head of Equity Research   Alan Hargreaves *Director, Head of Equity Reasearch*

Syndicated Lending
Loan-Related Activities
Project Finance   Andrew Davis *Director, Joint Head of Project Finance & Advisory*
    Erwin Elstermann *Director, Joint Head of Project Finance & Advisory*

Euromoney Directory 1999   35

AUSTRALIA (+61)   www.euromoneydirectory.com

ABN AMRO Australia Limited (cont)
Risk Management
Head of Risk Management   Ray Henry
                                 David Dawes *Director, Head of Futures*

Corporate Finance / M&A Advisory
Head of Corporate Finance   Simon Mordant *Director, Joint Head of Corporate Finance*
                                   Peter Hunt *Director, Joint Head of Corporate Finance*

Asset Management
Head   John Hartshorn *Director, Head of Asset Management*

Administration
Head of Administration   Toni Barnes *Director, Operations & Administration*
Head of Marketing   Elizabeth Brand *Director, Marketing Services*

Technology & Systems
                                   Linton Scott *Director, IT*

Compliance
                                   Kirk Hanson *Head of Compliance & Audit*

Accounts / Audit
                                   Steve Kinsella *Chief Financial Officer*

Other (Administration)
Human Resources   Karen Robinson *Director*

ABN AMRO Bank NV
Level 24, 255 George Street, Sydney, New South Wales 2000
Tel: (2) 9259 5711 Fax: (2) 9259 5777

AMP Securities Pty Limited
Level 16, AMP Building, 33 Alfred Street, Sydney, New South Wales 2000
Tel: (2) 9257 5428; (2) 9257 6716 Fax: (2) 9257 9799

Equity Capital Markets
Equity Repo / Securities Lending
Marketing & Product Development   Michelle Dyer *Director* ☎ **9257 5238** E michelle_dyer@invest.amp.com.au

ANZ Investment Bank - Equities Division
Level 10, 530 Collins, Melbourne, Victoria 3000
Tel: (3) 9205 1834 Fax: (3) 9629 2496 Telex: 33228

Equity Capital Markets
Tel: 9205 1988

Equity Repo / Securities Lending
Marketing & Product Development   Stephen Dear *Business Development Analyst* ☎ **9205 1510**
                                           E szd@anzsec.com.au

Arab Bank Australia Limited   Subsidiary Company
Formerly known as: Arab Australia Limited
Level 9, 200 George Street, Sydney, New South Wales 2000
Tel: (2) 9377 8900 Fax: (2) 9221 5428 Telex: AA120520

Senior Executive Officers
Chief Executive Officer   Jack Beighton *Managing Director* ☎ **9377 8901**
Financial Director   Gary Dundas *Financial Controller* ☎ **9377 8931**
Treasurer   Christopher Thompson *Chief Dealer* ☎ **9377 8954**

Others (Senior Executives)
Chief Manager   James Wakim *Retail & Commercial Banking* ☎ **9377 8903**

Administration
                                 Chor Hor Choo *Manager, Information Technology* ☎ **9377 8946**

www.euromoneydirectory.com   AUSTRALIA (+61)

The Asahi Bank Limited
Full Branch Office

5th Floor, 25 Bligh Street, Sydney, New South Wales NSW 2000
Tel: (2) 9221 5511 Fax: (2) 9221 3337 Telex: AA170199 ASHSY
Website: www.asahibank.co.jp

Senior Executive Officers
General Manager   Fumihiro Fukuda

Australia & New Zealand Banking Group Limited

100 Queen Street, Melbourne, Victoria 3000
PO Box 537E, Melbourne, Victoria 3001
Tel: (3) 9273 5555 Fax: (3) 9273 4161 Telex: AA68210 ANZBANK Swift: ANZB AU 3M

Senior Executive Officers
Chief Executive Officer   John McFarlane
Financial Director   Peter Marriott

Syndicated Lending
Loan-Related Activities
Trade Finance   John Winders *Group General Manager, International* ⊤ 9273 2220

Other Departments
Commodities / Bullion   Albert Burgio *General Manager, International Services* ⊤ 9273 1152
Correspondent Banking   Jeffrey Clarkin *General Manager* ⊤ 9273 1907

Administration
Head of Marketing   Leeshing Xu *Marketing Support Officer* ⊤ 3273 1165 F 9273 2864

Australian Guarantee Corporation Limited
Head Office

Alternative trading name: AGC
Level 14, AGC House, 130 Phillip Street, Sydney, New South Wales 2000
Tel: (2) 9234 1122 Fax: (2) 9234 1225
Website: www.agc.com.au

Senior Executive Officers
Chairman   Bob Joss ⊤ 9226 3004
Chief Executive Officer   Richard Thomas *Managing Director* ⊤ 9234 1155
Financial Director   Peter George *Chief Manager, Finance* ⊤ 9234 1130
Chief Operating Officer   John Malouf *Executive Director* ⊤ 9234 1077
General Manager   Ron O'Neil ⊤ 9234 1208
Secretary   Ron Matthews ⊤ 9234 1103

BA Australia Limited
Head Office

Formerly known as: Bank of America Australia Limited
Level 63, MLC Centre, 19 Martin Place, Sydney, New South Wales 2000
PO Box 490, Sydney, New South Wales
Tel: (2) 9931 4200 Fax: (2) 9931 1023 Telex: AA25041 Swift: BOFA AU 2X
Website: www.bofa.com

Senior Executive Officers
Chairman   Bryce Wauchope
Chief Executive Officer   Terry Francis *Country Manager*
Financial Director   Warren Whitley *Financial Controller*
Treasurer   Mark Glover
Financial Controller   Warren Whitley

Others (Senior Executives)
                                   Ted Jenkel
                                   Robert Morrow

General-Lending (DCM, SL)
Head of Corporate Banking   Robert Spee *Corporate Banking - Melbourne*
                                   Ted Jenkel *Credit*
                                   Geoff Robb *Corporate Banking - Sydney*
                                   Graham Brown

Debt Capital Markets / Fixed Income
Bonds - General
Securities Origination   John Davenport

AUSTRALIA (+61)　　　　　　www.euromoneydirectory.com

BA Australia Limited (cont)
Syndicated Lending
Loan-Related Activities
Trade Finance　　　　　　　　　　　　　Trevor Perera
Project Finance; Project Finance　　　　　John O'Neil
Corporate Finance / M&A Advisory
Head of Corporate Finance　　　　　　　Geoff Robb
Other Departments
Chief Credit Officer　　　　　　　　　　Ted Jenkel
Cash Management　　　　　　　　　　　Roger Yeo
Administration
Head of Administration　　　　　　　　　Tony Dowling
Technology & Systems
　　　　　　　　　　　　　　　　　　　Frank Venditti
Compliance
　　　　　　　　　　　　　　　　　　　Mary-Lynn Ladbrooke
Other (Administration)
Human Resources　　　　　　　　　　　Marilyn Johnston *Human Resources Manager*

Bank Leumi Le Israel BM
43rd Floor, Nauru House, 80 Collins Street, Melbourne, Victoria 3001
PO Box 1513N, GPO
Tel: (3) 9654 2696 Fax: (3) 9650 6473
Senior Executive Officers
Chief Representative　　　　　　　　　　Ephraim Avigdori

Bank of New York - Inter Maritime Bank, Geneva
Representative Office
Level 5, 151 Macquarie Street, Sydney, New South Wales 2000
Tel: (2) 9252 0668 Fax: (2) 9252 0669
Senior Executive Officers
Representative　　　　　　　　　　　　Winston Yuen

Bank of Queensland Limited
Head Office
229 Elizabeth Street, Brisbane, Queensland 4000
GPO Box 898, Brisbane, Queensland 4001
Tel: (7) 3212 3333 Fax: (7) 3212 3399
Senior Executive Officers
Chairman　　　　　　　　　　　　　　　Neil Roberts ☎ 3212 3220
Chief Executive Officer　　　　　　　　　John Dawson ☎ 3212 3211
Financial Director　　　　　　　　　　　Bruce Wilson *General Manager, Finance* ☎ 3212 3213
Chief Operating Officer　　　　　　　　　David Jeffries *Deputy Chief Executive* ☎ 3212 3212
Treasurer　　　　　　　　　　　　　　　Len Stone *Head of Treasury* ☎ 3212 3553 F 3212 3418
International Division　　　　　　　　　Howard Smith *Manager, International Banking* ☎ 3212 3117 F 3212 3419
Syndicated Lending
Loan-Related Activities
Trade Finance　　　　　　　　　　　　　Howard Smith *Manager, International Banking* ☎ 3212 3117 F 3212 3419
Leasing & Asset Finance　　　　　　　　Ian Whittle *General Manager, Business* ☎ 3212 3500
Money Markets
Global Head　　　　　　　　　　　　　Len Stone *Head of Treasury* ☎ 3212 3553 F 3212 3418
Wholesale Deposits
Marketing; Head of Sales　　　　　　　　Tim Ledingham *Manager, Institutional Dealings* ☎ 3212 3342
Foreign Exchange
Global Head　　　　　　　　　　　　　Howard Smith *Manager, International Banking* ☎ 3212 3117 F 3212 3419
Risk Management
Global Head　　　　　　　　　　　　　Bruce Wilson *General Manager, Finance* ☎ 3212 3213
Fixed Income Derivatives / Risk Management
Global Head　　　　　　　　　　　　　Bruce Wilson *General Manager, Finance* ☎ 3212 3213
IR Swaps Sales / Marketing　　　　　　　Tim Ledingham *Manager, Institutional Dealings* ☎ 3212 3342

38 Euromoney Directory 1999

www.euromoneydirectory.com   **AUSTRALIA (+61)**

Settlement / Clearing
Regional Head; Fixed-Income Settlement   Liam Murphy *Accounting* ☎ 3212 3295 📠 3212 3402

Bank SA
Head Office

97 King William Street, Adelaide, South Australia 5000
Tel: (8) 8210 4411 **Fax**: (8) 8210 4903

Senior Executive Officers
Managing Director / General Manager   Lou Morris ☎ 8210 4538 📠 8210 4903

Bank of Tokyo-Mitsubishi (Australia) Limited
Subsidiary Company

Level 25, Gateway, 1 Macquarie Place, Sydney, New South Wales 2000
Tel: (2) 9296 1111 **Fax**: (2) 9247 4266 **Telex**: AA73354 **Swift**: BOTK AU 2X

Senior Executive Officers
Managing Director   Hisao Yokoyama
Deputy Managing Director   Norio Takeda
Chief Executive Officer   Tomonobu Kobayashi *Deputy Managing Director*
Financial Director   Yoichi Tsukada *General Manager, Corporate*
Chief Operating Officer   Brian Donnelly *General Manager, Administration*
Treasurer   Keiichi Voagawa *Deputy Managing Director*
General Manager, Operations   Oliver Mak

Syndicated Lending
Country Head of Origination; Head of   Yoichi Tsukada *General Manager, Corporate*
Syndication; Head of Trading; Recovery

Loan-Related Activities
Trade Finance   Gianni Paludetto *Manager, International*
Project Finance; Structured Trade Finance   Victor Soh *Senior Manager*

Money Markets
Regional Head   Kenny Lau *Senior Manager*

Domestic Commercial Paper
Head of Origination; Head of Sales; Head of   Kenny Lau *Senior Manager*
Trading

Eurocommercial Paper
Head of Origination; Head of Sales; Head of   Kenny Lau *Senior Manager*
Trading

Foreign Exchange
Regional Head   Gerry Teo *Chief Manager*
Corporate Sales   Antoinette Balog *Senior Manager*
Head of Trading   Roger Chan *Manager*

Risk Management
Regional Head   Leslie Leong *Senior Manager*

Fixed Income Derivatives / Risk Management
Regional Head   Leslie Leong *Senior Manager*

Foreign Exchange Derivatives / Risk Management
Cross-Currency Swaps, Sales / Marketing   Kenny Lau *Senior Manager*
Cross-Currency Swaps, Trading   Leslie Leong *Senior Manager*

Corporate Finance / M&A Advisory
Regional Head   John Murray *Manager*

Global Custody
Country Head   Simon Hindson *Manager*

Other Departments
Correspondent Banking   Gianni Paludetto *Manager, International*

Administration

Technology & Systems
    Raymond Lau *Manager EDP*

Legal / In-House Counsel
    Bret Lee *Manager*

AUSTRALIA (+61)   www.euromoneydirectory.com

Bank of Valletta plc
Representative Office

Suite 2, Ground Floor, Wyoming Building, 175 Macquarie Street, Sydney, New South Wales 2000
Tel: (2) 9231 5102; (2) 9233 8703 Fax: (2) 9231 4919

Senior Executive Officers
Head   Emmanuel Ciappara

Bank of Western Australia Limited
Head Office

Alternative trading name: BankWest
BankWest Tower, 108 St Georges Terrace, Perth, Western Australia 6000
Tel: (8) 9449 7003; (8) 9449 7000 Fax: (8) 9449 6444; (8) 9449 6855 Telex: 92417 Swift: BKWA AU 6P
Reuters: BKWA Telerate: 2640
Website: www.bankwest.com.au

Senior Executive Officers
Chairman   Ian Mackenzie ☎ **9449 6269** 🖷 **9449 6570**
Financial Director   Barry Nazer *GM, Finance & Planning* ☎ **9449 6807** 🖷 **9449 6570**
Treasurer   Gary Purtill *Bank Treasurer* ☎ **9449 6372** 🖷 **9449 6855**
Managing Director   Terry Budge ☎ **9449 6258** 🖷 **9449 6570**

Debt Capital Markets / Fixed Income
Global Head   Peter Latham *Senior Manager, Funding & Liquidity* ☎ **9449 6406**
                                                  🖷 **9449 6855**

Syndicated Lending

Loan-Related Activities
Trade Finance   Arthur Tam *Head of International Banking* ☎ **9449 6134** 🖷 **9449 6825**

Money Markets
Global Head   Philip Webster *Manager, Money Market & Liquidity* ☎ **9449 7676**
                                                  🖷 **9449 6555**

Domestic Commercial Paper
Head of Origination   Lisa Webb *Senior Dealer, Sydney* ☎ **(2) 9338 2242** 🖷 **(2) 9338 2280**

Foreign Exchange
Country Head   Matt Lawson *Head of Financial Markets* ☎ **9449 7600** 🖷 **9449 6555**
Head of Trading   Murray Stewart *Senior Manager, Trading* ☎ **9449 7627** 🖷 **9449 6555**
                                                  Paul Dugmore *Manager Foreign Exchange* ☎ **9449 7679** 🖷 **9449 6555**

Risk Management
Global Head   Craig O'Brien *Senior Dealer, IR & FX Derivatives* ☎ **9449 7672** 🖷 **9449 6555**

Fixed Income Derivatives / Risk Management
IR Swaps Trading   Paul Woodward *Senior Dealer, IR & FX Derivatives* ☎ **9449 7675**
                                                  🖷 **9449 6555**

Corporate Finance / M&A Advisory
Global Head   Peter Jackson *GM, Corporate & Interstate Banking* ☎ **9449 6145**
                                                  🖷 **9449 6818**

Settlement / Clearing
Regional Head   Tom Branch *Manager, Operations* ☎ **9449 6824** 🖷 **9449 6444**

Other Departments
Commodities / Bullion   Chris Hunt *Manager, Bullion Services* ☎ **9449 7671** 🖷 **9449 6555**

Administration

Legal / In-House Counsel
                                                  Mahmood Fadjiar *Legal Advisor* ☎ **9449 6579** 🖷 **9449 7455**

Compliance
                                                  Diane Browning *Head of Legal & Compliance* ☎ **9449 6161** 🖷 **9449 7455**

Public Relations
Group Public Affairs   Ray Jordan *Manager* ☎ **9449 6305** 🖷 **9449 6122**

www.euromoneydirectory.com   AUSTRALIA (+61)

Bankers Trust Australia Limited
Subsidiary Company

Level 15, The Chifley Tower, 2 Chifley Square, Sydney, New South Wales 2000
PO Box H 193, Australia Square, Sydney, New South Wales 2000
Tel: (2) 9259 9244 Fax: (2) 9259 9800 Telex: AA95110
Website: www.bankerstrust.com.au

Senior Executive Officers
Chief Executive Officer   Rob Ferguson *Managing Director*
Financial Director   Terry Williamson *Chief Financial Officer*
Company Secretary   Cameron Paterson
Others (Senior Executives)
Head of Funds Management   Ian Martin
General-Investment
Head of Investment   Gavin Walker *Head of Investment Banking*

Banque Worms
Representative Office

5 Crewe Place, Rosebery, Sydney, New South Wales 2018
Tel: (2) 9663 4277 Fax: (2) 9663 3155

Senior Executive Officers
Representative   M H Carriol

Baring Brothers Burrows & Co Limited
Head Office

Level 9, 7 Macquarie Place, Sydney NSW, New South Wales 2000
PO Box R537, Royal Exchange, Sydney, New South Wales 1225
Tel: (2) 9247 1222 Fax: (2) 9247 7040 Email: clay_obrien@barings.com.au

Senior Executive Officers
Executive Chairman   Mark Burrows
Director   Jeff White
Director   Clay O'Brien
Accountant   Stephen Lloyd

Debt Capital Markets / Fixed Income
Department: Furman Selz, International Sales
Level 67, MLC Centre, Sydney, New South Wales
Tel: +61 (2) 9238 2286 Fax: +61 (2) 9238 2285
Head of Debt Capital Markets   Gary Wilson

BBL Australia Limited

Level 4, 347 Kent Street, Sydney, New South Wales 2000
GPO Box 5309, Sydney, New South Wales 2001
Tel: (2) 9234 8555 Fax: (2) 9234 8885 Telex: AA176582 BBLASD Swift: BBRU AU 2S

Senior Executive Officers
Managing Director   Bruce Foy

Cedef Assets Management Limited

Level 32, Grosvenor Place, 225 George Street, Sydney, New South Wales
Tel: (2) 9241 2701
Administration Tel: 9241 2731; Asset Swaps & Credit Derivatives Tel: 9241 2701

Senior Executive Officers
Managing Director   Kevin Beaman

The Chase Manhattan Bank
Full Branch Office

Levels 35 (Reception), AAP Centre, 259 George Street, Sydney, New South Wales 2000
Tel: (2) 9250 4111 Fax: (2) 9250 4554 Telex: 176117

Senior Executive Officers
Chief Executive Officer   Scott Reid *Managing Director*
Financial Director   Peter Corea *Director of Finance*

AUSTRALIA (+61)   www.euromoneydirectory.com

The Chase Manhattan Bank (cont)

Others (Senior Executives)
Chase Treasury Solutions   Maree Patterson *Director, Chase Treasury Solutions*

Syndicated Lending
Global Investment Banking Group   Paul Bartlett *Director (Country Head)* [T] **9250 4434** [F] **9250 4517**

Loan-Related Activities
Trade Finance   Sol Solomon *Director, Global Trade Finance*

Risk Management
Global Markets Group   David Dagg *Director* [T] **9250 4370** [F] **9250 4928**

Corporate Finance / M&A Advisory
Department: Global Corporate Finance Group
Country Head   Stephen Brimo *Director*

Global Custody
Department: Global Investor Services
Regional Head   Michael Hamar
Country Head   Laurence Bailey *Director*

Administration
Legal / In-House Counsel
    David Perkins *Legal Counsel*

Public Relations
    Jenny Moore *Communications & Public Relations Officer* [T] **9250 4545**
    [F] **9250 4531** [E] **jennymoore@chase.com**

Citibank NA   Full Branch Office

Level 12, 1 Margaret Street, Sydney, New South Wales 2000
Tel: (2) 9239 9100 **Fax:** (2) 9239 9690 **Telex:** 26181 **Reuters:** CISY **Telerate:** 2812
Corporate Dealers & Overnight Desk **Tel:** 9239 0844
Website: www.globalmarkets.citibank.com

Senior Executive Officers
Chairman   Tom McKeon [T] **9239 9668**
Financial Director   Bernard Rouault *Financial Controller* [T] **9239 9484**
Treasurer   Tom Pragastis *Head of Financial Markets* [T] **9239 9854**
Business Head   Bill Ferguson [T] **9239 9661**

Syndicated Lending
Loan-Related Activities
Structured Trade Finance; Leasing & Asset Finance   Shane Taylor [T] **9239 5885**

Money Markets
Tel: 9238 0566 **Fax:** 9239 9690
Head of Money Markets   Michael Cunningham *Money Markets, Funding* [T] **9239 9908**

Foreign Exchange
Tel: 9239 0755 **Fax:** 9239 9690 **Reuters:** CISA
Head of Foreign Exchange   Steve Shuster *Head, FX* [T] **9239 9561**
Head of Institutional Sales; Corporate Sales   Bernard Sinniah *Head, Marketing - FX & IR Products* [T] **9239 9435**
Head of Trading   Steve Shuster *Head, FX* [T] **9239 9561**

FX Traders / Sales People
    Andrew DeSouza *Head, FX Forward Trading* [T] **9239 9434**
    Chris Wray *Head, FX Spot Trading* [T] **9239 9474**

Risk Management
Reuters: CISB
Head of Sales   Bernard Sinniah *Head, Marketing - FX & IR Products* [T] **9239 9435**
Trading   Charles Finkelstein *Bond & Derivatives Trading Head* [T] **9239 9950**
IR Swaps Sales / Marketing   Diana Lollato [T] **9239 9435**

Foreign Exchange Derivatives / Risk Management
Cross-Currency Swaps, Sales / Marketing;   Bernard Sinniah *Head, Marketing - FX & IR Products* [T] **9239 9435**
Vanilla FX option Sales

Exotic Options (Barriers, Range, Timers, Digitals, Faders etc)
Sales   Bernard Sinniah *Head, Marketing - FX & IR Products* [T] **9239 9435**

OTC Commodity Derivatives
Head   Carlos Ranguis [T] **9239 9955**
Sales   Sean Mulhearn *Head, Derivative Sales* [T] **9239 9432**

OTC Credit Derivatives
Head   Bernard Sinniah *Head, Marketing - FX & IR Products* [T] **9239 9435**

www.euromoneydirectory.com　　　　　AUSTRALIA (+61)

Settlement / Clearing
Country Head
Equity Settlement; Derivatives Settlement;　　Pauline Soon ☎ **9239 9456**
Foreign Exchange Settlement; Operations;　　John Duckworth ☎ **9239 9411**
Back-Office
Other Departments
Commodities / Bullion　　Carlos Ranguis ☎ **9239 9955**
Administration
Technology & Systems
　　Himanshu Argarwal ☎ **9239 9930**
Legal / In-House Counsel
　　Tom O'Callaghan *Legal Counsel* ☎ **9239 9648**
Compliance
　　Nick Stramondanoli

Commerzbank AG   Representative Office
Suite 5301, MLC Centre, 19/29 Martin Place, Sydney, New South Wales 2000
Tel: (2) 9221 5700 Fax: (2) 9221 5605 Telex: 24026 COBANK
Senior Executive Officers
Representative　　Werner Menges

Commonwealth Bank of Australia   Head Office
Level 6, 48 Martin Place, Sydney, New South Wales 1155
GPO Box 2719, Sydney, New South Wales 2001
Tel: (2) 9378 2000; (2) 9378 2638 Fax: (2) 9378 3317; (2) 9378 2344 Telex: 120345; 120267 Swift: CTBA AU 2S
Email: bickerba@cba.com.au Reuters: CBAA-C (Monitor) Telerate: 2646
General Telex: 120267; Reuters: CBAB; CBAC
Website: www.commbank.com.au

Senior Executive Officers
Financial Director　　Michael Ulmer *Group General Manager*
Managing Director　　David Murray
Company Secretary　　John Hatton
Others (Senior Executives)
Global Trading　　Paul Riordan *Head* ☎ **9378 0592**
Financial Markets, Distribution　　Neil Schafer *Head* ☎ **9312 0600**
General-Investment
Head of Investment　　Michael Katz *Head* ☎ **9378 3900**
General - Treasury
Head of Treasury　　Mark Emery *Head of Treasury Services* ☎ **9312 0464**
Relationship Manager
Institutional Banking　　Michael Katz *Head* ☎ **9378 3900**
Debt Capital Markets / Fixed Income
Department: Fixed Interest Securities (Trading)
Head of Fixed Income Sales　　Ian Burnett *Head of Interest Rate Product Distribution* ☎ **9235 0122**
Head of Fixed Income Trading　　Rod Lewis *Global Trading Manager, Fixed Interest Securities* ☎ **9235 0122**
Libor-Based / Floating-Rate Products
FRN Origination　　Wayne Hoy *Head of Origination* ☎ **9312 0760**
FRN Sales　　Ian Burnett *Head of Interest Rate Product Distribution* ☎ **9235 0122**
Asset-Backed Securities / Securitization
Global Head　　Lyn Cobley *Head of Securitization* ☎ **9378 3331**
Mortgage-Backed Securities
Global Head　　Lyn Cobley *Head of Securitization* ☎ **9378 3331**
Fixed-Income Repo
Head of Repo　　Kate Murray *Manager, Repo Trading* ☎ **9235 0122**
Equity Capital Markets
Head of Equity Capital Markets　　John Beggs *Head of Equities* ☎ **9675 4846**
Other (Domestic Equities)
Infrastructure Equity　　Darce Corsie *VP, Equity Finance* ☎ **9378 2683**
Equity Repo / Securities Lending
Marketing　　Kate Murray *Manager, Repo Trading* ☎ **9235 0122**

Euromoney Directory 1999   43

AUSTRALIA (+61) www.euromoneydirectory.com

Commonwealth Bank of Australia (cont)
Syndicated Lending
Head of Origination — Wayne Hoy *Head of Origination* ☏ **9312 0760**
Head of Syndication — Gary Deadman *Head of Syndication*

Money Markets
Head of Money Markets — Ken Louden *Global Trading Manager, Money Markets*
Regional Head — John Martin *Head, Financial Markets - USA* ☏ **+1 (212) 336 7734**

Foreign Exchange
Tel: (2) 9312 0740 Telex: CBAA, CBAB, CMAC
Corporate Sales — Peter Prowse *Global Head, FX Distribution* ☏ **9675 6725**
Head of Trading — Rick Lloyd *Global Trading Manager, Spot FX* ☏ **9312 0740**

FX Traders / Sales People
Foreign Exchange Options — Luke Duffi *Chief Dealer* ☏ **9312 0683**
Corporate Foreign Exchange Distribution — Jon Sutton *Senior Manager* ☏ **9312 0137**
Foreign Exchange Funds Distribution — Kurt Magnus *Senior Manager* ☏ **9312 0766**
Commercial Foreign Exchange Distribution — Dave Hillhouse *Senior Manager* ☏ **9312 0137**
Futures — Rod Thomas *Head* ☏ **9312 0555**

Risk Management
Global Head — Mick Leonard *Head* ☏ **9675 7408**
Country Head — Rob Verlander *Head of Distribution, Europe* ☏ **+44 (171) 329 6444**
Debra Hazelton *Treasurer - Japan* ☏ **+81 (3) 5400 7277**
Andrew Fung *Chief Manager, Capital Markets, HK* ☏ **+852 2844 7529**

Fixed Income Derivatives / Risk Management
Head of Sales — Steven Bigg *Senior Manager, Financial Engineering Group* ☏ **9312 0377**
Trading — Peter Burgess *Global Trading Manager, Derivatives*

Settlement / Clearing
Head of Settlement / Clearing — Kevin O'Sullivan *Head, Financial Markets Operations* ☏ **9312 0515**
Operations — Paul Tabbiner *Senior Manager* ☏ **9312 0668**

Global Custody
Head of Global Custody — David Lawler *Financial Controller* ☏ **9378 2900**

Asset Management
Head — Shaun Mays *Chief Investment Officer* ☏ **9378 4784**

Other Departments
Commodities / Bullion — Greg Madden *Head, Precious Metals & Commodities* ☏ **9312 0700**
Chief Credit Officer — Mick Leonard ☏ **9312 2944**
Correspondent Banking — Drone Chowdry *Vice President, Business Development* ☏ **9312 0973**

Administration
Legal / In-House Counsel
Chief Solicitor — Les Taylor ☏ **9378 4709**

Public Relations
Carolyn Kerr *Head of Investor Relations* ☏ **9378 2747**

Cooperatieve Centrale Raiffeisen-Boerenleenbank BA
Full Branch Office

Alternative trading name: Rabobank
Level 7, 115 Pitt Street, Sydney, New South Wales 2000
Tel: (2) 9234 4200 Fax: (2) 9233 1436; (2) 9234 4211 Telex: AA22619 Swift: RABO AU SS Reuters: RABA

Senior Executive Officers
Chief Executive Officer — Cornelis Broekhuyse
Chief Operating Officer — David Owen *GM, Group Operations*

Others (Senior Executives)
Information Technology — John Pascoe *General Manager*
Structured Finance — Andrew Davison *General Manager*

General-Lending (DCM, SL)
Head of Corporate Banking — Ab Gillhuis *General Manager, Corporate Banking*

General - Treasury
Head of Treasury — Andrew Quoyle *Head, IR Risk Management*

Relationship Manager
Residential — Brian Rowe *General Manager*
New Zealand — Jaap Klep *General Manager*
Rural — Steve Morgan *General Manager*

www.euromoneydirectory.com   **AUSTRALIA (+61)**

Debt Capital Markets / Fixed Income
Department: New Issue Syndication
Other (Libor-Based / Floating Rate Products)
Fixed Rate / Straights   Andrew Quoyle *Head, IR Risk Management*
FRNs / VRNs / FRAs   John Rollings *Chief Dealer, IR Risk Management*
Settlements   Sjaak Verschoor *Senior Manager, Operations* ☏ **9234 4233**
Private Placements
Head of Origination   Bonnie Fitzgibbon *Senior Manager, Treasury Corporate Sales*
Syndicated Lending
Head of Credit Committee   Philip Hislop *General Manager, Credit*
Other (Trade Finance)
Structured Finance   Andrew Davison *General Manager*
Money Markets
Eurocommercial Paper
Head of Origination   John Rollings *Chief Dealer, IR Risk Management*
Other (Wholesale Deposits)
Euronotes, CDs - Origination   John Rollings *Chief Dealer, IR Risk Management*
Risk Management
Fixed Income Derivatives / Risk Management
IR Swaps Sales / Marketing   John Rollings *Chief Dealer, IR Risk Management*
Foreign Exchange Derivatives / Risk Management
Cross-Currency Swaps, Sales / Marketing   John Rollings *Chief Dealer, IR Risk Management*
Settlement / Clearing
Country Head   Sjaak Verschoor *Senior Manager, Operations* ☏ **9234 4233**
Administration
Technology & Systems
Information Technology   John Pascoe *General Manager*
Legal / In-House Counsel
    Gregory Kelly *Group Secretary & Chief Manager, Legal*
Public Relations
    Anne Lenehan *Manager*

Credit Suisse First Boston   Broker/Dealer

Gateway Level 31, One Macquarie Place, Sydney, New South Wales NSW 2000
Tel: (2) 9394 4400 **Fax:** (2) 9394 4382

Debt Capital Markets / Fixed Income
Fixed-Income Repo
Marketing & Product Development   Eigen Kaji *Vice President* ✉ **eigen.kaji@csfb.com**
Trading   Graeme Colloff *Vice President* ✉ **graeme.colloff@csfb.com**

The Dai-Ichi Kangyo Bank Limited

Level 57, MLC Centre, 29 Martin Place, Sydney, New South Wales 2000
GPO Box 4090, Sydney, New South Wales 2001
Tel: (2) 9233 8400 **Fax:** (2) 9235 1263 **Telex:** AA22685 DKBSYD **Reuters:** DKAA

Senior Executive Officers
Managing Director / General Manager   Toshiro Ikehara
Others (Senior Executives)
Deputy General Manager   Kazumasa Otani
General - Treasury
Head of Treasury   Dan East *Chief Manager, Treasury*
Risk Management
Head of Risk Management   Fumio Matsuzawa *Risk Controller*
Corporate Finance / M&A Advisory
Head of Corporate Finance   Tetsuya Nakamura *Chief Manager*
Settlement / Clearing
Operations   Neil Leow *Chief Manager, Operations*
Administration
Accounts / Audit
Accounting & Administration   Phillip Pragasam *Chief Manager*
Internal Auditor   Karen Chan *Internal Auditor*

AUSTRALIA (+61)   www.euromoneydirectory.com

Daiwa Securities Australia Limited

Alternative trading name: Daiwa Securities Stockbroking Limited
Level 48, Nauru House, 80 Collins Street, Melbourne, Victoria 3000
Tel: (3) 9280 1300 **Fax:** (3) 9650 7752 **Telex:** 152198 **Bloomberg:** MAILER

Senior Executive Officers
Chairman & President   H Kondo
Managing Director   John S Chambers

Equity Capital Markets
Head of Equity Capital Markets   John S Chambers *Managing Director*

Syndicated Lending
Head of Origination   Nicholas Palaskas *General Manager, Capital Markets*

Administration
Technology & Systems
                                     Meg Smith *IT Administrator*
Accounts / Audit
                                     Lynette Board *Financial Controller*

Deutsche Bank AG   Full Branch Office

Level 23, 333 Collins Street, Melbourne, Victoria 3000
Tel: (3) 9270 4444; (3) 9629 6710 **Fax:** (3) 9270 4451 **Telex:** AA136122 DBAL **Swift:** DEUT AU 2S

Senior Executive Officers
General-Lending (DCM, SL)
Head of Corporate Banking   Paul Davies *Chief Manager, Corporate Banking*

Deutsche Bank AG   Full Branch Office

225 George Street, Sydney, New South Wales 2001
Tel: (2) 9258 1234

Senior Executive Officers
Department: Senior Executives: Global Corporates & Institutions

Others (Senior Executives)
Head of Investment Banking   Josef Ackermann
Head of Global Markets   Edson Mitchell
Head of Equities   Michael Philipp
Head of Risk Management   Hugo Banziger
Head of Global Banking Services   Juergen Fitschen
Head of Structured Finance   Gavin Lickley
Head of IT / Operations   Marc Sternfeld

Debt Capital Markets / Fixed Income
Tel: 9247 7177 **Fax:** 9258 3632

Fixed-Income Repo
Head of Repo   Lou Ghiradello *Head of Money Market / Repo* ☏ **9258 1460**
                                     ✉ lou.ghiradello@db.com
Trading   Rod Everitt *Repo Trader*
                                     Bill Reeks *Head of Money Markets / Trader* ✉ bill.reeks@db.com
                                     Pamela Carr *Repo Trader*
                                     Jeff Weiss *Repo Trader*

Deutsche Capital Markets Australia Limited   Head Office

Formerly known as: Deutsche Morgan Grenfell Australia Limited
Level 18, Grosvenor Place, 225 George Street, Sydney, New South Wales 2000
GPO Box 7033, Sydney, New South Wales 1170
Tel: (2) 9258 1234 **Fax:** (2) 9258 1170; (2) 9258 1401

Senior Executive Officers
Chairman   Maurice L Newman
Chief Executive Officer   Klaus Albrecht *Chief Executive Officer*
Chief Operating Officer   Sue Griffin *Chief Operating Officer*
Company Secretary   Phil Costa

www.euromoneydirectory.com　　　AUSTRALIA (+61)

Dresdner Bank AG Representative Office

Level 18, 367 Collins Street, Melbourne, Victoria 3000
Tel: (3) 9629 1701 Fax: (3) 9629 2386

Senior Executive Officers
Chief Representative　　　　　　　　　Viktor von Gleichenstern
Assistant Representative　　　　　　　Royston Fish

Dresdner Kleinwort Benson Australia Full Branch Office

Alternative trading name: Dresdner Bank AG Australian Branch
Formerly known as: Dresdner Australia Limited
Level 20, 2 Market Street, Sydney, New South Wales 2000
Tel: (2) 9286 2088 Fax: (2) 9286 2098 Swift: DRES AU 2S Reuters: DRSA-B

Senior Executive Officers
Managing Director　　　　　　　　　　John Dawson ☏ **9286 2088**
Deputy Managing Director　　　　　　Ralf Zimpel ☏ **9286 2088**
Deputy Managing Director　　　　　　Julie Bellingham ☏ **9286 2088**
General Counsel　　　　　　　　　　　John Prineas ☏ **9286 2088**
Chief Representative　　　　　　　　　Viktot von Gueichenstern ☏ **(3) 9629 1701**

Debt Capital Markets / Fixed Income
Department: Global Markets
Tel: 9283 2211 Fax: 9286 2150 Reuters: DRSA
Head of Fixed Income Sales　　　　　David O'Hanlon *Associate Director, International Bonds* ☏ **9283 2211**
Head of Fixed Income Trading　　　　Terry Green *Associate Director, Fixed Income* ☏ **9286 2136**

Domestic Government Bonds
Head of Sales　　　　　　　　　　　　David O'Hanlon *Associate Director, International Bonds* ☏ **9283 2211**
Head of Origination; Head of Syndication　Lindsay Skardoon *Associate Director, Capital Markets* ☏ **9283 2211**

Eurobonds
Head of Sales　　　　　　　　　　　　David O'Hanlon *Associate Director, International Bonds* ☏ **9283 2211**

Emerging Market Bonds
Head of Sales　　　　　　　　　　　　David O'Hanlon *Associate Director, International Bonds* ☏ **9283 2211**

Libor-Based / Floating-Rate Products
FRN Sales　　　　　　　　　　　　　　David O'Hanlon *Associate Director, International Bonds* ☏ **9283 2211**
Asset Swaps　　　　　　　　　　　　　Lindsay Skardoon *Associate Director, Capital Markets* ☏ **9283 2211**
Asset Swaps (Sales)　　　　　　　　　David O'Hanlon *Associate Director, International Bonds* ☏ **9283 2211**

Fixed-Income Repo
Head of Repo　　　　　　　　　　　　Mark Tkocz *Dealer* ☏ **9286 2900**
Matched Book Manager　　　　　　　Chris Bell *Director, Treasury* ☏ **9286 2900**

Fixed-Income Research
Head of Fixed Income　　　　　　　　Rob Henderson *Chief Economist* ☏ **9286 2192**
Head of Credit Research　　　　　　　Klaus Isenbeck *Director, Credit* ☏ **9286 2088**

Syndicated Lending
Tel: 9286 2088
Head of Syndicated Lending; Head of　Julie Bellingham *Deputy Managing Director* ☏ **9286 2088**
Origination; Head of Syndication
Head of Credit Committee　　　　　　Ralf Zimpel *Deputy Managing Director* ☏ **9286 2088**

Loan-Related Activities
Project Finance　　　　　　　　　　　Alastair Banfield *Director* ☏ **9286 2088**
Structured Trade Finance　　　　　　Julie Bellingham *Deputy Managing Director* ☏ **9286 2088**

Other (Trade Finance)
Resources Finance　　　　　　　　　Alastair Banfield *Director* ☏ **9286 2088**
Structured Finance　　　　　　　　　Rod McPherson *Director* ☏ **9286 2088**

Money Markets
Tel: 9286 2900 Fax: 9286 2150
Country Head　　　　　　　　　　　　Chris Bell *Director, Treasury* ☏ **9286 2900**

Domestic Commercial Paper
Head of Origination　　　　　　　　　Lindsay Skardoon *Associate Director, Capital Markets* ☏ **9283 2211**
Head of Sales; Head of Trading　　　Chris Bell *Director, Treasury* ☏ **9286 2900**

Wholesale Deposits
Marketing; Head of Sales　　　　　　Chris Bell *Director, Treasury* ☏ **9286 2900**

Foreign Exchange
Tel: 9283 2211 Fax: 9286 2150
Head of Foreign Exchange　　　　　　Rob Graham *Director, MRM* ☏ **9286 2136**
Head of Institutional Sales　　　　　　Michael Lee *Associate Director, SRM* ☏ **(3) 9629 8764**

AUSTRALIA (+61)

www.euromoneydirectory.com

Dresdner Kleinwort Benson Australia (cont)

Foreign Exchange (cont)

Corporate Sales
Head of Trading

Jenny Piper *Associate Director, Public Relations* ☎ **9286 2088**
Rob Graham *Director, MRM* ☎ **9286 2136**

FX Traders / Sales People
A$
A$ Sales
FX Sales

Ian Rutherford *Senior Dealer* ☎ **9283 2200**
Michael Lee *Associate Director, SRM* ☎ **(3) 9629 8164**
Rob Hollonds *Director, SRM* ☎ **9283 2211**
Tony Laycock *Manager, SRM* ☎ **(3) 9629 8164**
Rohan Clarke *Senior Dealer, SRM* ☎ **9283 2211**

Risk Management

Department: Market Risk Management
Tel: 9286 2136 **Fax:** 9286 2150
Country Head

John Dawson *Managing Director* ☎ **9286 2088**

Fixed Income Derivatives / Risk Management
Country Head
Head of Sales
Trading
IR Swaps Sales / Marketing
IR Swaps Trading
IR Options Sales / Marketing
IR Options Trading

Rob Graham *Director, MRM* ☎ **9286 2136**
David O'Hanlon *Associate Director, International Bonds* ☎ **9283 2211**
Terry Green *Associate Director, Fixed Income* ☎ **9286 2136**
Rob Hollonds *Director, SRM* ☎ **9283 2211**
Rob Graham *Director, MRM* ☎ **9286 2136**
Rob Hollonds *Director, SRM* ☎ **9283 2211**
Rob Graham *Director, MRM* ☎ **9286 2136**

Foreign Exchange Derivatives / Risk Management
Spot / Forwards Sales; Spot / Forwards Trading
Cross-Currency Swaps, Sales / Marketing
Cross-Currency Swaps, Trading
Vanilla FX option Sales
Vanilla FX option Trading

Rob Graham *Director, MRM* ☎ **9286 2136**
Rob Hollonds *Director, SRM* ☎ **9283 2211**
Rob Graham *Director, MRM* ☎ **9286 2136**
Rob Hollonds *Director, SRM* ☎ **9283 2211**
Rob Graham *Director, MRM* ☎ **9286 2136**

Other Currency Swap / FX Options Personnel

Tony Laycock *Manager, SRM* ☎ **(3) 9629 8164**
Marcus Taylor *Dealer, Options* ☎ **9283 2200**
Rohan Clarke *Senior Dealer, SRM* ☎ **9283 2211**

OTC Equity Derivatives
Sales
Trading

Rob Hollonds *Director, SRM* ☎ **9283 2211**
Tony Laycock *Manager, SRM* ☎ **(3) 9629 8164**

OTC Commodity Derivatives
Head
Sales

Trading

Paul Lee *Director, Commodities* ☎ **9286 2130**
Jeff Duncan-Nagy *Associate Director, Commodities* ☎ **9286 2130**
Paul Thomas *Senior Dealer* ☎ **9286 2130**
Paul Lee *Director, Commodities* ☎ **9286 2130**
Rohin Furtado *Director, Base Metals* ☎ **9286 2088**

OTC Credit Derivatives
Head

Lindsay Skardoon *Associate Director, Capital Markets* ☎ **9283 2211**

Settlement / Clearing

Tel: 9286 2000 **Fax:** 9286 2028
Head of Settlement / Clearing; Fixed-Income Settlement; Derivatives Settlement; Foreign Exchange Settlement; Operations

Les Andrews *Director, Operations* ☎ **9286 2001**

Other Departments

Commodities / Bullion

John Dawson *Managing Director* ☎ **9286 2088**
Rohin Furtado *Director, Base Metals* ☎ **9286 2088**
Klaus Isenbeck *Director, Credit* ☎ **9286 2088**
Viktot von Gueichenstein ☎ **(3) 9629 1701**

Chief Credit Officer
Correspondent Banking

Administration

Head of Administration
Business Development

Jenny Pearce *Manager, Administration* ☎ **9286 2061**
Jenny Piper *Associate Director, Public Relations* ☎ **9286 2088**

Technology & Systems

Greg Gilmour *Associate Director, IT* ☎ **9286 2088**

Legal / In-House Counsel

John Prineas *General Counsel* ☎ **9286 2088**

Compliance

John Prineas *General Counsel* ☎ **9286 2088**

Public Relations

Jenny Piper *Associate Director, Public Relations* ☎ **9286 2088**

Accounts / Audit

Tim McGrath *Financial Controller* ☎ **9286 2088**

www.euromoneydirectory.com AUSTRALIA (+61)

Other (Administration)
Marketing Jenny Piper *Associate Director, Public Relations* ☏ **9286 2088**

E L & C Baillieu Stockbrokering Limited
Head Office

Formerly known as: E L & C Baillieu Limited
27th Level, 360 Collins Street, Melbourne, Victoria 3000
PO Box 48, Collins Street West, Melbourne, Victoria 8007
Tel: (3) 9602 9222 **Fax:** (3) 9602 2350 **Telex:** 30157 **Email:** baillieu@baillieu.com.au
Website: www.baillieu.com.au.

Senior Executive Officers
Chairman Malcolm Brodie
Chief Executive Officer Ronald Hay *Chairman, Management Committee*
Finance Director Gavin Powell

Erste Bank
Representative Office

Formerly known as: GiroCredit Bank Aktiengesellschaft der Sparkassen
Level 19, Gateway Building, 1 Macquarie Place, Sydney, New South Wales 2000
Tel: (2) 9251 9588 **Fax:** (2) 9251 9355

Senior Executive Officers
Head, Asia Pacific Region Errol Carr
General Manager Paul Mazzola

The Export-Import Bank of Japan
Representative Office

Suite 2501, Level 25, Gateway 1, Macquarie Place, Sydney, New South Wales 2000
Tel: (2) 9241 1388; (2) 9241 1389 **Fax:** (2) 9231 1053 **Email:** eximnaga@dot.net.au
Website: www.japanexim.go.jp

Senior Executive Officers
Chief Representative Masaki Yuzawa

Financial Security Assurance Inc
Representative Office

Hambros House, 167 Macquarie Street, Sydney, New South Wales 2000
Tel: (2) 9221 8533 **Fax:** (2) 9223 8629

Senior Executive Officers
Representative Peter Wedgewood

Goldman Sachs Australia LLC

Level 48, Governor Phillip Tower, 1 Farrer Place, Sydney, New South Wales
Tel: (2) 9320 1000 **Fax:** (2) 9320 1009

Senior Executive Officers
Chairman & Managing Director Malcolm B Turnbull

HongkongBank of Australia Limited
Subsidiary Company

Level 10, 1 O'Connell Street, Sydney, New South Wales 2000
Tel: (2) 9255 2888 **Fax:** (2) 9255 2332 **Telex:** AA24856 HKBASY **Swift:** HKBA AU 2SA SYD **Reuters:** HKBA

Senior Executive Officers
Chairman David Say
Chief Executive Officer Chris Crook
Financial Director Gary McLennan *Chief Financial Officer*
Treasurer Graeme Bricknell
Managing Director Stuart Davis
Company Secretary Stephen Mckeane

Others (Senior Executives)
Director David Eldon
Ric Charlton
Richard Hein
Aman Mehta

AUSTRALIA (+61)   www.euromoneydirectory.com

HongkongBank of Australia Limited (cont)
General-Lending (DCM, SL)
Head of Corporate Banking   Kieran Marnell
Relationship Manager
                                    David Tunnicliffe *Head of Personal Banking*
Syndicated Lending
Other (Trade Finance)
Head of Trade Services   Alan Wilson
Money Markets
Head of Money Markets   Chris Compton *Manager*
Foreign Exchange
Head of Foreign Exchange   Kim Elliott *Manager*
Head of Institutional Sales   Agnes Vas
Corporate Sales   Nisha Karan
Head of Trading   Dale Felton
Corporate Finance / M&A Advisory
Head of Corporate Finance   Tony O'Sullivan
Global Custody
Regional Head   Garry Richmond
Other Departments
Chief Credit Officer   Bruce Strang
Correspondent Banking   Kieran Marnell
Administration
Legal / In-House Counsel
                                    Andrew Jackson
Compliance
                                    Andrew Jackson
Public Relations
Public Affairs   Joanna Munro *Manager*
Accounts / Audit
Audit   Graham Thomson
Other (Administration)
Marketing   Andrew Carruthers *Manager*

HSBC Asset Management Australia Limited
Levels 29 & 30, 140 William Street, Melbourne, Victoria 3000
PO Box 291, Market Street, Melbourne, Victoria 8007
Tel: (3) 9225 3000 **Fax:** (3) 9225 3195 **Telex:** AA152145 WIMLM
Senior Executive Officers
Chairman   J J D'Arcy
Managing Director / General Manager D I Stevens

ING Bank NV   Full Branch Office
Alternative trading name: ING Barings
Level 1, 347 Kent Street, Sydney, New South Wales 2001
Tel: (2) 9234 8426 **Fax:** (2) 9290 3693; (2) 9299 7905 **Telex:** 20005 **Swift:** INGAU25 **Email:** ingtreasury@bigpond.com
Senior Executive Officers
Chief Executive Officer   Vaughn Richtor *Country Banking Officer* ☎ **9234 7110**
Financial Director   John Horn *Financial Controller* ☎ **9234 8449**
Treasurer   Glenn Baker *Head of Treasury* ☎ **9234 7119**
International Division   Rene Wegers *Head of Corporate Banking* ☎ **9234 7270**
Syndicated Lending
Loan-Related Activities
Trade Finance   Andrea Govaert *Manager, Trade & Commodity Finance* ☎ **9234 7191**
Project Finance   Mike Klemme *Vice President* ☎ **9234 7159**
Money Markets
Tel: 9234 7149 **Fax:** 9290 3683 **Telex:** 20005
Country Head   Glenn Baker *Head of Treasury* ☎ **9234 7119**
Risk Management
Country Head   John Hickey *Head* ☎ **9234 7163**

50   Euromoney Directory 1999

www.euromoneydirectory.com　　　AUSTRALIA (+61)

Settlement / Clearing
Country Head　　　　　　　　　　Karen Knight *Supervisor* ☏ **9234 7125**
Operations　　　　　　　　　　　　Robert Attanasio *Manager* ☏ **9234 7169**
Other　　　　　　　　　　　　　　David Lim *Manager, TCF Settlements* ☏ **9234 7159**
Administration
Accounts / Audit
Internal Auditor　　　　　　　　　Alk Leow *Internal Auditor* ☏ **9234 7102**

ING Mercantile Mutual Bank　　　　　　　　Subsidiary Company

Level 1, 347 Kent Street, Sydney, New South Wales 2001
GPO Box 4094, Sydney, New South Wales 2001
Tel: (2) 9234 8426 **Fax:** (2) 9290 3683 **Telex:** 20005 **Swift:** INGBAU25 **Email:** ingtreasury@bigpond.com

Senior Executive Officers
Chief Executive Officer　　　　　　Vaughn Richtor *General Manager* ☏ **9234 7110**
Financial Director　　　　　　　　John Horn *Financial Controller* ☏ **9234 8449**
Treasurer　　　　　　　　　　　　Glenn Baker *Head of Treasury* ☏ **9234 7119**
General Manager, Commercial Banking　Royal Moore ☏ **9234 8450**

Money Markets
Tel: 9234 7149 **Fax:** 9290 3683 **Telex:** 20005
Country Head　　　　　　　　　　Glenn Baker *Head of Treasury* ☏ **9234 7119**

Risk Management
Country Head　　　　　　　　　　John Hickey *Head* ☏ **9234 7163**

Settlement / Clearing
Country Head　　　　　　　　　　Karen Knight *Supervisor* ☏ **9234 7125**
Settlement (General)　　　　　　　Robert Attanasio *Manager, Business Support Services* ☏ **9234 7169**

Administration
Accounts / Audit
Internal Auditor　　　　　　　　　Alk Leow ☏ **9234 7102**

Intercapital plc

Level 33, AMP Centre, 50 Bridge Street, Sydney, New South Wales 2000
Tel: (2) 9233 5733 **Fax:** (2) 9233 5275

Senior Executive Officers
Others (Senior Executives)
　　　　　　　　　　　　　　　　George Macdonald

KEB Australia Limited　　　　　　　　Subsidiary Company

Level 4, NAB House, 255 George Street, Sydney, New South Wales 2000
Tel: (2) 9251 3355; (2) 9241 1988 **Fax:** (2) 9251 3853; (2) 9251 3451 **Telex:** AA24932 **Swift:** KOEX AU 2S
Email: admin@keba.com.au

Senior Executive Officers
Managing Director　　　　　　　　Kee Jong Chung
Executive Director　　　　　　　　Chae-Ok Kim
Chief Executive Officer　　　　　　Yoon-Sup Maeng *Chief Manager*
Financial Director　　　　　　　　Hee Cheon Oh *Senior Manager*

LTCB Australia Limited　　　　　　　　Subsidiary Company

34th Level, Tower Building, Australia Square, Sydney, New South Wales 2000
Tel: (2) 9251 3544 **Fax:** (2) 9235 0162

Senior Executive Officers
Chairman　　　　　　　　　　　　Kazuhide Koshiishi
Treasurer　　　　　　　　　　　　Raymond Orr
Managing Director　　　　　　　　Hiroshi Nakamura

Euromoney Directory 1999　　**51**

AUSTRALIA (+61)   www.euromoneydirectory.com

Macquarie Bank Limited — Head Office

Formerly known as: Hill Samuel Australia Limited
Level 22, 20 Bond Street, Sydney, New South Wales 2000
Tel: (2) 9237 3126 **Fax:** (2) 9237 6882 **Telex:** 122246 **Swift:** MACQ AU 2S **Reuters:** MBL
Website: www.macquarie.com.au

Senior Executive Officers
Executive Chairman	David Clarke ☏ **9237 3413**
Chief Executive Officer	Allan Moss *Managing Director & Chief Executive* ☏ **9237 3483**
	Richard Sheppard *Executive Director* ☏ **9237 3183**
Financial Director	Greg Ward *Division Director* ☏ **9237 3087**
Treasurer	Paul Robertson *Executive Director* ☏ **9237 3371**

Others (Senior Executives)
Investment Services Group	David Adams *Executive Director* ☏ **9237 3436**
Treasury & Commodities Group	Andrew Downe *Executive Director* ☏ **9237 3036**
Equities Group	Richard Jenkins *Executive Director* ☏ **9237 3811**
Corporate Finance Group	Laurie Cox *Joint Chairman* ☏ **9237 3869**
	Mark Johnson ☏ **9237 3869**
Banking & Property	Bill Moss *Executive Director*

Debt Capital Markets / Fixed Income
Department: Structured, Corporate & Infrastructure Group
Tel: 9237 4028
Global Head	Nicholas Moore *Executive Director*
Regional Head	Els Termaat *Division Director* ☏ **9237 4245**

Mortgage-Backed Securities
Global Head	Tony Gill *Executive Director* ☏ **9237 6363**

Syndicated Lending
Department: Loan-Related Activities

Loan-Related Activities
Leasing & Asset Finance	Russell Leslie *Executive Director* ☏ **9237 3537**
	Charles Wheeler *Executive Director* ☏ **9237 3323**

Money Markets
Tel: 9237 3371 **Fax:** 9237 4227
Global Head	Paul Robertson *Executive Director* ☏ **9237 3371**

Domestic Commercial Paper
Head of Sales; Head of Trading	Liz Morell *Manager* ☏ **9237 3382**

Eurocommercial Paper
Head of Sales; Head of Trading	Craig Shapiro *Associate Director* ☏ **9237 3375**

Wholesale Deposits
Marketing; Head of Sales	Liz Morell *Manager* ☏ **9237 3382**

Foreign Exchange
Global Head; Corporate Sales	Simon Wright *Executive Director* ☏ **9237 4777**
Head of Trading	Guy Reynolds *Division Director* ☏ **9237 4996**

Risk Management
Global Head	Simon Wright *Executive Director* ☏ **9237 4777**

Fixed Income Derivatives / Risk Management
IR Swaps Trading	David Finnimore *Associate Director* ☏ **9237 3385**

Foreign Exchange Derivatives / Risk Management
Cross-Currency Swaps, Trading	Alexander Gow *Associate Director* ☏ **9237 4777**
Vanilla FX option Trading	David Bavin *Division Director* ☏ **9237 4777**

Exotic Options (Barriers, Range, Timers, Digitals, Faders etc)
Trading	David Bavin *Division Director* ☏ **9237 4777**

OTC Equity Derivatives
Trading	Ottmar Weiss *Executive Director* ☏ **9237 3980**

OTC Commodity Derivatives
Trading	Ross Ryan *Executive Director* ☏ **9237 4178**

Exchange-Traded Derivatives
Global Head	Ottmar Weiss *Executive Director* ☏ **9237 3980**

Corporate Finance / M&A Advisory
Global Head	Alastair Lucas *Executive Director* ☏ **9655 8134**

Settlement / Clearing
Regional Head	Julie Milton *Division Director* ☏ **9237 3319**
Equity Settlement	Mike McCarthy *Division Director* ☏ **9237 3688**
Foreign Exchange Settlement	Julie Milton *Division Director* ☏ **9237 3319**

www.euromoneydirectory.com　　　AUSTRALIA (+61)

Other Departments
Commodities / Bullion
Private Banking
Correspondent Banking

Warwick Morris *Executive Director* ☎ **9237 6205**
Tony Bates *Associate Director* ☎ **9237 4785**
Sarah Harrington *Associate Director* ☎ **9237 3355**

Administration
Technology & Systems

Gail Burke *Executive Director* ☎ **9237 3457**

Legal / In-House Counsel

Andrew Harding *Division Director* ☎ **9237 4205**

Compliance

Cheryl Sefton *Manager* ☎ **9237 3915**

Public Relations

Michelle Innis *Associate Director* ☎ **9237 4102**

Merrill Lynch Australia PTY Limited　　Subsidiary Company

Level 39, 120 Collins Street, Melbourne, Victoria 3000
Tel: (3) 9659 2222 **Fax:** (3) 9659 2696
Website: www.ml.com

Merrill Lynch Australia PTY Limited　　Subsidiary Company

Level 49, MLC Centre, 19-29 Martin Place, Sydney, New South Wales 2000
Tel: (2) 9225 6503 **Fax:** (2) 9225 6797; (2) 9225 6655 **Telex:** AA 24498
Debt Capital Markets / Fixed Income
Department: Merrill Lynch International (Australia) Ltd
Tel: 9225 6666 **Fax:** 9225 6678

Fixed-Income Repo
Head of Repo　　　　　　　　　　Tim Martin *Director*
Trading　　　　　　　　　　　　Jo Henderson *Vice President*

Midland Bank plc　　Full Branch Office

Level 7, 1 O'Connell Street, Sydney, New South Wales 2001
Tel: (2) 9225 2888 **Fax:** (2) 9225 2332

Senior Executive Officers
Others (Senior Executives)
　　　　　　　　　　　　　　C Crook *Senior Officer*

Debt Capital Markets / Fixed Income
Tel: 9255 2001 **Fax:** 9255 2205

Fixed-Income Repo
Head of Repo　　　　　　　　　　Chris Ewin *Treasurer* ☎ **9255 2009**
Trading　　　　　　　　　　　　Maurice Earhart *Head, Fixed Interest*
　　　　　　　　　　　　　　Luke Muttdon *Manager, Fixed Interest Trading*
　　　　　　　　　　　　　　Samantha Ridler *Dealer, Repo*
　　　　　　　　　　　　　　Ian Hamilton *Manager, Fixed Interest Sales*
　　　　　　　　　　　　　　Andrew Koczanowski *Senior Money Market Dealer*

Mitsubishi Trust Australia Limited

Level 27, The Chifley Tower, 2 Chifley Square, Sydney, New South Wales 2000
Tel: (2) 9221 5455 **Fax:** (2) 9233 3795 **Telex:** AA73388 MTBCSY **Reuters:** MTAL
Dealers **Tel:** (2) 9221 6044

Senior Executive Officers
Chairman　　　　　　　　　　　Kuniyasu Yamada
Treasurer　　　　　　　　　　　Masuhiro Yamamoto
Managing Director　　　　　　　　Tsuyoshi Aoki
General Manager, Corporate　　　　Yoichi Takahashi
Company Secretary　　　　　　　Garry Bloore

Euromoney Directory 1999　53

AUSTRALIA (+61)　　　　www.euromoneydirectory.com

Natexis Banque - BFCE
Representative Office

Formerly known as: Banque Française du Commerce Extérieur
45th Floor, 55 Collins Street, Melbourne, Victoria 8003
PO Box 18094, Melbourne, Victoria 8003
Tel: (3) 9650 3111 Fax: (3) 9650 5448

Senior Executive Officers
Chief Executive Officer　　　　Sandy Clark *Delegate*

National Australia Bank

5th Floor, 271 Collins Street, Melbourne, Victoria 3000
GPO Box 1406M, Melbourne, Victoria 3000
Tel: (3) 9659 6111 Fax: (3) 9659 7922 Telex: 33050 Swift: NATA AU33 03X

Debt Capital Markets / Fixed Income
Department: National Australia Bank Custodian Services
Tel: 9659 6222 Fax: 9659 7922

Fixed-Income Repo
Head of Repo　　　　Tony O'Grady *General Manager* ☏ **9659 6561**

Equity Capital Markets
Fax: 6959 6999
Head of Equity Capital Markets　　Tony O'Grady *General Manager* ☏ **9659 6561**
Head of Sales　　　　Patrick Liddy *Head of Sales & Marketing* ☏ **9659 6357**

Equity Repo / Securities Lending
Head　　　　Tony O'Grady *General Manager* ☏ **9659 6561**
Marketing & Product Development　Patrick Liddy *Head of Sales & Marketing* ☏ **9659 6357**

Global Custody
Department: National Australia Bank Custodian Services
Tel: 9659 6222 Fax: 9659 7922
Regional Head　　　　John Treloar *Executive Head Global Securities* ☏ **9659 6317** F **9659 6999**
　　　　　　　　　　✉ john_treloar@nag.national.com.au

Other (Global Custody)
　　　　　　　　　　Richard Simmons ☏ **9659 6580**

National Australia Bank Limited
Head Office

24th Floor, 500 Bourke Street, Melbourne, Victoria 3000
PO Box 84A, Melbourne, Victoria 3001
Tel: (3) 9641 3500 Fax: (3) 9641 4916 Telex: AA 30241 / AA30490 NATAUS Swift: NATAAU 33033 Reuters: NABA
Website: www.national.com.au

Senior Executive Officers
Chairman　　　　　　　　Mark Rayner
Chief Executive Officer　　　Donald Argus *MD & CEO*
Financial Director　　　　　Robert Prowse *CFO*
Treasurer　　　　　　　　Mike Aynsley *General Manager, Group Treasury*
Company Secretary　　　　Gary Nolan

Others (Senior Executives)
Business & Personal　　　　Glenn Barnes *Executive General Manager*
Technology　　　　　　　Michael Coomer *Chief Information Officer*
Legal　　　　　　　　　David Krasnosbein *Group General Legal Counsel*
Asia　　　　　　　　　　Michael Liley *Group General Manager, Asia*
Personnel　　　　　　　Grant Steel *Executive GM, Human Resources*
Payments　　　　　　　Peter Thomas *Group General Manager, Global Payments*

General-Lending (DCM, SL)
Head of Corporate Banking　　Mike Soden *Executive GM, Global Wholesale & Financial Service*

Foreign Exchange
Head of Foreign Exchange　　Colin Campbell *Head of Treasury*
Head of Institutional Sales　　Chris Herde *General Manager, Institutions*

Risk Management
Head of Risk Management　　Robert Miller *Executive General Manager*

Fixed Income Derivatives / Risk Management
Head of Sales　　　　　　Peter Anderson *Head of Derivative Markets*

Settlement / Clearing
Head of Settlement / Clearing　Ray Terkelsen *Head of Operations*

www.euromoneydirectory.com AUSTRALIA (+61)

Global Custody
Department: National Australia Custodian Services
Head of Global Custody Tony O' Grady *General Manager*

Other Departments
Private Banking David Jones *General Manager, Private Banking*

Administration
Technology & Systems
 Michael Coomer *Chief Information Officer*

Legal / In-House Counsel
 David Krasnosbein *Group General Legal Counsel*

Public Relations
 Michael Liley *Group General Manager, Asia*

Other (Administration)
Personnel Grant Steel *Executive GM, Human Resources*

National Bank of Greece — Representative Office
114 William Street, Melbourne, Victoria 3000
Tel: (3) 9670 0563 **Fax:** (3) 9642 1451 **Telex:** AA35687

Senior Executive Officers
Representative John Marakis

National Bank of Greece — Representative Office
37 Pitt Street, Sydney, New South Wales 2000
Tel: (2) 9247 7456 **Fax:** (2) 9251 4321 **Telex:** AA25209

Senior Executive Officers
Chief Representative L A Frangos

National Mutual Funds Management Limited
Level 13, 447 Collins Street, Melbourne, Victoria 3000
Tel: (3) 9617 2400 **Fax:** (3) 9617 2360 **Swift:** NMFM AU 3M **Email:** scottm@nmfm.com.au
Website: www.nmfm.com.au

Debt Capital Markets / Fixed Income
Fixed-Income Repo
Marketing & Product Development Nick Vamvakas *Fixed Interest Dealer* ☎ 9617 2730
Trading Rachel Edwardes *Cash Dealer / Repo*
 Wendy Hughes *Short Bonds / Repo*

Equity Capital Markets
Equity Repo / Securities Lending
Head Mark Armour *Managing Director* ☎ 9617 2400 ℻ 9617 2360
Marketing & Product Development Cameron Simpson *Manager of Operations* ☎ 9617 2856
  ✉ camerons@nmfm.com.au
Marketing John Nairn *Executive Director, Marketing* ☎ 9617 2901
Head of Trading Gail Logan *Trading, Bookings*
 Enza Tsagros *Dealing Assistant*
 Hugo Graves *Australian Equity Dealing Manager* ☎ 9617 2979 ℻ 9617 2337

New South Wales Treasury Corporation — Head Office
Level 22, Governor Phillip Tower, 1 Farrer Place, Sydney, New South Wales 2000
Tel: (2) 9325 9325 **Fax:** (2) 9325 9333; (2) 9325 9355 **Telex:** AA127551 **Email:** generalq@tcorp.nsw.gov.au
Website: www.tcorp.nsw.gov.au

Senior Executive Officers
Chairman John Pierce
Chief Executive Officer Wayne Jarman
Financial Director Peter Lucas *General Manager, Finance & Admin.*
Treasurer Stephen Knight *General Manager, Treasury*

Debt Capital Markets / Fixed Income
Regional Head Stephen Knight *State Head*
Domestic Government Bonds
Head of Sales Stephen Knight *General Manager, Treasury*

AUSTRALIA (+61)　　　　　　www.euromoneydirectory.com

New South Wales Treasury Corporation (cont)

Eurobonds
Head of Sales　　　　　　　　　　Stephen Knight *General Manager, Treasury*

Libor-Based / Floating-Rate Products
FRN Sales　　　　　　　　　　　　Stephen Knight *General Manager, Treasury*

Medium-Term Notes
Head of Sales　　　　　　　　　　Stephen Knight *General Manager, Treasury*

Fixed-Income Repo
Sales　　　　　　　　　　　　　　Stephen Knight *General Manager, Treasury*

Syndicated Lending
Loan-Related Activities
Project Finance　　　　　　　　　Oliver Bedford *General Manager, Client Services*

Money Markets
Country Head　　　　　　　　　　Stephen Knight *General Manager, Treasury*

Risk Management
Country Head　　　　　　　　　　Serge Olivieri *Manager & Risk Compliance*

Fixed Income Derivatives / Risk Management
Country Head　　　　　　　　　　Serge Olivieri *Manager & Risk Compliance*

OTC Commodity Derivatives
Sales　　　　　　　　　　　　　　Stephen Knight *General Manager, Treasury*

OTC Credit Derivatives
Head of Sales　　　　　　　　　　Stephen Knight *General Manager, Treasury*

Exchange-Traded Derivatives
Regional Head　　　　　　　　　 Stephen Knight *General Manager, Treasury*

Corporate Finance / M&A Advisory
Country Head　　　　　　　　　　Oliver Bedford *General Manager, Client Services*

Settlement / Clearing
Country Head　　　　　　　　　　Eva Inatey *Chief Manager*

Global Custody
Country Head　　　　　　　　　　Eva Inatey *Chief Manager*

Administration
Technology & Systems
　　　　　　　　　　　　　　　　Manuel Urbiztondo *Chief Manager, IT*

Legal / In-House Counsel
　　　　　　　　　　　　　　　　Scott Mannix

Compliance
　　　　　　　　　　　　　　　　Serge Olivieri *Manager & Risk Compliance*

Public Relations
　　　　　　　　　　　　　　　　Victoria Sue *Manager, Communications*

Nikko Securities (Australia) Limited　　　　　　Subsidiary Company

Level 36, Chifley Tower, 2 Chifley Square, Sydney, New South Wales 2000
Tel: (2) 9229 2800 **Fax**: (2) 9221 5634 **Telex**: 171618

Senior Executive Officers
Chief Executive Officer　　　　　　Robert Simms *Managing Director* ☎ **9229 2822**
Deputy Managing Director　　　　 Toshio Fukuhara ☎ **9229 2801**

Settlement / Clearing
Country Head　　　　　　　　　　Andy Kung *Settlements Manager* ☎ **9229 2812**

Administration
Head of Administration　　　　　　Mandy Jankowski *Administrator* ☎ **9229 2811**

Accounts / Audit
　　　　　　　　　　　　　　　　Chie Kakami ☎ **9229 2813**

NM Rothschild & Sons (Australia) Limited

10th Floor, 1 Collins Street, Melbourne, Victoria 3000
Tel: (3) 9654 4900 **Fax**: (3) 9654 4961 **Telex**: 34180

56　Euromoney Directory 1999

www.euromoneydirectory.com   AUSTRALIA (+61)

NM Rothschild & Sons (Australia) Limited

Level 24, Exchange Plaza, 2 The Esplanade, Perth, Western Australia
Tel: (8) 9268 4600 **Fax:** (8) 9268 4646 **Telex:** 197319

NM Rothschild & Sons (Australia) Limited   Head Office

Level 15, 1 O'Connell Street, Sydney, New South Wales NSW 2000
PO Box R237, Royal Exchange, Sydney, New South Wales 2000
Tel: (2) 9323 2000 **Fax:** (2) 9323 2323 **Telex:** AA121295 **Reuters:** RALA

Senior Executive Officers
Chairman   Philip Brass
Chief Executive Officer   Richard Lee
Financial Director   Ian Jew
Company Secretary   Michael Pickering

Others (Senior Executives)
Head of Banking   Geoffrey Hodgkinson

General-Investment
Head of Investment   Ronnie Beevor *Head of Investment Banking*

General - Treasury
Head of Treasury   Geoffrey P Spice

Administration
Legal / In-House Counsel
    Michael Pickering

NM Rothschild Australia Holdings Pty Limited

Level 15, 1 O'Connell Street, Sydney, New South Wales 2000
PO Box R237, Royal Exchange, Sydney, New South Wales 2001
Tel: (2) 9323 2000 **Fax:** (2) 9323 2323 **Telex:** 121295 **Reuters:** RALA

Senior Executive Officers
Chairman   Evelyn de Rothschild
Chief Executive Officer   R J Lee

Nomura Australia Limited   Subsidiary Company

Level 32, Colonial Centre, 52 Martin Place, Sydney, New South Wales 2000
Tel: (2) 9321 3500 **Fax:** (2) 9321 3599 **Telex:** AA171219

Senior Executive Officers
Chairman   Daisuke Takeuchi
Managing Director   Naoki Matsuzumi
Deputy Managing Director   Yasuhiro Takama
Director   Nobuyori Yamashita

Ord Minnett   Head Office

Level 25, 225 George Street, Grosvenor Place, Sydney, New South Wales 2000
GPO Box 3804, Sydney, New South Wales 2001
Tel: (2) 9220 1333; (2) 9220 1555 **Fax:** (2) 9220 1310

Senior Executive Officers
Chairman   Peter Mason
Financial Director   Peter Herington
Managing Director   Christopher Gorman

Corporate Finance / M&A Advisory
Head of Corporate Finance   Neil Johnson

AUSTRALIA (+61)   www.euromoneydirectory.com

Oversea-Chinese Banking Corporation
Full Branch Office

Level 2, 75 Castlereagh Street, Sydney, New South Wales 2000
Tel: (2) 9235 2022 **Fax:** (2) 9221 4360 **Telex:** AA 74295 **Swift:** OCBC AU 2S

Senior Executive Officers
Chief Executive Officer Sing Yik Ong *General Manager*
Treasurer Freddie Wong *Head of Treasury*

Overseas Union Bank Limited

12th Floor, Overseas Union Bank Building, 53 Martin Place, Sydney, New South Wales 2000
Tel: (2) 9233 4211 **Fax:** (2) 9233 6492 **Telex:** 75872 OUBAUS

Senior Executive Officers
Regional Head, Australia - New Zealand Peter H Mackinlay [E] petermackinlay@oub.com.au
General-Lending (DCM, SL)
Head of Corporate Banking James Teh [E] jamesteh@oub.com.au
General-Investment
Head of Investment Ronald Griffin [E] rongriffin@oub.com.au
General - Treasury
Head of Treasury Mark Cheng [E] markcheng@oub.com.au
Settlement / Clearing
Operations Iain Walker [E] iainwalker@oub.com.au
Other Departments
Chief Credit Officer Pius Lau *Head, Credit Administration* [E] piuslau@oub.com.au
Administration
Head of Administration Kacey Lim [E] kaceylim@oub.com.au

Paterson Ord Minnett Limited
Head Office

Level 23, Exchange Plaza, 2 The Esplanade, Perth, Western Australia 6000
GPO Box W2024, Perth, Western Australia 6001
Tel: (8) 9263 1111 **Fax:** (8) 9325 6452 **Telex:** AA92141 **Email:** paterson@patersonord.com.au
Website: www.patersonord.com.au

Senior Executive Officers
Executive Chairman Michael Manford [T] **9263 1257** [F] **9325 6114**
General Manager Tim Platts [T] **9263 1223** [F] **9325 6452**
Others (Senior Executives)
Institutions Peter Diamond *Executive Director* [T] **9263 1259** [F] **9421 1335**
Jay Hughes *Executive Director* [T] **9263 1270** [F] **9325 7189**
Andrew McKenzie *Executive Director* [T] **9263 1263** [F] **9421 1335**
Head of Corporate Peter Unsworth *Executive Director* [T] **9263 1211** [F] **9325 5123**
Equity Capital Markets
Head of Research Greg Chessell *Resource Analyst* [T] **9263 1244**
Andrew Clayton *Resource Analyst* [T] **9263 1202**
Greg Galton *Retail Strategy* [T] **9263 1189**
Steve Suelski *Industrial Analyst* [T] **9263 1262**
Phillip Zammit *Industrial Analyst* [T] **9263 1195**
Brian Eley *Head* [T] **9263 1248**
International Equities
Head of Sales Jay Hughes *Executive Director* [T] **9263 1270** [F] **9325 7189**
Head of Trading Peter Diamond *Executive Director* [T] **9263 1259** [F] **9421 1335**
Warrants
Head of Trading Derek Jones *Advisor* [T] **9263 1239**
Money Markets
Head of Money Markets Terri Lovett *Manager* [T] **9263 1121** [F] **9325 6452**
Risk Management
Foreign Exchange Derivatives / Risk Management
Global Head Sally Voce *Manager* [T] **9263 1144** [F] **9325 6452**
Settlement / Clearing
Head of Settlement / Clearing Jo Beveridge *Manager* [T] **9263 1212** [F] **9325 1086**
Operations Tim Platts *General Manager* [T] **9263 1223** [F] **9325 6452**

www.euromoneydirectory.com   **AUSTRALIA (+61)**

Asset Management
Head
Portfolio Management

Aaron Constantine *Executive Director* T 9263 1267 F 9325 6114
Cindy Eliassen *Manager* T 9263 1177 F 9325 6452

Other (Asset Management)

Melanie Brown *Manager* T 9263 1206 F 9325 6452

Other Departments
Private Banking

Murray McGill *Executive Director* T 9263 1235 F 9325 6452

Administration
Head of Administration

Joan Warren *Manager* T 9263 1203 F 9325 6452

Potter Warburg Securities Pty Limited

Level 8, 530 Collins Street, Melbourne, Victoria 3000
Tel: (3) 9242 6100 **Fax:** (3) 9242 6284

Senior Executive Officers
Others (Senior Executives)
Private Client Services

Marcel Kreis *Managing Director*
Rene Mottas *Head*

Primary Industry Bank of Australia Limited   Head Office

Level 7, 115 Pitt Street, Sydney, New South Wales 2000
Tel: (2) 9234 4200 **Fax:** (2) 9221 6218; (2) 9233 1436 **Telex:** AA123495 PIBA **Reuters:** PIBS

Senior Executive Officers
Chairman
Deputy Chairman
Financial Director
Chief Operating Officer
Managing Director

Henri Gentis
Cornelis Broekhuyse
Tony Li *Chief Manager, Financial Control*
David Owen *GM, Group Operations*
Beverley Walters

Others (Senior Executives)
Information Technology
Structured Finance

John Pascoe *GM, Information Technology*
Andrew Davison *General Manager*

General-Lending (DCM, SL)
Head of Corporate Banking

Ab Gillhaus *General Manager, Corporate Banking*

General - Treasury
Head of Treasury

Andrew Quoyle *Head of Treasury*

Relationship Manager
Residential
New Zealand
Rural

Brian Rowe *General Manager*
Jaap Kelp *General Manager*
Steve Morgan *General Manager*

Debt Capital Markets / Fixed Income
Department: Capital Markets Eurobonds

Bonds - General
New Issue Syndication Fixed Rate / Straights
FRNs / VRNs / FRAs
Settlements

Andrew Quoyle *Head of Treasury*
John Rollings *Chief Dealer, IR Risk Management*
Sjaak Verschoor *Senior Manager, Operations* T 9234 4233

Private Placements
Head of Origination

Bonnie Fitzgibbon *Senior Manager, Treasury Corporate Sales*

Syndicated Lending
Head of Credit Committee

Philip Hislop *General Manager, Credit*

Other (Trade Finance)
Structured Finance

Andrew Davison *General Manager*

Money Markets

Eurocommercial Paper
Head of Origination

John Rollings *Chief Dealer, IR Risk Management*

Other (Wholesale Deposits)
Euronotes, CDs - Origination

John Rollings *Chief Dealer, IR Risk Management*

Risk Management

Other Currency Swap / FX Options Personnel
Interest & Currency Swaps

John Rollings *Chief Dealer, IR Risk Management*

Settlement / Clearing
Country Head

Sjaak Verschoor *Senior Manager, Operations* T 9234 4233

Euromoney Directory 1999   **59**

AUSTRALIA (+61) www.euromoneydirectory.com

Primary Industry Bank of Australia Limited (cont)
Administration
Technology & Systems
    John Pascoe *GM, Information Technology*
Legal / In-House Counsel
    Gregory Kelly *Group Secretary & Chief Manager, Legal*
Public Relations
    Anne Lenehan *Manager*

Queensland Treasury Corporation
Head Office

Level 14, Queensland Minerals & Energy Centre, 61 Mary Street, Brisbane, Queensland 4000
Tel: (7) 3842 4600; (7) 3842 4771 Fax: (7) 3221 4122; (7) 3221 2410 Reuters: QTC 1 Telerate: 22741
Bloomberg: QTC "go"
Website: www.qtc.qld.gov.au

Senior Executive Officers
Chairman   Leo Hielscher ☎ **384 24620**
Chief Executive Officer   Stephen Rochester ☎ **384 24610**
Debt Capital Markets / Fixed Income
Global Head   Neville Ide *Director, Financial Markets* ☎ **384 24700**

Rabo Australia Limited
Subsidiary Company

Level 10, Challis House, 4 Martin Place, Sydney, New South Wales 2000
Tel: (2) 9223 9999 Fax: (2) 9231 0007 Telex: AA22619 Swift: RABO AU 2S

Senior Executive Officers
Chairman   Henri Gentis
Chief Executive Officer   Cornelis Broekhuyse ☎ **9234 4200**
Financial Director   Tony Li *Chief Manager, Financial Control* ☎ **9234 4200**
Chief Operating Officer   David Owen *GM, Group Operations* ☎ **9234 4200**
Managing Director   Beverley Walters ☎ **9234 4200**

Others (Senior Executives)
Structured Finance   Andrew Davison *General Manager*
Information Technology   John Pascoe *GM, Information Technology* ☎ **9234 4200**

General-Lending (DCM, SL)
Head of Corporate Banking   Ab Gillhaus *General Manager, Corporate Banking*

General - Treasury
Head of Treasury   Andrew Quoyle *Head of Treasury* ☎ **9234 4200**

Relationship Manager
Residential   Brian Rowe *General Manager*
New Zealand   Jaap Klep *General Manager*
Rural   Steve Morgan *General Manager*

Debt Capital Markets / Fixed Income
Department: Capital Markets Eurobonds

Bonds - General
FRNs / VRNs / FRAs   John Rollings *Chief Dealer, IR Risk Management* ☎ **9234 4200**
New Issue Syndication Fixed Rate / Straights   Andrew Quoyle *Head of Treasury* ☎ **9234 4200**
Settlements   Sjaak Verschoor *Senior Manager, Operations* ☎ **9234 4233**

Private Placements
Head of Origination   Bonnie Fitzgibbon *Snr Manager, Treasury Corporate Sales* ☎ **9234 4200**

Syndicated Lending
Head of Credit Committee   Philip Hislop *General Manager, Credit*

Other (Trade Finance)
Structured Finance   Andrew Davison *General Manager*

Money Markets
Eurocommercial Paper
Head of Origination   Ian Hastings *Interest Rates* ☎ **9234 4200**
     John Rollings *Chief Dealer, IR Risk Management* ☎ **9234 4200**

Other (Wholesale Deposits)
Euronotes, CDs - Origination   Ian Hastings *Interest Rates* ☎ **9234 4200**
     John Rollings *Chief Dealer, IR Risk Management* ☎ **9234 4200**

www.euromoneydirectory.com   AUSTRALIA (+61)

Risk Management
Other Currency Swap / FX Options Personnel
Interest & Currency Swaps   John Rollings *Chief Dealer, IR Risk Management* ☎ **9234 4200**
Settlement / Clearing
Country Head   Sjaak Verschoor *Senior Manager, Operations* ☎ **9234 4233**
Administration
Technology & Systems
                                     John Pascoe *GM, Information Technology* ☎ **9234 4200**
Legal / In-House Counsel
                                     Gregory Kelly *Group Secretary & Chief Manager, Legal* ☎ **9234 4200**
Public Relations
                                     Anne Leneham *Manager* ☎ **9234 4200**

Republic Mase Australia Limited   Subsidiary Company

Level 6, AMP Centre, 50 Bridge Street, Sydney, New South Wales 2000
Tel: (2) 9233 8566 **Fax:** (2) 9235 0950 **Telex:** AA73965 **Reuters:** MASE (Monitor)
Reuters: MASA (Dealing)
Website: www.rnb.com

Senior Executive Officers
Treasurer   Mark McGowen *Treasurer*
Managing Director   Daniel Mahni
Foreign Exchange
Tel: 9233 3944 **Fax:** 9233 8479
Corporate Sales   Blake Jensen
Head of Trading   Matt Harper
Other Departments
Commodities / Bullion   Eric Doutrebrand ☎ **9233 3944**
                                     Nick Socratous ☎ **9233 3944**

Rothschild Australia Asset Management Limited   Head Office

Level 15, 1 O'Connell Street, Sydney, New South Wales 2000
PO Box R253, Sydney, New South Wales 2000
Tel: (2) 9323 2000 **Fax:** (2) 9323 2323 **Telex:** AA121295

Senior Executive Officers
Chairman   Gordon Scott
Financial Director   Peter Loosmore *Financial Controller*
Managing Director   Peter Martin
Company Secretary   Michael Pickering

Others (Senior Executives)
Director of Investment Management Jonathan Pain
Director of Business Services   John Tuxworth
Director of Institutional Buisness Carol Austin
Director of Legal & Compliance   Daryl Hawkey

Salomon Smith Barney Australia Securities Pty Limited

Full Branch Office

Level 16, Grosvenor Place, 225 George Street, Sydney, New South Wales 2000
PO Box N298, Grosvenor Place, Sydney, New South Wales 1220
Tel: (2) 9321 4000 **Fax:** (2) 9251 5468 **Bloomberg:** SSBR
Corporate Dealers Tel: 576 2403; **Fax:** 576 2403
Website: www.ssmb.com.au

Senior Executive Officers
Chief Executive Officer   Peter St George ☎ **9321 4000** 📠 **9321 4072**
MD, Head of Australia / NZ Equities Rob Thomas ☎ **9321 4054** 📠 **9321 4346**
MD, Deputy Head of Australia / NZ Equities Malcolm Sinclair ☎ **9321 4321**
Director of Compliance & Company Secretary Victoria Weekes ☎ **9321 4004** 📠 **9251 2997**

General-Investment
Head of Investment   Trevor Rowe *Chairman, Investment Banking* ☎ **9321 4000** 📠 **9321 4050**

Euromoney Directory 1999   61

AUSTRALIA (+61)   www.euromoneydirectory.com

Salomon Smith Barney Australia Securities Pty Limited (cont)

Debt Capital Markets / Fixed Income
Department: Fixed Income Division

Head of Fixed Income — Bryan Davies *Managing Director & Head of Fixed Income* [T] **9321 4356** [F] **9241 5231**

Head of Fixed Income Sales; Head of Fixed Income Trading — Jeff Jerbett-Smith *Head of Sales & Trading* [T] **9321 4582** [F] **9247 1096**

Government Bonds
Head of Sales — Vincent LoBlanco [T] **9321 4938** [F] **9251 2198**
Head of Trading — Andrew Cameron [T] **9321 4562** [F] **9251 2198**

Equity Capital Markets
Department: Institutional Sales
Tel: 9321 4000 **Fax:** 9247 1126 **Telex:** SSBARN AA27455

Head of Equity Capital Markets — Richard Moore [T] **9321 4892** [F] **9321 4454**
Mark Bartels [T] **9268 9132** [F] **9268 9118**

Domestic Equities
Head of Sales — Phil Schofield *Director, Head of Sales (Sydney)* [T] **9231 4000** [F] **9247 1126**
Peter Halstead *Director, Head of Sales (Melbourne)* [T] **(3) 9268 9157** [F] **(3) 9268 9118**

Head of Trading — Luke Randell *Director, Head of Derivative Sales & Trading* [T] **9321 4000** [F] **9251 5468**

International Equities
Head of Sales — Tim Wilkinson *Director, Head of International Equities* [T] **9321 4434** [F] **9252 2081**

Equity Research
Head of Equity Research — Mark Foulton *Managing Director & Head of Research* [T] **9321 4327**

Convertibles / Equity-Linked
Head of Sales; Head of Trading — Luke Randell *Director, Head of Derivative Sales & Trading* [T] **9321 4000** [F] **9251 5468**

Risk Management
OTC Equity Derivatives
Sales; Trading — Luke Randell *Director, Head of Derivative Sales & Trading* [T] **9321 4000** [F] **9251 5468**

The Sanwa Bank Limited — Representative Office

Level 30, AMP Centre, 50 Bridge Street, Sydney, New South Wales
Tel: (2) 9364 6565 **Fax:** (2) 9364 6570 **Telex:** 122277

Senior Executive Officers
Representative — Hiroyuki Ogawa

Schroders Australia Limited — Subsidiary Company

Level 31, Grosvenor Place, 225 George Street, Sydney, New South Wales 2000
Tel: (2) 9258 9500 **Fax:** (2) 9251 5353 **Swift:** SCHR AU 2S **Reuters:** SCHA
Website: www.schroders.com

Senior Executive Officers
Chief Executive Officer — Kerry Smith
Financial Director — Rayna Watson *Group Financial Controller*

Others (Senior Executives)
Andrew Peden *Head of Financial Markets*

General-Investment
Head of Investment — Michael Gordon *Joint Head, Investment Management*
Stephen Nevitt *Joint Head, Investment Management*

Syndicated Lending
Property — David Allott *Joint Head, Property*
John Kelleher *Joint Head, Property*

Corporate Finance / M&A Advisory
Country Head — David Lowes *Head, Corporate Finance*

Administration
Technology & Systems — Scott Ashhurst *Head, Information Technology*

www.euromoneydirectory.com AUSTRALIA (+61)

Other (Administration)
Librarian Anne Tattershall
Human Resources Patricia Pithers *Head, Human Resources*

SG Hambros Australia Limited — Subsidiary Company

Hambros House, 167 Macquarie Street, Sydney, New South Wales 2000
Tel: (2) 9373 0300 **Fax:** (2) 9233 4302 **Telex:** AA 2431 HAMBROA **Email:** hcfsyd@hambros.com.au **Reuters:** HAMA

Senior Executive Officers
Chief Executive Officer Richard Sommerville *Managing Director*
Company Secretary Sean Rahilly

Debt Capital Markets / Fixed Income

Fixed-Income Repo
Head of Repo Rod Ireland *Director, Fixed Interest*

Corporate Finance / M&A Advisory
Global Head Richard Sommerville *Managing Director*

Other (Corporate Finance)
Ian Cameron-Smith *Director, Corporate Finance*
Colin Richardson *Director, Corporate Finance*
David Williams *Director, Corporate Finance*

Société Générale Australia Limited — Subsidiary Company

Alternative trading name: SG Australia
400 George Street, Sydney, New South Wales 2000
Tel: (2) 9350 7400 **Fax:** (2) 9235 3941 **Telex:** AA71982 **Email:** sglib@zip.com **Reuters:** SGAA
Website: www.socgen.com

Senior Executive Officers
Managing Director Michael Macagno
Deputy Managing Director Edouard-Malo Henry
Chief Operating Officer Andre Gourret *Director of Administration*
Treasurer John Harvey *Group Treasurer* ☎ **9350 7577**
Company Secretary & Compliance Officer Sean Rahilly

Debt Capital Markets / Fixed Income
Tel: 9233 1244 **Fax:** 9223 3396
Head of Fixed Income; Head of Fixed Income Trading Philip Coates *Head of Credit Trading* ☎ **9233 1244**

Government Bonds
Head of Trading Andrew Wardle *Head of Derivatives Trading*

Eurobonds
Head of Trading Philip Coates *Head of Credit Trading* ☎ **9233 1244**

Emerging Market Bonds
Head of Trading Philip Coates *Head of Credit Trading* ☎ **9233 1244**

Libor-Based / Floating-Rate Products
FRN Trading; Asset Swaps Philip Coates *Head of Credit Trading* ☎ **9233 1244**

Fixed-Income Repo
Head of Repo; Matched Book Manager Anthony Bell *Chief Dealer, Money Markets* ☎ **9233 4422**
Sales Jonathan Cattana *Senior Manager, Sales & Distribution MM* ☎ **9233 4422**

Syndicated Lending
Department: Corporate Finance
Tel: 9350 7400
Head of Origination Peter Donkin *Director, Corporate Finance* ☎ **9350 7474**
Head of Syndication Michael Lang *Director, Corporate Finance* ☎ **9350 7427**
Head of Credit Committee Peter Edward *Director of Credit* ☎ **9350 9365**

Loan-Related Activities
Trade Finance John Wyndham *Associate Director, Trade Finance* ☎ **9350 7462**
Project Finance Ian Mitchell *Director, Project Finance* ☎ **9350 7423**
Structured Trade Finance Greg Medcraft *Director, Structured Finance* ☎ **9350 7568**
Leasing & Asset Finance Barry Clarke *Director, Asset-Based Finance* ☎ **9350 7420**

Money Markets
Tel: 9233 4422 **Fax:** 9223 3396
Country Head Stuart Hudson *Associate Director, Head of Money Markets*

Domestic Commercial Paper
Head of Origination Stuart Hudson *Associate Director, Head of Money Markets*
Head of Sales Jonathan Cattana *Senior Manager, Sales & Distribution MM* ☎ **9233 4422**

Euromoney Directory 1999 63

AUSTRALIA (+61)　　　　　　www.euromoneydirectory.com

Société Générale Australia Limited (cont)
Domestic Commercial Paper (cont)
Head of Trading　　　　　　Anthony Bell *Chief Dealer, Money Markets* ☎ 9233 4422
Eurocommercial Paper
Head of Origination; Head of Sales　　　　Stuart Hudson *Associate Director, Head of Money Markets*
Head of Trading　　　　　　Daniel Cortis *Chief Dealer, Money Markets*
Wholesale Deposits
Marketing　　　　　　Stuart Hudson *Associate Director, Head of Money Markets*
Head of Sales　　　　　　Jonathan Cattana *Senior Manager, Sales & Distribution MM* ☎ 9233 4422
Foreign Exchange
Tel: 9232 7200 **Fax:** 9223 3296
Country Head　　　　　　John Harvey *Group Treasurer* ☎ 9350 7577
Head of Institutional Sales; Corporate Sales　　　Keith Faassen *Head, Treasury Client Services* ☎ 9223 1299
Head of Trading　　　　　　Michael O'Rourke *Head of Forex*
FX Traders / Sales People
　　　　　　　　Andrew Pether *Junior Dealer, Forex*
All Currencies　　　　　　Mark Austin *Senior Dealer, Forex*
　　　　　　　　Dean Rose *Chief Dealer, FX*
Risk Management
Country Head　　　　　　Jeran-Claude Gracia *Director, Operations & Administration* ☎ 9350 7559
Fixed Income Derivatives / Risk Management
Trading　　　　　　Andrew Wardle *Head of Derivatives Trading*
IR Swaps Sales / Marketing　　　Kevin Francis *Chief Manager Marketing, CM* ☎ 9233 1244
IR Swaps Trading　　　　　　Philip Coates *Head of Credit Trading* ☎ 9233 1244
IR Options Sales / Marketing　　　Maroussia L'Huillier *Senior Manager Marketing, CM* ☎ 9233 1244
IR Options Trading　　　　　　Robert Reilly *Dealer, Capital Markets* ☎ 9233 1244
Foreign Exchange Derivatives / Risk Management
Cross-Currency Swaps, Sales / Marketing　　　Kevin Francis *Chief Manager Marketing, CM* ☎ 9233 1244
Cross-Currency Swaps, Trading　　　Andrew Wardle *Head of Derivatives Trading*
Other Currency Swap / FX Options Personnel
　　　　　　　　Robert Reilly *Dealer, Capital Markets* ☎ 9233 1244
　　　　　　　　Philip Coates *Head of Credit Trading* ☎ 9233 1244
OTC Commodity Derivatives
Sales　　　　　　Andrew Dixon *Marketing Manager, Commodity Derivatives* ☎ 9232 3811
Trading　　　　　　Christopher Renaud *Manager, Commodity Derivatives* ☎ 9232 3811
OTC Credit Derivatives
Head　　　　　　Philip Coates *Head of Credit Trading* ☎ 9233 1244
Head of Sales; Head of Trading　　　Gregory Piercy *Associate Director, Capital Markets*
Settlement / Clearing
Country Head; Equity Settlement; Fixed-Income　　Elizabeth Brown *Senior Manager, Settlements* ☎ 9350 7547
Settlement; Derivatives Settlement; Foreign
Exchange Settlement
Other Departments
Commodities / Bullion　　　　Christopher Renaud *Manager, Commodity Derivatives* ☎ 9232 3811
Administration
Technology & Systems
　　　　　　　　Desiree Lim *Associate Director, Information Services* ☎ 9350 9555
Legal / In-House Counsel
　　　　　　　　Peter Lawrence *Company Secretary, Associate Director, Legal*
　　　　　　　　☎ 9350 9430

St George Bank Limited　　　　　　　　　　　　Head Office

4-16 Montgomery Street, Kogarah, Sydney, New South Wales 2217
Tel: (2) 9952 1111 **Fax:** (2) 9952 1060 **Reuters:** STGEORGE
Website: www.stgeorge.com.au

Senior Executive Officers
Chairman　　　　　　Frank Conroy
Chief Executive Officer　　　Edward O'Neal
Financial Director　　　　Steve McKerihan *Chief Financial Officer*
Treasurer　　　　　　Gregory Bartlett *Chief GM, Group Treasury & Capital Mkts* ☎ 9320 5555
Company Secretary　　　Paul Gibbeson
Others (Senior Executives)
Integration　　　　　　Chris Gillies *General Manager* ☎ 130 036 2555
　　　　　　　　Mike Daly *Head* ☎ 130 036 2555

64　Euromoney Directory 1999

www.euromoneydirectory.com AUSTRALIA (+61)

Others (Senior Executives) (cont)
Commercial Banking
Retail Banking
Bank SA
Sealcorp

Kerry Gilbert *Chief General Manager* ☏ **130 036 2555**
Keith Ward *Head*
Lou Morris *Managing Director* ☏ **+61 (8) 8210 4411**
Irene Lee *Chief Executive Officer* ☏ **9320 0200**

General-Lending (DCM, SL)
Head of Corporate Banking

Kerry Gilbert *Chief GM, Commercial Banking* ☏ **130 036 2555**
Graham Broome *General Manager, Group Credit* ☏ **130 036 2555**

Relationship Manager
BankSA

Terence Jay *Managing Director* ☏ **+61 (8) 8210 4411**

Debt Capital Markets / Fixed Income
Level 11, 55 Market Street, Sydney, New South Wales 2000
Tel: +61 (2) 9320 5555 **Fax:** +61 (2) 9320 5586
Global Head

Jeff Sheehan *Chief Manager, Capital Markets* ☏ **9320 5510**
✉ **sheehan_j@stgeorge.com.au**

Country Head

Narindar Bhavnani *Executive Manager, Capital Markets* ☏ **9320 5546**
✉ **bhavnani_n@stgeorge.com.au**

Domestic Government Bonds
Head of Sales
Head of Trading

Ian Hamilton *Senior Manager* ☏ **9267 4214**
Paul Wilkinson *Senior Manager, Fixed Interest* ☏ **9261 3355**

Eurobonds
Head of Origination

Jeff Sheehan *Chief Manager, Capital Markets* ☏ **9320 5510**
✉ **sheehan_j@stgeorge.com.au**

Libor-Based / Floating-Rate Products
FRN Origination

Jeff Sheehan *Chief Manager, Capital Markets* ☏ **9320 5510**
✉ **sheehan_j@stgeorge.com.au**

Medium-Term Notes
Head of Origination

Jeff Sheehan *Chief Manager, Capital Markets* ☏ **9320 5510**
✉ **sheehan_j@stgeorge.com.au**

Private Placements
Head of Origination

Jeff Sheehan *Chief Manager, Capital Markets* ☏ **9320 5510**
✉ **sheehan_j@stgeorge.com.au**

Asset-Backed Securities / Securitization
Global Head

Peter Gow *Chief Manager, Structured Investments* ☏ **9320 5503**

Mortgage-Backed Securities
Global Head
Regional Head

Peter Gow *Chief Manager, Structured Investments* ☏ **9320 5503**
Roger Desmarchelier *Executive Manager, Securitization* ☏ **9320 5605**

Fixed-Income Repo
Head of Repo

Warwick Overton *Dealer* ☏ **9320 5615**

Syndicated Lending
Loan-Related Activities
Trade Finance
Project Finance; Leasing & Asset Finance

Ian Saggus *National Manager, Trade Operations* ☏ **9236 3660**
Peter Gow *Chief Manager, Structured Investments* ☏ **9320 5503**

Money Markets
Level 11, 55 Market Street, Sydney, New South Wales
Tel: +61 (2) 9320 5555 **Fax:** +61 (2) 9320 5588
Global Head
Country Head

Gregory Kenny *Chief Manager, Financial Markets* ☏ **9320 5507**
Peter Fitzgerald *Head of Money Markets* ☏ **9267 4214**

Domestic Commercial Paper
Head of Origination

Tracey Logan *Senior Manager, Distribution* ☏ **9261 3355**

Eurocommercial Paper
Head of Origination

Tracey Logan *Senior Manager, Distribution* ☏ **9261 3355**

Wholesale Deposits
Marketing

Tony Kitchen *Manager, Banking Services* ☏ **9320 5594**

Foreign Exchange
Level 11, 55 Market Street, Sydney, New South Wales
Tel: +61 (2) 9320 5555 **Fax:** +61 (2) 9320 5588
Country Head
Corporate Sales
Head of Trading

Craig Busch *Head of Forex* ☏ **9261 3484**
Terry Carr *Senior Manager, FX Sales* ☏ **9267 9655**
Stuart Moore *Manager, FX Trading* ☏ **9261 3484**

Risk Management
Level 11, 55 Market Street, Sydney, New South Wales
Tel: +61 (2) 9320 5555 **Fax:** +61 (2) 9320 5588
Fixed Income Derivatives / Risk Management
Country Head

Warwick McCarthy *Senior Manager, Swaps* ☏ **9267 4214**

AUSTRALIA (+61) www.euromoneydirectory.com

St George Bank Limited (cont)
Settlement / Clearing
Level 12, 55 Market Street, Sydney, New South Wales
Tel: +61 (2) 9320 5555 Fax: +61 (2) 9320 5589

Regional Head — Shirley Wilson *Chief Manager, Treasury Operations & Accounting* ☏ 9320 5511
Country Head — Susan Bennett *Senior Manager, Derivatives & MM Operations* ☏ 9320 5542

Asset Management
Department: Advance Asset Management Limited
Level 10, 182 George Street, Sydney, New South Wales 2000
Tel: +61 9236 2000 Fax: +61 9231 1673

Head — Russell Hooper *Managing Director*
Investment Funds — Malcolm Robertson *Head of Investments*

Other (Asset Management)
External Sales — James Banfield *Head*
Head — Russell Hooper *Managing Director* ☏ 9236 2000

Other Departments
Chief Credit Officer — Graham Broome *General Manager, Group Credit* ☏ 130 036 2555
Correspondent Banking — Shirley Wilson *Chief Manager, Treasury Operations & Accounting* ☏ 9320 5511

Administration
Technology & Systems
Treasury Technology — Peter Downs *Manager* ☏ 9320 5523
Legal / In-House Counsel
— Tim Norling *General Counsel* ☏ 130 036 2555

Public Relations
Corporate Relations — Adam Cooke *Manager* ☏ 9952 1249
Other (Administration)
Human Resources — Anne Ellison *Chief General Manager*

Standard Chartered Bank Australia Limited   Subsidiary Company
11th Floor, George Street, Sydney, New South Wales 2000
Tel: (2) 9232 6599 Fax: (2) 9232 9345; (2) 9232 9304 Telex: AA122363 SCBAUS Swift: SCBL AU 2S Reuters: SCBA

Senior Executive Officers
Chairman — Bruce Macklin
Chief Executive Officer — David Manson ☏ 9232 9306
Financial Director — Nicholas Wu *Country Head, Finance* ☏ 9232 9369
Chief Operating Officer — Peter Cain *Head of Operations* ☏ 9224 8630
Treasurer — Guy Beale ☏ 9224 8646 F: 9224 8666
Company Secretary — Varuni De Silva ☏ 9232 9385

Others (Senior Executives)
Head of Treasury Operations — Matthew Yeung ☏ 9224 8623

General-Lending (DCM, SL)
Head of Corporate Banking — Michael Dowling *Corporate Banking - Sydney* ☏ 9224 8598
John Love *Corporate Banking - Melbourne* ☏ 9654 3177

Money Markets
Head of Money Markets — Christopher Nielson *Senior Dealer* ☏ 9252 2255 F: 9224 8666

Foreign Exchange
Corporate Sales — Steve Hull *Senior Manager, Treasury* ☏ 9252 2244
Head of Trading — Michael Adland *Senior Manager, FX Trading* ☏ 9252 2366
FX Traders / Sales People
— Chris Tyson *Senior Dealer, Spot* ☏ 9252 2366
Donna Degli-Innocenti *Senior Dealer, Corporate* ☏ 9252 2244
James Asher *Int'l Private Investors* ☏ 9252 2366

Settlement / Clearing
Back-Office — Matthew Yeung *Head of Treasury Operations* ☏ 9224 8623 F: 9290 1418
Other Departments
Correspondent Banking — John Plumridge *Country Executive, Institutional Banking* ☏ 9224 8529
Administration
Head of Administration — Peter Cain *Head of Operations* ☏ 9224 8630
Technology & Systems
— Phil Smith *Local Service Manager, GTS* ☏ 9232 9379

66 Euromoney Directory 1999

www.euromoneydirectory.com AUSTRALIA (+61)

Compliance
Varuni De Silva *Company Secretary* ☏ **9232 9385**

State Street Bank & Trust Company
Full Branch Office
Level 64, MLC Centre, 19-29 Martin Place, Sydney, New South Wales 2090
Tel: (2) 9323 6500 **Fax:** (2) 9323 6540
Website: www.statestreet.com

Debt Capital Markets / Fixed Income
Department: Global Securiteis Lending
Government Bonds
Head of Sales — Christopher Taylor ☏ **9323 6510**
Head of Trading — Jeffrey Brewer ☏ **9323 6582**
Fixed-Income Repo
Head of Repo; Trading — Jeffrey Brewer ☏ **9323 6582**
Other — Alev Yard ☏ **9323 6586**

Equity Capital Markets
Department: Global Securities Lending
Equity Repo / Securities Lending
Head — Chris Taylor ☏ **9323 6510**
Head of Trading — Jeffrey Brewer ☏ **9323 6582**

Foreign Exchange
Tel: 9231 1300 **Fax:** 9323 6541
Head of Foreign Exchange — Ian Martin *Treasury Manager* ☏ **9323 6580**
Head of Institutional Sales — Ian Battye *Vice President* ☏ **9323 6550**
Michele Hardeman *Assistant Vice President* ☏ **9323 6550**

FX Traders / Sales People
Trading — Mark Payne *Assistant Vice President* ☏ **9231 1300**
Sales — Michele Hardeman *Assistant Vice President* ☏ **9323 6550**

Global Custody
Tel: 9323 6166 **Fax:** 9323 6666
Regional Head — John M Brown

Sumitomo International Finance Australia Limited
Subsidiary Company
Level 45, Melbourne Central, 360 Elizabeth Street, Melbourne, Victoria 3000
Tel: (3) 9639 2777 **Fax:** (3) 9689 2547 **Telex:** AA34638

Senior Executive Officers
Senior Manager & Head — Ross Land

Sumitomo International Finance Australia Limited
Subsidiary Company
Level 40, The Chifley Tower, 2 Chifley Square, Sydney, New South Wales 2000
Tel: (2) 9376 1800 **Fax:** (2) 9376 1863 **Telex:** AA24091 **Email:** sifasy@ozmail.com.au **Reuters:** SIFA
Foreign Exchange Tel: (2) 9231 0522; **Money Market Tel:** (2) 9231 0322

Senior Executive Officers
Chairman — Hugh Dixson
Director — Shunichi Okuyama
Managing Director — Yasuo Mitzobuchi
Senior Manager, Planning & Company Secretary — Takaaki Otani

General-Lending (DCM, SL)
Head of Corporate Banking — Takaaki Otani *Senior Manager, Head of Credit*
General - Treasury
Head of Treasury — Peter Mordaunt *Senior Manager, Head of Tresury*
Syndicated Lending
Loan-Related Activities
Project Finance — Tony Morgan *Senior Manager & Head*
Corporate Finance / M&A Advisory
Global Head — Ian Lewis *Senior Manager, Head, Corporate Finance*

Euromoney Directory 1999 **67**

AUSTRALIA (+61)

TFS Australia PTY Limited

Level 19, 25 Bligh Street, Sydney, New South Wales 2000
Tel: (2) 9233 6611 Fax: (2) 9233 1866

Senior Executive Officers
Director — Dennis Trappit

Others (Senior Executives)
Trevor Conway *Senior Broker*

Tokai Australia Finance Corporation Limited — Subsidiary Company

Level 19, Colonial. Centre, 52 Martin Place, Sydney, New South Wales 2000
Tel: (2) 9231 6599 Fax: (2) 9221 1775 Telex: 176327 TAFCOL
Dealing Tel: (2) 9221 1277; Fax: (2) 9223 5465; Telex: 176328 TAFCOL

Senior Executive Officers
Chairman — Satoru Nishigaki
Managing Director — Yukio Sakai
Director — Tomio Tanaka
Director — Kyosuke Watanabe
Deputy Managing Director — Hiroto Aoyama

Others (Senior Executives)
Australian & International Business
Florian Wieser *Chief Manager*
Mikihisa Imoto *Corporate Relations Executive*
Robert Noylan *Manager*

General-Lending (DCM, SL)
Head of Corporate Banking — Tsutomu Minato *Chief Manager, Japanese Business*

General - Treasury
Head of Treasury — Yasuhi Usuda *Chief Manager*

Money Markets
Department: Treasury
Country Head — Yasuhi Usuda *Chief Manager*
Joanne Rains *Manager, Money Market*

Administration
Department: Administration & Operations
Head of Administration — Peter Peate *General Manager & Secretary*

Accounts / Audit
Cecilia Cheung *Chief Accountant*

Other (Administration)
Operations — Simon Cormack *Manager*

The Tokai Bank Limited — Representative Office

Level 52 Rialto, 525 Collins Street, Melbourne, Victoria 3000
Tel: (3) 9629 4540 Fax: (3) 9629 3509 Telex: 39744 TOKMEL

Senior Executive Officers
Chief Representative — Toyoharu Akiyama

General-Lending (DCM, SL)
Head of Corporate Banking — Tat Lim Choo *Senior Manager*

Toronto-Dominion Australia Limited — Head Office

Level 36, 385 Bourke Street, Melbourne, Victoria 3000
Tel: (3) 9602 1344 Fax: (3) 9602 3155 Telex: 32316 Swift: TDOM AU 3M

Senior Executive Officers
Managing Director — Wade Jacobson
Financial Director — Peter Bell *Associate Director, Finance & Administration*
Treasurer — Geoff Oberg *Director & Vice President* ☎ 9619 8888

Debt Capital Markets / Fixed Income
Level 24, 9 Castlereagh Street, Sydney, New South Wales 2000
Tel: +61 (2) 9619 8888 Fax: +61 (2) 9619 8800

Domestic Government Bonds
Head of Sales — Chris Pashley *Director & Vice President* ☎ 9619 8866

www.euromoneydirectory.com AUSTRALIA (+61)

Eurobonds
Head of Origination Geoff Oberg *Director & Vice President* ☏ **9619 8888**
Head of Sales Chris Pashley *Director & Vice President* ☏ **9619 8866**

Syndicated Lending
Head of Syndication Geoff Luxton *Associate Director, Corporate Finance*

Loan-Related Activities
Project Finance Wade Jacobson *Managing Director*

Money Markets
Country Head John Palamara *Vice President* ☏ **(2) 9619 8844**

Domestic Commercial Paper
Head of Origination John Palamara *Vice President* ☏ **(2) 9619 8844**

Foreign Exchange
Corporate Sales Mano Paul *Vice President* ☏ **(2) 9619 8833**

FX Traders / Sales People
Spot Chris Wells *Vice President* ☏ **(2) 9619 8833**
Forwards Mark O'Brien *Vice President* ☏ **(2) 9619 8833**

Risk Management
Country Head Peter Bell *Associate Director, Finance & Administration*

Corporate Finance / M&A Advisory
Country Head Wade Jacobson *Managing Director*

Settlement / Clearing
Country Head David Shaw *Manager, Corporate & Treasury Servic*

Administration

Technology & Systems
  John Alvey *Manager, Systems*

Legal / In-House Counsel
  Paul Mulderry *General Counsel and Secretary*

Compliance
  Peter Bell *Associate Director, Finance & Administration*

Toyo Trust Australia Limited Subsidiary Company

Level 19, AMP Centre, 50 Bridge Street, Sydney, New South Wales 2000
Tel: (2) 9233 3077 **Fax:** (2) 9235 0547 **Telex:** AA72553 TYTAUS

Senior Executive Officers
Managing Director Takashi Kawaguchi

Administration
Head of Administration Andy Chow *Senior Manager*

Accounts / Audit
  Andy Chow *Senior Manager*

UBS Brinson

Level 45 Governor Phillip Tower, 1 Farrer Place, Sydney, New South Wales 2000
Tel: (2) 9324 3100 **Fax:** (2) 9324 3245

Senior Executive Officers
Chief Executive Officer John Fraser *Executive Chairman & CEO, UBS Brinson*

UOB Australia Limited Subsidiary Company

Level 9, 32 Martin Place, Sydney, New South Wales 2000
Tel: (2) 9221 1924 **Fax:** (2) 9221 1541 **Telex:** AA 73507 **Swift:** UOVB AU 2S

Senior Executive Officers
Director & General Manager Lian Khee Wang

AUSTRALIA (+61)   www.euromoneydirectory.com

Warburg Dillon Read Australia Limited

Level 8, 530 Collins Street, Melbourne, Victoria 3000
PO Box 1328L, Melbourne, Victoria 3000
Tel: (3) 9242 6100 Fax: (3) 9242 6210

Senior Executive Officers
Others (Senior Executives)
    C Standish *CEO Asia / Pacific*
    B Gurry *Chairman*

Equity Capital Markets
Head of Equity Capital Markets   B Paton

Equity Research
Head of Equity Research   J King

Warburg Dillon Read Australia Limited

Level 25, Governor Phillip Tower, 1 Farrer Place, Sydney, New South Wales 2000
GPO Box 4151, Sydney, New South Wales 2001
Tel: (2) 9324 2000 Fax: (2) 9324 2001 Telex: AA22553 Swift: SBCOAU2S

Senior Executive Officers
Chief Executive Officer   C W Dickinson *Managing Director & CEO, Australia / NZ*

Debt Capital Markets / Fixed Income
Department: Rates

Bonds - General
    J Lechte *Government and Derivative Trading*
    P Broughton *Derivative Products, Swaps & Options*
    S Mitchell *Head of Rates - Australia*
    M Langsworth *Head of Debt Capital Markets - Australia*
    T Perkins *Head of Asset Backed Finance*
    C Roden *Credit and Structured Products Trading*

Equity Capital Markets
Department: Equities
Country Head   R Aboud *Head, Equities-Australia*

Other (Domestic Equities)
    S Finemore *Head of Equities Trading & Derivatives - Australia*
Equities & Derivatives Distribution   A Normington *Head of Equity Sales - Australia*

Foreign Exchange
Country Head   J Radinoff *Head of Foreign Exchange - Australia*

FX Traders / Sales People
    C Andrews *Precious Metals Sales*

Corporate Finance / M&A Advisory
Country Head   A Pridham *Head of Corporate Finance*

Other Departments
Economic Research   Mark Rider *Chief Economist*

Administration
Department: Departments

Technology & Systems
Information Technology - Australia   S Coleman *Head*

Legal / In-House Counsel
    C Madden

Compliance
    C Madden

Corporate Communications
    M Cole

Other (Administration)
Human Resources - Australia   S Bensted
Financial Control   N Campbell
Chief Operating Officer, Asia / Pacific   I Holyman

www.euromoneydirectory.com   AUSTRALIA (+61)

JB Were & Son
Head Office   A

Alternative trading name: Were Stockbroking Limited
17th Floor, 101 Collins Street, Melbourne, Victoria 3000
PO Box 20505, Melbourne, Victoria 3000
Tel: (3) 9679 1111 Fax: (3) 9679 1330; (3) 9679 1112
Website: www.jbwere.com.au

Senior Executive Officers
Chairman   Terence Campbell

Others (Senior Executives)
Were Stockbroking   John Paterson *Managing Director* ☏ **9679 1421**
Were Capital Markets   Ross Barker *Managing Director*
    Paul Sundberg *General Manager*
Head of Research   Craig Drummond *Director*
Sydney Branch   Guy Paynter *Director*

Debt Capital Markets / Fixed Income
Department: JB Were Capital Markets
Tel: 9679 1444 Fax: 9679 1522
Head of Fixed Income   John Fittock
Head of Fixed Income Trading   Roy Keenan

Equity Capital Markets
Department: Were Stockbroking Limited
Head of Equity Capital Markets   John Paterson *Managing Director* ☏ **9679 1421**
Head of Sales   Peter Wade *Director, International Sales*
Head of Trading   Graeme Linton *Director*

Domestic Equities
Head of Sales   John Bryson *Retail Sales* ☏ **9679 1455**
Head of Research   Justin Anter ☏ **9679 1425**

Other (Domestic Equities)
Institutional Sales   Rob Evans ☏ **9679 1431**

International Equities
Head of Sales   Peter Wade *Director, International Sales*

Equity Repo / Securities Lending
Head   Rowan Fell *Manager, Equity Finance*

Risk Management
Country Head   Paul Sundbery *Chairman, Risk Committee*

Corporate Finance / M&A Advisory

Other (Corporate Finance)
Chief Executive Officer   John Paterson *Managing Director* ☏ **9679 1421**

Settlement / Clearing
Operations   Andrea Broom *Manager, Operations*

Global Custody
Department: Custody & Administration
Tel: 9679 1444 Fax: 9679 1322
Regional Head   Chris Despotelis *Manager* ☏ **9679 1283**

Other (Global Custody)
Investment Services   Barry Whitehead *Manager* ☏ **9679 1292**

Asset Management
Head   Ross Barker *Managing Director*

Other Departments
Economic Research   Craig Drummond *Head of Research*

Administration
Head of Administration   Andrea Broom *Manager, Operations*

Technology & Systems
    Peter Yarrington *Chief Investment Officer, IT* ☏ **9679 1966**

Legal / In-House Counsel
    Lisa Gay *Corporate Counsel*

Compliance
    Lisa Gay *Corporate Counsel*

AUSTRALIA (+61) www.euromoneydirectory.com

Westdeutsche Landesbank Girozentrale — Full Branch Office

Alternative trading name: WestLB
Level 29, 60 Margaret Street, Sydney, New South Wales 2000
Tel: (2) 9777 9900 **Fax:** (2) 9777 9911 **Swift:** WELA AU 2S **Email:** westlb@zeta.org.au **Reuters:** WDLA

Senior Executive Officers
SVP & General Manager — Günter Richert ☏ **9777 9910**

Syndicated Lending
Head of Origination — Anthony Boland *Vice President, Corporate Finance* ☏ **9777 9906**
Bruce MacFarlane *Vice President, Corporate Finance* ☏ **9777 9905**

Loan-Related Activities
Project Finance — Peter Mathews *Head of Structured Finance* ☏ **9777 9908**

Money Markets
Tel: 9777 9927 **Fax:** 9777 9963
Head of Money Markets — Sean Saxon *VP & Head of Treasury* ☏ **9777 9946**

Wholesale Deposits
Head of Sales — Paul Webb *Senior Dealer* ☏ **9777 9953**

Foreign Exchange
Tel: 9777 9926 **Fax:** 9777 9963
Head of Foreign Exchange — Sean Saxon *VP & Head of Treasury* ☏ **9777 9946**
Corporate Sales — John Basile *Head of FX Sales* ☏ **9777 9950**
Head of Trading — Chris Knight *Senior Dealer* ☏ **9777 9947**

FX Traders / Sales People
Precious Metals — Tony Gamson *Head of Precious Metals* ☏ **9777 9952**

Risk Management
Head of Risk Management — David Tattam *VP & Head of Operations* ☏ **9777 9913**

Corporate Finance / M&A Advisory
Tel: 9777 9922 **Fax:** 9777 9911
Country Head — Günter Richert *SVP & General Manager* ☏ **9777 9910**
Peter Clermont *SVP & General Manager* ☏ **9777 9920**

Settlement / Clearing
Tel: 9777 9923 **Fax:** 9777 8020
Head of Settlement / Clearing — Kerry Farelly *Manager, Settlements* ☏ **9777 9957**

Other Departments
Chief Credit Officer — Perry Cecilio *VP & Head of Credit* ☏ **9777 9912**

WestLB Securities Australia Limited — Subsidiary Company

Level 29, 60 Margaret Street, Sydney, New South Wales 2000
Tel: (2) 9777 9977 **Fax:** (2) 9777 9975 **Email:** westlbsal@wr.com.au **Reuters:** WESTLB

Senior Executive Officers
Chairman — Johannes Ringel

Others (Senior Executives)
Marcus von Busse *Director*

Westpac Banking Corporation — Head Office

Level 9, 255 Elizabeth Street, Sydney, New South Wales 2000
GPO Box 1, Sydney, New South Wales 2001
Tel: (2) 9226 3311 **Fax:** (2) 9220 3553 **Swift:** WPAC AU 2S **Email:** westpac@westpac.com.au
Website: www.westpac.com.au

Senior Executive Officers
Chief Executive Officer — Robert L Joss *Managing Director and CEO* ☏ **9226 3001**
Financial Director — Patrick Handley *Group Executive & CFO* ☏ **9226 3377**
Treasurer — Marten Touw *Group Treasurer* ☏ **9226 1065**
Group Executive, Human Resources — Avery Duff ☏ **9226 1837**
Group Executive, Institutional Banking Group — David Morgan ☏ **9226 3649**
Director of Strategy — Helen Nugent ☏ **9226 3020**
Group Executive & Chief Credit Officer — Robert Nimmo ☏ **9226 3026**
Group Secretary & General Counsel — Bettie McNee ☏ **9226 3584**

Others (Senior Executives)
Australian Guarantee Corporation — Richard Thomas *Managing Director* ☏ **9234 1155**

72 Euromoney Directory 1999

www.euromoneydirectory.com   AUSTRALIA (+61)

Department: Australian Banking Group
Others (Senior Executives)
　　　　　　　　　　　　　　　　　Loran Fite *Chief Information Officer* ☏ **9226 3761**
Financial Services　　　　　　　David Fite *Managing Director* ☏ **9226 2646**
New South Wales　　　　　　　Mike Hawker *Chief Executive* ☏ **9260 6566**
Challenge Bank　　　　　　　　Tony Howarth *Chief Executive* ☏ **(9) 426 2300**
Queensland　　　　　　　　　　David Liddy *Chief Executive* ☏ **(7) 3227 2300**

Department: Institutional and International Banking Group
Relationship Manager
Asia　　　　　　　　　　　　　Tony Mathers *General Manager* ☏ **+65 530 9520**
　　　　　　　　　　　　　　　　Jake Williams *General Manager* ☏ **9284 9209**
Europe　　　　　　　　　　　　Jim Tate *General Manager* ☏ **+44 (171) 621 7007**
Americas　　　　　　　　　　　Sally Herman *SVP & Country Manager* ☏ **+1 (212) 551 1801**
New Zealand　　　　　　　　　Harry Price *Chief Executive* ☏ **+64 (4) 498 1150**
Pacific Regional Banking　　　Bruce Alexander *Chief Executive* ☏ **9226 1332**
Corporate Finance & Financial Markets　　David Wills *General Manager* ☏ **9284 8600**
Property Finance　　　　　　　Garry Rothwell *General Manager* ☏ **9226 4162**
Global Transaction & Treasury Solutions　Leslie Martin *Chief Operations Officer* ☏ **9272 1702**
Credit　　　　　　　　　　　　Jim Coleman *General Manager* ☏ **9284 9158**
Finance　　　　　　　　　　　Chris Skilton *General Manager* ☏ **9277 1337**
Human Resources　　　　　　Amanda Revis *General Manager* ☏ **9216 0541**
Marketing & Knowledge Management　Mark Veyret *General Manager* ☏ **9284 8753**

Debt Capital Markets / Fixed Income
Domestic Government Bonds
Head of Sales　　　　　　　　Nicholas Fyffe *Senior Manager, Insitutional Distribution* ☏ **9284 8427**
Head of Trading　　　　　　　Damien McColough *Manager, Strategy* ☏ **9284 8427**
　　　　　　　　　　　　　　　　Anthony Robson *Chief Dealer, Fixed Interest* ☏ **9284 8430**

Asset-Backed Securities / Securitization
Head of Trading　　　　　　　Cathryn Carver *Global Head of Capital Raising* ☏ **9284 8611**

Fixed-Income Repo
Head of Repo　　　　　　　　Neil Easton *Dealer* ☏ **9284 8430**

Equity Capital Markets
Domestic Equities
Head of Origination　　　　　James Wall *Senior Manager, Product Development* ☏ **9284 9266**

Syndicated Lending
Global Head　　　　　　　　　Angela Mentis *Head, Syndications & Agency* ☏ **9284 8614**

Other (Trade Finance)
Property　　　　　　　　　　　Gary Berrell *Trader* ☏ **9284 8707**

Money Markets
Global Head　　　　　　　　　Ross Campbell *Manager, Australian Money Markets* ☏ **9284 8965**

Domestic Commercial Paper
Head of Origination　　　　　Mike Anderson *Manager* ☏ **9284 8406**

Eurocommercial Paper
Head of Origination　　　　　Iain Stowart *Head of Capital Markets (Australasia)* ☏ **+44 (171) 621 7615**

Foreign Exchange
Global Head　　　　　　　　　Phil Coffey *Head* ☏ **9284 8610**

FX Traders / Sales People
On-Shore Corporates & Institutions　Mark Whelan *Head* ☏ **+61 (3) 9608 4215**

Risk Management
Global Head　　　　　　　　　Bill Wilson *Head* ☏ **9284 8025**
Regional Head　　　　　　　　Ray Gunston *Head of Trading & Risk Operations* ☏ **+61 (3) 9608 3394**

Fixed Income Derivatives / Risk Management
Global Head　　　　　　　　　Mike D'Silva *Senior Manager, Corporate Distribution* ☏ **9284 8598**
IR Swaps Sales / Marketing　Brendan Smith *Chief Dealer, Swaps* ☏ **9284 8511**
IR Options Sales / Marketing　Gavin McLaren *Chief Dealer, IR Options* ☏ **9284 8499**

Foreign Exchange Derivatives / Risk Management
Global Head　　　　　　　　　Russel Armstrong *Head, Derivatives* ☏ **9284 8201**
Spot / Forwards Sales　　　　Peter McGrath *Chief Dealer, Spot FX* ☏ **9284 8445**
Spot / Forwards Trading　　　David Jones *Chief Dealer, Forward Trading FX* ☏ **+44 (171) 621 7680**
　　　　　　　　　　　　　　　　Graham Edie *Chief Dealer, Short-Term IR* ☏ **+64 (4) 498 1237**
　　　　　　　　　　　　　　　　Rob Colla *Chief Dealer, Forward Trading FX* ☏ **9284 8435**
Cross-Currency Swaps, Sales / Marketing　Brett Darley *Product Head, Currency Derivatives* ☏ **9284 8411**

Other Currency Swap / FX Options Personnel
Currency & Commodity Derivatives　Simon Bassett *Head of Currency & Commodity Derivatives* ☏ **9284 8411**
　　　　　　　　　　　　　　　　Trevor Nicholson *Manager, Currency & Commodity Derivatives*
　　　　　　　　　　　　　　　　☏ **9284 8411**

AUSTRALIA (+61)	www.euromoneydirectory.com

Westpac Banking Corporation (cont)

Exotic Options (Barriers, Range, Timers, Digitals, Faders etc)
Trading	Barry O'Malley Senior Dealer, Corporate FX ☎ 9284 8456
OTC Commodity Derivatives
Sales	Paul Horsten Manager, Commodity Risk ☎ 9284 8607
OTC Credit Derivatives
Global Head	Greg Mizon Head, Financing Products ☎ 9284 8397
Corporate Finance / M&A Advisory
Other (Corporate Finance)
Structured Finance	Mark Woodward Head ☎ 9284 9275
Project Advisory & Finance	Michael Kerslake Head ☎ 9284 9237
Capital Markets	David Hurford Joint Head ☎ 9284 9388
	Chris Rand Joint Head ☎ +852 2842 9986
Corporate Advisory	Adrian Palser Chief Manager ☎ 9284 9149
Victoria	Andrew Hall Chief Manager ☎ (3) 9608 3689
New Zealand	John Mandeno Chief Manager ☎ +64 (9) 367 3824
Corporate Finance - Singapore	Richard Ng Head ☎ +65 530 9524
Financial Markets - New Zealand	Stephen Moir General Manager ☎ +64 (4) 498 1534
Debt Securities, Asia	Steve Lambert Head ☎ +852 2842 9986
Japan	Harry Rosario Country Head ☎ +81 (3) 3592 0886
Settlement / Clearing
Operations	Lyn Lennard Head ☎ 9272 1510
	Jodie Way Assistant Manager, Currency Operations ☎ 9284 8561
	Michael Rosslind Manager, Derivative Sales ☎ 9284 9461
	Martin Stockley-Smith Head, Global FX Markets Delivery ☎ 9284 8514
	Craig Buckley Manager, Global Securities Operations ☎ 9284 8834
Administration
Technology & Systems
IB Technology	David Backley Head ☎ 9284 8036
Legal / In-House Counsel
FM Legal & Compliance	Justin Moses Counsel & Head ☎ 9284 8852
Public Relations
Media Relations ABG	Megan Donald Manager ☎ 9226 3443
Media Relations IIBG	Peter Vicary Manager ☎ 9284 8221
Other (Administration)
Public Affairs	Owen van der Wall Director ☎ 9226 3005

Westpac Custodian Nominees Limited

Level 8, 50 Pitt Street, Sydney, New South Wales 2000
Tel: (2) 9260 7365; (2) 9220 4166 **Telex:** AA20122 **Swift:** WPAC AU2S NOM **Email:** jhaywood@westpac.com.au
Website: www.westpac.com.au

Equity Capital Markets
Equity Repo / Securities Lending
Head	John Drinkall Manager ☎ 9260 7207 📠 9220 4116
Head of Trading	Leanne Gardner Lending Officer

## Yasuda Trust Australia Limited	Subsidiary Company

Level 38, Tower Building, Australia Square, Sydney, New South Wales 2000
Tel: (2) 9251 3344 **Fax:** (2) 9233 8359 **Telex:** AA71170 YTBC **Reuters:** YTAS

Senior Executive Officers
Chairman & Non-Executive Director	Isamu Kuwako
Managing Director	Mitsuro Ohashi
Director	Hirofumi Shikano
Director	Kenji Ishii
Company Secretary	John Lewis

General - Treasury
Head of Treasury	Kenji Ishii Director

Debt Capital Markets / Fixed Income
Bonds - General
	Hirofumi Shikano Manager

74   Euromoney Directory 1999

AUSTRIA (+43)

Money Markets

Eurocommercial Paper
Head of Sales — Kenji Ishii *Dealer*

Money Markets - General
Cash — Cameron Fisher *Dealer*

Foreign Exchange

FX Traders / Sales People — Kenji Ishii *Dealer*

Risk Management

Foreign Exchange Derivatives / Risk Management
Cross-Currency Swaps, Sales / Marketing — Kenji Ishii *Director*

Settlement / Clearing
Foreign Exchange Settlement — John Lewis *Manager, Back-Office Settlements*

Administration
Head of Administration — John Lewis *Financial Controller*

Accounts / Audit
Accounting — John Lewis *Financial Controller*

AUSTRIA
(+43)

Oesterreichische Nationalbank — Central Bank

Otto Wagner Platz 3, A-1090 Vienna
PO Box 61, A-1011 Vienna
Tel: (1) 40420 0; (1) 40420 6666 **Fax:** (1) 40420 6699 **Telex:** 114669 **Swift:** NABA AT WW **Cable:** DEVISENLEITUNG
Telex: 114778
Website: www.oenb.co.at

Senior Executive Officers
President — Klaus Liebscher **40420 9000**
Chief Executive Officer — Adolf Wala *Central Bank Policy Dept Director* **40420 6000**
Secretariat of the President — Wolfgang Ippisch **40420 9100**

Others (Senior Executives)
First Vice President — Erich Göttlicher **40420 9001**
Second Vice President — Karl Werner Rüsch **40420 9002**
General Secretariat — Peter Achleitner *Director* **40420 6001**

Relationship Manager
Economics and Financial Markets — Andreas Ittner *Director* **40420 3002**

Other Departments
Liquidity Management — Wolfgang Duchatczek *Executive Director* **40420 2000**
Peter Zöllner *Treasury Director* **40420 4001**
Josef Kratochvil *Director, Organization and Internal Services* **40420 2001**
Aurel Schubert *Statistics Director* **40420 2003**
Economic Research — Gertrude Tumpel-Gugerell *Executive Director* **40420 3000**
Helmut Pech *Director* **40420 7002**

Administration

Technology & Systems
Money, Payment Systems, and Information — Erwin Tischler *Executive Director* **40420 1000**

Legal / In-House Counsel
Legal Matters & Management of Equity Interests — Bruno Gruber **40420 6003**

Accounts / Audit
Accounting — Michael Wolf *Director* **40420 6002**

Other (Administration)
Payment Systems and Information Technology — Wolfgang Pernkopf *Director* **40420 1001**

AUSTRIA (+43) www.euromoneydirectory.com

Allgemeine Sparkasse Oberösterreich
Bankaktiengesellschaft
Head Office

Promenade 11/13, A-4020 Linz
PO Box 92, A-4041 Linz
Tel: (732) 7391 0 Fax: (732) 7391 832 Swift: ASPK AT 2L Reuters: ASKX
Website: www.ask.co.at

Senior Executive Officers
President	Ernst Ertl
Treasurer	Johann Penzenstadler ☎ **7391 2130**
Director of the Board	Michael Martinek
Director of the Board	Manfred Reitinger
Director of the Board	Markus Limberger
International Division	Alois Obermair *Senior Manager* ☎ **7391 2675**

General - Treasury
Head of Treasury	Wolfgang Sachsenhofer ☎ **7391 2691**

Debt Capital Markets / Fixed Income
Head of Debt Capital Markets	Kurt Waldmann ☎ **7391 2128**

Equity Capital Markets

Domestic Equities
Head of Sales	Johann Hennebichler *Head* ☎ **7391 2716**

Syndicated Lending
Country Head	Harald Lietz ☎ **7391 2711**

Loan-Related Activities
Trade Finance	Harald Musileck ☎ **7391 2712**
	Harald Lietz ☎ **7391 2711**

Money Markets
Head of Money Markets	Wolfgang Sachsenhofer ☎ **7391 2691**

Money Markets - General
	Frantz Praschl *Dealer* ☎ **7391 2686**

Foreign Exchange
Head of Foreign Exchange	Wolfgang Sachsenhofer ☎ **7391 2691**

FX Traders / Sales People
	Maximillian Pointner ☎ **7391 3692**

Risk Management
Head of Risk Management	Alois Obermair *Senior Manager* ☎ **7391 2675**

Settlement / Clearing
Head of Settlement / Clearing	Manfred Köck ☎ **7391 2871**

Other Departments
Correspondent Banking	Alois Obermair *Senior Manager* ☎ **7391 2675**

Anglo Irish Bank (Austria) AG

Formerly known as: Royal Trust Bank (Austria) AG

Rathausstrasse 20, A-1011 Vienna
PO Box 306, A-1011 Vienna
Tel: (1) 406 6161 Fax: (1) 405 8142 Telex: 114911 AIB A Swift: ANGO AT WW Email: anglo@via.at

Senior Executive Officers
Chairman	Terence A Carroll
Chief Executive Officer	Erich Pitak

Banco do Brasil AG

Tegetthoffstrasse 4, A-1010 Vienna
Tel: (1) 512 6663 0 Fax: (1) 512 1042 Swift: BRAS AT WW Reuters: BDBV (Dealing)

Senior Executive Officers
Chairman of the Board	Sérgio Ribas-Câmara
Member of the Board	Benno Mallmann
International Division	Boaventura Ribeiro ☎ **512 6663 24**

General - Treasury
Head of Treasury	Boaventura Ribeiro ☎ **512 6663 24**

www.euromoneydirectory.com   AUSTRIA (+43)

Settlement / Clearing
Other
Boaventura Ribeiro *Documentary Payments* ☏ **512 6663 24**
Michaela Schindelar *Documentary Payments* ☏ **512 6663 25**
Irina Bauer *Documentary Payments* ☏ **512 6663 28**
Astrid Fajt *Documentary Payments* ☏ **512 6663 26**
Maria José Barile *Documentary Payments* ☏ **512 6663 33**
Maria Kunert *Documentary Payments* ☏ **512 6663 27**
Jorge Moreno *Documentary Payments* ☏ **512 6668 16**
Dagmar Beranek *Clean Payments* ☏ **512 6663 31**
Andrea Litschauer *Clean Payments* ☏ **512 6663 42**

Other Departments
Proprietary Trading
Michaela Schindelar *Dealer* ☏ **512 6663 25**
Maria Kunert *Dealer* ☏ **512 6663 27**
Correspondent Banking
Tatjana Kordik ☏ **512 6663 13**

Bank Austria Aktiengesellschaft   Head Office
Vordere Zollamtsstrasse 13, A-1030 Vienna
PO Box 35, A-1011 Vienna
Tel: (1) 71191 0 **Fax:** (1) 71191 56155 **Telex:** 115561 BKAUA **Swift:** BKAU AT WW **Reuters:** BAUS
Website: www.bankaustria.at

Senior Executive Officers
Chairman of the Board & CEO   Gerhard Randa ☏ **71191 57000** 🖷 **71191 57800**
President of The Supervisory Board   Siegfried Sellitsch ☏ **71191 52205**
Chief Executive Officer   Gerhard Randa *Chairman of the Board & CEO* ☏ **71191 57000**
🖷 **71191 57800**
Karl Samstag *Deputy Chief Executive Officer* ☏ **71191 52418** 🖷 **71191 52934**
Financial Director   Franz Gerhard Kolarik *General Manager* ☏ **71191 59500** 🖷 **71191 59502**
Treasurer   Peter Fischer *General Manager* ☏ **71191 82001** 🖷 **71191 8205**
International Division   Franz Hörhager *General Manager* ☏ **71191 56460** 🖷 **71191 56465**
Others (Senior Executives)
Member of the Board   Friedrich Kadrnoska *Managing Director* ☏ **71191 56151** 🖷 **71191 56154**
Wolfgang Haller *Managing Director* ☏ **71191 53050** 🖷 **71191 52058**
Heinz Gehl *Managing Director* ☏ **71191 52050** 🖷 **71191 52110**
Franz Zwickl *Managing Director* ☏ **71191 53131** 🖷 **71191 53135**
Gerhard Novy *Managing Director* ☏ **71191 53131** 🖷 **71191 41004**

General-Lending (DCM, SL)
Head of Corporate Banking   Wolfgang Feuchtmüller *General Manager* ☏ **71191 56800** 🖷 **71191 56813**
Debt Capital Markets / Fixed Income
Emerging Market Bonds
Head of Emerging Markets   Franz Hörhager *General Manager* ☏ **71191 56460** 🖷 **71191 56465**
Money Markets
Tel: 71191 82700 **Fax:** 71191 82747 **Reuters:** BAUM, BAUX **Telex:** 134279
Head of Money Markets   Armin Steppan *General Manager* ☏ **71191 82799**
Eurocommercial Paper
Head of Sales   Stephen Rushton *Manager* ☏ **71191 82740**
Wholesale Deposits
Marketing   Armin Steppan *General Manager* ☏ **71191 82799**
Foreign Exchange
Head of Foreign Exchange   Josef Meyer *General Manager* ☏ **71191 82901**
FX Traders / Sales People
Ludwig Fischer *Senior Manager* ☏ **71191 82920**
Franz Gruber *Deputy General Manager* ☏ **71191 82902**
Martin Neuhold *Senior Manager* ☏ **71191 82910**

Risk Management
Head of Risk Management   Johann Strobl *General Manager* ☏ **71191 31333** 🖷 **71191 46960**
Other Currency Swap / FX Options Personnel
FX Options   Gerald Podhorsky *Deputy General Manager* ☏ **71191 82851**
Settlement / Clearing
Tel: 71191 82200 **Fax:** 71191 82210
Head of Settlement / Clearing   Gerhard Dinhopl ☏ **71191 82200** 🖷 **71191 82210**
Global Custody
Head of Global Custody   Karl Bruck *General Manager* ☏ **71191 52638** 🖷 **71191 52610**
Asset Management
Head   Ruth Iwonski-Bozo ☏ **71191 56500**

Euromoney Directory 1999   77

AUSTRIA (+43) www.euromoneydirectory.com

Bank Austria Aktiengesellschaft (cont)

Other Departments
Commodities / Bullion — Peter Caporale *Senior Manager* ☎ 71191 82880 ℻ 71191 82890
Private Banking — Stefan Zapotocky *General Manager* ☎ 71191 55700
Correspondent Banking — Peter Scheithauer *General Manager* ☎ 71191 56210 ℻ 71191 56212

Administration
Head of Marketing — Josef Hruby *General Manager* ☎ 71191 56000 ℻ 71191 56019

Technology & Systems
Walter Zdrazil *Advisor to the Board* ☎ 71191 51590 ℻ 71191 55644

Legal / In-House Counsel
Kurt Hejc *General Manager* ☎ 71191 52390 ℻ 71191 51037

Compliance
Helmuth Hietzker *Advisor* ☎ 71191 57830 ℻ 71191 57838

Public Relations
Heimo Hackel *Head* ☎ 71191 57007 ℻ 71191 56149
Karl Mauk *Manager, International Public Relations* ☎ 71191 51373 ℻ 71191 52807

Corporate Communications
Karl Pour *General Manager* ☎ 71191 52218 ℻ 71191 52026

Bank Austria Creditanstalt International AG — Head Office

Alternative trading name: BA/CA International AG
Am Hof 2, A-1010 Vienna
Tel: (1) 536 360 **Fax:** (1) 71191 ext 52872

Senior Executive Officers
Chairman of the Managing Board — Gerhard Randa
Deputy Chairman of the Managing Board — Alarich Fenyves
President of The Supervisory Board — Siegfried Sellitsch

Others (Senior Executives)
Members of the Managing Board — Erich Hampel *Managing Director*
Franz Hörhager *Managing Director*
Gerhard Novy *Managing Director*
Karl Samstag *Managing Director*
Alois Steinbichler *Managing Director*
General Management — Heinrich Geyer *General Manager*
Gertrude Pils *General Manager*

General-Lending (DCM, SL)
Head of Corporate Banking — Alois Steinbichler *Managing Director*
Heinrich Geyer *General Manager*

General-Investment
Head of Investment — Alarich Fenyves *Deputy Chairman of the Managing Board*

Debt Capital Markets / Fixed Income
Emerging Market Bonds
Head of Emerging Markets — Ulf Lichtenberg *Head of Department*

Corporate Finance / M&A Advisory
Head of Corporate Finance — Michael Neumayr *Head of Department*

Settlement / Clearing
Head of Settlement / Clearing — Silvia Svoboda

Administration

Technology & Systems
Christian Bruckner *Head of International Operations Management*
Johannes Majer *Chief Expert*

Corporate Communications
Sonja Wilfling *Head of Corporate Communications*

Bank der Österreichischen Postsparkasse AG — Head Office

Wipplingerstrasse 1, A-1010 Vienna
Tel: (1) 53163 0 **Fax:** (1) 535 1358 **Telex:** 112755

Senior Executive Officers
Chairman — Frisch Helmut ☎ 53163 1300
President — Max Kothbauer ☎ 53163 1000
Chief Executive Officer — Karl Stoss ☎ 53163 1100

www.euromoneydirectory.com   AUSTRIA (+43)

Bank für Arbeit und Wirtschaft AG   Head Office A

Seitzergasse 2/4, A-1010 Vienna
Tel: (1) 53453 0 **Fax:** (1) 53453 2840 **Telex:** 115311/3 BAWAG A **Swift:** BAWA AT WW **Reuters:** BAWX; BAWV; BAWM
Website: www.bawag.com

Senior Executive Officers
Director General & Chairman, Managing Board Helmut Elsner
Treasurer Horst Leichtfried *Director* ☎ **53453 2850**
  Thomas Hackl *Director* ☎ **53453 2951**

Debt Capital Markets / Fixed Income
Global Head Roland Lotterstätter *Manager* ☎ **53453 2951**
Domestic Government Bonds
Head of Sales Heinz Karasek ☎ **53453 2368**
Eurobonds
Head of Sales Heinz Karasek ☎ **53453 2368**
Head of Trading Roland Lotterstätter *Manager* ☎ **53453 2951**
Trading (Sovereigns) Thomas Heiss *Dealer* ☎ **53453 3030**

Equity Capital Markets
Global Head Peter Deszar *Director* ☎ **53453 2951**
Domestic Equities
Head of Sales Peter Erlsbacher *Vice President* ☎ **53453 2525**
Head of Trading Christian Kraus ☎ **53453 2885**
International Equities
Head of Sales Peter Erlsbacher *Vice President* ☎ **53453 2525**

Money Markets
Tel: 535 3685 **Fax:** 5345 32620
Global Head Horst Leichtfried *Director* ☎ **53453 2850**
Regional Head Peter Roth *Manager* ☎ **535 3685**
Other (Wholesale Deposits)
Trading Monika Ottenschläger *Assistant Manager* ☎ **535 3685**

Foreign Exchange
Global Head Horst Leichtfried *Director* ☎ **53453 2850**
Country Head Heinz Hörmann *Assistant Director* ☎ **533 1751**
Corporate Sales Josef Pongratz *Manager* ☎ **535 0700**
FX Traders / Sales People
  Johannes Nagy *Dealer* ☎ **533 1751**
  Franz Hladovec *Dealer* ☎ **533 1751**
  Robert Mirnigg *Dealer* ☎ **533 1751**
  Mario Tieff *Dealer* ☎ **533 1751**

Risk Management
Country Head Roland Lotterstätter *Manager* ☎ **53453 2951**
IR Swaps Sales / Marketing Helmut Flieh *Manager* ☎ **535 0705**
IR Swaps Trading Ingrid Baxa *Dealer* ☎ **535 0705**
Foreign Exchange Derivatives / Risk Management
Vanilla FX option Trading Klaus Mlakar *Dealer* ☎ **535 0705**

Settlement / Clearing
Fax: 5345 32620
Equity Settlement; Fixed-Income Settlement Walter Grill *Manager* ☎ **53453 2539**
Derivatives Settlement; Foreign Exchange Settlement Monika Weinhengst ☎ **53453 2446**

Bank für Kärnten und Steiermark AG   Head Office

Alternative trading name: BKS 3Banken Gruppe
Formerly known as: Bank Für Kärnten AG

St Veiter Ring 43, A-9010 Klagenfurt, Carinthia
PO Box 499, A-9020 Klagenfurt, Carinthia
Tel: (463) 5858 0; (463) 5858 800 **Fax:** (463) 5858 803; (463) 5858 841 **Telex:** 75315207 **Swift:** BFKK AT 2K
Email: bks@bks.at **Reuters:** BKSK
Website: www.bks.at

Senior Executive Officers
Member of the Management Board Heimo Penker ☎ **5858 612**
Member of the Management Board Markus Orsini-Rosenberg ☎ **5858 602**

Euromoney Directory 1999 79

AUSTRIA (+43)　　　　　　　www.euromoneydirectory.com

Bank für Kärnten und Steiermark AG (cont)
Senior Executive Officers (cont)

International Division	Josef Morak *Head, International & Treasury* ☎ 5858 800
General - Treasury	
Head of Treasury	Josef Morak *Head, International & Treasury* ☎ 5858 800
Debt Capital Markets / Fixed Income	
Head of Fixed Income	Dieter Dreier
Equity Capital Markets	
Head of Equity Capital Markets	Dieter Dreier
Money Markets	
Head of Money Markets	Dieter Dreier
Foreign Exchange	
Head of Foreign Exchange	Dieter Dreier

Bank für Tirol und Vorarlberg AG   Head Office

Erlerstrasse 5-9, A-6020 Innsbruck
PO Box 573, A-6021 Innsbruck
Tel: (512) 5333 0 **Fax:** (512) 5333 509 **Swift:** BTVA AT 22 **Email:** banking.relations@btv.at **Reuters:** BTVA
Website: www.btv.at

Senior Executive Officers

Director	Peter Gaugg ☎ 5333 110 📠 5333 133
Director	Matthias Moncher ☎ 5333 120 📠 5333 133
General - Treasury	
Head of Treasury	Dietmar Strigl ☎ 5333 600
Debt Capital Markets / Fixed Income	
Head of Fixed Income	Richard Altstätter ☎ 5333 736 📠 5333 488
Domestic Government Bonds	
Head of Trading	Manfred Unterwurzacher *Trader* ☎ 5333 781
	Richard Altstätter ☎ 5333 736 📠 5333 488
Eurobonds	
Head of Trading	Martin Kuttner *Trader* ☎ 5333 734
Equity Capital Markets	
Head of Equity Capital Markets	Richard Altstätter ☎ 5333 736 📠 5333 488
Syndicated Lending	
Head of Syndication	Bernhard Huber ☎ 5333 800 📠 5333 811
Money Markets	
Head of Money Markets	Bernhard Huber ☎ 5333 800 📠 5333 811
Foreign Exchange	
Head of Foreign Exchange	Bernhard Huber ☎ 5333 800 📠 5333 811
Settlement / Clearing	
Settlement (General)	Monika Kofler ☎ 5333 496
Other Departments	
Correspondent Banking	Thomas Held ☎ 5333 504 📠 5333 509

Bank Gutmann Aktiengesellschaft   Head Office

Schwarzenbergplatz 16, 1011 Vienna
Tel: (1) 5022 0 **Fax:** (1) 5022 0249 **Telex:** 136506 **Swift:** GUTB AT WW **Email:** sept.maier@bankgutmann.co.at
Cable: GUTBANK VIENNA

Senior Executive Officers

Chairman	Emil Alexander Kahane
Manager	Walter Dawid
Manager	Rudolf Stahl
Manager	Anton Fink

Settlement / Clearing

Operations	Adolf Hengtschläger *Head*

80　Euromoney Directory 1999

www.euromoneydirectory.com   AUSTRIA (+43)

The Bank of Tokyo-Mitsubishi Limited   Full Branch Office

Schwarzenbergplatz 16/2, A-1015 Vienna
Tel: (1) 502 6213; (1) 502 6220 Fax: (1) 502 6250; (1) 502 6255
Senior Executive Officers
General Manager   Michio Ito

Bank Winter & Co AG   Head Office

Singerstrasse 10, A-1010 Vienna
Tel: (1) 51504 0 Fax: (1) 51504 213 Telex: 135858 WINTL Swift: WISM AT WW Reuters: BHWX
Senior Executive Officers
Chairman & Chief Executive   Thomas Moskovics ☏ **51504 251**
Treasurer   Raimund Fastenbauer *Treasurer* ☏ **51504 277**
Managing Director   Herbert Spitznagel ☏ **51504 258**
Syndicated Lending
Global Head   Thomas Moskovics *Chairman & Chief Executive* ☏ **51504 251**
Money Markets
Global Head   Raimund Fastenbauer *Treasurer* ☏ **51504 277**
Foreign Exchange
Global Head   Raimund Fastenbauer *Treasurer* ☏ **51504 277**
Administration
Other (Administration)
International Banking Relations   Henry Klausner *Managing Director* ☏ **51504 217**

Bankhaus Krentschker & Co   Head Office

Am Eisernen Tor 3, A-8010 Graz
PO Box 846, A-8010 Graz
Tel: (316) 8030 0 Fax: (316) 8030 949 Telex: 311411 Swift: KREC AT 2G Email: oberleitnerp@krentschker.at
Senior Executive Officers
Chairman of the Executive Board   Jörg Bruckbauer
Member of the Executive Board   Georg Wolf-Schönach
International Division   Hans Peter Oberleitner *Head of International Payments*
Foreign Exchange
Head of Foreign Exchange   Britta Sewera
Other Departments
Correspondent Banking   Gudrun Morbitzer *Head*

BULBANK   Representative Office

Kartner Ring 5-7/305, A-1010 Vienna
Tel: (1) 51331 82 Fax: (1) 51331 8275 Telex: 115728
Senior Executive Officers
Representative   Zdravko Milev

CA IB Investmentbank AG   Subsidiary Company

Formerly known as: Bank Austria Investment Bank AG
Nibelungenasse 15, A-1011 Vienna
Tel: (1) 58884 0 Fax: (1) 58542 42 Email: ca-ib@ca-ib.com
Senior Executive Officers
Chairman & CEO   Willi Hemetsberger ☏ **58884 2000**
Financial Director   Helmut Horvath *CFO & Deputy Chairman*
Assistant Director   Henriette Svatek ☏ **58884 2090**
Equity Capital Markets
Domestic Equities
Head of Trading   Gerald Hoenigsberger *Director* ☏ **58884 2421**
International Equities
Head of Sales   Fritz Schweiger *Managing Director*
Gyula Schuch *Managing Director* ☏ **+44 (171) 600 4250**

AUSTRIA (+43)　　　　　　　www.euromoneydirectory.com

CA IB Investmentbank AG (cont)

Equity Research
Head of Equity Research　　　　Dan Wison *Managing Director* ☎ +44 (171) 600 4250

Syndicated Lending
Loan-Related Activities
Project Finance　　　　John Kramer *CEO* ☎ +44 (181) 878 6627

Risk Management
Head of Risk Management　　　　Christian Schmid *Assistant Director* ☎ 58884 2132

OTC Equity Derivatives
Head　　　　Gerhard Kalchgruber ☎ 58884 2414

Asset Management
Head　　　　Etienne D'Arenberg *Director* ☎ 58884 2031

Administration
Head of Administration　　　　Lukas Bonelli *Director* ☎ 58884 2210

Technology & Systems
　　　　Christian Kramer *Operations Director* ☎ 58884 2300

Legal / In-House Counsel
　　　　Henriette Svatek *Assistant Director* ☎ 58884 2090

Compliance
　　　　Linda Davies *Director* ☎ +44 (171) 309 7892

Public Relations
　　　　Veronika Fischer-Kief ☎ 58884 2121 F 58884 6104

Corporate Communications
　　　　Veronika Fischer-Kief ☎ 58884 2121 F 58884 6104

Accounts / Audit
　　　　Kurt Bachinger *Managing Director* ☎ 58884 2150

CDI-AManda GmbH　　　　　　　　　　Head Office

Formerly known as: AMandA Beteiligungsberatung GmbH
Schellinggasse 7, A-1010 Vienna
Tel: (1) 512 9372; (1) 512 4631 **Fax:** (1) 513 8191
Website: www.cdi-amanda.com

Senior Executive Officers
President & CEO　　　　Harald C Klien

Centro Internationale Handelsbank AG　　　　Head Office

Alternative trading name: Centrobank
Tegetthoffstrasse 2, A-1015 Vienna
PO Box 272, A-1015 Vienna
Tel: (1) 51520 0 **Fax:** (1) 513 4396 **Telex:** 136990 CENT A **Swift:** CENB AT WW **Email:** general@centrobank.com
Reuters: CENV
Website: www.centrobank.com

Senior Executive Officers
Chairman, Executive Board　　　　Gerhard Vogt

Others (Senior Executives)
　　　　Christian F Sperk *Member of the Executive Board*
　　　　Jerzy Plusa *Member of the Executive Board*

General-Investment
Head of Investment　　　　Michael Kalwil *Senior Manager*

General - Treasury
Head of Treasury　　　　Paul D Stodola *Director*

Debt Capital Markets / Fixed Income
Head of Debt Capital Markets　　　　Michael Spiss *Director, Securities & Derivatives*
Head of Fixed Income Trading　　　　Wilhelm Celeda *Senior Manager*

Syndicated Lending
Department: Credit Department
Head of Syndicated Lending　　　　John Dinhobel *Director, Credit Department*
Head of Syndication　　　　Gerhard Berger *Senior Manager*
　　　　Wolfgang Hofer *Deputy Director*

Loan-Related Activities
Trade Finance — Wolfgang Hofer *Deputy Director*
Gerhard Berger *Senior Manager*
Project Finance — Wolfgang Hofer *Deputy Director*
Other (Trade Finance)
Guarantees — Wolfgang Hofer *Deputy Director*
Gerhard Berger *Senior Manager*
Forfaiting — Wolfgang Hofer *Deputy Director*
Gerhard Berger *Senior Manager*
Countertrade, Offset, Barter, & Buy Back — Maria Janisch *Director*
Letters of Credit — Irene Kammerhofer *Director*

Money Markets
Global Head
Country Head — Paul D Stodola *Director*
Beatrix Stark *Manager*
Michael Hensel *Manager*

Foreign Exchange
Global Head
Country Head — Paul D Stodola *Director*
Beatrix Stark *Manager*
Michael Hensel *Manager*

Risk Management
Fixed Income Derivatives / Risk Management
Country Head — Michael Spiss *Director, Securities & Derivatives*
Trading — Wilhelm Celeda *Senior Manager*

Asset Management
Head — Manfred Ditz *Senior Manager*

Other Departments
Private Banking — Wolfgang Knapp *Senior Manager*
Correspondent Banking — Paul D Stodola *Director*

Administration
Head of Administration — Eva Marchart *Director*

Accounts / Audit
Accounting — Peter Jantscher *Senior Manager*

Citibank International plc
Full Branch Office

Schwarzenbertplatz 3, A-1010 Vienna
PO Box 90, A-1015 Vienna
Tel: (1) 717 170 **Fax:** (1) 713 9206 **Reuters:** CITV

Senior Executive Officers
Chief Executive Officer — Alberretcht Staecker ☏ **71717 400**

General - Treasury
Head of Treasury — Gunter Woinera *Country Treasurer* ☏ **71717 401**

Constantia Privatbank AG
Head Office

Opernring 17, A-1010 Vienna
Tel: (1) 58875 0 **Fax:** (1) 58875 90 **Email:** mr@constantia.co.at
Website: www.constantia.co.at

Senior Executive Officers
Chairman — Christoph Kraus ☏ **58875 100** F **58875 333**
President — Karl Petrikovics ☏ **58875 200** F **58875 90**
Chief Operating Officer — Gottfried Landrock ☏ **58875 300**
Treasurer — Peter Thomayer ☏ **4075084 27**

Relationship Manager
Head of Portfolio Management — Harald Holzer ☏ **58875 160**

Debt Capital Markets / Fixed Income
Domestic Government Bonds
Head of Trading — Harald Besser ☏ **58875 140**
Hannes Pruckner ☏ **58875 180**

Eurobonds
Head of Trading — Johann Pruckner ☏ **58875 180**
Harald Besser ☏ **58875 140**

Medium-Term Notes
Head of Structuring — Harald Holzer ☏ **58875 160**

AUSTRIA (+43)

www.euromoneydirectory.com

Constantia Privatbank AG (cont)

Private Placements
Head of Structuring — Harald Holzer ☏ 58875 160

Fixed-Income Repo
Head of Repo — Andreas Weidinger ☏ 58875 184

Equity Capital Markets
Domestic Equities
Head of Trading — Josef Stadler ☏ 58875 150

International Equities
Head of Trading — Josef Stadler ☏ 58875 150 F 58875 90
Guenter Leonhartsberger ☏ 58875 151

Money Markets
Global Head — Andreas Weidinger ☏ 58875 184

Foreign Exchange
Head of Trading — Barbara Maurer ☏ 58875 143

Corporate Finance / M&A Advisory
Tel: 58875 ext 406
Global Head — Norbert Doll *Managing Director*
Regional Head — Stephan Zoechling *Director* ☏ 58875 182

Settlement / Clearing
Head of Settlement / Clearing — Andrea Pussich ☏ 58875 351
Karin Magenschab ☏ 58875 321

Administration
Head of Administration — Gottfried Landrock ☏ 58875 300 F 58875 390

Compliance
Wolfgang Ledl ☏ 4075084 42

Public Relations
Martina Reim ☏ 58875 103

Other (Administration)
Marketing — Norbert Gertner ☏ 58875 402 F 58875 490

Crédit Lyonnais Bank (Austria) AG
Subsidiary Company

Wallnerstrasse 8, A-1010 Vienna
Tel: (1) 53150 0 Fax: (1) 53150 50; (1) 53150 54 Swift: CRLY AT WW Email: clwien@via.at Reuters: CLYV
Website: www.creditlyonnais.at

Senior Executive Officers
General Manager — Pascal Grundrich ☏ 53150 100

Others (Senior Executives)
Institutional Banking — Nassif Chehab *Head* ☏ 53150 228

Foreign Exchange
FX Treasury — Manfred Heller ☏ 53150 266
FX & Derivative Sales — Alexander Burian ☏ 53150 265
FX Sales — Thomas Brand ☏ 53150 268

Corporate Finance / M&A Advisory
Country Head — Nassif Chehab *Head* ☏ 53150 228

Other Departments
Private Banking — Ernst Traun *Senior Manager, Private Banking* ☏ 53150 110
Correspondent Banking — Nassif Chehab *Head* ☏ 53150 228

Administration
Technology & Systems
Sujata Bhatt *Senior Manager, Administration* ☏ 53150 300

Legal / In-House Counsel
Sujata Bhatt *Senior Manager, Administration* ☏ 53150 300

Compliance
Sujata Bhatt *Senior Manager, Administration* ☏ 53150 300

Public Relations
Sujata Bhatt *Senior Manager, Administration* ☏ 53150 300

www.euromoneydirectory.com　　　　AUSTRIA (+43)

Creditanstalt AG　　　　　　　　　　　　　　　　Head Office

Julius Tandler Platz 3, A-1090 Vienna
Tel: (1) 53131 0; (1) 31333 0 Telex: 134228 CAEK Swift: CABV AT WW
Website: www.creditanstalt.co.at

Senior Executive Officers
Treasurer　　　　　　　　　　　Patrick Butler *General Manager, Treasury* ☏ 31333 16700
　　　　　　　　　　　　　　　　　E patrick.butler@creditanstalt.co.at

Debt Capital Markets / Fixed Income
Regional Head　　　　　　　　　Peter Harold *Senior Manager* ☏ 31333 6801

Domestic Government Bonds
Head of Trading　　　　　　　　Hugo Neuhold *Manager* ☏ 31333 82560
Head of Research　　　　　　　Heinz Bednar *Manager* ☏ 31333 6890

Eurobonds
Head of Origination; Head of Syndication　Philippe Kogler *Manager* ☏ 31333 6770
Head of Trading　　　　　　　　Harald Kreuzhair *Deputy Manager* ☏ 31333 82660
Head of Research　　　　　　　Heinz Dednar *Manager* ☏ 31333 6890
Trading (Sovereigns)　　　　　　Harald Kreuzhair *Deputy Manager* ☏ 31333 82660
Trading (Corporates); Trading (High-yield)　Georg Kopecek *Trader* ☏ 31333 82610

Emerging Market Bonds
Head of Origination; Head of Syndication　Philippe Kogler *Manager* ☏ 31333 6770
Head of Sales; Head of Trading　　Harald Kreuzhair *Deputy Manager* ☏ 31333 82660
Head of Research　　　　　　　Heinz Bednar *Manager* ☏ 31333 6890

Fixed-Income Repo
Head of Repo　　　　　　　　　Hugo Neuhold *Manager* ☏ 31333 82560
Matched Book Manager　　　　Christine Gruber *Assistant Manager* ☏ 31333 82500

Equity Capital Markets
Equity Repo / Securities Lending
Head of Trading　　　　　　　　Hugo Neuhold *Manager* ☏ 31333 82560

Money Markets
Regional Head　　　　　　　　　Armin Steppan *Senior Manager, Chief Dealer* ☏ 31333 82300
　　　　　　　　　　　　　　　　　E armin.steppan@creditanstalt.co.at

Eurocommercial Paper
Head of Origination　　　　　　Armin Steppan *Senior Manager, Chief Dealer* ☏ 31333 82300
　　　　　　　　　　　　　　　　　E armin.steppan@creditanstalt.co.at
Head of Trading　　　　　　　　Stephen Rushton *Manager* ☏ 31333 82300
　　　　　　　　　　　　　　　　　E stephen.rushton@creditanstalt.co.at

Risk Management
Fixed Income Derivatives / Risk Management
Regional Head　　　　　　　　　Hugo Neuhold *Manager* ☏ 31333 82560

Deutsche Bank AG　　　　　　　　　　　　　　Full Branch Office

Univeritätsplatz 3, Getreidegasse 31, A-5010 Salzburg
Tel: (662) 8491 710 Fax: (662) 8491 715

Deutsche Bank AG　　　　　　　　　　　　　　Full Branch Office

Hohenstauffengasse 4, A-1010 Vienna
PO Box 8, A-1013 Vienna
Tel: (1) 53181 0 Fax: (1) 53181 14 Telex: 114183 Swift: DEUT AT WW Cable: DEUTBANK WIEN
Corporate Banking Tel: 53181 171; Fax: 532 1201; Credit Control Tel: 53181 181; Fax: 532 1201; Foreign
Exchange Tel: 53181 212; Mangement Tel: 53181 105; Fax: 533 9459; Private Banking Tel: 53181 240;
Fax: 53181 19; Securities Trading/Foreign Exchange Tel: 53181 203; Fax: 535 2661; Security Settlement
Tel: 53181 314; Fax: 53181 422; Stock Exchange Tel: 53181 203; Fax: 535 2661
Website: www.deutsche-bank.de

Senior Executive Officers
Chief Operating Officer　　　　Michael Recknagel ☏ 53181 300 E 53354 28
Managing Director　　　　　　Wolfgang Habermayer ☏ 53181 105
Managing Director　　　　　　Claude Sadeler ☏ 53181 100
Company Secretary　　　　　　Gunda Pfingstner ☏ 53181 112

General-Lending (DCM, SL)
Head of Corporate Banking　　Throsten Paul ☏ 53181 171

Euromoney Directory 1999　　85

AUSTRIA (+43)

Deutsche Bank AG (cont)

General-Investment
Head of Investment — Wolfgang Habermayer *Managing Director* ☏ 53181 105

Debt Capital Markets / Fixed Income
Head of Fixed Income — Franz Bartmann ☏ 53181 212

Equity Capital Markets
Head of Equity Capital Markets — Eduard Berger ☏ 53181 203

Syndicated Lending

Loan-Related Activities
Trade Finance — Barbara Dorner ☏ 53181 319

Money Markets
Head of Money Markets — Friedrich Hondl ☏ 53181 234

Foreign Exchange
Head of Foreign Exchange — Friedrich Hondl ☏ 53181 234

Settlement / Clearing
Head of Settlement / Clearing — Michael Recknagel ☏ 53181 300 F 53354 28

Asset Management
Head — Andreas Varnavides ☏ 53181 150

Other Departments
Chief Credit Officer — Thomas Blumenthal ☏ 53181 181
Private Banking — Frank Heinsohn ☏ 53181 240
Cash Management — Rainer Derx ☏ 53181 167

Administration
Head of Administration — Michael Recknagel ☏ 53181 300 F 53354 28
Head of Marketing — Vera Millauer ☏ 53181 111

Legal / In-House Counsel
— Thomas Blumenthal ☏ 53181 181

Public Relations
— Vera Millauer ☏ 53181 111

Diskont Bank AG — Head Office

Formerly known as: EffectInvest Bank AG

Haas Haus, Stephansplatz 12, A-1010 Vienna
PO Box 588, A-1011 Vienna
Tel: (1) 53180 0 **Fax:** (1) 53180 280 **Telex:** 7531 2628 **Email:** headoffice@diskontbank.com
Website: www.diskontbank.com

Senior Executive Officers
Treasurer — Dr Alfred Fuhrmann *General Manager* ☏ 53180 204
Managing Director — Martina Szeikovich ☏ 53180 203
Assistant — Susanne Scholz-Oeztuerk ☏ 53180 204

Debt Capital Markets / Fixed Income
Head of Fixed Income — Dr Alfred Fuhrmann *General Manager* ☏ 53180 204

Emerging Market Bonds
Head of Emerging Markets — Dr Alfred Fuhrmann *General Manager* ☏ 53180 204

Settlement / Clearing
Head of Settlement / Clearing — Norbert Maier ☏ 53180 341 F 53180 380

Global Custody
Head of Global Custody — Norbert Maier ☏ 53180 341 F 53180 380

Asset Management
Head — Michael Leiner ☏ 53180 204

Other Departments
Correspondent Banking — Martina Szeikovich *Managing Director* ☏ 53180 203

Administration
Head of Marketing — Dr Alfred Fuhrmann *General Manager* ☏ 53180 204

Technology & Systems
— Mario Weitenbacher ☏ 53180 610 F 53180 380

Compliance
— Joachim Shelton-Stefani ☏ 53180 334

Public Relations
— Dr Alfred Fuhrmann *General Manager* ☏ 53180 204

www.euromoneydirectory.com AUSTRIA (+43)

Donau-Bank AG Head Office A

Parkring 6, A-1010 Vienna
PO Box 1451, A-1011 Vienna
Tel: (1) 51535 0 **Fax:** (1) 51535 297 **Telex:** 116473 DOFOR A **Swift:** DOBA AT WW **Reuters:** DOBV

Senior Executive Officers
Chairman of the Board
Board Member
International Division

Andrei E. Tchetyrkine
Otto Dracka
Hildergard Kait *Head of International Division*

Others (Senior Executives)
Supervisory Board

Dmitri V. Tulin *Chairman*
Pavel E. Mntzakanov *Deputy Chairman*
Konstantin D. Lubenchenko *Deputy Chairman*

Works Council of the Donau-Bank AG

Friedrich Heider *Chairman*
Helmut Hruby *Chairman*

General-Lending (DCM, SL)
Head of Corporate Banking

Valery V. Liakin *Director, Credit Department*
Daniela Ganster *Holder of Procuration, Credit Department*

General - Treasury
Head of Treasury

Evgueni V. Tikhonov *Director, Treasury*
Friedrich Traxler *Holder of Procuration, Treasury*

Foreign Exchange
Head of Foreign Exchange

Evgueni V. Tikhonov *Director, Treasury*
Friedrich Traxler *Holder of Procuration, Treasury*

Other Departments
Correspondent Banking

Hildergard Kait *Head of International Division*

Administration
Accounts / Audit

Gerhard Martin *Holder of Procuration, Accountancy*

Erste Bank der Österreichischen Sparkassen AG Head Office

Formerly known as: Die Erste Österreichische Spar-Casse-Bank AG & GiroCredit Bank AG der Sparkassen
Graben 21, A-1010 Vienna
PO Box 162, Vienna
Tel: (1) 53100 0; (1) 71194 0 **Fax:** (1) 53100 2272; (1) 713 7052 **Telex:** 114012 **Swift:** ESPK AT WW
Email: service.center@erstebank.at **Reuters:** OERO **Telex:** 133006 **Telex:** 132591; **Syndicated Lending**
Tel: 53100 1267; 71194 9102; **Fax:** 712 9665; **Reuters:** OERV; OERN; GOWV; GOVM
Website: www.erstebank.at

Senior Executive Officers
Chairman
Chief Executive Officer

Herbert Schimetschek ⓣ **21175 0** ⓕ **21175 1001**
Andreas Treichl *Managing Director & Chief Executive* ⓣ **53100 1123**
ⓕ **53100 1533**

Financial Director
Chief Operating Officer
Treasurer
Managing Director & Chief Executive
Company Secretary
International Division

Rudolf Penz ⓣ **53100 3755** ⓕ **53100 1417**
Georg Tucek ⓣ **53100 2442** ⓕ **53100 2314**
Reinhard Ortner ⓣ **53100 1584** ⓕ **53100 1417**
Andreas Treichl ⓣ **53100 1123** ⓕ **53100 1533**
Bernhard Spalt ⓣ **53100 6383** ⓕ **53100 2766**
Christian Goreth *General Manager & Head, International Dept.*
ⓣ **71194 2800** ⓕ **712 9652**

Others (Senior Executives)
Emerging Markets

Otto Ilchmann ⓣ **71194 2701** ⓕ **71194 2714**

General-Lending (DCM, SL)
Head of Corporate Banking

Elisabeth Bleyleben-Koren ⓣ **53100 1367** ⓕ **53100 1506**

General-Investment
Head of Investment

Reinhard Ortner ⓣ **53100 1584** ⓕ **53100 1417**

Debt Capital Markets / Fixed Income
Department: Treasury Trade & Sales
Global Head
Head of Fixed Income Sales
Head of Fixed Income Trading

Manfred Stagl *Global Head of Trading* ⓣ **53100 1392** ⓕ **53100 1521**
Guenther Toifl *Senior Vice President* ⓣ **53100 1810** ⓕ **53100 1895**
Sepp-Dieter Kernmayer *Senior Vice President* ⓣ **71194 3300** ⓕ **71194 2707**

Government Bonds
Head of Sales
Head of Trading
Head of Syndication; Head of Origination

Robert Hengl *Head of Sales* ⓣ **71194 5940** ⓕ **703 6078**
Werner Schorn *Head of Trading* ⓣ **71194 3430** ⓕ **703 6078**
Siegfried Hölz ⓣ **71194 5020** ⓕ **71194 5050**

Euromoney Directory 1999 87

AUSTRIA (+43)   www.euromoneydirectory.com

Erste Bank der Österreichischen Sparkassen AG (cont)

Eurobonds
Head of Sales   Robert Hengl *Head of Sales* ☏ 71194 5940 ⒡ 703 6078
Head of Trading   Werner Schorn *Head of Trading* ☏ 71194 3430 ⒡ 703 6078

Emerging Market Bonds
Head of Sales   Robert Hengl *Head of Sales* ☏ 71194 5940 ⒡ 703 6078
Head of Trading   Josef Leithner ☏ 71194 3650 ⒡ 713 6078

Libor-Based / Floating-Rate Products
FRN Sales   Robert Hengl *Head of Sales* ☏ 71194 5940 ⒡ 703 6078
FRN Trading   Werner Schorn *Head of Trading* ☏ 71194 3430 ⒡ 703 6078
Asset Swaps   Josef Pfleger *Assistant Vice President* ☏ 71194 8798 ⒡ 71194 2670

Fixed-Income Repo
Head of Repo   Werner Schorn *Head of Trading* ☏ 71194 3430 ⒡ 703 6078

Fixed-Income Research
Head of Fixed Income   Friedrich Hostboeck ☏ 53100 1902 ⒡ 53100 3016

Equity Capital Markets
Department: Treasury Trade & Sales
Tel: 53100 1392 **Fax:** 53100 1521
Global Head   Peter Nowak *Global Head, Capital Markets* ☏ 71194 9300 ⒡ 71194 3409
Country Head   Manfred Stagl *Global Head of Trading* ☏ 53100 1392 ⒡ 53100 1521
Head of Sales   Guenther Toifl *Senior Vice President* ☏ 53100 1810 ⒡ 53100 1895
Head of Trading   Sepp-Dieter Kernmayer *Senior Vice President* ☏ 71194 3300 ⒡ 71194 2707

Domestic Equities
Head of Origination   Siegfried Mörz *Head, New Issues* ☏ 71194 5020 ⒡ 71194 5030
Head of Sales   Hans-Juergen Egerling *Vice President* ☏ 53100 1842 ⒡ 53100 1595
Head of Trading   Doris Sykora *Head of Trading* ☏ 53100 1000 ⒡ 53100 1991

International Equities
Head of Sales   Hans-Juergen Egerling *Vice President* ☏ 53100 1842 ⒡ 53100 1595
Head of Trading   Doris Sykora *Head of Trading* ☏ 53100 1000 ⒡ 53100 1991

Equity Research
Head of Equity Research   Friedrich Hostboeck ☏ 53100 1902 ⒡ 53100 3016

Equity Repo / Securities Lending
Head   Werner Schorn *Head of Trading* ☏ 71194 3430 ⒡ 703 6078

Syndicated Lending
Head of Origination   Carmen Rothmüller *Head, International Corporate Finance* ☏ 71194 2807 ⒡ 71194 3097

Loan-Related Activities
Trade Finance   Werner Markl ☏ 53100 3871 ⒡ 53100 3880
Project Finance   Richard Wollein ☏ 53100 6508 ⒡ 53100 3460

Money Markets
Tel: 53100 1530 **Fax:** 53100 3422 **Reuters:** EGAM
Head of Money Markets   Heinz Herkner ☏ 53100 1530 ⒡ 53100 1505

Foreign Exchange
Head of Foreign Exchange   Leopold Sokolicek *Vice President* ☏ 71194 5920 ⒡ 71194 5855
Head of Institutional Sales; Corporate Sales   Matthias Bauer *Vice President* ☏ 71194 5610 ⒡ 71194 5655
Head of Trading   Leopold Sokolicek *Vice President* ☏ 71194 5920 ⒡ 71194 5855

Risk Management
Head of Risk Management   Christoph Wiesmayr *Head, Central Risk Management* ☏ 71194 9049 ⒡ 71194 9059

Corporate Finance / M&A Advisory
Head of Corporate Finance   Elisabeth Bleyleben-Koren ☏ 53100 1367 ⒡ 53100 1506

Settlement / Clearing
Head of Settlement / Clearing   Wolfgang Aubrunner ☏ 53100 1819 ⒡ 53100 2840

Global Custody
Head of Global Custody   Monika Huber ☏ 53100 6346 ⒡ 53100 6347

Asset Management
Head   Wolfgang Traindl ☏ 53100 3066 ⒡ 53100 3073

Other Departments
Chief Credit Officer   Frank-Michael Beitz *International* ☏ 71194 2702 ⒡ 71194 2713
    Walter Schmidt *Domestic* ☏ 53100 1353 ⒡ 53100 9537
Private Banking   Ernst Karner ☏ 71194 1715 ⒡ 71194 9400
Correspondent Banking   Manfred Sieber ☏ 53100 1153 ⒡ 53100 1670
Cash Management   Heinz Herkner ☏ 53100 1530 ⒡ 53100 1505

www.euromoneydirectory.com   AUSTRIA (+43)

Administration
Head of Administration   Karl Kleedorfer ☏ 71194 6700 🖷 71194 3585
Head of Marketing   Gerturde Sobotka-Hirnthaler ☏ 71141 141 🖷 71141 145

Technology & Systems
Georg Tucek ☏ 53100 2442 🖷 53100 2314

Legal / In-House Counsel
Erich Rebholz ☏ 71194 2175 🖷 71194 3762

Compliance
Johannes Häusler ☏ 71194 3510 🖷 71194 3502

Public Relations
Michael Ikrath ☏ 53100 2903 🖷 53100 2677

Accounts / Audit
Helmut Schalko ☏ 71194 8500 🖷 71194 3111

HYPO-Bausparkasse AG   Subsidiary Company
Saquingasse 16-18, A-1030 Vienna
Tel: (1) 79742 0 **Fax:** (1) 79742 42

ING Barings   Full Branch Office
Neuer Markt 2, PO Box 152, A-1011 Vienna
Tel: (1) 514 620 **Fax:** (1) 5146 2900 **Telex:** 112393 INGB VI **Swift:** INGBV AT WW **Reuters:** INGV

Senior Executive Officers
General Manager   Burkhard Klein

Others (Senior Executives)
Leasing   Steffen Heinrich *Manager*

Investmentbank Austria AG   Head Office
Nibelungengasse 15, PO Box 866, A-1010 Vienna
Tel: (1) 5888 4 **Fax:** (1) 585 4242 **Telex:** 112884

Debt Capital Markets / Fixed Income
Domestic Government Bonds
Head of Sales   Michael Buhl
Head of Trading   Gerald Honigsberger
   Rene Prinz

Equity Capital Markets
Domestic Equities
Head of Origination   Villy Hemegesberger
Head of Sales   Michael Buhl
Head of Trading   Gerald Honigsberger
   Rene Prinz

Settlement / Clearing
Operations   Christian Kramer

Kärntner Landes-und-Hypothekenbank AG   Head Office
Alternative trading name: Hypo Alpe-Adria-Bank
Domgasse 5, A-9020 Klagenfurt, Carinthia
Tel: (463) 5866 0 **Fax:** (463) 5860 50 **Telex:** 140-422473 **Swift:** KLAB AT 2K **Email:** market@hypo.co.at
Reuters: KLHA
Website: www.hypo-alpe-adria.com

Senior Executive Officers
Chairman of the Supervisory Board   Herbert Koch
Treasurer   Dietmar Falschlehner ☏ 5860 286
Board of Management   Wolfgang Kulterer ☏ 5860 100
Board of Management   Jörg Schuster ☏ 5860 200
International Division   Günter Striedinger ☏ 5860 207
Public Relations   Karl Isak ☏ 55991 🖷 55991 56

General-Investment
Head of Investment   Anton Sgaga ☏ 5860 294

AUSTRIA (+43)　　　　　　　　www.euromoneydirectory.com

Kärntner Landes-und-Hypothekenbank AG (cont)
Debt Capital Markets / Fixed Income
Emerging Market Bonds
Head of Emerging Markets　　　　　Anton Sgaga ☎ 5860 294
Equity Capital Markets
Head of Equity Capital Markets　　　Herbert Manhartseder ☎ 5860 413
Money Markets
Head of Money Markets　　　　　　Dietmar Falschlehner ☎ 5860 286
Settlement / Clearing
Head of Settlement / Clearing　　　　Herbert Gollinger ☎ 5860 297
Asset Management
Head　　　　　　　　　　　　　　Günther Bamberger ☎ 242307 20
Administration
Business Development　　　　　　Herbert Manhartseder ☎ 5860 413
Head of Marketing　　　　　　　　Karl Isak *Public Relations* ☎ 55991 F 55991 56
Technology & Systems
　　　　　　　　　　　　　　　　Erwin Sucher ☎ 5860 300
Legal / In-House Counsel
Legal Department　　　　　　　　Hans-Dieter Kerstnig ☎ 5860 226
Compliance
　　　　　　　　　　　　　　　　Hans-Dieter Kerstnig ☎ 5860 226
Public Relations
　　　　　　　　　　　　　　　　Karl Isak *Public Relations* ☎ 55991 F 55991 56
Accounts / Audit
Auditing & Controlling　　　　　　Herbert Manhartseder ☎ 5860 413

Landes-Hypothekenbank Tirol　　　　　　　　　　　Head Office

Meranerstraße 8, A-6020 Innsbruck
Tel: (512) 5911 0 **Fax:** (512) 5911 2121 **Telex:** 533899 AUSTRIA **Swift:** HYPT AT 22

Senior Executive Officers
Chairman　　　　　　　　　　　　Helmut Fröhlich ☎ 5911 2102
Financial Director　　　　　　　　Siegfried Rainer-Theurl ☎ 5911 2104
Chief Operating Officer　　　　　　Walter Mair ☎ 5911 3200
Treasurer　　　　　　　　　　　　Werner Pfeifer ☎ 5911 3400

Debt Capital Markets / Fixed Income
Global Head　　　　　　　　　　　Hans-Peter Hörtnagl ☎ 5911 3436
Domestic Government Bonds
Head of Trading　　　　　　　　　　Anton Staudacher ☎ 5911 3461
Eurobonds
Head of Trading　　　　　　　　　　Ulla Ruggenthaler-Zobler ☎ 5911 3481
Libor-Based / Floating-Rate Products
FRN Origination　　　　　　　　　　Anton Staudacher ☎ 5911 3461
Asset Swaps　　　　　　　　　　　Hans-Peter Hörtnagl ☎ 5911 3436
Private Placements
Head of Origination; Head of Sales; Head of　　Hans-Peter Hörtnagl ☎ 5911 3436
Structuring
Asset-Backed Securities / Securitization
Global Head　　　　　　　　　　　　Anton Staudacher ☎ 5911 3461

Equity Capital Markets
Global Head　　　　　　　　　　　Hans-Peter Hörtnagl ☎ 5911 3436
Domestic Equities
Head of Trading　　　　　　　　　　Manfred Kirchmair ☎ 5911 3488
International Equities
Head of Trading　　　　　　　　　　Walter Egger ☎ 5911 3466

Money Markets
Global Head　　　　　　　　　　　Hans-Peter Hörtnagl ☎ 5911 3436
Eurocommercial Paper
Head of Sales　　　　　　　　　　　Siegfried Draxl ☎ 5911 3483

Foreign Exchange
Global Head　　　　　　　　　　　Hans-Peter Hörtnagl ☎ 5911 3436

www.euromoneydirectory.com							AUSTRIA (+43)

FX Traders / Sales People
 Stefan Nagiller ☏ 5911 3486
 Daniel Plattner ☏ 5911 3477

Risk Management
Global Head Werner Pfeifer ☏ 5911 3400

Fixed Income Derivatives / Risk Management
Global Head Hans-Peter Hörtnagl ☏ 5911 3436
IR Swaps Trading; IR Options Trading Manfred Kirchmair ☏ 5911 3488

Foreign Exchange Derivatives / Risk Management
Cross-Currency Swaps, Trading; Vanilla FX option Sales Manfred Kirchmair ☏ 5911 3488

OTC Equity Derivatives
Trading Anton Staudacher ☏ 5911 3461

Settlement / Clearing
Regional Head Christian Kröll ☏ 5911 3423
Equity Settlement Günther Lutz ☏ 5911 3443
Derivatives Settlement; Foreign Exchange Settlement Isabella Ingruber ☏ 5911 3405

Global Custody
Regional Head Günther Lutz ☏ 5911 3443
Country Head Günther Netzer ☏ 5911 3454

Other (Global Custody)
 Helene Peer ☏ 5911 3456

Meinl Bank AG

Bauernmarkt 1, A-1014 Vienna
PO Box 99, Vienna
Tel: (1) 531 880 **Fax:** (1) 531 8844

Senior Executive Officers
Chairman Anton Osond
General Manager Julius Meinl
General Manager Wolfgang Samesch
General Manager Herbert Kofler
Assistant Manager Herbert Kräutelhofer

Merrill Lynch (Austria) AG Subsidiary Company

Wallnerstrasse 4, A-1010 Vienna
Tel: (1) 53140 **Fax:** (1) 535 0227 **Telex:** 136332

Senior Executive Officers
Managing Director Johann P Weisenhorn

The Nomura Securities Co Limited Representative Office

Kaertner Ring 5-7, Kaertnerringhof 2 Floor, A-1010 Vienna
Tel: (1) 513 2322 **Fax:** (1) 513 2321 **Email:** rep.office@nomuravie.co.at

Senior Executive Officers
Chief Representative Michio Chano ☏ 513 2314 ℱ 513 2313

Oberbank Head Office

Formerly known as: Bank für Oberosterreich und Salzburg
PO Box 60, Untere Donaulände 28, A-4010 Linz
Tel: (732) 7802 0 **Fax:** (732) 785 817; (732) 785 804
Website: www.oberbank.at

Senior Executive Officers
Chairman Hermann Bell
Deputy Chairman Josef Kneidinger

Others (Senior Executives)
 Erich Kleibel *Director*
 Franz Gasselsberger *Director*

Euromoney Directory 1999 **91**

AUSTRIA (+43)　　　　　　　www.euromoneydirectory.com

Oberbank (cont)

General - Treasury
Head of Treasury　　　　　　　Helmut Edlbauer *General Manager, Treasury* ☎ 7802 2630
　　　　　　　　　　　　　　　Manfred Leitner *Deputy General Manager, Treasury* ☎ 7802 2631
　　　　　　　　　　　　　　　📠 773 980

Department: Banking Relations & Payments
Senior General Manager　　　　Franz Novotny ☎ 7802 2300
Deputy General Manager　　　　Helmut Lanegger ☎ 7802 2301　📠 772 701

Others (Senior Executives)
Banking Relations; International Payments　Florian Hagenauer *Manager* ☎ 7802 2320　📠 785 804
Domestic Payments　　　　　　Johanna Wasserbauer *Manager* ☎ 7802 2100　📠 785 806

Debt Capital Markets / Fixed Income
Reuters: OBKA-G, OBKB-G

Bonds - General
Securities Dealing Fixed Income　Max Koblmüller *Manager* ☎ 7802 2633　📠 776 511

Equity Capital Markets
Reuters: OBKH-J

Domestic Equities
Head of Trading　　　　　　　Robert Musner *Manager* ☎ 7802 2642　📠 776 511

Syndicated Lending
Department: Financing
Country Head　　　　　　　　Günther Ramusch *Senior General Manager* ☎ 7802 2500
　　　　　　　　　　　　　　　Manfred Weissmann *Deputy General Manager* ☎ 7802 2501　📠 796 633

Other (Syndicated Lending)
International Loans　　　　　　Wolfgang Kappl *Manager* ☎ 7802 2305　📠 785 800

Other (Trade Finance)
Subsidized Financing　　　　　Ferdinand Sieber *Manager* ☎ 7802 2575　📠 785 805
Trade Finance & Documentary Business　Claudia Raml *Manager* ☎ 7802 2570　📠 785 802

Money Markets
Reuters: OBKX, OBKL
Money Market Dealing　　　　　Hans Hamberger *Manager* ☎ 7802 2226　📠 776 511

Foreign Exchange
Reuters: OBKX, OBKL

FX Traders / Sales People
　　　　　　　　　　　　　　　Franz Schnell *Manager* ☎ 7802 2330　📠 776 511

Asset Management
Department: Securities
Head　　　　　　　　　　　　Reinhold Reisinger *General Manager* ☎ 7802 7270
　　　　　　　　　　　　　　　Peter Kottbauer *Deputy General Manager* ☎ 7802 7271　📠 795 275
Portfolio Management　　　　　Alois Wögerbauer ☎ 7802 7424　📠 785 816

Other (Asset Management)
Sales　　　　　　　　　　　　Erich Stadlberger *Manager* ☎ 7802 7384　📠 785 814
Administration　　　　　　　　Elfriede Domnanich *Manager* ☎ 7802 7276　📠 778 940

Oberösterreichische Landesbank AG　　　　　　　　　　Head Office

Alternative trading name: Hypo-Bank
　　　　　　　　　　Landstrasse 38, A-4010 Linz
　　　Tel: (732) 7639 0　Fax: (732) 7639 205　Swift: OBLA AT 2L
　　　　　　　　　　Website: www.hypo.at

Senior Executive Officers
President　　　　　　　　　　Wolfgang Stampfi
Managing Director / General Manager　Josef Kolmhofer
International Division　　　　　Herbert Ackerl

Foreign Exchange
Head of Foreign Exchange　　　Herbert Ackerl

Other Departments
Correspondent Banking　　　　Friedrich Wiesinger

www.euromoneydirectory.com   AUSTRIA (+43)

Österreichische Investitionskredit AG   Head Office   **A**

Renngasse 10, A-1013 Vienna
Tel: (1) 53135 0 **Fax:** (1) 53135 990 **Telex:** 111619 **Swift:** OEINATWW **Email:** invest@investkredit.at
Cable: INVESTCRED
Website: www.investkredit.at

Senior Executive Officers
President — Anton Osond [T] **53135 101** [F] **53135 990**
Chief Executive Officer — Alfred Reiter [T] **53135 103** [F] **53135 993**
Treasurer — Peter Tschusch [T] **53135 140** [F] **53135 989**
Company Secretary — Margot Binder [T] **53135 111** [F] **53135 990**
International Division — Walter Anscheringer *Department Head* [T] **53135 352** [F] **53135 909**

Foreign Exchange
Head of Foreign Exchange — Martin Kernstock [T] **53135 152** [F] **53135 989**

Corporate Finance / M&A Advisory
Head of Corporate Finance — Gerhard Ehringer [T] **53135 260** [F] **53135 929**

Settlement / Clearing
Head of Settlement / Clearing — Ferdinand Dietersdorfer [T] **53135 142** [F] **53135 989**

Asset Management
Head — Rita Hochgatterer [T] **53135 141** [F] **53135 989**

Administration
Technology & Systems — Julius Gauguch [T] **53135 330** [F] **53135 969**

Public Relations
PR & Marketing — Hannah Rieger [T] **53135 112** [F] **53135 990**

Österreichische Postsparkasse Aktiengesellschaft   Head Office

Georg-Coch-Platz 2, A-1018 Vienna
Tel: (1) 51400 0 **Fax:** (1) 51400 1700 **Telex:** 111663 **Swift:** OPSK AT WW **Reuters:** PSKV
Website: www.psk.co.at/psk

Senior Executive Officers
President — Helmut Frisch [T] **51400 1300**
Chief Executive Officer — Max Kothbauer [T] **51400 1000**
Treasurer — Gottfried Halbwidl [T] **51400 2800**
International Division — Günter Krottenmüller [T] **51400 2900**

Others (Senior Executives)
Member of the Board — Karl Stoss *Deputy Chairman* [T] **51400 1100**

Debt Capital Markets / Fixed Income
Department: Trading
Tel: 51400 2845 **Fax:** 51400 1774

Domestic Government Bonds
Head of Sales — Josef Gollowitzer [T] **51400 2838**

Eurobonds
Head of Sales — Josef Gollowitzer [T] **51400 2838**

Money Markets
Tel: 51400 2966 **Fax:** 51400 1761
Global Head — Gerhard Bösch [T] **51400ext2830**

Foreign Exchange
Tel: 51400 2955 **Fax:** 51400 1791
Corporate Sales — Veronika Poinstingl [T] **51400 2955**

Risk Management
Tel: 51400 3821 **Fax:** 51400 1730
Global Head — Otto Karasek [T] **51400 2821**

Other (Equity Derivatives) — Heinrich Jirku [T] **51400 2955**

Settlement / Clearing
Tel: 51400 3811 **Fax:** 51400 1775
Foreign Exchange Settlement — Anneliese Blasl-Müller [T] **51400 2811**

Other Departments
Chief Credit Officer — Harald Machat [T] **51400 2820**
Correspondent Banking — Franz-Peter Pairitsch [T] **51400 2910**

AUSTRIA (+43)　　　　　　　www.euromoneydirectory.com

Österreichische Postsparkasse Aktiengesellschaft (cont)
Administration
Head of Marketing　　　　　　　Manfred Feichter ☏ 51400 2080
Technology & Systems
　　　　　　　　　　　　　　　　Christoph Bösch ☏ 51400 2200
Legal / In-House Counsel
　　　　　　　　　　　　　　　　Klaus Wenda ☏ 51400 2020
Compliance
　　　　　　　　　　　　　　　　Karl Vogl ☏ 51400 2040
Public Relations
　　　　　　　　　　　　　　　　Georgia Schütz-Spörl ☏ 51400 2010
Accounts / Audit
　　　　　　　　　　　　　　　　Wolfgang Sützl ☏ 51400 2060

Österreichische Volksbanken AG　　　　　　　　　　　Head Office
Peregringasse 3, A-1090 Vienna
PO Box 95, A-1011 Vienna
Tel: (1) 31340 0 **Fax:** (1) 31340 3430; (1) 31340 3125 **Telex:** 134206 **Swift:** VBOE AT WW **Reuters:** OVAG

Senior Executive Officers
Chairman & Chief Executive　　　　Robert Mädl ☏ 31340 3332
President　　　　　　　　　　　　Gerhard Ortner
Chief Executive Officer　　　　　　Robert Mädl *Chairman & Chief Executive* ☏ 31340 3332
Treasurer　　　　　　　　　　　　Herbert Skok *Director, Head of Trading* ☏ 31340 3368
Deputy Chairman　　　　　　　　Klaus Thalhammer ☏ 31340 3431

Debt Capital Markets / Fixed Income
Tel: 31340 3806 **Fax:** 31340 3125
Global Head　　　　　　　　　　Herbert Skok *Director, Head of Trading* ☏ 31340 3368

Domestic Government Bonds
Head of Sales; Head of Trading　　Martin Fuchsbauer *Head, Bond Trading* ☏ 31340 3806
Head of Research　　　　　　　　Andreas Mäutner *Head, New Issues* ☏ 31340 3424

Eurobonds
Head of Origination; Head of Syndication　Andreas Mäutner *Head, New Issues* ☏ 31340 3424
Head of Trading　　　　　　　　Martin Fuchsbauer *Head, Bond Trading* ☏ 31340 3806

Libor-Based / Floating-Rate Products
FRN Origination　　　　　　　　Thomas Biedermann *Vice President* ☏ 31340 3178
FRN Sales　　　　　　　　　　　Johann Filler *Manager* ☏ 31340 3696

Private Placements
Head of Origination; Head of Structuring　Andreas Mäutner *Head, New Issues* ☏ 31340 3424

Equity Capital Markets
Tel: 31340 3714 **Fax:** 31340 3125
Global Head　　　　　　　　　　Herbert Skok *Director, Head of Trading* ☏ 31340 3368

Domestic Equities
Head of Trading　　　　　　　　Christoph Mayrhofer ☏ 31340 3701
Head of Research　　　　　　　　Andreas Mäutner *Head, New Issues* ☏ 31340 3424

International Equities
Head of Syndication　　　　　　Andreas Mäutner *Head, New Issues* ☏ 31340 3424
Head of Trading　　　　　　　　Christoph Mayrhofer ☏ 31340 3701

Warrants
Head of Trading　　　　　　　　Christoph Mayrhofer ☏ 31340 3701

Syndicated Lending
Global Head　　　　　　　　　　Michael Oberhummer *Head, Int'l Finance* ☏ 31340 3461
Head of Syndication　　　　　　Thomas Biedermann *Vice President* ☏ 31340 3178

Money Markets
Tel: 310 9720 **Fax:** 31340 3430
Global Head　　　　　　　　　　Franz Schleifer *Chief Dealer* ☏ 31340 3500

Foreign Exchange
Tel: 31340 3490 **Fax:** 31340 3430
Global Head　　　　　　　　　　Herbert Skok *Director, Head of Trading* ☏ 31340 3368
Head of Trading　　　　　　　　Franz Schleifer *Chief Dealer* ☏ 31340 3500

Risk Management
Global Head　　　　　　　　　　Erich Kaschnigg *Vice President* ☏ 31340 3267

Fixed Income Derivatives / Risk Management
IR Swaps Trading; IR Options Trading　Franz Schleifer *Chief Dealer* ☏ 31340 3500

www.euromoneydirectory.com AUSTRIA (+43)

Foreign Exchange Derivatives / Risk Management
Vanilla FX option Sales; Vanilla FX option Tanja Duscher *Assistant Manager* ☏ **31340 3494**
Trading

Corporate Finance / M&A Advisory
Tel: 31340 3490 **Fax:** 31340 3430
Global Head Alfred Raidl *Manager, Corporate* ☏ **31340 3499**

Settlement / Clearing
Regional Head Herbert Henninger *Head of Operations* ☏ **31340 3620**
Equity Settlement Ulrike Zach *Assistant Manager* ☏ **31340 3393**
Derivatives Settlement Robert Zwickl *FX & MM Settlement Manager* ☏ **31340 3462**

Other Departments
Commodities / Bullion Gerhard Heinrich *Manager, Notes & Bullions* ☏ **31340 3506**
Correspondent Banking Renate Bernthaler *Head* ☏ **31340 3197**

Administration
Compliance
  Othmar Schmid *Director* ☏ **31340 3291**

Public Relations
  Ernst Ahammer *Director* ☏ **31340 3365**

Privatinvest Bank AG   Head Office

Griesgasse 11, A-5020 Salzburg
Postfach 16, A-5010 Salzburg
Tel: (662) 8048 0 **Fax:** (662) 8048 334 **Telex:** 63 3267 PIAG A **Swift:** PIAG AT 2S **Email:** piag@aon.at

Senior Executive Officers
MD / Speaker of the Board Reimund Ziegler ☏ **8048 203**
MD / Speaker of the Board Hermann J Reif ☏ **8048 211**

General-Investment
Head of Investment Johann Eder *Investment Manager* ☏ **8048 275**
  Ferdinand Pürner *Investment Manager* ☏ **8048 280**
  Wolfgang Gugg *Investment Manager* ☏ **8048 290**
  Monika Geisseder *Investment Manager* ☏ **8048 299**

Debt Capital Markets / Fixed Income
Asset-Backed Securities / Securitization
Head of Trading Helga Schwab ☏ **8048 277**

Money Markets
Global Head Walter Romagna ☏ **8048 260**

Foreign Exchange
Global Head Walter Romagna ☏ **8048 260**

Quelle Bank CA Steinhäusser AG   Head Office

Kornstrasse 4, A-4060 Linz
Tel: (732) 6867 0; (7111) 7112 **Fax:** (732) 6867 150 **Email:** email@quelle-bank.at
Website: www.quelle-bank.at

Senior Executive Officers
Chairman Karl-Heinz Stoiber ☏ **6867 100**
Chairman Bernd Schadrack ☏ **6867 100**
President Johannes Verbunt
Financial Director Werner Pürstinger ☏ **6867 111**

Other Departments
Private Banking Josef Breitschopf ☏ **6867 200**

Administration
Head of Marketing Klaus Lienerbrünn ☏ **6867 121**

Technology & Systems
  Dietmar Kirchweger ☏ **6867 131**

Public Relations
  Stefan Donacz ☏ **(1) 985 6659**

AUSTRIA (+43) www.euromoneydirectory.com

Raiffeisenlandesbank Niederösterreich-Wien GmbH

Friedrich-Wilhelm-Raiffeisen-Platz 1, A-1020 Vienna
PO Box 991, A-1011 Vienna
Tel: (1) 21136 0 **Fax:** (1) 21136 2223 **Telex:** 116760 RAIFFEISEN WIEN **Swift:** RLNW AT WW
Website: www.rlbnoew.at

Senior Executive Officers
Chairman Christian Konrad
First Deputy Chairman Karl Nigl
Second Deputy Chairman Franz Romeder
General Manager Peter Püspök
Deputy General Manager Erwin Hamseder

Others (Senior Executives)
Walter Grün *Executive*
Anton Bodenstein *Member of the Management Board*
Karl Buchinger *Member of the Management Board*
Eduard Ceidl *Member of the Management Board*
Leopold Danzer *Member of the Management Board*
Karl Fenth *Member of the Management Board*
Anneliesc Fuchs *Member of the Management Board*
Rudolf Glösmann *Member of the Management Board*
Gottfried Holzer *Member of the Management Board*
Karl Kloucek *Member of the Management Board*
Hubert Mayrhofer *Member of the Management Board*
Franz Schall *Member of the Management Board*
Johann Schellenbacher *Member of the Management Board*
Alfred Schuster *Member of the Management Board*
Adolf Steiner *Member of the Management Board*
Franz Tröster *Member of the Management Board*
Leopold Unterleuthner *Member of the Management Board*
Johann Wiesbauer *Member of the Management Board*
Alois Zach *Member of the Management Board*
Theodor Zeh *Member of the Management Board*

Foreign Exchange
Head of Foreign Exchange Christian Ratz
  Josef Mantler

Raiffeisenlandesbank Oberösterreich Head Office

Raiffeisenplatz 1, A-4021 Linz
Tel: (732) 6596 0 **Fax:** (732) 6596 2995
Website: www.raiffeisen.at/rbgooe

Senior Executive Officers
Chairman Helmut Angermeier ☏ **6596 2098**
Treasurer Alois Mayrhofer *Head of Asset & Liability Management* ☏ **6596 2900**
Chairman of the Managing Board Ludwig Scharinger
Deputy Chairman of the Managing Board Hans Schilcher

Debt Capital Markets / Fixed Income
Global Head Jürgen Graffonara *Head of Securities Trading* ☏ **6596 2960**
Domestic Government Bonds
Head of Sales Jürgen Graffonara *Head of Securities Trading* ☏ **6596 2960**
Head of Trading Wolfgang Aschenwald *Head of Fixed Income Trading* ☏ **6596 2968**
Eurobonds
Head of Origination; Head of Syndication Andreas Hahn ☏ **6596 5112**
Head of Sales Jürgen Graffonara *Head of Securities Trading* ☏ **6596 2960**
Head of Trading Wolfgang Aschenwald *Head of Fixed Income Trading* ☏ **6596 2968**

Raiffeisenverband Salzburg Head Office

Schwarzstrasse 13/15, A-5024 Salzburg
Tel: (662) 8886 0 **Fax:** (662) 8886 525 **Telex:** 633399 **Swift:** RVSA AT 2S

Senior Executive Officers
Chairman & General Manager Manfred Holztrattner ☏ **8886 1000** 🖷 **8886 202**
Financial Director Herbert Winter-Steller *Director* ☏ **8886 2000** 🖷 **8886 245**
International Division Erich Ortner *Director & Head* ☏ **8886 5100** 🖷 **8886 524**
  Friedrich Zehentner *Deputy Head* ☏ **8886 5200** 🖷 **8886 524**

www.euromoneydirectory.com   **AUSTRIA (+43)**

Senior Executive Officers (cont)
Hans Schinwald *Director, Int'l Division & Securities* ☎ **8886 4000**
🖷 **8886 525**

Others (Senior Executives)
Credit & Branch Offices   Werner Wiltsch *Director* ☎ **8886 3000** 🖷 **8886 384**

Syndicated Lending
Head of Credit Committee   Rudolf Brauer *Director & Head* ☎ **8886 3100** 🖷 **8886 384**

Foreign Exchange
Country Head   Andreas Dauer *Manager* ☎ **8886 5460** 🖷 **8886 423**

Other Departments
Correspondent Banking   Fritz Buchmüller *Manager* ☎ **8886 5170** 🖷 **8886 524**

RZB   Head Office

Am Stadtpark 9, A-1030 Vienna
Tel: (1) 71707 0 **Fax:** (1) 71707 1715 **Telex:** 136989
Website: www.rzb.co.at/rzb

Senior Executive Officers
Chairman   Christian Konrad ☎ **71707 1210**
President   Walter Rothensteiner ☎ **71707 2420**
Financial Director   Hellfried Marek ☎ **71707 1306**
Treasurer   Heinrich Schaller ☎ **71707 1707**

Debt Capital Markets / Fixed Income
Global Head   Gerhard Grund ☎ **71707 1768**

Domestic Government Bonds
Head of Sales; Head of Trading   Christian Saeckl ☎ **71707 3347**
Head of Research   Peter Weigl ☎ **71707 1516**

Eurobonds
Head of Origination; Head of Syndication   Ernst Rosi ☎ **71707 1735**
Head of Sales; Head of Trading   Christian Saeckl ☎ **71707 3347**
Head of Research   Peter Weigl ☎ **71707 1516**
Trading - Sovereigns, Corporates, High-yield   Christian Saeckl ☎ **71707 3347**

Libor-Based / Floating-Rate Products
FRN Origination   Ernst Rosi ☎ **71707 1735**
FRN Sales   Christian Saeckl ☎ **71707 3347**
Asset Swaps   Robert Kliesspiess ☎ **71707 3769**

Medium-Term Notes
Head of Origination   Ernst Rosi ☎ **71707 1735**
Head of Structuring   Nicolaus Hagleitner ☎ **71707 1467**
Head of Sales   Christian Saeckl ☎ **71707 3347**

Private Placements
Head of Origination   Ernst Rosi ☎ **71707 1735**
Head of Sales   Christian Saeckl ☎ **71707 3347**
Head of Structuring   Nicolaus Hagleitner ☎ **71707 1467**

Fixed-Income Repo
Head of Repo   Johannes Weninger ☎ **71707 1755**
Sales   Karl Bucher ☎ **71707 1774**

Equity Capital Markets
Global Head   Gerhard Grund ☎ **71707 1768**

Domestic Equities
Head of Origination; Head of Syndication   Ernst Rosi ☎ **71707 1735**
Head of Sales; Head of Trading   Christian Saeckl ☎ **71707 3347**
Head of Research   Peter Weigl ☎ **71707 1516**

International Equities
Head of Origination; Head of Syndication   Ernst Rosi ☎ **71707 1735**
Head of Sales; Head of Trading   Christian Saeckl ☎ **71707 3347**
Head of Research   Peter Weigl ☎ **71707 1516**

Equity Repo / Securities Lending
Head   Johannes Weninger ☎ **71707 1755**

Money Markets
Global Head   Heinz Schaller ☎ **71707 1707**

Foreign Exchange
Global Head   Heinz Schaller ☎ **71707 1707**
Head of Institutional Sales; Corporate Sales   Walter Gleissinger ☎ **71707 3322**
Head of Trading   Gerhard Herda ☎ **71707 1280**

AUSTRIA (+43) www.euromoneydirectory.com

RZB (cont)
Risk Management

Fixed Income Derivatives / Risk Management
Global Head — Heinz Schaller ☎ **71707 1707**
IR Swaps Sales / Marketing — Walter Gleissinger ☎ **71707 3322**
IR Swaps Trading — Lilo Buchgraber ☎ **71707 1294**

Foreign Exchange Derivatives / Risk Management
Cross-Currency Swaps, Sales / Marketing — Werner Pelzmann ☎ **71707 1793**
Cross-Currency Swaps, Trading — Lilo Buchgraber ☎ **71707 1294**
Vanilla FX Option Sales — Werner Pelzmann ☎ **71707 1793**
Vanilla FX Option Trading — Gerhard Herda ☎ **71707 1280**

OTC Equity Derivatives
Sales — Malleras Siller ☎ **71707 3340**
Trading — Hannes Reisinger ☎ **71707 3335**

Settlement / Clearing
Derivatives Settlement — Ernst Steiger
Foreign Exchange Settlement — Werner Holy

Other Departments
Correspondent Banking — Heinz Hoedl

Administration
Technology & Systems
— Julius Schauderhuber

Compliance
— Friedrich Sommer

Salzburger Kredit-und Wechselbank AG   Subsidiary Company
Makartplatz 3, PO Box 24, A-5024 Salzburg
Tel: (662) 8684 0

Schoellerbank Aktiengesellschaft   Head Office
Formerly known as: Schoeller & Co Bankaktiengesellschaft
Renngasse 1-3, A-1010 Vienna
Tel: (1) 53471 0 Fax: (1) 533 4390 Telex: 114219 SCHOE A Swift: SCHO AT WW

Senior Executive Officers

Others (Senior Executives)
Michael von Medem *Member, Management Board* ☎ **53471 257**
Manfred Mautner Markhof *Member, Management Board* ☎ **53471 255**

General-Lending (DCM, SL)
Head of Corporate Banking — Klaus Windischbauer *Manager* ☎ **53471 296**
Christoph Staelin *Manager* ☎ **(662) 88559 20**

Syndicated Lending
Trade Finance — Norbert Schran *Senior Manager* ☎ **53471 432**

Money Markets
Global Head — Erich Stejskal *Manager* ☎ **53471 480**

Foreign Exchange
Global Head — Gustav Rakovsky *Manager* ☎ **53471 454**

Risk Management
Global Head — Helmut Pitsch *Senior Manager* ☎ **53471 634**

Corporate Finance / M&A Advisory
Global Head — Helmut Pitsch *Senior Manager* ☎ **53471 634**

Settlement / Clearing
Operations — Peter Heiling *Senior Manager* ☎ **53471 393**

Other Departments
Private Banking — Alexander Götzinger *Manager* ☎ **53471 560**
Correspondent Banking — Norbert Schran *Senior Manager* ☎ **53471 432**

www.euromoneydirectory.com AUSTRIA (+43)

Société Générale Zweigniederlassung Wien — Full Branch Office   A

Alternative trading name: SG
Formerly known as: Société Générale (Austria) Bank AG
Prinz-Eugen-Strasse 32, A-1040 Vienna
PO Box 82, A-1041 Vienna
Tel: (1) 50695 0 **Fax:** (1) 50695 95 **Telex:** 133766 **Swift:** SGAB AT WW **Reuters:** SOGV
Website: www.socgen.com

Senior Executive Officers
Financial Director — Reinhard Dauböck *Head of Administration* ☎ **50695 30**
Treasurer — Emil Steiner *Head of Dealing Room* ☎ **50695 80**
General Manager — Dieter Dulias

General-Lending (DCM, SL)
Head of Corporate Banking — George Buxbaum ☎ **50695 45**

Syndicated Lending
Head of Syndication — Danièle Walther ☎ **50695 26**
Sandra Neumayr ☎ **50695 27**

Loan-Related Activities
Trade Finance; Project Finance — Danièle Walther ☎ **50695 26**

Foreign Exchange
Telex: 136292
Head of Foreign Exchange — Emil Steiner *Head of Dealing Room* ☎ **50695 80**

Risk Management
Head of Risk Management — Reinhard Dauböck *Head of Administration* ☎ **50695 30**

Settlement / Clearing
Head of Settlement / Clearing — Alexandra Golosetti ☎ **50695 28**

Other Departments
Correspondent Banking — Rudolf Bruckner ☎ **50695 44**

Administration
Head of Administration — Reinhard Dauböck *Head of Administration* ☎ **50695 30**

Steiermärkische Bank und Sparkassen AG — Head Office

Alternative trading name: Bank Styria
Rathaus, Sparkassenplatz 4, A-8010 Graz
Tel: (316) 8033 0 **Fax:** (316) 8033 2999 **Telex:** 311280 **Swift:** STSP AT 2G **Email:** bankstyria@bankstyria.co.at
Reuters: GRAZ

Senior Executive Officers
President — Ernst Hoeller
Chief Executive Officer — Josef Kassler
Treasurer — Harald Seyer ☎ **8033 4471**
International Division — Franz Mally ☎ **8033 5272**

Money Markets
Head of Money Markets — Volker Wetschnig
Birgidd Kadanik

Foreign Exchange
Global Head — Volker Wetschnig
Birgidd Kadanik

Other Departments
Commodities / Bullion — Ernst Stelzmann ☎ **8033 5280**
Private Banking — Werner Schmidt *Director* ☎ **8033 4021**
Correspondent Banking — Martina Schleich ☎ **8033 4048**

Administration
Technology & Systems — Helmut Vanek *Director* ☎ **8033 4440**

Legal / In-House Counsel
Dr Stuerzer *Syndikus* ☎ **8033 4306**

Public Relations
Barbara Kunzfeld-Muhi ☎ **8033 4055**

Euromoney Directory 1999   **99**

AUSTRIA (+43) www.euromoneydirectory.com

Tiroler Sparkasse Bank Aktiengesellschaft Innsbruck
Head Office

Sparkassenplatz 1, A-6020 Innsbruck
Tel: (512) 591 0 Fax: (512) 591 2519; (512) 591 0720 Telex: 533773 SPIFX A Swift: SPIH AT 22 Reuters: SPKI

Senior Executive Officers
General Director   Ernst Wunderbaldinger [T] 591 0110 [F] 591 0115
Chairperson, Supervisory Board Ivo Greiter [T] 591 0110
Chief Executive Officer   Ernst Wunderbaldinger *General Director* [T] 591 0110 [F] 591 0115
Financial Director   Reiner Splechtna *Director* [T] 591 0103
Treasurer   Gernot Deutschmann [T] 590 530

Debt Capital Markets / Fixed Income
Head of Fixed Income   Gernot Deutschmann [T] 590 530

Syndicated Lending
Head of Syndicated Lending   Herbert Kuess [T] 591 0755

Loan-Related Activities
Trade Finance; Project Finance Herbert Kuess [T] 591 0755

Money Markets
Head of Money Markets   Gernot Deutschmann [T] 590 530

Foreign Exchange
Head of Foreign Exchange   Gernot Deutschmann [T] 590 530

The Tokai Bank Limited
Representative Office

4th Floor, Schwarzenbergplatz 16, A-1070 Vienna
Tel: (1) 5012 8150 Fax: (1) 5012 8333

Senior Executive Officers
Chief Representative   Toru Kojima

Vorarlberger Landes-und Hypothekenbank

Hypo-Passage 1, A-6900 Bregenz
Tel: (5574) 414 0 Fax: (5574) 414 457
Website: www.hypovbg.at

Senior Executive Officers
Chairman of the Board   Kurt Rupp
President   Jodok Simma
Chief Executive Officer   Ernst Stadelman *Vice President*
                                Johannes Hefel *Vice President*

Welser Volksbank rGmbH
Head Office

Eisenhowerstraße 32, A-4600 Wels
PO Box 190, A-4601 Wels
Tel: (7242) 495 0 Fax: (7242) 495 97 Swift: VBWE AT 2W

Senior Executive Officers
Chairman   Josef Steinböck
Managing Director   Hans Mayr [T] 495 250
International Division   Alfred Radinger [T] 495 232

General-Lending (DCM, SL)
Head of Corporate Banking   Werner Deixler [T] 495 260

Equity Capital Markets
Equity Repo / Securities Lending
Head   Christian Ernst [T] 495 234

Foreign Exchange
Head of Foreign Exchange   Christianne Ikonen [T] 495 287

Corporate Finance / M&A Advisory
Global Head   Werner Deixler [T] 495 260

Asset Management
Head   Manfred Part [T] 495 281

Other Departments
Private Banking
Correspondent Banking
Cash Management
Administration
Head of Marketing
Technology & Systems

Accounts / Audit

Gerhard Niklas ☏ 495 226
Günter Wiplinger ☏ 495 289
Klaus Hatheier ☏ 495 229

Rudolf Kotzian ☏ 495 240

Christian Mayr ☏ 495 200

Hubert Alt ☏ 495 205

AZERBAIJAN (+994)

National Bank of Azerbaijan 🏛 Central Bank

19 Bul Bul Avenue, Baku, 370070
Tel: 935 058 Fax: 935 541 Telex: 142163 Swift: NABZ AZ 2X

Senior Executive Officers
Chairman of the Board
First Deputy Chairman
Deputy Chairman
Deputy Chairman
Deputy Chairman

Others (Senior Executives)
Head, Bank Licensing
Head, Banking Supervisioin
Head, Economics & Statistics
Head, Reserves Management

Foreign Exchange
Head of Foreign Exchange

Settlement / Clearing
Head of Settlement / Clearing

Administration
Head of Administration

Accounts / Audit
Head, Accountancy

Elman Rustamov ☏ 935 058 ext 201
Alim Guliyev ☏ 935 058 ext 206
Abdulla Malik Aslanov ☏ 935 058 ext 204
Abuffaz Akhoundov ☏ 935 058 ext 205
Vadim Khubanov ☏ 935 058 ext 245

Zakiz Kazimov ☏ 935 058 ext 223
Namik Samedov ☏ 935 058 ext 208
Avtandil Babayev ☏ 935 058 ext 212
Shakhmar Movsumov ☏ 935 058 ext 319

Samiz Shazifov ☏ 935 058 ext 213

Razim Veliyev ☏ 935 058 ext 230

Mustafa Mustafayev ☏ 935 058 ext 211

Aliya Vezikova *Chief Accountant* ☏ 935 058 ext 217

European Bank for Reconstruction & Development
Representative Office

5 Sabir Street, Baku, 370004
Tel: (12) 971 014 Fax: (12) 971 019

Senior Executive Officers
Mission Advisor

Murat Yildiran

BAHAMAS (+1)

The Central Bank of the Bahamas 🏛 Central Bank

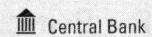

Formerly known as: Bahamas Monetary Authority
PO Box N-4868, Nassau
Tel: (242) 322 2193/6; (242) 302 2600 Fax: (242) 322 4321 Telex: 20115 Swift: CBBH BS NS
Email: centralbankbah@mail.batelnet.bs
Extra Telex: 20242

Senior Executive Officers
Governor
Deputy Governor

Julian Francis
Wendy Craigg

BAHAMAS (+1)   www.euromoneydirectory.com

The Central Bank of the Bahamas (cont)

General-Investment
Head of Investment   Sherman Cecile *Manager, Banking*

Debt Capital Markets / Fixed Income
Department: Banking
Tel: 322 2193 Fax: 322 4321 Telex: 20115, 20242
Head of Fixed Income Sales   Cecile Sherman *Banking Manager*

Corporate Finance / M&A Advisory
Head of Corporate Finance   Henderson Wilson *Manager, Accounts*

Settlement / Clearing
Fax: 322 4321 Telex: 20115
Head of Settlement / Clearing   Sherman Cecile *Manager, Banking*

Administration

Technology & Systems
    Bert Sherman *Manager, Computer*

Compliance
    Iqbal Singh *Manager, Bank Supervision*

Public Relations
    W Lester Bowleg *Manager, Human Resources*

Corporate Communications
    Henderson Wilson *Manager, Accounts*

CIBC Trust Company (Bahamas) Limited   Subsidiary Company

PO Box N-3933, Nassau
Tel: (242) 323 3314 Fax: (242) 328 2102 Telex: 20343 Swift: CIBC BS NS ATST

Senior Executive Officers
Managing Director   Christopher F Richmond

Credit Suisse (Bahamas) Limited   Subsidiary Company

4th Floor, Bahamas Financial Center, Shirley & Charlotte Street, Nassau
PO Box N-4928, Nassau
Tel: (242) 322 8345; (242) 356 8100 Fax: (242) 326 6589 Telex: 20178 Swift: CRES BS NS AN

Senior Executive Officers
Chief Executive Officer
Chief Operating Officer   Gregory H Bethel *Managing Director*
    Carl M Albury *Senior Manager*

Foreign Exchange
Head of Trading   Stephen Duncombe *Manager*

Settlement / Clearing
Equity Settlement   Marcel Knecht *Supervisor*

Other Departments
Private Banking   Alfred Notter *Senior Manager*

The Deltec Banking Corporation Limited   Head Office

Deltec House, Lyford Cay, Nassau NP
PO Box N-3229, Nassau
Tel: (242) 302 4100 Fax: (242) 362 4623 Telex: 20 101 PANDELTEC

Senior Executive Officers
Chairman & Chief Executive   David P McNaughton
Financial Director   Terry Girling
Chief Operating Officer; Treasurer   Gordon Bradshaw
Managing Director / General Manager   Jennifer Rahming

BAHAMAS (+1)

ENI International Bank Limited — Head Office

IBM Building, East Bay Street, Nassau
PO Box SS-6377, Nassau
Tel: (242) 322 1928 **Fax:** (242) 323 8600 **Telex:** 20105, 20221 ENIBANK

Senior Executive Officers
Chairman & President — Franco Luigi
Deputy Chairman & MD — Diego Munafo'
Financial Director — Sergio Paolucci

Syndicated Lending

Other (Trade Finance)
Documentary Credits — Luisa Borgogno

Foreign Exchange
Department: Foreign Exchange & Treasury
Global Head — Annie Simon

Other Departments
Correspondent Banking — Stefano Gili

Administration
Head of Administration — Giovanni Quagliero *Manager, Administration & Control*

Leu Trust & Banking (Bahamas) Limited — Subsidiary Company

2nd Floor, Norfolk House, Frederick Street, Nassau
PO Box N-3926, Nassau
Tel: (242) 326 5054 **Fax:** (242) 323 8828 **Swift:** LEUZ BS NS

Senior Executive Officers
President of the Executive Board — Reto Donatsch ☎ +1 (219) 2377 2875
Managing Director — Gregor Maissen ☎ 326 5054

Other Departments
Private Banking — Adolfo Miranda *Private Banking Manager* ☎ 328 1444

Administration
Legal / In-House Counsel
Tery Bellot *Company & Trust Manager* ☎ 328 1441

Public Relations
Sheena Dawkins *Assistant Treasurer*

The Royal Bank of Scotland International Limited

Subsidiary Company

3rd Floor, Bahamas Financial Centre, Shirley & Charlotte Streets, Nassau
PO Box N-3045, Nassau
Tel: (242) 322 4643 **Fax:** (242) 326 7559 **Swift:** RBOS CH 22

Senior Executive Officers
Managing Director — David Barron

UNIBANCO-União de Bancos Brasileiros SA — Full Branch Office

3rd Floor, Bank America House, 308 East Bay Street, Nassau
PO Box SS-6387, Nassau
Tel: (242) 394 5940; (242) 394 8316 **Fax:** (242) 394 8180; (242) 394 8181 **Telex:** 20335 **Swift:** UBBRBSNS

Senior Executive Officers
Financial Director — Alain Newry *Financial Comptroller*
Managing Director — Augosto Rocha
Deputy General Manager — Jose Maciel
Manager — Adilson Lopes

BAHRAIN (+973) www.euromoneydirectory.com

BAHRAIN
(+973)

Bahrain Monetary Agency — Central Bank
PO Box 27, Manama
Tel: 535 535 Fax: 534 170 Telex: BN 8295 BAHMON Email: bmalbr@batelco.com.bh
Website: www.bma.gov.bh

Senior Executive Officers
Prime Minister — Khalifa Bin Sulman Al Khalifa
Deputy Chairman, Finance & National Economy — Ibrahim Abdul Karim Mohammed
Governor — Abdulla Hassan Saif ☏ 529 500 F 537 799
Deputy Governor — Abdulla Bin Khalifa Al Khalifa ☏ 529 529 F 533 342

Others (Senior Executives)
Board of Directors — Abdul Rahman Taqi *Member*
Abdul Rahman Al Moayyed *Member*
Mohammed Jawad Al Modaifa'a *Member*
Head, Management Services — Naser M Y Al Belooshi *Executive Director* ☏ 529 305 F 531 115
Head, Banking Control — Khalid A Ateeq *Executive Director* ☏ 529 400 F 532 605
Head, Banking Operations — Khalid Abdulla Al Bassam *Executive Director* ☏ 529 200 F 533 776
Head, Currency Issue — Abbas Mahmoud Radhi *Director* ☏ 529 700 F 536 164
Head, Banking Services — Salman K Al Khalifa *Director* ☏ 529 206 F 532 050
Head, Financial Institutions Supervision — Anwar Khalifa Al Sadah *Director* ☏ 529 444 F 532 605
Head, Bank Supervision — Khalid Hamad Abdul Rahman *Director* ☏ 529 404 F 532 605
Head, Inspection — Whaleed Rashdan *Director* ☏ 529 420 F 532 605
Monetary Affairs — John A Howard *Advisor* ☏ 529 557 F 533 342
Economic Affairs — Bakri A Bashir *Advisor* ☏ 529 560 F 533 981

Asset Management
Investment Funds — Ahmed Isa Al Somaim *Director, Investment Directorate* ☏ 529 203 F 534 170

Other Departments
Economic Research — Abdul Rahman A Saif *Director* ☏ 529 303 F 532 274
John F Wilson *Advisor* ☏ 529 342 F 532 274

Administration
Head of Administration — Nabeel Hussain Mattar *Director, Administration Directorate* ☏ 529 310 F 530 399

Technology & Systems
Computer Services — Yousif R Al Fadhel *Director* ☏ 529 223 F 536 246

Legal / In-House Counsel
Legal Affairs — Bernadette M Doyle *Advisor* ☏ 529 531 F 533 981

Accounts / Audit
Accounts Directorate — Raqia Ebrahim Bardooli *Director* ☏ 529 323 F 530 399

ABC Islamic Bank — Head Office
ABC Tower, Diplomatic Area, PO Box 2808, Manama
Tel: 532 235 Fax: 533 163 Swift: 9432 ABCBAH BN

Senior Executive Officers
Director — Adnan A Yousif

Others (Senior Executives)
ABC London — Abdulmagid Breish *Member, Board of Directors*
ABC Jordon — Jawad Hadid *Member, Board of Directors*

General - Treasury
Head of Treasury — Essam El Wakil

ABN AMRO Bank NV — Full Branch Office
PO Box 350, Car Park Building, Al-Furdah Avenue, Manama
Tel: 225 420 Fax: 226 641 Telex: 8356 Swift: ABNA BH BM Reuters: ABNB (Monitor), Cable: BANCOLANDA

Senior Executive Officers
Chief Executive Officer — G Leot Kniphorst *General Manager* ☏ 224 309 F 214 751
Treasurer — Ahmed Ali Hassan *Manager, Treasury* ☏ 227 744 F 227 593

BAHRAIN (+973)

General-Lending (DCM, SL)	
Head of Corporate Banking	Robert Timmers *Division Manager* ☎ 210 056 F 226 641
Relationship Manager	
Global Islamic Financial Services	Richard Duncan *Manager* ☎ 224 896 F 224 318
Syndicated Lending	
Loan-Related Activities	
Trade Finance	Ahmed Matter *Marketing Manager, Trade Finance* ☎ 213 264 F 226 641
Risk Management	
Head of Risk Management	Austin Sequeira ☎ 211 372 F 226 641
Settlement / Clearing	
Operations	Abdul Nabi Sarhan *Treasury - Back-Office* ☎ 215 672 F 226 641
	Hassan Ashoor ☎ 210 592 F 226 641
Other Departments	
Private Banking	Ehab Amiri *Manager* ☎ 224 023 F 227 593
Administration	
Head of Administration	Bansi Sumathi ☎ 224 319 F 226 641
Technology & Systems	
	T S Chandra
Accounts / Audit	
Internal Auditor	N Jairaj
Other (Administration)	
Marketing	Adel Al Mannai *Manager* ☎ 213 592 F 226 641

Al-Ahli Commercial Bank BSC — Head Office

Bahrain Car Park Building, 126 Government Avenue, Manama, AHLI
PO Box 5941, Manama
Tel: 224 333 **Fax:** 224 322 **Telex:** 9130, 9130 AHLICO BN **Swift:** AHCB BH BM **Email:** alahli@al-alahlibank.com
Reuters: AHLI
Website: www.al-ahlibank.com

Senior Executive Officers
Chairman of the Board — Mohammed Yousif Jalal
First Deputy Chairman — Mohammed Abdulla Al Mannai
Second Deputy Chairman — Nooruddin A Nooruddin

Others (Senior Executives)
International Banking — Salah Murad *Senior Manager*
Board of Directors — Mohammed A Ghaffer Al Alawi *Director*
Jassim Mohammed Murad *Director*
Fuad Kanoo *Director*
A Rahman Jamsheer *Director*
Mohammed Hussain Yateem *Director*
Ali Bin Ebralum Abdul A'Al *Director*
Adel Abdulla Fakhro *Director*
Executive Management — Michael Fuller *Chief Executive*
Sabah Al-Moaayyed *First Deputy Chief Executive*
A Rahman Fakhro *Deputy Chief Executive*
Corporate / International Banking — Saleh Murad *Senior Manager* ☎ 209 109
Commercial Banking — Abdulla Al Amer *Assistant General Manager* ☎ 209 177
Retail Banking — Keith Williams *Head* ☎ 290 170
Man-Ahli Investment Bank — Antoine Massad *Managing Director* ☎ 224 317

Debt Capital Markets / Fixed Income
Department: Capital Markets, Foreign Exchange, Derivatives
Country Head — Jawad Nasser ☎ 224 317

Risk Management
Department: Credit Control & Risk Management
Head of Risk Management — Jai Menon *Assistant General Manager* ☎ 209 139

Settlement / Clearing
Operations — Sanjeev Baijal *Financial Controller* ☎ 209 117

Administration
Head of Marketing — Sadek Karam *Head* ☎ 209 104

Other (Administration)
Human Resources — Howard Winters *Senior Manager* ☎ 209 175

BAHRAIN (+973)   www.euromoneydirectory.com

ALUBAF Arab International Bank EC
Head Office

UGB Tower, Diplomatic Area, PO Box 11529, Manama
Tel: 531 212 Fax: 523 100 Telex: 9671 ALUBAF BN

Senior Executive Officers
Chairman — Rashid Al-Zayani
Vice Chairman & Chairman, Executive Committee — Mohammed Abduljawad
Deputy General Manager — Ramadan Mohammed Omeish
AGM & Secretary — Mutasim Mahmassani

ANZ Grindlays Bank plc
Full Branch Office

1st Floor, Manama Centre, Manama
PO Box 5793, Manama
Tel: 224 210 Fax: 224 478 Telex: 8723 GRNOBU BN

Senior Executive Officers
Director, ANZ Investment Banking — Stephen J Atkinson

Others (Senior Executives)
Global Islamic Finance — Tahir Chaudhary *Manager*
Transportation Finance, IME & South Asia — Sven Dybdahl *Regional Head*

Arab Banking Corporation (BSC)
Head Office

ABC Tower, Diplomatic Area, PO Box 5698, Manama
PO Box 5698, Manama
Tel: 532 235 Fax: 533 163; 533 062 Telex: 9432 ABCBAH BAH Swift: ABCOBHBM Reuters: ABCZ
FX Tel: 53 3155
Website: www.arabbanking.com

Senior Executive Officers
Chairman — Abdul Mohsen Al-Hunaif
President & Chief Executive Officer — Ghazi Abdul-Jawad ☎ **523 200**
Treasurer — Mark Leonard *Global Treasurer* ☎ **533 043**
SVP & GM, Bahrain Main Branch — Mohamed S Khleif
International Division — George Morton *First Vice President* ☎ **523 319**

General-Lending (DCM, SL)
Head of Corporate Banking — Hussam Abu Suud *First Vice President* ☎ **523 262**

General-Investment
Head of Investment — Omar El-Abd *SVP, Investment Coordinator* ☎ **533 302**

General - Treasury
Head of Treasury — Essam El Wakil *FVP, Head of Treasury & Marketable Securities* ☎ **532 933**

Debt Capital Markets / Fixed Income
Head of Fixed Income — Fuad Zeidan *FVP, Head of Investment Management* ☎ **533 169**

Government Bonds
Head of Trading — Fuad Zeidan *FVP, Head of Investment Management* ☎ **533 169**

Emerging Market Bonds
Head of Emerging Markets — Fuad Zeidan *FVP, Head of Investment Management* ☎ **533 169**

Libor-Based / Floating-Rate Products
FRN Trading — Fuad Zeidan *FVP, Head of Investment Management* ☎ **533 169**

Fixed-Income Repo
Head of Repo — Fuad Zeidan *FVP, Head of Investment Management* ☎ **533 169**

Equity Capital Markets
Department: Equities
Tel: 533 169 Fax: 532 164
Head of Trading — Anwar Abdulrahman *Manager* ☎ **533 169**

Domestic Equities
Head of Trading — Abdul Hameed Naqi *Deputy Manager* ☎ **226 848**

Other (Domestic Equities)
Head of ABC Securities W.L.L. — Yousif AlDhaen *General Manager* ☎ **523 203**
Anwar Abdulrahman *Manager* ☎ **533 169**

Risk Management
Head of Risk Management — Abhijit Choudury *VP, Credit Risk Control & Policy* ☎ **523 288**

www.euromoneydirectory.com   BAHRAIN (+973)

Other Departments
Chief Credit Officer   Ron Upstone *FVP, Senior Credit Officer & Head*
Administration
Head of Administration   Hatem Abou Said *EVP, Chief Administrative Officer* ☎ **523 207**
Technology & Systems
Global Information Technology   Sael F Al Waary *First Vice President & Head* ☎ **523 707**
Legal / In-House Counsel
Legal Affairs   Mounir Ben Slimane *Legal Counsel & Head* ☎ **523 371**
Corporate Communications
   Sami Dannish *Vice President & Head* ☎ **523 204**
Accounts / Audit
Internal Audit   Prasad Abraham *First Vice President & Head* ☎ **523 387**

The Arab Investment Company   Head Office

4th Floor, Standard Chartered Bank Building, Government Avenue, Manama
Tel: 227 126 **Fax:** 225 007 **Telex:** 8334TAIC BN, 7055 TAIC FX **Swift:** TAIQ BH BM **Reuters:** TAIC-L **Cable:** AMWAL
Dealers Tel: 22 8146

Senior Executive Officers
Chairman   Muhammad S Al-Jasser
Vice Chairman   Fahd Rashid Al-Ebrahim
Chief Executive Officer   Ali Al-Shiddi *Assistant Director General*
   Saleh Al-Humaidan *Director General*
Financial Director   Abdul Wahid Mearza *Director of Finance*
General Manager, OBU, Bahrain   Faisal M Al-Alwan

Others (Senior Executives)
Islamic Banking   Sulieman Walhad *Manager* ☎ **214 312** 🖷 **214 514**

Debt Capital Markets / Fixed Income
Tel: 228 146 **Fax:** 215 054
Global Head   Sami Rais *Senior Manager*
Regional Head   Ibrahim Radhi *Manager*
Country Head   Dana Al-Tajer *Assistant Manager*

Bonds - General
New Issue Syndication   Sami Rais *Senior Manager*
   Ibrahim Radhi *Manager*
   Dana Al-Tajer *Assistant Manager*

Private Placements
Head of Origination   Sami Rais *Senior Manager*
Head of Sales   Aqeel Al-Owed *Manager*
Head of Structuring   Sami Rajab *Manager*
   Nestor Ang *Assistant Manager*

Syndicated Lending
Other (Syndicated Lending)
Loans & Facilities   Nabil Hamdan *Senior Manager* ☎ **214 286**

Loan-Related Activities
Trade Finance   Mohammed Atti *Senior Manager* ☎ **225 014**

Other (Trade Finance)
Forfaiting   Mohammed Atti *Senior Manager* ☎ **225 014**

Money Markets
Tel: 228 146 **Fax:** 215 064
Head of Money Markets   Sami Rais *Senior Manager*

Other (Wholesale Deposits)
   Aqeel Al-Owed *Manager*
   Sami Rajab *Manager*
   Nestor Ang *Assistant Manager*

Foreign Exchange
Tel: 228 146 **Fax:** 215 064
Head of Foreign Exchange   Sami Rais *Senior Manager*

FX Traders / Sales People
   Aqeel Al-Owed *Manager*
   Sami Rajab *Manager*
   Nestor Ang *Assistant Manager*

BAHRAIN (+973)   www.euromoneydirectory.com

The Arab Investment Company (cont)
Risk Management
Department: Interest & Currency Swaps
Fax: 215 064
Head of Risk Management   Sami Rais *Senior Manager*
Other (FI Derivatives)
                                Aqeel Al-Owed *Manager*
                                Sami Rajab *Manager*
Corporate Finance / M&A Advisory
Head of Corporate Finance   Fahad Naseeb *Manager* ☎ 211 752 ℱ 214 514
Settlement / Clearing
Operations   Navinsing Mareeachalee *Senior Manager* ☎ 225 048
Administration
Head of Administration   Ziad Bachnak *Senior Manager, Administration & Finance* ☎ 224 997
                                ℱ 215 064
Business Development   Kamal El Zubeir ☎ 225 039

Bahrain International Bank EC   Head Office
Sheraton Complex, Manama
PO Box 5016, Manama
Tel: 538 777 **Fax:** 534 833; 535 141 **Telex:** 9832 BIB BN **Reuters:** BIBN (Monitor)
Website: www.dilmun.com

Senior Executive Officers
Chairman of the Board   Faisal Al Marzook
Vice Chairman of the Board   Sami Kaiksow
Chief Executive Officer   Robin McIlvenny
                                David J Mathies,Jr *Deputy Chief Executive*
Financial Director   Sameer Al Aradi *Chief Financial Officer*
General-Investment
Head of Investment   James Conlon *MD, Merchant Banking*
                                Victor Kiarsis *MD, Merchant Banking*
                                Stephen Mallet *MD, Merchant Banking*
                                Benjamin Bach *Director, Merchant Banking*
                                Ruth Eaton *Director, Merchant Banking*
                                Paul Murphy *Director, Merchant Banking*
                                Nick Sutton *MD, Real Estate*
                                Christopher Ford *Assistant Director, Real Estate*
                                David Jansen *MD, Investment Securities*
                                Tom Buchanan *Director, Investment Securities*

General - Treasury
Head of Treasury   Cassim Docrat *Director, Treasury & Financial Institutions*
                                Abdul Aziz A Nabi *Chief Dealer*

Debt Capital Markets / Fixed Income
Non-Domestic Government Bonds
                                David Jansen *MD, Investment Securities*
Eurobonds
Head of Origination   David Jansen *MD, Investment Securities*
Libor-Based / Floating-Rate Products
FRN Origination   David Jansen *MD, Investment Securities*
Medium-Term Notes
Head of Origination   David Jansen *MD, Investment Securities*
Private Placements
Head of Origination   James Conlon *MD, Investment Securities*
                                Victor Kiarsis *MD, Merchant Banking*
                                Stephen Mallet *MD, Merchant Banking*

Asset-Backed Securities / Securitization
Global Head   David Jansen *MD, Investment Securities*
Head of Trading   Tom Buchanan *Director, Investment Securities*
Mortgage-Backed Securities
Global Head   David Jansen *MD, Investment Securities*
Fixed-Income Repo
Head of Repo   David Jansen *MD, Investment Securities*

www.euromoneydirectory.com BAHRAIN (+973)

Equity Capital Markets
Other (International Equity)
US Equities, Origination — David Jansen *MD, Investment Securities*
Int'l Equities / Private Placement — James Conlon *MD, Investment Securities*
Stephen Mallet *MD, Merchant Banking*
Victor Kiarsis *MD, Merchant Banking*

Convertibles / Equity-Linked
Head of Origination — James Conlon *MD, Merchant Banking*
Head of Syndication — Stephen Mallet *MD, Merchant Banking*
Head of Sales — Victor Kiarsis *MD, Merchant Banking*

Warrants
Head of Sales — James Conlon *MD, Merchant Banking*
Victor Kiarsis *MD, Merchant Banking*
Head of Trading — Stephen Mallet *MD, Merchant Banking*

Syndicated Lending
Other (Trade Finance)
Asset Liabilities Management — Cassim Docrat *Director, Treasury & Financial Institutions*
Real Estate — Nick Sutton *MD, Real Estate*

Money Markets
Country Head — A Aziz A Nabi

Eurocommercial Paper
Head of Origination — David Jansen *MD, Investment Securities*

Risk Management
Global Head — William Khouri *Managing Director*
Regional Head — Deepa Chandrasekhar *Assistant Director*

Corporate Finance / M&A Advisory
Other (Corporate Finance)
Ali Mansoori *Director*
Faisel Hoodbhoy *Director, Corporate Finance*
Firas Shehab *Assistant Director*

Settlement / Clearing
Regional Head; Operations — Naeem Karmustaji *Director*
Operations — Jalal Haji *Assistant Director*

Global Custody
Regional Head — David Jansen *MD, Investment Securities*

Other Departments
Proprietary Trading — Nick Sutton *MD, Real Estate*
Correspondent Banking — Cassim Docrat *Director, Treasury & Financial Institutions*

Administration
Head of Marketing — Abdul Razak Jawahery *Director*
Mohamed Nooruddin *Director, Head of Marketing*
George Kardouche *Senior Adviser*

Technology & Systems
Neal Lowson *Director, IT*

Public Relations
Media — Abdul Razak Jawahery *Director*

Accounts / Audit
Internal Audit — Khalid Abdul Karim *Director*

Bahrain Middle East Bank (EC)   Head Office

BMB Centre, Diplomatic Area, Manama
PO Box 797, Manama
Tel: 532 345 **Fax:** 530 526; 530 987 **Telex:** 9706 BMB BN **Reuters:** BMBB; BMBC; BMBD **Cable:** BMB
Reuters: BMBC; BMBD

Senior Executive Officers
Chairman — Abdul Rahman Al-Ateeqi ☎ 528 101
Vice Chairman — Ebrahim Al-Khalifa
Chief Executive Officer — Albert I Kittaneh *Chief Executive* ☎ 528 101
Chief Operating Officer — Abdul Aziz Abdul Malik *AGM, Operations* ☎ 528 111
Treasurer — Georges N Zouein *AGM, Treasury* ☎ 528 123 F 533 704
Executive Vice President — Stewart Hay ☎ 528 111
Senior Representative, UK — David Brunskill ☎ +44 (171) 236 0413 F +44 (171) 236 0409

Euromoney Directory 1999   109

BAHRAIN (+973)

www.euromoneydirectory.com

Bahrain Middle East Bank (EC) (cont)

General-Investment
Head of Investment — Robert Moxon *Executive Vice President, Investments* T 528 140 F 530 636
Alwaleed Kamal *Senior Vice President, Investor Marketing* T 528 161
F 536 312

Debt Capital Markets / Fixed Income
Head of Fixed Income — Georges N Zouein *AGM, Treasury* T 528 123 F 533 704

Government Bonds
Head of Trading — Dominic Bullman *Assistant Vice President* T 528 544 F 533 704

Emerging Market Bonds
Head of Trading — Samer Alabed *AVP, Treasury* T 528 543 F 533 704

Fixed-Income Repo
Head of Trading — Dominic Bullman *Assistant Vice President* T 528 544 F 533 704
Other — Samer Alabed *AVP, Treasury* T 528 543 F 533 704

Equity Capital Markets
Head of Equity Capital Markets — Robert Moxon *Executive Vice President* T 528 140 F 530 636
Head of Trading — Bassam Khoury T 258 151 F 530 636

International Equities
Head of Trading — Robert Moxon *Executive Vice President* T 528 140 F 530 636

Equity Research
Head of Equity Research — Robert Moxon *Executive Vice President* T 528 140 F 530 636

Convertibles / Equity-Linked
Head of Trading — Robert Moxon *Executive Vice President* T 528 140 F 530 636

Money Markets
Head of Money Markets — Georges N Zouein *AGM, Treasury* T 528 123 F 533 704

Foreign Exchange
Head of Foreign Exchange — Georges N Zouein *AGM, Treasury* T 528 123 F 533 704
Head of Trading — Fadhel Makhlooq *Assistant Vice President* T 528 542 F 533 704

FX Traders / Sales People
Rula Jumblat *Manager* T 528 141 F 533 704
Samer Batshoun *Assistant Manager* T 528 164 F 530 636

Risk Management
Head of Risk Management — K S Ganesh *VP, Risk Management* T 528 138 F 536 312

Fixed Income Derivatives / Risk Management
Trading — Georges N Zouein *AGM, Treasury* T 528 123 F 533 704

Foreign Exchange Derivatives / Risk Management
Spot / Forwards Trading — Georges N Zouein *AGM, Treasury* T 528 123 F 533 704

OTC Equity Derivatives
Trading — Robert Moxon *Executive Vice President* T 528 140 F 530 636

Corporate Finance / M&A Advisory
Head of Corporate Finance — Stewart Hay *Executive Vice President* T 528 111

Settlement / Clearing
Head of Settlement / Clearing; Equity
Settlement; Fixed-Income Settlement;
Operations — Mohammed Al-Mogla T 528 120 F 530 526

Other Departments
Correspondent Banking — Georges N Zouein *AGM, Treasury* T 528 123 F 533 704
Cash Management — Abdul Aziz Abdul Malik *AGM, Operations* T 528 111

Administration
Head of Administration — Mohammed Al-Shaikh T 528 119
Business Development; Head of Marketing — Alwaleed Kamal *Senior Vice President, Investor Marketing* T 528 161
F 536 312

Technology & Systems
Information Technology — Naresh Kumaran *Manager* T 528 148

Legal / In-House Counsel
Tala Fakhro *Manager, Corporate Finance* T 528 157

Compliance
Ravi Khot *Group Financial Controller* T 528 117

Public Relations
Haya Abuzeid *SVP, Corporate Communications* T 528 102

Corporate Communications
Haya Abuzeid *SVP, Corporate Communications* T 528 102

Accounts / Audit
Warqa Roohani T 528 116

The Bahraini Saudi Bank BSC — Head Office

PO Box 1159, Manama
Tel: 211 010 **Fax:** 210 989 **Telex:** 7232 BASB BN **Swift:** BSAU BH BM

Senior Executive Officers
Chairman	Ebrahim Bin Hamad Al-Khalifa
Vice Chairman	Fahad M Al Athel
General Manager	Mansoor Al Sayed

General - Treasury
Head of Treasury — Ali M Qahtan *Assistant General Manager, Treasury*

Money Markets
Head of Money Markets — Ali M Qahtan *Assistant General Manager, Treasury*

Foreign Exchange
Head of Foreign Exchange — Ali M Qahtan *Assistant General Manager, Treasury*

Risk Management
Head of Risk Management — Arunava Banerjee *Assistant General Manager, Corporate Banking*

Corporate Finance / M&A Advisory
Head of Corporate Finance — Arunava Banerjee *Assistant General Manager, Corporate Banking*

Settlement / Clearing
Head of Settlement / Clearing; Operations — Satya Dayanand *Assistant General Manager, Corporate Banking*
Operations — S G Sankara Raman *Assistant General Manager, Corporate Banking*

Administration
Head of Administration — Satya Dayanand *Assistant General Manager, Corporate Banking*

Technology & Systems
Technology & Software — Satya Dayanand *Assistant General Manager, Corporate Banking*

Public Relations
Satya Dayanand *Assistant General Manager, Corporate Banking*

Corporate Communications
Corporate Communications & Advertising — Satya Dayanand *Assistant General Manager, Corporate Banking*

Bank of Bahrain and Kuwait BSC — Head Office

43 Government Avenue, Manama, 305
PO Box 597, Manama, 305
Tel: 223 388 **Fax:** 229 822 **Telex:** 8919 BAKUBK BN **Swift:** BBKU BH BM **Email:** bbkrbd@batelco.com.bh
Reuters: BBKB **Cable:** BAHKUBANK
Website: www.bbkonline.com

Senior Executive Officers
Chairman — Rashid Al-Zayani T **223 388** F **229 822**
Chief Executive Officer — Murad Murad *General Manager & Chief Executive Officer* T **207 555** F **229 199**
Financial Director — Farid Al-Mulla *DGM, Business Group* T **207 473** F **229 199**
Chief Operating Officer — Peter Stevenson *DGM, Support Group* T **207 413** F **229 199**
Treasurer — Jeremy Jacquet *Treasurer* T **207 551** F **213 561**
General Manager & Chief Executive Officer — Murad Murad T **207 555** F **229 199**
Board Secretary — Saad Al-Hooti T **207 464** F **229 199**
International Division — Shahriar Khoshabi *AGM, International Banking* T **207 446** F **213 370**

Others (Senior Executives)
Head of Finance — Yousif Khalaf *AGM, Risk & Financial Control* T **207 434** F **215 994**
Head of Human Resources & Administration — A Hussain Bustani *AGM, Human Resources & Administration* T **207 442** F **228 200**
Head of Central Processing — A Wahid Noor *AGM, Central Processing* T **207 410** F **229 199**
Head of IT — A Rahman Hussain *AGM, IT* T **207 224** F **229 722**

General-Lending (DCM, SL)
Head of Corporate Banking — Jamal Hijres *AGM, Corporate Banking* T **207 474** F **213 371**

General-Investment
Head of Investment — Ibrahim Buhindi *AGM, Treasury & Investments* T **207 444** F **213 561**

Debt Capital Markets / Fixed Income
Head of Fixed Income; Head of Fixed Income Sales; Head of Fixed Income Trading — Suhail Hajee *Senior Manager* T **207 567** F **210 387**

Government Bonds
Head of Trading — Suhail Hajee *Senior Manager* T **207 567** F **210 387**

Eurobonds
Head of Trading — Suhail Hajee *Senior Manager* T **207 567** F **210 387**

BAHRAIN (+973)

www.euromoneydirectory.com

Bank of Bahrain and Kuwait BSC (cont)

Emerging Market Bonds
Head of Emerging Markets — Amit Kumar *Senior Manager* T 207 503 F 213 370

Libor-Based / Floating-Rate Products
FRN Trading; Asset Swaps — Jeremy Jacquet *Treasurer* T 207 551 F 213 561

Fixed-Income Research
Head of Fixed Income — Suhail Hajee *Senior Manager* T 207 567 F 210 387

Equity Capital Markets
Head of Equity Capital Markets — Suhail Hajee *Senior Manager* T 207 567 F 210 387

International Equities
Head of Trading — Suhail Hajee *Senior Manager* T 207 567 F 210 387

Equity Research
Head of Equity Research — Suhail Hajee *Senior Manager* T 207 567 F 210 387

Convertibles / Equity-Linked
Head of Trading — Suhail Hajee *Senior Manager* T 207 567 F 210 387

Syndicated Lending
Tel: 223 388 Fax: 213 370
Head of Syndication — Amit Kumar *Senior Manager* T 207 503 F 213 370

Loan-Related Activities
Trade Finance — Mahmood A Aziz *Senior Manager* T 207 430 F 227 727
Project Finance — Jamal Hijres *AGM, Corporate Banking* T 207 474 F 213 371

Money Markets
Head of Money Markets — Jeremy Jacquet *Treasurer* T 207 551 F 213 561

Foreign Exchange
Tel: 223 388 Fax: 213 561 Reuters: BBKB Telex: 8919 BAKUBK BN
Head of Foreign Exchange; Head of Institutional Sales; Corporate Sales; Head of Trading — Jalal Al Hussaini *Chief Dealer* T 227 441 F 213 561

Risk Management
Tel: 223 388 Fax: 229 822 Reuters: BBKB Telex: 8919 BAKUBK BN
Head of Risk Management — A Mannan Al Bastaki *Senior Manager* T 207 449 F 229 822

Settlement / Clearing
Tel: 223 388 Fax: 229 822 Reuters: BBKB Telex: 8919 BAKUBK BN
Head of Settlement / Clearing; Equity Settlement; Fixed-Income Settlement — Reyadh Sater *Senior Manager* T 207 432 F 229 822
Back-Office — Mahdi A Nabi *Manager* T 207 447 F 213 561

Asset Management
Head — Suhail Hajee *Senior Manager* T 207 567 F 210 387

Other Departments
Chief Credit Officer — Yousif Khalaf *AGM, Risk & Financial Control* T 207 434 F 215 994
Private Banking — Ahmed Al-Banna *AGM, Retail Banking* T 207 456 F 213 369
Correspondent Banking — Khalifa Nayem *Manager* T 207 550 F 213 370

Administration
Head of Administration — A Hussain Bustani *AGM, Human Resources & Administration* T 207 442 F 228 200
Business Development — A Nasser A Rahman *Manager* T 207 407 F 225 109

Technology & Systems
A Rahman Hussain *AGM, IT* T 207 224 F 229 822

Legal / In-House Counsel
Ismail Fakhri *Manager* T 20 7484 F 21 5994

Accounts / Audit
Raouf Azraq *Senior Manager* T 207 572 F 225 703

Bank of Bermuda Limited — Representative Office

Suite 3, 6th Floor, Bahrain Commercial Centre, Essa Al Khabeer Road, PO Box 11265, Manama, 316
Tel: 535 100 Fax: 533 266

Senior Executive Officers
Vice President — Thomas J B Kelly

www.euromoneydirectory.com   BAHRAIN (+973)

Bank Melli Iran
Full Branch Office
City Centre, Government Road, Manama
PO Box 785, Manama
Tel: 229 910 Fax: 224 402 Telex: 8266

Senior Executive Officers
General Manager   Ali Asghar Kamali Roosta

Bankers Trust Company
Representative Office
Entrance 4, 1st Floor, Manama Center, PO Box 5905, Manama
Tel: 229 966 Fax: 229 991 Telex: 9020 BN

Senior Executive Officers
VP & Representative   Salman Hussain

BNP Bahrain
Full Branch Office
BKIC House, Diplomatic Area, Manama
PO Box 5253, Manama
Tel: 531 152 Fax: 531 237 Telex: 8595 (General), 8596 (Dealers), Swift: BNPA BH BM Reuters: BNPB (Dealing)
Dealers Tel: 531 116; Equities Tel: 533 978; Representative Office Tel: 536 301

Senior Executive Officers
General Manager   Jean-Christophe Durand
Deputy General Manager   Eric Morin

Others (Senior Executives)
Administration & Financial Control   Alok Gupta *Manager*

General - Treasury
Head of Treasury   Glyn Davies *Treasury Manager*

Equity Capital Markets
Department: Treasury - Dealing Room
Global Head   Glyn Davies *Treasury Manager*
Regional Head   Thomas Johansen *Chief Dealer*

Other (Domestic Equities)
Gulf Currencies   Hameed Aryan *Chief Dealer*
Corporate   Fahima Sharif *Chief Dealer*
    Ali Al Sharif *Senior Dealer*
Islamic Operations   Hussain Al-Mukhareq *Chief Dealer*
Dealer   Eric Josserand *Senior Dealer*
Options Operations   Taher Al Sharif *Dealer*

Other (International Equity)
European Securities   Nabil Traboulsi *Manager*
US Securities   Mark Royal Sorensen *Manager*
Asian Securities   Mani George Kuttickal *Manager*

Administration

Other (Administration)
Administration & Financial Control   Alok Gupta *Manager*

The British Bank of the Middle East
Full Branch Office
93 Al Khalifa Avenue, Manama, 304
PO Box 57, Manama, 304
Tel: 223 254; 224 555 Fax: 222 770; 226 822 Telex: 8230 BBME BN Swift: BBME BH BX
Email: bbmemnm@batelco.com.bh
Website: www.britishbank.com

Senior Executive Officers
Chief Executive Officer   Saleh S AlKowary

Global Custody
Country Head   T T Bhat *Manager, Treasury & Securities*

Euromoney Directory 1999   113

BAHRAIN (+973)   www.euromoneydirectory.com

The Chase Manhattan Bank
4th Floor, Bahrain Commercial Complex, PO Box 368, Government Road, Manama
Tel: 535 388 Fax: 535 135 Telex: 8286 CMBBAH BN
Senior Executive Officers
Managing Director, Area Manager Gulf   John Elkhair ☎ 522 760 ℻ 522 751
Managing Director, Middle East Region   Mahmoud Difrawy ☎ 522 700 ℻ 535 149

Citi Isalmic Investment Bank EC   Head Office
Bab-Al-Bahrain Building, Government Road, PO Box 3199, Manama
Tel: 210 411 Fax: 228 900 Telex: 8225 CITIBAK BN
Senior Executive Officers
Chairman   Mohammed Al-Shroogi ☎ 207 650
Chief Operating Officer   Gilbert Noronha Senior Operations Officer ☎ 207 689
Treasurer   Umesh Jagtiani ☎ 224 735
Others (Senior Executives)
Acting General Manager   Salman Younis ☎ 207 669
Administration
Head of Marketing   Aref Al-Kooheji Head ☎ 207 686

Citibank NA   Full Branch Office
Bab-Al-Bahrain Building, Government Road, PO Box 548, Manama
Tel: 223 344 Fax: 211 323; 215 308, 213 298 Telex: 8225 CITIBAK BN
Senior Executive Officers
Chief Executive Officer   Mohammed Al-Shroogi Middle East Regional Director ☎ 207 650
Financial Director   Monaim Bastaki Financial Control ☎ 207 679
Chief Operating Officer   Gilbert Noronha Senior Operations Officer ☎ 207 689
Treasurer   Umesh Jagtiani ☎ 224 735
Others (Senior Executives)
Chief of Staff   Shirish Trivedi ☎ 207 660
General-Lending (DCM, SL)
Head of Corporate Banking   Mohammed Al-Shroogi Middle East Regional Director ☎ 207 650
Relationship Manager
Financial Institutions   Raj Dvivedi ☎ 207 646
       Wagdi Rabbat Head ☎ 207 642
Debt Capital Markets / Fixed Income
Department: Debt, Derivatives & FX
Head of Debt Capital Markets   Sanjay Bagga Unit Head
Syndicated Lending
Head of Syndicated Lending   Wagdi Rabbat Head ☎ 207 642
Money Markets
Head of Money Markets   Nabil Khemiri Unit Head
Foreign Exchange
Head of Foreign Exchange   Mohammed Al-Shroogi ☎ 247 650
Risk Management
Head of Risk Management   Raj Jajaram Head
Foreign Exchange Derivatives / Risk Management
Global Head   Umesh Jagtiani ☎ 247 629
Corporate Finance / M&A Advisory
Head of Corporate Finance   Wagdi Rabbat Head ☎ 207 642
Settlement / Clearing
Head of Settlement / Clearing   Gilbert Noronha Senior Operations Officer ☎ 207 689
Operations   R Jaidev Transaction Services Head
Other Departments
Cash Management   Hani Al Maskati Head ☎ 207 605
Administration
Public Relations
       Adel Al-Shroogi Officer ☎ 207 699
Other (Administration)
Human Resources   Abdulla Edham Officer ☎ 207 662
Customer Services Group   Fuad Taqi ☎ 207 682

BAHRAIN (+973)

Citicorp Investment Bank Limited
Subsidiary Company

Commercial Building, Government Road, PO Box 2465, Manama
Tel: 274 117; 247 671 (Direct) **Fax:** 243 027 **Telex:** 8225 CITIBK BN **Reuters:** CBAH

Senior Executive Officers
Others (Senior Executives)
Vice President — Mohammed Al-Shroogi *VP & Head, Investment Banking*

Commerzbank AG
Representative Office

4th Floor, UGB Tower, Diplomatic Area, Manama
PO Box 11800, Manama
Tel: 531 431; 531 432 **Fax:** 531 435 **Email:** commerz@batelco.com.bh

Senior Executive Officers
Chief Representative — Ralph Nitzgen

Credit Suisse
Representative Office

Bahrain Chamber of Commerce & Industry Building, King Faisal Highway, Manama
PO Box 5100, Manama
Tel: 225 823 **Fax:** 213 118 **Telex:** 8426 CREDRP

Senior Executive Officers
Senior Representative — Jean-Marie Hoffman

The Dai-Ichi Kangyo Bank Limited
Representative Office

2nd Floor, Part IV, Manama Centre, Manama
PO Box 26891, Manama
Tel: 224 522; 226 937 **Fax:** 224 566 **Telex:** 9419 DKB BAH

Senior Executive Officers
Chief Representative — Shuichi Sato
Representative — Shigeo Uesugi

Daiwa Middle East EC
Subsidiary Company

Alternative trading name: Daiwa Bahrain
7th Floor, The Tower, Bahrain Commercial Complex, Government Road, PO Box 30069, Manama
Tel: 534 452 (Investment); 535 185 (Admin) **Fax:** 535 113 (Investment); 531 560 (Admin) **Telex:** 9691 DIWSEC BN
Email: daiwabah@batelco.com **Bloomberg:** ALI MONFEREDY
General Telex: 9692 DIWSEC BN

Senior Executive Officers
Chairman & Director — Nagayaoshi Miyata ☎ +44 (171) 548 8080
Financial Director — Rosario Almeida *Manager, Banking & Administration*
Managing Director — Yoshiki Koga

General-Investment
Head of Investment — Ali Monferedy *Head of Investment Department*

Debt Capital Markets / Fixed Income
Department: Investment Department
Head of Fixed Income Sales; Head of Fixed Income Trading — Ali Monferedy *Head of Investment Department*

Eurobonds
Head of Sales; Head of Trading — Ali Monferedy *Head of Investment Department*

Emerging Market Bonds
Head of Emerging Markets — Ali Monferedy *Head of Investment Department*

Equity Capital Markets
Department: Investment Department
Head of Sales; Head of Trading — Ali Monferedy *Head of Investment Department*

International Equities
Head of Sales; Head of Trading — Ali Monferedy *Head of Investment Department*

Other (International Equity)
European Equity Desk — Peter Brown *Investment Officer*
Japanese Equity Desk — Hideki Matsuno *Assistant Manager, Investment*

Euromoney Directory 1999 115

BAHRAIN (+973)   www.euromoneydirectory.com

Daiwa Middle East EC (cont)
Other (International Equity) (cont)
European Equity Desk
Asian / American Desk

Tariq Al-Samahiji *Investment Officer*
Ali Monferedy *Head of Investment Department*
Roy Thomas *Investment Officer*

Convertibles / Equity-Linked
Head of Sales; Head of Trading   Ali Monferedy *Head of Investment Department*

Money Markets
Head of Money Markets   Rosario Almeida *Manager, Banking & Administration*

Wholesale Deposits
Marketing   Junichi Shirahama *Assistant Manager, Banking & Administration*
Head of Sales   Zainab Al Safar *Head of Settlements*

Foreign Exchange
Global Head   Rosario Almeida *Manager, Banking & Administration*

FX Traders / Sales People
            Junichi Shirahama *Assistant Manager, Banking & Administration*
            Zainab Al Safar *Head of Settlements*

Risk Management
Head of Risk Management   Rosario Almeida *Manager, Banking & Administration*

Settlement / Clearing
Head of Settlement / Clearing; Equity   Zainab Al Safar *Head of Settlements*
Settlement
Operations; Back-Office   Junichi Shirahama *Assistant Manager, Banking & Administration*

Global Custody
Head of Global Custody   Junichi Shirahama *Assistant Manager, Banking & Administration*

Other Departments
Chief Credit Officer; Correspondent Banking;   Rosario Almeida *Manager, Banking & Administration*
Cash Management

Administration
Head of Administration   Rosario Almeida *Manager, Banking & Administration*
Business Development   Yoshiki Koga *Managing Director*
Head of Marketing   Ali Monferedy *Head of Investment Department*

Technology & Systems
            Rosario Almeida *Manager, Banking & Administration*

Legal / In-House Counsel
            Rosario Almeida *Manager, Banking & Administration*

Compliance
            Rosario Almeida *Manager, Banking & Administration*

Public Relations
            Vivian Penaflor *Executive Secretary*

Accounts / Audit
            Ali Essa Marzooq *Head of Accounts*

Deutsche Bank AG   Representative Office
6th Floor, Entrance 1, Manama Centre, Manama
PO Box 20619, Manama
Tel: 227 630 **Fax:** 224 437 **Telex:** 8493 DEUTBK BN

Faysal Islamic Bank of Bahrain EC   Head Office
Chamber of Commerce Building, King Faisal Highway, Manama
PO Box 3005, Manama
Tel: 227 040 **Fax:** 224 872; 210 118 **Telex:** 9270 FAISBK BN **Email:** fibbrn@batelco.com.bh **Cable:** MASFASLAM
Telex: 9411 FAIFX BN

Senior Executive Officers
Chairman   Mohammed Al-Saud
Deputy Chairman   Ahmad Salah Jamjoom
Deputy Chairman   Abdullah Ahmad Zainal Ali-Reza
President & CEO   Nabil A Nassief
Financial Director   Rizwan Sayed *Financial Controller*

General-Lending (DCM, SL)
Head of Corporate Banking   Mohamed Bucheerei *Senior Vice President*

www.euromoneydirectory.com BAHRAIN (+973)

Debt Capital Markets / Fixed Income
Department: Capital Markets & Dealing
Global Head — Mohammed Tariq *Executive Vice President*
Regional Head — Arsalan El-Guindy *Senior Vice President*
Country Head — Khalid Al-Gattan *Assistant Vice President & Dealer*

Equity Capital Markets
Head of Equity Capital Markets — Juma Abull *Senior Vice President*

Syndicated Lending
Loan-Related Activities
Trade Finance — Matdial Ansari *Resident Vice President*

Risk Management
Head of Risk Management — Akbar Chughtai *Executive Vice President*

Settlement / Clearing
Operations — Rizwan Sayed *Financial Controller*
Abdul Rahman Shehab *Executive Vice President*

Other Departments
Correspondent Banking — Youssef Shaheed *Senior Vice President*

Administration
Head of Administration — Abdul Rahim *Resident Vice President*
Head of Marketing — Abdul Aziz Al-Mutlaq *Senior Vice President*

Technology & Systems
Information Technology — Anwar Lutfullah *Executive Vice President*

Legal / In-House Counsel
M Fateh Al-Madani *Senior Vice President*

Accounts / Audit
Audit — Mian Mansoor Mannan

Flemings   Full Branch Office

Formerly known as: Robert Fleming Holdings Limited
10th Floor, Bahrain Commercial Complex, PO Box 2467, Manama
Tel: 535 152 **Fax:** 535 121 **Telex:** 7356 RFLEM BN **Reuters:** ROFX, RFBG, RFGH; FFML-O (Fleming Flagship Fund Prices); JFUT-X (Jardine Fleming UT Prices)

Senior Executive Officers
Director, GCC — Mark Lawson-Statham

Others (Senior Executives)
Retail Banking — Nikki Birch *Sales Manager*

General-Investment
Head of Investment — Patrick Grant *Manager*

Administration
Other (Administration)
Fund Marketing — Simon Barclay-Brown *Manager*

The Fuji Bank Limited   Representative Office

Part 4, Manama Centre, Government Road, PO Box 26899, Manama
Tel: 224 158 **Fax:** 224 818

Senior Executive Officers
Chief Representative for Middle East — Hiroshi Toriba

Gulf International Bank BSC   Head Office

Alternative trading name: GIB
Al-Dowali Building, 3 Palace Avenue, Manama
PO Box 1017, Manama
Tel: 534 000 **Fax:** 522 633 **Telex:** 8802 DOWALI BN **Swift:** GULF BH BM **Email:** giblib@batelco.com.bh
Reuters: GIBB **Cable:** GINTBANK
Reuters: GIBC; GIBD; GIBE
Website: www.gibonline.com

Senior Executive Officers
Chairman — Ibrahim Abdul-Karim ☎ **522 500**
Vice Chairman — Khaled Al-Fayez ☎ **522 500**

BAHRAIN (+973) www.euromoneydirectory.com

Gulf International Bank BSC (cont)
Senior Executive Officers (cont)
Chief Executive Officer Mohannad T Farouky
 Abdullah El-Kuwaiz *General Manager* ☎ **522 444**
Financial Director Anthony James *EVP & Financial Controller* ☎ **522 610**
Chief Operating Officer Antony Maw *EVP, Operations & Admin Group Head* ☎ **522 572**
Treasurer Bachir Barbir *Assistant General Manager* ☎ **522 526**

Debt Capital Markets / Fixed Income
Global Head Bachir Barbir *Assistant General Manager* ☎ **522 526**

Eurobonds
Head of Trading; Trading - Sovereigns, Mahmood Fikree *Vice President* ☎ **533 188**
Corporates, High-yield

Libor-Based / Floating-Rate Products
FRN Origination; Asset Swaps Mahmood Fikree *Vice President* ☎ **533 188**

Asset-Backed Securities / Securitization
Global Head Bachir Barbir *Assistant General Manager* ☎ **522 526**
Head of Trading Mahmood Fikree *Vice President* ☎ **533 188**

Mortgage-Backed Securities
Global Head Bachir Barbir *Assistant General Manager* ☎ **522 526**
Head of Trading Mahmood Fikree *Vice President* ☎ **533 188**

Fixed-Income Repo
Head of Repo Sunil Dattani *Vice President* ☎ **522 521**
Matched Book Manager Yaser Humaidan *Manager* ☎ **522 521**

Syndicated Lending
Global Head Farouky Mohannad *Chief Economist & Head of Research* ☎ **522 452**
Regional Head Atef Sakr *EVP & Middle East Head* ☎ **522 541**
Head of Origination Ameeri Abbas *SVP, Corporate Banking* ☎ **522 545**
Head of Syndication Abdul-Ghani Hassan *SVP, Financial Institutions & Syndication* ☎ **522 418**
Head of Trading Ihsan Munawar *VP, Syndication Unit* ☎ **522 485**
Head of Credit Committee Ebrahim Shabudin *Executive Vice President* ☎ **522 450**

Loan-Related Activities
Trade Finance Atef Sakr *EVP & Middle East Head* ☎ **522 541**
 Ameeri Abbas *SVP, Corporate Banking* ☎ **522 545**
Project Finance Atef Sakr *EVP & Middle East Head* ☎ **522 541**
 Aditya Srivastava *Vice President* ☎ **522 546**
Structured Trade Finance Atef Sakr *EVP & Middle East Head* ☎ **522 541**
 Aditya Srivastava *Vice President* ☎ **522 546**
Leasing & Asset Finance Atef Sakr *EVP & Middle East Head* ☎ **522 541**
 Aditya Srivastava *Vice President* ☎ **522 546**

Money Markets
Tel: 522 600/530 030 **Fax:** 522 636
Global Head Essa Abu-Al-Fateh *Vice President & Treasurer* ☎ **522 478**

Eurocommercial Paper
Head of Sales Nasreen Khunji *Vice President* ☎ **522 622**
Head of Trading Abdulla Haji *Vice President* ☎ **522 600**

Wholesale Deposits
Marketing Salman Al-Zayani *Senior Vice President* ☎ **522 622**

Foreign Exchange
Global Head Brian Donkin *Vice President* ☎ **522 456**
Head of Trading Rashid Al-Ahmed *Vice President* ☎ **522 456**

FX Traders / Sales People
 Hameed Janahi *Manager* ☎ **522 456**
 Younis Turabi *Vice President* ☎ **522 456**

Risk Management
Other Currency Swap / FX Options Personnel
Currency Swap Fadhel Hamad *Assistant Vice President* ☎ **522 600**
Forex Options Younis Turabi *Vice President* ☎ **522 456**

Corporate Finance / M&A Advisory
Department: Corporate & Finance Banking Division
Global Head Farouky Mohannad *Chief Economist & Head of Research* ☎ **522 452**
Regional Head Atef Sakr *EVP & Middle East Head* ☎ **522 541**
Country Head Ameeri Abbas *SVP, Corporate Banking* ☎ **522 545**

www.euromoneydirectory.com   BAHRAIN (+973)

Settlement / Clearing
Department: Product Processing Division
Regional Head — Ali Buhejji *Vice President* ☎ **522 537**
Country Head — Ebrahim Omaigan *Vice President* ☎ **522 534**
Equity Settlement; Fixed-Income Settlement — Alia Al-Amir *Assistant Vice President* ☎ **522 525**
Derivatives Settlement — Yousif Bumjaid *Assistant Vice President* ☎ **522 539**
Foreign Exchange Settlement — Aqeel Al-Ansari *Manager* ☎ **522 583**

Global Custody
Department: Product Processing Division
Regional Head — Ali Buhejji *Vice President* ☎ **522 537**

Asset Management
Other (Asset Management)
Assest & Liabilaties — Bachir A Barbir *Assistant General Manager*
Anthony James *Executive Vice President*

Other Departments
Chief Credit Officer — Ebrahim Shabudin *Executive Vice President* ☎ **522 450**
Correspondent Banking — Ali Buhejji *Vice President* ☎ **522 537**

Administration
Head of Administration — Antony Maw *Executive Vice President*
Head of Marketing — Atef E Sakr *EVP, Middle East Marketing Area*

Technology & Systems
Jameel Al-Sairafi *Vice President* ☎ **522 442**

Public Relations
Abdul Elah Al-Amer *Vice President* ☎ **522 498**

Accounts / Audit
Audit Division — Masood Zafar *Executive Vice President*

Gulf Monetary Group   Head Office
Formerly known as: Pearl Investment Co
Government Street, Unitay House, Manama
PO Box 5809, Manama
Tel: 224 677; 228 722 **Fax:** 210 606

Senior Executive Officers
Chairman — Abdul Mohsin Al-Meshaan
Chief Executive Officer — Rasheed Al-Abdul Jader *Managing Director & Chief Executive*
Assistant Vice President — Khalid Al-Bassam

The Hongkong & Shanghai Banking Corporation Limited
Full Branch Office

Mezzanine Floor, British Bank Building, Road #718, Muharraq, 207
Tel: 336 992; 336 995 **Fax:** 325 563 **Telex:** 9666 HSBCG BN

Senior Executive Officers
Manager — K H D Leelananda ☎ **325 304**

General-Lending (DCM, SL)
Head of Corporate Banking — C S Goswami *Manager, Credit* ☎ **331 688**

General - Treasury
Head of Treasury — T T Bhat *Manager, FX & Treasury*

Settlement / Clearing
Operations — D K de S Wijeyeratne *Financial Controller* ☎ **332 045**

The Industrial Bank of Japan Limited   Representative Office

4th Floor, Manama Centre, Entrance 4, Manama
PO Box 5759, Manama
Tel: 228 868; 228 869 **Fax:** 224 828 **Telex:** 9775 IBJBAH BN

Senior Executive Officers
Others (Senior Executives)
Chief Representative for the Middle East — Toshihiro Kodama ☎ **228 868**
Toshiya Sasagawa ☎ **228 869**

Euromoney Directory 1999   119

BAHRAIN (+973)   www.euromoneydirectory.com

INVESTCORP Bank EC
Head Office

Investcorp House, PO Box 6340, Manama
Tel: 532 000 Fax: 530 816 Telex: 9664 INCORP BN
Website: www.investcorp.com

Senior Executive Officers
Chairman — Abdul-Rahman Sali Al-Ateeqi
President & Chief Executive Officer — Nemir Amin Kirdar
Financial Director — Gary S Long *Chief Financial Officer*
Treasurer — Ibrahim E Gharghour *Head, Corporate Treasury*
Company Secretary — Salman A Abbasi

Administration
Head of Administration — Lawrence B Kessler *Chief Administrative Officer*

Technology & Systems
Technology / IT — Steve Ritchie *Head*

Legal / In-House Counsel
Lawrence B Kessler *Chief Administrative Officer*

Compliance
Lawrence B Kessler *Chief Administrative Officer*

Corporate Communications
Joanne Crosland *Head*

Accounts / Audit
Gary S Long *Chief Financial Officer*

INVESTCORP Trading Limited
Subsidiary Company

Diplomatic Area, PO Box 5340, Manama
Tel: 532 000; 531 011 Fax: 530 816 Telex: 8573/ 9664

Settlement / Clearing
Settlement (General) — Mohammed A Rahman ☎ 525 118

Administration

Compliance
Anthony Robinson *Head, Compliance*

RP Martin (Bahrain) WLL
Head Office

3rd Floor, Yateem Centre, Manama
PO Box 5496, Manama
Tel: 225 100; 228 449 Fax: 210 035 Telex: 8533 Reuters: RPMB Telex: 8720

Senior Executive Officers
General Manager — Yousef Baluchi

Merrill Lynch International Bank Limited
Subsidiary Company

4th Floor, Bahrain BMB Building, Diplomatic Area, PO Box 10399, Manama
Tel: 530 260 Fax: 530 245

Senior Executive Officers
Chief Executive Officer — Bruno Daher *Resident Executive Director*

National Bank of Bahrain
Head Office

NBB Tower, Government Avenue, PO Box 106, Manama
Tel: 228 800 Fax: 228 998; 213 503 Telex: 8242 NATBNK BN Swift: NBOB BH BM Email: nbb@nbbonline.com
Reuters: NBBB/NBFX Telerate: 2087
Website: www.nbbonline.com

Senior Executive Officers
Chairman — Abdulla Kanoo ☎ 228 800
Treasurer — Hussain Al Hussaini *AGM, Treasury & Capital Markets* ☎ 205 570
Managing Director — Hassan Juma
General Manager — Abdul Razak Hassan

120 Euromoney Directory 1999

www.euromoneydirectory.com BAHRAIN (+973)

Debt Capital Markets / Fixed Income
Department: Portfolio Management Unit
Tel: 214 942 **Fax**: 213 503 **Telex**: 8899
Global Head — Sami Radi *Manager* ☏ 214 942
Equity Capital Markets
Department: Portfolio Management Unit
Tel: 214 942 **Fax**: 213 503
Head of Equity Capital Markets — Aidan Synnott *Manager* ☏ 214 942
Syndicated Lending
Tel: 205 412 **Fax**: 211 494
Head of Syndication — Sten Oedman ☏ 205 509
Loan-Related Activities
Trade Finance — Sten Oedman ☏ 205 509
Project Finance — A Rahman Mohammed ☏ 205 454
Money Markets
Tel: 214 941 **Fax**: 213 503 **Reuters**: NBBB **Telex**: 8899
Head of Money Markets — Hassan Haji *Manager* ☏ 214 941
Foreign Exchange
Tel: 214 940 **Fax**: 213 503 **Reuters**: NBFX **Telex**: 8899
Head of Foreign Exchange — Mohamed Ebrahim *Senior Manager* ☏ 214 940
Other Departments
Chief Credit Officer — Raui Krishnan ☏ 205 652
Correspondent Banking — Sten Oedman ☏ 205 509
Administration
Head of Administration — Ahmed Rahim *AGM, Corporate Services* ☏ 205 357
Technology & Systems
IT — Kiran Shah *Senior Manager* ☏ 205 541
Public Relations
Ahmen Maumoon ☏ 205 507
Accounts / Audit
Internal Control — Khalil Haji *Assistant General Manager* ☏ 205 305

Nikko Europe Plc (Middle East Branch) Subsidiary Company
3rd Floor, Unitag House, Manama
PO Box 5510, Manama
Tel: 225 750 **Fax**: 224 688 **Telex**: 9619 NIKKO BN

Senior Executive Officers
Regional Executive & General Manager — Hidehiko Inoue
Administration
Head of Administration — T.S. Mahadevan *Manager*
Shinichi Toya *Deputy General Manager*
Gopal Pathak *Assistant Manager*

Nomura Investment Banking (Middle East) EC Subsidiary Company
10th & 11th Floors, BMB Centre, Diplomatic Area, PO Box 26893, Manama
Tel: 530 531 **Fax**: 530 365 **Telex**: 9070 NOMURA BN

Senior Executive Officers
Chairman — Max C Chapman Jr.
Deputy Chairman & President — Yasutomi Akabori
Director, Administration & Accounting — Hideaki Kojima
Director, Investment & Asset Management — Risaku Sakai
Settlement / Clearing
Head of Settlement / Clearing — Shuichi Kono *Manager, Settlements*
Operations — Dawood H A Abdulla *Deputy Manager, Front Operations*
Asset Management
Department: Investment & Asset Management Department
Head — Risaku Sakai *Director, Investment & Asset Management*
Tomoyuki Funabiki *Manager*

Other (Asset Management)
Masaru Tokiwa *Manager, Investment*
Daisuke Mototani *Manager, Investment*
Atsushi Ichii *Deputy Manager, Investment*
Mohammed Al Ghasrah *Deputy Manager, Investment*

BAHRAIN (+973)　　　　　　　www.euromoneydirectory.com

Nomura Investment Banking (Middle East) EC (cont)
Other (Asset Management) (cont)
　　　　　　　　　　　　　　Ali Ebrahim Al Mallah *Deputy Manager, Investment*
Administration
Head of Administration　　　　Hideaki Kojima *Director, Administration & Accounting*
Accounts / Audit
Accounts　　　　　　　　　　Masashi Yamada *Manager*

The Sakura Bank Limited　　　　　　　　　　　Representative Office

3rd Floor, Part II, Manama Centre, Government Road, PO Box 26859, Manama
Tel: 224 805 **Fax:** 224 784 **Telex:** 9427 MITKBK BN

Senior Executive Officers
Chief Representative　　　　　Yasuhiro Kanehira
Manager　　　　　　　　　　Abdulla Majed Ali

Saudi National Commercial Bank (OBU)　　　　Full Branch Office

Diplomat Tower, Diplomatic Area, PO Box 10363, Manama
Tel: 531 182; 531 183 (Forex) **Fax:** 530 657 **Telex:** 9298 NCBGX BN (General) **Reuters:** NCBB (Monitor)
Telex: 9299 NCBGX BN

Senior Executive Officers
Chief Executive Officer　　　　Saleh H A Hussain *General Manager*
Treasurer　　　　　　　　　　Yousif Al-Hamden
Others (Senior Executives)
Internal & Financial Control　　Adnan Hashim *Manager*
General-Lending (DCM, SL)
Head of Corporate Banking　　Ebrahim Shehabi *SVP, Corporate*
General - Treasury
Head of Treasury　　　　　　Ahmed Ismail *Senior Dealer*
　　　　　　　　　　　　　　Javed Pordhan *Chief Dealer*
Settlement / Clearing
Operations　　　　　　　　　P L Alagappan *VP, Operations & Administration*
Administration
Head of Administration　　　　Khalil Kooheji *Manager, Personnel & Admin*

Standard Chartered Bank　　　　　　　　　　Full Branch Office

Government Road, PO Box 29, Manama
Tel: 223 636 **Fax:** 225 001 **Telex:** 8385 **Swift:** SCBL BH BM A XXX **Email:** scbbahra@mhs.compuserve.com
Reuters: SCXB

Senior Executive Officers
Chief Executive Officer　　　　Rupert Keeley ☎ **225 032**

The Sumitomo Bank Limited　　　　　　　　　Representative Office

Entrance 3, 4th Floor, 406/407 Manama Centre, Government Road, PO Box 20483, Manama
Tel: 223 211 **Fax:** 224 424 **Telex:** 9301

Senior Executive Officers
Chief Representative　　　　　Isa Shehabi

The Tokai Bank Limited　　　　　　　　　　　Representative Office

Room 302, 3rd Floor, Part 1, Manama Centre, Government Road, Manama
PO Box 2217, Manama
Tel: 224 121 **Fax:** 224 436 **Telex:** 7361 TOKBAH BN

Senior Executive Officers
Chief Representative　　　　　Hiroshi Tamano

www.euromoneydirectory.com   BANGLADESH (+880)

UBS AG
Representative Office

5th Floor, Bahrain Commercial Complex, (Sheraton Tower), PO Box 5560, Manama
Tel: 533 303 Fax: 524 224 Telex: 9248 Cable: SWISSBANK
Website: www.ubs.com

Senior Executive Officers
Senior Representative   Hans Röthlisberger ☎ **524 222**

United Gulf Bank (BSC) EC
Head Office

UGB Tower, Diplomatic Area, PO Box 5964, Manama
Tel: 533 233 Fax: 533 137 Telex: 9556 UGBADM Swift: UGUB BH BM Reuters: UGBB

Senior Executive Officers
Chairman   Faisal Al-Ayyar
Managing Director   Masaud Hayat
General Manager   Mohammad Haroon

Others (Senior Executives)
Deputy Chairman   Hamad Al-Sabah

General - Treasury
Head of Treasury   Fayeq Hussain *Vice President, Treasury* ☎ **533 500**

Administration
Accounts / Audit
Accounts & EDP   Sawsan Siddiqi *Vice President*

Other (Administration)
Administration & Operations   Ali Al-Laith *Vice President*

Yapi ve Kredi Bankasi AS
Offshore Banking Unit

Alternative trading name: Yapi Kredi Bank
2nd Floor, Bahrain Development Bank Building, Road 1703, Diplomatic Area, Manama
PO Box 10615, Manama
Tel: 530 313; 530 312 Fax: 530 311 Telex: 9931 YAPIBAH BN Tel: 530 310; Telex: 9935 YAPIBAH BN

Senior Executive Officers
Chief Executive Officer   Sabah Tuzcu *Branch Manager*
Financial Director   Can Yildir *Assistant Manager*
Chief Operating Officer   Turan Ungor *Assistant Manager*
Treasurer   Cantekin Yildirimer
Executive Secretary   Anne Suba

BANGLADESH
(+880)

Bangladesh Krishi Bank
Head Office

Formerly known as: Agriculture Development Bank of Pakistan
Krishi Bank Bhabon, 83/85 Motijheel C/A, Dhaka 1000
Tel: (2) 955 3028 Fax: (2) 956 1211 Telex: 642526 BKB BJ

Senior Executive Officers
Chairman   Mirza A Jalil ☎ **956 1347**
Chief Executive Officer   Shoaid Ahmed *Managing Director* ☎ **956 1348**

Debt Capital Markets / Fixed Income
Department: Central Accounts & Fund Management 1
Global Head   Sushan Ulandra Shaha *Deputy General Manager* ☎ **955 7931**

Syndicated Lending
Loan-Related Activities
Project Finance   Md Liakatali Khan ☎ **955 7988**

Foreign Exchange
Department: International Department
Global Head   Raihana Aneesa Yusuf Ali *Deputy General Manager* ☎ **955 3028**

BANGLADESH (+880)　　　　　　www.euromoneydirectory.com

Bangladesh Krishi Bank (cont)

Settlement / Clearing
Department: International Department
Regional Head　　　　　　　　　Raihana Aneesa Yusuf Ali *Deputy General Manager* ☏ 955 3028

Other Departments
Correspondent Banking　　　　　Raihana Aneesa Yusuf Ali *Deputy General Manager* ☏ 955 3028

Administration

Public Relations
　　　　　　　　　　　　　　　　Md Fazlul Kabir *Chief Public Relations Officer* ☏ 955 8609

Janata Bank　　　　　　　　　　　　　　　　　　　　　　　　Head Office
110 Motijheel Commercial Area, Dhaka 1000
PO Box 468, Dhaka 1000
Tel: (2) 956 6443; (2) 956 6442 Fax: (2) 956 4644 Telex: 675840 JBD BJ

Senior Executive Officers
Managing Director　　　　　　　H A Hashem

Other Departments
Correspondent Banking　　　　　Ghiasuddin Azhar Yusuf *Deputy General Manager*

National Bank Limited　　　　　　　　　　　　　　　　　　　Head Office
18 Dilkusha Commercial Area, Dhaka 1000
PO Box 3424, Dhaka 1000
Tel: (2) 956 1201; (2) 955 7045 Fax: (2) 956 3953; (2) 956 9404 Telex: 642791 NBLHO BJ Email: nblho@citechco.net
Telerate: 642791 NBL HO BJ. Cable: NATIONALBANK, DHAKA.

Senior Executive Officers
Chairman　　　　　　　　　　　Abdul Awal ☏ 956 3952 ℻ 868 861
CEO　　　　　　　　　　　　　Sarwaruzzaman Khan ☏ 955 1201 ℻ 956 9404
Company Secretary　　　　　　　Solaiman Mojlish ☏ 955 1176
International Division　　　　　　Lakiotullah Mohd ☏ 955 7045

Administration
Head of Administration　　　　　Ziaur Rahman ☏ 956 8493
Head of Marketing　　　　　　　Salam Bhuiyan ☏ 955 0216

Technology & Systems
　　　　　　　　　　　　　　　　Abdul Wali ☏ 955 7658

Public Relations
　　　　　　　　　　　　　　　　Atm Afsar ☏ 955 2733

Accounts / Audit
　　　　　　　　　　　　　　　　Sr Alamgir ☏ 955 4314

Pangaea Partners (Bangladesh) Limited　　　　　　　　　Subsidiary Company
74 Road 11, Block D, Banani, Dhaka 1213
Tel: (2) 881 207
Website: www.pangaeapartners.com

Senior Executive Officers
Managing Director　　　　　　　Irshadul Islam ℇ iislam@citechco.net

Société Générale
BSL Office Complex, Sheraton Hotel Annex, 1 Minto Road, Ramna, Dhaka 1000
Tel: (2) 933 5601; (2) 933 5602 Fax: (2) 933 5612

www.euromoneydirectory.com BELARUS (+375)

Standard Chartered Equitor
Full Branch Office

Standard Chartered Bank, Box 536, 18-20 Motijheel Commercial Area, Dhaka 1000
Tel: (2) 956 1465 ext 115 **Fax:** (2) 956 1457 **Telex:** 675859 SCBDAC/632412 SCBDKBJ **Swift:** SCBL BD DXXXXX
Website: www.equitor.com

Senior Executive Officers
Chief Executive Officer   Geoffrey Williams ☎ **956 1713**
Financial Director   Mahbubul Alam *Head of Finance* ☎ **956 7831**
General-Lending (DCM, SL)
Head of Corporate Banking   S.A.A Masrur *Head, Corporate Banking* ☎ **956 1441**
General - Treasury
Head of Treasury   Mamun Ur Rashid ☎ **956 1484**
Global Custody
Department: Standard Chartered Equitor
Fax: 956 1494
Regional Head   Arunangshu Dutta *Manager, Custodial Services*

BARBADOS
(+1 246)

Central Bank of Barbados
🏛 Central Bank

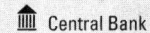

Tom Adams Financial Centre, Church Village, Bridgetown
Tel: 436 6870 **Fax:** 427 9559 **Telex:** 2251 CENBANK WB **Email:** cbb.libr@caribsurf.com

Senior Executive Officers
Governor   Winston Cox
Deputy Governor   Marion Williams
Deputy Governor   Delisle Worrell
Secretary   Adrian Clarke
Others (Senior Executives)
Head, Banking Supervision   Victor Springeys *Director*
                                   Ian Carrington *Director*
Head, Economics & Statistics   Daniel Boamah *Director*
Foreign Exchange
Head of Foreign Exchange   Kenneth Brathwaite *Director*
Administration
Public Relations
                                   Carl Moore *Public Affairs Officer* ☎ **436 0870**
Accounts / Audit
Head, Accountancy   Michael Carrington *Financial Controller*

BELARUS
(+375)

National Bank of the Republic of Belarus
🏛 Central Bank

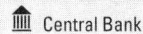

20 F Skorine Avenue, 220008 Minsk
Tel: (17) 227 6431; (17) 227 6658 **Fax:** (17) 227 4879 **Telex:** 252449 BELAR BY **Telerate:** NBRB BY 2X

Senior Executive Officers
Chairman of the Board   Petr Prokopovich ☎ **229 2384**
First Deputy   Natalya Alexseeva ☎ **227 1801**
Others (Senior Executives)
Head, Bank Licensing   Ludmila Takunmova ☎ **229 2173**
Head, Banking Supervision   Valentina Grigorovich ☎ **222 3995**
Head, Economics & Statistics   Yury Vlaskin ☎ **229 2888**
Head, Reserves Management   Vladimir Savenok ☎ **227 7625**
Foreign Exchange
Head of Foreign Exchange   Nikolay Luzgin ☎ **227 7463**
Settlement / Clearing
Head of Settlement / Clearing   Vladimir Zhukov ☎ **223 4464**

Euromoney Directory 1999 **125**

BELARUS (+375) www.euromoneydirectory.com

National Bank of the Republic of Belarus (cont)

Administration
Head of Administration Nikolay Zalevskiy ☎ **227 7471**

Technology & Systems
  Natalya Menkh ☎ **227 1137**

Public Relations
  Anatoly Drozdov ☎ **223 9890**

Accounts / Audit
Head, Accountancy Leongina Erokhovets ☎ **227 7136**

Absolutbank   Head Office
115 F Skoriny Avenue, 220014 Minsk
Tel: (172) 642 443; (172) 643 780 **Fax:** (172) 642 443; (172) 643 780 **Telex:** 252696 ABSOL BY
General Tel: 636 080; 100 092

Senior Executive Officers
Chairman of the Board Daniil P Svirid
First Deputy Chairman Vladimir V Stcherbo
Deputy Chairman Andrei G Shkiritch
Deputy Chairman Dmitry V Gladky
President Alexander D Demenok

Administration

Accounts / Audit
Accounting & Book-Keeping Galina G Lascvitch
  Tamara K Jakzhik

Belagroprombank   Head Office
24 Olshevskogo Street, 220073 Minsk
Tel: (17) 228 5513 **Fax:** (17) 228 5513 **Telex:** 252514 APBBRB BY **Swift:** BAPP BY 2X **Reuters:** BAGR
Telerate: 56782

Senior Executive Officers
Chairman Alexander Gavrushev ☎ **250 3959**
Financial Director Maria Shapovalova ☎ **228 5800**
Treasurer Andrey Zhitny ☎ **228 5206**

Other Departments
Correspondent Banking Svetlana Shpilevskaya ☎ **228 5402**

Administration

Technology & Systems
  Oleg Babinets ☎ **228 5705**

Legal / In-House Counsel
  Nikolay Grushevsky ☎ **228 5516**

Belarussian Bank of Development   Head Office
Formerly known as: Belarussian Investment Bank
2 Melnikaite Street, 220004 Minsk
Tel: (172) 238 724 **Fax:** (172) 239 396 **Email:** bbr@belinv.minsk.by

Senior Executive Officers
Chairman Alexander Rutkovski ☎ **239 396**
Chief Executive Officer Sergei Usarov *Vice Chairman* ☎ **201 108**
Financial Director Igor Lyskovets *Vice Chairman* ☎ **267 945**
International Division Vasily Chekanov ☎ **239 816**

Others (Senior Executives)
International Department Alexei Shkadarevich ☎ **260 959** 🖷 **209 820**

126 Euromoney Directory 1999

www.euromoneydirectory.com   BELARUS (+375)

Belarussian Exchange Bank   Head Office

Alternative trading name: Belarus Exchange Bank
48a Surganova Street, 220013 Minsk
Tel: (17) 232 4786 **Fax:** (17) 232 6700; (17) 232 5033 **Telex:** 252661 ECHB BY **Swift:** BEXB BY 22
Email: kuzar@exchbank.org.by **Reuters:** BEBM

Senior Executive Officers
Chairman of the Board	Vladimir Evtuch
Chief Executive Officer	Pavel Dick *Director & CEO*
Chief Operating Officer	Vasily Senko *Chief Accountant* ☏ **231 9827**
Treasurer	Victor Samarin *Chief Treasurer* ☏ **232 2136**

Debt Capital Markets / Fixed Income
Department: Securities Trading Department
Head of Fixed Income Sales — Alexandr Kuvashov ☏ **232 4814**

Government Bonds
Head of Trading — Andrey Davidchik ☏ **232 6601**

Equity Capital Markets
Head of Equity Capital Markets — Alexandr Kuvashov ☏ **232 4814**

Syndicated Lending
Head of Trading — Tatiana Gorodnikova *Head of Loan Department* ☏ **239 3047**

Money Markets
Head of Money Markets — Denis Voronkov *Head, Currency Treasury Section* ☏ **232 4924**

Foreign Exchange
Head of Foreign Exchange — Dmitry Kepet *Head, Currency Department* ☏ **231 6786**
Head of Trading — Vasily Barsukov *Head, Foreign Exchange Desk* ☏ **231 9914**

Risk Management
Fixed Income Derivatives / Risk Management
Head of Sales — Victor Samarin *Chief Treasurer* ☏ **232 2136**

Settlement / Clearing
International Payments — Valery Krokun *Head* ☏ **232 6765**

Other Departments
Correspondent Banking — Oleg Rubanov *Head* ☏ **232 6679**

Joint Stock Company 'Belkombank'   Head Office

Formerly known as: Brestcombank & Komplexbank
4th Floor, 43 Mogllevskaya Street, 220007 Minsk
Tel: (172) 292 721; (172) 292 781 **Fax:** (172) 292 196; (172) 104 202 **Swift:** BEKBBY2X

Senior Executive Officers
Chairman of the Board	Alexander Kirnozhitsky ☏ **292 721**
Deputy Chairman of the Board	Vladima Navaako
Deputy Chairman of the Board	Gallina Stotskayo ☏ **292 448**
Chief Executive Officer	Sergey Mokoain *Deputy Chairman of the Board* ☏ **291 699**
Chief Operating Officer	Tatyana Kozlova ☏ **768 976**
Managing Director	Vladimir Strok ☏ **292 063**
Company Secretary	Elena Pavlikovskaya ☏ **292 721**

Debt Capital Markets / Fixed Income
Tel: 375 172 **Fax:** 292 421
Head of Debt Capital Markets — Vladimir Strok *Managing Director* ☏ **292 068**

Government Bonds
Head of Sales — Alexey Popkov *Head of Bonds & Securities* ☏ **104 201**

Fixed-Income Repo
Head of Repo — Olga Tarasevitch *Chief Economist of Fixed Income Reporting Dept* ☏ **291 675**

Equity Capital Markets
Head of Equity Capital Markets — Alexey Popkov *Head of Bonds & Securities* ☏ **104 201**
Head of Trading — Taisia Tryntova *Chief Economist* ☏ **104 201**

Syndicated Lending
Head of Origination — Sergey Doroshevitch *Chief Economist* ☏ **280 847**
Head of Trading — Elena Plakhotnikova *Head of Management for Crediting & Lending* ☏ **260 780**

Euromoney Directory 1999   **127**

BELARUS (+375)　　　www.euromoneydirectory.com

Joint Stock Company 'Belkombank' (cont)

Foreign Exchange
Tel: 292 357　Fax: 260 992
Head of Foreign Exchange　　Sergy Parlyukevitch Head of Money Market Operations Dept

FX Traders / Sales People
　　Maxim Vazhnik Chief Economist T 768 508
　　Nadeszkala Smetirnova Dealer T 227 6798

Risk Management
Tel: 291 670　Fax: 292 194
Head of Risk Management　　Tatyana Shulpenkova Mgmt for Economic Analysis & Consolidated Research T 291 670

Settlement / Clearing
Tel: 104 202
Head of Settlement / Clearing　　Tatyana Klemantovitch Head of Settlement & Clearing
Back-Office　　Elena Kovalevskaya

Global Custody
Head of Global Custody　　Yuri Netchaev T 104 205　F 276 291

Other Departments
Correspondent Banking　　Irina Orlova T 292 357
Cash Management　　Irina Konoplitskaya T 291 649

Administration

Technology & Systems
Data Processing　　Natalya Bulbach Head T 292 285

Legal / In-House Counsel
　　Irina Scherbak T 292 530

Public Relations
　　Tatyana Kozlova

Accounts / Audit
Head of Internal Audit Departments　　Vasily Petrov

Belpromstroibank

Alternative trading name: Belarusion Joint-Stock Commercial Bank for Industry and Construction
6 Boulevard Lunacharskogo, 220678 Minsk
Tel: (172) 329 748; (172) 101 314　Fax: (172) 314 476; (172) 100 342　Telex: 252410 AVAL　Swift: BPSB BY 2X
Email: teletype@belpsb.minsk.by　Reuters: BEPS
Website: www.belpsb.minsk.by

Senior Executive Officers
General Director　　Nikolay Y Rakov T 133 993
First Deputy General Director　　Anatoly I Gapeenkov T 316 541

Others (Senior Executives)
　　Anatoly P Dudkin Deputy General Director T 318 902
　　Alexander I Naumenko Deputy General Director T 317 901

General - Treasury
Head of Treasury　　Alla N Dubetenetskaya Treasury Director T 175 687

Syndicated Lending

Loan-Related Activities
Leasing & Asset Finance　　Stanislav I Romash Head, Leasing and Innovations Dept. T 333 340

Other (Trade Finance)
International and Domestic Credits　　Nadezhda F Bolshinskaya Deputy Director T 326 143

Money Markets
Global Head　　Stanislav K Zalenskiy Head, FX & Money Markets T 175 691

Foreign Exchange
Global Head　　Stanislav K Zalenskiy Head, FX & Money Markets T 175 691

Settlement / Clearing
Regional Head　　Tamara I Zhevnyak First Deputy Director T 334 711

Other Departments
Correspondent Banking　　Gailna I Mikhalskaya Head, Correspondent Banking T 329 748

www.euromoneydirectory.com   BELARUS (+375)

Belvnesheconombank
Head Office

32 Miasnikova Street, 220050 Minsk
Tel: (172) 381 140; (172) 381 239 Fax: (172) 264 809 Telex: 252194 BVB BY Swift: BELB BY 2X Reuters: BELB

Senior Executive Officers
President — Georgi Egorov ☏ 269 757
Financial Director — Zinaida Kushnerova *Finance Director & Chief Accountant* ☏ 203 971
Treasurer — Sergei Shtcherbak *Vice President & Director* ☏ 381 101
Head & Senior Assistant to President — Vyacheslav Vysevka ☏ 381 108

Others (Senior Executives)
Economics — Iossif Manenok *Vice President* ☏ 269 758
Retail Banking — Ludmila Filipovich *Vice President & Director* ☏ 269 633
Strategic Planning — Anatoly Bondarev *Director* ☏ 203 325
Banking Technology — Evgeni Daoud *Director* ☏ 269 377
Cons & Logistics — Grigory Tishkevich *Director* ☏ 208 969
Credits & Project Financing — Irina Petrovskaya *Head of Division* ☏ 208 194
Internal Audit — Svetlana Zhuravliova *Head of Division* ☏ 264 312
Administration — Stepan Brishtelev *Director* ☏ 381 118
Gomel Regional Bank — Mikhail Lesun *Manager* ☏ +375 (23) 253 7120
International Banking — Dmitri Kourotchkin *Director of Equities* ☏ 381 106

Debt Capital Markets / Fixed Income
Global Head — Nikolai Golovko *Division Head* ☏ 200 062

Domestic Government Bonds
Head of Sales — Nikolai Golovko *Division Head* ☏ 200 062

Non-Domestic Government Bonds
— Nikolai Golovko *Division Head* ☏ 200 062

Eurobonds
Head of Trading — Nikolai Golovko *Division Head* ☏ 200 062

Medium-Term Notes
Head of Trading — Nikolai Golovko *Division Head* ☏ 200 062

Fixed-Income Repo
Head of Repo — Nikolai Golovko *Division Head* ☏ 200 062

Equity Capital Markets
Equity Repo / Securities Lending
Marketing — Nikolai Golovko *Division Head* ☏ 200 062

Syndicated Lending
Loan-Related Activities
Trade Finance — Yuri Tiavlovsky ☏ 200 823
Project Finance — Irina Petrovskaya *Head of Division* ☏ 208 194

Money Markets
Domestic Commercial Paper
Head of Trading — Nikolai Golovko *Division Head* ☏ 200 062

Foreign Exchange
Head of Trading — Nikolai Golovko *Division Head* ☏ 200 062

FX Traders / Sales People
— Andrei Romanenko *Deputy Department Head* ☏ 381 258

Risk Management
Global Head — Nikolai Golovko *Division Head* ☏ 200 062

Foreign Exchange Derivatives / Risk Management
Cross-Currency Swaps, Sales / Marketing; — Oleg Borzenkov *Head of Department* ☏ 381 162
Cross-Currency Swaps, Trading

Corporate Finance / M&A Advisory
Private Equity — Anatoly Bondarev *Director* ☏ 203 325

Settlement / Clearing
Fixed-Income Settlement — Nikolai Golovko *Division Head* ☏ 200 062
Operations — Grigory Tishkevich *Director* ☏ 208 969

Global Custody
Country Head — Nikolai Golovko *Division Head* ☏ 200 062

Other Departments
Private Banking — Maria Zhiglian *Division Head* ☏ 381 124
Correspondent Banking — Victor Loukiantchik *Division Head* ☏ 381 190

Euromoney Directory 1999   129

BELARUS (+375) www.euromoneydirectory.com

Belvnesheconombank (cont)
Administration
Head of Administration Stepan Brishtelev *Director* ☎ 381 118
Technology & Systems
 Vitali Troushko *Head of Department* ☎ 381 123
Legal / In-House Counsel
 Alexandre Bouben *Head of Section* ☎ 381 197
Legal Services Rostislav Krivitsky ☎ 264 482
Public Relations
 Yuri Gais *Head of Section* ☎ 381 197
Accounts / Audit
Internal Audit Svetlana Zhuravliova *Head of Division* ☎ 264 312
 Zinaida Kushnerova *Finance Director & Chief Accountant* ☎ 203 971
Corporate Accounts Natalia Pesotskaya ☎ 202 992
Other (Administration)
Human Resources Vladimir Zhourba ☎ 381 210

Commerzbank AG
Representative Office
Tschitscherin Street 21, Zimmer 601, 220029 Minsk
Tel: (17) 239 4688; (17) 276 1617 **Fax:** (17) 210 1119
Senior Executive Officers
Representative Helmut Fescher

European Bank for Reconstruction & Development
Representative Office
Gertsena 2, 220030 Minsk
Tel: (17) 220 1537 **Fax:** (17) 211 0410
Senior Executive Officers
Resident Representative Allan Popoff

Priorbank
Head Office
31A V Khoruzhey Street, 220002 Minsk
Tel: (17) 269 0964; (17) 234 0135 **Fax:** (17) 234 1554; (17) 234 8072 **Telex:** 681252268 PRIOR BY **Swift:** PJCB BY 2X
Reuters: PRBM
Senior Executive Officers
Chairman & Chief Executive Sergei Kostyuchenko ☎ 234 0135
President Mikhail Lavrinovitch
Financial Director Victor Markovsky *Director* ☎ 234 7756
Treasurer Mikhail Provorov *Head of Treasury* ☎ 210 1079
Debt Capital Markets / Fixed Income
Domestic Government Bonds
Head of Sales Alexander Silivonetz *Deputy Head of Securities* ☎ 210 1140
Equity Capital Markets
Domestic Equities
Head of Sales Oleg Kurmaev *Head of Investment Department* ☎ 210 1063
Syndicated Lending
Global Head Victor Gvozdev *Head of Lending* ☎ 234 3722
Loan-Related Activities
Project Finance Oleg Kurmaev *Head of Investment Department* ☎ 210 1063
Leasing & Asset Finance Algerdas Tabatadze *Director 'Priorleasing'* ☎ 239 7378
Money Markets
Global Head Olga Danilevich *Manager, Forex & MM* ☎ 210 1079
Wholesale Deposits
Marketing Olga Danilevich *Manager, Forex & MM* ☎ 210 1079
Foreign Exchange
Global Head Olga Danilevich *Manager, Forex & MM* ☎ 210 1079
FX Traders / Sales People
DM Igor Piskunov *Dealer* ☎ 210 1079
US$; Others Alexander Polischuk *Dealer* ☎ 210 1079

www.euromoneydirectory.com   BELGIUM (+32)

Risk Management
Department: Risk & Liquidity Management Department
Global Head   Zoya Yarmosh *Head* ☏ 269 0967

Corporate Finance / M&A Advisory
Global Head   Valentin Treschov *Deputy Chairman* ☏ 234 6825

Settlement / Clearing
Regional Head   Oleg Savin *Head of International Payments* ☏ 210 1059

Other Departments
Private Banking   Gennady Zinovkin *Deputy Chairman* ☏ 234 9940

Administration
Technology & Systems
    Victor Kvach *Head of IT* ☏ 234 7374

Legal / In-House Counsel
    Tatyana Lyahovetz *Head of Legal Dept* ☏ 210 1071

Compliance
    Zoya Yarmosh *Head* ☏ 269 0967

Public Relations
    Yuri Slepich *Head of Secretariat* ☏ 234 0135

BELGIUM
(+32)

Banque Nationale de Belgique SA   🏛 Central Bank

Alternative trading name: Nationale Bank van België
Boulevard de Berlaimont 14, B-1000 Brussels
Tel: (2) 221 2111 **Fax:** (2) 221 3100 **Telex:** 21105 BNBSG D **Swift:** NBBE BE BB **Email:** secretariat@bnbb.be
Cable: BANKIONALE BRUSSELS
Board of Directors Fax: (2) 221 3101; **Telex:** 21355 BKNLE B
Website: www.nbb.be; www.bnb.be; www.nationalebank.be

Senior Executive Officers
Governor   Alfons Verplaetse

Others (Senior Executives)
    William Fraeys *Vice Governor*
    Jean-Pierre Pauwels *Director*
    Guy Quaden *Director*
    Jean-Jacques Rey *Director*
    Robert Reynders *Director*
    Serge Bertholomé *Treasurer*
    Marcia de Wachter *Secretary*

ABN AMRO Bank (België) NV   Full Branch Office

Frankrijklei 121, B-2018 Antwerp
Tel: (3) 222 0411 **Fax:** (3) 231 9608 **Telex:** 27040

Senior Executive Officers
Others (Senior Executives)
Dutch Desk   D Rossèl *Senior Manager*

ABN AMRO Bank NV   Full Branch Office

Pelikaanstraat 70/76, B-2018 Antwerp
Tel: (3) 222 0291 **Fax:** (3) 234 3143

Senior Executive Officers
General Manager   Peter Gross

Euromoney Directory 1999   **131**

BELGIUM (+32) www.euromoneydirectory.com

EUROWEEK Online
http://www.euroweek.com

Euroweek is the definitive guide to the world's capital markets. With comprehensive coverage of international bonds, syndicated loans, international equity, derivative products, emerging markets, MTNs and structured finance deals, *Euroweek*'s coverage is second to none.

Speed of information is increasingly important for the capital markets professional. *Euroweek* is meeting this demand with an online version of the newspaper published as the printed version goes to press. Access to archived copies of *Euroweek* and its associated publications is also available through comprehensive search facilities.

For a free trial to the Euroweek web site, or for more information, contact Matt Morgan on +44 171-779 8972 or email mmorgan@dial.pipex.com

☐ **Euroweek Premium subscription** (print copy **plus** Euroweek Online) **$4,545 (£2,745 UK only)**
☐ **Euroweek print copy only $3,950 (£2,350 UK only)**

I wish to order .... subscriptions

Name (Mr/Ms etc)...............................

Job title..

Company..

Address..
....
....

Post/Zip code ....

Signature..

Date ....

Name...

Job title...

METHOD OF PAYMENT
Cheque enclosed and made payable to:
Euromoney Publications plc
☐ Invoice — Name
☐ Amex card no
☐☐☐☐ ☐☐☐☐ ☐☐☐☐ ☐☐☐
Expiry date ☐☐☐☐

Please complete and return to:
Matt Morgan
Euroweek
Nestor House, Playhouse Yard,
London EC4V 5EX
Tel: +44 171-779 8972   Fax: +44 171-779 8585

www.euromoneydirectory.com   BELGIUM (+32)

ABN AMRO Bank NV
Full Branch Office

Rengtlaan 53, B-1000 Brussels
Tel: (2) 546 0460 **Fax:** (2) 546 0400 **Telex:** 27040 **Swift:** ABNA BE BB **Reuters:** ABBR
Website: www.abnamro.be

Senior Executive Officers
Chairman	J Koopman
Director	J J W Zweegers
Financial Director	Luc Verhoeven
Chief Operating Officer	Kenneth Lam
Treasurer	Paul Groothuis
Managing Director	L Marchal
Managing Director	P V Callenfels

Others (Senior Executives)
Dutch Desk	D Ròssel *Business Unit Manager*
Global & Institutionals	E Thoelen *Business Unit Manager*
Corporate Banking	F Verdeemen *Business Unit Manager*
Private Banking	C Guépin *Business Unit Manager*
Diamond	F Hanard *Business Unit Manager*
Structured Finance	M van Balen *Product Unit Manager*

General - Treasury
Head of Treasury	P Groothuis *Treasury*

Debt Capital Markets / Fixed Income
Tel: 546 0460 **Fax:** 546 0410

Fixed-Income Repo
Trading	Martine Aerts *Trading, Bfr*

Syndicated Lending
Loan-Related Activities
Structured Trade Finance	M van Balen *Product Unit Manager*

Settlement / Clearing
Operations	M Sirjacobs

Other Departments
Private Banking	C Guépin *Business Unit Manager*
Correspondent Banking	Toon van Paesschen

Administration
Technology & Systems
Kenneth Lam

Legal / In-House Counsel
Andre de Keere

Compliance
Gert Dillen

Public Relations
Dominique Steenbeek

Corporate Communications
Dominique Steenbeek

Accounts / Audit
Gert Dillen

Other (Administration)
Marketing	D Steenbeek
Information & Organization	K Lam
Personnel Division	L Nys

Antwerpse Diamantbank NV
Head Office

Pelikaanstraat 54, B-2018 Antwerp
Tel: (3) 204 7204 **Fax:** (3) 233 9095 **Telex:** 31673 **Swift:** ADIA BE

Senior Executive Officers
Chairman	Jan Vanhevel
Chairman, Executive Committee	Paul C Goris
Member, Executive Committee	Pierre De Bosscher
Member, Executive Committee	Leopold A Bollaerts

General-Lending (DCM, SL)
Head of Corporate Banking	Willy Laeremans *Head of Credit*

BELGIUM (+32) www.euromoneydirectory.com

Antwerpse Diamantbank NV (cont)
Relationship Manager
Bank Relations   Pierre De Bosscher *Member, Executive Committee*
Administration
Head of Administration   Stéphane Vinogradoff *Head of Administration*
Technology & Systems
Finance & IT   Frank De Houwer *Head*
Other (Administration)
Commercial   Jean van der Donckt *Head*

Artesia Bank   Head Office

Formerly known as: Banque Paribas Belgique SA
WTC Tower 1, Building Emile Jacqmain 162, B-1000 Brussels
Tel: (2) 204 4111 **Fax:** (2) 203 2014 **Swift:** PARB BE BB **Reuters:** PBXD **Telerate:** 8509; 8508
Willem Mosen **Tel:** 204 4390; **Reuters:** PBCX; PARB
Website: www.artesia.be

Senior Executive Officers
Chairman   Willem Mosen ☏ **204 4612**
Chief Executive Officer   Philippe Romagnoli *Chairman* ☏ **204 4390**
Financial Director   Luc Vanden Bussche ☏ **204 4533**
Chief Operating Officer   Philippe Sterno ☏ **204 4776**
Chairman   Philippe Romagnoli ☏ **204 4390**
Secretary General   Erik Swaelen
Others (Senior Executives)
                                      Christian Pinte
                                      Geert Dauwe

General-Lending (DCM, SL)
Head of Corporate Banking   René Avonts
General-Investment
Head of Investment   René Avonts
Debt Capital Markets / Fixed Income
Tel: 204 5035 **Fax:** 204 4864
Global Head   Eric Le Vernoye ☏ **204 4820**
Government Bonds
Head of Sales   Eric Aeyels ☏ **204 4797**
Head of Trading   Geert Van De Walle ☏ **204 4389**
Eurobonds
Head of Origination   Geert Van De Walle ☏ **204 4389**
Head of Sales   Wouter Van Roste ☏ **204 4190**
Head of Trading   Paul Van Geert ☏ **204 4469**
Fixed-Income Repo
Head of Repo   Yvonne Sigrist ☏ **204 4025**
Equity Capital Markets
Tel: 204 5152 **Fax:** 204 4921
Head of Equity Capital Markets   Eric Le Vernoye ☏ **204 4820**
Domestic Equities
Head of Sales; Head of Trading   Etienne Deklippel ☏ **204 4468**
International Equities
Head of Origination   Stefaan Decraene ☏ **204 4448**
Head of Trading   Etienne Deklippel ☏ **204 4468**
Convertibles / Equity-Linked
Head of Trading   Etienne Deklippel ☏ **204 4468**
Syndicated Lending
Tel: 204 5078 **Fax:** 204 4921
Head of Trading   Francois Saverys ☏ **204 4432**
Loan-Related Activities
Trade Finance   Karl Thirion *Trade Finance (Short Term)* ☏ **204 4446**
                                      Wim Lievens *Trade Finance (Medium Term)* ☏ **204 4653**
Money Markets
Tel: 204 5068 **Fax:** 204 4913
Global Head   Alain Engel ☏ **204 4532**
Eurocommercial Paper
Head of Sales   Filip Lambrechts ☏ **204 4372**

www.euromoneydirectory.com   BELGIUM (+32)

Foreign Exchange
Tel: 204 5368 Fax: 204 4920
Head of Foreign Exchange — Geert Van De Walle ☎ **204 4389**
Corporate Sales — Wouter Van Roste ☎ **204 4190**
Head of Trading — Serge Berger ☎ **204 4196**

FX Traders / Sales People
Short Term — Norbert Van Assche ☎ **204 4848**

Risk Management
Foreign Exchange Derivatives / Risk Management
Cross-Currency Swaps, Sales / Marketing — Wouter Van Roste ☎ **204 4190**
Cross-Currency Swaps, Trading — Frans Caes ☎ **204 4471**
Vanilla FX option Sales — Wouter Van Roste ☎ **204 4190**
Vanilla FX option Trading — Peter Verplancke ☎ **204 4353**

Exotic Options (Barriers, Range, Timers, Digitals, Faders etc)
Sales — Wouter Van Roste ☎ **204 4190**
Trading — Regina Spierings ☎ **204 4166**

Settlement / Clearing
Tel: 204 5030 Fax: 204 4079
Equity Settlement; Fixed-Income Settlement — Charles Guissard ☎ **204 4300**

Other Departments
Correspondent Banking — Karl Thirion *Trade Finance (Short Term)* ☎ **204 4446**

Administration
Compliance
Eric De Gyns ☎ **204 4597**

Public Relations
Anne Sterkmans ☎ **204 4787**

ASLK-CGER Bank   Head Office

FORTIS
Solid partners, flexible solutions

is part of the Fortis group

Wolvengracht 48, 48 Rue Fossé-aux-Loups, B-1000 Brussels
PO Box 1436, B-1000 Brussels
Tel: (2) 228 6111 **Fax:** (2) 228 7199 **Telex:** 26860 CGEASK B **Swift:** CGAK BE BB
Email: webmaster@aslk.be & webmaster@cger.be
Website: www.aslk.be & www.cger.be

Senior Executive Officers
Chairman & Chief Executive — Karel De Boeck ☎ **228 7860**
Treasurer — Olivier Casse *Senior General Manager* ☎ **228 6695**

General-Lending (DCM, SL)
Head of Corporate Banking — Wilfried Van Dooren *Managing Director* ☎ **228 1207**

General-Investment
Head of Investment — Roger Cocquyt *Managing Director* ☎ **228 6069**

Debt Capital Markets / Fixed Income
Department: Service Dealing Room - Capital Markets
Fax: 228 8816
Country Head
Head of Fixed Income Trading — André Habay ☎ **228 9509**
 — Danny Van Wesemael ☎ **228 6063**

Bonds - General
Luc Collard *Dealer* ☎ **228 8213**
Rita Plaete *Dealer* ☎ **228 6104**
Raf Dammekens *Dealer* ☎ **228 9812**
Peter Grijseels *Dealer* ☎ **228 9590**
Geert Kesteleyn *Dealer* ☎ **228 9812**
Eddy Reynebeau *Dealer* ☎ **228 7114**

BELGIUM (+32)   www.euromoneydirectory.com

ASLK-CGER Bank (cont)

Fixed-Income Repo
Head of Repo — Willem Goubert ☎ 228 6986
Marketing & Product Development — Stéphane Habousha *Product Management* ☎ 228 1840

Fixed-Income Research
Head of Fixed Income — Walter Van Nieuwenhove *Senior Manager* ☎ 228 6058

Equity Capital Markets
Head of Trading — Luc Zuallaert *Chief Trader* ☎ 228 6597

Other (Domestic Equities)
Guy Noerens *Trader* ☎ 228 9402
Patrick Santels *Trader* ☎ 228 8646 F 228 8816

Syndicated Lending
Trade Finance — Guy De Koninck *Senior Manager* ☎ 228 8542 F 228 9134

Money Markets
Tel: 228 6986 Fax: 228 9954 Reuters: AKCG
Head of Money Markets — Willem Goubert ☎ 228 6986

Money Markets - General
Money Markets - BEF — Monique Perremans *Dealer* ☎ 228 9543
Gilles De Coster *Dealer* ☎ 228 9989
Money Markets - CCY — Françoise De Craecker *Dealer* ☎ 228 6985
Marc De Bosscher *Dealer* ☎ 228 9962
Marie Joveneau *Dealer* ☎ 228 6592
Thierry Warnotte *Dealer* ☎ 228 8985
Marie-Christine Naud *Dealer* ☎ 228 8500

Foreign Exchange
Department: Corporate & Sales
Country Head — Henk Raison *Executive Manager* ☎ 228 8697

FX Traders / Sales People
Corporate — Willem Seynnaeve *Dealer* ☎ 228 1359
Nathalie Catala *Dealer* ☎ 228 1748
Daniel Dubois *Dealer* ☎ 228 9255
Martine Van Sinay *Dealer* ☎ 228 7944
Arlette Vandeneucker *Dealer* ☎ 228 8458
Steven Meuldermans *Dealer* ☎ 228 7971
Anne Lejeune *Dealer* ☎ 228 9692
Jozef De Koster *Dealer* ☎ 228 1734
Eric Baens *Dealer* ☎ 228 1783 F 228 5925
Marc Sollie *Sales* ☎ 228 9254
Eddy Vonckx *Sales* ☎ 228 8757
François-Xavier Cabay *Sales* ☎ 228 5908
Wim D'Heere *Sales* ☎ 228 7410

Department: Service Dealing Room - FX & Money Markets
Reuters: ASLB
Head of Foreign Exchange — Willem Goubert ☎ 228 6986
Spot / Forwards Trading — Willy Deboeck ☎ 228 6987
Jacqueline Lipenga ☎ 228 8647
Henry Van Garl ☎ 228 8647

Risk Management
Department: Service Dealing Room - Capital Markets
Tel: 228 6085 Fax: 228 9430
Head of Risk Management — Olivier Casse *Senior General Manager* ☎ 228 6695
André Habay ☎ 228 9509

Fixed Income Derivatives / Risk Management
Head of Sales — Wim D'Heere *Sales* ☎ 228 7410
Trading — Didier Engels *Dealer* ☎ 228 6363
Jean-Marie Bertin ☎ 228 9864
Christophe Rodrigues ☎ 228 9868 F 228 5925
IR Swaps Sales / Marketing — Dirk Peeters *Senior Manager* ☎ 228 8482
Department: Service Dealing Room - FX & Money Markets
Head of Risk Management — Willem Goubert ☎ 228 6986

Foreign Exchange Derivatives / Risk Management
Cross-Currency Swaps, Trading — Marnix Barbiers ☎ 228 8930
Rudy Maes ☎ 228 9661

Settlement / Clearing
Tel: 228 7807 Fax: 228 9430
Fixed-Income Settlement — Bart Baudewyn *Senior Manager & Head of Fixed-Income Settlement*
☎ 228 9909

www.euromoneydirectory.com BELGIUM (+32)

Global Custody
Tel: 228 5621 **Fax:** 228 8119
Head of Global Custody Joseph Duplicy *Deputy General Manager* ☏ **228 5621**
Other (Global Custody)
  Rik Wittemans *Executive Manager*

Asset Management
Department: Asset Building
Fax: 228 9750
Head Ralf Bauer ☏ **228 8150**
Other (Asset Management)
  Stefaan De Doncker ☏ **228 8337**
  Jan Vanermen ☏ **228 8406**

Other Departments
Private Banking Freddy Van den Spiegel *General Manager* ☏ **228 6547** F **228 7066**
Correspondent Banking Paul André Meyers *Executive Manager* ☏ **228 8952** F **228 9863**

Austrian National Bank Representative Office
Avenue de Cortenbergh 30, B-1040 Brussels
Tel: (2) 285 4842 **Fax:** (2) 285 4848

Senior Executive Officers
Chief Representative Daniela Bankier

BACOB Bank Head Office
Rue de Trèves 25, B-1040 Brussels
Tel: (2) 285 3798; (2) 282 5050 **Fax:** (2) 285 3502; (2) 285 1570 **Telex:** 62199 **Swift:** BACB BE BB
Email: bacob@bacob.be **Reuters:** BACB **Telerate:** 3900 **Cable:** 62199
Reuters: BACD
Website: www.bacob.be

Senior Executive Officers
Head of Financial Markets Dirk Vanderschrick ☏ **285 3799** F **285 3502**
Others (Senior Executives)
Member of the Management Committee Guido Allegaert ☏ **285 2020**
  Rik Duyck ☏ **285 2020**
  Claude Piret ☏ **285 2020**
Secretary Pros Gielen *Secretary* ☏ **285 2020**

Debt Capital Markets / Fixed Income
Tel: 282 3780 **Fax:** 285 3502
Head of Fixed Income Gert Wauters *Head, Capital Markets* ☏ **285 3780**
Head of Fixed Income Sales Evelyne Pierre ☏ **282 5648**

Libor-Based / Floating-Rate Products
Asset Swaps Kobe Van Der Straeten *Investment Portfolio Manager* ☏ **285 3771**

Asset-Backed Securities / Securitization
Head of Trading Patrick Van Den Eynde *Head of Securitization* ☏ **285 3750**

Fixed-Income Repo
Head of Repo Johan Evenepoel *Chief Dealer* ☏ **282 5001** E joevenep@bacob.be
Trading Veerle Deprins *Dealer*
  Jeffrey van Impe *Dealer* E jevimpe@bacob.be

Money Markets
Tel: 285 3760 **Fax:** 285 3502
Head of Money Markets Johan Evenepoel *Chief Dealer* ☏ **282 5001** E joevenep@bacob.be

Risk Management
Other Currency Swap / FX Options Personnel
IR Swaps Trading Ellen Van Steen *Portfolio Manager* ☏ **282 5600**

Administration
Technology & Systems
IT & Project Support Pascal van de Neirssche *Head* ☏ **285 3732**

Legal / In-House Counsel
  Arianne Vanden Berghe *Legal & Compliance Manager* ☏ **285 3749**

Compliance
  Arianne Vanden Berghe *Legal & Compliance Manager* ☏ **285 3749**

BELGIUM (+32)   www.euromoneydirectory.com

Banca Nazionale del Lavoro SpA   Representative Office

Avenue Louise 66, Bte 6, B-1050 Brussels
Tel: (2) 513 7610 Fax: (2) 513 1802 Telex: 26001 LAVORO B Email: banca.nazionale.del.lavoro@skynet.be

Senior Executive Officers
Chief Representative   Aldo Costa

Banca Popolare di Novara Scrl   Representative Office

Rue de l'Industrie 40, B-1040 Brussels
Tel: (2) 513 6713 Fax: (2) 513 3470

Senior Executive Officers
Representative   Paolo Clarotti

Banco do Brasil (Europe) NV/SA

14/16 Rue du Trône, B-1000 Brussels
Tel: (2) 289 5211 Fax: (2) 511 9185 Telex: 63104 BBBRUX Swift: BRAS BE BB Reuters: BBEU (Dealing)

Senior Executive Officers
President   Akira Ensiki
General Manager   Chevenno Alvares

Foreign Exchange
Head of Foreign Exchange   R Delbare

Other Departments
Private Banking   E Rousselle *Head* ☏ 289 5213

Administration
Head of Administration   Chevenno Alvares *General Manager*

Banco Exterior de España Sucursal en Bélgica   Full Branch Office

Formerly known as: Banco Exterior Bélgica SA
Avenue des Arts 43, B-1040 Brussels
Tel: (2) 512 3262 Fax: (2) 512 8531; (2) 512 9318 Telex: 22746 BESBRU B Swift: EXTE BE BB Reuters: BEXB
Cable: BANESBRUS

Senior Executive Officers
Treasurer   Cándido López Márquez *General Sud-Director*
General Manager   Ferrán Campos Fortuny

Others (Senior Executives)
     Cándido López Márquez *General Sud-Director*

Debt Capital Markets / Fixed Income
Domestic Government Bonds
Head of Sales   Javier Esharri *Institutional Head*

Administration
Head of Administration   Eddy Chabert *Administrative Director*

Bank of America NT & SA   Full Branch Office

Uitbreidingstraat 180, Box 6, Berchem, B-2600 Antwerp
Tel: (3) 280 4211 Fax: (3) 239 6109 Telex: 31076, 35324 BOFAEX B Swift: BOFA BE 3X Reuters: BANB (Dealing)

Senior Executive Officers
VP & Regional Manager - Benelux   Willem Nijboer
Treasurer   Wilfried Damman *VP & Country Treasurer* ☏ 280 4419

Others (Senior Executives)
     Margaret Frances Eelen *VP, Country Operations Officer* ☏ 280 4380

Relationship Manager
     Henk Cottenie *Vice President Relationship Manager* ☏ 280 4205

www.euromoneydirectory.com   BELGIUM (+32)

Bank of America NT & SA   Full Branch Office
Van Nieuwenhuyselaan 6, B-1160 Brussels
Tel: (2) 663 2100 Fax: (2) 663 2150

Senior Executive Officers
Vice President   Richard Challinor

Bank Austria Creditanstalt AG   Representative Office
Avenue de Cortenbergh 89, Box 6, B-1000 Brussels
Tel: (2) 735 4122 Fax: (2) 736 9816

Senior Executive Officers
Chief Representative   Peter Rieger [E] peter.rieger@pophost.eunet.be

Bank Brussels Lambert   Subsidiary Company
Avenue Marnix 24, B-1000 Brussels
Cours Saint-Michel 60, B-1040 Brussels
Tel: (2) 547 2111 Fax: (2) 547 3344 Telex: 21421 BBL B Swift: BBRU BE BB 010 Email: ctp.cno@bbl.be
Reuters: BBL/MENU Cable: BRUXELAT
General Telex: 21742 BBL B; General Telex: 26392 BBL B; General Telex: 63965 BBL B
Website: www.bbl.be

Senior Executive Officers
Chairman of the Board of Directors   Jacques Moulaert
President & CEO   Michel Tilmant
Financial Director   Jean-Pierrre Wellens *Chairman, Financial Markets Committee*
                                                 Robert Van Hoofstat *Internal Financial Management*
Secretary General   André de Kerchove
International Division   Giselbert Schmidburg *Head, International Banking*

Others (Senior Executives)
Head of Emerging Markets   Jacques Valentin *DEP GM International Banking*
Global Head, Financial Markets   Peter Horstmann *Forex, Proprietary Trading & International Network*
International Network Management   Pierre Heilporn *Head*

General-Lending (DCM, SL)
Head of Corporate Banking   Jacques Van Rymenant

General-Investment
Head of Investment   Arnaud Laviolette *Joint Head of Investment Banking* [T] **547 7493**
                                                 Jos Behiels *Joint Head of Investment Banking* [T] **547 3487**

General - Treasury
Head of Treasury   Eric Boyer de la Giroday *Treasury & Capital Markets*

Debt Capital Markets / Fixed Income
Department: ING Barings / BBL
Tel: 547 2963 Fax: 547 2922
Head of Debt Capital Markets   Eric Boyer de la Giroday *Chairman*
Global Head   Philippe Follebouckt *Head of Capital Markets* [T] **547 3611**

Government Bonds
Head of Sales   Karl Pittevils *Head, Institutional Sales* [T] **547 3371**
Head of Trading   Gunter Fluyt [T] **547 2868**

Emerging Market Bonds
Head of Emerging Markets   Jacques Valentin *DEP GM International Banking*

Fixed-Income Repo
Head of Repo   Eric Hollanders *DGM, International Banking Department* [T] **547 3319**
                                                 [F] **547 2315**
Marketing & Product Development   Jan Van de Vyvere [T] **547 3384**
                                                 Marc Seidemann [T] **547 3901**

Equity Capital Markets
Head of Equity Capital Markets   Eric Boyer de la Giroday *Treasury & Capital Markets*

Domestic Equities
Head of Origination   Arnaud Laviolette *Joint Head of Investment Banking* [T] **547 7493**
                                                 Jos Behiels *Joint Head of Investment Banking* [T] **547 3487**
Head of Syndication   Philippe Follebouckt *Head of Capital Markets* [T] **547 3611**
Head of Sales   Karl Pittevils *Head, Institutional Sales* [T] **547 3371**

BELGIUM (+32)   www.euromoneydirectory.com

Bank Brussels Lambert (cont)

Equity Repo / Securities Lending
Head — Eric Hollanders *DEPGM International Banking* ☎ **547 3319** F **547 2315**
Marketing — Jan Van de Vyvere ☎ **547 3384**
Marc Seidemann ☎ **547 3901**

Syndicated Lending
Loan-Related Activities
Trade Finance; Project Finance — Jacques Samoy *Project & Export Finance* ☎ **547 2850**

Money Markets
Fax: 547 2922
Other — Jacques Goffaux *Desk Manager* ☎ **547 3512**
Robert Peeters *Desk Manager* ☎ **547 3233**

Domestic Commercial Paper
Head of Origination — François De Witt *Senior Manager, Corporate Banking* ☎ **547 8148**
Head of Sales — Karl Pittevils *Head, Institutional Sales* ☎ **547 3371**

Foreign Exchange
Tel: 547 3388 Fax: 547 2922
Head of Foreign Exchange — Peter Horstmann *Forex, Proprietary Trading & International Network*
Country Head — Donat Wattelet *Desk Manager* ☎ **547 2614**
Head of Sales — Josine Kamerling *Head, Corporate Advice & Distribution* ☎ **547 3078**

Risk Management
Department: Market Risk Management
Tel: 547 2455 Fax: 547 3096
Global Head — Jean-Pierre Straet *Head, Financial Markets Support*
Regional Head — Arnaud Laviolette *Joint Head of Investment Banking* ☎ **547 7493**
Jos Behiels *Joint Head of Investment Banking* ☎ **547 3487**

Corporate Finance / M&A Advisory
Head of Corporate Finance — Georges Walckiers
Head of Mergers & Acquisition — Arnaud Laviolette *Joint Head of Investment Banking* ☎ **547 7493**
Jos Behiels *Joint Head of Investment Banking* ☎ **547 3487**

Settlement / Clearing
Tel: 738 2111 Fax: 738 2714
Head of Settlement / Clearing — Karel Broothaers *Head of Cash & Securities Administration* ☎ **738 6186**
Equity Settlement; Fixed-Income Settlement — Christian De Jonghe *Domestic & Foreign Settlement* ☎ **738 3392**
Back-Office — Karel Broothaers *Head of Cash & Securities Administration* ☎ **738 6186**

Global Custody
Tel: 738 2111 Fax: 738 2714
Head of Global Custody — Karel Broothaers *Head of Cash & Securities Administration* ☎ **738 6186**

Asset Management
Head — Michel de Crayencour *Head of Asset Management*

Other Departments
Proprietary Trading — Peter Horstmann *Forex, Proprietary Trading & International Network*
Chief Credit Officer — Jean-Marie Van Overstraeten *Credit Department*
Private Banking — Michel de Crayencour *Head of Asset Management*
Correspondent Banking — Giselbert Schmidburg *Head, International Banking*
Cash Management — Eric Hollanders *DEPGM International Banking* ☎ **547 3319** F **547 2315**

Administration
Head of Marketing — Oliver de Broqueville ☎ **738 6220**

Technology & Systems
Organisation & Information Technology — Michel Callier ☎ **738 3176**

Legal / In-House Counsel
Legal & Fiscal Affairs — Eric de Baenst ☎ **547 3982**

Compliance
Eric de Baenst ☎ **547 3982**

Public Relations
Communications — Noël Dor *General Secretariat* ☎ **547 2094**

Corporate Communications
Marie-Christine Leys *Corporate Communication Officer* ☎ **547 2637**
F **547 3844**

Accounts / Audit
Internal Audit Department — Réginald Thiry *Head* ☎ **547 8161**

www.euromoneydirectory.com   BELGIUM (+32)

Bank Degroof
Head Office

Rue de l'Industrie 44, B-1040 Brussels
Tel: (2) 287 9111 **Fax:** (2) 230 6700 **Telex:** 21317 **Swift:** DEGR BE BB

B

Senior Executive Officers
Managing Partner   Alain Philippson
Managing Partner   Claude Fontaine
Chief Executive Officer   Alain Schockert *Managing Partner*
Financial Director   Alain Siaens *Managing Partner*
Chief Operating Officer   Regnier Haegelsteen *Managing Partner*
Managing Director   Yves Dallemagne
Managing Director   Pierre-Paul de Schrevel
Managing Director   Ger Rooze
MD & Secretary General of the Group   Marc Giboux

Debt Capital Markets / Fixed Income
Global Head   Yves Dallemagne *Managing Director*
Regional Head   Gautier Bataille

Domestic Government Bonds
Head of Sales   Jean-Marc Michelet

Equity Capital Markets
Domestic Equities
Head of Sales   Damien Crispiels
Head of Trading   Michel Guillaume
Head of Research   Mireille Walravens

Other (Domestic Equities)
                                                          Sylvie De Cooman

Equity Repo / Securities Lending
Marketing   Sylvie De Cooman

Money Markets
Global Head   Alain Strapart
Regional Head   Arlette Verfaillie

Foreign Exchange
Global Head   Daniel Verschaeve

Risk Management
OTC Equity Derivatives
Sales   Damien Crispiels

Other Departments
Private Banking   Pierre-Paul de Schrevel *Managing Director*
Correspondent Banking   Alain Lacourt

Administration
Technology & Systems
                                                          Jo de Jamblinne de Meux

Legal / In-House Counsel
                                                          Anne Winckelmans *Head*

Public Relations
Marketing & Communications   Anne Vierstraete *Head*

The Bank of Tokyo-Mitsubishi Limited
Full Branch Office

Avenue des Arts 58, Bte 1, B-1000 Brussels
Tel: (2) 551 4411 **Fax:** (2) 551 4599 **Telex:** 22158 TOHBK B **Swift:** BOTK BEBX **Reuters:** BOTX

Senior Executive Officers
General Manager   Susumu Oki
Deputy General Manager   Kenichi Oshima

Syndicated Lending
Fax: 551 4597
Head of Trading   Kazutake Kobayashi *Manager, Head of Department* ☏ 551 4420

Foreign Exchange
Fax: 551 4597
Head of Foreign Exchange   Ryuya Koshimae *Manager, Head of Department* ☏ 551 4441

Risk Management
Head of Risk Management   Marc Albert *Manager* ☏ 551 4443

Euromoney Directory 1999   **141**

BELGIUM (+32) www.euromoneydirectory.com

The Bank of Tokyo-Mitsubishi Limited (cont)
Settlement / Clearing
Fax: 551 4450
Regional Head   Agathe Housiaux *Manager, Head of Department* ☎ **551 4460**
Global Custody
Head of Global Custody   Agathe Housiaux *Manager, Head of Department* ☎ **551 4460**
Other Departments
Correspondent Banking   Leopold Ons *Manager, Head of Department* ☎ **551 4430**
Administration
Head of Administration   Francine Ruelle *Manager, Head of Department* ☎ **551 4520**
Technology & Systems
                                            Sidney Comeyne *Manager, Head of Department* ☎ **551 4530**
Compliance
                                            Claude Ermans *Senior Manager, Human Resources* ☎ **551 4403**
Public Relations
                                            Claude Ermans *Senior Manager, Human Resources* ☎ **551 4403**
Accounts / Audit
                                            Michel Proult *Manager, Head of Department* ☎ **551 4500**

Bank of Yokohama (Europe) SA   Subsidiary Company
Avenue Louise 287, Box 1, B-1050 Brussels
Tel: (2) 648 8285 **Fax:** (2) 648 3148; (2) 647 7277 **Telex:** 21709 **Reuters:** BOYB
Senior Executive Officers
Managing Director & General Manager   Akio Kawachi
Others (Senior Executives)
                                            Harumichi Oishi *Director & Deputy General Manager*
                                            Osamu Moribe *Director & Manager*
Debt Capital Markets / Fixed Income
Eurobonds
Head of Syndication; Head of Sales; Head of Harumichi Oishi *Director & Deputy General Manager*
Trading
Bonds - General
Sales   Geert Seeldrayers *Assistant Manager*
                                            Mayumi Saishu *Assistant Manager*
Underwriting   Harumichi Oishi *Director & Deputy General Manager*
Syndicated Lending
Head of Origination   Naomi Goto *Manager*
Risk Management
Foreign Exchange Derivatives / Risk Management
Cross-Currency Swaps, Sales / Marketing;   Naomi Goto *Manager*
Cross-Currency Swaps, Trading
Settlement / Clearing
Settlement (General); Operations   Annick Dandois
Administration
Head of Administration   Osamu Moribe *Director & Manager*

Banque Belgolaise SA   Head Office
Cantersteen 1, PO Box 807, B-1000 Brussels
Tel: (2) 551 7211 **Fax:** (2) 551 7515 **Telex:** 21375, 62543 **Swift:** BLGO BE BB **Cable:** BELGOLAISE

Banque Delen & de Schaetzen SA   Head Office
Jan Van Rijswijcklaan 184, B-2020 Antwerp
Tel: (3) 244 5566 **Fax:** (3) 216 0491; (3) 216 1957 **Telex:** 41283 SCHTZN B
Senior Executive Officers
Managing Director / General Manager   Jacques Delen
Managing Director / General Manager   Paul De Winter
Managing Director / General Manager   Thierry Maertens de Noordhout

Banque Dewaay SA
Head Office

Alternative trading name: Dewaay
Boulevard Anspach 1, Box 39, B-1000 Brussels
Tel: (2) 227 8811 **Fax:** (2) 227 8928 **Telex:** 21 325 **Swift:** DEWABE BB **Telerate:** DEWI

Senior Executive Officers
President — Henri Servais

Others (Senior Executives)
— André Beier
— Guy Kleynen
— Michel Bragard

Debt Capital Markets / Fixed Income
Department: Fixed Income
Country Head — Henri Servais

Bonds - General
Belgian — Georges Delcroix
Foreign — Alain Servais

Equity Capital Markets
Domestic Equities
Head of Sales — André Beier

International Equities
Head of Trading — Henri Servais
— Claude Dandois
— Herman de Decker

Syndicated Lending
Structured Finance & Legal — Guy Kleynen

Asset Management
Department: Private Portfolio Management
Portfolio Management — Michel Bragard
— François Klinkemallie

Other (Asset Management)
Institutional Portfolio Management — Danièle Barthelemy

Banque Européenne pour l'Amérique Latine (BEAL) SA
Head Office

Chaussée de la Hulpe 166, B-1170 Brussels
Tel: (2) 663 6900 **Fax:** (2) 663 6909 **Telex:** 22431 BEALB

Senior Executive Officers
Managing Director — Horst R Magiera [T] 663 6900
Managing Director — Philip Wykes [T] 663 6800 [F] 663 6809

Banque Nagelmackers 1747 SA
Head Office

Avenue De L' Astronomie 23, B-1210 Brussels
Tel: (2) 229 7600 **Fax:** (2) 229 7699 **Telex:** 21612 **Swift:** BNAG BE BB

Senior Executive Officers
Chairman — Jean-Louis Luyckx
Financial Director — Peter de Proft
Chief Operating Officer — Aymon Detroch

Asset Management
Head — Marc Moles Le Bailly

Administration
Head of Marketing — Ronald Elskens

Technology & Systems
— Anne Gauthier

Legal / In-House Counsel
— Christine Orban

Public Relations
— Frank Jacobs

BELGIUM (+32)   www.euromoneydirectory.com

Banque Nationale de Paris SA — Full Branch Office
Formerly known as: BNP
Boulevard du Regent 47/48, B-1000 Brussels
Tel: (2) 518 0811 Fax: (2) 518 0934; (2) 513 1244 Telex: 21628 Swift: BNPA BE BB

Senior Executive Officers
Director General Hubert Reynier ☎ **518 0801**
Secretary General Olivier Thiry ☎ **518 0804**

Others (Senior Executives)
Market Sales & Trading Room Fabiano Gervasi ☎ **518 0835**

General-Lending (DCM, SL)
Head of Corporate Banking Hugo Baetens *Director, Commercial Banking* ☎ **518 0805**

General-Investment
Head of Investment Patrick Limbos *Structured Finance* ☎ **518 0869**

Administration
Legal / In-House Counsel
Christian Wilmet *Legal Affairs and Fiscals* ☎ **518 0995**

BCH Benelux SA — Subsidiary Company
Formerly known as: Central Hispano Benelux SA
227 rue de la Loi, B-1040 Brussels
Tel: (2) 286 5411 Fax: (2) 230 5232; (2) 230 0940 Telex: 21219 BHABR B Swift: CENTBEBB Reuters: BHAB

Senior Executive Officers
Treasurer Segundo Herranz *Head of Trading*
Managing Director Miguel Sanchez Tovar
General Manager Jacques Barbier

General-Lending (DCM, SL)
Head of Corporate Banking Jacques-Yves Janssens *Assistant Manager*

General-Investment
Head of Investment Pedre Tapia *Assistant Manager*

Syndicated Lending
Loan-Related Activities
Structured Trade Finance Philippe Duyckaerts *Proxy Holder*

Administration
Head of Administration Pina Smeets *Administrative Assistant*

Belgo-Factors NV — Head Office
Steenweg op Tielen 51, B-2300 Turnhout
Tel: (14) 405 411 Fax: (14) 405 600 Telex: 31045

Senior Executive Officers
Managing Director Dirk Driessens

Byblos Bank Europe SA — Head Office
Formerly known as: Byblos Bank Belgium SA
Rue Montoyer 10/B 3, B-1000 Brussels
Tel: (2) 551 0020 Fax: (2) 513 0526 Telex: 63461 BYBLOS B Swift: BYBB BE BB Email: byblos-it@pophost.eunet.be

Senior Executive Officers
Chief Executive Officer Najah L Salem *Managing Director*
Financial Director Elie A Bassil *Director & Finance Manager*
Director & General Manager Nicholas E Robinson
International Division Sélim C Haddad *Deputy Manager, International Dept*

Others (Senior Executives)
Daniel Ribant *Director & Credit Manager*

Syndicated Lending
Other (Trade Finance)
Letters of Credit Isabelle Ippersiel *Head, LC Dept.*

Foreign Exchange
Tel: (2) 513 7645 Telex: 62617 BYBLEX B
Global Head Georges Khneysser *Chief Dealer & Treasurer*

144 Euromoney Directory 1999

BELGIUM (+32)

Other Departments
Chief Credit Officer   Raymond Letayf *Head of Credit Department*

CARIPLO SA - Cassa di Risparmio delle Provincie Lombarde SpA
Representative Office
Avenue Louise 250, Box 63, B-1050 Brussels
Tel: (2) 640 0080 **Fax:** (2) 640 2674

Senior Executive Officers
Representative, Benelux & EU   Antonio Kuciukyan

The Chase Manhattan Bank
Full Branch Office
Blue Tower, Avenue Louise 326, Box 51, B-1050 Brussels
Tel: (2) 629 5811 **Fax:** (2) 629 5850 **Swift:** CHBIS BE BX

Senior Executive Officers
Senior Chase Officer   Benoît Struye de Swielande ☎ **629 5831** 🖷 **629 5850**

Settlement / Clearing
Other (Settlement & Clearing)
Operations & Finance   Noël Boullart *Senior Finance Officer* ☎ **629 5836** 🖷 **629 5837**

Citibank NA
Full Branch Office
Boulevard General Jacques 263 G, B-1050 Brussels
Tel: (2) 626 5111; (2) 644 9310 **Fax:** (2) 626 5575 **Telex:** 65100 **Cable:** CITIBANK BRU
Website: www.citibank.com

Senior Executive Officers
Managing Director / General Manager   Michael M Roberts ☎ **626 6277** 🖷 **626 5580**

General - Treasury
Head of Treasury   Paul Vandeperre *Financial Investment Advisor* ☎ **626 6119**

Money Markets
Money Markets - General
   Paul Vandeperre *Financial Investment Advisor* ☎ **626 6119**

Administration
Corporate Communications
   Guy Hendrix ☎ **626 5527** 🖷 **626 5598**

Citibank SA (Global Consumer)
Boulevard General Jacques 263 G, B-1050 Brussels
Tel: (2) 626 5111; (2) 626 5151
Website: www.citibank.be

Senior Executive Officers
Chairman   Victor Toledo ☎ **626 5507** 🖷 **626 5601**
Financial Director   Jose de Penaranda *Chief Financial Officer*
Business Manager   Victor Toledo ☎ **626 5507**
Company Secretary   Ria de Rudder ☎ **626 5507**

Administration
Legal / In-House Counsel
   Christian Vergaert ☎ **626 5393** 🖷 **626 5572**

Corporate Communications
   Guy Hendrix ☎ **626 5527** 🖷 **626 5598**

Commerzbank AG
Boulevard Louis Schmidt 87, B-1040 Brussels
Tel: (2) 743 1811 **Fax:** (2) 743 1800 **Telex:** 62790 **Swift:** COBA BE BX

Senior Executive Officers
General Manager   Thomas Elshorst
Treasurer   H Wiebe

BELGIUM (+32) www.euromoneydirectory.com

Commerzbank AG (cont)
Administration
Head of Administration Franz Braun *Head*

Crédit Commercial de France

Avenue des Arts 46, B-1000 Brussels
Tel: (2) 512 9170 **Fax:** (2) 513 0516 **Telex:** 63274 **Swift:** CCFR BE BB **Email:** ccfbxl@ccf.arc.be **Reuters:** CCFB

Senior Executive Officers
Financial Director Marc Van Wambeke
Chief Operating Officer Christine De Greef
Treasurer Anne Herlemont ☏ **513 9160**
Managing Director / General Manager Bernard de Bellefroid

General-Lending (DCM, SL)
Head of Corporate Banking Kathleen van Rijckevorsel

Risk Management
Country Head Thierry Larose *Head of Derivatives* ☏ **513 9160**

Other Departments
Chief Credit Officer Chantal Peters

Administration
Legal / In-House Counsel
  Chantal Peters

Crédit Communal de Belgique Head Office

Boulevard Pacheco 44, B-1000 Brussels
Tel: (2) 222 1111 **Fax:** (2) 222 5504 **Telex:** 26354 **Swift:** GKCC BE BB **Reuters:** COMU

Senior Executive Officers
Chairman of the Management Committee François Narmon
Financial Director Paul Vanzeveren *Member, Management Committee*
GM, Treasury & Capital Markets Gerrit van Daele

General-Investment
Head of Investment Geert Junius *Deputy General Manager*

Debt Capital Markets / Fixed Income
Reuters: COMB, COMS, COMU
Head of Fixed Income Trading Marc Duckens ☏ **250 7008**

Domestic Government Bonds
Head of Sales Albert Girboux ☏ **250 7299**
Head of Trading Marc Duckens ☏ **250 7008**

Eurobonds
Head of Sales Marc Henry ☏ **250 7451**

Libor-Based / Floating-Rate Products
Asset Swaps Geert Junius ☏ **222 4680**

Fixed-Income Repo
Head of Repo Albert Girboux ☏ **250 7299**

Fixed-Income Research
Head of Fixed Income Francoise Bernard ☏ **250 7070**

Equity Capital Markets
Domestic Equities
Head of Trading William de Smet *Equity Trader* ☏ **250 7005**

Syndicated Lending
Head of Syndication Geert Junius ☏ **222 4680**

Loan-Related Activities
Project Finance François Greindl ☏ **222 3613**

Money Markets
Reuters: COMU
Head of Money Markets Erik Van Damme *Head* ☏ **222 5518**

Foreign Exchange
Reuters: COMS
Head of Trading Serge Van De Velde ☏ **250 7801**

146 Euromoney Directory 1999

www.euromoneydirectory.com					BELGIUM (+32)

Risk Management
Head of Risk Management				Michel Bolle *General Manager* ☎ 222 5116
Other (FI Derivatives)
Head of Swaps / Options				Manuel Hulet ☎ 250 7006
OTC Credit Derivatives
Country Head						Geert Junius ☎ 222 4680
Settlement / Clearing
Head of Settlement / Clearing				Jos Vermeulen ☎ 222 4021
Fixed-Income Settlement				Joelle Van Gulck ☎ 222 6049
Global Custody
Head of Global Custody				Christian Maertens ☎ 222 3235
Asset Management
Head							Jean-Yves Maldague ☎ 222 3301
Other Departments
Private Banking					Jean-Yves Maldague ☎ 222 3301
Correspondent Banking					Bruno De Decker ☎ 222 3214
Cash Management					Wilfred Herremans ☎ 250 7720
Administration
Legal / In-House Counsel
							Tanguy Van De Werve ☎ 222 6336
Compliance
							Tanguy Van De Werve ☎ 222 6336

## Crédit Général SA de Banque						Head Office
5 Grand'Place, B-1000 Brussels
Tel: (2) 547 1211 **Fax:** (2) 547 1110 **Telex:** 25059 **Swift:** CREG BE BB **Reuters:** CGBB
Senior Executive Officers
President						Ch Deleu

## Crédit Lyonnais Belgium SA						Bank Subsidiary
17 Avenue Marnix, B-1000 Brussels
Tel: (2) 516 0813; (2) 551 6511 **Fax:** (2) 516 0694; (2) 551 6666 **Telex:** 20227 **Reuters:** CLYC
Senior Executive Officers
General Director					Philippe Cloes ☎ 516 0600
Chief Operating Officer				Juan De Vinck *Head of Fund Management* ☎ 516 0307
Treasurer						Tanguy de Villenfagne *Manager, Treasury & Capital Markets* ☎ 516 0590
Administrator						Tanguy de Villenfagne ☎ 516 0595
Debt Capital Markets / Fixed Income
Telex: 20227B CREDI B
Fixed-Income Repo
Head of Repo; Matched Book Manager;			Thierry Ponet *Head of Belgian Trading*
Trading
Trading						Alain Dewatine
							Jean-Philippe Guignon *Trader* ☎ 516 0883
							Gaetan Dumon
Sales							Jean-Philippe Guignon *Trader* ☎ 516 0883
Equity Capital Markets
Equity Repo / Securities Lending
Head							Thierry Ponet *Head of Belgian Trading*
Head of Trading					Jean-Philippe Guignon *Trader* ☎ 516 0883
							Alain Dewatine
							Frank Fogiel *Trader* ☎ 516 0838

## Crédit Professional SA						Head Office
Formerly known as: Caisse Nationale de Crédit Professional SA
Boulevard de Waterloo 16, B-1000 Brussels
Tel: (2) 289 8989 **Fax:** (2) 289 8990 **Telerate:** 17766 **Bloomberg:** ELMAR HEYMAN
Senior Executive Officers
Chairman						Thierry Faut ☎ 289 8001
Treasurer						Jean-Marie Colette ☎ 289 8713 ⨍ 289 8997
International Division				Thierry Faut ☎ 289 8001

Euromoney Directory 1999   **147**

BELGIUM (+32)

Crédit Professional SA (cont)
Debt Capital Markets / Fixed Income
Head of Debt Capital Markets   Elmar Heyman ☎ 289 8711 ℻ 289 8997 ℡ elm@flexibank.be
Fixed-Income Repo
Trading   Dany Lomeux *Short-Term Derivatives* ☎ 289 8740
Equity Capital Markets
Head of Equity Capital Markets   Elmar Heyman ☎ 289 8711 ℻ 289 8997 ℡ elm@flexibank.be
Money Markets
Head of Money Markets   Jean-Marie Colette ☎ 289 8713 ℻ 289 8997
Other   Erve Bernard *Trader* ☎ 289 8740
Foreign Exchange
Head of Foreign Exchange   Jean-Marie Colette ☎ 289 8713 ℻ 289 8997
Head of Trading   Erve Bernard *Trader* ☎ 289 8740
Risk Management
Fixed Income Derivatives / Risk Management
Trading   Dany Lomeux *Short-Term Derivatives* ☎ 289 8740

Deutsche Bank AG   Full Branch Office
Arenbergstraat 23, B-2000 Antwerp
PO Box 228, Antwerp
Tel: (3) 220 0011 **Fax:** (3) 226 2018 **Telex:** 71549 DEUTBANK

Deutsche Bank AG   Full Branch Office
Boulevard du Souverain 100, B-1170 Brussels
Tel: (2) 674 3711; (2) 674 3782 **Fax:** (2) 674 3811; (2) 674 3704 **Telex:** 63708 DEUTBANK **Swift:** DEUT BE BE

Dewaay Broking SA   Head Office
Ragui House, Place de Brouckère 12, B-1000 Brussels
Tel: (2) 219 2490; (2) 219 3320 **Fax:** (2) 219 7665 **Telex:** 25417

Senior Executive Officers
Partner   Emile Servranckx ☎ 213 06 21
Foreign Exchange Manager   Theo Ghÿs
Foreign Exchange
Department: FX Broker
Global Head   Emile Servranckx *Partner* ☎ 213 06 21
FX Traders / Sales People
Deposits   S Bakalli *Chief*
IRS / FRA   H Garré *Chief*
   Theo Ghÿs *Foreign Exchange Manager*

ES-Finance SA/NV
Sterrenkundelaan 14, Av De L'Astronomie, B-1210 Brussels
Tel: (2) 228 8963 **Fax:** (2) 228 6773

Senior Executive Officers
Chairman   Wilfred Van Dooren
Managing Director   François F Voorhelst

Euroclear Operations Centre   Head Office
Boulevard Emile Jacqmain 151, B-1210 Brussels
Tel: (2) 224 1211 **Fax:** (2) 224 2041 **Telex:** 61025 MGTEC B **Swift:** MGTC BE BE ECL **Reuters:** ECLEAR01-02-03
Telerate: 3274-6
Website: www.euroclear.com

Senior Executive Officers
Financial Director   Theo Van Engeland *VP, Finance* ☎ 224 4921 ℻ 224 2649
Managing Director & General Manager   Luc Bomans ☎ 224 1300 ℻ 224 1301

www.euromoneydirectory.com   BELGIUM (+32)

Others (Senior Executives)
Resident Counsel   Luigi L De Ghenghi *Vice President* ☏ **224 1444** 🖷 **224 2568**
Market Services   Ignace R Combes *Managing Director* ☏ **224 2620** 🖷 **224 2041**
Domestic Securities Division   Pierre Francotte *Managing Director* ☏ **224 1140** 🖷 **224 2694**
International Securities Division   Pierre Slechten *Managing Director* ☏ **224 1424** 🖷 **224 2880**
Commercial Division   Martine Dinne *Managing Director* ☏ **224 1456** 🖷 **224 2521**
Information Technology   Michael Pilkington *Vice President* ☏ **224 1220** 🖷 **224 1876**
EMU Transition Coordination   Yves Poullet *Vice President* ☏ **224 1883** 🖷 **224 4529**
Cash Services   Erik Cauwenbergh *Vice President* ☏ **224 1478** 🖷 **224 2041**

Debt Capital Markets / Fixed Income
Tel: 224 2577 **Telex:** 224 2041

Fixed-Income Repo
Marketing & Product Development   Jo Van de Velde *Vice President* ☏ **224 2744**
                                    Philippe Verriest *Associate* ☏ **224 2577**
                                    Boi Ai Giang *Associate* ☏ **224 2732**

Equity Capital Markets
Telex: 224 2041

Equity Repo / Securities Lending
Head   Ignace R Combes *Managing Director* ☏ **224 2620** 🖷 **224 2041**
Marketing & Product Development   Mireille Lebrun ☏ **224 2325**
                                    Annette Brandt *Vice President, Securities Lending* ☏ **224 1360**
                                    Michel Boving *Associate, Triparty Securities Lending* ☏ **224 2715**
                                    Marc Vermeylen *Associate, Triparty Secured Loans* ☏ **224 2870**

Risk Management
Global Head   Peter Sucaet *Vice President* ☏ **224 4624** 🖷 **224 2979**

Administration
Corporate Communications
Corporate Communications   Denis Peters *Vice President* ☏ **224 2618** 🖷 **224 2433**

Accounts / Audit
                                    Niall Byrne *Vice President* ☏ **224 4905** 🖷 **224 1876**

Other (Administration)
Human Resources   Guy Schuermans *Vice President* ☏ **224 1306** 🖷 **224 2309**

Eurolease SA/NV   Head Office

Rue des Colonies 62, B-1000 Brussels
Tel: (2) 506 0211 **Fax:** (2) 511 9960

Senior Executive Officers
Chairman & President   Jean-Jacques Verdickt
Financial Director; Treasurer   Philippe De Vos *Financial & Administrative Director*
Managing Director / General Manager Ronnie Richardson

Others (Senior Executives)
                                    Dirk Boeykens *Commercial Director*
Real Estate   François De Cort *Commercial Director*
Credit Department   Marc Flamee *Director*

Other Departments
Chief Credit Officer   Marc Flamee *Director*

Administration
Head of Administration   Philippe De Vos *Financial & Administrative Director*

Public Relations
                                    Dirk Boeykens *Commercial Director*

Other (Administration)
Marketing   Dirk Boeykens *Commercial Director*

Finacor et Associés SA   Subsidiary Company

Rue des Colonies 52, B-1000 Brussels
Tel: (2) 219 1180 **Fax:** (2) 219 7669 **Telex:** 26229 FINCOR B **Email:** straven@elysee.finacor.fr **Telerate:** 8500-8506/
42670

Senior Executive Officers
Others (Senior Executives)
Management   Corneel Van Den Branden *General Manager*
                                    Philippe Vanommeslaeghe *Assistant General Manager*

Euromoney Directory 1999   **149**

BELGIUM (+32) www.euromoneydirectory.com

Finacor et Associés SA (cont)
Debt Capital Markets / Fixed Income
Department: Belgian Bond Market
Tel: 219 0832

Domestic Government Bonds
Head of Trading Jean-Louis Muylaert
  Philippe Miles
  Rudi Cornelis

Fixed-Income Repo
Head of Repo Philippe Van Ommeslaghe *AG Manager* ☏ **219 7414**
Trading Sandra De Cubber *Trader*
  Nathalie Allaert *Trader* ☏ **219 8181**
  Eric Allaert *Trader*
  J Marie Galloy *Trader*
  J Louis Manderfelt *Trader*

Money Markets
Department: Belgian Money Market
Tel: 219 8181 Fax: 219 7669 Reuters: FICO-Q, ICOR-W
Country Head Nathalie Allaert *Trader* ☏ **219 8181**

Money Markets - General
  Jean Marie Galloy
  Sandra De Cubber *Trader*
  Jean-Louis Manderfelt
  Eric Minnen
  Julie Neville
  Jean-François Rooman
  Véronique Van Moer
  Eric Allaert
  Ann De Lange
Department: International Money Market
Country Head Anko Wentholt

Money Markets - General
  Hartley Bates
  Pierre De Vos
  Kris Jacobs
  Jean-Louis Van Acker
  Susan Cauldwell
  Giuseppe Noto
  Jan Proesmans
  Jean-Paul Dermine
  Philippe Rep
  David Baker

Risk Management
Spot / Forwards Trading Emmanuel de Brouchoven *Spot Dealer*
  Emmanuel Ghyssens *Spot Dealer*
  Donald Van Der Fraenen *Spot Dealer*
  Guy Annoni *Spot Dealer*

Settlement / Clearing
Settlement (General) Hilde Vanden Bossche *Back-Office*
  Béatrice Danau *Back-Office*

Administration

Accounts / Audit
Internal Audit Hans Maertens

Other (Administration)
Secretariat Sylvie Tossyn
  Michèle Gerard
  Yolande Frey
Information Christian Straven
  Olivier Collon
  Stéphane Juillet

Fortis Investments Belgium NV/SA

Rue Du Marais 2, B-1000 Brussels
Tel: (2) 228 2800 Fax: (2) 228 2801

Senior Executive Officers
President of the Executive Committee   Freddy Van den Spiegel ☎ **228 6547** F **228 7066**
Chief Executive Officer   Joseph Hönen *Vice President, Executive Commitee* ☎ **228 2930** F **228 2804**
Managing Director   Christian Fabert ☎ **228 2805** F **228 2929**
Managing Director   Jean Paul Gruslin ☎ **228 2967** F **228 2973**
General Secretary   Dominique Lienart ☎ **228 9488** F **228 2999**

Others (Senior Executives)
Internal Control   Johan Huylebroeck *Internal Control* ☎ **288 7800** F **288 2999**
Methods & Development   Germain Lanneau *Head of Department* ☎ **288 2810** F **288 2999**

Debt Capital Markets / Fixed Income
Department: Stockbroking
Head of Debt Capital Markets   Marc Putteman *Coordinator Stockbrocking* ☎ **228 2900** F **228 2901**
Head of Fixed Income   Frédéric Peemans *Senior Portfolio Manager, Head of Fixed Income*
☎ **228 6711** F **228 2922**

Equity Capital Markets
Department: Stockbroking
Head of Equity Capital Markets   Marc Putteman *Coordinator Stockbrocking* ☎ **228 2900** F **228 2901**
Head of Equity Capital Markets   Etienne Beckers *Senior Portfolio Manager, Head of Equities* ☎ **228 7246**
F **228 5841**

Settlement / Clearing
Head of Settlement / Clearing   Philippe Mouffe *Co-ordinator Middle Office* ☎ **228 6400** F **228 8227**
Back-Office   Marc Herman *Head, Middle / Back Office* ☎ **228 2971** F **228 2974**
Eddy Gaffin *Head, Middle / Back Office* ☎ **228 8678** F **228 8498**

Asset Management
Head   Kris Vanderstede *Chief Investment Officer* ☎ **228 8814** F **228 2922**

Other (Asset Management)
Equity & OPC   Etienne Beckers *Senior Portfolio Manager, Head of Equities* ☎ **228 7246**
F **228 5841**
Grégoire Delouche *Portfolio Manager* ☎ **228 5849** F **228 5841**
Bart Geukens *Portfolio Manager* ☎ **228 2852** F **228 5841**
Rudy Vandorpe *Portfolio Manager* ☎ **228 5738** F **228 5841**
Belgian Asset & Group AG   Dorothée Richard *Senior Portfolio Manager* ☎ **228 2850** F **228 2877**
Anne-Marie Léonard *Junior Portfolio Manager* ☎ **228 2854** F **228 2877**
Fixed Income & OPC   Frédéric Peemans *Senior Portfolio Manager, Head of Fixed Income*
☎ **228 6711** F **228 2922**
Bernard Dellége *Portfolio Manager* ☎ **228 2873** F **228 2922**
Institutionals   Yves Van Langenhove *Senior Portfolio Manager* ☎ **228 8650** F **228 2877**
Christian Truyens *Senior Portfolio Manager* ☎ **228 7818** F **228 2877**

Department: Group Asset
Head   Luc Van Den Meersschaut ☎ **228 7694** F **228 8498**
Portfolio Management   Philippe Lhoest *Senior Investment Manager* ☎ **228 2969** F **228 2973**

Other Departments
Private Banking   Philippe Masson *Senior Portfolio Manager* ☎ **228 2848** F **228 2929**
Eric De Maeyer *Sales Manager* ☎ **228 2889** F **228 2929**
Economic Research   Werner Huysmans *Senior Analyst, Coordinator Research* ☎ **228 9387**
F **228 5514**

Administration
Head of Administration   Bertrand Veldekens *Head, Central Administration* ☎ **228 2828** F **228 2878**

Accounts / Audit
Accounting & Logistics   Alain Louckx *Accounting Manager* ☎ **208 2824** F **288 2801**
Department: Product Development Research & Communication
Fax: +32 (2) 228 5514
Business Development   Dirk De Batseller *Chief Strategist, Head of Department* ☎ **228 8687**
Philippe De Brouwer *Coordinator Product & Concept Development*
☎ **228 2812**

Corporate Communications
Coordinator Communication   Dirk Huyghe ☎ **228 7357**

BELGIUM (+32)　　　www.euromoneydirectory.com

Generale Bank
Head Office

Montagne du Parc 3, B-1000 Brussels
Tel: (2) 565 1111 **Fax:** (2) 565 4222 **Telex:** 21283 geba b **Swift:** GEBA BE BB **Email:** info@gbank.be **Reuters:** GBBS
Telerate: GBBO/GFDU
Reuters: GBBT; GBBM; GBBF
Website: www.gbank.be

Senior Executive Officers
Chairman of Board of Directors — Maurice Lippens
Chief Executive Officer — Herman Verwilst *MD & CEO*
Treasurer — René Myncke *General Manager* ☎ **565 6222**
Managing Director — Jean-Jacques Verdickt
Managing Director — Karel De Boeck
Managing Director — André Bergen
Managing Director — Erik van de Merwe
Managing Director — Johan Tack
Secretary General — Luc Willemyns
International Division — Luc Delvaux *General Manager* ☎ **565 3500**

General-Lending (DCM, SL)
Head of Corporate Banking — Paul Dor *General Manager* ☎ **518 2000**

General-Investment
Head of Investment — Francis Van der Hoydonck *Manager* ☎ **565 3562**

Debt Capital Markets / Fixed Income
Department: Fixed Income
Tel: 565 6014 **Fax:** 565 6231
Head of Fixed Income — Ludwig Coppens *Manager of Fixed-Income*

Government Bonds
Head of Sales — Thierry Lengelé *Head, Institutional Sales* ☎ **565 7470**
Head of Trading — Mario Van Hemelryk *Head, Domestic Trading* ☎ **565 7400**
Head of Syndication — Jacques Romainville *Head of Syndication* ☎ **565 6001**

Eurobonds
Head of Sales — Roger Rosier *Head, Retail Sales & Research* ☎ **565 7550**
Head of Trading — Geert Van der Heyden *Head, International Trading* ☎ **565 7420**

Fixed-Income Repo
Head of Repo — Godfried De Vidts *Senior Dealer, Repo* ☎ **565 7248**

Equity Capital Markets
Department: Equities
Tel: 565 6090 **Fax:** 565 6248
Global Head — Daniel de Meeûs *Manager, Equities*

Domestic Equities
Head of Syndication — Thierry Desgain *Head of Syndication* ☎ **565 7540**
Head of Sales — Wim Van Dyck *Head of Sales & Research* ☎ **565 7650**
Head of Trading — Frédéric Van Gheluwe *Head, Trading Derivatives* ☎ **565 7640**

International Equities
Head of Syndication — Thierry Desgain *Head of Syndication* ☎ **565 7540**
Head of Sales — Wim Van Dyck *Head of Sales & Research* ☎ **565 7650**
Head of Trading — Frédéric Van Gheluwe *Head, Trading Derivatives* ☎ **565 7640**

Equity Research
Head of Equity Research — Wim Van Dyck *Head of Sales & Research* ☎ **565 7650**

Syndicated Lending
Fax: 565 4284
Head of Syndication — Herman Coppens *Head, Structured Finance* ☎ **565 2872**

Loan-Related Activities
Trade Finance — Xavier d'Harveng *Manager* ☎ **565 2555**

Money Markets
Tel: 565 6020 **Fax:** 565 6280
Head of Money Markets — Jos Dekeukeleire *Manager, Sales & Trading*

Domestic Commercial Paper
Head of Sales — Roger Rosier *Head, Retail Sales & Research* ☎ **565 7550**

Eurocommercial Paper
Head of Sales — Roger Rosier *Head, Retail Sales & Research* ☎ **565 7550**

Foreign Exchange
Tel: 565 6020 **Fax:** 565 6230
Head of Foreign Exchange — Jos Dekeukeleire *Manager, Sales & Trading*
Head of Institutional Sales — Alex Devroye ☎ **565 6027**

152　Euromoney Directory 1999

www.euromoneydirectory.com BELGIUM (+32)

Risk Management
Tel: 565 6210
Head of Risk Management   Guido Verbaet *Manager, General Services*
Corporate Finance / M&A Advisory
Head of Corporate Finance   Francis Van der Hoydonck *Manager* ☏ **565 3562**
Asset Management
Head   Alain Wicker *General Manager*
Other Departments
Chief Credit Officer   Jean-Maxine Stengers *General Manager* ☏ **565 2502**
Private Banking   Pierre de Donnea *Manager* ☏ **773 3200**
Correspondent Banking   Jean-Marie de Baerdemaeker *Head of Financial Institutions* ☏ **565 2067**
Administration
Head of Marketing   Paul Lembrechts *General Manager* ☏ **565 2324**
Technology & Systems
                                           Henri Franken *General Manager* ☏ **565 4748**
Legal / In-House Counsel
                                           Charles-Ghislain Winandy *General Manager* ☏ **565 2074**
Compliance
                                           Henri Huet *General Manager* ☏ **565 2860**
Public Relations
                                           Kathleen Steel *Manager* ☏ **565 2266**
Other (Administration)
Information Services   Jacques Godet *General Manager* ☏ **565 6161**
Human Resources   Nadine Lemaitre *General Manager* ☏ **565 2082**
Planning, Systems Plan, Facility Mgmt &   Rosa Van Elegem *General Manager* ☏ **565 4186**
Security
Central Management   Godfried Willems *General Manager* ☏ **565 2371**

ING Baring Private Bank   Full Branch Office
Eggestraat 30, B-2610 Antwerp Morstel
Tel: (3) 449 3321 Fax: (3) 449 6704
Senior Executive Officers
Manager   Peter van der Voort van Zijp
Relationship Manager
                                           Marienus Molier
Other Departments
Private Banking   Rob Moonen *Manager*

ING Barings   Full Branch Office
De Lignestraat 1, B-1000 Brussels
Tel: (2) 229 8711 Fax: (2) 229 8810; (2) 229 8710 Telex: 21780 Swift: INGB BE BB
Extra Telex: 24191
Senior Executive Officers
General Manager   Peter van der Voort van Zijp
General Manager   Gilbert Colonna
Others (Senior Executives)
Financial Director   Z Duvaterkeyn
General-Lending (DCM, SL)
Head of Corporate Banking   Robert Maurissen *Head* ☏ **738 4728**
Other Departments
Department: ING Baring Private Bank
Private Banking   Eddy Willo *General Manager*

ING Belgium
24 Avenue Marnix, 1000 Brussels
Tel: (2) 547 2111 Fax: (2) 547 3544
Senior Executive Officers
Chairman   M Tilmant

Euromoney Directory 1999   **153**

BELGIUM (+32) www.euromoneydirectory.com

Interfinance SA
Head Office

222 Avenue de Tervuren, B-1150 Brussels
Tel: (2) 763 0960 **Fax:** (2) 770 3353 **Reuters:** STAT

Senior Executive Officers
Chairman & Chief Executive Officer — A Ferreira

Others (Senior Executives)
Finn Ellingsen
Claude Lai
P Ferreira

Administration
Head of Administration — A Mues

Technology & Systems
M Houpperoz

Accounts / Audit
K Massie

International Securities SA
Head Office

Rue de Namur 43/7, B-1000 Brussels
Tel: (2) 511 1895 **Fax:** (2) 511 2811 **Telex:** 23083

Senior Executive Officers
Chief Executive Officer — Pierre Geismar *Managing Director*
Proxy Holder — Nicole Siffredi

Debt Capital Markets / Fixed Income
Eurobonds
Head of Trading — Pierre Geismar *Managing Director*

Equity Capital Markets
International Equities
Head of Trading — Pierre Geismar *Managing Director*

Settlement / Clearing
Regional Head — Nicole Siffredi *Proxy Holder*
Equity Settlement — Ingrid Verbraeken
Marie Ferreiro

Fixed-Income Settlement — Ingrid Verbraeken
Marie Ferreiro

Ippa Bank NV
Head Office

Formerly known as: Bank Ippa NV

23 Boulevard du Souverain, B-1170 Brussels
Tel: (2) 678 6911 **Fax:** (2) 678 6605 **Telex:** 26594-63978 **Swift:** IPPA BE 22 **Reuters:** IPPA
Website: www.ippa.be

Senior Executive Officers
Chairman — Patrick de Courcel
Managing Director — Albert Van Houtte
Financial Director — Jean-Claude Mertens *Director*
Treasurer — Vincent de Smet *Head of Department*

Debt Capital Markets / Fixed Income
Head of Fixed Income — Wim Weyers *Section Head*

Government Bonds
Head of Sales — Eddy Van Santvoort *Portfolio Manager*
Head of Trading — Wim Weyers *Section Head*
Head of Syndication — Eddy Van Santvoort *Portfolio Manager*

Eurobonds
Head of Sales — Robert Deckers *Dealer*
Head of Trading — Denis Van Bauwel *Dealer*

Libor-Based / Floating-Rate Products
FRN Sales; Asset Swaps — Emmanuel Dendauw *Portfolio Manager*

Syndicated Lending
Head of Syndication — Eddy Van Santvoort *Portfolio Manager*

154 Euromoney Directory 1999

www.euromoneydirectory.com BELGIUM (+32)

Money Markets
Tel: 678 6940
Head of Money Markets Marc Renard *Section Head*

Wholesale Deposits
Marketing Hugo Van Geert *Section Head*

Foreign Exchange
Head of Foreign Exchange Vincent Gyselinck *Section Head*

Risk Management
Head of Risk Management Guy Begasse *Head of Department*

Settlement / Clearing
Back-Office Rene Van Thillo *Back Office Manager*

Asset Management
Head Alain Wauthier *ALM Manager*

Other Departments
Correspondent Banking Philippe Marinus *Head of Correspondent Banking*

Administration
Head of Administration Rene Van Thillo *Back Office Manager*

Joyo Bank (Europe) SA Subsidiary Company
Avenue Louise 283, Box 4, B-1050 Brussels
Tel: (2) 647 5660 **Fax:** (2) 647 9159 **Telex:** 24.199 **Reuters:** 200 27682 **Telerate:** 200 27578
Bloomberg: +32 (2) 644 4438

Senior Executive Officers
Managing Director Michio Tochigi

Money Markets
Head of Money Markets Hiroyuki Kawada *Manager*

Foreign Exchange
Head of Foreign Exchange Hiroyuki Kawada *Manager*

Settlement / Clearing
Head of Settlement / Clearing Katsuhiro Noda *Manager*

Administration
Head of Administration Ritsuo Sasajima *Deputy Managing Director*

Accounts / Audit
Danny Serckx *Accounting Manager*

KBC Bank
Arenbergstraat 7, B-1000 Brussels
Tel: (2) 546 4111 **Fax:** (2) 422 8131 **Telex:** 21207/61402 KBCOMP B **Swift:** KRED BE BB **Email:** v20615@kb.be
Telerate: 3620, 3265/7, 21444 **Cable:** CREDITBANK
Reuters: KRBX (Forex); KBXE (ECU); KRBA-N (Eurobond Trading); KBBO-R (Primary Dealer OLO);
KRBI-J (Belgian Stock Market); KRBK-N
Website: www.kb.be

Senior Executive Officers
Chairman of Board of Directors Andreas de Keersmaeker ☐ **546 4769**
President Marcel Cockaerts ☐ **546 4925**
Managing Director Rudy Broechaert ☐ **546 4523**
Managing Director Herman Agneessens ☐ **546 5770**
Managing Director Jan Van Hevel ☐ **546 4201**
Managing Director Luc Philips ☐ **546 5300**
Managing Director Remi Vermeiren ☐ **546 4913**

Relationship Manager
Central Division Multinationals Pieter Vandendriesche *General Manager* ☐ **546 4080**
Jean-Pierre Vijverman *Deputy General Director* ☐ **546 6300**

Debt Capital Markets / Fixed Income
Tel: 546 4010 Fax: 546 6022

Domestic Government Bonds
Head of Trading Danny Swinnen *Head, Government Bonds* ☐ **546 4613**

Eurobonds
Head of Origination; Head of Syndication Jacques Vandenberghan *Head, New Issues* ☐ **546 4702**
Head of Sales Ann Pieraerts *Head, Institutional Sales* ☐ **546 4625**
Head of Trading Tinny Hasendonckx *Head, Eurobond Trading* ☐ **546 4810**

Euromoney Directory 1999 **155**

BELGIUM (+32)   www.euromoneydirectory.com

KBC Bank (cont)

Fixed-Income Repo
Head of Repo — Christophe Finck *Repos* ☎ 546 4487 ℻ 546 5160
Trading — Guy De Munck

Syndicated Lending
Head of Syndication — Erik Feys *Head of Syndication* ☎ 546 4591

Loan-Related Activities
Trade Finance — Ian D Brigden *SVP & General Manager* ☎ +44 (171) 256 4891
Malcolm D Watson *FVP & Regional Manager, Europe* ☎ +44 (171) 256 4891
Carmen Rodriguez *First Vice President* ☎ +34 (1) 598 3588
Bartel Puelinckx *Manager* ☎ 546 6222

Project Finance — Cormac O'Rourke *GM & Regional Head, Europe* ☎ +353 (1) 603 5406
Eric McCartney *GM & Regional Head, Americas* ☎ +1 (212) 541 0706
℻ +1 (212) 541 0666
Peter Barrett *GM & Regional Head, Asia* ☎ +353 (1) 603 5404
℻ +353 (1) 670 0855
Gert Dekeyser *Project Finance Manager* ☎ 546 5933 ℻ 546 5108
Robert Tam *Senior Manager* ☎ +852 2879 3409 ℻ +852 2879 3418
Liam Donlon *Managing Director* ☎ +353 (1) 603 5439 ℻ +353 (1) 670 0855

Structured Trade Finance — Ian D Brigden *SVP & General Manager* ☎ +44 (171) 256 4891
Malcolm D Watson *FVP & Regional Manager, Europe* ☎ +44 (171) 256 4891
Carmen Rodriguez *First Vice President* ☎ +34 (1) 598 3588
Bartel Puelinckx *Manager* ☎ 546 6222

Risk Management
Tel: 546 4386 Fax: 546 4046
Global Head — Maurits Verherstraeten *Risk Manager* ☎ 546 4308 ✉ u11897@kb.be
Regional Head — Pat Garrity *Risk Manager* ☎ +1 (212) 541 0600

Fixed Income Derivatives / Risk Management
Global Head — Willy Kestens ☎ 546 4181
Country Head — Pierre Deheegher ☎ 546 4483
IR Swaps Sales / Marketing — Paul Goossens ☎ 546 4031
IR Swaps Trading — Koen Van Baarle ☎ 546 5131
IR Options Sales / Marketing — Paul Goossens ☎ 546 4031
IR Options Trading — Jos Cornelissen ☎ 546 4378

Foreign Exchange Derivatives / Risk Management
Cross-Currency Swaps, Sales / Marketing — Paul Goossens ☎ 546 4031
Cross-Currency Swaps, Trading — Fabrice Schelback ☎ 546 4938
Vanilla FX option Sales — Paul Goossens ☎ 546 4031
Vanilla FX option Trading — Jos Cornelissen ☎ 546 4378

Other Currency Swap / FX Options Personnel
Philip Desmet ☎ 546 4310
Geert De Koninck ☎ 546 5315
Kris Bauters ☎ 546 4168
Antoine Scheirlinck ☎ 546 4309
Mark Haynes ☎ 546 4309

Exchange-Traded Derivatives
Global Head — Peter Hannes *Head, Clearing Derivatives* ☎ 546 4002

Settlement / Clearing
Equity Settlement — Jean-Pierre Van Wesemael *Head of Operations* ☎ 546 4003
✉ jean-pierre.vanwesemael@kb.be
Derivatives Settlement — Peter Hannes *Head, Clearing Derivatives* ☎ 546 4002
Foreign Exchange Settlement — Freddy Stoop *Head, Enquiries* ☎ 546 4680

Other Departments
Correspondent Banking — Patrick Daems *GM, International Directorate* ☎ 546 5777

Administration

Legal / In-House Counsel

Legal Advice & Accounting — Veerle Vercaigne *Senior Legal Counsel* ☎ 546 6146
Gerrit Callaerts ☎ 546 4872
Nathalie Vermassen *Legal Counsel* ☎ 546 5075
Geert De Greef *Legal Counsel* ☎ 546 4894
Mark Hillewaere *Legal Counsel* ☎ 546 4388

Accounts / Audit
Accounting Support Service — Dirk De Bleser *Head of Accounting & Reporting* ☎ 546 4276

Other (Administration)
Secretariat — Gaston Vangramberen *Head* ☎ 546 5932

www.euromoneydirectory.com BELGIUM (+32)

KBC Securities
Vondelstraat 15, B-2060 Antwerp
Tel: (3) 213 6900 Fax: (3) 226 0038; (3) 226 8373

Senior Executive Officers
Chairman Luc Philips
Chief Executive Officer Michel Vanderkeilen *Managing Director* [T] **(2) 429 5221** [F] **(2) 429 6373**
Managing Director Luc Aspeslagh [T] **(2) 429 5824** [F] **(2) 429 6373**
Managing Director Franky Depickere [T] **(2) 505 9395** [F] **(2) 514 0001**

Equity Capital Markets
Department: Head Office
Place Sainte-Gudule 14, B-1000 Brussels
Tel: +32 (2) 429 4404 Fax: +32 (2) 429 5385

Domestic Equities
Head of Trading Eric Mouling
 Dirk Marckx

Other (Domestic Equities)
Equity Sales & Advice Peiter Hofman
 Koen Hoffman
 Serge Van Heurck
 Michel Van Meerbeek

Equity Research
Head of Equity Research Luc Van Hecke *Department Manager* [T] **(2) 429 4161** [F] **(2) 429 4707**
Analyst Ruth Devenyns *Biotechnology* [T] **(2) 429 5751**
 Kurt Janssens *Telecommunication* [T] **(2) 429 2962**
 Caroline Lauwers *Retail, Holdings* [T] **(2) 429 4088**
 Serge Pattyn *Industrials* [T] **(2) 429 5378**
 Filip Platteeuw *Utilities* [T] **(2) 429 5750**
 Nathalie Sierens *Industrials (small caps.)* [T] **(2) 429 2964**
 Kurt Kegels *Industrials (small caps.)* [T] **(2) 429 3189**
 Michel Vanderlinden *Generalist* [T] **(2) 429 2965**
 Sylvie Van Houtte *High Tech* [T] **(2) 429 6490**
 Philippe Verschuere *Industrials* [T] **(2) 429 4174**
 Pascale Weber *Construction* [T] **(2) 429 4106**

Other (International Equity)
Market Maker Johan Segers [T] **(2) 429 5566**
 Alain Verwimp [T] **(2) 429 5566**
 Kurt Gyselinck [T] **(2) 429 5566**
Broker Patrick Sonck [T] **(2) 429 5577**
 Pascal Burm [T] **(2) 429 5577**

Risk Management

OTC Equity Derivatives
Sales Bruno Tuybens [T] **(2) 429 4859**
 Patricia Van Roosbroeck

Other (Equity Derivatives)
Market Maker Options Hélène Goessaert
 Walter Schoenmaekers
 Bart De Sutter
Market Maker Futures Michael Franklin [T] **(2) 429 5144**

Corporate Finance / M&A Advisory
Head of Corporate Finance Bruno Accou [T] **(2) 505 9063**

Other (Corporate Finance)
Advisor Wilbert De Leyn [T] **(2) 429 4651**
 Leen De Smet [T] **(2) 429 4857**
 Eric De Munter [T] **(2) 505 9356**
 Charlotte Desot [T] **(2) 505 9029**
 Christophe Heerinckx [T] **(2) 505 9116**
 Pierre Nossent [T] **(2) 505 9115**
 Bernard Orban [T] **(2) 505 9394**
 Carine Tourneur [T] **(2) 505 9035**
 Marc Van Acoleyen [T] **(2) 505 9025**
 Floris Vansina [T] **(2) 429 5174**

Euromoney Directory 1999 **157**

BELGIUM (+32) www.euromoneydirectory.com

Lloyds Bank plc
Full Branch Office

2 Avenue de Tervueren, B-1040 Brussels
Tel: (2) 739 5811 **Fax:** (2) 733 1107 **Swift:** LOYDBEBB **Email:** lloydsbank@lloyds.be **Reuters:** LOYB

Senior Executive Officers
Chief Executive Officer	Brian Brown *Principal Manager* ☏ **739 5937**
Chief Operating Officer	George Hartwell *Manager, Support Services* ☏ **739 5938**
Manager, Flanders	Michael Coppe ☏ **(3) 202 5200**

Debt Capital Markets / Fixed Income
Eurobonds
Head of Sales — Jo Roesen *Senior Manager, Corporate* ☏ **739 5933**

Libor-Based / Floating-Rate Products
FRN Trading; Asset Swaps — Jo Roesen *Senior Manager, Corporate* ☏ **739 5933**

Syndicated Lending
Head of Origination — Jo Roesen *Senior Manager, Corporate* ☏ **739 5933**
Head of Trading — Michael Coppe *Manager, Flanders* ☏ **(3) 202 5200**

Loan-Related Activities
Trade Finance — Bernard van Nevel *Senior Manager, International Trade Finance* ☏ **739 5942**
Luc van Leeuwe *Manager, Corporate* ☏ **(3) 232 5202**
Francesco Gesa *Corporate Manager* ☏ **739 5945**
Project Finance — Jo Roesen *Senior Manager, Corporate* ☏ **739 5933**

Money Markets
Head of Money Markets — Jan van Cauwenberghe *Manager, Treasury* ☏ **737 0105**

Wholesale Deposits
Marketing — Serge Kasaba *Head of Money Markets* ☏ **737 0108**

Foreign Exchange
Head of Foreign Exchange — Jan van Cauwenberghe *Manager, Treasury* ☏ **737 0105**
Head of Institutional Sales; Corporate Sales — Jean-Pierre van der Wilt *Head of Corporate Dealing* ☏ **737 0106**

Risk Management
Head of Risk Management — Patrick Goyens de Heusch *Manager, Risk Control* ☏ **739 5939**

Settlement / Clearing
Head of Settlement / Clearing — Ian Horspool *Head of Settlements* ☏ **739 5831**

Global Custody
Country Head — Martine Masuy *Head of Custody* ☏ **739 5804**

Administration
Technology & Systems
IT & Communications — Danny Callaert *Manager* ☏ **739 5825**

Compliance
Dominique Bailly *Assistant Manager Credit Control* ☏ **739 5902**

LOCABEL SA
Head Office

Avenue de Cortenbergh 71, B-1000 Brussels
Tel: (2) 739 6411 **Fax:** (2) 739 6435; (2) 739 6401 **Email:** rocabel@skypno.be

Senior Executive Officers
Chairman	Luc Vandewalle
Chief Executive Officer	Alain Vervaet
Chief Operating Officer	Jan Ingelbrecht
Treasurer	Stephane Gillisjans
Company Secretary	Michel Carlier

Administration
Head of Administration	Jean Marie Gilbert
Business Development	Patrick Beselaere
Head of Marketing	Michel Rolans

Technology & Systems
Yuon Delaby

Legal / In-House Counsel
Pierre Etienne Sacre

Public Relations
Edithe Sacre

Accounts / Audit
Egidio Donatella

www.euromoneydirectory.com	BELGIUM (+32)

Mitsubishi Trust & Banking Corporation (Europe) SA Head Office

Boulevard du Regent 40, B-1000 Brussels
Tel: (2) 511 2200 Telex: 69021

Senior Executive Officers
Managing Director	Shigeo Sekijima

Debt Capital Markets / Fixed Income
Global Head	Susumu Mimura *Director & Deputy General Manager*

Eurobonds
Head of Origination	Susumu Mimura *Director & Deputy General Manager*
	Frans Depoorter *Assistant Manager*

Bonds - General
	Hiroaki Matsuyama *Manager*

Risk Management
Global Head	Susumu Mimura *Director & Deputy General Manager*

Corporate Finance / M&A Advisory
Global Head	Takashi Masuyama *Deputy Director & General Manager*
	Frans Depoorter *Assistant Manager*

Other Departments
Correspondent Banking	Susumu Mimura *Director & Deputy General Manager*

Administration
Head of Administration	Susumu Mimura *Director & Deputy General Manager*

Compliance
	Hiroaki Matsuyama *Manager*

Ogaki Kyoritsu Bank (Europe)   Subsidiary Company

287 Avenue Louise, Box 9, B-1050 Brussels
Tel: (2) 640 6340 Fax: (2) 640 9524 Telex: 20130 Email: okbbrs@club.immet.be

Senior Executive Officers
General Manager	Hidashi Mori
General Affairs Department	K Tsâm Nguyen

Debt Capital Markets / Fixed Income
Head of Fixed Income; Head of Fixed Income	Masahiro Ogawa *Deputy General Manager*
Sales; Head of Fixed Income Trading

Government Bonds
Head of Sales	Masahiro Ogawa *Deputy General Manager*

Syndicated Lending
Head of Trading	Koji Kubota *Manager*

Administration
Head of Administration	Masahiro Ogawa *Deputy General Manager*

Technology & Systems
	Masahiro Ogawa *Deputy General Manager*

Public Relations
	Masahiro Ogawa *Deputy General Manager*

Accounts / Audit
	Masahiro Ogawa *Deputy General Manager*

Parfibank   Head Office

Formerly known as: The Long-Term Credit Bank of Japan (Europe) SA
Boulevard du Régent 40, B-1000 Brussels
Tel: (2) 513 9020 Fax: (2) 512 7320 Telex: 61403

Senior Executive Officers
Managing Director	S Frei
Managing Director & General Manager	R Deras

Foreign Exchange
Head of Trading	P Hansquine *Chief Dealer*

Corporate Finance / M&A Advisory
Global Head	G Goesaert *Senior Adviser*

Euromoney Directory 1999   159

BELGIUM (+32) www.euromoneydirectory.com

Parfibank (cont)
Administration
Head of Administration   R Deras *General Manager*
Other (Administration)
Business Promotion   G Goesaert *Senior Adviser*

Petercam Institutional Bonds (PIB) Subsidiary Company
19 Place Sainte Gudule, B-1000 Brussels
Tel: (2) 229 6200 Fax: (2) 229 6222 Reuters: PIBONDS

Senior Executive Officers
President   Georges Caballé ☏ 229 6551
Managing Director   Herve Coppens D' Eeckenbrugge ☏ 229 6203
Managing Director   Alexandre De Groote ☏ 229 6204

Debt Capital Markets / Fixed Income
Head of Fixed Income   Herve Coppens D' Eeckenbrugge *Managing Director* ☏ 229 6203
                                       Alexandre De Groote *Managing Director* ☏ 229 6204

Settlement / Clearing
Fixed-Income Settlement   Thierry Vah Landuyt ☏ 229 6207
Operations   Monique Moerman ☏ 229 6200

Petercam SA Head Office
Place Sainte-Gudule 19, B-1000 Brussels B-1000 Brussels
Tel: (2) 229 6311 Fax: (2) 229 6598 Telex: 21353, 21354
Website: www.petercam.be

Senior Executive Officers
Tel: 229 6311 Fax: 229 6598

Others (Senior Executives)
                                       Jean Peterbroeck *Partner*
                                       Baudouin du Parc *Partner*
                                       William Vanderfelt *Partner*
                                       Pierre Drion *Partner*
                                       Michel Peterbroeck *Partner*
                                       Philippe Huens *Partner*
                                       Georges Caballé *Partner*
                                       Dirk Van den Broeck *Partner*
                                       Marc Ooms *Partner*
                                       Léopold d'oultrement *Partner*
                                       Marc Janssens *Partner*
                                       Eric Struye *Partner*
                                       Pierre Lebeau *Partner*
                                       Guy Lerminiaux *Partner*
                                       Johnny Debuysscher *Partner*
                                       Marc Debrouwer *Director*

Debt Capital Markets / Fixed Income
Tel: 229 6311 Fax: 229 6545
Head of Fixed Income; Head of Fixed Income   Georges Caballé *Partner*
Sales; Head of Fixed Income Trading

Government Bonds
Head of Sales
                                       Hervé Coppens *Manager* ☏ 229 6203
                                       Alexandre De Groote *Manager* ☏ 229 6204

Eurobonds
Head of Sales   John Lumley *Trader* ☏ 229 6514
Head of Trading   Luc Ory *Trader* ☏ 229 6465

Fixed-Income Research
Head of Fixed Income   Johny De Buysscher *Partner* ☏ 229 6449

Equity Capital Markets
Department: Institutional Research and Sales
Tel: 229 6311 Fax: 229 6545

Domestic Equities
Head of Sales   William Vanderfelt *Partner*
Head of Trading   Michel Peterbroeck *Partner*

Other (Domestic Equities)
                                       Marc Janssens *Partner*

www.euromoneydirectory.com BELGIUM (+32)

Equity Research
Head of Equity Research   Marc Debrouwer *Director*
Department: EASDAQ
19 Place Sainte Gudule, Brussels
Head of Sales   Alain Berckmans *Easdaq, Sales & Trading* ☏ **229 6618**
Head of Trading   Stefan Pelckmans *Easdaq, Sales & Trading* ☏ **229 6623**

Foreign Exchange
Tel: 229 6570 Fax: 229 6669 Reuters: CAMR
Head of Foreign Exchange   Francis Heymans *General Manager* ☏ **229 6467**
Head of Trading   Rudi Beke *Head of Trading* ☏ **229 6570**
FX Traders / Sales People
                                Eddy Ceuppens *Trader* ☏ **229 6570**

Risk Management
Tel: 229 6324 Fax: 229 6545
Head of Risk Management   Eric Struye *Partner*

Fixed Income Derivatives / Risk Management
Head of Sales   Eric Struye *Partner*

OTC Equity Derivatives
Head   François Ducuroir *Sales Derivative Products* ☏ **229 6475**
Trading   Christophe Beuvain *Head Trader* ☏ **229 6471**

Other (Equity Derivatives)
                                Alexis Maenhout *Trader* ☏ **229 6550**

Exchange-Traded Derivatives
Head   Christophe Beuvain *Head Trader* ☏ **229 6471**

Settlement / Clearing
Head of Settlement / Clearing   Christian Liegois ☏ **229 6531**
Equity Settlement; Fixed-Income Settlement Ann Van Severen ☏ **229 6440**
Operations; Back-Office   Pierre Hart ☏ **229 6464**

Asset Management
Head   Leopold d'Oultremont *Partner*

Other Departments
Cash Management   Fernand Saegerman *Treasurer* ☏ **229 6574**

Administration
Head of Administration   Pierre Hart ☏ **229 6464**

Technology & Systems
                                Jean-Pierre Diepenrijkx ☏ **229 6411**

Legal / In-House Counsel
                                Philippe Huens *Partner*

Compliance
                                Hans Standaert ☏ **229 6463**

Public Relations
                                Catherine Lejeune ☏ **229 6613**

Accounts / Audit
Accounts   Hans Standaert ☏ **229 6463**
Audit   Sylvie Huret ☏ **229 6680**

Prudential-Bache International Limited (Brussels) Full Branch Office

Formerly known as: Prudential-Bache Securities (Brussels) Inc
Chaussée de la Hulpe 130, B-1000 Brussels
Tel: (2) 661 2211 Fax: (2) 672 6224

Senior Executive Officers
Chief Executive Officer   Geoffroy de Robiano *Director & Branch Manager*
Chief Operating Officer   Hilary Stone *Operations Manager*
Associate Manager   Geert Roggeman

The Sanwa Bank Limited   Full Branch Office

Avenue des Arts 53/54, B-1000 Brussels
Tel: (2) 507 1211 Fax: (2) 513 4381

Senior Executive Officers
General Manager   Yutaka Kitamura

BELGIUM (+32) www.euromoneydirectory.com

Shizuoka Bank (Europe) SA
Subsidiary Company

283 Avenue Louise, B-1050 Brussels
Box 13, Brussels
Tel: (2) 646 0470 **Fax:** (2) 646 2462 **Telex:** 23330 SHIZBR B

Senior Executive Officers
Managing Director & General Manager   Nobuyuki Ishida

Debt Capital Markets / Fixed Income
Head of Debt Capital Markets   Misao Nagakura *Deputy Managing Director & Deputy General Manager*
   ☎ 646 0376

Equity Capital Markets
Head of Equity Capital Markets   Misao Nagakura *Deputy Managing Director & Deputy General Manager*
   ☎ 646 0376

Syndicated Lending
Head of Syndicated Lending   Misao Nagakura *Deputy Managing Director & Deputy General Manager*
   ☎ 646 0376

Money Markets
Head of Money Markets   Misao Nagakura *Deputy Managing Director & Deputy General Manager*
   ☎ 646 0376

Foreign Exchange
Head of Foreign Exchange   Misao Nagakura *Deputy Managing Director & Deputy General Manager*
   ☎ 646 0376

Risk Management
Head of Risk Management   Masahiko Nagakura *Manager*

Settlement / Clearing
Head of Settlement / Clearing   Pierre Loedts *Manager*

SIBEKA - Société d'Entreprise et d'Investissements, SA
Head Office

Formerly known as: Entreprise Investissements

Rue Royale 52, B-1000 Brussels
Tel: (2) 510 0211 **Fax:** (2) 514 1393

Senior Executive Officers
Chairman   Etienne Davignon
Managing Director   Etienne Denis

Administration
Head of Administration   Michel Alloo *Administrative Director*

Smeets Securities NV

Formerly known as: Smeets, Verbaet & Co NV

Kipdorp 10/12, B-2000 Antwerp
Tel: (3) 204 7777 **Fax:** (3) 204 7778 **Telex:** 71466 **Email:** smeets.verbaet@pophost.eunet.be **Bloomberg:** smee

Senior Executive Officers
Chairman   Dirk Bruneel

Others (Senior Executives)
   Benoît Wetterwulghe *Manager*
   Geoffroy Vermeire *Manager*
   Dick Stalanhoef *Manager*
   Walter Vanderbeken *Manager*

Société Générale
Full Branch Office

Tour Bastion, Place du Champ de Mars 5, B-1000 Brussels
Tel: (2) 506 6511 **Fax:** (2) 512 0872 **Telex:** 63405 **Swift:** SGABBEB2 **Email:** marie.coppola@skynet.be

Senior Executive Officers
Chief Executive Officer   J P Ducroquet *CEO, Belgium & Netherlands*
Chief Operating Officer   D Lefevre
Managing Director   J Jarry

General - Treasury
Head of Treasury   D Averoldi *Manager, Treasury & Foreign Exchange*

www.euromoneydirectory.com   BELGIUM (+32)

Syndicated Lending
Loan-Related Activities
Structured Trade Finance   J Zimmermann *Structured Finance Manager*
Other (Trade Finance)
Export Finance   I Backaert *Manager*
                                          G Declercq *Manager*
Money Markets
Currencies Sales   M Quaeghebeur *Dealer*
Foreign Exchange
Department: Treasury & Foreign Exchange
Head of Foreign Exchange   D Averoldi *Manager, Treasury & Foreign Exchange*
FX Traders / Sales People
                                          R Backx *Deputy Manager, Treasury & Foreign Exchange*
                                          F Farina *Deputy Manager, Treasury & Foreign Exchange*
Corporate Dealer   B van der Mussell
                                          C Dedonder
Corporate Finance / M&A Advisory
Corporate Finance Advisor   L Wullaerts
Settlement / Clearing
Back-Office   J Jemine *Head*
Administration
Other (Administration)
Banking Services   P De Jaegere *Manager*
                                          P Demoiny *Officer*

State Street Bank & Trust Company   Representative Office
Chausée de Wavre 1789, B-1160 Brussels
Tel: (2) 663 2036 Fax: (2) 672 2077

Senior Executive Officers
Managing Director   Jean-François Schock ⊤ **663 2037**
Global Custody
Tel: 663 2030 Fax: 673 9863
Head of Global Custody   Michel Bertrand *Vice President* ⊤ **663 2035**
Administration
Head of Marketing   Benoit Fally *Marketing Director* ⊤ **663 2038**

State Street Global Advisors Brussels   Full Branch Office
Chaussee de Wavre 1789, B-1160 Brussels
Tel: (2) 663 2036 Fax: (2) 672 2077

Senior Executive Officers
Managing Director   Jean-François Schock ⊤ **663 2037** F **672 2077**
                                          E **jean-francois_schock@ssga.statestreet.com**

Asset Management
Head   Jean-François Schock *Managing Director* ⊤ **663 2037** F **672 2077**
                                          E **jean-francois_schock@ssga.statestreet.com**

Other (Asset Management)
                                          Michel Bertrand *Vice President* ⊤ **663 2033** F **673 9863**
                                          E **mbertrand@statestreet.com**

The Sumitomo Bank Limited   Full Branch Office
Avenue des Arts 58, Bte 18, B-1000 Brussels
Tel: (2) 551 5000 Fax: (2) 513 4100 Telex: 26416 (General) 62684 (Treasury) Swift: SMIT BB BX
Reuters: SUMB (Money)

Senior Executive Officers
General Manager   M Nishimoto ⊤ **551 5101** E **masayoshi.nishimoto@be.sumitomobank.com**
Joint General Manager   R Fujimoto ⊤ **551 5102** E **ryuzaburo.fujimoto@be.sumitomobank.com**
Joint General Manager   P Grosjean ⊤ **551 5103** E **paul.grosjean@be.sumitomobank.com**
Deputy General Manager   J Chen ⊤ **551 5105** E **jean.chen@be.sumitomobank.com**
Deputy General Manager   P Devos ⊤ **551 5111** E **philippe.devos@be.sumitomobank.com**

BELGIUM (+32) www.euromoneydirectory.com

The Sumitomo Bank Limited (cont)
General - Treasury
Head of Treasury J Chen *Deputy General Manager* ☏ 551 5105
 E jean.chen@be.sumitomobank.com
 N Shidao *AGM, Treasury & Derivatives* ☏ 551 5132
 E naoaki.shidao@be.sumitobank.com
 J L Renard *Assistant Manager, Treasury & Derivatives* ☏ 551 5133
 E jeanluc.renard@be.sumitobank.com

Syndicated Lending
Other (Syndicated Lending)
Loan & Remittance D Rutten *Assistant Manager* ☏ 551 5171
 E daniel.rutten@be.sumitomobank.com
 F Bouchat *Officer* ☏ 551 5175 E francoise.bouchat@be.sumitomobank.com

Administration
Business Development P Devos *Deputy General Manager* ☏ 551 5111
 E philippe.devos@be.sumitomobank.com
 Y Kubo *Assistant Manager, Business Promotion* ☏ 551 5122
 E yuji.kubo@be.sumitomobank.com
 T Tagnit-Hamou ☏ 551 5113 E thomas.tagnithamou@be.sumitomobank.com
 I Vandersnickt *Officer* ☏ 551 5114
 E isabelle.vandersnickt@be,sumitomobank.com

Technology & Systems
Electronic Data Processing P Vallez *Officer* ☏ 551 5151 E philippe.vallez@be.sumitomobank.com
Accounts / Audit
Accounting K Karabalis *Assistant Manager* ☏ 551 5141
 E constantin.karabalis@be.sumitomobank.com

Other (Administration)
Foreign D Rutten *Assistant Manager* ☏ 551 5171
 E daniel.rutten@be.sumitomobank.com
General Affairs, Personnel S Rowies *Officer* ☏ 551 5191 E sabine.rowies@be.sumitomobank.com

The Tokai Bank Limited Representative Office
Avenue Louise 283, B-1050 Brussels
Tel: (2) 646 7940 **Fax:** (2) 646 8690 **Telex:** 20446 TOKAI B
Senior Executive Officers
Chief Representative Naoya Hisada

Tullett & Tokyo Forex (Belgium) SA Subsidiary Company
Avenue Molière 114, B-1190 Brussels
Tel: (2) 348 8700; (2) 349 7700 **Fax:** (2) 344 3655 **Telex:** 25555 **Reuters:** TTFX, TTFB
Senior Executive Officers
Managing Director Patrick Annez de Taboada
Foreign Exchange
Department: Dollar, Euro, Currencies, Crosses
FX Traders / Sales People
 Daniel Kerkhove ☏ 348 8610
 Michel Santos Moro ☏ 348 8617
 Graham Axe ☏ 348 8614
 Robert Harvey ☏ 348 8614
 Didier Martin ☏ 348 8612
 Claude Colin ☏ 348 8615
 Benoît Herman ☏ 348 8613
 Alain Ecker ☏ 348 8620
 Patrick Gardiner ☏ 348 8621
 Steve Adkins ☏ 348 8618
Reuter Dealing Helena Van Genechten *Dealer* ☏ 348 8639
Risk Management
Other Currency Swap / FX Options Personnel
Short Swaps & FRAs Alain Jungers *Deputy Managing Director* ☏ 348 8652 E 344 3655
 Jean-Louis Ecker *Director* ☏ 348 8654 E 344 3655

Other (Exchange-Traded Derivatives)
Global Trading Desk - Non Euro-Derivatives Jean-Louis Ecker *Director* ☏ 348 8654 E 344 3655
 Philippe Leneeuw ☏ 348 8630

www.euromoneydirectory.com   BELGIUM (+32)

Other (Exchange-Traded Derivatives) (cont)
Alain De Potter ☎ 348 8642
Patricia Perrault ☎ 348 8682
Alain Jungers *Deputy Managing Director* ☎ 348 8652 F 344 3655

Türkiye Vakiflar Bankasi TAO   Representative Office
19 Chausse de Haech, B-1210 Brussels
Tel: (2) 219 3700 **Fax:** (2) 219 9839
Senior Executive Officers
Representative   M Ugur Cokdogan

Union Européenne de CIC
Square de Meeûs 37, B-1040 Brussels
Tel: (2) 511 2358 **Fax:** (2) 514 1031 **Email:** cic.banques.bruxelles@skynet.be
Senior Executive Officers
Representative   Yolande van der Bruggen

United Taiwan Bank   Head Office
Avenue des Arts 27, B-1040 Brussels
Tel: (2) 230 5359 **Fax:** (2) 230 0470 **Telex:** 21795 UTBBR B **Email:** sky51593@skynet.be
Senior Executive Officers
President   Ming-Chung Tseng
Treasurer   Philippe Chen *Manager & Dealer* ☎ 230 1822
Managing Director   Yih-Ho Huang
Deputy Managing Director   Samuel Chen

Others (Senior Executives)
Advisor   Max Osterrieth
Business Operation   Lawrence Chang *Manager*

Debt Capital Markets / Fixed Income
Tel: 230 1822 **Fax:** 230 0470
Head of Fixed Income; Head of Fixed Income Sales; Head of Fixed Income Trading   Philippe Chen *Manager & Dealer* ☎ 230 1822

Government Bonds
Head of Trading   Philippe Chen *Manager & Dealer* ☎ 230 1822

Eurobonds
Head of Trading   Philippe Chen *Dealer & Manager* ☎ 230 1822

Emerging Market Bonds
Head of Emerging Markets   Philippe Chen *Manager & Dealer* ☎ 230 1822
Head of Trading   Philippe Chen *Dealer & Manager* ☎ 230 1822

Libor-Based / Floating-Rate Products
FRN Trading   Philippe Chen *Manager & Dealer* ☎ 230 1822
Asset Swaps   Philippe Chen *Dealer & Manager* ☎ 230 1822

Fixed-Income Repo
Head of Repo; Head of Trading   Philippe Chen *Dealer & Manager* ☎ 230 1822

Fixed-Income Research
Head of Fixed Income   Philippe Chen *Manager & Dealer* ☎ 230 1822
Head of Credit Research   Lawrence Chang *Manager*

Syndicated Lending
Head of Syndication   Lawrence Chang *Manager*

Loan-Related Activities
Trade Finance; Project Finance   Lawrence Chang *Manager*

Money Markets
Tel: 230 1822
Head of Money Markets   Philippe Chen *Manager & Dealer* ☎ 230 1822

Domestic Commercial Paper
Head of Trading   Philippe Chen *Dealer & Manager* ☎ 230 1822

Eurocommercial Paper
Head of Trading   Philippe Chen *Dealer & Manager* ☎ 230 1822

BELGIUM (+32) www.euromoneydirectory.com

United Taiwan Bank (cont)
Foreign Exchange
Tel: 230 1822
Head of Trading   Philippe Chen *Dealer & Manager* ☎ **230 1822**
Risk Management
Head of Risk Management   Samuel Chen *Deputy Managing Director*
Fixed Income Derivatives / Risk Management
IR Swaps Trading   Samuel Chen *Deputy Managing Director*
Foreign Exchange Derivatives / Risk Management
Spot / Forwards Trading   Samuel Chen *Deputy Managing Director*
OTC Credit Derivatives
Head of Trading   Samuel Chen *Deputy Managing Director*
Exchange-Traded Derivatives
Head   Samuel Chen *Deputy Managing Director*
Settlement / Clearing
Fixed-Income Settlement; Derivatives   Eva Huang *Manager*
Settlement; Foreign Exchange Settlement
Other Departments
Correspondent Banking   Philippe Chen *Manager & Dealer* ☎ **230 1822**
Administration
Head of Administration   Eva Huang *Manager*
Business Development   Lawrence Chang *Manager*
Technology & Systems
                                               Eva Huang *Manager*
Accounts / Audit
Accounts   Adolfo Flores Canton *Assistant Manager*

De Vaderlandsche Spaarbank — Subsidiary Company

Oesguinlei 92, B-2018 Antwerp
Tel: (3) 244 6931 Fax: (3) 244 6698
Senior Executive Officers
Managing Director   Mr Piirlink

Westdeutsche Landesbank — Full Branch Office

Chaussée de la Hulpe 166, B-1170 Brussels
Tel: (2) 663 6800 Fax: (2) 663 6859
Senior Executive Officers
General Manager   Philip Wykes
General Manager   Horst R Magiera
General-Lending (DCM, SL)
Head of Corporate Banking   Mark W Couvreur *Corporate Banking*
                                               Michael Jadot *Corporate Banking*
                                               Francois Monnaert *Corporate Banking*

BELIZE
(+501)

Central Bank of Belize — Central Bank

PO Box 852, Belize City
Tel: (2) 77216 Fax: (2) 76113 Telex: 225 MONETARY BZ
Senior Executive Officers
Governor   Keith Arnold
Deputy Governor   Yvette Alvarez
Company Secretary   Cecile Reyes
Others (Senior Executives)
Finance Department   Dwain Davis *Manager*
Banking & Currency Department   Marilyn Gardiner *Manager*
Other Departments
Economic Research   Sydney Campbell *Manager*

Administration
Head of Administration Cecile Reyes
Other (Administration)
Human Resources Carol Hyde *Manager*
Chief of Security Kent Haylock

BENIN
(+229)

Banque Centrale des Etats de l'Afrique de l'Ouest Central Bank
PO Box 325, Cotonou
Tel: 312 466; 312 467 **Fax:** 312 465 **Telex:** 5211 BCEAO COTONOU
Senior Executive Officers
Country Director Paulin Cossi
Branch Director Idriss Lyassou Daouda

BERMUDA
(+1 441)

Bermuda Monetary Authority Central Bank
Burnaby House, 26 Burnaby Street, Hamilton, HM 12
PO Box HM 2447, Hamilton, HM JX
Tel: 295 5278 **Fax:** 292 7371 **Telex:** 3567 BEEMA BA **Email:** info@bma.bm
Website: www.bma.bm

Senior Executive Officers
Chairman Mansfield H Brock Jr
General Manager Malcolm E Williams
Others (Senior Executives)
Head, Banking Supervision Colin Furr
Head, Economics & Statistics John Hill
Head, Reserves Management Lori Blackwood
Head, Investment Services Supervision Mark Crockwell
Administration
Head of Administration Marcia Woolridge-Allwood
Technology & Systems
Philip Chadwick
Accounts / Audit
Head, Accountancy Deborah Blakeney de-Shield

The Bank of Bermuda Limited Head Office
6 Front Street, Hamilton, HM 11
Tel: 295 4000 **Fax:** 295 7093; 299 6565 **Telex:** BA 3599 **Swift:** BBDA BM HM
Website: www.bankofbermuda.com

Senior Executive Officers
President & Chief Executive Officer Henry B Smith
Financial Director Edward H Gomez *Senior Vice President & Chief Financial Officer*
Others (Senior Executives)
Executive Management Cummings V Zuill *Senior Vice President*
Alan F Richardson *Senior Vice President*
Hed of Operations Martin Lancaster *Senior Vice President*
Europe Austin J O'Connor *Senior Vice President*
General-Investment
Head of Investment Wayne P Chapman *Senior Vice President, Investment Services*
General - Treasury
Head of Treasury Alan Kershaw *SVP & Head of Treasury*
Relationship Manager
Corporate Clients Luis A Douglas *Senior Executive Vice President*
Private Clients John A Hawkins *Senior Executive Vice President*

BERMUDA (+1 441)   www.euromoneydirectory.com

The Bank of Bermuda Limited (cont)
Relationship Manager (cont)
Private Client Services   Karen M Malcolm *Senior Vice President*
Private Clients, Europe   Peter M C Hodsen *Senior Vice President*
Private Clients, Asia   Paul T O'Neill *Senior Vice President*
Corporate Trust   J Christopher Wilcockson *Senior Vice President*

Equity Capital Markets
Equity Repo / Securities Lending
Head   David Smith *Senior Vice President*
Marketing & Product Development   Anthony T Riker *Manager, Securities Lending* ☏ 299 5117 F 299 6565

Risk Management
Global Head   Peter W McClean *Senior Vice President*

Corporate Finance / M&A Advisory
Head of Corporate Finance   David T Smith *SVP, Corporate Trust* ☏ 299 5205

Settlement / Clearing
Operations   Peter W Le Noury *EVP, Systems & Operations*

Global Custody
Other (Global Custody)
Singapore   Nigel Stead *Managing Director* ☏ +65 534 1900
Channel Islands   Richard Corbin *Global Custody Manager* ☏ +44 (1481) 707 020
Isle of Man   June Watson *General Manager* ☏ +44 (1624) 637 777
Hong Kong   Kim Downs *Marketing Manager* ☏ +852 2847 1113
Luxembourg   Daraius Nawroze *Network Manager - Europe* ☏ +352 404 6342
Treasury   Michael McCarthy *Head of Global Network Management*

Asset Management
Head   Alan Kershaw *SVP & Head of Treasury*
Other (Asset Management)
   Christopher J Tribley *Vice President* ☏ 229 6255

Administration
Head of Administration   Barry L Shailer *EVP, Retail Banking & Administration* ☏ 299 5372
Accounts / Audit
Internal Audit   Garry W Musy *Vice President*
Other (Administration)
Human Resources   Mark S P Perreault *Senior Vice President*

The Bank of NT Butterfield & Son Limited   Head Office

65 Front Street, Hamilton, HM 12
PO Box HM 195, Hamilton, HM AX
Tel: 295 1111 **Fax:** 292 4365 **Telex:** 3211 FIELD BA **Swift:** BNTB BM HM **Email:** bntb@ibl.bm
Cable: FIELD BERMUDA
Website: www.bankofbutterfield.com

Senior Executive Officers
Chairman of the Board   James A C King
CEO   M Calum Johnston
Executive Vice President   Graham C Brooks
Financial Director   Richard J Ferrett *Chief Financial Officer*
Secretary to the Board   Peter J M Rodger

Others (Senior Executives)
Information Systems   William G Francis II *Senior Vice President*
Treasury & Capital Markets   Richard A Gonzales *Senior Vice President*
Customer & Staff Relations   Janet M Nearon *Senior Vice President*
Human Resources   Patricia G Bean *Senior Vice President*
Credit   David M Brierley *Senior Vice President*
Finance & Planning   Ronald E Simmons *Senior Vice President*

General - Treasury
Head of Treasury   Richard A Gonzales *Treasury & Capital Markets*

Settlement / Clearing
Operations   C Wendell Emery *Executive Vice President*

Asset Management
Head   Peter G Wignall *Senior Vice President*

Administration
Legal / In-House Counsel
   Peter J M Rodger *Group Legal Adviser*

www.euromoneydirectory.com   BERMUDA (+1 441)

Bermuda Commercial Bank Limited
Head Office

Bermuda Commercial Bank Building, 44 Church Street, Hamilton, HM 12
PO Box HM 1748, Hamilton, HMGX
Tel: 295 5678 **Fax**: 295 8091 **Telex**: 3336 COMBK BA **Swift**: BPBK BM HM **Reuters**: BCBB

Senior Executive Officers
Chairman   John Chr M A M Deuss
Managing Director   Peter Roberts

Others (Senior Executives)
Global Custody   Sheila Brown *General Manager*
Inter'l Corp. Management of Bermuda   Georges Boivin *General Manager*
International Trust Company of Bermuda   Tony Keywood *General Manager*

General-Lending (DCM, SL)
Head of Corporate Banking   Manuel Yglesias *General Manager*

Money Markets
Global Head   Gregory Summers

Administration
Head of Marketing   Lynne Taylor ☎ 299 2856

Corporate Communications
                                           Lynne Taylor *Corporate Client Liaison Officer* ☎ 299 2856

Bermuda International Investment Management Limited (BIIML)

Compass Point, 9 Bermudiana Road, Hamilton, HM 11
Tel: 299 5700 **Fax**: 299 6536; 299 6537 **Telex**: BA3212 **Swift**: BBDA BM HM **Cable**: BANCO BERMUDA

Senior Executive Officers

General-Investment
Head of Investment   Wayne P Chapman *Senior Vice President, Investments* ☎ 299 6518
                                           ℻ 299 6518 ✉ chapmawp@bankofbermuda.com

Refco Capital Markets Limited

12 Bermudiana Road, Hamilton, HM 11
Tel: 295 6960 **Fax**: 292 0090

Debt Capital Markets / Fixed Income

Fixed-Income Repo
Trading   Thomas Yorke *Vice President*

Equity Capital Markets

Equity Repo / Securities Lending
Head   Martin Loftus *Senior Vice President* ☎ 693 7856 ℻ 390 8778
Marketing   Edward Reid *Vice President* ☎ +1 (212) 693 7069 ℻ +1 (212) 693 7730

Euromoney Directory 1999   169

BHUTAN (+975)

Royal Monetary Authority of Bhutan
🏛 Central Bank

PO Box 154, Thimphu
Tel: 23111; 23112 Fax: 22847 Telex: 206 RMATPU BT

Senior Executive Officers
Finance Minister — Dorji Tshering
Treasurer — Namgay Tshering *Treasurer*
Managing Director — Sonam Wangchuk ☎ **23110**

Others (Senior Executives)
Head, Banking Supervision — Pema Tshering
Head, Economics & Statistics — Penjore
Head, Reserves Management — Chador Tshering

Foreign Exchange
Head of Foreign Exchange — Chador Tshering

Settlement / Clearing
Head of Settlement / Clearing — Penjore

Administration
Head of Administration — Dechen Tshering *Deputy Managing Director*

Technology & Systems
K S Dem *Computer Programmer*

Accounts / Audit
Head, Accountancy — Jai Narayan *Chief, Banking Division*

BOLIVIA (+591)

Banco Central de Bolivia
🏛 Central Bank

Calle Ayacucho esquina Mercado, La Paz
PO Box 3118, La Paz
Tel: (2) 374 151 Fax: (2) 392 398; (2) 391 563 Telex: 3255 NAVLANA Swift: BCEBBOLPA
Email: sgrde@mail.bcb.gov.bo Bloomberg: YES

Senior Executive Officers
President — Juan Antonio Morales
General Secretary — Victor Marquez Ostria
General Manager — Jaime Valencia
International Division — David Espinosa *Manager*

Debt Capital Markets / Fixed Income
Tel: 374 151 Fax: 377 119
Country Head — Rodolfo Sucre *Manager*

Government Bonds
Head of Sales — Rodolfo Sucre *Manager*

Fixed-Income Repo
Head of Repo — Rodolfo Sucre *Manager*

Equity Capital Markets
Country Head — Rodolfo Sucre *Manager*

Foreign Exchange
Fax: 391 563
Head of Foreign Exchange; Head of Trading — Oscar Ferrufino *Department Head*

Settlement / Clearing
Head of Settlement / Clearing — Eduardo Navarro *Manager, Operations*

Other Departments
Economic Research — Javier Comboni *Manager*

Administration
Head of Administration — Hugo Meneses *Administration Manager*

Technology & Systems
Gonzalo Riveros *Manager*

Legal / In-House Counsel
Fernando Rollano *Manager*

Public Relations
Luz Coca de Peña *Public Relations Officer*

Accounts / Audit
Audit — Javier Cachi Vásquez *Manager*
Accounting — Alberto Loayza *Manager, Accounting*

Banco Mercantil SA — Head Office

Ayacucho esquina Mercado 277, La Paz
PO Box 423, La Paz
Tel: (2) 315 131 **Fax:** (2) 391 442 **Telex:** 2270, 2586, 2481 **Swift:** MERB BO LX **Email:** bercant@caoba.entelnet.bo
Website: www.mercantil.com.bo

Senior Executive Officers
President — Javier Zuazo
Chief Executive Officer — Emilio Unzueta *Executive Vice President*
Financial Director — Juan Carlos Salaves *Commercial Vice President*
Chief Operating Officer — Marcelo Diez De Medina *Vice President, Operations*
Treasurer — Fernando Gutierrez *VP, International Affairs*

Banco Santa Cruz SA — Head Office

Formerly known as: BCH, Banco Central Hispano Americano
Calle Junin 154, Santa Cruz
Tel: (3) 369 911 **Fax:** (3) 350 114 **Telex:** 4230 BANCRUZ BV **Swift:** BSCZ BO 2X **Email:** bancruz@mail.com.bo

Senior Executive Officers
Chief Executive Officer — Alfonso Alvarez *General Manager*
Financial Director — Ismael Serrate *General Manager, Finance* ☎ **35 1534**
Chief Operating Officer — Jorge Chahin *General Manager, Operations*

Other Departments
Private Banking — Eduardo Bustos *Chief*
Correspondent Banking — Ronald Gutierrez *Manager, International*

Administration
Technology & Systems
Arturo Suaman *General Manager, Systems*

Legal / In-House Counsel
Roger Robles *Legal Assessor*

Public Relations
Jose Edgardo Cuellar *Deputy Manager, Markets* ☎ **351 534**

BOSNIA-HERZEGOVINA
(+387)

Central Bank of Bosnia & Herzegovina — Central Bank

Marsala Tita 25, Sarajevo, 71000
Tel: (71) 664 548 **Fax:** (71) 201 517 **Telex:** 41101

Senior Executive Officers
Governor — Peter Nicholl ☎ **210 518**
Vice Governor — Dragan Kovacevic ☎ **444 797**
Vice Governor — Enver Backovic ☎ **664 230**
Vice Governor — Ljubisa Vladusic ☎ **786 296**
General Secretary — Mehmed Šehic ☎ **214 322**

Others (Senior Executives)
Obrad Pitjak *Comptroller General* ☎ **663 315**
Anton Salapic *Deputy Comptroller* ☎ **522 505**
Amina Sofradzija *Deputy Comptroller* ☎ **522 505**
Milosija Drakulic *Deputy Comptroller* ☎ **786 296**

Head, Statistics — Ljiljana Marjanovic ☎ **787 153**
Head, Balance of Payments — Novo Cicovic ☎ **786 296**
General Cashier — Silvestar Lincender ☎ **214 317**
Head, International & Domestic Banking — Zuhdija Fetahovic ☎ **470 592**

Euromoney Directory 1999 171

BOSNIA-HERZEGOVINA (+387)   www.euromoneydirectory.com

Central Bank of Bosnia & Herzegovina (cont)
Others (Senior Executives) (cont)
Head, Institutional Financial Institutions   Meliha Jusic ☎ 533 638
Head, Market Evaluation   Jasmina Halilbegovic ☎ 214 337
Administration
Head, Information Technology   Nazif Husovic ☎ 214 332
Accounts / Audit
Chief Accountant   Ninoslav Gregovic ☎ 668 168
Other (Administration)
Head, Human Resources   Anda Bijeljac ☎ 668 206

BOTSWANA
(+267)

Bank of Botswana   🏛 Central Bank
Private Bag 154, Gaborone
Tel: 360 6006 Fax: 371 231 Telex: 2448 BD
Senior Executive Officers
Governor   Baledzi Gaolathe ☎ 351 919
Deputy Governor   Julia Majaha-Jartby ☎ 371 463
Deputy Governor   Unah Mohohlo ☎ 351 399
Board Secretary   Eweste Rakhudu ☎ 360 6217
Others (Senior Executives)
Head, Bank Licensing; Head, Banking Supervision   Moses Pelaelo *Director, Financial Institutions* ☎ 360 6368
Head, Economics & Statistics   Jay Salkin *Director, Research* ☎ 313 851
Head, Reserves Management   Oduetse Motshidisi *Director, International* ☎ 351 795
Foreign Exchange
Head of Foreign Exchange   Oduetse Motshidisi *Director, International* ☎ 351 795
Settlement / Clearing
Head of Settlement / Clearing   Gabriel Hobona *Director, Banking* ☎ 374 171
Administration
Head of Administration   Oabile Mabusa *Director* ☎ 302 156
Technology & Systems
     Chris Jackson *Deputy Director* ☎ 360 6312
Public Relations
     Binkie Kerileng *Public Relations Officer* ☎ 360 382
Accounts / Audit
Head, Accountancy   Nozipho Mabe *Director, Finance* ☎ 313 853

Stanbic Bank Botswana Limited
Private Bag 00168, Gaborone
Tel: 301 600 Fax: 300 171 Telex: 2562 BD Swift: UBBL BW GX

BRAZIL
(+55)

Agora CTVM SA   Head Office
Rua Professor Arthur Ramos 140, Leblon, Rio de Janeiro RJ 22441-110
Tel: (21) 512 6000 Fax: (21) 512 7767 Email: honigman@agoractvm.com.br
Senior Executive Officers
Chairman   Selmo Nissenbaum

www.euromoneydirectory.com BRAZIL (+55)

The Asahi Bank Limited
Representative Office
18° andar, Avenida Paulista 1938, São Paulo SP 01310-200
Tel: (11) 285 5417; (11) 287 7622 **Fax:** (11) 283 4078 **Telex:** 1133877 ASAH
Senior Executive Officers
Chief Representative   Hitoshi Suzuki

Atlantic Rating Limited
Formerly known as: Atlantic Capital Limited
Rua Pedroso Alvarenga 1284/12, São Paulo SP 04531-004
Tel: (11) 852 6166 **Fax:** (11) 853 5802 **Email:** info@atlanticrating.com.br
Senior Executive Officers
President   Paul L Bydalek

Australia & New Zealand Banking Group Limited
Representative Office
Avenida Nilo Pecanha, 50 grupo 810, Rio de Janeiro RJ 20090-003
Tel: (21) 518 2990 **Fax:** (21) 518 3213
Senior Executive Officers
Group Representative & Country Head,   Peter Mason

Australia & New Zealand Banking Group Limited
Representative Office
Rua Tenente Negráo 140, 4° andar, São Paulo SP 04530-030
Tel: (11) 829 0737 **Fax:** (11) 829 3071
Senior Executive Officers
Manager   Luciana Bioga

Banco ABC Brasil SA
Subsidiary Company
Formerly known as: Banco ABC-Roma SA
Avenida Paulista 37, 15° andar, São Paulo SP 01311-902
Tel: (11) 3170 2000 **Fax:** (11) 3170 2079; (11) 3170 2015 **Telex:** 1130298
Senior Executive Officers
President & CEO   Tito Henrique da Silva Neto ☏ **3170ext2268**
Chief Executive Officer   Anis Chacur Neto *Director Vice President* ☏ **3170ext2274**
Financial Director   Alfredo Neves P Moraes *Director Vice President* ☏ **3170ext2270**
Chief Operating Officer   Edgar Azevedo Uchôa *Director Vice President* ☏ **3170 2325**
Treasurer   José Eduardo Cintra Laloni *Director Vice President* ☏ **3170ext2253**
Director   Walter de A Fernandes ☏ **3170ext2235**

Debt Capital Markets / Fixed Income
Global Head   Paulo de Lara Campos *Deputy Director* ☏ **3170 2141**
Head of Fixed Income   Sergio Lulia Jacob *Director* ☏ **3170ext2347**

Government Bonds
Head of Sales   Waudir Reis *Deputy Director* ☏ **3170 2282**

Eurobonds
Head of Origination   Paulo de Lara Campos *Deputy Director* ☏ **3170 2141**
Head of Syndication   José Augusto de N Carvalho *Manager* ☏ **3170 2132**
Head of Sales   Paolo Rogerio Moreira *Deputy Director* ☏ **3170 2130**
Head of Trading   Paulo de Lara Campos *Deputy Director* ☏ **3170 2141**
Head of Research   Young Man To *Deputy Director* ☏ **3170 2133**
Trading - Sovereigns, Corporates, High-yield   Paulo de Lara Campos *Deputy Director* ☏ **3170 2141**

Libor-Based / Floating-Rate Products
FRN Origination   João Carlos G da Silva *Deputy Director* ☏ **3170 2289**
FRN Sales   Paolo Rogerio Moreira *Deputy Director* ☏ **3170 2130**
Asset Swaps   Paulo de Lara Campos *Deputy Director* ☏ **3170 2141**

Medium-Term Notes
Head of Origination   João Carlos G da Silva *Deputy Director* ☏ **3170 2289**
Head of Structuring   José Augusto de N Carvalho *Manager* ☏ **3170 2132**

Euromoney Directory 1999   **173**

BRAZIL (+55)

Banco ABC Brasil SA (cont)
Medium-Term Notes (cont)
Head of Sales — Paulo Rogério Moreira *Deputy Director* ☎ **3170 2130**
Private Placements
Head of Origination — João Carlos G da Silva *Deputy Director* ☎ **3170 2289**
Head of Sales — José Augusto de N Carvalho *Manager* ☎ **3170 2132**
Head of Structuring — Paulo Rogério Moreira *Deputy Director* ☎ **3170 2130**
Fixed-Income Repo
Head of Repo — Paolo de Lara Campos *Deputy Director* ☎ **3170 2141**
Equity Capital Markets
Domestic Equities
Head of Sales — Wandir Reis *Deputy Director* ☎ **3170 2282**
Head of Research — Young Man To *Deputy Director* ☎ **3170 2133**
Equity Research
Head of Equity Research — Ronaldo de Oliveira Valsani *Deputy Director* ☎ **3170 2178**
Syndicated Lending
Head of Trading — Edgar Azevedo Uchôa *Director Vice President* ☎ **3170 2325**
Paolo Bartczak *Deputy Director* ☎ **3170 2260**
Angela Martins *Deputy Director* ☎ **3170 2136**

Money Markets
Domestic Commercial Paper
Head of Sales — Nelson Rosa ☎ **3170 2177**
Eurocommercial Paper
Head of Sales — Paolo Rogerio Moreira *Deputy Director* ☎ **3170 2130**
Head of Trading — Paulo de Lara Campos *Deputy Director* ☎ **3170 2141**

Foreign Exchange
Head of Foreign Exchange — Marcel Palanch *Director* ☎ **3170 2342**
Head of Trading — Luis Otavio Vilella de Andrade *Deputy Director* ☎ **3170 2343**
FX Traders / Sales People
Marcelo Belloto *Manager* ☎ **3170 2353**

Risk Management
Head of Risk Management — Maria Aparecida Pinto *Deputy Director* ☎ **3170 2238**
Foreign Exchange Derivatives / Risk Management
Cross-Currency Swaps, Sales / Marketing; Cross-Currency Swaps, Trading; Vanilla FX option Sales; Vanilla FX option Trading — Paulo de Lara Campos *Deputy Director* ☎ **3170 2141**

Corporate Finance / M&A Advisory
Global Head — Anis Chacur Neto *Director Vice President* ☎ **3170ext2274**

Settlement / Clearing
Regional Head — Walter de A Fernandes *Director* ☎ **3170ext2235**

Banco ABN AMRO — Subsidiary Company
Rua Verbo Divino 1711, 1° andar, São Paulo SP 04719-002
Tel: (11) 5180 6000 Fax: (11) 5181 2500

Senior Executive Officers
President — Fabio Barbosa
Treasurer — Marcelo Iacovone *Executive Director*

General-Lending (DCM, SL)
Head of Corporate Banking — Francisco di Roberto *Executive Director* ☎ **5180 6205** 📠 **5180 6790**

General-Investment
Head of Investment — Michiel van Schaardenburg *Executive Director* ☎ **5180 6752**

Debt Capital Markets / Fixed Income
Head of Fixed Income — José Luiz Gavião *Director* ☎ **5180 6208**

Equity Capital Markets
Head of Equity Capital Markets — Luiz Reis *Director* ☎ **5180 6208**

Syndicated Lending
Loan-Related Activities
Trade Finance — Renato Faria *Director* ☎ **5180 6766**
Project Finance — Paul Witsiers *Director* ☎ **5180 6208**

Corporate Finance / M&A Advisory
Head of Corporate Finance — Michiel van Schaardenburg *Executive Director* ☎ **5180 6752**

www.euromoneydirectory.com BRAZIL (+55)

Global Custody
Regional Head Daniela Laub *Officer* ☏ 525 6193 ✉ daniela.laub@abnamro.com
 Andrea Bastazini ☏ 525 6194
Asset Management
Head Luiz Maia *Executive Director* ☏ 5180 6700
Other Departments
Private Banking Mario Julio Lima *Director* ☏ 5180 6206
Correspondent Banking Fernando Ribeiro *Director* ☏ 5180 6790
Cash Management Milton Nakamura ☏ 5180 6752

Banco da Amazônia SA   Head Office

Avenida Presidente Vargas 800, Belém Para 66017-000
PO Box 1616, Belém Para 66017-000
Tel: (91) 223 0678 **Fax:** (91) 223 5403 **Telex:** 911191 **Swift:** AMAB BR N1

Senior Executive Officers
Chairman Alberto de Almeida Pais
President Flora Valldares Coelho
Financial Director Carlos Jorgi Oliveira
Others (Senior Executives)
GM, Commercial Area Jose Martins
Director, Commerce & Industry Jorge Nemetala
Debt Capital Markets / Fixed Income
Department: Trading Department
Tel: 223 4636
Other Eduardo H S Guimaraes *Chief Dealer*

Banco América do Sul SA   Head Office

Avenida Brigadeiro Luis Antonio 2020, 8°/9° andar, São Paulo SP 01318-911
Tel: (11) 281 1511 **Fax:** (11) 281 1015 **Telex:** 11-21354 **Swift:** BCAS BR SP
Website: www.bas.com.br

Senior Executive Officers
Superintendent Director Yves-Louis J Lejeune

Banco Bandeirantes SA   Head Office

Rua Boa Vista 162, 13° andar, Centro, São Paulo SP 01014-902
Tel: (11) 233 7961 **Fax:** (11) 239 5975 **Telex:** 11 22009 BCBC BR **Swift:** BBAN BR SP

Senior Executive Officers
Chairman Antonio Tomás Correia
President Carlos Tragelho
Chief Executive Officer Antonio Almeida Porto *General Director*
International Division Fausto V G Neto *Director*
Foreign Exchange
Tel: (11) 233 7676 **Fax:** (11) 233 5252
Global Head Arilton Dias *Director*
Other Departments
Correspondent Banking Fausto Vaz Guimaraes Neto *Director*

Banco BBA Creditanstalt SA   Head Office

Avenida Paulista 37, 20° andar, São Paulo SP 01311-902
PO Box 5581, São Paulo SP
Tel: (11) 281 8000 **Fax:** (11) 281 8172 **Telex:** 1131607 **Swift:** CBBA BR SP **Email:** bancobba@bba.com.br
Website: www.bba.com.br

Senior Executive Officers
President Fernão Bracher ☏ 281 8210
Vice President Antonio Beltran ☏ 281 8212
Chief Executive Officer Candido Brachter ☏ 281 8817
Treasurer Luiz Fernando Figueiredo ☏ 281 8040
Company Secretary Fatima Jacomino ☏ 281 8210

Euromoney Directory 1999 **175**

BRAZIL (+55)　　　　　　　www.euromoneydirectory.com

Banco BBA Creditanstalt SA (cont)

General-Investment
Head of Investment　　　　　　　　　　　Heinz Gruber *Director, Emerging Markets* ☎ 281 8208

Equity Capital Markets
Head of Equity Capital Markets　　　　　　Percio Souza ☎ 281 8270

Foreign Exchange
Head of Foreign Exchange　　　　　　　　Armando Pinto ☎ 281 8043

Asset Management
Head　　　　　　　　　　　　　　　　　　Francisco Pinot ☎ 3178 8576

Other Departments
Private Banking　　　　　　　　　　　　　Luiz Hess Borges ☎ 281 8389
Correspondent Banking　　　　　　　　　Sveana Herzka ☎ 281 8223

Administration
Head of Administration　　　　　　　　　José Irineu Braga ☎ 281 8238
Head of Marketing　　　　　　　　　　　Márcia Leal ☎ 281 8150

Technology & Systems
　　　　　　　　　　　　　　　　　　　　Claudio Aleksitch ☎ 281 8093

Public Relations
　　　　　　　　　　　　　　　　　　　　Márcia Leal ☎ 281 8150

Accounts / Audit
　　　　　　　　　　　　　　　　　　　　Geraldo Frei ☎ 281 8056

Banco BMG SA

Alameda Santos 2335 - 3rd Floor, São Paulo SP 1419-002
Tel: (11) 3067 2228 **Fax:** (11) 3067 2215

Senior Executive Officers
Chief Executive Officer　　　　　　　　　Ricardo Della Santina Torres

Equity Capital Markets
Country Head　　　　　　　　　　　　　Celio Afonso da Silva *Executive Director* ☎ 290 3700 ℻ 290 3168

Money Markets
Regional Head　　　　　　　　　　　　　Nelson Costa Correa *Director* ☎ 3067 2288 ℻ 3067 2014

Risk Management
Country Head　　　　　　　　　　　　　Jacques Rodarte *Head* ☎ 290 3343 ℻ 290 3218

Settlement / Clearing
Country Head　　　　　　　　　　　　　Edezio Grande *Administrative Supervisor* ☎ 3067 2120 ℻ 3067 2092

Banco Boavista　　　　　　　　　　　　　　　　　　　　　　　　　　　Head Office

Praça Pio X 118, Centro, Rio de Janeiro RJ 20091-040
Tel: (21) 211 1646 **Fax:** (21) 211 1373 **Telex:** 21211858 **Swift:** BCBV BR RJ **Email:** bvista@ibm.net
Cable: VISTABANCO

Senior Executive Officers
President　　　　　　　　　　　　　　　Jose Miranda
International Division　　　　　　　　　Cristiano Gomes *Executive Director*
　　　　　　　　　　　　　　　　　　　Paulo Narcelo *Director of International Division*

Debt Capital Markets / Fixed Income
Head of Debt Capital Markets　　　　　　Claudia Hausner *Director, International Capital Markets* ☎ (11) 534 7400
　　　　　　　　　　　　　　　　　　　Francisco Cary *Executive Director, Investment Banking* ☎ 211 1711

Equity Capital Markets
Head of Equity Capital Markets　　　　　Claudia Hausner *Director, International Capital Markets* ☎ (11) 534 7400
　　　　　　　　　　　　　　　　　　　Francisco Cary *Executive Director, Investment Banking* ☎ 211 1711

Syndicated Lending
Loan-Related Activities
Trade Finance　　　　　　　　　　　　　Cristiano Gomes *Executive Director*

Foreign Exchange
Head of Foreign Exchange　　　　　　　Carlos Alberto Mazolli ☎ (11) 534 7371

Other Departments
Correspondent Banking　　　　　　　　Leticia Visconti *Manager*

www.euromoneydirectory.com   BRAZIL (+55)

Banco Boavista Interatlântico SA   Head Office

Avenida Roque Petroni Junior 999, 3º andar, Morumbi, São Paulo SP 04707-910
Tel: (11) 5189 7444
Website: www.boavista.com.br

Senior Executive Officers
President — José Luiz Silveira Miranda

Debt Capital Markets / Fixed Income
Global Head — Claudia H Burlamaqui ☏ **5189 7370**

Equity Capital Markets
Global Head — Marcelo V de Araujo ☏ **5189 7378**

Syndicated Lending
Global Head — Jose Carlos Mendes ☏ **5189 7372**

Money Markets
Global Head — Luiz Alberto Marques ☏ **5189 7350**

Foreign Exchange
Global Head — Carlos Alberto Mazzoli ☏ **5189 7371**

Risk Management
Global Head — Luiz Henrique Lobo ☏ **(21) 211 1563**

Corporate Finance / M&A Advisory
Global Head — Francisco Cary ☏ **(21) 211 1711**

Settlement / Clearing
Regional Head — Jorge Miranda ☏ **(21) 211 1711**

Banco Bozano, Simonsen SA   Head Office

Avenida Rio Branco 138, Rio de Janeiro RJ 20057-900
Tel: (21) 508 4000 Fax: (21) 508 4053 Telex: 22963 BOZS Swift: BBSI BR RJ Email: info@bozano.com.br
Bloomberg: S/N 235408.4
General Telex: 2134422
Website: www.bozano.com.br

Senior Executive Officers
Chief Executive Officer — Paulo Ferraz ℻ **508 4611** ✉ pferraz@bozano.com.br
Financial Director — Sergio Eraldo Salles Pinto *Controller* ☏ **508 4711**
Chief Operating Officer — Alvaro Lopes *Executive Vice President* ☏ **508 4090**
✉ alvaro@bozano.com.br
Treasurer — Roberto Gaspar *Director* ☏ **508 4453** ✉ gaspar@bozano.com.br
International Division — Armando Almeida *International Area Director* ☏ **508 4453**
✉ almeida@bozano.com.br

Debt Capital Markets / Fixed Income
Head of Fixed Income — Armando Almeida *International Area Director* ☏ **508 4453**
✉ almeida@bozano.com.br
Head of Fixed Income Trading — Roberto Gaspar *Director* ☏ **508 4453** ✉ gaspar@bozano.com.br

Domestic Government Bonds
Head of Trading — Roberto Gaspar *Director* ☏ **508 4453** ✉ gaspar@bozano.com.br
Head of Origination — Paulo Carneiro ☏ **(11) 245 8170**
Head of Syndication — Arnóbio Aladim *Director* ☏ **508 4453** ✉ aladim@bozano.com.br

Eurobonds
Head of Sales; Head of Trading — Armando Almeida *International Area Director* ☏ **508 4453**
✉ almeida@bozano.com.br

Emerging Market Bonds
Head of Sales — Armando Almeida *International Area Director* ☏ **508 4453**
✉ almeida@bozano.com.br
Head of Trading — Roberto Gaspar *Director* ☏ **508 4453** ✉ gaspar@bozano.com.br

Libor-Based / Floating-Rate Products
FRN Sales — Armando Almeida *International Area Director* ☏ **508 4453**
✉ almeida@bozano.com.br
FRN Trading; Asset Swaps — Roberto Gaspar *Director* ☏ **508 4453** ✉ gaspar@bozano.com.br

Fixed-Income Repo
Head of Repo — Roberto Gaspar *Director* ☏ **508 4453** ✉ gaspar@bozano.com.br
Marketing & Product Development — Armando Almeida *International Area Director* ☏ **508 4453**
✉ almeida@bozano.com.br
Head of Trading — Roberto Gaspar *Director* ☏ **508 4453** ✉ gaspar@bozano.com.br

BRAZIL (+55) www.euromoneydirectory.com

Banco Bozano, Simonsen SA (cont)

Fixed-Income Research
Head of Fixed Income — Armando Almeida *International Area Director* ⊤ 508 4453
  E almeida@bozano.com.br
Head of Credit Research — Geoffrey Langlands *Director* ⊤ 508 4247 F 508 4199
  E geoffrey@bozano.com.br

Equity Capital Markets
Head of Equity Capital Markets — Luis Alberto Reategui *Director* ⊤ +1 (212) 869 1234 F +1 (212) 869 3654
  E lobato@bozano.com.br
Head of Sales — Arnóbio Aladim *Director* ⊤ 508 4453 E aladim@bozano.com.br
Head of Trading — Roberto Gaspar *Director* ⊤ 508 4453 E gaspar@bozano.com.br

Domestic Equities
Head of Sales — Arnóbio Aladim *Director* ⊤ 508 4453 E aladim@bozano.com.br
  Heitor Souza Lima *Sales* ⊤ 508 4550 E heitor@bozano.com.br
  Quentin J Lewis *Sales* ⊤ 508 4550 E quentin@bozano.com.br
  Robert Drummond *Sales* ⊤ 508 4550 E drummond@bozano.com.br
Head of Trading — Roberto Gaspar *Director* ⊤ 508 4453 E gaspar@bozano.com.br
  Dave Sharp *Trader* ⊤ 508 4020 E dave@bozano.com.br
  Rafael Parga *Trader* ⊤ 508 4020 E parga@bozano.com.br
  Sérgio Ramos Yoshino *Trader* ⊤ 508 4020 E sergior@bozano.com.br
  Ulf Petterson *Trader* ⊤ 508 4020

International Equities
Head of Sales — Luis Alberto Reategui *Director* ⊤ +1 (212) 869 1234 F +1 (212) 869 3654
  E lobato@bozano.com.br
  Heitor Souza Lima *Sales* ⊤ 508 4550 E heitor@bozano.com.br
  Quentin J Lewis *Sales* ⊤ 508 4550 E quentin@bozano.com.br
  Robert Drummond *Sales* ⊤ 508 4550 E drummond@bozano.com.br
Head of Trading — Antonio Coury ⊤ +44 (171) 456 7200

Equity Research
Global Head — Geoffrey Langlands *Director* ⊤ 508 4247 F 508 4199
  E geoffrey@bozano.com.br

Convertibles / Equity-Linked
Head of Trading — Sergio Castro ⊤ 508 4296

Syndicated Lending
Head of Origination — Luis Fernando Rezende *Director, Corporate Finance* ⊤ 245 8170
  E lfar@bozano.com.br
Head of Syndication — Arnóbio Aladim *Director* ⊤ 508 4453 E aladim@bozano.com.br
Head of Trading — Roberto Gaspar *Director* ⊤ 508 4453 E gaspar@bozano.com.br

Loan-Related Activities
Trade Finance — Armando Almeida *International Area Director* ⊤ 508 4453
  E almeida@bozano.com.br
Project Finance — Vitor Hallack ⊤ 508 4606 E hallack@bozano.com.br

Money Markets
Head of Money Markets — Roberto Gaspar *Director* ⊤ 508 4453 E gaspar@bozano.com.br

Domestic Commercial Paper
Head of Sales — Arnóbio Aladim *Director* ⊤ 508 4453 E aladim@bozano.com.br
Head of Trading — Roberto Gaspar *Director* ⊤ 508 4453 E gaspar@bozano.com.br

Eurocommercial Paper
Head of Sales — Armando Almeida *International Area Director* ⊤ 508 4453
  E almeida@bozano.com.br
Head of Trading — Roberto Gaspar *Director* ⊤ 508 4453 E gaspar@bozano.com.br

Wholesale Deposits
Marketing — Raul Rosenthal ⊤ (11) 245 8170
Head of Sales — Marcio Barbosa ⊤ (11) 245 8170

Foreign Exchange
Head of Foreign Exchange — Roberto Gaspar *Director* ⊤ 508 4453 E gaspar@bozano.com.br
Head of Institutional Sales — Armando Almeida *International Area Director* ⊤ 508 4453
  E almeida@bozano.com.br
Corporate Sales — Marcio Barbosa ⊤ (11) 245 8170
Head of Trading — Roberto Gaspar *Director* ⊤ 508 4453 E gaspar@bozano.com.br

Risk Management
Head of Risk Management — Fernando Penteado *Director* ⊤ 508 4453 E penteado@bozano.com.br

OTC Equity Derivatives
Trading — Fernando Penteado *Director* ⊤ 508 4453 E penteado@bozano.com.br

OTC Commodity Derivatives
Head — Roberto Gaspar *Director* ⊤ 508 4453 E gaspar@bozano.com.br

www.euromoneydirectory.com   BRAZIL (+55)

OTC Credit Derivatives
Head   Fernando Penteado *Director* ☎ **508 4453** ℰ **penteado@bozano.com.br**
Settlement / Clearing
Tel: 508 4568
Head of Settlement / Clearing   Evilasio Vitoriano ☎ **508 4568**
Equity Settlement; Fixed-Income Settlement;   Manoel Alberto ☎ **508 4568**
Operations; Back-Office
Asset Management
Head   Vitor Duarte ☎ **508 4310**
Other Departments
Chief Credit Officer   Alexandre Costa ☎ **508 4355**
Correspondent Banking   Armando Almeida *International Area Director* ☎ **508 4453**
                                                ℰ **almeida@bozano.com.br**

Administration
Head of Administration   Lucio Beleza ☎ **508 4568**
Head of Marketing   Raul Rosenthal ☎ **(11) 245 8170**
Technology & Systems
                                                Carlos Ripper ☎ **508 4582**
Legal / In-House Counsel
                                                Luiz Fernando Freitas *Director* ☎ **508 4190** ℰ **luizf@bozano.com.br**
Compliance
                                                Lucio Beleza ☎ **508 4568**
Public Relations
                                                Olinda Campos *Manager, Marketing* ☎ **508 4068**
Accounts / Audit
                                                Sergio Eraldo Salles Pinto *Controller* ☎ **508 4711**

Banco Bradesco SA   Head Office

Avenida Ipiranga 282, São Paulo SP 01046-920
PO Box 1250, São Paulo SP
Tel: (11) 235 9566 **Fax:** (11) 235 9161 **Swift:** BBDE BR SP OCO
International Division **Tel:** 235 9279

Senior Executive Officers
Chairman   Lázaro de Mello Brandao
Managing Director / General Manager   Antonio Bornia
International Division   Jose Guilherme
Foreign Exchange
Tel: 235 9509
Head of Foreign Exchange   Aldo Alvis Adorno

Banco do Brasil SA   Head Office

SBS Quadra 5, Bloco C Edificio Sede III 24° andar, Brasilia 70089-900
Tel: (61) 310 3400 **Fax:** (61) 310 2563
Website: www.bancobrasil.com.br

Senior Executive Officers
Chairman   Pedro Parente ☎ **314 4713**
President & CEO   Paulo Ximenes
Financial Director   Carlos Caetano *Finance Director* ☎ **310 3406**
Chief Operating Officer   Evandro Oliveira *Superintendent Executive* ☎ **(21) 808 3626**
Treasurer   Arnaldo Vollet *Treasurer* ☎ **(21) 808 3580**
Executive Manager   Carlos André ☎ **(21) 808 3626**
General Manager   Wiliam Cavalcanti ☎ **(21) 808 3626**
General Manager   Sergio Mamede ☎ **(21) 272 7049**
Debt Capital Markets / Fixed Income
Medium-Term Notes
Head of Origination; Head of Structuring   Carlos André *Executive Manager* ☎ **(21) 808 3626**
Head of Sales   Délcio Blajfeder *Executive Director* ☎ **+44 (171) 216 4200**
Private Placements
Head of Origination   Carlos André *Executive Manager* ☎ **(21) 808 3626**
Head of Sales   Délcio Blajfeder *Executive Director* ☎ **+44 (171) 216 4200**
Asset-Backed Securities / Securitization
Global Head   Roberto de Camilo ☎ **(11) 3066 9002**
Regional Head   Augusto Braúna *General Manager* ☎ **(11) 3066 9002**

Euromoney Directory 1999   **179**

BRAZIL (+55)   www.euromoneydirectory.com

Banco do Brasil SA (cont)

Mortgage-Backed Securities
Global Head — Ricardo Paranhos *Manager* ☎ +1 (212) 626 7022

Equity Capital Markets
Tel: (21) 808 3626 Fax: (21) 240 3357
Global Head — Evandro Oliveira *Superintendent Executive* ☎ (21) 808 3626
Regional Head — Carlos André *General Manager*
Country Head — Ricardo Adenes *Manager* ☎ (21) 808 3522

Domestic Equities
Head of Origination; Head of Syndication; Head of Sales — Ricardo Adenes *Manager* ☎ (21) 808 3522
Head of Trading — Ari Sarmento *Manager* ☎ (21) 808 3522
Head of Research — Maria Celia Juannes *Manager*

International Equities
Head of Origination — Carlos André *Executive Manager* ☎ (21) 808 3626

Syndicated Lending

Loan-Related Activities
Trade Finance; Project Finance; Structured Trade Finance; Leasing & Asset Finance — Rubens Amaral *General Manager* ☎ (11) 3066 9004

Money Markets

Global Head — Arnaldo Vollet *Treasurer* ☎ (21) 808 3580
Regional Head — Armênio Saburgueiro *Manager* ☎ (21) 808 3580

Domestic Commercial Paper
Head of Origination — Ricardo Adenes *Manager* ☎ (21) 808 3522
Head of Trading — Ari Sarmento *Manager* ☎ (21) 808 3522

Eurocommercial Paper
Head of Origination — Carlos André *Executive Manager* ☎ (21) 808 3626
Head of Sales — Délcio Blajfeder *Executive Director* ☎ +44 (171) 216 4200

Wholesale Deposits
Marketing; Head of Sales — Natanael Castro *Manager* ☎ 310 1300

Foreign Exchange

Global Head — Wolney Ferreira *Manager* ☎ +1 (212) 626 7022
Regional Head — Carlos Alberto Alvarenga *Manager* ☎ +44 (171) 606 7022

Risk Management

Global Head — Luiz Tarquínio *Superintendent Executive* ☎ 310 3980
Regional Head — Edson Tanigaki *General Manager* ☎ 310 3980

Other Currency Swap / FX Options Personnel
Dealing Room — Sérgio Mattos *Trader* ☎ (21) 532 2900
Trading — Pédro Machado *FX Dealer* ☎ (21) 532 2900

Corporate Finance / M&A Advisory

Tel: (21) 808 3626 Fax: (21) 240 3357
Head of Mergers & Acquisition — Walter Furtado *Manager* ☎ (21) 272 7714
Global Head — Evandro Oliveira *Superintendent Executive* ☎ (21) 808 3626

Other (Corporate Finance)
General Manager — Carlos André *Executive Manager* ☎ (21) 808 3626
Local Debt / Equity — Ricardo Adenes *Manager* ☎ (21) 808 3522
International Debt Origination — Marco Antonio Pereira *Manager* ☎ (21) 808 3625
International Debt Sales — Délcio Blajfeder *Executive Director* ☎ +44 (171) 216 4200
Trading Head — Ari Sarmento *Manager* ☎ (21) 808 3522
Research Head — Maria Celia Juannes *Manager*

Other Departments

Proprietary Trading — Luiz Siqueira *Manager* ☎ 310 4540
Correspondent Banking — José Magalhães *Manager* ☎ (11) 3066 9080

Administration

Technology & Systems
Rui Barroso *Manager* ☎ 310 6601

Legal / In-House Counsel
João Noronha *Manager* ☎ 310 3100

www.euromoneydirectory.com BRAZIL (+55)

Banco CCF Brasil SA — Head Office

Avenida Brigadeiro Faria Lima 3064, 1°, 2° e 3° andares, São Paulo SP 01451-020
Tel: (11) 827 5500; (11) 827 5523 Fax: (11) 827 5097; (11) 827 5187 Telex: 36728 Swift: CCF BR SP
Email: corporate@ccfbrasil.com.br

Senior Executive Officers
Chief Executive Officer — Bernard Mencier T 827 5573 F 827 5299
International Division — Deborah Stern Vietas *Executive Vice President* T 827 5293 F 827 5097

Others (Senior Executives)
General-Lending (DCM, SL)
Head of Corporate Banking — Deborah Stern Vietas *Executive Vice President* T 827 5293 F 827 5097
General - Treasury
Head of Treasury — Carlos Calabresi *EVP, Treasury & Derivatives* T 827 5166 F 827 5083
Relationship Manager
Corporate Relationship — José Luiz Lima *Deputy Director* T 827 5714 F 827 5187
Insurance Brokerage — Alberto Fernandes T 827 5338

Debt Capital Markets / Fixed Income
Country Head — Gilberto Miyamoto *Manager* T 827 5507

Syndicated Lending
Loan-Related Activities
Trade Finance — Hitosi Hassegawa *Director* T 827 5503
Other (Trade Finance)
Leasing — Jorg Henning Dornbusch T 827 5137

Money Markets
Brazilian Desk — Juliana Bonfá T +1 (212) 848 0543 F +1 (212) 832 7469
Cesar Figueiredo *Director* T +1 (212) 848 0543 F +1 (212) 832 7469

Foreign Exchange
Country Head — Monica Junqueira *Manager* T 827 5011 F 827 5097

Corporate Finance / M&A Advisory
Head of Mergers & Acquisition — François Legleve *Director* T 827 5076 F 827 5021

Asset Management
Head — Marcelo F Ginfrida *Executive Vice President* T 827 5347 F 827 5088
Other (Asset Management)
Pension Fund Management — Paulo Bittencourt *Director* T 827 5241 F 827 5819

Other Departments
Private Banking — Hiram Maisonnave *Director* T 827 5105 F 827 5089
Correspondent Banking — Vera Gillaux *Assistant Director* T 827 5971 F 827 5097

Banco Cidade S/A — Head Office

Praça Dom José Gaspar 134, São Paulo SP 01047-010
Tel: (11) 3150 5000; (11) 3150 4333 Fax: (11) 255 4176 Telex: 22198 Swift: BCSP BR SP
Email: we@bancocidade.com.br Reuters: CIDADE
Website: www.bancocidade.com.br

Senior Executive Officers
President — Edmundo Safdié
Chief Executive Officer — Victor Manuel Malhao Souza *Managing Director* T 3150 4939
E supger@bancocidade.com.br
Financial Director — Gilberto M Meiches *Director, Financial Markets* T 3150 4571
E dirfi@bancocidade.com.br
Managing Director / General Manager — Antonio Corréa Bosco T 3150 4501 E diadm@bancocidade.com.br

Debt Capital Markets / Fixed Income
Global Head — Ricardo Simone Pereira *Manager, Capital Markets* T 3150 4344
E capmark@bancocidade.com.br

Equity Capital Markets
Global Head — Thomas D Taterka *Manager* T 3150 4365 E mesap@bancocidade.com.br

Money Markets
Global Head — Darci Beato Jr. *Manager, Financial Resources* T 3150 4333
E mesacap@bancocidade.com.br

Foreign Exchange
Global Head — Vitor A Carvalho *FX Manager* T 3150 4576 E cambio@bancocidade.com.br

Risk Management
Global Head — Antonio Corréa Bosco T 3150 4501 E diadm@bancocidade.com.br

Euromoney Directory 1999   **181**

BRAZIL (+55) www.euromoneydirectory.com

Banco Cidade S/A (cont)
Corporate Finance / M&A Advisory
Global Head   Isaac Khafif *Director, Corporate Finance* T 3150 4390
                                  E diacorp@bancocidade.com.br
Settlement / Clearing
Regional Head   Fabio A Caputo T 3150 4344 E capmark@bancocidade.com.br

Banco Comercial Uruguai SA   Subsidiary Company
Rua Uruguai 171, Centro, Porto Alegre 90010-140
Tel: (51) 228 9118 Fax: (51) 228 5703; (51) 228 9118
Senior Executive Officers
Financial Director   Ricardo Porto *General Director*

Banco de Crédito Nacional SA   Full Branch Office
Alternative trading name: BCN
Rua Boa Vista 208, São Paulo SP 01014-904
Tel: (11) 244 1890; (11) 244 1221 Fax: (11) 3105 6892; (11) 244 1373 Telex: 21284 Swift: SBCN BRSP
Website: www.bcn.com.br
Senior Executive Officers
Chairman   Lazaro de Mello Brandão
Vice Chairman   Pedro Conde
President   Marcio A Laurelli Cypriano
Vice President   José L Acar Pedro
Vice President   Julio de S Carvalho de Araújo
Vice President   Norberto Pinto Barbedo
International Division   Joao de Freitas *Director*
                                  Valter Crescente *Director*

Other Departments
Correspondent Banking   Esther A T Barzilay *Manager, International Division*

Banco do Estado do Rio Grande do Sul SA   Head Office
Rua Capitão Montanha 177, Porto Alegre 90010-040
Tel: (51) 215 1515 Fax: (51) 215 1715 Telex: 512474 BERS BR Swift: BRGS BR RS
Website: www.banrisul.com.br
Senior Executive Officers
Chairman   Aquiles Vieira T 215 1317
President   Ricardo Russowsky T 215 2901
Financial Director   Jose Martello *Finance Director* T 215 2864

Banco do Estado de São Paulo SA - Banespa   Head Office
Alternative trading name: BANESPA
Praça Antonio Prado 6, 6: andar, São Paulo SP 01062-900
Rua João Brícola 32, 7: andar, São Paulo SP 01062-900
Tel: (11) 249 7141; (11) 249 9090 Fax: (11) 249 1330; (11) 239 2414 Swift: BESPBRSPADM
Email: ariodang@banespa.com.br Reuters: BRSP
Senior Executive Officers
Chairman   João Alberto Magro
Financial Director; Chief Operating Officer Ariovaldo D'Angelo *Investor Relations Manager* T 249 9022 F 249 8304
Treasurer   Luiz Roberto Belfiore Saura *Department Director* T 249 9022 F 249 8304
International Division   Marcello Peron Pereira *Head* T 249 7077 F 249 8022

Others (Senior Executives)
Head, Emerging Markets   Luiz Roberto Belfiore Saura *Department Director* T 249 9022 F 249 8304

General-Investment
Head of Investment   Benigno Bernardes Correa *Head, Investment Banking* T 249 7972
                                  F 249 7994

Department: Executive Board of Directors
President   João Alberto Magro

182 Euromoney Directory 1999

www.euromoneydirectory.com   BRAZIL (+55)

Others (Senior Executives)
IRD-Investor Relations Director — Ariovaldo D'Angelo *Investor Relations Manager* T 249 9022 F 249 8304
Directors — Antonio José Barreto de Paiva T 249 7099 F 249 1130
José Antonio Guarnieri *Director* T 249 7404 F 249 1160
Jayme Cardoso Júnior T 249 7216 F 232 1959
Hélcio Gaspar T 249 7581 F 604 0871
Pedro Ulisses Siqueira T 249 9070 F 604 0871
Edmundo de Paulo T 249 7177 F 232 6085
Paulo Renato dos Santos T 249 8444 F 249 1300
Edson Luiz Domingues T 249 7146 F 232 1948
Ricardo Franco Coelho T 249 7010 F 249 7350

Debt Capital Markets / Fixed Income
Emerging Market Bonds
Head of Emerging Markets — Luiz Roberto Belfiore Saura *Department Director* T 249 9022 F 249 8304
Equity Capital Markets
Head of Equity Capital Markets — Luiz Roberto Belfiore Saura *Department Director* T 249 9022 F 249 8304
Equity Repo / Securities Lending
Head — Luiz Roberto Belfiore Saura *Department Director* T 249 9022 F 249 8304
Syndicated Lending
Head of Origination — Benigno Bernardes Correa *Head, Investment Banking* T 249 7972 F 249 7994
Head of Syndication — Primo Aldrigue Júnior *Head* T 249 9049 F 249 1012
Carlos Eduardo de Oliveira *Head* T 249 8652 F 232 8451
Benigno Bernardes Correa *Head, Investment Banking* T 249 7972 F 249 7994

Money Markets
Head of Money Markets — Gilson de Lima Garófalo *Head* T 249 7394 F 249 1073
Foreign Exchange
Head of Foreign Exchange — Marcello Peron Pereira *Head* T 249 7077 F 249 8022
Settlement / Clearing
Head of Settlement / Clearing — Carlos Roberto Zogbi *Head* T 837 2221 F 837 2697
Global Custody
Head of Global Custody — Luiz Roberto Belfiore Saura *Department Director* T 249 9022 F 249 8304
Asset Management
Head — Luiz Roberto Belfiore Saura *Department Director* T 249 9022 F 249 8304
Francisco Mendes de Oliveira T 248 1130 F 248 1298

Other Departments
Commodities / Bullion — Primo Aldrigue Júnior *Head* T 249 9049 F 249 10120
Correspondent Banking — José Jorge Casseb *Head* T 248 1992 F 248 1988
Administration
Business Development — José Antonio Guarnieri *Director* T 249 7404 F 249 1160
Head of Marketing — Mário Carlos Ferreira *Head* T 249 7250 F 249 7870
Technology & Systems
Carlos Roberto Zogbi *Head* T 837 2221 F 837 2697
Luiz Francisco Oliveira *Head* T 249 9339 F 249 1235
Luiz Antonio Maraccini *Head* T 837 2669 F 837 2697

Legal / In-House Counsel
Silvânio Covas *Head* T 248 1598 F 248 1659
Compliance
Luiz Francisco Oliveira *Head* T 249 9339 F 249 1235
Public Relations
Mario Carlos Ferreira *Head* T 249 7250 F 249 7870
Accounts / Audit
Antonio Carlos Rodrigues *Head* T 248 1350 F 248 1139
Sérgio Eduardo Calvo Carrasco *Head* T 249 9083 F 249 7436

Banco Europeu para América Latina (BEAL) SA Subsidiary Company

Alternative trading name: WestLB Banco Europeu & BEAL
Avenida Eng Luiz Carlos Berrini 716, 7°/10° andar, São Paulo SP 04571-000
Tel: (11) 5504 9844 **Fax:** (11) 5504 9933 **Telex:** 1156085 **Email:** banpeu@embratel.net.br
Website: www.westlb.com

Senior Executive Officers
General Manager — Moses Dodo
Financial Director — Carlos Alberto Melo *Deputy General Manager*

Euromoney Directory 1999   **183**

BRAZIL (+55)   www.euromoneydirectory.com

Banco Excel Economico SA
Formerly known as: Excel Banco
Rua Cincinato Braga 340, 15° andar, São Paulo SP SP 01333-010
Tel: (11) 247 5333 **Fax:** (11) 243 3016
International Department **Tel:** 243 1012

Senior Executive Officers
President   Ezekuiel Nasser
International Division   Sergio Peirao *Executive Director*

Debt Capital Markets / Fixed Income
Tel: 243 3025 **Fax:** 243 3026
Head of Debt Capital Markets   Luiz França *Director, International Capital Markets*

Equity Capital Markets
Tel: 243 3025 **Fax:** 243 3026
Head of Equity Capital Markets   Luiz França *Director, International Capital Markets*

Banco Icatu SA   Head Office
Avenida Presidente Wilson 231, Down Town, Rio de Janeiro RJ 20030-021
Tel: (21) 217 1300 **Fax:** (21) 804 8600

Senior Executive Officers
Managing Director / General Manager   Luis de Avillez

Debt Capital Markets / Fixed Income
Department: Capital Markets
Marketing   Jorge Garcia Garcia *Head of Marketing*

Banco Industrial e Comercial SA   Head Office
Rua Boa Vista 192, São Paulo SP 01014-030
Tel: (11) 237 6873 **Fax:** (11) 607 5290 **Telex:** 21344 **Swift:** BICB RSP **Email:** bicdinke@uol.com.br
Reuters: BICB, BRSP
Website: www.bicbanco.com.br

Senior Executive Officers
Chairman   Francisco Humberto Bezarra ☏ **211 5740**
President   José Bezarra de Menezes ☏ **237 6833**
Financial Director   Paulo Mallmann ☏ **237 6954**
Vice President   Jose Adauto Bezerra Jr ☏ **237 6812**
Managing Director / General Manager   Valmir Rosa Torres
International Division   Carlos A K Brigagao *Director* ☏ **237 6873**

Others (Senior Executives)
                                         Claudio G Good *Executive Director* ☏ **292 7744**
                                         Sebastio Ghidetti *Executive Director* ☏ **237 6761**
                                         Khalil Kfouri *Regional Director* ☏ **237 6877**

General-Investment
Head of Investment   Carlos A K Brigagao *Director* ☏ **237 6873**

Debt Capital Markets / Fixed Income
Head of Debt Capital Markets; Head of Fixed   Carlos A K Brigagao *Director* ☏ **237 6873**
Income Sales; Head of Fixed Income Trading

Government Bonds
Head of Sales   Sergio Marcelino *Deputy Director* ☏ **237 6867**
Head of Trading; Head of Syndication; Head of   Sergio Marceiino *Deputy Director* ☏ **237 6867**
Origination

Eurobonds
Head of Sales; Head of Trading   Carlos A K Brigagao *Director* ☏ **237 6873**

Syndicated Lending
Head of Trading; Recovery; Head of Credit   Carlos A K Brigagao *Director* ☏ **237 6873**
Committee

Loan-Related Activities
Trade Finance   Edgard Almgida *Senior Officer* ☏ **237 6834**

Foreign Exchange
Head of Foreign Exchange   Marco Antonid Dias *Manager* ☏ **237 6126**

www.euromoneydirectory.com BRAZIL (+55)

Risk Management
Head of Risk Management Sergio Marubayashi *Director* ☎ **237 6968**

Other Currency Swap / FX Options Personnel
Head of C. Swaps Marco Antonid Dias *Manager* ☎ **237 6126**

Other Departments
Correspondent Banking Maria Fernanda Giacchetti *Manager* ☎ **237 6904**

Administration
Head of Administration Jose Adauto Bezerra Jr *Vice President* ☎ **237 6812**
Business Development Claudio Korody *Director* ☎ **237 6875**

Technology & Systems
  Carlos Schiliro *Director* ☎ **237 6771**

Legal / In-House Counsel
  Eugenio Collares *Superintendent* ☎ **237 6767**

Accounts / Audit
  Vicente Terencio *Superintendent* ☎ **237 6754**

Banco Inter-Atlantico SA
3rd Floor, Avenida Roque Petroni Jr 999, São Paulo SP 04707-910
Tel: (11) 534 7444; (11) 534 7374 **Fax:** (11) 534 7424

Banco de Investimentos Garantia SA Head Office
Avenida Brig Fara Lima 3064/13, São Paulo SP 01451-000
Tel: (11) 821 6000 **Fax:** (11) 821 6900

Senior Executive Officers
Financial Director Luis Alberto Mendes Rodrigues *Finance Director*
Chief Operating Officer Marcelo Pinto Duarte Barbará

Equity Capital Markets
Domestic Equities
Head of Origination Fernando Antonio Botelho Prado *Director*

Corporate Finance / M&A Advisory
Global Head Roger Ian Wright *Director, Corporate Finance*

Banco Itaú SA Subsidiary Company
Rua Boa Vista 176, São Paulo SP 01092-900
Tel: (11) 237 3000 **Fax:** (11) 277 104 **Telex:** 1113044 **Swift:** ITAU BRSP

Banco Marka Head Office
20th floor, 231 Avenida Presidente Wilson, Rio de Janeiro RJ 20030-021
Tel: (21) 217 7788 **Fax:** (21) 217 7878 **Reuters:** MARKA
Website: www.marka.com.br

Senior Executive Officers
Chairman Salvatore Cacciola ☎ **217 7777**
Chief Executive Officer Luiz Fernando Fleury ☎ **217 7785**
Treasurer Antonio Dupim ☎ **217 7730**

Debt Capital Markets / Fixed Income
Av. Juscelino Kubitschek, 50/ 4 andar, São Paulo SP 04543-000
Global Head Carlos Gradim ☎ **(11) 3040ext4644**
Country Head Gilberto Giberti *Head of Sales* ☎ **(11) 3040 4646**

Settlement / Clearing
Country Head Gustavo Freitas *Head, Settlements & Clearing* ☎ **217 7760**

Administration
Legal / In-House Counsel
  Cinthia Souza *Head, Legal Department* ☎ **217 7888**

Euromoney Directory 1999 **185**

BRAZIL (+55)　　　　　　www.euromoneydirectory.com

Banco Mercantil de São Paulo SA FINASA
Head Office

Avenida Paulista, 1450, São Paulo SP 01310-917
PO Box 4077, São Paulo SP
Tel: (11) 252 2121 **Fax:** (11) 284 3312 **Telex:** 11 37 701 **Swift:** BMSP BR SP **Email:** fimasa@fimasa.com.br
Website: www.finasa.com.br

Senior Executive Officers
Chairman, President & CEO　　　　　　Gastão Eduardo de Buneo Vidigal
International Division　　　　　　Regis Soulas *Director & SVP, International Relations*
　　　　　　João Figueiredo Filho *Director & SVP, International & Corporate Banking*

Others (Senior Executives)
　　　　　　Luiz Carlos da Costa Carvalho *Director & SVP, Budget*
　　　　　　Léo do Amaral *Director & SVP, Private Banking*
　　　　　　Raul Carlos Pereira Baretto

General-Lending (DCM, SL)
Head of Corporate Banking　　　　　　João Figueiredo Filho *Director & SVP, International & Corporate Banking*
General - Treasury
Head of Treasury　　　　　　Raul Carlos Pereira Barretto *Director & SVP, Treasury*
Other Departments
Private Banking　　　　　　Léo do Amaral *Director & SVP, Private Banking*
Correspondent Banking　　　　　　Liam Gallagher *Director, Operations* ☐ **252 2944**

Banco Meridional do Brasil SA
Head Office

Rua Sete de Setembro 1028, 3° andar, Porto Alegre 90010-191
Tel: (51) 225 6088 **Fax:** (51) 287 5769 **Swift:** BMEB BR RS

Senior Executive Officers
General Manager　　　　　　Mauricio Caetano
Foreign Exchange
Head of Foreign Exchange　　　　　　Andrè de Oliveira *Manager*

Banco do Nordeste
Head Office

Alternative trading name: Banco do Nordeste do Brasil SA
Av Paranjana 5700, Fortaleza Ceará 60035-210
Caixa Postal 628, Fortaleza Ceará
Tel: (85) 299 3012; (85) 299 3017 **Fax:** (85) 299 3258 **Telex:** 0851105 **Swift:** BNBR BR CF A
Email: info@bauconondiste.gov.br
Website: www.banconordeste.gov.br

Senior Executive Officers
President　　　　　　Byron Queiroz ☐ **299 3041**
Chief Executive Officer　　　　　　Siluana Parente ☐ **299 3050**
Financial Director　　　　　　Osmundo Evangelista Rebouças *Director* ☐ **299 3093**
Treasurer　　　　　　Lucenildo Piuentel *Treasurer* ☐ **299 3661**
International Division　　　　　　Alexandre Cabnal *Director* ☐ **299 3012**

Debt Capital Markets / Fixed Income
Eurobonds
Head of Origination　　　　　　Alexandre Cabral *Manager, International Finance*
Head of Sales　　　　　　Francisco Rabelo *Manager, Project Finance* ☐ **299 3228**

Syndicated Lending
Loan-Related Activities
Project Finance　　　　　　Francisco Rabelo *Manager, Project Finance* ☐ **299 3228**

Corporate Finance / M&A Advisory
Global Head　　　　　　Alexandre Cabral *Manager, International Finance*

Administration
Head of Administration　　　　　　Paulo Carvalho ☐ **299 3058**

Technology & Systems
　　　　　　Valdemar Barnos ☐ **299 3059**

Legal / In-House Counsel
　　　　　　Everaldo Maia ☐ **299 3084**

Public Relations
　　　　　　Eliane Brasil ☐ **299 3082**

www.euromoneydirectory.com　　　　　　　　BRAZIL (+55)

Accounts / Audit
　　　　　　　　　　　　Joaquim Barnos ☎ 299 3056
Other (Administration)
　　　　　　　　　　　　Rita Valente ☎ 299 3063

Banco Pactual SA　　　　　　　　　　　　　　　　　Head Office

Avenida República do Chile 230, 29° andar, Centro, Rio de Janeiro RJ 20031-170
Tel: (21) 514 9600; (21) 588 4900 **Fax:** (21) 514 8600 **Telex:** 34850 **Email:** pimenta@pactual.com.br
Bloomberg: PCTL; PCTF
Website: www.pactual.com.br

Senior Executive Officers
Chairman　　　　　　　　　　　Luiz Cezar Fernandes
President　　　　　　　　　　　Eduardo Plass
Financial Director　　　　　　　Marcelo Ferfaty *Executive Director*
Managing Director　　　　　　　José Mario Caldas Osorio
International Division　　　　　Gerrit Tames

General-Lending (DCM, SL)
Head of Corporate Banking　　　André Schwartz

Debt Capital Markets / Fixed Income
Head of Fixed Income　　　　　　André Esteves

Equity Capital Markets
Head of Equity Capital Markets　Marciliano de Freitas

Foreign Exchange
Head of Foreign Exchange　　　　Paulo Fernando de Oliveira

Corporate Finance / M&A Advisory
Global Head　　　　　　　　　　Paulo Bilyk

Other Departments
Private Banking　　　　　　　　André Esteves

Administration
Head of Administration　　　　　Daniele de Mattos

Technology & Systems
　　　　　　　　　　　　　　　　Sami Haddad

Legal / In-House Counsel
　　　　　　　　　　　　　　　　Silvia Bugelli

Banco Real SA　　　　　　　　　　　　　　　　　　Head Office

Avenida Paulista 1374, 3° andar, São Paulo SP 01310-916
Tel: (11) 285 5645; (11) 3174 9754 **Fax:** (11) 3174 9234; (11) 3174 9145 **Telex:** 1131811 **Swift:** REAL BR SP
Website: www.real.com.br

Senior Executive Officers
Chairman　　　　　　　　　　　　Aloysio Faria ☎ 285 4998
President & CEO　　　　　　　　Paulo Ribeiro ☎ 3174 2133
Financial Director　　　　　　　Renê Aduan *Executive Director* ☎ 288 4674
Chief Operating Officer　　　　Flamarion Nunes *Executive Director* ☎ 3174 9601
Treasurer　　　　　　　　　　　Cacildo Rocha *Director* ☎ 285 4722

Debt Capital Markets / Fixed Income
Global Head　　　　　　　　　　Luiz Felipe Motta *Director, Corporate Finance* ☎ 3174 9269

Domestic Government Bonds
Head of Sales　　　　　　　　　Ivan Dumond *General Manager* ☎ 253 1900

Eurobonds
Head of Origination　　　　　　Sellers McKee *General Manager* ☎ 3174 9703

Libor-Based / Floating-Rate Products
FRN Origination　　　　　　　　Sellers McKee *General Manager* ☎ 3174 9703

Medium-Term Notes
Head of Origination　　　　　　Sellers McKee *General Manager* ☎ 3174 9703

Private Placements
Head of Origination　　　　　　Sellers McKee *General Manager* ☎ 3174 9703

Asset-Backed Securities / Securitization
Global Head　　　　　　　　　　Sellers McKee *General Manager* ☎ 3174 9703

Mortgage-Backed Securities
Global Head　　　　　　　　　　Sellers McKee *General Manager* ☎ 3174 9703

BRAZIL (+55)　　　　　　　www.euromoneydirectory.com

Banco Real SA (cont)

Fixed-Income Repo
Head of Repo　　　　　　　　　Ivan Dumond *General Manager* ☎ 253 1900
Equity Capital Markets
Global Head　　　　　　　　　Sellers McKee *General Manager* ☎ 3174 9703
Domestic Equities
Head of Origination　　　　　　José Carlos Galante *General Manager* ☎ 3174 9136
International Equities
Head of Origination　　　　　　Luiz Felipe Motta *Director, Corporate Finance* ☎ 3174 9269
Convertibles / Equity-Linked
Head of Origination　　　　　　Luiz Felipe Motta *Director, Corporate Finance* ☎ 3174 9269
Syndicated Lending
Loan-Related Activities
Trade Finance　　　　　　　　Angelina Sposito *General Manager* ☎ 3174 9794
Money Markets
Global Head　　　　　　　　　Ivan Dumond *General Manager* ☎ 253 1900
Domestic Commercial Paper
Head of Origination　　　　　　Fernando Spinetti *General Manager* ☎ 251 9136
Eurocommercial Paper
Head of Origination　　　　　　Sellers McKee *General Manager* ☎ 3174 9703
Wholesale Deposits
Marketing　　　　　　　　　　Ivan Dumond *General Manager* ☎ 253 1900
Foreign Exchange
Global Head　　　　　　　　　Francisco Lage *Manager* ☎ 253 1900
Risk Management
Global Head　　　　　　　　　Renê Aduan *Executive Director* ☎ 288 4674
Other Currency Swap / FX Options Personnel
　　　　　　　　　　　　　　Sellers McKee *General Manager* ☎ 3174 9703
Corporate Finance / M&A Advisory
Global Head　　　　　　　　　Nelson Andrade *General Manager* ☎ 3174 9703
Other Departments
Private Banking　　　　　　　Fernando Moura *Executive Officer* ☎ 251 9046
Correspondent Banking　　　　Sebastião Cunha *Director, Institutional Division* ☎ 285 5645
Administration
Technology & Systems
　　　　　　　　　　　　　　Adilson Herrero *Director, Technology & Infrastructure System* ☎ 251 5140
Legal / In-House Counsel
　　　　　　　　　　　　　　Mauro Moraes *Director* ☎ 251 9650
Compliance
　　　　　　　　　　　　　　Flamarion Nunes *Executive Director* ☎ 3174 9601
Public Relations
　　　　　　　　　　　　　　Ricardo Gribel *Executive Officer* ☎ 287 8682

Banco Republic National Bank of New York (Brasil) SA
Subsidiary Company

Alternative trading name: Republic National Bank
Avenida Paulista 1842, 10° andar Cjtos 106/107, Torre Norte, São Paulo SP 01310-200
Tel: (11) 235 1985; (11) 253 1985 **Fax:** (11) 283 4228; (11) 287 7081
Senior Executive Officers
President　　　　　　　　　　Oscar Marques
Chief Executive Officer　　　　Miriam Saintive *Executive Director*
Financial Director　　　　　　Julio Ferreira
Chief Operating Officer　　　　Eduardo Saito

Banco Safra SA
Head Office

Avenida Paulista 2100, São Paulo SP 01310-930
Tel: (11) 3175 7575 **Fax:** (11) 3175 8532 **Telex:** 37742 **Swift:** SAFR BR SP
Senior Executive Officers
President　　　　　　　　　　Carlos Alberto Vieira ☎ **(21) 216 2808**
Treasurer　　　　　　　　　　João C Tourinho *Director* ☎ **3175 7579**

188　Euromoney Directory 1999

www.euromoneydirectory.com BRAZIL (+55)

Debt Capital Markets / Fixed Income	
Global Head	João C Tourinho *Director* ☎ **3175 7579**
Eurobonds	
Head of Origination	Marcos Grodetzky *Director, International* ☎ **3175 8502**
Syndicated Lending	
Loan-Related Activities	
Trade Finance	Carlos A dos Santos *Superintendent* ☎ **3175 3590**
Money Markets	
Head of Origination	Marcos Grodetzky *Director, International* ☎ **3175 8502**
Foreign Exchange	
Tel: 3175 7717 **Fax:** 3175 7401	
Global Head	Walter Piacsek *Director, Planning & Control* ☎ **3175 8717**
Other Departments	
Correspondent Banking	Carlos A dos Santos *Superintendent* ☎ **3175 3590**
Administration	
Technology & Systems	
	Luiz C Zambaldi *Director* ☎ **3175 7427**

Banco Santander Brasil SA — Subsidiary Company

Alternative trading name: Banco Santander Noroeste
Formerly known as: Banco Geral do Comércio SA / Banco Noroeste SA
R Amador Bueno 474, São Paulo SP 04752-000
Tel: (11) 538 6000 **Fax:** (11) 538 8430 **Telex:** 11157559

Senior Executive Officers
President	António Horta Osório ☎ **538 8722**
Vice President	Aurélio Velo Vallejo ☎ **538 8706**
Vice President	José de Paiva Ferreira ☎ **538 8181**
Vice President	Leocádio Geraldo Rocha ☎ **538 6175**
Vice President	Miguel de Campos Pereira Bragança ☎ **828 7379**
Financial Director	João Ermida ☎ **538 8459**
Treasurer	Gustavo Murgel ☎ **538 8791**
International Division	Luis Carlos Cantidio ☎ **538 8554**

General-Lending (DCM, SL)
Head of Corporate Banking   Walter Shinomata ☎ **538 8776**

General-Investment
Head of Investment   Miguel de Campos Pereira Bragança *Global Head of Investment Banking* ☎ **538 7379**

Corporate Finance / M&A Advisory
Global Head   Walter Shinomata ☎ **538 8776**

Banco Santos SA — Head Office

Avenida Paulista, 1842, 4,5,6 and 7° andars, Torre Norte, São Paulo SP 01310-200
Tel: (11) 269 6000; (11) 269 6004 **Fax:** (11) 283 2701

Senior Executive Officers
President	Edemar Ferreira ☎ **(11) 269 6001**
Chief Executive Officer	Mario Martinelli *Executive Director* ☎ **(11) 269 6004**
Treasurer	Guimaraes Eduardo ☎ **(11) 269 6005**
International Division	Grinberg Regina ☎ **269 6195**

Others (Senior Executives)
Operations Director   Alvaro Cabral

Banco Sudameris Brasil SA — Subsidiary Company

Avenida Paulista 1000, São Paulo SP 01310-912
PO Box 3481, São Paulo SP 01060
Tel: (11) 3170 9633 **Fax:** (11) 3170 1239 **Telex:** 1130517 SUDM BR **Swift:** SUDM BR SP SPO
Website: www.sudameris.com.br

Senior Executive Officers
Chief Executive Officer	Giovanni Urizio ☎ **3170 9200**
Treasurer; International Division	João Luiz Pasqual *Deputy Executive Director* ☎ **3170 9209**

Euromoney Directory 1999 **189**

BRAZIL (+55)   www.euromoneydirectory.com

Banco Sudameris Brasil SA (cont)
Debt Capital Markets / Fixed Income
Global Head   Humberto Casagrande Neto *Director* ☎ **5504 6016**
Equity Capital Markets
Global Head   Humberto Casagrande Neto *Director* ☎ **5504 6016**
Syndicated Lending
Loan-Related Activities
Trade Finance   Sandra W Crocco *Senior Manager* ☎ **3170 9251**
Foreign Exchange
Global Head   Afonso F Santos *Senior Manager* ☎ **3170 9254**
Other Departments
Correspondent Banking   Sandra W Crocco *Senior Manager* ☎ **3170 9251**

Banco Sul America SA   Head Office
Avenida Presidente Juscelino Kubitschek 1830, Torre II, 7° andar, São Paulo SP 04543-900
Tel: (11) 3779 4800 **Fax:** (11) 829 7914; (11) 820 0717 **Telex:** 11 32308 **Email:** infobsa.com.br **Reuters:** SULAM
Bloomberg: BSA
Website: www.bsa.com.br

Senior Executive Officers
Chairman & President   Rony Lyrio
Vice Chairman   Roberto T da Costa ☎ **3779 4931**
Chief Executive Officer   Felipe Cavalcanti *Executive Vice President* ☎ **3779 4964**
Financial Director   Renato Russo *Financial Director & Treasurer* ☎ **3779 4957**
Chief Operating Officer   Domingos Carelli Netto *Vice President* ☎ **3779 4967**
Treasurer   Renato Russo *Financial Director & Treasurer* ☎ **3779 4957**
International Division   Robert Linton *Head of Foreign Operations* ☎ **3779 4844**
Relationship Manager
Cayman Office   Eduardo D'Angelo ☎ **+345 949 0855**
Financial Institutions   Lauro Campos ☎ **828 1892**
Market Relationship   Ronaldo Magalhaes *Director & Head* ☎ **828 1958**
   Arthur Prado *Sales* ☎ **828 1855**
   Vinicius Bari *Sales* ☎ **828 1899**

Debt Capital Markets / Fixed Income
Department: Fixed Income
Domestic Government Bonds
Head of Trading   Antonio Manoel Caeiro ☎ **828 1966**
Fixed-Income Research
Global Head   Fabio Anderaos ☎ **828 1824**
Equity Capital Markets
Equity Research
Global Head   Fabio Anderaos ☎ **828 1824**
Foreign Exchange
Corporate Sales   Leopoldo Barreto ☎ **828 1835**
Risk Management
Tel: 828 1934 **Fax:** 820 0717
Country Head   Mailson Hykavei *Funding*
   Renato Russo *Financial Director & Treasurer* ☎ **3779 4957**
OTC Equity Derivatives
Head   Paulo Roberto Ramos ☎ **828 1861**
Corporate Finance / M&A Advisory
Head of Corporate Finance   Helektra Karnakis ☎ **3779 4951**
Asset Management
Tel: 828 1831 **Fax:** 829 3384
Portfolio Management   Luiz Carlos Simão *Head* ☎ **3779 4968**
Other (Asset Management)
Asset Manangement Sales   Ronaldo Magalhães *Head* ☎ **3779 4958**
Administration
Legal / In-House Counsel
   Tito Livio
Other (Administration)
Products Development   Enio Fukai ☎ **828 1889**
Information Support   Maria Forbes ☎ **828 1885**
Marketing   Roberta Lima ☎ **828 1947**

www.euromoneydirectory.com　　　BRAZIL (+55)

Banco Sumitomo Brasileiro SA — Subsidiary Company

Avenida Paulista 949, 1° andar, São Paulo SP 01311-917
Tel: (11) 3178 8000 Fax: (11) 253 2704; (11) 289 6996 Swift: SUBR BR SP

Senior Executive Officers
President　　　　　　　　　　　Nobuhisa Hasegawa ☎ **3178 8001**
Vice President　　　　　　　　　Taiichi Oketani ☎ **3178 8002**
Vice President　　　　　　　　　Yasuhiro Obana ☎ **3178 8011**

Others (Senior Executives)
Director　　　　　　　　　　　　Taturo Nakamura ☎ **3178 8105**
　　　　　　　　　　　　　　　　Takumi Kamijo ☎ **3178 8014**

Foreign Exchange
Tel: 3178 8150 Fax: 253 2704
Head of Foreign Exchange　　　Yochinobu Murackami ☎ **3178 8125**

Other Departments
Correspondent Banking　　　　Vanderlei Teixeira *General Manager* ☎ **3178 8150**

Banco Votorantim

16th Floor, Avenida Roque Petroni Jr, Vila Gertrudes, São Paulo SP 04708000
Tel: (11) 536 1700; (11) 536 1722 Fax: (11) 536 1900

The Bank of Tokyo-Mitsubishi Limited

Praia de Botafogo 228, 8° andar, Sector B, Botafogo, Rio de Janeiro RJ 22359 900
Tel: (21) 552 0794 Fax: (21) 551 6648 Email: samy@uninet.com.br

Senior Executive Officers
Chief Representative　　　　　Masami Tsutsumimoto

Camara de Liquidacao e Custodia — Head Office

Alternative trading name: CLC
Praça XV de Novembro 20, 7° andar, Rio de Janeiro RJ 20010-120
Tel: (21) 514 1890 Fax: (21) 514 1891 Telex: 35104 Swift: CLCB BR RJ Email: clc@clc.com.br
Website: www.clc.com.br

Senior Executive Officers
President　　　　　　　　　　　Luiz Motta Veiga
Managing Director　　　　　　　João Fraga

Equity Capital Markets

Equity Repo / Securities Lending
Head　　　　　　　　　　　　　Jorge Marques *Securities Lending Assistant* ☎ **514 1896** 📠 **221 2768**

Settlement / Clearing
Head of Settlement / Clearing　Nirvando Diniz *Manager, Settlement & Clearing* ☎ **514 1879** 📠 **221 2768**

Global Custody
Head of Global Custody　　　　Paulo Malafaia *Custody Director* ☎ **514 1023**

Administration
Head of Administration　　　　Umberto Oliveira ☎ **514 1846**
Business Development　　　　Alexandre Silveira *Product Manager* ☎ **514 1196** 📠 **514 1185**

Citibank NA — Full Branch Office

3rd Floor, Avenida Paulista 1111, São Paulo SP 01311-920
Tel: (11) 576 1000 Fax: (11) 576 1143 Telex: 6735455 Swift: CITI US33 BRR
Corporate Dealers Tel: 576 2403

Foreign Exchange
Global Head　　　　　　　　　Luis Candiota ☎ **576 1484**

FX Traders / Sales People
Customer FX Head　　　　　　Jose Antonio Coelho da Costa ☎ **576 2666**

Settlement / Clearing
Operations　　　　　　　　　Angelim Curiel *Transaction Services Head* ☎ **576 1409**

Euromoney Directory 1999　**191**

BRAZIL (+55) www.euromoneydirectory.com

Citibank NA (cont)
Global Custody
Regional Head Pedro Guerra ☏ 576 1203 ✉ 576 2369

Clariden Brasil Ltda Subsidiary Company
Avenida Brigadeiro Faria Lima 1276/Cj 42, Jardim Paulistano, São Paulo SP 01452-000
Tel: (11) 867 8011 Fax: (11) 816 3841
Senior Executive Officers
Managing Director Stefan Kron

Commerzbank Rio de Janeiro Serviços Ltda Representative Office
Avenida Rio Branco 123, Conjunto 706, Rio de Janeiro RJ 20040-005
Caixa Postal 910, Rio de Janeiro RJ 20001-970
Tel: (21) 231 0623 Fax: (21) 224 7316 Telex: 2121430 COBA BR
Senior Executive Officers
Representative Carsten Kayatz

Commerzbank São Paulo Serviços Ltda Representative Office
Rua Pedroso Alvarenga 1208, 16° andar, São Paulo SP 04531-911
PO Box 2951, São Paulo SP SP 01064-970
Tel: (11) 852 8055 Fax: (11) 853 9790 Telex: 11-33378 COBA BR
Senior Executive Officers
Representative Arno Noellenburg

Corretora Patente SA CVM Subsidiary Company
Alternative trading name: Patente
Avenida Paulista 1106, 7° andar, São Paulo SP 01310-914
Tel: (11) 886 9600; (11) 886 9840 Fax: (11) 886 9700 Email: secre@patente.com.br
Senior Executive Officers
Financial Director Ricardo Amaral *Director*
Director Manoel Francisco Pires da Costa
Director Luiz Fernando Nazarian
General-Investment
Head of Investment Jayme Alves Nero *Assistant Director* ☏ 886 9771
Debt Capital Markets / Fixed Income
Head of Fixed Income Marcelo Tadeu Ferreira *Operational Manager* ☏ 886 9773
Equity Capital Markets
Head of Equity Capital Markets Martin Arranz *Manager, Open Market* ☏ 886 9773
Administration
Head of Administration Flávio Bartalotti *Administration Manager* ☏ 886 9669
Compliance
 Ubiratan Ribeiro *Controller* ☏ 886 9637

Crédit Lyonnais Brazil Representative Office
Avenida Brigadeiro Faria Lima 1355, 21° andar, São Paulo SP 01452-919
Tel: (11) 3030 7811 Fax: (11) 3030 7900
Senior Executive Officers
Chief Representative Christian Pehuet ☏ 3030 7800
Debt Capital Markets / Fixed Income
Country Head Cristo Kirhakos ☏ 3030 7851
Equity Capital Markets
Country Head Alex Rabinowitz ☏ 3030 7815
Corporate Finance / M&A Advisory
Country Head Cristo Kirhakos ☏ 3030 7851

192 Euromoney Directory 1999

BRAZIL (+55)

Other Departments
Private Banking — Georges Roy 3030 7800
Correspondent Banking — Marco de Oliveira 3030 7858

Credit Suisse
Representative Office

Avenida Rio Branco 108, 27° andar, Rio de Janeiro RJ 20040-001
Caixa Postal 1250, Rio de Janeiro RJ
Tel: (21) 507 1107 **Fax:** (21) 507 2398 **Telex:** 32531

Senior Executive Officers
Senior Officer — Felix Reto Jungen
Senior Officer — Silvano Alberto Bernasconi
Senior Officer — Silvio Christian Clavadetscher
Senior Officer — Alex Harry Haegler

Den norske Bank AS
Representative Office

Caixa Postale 1620, Rio de Janeiro RJ 20001-970
Tel: (21) 285 1795 **Fax:** (21) 205 0581

Senior Executive Officers
Representative — Tom M Ringseth

Deutsche Bank
Full Branch Office

Rua Alexandre Dumas, 2200 Ander, Chacara Santo Antonio, São Paulo SP 04717-910
Caixa Postal 55192, São Paulo SP 04799-970
Tel: (11) 5189 5000 **Fax:** (11) 5189 5100 **Telex:** 1153251 DBSPBR **Swift:** DEUT BR SP SPO **Cable:** DEUTB
Client Relationship Management **Fax:** 5189 5135; Corporate & Institutional Banking **Fax:** 5189 5150; DB Capital Investment **Fax:** 5189 5140; DMG - Capital Markets **Fax:** 5189 5150; DMG - Equities **Fax:** 5189 5161; DMG - Executive Diretory **Fax:** 5189 5191; DMG - Global Markets **Fax:** 5189 5120; DMG - M&A **Fax:** 5189 5160; DMG - Research **Fax:** 5189 5265; DMG - Traders **Fax:** 5189 5161; Executive Director **Fax:** 5189 5125; Financial Institutions **Fax:** 5189 5140; International Trade Finance **Fax:** 5189 5115; Legal Dept/Compliance **Fax:** 5189 5287; Organziation & EDP **Fax:** 5189 5130; Private Banking **Fax:** 5189 5175; Resources & Controlling **Fax:** 5189 5115
Website: www.deutsche-bank.de

Senior Executive Officers
Managing Director / General Manager — Manfred Hamburger

Deutsche Bank AG
Full Branch Office

Avenida Carlos, Gomes, 651-Cong 902, Porto Alegre 90480-003
Tel: (51) 328 2828 **Fax:** (51) 328 3811 **Telex:** 520450 **Swift:** DEUT BR SP PAE

Deutsche Bank SA
Full Branch Office

Rua dos Inconfidentes 1076, 13° andar, Belo Horizonte MG 30140-120
Tel: (31) 261 4555 **Fax:** (31) 261 5090 **Swift:** DEUT BR SP BHE

Deutsche Bank SA
Full Branch Office

Rua Pasteur 463, 2° andar, conj 201, Curitiba PR 80250-080
Tel: (41) 342 6176 **Fax:** (41) 243 9207

Deutsche Bank SA
Full Branch Office

Avenida Rio Branco 1, 16° andar, Rio de Janeiro RJ 20090-003
Tel: (21) 550 8050 **Fax:** (21) 550 8059 **Swift:** DEUT BR SP RJO

BRAZIL (+55)　　　　　　　www.euromoneydirectory.com

DG BANK
Representative Office

Rua Sansão Alves dos Santos 433, 3°andar/conj 32, Edificio Hormino Maia, São Paulo SP 04571-090
Tel: (11) 5505 1087; (11) 5505 1077 Fax: (11) 5505 0274

Senior Executive Officers
Representative　　　　　　　　　Christian E Königsfeld

Dresdner Bank Brasil
Full Branch Office

1/2nd Floors, Rua Verbo Divino 1488, São Paulo SP 04719-904
Tel: (11) 5188 6700 Fax: (11) 5188 6900 Telex: 5320718 Swift: DRES BR SP
Website: www.brain.dresdnerbank.de

Senior Executive Officers
Chairman & Managing Director　　　Winston Fritsch
Vice Chairman　　　　　　　　　　　Günther Leopold Matter
Managing Director　　　　　　　　　João Pinheiro Nogueira Batista

Others (Senior Executives)
　　　　　　　　　　　　　　　　　Uwe A H Mossakowski *Vice Director, Credit Division*

General-Lending (DCM, SL)
Head of Corporate Banking　　　　　Ricardo Cohen *Vice Director, Corporate Banking*

General - Treasury
Head of Treasury　　　　　　　　　André Weber *Manager*

Relationship Manager
Foreign Funding　　　　　　　　　Marina Martini Ribeiro *Manager*

Equity Capital Markets
Global Head　　　　　　　　　　　Uwe J Niederberger *Vice Director*

Syndicated Lending
Head of Credit Committee　　　　　Uwe A H Mossakowski *Vice Director, Credit Division*

Loan-Related Activities
Project Finance　　　　　　　　　Jon D. Boles *Vice Director*
Structured Trade Finance　　　　　Klaus Heritt *Vice Director*

Settlement / Clearing
Operations　　　　　　　　　　　Luciano Fantin *Manager*

Administration

Accounts / Audit
Auditing Division　　　　　　　　Luciano Fantin *Manager*

Other (Administration)
Human Resources Division　　　　Alda C Kuznecov *Manager*

Robert Fleming do Brasil Ltdo
Subsidiary Company

Avenida Brigadeiro Faria Lima 1279, 4° andar, São Paulo SP 01451-001
Tel: (11) 870 1777 Fax: (11) 870 1778; (11) 815 2213

The Fuji Bank Limited
Representative Office

Avenida Brigadeiro Luiz Antonio 2020, 10° andar, São Paulo SP 01318-911
Tel: (11) 289 1812; (11) 287 1472 Fax: (11) 287 7867

Senior Executive Officers
Chief Representative　　　　　　　Kazuo Sano

HypoVereinsbank
Representative Office

Rua da Assembleia 10, Cojunto 2701, Rio de Janeiro RJ 20119-900
Caixa Postale 2996, Rio de Janeiro RJ 20001-970
Tel: (21) 531 2716 Fax: (21) 531 1227

www.euromoneydirectory.com BRAZIL (+55)

The Industrial Bank of Japan Limited — Representative Office
Avenida Paulista 1842, 22° andar, Conjunto 228, São Paulo SP 1310-200
Tel: (11) 289 2666 **Fax:** (11) 251 4241 **Telex:** 11 36655 IBJA BR

Senior Executive Officers
Representative — Koji Adachi
Representative — Marcos Yasuzawa

ING Baring Corretora de Valores Mobiliáros — Subsidiary Company
Avenida Brigadeiro Faria Lima 3064, 8° andar, São Paulo SP 01451-000
Tel: (11) 827 6000 **Fax:** (11) 827 6464

Senior Executive Officers
Country Manager — Carlos Craide

ING Barings — Full Branch Office
Avenida Brigadeiro Faria Lima 3064, 8° andar, São Paulo SP 01451-020
Tel: (11) 827 6000 **Fax:** (11) 827 6464 **Telex:** 1130817; 1131064 ING BR **Swift:** INGB BR SP
Extra Telex: 130817 INGB BR; **Extra Telex:** 1131064 INGB BR

Senior Executive Officers
Country Manager — Carlos Craide [T] **827 6256** [F] **827 6164** [E] **carlos.craide@ing-barings.com.br**
Department: Investment Management
Avenida Brigadeiro Faria Lima 3064, 10° andar, São Paulo SP
Tel: +55 (11) 827 6055 **Fax:** +55 (11) 827 8055

General-Investment
Head of Investment — Ricardo Leonardos *General Manager*

Debt Capital Markets / Fixed Income
Head of Debt Capital Markets — Deiwes Rubira *Managing Director* [T] **827 6278** [F] **827 6127**
Romolo Nigro *Senior Vice President* [T] **827 6229** [F] **827 6045**
[E] **romolo.nigro@ing-barings.com.br**
Head of Fixed Income Sales — Fabio Amorosino *Vice President* [T] **827 6245** [F] **8270 6045**
[E] **fabio.amorosino@ing-barings.com.br**

Eurobonds
Head of Origination — José Berenguer [T] **827 6228**
Head of Sales — Romolo Nigro *Senior Vice President* [T] **827 6229** [F] **827 6045**
[E] **romolo.nigro@ing-barings.com.br**
Head of Trading — Pedro Barbosa [T] **827 6245**

Fixed-Income Research
Head of Credit Research — Carlos J de Faria *AVP, Economist* [T] **827 6131** [F] **827 6042**
[E] **josé.faria@ing-barings.com.br**
Guilherme Abbud *Junior Economist* [T] **827 6128**
Analyst — Fábio Motta *Vice President* [T] **827 8322** [F] **827 8120**
[E] **fabio.motta@ing-barings.com.br**
Mauro Schneider *Vice President* [T] **827 6304** [F] **827 6042**
[E] **mauro.schneider@ing-barings.com.br**

Equity Capital Markets
Domestic Equities
Head of Origination — Luciano Camargo *Head, Equity Broking, Trading & Sales* [T] **827 6545**
[E] **luciano.camargo@ing-barings.com.br**
Head of Trading — Fábio Penteado *Equity Broking, Trading & Sales* [T] **827 6547**
[E] **fabio.penteado@ing-barings.com.br**
Fabio Alcantara *Equity Broking, Trading & Sales* [T] **827 6536**
[E] **fabio.alcantara@ing-barings.com.br**
Sergio Ayrosa *Equity Broking, Trading & Sales* [T] **827 6534**
[E] **sergio.ayrosa@ing-barings.com.br**
Andrea Chamma *Equity Broking, Trading & Sales* [T] **827 6587**
[E] **andrea.chamma@ing-barings.com**

International Equities
Head of Origination — Luciano Camargo *Head, Equity Broking, Trading & Sales* [T] **827 6545**
[E] **luciano.camargo@ing-barings.com.br**
Head of Trading — Fábio Penteado *Equity Broking, Trading & Sales* [T] **827 6547**
[E] **fabio.penteado@ing-barings.com.br**

BRAZIL (+55)　　　www.euromoneydirectory.com

ING Barings (cont)
International Equities (cont)

Fabio Alcantara *Equity Broking, Trading & Sales* ☏ **827 6536**
🖃 **fabio.alcantara@ing-barings.com.br**
Sergio Ayrosa *Equity Broking, Trading & Sales* ☏ **827 6534**
🖃 **sergio.ayrosa@ing-barings.com.br**
Andrea Chamma *Equity Broking, Trading & Sales* ☏ **827 6587**
🖃 **andrea.chamma@ing-barings.com**

Equity Research
Regional Head　　　Paulo Vasconcellos *Head of Research* ☏ **827 6581**
　　　　　　　　　🖃 **paulo.vasconcellos@ing-barings.com.br**

Other (Equity Research)
Steel　　　Mirela Rappaport *Analyst* ☏ **827 6572**
　　　　🖃 **mirela.rappaport@ing-barings.com.br**
Telecoms　　　Vera Rossi *Analyst* ☏ **827 6505** 🖃 **vera.rossi@ing-barings.com.br**
Consumer Durables, Capital Goods, Auto Parts　　Thomas Atkinson *Analyst* ☏ **827 6336** 🖃 **thomas.atkinson@ing-barings.com**
Electric Utilities　　　Charles Barnett *Analyst* ☏ **827 6502** 🖃 **charles.barnett@ing-barings.com.br**
Oil & Gas / Chemicals　　　Ana Zagato *Analyst* ☏ **827 6583** 🖃 **ana.zagatto@ing-barings.com**
Retail　　　Flavia Cipovicci *Analyst* ☏ **827 6506** 🖃 **flavia.cipovicci@ing-barings.com.br**
Electric Utilities　　　Francisco Navarrete *Junior Analyst* ☏ **827 6504**
　　　　🖃 **francisco.navarrete@ing-barings.com.br**

Other Departments
Economic Research　　　José Carlos De Faria *Economist* ☏ **827 6131**
　　　　🖃 **jose.faria@ing-barings.com.br**
　　　　Guilherme Abbud *Junior Economist* ☏ **827 6128**
　　　　Mauro Schneider *Senior Economist* ☏ **827 6394**

ING Investment Management

Avenue Brigadeiro Faria Lima 3014, 10° andar, São Paulo SP 01451-000
Tel: (11) 827 6055 Fax: (11) 827 8055

Senior Executive Officers
Managing Director / General Manager　　　Ricardo Leonardos

ING Serviços Ltda　　　　　　　　　　　　　　　Representative Office

Suite 3302, Avenida Almirante Barroso 52, Rio de Janeiro RJ 20031-000
Tel: (21) 532 2216 Fax: (21) 220 9675

Senior Executive Officers
Representative　　　Augusto E Lins

International Finance Corporation　　　　　　　Representative Office

Room 103, Rua Guararapes 2064, 10° andar, São Paulo SP 04561-004
Tel: (11) 5505 1629 Fax: (11) 5505 3073 Cable: CORINTFIN

Senior Executive Officers
Resident Representative　　　R Bruce Leighton

Lloyds Bank plc　　　　　　　　　　　　　　　Full Branch Office

Avenida Jurubatuba 73, 4°/10° andares, São Paulo SP 04583-900
Tel: (11) 5504 6855; (11) 5504 6249 Fax: (11) 5504 6403; (11) 5504 6373 Swift: LLOYD BRSP
Email: lloydsbank.br@lloydsbank.com.br
Website: www.lloydsbank.com.br

Senior Executive Officers
Chief Executive Officer　　　Frederick H Gibbs *Regional Director, Latin America-South Region*
　　　　　　　　　　　　☏ **5504 6701**
Financial Director　　　Carlos Candido da Silva *Senior Manager, Financial Division* ☏ **5504 6269**
General Manager, Brazil　　　David V Thomas ☏ **5504 6234**

Others (Senior Executives)
Financial Resources & Products　　　Leonard Plant *Assistant General Manager* ☏ **5504 6913**
Commercial Area　　　Roberto Paschoali *Assistant General Manager* ☏ **5504 6913**

www.euromoneydirectory.com						BRAZIL (+55)

General-Lending (DCM, SL)
Head of Corporate Banking		Antonio L Morad *Senior Manager, Corporate & Investment Banking*
					☎ 5504 6571

General - Treasury
Head of Treasury			Reinaldo Le Grazie *Senior Manager* ☎ 5504 6302

Global Custody
Regional Head				Monica Santos ☎ 5504 6849

Other (Global Custody)
US					Neusa Bulcão ☎ +1 (212) 607 5329 F +1 (212) 607 4969
UK					Sergio Gullo ☎ +44 (171) 661 4629

Other Departments
Chief Credit Officer			Nilton Santos ☎ 5504 6293
Private Banking			Dilson Oliveira *Senior Manager* ☎ 5504 6950
Debt Recovery / Restructuring		Paulos F Raus ☎ 5504 6293

Administration
Head of Marketing			Marisa Nannini *Manager* ☎ 5504 6456

Technology & Systems
					Luiz Roberto Amato *Manager* ☎ 5504 6488

Legal / In-House Counsel
					Guilherme Oliveira *Senior Manager* ☎ 5504 6405

Corporate Communications
International Marketing		Marisa Nannini *Manager* ☎ 5504 6456

Accounts / Audit
Audit					Alexandre Kealman *Manager* ☎ 5504 6922

Other (Administration)
Human Resource			Monica Bighe *Manager* ☎ 5504 6809
Distribution				Lucio Moura Neto *Manager* ☎ 5504 6957

# London Forfaiting do Brasil Ltda					Subsidiary Company

Avenida das Nacoes Unidas 12551, World Trade Center, 17° andar, São Paulo SP 04578-903
Tel: (11) 3043 7197; (11) 3043 7198 **Fax:** (11) 3043 7249 **Email:** lfc.brasil@forfaiting.com.br

Senior Executive Officers
Managing Director			Donald Marsjanik

Others (Senior Executives)
					Gilberto Yamamuro *Manager*

# Merita Bank Plc/Nordbanken AB (publ)				Representative Office

Rua Oscar Freire 379-cj 122, São Paulo SP 01426-001
Tel: (11) 881 9499 **Fax:** (11) 881 9368 **Email:** merita.nordbanken@br2001.com.br

Senior Executive Officers
Representative			Alexandra Kettis

# Merrill Lynch									Full Branch Office

Edificio Centro Cultural de Brasil, Av Presidente Wilson 231 C: 1801, Rio de Janeiro RJ 20030-021
Tel: (21) 3175 4078 **Fax:** (21) 3175 4045
Website: www.ml.com

# Midland Bank plc								Representative Office

Avenida das Nações Unidas 11541, 10° andar, São Paulo SP 04578-00
Tel: (11) 5504 4213 **Fax:** (11) 5504 4212

Senior Executive Officers
Group Representative			Frank Legori
Group Representative			Harvey Lawson

Euromoney Directory 1999   **197**

BRAZIL (+55) www.euromoneydirectory.com

Royal Bank of Canada
Representative Office

Avenida Paulista 460, 14° andar, São Paulo SP 01310-904
Tel: (11) 289 3911 Fax: (11) 284 0508

Senior Executive Officers
VP & Representative Duarte M Miranda ⓔ duarte.miranda@royalbank.com
Others (Senior Executives)
Deputy Country Manager Juan M Lahens ⓔ juan.lahens@royalbank.com
General-Lending (DCM, SL)
Head of Corporate Banking Rui Y Matsuda ⓔ rui.matsuda@royalbank.com
Other Departments
Correspondent Banking Claudia M Leao *Manager* ⓣ 289 3110 ⓔ claudia.leao@royalbank.com

The Sakura Bank Limited

12° andar, 1274 Avenida Paulista, Conjunto 31, Bela Vista, São Paulo SP
Tel: (11) 283 0844 Fax: (11) 251 0054; (11) 251 3811 Telex: 01122864 MITK BR

Senior Executive Officers
Chief Representative Tatsuo Usami

The Sanwa Bank Limited
Representative Office

Avenida Ipiranga 282, 3° andar, Centro, São Paulo SP 01046-010
Tel: (11) 235 9488; (11) 256 1144 Fax: (11) 257 2740 Telex: 1130050 SANW

Senior Executive Officers
Chief Representative Taro Kawamura ⓣ 257 1481

Standard Chartered Bank
Representative Office

Rua da Ajuda 35, Cobertura-31° andar, Rio de Janeiro RJ 20040-000
Tel: (21) 262 4172 Fax: (21) 220 9735

Senior Executive Officers
SVP & Country Manager Elizabeth M Henshaw

The Tokai Bank Limited
Representative Office

Rua Libero Badaro 377, Sala 910, São Paulo SP 01009
Tel: (11) 3106 9071 Fax: (11) 3106 3896 Telex: 1135366 TASL BR

Senior Executive Officers
Chief Representative Akira Tsunekawa

UNIBANCO-União de Bancos Brasileiros SA
Head Office

15th Floor, 891 Eusebio Matoso Avenue, São Paulo SP 05423-901
PO Box 8185, São Paulo SP
Tel: (11) 867 1313; (11) 867 1626 Fax: (11) 813 6182; (11) 867 4830 Email: ubbir@ibm.net Cable: UNIBANCO
Website: www.unibanco.com.br

Senior Executive Officers
Chairman of the Board Pedro Moreira Salles ⓣ 867 4421 ⓕ 814 8506
Financial Director Cesar Sizenando *CFO* ⓣ 867 4400 ⓕ 816 6400
Others (Senior Executives)
President Wholesale Banking Fernando Sotelino ⓣ 867 1144 ⓕ 814 8506
President Retail Banking Joaquim Francisco Castro Neto ⓣ 867 4222 ⓕ 814 8506
Vice Chairman of the Board Tomas Zinner ⓣ 867 4747 ⓕ 814 8506
President of Unibanco Holdings Israel Vainboim *Member of the Board* ⓣ 867 4444
Administration & Technology Adalberto de Moracs Schettert *Executive Vice President* ⓣ 867 4913
 ⓕ 816 6400
Private Banking Celso Scaramuzza *Executive Vice President* ⓣ 867 4228 ⓕ 816 6400
Retail Banking Danilo Mansur *Executive Vice President* ⓣ 867 4832 ⓕ 814 8506
Credit Corporate Aldo José Facin *Executive Director* ⓣ 867 1928 ⓕ 867 4823
Branches Network Alvaro Sergio do Vale *Executive Director* ⓣ 216 3086 ⓕ 216 3585
Technology Elio Boccia *Executive Director* ⓣ 867 1407 ⓕ 867 1378

Others (Senior Executives) (cont)
Products
Legal Department
Investment Banking

International Area & Treasury
Japan Desk
Marketing Department
German Desk
Corporate Banking

Debt Capital Markets / Fixed Income
Global Head

Country Head
Domestic Government Bonds
Head of Sales

Eurobonds
Head of Origination; Head of Syndication
Head of Sales
Head of Research
Trading - Sovereigns, Corporates, High-yield
Bonds - General
International Capital Markets
Libor-Based / Floating-Rate Products
FRN Origination
FRN Sales; Asset Swaps; Asset Swaps (Sales)
Medium-Term Notes
Head of Origination; Head of Structuring
Head of Sales
Private Placements
Head of Origination
Head of Sales
Head of Structuring
Asset-Backed Securities / Securitization
Global Head
Mortgage-Backed Securities
Global Head

Equity Capital Markets
Head of Equity Capital Markets

Domestic Equities
Head of Origination
Head of Syndication

Head of Sales

Head of Trading
Head of Research
Convertibles / Equity-Linked
Head of Origination
Head of Syndication

Head of Sales

Syndicated Lending
Global Head

Head of Syndication

Loan-Related Activities
Trade Finance
Project Finance
Structured Trade Finance
Leasing & Asset Finance

Geraldo Travaglia *Executive Director* T 867 1706 F 867 4337
Gilberto VB Prado *Executive Director* T 867 4685 F 867 4967
Murilo Kammer *Executive Director, Corporate Finance* T 867 1426
F 867 4823
Sérgio Zappa *Executive Director* T 867 4850 F 815 1151
Takeshi Watanabe *Executive Director* T 238 7839 F 238 7900
Walter Henrique Schmidt *Executive Director* T 867 1038 F 867 4823
Wilhelm Peter Zeise *Executive Director* T 867 4705 F 867 1226
Alvaro Sá Freire *Executive Director* T 867 1636 F 867 4823

Murilo Kammer *Executive Director, Corporate Finance* T 867 1426
F 867 4823
Marcio Guedes *Director, Corporate Finance* T 867 1246 F 867 4823

Dauro Zaltman *Director, Domestic Sales & Distribution* T 867 1616
F 813 2675

Luiz Mauricio Jardim *Director, Corporate Finance* T 867 4850 F 815 1151
Pedro Bastos *Director, Asset Trading* T 867 4064 F 867 4408
Flavio Dania *Director, Research* T 867 1622 F 813 2675
Luiz Mauricio Jardim *Director, Asset Trading* T 867 4850 F 815 1151

Luiz Mauricio Jardim *Director, Asset Trading* T 867 4850 F 815 1151

Marcio Guedes *Director, Corporate Finance* T 867 1246 F 867 4823
Luiz Mauricio Jardim *Director, Asset Trading* T 867 4850 F 815 1151

Marcio Guedes *Director, Corporate Finance* T 867 1246 F 867 4823
Daniel Kenna *Superintendent* T 867 4993 F 813 2675

Marcio Guedes *Director, Corporate Finance* T 867 1246 F 867 4823
Daniel Kenna *Superintendent* T 867 4993 F 813 2675
Marcio Guedes *Director, Corporate Finance* T 867 1246 F 867 4823

Marcio Guedes *Director, Corporate Finance* T 867 1246 F 867 4823

Marcio Guedes *Director, Corporate Finance* T 867 1246 F 867 4823

Murilo Kammer *Executive Director, Corporate Finance* T 867 1426
F 867 4823
Gustava Heller *Director, Corporate Finance* T 867 1799 F 813 2675

Gustava Heller *Director, Corporate Finance* T 867 1799 F 813 2675
Dauro Zaltman *Director, Domestic Sales & Distribution* T 867 1616
F 813 2675
Pedro Bastos *Director, Int'l & Domestic Sales & Distribution* T 867 4065
F 867 4408
Luiz Mauricio Jardim *Director, Asset Trading* T 867 4850 F 815 1151
Flavio Dania *Director, Macro Economic Research* T 867 1622 F 813 2675

Gustava Heller *Director, Corporate Finance* T 867 1799 F 813 2675
Dauro Zaltman *Director, Domestic Sales & Distribution* T 867 1616
F 813 2675
Pedro Bastos *Director, Int'l & Domestic Sales & Distribution* T 867 4065
F 867 4408

Sergio Zappa *Executive Director, International Area & Treasury*
T 867 4850 F 815 1151
Luiz Mauricio Jardim *Director, International Capital Markets* T 867 4850
F 815 1151
Luiz Mauricio Jardim *Director, Asset Trading* T 867 4850 F 815 1151

Angelo Vasconcellos *Director, Forex Trading* T 867 4180 F 813 7972
Adhemar Kajita *Superintendent, Corporate Finance* T 867 4235 F 867 4823
Carlos Catraio *Director, Correspondent Banking* T 867 1611 F 814 0528
Daniro Kahil *Director, Corporate Products* T 867 1444 F 238 7882

Euromoney Directory 1999 199

BRAZIL (+55)　　　　　　　www.euromoneydirectory.com

UNIBANCO-União de Bancos Brasileiros SA (cont)

Money Markets
Global Head　　　　　　　　　　Sergio Zappa *Director, Treasury* ☏ **867 4850** 🖷 **815 1151**
Country Head　　　　　　　　　Reinaldo Rios *Director* ☏ **867 1234** 🖷 **813 7972**

Domestic Commercial Paper
Head of Origination　　　　　　Marcio Guedes *Director, Corporate Finance* ☏ **867 1246** 🖷 **867 4823**
Head of Sales　　　　　　　　　Pedro Bastos *Director, Domestic Sales & Distribution* ☏ **867 4064**
　　　　　　　　　　　　　　　🖷 **867 4408**

Eurocommercial Paper
Head of Origination　　　　　　Luiz Mauricio Jardim *Director, Corporate Finance* ☏ **867 4850** 🖷 **815 1151**

Foreign Exchange
Global Head　　　　　　　　　　Sergio Zappa *Executive Director, Forex Trading* ☏ **867 4850** 🖷 **815 1151**
Head of Institutional Sales; Corporate Sales;　Angelo Vasconcellos *Director, Forex Trading* ☏ **867 4180** 🖷 **813 7972**
Head of Trading

Risk Management
Global Head　　　　　　　　　　Cesar Sizenando *CFO, Credit & Risk Management* ☏ **867 4400** 🖷 **816 6400**
Regional Head　　　　　　　　　Fernando Pinheiro *Superintendent, Risk Management* ☏ **867 1805**
　　　　　　　　　　　　　　　🖷 **867 4276**

Fixed Income Derivatives / Risk Management
Global Head　　　　　　　　　　Cesar Sizenando *CFO, Credit & Risk Management* ☏ **867 4400** 🖷 **816 6400**

Foreign Exchange Derivatives / Risk Management
Cross-Currency Swaps, Sales / Marketing　Fernando Pinheiro *Superintendent, Risk Management* ☏ **867 1805**
　　　　　　　　　　　　　　　🖷 **867 4276**

Corporate Finance / M&A Advisory
Global Head　　　　　　　　　　Murilo Kammer *Executive Director, Investment Banking* ☏ **867 1426**
　　　　　　　　　　　　　　　🖷 **867 4823**
Regional Head　　　　　　　　　Eduardo Luzio *Superintendent, M&A* ☏ **867 1548**

Settlement / Clearing
Regional Head　　　　　　　　　Jamil Farath *Director, Investor Services* ☏ **867 4554** 🖷 **867 4408**

Other Departments
Proprietary Trading; Private Banking　　Celso Scaramuzza *EVP, Private Banking* ☏ **867 4228** 🖷 **816 6400**
Correspondent Banking　　　　　Carlos Catraio *Director, Correspondent Banking* ☏ **867 1611** 🖷 **814 0528**
　　　　　　　　　　　　　　　Francisco Castro Limo *Director, Correspondent Banking* ☏ **867 1611**

Administration
Technology & Systems
　　　　　　　　　　　　　　　Adalberto de Moracs Schettert *Executive Vice President* ☏ **867 4913**
　　　　　　　　　　　　　　　🖷 **816 6400**

Legal / In-House Counsel
　　　　　　　　　　　　　　　Gilberto VB Prado *Executive Director* ☏ **867 4685** 🖷 **867 4967**

Other (Administration)
Investor Relations　　　　　　　Julia H. Reid *Superintendent, Investor Relations* ☏ **867 1313** 🖷 **813 6182**

Union Européenne de CIC　　　　　　　　　　　　　　Representative Office

Avenida Paulista 2073, São Paulo SP 01311-940
Tel: (11) 251 1421 **Fax:** (11) 288 7468

Senior Executive Officers
Chief Representative　　　　　　Alain Costilhes ☏ **251 1421**

BRUNEI
(+673)

Brunei Currency Board　　　　　　　　　　　　　　🏛 Central Bank

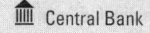

Old Secretariat Building, Ministry of Finance, Bandar Seri Begawan, 1906
Tel: (2) 224 022; (2) 224 032 **Fax:** (2) 241 559 **Telex:** 2622 WANGBRU

Senior Executive Officers
Secretary　　　　　　　　　　　Mahadi Ibrahim ☏ **222 095**

Others (Senior Executives)
Head, Banking Supervisioni　　　Khalid Ghazali *Director, Financial Institutions* ☏ **239 226**

Settlement / Clearing
Operations　　　　　　　　　　　Hoe Siang Teo *Financial Officer*

www.euromoneydirectory.com   BULGARIA (+359)

Administration
Head of Administration   Osman Tengah
Head of Marketing   Suraya Jaidin
Accounts / Audit
Head, Accountancy   Tsueing Yap *Financial Officer*

BULGARIA
(+359)

Bulgarian National Bank   🏛 Central Bank
1 Alexander Battenberg Square, BG-1000 Sofia
Tel: (2) 855 1 **Fax:** (2) 980 2425; (2) 980 6493 **Telex:** 24090 BNB BG **Swift:** BNBG BG SF **Reuters:** NBOB
Telerate: 39618, 41179, 41340 **Telex:** 24091 BNB BG; **Reuters:** BGBNB1-4; BGBNB7

Senior Executive Officers
Governor   Svetoslav Gavriiski
General Secretary   Velizar Stoilov ☎ **886 1592**

Others (Senior Executives)
                                      Roumen Avramov *Member of the Management Board*
                                      Garabed Minassian *Member of the Management Board*
                                      Georgi Petrov *Member of the Management Board*
Banking Department   Valentin Tsvetanov *Deputy Governor* ☎ **886 1799**
Issue Department   Martin Zaimov *Deputy Governor* ☎ **886 1201**
Banking Supervision Department   Emilia Milanova *Deputy Governor* ☎ **886 1208**
Fiscal Services Department   Nikolina Mitcheva ☎ **886 1530**

Administration

Legal / In-House Counsel
Chief Legal Advisor   Dimitar Ananiev ☎ **886 1277**

Public Relations
Protocol & Press Office   Georgi Atanassoff ☎ **886 1203**

Other (Administration)
Personnel Management   Christina Milanova ☎ **886 1361**

Bayerisch-Bulgarische Handelsbank   Subsidiary Company
36 Alabin Straße, BG-1000 Sofia
Tel: (2) 981 0500; (2) 980 3303 **Fax:** (2) 980 5313

Equity Capital Markets

Equity Repo / Securities Lending
Marketing & Product Development   Peter Schönenberger *Vice President* ☎ **437 4184**

BNP-Dresdner Bank (Bulgaria) AD   Subsidiary Company
11 Narodno Sabranie Square, BG-1000 Sofia
PO Box 11, Sofia
Tel: (2) 980 1237; (2) 980 8870 **Fax:** (2) 981 6991 **Telex:** 06722295 **Swift:** BNDB BG SX
Email: pobox@bnpdreba.ttm.bg **Reuters:** BSBD **Telerate:** 41337

Senior Executive Officers
General Manager   Xavier de Beausse
Deputy General Manager   Werner Fick ☎ **981 3920**
International Division   Vladimir Georgiev *International Manager*

Others (Senior Executives)
                                      Alberto Suarez *Credit Manager*
                                      Daniel Bobelet *Operation Manager*

General-Lending (DCM, SL)
Head of Corporate Banking   Stefan Dachsel *Corporate Manager*

General - Treasury
Head of Treasury   Ivaylo Liubomirov *Treasury Manager*

BULGARIA (+359)　　　　　www.euromoneydirectory.com

BULBANK Ltd
Head Office

BULBANK Ltd.
7 Sveta Nedelya Square, BG-1000 Sofia
Tel: (2) 9841 1111 Fax: (2) 988 4636; (2) 988 5370 Telex: 22031 Swift: BFTB BG SF Email: info@sof.bulbank.bg
Reuters: BULB
Website: www.bulbank.bg

Senior Executive Officers
Chairman & Chief Executive　　　　　Chavdar Kantchev
Deputy Chairman　　　　　　　　　　Ventsislav Antonov
Chief Executive Officer　　　　　　　 Chavdar Kantchev *Chairman & Chief Executive*

Others (Senior Executives)

Dimiter Atanassov *Member of the Board & Managing Director*
Plamen Oresharski *Member of the Board*
Kiril Kalinov *Member of the Board & Executive Vice President*
Anton Saldjiiski *Member of the Board*
Kiril Stefanov *Member of the Board & Executive Vice President*

General - Treasury
Head of Treasury　　　　　　　　　 Kalinka Kirova *Manager, Treasury* ☎ **9841 2560** ℻ **981 9171**

Settlement / Clearing
Settlement (General)　　　　　　　　Petar Kalinov *Manager, International Payments & Investigations*
　　　　　　　　　　　　　　　　　　☎ **9841 2328**

Global Custody
Head of Global Custody　　　　　　　Radostina Radeva *Manager* ☎ **29841 2420**

Other Departments
Correspondent Banking　　　　　　　 Slavyana Kalaidjieva *Manager* ☎ **9841 2282**

Bulgarian Post Bank Limited
Head Office

1 Bulgaria Square, BG-1414 Sofia
Tel: (2) 963 2104; (2) 963 2105 Fax: (2) 963 0482 Telex: 22290 Swift: BPBI BG SF Email: intldiv@postbank.bg
Reuters: BPBB Telerate: 38266

Senior Executive Officers
Chairman, Board of Directors & Executive　　Vladimir Vladimirov ☎ **963 4461**
Financial Director　　　　　　　　　　　　　Reni Petkova *Member & Director* ☎ **981 2175**
Chief Operating Officer　　　　　　　　　　 Evgeni Todorov *Director & Member of the Board* ☎ **963 1275**
Company Secretary　　　　　　　　　　　　Jordan Trenkov ☎ **963 2871**
International Division　　　　　　　　　　　Irena Mildova ☎ **963 0478**

Others (Senior Executives)
Head of Economic Research & Analysis Div　Teodora Stoyanova ☎ **963 2104 ext 541**
Head Local Currancy Div　　　　　　　　　 Andrei Andreev ☎ **951 6839**
Head Money & Capital Markets Division　　 Assen Yagodin *Head, MM & Government Securities Div* ☎ **951 6835**
Treasury & FX Division　　　　　　　　　　 Detelina Georgieva *Senior Expert* ☎ **963 4043**

Debt Capital Markets / Fixed Income
Global Head　　　　　　　　　　　　　　　 Assen Yagodin *Head, MM & Government Securities Div* ☎ **951 6835**

Domestic Government Bonds
Head of Sales　　　　　　　　　　　　　　 Ivan Valchev *Senior Expert* ☎ **951 6835**

Syndicated Lending
Global Head of Credit Committee　　　　　 Krasimira Saeva *Head of Loan Department* ☎ **963 0467**

Foreign Exchange
Global Head　　　　　　　　　　　　　　　 Ivaylo Lubomirov *Head, Treasury & Forex Division* ☎ **963 0081**

FX Traders / Sales People
Local currency operations　　　　　　　　　Andrei Andreev *Head* ☎ **951 6839**

Other Departments
Chief Credit Officer　　　　　　　　　　　　Krasimira Saeva *Head of Loan Department* ☎ **963 0467**
Correspondent Banking　　　　　　　　　　Vassil Cherpokov ☎ **963 3644**

Administration

Technology & Systems
　　　　　　　　　　　　　　　　　　　　　 Jordan Trenkov ☎ **963 2871**

Legal / In-House Counsel
　　　　　　　　　　　　　　　　　　　　　 Lachezar Tchuturkov *Head of Division* ☎ **963 0474**

Public Relations
　　　　　　　　　　　　　　　　　　　　　 Silva Maximova ☎ **963 0091**

www.euromoneydirectory.com BULGARIA (+359)

Accounts / Audit
Marina Kozovska ☎ 963 4066

Other (Administration)
Business Development Veselin Martchovski ☎ 963 2015

B

Bulgarian Russian Investment Bank plc
Head Office

Alternative trading name: BRIBank
11A Saborna Street, BG-1000 Sofia
Tel: (2) 860 7240; (2) 860 7301 **Fax:** (2) 981 2526; (2) 981 9453 **Telex:** 23008 BRIB BG **Swift:** BUIB BG SF
Email: postmaster@hq.bribank.bg **Reuters:** BRIB

Senior Executive Officers
Chairman of the Board	Krassimir Angarski
Chief Executive Officer	Vladimir Penchev *Executive Director* ☎ 860 7308
	Jordon Donchev *Executive Director* ☎ 981 0530
Chief Operating Officer	Svetoslav Bojilov *Procurator* ☎ 860 1750
Procurator	Ivan Nenkov ☎ 8858 4680
Trade Representative	Konstantin Nenov ☎ 8853 2260
Trade Representative	Hristina Filipova ☎ 981 1747
Secretary	Meglena Parvanova ☎ 981 6990
International Division	Georgy Dimitrov *Head of International Payments* ☎ 980 1634
Trade Representative	Rositsa Lisitchkova ☎ 981 2151
Relationship Manager	
International Payments	Mincho Mihov *Chief* ☎ 860 7210

Debt Capital Markets / Fixed Income
Department: Foreign Exchange & Securities Trading
Tel: 981 6929 **Fax:** 981 9453
Head of Fixed Income Trading Anastas Petrov *Head of Trading* ☎ 981 6929

Government Bonds
Head of Trading Anastas Petrov *Head of Trading* ☎ 981 6929

Emerging Market Bonds
Head of Trading Anastas Petrov *Head of Trading* ☎ 981 6929

Fixed-Income Research
Head of Fixed Income Stefan Iliev *Head of Research* ☎ 860 7234

Equity Capital Markets
Equity Research
Country Head Danail Kamenov *Head of Research* ☎ 860 7371 📠 981 3800

Money Markets
Tel: 981 6929 **Fax:** 981 9453 **Reuters:** BRIB
Head of Money Markets Anastas Petrov *Head of Trading* ☎ 981 6929

Foreign Exchange
Tel: 980 8939 **Reuters:** BRIB
Head of Foreign Exchange Encho Staikov *Dealer* ☎ 980 8939
Global Head Plamen Milkov ☎ 981 0525

FX Traders / Sales People
Dimitar Dmitrov *Dealer* ☎ 980 8939

Risk Management
Foreign Exchange Derivatives / Risk Management
Cross-Currency Swaps, Sales / Marketing Sasho Petrov *Dealer* ☎ 860 7224
Encho Staikov *Dealer* ☎ 980 8939
Boyan Milenkov *Dealer* ☎ 860 7219
Cross-Currency Swaps, Trading Sasho Petrov *Dealer* ☎ 860 7224
Encho Staikov *Dealer* ☎ 980 8939
Boyan Milenkov *Dealer* ☎ 860 7219

Exotic Options (Barriers, Range, Timers, Digitals, Faders etc)
Sales Ivan Nenkov *Procurator* ☎ 8858 4680

Asset Management
Head Ivo Stoikov *Head of Asset Management* ☎ 980 7019

Other Departments
Correspondent Banking Boriana Marinova *Expert* ☎ 860 7213
Cash Management Goergy Milenkov ☎ 860 7233

Administration
Technology & Systems
IT Division Ivo Popov ☎ 981 7019

➡

Euromoney Directory 1999 **203**

BULGARIA (+359)   www.euromoneydirectory.com

Bulgarian Russian Investment Bank plc (cont)
Legal / In-House Counsel
　　　　Maria Rashkova ☏ 980 8955
Public Relations
　　　　Teodora Angelova ☏ 980 7735
Accounts / Audit
　　　　Dafin Sredkov *Internal Control* ☏ 860 7420

Central Cooperative Bank   Head Office
103 Rakovski Street, BG-1000 Sofia
Tel: (2) 9844 3237; (2) 9844 3241 **Fax:** (2) 9844 3202; (2) 83 5453 **Telex:** 24066 CCB **Swift:** CECB BG SF
Reuters: CCBS

Senior Executive Officers
Chairman & Chief Executive　　　　Stoyan Alexandrov ☏ **987 4007**
Executive Director　　　　　　　　Dimitar Kostov ☏ **981 0977**
Chief Executive Officer　　　　　　Yuei Popov *Executive Director* ☏ **980 4387**
International Division　　　　　　Tzvetan Vassilev ☏ **9844 3229**
General - Treasury
Head of Treasury　　　　　　　　Veronika Gecheva *Director of Treasury Department* ☏ **9844 3244**
Debt Capital Markets / Fixed Income
Head of Sales　　　　　　　　　　Orlin Rusev *Director, MM & Domestic Gov't Bonds* ☏ **9844 3235**
Equity Capital Markets
Domestic Equities
Head of Sales　　　　　　　　　　Ljubomir Hristov
Syndicated Lending
Head of Credit Committee　　　　Georgi Bojinov ☏ **9844 3686**
Loan-Related Activities
Trade Finance　　　　　　　　　　Metodi Tachev *Head of L / C Department* ☏ **9844 3238**
Money Markets
Global Head　　　　　　　　　　Orlin Rusev *Director, MM & Domestic Gov't Bonds* ☏ **9844 3235**
Foreign Exchange
Tel: 9844 3250 **Reuters:** CCBS
Head of Foreign Exchange　　　　Docho Karadochev *Director, Foreign Exchange* ☏ **9844 3250** 🖷 **987 1948**
Other Departments
Chief Credit Officer　　　　　　　Georgi Bojinov ☏ **9844 3686**
Correspondent Banking　　　　　Emil Hristov ☏ **9844 3237** 🖷 **9844 3202**
Other Departments
International Payments Department　Ilian Zafirov *Director* ☏ **9844 3241**
Administration
Head of Administration　　　　　Tarpo Bojilov *Head of Administration* ☏ **9844 3221**
Legal / In-House Counsel
　　　　　　　　　　　　　　　Ivo Goranov ☏ **9844 3685**

Commercial Bank Biochim plc   Head Office
1 Ivan Vazov Street, BG-1040 Sofia
Tel: (2) 861 69 **Fax:** (2) 981 9151; (2) 988 1147 **Telex:** 23921 **Swift:** CBBI BG SF **Reuters:** CBBB
General Telex: 24757
Website: www.biochim.bg

Senior Executive Officers
Chairman of the Management Board　Evgeni Chachev ☏ **987 5283** 🖷 **981 9360**
Chief Executive Officer　　　　　　Tencho Tenev *Executive Director* ☏ **980 6506**
Financial Director　　　　　　　　Krassimir Koev *Executive Director* ☏ **980 5741**
Chief Operating Officer　　　　　　Tsvetan Tsekov *Executive Director* ☏ **980 6542**
Treasurer　　　　　　　　　　　Ventzislav Lubomirov *Chief of Markets & Investments Division* ☏ **987 8984**
International Division　　　　　　Philip Alev *Chief of International Operations Division* ☏ **980 6510**
Debt Capital Markets / Fixed Income
Department: Investment & Privatisation Department
Tel: 980 6537 **Fax:** 988 1147
Head of Fixed Income　　　　　　Ventzislav Lubomirov ☏ **987 8984**
Government Bonds
Head of Trading　　　　　　　　Kamen Kalchev *Chief Dealer* ☏ **981 1483**

204　Euromoney Directory 1999

www.euromoneydirectory.com　　　　**BULGARIA (+359)**

Emerging Market Bonds
Head of Trading　　　　　　　　　Dimiter Koutelov *Securities Dealer* T **861 6570**
Equity Capital Markets
Head of Equity Capital Markets　　Sava Stoynov T **981 1472** F **980 6537**
Domestic Equities
Head of Trading　　　　　　　　　Krassimir Marinov *Broker* T **981 1472**
Money Markets
Head of Money Markets　　　　　　Roumen Denkov *Dealer* T **980 0641**
Foreign Exchange
Tel: 980 4944 **Fax:** 988 1147
Head of Trading　　　　　　　　　George Kissov *Chief Dealer* T **861 6570**
FX Traders / Sales People
　　　　　　　　　　　　　　　　　Vladimir Tenev *Dealer* T **980 4944**
　　　　　　　　　　　　　　　　　Ivo Nikolov *Dealer* T **980 4946**
Settlement / Clearing
Operations; Back-Office　　　　　Elena Gerdjeva *Head* T **980 3736**
Other Departments
Correspondent Banking　　　　　　Stefan Stoev *Head* T **980 4926** F **988 1147**
Administration
Head of Administration　　　　　Ludmilla Stoeva T **980 6514**
Business Development　　　　　　Galina Gavrailova *Head of Department* T **980 5719**
Technology & Systems
　　　　　　　　　　　　　　　　　Ognian Drenski *Director* T **981 9149**
Legal / In-House Counsel
　　　　　　　　　　　　　　　　　Ivan Kolev *Director* T **980 6533**
Public Relations
　　　　　　　　　　　　　　　　　Stanka Dineva T **980 0420**
Accounts / Audit
　　　　　　　　　　　　　　　　　Todor Hristoskov *Chief Accountant* T **988 4406**

Commercial Bank Expressbank AD　　　　　　　　　　　Head Office

Alternative trading name: Expressbank
　　　　　　　　　　92 VI Varnenchik Boulevard, BG-9000 Varna
Tel: (52) 660 0; (52) 600 480 **Fax:** (52) 601 601 **Telex:** 77303 **Swift:** TTBB BG 22 **Reuters:** TBVB
Senior Executive Officers
Executive Director　　　　　　　Ivan Konstantinov T **601 681**
Company Secretary　　　　　　　Georgi Appostolov T **601 688**
International Division　　　　　Simeon Gospodinov T **601 382**
Others (Senior Executives)
Executive Director　　　　　　　Maria Dobreva *Executive Director* T **601 683**
　　　　　　　　　　　　　　　　　Krassimir Zhilov *Executive Director* T **601 383**
Head of Financial Analysis　　　Plamen Dobrev *Head of Credit* T **601 548**
Expert Documentary Payments　　Emilian Blagoichev T **600 471**
Expert Guarantees　　　　　　　Nedyalka Nikolova T **600 471**
Expert Cheque Clearing Services　Galina Doichinova T **600 0 ext 547**
General - Treasury
Head of Treasury　　　　　　　　Rumyana Petrova *Head of Treasury Division*
Money Markets
Head of Money Markets　　　　　Penka Stefanova *Expert* T **601 549**
Foreign Exchange
Head of Foreign Exchange　　　　Todor Todorov *Chief FX Dealer* T **602 368**
Other Departments
Chief Credit Officer　　　　　　Plamen Dobrev *Head of Credit* T **601 548**
Correspondent Banking　　　　　Yuri Loutchev T **600 0 ext 549**
Administration
Head of Marketing　　　　　　　Lyudmila Dimitrova T **600 241**
Technology & Systems
　　　　　　　　　　　　　　　　　Yanosh Ivanov *Head of Department* T **602 364**
Public Relations
　　　　　　　　　　　　　　　　　Lyudmila Dimitrova T **600 241**
Accounts / Audit
　　　　　　　　　　　　　　　　　Keratsa Dimova *Chief Accountant* T **601 393**

BULGARIA (+359)   www.euromoneydirectory.com

Credit Bank plc
Head Office

3 Angel Kanchev Street, BG-1000 Sofia
Tel: (2) 980 0074; (2) 981 0113 **Fax:** (2) 981 6398; (2) 981 8905 **Telex:** 24600 **Swift:** CRBGBGSF
Email: credit-bank-plc-sofia@ibm.net **Reuters:** CBSF

Senior Executive Officers
Chairman of the Managing Board — Ivailo Bojkov ☏ **981 8914**
Chief Executive Officer — Vladimir Bonev *Executive Director* ☏ **981 8903**
                         Milcho Vassilev *Executive Director* ☏ **981 6406**
Financial Director — Mihael Djambazov *Chief Accountant* ☏ **987 1585**
Treasurer — Volodia Voisky *Bank Liquidity & Capital Markets* ☏ **981 8903**
Deputy Managing Director — Vesselin Blagoev ☏ **980 7306**

Equity Capital Markets
Tel: 981 8903 **Fax:** 875 567
Global Head — Volodia Voisky *Bank Liquidity & Capital Markets* ☏ **981 8903**

Money Markets
Tel: 981 8903 **Fax:** 875 567
Global Head — Volodia Voisky *Bank Liquidity & Capital Markets* ☏ **981 8903**

Foreign Exchange
Tel: 981 8920 **Fax:** 981 6407
Global Head — Peter Novkov *Chief Dealer* ☏ **981 8920**

Risk Management
Foreign Exchange Derivatives / Risk Management
Cross-Currency Swaps, Sales / Marketing — Peter Novkov *Chief Dealer* ☏ **981 8920**
Cross-Currency Swaps, Trading — Nanko Kolev *Dealer* ☏ **981 8920**

Other Departments
Correspondent Banking — Krassimira Radoulova *Manager, International Department* ☏ **987 6141**
                       Ivan Garistov *Manager, International Department* ☏ **987 6141**

Administration
Technology & Systems
                       Ginka Petrova *Director, IT* ☏ **980 5291**

Legal / In-House Counsel
                       Bistra Panova ☏ **980 2081**

Public Relations
                       Vesselin Blagoev *Deputy Managing Director* ☏ **980 7306**

European Bank for Reconstruction & Development
Representative Office

17 Moskovska Street, BG-1000 Sofia
Tel: (2) 987 6611 **Fax:** (2) 981 5336

Senior Executive Officers
Resident Representative — Jean-Marc Peterschmitt

First East International Bank

10 Legue Street, BG-1000 Sofia
Tel: (2) 980 3322; (2) 84759 **Fax:** (2) 801 221 **Telex:** 23319 FEIBSFBG **Swift:** FEIB BG SF **Reuters:** FEIB

Senior Executive Officers
Chairman & President — Anna Sabeva ☏ **988 5185**
Chief Executive Officer — Rossitsa Tosheva *Executive Director* ☏ **981 4840**
Financial Director — Anton Gatchev *Chief Accountant* ☏ **987 9269**
Treasurer — Borislav Chilikov *Director, Treasury* ☏ **883 122**
International Division — Ira Zlatanova *Director, International Division* ☏ **803 957**

Money Markets
Tel: 91137 **Fax:** 981 2333
Head of Money Markets — Valeri Raykov *Head, FX & Money Markets*

Other Departments
Correspondent Banking — Boryana Sirakova ☏ **803 865**
Cash Management — Plamen Todorov *Foreign Exchange, Cash Management* ☏ **980 0095**

206   Euromoney Directory 1999

BULGARIA (+359)

Administration
Head of Administration   Kostadin Spassov *General Secretary* ☏ 980 9922

Technology & Systems
Valentin Iliev *Director, IT Department* ☏ 845 5171

First Investment Bank Limited   Head Office
10 Stefan Karadja Str, BG-1000 Sofia
Tel: (2) 910 01 **Fax:** (2) 980 5033 **Telex:** 25 085 **Swift:** FINVBGSF **Email:** fib@fibankbg **Reuters:** BFIB

Senior Executive Officers
Executive Director   Ivaylo Mutafchiev ☏ 980 2442
Executive Director   Tzeko Minev ☏ 981 1881
Financial Director   Bozhidar Grigorov *Chief Accountant* ☏ 980 3017
Treasurer   Ognian Yordanov *Chief Treasurer* ☏ 981 5911
Company Secretary   Sirma Arnaudova ☏ 91001
International Division   Maya Georgieva *Executive Director, Head of International Loan Dep*
                               ☏ 981 3091

Debt Capital Markets / Fixed Income
Tel: 980 8257 **Fax:** 981 0269
Head of Fixed Income   Victor Metchkarov *Chief Dealer* ☏ 980 8659
Head of Fixed Income Sales   Damian Georgiev *Dealer, Capital Markets* ☏ 980 1212
Head of Fixed Income Trading Vladimir Mintchev *Dealer, Money Markets* ☏ 980 8659

Domestic Government Bonds
Head of Sales   Damian Georgiev *Dealer, Capital Markets* ☏ 980 1212
Head of Trading   Vladimir Mintchev *Dealer, Money Markets* ☏ 980 8659
Head of Research   Victor Metchkarov *Chief Dealer* ☏ 980 8659

Non-Domestic Government Bonds
Bulgarian Brady Bonds (USD); US Treasury   Victor Metchkarov *Chief Dealer* ☏ 980 8659
Bonds

Equity Capital Markets
Head of Equity Capital Markets   Maria Sharlandjieva *Dealer* ☏ 980 1212

Syndicated Lending
Global Head   Matthew Mateev *Director, Credit Department* ☏ 981 1075

Loan-Related Activities
Trade Finance; Project Finance   Matthew Mateev *Director, Credit Department* ☏ 981 1075

Money Markets
Tel: 980 9465 **Fax:** 981 0269
Head of Money Markets   Jordan Skortchev *Chief Dealer, FX* ☏ 980 9465

Wholesale Deposits
Head of Sales   Nikolay Dragomiretzki *FX Dealer* ☏ 980 9869

Foreign Exchange
Tel: 980 9465 **Fax:** 981 0269
Global Head   Jordan Skortchev *Chief Dealer, FX* ☏ 980 9465
Regional Head   Nikolay Dragomiretzki *FX Dealer* ☏ 980 9869
Corporate Sales   Albena Grigorova *FX Dealer* ☏ 980 9869

Settlement / Clearing
Head of Settlement / Clearing   Ognian Yordanov *Chief Treasurer* ☏ 981 5911

Other Departments
Chief Credit Officer   Matthew Mateev *Executive Director, Head of Loan Department* ☏ 981 1075
Correspondent Banking   Maya Georgieva *Executive Director, Head of International Loan Dep*
                               ☏ 981 3091
Cash Management   Bozhidar Grigorov *Chief Accountant* ☏ 980 3017

Administration
Head of Administration   Mariana Shivarova ☏ 980 7451
Business Development; Head of Marketing   Rumen Nanov *Director* ☏ 981 5509

Legal / In-House Counsel
                               Lazar Iliev *Chief Legal Advisor* ☏ 980 0673

Euromoney Directory 1999   **207**

BULGARIA (+359)   www.euromoneydirectory.com

ING Barings
Full Branch Office

7 Vassil Levski Street, BG-1000 Sofia
PO Box 1652, BG-1000 Sofia
Tel: (2) 980 9303; (2) 980 2039 **Fax:** (2) 981 4111 **Telex:** 25156 INGBSOF BG **Swift:** INGB BG SF **Reuters:** SING

Senior Executive Officers
Chief Executive Officer — Thomas G Muzoz *Country Manager*
Peter Rolls *Deputy General Manager*
Financial Director — Diana Miteva *Financial Controller*
Chief Operating Officer — Maarten De Jong *Operations Manager*
Treasurer — Nikolay Stoykov *Treasury Manager* T 980 8063 F 981 5323

Equity Capital Markets
Country Head — Nikolay Stoykov *Treasury Manager* T 980 8063 F 981 5323

Domestic Equities
Head of Research — Roumyana Sotirova

Money Markets
Country Head — Roumen Galabinov T 980 8517

Foreign Exchange
Head of Institutional Sales — Evelina Miltenova T 980 8517
Corporate Sales — Vladimir Popov T 980 8517
Head of Trading — Evelina Miltenova T 980 8517

Risk Management
Country Head — G Athlina *Head, Risk Management*

Global Custody
Country Head — E Beloeva *Head of Custody*

ING Barings

2A Gabrovo Street, BG-9000 Varna
Tel: (52) 665 1100 **Fax:** (52) 665 1190 **Telex:** 77221 INGVAR BG

Senior Executive Officers
Manager — Orlin Toddorov

Ionian Bank

20 Alexander Stamboliisky Boulevard, BG-1000 Sofia
Tel: (2) 981 6554 **Fax:** (2) 981 7779 **Telex:** 24737 IONSOF

Senior Executive Officers
Others (Senior Executives)
Anastasios Stefis *Manager*

Raiffeisenbank (Bulgaria) AD
Subsidiary Company

18/20 Gogol Street, BG-1504 Sofia
PO Box 220, Central Post Office, BG-1000 Sofia
Tel: (2) 919 859 **Fax:** (2) 943 4528 **Telex:** 22006 **Swift:** RZBB BG SF **Reuters:** RBBS

Senior Executive Officers
Chairman of the Management Board — Douglas Dryden T 9198 5541
Chief Executive Officer — Momtchil Andreev *Executive GM & Member of the Board* T 9198 5561
Chief Operating Officer — David Halstead *Executive GM & Member of the Board* T 9198 5241
Treasurer — Albert Trayner T 9198 5441
International Division — Silvana Grancharova T 9198 5431

General-Investment
Head of Investment — Albert Trayner T 9198 5441

Debt Capital Markets / Fixed Income
Department: Treasury & Capital Markets Division
Tel: 9198 5451 **Fax:** 943 4527 **Telex:** 22350
Head of Fixed Income — Katerina Maksimova *Head of Debt Trading* T 9198 5456

Fixed-Income Research
Head of Fixed Income — Dessislava Mihaylova *Fixed Income Analyst* T 9198 5414

208 Euromoney Directory 1999

BULGARIA (+359)

Equity Capital Markets
Department: Treasury & Capital Markets Division
Tel: 9198 5451 Fax: 943 4527
Head of Equity Capital Markets   Kiril Georgiev *Chief Dealer* ☏ **9198 5451** 🖷 **943 4527**
Head of Sales   Nikolai Simeonov *Equities Dealer* ☏ **9198 5452**

Equity Research
Head of Equity Research   Nadia Nedelcheva *Equity Analyst* ☏ **9198 5419**

Syndicated Lending
Loan-Related Activities
Trade Finance; Project Finance   David Halstead *Executive GM & Member of the Board* ☏ **9198 5241**

Money Markets
Tel: 9198 5455 Fax: 943 4527
Head of Money Markets   Vladimir Rogatchev *Senior Money Market Dealer* ☏ **9198 5455**

Foreign Exchange
Tel: 9198 5451 Fax: 943 4527
Head of Foreign Exchange   Bojidar Kounov ☏ **9198 5454**
Head of Institutional Sales; Corporate Sales;   Vassil Kotsev ☏ **9198 5453**
Head of Trading

Settlement / Clearing
Tel: 9198 5223 Fax: 943 4528
Equity Settlement; Fixed-Income Settlement   Spas Vidarkinski ☏ **9198 5223** 🖷 **943 4528**

Other Departments
Correspondent Banking   Silvana Grancharova ☏ **9198 5431**

Société Générale   Representative Office
36 rue Dragan Tsankov, BG-1040 Sofia
Tel: (2) 971 2964 Fax: (2) 971 2978 Telex: 22010 Swift: SOGE BGSF Email: socgen@exo.net
Website: www.socgen.com

State Savings Bank   Head Office
19 Moskovska Street, BG-1040 Sofia
Tel: (2) 988 1041 Fax: (2) 980 6477 Telex: 25043 CU DSK BG Swift: STSA BG SF

Senior Executive Officers
Chairman & President   Spass Dimitrov ☏ **988 1426** 🖷 **980 2055**
Financial Director   Strahil Videnov *Chief Accountant* ☏ **980 1649**

Others (Senior Executives)
Vice President   Ivan Iskrov *Vice President* ☏ **980 6109** 🖷 **980 8462**
    Violina Marinova *Vice President* ☏ **980 5263** 🖷 **980 2069**
    Assen Drumev *Vice President* ☏ **988 5136**

Debt Capital Markets / Fixed Income
Head of Fixed Income   Mario Anastasov *Head of Financial Markets & Liquidity Department*
    ☏ **980 8064**

Fixed-Income Repo
Head of Repo   Mario Anastasov *Head of Financial Markets & Liquidity Department*
    ☏ **980 8064**

Equity Capital Markets
Head of Equity Capital Markets   Mario Anastasov *Head of Financial Markets & Liquidity Department*
    ☏ **980 8064**

Other (Domestic Equities)
Head of Loan Origination   Anastasia Vasileva *Head of Credit Department* ☏ **980 4866**

Equity Repo / Securities Lending
Head   Mario Anastasov *Head of Financial Markets & Liquidity Department*
    ☏ **980 8064**

Syndicated Lending
Head of Origination   Anastasia Vasileva *Head of Credit Department* ☏ **980 4866**

Money Markets
Head of Money Markets   Mario Anastasov *Head of Financial Markets & Liquidity Department*
    ☏ **980 8064**

Foreign Exchange
Head of Foreign Exchange   Mario Anastasov *Head of Financial Markets & Liquidity Department*
    ☏ **980 8064**

BULGARIA (+359)   www.euromoneydirectory.com

State Savings Bank (cont)
Settlement / Clearing
Head of Settlement / Clearing   Mario Anastasov *Head of Financial Markets & Liquidity Department*
☎ 980 8064

Other Departments
Chief Credit Officer   Anastasia Vasileva *Head of Credit Department* ☎ 980 4866
Correspondent Banking   Svetlana Tsanova ☎ 981 9414
Cash Management   Strahil Videnov *Chief Accountant* ☎ 980 1649

Administration
Head of Administration   Ventseslav Medarski ☎ 980 8168

Technology & Systems
   Leonid Dimov *Head of Information Technology* ☎ 980 9672

Legal / In-House Counsel
   Diana Andonova *Head of Legal Dept* ☎ 980 8496

Public Relations
   Neli Markova ☎ 988 1041

Accounts / Audit
   Veselin Andreev *Head of Internal Audit Division* ☎ 873 715 ext 198

Other (Administration)
International Cooperation Division   Emilia Stoyanova ☎ 981 0073

United Bulgarian Bank AD   Head Office

5 Sveta Sofia Street, BG-1000 Sofia
Tel: (2) 847 090; (2) 318 192 **Fax:** (2) 880 822; (2) 334 001 **Telex:** 25298; 25299 **Swift:** STRB BG SF
Email: admin@main.ubb.bg **Reuters:** UBBK

Senior Executive Officers
Chairman of Board of Directors   Pierre Mellinger
Chief Executive Officer   Stilian Vatev ☎ 8470 2233 📠 8470 2209
Managing Director / General Manager   Radka Toncheva ☎ 8470 2232 📠 8470 2209
International Division   Plamen Mateev *Head of International PR, & Secretariat Department*
☎ 8470 2330

Others (Senior Executives)
Branch Management Division   Luchia Karachorova *Chief* ☎ 3322 3507

General - Treasury
Head of Treasury   Marln Atov *Chief* ☎ 8470 2421

Debt Capital Markets / Fixed Income
Global Head   Velko Velkov ☎ 8470 2453

Equity Capital Markets
Global Head   Velko Velkov ☎ 8470 2453

Syndicated Lending
Head of Credit Committee   Andrey Nikolov *Chief of Credit Management Division* ☎ 8470 2336

Loan-Related Activities
Trade Finance   Galya Petkova ☎ 8470 2310

Risk Management
Global Head   Stoyan Stoyanov *Chief* ☎ 8470 2116

Settlement / Clearing
Operations   Dimitar Shumarov *Chief of Financial Control* ☎ 8470 2640

Other Departments
Correspondent Banking   Damyan Damyanov *Head* ☎ 8470 2341

Administration
Head of Administration   Anton Lazarov *Chief of Central Services* ☎ 3322 3241

Technology & Systems
IT Division   Nikola Raykovski *Chief* ☎ 8470 2710

Legal / In-House Counsel
   Vanya Piskova *Chief* ☎ 8470 2117

Public Relations
   Plamen Mateev *Head of International PR, & Secretariat Department*
☎ 8470 2330

Other (Administration)
Human Resources   Rumyana Barova *Chief* ☎ 3322 3246
Strategic Planning, Marketing, & Advertising   Penka Nedyalkova *Chief* ☎ 3322 3248

BURKINA FASO
(+226)

Banque Centrale des Etats de l'Afrique de l'Ouest   🏛 Central Bank

PO Box 356, Ouagadougou
Tel: 306 015; 306 016 **Fax**: 310 122 **Telex**: 5205

Senior Executive Officers
Country Director   Moussa Kone
Branch Director   Sosthène Bambara

BURUNDI
(+257)

Banque de la Republique du Burundi   Representative Office

Avenue du Gouvernement, Bujumbura
Tel: 225 142 **Fax**: 223 128 **Telex**: 5071 **Telex**: 5072

Senior Executive Officers
Governor   Mathias Sinamenye ☎ **222 744**
Vice Governor   Emmanuel Ndayiragije ☎ **222 763**
Vice Governor   Charles Karikurubu ☎ **222 259**
Treasurer   Eustache Barukinamwo ☎ **222 517**

Others (Senior Executives)
Head, Bank Licensing   Libérata Kiburago ☎ **226 103**
Head, Banking Supervision   Yves Ntivumbura ☎ **224 226**
Head, Economics & Statistics   Bonaventure Sota ☎ **222 745**
Head, Reserves Management   Consolata Nkurikiye ☎ **222 732**

Foreign Exchange
Head of Foreign Exchange   Spès Baransata ☎ **222 805**

Settlement / Clearing
Head of Settlement / Clearing   Denisè Nizigama ☎ **226 616**

Administration
Head of Administration   Rose Buyoya ☎ **225 095**

Accounts / Audit
Head, Accountancy   Anaclet Ndabadugaritse ☎ **225 973**

CANADA
(+1)

Bank of Canada   🏛 Central Bank

234 Wellington Street, Ottawa, Ontario K1A 0G9
Tel: (613) 782 8111 **Fax**: (613) 782 8655 **Telex**: 4515 BANKCDA OTI **Swift**: BCAN CA 22
Website: www.bank-banque-canada.ca

Senior Executive Officers
Governor   Gordon G Thiessen
Senior Deputy Govenor   Bernard Bonin
Deputy Governor   W Paul Jenkins
Deputy Governor   Tim E Noël
Deputy Governor   Sheryl Kennedy
Deputy Governor   Charles Freedman
Corporate Secretary   L Theodore Requard
International Division   J D Murray

Others (Senior Executives)
Banking Operations   B J D M Schwab
Financial Markets   R M Parker

Debt Capital Markets / Fixed Income
Department: Government Securities Services
Global Head   R L Flett

CANADA (+1) www.euromoneydirectory.com

Bank of Canada (cont)
Other Departments
Economic Research
D J Longworth
J G Selody

Administration
Head of Administration
J Cosier *Head of Management Services*

Technology & Systems
Systems Management Services
J J Otterspoor

Legal / In-House Counsel
D M Duffy *General Counsel*

Corporate Communications
Communications Services
B Yemen

Accounts / Audit
P Koppe *Auditor*
Donald D Lusby *Chief Accountant*

Other (Administration)
Human Resources
R A J Julien *Director*

Banca Commerciale Italiana of Canada — Subsidiary Company
Suite 1800, 130 Adelaide Street West, Toronto, Ontario M5H 3P5
Tel: (416) 366 8101; (416) 585 2660 **Fax:** (416) 366 7675 **Telex:** 0622977 BCI CANADA TOR **Swift:** BCIT CA TT

Senior Executive Officers
Chairman
President & Chief Executive Officer
Financial Director
Treasurer
Donald Smith
Gennaro Stammati
Antonello Dessanti *VP, Chief Accountant & Compliance Officer*
Gary Reid *Vice President*

Others (Senior Executives)
Retail Banking
Commercial Banking
Liz Stamsell *Assistant Vice President*
Barry Campbell *Assistant Vice President*

General-Lending (DCM, SL)
Head of Corporate Banking
John Gundy *Assistant Vice President*

Administration
Head of Marketing
Sam Febbraro *Senior Manager*

Technology & Systems
Brian Michell *Assistant Vice President*

Legal / In-House Counsel
General Counsel
David Grad *Vice President & Secretary*

Compliance
Antonello Dessanti *VP, Chief Accountant & Compliance Officer*

Public Relations
Madeline Zito *Assistant Vice President*

Bank of America Canada — Subsidiary Company
200 Front Street West, Toronto, Ontario M5V 3L2
Tel: (416) 349 4100

Senior Executive Officers
President & Chief Executive Officer
Financial Director
Treasurer
Alfred P Buhler ☎ **349 5341**
Brian Wilson *Vice President & CFO* ☎ **349 5329**
Stephen Lobb *SVP & Treasurer* ☎ **349 4050**

Debt Capital Markets / Fixed Income
Fixed-Income Repo
Head of Repo
Garry Rennie *VP, Repos / Funding* ☎ **349 5489**

Money Markets
Country Head
Brent Shields *Vice President* ☎ **349 5489**

Foreign Exchange
Head of Trading
Jack Castigleone *VP, FX Trading* ☎ **349 5489**

Risk Management
Country Head
David Tanko *VP & Director, Risk Management* ☎ **349 5471**

Fixed Income Derivatives / Risk Management
IR Swaps Sales / Marketing
IR Swaps Trading
Greg Young *VP, Head of Institutional Marketing* ☎ **349 4060**
Lori Wilson *VP, Manager, Interest Rate Risk* ☎ **349 5263**

Fixed Income Derivatives / Risk Management (cont)
IR Options Trading　　　　　　　　　Rasheed Saleuddin *VP, Head of Structuring & Options* ☏ **349 5483**
Foreign Exchange Derivatives / Risk Management
Cross-Currency Swaps, Sales / Marketing　　Ray Williams *VP, Derivatives Marketing* ☏ **349 4060**
Cross-Currency Swaps, Trading　　　　Michael Breen *VP, Head of Swaps Trading* ☏ **349 5278**
OTC Equity Derivatives
Trading　　　　　　　　　　　　　Rasheed Saleuddin *VP, Head of Structuring & Options* ☏ **349 5483**

Bank of China (Canada)　　　　　　　　　　　　　　Subsidiary Company

Suite 3740, 161 Bay Street, BCE Place, Toronto, Ontario M5J 2S1
Tel: (416) 362 2991 **Fax:** (416) 362 3047 **Telex:** 06217598BOCC TOR **Swift:** BKCHCATT **Reuters:** BOCC

Senior Executive Officers
President & CEO　　　　　　　　　　Rubai Giu
Treasurer　　　　　　　　　　　　Raymond So *Manager*

Money Markets
Tel: 362 5659 **Fax:** 362 3047
Country Head　　　　　　　　　　　Raymond So *Manager* ☏ **362 5659**

Foreign Exchange
Head of Trading　　　　　　　　　　Raymond So *Manager* ☏ **362 5659**

Bank Hapoalim BM　　　　　　　　　　　　　　　Representative Office

Suite 303, 3910 Bathurst Street, Downsview, Ontario M3H 5Z3
Tel: (416) 398 4250 **Fax:** (416) 398 4246

Senior Executive Officers
Chief Representative　　　　　　　　Rafi Ben Ami

Bank Hapoalim BM　　　　　　　　　　　　　　　Representative Office

Suite 1470, 3400 de Maisonneuve Boulevard West, Montreal, Quebec H3Z 3B8
Tel: (514) 935 1128 **Fax:** (514) 935 1129

Senior Executive Officers
Chief Representative　　　　　　　　Eli Shalit

Bank of Montreal　　　　　　　　　　　　　　　　　Head Office

1 First Canadian Place, 100 King Street West, Toronto, Ontario M5X 1A1
PO Box 1, Toronto, Ontario M5X 1A1
Tel: (800) 555 3000; (416) 927 6000 **Fax:** (416) 927 5543 **Email:** info@bmo.com
Website: www.bmo.com

Senior Executive Officers
Chairman & Chief Executive　　　　　Matthew W Barrett ☏ **867 4686**
President & COO　　　　　　　　　　F Anthony Comper ☏ **867 7654**
Chief Executive Officer　　　　　　　Matthew W Barrett *Chairman & Chief Executive* ☏ **867 4686**
Financial Director　　　　　　　　　Robert B Wells *EVP & Chief Financial Officer* ☏ **867 4010**
Chief Operating Officer　　　　　　　F Anthony Comper *President & COO* ☏ **867 7654**
Treasurer　　　　　　　　　　　　Yvan J P Bourdeau *EVP & Head, Global Treasury Group* ☏ **867 7649**
VP & Corporate Secretary　　　　　　Vlema J Jones ☏ **867 6782**

Others (Senior Executives)
Commercial Financial Services　　　　Ronald G Rogers *Vice Chairman* ☏ **927 6460**
Electronic Financial Services　　　　　Jeffrey S Chisholm *Vice Chairman* ☏ **927 5790**
Harris Bankcorp, Inc.　　　　　　　　Alan G McNally *Chairman & Chief Executive* ☏ **(312) 461 6541**
Corporate Services & Organizational
Development　　　　　　　　　　　Gary S Dibb *Vice Chairman* ☏ **867 7740**
　　　　　　　　　　　　　　　　Keith O Dorricott *Vice Chairman, Corporate Services*
Mexico & Latin America　　　　　　　Carlos E Garin *Executive Vice President* ☏ **+52 (5) 201 0929**

General-Lending (DCM, SL)
Head of Corporate Banking　　　　　Brian J Steck *Vice Chairman, Corporate & Investment Banking* ☏ **867 6663**

Debt Capital Markets / Fixed Income
Global Head　　　　　　　　　　　Jim Beqaj *Vice Chairman, Global Debt Capital Markets* ☏ **359 5444**
Head of Fixed Income Sales　　　　　Michael Bowen *VP & Director, Institutional FI Sales* ☏ **359 4507**
Head of Fixed Income Trading　　　　Jim Schut *VP & Director, Institutional FI Trading* ☏ **359 7021**

CANADA (+1)

www.euromoneydirectory.com

Bank of Montreal (cont)

Government Bonds
Head of Sales; Head of Trading — Chris Tremaine *EVP & Director, NBSI Capital Markets* ☎ **(212) 702 1266**
Head of Syndication — Coleen Campbell *VP & Director, Debt Capital Markets* ☎ **359 5690**
Head of Origination — Mark Roche *Managing Director, Debt Capital Markets*

Eurobonds
Head of Sales; Head of Trading — John Keogh *Managing Director, International Capital Markets* ☎ **+44 (171) 570 7023**

Fixed-Income Repo
Head of Trading — Chris Tremaine *EVP & Director, NBSI Capital Markets* ☎ **(212) 702 1266**
Nick Pyle *Managing Director, Money Markets* ☎ **867 5941**

Fixed-Income Research
Head of Fixed Income — Sherry Cooper *Chief Economist* ☎ **359 4112**

Equity Capital Markets
Tel: 359 4142 **Fax:** 359 4933
Head of Equity Capital Markets; Head of Sales; Head of Trading — Barry Cooper *Vice Chairman, Global Institutional Equity*

Domestic Equities
Head of Sales — Richard Carl *SVP, Sales & Equity Trading* ☎ **359 6563**
Head of Trading — Eric Tripp *SVP, Equity Derivatives & Trading* ☎ **359 4339**

International Equities
Head of Sales; Head of Trading — Hans Queissner *SVP, Institutional Equity, Europe* ☎ **+44 (171) 246 5411**

Equity Research
Head of Equity Research — Jonathon Cunningham *EVP & Director, Research* ☎ **359 5194**

Convertibles / Equity-Linked
Head of Sales; Head of Trading — Eric Tripp *SVP, Equity Derivatives & Trading* ☎ **359 4339**

Equity Repo / Securities Lending
Head of Trading — Michelle Peacock *Director, Prime Brokerage & Risk Management* ☎ **359 4147**

Syndicated Lending
Head of Origination — Mark Roche *Managing Director, Debt Capital Markets*
Head of Syndication — Coleen Campbell *VP & Director, Debt Capital Markets* ☎ **359 5690**
Head of Trading — Nick Pyle *Managing Director, Money Markets* ☎ **867 5941**

Loan-Related Activities
Trade Finance — Peter Wren *Managing Director* ☎ **867 6412**
Project Finance — Barry Pollock *Managing Director, Global Project Finance* ☎ **867 2871**

Money Markets
Tel: 867 5940 **Fax:** 867 7371
Head of Money Markets — Nick Pyle *Managing Director, Money Markets* ☎ **867 5941**

Domestic Commercial Paper
Head of Sales — Nick Pyle *Managing Director, Money Markets* ☎ **867 5941**

Foreign Exchange
Tel: (312) 845 4060 **Fax:** (312) 845 4158
Head of Foreign Exchange — Jamie Thorsen *SVP, Global Foreign Exchange*
Head of Institutional Sales — Trevor Woodland
Head of Trading — Donald G Lloyd

Risk Management
Tel: 643 2462 **Fax:** 643 2475
Head of Risk Management — Michel G Maila *EVP, Risk Management Group*

Fixed Income Derivatives / Risk Management
Head of Sales — Kevin Holme
Trading — Mark Caplan

Foreign Exchange Derivatives / Risk Management
Country Head — David Faller *Head of Sales*

OTC Equity Derivatives
Sales — Eric Tripp *SVP, Equity Derivatives & Trading* ☎ **359 4339**

OTC Commodity Derivatives
Head — Rick Nason

Settlement / Clearing
Tel: (514) 877 1185 **Fax:** (514) 877 1547
Head of Settlement / Clearing — Terry Ceretti *VP, International / Treasury Operations*
Equity Settlement — Barry Cooper *Vice Chairman, Global Institutional Equity*
Fixed-Income Settlement — Charlie Moses

Asset Management
Head — Terry A Jackson *EVP, Asset Management Services* ☎ **867 7260**

214   Euromoney Directory 1999

www.euromoneydirectory.com CANADA (+1)

Other Departments
Private Banking Terry A Jackson *EVP, Asset Management Services* ☏ **867 7260**
Correspondent Banking Robert Tetley *SVP, Banking Operations* ☏ **927 5867**
Administration
Department: Corporate Services
Head of Marketing George D Bothwell *SVP, Public Affairs* ☏ **927 2827**
Technology & Systems
  Lloyd F Darlington *Chief Technology Officer & GM, Operations* ☏ **927 5566**
Legal / In-House Counsel
  Dereck M Jones *SVP & General Counsel* ☏ **867 7721**
Compliance
  Glenn B Higginbotham *VP, Corporate Compliance* ☏ **867 4070**
Public Relations
  George D Bothwell *SVP, Public Affairs* ☏ **927 2827**
Accounts / Audit
  Johanne M Totta *SVP & Chief Auditor* ☏ **643 1700**

Bank of Tokyo-Mitsubishi (Canada)

Suite 2780, Tour Banque Nationale, 600 de la Gauchetiere Street W, Montreal, Quebec H3B 4L8
Tel: (514) 875 9261 **Fax:** (514) 875 9392 **Telex:** 556 0946 **Cable:** TMBANK MTL
Senior Executive Officers
VP & General Manager - Montreal Amos W Simpson

Bank of Tokyo-Mitsubishi (Canada) Subsidiary Company

Suite 2100, South Tower, PO Box 42, Royal Bank Plaza, Toronto, Ontario M5J 2JL
Tel: (416) 865 0220 **Fax:** (416) 865 9511; (416) 865 0196 **Telex:** 065 24440 **Swift:** BOTK CA TX **Reuters:** TMTR
  Cable: TMBANK TOR
Senior Executive Officers
President & Chief Executive Officer Hiroshi Degawa
Chief Operating Officer Yoshio Saihara *Executive Vice President*
Others (Senior Executives)
  Angelo Bisutti *Vice President*
  David C A Frost *Senior Vice President*
  Doreen Durham *Vice President*
  Jun Buktaw *Vice President*
  Masakazu Mizutani *VP & Chief Trader*
  Tetsuya Ohashi *Vice President*
  Natsuki Sato *Vice President*
  Wataru Tanaka *Vice President*
  Ted Vanderlaan *Vice President*
  Sadachika Yoshioka *Vice President*
  Klement Choi *Vice President*
Money Markets
Country Head Masakazu Mizutani *VP & Chief Trader*
Foreign Exchange
Country Head Masakazu Mizutani *VP & Chief Trader*

Bank of Tokyo-Mitsubishi (Canada)

2410 Park Place, 666 Burrard Street, Vancouver, British Columbia V6C 3L1
Tel: (604) 691 7300 **Fax:** (604) 691 7311 **Telex:** 455520 **Swift:** BOTK CA TX VCR **Cable:** TMBANK VCR
Senior Executive Officers
EVP & General Manager - Vancouver Ken Asukai
Others (Senior Executives)
  Ivan J Hopkins *Vice President - Vancouver*
  Norio Fujimoto *Vice President - Vancouver*
  Davis Stewart *Vice President - Vancouver*
  Hiroyuki Yamazaki *Vice President - Vancouver*

CANADA (+1)   www.euromoneydirectory.com

Banque Nationale de Paris (Canada)   Subsidiary Company

1981 McGill College Avenue, Montreal, Quebec H3A 2W8
Tel: (514) 285 6000 **Fax:** (514) 285 6278 **Telex:** 0527137 **Swift:** BNPA CA MM **Email:** bnpcando@generation.net

Senior Executive Officers
General Manager   Robert Amzallag
General - Treasury
Head of Treasury   Daniel Grenier ☎ 285 6253
Syndicated Lending
Loan-Related Activities
Trade Finance   Philippe Bouyaud ☎ 285 2952
Project Finance   Vincent Joli-Coueur ☎ 285 2904

BMO Nesbitt Burns Inc

3rd Floor Podium, 1 First Canadian Place, PO Box 150, Toronto, Ontario M5X 1H3
Tel: (416) 359 4000 **Fax:** (416) 359 4844; (416) 359 5193 **Telex:** 06524455 NESTOM

Senior Executive Officers
Chairman   Brian J Steck
President   John McNaughton
Financial Director   Barbara Stymiest

Debt Capital Markets / Fixed Income
Tel: 867 5940 **Fax:** 867 7371

Fixed-Income Repo
Marketing & Product Development   Jamie Grant *Associate Repo Trader* ☎ 867 5940 ✉ 867 7371
Trading   Greg King *Director & Head Repo Trader* ☎ 867 5940 ✉ gking@bmo.com
   John Davidson *Trader*
   Jamie Grant *Associate Repo Trader* ☎ 867 5940 ✉ 867 7371
   Terry Morgan *Trader*
   Andrew Jones *Trader*

Equity Capital Markets
Equity Repo / Securities Lending
Head; Marketing & Product Development   Michelle Peacock *Director*
Head of Trading   Gary Bramfitt *Trader*
   Karen Jardim *Trader*
   Carmen De Federico *Trader* ☎ 359 4493

Administration
Other (Administration)
Human Resources   Susan Marineau *Manager* ☎ 359 7486

Brockhouse & Cooper Inc   Head Office

Suite 4025, 1250 Boulevard René Levesque West, Montreal, Quebec H3B 4W8
Tel: (514) 932 7171 **Fax:** (514) 932 8288 **Telex:** 0525412

Senior Executive Officers
Chairman   J E Brockhouse
President   R L Cooper

Bunting Warburg Inc

Suite 2510, 1010 Sherbrooke Street West, Montreal, Quebec H3A 2R7
Tel: (514) 842 8726 **Fax:** (514) 842 8720

Senior Executive Officers
Others (Senior Executives)
Unit Head   F W Molson

Bunting Warburg Inc

Suite 4100, BCE Place, 161 Bay Street, Toronto, Ontario M5J 2S1
PO Box 617, Toronto, Ontario
Tel: (416) 364 3293 **Fax:** (416) 364 1976

www.euromoneydirectory.com   CANADA (+1)

Equity Capital Markets
Department: Equities
Country Head — J M Estey

Other (Domestic Equities)
Equities Proprietary Trading — G D Finkle
M J Lawrance

Corporate Finance / M&A Advisory
Country Head — D C W Macdonald

Bunting Warburg Inc

Suite 3314, 1055 Dunsmuir Street, Vancouver, British Columbia V7X 1L4
PO Box 49332, Vancouver, British Columbia
Tel: (604) 682 0791 **Fax:** (604) 681 4220

Senior Executive Officers
Others (Senior Executives)
Unit Head — D A Hendry

Caisse Centrale Desjardins

Suite 2822, 1 Complexe Desjardins, Montreal, Quebec H5B 1B3
Tel: (514) 281 7070 **Fax:** (514) 281 7083 **Telex:** 05561688 **Swift:** CCDQ CA MM **Reuters:** CCDX
Website: www.desjardins.com

Senior Executive Officers
President & Chief Executive Officer — Jean-Guy Langelier
Chief Operating Officer — Rénald Boucher
General Manager — Camil Laforge
SVP & General Manager — Albert Ouellet
SVP & General Manager — Régis Robin
SVP & General Manager — Yves Lavoie
SVP & General Manager — André Talbot
EVP & General Manager — Bruno Morin
VP & General Manager — Jacques Landry
Director — Marcel Busque
Director — Robert Guerriero
General Manager — Michel Latour
General Manager — Bertrand Laferrière
General Manager — Paul Lemieux
General Manager — Gilles Lafleur

Others (Senior Executives)
Michel Jourdain *SVP, Federation Services*
Denis Séguin *Assistant to the President*

General-Lending (DCM, SL)
Head of Corporate Banking — André Bellefeuille *SVP, Financing & Banking Services*
James McLeod *VP, Financing & Banking Services*
Sylvain Gascon *VP, Financing & Banking Services*
Paul Goulet *VP, Financing & Banking Services*
Christian St-Arnaud *VP, Financing & Banking Services*

General - Treasury
Head of Treasury — Alfred Pfeiffer *SVP, Treasury & Brokerage Services*
Bernard Venne *VP, Treasury & Investment*

Syndicated Lending
Head of Credit Committee — Michel Paradis *Vice President, Credit*

Risk Management
Fixed Income Derivatives / Risk Management
Country Head — Jacques Descôteaux *VP, Brokerage & Derivative Products*

Administration
Head of Administration — Huu Trung Nguyen *Senior Vice President*

Legal / In-House Counsel
Gilles Lapierre *Assistant Secretary & VP*

CANADA (+1)   www.euromoneydirectory.com

Canada Trust Company
Head Office

34th Floor, 161 Bay Street, Toronto, Ontario M5J 2T2
Tel: (416) 361 8000 Fax: (416) 361 8202
Website: www.canadatrust.com

Senior Executive Officers
Chairman   Purdy Crawford
President & Chief Executive Officer   W Edmund Clark ☎ **361 8365**
Financial Director   Paul Derksen *EVP & Chief Financial Officer* ☎ **361 8167**
Treasurer   Alan Jette *SVP, Treasury & Risk Management* ☎ **361 4826**

Debt Capital Markets / Fixed Income
Global Head   Andrew Kriegler *AVP, Funding Securities* ☎ **681 6427**

Eurobonds
Head of Origination   Bob Shatka *Manager, Public Finance* ☎ **361 8286**

Medium-Term Notes
Head of Origination   Bob Shatka *Manager, Public Finance* ☎ **361 8286**

Private Placements
Head of Origination   Bob Shatka *Manager, Public Finance* ☎ **361 8286**

Asset-Backed Securities / Securitization
Global Head   Andrew Kriegler *AVP, Funding Securities* ☎ **681 6427**

Mortgage-Backed Securities
Global Head   Andrew Kriegler *AVP, Funding Securities* ☎ **681 6427**

Fixed-Income Repo
Head of Repo   Lynne McMullen *Fixed-Income Trader* ☎ **361 4926**

Equity Capital Markets
Global Head   Andrew Kriegler *AVP, Funding Securities* ☎ **681 6427**

Domestic Equities
Head of Origination   Bob Shatka *Manager, Public Finance* ☎ **361 8286**

International Equities
Head of Origination   Bob Shatka *Manager, Public Finance* ☎ **361 8286**

Syndicated Lending
Loan-Related Activities
Leasing & Asset Finance   Mike Lough *Manager, Structured Finance* ☎ **361 4967**

Money Markets
Global Head   Dianne McPherson *Manager, Money Market* ☎ **361 8413**

Domestic Commercial Paper
Head of Origination   Dianne McPherson *Manager, Money Market* ☎ **361 8413**

Wholesale Deposits
Head of Sales   Bob Shatka *Manager, Public Finance* ☎ **361 8286**

Foreign Exchange
Global Head   Anne-Marie Ftohogiannis *Forex Risk Manager* ☎ **361 8414**

Risk Management
Global Head   Alan Jette *SVP, Treasury & Risk Management* ☎ **361 4826**

Fixed Income Derivatives / Risk Management
Global Head   Diane McPlanson *Manager, Money Market* ☎ **361 8413**
IR Swaps Trading   Jun Lin *Manager, Risk Position* ☎ **361 8572**
IR Options Trading   Helen Dong *Manager, Risk Position* ☎ **361 8285**

Foreign Exchange Derivatives / Risk Management
Cross-Currency Swaps, Trading   Anne-Marie Ftohogiannis *Forex Risk Manager* ☎ **361 8414**

Corporate Finance / M&A Advisory
Global Head   Paul Derksen *EVP & Chief Financial Officer* ☎ **361 8167**

Settlement / Clearing
Regional Head   Mark Feekery *AVP, Global Securities Operations* ☎ **361 8175**

Other Departments
Private Banking   Gary Brent *President & CEO, CTIMG* ☎ **869 6024**
Correspondent Banking   Richard Siu *AVP, Global Banking Services* ☎ **361 8012**

Administration
Technology & Systems
     Mike Woeller *EVP, Banking & Direct Information Services* ☎ **(519) 663 1597**

Legal / In-House Counsel
     Diane Walker *EVP, Corporate Resources* ☎ **361 4941**

Compliance
Chief Compliance Officer   Brigitte Geisler *VP, Associate General Counsel* ☎ **681 2386**

Corporate Communications
Diane Smith-Sanderson *VP, Advertising & Corporate Communications* ☏ 361 8523

Canadian Western Bank

Suite 2300, 10303 Jasper Avenue, Edmonton, Alberta T5J 3X6
Tel: (403) 423 8888 **Fax:** (403) 423 8897 **Email:** grahamg@telusplanet.net
Website: www.cwbank.com

Senior Executive Officers
Chairman — Jack C Donald
President & Chief Executive Officer — Larry M Pollock
Financial Director — Tracey C Ball *Chief Financial Officer*
Treasurer — Allister McPherson *Senior VP, Treasury & Operations*

Others (Senior Executives)
William J Addington *SVP, Corporate & Strategic Operations*

The Chase Manhattan Bank of Canada   *Subsidiary Company*

Suite 6900, 100 King Street West, Toronto, Ontario M5X 1A4
PO Box 106, Toronto, Ontario M5X 1A4
Tel: (416) 216 4100 **Fax:** (416) 216 4166

Senior Executive Officers
Chairman, President & CEO — Dale G Blue ☏ 216 4141
Financial Director — Ralph C Kern *VP & Chief Administrative Officer* ☏ 216 4131
Treasurer — Albert Williams *VP & Treasurer* ☏ 216 4114

CIBC Mellon Global Securities Services Co

4th Floor, 320 Bay Street, Toronto, Ontario M5H 4A6
Tel: (416) 643 5400 **Fax:** (416) 643 5132
Website: www.cibcmellon.com

Debt Capital Markets / Fixed Income

Fixed-Income Repo
Marketing & Product Development — James Slater *Head of Capital Markets* ☏ 643 5130
✉ slaterj@cicbcmellon.com
Trading — Robert Chiuch *International Securities Lending*
Trevor Carlin *Fixed Income Securities Lending*
Charles Murray *Domestic Equity Securities Lending*
Ken Latta *Fixed Income Securities Lending*

Equity Capital Markets

Equity Repo / Securities Lending
Head; Marketing & Product Development — James Slater *Head of Capital Markets* ☏ 643 5130
✉ slaterj@cicbcmellon.com
Head of Trading — Robert Chiuch *Global Trading*
Trevor Carlin *Fixed Income Securities Lending*
Rob Ferguson *Equities / Fixed Income*
Ken Latta *Fixed Income Securities Lending*
Charles Murray *Domestic Equity Securities Lending*

CIBC Wood Gundy Securities Inc

PO Box 500, BCE Place, 161 Bay Street, Toronto, Ontario M5J 2S8
Tel: (416) 594 8301; (416) 594 8400 **Fax:** (416) 594 8722

Debt Capital Markets / Fixed Income
Tel: 594 8512 **Fax:** 594 8336

Fixed-Income Repo
Head of Repo; Marketing & Product Development — Tesse Parigoris *Managing Director* ☏ 594 8512
Trading — Michael Surmak *Director*
Janet Richardson *Associate*
Neil Williams *Director*

CANADA (+1) www.euromoneydirectory.com

CIBC Wood Gundy Securities Inc (cont)
Equity Capital Markets
Equity Repo / Securities Lending
Head Jim Lailey
Head of Trading Paul Varey
  John MacDonald
  Tim Reid

CIBC World Markets Head Office
161 Bay Street, Toronto, Ontario M5J 2S8
PO Box 500, Toronto, Ontario
Tel: (416) 594 7000
Website: www.cibc.com

Senior Executive Officers
President & Managing Director John Hunkin
Managing Director Michael Rolle
Managing Director Gerry McCaughey
Managing Director Matthew Singleton
Managing Director Ron Lalonde
Managing Director Joe Mirza
Managing Director David Kassie
Managing Director Wayne Fox

General-Lending (DCM, SL)
Head of Corporate Banking David Kassie *Managing Director* ☎ **595 8034**

General-Investment
Head of Investment David Kassie *Managing Director* ☎ **595 8034**

Debt Capital Markets / Fixed Income
Department: Debt Capital Markets / Fixed Income / Money Markets
Global Head Steve McGirr *Managing Director & Vice Chairman* ☎ **594 7070**
Head of Fixed Income Sales Phipps Lounsbery *Managing Director*
Head of Fixed Income Trading Brian Thibideau *Managing Director*

Government Bonds
Head of Syndication Peter McLernon *Managing Director & Head of Canadian Syndication*
Head of Origination David Leith *Managing Director*

Eurobonds
Head of Sales Robert Edge *Managing Director*
Head of Trading Martin Shaw *Managing Director*

Fixed-Income Research
Global Head Peter Martin *Managing Director* ☎ **594 8698**

Equity Capital Markets
Department: Global Institutional Equities
Global Head Brian Shaw *Managing Director* ☎ **594 8558**
  Tom Gallagher *Managing Director* ☎ **667 7387**

Foreign Exchange
Global Head Michael Horrocks *Managing Director* ☎ **594 8305**

Risk Management
Regional Head Robert Mark *Executive Vice President* ☎ **956 6912**

Global Custody
Country Head Doug Nowers *Managing Director* ☎ **643 5100**

Administration
Head of Marketing Debra Douglas *Managing Director* ☎ **+1 (212) 856 4009**

Technology & Systems
  Peter Clark

Compliance
  Eric Young

Public Relations
  Debra Douglas *Managing Director* ☎ **+1 (212) 856 4009**

Other (Administration)
Infrastructure Ron Lalonde *Managing Director*

220 Euromoney Directory 1999

www.euromoneydirectory.com CANADA (+1)

Citibank NA
Full Branch Office

Suite 1900, Citibank Place, 123 Front Street West, Toronto, Ontario M5J 2M3
10th Floor, 1 Toronto Street, Toronto, Ontario M5C 2V6
Tel: (416) 947 5500 **Telex:** 0623 626 **Swift:** CITI CA TT

Senior Executive Officers
Chief Executive Officer Paul Labbe ☎ **947 5560**
Financial Director Kenneth Flynn *Country Corporate Officer* ☎ **947 5620**

Equity Capital Markets
Equity Repo / Securities Lending
Head Micky Butler *World Wide Securities Division Executive* ☎ **947 5843**
 F **947 5281**

Foreign Exchange
Corporate Sales Len Campbell ☎ **947 5748**

Corporate Finance / M&A Advisory
Other (Corporate Finance)
Structured Finance Head Derek Johnston ☎ **947 5298**

Global Custody
Country Head Micky Butler ☎ **947 5843** F **947 5281**

Commerzbank AG
Representative Office

Suite 3190, South Tower, Royal Bank Plaza, Toronto, Ontario M5J 2J4
PO Box 191, Toronto, Ontario M5J 2J4
Tel: (416) 865 0492 **Fax:** (416) 367 1090

Senior Executive Officers
Representative Werner E Samuel

Credifinance Securities Limited
Head Office

Suite 3303, 130 Adelaide Street West, Toronto, Ontario M5H 3P5
Tel: (416) 955 0159 **Fax:** (416) 364 1522 **Telex:** 06218013

Senior Executive Officers
Chairman Georges Benarroch
Chief Operating Officer Ann Glover

Crédit Lyonnais Canada
Head Office

18th Floor, 2000 Mansfield Street, Montreal, Quebec H3A 3A6
Tel: (514) 288 4848 **Fax:** (514) 288 5679 **Telex:** 05 25245 **Swift:** CRLY CA MM

Senior Executive Officers
President & Chief Executive Officer Thierry Hauret ☎ **499 8782**
Financial Director Louis Bastien *Vice President, Administration* ☎ **499 8760**
Treasurer Robert Audet *Vice President & Treasurer* ☎ **499 8214**

Debt Capital Markets / Fixed Income
Asset-Backed Securities / Securitization
Global Head Blake Colvin *VP, Corporate Banking* ☎ **(416) 202 6504**

Fixed-Income Repo
Head of Repo Amine Marrat *Head of Fixed-Income Desk* ☎ **499 8242**

Syndicated Lending
Loan-Related Activities
Trade Finance Louis Bourdon *AVP, Operations* ☎ **499 8204**

Money Markets
Global Head Robert Van Buskirk *AVP, Money Markets* ☎ **499 8218**

Wholesale Deposits
Marketing George Bitsakis *Arbitragiste Principal Force de Vent* ☎ **499 8221**

Foreign Exchange
Global Head Robert Audet *Vice President & Treasurer* ☎ **499 8214**

FX Traders / Sales People
 Robert Block ☎ **(416) 202 6526**
 Stephen Wiencke ☎ **499 8243**

Euromoney Directory 1999 **221**

CANADA (+1)   www.euromoneydirectory.com

Crédit Lyonnais Canada (cont)
FX Traders / Sales People (cont)
Michelle Heaphy ☎ (416) 202 6526
Michel Nahmany ☎ 499 8223
Risk Management
Global Head   Robert Massicotte *VP, Risk Management* ☎ 499 8789
Settlement / Clearing
Regional Head   Louis Bourdon *AVP, Operations* ☎ 499 8204
Administration
Technology & Systems
Information Management   Joseph Bejjani *Manager* ☎ 499 8773

Crédit Suisse First Boston Canada
Subsidiary Company

Formerly known as: Crédit Suisse Canada
Suite 1300, 525 University Avenue, Toronto, Ontario M5G 2K6
Tel: (416) 351 3500; (416) 351 1600 **Fax:** (416) 351 3630; (416) 351 3560 **Telex:** 06 524069 **Swift:** CRES CA TT
Website: www.csfb.com

Senior Executive Officers
Chairman & President   Thomas Barber ☎ 351 3623
Financial Director   Bruce Wetherly ☎ 351 3608
Equity Capital Markets
Head of Sales   Jim Houston ☎ 351 3679
            Ken Teslia
Head of Trading   Tony Oram ☎ 351 3682
Equity Research
Head of Equity Research Robert Goff ☎ 351 3543
Syndicated Lending
Head of Syndication   Colleen Paige ☎ 351 3553
Money Markets
Head of Money Markets Lindsay Glass ☎ +1 (212) 325 5540
Risk Management
Head of Risk Management Graham Hunt ☎ +1 (212) 325 2242
Other Departments
Chief Credit Officer   Graham Hunt ☎ +1 (212) 325 2242
Administration
Technology & Systems
            Tony Mo ☎ 351 3490
Compliance
            Ken Redpath ☎ 351 3561
Accounts / Audit
            Bruce Wetherly ☎ 351 3608

Dai-Ichi Kangyo Bank (Canada)
Subsidiary Company

PO Box 295, Suite 5025, Commerce Court West, Toronto, Ontario M5L 1H9
Tel: (416) 365 9666 **Fax:** (416) 365 7314 **Telex:** 0622404
Senior Executive Officers
Chairman   H Ikeda
President   M Matsuzawa

Darier Hentsch Canada Inc
Full Branch Office

3655 Redpath, Montreal, Quebec H3G 2G9
Tel: (514) 288 2991 **Fax:** (514) 288 9780 **Swift:** DACO CA MX **Telerate:** telecourse-DHMBI 105
Senior Executive Officers
President   Pierre Trahan
Chief Executive Officer Alan Griffin *Vice President & Head of Trading*
Debt Capital Markets / Fixed Income
Head of Debt Capital Markets Alan Griffin *Vice President & Head of Trading*
Domestic Government Bonds
Head of Trading   Karen Chopko *Trader*

Eurobonds
Head of Trading   Karen Chopko *Trader*

Equity Capital Markets
Head of Equity Capital Markets   Alan Griffin *Vice President & Head of Trading*

Domestic Equities
Head of Trading   Karen Chopko *Trader*

International Equities
Head of Trading   Karen Chopko *Trader*

Money Markets
Department: Trading purposes only - Client
Head of Money Markets   Alan Griffin *Vice President & Head of Trading*

Foreign Exchange
Head of Foreign Exchange   Alan Griffin *Vice President & Head of Trading*

Risk Management
OTC Equity Derivatives
Head   Alan Griffin *Vice President & Head of Trading*
Trading   Karen Chopko *Trader*

Settlement / Clearing
Equity Settlement   Nancy Speight *Settlement Coordinator*
Foreign Exchange Settlement   Alain Coulombe *Exchange Coordinator*

Global Custody
Head of Global Custody   Alan Griffin *Vice President & Head of Trading*

Other Departments
Private Banking   Peter Pfiffner *President* ☏ **288 2991**

Administration
Technology & Systems
    Jean Pierre Nicollin *Vice President, Systems*

Desjardins Trust

1 Complexe Desjardins, CP 34, Montreal, Quebec H5B 1E4
Tel: (514) 286 5944 Fax: (514) 286 3664; (514) 286 3108
Corporate Dealers Tel: 576 2403

Debt Capital Markets / Fixed Income
Fixed-Income Repo
Trading   James Burdick *Director, Financial Markets*
    Denis Boisjoli *Securities Lending Agent*
    Daniel Lajoie *Securities Lending Agent*

Equity Capital Markets
Equity Repo / Securities Lending
Head   Pierre Payeur *Vice President & Treasurer* ☏ **286 3474**
Head of Trading   Daniel Lajoie *Securities Lending Agent*
    Denis Boisjoli *Securities Lending Agent*

Deutsche Bank Canada   Subsidiary Company

Suite 1100, 222 Bay Street, PO Box 196, Toronto, Ontario M5K 1H6
Tel: (416) 682 8400; (416) 682 8030 Fax: (416) 682 8484; (416) 682 8048 Telex: 06218479 Swift: DEUT CA TT
Cable: DEUTSHBANK TOR
Foreign Exchange & Money Market Tel: 682 8370

Senior Executive Officers
Chairman   Michael Rassmann
Chief Executive Officer   Doug Byers

Debt Capital Markets / Fixed Income
Fixed-Income Repo
Head of Repo   Dennis Bernhard *Head of Money Market / Repo*
Trading   Ross Smellie *Vice President / Head Repo Trader*
    Heather Steer *Assistant Trader*

CANADA (+1)   www.euromoneydirectory.com

Deutsche Morgan Grenfell Canada Limited — Subsidiary Company
Suite 1100, Toronto-Dominion Centre, 222 Bay Street, PO Box 64, Toronto, Ontario M5K 1E7
Tel: (416) 682 8000 Fax: (416) 682 8383 Telex: 06-219714

Dresdner Bank Canada — Subsidiary Company
Suite 1700, Exchange Tower, 2 First Canadian Place, Toronto, Ontario M5X 1E3
PO Box 430, First Canadian Place Postal, Toronto, Ontario
Tel: (416) 369 8300 Fax: (416) 369 8362 Swift: DRES CA TX Reuters: DRCN

Senior Executive Officers
President & Chief Executive Officer David N Brandt

General-Lending (DCM, SL)
Head of Corporate Banking Uwe Seedorf *SVP, Corporate Banking*
  W Brian West *VP, Corporate Banking*
  John Walenta *VP, Corporate Banking*
  Gerhard Ziepa *VP, Corporate Banking*

General - Treasury
Head of Treasury Paul Darling *Vice President*

Risk Management
Global Head Nicole Juncker *Vice President*

Settlement / Clearing
Operations J Dario Murkovic *VP, Controlling & Operations*

Euro Brokers Canada Limited — Subsidiary Company
Suite 1110, 141 Adelaide Street West, Toronto, Ontario M5H 3L5
Tel: (416) 941 9506; (416) 594 3600 Fax: (416) 594 3614

Senior Executive Officers
CEO David Coomber
Treasurer Jeannette Wiltse *SVP & Secretary, Treasurer* ☎ 594 3616

Export Development Corporation — Head Office
Alternative trading name: EDC
151 O'Connor Street, Ottawa, Ontario K1A 1K3
Tel: (613) 598 2500 Fax: (613) 237 2690 Telex: 053-4136 EXCREDCORP OTT
Trading & Treasury Tel: 598 2800; Fax: 563 8834
Website: www.edc.ca

Senior Executive Officers
President & CEO A Ian Gillespie ☎ 598 2950 📠 598 6899 ✉ gillia@edc1.ca
Chief Executive Officer A Ian Gillespie *President & CEO* ☎ 598 2950 📠 598 6899 ✉ gillia@edc1.ca
Financial Director P Allen *SVP & CFO* ☎ 598 8662 📠 598 3120 ✉ allepe@edc2.edc.ca
Treasurer R G C Marshall *SVP & Treasurer* ☎ 598 2822 📠 563 8834
  ✉ marscl@edc2.edc.ca

General-Lending (DCM, SL)
Head of Corporate Banking J F Gagan *VP & Corporate Controller* ☎ 598 2938 📠 598 6672
  ✉ gagjo@edc2.edc.ca

Debt Capital Markets / Fixed Income
Global Head M MacDougall *VP & Assistant Treasurer* ☎ 598 2800 📠 563 8834
  ✉ macdma@edc2.edc.ca

Risk Management
Head of Risk Management D Dmytryk *Assistant Treasurer, Treasury Risk* ☎ 598 2862 📠 563 8834
  ✉ dmytda@edc2.edc.ca

Settlement / Clearing
Settlement (General) M Hodgkinson *Treasury Manager, Cash Admin & Settlements* ☎ 598 2830
  📠 563 8834 ✉ hodgma@edc2.edc.ca
Operations A Young *Assistant Treasurer, Treasury Operations* ☎ 598 2763 📠 563 8834
  ✉ younan@edc2.edc.ca

www.euromoneydirectory.com   CANADA (+1)

First Chicago NBD Bank Canada   Subsidiary Company

Suite 4240, BCE Place, PO Box 613, Mail Code Suite 5053, 161 Bay Street, Toronto, Ontario M5J 2S1
PO Box 613, Toronto, Ontario 5053 (Mail Code)
Tel: (416) 865 0466 Fax: (416) 363 7574 Telex: 06218722 NBDCDNTOR Swift: NBDD CA TT Cable: NATIONBANK

Senior Executive Officers
Chairman — James McNamee II
Unit Head - President — William J Buchanan

General-Lending (DCM, SL)
Head of Corporate Banking —
Jeremiah A Hynes III *Credit Officer*
Dwayne G Wesley *Finance*
William J Buchanan *Head, Corporate Markets*
Janet A Beadle *Banker, Corporate Markets*
Colleen H Delaney *Underwriter, Credit Products*
Mike C Bauer *Banker, Corporate Markets*
Michael N Tam *Underwriter, Credit Products*
Ruth J Halperin *Operations & Corporate Banking*

General - Treasury
Head of Treasury — Peter J Evans *Head*

Foreign Exchange
Department: Funding, Arbitrage, Money Markets, Foreign Exchange
Country Head — Peter J Evans *Head*

FX Traders / Sales People
FX Spot & Forward — Michael K Hawie

Settlement / Clearing
Operations — Ruth J Halperin *Operations & Corporate Banking*

Other Departments
Cash Management — Deborah E Booth

Administration
Other (Administration)
Finance & Human Resources — Dwayne G Wesley *Finance*

First Marathon Securities Limited

Suite 3200, The Exchange Tower, 2 First Canadian Place, Toronto, Ontario M5X 1J9
Tel: (416) 869 6416 Fax: (416) 864 6404; (416) 869 8002 Email: mnewallo@fmarathon.com
Website: www.fmarathon.com

Debt Capital Markets / Fixed Income
Fixed-Income Repo
Trading — Franklyn McRay

Equity Capital Markets
Equity Repo / Securities Lending
Head of Trading —
Graham Dyke *Trading*
Madhvi Patel *Trading*

Fuji Bank Canada   Subsidiary Company

Suite 2800, BCE Place, Canada Trust Tower, 161 Bay Street, Toronto, Ontario M5J 2S1
PO Box 609, Toronto, Ontario M5J 2S1
Tel: (416) 865 1020 Fax: (416) 865 9618 Swift: FUJI CA TT

Senior Executive Officers
Chairman — Soichi Hirabayashi
President & Chief Executive Officer — Kuninori Tanabe ☏ **814 2950**
Executive Vice President — Nobuaki Onishi ☏ **814 2960**
EVP & Chief Accountant — John Tan ☏ **814 2955**
AVP & Corporate Secretary — Nelly Pires ☏ **814 2957**

Syndicated Lending
Head of Origination —
Daniel Lee *Senior Vice President* ☏ **814 2961**
Hiroaki Watanabe *Vice President* ☏ **814 2975**

Money Markets
Head of Money Markets — Yutaka Miyajima *VP, Treasury*

Other Departments
Chief Credit Officer — Daniel Lee *Senior Vice President* ☏ **814 2961**

CANADA (+1)   www.euromoneydirectory.com

Fuji Bank Canada (cont)
Administration
Head of Administration   Masatoshe Eiryu *Vice President* ☏ **814 2957**
Compliance
   John Tan *EVP & Chief Accountant* ☏ **814 2955**
Accounts / Audit
   John Tan *EVP & Chief Accountant* ☏ **814 2955**

Goldman Sachs Canada   Subsidiary Company

600 Boulevard de Maisonneuve Ouest, Bureau 2350, Montreal, Quebec H3A 3J2
Tel: (514) 499 1510 **Fax:** (514) 499 9008

Senior Executive Officers
Vice President & Manager   Steven Shelton
Administration
Head of Administration   Ruby Fernandes

Goldman Sachs Canada   Subsidiary Company

Suite 1201, 150 King Street West, Toronto, Ontario M5H 1J9
Tel: (416) 343 8900 **Fax:** (416) 343 8792 **Telex:** 0622033 GOLDCANADA TOR

Senior Executive Officers
Chairman & Chief Executive   John P Curtin Jr
President   James T Kiernan Jr
Vice President   James R Cahill
Chief Executive Officer   John P Curtin Jr *Chairman & Chief Executive*
Managing Director / General Manager   James T Kiernan Jr
Administration
Head of Administration   Ruby Fernandes

Goldman Sachs Canada   Subsidiary Company

200 Burrard Street, Suite 1630, Water Front Centre, Vancouver, British Columbia V6C 3L6
Tel: (604) 257 1301 **Fax:** (604) 257 1300

Senior Executive Officers
Vice President & Manager   Michael Hicks

Gordon Capital Corporation

Box 67, Suite 5300, TD Tower, Toronto-Dominion Centre, Toronto, Ontario M5K 1E7
Tel: (416) 364 9393; (416) 868 5480 **Fax:** (416) 868 0445 **Telex:** 0622118

Equity Capital Markets
Equity Repo / Securities Lending
Head   Nino Guercio *Head Securities Lending Trader*
   ✉ nguercio@gordoncapital.com
Head of Trading   Taras Sidorenko *Securities Lending Trader*

Harlow Meyer Savage Canada   Subsidiary Company

Suite 300, One Richmond Street West, Toronto, Ontario M5H 3W4
Tel: (416) 864 7600 **Fax:** (416) 864 7610 **Telex:** 06218686 **Reuters:** HMST

Senior Executive Officers
Chief Executive Officer   Robert I McCully
Financial Director   Madrie A Secord *Chief Financial Officer*
Managing Director   Alexander D Stewart ☏ **864 7604**
Foreign Exchange
Head of Trading   Alexander D Stewart *Managing Director* ☏ **864 7604**
FX Traders / Sales People
   Alex Roome *Managing Director* ☏ **864 7603**
   Kevin Armstrong *Manager* ☏ **864 7603**

www.euromoneydirectory.com		CANADA (+1)

Hongkong Bank of Canada

70 York Street, Toronto, Ontario M5J 1S9
Tel: (416) 868 8000 Fax: (416) 868 3819 Email: info@hkbc.com
Website: www.hkbc.com

Senior Executive Officers
Senior Executive Vice President	J L Gordon

General-Lending (DCM, SL)
Head of Corporate Banking	R J Ross Vice President, Corporate Banking

General-Investment
Head of Investment	J Book Vice President, Investment Services

General - Treasury
Head of Treasury	J B Meredith Senior Vice President

Relationship Manager
Financial Services	J F Mahaffy Senior Vice President

Syndicated Lending

Other (Trade Finance)
International Trade	P H C Blondel Vice President

Risk Management

Other (FI Derivatives)
Risk Management and Credit Services	J B Howden Vice President
Credit East	W McLaney Vice President

Hongkong Bank of Canada

885 West Georgia Street, Vancouver, British Columbia V6C 3E9
Tel: (604) 685 1000 Fax: (604) 641 1849 Telex: 04507750 HONGGRO Email: info@hkbc.com
Website: www.hkbc.com

Senior Executive Officers
President & Chief Executive Officer	W R P Dalton
Chief Executive Officer	Y A Nasr Deputy Chief Executive Officer
Chief Operating Officer	M J G Glynn

Others (Senior Executives)
	B A Giacomazzi Chief Credit Officer
	J T Mould Chief Financial Officer

Relationship Manager
Financial Services Systems	H Koa Vice President
Banking Systems	R M Leury Vice President

Other Departments
Economic Research	D E Bond Chief Economist

Administration

Technology & Systems
Distribution Systems	S P O'Sullivan Senior Vice President
Group Systems Development Centre	A H Tong Senior Vice President
Distribution Systems	L S Bailey Vice President

Legal / In-House Counsel
Legal Counsel & Company Secretary	M Miller Vice President

Accounts / Audit
Chief Auditor	D M Sargeant Vice President
Chief Accountant	C J Young Vice President

Other (Administration)
Human Resources	S R Babani Senior Vice President
Services	R Morgan Senior Vice President
Government & Public Affairs	D E Bond Vice President
Marketing	J G S McCulloch Vice President
Strategic Development & Financial Management	K C Matheson Vice President
Hongkong Bank Leasing	M J Stevulak Vice President

Euromoney Directory 1999   **227**

CANADA (+1) www.euromoneydirectory.com

The Industrial Bank of Japan (Canada)
Head Office

Suite 1102, PO Box 29, 100 Yonge Street, Toronto, Ontario M5C 2W1
Tel: (416) 365 9550 Fax: (416) 367 3452 Telex: 233775039 Email: ibjctor@netcom.ca

Senior Executive Officers
Chairman   Yoh Kurosawa ☎ +81 (3) 3214 1111
President & Chief Executive Officer   Mitsuo Iwamoto
Financial Director   Howard Bennett *EVP, Chief Accountant & Secretary*
Chief Operating Officer   Toru Irie *Executive Vice President*
Treasurer   Hiromasa Okada *Chief Trader*

Debt Capital Markets / Fixed Income
Libor-Based / Floating-Rate Products
FRN Origination; FRN Sales; Asset Swaps;   Toru Irie *Executive Vice President*
Asset Swaps (Sales)
Asset-Backed Securities / Securitization
Regional Head   Toru Irie *Executive Vice President*
Head of Trading   Hiromasa Okada *Chief Trader*

Syndicated Lending
Tel: 365 9550 Fax: 367 3452
Country Head of Origination; Head of   Toru Irie *Executive Vice President*
Syndication
Loan-Related Activities
Trade Finance; Project Finance; Structured   Toru Irie *Executive Vice President*
Trade Finance

Money Markets
Tel: 365 9550 Fax: 367 3452
Country Head   Toru Irie *Executive Vice President*
Domestic Commercial Paper
Head of Origination; Head of Sales; Head of   Toru Irie *Executive Vice President*
Trading

Foreign Exchange
Tel: 365 9550 Fax: 367 3452
Country Head of Institutional Sales; Corporate Toru Irie *Executive Vice President*
Sales
Head of Trading   Hiromasa Okada *Chief Trader*

Risk Management
Global Head   Toru Irie *Executive Vice President*
Fixed Income Derivatives / Risk Management
Country Head; IR Swaps Sales / Marketing; IR Toru Irie *Executive Vice President*
Swaps Trading; IR Options Sales / Marketing;
IR Options Trading
Foreign Exchange Derivatives / Risk Management
Cross-Currency Swaps, Sales / Marketing;   Toru Irie *Executive Vice President*
Cross-Currency Swaps, Trading; Vanilla FX
option Sales; Vanilla FX option Trading

Settlement / Clearing
Regional Head   Frances Hills *Assistant Manager Operations*

Administration
Technology & Systems
                                              Howard Bennett *EVP, Chief Accountant & Secretary*

ING Bank of Canada
Subsidiary Company

Suite 900, 9th Floor, 111 Gordon Baker Road, North York, Ontario M2H 3RI
Tel: (416) 497 5157 Fax: (416) 758 5215

Senior Executive Officers
President & CEO   Arkadi Kuhlmann

ING Direct

Suite 900, 9th Floor, 111 Gordon Baker Road, Toronto, Ontario M2H 3RI
Tel: (416) 758 5200 Fax: (416) 758 5201

Senior Executive Officers
President & CEO   Arkadi Kuhlmann

www.euromoneydirectory.com   CANADA (+1)

Laurentian Bank of Canada
Head Office

1981 McGill College Avenue, Montreal, Quebec H3A 3K3
Tel: (514) 284 7922; (514) 522 6306 **Fax:** (514) 284 4075; (514) 284 2426 **Telex:** 524217 LAURENTBANK
Swift: BLCM CA MM **Reuters:** LRTN
Website: www.laurentianbank.com

Senior Executive Officers
Chairman
President & Chief Executive Officer
Financial Director
Treasurer

Executive Vice President

Others (Senior Executives)
Retail Banking
General-Lending (DCM, SL)
Head of Corporate Banking

Debt Capital Markets / Fixed Income
Tel: 284 7548 **Fax:** 284 3396
Global Head
Domestic Government Bonds
Head of Sales
Head of Trading
Head of Research
Medium-Term Notes
Head of Origination
Asset-Backed Securities / Securitization
Global Head
Fixed-Income Repo
Matched Book Manager
Syndicated Lending
Global Head
Loan-Related Activities
Trade Finance
Other (Trade Finance)
Real Estate Financing
Money Markets
Fax: 284 5924
Global Head
Wholesale Deposits
Marketing
Foreign Exchange
Fax: 284 5924
Head of Institutional Sales
Head of Trading
Risk Management
Global Head
Fixed Income Derivatives / Risk Management
Global Head
Corporate Finance / M&A Advisory
Global Head
Private Equity
Settlement / Clearing
Fax: 284 7983
Regional Head
Global Custody
Regional Head
Asset Management
Investment Funds
Other Departments
Proprietary Trading
Private Banking
Correspondent Banking
Global Trust

Jeanine Guillevin-Wood
Henri-Paul Rousseau ⓣ **284 7967**
Robert Cardinal *SVP, Finance & CFO* ⓣ **284 7535**
André Dubuc *SVP, Treasury Risk Mgmt & Strategic Development*
ⓣ **284 7562** ⓕ **284 3396**
Louis Bernard

Gilles Godbout *Executive Vice President*

André Scott *Vice President, Credit*
Richard Guay *EVP, Commercial & Corporate Banking*

Bernard Piché *SVP, Brokerage Operations & CM* ⓣ **284 6932**

Claude Lepage *VP, Institutional Fixed-Income* ⓣ **350 2904** ⓕ **350 2897**
Jean Bordeleau *Vice President, Trading* ⓣ **350 2904** ⓕ **350 2897**
Clément Gignac *EVP, Research* ⓣ **350 2904** ⓕ **350 2897**

Pierre Bélanger ⓣ **350 2904** ⓕ **350 2987**

Michel Richard *VP, Corporate Finance* ⓣ **350 2863** ⓕ **350 2918**

Philippe Fournier *Trader, Repo* ⓣ **350 2904** ⓕ **350 2987**

Jean-Louis Mongrain *SVP, Corporate Finance & Investment*

Susan Fotopoulos *Manager* ⓣ **350 2860**

Paul Hurtubise *Senior Vice President*

Antoine Abraham *Manager* ⓣ **350 2901**

Antoine Abraham *Manager* ⓣ **350 2901**

Antoine Abraham *Manager* ⓣ **350 2901**
Normand Faubert *Manager, FX* ⓣ **350 2901**

Réjean Robitaille *VP & Deputy General Manager* ⓣ **284 6908** ⓕ **284 7918**

Réjean Robitaille *VP & Deputy General Manager* ⓣ **284 6908** ⓕ **284 7918**

Michel Richard *VP, Corporate Finance* ⓣ **350 2863** ⓕ **350 2918**
Paul Tardif *Senior Vice President*

André Richard *Manager*

Caroline Beaudoin *Senior Manager, Securities* ⓣ **284 4668**

Paul Tardif *Senior Vice President*

Jean Bordeleau *Vice President, Trading* ⓣ **350 2904** ⓕ **350 2897**
Marcel Bédard *Senior Manager* ⓣ **284 4002**
Martine Mounier *Manager* ⓣ **284 5971**
Paul Tardif *Senior Vice President*

Euromoney Directory 1999   **229**

Laurentian Bank of Canada (cont)

Administration
Head of Administration — Louis Bernard *Executive Vice President*

Technology & Systems
Technology & Corporate System — V.P. Pham *Vice President* ☎ **284 4521**
Louis Bernard *Executive Vice President*

Legal / In-House Counsel
Lorraine Pilon *VP, Legal Affairs, Secretary's Office* ☎ **284 7160** Fax **284 3396**

Compliance
Sophie Lussier *Counsellor* ☎ **284 3969** Fax **284 3396**

Public Relations
Advertising, Marketing & Public Relations — Danielle St-Denis *Vice President* ☎ **284 3917**

Other (Administration)
Human Resources — Robert Teasdale *Senior Vice President*
General Affairs — Robert S. Robson *Executive Vice President*
Laurentian Trust — Paul Tardif *Senior Vice President*
International Services — Susan Fotopoulos *Manager* ☎ **350 2860**

Lévesque Beaubien Geoffrion Inc
Broker/Dealer

Suite 600, 121 King Street West, Toronto, Ontario M5H 3T9
Tel: (416) 865 7442 **Fax:** (416) 865 7608

Debt Capital Markets / Fixed Income
Fixed-Income Repo
Head of Repo
Marketing & Product Development
Trading

Daniel C Duggan *Repo Trader*
Daniel C Duggan *Manager*
Daniel C Duggan *Repo Trader*
Mary Spadafora *Repo Trader*
Dave Duggan *Repo Trader*

Equity Capital Markets
Equity Repo / Securities Lending
Head
Head of Trading

Daniel C Duggan *Repo Trader*
Dave Duggan *Repo Trader*

The Long-Term Credit Bank of Japan Limited
Representative Office

Suite 3710, 161 Bay Street, Toronto, Ontario M5J 2S1
PO Box 616, Toronto, Ontario M5J 2S1
Tel: (416) 865 0711 **Fax:** (416) 366 0950

Senior Executive Officers
Chief Representative & SVP — Makoto Tatebayashi
VP & Representative — Nigel Sharpley

Merrill Lynch Canada Inc
Full Branch Office

Suite 1650, South West Bow Valley Square, 250 6th Avenue, Calgary, Alberta T2P 3H7
Tel: (403) 231 7500 **Fax:** (403) 237 7372

Merrill Lynch Canada Inc
Full Branch Office

Suite 2500, Place Montreal Trust, 1800 McGill College Avenue, Montreal, Quebec H3A 3J6
31st Floor, 1250 Renaoe-Levesque, Boulevard West, Montreal, Quebec H3B 4W8
Tel: (514) 982 2700 **Fax:** (514) 982 2729; (514) 846 3591

Merrill Lynch Canada Inc
Subsidiary Company

Merrill Lynch Canada Tower, 200 King Street West, Toronto, Ontario M5H 3W3
Tel: (416) 586 6000; (416) 586 6450 **Fax:** (416) 586 6402

Senior Executive Officers
Chairman — Robert Grandy
President — Paul Thomas

www.euromoneydirectory.com CANADA (+1)

Debt Capital Markets / Fixed Income
Tel: 586 6619 Fax: 586 6687

Fixed-Income Repo
Head of Repo
Marketing & Product Development
Trading

Craig Aubrey *Desk Head* T 586 6620
Joanne Feekery *Repo Sales*
Craig Aubrey *Desk Head* T 586 6620
Geoff Denton *Vice President & Repo Trader*
Todd Evans *Repo Trader*
Adam Mann *Repo Trader*

National Bank of Canada — Head Office
600 de la Gauchetiere West, Montreal, Quebec H3B 4L2
Tel: (514) 394 5000; (800) 361 8688 Reuters: NBCM

Senior Executive Officers
Chairman of the Board & CEO
President & Chief Operating Officer
Chief Executive Officer
Financial Director
Chief Operating Officer
Treasurer

International Division

Others (Senior Executives)

André Bérard T 394 6547 F 394 8377
Léon Courville T 394 6559 F 394 8434
André Bérard *Chairman of the Board & CEO* T 394 6547 F 394 8377
Michel Labonté *SVP, Finance & Operations*
Léon Courville *President & Chief Operating Officer* T 394 6559 F 394 8434
Jean Turmel *SEVP, Treasury, Brokerage & Corporate Banking* T 394 6399 F 394 4341
Gaby Touma *SVP, International Division* T 394 6713 F 394 8276

Gilles Bissonette *SVP, Banking & Operations* T 646 3897 F 646 6559
Jules G Gagné *SVP, Electronic Networks* T 394 6565 F 394 8947
Jean Houde *SVP, Banking & Retail Markets* T 394 8778 F 394 6553
Tony P Meti *SVP, Banking & Commercial Markets* T 394 6638 F 394 6553

General-Lending (DCM, SL)
Head of Corporate Banking

General - Treasury
Head of Treasury

Mario Lecaldare *SVP, Corporate Banking, Canada* T 394 6713 F 394 6073

Louis Vachon *SVP, Treasury & Financial Markets* T 394 6408 F 394 6268

Foreign Exchange
Tel: 394 8237 Fax: 394 8635 Reuters: NBCFXO
Head of Foreign Exchange
Head of Institutional Sales

Head of Trading

Martin Ouellet *VP, Treasury & Financial Markets* T 394 8974
Steve Demers *Manager, Foreign Exchange & Derivative Products* T 394 8875
Jacques Tessier *Chief Dealer & Manager, Foreign Exchange* T 394 8237

Risk Management
Fax: 394 8635
Head of Risk Management

Louis Beaudoin *Manager, Risk Management* T 394 5819 F 394 6268

Fixed Income Derivatives / Risk Management
Head of Sales

Trading

Steve Demers *Manager, Foreign Exchange & Derivative Products* T 394 8875
Richard Poirier *Senior Trader* T 394 8237

OTC Equity Derivatives
Sales

André Forcier *Manager, Equity Derivatives* T 394 8561

Corporate Finance / M&A Advisory
Head of Corporate Finance

Réal Raymond *SEVP, Corporate Finance* T 390 7370 F 879 5142

Settlement / Clearing
Head of Settlement / Clearing
Equity Settlement; Fixed-Income Settlement;
Operations; Back-Office

Guy Bérard *VP, Risk Management & Administration* T 394 8368
Lynda Lupien *Manager, Treasury Operations* T 394 8020

Global Custody
Department: NBC Clearing
Head of Global Custody

Yvan Naud *President* T 879 2412

Asset Management
Department: NATCAN
Head

Michel Tremblay *President* T 871 7601

Other Departments
Chief Credit Officer
Correspondent Banking
Cash Management

Patricia Curadeau-Grou *SVP, Credit* T 394 6619
Alistair Sinclair *Senior Manager, Corporate Banking* T 394 8053
Benoit Dagenais *Manager, LVTS / Cash Management* T 397 5843

Euromoney Directory 1999 231

CANADA (+1)　　　　　　www.euromoneydirectory.com

National Bank of Canada (cont)
Administration
Head of Administration　　　　Regina Kudzma *Controller* ☎ **394 6386**

Technology & Systems
　　　　　　　　　　　　　Jean-Marc Denault *Manager, IT* ☎ **394 8818**

Legal / In-House Counsel
　　　　　　　　　　　　　Francois Bourassa *Senior Legal Counsel* ☎ **394 8370**

Compliance
　　　　　　　　　　　　　Guy Bérard *VP, Risk Management & Administration* ☎ **394 8368**

Corporate Communications
　　　　　　　　　　　　　Regina Kudzma *Controller* ☎ **394 6386**

National Bank of Greece (Canada)　　　　　　Head Office
Suite 200, 1170 Place du Frère André, Montreal, Quebec H3B 3C6
Tel: (514) 954 1522 Fax: (514) 954 1620 Telex: 0524196 Swift: ETHN CA MM ADM

Senior Executive Officers
Chairman & President　　　　　　Theodore Karatzas
Chief Executive Officer　　　　　Nicholas Avgoustakis
Financial Director　　　　　　　Demetris J Yantsulis *SVP, Finance & Operations*
Treasurer　　　　　　　　　　　James Tsalikis ☎ **866 2286**

Administration

Corporate Communications
Corporate Affairs　　　　　　　R W B White *Senior Vice President*

NM Rothschild & Sons Canada Limited　　　　Subsidiary Company
Formerly known as: Rothschild Canada Limited
Suite 3800, 1 First Canadian Place, Toronto, Ontario M5X 1B1
PO Box 77, Toronto, Ontario M5X 1B1
Tel: (416) 369 9600 Fax: (416) 864 1261; (416) 863 6746

Senior Executive Officers
Chairman　　　　　　　　　　　　David de Rothschild
President & Chief Executive Officer　H Garfield Emerson ☎ **369 2634**
Chief Operating Officer　　　　　R Peter Gillen *Vice Chairman*
Managing Director　　　　　　　E R Giacomelli
Managing Director　　　　　　　Gordon Bogden
Managing Director　　　　　　　George Kitching
Managing Director & Secretary　　Mark A Hill

Others (Senior Executives)
　　　　　　　　　　　　　　　David Bell *Vice President*
　　　　　　　　　　　　　　　Susan Wood *Vice President*
　　　　　　　　　　　　　　　Stephen Shapiro *Vice President*

Nomura Canada Inc　　　　　　　　　　　　Subsidiary Company
PO Box 434, Suite 5830, 1 First Canadian Place, Toronto, Ontario M5X 1E3
Tel: (416) 868 1683 Fax: (416) 359 8956

Senior Executive Officers
President & Chief Executive Officer　Thomas K Wu ☎ **359 8990**

Equity Capital Markets
Department: Equity Trading
Tel: 868 6210 Fax: 359 8984
Head of Trading　　　　　　　　Michael Cappuccio *Equity Trader*

Equity Repo / Securities Lending
Head　　　　　　　　　　　　　Peter Abric *Equity Finance Trader*

Paribas Bank of Canada

Suite 4100, Royal Trust Tower, Toronto Dominion Centre, Toronto, Ontario M5K 1N8
PO Box 31
Tel: (416) 365 9600; (416) 365 7418 **Fax:** (416) 947 0086 **Telex:** 06218612

Senior Executive Officers
President — Edward Speal E edward_speal@paribas.com

Administration
Head of Administration — Fanny Ng *Administrative Assistant* T 365 6733 F 947 0086
E fanny_ng@paribas.com

Pope & Company
Head Office

15 Duncan Street, Toronto, Ontario M5H 3P9
Tel: (416) 593 5537; (416) 593 5535 **Fax:** (416) 593 5099 **Email:** popebank@compuserve.com

Senior Executive Officers
Chief Executive Officer — Francis Pope *Chief Executive Officer* T 593 5535
Financial Director — Richard Munro *Chief Finance Officer* T 593 5540

Equity Capital Markets
Head of Trading — Bill Owens *Head Trader* T 593 5537

Money Markets
Head of Money Markets — Katherine Frida *Manager* T 593 5536

Settlement / Clearing
Country Head — Jean O'Hagen *Manager* T 593 5540

Power Financial Corporation
Subsidiary Company

751 Victoria Square, Montreal, Quebec H2Y 2J3
Tel: (514) 286 7430; (514) 286 7400 **Fax:** (514) 286 7424

Senior Executive Officers
Chairman — Paul Desmarais Jr
President & Chief Executive Officer — Robert Gratton
Financial Director — Michel Plessis-Bélair *EVP & Chief Financial Officer*
Treasurer — Monique Létourneau
Company Secretary — Edward Johnson

Prebon Yamane (Canada) Limited
Full Branch Office

Suite 301, PO Box 20, 1 Toronto Street, Toronto, Ontario M5C 2V6
Tel: (416) 941 0600 **Fax:** (416) 941 0607 **Telex:** 0622377

Senior Executive Officers
Managing Director — Denis Marcotte T 941 0545
Financial Director — Christine Bourne *Controller* T 941 0628

Debt Capital Markets / Fixed Income
Tel: 941 0614 **Fax:** 941 0607
Country Head — Frank Klotz *Senior Vice President*

Domestic Government Bonds
Head of Sales — Karel Tomes *Senior Vice President* T 941 0619

Fixed-Income Repo
Head of Repo — Gary Kirk *Senior Vice President* T 941 0618

Money Markets
Tel: 941 0616 **Fax:** 941 0601
Country Head — Paul Paquette *Vice President*

Foreign Exchange
Tel: 941 0612
Country Head — Nick Abrahams *Senior Vice President* T 941 0612

Administration

Technology & Systems — John Schoon *Manager, IT & Communication* T 941 0625

Other (Administration)
CAGE — Sam Schiavone *Manager* T 941 0624
Accounts Receivable — Jane Clarke *Manager* T 941 0629

CANADA (+1) www.euromoneydirectory.com

RBC Dominion Securities Inc — Head Office

Alternative trading name: Royal Bank of Canada
PO Box 50, 2nd Floor, South Tower, Royal Bank Plaza, Toronto, Ontario M5J 2WJ
Tel: (416) 842 2000 Fax: (416) 842 8044

Senior Executive Officers
Honorary Chairman — George T Richardson
Chairman, CEO & Director — Anthony Fell
President, COO & Director — W Reay Mackay
Financial Director — David O Hawkey *VP, CFO & Director*

Others (Senior Executives)
Charles M Winograd *Deputy Chairman & Director*
Bryce W Douglas *Deputy Chairman & Director*
Mark L Cullen *Vice Chairman & Director*
Thomas F Rahilly *Vice Chairman & Director*
Michael H Wilson *Vice Chairman & Director*
K Michael Edwards *EVP & Director*

Debt Capital Markets / Fixed Income
Global Head — Andy Pringle *Head of Capital Markets* [T] **842 6333**

Fixed-Income Repo
Head of Repo
Trading
Robert Nobrega *Director* [T] **842 6430** [F] **842 6377**
Scott Bryson *Vice President & Repo Trader*
Robert Perry *Vice President & Repo Trader*
Dave Sweeny *Vice President & Repo Trader*
Rob Jarvis *Vice President & Repo Trader*
Gord Pearce *Vice President & Repo Trader*
Jason Ellis *Vice President & Repo Trader*
Terry Upham *Vice President & Repo Trader*
John Kuntz *Vice President & Repo Trader*

Equity Capital Markets
Global Head — Andy Pringle *Head of Capital Markets* [T] **842 6333**

Equity Repo / Securities Lending
Head — Kevin Douclet *Vice President* [T] **842 6430** [F] **842 4345**
[E] **kdouclet@rbcds.com**
Head of Trading — Andrew Thornhill *CFA, Trader*

Syndicated Lending
Global Head — Robert Nobrega *Vice President & Director* [T] **842 6430**

Money Markets
Global Head — Peter Dymott *Vice President* [T] **482 6222**

Foreign Exchange
Global Head — Peter Dymott *Vice President* [T] **482 6222**
George Brazil *Vice President* [T] **482 6222** [F] **482 6262**

Administration
Compliance
Michael D Sharpe *Vice President*

Republic National Bank of New York (Canada) — Bank Subsidiary

1981 McGill College Avenue, Montreal, Quebec H3A 3A9
Tel: (514) 288 5551; (514) 288 0393 Fax: (514) 286 4577 Telex: 055 60059 Swift: BLIC CA MN Reuters: RNBC
Website: www.rnb.com

Senior Executive Officers
Chairman — Ezekiel Schouela
President — Allan Schouela
Treasurer — Simon Wahed *Executive Vice President*
International Division — Elizabeth Pereira *Manager*

Others (Senior Executives)
Commercial Banking — Olive Dunn *Senior Vice President*

General-Lending (DCM, SL)
Head of Corporate Banking — Jack Spitz *Representative, Toronto Office* [T] **(416) 789 7981**

General - Treasury
Head of Treasury — Simon Wahed *Executive Vice President*

Debt Capital Markets / Fixed Income
Head of Debt Capital Markets — Simon Wahed *Executive Vice President*

Syndicated Lending
Other (Trade Finance)
Letters of Credit
Real Estate & Property Finance

Bina Romita *Manager*
David M Schoucla *Executive Vice President*

Money Markets
Other (Wholesale Deposits)
CDs & Eurocurrency Sales

Alain Baisle
Alain Hage

Foreign Exchange
Head of Foreign Exchange
Head of Institutional Sales

Simon Wahed *Executive Vice President*
Howard Chin *Institutional Desk*

FX Traders / Sales People
Chief Dealer
Options & Forwards

Steve Boucouvalas *Executive Vice President*
Antoine Lessard *Vice President*

Settlement / Clearing
Foreign Exchange Settlement

Marc Hopkins ☏ **(514) 286 4561**

Other Departments
Private Banking

Jack Spitz *Representative, Toronto Office* ☏ **(416) 789 7981**

Administration
Head of Administration

Patrick Bubendorff *Vice President*

Technology & Systems

Guy Motard *Manager*

Legal / In-House Counsel

Christianne Filiatrault *Vice President*

Compliance

Ann Bernstein

Royal Bank of Canada
Full Branch Office

1 Place Ville Marie, Montreal, Quebec H3C 3A9
PO Box 6001, Montreal, Quebec H3C 3A9
Tel: (514) 874 2110; (514) 874 2110 **Telex:** 05561086

The Royal Bank of Canada
Full Branch Office

200 Bay Street, Toronto, Ontario M5J 2J5
Tel: (416) 974 3940 **Telex:** 06217897 **Reuters:** +RBCO (Non-C$ Op

Senior Executive Officers
President

Paul Taylor

Debt Capital Markets / Fixed Income
Fixed-Income Repo
Head of Repo
Trading

Bob Nobrega *Vice President & Director* ☏ **842 6430** 📠 **842 6377**
Dave Sweeny *Vice President*
Scott Bryson *Sales*
Robert Perry *VP, Sales*
Gord Pearce *Trader*
Jason Ellis *Trader*
Terry Upham *Trader*
John Kuntz *Trader*

Royal Trust Corporation of Canada

Global Securities Services, 35th Floor, Royal Trust Tower, Toronto, Ontario M5W 1P9
PO Box 7500, Station A, Toronto, Ontario
Tel: (416) 955 3355; (416) 955 5555 **Fax:** (416) 955 3377; (416) 955 5501 **Telex:** 929670 **Swift:** RTBB GB 2L
Website: www.royalbank.com/english/gss

Debt Capital Markets / Fixed Income
Tel: 955 5500 **Fax:** 955 6483

Fixed-Income Repo
Head of Repo

Marketing & Product Development

Frederick Francis *VP, Global Securities & Lending Services*
✉ **frederick.francis@royalbank.com**
Allan Kaufman *Director & Product Manager* ☏ **955 5553**

CANADA (+1)   www.euromoneydirectory.com

Royal Trust Corporation of Canada (cont)
Fixed-Income Repo (cont)

	Warren Maynard *Head of Global Sales & Marketing* ☎ 955 5400
	Ⓔ **warren.maynard@royalbank.com**
	Cathy Meaney *Marketing Manager* ☎ 955 3386
	Ⓔ **cathy.meaney@royalbank.com**
Trading	Yvonne Wyllie *Head, Global Trading* ☎ 955 5500
	Ⓔ **yvonne.wyllie@royalbank.com**
	Carmen Cotter
	Nick Thomas *Head of Securities Lending, Europe* ☎ +44 (171) 653 4182
	Ⓕ +44 (171) 489 1195 Ⓔ **thomasni@rbcel.com**
	Paul Bertrand
	Scott Logan *Trader, Asian Desk*
	Luisa Starns *Trader, Europe Desk*
	Jeff Tkachuk
	David Williams
	Phil Zywot

Equity Capital Markets
Equity Repo / Securities Lending

Head	Frederick Francis *VP, Global Securities & Lending Services*
	Ⓔ **frederick.francis@royalbank.com**
	Susan Pike *Director, Operations* ☎ 955 5557 Ⓔ **susan.pike@royalbank.com**
Marketing & Product Development	Allan Kaufman *Director & Product Manager* ☎ 955 5553
	Ⓔ **allan.kaaufman@royalbank.com**
	Warren Maynard *Head, Global Sales & Marketing* ☎ 955 5525
	Ⓔ **warren.maynard@royalbank.com**
	Cathy Meaney *Marketing Manager* ☎ 955 3386
	Ⓔ **cathy.meaney@royalbank.com**
Marketing	Warren Maynard *Head of Global Sales & Marketing* ☎ 955 5400
	Ⓔ **warren.maynard@royalbank.com**
	Warren Maynard *Head, Global Sales & Marketing* ☎ 955 5525
	Ⓔ **warren.maynard@royalbank.com**
Head of Prime Brokerage	Susan Pike *Director, Operations* ☎ 955 5557 Ⓔ **susan.pike@royalbank.com**
Head of Trading	David Williams
	Phil Zywot
	Carmen Cotter
	Scott Logan *Trader, Asian Desk*
	Claude Robillard *Trader, International Equities*
	Laura Torrance *Trader, International Equities*
	James Bowes *Trader, Canadian Equities*

Global Custody

Regional Head	Robert T Wright *Vice President, Sales* ☎ 955 3355 Ⓕ 955 3377
	Ⓔ **rwright@royaltrust.com**

Sakura Bank (Canada) — Subsidiary Company

Suite 3601, Commerce Court West, Toronto, Ontario M5L 1B9
PO Box 59, Toronto, Ontario M5L 1B9
Tel: (416) 369 8531 **Fax:** (416) 369 0268 **Telex:** 0623400 **Reuters:** MTKT

Senior Executive Officers
Chairman — Takao Umino
President & Chief Executive Officer — Naoki Asaumi
Financial Director — Toshio Ueda *Executive Vice President & Chief Financial Officer*
Treasurer — Hideo Kobayashi *Vice President*
Vice President — Eddy Yao

General-Lending (DCM, SL)
Head of Corporate Banking — Kazuo Nakakuma *Vice President*

Syndicated Lending
Head of Syndication — Elwood Langley *Vice President*

Money Markets
Head of Money Markets — Hideo Kobayashi *Vice President*

Foreign Exchange
Head of Foreign Exchange — Hideo Kobayashi *Vice President*

Corporate Finance / M&A Advisory
Head of Corporate Finance — Kazuo Nakakuma *Vice President*

Settlement / Clearing
Head of Settlement / Clearing — Eddy Yao *Vice President*

Other Departments
Cash Management
Administration
Head of Administration
Business Development
Technology & Systems

Compliance

Accounts / Audit

Hideo Kobayashi *Vice President*

Peter Wu *Vice President*
Kazuo Nakakuma *Vice President*

Peter Wu *Vice President*

Toshio Ueda *Executive Vice President & Chief Financial Officer*

Peter Wu *Vice President*

Scotia Capital Markets
Subsidiary Company

Alternative trading name: The Bank of Nova Scotia & ScotiaMcleod Inc
68th Floor, 40 King Street West, Toronto, Ontario M5W 2X6
PO Box 4085, Station A, Toronto, Ontario M5W 2X6
Tel: (416) 863 7411 **Fax:** (416) 862 3052 **Telex:** 06524250
Reuters: MYIA-B (Equity Prices); MXWJ (Economics); MYWA, MYWG-H (Money Markets);
BNST (Forex Dealing); GOLD (Precious Metals)
Website: www.scotiacapital.com

Senior Executive Officers
Chairman & Chief Executive Officer
Deputy Chairman
Deputy Chairman
Deputy Chairman
Financial Director

W D Wilson
G J Homer
R E Lint
D F Sullivan
C M Johnston *Chief Financial Officer*

Others (Senior Executives)
Global Trading (Co-Head)

Western Canada
European Operations
Asian Operations
Quebec Region
USA Operations

T A Healy *Managing Director*
C J Schumacher *Managing Director*
I D Bruce *Managing Director & Head*
K R Ray *Head*
I A Berry *Head*
J O Nadeau *Head*
F E Price *Head*

General-Investment
Head of Investment

S A Martin *MD & Head, Investment Banking*

Relationship Manager
Head of Corporate & Institutional Client Services

B J Porter *Managing Director*

Debt Capital Markets / Fixed Income
Fax: 862 3001
Head of Fixed Income

J F Madden *Managing Director*

Fixed-Income Repo
Trading

Taylor Moore *Associate Director, Repo Trading*
Bradford Ellies *Associate Director, Repo Trading*
Chris Thomas *Associate Director, Repo Sales*

Equity Capital Markets
Other (Domestic Equities)
Institutional Equity

L R Lewis *Co-Head*
J W Mountain *Co-Head*

Equity Research
Head of Equity Research

L Ward *Managing Director*

Foreign Exchange
Head of Foreign Exchange

B M Wainstein *Managing Director*

Risk Management
Other (Exchange-Traded Derivatives)
Derivative Products

C J Schumacher *Managing Director*

Corporate Finance / M&A Advisory
Head of Mergers & Acquisition

W N Gula *Managing Director*

Other Departments
Commodities / Bullion
Private Banking

L J Scott *MD & Global Head, Precious & Base Metals*
J M Werry *MD & Head of Private Client Financial Services*

CANADA (+1)　　　　　　　www.euromoneydirectory.com

Scotia Capital Markets (cont)
Administration
Head of Administration　　　　　M I Greenspan *Chief Administrative Officer & Head*

Compliance
　　　　　　　　　　　　　　　J C Smart *Head*

Other (Administration)
Human Resources　　　　　　　R G Woods *Head*

Scotiabank
Subsidiary Company

Alternative trading name: The Bank of Nova Scotia
Scotia Plaza, 44 King Street West, Toronto, Ontario M5H 1H1
Tel: (416) 866 6161 Fax: (416) 866 3750 Telex: WUI 6719400 Swift: NOSC CA TT Email: email@scotiabank.ca
Website: www.scotiabank.ca

Senior Executive Officers
Chairman & CEO, Scotia Capital Markets　　　W David Wilson
Chairman & Chief Executive　　　　　　　　　Peter C Godsoe
Vice Chairman, Wealth Management & Int'l Banking　　　Richard E Waugh
SEVP, Global Risk Management　　　　　　　　John F M Crean
President　　　　　　　　　　　　　　　　　　Bruce R Birmingham
Financial Director　　　　　　　　　　　　　Sarabjit S Marwah *EVP & Chief Financial Officer*
Treasurer　　　　　　　　　　　　　　　　　Robert L Brooks *EVP & Group Treasurer*

Others (Senior Executives)
Grupo Financiero Inverlat, Mexico　　　　　William P Sutton *Executive Vice President*
Branch Banking & Alternate Delivery Channels　Robert W Chisholm *Vice Chairman*

General-Investment
Head of Investment　　　　　　　　　　　　Barry R F Luter *EVP, Corporate Banking*
　　　　　　　　　　　　　　　　　　　　　S Dennis N Belcher *EVP, Investment Bnkg Credit & Credit Policy*

Other Departments
Private Banking　　　　　　　　　　　　　J Rory MacDonald *Senior Vice President*
Correspondent Banking　　　　　　　　　　Timothy Plumptre *Senior Vice President* ☎ 866 3757

Administration
Legal / In-House Counsel
　　　　　　　　　　　　　　　　　　　　George Whyte *SVP & General Counsel* ☎ 866 6967

Compliance
　　　　　　　　　　　　　　　　　　　　Louise Cannon *Senior Vice President* ☎ 866 7033

Public Relations
　　　　　　　　　　　　　　　　　　　　Sandra Stewart *Vice President* ☎ 866 7238

Other (Administration)
Human Resources　　　　　　　　　　　　　Sylvia D Chrominska *Executive Vice President*

State Bank of India (Canada)
Subsidiary Company

200 Bay Street, Royal Bank Plaza, #1600 North Tower, Toronto, Ontario M5J 2J2
PO Box 81, Suite 1600, Toronto, Ontario M5J 2J2
Tel: (416) 865 0414 Fax: (416) 865 0324 Reuters: SBIT

The Sumitomo Trust & Banking Company Limited
Representative Office

Suite 6920, 1 First Canadian Place, Toronto, Ontario M5X 1E3
PO Box 439, Toronto, Ontario M5X 1E3
Tel: (416) 364 8111 Fax: (416) 367 3269

Senior Executive Officers
Senior Vice President & Representive　　　　Gordon Herington

www.euromoneydirectory.com   CANADA (+1)

TD Securities
7th Floor, Ernst & Young Tower, 222 Bay Street, Toronto, Ontario M5K 1A2
Tel: (416) 982 6109 Fax: (416) 944 3378

Senior Executive Officers
Vice Chairman   Duncan Gibson ☎ **982 8877**

Debt Capital Markets / Fixed Income
Fixed-Income Repo
Trading   Santo Cesario *Vice President, Financing Group*
Lynda Edgar *Senior Dealer, Financing Group*
Mario Reffo *Vice President, Financing Group*
Frank McGillicuddy *Dealer, Financing Group*
David Zavitz *Dealer, Financing Group*

Equity Capital Markets
Equity Repo / Securities Lending
Head   Joseph Serpe *Managing Director, Fixed Income* ☎ **307 8331** 📠 **983 3378**
Head of Trading   Santo Cesario *Vice President, Financing Group*
Lynda Edgar *Senior Dealer, Financing Group*
Frank McGillicuddy *Dealer, Financing Group*
Kevin Smith *Manager of Securities Lending & Borrowing Finance*
Mario Reffo *Vice President, Financing Group*
David Zavitz *Dealer, Financing Group*

Thomas Cook Currency Services Inc
15th Floor, 100 Yonge Street, Toronto, Ontario
Tel: (416) 359 3700 Fax: (416) 359 3670 Swift: COOK CA TT

Senior Executive Officers
President   Garry MacDonald

Tokai Bank Canada   Subsidiary Company
Box 84, Suite 2401, Sun Life Centre, 150 King Street West, Toronto, Ontario M5H 1J9
Tel: (416) 597 2210 Fax: (416) 591 7415 Telex: 623890 TOKAIBANK

Senior Executive Officers
President   Ryuji Kurihara

The Toronto-Dominion Bank   Head Office
55 King Street West & Bay Street, Toronto, Ontario M5K 1A2
PO Box 1, Toronto-Dominion Centre, Toronto, Ontario
Tel: (416) 982 8222 Fax: (416) 944 6931 Telex: 06524267 Cable: TORBADOM TOR
Website: www.tdbank.ca

Senior Executive Officers
Chairman   A Charles Baillie
Chief Executive Officer   A Charles Baillie
Financial Director   Dan Marinangeli
Chief Operating Officer   Michael A Foulkes

Other Departments
Proprietary Trading   Bimal Morjaria *Vice President & Director*

Administration

Legal / In-House Counsel
    R Glenn Bumstead *Senior Vice President*

Compliance
    Christopher A Montague *Senior Vice President*

Public Relations
    Heather Conway *Senior Vice President*

Other (Administration)
Private Client Services   Merle Kriss *Vice President*

Euromoney Directory 1999   **239**

CANADA (+1) www.euromoneydirectory.com

UBS Bank (Canada)

154 University Avenue, Toronto, Ontario M5H 3Z4
Tel: (416) 343 1800 Fax: (416) 343 1900

Senior Executive Officers
Others (Senior Executives)
Senior Executive Officer B Guldimann

UBS Trust (Canada)

Suite 2360, 1501 Avenue McGill Collège, Montreal, Quebec H3A 3M8
Tel: (514) 845 8828 Fax: (514) 985 8129

Other Departments
Private Banking R Delacombaz

UBS Trust (Canada)

154 University Avenue, Toronto, Ontario M5H 3Z4
Tel: (416) 343 1800 Fax: (416) 203 4303

Senior Executive Officers
Others (Senior Executives)
Senior Executive Officer B Guldimann

UBS Trust (Canada)

Suite 650, 999 West Hastings Street, Vancouver, British Columbia V6C 2W2
Tel: (604) 669 5570 Fax: (604) 669 7521

Other Departments
Private Banking H R Bolz

Westdeutsche Landesbank Girozentrale — Representative Office

Suite 1704, 95 Wellington Street West, Toronto, Ontario M5J 2N7
Tel: (416) 869 1085 Fax: (416) 869 0771

Senior Executive Officers
Vice President Lindsay LaRoche

CAPE VERDE ISLANDS
(+238)

Banco de Cabo Verde — Central Bank

Avenida Amílcar Cabral, PO Box 101, Praia
Tel: 615 530; 615 529 Fax: 614 447 Telex: 6050 BANCO CV Tel: 61 5541

Senior Executive Officers
Governor & Chairman Oswaldo Miguel Sequeira
Deputy Governor António Hilário Cruz

Others (Senior Executives)

Vasco Marta *Executive Director*
Bank Licensing & Supervision Maria Encarnação Rocha *Executive Director*
Statistics & Economic Research Carlos Rocha *Director*
Banking Supervision Valentim Pinto *Director*
Treasury, Accounting & Administration Abraão Lima *Director*
Human Resources & Computing José Manuel Veiga *Director*
Credit & Foreign Relations António Péricles Silva *Director*
Loan Recovery Administration Manuel Costa *Director*
Legal Issues Raquel Medina *Co-ordinator*

240 Euromoney Directory 1999

CAYMAN ISLANDS
(+1 345)

Cayman Islands Monetary Authority
Central Bank

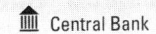

PO Box 10052APO, Georgetown
Tel: 949 7089 Fax: 949 2532; 945 1145
Website: www.cimoney.com.ky

Senior Executive Officers
Chairman — George McCarthy ☏ **949 7900**
Financial Director — Don Seymour *Financial Controller* ✉ d.seymour@cimoney.com.ky
Managing Director — Neville Grant ✉ n.grant@cimoney.com.ky
General Manager — Cindy Bush ✉ d.seymour@cimoney.com.ky

Others (Senior Executives)
Head, Insurance Supervision — William McCullough ✉ w.mccullough@cimoney.com.ky
Head, Policy & Research — Mitchell Scott ✉ m.scott@cimoney.com.ky

Administration
Neil Glasson *Manager, Information Technology*
✉ n.glasson@cimoney.com.ky

Cayman National Bank
Subsidiary Company

200 Elgin Avenue, Georgetown
PO Box 1097 GT, Georgetown
Tel: 949 4655 Fax: 949 7506 Telex: 4313 CNBBANK CP

Senior Executive Officers
Chairman & Chief Executive — Eric Crutchley ☏ **949 7416**
President — Chris Gunby ☏ **949 7100**
Chief Executive Officer — Eric Crutchley *Chairman & Chief Executive* ☏ **949 7416**

Cayman National Trust Co Limited
Subsidiary Company

PO Box 1790, Cayman National Building, Georgetown
Tel: 949 0445 Fax: 949 9557 Email: cntrust@candw.ky

Senior Executive Officers
President — John Law
Chief Executive Officer — Philip Sutcliffe *Senior Vice President*
Financial Director — Julie Arnall *Senior Vice President*

Merrill Lynch Bank & Trust Co Limited
Full Branch Office

5th Floor, Dr Roy's Drive, Georgetown, Grand Cayman
PO Box 1164, Georgetown, Grand Cayman
Tel: 949 8206 Fax: 949 8895
Website: www.ml.com

State Street Cayman Trust
Offshore Banking Unit

2nd Floor Elizabethean Square, Georgetown
Tel: 949 6644 Fax: 949 3181

Global Custody
Country Head — Jaqueline Henning

CHANNEL ISLANDS (+44)

CHANNEL ISLANDS
(+44)

Abbey National Treasury International Limited — Full Branch Office

International House, 41, The Parade, St Helier, Jersey JE4 8XG
PO Box 545, St Helier, Jersey JE4 8XG
Tel: (1534) 885 000 Fax: (1534) 885 050

Senior Executive Officers
Chairman — Graham Long
Deputy Chairman — Peter Donne Davis ☎ **885 088**
Chief Executive Officer — Ian Burns *Chief Executive* ☎ **885 008**

Others (Senior Executives)
Steve Withers *Dealer* ☎ **617 673**

Settlement / Clearing
Operations — David Siddall ☎ **885 044**

Ansbacher (Guernsey) Limited — Subsidiary Company

PO Box 79, La Plaiderie House, La Plaiderie, St Peter Port, Guernsey GY1 3DQ
Tel: (1481) 726 421 Fax: (1481) 726 526 Telex: 4191524 ANSBCH G Reuters: Recipient

Senior Executive Officers
Chairman — Peter N Scaife
Managing Director — Kevin M McAuliffe

Others (Senior Executives)
Director — Robert D Bannister
Barbara A Le Gallez *Head of Banking*
Peter St J Warry
Non-Executive — L C Morgan
J N van Leuven
Kenneth Tucknott *Assistant Director*

Other Departments
Private Banking — Keith Pleasant *Banking Manager*

Ansbacher (Jersey) Limited — Subsidiary Company

Formerly known as: Westpac Banking Corporation (Jersey) Limited
7/11 Britannia Place, Bath Street, St Helier, Jersey JE4 8US
Tel: (1534) 504 504 Fax: (1534) 504 575 Telex: 4192438 Swift: ANSL JE SH

Senior Executive Officers
Chief Executive Officer — Brian Frith *Managing Director*
Financial Director — Dennis Rainbow *Finance Director*

General-Lending (DCM, SL)
Head of Corporate Banking — Michael Meloy *Banking Director* ☎ **504 505**

Foreign Exchange
Head of Foreign Exchange — Michael Meloy *Banking Director* ☎ **504 505**

ANZ Bank (Guernsey) Limited — Subsidiary Company

Frances House, Sir William Place, St Peter Port, Guernsey GYI 4ES
PO Box 153, St Peter Port, Guernsey GY1 4ES
Tel: (1481) 726 771 Fax: (1481) 727 851 Telex: 4191663 Email: judyd@anz.com Reuters: GBJL Cable: ANZBANK
Website: www.pb.grindlays.com

Senior Executive Officers
Managing Director & GM, Channel Islands — Brian Human

Money Markets
Tel: 726 050 Reuters: ANZC
Country Head — Nigel Gallienne *Senior Manager, Treasury* ☎ **72 6050**

242 Euromoney Directory 1999

www.euromoneydirectory.com CHANNEL ISLANDS (+44)

ANZ Grindlays Bank (Jersey) Limited
Subsidiary Company

Formerly known as: Grindlays Bank (Jersey) Limited
West House, West's Centre, Peter Street, St Helier, Jersey JE4 8PT
Tel: (1534) 874 248 **Fax:** (1534) 877 695 **Telex:** 4192062

Senior Executive Officers
Managing Director   B Human

Bank of Bermuda (Guernsey) Limited
Offshore Banking Unit

Bermuda House, St Julian's Avenue, St Peter Port, Guernsey
PO Box 208, St Peter Port, Guernsey GY1 3NF
Tel: (1481) 707 000 **Fax:** (1481) 726 987 **Telex:** 4191502 BKBDGY G **Swift:** BBDA GG SX **Reuters:** BOBG
Telerate: Recipient

Senior Executive Officers
Managing Director / General Manager   Peter Hodfon

General-Lending (DCM, SL)
Head of Corporate Banking   David Purdy *Manager, Banking*

General - Treasury
Head of Treasury   Tom Lees

Relationship Manager
Personal Trust & Company Management   Talmai Morgan *Manager*

Global Custody
Regional Head   Richard J Corbin *Manager*

Other (Global Custody)
Fund Management   Barry Carroll

Bank Brussels Lambert (Jersey) Limited
Subsidiary Company

Alternative trading name: Bank Brussels Lambert Trust Company (Jersey) Limited
Huguenot House, 28 La Motte Street, St Helier, Jersey JE2 4SZ
Tel: (1534) 880 888 **Fax:** (1534) 880 777 **Telex:** 4192336 BBL SCI G

Senior Executive Officers
Others (Senior Executives)
BBL Units   Jacques Favre *Head*

Bank of Scotland
Offshore Banking Unit

Eagle House, 4 Don Road, St Helier, Jersey JE4 8XU
PO Box 588, St Helier, Jersey JE4 8XU
Tel: (1534) 825 000; (1534) 825 002 **Fax:** (1534) 738 633; (1534) 737 506 **Telex:** 4192457 BOSINJ G
Email: bkscotje@itl.net

Senior Executive Officers
Director of Offshore Banking   Tony Brian

Barings (Guernsey) Limited
Subsidiary Company

Formerly known as: Baring Brothers (Guernsey) Limited
Arnold House, St Julian's Avenue, St Peter Port, Guernsey GY1 3DA
Tel: (1481) 726 541 **Fax:** (1481) 720 132 **Telex:** 4191606 **Swift:** BBCO GG SP

Senior Executive Officers
Chairman   P P Walsh
Chief Executive Officer   J L Burton *Managing Director*
Financial Director   S J Lawson *Finance Manager*

Others (Senior Executives)
   S R Watts *Banking Director*
Investment Banking   W N Collins *Director*

General-Lending (DCM, SL)
Head of Corporate Banking   K J Stabbington *Deputy Manager, Corporate Banking*

Euromoney Directory 1999   243

CHANNEL ISLANDS (+44)   www.euromoneydirectory.com

Barings (Guernsey) Limited (cont)
Money Markets
Money Markets - General
Money Markets & CDs
    C Mallandaine *Manager, Trading*
    D Le Tissier *Dealer*

Foreign Exchange
FX Traders / Sales People
    N Laine *Dealer*
    R Jones *Dealer*

Settlement / Clearing
Foreign Exchange Settlement
    K Day *Manager, Back-Office Settlements*

Global Custody
Other (Global Custody)
Custodian Banking
    S Baker *Manager*

Other Departments
Private Banking
    J N Ward *Manager*

Administration
Technology & Systems
    P Dumont *Director*

Legal / In-House Counsel
    C Rich *Advocate*

Compliance
    H England *Assistant Manager*

BBV Privanza Bank (Jersey) Limited — Subsidiary Company

Formerly known as: Bilbao Vizcaya Bank (Jersey) Limited
2 Mulcaster Street, St Helier, Jersey JE2 3NJ
Tel: (1534) 511 200 Fax: (1534) 511 201 Telex: 4192042 Swift: BBVIJESH

Senior Executive Officers
Chairman — Gervasio Collar
Financial Director — Francisco Moya *Operations Manager*
Treasurer — Javier Escoda *Investment Manager*
Managing Director — Manuel Lopez

Other Departments
Private Banking — Miguel Rufian *Assistant General Manager*

Administration
Technology & Systems — Alistair Viel

Compliance — Francis Torrell

Bermuda Trust (Jersey) Limited — Subsidiary Company

Bermuda House, Green Street, St Helier, Jersey JE4 8TG
PO Box 284, Jersey
Tel: (1534) 814 400 Fax: (1534) 814 474

Senior Executive Officers
Chairman — Henry B Smith
Managing Director — J H Ruddy

Others (Senior Executives)
Director — M R E Todd *Director of Trust Services*

Settlement / Clearing
Operations — K J Ponter *Operation Manager*

BHF-Bank (Jersey) Limited — Subsidiary Company

6 Wests Centre, St Helier, Jersey JE2 4ST
Tel: (1534) 879 044 Fax: (1534) 879 246

Senior Executive Officers
Manager — John M Alcock

Bridport & Co (Jersey) Limited
Subsidiary Company
60/62 Halkett Place, St Helier, Jersey JE2 4WG
Tel: (1534) 887 448 **Fax:** (1534) 887 805 **Telex:** 425007 BRI CH
Senior Executive Officers
Manager   Mark Robinson

The British Bank of the Middle East
Head Office
1 Grenville Street, St Helier, Jersey JE2 8UB
PO Box 315, St Helier, Jersey JE4 8UB
Tel: (1534) 606 512 **Fax:** (1534) 606 149 **Telex:** 4192254
Senior Executive Officers
Chairman   John Bond
Others (Senior Executives)
Board of Directors   A Dixon
J A P Hill
A Mehta
R Stock
Abdul-Jalil Yousuf
C J M Keirle
A A Flockhart
Mike Bussey
J Tibbo
Abdel Salam el Anwar

BZW Securities Limited
Subsidiary Company
Formerly known as: Barclays de Zoete Wedd Securities Limited
4th Floor, Harbour House, South Esplanade, St Peter Port, Guernsey GY1 1AP
Tel: (1481) 713 997 **Fax:** (1481) 714 111
Senior Executive Officers
Director   Lena Chesney

Cantrade Private Bank Switzerland (CI) Limited
Subsidiary Company
24 Union Street, St Helier, Jersey JE4 8UJ
PO Box 350, St Helier, Jersey JE4 8UJ
Tel: (1534) 611 200 **Fax:** (1534) 611 399
Senior Executive Officers
Chairman   Thomas Schlieper
Treasurer   Mike McKenna ☎ **611 295**
Managing Director   Johann-Georg Bärlocher ☎ **611 301**
Company Secretary   Mike McLoughlin ☎ **611 302**
Other Departments
Private Banking   Neil Buesnel *Head, Private Banking* ☎ **611 323**

Channel Islands Money Brokers Limited
2 La Chasse, St Helier, Jersey JE2 4UE
Tel: (1534) 37508; (1534) 285 999 **Fax:** (1534) 36112 **Telex:** 4192128 CIMB J **Reuters:** CIMB
Senior Executive Officers
Chief Executive Officer   P S Cruickshank
Managing Director / General Manager   D V Pallot

Channel Islands Money Brokers Limited
Full Branch Office
Suites 7 & 8, Grove House, Le Bordage, St Peter Port, Guernsey GY1 1DB
Tel: (1481) 726 026 **Fax:** (1481) 722 764 **Telex:** 4191552 CIMBL G **Reuters:** CIGY
Senior Executive Officers
Director   Stephen Kail ☎ **710 796**

CHANNEL ISLANDS (+44)   www.euromoneydirectory.com

Chase Bank & Trust Company (CI) Limited Subsidiary Company

Chase House, Grenville Street, PO Box 289, St Helier, Jersey JE4 8TH
Tel: (1534) 626 262 Fax: (1534) 626 301 Telex: 4192209 CHASJY G

Senior Executive Officers
Senior Officer   Catherine E Lenz ☏ **626 335** F **68906**
Others (Senior Executives)
Fiduciary Oversight   Keith Graham *Vice President* ☏ **626 460** F **68906**
Settlement / Clearing
Operations   Terry A Heulin *Operations & Financial Management*
                                            Jenny Swan *Operations & Financial Management*
Other Departments
Global Trust   Larry Ingraham *General Manager, Trust*
                                            Anne Williams *Senior Trust Manager*
                                            Hazel Altham *Senior Trust Manager*
                                            Edward Lee *Senior Trust Manager*

The Chase Manhattan Bank Full Branch Office

PO Box 127, Chase House, Grenville Street, St Helier, Jersey JE4 8QH
Tel: (1534) 626 262 Fax: (1534) 626 301 Telex: 4192209 CHASJY G Swift: CHAS JE SX

Senior Executive Officers
Senior Officer   Catherine E Lenz ☏ **626 335** F **68906**
Settlement / Clearing
Operations   Terence A Huelin *VP, Operations & Financial Management* ☏ **626 272**
                                            Mark Chapman *Vice President, Operations*
Global Custody
Head of Global Custody   Ian N Blackburn *Vice President* ☏ **626 200**
Other Departments
Private Banking   Ian Blackman *Vice President*
                                            John Eddy *Vice President*
                                            Stuart Hornby *Vice President*

Citibank (Channel Islands) Limited Subsidiary Company

38 Esplanade, St Helier, Jersey JE4 8QB
PO Box 104, St Helier, Jersey
Tel: (1534) 608 000 Fax: (1534) 608 291 Telex: 4192313 Swift: CITI JE SXL Reuters: CICI (Dealing)

Senior Executive Officers
Chairman   Clive Jones
Treasurer   Phil Morris *Head, Treasury & Forex Division* ☏ **608 250**
Foreign Exchange
Head of Foreign Exchange   Phil Morris *Head, Treasury & Forex Division* ☏ **608 250**

Credit Suisse (Guernsey) Limited Subsidiary Company

Helvetia Court, South Esplanade, St Peter Port, Guernsey GY1 3YJ
PO Box 368, St Peter Port, Guernsey GY1 3YJ
Tel: (1481) 719 000 Fax: (1481) 724 676 Telex: 4191228 Swift: CRES GG SP

Senior Executive Officers
Treasurer   Roger Rimann
Managing Director   Albert F Good
Others (Senior Executives)
                                            Geoff Marson *Head of Securities Products*
Debt Capital Markets / Fixed Income
Department: Securities Sales & Execution
Head of Fixed Income   Lynne Roberts
Equity Capital Markets
Department: Securities Sales & Execution
Head of Equity Capital Markets   Shaun Le Messurier *Head of Securities Sales & Execution*

www.euromoneydirectory.com   CHANNEL ISLANDS (+44)

Money Markets
Department: Sales & Execution
Other   Will Davey
                                       Debbie Ashwell

Foreign Exchange
Department: Sales & Execution
Head of Foreign Exchange   John Marquis

Risk Management
Head of Risk Management   Frank Coppolo *Head of Credit & Risk Analysis*

Asset Management
Head   Rachael Bearder

Deutsche Morgan Grenfell (CI) Limited   Subsidiary Company

Formerly known as: Morgan Grenfell (CI) Limited
PO Box 727, St Paul's Gate, New Street, St Helier, Jersey JE4 8ZB
Tel: (1534) 889 900 **Fax:** (1534) 889 911 **Telex:** 4192007 MG JSY G **Reuters:** MGJY

Senior Executive Officers
Chairman   Philip E Smith
Managing Director   John C Boothman
Others (Senior Executives)
                                       P J Pichler *Finance & Resources*
                                       David A Endacott *Administration*
                                       Gordon C Fitzjohn *Fund Administration, Corporate & Trustee Services*
                                       Gus Meyer *Treasury & Banking*

General-Lending (DCM, SL)
Head of Corporate Banking   Mark J Wildman *Senior Assistant Director, Lending*
                                       Martin Hughes *Manager, Lending*

Money Markets
Department: Capital Markets
Global Head   Mark Osment *Assistant Director*

Money Markets - General
                                       Darren Langlois *Dealer*
                                       Andrew Falle *Senior Dealer*

Foreign Exchange
Global Head   Kevin Moore *Assistant Director*
FX Traders / Sales People
                                       Philip Harvey *Dealer*

Settlement / Clearing
Operations   Caroline Clayden *Manager, Banking Operations*
                                       James Hodges *Banking Operations*

Global Custody
Regional Head   Joan Finch *Senior Assistant Director*

Asset Management
Portfolio Management   Ryan Harrison *Manager*

Deutsche Morgan Grenfell (CI) Limited - Guernsey
Subsidiary Company

Formerly known as: Morgan Grenfell (CI) Limited - Guernsey
Morgan Grenfell House, 424 Lefevre Street, St Peter Port, Guernsey GY1 3WT
PO Box 96, St Peter Port, Guernsey
Tel: (1481) 726 383 **Fax:** (1481) 702 001 **Telex:** 4191609 MG CIG G

Senior Executive Officers
Managing Director   Roger E Alcock
Director, Fiduciary Services   John K Blewett
Others (Senior Executives)
Business Development   Gerry Morrissey *Senior Associate Director & Head*

General-Lending (DCM, SL)
Head of Corporate Banking   Nigel B Corbin *Senior Associate Director & Head of Banking*

General - Treasury
Head of Treasury   Nigel B Corbin *Senior Associate Director, Treasury & Credit*

CHANNEL ISLANDS (+44)   www.euromoneydirectory.com

Deutsche Morgan Grenfell (CI) Limited - Guernsey (cont)
Foreign Exchange
Tel: 716228
Global Head   M R C Bisson *Senior Manager*
Regional Head   R Hughes *Assistant Manager*
Global Custody
Other (Global Custody)
Custodian Banking   M R C Bisson *Senior Manager*
Other Departments
Correspondent Banking   M R C Bisson *Senior Manager*

EFG Private Bank (Channel Islands) Limited — Subsidiary Company

Formerly known as: The Private Bank & Trust Company (Guernsey) Limited
Sarnia House, Le Truchot, St Peter Port, Guernsey GYI 4NN
PO Box 603, St Peter Port, Guernsey GYI 4NN
Tel: (1481) 723 432 **Fax:** (1481) 723 488 **Telex:** 4191122

Senior Executive Officers
Chairman   Harry Taylor CBE
Managing Director   Owen Bourgaize
Banking Director   Michael De Jersey
Trust Director   James Bottomley
Settlement / Clearing
Operations   Andy Scott *Manager, Operations*
Other Departments
Correspondent Banking   Chris Rowe *Manager, Banking*

Flemings (Jersey) Limited — Subsidiary Company

28 New Street, St Helier, Jersey JE2 3TE
Tel: (1534) 887 889 **Fax:** (1534) 509 725

Senior Executive Officers
General-Lending (DCM, SL)
Head of Corporate Banking   Nicholas Owen *Head, Offshore Banking*
Money Markets
Country Head   Kevin Moore *Head*
Global Custody
Other (Global Custody)
Custodian & Trustee   Geoffrey Foulerton *Manager*

Guernsey International Fund Managers Limited — Head Office

Barfield House, St Julian Avenue, St Peter Port, Guernsey GY1 3QL
PO Box 255, St Peter Port, Guernsey GY1 3QL
Tel: (1481) 710 651 **Fax:** (1481) 710 285

Senior Executive Officers
Managing Director   C M W Hill
Deputy Managing Director   Mark N Huntley

Guinness Mahon Guernsey Limited — Subsidiary Company

PO Box 188, La Vieille Cour, St Peter Port, Guernsey GY1 3LP
Tel: (1481) 723 506 **Fax:** (1481) 720 844 **Telex:** 4191482 **Swift:** GMGU GG SP **Reuters:** GMGY

Senior Executive Officers
Chairman   S H Wells
Director, Treasury   B L Cumner
Financial Director   Steven D Henry *Director, Finance*
Managing Director   Carol Goodwin
Director & Company Secretary   Steven D Henry
Foreign Exchange
Head of Trading   B L Cumner *Director, Treasury*

Other Departments
Private Banking H K Kelling *Manager*

Hill Samuel Bank (Jersey) Limited
Subsidiary Company

PO Box 63, 7 Bond Street, St Helier, Jersey JE4 8PH
Tel: (1534) 604 604 **Fax:** (1534) 604 606 **Swift:** HSAM JE SH **Email:** hsj@hillsamjsy.co.uk

Senior Executive Officers
Chairman A R Jesseman
Managing Director T L Slattery
Company Secretary M Le Masurier

Others (Senior Executives)
 D Hunt *Director*

ING Baring Private Bank

PO Box 486 Arnold House, St Julian's House, St Peter Port, Guernsey GY1 6BW
Tel: (1481) 717 505 **Fax:** (1481) 717 506 **Telex:** 4191120 INGB G

Senior Executive Officers
General Manager Jeffrey Burton

ING Trust (Jersey) Limited
Subsidiary Company

Kensington Chambers, 46/50 Kensington Place, St Helier, Jersey JE2 3PE
Tel: (1534) 608 080 **Fax:** (1534) 607 060 **Email:** bart.wijsmuller@ingbank.com

Senior Executive Officers
General Manager Bart Wijsmuller

Kleinwort Benson (Jersey) Limited
Subsidiary Company

PO Box 76, Wests Centre, St Helier, Jersey JE4 8PQ
Tel: (1534) 613 000 **Fax:** (1534) 613 141 **Telex:** 4192284 **Swift:** KBEN JE SH **Cable:** KLEINWORT JERSEY

Senior Executive Officers
Chief Executive Officer Richard Robins
Financial Director Ronald Hendry ☏ **(1481) 727 111**
General Manager, Development Angus Taylor
General Manager, Administration Sandra Platts ☏ **613 060**

Money Markets
Global Head Paul Rioda *Head of Treasury* ☏ **613 015**

Foreign Exchange
Global Head Paul Rioda *Head of Treasury* ☏ **613 015**

FX Traders / Sales People
All Mark Rondel
 Nigel Lawrence
 Sebaotian Volpe

Settlement / Clearing
Regional Head Nick Freeland *Head, International Settlements* ☏ **613 188**

Other Departments
Private Banking Hamish Kean *Head of Banking* ☏ **613 063**

Administration

Technology & Systems
 Brian Vickers *Head, Information Systems* ☏ **613 107**

Corporate Communications
 Sandra Platts *General Manager, Administration* ☏ **613 060**

CHANNEL ISLANDS (+44)   www.euromoneydirectory.com

Lazard Brothers & Co (Jersey) Limited
Subsidiary Company

Lazard House, 2/6 Church Street, St Helier, Jersey JE4 8QD
PO Box 108, St Helier, Jersey JE4 8QD
Tel: (1534) 620 620 Fax: (1534) 620 621 Telex: 4192154 Swift: LAZL JE SH

Senior Executive Officers
Chairman   Neil Lukes
Chief Executive Officer   Michael Fornara *Deputy Chairman*
Chief Operating Officer   Ayaz Siddiqui *Chief Operating Officer*
                                        Martyn Samphier *Director*
Managing Director   Peter Williams
Secretary   Mark Grigg

Leopold Joseph & Sons (Guernsey) Limited
Subsidiary Company

Albert House, South Esplanade, St Peter Port, Guernsey GY1 3QB
PO Box 244, St Peter Port, Guernsey
Tel: (1481) 712 771 Fax: (1481) 727 025 Telex: 4191505 Email: info@leopoldjoseph.com

Senior Executive Officers
Managing Director   Roger Carter

Others (Senior Executives)
Operations   Andrew Guille *Director, Operations*
Banking   Christopher Wakefield *Director, Banking*

Debt Capital Markets / Fixed Income
Department: Investment Management
Head of Fixed Income   Matthew Hulme *Assistant Director, Investments*

Equity Capital Markets
Department: Investment Management
Head of Equity Capital Markets   Matthew Hulme *Assistant Director, Investments*

Money Markets
Head of Money Markets   Jeff Swain *Assistant Director, Banking*

Foreign Exchange
Head of Foreign Exchange   Susan Reeves *Manager, Dealing*

Settlement / Clearing
Head of Settlement / Clearing   Mike Webber *Manager, Investment Administration*

Global Custody
Head of Global Custody   Mike Webber *Manager, Investment Administration*

Administration
Accounts / Audit
                                        Julie Gibson *Manager, Finance*

Other (Administration)
Business Development & Marketing   Christopher Wakefield *Director, Banking*

Lloyds Private Banking (Channel Islands) Limited
Subsidiary Company

Waterloo House, Don Street, St Helier, Jersey JE4 8ZG
PO Box 195, St Helier, Jersey JE4 8RS
Tel: (1534) 284 360 Fax: (1534) 284 035 Telex: 888301 LOYDLNG

Senior Executive Officers
General Manager   J A Hatcher

Lloyds TSB Bank (Jersey) Limited
Subsidiary Company

25 New Street, St Helier, Jersey JE4 8RG
Tel: (1534) 503 000 Fax: (1534) 503 047 Telex: 4192164 TSB CI G

Senior Executive Officers
Director, Offshore Banking   A R Jesseman
Chief Executive Officer   M J Smith *Island Director*
Company Secretary   J Le Suer

www.euromoneydirectory.com CHANNEL ISLANDS (+44)

Others (Senior Executives)
R T McGinnigle *Director*
N W Battersby *Director*
M Coombes *Director*

Administration
Accounts / Audit
W J McLaughlin *Chief Accountant*

Management International (Guernsey) Limited   Subsidiary Company

PO Box 208, Bermuda House, St Julian's Avenue, St Peter Port, Guernsey
Tel: (1481) 707 000 **Fax:** (1481) 726 987 **Telex:** 4191502 BKBDGY **Reuters:** BOBG

Senior Executive Officers
Managing Director   Barry Carroll

Matheson Securities (Channel Islands) Limited   Head Office

4th Floor, 38 Esplanade, St Helier, Jersey JE4 8RF
PO Box 177, St Helier, Jersey JE4 8RF
Tel: (1534) 876 222 **Fax:** (1534) 30185 **Telex:** 4192287 MATJSY **Email:** msciljsy@itl.net **Bloomberg:** MSCIL

Senior Executive Officers
Managing Director   Grahame Lovett

Others (Senior Executives)
Nigel Cuming *Head, Portfolio Management*
Christopher Huelin *Head of Fixed Interest* ☏ **38115**
Richard Mason *Head of Equities*
Guy O'Connor *Head of Business Development*

Debt Capital Markets / Fixed Income
Head of Fixed Income   Christopher Huelin *Head of Fixed Interest* ☏ **38115**

Government Bonds
Head of Sales   Spencer Mariscal *Institutional Sales* ☏ **38115**
Head of Trading   Christopher Huelin *Head of Fixed Interest* ☏ **38115**

Eurobonds
Head of Sales   Spencer Mariscal *Institutional Sales* ☏ **38115**
Head of Trading   Christopher Huelin *Head of Fixed Interest* ☏ **38115**

Emerging Market Bonds
Head of Sales   Spencer Mariscal *Institutional Sales* ☏ **38115**
Head of Trading   Christopher Huelin *Head of Fixed Interest* ☏ **38115**

Libor-Based / Floating-Rate Products
FRN Sales   Spencer Mariscal *Institutional Sales* ☏ **38115**

Fixed-Income Research
Head of Fixed Income   Christopher Huelin *Head of Fixed Interest* ☏ **38115**

Equity Capital Markets
Department: Equity Trading & Sales
Tel: 30858 **Fax:** 30685
Head of Sales; Head of Trading   Richard Mason *Head, Equity Trading*

Domestic Equities
Head of Sales   Richard Mason *Head, Equity Trading*

International Equities
Head of Sales   Richard Mason *Head, Equity Trading*

Equity Research
Head of Equity Research   Richard Mason *Head, Equity Trading*

Convertibles / Equity-Linked
Head of Sales   Spencer Mariscal *Institutional Sales* ☏ **38115**

Equity Repo / Securities Lending
Head   Ian Ireland *Business Development*
Marketing & Product Development   Guy O'Connor *Business Development*

Syndicated Lending
Loan-Related Activities
Trade Finance   Sue Allen *Head of Operations*
Project Finance   Sue Allen *Head of Operations*

Risk Management
OTC Equity Derivatives
Sales; Trading   Scott Spencer ☏ **38115**

CHANNEL ISLANDS (+44)	www.euromoneydirectory.com

Matheson Securities (Channel Islands) Limited (cont)
Other (Equity Derivatives)
                                Scott Spencer ☎ **38115**

Settlement / Clearing
Head of Settlement / Clearing   Sue Allen *Head of Operations*
Equity Settlement   Sue Allen *Head of Operations*
Fixed-Income Settlement   Sue Allen *Head of Operations*
Back-Office   Sue Allen *Head of Operations*

Global Custody
Head of Global Custody   Sue Allen *Head of Operations*

Asset Management
Head   Sue Allen *Head of Operations*
Portfolio Management   Chris Huelin *Fixed Interest*
                                Nigel Cuming *Head, Portfolio Management*
                                Francis Clayton
                                Alan Orchard
                                John Conlon
                                Glen Coxon

Other Departments
Commodities / Bullion; Chief Credit Officer   Sue Allen *Head of Operations*
Correspondent Banking; Cash Management   Sue Allen *Head of Operations*

Administration
Compliance
                                Ann Mulvin
                                Paul Martin

MeesPierson (CI) Limited
Bordage House, Le Bordage, St Peter Port, Guernsey GY1 3QT
PO Box 253, St Peter Port, Guernsey GY1 3QT
Tel: (1481) 708 708 **Fax:** (1481) 710 665 **Telex:** 4191564 **Swift:** MEES GG SP **Email:** mpci@itl.net

Senior Executive Officers
Managing Director / General Manager   Paul Backhouse

Mercury Asset Management Channel Islands Limited
Subsidiary Company

Forum House, Grenville Street, St Helier, Jersey JE4 8RL
Tel: (1534) 600 600 **Fax:** (1534) 600 687

Senior Executive Officers
Chairman   F D S Rosier
Managing Director   F P LeFeuvre

Others (Senior Executives)
                                J Gillespie *Director*

Midland Bank Offshore Limited
Subsidiary Company

Formerly known as: Midland Bank International Finance Corporation Limited
PO Box 26, 28/34 Hill Street, St Helier, Jersey JE4 8NR
Tel: (1534) 606 000 **Fax:** (1534) 606 090 **Telex:** 4192098

Senior Executive Officers
Chief Executive Officer   B P McDonagh *CEO, Offshore Islands*
                                P J Austin *Deputy CEO, Offshore Islands*

Midland Bank Offshore Limited
Subsidiary Company

PO Box 315, Weighbridge House, Lower Pollet, St Peter Port, Guernsey GY1 3TQ
Tel: (1481) 717 717 **Fax:** (1481) 717 820

Senior Executive Officers
Others (Senior Executives)
                                G J Davies *Area Manager*

www.euromoneydirectory.com CHANNEL ISLANDS (+44)

Rabobank Guernsey Limited
Subsidiary Company

Holland House, 1 St Julian's Avenue, St Peter Port, Guernsey GY1 3UY
PO Box 348, St Peter Port, Guernsey GY1 3UY
Tel: (1481) 725 147 **Fax:** (1481) 725 157 **Swift:** RABO GG SP **Email:** rabobank@guernsey.net

Senior Executive Officers
Chief Executive Officer   Andrew M J Courtney *Director*
Managing Director   Ronald Van Beek

RBSI Custody Bank Limited
Subsidiary Company

PO Box 451, Liberté House, La Motte Street, St Helier, Jersey JE4 5RL
Tel: (1534) 286 000 **Fax:** (1534) 286 070 **Telex:** 4192251 RBSICG **Swift:** SGWL JE SX **Reuters:** RBSC

Senior Executive Officers
Chairman   C I McPhail
Managing Director   Derek Ferguson ☎ **286 001**

Republic National Bank of New York (Guernsey) Limited
Subsidiary Company

Rue du Pré, St Peter Port, Guernsey GY1 1LU
Tel: (1481) 710 901 **Fax:** (1481) 711 824 **Telex:** 4191123 RNBCIG

Senior Executive Officers
Chairman   Andrew Pucher
Treasurer   Peter Kenel
Managing Director   Gary Miller
Managing Director - Funds   Paul Wrench
Managing Director - Trusts   Brian Horsepool

Others (Senior Executives)
                                  Peter Kenel *Director & Chief Credit Officer*

Debt Capital Markets / Fixed Income
Asset-Backed Securities / Securitization
Global Head   Gary Wade *Manager, Securities*

Money Markets
Department: Capital Markets - Money Markets
Money Markets - General
Eurocurrency Deposits - Trading   Phillip Lee

Foreign Exchange
Department: Capital Markets - Money Markets
FX Traders / Sales People
FX - Trading   Paul Lawrence

Other Departments
Correspondent Banking   Judi Lees *Manager*

NM Rothschild & Sons (CI) Limited
Subsidiary Company

St Julian's Court, St Julian's Avenue, St Peter Port, Guernsey GY1 3BP
Tel: (1481) 713 713 **Fax:** (1481) 727 705 **Telex:** 888031 NMR G **Swift:** ROTH GG SP **Reuters:** NMRA (Monitor); NMRG (Dealing)

Senior Executive Officers
Financial Director   Peter Rose *Finance Director*

Debt Capital Markets / Fixed Income
Global Head   Andrew R Clarke *Assistant Director* ☎ **728 016**

Money Markets
Other (Wholesale Deposits)
Eurocurrency Deposits-Origination Darren Heathcote *Dealer*

Foreign Exchange
FX Traders / Sales People
                                  Steven Moody *Dealer* ☎ **727 301**

Settlement / Clearing
Foreign Exchange Settlement   Michael Thomson *Assistant Director*

Euromoney Directory 1999 253

CHANNEL ISLANDS (+44)   www.euromoneydirectory.com

NM Rothschild & Sons (CI) Limited (cont)
Other Departments
Private Banking   Sara Jonkmans *Manager*
Administration
Technology & Systems
                                     Andrew Dimelow *Manager*

Rothschild Bank Switzerland (CI) Limited   Subsidiary Company
PO Box 330, St. Julian's Court, St. Julian's Avenue, St Peter Port, Guernsey GY1 3BP
Tel: (1481) 710 521 Fax: (1481) 711 272 Telex: 4191219 ROTH CI Email: rothswtz@guernsey.net
Senior Executive Officers
Managing Director   Paul Meader

Rothschild Trust Guernsey Limited   Subsidiary Company
PO Box 472, St Peters House, Le Bordage, St Peter Port, Guernsey GY1 6AX
Tel: (1481) 707 800 Fax: (1481) 712 686
Senior Executive Officers
Managing Director   David Allison

Royal Bank of Canada (Channel Islands) Limited
Subsidiary Company
PO Box 48, Canada Court, Upland Road, St Peter Port, Guernsey GY1 3BQ
Tel: (1481) 723 021 Fax: (1481) 723 524 Telex: 4191527 Swift: ROYC GG SP Reuters: RBCI
Website: www.royalbankci.com

Senior Executive Officers
Chairman & Chief Executive   Tony Webb
Managing Director   Ansel Holder
Secretary   Peter Hanna
Others (Senior Executives)
Institutional Management & Corporate Sales   Roger Arundale *Senior Manager*
Trust, Sales & Marketing   John West *Senior Manager*
Money Markets
Country Head   Adrian Bailey *Manager, Money Market*
Foreign Exchange
Head of Trading   Andrew Gent *Manager, Trading*
Settlement / Clearing
Country Head   Alan Hunt *Manager, Treasury Operations*
Global Custody
Country Head   Frank Bichard *Senior Manager*
Asset Management
Head   John Prow *Senior Manager, Investment Management*
Other Departments
Chief Credit Officer   Steve Burt *Manager, Credit*
Global Trust   Ian Kelley *Manager, Trust Services*
                                     Andrew Lindsay *Manager, Institutional Management*
                                     Steve Fell *Manager, Institutional Sales*
                                     John Renouf *Manager, Offshore Funds*

Administration
Technology & Systems
                                     Ellen Chalmers *Senior Manager, Systems*
Compliance
                                     John Bihet *Manager*
Accounts / Audit
Audit   John Bihet *Manager*
Other (Administration)
Human Resources   David Leafe *Manager*
Marketing & Insurance Services   Stephen Harding *Manager*
Corporate Services   Andrew Marquis *Manager*

www.euromoneydirectory.com CHANNEL ISLANDS (+44)

Royal Bank of Canada (Jersey) Limited
Subsidiary Company

Formerly known as: Royal Trust Bank (Jersey) Limited
PO Box 194, 19/21 Broad Street, St Helier, Jersey JE4 8RR
Tel: (1534) 27441 Fax: (1534) 32513 Telex: 4192351 RBCJSY Swift: ROYC JE SH Reuters: RTBJ

Senior Executive Officers
Chairman	Tony Webb
Managing Director & Vice President	T C Sears
Director & Company Secretary	George W Dick

Others (Senior Executives)
Global Private Banking	M J Lagopoulos *Senior Vice President*
	R E Stanley
	T J Betley
	A E Holder

General-Lending (DCM, SL)
Head of Corporate Banking	Christopher Blampied *Senior Manager, Banking*

General - Treasury
Head of Treasury	Steve Gavey *Manager, Treasury Administration*
	Mo Matthews *Manager, Treasury*

Corporate Finance / M&A Advisory
Global Head	George W Dick *Senior Manager, Corporate Finance I*

Settlement / Clearing
Operations	Michael S Broughton *Senior Manager, Systems & Operations*

Administration
Other (Administration)
New Business	Steve Bealey *Manager*

The Royal Bank of Scotland International Limited
Subsidiary Company

Royal Bank House, 71 Bath Street, PO Box 64, St Helier, Jersey JE4 8PJ
Tel: (1534) 285 200 Fax: (1534) 285 222 Telex: 4192486 Swift: RBOS JE SX Reuters: RBSJ

Senior Executive Officers
Chairman	G A Schofield
Chief Executive Officer	C I McPhail

Others (Senior Executives)
	J Paton *Director, Jersey*

The Royal Bank of Scotland International Limited
Subsidiary Company

22 High Street, PO Box 62, St Peter Port, Guernsey GY1 4BQ
Tel: (1481) 710 051 Fax: (1481) 723 689

Senior Executive Officers
Others (Senior Executives)
	A F Rodger *Director, Guernsey*

Royal Trust Asset Management (CI) Limited
Subsidiary Company

PO Box 194, 19-21 Broad Street, St Helier, Jersey JE4 8RR
Tel: (1534) 27441 Fax: (1534) 24760 Telex: 4192465
Website: www.royalbank.com/english/gpb

Senior Executive Officers
Chairman	A H Webb
SVP, Global Private Banking	M J Lagopoulos
MD & Vice President	Tom Sears
Director & Company Secretary	G W Dick

Others (Senior Executives)
	K E Rayner *Senior Manager*

General-Investment
Head of Investment	Andrew Buchanan *Senior Manager, Investments*

CHANNEL ISLANDS (+44)   www.euromoneydirectory.com

Royal Trust Asset Management (CI) Limited (cont)
Corporate Finance / M&A Advisory
Global Head
George W Dick *Senior Manager, Corporate Finance I*
Settlement / Clearing
Operations
Tony Bickley *Senior Manager*
Other Departments
Global Trust
Kenneth E Rayner *Senior Manager, Trust Services*

Schroders (CI) Limited   Full Branch Office
PO Box 284, Bermuda House, Green Street, St Helier, Jersey JE4 9TG
Tel: (1534) 630 825 Fax: (1534) 630 826
Senior Executive Officers
Director
Gregor Allan

Schroders (CI) Limited   Subsidiary Company
Sarnia House, Le Truchot, St Peter Port, Guernsey GY1 3UF
PO Box 334, St Peter Port, Guernsey GY1 3UF
Tel: (1481) 703 700 Fax: (1481) 703 600 Email: scil@schroders.com
Senior Executive Officers
Chief Executive Officer
Richard Crowder *Managing Director*
Financial Director
Richard Battey *Director*
Others (Senior Executives)
Jamie Dorrien Smith *Director*
Chris Sherwell *Director*

SG Hambros Bank & Trust Company (Guernsey) Limited
Subsidiary Company
St Julian's Court, St Julian's Avenue, PO Box 86, St Peter Port, Guernsey GY1 3AE
Tel: (1481) 728 181 Fax: (1481) 710 742; (1481) 727 139 Telex: 4191110
Senior Executive Officers
Others (Senior Executives)
Bank
Ian Marsh *Director*
Trust
J C Loveless *Director*

Soditic Finance Limited   Subsidiary Company
18/20 Dumaresq Street, St Helier, Jersey JE2 3RL
Tel: (1534) 515 515 Fax: (1534) 515 516 Telex: 4192411 SODT G
Senior Executive Officers
Managing Director
Ronald M Adair 515 525 ron_adair@soditic.co.uk

Standard Chartered Bank (CI) Limited   Subsidiary Company
Standard Chartered House, Conway Street, St Helier, Jersey JE4 8PY
PO Box 89, St Helier, Jersey JE4 8PY
Tel: (1534) 507 000 Fax: (1534) 507 111 Telex: 4192013 SCBJSY G Swift: SCBL GB 2L SCO Cable: STANCHART
Senior Executive Officers
Managing Director
C Dickinson
Others (Senior Executives)
G J Buckland *Director*
C M Steer *Director*
P Paillart *Director*
B C Le Cuirot *Director*
M J Lezala *Director*
F P Saarloos *Director*

www.euromoneydirectory.com   CHILE (+56)

UBS AG
Full Branch Office
PO Box 350, 4 Union Street, St Helier, Jersey JE4 8U
Tel: (1534) 611 300 Fax: (1534) 611 399
Senior Executive Officers
Others (Senior Executives)
Unit Head   J G Bärlocher *Unit Head*

Union Bancaire Privée
PO Box 526, St Helier, Jersey JE4 5UH
Tel: (1534) 488 0949 Fax: (1534) 488 0950 Telex: 419 2234
Senior Executive Officers
Others (Senior Executives)
Member of Senior Management   Alex Hacker

CHILE (+56)

ABN AMRO Bank NV
Full Branch Office
Nueva York 33, Santiago
Tel: (2) 671 5776 Fax: (2) 672 2696 Telex: 240017
Senior Executive Officers
Chairman   Floris G H Dockers
Treasurer   Eduardo Martinez *Treasurer & Manager*
Country Manager   Félix A Van Kleef
General-Lending (DCM, SL)
Head of Corporate Banking   Adolfo Vial *Corporate Banking Manager*
Settlement / Clearing
Operations   Eduardo Schätzke *Manager*
Asset Management
Head   Mauricio Danús Laucirica

Banco de A Edwards
Head Office
Huérfanos 740, Santiago
Tel: (2) 388 3000 Fax: (2) 388 4163; (2) 388 3722 Telex: 441160 BANEX CZ Swift: BAED CL RM 320
Senior Executive Officers
Chairman   Sergio de Castro S ☎ **388 4019**
Vice Chairman   Jacob Ergas E
Chief Executive Officer   Gustavo Favre D *General Manager* ☎ **388 4006**
Financial Director   Julio Guzman ☎ **388 3710**
Chief Operating Officer   Guido Silva ☎ **388 4320**
General Manager   Gustavo Favre D ☎ **388 4006**
International Division   Julio Guzmán *International Division Director*
General-Lending (DCM, SL)
Head of Corporate Banking   Domingo Amunategui *Commercial & Corporate Banking Director*
Administration
Public Relations
                                       Jacqueline Barrio

Banco BICE
Head Office
Teatinos 220, Santiago
Tel: (2) 692 2000 Fax: (2) 696 5324 Telex: 645195 BICE CT Swift: BICE CL RM Email: mvial@bice.cl Reuters: BICE
Website: www.bice.cl
Senior Executive Officers
Chairman   Gonzalo Valdes ☎ **692 2029**
Chief Executive Officer   Cristian Eyzaguirre ☎ **692 2230**

CHILE (+56)

Banco BICE (cont)
Senior Executive Officers (cont)

Financial Director — Carlos Budge ☎ **692 2100**
Chief Operating Officer — Alejandro Fernandez ☎ **629 2302**

General-Lending (DCM, SL)
Head of Corporate Banking — Juan Antonio Minassian ☎ **692 2095** 📠 **696 5324**

General-Investment
Head of Investment — Fernando Alvear ☎ **692 2602**

Debt Capital Markets / Fixed Income
Head of Fixed Income — Andres Perez ☎ **692 2112**
Head of Fixed Income Trading — Jose Miguel Irarrazaval ☎ **692 2804**

Government Bonds
Head of Trading — Andres Perez ☎ **692 2112**
Head of Syndication — Jose Miguel Irarrazaval ☎ **692 2804**

Equity Capital Markets
Department: **Bice Corredores de Bolsa SA**
Tel: 692 2800 **Fax**: 692 2831
Head of Equity Capital Markets — Jose Miguel Irarrazaval ☎ **692 2804**
Head of Sales — Ramiro Fernandez ☎ **692 2805**
Head of Trading — Luis Alberto Keitel ☎ **692 2815**

Domestic Equities
Head of Sales — Ramiro Fernandez ☎ **692 2805**

Syndicated Lending

Loan-Related Activities
Trade Finance — Jaime Lara ☎ **692 2208**
Project Finance — Joaquin Izcue ☎ **692 2202**

Foreign Exchange
Head of Foreign Exchange — Carlos Budge ☎ **692 2100**
Head of Institutional Sales — Claudio Lopez ☎ **692 2114**
Corporate Sales — Cristian Pinto ☎ **692 2803**
Head of Trading — Ramiro Soffia ☎ **692 2801**

Risk Management

Fixed Income Derivatives / Risk Management
Head of Sales — Claudio Lopez ☎ **692 2114**
Trading — Cristian Pinto ☎ **692 2808**

Corporate Finance / M&A Advisory
Head of Corporate Finance — Luis Alberto Cruz ☎ **692 2214**

Asset Management
Head — Claudio Baldovino ☎ **692 2728**

Other Departments
Chief Credit Officer — Jose Luis Arbildua ☎ **692 2033**
Correspondent Banking — Carlos Klapp ☎ **692 2215**
Cash Management — Juan Elizalde ☎ **692 2113**

Administration
Head of Administration — Raimundo Valdes ☎ **692 2991**
Business Development — Joaquin Izcue ☎ **692 2202**
Head of Marketing — Marilu Vial ☎ **692 2014**

Technology & Systems
Jeronimo Garcia ☎ **692 2108**

Legal / In-House Counsel
Patricio Fuentes ☎ **692 2004**

Compliance
Jose Luis Arbildua ☎ **692 2033**

Public Relations
Marilu Vial ☎ **692 2014**

Accounts / Audit
Fernando Garcia ☎ **692 2306**

Banco de Boston — Full Branch Office

Moneda 799, Santiago, 1946
Tel: (2) 686 0000 **Fax**: (2) 686 0760; (2) 686 0770

www.euromoneydirectory.com   CHILE (+56)

Banco do Brasil SA
Full Branch Office

Apoquindo 3001, Las Condes, Santiago
Casilla de Correo 9396, Santiago
Tel: (2) 336 3001 Fax: (2) 336 3005

Senior Executive Officers
General Manager — Lincoln Barros de Souza
Others (Senior Executives)
Rui Barboza Pereiro *Deputy General Manager*

Administration
Other (Administration)
Commercial Banking — Héctor Fabio Muñoz

Banco de Chile
Head Office

Ahumada 251, Santiago 1
PO Box 151-D, Santiago 1
Tel: (2) 637 1111 Fax: (2) 637 3434 Telex: 24040479 BCHIL CL Swift: BCHI CL RM
Website: www.bancochile.cl

Senior Executive Officers
Chairman of the Board — Adolfo Rojas ☎ **637 2280**
Chief Executive Officer — Segismundo Schulin-Zeuthen *Chief Executive Officer* ☎ **637 3232**
Financial Director — Arturo Concha *Chief Financial Officer* ☎ **637 3197**
Chief Operating Officer — Miguel Luis Leonvendagar *Chief Operating Officer* ☎ **637 3104**
International Division — David Orrego *International Division Director* ☎ **637 2440**

General-Lending (DCM, SL)
Head of Corporate Banking — Jorge Buzzoni *Corporate Banking Director* ☎ **637 2634**

Foreign Exchange
Head of Trading — Cristian Del Solar *VP & Manager, Treasury* ☎ **637 2128**
FX Traders / Sales People
Franco Albertini *Manager, Foreign Trading* ☎ **637 4010**
Mario Diaz ☎ **637 2301**

Corporate Finance / M&A Advisory
Head of Corporate Finance — Jorge Buzzoni *Corporate Banking Director* ☎ **637 2634**

Other Departments
Correspondent Banking — Karen Ergas *VP & Manager, Correspondent Banking* ☎ **637 2285**

Administration
Business Development — Arturo Tagle
Head of Marketing — Osvaldo Iturriaga

Legal / In-House Counsel
Ricardo Dell'Orto *Chief Legal Counsel* ☎ **637 2580**

Banco de Crédito e Inversiones
Head Office

Huérfanos 1134, Santiago
Tel: (2) 696 6633; (2) 692 7000 Fax: (2) 699 0729; (2) 695 3775 Telex: 241356 CREDI CL Swift: CRED CL RM
Cable: BANCREDITO
Website: www.bci.cl

Senior Executive Officers
Chairman — Luis Enrique Yarur ☎ **696 6121**
Chief Executive Officer — G Lionel Olavarria *General Manager* ☎ **671 3651**
Financial Director — Mario Gomez *Manager, Commercial Banking* ☎ **692 7601**
Chief Operating Officer — Mario Gaete *Area Manager, Operations & Technology* ☎ **692 7501**
General Manager — G Lionel Olavarria ☎ **671 3651**
International Division — Ricardo Gabler *Manager, International* ☎ **672 6201**
Others (Senior Executives)
Graciela Duran *Comptroller* ☎ **696 6633**
Adviser to Chairman — Humberto Bejares *General Manager* ☎ **696 6633**
Commercial Banking — Rodrigo Junco *Manager* ☎ **692 7311**

General-Lending (DCM, SL)
Head of Corporate Banking — José Isla *Manager, Corporate Banking* ☎ **692 8533**

General-Investment
Head of Investment — Gonzalo Elizalde *Manager* ☎ **692 7301**

CHILE (+56)   www.euromoneydirectory.com

Banco de Crédito e Inversiones (cont)
Syndicated Lending
Loan-Related Activities
Trade Finance — Fernando Ahumada ☎ 692 8700
Project Finance — Gonzalo Elizalde *Manager* ☎ 692 7301

Money Markets
Head of Money Markets — Alberto Potin

Domestic Commercial Paper
Head of Sales; Head of Trading — Alberto Potin

Foreign Exchange
Head of Foreign Exchange — Alberto Potin
Corporate Sales — Jorge Barrenechea

Risk Management
Head of Risk Management — Andrés Atala *Commercial Banking Director* ☎ 692 7601

Foreign Exchange Derivatives / Risk Management
Vanilla FX option Sales; Vanilla FX option Trading — Jacques Lagas

OTC Equity Derivatives
Sales; Trading — Jacques Lagas

Other (Exchange-Traded Derivatives) — Jacques Lagas

OTC Credit Derivatives
Head — Jacques Lagas

Exchange-Traded Derivatives
Regional Head — Jacques Lagas

Corporate Finance / M&A Advisory
Head of Corporate Finance — Mario Gomez *Manager, Commercial Banking* ☎ 692 7601

Settlement / Clearing
Operations — Osvaldo Romero *Manager*
Adolfo García-Huidobro *Manager, Planning* ☎ 692 7311

Asset Management
Head — Gerardo Spoerer

Other Departments
Private Banking — Abraham Romero *Manager* ☎ 692 8739
Correspondent Banking — Ricardo Gabler *Manager, International* ☎ 672 6201

Administration
Head of Administration — Mario Gaete *Area Manager, Operations & Technology* ☎ 692 7501
Head of Marketing — Nicolas Diban

Technology & Systems
Mario Gaete *Area Manager, Operations & Technology* ☎ 692 7501

Legal / In-House Counsel
Pedro Balla

Public Relations
Tatiana Velez

Other (Administration)
Human Resources — Patricio Silva *Manager*

Banco del Desarrollo — Head Office

Avenida Bernardo O'Higgins 949, piso 3°, Santiago
PO Box 320-V, Santiago
Tel: (2) 674 5000; (2) 672 1897 **Fax:** (2) 671 5616

Senior Executive Officers
President — Vicente Caruz
General Manager — Hugo Trivelly
International Division — Roberto Senerman Finkelstein *Divisional Manager* ☎ 671 6646

Others (Senior Executives)
Nicolás Flaño Calderón *Director*
Alberto Etchegaray Aubry *Director*
Jean Luc Orsi *Director*
Sergio Molina Silva *Director*

General-Lending (DCM, SL)
Head of Corporate Banking — Roberto Senerman Finkelstein *Divisional Manager* ☎ 671 6646

www.euromoneydirectory.com   CHILE (+56)

Administration
Other (Administration)
Commercial Banking   José Massaro Olmeño *Divisional Manager* ☎ **639 4790**

Banco del Estado de Chile
Head Office

Avenida Libertador Bernardo O'Higgins 1111, Santiago
PO Box 21, Casilla 240-V, Santiago
Tel: (2) 670 7000; (2) 670 6140 **Fax:** (2) 670 6964; (2) 698 3299 **Telex:** 440133 **Swift:** BECH CL RM

Senior Executive Officers
Chairman   Andrés Sanfuentes Vergara ☎ **670 5005**
Financial Director   Orlando Guastavino I *General Manager*
Managing Director / General Manager   José Manuel Mena Valencia ☎ **670 5035**
International Division   Felipe Perucci Lezaeta *International Business Manager* ☎ **670 7512**

Others (Senior Executives)
                              Marco Colodro H *Vice Chairman*

Debt Capital Markets / Fixed Income
Mortgage-Backed Securities
Global Head   Carlos Espinosa

Syndicated Lending
Other (Syndicated Lending)
Letters of Credit   Luis Hernández G *Manager*

Settlement / Clearing
Operations   Fernando León *Manager*

Administration
Head of Administration   Orlando Guastavino I *General Manager*

Technology & Systems
                              Fernando León *Manager*

Legal / In-House Counsel
                              Matias Moreno *Lawyer*
                              Alberto Chacón O *Chief Lawyer*

Public Relations
                              Jorge Fernandez

Other (Administration)
                              Horacio de la Maza

Banco do Estado de São Paulo SA - BANESPA
Full Branch Office

Alternative trading name: BANESPA
Agustinas 1451, Santiago
Casilla de Correo 94 D, Correo Central, Santiago
Tel: (2) 695 1307 **Fax:** (2) 672 2459

Senior Executive Officers
General Manager   José Rocilo Sampaio da Cruz

Banco Europeo para America Latina (BEAL) SA
Representative Office

Miraflores 178, piso 14°, Oficina 1401, Santiago
Tel: (2) 639 6133; (2) 639 7137 **Fax:** (2) 633 9862 **Email:** beal@entelchile.net

Senior Executive Officers
Representative   Rodrigo Schele Kenkel

Banco de la Nación Argentina
Full Branch Office

Morandé 223/239, Santiago
Tel: (2) 696 6935; (2) 672 7768 **Fax:** (2) 698 7341 **Telex:** 240968 BNACL

Senior Executive Officers
General Manager   Jorge Humberto Rossi

CHILE (+56)   www.euromoneydirectory.com

Banco Santander - Chile
Full Branch Office

Formerly known as: Banco Osorno y la Unión
Bandera 140, Santiago
Casilla de Correo 57-D, Santiago
Tel: (2) 320 2000 **Fax:** (2) 661 8877; (2) 672 3166 **Swift:** BDER CL RM

Senior Executive Officers
General Manager   Oscar Von Chrismar

Others (Senior Executives)
    Mauricio Larrain *Vice President*

General-Lending (DCM, SL)
Head of Corporate Banking   Fernando Massú *Divisional Manager*
    Ignacio Ruiz-Tagle *Commercial Banking Manager*

Administration
Head of Marketing   Eduardo Opazo *Divisional Manager*

Corporate Communications
    Eduardo Opazo *Divisional Manager*

Other (Administration)
Commercial Banking   Ignacio Ruiz-Tagle *Commercial Banking Manager*

Banco Santiago
Head Office

Formerly known as: Banco O'Higgins
Bandera 201, Santiago
Casilla 14437, Correo 21, Santiago
Tel: (2) 630 4000 **Fax:** (2) 672 5825 **Cable:** BANGINS

Senior Executive Officers
Chairman   Andronico Luksic
Financial Director   Gustavo Rosselot
Chief Operating Officer   Alberto Salinas
Vice Chairman   Fernando Cañas B
International Division   Enrique Marshall R *Manager*

Others (Senior Executives)
Advisor to the CEO   Egidio Calzón *Comptroller*

Relationship Manager
Head of Investor Relations   Desiree Souldre ☎ **648 4711**

Syndicated Lending
Head of Credit Committee   Fernando Valdivieso *Credit Manager*

Risk Management
Head of Risk Management   Fernando Valdivieso *Credit Manager*

Other Departments
Economic Research   Samuel Arancibia *Research Manager*

Administration
Legal / In-House Counsel
    Juan Pedro Santa María P

Compliance
    Egidio Calzón *Comptroller*

Banco Security
Head Office

Agustinas 621, Santiago
Casilla de Correo 13312-21, Santiago
Tel: (2) 270 4000 **Fax:** (2) 270 4003; (2) 270 4013

Senior Executive Officers
President   Francisco Silva Silva
General Manager   Ramón Eluchans Olivares
International Division   Roland Jacob Díaz *International Division Director*

General-Lending (DCM, SL)
Head of Corporate Banking   Cristian Valdés B *Corporate Banking Manager*
    Christian Sinclair M *Corporate Banking Manager*

CHILE (+56)

Debt Capital Markets / Fixed Income
Tel: 270 4319
Head of Debt Capital Markets — Bonifiacio Bilbao
Head of Fixed Income Trading — Ignacio de Vicenti

Equity Capital Markets
Tel: 270 4319
Head of Equity Capital Markets — Bonifiacio Bilbao
Head of Trading — Nicola Ugarti

Money Markets
Tel: 270 4319
Head of Money Markets — Bonifiacio Bilbao

Money Markets - General
Trading — Ricardo Turner

Foreign Exchange
Tel: 270 4319
Head of Foreign Exchange — Bonifiacio Bilbao
Head of Trading — Matias Errasuiz

Risk Management
Tel: 270 4319
Head of Risk Management — Bonifiacio Bilbao
Claudio Izzo *Derivatives Trading*

Banco Sud Americano — Head Office

Morandé 226, Santiago
PO Box 90-D, Santiago
Tel: (2) 692 6000 Fax: (2) 692 6570 Telex: 240954 BSA CL Swift: BKSA CL RM
Website: www.bsa.cl

Senior Executive Officers
President — José Borda ☎ **692 6300**
Chief Executive Officer — Juan Luis Köstner *General Manager* ☎ **692 6402**
Financial Director — Joaquin Lagos *Assistant General Manager* ☎ **692 6401**
General Manager — Juan Luis Köstner ☎ **692 6402**

General-Investment
Head of Investment — Eduardo Orpis *Manager, Corporate Finance* ☎ **692 6505**

Debt Capital Markets / Fixed Income
Department: Corporate Finance
Head of Debt Capital Markets; Head of Fixed Income Sales; Head of Fixed Income Trading — Eugenio Echeverría *Assistant Manager* ☎ **692 6550** F **692 6581**

Government Bonds
Head of Sales — Eugenio Echeverría *Assistant Manager* ☎ **692 6550** F **692 6581**
Head of Syndication — Juan Pablo Silva ☎ **692 6550** F **692 6581**

Fixed-Income Repo
Head of Repo — Eugenio Echeverría *Assistant Manager* ☎ **692 6550** F **692 6581**

Equity Capital Markets
Department: Coriledores de Bolsa Sud americano SA
Tel: 692 5701
Head of Equity Capital Markets
Head of Sales; Head of Trading — Carlos Serrano *General Manager*
 Claudio Raglianto *Finance Manager* ☎ **692 5702**

Domestic Equities
Head of Sales; Head of Trading — Claudio Raglianto *Finance Manager* ☎ **692 5702**

Equity Research
Head of Equity Research — Miguel Canales

Syndicated Lending
Head of Trading — Alfonso Straub *Manager* ☎ **692 6200**

Loan-Related Activities
Trade Finance — Eduardo Orpis *Manager, Corporate Finance* ☎ **692 6505**

Money Markets
Head of Money Markets — Eduardo Orpis *Manager, Corporate Finance* ☎ **692 6505**

Domestic Commercial Paper
Head of Sales; Head of Trading — Juan Pablo Silva ☎ **692 6550** F **692 6581**

Wholesale Deposits
Marketing; Head of Sales — Eugenio Echeverría *Assistant Manager* ☎ **692 6550** F **692 6581**

Euromoney Directory 1999   **263**

CHILE (+56) www.euromoneydirectory.com

Banco Sud Americano (cont)
Foreign Exchange
Tel: 692 6540 Fax: 692 6581
Head of Foreign Exchange; Head of Institutional Sales; Corporate Sales; Head of Trading — Juan Silva *Deputy Manager, FX*
FX Traders / Sales People
　　Cristian Troncoso
　　Pedro Gaete

Risk Management
Tel: 692 6580 Fax: 692 6581
Head of Sales; Trading — Vivian Clarke *Deputy General Manager*
Other (FI Derivatives) — Vivian Clarke *Deputy General Manager*
Foreign Exchange Derivatives / Risk Management
Country Head — Vivian Clarke *Deputy General Manager*
Other Currency Swap / FX Options Personnel — Vivian Clarke *Deputy General Manager*

Corporate Finance / M&A Advisory
Head of Corporate Finance — Eduardo Orpis *Manager, Corporate Finance* ☎ **692 6505**

Settlement / Clearing
Tel: 692 6511 Fax: 692 6581
Head of Settlement / Clearing; Fixed-Income Settlement; Operations — Aldo Urrutia ☎ **692 5539** 🖷 **692 6507**

Asset Management
Head — Joaquin Lagos *Assistant General Manager* ☎ **692 6401**

Other Departments
Chief Credit Officer — Alfonso Straub *Manager* ☎ **692 6200**
Correspondent Banking — Patricio Carvallo
Cash Management — Eugenio Echeverría *Assistant Manager* ☎ **692 6550** 🖷 **692 6581**

Banco Sudameris　　　　　　　　　　　Full Branch Office
Huérfanos 699, Santiago
Casilla de Correo 402 V-21, Santiago
Tel: (2) 638 1514 Fax: (2) 633 0957 Telex: 340499 SUDAM CK Swift: BSUD CL RM

Senior Executive Officers
General Manager — Alberto Cordero di Montezemolo
Others (Senior Executives)
　　Giuseppe Falcone *Assistant Manager*

General-Lending (DCM, SL)
Head of Corporate Banking — Georges V de Conchard *Head, Corporate Banking*

Syndicated Lending
Aircraft / Aerospace Finance; Leasing & Asset Finance — José A Camiruaga

Other (Trade Finance)
Forfaiting, Letters of Credit & — Leonardo Fuentalba *Officer*

Foreign Exchange
Country Head — José Antonio Chahin *Manager*

Risk Management
Exchange-Traded Derivatives
FX Futures — José Antonio Chahin *Manager*

Settlement / Clearing
Operations — Giuseppe Falcone *Assistant Manager*

Other Departments
Correspondent Banking — Leonardo Fuentalba *Officer*

Administration
Head of Administration — Giuseppe Falcone *Assistant Manager*

Technology & Systems
　　Eduardo Letelier

Legal / In-House Counsel
　　Ricardo Edwards

Other (Administration)
Human Resources — Andrés Juri
Commercial Banking — Georges V de Conchard *Head, Corporate Banking*

Banedwards SA Corredores de Bolsa
Subsidiary Company

59 Ahumada Street, piso 3°, Santiago
Tel: (2) 510 8300 Fax: (2) 510 8339

Senior Executive Officers
President — Alfredo Prieto
Chief Executive Officer — Andrés Valenzuela *Gerente General* 🕿 **510 8310**
Financial Director — Jose de la Sotta *Gerente Finanzos* 🕿 **510 8310**
Chief Operating Officer — Pedro Caeorla *Gerente Oporaciones* 🕿 **510 8272**

BANEFE
Head Office

Formerly known as: Financiera Fusa SA

Tenderini 115, Santiago-Centro, Santiago
Tel: (2) 672 8581 Fax: (2) 639 7233

Senior Executive Officers
General Manager — Susana Tonda

Bank of America NT & SA

Alcánatara 200, piso 7°, Las Condes, Santiago
Tel: (2) 243 7210; (2) 243 7209 Fax: (2) 243 7393 Telex: 441188 BKMER CL

Senior Executive Officers
Managing Director — Marco A Gomez ✉ marco.a.gomez@bankamerica.com

The Bank of Tokyo-Mitsubishi Limited
Full Branch Office

Avenida El Bosque 130, piso 11°, Las Condes, Santiago
Tel: (2) 203 1180 Fax: (2) 203 1190 Telex: 441276

Senior Executive Officers
Managing Director / General Manager — Yorikatsu Yoshida
International Division — Juan Barticevic *International Division Director*

Others (Senior Executives)
Shigeomi Ogata *Deputy General Manager*

General-Lending (DCM, SL)
Head of Corporate Banking — Enrique Olivares *Corporate Banking Director*

Berliner Bank AG
Representative Office

Huérfanos 835, Oficina 704, Santiago
Tel: (2) 633 6477; (2) 639 8896 Fax: (2) 633 6477

Senior Executive Officers
Representative — Juan Antonio Garcia Sánchez

BICE Fondos Mutuos SA
Head Office

Teatinos 220, Santiago
Tel: (2) 692 2000 Fax: (2) 696 5324 Telex: 645197 BECE

Senior Executive Officers
General Manager — José Pedro Balmaceda

The Chase Manhattan Bank
Representative Office

Agustinas 1235, piso 5°, Santiago
Casilla de Correo 9192, Santiago
Tel: (2) 699 0068 Fax: (2) 690 5177

Senior Executive Officers

Others (Senior Executives)
Hernán Isotta *Vice President*
Institutional Banking — Eugenio Simón *Vice President*

CHILE (+56)

The Chase Manhattan Bank (cont)
Debt Capital Markets / Fixed Income
Head of Debt Capital Markets — Vicente Monge *Vice President*
Equity Capital Markets
Head of Equity Capital Markets — Vicente Monge *Vice President*

CIGNA International Investment Advisors Limited   Full Branch Office

Nueva York 80, piso 11°, Santiago
Tel: (2) 675 9095 Fax: (2) 675 9094

Senior Executive Officers
General-Investment
Head of Investment — Jaime Barros Cresta *Investment Director*

Citibank NA   Full Branch Office

Ahumada 48, 2nd Floor, Santiago
Tel: (2) 338 3000 Fax: (2) 338 2839 **Reuters:** CICH

Senior Executive Officers
General-Lending (DCM, SL)
Head of Corporate Banking — Francisco Leon ☎ **338 8217**
Debt Capital Markets / Fixed Income
Country Head — Francisco Leon ☎ **338 8217**
Equity Capital Markets
Country Head — Francisco Leon ☎ **338 8217**
Foreign Exchange
Global Head — Rodrigo Alvarez ☎ **338 8110**
Settlement / Clearing
Operations — Alvaro Valenzuela *Transaction Services Head* ☎ **338 8082** F **690 8710**
Global Custody
Regional Head — Alvaro Valenzuela *Transaction Services Head* ☎ **338 8082** F **690 8710**

Corp Banca   Head Office

Formerly known as: Banco Concepcion
Huerfanos 1072, Santiago, 80 D
PO Box 80-D, Santiago
Tel: (2) 696 7192; (2) 687 8000 Fax: (2) 696 5763 Telex: 441245 CONBC CK Swift: CONB CL RM
Email: fburgos@corpgroup.cl
Website: www.corpbanca.cl

Senior Executive Officers
Chairman of the Board — Carlos Abumohor ☎ **698 2566**
Vice Chairman of the Board — Alvaro Saieh ☎ **672 4858**
Chief Executive Officer — Jorge Selume ☎ **696 7323**
Financial Director — Christian Schiessler
Chief Operating Officer — Juan Carlos Corral ☎ **687 8000**

Others (Senior Executives)
Head, Commercial Division — Marcelo Achondo

General-Lending (DCM, SL)
Head of Corporate Banking — José Francisco Sanchez

Corporate Finance / M&A Advisory
Head of Corporate Finance — Christian Schiessler

Administration
Other (Administration)
Head, Human Resources — Luis Aguila

www.euromoneydirectory.com CHILE (+56)

Crédit Commercial de France
Representative Office

Andrés de Fuensalida 17, Oficina 34, Santiago
Tel: (2) 231 9012 **Fax:** (2) 231 5314 **Telex:** 247291 FASCO CL

Senior Executive Officers
Chief Representative Francisco Sáez C

Deutsche Bank AG
Representative Office

Coyancura 2283, Oficina 1101, piso 11°, Santiago
Casilla de Correo 3897, Santiago
Tel: (2) 335 1355 **Fax:** (2) 335 1360 **Telex:** 240542 DB SGO CL **Cable:** DEUTBANK

Dresdner Bank Lateinamerika
Representative Office

Huérfanos 1219, Entrepiso, Santiago
Casilla 9972, Santiago
Tel: (2) 688 0411 **Fax:** (2) 688 0422

Senior Executive Officers
Representative Rodolfo Kempter

Dresdner Banque Nationale de Paris
Subsidiary Company

Formerly known as: Deutsch Suedamerikanische Bank AG
Huérfanos 1219, Santiago
PO Box 10492, Santiago
Tel: (2) 731 4444 **Fax:** (2) 671 3307 **Telex:** 645341 DRESBK CL **Swift:** DRES CL RM **Email:** dresbnp@chilesat.net

Senior Executive Officers
President Andrés Bianchi ☎ **731 4233**
General Manager Ewald Doerner ☎ **731 4238**
International Division Miguel Angel Delpin *International Manager* ☎ **731 4268**
Deputy General Manager Francis Hartmann ☎ **731 4279**

General-Lending (DCM, SL)
Head of Corporate Banking Alfonso Piriz *Corporate Manager* ☎ **731 4210**

Foreign Exchange
Tel: 731 4268 **Fax:** 698 5961 **Telex:** 645347 DRESBK CL
Head of Foreign Exchange Benjamín Diaz *Chief of Foreign Exchange Dept.* ☎ **731 4299**

Risk Management
Tel: 731 4226 **Fax:** 672 0373 **Telex:** 340311 DRESBK CK
Head of Risk Management Patricia Peña ☎ **2731 4226**

Other Departments
Correspondent Banking Aldo Reganaz ☎ **731 4267**

Administration
Head of Administration Enrique Doberti *Manager* ☎ **731 4216**

Technology & Systems
 German Barbosa *System Manager* ☎ **731 4221**

Accounts / Audit
 Mario Cabello *Accounting* ☎ **731 4241**

ING Baring Fiseco

Avenida El Bosque Norte 0440, Oficina 1301, Las Condes, Santiago
Tel: (2) 203 5363 **Fax:** (2) 203 5364; (2) 203 5237 **Telex:** 341244 INGB CK

Senior Executive Officers
Managing Director / General Manager Michel Iselin

Euromoney Directory 1999 **267**

CHILE (+56) www.euromoneydirectory.com

ING Barings
Representative Office

Avenida Nueva Tajamar 555, Oficina 802, piso 8° Torre Costanera, World Trade Centre Building, Las Condes, Santiago
Tel: (2) 330 0600 Fax: (2) 330 0650 Telex: 341244 INGB CK Swift: INGB CL RM

Senior Executive Officers
Representative   German Tagle

Inversiones Deutsche Morgan Grenfell SA
Subsidiary Company

Formerly known as: Morgan Grenfell & Co
Coyancura 2283, Oficina 1101, piso 11°, Santiago
Tel: (2) 335 2046 Fax: (2) 335 2047

Kleinwort Benson Limited
Representative Office

Enrique Foster Sur 39, piso 8°, Las Condes, Santiago
Tel: (2) 234 1976 Fax: (2) 234 2506

Senior Executive Officers
Others (Senior Executives)
Director   Francisco Gutiérrez

Leasing Andino SA
Head Office

Moneda 970, piso 8°, Santiago, 340 V
Tel: (2) 250 0416; (2) 250 0413 Fax: (2) 695 6147; (2) 250 0392

Senior Executive Officers
President & Chairman, Board of Directors   Adolfo Rojas Gandulfo
Chief Executive Officer   Julio Acevedo Acuña
Financial Director   Juan Rius García *Chief Financial Officer*

Others (Senior Executives)
                                            Yujl Nishioka *Vice President of the Board*

Merrill Lynch Chile SA
Representative Office

Alcantara 200, piso 6, Santiago
Tel: (2) 369 5627 Fax: (2) 369 5657 Email: fzavala@ctcreuna.cl
Website: www.ml.com

Senior Executive Officers
General-Investment
Head of Investment   Fernando Zavala *Relationship Manager*
Administration
Head of Administration   Paulina Ureta *Office Manager*

Midland Bank plc
Representative Office

Miraflores 222, piso 18°, Santiago
Tel: (2) 632 3202 Fax: (2) 633 8458

Senior Executive Officers
Group Representative   P Stickland

Republic National Bank of New York
Full Branch Office

Huérfanos 1060, Santiago
Tel: (2) 695 2002 Fax: (2) 698 7512 Swift: BLIC CL RM
Website: www.rnb.com

Senior Executive Officers
Executive Vice President   Alberto Muchnick
SVP & Co-General Manager   Emilio Drullinsky
SVP & Co-General Manager   Simon Dahan

Santander Investment
Subsidiary Company

Alternative trading name: Sanander Corredora de Aciones
Piso 16, Avenida Andres Bello 2777, Las Condes, Santiago
Tel: (2) 336 3300 **Fax:** (2) 203 3167

Senior Executive Officers
General Manager & Chief Dealer   Alonso Moreno

Debt Capital Markets / Fixed Income
Tel: 336 3405
Head of Debt Capital Markets   Alonso Moreno *General Manager & Chief Dealer*
Head of Fixed Income Trading   Christian Paul

Equity Capital Markets
Tel: 336 3405
Head of Equity Capital Markets   Alonso Moreno *General Manager & Chief Dealer*
Head of Trading   Guillermo Tagle

Money Markets
Tel: 336 3405
Head of Money Markets   Alonso Moreno *General Manager & Chief Dealer*

Domestic Commercial Paper
Head of Trading   Patricio Aliaga

Foreign Exchange
Tel: 336 3405
Head of Foreign Exchange   Alonso Moreno *General Manager & Chief Dealer*
Head of Trading   Sergio Carlesi

Risk Management
Tel: 336 3405
Head of Risk Management   Alonso Moreno *General Manager & Chief Dealer*
Country Head   Phelipe Rodriguez *Derivatives Trading*

Société Générale
Representative Office

San Sebastian 2807, Of 413, Las Condes, Santiago
Tel: (2) 233 8126 **Fax:** (2) 334 1223
Website: www.socgen.com

Sudameris Agencia de Valores Ltda - Santiago

Huérfanos 669, piso 2°, Santiago
Tel: (2) 633 4434 **Fax:** (2) 639 6334 **Telex:** 340499 SUDAM CK

Senior Executive Officers
Manager   Belisario A Flores

CHINA
(+86)

Agricultural Bank of China

No Jia 23, Fu Xing Road, Beijing 100036
Tel: (10) 6821 6807; (10) 6841 3128 **Fax:** (10) 6829 7160 **Telex:** 22017 ABC CN **Swift:** ABOC CN BJ **Reuters:** ABCI

Senior Executive Officers
Chairman   Jiliang Shi
International Division   Tang Jianbang *General Manager*

Foreign Exchange
Head of Foreign Exchange   Lui Xing

Administration
Head of Administration   Faa Gang *Office Administration*

CHINA (+86) www.euromoneydirectory.com

The Asahi Bank Limited
Suite 2513, China World Tower, China World Trade Centre, 1 Jianguomenwai Avenue, Beijing
Tel: (10) 6505 1337 Fax: (10) 6505 1338 Telex: 22707 ASHBJ
Senior Executive Officers
Chief Representative   Yadoru Amano

The Asahi Bank Limited
Room 1436, Fuzhou Lakeside Hotel, 1 Hu Bin Road, Fuzhou, Fujian
Tel: (591) 783 9888 Fax: (591) 783 6000
Senior Executive Officers
Chief Representative   Yukihiro Komai

The Asahi Bank Limited Representative Office
5th Floor, Hua-He International Leasing Building, 121 Yan An San Road, Quingdao, Shangdong Province
Tel: (532) 387 1239 Fax: (532) 387 1322 Telex: 321073 ASHQD
Senior Executive Officers
Chief Representative   Kazuomi Yamada

The Asahi Bank Limited
Room 1403, Shanghai International Trade Center, 2200 Yan-an Road (West), Shanghai 200335
Tel: (21) 6275 8111 Fax: (21) 6270 2701 Telex: 337238 ASHSH CN
Senior Executive Officers
General Manager   Hiroshi Fujita

Banca Nazionale del Lavoro SpA Representative Office
10th Floor, Office 2, CITIC Building, 19 Jianguomenwai Dajie, Beijing 100004
Tel: (10) 6500 4212; (10) 6500 6412 Fax: (10) 6500 3507 Telex: 22567 BNL CN Email: bnl@bj.col.com.cn
Senior Executive Officers
Chief Representative   Renzo Franceschini

Banco Exterior de España SA Representative Office
Room 1007, SCITECH Tower, 22 Jianguomenwai Dajie, Beijing 100004
Tel: (10) 6512 3838 Fax: (10) 6512 3765 Email: bexpekin@sw.com.cn
Senior Executive Officers
Chief Representative   Victor Ochoa

Bank Brussels Lambert Representative Office
Beijing Lufthansa Cener, Unit C317, 50 Liangmaqiao Road, Chaoyang District, Beijing 100016
Tel: (10) 6463 7961; (10) 6463 7926 Fax: (10) 6463 7985
Senior Executive Officers
Chief Representative   Dave Deruytter

Bank of China Head Office
410 Fu Cheng Men Nei Dajie, Beijing 100818
Tel: (10) 0001 0088 Fax: (10) 6601 6869 Telex: 22254 BCHO CN Swift: BKCH CH BJ
Senior Executive Officers
Chairman   Xuebing Wang
Treasurer   Guang Bei He ☎ 6602 2681
Managing Director   Ping Yue
International Division   Yang Xin Huang ☎ 6601 1830
General-Lending (DCM, SL)
Head of Corporate Banking   Gang Xu ☎ 6834 3050

270   Euromoney Directory 1999

www.euromoneydirectory.com   CHINA (+86)

Syndicated Lending
Trade Finance   Jian Bao Shan ☎ 6601 6688
Corporate Finance / M&A Advisory
Head of Corporate Finance Gang Xu ☎ 6834 3050
Settlement / Clearing
Head of Settlement / Clearing Lan Li ☎ 6602 5817
Other Departments
Correspondent Banking   Yang Xin Huang ☎ 6601 1830
Administration
Legal / In-House Counsel
                             Yong Tang Wang

Public Relations
                             Chang Chen Qu ☎ 6601 1837

Bank of Communications   Head Office
18 Xian Xia Road, Shanghai 200336
Tel: (21) 6275 1234 **Fax:** (21) 6275 6784 **Telex:** 337340 **Swift:** COMM CN SH **Reuters:** BCOH
Website: www.bankcomm.com
Senior Executive Officers
Chairman   Jieyan Yin
President   Mingguan Wang
Chief Executive Officer   Mingguan Wang *President*
Managing Director   Qiao Wei
Managing Director   Wu Jian
Managing Director   Yin Baoyu

The Bank of East Asia Limited
Ground/3rd Floors, Metro Plaza, 183 Tian He Bei Road, Guangzhou
Tel: (20) 8755 1892 **Fax:** (20) 8755 3938 **Telex:** 440726 BEAGZ CN **Swift:** BEAS CN SHA GZU
Senior Executive Officers
Managing Director / General Manager   Raymond Chang Wai Yan

The Bank of East Asia Limited
The Bank of East Asia Building, 299 Szechuen Road Central, Shanghai 200002
Tel: (21) 6323 3518 **Fax:** (21) 6321 7617 **Telex:** 33678 BEAPX CN
Senior Executive Officers
General Manager   Timmy Leung Tat Man

The Bank of East Asia Limited
Ground Floor, Hai Yan Commercial Building, Jia Bin Road, Shenzhen
Tel: (755) 222 9680 **Fax:** (755) 222 9681 **Telex:** 420375 BEASZ CN
Senior Executive Officers
General Manager   Tang Sing Yu

The Bank of Yokohama Limited   Representative Office
2209 China World Tower, China World Trade Center, No 1, Jianguomenwai Avenue, Beijing
Tel: (10) 6505 1157 **Fax:** (10) 6505 1158 **Cable:** HAMABANK
Senior Executive Officers
Chief Representative   Sumio Ai

The Bank of Yokohama Limited   Representative Office
Room No 1411, Ruijin Building, 205 Mao Ming Nanlu, Shanghai
Tel: (21) 6472 5930 **Fax:** (21) 6472 9255
Senior Executive Officers
Chief Representative   Hitoshi Uemura

CHINA (+86)   www.euromoneydirectory.com

Barclays Bank plc
Representative Office

Alternative trading name: Barclays Capital
Room 1211, SCITE Tower, 22 Jianguomenwai Dajie, Beijing 100004
Tel: (10) 6512 2288; (10) 6512 7804 Fax: (10) 6512 7889

Senior Executive Officers
Chief Representative   Helen Fei

Bear Stearns Beijing Representative Office
Representative Office

Level 09, Units 23-24, China World Tower, #1 Jianguomenwai Dajie, Beijing 100004
Tel: (10) 6505 5101; (10) 6505 5101 Fax: (10) 6505 5203
Website: www.bearsteans.com

Canadian Imperial Bank of Commerce
Representative Office

Rooms 201/2, International Club, Jianguomenwai Dajie, Beijing 100020
Tel: (10) 6532 3164 Fax: (10) 6532 5385

Senior Executive Officers
Resident Representative   Zhong-Hua Guo

CARIPLO - Cassa di Risparmio delle Provincie Lombarde SpA
Representative Office

Unit S21 Beijing Lufthansa Centre, No 50 Liang Ma Qiao Road, Chaoyang District, Beijing 100016
Tel: (10) 6465 1057; (10) 6463 1058 Fax: (10) 6465 3338 Telex: 210287 CRPLP CN

Senior Executive Officers
Representative   Roberto Bisagno

The Chase Manhattan Bank
Representative Office

5th Floor, Fullink Plaza, 18 Chaoyangmenwai Avenue, Chaoyang District, Beijing 100020
Tel: (10) 6588 1039; (10) 6588 1040 Fax: (10) 6588 1048; (10) 6588 1049

Senior Executive Officers
Senior Country Officer   Christian Murck

The Chase Manhattan Bank
Full Branch Office

Suite 700A, The Shanghai Centre, 1376 Nanjing Road West, Shanghai 200040
Tel: (21) 6279 7288; (21) 6279 7218 Fax: (21) 6279 8101 Telex: 33258 CHASE CN

Senior Executive Officers
Others (Senior Executives)
Branch Manager   Peter Shay *Vice President*

China Investment Bank
Head Office

1 Fuchengmenwai Street, Beijing 100037
Tel: (10) 6836 4987; (10) 6836 4984 Fax: (10) 6836 4959; (10) 6836 4960 Telex: 22537 CIB CN Swift: IBDC CN BJ
Reuters: CIBD

Senior Executive Officers
Chairman   Xiaochuan Zhou
President   Dawei Liu
International Division   Yansong Jiang ☎ 6836 4984 📠 6836 4959

Others (Senior Executives)
Executive Vice President   Yufeng Zhu
Kerang Qin
Shijing Jiao
Xiaofan Sun

www.euromoneydirectory.com   CHINA (+86)

Money Markets
Tel: 6836 4996 Fax: 6836 4991 Telex: 222947, 221112
Head of Money Markets   Ruian Zhao *General Manager*

China Merchants Bank   Head Office

2 Shennan Road C, Shenzhen 518031
Tel: (755) 229 0000; (755) 322 4905 Fax: (755) 321 4556; (755) 322 4976 Telex: 420034 CMBHO Swift: CMBC CN BS
Reuters: CMHO
Website: www.cmbchina.com

Senior Executive Officers
Chairman	Songjin Liu
President	Shizhen Wang ☏ **224 2101**
Chief Operating Officer	Jianhua Wan *Executive Vice President* ☏ **224 3588**
Assistant President	Junzhi Shi ☏ **322 0980**

Syndicated Lending
Tel: 224 2096 Fax: 219 0010 Telex: 420035 CMBHOCN
Head of Syndication; Head of Trading   Jianwei Huang *Deputy General Manager*

Loan-Related Activities
Trade Finance	Shaojun Wang *Manager* ☏ **321 5443**
Project Finance	Jianwei Huang *Deputy General Manager*

Money Markets
Tel: 322 0984 Fax: 322 0990
Head of Money Markets   Yeging Wang *Manager*

Foreign Exchange
Tel: 322 0984 Fax: 322 0990 Telex: 420035 CMBHOCN
Head of Foreign Exchange   Yeging Wang *Manager*

Settlement / Clearing
Tel: 322 4996 Fax: 322 0990 Telex: 420035 CMBHOCN
Head of Settlement / Clearing; Operations; Back-Office   Yao Jian *Manager*

Other Departments
Correspondent Banking   Kevin Liu ☏ **322 4905**

Administration
Head of Administration   Nanqing Li *Head* ☏ **224 2100**

Accounts / Audit
     Rongli Guo ☏ **219 0021** 🖷 **229 0059**

Cho Hung Bank   Full Branch Office

1901, Tianjin International Building, 75 Nanjing Road, Heping District, Tianjin 300050
Tel: (22) 2339 4070; (22) 2339 4077 Fax: (22) 2339 4043 Telex: 234190 CHO BANK Swift: CHOH CN BT

Senior Executive Officers
General Manager   Young Pyo Kim ☏ **2311 4442**

CITIC Industrial Bank   Head Office

Block C, Fuhua Mansion, 8 Chaoyangmenbei Dajie, Dongcheng District, Beijing 100027
Tel: (10) 6554 1158; (10) 6500 1168 Fax: (10) 6554 1671; (10) 6554 1672 Telex: 210716 CIBAD CN Swift: CIBK CN BJ
Reuters: CTIB

Senior Executive Officers
Chairman	Yuncheng Hong ☏ **6554 1088**
President	Jianzhong Dou ☏ **6554 1088**

Debt Capital Markets / Fixed Income
Department: Capital Markets Group
Tel: 6554 1189 Fax: 6554 2273
Global Head   Chuanchun Jiang *General Manager* ☏ **6554 2296**

Syndicated Lending
Department: Credit & Loan Department
Global Head   Qiang Zhang *General Manager* ☏ **6554 1268**

Loan-Related Activities
Trade Finance   Xuejun Wang *Deputy General Manager* ☏ **6554 1229**

CHINA (+86)　　　　　　　www.euromoneydirectory.com

CITIC Industrial Bank (cont)
Money Markets
Department: Treasury Department
Tel: 6554 2295 **Fax:** 6554 2294
Global Head　　　　　　　　　　　Desheng Lai *Deputy General Manager* ☏ **6554 2289**
Foreign Exchange
Global Head　　　　　　　　　　　Desheng Lai *Deputy General Manager* ☏ **6554 2289**
Risk Management
Department: Credit Control Department
Global Head　　　　　　　　　　　Jianlin Sun *Deputy General Manager* ☏ **6554 1321**
Settlement / Clearing
Department: Clearing Center
Regional Head　　　　　　　　　　Feiyao Xia *General Manager* ☏ **6554 1275**
Other Departments
Correspondent Banking　　　　　　Jian Zhang *Deputy General Manager* ☏ **6554 1891**

Commerzbank AG　　　　　　　　　　　　　　　　　Representative Office
8-4 CITIC Building, 19 Jianguomenwai Dajie, Beijing 100004
Tel: (10) 6500 4959; (10) 6500 3703 **Fax:** (10) 6500 3161 **Telex:** 22628 CBPEK CN
Senior Executive Officers
VP & Chief Representative　　　　Michael M Reichel

Compagnie Financière Tradition　　　　　　　　Representative Office
Room 4015, Beijing Toronto Hotel, 3 Jianguomenwai Dajie, Beijing 100020
Tel: (10) 6594 1873 **Fax:** (10) 6594 1873
Senior Executive Officers
Assistant Representative　　　　　Huang Wei

Crédit Agricole Indosuez　　　　　　　　　　　　Representative Office
Formerly known as: Banque Indosuez
Room 1205, CITIC Building, 19 Jianguomenwai Dajie, Beijing 100004
Tel: (10) 6500 3574; (10) 6513 9747 **Fax:** (10) 6500 4930 **Telex:** 22909 BISPK CN
Senior Executive Officers
Chief Representative　　　　　　　Patrick Herbert

Crédit Agricole Indosuez　　　　　　　　　　　　　　Full Branch Office
Formerly known as: Banque Indosuez
Room 214, Aether Square, 986 Jie Fang Bei Road, Guangzhou 510030
Tel: (20) 8669 3303; (20) 8669 3181 **Fax:** (20) 8669 3202; (20) 8669 3312 **Telex:** 440794 BISGZ CN
Senior Executive Officers
General Manager　　　　　　　　　Yu May Wong
Foreign Exchange
Head of Foreign Exchange　　　　Zhi Qin Dai *Dealer*
Administration
Head of Administration　　　　　　Ting Kwan Cheng *Senior Manager*

Crédit Agricole Indosuez　　　　　　　　　　　　　　Full Branch Office
Formerly known as: Banque Indosuez
1704-1707 Marine Tower, 1 Pudong Avenue, Pudong New Area, Shanghai 200120
Tel: (21) 5879 5559 **Fax:** (21) 5879 4379; (21) 5879 4393 **Telex:** 33130 **Reuters:** IDSH
Senior Executive Officers
Chief Executive Officer　　　　　　Jean-Pierre Raynaud *General Manager* ☏ **5879 4386**
Chief Operating Officer　　　　　　Richard Groves ☏ **5879 4262**
Treasurer　　　　　　　　　　　　　Frederick Ng ☏ **5879 7816**
Deputy General Manager　　　　　Alan Liu ☏ **5879 0285**
International Division　　　　　　　John Fok *Manager, Trade Finance*

www.euromoneydirectory.com   CHINA (+86)

Equity Capital Markets
Domestic Equities
Head of Origination — Dominic Yee *Manager*
Syndicated Lending
Loan-Related Activities
Trade Finance — John Fok *Manager, Trade Finance*
Risk Management
Country Head — Tang Loaec *Vice President*

Crédit Agricole Indosuez — Full Branch Office

Formerly known as: Banque Indosuez
Room 320, Century Plaza Hotel, 1 Chun Feng Road, Shenzhen 518001
Tel: (755) 232 8930; (755) 232 8931 **Fax:** (755) 232 3023 **Telex:** 420569 BISSZ CN

Senior Executive Officers
Branch Manager — Philip Lian Fei Zhu ☏ **234 3511**
Settlement / Clearing
Operations — Thomas Shiu Lam Yip *Operations Manager* ☏ **233 9085**
Administration
Head of Marketing — Yan Chen *Marketing Officer* ☏ **232 8930**
Accounts / Audit
Accounts — Kent Jian Chan *Senior Officer* ☏ **234 6505**

The Dai-Ichi Kangyo Bank Limited — Full Branch Office

6th Floor, Senmao Building, 4 Zhongshan Road 147, Xigang District, Dalian
Tel: (411) 360 2543; (411) 360 2546 **Fax:** (411) 360 2570; (411) 360 2605 **Telex:** 86416 DKBDL CN

The Dai-Ichi Kangyo Bank Limited

Room 915, East Ocean Building Hotel, 1 Building, Zhongshan Road, Xiamen, Fujian
Tel: (592) 202 1111 **Fax:** (592) 205 8150

The Dai-Ichi Kangyo Bank Limited — Full Branch Office

25th Floor, Shanghai Senmao International Building, 101 Yincheng East Road, Pudong New Area, Shanghai
Tel: (21) 6841 0001 **Fax:** (21) 6841 0002 **Telex:** 33302 DKBSH CN
Website: www.dkb.co.jp

Senior Executive Officers
Managing Director / General Manager — Kunihiko Okabe

The Daiwa Bank Limited — Representative Office

Room 1118, Beijing Fortune Building, 5 Dong Sanhuan Beilu, Chaoyang District, Beijing 100004
Tel: (10) 6590 8500; (10) 6590 8501 **Fax:** (10) 6590 8502 **Telex:** 210553 DWBKB CN

Senior Executive Officers
Chief Representative — Sumio Hayashi

The Daiwa Bank Limited — Representative Office

Room 1032, The Garden Tower, 368 Huanshi Dong Lu, Guangzhou 510064
Tel: (20) 8384 0125 **Fax:** (20) 8384 0553 **Telex:** 440915 DAIWA

Senior Executive Officers
Chief Representative — Gen Kataoka

CHINA (+86)　　　www.euromoneydirectory.com

The Daiwa Bank Limited
Full Branch Office

Room 2709, Shangai International Trade Centre, 2200 Yan An Xi Lu, Shanghai
Tel: (21) 6275 5198 Fax: (21) 6275 5229 Telex: 33514

Senior Executive Officers
General Manager　　　　　　　　Chiaki Maeda
Deputy General Manager　　　　　Nobuhisa Ishizaki

Den norske Bank
Representative Office

Rooms 124/6 Jianguo Hotel, 5 Jianguomenwai dajie, Beijing 100020
Tel: (10) 501 1902 Fax: (10) 501 1909

Senior Executive Officers
Chief Representative　　　　　　John Hjelset

Deutsche Bank AG
Representative Office

2620/24 China World Tower, China World Trade Center, 1 Jianguomenwai dajie, Beijing 100004
Tel: (10) 6505 2305; (10) 6505 2306 Fax: (10) 6505 2304 Telex: 22572 DBPRC CN Cable: DEUTBANK BEIJING

Deutsche Bank AG
Representative Office

Room 809/11, Main Building, GITIC Plaza, 339 Huanshi Dong Lu, Guangzhou 510098
Tel: (20) 8331 2998 Fax: (20) 8331 1558; (20) 8331 1640 Telex: 441630 DBGZ CN

Deutsche Bank AG
Representative Office

Room 2501/2, 25th Floor, Guangming Mansion, 2 Jin Ling Road (East), Shanghai 200002
Tel: (21) 6323 9857 Fax: (21) 6323 9858

DG BANK
Representative Office

Room 23-E, CITIC Building, 19, Jianguomenwai Street, Beijing 100004
Tel: (10) 6500 6332 Fax: (10) 6500 6333

Senior Executive Officers
Representative　　　　　　　　　Lunzhang Dai

DG BANK
Representative Office

Room 510, Bund Centre Building, 555 Zhongshan East Road, Shanghai 200010
Tel: (21) 6320 0100 Fax: (21) 6320 0221

Senior Executive Officers
Representative　　　　　　　　　Holger Wessling

Generale Bank
Representative Office

Zijin Guest House 3, 9 Chong Wenmen Xidajie, Beijing 100005
Tel: (10) 6513 3310; (10) 6513 3394 Fax: (10) 6512 9180 Telex: 22697 SGBJ CN

Senior Executive Officers
Chief Representative　　　　　　Dominique Casier
Assistant Chief Representative　　Jie Wang

Others (Senior Executives)

Jia-Rui Feng *Administrative Assistant*
Yi Juan Huang *Commercial Assistant*
Wen-Li Qiu *Executive Assistant*

Guangdong Development Bank — Head Office

83 Nonglinxia Road, Guangzhou 510080
Tel: (20) 8731 0888 Fax: (20) 8731 0779 Swift: GDBK CN 22 Reuters: DEVE

Senior Executive Officers
Chairman — Chixin Wu ☎ 8731 0888 ext 2925
President — Ruohong Li ☎ 8731 0888 ext 2925
Financial Director — Fei Sun *General Manager* ☎ 8731 0620
Treasurer — Huang Tang *Deputy Manager* ☎ 8731 0568
International Division — Lianming Zheng *General Manager* ☎ 8731 0779

Other Departments
Correspondent Banking — Poebe Weng *Deputy Manager* ☎ 8731 0905

HypoVereinsbank — Representative Office

Unit 10-10 Landmark Tower, Beijing 100004
Tel: (10) 6590 0105; (10) 6590 0106 Fax: (10) 6590 0110

HypoVereinsbank — Representative Office

Suite 1808, Shanghai International Trade Centre, 2200 Yan An Road (West), Shanghai 200335
Tel: (21) 6278 0120 Fax: (21) 6278 0121

The Industrial & Commercial Bank of China

55 Fuxingmennei Avenue, Xicheng District, Beijing 100031
Tel: (10) 6610 6114; (10) 6610 7156 Fax: (10) 6610 6053; (10) 6610 6044 Telex: 22770 Swift: ICBK CN BJ
Website: www.icbc.com.ch

Senior Executive Officers
Chairman & President — Liu Tinghuan
International Division — Zhang Jianguo

Others (Senior Executives)
Yang Zilin *Vice Chairman & Deputy President*
Tian Ruizhang *Vice Chairman & Deputy President*
Li Lihui *Executive Director & Deputy President*
Xie Duyang *Executive Director & Deputy President*
Yang Kaisheng *Executive Director & Deputy President*
Chen Keru *Executive Director*
Zhang Furong *Executive Vice President*
Dong Dongqing *Executive Vice President*

Syndicated Lending
Loan-Related Activities
Trade Finance — Qin Lei *Senior Manager* ☎ 6610 6022
Project Finance — Zhang Shiming *General Manager*

Money Markets
Head of Money Markets — Shen Shisheng *Deputy General Manager* ☎ 6821 7428

Other Departments
Correspondent Banking — Gao Ming *Senior Manager* ☎ 6610 6071

The Industrial Bank of Japan Limited — Full Branch Office

8th Floor, Senmao Building, 147 Zhong Shan Lu, Xi Gang Qu, Dalian 116011
Tel: (411) 369 2712 Fax: (411) 360 3581 Telex: 86212 IBJDL CN

Senior Executive Officers
General Manager — Atsushi Endo

The Industrial Bank of Japan Limited — Full Branch Office

Room 1601, Shanghai International Trade Center, 2200 Yan an Road (West), Shanghai 200335
Tel: (21) 6275 1111 Fax: (21) 6275 1769

Senior Executive Officers
General Manager — Kiyoshige Akamatsu

Euromoney Directory 1999 277

CHINA (+86)   www.euromoneydirectory.com

The Industrial Bank of Japan Limited
Full Branch Office

Room 401 Marine Tower, 1 Pudong Avenue, Pudong New Area, Shanghai 200120
Tel: (21) 5879 0611 Fax: (21) 5879 0600 Telex: 33144 IBJSH CN Swift: IBJT CN SH

Senior Executive Officers
General Manager   Kiyoshige Akamatsu

ING Baring Securities (China)
Representative Office

Suite 538, East Tower, The Shanghai Centre, 1376 Nanjing West Road, Shanghai 200040
Tel: (21) 6279 7161; (21) 6279 7163 Fax: (21) 6279 7160; (21) 6279 8621
Extra Tel: 6279 7162; Fax: 6279 7171

Senior Executive Officers
Head of Equities   Hoong Yik-Luen

ING Barings
Representative Office

Room 1510, Landmark Building, 8 North Dongsanhuan Road, Beijing 100004
Tel: (10) 6590 0955; (10) 6590 0954 Fax: (10) 6590 0957; (10) 6590 0956 Telex: 211248 INGCL CN

Senior Executive Officers
Country Manager   Jan Bosma ☏ 6590 0950
Representative   Benby Chan ☏ 6590 0943
Department: ING Consultants
Room 1509, Landmark Building No.8 North Dongsanhuan Road, Beijing
Tel: +86 (10) 659 0954 Fax: +86 (10) 659 0956

Others (Senior Executives)
Contact Person   Banby Chan

ING Barings
Representative Office

Room 1246-7 Garden Tower, Garden Hotel, 368 Huan Shi Dong Road, Guangzhou 510064
Tel: (20) 8387 8866; (20) 8387 8862 Fax: (20) 8387 8889 Telex: NZ21453
Extra Tel: 8333 8999 1247

Senior Executive Officers
Representative   David Wu

ING Barings
Full Branch Office

2nd Floor, Central Place, 16 Henan Road South, Shanghai 200002
Tel: (21) 6355 6006 Fax: (21) 6355 7005 Telex: 08533088 INGH CN

Senior Executive Officers
General Manager   Douglas Red

ING Barings
Representative Office

Room 328, Liaoning Hotel, No. 97, Zhongshan Street, Heiping District, Shenyang 11001
Tel: (24) 2383 9166 328; (24) 2340 9388 Fax: (24) 2340 3188

Senior Executive Officers
Representative   Amin Ng

ING Barings
Full Branch Office

32nd Floor, Shenzen Development Centre, Renminnan Road, Shenzhen 518001
Tel: (755) 229 9775 Fax: (755) 229 8239; (755) 222 4432 Telex: 420047 INGSZ

Senior Executive Officers
General Manager   Frank Lam ☏ 229 8250
Assistant General Manager   Benjamin Ng

ING Barings
Full Branch Office

19 Hubin Bei Road, 07-01 United Overseas Bank Building, Xiamen 361012, Fujian Province
Tel: (592) 511 3338 **Fax:** (592) 509 9098 **Telex:** 93108 INGXM CN

Senior Executive Officers
General Manager   Philip Lum

International Finance Corporation
Representative Office

Tower B, 9th Floor, Fuhma Mansion, 8 Chasyangmen Beidajie, Dongcheng District, Beijing 100027
Tel: (10) 6554 4191 **Fax:** (10) 6554 4192
Website: www.ifc.org

Senior Executive Officers
Chief of Mission   Davin Mackenzie

Jardine Fleming Securities Limited
Representative Office

9/F Jiu Shi Fu Xing Mansion, 918 Huai Hai Zhong Road, Shanghai 200020
Tel: (21) 6415 0828 **Fax:** (21) 6415 0622

Senior Executive Officers
Chief Representative   William Tenison

The Joyo Bank Limited
Representative Office

Room 1901, Shanghai International Trade Centre, 2200 Yan An Road (West), Shanghai 200335
Tel: (21) 6209 0258 **Fax:** (21) 6209 0508

The Long-Term Credit Bank of Japan Limited
Representative Office

34-2 Jing Guang Centre, Hujialou, Chaoyang-qu, Beijing
Tel: (10) 6597 3560 **Fax:** (10) 6597 4561

The Long-Term Credit Bank of Japan Limited
Full Branch Office

Suite 550, The American International Centre at Shanghai, 1376 Nanjing Road West, Shanghai
Tel: (21) 6279 8855 **Fax:** (21) 6279 8856

Merita Bank Plc/Nordbanken AB (publ)
Representative Office

Room 721, Beijing Fortune Building, 5 North Dongsanhuan Road, Beijing 100004
Tel: (10) 6590 9070 **Fax:** (10) 6590 9073

Senior Executive Officers
Representative   Todor Panayotov

Merrill Lynch International Incorporated
Representative Office

Suite 3301-3302, China World Tower, World Trade Centre, 1 Jianguomenwai dajie, Beijing 100004
Tel: (10) 6505 0290 **Fax:** (10) 6505 0278

Merrill Lynch International Incorporated
Subsidiary Company

Suite 308, West Tower, Shanghai Centre, 1376 Nanjing West Road, Shanghai 200040
Tel: (21) 6279 7032 **Fax:** (21) 6279 7031

Other Departments
Department: Financial Markets
Other Departments
Financial Markets   Patrick Lo *Dealer*

CHINA (+86)   www.euromoneydirectory.com

The Nikko Securities Co Limited — Representative Office
Room 2503, 25th Floor, CITIC Building, 19 Jianguomenwai dajie, Beijing
Tel: (10) 6500 4402; (10) 6592 7722 Fax: (10) 6500 3417 Telex: 22941
Senior Executive Officers
Chief Representative   Hideki Yamamoto ✉ yamahide@public.east.cn.net

Overseas Union Bank Limited — Representative Office
No. 3, Quin Men East Street, Beijing Capital Hotel, Beijing 100006
Tel: (10) 6512 9988 Fax: (10) 6512 0324
Senior Executive Officers
Chief Representative   Ang Hoon Seng

Overseas Union Bank Limited — Full Branch Office
Room 305, Century Plaza Hotel, Kin Chit Road, Shenzhen 518001
Tel: (755) 232 2755 Fax: (755) 234 3512
Senior Executive Officers
Vice President & Manager   Wu Ser Wah

Paribas — Representative Office
Suite 1622, Beijing Hotel, 33 Chang An Avenue, Beijing 100004
Tel: (10) 6513 3990 Fax: (10) 6513 7430
Senior Executive Officers
Head of Territory for China   Jean Michel Piveteau

Paribas — Representative Office
Suite 409, Block C, China Hotel Office Tower, Guangzhou 510015
Tel: (20) 8666 4094 Fax: (20) 8668 2395
Senior Executive Officers
Senior Officer   Jonathan Lin

Paribas — Full Branch Office
31st Floor, China Merchants Tower, 66 Lujiazui Road, Shanghai 200120
Tel: (21) 5879 7725 Fax: (21) 5882 6780
Senior Executive Officers
General Manager   Pierre Imhof

Royal Bank of Canada — Representative Office
Units 18/20, Level 6, China World Tower, China World Trade Centre, 1 Jianguomenwai Avenue, Beijing 100004
Tel: (10) 6505 0358 Fax: (10) 6505 4206

The Sakura Bank Limited — Representative Office
3rd Floor, Changfugong Office Building, A-26, Jianguomenwai Dajie, Chaoyang-Qu, Beijing
Tel: (10) 6513 9018; (10) 6513 9253 Fax: (10) 6513 9019 Telex: 22676 MTKBJ CN
Senior Executive Officers
Chief Representative   Yoichi Fujikura

www.euromoneydirectory.com   CHINA (+86)

The Sakura Bank Limited
Representative Office
17th Floor, Senmao Building, 147 Zhongshan Road, XI Gang District, Dalian
Tel: (411) 360 6161 Fax: (411) 360 7171 Telex: 86341 MTKDL CN
Senior Executive Officers
Chief Representative   Takashi Hirata

The Sakura Bank Limited
Full Branch Office
7th Floor, Room 701-704 Main Building, Guangdong International Hotel, 339 Huanshi Dong Lu, Guangzhou
Tel: (20) 8331 1111 Fax: (20) 8331 1932; (20) 8331 1923 Telex: 440916 MTKGZ CN
Senior Executive Officers
General Manager   Yuji Tsujino

The Sakura Bank Limited
Full Branch Office
41st Floor, Shanghai Senmao International Building, 101 Yin Cheng East Road, Pudong New Area, Shanghai 200120
Tel: (21) 6841 3111 Fax: (21) 6841 0650; (21) 6841 4113 Telex: 33540 MITKBKSH C
Senior Executive Officers
General Manager   Hiroshi Shigeta

The Sakura Bank Limited
Full Branch Office
Room 1210, Tianjin International Building, 75 Nanjing Lu, Tianjin
Tel: (22) 2330 3334 Fax: (22) 2331 3834 Telex: 23248 MTKTJ CN
Senior Executive Officers
General Manager   Kenji Kato

Shanghai International Finance Company Limited
Head Office
2301 World Trade Tower, 500 Guangdong Road, Shanghai 200001
Tel: (21) 6350 2020 Fax: (21) 6350 0202 Telex: 33224 SIFCO CN
Senior Executive Officers
Chairman of the Board   Jiasheng Xu ☏ 6321 3400
Others (Senior Executives)
Director   Fook Por Wong *Deputy General Manager*
                                         Ling Di Chen *Deputy General Manager*
                                         Zong Xue Zeng *Deputy General Manager*

SocGen-Crosby
Subsidiary Company
Room 210, Office Tower, Beijing Asia Jinjiang Mansion, 8 Xinzhong Xi Jie, Gongti Bei Lu, Beijing 100027
Tel: (10) 6500 7510 Fax: (10) 6500 7466
Equity Capital Markets
Equity Research
Regional Head   Raymond Jook *Head of Research* ☏ +852 2166 4340 ✉ +852 2166 4662
                                         ✉ raymond_jook@socgen-crosby.com

Other (Equity Research)
China Economy   Hu Biliang *Senior Economist* ✉ hu_biliang@socgen-crosby.com

Société Générale
Full Branch Office
Room 304, 3rd Floor, Century Plaza Hotel, 1 Chun Feng Lu, Shenzhen
Tel: (755) 233 8930; (755) 232 8645 Fax: (755) 232 8646 Telex: 420290 SGZB CN Cable: SOCGEN SHENZHEN
Senior Executive Officers
General Manager   David Cheung
Others (Senior Executives)
Operation Manager   Jack Cheng
Senior Credit & Marketing Manager   Jonathan Lam

Euromoney Directory 1999   **281**

CHINA (+86) www.euromoneydirectory.com

Standard Chartered Bank
Full Branch Office
35/F China Merchants Tower, 66 Lujilazui Lu, Pudong District, Shanghai 200120
Tel: (21) 5887 1230 Fax: (21) 5876 9989
Senior Executive Officers
Chief Executive Officer   Lance Browne

Svenska Handelsbanken
Representative Office
Room 22D, CITIC Building, 19 Jianguomenwai Dajie, Beijing 100004
Tel: (10) 6500 4310; (10) 6500 3435 Fax: (10) 6512 6692 Telex: 22910 SHBBJ Email: shbbj@public3.bta.net.cn
Senior Executive Officers
Chief Representative   Johan Andren

The Tokai Bank Limited
Representative Office
Room 3202, Jing Guang Centre, Hujialou, Chaoyang District, Beijing
Tel: (10) 6500 2506 Fax: (10) 6597 3079 Telex: 22901 TOKAI CN
Senior Executive Officers
Chief Representative   Makoto Sugahara

The Tokai Bank Limited
Representative Office
Room 510, China Hotel Office Tower, Liu Hua Lu, Guangzhou
Tel: (20) 8667 7731 Fax: (20) 8667 7720 Telex: 44685 TOKAI CN
Senior Executive Officers
Chief Representative   Tetsuya Tsunekawa

The Tokai Bank Limited
Full Branch Office
18 Floor, Nextage Business Center No. 1111, Pudong South Road, Pudong New District, Shanghai
Tel: (21) 5830 6570 Fax: (21) 5830 6450 Telex: 33533 TOKSH A CN
Senior Executive Officers
General Manager   Toshihiro Ikeda

The Tokai Bank Limited
Full Branch Office
Room 811, Tianjin International Building, 75 Nanjing Lu, Tianjin
Tel: (22) 2330 4852 Fax: (22) 2330 4660 Telex: 234203 TOKAI CN
Senior Executive Officers
General Manager   Shigenobu Omori

UBS AG
Representative Office
3624 & 1610 China World Tower, 1 Jianguomenwai dajie, Beijing 100004
Tel: (10) 6505 2213/14/15; (10) 6505 2283/84/85 Fax: (10) 6505 1179; (10) 6505 6505
Senior Executive Officers
Chief Representative   C Li
Syndicated Lending
Other (Syndicated Lending)
Liability Marketing & Syndicate   R Wang
Other (Trade Finance)
Global Trade Finance   Patrick Freymond
   Ling Wang
   Yan Lin Gao

www.euromoneydirectory.com   CHINA (+86)

UBS AG
Representative Office
8th Floor, Room 812-3, Shanghai International Trade Centre, 2200 Yan An Road West, Shanghai 200335
Tel: (21) 6219 9208/10 Fax: (21) 6219 9188
Senior Executive Officers
Chief Representative   Gu Qi

Unibank A/S
Representative Office
Room 1607, Landmark Tower, 8 North Dongsanhuan Road, Beijing 100004
Tel: (10) 6501 1904 Fax: (10) 6501 1911
Senior Executive Officers
Chief Representative   Ronnie Zhang

Warburg Dillon Read (Asia) Limited
Representative Office
3625 & 1610 China World Tower, 1 Jian Guo Men Wai Avenue, Beijing 100004
Tel: (10) 6505 2215; (10) 6505 2283/84/85 Fax: (10) 6505 1179; (10) 6505 2286
Senior Executive Officers
Chief Representative   Y Kai
Corporate Finance / M&A Advisory
Other (Corporate Finance)
                              R X Yan
                              L M Z Yu

Warburg Dillon Read (Asia) Limited
Representative Office
8th Floor, Room 812-3, Shanghai International Trade Centre, 2200 Yan An Road West, Shanghai 200335
Tel: (21) 6219 9208; (21) 6219 9210 Fax: (21) 6219 9188
Senior Executive Officers
Chief Representative   Eva Hua

Westdeutsche Landesbank
Representative Office
Suite C613, Beijing Lufthansa Centre, 50 Liang Ma Qiao Road, Chaoyang District, Beijing
Tel: (10) 6465 1936 Fax: (10) 6465 1912
Senior Executive Officers
Representative   Viktor Utermann

Westpac Banking Corporation
Representative Office
Suite 506, SCITE Tower, 22 Jianguomenwai Dajie, Beijing 100004
Tel: (10) 6512 2288 ext 506 Fax: (10) 6512 3780 Email: chihao@sw.com.cn
Senior Executive Officers
Chief Representative   Frank H Chi ▣ **6512 3465**

Xiamen International Bank
10 Hu Bin Road North, Xiamen, Fujian Province
Tel: (592) 202 1780 Fax: (592) 202 1192 Telex: 93062 INTBK CN
Senior Executive Officers
Chairman   Li Li Hui
Vice Chairman   Chen Gui Zong
Vice Chairman   Chen Zong Lin
Vice Chairman   Henry Peters
President   Eugene Ho

COLOMBIA (+57)   www.euromoneydirectory.com

COLOMBIA
(+57)

Banco Anglo Colombiano
Subsidiary Company

Carrera 8 15-46, Santafé de Bogotá
PO Box 3532, Santafé de Bogotá
Tel: (1) 334 5088; (1) 284 1879 **Fax:** (1) 286 1383; (1) 341 9144 **Telex:** 44884 **Swift:** ANGL CO BB
Email: anglomer@impsat.net.co **Reuters:** BANG
Website: www.bancoanglocolombiano.com

Senior Executive Officers
President of the Board — Frederick Gibbs
President — David J Hutchinson
Financial Director — Alba Rojas *Executive VP, Finance*
Secretary General — Boris Hernandez
International Division — Nicholas J Bruce *VP, International & Credit*

Administration
Head of Administration — Roberto N Jones *Executive VP, Administration*

Banco Atlántico
Representative Office

Carrera 7A, 26-20, piso 15°, Santafé de Bogotá
Tel: (1) 287 9774; (1) 287 9650 **Fax:** (1) 287 6320

Senior Executive Officers
Representative — Rodrigo de Sagarminaga

Banco de Bogotá
Head Office

Calle 36, 7-47, Bogota, AA 3416
Tel: (1) 288 1188 **Fax:** (1) 338 3308 **Telex:** 44624 **Swift:** BBOG CO BBA **Reuters:** BBTA

Senior Executive Officers
President — Alejandro Figueroa ☎ **338 3396** 📠 **288 4590**
Chief Executive Officer — Juan M Robledo *Executive Vice President* ☎ **338 3408**
Financial Director — Maria L Rojas *VP, Finance* ☎ **338 3415** 📠 **338 3406**
Treasurer — Diana P Valderrama *Treasury Manager* ☎ **288 1188 ext 1336**
General Secretary — Octavio Gutiérrez ☎ **288 2581** 📠 **288 4590**
International Division — Germán Salazar *VP, International & Treasury* ☎ **338 3405**

Foreign Exchange
Head of Foreign Exchange — Victor Guerrero *FX Manager* ☎ **338 3304** 📠 **338 3370**
Head of Trading — Ruth Duénas *Assistant* ☎ **287 4408**

FX Traders / Sales People
Patricia Ardila *Trader* ☎ **288 1188 ext 1799**
Ximena Carrillo *Trader* ☎ **288 1188 ext 1295**
Juan P Cajigas *Trader* ☎ **288 1188 ext 1548**

Risk Management
Head of Risk Management — Guillermo Topa *Risk Manager* ☎ **287 4145** 📠 **338 3370**

Fixed Income Derivatives / Risk Management
Head of Sales — Martha Moreno *Manager, Derivatives* ☎ **338 3304**

Other (FI Derivatives)
Martha Moreno *Manager, Derivatives* ☎ **338 3304**

Foreign Exchange Derivatives / Risk Management
Spot / Forwards Sales — Martha Moreno *Manager, Derivatives* ☎ **338 3304**

OTC Equity Derivatives
Sales — Martha Moreno *Manager, Derivatives* ☎ **338 3304**

Global Custody
Head of Global Custody — Consuelo Franco *Chief of Global Custody* ☎ **288 1188 ext 1604**

Asset Management
Head — Mario A Gonzalez ☎ **288 1188 ext 1496**

Other Departments
Chief Credit Officer — German Michelson *VP, Credit* ☎ **338 3401**
Correspondent Banking — Camilo Pombo *Manager, International Business* ☎ **340 1100** 📠 **320 1266**

www.euromoneydirectory.com   COLOMBIA (+57)

Administration
Head of Administration   Luis C Moreno *VP, Administration* ☏ **338 3373** 🖷 **285 7630**
Business Development   Juan M Robledo *Executive Vice President* ☏ **338 3408**
Head of Marketing   Adriana Sarmiento *VP, Marketing* ☏ **338 3407** 🖷 **285 7630**

Technology & Systems
    Augusto Barrera *VP, Technology* ☏ **338 3423** 🖷 **285 7630**

Legal / In-House Counsel
    Maria M Copello *Legal Advisor* ☏ **288 2382** 🖷 **288 4590**

Compliance
    Hernando Pérez *Director, Compliance* ☏ **338 3076**

Accounts / Audit
    Avelino Gonzalez *Manager, Accounting* ☏ **288 1188 ext 1102** 🖷 **338 3406**

Banco de Colombia   Head Office
Calle 30A, 6-38, piso 10°, Santafé de Bogotá DC
Apartado Aéreo 6836, Santafé de Bogotá DC
Tel: (1) 288 6866 **Fax:** (1) 285 3231

Senior Executive Officers
Financial Director   Jaime Velasquez

Banco Colpatria   Head Office
Carrera 7, 24-89, Bogota
Tel: (1) 561 2777 **Fax:** (1) 561 2762 **Swift:** COLP CO BB

Senior Executive Officers
President   Eduardo Pacheco ☏ **334 0600** 🖷 **334 0605**
Chief Executive Officer   Santiago Perdomo *Executive Vice President* ☏ **334 3351**
Financial Director   Daniel Gomez *Vice President, Investment* ☏ **523 0350**
Chief Operating Officer   Fabio Zuluaga *Vice President, Technology* ☏ **334 0600** 🖷 **334 0605**
Treasurer   Jorge Rojas *Manager, Treasury* ☏ **523 0316**
Secretary General   Jaime Santos ☏ **334 0600**
International Division   Juanita Gomez *International Manager* ☏ **341 7490**

General-Lending (DCM, SL)
Head of Corporate Banking   Clara Riaño *Manager* ☏ **286 4666**

General-Investment
Head of Investment   Daniel Gomez *Vice President, Investment* ☏ **523 0350**

Debt Capital Markets / Fixed Income
Tel: 523 0330 **Fax:** 523 0340

Government Bonds
Head of Sales   Elsa Salgado *Director*
Head of Trading   Mauricio Duque *Trader*

Fixed-Income Repo
Head of Repo   Elsa Salgado *Director*

Syndicated Lending

Loan-Related Activities
Trade Finance   Daniel Gomez *Vice President, Investment* ☏ **523 0350**

Foreign Exchange
Head of Trading   Fernanda Parra *Head Trader* ☏ **523 0330** 🖷 **523 0340**

FX Traders / Sales People
    Armando Cruz *Trader* ☏ **523 0353**

Risk Management
Head of Risk Management   Alexandra Castillo *Risk Manager* ☏ **523 0330** 🖷 **523 0340**

Corporate Finance / M&A Advisory
Head of Corporate Finance   Daniel Gomez *Vice President, Investment* ☏ **523 0350**

Settlement / Clearing
Head of Settlement / Clearing   Carlos Luna *Office Support Manager* ☏ **334 0600**
Back-Office   Cristina Coral *Manager* ☏ **334 0600** 🖷 **334 0605**

Asset Management
Head   Santiago Rodriguez *Asset Manager* ☏ **334 0600**

Other Departments
Chief Credit Officer   Jorge Camargo *Vice President, Credit* ☏ **334 0600**
Private Banking   Jaime A Upegui *Vice President, Private Banking* ☏ **334 0600**
Correspondent Banking   Daniel Pardo de Brigard *Head* ☏ **561 2777**

COLOMBIA (+57)   www.euromoneydirectory.com

Banco Colpatria (cont)
Administration
Head of Administration Ricardo Sanchez *Vice President, Operations* ☏ **334 0600**
Business Development   Juan Antonio Montoya *Vice President, Commercial Banking* ☏ **334 0600**
Head of Marketing   Martha H Diaz *Vice President, Marketing* ☏ **334 0600**
Technology & Systems
                         Fabio Zuluaga *Vice President, Technology* ☏ **334 0600** 🖷 **334 0605**
Legal / In-House Counsel
                         Jaime Santos *Secretary General* ☏ **334 0600**
Public Relations
                         Martha H Diaz *Vice President, Marketing* ☏ **334 0600**
Accounts / Audit
                         Ricardo Arbelaez *Vice President, Audit Division* ☏ **334 0600**

Banco de Comercio Exterior de Colombia   Head Office
Alternative trading name: Bancoldex
Calle 28, N° 13A-15, piso 40°, Santafé de Bogotá
Tel: (1) 341 0677 **Fax:** (1) 282 5071
Senior Executive Officers
President   Miguel Gomez
Financial Director   Sergio Calderon *Financial Vice President*
International Division Gustavo Ardila Latiff *International Commercial Manager*
Others (Senior Executives)
                         Marta Isabel Vergara E *Commercial Vice President*
Risk Management
Country Head   Andrea Willner G

Banco de Crédito   Head Office
Calle 27, 6-48, Santafé de Bogotá DC
Tel: (1) 286 8400; (1) 286 1771 **Fax:** (1) 286 6850; (1) 286 7256 **Telex:** 44789 **Swift:** BCTO CO BB
Senior Executive Officers
President & CEO   Luis Fernando Mesa
Executive Committee President Anthony J Heeb
Chief Executive Officer   Luis Fernando Mesa *President & CEO*
Financial Director   Carlos Squerra *Financial Vice President*
Chief Operating Officer   Alex Barraza *Operative Vice President*
Others (Senior Executives)
                             Fidel Cortés *Commercial Vice President*
General-Lending (DCM, SL)
Head of Corporate Banking Carlos Squerra *Financial Vice President*
Administration
Head of Administration   Carmiña Ferro *Administrative Vice President*

Banco Exterior de los Andes y de España SA   Representative Office
Calle 74, 6-65, Santafé de Bogotá
Apartado Aéreo 241247, Santafé de Bogotá
Tel: (1) 217 7200 **Fax:** (1) 345 3197

Banco Nacional del Comercio   Head Office
Calle 72, N° 7-64, piso 10°, Santafé de Bogotá
Tel: (1) 210 1600 **Fax:** (1) 346 2521
Senior Executive Officers
President   Hernando Quesada Piedrahita
Financial Director   Jaime Hernández Bohorquez *Financial Vice President*
Administration
Public Relations
                         Isabel Cristina Sierra de Mercadeo ☏ **310 7404** 🖷 **310 7410**

COLOMBIA (+57)

Banco de Occidente
Head Office

Carrera 4, No 7 - 61, Cali, Valle del Cauca
Apartado Aéreo 7607, Cali, Valle del Cauca
Tel: (2) 886 1111 Fax: (2) 886 1297 Telex: 51255 Swift: OCCI CO BC XXX Email: banoccdi@col2telecom.com.co
Website: www.bancooccidente.com.co

Senior Executive Officers
President   Efrain Otero ☏ 884 1370
Chief Executive Officer   Gerardo Silva *Commercial Vice President* ☏ 884 1346
Financial Director   Bernardo Escobar *Financial Vice President* ☏ 884 1346
Chief Operating Officer   Gabriel Roberto Gomez *Operations Vice President* ☏ 884 1346
Treasurer   Johnny Sabogal *Treasury Manager*
International Division   Patricia Camargo *International Division Manager* ☏ 886 1118

General-Lending (DCM, SL)
Head of Corporate Banking   Mauricio Celin *Corporate Banking Manager*

General-Investment
Head of Investment   Mauricio Cepeda *Investment Banking Manager*

Foreign Exchange
Tel: (2) 886 1111 ext 1435 Fax: (2) 886 1292
Head of Foreign Exchange   Johnny Sabogal *Treasury Manager*
Head of Sales   Juan Pablo Amaya *Cash Management, Deputy Manager*

Other Departments
Chief Credit Officer   Carlos Santander *Credit Manager*
Correspondent Banking   Marcela Bonero *Correspondent Bank Director* ☏ 886 1117
Cash Management   Juan Pablo Amaya *Cash Management, Deputy Manager*

Banco Popular
Head Office

Calle 17, 7-43, piso 3°, Santafé de Bogotá
Tel: (1) 281 5130; (1) 284 9114 Fax: (1) 281 9448; (1) 282 4246 Telex: 44420 BANP CO Swift: BPOP CO BBA
Email: bpopuvpi@colomsat.net.co
Website: www.bancopopular.com.co

Senior Executive Officers
President   Hernando Rincon
Vice President   Maria Christina Vargas
Treasurer   Sergio Penagos
International Division   Hernando Vivas *Manager*
                                   Serafin Betancourt *International Business*
                                   Myriam Patino *International Operations*
                                   Maria Cristina Vargas *International Vice President*

Others (Senior Executives)
Board of Directors   Luis Carlos Sarmiento
                                   Edgar Velez
                                   Fabio Villegas
                                   Alvaro Jaramillo
                                   Enrique Gomez
                                   Mario Carvajalino
                                   Juan Guillermo Serna
                                   Alvaro Cala
                                   Julio Leonzo Alvarez

Foreign Exchange
Country Head   Mauricio Zuniga

Other Departments
Correspondent Banking   Héctor Urbano *Director*

Banco Real de Colombia
Head Office

Carrera 7, 33-80, Santafé de Bogotá
Apartado Aéreo 034262, Santafé de Bogotá
Tel: (1) 287 9300; (1) 285 0763 Fax: (1) 287 0507 Telex: 03544688

Senior Executive Officers
President   Paulo Cezar Da Rocha Dias
General Manager   José Roberto do Nascimento
International Division   Romario Albef

Euromoney Directory 1999   287

COLOMBIA (+57)   www.euromoneydirectory.com

Banco Real de Colombia (cont)
General-Lending (DCM, SL)
Head of Corporate Banking   Ivan Rodriguez Carrizosa *Commercial Banking Director*

Banco Sudameris Colombia
Carrera 11, No. 94 A 03, piso 5°, Santafé de Bogotá
Tel: (1) 636 8785 Fax: (1) 636 7702
Senior Executive Officers
Managing Director / General Manager   Giancarlo Panicucci

Banco Union Colombiano
Carrera 7, 71-52, piso 2°, Santafé de Bogotá, 3438
Tel: (1) 312 0411 Fax: (1) 312 0053; (1) 312 0836 Telex: 45191 Swift: UNIC CO BB Email: unionbca@cablenet.co
Reuters: BUNI
Senior Executive Officers
Chairman & President   Jose Joaquin Casas
President   Guillermo Villaveces ☎ 312 0839

Banque Sudameris
Representative Office
Calle 93 B, Piso 12-18°, Oficina 302, Apartado Aéreo 3440, Santafé de Bogotá
Tel: (1) 635 8801 Fax: (1) 635 8823 Email: misaja@andinet.com
Senior Executive Officers
Assistant Representative   Marco Isaja

Barclays Bank plc
Representative Office
Carrera 7, 72-13, piso 4°, Santafé de Bogotá
PO Box 35408, Santafé de Bogotá
Tel: (1) 312 8966 Fax: (1) 255 5451 Cable: BARCLAYREP
Senior Executive Officers
Representative   Roberto Brigard

BBV - Banco Ganadero SA
Head Office
Formerly known as: Banco Ganadero SA
Carrera 9, 72-21, Santafé de Bogotá
PO Box 53859, Santafé de Bogotá
Tel: (1) 312 4666; (1) 347 1600 Fax: (1) 211 0727 Swift: GERO CO BB
Senior Executive Officers
Executive President   José Maria Ayala Vargas ☎ 312 4666 ext 2054 📠 235 9829
Chief Executive Officer   José Maria Ayala Vargas *Executive President* ☎ 312 4666 ext 2054 📠 235 9829
Financial Director   Manuel Saenz Mayoral *Executive Vice President* ☎ 312 4666 ext 2068 📠 321 5724
General Secretary   Hernan Dario Zea Llanos ☎ 312 4666 ext 1105 📠 235 9829
International Division   Carlos Gorria *Executive Vice President* ☎ 312 4666 ext 2067
Executive Vice President   Carlos Vergara G ☎ 312 4666 ext 1901 📠 235 8980
General-Lending (DCM, SL)
Head of Corporate Banking   Carlos Vergara G *Executive Vice President* ☎ 312 4666 ext 1901 📠 235 8980
Debt Capital Markets / Fixed Income
Fixed-Income Repo
Head of Repo   Javier Gonzalez de Alcala *VP, Treasury* ☎ 312 4666 ext 1534 📠 210 4973
Equity Capital Markets
Global Head   Carlos Gorria *Executive Vice President* ☎ 312 4666 ext 2067

www.euromoneydirectory.com   COLOMBIA (+57)

Syndicated Lending
Head of Syndication   Carlos Gorria *Executive Vice President* ☎ 312 4666 ext 2067
Loan-Related Activities
Trade Finance   Jorge González Suárez *VP, International & Finance* ☎ 312 4666 ext1501
     F 211 6769
Project Finance   Carlos Gorria *Executive Vice President* ☎ 312 4666 ext 2067
Money Markets
Head of Money Markets   Carlos Gorria *Executive Vice President* ☎ 312 4666 ext 2067
Foreign Exchange
Head of Foreign Exchange   Javier Gonzalez de Alcala *VP, Treasury* ☎ 312 4666 ext 1534 F 210 4973
Global Custody
Head of Global Custody   Alfredo Murillo *Manager, Back Office* ☎ 312 4666 ext 1549 F 210 4973
Other Departments
Correspondent Banking   Stela Navas Rueda *Manager, Correspondent Banking* ☎ 312 4666 ext1507
     F 211 0727
Cash Management   Jorge González Suárez *VP, International & Finance* ☎ 312 4666 ext1501
     F 211 6769

Administration
Head of Administration   Alejandro Torres *EVP, Administration* ☎ 312 4666 ext 1105
Business Development   Carlos Gorria *Executive Vice President* ☎ 312 4666 ext 2067
Technology & Systems
     Mariano Ferrer Pascual *Vice President* ☎ 312 4666 ext 2062

Legal / In-House Counsel
Law Department   Alejandro Gomez *Manager* ☎ 312 4666 ext 1125
Accounts / Audit
Audit   Javier Gutierrez *Manager* ☎ 312 4666 ext 1803

Citibank Colombia   Full Branch Office

Carrera 9a 99-02, piso 1°, Santafé de Bogotá
Casilla de Correo 4134, Santafé de Bogotá
Tel: (1) 618 4155 **Fax:** (1) 621 5618 **Telex:** 44329

Senior Executive Officers
President   Eric R Mayer ☎ 618 2570 F 618 2434
Chief Operating Officer   Martha Zamudio ☎ 639 4098
Treasurer   Alvaro Jaramillo ☎ 618 2204/2241
General - Treasury
Head of Treasury   Alvaro Jaramillo ☎ 618 2204/2241
Debt Capital Markets / Fixed Income
Country Head   Alvaro Jaramillo ☎ 618 2204/2241
Equity Capital Markets
Country Head   Alvaro Jaramillo ☎ 618 2204/2241
Money Markets
Country Head   Alvaro Jaramillo ☎ 618 2204/2241
Foreign Exchange
Global Head   Maria Hilda Rodriguez ☎ 618 2271
Risk Management
Foreign Exchange Derivatives / Risk Management
Global Head   Felipe Fardi ☎ 618 2246

Corporacion Financiera Nacional y Suramericana SA
Head Office

Alternative trading name: Corfinsura
Carrera 43A, 3-101, Avenida el Poblado, Medellín
Apartado Aereo 1039, Medellín
Tel: (4) 266 5511 **Fax:** (4) 266 5376; (4) 268 4386 **Telex:** 66789 **Swift:** CFSU CO BB
Website: www.corfinsura.com.co

Senior Executive Officers
President   Carlos Enrique Piedrahita
Financial Director   Alba Luz Hoyos *Vice President, Finance*
Chief Operating Officer   Rodrigo Isaza *Vice President, Administration*
Treasurer   Jorge Tabares *General Treasurer* ☎ 311 3500

COLOMBIA (+57) www.euromoneydirectory.com

Corporacion Financiera Nacional y Suramericana SA (cont)
Senior Executive Officers (cont)
Secretary General Margarita Mesa
General-Investment
Head of Investment Sergio Restrepo *Vice President, Investment Banking*
Department: Headquarters in Bogota
Calle 72, 8-24, piso 2°, Bogota
Tel: +57 (1) 310 0355
International Division Jose Humberto Acosta
Administration
Head of Administration Rodrigo Isaza *Vice President, Administration*
Technology & Systems
Technology Rodrigo Velasquez *Vice President, Technology*

Deutsche Bank AG Representative Office
Carrera 7, No 71-52, Torre A, Oficina 805, Santafé de Bogotá DC
Apartado Aéreo 8597, Santafé de Bogotá
Tel: (1) 312 0428; (1) 312 0432 **Fax:** (1) 312 0435
Senior Executive Officers
Representative Hartwig Krieg
Others (Senior Executives)
 Nikolaus Lerner *Assistant Representative*

Deutsche Morgan Grenfell (Andes) Ltda Full Branch Office
Formerly known as: Morgan Grenfell (Andes) Limited
Carrera 7, 71-52, Oficina 704, Torre A, piso 7°, Santafé de Bogotá
Tel: (1) 312 0347; (1) 312 0348 **Fax:** (1) 312 0867
Senior Executive Officers
Managing Director & Representative, Eduardo Barco Canal
Corporate Finance / M&A Advisory
Country Head Mauricio Ramos *Assistant Director*

Dresdner Bank Lateinamerika AG Representative Office
Formerly known as: Deutsch-Südamerikanische Bank AG/Dresdner Bank AG
Carrera 9, 74-08, Oficina 1202, Edificio Profinanzas, Santafé de Bogotá
Tel: (1) 217 7721; (1) 254 8650 **Fax:** (1) 210 2561
Senior Executive Officers
Representative Carlos A Schaefer ☏ **217 7721**
Joint Representative Ingo F Josenhans ☏ **254 8650**
Joint Representative Narda Ramírez ☏ **254 8650**

The Export-Import Bank of Japan Representative Office
Calle 100, 8A-55, Oficina 715, World Trade Center, Torre C, Santafé de Bogotá
Apartado Aereo 241432, Santafé de Bogotá
Tel: (1) 621 1828; (1) 621 1878 **Fax:** (1) 610 7293
Senior Executive Officers
First Representative Yoshio Matsumura

HypoVereinsbank Full Branch Office
Calle 114, 9-45, Torre B, Oficina 1109, Teleport Busines Park, Bogota
Tel: (1) 629 3594; (1) 629 3608 **Fax:** (1) 629 3620

Ibero Platina Bank AG Representative Office
Carrera 15 No 106-64, Apartado Aéreo 25 11 95, Santafé de Bogotá
Tel: (1) 214 0573; (1) 215 9267 **Fax:** (1) 215 9163 **Email:** pbg@cable.net.co **Tel:** (1) 215 9037

www.euromoneydirectory.com CONGO, DEMOCRATIC REPUBLIC (+243)

ING Barings
Carrera 9 No 76-49, Piso 7°& 8°, Bogota
Tel: (1) 317 6162 Fax: (1) 317 6777

Senior Executive Officers
Country Manager   Bernardo Vargas

Lloyds Bank plc   Full Branch Office
Carrera 8, 15-46, piso 3°, Santafé de Bogotá
Apartado Aéreo 4040, Santafé de Bogotá
Tel: (1) 281 5857; (1) 334 5088 Fax: (1) 281 8648 Telex: 44884 ANGL CO Cable: LBICO

Senior Executive Officers
Representative   Scott Donald

Midland Bank plc   Representative Office
Carrera 11 86-32, Oficina 702, Santafé de Bogotá
PO Box 54562, Santafé de Bogotá
Tel: (1) 218 3894 Fax: (1) 622 6986

Senior Executive Officers
Representative   H Jaramillo

Société Générale
Torre B Edificio Avenida Chile, Of 602, Carrera 7 n-71-21, Bogota
Tel: (1) 317 4707; (1) 317 4496 Fax: (1) 317 4720
Website: www.socgen.com

Standard Chartered Bank   Representative Office
#74-08 Carrera 9, Oficina 1005, Santafé de Bogotá
Tel: (1) 211 4496 Fax: (1) 217 5282

Senior Executive Officers
VP & Deputy Representative   Camilio Martinez

The World Bank   Full Branch Office
Diagonal 35, 5-98, Santafé de Bogotá
Tel: (1) 320 3577 Fax: (1) 245 5744

Senior Executive Officers
Resident Representative   Félipe Sáez

CONGO, DEMOCRATIC REPUBLIC
(+243)

Citibank (Zaïre)   Subsidiary Company
Coin des Av Colonel Lukesa et Ngongo-Lutete, Gombe, Kinshasa 1
Tel: (12) 20555 Fax: (88) 04156 Telex: 21622 CTBKZR

Senior Executive Officers
President   Divinda Sivi ☏ **40015**
Chief Executive Officer   Mulongo Masangu Country Corporate Officer ☏ **20555**
Treasurer   Losembe Botumbe ☏ **41184**
                                   Kamanzi Muhindo ☏ **20168**

General-Lending (DCM, SL)
Head of Corporate Banking   Gaby Lopez ☏ **20557**

Debt Capital Markets / Fixed Income
Country Head   Michael Losembe Transaction Services Head ☏ **41184**

Euromoney Directory 1999 **291**

CONGO, DEMOCRATIC REPUBLIC (+243) www.euromoneydirectory.com

Citibank (Zaïre) (cont)
Equity Capital Markets
Country Head   Michael Losembe *Transaction Services Head* ☏ **41184**
Syndicated Lending
Country Head   Michael Losembe *Transaction Services Head* ☏ **41184**
Money Markets
Country Head   Michael Losembe *Transaction Services Head* ☏ **41184**
Settlement / Clearing
Operations   Michael Losembe *Transaction Services Head* ☏ **41184**

Stanbic Bank Congo sarl

12 Avenida de la Mongala, Kinshasa
BP 16297, Kinshasa 1
Tel: (88) 48445; (88) 43453 **Fax:** (88) 46216

Senior Executive Officers
Managing Director   J S Callaghan ☏ **41984**
General - Treasury
Head of Treasury   M Arend *Manager, Treasury* ☏ **43453**

COSTA RICA
(+506)

Citibank NA   Full Branch Office

Oficentro Ejecutivo La Sabana, 50 Sur Contraloria Gen de la Republica, Building 3, piso 1°, Sabana Sur, San José
Tel: (2) 961 494 **Fax:** (2) 52458

Senior Executive Officers
Treasurer   Ruben Gonzales
General Manager   Henry Comber
Foreign Exchange
Head of Trading   Mariano Campos
Settlement / Clearing
Operations   Jorge Monge *Transaction Services Head*

Ibero Platina Bank AG

Formerly known as: Ibero-Amerika Bank AG
Calle 29 Avenida 10, San José
Apartado 5548, San José, 1000
Tel: 253 8895 **Fax:** 234 2589 **Email:** rfischer@sol.racsa.co.cr

Senior Executive Officers
Chief Executive Officer   Ralf Fischer *Country Manager*

Scotiabank de Costa Rica SA   Subsidiary Company

Formerly known as: Banco Mercantil de Costa Rica SA
Calle 0-2, Avenida Primera, San José, 1000
PO Box 5395, San José, 1000
Tel: 287 8700; 287 8701 **Fax:** 255 3076; 255 3142 **Telex:** 2718 CREDIT CR **Swift:** NOSC CR SJ
Email: scotiagg@sol.racsa.co.cr

Senior Executive Officers
Chairman   Roberth Pitfield
General Manager   Alberto Tarabotto
Others (Senior Executives)
    Andres Vega *Finance Manager* ☏ **287 8710**
General-Lending (DCM, SL)
Head of Corporate Banking   Nestor Vale *Commercial Banking Manager* ☏ **287 8704**

www.euromoneydirectory.com   CROATIA (+385)

Administration
Head of Administration   John Caldwell *Assistant General Manager* ☏ **287 8707**

COTE D'IVOIRE
(+225)

Banque Centrale des Etats de l'Afrique de l'Ouest 🏛 Central Bank
PO Box 01 1769, Abidjan 01
Tel: 210 466; 219 070 **Fax:** 222 852 **Telex:** 23474 BC ABJ CI

Senior Executive Officers
Country Director   Tiémoko Meyliet Kone
Branch Director   Souleymane Cisse

Citibank NA
Full Branch Office

Immeuble Botreau-Roussel, 28 Avenue Delafosse, Abidjan 01
PO Box 3698, Abidjan 01
Tel: 209 000 **Fax:** 211 687; 217 685 **Telex:** 22121
Dealing Room Tel: 209 080; 209 081

Senior Executive Officers
Chief Executive Officer   Mark H Wiessing *Country Corporate Officer* ☏ **209 010**
Financial Director   Felix Bikpo
Chief Operating Officer   Klaus-Peter Schulze *Senior Operations Officer* ☏ **209 120**
Treasurer   Michel Losembe *Country Treasurer* ☏ **209 080**

Others (Senior Executives)
Khady N'Diaye *Trader* ☏ **209 081**

General-Lending (DCM, SL)
Head of Corporate Banking   Sylvain Yangni-Angate

Debt Capital Markets / Fixed Income
Country Head   Jean N'Sele *Head, Corporate Finance* ☏ **209 075**

Equity Capital Markets
Country Head   Pascal Djereke *Head* ☏ **209 070**

Syndicated Lending
Country Head   Jean N'Sele *Head, Corporate Finance* ☏ **209 075**

Societe Generale de Banques en Cote d'Ivoire
5 & 7 Avenue Joseph Anoma 01, 01 BP 1355, Abidjan 01
Tel: 201 234 **Fax:** 201 492
Website: www.socgen.com

CROATIA
(+385)

Hrvatska narodna banka
🏛 Central Bank

Alternative trading name: Croatian National Bank
Formerly known as: Narodna banka Hrvatske

Trg Burze 3, 10000 Zagreb
Tel: (1) 456 4555 **Fax:** (1) 461 0591 **Telex:** 22569 NB ZG RH **Swift:** NBHR HR 2X **Reuters:** NBHH **Bloomberg:** HNB
Cable: NARODNA BANKA
Website: www.hnb.hr

Senior Executive Officers
Governor   Marko Škreb ☏ **456 4567** F **455 0598**
Deputy Governor   Zdravko Rogic ☏ **456 4562** F **456 4733**
Vice Governor   Relja Martic ☏ **456 4606** F **455 0598**
Department: International Department
International Division   Jadranka Granic *Executive Director* ☏ **456 4548** F **456 4704**

Euromoney Directory 1999   **293**

CROATIA (+385)　　　　　　　www.euromoneydirectory.com

Hrvatska narodna banka (cont)

Money Markets
Head of Money Markets　　　　　　Adolf Matejka *Executive Director* ℡ **456 4664**

Foreign Exchange
Head of Foreign Exchange　　　　　Jadranka Marušic *Director* ℡ **456 4844** F **466 4651**

Other Departments
Correspondent Banking　　　　　　Maja Landsman *Director, International Banking* ℡ **456 4551** F **456 4704**

Administration
Technology & Systems
　　　　　　　　　　　　　　　　Petar Curkovic *Executive Director* ℡ **456 4757** F **456 4778**

Legal / In-House Counsel
　　　　　　　　　　　　　　　　Marjan Klanac *Director* ℡ **456 4859** F **456 4874**

Public Relations
　　　　　　　　　　　　　　　　Ruzica Vuger *Advisor* ℡ **456 4578** F **461 0587**

Accounts / Audit
Internal Audit　　　　　　　　　　Ivica Prga *Director* ℡ **456 4608**
Accounts　　　　　　　　　　　　Durda Haramija ℡ **456 4680** F **455 0594**

Alpe Jadran banka dd　　　　　　　　　　　　　　　　　　Head Office

Starceviceva 1, HR-21000 Split
Tel: (21) 305 305; (21) 305 303 **Fax:** (21) 305 306; (21) 305 345 **Telex:** 26647 AJBANK RH **Swift:** AJBK HR 2X
Email: ajb@ajb.tel.ur

Senior Executive Officers
President of the Management Board　　Pero Perišic ℡ **305 205** F **305 206**
International Division　　　　　　　　Anita Filipovic *Manager of International Division* ℡ **305 300** F **305 306**

Others (Senior Executives)
　　　　　　　　　　　　　　　　Mladen Garabic *Member of the Management Board* ℡ **305 300** F **305 306**
　　　　　　　　　　　　　　　　Frane Galzina
　　　　　　　　　　　　　　　　Tonci Koludrovic
　　　　　　　　　　　　　　　　Mirela Malcak *Accounting Manager*

General-Lending (DCM, SL)
Head of Corporate Banking　　　　　Anica Duplancic *Manager of Kuna Funds & Placements*

Other Departments
Private Banking　　　　　　　　　Marija Juric *Head of Retail Division* ℡ **305 326** F **305 306**

Auctor Securities doo　　　　　　　　　　　　　　　　　Head Office

Palmoticeva 2, 10000 Zagreb
Tel: (1) 481 4139; (1) 481 4149 **Fax:** (1) 481 4143

Senior Executive Officers
Chairman of the Board of Directors　　Nened Pavletic E **npavleti@auctor.hr**

Debt Capital Markets / Fixed Income
Global Head　　　　　　　　　　　Nened Pavletic *Chairman of the Board of Directors* E **npavleti@auctor.hr**

Asset-Backed Securities / Securitization
Global Head　　　　　　　　　　　Michael Glazer *Director* E **mglazer@auctor.hr**

Equity Capital Markets
Global Head　　　　　　　　　　　Marijan Palic *Director* E **mpalic1@auctor.hr**

Corporate Finance / M&A Advisory
Global Head　　　　　　　　　　　Michael Glazer *Director* E **mglazer@auctor.hr**

Settlement / Clearing
Regional Head　　　　　　　　　　Snjiezana Kuhtic *Head, Back Office* E **skuhtic@auctor.hr**

Other Departments
Proprietary Trading　　　　　　　　Branka Cempuh *Chief Trader* E **bcempuh@auctor.hr**

Administration
Legal / In-House Counsel
　　　　　　　　　　　　　　　　Vladimira Jerkovic *Legal Advisor* E **vjerkovic@auctor.hr**

Compliance
　　　　　　　　　　　　　　　　Vladimira Jerkovic *Legal Advisor* E **vjerkovic@auctor.hr**

Public Relations
　　　　　　　　　　　　　　　　Michael Glazer *Director* E **mglazer@auctor.hr**

www.euromoneydirectory.com   CROATIA (+385)

Bank Austria Creditanstalt Croatia dd
Subsidiary Company

Jurisiceva 2, 10000 Zagreb
Tel: (1) 480 0777; (1) 480 0757 **Fax:** (1) 480 0899; (1) 480 0891 **Telex:** 21650 BKAUHR **Swift:** BKAU HR 2X
Email: bac_operations@zg.tel.hr

Senior Executive Officers
Chairman of the Board   Johchim Reitmrier
Deputy Chairman of the Board   Joran Gazivoda
Treasurer   Zvonko Ivanušic
Others (Senior Executives)
Member of the Board   Ivo Bilic *Director*
Settlement / Clearing
Operations   Igor Hein *Head*
Administration
Legal / In-House Counsel
Legal Advisor   Boris Kalajdzic

Croatia banka dd, Zagreb
Head Office

Kvaternikov trg 9, 10000 Zagreb
Tel: (1) 239 1111 **Fax:** (1) 233 2470; (1) 239 1169 **Telex:** 21146 CB ZG RH **Swift:** CROA HR 2X
Website: www.open.hr/com/crobanka/

Senior Executive Officers
Chairman of the Supervisory Board   Krunoslav Covic
President of the Managing Board   Ivan Tarle [T] 233 8140
Treasurer   Marko Gabela *Director* [T] 239 1114 [F] 233 2470
Others (Senior Executives)
International Division   Vesna Sojat *Director* [T] 239 1273 [F] 239 1158
Administration
Head of Marketing   Marijan Maricic *Director* [T] 239 1127 [F] 233 2470
Technology & Systems
                                                Zlato Mandaric [T] 239 1111
Legal / In-House Counsel
                                                Ivan Grgic [T] 239 1130
Public Relations
                                                Goran Kauzlaric *Assistant Manager, Marketing & Public Relations*
                                                [T] 239 1254 [F] 239 1157

Dalmatinska Banka dd
Head Office

Trg Sv Stošije 3, 23000 Zadar
Tel: (23) 311 311 **Fax:** (23) 437 867 **Telex:** 27224 **Swift:** DBZD HR 2X **Reuters:** DBZH **Telerate:** DBZH

Senior Executive Officers
Chairman, Management Board   Zdravko Bubalo [T] 312 752
Financial Director   Anka Jagic *General Manager Finance* [T] 433 737
Chief Operating Officer   Mira Magaš *General Manager* [T] 437 784
Treasurer   Zorislav Vidovic *General Manager, Treasury* [T] 313 969
International Division   Ana Maricic *General Manager* [T] 437 113
Others (Senior Executives)
                                                Darinko Pupovac *Member of the Management Board* [T] 311 772
                                                Jadranka Gotovac *Member of the Management Board* [T] (01) 433 8454
General-Lending (DCM, SL)
Head of Corporate Banking   Jadranka Škific
Syndicated Lending
Trade Finance   Ranka Ivaniševic *Manager, International Payments & Investigations*
                                                [T] 437 910
Foreign Exchange
Head of Foreign Exchange   Neven Majica *Manager* [T] 437 367
FX Traders / Sales People
                                                Marina Kozul *Manager, Treasury* [T] 313 969
                                                Mirjana Dukic *Chief Dealer* [T] 437 367
Risk Management
Head of Risk Management   Helena Banjad [T] 315 275

Euromoney Directory 1999   **295**

CROATIA (+385) www.euromoneydirectory.com

Dalmatinska Banka dd (cont)

Other Departments
Correspondent Banking

Milutin Šaponja *Manager, Int'l Finance & Correspondent Banking*
☎ 437 113

Administration
Business Development

Damira Burchi *General Manager* ☎ 312 536

Technology & Systems

Marina Bozicev *General Manager* ☎ 212 772

Legal / In-House Counsel

Milan Petricic *General Manager* ☎ 437 862

Deutsche Bank AG
Representative Office

Hotel Sheraton - Kneza Borne 2, 10000 Zagreb
Tel: (1) 430 640 **Fax:** (1) 432 749

Senior Executive Officers
Representative Nikola Carevic

Dubrovacka banka dd
Head Office

Put Republike 9, 20000 Dubrovnik
PO Box 69, Dubrovnik
Tel: (20) 431 366; (20) 412 388 **Fax:** (20) 411 035; (20) 413 589 **Swift:** DUBA HR 2X **Email:** dubank@dubank.hr
Website: www.dubank.hr

Senior Executive Officers
Chief Executive Officer Niko Koncul *Chief Executive Officer*
Chief Operating Officer Niko Matusic *Chief Operating Officer*
International Division Ruzica Cvjetenovic *Head*

Others (Senior Executives)
Assistant Executive Adviser Vlaho Sutic
  Jadranka Kristic

General-Lending (DCM, SL)
Head of Corporate Banking Duro Damjanovic

General-Investment
Head of Investment Velimir Tomasic

Foreign Exchange
Head of Foreign Exchange Andelka Rana *Head, Foreign Exchange*

Settlement / Clearing
Other Milica Borkovic *Head, Foreign Payments*

Other Departments
Private Banking Mirjana Pccotic *Head of Retail Banking*

Administration
Head of Marketing Niko Matusic *Chief Operating Officer*

Public Relations
  Nives Kera *PR Manager* ☎ 413 589

Other (Administration)
Chief Information Officer Ivan Vilovic

European Bank for Reconstruction & Development
Representative Office

5th Floor, Petrinjska 59, 10000 Zagreb
Tel: (1) 481 2400 **Fax:** (1) 481 9468

Senior Executive Officers
Resident Representative Juliet Stubican

www.euromoneydirectory.com   CROATIA (+385)

Glumina Banka dd
Head Office

PO Box 215, Trpinjska 9, 10000 Zagreb
Tel: (1) 239 4444 **Fax:** (1) 239 5706 **Telex:** 21108 GLUMBA RH **Swift:** GLUM HR 22 **Email:** glumban@zg.tel.hr
Reuters: GBZH (Dealing)

Senior Executive Officers
President, Management Board — Marko Marcinko ☎ **239 4502**

Syndicated Lending
Loan-Related Activities
Trade Finance; Project Finance — Mitchelle Brajdic *Member, Management Board* ☎ **239 4507**
✉ mbrajdic@open.hr

Money Markets
Department: Treasury
Fax: 230 3563
Global Head — Majda Fistrek *Head of Treasury* ☎ **230 0211**

Domestic Commercial Paper
Head of Origination — Majda Fistrek *Head of Treasury* ☎ **230 0211**

Wholesale Deposits
Marketing; Head of Sales — Majda Fistrek *Head of Treasury* ☎ **230 0211**

Foreign Exchange
Department: International Division
Tel: 239 4506 **Fax:** 233 7595
Global Head — Sandra Zubcic ☎ **239 4506**

Risk Management
Department: International Division
Global Head — Sandra Zubcic ☎ **239 4506**

OTC Equity Derivatives
Sales; Trading — Tatjana Turza *Head, Securities Trading* ☎ **239 4411**

Corporate Finance / M&A Advisory
Department: International Banking
Tel: 239 5706 **Fax:** 230 3562
Global Head — Mitchelle Brajdic *Member, Management Board* ☎ **239 4507**
✉ mbrajdic@open.hr

Settlement / Clearing
Department: HRK Payment Operations & International Division
Regional Head — Majda Fistrek *Head of Treasury* ☎ **230 0211**
Foreign Exchange Settlement — Sandra Zubcic ☎ **239 4506**

Other Departments
Private Banking — Dennis Gudasic *Head, Retail Banking* ☎ **239 4512**
Correspondent Banking — Mitchelle Brajdic *Member, Management Board* ☎ **239 4507**
✉ mbrajdic@open.hr

Administration
Technology & Systems — Milivoj Obradovic *Head, EDP* ✉ omilivoj@open.hr

Legal / In-House Counsel — Ivan Bidin *Chief Legal Officer*

Compliance — Rade Cvjeticanin *Internal Analysis* ☎ **239 4431**

Public Relations — Ankica Mamic *Marketing Director* ☎ **239 4501** ✉ amamic@open.hr

Gospodarsko Kreditna banka dd
Head Office

Draskopiceva 58, 10000 Zagreb
Tel: (1) 480 2555 **Fax:** (1) 480 2577; (1) 481 5154 **Swift:** CCBZ HR 2X

Senior Executive Officers
President of the Managing Board — Izidor Sucic ☎ **480 2551**
Financial Director — Branko Petanjek *Member of the Management Board* ☎ **480 2564**
International Division — Jasna Fumagalli *Member of the Management Board* ☎ **480 2553**

General-Lending (DCM, SL)
Head of Corporate Banking — Zvjezdana Stipic *Executive Director, Credit Sector* ☎ **480 2552**

CROATIA (+385) www.euromoneydirectory.com

Gospodarsko Kreditna banka dd (cont)
Foreign Exchange
FX Traders / Sales People
Dealer Suzana Sucic ☏ 480 2557
  Vatroslav Jukic ☏ 480 2557

Hypo Banka Croatia   Full Branch Office
Koturaška 47, 10000 Zagreb
Tel: (1) 610 3666 **Fax:** (1) 610 3555 **Swift:** KLHB HR 22 **Email:** hypo@hypo.hr
Website: www.hypo.hr

Senior Executive Officers
Chairman	Wolfgang Kulterer
Chairman of the Board	Günter Striedinger ☏ 610 3500
Treasurer	Dieter Starc ☏ 610 3501
Member of the Board	Heinz Truskaller ☏ 610 3501
Company Secretary	Vesna Goja ☏ 610 3505
International Division	Robert Weissenberger ☏ 610 3565

General-Lending (DCM, SL)
Head of Corporate Banking Kurt Makula ☏ 610 3542

General-Investment
Head of Investment Gerhard Greimer *Global Head of Investment Banking* ☏ 610 3531

Money Markets
Tel: 610 3550 **Fax:** 610 3626
Head of Money Markets Slavka Megla- Reljic

Foreign Exchange
Tel: 610 3560 **Fax:** 610 3626
Head of Foreign Exchange Darko Umic ☏ 610 3560

Risk Management
Tel: 610 3500
Head of Risk Management Igor Kodzoman

Corporate Finance / M&A Advisory
Global Head Kurt Makula ☏ 610 3542

Settlement / Clearing
Head of Settlement / Clearing Robert Weissenberger ☏ 610 3565

Global Custody
Head of Global Custody Gerhard Greimer *Global Head of Investment Banking* ☏ 610 3531

Other Departments
Private Banking	Evelyan Schury ☏ 610 3510
Correspondent Banking	Lena Radovic ☏ 610 3556
Cash Management	Darko Umic ☏ 610 3560

Administration
Head of Administration	Ernst Fanzott ☏ 610 3595
Head of Marketing	Lidija Bunta ☏ 610 3602

Technology & Systems
  Zeljko Brkic ☏ 610 3610

Legal / In-House Counsel
  Robert Hrsak ☏ 610 3525

Public Relations
  Ernst Fanzott ☏ 610 3595

Accounts / Audit
  Bratislav Stanic ☏ 610 3640

Istarska Kreditna banka Umag dd   Head Office
Ernesta Milosa 1, PO Box 103, 52470 Umag
Tel: (52) 741 622 **Fax:** (52) 741 275 **Telex:** 24745 IKB RH **Swift:** ISKB HR 2X

Senior Executive Officers
Chairman, Management Board Miro Dodic

Others (Senior Executives)
Member of the Management Board Ivan Petrokov *Investments & Commercial Banking*

CROATIA (+385)

General-Lending (DCM, SL)
Head of Corporate Banking — Ivan Petrokov *Investments & Commercial Banking*
Anton Belusic *Head, Credit & International Division*

General-Investment
Head of Investment — Ivan Petrokov *Investments & Commercial Banking*

General - Treasury
Head of Treasury — Klaudija Paljuh *Head, Treasury Div & Mgr, Domestic Treasury*

Relationship Manager
International Payments — Vesna Crnkovic *Manager*

Syndicated Lending

Loan-Related Activities
Trade Finance — Ruzica Bosnjak *Manager, Loans & Trade Finance*

Foreign Exchange
Global Head — Vesna Peovic *Manager*

Risk Management
Country Head — Jakov Brajkovic *Manager, Credit Risk Management*

Jadranska banka dd — Head Office

Ante Starcevica 4, 22000 Sibenik
Tel: (22) 334 244; (22) 334 880 **Fax:** (22) 335 881 **Telex:** 27635 JB SBK **Swift:** JADR HR 2X

Senior Executive Officers
General Manager — Ivo Sinko [T] 334 234 [F] 331 798
International Division — Lidvina Mandic [T] 334 244 [F] 335 881

Karlovacka banka

IG Kovacica 1, 47000 Karlovac
Tel: (47) 223 333; (47) 222 040 **Fax:** (47) 220 653; (47) 224 157 **Telex:** 23712 KBK RH **Swift:** KALC HR 2X

Senior Executive Officers
President of the Board — Vladimir Tvrdinic [T] 223 333 [F] 220 653

Others (Senior Executives)
Board Member — Mijo Bursic [T] 224 042 [F] 223 274
Sandra Cvitesic [T] 611 540 [F] 220 653
Danko Seiter [T] 611 540 [F] 220 653
Loans — Irena Vrbanic *Manager* [T] 224 042 [F] 223 274
Retail — Bozena Zitko *Manager* [T] 224 308 [F] 220 440

General - Treasury
Head of Treasury — Marijana Reskovac *Manager* [T] 222 040 [F] 224 157

Equity Capital Markets
Head of Equity Capital Markets — Marianna Reskovac [T] 223 851

Money Markets
Head of Money Markets — Dubravka Smerdely *Manager* [T] 220 650

Foreign Exchange
Head of Foreign Exchange — Jasna Brezovic *Head* [T] 224 052 [F] 611 021

Risk Management
Head of Risk Management — Marianna Reskovac [T] 223 851

Other Departments
Correspondent Banking — Jasna Brezovic *Head* [T] 224 052 [F] 611 021

Administration
Head of Administration — Danko Seiter *Member of the Board* [T] 611 540
Stevo Poljak *Head* [T] 220 894

Privredna banka Zagreb dd — Head Office

Rackoga 6, 10001 Zagreb
PO Box 1032, 10001 Zagreb
Tel: (1) 455 0822 **Fax:** (1) 461 0477 **Telex:** 21120 **Swift:** PBZG HR 2X **Reuters:** PBZH

Senior Executive Officers
President & Chief Executive Officer — Bozo Prka [T] 461 0401 [F] 455 2597
Financial Director — Ivan Gerovac *Member, Finance & Control* [T] 455 2043 [F] 455 2049
Treasurer — Drazenko Pavlinic *Executive Director* [T] 461 0472 [F] 461 0397
International Division — Jadranka Primorac *Executive Director* [T] 461 0403 [F] 461 0477

Euromoney Directory 1999   **299**

CROATIA (+385)

Privredna banka Zagreb dd (cont)

General-Lending (DCM, SL)
Head of Corporate Banking — Hrvoje Matezovic *Executive Director* ☎ 461 0429 Ⓕ 455 0532
Sanja Boronic *Chief Manager, Int'l Loans & Guarantees* ☎ 461 1416 Ⓕ 461 1308
Franjo Filipovic *Member, Corporate Banking / International* ☎ 461 0437 Ⓕ 461 0431

General-Investment
Head of Investment — Drazen Vrbelic *Executive Director, Loans & Investment* ☎ 461 0438 Ⓕ 461 0477
Ivan Krolo *General Manager, Investment Banking* ☎ 455 2046 Ⓕ 455 2053

General - Treasury
Head of Treasury — Drazenko Pavlinic *Executive Director* ☎ 461 0472 Ⓕ 461 0397
Robert Mamic *Deputy* ☎ 461 0472 Ⓕ 461 0397

Debt Capital Markets / Fixed Income
Head of Fixed Income; Head of Fixed Income Sales — Jure Zubak *Head of Trading* ☎ 484 3124 Ⓕ 484 3113

Equity Capital Markets
Head of Equity Capital Markets; Head of Sales — Jure Zubak *Head of Trading* ☎ 484 3124 Ⓕ 484 3113

Domestic Equities
Head of Sales — Jure Zubak *Head of Trading* ☎ 484 3124 Ⓕ 484 3113

Equity Research
Global Head — Jasna Meter *Officer* ☎ 484 3955 Ⓕ 484 3125

Syndicated Lending
Head of Syndication — Jadranka Primorac *Executive Director* ☎ 461 0403 Ⓕ 461 0437

Other (Syndicated Lending) — Drazen Vrbelic *Executive Director, Loans & Investment* ☎ 461 0438 Ⓕ 461 0477

Loan-Related Activities
Project Finance — Miroslav Gregurex *Head, Project Finance* ☎ 484 3126 Ⓕ 484 3125

Foreign Exchange
Tel: 455 2196 Fax: 461 0266
Regional Head — Lina Tuda *Chief Dealer* ☎ 461 0267

Corporate Finance / M&A Advisory
Head of Corporate Finance — Martin O Hutchinson *Executive Director* ☎ 484 3470 Ⓕ 461 0448

Settlement / Clearing
Fax: 469 0497
Equity Settlement — Katica Mandic *Custody Officer* ☎ 484 3124 Ⓕ 484 3113
Fixed-Income Settlement — Dubravko Katalinic *Custody Officer* ☎ 484 3124 Ⓕ 484 3113
Operations — Ivica Odorijan *Manager, Back Office* ☎ 455 2596 Ⓕ 461 0266
Vesna Mlinarek *Chief Manager, Int'l Operations* ☎ 455 2394 Ⓕ 455 0078

Global Custody
Regional Head — Dubravko Stimac *Head* ☎ 484 3116 Ⓕ 484 3113

Asset Management
Head — Josip Proteca *Executive Director, Investment Management* ☎ 484 3120 Ⓕ 484 3125

Other Departments
Private Banking — Josip Proteca *Executive Director, Investment Management* ☎ 484 3120 Ⓕ 484 3125
Correspondent Banking — Jadranka Peloza *Head, Correspondent Banking* ☎ 455 0206 Ⓕ 461 0283

Administration
Head of Administration — Bojana Cosic *Executive Director* ☎ 611 5502 Ⓕ 611 5118

Technology & Systems
IT Division — Zoran Simunic *Executive Director* ☎ 467 7823 Ⓕ 467 7770

Legal / In-House Counsel
Legal Affairs Division — Stjepan Brcic *Executive Director* ☎ 461 1417 Ⓕ 461 1401

Accounts / Audit
Accounting Division — Ivan Jarcevic *Executive Director* ☎ 536 3306 Ⓕ 611 4094
Financial Control Division — Franka Barbic *Executive Director* ☎ 337 111 Ⓕ 611 0378
Internal Control & Audit Division — Ana Vrdoljak *Deputy to CEO, General Admin* ☎ 615 5537 Ⓕ 611 7682

Other (Administration)
Group Support — Nediljko Matic *Member* ☎ 461 0458 Ⓕ 461 0466

www.euromoneydirectory.com CROATIA (+385)

Riadria Banka dd
Head Office

D Sporera 3, 51000 Rijeka
Tel: (51) 339 111; (51) 330 018 **Fax:** (51) 211 093; (51) 336 550 **Telex:** 24161 **Swift:** ADRI HR 2X

Senior Executive Officers
President & Chief Executive Officer Mlaben Stic ☎ **330 018**

Rijecka Banka dd

Jadranski trg 3a, 51000 Rijeka
Tel: (51) 208 211 **Fax:** (51) 330 525; (51) 331 880 **Telex:** 24143 BANKOM RH **Swift:** RBRI HR 2X

Senior Executive Officers
Chairman of the Board Ivan Štokic ☎ **213 392** 🖷 **330 525**
Treasurer Borislav Perozic *Member of the Board* ☎ **212 242** 🖷 **330 525**
Management Board Coordinator Ornela Vuškovic-Kosier ☎ **208 315**
International Division Drazen Kurpis *International Division Director* ☎ **335 139** 🖷 **333 182**

Others (Senior Executives)
Emerging Markets Ana Vlastelic *Divisional Director* ☎ **208 354** 🖷 **333 297**

General-Lending (DCM, SL)
Head of Corporate Banking Borislav Perozic *Member of the Board* ☎ **212 242** 🖷 **330 525**

General-Investment
Head of Investment Borislav Perozic *Member of the Board* ☎ **212 242** 🖷 **330 525**

Debt Capital Markets / Fixed Income
Domestic Government Bonds
Head of Sales; Head of Trading; Head of Research Mladenka Milkovic *Manager of Securities* ☎ **208 187**

Equity Capital Markets
Head of Equity Capital Markets Mladenka Milkovic *Manager of Securities* ☎ **208 187**

Syndicated Lending
Head of Syndication Ana Vlastelic *Divisional Director* ☎ **208 354** 🖷 **333 297**

Loan-Related Activities
Trade Finance; Project Finance Masa Pelcic *Director, International Loans & Guarantees* ☎ **208 194** 🖷 **214 954**

Money Markets
Head of Money Markets Mile Tankosic *Director, Foreign Exchange* ☎ **208 191** 🖷 **214 426**

Foreign Exchange
Head of Foreign Exchange Mile Tankosic *Director, Foreign Exchange* ☎ **208 191** 🖷 **214 426**

Corporate Finance / M&A Advisory
Head of Corporate Finance Borislav Perozic *Member of the Board* ☎ **212 242** 🖷 **330 525**

Settlement / Clearing
Head of Settlement / Clearing Mile Tankosic *Director, Foreign Exchange* ☎ **208 191** 🖷 **214 426**

Asset Management
Head Jacinta Brusich *Treasury Division Director* ☎ **330 804** 🖷 **214 426**

Other Departments
Private Banking Borislav Perozic *Member of the Board* ☎ **212 242** 🖷 **330 525**
Correspondent Banking Krsto Juric *Manager* ☎ **208 036** 🖷 **333 182**
Cash Management Mile Tankosic *Director, Foreign Exchange* ☎ **208 191** 🖷 **214 426**

Administration
Head of Administration; Head of Marketing Ivan Prpic ☎ **212 179** 🖷 **206 410**

Technology & Systems
Antun Jurman *Member of the Board* ☎ **213 300** 🖷 **200 278**

Public Relations
Ornela Vuškovic-Kosier *Management Board Coordinator* ☎ **208 315**

Accounts / Audit
Davorka Themel ☎ **208 415**

Société Générale

4th Floor, Ulica Alexandera Von Humboldta 4B, 1000 Zagreb
Tel: (1) 615 9200; (1) 615 9206 **Fax:** (1) 615 9197

CROATIA (+385)   www.euromoneydirectory.com

Splitska banka dd
Head Office

Rudera Boskovica 16, 21000 Split
Tel: (21) 370 500 **Fax:** (21) 370 541 **Telex:** 26252, 26161 STBANK RH **Swift:** SPLI HR 2X **Reuters:** SBSH

Senior Executive Officers
President, Management Board — Tomo Bolotin
Member of Management Board — Pero Vrdoljak
Member of Management Board — Jerislav Kustera
International Division — Mihovil Sodan *General Manager*
Jadranka Bodlovic *Assistant General Manager*
Ivica Srdelic *Assistant General Manager*

General-Lending (DCM, SL)
Head of Corporate Banking — Maja Luetic *Chief Manager, Credit & Guarantees*
Syndicated Lending
Other (Trade Finance)
Int'l Payments & Doc Operations — Arinka Vujevic *Chief Manager*
Foreign Exchange
Global Head — Tomislav Vorkapic *Chief Manager*
Other Departments
Correspondent Banking — Anka Drazic-Segrt *Manager*
Administration
Technology & Systems
Dada Narkovic *General Manager*

Trgovacka banka dd Zagreb
Head Office

Varsavska 3/5, 10000 Zagreb
Tel: (1) 456 1999; (1) 456 1901 **Fax:** (1) 456 1900 **Telex:** 22370 TB RH **Swift:** TRGB HR 2X

Senior Executive Officers
Chairman — Davor Matas ☎ **456 1901**
Chief Executive Officer — Boris Ninic ☎ **456 1901**
Financial Director — Boris Centner ☎ **456 1902**
Chief Operating Officer — Tomislav Vuic ☎ **456 1941**
Treasurer — Sladana Jagar ☎ **456 1951**
Managing Director / General Manager — Boris Ninic ☎ **456 1901**

Debt Capital Markets / Fixed Income
Domestic Government Bonds
Head of Trading — Zoenka Butkovic ☎ **456 1945**
Eurobonds
Head of Origination — Dino Jankovic ☎ **456 1961**
Head of Trading — Vitomir Palinec ☎ **456 1944**

Foreign Exchange
Global Head — Marko Oraskovic
Global Custody
Other (Global Custody)
Tajana Tomasevic ☎ **456 1911**

Other Departments
Private Banking — Dragica Hakalovic ☎ **456 1938**
Correspondent Banking — Vlasta Novak ☎ **456 1931**
Administration
Public Relations
Tomislav Uuic ☎ **456 1941**

Varazdinska banka dd

P Preradovica 17, 42000 Varazdin
Tel: (42) 106 0 **Fax:** (42) 106 146 **Swift:** VBDD HR 2X **Reuters:** VBVH
Website: www.banka.hr

Senior Executive Officers
President — Mato Lukinic ☎ **106 100**
International Division — Bozidar Grobotek *Executive Director* ☎ **106 300**

www.euromoneydirectory.com CROATIA (+385)

Others (Senior Executives)
Stjepan Bunic *Vice President* ☏ **106 124**
Branimir Greguric *Executive Director* ☏ **+385 (1) 428 175**
Head, Emerging Markets Pavao Parat *Member of the Board* ☏ **106 130**
General-Lending (DCM, SL)
Head of Corporate Banking Jadranka Vugrinec *Executive Director* ☏ **106 120**
Money Markets
Tel: 106 371 **Fax:** 55 114
Head of Money Markets Zvonimir Jasek *Manager* ☏ **106 350**
Foreign Exchange
Tel: 106 371 **Fax:** 55 114
Head of Foreign Exchange Zvonimir Jasek *Manager* ☏ **106 350**
Head of Trading Vesna Rajkovic *Chief Dealer*
FX Traders / Sales People
Ljiljana Grgec *Dealer*
Jasminka Prasnicki *Dealer*

Administration
Head of Administration Zeljko Filipovic *Executive Director* ☏ **106 220**
Technology & Systems
Nevon Marusevec *Executive Director* ☏ **106 500**
Legal / In-House Counsel
Lidia Belamakic *Manager* ☏ **106 115**

Zagrebacka banka - Pomorska banka dd Split   Head Office
Ivana Gundulica 26A, HR-21000 Split
Tel: (21) 352 222; (21) 352 352 **Fax:** (21) 357 079; (21) 357 080 **Telex:** 26333 ZGPBK **Swift:** ZAPO HR 22
Senior Executive Officers
President of the Management Board Mladen Rakelic ☏ **352 200** F **357 069**
Financial Director Ruza Perkovic *Finance Division Director* ☏ **352 302** F **357 079**
Chief Operating Officer Ante Blazevic *Member, Management Board* ☏ **352 352** F **357 069**
Treasurer Katja Vukojevic *Director, Treasury Division* ☏ **352 396** F **357 069**
International Division Nada Matkovic *Director, International Division* ☏ **352 288** F **352 242**
Syndicated Lending
Global Head Marija Gojo *Corporate Lending Division Director* ☏ **352 291** F **352 242**
Head of Credit Committee Mladen Rakelic *President of the Management Board* ☏ **352 200** F **357 069**
Loan-Related Activities
Trade Finance Marija Gojo *Corporate Lending Division Director* ☏ **352 291** F **352 242**
Money Markets
Global Head Zemira Jeglic *Head, Money Markets* ☏ **352 331** F **357 069**
Foreign Exchange
Global Head Jadranka Milas *Head, Foreign Exchange* ☏ **352 236** F **357 069**
Settlement / Clearing
Foreign Exchange Settlement Nada Matkovic *Director, International Division* ☏ **352 288** F **352 242**
Other Departments
Private Banking Tonci Jakovcevic *Retail Division Director* ☏ **352 268** F **357 069**
Correspondent Banking Nives Borovic-Defilippis *Manager, International Department* ☏ **352 390**
F **357 079**
Administration
Technology & Systems
Frano Kucer *Division Director* ☏ **352 232** F **357 079**
Legal / In-House Counsel
Arijana Munitic *Manager* ☏ **352 272** F **357 079**
Compliance
Ruza Perkovic *Finance Division Director* ☏ **352 302** F **357 079**

Zagrebacka banka dd   Head Office
Paromlinska 2, 10000 Zagreb
Tel: (1) 610 4000 **Fax:** (1) 536 286 **Telex:** 21211 ZABA RH **Swift:** ZABA HR 2X **Reuters:** ZBZH **Telerate:** 38265 58117
Foreign Exchange & Money Market **Tel:** 682 8370; **Fax:** 682 8370; **Reuters:** ZABA 01
Senior Executive Officers
Chairman, Management Board Franjo Lukovic ☏ **610 4146**
Vice Chairman Nikola Kalinic ☏ **610 4117**

Euromoney Directory 1999   **303**

CROATIA (+385)　　　　　　www.euromoneydirectory.com

Zagrebacka banka dd (cont)
Senior Executive Officers (cont)
Treasurer　　　　　　　　　　　Tomica Pustišek *Director, Treasury Division* ☏ **610 4196**
International Division　　　　　　Milivoj Goldštajn ☏ **617 6264**
Others *(Senior Executives)*
Management Board　　　　　　Zvonimir Jurjevic *Member* ☏ **481 3916**
　　　　　　　　　　　　　　　Sanja Rendulic *Member* ☏ **610 4401**

General-Lending (DCM, SL)
Head of Corporate Banking　　　Damir Odak *Director* ☏ **610 4087**
General-Investment
Head of Investment　　　　　　Duilio Belic *Director* ☏ **610 4215**
Debt Capital Markets / Fixed Income
Department: Treasury Division Trading Dept
Tel: 610 4710 **Fax:** 610 4859
Head of Fixed Income　　　　　Ana Šoštaric
Head of Fixed Income Sales　　 Nikolina Slavujevic *Assistant Director*
Eurobonds
Head of Origination　　　　　　Nikolina Slavujevic *Assistant Director*
Head of Sales　　　　　　　　 Ana Sostaric ☏ **610 4710**
Head of Trading　　　　　　　 Vesna Petrak-Drljanovcan ☏ **610 4499**
Equity Capital Markets
Head of Sales　　　　　　　　 Davorka Zupic ☏ **610 4295**
Head of Trading　　　　　　　 Tomislav Ticic ☏ **610 4507**
Equity Research
Head of Equity Research　　　　Nenad Bakic ☏ **610 4220**
Syndicated Lending
Head of Syndicated Lending　　 Milivoj Goldštajn ☏ **617 6264**
Money Markets
Reuters: ZABA 03
Head of Money Markets　　　　 Vesna Petrak-Drljanovcan ☏ **610 4499**
Foreign Exchange
Reuters: ZABA 02
Head of Foreign Exchange　　　 Mladen Miler ☏ **610 4503**
FX Traders / Sales People
　　　　　　　　　　　　　　　Zrinka Kavel ☏ **610 4502**
　　　　　　　　　　　　　　　Darinka Lovrec ☏ **610 4501**
Risk Management
Head of Risk Management　　　 Renata Babic ☏ **610 4037**
Settlement / Clearing
Head of Settlement / Clearing　　Mira Tomicic ☏ **610 4377**
Global Custody
Head of Global Custody　　　　 Jadranka Egíc *Senior Officer* ☏ **610 4724**
Other Departments
Correspondent Banking　　　　 Jadranka Popovic Tumpa ☏ **630 5408**
Administration
Technology & Systems
IT Division　　　　　　　　　 Goran Padjen *Director* ☏ **610 4289**
Legal / In-House Counsel
　　　　　　　　　　　　　　　Igor Tepšic *Manager Legal Division* ☏ **630 5494**

CUBA
(+53)

Banco Central de Cuba　　　　　　　　　　　🏛 Central Bank
Cuba 402, Lamparilla y Amargura, Havana
Tel: (7) 338 003; (7) 622 616 **Fax:** (7) 666 601; (7) 634 061 **Telex:** 511823 **Swift:** BCCU CU HH
Senior Executive Officers
Minister-President　　　　　　 Francisco Soberón
Vice President　　　　　　　　 Sergio Plasencia ☏ **625 545**
Vice President　　　　　　　　 Jacobo Peison ☏ **622 616**
Vice President　　　　　　　　 Gustavo Roca ☏ **625 544**

Senior Executive Officers (cont)
Chief Executive Officer
Treasurer
Secretary

Others (Senior Executives)
Chief Cashier
Banking Supervision
Economics & Statistics
Reserves Management

Debt Capital Markets / Fixed Income
Government Bonds
Head of Origination

Foreign Exchange
Head of Foreign Exchange

Settlement / Clearing
Head of Settlement / Clearing

Administration
Head of Administration

Technology & Systems

Public Relations

Accounts / Audit
Accountancy

Benigno Regueira *Director* ☏ **628 589**
Nélson Argüelles *Director* ☏ **335 744**
Julio Fernández ☏ **665 344**

Tomás Lorenzo *Director* ☏ **669 234**
Esteban Martel *Supervisor* ☏ **616 519**
José M Sánchez *Director* ☏ **634 963**
Juana L Delgado *Director, Operations* ☏ **629 562**

Juana L Delgado *Director, Operations* ☏ **629 562**

Juana L Delgado *Director, Operations* ☏ **629 562**

Juana L Delgado *Director, Operations* ☏ **629 562**

Gustavo Roca *Vice President* ☏ **625 544**

Jorge Barrera ☏ **338 352**

Gustavo Roca *Vice President* ☏ **625 544**

Jorge Torres *Director* ☏ **628 280**

ING Barings
Representative Office

Quinta Avenida 6407, Esquina 66, Miramar Playa, Havana
Tel: (7) 240 420; (7) 240 419 **Fax:** (7) 240 472; (7) 240 422

Senior Executive Officers
Country Manager

Peter Bombeld ☏ **240 421** ✉ **bombeld@hotmail.com**

CYPRUS
(+357)

Central Bank of Cyprus
Central Bank

PO Box 5529, CY-1395 Nicosia
Tel: (2) 379 800 **Fax:** (2) 378 153 **Telex:** 2424 **Swift:** CBCY CY 2N **Email:** cbcinfo@centralbank.gov.cy
Reuters: CBCY **Telerate:** 39691 **Telex:** 2228
Website: www.centralbank.gov.cy

Senior Executive Officers
Governor

Afxentis Afxentiou ☏ **394 444** ℱ **378 151** ✉ **acafxent@centralbank.gov.cy**

Debt Capital Markets / Fixed Income
Department: Domestic Banking Operations Department
Tel: 394 146 **Fax:** 378 150
Global Head

George Thoma *Manager, Domestic Debt* ☏ **394 144**
✉ **gtthoma@centralbank.gov.cy**

Domestic Government Bonds
Head of Sales; Head of Trading; Head of Research
Department: International Division
Fax: +357 378 070
Global Head

Maria Othonos *Senior Officer* ☏ **394 189** ℱ **378 053**
✉ **issect@centralbank.gov.gy**

Iacovos Pashos *Senior Manager, Foreign Debt* ☏ **394 278** ℱ **378 070**
✉ **isapashos@centralbank.gov.cy**

Medium-Term Notes
Head of Sales

Ioannis Ioannou *Assistant Manager* ☏ **394 282**
✉ **igioanno@centralbank.gov.cy**

Private Placements
Head of Sales

Ioannis Ioannou *Assistant Manager* ☏ **394 282**
✉ **igioanno@centralbank.gov.cy**

CYPRUS (+357)   www.euromoneydirectory.com

Central Bank of Cyprus (cont)

Fixed-Income Repo
Head of Repo — Kyriacos Stavrou *Senior Officer* ☏ 394 326 ✉ idmor@centralbank.gov.cy

Syndicated Lending
Department: International Division
Global Head — Iacovos Pashos *Senior Manager, Foreign Debt* ☏ 394 278 ℱ 378 070
✉ isapashos@centralbank.gov.cy

Money Markets
Department: International Division
Global Head — Iacovos Pashos *Senior Manager, Foreign Debt* ☏ 394 278 ℱ 378 070
✉ isapashos@centralbank.gov.cy

Eurocommercial Paper
Head of Sales — Ioannis Ioannou *Assistant Manager* ☏ 394 282
✉ igioanno@centralbank.gov.cy

Wholesale Deposits
Marketing — Kyriacos Stavrou *Senior Officer* ☏ 394 326 ✉ idmor@centralbank.gov.cy

Foreign Exchange
Department: International Division
Global Head — Iacovos Pashos *Senior Manager, Foreign Debt* ☏ 394 278 ℱ 378 070
✉ isapashos@centralbank.gov.cy
Head of Institutional Sales; Head of Trading — Kyriacos Stavrou *Senior Officer* ☏ 394 326 ✉ idmor@centralbank.gov.cy

Risk Management
Department: International Division
Global Head — Iacovos Pashos *Senior Manager, Foreign Debt* ☏ 394 278 ℱ 378 070
✉ isapashos@centralbank.gov.cy

Fixed Income Derivatives / Risk Management
Global Head — Iacovos Pashos *Senior Manager, Foreign Debt* ☏ 394 278 ℱ 378 070
✉ isapashos@centralbank.gov.cy
IR Swaps Trading — Ioannis Ioannou *Assistant Manager* ☏ 394 282
✉ igioanno@centralbank.gov.cy

Foreign Exchange Derivatives / Risk Management
Cross-Currency Swaps, Sales / Marketing — Ioannis Ioannou *Assistant Manager* ☏ 394 282
✉ igioanno@centralbank.gov.cy

Settlement / Clearing
Department: International Division
Fixed-Income Settlement — George Kamperis *Senior Officer* ☏ 394 321 ℱ 378 070
✉ ideos@centralbank.gov.cy
Derivatives Settlement — Ioannis Ioannou *Assistant Manager* ☏ 394 282
✉ igioanno@centralbank.gov.cy
Foreign Exchange Settlement — George Kamperis *Senior Officer* ☏ 394 321 ℱ 378 070
✉ ideos@centralbank.gov.cy

Agropromstroybank   Full Branch Office

Maximos Court B, Leontiou A Street 17, PO Box 5297, CY-3820 Limassol
Tel: (5) 384 747; (5) 384 224 **Fax:** (5) 384 858 **Telex:** 5065 APSBCBU CY

Senior Executive Officers
General Manager — A Mokhonko
Deputy General Manager — V Bogdanovski

Administration
Accounts / Audit
N G Tabri *Chief Accountant*

Alpha Bank Limited   Subsidiary Company

PO Box 1661, Lombard House, Corner of Chilon & Gladstone Streets, Stylianos Lenas Square, Nicosia
Tel: (2) 474 333 **Fax:** (2) 457 870 **Telex:** 2262 LOMBRD CY **Swift:** NWBK CY 2N

Senior Executive Officers
Chairman — M G Colokassides
Managing Director — E P Ioannou

Others (Senior Executives)
G M H Keheyan *Member, Board of Directors*

General-Lending (DCM, SL)
Head of Corporate Banking — A Demetriades *Director, Corporate & Int'l Banking*

Arab Jordan Investment Bank SA
Full Branch Office

Libra Tower, 23 Olympion Street, PO Box 4384, CY-3035 Limassol
Tel: (5) 351 351 **Fax:** (5) 360 151 **Telex:** 3809 AJIB CY **Swift:** AJIB CY 2I **Email:** ajib@logos.cy.net
Reuters: AJIC (Dealing) **Telex:** 4029 AJIB CY
Website: www.ajib.com.

Senior Executive Officers
Senior Manager   Abed Abu Dayeh

Bank of Beirut & the Arab Countries SAL
Full Branch Office

1st Floor, Emelle Building, 135 Archbishop Makarios III Avenue, Limassol
PO Box 6201, CY-3305 Limassol
Tel: (5) 381 290 **Fax:** (5) 381 584 **Telex:** 5444 BBAC CY

Senior Executive Officers
Managing Director / General Manager   Omar S Saab

Other Departments
Department: Financial Markets
Tel: 381 481

Other Departments
Chief Dealer, Financial Markets   Elie Tabet

Bank of Cyprus Limited
Head Office

51 Stassinos Street, Ayia Paraskevi, Strovolos, CY-1599 Nicosia
PO Box 1472, Strovolos, CY-1599 Nicosia
Tel: (2) 378 0000 **Fax:** (2) 378 111 **Telex:** 2451 KYPRIAKI CY **Swift:** BCYP CY 2N **Email:** ingo@cy.bankofcyprus.com
Cable: KYPRIAKI
Website: www.bankofcyprus.com

Senior Executive Officers
Chairman   Solon Triantafyllides [T] 372 107 [F] 378 456
Chief Executive Officer   Christos Pantzaris *Chief Executive* [T] 372 108 [F] 378 234
Financial Director   Christis Hadjimitsis *Financial Controller* [T] 372 127 [F] 378 112
Group Chief General Manager   Evdokimos Xenophontos [T] 372 110 [F] 378 767

Others (Senior Executives)
Group GM   Antonis Jacouris *Support Services* [T] 372 105 [F] 378 320
                                       [E] gm.support@cy.bankofcyprus.com
                                       Yiannis Kypri *Finance & Treasury* [T] 372 126 [F] 379 655
                                       [E] yiannis.kypri@cy.bankofcypris.com
                                       Costakis Ioannides *Bank of Cyprus (London)* [T] +44 (171) 304 5831
                                       [F] +44 (171) 323 0299
                                       Vasos Shiarly *Branch / Retail Banking* [T] 372 224 [F] 378 469
                                       Charilaos Stavrakis *International Banking Services* [T] 372 263 [F] 378 325
                                       Andreas Eliades *Bank of Cyprus (Greece)* [T] +30 (1) 338 4201
                                       [F] +30 (1) 641 8809
                                       George Charalambous *General Manager* [T] 372 112 [F] 378 320

General-Lending (DCM, SL)
Head of Corporate Banking   Charalambos Charalambides *Group General Manager* [T] 372 173 [F] 378 111

Debt Capital Markets / Fixed Income
Global Head   Socrates Solomides *General Manager, CISCO (Subsidiary)* [T] 751 535
                                       [F] 755 481 [E] cisco@dionysos.bankofcyprus.com.cy

Equity Capital Markets
Global Head   Socrates Solomides *General Manager, CISCO (Subsidiary)* [T] 751 535
                                       [F] 755 481 [E] cisco@dionysos.bankofcyprus.com.cy

Risk Management
Head of Risk Management   George Charalambous *Credit Risk Management* [T] 372 112 [F] 378 320

Settlement / Clearing
Operations   George Charalambous *General Manager* [T] 372 112 [F] 378 320

Global Custody
Department: Custody Services
Regional Head   Phofis Photiou *Head* [T] 751 014 [F] 750 257

CYPRUS (+357) www.euromoneydirectory.com

Bank of Cyprus Limited (cont)
Administration
Head of Administration　　　　　　　　Antonis Jacouris *Support Services* ☎ 372 105 🖷 378 320
　　　　　　　　　　　　　　　　　📧 gm.support@cy.bankofcyprus.com

Legal / In-House Counsel
Internal Legal Advisor　　　　　　　　Andreas Ioannides *Senior Manager* ☎ 372 305 🖷 237 8322

Accounts / Audit
Group Internal Auditor　　　　　　　　Stelios Christodoulou *Senior Manager* ☎ 372 203 🖷 378 247

Banque du Liban et d'Outre-Mer SAL　　　　　　　　Offshore Banking Unit

P Lordos Center - Roundabout, PO Box 3243, CY-3301 Limassol
PO Box 3493, CY-3303 Limassol
Tel: (5) 376 433 **Fax:** (5) 376 292 **Telex:** 4424, 5232 BLOM CY

Senior Executive Officers
Manager　　　　　　　　　　　　　　Simon Farah

Banque Nationale de Paris - Intercontinentale SA
Offshore Banking Unit

Hanseatic House, 111 Spyrou Araouzou Avenue, CY-3600 Limassol
PO Box 58, Limassol
Tel: (5) 360 166; (5) 360 883 **Fax:** (5) 376 519; (5) 346 407 **Telex:** 5519 BNPT CY **Swift:** BNPI CY 2I
Email: bnpcy@cytanet.comm.cy **Telex:** 5941 BNPT CY

Senior Executive Officers
Chief Executive Officer　　　　　　　Yannik Chauvin *General Manager* ☎ 373 607
Treasurer　　　　　　　　　　　　　Robert Tinus ☎ 345 876

General-Lending (DCM, SL)
Head of Corporate Banking　　　　　Georges Ghantous *Corporate Manager* ☎ 346 109
　　　　　　　　　　　　　　　　　Ghassan Zaloum *Corporate Manager* ☎ 359 868

Other Departments
Private Banking　　　　　　　　　　Hartmut Clasen ☎ 370 890

Administration
Head of Administration　　　　　　　Olivier Decock *Secretary General* ☎ 360 166

Barclays Bank plc　　　　　　　　　　　　　　　　　　Full Branch Office

2nd & 3rd Floors, 88 Dighenis Akritas Avenue, CY-1644 Nicosia
PO Box 7320, CY-1644 Nicosia
Tel: (2) 764 777 **Fax:** (2) 754 233 **Telex:** 5200 BAROBU CY **Swift:** BARC CY NN

Senior Executive Officers
Senior Manager　　　　　　　　　　Clive Britton
Manager　　　　　　　　　　　　　Robert Miller

Syndicated Lending

Loan-Related Activities
Trade Finance　　　　　　　　　　Tony Nicolaides *Head, Trade Services*

Foreign Exchange

FX Traders / Sales People
Dealing Room　　　　　　　　　　Anna Kyriakides *Dealer*

Risk Management
Country Head　　　　　　　　　　Clive Britton *Senior Manager*

Administration

Technology & Systems
　　　　　　　　　　　　　　　　Xenia Phanartzis *Head of IT*

308　Euromoney Directory 1999

www.euromoneydirectory.com CYPRUS (+357)

Commercial Bank of Greece
Full Branch Office

4 Ionos Street, 1 Iona Nicolaou Street, Nicosia
Tel: (2) 363 727; (2) 363 646 **Fax:** (2) 473 923
Foreign Exchange & Money Market **Tel:** 682 8370

Senior Executive Officers
Manager Ph Gavris
Country Manager G Kantianis

Co-Operative Central Bank Limited
Head Office

8 Gregoris Afxentiou Street, PO Box 4537, CY-1389 Nicosia
Tel: (2) 672 921 **Fax:** (2) 673 088 **Telex:** 2313 COBANK CY **Telex:** 4799 COBFOR CY

Senior Executive Officers
Chairman A Soteriades
Chief Executive Officer D Pitsillides

Others (Senior Executives)
Board D Stavrou
 Y Yiannaki
 G Iosif
 K Nicolaides
 D Pipis
 A Papademetris

The Cyprus Popular Bank Limited
Head Office

Popular Bank Building, 154 Limassol Avenue, CY-1598 Nicosia
PO Box 2032, CY-1598 Nicosia
Tel: (2) 752 000; (2) 813 000 **Fax:** (2) 811 498 **Telex:** 3362 **Swift:** LIKI CY 2N **Email:** laiki.teleservice@ibm.net
Reuters: BAPO **Telerate:** 39693
Website: www.cypruspopularbank.com

Senior Executive Officers
Chairman & Chief Executive Officer Kikis Lazarides ☏ **811 001**
Financial Director Andreas Papavasiliou *Executive Director* ☏ **811 051**
Chief Operating Officer Nicos Hadjinicolaou *Executive Director Domestic Banking* ☏ **811 101**
Treasurer Kyriacos Constantinou *Manager, Treasury* ☏ **811 301**
Divisional Director International Banking Rena Rouvithapanou ☏ **811 123**

Debt Capital Markets / Fixed Income
Tel: 512 526 **Fax:** 811 498
Global Head Costas Argyrides ☏ **811 383**

Domestic Government Bonds
Head of Sales Michalis Athanasiou ☏ **811 384**

Eurobonds
Head of Origination Costas Argyrides ☏ **811 383**

Medium-Term Notes
Head of Origination Michalis Athanasiou ☏ **811 384**

Fixed-Income Repo
Head of Repo Costas Argyrides ☏ **811 383**

Equity Capital Markets
Department: Laiki Investments
Silver House, 54 Griva Digheni Avenue, PO Box 5065, CY-1306 Nicosia
Tel: +357 (2) 663 212 **Fax:** +357 (2) 663 554
Global Head Lepteris Papaheracleous *Manager* ☏ **812 131**

Domestic Equities
Head of Sales Charis Savvides ☏ **812 136**
Head of Trading Costas Anastasiades ☏ **812 132**
Head of Research Stelios Marcoulis ☏ **812 134**

Syndicated Lending
Tel: 811 251 **Fax:** 811 496
Global Head Michalis Louis ☏ **811 251**

Money Markets
Tel: 512 526 **Fax:** 811 498
Global Head Andri Chasou ☏ **811 385**

CYPRUS (+357)   www.euromoneydirectory.com

The Cyprus Popular Bank Limited (cont)
Foreign Exchange
Tel: 512 528 **Fax**: 811 498
Global Head
Regional Head   Chris Orphanou ☎ **811 387**
Country Head   Photoula Vosrou ☎ **811 386**
Head of Institutional Sales   Polly Agrotis ☎ **811 389**
Corporate Sales   Katerina Ktorides ☎ **811 388**
                                 George Stephanides ☎ **811 390**
Risk Management
Tel: 811 255 **Fax**: 811 496
Global Head   Achileas Malliuta ☎ **811 255**
Settlement / Clearing
Regional Head   Soteris Charalambou ☎ **811 312**
Other Departments
Proprietary Trading   Philippos Philippou ☎ **811 382**
Private Banking   Savvas Savvides ☎ **812 110**
Correspondent Banking   Era Michaelides ☎ **811 256**
Administration
Technology & Systems
                                 Panicos Michael ☎ **812 474**
Legal / In-House Counsel
                                 Savvas Christodoulou ☎ **811 164**
Public Relations
                                 Andreas Stylianou Manager, Press Office ☎ **811 053**

Federal Bank of the Middle East
Megaron Lavinia, Santa Rosa Avenue, CY-1391 Nicosia
PO Box 5566, CY-1391 Nicosia
Tel: (2) 761 751 **Fax**: (2) 769 497 **Telex**: 4677 FBMAN **Swift**: FBME CY 2N **Reuters**: FBMX
Cable: FEDMEBANK NICOSI
Foreign Exchange Tel: 761 620

Senior Executive Officers
Chairman   Ayoub-Farid M Saab
Chief Executive Officer   James V Hoey
Treasurer   A R Wazzi
Senior Vice President   Sean C Hickey

Hellenic Bank Limited   Head Office
92 Dhigenis Akritas Avenue, PO Box 4747, CY-1394 Nicosia
Tel: (2) 767 755 **Fax**: (2) 760 336 **Telex**: 3311 HELLENIC CY **Swift**: HEBA CY 2NA **Reuters**: HBCY

Senior Executive Officers
Chairman & Chief Executive   Panos Chr Ghalanos
Vice Chairman   Constantinos S Lozides
Financial Director   Panikos Malekos Group Chief Financial Officer
Assistant General Manager   John Epaminondou
AGM & Company Secretary   Pieris Theodorou
International Division   Kyriakos Papadopoulos Manager, International Banking
General - Treasury
Head of Treasury   Kyriakos Papadopoulos Manager, Treasury
Relationship Manager
Group Chief Inspector   Andreas Palmas
Other Departments
Correspondent Banking   Panikos Malekos Group Chief Financial Officer
Administration
Head of Administration   George Papadopoulos Senior Manager
Technology & Systems
Information Technology   Thomas Stylianou Senior Manager
Accounts / Audit
                                 Andreas Triantafyllides Chief Credit Auditor
Other (Administration)
Planning & Research   Marios Clerides Senior Manager
Personnel   Miltiades Tingherides Senior Manager

www.euromoneydirectory.com   CYPRUS (+357)

HSBC Investment Bank Cyprus Limited
Subsidiary Company

Dositheou 7, Block C, 3rd Floor, Nicosia
PO Box 5718, CY-1311 Nicosia
Tel: (2) 376 116 Fax: (2) 376 121 Telex: 4980 HICL CY Swift: HICL CY 2X Reuters: HIBC

Senior Executive Officers
Managing Director
International Division   T Taoushanis
                                      T Taoushanis *Managing Director*

Debt Capital Markets / Fixed Income
Department: Capital Markets
Global Head   Maria Theodorou *Manager, Treasury*

Syndicated Lending
Head of Syndication   N Michaelides *Credit Officer*
                                      A Koehle *Credit Officer*

Foreign Exchange
Global Head   Maria Theodorou *Manager, Treasury*
FX Traders / Sales People
                                      R Shnoudeh *Dealer*
                                      N McGill *Dealer*

Risk Management
Global Head   T Taoushanis *Managing Director*

Corporate Finance / M&A Advisory
Global Head   T Taoushanis *Managing Director*

Settlement / Clearing
Settlement (General)   Y Antoniou *Settlement Officer*

Other Departments
Private Banking   A Michaelides *Private Banking Officer*

Administration
Head of Administration   A. Antoniades *Manager*

Inkombank
Offshore Banking Unit

Karmazi House, 67 Spyros Araouzos Street, CY-3036 Limassol
PO Box 3349, CY-3302 Limassol
Tel: (5) 745 494 Fax: (5) 747 067 Telex: 5817 INKOM CY Swift: INCO CY 2N Reuters: INCY

Senior Executive Officers
General Manager   A Krokhin

Debt Capital Markets / Fixed Income
Country Head   K Ossipov *Chief Dealer*

Syndicated Lending
Country Head   N Tchepourin *Manager, Customer Services*

Money Markets
Country Head   K Ossipov *Chief Dealer*

Corporate Finance / M&A Advisory
Global Head   N Tchepourin *Manager, Customer Services*

Settlement / Clearing
Country Head   M Assalieva *Manager, Funds Transfers*

Jordan National Bank plc
Full Branch Office

2nd Floor, Pecora Tower, 1 Anexartissias Street, CY-3303 Limassol
PO Box 3587, CY-3303 Limassol
Tel: (5) 356 669 Fax: (5) 356 673 Telex: 3547 Swift: JONB CY 2I Email: jnb@cytanet.com.cy Reuters: JNBC
General Telex: 4103 AHLIBK CY; General Telex: 5471 AHLIBK CY; Foreign Exchange & Money Market
Tel: 371 118; Fax: 35 6673; Telex: 6257 AHLIFX CY
Website: www.ahli.com

Senior Executive Officers
Regional Manager   Khalil A Nasr ☎ **344 088**

Others (Senior Executives)
Operations   Alfred Abu Manneh *Deputy Manager*

Syndicated Lending
Head of Credit Committee   Walid Ghoulmieh *Assistant Manager*

CYPRUS (+357)   www.euromoneydirectory.com

Karic Banka dd
Full Branch Office

66 Archiepiskopou Makariou, Cronos Court, CY 1640 Nicosia
PO Box 6522, Nicosia
Tel: (2) 374 977; (2) 374 980 Fax: (2) 374 151 Telex: 6510 QFS CY

Senior Executive Officers
President   Sreten Karic
Financial Director   Muhamed Mulhacha
Managing Director   Biljana Camilovic
International Division   Layia Hadjiantoniou

General-Investment
Head of Investment   Eleni Averkiou

London Forfaiting Cyprus Limited
Subsidiary Company

Lophitis Business Centre, PO Box 1658, 28 October Street, CY-3035 Limassol
Tel: (5) 344 445 Fax: (5) 344 091 Telex: 4513 LFA CY Email: lfa@dial.cylink.com.cy

Senior Executive Officers
Chief Executive Officer   Victor Papadopoulos *Chief Executive*

Syndicated Lending
Department: Forfaiting, Loans Syndication, Capital Markets Trading

Other (Trade Finance)
                                    Geert Declerck *Managing Director*
                                    Sophocles Parapanos *Managing Director*
                                    Kypros Papatheodoulou *Associate Director*
                                    Costas Stylianou *Associate Director*
                                    George Kalathias *Senior Manager*
                                    Olga Sophocleous *Assistant Manager*
                                    Yiannis Televantides *Assistant Manager*
Loans Administration   Angela Chrysostomou *Director*
                                    Maria Karamanou *Senior Manager*
                                    Christina Christophi *Manager*

Administration

Accounts / Audit
Accounts   Kyriakos Rialas *Finance Director*
                                    George Demetriades *Associate Director*

Other (Administration)
Personnel & Administration   Veeny Hadjimilti *Director & Company Secretary*

National Bank of Greece (Cyprus) Limited
Head Office

2nd Floor, Galaxias Centre, 36 Ayias Elenis Street, CY-1061 Nicosia
Tel: (2) 840 000 Fax: (2) 758 090 Telex: 3956 NBG CY Swift: ETHN CY 2N Reuters: NBCY Cable: ETHNOMAK
Foreign Exchange & Money Market Tel: 682 8370

Senior Executive Officers
Chairman, Board of Directors   Th Karatzas
General Manager   M St Joannides
General Manager   K Kyriakides
General Manager   M Tagaroulias

Others (Senior Executives)
                                    N Karamouzis *Member, Board of Directors*
                                    Th Pantalakis *Member, Board of Directors*
                                    M Tagaroulias *Member, Board of Directors*
                                    N Koutsos *Member, Board of Directors*
                                    M Kolakides *Member, Board of Directors*
                                    T Lefkaritis *Member, Board of Directors*
                                    F Epifaniou *Member, Board of Directors*
                                    A Triantafyllides *Member, Board of Directors*

CZECH REPUBLIC (+420)

Russian Commercial Bank (Cyprus) Limited
Head Office

2 Amathuntos Street, CY-3310 Limassol
PO Box 6868, CY-3310 Limassol
Tel: (5) 342 190 **Fax:** (5) 342 192 **Telex:** 4561 **Swift:** RCBL CY 2I **Reuters:** RCBL **Cable:** RUSCOMBANK-LIMASSOL

Senior Executive Officers
Chairman — Dimitry Tulin
General Manager — Yury Babkin

Société Générale Cyprus Limited
Subsidiary Company

7/9 Grivas Dighenis Avenue, CY-2080 Nicosia
PO Box 8560, CY-2080 Nicosia
Tel: (2) 764 885 **Fax:** (2) 764 471

Senior Executive Officers
Chairman — Maurice Sehnaoui
General Manager — Gérard Malhamé

General-Lending (DCM, SL)
Head of Corporate Banking — Elenitsa Petri *Assistant Manager, Credit*

Foreign Exchange
Global Head — Jack Georgiou *Marketing Manager*

Settlement / Clearing
Operations — Kety Symeonidou *Head, L / C & L / G*

Administration
Head of Administration — Abed Jomaa *Manager, Financial Controller*

Universal Savings Bank Limited
Head Office

Alternative trading name: Universal Bank
Formerly known as: Yialdusa Savings Bank Limited

6A Kennedy Avenue, CY-2080 Nicosia
PO Box 8510, CY-2080 Nicosia
Tel: (2) 764 111; (2) 327 222 **Fax:** (2) 767 175; (2) 321 729 **Telex:** 2720 UNITELX **Swift:** UNVK CY 2N
Email: offshore@usb.com.cy
Website: www.usb.com.cy

Senior Executive Officers
Chairman — George Syrimis
General Manager — George Makariou
Secretary — Michalis Kleopas
International Division — Demetris Christou *Manager, Domestic Bank & Sales* 🕾 763 922

Others (Senior Executives)
Andreas Georgiov *Executive Vice Chairman* 🕾 327 222

General-Lending (DCM, SL)
Head of Corporate Banking — Stelios Alexandrou *Manager, Business & Retail Banking* 🕾 667 633

CZECH REPUBLIC
(+420)

Ceská národní banka
Central Bank

Na príkope 28, 110 03 Prague
Tel: (2) 2441 1111 **Fax:** (2) 2441 3708; (2) 24417865 **Telex:** 121555 **Swift:** CNBA CZ PP **Reuters:** CZSB
Cable: CENABA
Reuters: CZSC

Senior Executive Officers
Vice Governor — Pavel Kysilka
Vice Governor — Jan Vit
Chief Executive Officer — Miroslav Hrncir *Chief Executive Director*
Ota Kaftan *Chief Executive Director*
Ludek Niedermayer *Chief Executive Director*
Jirí Pospíšil *Chief Executive Director*

CZECH REPUBLIC (+420)

Česká národní banka (cont)
Senior Executive Officers (cont)

Jan Hampl *Senior Executive Director*
Josef Vanzura *Senior Executive Director*

Others (Senior Executives)
Head, Inspection
Head, Monetary Policy
Head, Statistics
Head, CNB Budget
Head, Banking Transactions
Head, Transactions Support
Head, Substandard Transactions
Head, Currency
Head, Banking Supervision Policy
Head, Banking Supervision I
Head, Banking Supervision II
Head, Institute of Economy

Jirí Zimola *Executive Director*
Petr Vojtíšek *Executive Director*
Richard Pavelka *Executive Director*
Marian Mayer *Executive Director*
Jirí Koliha *Executive Director*
Jirí Klumpar *Executive Director*
Ladislav Reznícek *Executive Director*
Leopold Surga *Executive Director*
Vera Mašindová *Executive Director*
Vladimír Krejca *Executive Director*
Pavel Racocha *Executive Director*
Jan Klacek *Executive Director*

Relationship Manager
Head, International Relations

Petr Procházka *Executive Director*

Risk Management
Head of Risk Management

Jirí Klumpar *Executive Director*

Administration
Head of Administration

Michal Šatra *Executive Director*

Technology & Systems
Head, Information Systems
Head, Automation

Jirí Nosál *Executive Director*
Jirí Strach *Executive Director*

Legal / In-House Counsel
Legal Services

Jaromír Vlcek *Executive Director*

Public Relations

Martin Švehla *Executive Director*

Accounts / Audit
Head, Accounting & Payment Systems
Head, Internal Audit

Vratislav Hübner *Executive Director*
Jirí Zimola *Executive Director*

Other (Administration)
Head, Personnel & Bank Organisation

Vera Nepimachová *Executive Director*

ABN AMRO Bank NV — Representative Office

Brandlova 4, PO Box 266, 601 00 Brno
Tel: (5) 4221 9959/61 **Fax:** (5) 4221 5826

Senior Executive Officers
Manager

Igor D Pakan

ABN AMRO Bank NV — Full Branch Office

Lazarska 3, 111 21 Prague 1
PO Box 773, 111 21 Prague 1
Tel: (2) 4405 1111; (2) 4405 1132 **Fax:** (2) 4405 2222 **Telex:** 122295 AABC **Swift:** ABNA CZ PP

Senior Executive Officers
Country Manager
Senior Adviser
Financial Director
Treasurer
International Division

Rob den Heggeler ☏ **4405 2334**
Jaromir Zahradnik ☏ **4405 2335**
Martin Sauer *Head, Corporate Banking* ☏ **4405 2351**
Zdenek Jandus ☏ **4405 3111**
Felko Truijens ☏ **4405 2319**

Equity Capital Markets
Head of Equity Capital Markets

Ludvik Vacek *Head, Equity* ☏ **4405 2500**

AR Stavební sporitelna as — Head Office

Neklanova 38, 128 00 Prague 2
Tel: (2) 290 303 **Fax:** (2) 296 174

Senior Executive Officers
General Director

Václav Soukup

www.euromoneydirectory.com   CZECH REPUBLIC (+420)

Banka Haná as
Head Office

Rooseveltova 10, 60158 Brno
Tel: (5) 4221 5675; (5) 4221 2480 Fax: (5) 4221 5680

Senior Executive Officers
Chairman of the Board of Directors   Mr Ohlidal

Banque Paribas
Representative Office

Biskupská 13, 110 00 Prague 1
Tel: (2) 232 1161; (2) 232 8107 Fax: (2) 232 1839

Senior Executive Officers
Chief Representative   Aleš Musil

Barclays Bank plc
Representative Office

Palác Myslbek, Ná prikope 21, 117 19 Prague 1
Tel: (2) 2422 9872; (2) 2422 7994 Fax: (2) 2422 9890
Foreign Exchange & Money Market Tel: 682 8370

Senior Executive Officers
Representative   Jan Hasek

Bayerische Landesbank Girozentrale
Representative Office

U Prasné Brány 3, 110 00 Prague 1
Tel: (2) 2481 0886 Fax: (2) 231 6518

Senior Executive Officers
Chief Representative   Kurt Olbert

BNP-Dresdner Bank (CR) as
Subsidiary Company

Vitezna 1, 150 00 Prague 5
Tel: (2) 5731 0190 Fax: (2) 5700 6200

Senior Executive Officers
General Manager   Mr Beck

Cassa di Risparmio di Trieste - Banca SpA
Representative Office

Belehradská 132, 120 84 Prague 2
Tel: (2) 2109 1000 Fax: (2) 2109 1300

Senior Executive Officers
Representative   Mrs Zelpletova

Ceská Sporitelna as
Head Office

Na Príkope 29, 113 98 Prague 1
Tel: (2) 6107 1111 Fax: (2) 6107 3006; (2) 6107 3007 Telex: 121010 SPDBC Swift: CSPO CZ PP Reuters: CZSB
General Telex: 121624 SPDBC; General Telex: 121605 SPDBC; Reuters: CSPS
Website: www.csas.cz

Senior Executive Officers
Chairman of the Board & CEO   Jaroslav Klapal ☎ 6107 3500
Chief Executive Officer   Jaroslav Klapal Chairman of the Board & CEO ☎ 6107 3500
Company Secretary   Tomáš Pribyl ☎ 6107 3499 F 6107 3007
International Division   Michal Krišlo Director, Commercial Banking ☎ 2200 4500 F 2422 4546

General-Lending (DCM, SL)
Head of Corporate Banking   Michal Krišlo Director, Commercial Banking ☎ 2200 4500 F 2422 4546

General-Investment
Head of Investment   Petr Hlavácek Director, Investment Banking ☎ 2422 1201 F 2422 0300

Debt Capital Markets / Fixed Income
Head of Fixed Income   Petr Hlavácek Director, Investment Banking ☎ 2422 1201 F 2422 0300

CZECH REPUBLIC (+420)   www.euromoneydirectory.com

Ceská Sporitelna as (cont)

Fixed-Income Repo
Head of Repo   Petr Hlavácek *Director, Investment Banking* ☎ 2422 1201 F 2422 0300

Equity Capital Markets
Head of Equity Capital Markets   Petr Hlavácek *Director, Investment Banking* ☎ 2422 1201 F 2422 0300

Equity Repo / Securities Lending
Head   Petr Hlavácek *Director, Investment Banking* ☎ 2422 1201 F 2422 0300

Syndicated Lending
Head of Syndicated Lending; Head of Origination   Luboš Fridrich *Director, Credit Assessment & Approval* ☎ 6107 3156 F 6107 3273

Loan-Related Activities
Project Finance   Michal Krišlo *Director, Commercial Banking* ☎ 2200 4500 F 2422 4546

Money Markets
Head of Money Markets   Roman Mentlík *Director, Treasury Trading & Sales* ☎ 2422 0977 F 2421 6522

Foreign Exchange
Head of Foreign Exchange   Roman Mentlík *Director, Treasury Trading & Sales* ☎ 2422 0977 F 2421 6522

Corporate Finance / M&A Advisory
Head of Corporate Finance   Helena Riedelová *Director of Finance* ☎ 6107 4495 F 6107 4211

Settlement / Clearing
Head of Settlement / Clearing   Roman Mentlík *Director, Treasury Trading & Sales* ☎ 2422 0977 F 2421 6522

Global Custody
Head of Global Custody   Jaroslava Studenovská *Director, Trade Settlement* ☎ 2499 5806

Asset Management
Head   Pavel Cetkovský *Director, Assets & Liabilities* ☎ 2421 5675 F 2422 2499

Other Departments
Chief Credit Officer   Luboš Fridrich *Director, Credit Assessment & Approval* ☎ 6107 3156 F 6107 3273

Private Banking   Miroslav Vágner *Director, Retail Banking* ☎ 6107 4500 F 6107 4074
Correspondent Banking   Vera Brázová *Manager, Correspondent Banking* ☎ 2200 4507 F 2423 1775
Cash Management   Roman Mentlík *Director, Treasury Trading & Sales* ☎ 2422 0977 F 2421 6522

Administration
Head of Administration   Tomáš Pribyl ☎ 6107 3499 F 6107 3007

Technology & Systems
Information Technology   Josef Vacek *Director* ☎ 232 0820 F 232 8196

Legal / In-House Counsel
    Petr Liška *Director, Legal Affairs* ☎ 6107 3476 F 6107 3073

Public Relations
Public Relations & Advertising   Alena Kindová *Director* ☎ 6107 4460 F 61073157

Accounts / Audit
Internal Audit & Control   Bohuslav Poduška *Director* ☎ 6107 2508 F 6107 2294

Ceskomoravská Hypotecni banka as   Head Office

Formerly known as: Regiobanka, as
Budéjovicka 1, 140 00 Prague 4
Tel: (2) 6112 1111; (2) 6112 2831 **Fax:** (2) 6112 2563; (2) 6112 2833 **Email:** hypo@pha.pvtnet.cz

Senior Executive Officers
Chief Executive Officer   Pavel Ševcík ☎ 6112 2830
Financial Director   Rudolf Kostka *Senior Manager* ☎ 6112 2843
Company Secretary   Jitka Silhavá ☎ 6112 2831
Manager   Frantisek Pavelka ☎ 6112 2834

Syndicated Lending
Head of Origination   Libor Ostatek *Senior Manager* ☎ 6112 2898

Loan-Related Activities
Project Finance   Jana Zahradkova *Senior Manager* ☎ 6112 2886

Money Markets
Head of Money Markets   Pavel Holecka *Senior Manager* ☎ 6112 2839

Corporate Finance / M&A Advisory
Head of Corporate Finance   Ladislav Koucký *Senior Manager* ☎ 6112 2887

www.euromoneydirectory.com			CZECH REPUBLIC (+420)

Settlement / Clearing
Head of Settlement / Clearing		Josef Polidar *Manager* ☏ **(49) 506 2304**
Asset Management
Head		Jirí Mazuch *Manager* ☏ **6112 2855**
Other Departments
Chief Credit Officer		Znenek Kúril *Manager* ☏ **6112 2718**
Correspondent Banking		Rudolf Kostka *Senior Manager* ☏ **6112 2843**
Administration
Head of Marketing		Kamila Reznickerá *Manager* ☏ **6112 2891**
Technology & Systems
		Ivan Gavran *Manager* ☏ **6112 2844**
Public Relations
		Frantisek Pavelka *Manager* ☏ **6112 2834**
Accounts / Audit
		Jan Kondta *Manager* ☏ **6112 2838**

## Ceskoslovenská Obchodni Banka as			Head Office
Na Prikope 14, 115 20 Prague 1
Tel: (2) 2411 1111 **Fax:** (2) 2422 5049 **Telex:** 122201 COB **Swift:** CEKO CZ PP
Website: www.csob.cz

Senior Executive Officers
Chairman, Board of Directors, GM		Pavel Kavánek ☏ **2411 2000** 📠 **2422 5282**
Chief Executive Officer		Josef Tauber *Vice Chairman, Board of Directors & SEO* ☏ **2411 2006**
		📠 **2422 3941**
Financial Director		Rudolf Autner *Member, Board of Directors & SEO* ☏ **2411 2028**
		📠 **2421 7554**
Treasurer		Petr Chvojka *Chief Economist* ☏ **2411 2024** 📠 **2424 3574**
Others (Senior Executives)
Strategic Projects		Jan Lamser *Member, Board of Directors & SEO* ☏ **2411 2128** 📠 **2421 8465**
General-Lending (DCM, SL)
Head of Corporate Banking		Vladimír Stanura *Member, Board of Directors, SEO, Corp Bnkg*
		☏ **2411 2008** 📠 **2422 4556**
		Petr Knapp *Member, Board of Directors, SEO Credits* ☏ **6135 2660**
		📠 **6135 2832**
		Jan Blaho *Chief Manager, Corporate Banking* ☏ **2411 2070** 📠 **2424 3574**

General-Investment
Head of Investment		Petr Lasek *Chief Manager, Capital Investments* ☏ **6135 3608** 📠 **6135 3333**
		René Smerda *Chief Manager, Funds* ☏ **6135 3100** 📠 **6135 3358**

Relationship Manager
Bilateral Agreements & Debt Trading		Antonín Petersky *Chief Manager* ☏ **2411 2074** 📠 **2411 2212**
Financial Institutions		Miloslav Dudek *Chief Manager* ☏ **2411 2065** 📠 **2424 3515**
Office of the Board		Tomáš Bergmann *Chief Manager* ☏ **2411 2042** 📠 **2421 8465**
Debt Capital Markets / Fixed Income
Domestic Government Bonds
Head of Sales		Pavel Cech *Director, Primary Markets* ☏ **6135 3311** 📠 **6135 3330**
Non-Domestic Government Bonds
		Pavel Cech *Director, Primary Markets* ☏ **6135 3311** 📠 **6135 3330**

Fixed-Income Research
Head of Credit Research		Josef Kovalovsky *Acting Chief Manager* ☏ **6135 4000** 📠 **266 086**
Equity Capital Markets
Global Head		Radovan Tlamsa *Managing Director* ☏ **6135 4000** 📠 **266 086**
Other (Domestic Equities)
Capital Markets Research		Josef Kovalovsky *Acting Chief Manager* ☏ **6135 4000** 📠 **266 086**
Syndicated Lending
Global Head		Ivan Horák *Chief Manager, Loans & Syndications* ☏ **2411 2063** 📠 **2421 9989**
Loan-Related Activities
Project Finance		Lenka Kostraounova *Chief Manager, Project Finance* ☏ **6135 2670**
		📠 **6135 2835**

Other (Trade Finance)
Export / Import Finance		Jana Svabenská *Chief Manager* ☏ **2411 2304** 📠 **2422 0582**
Money Markets
Global Head		Tomás Novák *Chief Manager, FX & MM* ☏ **6135 3550** 📠 **6135 3324**

CZECH REPUBLIC (+420)   www.euromoneydirectory.com

Ceskoslovenská Obchodní Banka as (cont)

Money Markets - General
Brokerage   Jan Barta *Acting Chief Manager* T 6135 3540 F 6135 3324

Foreign Exchange
Global Head   Tomás Novák *Chief Manager, FX & MM* T 6135 3550 F 6135 3324

Risk Management
Global Head   Roman Somol *Chief Manager, Risk Management* T 6135 3000 F 6135 3326

Corporate Finance / M&A Advisory
Global Head   Jan Blaho *Chief Manager, Corporate Banking* T 2411 2070 F 2424 3574

Settlement / Clearing
Settlement (General)   Jirí Beránek *Chief Manager, Banking Support Services* T 2411 2018 F 232 7562
Operations   Jirina Horáková *Acting Chief Manager* T 6135 4504 F 6135 4811
Back-Office   Josef Sincák *Chief Manager, Financial Markets* T 6135 4011 F 266 086
Other   Ladislav Vašku *Chief Manager, Financial Markets* T 6135 3601 F 6135 3802

Global Custody
Other (Global Custody)
Safe Custody   Radovan Tlamsa *Managing Director* T 6135 4000 F 266 086

Other Departments
Correspondent Banking   Ivo Novotný *Chief Manager* T 2411 2049 F 2423 6262
Economic Research   Petr Vojácek *Chief Manager* T 6135 2740 F 6125 2850
Debt Recovery / Restructuring   Jirí Michalicka *Chief Manager* T 6135 2690 F 6135 2840

Administration
Head of Marketing   Helena Cetlová *Acting Chief Manager* T 2411 2012 F 2411 2417

Technology & Systems
    Pavel Holec *Chief Manager, IT* T 6135 4500 F 6135 5353
Management Information System   Vladimír Letko *Chief Manager* T 6135 2580 F 6135 2820

Legal / In-House Counsel
    Karel Kaloc *Chief Manager* T 6135 4002 F 261228

Public Relations
    Milan Tománek *Manager, Communications* T 2411 2030

Corporate Communications
Communications   Milan Tománek *Manager* T 2411 2030 F 2411 2240

Accounts / Audit
Accounting   Vitezlav Vojácek *Chief Manager* T 6135 2500 F 6135 2800
Internal Audit   Ladislav Kopecky *Chief Manager* T 6135 4006 F 262 634
Cost Management   Hana Stríbrna *Chief Manager* T 6135 2750 F 6135 2855

Other (Administration)
Personnel   Petr Richter *Chief Manager* T 6135 4502 F 2421 0631
Administration of Ceded Receivables   Miloslav Hynek *Chief Manager* T 6671 0220 F 6671 0061
Strategy   Vera Svobodová *Manager* T 2411 2022 F 2424 3522

The Chase Manhattan Bank   Representative Office

Karlova 27, 110 00 Prague 1
Tel: (2) 2423 4311; (2) 2423 4313 **Fax:** (2) 2423 4314

Senior Executive Officers
Others (Senior Executives)
Senior Country Officer   Roger E Kodat *Vice President*

Corporate Finance / M&A Advisory
Global Head   Martin Pasek *Associate*

Administration
Head of Administration   Sarka Navratilova *Office Manager*

Citibank ac   Subsidiary Company

Evropska 178, 16 640 Prague 6
Tel: (2) 2430 4111 **Fax:** (2) 2430 4611 **Telex:** 122196 CITIC **Swift:** CITI CS PX **Reuters:** CICZ; CSFR

Senior Executive Officers
General Manager   Akshaya Bhargava T 2430 4222
Financial Director   Frank Slacik T 2430 4242
Treasurer   Scott Riedel *Head of Sales & Trading* T 2430 4422

www.euromoneydirectory.com CZECH REPUBLIC (+420)

Equity Capital Markets
Head of Sales; Head of Trading — Scott Riedel *Head of Sales & Trading* ☏ **2430 4422**
Domestic Equities
Head of Sales; Head of Trading — Petr Opocensky ☏ **2430 4425**
Syndicated Lending
Head of Origination; Head of Syndication — William Rocca ☏ **2430 4383**
Loan-Related Activities
Trade Finance — Michael Nebesky ☏ **2430 4382**
Project Finance — William Rocca ☏ **2430 4383**
Foreign Exchange
Country Head — Lubos Jancosek ☏ **2430 4449**
Risk Management
Country Head — Terrance Kyle ☏ **2430 4332**
Global Custody
Country Head — Frantisek Máslo ☏ **2430 4454**
Asset Management
Head — Radek Vaura ☏ **2430 4454**
Other Departments
Chief Credit Officer — Terrance Kyle ☏ **2430 4332**
Correspondent Banking — Frantisek Máslo ☏ **2430 4454**
Cash Management — Jean Murphy ☏ **2430 4443**
Administration
Technology & Systems — Jiri Hladik ☏ **2430 4541**

Legal / In-House Counsel — Radomil Stumpa ☏ **2430 4224**

Compliance — Cari Votava ☏ **2430 4228**

Public Relations — Katerina Kurkova *Officer* ☏ **2430 4328**

Accounts / Audit — Miroslav Škoda ☏ **2430 4514**

Citicorp Investment Company

Europska 178, 160 70 Praha 6, 16670 Prague
Tel: (2) 2430 4843 **Fax:** (2) 2430 4616
Senior Executive Officers
Chief Executive Officer — Tomas Strnad *Director* ☏ **2430 4415**
Administration
Head of Administration — Daniela Harlasova ☏ **2430 4474**

Commerzbank AG   Full Branch Office

Jugoslávská 1, 120 21 Prague 2
Tel: (2) 2119 3111 **Fax:** (2) 2119 3699 **Telex:** 121502 COMMC **Swift:** COBA CZ PX XXX
Email: commerz@commerzbank.anet.cz **Reuters:** CBPR, CZBG
Senior Executive Officers
Chief Executive Officer — Nicholas Teller *Branch Director* ☏ **2119 3125**
Wilhelm Nüse *Branch Director* ☏ **2119 3115** 🖷 **2119 3140**
Treasurer — Jaromír Hronek *Head of Treasury* ☏ **2119 3150** 🖷 **2119 3169**
✉ hronek@commerzbank.cz

Debt Capital Markets / Fixed Income
Domestic Government Bonds
Head of Sales — Jaromír Hronek *Head of Treasury* ☏ **2119 3150** 🖷 **2119 3169**
✉ hronek@commerzbank.cz

Syndicated Lending
Fax: 2119 3239
Regional Head — Petr Vozka *Head, Corporate Banking* ☏ **2119 3210**
Oliver Sipeer *Head, Corporate Banking* ☏ **2119 3200**
Head of Origination; Head of Syndication — John N. Webster ☏ **2119 3232**

Euromoney Directory 1999   **319**

CZECH REPUBLIC (+420) www.euromoneydirectory.com

Commerzbank AG (cont)

Loan-Related Activities
Trade Finance — Ralph Klose *Head, Trade Finance* ☎ 2119 3270
Project Finance — Petr Vozka *Head, Corporate Banking* ☎ 2119 3210
Oliver Sipeer *Head, Corporate Banking* ☎ 2119 3200
Leasing & Asset Finance — Petr Vozka *Head, Corporate Banking* ☎ 2119 3210
Oliver Sipeer *Head, Corporate Banking* ☎ 2119 3200

Money Markets
Regional Head — Jaromír Hronek *Head of Treasury* ☎ 2119 3150 ℻ 2119 3169
✉ hronek@commerzbank.cz

Foreign Exchange
Regional Head — Jaromír Hronek *Head of Treasury* ☎ 2119 3150 ℻ 2119 3169
✉ hronek@commerzbank.cz

FX Traders / Sales People
FXI CZK — Tomás Hohl ☎ 2119 3158 ℻ 2119 3169

Risk Management
Regional Head — Petr Vozka *Head, Corporate Banking* ☎ 2119 3210
Oliver Sipeer *Head, Corporate Banking* ☎ 2119 3200

Fixed Income Derivatives / Risk Management
Regional Head; IR Swaps Sales / Marketing — Jaromír Hronek *Head of Treasury* ☎ 2119 3150 ℻ 2119 3169
✉ hronek@commerzbank.cz

Foreign Exchange Derivatives / Risk Management
Cross-Currency Swaps, Sales / Marketing — Jaromír Hronek *Head of Treasury* ☎ 2119 3150 ℻ 2119 3169
✉ hronek@commerzbank.cz
Cross-Currency Swaps, Trading; Vanilla FX option Sales — Martin Kischer ☎ 2119 3153 ℻ 2119 3169

Corporate Finance / M&A Advisory
Fax: 2119 3239
Regional Head — Petr Vozka *Head, Corporate Banking* ☎ 2119 3210
Martin Herrmann *Head, Investment Banking* ☎ 2119 3350
Oliver Sipeer *Head, Corporate Banking* ☎ 2119 3200

Global Custody
Country Head — Renata Zaludova *Custody Manager* ☎ 2119 3370 ℻ 2119 3379
✉ renata.zaludova@commerzbank.cz

Other Departments
Private Banking — Ines Schober *Head of Private Banking* ☎ 2119 3300 ℻ 2119 3509
Correspondent Banking — Ralph Klose *Head, Trade Finance* ☎ 2119 3270

Administration
Technology & Systems
Zdenek Blazek ☎ 2119 3571 ℻ 2119 3579

Public Relations
Iva Gottliebová ☎ 2119 3330 ℻ 2119 3339

Commerzbank Capital Markets (Eastern Europe) as

Subsidiary Company

Alternative trading name: Commerzbank Capital Markets
Myslikova 31, 110 00 Prague 1
Tel: (2) 2190 8111 **Fax:** (2) 2190 8119
Website: www.commerzbank-capital-markets.cz

Senior Executive Officers
Member of the Board of Managing Directors — Klaus Patig ☎ 1362 2973 ✉ klaus.patig@ccme.cz
Managing Director — John J Vax ☎ 2190 8500 ✉ john.vax@ccme.cz
Managing Director — Volker Widdel ☎ 2190 8200 ✉ volker.widdel@ccme.cz

Debt Capital Markets / Fixed Income
Head of Fixed Income — Bernd Kuehl *Trader* ☎ 2190 8511 ✉ bernd.kuehl@ccme.cz

Settlement / Clearing
Head of Settlement / Clearing — John Halls *Settlements Manager* ☎ 2190 8230 ✉ john.halls@ccme.cz

Administration
Head of Administration — Helmut Mazuch *Head of Administration* ☎ 2190 8210
✉ helmut.mazuch@ccme.cz

Accounts / Audit
Steve Withers *Accounting Manager* ☎ 2190 8240
✉ steve.withers@ccme.cz

www.euromoneydirectory.com   CZECH REPUBLIC (+420)

Credit Suisse First Boston (Prague) as
Subsidiary Company
Staromestské námestí 15, 110 00 Prague 1
Tel: (2) 2481 0937 Fax: (2) 2481 0996
Senior Executive Officers
Director   Michal Susak

Deutsche Bank
Full Branch Office
Jungmannova 34, 110 00 Prague 1
PO Box 829, 111 21 Prague 1
Tel: (2) 2119 1111 Fax: (2) 2422 5727 Telex: 123164 Swift: DEUT CZ PX
Controlling Fax: 2409 8260; Corporate Banking Fax: 2119 1222; Global Markets - FX/Sales Fax: 2409 8260; Global Markets - Money Market/Repo Tel: 2688 5757 ext 5903; Group Services Fax: 2409 8260; Mangement Fax: 2119 1411; Personnel Fax: 2421 0275; Trade Finance Fax: 2119 1255
Website: www.deutshe-bank.de
Senior Executive Officers
Director   Thomas Haag
Director   Jaroslav Kudena

European Bank for Reconstruction & Development
Representative Office
Karlova 27, 110 00 Prague 1
Tel: (2) 2423 9070 Fax: (2) 2423 3077
Senior Executive Officers
Senior Banker & Co-Head   Igor Ocka
Senior Banker & Co-Head   Joaquin Gefaell

Expandia Bank as
Head Office
Formerly known as: Zemská banka as
Ovocnydrh 8, 11 000 Prague
Tel: (2) 2211 5222 Fax: (2) 2211 5300
Senior Executive Officers
General Manager   Jan Kala

Fleming Investment Management Limited
Subsidiary Company
Celdni 19, 110 00 Prague
Tel: (2) 2481 2711 Fax: (2) 2481 1487

Foresbank as
Head Office
Prílucká 360, 760 01 Zlin
Tel: (67) 762 6100; (67) 762 6102 Fax: (67) 721 0833; (67) 762 6344 Telex: CZ62701 FORES C Swift: FORA CZ 22
Senior Executive Officers
Chairman   Radomír Satinský
Vice Chairman   Roman Vybíral
Vice Chairman   Miroslav Kucera
Financial Director   Helena Peskova *Chief Financial Officer*
Treasurer   Smejkal Zbysek
International Division   Pavol Capka *Director, Foreign Department*
General - Treasury
Head of Treasury   Helena Peskova *Treasury*
Debt Capital Markets / Fixed Income
Global Head   Dagmar Tomková *Manager*
Bonds - General
Domestic Securities - Origination   Mikel Zdenek *Trader*
                                      Pavel Kochta *Sales*
Domestic Securities - Syndication   Petra Rybnícková *Sales*

Euromoney Directory 1999   **321**

CZECH REPUBLIC (+420)　　　www.euromoneydirectory.com

Foresbank as (cont)
Foreign Exchange
Global Head　　　　　　　　　Ruzena Skokánková Manager
　　　　　　　　　　　　　　　Tomás Omelka Manager
Risk Management
Other (Exchange-Traded Derivatives)
Forfaiting, Factoring & Countertrade　　Roman Vybíral Vice Chairman
Corporate Finance / M&A Advisory
Global Head　　　　　　　　　Roman Vybíral Vice Chairman
Settlement / Clearing
Country Head　　　　　　　　Jiri Pala
Electronic Banking　　　　　　Tomás Rosi Director, MIS
Other Departments
Correspondent Banking　　　　Ivana Rosselová
Economic Research　　　　　　Helena Peskova Chief Financial Officer
Administration
Technology & Systems
　　　　　　　　　　　　　　　Tomás Rosi Director, MIS
Public Relations
　　　　　　　　　　　　　　　Mikel Zdenek Director, Marketing
Corporate Communications
　　　　　　　　　　　　　　　Mikel Zdenek Director, Marketing
Other (Administration)
Human Resources　　　　　　　Julie Zaydlarová Director, Personnel

Generale Bank   Representative Office
Oettingen Palace, Josefská 6, 118 00 Prague 1
Tel: (2) 534 759; (2) 548 376 **Fax:** (2) 538 895
Senior Executive Officers
Chief Representative　　　　　Ilona Toufarová

HYPO Bank CZ as   Subsidiary Company
Stepánská 27 & 33, 110 00 Prague 1
Tel: (2) 2110 6200 **Fax:** (2) 2110 6112 **Telex:** 122821 HYPO C **Swift:** HYPO CZ PP
Senior Executive Officers
Financial Director　　　　　　Mrs. Rehakova
Treasurer　　　　　　　　　　Milan Dubecky ☎ 2110 6400
Member, Board of Managing Directors　Ivan Cernohorsky ☎ 2110 6203
Member, Board of Managing Directors　Raimund P Zikeli

HypoVereinsbank (CZ) as   Subsidiary Company
Formerly known as: Vereinsbank (CZ) as
Italská 24, 12 149 Prague 2
Italská 24, P.O.Box 70, 12149 Prague
Tel: (2) 2209 1111 **Fax:** (2) 2225 1158 **Swift:** BVBE CZ PP **Reuters:** BVCS
Senior Executive Officers
Chairman　　　　　　　　　　Hans-Peter Horster ☎ 2209 1377 🖷 2225 0821
Others (Senior Executives)
Member of the Board　　　　　Karel Kratina ☎ 2209 1213 🖷 2225 1158
　　　　　　　　　　　　　　　David Svojitka ☎ 2209 1550 🖷 2225 2316
　　　　　　　　　　　　　　　Ivan Cernohorsky ☎ 2209 1111 🖷 2225 1158
Debt Capital Markets / Fixed Income
Fax: 2225 2316
Head of Fixed Income　　　　　Jirí Caldr ☎ 2209 1515
Head of Fixed Income Sales　　Jirí Caldr ☎ 2209 1515
Head of Fixed Income Trading　Jirí Caldr ☎ 2209 1515
Medium-Term Notes
Head of Sales　　　　　　　　Jirí Caldr ☎ 2209 1515
Head of Trading　　　　　　　Jirí Caldr ☎ 2209 1515

www.euromoneydirectory.com CZECH REPUBLIC (+420)

Mortgage-Backed Securities
Global Head Hana Jakubová ☎ 2209 1396

Syndicated Lending
Fax: 2225 1158
Head of Origination; Head of Syndication; Head of Trading Vaclav Vitha ☎ 2209 1214

Loan-Related Activities
Project Finance Vaclav Vitha ☎ 2209 1214
Structured Trade Finance Ulrich Burghardt ☎ 2209 1212 Ⓕ 2225 1158

Money Markets
Fax: 2225 2316
Global Head Martin Bláha ☎ 2209 1513 Ⓕ 2225 2316

Foreign Exchange
Global Head Martin Bláha ☎ 2209 1513 Ⓕ 2225 2316
Head of Institutional Sales Karel Jelínek ☎ 2209 1507
Corporate Sales; Head of Trading Milan Chupek ☎ 2209 1511

FX Traders / Sales People
Michaela Dostalová ☎ 2209 1509

Risk Management
Global Head Dietrich Bräuchle ☎ 2209 1222 Ⓕ 2225 1153

Foreign Exchange Derivatives / Risk Management
Cross-Currency Swaps, Sales / Marketing; Cross-Currency Swaps, Trading Martin Bláha ☎ 2209 1513 Ⓕ 2225 2316

Corporate Finance / M&A Advisory
Global Head Ulrich Burghardt ☎ 2209 1212 Ⓕ 2225 1158

Settlement / Clearing
Head of Settlement / Clearing Gavrilo Vucic ☎ 2209 1111 Ⓕ 2225 2316

Global Custody
Other (Global Custody)
Jana Hrabalová ☎ 2209 1238 Ⓕ 2225 2316

IC Banka as
Head Office

Pobrezni 3, 18 600 Prague 8
Tel: (2) 232 6508/9; (2) 232 6551/2 **Fax:** (2) 232 6549 **Telex:** 121816 ICBN C

Senior Executive Officers
Managing Director / General Manager Martin Houda ☎ 232 6502

ING Baring Capital Markets
Full Branch Office

9th Floor, Tower A, International Business Centre, Pobrezni 3, 186 00 Prague 8
Tel: (2) 232 0000 **Fax:** (2) 232 0026; (2) 2483 5061

Senior Executive Officers

General-Investment
Head of Investment Kent Holt *Director, Investment Banking* ☎ 2186 6420

Debt Capital Markets / Fixed Income
Head of Fixed Income Jan Mareš ☎ 2186 6425

Equity Capital Markets
Head of Equity Capital Markets Tomaš Horacek ☎ 2186 6426

ING Barings
Representative Office

IBC Building, Príkop 4, 602 00 Brno
Tel: (5) 4517 6240 **Fax:** (5) 4517 6240

Senior Executive Officers
Representative Zbyn K Dostál

Euromoney Directory 1999 **323**

CZECH REPUBLIC (+420)   www.euromoneydirectory.com

ING Barings
Representative Office

Moskevská 637/06, 460 01 Liberec
Tel: (48) 510 2159 Fax: (48) 510 0147

Senior Executive Officers
Manager   Milan Radkovic

ING Barings
Full Branch Office

Tower A, 9th Floor, International Business Center, Pobrizn 3, 186 00 Prague 8
Tel: (2) 232 0000 Fax: (2) 232 0026 Telex: 121913 INGB C Swift: INGB CZ PP Reuters: INCZ

Senior Executive Officers
Country Manager   Jan Struz

Others (Senior Executives)
   Jan Willem Overwater *Deputy General Manager*

Corporate Finance / M&A Advisory
Department: ING Baring Capital Markets
Fax: 2483 5061

Other (Corporate Finance)
Corporate Finance / Equity Brokerage & Trading   Igor Kocmnek

Other Departments
Department: ING Baring Private Bank
Private Banking   Jana H Florianova ℱ **2483 5011**

Interbanka as
Head Office

Václavské námestím 40, 110 00 Prague 1
Tel: (2) 2440 6111; (2) 2440 6215 Fax: (2) 2421 5591; (2) 2440 6343 Telex: 121181 INTB C Swift: INPA CZ PP Reuters: IBPR

Senior Executive Officers
Chairman & Chief Executive Officer   Vladimir Kolman ☎ **2440 6216**
Treasurer   Dušan Ordelt *Head of Treasury* ☎ **2440 6220**
Corporate & Fixed Income   Vlastimil Gencur ☎ **2440 6245**
General Secretary   Václav Prokeš ☎ **2440 6228**

Syndicated Lending
Tel: 2440 6313 Fax: 2440 6343
Head of Syndication   Richard Hlavaty *Senior Manager*

Money Markets
Fax: 2440 6343
Global Head   Dušan Ordelt *Head of Treasury* ☎ **2440 6220**

Foreign Exchange
Tel: 2440 6224 Fax: 2440 8291
Global Head   Radoslav Maxa *Senior Manager*

Risk Management
Tel: 2440 6208 Fax: 2440 8291
Global Head   Miroslava Habigtova

Other Departments
Private Banking   Tamara Narovcova ☎ **2440 6259**

International Finance Corporation
Representative Office

Husova 5, 110 00 Prague 1
Tel: (2) 2440 1402 Fax: (2) 2440 1410

Senior Executive Officers
Chief Representative   Milos Vecera

www.euromoneydirectory.com CZECH REPUBLIC (+420)

Investicní a Postovní banka as
Head Office

Senovázné námestím 32, 114 03 Prague 1
Tel: (2) 2401 1111 **Fax:** (2) 2424 4035; (2) 2424 4274 **Telex:** 122459 INRBC **Swift:** INBA CZ PP **Email:** info@ipb.cz
General Telex: 121445
Website: www.ipb.cz

Senior Executive Officers
Chairman   Jan Klacek
Vice Chairman   Libor Procházka
Financial Director   Stanislav Maxa *Senior Director*

Others (Senior Executives)
Member of the Board   Aladár Blaas ☏ **2204 2014**
                                                  Jirí Fárek ☏ **2204 2036**
                                                  Jirí Fabián
                                                  Alfréd Šebek ☏ **2204 2078**
                                                  Josef Horák
IPB Group Strategic Plan Management   Helena Jensová *Senior Director* ☏ **2204 2011**
Capital Operations   Jan Chalupa *Senior Director*
Banking Operations Division   Lubomír Štěpánik *Senior Director*
Postal Savings Bank   Jiñ Tydlacka *Senior Director*
Payments Division   Jitka Pantucková *Senior Director*

General-Investment
Head of Investment   Karel Haushalter *Senior Director* ☏ **2204 2034**

General - Treasury
Head of Treasury   Josef Ondrácek *Senior Director, Treasury* ☏ **2204 2017**

Foreign Exchange
Head of Foreign Exchange   Pavel Linhart *Senior Director* ☏ **2204 4806**

Administration
Technology & Systems
Management Systems Information Services   Jirí Samek *Senior Director, Credit Risk Management* ☏ **2204 2022**

Other (Administration)
Payments   Marie Marvanová *Senior Director* ☏ **2204 2042**

KBC Bank NV
Representative Office

Formerly known as: Kredietbank NV
Senovázné nám 19, 111 21 Prague 1
PO Box 473, 111 21 Prague
Tel: (2) 21616 101; (2) 21616 301 **Fax:** (2) 21616 302 **Email:** kbcbank@iol.cz

Senior Executive Officers
Senior Representative   Paul Vanoverloop
Representative   Marek Loula

Komercní banka as
Head Office

Formerly known as: KB
Na Príkope 33, PO Box 839, 114 07 Prague 1
Tel: (2) 2243 2111 **Fax:** (2) 2424 3020; (2) 2424 6035 **Telex:** 121831 **Swift:** KOMB CZ PP
Email: group_strategy@koba.cz **Reuters:** KOBA; KOBB; KOBC
Website: www.koba.cz

Senior Executive Officers
Chairman   Jan Kollert ☏ **2243 2031**
Chief Executive Officer   Jan Kollert ☏ **2243 2031**
Financial Director; Treasurer   Miroslav Sulai *Executive Director* ☏ **2189 2022**
Department Director   Ditmar Vladimír ☏ **2243 2105**
International Division   Vladimír Zácek *Department Director* ☏ **2119 2406**

Others (Senior Executives)
Retail Banking (Global Head)   Martin Škopek *Executive Director*
Payment Services Division   Otakar Schlossberger *Department Director* ☏ **2243 3021**

General-Lending (DCM, SL)
Head of Corporate Banking   Miroslaz Cermák ☏ **2243 6200**

General-Investment
Head of Investment   Lubor Zalman *Executive Director* ☏ **2243 6213**

CZECH REPUBLIC (+420)   www.euromoneydirectory.com

Komercní banka as (cont)
Debt Capital Markets / Fixed Income
Tel: 2200 8501 Fax: 2200 8690
Head of Fixed Income Trading   Nadezda Libnarová ☏ 2200 8239
Equity Capital Markets
Tel: 2200 8501 Fax: 2200 8690
Head of Trading   František Vencl ☏ 220 8226
Syndicated Lending
Tel: 2119 2406 Fax: 2421 9390
Head of Trading   Vladimir Zácek Director ☏ 2119 2406
Loan-Related Activities
Project Finance   Petr Kohout Department Director ☏ 2163 7240
Money Markets
Tel: 2200 8245 Fax: 2200 8691
Head of Money Markets   Richard Tykal Chief Dealer ☏ 2200 8245
Foreign Exchange
Head of Foreign Exchange   Tomáš Becvár Manager ☏ 2200 8215
Risk Management
Tel: 2200 8501 Fax: 2200 5690
Head of Risk Management   Josef Snopek Executive Director
      Roman Pospísil Department Director ☏ 2200 8501
Corporate Finance / M&A Advisory
Head of Corporate Finance   Radomír Lasák ☏ 2243 6200
Settlement / Clearing
Fax: 2421 3406
Head of Settlement / Clearing   David Buzga Department Director ☏ 2243 6221
Asset Management
Head   Jirí Šperl Department Director ☏ 2243 5046
Other Departments
Private Banking   Ales Mamica ☏ 2189 3397
Correspondent Banking   Martina Motlová Department Director ☏ 2119 2400
Debt Recovery / Restructuring   Oldrich Dobrý Executive Director ☏ 2243 2052
Administration
Head of Administration   Miloslav Šum Executive Director ☏ 2243 2020
Technology & Systems
Information Services   Miroslav Skorpík Executive Director ☏ 2243 3029
Legal / In-House Counsel
      Jirí Cerný Department Director ☏ 2402 2070
Public Relations
      Miloš Ruzicka ☏ 2243 2158
Accounts / Audit
      Karel Kafka Department Director ☏ 2423 4268
Other (Administration)
Human Resources Division   Václav Talír General Director ☏ 2119 2502

Konsolidacni banka Praha spú
Head Office

Janovského 438/2, 170 06 Prague 7
Tel: (2) 2014 1111 **Fax:** (2) 3337 0033 **Telex:** 122931 KOBP C **Swift:** KOBP CZ PP **Reuters:** KOBP
Website: www.kobp.cz

Senior Executive Officers
Chief Executive Officer   Libor Löfler ☏ 2014 2070
Financial Director   Dagmar Polanská ☏ 2014 3663
Treasurer   Ivan Duda ☏ 2014 3006

Landesbank Hessen-Thüringen Girozentrale
Representative Office

U Prasné brány 3, 110 00 Prague 1
Tel: (2) 2481 0886 **Fax:** (2) 231 6518

Senior Executive Officers
Representative   Kurt Olbert

326   Euromoney Directory 1999

www.euromoneydirectory.com   CZECH REPUBLIC (+420)

London Forfaiting Praha sro
Subsidiary Company

Trziste 13, 118 00 Prague 1
Tel: (2) 530 520; (2) 530 534 Fax: (2) 530 887

Senior Executive Officers
Managing Director   Dalibor Hanka

Others (Senior Executives)
                                   Tomáš Nymburský *Senior Manager*
                                   Adriana Vojtechová *Manager*
                                   František Zverina *Manager*
                                   Lubos Chyba *Assistant Manager*
                                   Petra Vavrova *Assistant*

Moravia Banka as
Head Office

Palackého 133, 738 02 Frydek-Místek
PO Box 88, 738 02 Frydek-Místek
Tel: (658) 606 111 Fax: (658) 606 225 Telex: 52171 MOBA C Swift: MOBA CZ 22 Email: international@moba.cz
Website: www.moba.cz

Senior Executive Officers
Chairman   Petr Gerlich
Chief Executive Officer   Jirí Barton
Chief Operating Officer   Kamila Jemelikova [T] **606 240**
Company Secretary   Martina Bílková [T] **606 222**
International Division   Rudolf Tauchman

Syndicated Lending

Loan-Related Activities
Trade Finance   Roman Gorgoš [T] **606 250** [F] **606 245**

Money Markets
Global Head   Emilia Matilcaková *Director* [T] **606 320** [F] **606 325**

Foreign Exchange
Global Head   Emilia Matilcaková *Director* [T] **606 320** [F] **606 325**

Risk Management
Tel: 606 228 Fax: 606 111
Head of Risk Management   Richard Woš

Corporate Finance / M&A Advisory

Other (Corporate Finance)
                                   Jan Rainisch *Director*

Other Departments
Correspondent Banking   Markéta Glajcová [T] **606 258** [F] **606 245**

Nomura International plc
Representative Office

Husova 5, 110 00 Prague 1
Tel: (2) 2440 1444 Fax: (2) 2424 8648

Senior Executive Officers
Chief Representative   Eiichi Yumoto

Norddeutsche Landesbank Girozentrale SRN
Representative Office

U Prasné Brány 3, 110 00 Prague 1
Tel: (2) 2481 0886 Fax: (2) 231 6518

Senior Executive Officers
Chief Representative   Kurt Olbert

Nova Ljubljanska banka dd
Representative Office

Na Príkope 6, 110 00 Prague 1
Tel: (2) 2422 5858; (2) 2422 2869 Fax: (2) 2422 5917

Senior Executive Officers
Resident Representative   Stefan Loncnar

Euromoney Directory 1999   **327**

CZECH REPUBLIC (+420)   www.euromoneydirectory.com

OB Aval
Head Office

Americká 16, 120 00 Prague 2
Tel: (2) 251 342; (2) 251 517 **Fax:** (2) 691 0466 **Email:** obaval@comp.cz

Senior Executive Officers
Chief Executive Officer   Pavel Mosna *Senior Chief Executive & MD* 🕾 **(2) 691 1787**

Patria Asset Management as

Alternative trading name: PAM

Husova 5, 110 00 Prague 1
Tel: (2) 2424 8770; (2) 2424 8752 **Fax:** (2) 2424 8744; (2) 2424 8769 **Email:** info@patria.cz
Website: www.patria-finance.com

Senior Executive Officers
Managing Director   Miroslav Dvorák
Deputy   Slávka Sehnalova

Others (Senior Executives)
    Sabina Surá *Assistant*

Patria Finance as
Head Office

Husova 5, 110 00 Prague 1
Tel: (2) 2424 8770 **Fax:** (2) 2424 8744 **Email:** info@patria.cz **Reuters:** PTRR-Z **Bloomberg:** PATR
Website: www.patria-finance.com

Senior Executive Officers
Chairman   Zdenek Bakala
Financial Director   Roger de Backker *Chief Financial Controller*
Treasurer   Jan Brozík *Head of Fixed Income*

Debt Capital Markets / Fixed Income
Head of Debt Capital Markets   Jan Brozík *Head of Fixed Income*

Equity Capital Markets
Head of Equity Capital Markets   Marco Anderegg 📧 **anderegg@patria.cz**

Corporate Finance / M&A Advisory
Head of Corporate Finance   Petr Motloch

Settlement / Clearing
Head of Settlement / Clearing   Natalie Vlóková

Asset Management
Head   Miroslav Dvorak *Managing Director*

Administration
Technology & Systems
    Petr Hons

Legal / In-House Counsel
In-House Counsel   Marek Belsán

Plzenská banka as
Head Office

nám Republiky 16, PO Box 322, 30622 Plzen
Tel: (19) 723 5354 **Fax:** (19) 723 5330

Senior Executive Officers
Manager   Eva Krizová

Pragobanka as
Head Office

Vinohradská 230, 100 00 Prague 10
Tel: (2) 6700 7111 **Fax:** (2) 6700 7255 **Telex:** 121776 PGBA **Swift:** PGBA CZ PP **Reuters:** PGBA

Senior Executive Officers
Chairman & Chief Executive Officer   Štefan Veselovský
Financial Director   Daniel Nedeliak
Treasurer   Josef Duchácek
International Division   Pavel Langr

www.euromoneydirectory.com   CZECH REPUBLIC (+420)

Others (Senior Executives)
Irena Bobková
Petr Kunštát
Jiří Rozinek

General-Lending (DCM, SL)
Head of Corporate Banking   Pavel Langr

General-Investment
Head of Investment   Pavel Langr

Other Departments
Private Banking   Pavel Langr

První Mestká Banka as
Head Office

Formerly known as: Royal Banka CS as
Malé Námestí 11, 111 21 Prague 1
PO Box 897, 111 21 Prague 1
Tel: (2) 2161 1200; (2) 2161 1202 **Fax:** (2) 2161 1497; (2) 2161 1498 **Telex:** 121515 PMB DC **Swift:** PMBP CZ PP
Reuters: PMBA
Website: www.pmb.cz

Senior Executive Officers
Chairman & General Manager   Leoš Pýtr ☎ **2161 1200 ext 200**
Treasurer   Zdenek Lust *Chief Manager* ☎ **2161 1200 ext 403**
Chairman & General Manager   Leoš Pýtr ☎ **2161 1200 ext 200**
International Division   Vladimír Gulla *Deputy Chairman & General Manager* ☎ **2161 1200 ext 319**

Debt Capital Markets / Fixed Income
Head of Fixed Income   Vladimír Gulla *Deputy Chairman & General Manager* ☎ **2161 1200 ext 319**

Equity Capital Markets
Global Head   Jaruslav Zák *Chief Manager* ☎ **2161 1200 ext 304**

Syndicated Lending
Head of Origination; Head of Syndication   Tomáš Pakosta *Chief Manager* ☎ **2161 1200 ext 344**

Loan-Related Activities
Trade Finance   Pavel Boháček *Chief Manager* ☎ **2161 1200 ext 230**
Project Finance   Tomáš Pakosta *Chief Manager* ☎ **2161 1200 ext 344**

Money Markets
Head of Money Markets   Zdenek Lust *Chief Manager* ☎ **2161 1200 ext 403**

Foreign Exchange
Head of Foreign Exchange   Zdenek Lust *Chief Manager* ☎ **2161 1200 ext 403**

Other Departments
Correspondent Banking   Vera Platilová *Senior Officer* ☎ **2161 1200 ext 409**

Raiffeisenbank as
Head Office

Vodickova 38, 110 00 Prague 1
PO Box 563, 111 21 Prague
Tel: (2) 2423 1270; (2) 2423 1280 **Fax:** (2) 2423 1278 **Telex:** 123160 RZBP C **Swift:** RZBC CZ PP
Email: raiffeisenbank@rb.cz **Reuters:** RAIF

Senior Executive Officers
Chairman   John D. Harris ☎ **2440 7101**
Chief Operating Officer   Pierre Brisse *Head of Operations* ☎ **2440 7202**
Treasurer   Petr Tomek *Head of Treasury* ☎ **2440 7141**
Executive Director   Jan Vlachy ☎ **2440 7101**
International Division   Pavel Trcka *Division Manager* ☎ **2440 7114**

General-Lending (DCM, SL)
Head of Corporate Banking   Petr Dedek *Division Manager* ☎ **2440 7258**

General-Investment
Head of Investment   Pavel Trcka *Division Manager* ☎ **2440 7114**

Syndicated Lending

Loan-Related Activities
Trade Finance   Iva Soltysova *Head* ☎ **2440 7147**
Project Finance   Jan Rydl *Head, Structured Finance* ☎ **2440 7133**

Foreign Exchange
Head of Foreign Exchange   Petr Tomek *Head of Treasury* ☎ **2440 7141**

CZECH REPUBLIC (+420) www.euromoneydirectory.com

Raiffeisenbank as (cont)

Risk Management
Head of Risk Management — Michael Grahammer *Head of Risk Management* ☎ 2440 7289

Settlement / Clearing
Head of Settlement / Clearing — Pierre Brisse *Head of Operations* ☎ 2440 7202

Global Custody
Head of Global Custody — Radek Novotný *Head of Operations* ☎ 2440 7118

Asset Management
Portfolio Management — Jan Rydl ☎ 2440 7114

Other Departments
Correspondent Banking — Pavel Trcka *Division Manager* ☎ 2440 7114
Cash Management — Pavel Sikora *Head, Cash Management* ☎ 2440 7185

Administration
Technology & Systems
Vladimir Vagner *Head of Systems* ☎ 2440 7190

Legal / In-House Counsel
Juraj Szabõ *Head of Legal Department* ☎ 2440 7108

Compliance
Ivan Zemlicka *Internal Auditor* ☎ 2440 7183

Public Relations
Martin Kupka *Head of Strategy and Research* ☎ 2440 7278

Schmidtbank Hof / Saale — Representative Office

Moskevská 2, 360 21 Karlovy Vary
Tel: (17) 322 4509 **Fax:** (17) 322 4102

Senior Executive Officers
Representative — Petr Pultar

Schmidtbank Hof / Saale — Representative Office

Sedláčkova 11, 301 11 Plzen
Tel: (19) 722 7196 **Fax:** (19) 722 7231

Senior Executive Officers
Representative — Petr Pultar

Société Générale — Full Branch Office

Smetanovo nám 1, 702 00 Ostrava 1
Tel: (69) 611 2017; (69) 611 2018 **Fax:** (69) 612 1904 **Email:** martin.pistak@socgen.com

Senior Executive Officers
Head — Martin Pisták

Société Générale — Full Branch Office

Formerly known as: Société Générale Komercní Banka AS SGKB & Société Générale Banka as SGB
Pobrezní 3, 186 00 Prague 8
Tel: (2) 2483 2300 **Fax:** (2) 2483 2487 **Telex:** 122735 SOGE **Swift:** SOGE CZ PP **Reuters:** SGPG **Telex:** 123385 SOGE;
Reuters: SGPR (Dealing)

Senior Executive Officers
Chief Executive Officer
Chief Operating Officer
Managing Director
Managing Director, Capital Markets

Claude Blanot *Chief Executive Officer*
Lionel Ridé *Chief Operating Officer*
Matús Púll
Lars Hakanson

General-Lending (DCM, SL)
Head of Corporate Banking — Luc Delaunay *Managing Director*

Debt Capital Markets / Fixed Income
Department: Dealing Room
Head of Debt Capital Markets — Lars Hakanson *Managing Director, Capital Markets*
Head of Fixed Income Sales — Milos Kral *Head, Corporate Desk*
Head of Fixed Income Trading — Ivan Varga *Head, Traders*

www.euromoneydirectory.com CZECH REPUBLIC (+420)

Syndicated Lending
Other (Syndicated Lending)
Loan Administration   Iva Berková *Head*

Loan-Related Activities
Trade Finance   Milada Kubernátová *Head*

Other (Trade Finance)
Letters of Guarantee   Jindra Fridrichová *Head*
Letters of Credit   Vera Langrová *Head*
Forfaiting & ST Export Financing   Andrea Strauchová *Head*
Export Project Finance   Jirí Vorác *Head*
Marketing   Dagmar Lomecká *Head*

Risk Management
Country Head   Hervé Bel *Head, Risk Control*
                                        Frantisek Reich *Head, Risk Assessment*

Corporate Finance / M&A Advisory
Country Head   Milan Tuma *Head*

Settlement / Clearing
Settlement (General)   Simona Azilinova *Head, Treasury Operations*
Department: Cash & Transfer
Other   Andrea Klímová *Head, Domestic Transfers*
                                        Miroslava Pešková *Head, International Transfers*
                                        Roman Bílý *Head, Cash Desk*

Other Departments
Correspondent Banking   Simona Sobotková *Commercial Manager, Correspondent Banking*

Administration
Head of Administration   Dagmar Bydzovoská
                                        Jitka Vojtová *Head, General Administration*

Technology & Systems
Computer   Tomáš Klíma *Head, EDP*

Legal / In-House Counsel
                                        Iva Stepánková *Head, Legal Advisers*

Compliance
Management Control   Pierre Meme *Head*

Accounts / Audit
Internal Audit   Anna Horácková *Head*
                                        Zora Procházkova *Head, Commercial Managers*
                                        Markéta Nováková *Commercial Manager*
                                        Petr Pastyrík *Commercial Manager*
Accounting   Josef Král *Head*

Other (Administration)
SWIFT   Tomáš Pithart *Head*
Personnel   Milena Ortová *Head*

Société Générale Banka   Full Branch Office
Príkop 8, 604 60 Brno
Tel: (5) 4521 5908 Fax: (5) 4521 5909

Senior Executive Officers
Head   Tomás Hron

Others (Senior Executives)
                                        Jurmil Vlach *Regional Manager*

Union banka as   Head Office
30 dubna no 35, 702 00 Ostrava
Tel: (69) 610 8111 Fax: (69) 211 586 Telex: 121949 UNBO C Swift: UNBA CZ 22
Website: www.union.cz

Senior Executive Officers
Chairman & President   Marie Parmová
Chief Executive Officer   Jozef Dejcík ☏ **610 8208**
Financial Director   Tomas Seidler ☏ **610 8325**
Treasurer   Jiri Adamec ☏ **(2) 2201 8306**
Company Secretary   Ivan Kupa ☏ **610 8265**

CZECH REPUBLIC (+420)   www.euromoneydirectory.com

Union banka as (cont)
Administration
Public Relations
Press Office   Josef Rericha T 615 6251 F 612 4043

Union Européenne de CIC   Representative Office

Alternative trading name: CIC Banques/ L'Union Européenne de CIC
Vodickova 17, 110 00 Prague 1
Tel: (2) 2494 7579 **Fax:** (2) 2494 6966
Senior Executive Officers
Representative   Ivan Panak

Universal banka as   Head Office

PO Box 775, Senovázné Nam 4, 111 21 Prague
Tel: (2) 2421 2902 **Fax:** (2) 2421 2899 **Email:** jan.ringelhan@univ.cz **Reuters:** UNVR
Senior Executive Officers
Chairman & General Manager   Jan Rolc T 2218 9224
Chief Operating Officer   Ladislav Kubícek *Deputy General Manager* T 2218 9210
Treasurer   Jan Ringelhán *Head of A & L Management* T (47) 523 2291
Chairman & General Manager   Jan Rolc T 2218 9224
Company Secretary   Zdenek Zedník T 2218 9203
General-Investment
Head of Investment   Markéta Hlavicová *Head, Investment Banking & Money Markets*
    T 2218 9303 F 2421 2976
Debt Capital Markets / Fixed Income
Head of Fixed Income   Igor Bezdek T 2218 9305
Equity Capital Markets
Head of Equity Capital Markets   Martin Stolfa T 2218 9307
Syndicated Lending
Head of Origination   Josef Styblík *Head, Commerce Department* T 2218 9431
Money Markets
Head of Money Markets   Pavel Novotný *Head of Money Markets* T 2218 9304 F 267 217
Foreign Exchange
Head of Foreign Exchange   Pavel Novotný *Head of Money Markets* T 2218 9304 F 267 217
Settlement / Clearing
Head of Settlement / Clearing   Zdenka Machová *Head of Accounting* T +420 (47) 523 2275
Other Departments
Chief Credit Officer   Stanislav Ovešlo T 2218 9436
Private Banking   Bozena Formánková *Head, Banking Services Department* T (47) 523 2260
Correspondent Banking   Katerina Pavlícková T (47) 523 2213
Administration
Head of Marketing   Monika Krízová T (47) 523 2259
Technology & Systems
Informatics Department   Roman Jiroudek *Head* T (47) 523 2258
Legal / In-House Counsel
Legal Services   Hana Klempová *Head* T (47) 523 2251
Accounts / Audit
Internal Audit   Jaroslava Prazáková *Head* T (47) 523 2256

Volksbank as   Full Branch Office

Heršpická 5, 658 26 Brno
PO Box 226, 658 26 Brno
Tel: (5) 4352 5111; (5) 4352 5456 **Fax:** (5) 4352 5555 **Swift:** VBOECZ2X **Email:** mail@volksbank.cz
Senior Executive Officers
Chief Executive Officer   Johann Lurf T 4352 5456 F 4352 5556 E lurf@volksbank.cz
Others (Senior Executives)
Member of Management Board   Karl Schinagl T 4352 5705 F 4352 5552 E schinagl@volksbank.cz
    Herbert Skok T 4352 5705 F 4352 5552 E skok@voksbank.cz
Director of Payments   Ivana Beltramová T 4352 5329 F 4352 5552 E beltramova@volksbank.cz
Controller   Andrea Krupková T 4352 5438 F 4352 5556 E krupkova@volksbank.cz

www.euromoneydirectory.com CZECH REPUBLIC (+420)

General - Treasury
Head of Treasury Radovan Zednícek T 4352 5702 F 4352 5554 E zednicek@volksbank.cz
Asset Management
Head Helmut Rührer T 4352 5445 F 4352 5556 E ruhrer@volksbank.cz
Administration
Head of Marketing Jana Šafránková T 43525309 F 4352 5552 E safrankova@volksbank.cz
Technology & Systems
  Tomáš Zeman T 4352 5656 F 4352 5554 E zeman@volksbank.cz

Legal / In-House Counsel
Legal Aleš Vymazal T 4352 5215 F 4352 5555
Public Relations
Human Resources Zbyněk Pospíšek T 4352 5426 F 4352 5556 E popisek@volksbank.cz
Accounts / Audit
Internal Auditing Zdenek Laudát T 43525423 F 43525556 E laudat@volksbank.cz
Accountant Libuše Ohnisková T 4352 5307 F 4352 5552 E ohniskova@volksbank.cz
Other (Administration)
Organization Milana Niedermayerová T 4352 5318 F 4352 5554
  E niedermayerova@volksbank.cz
Statistics Bohuslav Donar T 4352 5439 F 4352 5556 E donar@volksbank.cz

Všeobecná úverová banka as Full Branch Office

Celetná 31, 111 21 Prague 1
Tel: (2) 2421 9891; (2) 232 3776 **Fax:** (2) 232 8796; (2) 231 0206 **Email:** vubnuibm@ms.anet.cz
Senior Executive Officers
Branch Director Jan Vinter
Deputy Branch Manager Pavol Malickay

Westdeutsche Landesbank Girozentrale Representative Office

Králodvorská 13, 110 00 Prague 1
Tel: (2) 232 3484; (2) 232 2010 **Fax:** (2) 231 4205 **Email:** repre@westlb.cz
Senior Executive Officers
Representative Robert Hessenberger
Administration
Head of Administration Miriana Panska
Head of Marketing Magda Rejentova *Marketing Officer*

Wood & Company Head Office

Martinska 4, 110 00 Prague 1
Tel: (2) 2422 7731 **Fax:** (2) 2422 7759 **Email:** wood@wood.com **Reuters:** WOCO **Bloomberg:** BLOOM: WOOD
Website: www.wood.com
Senior Executive Officers
Chairman Preston Rabl
Chief Executive Officer Richard Wood *Managing Director*
Financial Director Trevor Pettifar
General Manager Jan Sykora
Others (Senior Executives)
Head of Research Vladimir Jaros
Marketing / PR Mark Rutherford *Marketing Manager*
Funds Management Mark Sanders
Equity Capital Markets
Department: Equity Capital Markets
Tel: 695 0746 **Fax:** 695 0505
Head of Equity Capital Markets Mikolaj Dietrich
International Equities
Head of Sales Christopher Fitzwilliam - Lay *Director of Sales*
Head of Trading Alexander Angell *Director of Trading*
Equity Research
Head of Equity Research Vladimir Jaros
Settlement / Clearing
Head of Settlement / Clearing Peter Musil

Euromoney Directory 1999 **333**

CZECH REPUBLIC (+420)   www.euromoneydirectory.com

Wood & Company (cont)
Administration
Legal / In-House Counsel
　　　　　　　　　　　　　Lenka Malouskova *Head of Compliance*
Compliance
　　　　　　　　　　　　　Lenka Malouskova *Head of Compliance*

Zivnostenská Banka AS   Head Office

Na Príkopé 20, 113 80 Prague 1
PO Box 421, 113 80 Prague 1
Tel: (2) 2412 1111 **Fax:** (2) 2412 5555 **Telex:** 122313 ZIBA C **Swift:** ZIBA CZ PP **Email:** info@ziba.cz
Website: www.ziba.cz

Senior Executive Officers
Chairman, Board of Directors 　　Jiri Kunert ☎ 2412 1001 📠 2422 5140
Chief Executive Officer 　　　　　Jiri Kunert *Chairman, Board of Directors* ☎ 2412 1001 📠 2422 5140
Company Secretary 　　　　　　　Jirina Roubícková ☎ 2412 1001 📠 2422 5140
General-Lending (DCM, SL)
Head of Corporate Banking 　　　Pavel Chlumský *Managing Director* ☎ 2412 7107 📠 2412 7172
General-Investment
Head of Investment 　　　　　　　Peter K Medlock *Managing Director* ☎ 2412 8501 📠 2412 8505
Equity Capital Markets
Equity Research
Head of Equity Research 　　　　Pavel Sobíšek *Management* ☎ 2412 7212 📠 2412 8505
Syndicated Lending
Loan-Related Activities
Trade Finance; Project Finance 　Petr Merezko *Director, Structured Finance* ☎ 2412 7512 📠 2412 7273
Money Markets
Global Head 　　　　　　　　　　Peter K Medlock *Managing Director* ☎ 2412 8501 📠 2412 8505
Foreign Exchange
Global Head 　　　　　　　　　　Peter K Medlock *Managing Director* ☎ 2412 8501 📠 2412 8505
Settlement / Clearing
Head of Settlement / Clearing 　　Miraslav Matoušek *Director, Operations* ☎ 2412 1032 📠 2412 8282
Global Custody
Head of Global Custody 　　　　　Petra Mecavová *Manager* ☎ 2412 8140 📠 2412 7474 📧 mecavova@ziba.cz
Other Departments
Private Banking 　　　　　　　　Martin Kuyl *Managing Director* ☎ 2412 7245 📠 2412 7474
Correspondent Banking 　　　　　Miloslava Kalfusová *Director* ☎ 2412 8401 📠 2412 8484
Administration
Technology & Systems
　　　　　　　　　　　　　　　　Martin Pilecký *Director* ☎ 2412 5001 📠 2412 5252
Legal / In-House Counsel
　　　　　　　　　　　　　　　　Ivana Buresová *Director, Legal Affairs* ☎ 2412 3001 📠 2412 1313
Public Relations
　　　　　　　　　　　　　　　　Karel Jezek *Manager* ☎ 2412 1007 📠 2512 1717
Accounts / Audit
　　　　　　　　　　　　　　　　Anna Smutná *Director, Finance Division* ☎ 2512 4001 📠 2412 4040

DENMARK
(+45)

Danmarks Nationalbank   🏛 Central Bank

Havnegade 5, DK-1093 Copenhagen
Tel: 3363 6363 **Fax:** 3363 7103 **Telex:** 27051
Website: www.nationalbanken.dk

Senior Executive Officers
Governor & Chairman 　　　　　Bodil Nyboe Andersen
Governor 　　　　　　　　　　　Torben Nielsen
Board of Governors 　　　　　　Jens Thomsen
Secretariat 　　　　　　　　　　Kirsten Mordhorst

334　Euromoney Directory 1999

Senior Executive Officers (cont)
International Division   Benny Andersen *Head of International Department*

Others (Senior Executives)
Financial Markets   Jørgen Ovi *Assistant Governor*
Ib Hansen *Head of Department*
Ove Sten Jensen *Head of Department*

Settlement / Clearing
Operations   Ole Christian Hansen *Head of Market Operations*
Frank Nielsen *Head of Market Operations*
Niels Erik Sørensen *Head of Market Operations*
Hans Denkov *Assistant Director, Market Operations*

Other Departments
Economic Research   Hugo Frey Jensen *Head of Department*
Anders Møller Christensen *Director*

Administration
Technology & Systems
Information Technology   Jørgen Petersen *Assistant Head of Department*
Leif Kjærgaard *Head of IT*

Legal / In-House Counsel
Legal Section   Kirsten Rohde Jensen *Assistant Head of Department*

Accounts / Audit
Accounting   Kjeld Røhl *Chief Accountant*
Viggo Sørensen *Head of Department*
Audit   Henrik Larsen *Chief Auditor*

Other (Administration)
Cash Department   Tage Heering *Chief Cashier*
Payment Systems   Jesper Berg *Head of Payment Systems*
Personnel & Organizational   Flemming Farup *Head of Personnel*
Statistics   John Larsen *Head of Statistics*
Jens Hjorth Hald *Advisor*

ABN AMRO Bank   Full Branch Office
Midtermolen 7, PO Box 2575, DK-2100 Copenhagen O
PO Box 2575, DK-2100 Copenhagen O
Tel: 3544 3544 **Fax:** 3544 3535 **Telex:** 16518 **Swift:** ABNA DK KK AXXX

Senior Executive Officers
Country Manager   Robert Lindo

Others (Senior Executives)
Commercial   F Mortensen *Senior Vice President*

General - Treasury
Head of Treasury   T Helstrup *SVP & Head of Treasury*

Debt Capital Markets / Fixed Income
Head of Fixed Income   F Meere *Senior Vice President*
Head of Fixed Income Trading   L Kofoed *Vice President*

Fixed-Income Repo
Head of Repo   Bo Aagaard *Vice President*
Trading   Lene Nielsen *Trading*
Kim Jakobsen *Trading*

Alfred Berg Bank A/S   Full Branch Office
Amaliegade 35, DK-1256 Copenhagen
Tel: 3396 1000 **Fax:** 3396 1100 **Telex:** 16894

Senior Executive Officers
Chief Executive Officer   Claus Gregersen
Financial Director   Per Kold Anker *Finance Director*

Equity Capital Markets
Head of Equity Capital Markets   Henrik Heideby

Domestic Equities
Head of Syndication   Edward Plumbly
Head of Sales   Michael Dam
Head of Trading   John Lauritsen
Head of Research   Torben Danielsen

DENMARK (+45)   www.euromoneydirectory.com

Alfred Berg Bank A/S (cont)

International Equities
Head of Sales   Jack Austern

Corporate Finance / M&A Advisory
Head of Corporate Finance   Henrik Heideby

Settlement / Clearing
Head of Settlement / Clearing   Ilze Kazeks

Administration

Legal / In-House Counsel
                                           Per Kold Anker *Finance Director*

Alm Brand Bank   Head Office

Jarmers Plads 7, DK-1551 Copenhagen V
Tel: 3330 7030 **Fax:** 3314 1188 **Telex:** 16858 ALMBK DK **Swift:** ALMB DK KK

Debt Capital Markets / Fixed Income
Head of Debt Capital Markets   Brian Kudsk *General Manager*

Domestic Government Bonds
Head of Sales   Brian Kudsk *General Manager*
Head of Trading   Jan Olufsen *Trader*

Medium-Term Notes
Head of Trading   Jan Olufsen *Trader*

Asset-Backed Securities / Securitization
Head of Trading   Jan Olufsen *Trader*

Equity Capital Markets
Head of Equity Capital Markets   Johnny Madsen *Head*

International Equities
Head of Origination; Head of Sales   Kristian Klinge

Convertibles / Equity-Linked
Head of Sales; Head of Trading   Brian Kudsk *General Manager*

Money Markets
Head of Money Markets   Ken Samuelsen *Manager*

Eurocommercial Paper
Head of Trading   Ken Samuelsen *Manager*

Other (Wholesale Deposits)
Eurocurrency Deposits; Euronotes, CDs   Ken Samuelsen *Manager*

Foreign Exchange
Head of Foreign Exchange   Thomas Kortbech
Regional Head   Ken Samuelsen *Manager*

Risk Management
Head of Risk Management   Kristian Myrup *Manager*

Fixed Income Derivatives / Risk Management
IR Swaps Trading   Mads Hørberg *Manager*

Foreign Exchange Derivatives / Risk Management
Cross-Currency Swaps, Trading   Kristian Myrup *Manager*

Other (Exchange-Traded Derivatives)
IR Derivatives   Jan Olufsen *Trader*
Equity Derivitaves   Ken Samuelsen *Manager*

Exchange-Traded Derivatives
FX Futures   -   Ken Samuelsen *Manager*
FX Options   Ken Samuelsen *Manager*

Settlement / Clearing
Head of Settlement / Clearing   Kirsten Bang *Head*

Amagerbanken A/S
Head Office

Amagerbrogade 25, DK-2300 Copenhagen
Tel: 3295 6090; 3295 0598 **Fax:** 3254 4534 **Telex:** 31262 AMABK DK **Swift:** AMBK DK KK
Cable: AMAGERBANKEN COPENHAGEN
Banknotes Tel: 3157 1717; **Domestic Market Investment Tel:** 3295 2416; **Forex Tel:** 3295 1698; **International Bonds & Shares Tel:** 3254 5060; **Reuters:** AMCA-B (Domestic Market Investment); AMAG (Forex)

Senior Executive Officers
Chief Executive Officer   Knud Christensen
Managing Director   Bent Schön Hansen
International Division   Peder Krag *EVP, Treasury & International Division*

General - Treasury
Head of Treasury   Peder Krag *EVP, Treasury & International Division*

Money Markets
Money Markets - General
Banknotes   Jørgen Petersen *Manager*

Foreign Exchange
Global Head   Peder Krag *EVP, Treasury & International Division*
FX Traders / Sales People
Chief Dealer   Flemming Rasmussen

Settlement / Clearing
Settlement (General)   Øyvind Egelund *Head of Settlements*

Administration
Other (Administration)
Foreign Department   Robert G Olsen *Manager*
Commercial Clients   Jeppe Kjærgaard

Amtssparekassen Fyn A/S
Head Office

Vestre Stationsvej 7, DK-5100 Odense C
Tel: 6614 0474 **Fax:** 6614 7995 **Telex:** 59778 AMSPAR DK **Swift:** AMSP DK 22 **Reuters:** AMSP (Dealing)

Senior Executive Officers
Others (Senior Executives)
    Kaj O Mortensen *Executive Vice President*
    Erik G Hansen *Vice President & Head of Sales*

Debt Capital Markets / Fixed Income
Head of Debt Capital Markets   Kaj O Mortensen *Executive Vice President*

Domestic Government Bonds
Head of Sales   Erik G Hansen *Vice President* 6612 6066
Head of Trading   Jan Stentoft *Head of Interbank Relations* 6613 4698
Head of Research   Allan Andreasen *Chief Analyst*

Eurobonds
Head of Sales   Erik G Hansen *Vice President* 6612 6066
Head of Trading   Jorgen M Hansen *Senior Manager* 6612 6648

Asset-Backed Securities / Securitization
Global Head   Erik G Hansen *Vice President* 6612 6066

Mortgage-Backed Securities
Global Head   Erik G Hansen *Vice President* 6612 6066
Head of Trading   Peter Brink *Senior Trader* 6612 0093

Fixed-Income Repo
Head of Repo   Jan Stentoft *Head of Interbank Relations* 6613 4698

Equity Capital Markets
Global Head   Erik G Hansen *Vice President* 6612 6066

Domestic Equities
Head of Sales   Per Hunniche *Senior Dealer* 6613 5470
Head of Research   Lars Jorgen Rasmussen *Head of Research* 6614 0431

Money Markets
Global Head   Kaj O Mortensen *Executive Vice President*
Country Head   Jan Stentoft *Head of Interbank Relations* 6613 4698

DENMARK (+45) www.euromoneydirectory.com

Amtssparekassen Fyn A/S (cont)
Foreign Exchange
Global Head Jan Stentoft *Head of Interbank Relations* ☎ **6613 4698**

FX Traders / Sales People
All Currencies Mikael Slot *Senior Dealer* ☎ **6590 8480**
Henrik Fauerby *Senior Dealer* ☎ **6613 4363**

Risk Management
Tel: 6614 0474 Fax: 6614 7995
Head of Risk Management Allan Andreasen *Chief Analyst*

Fixed Income Derivatives / Risk Management
Global Head Jan Stentoft *Head of Interbank Relations* ☎ **6613 4698**
IR Swaps Trading Kurt Madsen *Senior Dealer* ☎ **6590 8480**

Settlement / Clearing
Head of Settlement / Clearing Jes Moller Madsen *Head of Settlements*

Other Departments
Correspondent Banking Karl Therkildsen *Foreign Manager*

Administration

Technology & Systems
Technology & Systems Peter Olsen *Area Manager*

Compliance
  Jorn Thomsen *Legal Advisor*

Public Relations
  Kurt Jensen *Area Manager*

A/S Arbejdernes Landsbank   Head Office

Vesterbrogade 5, DK-1502 Copenhagen V
Tel: 3338 8000 Fax: 3338 8910 Telex: 15633 Swift: ALBA DK KK

Senior Executive Officers
Chairman Anton Johannsen
Managing Director / General Manager Ernst Midtgaard

Bank of Copenhagen   Head Office

Alternative trading name: Den Københavnske Bank A/S
Oestergade 4/6, DK-1100 Copenhagen K
Tel: 3311 1515; 3315 7415 Fax: 3332 6004 Telex: 15977, 15168 Swift: BCPH DK KK Cable: BANCOP

Senior Executive Officers
Chairman Ingemar Gustafsson
President & Chief Executive Officer Jörgen Lamp
General Manager Kristian Biel

Others (Senior Executives)
Finance & Accounting, Credits Kristian Biel *General Manager*

General - Treasury
Head of Treasury Palle Sørensen *Manager, Foreign Dept & Treasury*
  Ole Thomsen *Account Manager*

Debt Capital Markets / Fixed Income

Asset-Backed Securities / Securitization
Head of Trading Jesper Niclsen *Manager, Securities Department*

Asset Management
Portfolio Management Palle Sørensen *Manager*

Other Departments
Correspondent Banking Palle Sørensen *Manager*

www.euromoneydirectory.com   DENMARK (+45)

BG BANK A/S
Head Office

Formerly known as: Bikuben Girobank A/S
Alternative trading name: BG Markets
10 Højbro Plads, DK-1017 Copenhagen K
Tel: 4330 3030 **Fax:** 4330 6161 **Telex:** 21571 BGMKTS DK **Reuters:** BGBONDS1 **Bloomberg:** BG
Reuters: BGBONDS2
Website: www.bgbank.dk

Senior Executive Officers
Chairman   Peter Højzland
Chief Executive Officer   Henrik Thufoson
Financial Director   Henning Skovlund *Managing Director*
Treasurer   Søren Kaare Anderson *Managing Director*

Others (Senior Executives)
Head of Research   Keld Holm ☏ **4330 5137**

Debt Capital Markets / Fixed Income
Fax: 3312 7756
Head of Fixed Income Sales   Frank Fryd Petersen ☏ **4330 5154**
Head of Fixed Income Trading   Svend Pedersen ☏ **4330 5308**

Government Bonds
Head of Sales   Frank Fryd Petersen ☏ **4330 5154**
Head of Trading   Erik Bladt ☏ **4330 5146**
Head of Syndication   Lars Egedoc ☏ **4330 5568**

Libor-Based / Floating-Rate Products
FRN Trading   Ole Lindholt ☏ **4330 5250**

Fixed-Income Repo
Head of Repo   Ole Lindholt ☏ **4330 5250**

Fixed-Income Research
Head of Fixed Income   Torben Elkjaer ☏ **4330 6048**

Equity Capital Markets
Tel: 3391 0106 **Fax:** 3312 7756 **Reuters:** BGEQUITIES
Head of Equity Capital Markets   Claus Andersen

Other (International Equity)
Scandinavian Equities   Ove Jensen

Equity Research
Head of Equity Research   Torsten Hagen Jørgensen ☏ **4330 6099**

Syndicated Lending
Fax: 4330 5571 **Reuters:** BGMONEY
Head of Syndication   Jørgen Blaunfeldt ☏ **4330 5572**

Money Markets
Head of Money Markets   Ole Lindholdt ☏ **4330 5250**

Foreign Exchange
Head of Foreign Exchange   Niels Windekilde *Manager* ☏ **4330 5200**
Regional Head   Åge Lundager *Chief Dealer* ☏ **4330 5216**

Corporate Finance / M&A Advisory
Head of Corporate Finance   Frank Halborg ☏ **4330 5900**

Settlement / Clearing
Head of Settlement / Clearing   Ole Bjerre ☏ **4330 6277**

Administration
Compliance
                                    Michael Vovoelbo ☏ **4330 6170**

Bikuben Girobank A/S
Head Office

Højbro Plads 10, DK 1200 Copenhagen
Tel: 4330 3030 **Swift:** BIKU DK KK **Cable:** BIKUBEN

Senior Executive Officers
Chief Executive Officer   Henrik Thufason ☏ **4330 7000**
Treasurer   Søren Kaare-Andersen *Executive Vice President* ☏ **4330 6000**

Settlement / Clearing
Regional Head   Ingolf Skafte ☏ **4330 5198**
Equity Settlement   Annegrethe Tybring ☏ **4330 6277**
Foreign Exchange Settlement   Ingolf Skafte ☏ **4330 5198**

Euromoney Directory 1999   **339**

DENMARK (+45)   www.euromoneydirectory.com

Bikuben Girobank A/S (cont)

Global Custody
Regional Head   Annegrethe Tybring ☎ 4330 6277

Other Departments
Private Banking   Torkel Olrik ☎ 4330 7350
Correspondent Banking   Jens Niemann Olesen ☎ 4330 5040

Administration
Legal / In-House Counsel

     Marianne Majbrink ☎ 4330 6170

Public Relations

     Rene La Cour Sell ☎ 4330 7310

Carnegie Bank A/S   Head Office

Carnegie

Overgaden neden Vandet 9 B, DK-1414 Copenhagen K
PO Box 1935, DK-1414 Copenhagen K
Tel: 3288 0200 **Fax:** 3296 1022 **Telex:** 21387 DK **Swift:** CAJB DK KK BIC **Reuters:** CARN 12-14 **Telerate:** 20876-8
Bloomberg: CABK
Website: www.carnegie.dk

Senior Executive Officers
Chairman of the Board   Lars Bertram ☎ +46 (8) 676 8595 ✉ larber@carnegie.se
Chief Executive Officer   Niels Roth ☎ 3288 0211 ✉ nielsr@carnegie.dk
Financial Director   Niels Olsen ☎ 3288 0236 ✉ nolsen@carnegie.dk
Treasurer   Brian Sonne Friis ☎ 3288 0235 ✉ bsfriis@carnegie.dk
Managing Director / General Manager   Niels Roth ☎ 3288 0211 ✉ nielsr@carnegie.dk

Debt Capital Markets / Fixed Income
Head of Debt Capital Markets; Head of Fixed
Income Sales; Head of Fixed Income Trading   Thor Bendixen ☎ 3288 0250 ✉ thor@carnegie.dk

Fixed-Income Repo
Head of Repo; Marketing & Product
Development; Head of Trading   Thor Bendixen ☎ 3288 0250 ✉ thor@carnegie.dk

Fixed-Income Research
Head of Fixed Income   Frank V Velling ☎ 3288 0233

Equity Capital Markets
Country Head of Sales; Head of Trading   Ole Christiansen ☎ 3288 0292 ✉ olechr@carnegie.dk

Domestic Equities
Head of Sales; Head of Trading   Ole Christiansen ☎ 3288 0292 ✉ olechr@carnegie.dk

International Equities
Head of Sales   Søren Rasmussen ☎ 3288 0268 ✉ srasmussen@carnegie.dk

Equity Research
Head of Equity Research   Per Hillebrandt ☎ 3288 0274 ✉ phillebran@carnegie.dk

Convertibles / Equity-Linked
Head of Sales; Head of Trading   Jacob Bro Eriksen ☎ 3288 0260 ✉ jberiksen@carnegie.dk

Risk Management
Fixed Income Derivatives / Risk Management
Head of Sales; Trading   Thor Bendixen ☎ 3288 0250 ✉ thor@carnegie.dk

Corporate Finance / M&A Advisory
Global Head   Kim Bøttkjær ☎ 3288 0213 ✉ kbottkjaer@carnegie.dk

Settlement / Clearing
Tel: 3288 0200 **Fax:** 3296 0266
Country Head; Equity Settlement; Fixed-Income
Settlement   Hanne Gall ☎ 3288 0212 ✉ hgall@carnegie.dk

Global Custody
Regional Head   Poul Erik Jensen ☎ 3288 0208 ✉ pejensen@Carnegie.dk

Administration
Head of Administration   Niels Olsen ☎ 3288 0236 ✉ nolsen@carnegie.dk

Technology & Systems

     Jacob Sander ☎ 3288 0219 ✉ jsander@carnegie.dk

www.euromoneydirectory.com   DENMARK (+45)

Compliance
Niels Olsen ☎ **3288 0236** ✉ nolsen@carnegie.dk

Citibank International plc
Full Branch Office

HC Andersens Boulevard 12, DK-1553 Copenhagen V
PO Box 243, DK-1502 Copenhagen V
Tel: 3363 8383; 3363 8374 (Treasury) **Fax:** 3363 8333 **Telex:** 27554 **Swift:** CITI DK KK **Reuters:** CICO
Cable: CITIBANK COPENHAGEN
Reuters: CIAO

Senior Executive Officers
Managing Director & Country Head   Ineke Bussemaker

Others (Senior Executives)
Head of Treasury   Susanne Poulsen *VP & Chief Dealer, Treasury Customer Unit*
Treasury Customer Unit   Henrik Bønnelykke *Vice President & Dealer*
                                            David Goddard *Vice President & Dealer*
                                            Ulrik Funch Holm *Manager & Dealer*

Foreign Exchange
Corporate Sales   Susanne Poulsen ☎ **3393 1093** 📠 **3363 8373**

Settlement / Clearing
Settlement (General)   Mette Jørgensen *Back-Office Settlements*
                                            Jan Arvedsen *Back-Office Settlements*
Operations   Per Bering Sørensen *Head of Operations*

Administration
Head of Administration   Per Bering Sørensen *Head of Operations*

Other (Administration)
Marketing   Steffen Bach *Vice President*
                                            John Erik Stern-Peltz *Vice President, Marketing*

Codan Bank A/S
Head Office

24 Borgergade, DK-1790 Copenhagen
Tel: 3355 6666; 3355 4509 **Fax:** 3355 6667; 3355 2330 **Telex:** 22396 CODA DK **Swift:** CODA DK KK **Reuters:** CODA
Telerate: 8557 **Telex:** 8588
Website: www.codam.com

Senior Executive Officers
Chairman, Board of Directors   Henrik Christrup
Deputy Chairman, Board of Directors   Søren Theilgaard
Chief Executive Officer   Jens Ole Pedersen *Chief Executive, Board of Management*
VP, Management Secretariat & Marketing   Lene Kjærbo

Others (Senior Executives)
                                            Niels Harding Bressendorff *Senior Vice President*
                                            Thorkild Kokholm *Board of Management*
Codan Konto Service   Susanne Jensen *Vice President*
Pension Schemes   Niels Bressendorff *Senior Vice President*
Accounting   John Arthur Lind *Chief Accountant*
Securities   Hans Skytte Pedersen *Senior Vice President* ☎ **3355 2702**
Asset Management   Arne Rasmussen *Senior Vice President* ☎ **3355 4500**
International Relations   Per Hellmund *Vice President* ☎ **3355 4509**

General-Lending (DCM, SL)
Head of Corporate Banking   Flemming Ahrent Pedersen *SVP, Credit Dept & Staff Bank*

Debt Capital Markets / Fixed Income
Global Head   Niels Jacobsgaard *Head, Fixed Income* ☎ **3355 2390**
                                            Merete Hyldmar *Head* ☎ **3355 2169**

Domestic Government Bonds
Head of Sales   Niels Staerup ☎ **3355 4547**
                                            Peter Christensen ☎ **3355 4703**

Non-Domestic Government Bonds
International Sales   Morten Dresling ☎ **3355 4530**
                                            Peter Baumann ☎ **3355 4529**
                                            Pieter van der Noordaa ☎ **3355 2391**

Bonds - General
Bond Sales   Peter Bo Kiaer *Market-Maker* ☎ **3355 4757**
                                            René Jaeger Nielsen *Market-Maker* ☎ **3355 2151**

Euromoney Directory 1999   **341**

DENMARK (+45)

www.euromoneydirectory.com

Codan Bank A/S (cont)
Bonds - General (cont)

Svend Petersen *Market-Maker* ☎ **3355 4872**
Kai Lindberg *Strategist* ☎ **3355 2158**
Torben Jansen *Controller* ☎ **3355 2124**
Lisbeth Ramloese *Controller* ☎ **3355 2154**

Fixed-Income Research
Global Head

Geert Ditlev Kunde *Vice President* ☎ **3355 4532**

Equity Capital Markets
Domestic Equities
Head of Sales

Jesper Alsing *Vice President* ☎ **3355 4759**
Lars Braemer ☎ **3355 4780**
Henrik Pedersen ☎ **3355 4764**
Christian Strandgaard ☎ **3355 2164**
Jesper Thomsen ☎ **3355 4765**

International Equities
Head of Sales

Jesper Alsing *Vice President* ☎ **3355 4759**
Lars Braemer ☎ **3355 4780**
Henrik Pedersen ☎ **3355 4764**
Christian Strandgaard ☎ **3355 2164**
Jesper Thomsen ☎ **3355 4765**

Equity Research
Country Head

Karsten V Hansen ☎ **3355 2126**

Other (Equity Research)

Stig Andersen ☎ **3355 2166**
Susanne Forsingdal ☎ **3355 2162**
Soeren Krohn ☎ **3355 2165**

Money Markets
Global Head

Hans Skytte Pedersen *Senior Vice President* ☎ **3355 2702**

Foreign Exchange
Spot / Forwards Trading

Henrik Tolmark *Vice President* ☎ **3355 4751**
Troels Nielsen ☎ **3355 4752**

Risk Management
Other Currency Swap / FX Options Personnel
Money Markets & Forwards

Flemming Elhoej *Deposits & Forwards* ☎ **3355 4754**
Benny Christensen *Deposits & Forwards* ☎ **3355 4511**
Annemette Jessen *Money Markets* ☎ **3355 4546**

Settlement / Clearing
Telex: 22396 CODA DK
Head of Settlement / Clearing
Settlement (General)

Claus Kehler *Head, Settlements, Custody & Clearing* ☎ **3355 2339**
Henriette Hyldstrup Larsen ☎ **3355 4521**
Mette Jepp *Domestic Treasurer* ☎ **3355 2449**
Malene Sorensen *International* ☎ **3355 4521**
Irene Dyfort *International* ☎ **3355 2762**

Global Custody
Head of Global Custody

Claus Kehler *Head, Settlements, Custody & Clearing* ☎ **3355 2339**

Other (Global Custody)
Custody Services

Lone Christensen ☎ **3355 4762**
Alex Jensen ☎ **3355 2242**
Frans Madsen ☎ **3355 4579**
Alice Petersen ☎ **3355 4701**

Asset Management
Fax: 3314 9626
Head

Arne Rasmussen *Senior Vice President* ☎ **3355 4500**

Other (Asset Management)
High Net Worth Individuals

Birgitte Thranegaard ☎ **3355 2317**
Per Hellmund *Area Manager, International Relations* ☎ **3355 4509**
℻ **3355 2330**

Asset Management

John Boedker *Product Manager* ☎ **3355 4576**
Vivan Dahlgaard ☎ **3355 2713**
Finn Holmer *Human Resources* ☎ **3355 4537**

Sales

Jens Kruse *Portfolio Manager* ☎ **3355 2714**

Trust Funds

Ove Pedersen ☎ **3355 2338**

Other Departments
Correspondent Banking
Economic Research

Per Hellmund *Vice President* ☎ **3355 4509**
Peter Schlaikjer Bruhn *Macroeconomic Research* ☎ **3355 2132**
Kai Lindberg *VP, Macroeconomic Research* ☎ **3355 2173**

www.euromoneydirectory.com　　　　DENMARK (+45)

Administration
Accounts / Audit
　　　　　　　　　John Arthur Lind *Chief Accountant*

Commerzbank AG
Representative Office
Radhuspladsen 4, DK-1550 Copenhagen
Tel: 3315 2236 Fax: 3315 3105
Senior Executive Officers
Senior Vice President　　　　Wilfried A Reschke

Crédit Agricole Indosuez
Representative Office
Formerly known as: Banque Indosuez
Bredgade 20, DK-1260 Copenhagen K
Tel: 3391 1422 Fax: 3391 2070
Senior Executive Officers
Representative　　　　Valérie Lambel-Reinholdt

Danish Securities Dealers Association
Amaliegade 7, DK-1256 Copenhagen K
PO Box 1003, DK-1256 Copenhagen
Tel: 3332 7411 Fax: 3332 9411 Email: sekr@borsmaeglerforening.dk

Danish Ship Finance
Head Office
Alternative trading name: Danmarks Skibskreditfond
Formerly known as: The Ship Credit Fund of Denmark
Sankt Annæ Plads 1-3, DK-1250 Copenhagen K
PO Box 3028, D-1021 Copenhagen K
Tel: 3333 9333 Fax: 3333 9366 Telex: 16757 Email: danmarks@skibskredit.dk
Senior Executive Officers
Chairman　　　　Thorleif Krarup
Managing Director　　　　Bo Jagd
Chief Executive Officer　　　　Stig Kaare Lyngsie *Senior Vice President*
Financial Director　　　　Per Schnack *Senior Vice President*
Treasurer　　　　Erling Garrelts *Vice President*
Managing Director　　　　Bo Jagd
Others (Senior Executives)
Head of Credit Department　　　　Denis Dønbo *Senior Vice President*
Syndicated Lending
Head of Origination　　　　Erik Nielsen *Vice President*
Head of Syndication　　　　Stig Kaare Lyngsie *Senior Vice President*
Head of Trading　　　　Erik Nielsen *Vice President*
Loan-Related Activities
Project Finance　　　　Stig Kaare Lyngsie *Senior Vice President*
Other Departments
Chief Credit Officer　　　　Denis Dønbo *Senior Vice President*
Administration
Head of Administration　　　　Erling Garrelts *Vice President*
Head of Marketing　　　　Stig Kaare Lyngsie *Senior Vice President*

Den Danske Bank
Head Office
Holmens Kanal 2-12, DK-1092 Copenhagen
Tel: 3344 0000; 3310 1088 Fax: 3918 5873 Telex: 27000 DDB DK Swift: DABA DK KK Telerate: 3305
Cable: DENDANSKE
Reuters: DDBA (Forex & Money Market Monitor); DANP (Equities); DANQ (Equities)
Website: www.danskebank.dk
Senior Executive Officers
Chairman　　　　Peter Straarup

Euromoney Directory 1999　**343**

DENMARK (+45)   www.euromoneydirectory.com

Den Danske Bank (cont)
Others (Senior Executives)
Member   Karsten Knüdsen
                      Søren Møller Nielsen
                      Jakob Brogaard
                      Jens Otto Veile

Diskontobanken A/S   Head Office
Axeltorv 4, DK-4700 Næstved
Tel: 5578 7878 **Fax:** 5578 7920 **Telex:** 46227 DISKBK DK **Swift:** DIBA DK 22
Website: www.diskontobank.dk

Senior Executive Officers
Chairman   Georg Knüdsen
Managing Director   Claús Schroll

Other Departments
Private Banking   Flemming Jensen
Correspondent Banking   Anne Grete Christiansen

Administration
Public Relations
                        Arne Hojbo

Djurslands Bank A/S   Head Office
5 Torvet, DK-8500 Grenaa
Tel: 8632 1555 **Fax:** 8632 7577 **Telex:** 63488 DJURS DK **Swift:** DJUR DK 22

Senior Executive Officers
Chairman   Erik Wiedemann
Managing Director   Vagn Stenager

Other Departments
Correspondent Banking   Flemming Boettcher *Foreign Manager*

A/S Egnsbank Nord   Head Office
Jernbanegade 4/6, PO Box 701, DK-9900 Frederikshavn
Tel: 9921 2223 **Fax:** 9921 2267 **Telex:** 67102 EBANFB DK **Swift:** EBAN DK 22 **Cable:** HAVNBANK

Senior Executive Officers
Chairman   Hans Jorgen Kaptain
General Manager   Jens Ole Jensen
Chief Executive Officer Ole Kristensen *General Manager*

Foreign Exchange
Head of Foreign Exchange   Susanne L Vinther *Manager* ☏ 9921 2255

Other Departments
Correspondent Banking   Eigil Gronkjær *Manager* ☏ 9921 2250

Finansrådet - Danske Pengeinstitutters Forening   Head Office
Alternative trading name: Danish Bankers Association
Amaliegade 7, DK-1256 Copenhagen K
Tel: 3312 0200 **Fax:** 3393 0260 **Email:** f@finansraadet.dk

Senior Executive Officers
Chairman   Peter Straarup
Vice Chairman   Thorleif Krarup
Deputy Chairman   Jacob Leth
Deputy Chairman   Henrik Thufason
Managing Director   Lars Barfoed

www.euromoneydirectory.com   DENMARK (+45)

Gudme Raaschou Investment Bankers Limited
Head Office
Østergade 13, DK-1100 Copenhagen K
Tel: 3348 9000 **Telex:** 15071 DK
Administration - After Hours Tel: 3349 9140; **Corporate Finance Fax:** 3348 9021; **Corporate Finance - After Hours Tel:** 3348 9020; **EDP - After Hours Tel:** 3348 9150; **International Capital Markets Fax:** 3348 9129; **International Capital Markets - After Hours Tel:** 3348 9120; **Portfolio Management Fax:** 3348 9184; **Portfolio Management - After Hours Tel:** 3348 9040; **Stocks & Shares Fax:** 3348 9096

Senior Executive Officers
Managing Director	Kåre B Dullum
Director	Knud J Strange
Director, International Capital Markets	Aage Jacobsen
Director	Per Skovsted
Company Secretary	Annie Voller

Others (Senior Executives)
Board of Directors   Hans Cavalli-Björkmann
                      Kåre Stolt
                      Eigil Pedersen
                      Kurt Bjørndal
                      Niels Antonsen

Debt Capital Markets / Fixed Income
Eurobonds
Head of Origination   Niels Aavild *Senior Vice President*
                       Andrej Makar *Vice President*

Bonds - General
Domestic Bonds   Niels Aavild *Senior Vice President*
                  Andrej Makar *Vice President*
                  Jøregen Haderup *Vice President*
                  Peter Elgaard *Vice President*

New Issue Syndicates   Aage Jacobsen *Director, International Capital Markets*
                        Henrik Ankjer-Jensen *Vice President*
                        Torben Lykke Hansen *Vice President*
                        Thomas Hinnerskov *Vice President*
                        Henrik Kappel *Vice President*

Libor-Based / Floating-Rate Products
Asset Swaps   Henrik Ankjer-Jensen *Vice President*
               Torben Lykke Hansen *Vice President*
               Thomas Hinnerskov *Vice President*
               Aage Jacobsen *Director, International Capital Markets*
               Henrik Kappel *Vice President*

Private Placements
Head of Origination   Henrik Ankjer-Jensen *Vice President*
                       Aage Jacobsen *Director, International Capital Markets*
                       Torben Lykke Hansen *Vice President*
                       Thomas Hinnerskov *Vice President*
                       Henrik Kappel *Vice President*

Equity Capital Markets
Domestic Equities
Head of Origination   Lars Perch-Nielsen *Director*
                       Poul Antonsen *Dealer*
                       Henrik Madsen *Dealer*

International Equities
Head of Origination   Morten Schou *Senior Vice President*

Corporate Finance / M&A Advisory
Department: Corporate Finance
Global Head   Stiin Christian Nielsen *Director*

Other (Corporate Finance)
    Thomas Krantz *Vice President*
    Allan Reimann *Vice President*
    Søren Mølbak *Vice President*
    John Jensen *Vice President*

Settlement / Clearing
Settlement (General)   Connie Severin *Back-Office Settlements - Domestic*
                        Rikke Høberg *Back-Office Settlements - Domestic*
                        Jette Mertins *Back-Office Settlements - Domestic*
                        Lotte Halse *Back-Office Settlements - International*

DENMARK (+45)　　　　www.euromoneydirectory.com

Gudme Raaschou Investment Bankers Limited (cont)
Asset Management
Portfolio Management　　　　Per Skovsted *Director*
　　　　　　　　　　　　　　Morten Schou *Senior Vice President*
　　　　　　　　　　　　　　Jens Honoré *Vice President*
　　　　　　　　　　　　　　Claus Hector Kjær *Vice President*
　　　　　　　　　　　　　　Lars Holm *Senior Vice President*
　　　　　　　　　　　　　　Janet Rasmussen *Secretary*

A/S Haandværkerbanken　　　　　　　　　　　　　Head Office

Jernbanegade 9, DK-4700 Næstved
Tel: 5578 0111 Fax: 5578 0122 Telex: 46255 Swift: HAHA DK 21
Website: www.haandvaerkerbanken.dk

Senior Executive Officers
Chairman　　　　　　　　　　　Hans Fossing Nielsen
Managing Director / General Manager　Hermann Höhrmann

Debt Capital Markets / Fixed Income
Domestic Government Bonds
Head of Trading　　　　　　　　Flemming Joergensen *Head Clerk* ☏ **5578 0141**
　　　　　　　　　　　　　　　✉ finans@haandvaerkerbanken.dk

Money Markets
Domestic Commercial Paper
Head of Trading　　　　　　　　Flemming Joergensen *Head Clerk* ☏ **5578 0141**
　　　　　　　　　　　　　　　✉ finans@haandvaerkerbanken.dk

Foreign Exchange
Head of Trading　　　　　　　　Flemming Joergensen *Head Clerk* ☏ **5578 0141**
　　　　　　　　　　　　　　　✉ finans@haandvaerkerbanken.dk

Other Departments
Private Banking　　　　　　　　Benny Mieszczak *Confidential Clerk* ☏ **5578 0140**
Correspondent Banking　　　　　Flemming Joergensen *Head Clerk* ☏ **5578 0141**
　　　　　　　　　　　　　　　✉ finans@haandvaerkerbanken.dk

Administration
Technology & Systems
　　　　　　　　　　　　　　　Mogens Pedersen *Head Clerk* ☏ **5578 0145**

Compliance
　　　　　　　　　　　　　　　Steen Loevgreen *Head Accountant* ☏ **5578 0148**

Public Relations
　　　　　　　　　　　　　　　Hans Verner Larsen *Assistant Director* ☏ **5578 0123**

Intercapital plc

Vestergade 33, DK-1456 Copenhagen K
Tel: 3315 5333 Fax: 3313 2504

Senior Executive Officers
Others (Senior Executives)
　　　　　　　　　　　　　　　Erling Schiøtz

A/S Jyske Bank　　　　　　　　　　　　　　　　Head Office

Vestergade 8-16, DK-8600 Silkeborg
Vesterbrogade 9, DK-1780 Copenhagen V
Tel: 3378 7650; 8922 2222 Fax: 3378 7634 Swift: JYBA DK KK
Website: www.jyskebank.dk

Senior Executive Officers
Chairman　　　　　　　　　　　Leon Rasmussen
Chief Executive Officer　　　　　Anders Dam ☏ **8922 2000**
Financial Director　　　　　　　Poul Thorhauge ☏ **8922 2136**
International Division　　　　　Per M Poulsen

346　Euromoney Directory 1999

www.euromoneydirectory.com   DENMARK (+45)

LB Kiel
Full Branch Office

Alternative trading name: Landesbank Schleswig-Holstein Girozentrale
Holmens Kanal 7, DK-1020 Copenhagen K
PO Box 1600, DK-1020 Copenhagen
Tel: 3395 0730; 3395 0100 **Fax:** 3395 0795 **Telex:** 27228 KILA DK **Reuters:** KICO
General Tel 3: **Tel:** 3595 0730

Senior Executive Officers
General Manager	Ulrich W Ellerbeck ☏ **3395 0101**
General Manager	Flemming Jensen ☏ **3395 0718**

Debt Capital Markets / Fixed Income
Tel: 3395 0730 **Fax:** 3395 0795
Head of Fixed Income	Niels Aavid
Head of Fixed Income Sales	Jens Lohfert Jørgensen ☏ **3395 0731**
Head of Fixed Income Trading	Ken Øxby ☏ **3395 0733**

Government Bonds
Head of Sales	Jens Lohfert Jørgensen ☏ **3395 0731**
Head of Trading	Ken Øxby ☏ **3395 0733**

Eurobonds
Head of Sales; Head of Trading	Peter Elgaard Madsen

Libor-Based / Floating-Rate Products
FRN Sales; FRN Trading; Asset Swaps; Asset Swaps (Sales)	Jorgen Sichelkow ☏ **3395 0713**

Fixed-Income Repo
Head of Repo	Peter Hamann ☏ **3395 0712**

Fixed-Income Research
Head of Fixed Income	Niels Antonsen

Syndicated Lending
Head of Syndication	Poul Therkelsen *Senior Officer* ☏ **3395 0133**

Money Markets
Head of Money Markets	Peter Hamann ☏ **3395 0712**

Foreign Exchange
Head of Foreign Exchange	Peter Hamann ☏ **3395 0712**

Corporate Finance / M&A Advisory
Head of Corporate Finance	Niels Troen *Senior Officer* ☏ **3395 0171**

Settlement / Clearing
Country Head	Mette Hamilton ☏ **3395 0763**
	Axel Koch ☏ **3395 0763**
	Charlotte Nilsson ☏ **3395 0763**
Operations	Niels Sindberg *Senior Officer, General Operations* ☏ **3395 0780**

Lollands Bank

Nybrogade 3, DK-4900 Nakskov
Tel: 5392 1133 **Fax:** 5495 1133 **Telex:** 47542 LOBANK DK **Email:** lb@lollandsbank.dk
Website: www.lollandsbank.dk

Senior Executive Officers
Managing Director / General Manager	Ebbe Helmer Nielsen

Midtbank AS
Head Office

2 Øestergade, DK-7400 Herning
Tel: 9626 2626 **Fax:** 9626 2898 **Telex:** 62142 **Swift:** MIBA DK 22 **Email:** midtbank@midtbank.dk
Reuters: MIDTBANK
Website: www.midtbank.dk

Senior Executive Officers
Chairman of the Board	Gunnar Pedersen ☏ **9626 2801**
Chief Executive Officer	Steen Hove *Chief General Manager* ☏ **9626 2800**
	Bjarne Degn *General Manager* ☏ **9626 2810**

Others (Senior Executives)
Foreign Department	Anders Frederiksen *Manager* ☏ **9628 2870**
	Anders Kjaer *Foreign Exchange Manager* ☏ **9626 2860**
	Erik Thomsen *Deputy General Manager* ☏ **9626 2820**

Euromoney Directory 1999   **347**

DENMARK (+45)   www.euromoneydirectory.com

Midtbank AS (cont)
Debt Capital Markets / Fixed Income
Department: MidtBØRS
Tel: 9721 2100 Fax: 9626 2868
Global Head   Ole Nørgaard *Manager, Investment* ☏ **9626 2845**

Domestic Government Bonds
Head of Trading   Claus Gade *Assistant Manager* ☏ **9626 2840**
Head of Research   Erik Andreasen *Dealer* ☏ **9626 2831**

Non-Domestic Government Bonds
                                          Jesper Poulsen *Dealer* ☏ **9626 2835**
                                          Erik Andreasen *Dealer* ☏ **9626 2831**

Eurobonds
Head of Origination; Head of Syndication; Head   Erik Andreasen *Dealer* ☏ **9626 2831**
of Sales; Head of Trading; Head of Research;
Trading - Sovereigns, Corporates, High-yield

Asset-Backed Securities / Securitization
Global Head   Erik Andreasen *Dealer* ☏ **9626 2831**

Mortgage-Backed Securities
Global Head   Erik Andreasen *Dealer* ☏ **9626 2831**

Fixed-Income Repo
Head of Repo   Erik Andreasen *Dealer* ☏ **9626 2831**

Equity Capital Markets
Global Head   Ole Nørgaard *Manager, Investment* ☏ **9626 2845**

Domestic Equities
Head of Sales   Claus Gade *Assistant Manager* ☏ **9626 2840**
Head of Trading   Ole Nielsen *Dealer* ☏ **9626 2844**
Head of Research   John Christensen *Analyst* ☏ **9626 2849**

International Equities
Head of Trading   Jesper Poulsen *Dealer* ☏ **9626 2835**
Head of Research   John Christensen *Analyst* ☏ **9626 2849**

Equity Repo / Securities Lending
Head of Trading   Ole Nielsen *Dealer* ☏ **9626 2844**

Syndicated Lending
Tel: 9722 5533 Fax: 9626 2869
Global Head   Anders Kjaer *Foreign Exchange Manager* ☏ **9626 2860**

Foreign Exchange
Tel: 9722 5533 Fax: 9626 2869 **Reuters:** MABA
Head of Foreign Exchange   Anders Kjaer *Foreign Exchange Manager* ☏ **9626 2860**

Settlement / Clearing
Regional Head   Liselotte Aarenstrup *Senior Assistant Manager* ☏ **9626 2847**
Equity Settlement; Fixed-Income Settlement   Kirsten Raben *Bank Assistant* ☏ **9626 2846**
Derivatives Settlement; Foreign Exchange   Irene Fromberg *Bank Assistant* ☏ **9626 2838**
Settlement

Global Custody
Head of Global Custody   Liselotte Aarenstrup *Senior Assistant Manager* ☏ **9626 2847**

Other (Global Custody)
                                          Ellen Kjaer *Bank Assistant* ☏ **9626 2837**

Other Departments
Correspondent Banking   Gitte Nielsen *Manager* ☏ **9626 2878**

Administration
Technology & Systems
                                          Ole Christensen *Manager, IT* ☏ **9626 2728**

Legal / In-House Counsel
                                          N H Neermark *Chief Lawyer* ☏ **9626 2690**

Public Relations
                                          Børge Thomsen *Marketing Director* ☏ **9626 2660**

Accounts / Audit
                                          Peder Grandelag *Manager* ☏ **9626 2680**

Other (Administration)
Business Development   Erik Juul *Manager, Organization Department* ☏ **9626 2740**

www.euromoneydirectory.com DENMARK (+45)

Morsø Bank
Head Office

Algade 2, DK-7900 Nykobing Mors
Tel: 9772 1400; 9772 1600 **Fax:** 9772 3193; 9772 5837 **Swift:** MORB DK 22 **Email:** algade2@morsbank.dk
Website: www.morsbank.dk

The Mortgage Bank of Denmark
Head Office

Alternative trading name: Financial Administration Agency of the Kingdom of Denmark
4 Landgreven, DK-1301 Copenhagen K
Tel: 3392 8000 **Fax:** 3311 4380 **Telex:** 16323 MOBANK DK **Email:** hypotekbanken@hyp.dk
Website: www.hypotekbanken.dk

Senior Executive Officers
Chairman — Karstne Olsen
Chief Executive Officer — Hans Henrik H Øslergaard *Managing Director & Chief Executive*
Managing Director — Lars Tybjerg E **ljt@hyp.dk**
Debt Capital Markets / Fixed Income
Head of Debt Capital Markets — Marianne Ziirsen *Head of Division* E **mzi@hyp.dk**

Nordbanken AB (publ)
Full Branch Office

St Regnegade 5, DK-1110 Copenhagen K
Tel: 3391 1000 **Fax:** 3391 1004

Senior Executive Officers
General Manager — Ann-Britt Elvstad

A/S Nordvestbank
Head Office

Torvet 4/5, DK-7620 Lemvig
Tel: 9663 0777 **Fax:** 9663 0700 **Telex:** 66536 **Swift:** NOLE DK 22

Senior Executive Officers
Chairman — Peter Grankaer
Managing Director — Jorgen Holt

A/S Nørresundby Bank
Head Office

Torvet 4, DK-9400 Nørresundby
PO Box 200, DK-9400 Nørresundby
Tel: 9817 3333 **Fax:** 9819 1878 **Telex:** 69376 NRSBK DK **Swift:** NRSB DK 24 **Cable:** NORRESUNDBYBANK

Senior Executive Officers
Chairman — Kjeld Kolind Jensen
Managing Director — Andreas Rasmussen
Managing Director — Finn Øst Andersson
General Manager, International — Claus Kongsgaard

Nykredit A/S
Head Office

Bredgade 40, DK-1021 Copenhagen K
PO Box 1172, DK-1010 Copenhagen K
Tel: 3342 1000; 3342 1800 **Fax:** 3342 1002; 3342 1801 **Bloomberg:** Nykredit
Website: www.nykredit.dk

Senior Executive Officers
Chairman — Axel Ladegaard Jensen
Chief Executive Officer — Mogens Munk Rasmussen *Group Chief Executive*
Financial Director — Asger Hansen *Executive Vice President*
Treasurer — Soren Holm *Executive Vice President*
Group Managing Director — Peter Engberg Jensen
Group Managing Director — Per Lodegard
Group Managing Director — Henning Kruse Petersen

Euromoney Directory 1999 **349**

DENMARK (+45)   www.euromoneydirectory.com

Nykredit A/S (cont)

Debt Capital Markets / Fixed Income
Department: Treasury
Head of Fixed Income — Kim Duus *Managing Director*
Head of Fixed Income Sales — Thomas Ververd *First Vice President*
Head of Fixed Income Trading — Anders Brusendorff *First Vice President*

Government Bonds
Head of Sales — Jesper Brams *Chief Dealer*
Head of Trading — Henning Als Jensen *Chief Dealer*

Eurobonds
Head of Sales — Jeremy John Spinney *Chief Dealer*

Libor-Based / Floating-Rate Products
FRN Sales — Jeremy John Spinney *Chief Dealer*

Fixed-Income Repo
Head of Repo — Per de la Motte Olsen *Chief Dealer*

Fixed-Income Research
Head of Fixed Income — Birger Durhuus *Chief Analyst*

Equity Capital Markets
Head of Equity Capital Markets — Jan Correll *First Vice President*

Domestic Equities
Head of Sales — Jan Correll *First Vice President*

International Equities
Head of Sales — Jan Correll *First Vice President*

Equity Research
Head of Equity Research — Michael Henicke *Chief Analyst*

Money Markets
Head of Money Markets — Per de la Motte Olsen *Chief Dealer*

Foreign Exchange
Head of Foreign Exchange — Soren Klitholm *Chief Dealer*

Risk Management
Head of Risk Management — Lars Eibeholm *Vice President*

Settlement / Clearing
Head of Settlement / Clearing — Sten Lawaetz *First Vice President*

Asset Management
Head — Tommy Christensen

Administration
Technology & Systems — Jorgen Wohnsen *Executive Vice President*

Public Relations — Henrik Hougaard *Senior Vice President*

Nykredit Bank A/S   Head Office

Alternative trading name: Nykredit Markets A/S
Bredgade 40, DK-1010 Copenhagen K
PO Box 1172, DK-1010 Copenhagen K
Tel: 3342 1800 **Fax:** 3342 1806 **Email:** nykreditbank@nykredit.dk **Reuters:** NYKREDIT **Bloomberg:** nykredit
Website: www.nykredit.dk

Senior Executive Officers
Group Managing Director — Henning Kruse Pedersen ☎ **3342 1510**
Chief Executive Officer — Hans Møller Christensen *Managing Director* ☎ **3342 1990**
Financial Director — Bent Fredriksen *Chief Financial Officer* ☎ **3342 1848**
Head of Secretariat — Inge Stig Nielsen ☎ **3342 1991**

General-Lending (DCM, SL)
Head of Corporate Banking — Jens Smedegaard *First Vice President* ☎ **3342 1926**

General-Investment
Head of Investment — Kim Duus *Managing Director* ☎ **3342 1025**

Debt Capital Markets / Fixed Income
Head of Fixed Income — Anders Brusendorff *First Vice President* ☎ **3342 1050**

Fixed-Income Repo
Head of Repo — Anders Brusendorff *First Vice President* ☎ **3342 1050**

Equity Capital Markets
Head of Equity Capital Markets — Jan Correll *First Vice President* ☎ **3342 1860**

www.euromoneydirectory.com　　　　　　DENMARK (+45)

Syndicated Lending
Loan-Related Activities
Trade Finance　　　　　　　　　　　　Anders Brusendorff *First Vice President* ☏ **3342 1050**
Money Markets
Head of Money Markets　　　　　　　Lars Eibeholm *Chief Dealer* ☏ **3342 1170**
Foreign Exchange
Head of Foreign Exchange　　　　　　Søren Klitholm *Chief Dealer* ☏ **3342 1830**
Corporate Finance / M&A Advisory
Head of Corporate Finance　　　　　　Anders Christensen *First Vice President* ☏ **3342 1850**
Settlement / Clearing
Head of Settlement / Clearing　　　　Sten Lawaetz *First Vice President* ☏ **3342 1035**
Global Custody
Head of Global Custody　　　　　　　Sten Lawaetz *First Vice President* ☏ **3342 1035**
Asset Management
Head　　　　　　　　　　　　　　　Kjeld Oeberg *Senior Executive Vice President* ☏ **3342 1020**
Other Departments
Chief Credit Officer　　　　　　　　Tom Ahrenst *Senior Vice President* ☏ **3342 1953**
Private Banking　　　　　　　　　　Jes Klausby *Managing Director* ☏ **3342 1905**
Correspondent Banking　　　　　　Hans Christian Overbeck *First Vice President* ☏ **3342 1955**
Administration
Head of Administration; Business Development　Tonny T Andersen *First Vice President* ☏ **3342 1900**
Head of Marketing　　　　　　　　　Tonny T Andersen *First Vice President* ☏ **3342 1900**
Technology & Systems
　　　　　　　　　　　　　　　　　Thomas Andgren *Vice President* ☏ **3342 1939**
Legal / In-House Counsel
　　　　　　　　　　　　　　　　　Elisabeth Stamer *Chief Legal Advisor* ☏ **3342 1938**
Public Relations
　　　　　　　　　　　　　　　　　Tonny T Andersen *First Vice President* ☏ **3342 1900**
Accounts / Audit
Internal Audit　　　　　　　　　　　Lars Ellyton *Deputy Head* ☏ **3342 1980**

Realkredit Danmark A/S　　　　　　　　　　　　　　　　　Head Office

Formerly known as: Kreditforeningen Danmark
Jarmers Plads 2, DK-1590 Copenhagen
Tel: 3312 5290 **Fax:** 3688 2149 **Telex:** 19957 KDMARK DK **Email:** rd@rd.dk
Website: www.rd.dk

Senior Executive Officers
Chairman of the Supervisory Board　　Jørgen Nue'Møller ☏ **3157 1930**
Chief Executive Officer　　　　　　　Kjeld Jørgensen *Chief Executive Director*
Financial Director　　　　　　　　　Sven Holm *Executive Director*
　　　　　　　　　　　　　　　　　Per Helle *Executive Director*
Treasurer　　　　　　　　　　　　　Sven-Karsten Topp *Director of Treasury Department*
　　　　　　　　　　　　　　　　　Flemming Børreskov *Executive Director*
Director　　　　　　　　　　　　　Finn Bartholdy

Others (Senior Executives)
Director　　　　　　　　　　　　　Thomas Dywremose
　　　　　　　　　　　　　　　　　Bent Fjord
　　　　　　　　　　　　　　　　　Erik V Madsen

General-Lending (DCM, SL)
Head of Corporate Banking　　　　　Jørgen Bo Andersen *Director*
Debt Capital Markets / Fixed Income
Department: Treasury & Markets
Fax: 3688 2401
Head of Fixed Income Trading　　　　Peter Johansen F **3688 2403**
Equity Capital Markets
Department: Treasury & Markets
Fax: 3688 2401
Head of Trading　　　　　　　　　　Peter Johansen F **3688 2403**
Risk Management
Fax: 3688 2401
Head of Risk Management　　　　　Henrik Jepsen *Head of Research*

Euromoney Directory 1999　**351**

DENMARK (+45)　　　　　　　www.euromoneydirectory.com

RealKredit Danmark A/S (cont)

Settlement / Clearing
Fax: 3688 2401
Head of Settlement / Clearing　　　Jan Sindai *Head of Administration & Settlements*

Other Departments
Chief Credit Officer　　　　　　　　Borger Borgersen *Director*

Administration
Business Development　　　　　　Bjarne Graven Larsen *Director*
Head of Marketing　　　　　　　　Thomas Dywremose

Technology & Systems
　　　　　　　　　　　　　　　　Knud Rasmussen *Director*

Legal / In-House Counsel
　　　　　　　　　　　　　　　　Nils Guttenberg *Director*

Public Relations
　　　　　　　　　　　　　　　　Troels Brøndsted *Director*

Accounts / Audit
　　　　　　　　　　　　　　　　Lars D Sørensen *Director*

Ringkjøbing Landbobank A/S　　　　　　　Head Office

Torvet 1, DK-6950 Ringkobing
Tel: 9732 1166 **Fax:** 9732 1818; 9975 1256 **Telex:** 60385 **Swift:** RING DK 22

Senior Executive Officers
Chairman　　　　　　　　　　　　Kr Ole Kristensen
President　　　　　　　　　　　　Verner Ebdrup
Managing Director / General Manager　Bent Naur Kristensen

Debt Capital Markets / Fixed Income

Domestic Government Bonds
Head of Sales　　　　　　　　　　Toben Viuf ☎ **9975 1296**
Head of Trading　　　　　　　　　Hans Ronberg ☎ **9975 1295**

Money Markets
Tel: 9975 1275 Fax: 9975 1256
Global Head　　　　　　　　　　　Jorgen Josephsen ☎ **9975 1275**

Domestic Commercial Paper
Head of Origination　　　　　　　　Toben Viuf ☎ **9975 1296**

Foreign Exchange
Tel: 9732 1818 Fax: 9732 1818
Global Head　　　　　　　　　　　Jorgen Hojgaard

Global Custody
Tel: 9975 1296
Regional Head　　　　　　　　　　Toben Viuf ☎ **9975 1296**

Other Departments
Correspondent Banking　　　　　　Jorgen Hojgaard

Administration

Technology & Systems
　　　　　　　　　　　　　　　　Mogens Rud ☎ **9975 1260**

Public Relations
　　　　　　　　　　　　　　　　Peder Dahl ☎ **9975 1258**

Salling Bank A/S

Frederiksgade 6, DK-7800 Skive
Tel: 9752 3366 **Fax:** 9751 0696 **Telex:** 66726 SALLBK DK **Swift:** SALL DK 22

Senior Executive Officers
Managing Director / General Manager　Peter Vinther Christensen

www.euromoneydirectory.com   DENMARK (+45)

Spar Nord Bank
Head Office

4 Karlskogavej, DK-9200 Aalborg SV
PO Box 162, DK-9100 Aalborg
Tel: 9634 4000 **Fax:** 9634 4560; 9634 4575 **Telex:** 69662 SPANO DK **Swift:** SPNO DK 22 **Reuters:** SBNN; SBNX
Website: www.spanord.dk

Senior Executive Officers
Chairman — Poul Lauridsen
Treasurer — Peter Westphal *Senior Vice President* ☏ **9634 4052**
Managing Director / General Manager — Ole Jørgensen ☏ **9634 4016**

Debt Capital Markets / Fixed Income
Domestic Government Bonds
Head of Trading — Lars Rolighed ☏ **9634 4169**

Equity Capital Markets
Domestic Equities
Head of Trading — Peter Møller ☏ **9634 4166**

Syndicated Lending
Head of Trading — Jan Gerhardt ☏ **9634 4177**

Money Markets
Head of Money Markets — Jan Poulsen ☏ **9634 4436**

Risk Management
Head of Risk Management — Michael Blirup ☏ **9634 4043**

Settlement / Clearing
Head of Settlement / Clearing — Thorkild Mathiasen ☏ **9634 4145**

Sydbank A/S
Head Office

Kirkeplades, DK-6200 Aabeuraa
PO Box 169, DK-6200 Aabeuraa
Tel: 7436 3636 **Fax:** 7436 3549 **Telex:** 52414 **Swift:** SYBK DK 22 **Email:** intl@sydbank.dk **Reuters:** SYDF
Telerate: 20895 **Bloomberg:** SYDB
Reuters: SYDBANK 1/2
Website: www.sydbank.com

Senior Executive Officers
Chairman — Vagn Jacobsen
Chief Executive Officer — Carsten Andersen *CEO* ☏ **7436 2000**
Financial Director — Mogens Sandbaek *General Manager* ☏ **7436 2400**
General Manager — Mogens Asmund ☏ **7436 2050**
International Division — N H Nordstroem *General Manager* ☏ **7436 3200**

Debt Capital Markets / Fixed Income
Department: Fixed Income
Tel: 7436 4650 **Fax:** 7436 3570
Head of Fixed Income — Lars Bolding *Senior Manager* ☏ **7436 4624**
Head of Fixed Income Sales — Kim Otte *Manager* ☏ **7436 4621**
Head of Fixed Income Trading — Holger Kristensen *Chief Dealer* ☏ **7436 4611**

Equity Capital Markets
Department: Equities
Tel: 7436 4493 **Fax:** 7436 3578
Head of Equity Capital Markets — Bendt Heidner *Senior Manager* ☏ **7436 4450**
Head of Sales — Preben Hansen *Manager* ☏ **7436 4450**
Head of Trading — Joern Jakobsen *Manager* ☏ **7436 4465**

Equity Research
Head of Equity Research — Christian Kirk-Thomsen *Senior Analyst* ☏ **7436 4464**

Syndicated Lending
Loan-Related Activities
Trade Finance — Ellen Bech Jensen *Senior Manager* ☏ **7436 3210**

Money Markets
Fax: 7436 3575
Head of Money Markets — Kaj Christensen *Senior Manager* ☏ **7436 3715**

Euromoney Directory 1999   **353**

DENMARK (+45)   www.euromoneydirectory.com

Sydbank A/S (cont)

Foreign Exchange
Tel: 7436 3737 Fax: 7436 3575 Telex: 52188
Head of Foreign Exchange   Erling Carlsson *Senior Manager* ☎ **7436 4158**

FX Traders / Sales People
Spot   Paul Jespersen *Chief Dealer* ☎ **7436 3706**

Risk Management
Department: Foreign Exchange Derivatives
Tel: 7436 3737 Fax: 7436 3575 Telex: 52188

Foreign Exchange Derivatives / Risk Management
Country Head   Jan Schack Soerensen *Manager* ☎ **7436 3700**

Corporate Finance / M&A Advisory
Head of Corporate Finance   Knud Kristensen *General Manager* ☎ **7436 5000**

Settlement / Clearing
Head of Settlement / Clearing   Egon Rohden *Senior Manager* ☎ **7436 4340**

Global Custody
Head of Global Custody   Egon Rohden *Senior Manager* ☎ **7436 4340**

Other Departments
Correspondent Banking   N H Nordstroem *General Manager* ☎ **7436 3200**

Administration
Head of Administration   Mogens Asmund *General Manager* ☎ **7436 2050**

Legal / In-House Counsel
                                         Karen Froesig *Head of Legal Department* ☎ **7436 2070**

Public Relations
                                         Steen Kernfelt *Head of Marketing & Sales* ☎ **7436 2600**

Accounts / Audit
                                         Ole Kirkbak *Head of Internal Audit* ☎ **7436 3100**

Topdanmark A/S   Head Office

Borupvang 4, DK-2750 Ballerup
Tel: 4468 3311 Fax: 4468 1906

Senior Executive Officers
Chairman   Klaus Bonde Larsen
Chief Executive Officer   Michael Pram Rasmussen
Managing Director   Poul Almlund
Managing Director   Leif Larsen

General - Treasury
Head of Treasury   Lars Thykier *General Manager*

Debt Capital Markets / Fixed Income
Head of Sales; Head of Trading   Niels Larsen *Trader*

Foreign Exchange

FX Traders / Sales People
                                         Niels Larsen *Trader*

Risk Management

Other Currency Swap / FX Options Personnel
Risk Management   Lars Thykier *General Manager*

Corporate Finance / M&A Advisory

Other (Corporate Finance)
Corporate Finance   Poul Almlund *Managing Director*

Administration
                                         Niels Lillemose *General Manager*

Legal / In-House Counsel
                                         Birgit Sevel *Deputy General Manager*

Corporate Communications
                                         Steffen Heegaard *Deputy General Manager*

www.euromoneydirectory.com DOMINICAN REPUBLIC (+1 809)

Unibank A/S

Helgeshoj Alle 33, DK-1786 Copenhagen V
Tel: 3333 3333 **Fax:** 3333 1031 **Telex:** 27543 UNIB DK **Swift:** UNIB DK KK **Reuters:** UNIC **Cable:** UNIBANK
Website: www.unibank.dk

Senior Executive Officers
Chairman   Thorleif Krarup
Deputy Chairman & CEO   Lars Eskesen
Chief Executive Officer   Preben Kendal
Managing Director / General Manager   Jorn Kristian Jensen

DJIBOUTI
(+253)

Banque Nationale de Djibouti   🏛 Central Bank

PO Box 2118, Djibouti
Tel: 352 751 **Fax:** 356 288 **Telex:** 5838 DJ **Cable:** DJIBOUTIBANK

Senior Executive Officers
Governor   Djama M Haid
Financial Director   Ahmed Osman

Others (Senior Executives)
Chief Cashier   Hisham A Taher
Head, Banking Supervision   Houmea Abdou

DOMINICAN REPUBLIC
(+1 809)

Banco Central de la República Dominicana   🏛 Central Bank

Calle Pedro Henríquez Ureña, esquina Leopoldo Navarro, Santo Domingo
PO Box 1347, Santo Domingo
Tel: 221 9111 **Fax:** 686 7488 **Telex:** ITT: 3460052 BANCEN **Swift:** BCRD DO SX
Website: www.bancentral.gov.do

Senior Executive Officers
Governor   Héctor Valdez ☏ 688 2011 F 687 8087
Financial Director   Angelica Fondeur ☏ 688 2939 F 686 0989
Treasurer   María Rodríguez ☏ 682 8269 F 682 2985
General Manager   Rafael Alcántara ☏ 685 4312
Bank Secretary   Miguel Reyes ☏ 687 1416 F 688 3280
International Division   Clarissa de la Rocha Director, International Division ☏ 686 3334 F 686 7793

Others (Senior Executives)
Department of Monetary Programming   José A Guerrero Director ☏ 682 3887 F 682 7666
National Account Department   Olga Diaz Director ☏ 685 0783 F 682 7666

Administration
Head of Administration   Carlos Gutiérrez Director, Administration ☏ 682 0559 F 686 1115

Technology & Systems
System & Tecnology Department   Renato González Director ☏ 686 5884

Legal / In-House Counsel
                                     Luis M Piña Legal Counsel ☏ 682 6565 F 685 7585

Public Relations
Communication Department   Ricardo Rojas ☏ 682 1622 F 687 9491

Accounts / Audit
Accounting Department   Tomás Aybar Director ☏ 689 2020 F 688 0558

Euromoney Directory 1999   **355**

DOMINICAN REPUBLIC (+1 809)   www.euromoneydirectory.com

The Bank of Nova Scotia
Full Branch Office
Avenida John F Kennedy esquina Lope de Vega, Santo Domingo
Tel: 544 1700 Fax: 542 6302

Senior Executive Officers
Others (Senior Executives)
Ariel D Pérez A *Vice President*

Citibank NA
Full Branch Office
Citibank Building, Piso 4°, John F Kennedy N° 1, Santo Domingo
Tel: 566 5611 Fax: 567 2255

Senior Executive Officers
Chief Executive Officer — Henry Comber *Country Corporate Officer* ☎ **566 2403**
Treasurer — Manuel Caceres ☎ **566 2425**

General-Lending (DCM, SL)
Head of Corporate Banking — Lynn Snuffer *Head of Corporate Banking* ☎ **566 2430**

ECUADOR
(+593)

Banco Central del Ecuador
🏛 Central Bank
Avenida 10 de Agosto y Brinceno, Quito
Tel: (2) 582 577; (2) 572 522 Fax: (2) 580 158 Telex: 2175 BANCEN ED Swift: BCEN EC EQ
Website: www.bce.fin.ec

Senior Executive Officers
Governor & General Manager — Fidel Jaramillo ☎ **582 571**
Deputy Governor — Mauricio Yépez ☎ **580 152**
Chief Executive Officer — Mauricio Valencia *Executive Director* ☎ **580 155**
Treasurer — Rosa M Guyerrero ☎ **580 619**
Secretary — Carlos Landázuri ☎ **580 637**

Others (Senior Executives)
Head, Banking Supervision — Miguel Dávila ☎ **580 972**

Other Departments
Economic Research — José Samaniego *Head of Research* ☎ **580 156**

Administration
Head of Administration — luis Guzmán ☎ **580 596**

Technology & Systems
David Balarezo ☎ **582 577**

Public Relations
Alba pico ☎ **514 031**

Accounts / Audit
Head, Accountancy — Patricio Proaño ☎ **584 918**

ABN AMRO Bank SA
Full Branch Office
Avenida Amazonas 4272 y Villalengua, Quito
Tel: (2) 440 450; (2) 266 666 Fax: (2) 443 151

Senior Executive Officers
Country Manager — J J M Martinot

General-Lending (DCM, SL)
Head of Corporate Banking — Alejandro Peré *Corporate Banking Director*

356 Euromoney Directory 1999

ECUADOR (+593)

Banco Bolivariano CA — Head Office
Junin 200 y Panama, Guayaquil, 09-01-10184
Tel: (4) 560 799; (4) 562 277 **Fax:** (4) 566 450; (4) 566 378 **Telex:** 43659 **Swift:** BBOL EC EG

Senior Executive Officers
Chairman of the Board — Jose Salazar
Chief Executive Officer — Miguel Babra
Financial Director — Vicenze Vallarino *Manager, Financial Planning*
Treasurer — Aldo Bruzzone
Corporate Secretary — Enrique Valle
International Division — Ceclia Lopez

General-Lending (DCM, SL)
Head of Corporate Banking — Fernando Salazar *VP, Commercial Banking*

Administration
Head of Marketing — Carlos Guzman *Marketing Manager*

Technology & Systems
Gustavo Molina *Systems Manager*

Legal / In-House Counsel
Enrique Valle *Corporate Secretary*

Crédit Commercial de France — Representative Office
Avenida 12 de Octubre 476 y Pasaje Treviño, Quito, 1707 9022
Tel: (2) 230 713; (2) 549 058 **Fax:** (2) 898 696 **Telex:** 22401 MARGOY ED

Senior Executive Officers
Manager — Marcel Goyeneche

Depósito Centralizado de Valores SA — Head Office
Alternative trading name: DECEVALE
G Córdova 1004 y P Icaza, Edificio Alpeca, piso 10, Guayaquil, 09-01-10116
Tel: (4) 560 302 **Fax:** (4) 564 170 **Swift:** DEVE EC EG **Email:** decevale@telconet.net

Senior Executive Officers
President — Rodolfo Kronfle
General Manager — Raúl Bejarano

Administration
Head of Administration — Aldolfo Barniol *Administration Manager*

Technology & Systems
Julio Ordoñez *Sub Manager*

Compliance
Luis Moyano *Sub Manager*

Deutsche Morgan Grenfell — Representative Office
Formerly known as: Morgan Grenfell & Co Limited
3rd Floor, 12 de Octubre 2139 y Avenida Colón, Quito
Tel: (2) 568 096; (2) 569 166 **Fax:** (2) 569 167

Senior Executive Officers
Representative — Ramiro Ponce Almeida

Filanbanco SA — Head Office
Avenida 9 de Octubre 203 y Pichincha, Guayaquil, 09-01-1303
Tel: (4) 322 780 **Fax:** (4) 326 916; (4) 329 217 **Telex:** 041373 FILBAN ED **Swift:** FILA EC EG
Website: www.filanbanco.com

Senior Executive Officers
Executive President — Roberto Isaias
Chief Executive Officer — Juan Franco *General Manager*
International Division — Maria del Carmen de Morla *Vice President*

Others (Senior Executives)
Security Division — Miguel Montalvo *Vice President*

ECUADOR (+593)　　　　　www.euromoneydirectory.com

Filanbanco SA (cont)

General-Lending (DCM, SL)
Head of Corporate Banking　　　　　Julio Egas *Manager, Financial Corporate Business*

Settlement / Clearing
Operations　　　　　Roberto Gavilanes *Vice President*

Administration

Accounts / Audit
　　　　　Gaston Garcia *General Auditor*

Other (Administration)
Development Division　　　　　Alfredo Ochoa *Vice President*
Marketing Division　　　　　Rolando Lebed *Vice President*

ING Barings
Piso 22° Oficina 7, Edificio La Previsora, Avenida 9 Octubre 100 y Malecon, Guayaquil
Tel: (4) 518 957 Fax: (4) 518 958

Senior Executive Officers
Manager　　　　　Ignacio Roca

ING Barings　　　　　Full Branch Office
Piso 6°, Edificio Centro Financiero, Avenida Amazonas 4545 y Pereira, Quito
PO Box 1717 1025, Quito
Tel: (2) 981 650; (2) 981 670 Fax: (2) 981 665 Swift: INGB EC EQ Reuters: INGQ

Senior Executive Officers
Chief Executive Officer　　　　　Luis Pérez *General Manager*
Financial Director　　　　　Vicente Silva *Financial Controller*
Treasurer　　　　　Patricio Puga *Head of Treasury & Markets*

General-Lending (DCM, SL)
Head of Corporate Banking　　　　　Eduardo Checa *Corporate Manager*

General-Investment
Head of Investment　　　　　Eduardo Checa *Corporate Manager*

Debt Capital Markets / Fixed Income
Head of Fixed Income　　　　　Patricio Puga *Head of Treasury & Markets*

Libor-Based / Floating-Rate Products
Asset Swaps　　　　　Patricio Puga *Head of Treasury & Markets*

Foreign Exchange
Head of Foreign Exchange; Head of Sales;　　　　　Patricio Puga *Head of Treasury & Markets*
Head of Trading

Risk Management
Country Head　　　　　Cecilia Villota *Risk Manager*

Corporate Finance / M&A Advisory
Head of Corporate Finance　　　　　Eduardo Checa *Corporate Manager*

Administration

Other (Administration)
Commercial Banking　　　　　Debra Gentz *Account Officer*

The World Bank　　　　　Representative Office
Calle Juan León Mera 130 y Avenida Patria, Edificio Corporación Financiera Nacional, piso 6°, Quito
Tel: (2) 566 861 Fax: (2) 566 862

Senior Executive Officers
Chief Operating Officer　　　　　Marcelo Romero *Operations Officer*

EGYPT
(+20)

Alwatany Bank of Egypt — Head Office
13 Semar Street, Dr Fouad Mohy El Din Square, Gameat El Dewal El Arabia, Mohandissen, Giza
PO Box 63, Mohandessin, Giza, 12655
Tel: (2) 338 8916; (2) 338 8917 **Fax:** (2) 337 9302 **Telex:** 93268 WATAN UN **Swift:** WABA EG CX
Email: watany@alwatany.com.eg **Reuters:** WBOE (Dealing)
General Telex: 21108 WATAN UN; **International Capital Markets Tel:** 3348 9129
Website: www.alwatany.com.eg

Senior Executive Officers
Chairman	Adel Hussein Ezzy
Managing Director	Nabil Ahmed Gouda El Sahar
General Manager	Farouk Abdou
General Manager	Ahmed Koura
General Manager	Abd Alhakeem Abou Alam
International Division	Farouk Abdou *General Manager*

Money Markets
Global Head — Laila Fahmy *Manager* 336 2779

Foreign Exchange
Global Head — Laila Fahmy *Manager* 336 2779

Other Departments
Correspondent Banking — Manal Hassan *Deputy Manager*

Administration
Head of Administration — Ismail Adam *Deputy General Manager*

Other (Administration)
Foreign Relations — Ahmed Belal *Manager*

Arab African International Bank — Head Office
5 Midan Al Saray Al Koubra, Garden City, Cairo
PO Box 60, Magless El Shaab, Cairo, 11516
Tel: (2) 354 5094; (2) 354 5096 **Fax:** (2) 355 8493 **Telex:** 93531 AAIB UN **Swift:** ARAI EG CX **Reuters:** AAFE
Cable: ARABAFRO HO
General Telex: 21566 AAIB UN

Senior Executive Officers
Chairman — Fahed M Al Rashed

Others (Senior Executives)
Member of the Board —
Gamal H Mubarak *Director*
Mahmoud A Al Noury *Director*
Badr Salman Al Rashoud *Director*
Abdullah Abdel Aziz Al Qandy *Director*
Faika M El Refaie *Director*
Mohamed Saad Bader *Director*
Salah El Din El Baroudi *General Secretary to the Board*

General-Investment
Head of Investment —
Hassan Abdalla *Deputy General Manager*
Hany Seif El Nasr *AGM, Investment & Portfolio Control*

General - Treasury
Head of Treasury — Hassan Abdalla *Deputy General Manager*

Relationship Manager
Financial Institutions — Hany Hassan *Assistant General Manager*

Risk Management
Head of Risk Management — Sahar El Damati *Deputy General Manager*

Asset Management
Portfolio Management —
Hassan Abdalla *Deputy General Manager*
Hany Seif El Nasr *AGM, Investment & Portfolio Control*

EGYPT (+20)   www.euromoneydirectory.com

Arab International Bank
Head Office

35 Abdel Khalek Sarwat Street, Cairo
Tel: (2) 391 8794; (2) 391 6391 Fax: (2) 391 6233 Telex: 92079 AIB Swift: ARIB EG CX 001 Reuters: AIBC
Cable: ARABINBANK Tel: 391 6492; 391 8020; Telex: 92098

Senior Executive Officers
Chairman   Moustafa Khalil ☏ **390 5765**
Chief Executive Officer   Aly Dabbons *Managing Director* ☏ **391 0072**
    Mohamed Layas *Managing Director* ☏ **391 7895**
Acting General Manager   Atef Ibrahim ☏ **574 4258** F **574 5248**
Assistant General Manager   Nadia Fouad ☏ **390 5765**
International Division   Mohamed El Deeb *General Manager* ☏ **391 9302**

General-Investment
Head of Investment   Atef Ibrahim *Acting General Manager* ☏ **574 4258** F **574 5248**

Debt Capital Markets / Fixed Income
Department: International Financial Markets
Tel: 580 3066/7 Telex: 21317
Head of Debt Capital Markets; Head of Fixed   Atef Ibrahim *Acting General Manager* ☏ **574 4258** F **574 5248**
Income Sales; Head of Fixed Income Trading

Government Bonds
Head of Sales; Head of Trading   Mohamed Shaaben *Manager* ☏ **574 4256** F **574 5680**

Eurobonds
Head of Sales; Head of Trading   Mohamed Shaaben *Manager* ☏ **574 4256** F **574 5680**

Emerging Market Bonds
Head of Emerging Markets; Head of Sales;   Samia Zanfali *Assistant General Manager* ☏ **393 8176**
Head of Trading

Libor-Based / Floating-Rate Products
FRN Sales; FRN Trading   Mohamed Shaaben *Manager* ☏ **574 4256** F **574 5680**

Fixed-Income Repo
Head of Repo; Head of Trading   Mohamed Shaaben *Manager* ☏ **574 4256** F **574 5680**

Equity Capital Markets
Department: International Finacial Markets
Tel: 580 3066/7 Telex: 21317
Head of Equity Capital Markets; Head of Sales;   Atef Ibrahim *Acting General Manager* ☏ **574 4258** F **574 5248**
Head of Trading

Domestic Equities
Head of Sales; Head of Trading   Mohamed Shaaben *Manager* ☏ **574 4256** F **574 5680**

International Equities
Head of Sales; Head of Trading   Mohamed Shaaben *Manager* ☏ **574 4256** F **574 5680**

Convertibles / Equity-Linked
Head of Sales; Head of Trading   Mohamed Shaaben *Manager* ☏ **574 4256** F **574 5680**

Syndicated Lending
Head of Origination; Head of Syndication; Head   Samia Zanfali *Assistant General Manager* ☏ **393 8176**
of Trading

Money Markets
Head of Money Markets   Ahmed Nassef *Chief Manager* ☏ **574 5275** F **574 5277**

Foreign Exchange
Head of Foreign Exchange; Head of Institutional   Ahmed Nassef *Chief Manager* ☏ **574 5275** F **574 5277**
Sales; Corporate Sales; Head of Trading

Risk Management
Head of Risk Management   Atef Ibrahim *Acting General Manager* ☏ **574 4258** F **574 5248**

Settlement / Clearing
Head of Settlement / Clearing; Equity   Mohamed Hagin *Manager* ☏ **574 4256** F **574 5680**
Settlement; Fixed-Income Settlement; Back-
Office

Other Departments
Correspondent Banking   Hanaa Islamboli *Assistant General Manager*
Cash Management   Mohamed El Deeb *General Manager* ☏ **391 9302**

Administration
Head of Administration   Saher Abul Ezz *Assistant General Manager*
Head of Marketing   Walid Salah *Assistant General Manager*

Technology & Systems
    Moncef Ali *Assistant General Manager*

Legal / In-House Counsel
    Ghanem Ali *Assistant General Manager*

www.euromoneydirectory.com EGYPT (+20)

Compliance
Ghanem Ali *Assistant General Manager*
Public Relations
Essam Dabbous *Assistant General Manager*
Accounts / Audit
Yazid Dessouky *Assistant General Manager*

Arab Investment Bank — Head Office

Cairo Sky Boulevard, 8 Abd El-Khalek Sarwat Street, Cairo
PO Box 826, Cairo
Tel: (2) 770 376; (2) 760 031 **Fax:** (2) 770 329 **Telex:** 20191 INVBK UN **Cable:** INVESBANK CAIRO

Senior Executive Officers
Chairman
Mohamed Ahmed El Razaz
GM, Supervising Central Departments
Abdul Halim Amin
General Manager, Cairo Branch
Mohamed Abdul Hamid Mahmoud

General-Lending (DCM, SL)
Head of Corporate Banking
Osama El Shabrawy *GM, Loans Department* ☎ **770 354**
Abdul Hamid Ahmed El Gohary *GM, Central Credit*

General-Investment
Head of Investment
Hussein Beshir Selim *GM, Investment Department*

Relationship Manager
Follow Up Branches
Abdul Hamid Ahmed El Gohary *GM, Central Credit*
Islamic Branches
Ashraf Mohamed El Salamony *General Manager*
Affiliated Companies
Fikry Philip Bassily *Assistant General Manager*

Debt Capital Markets / Fixed Income
Domestic Government Bonds
Head of Sales; Head of Trading
Hussein Beshir Selim *Government Securities* ☎ **579 0311**

Syndicated Lending
Head of Syndication
Osama El Shabrawy *GM, Loans Department* ☎ **770 354**

Foreign Exchange
Country Head
Inas H Gameh *Manager* ☎ **777 176** **F 575 9262**

Administration
Head of Administration
Mohamed Mamdruh Mustafa *Manager* ☎ **579 1250**

Technology & Systems
Magdi Badr El Din *General Manager* ☎ **575 9261**

Legal / In-House Counsel
Osama Mazwouna *Manager* ☎ **575 9254**

Other (Administration)
Office Departments
Mohamed Adel Abdel Hamid Eissa *GM & Supervisor Head* ☎ **578 1680**

Bank of Commerce & Development (Al Tegaryoon) — Head Office

13, 26th July Street, Sphinx Square, Mohandessin, Cairo
PO Box 1373, Cairo
Tel: (2) 347 2056; (2) 347 5584 **Fax:** (2) 344 7537; (2) 345 0581 **Telex:** 21607 BCD UN **Swift:** BCDE EG CA
Reuters: BCDE
General Tel: 347 2063; 302 8156; **Telex:** 93408 BCDUN; **General Telex:** 21530 BCDUN

Senior Executive Officers
Chairman & Managing Director
Samir El Kasry
Treasurer
Mahmoud Zaki *Treasurer & Manager International Relations* ☎ **303 2209**
GM & Member, Board of Directors
Ahmed Fawzi El Shahed
International Division
Youssef Harhash *DGM, International Division*

Bankers Trust Company — Representative Office

Semiramis Inter-Continental Hotel, 1 Kamel El Shinawy Street, Garden City, Cairo
Tel: (2) 354 4817

Senior Executive Officers
Representative
Neveen Hossam El Din

Euromoney Directory 1999 **361**

EGYPT (+20)   www.euromoneydirectory.com

Banque du Caire   Head Office

30 Roushdy Street, Abdin, Cairo, 11511
PO Box 1495, Cairo
Tel: (2) 390 4554 **Fax:** (2) 390 8992 **Telex:** 21944 BNKHR UN **Swift:** BCAI EG CXX

Senior Executive Officers
Chairman   Mohamed Abo El Fath
Chief Executive Officer   Mofida El Dahaby *Executive General Manager*
Deputy Chairman   Hassan Mamdouh
General Manager   Kamal H Bishara
International Division   Suzanne Samy *Deputy General Manager*

General-Investment
Head of Investment   Soher El Sayed *Executive General Manager*

Equity Capital Markets
Equity Repo / Securities Lending
Head   Soher El Sayed *Executive General Manager*

Syndicated Lending
Loan-Related Activities
Trade Finance   Abd El Rahman Zahran *Manager*

Money Markets
Head of Money Markets   Nadia Boushra *Manager*

Foreign Exchange
Head of Foreign Exchange   Nevine El Shafei *Manager*

Other Departments
Correspondent Banking   Mohamed El Sammak *Manager*

Banque du Caire Barclays International SAE   Subsidiary Company

12 Midan El Sheikh Youssef, Garden City, Cairo
PO Box 110, Maglis El Shaab, Cairo
Tel: (2) 354 2195; (2) 354 9415 **Fax:** (2) 355 2746 **Telex:** 92343 CABAR UN **Swift:** BCBI EG CX
Reuters: CBIE (Monitor) **Cable:** CAIBARINT **Telex:** 93734 CABAR UN

Senior Executive Officers
Chairman   Mohamed Abo El Fath
Joint Managing Director   Egidio Giles Cutayar ☎ 355 6833
Joint Managing Director   Youssef Ezz El Din Esmat

Foreign Exchange
Head of Foreign Exchange   Karam Soliman *Deputy Senior Manager, Treasury* ☎ 354 0431 📠 355 6186

Risk Management
Global Head   Alan Causer *Assistant General Manager*

Corporate Finance / M&A Advisory
Country Head   Tony Minss *Senior Manager*

Other (Corporate Finance)
Marketing   Wafaa Zaklama *Senior Manager*

Settlement / Clearing
Operations   Dawoud M. Mahmoud *Senior Manager*
                                      El Sayed Zahran *Assistant General Manager*

Administration
Technology & Systems
Computer Department   Mohamed Ahmed *Senior Manager*

Accounts / Audit
Auditing   Moustafa Hamza *Senior Manager*

Banque du Caire et de Paris SAE   Subsidiary Company

3 Latin America Street, Garden City, Cairo, 11511
PO Box 2441, Ataba, Garden City, Cairo, 11511
Tel: (2) 354 8323; (2) 354 8325 **Fax:** (2) 354 0619 **Telex:** 93722 BACAP UN

Senior Executive Officers
Managing Director   Mr Vermenouze
Treasurer   Mrs Shadia *Head of Treasury*

www.euromoneydirectory.com EGYPT (+20)

Debt Capital Markets / Fixed Income
Marketing Mrs Souraya *Marketing*

Risk Management
Head of Risk Management Mr Voisin *Head*

Banque Misr — Head Office
151 Mohamed Farid Street, Cairo
Tel: (2) 391 2711; (2) 391 2106 **Fax:** (2) 391 9779 **Telex:** 92242 BANSR UN **Email:** staff@banquemisr.com
Website: www.banquemisr.com

Senior Executive Officers
Chairman	Essam El-Din El-Ahmady
Deputy Chairman	Bahaa El-Din Helmy Ismail
Deputy Chairman	Mahmoud Ali Bedeir
Managing Director	Ahmed Metwalli Hussein
Managing Director	Fouad Abdel Latif Hussein

Others (Senior Executives)
Sofi Hassan Abou Taleb *Member*
Ahmed Sorour Mohamed *Member*
Mohamed Abbas Hegazi *Member*

Berliner Bank AG — Representative Office
6th Floor, Apartment 36, 17 Kasr El Nil Street, Cairo
Tel: (2) 393 7978; (2) 392 1872 **Fax:** (2) 393 0526

Senior Executive Officers

Others (Senior Executives)
Sameh F Makram-Ebeid *Advisor* ☎ 390 9926 ✉ sme@ie-eg.com

The Chase Manhattan Bank — Full Branch Office
3 Ahmed Nessim Street, Giza, Cairo
PO Box 1962, Cairo
Tel: (2) 361 0393 **Fax:** (2) 361 0498

Senior Executive Officers
Senior Country Officer Mahmoud Abdel Latif

Citibank NA — Full Branch Office
4 Ahmed Pasha Street, Garden City, Cairo
PO Box 188, Cairo
Tel: (2) 355 1873; (2) 355 1874 **Fax:** (2) 355 7743 **Telex:** 20702 CITEX UN

Senior Executive Officers
Treasurer Zeinab Hashim *Country Treasurer* ☎ 356 2058
Ghada El Bialy *Deputy Treasurer* ☎ 356 2085

Debt Capital Markets / Fixed Income
Country Head Salman Butt *Head of Capital Markets* ☎ 597 0505

Equity Capital Markets
Country Head Salman Butt *Head of Capital Markets* ☎ 597 0505

Syndicated Lending
Country Head Mona Yassin *Head, Commercial Loans* ☎ 597 0531

Foreign Exchange
Country Head Zeinab Hashim *Country Treasurer* ☎ 356 2058
Ghada El Bialy *Deputy Treasurer* ☎ 356 2085

EGYPT (+20)　　　　　www.euromoneydirectory.com

Commercial International Bank (Egypt) SAE　　　　　Head Office
PO Box 2430, Nile Tower Building, 21/23 Giza Street, Giza
Tel: (2) 570 3043 **Fax:** (2) 570 3172; (2) 570 2691 **Telex:** 92394 CNBCA UN **Swift:** CIBE EG CX
Reuters: CIBE (Dealing) **Telex:** 20201 CNBCZ UN; **Reuters:** COIB (Monitor)

Senior Executive Officers
Chairman & Managing Director　　　　　Mahmoud Abdel Aziz
Vice Chairman & MD　　　　　Mahmoud Helal
Managing Director　　　　　Adel El Labban
International Division　　　　　Mohamed Shahbou *GM, Foreign Department*

General-Lending (DCM, SL)
Head of Corporate Banking　　　　　Hala Fayek *GM, Corporate Banking Group*

Relationship Manager
Staff Credit　　　　　Sahar El Sallab *General Manager*
Branches Group　　　　　Mohamed El Khouly *General Manager*

Debt Capital Markets / Fixed Income
Global Head　　　　　Adel El Labban *Managing Director*

Equity Capital Markets
Global Head　　　　　Adel El Labban *Managing Director*

Syndicated Lending
Global Head　　　　　Adel El Labban *Managing Director*

Money Markets
Global Head　　　　　Adel El Labban *Managing Director*

Foreign Exchange
Global Head　　　　　Adel El Labban *Managing Director*

Risk Management
Global Head　　　　　Sahar El Sallab *General Manager*

Corporate Finance / M&A Advisory
Global Head　　　　　Adel El Labban *Managing Director*

Settlement / Clearing
Regional Head　　　　　Mohamed El Prince *General Manager*
Operations　　　　　Mahmoud Anwar *GM, Financial Control & Administration*

Administration
Head of Administration　　　　　Mahmoud Anwar *GM, Financial Control & Administration*

Technology & Systems
Electronic Data Processing & Banking Systems　　　　　Mohamed El Prince *General Manager*

Accounts / Audit
Internal Audit　　　　　Mohamed El Turky *General Manager*

Commercial International Investment Company SAE
9 Mohamed Fahmy Street, Garden City, Cairo
Tel: (2) 594 3876; (2) 594 3877 **Fax:** (2) 594 3869

Senior Executive Officers
Financial Director　　　　　Ahmad S Abdallah *Financial Controller*
Managing Director　　　　　Yasser H El Mallawany
Executive Director　　　　　Neveen O El Shafei
Executive Director　　　　　Amr A El Garhy
Associate Director　　　　　Amr N Sheta
Associate Director　　　　　Hossam M Rageh

Others (Senior Executives)
Trading & Settlement　　　　　Mohamed S Bendary *Manager*

General-Investment
Head of Investment　　　　　Ayman S El Gammal *Executive Director*

Equity Capital Markets
Head of Equity Capital Markets　　　　　Ayman S El Gammal *Executive Director*

Corporate Finance / M&A Advisory
Head of Corporate Finance　　　　　Amr A El Garhy *Executive Director*
　　　　　Ayman S El Gammal *Executive Director*

The Definition of Banking in Egypt

EGYPT (+20)   www.euromoneydirectory.com

Commerzbank AG — Representative Office

22nd Floor, Banque Misr Tower, 153 Mohamed Farid Street, Cairo
PO Box 1944, Cairo, 11511
Tel: (2) 393 1661; (2) 390 7242 Fax: (2) 392 3718 Telex: 92194 CBK UN

Senior Executive Officers
Representative — Wilhelm Grethe

Crédit Agricole Indosuez — Representative Office

Formerly known as: Banque Indosuez

9 Mariette Pacha Street, Tahrir Square, Cairo
PO Box 175, Magless El Shaab, Cairo
Tel: (2) 575 5960; (2) 770 871 Fax: (2) 771 011

Senior Executive Officers
Manager — M Zalat

Crédit Commercial de France — Representative Office

4th Floor, Apartment 27, 26 Mahmoud Bassouin Street, Cairo
PO Box 2687, Cairo, 11511
Tel: (2) 574 0441; (2) 575 2980 Fax: (2) 777 603 Telex: 92687 CCF UN

Senior Executive Officers
Representative, Middle East — Jean-Pierre Levallois
Representative — Aida Rezkalla

Credit Suisse — Representative Office

32 Haroon Street, Dokki, Giza
PO Box 224, Dokki, Giza
Tel: (2) 360 0512; (2) 360 7865 Fax: (2) 348 5237

Senior Executive Officers
Senior Representative — Antonio F Lafranchi
Representative — Alain Ucari
Representative — Hala Hammad
Representative — Colette A Atallah

Credit Suisse First Boston — Full Branch Office

32 Haroon Street, Dokki, Giza
PO Box 224, Dokki, Giza
Tel: (2) 349 9760 Fax: (2) 361 5136 Telex: 94128 CSFB UN Telex: 20853 CSFB UN

Senior Executive Officers
Branch Manager — Magdi Hanna

Debt Capital Markets / Fixed Income
Country Head — Mohamed Feif El Nasr *Country Manager*

Settlement / Clearing
Tel: (2) 349 9760 Fax: (2) 361 5136
Operations — René Müller *Manager*

Administration
Other (Administration)
Commercial — Daniel Niggli *Manager*

Delta International Bank — Head Office

1113 Corniche El-Nil Street, PO Box 1159, Cairo, 11511
Tel: (2) 575 3492 Fax: (2) 762 851; (2) 574 3403 Telex: 93833 DIBHO UN Swift: DEIB EG CX Reuters: DIBE

Senior Executive Officers
Chairman & Managing Director — Aly Mohamed Negm
Treasurer — Hossam Osman

www.euromoneydirectory.com EGYPT (+20)

Others (Senior Executives)
GM, Finance & International Relations   Ismail Shaker
Debt Capital Markets / Fixed Income
Department: Financial Markets
Global Head   Yihia Saad *Finance & Investment*

Deutsche Bank AG
Representative Office

23 Kasr El Nil Street, Cairo
PO Box 2306, Cairo
Tel: (2) 392 1373; (2) 392 2341 **Telex**: 92306 DEUCAI UN **Cable**: DEUTBANK

EFG-Hermes
Head Office

55 Charles de Gaulle Street, Giza, Cairo
Tel: (2) 571 7846; (2) 571 7848 **Fax**: (2) 571 6121 **Reuters**: EFGS; HRMT
Website: www.efg-hermes.com

Senior Executive Officers
Chairman   Mohamed Taymour ☎ **338 3626**
General-Investment
Head of Investment   Ali El-Tahry
Debt Capital Markets / Fixed Income
Head of Fixed Income Sales   Mostafa El Assal *Head of Fixed Income*
Equity Capital Markets
Department: Securities Brokerage
Head of Equity Capital Markets   Ahmed Heakal *Head of Brokerage*
Equity Research
Head of Equity Research   Amur El-Kadi ☎ **336 1566**
Corporate Finance / M&A Advisory
Head of Corporate Finance   Hassan Heakal
Settlement / Clearing
Head of Settlement / Clearing   Ramsey Zaki
Asset Management
Investment Funds   Alladin El-Saboa ☎ **336 1045**
Portfolio Management   Hisham Tawfik ☎ **336 5960**

Egypt Arab African Bank SAE
Head Office

5 Midan El Saray El Koubra, Garden City, Cairo
PO Box 61, Magless El Shaab, Cairo
Tel: (2) 355 1513; (2) 355 0948 **Fax**: (2) 355 6239 **Telex**: 20965 EAAB UN **Swift**: EAAB EG CX
Email: eaab10@eaab.com.eg **Cable**: egyrabaf
International Capital Markets Tel: 3348 9129 **Telex**: 93505 EAAB UN **Telex**: 21600 EAAB UN

Senior Executive Officers
Chairman & Managing Director   Ali Mahmoud Seif
Chief Executive Officer   Ali Ezz-El-Din *CEO, Treasurer & GM*
Deputy Managing Director   Fathy Sebai Mansour
International Division   Ali Ezz-El-Din *General Manager*
Others (Senior Executives)
    Mokhtar Zayed *Manager, Foreign Department*
    Hassan Samir Abdel Moneim *DGM, I / C Dept*
General-Lending (DCM, SL)
Head of Corporate Banking   Mohamed Ibrahim El Badawy *DGM, Financial*
    Emad Abd El Kader *Deputy General Manager, Credit*
Syndicated Lending
Other (Trade Finance)
Letters of Credit   Hassan Samir Abdel Monem *Deputy General Manager*
Foreign Exchange
Global Head   Fawkeya El Guiziry *Manager*
FX Traders / Sales People
    Maysa Hussain *Dealer*
    Mona El Sharkawi *Dealer*
    Hisham Ghoneim *Dealer*

EGYPT (+20) www.euromoneydirectory.com

Egypt Arab African Bank SAE (cont)

Settlement / Clearing
Electronic Banking — Youssef Sharara *Deputy General Manager*

Other Departments
Chief Credit Officer — Emad Abdel Kader *Deputy General Manager*
Correspondent Banking — Ahmed Mokhtar Zayed *Manager, Foreign Relations*

Administration
Head of Administration — Mohamed Abou Ward *General Manager*
Head of Marketing — Nadea Mahmoud Fahmy *Deputy General Manager*

Technology & Systems
EDP — Youssif Kamel Sharara *General Manager*

Legal / In-House Counsel
Legal Affairs — Said El Sayed Rakha *General Manager*

Egyptian American Bank — Full Branch Office

Alternative trading name: EAB
4 & 6 Hassan Sabri Street, Zamalek, Cairo, 11511
PO Box 1825, Zamalek, Cairo, 11511
Tel: (2) 340 0063; (2) 341 6150 **Fax:** (2) 342 0265; (2) 340 9430 **Telex:** 92683 EGAMB UN **Swift:** EAMB EG CX
Email: tascano@eab-online.com **Reuters:** EABE
Foreign Exchange Tel: 340 0132; **Fax:** 340 1715; **Telex:** 20994 EGAMB UN
Website: www.eab-online.com

Senior Executive Officers
Chairman — Abdel Karim Abdel Hamid
Vice Chairman — Francis Stankard
Chief Executive Officer — James D Vaughn *Managing Director* 339 1509
Financial Director — Amr Tawfik *Financial Controller* 339 1502
Treasurer — Mohamed Taha *General Manager* 339 1560
Senior General Manager — Fatma Lotfy 339 1575
Senior General Manager — Tito Ascano 339 1511
Secretary to the Board — Hala Ragab 339 1550
International Division — Amr Abbas *Executive Manager* 339 1734

General-Lending (DCM, SL)
Head of Corporate Banking — Ahmed El Savyad *General Manager, Credit* 339 1560
Khaled El Badrawi *General Manager* 339 1652

General-Investment
Head of Investment — Azza Aziz *Executive General Manager* 391 5374

General - Treasury
Head of Treasury — Mohamed Taha *General Manager*

Syndicated Lending
Loan-Related Activities
Trade Finance — Amr Abbas *Manager* 339 1755
Shipping Finance — Mahmoud Eid *DGM, Delta Group / Shipping*

Money Markets
Country Head — Mohamed Taha *General Manager* 339 1560

Risk Management
Tel: 340 0132 **Fax:** 340 1715
Country Head — Mohamed Taha Mostafa *General Manager*

Corporate Finance / M&A Advisory
Head of Corporate Finance — Fatma Lotfy *Senior General Manager* 339 1575

Settlement / Clearing
Country Head — Ihab Ezzat *Senior Manager* 339 1504

Other Departments
Private Banking — Adel Kabil *General Manager* 594 1940
Correspondent Banking — Emad Rashad 339 1757

Administration
Head of Administration — Tito Ascano *Senior General Manager* 339 1511

Technology & Systems
Sherif Samy Aguib *Deputy General Manager* 339 1515

Legal / In-House Counsel
Hala Ragab *Secretary to the Board* 339 1550

Corporate Communications
Communications & Advertising — Ihab Badran *Deputy General Manager* 339 1662

www.euromoneydirectory.com EGYPT (+20)

Accounts / Audit
Audit — Gamil William *General Manager* ☎ 339 1569

Other (Administration)
Financial Administration — Amr Tawfik *Financial Controller* ☎ 339 1502
Human Resources — Ashraf Bebars *Deputy General Manager* ☎ 339 1562

Egyptian British Bank
Bank Subsidiary

Aboul Feda Building, 3 Aboul Feda Street, Zamalek, Cairo
PO Box 126D, Zamalek, Cairo
Tel: (2) 340 4849; (2) 340 9186 **Fax:** (2) 341 4010 **Telex:** 20505 EBBHO UN **Swift:** EBBK EG CX **Reuters:** EBBE
Cable: HONEGBANK **Tel:** 340 9286; **Telex:** 20471 HKEB UN

Senior Executive Officers
Managing Director — Abdel Salam El Anwar
Deputy Managing Director — T S T Major
Deputy General Manager — Assaad M Assaad

Others (Senior Executives)
Mohamed Abdel Moneim *General Manager, Branches*

General-Lending (DCM, SL)
Head of Corporate Banking — Mounir El Zahid *General Manager, Corporate Banking*
Tarek Helmy *Assistant General Manager*
Nevine Taher *Assistant General Manager*
Rafi Kassem *Senior Manager*
Shadia Sisalem *Deputy Senior Manager*

General - Treasury
Head of Treasury — Samy Safwat *Manager*

Debt Capital Markets / Fixed Income
Country Head — Tarek Afifi *Manager, Securities*

Equity Capital Markets
Country Head — Tarek Afifi *Manager, Securities*

Syndicated Lending

Other (Syndicated Lending)
Manager Card Product Department — Salah Helmy

Loan-Related Activities
Trade Finance — Manal Ghaly *Manager, Import / Export*

Other (Trade Finance)
Credit Control & Credit Administration — Halla Sakr *Assistant General Manager*

Money Markets

Wholesale Deposits
Marketing — Iman Eid *Manager, Guarantees / Bills*

Settlement / Clearing
Operations — Khaled Emam *Senior Manager, Financial Control*
Khaled Younes *Manager, Operational Training*
Lamia El Bahi *Manager, Financial Control*
Lamia Rabie *Manager, Operations Support*

Administration
Head of Administration — Nabil Sobhi *Deputy Senior Manager*

Technology & Systems
Technical Services — Hania Sadek *Senior Manager*

Legal / In-House Counsel
Medhat Refaat *Senior Manager*

Public Relations
Bank Secretary / Shareholders Relations / Advertising — Inas Anwar

Accounts / Audit
Internal Audit — Alaa El Gharably *Assistant General Manager*

Other (Administration)
Business Support — Hany Aboul Fotouh *Manager*
Human Resources — Khaireya Kandil *Senior Manager*
Cables — Gamal El Laicy *Manager*
Product Development — Adel Ghanem *Deputy Senior Manager*

EGYPT (+20)   www.euromoneydirectory.com

Export Development Bank of Egypt   Head Office

10 Talaat Harb Street, Cairo
Tel: (2) 777 003; (2) 769 854 **Fax:** (2) 774 553 **Telex:** 20850 **Swift:** EXDE EG CXA **Reuters:** EDBE **Telex:** 20872

Senior Executive Officers
Chairman, President & CEO   Mahmoud Mohamed Mahmoud
Vice Chairman   Salah Fahmy ☏ **761 153**
Financial Director   Salwa Mansour General Manager
General Manager   Hamdi Moussa

Debt Capital Markets / Fixed Income
Global Head   Salwa Mansour General Manager

Equity Capital Markets
Global Head   Salwa Mansour General Manager
Regional Head   Mahmoud Negm Deputy General Manager ☏ **578 2589**

Syndicated Lending
Global Head   Mokhtar EL Gamal General Manager

Loan-Related Activities
Trade Finance   Mokhtar EL Gamal General Manager
Project Finance   Faten Hamouda General Manager

Money Markets
Global Head   Salwa Mansour General Manager
                                         Mohamed Abdul Barry Manager

Foreign Exchange
Global Head   Salwa Mansour General Manager
                                         Khaled Amin Manager ☏ **578 2573**

Risk Management
Global Head   Mokhtar EL Gamal General Manager

Corporate Finance / M&A Advisory
Global Head   Mokhtar EL Gamal General Manager

Settlement / Clearing
Regional Head   Hamdi Moussa General Manager

Other Departments
Correspondent Banking   Ashraf Abou Alam Deputy General Manager

Administration
Technology & Systems
                                         Reda Askar General Manager

Legal / In-House Counsel
                                         Essam EL Kassaby Consultant

Public Relations
                                         Hassan Ezz Eldin General Manager

Faisal Islamic Bank of Egypt   Head Office

1113 Kournich El-Nil Street, Cairo
PO Box 2446, Cairo
Tel: (2) 575 3109; (2) 575 3165 **Fax:** (2) 777 301 **Telex:** 93877 **Telex:** 93878

Senior Executive Officers
Chairman   Prince Mohammed Al-Faisal Al-Saud
Vice Chairman   Ahmed Thabet Oweida
Governor   Abdelhamid Aboumoussa

Misr America International Bank   Head Office

12 Nadi El Seid Street, Dokki-Giza, Cairo
PO Box 1003-11511, Cairo
Tel: (2) 361 6623; (2) 361 6627 **Fax:** (2) 361 6610 **Telex:** 21505 MAIBQ UN **Swift:** MAME EG CX

Senior Executive Officers
Chairman & Managing Director   Yousry Moustafa ☏ **361 6634**
Chief Executive Officer   Mamdouh Abou Alam Chief Executive Officer & General Manager
                                         ☏ **361 66634** 🖷 **336 4182**
Financial Director   Fadel Hegazi ☏ **361 6623**
Treasurer   Raouf Kidwani ☏ **336 4184**

370 Euromoney Directory 1999

Senior Executive Officers (cont)
Chairman & Managing Director   Yousry Moustafa ☎ 361 6634
Chief Executive Officer & General Manager   Mamdouh Abou Alam ☎ 361 66634 F 336 4182
International Division   Mohamed El Deknawi ☎ 360 9758

Others (Senior Executives)
Assistant GM, PR & Marketing   Sayed Hussein ☎ 348 3179
Assistant GM, Systems   Abdel Hamid Solimam ☎ 361 6628
Assistant GM, Operations   Yousry Moussa ☎ 335 6811
Assistant GM, Cairo Branch   Sayed El Khatib ☎ 258 8446
Assistant Gm, Treasury   Raouf Kidwani ☎ 336 4184
Assistant GM, Alexandria & Delta Branch   Zaki El Gezeri ☎ (34) 920 661

General-Lending (DCM, SL)
Head of Corporate Banking   Ashraf Abd El Gelil ☎ 348 3179

General-Investment
Head of Investment   Ali Nasser ☎ 336 5105

Administration
Head of Administration   Mohamed Mitkees *Administration Manager* ☎ 360 9758 F 361 6623

Misr Exterior Bank Head Office

Cairo Plaza Building, Corniche El Nil St Boulaq, Cairo
Tel: (2) 778 552; (2) 778 701 **Fax:** (2) 762 806 **Telex:** 21616 **Email:** meb2@rite.com **Cable:** EXTEBANISR

Senior Executive Officers
Executive Chairman   Mohamed Nabil Ibrahim
Deputy Chairman, GM & Managing Director   Abdallah Abdel Fattah Tayel
Chief General Manager   Mohamed Abul Kassem

Others (Senior Executives)
Member, Board of Directors   Onsi Sawiras
                                            Mohamed Abdel Razek Anwar

General-Lending (DCM, SL)
Head of Corporate Banking   Abdel Halim El Fayoumi *General Manager, Credit*

Debt Capital Markets / Fixed Income
Global Head   Sayed Abdel Halim Emira *GM & Head, Capital Markets*

Syndicated Lending
Global Head   Rashad Abdel Gawad *General Manager*

Money Markets
Global Head   Helmi El Shayeb *Assistant General Manager & Head*

Foreign Exchange
Global Head   Helmi El Shayeb *Assistant General Manager & Head*

Corporate Finance / M&A Advisory
Department: MEFI (Misr Exterior Financial Investments Co)
Global Head   Onsi Sawiras

Other (Corporate Finance)
Public Offerings, Flotation Management;   Onsi Sawiras
Underwriting, Portfolio Management

Other Departments
Correspondent Banking   Helmi El Shayeb *Assistant General Manager & Head*

Misr Iran Development Bank Head Office

The Nile Tower, 21 Charles de Gaulle Avenue, Cairo
PO Box 219, Cairo, 12612
Tel: (2) 572 7311 **Fax:** (2) 570 1185 **Telex:** 20474 **Swift:** MIDB EG CX **Email:** midb@mst1.mist.eg.com
Cable: MIRBANK **Telex:** 21407

Senior Executive Officers
Chairman & Managing Director   Mahmoud Hamed
Financial Director   Mahmoud Ibrahim
Managing Director   Al-Motaz Bellah Mansour

Others (Senior Executives)
Credit & Investment Follow-Up   Ahmed Abdel Moneim *First Deputy General Manager* ☎ 570 3527

General-Lending (DCM, SL)
Head of Corporate Banking   Mahmoud Ibrahim Hassan *AGM, Financial Affairs* ☎ 570 1186
                                            Moustafa Khalil Ibrahim *First DGM, Banking Affairs (Mandated)* ☎ 570 3447 ➡
                                            Mohamed Abdel Latif *AGM, Credit*

EGYPT (+20)　　　　　　　　　www.euromoneydirectory.com

Misr Iran Development Bank (cont)
Debt Capital Markets / Fixed Income
Global Head　　　　　　　　Hossam El Guindi *AGM, Capital Market, Finance & Marketing* ☏ **570 3460**
　　　　　　　　　　　　　　🖷 **568 3379**
Syndicated Lending
Global Head　　　　　　　　Yousri Hamed *AGM, Loans Syndication*
Other (Syndicated Lending)
Credit Affairs　　　　　　　Adel Oweis *First Deputy General Manager* ☏ **570 3531**
Settlement / Clearing
Operations　　　　　　　　　Adham Fouad Abbas *Snr Adviser, Planning Inspection & Information*
Other Departments
Economic Research　　　　　Salwa Abdel Ghani *AGM, Research Affairs* ☏ **572 7056**
Other Departments
Treasury & Dealing Affairs　　Mahmoud Shafei *Assistant General Manager*
Finance & Follow Up Affairs　 Samir El Selouki *Assistant General Manager*
Administration
Data Information System　　　Moustafa Abdel Kader *Deputy General Manager* ☏ **570 3445**
　　　　　　　　　　　　　　Shaaben Hussein Halawy *Assistant General Manager*

Legal / In-House Counsel
　　　　　　　　　　　　　　Hussein Toema *Legal Consultant* ☏ **570 3448**
Legal Affairs　　　　　　　　Shaaban Hussein Halawy *Assistant General Manager*
　　　　　　　　　　　　　　Saber Ammar *Assistant General Manager* ☏ **572 1023**
Other (Administration)
Services　　　　　　　　　　Al Sayed El Sheneoufy *Deputy General Manager* ☏ **571 7807**
Foreign Relations　　　　　　Hoda Shoukry *Assistant General Manager* ☏ **570 3462** 🖷 **570 1191**
Internal Services　　　　　　Fatima Sharifa Sayed Ahmed *Assistant General Manager* ☏ **570 3529**
Human Resources　　　　　　Hamada Al Kareh *Assistant General Manager*

Misr Romanian Bank SAE　　　　　　　　　　　　　　　　　　　　Head Office

54 Lebnan Street, Mohandeseen, Giza
PO Box 144, Mohandeseen, Cairo
Tel: (2) 303 9825 **Fax:** (2) 303 9804 **Telex:** 21573 MRB UN **Swift:** MRBA EG CX **Email:** mrbeg@ie-eg.com
Reuters: MRBE **Cable:** ROMISBANK

Senior Executive Officers
Chairman　　　　　　　　　　Bahaa Eldin Helmy Ismail
Deputy Chairman & MD　　　　Abdel Monem Sayed Nada
Deputy Chairman & MD　　　　Lungu Dumitru
General Manager　　　　　　　Mircea Moisescu
General Manager　　　　　　　Abdel Rahman Baraka
International Division　　　　　Lungu Dumitru *Deputy Chairman & MD*

Mohandes Bank　　　　　　　　　　　　　　　　　　　　　　　　　Head Office

3, 5 Mossadek Street, Dokki, Giza
PO Box 170, Dokki, Giza
Tel: (2) 336 2760; (2) 336 2761 **Fax:** (2) 336 2741 **Telex:** 93407 MBAZ UN **Cable:** HANDES BANK
General Tel: 336 2762; **Telex:** 20762 MB UN

Senior Executive Officers
Chairman　　　　　　　　　　Hussein Fayek Sabbour
Managing Director　　　　　　Mohamed Adel El Sayed Hashish
Others (Senior Executives)
Board of Directors　　　　　　Ahmed Ali Mazen *Member*
　　　　　　　　　　　　　　Mohamed Mohi El Din El Tayeb *Member*
　　　　　　　　　　　　　　Mohamed Bahaa El Din *Member*
　　　　　　　　　　　　　　Ibrahim Ismail El Far *Member*
　　　　　　　　　　　　　　Mohamed Shafek Mansour *Member*
　　　　　　　　　　　　　　Yehia Shebl Saoudi *Member*
　　　　　　　　　　　　　　EL Shabrawy Mohamed El Feky *Member*
　　　　　　　　　　　　　　Mohamed Mohamed Gad Allah *Member*
　　　　　　　　　　　　　　Soad Mahmoud Ahmed *Member*

General-Lending (DCM, SL)
Head of Corporate Banking　　Mohamad Zohier Fahmy *DGM, Financial*
　　　　　　　　　　　　　　Abdel Aziz El Sayed *Deputy General Manager, Credit*

www.euromoneydirectory.com　　　　　　　　　　　　EGYPT (+20)

Relationship Manager
Foreign Relations　　　　　　　　Madiha Aly Sabri *Assistant General Manager*
Syndicated Lending
Other (Trade Finance)
Letters of Credit & Guarantees　　Kamal Ramadan Ibrahim *AGM*
Foreign Exchange
Head of Foreign Exchange　　　　Mohamed Nagi Abbas *Manager*
Administration
Head of Administration　　　　　Ahmed El Sadek Halawa *DGM*
Head of Marketing　　　　　　　Elham Ahmed Shoukry *DGM*

National Bank of Abu Dhabi　　　　　　　　　　　Full Branch Office

18th Floor, Nile Tower Building, 21 Giza Street, Cairo
Tel: (2) 573 7174; (2) 360 9724 **Fax:** (2) 572 4640; (2) 571 7584 **Telex:** 20774 BNZAB **Swift:** NBAD EG CA GIZ
Telex: 20734 BNZAB

Senior Executive Officers
AGM, Egypt　　　　　　　　　　Abdel Aziz Al Assar
Financial Director　　　　　　　Sarwat Nasr Debbana *Financial Controller*
Other Departments
Chief Credit Officer　　　　　　Magdi Aziz *Manager* ☎ **573 7331**
Administration
Head of Marketing　　　　　　　Amr Gaber *Manager*

National Bank of Egypt　　　　　　　　　　　　　Head Office

Alternative trading name: NBE
National Bank of Egypt Tower, 1187 Corniche El Nil, Cairo
PO Box 11611, Cairo
Tel: (2) 574 9101; (2) 574 8890 **Fax:** (2) 574 7159; (2) 574 6858 **Telex:** 20069 NBE UN **Email:** nbe@idsc.gov.eg
Website: www.nbe.com.eg

Senior Executive Officers
Chairman　　　　　　　　　　　Mahmoud Abdel Aziz ☎ **574 6000**
Deputy Chairman　　　　　　　Mohamed El Halawany ☎ **574 6900**
Deputy Chairman　　　　　　　Ahmed Abdel Rahman ☎ **574 9830**
Chief Executive Officer　　　　Hussein Hussein *Executive General Manager* ☎ **574 7682**
　　　　　　　　　　　　　　　Hafez El Ghandour *Executive General Manager* ☎ **574 8890**
　　　　　　　　　　　　　　　Mokhtar Abdel Rahman *Executive General Manager* ☎ **574 8116**
　　　　　　　　　　　　　　　Mohamed Gomaa *Executive General Manager* ☎ **574 7521**
　　　　　　　　　　　　　　　Fathi Ali *Executive General Manager* ☎ **578 5811**
　　　　　　　　　　　　　　　Abbas Samaha *Executive General Manager* ☎ **574 9045**
Financial Director　　　　　　Ahmed Abu Bakr *Executive General Manager* ☎ **574 8901**
Treasurer　　　　　　　　　　Ahmed Diaa El Din *GM, Member of the Board* ☎ **574 7524**
GM, Member of the Board　　Afaf Maged ☎ **574 9540**

Debt Capital Markets / Fixed Income
Head of Fixed Income　　　　　Mohamed Hasaneen *General Manager, Securities Dept* ☎ **578 4101**
Equity Capital Markets
Head of Equity Capital Markets　Mohamed Guendy ☎ **574 8395**
Syndicated Lending
Loan-Related Activities
Trade Finance　　　　　　　　Boshra Beshara *General Manager* ☎ **390 2152**
Project Finance　　　　　　　Ahmed Abu Bakr *Executive General Manager* ☎ **574 8901**
Money Markets
Head of Money Markets　　　　Yaser Abdou *Head, Money Markets* ☎ **574 7170** F **574 6060**
Foreign Exchange
Head of Foreign Exchange　　　Ahmed El Sherbiny *Head, Foreign Exchange* ☎ **574 7170** F **574 6060**

Euromoney Directory 1999　**373**

EGYPT (+20)

National Bank for Development
Head Office

5 (A) El Borsa El Gededa Street, Cairo, 11511
Tel: (2) 392 3528; (2) 392 23245 Fax: (2) 393 6719

Senior Executive Officers
Chairman　　　　　　　　　　　　　Mohamed Zaki El Oraby
General Manager　　　　　　　　　Mohamed K Hammad
General Manager　　　　　　　　　Mansour M Mansour
General Manager　　　　　　　　　Abdel Fattah A Salem
General Manager　　　　　　　　　Mamdouh A Sherbiny
International Division　　　　　　Sayed Zaky Ibrahim Manager

Relationship Manager
Financial Affairs　　　　　　　　　Mohamed T Karara Deputy General Manager

Debt Capital Markets / Fixed Income
Department: Financial Markets
Other　　　　　　　　　　　　　　Ezzat Abdab Halim Head of Trading ☏ 390 9734

Syndicated Lending

Other (Trade Finance)
Letters of Credit　　　　　　　　Mohamed R Ismail Deputy General Manager

Foreign Exchange
Head of Trading　　　　　　　　Mr Abdfattah

National Société Générale Bank SAE

10 Talaat Harb Street, Evergreen Building, PO Box 2664, Cairo
Tel: (2) 574 9376; (2) 574 9382 Fax: (2) 776 249

Nile Bank Cairo
Head Office

35 Ramses Street, Abdel Moneim Riad Square, Cairo
PO Box 2741, Cairo
Tel: (2) 574 1417; (2) 574 3502 Fax: (2) 575 6296 Telex: 22344 BANIL UN Swift: NILE EG CX
Email: nilebank@egyptonline.com Cable: NILBANGYPT

Senior Executive Officers
Chairman & Managing Director　　　Issa El Ayouty ☏ 575 3640
Managing Director　　　　　　　　Mohamed Hassan El Sabagh ☏ 575 3640
Secretary General & GM, Foreign Dept　Madiha Gaber ℻ 575 6296

Foreign Exchange
Global Head　　　　　　　　　　Nahed Elwy Manager ℻ 578 9187

Administration
Other (Administration)
Foreign Department　　　　　　Madiha Gaber Secretary General & GM, Foreign Dept ℻ 575 6296
　　　　　　　　　　　　　　　Assem Abdel Mohsen Manager ℻ 575 6296

Nordbanken AB (publ)
Agency

6th Floor, Apt 36, 17, Kasr el Nil Street, Cairo
Tel: (2) 393 7978 Fax: (2) 393 0526

Senior Executive Officers
Others (Senior Executives)
　　　　　　　　　　　　　　　Sameh F Makram-Ebeid Agent

State Bank of India
Representative Office

15 Kamel El Shinawy Street, Garden City, Cairo
Tel: (2) 354 2522 Fax: (2) 354 3504 Email: sbi@link.com.eg

Senior Executive Officers
Area Representative　　　　　　Adesh Saxena

www.euromoneydirectory.com   EL SALVADOR (+503)

The Sumitomo Bank Limited
Representative Office
12th Floor, Nile Tower Building, 21/23 Giza Street, Giza, Cairo
Tel: (2) 570 3644 **Fax:** (2) 570 3655
Senior Executive Officers
Chief Representative   Junichi Ikeno

The World Bank
Full Branch Office
Alternative trading name: International Bank for Reconstruction & Development
15th Floor, World Trade Center, 1191 Corniche El-Nil, Cairo
Tel: (2) 574 1670; (2) 574 1671 **Fax:** (2) 574 1676
Senior Executive Officers
Country Director   Khalid Ikram

EL SALVADOR
(+503)

Banco Central de Reserva de El Salvador
Central Bank
Alameda Juan Pablo II, y 15 Avenida Norte, San Salvador
Tel: 281 8000; 281 8001 **Fax:** 281 8011; 281 8113 **Telex:** 20088 **Swift:** CENR SV SS **Telex:** 20188
Website: www.bcr.gob.sv
Senior Executive Officers
President   Roberto Orellana ☏ **281 8402**
Vice President   Mauricio Gallardo ☏ **281 8406**
Vice President   Gino Bettaglio ☏ **281 8409**
Treasurer   Marco Tulio Rodríguez *Treasury Manager* ☏ **281 8803**
Others (Senior Executives)
Head, Banking Supervision   Francisco López *Manager, Financial Systems* ☏ **281 8176**
Head, Economics & Statistics   Rafael Barraza ☏ **281 8197**
Foreign Exchange
Head of Foreign Exchange   Carmen de Alemán *International Manager*
Administration
Head of Administration   Rafael Avillar *Manager, Administration* ☏ **281 8147**
Technology & Systems
     Oscar Quintanilla *Manager* ☏ **281 8008**
Public Relations
     María Luisa de Castro *Manager, Communications* ☏ **281 8120**

Banco Cuscatlan
Head Office
Km 10 Carretera a Santa Tecla, Edificio Pirámide Cuscatlán, San Salvador, 06626
Tel: 228 7777; 229 3006 **Fax:** 229 2168; 228 6687 **Telex:** 404290990
Senior Executive Officers
President   Mauricio Samayoa
Financial Director   Eduardo Quevedo
Managing Director / General Manager   Aturo Renderos
Foreign Exchange
Global Head   Tomás Yánez *International Manager* ☏ **229 3006**
Risk Management
Head of Risk Management   Maria Antonia Casanova

Banco Desarrollo SA
Head Office
Formerly known as: Banco de Desarrollo e Inversión
67 Avenida Norte 7 Boulevard San Antonio Abad, Plaza Las Américas, San Salvador
Tel: 298 6488; 224 0511 **Fax:** 224 2003; 298 6488 ext 427 **Telex:** 2026 **Email:** desarrollomail@ejje.com **Telex:** 2031-9
Senior Executive Officers
President   José Antonio Salaverría
Chief Executive Officer   Ricardo Morán *Executive Director*

EL SALVADOR (+503)

Banco Desarrollo SA (cont)
Senior Executive Officers (cont)
General Manager
International Division
    Bruno Wyld
    Sandra de Munguía *International Division Manager*

Administration
Head of Administration   Delmy Arrazzate *Administrative Manager*
Business Development   Claudia Hasfura *Commercial Manager* ☎ **264 1300**
Head of Marketing   Pedro Escalón *Marketing Manager*

Technology & Systems
    Eduardo Escalante *Systems Manager*

Legal / In-House Counsel
    Samuel Castro *Legal Manager*

Compliance
    Herbert Rico *Method & Organization Manager*

Accounts / Audit
    Carlos Alegría *Operations Manager*

Banco Santander SA — Representative Office
Calle la Reforma 183, Apartamento B, Colonia San Benito, San Salvador
Tel: 224 1099 **Fax:** 298 5877

Senior Executive Officers
Representative   María Laura Baires

Citibank NA — Full Branch Office
Alameda Dr Manuel Enrique Araujo, Kilómetro 4, Complejo Century Plaza, Edificio B, San Salvador
Tel: 224 3011; 224 3355 **Fax:** 224 2906

Senior Executive Officers
Chief Executive Officer   Steven Puig *Vice President & Country Corporate Officer* ☎ **245 1850** 📠 **245 1342**
Treasurer   Rafael Alfarc *Resident Vice President* ☎ **245 1850** 📠 **245 1342**

Ibero Platina Bank AG — Representative Office
Edif Gran Plaza, Local 101, Boulevard El Hipódromo, Colonia San Benito, San Salvador
Tel: 245 1101; 279 0418 **Fax:** 245 3254 **Email:** pbg@netcomsa.com **Tel:** 279 0428

ESTONIA
(+372)

Eesti Pank/Bank of Estonia — Central Bank
13 Estonia Pst, EE-0100 Tallinn
Tel: 631 0911 **Fax:** 631 0836 **Telex:** 173146 EPANK EE **Swift:** EPBE EE 2X **Reuters:** ESTI-L **Telerate:** 56772
Website: www.ee/epbe/

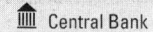

Senior Executive Officers
Chairman of the Board   Mart Sõrg ☎ **631 0844**
President   Vahur Kraft ☎ **631 0810**
Treasurer   Valdur Laid *Financial Markets Dept* ☎ **631 0960**

www.euromoneydirectory.com   ESTONIA (+372)

AS Eesti Uhispank
Head Office

Alternative trading name: Union Bank of Estonia
Tartu mnt 13, EE-0001 Tallinn
Roosikrantsi 2, EE-0001 Tallinn
Tel: 610 4100; 631 0100 **Fax:** 610 4102; 631 0122 **Telex:** 173006 UNION EE **Swift:** EEUH EE 2X
Email: postkast@eyp.ee **Reuters:** UBEX **Telerate:** 56770
Reuters: UNEE (Dealing)
Website: www.eyp.ee

Senior Executive Officers
Chairman of the Supervisory Board   Aare Urm ☎ **610 4300**
President   Ain Hanschmidt ☎ **610 4300**
Chief Executive Officer   Lembit Kitter *Vice President* ☎ **610 4300**
Financial Director   Ulo Suurkask *VP, Head of Finance Division* ☎ **611 0350**
Treasurer   Alo Alunurm *Director of Treasury Department* ☎ **631 0190**
Assistant   Inga Toomingas ☎ **610 4301**
International Division   Margus Schults *VP, Head of International Banking Division* ☎ **611 0600**

General-Lending (DCM, SL)
Head of Corporate Banking   Ott Karolin *VP, Head of Credit & Corporate Banking Division* ☎ **611 0650**

General-Investment
Head of Investment   Targo Raus *VP, Head of Investment Banking Division* ☎ **611 0810**

Debt Capital Markets / Fixed Income
Head of Fixed Income   Alo Alunurm *Director of Treasury Department* ☎ **631 0190**

Fixed-Income Repo
Head of Repo   Alo Alunurm *Director of Treasury Department* ☎ **631 0190**

Equity Capital Markets
Head of Equity Capital Markets   Toomas Tsopp *Director of Capital Markets Division* ☎ **611 0801**

Equity Repo / Securities Lending
Head   Toomas Tsopp *Director of Capital Markets Division* ☎ **611 0801**

Syndicated Lending
Head of Syndication   Margus Kangro *Director of Corporate Finance Division* ☎ **611 0631**

Loan-Related Activities
Trade Finance   Tatjana Nabokova *Head of Trade Finance Department* ☎ **631 0183**
Project Finance   Margus Kangro *Director of Corporate Finance Division* ☎ **611 0631**

Money Markets
Head of Money Markets   Andres Ojamaa *Head of Money Markets* ☎ **611 0617**

Foreign Exchange
Head of Foreign Exchange   Ulle Mathiesen *Head of Foreign Exchange Markets* ☎ **611 0616**

Corporate Finance / M&A Advisory
Head of Corporate Finance   Margus Kangro *Director of Corporate Finance Division* ☎ **611 0631**

Settlement / Clearing
Head of Settlement / Clearing   Virge Kärsten *Head of Settlement Department* ☎ **611 0455**

Global Custody
Head of Global Custody   Katrin Tur *Head of Depositary* ☎ **611 0642**

Other Departments
Chief Credit Officer   Ott Karolin *VP, Head of Credit & Corporate Banking Division* ☎ **611 0650**
Private Banking   Toivo Annus *VP, Head of Branch Management* ☎ **610 4200**
Correspondent Banking   Eerika Vaikmäe-Koit *Head of Correspondent Banking* ☎ **611 0600**
Cash Management   Heidi Tamm *Chief Cashier* ☎ **631 0224**

Administration
Head of Administration   Leho Lugna *Director of Administration* ☎ **610 4500**
Business Development; Head of Marketing   Jürgen Lamp *VP, Head of Organisation & Strategic Division* ☎ **610 4674**

Technology & Systems
Andres Keevallik *VP, Head of Information Technology* ☎ **610 4404**

Legal / In-House Counsel
Livia Toomik *Head of Legal & Compliance* ☎ **610 4404**

Compliance
Livia Toomik *Head of Legal & Compliance* ☎ **610 4404**

Public Relations
Janek Mäggi *VP, Head of Public Relations Department* ☎ **610 4334**

Accounts / Audit
Ülle Pärna *Head of Internal Audit Division* ☎ **611 0126**

ESTONIA (+372)   www.euromoneydirectory.com

AS Era Pank Limited
Head Office

Vallikraavi 2, EE-51014 Tartu
Tel: (7) 440 400; (7) 440 401 Fax: (7) 440 404 Telex: 173133 ERABN EE Swift: ERAP EE 2X Email: erap@proinv.ee
Reuters: ERAE
Website: www.erapank.ee

Senior Executive Officers
Chairman of the Board — Jaak Kiiker
Financial Director — Peep Akkel *Director, Finance Division*
Treasurer — Vivika Tael *Head, MM & Forex Dept* ☎ **440 430**
International Division — Ave Hussar *Head, International Relations Department*

Others (Senior Executives)
Rauno Kallas *Head, Loan Division*

Syndicated Lending
Country Head — Rauno Kallas *Head, Loan Division*

Loan-Related Activities
Trade Finance — Karin Ossipova *Specialist, Documentary Payments*

Money Markets
Global Head — Vivika Tael *Head, MM & Forex Dept* ☎ **440 430**

Domestic Commercial Paper
Head of Sales — Madis Jaaniste *Broker* ☎ **440 449**
Head of Trading — Raimond Russak *Broker* ☎ **440 439**

Foreign Exchange
Global Head — Vivika Tael *Head, MM & Forex Dept* ☎ **440 430**
Head of Trading — Herdis Kirk *FX Dealer* ☎ **440 431**

Other Departments
Private Banking — Indrek Lass *Customer Service*

Administration
Head of Marketing — Signe Kaurson *Marketing Director*

Technology & Systems
Mart Kallaste *IT Director*

Estonian Forexbank
Head Office

Narva maantee 11, EE-15015 Tallinn
PO Box 19, EE-10502 Tallinn
Tel: 630 2100; 630 2230 Fax: 630 2200 Telex: 173810 FOREX EE Swift: FORE EE 2X Email: bank@forex.ee
Website: www.forex.ee

Senior Executive Officers
Chairman — Härmo Värk
Financial Director — Priit Perens *Director of Finance* ☎ **630 2101**

Others (Senior Executives)
Business Banking — Kaido Kangur *Director*
Personal Banking — Erki Urva *Director* ☎ **630 2101**
Financial Markets — Kalle Norberg *Director of Financial Markets*

General-Lending (DCM, SL)
Head of Corporate Banking — Tauno Vanaselja *Director*

European Bank for Reconstruction & Development
Full Branch Office

Roosaskrnse 11, EE-0001 Tallinn
Tel: 641 8548 Fax: 641 8552

Senior Executive Officers

Others (Senior Executives)
Head of Office — Jonathan Harfield

www.euromoneydirectory.com ESTONIA (+372)

EVEA Bank Limited
Head Office

Pronksi 19, EE-15159 Tallinn
Tel: 667 1200 **Fax:** 667 1033 **Telex:** 173184 EVEA EE **Swift:** EVBA EE 2X **Email:** info@evb.ee **Reuters:** EVEA
Website: www.evb.ee

Senior Executive Officers
Chairman   Boris Špungin
Financial Director   Mati Kanarik
Chief Operating Officer   Anatoli Beilinson *Credit & Marketing Manager*
Treasurer   Aivar Riimets *Head of Financial Markets*
Company Secretary   Malle Enok
International Division   Endel Mustjogi

Debt Capital Markets / Fixed Income
Eurobonds
Head of Sales   Aivar Riimets *Head of Financial Markets*

Money Markets
Head of Money Markets   Aivar Riimets *Head of Financial Markets*

Other Departments
Chief Credit Officer   Antti Vinnal *Head of Loan Department*
Correspondent Banking   Endel Mustjogi
Cash Management   Heikki Kebbinau

Administration
Head of Administration   Moissei Jankelevitš *Administration Director*
Head of Marketing   Lidia Levtšenko *Head of Marketing Department*

Technology & Systems
                                    Leonid Orehhov *Head of IT Division*

Legal / In-House Counsel
                                    Riivo Sinijärv *Advisor*
                                    Peeyer Allikvere *Advisor*

Public Relations
                                    Gennadi Gramberg

Accounts / Audit
Chief Accountant   Anne Torva

Hansa Investments Group
Head Office

Kreutzwaldi 4, EE-0001 Tallinn
Tel: 640 0400; 640 0402 **Fax:** 640 0401; 640 0403
Website: www.hansa.ee/invest

Senior Executive Officers
Chairman of the Board   Joakim Helenius ☏ **509 1282**
Chief Executive Officer   Ben Wilson *Executive Director* ☏ **+371 732 2011**
Financial Director   John Wilson *Director, Sales & Trading* ☏ **640 0415**
Treasurer   Mare Eltermann *Corporate Administrator* ☏ **640 0495**
Managing Director   Piret Raudsepp ☏ **640 0404**

Relationship Manager
Investor Relations   Paul-Endel Luedig *Director* ☏ **640 0416**

Debt Capital Markets / Fixed Income
Department: Hansa Investment Managerment
Fax: 640 0426
Global Head   Aadu Oja *Managing Director* ☏ **640 0420**

Private Placements
Head of Origination   Piret Raudsepp *Managing Director* ☏ **640 0404**
Head of Sales   John Wilson *Director, Sales & Trading* ☏ **640 0415**
Head of Structuring   Piret Raudsepp *Managing Director* ☏ **640 0404**

Asset-Backed Securities / Securitization
Global Head   Ben Wilson *Executive Director* ☏ **+371 732 2011**
Regional Head   Tarmo Juristo *Associate Director* ☏ **640 0407**
Head of Trading   John Wilson *Director, Sales & Trading* ☏ **640 0415**

Mortgage-Backed Securities
Global Head   Ben Wilson *Executive Director* ☏ **+371 732 2011**
Regional Head   Tarmo Juristo *Associate Director* ☏ **640 0407**
Head of Trading   John Wilson *Director, Sales & Trading* ☏ **640 0415**

ESTONIA (+372)　　　　　　　　www.euromoneydirectory.com

Hansa Investments Group (cont)

Fixed-Income Research
Analyst　　　　　　　　　　　　　Viktor Karpov *Asset Management Analyst* ☏ **640 0421**
　　　　　　　　　　　　　　　　Inga Mathiesen *Asset Management Analyst* ☏ **640 0421**

Equity Capital Markets
Global Head　　　　　　　　　　Ben Wilson *Executive Director* ☏ **+371 732 2011**
Country Head　　　　　　　　　 Piret Raudsepp *Managing Director* ☏ **640 0404**

Domestic Equities
Head of Origination; Head of Syndication　Piret Raudsepp *Managing Director* ☏ **640 0404**
Head of Sales　　　　　　　　　John Wilson *Director, Sales & Trading* ☏ **640 0415**
Head of Trading　　　　　　　　Paul-Endel Luedig *Director* ☏ **640 0416**

Other (Domestic Equities)
Corporate Finance　　　　　　　Lenno Ruut *Associate Director* ☏ **640 0413**
　　　　　　　　　　　　　　　　Triin Palge *Analyst* ☏ **640 0410**
　　　　　　　　　　　　　　　　Anneli Simm *Analyst* ☏ **640 0409**
　　　　　　　　　　　　　　　　Rasmus Kurm *Analyst* ☏ **640 0411**
　　　　　　　　　　　　　　　　Laire Puhmaste *Analyst* ☏ **640 0412**
　　　　　　　　　　　　　　　　Kristel Kivinurm *Analyst* ☏ **640 0408**

Money Markets
Department: Hansa Investment Management
Fax: 640 0426
Global Head　　　　　　　　　　Aadu Oja *Managing Director* ☏ **640 0420**

Risk Management
Department: Hansa Investment Management
Tel: 640 0420 Fax: 640 0426
Global Head　　　　　　　　　　Aadu Oja *Managing Director* ☏ **640 0420**

Fixed Income Derivatives / Risk Management
Global Head　　　　　　　　　　Aadu Oja *Managing Director* ☏ **640 0420**

Corporate Finance / M&A Advisory
Global Head　　　　　　　　　　Ben Wilson *Executive Director* ☏ **+371 732 2011**
Country Head　　　　　　　　　 Piret Raudsepp *Managing Director* ☏ **640 0404**

Other (Corporate Finance)
Domestic Equity　　　　　　　　Lenno Ruut *Associate Director* ☏ **640 0413**
　　　　　　　　　　　　　　　　Triin Palge *Analyst* ☏ **640 0410**
　　　　　　　　　　　　　　　　Anneli Simm *Analyst* ☏ **640 0409**
　　　　　　　　　　　　　　　　Rasmus Kurm *Analyst* ☏ **640 0411**
　　　　　　　　　　　　　　　　Laire Puhmaste *Analyst* ☏ **640 0412**
　　　　　　　　　　　　　　　　Kristel Kivinurm *Analyst* ☏ **640 0408**

Settlement / Clearing
Regional Head　　　　　　　　　Ben Wilson *Executive Director* ☏ **+371 732 2011**
Equity Settlement　　　　　　　 John Wilson *Director, Sales & Trading* ☏ **640 0415**

Hansabank　　　　　　　　　　　　　　　　　　　　　　　　Head Office

8 Liivalaia Street, EE-0001 Tallinn
Tel: 631 0310 Fax: 631 0410 Telex: 173005 HABA EE Swift: HABA EE 2X
Website: www.hansa.ee

Senior Executive Officers
Chairman of the Board, Hansabank & CEO　Jüri Môis ☏ **631 0320** F **631 0434**
Chief Executive Officer　　　　　Indrek Neivelt *Member of the Board, Hansabank Estonia* ☏ **631 0372**
　　　　　　　　　　　　　　　　F **631 0434**
Vice Chairman, MD, Hansabank Markets　Rain Lohmus ☏ **631 0323** F **626 0545**
Member of the Board & Managing Director　Gerd Müller ☏ **631 0307** F **626 0557**
Member of the Board & Managing Director　Tonis Sildmäe ☏ **631 0304** F **631 0444**
Member of the Board & Managing Director　Tiina Mois ☏ **631 0407** F **626 0550**

Debt Capital Markets / Fixed Income
Reuters: 631 0323 Telex: 626 0545
Global Head　　　　　　　　　　Erkki Raasuke *Head of Department* ☏ **631 0472** E **e.raasuke@hansa.ee**

Domestic Government Bonds
Head of Sales　　　　　　　　　Lauri Kärner ☏ **631 0467** F **626 0545** E **l.karner@hansa.ee**
Head of Trading　　　　　　　　Erkki Raasuke *Head of Department* ☏ **631 0472** E **e.raasuke@hansa.ee**

Equity Capital Markets
Tel: 631 0323 Fax: 626 0545 Reuters: HANS
Global Head　　　　　　　　　　Tonu Pekk *Head* ☏ **631 0362**

www.euromoneydirectory.com ESTONIA (+372)

Domestic Equities
Head of Sales — Märt Meerits *Stock Broker* ☏ **626 0652**
Head of Trading — Märt Meerits *Senior Trader* ☏ **626 0652** E m.meerits@hansa.ee
Head of Research — Heikki Källu *Analyst* ☏ **626 0664** E h.kallu@hansa.ee

International Equities
Head of Sales — Megan Stifel *Head of Equity Sales* ☏ **626 0667** E m.stifel@hansa.ee

Syndicated Lending
Department: Credit Division
Tel: 631 0325 **Fax:** 631 0232

Loan-Related Activities
Trade Finance — Mait Koldits *Senior Manager* ☏ **626 0631**
Project Finance — Andri Hobemägi *Director* ☏ **631 0453**
Leasing & Asset Finance — Mart Tooming *Managing Director* ☏ **631 0495**

Foreign Exchange
Tel: 631 0323 **Fax:** 626 0545
Global Head — Art Lestberg *Head* ☏ **631 0467**

FX Traders / Sales People
Volatilities — Tonis Haavel *Chief Dealer, Volatilities* ☏ **631 0457**
Darius Gecevicius *Dealer* ☏ **626 0655**

Risk Management
Tel: 631 0323 **Fax:** 626 0545
Global Head — Kersti Allik *Head, Risk Management & Technologies* ☏ **626 0563**

Corporate Finance / M&A Advisory
Tel: 631 0347 **Fax:** 626 0557
Global Head — Ivo Kasak *Director, Corporate Finance* ☏ **631 0330** F **631 0322**
Gerd Müller *Member of the Board & Managing Director* ☏ **631 0307** F **626 0557**

Settlement / Clearing
Department: Back Office Settlements
Regional Head — Pille Parikas *Back-Office, Manager* ☏ **631 0306** F **626 0545**
Maie Oispuu *Head, International Operations* ☏ **631 0357** F **631 1693**

Global Custody
Tel: 631 0323 **Fax:** 626 0545
Regional Head — Tuuli Viilup *Manager, Securities Services* ☏ **631 0348** F **626 0822** E t.viilup@hansa.ee

Other Departments
Correspondent Banking — Terli Juhani *Manager* ☏ **631 0338** F **626 0545**

Administration
Head of Administration — Tiina Mois *Member of the Board & Managing Director* ☏ **631 0407** F **626 0550**

Technology & Systems
IT Division — Tonis Sildmäe *Member of the Board & Managing Director* ☏ **631 0304** F **631 0444**

Legal / In-House Counsel
Kaidar Sultson *Head* ☏ **631 0492** F **631 0322**

Compliance
Joel Aasmäe *Officer* ☏ **631 0331** F **626 0545**

Public Relations
Human Resources — Agve Aasma *Head* ☏ **631 0487** F **626 0550**
Marketing & Public Relations — Kai Vahe *Head* ☏ **631 0405** F **626 0557**

Leonia Bank Representative Office

Formerly known as: Postipankki
7th Floor, Liivalaia 14, EE-0100 Tallinn
Tel: 646 1090 **Fax:** 646 1093

Senior Executive Officers
Chief Representative — Sirkka Tounonen

Merita Bank Plc Full Branch Office

Harju 6, EE-0001 Tallinn
Tel: 628 3200 **Fax:** 628 3201 **Email:** tallinn@merita.ee

Senior Executive Officers
General Manager — Heikki Viitanen

Euromoney Directory 1999 **381**

ESTONIA (+372) www.euromoneydirectory.com

Talinvest Suprema Securities
Head Office
Pärnu mnt. 10, EE-10148 Tallinn
Tel: 640 5700 Fax: 640 5701
Senior Executive Officers
Managing Director / General Manager Henrik Igasta

ETHIOPIA
(+251)

National Bank of Ethiopia
Central Bank
Unity Square, Addis Ababa 5550
Tel: (1) 517 430 Fax: (1) 514 588 Telex: 21020
Senior Executive Officers
Governor Teklewold Atnafu ☏ 513 859
Vice Governor Alemseged Assefa ☏ 513 858
Treasurer Ahmed Seid ☏ 511 456
International Division Seife Desta *Manager, Foreign Banking* ☏ 515 579
Others (Senior Executives)
 Bekele Wolde *Executive Assistant* ☏ 514 893
Head, Banking Supervision Lakew Lema ☏ 513 857
Head, Banking & Insurance Institute Girma Seyoum *Director* ☏ 510 359
Saving & Credit Cooperative Department Maaza Beyene *Head* ☏ 513 667
Foreign Exchange
Head of Foreign Exchange Mekonnen Kahsay ☏ 511 425
Other Departments
Economic Research Ibrahim Abdulahi *Director, Economic Research* ☏ 514 792
Administration
Head of Administration Tiruneh Nitafa *Manager* ☏ 510 235
Technology & Systems
EDP Centre Tesfaye Teshome *Head* ☏ 511 750
Legal / In-House Counsel
Head, Legal Service Eshetu Irana ☏ 515 725
Accounts / Audit
Head, Accountancy Mohammed Hassen ☏ 517 069
Head, Audit Rebecca Bekele ☏ 510 416

Commercial Bank of Ethiopia
Head Office
Unity Square, Addis Ababa 255
Tel: (1) 511 271 Fax: (1) 514 522
Senior Executive Officers
Chairman of the Board Philipos W Mariam
President Tilahun Abbay
Chief Executive Officer Alazar Dessie *EVP & Operations*
Financial Director Hailu Legesse *Credit & Risk Manager*
Treasurer Asrat Getaneh *AVP, Finance*
Syndicated Lending
Department: Accounts - Finance
Head of Syndication Hailu Legesse *Credit & Risk Manager*
Loan-Related Activities
Trade Finance Eprem Negash *AVP, Credit Review & Risk Management*
Project Finance Mulugeta G Medhin *AVP, Credit Analysis & Appraisal*
Foreign Exchange
Department: International Banking Department
Global Head Jarso Kara *Manager*
Risk Management
Country Head Eprem Negash *AVP, Credit Review & Risk Management*

The World Bank
Representative Office

Alternative trading name: International Bank for Reconstruction & Development
Africa Avenue, Bole, Addis Ababa
PO Box 5515, Addis Ababa
Tel: (1) 514 200 **Fax:** (1) 511 441 **Telex:** 21154 **Cable:** INTBAFRAD

Senior Executive Officers
Representative   Niger Roberts

FIJI
(+679)

Reserve Bank of Fiji
Central Bank

Formerly known as: Central Monetary Authority of Fiji
Private Mail Bag, Suva
Tel: 313 611 **Fax:** 301 688; 307 210 **Telex:** 2164 FJ **Email:** rbf@is.cin.fj

Senior Executive Officers
Governor   Ratu Jone Kubuabola
Deputy Governor   Sada Reddy
General Manager   Eroni Mavoa

Others (Senior Executives)
Head, Economics   Steven Morling *Chief Manager*
Head, Financial Institutions   Inia Naiyaga *Chief Manager*
Head, Financial Markets   Barry Whiteside *Chief Manager*
Head, Currency & Corporate Services   Lorraine Seeto *Chief Manager*

Foreign Exchange
Head of Foreign Exchange   Barry Whiteside

FX Traders / Sales People
NZ$ / ¥
US$ Frazine Dutta *Investment Officer*
A$ / SGB   Villiame Caniogo *Investment Officer*
       Dennis Murray *Investment Officer*

Settlement / Clearing
Head of Settlement / Clearing   Lorraine Seeto *Chief Manager*
Fixed-Income Settlement; Foreign Exchange Settlement   Salote Lomaloma *Assistant Manager, Settlements*

Administration

Technology & Systems
       Anil Patel *Manager, IT*

Public Relations
       Eroni Mavoa *General Manager*

Fiji Development Bank
Head Office

Development Bank Centre, 360 Victoria Parade, Suva
PO Box 104, Suva
Tel: 314 866 **Fax:** 314 886

Senior Executive Officers
Chairman of the Board   Charles Walker
Chief Executive Officer   Isoa Kaloumaira *Managing Director*
Financial Director   Semi Tukana *General Manager, Finance*
Chief Operating Officer   Umarji Musa *General Manager, Operations*
Treasurer   Kee Fong *Manager, Finance*

Administration

Legal / In-House Counsel
       Tevita Madigibuli *Officer-in-Charge*

Public Relations
       Raijeli Nicole *Officer*

FIJI (+679)   www.euromoneydirectory.com

National Bank of Fiji
Head Office

Provident Plaza One, 33 Ellery Street, Level 3, Modules 1 & 2, Suva
PO Box 1166, Suva
Tel: 303 499 Fax: 302 190; 300 920 Telex: 2135 FIJIBANK FJ Swift: NBFI FJ FJ

Senior Executive Officers
Chairman — Lionel Yee
Chief Operating Officer — J M Konusi Head of Operations

Others (Senior Executives)
Corporate Services — R Singh
Credit — R Lal
Finance & Planning — I Moliciri Manager

General - Treasury
Head of Treasury — I Cakau Manager, International / Treasury ☎ 301 461 ℻ 303 217

Administration
Other (Administration)
Management Information Systems — M Vaurasi ☎ 302 982 ℻ 312 556

FINLAND
(+358)

Suomen Pankki-Finlands Bank
Central Bank

Alternative trading name: Bank of Finland
PO Box 160, FIN-00101 Helsinki
Tel: (9) 1831 Fax: (9) 174 872 Telex: 121224 SPFB SF Swift: SPFB FI HH Reuters: HELX; SPFB-K
Website: www.bof.fi

Senior Executive Officers
Chairman — Sirkka Hämäläinen
Member of the Board — Esko Ollila
Member of the Board — Matti Vanhala
Member of the Board — Matti Louekoski
Member of the Board — Matti Korhonen
Secretary of the Board — Heikki T Hämäläinen

Others (Senior Executives)
Chief Cashier — Antti Heinonen
Head, Monetary Policy — Pentti Pikkarainen
Head, Economics — Antti Suvanto
Head, Market Operations — Markus Fogelholm
Head, Financial Markets — Heikki Hoskenkylä
Head, International Secretariat — Kjell Peter Söderlund

Settlement / Clearing
Head of Settlement / Clearing — Raimo Hyvärinen

Other Departments
Economic Research — Juha Tarkka Head of Research

Administration
Head of Administration — Urpo Levo

Technology & Systems
Information Services — Martti Lehtonen
Information Technology — Pertti Simola

Legal / In-House Counsel
Head, Legal Affairs — Arno Lindgren

Corporate Communications
Communications — Antti Juusela Head

Accounts / Audit
Head, Accountancy — Ossi Leppänen
Internal Audit — Taina Kivelä

Other (Administration)
Personnel — Aura Laento
Publication & Language Services — Antero Arimo

384 Euromoney Directory 1999

iCB

the magazine for Global Transactions Services

**Call +44 171 779 8043, or
email nstainthorpe@euromoneyplc.com
now for a FREE TRIAL SUBSCRIPTION
and further information.**

- iCB is essential reading for anyone involved in wholesale financial services such as Custodians, Fund Managers, Broker/Dealers, Correspondent Bankers and Clearing Organisations.

- Over the last 15 years iCB has provided insightful news and analysis on the securities and payments industries.

- iCB is the only magazine dedicated to reporting on: Custody, Clearing, Payments, Technology and Regulations.

FINLAND (+358) www.euromoneydirectory.com

Ålandsbanken AB
Head Office

Alternative trading name: Bank of Åland Ltd
Nygatan 2, FIN-22100 Mariehamn
PO Box 3, Mariehamn
Tel: (204) 29011 **Fax:** (204) 291 228 **Telex:** 63157 ABINT FI **Swift:** AABA FI 22 **Email:** info@alandsbanken.fi
Reuters: ALMA **Telerate:** 20793
Website: www.alandsbanken.fi

Senior Executive Officers
Chairman & Chief Executive   Folke Husell ☏ 291 239
Vice Chairman & General Manager   Peter Grönlund
General Manager   Jan Tallqvist ☏ 293 652
General Manager, Administration   Lennart Haglund ☏ 291 401
General Manager, Branch Offices   Edgar Vickström ☏ 291 182
General Manager   Lars Donner

General-Investment
Head of Investment   Carl Magnus Gardberg *Investment Manager*

Relationship Manager
Foreign Payments   Gun-Marie Sandell *Supervisor*

Debt Capital Markets / Fixed Income
Department: Capital & Treasury Markets
Global Head   Bengt Lundberg *Department Manager* ☏ 291 188 ℻ 291 551

Domestic Government Bonds
Head of Sales   Carl Magnus Gardberg *Investment Manager*
Head of Trading   Tom Signell *Dealer*
                                          Tuula-Riitta Nyström *Dealer*

Bonds - General
Eurobonds   Carl Magnus Gardberg *Investment Manager*

Libor-Based / Floating-Rate Products
FRN Origination   Carl Magnus Gardberg *Investment Manager*

Equity Capital Markets
Global Head   Carl Magnus Gardberg *Investment Manager*

Convertibles / Equity-Linked
Head of Origination   Carl Magnus Gardberg *Investment Manager*

Syndicated Lending
Country Head   Lars Donner *General Manager*

Other (Syndicated Lending)
Letters of Credit; Documentary Credits   Gun-Marie Sandell *Supervisor*

Loan-Related Activities
Trade Finance   Gun-Marie Sandell *Supervisor*

Money Markets
Global Head   Bengt Lundberg *Department Manager* ☏ 291 188 ℻ 291 551

Other (Wholesale Deposits)
Eurocurrency Deposits   Tom Signell *Dealer*
                                          Tuula-Riitta Nyström *Dealer*
                                          Inger Holmström *Dealer*
                                          Ulla Berglund *Dealer*

Foreign Exchange
FX Traders / Sales People
                                          Inger Holmström *Dealer*
                                          Ulla Berglund *Dealer*

Risk Management
IR Swaps Trading   Tom Signell *Dealer*
                                          Tuula-Riitta Nyström *Dealer*

Foreign Exchange Derivatives / Risk Management
Cross-Currency Swaps, Trading   Tom Signell *Dealer*
                                          Tuula-Riitta Nyström *Dealer*

Other Currency Swap / FX Options Personnel
Eurocurrency Swaps   Ulla Berglund *Dealer*
                                          Inger Holmström *Dealer*

Settlement / Clearing
Settlement (General)   Bernt-Johan Jansson *Department Manager*
                                          Siw Sommarlund *Bank Guarantees*
Electronic Banking   Björn Tennström *Manager*

www.euromoneydirectory.com　　　　　　　　　　　FINLAND (+358)

Other Departments
Correspondent Banking　　　　　　　Peter Grönlund *Vice Chairman & General Manager*
Global Trust　　　　　　　　　　　　　Lars Donner *General Manager*
Economic Research　　　　　　　　　Danny Lindqvist
Administration
Head of Administration　　　　　　　Lennart Haglund *General Manager, Administration* ☏ **291 401**
Head of Marketing　　　　　　　　　Tiina Sovela-Björklund *Manager*
Technology & Systems
　　　　　　　　　　　　　　　　　　　Eva Wahlberg *Manager*
Legal / In-House Counsel
　　　　　　　　　　　　　　　　　　　Dan-Erik Woivalin *Manager*
Public Relations
Human Resources　　　　　　　　　　Gunilla Blomroos *Manager*
Accounts / Audit
Internal Audit　　　　　　　　　　　Tom Pettersson *Manager*
Other (Administration)
International & Securities Administration　　Thomas Nordlund *Dept Manager, Back-Office Settlements*
Security　　　　　　　　　　　　　　Ulrica Lindström *Manager*
Administration　　　　　　　　　　　Bernt-Johan Jansson *Department Manager*

Arctos Securities Limited

Aleksanterinkatu 44, FIN-00100 Helsinki
Tel: (9) 54993 00 **Fax**: (9) 54993 333 **Telex**: 126271 ARC FI
Website: www.arctos.fi

Senior Executive Officers
Managing Director　　　　　　　　　Jakka Laukkenen ☏ **54993 320**
Financial Director　　　　　　　　　Pekka Vaisönen ☏ **54993 445**

Alfred Berg Finland Oy Ab   Head Office

Kluuvikatu 3, FIN-00100 Helsinki
Tel: (9) 22832 1 **Fax**: (9) 22832 283; (9) 22832 282 **Telex**: 126314 BERG FI
Website: www.alfredberg.fi

Senior Executive Officers
Chairman　　　　　　　　　　　　　Lars Wedenborn
President　　　　　　　　　　　　　Robert Sergelius ☏ **22832 710** 🖷 **22832 790**
Chief Executive Officer　　　　　　　Jaana Pohjanheimo *Controller* ☏ **22832 714** 🖷 **22832 790**
Debt Capital Markets / Fixed Income
Tel: 22832 300 **Fax**: 22832 283
Country Head　　　　　　　　　　　Anders Ehrstrom ☏ **22832 709**
Domestic Government Bonds
Head of Sales　　　　　　　　　　　Antti Rikka ☏ **22832 350**
Head of Trading　　　　　　　　　　Staffan Hansér ☏ **22832 451**
Head of Research　　　　　　　　　Sampsa Laine ☏ **22832 732**
Equity Capital Markets
Tel: 22832 200 **Fax**: 22832 283
Country Head　　　　　　　　　　　Marco Granskog *Head of Sales* ☏ **22832 450**
Domestic Equities
Head of Sales　　　　　　　　　　　Marco Granskog *Head of Sales* ☏ **22832 450**
Head of Trading　　　　　　　　　　Juha Vähäpassi ☏ **22832 452**
Head of Research　　　　　　　　　Robert Sergelius ☏ **22832 710**
Risk Management
Country Head　　　　　　　　　　　Jaana Pohjanheimo *Controller* ☏ **22832 714** 🖷 **22832 790**
Corporate Finance / M&A Advisory
Tel: 22832 500 **Fax**: 22832 582
Country Head　　　　　　　　　　　Klaus Oehlandt ☏ **22832 515**
Settlement / Clearing
Fax: 22832 382
Country Head; Equity Settlement　　Ulla Heikkinen ☏ **22832 747**
Fixed-Income Settlement　　　　　　Katriina Tammisto ☏ **22832 752**

Euromoney Directory 1999　**387**

FINLAND (+358)　　　　　　www.euromoneydirectory.com

Carnegie Asset Management Finland Limited　　Subsidiary Company

Etela Espanadi 12, FIN-00130 Helsinki
Tel: (9) 61871 1; (9) 61871 400 **Fax:** (9) 61871 401; (9) 61871 402 **Email:** sijo@carnegie.fi
Website: www.carnegie.fi

Senior Executive Officers
Managing Director　　　　　　　　　　Jorma Saine ☎ **61871 411**
Others (Senior Executives)
Carnegie Fund Company Finland Ltd　　　Kai Luotonen *Managing Director* ☎ **61871 421**
　　　　　　　　　　　　　　　　　　　Kaj Olof Lindgren *Head, Sales & Marketing* ☎ **61871 432**
Asset Management
Portfolio Management　　　　　　　　　Karri Alameri *Portfolio Manager, Equities*
　　　　　　　　　　　　　　　　　　　Timo Penttal *Portfolio Manager, Equities*
　　　　　　　　　　　　　　　　　　　Jarmo Stirldeinen *Portfolio Manager, Fixed-Income*
　　　　　　　　　　　　　　　　　　　Kim Jansson *Portfolio Manager, Fixed-Income*
Administration
Head of Administration　　　　　　　　Jukka Rasanen *Head of Administration* ☎ **61871 452**

Citibank International plc　　　　　　　　　　　　　　　　　Full Branch Office

Aleksanterinkatu 48 A, FIN-00101 Helsinki
PO Box 980, FIN-00101 Helsinki
Tel: (9) 34887 1 **Fax:** (9) 34887 388 **Telex:** 121984 **Swift:** CITI FI HX

Senior Executive Officers
Managing Director　　　　　　　　　　Stephen L Dwyre ☎ **34887 200**
Financial Director　　　　　　　　　　Anneli Brummer *FI Head* ☎ **34887 220**
Chief Operating Officer　　　　　　　　Stefan Einarsson *Infrastructure Head* ☎ **34887 250**
Treasurer　　　　　　　　　　　　　　Veli-Matti Jaatinen *Treasury Head* ☎ **34887 300**
Relationship Manager
Forest Products　　　　　　　　　　　Juhani Numminen *Deputy Managing Director* ☎ **34887 201**
Foreign Exchange
Corporate Sales　　　　　　　　　　　Veli-Matti Jaatinen ☎ **17338 226**

DAVY-Protos Stockbrokers Limited　　　　　　　　　　　Head Office

Formerly known as: Protos Stockbrokers Limited
Aleksanterinkatu 48 A, FIN-00100 Helsinki
PO Box 334, FIN-00101 Helsinki
Tel: (9) 1733 9301 **Fax:** (9) 651 093 **Telex:** 126184 PTS FI **Reuters:** PRTS **Bloomberg:** PSFI

Den Danske Bank Aktieselskab　　　　　　　　　　　　Full Branch Office

Aleksanterinkatu 44, PO Box 993, FIN-00101 Helsinki
Tel: (9) 7514 5000 **Fax:** (9) 7514 5050 **Swift:** DABA FI HX

Senior Executive Officers
Chief Executive Officer　　　　　　　　Heikki Palosuo *General Manager*
Deputy General Manager　　　　　　　Per Hovgaard

ENSO Group

Kanavaranta 1, FIN-00101 Helsinki
Tel: (20) 462 6131 **Fax:** (20) 462 1267

Leonia Corporate Bank plc

Formerly known as: Finnish Export Credit Ltd
Etaläesplanadi 8, FIN-00007 Helsinki
Tel: (204) 2511 **Fax:** (9) 174 819 **Telex:** 121893 FEC FI

Senior Executive Officers
Chief Executive Officer　　　　　　　　Harri Hollmen ☎ **254 112** 📠 **254 121**
President　　　　　　　　　　　　　　Orvo Siimesto ☎ **254 130** 📠 **257 345**

www.euromoneydirectory.com　　　　　　　　　FINLAND (+358)

Relationship Manager
Products　　　　　　　　　　　Matti Virtanen *Executive Vice President* ☏ 254 210
Administration
Public Relations
Customer Relations　　　　　　　Matti Copeland *Executive Vice President* ☏ 253 860

Leonia plc

Eteläesplanadi 8, FIN-00007 Helsinki
Tel: (204) 2511 **Fax:** (204) 252 608 **Email:** forename.lastname@leonia.fi
Website: www.leonia.fi

Senior Executive Officers
Chairman　　　　　　　　　　　Eino Keinänen ☏ 254 111 [F] 255 251
Chief Executive Officer　　　　　 Harri Hollhén ☏ 254 112 [F] 254 121
International Division　　　　　　Jussi Osola *Executive Vice President*

General-Lending (DCM, SL)
Head of Corporate Banking　　　　Ilkka Hallavo *Executive Vice President*

General - Treasury
Head of Treasury　　　　　　　　Jussi Osola *Executive Vice President*
Department: Baltic Countries
Chief Representative　　　　　　 Sirkka Tuononen

Debt Capital Markets / Fixed Income
Department: Leonia Markets
Head of Fixed Income　　　　　　Kai Brander *First Vice President*
Head of Fixed Income Sales　　　 Matti Villikka *Senior Vice President*
Head of Fixed Income Trading　　 Risto Tornivaara *Senior Vice President, Trading*

Government Bonds
Head of Trading　　　　　　　　 Ismo Hokkanen *Chief Dealer*
　　　　　　　　　　　　　　　　Jouni Parviainen *Chief Dealer*

Eurobonds
Head of Trading　　　　　　　　 Ismo Hokkanen *Chief Dealer*
　　　　　　　　　　　　　　　　Jouni Parviainen *Chief Dealer*

Equity Capital Markets
Department: Leonia Markets
Global Head　　　　　　　　　　 Kai Brander *First Vice President*
Head of Sales　　　　　　　　　　Matti Villikka *Senior Vice President*
Head of Trading　　　　　　　　　Risto Tornivaara *Senior Vice President, Trading*
　　　　　　　　　　　　　　　　Petri Nurmi *Assistant Vice President*
　　　　　　　　　　　　　　　　Timo Huttunen *Assistant Vice President*

Domestic Equities
Head of Sales　　　　　　　　　　Mika Kivinen
　　　　　　　　　　　　　　　　Petri Korpineva
　　　　　　　　　　　　　　　　Pasi Käkelä
Head of Research　　　　　　　　 Mika Kivinen
　　　　　　　　　　　　　　　　Petri Korpineva
　　　　　　　　　　　　　　　　Pasi Käkelä

Money Markets
Department: Leonia Markets
Head of Money Markets　　　　　 Karin Martin *Vice President*

Foreign Exchange
Department: Leonia Markets
Global Head　　　　　　　　　　 Hannu Heinonen *First Vice President*
Corporate Sales　　　　　　　　　Veikko Virtanen *Director, Large Corporates Sales*
Head of Trading　　　　　　　　　Heikki Nordman *Chief Dealer*
　　　　　　　　　　　　　　　　Jyrki Tavaila *Chief Dealer, Emerging Markets*
　　　　　　　　　　　　　　　　Kari Koivula *Chief Dealer, Emerging Markets*

Risk Management
Department: Leonia Markets
Fixed Income Derivatives / Risk Management
Trading　　　　　　　　　　　　 Ismo Hokkanen *Chief Dealer*
　　　　　　　　　　　　　　　　Jouni Parviainen *Chief Dealer*
IR Swaps Trading　　　　　　　　Petri Viertiö *VP, Financial Engineering & Swaps*

Foreign Exchange Derivatives / Risk Management
Country Head　　　　　　　　　　Veikko Virtanen *Director, Large Corporates Sales*
Spot / Forwards Trading　　　　　 Tuula Koskimäki *Chief Dealer, Forwards*
Vanilla FX option Trading　　　　 Oskar Rewell *Chief Dealer, Options*

FINLAND (+358)   www.euromoneydirectory.com

Leonia plc (cont)
Asset Management
Head   Tomi Dahlberg *SVP, Asset & Liability Management*
Other Departments
Private Banking   Maarit Näkyvä *Executive Vice President*

London Forfaiting Company plc   Representative Office
World Trade Center, Aleksanterinkatu 17, FIN-00101 Helsinki
PO Box 800, FIN-00101 Helsinki
Tel: (9) 6969 2244 **Fax:** (9) 6969 2240 **Email:** lfc@wtc.fi

Senior Executive Officers
Representative   Matti Liedes
Others (Senior Executives)
                                  Keijo Kivilmoma *Senior Manager*
                                  Topi Tajakka *Manager*

Mandatum Bank Plc
Formerly known as: Interbank Limited
Bulevardi 10, FIN-00120 Helsinki
PO Box 152, FIN-00121 Helsinki
Tel: (9) 166 721 **Fax:** (9) 632 705 **Telex:** 126313 INSEC FI **Swift:** INTK FI HH
Website: www.mandatum.fi

Senior Executive Officers
Chairman of the Board   Björn Wahlroos
Vice Chairman & Managing Director Paavo Prepula
Financial Director   Patrick Lapveteläinen *Chief Financial Officer & Member of the Board*
Others (Senior Executives)
Board of Directors   Kurt Lundmark
                                  Jerker Molander
                                  Lars-Olof Staffans
                                  Sten Eklundh
                                  Ilona Ervasti-Vaintola

General - Treasury
Head of Treasury   Patrick Lapveteläinen *Director, International & Treasury*
Relationship Manager
Credit   Heikki Simola *Bank Director*
Debt Capital Markets / Fixed Income
Country Head   Patrick Lapveteläinen
Bonds - General
                                  Pekka Moisio *Chief Dealer*
                                  Harri Piipponen *Dealer*
                                  Christian Brade *Dealer*
Medium-Term Notes
Head of Sales   Harri Piipponen
Department: Government Securities & Municipal Bonds
Domestic Government Bonds
Head of Sales   Pekka Moisio
Head of Trading   Patrick Lapveteläinen
Department: Domestic Securities
Domestic Government Bonds
Head of Trading   Patrick Lapveteläinen
Money Markets
Money Markets - General
CDs   Christian Brade *Sales*
                                  Pekka Moisio *Trading*

Foreign Exchange
Country Head   Patrick Lapveteläinen *Manager*
Head of Trading   Harri Piipponen *Dealer*
Settlement / Clearing
Foreign Exchange Settlement   Marjatta Peisanen *Manager*

www.euromoneydirectory.com FINLAND (+358)

Global Custody
Other (Global Custody)
Custodian Banking Marjatta Peisanen *Manager*
Asset Management
Funds Management Reijo Manninen *Fund Manager*
Other Departments
Correspondent Banking Leena Mäkinen
Administration
Head of Administration Marjatta Peisanen *Manager*
Technology & Systems
Technology & Software Jari Julin *IT Director*
Legal / In-House Counsel
Legal Counsel Timo Rikkonen *Lawyer*
Public Relations
 Liisa Scmidt *Executive Secretary*
Corporate Communications
 Liisa Scmidt *Executive Secretary*
Other (Administration)
Corporate Marketing Kirsi Lempinen *Marketing Manager*
Marketing Department Anna-Mari Patrakka *Assistant*

MB Finance Limited

Alternative trading name: MB Corporate Finance Limited
Fabianinkatu 23, FIN-00130 Helsinki
Tel: (9) 13101 1 **Fax:** (9) 13101 310

Senior Executive Officers
Managing Director Juhani Suomela
Corporate Finance / M&A Advisory
Private Equity Matti Mertsola *Private Equity & Mezzanine*
 Kari Rytkönen *Private Equity & Mezzanine*

Merita Bank Plc   Head Office

Aleksanterinkatu 30, FIN-00100 Helsinki
PO Box 84, FIN-00020 Merita
Tel: (9) 1651; (9) 1654 3968 **Fax:** (9) 1654 2838 **Telex:** MRIT FI 124407 **Swift:** MRIT FI HH **Reuters:** MERITA
Website: www.merita.fi

Senior Executive Officers
Chairman of the Board & CEO Vesa Vainio
Vice Chairman Jacob Palmstierna
President & Chief Executive Officer Hans Dalborg
Treasurer Fanny Borgström *Senior Vice President*
 Sven-Åke Johansson *Treasury & Real Estate*
International Division K G Lindvall *Executive Vice President*

Others (Senior Executives)
Retail Banking Markku Pohjola *Managing Director*
Corporate Division Jorma Laakkonen *Executive Vice President*
Consumer Banking Eino Halonen *Executive Vice President*
Markets Jussi Laitinen *Executive Vice President*
Credit Policy & Credit Control Claes Östberg *Executive Vice President*
International Products Kari Kangas *Senior Vice President*
Trading Pirjo Jääskeläinen *First Vice President*
International Payment Services Kari Pulkkinen *First Vice President*

General-Lending (DCM, SL)
Head of Corporate Banking Kari Jordan *EVP, Commercial Banking*
 Carl-Johan Granvik *Managing Director, Corporate Bank*
 Martti Huhtamäki *EVP, Finance*

General-Investment
Head of Investment Hari Hallmén *Managing Director, Investment Banking*

Debt Capital Markets / Fixed Income
Global Head Jussi Laitinen *EVP, Trading and Capital Markets*

FINLAND (+358)   www.euromoneydirectory.com

Merita Bank Plc (cont)
Fixed-Income Repo
Head of Repo
Trading

Jussi Laiting *Executive Vice President* ☎ 1655 9005 🖷 726 1313
Jyri Tanskanen *Trading*
Thomas Begley *Vice President*

Equity Capital Markets
Equity Repo / Securities Lending
Head
Head of Trading

Thomas Begley *Vice President*
Jyri Tanskanen *Trading*

Syndicated Lending
Other (Trade Finance)
Real Estate

Heikki Hyppönen *Executive Vice President*

Other Departments
Correspondent Banking

Bo Harald *EVP, Network Banking and Domestic Payments*

Administration
Head of Administration

Ari Laakso *Executive Vice President*

Technology & Systems
Information Technology & Strategic Analysis

Kalevi Kontinen *Executive Vice President*

Accounts / Audit
Accounting & Control

Arne Liljedahl *Executive Vice President*

Other (Administration)
Production, Productivity and Net

Harri Sailas *Executive Vice President*

Nordic Investment Bank   Head Office
PO Box 249, FIN-00171 Helsinki
Tel: (9) 1800 1 **Fax:** (9) 1800 210 **Telex:** 122121 NIB FI **Swift:** NOIN FI HH

Senior Executive Officers
Chairman of the Board
President & CEO
Financial Director; Treasurer

Ib Katznelson
Jón Sigurdsson
Bo Heide-Ottosen *EVP, CFO & Treasurer*

Others (Senior Executives)

Erkki Karmila *Executive Vice President*
Carl Löwenhielm *Executive Vice President*
Juha Kotajoki *SVP, Risk Management*
Siv Hellén *SVP & General Counsel*
Oddvar Sten Rønsen *SVP, Appraisal Dept*
Eivind Dingstad *Senior Vice President*

General - Treasury
Head of Treasury

Torben Nielsen *Vice President*

Debt Capital Markets / Fixed Income
Department: Fixed Income and Swaps
Regional Head

Patrik Wainio *Senior Dealer*

Fixed-Income Research
Analyst

Jon Thorsteinsson *Financial Analyst*

Syndicated Lending
Department: Funding and Syndication
Regional Head

Søren Elbech *Deputy Head of Funding*

Other (Syndicated Lending)

Ulrik Ross *Funding Officer*

Money Markets
Department: Money Market and Foreign Exchange
Global Head
Other

Birgitta Lipponen *Manager*
Samu Slotte *Dealer*

Risk Management
Global Head

Juha Kotajoki *SVP, Risk Management*

Settlement / Clearing
Regional Head

Lena Moksi *Head, Back Office*

Administration
Legal / In-House Counsel

Siv Hellén *SVP & General Counsel*
Åse Nilsson *Vice President, Senior Counsel*
Sten Holmberg *Legal Counsel*

392 Euromoney Directory 1999

www.euromoneydirectory.com　　　　　　　　　　　　FINLAND (+358)

Public Relations
　　　　　　　　Christian Söderström *Information Manager*

Okobank Limited　　　　　　　　　　　　　　　　Subsidiary Company

Teollisuuskatu 18, FIN-00510 Helsinki
PO Box 308, FIN-00101 Helsinki
Tel: (9) 404 1 **Fax:** (9) 404 2002 **Telex:** 124714 OKO HE FI **Swift:** OKOY FI HH **Reuters:** OKOH
Website: www.osuuspankki.fi

Senior Executive Officers
Chairman & Chief Executive Officer　　Antti Tanskanen
Managing Director　　　　　　　　　　　Mikael Silvennoinen
Financial Director　　　　　　　　　　　Timo Ritakallio *Executive Director* ☎ **404 4322** 🖷 **404 2219**
Treasurer　　　　　　　　　　　　　　　Jorma Alanne *Director*
Director　　　　　　　　　　　　　　　　Markku Koponen ☎ **404 2648** 🖷 **404 2135**
International Division　　　　　　　　　Timo Ritakallio *Executive Director* ☎ **404 4322** 🖷 **404 2219**

Others (Senior Executives)
　　　　　　　　　　　　　　　　　　　　Kari Kukka *Director, International Funding* ☎ **404 2865** 🖷 **404 2616**

General-Lending (DCM, SL)
Head of Corporate Banking　　　　　　Timo Ritakallio *Executive Director* ☎ **404 4322** 🖷 **404 2219**

General-Investment
Head of Investment　　　　　　　　　　Juhani Elomaa *Executive Director* ☎ **404 4433** 🖷 **404 2679**

Debt Capital Markets / Fixed Income
Global Head　　　　　　　　　　　　　Antti Heinonen *Head of Trading* ☎ **404 4286** 🖷 **404 2149**

Domestic Government Bonds
Head of Sales　　　　　　　　　　　　Heikki Pelto-Arvo *Manager* ☎ **404 4301**
Head of Trading　　　　　　　　　　　Timo Leskinen *Manager* ☎ **404 2850**
Head of Research　　　　　　　　　　Teppo Koivisto *Head Analyst* ☎ **404 4284**

Eurobonds
Head of Sales　　　　　　　　　　　　Heikki Pelto-Arvo *Manager* ☎ **404 4301**
Head of Trading　　　　　　　　　　　Matti Kuhakoski *Manager* ☎ **404 2221**
Head of Research　　　　　　　　　　Teppo Koivisto *Head Analyst* ☎ **404 4284**

Asset-Backed Securities / Securitization
Global Head　　　　　　　　　　　　　Matti Kuhakoski *Manager* ☎ **404 2221**

Mortgage-Backed Securities
Global Head　　　　　　　　　　　　　Matti Kuhakoski *Manager* ☎ **404 2221**

Fixed-Income Repo
Head of Repo　　　　　　　　　　　　Matti Hannuksela *Manager* ☎ **404 4062**

Equity Capital Markets
Global Head　　　　　　　　　　　　　Juhani Elomaa *Executive Director* ☎ **404 4433** 🖷 **404 2679**

Domestic Equities
Head of Sales　　　　　　　　　　　　Risto Murto *Manager* ☎ **404 4434**
Head of Trading　　　　　　　　　　　Esa Nurkka *Chief Dealer* ☎ **404 4366**
Head of Research　　　　　　　　　　Risto Murto *Manager* ☎ **404 4434**

International Equities
Head of Trading　　　　　　　　　　　Annika Knekt-Ahtinen *Dealer* ☎ **404 4554**

Equity Repo / Securities Lending
Head of Trading　　　　　　　　　　　Jari Vikström *Dealer* ☎ **404 4365**

Syndicated Lending
Loan-Related Activities
Trade Finance　　　　　　　　　　　　Jarmo Viitanen *Director* ☎ **404 2251**

Money Markets
Global Head　　　　　　　　　　　　　Antti Heinonen *Head of Trading* ☎ **404 4286** 🖷 **404 2149**

Domestic Commercial Paper
Head of Sales　　　　　　　　　　　　Heikki Pelto-Arvo *Manager* ☎ **404 4301**
Head of Trading　　　　　　　　　　　Reima Rytsölä *Manager* ☎ **404 2788**

Eurocommercial Paper
Head of Sales　　　　　　　　　　　　Heikki Pelto-Arvo *Manager* ☎ **404 4301**
Head of Trading　　　　　　　　　　　Reima Rytsölä *Manager* ☎ **404 2788**

Foreign Exchange
Global Head　　　　　　　　　　　　　Antti Heinonen *Head of Trading* ☎ **404 4286** 🖷 **404 2149**
Head of Institutional Sales　　　　　　Mika Uusi-Pantti *Manager* ☎ **404 2514**
Corporate Sales　　　　　　　　　　　Heikki Pelto-Arvo *Manager* ☎ **404 4301**
Head of Trading　　　　　　　　　　　Mika Uusi-Pantti *Manager* ☎ **404 2514**

FINLAND (+358)   www.euromoneydirectory.com

Okobank Limited (cont)
Risk Management
Fixed Income Derivatives / Risk Management
Global Head   Antti Heinonen *Head of Trading* T **404 4286** F **404 2149**
IR Swaps Sales / Marketing; IR Swaps Trading;   Jouni Salmenkivi *Manager* T **404 4280**
IR Options Sales / Marketing; IR Options
Trading

Foreign Exchange Derivatives / Risk Management
Cross-Currency Swaps, Trading   Mikko Räsänen *Chief Dealer* T **404 2996**
Vanilla FX option Sales; Vanilla FX option   Janne Sumusalo *Chief Dealer* T **404 4355**
Trading

Exotic Options (Barriers, Range, Timers, Digitals, Faders etc)
Trading   Janne Sumusalo *Chief Dealer* T **404 4355**

Corporate Finance / M&A Advisory
Head of Corporate Finance   Juhani Elomaa *Executive Director* T **404 4433** F **404 2679**

Settlement / Clearing
Equity Settlement   Marja Ben-Cheikh *Manager* T **404 4378**
Fixed-Income Settlement; Foreign Exchange   Mirja Railo *Manager* T **404 4593**
Settlement

Global Custody
Department: Group Financial Services
Regional Head   Mikko Hyttinen *Director* T **404 2211**
Country Head   Kaija Seitsamo *Manager* T **404 4568**
Other (Global Custody)
    Jopi Sairio *Assistant Manager* T **404 2350**

Other Departments
Financial Institutions   Kyllikki Pankakoski *Senior Manager* T **404 2960**

Administration
Legal / In-House Counsel
    Jari Jaulimo *Manager* T **404 4380**

Public Relations
    Esko Roos *Manager* T **404 2573** F **404 2135**

Opstock Securities Limited   Subsidiary Company
Teollisuuskatu 1B, FIN-00101 Helsinki
PO Box 362, FIN-00101 Helsinki
Tel: (9) 404 65

Senior Executive Officers
Chief Executive Officer   Juhani Elomaa T **404 4433**

Equity Capital Markets
Head of Equity Capital Markets   Risto Murto T **404 4434**

Equity Repo / Securities Lending
Head of Prime Brokerage   Risto Murto T **404 4434**

Skandinaviska Enskilda Banken AB   Full Branch Office
Unioninkatu 30, FIN-00101 Helsinki
PO Box 630, FIN-00101 Helsinki
Tel: (9) 6162 8000 Fax: (9) 171 056 Reuters: SEHX Bloomberg: SEB HELSINKI
Website: www.sebweb1.sebank.se

Debt Capital Markets / Fixed Income
Head of Fixed Income   Olli Enqvist T **6162 8600** F **6162 8690**

Emerging Market Bonds
Head of Emerging Markets   Jari Sorri T **6162 8615** F **6162 8690**

Money Markets
Head of Money Markets   Pekka Moisio T **6162 8670** F **6162 8690**

Foreign Exchange
Head of Foreign Exchange   Olli Enqvist T **6162 8600** F **6162 8690**

Administration
Head of Administration   Lennart Bröderman T **6162 8010** F **6162 8059**

Legal / In-House Counsel
Legal Counsel   Leena Siirala T **6162 8102** F **6162 8070**

www.euromoneydirectory.com FRANCE (+33)

Compliance
　　　　　　　　　Leena Siirala ☎ 6162 8102 🖷 6162 8070

Svenska Handelsbanken
Full Branch Office

Eteläranta 8, FIN-00130 Helsinki
PO Box 315, FIN-00131 Helsinki
Tel: (10) 44411; (9) 16677 1 **Telex:** 125003 SHB FI **Reuters:** SVEI **Telerate:** 6284 FX, 8618 MM
Reuters: SVEH

Senior Executive Officers
Chief Executive Officer　　　　　　　Carl-Axel Olsson
Treasurer　　　　　　　　　　　　　Holger Schauman *Head of Treasury*

Debt Capital Markets / Fixed Income
Regional Head　　　　　　　　　　　Pasi Heinard *Debt Capital Market* ☎ 444 2434

Domestic Government Bonds
Head of Sales　　　　　　　　　　　Tomi Närhinen *Head* ☎ 444 2547

Equity Capital Markets
Regional Head　　　　　　　　　　　Patrik Hertsberg *Head of Equities* ☎ 444 2237

Domestic Equities
Head of Sales; Head of Trading　　　Patrik Hertsberg *Head of Equities* ☎ 444 2237

International Equities
Head of Sales; Head of Trading　　　Patrik Hertsberg *Head of Equities* ☎ 444 2237

Money Markets
Wholesale Deposits
Head of Sales　　　　　　　　　　　Tomi Närhinen *Head* ☎ 444 2547

Corporate Finance / M&A Advisory
Regional Head　　　　　　　　　　　Markus Gylling *Head, Corporate Finance* ☎ 444 2401

Settlement / Clearing
Regional Head　　　　　　　　　　　Mirjam Koljonen *Head of Trading Services* ☎ 444 2346
Equity Settlement　　　　　　　　　Matti Sulamaa ☎ 444 2338
Fixed-Income Settlement; Derivatives　Mirjam Koljonen *Head of Trading Services* ☎ 444 2346
Settlement; Foreign Exchange Settlement

Williams de Broë Pankkiiriliike Oy
Subsidiary Company

Pohjoisesplanadi 25A, FIN-00100 Helsinki
Tel: (9) 622 0440 **Fax:** (9) 622 3340

Senior Executive Officers
General Manager　　　　　　　　　Antti Manpila

FRANCE
(+33)

Banque de France
🏛 Central Bank

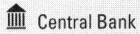

39 rue Croix des Petits Champs, F-75001 Paris
PO Box 140-01, F-75049 Paris Cedex 01
Tel: (1) 42 92 42 92 **Fax:** (1) 42 96 04 23 **Telex:** 220932

Senior Executive Officers
Governor　　　　　　　　　　　　Jean-Claude Trichet
Deputy Governor　　　　　　　　　Denis Ferman
Deputy Governor　　　　　　　　　Howé Hannain

Abbey National Treasury Services
Full Branch Office

163/165 Avenue Charles de Gaulle, F-92200 Neuilly-sur-Seine
Tel: (1) 46 37 10 40 **Fax:** (1) 46 37 51 38

Senior Executive Officers
Manager, Treasury　　　　　　　　Michel Elleboode ☎ 46 41 08 08

FRANCE (+33)   www.euromoneydirectory.com

ABN AMRO Fixed Income France
Formerly known as: ABN AMRO Finance SA
65 rue de Courcelles, F-75388 Paris Cedex 08
Tel: (1) 44 29 89 53 Fax: (1) 44 29 89 59 Telex: 643436 Reuters: AAFIMENU

ABS Banque
Formerly known as: Banque Internationale de Gestion et de Trésorerie
46 Avenue Kleber, F-75116 Paris
Tel: (1) 45 01 40 00 Fax: (1) 45 01 40 35

Senior Executive Officers
President   Xavier de Bayser

AKBANK TAS   Representative Office
5 rue de Rome, F-75008 Paris
Tel: (1) 45 22 94 11 Fax: (1) 45 22 94 12

Senior Executive Officers
Representative   Oral Oguz

American Express Bank (France) SA   Subsidiary Company
11 rue Scribe, F-75009 Paris
Tel: (1) 47 14 50 00 Fax: (1) 42 68 17 17 Telex: 290177

Senior Executive Officers
President   Piero Grandi [T] 47 14 51 95
General Manager   Gordon Joost [T] 47 14 51 93

Apax Partners & Cie Finance SA   Head Office
45 Avenue Kléber, F-75784 Paris Cedex 16
Tel: (1) 45 53 01 32 Fax: (1) 47 55 05 84

Senior Executive Officers
Co-President / Partner   Wladimir Mollof [E] w.mollof@apax-partners.fr
Co-President / Partner   Jacqueline Henry
Co-President / Partner   Maurice Tchenio

Debt Capital Markets / Fixed Income

Private Placements
Head of Origination   Wladimir Mollof *Co-President / Partner* [E] w.mollof@apax-partners.fr

Corporate Finance / M&A Advisory
Head of Corporate Finance   Wladimir Mollof *Co-President / Partner* [E] w.mollof@apax-partners.fr
Regional Head   Jacqueline Henry *Co-President / Partner*

Aurel SA   Head Office
Formerly known as: Aurel Finance
Washington Plaza, 29 rue de Berri, F-75408 Paris Cedex 08
Tel: (1) 53 89 53 89; (1) 53 89 53 70 Fax: (1) 53 89 53 80; (1) 53 89 53 99 Telex: 651389 F Reuters: LDCO
Bloomberg: AURE
Reuters: LDCP; LDCQ
Website: www.aurel.fr

Senior Executive Officers
President of the Board of Directors Jean-Marc Teurquetil [T] 53 89 53 90 [F] 53 89 53 92
Financial Director   Sophie Langlois *Member of the Board* [T] 53 89 53 83 [F] 53 89 53 96
Chief Operating Officer   Jean-Daniel Cohen *Member of the Board* [T] 53 89 53 54 [F] 53 89 73 92
                                     Jérôme Frank *Member of the Board* [T] 53 89 53 93 [F] 53 89 73 93
Treasurer   Marie-Pierre Fradin [T] 53 89 53 44 [F] 53 89 73 90

www.euromoneydirectory.com　　　　　　FRANCE (+33)

Debt Capital Markets / Fixed Income
Tel: 53 89 53 89 Fax: 53 89 73 90
Domestic Government Bonds
Head of Sales　　　　　　　　Laurent Zerbib *Head* ☎ 53 89 53 02
　　　　　　　　　　　　　　Alain Pestre ☎ 53 89 53 03
Head of Trading　　　　　　Olivier Scialom ☎ 53 89 53 31
Eurobonds
Head of Sales　　　　　　　Laurent Zerbib *Head* ☎ 53 89 53 02
　　　　　　　　　　　　　　Alain Pestre ☎ 53 89 53 03
Head of Trading　　　　　　Frank Bekaert ☎ 53 89 53 30
Fixed-Income Repo
Head of Repo　　　　　　　Marie-Pierre Fradin ☎ 53 89 53 44 F 53 89 73 90
Fixed-Income Research
Head of Fixed Income　　　Régis Khaber ☎ 53 89 53 53 F 53 89 53 80
Head of Credit Research　　Karen Kharmandarian ☎ 53 89 53 82 F 53 89 53 98

Equity Capital Markets
Domestic Equities
Head of Origination　　　　Eric Parent *Head of New Issue* ☎ 53 89 73 10 F 53 89 73 37
Head of Sales　　　　　　　Olivier Balva ☎ 53 89 53 41
　　　　　　　　　　　　　　Murielle Plavis ☎ 53 89 53 46
　　　　　　　　　　　　　　Sarah Thirion ☎ 53 89 53 22

Equity Research
Head of Equity Research　　Guillaume Le Floch ☎ 53 89 73 43 F 53 89 53 98
Convertibles / Equity-Linked
Head of Sales　　　　　　　Didier Buniak ☎ 53 89 53 08 F 53 89 53 98
Head of Trading　　　　　　Christophe Lepitre ☎ 53 89 53 17 F 53 89 53 98

Settlement / Clearing
Head of Settlement / Clearing　Christian De La Touanne ☎ 53 89 53 79

Administration
Head of Administration　　　Sophie Langlois *Member of the Board* ☎ 53 89 53 83 F 53 89 53 96

Technology & Systems
　　　　　　　　　　　　　　Patrick Reynaud ☎ 53 89 53 55 F 53 89 53 99

Compliance
　　　　　　　　　　　　　　Sophie Langlois *Member of the Board* ☎ 53 89 53 83 F 53 89 53 96

Accounts / Audit
　　　　　　　　　　　　　　Antonio Cordoba ☎ 53 89 53 66

Australia & New Zealand Banking Group Limited
6 rue de Berri, F-75008 Paris
Tel: (1) 40 75 05 37 Fax: (1) 40 75 05 46 Telex: 643311 Swift: ANZB FR PP

Senior Executive Officers
Managing Director / General Manager　　Maurice J-P Lemoine
Others (Senior Executives)
Global Structured Finance　　Philippe Cassiers *Director*
Operations　　　　　　　　　Evelyn Gauthier *Manager*

Austrian National Bank　　　　　　　　　　　Representative Office
3 rue Albéric-Magnard, F-75116 Paris
Tel: (1) 53 92 23 39 Fax: (1) 45 24 42 49 Telex: 611946

Senior Executive Officers
Chief Representative　　　　Stefan Huemer

Banca Popolare di Novara　　　　　　　　　Representative Office
56 rue de Provence, F-75439 Paris Cedex 09
Tel: (1) 40 16 10 93 Fax: (1) 40 16 11 67

Senior Executive Officers
Representative　　　　　　　Bernard Giraud

Euromoney Directory 1999　397

FRANCE (+33)   www.euromoneydirectory.com

Banca di Roma SpA
Full Branch Office

21 Avenue George V, F-75008 Paris Entre Rios
Tel: (1) 49 52 69 52 **Fax:** (1) 49 52 69 84 **Swift:** BROM FR PP **Reuters:** ROMP

Senior Executive Officers
Director — Alessandro Agnolucci

Others (Senior Executives)
Roberto Larini

General-Lending (DCM, SL)
Head of Corporate Banking — Roberto Larini

General - Treasury
Head of Treasury — Bruno Avallone

Debt Capital Markets / Fixed Income
Eurobonds
Head of Syndication — Roberto Larini
José-Marc Vincentelli

Foreign Exchange
Global Head — Bruno Avallone

Settlement / Clearing
Settlement (General); Operations — Claude Bakhashe

Administration
Accounts / Audit — Claude Bakhashe

Banco Bilbao Vizcaya
Full Branch Office

29 Avenue de l'Opéra, F-75001 Paris
Tel: (1) 44 86 83 00; (1) 44 88 83 04 **Fax:** (1) 44 86 84 88; (1) 44 88 84 89 **Telex:** 670444 BBV PAR **Swift:** BBVI FR PP

Senior Executive Officers
Chairman — Mr Eguiluz ☎ 44 88 83 89
Financial Director; Chief Operating Officer — Armando Pastor *Assistant Director* ☎ 44 86 83 32
Treasurer — B Hurlin ☎ 44 86 83 23

Debt Capital Markets / Fixed Income
Global Head — M Sánchez ☎ 44 88 83 53 F 44 88 84 59

Eurobonds
Head of Syndication — M Sánchez ☎ 44 88 83 53 F 44 88 84 59

Syndicated Lending
Loan-Related Activities
Trade Finance — Raymond Raoul ☎ 44 86 83 30 E raoul.raymond@gruppobbv.com
Project Finance; Structured Trade Finance; Leasing & Asset Finance — M Sánchez ☎ 44 88 83 53 F 44 88 84 59

Other Departments
Private Banking — C Honrado *Assistant Director* ☎ 44 88 83 38
Correspondent Banking — Armando Pastor *Assistant Director* ☎ 44 86 83 32

Administration
Technology & Systems
E.D.P. — Antonio Castaner ☎ 44 86 83 03

Legal / In-House Counsel
A Bensoussan ☎ 44 86 83 58

Accounts / Audit
M Angel Torrijos ☎ 44 88 83 03

Banco Espirito Santo
Representative Office

45 Avenue Georges Mandel, F-75116 Paris
Tel: (1) 44 34 49 00 **Fax:** (1) 44 34 49 49

Senior Executive Officers
Representative — Luis Cervantes

398 Euromoney Directory 1999

www.euromoneydirectory.com   FRANCE (+33)

Bank Austria Creditanstalt International AG   Representative Office

Formerly known as: Bank Austria AG
7 Place Vendôme, F-75001 Paris
Tel: (1) 42 60 70 80 **Fax**: (1) 42 60 09 65 **Email**: ba-ca.paris@wanadoo.fr

Senior Executive Officers
Chief Representative   Didier Harand

Bank of China   Full Branch Office

52 bis rue Laffitte, F-75009 Paris
Tel: (1) 49 70 13 70 **Fax**: (1) 49 70 13 72 **Telex**: 202602

Senior Executive Officers
General Manager   Lingun Yang

Others (Senior Executives)
                              Du Ai Fang *Assistant General Manager*

Bank Melli Iran   Full Branch Office

43 Avenue Montaigne, F-75008 Paris
Tel: (1) 47 23 78 57 **Fax**: (1) 47 20 74 21 **Telex**: 641506 **Swift**: MELI FR PP

Senior Executive Officers
General Manager   Amir Ali Taghati

Others (Senior Executives)
                              Mohammadi Amiri *Assistant Manager*

Bank Polska Kasa Opieki SA   Full Branch Office

23 rue Taitbout, F-75009 Paris
Tel: (1) 48 01 34 34 **Fax**: (1) 42 47 15 38 **Telex**: 285636 POLFORX

Senior Executive Officers
General Manager   Ireneusz Chodorek

Bank Saderat Iran   Full Branch Office

16 rue de la Paix, F-75002 Paris
Tel: (1) 42 61 79 51 **Fax**: (1) 42 61 61 53 **Telex**: 220287 SADER

Senior Executive Officers
General Manager   Shahram Razavi

Foreign Exchange
Head of Trading   Jean-Louis Methia *Trader*

Bank Tejarat   Full Branch Office

124/126 rue de Provence, F-75008 Paris
Tel: (1) 44 70 78 44 **Fax**: (1) 40 08 06 55 **Telex**: 281973 BKTU OJ

Senior Executive Officers
General Manager   M Mehriari

Others (Senior Executives)
                              M Davoud *Assistant Manager*

Administration
Accounts / Audit
Audit   M Marvian *Adviser & Auditor*

Euromoney Directory 1999   **399**

FRANCE (+33)   www.euromoneydirectory.com

The Bank of Tokyo-Mitsubishi (France) SA — Subsidiary Company

Formerly known as: Banque Européenne de Tokyo SA
4-8 rue Sainte Anne, F-75001 Paris
Tel: (1) 49 26 49 30 **Fax:** (1) 42 60 98 83 **Telex:** BTM PR A 210436F **Swift:** BOTK FR PX

Senior Executive Officers
President & General Manager — Mr Yoshida

Others (Senior Executives)
Mr Sato *Deputy General Manager*
Yoshihiro Ota *Deputy General Manager*
Claude Meyer *Deputy General Manager*
Alain G Menoncin *Deputy General Manager*

Debt Capital Markets / Fixed Income
Country Head — Mr Tanada *Manager*

Equity Capital Markets
Country Head — Mr Tanada *Manager*

Syndicated Lending
Head of Origination; Head of Syndication — Claude Meyer *Deputy General Manager*

Money Markets
Country Head — Mr Tanada *Manager*

Administration
Head of Administration — Takuya Sugitani

Banque AIG — Head Office

46 rue de Bassano, F-75008 Paris
Tel: (1) 49 52 36 00 **Fax:** (1) 47 20 43 05

Senior Executive Officers
President — Mauro Gabriele
Financial Director — Jean-Pierre Pacaud *Director General / CFO*

Banque Audi (France) SA — Head Office

73, avenue des Champs-Elysées, F-75008 Paris
Tel: (1) 53 83 50 00 **Fax:** (1) 42 56 09 74 **Telex:** 650380 AUDIB **Swift:** AUDI FR PP
Email: banqueaudifrance@compuserve.com

Senior Executive Officers
Chairman — Raymond Audi
General Manager — Yves Kuehn ☎ 53 83 50 39
International Division — Shérine Audi *Deputy General Manager* ☎ 53 83 50 01

Syndicated Lending

Loan-Related Activities
Trade Finance — Michel Mehanna *Fondé de Pouvoirs* ☎ 53 83 50 04

Money Markets
Head of Money Markets — Joe Ferran *Manager* ☎ 53 83 50 10

Foreign Exchange
Head of Foreign Exchange — Joe Ferran *Manager* ☎ 53 83 50 10

Risk Management
Head of Risk Management — Shérine Audi *Deputy General Manager* ☎ 53 83 50 01

Settlement / Clearing
Head of Settlement / Clearing — Dominique Tondoux *Fondé de Pouvoirs* ☎ 53 83 50 31

Other Departments
Chief Credit Officer; Correspondent Banking — Shérine Audi *Deputy General Manager* ☎ 53 83 50 01

Administration
Head of Administration — Dominique Giraud ☎ 53 83 50 32

Technology & Systems
Phillippe Bremont ☎ 53 83 50 26

Accounts / Audit
Dominique Tondoux *Fondé de Pouvoirs* ☎ 53 83 50 31

www.euromoneydirectory.com   FRANCE (+33)

Banque Banorabe SA
Head Office

38-40 Avenue des Champs-Elysées, F-75008 Paris
Tel: (1) 44 95 06 06 Fax: (1) 44 95 06 00 Telex: 644401 BANOPAR Swift: BANO FR PP
Email: banorabe.paris@wanadoo.fr Reuters: BANO Telex: 644402 BANOPAR

Senior Executive Officers
Chairman & General Manager — Naaman Azhari
Chief Executive Officer — Amine Awad *Deputy General Manager*
Financial Director — Gilbert Moine *Senior Manager*
Chief Operating Officer — Amr Azhari *Senior Executive Officer*
Treasurer — Raymond Baharian *Chief Dealer*
Deputy General Manager — Amine Awad
Senior Manager — Gilbert Moine
International Division — Amine Awad *Deputy General Manager*

Syndicated Lending

Loan-Related Activities
Trade Finance; Project Finance — Amine Awad *Deputy General Manager*

Money Markets
Tel: 44 95 06 36 Fax: 44 95 06 00 Reuters: BANO Telex: 644456 BANOPAR
Head of Money Markets — Raymond Baharian *Chief Dealer*

Foreign Exchange
Tel: 44 95 06 36 Telex: 644456 BANOPAR
Head of Foreign Exchange — Raymond Baharian *Chief Dealer*

FX Traders / Sales People
Charbel Makhlouf *Dealer*

Global Custody
Head of Global Custody — Amine Awad *Deputy General Manager*

Other Departments
Chief Credit Officer; Correspondent Banking — Amine Awad *Deputy General Manager*

Administration
Head of Administration — Gilbert Moine *Senior Manager*
Head of Marketing — Amine Awad *Deputy General Manager*

Technology & Systems
Jacques Pruvost *Head, EDP DPT*

Public Relations
Amr Azhari *Senior Executive Officer*

Banque Bruxelles Lambert France
Head Office

85-91, rue du Faubourg Saint Honoré, F-75008 Paris
Tel: (1) 55 27 70 00 Fax: (1) 55 27 77 77 Telex: 210024 Swift: BBRU FR PP

Senior Executive Officers
Chairman — Michel Tilmant
Chief Executive Officer — John Gielen
Financial Director — Maria Fuentes
General Manager — Guy Beniada

General-Lending (DCM, SL)
Head of Corporate Banking — Robert de Tinguy

Debt Capital Markets / Fixed Income
Head of Debt Capital Markets — Marc Eichinger

Equity Capital Markets
Head of Equity Capital Markets — Michel Behar
Head of Sales — Vincent Lutreau

Equity Research
Head of Equity Research — Laurent Saint Aubin

Money Markets
Head of Money Markets — Marc Eichinger

Foreign Exchange
Head of Foreign Exchange — Marc Eichinger
Head of Institutional Sales; Corporate Sales — Philippe Richard

Euromoney Directory 1999   **401**

FRANCE (+33)   www.euromoneydirectory.com

Banque Commerciale pour l'Europe du Nord-Eurobank
79/81 Boulevard Haussmann, F-75382 Paris Cedex 08
Tel: (1) 40 06 43 21 **Fax:** (1) 40 06 48 48 **Telex:** 280200 F EUROB **Swift:** EURO FR PP **Reuters:** BCEN (General)
Senior Executive Officers
Chairman of the Supervisory Board   Iouri Ponomarev
Chairman Executive Board   Anolreï Movtchan

Banque Courtois   Head Office
33 Rue de Rémusat, F-31000 Toulouse
Tel: (5) 61 10 84 84 **Fax:** (5) 61 10 84 85 **Telex:** 531580 F COURBAN
Senior Executive Officers
President   Marc Batave
Vice President   Dominique Chastel

Banque CPR   Head Office
Alternative trading name: Compagnie Parisienne de Réescompte
Formerly known as: Banque CGM
30 rue Saint Georges, F-75312 Paris Cedex 09
Tel: (1) 45 96 20 00 **Fax:** (1) 45 96 25 55 **Telex:** 282511F **Swift:** CPRE FR PP **Email:** dircom@cpr.fr
Reuters: CPRMENU **Telerate:** 2545
Website: www.cpr.fr

Senior Executive Officers
Chairman & President   Henri Cukierman ☎ 45 96 27 53 ✉ hcukierman@cpr.fr
Chief Executive Officer   Philippe Delienne ☎ 45 96 21 02 ✉ pdelienne@cpr.fr
Financial Director   Philippe Crénin ☎ 45 96 24 45 ✉ pcrenin@cpr.fr
Chief Operating Officer   Olivier Mirat *Chief Operating Officer* ☎ 45 96 24 32 ✉ omirat@cpr.fr
   Henri Michel Tranchimand *Chief Operating Officer* ☎ 45 96 21 77
   ✉ htranchimand@cpr.fr

Debt Capital Markets / Fixed Income
Department: CPR Finance
Global Head   Henri Michel Tranchimand ☎ 45 96 21 77 ✉ htranchimand@cpr.fr

Domestic Government Bonds
Head of Sales   Olivier Régis *Sales* ☎ 45 96 21 99 ✉ oregis@cpr.fr
Head of Trading   Marc Botter *Trading* ☎ 45 96 72 10 ✉ mbotter@cpr.fr

Non-Domestic Government Bonds
Non-Domestic Government Bonds   Olivier Régis *Sales* ☎ 45 96 21 99 ✉ oregis@cpr.fr
Fixed Income, Primary & Secondary Market   Jean Louis Bertrand ☎ 45 96 22 22 ✉ jbertrand@cpr.fr
Non-Domestic Government Bonds   Marc Botter *Trading* ☎ 45 96 72 10 ✉ mbotter@cpr.fr

Eurobonds
Head of Origination   Richard Tuffier ☎ 45 96 72 39 ✉ rtuffier@cpr.fr
Head of Syndication   Thierry Cherbit ☎ 45 96 23 30 ✉ tcherbit@cpr.fr
Head of Sales   Olivier Régis *Sales* ☎ 45 96 21 99 ✉ oregis@cpr.fr
Head of Trading   Thierry Cherbit ☎ 45 96 23 30 ✉ tcherbit@cpr.fr

Libor-Based / Floating-Rate Products
FRN Trading   Francis Perrin ☎ 45 96 72 72 ✉ fperrin@cpr.fr

Fixed-Income Repo
Head of Repo   Dominique Roux ☎ 45 96 72 16 ✉ droux@cpr.fr

Equity Capital Markets
Department: CPR Finance
Global Head   Henri Michel Tranchimand ☎ 45 96 21 77 ✉ htranchimand@cpr.fr

Domestic Equities
Head of Origination   François Beaufine-Ducrocq ☎ 45 96 71 88 ✉ fbeaufine-ducrocq@cpr.fr
Head of Sales   Alexandre Tokay ☎ 45 96 17 71 ✉ atokay@cpr.fr
Head of Trading   Jacques Bocquet ☎ 45 96 22 39 ✉ jbocquet@cpr.fr
Head of Research   Guillaume Beau ☎ 45 96 23 41 ✉ gbeau@cpr.fr

Other (Domestic Equities)
Equities   Guillaume Beau ☎ 45 96 23 41 ✉ gbeau@cpr.fr

Convertibles / Equity-Linked
Head of Origination   François Beaufine-Ducrocq ☎ 45 96 71 88 ✉ fbeaufine-ducrocq@cpr.fr
Head of Sales   Frédéric Barge ☎ 45 96 17 08 ✉ fbarge@cpr.fr

www.euromoneydirectory.com   FRANCE (+33)

Warrants
Head of Sales   Fredéric Barge ☏ 45 96 17 08 ✉ fbarge@cpr.fr

Equity Repo / Securities Lending
Marketing   Letteria Barbaro-Bour ☏ 45 96 25 91 ✉ lbarbaro-bour@cpr.fr
Xavier Clément ☏ 45 96 21 84 ✉ xclement@cpr.fr

Money Markets
Department: CPR Finance
Global Head   Henri Michel Tranchimand ☏ 45 96 21 77 ✉ htranchimand@cpr.fr

Domestic Commercial Paper
Head of Origination   Dominique Roux ☏ 45 96 72 16 ✉ droux@cpr.fr
Head of Sales   Olivier Régis *Sales* ☏ 45 96 21 99 ✉ oregis@cpr.fr
Head of Trading   Dominique Roux ☏ 45 96 72 16 ✉ droux@cpr.fr

Foreign Exchange
Department: CPR Finance
Global Head   Henri Michel Tranchimand ☏ 45 96 21 77 ✉ htranchimand@cpr.fr

Risk Management
Global Head   Bernard Crutz ☏ 45 96 70 74 ✉ bcrutz@cpr.fr

Fixed Income Derivatives / Risk Management
Global Head   Dominique Daridan ☏ 45 96 70 37 ✉ ddaridan@cpr.fr

Settlement / Clearing
Country Head   Christophe Couturier *Head* ☏ 45 96 27 08 ✉ ccouturier@cpr.fr
Equity Settlement   Christophe Le Gac ☏ 45 96 16 85 ✉ clegac@cpr.fr
Fixed-Income Settlement   Bernard Lupette ☏ 45 96 72 34 ✉ blupette@cpr.fr

Other Departments
Private Banking   Olivier de Conihout ☏ 45 96 25 64 ✉ odeconihout@cpr.fr
Correspondent Banking   Olivier Mirat *Chief Operating Officer* ☏ 45 96 24 32 ✉ omirat@cpr.fr

Administration
Head of Marketing   Eric Langeard ☏ 45 96 25 00 ✉ elangeard@cpr.fr

Technology & Systems   Christophe Couturier *Head* ☏ 45 96 27 08 ✉ ccouturier@cpr.fr

Legal / In-House Counsel   Agnès Bisciglia ☏ 45 96 24 79 ✉ abisciglia@cpr.fr

Banque du Louvre   Head Office

139 Boulevard Haussmann, F-75008 Paris
Tel: (1) 44 35 77 77 **Fax:** (1) 44 35 78 78

Senior Executive Officers
Chairman   Guillaume Dard
Managing Director   Hugues Riché
Managing Director   Christian Guilloux
Vice Managing Director   Wladimir Taittinger
General Manager   Cécile Barjak
Corporate Secretary   Catherine Cornemillot

Settlement / Clearing
Regional Head   Cécile Barjak

Global Custody
Regional Head   Cécile Barjak

Other Departments
Private Banking   Hugues Riché *Managing Director*

Administration
Public Relations   Anne-Françoise de Charry

Banque Dupuy de Parseval   Head Office

10 rue Général de Gaulle, F-34200 Sete
Tel: (4) 67 46 29 30 **Fax:** (4) 67 74 14 77

Senior Executive Officers
General Manager   Philippe Dupuy

FRANCE (+33)   www.euromoneydirectory.com

Banque Fédérative du Crédit Mutuel
Head Office

6, rue de Ventadour, F-75001 Paris
Tel: (1) 44 58 42 00 **Fax:** (1) 44 58 41 45 **Telex:** 214316 **Swift:** BFCM FR 2A **Reuters:** BFED (Dealing)

Senior Executive Officers
President — Etienne Pflinlin [T] (3) 88 14 88 14
Chief Executive Officer — Michel Lucas [T] (3) 88 14 88 14
Financial Director — Christian Klein [T] 44 58 42 40
Chief Operating Officer — Claude Brun [T] (3) 88 14 70 01
Treasurer — Christian Ander [T] 44 58 41 01

General-Lending (DCM, SL)
Head of Corporate Banking — Jean Lacaze [T] 44 58 42 30

Debt Capital Markets / Fixed Income
Eurobonds
Head of Sales — Jean-Claude Poncin *Executive Vice President* [T] 44 58 42 43
Head of Trading — Joseph Broune *Vice President* [T] 44 58 41 16

Libor-Based / Floating-Rate Products
FRN Sales — Jean-Claude Poncin *Executive Vice President* [T] 44 58 42 43
Asset Swaps — Joseph Broune *Vice President* [T] 44 58 41 16
Asset Swaps (Sales) — Jean-Claude Poncin *Executive Vice President* [T] 44 58 42 43

Fixed-Income Repo
Head of Repo — Christian Ander [T] 44 58 41 01

Money Markets
Domestic Commercial Paper
Head of Sales — Patrick Volant *Vice President* [T] 44 58 41 08
Head of Trading — Eric Cuzzuloli *Vice President* [T] 44 58 41 04

Eurocommercial Paper
Head of Sales — Patrick Volant *Vice President* [T] 44 58 41 08
Head of Trading — Eric Cuzzuloli *Vice President* [T] 44 58 41 04

Wholesale Deposits
Head of Sales — Patrick Volant *Vice President* [T] 44 58 41 08

Foreign Exchange
Head of Trading — Patrick Volant *Vice President* [T] 44 58 41 08

Risk Management
Head of Risk Management — Christian Klein [T] 44 58 42 40

Other (FI Derivatives)
Head of Sales — Christian Ander [T] 44 58 41 01

Other Departments
Correspondent Banking — Jérôme Linder *First Vice President* [T] 44 58 41 02

Administration
Technology & Systems
— Claude Brun [T] (3) 88 14 70 01

Legal / In-House Counsel
— Philippe Coussieu *Executive Director* [T] (3) 88 14 71 91

Banque Française de l'Orient
Head Office

30 Avenue George V, F-75008 Paris
Tel: (1) 49 52 17 00 **Fax:** (1) 49 52 18 00 **Telex:** BFO 645500 F **Swift:** BFOR FR PP **Reuters:** BFOP

Senior Executive Officers
Chairman & Chief Executive — Bernard Vernhes [T] 49 52 17 02 [F] 49 52 17 10
Chief Executive Officer — Jean-Louis Sabet [T] 49 52 17 03 [F] 49 52 17 80
— Hadi Naffi *Executive Vice President* [T] 49 52 18 01 [F] 49 52 17 10
Chief Operating Officer — Claude Jeanbart [T] 49 52 18 08 [F] 49 52 17 70
Treasurer — Gaby Haddad [T] 47 20 83 16 [F] 49 52 17 19
Company Secretary — Bernard Calvet [T] 40 74 33 10 [F] 40 74 33 40

Others (Senior Executives)
Head of Emerging Markets — Wissam Elkhoury [T] 49 52 17 36 [F] 49 52 17 20

General-Lending (DCM, SL)
Head of Corporate Banking — Hadi Naffi *Executive Vice President* [T] 49 52 18 01 [F] 49 52 17 10

Syndicated Lending
Trade Finance — Antoine Abboud [T] 49 52 17 37 [F] 49 52 17 08

Money Markets
Head of Money Markets — Gaby Haddad [T] 47 20 83 16 [F] 49 52 17 19

www.euromoneydirectory.com   FRANCE (+33)

Foreign Exchange
Head of Foreign Exchange
Gaby Haddad ☏ 47 20 83 16 🗎 49 52 17 19
Settlement / Clearing
Head of Settlement / Clearing
Carole Xicluna ☏ 49 52 17 73 🗎 49 52 17 18
Global Custody
Head of Global Custody
Carole Xicluna ☏ 49 52 17 73 🗎 49 52 17 18
Asset Management
Head
Wissan Elkhoury ☏ 49 52 17 36 🗎 49 52 17 20
Other Departments
Chief Credit Officer
Nouhad Debs ☏ 49 52 18 80 🗎 49 52 17 13
Private Banking
Jean-Louis Sabet ☏ 49 52 17 03 🗎 49 52 17 80
Administration
Technology & Systems
Jean Ouba ☏ 40 74 33 30 🗎 40 74 33 50

Legal / In-House Counsel
Nahia Nouzannar ☏ 49 52 18 94

Compliance
Daniel Joly ☏ 49 52 18 06 🗎 49 52 45 33

Public Relations
Isabelle Sarkis ☏ 49 52 18 85 🗎 49 52 18 00

Accounts / Audit
Michel Ancel ☏ 40 74 33 12

Banque Franco Yougoslave
Head Office
18, rue de Filsilt, F-75017 Paris
Tel: (1) 53 81 90 70 **Fax:** (1) 42 67 13 70; (1) 53 81 90 70 **Telex:** 644060 YOUGFRA **Swift:** BAFY FR PP

Senior Executive Officers
President
André Lecomte
Chief Executive Officer
Olivier Seigneur *Director*
Money Markets
Head of Money Markets
Preshaj Milivosevic *Dealer*
Foreign Exchange
Head of Foreign Exchange
Ivana Radvlovic
Risk Management
Head of Risk Management
Ljiljana Avon *Deputy Director*
Administration
Legal / In-House Counsel
Dejan Babic *Legal Advisor*

Banque Hervet
127 Avenue Charles de Gaulle, F-92200 Paris
PO Box 154, F-92200 Neuilly-sur-Seine
Tel: (1) 46 40 90 00 **Fax:** (1) 46 40 92 77 **Telex:** 620433 **Swift:** BHVT FR PP

Senior Executive Officers
Chairman
Patrick Careil
Financial Director
Bernard Azoulay
Managing Director / General Manager
Alain Cadiou
International Division
Jean Hesbert

General-Lending (DCM, SL)
Head of Corporate Banking
Remi Steiner
Jean Yves Lefevre
Marcel Bonnier

Other Departments
Chief Credit Officer
Jean Naire Blot
Private Banking
Isabelle Desbons Lauvaux
Administration
Legal / In-House Counsel
Legal Affairs
Yves Desaedeleer
Accounts / Audit
Accounting Director
Jean-Francis Rouault

Euromoney Directory 1999   **405**

FRANCE (+33)   www.euromoneydirectory.com

Banque IBJ (France) SA
Head Office

42 rue Washington, Washington Plaza, F-75408 Paris Cedex 08
Tel: (1) 53 83 41 00 Fax: (1) 53 83 41 69 Telex: 642247

Senior Executive Officers
President — Takashi Watanabe

Others (Senior Executives)
Denis Faure *Assistant Director* ☎ 53 83 41 11

Debt Capital Markets / Fixed Income
Fixed-Income Repo
Head of Repo
Marketing & Product Development
Trading

Rodolf Lorfing *Director*
Denis Faure *Assistant Director* ☎ 53 83 41 11
Jerome Sabah *Trading*
Michaël Aissaoui *Trading*
Rudolf Lorfing *Director*

Equity Capital Markets
Telex: 216809

Equity Repo / Securities Lending
Head
Marketing
Head of Trading

Rudolf Lorfing *Director*
Denis Faure *Assistant Director* ☎ 53 83 41 11
Michaël Aissaoui *Trading*
Rudolf Lorfing *Director*
Jerome Sabah *Trading*

Banque Industrielle et Mobiliere Privée - BIMP
Head Office

39 rue d'Anjou, F-75008 Paris
Tel: (1) 40 06 60 00 Telex: MOBPRIV 285291F Swift: BIMP FR PP
Debt Capital Markets Fax: 40 06 60 75

Senior Executive Officers
President & General Director
Financial Director
Treasurer
General Secretary

Mr Huaf ☎ 40 06 60 01
Pierre Xavier Crociccmia *Chief Investment Officer* ☎ 40 06 60 05
Alban Dunod ☎ 40 06 62 95
Eric Le Corre ☎ 40 06 62 22

Settlement / Clearing
Regional Head — Andie Bichet *Director* ☎ 40 06 60 19

Global Custody
Regional Head — Andie Bichet *Director* ☎ 40 06 60 19

Other Departments
Private Banking
Correspondent Banking

Pierre Merceron *Director* ☎ 40 06 62 14
Andie Bichet *Director* ☎ 40 06 60 19

Administration

Technology & Systems
Maryvonne Guerin ☎ 40 06 61 03

Compliance
Philippe de Vaujuas ☎ 40 06 62 80

Banque Lehman Brothers SA
Subsidiary Company

21 rue Balzac, F-75406 Paris Cedex 08
Tel: (1) 53 89 30 00 Fax: (1) 53 89 31 30 Telex: 280677
Back Office Fax: 53 89 31 39; Dealing Room Fax: 53 89 31 35

Senior Executive Officers
Chairman & President
Vice President
Managing Director

Leopold Jeorger
Philippe Villin
Nicolas Pourcelet ☎ 53 89 30 81

Others (Senior Executives)
Barry D Zwicker *Chief Administrative Officer*

Debt Capital Markets / Fixed Income
Government Bonds
Head of Trading — Bruno Guérin *Head of Trading* ☎ 53 89 31 70

406 Euromoney Directory 1999

www.euromoneydirectory.com　　　　　　FRANCE (+33)

Non-Domestic Government Bonds
BTAN　　　　　　　　　　　　　　Guy Blommé ☎ 53 89 31 70
ECU / OAT　　　　　　　　　　　Romain Dumas ☎ 53 89 31 70

Bonds - General
Domestic Sales　　　　　　　　　Sandro Anchisi ☎ 53 89 30 81
　　　　　　　　　　　　　　　　Leila Benguezzou ☎ 53 89 30 81
　　　　　　　　　　　　　　　　Réza Ghodsi ☎ 53 89 30 81
　　　　　　　　　　　　　　　　François Girod ☎ 53 89 30 81
Head of Syndicate　　　　　　　Nicolas Pourcelet *Managing Director* ☎ 53 89 30 81
Head of New Issues　　　　　　Tim Skeet *Head of New Issue* ☎ +44 (171) 260 3094

Fixed-Income Repo
Trading　　　　　　　　　　　　Jeanne Bastien *Head, Treasury & Repo* ☎ 53 89 30 47 ☎ 53 89 31 35

Foreign Exchange

FX Traders / Sales People
　　　　　　　　　　　　　　　　Christopher Lalo ☎ 53 89 30 60

Risk Management
Department: Domestic Sales

Other Currency Swap / FX Options Personnel
Futures & Derivatives　　　　　Benoît Migeot *Head* ☎ 53 89 30 20
　　　　　　　　　　　　　　　　Cyril Paillard ☎ 53 89 30 20

Settlement / Clearing
Department: Back-Office
Operations　　　　　　　　　　Thierry Larroque *Head Financial Controller* ☎ 53 89 30 55
　　　　　　　　　　　　　　　　Cyrille Guilleux *Operations* ☎ 53 89 31 07

Banque Leumi France SA　　　　　　　　　　　　　　　Head Office
100 rue Réaumur, F-75002 Paris
Tel: (1) 40 13 53 53 **Fax:** (1) 40 26 29 07 **Telex:** 215054

Senior Executive Officers
General Manager　　　　　　　Leon Malowanczyk

Banque Misr　　　　　　　　　　　　　　　　　　　　Full Branch Office
9 rue Auber, F-75009 Paris
Tel: (1) 44 94 32 32 **Fax:** (1) 42 66 59 78 **Telex:** 281124 BANSR **Swift:** BMIS FR PP **Email:** euromisr@banquemisr.fr
Reuters: MISP

Senior Executive Officers
General Manager　　　　　　　Mohamed Sayed
Deputy General Manager　　　Bruno Baume

Syndicated Lending
Head of Syndicated Lending　　Khaled Dessouki

Money Markets
Head of Money Markets　　　　Alaa Azaz

Foreign Exchange
Head of Foreign Exchange　　　Essam Aly

Other Departments
Commodities / Bullion　　　　　Mohamed Kenawi *Manager*
Correspondent Banking　　　　Antoine Nassif *Fondé de Pouvoirs*

Administration

Technology & Systems
　　　　　　　　　　　　　　　　Alfred Dufresne *Manager*

Accounts / Audit
Accounts　　　　　　　　　　　Charbel Antoun
Audit　　　　　　　　　　　　　Reda Moussa

FRANCE (+33)   www.euromoneydirectory.com

Banque Nationale de Grèce (France) — Subsidiary Company

65 Avenue Franklin D Roosevelt, F-75008 Paris
PO Box 459, F-75336 Paris Cedex 08
Tel: (1) 53 77 02 02 **Fax:** (1) 42 89 27 50; (1) 53 76 04 80 **Telex:** 642010F **Swift:** BNGF FR PP **Reuters:** BNGF
Telerate: 2506

Senior Executive Officers
President — Theodoros Karatzas
Chief Executive Officer — Stavros Androutsopoulos ☏ 53 77 02 53
Treasurer — Jean-Paul Dufour *Treasury Manager* ☏ 42 56 06 15 F 45 63 08 75

General-Lending (DCM, SL)
Head of Corporate Banking — Jean Stergiou *Manager, Credit & Marketing* ☏ 53 77 02 27

Foreign Exchange
Global Head — Jean-Paul Dufour *Treasury Manager* ☏ 42 56 06 15 F 45 63 08 75

FX Traders / Sales People
Dealer — Dimitrios Politis

Other Departments
Correspondent Banking — Jean Sotiriadis *Deputy Manager* ☏ 53 77 02 72

Banque Nationale de Paris — Head Office

Alternative trading name: BNP

16 Boulevard des Italiens, F-75450 Paris Cedex 9
Tel: (1) 40 14 45 46 **Fax:** (1) 40 14 69 40; (1) 40 14 89 10 **Telex:** 280605 **Reuters:** BNBA-G (Bonds)
Cable: NATIOPAR PARIS
Government Bond Trading, JGB, Tokyo **Tel:** +81 (3) 5473 3637; Government Bond Trading, US Treasuries,
London **Tel:** +44 (171) 623 5990
Website: www.bnp.fr

Senior Executive Officers
Chairman of the Board & CEO — Michel Pébereau
President & Chief Operating Officer — Baudouin Prot
Chief Executive Officer — Michel Pébereau *Chairman of the Board & CEO*
Chief Operating Officer — Baudouin Prot *President & Chief Operating Officer*

Others (Senior Executives)
Group Executive Vice President — Georges Chodron de Courcel
Vivien Levy-Garboua
Advisor to the Chairman — Christian Aubin
Jacques Henri Wahl
Advisor to the Chairman, Asset Liability Mgt — Jean François Lepetit
Executive VP, Control & Finance — Philippe Bordenave
Executive VP, International Trade — Jacques Desponts
Executive VP, Operational & Technical support — Michel Passant
Executive VP, Human Resources — Bernard Lemée
Executive VP, Domestic Networks — Alain Moynot
Executive VP, Organisation & Information System — Hervé Gouezel
Executive VP, Structured Finance — Michel Konczaty
Executive VP, Management Audit & Inspection — Marc Lavergne
Executive VP, Marketing Products — Yves Martrenchar
Executive VP, Subsidiaries & Real Estate — Claude Porcherot
Executive VP, Risk Policy & Industry Research — Edouard Sautter
Executive VP, Banks & Risks — Jean Thomazeau
Executive VP, Development — Laurent Treca
Executive VP, Large Corporations & Institutions — Ervin Rosenberg
Corporate Communication & Advertising — Antoine Sire *General Management & Management Committee*

Debt Capital Markets / Fixed Income
Department: Forex & Interest Rate Markets: Global Fixed Income
Reuters: BNBA-G (Bonds)
Global Head — Jean Bernard Lafonta *Global Head, Foreign Exchange & Interest Rate Mark* ☏ 40 14 14 51
Other — Fabrice di Meglio *Global Head, Global Fixed Income* ☏ 40 14 03 34
Pierre Verdeil *General Secretary* ☏ 40 14 84 72

Government Bonds
Head of Trading — Denis Prouteau *Benchmark Markets* ☏ 40 14 03 34
Olivier Michel *Non-Benchmark Markets* ☏ 40 14 03 34

www.euromoneydirectory.com FRANCE (+33)

Domestic Government Bonds
Head of Trading   Stéphane Levy *FRF Treasury* ☎ 40 14 02 98

Non-Domestic Government Bonds
Trading, BTP, Italian Treasury   Renaud Labbe ☎ +39 (02) 7212 4258

Bonds - General
Arbitrage   Gilles Pradere ☎ 40 14 90 20
                                         Véronique Chauvin *Head, Institutional Bonds Sales* ☎ 40 14 61 95

Fixed-Income Repo
Trading   Fabienne Zamfiresco *Paris* ☎ 40 14 78 66
                                         Ian Forrest *London* ☎ +44 (171) 548 9410

Fixed-Income Research
Analyst   Bertrand Levoir *Research* ☎ 40 14 37 71
Department: FX & Interest Rate Mark.: Global Fixed Income Spread Markets
Global Head   Jean Bernard Lafonta *Global Head, Foreign Exchange & Interest Rate Mark* ☎ 40 14 14 51
                                         Eric Dumas ☎ 55 77 34 38

Bonds - General
Trading, Primary Markets   Laurent Attali ☎ 40 14 03 34
Origination, Paris   Bruno Merlin ☎ 40 14 06 22
Origination, London   Arianna Mezzotero ☎ +44 (171) 548 9501
Financial Engineering   Jean François Borgy ☎ 40 14 04 30
MTN   Bénédicte Cribier Guerin ☎ 40 14 22 86
Secondary Market, Paris   François Valette ☎ 40 14 33 45
Secondary Market, London   Christophe Gouelo ☎ +44 (171) 398 9413
Credit Research, London   Philippe Crate ☎ +44 (171) 772 9566
Department: Forex & Interest Rate Markets: Advisory & Development
Global Head   Jean Bernard Lafonta *Global Head, Foreign Exchange & Interest Rate Mark* ☎ 40 14 14 51
                                         Danièle Guedj *Advisory Services* ☎ 40 14 14 52
Other   Michel Cohen *Advisory Services* ☎ 40 14 57 37
                                         Laurent Bouaziz *Advisory Services*
                                         Jean Pierre Falgas *Development* ☎ 40 14 03 96
                                         Florence Karras *Development* ☎ 40 14 90 61
                                         Jean Yves De Vos *Development*
                                         Christophe Michelin *Financial & Budget Control* ☎ 40 14 29 17
Department: FX & Interest Rate Markets: Institutional Sales
Global Head   Philippe Guyot *Global Head, Institutional Sales* ☎ 55 77 34 38
Head of Fixed Income Sales   Véronique Chauvin *Head, Institutional Bonds Sales* ☎ 40 14 61 95
Other   Hugues Laqueille *Institutional Derivatives Sales* ☎ 40 14 77 81
                                         Francine Royer *Interest Rate & FX Markets* ☎ 40 14 67 09
                                         Henry Kedziora *Central & Supranational Banks* ☎ 40 14 77 18
Department: FX & Interest Rate Markets: European Corporate Sales
Global Head   Ligia Torres *Global Head, European Corporate Sales* ☎ 40 14 03 12
Other   Guylaine Dyevre *Corporate Sales* ☎ 40 14 22 72
                                         Christophe Moenne Loccoz *Corporate Sales* ☎ 48 01 35 79
                                         Solveig Bourgeois *French Network* ☎ 40 14 88 49
Department: FX & Interest Rate Markets: Global Market Research
Global Head   Nicole Theze *Global Head, Global Market Research* ☎ 40 14 14 99
Other   Cyril Beuzit *Fixed Income Strategies* ☎ 40 14 98 68
                                         René Defossez *Foreign Exchange Strategies* ☎ 40 14 26 23
                                         Claude Mattern *Technical Analysis* ☎ 40 14 44 40
                                         Christian Sene *Technical Analysis* ☎ 40 14 58 67

Equity Capital Markets
Department: BNP Equities
Global Head   Chantal Mazzacurati ☎ 40 14 39 46
                                         Yann Gerardin *Deputy Head* ☎ 40 14 51 13
Head of Sales   Laurent Cadieu *Head, European Brokerage* ☎ 40 14 07 10
Head of Trading   Chris Hipkins *Head of Trading* ☎ +44 (171) 398 9912
Other   Michel Royant *Head of Origination* ☎ 40 14 71 83
                                         Jean Marie Guillaume *Head of Origination* ☎ 40 14 34 43
                                         Joanna Darlington *Head, European Research* ☎ +44 (171) 772 9635
                                         Oliver Osty *Head, European Equity Derivatives* ☎ 40 14 77 16
                                         Rémi Frank *Global Head, Equity Derivatives Sales* ☎ 40 14 44 86
                                         Yann Muzika *Asian Equity Derivatives* ☎ +852 2810 0138
                                         Mike Selverian *Head, US Equity Derivatives* ☎ +1 (610) 995 1431

FRANCE (+33)   www.euromoneydirectory.com

Banque Nationale de Paris (cont)
Money Markets
Department: FX & Interest Rate Markets: Money Market & FX

Global Head	Jean Bernard Lafonta *Global Head, Foreign Exchange & Interest Rate Mark* ☎ 40 14 14 51
	Geoffroy Sartorius *Deputy Head, Foreign Exchange & Interest Rate Mark* ☎ 40 14 39 94
	Albert Bossuet *Global Head, Money Market & Foreign Exchange* ☎ 55 77 32 07
Other	Pierre Renom *Head, Money Markets* ☎ 40 14 58 05
	Claude Bertin *Co-Head, Money Market* ☎ +44 (171) 895 7070

Eurocommercial Paper
Head of Trading	Patrick Pernet *Trading* ☎ 40 14 57 93

Money Markets - General
FRF Euro	Patrick Chauvet ☎ 40 14 64 92
European Currencies	Didier Compere ☎ 40 14 67 76
	Gilles Perrin ☎ 40 14 06 35
Arbitrage	Gilles Garnier ☎ 40 14 02 68

Foreign Exchange
Department: FX & Interest Rate Markets: Money Market & FX

Global Head	Jean Bernard Lafonta *Global Head, Foreign Exchange & Interest Rate Mark* ☎ 40 14 14 51
	Geoffroy Sartorius *Deputy Head, Foreign Exchange & Interest Rate Mark* ☎ 40 14 39 94
	Albert Bossuet *Global Head, Money Market & Foreign Exchange* ☎ 55 77 32 07
Head of Trading	Henry Foch *Global Head, Foreign Exchange & FX Options* ☎ 40 14 58 04
	Philippe Ruiz ☎ 40 14 58 04
	Patrice Cohen *FX Options Trading* ☎ 40 14 67 76
	Kevin Murphy *FX Options Trading* ☎ +1 (610) 995 1568

FX Traders / Sales People
Foreign Exchange Strategy	René Defossez *Foreign Exchange Strategies* ☎ 40 14 26 23

Risk Management
Department: FX & Interest Rate Markets: Derivatives

Global Head	Jean Bernard Lafonta *Global Head, Foreign Exchange & Interest Rate Mark* ☎ 40 14 14 51

Fixed Income Derivatives / Risk Management
Global Head	Emmanuel Heurtier ☎ 40 14 39 94
	Emmanuel Heurtier ☎ +44 (171) 548 9482
Trading	Raphael Masgnaux *Head, Trading, London*
IR Swaps Trading	Alexis Viry ☎ 40 14 83 47
	Rémi Lefevre Moulenq ☎ +44 (171) 398 9402
IR Options Trading	Bertrand Arnaud ☎ 40 14 06 77
	Babek Saber ☎ +44 (171) 398 9402

Other (FI Derivatives)
Research	Nathalie Bouez ☎ 40 14 28 93
Legal Department	Gilles Kolifrath ☎ 40 14 13 21

Foreign Exchange Derivatives / Risk Management
Global Head	Henry Foch *Global Head, Foreign Exchange & FX Options* ☎ 40 14 58 04
Vanilla FX option Trading	Patrice Cohen *FX Options Trading* ☎ 40 14 67 76
	Kevin Murphy *FX Options Trading* ☎ +1 (610) 995 1568

Other (Exchange-Traded Derivatives)
	Hugues Laqueille *Institutional Derivatives Sales* ☎ 40 14 77 81

Banque de Neuflize, Schlumberger, Mallet   Head Office

3 Avenue Hoche, F-75008 Paris
Tel: (1) 53 53 11 12; (1) 49 15 70 74   **Fax:** (1) 53 53 11 20; (1) 49 15 70 87   **Telex:** 640653 F   **Swift:** NSMB FR PP

Senior Executive Officers
Chairman	Henri Moulard
Financial Director	Bertrand Leblanc

Equity Capital Markets
Equity Repo / Securities Lending
Head	Bernard J van de Ven *Senior Vice President* ☎ 53 53 11 10
Marketing & Product Development	Lionel Farcy *Vice President* ☎ 53 53 11 14 ✉ lionel.farcy@fr.abnamro.com
Marketing	Sylvie Moissenet-Merle *VP & Area Manager* ☎ 53 53 11 17
Head of Trading	Alexandre Questat *Trader, Term Repo Matchbook* ☎ 53 53 11 11

410 Euromoney Directory 1999

www.euromoneydirectory.com FRANCE (+33)

Banque Nomura France
Subsidiary Company
164 rue de Rivoli, F-75001 Paris
Tel: (1) 42 97 19 00 Fax: (1) 42 97 18 88 Telex: 213234
Senior Executive Officers
Directeur Yoshitaka Okuyama

Banque OBC Odier Bungener Courvoisier
57 Avenue d'Iéna, F-75116 Paris
Tel: (1) 45 02 40 00 Fax: (1) 45 00 77 79

Banque Parisienne de Credit
Head Office
56 rue de Châteaudun, F-75009 Paris
Tel: (1) 42 80 68 68 Fax: (1) 40 16 16 30 Telex: 280179 BAPAR F
Senior Executive Officers
Chief General Manager Guy Chartier
General Manager François Goulard

Banque Regionale du Nord
Full Branch Office
21 Place Jean Jaurés, F-62300 Lens
Tel: (3) 21 79 15 55 Fax: (3) 21 70 89 00
Senior Executive Officers
Manager Friederik Trouche-Brügger

Banque Regionale du Nord
Head Office
84 rue Nationale, F-59000 Lille
Tel: (3) 20 14 23 23 Fax: (3) 20 14 23 63 Telex: 110370 BARENOR F
Senior Executive Officers
Chairman Guy Chartier
Managing Director François Gagnaire

Banque Regionale du Nord
Full Branch Office
50 Boulevard du Gal de Gaulle, F-59100 Roubaix
Tel: (3) 20 81 98 68 Fax: (3) 20 73 59 16

Banque Regionale du Nord
Full Branch Office
2 Avenue des Denteileres, F-59308 Valenciennes Cedex
Tel: (3) 27 28 03 03 Fax: (3) 27 46 82 82
Senior Executive Officers
Manager Pascal Wallers

Banque Saradar France SA
49/51 Avenue George V, F-75008 Paris
Tel: (1) 44 43 44 43 Fax: (1) 47 23 99 20 Telex: 649091 Swift: SARF FR PP Reuters: SARP
Senior Executive Officers
Chairman Georges Batt
Managing Director / General Manager André Tyan

FRANCE (+33)   www.euromoneydirectory.com

Banque SBA

28 rue de Berri, F-75008 Paris
PO Box 7108, F-75008 Paris
Tel: (1) 45 62 72 88 Fax: (1) 53 93 25 98 Telex: 641960 F SOBAR Swift: SBAA FR PP Cable: SOBAR

Senior Executive Officers
Chairman   Mustafa Janoudi
General Manager   Renaud Devinat
Assistant General Manager   Fawaz Kabbara

Banque SOFIREC   Head Office

10 Avenue de la Grande Armée, F-75017 Paris
Tel: (1) 40 68 66 66 Fax: (1) 45 74 33 17 Telex: 280694

Senior Executive Officers
Chief Executive Officer   Pierre Audibert
Financial Director; Treasurer   Bernard Verdalle
Managing Director / General Manager   Jean Crapet [T] 40 68 66 66
Company Secretary   Mireille Miot [T] 48 16 63 03
International Division   Eric Hoffmeister [T] 40 68 66 70

Banque Sudameris

4 rue Meyerbeer, F-75009 Paris Cedex 09
PO Box 25109, F-75429 Paris Cedex 09
Tel: (1) 48 01 77 77 Fax: (1) 42 46 32 13 Telex: 283669 SUDIR F Swift: BSUD FR PP Email: infocom@sudameris.fr
Reuters: SUDP
Website: www.sudameris.fr

Senior Executive Officers
Chairman   Alberto Abelli
President & Chief Executive Officer   Enrico Meucci
First Executive Vice President & COO   Adriano Bisogni [T] 48 01 79 82
Executive Vice President   Patrick de Villemandy [T] 48 01 79 49
Executive Vice President   Alfonso Lanni [T] 48 01 78 81
First Vice President & Corporate Secretary   François Chanoit [T] 48 01 78 65

Others (Senior Executives)
Cross Border Risk Management; Financial   Natale Arculeo *Senior Vice President* [T] 48 01 78 50 [F] 40 22 90 57
Engineering

Debt Capital Markets / Fixed Income
Department: Capital Markets
Head of Debt Capital Markets   Frederic Phan *First Vice President* [T] 48 01 77 91 [F] 48 01 79 81

Equity Capital Markets
Head of Equity Capital Markets   Frederic Phan *First Vice President* [T] 48 01 77 91 [F] 48 01 79 81

Syndicated Lending

Other (Trade Finance)
Trade & Commodity Finance Operations   Michel Dupreuilh *First Vice President* [T] 48 01 79 10 [F] 48 00 08 07

Money Markets
Head of Money Markets   Brian De Freytas *Senior Vice President* [T] 48 01 77 80 [F] 48 00 08 07

Foreign Exchange
Head of Foreign Exchange   Brian De Freytas *Senior Vice President* [T] 48 01 77 80 [F] 48 00 08 07

Corporate Finance / M&A Advisory
Head of Corporate Finance   Robert Housset *Senior Vice President* [T] 48 01 78 74 [F] 48 01 78 85

Other Departments
Private Banking   Michel de Gironde *First Vice President* [T] 48 01 77 88 [F] 48 01 79 62
Correspondent Banking   Joël Berthoin *Officer* [T] 48 01 78 94 [F] 48 00 08 07

Administration
Business Development   Andrés Ezcurra *Senior Vice President* [T] 48 01 77 58 [F] 48 00 08 07

www.euromoneydirectory.com   FRANCE (+33)

Banque Trad-Crédit Lyonnais (France) SA
Subsidiary Company
38 Avenue de l'Opéra, F-75002 Paris
PO Box 6334, F-75063 Paris Cedex 02
Tel: (1) 44 56 24 50 **Fax:** (1) 42 68 07 64 **Telex:** 680720 **Cable:** CREDITRAD

Senior Executive Officers
President — Roger Hernandez
Managing Director — Gilbert Aknin
General Manager — Emile G Badra

Banque Vernes
Head Office

Alternative trading name: Vernes Gestion
15 rue des Pyramides, F-75026 Paris Cedex 01
Tel: (1) 44 86 80 00 **Fax:** (1) 44 86 82 82 **Telex:** 216458 **Swift:** VERN FR PP **Email:** cfoliot.banquevernes@fininfo.fr

Senior Executive Officers
President — Pierre Bruneau de la Salle ☎ 44 86 80 21
Chief Executive Officer — Christian Ginolhac *Director General* ☎ 44 86 80 24
Joël Scelo *Director General* ☎ 44 86 80 21
Treasurer — Philippe Malteste ☎ 44 86 81 66

Debt Capital Markets / Fixed Income
Global Head — Claudio Arenas *Sub Director* ☎ 44 86 81 29
✉ carenas.banquevernes@fininfo.fr

Domestic Government Bonds
Head of Sales — Claudio Arenas *Sub Director* ☎ 44 86 81 29
✉ carenas.banquevernes@fininfo.fr

Non-Domestic Government Bonds
Claude Steegman *Joint Director* ☎ 44 86 80 77

Equity Capital Markets
Global Head — Michel Moinecourt *Joint Director* ☎ 44 86 81 27

Domestic Equities
Head of Origination — Christian Jacquet *Sub Director* ☎ 44 86 81 33

Convertibles / Equity-Linked
Head of Origination — Christian Jacquet *Sub Director* ☎ 44 86 81 33

Money Markets
Global Head — Claudio Arenas *Sub Director* ☎ 44 86 81 29
✉ carenas.banquevernes@fininfo.fr

Foreign Exchange
Global Head — Philippe Malteste *Treasurer* ☎ 44 86 81 66

Corporate Finance / M&A Advisory
Global Head — Mathieu Dierstein *Joint Director* ☎ 44 86 81 57

Other Departments
Private Banking — Jean Oliver *Director* ☎ 44 86 81 41

Administration
Public Relations — M C Lanata *Sub Director* ☎ 44 86 82 42

Banque Worms
Tour Voltaire, 1 Place des Degrés, F-92059 Paris La Defense
Tel: (1) 49 07 50 50 **Fax:** (1) 49 07 59 11 **Telex:** 616023 BWOR **Swift:** BWOR FR PP

Senior Executive Officers
Department: Supervisory Board
Chairman — Henri de Castries
Vice Chairman — Daniel Durca
Member — Claude Fath
Member — Michel Pariat
Member — Jean Blondeau
Member — Jean-Marc Espalioux
Member — Patrick Fellous
Member — Jean-Pierre Halbron
Member — Nicolas Millotte
Member — Nicolas Noreau

Euromoney Directory 1999   413

FRANCE (+33)   www.euromoneydirectory.com

Banque Worms (cont)
Supervisory Board (cont)
Member	Jean-François Phélizon
Member	Albert Van Houtte
Secretary	Liliane Vimont

Department: Management Board
Chairman	Marc Vuillermet

Others (Senior Executives)
Investment Banking & Capital Markets	Marc Vuillermet
Private Clients	Frédéric de Pelleport *Managing Director*
Institutional Investors	Loïc de Rodellec *Managing Director*
Banking Systems & Operations	Maurice Duvert *Managing Director*
Risk Control, Asset / Liability Management	Benoît Salet *Managing Director*
	Sibylle Quéré-Becker *Secretary*

Debt Capital Markets / Fixed Income
Head of Debt Capital Markets	Marc Vuillermet

Equity Capital Markets
Head of Equity Capital Markets	Marc Vuillermet

Risk Management
Department: Risk Control, Asset / Liability Management
Head of Risk Management	Benoît Salet *Managing Director*

Administration
Head of Marketing	O Dillard

Legal / In-House Counsel
Legal Affairs	J-M Canac

Corporate Communications
	Sibylle Quéré-Becker *Secretary*

Accounts / Audit
Audit	C Lacan

Other (Administration)
Human Resources	M Tabary

Barclays Asset Management France *Subsidiary Company*
Formerly known as: Barclays Puget-Mahé Gestion SNC
Alternative trading name: Compagnie Financière Barclays de Zoete Wedd
21 Boulevard de la Madeleine, F-75001 Paris
Tel: (1) 44 58 32 32 **Fax:** (1) 44 58 31 31

Senior Executive Officers
Managing Director	Mr Lavignasse

Barclays Capital *Subsidiary Company*
Formerly known as: BZW Puget Mahé SA
21 Boulevard de la Madeleine, F-75038 Paris Cedex 01
Tel: (1) 44 58 32 32; (1) 44 58 31 71 **Fax:** (1) 44 58 31 31; (1) 44 58 31 70

Senior Executive Officers
General Director	Andrea Munari
General Director	Aurian D'Ursel

General-Investment
Head of Investment	Christian Bartholin *Managing Director of Investment Banking*

Barclays Capital Développement SA *Subsidiary Company*
19 Avenue de l'Opera, F-75001 Paris
Tel: (1) 53 45 11 50 **Fax:** (1) 53 45 11 70

Senior Executive Officers
Director	Gonzague De Blignères
Director	Charles Diehl

www.euromoneydirectory.com FRANCE (+33)

Barings France SA
Subsidiary Company

Formerly known as: Baring Brothers (France) SA
49 Avenue d'Iena, F-75116 Paris
Tel: (1) 53 67 11 11 **Fax:** (1) 53 67 11 22

Senior Executive Officers
Director General — Pierre Pâris

Corporate Finance / M&A Advisory
Head of Corporate Finance — Pierre Pâris *Director General*

Bayerische Hypo-und Vereinsbank AG
Full Branch Office

Alternative trading name: Hypovereinsbank
Formerly known as: Bayerische Vereinsbank AG
34 rue Pasquier, F-75008 Paris
Tel: (1) 43 12 14 14 **Fax:** (1) 43 12 14 44 **Telex:** 660947 **Swift:** BVBE FR PP **Email:** acpont@bloomberg.net
Reuters: HVBP **Bloomberg:** HVBR

Senior Executive Officers
Financial Director — Edgar Husser [T] 43 12 14 04 [F] 43 12 14 38
General Manager — Hartmut Roeske [T] 43 12 14 16 [F] 43 12 14 33
Deputy General Manager — Anne-Claude Pont [T] 43 12 14 74 [F] 43 12 14 29

General-Lending (DCM, SL)
Head of Corporate Banking — Jean Oastakian *Director* [T] 43 12 14 68

Debt Capital Markets / Fixed Income
Head of Fixed Income — Claude Wittezaele [T] 43 12 14 78 [F] 43 12 14 29

Syndicated Lending
Loan-Related Activities
Trade Finance — Rene Jacob [T] 43 12 14 32 [F] 43 12 14 66

Other (Trade Finance)
Real Estate — Serge Chauvin [T] 43 12 14 01 [F] 43 12 14 11

Money Markets
Head of Money Markets — Yann Passeron [T] 43 12 14 79 [F] 43 12 14 29

Settlement / Clearing
Head of Settlement / Clearing — Nadine Boyer [T] 43 12 14 18 [F] 43 12 14 00

Global Custody
Head of Global Custody — Christina Oudot [T] 43 12 14 59 [F] 43 12 14 38

Other Departments
Chief Credit Officer — Hildegarde Schnell [T] 43 12 14 10 [F] 43 12 14 55

Administration
Technology & Systems — Thierry Georgel [T] 43 12 14 60 [F] 43 12 14 29

BBL Lille SA
Subsidiary Company

Formerly known as: BBL Aviation SA
7 Boulevard Louis XIV, F-59042 Lille Cedex
Tel: (3) 20 62 11 19 **Fax:** (3) 20 52 64 45

Senior Executive Officers
Chairman — Alex Sauvage

BCEN-EUROBANK
Head Office

79-81 Boulevard Haussmann, F-75382 Paris Cedex 08
Tel: (1) 40 06 43 21 **Fax:** (1) 40 06 48 48 **Telex:** 280200 F

Senior Executive Officers
Chairman of the Supervisory Board — Iouri Ponomarev
Chairman — Andreï Moutchan

Others (Senior Executives)
Executive Board — Patrice Daudier de Cassini
Patrick Deloziere
Alexandre Elson

FRANCE (+33)　　　www.euromoneydirectory.com

Berliner Bank AG
Full Branch Office

Tour Voltaire, 1 Place des Degrés, F-82059 Paris
Tel: (1) 49 07 55 00 **Fax:** (1) 49 07 59 11

Senior Executive Officers
Senior Vice President　　　François Levasseur

BNP Arbitrage
Head Office

Salle des Marchés Actions, Third Floor, 20 Boulevard des Italiens, F-75009 Paris
Tel: (1) 40 14 02 42 **Fax:** (1) 40 14 14 95 **Swift:** BNAB FR PP

Senior Executive Officers
Chairman & Chief Executive Officer　　　Yann Gerardin
Chief Financial Officer　　　Jean Marie Savin

Equity Capital Markets
Equity Repo / Securities Lending
Head　　　Alexandre Mojaisky *Head of Securities Lending Desk* E amojaisk@bnp.fr
Head of Trading　　　Corine LaFrongne *Trader,FRF, HKD* T 40 14 03 51
　　　Fabrice Cohen *Trader, DEM, FRF, GBP, CHF* T 55 77 36 51
　　　Marie Claire Treanton *Trader, ITL, ESP,NLG,BEF,HKD* T 40 14 34 94

Risk Management
Country Head　　　Bertrand Meyer

BNP Finance
Subsidiary Company

20 Boulevard des Italiens, F-75002 Paris
Tel: (1) 40 14 78 66 **Fax:** (1) 40 20 86 80; (1) 40 14 23 31 **Telex:** 281366 **Swift:** BNPF FR PF

Senior Executive Officers
Chairman　　　Philippe Bordenave
Managing Director / General Manager　　　Geoffrey Sartorius

Debt Capital Markets / Fixed Income
Fixed-Income Repo
Marketing & Product Development　　　Albano Vincenzo T +44 (171) 283 3664 E vincenzo.albano@bmpgroup.com
Trading　　　Pascal Chauvier *Repo Trader on Ffr Government Bonds*
　　　Benoit Faillat *Assistant Trader*
　　　Patrice Palisson *Repo Trader on Ffr & ECU*
Sales　　　Fabienne Zamfiresco *Head of Repo*

BRED Banque Populaire
Head Office

Formerly known as: Banque Regionale d'Escompte et de Depots
18 Quai de la Rapée, F-75012 Paris F
Tel: (1) 48 98 60 00 **Fax:** (1) 40 04 71 57 **Telex:** 214844 BREDTU **Swift:** BRED FR PP **Email:** dcebred@bred.fr

Senior Executive Officers
Chairman　　　Steve Gentili
Chief Executive Officer　　　François-Xavier de Fournas
Financial Director　　　Yves Jacquot *Chief Financial Officer*
International Division　　　Mohamed Eddequiouaq *Head, International Division* T 40 04 77 33

Debt Capital Markets / Fixed Income
Head of Debt Capital Markets　　　Pierre Vedrines

Syndicated Lending
Head of Syndicated Lending　•　Mohamed Eddequiouaq *Head, International Division* T 40 04 77 33

Other Departments
Correspondent Banking　　　Mohamed Eddequiouaq *Head, International Division* T 40 04 77 33

Byblos Bank Belgium SA
Full Branch Office

15 rue Lord-Byron, F-75008 Paris
Tel: (1) 45 63 10 01 **Fax:** (1) 45 61 15 77 **Telex:** 640865 BYBLOS F

Senior Executive Officers
Manager　　　Alain Blumenkranz

416　Euromoney Directory 1999

www.euromoneydirectory.com   FRANCE (+33)

Others (Senior Executives)
Christelle Haddad-Roux *Assistant Manager*

Caisse Centrale des Banques Populaires   Head Office
115 rue Montmartre, F-75002 Paris
10-12 Avenue Winston Churchill, F-94577 Paris Cedex
Tel: (1) 40 39 30 00 **Fax:** (1) 40 39 40 01 **Telex:** 694200 **Swift:** CCBP FR PP PAR **Email:** international@ccbp.fr
Reuters: CCBP **Telex:** 680676 **Reuters:** CCDP
Website: www.ccbp.fr

Senior Executive Officers
Chairman   Jacques Delmas-Marsalet
Managing Director & Chief Executive   Paul Loriot

Others (Senior Executives)
Securities Processing, Payment Systems & Int'l   Luc André *Senior General Manager*
Banking   Dominique Alix *Senior General Manager*
International Division   Isolde Gatineau *Deputy General Manager*
                                                   François Schotte *Deputy General Manager*
Payment Systems   Alain Goldberg *General Manager*
Capital Markets   Bertrand Gaffet *Senior General Manager*
                                                   Serge Picard *Senior General Manager*

Relationship Manager
Payment Systems   Alain Goldberg *General Manager*

Debt Capital Markets / Fixed Income
Head of Debt Capital Markets   Bertrand Gaffet *Senior General Manager*
                                          Serge Picard *Senior General Manager*

Government Bonds
Head of Origination   Christophe Cazemajour *Deputy General Manager*

Fixed-Income Repo
Head of Trading   Daniel Sueur *Deputy General Manager*

Equity Capital Markets
Head of Equity Capital Markets   Nicolas Patel

Money Markets
Head of Money Markets   Daniel Sueur *Deputy General Manager*

Foreign Exchange
Head of Foreign Exchange   Nicolas Patel

Settlement / Clearing
Head of Settlement / Clearing   Alain Kessier *Deputy General Manager*

Caisse Centrale de Réescompte   Head Office
44 rue Washington, F-75008 Paris
Tel: (1) 49 53 20 00 **Fax:** (1) 42 25 60 48 **Telex:** 640425 **Swift:** CCER FR PP **Reuters:** CCRA-C
Website: www.ccpcm.com

Senior Executive Officers
Chairman of the Management Board   Daniel Terminet
Chief Executive Officer   Pierre Vincent *Member, Managing Board*

Others (Senior Executives)
Chairman Adviser   Hervé de Boysson *Chairman & CEO*
                                          Monique Muns *Company Secretary*

General-Lending (DCM, SL)
Head of Corporate Banking   Hervé de Boysson *Marketing & Commercial Banking*

General - Treasury
Head of Treasury   Thierry Gaube *Deputy Manager, Treasury*

Debt Capital Markets / Fixed Income
Department: Capital Markets
Global Head   Thierry Gaube *Deputy Manager*

Asset-Backed Securities / Securitization
Global Head   Pierre Vincent *Member, Managing Board*

Equity Capital Markets
Department: CCR Actions
Tel: 49 53 20 04 **Fax:** 49 53 20 19
Head of Equity Capital Markets   Hervé de Boysson *Chairman & CEO*

Euromoney Directory 1999 **417**

FRANCE (+33)　　　　　　　　www.euromoneydirectory.com

Caisse Centrale de Réescompte (cont)
Money Markets
Head of Money Markets　　　　　　　　Thierry Gaube *Deputy Manager*
Foreign Exchange
Head of Foreign Exchange　　　　　　　Thierry Gaube *Deputy Manager*
Risk Management
Exchange-Traded Derivatives
FX Futures; FX Options　　　　　　　　Thierry Gaube *Deputy Manager*
Asset Management
Department: CCR Gestion
Fax: 49 53 20 06
Head　　　　　　　　　　　　　　　　Hervé de Boysson *Adviser to the Chairman*
Department: CCR Patrimoine
Tel: (1) 49 53 21 00 Fax: (1) 49 53 20 23
Other (Asset Management)
Private Clients Fund Management　　　　Hervé de Boysson *Adviser to the Chairman*
Administration
Head of Marketing　　　　　　　　　　Hervé de Boysson *Adviser to the Chairman*

Caixa Geral de Depósitos　　　　　　　　　　　　　　　Full Branch Office
83 Avenue Marceau, F-75116 Paris
Tel: (1) 40 69 54 00 Fax: (1) 40 70 03 09; (1) 53 32 75 90 Telex: 640569 Swift: CGDI FR PP Reuters: CGDP

Senior Executive Officers
General Manager　　　　　　　　　　　Joaquim de Andrade Campos ☎ 40 69 54 07
Deputy General Manager　　　　　　　　Joaquim Neiva de Oliveira ☎ 42 69 54 04
Debt Capital Markets / Fixed Income
Tel: 47 20 87 35 Fax: 40 70 03 09
Global Head　　　　　　　　　　　　　Mario de Oliveira *Senior Manager* ☎ 40 69 54 51
Syndicated Lending
Tel: 47 20 87 35
Global Head　　　　　　　　　　　　　Mario de Oliveira *Senior Manager* ☎ 40 69 54 51
Money Markets
Tel: 47 20 87 35
Global Head　　　　　　　　　　　　　Mario de Oliveira *Senior Manager* ☎ 40 69 54 51
Foreign Exchange
Tel: 47 20 87 35
Global Head　　　　　　　　　　　　　Mario de Oliveira *Senior Manager* ☎ 40 69 54 51
Settlement / Clearing
Foreign Exchange Settlement　　　　　　René-Michel Criniere *Manager, Back Office* ☎ 40 69 54 53

James Capel SA　　　　　　　　　　　　　　　　　　Representative Office
20 bis Avenue Rapp, F-75332 Paris Cedex 07
Tel: (1) 44 42 70 00 Fax: (1) 44 42 77 77

Senior Executive Officers
Representative　　　　　　　　　　　　Pierre Bossef

Cariplo Banque SA　　　　　　　　　　　　　　　　　Subsidiary Company
40/42 rue la Boëtie, F-75008 Paris
Tel: (1) 44 13 41 34 Fax: (1) 42 25 20 64 Telex: CARIPAR 651045 F Swift: COIB FR PP

Senior Executive Officers
General Manager　　　　　　　　　　　G Galante

CDC Marchés　　　　　　　　　　　　　　　　　　　　Head Office
56 rue de Lille, F-75356 Paris Cedex 07
Tel: (1) 40 49 56 78 Fax: (1) 40 49 86 89 Swift: CDCM FR PP Reuters: CDC MENU

Senior Executive Officers
Chairman　　　　　　　　　　　　　　Isabelie Bouillot ☎ 40 49 54 50
Chief Executive Officer　　　　　　　　Anthony Orsatelli ☎ 40 49 78 81

418　Euromoney Directory 1999

FRANCE (+33)

Senior Executive Officers (cont)
Financial Director   Alain Prévot *Chief Financial & Administrative Officer* ☎ 40 49 26 01
                                      ☎ 40 49 72 48
Chief Operating Officer   Michel Bois ☎ 40 49 69 16
Debt Capital Markets / Fixed Income
Global Head   Nicolas Fourt ☎ 40 49 76 99
Country Head   Francis Bento ☎ +81 (3) 35 92 75 47
                                      Maxim Roche
                                      Martin Bouffard *CDC Frankfurt* ☎ +49 (69) 971 33383
                                      Ramine Rouhani ☎ +1 (212) 891 6170

Domestic Government Bonds
Head of Sales   Thierry Guinard ☎ 40 49 84 34
Head of Trading   Franck Butler ☎ 40 49 69 62
Head of Research   Patrick Artus ☎ 40 49 50 60
Non-Domestic Government Bonds
                                      Thomas Lay *CDC Frankfurt* ☎ +49 (69) 971 33363
                                      Luc Egnell ☎ 40 49 80 30

Eurobonds
Head of Syndication   Denis Krief ☎ 40 49 53 57
Head of Trading   Olivier Khayat *Co-Head, Debt Capital Markets* ☎ 40 49 11 22
                                      Olivier Allard ☎ 40 49 11 18

Bonds - General
German Credit   Hansjörg Paczschke *CDC Frankfurt* ☎ +49 (69) 971 133395
Fixed-Income Repo
Head of Repo   Michel Albertini ☎ 40 49 88 78
Matched Book Manager   Peter Nowicki *CDC New York* ☎ +1 (212) 891 6160
Equity Capital Markets
Department: CDC Marchés
3 rue Lafayette, F-75009 Paris
Global Head   Bernard Migus ☎ 40 49 77 04
Domestic Equities
Head of Origination   Jean Lanteri Laura ☎ 40 49 75 03
                                      Bernard Icard ☎ 40 49 79 42
Head of Syndication   François-Xavier Gilliot ☎ 40 49 62 38
Head of Sales   Stéphane About *Sales, CDC Bourse* ☎ 40 49 61 79
Head of Trading   Etienne Bur ☎ 40 49 63 76
Head of Research   Gilbert Ferrand ☎ 40 49 77 02
International Equities
Head of Origination   Jean Lanteri Laura ☎ 40 49 75 03
                                      Bernard Icard ☎ 40 49 79 42
Head of Syndication   François-Xavier Gilliot ☎ 40 49 62 38
Head of Sales   Stéphane About *Sales, CDC Bourse* ☎ 40 49 61 79
Head of Trading   Etienne Bur ☎ 40 49 63 76
Convertibles / Equity-Linked
Head of Origination   Bernard Migus ☎ 40 49 77 04
Head of Syndication   François-Xavier Gilliot ☎ 40 49 62 38
Head of Sales; Head of Trading   Etienne Bur ☎ 40 49 63 76
Equity Repo / Securities Lending
Marketing   Olivier Serouille ☎ 40 49 65 94
Money Markets
Global Head   Jean-Jacques Quellec ☎ 40 49 61 37
Domestic Commercial Paper
Head of Trading   Eric Chouteau ☎ 40 49 84 23
Eurocommercial Paper
Head of Trading   Eric Chouteau ☎ 40 49 84 23
Foreign Exchange
Global Head   Jeannot Conrad *Chief Dealer* ☎ 40 49 83 19
Risk Management
Global Head   Michel Bois ☎ 40 49 69 16
Regional Head   William Dellal *CDC, New York* ☎ +1 (212) 891 6100
Fixed Income Derivatives / Risk Management
Global Head   Stephane Kourganoff ☎ 40 49 84 29
Country Head   Victor Vasankht ☎ +1 (212) 891 0245
IR Swaps Sales / Marketing   Gwendoline Guerard des Lauriers ☎ 40 49 77 92
IR Swaps Trading   Guillaume Couzineau ☎ 40 49 13 25
IR Options Sales / Marketing   Gwendoline Guerard des Lauriers ☎ 40 49 77 92
IR Options Trading   Guillaume Couzineau ☎ 40 49 13 25

FRANCE (+33)   www.euromoneydirectory.com

CDC Marchés (cont)
Foreign Exchange Derivatives / Risk Management
Vanilla FX option Trading   Xin He ☎ 40 49 69 08
Settlement / Clearing
Regional Head   Michel Bois ☎ 40 49 69 16
Global Custody
Regional Head   Yvonnick Plaud ☎ 40 49 67 44
Asset Management
Investment Funds   Antoine Desjonquères *Funding Manager* ☎ 40 89 84 45
Other (Asset Management)
Asset & Liability Management   Kurt Jaïs Nielsen ☎ 40 49 71 53

The Chase Manhattan Bank — Full Branch Office
40/42 rue Washington, F-75008 Paris
Tel: (1) 53 77 10 00 **Fax:** (1) 53 77 14 49 **Swift:** CHAS FR PP
Senior Executive Officers
Others (Senior Executives)
Senior Country Officer   Jean-Olivier Bartholin *Senior Country Officer*

Cie Financiere Ottomane — Subsidiary Company
Formerly known as: Banque Ottomane
7 rue Meyerbeer, F-75009 Paris
Tel: (1) 47 42 67 05 **Fax:** (1) 47 42 88 57
Senior Executive Officers
Managing Director   P E Noyelle

Citibank SA — Full Branch Office
Citicenter, 19 Le Parvis, La Défense, F-92073 Paris Cedex 36
Tel: (1) 49 06 10 10 **Fax:** (1) 47 67 07 04 **Telex:** 614666
Senior Executive Officers
General Manager   Claude Jouven
Others (Senior Executives)
                                         Roland Voirin *Assistant General Manager*
General - Treasury
Head of Treasury   Paul Vandeperre ☎ 4906 1015
Foreign Exchange
Corporate Sales   Philippe Illien ☎ 4906 1130

Commerzbank AG — Full Branch Office
3 Place de l'Opéra, F-75002 Paris
PO Box 6512, F-75065 Paris Cedex 02
Tel: (1) 44 94 17 40 **Fax:** (1) 44 94 18 00; (1) 44 94 18 41 **Telex:** 680154
Senior Executive Officers
Others (Senior Executives)
Head of Branch   Burkhard Leffers *Executive Vice President* ☎ 44 94 17 01
                                         Michael Melcher *Executive Vice President* ☎ 44 94 17 02
Syndicated Lending
Head of Origination   Klaus-Dieter Heppenheimer *Senior Manager* ☎ 44 94 17 20
Head of Syndication   Fabrice Guesde *Manager* ☎ 44 94 17 30
Loan-Related Activities
Structured Trade Finance   Fabrice Guesde *Manager* ☎ 44 94 17 30
Other (Trade Finance)
Export Finance   Catherine Thevenet *Manager* ☎ 44 94 17 24
Money Markets
Regional Head   Jean-Charles Fernandez *Manager* ☎ 44 94 17 93
Money Markets - General
                                         Torsten Mix ☎ 44 94 17 97
                                         Hughes Wolke ☎ 44 94 17 94

www.euromoneydirectory.com	FRANCE (+33)

Money Markets - General (cont)
Heidi Eon ☎ 44 94 17 99

Foreign Exchange
Regional Head
Guy Seknadje *Manager* ☎ 44 94 77 45
Jean-Charles Fernandez *Manager* ☎ 44 94 17 93

FX Traders / Sales People
Stéphanie Lapras ☎ 44 94 17 96
Michel Levy ☎ 44 94 77 45
Fabio Madar ☎ 44 94 18 01
Christophe Migeon ☎ 44 94 18 02
Gilles Riquet ☎ 44 94 17 95

Administration
Ulrich Henninger *Manager* ☎ 44 94 17 07

Public Relations
René-Gilles Dechandol *Manager* ☎ 44 94 17 23

Compagnie d'Investissement et de Financement International
Head Office

Alternative trading name: CIFI SA
41 Avenue Montaigne, F-75008 Paris
Tel: (1) 47 20 07 39 **Fax:** (1) 47 20 98 21

Senior Executive Officers
General Manager
Michel Amsellem

Debt Capital Markets / Fixed Income
Global Head
Regional Head
Germain Giraud *Manager*
France Zeziola *Deputy Manager*

Corporate Finance / M&A Advisory
Global Head
Michel Amsellem *Manager, Corporate Finance*
Stephane de Kermoal *Manager, M&A*

Administration
Head of Administration
E Bitton *Manager*

Crédit Agricole Indosuez
Head Office

Formerly known as: Banque Indosuez
9 Quai du Président Paul Doumer, F-92400 Paris Courbevoie
Tel: (1) 41 89 00 00 **Fax:** (1) 41 89 49 07 **Telex:** INSU X 699600 F **Swift:** BSUI FR PP

Senior Executive Officers
Chairman, Supervisory Board	Lucien Douroux
Vice Chairman, Supervisory Board	Yves Barsalou
Chairman, Board of Mgt & Executive Cttee	Marc Antoine Autheman
Vice Chairman & GM, Board of Mgt &	Philippe Geslin
Executive Cttee
Vice Chairman & GM, Board of Mgt &	Philippe Guiral
Executive Cttee
GM, Board of Mgt & Executive Committee	Alain de Korsak
Executive Manager	Jean Charles Raindre ☎ 41 89 34 71 ℻ 41 89 25 93

Others (Senior Executives)
Member, Executive Committee	Andrew Watson *Senior Vice President, Debt & Forex* ☎ 41 89 25 21
	℻ 41 89 38 61
Senior Regional Officer Europe	Ariberto Fassati *Senior Vice President*
Senior Regional Officer for the Americas	Gilles de Margerie *Senior Vice President* ☎ 41 89 42 40 ℻ 41 89 18 98

General-Lending (DCM, SL)
Head of Corporate Banking	Jean Cheval *EVP, Asset Based, Corp. Bkg & Intl Commodities*
	☎ 41 89 38 09 ℻ 41 89 29 40

Debt Capital Markets / Fixed Income
Head of Debt Capital Markets	Andrew Watson *Senior Vice President, Debt & Forex* ☎ 41 89 25 21
	℻ 41 89 38 61
Global Head	Christian Laurenceau *Global Head, Treasury* ☎ 41 89 67 30 ℻ 41 89 48 64
	Henri Kuppers *Global Head, Bond Markets* ☎ 41 89 65 00 ℻ 41 89 65 50

Bonds - General
Short Term Trading	Thomas Gadenne *Global Head* ☎ 41 89 12 53 ℻ 41 89 48 64

FRANCE (+33)

www.euromoneydirectory.com

Crédit Agricole Indosuez (cont)

Emerging Market Bonds
Head of Emerging Markets — Alain de Korsak *GM, Board of Mgt & Executive Committee*

Equity Capital Markets
Global Head — Jean de Courcel *Executive Vice President, Equities* ☎ 41 89 79 49 📠 41 89 79 82
Regional Head — Vincent Hubert *Europe* ☎ 41 89 79 55 📠 41 89 70 60

Domestic Equities
Head of Syndication — François Silvain ☎ 41 89 71 11 📠 41 89 71 15

Other (International Equity)
Emerging Markets, Brazil — Marcos Lederman *Head, Emerging Markets, São Paulo, Brazil* ☎ +55 (11) 3178 4800 📠 +55 (11) 289 6559

Department: Crédit Agricole Indosuez Cheuvreux
Head of Sales — François Simon ☎ 41 89 73 62 📠 41 89 79 76
Head of Trading — Marc Couret ☎ 41 89 79 51 📠 41 89 79 83

Domestic Equities
Head of Research — François Simon ☎ 41 89 73 62 📠 41 89 79 76

International Equities
Head of Research — François Simon ☎ 41 89 73 62 📠 41 89 79 76

Syndicated Lending

Department: Corporate Banking - Europe
Head of Syndication — Jean Pierre Ludwig ☎ 41 89 20 99 📠 41 89 08 81
Head of Credit Committee — Jean Cheval *EVP, Asset Based, Corp. Bkg & Intl Commodities* ☎ 41 89 38 09 📠 41 89 29 40

Other (Syndicated Lending)
Corporate Banking France — Christian Ruggiu ☎ 41 89 32 36 📠 41 89 49 02
Corporate Banking Middle East — Henri Guillemin ☎ 41 89 35 95 📠 41 89 19 42
Corporate Banking Africa & Overseas Territories — Yves Guerin ☎ 41 89 45 13 📠 41 89 29 46
Corporate Banking United States (Chicago) — Alain Butzbach ☎ +1 (312) 372 9200 📠 +1 (312) 372 3724

Loan-Related Activities
Trade Finance; Trade Finance — Marc Tabouis *Project & International Finance, Export Finance* ☎ 41 89 35 13 📠 41 89 39 28
Aircraft / Aerospace Finance — Emmanuel Feld ☎ 41 89 34 25 📠 41 89 06 41
Shipping Finance — Boris Nachamkin *Senior Schipping Adviser* ☎ 41 89 34 78 📠 41 89 29 87
Jean Yves Gueritaud ☎ 41 89 60 74 📠 41 89 29 87
Project Finance — Jacques de Villaines *MD, Europe Project Finance* ☎ 44 20 38 92
Patrick Blanchard *MD, Asia Project Finance* ☎ +65 538 8466
Structured Trade Finance — Antoine Biais *Securitization & Structured Finance* ☎ 41 89 09 16 📠 41 89 19 48
Jacques Bourse *Head, Tax Lease* ☎ 41 89 03 07 📠 41 89 06 66
Bertrand Leveque *LBO, Acquisition Finance* ☎ 41 89 14 46 📠 41 89 06 36
Leasing & Asset Finance — Jean Clocheret *Leasing & Real Estate Services* ☎ 41 89 02 62 📠 41 89 2722
Patrice Dumas *Leasing & Real Estate Services* ☎ 41 89 34 75 📠 41 89 27 22

Foreign Exchange
Global Head — Nathalie Rachou *Head, Global FX & Currency Options* ☎ +44 (171) 971 4337 📠 +44 (171) 971 4535

Risk Management
Global Head — Martin de Waziers *Derivatives Products Group* ☎ 41 89 11 39 📠 41 89 19 71

Other (Exchange-Traded Derivatives)
Didier Varlet *Chairman, Chicago, Futures* ☎ +1 (312) 441 4200 📠 +1 (312) 441 4201

Corporate Finance / M&A Advisory
Head of Mergers & Acquisition; Global Head — Bertrand de Saint Remy *EVP, Corporate & Investment Banking* ☎ 41 89 60 72 📠 41 89 06 20
Acquistion Finance — Bertrand Leveque *LBO, Acquisition Finance* ☎ 41 89 14 46 📠 41 89 06 36

Settlement / Clearing
Country Head — Guillaume Fromont *First Vice President* ☎ 41 89 37 21 📠 41 89 29 64
Operations — Jean Jaques Picard *Senior Vice President* ☎ 41 89 49 25 📠 41 89 29 39

Global Custody
Country Head — Guillaume Fromont *First Vice President* ☎ 41 89 37 21 📠 41 89 29 64

Other Departments
Commodities / Bullion — Jean François Cahet ☎ 41 89 41 29 📠 41 89 08 77
Private Banking — Alain Seuge *Senior Vice President* ☎ 41 89 34 58 📠 41 89 19 05

Administration

Technology & Systems
Information System Division — Jean Jaques Picard *Senior Vice President* ☎ 41 89 49 25 📠 41 89 29 39

www.euromoneydirectory.com   FRANCE (+33)

Compliance
   Guy de La Presle *Executive Manager* ☎ 41 89 79 66 📠 41 89 79 68
Corporate Communications
Communications   Henri Balbaud *Senior Vice President*
Accounts / Audit
Financial Control Department   Gilles de Margerie *Senior Vice President* ☎ 41 89 42 40 📠 41 89 18 98
Other (Administration)
Human Resources   Henri Balbaud *Senior Vice President*
Relations with Crédit Agricole Regional Banks   Alain de Saignes *Executive Manager* ☎ 41 89 26 52 📠 41 89 49 99

Crédit Commercial de France   Head Office

103 Avenue des Champs Elysées, F-75008 Paris
Tel: (1) 40 70 70 40; (1) 40 70 24 35 **Fax:** (1) 40 70 70 09; (1) 40 70 75 76 **Telex:** 645300
Website: www.ccf.fr

Debt Capital Markets / Fixed Income
Global Head   Samir Assaf 📠 40 70 39 36
Head of Fixed Income   Olivier Gregoir ☎ 40 70 75 72 📠 40 70 27 69

Government Bonds
Head of Sales   Jean Louis Azoulay *Sales* ☎ 40 70 73 80 📠 40 70 21 14
   Hervé Souche *Sales* ☎ 40 70 73 94 📠 40 70 21 14
Head of Trading   Thibault de Roux *Head* ☎ 40 70 28 99
   Christophe Rivoire ☎ 40 70 21 39

Eurobonds
Head of Origination   Philippe Henry ☎ 40 70 29 30 📠 40 70 27 69
   Caroline Clermont Tonnerre ☎ 40 70 71 35 📠 40 70 27 69
   Philippe Guillot ☎ 40 70 21 36 📠 40 70 27 69
Head of Syndication   Jean Marc Mercier ☎ 40 70 78 01
   Benoît Arthuis ☎ 40 70 78 01 📠 40 70 27 69
Head of Sales   Florence Tardieu *Sales* ☎ 40 70 73 23 📠 40 70 21 14
   Skander Chabbi *Sales* ☎ 40 70 22 94 📠 40 70 21 14
Head of Trading   Philippe Peyrot *Secondary Trading* ☎ 40 70 77 74 📠 40 70 21 14
   Géraud Delteil *Secondary Trading* ☎ 40 70 00 37 📠 40 70 21 14

Libor-Based / Floating-Rate Products
Asset Swaps   Jean Michel Hannoun ☎ 40 70 27 96 📠 40 70 21 14

Asset-Backed Securities / Securitization
Head of Trading   Jean Eloi Dussartre ☎ 40 70 23 44 📠 40 70 27 69

Fixed-Income Repo
Trading   Jean Michel Meyer ☎ 40 70 32 04

Equity Capital Markets
Global Head   Samir Assaf 📠 40 70 39 36
Head of Trading   Christophe de Backer *Head, CCF Secuities* ☎ 40 70 27 31

Syndicated Lending
Head of Origination; Head of Syndication   Bertrand Grunenwald *Head* ☎ 40 70 21 70

Money Markets
Head of Money Markets   Alain Cousseau ☎ 40 70 57 23

Domestic Commercial Paper
Head of Trading   Alain de Fonteney ☎ 40 70 25 52

Foreign Exchange
Head of Foreign Exchange   Olivier Pacton ☎ 40 70 25 13
Head of Sales   Anita Kamal *Sales* ☎ 40 70 28 27
Head of Trading   Jean Christophe Gerard ☎ 40 70 25 13

Risk Management
Head of Risk Management   Thibault de Roux *Head* ☎ 40 70 28 99

Fixed Income Derivatives / Risk Management
Head of Sales   Xavier Boisseau *Sales* ☎ 40 70 71 01
Trading   Fabrice Garnier *Short-Term Derivatives* ☎ 40 70 30 79
   Michel Antonas *Long Term Derivatives* ☎ 40 70 59 90

Foreign Exchange Derivatives / Risk Management
Spot / Forwards Trading; Cross-Currency Swaps, Trading   Xavier Fouquerand ☎ 40 70 38 81

Other Departments
Economic Research   Valérie Plagnol *Market Research* ☎ 40 70 29 43
   Antoine Brunet *Market Research* ☎ 40 70 29 42

FRANCE (+33)   www.euromoneydirectory.com

Crédit du Nord — Head Office

5/9 Boulevard Haussmann, F-75009 Paris
PO Box 25309, F-75427 Paris Cedex 09
Tel: (1) 40 22 23 88 **Telex:** 285583 NORIB F **Swift:** NORD FR PP **Reuters:** CDNP

Senior Executive Officers
President — Bruno Flechez

Crédit Foncier de France SA — Head Office

19 rue des Capucines, F-75001 Paris
PO Box 65, F-75050 Paris Cedex 01
Tel: (1) 42 44 80 00 **Fax:** (1) 42 44 99 96 **Telex:** CRE FONC 220349 F

Senior Executive Officers
Governor — Jérôme Meyssonnier
Treasurer — Thierry Dufour

Others (Senior Executives)
Counsellor of the President — Régis de Laroulliere

Syndicated Lending
Head of Credit Committee — Claude Bousquet *Manager*

Settlement / Clearing
Operations — Thierry Dufour

Other Departments
Correspondent Banking — Yves Genevée

Administration

Technology & Systems
Information Systems — Dominique Thierry
Systems — Philippe Bompard *Manager*

Public Relations — Isabelle Goyard

Corporate Communications
— Patrick Corbion de la Tour
— Catherine Kock

Accounts / Audit
Inspection — Luc Roger
Audit — Claude Konzelmann

Other (Administration)
Commercial — Jacques Thunnissen *Manager*
Commercial Banking — Philippe Blanc
Human Resources — Colette Leger *Manager*
Client Relations — Philippe Bompard *Manager*
Fiscal — Jean-Paul Coutant

Crédit Industriel d'Alsace et de Lorraine - CIAL — Head Office

31 rue Jean Wenger-Valentin, F-67958 Strasbourg Cedex 9
Tel: (3) 88 37 61 23 **Fax:** (3) 88 37 71 81 **Reuters:** ALLO
Debt Capital Markets Email: dmt_oblig@cial.cicomore.fr **Equity Capital Markets Email:** dmt_action@cial.cicomore.fr **Foreign Exchange Email:** dmt_client@cial.cicomore.fr **Money Markets Email:** dmt_monet@cial.cicomore.fr
Website: www.cic-banques.fr/cial

Senior Executive Officers
Presidente Directeur Géneral — Jean Weber
Chief Operating Officer — Pierre Jackez *Directeur Général Adjoint*

Others (Senior Executives)
— Daniel Rohfritsch *Manager, FX*
— François Malnati *Manager, Correspondent Banking*

Debt Capital Markets / Fixed Income
Department: Debt Capital Markets / Fixed Income / Risk Management
Tel: 88 35 79 00 **Fax:** 88 37 71 93
Head of Fixed Income — Delphine Heckmann

www.euromoneydirectory.com FRANCE (+33)

Bonds - General
Swaps, Fixed Income Options & Exotics Trading

Dominique Capet ☏ 88 35 74 34
Pascal Kergoat ☏ 88 35 74 34
Emmanuel Gosselin
Bruno Lambert
Pierre Maugery-Pons

Equity Capital Markets
Department: Marchés actions e dérivés
Tel: 88 35 52 88
Head of Equity Capital Markets Frédéric Home ☏ 88 35 52 88
Other (Domestic Equities)

Fabrice Hermann *Trader*
Pascal Lallemand *Trader*
Romuald Lonni *Trader*
Jacky Schell *Trader*
Alain Schultz *Trader*
Hervé Bauer *Trader*

Other (International Equity)

Fabrice Hermann *Trader*
Pascal Lallemand *Trader*
Romuald Lonni *Trader*
Jacky Schell *Trader*
Alain Schultz *Trader*
Hervé Bauer *Trader*

Money Markets
Head of Money Markets Delphine Heckmann
Domestic Commercial Paper
Head of Trading Pascale Bendel *Head of Trading* ☏ 88 35 74 34
Money Markets - General

Dominique Heckel *Trader* ☏ 88 35 79 99
Laurent Albert *Trader* ☏ 88 35 74 34
Repo Danielle Eudeline ☏ 88 24 80 01
Foreign Exchange
Corporate Sales Jean-Marc Hauter *Head, Corporate Sales* ☏ 88 35 53 17
FX Traders / Sales People

Georges Goetzmann *Sales* ☏ 88 35 53 17
Anne-Christine Hering-Poyac *Sales* ☏ 88 35 54 24
Jacques Nizier *Sales* ☏ 88 35 54 24

Settlement / Clearing
Head of Settlement / Clearing Georges Vandermarliere *Manager, Back Office* ☏ 88 37 62 17 ☏ 88 37 71 58
Settlement (General) Fredy Mehl *Treasury Clearing* ☏ 88 37 61 78
Daniel Schnepp *Treasury Clearing* ☏ 88 37 70 15
Antoinette Rolling *Securities Clearing* ☏ 88 37 70 15

Administration
Technology & Systems
Jean-Charles Sabas

Legal / In-House Counsel
Jeannot Klein *Directeur Adjoint, Affaires Juridiques*

Public Relations
Jean Ketterer *Directeur Adjoint, Communication*

Crédit Local de France Dexia International   Head Office

Alternative trading name: Dexia Project and Public Finance International Bank
7-11 Quai Andrée Citroen, F-75901 Paris
PO BOX 1002, Paris Cedex 15
Tel: (1) 43 92 79 79 **Fax:** (1) 43 92 70 00

Debt Capital Markets / Fixed Income
Head of Fixed Income Trading Robert Benayoun ☏ 43 92 51 11
Government Bonds
Head of Origination Nelly Assouline ☏ 43 92 70 20
Money Markets
Money Markets - General
Trading Stephane Caminati ☏ 43 92 51 15

Euromoney Directory 1999 **425**

FRANCE (+33)　　　www.euromoneydirectory.com

Crédit Local de France Dexia International (cont)
Foreign Exchange
Head of Trading — Stephane Caminati ☎ 43 92 51 15
Risk Management
Other (Exchange-Traded Derivatives)
Derivatives Trading — Sephane Lefebvre ☎ 43 92 51 10
Asset Management
Portfolio Management — Robert Benayoun ☎ 43 92 51 11

Crédit Lyonnais Rouse (France) SNC — Full Branch Office
100 rue Reaumur, F-75002 Paris
Tel: (1) 42 95 48 99　Fax: (1) 42 95 60 65　Email: clrf@calva.net

Senior Executive Officers
General Manager — Arnaud Barbet-Massin ☎ 42 95 96 73
Risk Management
Exchange-Traded Derivatives
Regional Head — Nicholas I Stephens *Director, Financial Markets* ☎ 42 95 42 42　F 42 95 94 49

Settlement / Clearing
Country Head — Jocelyne Boone-Nikolaus *Director, Operations* ☎ 42 95 97 87
Administration
Technology & Systems — Philippe Sossah *Deputy Director* ☎ 42 95 55 99
Compliance — Cindy Elalouf *Compliance Officer* ☎ 42 95 16 63　F 42 95 55 32
Other (Administration)
Treasury / Billing — Butand Jounin *Deputy Director* ☎ 42 95 56 51　F 42 95 55 32

Crédit Lyonnais SA — Head Office
Capital Markets Division, 16 rue du 4 Septembre, F-75002 Paris
Tel: (1) 42 95 70 00　Fax: (1) 42 95 75 42; (1) 42 95 64 75　Telex: 615310 CRED　Cable: CREDIONAIS
Website: www.creditlyonnais.com

Senior Executive Officers
DGM, Head of Capital Markets — Chantal Lanchon ☎ 42 95 52 44
Debt Capital Markets / Fixed Income
Department: Fixed Income & Forex Division
Global Head — Marc Poli ☎ 49 24 75 24
Albéric de Saboulin *Deputy Manager* ☎ 42 95 87 13

Other (Fixed Income)
Fixed Income Origination — Philippe Terver ☎ 49 24 70 78
Marc Balgnières ☎ 49 24 70 73
Marc Faltheim ☎ 49 24 77 07
Barbara Horton ☎ 49 24 70 81
Arnaud Serougne ☎ 49 24 70 76
Fixed Income Syndication — Jérôme Nanty ☎ 42 95 26 94
Pierre Mouradian ☎ 49 24 70 41
Jean Marie Urquijo ☎ 49 24 70 72
Securitization — Bernard Flaven ☎ 42 95 45 45
Securitization - Banks — Jean Pierre de Cormis ☎ 42 95 24 61
Securitization - Companies — Daniel Guillot ☎ 42 95 13 13
Forex — Jean Alexandre ☎ 49 24 81 76
Warren Pinner ☎ +44 (171) 528 6168
Trading - TPS — Georges Fezenko ☎ 49 24 70 30
Treasury Short Term Trading — Daniel Gautrot ☎ 42 95 79 19
FRF Treasury — Eric Debry ☎ 49 24 70 20
Foreign Currencies Treasury — Joam Devos ☎ 49 24 70 90
Department: Trading & Bond Sales
Bonds - General
Bernard Fonbonne ☎ 49 24 70 50

Fixed-Income Repo
Head of Repo — Thomas Morand ☎ 49 24 76 40

426　Euromoney Directory 1999

www.euromoneydirectory.com   FRANCE (+33)

Department: Structured Products & High Yeld Distribution
High Yield / Junk Bonds
Head of Syndication   Nicolas Chaput ☏ 42 95 70 50
                                            Corinne Amirault ☏ 49 24 74 96
                                            Corinne Drogrey ☏ 49 24 70 53
                                            Antoine Gros ☏ 49 24 75 18
                                            Carole Miller ☏ 49 24 71 99
                                            Caroline Vilain ☏ 49 24 70 80
Head of Trading   Georges Goy *Structured Financing Markets* ☏ 42 95 61 00

Equity Capital Markets
Department: Equity Division
Domestic Equities
Head of Origination; Head of Syndication   Pierre Walter *Head* ☏ 42 95 70 02

Other (Domestic Equities)
French Equity   Alain Taillefer ☏ 49 24 83 31
                                            Myriam Karbache ☏ 49 24 83 32
French Market   Laurent Bourlard *French Market*
Trading   Ahmed Bhayat ☏ 49 24 83 09
                                            Jean-Michel Deville ☏ 49 24 80 63
                                            Vincent Godler ☏ 49 24 83 13
Sales (Institutionals)   Eric Beckerman ☏ 49 24 83 33
                                            Stéphanie Charles ☏ 49 24 83 33
                                            Constance Dutet ☏ 49 24 83 33
                                            Mohamed Idriss ☏ 49 24 83 33
                                            Alexandre Schneebeli ☏ 49 24 83 33
                                            Mohamed Souffir ☏ 49 24 83 33
Sales (Corporates)   Vincent Batailler ☏ 49 24 83 20
                                            Romain Rouet ☏ 49 24 83 19
                                            Yves Teszner ☏ 49 24 83 61

Other (International Equity)
Origination   Bernard Arock ☏ 42 95 61 69
                                            Alix Caudrillier ☏ 42 95 51 47
                                            Christophe Ramoisy ☏ 42 95 48 30
                                            Gilles Smertnik ☏ 42 95 30 99
Syndication   Loïc Bonete ☏ 42 95 54 13
                                            Eric Vorfeld ☏ +44 (171) 214 5108
European Brokerage   Michael Kerr-Dineen ☏ +44 (171) 214 5498
Management Control   Louis Marie Cordier ☏ 42 95 83 37
Equity & Indices Derivatives   Joël Jeuvell ☏ 42 95 92 40
Stock Lending & Borrowing   Alexandre Urwicz ☏ 49 24 83 30
Trading   Pascual Guezi ☏ 49 24 83 29
                                            Hossein Ardehali ☏ +44 (171) 214 5564
Equity & Indices Derivatives   Cyrille Liabeuf ☏ 42 95 92 31
Sales   François Bazin ☏ +44 (171) 214 5566
Research   Rachid Bouzouba ☏ +44 (171) 214 5729
Legal Documentation   Sarah Varlet ☏ 42 95 19 87
                                            Olivier Bedouet ☏ 42 95 16 20

Convertibles / Equity-Linked
Head of Trading   Joël Jeuvell ☏ 42 95 92 40

Other (Convertibles)
                                            Patrick Pilcer ☏ 49 24 81 76
                                            Jean Alexandre ☏ 49 24 81 76
                                            Frédéric Szerman ☏ 49 24 81 77
                                            Laurent Beruti ☏ 49 24 81 25
Trading   Christophe Havret ☏ 49 24 83 34
                                            Mike Ekaete ☏ +44 (171) 214 5606

Equity Repo / Securities Lending
Head   Alexandre Urwicz ☏ 49 24 83 30
Head of Trading   Pascual Guezi ☏ 49 24 83 29
                                            Hossein Ardehali ☏ +44 (171) 214 5564

Money Markets
Domestic Commercial Paper
Head of Trading   Daniel Gautrot ☏ 42 95 79 19
                                            Eric Debry ☏ 49 24 70 20

Eurocommercial Paper
Head of Trading   Daniel Gautrot ☏ 42 95 79 19
                                            Joam Devos ☏ 49 24 70 90

Euromoney Directory 1999   427

FRANCE (+33)   www.euromoneydirectory.com

Crédit Lyonnais SA (cont)
Foreign Exchange
Department: Money Markets & Foreign Exchange Instruments, Sales
Global Head   Christian de Laitre *Sales Coordinator* ☎ 49 24 70 90
FX Traders / Sales People
Corporates   Louis Michel Lavin ☎ 49 24 70 93
    Natalia Crofut ☎ 49 24 74 83
Central Banks   Patrick Cheula ☎ 49 24 70 54
Institutionals (Short Terms)   Sophie Lemoine ☎ 49 24 76 58
French Retail Network   Muriel Studer ☎ 49 24 70 71
Risk Management
Department: Fixed-Income & FX Division
Fixed Income Derivatives / Risk Management
Global Head   Guy Laffineur *Fixed Income Derivatives Products* ☎ 42 95 18 00
Head of Sales   Catherine Duvaud *Sales* ☎ 42 95 07 40
Trading   Benjamin Mellul ☎ 49 24 76 47
Other (FI Derivatives)
Research & Development   Christophe Michel ☎ 42 95 64 09
Domestic Corporates   Jean Sylvain Forneri ☎ 49 24 76 51
Enginering   Nicolas Dubourg ☎ 49 24 74 55
INA-CTC   Caroline Sautet ☎ 49 24 74 92

Credit Suisse First Boston France SA   Subsidiary Company

21 Boulevard de la Madeleine, F-75001 Paris
Tel: (1) 40 76 88 88   **Fax:** (1) 42 56 10 82   **Telex:** 210060 F   **Swift:** CRESFRPZ   **Reuters:** KS42D18   **Bloomberg:** 222565-2
Senior Executive Officers
President   Jean-Marc Forneri ☎ 40 76 88 82   ✉ 42 89 62 39
Managing Director   Eric Meyer ☎ 40 76 88 67   ✉ 40 76 09 90
Managing Director   Gilles de Dumast ☎ 55 04 11 11   ✉ 55 04 11 10

Crédit Suisse Hottinguer   Head Office

Formerly known as: Crédit Suisse (France) SA
38 rue de Provence, F-75009 Paris
Tel: (1) 49 70 58 00   **Fax:** (1) 49 70 58 80   **Telex:** 281641
Senior Executive Officers
Chairman of the Supervisory Board   Henri Hottinguer
Chief Executive Officer   Jean-Luc Peyrot
Others (Senior Executives)
Executive Board   Francois de Beco *Member*
    Frédéric Naître *Member*
    Jacques Bellany-Brown *Member*

Cyril Finance Gestion

2 rue des Italiens, F-75008 Paris
Tel: (1) 55 33 00 00   **Fax:** (1) 55 33 00 09
Senior Executive Officers
Chairman   M Laloyeau
General Manager   Didier Genet ☎ 55 33 00 04
Debt Capital Markets / Fixed Income
Head of Debt Capital Markets   Eric Molinie *Assistant General Manager* ☎ 55 33 00 61
    ✉ emolinie@cyrilfinance.com
Government Bonds
Head of Sales   Tony Ghorayeb *Sales* ☎ 55 33 00 65
Eurobonds
Head of Origination   Eric Molinie *Assistant General Manager* ☎ 55 33 00 61
    ✉ emolinie@cyrilfinance.com
Head of Sales   Tony Ghorayeb *Sales* ☎ 55 33 00 65
Equity Capital Markets
Head of Equity Capital Markets   Patrick Jacob *Manager* ☎ 55 33 00 09   pjacob@cyrilfinance.com
Asset Management
Portfolio Management   Christian Thonier ☎ 55 33 61 25

www.euromoneydirectory.com   FRANCE (+33)

The Dai-Ichi Kangyo Bank Limited
Full Branch Office
50 Avenue Montaigne, F-75008 Paris
PO Box 09, F-75362 Paris Cedex 08
Tel: (1) 42 99 62 00 **Fax:** (1) 42 99 62 75 **Telex:** 649595 DKBPR **Swift:** DKBL FR PP
Website: www.dkb.co.jp

Senior Executive Officers
General Manager   Shinji Fukumoto
Joint General Manager   Futoshi Okada

Daiwa Europe (France) SA
Subsidiary Company
26 Avenue des Champs-Elysées, F-75008 Paris
Tel: (1) 44 35 56 00 **Fax:** (1) 42 56 06 01 **Telex:** 643305

Senior Executive Officers
President & General Director   Shinji Karasawa
Treasurer   Takahiko Yoshino
Director General   Sumiyuki Akaiwa

Equity Capital Markets
Domestic Equities
Head of Sales   Toshiaki Honda
International Equities
Head of Sales   Shusuke Nakata
Convertibles / Equity-Linked
Head of Sales   Shusuke Nakata
Warrants
Head of Sales   Hugues Evain
Settlement / Clearing
Head of Settlement / Clearing Keiyuki Torada

Deutsche Bank AG
Full Branch Office
24 Avenue des Vosges, F-67000 Strasbourg
PO Box 433N/R7, F-67007 Strasbourg
Tel: (3) 88 25 75 75 **Fax:** (3) 88 35 46 97 **Telex:** 871075 DTBK

Senior Executive Officers
Others (Senior Executives)
                               Claude Fussler *Director*

Deutsche Bank France SNC
Subsidiary Company
3 Avenue de Friedland, F-75378 Paris Cedex 08
Tel: (1) 44 95 64 00 **Fax:** (1) 53 75 07 13 **Telex:** 644192 DEUTBANK
American Equities Fax: 53 75 22 65; Controlling Fax: 53 75 07 02; Corporate & Inst Banking - French Desk Fax: 53 75 07 07; Corporate & Inst Banking - International Desk Fax: 53 75 07 05; Credit Control Fax: 53 75 07 14; EDP Fax: 42 89 24 78; EDP Operating Fax: 53 75 07 16; Fixed Income - Front Office Fax: 53 75 07 08; Fixed Income - Future & Options/Matif Fax: 53 75 07 06; Funds Transfer Fax: 53 75 07 12; Investment Banking - Futures & Options Settlements Fax: 53 75 07 11; Investment Banking - Settlement Fax: 53 75 07 10; Legal Fax: 53 75 07 84; Management Corporate & Institutional Banking Fax: 53 75 07 13; Management Global Markets/Change - Money Market - Repo Fax: 53 75 07 15; Management Global Markets/ Fixed Income Fax: 53 75 08 07; Management Resources & Controlling Fax: 53 75 07 04; Organization Fax: 42 89 18 49; Personnel Fax: 53 75 07 03; Structured Finance Fax: 53 75 09 81

Senior Executive Officers
General Director   François-Xavier D'Aligny

DG BANK
Representative Office
112-114 Boulevard Haussmann, F-75008 Paris
Tel: (1) 42 93 00 42 **Fax:** (1) 42 94 80 48

Senior Executive Officers
Representative   Jean-Marie Kraft

FRANCE (+33)   www.euromoneydirectory.com

Donaldson, Lufkin & Jenrette International
Subsidiary Company

Centre Etoile St Honore, 21/25 rue Balzac, F-75406 Paris Cedex 08
Tel: (1) 53 75 85 47 Fax: (1) 53 75 85 30

Senior Executive Officers
Managing Director   Jean-Claude Gonneau ☎ 53 75 85 01
Others (Senior Executives)
Chief Operating Officer, Operations Manager   Pascale Voillot ☎ 53 75 85 21

Dresdner Bank AG
Representative Office

1 rue de Tilsitt, F-75008 Paris
Tel: (1) 45 63 07 00 Fax: (1) 45 63 47 80

Senior Executive Officers
Representative   Alexis Pillet-Will

Dresdner Kleinwort Benson (Marchés)
Head Office

Formerly known as: Banque Internationale de Placement
108 Boulevard Haussmann, F-75008 Paris
Tel: (1) 44 70 80 80 Fax: (1) 42 93 03 30 Telex: 660 002 Swift: BIPL FR PP FRF

Senior Executive Officers
Chairman, Executive Board   Jean-Louis Laurens ☎ 44 70 82 01
Member of the Executive Board   Bouafem Boukaiba ☎ 44 70 83 50
Member of the Executive Board   Dominique Ould-Ferhat ☎ 44 70 82 40
Member of the Executive Board   Alexis Piffet-Will ☎ 45 63 07 00 F 45 63 47 80
General Secretary   Jérôme Guiraud

Administration
Compliance
        Richard Dauchez *Compliance Officer*

Exane
Head Office

16 Avenue Matignon, F-75008 Paris
Tel: (1) 44 95 40 00 Fax: (1) 44 95 40 01
Website: www.exane.com

Senior Executive Officers
Chairman & Chief Executive Officer   Nicholas Chanut ☎ 44 95 40 45 F 42 89 43 10 E nicolas.chanut@exane.com
Financial Director   Henri Tran ☎ 44 95 35 53 F 44 95 40 01 E henry.tran@exane.com
Deputy Managing Director, Member of the Board   Philippe Sanlaville ☎ 44 95 41 41 F 42 89 43 10
        E philippe.sanlaville@exane.com
Deputy Managing Director   Bertrand Léonard ☎ 44 95 40 05 F 42 89 43 10
        E bertrand.leonard@exane.com
Deputy Managing Director   Hervé Ragagnon ☎ 44 95 40 11 F 40 76 05 83
        E herve.ragagnon@exane.com
Deputy Managing Director   Julien Schoenlaub ☎ 44 95 40 04 F 40 76 05 83
        E julien.schoenlaub@exane.com
Company Secretary   Marc Le Guern ☎ 44 95 40 39 F 42 89 36 27 E marc.le_guern@exane.com

Debt Capital Markets / Fixed Income
Bonds - General
Market Making & Arbitrage   Stéphane Egnell ☎ 44 95 41 42 F 42 89 43 10
        Cyril Mayer ☎ 44 95 41 46 F 42 89 43 10
Bonds Research   Emmanuel Raoul ☎ 44 95 41 83 F 42 89 36 69
        E emmanuel.raoul@exane.com

Equity Capital Markets
Head of Sales   Hervé Ragagnon *Deputy Managing Director* ☎ 44 95 40 11 F 40 76 05 83
        E herve.ragagnon@exane.com
        Julien Schoenlaub *Deputy Managing Director* ☎ 44 95 40 04 F 40 76 05 83
        E julien.schoenlaub@exane.com

Other (International Equity)
Market Making & Arbitrage   Stéphane Egnell ☎ 44 95 41 42 F 42 89 43 10
        Cyril Mayer ☎ 44 95 41 46 F 42 89 43 10

Equity Research
Head of Equity Research   Alain Kayayan ☎ 44 95 69 80 F 42 89 03 01 E alain.kayayan@exane.com

430 Euromoney Directory 1999

www.euromoneydirectory.com FRANCE (+33)

Risk Management
Other (Exchange-Traded Derivatives)
Derivatives Sales Bertrand Léonard *Deputy Managing Director* ☎ **44 95 40 05** 🖷 **42 89 43 10**
 🖃 **bertrand.leonard@exane.com**
Derivatives Research Gildas de Nercy ☎ **44 95 41 61** 🖷 **44 95 40 01**
 🖃 **gildas.de_nercy@exane.com**

Other Departments
Economic Research Vincent Mordrel *Strategy & Economic Research* ☎ **44 95 41 01**
 🖷 **42 89 03 01** 🖃 **vincent.mordrel@exane.com**

The Export-Import Bank of Japan
Representative Office

242 rue de Rivoli, F-75001 Paris
Tel: (1) 42 60 75 36 **Fax:** (1) 42 61 91 49

FIMAT International Banque
Head Office

50 Boulevard Haussmann, F-75439 Paris Cêdex 09
Tel: (1) 44 79 20 00 **Fax:** (1) 44 79 20 01 **Telex:** 290588 **Email:** fimat@fimat.com
Website: www.fimat.com

Senior Executive Officers
Managing Director Alain Bozzi
Risk Management
Head of Risk Management François Bloch *Group Risk Manager*
Settlement / Clearing
Operations Amaury de Villemandy ☎ **55 07 20 20**

Fimat Snc
Full Branch Office

50 Boulevard Haussmann, F-75439 Paris Cedex 09
Tel: (1) 55 07 20 20 **Fax:** (1) 55 07 20 21

Senior Executive Officers
General Manager Amaury de Villemandy

FIMATEX SA
Head Office

50 Boulevard Hauffmann, F-75439 Paris Cedex 9
Tel: (1) 55 07 20 20 **Fax:** (1) 55 07 22 21
Website: www.fimatex.fr

Senior Executive Officers
President Vincent Taupin
General Manager Laurent Cunin
Deputy General Manager Olivier de Montety

Finacor Group
Head Office

52 Avenue de Champs-Elysées, F-75008 Paris
Tel: (1) 40 74 15 15 **Fax:** (1) 42 89 25 49 **Telex:** 640067 FCOR

Senior Executive Officers
Chairman Pierre Lasserre
Managing Director Claude Ehlinger
Managing Director Alain Giraud
Deputy Managing Director Raoul Saada
Deputy Managing Director Olivier Stephanopoli

General - Treasury
Head of Treasury Françoise Herricher

Relationship Manager
Subsidiary & Correspondent Relationships Alain Beluche *International Director*

Debt Capital Markets / Fixed Income
Department: Capital Markets, Financor Peter, Finacor Ltd
Country Head Vernon Werge *Capital Market*

Euromoney Directory 1999 **431**

FRANCE (+33)

www.euromoneydirectory.com

Finacor Group (cont)

Bonds - General

Françoise Elson *Capital Market*

Other (Libor-Based / Floating Rate Products)
FRAs

Arash Adeli ☎ 53 76 71 15

Fixed-Income Repo
Head of Repo

Amaury Hervouet des Forges *Life Pensions / Repo* ☎ 40 74 18 32
Eric Millardet *Life Pensions / Repo*
Eric Marie Jacquet *Life Pensions / Repo*
Eduardus Wamerman *Life Pensions / Repo*

Department: Bonds - Finacor / Monecor
Tel: 40 74 02 34 **Fax:** 42 89 07 40 **Telex:** 650744
Global Head

Jean-Yves Jenty

Non-Domestic Government Bonds
Public Sector

Christian De Legge
Laurant Didier
Eric Deluga
Marie-Christine Fabiani

Primary Market

Georges Edouard

Bonds - General
Eurofrancs

Catherine Nahman
Olivier Gelernter
David Carenco ☎ 40 74 19 58

Eurobonds

Karine Levesque

Department: International Bonds - Finacor / Monecor
Tel: 42 89 35 80
Country Head

Christa Cochet

Bonds - General
Illiquid Structures Bonds

Nigel Mallander

Department: OATS - Financor Peter / Monecor
Tel: 40 74 03 94
Global Head

Frédéric Sola

Bonds - General
Government Bonds - OATS
OATS

Cyril Frenot
Vincent Gobillot
Olivier Rohart
Jérome Sulowski

Strips OAT

Jean-Michel Bonnafous ☎ 40 74 17 59
Michel Cuxac
Vincent Rohart

Treasury Bonds - BTANS

Jaime Gregoire ☎ 42 89 35 90
Marie-Noëlle Maes ☎ 42 89 35 90

BTAN

Frédérique Asseo
Jean Bruneau
Corine Khersis
Frédéric Mehta
Patrick Saada

Department: ECU Market - Finacor / Monecor
Global Head

Valérie Salomon
Cecile Beaugonin

Money Markets

Department: Domestic Money Market (Finacor Peter / Finacor Limited)
Tel: 42 89 35 91/3
Global Head

Raoul Saada *Long-Term Domestic Money Market*

Money Markets - General
Swaps / Ffr & Exchanges

Lee Bannon
Pascale Attuil
Robert Bou-Simon
Odilo Drouil
Jean-François Cohen
Richard Katz
Alexis Joachim
Celia Bernard
Paul-Olivier Martinot
Eric Massoulier
Franck Sebban

Swaps Ecu

Céline Ossana

432 Euromoney Directory 1999

www.euromoneydirectory.com　　　　　　　　　　　　　　FRANCE (+33)

Other (Wholesale Deposits)
Cash　　　　　　　　　　　　　　　Serge Lescoat ☏ **40 76 67 60**
　　　　　　　　　　　　　　　　　　Fadl Berbari
　　　　　　　　　　　　　　　　　　Arnaud Linard
　　　　　　　　　　　　　　　　　　Carole Bellanger
　　　　　　　　　　　　　　　　　　Corrine Le Perve
　　　　　　　　　　　　　　　　　　Charles Solta Hales

Department: International Money Market
Tel: 42 89 35 83 **Reuters:** FINW **Telex:** 650592
Global Head　　　　　　　　　　　Jean-Louis Bouthinon
Money Markets - General
　　　　　　　　　　　　　　　　　　William Asseline
　　　　　　　　　　　　　　　　　　Georges Akoka
　　　　　　　　　　　　　　　　　　Alain Dange
　　　　　　　　　　　　　　　　　　Emmanuel Demaury
　　　　　　　　　　　　　　　　　　Olivier Denoun
　　　　　　　　　　　　　　　　　　Philippe Fender
　　　　　　　　　　　　　　　　　　Rémi Goedkoop
　　　　　　　　　　　　　　　　　　Eric Grelet
　　　　　　　　　　　　　　　　　　Fabrice Hugues
　　　　　　　　　　　　　　　　　　Dominque Marnier
　　　　　　　　　　　　　　　　　　Eric Palomares
　　　　　　　　　　　　　　　　　　Laurent Sire
　　　　　　　　　　　　　　　　　　Guy Souet

Foreign Exchange
Department: Foreign Exchange - Finacor Peter
Tel: 42 89 35 82 **Reuters:** PETF **Telex:** 650566
FX Traders / Sales People
Cross　　　　　　　　　　　　　　　Michel Remond
DM / Ffr　　　　　　　　　　　　　Francis Grimbert
Cross　　　　　　　　　　　　　　　Christiane Ripoteau
US$ / Ffr　　　　　　　　　　　　Gérard Dardol
　　　　　　　　　　　　　　　　　　Jean Klein
　　　　　　　　　　　　　　　　　　Philippe Roussel

Risk Management
Department: Capital Markets, Finacor Peter, Finacor Ltd
Other (FI Derivatives)
IRS DM　　　　　　　　　　　　　Max Lehneiss ☏ **+44 (171) 403 9687**
　　　　　　　　　　　　　　　　　　Taki Ashida
　　　　　　　　　　　　　　　　　　Jonathan Churchill
　　　　　　　　　　　　　　　　　　James Davis
　　　　　　　　　　　　　　　　　　Cédric Holler
　　　　　　　　　　　　　　　　　　Françis Treece
　　　　　　　　　　　　　　　　　　Herbert Wenig
　　　　　　　　　　　　　　　　　　Colin Anderson
　　　　　　　　　　　　　　　　　　Stephen Francis
IRS Scandinavian　　　　　　　　Pat Cunninghan ☏ **+44 (171) 403 4269**
　　　　　　　　　　　　　　　　　　Georges Anderson
　　　　　　　　　　　　　　　　　　Vernon Werge *Capital Market*
　　　　　　　　　　　　　　　　　　Paul Owens
　　　　　　　　　　　　　　　　　　Damien Walsh
　　　　　　　　　　　　　　　　　　Grahame Dean
　　　　　　　　　　　　　　　　　　John Dovell
　　　　　　　　　　　　　　　　　　Peter Eliasen
　　　　　　　　　　　　　　　　　　David Shelley
　　　　　　　　　　　　　　　　　　Dereck Simpson
　　　　　　　　　　　　　　　　　　Ben White

Other Currency Swap / FX Options Personnel
Options Swaps Cap & Floor / Ffr & Exchanges　　Véronique Zimmermann-Paquet
Rate Swaps　　　　　　　　　　　Frédérique Bensaid
　　　　　　　　　　　　　　　　　　Carole Benaroya
　　　　　　　　　　　　　　　　　　Laurence Gay Molinas
Swaps Dollar / Ffr　　　　　　　Stéphen Petersen
Swaps Dollar / DM　　　　　　　Philippe Bertheau
　　　　　　　　　　　　　　　　　　Pascal Ruiz
Swaps Ecu / $　　　　　　　　　　Thierry Corbeau
OTC Options - Finacor Peter　　Thomas Valier ☏ **40 74 19 53**
　　　　　　　　　　　　　　　　　　Jean Chouraki

Other (Exchange-Traded Derivatives)
Arbitrage Futures　　　　　　　　Stéphane Leclerc ☏ **40 76 68 00** ☏ **42 89 37 66**

Euromoney Directory 1999　　**433**

FRANCE (+33)   www.euromoneydirectory.com

Finacor Group (cont)
Department: Financial Futures
Telex: 650766
Country Head — Jean-Luc Marechal ☎ 42 89 35 88
Alain Giraud *Managing Director*

Other (FI Derivatives)
French Financial Futures-Notionnel — Jean-Luc Marechal ☎ 42 89 35 88
French Financial Futures — Jérémy Lang
Martin Marchant
Xavier Massip
Options — Dominique Ponthieux
Pibor — Katixa Ribalka
Ecu — Jean-Jacques Ktorza
CAC40 — Jean-Luc Cohen
Jeremy Touati
Benjamin Jevons
François Manas
Thomas Perrot
CBOT — Cyril Castelli

Settlement / Clearing
Settlement (General) — Françoise Lacaze *Back-Office - Paris*
Patricia Marin *Back-Office - Paris*
Eileen Gavin *Back-Office - London*
Laurence Mallard *Back-Office, Domestic Money Market*
Jacqueline Chadoutaud *Back-Office, International Money Market*
Véronique Delestrain *Back-Office, International Money Market*
Catherine Glorion *Back-Office, International Money Market*
Philippe Dangin *Back-Office - Cedel / Euroclear* ☎ 40 74 16 62
Véronique Gasteau *Back-Office - SICOVAM* ☎ 40 74 17 23
Karim Khedimi *Back-Office - SICOVAM*
Catherine Carreto *Back-Office, Domestic Money Market* ☎ 40 74 16 36
Yves Pellettier *Back-Office - Strips OAT* ☎ 40 74 15 36
Laurence Langet *Back-Office - OTC Options* ☎ 40 74 16 28
Stephen Holt *Back-Office - Ecu Bonds* ☎ +44 (171) 940 6100
Marie-Carmen Perez *Back-Office - Futures & Options*
Karine Boulme *Back-Office - Futures & Options*
Catherine Crouzet *Back-Office - Futures & Options*
Muriel Attia *Back-Office - Financial Control-OTC Markets* ☎ 40 74 18 29
Operations — Olivier Dubois *Financial Control-Futures & Options*
Erwan Barbe *Financial Control - OTC Markets*
Denis Guipbaud *Controller*

Administration
Legal / In-House Counsel
Legal Affairs — Daniel Jessula
Accounts / Audit
Finance & Accounting — Olivier Stephanopoli *Deputy Managing Director*
Other (Administration)
Human Resources — Hugues Locoge
Technical Services — Angel Lara

Financial Security Assurance (UK) Limited — Subsidiary Company

116 rue la Boëtie, F-75008 Paris
Tel: (1) 42 56 72 22 **Fax:** (1) 42 56 72 26

Senior Executive Officers
Managing Director — Philippe Z Tromp
Others (Senior Executives)
Financial Guaranty Department — D Douglas Segars *Director*
Anne Wrobel *Assistant Vice President*

Robert Fleming (France) SA — Subsidiary Company

39/41 rue Cambon, F-75001 Paris
Tel: (1) 49 27 19 00 **Fax:** (1) 49 27 19 92 **Telex:** 216011

Senior Executive Officers
Financial Director — John Coles *Director*

434   Euromoney Directory 1999

Others (Senior Executives)
Head of Investment Banking / Paul Le Clerc *Director*

Fransabank (France) SA — Subsidiary Company
104 Avenue des Champs-Elysées, F-75008 Paris
Tel: (1) 53 76 84 00 **Fax:** (1) 45 63 57 00 **Telex:** 650841 F FRASA

Senior Executive Officers
Chairman / Adnan Kassar
General Manager / Pierre de Lavalette

The Fuji Bank Limited
26 Avenue des Champs-Elysées, F-75008 Paris
Tel: (1) 44 13 60 00 **Fax:** (1) 44 13 60 60; (1) 44 13 60 08 **Reuters:** FUJP

Senior Executive Officers
General Manager / Yoshihiro Sawada
Joint General Manager / Koichi Nakazawa
Joint General Manager / Jean-François Couturier

General-Lending (DCM, SL)
Head of Corporate Banking / Akira Nakayama *Manager, Credit Department I*
Ewen McDonald *Manager, Credit Department II*

General - Treasury
Head of Treasury / Masao Kanamaru *Manager, Treasury*

Settlement / Clearing
Operations / Alain Curtat *Manager*
Back-Office / Marie-France Chevalier *Manager*

Administration
Business Development / Shuichi Okada *Manager, Japanese Business Development Unit*
Bruno Lagarde *Manager, Business Development Department Group I*
Rogatien de Sesmaisons *Manager, Business Development Department Group II*

Technology & Systems
Electronic & Data Processing / Carlos Oliveira *Manager*

Accounts / Audit
Internal Audit / J M Genevois-Marlin

Other (Administration)
Accounting & Systems Organisation / Michio Noishiki *Manager*
Administration / Tatsuo Muromachi *Manager*

Goldman Sachs Paris Inc et Cie — Subsidiary Company
2 rue de Thann, F-75017 Paris
Tel: (1) 42 12 10 00 **Fax:** (1) 42 12 11 99

Senior Executive Officers
Managing Director / Reuben Jeffrey
Managing Director / Philippe Altuzarra

Hambrecht & Quist Euromarkets SA — Subsidiary Company
42 rue Washington, F-75408 Paris Cedex 08
Tel: (1) 56 59 82 00 **Fax:** (1) 45 59 82 19

Senior Executive Officers
President / Denis Mortier
Chief Executive Officer / James MacMillan-Scott
Financial Director / Muriel Roquejeoffre

Equity Capital Markets
Head of Equity Capital Markets / Bill Timken *Vice Chairman*

Domestic Equities
Head of Origination / Josh Rafner
Head of Sales / Malika Haddaolli *Manager, Institutional Sales*
Head of Trading / Michel Birnbaum *Senior Vice President*
Head of Research / Philippe Cramer *Co-Head*
Jean Pierre Geremy *Co-Head*

FRANCE (+33)　　　　　www.euromoneydirectory.com

Hambrecht & Quist Euromarkets SA (cont)
International Equities
Head of Origination　　　　　　　　　Josh Rafner
Head of Sales　　　　　　　　　　　　Malika Haddaolli *Manager, Institutional Sales*
Head of Trading　　　　　　　　　　　Michel Birnbaum *Senior Vice President*
Head of Research　　　　　　　　　　Philippe Cramer *Co-Head*
　　　　　　　　　　　　　　　　　　Jean Pierre Geremy *Co-Head*

Other (International Equity)
US Equities　　　　　　　　　　　　　Patrick Spencer *Manager, Institutional Sales*

Corporate Finance / M&A Advisory
Head of Corporate Finance　　　　　　David Golden
Regional Head　　　　　　　　　　　　Josh Rafner

Settlement / Clearing
Head of Settlement / Clearing　　　　　Michel Cassou *Operations Manager*

Administration
Technology & Systems
　　　　　　　　　　　　　　　　　　Benoit Delacrose *IT Consultant*

Public Relations
　　　　　　　　　　　　　　　　　　Carole Newman

HSBC Securities Contrepartie SA　　　　　　　　Representative Office

Formerly known as: HSBC Capel James SA
20 bis Avenue Rapp, F-75332 Paris Cedex 07
Tel: (1) 44 42 70 00 **Fax:** (1) 44 42 77 77 **Telex:** 202202

Senior Executive Officers
Managing Director　　　　　　　　　Pierre Bosset ☏ 44 42 76 20 ℻ 44 42 76 30

Ifabanque SA　　　　　　　　　　　　　　　　　　　　Head Office

39 Avenue Pierre 1er de Serbie, F-25708 Paris
PO Box 25708, F-75364 Paris Cedex 8
Tel: (1) 53 23 03 53 **Fax:** (1) 53 23 03 50 **Telex:** 642175 IFABK

Senior Executive Officers
Honorary Chairman　　　　　　　　　Louis-Amédée de Moustier
Chairman　　　　　　　　　　　　　　Edmond de la Haye Jousselin
Managing Director / General Manager　Christoph Grüninger

Others (Senior Executives)
Manager　　　　　　　　　　　　　　Jean de Lestrange
　　　　　　　　　　　　　　　　　　Michel Mercier
　　　　　　　　　　　　　　　　　　Richard Nottage
　　　　　　　　　　　　　　　　　　James von Claer
　　　　　　　　　　　　　　　　　　Jean de Tinguy du Pouët
　　　　　　　　　　　　　　　　　　Nicholas Hearn
　　　　　　　　　　　　　　　　　　Jacques van Zuylen
　　　　　　　　　　　　　　　　　　Ken Kinsey Quick
Treasurer　　　　　　　　　　　　　　Olivier Poussin
Assistant Treasurer　　　　　　　　　Danielle Trumeau

The Industrial Bank of Japan Limited　　　　　　Full Branch Office

Washington Plaza, 40 rue Washington, F-75408 Paris Cedex 08
Tel: (1) 53 83 40 00 **Fax:** (1) 53 83 40 99 **Telex:** 642105F KOGPA

Senior Executive Officers
General Manager　　　　　　　　　　Takashi Watanabe

ING Baring Securities (France)　　　　　　　　　Subsidiary Company

21 Boulevard de la Madeleine, F-75001 Paris
Tel: (1) 44 55 87 20 **Fax:** (1) 42 96 40 90 **Telex:** 240329 INGB F **Swift:** INGB FR PP

Senior Executive Officers
Others (Senior Executives)
　　　　　　　　　　　　　　　　　　Helen Coulthard *Administration Manager*

www.euromoneydirectory.com FRANCE (+33)

Equity Capital Markets
Other (International Equity)
Emerging Markets Intermediation   Helen Coulthard *Administration Manager*

ING Barings   Full Branch Office
21 Boulevard de la Madeleine, F-75001 Paris
Tel: (1) 44 55 88 99 **Fax:** (1) 42 96 40 90 **Telex:** 240329 **Swift:** INGB FR PP **Reuters:** INGP
Senior Executive Officers
Chief Executive Officer   Henri Courtheoux *Chief Operations Officer* 🕾 **44 55 88 66**
Treasurer   Giuseppe Barbaro *Chief Dealer* 🕾 **44 55 88 49**
General Manager   Dirk Jan van Swaay 🕾 **44 55 88 07**
Syndicated Lending
Head of Syndicated Lending   Bertrand Acker *Directeur de la Direction Bancaire* 🕾 **44 55 88 14**
Head of Credit Committee   Dirk Jan van Swaay *General Manager* 🕾 **44 55 88 07**
Loan-Related Activities
Project Finance   Bertrand Acker *Directeur de la Direction Bancaire* 🕾 **44 55 88 14**
Money Markets
Head of Money Markets   Giuseppe Barbaro *Chief Dealer* 🕾 **44 55 88 49**
Foreign Exchange
Head of Foreign Exchange   Giuseppe Barbaro *Chief Dealer* 🕾 **44 55 88 49**
Risk Management
Head of Risk Management   Jean-Paul Ribrioux *Risk Manager* 🕾 **44 55 88 27**
Corporate Finance / M&A Advisory
Head of Corporate Finance   Bertrand Acker *Directeur de la Direction Bancaire* 🕾 **44 55 88 14**
Administration
Technology & Systems
                                    Nicolas Bresset *Head of IT* 🕾 **44 55 89 03**
Compliance
                                    Pierre Lenoir *Internal Auditor* 🕾 **44 55 88 63**

Inter-American Development Bank   Representative Office
66 Avenue d'Iéna, F-75116 Paris
Tel: (1) 40 69 31 00 **Fax:** (1) 40 69 31 20
Senior Executive Officers
Special Representative   Andres Bajuk

Intermediate Capital Group   Representative Office
133 Boulevard Haussmann, F-75008 Paris
Tel: (1) 44 95 86 86 **Fax:** (1) 44 95 86 87
Senior Executive Officers
Others (Senior Executives)
                                    Christophe Evain *Director*

The International Commercial Bank of China   Full Branch Office
131/133 rue de Tolbiac, F-75013 Paris
Tel: (1) 44 23 08 68 **Fax:** (1) 45 82 18 44 **Telex:** 206715 ICBC FRP
Senior Executive Officers
VP & General Manager   Chien-Min Lan

International Finance Corporation   Representative Office
66 Avenue d'Iéna, F-75116 Paris
Tel: (1) 40 69 30 60 **Fax:** (1) 47 20 77 71 **Telex:** 620528 **Cable:** CORINTFIN
Senior Executive Officers
Special Representative   Vikas Thapar

Euromoney Directory 1999   **437**

FRANCE (+33)   www.euromoneydirectory.com

JP Morgan & Cie SA   Subsidiary Company

14 Place Vendôme, F-75001 Paris
Tel: (1) 40 15 45 00 Fax: (1) 40 15 49 55

Senior Executive Officers
Chief Executive Officer   Philippe Cagayette

KBC Bank   Full Branch Office

Formerly known as: Kredietbank France

32 Avenue de la Marne, F-59447 Wasquehal
Tel: (3) 20 11 61 11; (3) 20 11 61 22 Fax: (3) 20 11 61 19 Telex: 131 633 Swift: KRED FR PP

Senior Executive Officers
General Manager   Christine Van Rigsseghem
Administration
Legal / In-House Counsel
     Hubert Francois Marsal ☎ 20 11 61 58
Accounts / Audit
     Marc Aboukhalil ☎ 20 11 61 52

Kleinwort Benson France   Subsidiary Company

108 Boulevard Haussmann, F-75008 Paris
Tel: (1) 44 70 85 00; (1) 44 70 45 00 Fax: (1) 44 69 06 50; (1) 44 69 06 60 Telex: 280310 F

Senior Executive Officers
President Directeur General   Dimitri Lavaux ☎ 44 70 45 01
Financial Director   Claude Lambert *Directeur Financier* ☎ 44 70 85 31
Chief Operating Officer   Nigel Coles *Assistant Director* ☎ 44 70 85 32
Equity Capital Markets
Domestic Equities
Head of Sales   Dimitri Lavaux *President Directeur General* ☎ 44 70 45 01
Head of Trading   Darren Smith ☎ 44 70 45 25
International Equities
Head of Sales   Dimitri Lavaux *President Directeur General* ☎ 44 70 45 01
Settlement / Clearing
Tel: 44 70 85 51 Fax: 44 69 06 50
Head of Settlement / Clearing   Nigel Coles *Assistant Director* ☎ 44 70 85 32
Administration
Compliance
     Claude Lambert *Directeur Financier* ☎ 44 70 85 31

Korea Exchange Bank   Full Branch Office

17/19 Avenue Montaigne, F-75008 Paris
Tel: (1) 53 67 12 00 Fax: (1) 53 67 12 31; (1) 53 67 12 34 Telex: 640928 KOEXPA Swift: KOEX FR PP
Email: kebpr@club.internet.fr Cable: KOEXBANK PARIS

Senior Executive Officers
Treasurer   Soo-Hyun Baik
Managing Director   Yong-Eun Hahm
General Manager   Chan-Soo Kim
Others (Senior Executives)
Personnal Director   Hyun-Soo Kim
Debt Capital Markets / Fixed Income
Eurobonds
Head of Trading   Gustave Rubio
Money Markets
Head of Money Markets   Soo-Hyun Baik
Other Departments
Correspondent Banking   Georges Ziegelmeyer
Administration
Accounts / Audit
     Mi-Bang Romain

La Compagnie Financière Edmond de Rothschild

47 rue du Faubourg Saint-Honoré, F-75008 Paris
Tel: (1) 40 17 25 25 Fax: (1) 40 17 24 02

Senior Executive Officers
Chairman & CEO — Roger Cukierman
Representative — Ademaro Lanzara
Representative — Jean-Philippe Thierry

Others (Senior Executives)
Guy Grymberg *CEO*
Michel Jacob *CEO*
Pierre Palasi *Deputy CEO, Member of the Board*
Samuel Pinto *Deputy CEO & Fund Manager*
Jean-Louis Chemarin *Head of Information Technology*
Nicolas Giscar d'Estaing *Head of Private Portfolio Management*
Alain Benhamou *General Secretary*
Christophe Lauverqeon *Director*
François des Robert *Director, Institutional Investors Relations*

Landesbank Hessen-Thüringen Girozentrale   Representative Office

Alternative trading name: Helaba

40, rue la Pérouse, F-75116 Paris
Tel: (1) 40 67 77 22 Fax: (1) 40 67 91 53

Liberty Roussin SA   Subsidiary Company

89/91 rue du Faubourg Saint-Honoré, F-75008 Paris
Tel: (1) 49 24 19 00 Fax: (1) 42 66 51 10
Website: www.roussin.com

Senior Executive Officers
Chairman — Roderick Taylor
Honorary President — Jacques Roussin
General Manager — Dominique Roussin E **deproussin@roussin.com**
General Manager — Philippe Roussin

Debt Capital Markets / Fixed Income
Tel: 49 24 19 19
Head of Debt Capital Markets — Dominique Roussin *General Manager* E **deproussin@roussin.com**

Eurobonds
Head of Trading — Dominique Roussin *General Manager* E **deproussin@roussin.com**

Equity Capital Markets

International Equities
Head of Trading — Dominique Roussin *General Manager* E **deproussin@roussin.com**

Convertibles / Equity-Linked
Head of Trading — Dominique Roussin *General Manager* E **deproussin@roussin.com**

Warrants
Head of Trading — Dominique Roussin *General Manager* E **deproussin@roussin.com**

Money Markets
Tel: 49 24 19 06
Head of Money Markets — Philippe Roussin *General Manager*

Domestic Commercial Paper
Head of Trading — Serge Tavera T **49 24 19 10**

Eurocommercial Paper
Head of Trading — Serge Tavera T **49 24 19 10**

Foreign Exchange
Tel: 49 24 19 07
Head of Foreign Exchange — Stephane Dubé

Risk Management
Head of Risk Management — Roderick Taylor

Settlement / Clearing
Tel: 49 24 19 13
Regional Head — André Crepin *Head* E **backoffici@roussin.com**

FRANCE (+33) www.euromoneydirectory.com

London Forfaiting à Paris SA
Subsidiary Company

260 Boulevard Saint Germain, F-75007 Paris
Tel: (1) 40 62 61 90 **Fax:** (1) 40 62 61 91

Senior Executive Officers
Director General — Robert Duffau
Director — Pierre Gilles de Lupel
Manager — Didier Abbato

The Long-Term Credit Bank of Japan Limited
Full Branch Office

55/57 Boulevard Haussmann, F-75008 Paris
Tel: (1) 53 05 21 00 **Fax:** (1) 53 05 21 01

Senior Executive Officers
General Manager — Yoshiaki Hirai

Marceau Investissement
Head Office

Formerly known as: Delia Finance

10-12 Avenue de Messine, F-75008 Paris
Tel: (1) 40 74 25 25 **Fax:** (1) 40 74 25 00

Senior Executive Officers
President — Georges Pebereau
Managing Director / General Manager — Jean-Louis Roidot
Others (Senior Executives)
Board of Management — Tsunehiro Watabe

MATIF SA
Head Office

115 rue Réaumur, F-75002 Paris
Tel: (1) 40 28 82 82 **Fax:** (1) 40 28 80 01

Senior Executive Officers
President — Jean-François Theodore
Chief Executive Officer —
Jacques Werren *Deputy CEO, Business Development* ☎ 40 28 81 96
François-Guy Hamonic *Deputy CEO, Systems & Operations* ☎ 40 28 82 97
Patrich Stephan *Deputy CEO, Administration & Clearing* ☎ 40 28 82 04

Settlement / Clearing
Regional Head — Patrich Stephan *Deputy CEO, Administration & Clearing* ☎ 40 28 82 04
Operations — François-Guy Hamonic *Deputy CEO, Systems & Operations* ☎ 40 28 82 97

Administration
Head of Administration — Patrich Stephan *Deputy CEO, Administration & Clearing* ☎ 40 28 82 04
Other (Administration)
Jacques Werren *Deputy CEO, Business Development* ☎ 40 28 81 96

Meeschaert - Rousselle
Head Office

25 rue Balzac, F-75008 Paris
Tel: (1) 53 89 72 00 **Fax:** (1) 53 89 72 01 **Telex:** 660113

Senior Executive Officers
Chairman & Chief Executive — Michel Jollant
Chief Executive Officer — Michel Jollant *Chairman & Chief Executive*
Others (Senior Executives)
Arnaud Bricout *Executive Vice President*
Nick Adam *Executive Vice President*

Meijiseimei International France SA
Head Office

21 Boulevard de la Madeleine, F-75038 Paris Cedex 01
Tel: (1) 47 03 66 50 **Fax:** (1) 47 03 49 15

Senior Executive Officers
General Director — Hitoshi Suzuki

www.euromoneydirectory.com FRANCE (+33)

Mercury Capital Management
Subsidiary Company

48 Avenue Victor Hugo, F-75116 Paris
Tel: (1) 53 64 65 54 Fax: (1) 44 17 92 70

Senior Executive Officers
President   Stéphane Dokhan
Managing Director   Pascal Dokhan

Mercury Courtage Bancaire

48 Avenue Victor Hugo, F-75116 Paris
Tel: (1) 53 64 65 54 Fax: (1) 44 17 92 70

Senior Executive Officers
President   Stéphane Dokhan
Managing Director   Pascal Dokhan

Debt Capital Markets / Fixed Income
Fixed-Income Repo
Head of Repo   Steven Groslin

Settlement / Clearing
Settlement (General)   Florence Deneubourg *Back-Office*

Merrill Lynch Capital Markets
Full Branch Office

112 Avenue Kleber, F-75116 Paris
Tel: (1) 53 65 55 00; (1) 53 65 55 30 Fax: (1) 53 65 56 82; (1) 53 65 56 75 Telex: 645758 MERLSEC

Senior Executive Officers
President   Michel Fleuriet ☏ 53 65 58 60
Financial Director   Peter Kelk ☏ 53 65 58 25
Managing Director / General Manager Bruno de Pampelonne ☏ 53 65 58 80

Debt Capital Markets / Fixed Income
Head of Fixed Income; Head of Fixed Income   Bruno de Pampelonne ☏ 53 65 58 80
Sales; Head of Fixed Income Trading

Government Bonds
Head of Syndication   François Bleines ☏ 53 65 57 28

Equity Capital Markets
Tel: 53 65 58 72
Head of Equity Capital Markets; Head of Sales;   Henri Chermont ☏ 53 65 58 71
Head of Trading

Settlement / Clearing
Tel: 53 65 55 55
Head of Settlement / Clearing; Equity   Sophie d'Isidoro ☏ 53 65 58 96
Settlement; Fixed-Income Settlement;
Operations

Midland Bank SA
Subsidiary Company

20 bis Avenue Rapp, F-75332 Paris
Tel: (1) 44 42 70 00 Fax: (1) 44 42 77 77 Telex: 205530

Senior Executive Officers
President Director   R J Moseley
Chief Executive Officer   François Seurre

Morgan Guaranty Trust Company of New York
Full Branch Office

14 Place Vendôme, F-75001 Paris
PO Box 18, F-75021 Paris Cedex 01
Tel: (1) 40 15 45 00 Fax: (1) 40 15 44 77 Telex: 210841 Reuters: MGTP Cable: MORGANBANK

Senior Executive Officers
Chairman   Philippe Lagayette
International Division   Hérvé de Montlivault *Managing Director*

General-Investment
Head of Investment   Ivan Kerno

FRANCE (+33)   www.euromoneydirectory.com

Morgan Guaranty Trust Company of New York (cont)
Debt Capital Markets / Fixed Income
Fixed-Income Repo
Head of Repo
Trading
Frédérick Mouchel *Vice President* T 40 15 43 17 F 40 15 47 75
Nicolas Chanut *Associate*

Equity Capital Markets
Country Head Didier Saint-George

Money Markets
Country Head Frédérick Mouchel *Vice President* T 40 15 43 17 F 40 15 47 75

Settlement / Clearing
Country Head Caroline Tiberghien

Administration
Other (Administration)
Human Resources Guilloume Floquet *Managing Director*

Morgan Stanley SA — Subsidiary Company
25 rue Balzac, F-75008 Paris
Tel: (1) 53 77 70 00 **Fax:** (1) 53 77 70 99
Website: www.ms.com

Senior Executive Officers
President & Managing Director Patrice Vial
MD, Corporate Finance André H François-Poncet

Debt Capital Markets / Fixed Income
Domestic Government Bonds
Head of Sales Habib Achkar *Executive Director*
Head of Trading Pierre Mirat *Managing Director*
  Patrick George *Executive Director*

Eurobonds
Head of Syndication Pierre Massera *Vice President*
Head of Sales Habib Achkar *Executive Director*
Head of Trading Christophe Greffier *Vice President*

Fixed-Income Repo
Trading Ed Talisse *Principal Trader*
  Yohann Ignatiew *Trader*

Equity Capital Markets
Other (International Equity)
Equity Sales Olivier Haguenauer *Executive Director*
  Nicolas Wirz *Vice President*
Société de Bourse Chris Howland *Executive Director*

Corporate Finance / M&A Advisory
Country Head André H François-Poncet *MD, Corporate Finance*
  Pierre Pâris *MD, Corporate Finance*
  Gilles Graham *MD, Corporate Finance*
  Michael Zaoui *Managing Director, M&A*
  Vincent Gaillard *Executive Director, M&A*

Asset Management
Other (Asset Management)
Marketing François Sibilia *Vice President*

Natexis — Head Office
45 rue Saint Dominique, F-75007 Paris
Tel: (1) 48 00 48 00 **Fax:** (1) 48 00 41 51 **Telex:** 660370 **Swift:** BFCE FR PP

Senior Executive Officers
Chairman & Chief Executive Jacques Delmas Marsalet
Managing Director / General Manager Dominique Ferrero
Company Secretary Jean-François Colin de Verdiere
International Division Erik Lescar

Others (Senior Executives)
Commercial Banking France Jean François Prevost
Finance Olivier Schatz

442 Euromoney Directory 1999

www.euromoneydirectory.com FRANCE (+33)

Debt Capital Markets / Fixed Income
Head of Debt Capital Markets Jean Marie Jaccarini
Head of Fixed Income Jaques Omeyer ☏ 48 00 40 39

Emerging Market Bonds
Head of Emerging Markets Jaques Omeyer ☏ 48 00 40 39

Equity Capital Markets
Head of Equity Capital Markets Hervé Schricke ☏ 49 55 70 02

Syndicated Lending
Other (Trade Finance)
Specialized Financing Antoine Dargnies

Money Markets
Head of Money Markets Jan Paul Mallaivre ☏ 48 00 44 73

Foreign Exchange
Head of Foreign Exchange Jan Paul Mallaivre ☏ 48 00 44 73

Risk Management
Department: Risks
Head of Risk Management Yves Blaclard

Asset Management
Department: Financial Markets Asset Management & Brokerage
Head Gérard Gervais

Other Departments
Economic Research Dominique Vallet *Research & Strategy*

Administration
Technology & Systems
Information Technology Aline Bec

Legal / In-House Counsel
Legal Affairs & Tax Pierr Marie Tulli

Corporate Communications
 Philippe Perier

Other (Administration)
Organisation - Premises & Support Services François de Crecy
Human Resources Jean-François Masson

National Bank of Kuwait (International) plc   Full Branch Office

90 Avenue des Champs-Elysées, F-75008 Paris
Tel: (1) 43 59 99 49 **Fax:** (1) 45 62 95 76 **Telex:** 642528 NBKFR **Swift:** NBOK FR PP

Senior Executive Officers
Financial Director Laël Dufour *Director, Operations & Administration*
Director General Pierre Auba

Equity Capital Markets
Head of Equity Capital Markets Patricia Pinie *Director, Credit*

Syndicated Lending
Head of Syndicated Lending Patricia Pinie *Director, Credit*

Loan-Related Activities
Trade Finance; Structured Trade Finance Patricia Pinie *Director, Credit*

Money Markets
Head of Money Markets Carmen Jover

Foreign Exchange
Head of Foreign Exchange Carmen Jover

Risk Management
Fixed Income Derivatives / Risk Management
Regional Head Patricia Pinie *Director, Credit*

Foreign Exchange Derivatives / Risk Management
Cross-Currency Swaps, Trading Carmen Jover

Corporate Finance / M&A Advisory
Head of Corporate Finance Patricia Pinie *Director, Credit*

Settlement / Clearing
Head of Settlement / Clearing Guy Planquet

Euromoney Directory 1999   **443**

FRANCE (+33)   www.euromoneydirectory.com

Nova Ljubljanska banka dd
Representative Office
31 Avenue des Champs-Elysées, F-75008 Paris
Tel: (1) 42 25 12 58 **Fax:** (1) 42 56 30 43 **Telex:** 644863 LBREP F

Senior Executive Officers
SVP & Directeur   Anton Lavtar

Paribas

5 rue Duatin, F-75002 Paris
Tel: (1) 42 98 12 34 **Telex:** 210061 PARB **Cable:** PARIBAS
Website: www.paribas.com

Senior Executive Officers
Chairman, Management Board & Executive Committee — André Levy Lang
Chairman, Supervisory Board — Michel Francois Poncet
Financial Director — Jean Clamon *Member, Management Board & Executive Committee*
Secretary, Supervisory Board — Pierre Edouard Noyelle

Others (Senior Executives)
General Control — Philippe Dulac *Member, Management Board & Executive Committee*
Chairman, "Paribas Affaire Industrielles" — Amaury Daniel de Seze *Member, Management Board & Executive Committee*
Retail Financial Services — Bernard Müller *Member, Management Board & Executive Committee*

General-Lending (DCM, SL)
Head of Corporate Banking — Philippe Blavier *Member, Executive Committee*

General-Investment
Head of Investment — Amaury Daniel de Seze *Member, Management Board & Executive Committee*

Debt Capital Markets / Fixed Income
Head of Debt Capital Markets — Robert de Metz *Chief Executive Officer* T 42 98 67 06 F 42 98 15 60
Head of Fixed Income — Alec de Lezardiere T 42 98 10 60 F 42 98 44 19

Equity Capital Markets
Fax: 42 98 76 51
Head of Equity Capital Markets — Anthony Bourne T 42 98 66 32

Equity Repo / Securities Lending
Head — Dominique Hoenn *Member, Management Board* T 42 98 03 08 F 42 98 71 47

Syndicated Lending
Tel: 42 98 42 47 **Fax:** 42 98 13 00
Head of Syndicated Lending — Domenico Lellis

Money Markets
Head of Money Markets — Jean Eneman T 42 98 07 96 F 42 98 44 19

Foreign Exchange
Tel: 42 98 68 75 **Fax:** 42 98 66 83
Head of Foreign Exchange — Evrard Didier

Risk Management
Head of Risk Management — Dominique Hoenn *Member, Management Board* T 42 98 03 08 F 42 98 71 47

Corporate Finance / M&A Advisory
Head of Corporate Finance — Thierry Varene T 42 98 17 27 F 42 98 12 20

Asset Management
Head — Francois Debiesse T 42 98 04 96 F 42 98 06 82

Administration
Business Development — Amaury Daniel de Seze *Member, Management Board & Executive Committee*

Corporate Communications
Yves Marie Dalibard *Head of Communications* T 42 98 42 43 F 42 98 66 75

www.euromoneydirectory.com   FRANCE (+33)

Qatar National Bank SAQ
Full Branch Office
58 Avenue d'Iéna, F-75116 Paris
Tel: (1) 53 23 00 77 **Fax:** (1) 53 23 00 70 **Telex:** 641344 **Swift:** QNBA FR PP **Reuters:** QNBP

Senior Executive Officers
General Manager   Roland Chalhoub
Deputy General Manager   Luc Debieuvre

RBC Dominion Securities Inc
Full Branch Office
40 rue la Boegiet, F-75008 Paris
Tel: (1) 53 53 33 80 **Fax:** (1) 53 96 96 20 **Telex:** 282492

Senior Executive Officers
Manager   Alain Corbani

Republic National Bank of New York (France)
Subsidiary Company
20 Place Vendôme, F-75001 Paris
PO Box 2132, F-75021 Paris Cedex 01
Tel: (1) 44 86 18 61; (1) 42 60 05 62 **Telex:** 216307

Senior Executive Officers
President of the Board of Directors   Robert Sevin ☎ **44 86 18 61**
General Manager   Jacques Laoui ☎ **44 86 18 61**
General Manager   Gerard Cohen ☎ **93 15 25 25**

Royal St Georges Banque
Head Office
106 rue Saint Honore, F-75001 Paris
Tel: (1) 42 97 06 10 **Fax:** (1) 42 97 06 30 **Telex:** 282536

Senior Executive Officers
Chairman   Michael Graham Hoare

The Sakura Bank Limited
Full Branch Office
112 Avenue Kléber, F-75784 Paris Cedex 16
Tel: (1) 53 70 39 39 **Fax:** (1) 47 55 41 41 **Telex:** 640228

Senior Executive Officers
General Manager   Makiyo Narushima

Schelcher Prince Finance
Head Office
6 rue des Petits Pères, F-75002 Paris
Tel: (1) 42 44 40 04 **Fax:** (1) 53 29 31 93

Senior Executive Officers
President   Christian Prince
Chief Executive Officer   Jean François Vandroux *Manager* ☎ **53 29 31 83**

Debt Capital Markets / Fixed Income

Fixed-Income Repo
Head of Repo   Jean François Vandroux *Manager* ☎ **53 29 31 83**
Marketing & Product Development Sylvie Cayrol
Trading   Richard Gorniak
Trading; Sales   Sylvie Cayrol

Equity Capital Markets
Global Head   Jean François Vandroux *Manager* ☎ **53 29 31 83**

Settlement / Clearing
Settlement (General)   Corine Dupont

FRANCE (+33) www.euromoneydirectory.com

Skandinaviska Enskilda Banken

25 rue Balzac, F-75008 Paris
PO Box 125, Paris Cedex 08
Tel: (1) 53 83 19 50 **Fax:** (1) 42 89 63 60 **Telex:** 641301F SEB PAR
Website: www.sebank.se

Senior Executive Officers
General Manager   Mats Rönneskog ☏ **53 83 19 51** 🖷 **42 89 63 60**
✉ **mats.ronneskog@enskilda.se**

Société Bancaire de Paris   Head Office

45 Avenue Georges Mandel, F-75116 Paris
Tel: (1) 44 34 48 00 **Fax:** (1) 44 34 48 48 **Telex:** 643203F SOBANK **Swift:** SOBP FR PP

Senior Executive Officers
Chairman   Pierre Laffineur
Treasurer   José Manuel Fonseca Antunes
Managing Director / General Manager   Pedro Cudell

Société de Banque de l'Orleanais   Head Office

35 rue de la Bretonnerie, F-45006 Orleans Cedex 1
Tel: (2) 38 77 74 00 **Fax:** (2) 38 77 75 75

Senior Executive Officers
Chief General Manager   Thierry Boulan

Société Générale SA   Head Office

Alternative trading name: SG
Tour Société Générale, 17 Cours Valmy, F-92972 Paris La Défense Cedex
Tel: (1) 42 14 90 00 **Telerate:** 3217, 42231/52 (FX)
Reuters: SGMM (French Money Market); SOGE (FX & Deposit Rates); SGXO-V (Currency Options); SOCG (IR Swaps); SGFR (FRAs); SGOA-P (Financial Futures & Options); SGA-B; SGSC-R (Currency Warrants); SGEA (Equity Warrants & Structured Product); SOGA-D (Euronotes Trading); SGYA-X (IRs & Bond Warrants); SGHA-G (Bond Warrants); BSGC-D (French Treaury Bionds - BTF/BTAN); BSFG (Long OATS); BSGP-W (Stripped OATS); GENI-J (Structured Products); GENP-Q (Primary Domestic & Eurobonds); CFSA (IR Derivatives); CJSG (Caps, Floors, Swaptions); GENZ (Emerging Markets); SGHH-T (Commodity Warrants); SGDW (Equities - Derivatives World)
Website: www.socgen.com

Senior Executive Officers
Chairman   Daniel Bouton ☏ **42 14 36 48**
Chief Executive Officer   Patrick Duverger ☏ **42 13 81 85**
     Philippe Citerne ☏ **42 14 20 71**
Financial Director   Hervé Saint-Sauveur ☏ **42 14 38 51**
Others (Senior Executives)
Debt, Currencies, Commodities & Derivatives   Jean-Paul Oudet *Head* ☏ **42 13 69 97**
     Jean Dominjon *Deputy Head* ☏ **42 13 67 12**
Global Equities   Yves Tuloup *Head* ☏ **42 13 73 86**
Equity Corporate Finance   Peter Pantlin *Head* ☏ **42 13 78 34**
General-Lending (DCM, SL)
Head of Corporate Banking   Patrick Duverger ☏ **42 13 81 85**
General-Investment
Head of Investment   Jean-Pierre Marchand *Global Head* ☏ **42 14 62 16**
     Xavier Debonneuil *Deputy Global Head* ☏ **42 13 69 92**
     Jacques Bouhet *Deputy Global Head* ☏ **42 14 26 68**
Debt Capital Markets / Fixed Income
Department: Global Debt, Currencies, Commodities and Derivatives
Head of Fixed Income   Daniel Sfez ☏ **42 13 65 52**
Emerging Market Bonds
Head of Emerging Markets   Francis Repka ☏ **42 13 64 05**
Fixed-Income Research
Analyst   Philippe Ithurbide *Chief Economist* ☏ **42 13 61 27**

www.euromoneydirectory.com FRANCE (+33)

Equity Capital Markets
Department: Global Equities
Head of Sales Geoffroy De Beauregard *Head of Equity Distribution & Trading*
☎ 42 13 49 43

Domestic Equities
Head of Sales Jean-René De Fraguier *Head, Paris Equity Sales & Trading* ☎ 42 13 47 50

Equity Research
Head of Equity Research Paul Jackson ☎ 42 13 47 37

Convertibles / Equity-Linked
Head of Sales Philippe Halb ☎ 42 13 68 51

Other (Convertibles)
Jean-Claude Petard *Head of Convertibles Equity linked* ☎ 42 13 68 51

Foreign Exchange
Head of Foreign Exchange Douglas Plant ☎ 42 13 60 90

Risk Management
Department: Global Interest Rate Derivatives
Fixed Income Derivatives / Risk Management
Global Head Sébastien Cahen *Global Manager* ☎ 42 13 61 43
Regional Head Gilles Barret *Deputy Manager* ☎ 42 13 61 43

Other Departments
Commodities / Bullion François-Xavier Saint Macary *Global Manager* ☎ 42 13 86 21

Société Marseillaise de Crédit Head Office

75 rue Paradis, F-13006 Marseille
PO Box 1802, F-13221 Marseille Cedex 01
Tel: (4) 91 13 33 33 **Fax:** (4) 91 33 55 15 **Telex:** 430232 **Swift:** SMCT FR 2A **Email:** infos@smc.fr **Reuters:** MARP

Senior Executive Officers
Chairman Patrick Careil ☎ 91 13 55 31
Chief Executive Officer Patrick Careil ☎ 91 13 55 31
Financial Director Geneviève Gomez ☎ 91 13 55 59
Treasurer Christophe Brunie ☎ 91 13 32 68
International Division Jean-Michel Perrot *Head, International Division* ☎ 91 13 32 28 F 91 13 32 80

Money Markets
Fax: 91 13 55 07
Head of Money Markets Christophe Brunie ☎ 91 13 32 68

Foreign Exchange
Fax: 91 13 55 07
Head of Foreign Exchange Christophe Brunie ☎ 91 13 32 68

Risk Management
Fax: 91 13 32 40
Head of Risk Management Jean-Louis Chave ☎ 91 13 55 30

Corporate Finance / M&A Advisory
Fax: 91 13 32 25
Head of Corporate Finance Elisabeth Bertelli ☎ 91 29 95 52

Other Departments
Proprietary Trading Émmanuel Simonnet ☎ 91 29 95 42
Private Banking Alain Ferragut ☎ 91 13 33 18
Correspondent Banking Jean-Michel Perrot *Head, International Division* ☎ 91 13 32 28 F 91 13 32 80

Administration
Technology & Systems
Jean-Pierre Cresp ☎ 91 13 33 29

Legal / In-House Counsel
Jean Varnet ☎ 91 13 32 51

Public Relations
Nathalie Bossut ☎ 91 13 55 22

State Bank of India Full Branch Office

12/14 Rond Point des Champs Elysées, F-75015 Paris
Tel: (1) 53 77 23 00 **Fax:** (1) 53 77 28 50 **Swift:** SBIN FR PP **Reuters:** SBIP

Senior Executive Officers
Chief Executive Officer Surjit Banga ☎ 53 77 23 01

Euromoney Directory 1999 **447**

FRANCE (+33)   www.euromoneydirectory.com

State Bank of India (cont)
Other Departments
Private Banking   Vimla Madon *Commercial Secretary* ☎ 53 77 23 05
Administration
Compliance
                                 R Ravindran *Deputy Manager Compliance* ☎ 53 77 23 09

The Sumitomo Bank Limited
20 rue de la Ville-l'Evêque, F-75008 Paris
Tel: (1) 44 71 40 00 Fax: (1) 44 71 40 50 Telex: 281121
Senior Executive Officers
General Manager   Osamu Yamashita
Joint General Manager   Kazuto Shimizu
Deputy General Manager   René Roger

The Tokai Bank Limited   Full Branch Office
21 Boulevard de la Madeleine, F-75001 Paris
Tel: (1) 53 45 83 33 Fax: (1) 53 45 83 20 Telex: 280120 TOKBPAR
Senior Executive Officers
General Manager   Eiichi Aoyagi
Others (Senior Executives)
                                 Hiroshi Hoshino *Deputy General Manager*
General - Treasury
Head of Treasury   Makoto Yamashita *Manager*
Administration
Head of Administration   Frederic Pinon *Manager*

The Tokyo Sowa Bank Limited   Representative Office
15 rue Beaujon, F-75008 Paris
Tel: (1) 44 15 88 91 Fax: (1) 47 66 40 35
Senior Executive Officers
Chief Representative   Seiji Takatsuka

UBS Brinson SA
65 rue de Courcelles, F-75008 Paris
Tel: (1) 48 88 36 00 Fax: (1) 48 88 36 31
Senior Executive Officers
Senior Manager   P d'Anterroches

UFB Locabail   Head Office
14 rue Louis Blériot, F-92503 Rueil-Malmaison Cedex
PO Box 229, Rueil-Malmaison
Tel: (1) 41 42 60 60 Fax: (1) 41 42 77 21
Website: www.ufb.locabail.fr
Senior Executive Officers
Chairman   François Dambrine
Chief Executive Officer   Jacques Mallet

Union de Banques à Paris   Head Office
17-19 Place Etienne Pernet, F-75015 Paris
Tel: (1) 45 30 44 44 Fax: (1) 45 30 44 77 Telex: 206771 Reuters: UBPP
Senior Executive Officers
Chairman   Raymond Bert
General Manager   Jean-François Le Treïs

www.euromoneydirectory.com FRANCE (+33)

Union de Banques Arabes et Françaises - UBAF Head Office

190 Avenue Charles de Gaulle, F-92523 Neuilly-sur-Seine
Tel: (1) 46 40 61 01 Fax: (1) 40 88 30 25 Telex: 610334 Swift: UBAF FR PP

Senior Executive Officers
Chairman of the Management Board Guy de Jacquelot
Financial Director Thierry Lauret
Treasurer Tamer Assouad ☎ **46 40 65 94**
International Division Alphonse David *Arab World*
  Gerard Salord

Others (Senior Executives)
  Christiane Anfrie *Member of the Management Board*
  Aly El-Labban *Member of the Management Board*
  Bachir Sail *Member of the Management Board*

Debt Capital Markets / Fixed Income
Department: Capital Markets Division
Tel: 46 40 62 16 Fax: 46 40 65 23
Head of Debt Capital Markets Philippe Parant *Head, Treasury & Capital Markets Division* ☎ **46 40 64 17**

Emerging Market Bonds
Head Majid Mekouar *Emerging Markets Public Debts* ☎ **46 40 60 85**

Money Markets
Department: Treasury and Capital Markets Division
Tel: 47 38 19 19 Fax: 46 40 65 23
Head of Money Markets Philippe Parant *Head, Treasury & Capital Markets Division* ☎ **46 40 64 17**
Country Head Warant Baghdassarian ☎ **46 40 65 91**

Foreign Exchange
Tel: 47 38 19 19 Fax: 46 40 65 23
Head of Institutional Sales; Corporate Sales; Tamer Assouad ☎ **46 40 65 94**
Head of Trading

Risk Management
Tel: 46 40 62 85 Fax: 46 40 60 70
Head of Risk Management Brahim Achour *Head, Credit Policy & Risk Management* ☎ **46 40 64 20**

Administration
Head of Administration Jean Mathis
Business Development Gérard Salord *Europe & Americas*
  Alphonse David *Arab World*
  Rachid Sekak *Asian Network*
  Nouhad G Nassif *Merchant Banking & Islamic Banking*

Legal / In-House Counsel
Legal Affairs Department Lilia Ben-Khedder

Corporate Communications
Communications & Documentation Françoise Debray

Accounts / Audit
Internal Audit Vahé Kechichian

Other (Administration)
Human Resources Gérard Hersent

Union Européenne de CIC Head Office

Alternative trading name: Compagnie Financiere de CIC et de L'Union Europeenne
4 rue Gaillon, F-75107 Paris
Tel: (1) 42 66 70 00 Fax: (1) 42 66 78 39 Telex: 210942 Email: grogers@uecic.cicomore.com **Reuters:** CICBTF;
CICBTAN; CICOAT 1; CICOAT 2; BUBA; CICPUB 1

Senior Executive Officers
Chairman Michel Lucas
Treasurer Pierre André Guerillon ☎ **42 66 71 16**
General Manager Jean-Jacques Tamburini
International Division Henri Jacquand

Others (Senior Executives)
Global Head of Trading Bruno Julien-Laferriere ☎ **42 66 72 50**
Head of Sales Grant Rogers ☎ **42 66 72 40**
Global Head of Markets Cyril Le Touze ☎ **42 66 73 82**

Euromoney Directory 1999 **449**

FRANCE (+33)   www.euromoneydirectory.com

Union Européenne de CIC (cont)
Debt Capital Markets / Fixed Income
Tel: 42 66 72 50 Fax: 42 66 78 99

Government Bonds
Head of Sales   Claudine Presle ☎ 42 66 77 45
Head of Trading   Franck Launay ☎ 42 66 74 35

Equity Capital Markets
Department: Department Actions
Tel: 42 66 72 50 Fax: 42 66 78 99
Head of Sales   David Lenfant ☎ 42 66 71 76
Head of Trading   Jean Pierre Lardant ☎ 42 66 72 25

Syndicated Lending
Tel: 42 66 72 50 Fax: 42 66 78 99
Head of Origination   Susan Joly ☎ 42 66 70 71
Head of Syndication   Mark Grobien ☎ 42 66 74 53
Head of Trading   Jean Luc Baguet ☎ 42 66 72 30

Money Markets
Tel: 42 66 72 50 Fax: 42 66 78 99
Head of Money Markets   Pierre André Guerillon ☎ 42 66 71 16

Foreign Exchange
Head of Foreign Exchange   Pascal Chorain ☎ 42 66 79 32

Settlement / Clearing
Head of Settlement / Clearing Jean Claude Pinon ☎ 42 66 76 06

Administration
Head of Administration   Herve Bressan ☎ 42 66 71 77

Technology & Systems
                                 Jean-Claude Boutin

Public Relations
                                 Martin Damour

Via Banque SA   Head Office

10-12 rue Volney, F-75002 Paris
PO Box 27, F-75061 Paris Cedex 02
Tel: (1) 49 26 26 26 Fax: (1) 49 26 29 99 Telex: 220711 VIABA Swift: VIAB FR PP Email: via.banque@wanadoo.fr
Cable: CREDICOL PARIS

Senior Executive Officers
President   Philippe Toussaint
Director & General Manager   Roland de Montlivault

Others (Senior Executives)
Head, Capital Markets & Treasury   Antoine de Lacoste *Senior Vice President* ☎ 49 26 25 00
Legal & Accounting   Guillaume de Chalus *General Secretary* ☎ 49 26 29 53
Operations, Systems & Credit   Bruno Dupeyrat *Senior Vice President* ☎ 49 26 29 00

General-Lending (DCM, SL)
Head of Corporate Banking   Jean François Vitte *Vice General Manager* ☎ 49 26 29 58

Debt Capital Markets / Fixed Income
Head of Debt Capital Markets   Antoine de Lacoste *Senior Vice President* ☎ 49 26 25 00
Head of Fixed Income Trading   Philippe Delattre ☎ 49 26 25 54 F 49 26 29 99

Syndicated Lending
Head of Syndicated Lending   Jean François Vitte *Vice General Manager* ☎ 49 26 29 58
                                 Christel Prot ☎ 49 26 29 13

Settlement / Clearing
Operations   Christian Roux *Head* ☎ 49 26 27 22

Administration
Legal / In-House Counsel
Legal & Accounting   Guillaume de Chalus *General Secretary* ☎ 49 26 29 53

Other (Administration)
Operations, Systems & Credits Bruno Dupeyrat *Senior Vice President* ☎ 49 26 29 00

www.euromoneydirectory.com   FRANCE (+33)

Warburg Dillon Read (France) SA

65 rue de Courcelles, F-75008 Paris
Tel: (1) 48 88 33 44 Fax: (1) 40 53 07 07

Senior Executive Officers
Chairman	R Wojewodzki
Honorary Chairman	H van der Wyck
Vice Chairman	J L de Montesquiou
Director General, Country Head France	F Bacot
Director General	R Dawes
Director General	P Tibi
Director General	J B Toulouse

Debt Capital Markets / Fixed Income
Department: Rates

Bonds - General
Fixed Income Sales	E Bucaille
Origination	Michel Bernard
Exchange-Traded Derivatives	P Bartel

Equity Capital Markets
Department: Equities

Other (Domestic Equities)
Chief Executive	F Bacot
Corporate Broking	P Tibi
Distribution	O Hare
Trading	G Dick
Derivatives	F Potier
Research	M Mills

Corporate Finance / M&A Advisory
Country Head   J B Toulouse *Managing Director*

Wasserstein Perella (France) SA   Subsidiary Company

10 rue de la Paix, F-75002 Paris
Tel: (1) 44 58 91 15 Fax: (1) 42 96 91 15; (1) 42 96 91 16

Senior Executive Officers
Managing Director   Karine Curtis

Westdeutsche Landesbank (France) SA   Full Branch Office

6 rue Lamennois, F-75008 Paris
Tel: (1) 40 75 75 00 Fax: (1) 45 63 80 91; (1) 45 63 15 71 Telex: 650198 F Swift: WLBE FR PP

Senior Executive Officers
Chairman	Philippe Bouckaert
Chief Executive Officer	Ulrich Schröder *General Manager*
Treasurer	Antonio Pagano

Foreign Exchange
Head of Foreign Exchange   Patrick Centazzo

Other Departments
Correspondent Banking   Marie-Claude Petit

Administration
Legal / In-House Counsel
                         Angela Moreau

The World Bank   Full Branch Office

66 Avenue d'Iena, F-75116 Paris
Tel: (1) 40 69 30 00 Fax: (1) 47 23 74 36; (1) 40 69 30 69 Telex: 640651

Senior Executive Officers
Vice President   Jean François Reschard

FRANCE (+33)   www.euromoneydirectory.com

Württembergische Hypothekenbank AG
Full Branch Office
Avenue des Champs Élysées 119-121, F-75008 Paris
Tel: (1) 456 62 28 20 Fax: (1) 56 62 28 29

GABON
(+241)

Citibank NA
Full Branch Office
Boulevard Quaben & Rue Kringer, Libreville, 3940
PO Box 3940, Libreville
Tel: 733 000; 730 383 Fax: 733 786; 738 505 Telex: 5429 GO

Senior Executive Officers
Chief Executive Officer

Nuhad Saliba *Country Corporate Officer* 731 916
Wilson Chola *Senior Country Operations Officer* 731 032

Treasurer

Roland Etoughe *Acting Treasurer* 733 3784

General-Lending (DCM, SL)
Head of Corporate Banking

Christophe Jocktane-Lawson 733 785

Debt Capital Markets / Fixed Income
Country Head

Nat Johnson 733 195

Equity Capital Markets
Country Head

Nat Johnson 733 195

Syndicated Lending
Country Head

Nat Johnson 733 195

Loan-Related Activities
Project Finance; Structured Trade Finance

Christophe Jocktane-Lawson 733 785

Money Markets
Head of Money Markets

Roland Etoughe *Acting Treasurer* 733 3784

Foreign Exchange
Head of Foreign Exchange

Roland Etoughe *Acting Treasurer* 733 3784

Corporate Finance / M&A Advisory
Head of Corporate Finance

Christophe Jocktane-Lawson 733 785

Settlement / Clearing
Head of Settlement / Clearing

Cisse McRissouali *Operations Head* 733 000

Other Departments
Correspondent Banking
Cash Management

Gilbert Mue-Assoumou *Financial Institution Head* 733 000
Francis Zago 733 000

Administration
Head of Marketing

Christophe Jocktane-Lawson 733 785

Technology & Systems

Venant Diba *Data Centre Manager* 733 780

Compliance

Edgard Anon *Compliance Officer* 733 000

Public Relations

Christophe Jocktane-Lawson 733 785

Accounts / Audit

Edgard Anon *Compliance Officer* 733 000

GEORGIA
(+995)

National Bank of Georgia
Central Bank
3/5 Leonidze Street, 380005 Tbilisi
Tel: (32) 996 505; (32) 932 103 Fax: (32) 999 885 Telex: 212952 LEGAL SU Swift: BNIN GE 22

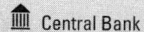

Senior Executive Officers
President   Irakli Managabze
Vice President   Givi Jigauri 998 069

www.euromoneydirectory.com GERMANY (+49)

Senior Executive Officers (cont)
Vice President　　　　　　　　　　　Merab Kakulia ☎ 932 103
Treasurer　　　　　　　　　　　　　Ivane Vakhtangishvili *Vice President* ☎ 921 810
Others (Senior Executives)
Head, Bank Licensing　　　　　　　Natia Mekabishvili ☎ 982 034
Head, Banking Supervision　　　　Levan Kistauki ☎ 996 041
Head, Economics & Statistics　　 Mzia Tepnadze ☎ 933 320
Head, Reserves Management　　　Samson Dhakadze ☎ 982 968
Foreign Exchange
Head of Foreign Exchange　　　　David Galegashvili ☎ 982 034
Settlement / Clearing
Head of Settlement / Clearing　　Waxtang Kareli ☎ 989 608
Administration
Accounts / Audit
Head, Accountancy　　　　　　　　Givi Gardaphadze ☎ 935 431

Deutsche Bank AG　　　　　　　　　　　　　　　　　Representative Office
3/5 Leonidze Street, 380027 Tbilisi
Tel: (32) 983 956 **Fax:** (32) 983 957 **Telex:** 212395 DBVT SU

GERMANY
(+49)

Deutsche Bundesbank　　　　　　　　　　　　　🏛 Central Bank
Wilhelm-Epstein-Strasse 14, D-60433 Frankfurt/Main
Tel: (69) 9566 1 **Fax:** (69) 560 1071 **Telex:** 41327 **Swift:** MARK DE FF **Email:** presse-information@bundesbank.de
International Telex: 414431
Website: www.bundesbank.de

Senior Executive Officers
President　　　　　　　　　　　　　Hans Tietmeyer
Deputy Governor　　　　　　　　　Jürgen Stark
Others (Senior Executives)
　　　　　　　　　　　　　　　　　Dieter Haferkamp *Member of the Directorate*
　　　　　　　　　　　　　　　　　Wendelin Hartmann *Member of the Directorate*
Land Central Bank of Bremen　　　　　　　　Helmut Hesse *President*
Land Central Bank in North Rhine-Westphalia　Reimut Jochimsen *President*
Land Central Bank in Rhineland-Palatinate　　Hans-Jürgen Koebnick *President*
Land Central Bank in Hamburg　　　　　　　Hans-Jürgen Krupp *President*
Land Central Bank in Berlin and Brandenburg　Klaus-Dieter Kühbacher *President*
Land Central Bank in Baden-Württemberg　　Guntram Palm *President*
Land Central Bank in Saxony & Thuringia　　Olaf Sievert *President*
Land Central Bank in Hesse　　　　　　　　 Ernst Welteke *President*
Land Central Bank in Bavaria　　　　　　　　Franz-Christoph Zeitler *President*

European Central Bank　　　　　　　　　　　　🏛 Central Bank
Alternative trading name: ECB
Kaiserstraße 29, D-60311 Frankfurt/Main
PO Box 160319, D-60066 Frankfurt/Main
Tel: (69) 1344 0 **Fax:** (69) 1344 6000 **Telex:** 411144 ecb d
Website: www.ecb.int

Senior Executive Officers
Department: Executive Board
President　　　　　　　　　　　　 Willem F Duisenberg
Vice President　　　　　　　　　　 Christian Noyer
Others (Senior Executives)
　　　　　　　　　　　　　　　　　Eugenio Domingo Solans *Member*
　　　　　　　　　　　　　　　　　Sirkka Hämäläinen *Member*
　　　　　　　　　　　　　　　　　Otmar Issing *Member*
　　　　　　　　　　　　　　　　　Tommaso Padoa-Schioppa *Member*

GERMANY (+49) www.euromoneydirectory.com

ABN AMRO Bank
Full Branch Office

Mainzer Landstrasse 65, D-60239 Frankfurt/Main
Tel: (69) 2690 00 **Fax:** (69) 2690 0999 **Telex:** 411222 **Swift:** ABNA DE FF **Reuters:** AABF 02-13
Website: www.abnamro.com

Senior Executive Officers
Country Manager & Chairman, Board of Mgt	Rolf Smit ☎ **2690 0503**
Managing Director	Udo Gerlach ☎ **2690 0611**

Others (Senior Executives)
Detlef Niezgodka *Member of Management Board* ☎ **2690 0701**
Ronald Teerlink *Member, Board of Management* ☎ **2690 0515**

Debt Capital Markets / Fixed Income
Department: Domestic Bonds & Pfandbriefe

Bonds - General
Syndication; Origination	Thomas Geller *Head, New Issues & Managing Director* ☎ **2690 0672**
Trading; Sales (all fixed-income)	Rainer Höfinghoff *Head, Fixed-Income & Managing Director* ☎ **2690 0634**

Medium-Term Notes
Head of Origination; Head of Structuring   Thomas Geller *Head, New Issues & Managing Director* ☎ **2690 0672**

Fixed-Income Repo
Head of Repo	Udo Gerlach *Managing Director* ☎ **2690 0611**
Sales	Jürgen Büscher ☎ **2690 0622**

Equity Capital Markets
Domestic Equities
Head of Sales	Peter Vutz *Managing Director* ☎ **2690 0652**
Head of Trading	Winfried Hauske *Managing Director* ☎ **2690 0651**
Head of Research	Peter Vutz *Managing Director* ☎ **2690 0652**

International Equities
Head of Sales	Peter Vutz *Managing Director* ☎ **2690 0652**
Head of Trading	Winfried Hauske *Managing Director* ☎ **2690 0651**
Head of Research	Peter Vutz *Managing Director* ☎ **2690 0652**

Warrants
Head of Sales; Head of Trading; Head of Research   Peter Vutz *Managing Director* ☎ **2690 0652**

Money Markets
Country Head   Udo Gerlach *Managing Director* ☎ **2690 0611**

Domestic Commercial Paper
Head of Origination	Thomas Geller *Head, New Issues & Managing Director* ☎ **2690 0672**
Head of Sales	Jürgen Büscher ☎ **2690 0622**

Eurocommercial Paper
Head of Origination	Thomas Geller *Head, New Issues & Managing Director* ☎ **2690 0672**
Head of Sales	Jürgen Büscher ☎ **2690 0622**

Wholesale Deposits
Marketing	Udo Gerlach *Managing Director* ☎ **2690 0611**
Head of Sales	Jürgen Büscher ☎ **2690 0622**

Foreign Exchange
Country Head	Udo Gerlach *Managing Director* ☎ **2690 0611**
Head of Institutional Sales	Dirk Petry ☎ **2690 0654**
Corporate Sales	Jürgen Büscher ☎ **2690 0622**
Head of Trading	Werner Eckert ☎ **2690 0617**

Risk Management
Global Head   Peter Janssen *Risk Manager* ☎ **2690 0601**

Foreign Exchange Derivatives / Risk Management
Vanilla FX option Sales   Ulf Schmücker ☎ **2690 0624**

Exotic Options (Barriers, Range, Timers, Digitals, Faders etc)
Sales   Ulf Schmücker ☎ **2690 0624**
Thorsten Konrad

OTC Equity Derivatives
Sales; Trading   Peter Vutz *Managing Director* ☎ **2690 0652**

Corporate Finance / M&A Advisory
Department: ABN AMRO Corporate Finance (Deutschland) GmbH
Mainzer Landstrasse 65, Frankfurt/Main
Tel: +49 (69) 2690 0721 **Fax:** +49 (69) 2690 0729

Global Head	Hugh Scott-Barnett ☎ **+44 (171) 374 1850**
Regional Head	Melville Mummert ☎ **2690 0720**
Country Head	Rolf Smit *Country Manager & Chairman, Board of Mgt* ☎ **2690 0503**

454   Euromoney Directory 1999

www.euromoneydirectory.com GERMANY (+49)

Settlement / Clearing
Regional Head   Jürgen Jud ☎ 2690 2030
Equity Settlement   Anja Finger *Assistant Vice President* ☎ 2690 0216
Derivatives Settlement   Johannes Rebscher *Assistant Vice President* ☎ 2690 0232
Foreign Exchange Settlement   Stephanie Endres *Assistant Vice President* ☎ 2690 0246
Global Custody
Regional Head   Jürgen Jud ☎ 2690 2030
Other (Global Custody)
                                           Angelika Hempen *Assistant Vice President* ☎ 2690 0221

AKA Ausfuhrkredit-Gmbh

Grosse Gallusstrasse 1/7, D-60311 Frankfurt/Main
PO Box 100163, D-60001 Frankfurt/Main
Tel: (69) 29891 00 **Fax:** (69) 29891 200 **Telex:** 411778 AKA **Email:** rrogowskil@compuserv.com
Telerate: AUSK DE FF **Cable:** ausfuhrkedit
Website: www.akabank.de

Senior Executive Officers
Chief Executive Officer   Hans-Jürgen Muth ☎ 29891 102 📠 29891 150
                                           Jurgen Strege ☎ 29891 103 📠 29891 150
Financial Director   Albert Schroter ☎ 29891 165
Settlement / Clearing
Head of Settlement / Clearing   Stefan Jaskulla ☎ 29891 177
Administration
Head of Administration   Thomas Egner ☎ 29891 218
Legal / In-House Counsel
                                           Marianne Motherby ☎ 29891 110

AKBANK TAS
Representative Office

Kaiser Strasse 9, D-60311 Frankfurt/Main
Tel: (69) 29717 0 **Fax:** (69) 29717 104 **Telex:** 412116 AKFFM D
Senior Executive Officers
Chief Representative   Altan Sanal

Allgemeine Deutsche Direktbank AG
Head Office

Baseler Strasse 27/31, D-60329 Frankfurt/Main
PO Box 110211, D-60037 Frankfurt/Main
Tel: (69) 272 2227 **Fax:** (69) 272 2244 **Email:** info@direktbank.de
Website: www.direktbank.de

Senior Executive Officers
Chairman   Bernhard Hafner
Others (Senior Executives)
                                           Bernd Weber *Director*
                                           Koen Beentjes *Director*

Allgemeine HypothekenBank
Head Office

Bockenheiner Landstrasse 25, D-60325 Frankfurt/Main
PO Box 170162, D-60075 Frankfurt/Main
Tel: (69) 7179 0 **Fax:** (69) 7179 100 **Reuters:** AHBA

Senior Executive Officers
Chairman, Board of Managing Directors   Horst Alexander Spitzkopf
Board of Managing Directors   Friedrich Geissel
Board of Managing Directors   Hans-Gerhard Grossmann
Debt Capital Markets / Fixed Income
Department: Treasury
Tel: 7179 414 **Fax:** 7179 416
Country Head   Wolfgang Bledau *Senior Vice President* ☎ 7179 400
                                           Werner Lorentz *First Vice President* ☎ 7179 402
                                           Stefan Goebel *Assistant Vice President* ☎ 7179 403

Euromoney Directory 1999   **455**

GERMANY (+49)　　　　　www.euromoneydirectory.com

Allgemeine HypothekenBank (cont)
Eurobonds
Head of Trading　　　　　Jochen Bonk ☎ 7179 404
　　　　　　　　　　　　　Carlo Barz ☎ 7179 405
　　　　　　　　　　　　　Nicole Keller ☎ 7179 406
　　　　　　　　　　　　　Mirko Gajdic ☎ 7179 409
　　　　　　　　　　　　　Thomas Gauder ☎ 7179 407

Syndicated Lending
Department: Real Estate and Property Finance
Tel: 7179 290

Other (Trade Finance)
　　　　　　　　　　　　　Peter Abel *Senior Vice President* ☎ 7179 240
　　　　　　　　　　　　　Leonhard Goebel *First Vice President* ☎ 7179 233

Settlement / Clearing
Department: Treasury Operations
Operations　　　　　　　　Wolfgang Hubl *First Vice President* ☎ 7179 223 F 7179 352

Arab Bank AG　　　　　　　　　　　　　　　　　　　　　　　　Head Office

Neue Mainzer Strasse 57, D-60311 Frankfurt/Main
PO Box 100127, D-60001 Frankfurt/Main
Tel: (69) 24259 0 Fax: (69) 235 471 Telex: 414249 Swift: ARAB DE FF Reuters: ARBF
Website: www.arabbank.com/branches/europe/germany

Senior Executive Officers
Chairman of the Supervisory Board　　Abdul Majeed Shoman
Managing Director and CEO　　　　　　Peter G Heinz ☎ 24259 323
Managing Director　　　　　　　　　　Wilfried Scheele ☎ 24259 315
International Division　　　　　　　　Horst Schneeweiss *Senior Manager* ☎ 24259 300
　　　　　　　　　　　　　　　　　　Peter Groemig *Director, Corporate & Int'l Banking* ☎ 24259 215

Others (Senior Executives)
Operations　　　　　　　　　　　　　Gerhard Eibelshaeuser *Senior Manager, Operations* ☎ 24259 326
General-Lending (DCM, SL)
Head of Corporate Banking　　　　　　Peter Groemig *Director, Corporate & Int'l Banking* ☎ 24259 215
General - Treasury
Head of Treasury　　　　　　　　　　　Horst Schaefer *Senior Manager, Treasurer* ☎ 24259 325

Arab Banking Corporation-Daus & Co GmbH　　　　　　　Subsidiary Company

Niedenau 13/19, D-60325 Frankfurt/Main
PO Box 170218, D-60076 Frankfurt/Main
Tel: (69) 71403 0 Fax: (69) 71403 350 Telex: 414894

Senior Executive Officers
Chairman　　　　　　　　　　　　　　Saleh M Al-Yousef
Vice Chairman　　　　　　　　　　　　Hatem Abou Said
General Manager　　　　　　　　　　　Jens-Ove Stier
General Manager　　　　　　　　　　　Jürgen Blumschein
International Division　　　　　　　　Osama Farag *Senior Vice President*

Debt Capital Markets / Fixed Income
Country Head　　　　　　　　　　　　Jürgen Wittayer *Senior Vice President*

Domestic Government Bonds
Head of Sales; Head of Trading　　　　Jan-Ove Flaellengsdal *Sales & Trading*
Eurobonds
Head of Trading　　　　　　　　　　　Reimer Thode
Bonds - General
Head, Eurocurrency Deposits　　　　　Horst Schäfer *Senior Vice President*

Syndicated Lending
Department: Loan Syndication / Asset Sales
Head of Origination　　　　　　　　　Eckhard Kolb *Vice President*

Other (Syndicated Lending)
Credit Risk Management　　　　　　　Parry Persaud *Senior Vice President*

Other (Trade Finance)
Forfaiting　　　　　　　　　　　　　　Tariq Amirzada *Assistant Vice President*
Letters of Credit & Documentary Credits　Hansjörg Wendling *Assistant Vice President*

Foreign Exchange
Country Head — Jürgen Wittayer *Senior Vice President*

Settlement / Clearing
Foreign Exchange Settlement Operations — Bodo Schmidt *Vice President*
Norbert Decker *Vice President*

Administration
Compliance — Norbert Decker *Vice President*

Other (Administration)
Human Resources — Christel Cox *Assistant Vice President*

Asahi Bank (Deutschland) GmbH — Subsidiary Company

Friedrich-Ebert-Anlage 49, Messeturm, D-60308 Frankfurt/Main
Tel: (69) 756 185 0 **Fax:** (69) 741 1774; (69) 741 0722 **Telex:** 4189170 ASHFD

Senior Executive Officers
President — Shinichi Nishino ☎ **756 185 20**
Deputy President — Jens Krause-Harder ☎ **756 185 31**

Debt Capital Markets / Fixed Income

Domestic Government Bonds
Head of Sales; Head of Trading — Masaru Kato *Senior Manager* ☎ **756 185 30**

Eurobonds
Head of Origination; Head of Syndication — Masaru Kato *Senior Manager* ☎ **756 185 30**

Equity Capital Markets

Convertibles / Equity-Linked
Head of Origination; Head of Syndication; Head of Sales; Head of Trading; Head of Research — Masaru Kato *Senior Manager* ☎ **756 185 30**

Warrants
Head of Sales; Head of Trading; Head of Research — Masaru Kato *Senior Manager* ☎ **756 185 30**

Money Markets
Country Head — Ritsuro Kunioka *Senior Manager* ☎ **756185 21**

Foreign Exchange
Head of Trading — Masaru Kato *Senior Manager* ☎ **756 185 30**

Settlement / Clearing
Regional Head — Ritsuro Kunioka *Senior Manager* ☎ **756185 21**

Other Departments
Correspondent Banking — Ritsuro Kunioka *Senior Manager* ☎ **756185 21**

The Asahi Bank Limited

Friedrich-Ebert-Anlage 49, Messeturm, 24th Floor, D-60308 Frankfurt/Main
Tel: (69) 756 185 0 **Fax:** (69) 741 1774 **Telex:** 4189170 ASHFD

Senior Executive Officers
Chief Representative — Shinichi Nishino

Asian Development Bank — Representative Office

Rahmhofstrasse 2/4, D-60001 Frankfurt/Main
PO Box 100147, Frankfurt/Main
Tel: (69) 9202 1488; (69) 9202 1481 **Fax:** (69) 9202 1499
Website: www.adberomail.asiandevbank.org

Senior Executive Officers
Representative — Keon-Woo Lee

GERMANY (+49)　　　　www.euromoneydirectory.com

Baden-Württembergische Bank AG　　　　Head Office

Kleiner Schloßplatz 11, D-70173 Stuttgart, Baden-Württemberg
PO Box 106014, D-70049 Stuttgart, Baden-Württemberg
Tel: (711) 180 0 **Fax:** (711) 209 4712; (711) 180 1000 **Telex:** 723919 BWS D **Swift:** BWBK DE 6S
Reuters: BWBS 01-09
Website: www.bw-bank.de

Senior Executive Officers
Chairman　　　　Frank Heintzeler
International Division　　　　Horst Mahr *Executive Vice President* 180 1820

Others (Senior Executives)
　　　　Horst Marschall *Member, Board of Management*

Debt Capital Markets / Fixed Income
Department: Capital Markets
Tubinger Straße 28, D-70049 Stuttgart, Baden-Württemberg
Tel: +49 (711) 180 2580 **Fax:** +49 (711) 180 1855
Global Head　　　　Wolf-Dieter Ihle *Executive Vice President* 180 1427 180 2489

Government Bonds
Head of Trading　　　　Edward Hubbard

Bonds - General
Jumbos　　　　Edward Hubbard

Fixed-Income Repo
Head of Trading　　　　Michael Strubel *Assistant Manager / Trader* 180 1494 180 1763

Equity Capital Markets
Department: Security Trading
Tel: 180 1494 Fax: 180 1855

Domestic Equities
Head of Origination　　　　Alfred Wuttke *Assistant Treasurer* 180 1778
　　　　Reinhard Schuster *Vice President* 180 1496
　　　　Peter Seibold *Assistant Treasurer* 180 1651

International Equities
Head of Origination　　　　Reinhard Schuster *Vice President* 180 1496
　　　　Rolf Bösenberg *Assistant Treasurer* 180 1563

Equity Repo / Securities Lending
Head of Trading　　　　Michael Strubel *Assistant Manager / Trader* 180 1494 180 1763

Syndicated Lending
Department: Money Market
Head of Origination　　　　Hansjörg Müller-Hermann *Senior Vice President & Head* 180 1407

Other (Trade Finance)
Asset Sales-Origination　　　　Hansjörg Müller-Hermann *Senior Vice President & Head* 180 1407

Money Markets
Head of Money Markets　　　　Helmut Schwander *Senior Vice President & Head* 180 1114

Money Markets - General
　　　　Helmut Staudinger *Assistant Vice President* 180 2910
Dealing　　　　Wolfram Krauter *Assistant Vice President*

Foreign Exchange
Global Head　　　　Helmut Schwander *Senior Vice President & Head* 180 1114
Head of Trading　　　　Klaus Michael Kizler *Vice President* 180 2920
Spot / Forwards Trading　　　　Susanne Abele *Assistant Treasurer*

Settlement / Clearing
Department: Security Trading
Settlement (General)　　　　Bernhard Odermatt *Assistant Vice President, Security Trading*
Operations　　　　Wolfgang Lubitz *Vice President & Head, Processing* 180 1703

Banca Nazionale del Lavoro SpA　　　　Representative Office

Goetheplatz 5, D-60313 Frankfurt/Main
Tel: (69) 289 858 **Fax:** (69) 296 202 **Telex:** 412703

Senior Executive Officers
Representative　　　　Andrea Duprè

Banca Popolare di Novara Scrl
Representative Office

Arndtstraße 34-36, D-60325 Frankfurt/Main
Tel: (69) 749 053 **Fax:** (69) 751 956

Senior Executive Officers
Representative   Maurizio Razeto

Banco Bilbao Vizcaya SA
Representative Office

Bettinastrasse 62, D-60325 Frankfurt/Main
Tel: (69) 743 810 **Fax:** (69) 743 2791

Senior Executive Officers
Others (Senior Executives)
     Franz Löhnert *Director*

Banco do Brasil SA
Full Branch Office

Neue Mainzer Strasse 75, D-60311 Frankfurt/Main
Tel: (69) 29909 0; (69) 29909 500 **Fax:** (69) 29909 222; (69) 131 0202 **Swift:** BRAS DE FF **Reuters:** BBFM
Tel: (69) 29909 550

Senior Executive Officers
Chief Executive Officer   Hanspeter Volk *Innenleiter* 🖃 **29909 103**
General Manager   Marino Spellmeier
Deputy General Manager   Jueci Pioner

Others (Senior Executives)
     Achim Klenner *Chief Dealer*

Money Markets
Global Head   Achim Klenner *Chief Dealer*

Foreign Exchange
Global Head   Achim Klenner *Chief Dealer*

Settlement / Clearing
Tel: 29909 600
Regional Head   Rüdiger Müller

Banco Espirito Santo
Representative Office

Bockenheimer Landstrasse 107, D-60325 Frankfurt/Main
Tel: (69) 743209 0; (69) 743209 3 **Fax:** (69) 743209 7

Senior Executive Officers
Representative   Alexander Schlitter

Bank Austria Creditanstalt International AG
Representative Office

Steinweg 8, D-60313 Frankfurt/Main
Tel: (69) 281 086 **Fax:** (69) 281 088

Senior Executive Officers
Chief Representative   Michael Lindner

Bank Brussels Lambert
Full Branch Office

An Lyskirchen 14, D-50676 Cologne
Tel: (221) 921 5150 **Fax:** (221) 240 3294

Senior Executive Officers
General Branch Manager   Hans Grudino

GERMANY (+49)　　　　www.euromoneydirectory.com

Bank of China
Full Branch Office

Bockenheimer Landstrasse 39, D-60325 Frankfurt/Main
PO Box 170143, D-60075 Frankfurt/Main
Tel: (69) 170 090 0 Fax: (69) 170 090 50 Telex: 416682 BOC FM

Senior Executive Officers
General Manager　　　　　　　　　　Shigan Zhao ☎ **170 090 22**

Bank Julius Bär (Deutschland) AG

Friedrich-Ebert-Anlage 49, D-60327 Frankfurt/Main
PO Box 150152, D-60061 Frankfurt/Main
Tel: (69) 75696 0 Fax: (69) 743 2511 Telex: 413081

Senior Executive Officers
Chairman　　　　　　　　　　Rudolf E Bär
Chief Executive Officer　　　　Karl-Heinz Arnold
Financial Director　　　　　　Eckhard Langenbach
Treasurer　　　　　　　　　　Dieter Danowski

Bank Melli Iran
Subsidiary Company

2 Holzbrücke, D-20459 Hamburg
PO Box 112129, D-20421 Hamburg
Tel: (40) 36000 0 Fax: (40) 36000 236 Telex: 211301 Swift: MELI DE HH

Senior Executive Officers
Chief Manager　　　　　　　　Theo Bosbach
Chief Manager　　　　　　　　Siavosh Naghshineh
Assistant Manager　　　　　　Mehran Dehghan

The Bank of New York
Full Branch Office

Niedenau 61-63, D-60325 Frankfurt/Main
PO Box 170324, D-60077 Frankfurt/Main
Tel: (69) 97151 0 Fax: (69) 721 798; (69) 97151 272 Telex: 416805/6 Swift: IRVT DE FX Reuters: BNYF
Website: www.bankofny.com

Senior Executive Officers
VP & General Manager　　　　Wolfgang Schaefer
General - Treasury
Head of Treasury　　　　　　　Gerhard Fehrer *Assistant Vice President*
Syndicated Lending
Loan-Related Activities
Trade Finance　　　　　　　　Yoram Matalon *VP & Manager, Marketing & Credit*
Other Departments
Correspondent Banking　　　　Marie-Luise Werner *Assistant Vice President* ☎ **97151 217**
Administration
Technology & Systems
　　　　　　　　　　　　　　Erich Fassing *VP & Operations Manager* ☎ **97151 218**

The Bank of Tokyo-Mitsubishi (Deutschland) AG
Head Office

Mainzer Landstrasse 16, D-60325 Frankfurt/Main
PO Box 102216, D-60284 Frankfurt/Main
Tel: (69) 7176 0 Fax: (69) 7176 280; (68) 7176 291 Telex: 413270 Swift: 3701 7019 Email: makoto.fato@t-mi.com

Senior Executive Officers
President　　　　　　　　　　Yutaka Watanabe ☎ **7176 318**
Managing Director　　　　　　Reiner Guthier ☎ **7176 373**
Managing Director　　　　　　Hiroyuki Mori ☎ **7176 420**
Debt Capital Markets / Fixed Income
Fax: 7176 291
Head of Debt Capital Markets　　Tadashi Mieki ☎ **7176 302**
Head of Fixed Income Sales　　Brian Tomlinson *Director, Head of Sales & Trading* ☎ **7176 380**

460　Euromoney Directory 1999

www.euromoneydirectory.com   **GERMANY (+49)**

Debt Capital Markets / Fixed Income (cont)

	Naoyuki Maekawa *Co-Head of Sales & Trading* ☏ **7176 308**
Head of Fixed Income Trading	Brian Tomlinson *Director, Head of Sales & Trading* ☏ **7176 380**
	Naoyuki Maekawa *Co-Head of Sales & Trading* ☏ **7176 308**

Bonds - General
Capital Markets Group   Keishi Urakami *Head of New Issue / Syndication* ☏ **7176 356**

Fixed-Income Repo
Head of Repo   Michael Lassmann *Vice President, Head of Repo Desk* ☏ **7176 385**
    ✉ michael.lassman@t-mi.com
Marketing & Product Development   Makoto Sato *Senior Vice President* ☏ **7176 248** ✉ **7176 364**
    ✉ makoto.sato@t-mi.com
Trading   Michael Lassmann *Vice President, Head of Repo Desk* ☏ **7176 385**
    ✉ michael.lassman@t-mi.com
    Gregor Oboth *Associate* ☏ **7176 384**

Equity Capital Markets
Fax: 7176 364
Head of Equity Capital Markets   Tadashi Mieki ☏ **7176 302**
Head of Sales   Brian Tomlinson *Director, Head of Sales & Trading* ☏ **7176 380**
    Naoyuki Maekawa *Co-Head of Sales & Trading* ☏ **7176 308**
Head of Trading   Brian Tomlinson *Director, Head of Sales & Trading* ☏ **7176 380**
    Naoyuki Maekawa *Co-Head of Sales & Trading* ☏ **7176 308**
Other   Keishi Urakami *Head of New Issue / Syndication* ☏ **7176 356**

Equity Repo / Securities Lending
Head   Michael Lassmann *Vice President, Head of Repo Desk* ☏ **7176 385**
    ✉ michael.lassman@t-mi.com
Marketing & Product Development; Marketing   Makoto Sato *Senior Vice President* ☏ **7176 248** ✉ **7176 364**
    ✉ sato@t-mi.com
Head of Trading   Gregor Oboth *Associate* ☏ **7176 384**

Money Markets
Global Head   Seiji Arizuka *Senior Manager*

Money Markets - General
Cash Desk   Elisabeth Gilsbach *Manager*
Derivative   Hans-Herbert Waschull *Manager*

Foreign Exchange
Global Head   Shinji Nohara *Senior Manager*

FX Traders / Sales People
Customer Desk   Alexander Blinkhorn *Manager*

Risk Management
Country Head   Gangolf Hirt *Manager*

Global Custody

Other (Global Custody)
Head of Custody   Makoto Sato *Director, Head of Custody Business* ☏ **7176 248** ✉ **7176 364**
    ✉ sato@t-mi.com

Asset Management
Portfolio Management   Issei Inou *Portfolio Manager* ☏ **7176 224**

Administration

Other (Administration)
Treasury Administration   Joachim Boucher *Assistant Manager*

Bankers Trust International plc   Full Branch Office
Grüneburgweg 16, D-60322 Frankfurt/Main
Tel: (69) 15301 0 **Fax:** (69) 15301 260 **Telex:** 413650

Administration

Compliance   Hartmut Hofmann *Head, Compliance*

GERMANY (+49)   www.euromoneydirectory.com

Bankgesellschaft Berlin AG
Head Office

Alexanderplatz 2, D-10178 Berlin
PO Box 110801, D-10838 Berlin
Tel: (30) 245 500 Fax: (30) 2456 6333 Swift: BEBE DE BG Reuters: BERA; BERD; BERE
Website: www.bankgesellschaft.de

Senior Executive Officers
Chairman, Supervisory Board — Edzard Reuter
Others (Senior Executives)
Board of Management
Wolfgang Rupf *Speaker*
Nobert Pawlowski
Hans Leukers
Leopold Tröbinger

General-Lending (DCM, SL)
Head of Corporate Banking
Peter König *Group Finances & Participations*
Willi Böhmer *Group Finances & Participations*

Debt Capital Markets / Fixed Income
Head of Fixed Income — Cord-Friedrich Köning

Domestic Government Bonds
Head of Trading
Georg-Heinrich Sieveking *Head, Money, Forex & Domestic Bond Trading*
T 2456 3100 F 2456 3150
Jochen Zimmermann *Head, Money, Forex & Domestic Bond Trading*
T 2456 3200
Frank-Michael Boenke *Head, Money, Forex & Domestic Bond Trading*
T 2456 3000 F 2456 3050

Eurobonds
Head of Trading
Heinz Dieter Gottschalk *Head* T 2456 6510 F 2456 6514

Libor-Based / Floating-Rate Products
Asset Swaps
Zoe Shaw T +44 (171) 572 6304 F +44 (171) 572 6796
Gerhard Richter T 2456 6513 F 2456 6514

Asset-Backed Securities / Securitization
Global Head
Gerhard Richter *Head, Asset-backed Transactions* T 2456 6513
F 2456 6514
Zoe Shaw *Head, Asset-backed Transactions* T +44 (171) 572 6304
F +44 (171) 572 6796

Equity Capital Markets
Global Head
Serge Demolière *Head, Equities & Equity Derivatives* T 2456 2428
F 2456 2488

Domestic Equities
Head of Sales
Bruno Schmidt-Voss *Institutional Equities*

Syndicated Lending
Global Head
Zoe Shaw *Head, Loan Syndication* T +44 (171) 572 6304
F +44 (171) 572 6796
Gerhard Richter *Head, Loan Syndication* T 2456 6513 F 2456 6514

Money Markets
Domestic Commercial Paper
Head of Trading
Georg-Heinrich Sieveking *Head, Money, Forex & Domestic Bond Trading*
T 2456 3100 F 2456 3150
Jochen Zimmermann *Head, Money, Forex & Domestic Bond Trading*
T 2456 3200
Frank-Michael Boenke *Head, Money, Forex & Domestic Bond Trading*
T 2456 3000 F 2456 3050

Foreign Exchange
Global Head
Georg-Heinrich Sieveking *Head, Money, Forex & Domestic Bond Trading*
T 2456 3100 F 2456 3150
Frank-Michael Boenke *Head, Money, Forex & Domestic Bond Trading*
T 2456 3000 F 2456 3050
Jochen Zimmermann *Head, Money, Forex & Domestic Bond Trading*
T 2456 3200

Risk Management
Global Head
Hadi Saidi *Head, Risk Management / Derivatives* T 2456 1222 F 2456 1217

Corporate Finance / M&A Advisory
Global Head
Erik Blahut *Head, Stock Sales & Co-ordination* T 2456 2777 F 2456 2788

Settlement / Clearing
Operations
Günter Salb *Group Organization*
Artur Fischer *Group Organization*

www.euromoneydirectory.com **GERMANY (+49)**

Asset Management
Other (Asset Management)
Asset Management Fonds BB-INVEST Tim Kettemann Head ☎ **2456 4515**
Asset & Liability Management Wolfgang Stöckel
Asset Management Fonds BB-INVEST Hans-Werner Wilms Head ☎ **2456 4511**
Asset Management Corporations BB-INVEST Tim Kettemann Head ☎ **2456 4515**
 Hans-Werner Wilms Head ☎ **2456 4511**

Other Departments
Chief Credit Officer Ulf Lassen Head of Credit
Economic Research Günter Laubner Head, Economics Division ☎ **2456 6110** 🖷 **2456 6113**
 Dietrich Beier Economics & Investor Relations

Administration
Legal / In-House Counsel
Group Legal Division Joachim Preussner

Corporate Communications
 Reinhard Fröhlich

Accounts / Audit
Risk Control Department Stefan Trägler
Group Auditing Heinrich Honerlage

Other (Administration)
Executive Service Hans-Joachim Bley
Group Human Resources Wolf-Joachim Sawahn
Corporate Marketing, Coordination Heinz Dieter Gottschalk Head ☎ **2456 6510** 🖷 **2456 6514**
Management Information, Division; Controlling Karl Friedrich Hirschhäuser Head ☎ **2456 5239** 🖷 **2456 6276**
Risk Monitoring
Controlling Wolfgang Pritische
Investor Relations Hans Hermann Mindermann

Bankhaus Carl F Plump & Co   Head Office
Am Markt 19, D-28195 Bremen
PO Box 102507, D-28025 Bremen
Tel: (421) 3685 0 **Fax:** (421) 3685 269 **Telex:** 244756 **Swift:** PLUM DE 29

Senior Executive Officers
Partner Jochen v Ciriacy-Wantrup
Managing Director / General Manager Wolfgang Kunze

Bankhaus Hermann Lampe KG   Head Office
Alternative trading name: Lampebank
10 Jägerhofstrasse, D-40479 Düsseldorf
PO Box 101442, D-40005 Düsseldorf
Tel: (211) 4952 0 **Fax:** (211) 491 2202 **Telex:** 8588594 LB D **Swift:** LAMP DE DD
Website: www.lampebank.de

Senior Executive Officers
Chairman Adolf Kracht
Chief Executive Officer Christian von Bassewitz Member of the Board ☎ **4952 391**
Chief Operating Officer Karl-Heinz Franke Member of the Board ☎ **4952 336**
Treasurer Hans-Jens Trelde Member of the Board ☎ **4952 281**
International Division Gerhard C Kappelhoff-Wulff Member of the Board ☎ **4952 235**

Others (Senior Executives)
Head of FX & Money Leonhard Uphues Director ☎ **4952 285**

Debt Capital Markets / Fixed Income
Head of Fixed Income Erwin Niehaus General Manager ☎ **4952 215**

Equity Capital Markets
Head of Equity Capital Markets Erwin Niehaus General Manager ☎ **4952 215**
Head of Trading Wolfgang Vogt Head ☎ **4952 213**

Equity Research
Head of Equity Research Christoph Schlienkamp ☎ **4952 311**

Money Markets
Head of Money Markets Wolfgang Bagusch Deputy Director ☎ **4952 282**
Other Peter Blenkle Derivatives Dealer ☎ **4952 286**

GERMANY (+49)

www.euromoneydirectory.com

Bankhaus Hermann Lampe KG (cont)

Foreign Exchange
Tel: 4952 460 **Fax:** 490 159
Head of Foreign Exchange — Angelika Knatz *Deputy Director* ☏ **4952 466**
Head of Institutional Sales — Armin Linge *Chief Trader* ☏ **4952 464**
Head of Trading — Thomas Neeman *Chief Trader* ☏ **4952 461**

Risk Management
Head of Risk Management — Thomas Welter ☏ **4952 444**

Settlement / Clearing
Head of Settlement / Clearing — Andreas Sanftenberg ☏ **4952 223**
Equity Settlement — Barbara Knopper *Holder of Procuration* ☏ **4952 478**

Other Departments
Chief Credit Officer — Willy Angerstein *General Manager* ☏ **4952 209**
Correspondent Banking — Günter Koch *Director* ☏ **4952 325**

Administration
Legal / In-House Counsel — Leonore Schäfer *Director* ☏ **4952 407**
Compliance — Jochen Schieke *Holder of Procuration* ☏ **4952 416**

Bankhaus Reuschel & Co — Head Office

Maximiliansplatz 13, D-80333 Munich, Bavaria
D-80285, Munich, Bavaria
Tel: (89) 2395 0 **Fax:** (89) 291 180 **Telex:** 524821

Settlement / Clearing
Settlement (General) — Ingrid Wimmer ☏ **239 5453**
Engelbert Faltermeier ☏ **239 5357**

Administration
Compliance — Rudolf Kriz *Head, Compliance*

Banque Générale du Luxembourg SA

Goethestrasse 10, D-60313 Frankfurt/Main
PO Box 100361, D-60003 Frankfurt/Main
Tel: (69) 929 110 0 **Fax:** (69) 929 110 50

Banque Sudameris

Westendstrasse 58/62, D-60325 Frankfurt/Main
Tel: (69) 975 680 **Fax:** (69) 745 204 **Telex:** 411752

Senior Executive Officers
Representative — Giuseppe Raimondi

Barclays Bank plc

Formerly known as: BZW Deutschland
Bockenheimer Landstrasse 38/40, D-60323 Frankfurt/Main
Tel: (69) 7161 00 **Fax:** (69) 7161 1099

Baring Brothers (Deutschland) GmbH — Subsidiary Company

Friedrichstrasse 2-6, D-60323 Frankfurt/Main
Tel: (69) 71904 0 **Fax:** (69) 71904 162

Senior Executive Officers
Managing Director — Jürgen B Rahn
Managing Director — Philip Meyer-Horn

Corporate Finance / M&A Advisory
Head of Corporate Finance — Jürgen B Rahn *Managing Director*

www.euromoneydirectory.com GERMANY (+49)

Bayerische Handelsbank AG Head Office

Von-der-Tann-Strasse 2, D-80539 Munich, Bavaria
Tel: (89) 28627 0 **Fax:** (89) 28627 304 **Reuters:** BHB01
Geschäftsbereich Passiv / Komunaldarlehen **Tel:** (89) 28627 324; **Fax:** (89) 28627 363; **Reuters:** BHB02; BHB03

Senior Executive Officers
Chairman Albrecht Schmidt
Member of the Executive Board Kurt Bonfig
Member of the Executive Board Manfred J Gottschaller
Member of the Executive Board Klaus Nolting
Member of the Executive Board Klaus Peter Pfeiffer

Bayerische Hypo-und Vereinsbank AG

Formerly known as: Bayerische Vereinsbank AG & Bayerische Hypotheken-und Wechsel Bank
Am Tucherpark 16, D-80538 Munich, Bavaria
Tel: (89) 378 0 **Fax:** (89) 338 029
Website: www.vereinsbank.de

Senior Executive Officers
Chairman Klaus Götte
Managing Director Egbert Eisele
Managing Director Peter Hoch
Managing Director Franz Huber
Managing Director Norbert Juchem
Managing Director Rainer Knoth
Managing Director Martin Kölsch
Managing Director Dieter Rampl
Managing Director Eberhard Rauch
Managing Director & Spokesman Albrecht Schmidt
Managing Director Stephan Schüller
Managing Director Martin Schütte
Managing Director Paul Siebertz
Managing Director Wolfgang Sprießler
Managing Director Josef F Wertshulte

Bayerische Landesanstalt für Aufbaufinanzierung Head Office

Königinstrasse 17, D-80539 Munich, Bavaria
Tel: (89) 2124 0 **Fax:** (89) 2124 2440 **Reuters:** BLFA
Website: www.lfa.de

Debt Capital Markets / Fixed Income
Tel: 2124 2333 **Fax:** 2124 2565
Global Head Peter Voglbauer *Bankdirektor*

Domestic Government Bonds
Head of Sales Peter Voglbauer *Bankdirektor*

Eurobonds
Head of Origination Peter Voglbauer *Bankdirektor*

Private Placements
Head of Origination Peter Voglbauer *Bankdirektor*

Syndicated Lending
Tel: 2124 2333
Global Head Peter Voglbauer *Bankdirektor*

Money Markets
Tel: 2124 2275 **Fax:** 2124 2565
Global Head Norbert Fritz

Risk Management
Tel: 2124 2438
Global Head Anton Stiegler *Bankdirektor*

Fixed Income Derivatives / Risk Management
Global Head Peter Voglbauer *Bankdirektor*
IR Swaps Sales / Marketing; IR Options Sales / Marketing Albert Brandl ☏ **2124 2346**

Settlement / Clearing
Fixed-Income Settlement; Derivatives Settlement; Foreign Exchange Settlement Siegfried Schmittner *Managing Director (CSIF)* ☏ **2124 2378**

Euromoney Directory 1999 **465**

GERMANY (+49) www.euromoneydirectory.com

Bayerische Landesbank Girozentrale Head Office
Brienner Strasse 18, D-80333 Munich, Bavaria
D-80277, Munich, Bavaria
Tel: (89) 2171 01 **Fax:** (89) 2171 3576; (89) 2171 3941 **Telex:** 5286270 **Swift:** BYLA DE MM **Reuters:** BLAX; BLAM; BAYA; BAYB
Website: www.bayernlb.de

Senior Executive Officers
Chairman, Board of Management Alfred Lehner

Others (Senior Executives)
Board of Management Gerold Brandt *Member*
  Peter Kahn *Member*
  Klaus Rauscher *Member*
  Werner Strohmayr *Member*
  Dietrich Wolf *Member*
  Eberhard Zinn *Member*

Department: Financial Institutions Division
Others (Senior Executives)
Head Michael von Hallwyl *Executive Vice President*
  Michael Stauder *Senior Vice President*
Far East, Australia, New Zealand; The Elaine Murphy *Assistant Vice President*
Americas, Caribbean, Central & Southern
Africa; Spain, Portugal, Germany
Europe (except Spain & Portugal); Israel, Bernhard Piesch *Senior Vice President*
Middle East, Northern Africa

Debt Capital Markets / Fixed Income
Department: Securities Division
Global Head Klaus Sturm *Executive Vice President* ⓣ **2171 3833**
  Florian Drexler *Senior Vice President* ⓣ **2171 3834**
Head of Fixed Income Jürgen Adamitza *Division Manager* ⓣ **2171 3330** ⓕ **2171 3305**
Head of Fixed Income Sales Georg Weißmann *Senior Vice President* ⓣ **2171 3253** ⓕ **2171 58253**
Head of Fixed Income Trading Günther Dillmann *First Vice President* ⓣ **(69) 71907 360** ⓕ **(69) 71907 152**

Government Bonds
Head of Sales Rainer Scholl *Senior Vice President* ⓣ **2171 3349** ⓕ **2171 58349**
Head of Trading Johannes Pfennig *Senior Vice President* ⓣ **2171 3289** ⓕ **2171 58289**

Eurobonds
Head of Sales Anton Walcher *First Vice President* ⓣ **2171 3264** ⓕ **2171 58264**
Head of Trading Günther Jäschke *First Vice President* ⓣ **2171 3254** ⓕ **2171 58254**

Bonds - General
Head, Short Term Desk Martin Hindelang *Vice President* ⓣ **2171 3276** ⓕ **2171 58276**
Head, Short Term Bonds Torsten Wieczorek ⓣ **2171 3294** ⓕ **2171 58294**

Emerging Market Bonds
Head of Sales Anton Wagner *First Vice President & Head* ⓣ **2171 3264** ⓕ **2171 58264**
Head of Trading Stefan Magerl *Head of Trading* ⓣ **2171 3314** ⓕ **2171 58314**

Fixed-Income Repo
Head of Repo Thomas Bachmeier *Chief Trader* ⓣ **2171 3293** ⓕ **2171 58293**
Department: New Issues
Global Head Hans Christoph Groscurth *Senior Executive Vice President*

Other (Fixed Income)
Japan, Korea Winfried Rohaus *Executive Vice President*
Asia / Pacific, Austria, Greece, Turkey Stephan Thiele *Vice President*
Spain, Portugal, Italy, Eastern Europe, Americas Werner Gerhardt *Senior Vice President*
Scandinavia, UK / Ireland, Switzerland Klaus Wrobel *Senior Vice President*
France, Benelux, Africa; Syndication Frederik Mehlitz *Vice President*
New Products Klaus Wrobel *Senior Vice President*
Debt Issuance Stefan Hauser *Vice President*

Non-Domestic Government Bonds
Documentation & Domestic Issues Bernd Wolpert *Senior Vice President*
  Siegfried Kupsch *Vice President*
  Franz Stadler *Vice President*

Asset-Backed Securities / Securitization
Regional Head Christoph Plattenteich *Assistant Vice President*

Equity Capital Markets
Department: Securities Trading & Sales
Head of Equity Capital Markets Jürgen Adamitza *Division Manager* ⓣ **2171 3330** ⓕ **2171 3305**
Global Head Matthias Voß *Division Manager*

www.euromoneydirectory.com GERMANY (+49)

Securities Trading & Sales (cont)

Head of Sales — Martin Hinkofer *Assistant Vice President* ☏ **2171 5492** 🖷 **2171 58492**
Head of Trading — Thomas Sickenberg *Vice President* ☏ **2171 3383** 🖷 **2171 58420**

Domestic Equities
Head of Sales — Zdenek Holly ☏ **2171 5491** 🖷 **2171 58491**
Head of Trading — Dietmar Birnkammer *Chief Trader* ☏ **2171 3355** 🖷 **2171 58362**

International Equities
Head of Sales; Head of Trading — Bernhard Hegel *Assistant Vice President* ☏ **2171 3386** 🖷 **2171 58420**

Convertibles / Equity-Linked
Head of Sales; Head of Trading — Alfred Mundner *Chief Trader* ☏ **2171 3388** 🖷 **2171 58388**

Syndicated Lending
Department: Structured Finance Division
Global Head — Klaus Zirkel *Executive Vice President & Head* ☏ **2171 3872** 🖷 **2171 3922**
✉ **Klaus.Zirkel@blb.de**
Georg Garner *Senior Vice President & Head* ☏ **2171 3861** 🖷 **2171 3922**
✉ **Georg.Garner@blb.de**

Loan-Related Activities
Trade Finance — Christoph Bräuning *First Vice President* ☏ **2171 3628** 🖷 **2171 3849**
✉ **Christoph.Braeuning@blb.de**
Claudia Groiss *Manager* ☏ **2171 3630** 🖷 **2171 3649**
✉ **Claudia.Groiss@blb.de**
Aircraft / Aerospace Finance; Shipping Finance — Rüdiger Fern *Senior Vice President* ☏ **2171 3767** 🖷 **2171 3763**
✉ **Ruediger.Fern@blb.de**
Project Finance — Kai Preugschal *First Vice President* ☏ **2171 3777** 🖷 **21713922**
✉ **Kai.Preugschal@blb.de**

Other (Trade Finance)
Credit & Administration — Klaus Brendl *First Vice President* ☏ **2171 3878** 🖷 **2171 3789**
✉ **Klaus.Brendl@blb.de**
Export Finance — Volker Kuntz *Senior Vice President* ☏ **2171 3965** 🖷 **2171 3789**
✉ **Volker.Kuntz@blb.de**
Satellite Finance — Rüdiger Fern *Senior Vice President* ☏ **2171 3767** 🖷 **2171 3763**
✉ **Ruediger.Fern@blb.de**

Money Markets

Global Head — Horst Gerhard Sauerer *Senior Vice President* ☏ **2171 3218**
Klaus Sturm *Executive Vice President* ☏ **2171 3833**
Florian Drexler *Senior Vice President* ☏ **2171 3834**
Country Head — Rudolf Hofbauer *FVP, Product Manager* ☏ **2171 3848**
Horst Gerhard Sauerer *Senior Vice President* ☏ **2171 3218**

Eurocommercial Paper
Head of Sales — Ms Legler ☏ **2171 8882**
Ms Suhling ☏ **2171 8882**

Money Markets - General
Joachim Hader *SVP, Sales Force, Saving Banks* ☏ **2171 3700**
Mr Berger *Chief Dealer, Saving Banks* ☏ **2171 3841**
Mr Hain *Sales, Saving Banks* ☏ **2171 3841**
Ms Janosch *Sales, Saving Banks* ☏ **2171 3841**
Ms Schilling *Sales, Saving Banks* ☏ **2171 3841**
Ms Urban *Sales, Saving Banks* ☏ **2171 3841**
Ms Wiesner *Sales, Saving Banks* ☏ **2171 3841**
Cash Management — Stefan Thoma *VP & Chief Dealer*
Mr Böhm
Mr Braun
Ms Huber
Sales Force Corporates — Hans-Günther Kroll *Senior Vice President* ☏ **2171 3722**
Mr Peter *VP, Chief Dealer* ☏ **2171 8540**
Prince Bartels *Assistant Vice President* ☏ **2171 8540**
Mr Schweiger *Assistant Vice President* ☏ **2171 8540**
Mr Ertl ☏ **2171 8540**
Mr Hertlein *AVP, Chief Dealer* ☏ **2171 3822**
Mr Grätz ☏ **2171 3822**
Mr Mitschke ☏ **2171 3822**
Mr Reisinger ☏ **2171 3822**
Ms Thomas ☏ **2171 3822**
Mr Fendl *VP, Chief Dealer* ☏ **2171 3202**
Ms Benz ☏ **2171 3202**
Ms Fähnrich ☏ **2171 3202**
Mr Lauerwald ☏ **2171 3202**
Ms Lück ☏ **2171 3202**
Ms Toth ☏ **2171 3202**

GERMANY (+49)　　　　　　　www.euromoneydirectory.com

Bayerische Landesbank Girozentrale (cont)
Wholesale Deposits
Head of Sales　　　　　　　　G Traber *AVP, Chief Dealer* ☎ **2171 3696**
　　　　　　　　　　　　　　　Mr Fichti ☎ **2171 3696**
　　　　　　　　　　　　　　　Mr Relnhardsstäfter ☎ **2171 3830**
　　　　　　　　　　　　　　　Angelika Zaigler *FVP & Chief Dealer* ☎ **2171 3830**
　　　　　　　　　　　　　　　Ms Kionke ☎ **2171 3830**

Foreign Exchange
Telex: 528232 (Forex & Deposits)
Global Head　　　　　　　　　Klaus Sturm *Executive Vice President* ☎ **2171 3833**
　　　　　　　　　　　　　　　Gerhard Schott *Senior Executive Vice President* ☎ **2171 3832**
Global Head; Country Head　　Florian Drexler *Senior Vice President* ☎ **2171 3834**
Head of Institutional Sales　　Joachim Hader *SVP, Sales Force, Saving Banks* ☎ **2171 3700**
　　　　　　　　　　　　　　　Mr Schmid *AVP, Chief Dealer, Saving Banks* ☎ **2171 3845**
　　　　　　　　　　　　　　　Ms Frischeisen *Sales, Saving Banks* ☎ **2171 3845**
　　　　　　　　　　　　　　　Mr Juhasz *Sales, Saving Banks* ☎ **2171 3845**
　　　　　　　　　　　　　　　Ms Wahrlich *Sales, Saving Banks* ☎ **2171 3845**
Corporate Sales　　　　　　　Hans-Günther Krolß *Senior Vice President* ☎ **2171 3722**
　　　　　　　　　　　　　　　Mr Peter *VP, Chief Dealer* ☎ **2171 8540**
　　　　　　　　　　　　　　　Prince Bartels *Assistant Vice President* ☎ **2171 8540**
　　　　　　　　　　　　　　　Mr Schweiger *Assistant Vice President* ☎ **2171 8540**
　　　　　　　　　　　　　　　Mr Ertl ☎ **2171 8540**
　　　　　　　　　　　　　　　Mr Hertlein *AVP, Chief Dealer* ☎ **2171 3822**
　　　　　　　　　　　　　　　Mr Grätz ☎ **2171 3822**
　　　　　　　　　　　　　　　Mr Mitschke ☎ **2171 3822**
　　　　　　　　　　　　　　　Mr Reisinger ☎ **2171 3822**
　　　　　　　　　　　　　　　Ms Thomas ☎ **2171 3822**
　　　　　　　　　　　　　　　Mr Fendl *VP, Chief Dealer* ☎ **2171 3202**
　　　　　　　　　　　　　　　Ms Benz ☎ **2171 3202**
　　　　　　　　　　　　　　　Ms Fähnrich ☎ **2171 3202**
　　　　　　　　　　　　　　　Mr Lauerwald ☎ **2171 3202**
　　　　　　　　　　　　　　　Ms Lück ☎ **2171 3202**
　　　　　　　　　　　　　　　Ms Toth ☎ **2171 3202**

FX Traders / Sales People
Spot Desk, Interbank　　　　　Mr Maier *AVP, Chief Dealer, Spot Desk Interbank* ☎ **2171 3810**
　　　　　　　　　　　　　　　Ms Schneider *Dealer, Spot Desk Interbank* ☎ **2171 3810**
　　　　　　　　　　　　　　　Mr Stern *Dealer, Spot Desk Interbank* ☎ **2171 3810**
　　　　　　　　　　　　　　　Ms Schukow *Dealer, Spot Desk Interbank* ☎ **2171 3810**
　　　　　　　　　　　　　　　Mr Raczek *Dealer, Spot Desk Interbank* ☎ **2171 3810**
　　　　　　　　　　　　　　　Mr Lehner *Dealer, Spot Desk Interbank* ☎ **2171 3810**
Spot Desk, Regional Banks　　Mr Borbe *VP, Chief Dealer, Spot Desk Regional Banks* ☎ **2171 3814**
　　　　　　　　　　　　　　　Mr Kaffka *Dealer, Spot Desk Regional Banks* ☎ **2171 3814**
　　　　　　　　　　　　　　　Mr Hofer *VP, Spot Desk Regional Banks* ☎ **2171 3814**

Risk Management
Global Head　　　　　　　　　Gerhard Schott *Senior Executive Vice President* ☎ **2171 3832**
　　　　　　　　　　　　　　　Klaus Sturm *Executive Vice President* ☎ **2171 3833**
Country Head　　　　　　　　Florian Drexler *Senior Vice President* ☎ **2171 3834**
　　　　　　　　　　　　　　　Johann Debert *FVP, Derivative Product Manager* ☎ **2171 2264**

Fixed Income Derivatives / Risk Management
Head of Sales　　　　　　　　Ms Kaeppel *Assistant Vice President* ☎ **2171 3697**
Trading　　　　　　　　　　　Jochen Winklharrer *AVP, Chief Dealer* ☎ **2171 3693**
　　　　　　　　　　　　　　　Mr Spahl ☎ **2171 3742**
　　　　　　　　　　　　　　　Mr Junkes ☎ **2171 3742**

Other (FI Derivatives)
Financial Engineering　　　　　Mr Rothhammer *AVP, Chief Dealer* ☎ **2171 3744**
　　　　　　　　　　　　　　　Mr Drexl ☎ **2171 3746**
Marketing　　　　　　　　　　Mr Morsh *Vice President* ☎ **2171 3699**
　　　　　　　　　　　　　　　Mr Fottner *Assistant Vice President* ☎ **2171 3699**
　　　　　　　　　　　　　　　Ms Kaeppel *Assistant Vice President* ☎ **2171 3697**

Foreign Exchange Derivatives / Risk Management
Spot / Forwards Trading　　　　G Kordick *AVP, Chief Dealer, FX Forwards* ☎ **2171 3818**
　　　　　　　　　　　　　　　Mr Kaeppel *AVP, FX Forwards* ☎ **2171 3818**
　　　　　　　　　　　　　　　E Macharzina *Dealer, FX Forwards* ☎ **2171 3818**
　　　　　　　　　　　　　　　Mr Scheld *Dealer, FX Forwards* ☎ **2171 3818**
Vanilla FX option Trading　　　Herbert Marxen *VP & Chief Dealer* ☎ **2171 3829**
　　　　　　　　　　　　　　　Christoph Albrecht *Assistant Vice President* ☎ **2171 3828**
　　　　　　　　　　　　　　　Mr Rechbauer ☎ **2171 3829**
　　　　　　　　　　　　　　　Ms Bichler ☎ **2171 3829**

www.euromoneydirectory.com GERMANY (+49)

OTC Commodity Derivatives
Trading   Mr Kraus *AVP, Chief Dealer* 🕾 **2171 3232**
                                   Mr Dick 🕾 **2171 3724**
                                   Mr Seldner 🕾 **2171 3724**
                                   Mr Frei 🕾 **2171 3724**

Other Departments
Commodities / Bullion   Mr Kraus *AVP, Chief Dealer* 🕾 **2171 3232**
                                   Mr Dick 🕾 **2171 3724**
                                   Mr Seldner 🕾 **2171 3724**
                                   Mr Frei 🕾 **2171 3724**

Berenberg Bank — Head Office
Alternative trading name: Joh Berenberg, Gossard & Co
Neuer Jungfernstieg 20, D-20354 Hamburg
PO Box 300547, D-20302 Hamburg
Tel: (40) 342 876 **Fax:** (40) 352 132 **Telex:** 215781 BEGO **Reuters:** BEGH **Telerate:** BEGO DE HH **Cable:** BERENBERG

Senior Executive Officers
Chairman   Christian Wilde
Partner   Joachim von Berenberg-Consbruch
Partner   Claus G Budelmann
Partner   Peter von Kap-Herr
Partner   Andreas M Odefey
Partner   Joachim H Wetzel
International Division   Rüdiger K Schultz

General-Investment
Head of Investment   Hans-Walter Peters 🕾 **3506 0418**

Money Markets
Head of Money Markets   Norbert Kruse 🕾 **3506 066**

Foreign Exchange
Head of Foreign Exchange   Norbert Kruse 🕾 **3506 066**

Other Departments
Chief Credit Officer   Jürgen Witt

BfG Bank AG — Head Office
Formerly known as: Bank für Gemeinwirtschaft AG
Mainzer Landstrasse 16, D-60325 Frankfurt/Main
Tel: (69) 258 0 **Fax:** (69) 258 6073 **Telex:** 4122122 **Swift:** BFGF DE FF **Reuters:** BFGA-D
Cable: BFGZENTRALE FRANKFURTMAI
Reuters: BFGG

Senior Executive Officers
Chairman, Board of Managing Directors   Karl-Heinz Hülsmann 🕾 **258 6028** 📠 **258 6026**
Board of Managing Directors   Patrick Fincker 🕾 **258 6012** 📠 **258 6026**
Board of Managing Directors   Michael A Kremer 🕾 **258 6018** 📠 **258 6566**
Board of Managing Directors   Ernst Maul 🕾 **258 6500** 📠 **258 6008**
Generalbevollmächtigte   Bernd Kiene 🕾 **258 5300** 📠 **258 5303**
Generalbevollmächtigte   Holger Tiedtke 🕾 **258 5400** 📠 **258 6213**

General-Lending (DCM, SL)
Head of Corporate Banking   Siegfried Schunack *VP, Corporate Banking* 🕾 **258 6220** 📠 **258 6479**
Department: Financial Institutions

Others (Senior Executives)
                                   Max A Lurz *SVP, Group Executive*

Relationship Manager
Hong Kong, Indonesia, Japan, Korea, Malaysia, Albert Kanschik *Dept Head & FVP* 🕾 **258 6878**
Philippines, S'pore, Taiwan, Thailand, Vietnam
Africa, Bangladesh, India, Iran, Pakistan; Sri Helmut Baumert *Vice President* 🕾 **258 6888**
Lanka, Turkey, Middle East

GERMANY (+49)

www.euromoneydirectory.com

BfG Bank AG (cont)

Relationship Manager (cont)

Credit Lyonnais Head Office & Network, France — Christa Elbacher-Dittrich *Vice President* ☎ **258 6837**
Austria, Central & E.Europe, Liechtenstein; — Harald Görtz *Vice President* ☎ **258 6838**
Switzerland, Poland, Romania, Slovak Republic; Slovenia, Yugoslavia
Australia, Caribbean, Central & South America; — Hinrich Garrels *First Vice President* ☎ **258 5294**
New Zealand, Pacific Islands
Benelux, Canada, Cyprus, Greece, Ireland, Italy; — Beverley-Ann Walls *Vice President* ☎ **258 5290**
Malta, Nordic Countries, Portugal, Spain, UK, USA

Debt Capital Markets / Fixed Income

Bonds - General
Bond Trading / Schuldscheine — Peter Winkel *Senior Vice President* ☎ **258 5200** F **258 5264**
Bonds, New Issues & Trading — Roland Ringelstetter *Vice President* ☎ **9727 1112** F **258 5264**
Martin Figge *Dealer* ☎ **9727 1104**
Gisela Timm *Dealer* ☎ **9727 1124**
Fixed-Income Sales — Ulrich Becker *Vice President* ☎ **9727 1110** F **258 5263**

Equity Capital Markets
Fax: 258 5209

Domestic Equities
Head of Sales — Stefan Euler *Sales-Trader* ☎ **258 7839**
Ute Jahns *Sales-Trader* ☎ **258 7848**
Christian Glowig *Sales-Trader* ☎ **258 7847**
Gerd-Uwe Petry *Assistant Vice President* ☎ **258 7844**
Head of Trading — Oliver Mettier ☎ **9727 1129**

Other (Domestic Equities)
New Issues — Uwe Isack ☎ **258 7729**

Warrants
Head of Sales — Renzo Sechi *Vice President* ☎ **258 7845**

Syndicated Lending

Other (Trade Finance)
Real Estate — Manfred Burkelc *Senior Vice President*

Money Markets
Department: Money Markets / Foreign Exchange / Derivatives
Country Head — Hannelore Plessow *SVP, Money Market, FX, Derivatives* ☎ **258 6780**

Money Markets - General
Domestic Money Markets — M Kornmann *Dealer* ☎ **9727 1196**
J Weber *Vice President* ☎ **9727 1196**
J Peters *Dealer* ☎ **9727 1196**
Euromarket — J Filter *Vice President* ☎ **9727 1206**
R Hermanns *Dealer* ☎ **9727 1206**
W Körber *Dealer* ☎ **9727 1206**
K Penschior *Dealer* ☎ **9727 1206**
A Weidenhammer *Dealer* ☎ **9727 1206**
H Cassens *Dealer* ☎ **9727 1206**

Foreign Exchange

FX Traders / Sales People
Chief Dealer — H J Oechsner *Vice President* ☎ **9727 1184**

Risk Management

Foreign Exchange Derivatives / Risk Management
Spot / Forwards Trading — I Mauer *Dealer, Currencies - Spot* ☎ **9727 1185/7**
T Boström *Dealer, Currencies - Spot* ☎ **9727 1185/7**
J Lörke *Dealer, Currencies - Spot* ☎ **9727 1885/7**
K H Schleiter *Dealer, Currencies - Forward* ☎ **9727 1208**
K Holscher *Dealer, Currencies - Forward* ☎ **9727 1193**

Other Currency Swap / FX Options Personnel
Options — F Ullrich *Dealer* ☎ **9727 1188**
M Schmidt *Dealer* ☎ **9727 1183**
Liquidity Trading Swaps — M Schwind *Dealer* ☎ **9727 1125**
T Gries *Broker* ☎ **9727 1174**
Futures & Options Brokerage — F Ménard *Head of Desk* ☎ **9727 1174**
M Kaiser *Head of Sales* ☎ **9727 1174**
Ch Oakley *Broker* ☎ **9727 1174**
Ch Bouton *Broker* ☎ **9727 1174**
F Ullrich *Dealer* ☎ **9727 1188**
B Thönges *Private Clients* ☎ **9727 1174**

www.euromoneydirectory.com					GERMANY (+49)

Other (Exchange-Traded Derivatives)
Sales / Customer Trading					W Hammerstein *Vice President* ☎ 9727 1159
									W Grebe *Dealer* ☎ 9727 1170
									U Denecke *Dealer* ☎ 9727 1172
									I Löcher *Dealer* ☎ 9727 1169
									H Junger *Dealer* ☎ 9727 1169
									J Müller *Dealer* ☎ 9727 1161
									Anja Kasper *Dealer* ☎ 9727 1162
									A Fernandez *Dealer* ☎ 9727 1173
Department: Treasury
Other (FI Derivatives)
									K Dahmann *Vice President* ☎ 258 6810
									A Overbeck *Risk Manager* ☎ 258 6846
									K Borgmeyer *Risk Manager* ☎ 258 6772
Other Departments
Economic Research						Heinrich Schaumburg *SVP, Communications & Economic Research*
									☎ 258 6400 F 258 6409
									Eberhard Unger *Vice President, Financial Analysis* ☎ 258 5214 F 258 5207

Administration
Public Relations
Public Information Office					Heinrich Schaumburg *SVP, Communications & Economic Research*
									☎ 258 6400 F 258 6409

BHF-BANK AG

Alternative trading name: Bank Aktiengesellschaft
					Bockenheimer Landstrasse 10, D-60323 Frankfurt/Main D-60302 Frankfurt/Main
		Tel: (69) 718 0 **Fax:** (69) 718 2296 **Telex:** 411 026 **Swift:** BHFB DE FF **Email:** debhfffm@ibmmail.com
					Reuters: BHFX (Monitor); BHFF (Dealing); BHFT (Dealing)

Senior Executive Officers
Others (Senior Executives)
									Tilo Paduch *Managing Director*
									Alfred Möckel *Managing Director*
									Roland Scharff *Managing Director*
									Dietmar Schmid *Managing Director*
									Louis Graf von Zech *Managing Director*
									Ralf-Hartmut Fiedler *Managing Director*
									Ernst Michel Kruse *Managing Director*

General-Lending (DCM, SL)
Head of Corporate Banking					Michael E Doyle *Management, Corporate Banking*
									Peter Dieckmann *Management, Corporate Banking*
									Sigurd Fischer-Güttich *Management, Corporate Banking*
									Tilo Paduch *Management, Corporate Banking*
									Ralf-Hartmut Fiedler *Managing Director*

Relationship Manager
Co-ordination Global Customers				Thomas Brücher
Spain, Andorra, Australia, N Zealand				Jürgen P Frank *Financial Institutions-OECD Countries*
Germany, Austria, Switzerland, Liechtenstein		Thomas Andreas *Financial Institutions-OECD Countries*
UK & Ireland							Antje Fricke *Financial Institutions-OECD Countries*
USA, Canada, Scandinavia, Finland, Iceland,			Michael Kleinschmidt *Financial Institutions-OECD Countries*
Japan
Italy, Portugal, Greece, Cyprus				Dirk Werthmann *Financial Institutions-OECD Countries*
France, Benelux Countries					Ruediger Mohrstedt *Financial Institutions-OECD Countries*
									Antje Fricke *Financial Institutions-OECD Countries*
Private Customers						Ulrich Lingenthal
Department: International Banking
Others (Senior Executives)
Central / E Europe, Israel, Turkey				Manfred Falkenmeier *Foreign Region I*
Macedonia, Serbia / Montenegro, CIS / Russia			Hans-Peter Romanowski *Foreign Region I*
Albania, Slovenia, Croatia, Bosnia-Herzegovina		André-Jean Cazabonne *Foreign Region I*
Bulgaria, Romania, Moldova					Hans-Peter Romanowski *Foreign Region I*
Czech & Slovak Republics, Poland, Hungary			Bernd Krückeberg *Foreign Region I*
Baltic States							Christine Löwe *Foreign Region I*
Latin America, East / West / Southern Africa			Bernd-Helmut Eichelbaum *Foreign Region II*
Argentina, Paraguay, Uruguay, Colombia;			Ingo Gerding *Foreign Region II*
Venezuela, Peru, Ecuador, Bolivia, Guayana;
Panama, Central America, Caribbean Countries

GERMANY (+49)

BHF-BANK AG (cont)
Others (Senior Executives) (cont)

Mexico, Brazil, Chile, Cuba	Juan Nicolas Pineros Petersen *Foreign Region II*
East & Southern Africa	Horst Schnoes *Foreign Region II*
	Sia-Homayun Mehr *Foreign Region II*
South Africa	Hansjörg Keßler *Foreign Region II*
Far East, Indian Sub-Continent, N.Africa,	Hans-Günter Wiesenack *Foreign Region III*
M.East; India, Iran, Sri Lanka, Morocco, Algeria, Tunis	
Bangladesh, Nepal, Pakistan	Lutz Dunker *Foreign Region III*
Brunei, Indonesia, Malaysia, Philippines, Vietnam	Ulf Hollstein *Foreign Region III*
Myanmar, S'pore, Thailand, N / S.Korea; Cambodia, Laos	Christian Hobrücker *Foreign Region III*
PR of China, HK, Taiwan, Macao	Paulo Bosbach *Foreign Region III*
Egypt, Libya, Bahrain, Iraq, Kuwait	Alf Sörensen *Foreign Region III*
	Marko Heimken *Foreign Region III*
Oman, Qatar, Saudi Arabia, UAE	Alf Sörensen *Foreign Region III*
	Marko Heimken *Foreign Region III*
Yemen, Syria, Jordan, Lebanon	Alf Sörensen *Foreign Region III*
	Marko Heimken *Foreign Region III*
Malta, Palestinian Self-Rule Areas	Alf Sörensen *Foreign Region III*
	Marko Heimken *Foreign Region III*

Debt Capital Markets / Fixed Income
Department: Fixed Income
Telex: 41226 BHF D
Global Head — Michael Hochgürtel

Domestic Government Bonds
Head of Trading — Michael Hochgürtel
Guido Schneider
Carl Albert Hellmann

Non-Domestic Government Bonds
Capital Market Products — Hans-Jürgen Moch *Capital Market Products*

Eurobonds
Head of Trading — Michael Hochgürtel

Bonds - General
Pfandbriefe / Schuldscheine — Bernhard Janz
Bond Sales — Thomas Knabe
Euro DM-Bonds — Dieter Baumgarten

Private Placements
Head of Structuring — Olav Klein *Asset Structuring*

Fixed-Income Repo
Marketing & Product Development; Trading — Astrid Dörr *Assistant Vice President* ☎ 718 3663 F 718 2815
Trading — Jörg Weirich *Assistant Treasurer*

Equity Capital Markets
Global Head — Christoph Arzt

Domestic Equities
Head of Sales — Rainer Jell
Head of Trading — Christoph Arzt

Other (Domestic Equities)
Market & Product Development — Rüdiger Wolf
Sales & Trading — Fritz-Karl Diehl

Other (International Equity)
Foreign Stocks — Marc Auth

Equity Research
Global Head — Volker Brandt

Equity Repo / Securities Lending
Head; Marketing & Product Development — Astrid Dörr *Assistant Vice President* ☎ 718 3663 F 718 2815
Head of Trading — Jörg Weirich *Assistant Treasurer*
Rainer Ackermann *Assistant Vice President*

Syndicated Lending

Loan-Related Activities
Trade Finance — Monika Millns *Trade & Commodity Finance*
Project Finance — Claus Peter *Structured & Project Finance*
Structured Trade Finance — Hansjörg Keßler *Foreign Region II*

www.euromoneydirectory.com   GERMANY (+49)

Other (Trade Finance)
Real Estate   Jörg Lienaerts
Financial Engineering   Joachim Käsler
Marketing Foreign Trade Products   Gerd Storm
Payments & Documentary Business   Dietmar Bernhard

Money Markets
Global Head   Thilo Schiering

Other (Wholesale Deposits)
Interbank Deposits & FRA / Futures   Jüregen Nebauer
Short-Term Liquidity   Rolf Köhler
Customer Desk   Monika Fischer

Foreign Exchange
Department: Financial Markets
Telex: 41235 BHF D
Global Head   Loukas Rizos *Head of Division*
                                                Alfred Möckel *Head of Division*
                                                Roland Scharff *Head of Division*

FX Traders / Sales People
FX Spot Arbitrage   Wilhelm Heuzeroth
Foreign Exchange   Hanns-Jürgen Roland
FX Forwards / Euromarket   Günter Hess
                                                Jörg Isselmann
FX Customer Desk   Gerd Müller
FX Currency Options   Eva Spitzlay
FX Technical Currency Analysis   Michael Schnirel

Risk Management
Department: Treasury & Capital Market Products
Global Head   Torsten Gebauer *Risk Management*

Fixed Income Derivatives / Risk Management
IR Options Trading   Robert Herlein

Other Currency Swap / FX Options Personnel
Advisory Group   Marius Revermann
Swaps & Arbitrage   Alexander Titsch-Rivero

OTC Equity Derivatives
Sales   Sabine Lehmann
                                                Gustav Gass

Corporate Finance / M&A Advisory
Department: Corporate Finance
Private Equity   Ulrich Fischer *Private Equity Funds*

Other (Corporate Finance)
New Issues / Equity   Michael Berg
                                                Thomas Brücher
                                                Rainer Lizon
Syndication   Manfred Soff
Listings   Günter Vogl
Regional / Sector Marketing Corp Finance   Axel Gollnick
M & A   Max Scheder-Bieschin

Asset Management
Head   Roland Kern *BHF Trust*
                                                Hans-Dieter Runte
                                                Bernd Witt *BHF Trust*
                                                Ruediger Ginsberg *BHF Capital Management*
Investment Funds   Hartwig Webersinke *Investment Research*
                                                Karl Stäcker *Mutual Funds*
                                                Hans-J Reinhart *Special Funds*

Other (Asset Management)
Business Development   Joachim Klinker
Asset Liability Management   Thomas Werndl
Capital Management   Hans-Dieter Runte
Frankfurt-Trust Investment-GmbH   Wolf-D Kaltenegger
                                                Wolfgang Seidel
                                                Hans-D Wehmeyer

Other Departments
Proprietary Trading   Josef Holzer
Private Banking   Emmerich Müller *Management, Private Banking*
                                                Louis Graf von Zech *Managing Director*
                                                Jörg Lienaerts *Management, Private Banking*
Economic Research   Hermann Remsperger *Economics*

Euromoney Directory 1999   473

GERMANY (+49) www.euromoneydirectory.com

Bremer Landesbank Kreditanstalt Oldenburg -Girozentrale-
Head Office

Domshof 26, D-28195 Bremen
D-28189, Bremen
Tel: (421) 332 0 **Fax:** (421) 332 2299; (421) 332 2322 **Telex:** 2402233/4 BLBD **Swift:** BRLA DE 22
Reuters: BRLA (Dealing)

Senior Executive Officers
Chairman   Peter Hasskamp
Vice Chairman   Axel Weber

Others (Senior Executives)
Board Member   Fritz Lütke-Uhlenbrock
                                        Horst-Günter Lucke

Debt Capital Markets / Fixed Income
Fax: 332 2494
Global Head   Dietrich Baensch *Senior Vice President*

Domestic Government Bonds
Head of Sales   Hermann Cordes ☏ **332 2461**
Head of Trading   Herfried Knief ☏ **332 2464**

Eurobonds
Head of Syndication   Fred Walther ☏ **332 2453**
Head of Sales   Hermann Cordes ☏ **332 2461**
Head of Trading   Herfried Knief ☏ **332 2464**
                                        Gunda Linke ☏ **332 2916**
Trading (Sovereigns)   Werner Meise ☏ **332 2463**

Libor-Based / Floating-Rate Products
FRN Sales   Hermann Cordes ☏ **332 2461**
Asset Swaps   Fred Walther ☏ **332 2453**
Asset Swaps (Sales)   Sandra Spieckermann

Medium-Term Notes
Head of Structuring   Fred Walther ☏ **332 2453**

Equity Capital Markets
Fax: 332 2494
Global Head   Dietrich Baensch *Senior Vice President*

Domestic Equities
Head of Syndication   Fred Walther ☏ **332 2453**
Head of Sales   Hermann Cordes ☏ **332 2461**
Head of Trading   Hans-Günter Prause ☏ **332 2468**
                                        Wolfgang Blöcker ☏ **332 2469**
                                        Herfried Knief ☏ **332 2464**

International Equities
Head of Syndication   Fred Walther ☏ **332 2453**
Head of Sales   Hermann Cordes ☏ **332 2461**
Head of Trading   Hans-Günter Prause ☏ **332 2468**
                                        Wolfgang Blöcker ☏ **332 2469**
                                        Herfried Knief ☏ **332 2464**

Warrants
Head of Sales   Hermann Cordes ☏ **332 2461**
Head of Trading   Herfried Knief ☏ **332 2464**

Equity Repo / Securities Lending
Head of Trading   Herfried Knief ☏ **332 2464**

Syndicated Lending
Global Head   Kirsten Discher *Senior Vice President* ☏ **332 2371**
Head of Syndication   Rainer Punke ☏ **332 2437**

Money Markets
Fax: 332 2020
Global Head   Jens Kurre ☏ **332 2271**

Money Markets - General
                                        Rüdiger von der Höh ☏ **332 2273**

Foreign Exchange
Fax: 332 2277
Global Head   Joachim Thein ☏ **332 2929**
Corporate Sales   Werner Prütt ☏ **332 2393**
Head of Trading   Thomas Greppmair ☏ **332 2394**
Spot / Forwards Trading   Detlef Bilke *Dealer, Spot FX* ☏ **332 2392**

GERMANY (+49)

Foreign Exchange (cont)

Tanja Böttjer *Dealer, Spot FX* ☏ **332 2598**
Eckart Brandsaeter *Dealer, Spot FX*

Risk Management
Fax: 332 2780
Global Head   Rolf Sander ☏ **332 2781**

Fixed Income Derivatives / Risk Management
Global Head   Rolf Sander ☏ **332 2781**
Trading   Uwe Harms ☏ **332 2622**

OTC Equity Derivatives
Trading   Timo Kamberger ☏ **332 2150**

Settlement / Clearing
Fax: 332 2516
Head of Settlement / Clearing   Karl-Heinz Heischmann *Senior Vice President*
Fixed-Income Settlement   Peter Kresin ☏ **332 2851**
Derivatives Settlement   Roman Malinowski ☏ **332 2641**

Other Departments
Private Banking   Harald Groppel *SVP, Private Banking* ☏ **332 2301**
Correspondent Banking   Kirsten Discher *Senior Vice President* ☏ **332 2371**

Administration

Technology & Systems
    Wolfgang Löffler *Senior Vice President* ☏ **332 2841**

Legal / In-House Counsel
    Arno Lehmann *Executive Vice President* ☏ **332 2291**

Compliance
    Klaus Kellner *Assistant Vice President* ☏ **332 2451**

Public Relations
    Wolfram Bottmann *Vice President* ☏ **332 2281**

BULBANK
Representative Office

21 Grosse Bochenheimerstraße, D-60313 Frankfurt/Main
Tel: (69) 283 247 **Fax:** (69) 282 157 **Telex:** 413586

Senior Executive Officers
Representative   Antony Tonev

Caisse Centrale des Banques Populaires
Representative Office

Rossmarkt 14, D-60311 Frankfurt/Main
Tel: (69) 920072 00 **Fax:** (69) 920072 19

Senior Executive Officers
Representative   Eric Véronneau

Caisse des Dépôts et Consignations GmbH

Bockenheimer Landstrasse 51-53, D-60325 Frankfurt/Main
Tel: (69) 97133 0 **Fax:** (69) 97133 100 **Telex:** 4170875 CDCD **Swift:** CDCF DE FX

Debt Capital Markets / Fixed Income

Fixed-Income Repo
Head of Repo   Thomas Lay *Head of Repo* ☏ **97133 363** 🖷 **97133 102** ✉ **tlay@cdc-gimbh.de**
Trading   Michael Teuber *Repo / Lending Trader*

Equity Capital Markets

Equity Repo / Securities Lending
Head   Thomas Lay *Head of Repo* ☏ **97133 363** 🖷 **97133 102** ✉ **tlay@cdc-gimbh.de**
Head of Trading   Frederic Topin *Repo / Lending Trader*
    Michael Teuber *Repo / Lending Trader*

GERMANY (+49)   www.euromoneydirectory.com

Carl Kliem & Co
Head Office

An der Hauptwache 7, D-60313 Frankfurt/Main
Tel: (69) 92016 0 Fax: (69) 289 968 Email: kliem@kliem.de Reuters: KLIM Bloomberg: KLIEM

Senior Executive Officers

Chairman & Chief Executive Officer	Karl Michel Kliem
Financial Director	Peter Schlör ☎ 92016 320
Managing Director	Gerhard Klose ☎ 92016 460
Managing Director	Jan-Peter Kolk ☎ 92016 440
Company Secretary	Ulla Lehnert ☎ 92016 313

Debt Capital Markets / Fixed Income

Head of Fixed Income	Rolf Seibold

Fixed-Income Repo

Head of Repo	Jürgen Lindner Senior Executive ☎ 92016 328
Head of Trading	Claire Bruckner Broker ☎ 92016 595
	Alexander Sahm Broker ☎ 92016 580

Equity Capital Markets

Equity Repo / Securities Lending

Head	Jürgen Lindner Senior Executive ☎ 92016 328
Head of Trading	Claire Bruckner Broker ☎ 92016 595
	Alexander Sahm Broker ☎ 92016 580

Money Markets

Country Head	Peter Recknagel Broker ☎ 92016 513 F 297 9977

Foreign Exchange

Fax: 284968

Head of Foreign Exchange	Jan-Peter Kolk Managing Director ☎ 92016 440
	Robert Matuszewski ☎ 92016 477

Settlement / Clearing

Head of Settlement / Clearing	Jürgen Wick ☎ 92016 331

Other Departments

Correspondent Banking	Jan-Peter Kolk Managing Director ☎ 92016 440

Administration

Technology & Systems

Fritz Sayler ☎ 92016 350

Compliance

Karl Michel Kliem Chairman & Chief Executive Officer

Accounts / Audit

Peter Schlör ☎ 92016 320

CDI - Corporate Development International
Subsidiary Company

Formerly known as: Amanda Industriebet GmbH

Hamburger Allee 49-53, D-60586 Frankfurt/Main
Tel: (69) 795 091 0 Fax: (69) 795 091 33
Website: www.cdi-germany.de

Senior Executive Officers

Supervisory Board	Harald Klien ☎ 728 451
Chief Executive Officer	Hans Mayer-Vellner
Financial Director	Wolfgang Dimmel ☎ +43 (1) 512 9372
Managing Director / General Manager	Ewald Kopplinger ☎ +43 (1) 512 9372

Chase Manhattan Bank AG
Subsidiary Company

Grüneburgweg 2, D-60322 Frankfurt/Main
D-60284, Frankfurt/Main
Tel: (69) 7158 1 Fax: (69) 7158 2209 Telex: 411625 Swift: CHAS DE FX

Senior Executive Officers

Chairman of the Supervisory Board	Mark S Garvin
Deputy Chairman	Bruce Hannon

Others (Senior Executives)

Supervisory Board	Thompson M Swayne
	Herbert F Aspbury
	Carl Schneppensiefer
	Susan Steuerwald

476   Euromoney Directory 1999

www.euromoneydirectory.com GERMANY (+49)

Others (Senior Executives) (cont)
Management Board	Rainer Ulrich Gebbe *Chairman, Frankfurt am Main*
	Günther Himpich
	Reimund Becker *VP, Member of the Board of Management*
	Sylvia Seignette
International	Rainer Ulrich Gebbe *Chairman & Senior Country Officer*

General - Treasury
Head of Treasury	Günther Himpich *Treasury*

Relationship Manager
Financial Institutions	Manfred H Liebchen *Vice President*
	Gerhard Stadler *Vice President*
Corporate Banking	Detlef A Tamke *Vice President, Credit*
	Heiko Neumann *Vice President, Credit*
	Walter Gross *Vice President, Credit*
	Miguel Holler *Assistant Treasurer, Commercial Banking*
	Wolgang Cremer *Assistant Vice President, Commercial Banking*

Syndicated Lending
Loan-Related Activities
Trade Finance	Thomas Fricke *Second Vice President*
	Iris Schröder *Vice President*
	Anil Walia *Vice President*
Project Finance	Michael Brüggemann *Vice President*

Money Markets
Department: Money Market & Securities

Money Markets - General
	Heike Keller *Assistant Treasurer*
	Steve Dicks *Vice President*
	Karsten Holste *Vice President*
	Silvia Müller *Vice President*

Corporate Finance / M&A Advisory
Department: Corporate Finance

Other (Corporate Finance)
	Sylvia Seignette *MD, Member of the Board of Management*
	Annette Baumgarten *Vice President*
	Claus M Bergmann *Vice President*
	Ingeborg Bretana *Vice President*
	Susheila Gross *Vice President*
	Volker Nied *Vice President*
	Robert Dickler *Vice President*
	Manfred Scheeder *Vice President*
	Ender Tanar *Second Vice President*
	Wolfgang Fasbender *Assistant Vice President*
Mergers & Acquisitions	Reimund Becker *VP, Member of the Board of Management*

Global Custody
Department: Global Investor Services

Other (Global Custody)
	Waltraud Rohrssen *Vice President*
	Gudrun Hartmann *Vice President*

Other Departments
Cash Management	Holly M Johnson *Vice President*
	Gabriele Hahn-Thimm *Vice President*
	Henry von Moltke *Vice President, DM Clearing*

Chase Manhattan Bank New York
Full Branch Office
Grüneburgweg 2, D-60322 Frankfurt/Main
Tel: (69) 7158 1 **Fax:** (69) 7158 2209

Senior Executive Officers
Managing Director	Rainer Ulrich Gebbe

Others (Senior Executives)
	Günter Himpich

GERMANY (+49)　　　　　　www.euromoneydirectory.com

Citibank AG
Subsidiary Company

Neue Mainzerstrasse 75, D-60311 Frankfurt/Main
PO Box 110333, D-60038 Frankfurt/Main
Tel: (69) 1366 0 **Fax:** (69) 1366 1113 **Telex:** 4189662 **Reuters:** CIWA; CIEF

Senior Executive Officers

Relationship Manager
Germany / Austria

Fritz Menzel *Market Manager*
Kadita Tshibaka *Division Director*

Debt Capital Markets / Fixed Income

Domestic Government Bonds
Head of Trading

Thomas Weidmann *Senior Trader*
Markus Alexander Flesch *Trader*
David Stroud *Trader*
Mats Ahl *Trader*
Törbjörn Hamnmark *Trader*
Georg Schraut *Trader*

Non-Domestic Government Bonds
European & Non-European Government Bonds

Solveig Kulas *Sales* ☎ **1366 3220**
Christian Röckemann *Sales* ☎ **1366 3220**
Jochen Wydra *Sales* ☎ **1366 3220**

Bonds - General
Structured Bonds

Vijaykumar Vankandari *Sales* ☎ **1366 3880**
Gregor Wolters *Sales* ☎ **1366 3881**
Ajay Chadha *Sales* ☎ **1366 3220**
Christian Röckemann *Sales* ☎ **1366 3220**

Private Placements
Head of Sales

Ajay Chadha *Sales* ☎ **1366 3220**
Christian Röckemann *Sales* ☎ **1366 3220**

Fixed-Income Repo
Marketing & Product Development
Trading

Sales

Markus-Alexander Flesch *Regional Vice President* ☎ **1366 3200**
Thomas Weidmann *Senior Trader*
Mats Ahl *Trader*
Markus-Alexander Flesch *Regional Vice President* ☎ **1366 3200**

Risk Management

Fixed Income Derivatives / Risk Management
IR Options Trading

Marcus Schnabel *Head* ☎ **1366 9320**

Foreign Exchange Derivatives / Risk Management
Vanilla FX option Trading

Roger Alan Krüger *Head, Currency Warrants* ☎ **1366 3900**

OTC Equity Derivatives
Trading

Marcus Schnabel *Head* ☎ **1366 9320**
Frank Langer *Trader* ☎ **1366 3930**
Thomas Bauer *Trader* ☎ **1366 3930**
Alexander Simon *Trader* ☎ **1366 3930**
Dieter Lendle *Trader* ☎ **1366 3930**
Frank Mühlhans *Trader* ☎ **1366 3930**

Other (Exchange-Traded Derivatives)
Equity Index Warrants

Marcus Schnabel *Head* ☎ **1366 9320**

OTC Credit Derivatives
Head of Sales

Head of Trading

Solveig Kulas *Sales* ☎ **1366 3220**
Peter Krembel *Sales* ☎ **1366 3220**
Thomas Weidmann *Senior Trader*

Corporate Finance / M&A Advisory

Other (Corporate Finance)
Global Automotive, Germany & Austria; Global
Automotive, Central & Eastern Europe
Corporate Finance / Asset Finance Group
Corporate Finance / Real Estate

Reimund Becker *Head* ☎ **1366 1426**

Jürgen Friedrich *Head* ☎ **1366 1259**
Ulrich Reiss *Head* ☎ **1366 1367**

478　Euromoney Directory 1999

www.euromoneydirectory.com   GERMANY (+49)

Commercial Bank of Greece (Germany) GmbH   Subsidiary Company
Muenchener Strasse 47, D-60329 Frankfurt/Main
PO Box 160323, D-60066 Frankfurt/Main
Tel: (69) 271 007 0 **Fax:** (69) 271 007 26 **Telex:** 416 642 CBG-D **Swift:** EMPO DE FF **Reuters:** CBGG

Senior Executive Officers
Chairman of the Supervisory Board   Georgios Michelis ☎ +30 (1) 321 0706
Managing Director   Athanasios Koudounas ☎ 271 007 37
Managing Director   Ioannis Papadimitriou ☎ 271 007 11
Managing Director   Hans Joachim Franke ☎ 271 007 10

Debt Capital Markets / Fixed Income
Department: International Finance
Global Head   Tayyab Bokhari Manager ☎ 271 007 56

Government Bonds
Head of Syndication   Tayyab Bokhari Manager ☎ 271 007 56

Emerging Market Bonds
Head of Emerging Markets   Tayyab Bokhari Manager ☎ 271 007 56

Libor-Based / Floating-Rate Products
FRN Origination   Tayyab Bokhari Manager ☎ 271 007 56

Fixed-Income Research
Head of Fixed Income; Head of Credit   Tayyab Bokhari Manager ☎ 271 007 56
Research

Syndicated Lending
Head of Syndication   Tayyab Bokhari Manager ☎ 271 007 56

Loan-Related Activities
Trade Finance   Andrea Becker Head of Settlements ☎ 271 007 80

Money Markets
Tel: 271 007 85 **Fax:** 271 007 95
Head of Money Markets   Olga Kefala Chief Dealer ☎ 271 007 85

Foreign Exchange
Tel: 271 007 85 **Fax:** 271 007 95
Head of Foreign Exchange; Head of Trading   Olga Kefala Chief Dealer ☎ 271 007 85

Risk Management
Tel: 271 007 56
Head of Risk Management   Tayyab Bokhari Manager ☎ 271 007 56

Settlement / Clearing
Tel: 271 007 80 **Fax:** 271 007 35
Head of Settlement / Clearing; Fixed-Income   Andrea Becker Head of Documentary Credits ☎ 271 007 80
Settlement; Back-Office

Other Departments
Chief Credit Officer   Wolfgang Stobbe Manager, Credit Policy & Supervision ☎ 271 007 28
Correspondent Banking   Tayyab Bokhari Manager ☎ 271 007 56

Administration
Technology & Systems
                                         Claus-Dieter Bergmann Manager EDP ☎ 271 007 68

Legal / In-House Counsel
                                         Panagiotis Spiliakos Legal Affairs Manager & Compliance Officer
                                         ☎ 271 007 20

Compliance
                                         Panagiotis Spiliakos Legal Affairs Manager & Compliance Officer
                                         ☎ 271 007 20

Public Relations
                                         Tayyab Bokhari Manager ☎ 271 007 56

Accounts / Audit
                                         Gerhard Carl Manager, Accounting ☎ 271 007 60

Commerzbank AG   Head Office
Kaiserplatz, D-60311 Frankfurt/Main
Tel: (69) 1362 0 **Fax:** (69) 285 389 **Email:** webmaster@commerzbank.de **Telerate:** Recipient
Website: www.commerzbank.com

Senior Executive Officers
Chairman, Supervisory Board   Walter Seipp
Chairman, Board of Managing Directors   Martin Kohlhaussen

Euromoney Directory 1999   479

GERMANY (+49)   www.euromoneydirectory.com

Commerzbank AG (cont)

Others (Senior Executives)

Asset Management	Erich Coenen *Managing Director*
Private Banking	Kurt Hochheuser *Managing Director*
Global Operations	Dietrich-Kurt Frowein *Managing Director*
Treasury	Peter Gloystein *Managing Director*
International Banking	Norbert Käsbeck *Managing Director*
Personnel	Jürgen Lemmer *Managing Director*
Global Bonds / Equities	Klaus-Peter Müller *Managing Director*
Compliance	Klaus Müller-Gabel *Managing Director*
	Klaus M Patig *Managing Director*
	Axel Ruedorffer *Managing Director*

General-Lending (DCM, SL)
Head of Corporate Banking   David R Savage *Senior Vice President*

General-Investment
Head of Investment   David R Savage *Senior Vice President*
    Bernhard Heye *International Finance & Investment Banking*

Relationship Manager
Relationship Management   Rüdiger von Eisenhart-Rothe

Debt Capital Markets / Fixed Income
Department: Global Bonds
Global Head   Regis Fraisse ☎ **1364 7617** 🖷 **1364 7631**
Head of Fixed Income Sales   Hans Strüder *Global Head of Sales* ☎ **+44 (171) 418 4894**
    🖷 **+44 (171) 570 4483**
Head of Fixed Income Trading   Andreas Gautsch ☎ **1362 9315** 🖷 **1362 9112**

Government Bonds
Head of Sales   Nico Diedrich ☎ **1362 3883** 🖷 **1362 9783**
Head of Origination   Wally Höfer-Neder ☎ **1362 3971** 🖷 **1362 9419**

Non-Domestic Government Bonds
Head of Benchmark Trading   Magnus Stenberg ☎ **1364 7710** 🖷 **1364 8923**

Eurobonds
Head of Trading   Carsten Samusch ☎ **1362 2878** 🖷 **1364 1135**

Emerging Market Bonds
Head of Emerging Markets; Head of Trading   Gary Sheldrake ☎ **+44 (171) 256 6400** 🖷 **+44 (171) 570 4666**

Fixed-Income Repo
Head of Repo   Manfred Bier *Head of Repo & Finance* ☎ **1362 8440** 🖷 **1364 7731**

Fixed-Income Research
Head of Fixed Income   Klaus Holschuh *Fixed Income Research and Marketing* ☎ **1362 3215**
    🖷 **1362 9097**

Equity Capital Markets
Head of Equity Capital Markets   Mark Eban
Head of Sales   Jacqueline O'Neill
Head of Trading   Phillip Wale

Equity Research
Head of Equity Research   Richard Jeer

Equity Repo / Securities Lending
Head   Paresh Shah
Head of Trading   John Kolb

Syndicated Lending
Loan-Related Activities
Trade Finance   Rainer Schmitges
Project Finance   Frank Schepp

Money Markets
Tel: 1362 3583 **Fax:** 1362 4029 **Reuters:** CBKJ
Head of Money Markets   Thomas Beul ☎ **1362 3583** 🖷 **1362 4029**

Foreign Exchange
Head of Foreign Exchange   Alfred Schorno ☎ **1362 9178** 🖷 **1362 3067**
Head of Sales   Christiana Sironi-Sommer *Head of Sales Europe* ☎ **1362 7341** 🖷 **1362 9334**
Head of Institutional Sales   René Hansvend *Head of Central Banks & Institutional Sales* ☎ **1362 7343**
    🖷 **1362 9334**

FX Traders / Sales People
    Andreas Rüger *Head of Spot Trading* ☎ **1362 7398** 🖷 **1362 9334**
    Michael Keubgen *Head of Forward Trading* ☎ **(211) 827 2471**
    🖷 **(211) 827 2513**

www.euromoneydirectory.com GERMANY (+49)

Risk Management
Other Currency Swap / FX Options Personnel
Market Risk   Willi Schwarz *Head of Market Risk Treasury* ⓣ **1362 9203** ⓕ **1364 0470**
Credit Risk   Jernot Kleckner *Head of Credit Risk Investment Banking* ⓣ **1362 8561**
                                          ⓕ **1362 9860**

OTC Equity Derivatives
Sales; Trading   Mark Richardson

Corporate Finance / M&A Advisory
Head of Corporate Finance   David R Savage *Senior Vice President*

Settlement / Clearing
Head of Settlement / Clearing   Gustav Adolf Schibbe
Equity Settlement; Fixed-Income Settlement Norbert Haber
Operations   Gerhard Orthwein
                                          Klaus-Peter Frohmüller *Organization*

Global Custody
Head of Global Custody   Gerhard Orthwein

Asset Management
Head   Heinz Hockmann

Other Departments
Commodities / Bullion   Rudolf Duttweiler *Senior Vice President*
Chief Credit Officer   Wolfgang Hartmann *Senior Vice President*
Private Banking   Heinz-Ludwig Wiedelmann *Senior Vice President*
Correspondent Banking   Jürgen Carlson *Senior Vice President*

Administration
Business Development   Wolfgang Hönig
Head of Marketing   Heinz-Ludwig Wiedelmann *Senior Vice President*

Technology & Systems
                                          Konrad Röntgen

Legal / In-House Counsel
                                          Joachim Appell

Compliance
                                          Hermann Beyer

Public Relations
                                          Ulrich Ramm *Senior Vice President*

Corporate Communications
                                          Ulrich Ramm

Accounts / Audit
                                          Wolfgang Möller
Internal Auditing   Lutz Kirchner
Accounting & Taxes   Wolfgang Möller

Other (Administration)
Human Resources Group Management   Gottfried-W von Waldthausen
Human Resources   Bernhard Heye

CoreStates Bank NA   Representative Office
Gänsemarkt 44, D-20354 Hamburg
Tel: (40) 345 135 **Fax:** (40) 3554 9550

Senior Executive Officers
VP & Representative   Ursula Schulz

Others (Senior Executives)
                                          Ronald Haverkorn *Vice President & Regional Manager*

Creditanstalt-Bankverein AG
Brienner Strasse 9, D-80333 Munich, Bavaria
Tel: (89) 290745 0 **Fax:** (89) 290745 89 **Swift:** CABV DE MX

Senior Executive Officers
Treasurer   Nils Fiebig

Euromoney Directory 1999 **481**

GERMANY (+49)　　　www.euromoneydirectory.com

Dai-Ichi Kangyo Bank (Deutschland) AG　Subsidiary Company

Mainzer Landstrasse 46, D-60325 Frankfurt/Main
PO Box 100663, D-60006 Frankfurt/Main
Tel: (69) 170 0050 **Fax:** (69) 9710 0630 **Telex:** 4175815 **Reuters:** GDKB-E
Website: www.dkb.co.jp

Senior Executive Officers
President　　　　　　　　　　　　Takeshi Honda
Managing Director / General Manager　Gerhard Müller

The Dai-Ichi Kangyo Bank Limited　Full Branch Office

Königsallee 60D, D-40212 Düsseldorf
PO Box 200229, D-40100 Düsseldorf
Tel: (211) 1302 0 **Fax:** (211) 324 935 **Telex:** 8588149 DKB D
Website: www.dkb.co.jp

Senior Executive Officers
Managing Director / General Manager　Yasushi Sugino

Daiwa Europe (Deutschland) GmbH　Subsidiary Company

Mainzer Landstrasse 16, D-60262 Frankfurt/Main
Tel: (69) 71708 0 **Fax:** (69) 723 744; (69) 723 349 **Telex:** 411336 DAIWA D **Reuters:** DDAA; DDAC; DDAX

Senior Executive Officers
Managing Director　　　　　　　　Wilfried Schmidt
Managing Director / General Manager　Detlef J Amonath

Debt Capital Markets / Fixed Income
Eurobonds
Head of Trading　　　　　　　　　Curtis Mundstock *Trader*

Bonds - General
Yen Securities　　　　　　　　　　Takao Inoue *Trader*
　　　　　　　　　　　　　　　　Martin Riepe *Trader*
　　　　　　　　　　　　　　　　Detlev Weber *Trader*
　　　　　　　　　　　　　　　　Terry Dedmon *Trader*

Equity Capital Markets
Domestic Equities
Head of Trading　　　　　　　　　Nobuaki Hori *Trader*
　　　　　　　　　　　　　　　　Yoshie Matsumura *Trader*
　　　　　　　　　　　　　　　　Sakiko Anzai *Trader*

Warrants
Head of Trading　　　　　　　　　Nobuaki Hori *Trader*
　　　　　　　　　　　　　　　　Yoshie Matsumura *Trader*
　　　　　　　　　　　　　　　　Sakiko Anzai *Trader*

Settlement / Clearing
Settlement (General)　　　　　　　Wolfram Alhusen
　　　　　　　　　　　　　　　　Martin Schneider
　　　　　　　　　　　　　　　　Reinhard Fries

Administration
Compliance
　　　　　　　　　　　　　　　　Frank Lipke *Head, Compliance*

Degussa Bank GmbH

Weissfrauenstrasse 9, PO Box 110533, D-60287 Frankfurt/Main
Tel: (69) 218 02 **Fax:** (69) 218 2770 **Telex:** 411395 DGBNK D **Swift:** DEGU DE FF

Senior Executive Officers
Managing Director / General Manager　Rudolf Horst ☎ **218 2218**
Managing Director / General Manager　Jürgen Eckert ☎ **218 3179**
Managing Director / General Manager　Klaus Grasenick ☎ **218 3687**

www.euromoneydirectory.com GERMANY (+49)

Delbrück & Co, Privatbankiers
Full Branch Office

Neue Mainzer Strasse 75, D-60311 Frankfurt/Main
Tel: (69) 1331 0 Fax: (69) 1331 121 Telex: 416580 Swift: DELB DE 33501 Reuters: DELB

Senior Executive Officers
Chief Executive Officer — Christian Ratjen *Managing Partner*
General Manager — Klaus Henkel ☎ **1331 230**

Debt Capital Markets / Fixed Income

Domestic Government Bonds
Head of Trading — Heinz Goergen ☎ **1331 221**

Eurobonds
Head of Trading — Heinz Goergen ☎ **1331 221**

Equity Capital Markets

Domestic Equities
Head of Trading — Heinz Goergen ☎ **1331 221**

Convertibles / Equity-Linked
Head of Trading — Heinz Goergen ☎ **1331 221**

Warrants
Head of Trading — Heinz Goergen ☎ **1331 221**

Syndicated Lending

Loan-Related Activities
Trade Finance — H-H Holtermann ☎ **1331 206**

Money Markets
Global Head — Herbert Gerlich ☎ **1331 217**

Foreign Exchange
Head of Trading — Wolfgang Reibesel ☎ **1331 211**

FX Traders / Sales People
All Currencies — Alain Steele ☎ **1331 211**

Risk Management
IR Swaps Trading; IR Options Trading — Wolfgang Reibesel ☎ **1331 211**

Foreign Exchange Derivatives / Risk Management
Cross-Currency Swaps, Trading; Vanilla FX option Trading — Wolfgang Reibesel ☎ **1331 211**

Other Currency Swap / FX Options Personnel
— Alain Steele ☎ **1331 211**

Exotic Options (Barriers, Range, Timers, Digitals, Faders etc)
Trading — Wolfgang Reibesel ☎ **1331 211**

OTC Equity Derivatives
Trading — Wolfgang Reibesel ☎ **1331 211**
       Alain Steele ☎ **1331 211**

OTC Credit Derivatives
Head of Trading — Wolfgang Reibesel ☎ **1331 211**

Settlement / Clearing
Equity Settlement; Fixed-Income Settlement — Peter Ring ☎ **1331 114**
Derivatives Settlement — W.R. Hanisch ☎ **1331 113**
Foreign Exchange Settlement — Klaus Trumpf ☎ **1331 118**

Other Departments
Private Banking — Friedrich Krämer ☎ **1331 244**
Correspondent Banking — H-H Holtermann ☎ **1331 206**

Den Danske Bank Aktieselskab
Full Branch Office

Georgsplatz 1, PO Box 101522, D-20010 Hamburg
Tel: (40) 328 1160 Fax: (40) 3281 1638 Telex: 2165842 DDB H Swift: DABA DE HH

Senior Executive Officers
Chief Executive Officer — Heinrich Zink *Chief General Manager*
Deputy General Manager — Thomas Kettner

Euromoney Directory 1999 483

GERMANY (+49)   www.euromoneydirectory.com

Den norske Bank ASA

Gerhofstrasse 18, D-20354 Hamburg
Tel: (40) 357 5200 Fax: (40) 357 52021

Senior Executive Officers
General Manager   Ola Landmark

Deutsch Türkische Bank AG   Head Office

Hochstrasse 52, D-60313 Frankfurt/Main
Tel: (69) 9200 240 Fax: (69) 9200 2455 Telex: 412028 DT BANK D Swift: DTBK DE FF Reuters: DTBF

Senior Executive Officers
General Manager   Ahmet V Biyik
General Manager   Dieter L Ahl

Deutsche Apotheker-und Ärztebank eG   Head Office

Emanuel-Leutze-Straße 8, D-40547 Düsseldorf
Tel: (211) 5998 0 Fax: (211) 5998 77 Telex: 8584330 DAD D Swift: DAAE DE DD

Senior Executive Officers
Chairman of the Executive Board   Michael Rosenfeld ☎ **5998 112**
Chairman of the Board of Directors   Wilhelm Osing

Others (Senior Executives)

Jürgen Helf *Member of the Executive Board* ☎ **5998 243**
Günter Preuß *Member of the Executive Board* ☎ **5998 130**
Rudolf Reil *Member of the Executive Board* ☎ **5998 120**
Werner Wimmer *Member of the Executive Board* ☎ **5998 135**

Deutsche Ausgleichsbank (DtA)   Agency

Ludwig-Erhard-Platz 3, D-53179 Bonn
Tel: (228) 831 0 Fax: (228) 831 2255 Telex: 885422
Website: www.dta.de

Senior Executive Officers
Chairman   Eckart von Reden ☎ **831 2222** 🖷 **831 2828**

General - Treasury
Head of Treasury   Robert Fassbender *Senior Vice President* ☎ **831 3200** 🖷 **831 2833**
                        Dirk Kuhman *Vice President* ☎ **831 2227** 🖷 **831 2114**

Debt Capital Markets / Fixed Income
Head of Debt Capital Markets   Robert Fassbender *Senior Vice President* ☎ **831 3200** 🖷 **831 2833**
                                    Juliane Pagel *Vice President* ☎ **831 3204** 🖷 **831 2833**

Eurobonds
Head of Origination   Juliane Pagel *Vice President* ☎ **831 3204** 🖷 **831 2833**

Administration

Corporate Communications
Investor Relations   Martina Doherty ☎ **831 2765** 🖷 **831 2833**

Other (Administration)
Transaction Management / Documentation   Dietmar Penzler *Senior Vice President* ☎ **831 2484** 🖷 **831 2850**
Documentation   Petra Hagmann *Assistant Vice President* ☎ **831 2225** 🖷 **831 2850**

Deutsche Bank AG   Full Branch Office

Otto-Suhr-Allee 6/16, D-10585 Berlin
Tel: (30) 3407 0; (30) 3407 2382 Telex: 181308

www.euromoneydirectory.com GERMANY (+49)

Deutsche Bank AG
Head Office
Grosse Gallusstrasse 10-14, D-60272 Frankfurt/Main
Tel: (69) 910 00 **Fax:** (69) 910 34227 **Swift:** DEUT DE FF **Reuters:** DEUF (Dealing) **Cable:** DEUTBANK

Senior Executive Officers
Department: Investment Banking Division
Tel: 910 35282

General-Investment
Head of Investment
    E Arent *Director*
    V Bloemer *Senior Associate Director*
    A Brunckhorst *Director*
    J Delbrück *Director*
    M Fahnauer *Director*
    G Hansel *Senior Associate Director*
    C Hauser *Senior Associate Director*
    R Henty *Senior Associate Director*
    U Kröger *Senior Associate Director*
    M Lepach *Director*
    P Lerbinger *Director*
    A Meyer *Senior Associate Director*
    M Prill *Director*
    J Raasch *Senior Associate Director*
    R Rhein *Director*
    J Ritter *Senior Associate Director*
    B Schinnerling *Director*
    W Steinmann *Director*
    R Stüsser *Director*
    W Suhl *Director*
    C Thun-Kohenstein *Director*
    H Wintzer *Director*

Department: Relationship Management

Relationship Manager
Co-Head Relationship Management
    Christian von Thun-Hohenstein *Managing Director*
    Michael Zitzmann *Managing Director*
    Alois Arens *Managing Director*
    Erhard Arent *Managing Director*
    Wolfgang Büsselberg *Managing Director*
    Jürgen Delbrück *Managing Director*
    Klaus Dintelmann *Managing Director*
    Bernhard-Klaus Dott *Managing Director*
    Martin Fahnauer *Managing Director*
    Frank Hoffmann *Managing Director*
    Bettina Langenberg *Managing Director*
    Michael Lepach *Managing Director*
    Joachim von Schorlerner *Managing Director*
    Matthias Schwierz *Managing Director*
    Rainer Stephan *Managing Director*
    Rudolph Stützle *Managing Director*

Department: Senior Executives: Global Corporates & Institutions

Others (Senior Executives)
Head of Investment Banking   Josef Ackermann
Head of Global Markets   Edson Mitchell
Head of Equities   Michael Philipp
Head of Risk Management   Hugo Banziger
Head of Global Banking Services   Juergen Fitschen
Head of Structured Finance   Gavin Lickley
Head of IT / Operations   Marc Sternfeld

Debt Capital Markets / Fixed Income
Global Head   H-W Voigt *Managing Director & Co-Head*

Domestic Government Bonds
Head of Sales
Head of Trading
    A Burnell *Director*
    L Bjurstroem *Director Global Markets*
    J Excell *Director Global Markets*
    U Ullrich *Director Global Markets*
    T Wania *Director Global Markets*
    K Wenzel *Director Global Markets*
    T Baumgart *Senior Assistant Director*
    A Bok *Senior Assistant Director*
    J Frey-Kinzinger *Senior Assistant Director*
    H Kron *Senior Assistant Director*

GERMANY (+49)

www.euromoneydirectory.com

Deutsche Bank AG (cont)
Domestic Government Bonds (cont)

T Zirjacks *Senior Assistant Director*
O Reitz *Senior Assistant Director*
P Wrench *Senior Assistant Director*
D Crapanzano *Assistant Director*
S Ericsson *Assistant Director*
J Franz *Assistant Director*
C Ringler *Assistant Director*
H Schäfer *Assistant Director*
A Chwatal

Bonds - General
Domestic Bonds - Trading

W Endriss *Director*
M Rank *Director*
W Wittich *Director*
K H Baron *Associate Director*
P Friedmann *Senior Associate Director*
L Gotthardt *Senior Associate Director*
T Mehler *Senior Associate Director*
U Stockey *Senior Associate Director*
J Dietze *Senior Associate Director*
J Hartmann *Associate Director*
D Brauch *Associate Director*
T Kopp *Associate Director*

Jumbo Trading
G Hudalla *Senior Associate Director*
Credit / Jumbo Trading
H-W Voigt *Managing Director & Co-Head*
Jumbo Trading
J Schmiedler *Associate Director*
D Burmeister *Associate Director*
C Linnert *Associate Director*

Credit Trading
E Teller *Director*
C Inderelst *Senior Associate Director*
T Koegel *Senior Associate Director*
L Thierolf *Senior Associate Director*
M Wilhelm *Senior Associate Director*
J Friese *Associate Director*
G Guldan *Associate Director*
F Schmiemann *Associate Director*

Structured Products Trading
H Heuer *Senior Associate Director*
H Hennings *Associate Director*

Low Yielders Trading
E Lotz *Director*
G Bree *Senior Associate Director*
B Gericke

Asset-Backed Securities / Securitization
Global Head

U Hack *Director*
H-J Fritz *Director*
P Rek *Director*

Fixed-Income Repo
Head of Repo
Petra Ritter *Senior Executive* ☎ **91036 909** 📠 **91035 449**
Trading
Damon Robbins *Trading*
Thomas Schwabe *Trading*
Paul Clark *Trading*
Shirley Sudlow *Trading*
Mario Kruger *Trading*

Department: Global Markets Sales
Global Head
C Ganssmüller *Managing Director*

Bonds - General
Banks
T Adam *Senior Assistant Director*
Fixed Income Sales Germany
K Ebert *Managing Director*
Banks
S Linker *Senior Assistant Director*
V Roesner *Senior Associate Director*
I Soehngen *Senior Associate Director*
I Heindel *Associate Director*
A Sahm *Associate Director*
A Schilling *Associate Director*
W Zielasny *Associate Director*

Insurance Companies
W Tripps *Director*
K Lehmayer *Senior Associate Director*
D Glang *Associate Director*

Funds
S Abshagen *Director*
B Herzberger *Senior Associate Director*

www.euromoneydirectory.com   GERMANY (+49)

Bonds - General (cont)

	F Huwe *Senior Assistant Director*
	M Krebs *Senior Associate Director*
	B Koch *Associate Director*
	T Weinast *Associate Director*
Institutionals	G Schelihas *Director*
	W Ratke *Associate Director*
Branches / Retail	H Kemm *Director*
	K Patz *Senior Associate Director*
	M Gelger *Associate Director*
	G Roskothen *Associate Director*
International Institutions	J Clenshaw *Director*
International Institutions / Central Banks	T Scherer *Director*
	C Friebertshaeuser *Senior Associate Director*
	G Kassenear *Associate Director*
	S Ungert
International Institutions / France / Belgium / Lux	M Bertrandie *Associate Director*
	N Dholani
International Institutions / Netherlands	M Evertsen *Senior Associate Director*
	A van der Spek *Associate Director*
International Institutions / Switzerland	J Collins
	E Scheidt
Middle Market Desk ex Germany	M Ebert *Director*
	C Bierholz *Associate Director*
	L Giaccomazzo *Associate Director*
	S Hummen *Associate Director*
	J Meighoemer *Associate Director*
	C Staal
Austria	M Gebert *Associate Director*
	A Siadak *Associate Director*
Eastern Europe	M Weiss *Director*

Fixed-Income Repo
Sales   Pierre Brinitzer *Marketing & Product Development*

Syndicated Lending
Global Head   Fritz E Kropatscheck *Director* T 910 33806 F 910 39755
                                                          E fritz.kropatscheck@db.com
                                                          Matthias Gaab *Director* T 910 33853 F 910 39755
                                                          E matthias.gaab@db.com
Regional Head   Achim Klüber *Director- Scandinavia* T 910 35855 F 910 38793
                                                          E achim.klueber@db.com
                                                          Goetz Laue *Director- Southern Europe, Middle East & Africa* T 910 33320
                                                          F 910 38793 E goetz.laue@db.com
                                                          Thomas Wolff *Associate Director- Eastern Europe* T 910 39759
                                                          F 910 38793 E thomas.wolff@db.com
                                                          Christof Mürb *Associate Director- Germany / Austria* T 910 39283
                                                          F 910 38793
                                                          Petra Sütter *Senior Associate Director- Switzerland* T 910 33659
                                                          F 910 38793 E petra.suetter@db.com
                                                          Olivier Cébélieu *Manager- France, Belgium, Netherlands & Luxembourg*
                                                          T 910 36721 F 910 38793 E olivier.cebelieu@db.com
Head of Syndication   Traugott Weber *Senior Associate Director* T 910 32421 F 910 32427
                                                          E traugott.weber@db.com
                                                          Reinhold Berger *Associate Director* T 910 32422 F 910 32427
                                                          E reinhold.berger@db.com
                                                          Arnd Beck *Executive* T 910 33259 F 910 32427 E arnd.beck@db.com
                                                          Sandra Schmies *Executive* T 910 32423 F 910 32427
                                                          E sandra.schimies@db.com
                                                          Harold Leenen T 910 36061 F 910 32427 E harold.leenen@db.com

Other (Syndicated Lending)
Leveraged Finance   Christoph Cleve *Director & Global Head* T 910 33819 F 910 38939
                                                          E christoph.cleve@db.com
                                                          Reiner Löslein *Director* T 910 30443 F 910 38939
                                                          E reiner.loeslein@db.com
                                                          Tim Zundel *Senior Associate Director* T 910 33814 F 910 38939
                                                          E tim.zundel@db.com

Loan-Related Activities
Project Finance   Hans Herold *Director, Head of Project & Export Finance* T 910 39767
                                                          F 910 34636 E hans.herold@db.com
                                                          Klaus Michalak *Director, Head of Oil & Gas Team* T 910 34893
                                                          F 910 34636 E klaus.michalak@db.com

GERMANY (+49)   www.euromoneydirectory.com

Deutsche Bank AG (cont)
Loan-Related Activities (cont)

    U Bergholz *Senior Associate Director*
    Alexander von Bethmann *Director, Head of Heavy & Other Industry*
    910 33742   910 34636   alexander.bethmann@db.com
    Matthias Moser *Director, Head of Infrastructure & Telecom*   910 36727
    910 38678   matthias.moser@db.com
    Peter Schultze-Rhonhof *Director, Head of Power*   910 31405   910 32617
    peter.schultze-rhonhof@db.com

Leasing & Asset Finance
    Georg Bachmaier *Director*   910 33283   910 33682
    georg-a.bachmaier@db.com
    Hans-Jürgen Fricke *Director*   910 35823   910 33682
    hans-juergen.fricke@db.com

Other (Trade Finance)
Special Products
    Thomas Pachmann *Director*   910 30370   910 39768
    thomas.pachmann@db.com
    Andreas Schwarz *Director*   910 33394   910 39766
    andreas.schwarz@db.com

Forfaiting & L / C Syndication
    Albert Traunthaler *Director*   910 33861   910 33805
    albert.traunthaler@db.com
    Alexander von Orloff *Senior Associate Director*   910 33861   910 33805
    alexander.orloff@db.com
    Gundula Schürmann *Executive*   910 33861   910 33805
    gundula.schuermann@db.com

Money Markets
Domestic Commercial Paper
Head of Origination
    A Stumpf *Associate Director*
    H Balzer *Associate Director*

Eurocommercial Paper
Head of Sales   R Lock *Associate Director*

Foreign Exchange
Department: Foreign Exchange Sales Germany
Global Head   W P Sandmann *Managing Director*
Head of Institutional Sales
    M Klein *Senior Associate Director*
    W Packeisen *Senior Associate Director*
    M Kiel *Associate Director*
    G Graff *Senior Associate Director*

Corporate Sales
    A Karthaus *Senior Associate Director*
    K Lieder *Associate Director*
    H Roesler *Associate Director*
    D Hempel *Senior Associate Director*

FX Traders / Sales People
Branch Sales & Service Desk
    F Schmidt
    P Hett *Senior Assistant Director*
    R Fischer *Associate Director*
    U Erbs *Associate Director*
    F Knatz *Associate Director*
    O Krämer *Associate Director*
    S Mück *Associate Director*
    H-W Selkat *Associate Director*
    D Volke *Associate Director*

Risk Management
Department: Foreign Exchange Sales Germany
Foreign Exchange Derivatives / Risk Management
Global Head
    J Harder *Senior Associate Director*
    R Probst *Assistant Director*
    M Klein *Senior Associate Director*

Vanilla FX option Sales
    T Hauschild *Associate Director*
    K Franzisky *Associate Director*

OTC Equity Derivatives
Head   C Wagner *Director*
Sales
    C Hecher *Senior Associate Director*
    F Groessel *Associate Director*
    R Asselmann *Associate Director*

Department: Relative Value Group Germany / Austria
Regional Head   Marzio Keiling *Managing Director*

Other (FI Derivatives)
Banks
    Dieter Bauermeister *Senior Associate Director*
    Maj-Britt Arndt *Director*

www.euromoneydirectory.com GERMANY (+49)

Other (FI Derivatives) (cont)
                    M Memmert *Assistant Director*
Corporates / States   W Heiss *Director*
                    Hasso Spielberg *Senior Associate Director*
Branches   G Kothe *Director*
                    M Lünzmann *Senior Associate Director*
Austria / Switzerland   M Haas

Other (Equity Derivatives)
Banks   Dieter Bauermeister *Senior Associate Director*
                    Maj-Britt Arndt *Director*
                    M Memmert *Assistant Director*
Corporates / States   W Heiss *Director*
                    Hasso Spielberg *Senior Associate Director*
Branches   G Kothe *Director*
                    M Lünzmann *Senior Associate Director*
Austria / Switzerland   M Haas

Global Custody
Department: Custody Services
Alfred-Herrhausen-Allee 16-24, Eschborn
Tel: +49 (69) 9106 6992 **Fax:** +49 (69) 9106 8824 **Telex:** 40751411

Other (Global Custody)
                    Stefan Gmuer [T] **9106 9922**
UK   Roger Booth [T] **+44 (171) 545 5380** [F] **+44 (171) 545 1359**
                    James Cassidy [T] **+44 (171) 545 5375** [F] **+44 (171) 545 1359**
                    Veronique Georg-Deligny [T] **+44 (171) 545 5376** [F] **+44 (171) 545 1359**

Other Departments
Proprietary Trading   N Kaiser *Senior Associate Director*
                    K Sterzik *Director*

Deutsche Bank AG - Deutsche Morgan Grenfell Full Branch Office
Königsallee 45/47, D-40189 Düsseldorf
Tel: (211) 883 0 **Fax:** (211) 883 9222 **Telex:** 8588281 **Reuters:** DBDA (Monitor) **Cable:** DEUTBANK

Deutsche Bau-und Bodenbank AG
Taunusanlage 8, D-60329 Frankfurt/Main
PO Box 100649, D-60006 Frankfurt/Main
Tel: (69) 27112 0 **Fax:** (69) 27112 206 **Telex:** 411926 DBBD

Senior Executive Officers
Department: Board of Directors

Others (Senior Executives)
                    Ulrich Claßen *Director* [T] **27112 211** [F] **27112 204**
                    Hannelore Baentsch *Director* [T] **27112 212** [F] **27112 204**
                    Hans Jochen Erlebach *Director* [T] **27112 217** [F] **27112 204**
                    Ruth Witzel *Director* [T] **27112 218** [F] **27112 204**
                    Peter Lammerskitten *Director* [T] **27112 209** [F] **27112 204**
                    Barbara Killinger *Director* [T] **27112 210** [F] **27112 204**
                    Thomas M Kolbeck *Director* [T] **27112 213** [F] **27112 204**
                    Beate Labends *Director* [T] **27112 214** [F] **27112 204**
                    Gerd Link *Secretariat* [T] **27112 221** [F] **27112 224**
                    Silke Jörg-Hanzsch *Secretariat* [T] **27112 222** [F] **27112 224**

General - Treasury
Head of Treasury   Michael Breyl [T] **27112 411** [F] **27112 409**
                    Ulrike Kamenik [T] **27112 418** [F] **27112 409**

Debt Capital Markets / Fixed Income
Government Bonds
Head of Origination   Werner Pues [T] **27112 371**
                    Brigitta Gans [T] **27112 372**

Bonds - General
Real Estate Bonds   Gretel Caspar [T] **27112 415** [F] **27112 509**
                    Anette Jäger [T] **27112 420** [F] **27112 509**
                    Phillip Keele [T] **27112 421** [F] **27112 509**
                    Sabine Knauf [T] **27112 416** [F] **27112 509**
                    Norbert Schulze [T] **27112 419** [F] **27112 509**

GERMANY (+49)	www.euromoneydirectory.com

Deutsche Bau-und Bodenbank AG (cont)
Other Departments
Global Trust	Peter Schaffner *Credit & Trust Management* T 27112 379 F 27112 257
	Heidi Wüst *Credit & Trust Management* T 27112 259 F 27112 257
Administration
Head of Marketing	Engelbert Maurer T 27112 518 F 27112 902
Legal / In-House Counsel
Legal Department	Hannelore Eichler T 27112 377 F 27112 236
Compliance
	Hans-Jörg Schmitt T 27112 364
Accounts / Audit
Accounts	Stefan Sander T 27112 273
	Michaela Frank T 27112 560
Other (Administration)
Personnel	Gerhard Böger T 27112 361 F 27112 208
	Maria B Varvelli T 27112 362 F 27112 208

Deutsche Börse Clearing AG

Börseplatz 7-11, D-60313 Frankfurt/Main
Tel: (69) 2101 0 Fax: (69) 2101 3981

Debt Capital Markets / Fixed Income
Tel: 2101 3180 Fax: 2101 4306
Fixed-Income Repo
Head of Repo	Michael Jung *Head of Securities Lending* T 2101 4814 F 2101 4307
	E michael_jung@exchange.de
Marketing & Product Development	Gerd Hortung *Senior Executive, Collateral Management* T 2101 4704
	F 2101 4504
Trading	Martin Greenleaf T 2101 3180 F 2101 4306
	Monika Seip

Equity Capital Markets
Equity Repo / Securities Lending
Marketing & Product Development	Meike Dieter *Head of Marketing & Sales* T 2101 5321 F 2101 3711
	E meite-dieter@exchange.de

Deutsche Genossenschaftsbank

Am Platz der Republik, Frankfurt/Main
Tel: (69) 7447 01; (69) 7447 1685

Debt Capital Markets / Fixed Income
Fixed-Income Repo
Marketing & Product Development	Michael Weigelt *First Vice President* T 7447 1223
Trading	Michael Weigelt *First Vice President*
	Vincent Fleuriet *Assistant Vice President*
	Berud Kesting *Assistant Vice President*
	Sebastian Vinao

Equity Capital Markets
Equity Repo / Securities Lending
Marketing & Product Development	Ralf Decker *Vice President*

Deutsche Girozentrale - Deutsche Kommunalbank   Head Office

Taunusanlage 10, D-60329 Frankfurt/Main
PO Box 110542, D-60040 Frankfurt/Main
Tel: (69) 2693 0 Fax: (69) 2693 2490 Telex: 414163 DGZA D (General/Int'l) Swift: DGZF DE FF
Reuters: DGZA-F (Monitor)
Economics & Information Fax: 2693ext2104; International Division Fax: 2693ext2170/1; Trading Division
Fax: 2693ext2472

Senior Executive Officers
Chairman of the Board	Ernst-Otto Sandvoss
International Division	Claus-Dieter Homann *EVP, International Division*

Dealing effectively with the accelerating pace of change in European markets has become one of the major challenges of our time. Although change often leads to

DGZ serves a select, demanding clientele of corporations and financial institutions as well as governments and government agencies.

EUROPEAN SAVOIR-FAIRE

QUALITY RESOURCES FOR CHANGING MARKETS

dramatic shifts in priorities and ways of conducting business, new problems caused by change invariably spawn new opportunities requiring the strength and resourcefulness of the financial community.

That's where Deutsche Girozentrale comes in. DGZ is a central institution of Germany's Savings Banks Organization, the country's largest banking sector. Backed by substantial resources plus proven knowhow on a European scale,

The Bank's service potential covers a broad range of wholesale commercial and investment banking capabilities, including syndicated fund-raising operations. Moreover, DGZ provides the full spectrum of Eurobanking services through branches in Berlin and Luxembourg as well as a subsidiary in Luxembourg.

If you are looking for a banking partner with quality resources for changing markets in Europe, have a talk with DGZ.

DGZ – the small team with big resources

Deutsche Girozentrale
·Deutsche Kommunalbank·
Frankfurt am Main/Berlin

nusanlage 10, D-60329 Frankfurt am Main, Tel.: (49) 69-26 93-0, Fax: (49) 69-26 93-2490; Bismarckstrasse 101, D-10625 Berlin, Tel.: (49) 30-31 59 67-0, Fax: (49) 30-31 59 67-30; Luxembourg Branch: Boulevard Royal, L-2449 Luxembourg, Tel.: (352) 47 43 60, Fax: (352) 46 24 77; DGZ International S.A.: 16, Boulevard Royal, L-2449 Luxembourg, Tel.: (352) 46 24 71-1, Fax: (352) 46 24 77

GERMANY (+49)

Deutsche Girozentrale - Deutsche Kommunalbank (cont)

Others (Senior Executives)
Trading Division
Member of the Board

Public Debt Division

Gerhard Schleif *Executive Vice President*
Dieter Goose *Member of the Board*
Hans-Joachim Reichert *Member of the Board*
Manfred Zass *Member of the Board*
Hans-Georg Welkenbach *Senior Vice President*

Relationship Manager
Business Origination

Jean-Philippe Gachet *First Vice President*

Debt Capital Markets / Fixed Income
Department: Public Debt Division
Country Head

Hans-Georg Welkenbach *Senior Vice President*

Non-Domestic Government Bonds
International Origination - Public Sector & Banks
Domestic Lending
Department: Central Office
Global Head

Jerome Diver *FVP, Public Debt Division*

Volker Mohr *VP, Public Debt Division*

Günter Diener *Senior Vice President*
Gerhard Schleif *Executive Vice President*
Thomas Hartmann *Senior Vice President*

Domestic Government Bonds
Head of Trading

Michael Alt *First Vice President*

Eurobonds
Head of Trading

Peter Kapfelsperger *Vice President*

Bonds - General
New Issues / Syndication

Tillmann Fabry *Assistant Vice President*
Axel Rosenberger *Vice President*

Equity Capital Markets
Global Head

Werner Diekötter *Vice President*

Domestic Equities
Head of Sales

Hans Mauersberg *Vice President*
Dieter Glöckner *Vice President*

Syndicated Lending
Department: International Division
Country Head

Claus-Dieter Homann *EVP, International Division*

Other (Syndicated Lending)
Loan Syndication

Nikolaus Hasslinger *Senior Vice President*

Loan-Related Activities
Project Finance

Stephan Wagner *Vice President*

Other (Trade Finance)
Structured Finance

Wolfgang Kämpken *VP, Export, Trade, Aircraft, Leasing*
Angelika Beyer *FVP, Export, Trade, Aircraft, Leasing*
Thomas Kramer *VP, Export, Trade, Aircraft, Leasing*

Money Markets
Central Money Market Desk

Lutz Faulwasser *First Vice President*

Foreign Exchange
Department: Trading Division

FX Traders / Sales People
FX & Eurodeposits

Ernst Pullmann *Vice President*

Risk Management
Department: Trading Division

OTC Credit Derivatives
Global Head

Andreas Bamberg *Vice President*

Exchange-Traded Derivatives
FX Futures; FX Options

Roland Schulz *Vice President*

Other Departments
Economic Research

Jürgen Jäger *VP, Investment Research*

www.euromoneydirectory.com GERMANY (+49)

Deutsche Handelsbank Aktiengesellschaft
Head Office

Jägerstrasse 49/50, D-10117 Berlin
PO Box 080151, D-10001 Berlin
Tel: (30) 20266 0 **Fax:** (30) 20266 285 **Telex:** 303746 **Swift:** DEHA DE BB

Senior Executive Officers
Chairman of the Board   Heinz Arno Wascheck ☎ **20266 345**
Treasurer   Bernhard Dieken *Head, Treasury & Trading Division* ☎ **20266 304**
Others (Senior Executives)
    Harald Strümpell *Member of the Board* ☎ **20266 300**

Deutsche Hypothekenbank AG
Head Office

Georgsplatz 8, D-30159 Hannover
Tel: (511) 3045 0 **Fax:** (511) 3045 459

Senior Executive Officers
Chairman   Wolfgang Strutz
Senior Manager   Jürgen Grieger ☎ **3045 314**
Senior Manager   Wolfgang Hollender ☎ **3045 313**
Senior Manager   Thomas V Tucher ☎ **3045 312**
Administration
Other (Administration)
Marketing   Jürgen Morr *Director* ☎ **3045 580**

Deutsche Postbank AG
Head Office

Alternative trading name: Postbank
Friedrich-Ebert-Allee 114-126, D-53113 Bonn
PO Box 4000, D-53105 Bonn
Tel: (228) 9200 **Fax:** (228) 2818 **Telex:** 885692 PBZE D **Swift:** PBNK DE PP **Email:** direkt@postbank.de
Website: www.postbank.de

Senior Executive Officers
Chairman   Dieter Boening
Treasurer   Uwe Nagel ☎ **920 5200**

Deutsche Schiffsbank AG
Head Office

Domshof 17, D-28195 Bremen
Tel: (421) 3609 0 **Fax:** (421) 323 539 **Telex:** 244870

Senior Executive Officers
Member, Board of Managing Directors   Rainhald Bohnhoff
Senior General Manager   Wulf-Peter Schiering

Deutsche Schiffsbank AG
Head Office

Katharinenstrasse 13, D-20457 Hamburg
Tel: (40) 37699 0 **Fax:** (40) 37699 178 **Telex:** 214029

Senior Executive Officers
Member, Board of Managing Directors   Jürgen Bentlage
Member, Board of Managing Directors   Jens Blöcker
Member, Board of Managing Directors   Henning Winter
Senior General Manager   Hans Christian Sienknecht

DG BANK
Head Office

Am Platz der Republik, D-60265 Frankfurt/Main
Tel: (69) 7447 01 **Fax:** (69) 7447 1685; (69) 7447 1688 **Telex:** 412291 **Swift:** GENO DE FF
Website: www.dgbank.de

Senior Executive Officers
Chairman   Bernd Thiemann

GERMANY (+49)

www.euromoneydirectory.com

DG BANK (cont)

General-Lending (DCM, SL)
Head of Corporate Banking — Ludger Schönecker *Head, Acquisition Finance* ☏ **7447 6021** 🖷 **7447 6098**

General-Investment
Head of Investment — Norbert Bräuer *Head, Investment Banking, Fixed Income & FX* ☏ **7447 2010**

General - Treasury
Head of Treasury — Arnd Stricker *Global Head, Treasury* ☏ **7447 2000** 🖷 **7447 6690**

Debt Capital Markets / Fixed Income
Global Head — Norbert Bräuer *Head, Investment Banking, Fixed Income & FX* ☏ **7447 2010**
Willi Ufer *Global Head, Capital Markets* ☏ **7447 6394** 🖷 **7447 6206**
Regional Head — Martin Ziesse *Head* ☏ **7447 2608** 🖷 **7447 3716**
Head of Fixed Income Sales — Ralf Winkelmann *Head, Bank Sales & Frequent Borrower Desk* ☏ **7447 6534**
Angela Janßen *Head, Bank Sales Germany* ☏ **7447 2999** 🖷 **7447 6550**
Hubert Dänner *Head, Bank Sales Europe* ☏ **7447 3432** 🖷 **7447 6869**
Head of Fixed Income Trading — Roland Zemelka *Head, Frequent Borrower Desk* ☏ **7447 4800** 🖷 **7447 7278**
Other — Steffen Dahmer *Head, Domestic Bank Bonds / SSD* ☏ **7447 1840** 🖷 **7447 6367**
Eckard Arndt *Head of Credit Trading* ☏ **7447 1732** 🖷 **7447 3716**
Uwe Engel *Head, Documentation* ☏ **7447 2142** 🖷 **7447 1906**
Ulrich Walter *Head, Structured Interest Rate Products, Trading* ☏ **7447 1100** 🖷 **7447 6889**
Axel Sauer *Head, Consulting Capital Markets* ☏ **7447 4821** 🖷 **7447 7278**
Götz Feldmann *Head, Institutional Sales Europe* ☏ **7447 2839** 🖷 **7447 6890**
Basilius Dan *Head, Institutional Sales New York* ☏ **+1 (212) 745 1697** 🖷 **+1 (212) 745 1616**
Yojiro Takahashi *Group Head, Institutional Sales Tokyo* ☏ **+81 (3) 860 5473** 🖷 **+81 (3) 860 4870**
Martin Finger *Head, Short Term Bonds* ☏ **7447 6072**

Government Bonds
Head of Syndication — Stefan Hess *Head of Debt Syndicate* ☏ **7447 7051** 🖷 **7447 2884**

Domestic Government Bonds
Head of Sales — Vitus Lohmann *Head, Domestic Bonds* ☏ **7447 1836** 🖷 **7447 6367**
Head of Trading — Micheal Klein *Head of Government Bonds* ☏ **7447 1313** 🖷 **7447 6889**

Non-Domestic Government Bonds
Sales Head — Gina Leu *Global Head, Institutional Sales* ☏ **7447 2839** 🖷 **7447 6890**
Trading Head — Oliver d'Oelsnitz *Head, Fixed Income Trading*

Eurobonds
Head of Syndication — Kevin Moule *Head, Debt Syndicate*
Head of Sales — Gina Leu *Global Head, Institutional Sales* ☏ **7447 2839** 🖷 **7447 6890**
Head of Trading — Detlef Giebe *Head, Eurobond Trading* ☏ **7447 1732** 🖷 **7447 6745**

Bonds - General
Short Term Products — Thomas Schumbert *Head of Trading* ☏ **7447 6860** 🖷 **7447 7258**

Libor-Based / Floating-Rate Products
FRN Trading — Thomas Schumbert *Head of Trading* ☏ **7447 6860** 🖷 **7447 7258**

Medium-Term Notes
Head of Origination — Axel Pohlücke *Head, Equity Origination, Corporates* ☏ **7447 2692** 🖷 **7447 2612**
Head of Sales — Thomas Schumbert *Head of Trading* ☏ **7447 6860** 🖷 **7447 7258**

Fixed-Income Repo
Head of Repo; Trading — Michael Weigelt *Trading* ☏ **7447 1223** 🖷 **7447 6889**
Trading — Bernd Kesting *Trading*
Laurenze Payet *Sales-France*

Fixed-Income Research
Head of Fixed Income — Rainer Lenz *Head, Sales Research* ☏ **7447 2839** 🖷 **7447 6890**

Equity Capital Markets
Global Head — Rolf Michael Betz *Head, Investment Banking, Equities & Struct. Fin.* ☏ **7447 2015** 🖷 **7447 4901**
Head of Sales; Head of Trading — Kurt Bürkin *Head, Equity Sales & Trading* ☏ **7447 6128** 🖷 **7447 4915**
Other — Dieter Falkenstein *Head, Equity Listing* ☏ **7447 7662** 🖷 **7447 2179**

Domestic Equities
Head of Origination — Hans Heinz Trobitz *Head, Equity Capital Markets* ☏ **7447 2607** 🖷 **7447 4901**
Günter Kreher *Head, Equity Origination, Small Caps* ☏ **7447 7850** 🖷 **7447 1236**

GERMANY (+49)

Domestic Equities (cont)

Alexander Neumann *Head, Equity Origination, Small Caps* ⓣ **7447 3980** ⓕ **7447 1236**
Elmar Thöne *Head, Equity Origination, Small Caps* ⓣ **7447 1351** ⓕ **7447 1236**
Wolfgang Lawrenz *Head, Equity Origination, Corporates* ⓣ **7447 2615** ⓕ **7447 2612**
Axel Pohlücke *Head, Equity Origination, Corporates* ⓣ **7447 2692** ⓕ **7447 2612**

Head of Syndication — Norbert Roth *Head, Equity Syndication* ⓣ **7447 2145** ⓕ **7447 7471**
Head of Sales — Hans-Jörg Schreiweis *Head, Equity Brokerage & Sales* ⓣ **7447 7103** ⓕ **7447 1233**
Lars Hille *Head, Equity Brokerage & Sales* ⓣ **7447 7498** ⓕ **7447 6151**
Head of Trading — Stephan Hink *Head, Equity Trading* ⓣ **7447 2632** ⓕ **7447 7406**
Head of Research — Sabine Bohn *Head, Equity Research* ⓣ **7447 7774** ⓕ **7447 2201**

International Equities
Head of Origination — Hans Heinz Trobitz *Head, Equity Capital Markets* ⓣ **7447 2607** ⓕ **7447 4901**
Wolfgang Lawrenz *Head, Equity Origination, Corporates* ⓣ **7447 2615** ⓕ **7447 2612**

Head of Syndication — Norbert Roth *Head, Equity Syndication* ⓣ **7447 2145** ⓕ **7447 7471**
Head of Sales — Kurt Bürkin *Head, Equity Sales & Trading* ⓣ **7447 6128** ⓕ **7447 4915**
Hans-Jörg Schreiweis *Head, Equity Brokerage & Sales* ⓣ **7447 7103** ⓕ **7447 1233**
Lars Hille *Head, Equity Brokerage & Sales* ⓣ **7447 7498** ⓕ **7447 6151**
Head of Trading — Kurt Bürkin *Head, Equity Sales & Trading* ⓣ **7447 6128** ⓕ **7447 4915**
Head of Research — Sturm Herbert *International Equities Research* ⓣ **7447 2953** ⓕ **7447 2201**

Other (International Equity)
Trading — Stephan Hink *Head* ⓣ **7447 2632** ⓕ **7447 7406**

Convertibles / Equity-Linked
Head of Origination — Hans Heinz Trobitz *Head, Equity Capital Markets* ⓣ **7447 2607** ⓕ **7447 4901**
Axel Pohlücke *Head, Equity Origination, Corporates* ⓣ **7447 2692** ⓕ **7447 2612**

Head of Syndication — Norbert Roth *Head, Equity Syndication* ⓣ **7447 2145** ⓕ **7447 7471**
Head of Sales — Hans-Jörg Schreiweis *Head, Equity Brokerage & Sales* ⓣ **7447 7103** ⓕ **7447 1233**
Kurt Bürkin *Head, Equity Sales & Trading* ⓣ **7447 6128** ⓕ **7447 4915**
Lars Hille *Head, Equity Brokerage & Sales* ⓣ **7447 7498** ⓕ **7447 6151**
Head of Trading — Stephan Hink *Head, Equity Trading* ⓣ **7447 2632** ⓕ **7447 7406**
Kurt Bürkin *Head, Equity Sales & Trading* ⓣ **7447 6128** ⓕ **7447 4915**
Head of Research — Sabine Bohn *Head, Equity Research* ⓣ **7447 7774** ⓕ **7447 2201**

Other (Convertibles)
Equity Listing — Dieter Falkenstein *Head, Equity Listing* ⓣ **7447 7662** ⓕ **7447 2179**

Warrants
Head of Sales; Head of Trading — Kurt Bürkin *Head, Equity Sales & Trading* ⓣ **7447 6128** ⓕ **7447 4915**
Head of Trading — Stephan Hink *Head, Equity Trading* ⓣ **7447 2632** ⓕ **7447 7406**
Head of Research — Andrea Kolander *Financial Analyst* ⓣ **7447 2215** ⓕ **7447 7003**
Thomas Schmiegel *Financial Analyst* ⓣ **7447 6972** ⓕ **7447 7003**

Others (Warrants)
Financial Engineering — Berthold Grünebaum *Co-ordinator* ⓣ **7447 7035** ⓕ **7447 7406**
Equity Listing — Dieter Falkenstein *Head, Equity Listing* ⓣ **7447 7662** ⓕ **7447 2179**

Equity Repo / Securities Lending
Head — Kurt Bürkin *Head, Equity Sales & Trading* ⓣ **7447 6128** ⓕ **7447 4915**
Head of Trading — Stephan Hink *Head, Equity Trading* ⓣ **7447 2632** ⓕ **7447 7406**

Money Markets
Global Head — Arnd Stricker *Global Head, Treasury* ⓣ **7447 2000** ⓕ **7447 6690**

Domestic Commercial Paper
Head of Origination — Axel Pohlücke *Head, Equity Origination, Corporates* ⓣ **7447 2692** ⓕ **7447 2612**
Head of Trading — Thomas Schumbert *Head of Trading* ⓣ **7447 6860** ⓕ **7447 7258**
Volker Schmidt *Global Head, Asset & Liability Management* ⓣ **7447 6071**

Eurocommercial Paper
Head of Origination — Axel Pohlücke *Head, Equity Origination, Corporates* ⓣ **7447 2692** ⓕ **7447 2612**
Head of Trading — Volker Schmidt *Global Head, Asset & Liability Management* ⓣ **7447 6071**
Thomas Schumbert *Head of Trading* ⓣ **7447 6860** ⓕ **7447 7258**

Money Markets - General
Trading — Michael Schneider *Global Head, Treasury* ⓣ **7447 1550** ⓕ **7447 6368**
Foreign Yield Curve & Forwards — Rolf Reichardt ⓣ **7447 4400**

GERMANY (+49)   www.euromoneydirectory.com

DG BANK (cont)

Foreign Exchange
Global Head   Nicky Naseem-Ahmed [T] 7447 7140 [F] 7447 7088
    Norbert Bräuer Head, Investment Banking, Fixed Income & FX
    [T] 7447 2010
Corporate Sales   Gert Kohlmüller Head of Sales [T] 7447 3659
    Hans-Joachim Gretscher Head, Sales, Non-Banks [T] 7447 1850
    [F] 7447 3982
    Marianne Höhler Head, Sales, Primary Banks [T] 7447 1216 [F] 7447 3982
Head of Trading   Ingo Köller Head of Spot Trading [T] 7447 7540
    Michael Rauhut Head, Sales Service [T] 7447 4442
FX Traders / Sales People
FX Option Trading   Michael Engbers Head [T] 7447 1650
Risk Management
IR Swaps Trading   Armin Kalisch Head, Swaps, Caps, Floors [T] 7447 2854 [F] 7447 6869
Foreign Exchange Derivatives / Risk Management
Vanilla FX option Trading   Jens Maskus Head, Money Markets Derivatives Trading [T] 7447 4441
    [F] 7447 6368
Other Currency Swap / FX Options Personnel
    Michael Engbers Head [T] 7447 1650
Exotic Options (Barriers, Range, Timers, Digitals, Faders etc)
Sales   Kurt Bürkin Head, Equity Sales & Trading [T] 7447 6128 [F] 7447 4915
Trading   Stephan Hink Head, Equity Trading [T] 7447 2632 [F] 7447 7406
    Kurt Bürkin Head, Equity Sales & Trading [T] 7447 6128 [F] 7447 4915
OTC Equity Derivatives
Head   Berthold Grünebaum Co-ordinator [T] 7447 7035 [F] 7447 7406
Sales; Trading   Kurt Bürkin Head, Equity Sales & Trading [T] 7447 6128 [F] 7447 4915
Trading   Stephan Hink Head, Equity Trading [T] 7447 2632 [F] 7447 7406
Other (Equity Derivatives)
Financial Engineering   Berthold Grünebaum Co-ordinator [T] 7447 7035 [F] 7447 7406
Research   Andrea Kolander Financial Analyst [T] 7447 2215 [F] 7447 7003
    Thomas Schmiegel Financial Analyst [T] 7447 6972 [F] 7447 7003
Other (Exchange-Traded Derivatives)
Short Term Derivatives   Jens Maskus Head, Money Markets Derivatives Trading [T] 7447 4441
    [F] 7447 6368
Corporate Finance / M&A Advisory
Global Head   Rolf Michael Betz Head, Investment Banking, Equities & Struct. Fin.
    [T] 7447 2015 [F] 7447 4901
Regional Head; Acquistion Finance   Ludger Schönecker Head, Acquisition Finance [T] 7447 6021 [F] 7447 6098
Other (Corporate Finance)
Structured Finance   Heinz-Werner Sichler Head [T] 7447 6612 [F] 7447 6098
Asset Management
Head   Volker Schmidt Global Head, Asset & Liability Management [T] 7447 6071

Dresdner Bank Lateinamerika AG   Subsidiary Company

Formerly known as: Deutsch-Südamerikanische Bank AG

Dresdner Bank Lateinamerika AG
vormals Deutsch-Südamerikanische Bank AG

Neuer Jungfernstieg 16, D-20354 Hamburg
Tel: (40) 3595 0 **Fax:** (40) 3595 3314 **Telex:** 2142360 DL D **Swift:** DRES DE HL **Reuters:** DSBH
Website: www.dbla.com

Senior Executive Officers
Chairman & Managing Director   Helmut Fröhlich
Treasurer   Wolfgang von Tronchin General Manager [T] 3595 3500
Managing Director   Udo H Gubitz
Managing Director   Holger F Sommer
Deputy Managing Director   Horst Herrmann
Debt Capital Markets / Fixed Income
Head of Debt Capital Markets   Klaus Fertig Manager [T] 3595 3643 [F] 3595 3644 [E] klaus.fertig@dbla.com
Money Markets
Head of Money Markets   Jens Sierk Assistant Manager [T] 3480 410 [F] 3595 3644
    [E] jens.sierk@dbla.com

www.euromoneydirectory.com   GERMANY (+49)

Foreign Exchange
Head of Foreign Exchange   Bernd Schulze *Manager* ☎ **3480 420** 🖷 **3595 3644**
✉ bernd.schulze@dbla.com

Drueker & Co GmbH   Head Office
Bockenheimer Landstrasse 98-100, D-60323 Frankfurt/Main
Tel: (69) 170 099 0 **Fax:** (69) 170 099 11 **Email:** jhopkins@druekerco.com

Senior Executive Officers
Managing Director   Siegfried L Drueker

Corporate Finance / M&A Advisory
Department: M & A Advisory / Corporate Finance
Global Head   Siegfried L Drueker *Managing Director*

Other (Corporate Finance)
   Lorenzo Gatti *Vice President*
   Joachim Beickler *Vice President*
   Ulrich Graebner *Vice President*

DSL Bank   Head Office
Kennedyallee 62/70, D-53175 Bonn
PO Box 200310, D-53133 Bonn
Tel: (228) 889 0 **Fax:** (228) 889 624 **Telex:** 8869973 DSL D **Swift:** DSLB DE 3D **Reuters:** DSLA-C
Website: www.dsl.bank.de

Senior Executive Officers
Speaker, Board of Managing Directors   Stefan Jütte

Others (Senior Executives)
   Ernst Seulen *Member of the Board of Managing Directors* ☎ **889 810**
   🖷 **889 906**
   Wolfgang Schnieder *Member of the Board of Managing Directors*
   Werner Albert Schuster *Member of the Board of Managing Directors*

Domestic Corporate Business   Rainald Schomburg *Director* ☎ **889 670** 🖷 **889 557**
Domestic Private Business / Housing Loans   Hans-Joachim Krafft *Director* ☎ **889 283** 🖷 **889 908**

General-Investment
Head of Investment   Peter Jansen *Director* ☎ **889 360** 🖷 **889 963**

Department: Supervisory Board
Chairman   Dieter Wendelstadt

Debt Capital Markets / Fixed Income
Tel: 889 307 **Fax:** 889 881
Head of Debt Capital Markets   Peter Jansen *Director* ☎ **889 360** 🖷 **889 963**
Head of Fixed Income Trading   Hartwig Oberfeld ☎ **889 213** 🖷 **889 982**
   Heinrich Häseling ☎ **889 218**

Domestic Government Bonds
Head of Trading   Hartwig Oberfeld ☎ **889 213** 🖷 **889 982**

Non-Domestic Government Bonds
Domestic Public Sector Financing   Albert Baudisch ☎ **889 389**
   Vera Ahrond ☎ **889 966**
   Georg Briele ☎ **889 444**
   Rainer Koch ☎ **889 687**
   Stefan Wald ☎ **889 439**

Eurobonds
Head of Origination; Head of Syndication   Monika Dahlmeyer *First Vice President* ☎ **889 307** 🖷 **889 881**
Head of Trading   Sabine Bosch ☎ **889 223** 🖷 **889 881**
   Ulrich Baumann ☎ **889 214**
   Claudia Dahm ☎ **889 287**
   Anke Dingler ☎ **889 590**
   Claudia Fuentes ☎ **889 590**

Bonds - General
Domestic Funding   Claudia Burgner ☎ **889 217** 🖷 **889 982**
   Wolfgang Mallwitz ☎ **889 224**
   Dietlinde Sieg ☎ **889 212**

Department: International Division
Head of Debt Capital Markets   Horst Willemse ☎ **889 866** 🖷 **889 884**
Other   Wolfgang Dahremöller *Administration* ☎ **889 745**
   Iris Beissel *Administration* ☎ **889 506**
   Heinz Harpers *Administration* ☎ **889 591**

GERMANY (+49)   www.euromoneydirectory.com

DSL Bank (cont)
International Division (cont)

                 Joachim Kluthausen *Administration* T 889 494
                 Martin Michaels *Administration* T 889 364
                 Martin Peters *Administration* T 889 694
                 Claudia Reifenrath *Administration* T 889 451

Government Bonds
Head of Origination   Roland Fuchs T 889 490

Syndicated Lending
Head of Syndicated Lending   Horst Willemse T 889 866 F 889 884

Loan-Related Activities
Project Finance   Horst Willemse T 889 866 F 889 884
Leasing & Asset Finance   Heiner Kubny T 889 125 F 889 908

Money Markets
Global Head   Peter Jansen *Director* T 889 360 F 889 963
                 Thomas Jost T 889 940 F 889 982

Money Markets - General

                 Sandra Malischewski T 889 543
                 Markus Schlömann T 889 112

Foreign Exchange
Head of Foreign Exchange   Thomas Jost T 889 940 F 889 982

FX Traders / Sales People

                 Sandra Malischewski T 889 543
                 Markus Schlömann T 889 112

Risk Management
Global Head   Peter Jansen *Director* T 889 360 F 889 963
                 Guido Behrendt *Manager* T 889 220 F 889 963

Other (FI Derivatives)
Derivatives / Security Investments   Martina Mertens T 889 221
                 Werner Selz T 889 159
                 Petra Widmaier T 889 691

Other Departments
Economic Research   Reinhard Hanse T 889 567 F 889 909

Administration
Legal / In-House Counsel

                 Monika Wenger *Director* T 889 680 F 889 885

Public Relations

                 Ingo Husemeyer T 889 243 F 889 909

EUROHYPO AG Europaische Hypothekenbank der Deutschen Bank
Head Office

Formerly known as: Frankfurter Hypothekenbank Centralboden
         Junghofstrasse 5/7, D-60311 Frankfurt/Main
         PO Box 100848, D-60008 Frankfurt/Main
Tel: (69) 29898 0 **Fax:** (69) 288 469 **Telex:** 411608 FHBF D **Email:** mailbox.eurohypo@db.com **Reuters:** FHCPFE 1-2
         Bloomberg: KASSULKE MESSAGE
         Website: www.eurohypo.com

Senior Executive Officers
Chairman   Carl L V Boehm-Bezing
Chief Executive Officer   Wolfgang H Jordan
                 Henning Sieh
                 Bernd Knobloch
                 Gerd Koidl
                 Joachim Plesser
                 Wilmar von Wentzky
                 Thomas Veit
Treasurer   Friedrich Munsberg
International Division   Claude Ramon

Debt Capital Markets / Fixed Income
Department: Pfandbriefe
Global Head   Henning Rasche *Manager*
Head of Fixed Income Sales   Hans Diel *Pfandbriefe Sales*

Syndicated Lending
Department: Real Estate Financing / Syndication
Country Head   Sylvia Renner
Administration
Legal / In-House Counsel
                               Hans-Joachim Horstnotte *General Counsel*

The Export-Import Bank of Japan   Representative Office
Taunustor 2, D-60311 Frankfurt/Main
Tel: (69) 238 577 0 **Fax:** (69) 238 577 10
Senior Executive Officers
Chief Representative   Kenji Hashimoto
Others (Senior Executives)
                          Tanja Beck *Secretary to the Chief Representative*

The Export-Import Bank of Korea   Representative Office
Zeppelinallee 65-67, D-60487 Frankfurt/Main
Tel: (69) 97783 0 **Fax:** (69) 97783 16
Senior Executive Officers
Chief Representative   Sung-Soo Lim

Finacor Deutschland GmbH   Subsidiary Company
Lenbachplatz 2a, D-80333 Munich, Bavaria
Tel: (89) 554 783 **Fax:** (89) 5502 9517 **Reuters:** FING (Dealing)
Debt Capital Markets / Fixed Income
Eurobonds
Head of Trading   Axel Breidenbach *Head*
                          Georg Traunfellner

Equity Capital Markets
Country Head   Gert Pfannenstiel
Domestic Equities
Head of Trading   Manfred Schmid
                          Christoph Kugler
                          Monika Selg

Finacor-Rabe AG   Subsidiary Company
Hochstraße 43, D-60313 Frankfurt/Main
Tel: (69) 294 879 **Fax:** (69) 294 207
Senior Executive Officers
Director   Patrice Morain
Others (Senior Executives)
Management   Gert Pfannenstiel
                          Klaus Schwantge

Debt Capital Markets / Fixed Income
Domestic Government Bonds
Head of Trading   Michael Puschmann *Head*
                          Jens Gerisch *Head*
                          Michael Mills *Head*
                          Dieter Schreder *Head*
                          Karina Jenckel
                          Jorg Banzhaf
                          Amar Abu Tir
                          Peter Buckendahl
                          Arek Classen
                          Bernd Finke
                          David Forbes Gower
                          Denis Labatut
                          Sabine Neu
                          Jorg Raabe

GERMANY (+49)   www.euromoneydirectory.com

Finacor-Rabe AG (cont)
Domestic Government Bonds (cont)

Andréas Schneider
Christoph Weiss
Heinz Wilke
Maren Zumkley

Eurobonds
Head of Trading

Michael Berger *Head* ☎ 290 761
Richard Worland *Head*
Stéfan Achhammer
Arndt Busshaus
Gabi Trapp

Equity Capital Markets
Country Head

Gert Pfannenstiel
Stephan Krust
Lothar Weinmann

Domestic Equities
Head of Trading

Thomas Brandt
George Carl
Ulrich Eichhon
Rudiger Fischer
Ralf Gelzenleuchter
Nicole Goodson
Mike Oakley
Christina Sack

Head of Research

Stefan Svinger

International Equities
Head of Trading

András Karolyi *Head*
Ali Cavli
Pia Steinmetz
Sabine Stier

Other (International Equity)
OTC / DTB Equities

Manuel Hiriart *Head*
Theo Lackman
Herve Reisser

Settlement / Clearing
Head of Settlement / Clearing
Back-Office

Isabelle Sanchez *Head* ☎ 290 343 [F] 290 346
Wilhelm Hernandez Sampere
Claudine Roullet
Stéphanie Wilms

Administration

Compliance

Helmut Büttel

First Commercial Bank   Full Branch Office

Kaiserstrasse 29, D-60311 Frankfurt/Main
Tel: (69) 239 631 **Fax:** (69) 237 678 **Swift:** FCBK DE FF

Senior Executive Officers
General Manager   Han-Hwei Lik
General Manager   Mathia Bleuer

Debt Capital Markets / Fixed Income

Other (Libor-Based / Floating Rate Products)
FRN Syndication

Hannes Dietrich *General Manager*
Rong-Ko Chen *Deputy General Manager*

Robert Fleming (Deutschland) GmbH
Subsidiary Company

Im Trutz Frankfurt 55, D-60322 Frankfurt/Main
PO Box 100857, D-60008 Frankfurt/Main
Tel: (69) 15209 100 **Fax:** (69) 557 871 **Telex:** 4170402
Website: www.flemings.com

Senior Executive Officers
Managing Director — Johannes Busch ☎ 15209 113 ✉ johannes.busch@flemings.com
Managing Director — Nicholas Jefcoat ☎ 15209 115 F 15209 456
✉ nicholas.jefcoat@flemings.com
Company Secretary — Concepcion Roldan ☎ 15209 152 F 15209 455

Administration
Head of Administration — Jeltje Brückel ☎ 15209 114 F 15209 455

Compliance
Jeltje Brückel ☎ 15209 114 F 15209 455

Frankfurt Bukarest Bank AG
Head Office

Westendstrasse 28, D-60325 Frankfurt/Main
PO Box 160362, D-60066 Frankfurt/Main
Tel: (69) 971 413 0 **Fax:** (69) 971 413 29 **Telex:** 413421 **Swift:** FRBU DE FF

Senior Executive Officers
Managing Director — Roderich Koch-Pausz ☎ 971 413 10
Managing Director — Gheorghe Neagu ☎ 971 413 12

Syndicated Lending
Global Head — Herbert Munz *Head of Loan Department* ☎ 971 413 50

Loan-Related Activities
Trade Finance — Heinz Kirig ☎ 971 413 20

Money Markets
Global Head — Wolfgang Maske ☎ 971 413 40

Foreign Exchange
Global Head — Wolfgang Maske ☎ 971 413 40

Other Departments
Correspondent Banking — Herbert Munz *Head of Loan Department* ☎ 971 413 50

Administration
Compliance
Martina Hofmann ☎ 971 413 15

Frankfurter Bodenkreditbank AG

Mendelssohnstraße 79, D-60325 Frankfurt/Main
PO Box 100832, D-60008 Frankfurt/Main
Tel: (69) 7577 1 **Fax:** (69) 7577 500; (69) 7577 215 **Email:** fbk@i-dial.de

Senior Executive Officers
Chairman of the Supervisory Board — Hans Møller-Christensen
Chairman of the Board — Hans Christian Drost
Member of the Board — Preben Riisberg Lund

Frankfurter Sparkasse
Head Office

Neue Mainzerstrasse 47-53, D-60255 Frankfurt/Main
PO Box 100822, D-60255 Frankfurt/Main
Tel: (69) 2641 0 **Fax:** (69) 2641 2900 **Telex:** 411506 **Swift:** FRAS DE FF
Website: www.fraspa18822.de

Senior Executive Officers
Chairman of the Managing Board — Klaus Wächter
Vice Chairman of the Managing Board — Gerhard Kittscher

Others (Senior Executives)
Gerhard Gritsch *Member of the Management Board*
Roland Hemmerich *Member of Management Board*

Department: International Banking
International Division — Bernd Kalkhof *Director, International Banking*

GERMANY (+49) www.euromoneydirectory.com

Frankfurter Sparkasse (cont)
Other Departments
Chief Credit Officer Michael Winkelman Director
Administration
Head of Administration Ernst Schäck Director
Head of Marketing Herbert Staub Director
Technology & Systems
Technology & Software Norbert Zander Director
Legal / In-House Counsel
Legal Counsel Christof Harbeke Director
Other (Administration)
Payment Transactions Ernst Schäck Director
Personnel Willi Grimm Director

GeldHandels GmbH HPC Head Office

Formerly known as: GeldHandels GmbH BBT - Interbanque
Rossmarkt 11, D-60311 Frankfurt/Main
Tel: (69) 92060 0 **Fax:** (69) 281 120 **Telex:** 412109 **Email:** geldhandel@germany.cerf.net **Reuters:** GEHX (Index),
Telex: 416714 **Telex:** 4175839 **Telex:** 4175988; **Reuters:** GEHA (Deposits Dealing); GEHB (IRS/FRAs Dealing)

Senior Executive Officers
Chairman Christian Prince
Others (Senior Executives)
  Norbert Pichler Director
  Joachim Kaupisch Director
  Peter Helmreich Authorized Signatory

Debt Capital Markets / Fixed Income
Tel: 92060 30
Other (Libor-Based / Floating Rate Products)
FRAs Norbert Pichler Director
  Marco Lovett Dealer
  Mark Gray Dealer
FRAs - Link Desk Thomas Walsh Dealer

Money Markets
Tel: 92060 20
Other (Wholesale Deposits)
Domestic Market Joachim Kaupisch Director
  Rüdiger Tabel Dealer
  Jürgen Pichlmaier Dealer
Euromarket Joachim Kaupisch Director
  Angela Schittko Dealer
  Daniel P Adams Dealer
  Gerhard Wolfahrt Dealer
Link Desk Andrew Wilson Manager ☏ 92060 50
  Christopher Baucke ☏ 92060 50
International Financing Department Jean-Michel Petit Dealer ☏ 92060 40

Risk Management
Fixed Income Derivatives / Risk Management
IR Swaps Trading Heinz Peter Helmreich Director ☏ 92060 40
  Michael Otto Dealer ☏ 92060 40
  Thomas Walsh Dealer
  Frédéric Salomon Dealer ☏ 92060 40

Settlement / Clearing
Settlement (General) Gaby Horlitz Back-Office
  Monika Rothe Back-Office
  Anke Rösler Back-Office

Generale Bank Niederlassung Deutschland Full Branch Office

Christophstraße 33/37, D-50670 Cologne
PO Box 101551, D-50455 Cologne
Tel: (221) 1611 0 **Fax:** (221) 1611 261 **Telex:** 8882414 GEBA D **Swift:** GEBA DE 33

Senior Executive Officers
Chief Executive Officer Gerard Buteneers General Manager ☏ 1611 310
Financial Director; Chief Operating Officer Bruno Groten Managing Director ☏ 1611 255

www.euromoneydirectory.com GERMANY (+49)

Senior Executive Officers (cont)
Treasurer   Reinhold Beisler *Manager* ☎ **1611 224**
Money Markets
Country Head   Reinhold Beisler *Manager* ☎ **1611 224**
Foreign Exchange
Country Head   Reinhold Beisler *Manager* ☎ **1611 224**

Goldman Sachs & Co oHG / Goldman Sachs & Co Finanz GmbH
Subsidiary Company

Friedrich-Ebert-Anlage 49, MesseTurm, D-60308 Frankfurt/Main
Tel: (69) 7532 1000 **Fax:** (69) 7532 2800

Senior Executive Officers
Managing Director   Stefan J Jentzsch
Managing Director   Scott B Kapnick
Managing Director   Paul M Achleitner

Others (Senior Executives)
                                          Ernst E Tschoeke *Executive Director*

Debt Capital Markets / Fixed Income
Department: Fixed Income Division
Country Head   Robert Jolliffe *Managing Director*

Equity Capital Markets
Department: Equities Division
Country Head   Gregory T Hoogkamp *Executive Director*

Settlement / Clearing
Operations   Paul H Burd *Exec Director, Operations, Technology, Finance*
                                          Ernst E Tschoeke *Executive Director*

Administration
Technology & Systems
Technology   Paul H Burd *Exec Director, Operations, Technology, Finance*
                                          Ernst E Tschoeke *Executive Director*

GZB-Bank Genossenschaftliche Zentralbank AG
Head Office

Heilbronner Strasse 41, D-70191 Stuttgart, Baden-Württemberg
PO Box 106019, D-70049 Stuttgart, Baden-Württemberg
Tel: (711) 940 0 **Fax:** (711) 940 2940 **Telex:** 7224430 GZ D **Swift:** GENO DE SG **Email:** geno@gzb.bank.de
Website: www.gzb-bank.de

Senior Executive Officers
Chairman of the Supervisory Board   Ernst Geprägs
Deputy Chairman of the Supervisory Board   Rainer Märklin
Managing Director   Helmut Koschka
Managing Director   Manfred Biehal
Managing Director   Dieter Wößner
Managing Director   Rudi Schühle
International Division   Martin Baugard *Director*
                                             Helmut Aydt *Director*

Others (Senior Executives)
Finance Director   Albrecht Merz *Director*

General-Investment
Head of Investment   Siegfried Schön *Director*

Debt Capital Markets / Fixed Income
Fax: 940 2941
Head of Fixed Income Trading   Carl-Alfons Maser *Director*

Domestic Government Bonds
Head of Trading   Manfred Häfner *Director*
Head of Research   Werner Löffler *Department Director*

Eurobonds
Head of Trading   Manfred Häfner *Director*
Head of Research   Werner Löffler *Department Director*

GERMANY (+49)   www.euromoneydirectory.com

GZB-Bank Genossenschaftliche Zentralbank AG (cont)
Equity Capital Markets
Fax: 940 3340
Domestic Equities
Head of Sales — Siegfried Schön *Director*
Head of Trading — Manfred Häfner *Director*
Head of Research — Werner Löffler *Department Director*
International Equities
Head of Sales — Siegfried Schön *Director*
Head of Trading — Manfred Häfner *Director*
Head of Research — Werner Löffler *Department Director*
Syndicated Lending
Loan-Related Activities
Trade Finance — Werner Bodenmüller *Department Director*
Other (Trade Finance)
Project Manger, Euro — Christian Richter
Foreign Exchange
Fax: 940 2942
Global Head — Werner Bodenmüller *Department Director*
Corporate Finance / M&A Advisory
Head of Corporate Finance — Günter Eulberg *Director*
Head of Mergers & Acquisition — Siegfried Schön *Director*
Settlement / Clearing
Fax: 940 3337
Country Head — Michael Steinback *Director, Domestic Payments*
Global Custody
Fax: 940 2953
Regional Head — Rolf Sauer *Department Director*
Administration
Head of Marketing — Hans Joachin Trö
Technology & Systems
Armin Jäger *Director*
Compliance
Stefan Allmendinger *Department Director*
Public Relations
Hans-Joachim Tröscher *Department Director*
Other (Administration)
Personnel Department — Manfred W Schmidt

Hamburger Sparkasse — Head Office
Adolphsplatz/Gr Burstah, D-20454 Hamburg
Tel: (40) 3579 0 **Fax:** (40) 3579 3418; (40) 3579 7334 **Telex:** 2162609 HSPD **Swift:** HASP DE HH XXX
Email: haspa@haspa.de **Reuters:** HSPA (Dealing) **Cable:** HASPA HAMBURG

Senior Executive Officers
Chairman — Klaus Asche
Chief Executive Officer — Friedhelm Steinberg *Deputy CEO, Board, Managing Directors*
Karl-Joachim Dreyer *Chief Executive Speaker, Board, MDs*
Board of Managing Directors — Jürgen Ullrich
Board of Managing Directors — Günter Wolfertz
Board of Managing Directors — Werner Matthews

Debt Capital Markets / Fixed Income
Bonds - General
Bond Trading — Peter Schaar *Assistant Manager*
Jens Hackstein *Assistant Manager*
Matthias Loll *Assistant Manager*
Eckhard Ochsenhof *Assistant Manager*

Asset-Backed Securities / Securitization
Global Head — Heinz Dreves *General Manager*
Carsten Hoever *Deputy General Manager*
Head of Trading — Axel Jensen *Senior Manager, Securities Trading*

Equity Capital Markets
Other (Domestic Equities)
Trading — Adalbert Czundy *Senior Manager* ☎ 3579 4710 📠 3579 7590

www.euromoneydirectory.com GERMANY (+49)

International Equities
Head of Origination Monika Leck *Assistant Manager*
　　　　　　　　　Kerstin Lange *Assistant Manager*

Syndicated Lending
Department: Foreign Department
Holstenwall 20, D-20454 Hamburg
Telex: 211827 HSP D

Other (Trade Finance)
　　　　　　　　　Günter Klenke *General Manager* ☎ **3579 7239** F **3579 7333**
　　　　　　　　　Klaus Kruse *Deputy General Manager* ☎ **3579 7243** F **3579 7333**
Documentary Business　Karl-Otto Murach *Manager* ☎ **3579 7508** F **3579 7238**
Import / Export Finance　Heinz J Westphal *Senior Manager* ☎ **3579 7296** F **3579 7192**
Documentary Business　Juan Pietrek *Assistant Manager* ☎ **3579 7493** F **3579 7238**
　　　　　　　　　Uwe Jacob *Assistant Manager* ☎ **3579 7485** F **3579 7238**
　　　　　　　　　Sylvia Meyer *Assistant Manager* ☎ **3579 7252** F **3579 7238**

Money Markets
Department: Trading Department
Ost-West-Straße 75, D-20454 Hamburg
Country Head　　　Adalbert Czundy *Senior Manager* ☎ **3579 4710** F **3579 7590**
Other　　　　　　Wolfgang Rothe *Assistant Manager* ☎ **3579 4711** F **3579 4782**
　　　　　　　　　Birgit Kühn *Assistant Manager* ☎ **3579 4712** F **3579 4782**

Foreign Exchange
Department: Trading Department
Ost-West-Straße 75, D-20454 Hamburg
Country Head　　　Adalbert Czundy *Senior Manager* ☎ **3579 4710** F **3579 7590**
Head of Trading　　Andreas Rudolph *Assistant Manager* ☎ **3579 7598** F **3579 4782**
　　　　　　　　　Arne Schildmann *Assistant Manager* ☎ **3579 7597** F **3579 4782**
　　　　　　　　　Westgard T Schulz *Assistant Manager* ☎ **3579 7599** F **3579 4782**

Settlement / Clearing
Foreign Exchange Settlement　Cornelia Siebke *Assistant Manager* ☎ **3579 7490** F **3579 7067**
　　　　　　　　　Winfried Kortüm *Assistant Manager* ☎ **3579 7265** F **3579 7067**
Other　　　　　　Uwe Pape *Senior Manager* ☎ **3579 7262** F **3579 7293**
　　　　　　　　　Elke Bendt *Assistant Manager* ☎ **3579 7222** F **3579 7293**

Other Departments
Correspondent Banking　Jens Haberkost *Manager* ☎ **3579 7528** F **3579 7334**

Administration

Accounts / Audit
Accounting　　　　Christoph Pfitzner *Manager* ☎ **3579 7259** F **3579 7232**
　　　　　　　　　Ortrud Kroh *Assistant Manager* ☎ **3579 7483** F **3579 7232**
　　　　　　　　　Petra Waldleben *Assistant Manager* ☎ **3579 7269** F **3579 7232**
　　　　　　　　　Bärbel Temps *Assistant Manager* ☎ **3579 7275** F **3579 7232**

Other (Administration)
Foreign　　　　　Günter Klenke *General Manager* ☎ **3579 7239** F **3579 7333**
　　　　　　　　　Klaus Kruse *Deputy General Manager* ☎ **3579 7243** F **3579 7333**

Hamburgische Landesbank - Girozentrale   Head Office

Gerhart-Hauptmann-Platz 50, D-20095 Hamburg
Tel: (40) 3333 0 **Fax:** (40) 3333 2707 **Telex:** 214510 HLD **Swift:** HALA DE HH **Email:** info@hamburglb.de
Reuters: HHLB **Cable:** LANDESBANK HAMBURG
International Telex: 214515; **Reuters:** HLHM
Website: www.hamburglb.de

Senior Executive Officers
Chairman, Board of Managing Directors　Alexander Stuhlmann ☎ **3333 2955** F **3333 1100**
Deputy Chairman, Board of Managing Directors　Peter Rieck ☎ **3333 2951** F **3333 3092**

Others (Senior Executives)
Director　　　　　Christian Baldenius *Board of Managing Directors* ☎ **3333 2953** F **3333 1101**
　　　　　　　　　Ulf Gänger *Board of Managing Directors* ☎ **3333 2952** F **3333 1101**
　　　　　　　　　Uwe Kruschinski *Board of Managing Directors* ☎ **3333 2954** F **3333 3092**

GERMANY (+49)   www.euromoneydirectory.com

Hanil Bank (Deutschland) GmbH
Subsidiary Company

Mainzer Landstrasse 46, D-60325 Frankfurt/Main
Tel: (69) 971 216 0 **Fax:** (69) 971 216 33 **Telex:** 416847 HNLBK D **Swift:** HANI DE FF

Senior Executive Officers
Managing Director   Hyun-Soo Park ☎ 971 216 11
Managing Director   Jürgen Klimm ☎ 971 216 10

Syndicated Lending
Country Head   Y C Kim *Manager* ☎ 971 216 23

Money Markets
Country Head   Y C Kim *Manager* ☎ 971 216 23

Other Departments
Correspondent Banking   Y C Kim *Manager* ☎ 971 216 23

Hauck & Aufhäuser Privatbankiers KGaA

Kaiserstraße 24, D-60311 Frankfurt/Main
Tel: (69) 2161 1 **Fax:** (69) 2161 340 **Telex:** 411061 **Swift:** HAUK DE FF

Senior Executive Officers
Others (Senior Executives)
Fully Liable Partners   Jörg-E Cramer *Managing Partner* ☎ 2161 400 F 2161 453
                             Peter Gatti *Managing Partner* ☎ 2161 220 F 2161 453
                             Alfred Junker *Managing Partner* ☎ 2393 2500 F 2393 2019
                             Helmut Schreyer *Managing Partner* ☎ 2393 2007 F 2393 2019

Hohenzollerische Landesbank-Kreissparkasse
Head Office

Leopoldplatz 5, D-72488 Sigmaringen, Baden Württemberg
PO Box 1454, Sigmaringen, Baden Württemberg
Tel: (7571) 103 0 **Fax:** (7571) 103 270; (7571) 103 264 **Telex:** 0732517 **Swift:** SOLA DE ST
Email: info@ksk-sigmaringen.de
Website: www.ksk-sigmaringen.de

Senior Executive Officers
Managing Director   Wolfgang Hahn
Deputy Managing Director   Reinhard Brunner
Deputy Managing Director   Lothar Wiedmann
Deputy Managing Director   Hubert Seiffer
General Manager   Ottmar Stoerkle
International Division   Albert Rebholz *Manager, Foreign Department*

Hypothekenbank in Essen AG
Head Office

Gildehofstrasse 1, D-45127 Essen
Tel: (201) 8135 0 **Fax:** (201) 8135 499; (201) 8135 399 **Email:** essenhyp@t-online.de
Website: www.essenhyp.de

Senior Executive Officers
Chairman   Hubert Schulte-Kemper ☎ 8135 301

Others (Senior Executives)
                             Wolfgang H Müller *Member of the Board of Managing Directors*
                             ☎ 8135 484
                             Erhard Tiemann *Member of the Board of Managing Directors* ☎ 8135 311
                             Gerhard Walter *Member of the Board of Managing Directors* ☎ 8315 321
                             Harald Pohl *Executive Vice President* ☎ 8135 407
                             Hans-Jürgen Kröncke *Executive Vice President* ☎ 8135 410

General Treasury
Head of Treasury   Thomas Kaysh *Head of Treasury* F 8135 360

Debt Capital Markets / Fixed Income
Global Head   Thomas Kaysh *Head of Treasury* F 8135 360
Country Head   Günther Pless F 8135 365
                             Heinrich Strack F 8135 366

Eurobonds
Head of Origination   Thomas Kaysh *Head of Treasury* F 8135 360

Libor-Based / Floating-Rate Products
FRN Origination — Thomas Kaysh Head of Treasury [E] 8135 360

Medium-Term Notes
Head of Origination — Thomas Kaysh Head of Treasury [E] 8135 360

Equity Capital Markets
Global Head — Norbert Boddenberg Director [T] 8135 515

Domestic Equities
Head of Origination — Norbert Boddenberg Director [T] 8135 515

Syndicated Lending
Global Head — Hans-Jürgen Kröncke Executive Vice President [T] 8135 410

Risk Management
Fixed Income Derivatives / Risk Management
Regional Head — Thomas Kaysh Head of Treasury [E] 8135 360

Administration
Thomas Reddig [T] 8135 402

Public Relations
Ute Gibbels [T] 8135 495

HypoVereinsbank (Bayerische Hypo und Vereinsbank AG)

Am Eisbach 3, D-80311 Munich, Bavaria
Tel: (89) 3781 2503; (89) 3781 3780 Fax: (89) 3781 3978 Email: name1.name2@hypovereinsbank.de

Debt Capital Markets / Fixed Income
Tel: 378 14193 Fax: 378 13978

Fixed-Income Repo
Marketing & Product Development — Claudia Schindler [T] 3781 4082 [E] claudia.schindler@hypovereinsbank.de
Trading — Peter Borowski Trader [T] 3781 4174
[E] peter.borowski@hypovereinsbank.de
Ines Weirich Assistant [T] 3781 4082 [E] ines.weirich@hypovereinsbank.de
Harald Endres Trader [T] 3781 7657 [E] harald.endres@hypovereinsbank.de
Harald Gay Trader [T] 3781 4158 [E] harald.gay@hypovereinsbank.de
Cornelia Lagers Trader [T] 3781 7653
[E] cornelia.lagers@hypovereinsbank.de
Arne Theia Trader [T] 3781 7655 [E] arne.theia@hypovereinsbank.de
Thomas Werkle Trader [T] 3781 4164
[E] thomas.werkle@hypovereinsbank.de

Equity Capital Markets
Tel: 3781 2503 Fax: 3781 3978

Equity Repo / Securities Lending
Marketing & Product Development — Claudia Schindler [T] 3781 4082 [E] claudia.schindler@hypovereinsbank.de

Ibero Platina Bank AG — Head Office

Formerly known as: Ibero-Amerika Bank AG

Domshof 14/15, D-28195 Bremen
PO Box 104509, D-28045 Bremen
Tel: (421) 3665 0 Fax: (421) 3665 260 Telex: 244273 Swift: IABK DE HB Email: iberobank@ibero.de

Senior Executive Officers
Member, Board of Managing Directors — Frank Bürsing [T] 3665 100 [F] 3665 111
Member, Board of Managing Directors — Christian v Mecklenburg [T] (40) 32902 34 [F] (40) 32902 45

Others (Senior Executives)
Treasurer — Dieter Noltenius Deputy Member, Board of Managing Directors [T] 3665 120 [F] 3665 111

Debt Capital Markets / Fixed Income
Department: Debt Capital Markets / Fixed-Income
Schäuenburgstrasse 32, D-20095, Hamburg
Fax: +49 (40) 32902 45
Global Head — Christian v Mecklenburg Member, Board of Managing Directors
[T] (40) 32902 34 [F] (40) 32902 45

Domestic Government Bonds
Head of Sales — Klaus Weber Manager [T] (40) 32902 23
Head of Trading — Sandra Labahn [T] (40) 32902 35

Non-Domestic Government Bonds
Guy Aufenacker [T] (40) 32902 37

GERMANY (+49) www.euromoneydirectory.com

Ibero Platina Bank AG (cont)

Eurobonds
Head of Sales — Michael Neben *Manager* ☏ **(40) 32902 38**
Head of Trading — Sandra Labahn ☏ **(40) 32902 35**

Money Markets
Tel: 3665 140 **Fax:** 3665 150
Global Head — Raymonders Stegemann *Manager* ☏ **3665 140**

Wholesale Deposits
Marketing — Raymonders Stegemann *Manager* ☏ **3665 140**
Department: Money Markets
Schauenburgerstrasse 32, 20095 Hamburg
Fax: +49 (40) 32902 45

Domestic Commercial Paper
Head of Sales — Klaus Weber *Manager* ☏ **(40) 32902 23**
Head of Trading — Sandra Labahn ☏ **(40) 32902 35**

Eurocommercial Paper
Head of Sales — Klaus Weber *Manager* ☏ **(40) 32902 23**
Head of Trading — Sandra Labahn ☏ **(40) 32902 35**

Foreign Exchange
Fax: 3665 150
Global Head — Dieter Noltenius *Deputy Member, Board of Managing Directors* ☏ **3665 120**
🖷 **3665 111**

FX Traders / Sales People
Volker Weber ☏ **3665 144**
Raymonders Stegemann *Manager* ☏ **3665 140**

Risk Management
Tel: 3665 140 **Fax:** 3665 150
Global Head — Dieter Noltenius *Deputy Member, Board of Managing Directors* ☏ **3665 120**
🖷 **3665 111**

Fixed Income Derivatives / Risk Management
Global Head; IR Swaps Sales / Marketing; IR — Raymonders Stegemann *Manager* ☏ **3665 140**
Swaps Trading; IR Options Sales / Marketing;
IR Options Trading

Foreign Exchange Derivatives / Risk Management
Cross-Currency Swaps, Sales / Marketing; — Raymonders Stegemann *Manager* ☏ **3665 140**
Cross-Currency Swaps, Trading

Other Currency Swap / FX Options Personnel
Raymonders Stegemann *Manager* ☏ **3665 140**

Settlement / Clearing
Department: Settlement / Clearing
Schauenburgerstrasse 32, D-20095 Hamburg
Tel: +49 (40) 32902 0 **Fax:** +49 (40) 32902 45
Regional Head — Monica Schlottau *Manager* ☏ **(40) 32902 15** 🖷 **(40) 32902 48**

IKB Deutsche Industriebank AG *Subsidiary Company*

Wilhelm-Bötzkes-Strasse 1, D-40474 Düsseldorf
PO Box 101118, D-40002 Düsseldorf
Tel: (211) 8221 0 **Fax:** (211) 8221 559
Website: www.ikb.de

Senior Executive Officers
Chairman — Alexander von Tippelskirch

Others (Senior Executives)
Board of Directors — Joachim Neupel
Stefan Ortseifen
Georg-Jesko von Puttkamer

General - Treasury
Head of Treasury — Winfried Reinke

Debt Capital Markets / Fixed Income
Head of Debt Capital Markets — Michael Brown *Director*
Gerd Neubeck *Director*

Other (Fixed Income)
Bernd Honermeyer *Dealer*
Gunter Schmidts *Dealer*
Gisbert Schulz *Dealer*

Equity Capital Markets
Head of Equity Capital Markets Gerd Neubeck *Director*
Administration
Public Relations
Investor Relations & Press Jörg Chittka ☎ **8221 4985**
 Gert Schmidt *Director*

Industriebank von Japan (Deutschland) AG   Full Branch Office
Immermannstrasse 45, D-40210 Düsseldorf
Tel: (211) 1683 0 **Fax:** (211) 365 602 **Telex:** 8582442
Senior Executive Officers
General Manager Mr Kitamura

Industriebank von Japan (Deutschland) AG   Subsidiary Company
Taunustor 2, D-60311 Frankfurt/Main
Tel: (69) 27282 0 **Fax:** (69) 27282 512 **Telex:** 414939 **Email:** info@ibjg.de **Reuters:** GIBJ-M
Senior Executive Officers
Chairman Tetsuo Narukawa
Debt Capital Markets / Fixed Income
Head of Fixed Income Keita Tanahashi *Deputy General Manager*
Money Markets
Head of Money Markets Naofumi Yamamura

ING Bank   Full Branch Office
Friedrichstrasse 2-6, D-60323 Frankfurt/Main
PO Box 170361, Frankfurt/Main
Tel: (69) 7169 0 **Fax:** (69) 7169 1550 **Telex:** 413408 INGB D **Swift:** INGB DE HH
Senior Executive Officers
Country Manager Gerald Bumharter
Others (Senior Executives)
Global Clients Peter Stappen *Deputy General Manager*

ING Barings Futures & Options Clearing Services
Escherheimer Landstrasse 10, 7th Floor, D-60322 Frankfurt/Main
Tel: (69) 5967 8314 **Fax:** (69) 5967 8377
Senior Executive Officers
Director Ab ter Horst

Intercapital plc
Stephanstrasse 3, D-60313 Frankfurt/Main
Tel: (69) 13 009 **Fax:** (69) 290 394
Senior Executive Officers
Others (Senior Executives)
 Hans Goehtz

INVESCO Asset Management Deutschland GmbH   Bank Subsidiary
Bleichstrasse 60/62, D-60313 Frankfurt/Main
Tel: (69) 29807 400 **Fax:** (69) 29807 178; (69) 29807 352 **Telex:** 410 190
Senior Executive Officers
Chairman, Supervisory Board Wolfgang Seiler ☎ **29807 226**
Chief Executive Officer Ralf Lochmüller ☎ **29807 239**
Managing Director / General Manager Volker H Friedrich

GERMANY (+49)   www.euromoneydirectory.com

INVESCO Asset Management Deutschland GmbH (cont)
Asset Management
Other (Asset Management)
Currency   Herwig Prielipp *Senior Portfolio Manager* ☎ **29807 187**
Bonds   Jörg Bartenstein *Senior Portfolio Manager* ☎ **29807 110**
                              Burkhard Allgeier *Portfolio Manager* ☎ **29807 234**
Equity Portfolio Management   Bernhard Langer *Head* ☎ **29807 310**
Equity   Rainer Buth *Senior Portfolio Manager* ☎ **29807 189**
                              Karl Fickel *Senior Portfolio Manager* ☎ **29807 312**
                              Torsten Haufe *Portfolio Manager* ☎ **29807 230**
                              Margit Bayer *Senior Portfolio Manager* ☎ **29807 256**
                              Michael Fraikin *Senior Portfolio Manager* ☎ **29807 138**

Other Departments
Economic Research   Rainer Schröder *Head, Macro Research* ☎ **29807 329**
                              Karl-Georg Bayer *Head, Quantitative Research* ☎ **29807 174**

Other Departments
Macro Quantitative Research   Rainer Schröder *Head, Macro Research* ☎ **29807 329**
                              Karl-Georg Bayer *Head, Quantitative Research* ☎ **29807 174**

INVESCO Bank Deutschland OHG   Subsidiary Company

Bleichstrasse 60/62, D-60313 Frankfurt/Main
PO Box 100354, D-60003 Frankfurt/Main
Tel: (69) 29807 0 **Fax:** (69) 29807 159 **Telex:** 4185862 **Swift:** BLFL DE FF **Email:** silke.roth@lgt-bank.com

Senior Executive Officers
Chairman   Wolfgang Seiler ☎ **29807 226**
Chief Executive Officer   Günter Goldhahn ☎ **29807 102**
Managing Director / General Manager   Ralf Lochmüller ☎ **29807 239**
Managing Director / General Manager   Volker Friedrich ☎ **29807 188**

The Japan Development Bank   Representative Office

Mainzer Landstrasse 46, D-60325 Frankfurt/Main
Tel: (69) 719 176 0 **Fax:** (69) 719 176 15 **Telex:** 412946 JDBF **Cable:** JADEBANK FRANKFU

Senior Executive Officers
Chief Representative   Yuichiro Miwa
Deputy Chief Representative   Senta Hoji
Representative   Michio Sugi

JP Morgan GmbH   Subsidiary Company

Börsenstrasse 2-4, D-60313 Frankfurt/Main
Tel: (69) 7124 0 **Fax:** (69) 7124 1306 **Telex:** 412802 JPM

Senior Executive Officers
Chairman   Dr Claus Löwe

Others (Senior Executives)
                                  Jochen Friedrich *Head of Markets* ☎ **7124 1353**

Debt Capital Markets / Fixed Income
Tel: 7124 1334 **Fax:** 7124 1242

Eurobonds
Head of Origination   Jörg Huber *Head, New Issue Syndication* ☎ **2160 1275**
Head of Sales   Jochen Friedrich *Head of Markets* ☎ **7124 1353**
                                  Claudia Schmidt *Sales* ☎ **2160 1106**
                                  Christian Neske *Sales* ☎ **2160 1362**
                                  Jürgen Grünewald *Sales* ☎ **2160 1211**
                                  Susanne Schlott *Sales* ☎ **2160 1364**
                                  Enrico Donato *Sales* ☎ **2160 1167**
                                  Frank Winter *Sales* ☎ **2160 1387**
                                  Marcus Kühnast *Sales* ☎ **2160 1451**
                                  Marcus Schüler *Emerging Markets* ☎ **2160 1541**
                                  Michael Zink *Sales* ☎ **2160 1110**
                                  Christian Spieler *Sales* ☎ **2160 1351**
                                  Gunnar Regier *Sales* ☎ **2160 1332**

www.euromoneydirectory.com   **GERMANY (+49)**

Equity Capital Markets
Tel: 7124 1334
Country Head   John Jetter *Managing Director*

Komercni banka   Representative Office

Westendstraße 21, D-60325 Frankfurt/Main
Tel: (69) 7409 70 **Fax:** (69) 7409 90 **Email:** kb-repoffice.de@t-online.de

Senior Executive Officers
Chief Representative   Pavel Bittner

Korea Development Bank (Deutschland) GmbH   Subsidiary Company

Rahmhofstrasse 4, D-60313 Frankfurt/Main
PO Box 101348, D-60013 Frankfurt/Main
Tel: (69) 920 713 0 **Fax:** (69) 920 713 99 **Telex:** 4189614 KDB D

Senior Executive Officers
Managing Director   Volker Gäthje
Managing Director   Myong-Kyu Lee
International Division   Woong Huh *Deputy Managing Director* ☎ **920 713 20**

General-Lending (DCM, SL)
Head of Corporate Banking   Joon-Seok Koh *Manager, Credit & Financing* ☎ **920 713 60**

General-Investment
Head of Investment   Norbert Kirches *Manager, Fund Mngt, New Issues, Bond Underwriting*
                                        ☎ **920 713 51**

Syndicated Lending

Loan-Related Activities
Trade Finance   Yong-Hwan Kim *Manager* ☎ **920 713 61**

Money Markets
Global Head   Jae-Ho Lee *Assistant Manager* ☎ **920 713 50**

Settlement / Clearing
Regional Head   Hak-Je Cho *Manager* ☎ **920 713 80**
Operations   Frank Ludwig ☎ **920 713 83**

Administration

Technology & Systems
                                        Du-Jin Chang ☎ **920 713 70**

Other (Administration)
Administration & Organization   Jae-Pih Shim ☎ **920 713 77**

Kredietbank-Bankverein AG   Head Office

Mendelssohnstrasse 75-77, D-60325 Frankfurt/Main
Tel: (69) 756 193 0 **Fax:** (69) 756 193 60; (69) 756 193 61 **Telex:** 411563 **Swift:** BANV DE HB **Reuters:** KBBF

Senior Executive Officers
Chief Executive Officer   Hendrik Scheerlinck
Treasurer   Mr Lang

Euromoney Directory 1999   **511**

GERMANY (+49)

Kreditanstalt für Wiederaufbau — Head Office

KfW

Palmengartenstrasse 5-9, D-60325 Frankfurt/Main
PO Box 111141, D-60046 Frankfurt/Main
Tel: (69) 7431 0 Fax: (69) 7431 2944 Telex: 4152560 KW D Swift: KFWI DE FF Email: kfw.vsb@kfw.de
Reuters: AVSU; AVSV
Website: www.kfw.de

Senior Executive Officers

Chairman of the Supervisory Board	Theo Waigel
Financial Director	Detlef Vogt *Chief Financial Officer* ☎ **7431 2263**
Treasurer	Gerhard Lewark *SVP & Treasurer* ☎ **7431 2296**
Board of Managing Directors	Hans W. Reich
Board of Managing Directors	Friedrich Voss
Spokesman, Board of Managing Directors	Gert Vogt ☎ **7431 2297**
Board of Managing Directors	Rudolf Klein

Debt Capital Markets / Fixed Income

Global Head	Gerhard Lewark *SVP & Treasurer* ☎ **7431 2296**

Bonds - General

German Capital Markets	Dieter Glüder *First Vice President* ☎ **7431 2080**
	Werner Steffens *Vice President* ☎ **7431 3230**
International Capital Markets	Frank Czichowski *First Vice President* ☎ **7431 2165**

Syndicated Lending

Other (Trade Finance)

Export & Project Finance	Heinrich Heims *Senior Vice President* ☎ **7431 2637**
	Peter Klaus *Senior Vice President* ☎ **7431 2728**

Money Markets

MM & Forex	Cherifa Larabi *Vice President* ☎ **7431 3242**
MM & German Capital Market	Dieter Glüder *First Vice President* ☎ **7431 2080**

Foreign Exchange

Global Head	Dieter Glüder *First Vice President* ☎ **7431 2080**

FX Traders / Sales People

All Currencies	Cherifa Larabi *Vice President* ☎ **7431 3242**

Risk Management

Other Currency Swap / FX Options Personnel

New Issues, Derivatives	Matthias Hartke *Vice President* ☎ **7431 4226**

Settlement / Clearing

Regional Head	Wolfgang Rossmeissl *First Vice President* ☎ **7431 2342**

Administration

Legal / In-House Counsel

	Ruediger Sass *Senior Vice President* ☎ **7431 2420**

Public Relations

	Gunther Braunig *Senior Vice President* ☎ **7431 2445**

Kreissparkasse Köln

Neumarkt 18-24, D-50667 Cologne
PO Box 102143, D-50461 Cologne
Tel: (221) 227 01; (221) 227 2561 Fax: (221) 227 3710 Telex: 8883226 COKS DE Swift: COKS DE 33
Email: info@ksk-koeln.de
Website: www.ksk-koeln.de

Senior Executive Officers

Chairman	Hans-Peter Krämer ☎ **227 2521** 📠 **227 3500**
Managing Director	Ingo Ellgering ☎ **227 2515** 📠 **227 3514**
Financial Director	Helmut Höfer *Managing Director* ☎ **227 2526** 📠 **227 3525**
Treasurer	Hans Seigner *Managing Director* ☎ **227 2512** 📠 **227 3511**
Managing Director	Dieter Stern ☎ **227 2519** 📠 **227 3518**
Managing Director	Axel Kraft ☎ **227 2448** 📠 **227 3440**

www.euromoneydirectory.com GERMANY (+49)

Senior Executive Officers (cont)
Managing Director
International Division Konrad Rüdelstein ☎ 227 2481 F 227 3401
Markus Kirschbaum *Manager* ☎ 227 2561 F 227 3710
Administration
Compliance
Harald Küchler ☎ 227 2380 F 227 3620

Landesbank Hessen-Thüringen Head Office
Junghofstraße 18-26, D-60297 Frankfurt/Main
Tel: (69) 9132 0 **Fax:** (69) 291 517 **Telex:** 4152910 GFD **Swift:** HELA DE FF
Website: www.helaba.de

Senior Executive Officers
Chairman Walter Schäfer ☎ 9132 2211 F 9132 4352
Relationship Manager
Multinational Corporations Jürgen Hofer ☎ 9132 2146 F 9132 2459
Financial Institutions Michael Pflitsch ☎ 9132 4838 F 9132 2635
Multinational Corporations Rainer Könner ☎ 9132 3811 F 9132 4201
Matthias Schultheis ☎ 9132 4860 F 9132 4866
Savings Banks Ulrich Kirchhoff ☎ 9132 3073 F 9132 2231
Municipal Corporations Hans-Georg Napp ☎ 9132 2378 F 9132 4090
Debt Capital Markets / Fixed Income
Head of Fixed Income Sales Sabine Glöckler *Treasury & Sales* ☎ 9132 1830 F 9132 3096
Domestic Government Bonds
Head of Trading Dieter Becker *Treasury & Sales* ☎ 9132 1800 F 9132 2288
Non-Domestic Government Bonds
Bund / Länder Detlef Menz ☎ 9132 1499 F 9132 3855
Eurobonds
Head of Origination Stefan Frank ☎ 9132 1429 F 9132 3855
Andreas Petrie ☎ 9132 2757 F 9132 3855
Fritz Kandora ☎ 9132 1427 F 9132 3855
Head of Trading Dieter Becker *Treasury & Sales* ☎ 9132 1800 F 9132 2288
Department: SparKassen - Sales
Global Head Michael Ruespeler ☎ 9132 4927 F 9132 3096
Equity Capital Markets
Head of Sales Axel Meisinger *Treasury & Sales* ☎ 9132 3149 F 9132 3096
Karl-Wilhelm Neeb *Treasury & Sales* ☎ 9132 3806 F 9132 3096
Head of Trading Ralph Bachmann ☎ 9132 3199 F 9132 3924
Syndicated Lending
Head of Syndication Antje Neussel ☎ 9132 1428 F 9132 3855
Other (Syndicated Lending)
Credit Secretariat Henning Schulz ☎ 9132 2173 F 9132 4379
Credit Analysis Dietrich-Jürgen Grün ☎ 9132 2350 F 9132 4379
Loan-Related Activities
Aircraft / Aerospace Finance Patrick Smyth *Head* ☎ 9132 4369 F 9132 4350
Shipping Finance Norbert Schuster ☎ 9132 4450 F 9132 4350
Project Finance Ulrich Pähler ☎ 9132 4848 F 9132 4350
Other (Trade Finance)
Structured Finance Norbert Schraad *General Manager* ☎ 9132 4365 F 9132 4350
Export Finance Jörg Hartmann ☎ 9132 2159
Department: Corporate Loans
Head of Syndicated Lending Dieter Thiel *General Manager* ☎ 9132 2178 F 9132 4136
Other (Syndicated Lending)
Loan Administration Adolf Schroeder ☎ 9132 2359 F 9132 4330
New Business Jürgen Frey ☎ 9132 2359 F 9132 4136
Ulrich Heseler ☎ 9132 2186 F 9132 4136
Josef Neuberger ☎ 9132 2121 F 9132 4136
Elke Oster ☎ 9132 2673 F 9132 4136

Money Markets
Country Head Helmut Kost *Treasury & Sales* ☎ 9132 1755 F 9132 3483
Erwin Jourdan *Sales* ☎ 9132 1700 F 9132 3096
Money Markets - General
Banknotes & Bullion - Trading Klaus Häring *Treasury & Sales* ☎ 9132 3568 F 9132 4167
Other (Wholesale Deposits)
Eurocurrency Market - Trading Klaus-Gunter Moeller *Treasury & Sales* ☎ 9132 1760 F 9132 3483

Euromoney Directory 1999 513

GERMANY (+49)

www.euromoneydirectory.com

Landesbank Hessen-Thüringen (cont)

Foreign Exchange
Corporate Sales — Dietmar Feistl *Treasury & Sales* T 9132 4926 F 9132 3096
Spot / Forwards Sales — Ottmar Schwarz *Treasury & Sales* T 9132 1750 F 9132 3096
Spot / Forwards Trading — Patrick Laub *Treasury & Sales* T 9132 1730 F 9132 4024
Folker Hellmeyer *Treasury & Sales* T 9132 1730 F 9132 4024
Thomas Reichl *Treasury & Sales* T 9132 1740 F 9132 3483

Risk Management
Foreign Exchange Derivatives / Risk Management
Country Head — Gerhard Heiler *Treasury & Sales* T 9132 1715 F 9132 3096
Michael Wegmann *Treasury & Sales* T 9132 1715 F 9132 3096

Other (Exchange-Traded Derivatives)
Capital Markets Derivatives Group-Origination — Christoph A. Schneider T 9132 1706 F 9132 4284

Exchange-Traded Derivatives
FX Futures — Caryl Krick *Futures - Frankfurt* T 9132 1833 F 9132 3096
FX Options — Markus Dieter *Treasury & Sales* T 9132 1745 F 9132 4024

Corporate Finance / M&A Advisory
Acquistion Finance — Marcus Nelgen T 9132 4396 F 9132 4350

Settlement / Clearing
Head of Settlement / Clearing — Otto wohl T 9132 3761 F 9132 4015
Derivatives Settlement — Harald Kornmann T 9132 3717 F 9132 3922
Operations — Michael Ruhrländer *General Manager* T 9132 3301 F 9132 3609
Borgis Reutzel *Organization* T 9132 5484 F 9132 3977
Helmut Schwarzkopf T 9132 4480 F 9132 3511

Department: Accounts Settlements
Head of Settlement / Clearing — Hans-Dieter Mees *General Manager* T 9132 3582 F 9132 4484
Other — Harald Gerbig *Account Maintenance* T 9132 3539 F 9132 4146
Gerhard Schneider *Payments Control* T 9132 2128 F 9132 3161

Global Custody

Other (Global Custody)
Master Agreements — Sanjoy Dutta T 9132 3211 F 9132 3922
Securities Administration — Dagmar Wünsch T 9132 3031 F 9132 2867
Herbert Fleckenstein T 9132 4133 F 9132 3701

Asset Management

Department: Asset / Liabilty Management
Head — Rainer Krick *GM, Treasury & Sales* T 9132 3709 F 9132 4416
Investment Funds — Peter Möller *Treasury & Sales* T 9132 1825 F 9132 3096

Other (Asset Management)
Interest Rate Management — Stefan Zayer *Treasury & Sales* T 9132 2887 F 9132 4416
New Issues / Funding — Jörg-Henrich Kranz *Treasury & Sales* T 9132 3092 F 9132 3177
Treasury Service — Hans-Volker Kurstedt *Treasury & Sales* T 9132 2122 F 9132 2449

Department: Helaba Trust
Bösenstraße 7-11, D-60313 Frankfurt/Main
Tel: +49 (69) 29970 0 **Fax:** +49 (69) 29970 194
Head — Herbert-Hans Grüntker *Managing Director* T 9132 4321 F 9132 4322
Karl-Heinz Schlotthauer *Managing Director* T 29970 102 F 29970 183
Portfolio Management — Gerhard Fusenig T 29970 121

Other (Asset Management)
Investment Research — Heinrich Peters T 29970 106

Department: Helaba Invest
Börsenstraße 7-11, D-60313 Frankfurt/Main
Tel: +49 (69) 29970 0 **Fax:** +49 (69) 29970 194
Head —
Bernd Appenzeller *Managing Director* T 29970 151
Uwe Trautmann *Managing Director* T 29970 150
Volker Westerborg *Managing Director* T 29970 159

Other Departments

Economic Research — Michael Heil T 9132 4189 F 9132 3511

Administration
Head of Administration — Joachim Mann T 9132 2001 F 9132 2890
Head of Marketing — Wolfgang Kuß T 9132 2877

Technology & Systems
Michael Ruhrländer *General Manager* T 9132 3301 F 9132 3609

Legal / In-House Counsel
Deitrich Rethorn *General Manager* T 9132 2200

Public Relations
Wolfgang Kuß T 9132 2877

www.euromoneydirectory.com　　　　GERMANY (+49)

Accounts / Audit
Internal Audit　　　　Wolfgang Glaab *General Manager* [T] 9132 2081 [F] 9132 2443

Landesbank Rheinland-Pfalz Girozentrale
Grosse Bleiche 54/56, D-55098 Mainz
Tel: (6131) 13 01 Fax: (6131) 13 2724 Telex: 4187885 Swift: MALA DE 55 550 Email: lrp@lrp.de Reuters: LBMM; LBMZ
Website: www.lrp.de

Senior Executive Officers
Chief Executive Officer　　　　Klaus G Adam *Chairman, Managing Board & CEO* [T] 13 2200 [F] 13 3133
Treasurer　　　　Heinz-Jürgen Rentsch *SEVP, Global Head Treasury, Trading* [T] 13 5701
　　　　[F] 13 5886
Executive Vice President　　　　Gundolf Reitmaier [T] 13 2710 [F] 13 3130
International Division　　　　Harald O Witte *Executive Vice President* [T] 13 2704 [F] 13 2713

Others (Senior Executives)
Vice Chairman　　　　Friedhelm Plogmann *Vice Chairman of the Managing Board* [T] 13 3496
　　　　[F] 13 3227
Member of the Managing Board　　　　Werner Fuchs [T] 13 2210 [F] 13 3188
　　　　Paul Kurt Schminke [T] 13 2213 [F] 13 3189

General-Investment
Head of Investment　　　　Gerhard Klimm *SEVP, Global Head Sales, Institutional Investors* [T] 13 5501
　　　　[F] 13 2223

Department: Business Promotion, Loan Syndication, Correspondent Banking

Others (Senior Executives)
Central & South America, Middle East; UK,　　　　Heinz-W Firmenich *Senior Vice President* [T] 13 2976 [F] 13 3327
Ireland, Benelux, Nordic Countries; Turkey,
India, Pakistan
Switzerland, N.America, Mexico, Africa,　　　　Herbert Geist *Senior Vice President* [T] 13 2207 [F] 13 3170
Germany
Austria, S. Europe, Asia, Australia, New　　　　Joachim Rosenzweig *Senior Vice President* [T] 13 2878 [F] 13 3327
Zealand
France, Eastern Europe　　　　Wolfgang Titz *Vice President* [T] 13 2720 [F] 13 2713

Debt Capital Markets / Fixed Income
Global Head　　　　Heinz-Jürgen Rentsch *SEVP, Global Head Treasury, Trading* [T] 13 5701
　　　　[F] 13 5886
　　　　Gerhard Klimm *SEVP, Global Head Sales, Institutional Investors* [T] 13 5501
　　　　[F] 13 2223
Head of Fixed Income; Head of Fixed Income　　　　Heinz-Jürgen Rentsch *SEVP, Global Head Treasury, Trading* [T] 13 5701
Trading　　　　[F] 13 5886

Domestic Government Bonds
Head of Sales　　　　Joachim Huefken *Vice President* [T] 13 5510 [F] 13 3143
Head of Trading　　　　Christian Ferchland *Vice President* [T] 13 5524 [F] 13 3143
Head of Research　　　　Manfred Wolter [T] 13 5520 [F] 13 3143
Head of Origination; Head of Syndication　　　　Manfred Steyer *Vice President* [T] 13 2591 [F] 13 3630

Non-Domestic Government Bonds
　　　　Nicole Kaufamnn *Vice President* [T] 13 5533 [F] 13 3143
　　　　Marc Halbroth *Manager* [T] 13 5536 [F] 13 3143

Eurobonds
Head of Origination; Head of Syndication　　　　Manfred Steyer *Vice President* [T] 13 2591 [F] 13 3630
Head of Sales　　　　Joachim Huefken *Vice President* [T] 13 5510 [F] 13 3143
Head of Trading　　　　Christian Ferchland *Vice President* [T] 13 5524 [F] 13 3143
Trading (Sovereigns)　　　　Marc Halbroth *Manager* [T] 13 5536 [F] 13 3143
Trading (Corporates)　　　　Nicole Kaufamnn *Vice President* [T] 13 5533 [F] 13 3143

Emerging Market Bonds
Head of Emerging Markets　　　　Christian Ferchland *Vice President* [T] 13 5524 [F] 13 3143
　　　　Heinz-Jürgen Rentsch *SEVP, Global Head Treasury, Trading* [T] 13 5701
　　　　[F] 13 5886
Head of Trading　　　　Christian Ferchland *Vice President* [T] 13 5524 [F] 13 3143

Libor-Based / Floating-Rate Products
FRN Origination　　　　Manfred Steyer *Vice President* [T] 13 2591 [F] 13 3630
FRN Sales　　　　Joachim Huefken *Vice President* [T] 13 5510 [F] 13 3143
FRN Trading; Asset Swaps　　　　Barbara Altherr-Müller *Vice President* [T] 13 5922

Medium-Term Notes
Head of Origination; Head of Structuring　　　　Manfred Steyer *Vice President* [T] 13 2591 [F] 13 3630

GERMANY (+49)

www.euromoneydirectory.com

Landesbank Rheinland-Pfalz Girozentrale (cont)

Asset-Backed Securities / Securitization
Global Head — Heinz-Jürgen Rentsch *SEVP, Global Head Treasury, Trading* ☎ **13 5701** 📠 **13 5886**
Head of Trading — Christian Ferchland *Vice President* ☎ **13 5524** 📠 **13 3143**

Fixed-Income Repo
Head of Repo — Heinz-Jürgen Rentsch *SEVP, Global Head Treasury, Trading* ☎ **13 5701** 📠 **13 5886**
Head of Trading — Dieter Schwab *Vice President* ☎ **13 5720**

Equity Capital Markets
Department: Equity Trading
Tel: 13 5610 **Fax:** 13 2219
Head of Equity Capital Markets — Detlev Klug *Senior Vice President*

Domestic Equities
Head of Origination; Head of Syndication — Detlev Klug *Senior Vice President*
Head of Sales — Thomas Nolten ☎ **13 5612**
Head of Trading — Jörg Zimmer *Manager* ☎ **13 5620**
Head of Research — Piers Nestler *Vice President* ☎ **13 3341**
Rainer Monetha *Assistant Vice President* ☎ **13 3340**

Other (Domestic Equities)
Savings Banks, Private Investors — Friedrich Daus *Assistant Vice President* ☎ **13 2649** 📠 **13 2574**

International Equities
Head of Origination; Head of Syndication — Detlev Klug *Senior Vice President*

Equity Research
Head of Equity Research — Hans Beth *Assistant Vice President* ☎ **13 2616** 📠 **13 2574**

Other (Equity Research)
Savings Banks, Private Investors — Winfried Schitter *Manager* ☎ **13 2534** 📠 **13 2574**
Thomas Hollenbach *Manager* ☎ **13 2339** 📠 **13 2574**
Michael Sachse ☎ **13 2286** 📠 **13 2574**
Steffen Neumann ☎ **13 3184** 📠 **13 2574**

Convertibles / Equity-Linked
Head of Origination; Head of Syndication — Manfred Steyer *Vice President* ☎ **13 2591** 📠 **13 3630**

Syndicated Lending
Tel: 13 2704 **Fax:** 13 2713
Global Head — Harald O Witte *Executive Vice President*

Loan-Related Activities
Trade Finance — Hans-Peter Gries *Assistant Vice President* ☎ **13 2292** 📠 **13 3170**
Project Finance — Harald O Witte *Executive Vice President*
Structured Trade Finance — Hans-Peter Gries *Assistant Vice President* ☎ **13 2292** 📠 **13 3170**
Leasing & Asset Finance — Klaus Dieter Scholtz *Executive Vice President* ☎ **13 2403** 📠 **13 2325**

Money Markets
Tel: 13 5701 **Fax:** 13 5886
Head of Money Markets — Heinz-Jürgen Rentsch *SEVP, Global Head Treasury, Trading* ☎ **13 5701** 📠 **13 5886**

Domestic Commercial Paper
Head of Sales; Head of Trading — Dieter Schwab *Vice President* ☎ **13 5720**

Foreign Exchange
Tel: 13 5701 **Fax:** 13 5886
Head of Foreign Exchange — Heinz-Jürgen Rentsch *SEVP, Global Head Treasury, Trading* ☎ **13 5701** 📠 **13 5886**

Head of Institutional Sales; Head of Trading — James Round *Vice President* ☎ **13 5824**

Risk Management
Tel: 13 5701 **Fax:** 13 5886
Head of Risk Management — Heinz-Jürgen Rentsch *SEVP, Global Head Treasury, Trading* ☎ **13 5701** 📠 **13 5886**

Fixed Income Derivatives / Risk Management
Trading — Barbara Altherr-Müller *Vice President* ☎ **13 5922**
IR Swaps Sales / Marketing — Joachim Huefken *Vice President* ☎ **13 5510** 📠 **13 3143**
IR Swaps Trading — Barbara Altherr-Müller *Vice President* ☎ **13 5922**
IR Options Sales / Marketing — Joachim Huefken *Vice President* ☎ **13 5510** 📠 **13 3143**
IR Options Trading — Barbara Altherr-Müller *Vice President* ☎ **13 5922**

Foreign Exchange Derivatives / Risk Management
Global Head — James Round *Vice President* ☎ **13 5824**

Corporate Finance / M&A Advisory
Global Head — Roland Poczka *Senior Executive Vice President* ☎ **13 2675** 📠 **13 2684**

www.euromoneydirectory.com GERMANY (+49)

Settlement / Clearing
Tel: 13 2587 Fax: 13 3343
Head of Settlement / Clearing Stefan Degen *Vice President* ☎ **13 3430**
Equity Settlement Ernst-Jürgen Deißroth *Assistant Vice President* ☎ **13 2709** F **13 3665**
Fixed-Income Settlement Ralf Peter Müller ☎ **13 2553** F **13 3664**

Global Custody
Regional Head Stefan Degen *Vice President* ☎ **13 3430**

Other Departments
Private Banking Hans-Joachim Roos *Vice President* ☎ **13 2293** F **13 2814**

Administration
Head of Administration Sascha Lueck *Assistant Vice President* ☎ **13 2227** F **13 2883**
Head of Marketing Jürgen Pitzer *Senior Vice President* ☎ **13 2816** F **13 2560**

Technology & Systems
Klaus Jaeger *Executive Vice President* ☎ **13 2994** F **13 2468**

Legal / In-House Counsel
Peter Keber *Head of Legal* ☎ **13 3438** F **13 3436**

Compliance
Herbert Glietsch *Assistant Vice President* ☎ **13 3446** F **13 3436**

Accounts / Audit
Norbert Havenith *Executive Vice President* ☎ **13 3443** F **13 3477**

Landesbank Saar Girozentrale   Head Office

Alternative trading name: SaarLB
Ursulinenstrasse 2, D-66111 Saarbrücken
Tel: (681) 383 01 **Fax:** (681) 383 11200 **Telex:** 4428733 **Swift:** SALA DE 55 **Email:** saarlb@aol.com
Website: www.saarlb.de

Senior Executive Officers
Chairman Ernst Lenz ☎ **383 1310**
Deputy Chairman Max Häring ☎ **383 1699**

Others (Senior Executives)
Georg Gräsel *Director* ☎ **383 1252**
Jürgen Müsch *Director* ☎ **383 1228**

Landesbank Sachsen Girozentrale   Head Office

Humboldtstraße 25, 04105 Leipzig
Tel: (341) 979 0 **Fax:** (341) 979 7979 **Telex:** 311395 LSLB D **Swift:** SXLB DE 8L
Website: www.sachsenlb.de

Senior Executive Officers
Chairman Michael Weiss
Vice Chairman Dieter Scheil
Treasurer Bernward Hoving ☎ **979 4240** F **979 4209**

Others (Senior Executives)
Board of Management Hans-Jürgen Klumpp
Eckhard Laible
General Representative Joachim Weinhold

Debt Capital Markets / Fixed Income
Country Head Wiliam Klein
Horst Wagner

Syndicated Lending
Loan-Related Activities
Project Finance Martin Tucholke ☎ **979 3160** F **979 3169**
Peter Ulrich ☎ **979 3210** F **979 3209**
Structured Trade Finance Baldur Vander ☎ **979 3132** F **979 3106**
Leasing & Asset Finance Manuela Zeitler ☎ **979 3360** F **979 3309**

Risk Management
Country Head Bernd Bonness

Asset Management
Tel: 979 4230 Fax: 979 4209
Head Thorsten Wölbern
Ingo Steffenhag

GERMANY (+49)   www.euromoneydirectory.com

Landesbank Sachsen Girozentrale (cont)
Other Departments
Chief Credit Officer Gerhard Sender ☏ 979 1520 F 979 1529
Economic Research Andreas Stehr ☏ 979 4238 F 979 4209
Administration
Other (Administration)
Personnel Wolfgang Behrens

Landesbank Schleswig-Holstein Girozentrale — Head Office

Martensdamm 6, D-24103 Kiel
PO Box 1122, D-24100 Kiel
Tel: (431) 900 01 **Fax:** (431) 900 2446 **Telex:** 292822 GZKI D **Email:** info@lb-kiel.de
Website: www.lb-kiel.de

Senior Executive Officers
International Division Rainer Lemor *Senior Vice President & Global Head, Foreign* ☏ 900 1537
General-Investment
Head of Investment Lutz Koopman *Senior Vice President* ☏ 900 1580 F 900 1627
Debt Capital Markets / Fixed Income
Tel: 900 1961 **Fax:** 900 1731
Global Head Wolfgang Delfs *Executive Vice President* ☏ 900 1960
Domestic Government Bonds
Head of Sales Ulrich Heilen *Vice President & Head* ☏ 900 1976
 Michael Aßmann *Assistant Vice President* ☏ 900 1976
Head of Trading Jan Striepke *Assistant Vice President* ☏ 900 1976
Eurobonds
Head of Origination Reinhard Sievers *Vice President* ☏ 900 1995
Head of Trading Peter Kalmutzke *Assistant Vice President* ☏ 900 1950
Libor-Based / Floating-Rate Products
FRN Origination; Asset Swaps Reinhard Sievers *Vice President* ☏ 900 1995
Medium-Term Notes
Head of Origination Reinhard Sievers *Vice President* ☏ 900 1995
Equity Capital Markets
Tel: 900 1961 **Fax:** 900 1731
Global Head Wolfgang Delfs *Executive Vice President* ☏ 900 1960
Domestic Equities
Head of Trading Rainer Petsch *Vice President* ☏ 900 1740
International Equities
Head of Origination Thomas Giesenhagen *Assistant Vice President* ☏ 900 2013
Head of Trading Klaus-Dieter Nebendahl ☏ 900 2012
Equity Research
Head of Equity Research Thomas Giesenhagen *Assistant Vice President* ☏ 900 2013
Syndicated Lending
Loan-Related Activities
Trade Finance Klaus-Volker Lenk *Assistant Vice President* ☏ 900 1572
Project Finance Klaus Bernhart *Senior Vice President* ☏ 900 1500
Structured Trade Finance Klaus-Volker Lenk *Assistant Vice President* ☏ 900 1572
Leasing & Asset Finance Klaus Bernhart *Senior Vice President* ☏ 900 1500
Other (Trade Finance)
Structured Finance; Transportation Finance Klaus Bernhart *Senior Vice President* ☏ 900 1500
Sovereign Banks Eckhart Kleber *Assistant Vice President* ☏ 900 1543
Foreign Corporates Utz Meyer-Reim *Assistant Vice President* ☏ 900 2783
Money Markets
Global Head Guenter Gerson *Senior Vice President* ☏ 900 2140
Country Head Michael Teich *Vice President & Head of Trading* ☏ 900 1963
Foreign Exchange
Global Head Guenter Gerson *Senior Vice President* ☏ 900 2140
Head of Trading Jörg Arndt *Vice President* ☏ 900 2160
Risk Management
Department: Derivatives
Fixed Income Derivatives / Risk Management
Global Head Reinhard Sievers *Vice President* ☏ 900 1995
IR Options Sales / Marketing Gebhard v Krosigk *Assistant Vice President* ☏ 900 2965
IR Options Trading Frank Kolkmann *Assistant Vice President* ☏ 900 2965

www.euromoneydirectory.com GERMANY (+49)

OTC Commodity Derivatives
Sales   Reinhard Sievers *Vice President* ☏ 900 1995
Corporate Finance / M&A Advisory
Global Head   Rainer Lemor *Senior Vice President & Global Head, Foreign* ☏ 900 1537
                                   Uwe Madsen *Executive Vice President & Global Head, Domestic*
                                   ☏ 900 1580
Other (Corporate Finance)
Structured Finance   Klaus Bernhart *Senior Vice President* ☏ 900 1500

Landesgirokasse   Head Office

Alternative trading name: LG Bank
Fritz-Elsas-Straße 31, D-70144 Stuttgart, Baden-Württemberg
Tel: (711) 124 0 **Fax:** (711) 124 3544; (711) 124 4144 **Telex:** 723868 **Swift:** LAGI DE 6S **Email:** kontakt@lgbank.de
Cable: LANDESGIROKASSE
Website: www.lgbank.de

Senior Executive Officers
Chairman & Chief Executive Officer   Thomas R Fischer
Financial Director   Roland Hahn *Executive Vice President, Finance*
Chief Operating Officer   Hasko Neumann *Executive Vice President, Operations*
Treasurer   Michael Hawighorst *Senior Vice President*
Managing Director   Thomas Fischer
Managing Director   Tilo Berlin
Managing Director   Joachim Schielke
Managing Director   Reinhold Schreiner
Managing Director   Hans Waschkowski
International Division   Hans-Ulrich Liebert *Senior Vice President*

Debt Capital Markets / Fixed Income
Department: Trading
Head of Debt Capital Markets   Michael Arends *Senior Vice President*
Equity Capital Markets
Head of Equity Capital Markets   Jürgen Prockl *Senior Vice President*
Syndicated Lending
Head of Syndicated Lending   Jürgen Prockl *Senior Vice President*
Money Markets
Head of Money Markets   Michael Arends *Senior Vice President*
Foreign Exchange
Head of Foreign Exchange   Michael Arends *Senior Vice President*
Risk Management
Head of Risk Management   Bernhard Krob *Senior Vice President*
Corporate Finance / M&A Advisory
Head of Corporate Finance   Jürgen Prockl *Senior Vice President*
Settlement / Clearing
Head of Settlement / Clearing   Hasko Neumann *Executive Vice President, Operations*
Global Custody
Head of Global Custody   Peter Jürgen Nowotny *Senior Vice President*
Other Departments
Chief Credit Officer   Matthias Peschke *Senior Vice President*
Private Banking   Karl-Heinz Hausch *Senior Vice President*
                                           Manfred Tratzki *Senior Vice President*
Correspondent Banking   Dietmar Pasitsch *Second Vice President*
Administration
Technology & Systems
                                           Rolf Peter Schultz *Senior Vice President*
Legal / In-House Counsel
Legal   Helmut Irion von Dincklage *Senior Vice President*
Compliance
                                           Albert Urnauer *Vice President*
Accounts / Audit
Audit   Hermann Ziegler *Senior Vice President*
Other (Administration)
Marketing   Klaus R Dorsch *Senior Vice President*

Euromoney Directory 1999 **519**

GERMANY (+49)   www.euromoneydirectory.com

Landwirtschaftliche Rentenbank   Head Office

Hochstrasse 2, D-60313 Frankfurt/Main
PO Box 101445, D-60014 Frankfurt/Main
Tel: (69) 2107 0 **Fax:** (69) 2107 444 **Telex:** 411414 **Swift:** LARE DE FF **Email:** office@rentenbank.de **Reuters:** LRBF; LRBG; LRBH

Senior Executive Officers
Chief Executive Officer   Hans Jürgen Ploog *MD & Member of the Board* ☎ **2107 259**
    Uwe Zimpelmann *MD & Member of the Board* ☎ **2107 260**
    Karl-Ingo Bruns *MD & Member of the Board* ☎ **2107 264**
Treasurer   Horst Reinhardt *Senior Vice President* ☎ **2107 277**

General - Treasury
Head of Treasury   Uwe Zimpelmann *MD & Member of the Board* ☎ **2107 260**

Debt Capital Markets / Fixed Income
Tel: 2107 269 **Fax:** 2107 454
Regional Head   Horst Reinhardt *Senior Vice President* ☎ **2107 277**
Country Head   Karl-Heinz Peiler *Vice President* ☎ **2107 269** F **2107 454**

Fixed-Income Repo
Head of Repo   Karl-Heinz Peiler *Vice President* ☎ **2107 269** F **2107 454**
Trading; Sales   Roger Wudy ☎ **2107 205**

Equity Capital Markets
Equity Repo / Securities Lending
Head   Karl-Heinz Peiler *Vice President* ☎ **2107 269** F **2107 454**
Head of Trading   Roger Wudy ☎ **2107 205**

Syndicated Lending
Tel: 2107 274 **Fax:** 2107 459
Global Head   Lothar Kuhfahl *Senior Vice President & Head* ☎ **2107 275**
Regional Head   Jürgen Wegner ☎ **2107 274**

Money Markets
Tel: 9204 5110 **Fax:** 2107 454
Global Head   Hartwig Völkel *Vice President & Head* ☎ **2107 233**

Settlement / Clearing
Tel: 2107 229 **Fax:** 2107 448
Regional Head   Helmut Bert *Vice President & Head* ☎ **2107 229**

L-BANK   Head Office

Alternative trading name: Landeskreditbank Baden-Württemberg
Schlossplatz 10/12, D-76113 Karlsruhe
Tel: (721) 150 0 **Fax:** (721) 150 1001

Senior Executive Officers
Chairman   Dietmar Sauer
Vice Chairman   Christian Brand
International Division   Christian Brand *International Business*
Department: International Funding & Investments
Fax: (721) 150 1098

Others (Senior Executives)
Management   Stephen Tribull *Director* ☎ **150 1209**
    Helmut Stermann *Deputy Director* ☎ **150 1541**
International Funding   Martina Pfirmann-Meier ☎ **150 3626**
    Kai Scholl ☎ **150 3647**
Investments   Boris Bindschädel ☎ **150 3684**
    Detlef Lang ☎ **150 3681**
Documentation   Claudia Prutscher ☎ **150 1186**
    Christa Elsäßer ☎ **150 1151**
    Christina Thomas ☎ **150 1584**
    Andreas Birk ☎ **150 1146**
Money Market DEM   Dagobert Hochrießer ☎ **150 3638**
    Katja Franke ☎ **150 3635**
Administration   Ulrike Schwarz ☎ **150 1107**
Department: Treasury
Fax: (721) 150 3600 **Reuters:** ELBA-F

Others (Senior Executives)
Management   Thomas Keller *Director* ☎ **150 1108**
    Lothar Mierisch *Deputy Director* ☎ **150 1348**

www.euromoneydirectory.com			GERMANY (+49)

Others (Senior Executives) (cont)
Swapdesk					Thomas Weimer T 150 3680
						Ulrike Scheef T 150 3680
						Peter Oellers T 150 3680
Swapdesk / Money Market FX			Pauliina Hautala T 150 3680
						Markus Schneider T 150 3680
Administration				Rita Müller T 150 1106 F 150 1098
Department: Interbank Business
Fax: 150 1188

Others (Senior Executives)
Management					Gerhard Probst *Director* T 150 1101
						Werner Becker *Deputy Director* T 150 1103

Relationship Manager
Interbank Lending				Karl-Heinz Finsterle T 150 3629
						Dirk Püttner T 150 3632
						Doris Hofmann T 150 3726
Administration				Monika Ganz T 150 1102

Debt Capital Markets / Fixed Income
Department: Bond Trading, Domestic Funding & Derivatives Trading
Tel: 150 2900 Fax: 150 2948
Country Head					Gerhard Fink *Deputy Director* T 122 2940
						Michael Greiner *Deputy Director* T 122 2920

Bonds - General
						Wolfgang Günther *Trading / Sales Team* T 122 2954
						Markus Beuttel *Trading / Sales Team* T 122 2957
						Sven Kienzle *Trading / Sales Team* T 122 2951
						Peter Kießling *Trading / Sales Team* T 122 2960
						Günther Mayer *Trading / Sales Team* T 122 2923
						Britta Midding *Trading / Sales Team* T 122 2963
						Jürgen Motzer *Trading / Sales Team* T 122 2966
						Patrick Reiling *Trading / Sales Team* T 122 2943
						Stefan Schmid *Trading / Sales Team* T 122 2926
						Alexandra Seubert *Trading / Sales Team* T 122 2917
						Georg Sindermann *Trading / Sales Team* T 122 2969

Department: Treasury Settlement
Bonds - General
*Syndicate Business, MTNs, Loans, Comission	Claudia Hübler *Deputy Head* T 150 1147 F 150 3792
Business*
						Mona Fütterer T 150 1198 F 150 3792
						Rabea Brecht T 150 1814 F 150 3792
						Wilma Emig T 150 1631 F 150 3792
						Sven Mammes T 150 3767 F 150 3792
						Roswitha Laible T 150 1161 F 150 3792
						Alexander Stelzner T 150 3916 F 150 3792

Settlement / Clearing
Department: Treasury Settlement
Head of Settlement / Clearing			Gerd Ziegler *Director* T 150 1152 F 150 1455
Derivatives Settlement			Frank Mahler *Derivatives Settlement Team* T 150 1383 F 150 1097
						Mark Klopler *Derivatives Settlement Team* T 150 3768 F 150 1097
						Andreas Kehnen *Derivatives Settlement Team* T 150 1337 F 150 1097
						Anke Kainka *Derivatives Settlement Team* T 150 1197 F 150 1097
						Petra Hofer *Derivatives Settlement Team* T 150 3918 F 150 1097
						Kai Heidler *Derivatives Settlement Team* T 150 3927 F 150 1097
						Sabine Liebich *Derivatives Settlement Team* T 150 3784 F 150 1097
Foreign Exchange Settlement			Sonja Ball *Head of Derivatives, Securities, MM & FX Settlemen*
						T 150 1172 F 150 1097
						Hendrik Pott *Derivatives, Securities, MM & FX Settlements* T 150 1853
						F 150 1097
						Daniela Schmid *Securities, MM & FX Settlements Team* T 150 3784
						F 150 1097
						Jörg Heymann *Securities, MM & FX Settlements Team* T 150 1169
						F 150 1097
						Isabella Paul *Securities, MM & FX Settlements Team* T 150 1179
						F 150 1097
Other						Christel Zimmermann *Head, Securities Settlements* T 150 1165 F 150 1280
						Jürgen Schäfer *Deputy Head, Securities Settlements* T 150 1626
						F 150 1280
						Christiane Mahovsky *Securities Settlements Team* T 150 1144 F 150 1280
						Waltraud Roth *Securities Settlements Team* T 150 1078 F 150 1280
						Sybille Lehmacher *Securities Settlements Team* T 150 1158 F 150 1280

Euromoney Directory 1999	521

GERMANY (+49)   www.euromoneydirectory.com

L-BANK (cont)
Treasury Settlement (cont)

Frank Sindlinger *Securities Settlements Team* ☎ **150 1155** ℻ **150 1280**
Andreas M Loosemore *Securities Settlements Team* ☎ **150 3771** ℻ **150 1280**
Irmgard Nagel *Securities Settlements Team* ☎ **150 1168** ℻ **150 1280**
Yvonne Brisbois *Settlement of Securities Lending & Repo* ☎ **150 3769** ℻ **150 1097**
Marion Fischer *Administration* ☎ **150 1190** ℻ **150 1097**

Lehman Brothers Bankhaus AG   Subsidiary Company

Grüneburgweg 18, D-60322 Frankfurt/Main
Tel: (69) 15307 0 **Fax:** (69) 15307 283 **Telex:** 411758
Website: www.lehmann.com

Senior Executive Officers
Managing Director   Frank F Beelitz ☎ **15307 101** ℻ **558 894**
Managing Director   Peter Coym ☎ **15307 116** ℻ **558 894**

Others (Senior Executives)
                             Helmut Olivier *Executive Director* ☎ **15307 172** ℻ **15307 283**

Debt Capital Markets / Fixed Income
Head of Debt Capital Markets   Helmut Olivier *Executive Director* ☎ **15307 172** ℻ **15307 283**
Head of Fixed Income   Matthias Wittenburg *Director* ☎ **15307 410** ℻ **15307 211**

Fixed-Income Repo
Trading   Mathias Zorn *Trader* ☎ **15307 340** ℻ **15307 211**
                             Rebecca Holz *Trader* ☎ **15307 340** ℻ **15307 211**

Lehman Brothers International (Europe)   Subsidiary Company

Grüneburgweg 18, D-60322 Frankfurt/Main
Tel: (69) 15307 0 **Fax:** (69) 15307 6860
Website: www.lehman.com

Senior Executive Officers
Executive Director, Head of Equity   Michael Broszeit ☎ **15307 140**
Director & Head, Fixed Income Sales   Michael Noelle-Wying

Debt Capital Markets / Fixed Income
Department: Fixed Income
Tel: 15307 350 **Fax:** 15307 211
Head of Fixed Income Sales   Michael Noelle-Wying *Director & Head, Fixed Income Sales*
                                 Oliver Berger *Director*
                                 Nicola Spanger *Director*

Bonds - General
Eurex Trading   Stephen Ronnie

Equity Capital Markets
Department: Equity
Fax: 15307 210
Head of Equity Capital Markets   Michael Broszeit *Executive Director, Head of Equity* ☎ **15307 140**
Head of Trading   Jürgen Jänsch *Director* ☎ **15307 156**
                                   Werner Kähs *Director* ☎ **15307 156**

International Equities
Head of Sales   Thomas Fischer *Director, European Equities Sales* ☎ **15307 155**
                             Andreas Radike *European Equities* ☎ **15307 161**
                             Robert Focken *European Equities* ☎ **15307 174**
                             Asmus Stohn *Director, Institutional Sales* ☎ **15307 271** ℻ **15307 230**
                             Eva Kleeberg *Institutional Sales* ☎ **15307 269** ℻ **15307 230**

Risk Management
Department: Equity
Fax: 15307 210

OTC Equity Derivatives
Sales   Lars Dieterle *Derivative Sales* ☎ **15307 141**
                             Panagiotis Michaloploulos *Derivative Sales* ☎ **15307 153**
                             Nouchine Shohreh *Derivative Sales* ☎ **15307 152**
Trading   Steven Mondelink *Derivative Trader* ☎ **15307 154**
                             Andreas Günther *Derivative Trader* ☎ **15307 151**

London Forfaiting Deutschland GmbH
Subsidiary Company

Niederrheinstrasse 23, D-40474 Düsseldorf
Tel: (211) 43030 40 **Fax:** (211) 43030 555 **Email:** lonforfaid@aol.com

Senior Executive Officers
Geschäftsführerin — Doris Yvonne Bloniarz

Others (Senior Executives)
Udo Schiffkowski *Director*
Hans Gerhard Becker *Director*
Reiner Jahn *Deputy Director*
Martina Dietrich *Manager*
Hans Grutza *Manager*
Christoph Mrozek *Manager*
Frank Toennies *Manager*

Maple Partners Bankhaus GmbH
Head Office

Feuerbachstrasse 26-32, D-60325 Frankfurt/Main
Tel: (69) 97166 0 **Fax:** (69) 97166 111 **Telex:** 413333FMAB D

Senior Executive Officers
Financial Director — Michael Bernhard *Finance Director*
Chief Operating Officer — Manfred Knochenhauer

Debt Capital Markets / Fixed Income
Tel: 97166 150 **Fax:** 97166 112

Fixed-Income Repo
Head of Repo — Wolfgang Schuck *Chief Executive Officer* [T] 97166 100 [F] 97166 111
Marketing & Product Development — Wolfgang Schuck *Chief Executive Officer*
Trading — Paul Hiob *Executive Vice President*
Peter Ertel *Vice President*
Andreas Henckell *Senior Vice President*
Christian Pfleger *Trading*

Money Markets
Country Head — Christian Pfleger *Trading*

Risk Management
Country Head — Jürgen Daume

Settlement / Clearing
Country Head — Martin Mönninger

MeesPierson (Germany)

Niederlassung Frankfurt, Barckhausstrasse 10, D-60325 Frankfurt/Main
Tel: (69) 715 870

Equity Capital Markets
Tel: 718 870

Equity Repo / Securities Lending
Head of Trading — Frank Hodyjas
Holgar Schmidt

Merrill Lynch Capital Markets Bank Limited
Full Branch Office

Neue Mainzer Strasse 75, D-60311 Frankfurt/Main
Tel: (69) 2994 0 **Fax:** (69) 2994 284

Senior Executive Officers
General Manager — Wolfgang Stern

Merrill Lynch International Bank Limited
Full Branch Office

Ulmenstrasse 30, D-60325 Frankfurt/Main
Tel: (69) 97117 0 **Fax:** (69) 97117 247; (69) 97117 292 **Telex:** 41237
Website: www.ml.com

GERMANY (+49)   www.euromoneydirectory.com

Merrill Lynch International Bank Limited — Subsidiary Company

Moehlstrasse 2, D-81675 Munich, Bavaria
Tel: (89) 41305 0 Fax: (89) 41305 150

Senior Executive Officers
Chief Executive Officer

Raoul A Graf *Resident Executive Director*

B Metzler seel Sohn & Co KGaA — Head Office

Grosse Gallusstrasse 18, D-60311 Frankfurt/Main
PO Box 200138, D-60605 Frankfurt/Main
Tel: (69) 2104 0 Fax: (69) 281 429 Telex: 412139 BMA Swift: METZ DE FF

Senior Executive Officers

Others (Senior Executives)

Norbert Enste *Managing Partner*
Udo von Klot-Heydenfeldt *Managing Partner*
Friedrich von Metzler *Managing Partner*
Hans Hermann Reschke *Managing Partner*

General-Lending (DCM, SL)
Head of Corporate Banking

Gerhard Heck *Director, Financial Markets* ☎ **2104 281**

Debt Capital Markets / Fixed Income
Global Head

Jürgen Röthig *Director & Head* ☎ **2104 4170**

Eurobonds
Head of Sales
Head of Trading

Uwe Müller-Kasporick *Head* ☎ **2104 366**
Heike Mueller *Head* ☎ **2104 614**

Fixed-Income Research
Global Head

Johannes Reich *Head* ☎ **2104 4175**

Equity Capital Markets
Head of Sales

Uwe Müller-Kasporick *Head* ☎ **2104 366**

Domestic Equities
Head of Trading

Werner Litzinger *Head* ☎ **2104 364**

Equity Research
Global Head

Johannes Reich *Head* ☎ **2104 4175**

Foreign Exchange
Global Head

Thomas Rost *Head* ☎ **2104 292**

FX Traders / Sales People
Trader

Harald Mathé ☎ **2104 289**
Bettina Jung ☎ **2104 291**
Lothar Springer ☎ **2104 282**
Annelore Stadtmueller ☎ **2104 274**
Andreas Zellmann ☎ **2104 610**

Risk Management
Global Head

Harald Illy *Head* ☎ **2104 294**

Settlement / Clearing
Settlement (General)
Operations

Gerhard Fuchs *Director, Operations & Back-Office Settlements* ☎ **2104 253**
Rainer Ewald *Head* ☎ **2104 256**

Other Departments
Private Banking
Correspondent Banking

Klaus-Peter Kirschbaum *Director* ☎ **2104 1511**
Gerhard Heck *Director, Financial Markets* ☎ **2104 281**
Jürgen Conradi *Director* ☎ **2104 685**

Administration

Technology & Systems
Information Technology

Kari Emil Fuhrmann *Director*

Other (Administration)
Personnel
Organisation
Customer Relations

Birgit Kiessler ☎ **2104 555**
Frank Allgeier ☎ **2104 306**
Jürgen Conradi *Director* ☎ **2104 685**

www.euromoneydirectory.com GERMANY (+49)

The Mitsubishi Trust & Banking Corporation — Representative Office
Eschersheimer Landstrasse 55, D-60322 Frankfurt/Main
Tel: (69) 257 9512 Fax: (69) 591 089

Senior Executive Officers
Chief Representative   Kensuke Yoshioka

Morgan Stanley Bank AG — Subsidiary Company
Rahmhofstrasse 2-4, D-60313 Frankfurt/Main
PO Box 101601, D-60313 Frankfurt/Main
Tel: (69) 2166 0 Fax: (69) 2166 2099 Telex: 412648
Website: www.ms.com

Senior Executive Officers
MD & Chairman, Management Board   Lutz R Raettig

Others (Senior Executives)
Member, Management Board   Hans Jörg Schüttler *Managing Director*
Friedrich von Nathusius
Benedikt von Schröder *Managing Director*

Debt Capital Markets / Fixed Income
Eurobonds
Head of Syndication   Hans Jörg Schüttler *Managing Director*

Equity Capital Markets
Other (Domestic Equities)
Equity Sales & Trading   Dietmar Schmitt *Executive Director*
Warrants
Head of Trading   Stefan Armbruster *Vice President*
Equity Repo / Securities Lending
Head of Trading   Heike Niesler

Corporate Finance / M&A Advisory
Regional Head   Lutz R Raettig *MD & Chairman, Management Board*
Other (Corporate Finance)
Benedikt von Schröder *Managing Director*
Rolf-Michael Gerner *Executive Director*
Jan Weidner *Executive Director*
Christian Bergmann *Vice President*

Asset Management
Head   Andreas Povel *Executive Director*

Administration
Compliance
Hanns Christoph Siebold *Vice President*
Other (Administration)
Controller   Patrick Klaedtke *Executive Director*

Muenchener Hypothekenbank eG — Head Office
Nussbaumstrasse 12, D-80336 Munich, Bavaria
Tel: (89) 5387 0 Fax: (89) 5387 150; (89) 5387 243
Website: www.muenchener-hyp.de

Senior Executive Officers
Professor   Willibald Folz
Treasurer   Richard Leib *Direktor* 5387 127

Debt Capital Markets / Fixed Income
Global Head   Richard Leib *Direktor* 5387 127
Bonds - General
Pfandbriefe   Richard Leib *Direktor* 5387 127
Fixed-Income Repo
Head of Repo   Retler Ochs *Assistant Director* 5887 105
Money Markets
Global Head   Richard Leib *Direktor* 5387 127

GERMANY (+49)   www.euromoneydirectory.com

Nassauische Sparkasse

Rheinstrasse 42/46, D-65185 Wiesbaden
PO Box 4460, D-65034 Wiesbaden
Tel: (611) 364 0 **Fax:** (611) 364 04999 **Telex:** 4186805 **Swift:** NASS DE 55 **Email:** naspa@t-online.de
Website: www.naspa.de

Senior Executive Officers
Chairman — Anton Mauerer
Managing Director / General Manager — Hartmut Boeckler

The National Commercial Bank — Representative Office

Wilhelm-Leuscher-Strasse 7, D-60329 Frankfurt/Main
Tel: (69) 250 181 **Fax:** (69) 239 137

Senior Executive Officers
Representative — Saleh Naoura

Nikko Bank (Deutschland) GmbH — Subsidiary Company

Kaiser Strausse 29, D-60311 Frankfurt/Main
Tel: (69) 238 5180 **Fax:** (60) 237 400 **Telex:** 41684

Senior Executive Officers
General Manager — Mr Öchsler

Nomura Bank (Deutschland) GmbH — Head Office

MesseTurm, D-60308 Frankfurt/Main
Tel: (69) 97508 0 **Fax:** (69) 97508 600 **Telex:** 413350-0 NO D **Swift:** NOMU DE FF

Nordbanken AB (publ) — Representative Office

Alter Wall 22, D-20457 Hamburg
Tel: (40) 3692 3135 **Fax:** (40) 3692 2555

Senior Executive Officers
Representative — Lars Hansson

Norddeutsche Hypotheken-und Wechselbank — Head Office

Domstraße 9, D-20033 Hamburg
PO Box 104828, D-20095 Hamburg
Tel: (40) 3086 0 **Fax:** (40) 3086 308 **Telex:** 210365 **Swift:** NOHY DE HH

Senior Executive Officers
Managing Director / General Manager — Joachim Schônine ☎ 3086 212
Managing Director / General Manager — Werner Schule ☎ 3086 211

Norddeutsche Landesbank Girozentrale NORD/LB — Head Office

Georgsplatz 1, D-30159 Hannover
Tel: (511) 361 0 **Fax:** (511) 361 2502; (511) 361 4440 **Telex:** 92160 GZH D **Swift:** NOLA DE 2H **Reuters:** NOLA
Economics & Information Fax: 2693ext2104
Website: www.nordlb.de

Senior Executive Officers
Deputy Chairman of the Managing Board — Dr. Hannes Rehm
Chairman, Board of Management — Manfred Bodin
International Division — Suen Herlyn *Executive Vice President*

Others (Senior Executives)

Hans Vieregge *Board of Management*
Günter Dunkel *Board of Management*
Klaus Schiersmann *Board of Management*
Werner Schildt *Board of Management*

www.euromoneydirectory.com GERMANY (+49)

Others (Senior Executives) (cont)

Jürgen Kösters *Board of Management*
Hans Armin Curdt *Board of Management*

General-Lending (DCM, SL)
Head of Corporate Banking

Hans Hartmann *EVP, Corporate Banking*

Debt Capital Markets / Fixed Income
Global Head

Hans-Joachim Habben *SVP, Capital Markets* ⊤ 361 2307 [F] 361 5238
[E] hans-joachim.habben@nordlb.de

Country Head

Werner Kellner *Senior Vice President* ⊤ 361 5300 [F] 361 5157

Government Bonds
Head of Trading

Mena ter Veen *Vice President* ⊤ 361 9640 [F] 361 5466
[E] mena.terveen@nordlb.de

Eurobonds
Head of Syndication

Axel Weidemann *Assistant Vice President* ⊤ 361 2760 [F] 361 5238
[E] axel.weidermann@norlb.de

Head of Sales

Hans-Joachim Habben *SVP, Capital Markets* ⊤ 361 2307 [F] 361 5238
[E] hans-joachim.habben@nordlb.de

Head of Trading

Carsten Schrader *Assistant Vice President* ⊤ 361 9640 [F] 361 5466
[E] carsten.schrader@nordlb.de
Günther Gradtke *Vice President* ⊤ 361 9660 [F] 361 5466
[E] guenther.gradtke@nordlb.de

Bonds - General
New Issues Syndication

Axel Weidemann *Assistant Vice President* ⊤ 361 2760 [F] 361 5238
[E] axel.weidermann@norlb.de

New Issues

Thomas Arendt *Vice President* ⊤ 361 4600 [F] 361 5238
[E] thomas.arendt@nordlb.de

Other (Emerging Markets Bonds)
Other Currencies

Günther Gradtke *Vice President* ⊤ 361 9660 [F] 361 5466
[E] guenther.gradtke@nordlb.de

Equity Capital Markets
Country Head

Wolfgang Matzen *Vice President* ⊤ 361 9481 [F] 361 5157
[E] wolfgang.matzen@nordlb.de
Werner Kellner *Senior Vice President* ⊤ 361 5300 [F] 361 5157

Domestic Equities
Head of Syndication

Thomas Arendt *Vice President* ⊤ 361 4600 [F] 361 5238
[E] thomas.arendt@nordlb.de

Foreign Exchange
Global Head

Wilfried Bock *Senior Vice President* ⊤ 361 2075 [F] 361 5420
[E] wilfried.bock@nordlb.de

FX Traders / Sales People

Manfred Bergherr *Vice President* ⊤ 361 9600 [F] 361 5420
[E] manfred.bergherr@nordlb.de
Wolfgang Schwenden *Vice President* ⊤ 361 9610 [F] 361 5420
[E] wolfgang.schwenden@nordlb.de

Risk Management
Global Head

Eckhard Fiene *Senior Vice President* ⊤ 361 2991 [F] 361 4184
[E] eckhard.fiene@nordlb.de

Exchange-Traded Derivatives
FX Futures

Manfred Bergherr *Vice President* ⊤ 361 9600 [F] 361 5420
[E] manfred.bergherr@nordlb.de

IR Futures

Thomas Krüger *Vice President* ⊤ 361 9660 [F] 361 5466
[E] thomas.krueger@nordlb.de

Other Departments
Economic Research

Sonning Bredemeier *Executive Vice President*

Administration
Legal / In-House Counsel

Eicke Florkowski *Senior Vice President*

Corporate Communications

Sonning Bredemeier *Executive Vice President*

Nova Ljubljanska banka dd

Representative Office

Oeder Weg 48, D-60318 Frankfurt/Main
Tel: (69) 555 055; (69) 554 371 **Fax:** (69) 557 817 **Email:** nlb-ffm@compuserve.com

Senior Executive Officers
SVP & Resident Representative

Matevz Pirnat

GERMANY (+49)   www.euromoneydirectory.com

Sal Oppenheim jr & Cie KGaA — Head Office

Unter Sachsenhausen 4, D-50667 Cologne
PO Box 102743, D-50467 Cologne
Tel: (221) 145 01 **Fax:** (221) 145 1512 **Telex:** 8882547 **Swift:** SOPP DE 3K **Reuters:** SALOPP **Telerate:** Recipient
Reuters: OPDF (Dealing)

Senior Executive Officers
Chairman & Partner, Private Banking — Graf von Krockow

Others (Senior Executives)
Asset Management — Detlef Bierbaum *Partner*
Financial Markets — Dieter Pfundt *Partner*
Corporate Banking — Hans Detlef Bösel *Partner*
Administration — Johannes Maret *Partner*
Chairman's Office — Johann von Behr

General-Lending (DCM, SL)
Head of Corporate Banking — Wolfgang Jensen *Division Manager*
Helmut Zahn *Division Manager*

Risk Management
Head of Risk Management — Hans-Christoph Lachmann *Head*

Corporate Finance / M&A Advisory
Head of Corporate Finance — Hans Dahm *Manager, Corporate Finance*

Asset Management
Head — Bernd Borgmeiere *Division Manager*
Hermann Alexander Schindler *Division Manager*

Other Departments
Private Banking — Christopher von Oppenheim *Division Manager*
Wulf Matthias *Division Manager*

Administration

Technology & Systems
Peter Fröhlich

Legal / In-House Counsel
Dieter Rehbein

Compliance
Franz-Josef Löffelsender

Public Relations
Johann von Behr

Accounts / Audit
Manfred Uthoff

Sal Oppenheim jr & Cie KGaA — Full Branch Office

Königsallee 98, D-40212 Düsseldorf
PO Box 104051, D-40031 Düsseldorf
Tel: (211) 139 900 **Fax:** (211) 134 208 **Telex:** 2233 **Swift:** SOPP DE DD **Reuters:** OPPD

Senior Executive Officers
Senior Manager — B Röttgers

Foreign Exchange
Department: Foreign Exchange and Bullion
Head of Foreign Exchange — H Plum *Manager & Chief Dealer*

FX Traders / Sales People
D Schulte *Deputy Chief Dealer*
N Ivens *Holder of Procuration*
H Müller *Holder of Procuration*
A Frotz *Dealer*

528 Euromoney Directory 1999

www.euromoneydirectory.com　　　　　　　　GERMANY (+49)

Sal Oppenheim jr & Cie KGaA　　　　　　Full Branch Office
Bockenheimer Landstrasse 20, D-60323 Frankfurt/Main
PO Box 170419, D-60078 Frankfurt/Main
Tel: (69) 7134 0 **Fax:** (69) 7134 5211 **Telex:** 411016 **Reuters:** OPPF (Dealing) **Telerate:** Recipient

Senior Executive Officers
Department: See Cologne (Head Office)

Others (Senior Executives)
Financial Markets　　　　　　　　　　　　Dieter Pfundt *Partner*
Financial Institutions　　　　　　　　　　　Manfred Caesar *Head*

Debt Capital Markets / Fixed Income
Global Head　　　　　　　　　　　　　　Norbert Wieneke *Divisonal Manager* ☎ **7134 5257**

Domestic Government Bonds
Head of Sales　　　　　　　　　　　　　Wolfgang Lenertz
Head of Trading　　　　　　　　　　　　Carolyn Bunten ☎ **7134 5511**
Head of Research　　　　　　　　　　　James Douglas ☎ **7134 5523**
Head of Origination　　　　　　　　　　Kersten Schmitz ☎ **7134 5161**
Head of Syndication　　　　　　　　　　Alexander Szewald ☎ **7134 5564**

Non-Domestic Government Bonds
Domestic Bank Debt　　　　　　　　　　Kurt Klauditz *Head of Trading* ☎ **7134 5508**
　　　　　　　　　　　　　　　　　　　Michael Lindner *Head of Sales* ☎ **7134 5446**

Eurobonds
Head of Origination　　　　　　　　　　Georg Felix von Lewinski ☎ **7134 5595**
Head of Syndication　　　　　　　　　　Kersten Schmitz ☎ **7134 5161**
Head of Trading　　　　　　　　　　　　Kurt Klauditz *Head of Trading* ☎ **7134 5508**

Bonds - General
Structured Bonds　　　　　　　　　　　Volker Bellinger *Head of Trading* ☎ **7134 5255**
　　　　　　　　　　　　　　　　　　　Wolfgang Schwarz *Head of Sales* ☎ **7134 5542**

Emerging Market Bonds
Head of Trading　　　　　　　　　　　　Kurt Klauditz *Head of Trading* ☎ **7134 5508**

Libor-Based / Floating-Rate Products
FRN Origination　　　　　　　　　　　　Georg Felix von Lewinski ☎ **7134 5595**
FRN Sales　　　　　　　　　　　　　　Kristian Klasen ☎ **7134 5307**
Asset Swaps　　　　　　　　　　　　　Frank Deller *Head* ☎ **7134 5324**
Asset Swaps (Sales)　　　　　　　　　Michael Lindner *Head of Sales* ☎ **7134 5446**

Fixed-Income Repo
Head of Repo　　　　　　　　　　　　Walter Kraushaar ☎ **7134 5535**
Marketing & Product Development　　　Gerhard Eibner
Trading　　　　　　　　　　　　　　　Holger Pfeiffer ☎ **7134 5289**
Sales　　　　　　　　　　　　　　　　Ralf Hilfrich ☎ **7134 5297**

Fixed-Income Research
Head of Fixed Income　　　　　　　　Norbert Braems

Equity Capital Markets
Head of Trading　　　　　　　　　　　Hans-Peter Schneider *Co-Head, Equity Capital Markets* ☎ **7134 5302**

Domestic Equities
Head of Syndication　　　　　　　　　Kersten Schmitz ☎ **7134 5161**
Head of Trading　　　　　　　　　　　Hans-Peter Schneider *Co-Head, Equity Capital Markets* ☎ **7134 5302**
Head of Research　　　　　　　　　　Hans-Dieter Schollbach ☎ **(221) 145 2216**

International Equities
Head of Trading　　　　　　　　　　　Jörg Peter Heyn ☎ **7134 2353**

Equity Research
Head of Equity Research　　　　　　　Ralf Conen

Warrants
Head of Trading　　　　　　　　　　　Hans-Peter Schneider *Co-Head, Equity Capital Markets* ☎ **7134 5302**

Equity Repo / Securities Lending
Head　　　　　　　　　　　　　　　　Holger Pfeiffer ☎ **7134 5289**
Marketing; Head of Trading　　　　　　Walter Kraushaar ☎ **7134 5535**

Money Markets
Global Head　　　　　　　　　　　　Gerhard Scherer ☎ **7134 5355**

Foreign Exchange
Head of Institutional Sales; Corporate Sales　　Reinhard Berben ☎ **7134 5480**
Head of Trading　　　　　　　　　　Hans-Willi Wolber ☎ **7134 5482**

Euromoney Directory 1999　**529**

GERMANY (+49) www.euromoneydirectory.com

Sal Oppenheim jr & Cie KGaA (cont)

Risk Management
Global Head — Hans-Christoph Lachmann ☏ (221) 145 1240

Fixed Income Derivatives / Risk Management
IR Swaps Sales / Marketing — Marcus Schulte ☏ 7134 5332
IR Swaps Trading; IR Options Trading — Frank Deller *Head* ☏ 7134 5324

Foreign Exchange Derivatives / Risk Management
Cross-Currency Swaps, Sales / Marketing — Frank Deller *Head* ☏ 7134 5324
Cross-Currency Swaps, Trading — Thomas Preiss ☏ 7134 5445
Tatjana Patz ☏ 7134 5204
Frank Deller *Head* ☏ 7134 5324
Vanilla FX option Sales — Reinhard Berben ☏ 7134 5480
Vanilla FX option Trading — Jan Schrader ☏ 7134 5554

Other Currency Swap / FX Options Personnel
Ralf Heller ☏ 7134 5486
Adrian Marcu ☏ 7134 5356
Marcus Friedrich ☏ 7134 5334

Exotic Options (Barriers, Range, Timers, Digitals, Faders etc)
Trading — Jan Schrader ☏ 7134 5554

OTC Equity Derivatives
Sales — Joachim Rohrmann
Trading — Joachim Klähn ☏ 7134 5475

Settlement / Clearing
Head of Settlement / Clearing — Hans-Christoph Lachmann ☏ (221) 145 1240

Other Departments
Private Banking — Wulf Matthias ☏ 7134 5316

Administration

Technology & Systems
Peter Fröhlich ☏ (221) 145 2312

Legal / In-House Counsel
Dieter Rehbein ☏ (221) 145 1455

Compliance
Franz-Josef Löffelsender ☏ (221) 145 1369

Public Relations
Anne-Marie Frey ☏ (221) 145 2564

Sal Oppenheim jr & Cie KGaA — Full Branch Office

Odeonsplatz 12, D-80539 Munich, Bavaria
Tel: (89) 290 074 0 **Fax:** (89) 290 074 29

Senior Executive Officers
Senior Manager — Klaus Wagner

Paribas Frankfurt — Agency

Alternative trading name: Banque Paribas (Deutschland) OHG
Grüneburgweg 14, D-60322 Frankfurt/Main
PO Box 100363, D-600003 Frankfurt/Main
Tel: (69) 15205 555; (69) 15205 429 **Fax:** (69) 15205 505; (69) 15205 312 **Telex:** 416296 **Swift:** PARDEFF
Reuters: PBFF

Senior Executive Officers
General Manager — Thierry de Loriol ☏ 15205 431
General Manager, Commercial Banking — Hans-Albert Kleine ☏ 15205 314

Others (Senior Executives)
Business Development — Marianne Gottwick ☏ 15205 361
Thierry de Loriol *General Manager* ☏ 15205 431
Axel Großkreutz ☏ 15205 382
Stefan Volk ☏ 15205 398
Friedrich W. von Pfeil ☏ 15205 361

Equity Capital Markets
Tel: 15205 358 **Fax:** 15205 312
Country Head — Roland Lienau *Head* ☏ 15205 405

GERMANY (+49)

Domestic Equities
Head of Sales — Stefan Hüttermann ☎ **15205 407**
Karl Justus ☎ **15205 426**
Eberhard C. Langer ☎ **15205 406**
Roland Lienau *Head* ☎ **15205 405**
Gérard O'Doherty ☎ **15205 409**
Head of Trading — Claudia Cholewa ☎ **15205 411**
Kay Riegelhof ☎ **15205 412**
Michael Hoffman ☎ **15205 432**
Head of Research — Julie Statham ☎ **15205 401**
Charlotte Frenzel ☎ **15205 443**

International Equities
Head of Sales — Stefan Hüttermann ☎ **15205 407**
Karl Justus ☎ **15205 426**
Roland Lienau *Head* ☎ **15205 405**
Eberhard C. Langer ☎ **15205 406**
Gérard O'Doherty ☎ **15205 409**
Head of Trading — Claudia Cholewa ☎ **15205 411**
Kay Riegelhof ☎ **15205 412**
Michael Hoffman ☎ **15205 432**
Head of Research — Julie Statham ☎ **15205 401**
Charlotte Frenzel ☎ **15205 443**

Equity Repo / Securities Lending
Head — Thomas Brand *Head of Sales* ☎ **15205 55** F **15205 505**
E thomas_brand@paribas.com
Marketing — Romauld Orange *Head of Securities Lending Activities* ☎ **15205 429**
F **15205 312** E romauld_orange@paribas.com

Syndicated Lending
Department: Commercial Banking
Country Head — Hans-Albert Kleine *General Manager, Commercial Banking* ☎ **15205 314**
Head of Credit Committee — Jean-Michel Barthel *Head, Credit Risk Controlling* ☎ **15205 319**

Other (Trade Finance)
Corporate Multinationals — Carsten Strohdeicher ☎ **15205 348**
Forfaiting — Reinhard Wille ☎ **15205 309**
Export — Otto Köhler ☎ **15205 248**
Acquisition Finance — Heinz-Joachim Drewitz ☎ **15205 395**
Loan Services & Foreign Dept. — Madeleine Beier ☎ **15205 212**

Corporate Finance / M&A Advisory
Department: M&A Advisory
Tel: 15205 304 **Fax:** 15205 334
Country Head — John Chapman *Head* ☎ **15205 302**

Other (Corporate Finance)
Jan Hebeler ☎ **15205 352**
Jean-Sebastien Dietsch ☎ **15205 273**
Berthold Müller ☎ **15205 301**
Ralph Neher ☎ **15205 303**

Settlement / Clearing
Country Head — Vincent Lecomte *Head* ☎ **15205 505**
Operations — Richard Bartholomew *Operations, Securities Services* ☎ **15205 318**
Luc Chauvet *Financial Management* ☎ **15205 274**

Global Custody
Department: Securities Services
Tel: 15205 513 **Fax:** 15205 550
Country Head — Vincent Lecomte *Head* ☎ **15205 505**

Other (Global Custody)
Sales — Thomas Brand *Head of Sales* ☎ **15205 555** F **15205 505**
E thomas_brand@paribas.com
Pascal Pommier *Business Controller* ☎ **15205 563**

Asset Management
Department: Paribas Asset Management
Tel: 15205 397 **Fax:** 15205 338
Head — Arnold Dohmen *Head* ☎ **15205 342**
Portfolio Management — Ekkhard von Knebel-Doeberitz *Dedicated Account / Management*
☎ **15205 354**

Other (Asset Management)
Third Party / Distribution — Arnold Dohmen *Head* ☎ **15205 342**

Paribas Frankfurt (cont)
Department: Asset Liabilities Management
Other (Asset Management)
Sales
    Lothar Frank *Head* ☎ **15205 423**
    Richard Marterner ☎ **15205 439**
    Christa Domnick ☎ **15205 424**

Administration
Department: Other Departments
Head of Administration   Klaus Waldowski ☎ **15205 228**
Technology & Systems
Technology   Peter Bilge ☎ **15205 280**
Legal / In-House Counsel
Legal / Compliance / Secretary General   Paul Opitz ☎ **15205 245**
Compliance
Legal / Compliance / Secretary General   Paul Opitz ☎ **15205 245**
Accounts / Audit
Internal Control   Heidemarie Neuendorff ☎ **15205 247**
Other (Administration)
Human Relations / Administration   Klaus Waldowski ☎ **15205 228**
Sovereign & Institutional Finance   Bernard Janvier ☎ **15205 370**

PMP GmbH Wertpapiermakler
Head Office

Liebfrauenberg 39, D-60313 Frankfurt/Main
Tel: (69) 20980 **Fax:** (69) 280 282 **Reuters:** PMPEURO01 **Bloomberg:** PMP <Go>

Senior Executive Officers
Geschäftsführer   Peter Hakenberg
Geschäftsführer   Stephan Mütz
Geschäftsführer   Rolf Ensberg

Debt Capital Markets / Fixed Income
Eurobonds
Head of Trading   Stephan Mütz *Geschäftsführer*
Mortgage-Backed Securities
Head of Trading   Rolf Ensberg *Geschäftsführer*

Administration
Compliance
     Peter Hakenberg *Geschäftsführer*

Prager Handelsbank AG
Head Office

Gutleutstrasse 32, D-60329 Frankfurt/Main
PO Box 160664, D-60069 Frankfurt/Main
Tel: (69) 27304 0 **Fax:** (69) 27304 105 **Telex:** 413651 **Swift:** PHBK DE FF

Senior Executive Officers
Chairman of the Supervisory Board   Josef Tauber
Vice Chairman of the Supervisory Board   Miloslav Dudek
MD, Member of the Management Board   Hannes Dietrich
MD, Member of the Management Board   Frantisek Sejnoha
MD, Member of the Management Board   Gerhard Rohnfelder
International Division   Cornelia Mayr-Rosendorff
     Horst Müller

Equity Capital Markets
Department: Capital Markets
Global Head   Jürgen Rogalla *Senior Officer*

Syndicated Lending
Department: Loan Syndication / Asset Sales
Head of Origination   Horst Müller
Loan-Related Activities
Trade Finance   Horst Müller
Other (Trade Finance)
Documentary Credits; Letters of Credit   Cornelia Mayr-Rosendorff

Foreign Exchange
Department: Foreign Exchange and Bullion
Global Head   Jürgen Rogalla *Senior Officer*

www.euromoneydirectory.com GERMANY (+49)

Other Departments
Correspondent Banking Jürgen Rogalla *Senior Officer*
Administration
Head of Administration Manfred Fiedler

Quelle Bank GmbH & Co
Karl-Martell-Str 60, D-90431 Nürnberg
Tel: (911) 149 2030 **Fax:** (911) 149 2180
Website: www.quelle-bank.de

Senior Executive Officers
Chairman Joannes Verbunt ☏ **149 1400**
Managing Director Marcel van Leeuwen ☏ **149 2161**
Managing Director Klaus Pedell ☏ **149 2222**
Managing Director Hermann Zeilinger ☏ **149 2169**
Relationship Manager
Marketing Director Werner Decker
Organisation Director Michael Hamm ☏ **149 2153**
Administration
Public Relations
 Silvia van Leeuwen ☏ **149 2155**
Other (Administration)
Personal Director Bernd Lämmermann ☏ **149 2165**

Rabobank Deutschland AG
Solmsstrasse 2-26, D-60486 Frankfurt/Main
PO Box 900749, D-60447 Frankfurt/Main
Tel: (69) 70790 011 **Fax:** (69) 7714 7 **Telex:** 416913 **Swift:** RABO DE FF **Reuters:** RBSK

Senior Executive Officers
Chairman Hanno W E Riedlin
Chief Executive Officer Albert D Sonntag
Managing Director / General Manager Anton Nillesen
Debt Capital Markets / Fixed Income
Tel: 7079 0011 **Fax:** 7733 07
Fixed-Income Repo
Trading Maria Garripoli

Royal Bank of Canada Europe Limited   Full Branch Office
Lyoner Strasse 15, D-60528 Frankfurt/Main
Tel: (69) 66905 0 **Fax:** (69) 66905 256 **Telex:** 4032160 RBCD **Swift:** ROYC GB 22

Senior Executive Officers
Chairman R E Stanley
Managing Director S R Douglas
General Manager & Chief Treasurer Heinrich Coenen
Deputy General Manager Doris Schließer
Others (Senior Executives)
Board of Directors C S Brown
 P M Cutts
 R P R Darwall-Smith
 H de Guitaut
 C J H Fisher
 M G Klingsick
 S G A Scammell
 G P Z Tatrallyay
 S W Walker

General-Lending (DCM, SL)
Head of Corporate Banking Konrad Tomica
 Wolfgang Wollstadt

Money Markets
Country Head Heinrich Coenen *General Manager & Chief Treasurer*
Foreign Exchange
Country Head Heinrich Coenen *General Manager & Chief Treasurer*

GERMANY (+49) www.euromoneydirectory.com

Sabanci Bank plc
Representative Office

Mainzer Landstrasse 39, D-60311 Frankfurt/Main
Tel: (69) 242 668 0 Fax: (69) 242 668 21
Website: www.sabanci-bank.co.uk

Senior Executive Officers
Director — Claus Peter Hühner
Manager — Atilla Torgay

Sakura Bank (Deutschland) GmbH
Subsidiary Company

Im Trutz Frankfurt 55, D-60322 Frankfurt/Main
PO Box 170443, D-60078 Frankfurt/Main
Tel: (69) 959 681 0 Fax: (69) 555 091 Telex: 4189077 SAKF D Reuters: SAKU Telex: 4175937 SAKF D

Senior Executive Officers
Managing Director — Yoshiharu Nakamura ☎ **959 681 14**
General Manager — Walter E Rückert ☎ **959 681 11**
Company Secretary — Yayoi Urasaki ☎ **959 681 71**

Debt Capital Markets / Fixed Income
Department: Trading / Sales (Bonds / Swaps / Futures)
Tel: 959 681 50
Head of Fixed Income Sales — Edward Pfeiffenberger *Joint Head, Trading / Sales* ☎ **959 681 51**
Head of Fixed Income Trading — Eckhard Sauter *Joint Head, Trading / Sales* ☎ **959 681 52**
Hans-Joachim Gille *Dealer* ☎ **959 681 54**

Syndicated Lending
Head of Trading — Hiroshi Ukena *Head of Syndication* ☎ **959 681 61**

Money Markets
Tel: 959 681 50
Global Head — Hans-Joachim Gille *Dealer* ☎ **959 681 54**
Country Head — Andreas Mayr *Trainee* ☎ **959 681 53**
Michael Gondolf *Authorized Dealer* ☎ **959 681 55**

Domestic Commercial Paper
Head of Sales — Edward Pfeiffenberger *Joint Head, Trading / Sales* ☎ **959 681 51**
Head of Trading — Eckhard Sauter *Joint Head, Trading / Sales* ☎ **959 681 52**

Eurocommercial Paper
Head of Trading — Michael Gondolf *Authorized Dealer* ☎ **959 681 55**
Andreas Mayr *Trainee* ☎ **959 681 53**

Risk Management
Tel: 959 681 30
Global Head — Marianne Hödl ☎ **959 681 32**

Settlement / Clearing
Tel: 959 681 20
Regional Head — Kerstin Sommer ☎ **959 681 22**

Global Custody
Tel: 959 681 20
Regional Head — Kerstin Sommer ☎ **959 681 22**

Administration
Head of Administration — Ronald E M Moore *Operations Manager* ☎ **959 681 31**

Technology & Systems
Ronald E M Moore *Operations Manager* ☎ **959 681 31**

Compliance
Ronald E M Moore *Operations Manager* ☎ **959 681 31**

Accounts / Audit
Marianne Hödl ☎ **959 681 32**

Salomon Smith Barney
Subsidiary Company

Kaiserstrasse 29, D-60311 Frankfurt/Main
PO Box 160654, D-60069 Frankfurt/Main
Tel: (69) 2607 0 Fax: (69) 2325 70 Telex: 4189107 Reuters: FFSC Telex: 4189117; Reuters: SOMO; FFSG

Senior Executive Officers
MD / Speaker of the Board — Hendrik Borggreve ☎ **2607 150**
MD / Speaker of the Board — Daniel R Lee ☎ **2607 101**
Financial Director — Hans Ostermair *Director & Member of the Board* ☎ **2607 200**

www.euromoneydirectory.com GERMANY (+49)

Debt Capital Markets / Fixed Income
Country Head
Head of Fixed Income Sales — Christian Holste *Director* ☎ 2607 356 ℻ 2607 125
Head of Fixed Income Trading — Marcus Guddat *Director* ☎ 2607 356 ℻ 2607 125

Juergen Guba *Vice President*

Domestic Government Bonds
Head of Sales; Head of Trading — Marcus Guddat *Director* ☎ 2607 356 ℻ 2607 125

Eurobonds
Head of Origination — Juergen Guba *Vice President*
Head of Syndication — Christel Winheim *Vice President*
Head of Sales — Christian Holste
Head of Trading — Marcus Guddat *Director* ☎ 2607 356 ℻ 2607 125

Fixed-Income Repo
Head of Repo; Matched Book Manager — Michael Braumöller *Vice President* ☎ 2607 330 ℻ 2607 371
 ✉ michael.braumoeller@frankfurt.sbi.com
Trading — Menko Jaekel *Trader*

Equity Capital Markets
Domestic Equities
Head of Sales — Bryon Gilliam *Vice President*
Head of Trading — Steffen Hohmeister

International Equities
Head of Sales — Vaneesa Tourle *Vice President*

Equity Repo / Securities Lending
Marketing — Michael Braumöller *Vice President* ☎ 2607 330 ℻ 2607 371
 ✉ michael.braumoeller@frankfurt.sbi.com
Head of Trading — Menko Jaekel *Trader*
Michael Braumöller *Vice President* ☎ 2607 330 ℻ 2607 371
 ✉ michael.braumoeller@frankfurt.sbi.com

Money Markets
Country Head — Michael Braumöller *Vice President* ☎ 2607 330 ℻ 2607 371
 ✉ michael.braumoeller@frankfurt.sbi.com

Corporate Finance / M&A Advisory
Country Head — Hendrik Borggreve *MD / Speaker of the Board* ☎ 2607 150

Settlement / Clearing
Country Head — Hans Ostermair *Director & Member of the Board* ☎ 2607 200

Administration
Technology & Systems
Dieter Visser *Assistant Director*

Legal / In-House Counsel
Edith Christoffer *Vice President*

Compliance
Michael Zollweg *Vice President*

Sanwa Bank (Deutschland) AG Head Office

Bockenheimer Landstrasse 51/53, D-60325 Frankfurt/Main
Tel: (69) 17009 40 **Fax:** (69) 172 588 **Telex:** 412892 **Bloomberg:** SGERMANY

Senior Executive Officers
President — Nobuyuki Kono ☎ 17009 4125
MD & General Manager — Erich Gonder ☎ 17009 4123

Debt Capital Markets / Fixed Income
Eurobonds
Head of Syndication; Head of Sales — Kota Ishii *Head of Syndicate* ☎ 17009 4108

Bonds - General
Pfandbrief Trading — Ingo Nix *Dealer* ☎ 17009 4104

Fixed-Income Research
Global Head — Nobuo Date *Economist* ☎ 17009 4105

Settlement / Clearing
Tel: 17009 4122
Regional Head — Dirk Nickchen ☎ 17009 4131
Fixed-Income Settlement — Gabriele Baumgarth ☎ 17009 4121

Administration
Technology & Systems
Gabriela Albers ☎ 17009 4135

Euromoney Directory 1999 535

GERMANY (+49) www.euromoneydirectory.com

Schiffshypothekenbank zu Lübeck AG — Subsidiary Company

Brandstwiete 1, D-20457 Hamburg
PO Box 110311, D-20403 Hamburg
Tel: (40) 3701 4646

Senior Executive Officers
Chairman of the Supervisory Board — Jürgen Krumnow
Managing Director — Torsten Wagner ☏ **3701 4615**
Managing Director — Tjark H Woydt ☏ **3701 3128**
Senior Counsel — L Peter Flug ☏ **3701 4640**
International Division — Annemarie Ehrhardt Director ☏ **3701 4633**

General-Lending (DCM, SL)
Head of Corporate Banking — Henrich Brandt von Fackh Director ☏ **3701 3275**
Gunda Steiner Director ☏ **3701 4636**

Corporate Finance / M&A Advisory
Head of Corporate Finance — Holger Hilmer Director ☏ **3701 3299**

Administration
Legal / In-House Counsel — L Peter Flug Senior Counsel ☏ **3701 4640**

Schröder Münchmeyer Hengst AG

Kurfürstendamm 185, D-10707 Berlin
PO Box 151340, D-10675 Berlin
Tel: (30) 884 882 0 **Fax:** (30) 884 882 30

Schröder Münchmeyer Hengst AG

Cecilienallee 11, D-40474 Düsseldorf
PO Box 104743, D-40038 Düsseldorf
Tel: (211) 47811 0 **Fax:** (211) 47811 24

Schröder Münchmeyer Hengst AG

Friedensstrasse 6-10, D-60311 Frankfurt/Main
PO Box 102042, D-60020 Frankfurt/Main
Tel: (69) 2179 0 **Fax:** (69) 2179 511

Senior Executive Officers
Others (Senior Executives)
A Muth Management Board
G Lehmann Management Board

Schröder Münchmeyer Hengst AG

Ballindamm 33, D-20095 Hamburg
PO Box 105903, D-20040 Hamburg
Tel: (40) 3295 0 **Fax:** (40) 3295 270

Schröder Münchmeyer Hengst AG

Maximilianstraße 14, D-80539 Munich, Bavaria
PO Box 101362, D-80087 Munich, Bavaria
Tel: (89) 290 912 0 **Fax:** (89) 290 912 15

Schröder Münchmeyer Hengst AG

Kaiserstraße 73, D-63065 Offenbach
PO Box 101761, D-63017 Offenbach
Tel: (69) 2179 0 **Fax:** (69) 2179 890

www.euromoneydirectory.com GERMANY (+49)

Schwäbische Bank AG
Head Office

Königstrasse 28, D-70173 Stuttgart, Baden-Württemberg
PO Box 104642, D-70041 Stuttgart, Baden-Württemberg
Tel: (711) 22922 0 **Fax:** (711) 221 698 **Telex:** 723812 **Swift:** BWBK DE 6S XXX
Email: service@schwaebische-bank.de
Website: www.schwaebische-bank.de

Senior Executive Officers
Chairman | Peter Linder [T] **22922 10**
Vice Chairman | Maximilian Wölfe [T] **22922 13**

Debt Capital Markets / Fixed Income
Head of Fixed Income Trading | Robert Klugmann [T] **22922 20**

Equity Capital Markets
Head of Trading | Peter Linder [T] **22922 10**

Syndicated Lending
Fax: 22922 39
Head of Trading | Maximilian Wölfe *Vice Chairman* [T] **22922 13**

Money Markets
Head of Money Markets | Robert Klugmann [T] **22922 20**

Foreign Exchange
Head of Foreign Exchange | Oliver Gehb [T] **22922 45**

Risk Management
Head of Risk Management | Werner Held [T] **22922 60**

Settlement / Clearing
Head of Settlement / Clearing | Klaus-Dieter Hahn [T] **22922 25**

Global Custody
Head of Global Custody | Peter Linder [T] **22922 10**

Other Departments
Chief Credit Officer | Maximilian Wölfe *Vice Chairman* [T] **22922 13**

Administration
Technology & Systems
 | Bertram Eisele [T] **22922 70** [F] **22922 73**

Legal / In-House Counsel
 | Hermut Naujoks [T] **22922 30** [F] **22922 39**

Compliance
 | Jörg Massek [T] **22922 63** [F] **22922 73**

SGZ-Bank AG
Head Office

46 Bockenheimer Anlage, D-60322 Frankfurt/Main D-60274 Frankfurt/Main
Tel: (69) 7139 0 **Fax:** (69) 7139 1309 **Telex:** 41525142 **Swift:** GENO DE 55 **Email:** info@sgz-bank.de **Reuters:** SGZF
Cable: SGZBANK
Website: www.sgz-bank.de

Senior Executive Officers
Chairman | Ulrich Brixner
Managing Director | Karl-Heinz Vollmer
Managing Director | Manfred Wächterhäuser
Managing Director | Heinz Hilgert
Managing Director | Dietrich Voigtländer

Debt Capital Markets / Fixed Income
Global Head | Rainer Holbach *Executive Vice President* [T] **7139 1216**

Domestic Government Bonds
Head of Sales | Matthias Hillmer *First Vice President* [T] **7139 1453**
Head of Trading | Erik Wredenhagen *First Vice President* [T] **7139 1833**

Non-Domestic Government Bonds
Sales; Trading | Bernd Hillingshauser *First Vice President* [T] **7139 1262**

Eurobonds
Head of Sales | Matthias Hillmer *First Vice President* [T] **7139 1453**
Head of Trading | Hans-Achim Scholl *First Vice President* [T] **7139 1274**

Bonds - General
Jumbo Bonds | Erik Wredenhagen *First Vice President* [T] **7139 1833**
Currency Bonds | Bernd Hillingshauser *First Vice President* [T] **7139 1262**

GERMANY (+49) www.euromoneydirectory.com

SGZ-Bank AG (cont)

Libor-Based / Floating-Rate Products
FRN Sales — Matthias Hillmer *First Vice President* ☏ **7139 1453**
FRN Trading — Thomas Kaltwasser *First Vice President* ☏ **7139 1881**

Fixed-Income Repo
Head of Repo — Willi Zinßer *Vice President* ☏ **7139 1287**

Equity Capital Markets
International Equities
Head of Sales; Head of Trading — Bernd Hillingshauser *First Vice President* ☏ **7139 1262**

Syndicated Lending
Tel: 7139 1481 **Fax:** 7139 1170
Global Head — Klaus Wenk *General Manager*
Head of Syndication — Marco Ernst *Manager* ☏ **7139 1736**

Loan-Related Activities
Trade Finance — Klaus Wenk *General Manager*
Project Finance — Heiko Staroßom *General Manager* ☏ **7139 1266**

Money Markets
Global Head — Wolfgang Köhler *General Manager* ☏ **7139 1688**
Regional Head — Willi Zinßer *Vice President* ☏ **7139 1287**

Foreign Exchange
Global Head — Wolfgang Köhler *General Manager* ☏ **7139 1688**
Regional Head — Bernhard Kuntz *First Vice President* ☏ **7139 85**

Risk Management
Global Head — Wolfgang Köhler *General Manager* ☏ **7139 1688**
Regional Head — Michael Schulze ☏ **7139 1167**

Fixed Income Derivatives / Risk Management
IR Swaps Sales / Marketing; IR Swaps Trading; IR Options Trading — Thomas Kaltwasser *First Vice President* ☏ **7139 1881**

Foreign Exchange Derivatives / Risk Management
Cross-Currency Swaps, Trading — Thomas Kaltwasser *First Vice President* ☏ **7139 1881**
Vanilla FX option Sales; Vanilla FX option Trading — Bernhard Kuntz *First Vice President* ☏ **7139 85**

Other Departments
Private Banking — Wolfgang Müller
Correspondent Banking — Klaus Wenk *General Manager*

Administration

Technology & Systems
Sigurt Bünte

Legal / In-House Counsel
Friedhelm Buthmann

Public Relations
Mathias Beers

Société Générale — Full Branch Office

Friedrichstrasse 71, D-10117 Berlin
Tel: (30) 209 465 00 **Fax:** (30) 209 465 01 **Telex:** 411029 A SOGED **Swift:** SOGE DE FF BER

Senior Executive Officers
President — Daniel Bouton
General Manager — Henri Bonnet ☏ (69) 7174 101 ✉ (69) 7174 109
Deputy General Manager — Klaus Stiefermann ☏ (69) 7174 111 ✉ (69) 7174 109

Others (Senior Executives)
Head of Branch — Jacques Bensen ☏ 209 465 11 ✉ 209 465 01

Société Générale — Full Branch Office

Unter Sachsenhausen 17/19, D-50667 Cologne
PO Box 103162, D-50471 Cologne
Tel: (221) 1622 0 **Fax:** (221) 1622 211 **Telex:** 411029 A SOGED **Swift:** SOGE DE FF KOE

Senior Executive Officers
President — Daniel Bouton
General Manager — Henri Bonnet ☏ (69) 7174 101 ✉ (69) 7174 109
Deputy General Manager — Klaus Stiefermann ☏ (69) 7174 111 ✉ (69) 7174 109

www.euromoneydirectory.com GERMANY (+49)

Others (Senior Executives)
Head of Branch   Jean Moulart ☎ **1622 218**

Société Générale   Full Branch Office

Mainzer Landstrasse 36, D-60325 Frankfurt/Main
PO Box 101935, D-60019 Frankfurt/Main
Tel: (69) 7174 0 **Fax:** (69) 7174 196 **Telex:** 411029 A SOGED **Swift:** SOGE DE FF

Senior Executive Officers
President   Daniel Bouton
General Manager   Henri Bonnet ☎ **7174 101** F **7174 109**
Deputy General Manager   Klaus Stiefermann ☎ **7174 111** F **7174 109**
Others (Senior Executives)
Head of Branch   Manfred Beck ☎ **7174 400** F **7174 139**

Société Générale   Full Branch Office

Jungfernstieg 7, D-20354 Hamburg
PO Box 300143, D-20301 Hamburg
Tel: (40) 356 001 0 **Fax:** (40) 356 001 17 **Telex:** 411029 SOGED **Swift:** SOGE DE FF HAM

Senior Executive Officers
President   Daniel Bouton
General Manager   Henri Bonnet ☎ **(69) 7174 101** F **(69) 7174 109**
Deputy General Manager   Klaus Stiefermann ☎ **(69) 7174 111** F **(69) 7174 109**
Others (Senior Executives)
Head of Branch   Christian Schmied ☎ **356 001 14**

Société Générale   Full Branch Office

Kaiserstrasse 160/162, D-76133 Karlsruhe
PO Box 111365, D-76063 Karlsruhe
Tel: (721) 1803 0 **Fax:** (721) 1803 99 **Telex:** 411029 A SOGED

Senior Executive Officers
President   Daniel Bouton
General Manager   Henri Bonnet ☎ **(69) 7147 101** F **(69) 7174 109**
Deputy General Manager   Klaus Stiefermann ☎ **(69) 7174 111** F **(69) 7174 109**
Others (Senior Executives)
Head of Branch   Romain Lillié ☎ **1803 14**

Société Générale   Full Branch Office

Kardinal-Faulhaber Strasse 14a, D-80333 Munich, Bavaria
PO Box 101262, D-80086 Munich, Bavaria
Tel: (89) 290 066 0 **Fax:** (89) 290 066 13 **Telex:** 411029 SOGED **Swift:** SOGE DE FF MUE

Senior Executive Officers
President   Daniel Bouton
General Manager   Henri Bonnet ☎ **(69) 7174 101** F **(69) 7174 109**
Deputy General Manager   Klaus Stiefermann ☎ **(69) 7174 111** F **(69) 7174 109**
Others (Senior Executives)
Head of Branch   Henri Zimmer ☎ **290 066 10**

Société Générale   Full Branch Office

Bahnhofstrasse 32, D-66111 Saarbrücken
PO Box 102851, D-66028 Saarbrücken
Tel: (681) 3018 0 **Fax:** (681) 3018 160 **Telex:** 411029 SOGED **Swift:** SOGE DD FF SAA

Senior Executive Officers
President   Daniel Bouton
General Manager   Henri Bonnet ☎ **(69) 7174 101** F **(69) 7174 109**
Deputy General Manager   Klaus Stiefermann ☎ **(69) 7174 111** F **(69) 7174 109**
Others (Senior Executives)
Head of Branch   Remy Chomski ☎ **3018 101**

GERMANY (+49)　　　　www.euromoneydirectory.com

Sparkasse Bad Hersfeld-Rotenburg

Dudenstrasse 15, D-36251 Bad Hersfeld
PO Box 1953, D-36251 Bad Hersfeld
Tel: (6621) 850 **Fax:** (6621) 85475 **Telex:** 0493314 **Swift:** HELA DE FF

Senior Executive Officers
Chairman　　　　　　　　　　　　　Hans Lapp [T] **(6621) 85101** [F] **(6621) 85159**

Sparkasse Bonn　　　　　　　　　　　　　　　　　　　　　　　　Head Office

Friedensplatz 1, D-53111 Bonn
Tel: (228) 606 0 **Fax:** (228) 606 1840 **Telex:** 886502 **Swift:** BONS DE 33 **Email:** info@sparkasse-bonn.de
Website: www.sparkasse-bonn.de

Senior Executive Officers
Chairman　　　　　　　　　　　　　Michael Kranz
Chief Executive Officer　　　　　　　Wolfgang Riedel
International Division　　　　　　　Georg Altenweger *Manager* [T] **606 1800**

General-Lending (DCM, SL)
Head of Corporate Banking　　　　　Benedikt Allen *Manager, Investment Banking* [T] **606 1710**

Sparkasse Krefeld

Ostwall 155, D-47798 Krefeld
Tel: (2151) 68 0 **Fax:** (2151) 68 2100 **Swift:** SPKR DE 33

Senior Executive Officers
Chairman　　　　　　　　　　　　　Dieter Pützhofen
Managing Director / General Manager　Wenzel Nass

Spütz AG　　　　　　　　　　　　　　　　　　　　　　　　　　Head Office

Blumenstrasse 14, D-40212 Düsseldorf
PO Box 104553, D-40212 Düsseldorf
Tel: (21) 1860 00 **Fax:** (21) 1860 112 **Email:** sartingen@sputz.de **Reuters:** SPUETZ **Bloomberg:** SARTINGEN
Website: www.sputz.de

Senior Executive Officers
Chairman　　　　　　　　　　　　　Werner Schwilling
Chief Executive Officer　　　　　　　Gerd Spütz
Managing Director　　　　　　　　　Volker Pyrtek
Global Head of Investment Banking　　Axel Sartingen [T] **8600 700**

General-Lending (DCM, SL)
Head of Corporate Banking　　　　　Andreas Schüeler [T] **(691) 3300**

General-Investment
Head of Investment　　　　　　　　Axel Sartingen *Global Head of Investment Banking* [T] **8600 700**

Debt Capital Markets / Fixed Income
Tel: 8600 400
Head of Fixed Income　　　　　　　Andreas Schüeler [T] **(691) 3300**
Head of Fixed Income Trading　　　　Axel Sartingen *Global Head of Investment Banking* [T] **8600 700**

Eurobonds
Head of Trading　　　　　　　　　　Andreas Schüeler [T] **(691) 3300**

Emerging Market Bonds
Head　　　　　　　　　　　　　　　Axel Sartingen *Global Head of Investment Banking* [T] **8600 700**

Fixed-Income Repo
Trading　　　　　　　　　　　　　　Ronald Hofmeïsder *Head of Trading*
　　　　　　　　　　　　　　　　　　Thomas Hainz
　　　　　　　　　　　　　　　　　　Colin Ward
　　　　　　　　　　　　　　　　　　Hans Peter van Wersch
　　　　　　　　　　　　　　　　　　Stephan Schimberg
　　　　　　　　　　　　　　　　　　Bernd Spengler
　　　　　　　　　　　　　　　　　　Peter Schaefer
　　　　　　　　　　　　　　　　　　Zoe Jahub
　　　　　　　　　　　　　　　　　　Justine Bouchot

www.euromoneydirectory.com   GERMANY (+49)

Equity Capital Markets
Tel: (691) 3300
Global Head   Christian Stachow
Settlement / Clearing
Country Head   Ute Windeck ☎ 8600 130

Stadtsparkasse Dortmund   Head Office

Freistuhl 2, D-44137 Dortmund
PO Box 105054, D-44047 Dortmund
Tel: (231) 183 0 **Fax:** (231) 183 295; (231) 183 3505 **Telex:** 8227390 **Swift:** DORT DE 33
Email: s-direkt@stadtsparkasse.dortmund.de
Website: www.sparkasse.dortmund.de

Senior Executive Officers
Chairman   Helmut Kohls ☎ 183 1001
Deputy Chairman   Horst Bremer ☎ 183 4001
Director   Klaus Marciniak ☎ 183 2001
Chief Executive Officer   Uwe Samulewicz *Director* ☎ 183 3001
International Division   Johannes Krispin *Head, International Department* ☎ 183 3501
Foreign Exchange
Head of Trading   Sylvia Endemann *Dealer, FX* ☎ 183 3531
Other Departments
Correspondent Banking   Martin Einhaus ☎ 183 3532

Stadtsparkasse Duisburg   Head Office

Königstrasse 23-25, D-47051 Duisberg, Northrhine-Westphalia
PO Box 101511, D-47015 Duisberg, Northrhine-Westphalia
Tel: (203) 28150 **Fax:** (203) 281 5888; (203) 281 5595 **Telex:** 855785 **Swift:** DUIS DE 33
Cable: stadtsparkasse duisburg

Senior Executive Officers
Chairman   Alfred Reifenberg ☎ 281 5581

Stadtsparkasse Hannover   Head Office

Raschplatz 4, D-30001 Hannover
PO Box 145, Hannover
Tel: (511) 346 0 **Fax:** (511) 346 2525; (511) 346 2389 **Telex:** 922315 HANS D **Swift:** HANS DE 2H
Email: ssk-hannover@t-online.de
Website: www.stadtsparkasse-hannover.de

Senior Executive Officers
Chairman, Board of Management Harald Quensen
Chairman, Supervisory Board   Herbert Schmalstieg
International Division   Arno Bach *Vice President* ☎ 346 2380
                                 Frank Börnert *Manager* ☎ 346 2391
                                 Wolfgang Schauzu *Assistant Manager* ☎ 346 2381
                                 Gerhard Lahmann ☎ 346 2382
                                 Martin Behrmann ☎ 346 2387

Stadtsparkasse Köln

Hahnenstrasse 57, D-50667 Cologne
PO Box 103544, D-50475 Cologne
Tel: (221) 2261 **Fax:** (221) 240 1324 **Telex:** 8882710 KLNA D **Swift:** COLS DE 33

Senior Executive Officers
Chairman   Gustav Adolf Schröder
Debt Capital Markets / Fixed Income
Country Head   arndt Hallmann *Head of Capital Markets*

Euromoney Directory 1999   **541**

GERMANY (+49)　　　　　www.euromoneydirectory.com

Stadtsparkasse München
Full Branch Office

Sparkassenstrasse 2, D-80331 Munich, Bavaria
Tel: (89) 2167 0 **Fax:** (89) 2167 5151; (89) 2167 6408 **Telex:** 5216200 **Swift:** SSKM DE MM
Website: www.sskmde

Senior Executive Officers
Chairman　　　　　　　　　　　　Josef Turiaux ☏ **2167 2200**
Chief Executive Officer　　　　　Josef Turiaux ☏ **2167 2200**
Financial Director　　　　　　　　Karlheinz Strobl ☏ **2167 7301**
International Division　　　　　　Walter Escherle ☏ **2167 5101**

Stadtsparkasse Nürnberg

Lorenzer Strasse 2, D-90327 Nürnberg
Tel: (911) 230 1 **Fax:** (911) 230 4752 **Telex:** 623221 **Email:** stadsparkasse-nuernberg@t-online.de
Website: www.stadsparkasse-nuernberg.de

Senior Executive Officers
Chairman　　　　　　　　　　　　　　　　　　Prof Hubert Weiler
Managing Director / General Manager　　　Theo Döbler
Managing Director / General Manager　　　Helmut Lohmann
International Division　　　　　　　　　　　　Maximillian Ganczarski

Stadtsparkasse Wuppertal
Head Office

Islandufer 15, D-42103 Wuppertal
PO Box 100340, D-42097 Wuppertal
Tel: (202) 488 2320 **Fax:** (202) 488 2660 **Telex:** 8592222 **Swift:** WUPS DE 33

Senior Executive Officers
General Manager　　　　　　Gerd Scholz
International Division　　　　Kurt Lichtenberg Manager, Foreign Department

Others (Senior Executives)
Manager　　　　　　　　　　　Peter H. Vaupel
　　　　　　　　　　　　　　　　Friedrich-Wilhelm Schäfer
　　　　　　　　　　　　　　　　Manfred Wickendick

Stopanska Banka AD
Representative Office

Porzellanhof Straße 4/III, Frankfurt/Main
Tel: (69) 285 792 **Fax:** (69) 284 624 **Telex:** 416779

Stuttgarter Bank AG
Head Office

Schloss-Strasse 21, D-70174 Stuttgart, Baden-Württemberg
PO Box 104441, 70039 Stuttgart, Baden-Württemberg
Tel: 711 181 0 **Fax:** 711 181 2497 **Telex:** 721860 stbd **Swift:** VOBA DE SS
Website: www.stuttgarter-bank.de

Senior Executive Officers
Chairman　　　　　　　　　　　Werner Isern
Chief Executive Officer　　　　Hans-Joachim Reissner Senior Executive Officer
　　　　　　　　　　　　　　　　　Karl-Armin Alberts Senior Executive Officer

Others (Senior Executives)
Senior Manager　　　　　　　Wolfgang Tresselt GM, International Department ☏ **711 181 2385**

Syndicated Lending

Loan-Related Activities
Trade Finance　　　　　　　　Wolfgang Tresselt GM, International Department ☏ **711 181 2385**

Other Departments
Correspondent Banking　　　Wolfgang Tresselt GM, International Department ☏ **711 181 2385**

www.euromoneydirectory.com   GERMANY (+49)

Südwestdeutsche Landesbank   Head Office

Alternative trading name: SüdwestLB
Am Hauptbahnhof 2, D-70173 Stuttgart, Baden-Württemberg
PO Box 106349, D-70049 Stuttgart, Baden-Württemberg
Tel: (711) 127 0 **Fax:** (711) 127 3000
Website: www.suedwestlb.de

Senior Executive Officers
Treasurer   Heiko Laib *Senior Executive Vice President*

Debt Capital Markets / Fixed Income
Global Head   Günter Einöder *Senior Vice President* ☎ **127 5305**
Regional Head   Kurt Camphausen *Senior Vice President* ☎ **127 5310**

Domestic Government Bonds
Head of Sales   Hubert Leist *Vice President* ☎ **127 5320**
Head of Trading   Reiner Meisnest *Vice President* ☎ **127 5351**

Non-Domestic Government Bonds
    Hans-Joachim Naderwitz *Vice President* ☎ **127 5340**

Eurobonds
Head of Sales; Head of Trading   Uwe Nunn *Vice President* ☎ **127 5380**
Head of Trading   Hans-Joachim Naderwitz *Vice President* ☎ **127 5340**

Bonds - General
International Funding   Eugene Yurist *Vice President* ☎ **127 5270**
OTC Bond Options & Bond Futures   Matthias Becher *Vice President* ☎ **127 5407**

Libor-Based / Floating-Rate Products
Asset Swaps   Jayant Govindia *Vice President* ☎ **+44 (171) 634 1813**
    Klaus Lederer *Vice President* ☎ **127 5250**

Fixed-Income Repo
Head of Repo   Torsten Biesel *Junior Vice President* ☎ **127 5316**

Equity Capital Markets
Tel: +49 (69) 29975 0 **Fax:** +49 (69) 29975 1560
Global Head   Michael Wasserhaas *Senior Vice President* ☎ **+49 (69) 2997 1519**

Domestic Equities
Head of Sales   Claus Messenzehl *Vice President* ☎ **+49 (69) 29975 1505**
Head of Trading   Michael Wallmeyer *Vice President* ☎ **+49 (69) 29975 1514**

Other (Domestic Equities)
    Hendrik Klein *Sales Trader*

Money Markets
Global Head   Peter Pawlik *Senior Vice President* ☎ **127 5200**

Wholesale Deposits
Head of Sales   Bernd Hellerich *Vice President* ☎ **127 5240**

Foreign Exchange
Department: Foreign Exchange / Money Markets
Tel: 127 5101 **Fax:** 127 5192
Global Head   Walter Maier *Senior Vice President* ☎ **127 5100**
Head of Institutional Sales; Corporate Sales   Gerhard Klink *Vice President* ☎ **127 5110**
Head of Trading   Thilo Adler *Vice President* ☎ **127 5160**

FX Traders / Sales People
Head of Forwards, MM   Thomas Hilderbrand *Vice President, Forwards* ☎ **127 5115**
Head of Spot   Ralf Elmer *Vice President, Spot FX* ☎ **127 5138**
IR Derivatives   Thomas Hilderbrand *Vice President, Forwards* ☎ **127 5115**

Risk Management
Global Head   Peter Pawlik *Senior Vice President* ☎ **127 5200**
IR Swaps Sales / Marketing; IR Swaps Trading   Martina Wemmer *Assistant Vice President* ☎ **127 5251**
IR Options Sales / Marketing   Rüdiger Ohnesorge *Vice President* ☎ **127 5280**

Foreign Exchange Derivatives / Risk Management
Spot / Forwards Trading   Thomas Hilderbrand *Vice President, Forwards* ☎ **127 5115**
    Ralf Elmer *Vice President, Spot FX* ☎ **127 5138**
Vanilla FX option Sales   Vincent Weevers ☎ **127 5554**
Vanilla FX option Trading   Armin Wendel ☎ **127 5554**

Exotic Options (Barriers, Range, Timers, Digitals, Faders etc)
Sales; Trading   Christoph Seegeret ☎ **127 5554**

GERMANY (+49) www.euromoneydirectory.com

The Sumitomo Bank Limited
Full Branch Office

Immermannstrasse 14/16, D-40210 Düsseldorf
Tel: (211) 3619 0 Fax: (211) 3619 236 Telex: 8587114

Senior Executive Officers
General Manager Christoph Nembach ☎ 3619 232
Chief Executive Officer Michael Oellers *Executive Director* ☎ 3619 256
Chief Operating Officer Peter Pasch *Joint General Manager* ☎ 3619 211
International Division Thomas Eichinger *Assistant Manager* ☎ 3619 222

Svenska Handelsbanken Niederlassung Frankfurt
Full Branch Office

Mittlerer Hasenpfad 25, D-60598 Frankfurt/Main
Tel: (69) 60506 0 Fax: (69) 60506 252 Telex: 414796 SHB D Swift: HAND DE FF

Senior Executive Officers
General Manager Pär-Ivan Pärson ☎ 60506 102 60506 257
Executive Secretary Gabriele Niemöller ☎ 60506 173 60506 257

Money Markets
Head of Money Markets Ulrich Evers ☎ 60506 290

Foreign Exchange
Head of Foreign Exchange Ulrich Evers ☎ 60506 290

Settlement / Clearing
Head of Settlement / Clearing Klaus-Dieter Timmas ☎ 60506 290

Other Departments
Chief Credit Officer Brigitta Bjelkström ☎ 60506 162
Cash Management Johan Condé ☎ 60506 106

Administration
Head of Administration Rudolf Wittmann ☎ 60506 141

Technology & Systems
 Anders Ahrencrantz ☎ 60506 110

Accounts / Audit
 Johan Bengtsson ☎ 60506 156

T Garanti Bankasi AS
Full Branch Office

Friedrich Ebert Strasse 45, D-40210 Düsseldorf
Tel: (211) 173 200 Fax: (211) 354 289

Senior Executive Officers
Managing Director Fahri Birincioglu
Managing Director H Jürgen Hassenpelug

Syndicated Lending
Head of Origination Tolga Bastak

Money Markets
Head of Money Markets Ebru Kutlu

Other Departments
Correspondent Banking Ebru Kutlu

TFS Derivatives GmbH
Subsidiary Company

Goethestrasse 7, D-60313 Frankfurt/Main
Tel: (69) 283 616 Fax: (69) 288 949 Reuters: 63680, 48460
Dealing Tel: 534 5160

Senior Executive Officers
Managing Director Helmut Gaussmann

Others (Senior Executives)
 Jeremy Cordrey *Broker*
 Marcus Croonen *Broker*
 Rabia-Nur Krettek *Assistant to the Managing Director*

www.euromoneydirectory.com　　　　　　　　GERMANY (+49)

The Tokai Bank Limited
Full Branch Office

Immermannstrasse 13, D-40210 Düsseldorf
Tel: (211) 164 760 **Fax:** (211) 162 282 **Telex:** 8586948 TKAD D

Senior Executive Officers
General Manager　　　　　　　　Yuji Matsumoto

The Tokai Bank Limited
Full Branch Office

Bockenheimer Landstrasse 51/53, D-60325 Frankfurt/Main
PO Box 170518, D-60079 Frankfurt/Main
Tel: (69) 724 909; (69) 719 197 0 **Fax:** (69) 725 609 **Telex:** 413 464 **Reuters:** TOKI

Senior Executive Officers
General Manager　　　　　　　　Yuji Matsumoto
General Manager　　　　　　　　Rudolf Bachfeld
Joint General Manager　　　　　　Naoyoshi Shibamoto

Others (Senior Executives)
Treasurer　　　　　　　　　　　Christoph Kalde *Manager* ☎ **724 975**

Money Markets
Global Head　　　　　　　　　　Christoph Kalde *Manager* ☎ **724 975**
Regional Head　　　　　　　　　Tatsuhiko Hayashi *Assistant Manager* ☎ **717 240**

Foreign Exchange
Global Head　　　　　　　　　　Christoph Kalde *Manager* ☎ **724 975**
Regional Head　　　　　　　　　Tatsuhiko Hayashi *Assistant Manager* ☎ **717 240**

Risk Management
Global Head　　　　　　　　　　M Miura *Manager* ☎ **719 197 32**

Trinkaus & Burkhardt KGaA
Head Office

Königsallee 21/23, D-40212 Düsseldorf
Tel: (211) 910 0 **Fax:** (211) 326 119 **Telex:** 8581490 **Swift:** TUBD DE DD **Reuters:** Trinkaus

Senior Executive Officers
Partner　　　　　　　　　　　　Herbert H Jacobi ☎ **910 2458**
Chief Executive Officer　　　　　Sieghardt Rometsch *Partner* ☎ **910 2802**
Financial Director　　　　　　　Wolfgang Haupt *Partner* ☎ **910 3068**
Treasurer　　　　　　　　　　　Harold Hörauf *Partner* ☎ **910 2762**

Debt Capital Markets / Fixed Income
Global Head　　　　　　　　　　Derk Brouwer *Director* ☎ **910 2089**

Domestic Government Bonds
Head of Sales　　　　　　　　　Andreas Höfner *Director* ☎ **910 2087**
Head of Trading　　　　　　　　Hermann Collmann *Director* ☎ **910 57**
Head of Research　　　　　　　Karen Kricks-Brunnlieb *Assistant Director* ☎ **910 2157**

Eurobonds
Head of Origination　　　　　　Detlef Müller-Witte *Director* ☎ **910 2919**
　　　　　　　　　　　　　　　　Wolfgang Ege *Director* ☎ **910 2360**
Head of Syndication　　　　　　Udo Schinz *Director* ☎ **910 2546**
Head of Sales　　　　　　　　　Andreas Höfner *Director* ☎ **910 2087**
Head of Trading　　　　　　　　Hermann Collmann *Director* ☎ **910 57**
Head of Research　　　　　　　Karen Kricks-Brunnlieb *Assistant Director* ☎ **910 2157**

Fixed-Income Repo
Head of Repo　　　　　　　　　Jörg Bunse *Manager* ☎ **910 610**

Equity Capital Markets

Domestic Equities
Head of Origination; Head of Syndication　Andreas Schmitz *Director* ☎ **910 3032**
Head of Sales　　　　　　　　　Manfred v. Oettingen *Director* ☎ **910 59**
Head of Trading　　　　　　　　Mark Cringle *Director* ☎ **910 63**
　　　　　　　　　　　　　　　　Klaus P Nowag *Director* ☎ **910 68**
Head of Research　　　　　　　Franz Schmidt *Director* ☎ **910 2629**

International Equities
Head of Sales　　　　　　　　　Dirk Meisel *Director* ☎ **910 68**
Head of Trading　　　　　　　　Manfred v. Oettingen *Director* ☎ **910 59**

Warrants
Head of Trading　　　　　　　　Hans-Jürgen Gilles *Director* ☎ **910 68**

GERMANY (+49)

www.euromoneydirectory.com

Trinkaus & Burkhardt KGaA (cont)

Equity Repo / Securities Lending
Head; Marketing; Head of Trading — Carola von Schmettow *Director* ☏ 910 2083

Syndicated Lending
Global Head — Klaus Haarmann *Director* ☏ 910 2421
Recovery — Wolfgang Haupt *Partner* ☏ 910 3068

Loan-Related Activities
Trade Finance — Bernd Hoffmann *Director* ☏ 910 2750

Money Markets
Global Head — Carola von Schmettow *Director* ☏ 910 2083

Wholesale Deposits
Marketing; Head of Sales — Andrea Lanzi *Assistant Director* ☏ 910 610

Foreign Exchange
Global Head — Thomas Schlömer *Director* ☏ 910 2145
Country Head of Institutional Sales — Helmut Klöpfer *Director* ☏ 910 58
Corporate Sales — Thomas Schlömer *Director* ☏ 910 2145

Risk Management
Global Head — Carola von Schmettow *Director* ☏ 910 2083

Fixed Income Derivatives / Risk Management
Global Head — Markus Mirbach *Director* ☏ 910 2960
IR Swaps Sales / Marketing — Andreas Höfner *Director* ☏ 910 2087
IR Swaps Trading — Markus Mirbach *Director* ☏ 910 2960
  Olaf Schlünder *Manager* ☏ 910 611
IR Options Sales / Marketing — Andreas Höfner *Director* ☏ 910 2087
IR Options Trading — Stefan Bataille *Manager* ☏ 910 611

Foreign Exchange Derivatives / Risk Management
Cross-Currency Swaps, Sales / Marketing — Andreas Höfner *Director* ☏ 910 2087
Vanilla FX option Sales — Helmut Klöpfer *Director* ☏ 910 58
Vanilla FX option Trading — Markus Bellers *Director* ☏ 910 2239

Exotic Options (Barriers, Range, Timers, Digitals, Faders etc)
Sales — Helmut Klöpfer *Director* ☏ 910 58
Trading — Markus Bellers *Director* ☏ 910 2239
  Frank Jordan *Director* ☏ 910 3028

OTC Equity Derivatives
Sales — Dirk Steiner *Assistant Director* ☏ 910 59
Trading — Mark Cringle *Director* ☏ 910 63

Corporate Finance / M&A Advisory
Global Head — Andreas Schmitz *Director* ☏ 910 3032

Settlement / Clearing
Regional Head — Dieter Zeißler *General Director* ☏ 910 2605
Equity Settlement; Fixed-Income Settlement — Heinz-Josef Claassen *Director* ☏ 910 2341
Derivatives Settlement — Victor Maessen *Director* ☏ 910 2464
Foreign Exchange Settlement — Winfried Gerst *Assistant Director* ☏ 910 2652

Global Custody
Regional Head — Heinz-Josef Claassen *Director* ☏ 910 2341

Other Departments
Proprietary Trading — Harold Hörauf *Partner* ☏ 910 2762
Private Banking — Frank Schäfer ☏ 910 2554
Correspondent Banking — Rolf Leydorf ☏ 910 2117

Administration

Technology & Systems
Paul Hagen *Managing Director* ☏ 910 2295

Legal / In-House Counsel
Günter Böttger *General Director* ☏ 910 2718

Compliance
Günter Böttger *General Director* ☏ 910 2718

Public Relations
Dietmar Viertel *Director* ☏ 910 2428

www.euromoneydirectory.com GERMANY (+49)

UBS Beteiligungs-GmbH & Co KG

Ulmenstrasse 30, D-60325 Frankfurt/Main
PO Box 170511, 60079 Frankfurt/Main
Tel: (69) 1369 0 Fax: (69) 1369 1366

Senior Executive Officers
Others (Senior Executives)

Hans Peter Peters *Chair*
Peter F Aarts *Managing Director*
Dominicus Freiherr von Mentzingen *Managing Director*
Andreas Muth *Managing Director*
Robert Mueller *Managing Director*
Wolfgang Weber *Managing Director*
Stefan Winter *Managing Director*

UBS Brinson Capital GmbH

Friedensstraße 6-10, D-60311 Frankfurt/Main
PO Box 102042, D-60020 Frankfurt/Main
Tel: (69) 2179 0 Fax: (69) 2179 511

Senior Executive Officers
Others (Senior Executives)
Senior Executive Officer   D Freiherr von Mentzingen *Management*

Union Européenne de CIC

Barckhausstraße 4, D-60325 Frankfurt/Main
Tel: (69) 971 4610 Fax: (69) 971 46113 Email: cic.frankfurt@t-online.de

Senior Executive Officers
Representative   André Wurtz

Vereins-und Westbank AG

Alter Wall 22, D-20457 Hamburg
Tel: (40) 3692 01 Fax: (40) 3692 2513 Telex: 215 1640, 216624 Swift: VUWB DE HH

Debt Capital Markets / Fixed Income

Fixed-Income Repo
Marketing & Product Development   Ingo Stechmann *Assistant Vice President*
Trading   Dirk Fröbe *Trader*

Equity Capital Markets
Tel: 3692 2326 Fax: 3692 2106 Telex: 21424

Equity Repo / Securities Lending
Marketing & Product Development; Head of   Ingo Stechmann *Assistant Vice President*
Prime Brokerage

Volksbank Hannover eG

Kurt-Schumacher-Strasse 19, D-30159 Hannover
PO Box 6227, D-30062 Hannover
Tel: (511) 1221 0; (511) 1221 220 Fax: (511) 1221 188 Swift: VOHA DE 2H Email: info@vbhan.de
Cable: VOLKSBANK HANOVE
Website: www.vbhan.de

Senior Executive Officers
Chairman   Walter Heitmüller

Euromoney Directory 1999   547

GERMANY (+49) www.euromoneydirectory.com

MM Warburg & Co Kommanditgesellschaft auf Aktien
Subsidiary Company

Ferdinandstraße 75, D-20095 Hamburg
D-20079, Hamburg
Tel: (40) 3282 0 **Fax:** (40) 3618 1000 **Telex:** 2162211 **Swift:** WBWC DE HH **Reuters:** MMWBO1-10
Cable: MMMWARBURGBANK
Reuters: WBEX (FX Dealing)
Website: www.mmwarburg.com

Senior Executive Officers
Chief Executive Officer — Christian Olearius *Managing Partner & Spokesman*
Max M Warburg *Managing Partner*
General Manager — Thomas Schult
General Manager International Division — Eberhard Krause
Jan Imbeck *Director*

Relationship Manager
Institutional Advisory — Wolf Mandt-Merck *Director*
Commercial Business — Henneke Lütgerath *General Manager*

Corporate Finance / M&A Advisory
Global Head — Henneke Lütgerath *General Manager*

Other Departments
Correspondent Banking — Helmut Katt *Associate Director* ☎ **3282 2521** 📠 **3618 1115**

Warburg Dillon Read AG

Ulmenstrasse 30, D-60325 Frankfurt/Main
PO Box 170511, D-60079 Frankfurt/Main
Tel: (69) 1369 0 **Fax:** (69) 1369 1366

Senior Executive Officers
Chairman / Speaker, Management Board — H P Peters

Others (Senior Executives)
Logistics — P Aarts *Management Board*
Corporate Finance — R Jaekel *Management Board*
Equities, Securities — S Winter *Management Board*

Debt Capital Markets / Fixed Income
Department: Rates

Bonds - General
Rates — G Rücker

Equity Capital Markets
Department: Equities

Other (Domestic Equities)
Equities — S Winter
N Bedford
H-G Raven

Others (Warrants)
Warrants — R Bellet

Syndicated Lending

Other (Trade Finance)
Global Trade Finance — R Roetheli

Risk Management

Other (Exchange-Traded Derivatives)
Credit Risk Management — H Suter

Corporate Finance / M&A Advisory

Other (Corporate Finance)
Corporate Finance — H P Peters
R Jaekel
A Klemm

548 Euromoney Directory 1999

www.euromoneydirectory.com GERMANY (+49)

Wasserstein Perella & Co Deutschland GmbH
Rahmhofstrasse 2/4, D-60303 Frankfurt/Main
Tel: (69) 242 5280 Fax: (69) 230 408

Senior Executive Officers
Managing Director — Walter Jack Helm

West Merchant Bank Limited
Full Branch Office

Königsalle 33, D-40212 Düsseldorf
Tel: (211) 826 08 Fax: (211) 826 6355

Senior Executive Officers
Branch Manager — Claus Dietrich Zanger ☎ **826 6467**

Others (Senior Executives)
Joachim von Brockhausen *Branch Manager* ☎ **826 2099**

Syndicated Lending
Loan-Related Activities
Leasing & Asset Finance — Claus Dietrich Zanger *Branch Manager* ☎ **826 6467**

Corporate Finance / M&A Advisory
Regional Head — Joachim von Brockhausen *Branch Manager* ☎ **826 2099**

Westdeutsche Landesbank Girozentrale
Head Office

Alternative trading name: WestLB

Herzogstraße 15, D-40217 Düsseldorf
Tel: (211) 826 01 Fax: (211) 826 6119 Telex: 858 1882
Website: www.westlb.de

Senior Executive Officers
Chairman of the Managing Board — Friedel Neuber
Vice Chairman, Managing Board — Hans Henning Offen
Vice Chairman, Managing Board — Wolf-Albrecht Prautzsch

Others (Senior Executives)
Adolf Franke *Member, Management Board*
Dieter Falke *Member, Management Board*
Rudolf Holdijk *Member, Management Board*
Johannes Ringel *Member, Management Board*
Gerhard Roggemann *Member, Management Board*
Jürgen Sengera *Member, Management Board*

West Merchant Bank — Richard Briance *Chief Executive* ☎ **+44 (171) 444 7333** 📠 **+44 (171) 626 9936**
Hans R Keller *Deputy Chief Executive* ☎ **+44 (171) 220 8592**
📠 **+44 (171) 444 7766**

Panmure Gordon — Mark Hodgkin *Chief Executive* ☎ **+44 (171) 860 3977** 📠 **+44 (171) 283 6837**

General - Treasury
Head of Treasury — Humphrey Percy *Head, Global Treasury* ☎ **+44 (171) 447 2101**
📠 **+44 (171) 374 8672**
Stefan Leusder *SVP & General Manager* ☎ **2292 504** 📠 **2292 507**
Friedrich Piaskowski *SVP, Treasury* ☎ **826 2627** 📠 **826 5282**

Westfalenbank AG
Head Office

Huestrasse 21/25, D-44787 Bochum
PO Box 102710, D-44787 Bochum
Tel: (234) 616 0 Fax: (234) 616 4400 Telex: 825825 Swift: WEBO DE 33

Senior Executive Officers
Chief Executive Officer — Walter Richly *Information Processing*
Peter Hilgenstock
Managing Director — Norbert Krupke ☎ **616 4542**
Managing Director — Dieter Wenserski
Deputy Managing Director — Karl-Heinz Engelhardt
International Division — Frank-Dieter Szibrowski *GM & Head of International Division* ☎ **616 4240**

Others (Senior Executives)
International Business — Norbert Krupke *Managing Director* ☎ **616 4542**

General-Lending (DCM, SL)
Head of Corporate Banking — Walter Richly *Credit*

GERMANY (+49)   www.euromoneydirectory.com

Westfalenbank AG (cont)

General - Treasury
Head of Treasury — Axel Frein *Head of Trading* ☎ 616 4230 📠 616 4106

Relationship Manager
Banking Relations / International Finance — Klaus Grafenhain *Assistant General Manager* ☎ 616 4437

Debt Capital Markets / Fixed Income
Department: Trading Department

Domestic Government Bonds
Head of Trading — Josef Remmert *Bond Trader* ☎ 616 4162 📠 616 4335

Eurobonds
Head of Trading — Josef Remmert *Bond Trader* ☎ 616 4162 📠 616 4335

Equity Capital Markets
Head of Trading — Dietmar Pongratz ☎ 616 4423 📠 616 4717

Syndicated Lending

Loan-Related Activities
Trade Finance — Frank-Dieter Szibrowski *Foreign Trade Services*
Ralf Theile *Assistant General Manager* ☎ 616 4294
Project Finance — Ulrich Clement *Assistant General Manager* ☎ 616 4489

Other (Trade Finance)
Forfaiting — Ralf Theile *Assistant General Manager* ☎ 616 4294
Documentary Business & Letters of Guarantee — Rüdiger Klemp *Senior Manager* ☎ 616 4236

Money Markets
Department: Trading Department

Money Markets - General
Money Market — Heinz-Jürgen Niemeyer ☎ 616 4327 📠 616 4289

Foreign Exchange
Department: Trading Department
Head of Trading — Jochen Pick ☎ 616 4461 📠 616 4289

Risk Management
Department: Trading Department

Other (FI Derivatives)
Interest Rate Management — Susanne Jeß ☎ 616 4314 📠 616 4289

Asset Management
Head — Volkmar Irrasch

Administration

Technology & Systems
Information Processing — Albert-Udo Stappert

Legal / In-House Counsel — Jürgen Kalfaus

Compliance — Berthold Cremer

Accounts / Audit
Auditing — Karl-Heinz Kolwitz

Other (Administration)
Services — Ernst Eder
Controlling / Personnel — Peter Hilgenstock

WGZ-Bank Westdeutsche Genossenschafts Zentralbank eG
Head Office

Ludwig-Erhard-Allee 20, D-40227 Düsseldorf
PO Box 101032, D-40001 Düsseldorf
Tel: (211) 778 00 Fax: (211) 778 1277 Telex: 858 6709 Swift: GENO DE DD Email: info@wgz-bank.de
Reuters: WGZD
Website: www.wgz-bank.de

Senior Executive Officers
Chairman of the Managing Board — Eberhard Heinke ☎ 778 1100
Chairman of the Supervisory Board — Günther Schartz ☎ 778 1103
Chief Executive Officer — Helmut Ruwisch *Member of the Management Board* ☎ 778 1116
Treasurer — Manfred Meissner *SVP, Head, Money & FX Trading* ☎ 778 2030
Member, Managing Board — Werner Boehnke ☎ 778 1101
Member, Managing Board — Hans-Georg Monssen ☎ 778 1102

GERMANY (+49)

Senior Executive Officers (cont)
Member, Managing Board — Dieter Pahlen ☏ 778 1107
Member, Managing Board — Hubert Piel ☏ 778 1108

Debt Capital Markets / Fixed Income
Department: Bond Trading
Tel: 778 2600 Fax: 778 2639
Global Head — Karl-Heinz Moll *Head, Securities Trading* ☏ 778 2600

Domestic Government Bonds
Head of Sales — Fokke-Tan Paradies *Vice President* ☏ 778 2700

Eurobonds
Head of Trading — Rainer Hagemann *Assistant Vice President* ☏ 778 2710

Bonds - General
Domestic Non-Government — Inge Huwe *Sales* ☏ 778 2700
Barbara Schmitt *Sales* ☏ 778 2700
Hagen Schmidt *Sales* ☏ 778 2700
Tim Groh *Trading* ☏ 778 2700
Wilfried Kux *Trading* ☏ 778 2700

Libor-Based / Floating-Rate Products
FRN Sales — Thomas Gehse ☏ 778 2700

Equity Capital Markets
Fax: 778 2698
Global Head — Peter Heidecker *Vice President* ☏ 778 2640

Domestic Equities
Head of Sales — Rainer Boguslawski *Assistant Vice President* ☏ 778 2666
Head of Trading — Hubert Hammes ☏ 778 2860

International Equities
Head of Sales — Rainer Boguslawski *Assistant Vice President* ☏ 778 2666
Head of Trading — Rainer Guildhuis *Assistant Vice President* ☏ 778 2670

Convertibles / Equity-Linked
Head of Sales — Rainer Boguslawski *Assistant Vice President* ☏ 778 2666
Head of Trading — Michael Hölscher ☏ 778 1348

Warrants
Head of Sales — Rainer Boguslawski *Assistant Vice President* ☏ 778 2666
Head of Trading — Marlene Krieger ☏ 778 2661

Equity Repo / Securities Lending
Head of Trading — Jan Finkernagel ☏ 778 2660

Syndicated Lending
Fax: 778 2404
Head of Syndicated Lending — Jürgen Schaumann *Vice President* ☏ 778 2501

Loan-Related Activities
Trade Finance; Project Finance — Jürgen Schaumann *Vice President* ☏ 778 2501

Money Markets
Fax: 778 2018
Global Head — Maren Prühs *Vice President* ☏ 778 2000

Foreign Exchange
Head of Foreign Exchange — Albert Wolfram *Vice President* ☏ 778 2010

Risk Management
OTC Equity Derivatives
Sales — Rainer Boguslawski *Assistant Vice President* ☏ 778 2666
Trading — Michael Hölscher ☏ 778 1348

Corporate Finance / M&A Advisory
Fax: 778 2315
Global Head — Willi Radloff *Senior Vice President* ☏ (251) 706 4350

Settlement / Clearing
Fax: 778 3017
Regional Head — Mrs Post-Schulz *Senior Vice President* ☏ 778 3000
Equity Settlement — Mr Kelzenberg *Assistant Vice President* ☏ 778 3051
Derivatives Settlement — Mr Knopf *Vice President* ☏ 778 3300
Foreign Exchange Settlement — Frauke Hedde *Assistant Vice President* ☏ 778 3311

Other Departments
Commodities / Bullion — Dieter Malcher *Bullion* ☏ 778 2410
Correspondent Banking — José-Julio Magalhaes *Vice President* ☏ 778 2500

Administration
Technology & Systems — Jens-Olaf Bartels *Senior Vice President* ☏ 778 1600

GERMANY (+49)   www.euromoneydirectory.com

WGZ-Bank Westdeutsche Genossenschafts Zentralbank eG (cont)

Legal / In-House Counsel
　　　　　　　　　　　Alfred Locklair *Senior Vice President* ☎ **778 1530**
Compliance
　　　　　　　　　　　Manfred Jorris *Vice President* ☎ **778 1570**
Public Relations
　　　　　　　　　　　Henning Hennies-Rautenberg *Senior Vice President* ☎ **778 3400**

Württembergische Hypothekenbank AG — Head Office

Alternative trading name: Württemberger Hypo
　　　　　Büchsenstraße 26, D-70174 Stuttgart, Baden-Württemberg
　　　Tel: (711) 2096 0 **Fax:** (711) 2096 345 **Telex:** 722045 **Reuters:** WHBS; WHBT; WHBU

Senior Executive Officers
Chief Executive Officer　　Jürgen Blumer *Chief Executive Officer* ☎ **2096 214**
Treasurer　　　　　　　　Markus Weick ☎ **2096 399**
Others (Senior Executives)
　　　　　　　　　　　Paul Eisele *Member of the Board*
　　　　　　　　　　　Horst Jochemczyk *Member of the Board*
　　　　　　　　　　　Friedrich-Wilhelm Ladda *Member of the Board*

Debt Capital Markets / Fixed Income
Global Head　　　　　　Markus Weick ☎ **2096 399**
　　　　　　　　　　　Bernd Dambacher ☎ **2096 312**

Settlement / Clearing
Regional Head　　　　　Andreas Wagner ☎ **2096 333**

Administration
Compliance
　　　　　　　　　　　Peter Schubert *Director* ☎ **2096 223**
Public Relations
　　　　　　　　　　　Christoph Prillwitz *Manager, Public Relations* ☎ **2096 367**

Wüstenrot Bank AG — Head Office

　　　　　　　　Intanbour 1, D-71630 Ludwigsburg
　　　Tel: (71) 4116 1 **Fax:** (71) 4116 3851; (71) 4190 2941 **Reuters:** WUES

Senior Executive Officers
Chief Executive Officer　　Soennich Lassahn
Financial Director　　　　Wolfgang Maile
Treasurer　　　　　　　　Norbert Metzger

Debt Capital Markets / Fixed Income
Department: Department WP
Global Head　　　　　　Karl Schuska *Director* ☎ **4116 2845**
Non-Domestic Government Bonds
　　　　　　　　　　　Karl Schuska *Director* ☎ **4116 2845**

GHANA
(+233)

Bank of Ghana — 🏛 Central Bank

　　　　　　　　　　PO Box 2674, Accra
　　Tel: (21) 666 902; (21) 666 174 **Fax:** (21) 666 996 **Telex:** 2052 **Swift:** BAGH GH AC

Senior Executive Officers
Governor　　　　　　　　Kwabena Duffuor ☎ **664 719**
Deputy Governor　　　　Emmanuel Ossei-Kumah ☎ **663 147**
Company Secretary　　　Alex Bernasko ☎ **662 395**

Others (Senior Executives)
Chief Cashier　　　　　　Phyllis Clottey ☎ **669 370**
Head, Bank Licensing; Head, Banking Supervision
　　　　　　　　　　　E Asiedu-Mante ☎ **665 034**
Head, Economics & Statistics　H A K Wampah ☎ **663 082**
Head, Public Debt　　　　Fred France ☎ **668 242**

552　Euromoney Directory 1999

www.euromoneydirectory.com GHANA (+233)

Others (Senior Executives) (cont)
Head, Non-Banking Financial Institutions D O Andah ☎ 664 815
Advisor to Governor S Morrison ☎ 664 993
Head, Financial Markets Teresa Ntim ☎ 667 734
Syndicated Lending
Other (Trade Finance)
Development Finance S P D Kotey ☎ 667 905
Foreign Exchange
Head of Foreign Exchange D A Seidu ☎ 664 523
Settlement / Clearing
Head of Settlement / Clearing D A Seidu ☎ 664 523
Other Departments
Economic Research H A K Wampah ☎ 663 082
Administration
Head of Administration S K Newton ☎ 664 479
Technology & Systems
Daniel Hagan ☎ 667 3731
Legal / In-House Counsel
Alex Bernasko ☎ 662 395
Public Relations
Public Relations Alex Bernasko ☎ 662 395
Information, Documentation & Publications S M A Adjetey ☎ 668 731
Accounts / Audit
Head, Accountancy S D K N Gavor ☎ 665 616
Head, Internal Audit Offei Bekoe ☎ 666 720
Other (Administration)
Support Services Adelaide Benneh ☎ 665 031

Merchant Bank Ghana Limited — Head Office

Merban House, 44 Kwame Nkrumah Avenue, PO Box 401, Accra
Tel: (21) 666 331; (21) 666 332 **Fax:** (21) 667 305; (21) 663 398 **Telex:** 2191 MERBAN GH **Swift:** MBGHGHAC
Email: merban-services@ighmail.com **Reuters:** NSAY
Website: www.ghanaclassifieds.com/merchantbank/index.html

Senior Executive Officers
Board of Directors Kobina Richardson
Chief Executive Officer Chris Nartey *Managing Director*
Chief Operating Officer David Ansah *Executive Director*
Treasurer Samuel Acquaye *Financial Controller*
General Manager Frank Beecham
Secretary to the Board Naa Shormeh Gyang
International Division Edward Obeng *Manager, Foreign Operations*
Others (Senior Executives)
General Manager, Special Duties Richard Tetteh
Head, Merchant Banking Paul Baah-Sackey ☎ 780 463
Head, Internal Control John Djanie ☎ 780464
Head, Corporate Relations Felicity Acquah
General-Lending (DCM, SL)
Head of Corporate Banking Emmanuel Ampofo *Manager, Credit Risk Management*
Equity Capital Markets
Head of Equity Capital Markets Yaw Sarpong ☎ 780 465
Corporate Finance / M&A Advisory
Global Head Paarock Vanpercy *Manager, Corporate Finance*
Other Departments
Chief Credit Officer Steve Asare *Manager, Credit*
Administration
Head of Administration Kojo Sallah ☎ 780 464
Business Development Charles Otoo
Technology & Systems
Isaac Owusu
Legal / In-House Counsel
Rachel Baddoo ☎ 667 307

Euromoney Directory 1999 553

GHANA (+233)   www.euromoneydirectory.com

SSB Bank Limited
Head Office

Alternative trading name: Social Security Bank
PO Box 13119, Accra
Tel: (21) 221 726; (21) 221 743 Fax: (21) 668 651; (21) 220 713 Telex: 2209/2693 SSB FRX Swift: SSEB GHA CA
Website: www.ssb.com.gh

Senior Executive Officers
Chief Executive Officer — Pryce Kojo Thompson *Managing Director*
Financial Director — Ben A Gogo *General Manager, Finance*
Chief Operating Officer — Richard Priestman *General Manager, Operations*
General Manager, Administration — Kofi Abu Labi

Debt Capital Markets / Fixed Income
Global Head — Stephen Opoku *Head of Treasury* 229 174

Syndicated Lending
Global Head — Daniel Nsiah *Chief of Credit Department*

Money Markets
Global Head — Stephen Opoku *Head of Treasury* 229 174

Foreign Exchange
Global Head — Akosua Kotey *Head, International Banking* 667 147

Corporate Finance / M&A Advisory
Global Head — Daniel Nsiah *Chief of Credit Department*

GIBRALTAR
(+350)

ABN AMRO Bank (Gibraltar) Limited
Full Branch Office

2/6 Main Street, Gibraltar
PO Box 100, Gibraltar
Tel: 79220 Fax: 78512 Telex: 2234 GK Swift: ABNA GI GI

Senior Executive Officers
Chairman — Dr Zwegers
Managing Director — A H Meudenberg

The Gibraltar Private Bank Limited

Suites 1 & 2, 10th Floor, International Commercial Centre, Main Street, Gibraltar
Tel: 73350 Fax: 73475 Telex: 2141 PRIVAT GK

Senior Executive Officers
Chief Executive Officer — Frederic Binder

Hispano Commerzbank (Gibraltar) Limited
Subsidiary Company

Formerly known as: Banco Hispano-Americano SA
Suite 14, 2nd Floor, Don House, 30/38 Main Street, Gibraltar
Tel: 74199 Fax: 74174; 41266 Telex: GK2152

Senior Executive Officers
Chief Executive Officer — Bernd von Oelffen *Chief Executive*
General Manager — Robert G Soper

Jyske Bank (Gibraltar) Limited
Subsidiary Company

76 Main Street, Gibraltar
PO Box 143, Gibraltar
Tel: 72782 Fax: 72732 Telex: 2215 GK Swift: JYBA GI GI Email: jyskebank@jyskebank.ltd.gi
Website: www.jyske-bank.dk/pbi

Senior Executive Officers
Managing Director — Petter Blondeau

Others (Senior Executives)
Soeren Mose *Deputy Managing Director*
George Santos *Deputy Managing Director*

Lloyds Bank plc
Full Branch Office

323 Main Street, Gibraltar
PO Box 482, Gibraltar
Tel: 77373 **Fax:** 70023 **Telex:** LOYD GI GI

Senior Executive Officers
Senior Manager   A D Langston

Republic National Bank of New York (Gibraltar) Limited
Subsidiary Company

Neptune House, Marina Bay, Gibraltar
PO Box 557, Gibraltar
Tel: 79374 **Fax:** 75684 **Telex:** 2291 **Swift:** BLIC GI LX

Senior Executive Officers
Chairman   A Pucher
Vice Chairman   W T Robinson
Chief Executive Officer   Y Benaim
International Division   J Shaughnessy *GM, Int'l & Private Banking*

Others (Senior Executives)
M Elia *Director*
L Robertson *Director*
G Hanselmann *Director*

Settlement / Clearing
Operations   M Bersier *Operations Manager*

Administration
Head of Administration   M Bersier *Operations Manager*

The Royal Bank of Scotland International Limited
Subsidiary Company

Formerly known as: The Royal Bank of Scotland (Gibraltar) Limited
PO Box 766, 1 Corral Road, Gibraltar
Tel: 73200 **Fax:** 70152 **Telex:** 2124 RBSGIB GK

Senior Executive Officers
General Manager   K Blight

Springfield Bank & Trust Limited
Head Office

PO Box 850, Suite 922, Europort, Gibraltar
Tel: 42670 **Fax:** 42676 **Telex:** 2123 SPRING GK

Senior Executive Officers
Chairman of the Board   Ronnie Chan
President & CEO   Jan Erikson
Financial Director   Steven McDonald
Chief Operating Officer   Jan Erikson *President & CEO*
Treasurer   Steven McDonald

GREECE
(+30)

Bank of Greece
🏛 Central Bank

21 E Venizelou Avenue, GR-102 50 Athens
Tel: (1) 320 1111 Fax: (1) 323 2239; (1) 323 2816 Telex: 215102 Swift: BNGR GR AA Email: bogescr@ath.forthnet.gr
Reuters: BGAC Cable: BANGRECE Telex: 215206 Telex: 215363; Reuters: BGAD; BGAH; BGAI; BGAJ; BGAK;
BGAL; BGAM; BGAN; BGRP

Senior Executive Officers
Governor — Lucas D Papademos ☎ 323 8096 F 323 3178
Deputy Governor — Panayotis A Thomopoulos ☎ 324 4624 F 323 1926
Deputy Governor — Nicholas C Gaganas ☎ 322 9886 F 322 2784
International Division — Mantha K Christou ☎ 322 0045 F 323 6746
Konstantinos G Argyropoulos ☎ 323 0439 F 323 2594

Others (Senior Executives)
Monetary Policy Council — Lucas D Papademos *Governor* ☎ 323 8096 F 323 3178
Nicholas D Paleocrassas ☎ 323 4747 F 323 3761
Panayotis A Thomopoulos *Deputy Governor* ☎ 324 4624 F 323 1926
Nicholas C Gaganas *Deputy Governor* ☎ 322 9886 F 322 2784
Antonious G Manzavinos ☎ 331 2639
Vassillios Sp Droukopoulos ☎ 324 7652 F 322 6371
Head, Banking Supervision — Iacovos P Vahaviolos ☎ 323 0640 F 325 4653
Relationship Manager
Government Financial Operations & Accounts — Nicholaos V Alexopoulos ☎ 323 3444 F 323 0018
International Banking Relations — Spyros P Papanicolaou ☎ 322 2790 F 324 5044
Foreign Exchange
Tel: 322 8139
Head of Foreign Exchange — Panayotis A Pliatsikas ☎ 323 2018 F 324 9789
Administration
Head of Administration — Ioannis Chr Sioros ☎ 322 8721 F 322 1007
Technology & Systems
Information Systems & Organisation — Elias I Kyriakantonakis ☎ 324 4696 F 323 0018
Legal / In-House Counsel
Phoebus Ch Christodoulou ☎ 322 8781 F 323 4902
Accounts / Audit
Accounts — Demetrios E Matsimanis ☎ 322 1911 F 325 5508
Internal Audit — Eleftherious K Messologitis ☎ 322 9692 F 322 1052

ALKE Stockbrokers SA
Head Office

Stadioy 33, GR-105 59 Athens
Tel: (1) 321 1801ext5 Fax: (1) 321 5012

Senior Executive Officers
Representative — Spiros Kotzambasis
Chief Operating Officer — Alberto Ghiringhelli *Manager of Operations*
Executive Secretary — Athina Goutoy

Others (Senior Executives)
George Kotzambasis *Chief Trader*
John Petrolekas *Head of Fixed Income*

Debt Capital Markets / Fixed Income
Department: Fixed Income Department
Head of Fixed Income; Head of Fixed Income Trading — John Petrolekas *Head of Fixed Income*

Equity Capital Markets
Department: Domestic Equity Capital Markets
Head of Equity Capital Markets; Head of Sales; Head of Trading — George Kotzambasis *Chief Trader*

Domestic Equities
Head of Sales — Alexander Zamkinos *Broker, Domestic Equities*

Money Markets
Head of Money Markets — John Petrolekas *Head of Fixed Income*

www.euromoneydirectory.com GREECE (+30)

Settlement / Clearing
Head of Settlement / Clearing Operations
Kyriakos Kyriakos
Alberto Ghiringhelli *Manager of Operations*

Global Custody
Head of Global Custody
Dimitris Daskalakos *Settlements - Securities*

Administration
Head of Administration
Alberto Ghiringhelli *Manager of Operations*

Technology & Systems
Evi Mourtopoulou *Head*

Legal / In-House Counsel
Stavros Afendras *Legal Advisor* ☎ **364 6679**

Compliance
Kyriakos Kyriakos

Accounts / Audit
Odysseas Livanios *Chief Accountant*

Alpha Brokerage AE
6 Dragatsaniou Street, GR-105 59 Athens
Tel: (1) 331 3314; (1) 323 4791 **Fax:** (1) 322 2224; (1) 323 4683 **Email:** alphabrokerg@hol.gr **Reuters:** ABGR

Senior Executive Officers
Chairman & Managing Director
Managing Director / General Manager
Michael Papathanassiou ☎ **326 2344** F **331 1193**
Vassilios Sarris ☎ **326 6428** F **331 1193**

Alpha Credit Bank
Head Office

40 Stadiou Street, GR-102 52 Athens
Tel: (1) 326 3000 **Fax:** (1) 326 5438 **Telex:** 218691 CCB GR **Swift:** CRBA GR AA **Email:** secretariat@alpha.gr
Website: www.alpha.gr

Senior Executive Officers
Chairman & Managing Director
Chief Executive Officer
Financial Director
Treasurer
Company Secretary
International Division

Yannis Costopoulos ☎ **326 2121**
Constantine Kyriacopoulos *Executive Director & CEO* ☎ **326 2222**
George Kontos *Manager, Finance Division* ☎ **326 4043**
Peter K J Sweden *Manager, Treasury* ☎ **326 4002**
Hector Verykios ☎ **326 2424**
Vassilios Karaindros ☎ **326 3838**

Others (Senior Executives)
Executive General Manager
Demetrios Mantzoynis ☎ **326 3737**
Spyros Filaretos *Assistant Manager* ☎ **326 4007**
Stephanos Karathanassis ☎ **326 2355**
Marinos Yannopoulos ☎ **326 2366**

General-Lending (DCM, SL)
Head of Corporate Banking
Spyros Filaretos *Assistant Manager* ☎ **326 4007**

Debt Capital Markets / Fixed Income
Tel: 326 4276
Global Head
Head of Fixed Income Sales
Head of Fixed Income Trading
Apostolos Saraferas *Assistant Manager* ☎ **326 4263**
Andrian Evans ☎ **+44 (171) 648 5000**
Emmanuel Arzinos *Chief Dealer*

Government Bonds
Head of Sales
Head of Trading

Andrian Evans ☎ **+44 (171) 648 5000**
Emmanuel Arzinos *Chief Dealer*
George Papparas *Dealer* ☎ **326 4268**
Yannis Monastiriotis *Chief Dealer* ☎ **326 4150**
Jeremy Downward *General Manager* ☎ **364 1210**

Head of Syndication
Head of Origination

Non-Domestic Government Bonds
Other Bond Dealer
George Papparas *Dealer* ☎ **326 4268**
Yannis Monostiviotis *Chief Dealer* ☎ **326 4150**

Eurobonds
Head of Origination; Head of Syndication
Head of Sales

Apostolos Saraferas *Assistant Manager* ☎ **326 4263**
Emmanuel Arzinos *Chief Dealer*
George Papparas *Dealer* ☎ **326 4268**
Emmanuel Arzinos *Chief Dealer*
George Papparas *Dealer* ☎ **326 4268**
Emmanuel Arzinos *Chief Dealer*

Head of Trading; Head of Research
Trading (Sovereigns)
Trading (Corporates)

Euromoney Directory 1999 **557**

GREECE (+30)

www.euromoneydirectory.com

Alpha Credit Bank (cont)

Libor-Based / Floating-Rate Products
FRN Origination — Apostolos Saraferas *Assistant Manager* ☎ **326 4263**
FRN Sales — Andrian Evans ☎ **+44 (171) 648 5000**
FRN Trading — Emmanuel Arzinos *Chief Dealer*
Asset Swaps — Apostolos Saraferas *Assistant Manager* ☎ **326 4263**
Asset Swaps (Sales) — Apostolos Pantis *Dealer* ☎ **326 4212**

Medium-Term Notes
Head of Origination — Apostolos Saraferas *Assistant Manager* ☎ **326 4263**

Private Placements
Head of Origination — Apostolos Saraferas *Assistant Manager* ☎ **326 4263**

Fixed-Income Repo
Head of Repo — Apostolos Saraferas *Assistant Manager* ☎ **326 4263**
Other — George Papparas *Dealer* ☎ **326 4268**

Fixed-Income Research
Head of Fixed Income — Michael Massourakis *Manager* ☎ **326 2828**
Head of Credit Research — Andreas Andreou *Manager* ☎ **326 2929**

Equity Capital Markets
Head of Equity Capital Markets — Artemis Theodoridis *General Manager* ☎ **322 6427**
Head of Sales — Dimitrios Verriopoulos *Assistant Manager* ☎ **322 6321**
Head of Trading — Dimitrios Verriopoulos *Dealer* ☎ **322 6321**

Domestic Equities
Head of Sales — Dimitrios Verriopoulos *Assistant Manager* ☎ **322 6321**

Convertibles / Equity-Linked
Head of Sales — Pavlos Vasdekis *Assistant Chief Dealer* ☎ **326 4272**

Warrants
Head of Sales — Apostolos Saraferas *Assistant Manager* ☎ **326 4263**
Head of Trading — Paul Vasdekis *Assistant Chief Dealer* ☎ **326 4265**

Syndicated Lending
Tel: 326 4276
Head of Syndicated Lending — Apostolos Saraferas *Assistant Manager* ☎ **326 4263**
Regional Head — Yannis Monostiviotis *Chief Dealer* ☎ **326 4150**
Head of Origination — Apostolos Saraferas *Assistant Manager* ☎ **326 4263**

Loan-Related Activities
Trade Finance; Project Finance — Jeremy Downward *General Manager* ☎ **364 1210**

Money Markets
Tel: 326 4158
Head of Money Markets — Panagiotis Panagiotopoulos *Assistant Manager* ☎ **326 4188**
Country Head — Anna Kalogeropoulou *Dealer* ☎ **326 4158**

Wholesale Deposits
Marketing; Head of Sales — Anna Kalogeropoulou *Dealer* ☎ **326 4158**

Foreign Exchange
Head of Foreign Exchange — Panagiotis Panagiotopoulos *Assistant Manager* ☎ **326 4188**
Head of Institutional Sales — Dimitrios Papaioannou *Chief Dealer* ☎ **326 4266**
Corporate Sales — Etstratios Bulmetis *Assistant Manager* ☎ **326 4007**
Head of Trading — Dimitrios Papaioannou *Chief Dealer* ☎ **326 4266**

FX Traders / Sales People
Dimitris Kakounis *Dealer* ☎ **326 4246**
Sotiria Diamaniopoulou *Dealer* ☎ **326 4246**

Risk Management
Head of Risk Management — Apostolos Saraferas *Assistant Manager* ☎ **326 4263**

Fixed Income Derivatives / Risk Management
Global Head — Apostolos Saraferas *Assistant Manager* ☎ **326 4263**
IR Options Sales / Marketing; IR Options Trading — Paul Vasdekis *Assistant Chief Dealer* ☎ **326 4265**

Foreign Exchange Derivatives / Risk Management
Cross-Currency Swaps, Trading — Emmanuel Arzinos *Chief Dealer*
Vanilla FX option Sales; Vanilla FX option Trading — Paul Vasdekis *Assistant Chief Dealer* ☎ **326 4265**

Other Currency Swap / FX Options Personnel
Apostolos Pantis *Dealer* ☎ **326 4273**
Kalomira Kousta *Dealer* ☎ **326 4272**

OTC Equity Derivatives
Sales — Apostolos Pantis *Dealer* ☎ **326 4273**
Trading — Paul Vasdekis *Assistant Chief Dealer* ☎ **326 4265**

www.euromoneydirectory.com GREECE (+30)

Exchange-Traded Derivatives
Head   Apostolos Saraferas *Assistant Manager* ☏ **326 4263**
Corporate Finance / M&A Advisory
Head of Corporate Finance   Spyros Filaretos *Assistant Manager* ☏ **326 4007**
Settlement / Clearing
Head of Settlement / Clearing   Olga Chatzi *Assistant Manager* ☏ **326 4250**
Fixed-Income Settlement   Sotiris Nicolaou *Head, FX Settlements* ☏ **326 4310**
Foreign Exchange Settlement; Operations   Maria Apostolidou *Head, FX Settlements* ☏ **326 4255**
Global Custody
Head of Global Custody   Ariadni Giryrgou ☏ **326 5520**
Asset Management
Head   Iason Karavassilis ☏ **729 3503**
Other Departments
Chief Credit Officer   Andreas Andreou *Manager* ☏ **326 2929**
Private Banking   Jason Karavassilis ☏ **729 3502**
Correspondent Banking   Vassilios Karaindros ☏ **326 3838**
Administration
Head of Marketing   Constantine Carayannis ☏ **326 3800**
Technology & Systems
                                            Michael Tsourgiannis ☏ **346 7600**
                                            Efstathlos Kaudyannis ☏ **345 7272**
Legal / In-House Counsel
                                            Theofanis Saxonis ☏ **326 7030**
Public Relations
                                            Aphrodite Bilioni ☏ **326 2430**

Alpha Trust Investment Services SA   Head Office
36 Amalias Avenue, GR-105 58 Athens
Tel: (1) 331 2942; (1) 331 2943 Fax: (1) 331 2941

Senior Executive Officers
Tel: 331 2941
Chairman   David Gibbs
Chief Executive Officer   Phaedon Tamvakakis *Managing Director*
General Manager   Theodore Krintas
Debt Capital Markets / Fixed Income
Department: Hambros Hellenic M.FM.C.
Tel: 331 2945 Fax: 331 2941
Country Head   Theodore Krintas *General Manager*
Equity Capital Markets
Department: Alpha Trust SA
Country Head   Apostolos Constaninidis
Domestic Equities
Head of Research   Nota Zagaris
Money Markets
Department: Hambros Hellenic M.F.M.C.
Country Head   Theodore Krintas *General Manager*
Risk Management
Fixed Income Derivatives / Risk Management
Country Head   Theodore Krintas *General Manager*

American Express Bank Limited   Full Branch Office
31 Panepistimiou Street, GR-102 26 Athens
Tel: (1) 322 4061ext5; (1) 329 0681ext6 Fax: (1) 329 0602; (1) 329 0604 Telex: 221084 Reuters: AMGR, AMXG

Senior Executive Officers
Country Manager   Gas Kostakis ☏ **329 0800**
Financial Director   George Drydakis *Financial Controller* ☏ **325 1190**
Chief Operating Officer   Brian Burt ☏ **323 7253**
Treasurer   John Podaras ☏ **322 4165**
Debt Capital Markets / Fixed Income
Fax: 329 0602 Reuters: AMGX
Head of Fixed Income Sales   Vassius Thomas *Head of Treasury Sales* ☏ **329 0682**

Euromoney Directory 1999 **559**

GREECE (+30) www.euromoneydirectory.com

American Express Bank Limited (cont)
Money Markets
Tel: 329 0685/6
Head of Money Markets — Vassius Thomas *Head of Treasury Sales* ☎ **329 0682**

Foreign Exchange
Tel: 329 0681
Head of Foreign Exchange — George Christofides ☎ **329 0681**

Settlement / Clearing
Tel: 329 0521
Head of Settlement / Clearing — Kostas Stefopoulos ☎ **329 0521**

Other Departments
Chief Credit Officer — Kostas Michalopoulos ☎ **323 7775**
Correspondent Banking — Michael Spitauotis ☎ **329 0702**

Administration
Compliance — Christos Zervos ☎ **329 0210**

Arab Bank plc — Full Branch Office
9 Vas Sofias & 1 Merlin Street, GR-10671 Athens
PO Box 30357, GR-10033 Athens
Tel: (1) 361 3113 Fax: (1) 361 3140 Telex: 219922 ARAB GR Swift: ARAB GR AA
General Telex: 219538 ARAB GR

Senior Executive Officers
Others (Senior Executives)
Branch Manager — George Koutsantonis
Deputy Manager — Sami Makarem

Banca Commerciale Italiana — Representative Office
3 Mitropoleos Street, GR-105 57 Athens
Tel: (1) 324 6014; (1) 324 6017 Fax: (1) 323 4125 Telex: 215864 BCI GR

Senior Executive Officers
Representative — Anastassios Andreou

Bank of Crete — Head Office
Alternative trading name: Cretabank
22 Voukourestiou Street, GR-106 71 Athens
Tel: (1) 360 6511/15; (1) 362 8301/4 Fax: (1) 364 1200 Telex: 225624 BOFK GR Swift: CRET GR AA
Cable: Cretabank Athens

Senior Executive Officers
Chairman & Managing Director — Kostas Georgakopoulos
Deputy General Manager — George Linos
Chief Executive Officer — Panagiotis Houdalakis *Deputy General Manager*
Dimitris Alexakis *Deputy General Manager*
Financial Director — Patroklos Sparis ☎ **323 3539**
International Division — Demitris Charalambakis *Director*

General-Investment
Head of Investment — Charalambos Kontaxis *Director, Investments & Stock Market Division*

General - Treasury
Head of Treasury — Demitris Charalambakis *Director*

Administration
Head of Administration — Anna Douliotis

Technology & Systems
E.D.P. Division — Dimitris Kallimanis *Director* ☎ **323 3482**

Legal / In-House Counsel — George Orfanidis *Director* ☎ **363 5029**

Public Relations — Anna Douliotis ✉ **360 2641**

560 Euromoney Directory 1999

www.euromoneydirectory.com GREECE (+30)

Banque Nationale de Paris
Full Branch Office

94 Vas Sofias Avenue, 1 Kerassoudos, GR-115 28 Athens
Tel: (1) 748 6700 **Fax:** (1) 748 6726 **Telex:** 210759 **Swift:** BNPA GR AA **Reuters:** BQNP **Telerate:** 41961

Senior Executive Officers
General Manager — Jean Claude Chaval ☎ **748 6700**
Deputy General Manager — Dimitris Katsoulis ☎ **748 6700**

Others (Senior Executives)
Anthony Halaris *Treasurer* ☎ **748 6640**

Debt Capital Markets / Fixed Income
Department: Securities Desk
Tel: 748 6640 **Fax:** 748 6726 **Telex:** 210759
Head of Fixed Income — Anthony Halaris *Treasurer* ☎ **748 6640**
Head of Fixed Income Sales — Kostas Zanetopoulos *Head of Sales*
Head of Fixed Income Trading — Dimitris Fetichiakos *Chief Dealer, Mon.Mrkts-Securities*

Government Bonds
Head of Sales — Kostas Zanetopoulos *Head of Sales*
Head of Trading — Dimitris Fetichiakos *Chief Dealer, Mon.Mrkts-Securities*

Syndicated Lending
Tel: 748 6700 **Fax:** 748 6726
Head of Syndication — Eva Economou *Assistant Corporate Manager* ☎ **748 6700**

Money Markets
Tel: 748 6640 **Fax:** 748 6726 **Reuters:** BQNP **Telex:** 218969
Head of Money Markets — Dimitris Eftichiakos *Chief Dealer* ☎ **748 6640**

Foreign Exchange
Tel: 748 6640 **Fax:** 748 6726 **Reuters:** BQNP
Head of Foreign Exchange — Makis Karatassios *Chief Dealer*
Head of Institutional Sales; Corporate Sales — Costas Zanetopoulos *Chief Dealer* ☎ **748 6640/5**

FX Traders / Sales People
Sales — Markela Economou *Senior Dealer* ☎ **748 6640**
Trader — Elias Papachristopoulos *Senior Dealer* ☎ **748 6640**
Sales — Lefki Zachariadou *Dealer* ☎ **748 6640/5**

Risk Management
Tel: 748 6700 **Fax:** 748 6726
Head of Risk Management — Jojet Papathanasiou *Risk Controller* ☎ **748 6700**

Other Currency Swap / FX Options Personnel
Trading — Nestor Panagos *Dealer* ☎ **748 6640**
Katerina Zevgoli *Dealer* ☎ **748 6640**

Settlement / Clearing
Tel: 748 6700 **Fax:** 748 6726, 748 9534
Head of Settlement / Clearing — Elpida Tsouchlari *Assistant Head*
Equity Settlement; Fixed-Income Settlement — Katerina Gerassimatou *Assistant Head*
Back-Office — Panagiota Theodororopoulou *Head*

Administration
Head of Administration — Joel Letoüde *General Secretariat*

Technology & Systems
Stelios Agelakis *Head, EDP*

Legal / In-House Counsel
George Kaniaris *Legal Officer*

Accounts / Audit
Panayotis Mitropoulos *Head of Accounting*

Barclays Bank plc
Full Branch Office

1 Kolokotroni Street, GR-100 33 Athens
PO Box 30375, GR-100 33 Athens
Tel: (1) 331 0580; (1) 331 0591 **Fax:** (1) 324 4589 **Telex:** 214136 BORCGRAA **Swift:** BARC GR AA BAS
Cable: BARCLATH

Senior Executive Officers
Chief Executive Officer — Chris Yabanas *General Manager*
Treasurer — Apostolos Skafidas *Manager, Treasury Trading & Investment*

General-Lending (DCM, SL)
Head of Corporate Banking — Dimitris Couris *Manager, Corporate Banking*

Euromoney Directory 1999 **561**

GREECE (+30)　　　　　www.euromoneydirectory.com

Barclays Bank plc (cont)

Risk Management
Head of Risk Management
　　John Kazas *Manager, Credit Risk*
　　Randy Z Hensley *Operational Risk Manager*

Settlement / Clearing
Operations
　　Periclis Kleftakis *Manager, Internal Support Unit*
　　Peter Michalopoulos *Financial Comptroller*

Global Custody
Regional Head
　　Helen Koutoula *Manager*

Administration
Head of Marketing
　　Katerina Ferentinou *Manager*

Technology & Systems
　　Takis Kapsalis *Manager, IT*

Legal / In-House Counsel
　　Takis Kommatas *Legal Advisor*

Accounts / Audit
　　Randy Z Hensley *Operational Risk Manager*

Other (Administration)
Product Development
Human Resources
Premises & Procurement
　　Katerina Ferentinou *Manager*
　　Caterina Papaspirou *Manager*
　　Theodore Xydias *Manager*

Beta Securities SA　　　　　　　　　　　　　Head Office

8 Fanarioton Street, GR-114 72 Athens
Tel: (1) 642 2331 **Fax:** (1) 644 7319

Senior Executive Officers
Chairman　　　　　　　　　Nicholas Ritsonis
Chief Executive Officer　　　　Evangelos Charatsis
Chief Operating Officer　　　　Grammatiki Kagouras
Treasurer　　　　　　　　　Panayotis Zamanis
General Manager　　　　　　George Kagouras
Company Secretary　　　　　Harikleia Dimou
International Division　　　　John Akontidis

Debt Capital Markets / Fixed Income
Head of Fixed Income　　　　Evangelos Charatsis

Emerging Market Bonds
Head of Emerging Markets　　Christina Akritidis

Equity Capital Markets
Head of Equity Capital Markets　Helen Siaperas

Foreign Exchange
Head of Foreign Exchange　　Panayiotis Sarris

Settlement / Clearing
Head of Settlement / Clearing　Helen Sotiropoulos

Global Custody
Head of Global Custody　　　Fei Roussakis

Other Departments
Private Banking　　　　　　Dimitris Martinis

Administration
Head of Marketing　　　　　Lilian Ioannidis

Legal / In-House Counsel
　　Elias Karandalis

Compliance
　　Pavlos Rigatos

Public Relations
　　Cleopatra Coudounis

Accounts / Audit
　　Georgia Galani

CARIPLO - Cassa di Risparmio delle Provincie Lombarde SpA
Representative Office

13 Panepistimiou Street, GR-105 64 Athens
Tel: (1) 325 0061; (1) 325 2222 **Fax:** (1) 325 0144 **Telex:** 210566 CRPL GR

Senior Executive Officers
Chief Representative   A Morelli

The Chase Manhattan Bank
Representative Office

95 Akti Miaouli, GR-185 10 Piraeus
Tel: (1) 429 0674; (1) 429 0678 **Fax:** (1) 429 0725

Senior Executive Officers
Others (Senior Executives)
Senior Officer   Achilleas Stergiou *Senior Officer*

Citibank NA
Full Branch Office

8 Othonos Street, GR-105 57 Athens
Tel: (1) 329 2117 **Fax:** (1) 324 0829 **Telex:** 22643842 CITB GR **Swift:** CITI GR AA **Reuters:** CITG (Dealing)

Senior Executive Officers
Country Corporate Officer   Takis Araboglou
Treasurer   A Petroutsas ☏ **324 0893**

Others (Senior Executives)
Head of Financial Markets   Peter Doukas ☏ **323 4848**
WCG   Ion Englesos *Head* ☏ **3292 397**

General-Lending (DCM, SL)
Head of Corporate Banking   Lito Ioannidou *Local Corporate Group Head* ☏ **3292 201**

Relationship Manager
FI / PS   Christos Asperidis *Head* ☏ **3292 398**

Debt Capital Markets / Fixed Income
Global Head   Andis Tostopoulos ☏ **323 4099**

Equity Capital Markets
Global Head   Andis Tostopoulos ☏ **323 4099**

Money Markets
Global Head   Costas Coulopadis ☏ **323 4603**

Foreign Exchange
Global Head   George Kofinakos ☏ **329 2372**
Country Head   Tony Gounaris ☏ **323 4873**

Commercial Bank of Greece SA
Head Office

Alternative trading name: Banque Commerciale de Grece

11 Sophokleous Street, GR-102 35 Athens
Tel: (1) 328 4000 **Fax:** (1) 325 3746; (1) 323 4333 **Telex:** 01 216545-9 CBHO GR **Swift:** EMPO GR AA **Reuters:** CGRE
Telerate: 8677, 8678, 44614 **Cable:** COMERZBANK ATHENS
Economics & Information **Tel:** 2693ext2104; **Fax:** 2693ext2104; **Reuters:** CBGA; CBGB; CBGC; CBOG; CGRD
Website: www.combank.gr

Senior Executive Officers
Chairman & Managing Director   Costas Georgoutsakos ☏ **328 4250** 🖷 **324 3508**
Vice Chairman   Konstantinos Stefanou
Treasurer   George Yeoryiou ☏ **328 4964** 🖷 **328 4808**
General Manager   George Michelis ☏ **324 4249** 🖷 **323 4304**
Manager   Grigorios Chryssikos ☏ **328 4403** 🖷 **322 4401**
International Division   Constantin Kanonis *DGM, International Banking Group* ☏ **328 4170** 🖷 **328 4589**

Others (Senior Executives)
Alexopoulos Panayotis *Member of the Board*
Andrigiannakis Michalis *Member of the Board*
Antonopoulou Theodora *Member of the Board*
Voudrouris Gerasimos *Member of the Board*

GREECE (+30)

Commercial Bank of Greece SA (cont)
Others (Senior Executives) (cont)

    Estratoglou Konstantinos *Member of the Board*
    Theocharakis Nikolaos *Member of the Board*
    Karagounis Dimitrios *Member of the Board*
    Kontellis Pavlos *Member of the Board*
    Makronikolakis Georgios *Member of the Board*
    Babanasis Stergios *Member of the Board*
    Bekiaris Andreas *Member of the Board*
    Mylonas Nikkolaos *Member of the Board*
    Papadionysiou Vasilios *Member of the Board*
    Spiliopoulos Georgios *Member of the Board*
    Spyridakis Ioannis *Member of the Board*
    Travlos Spyros *Member of the Board*

Institutional Banking Group
    Paraskevas Paraskevopoulos T **328 4728** F **324 8785**

General-Lending (DCM, SL)
Head of Corporate Banking
    Costas Dedousis *DGM, Corporate / Consumer Bnkg Group*
    Constantin Kanonis *DGM, International Banking Group* T **328 4170**
    F **328 4589**
    Panagis Petropoulos *Manager, Loan Suspence Division* T **328 3480**
    F **324 8353**
    Alekos Diamandopoulos *Manager, Credit Policy Division*

General-Investment
Head of Investment
    Panayiotis Yeoryiou *DGM, Investment Banking Group* T **328 4284**
    F **324 5001**

Syndicated Lending
Recovery
    Panagis Petropoulos *Manager, Loan Suspence Division* T **328 3480**
    F **324 8353**
Head of Credit Committee
    Alekos Diamandopoulos *Manager, Credit Policy Division*

Loan-Related Activities
Shipping Finance
    Konstantinos Ploubidis T **422 2758** F **422 6775**

Settlement / Clearing
Operations
    Petros Lirintzis *Manager, Strategic Planning & Management Info*
    Haralambos Perrakis *DGM, Strategic Planning, Marketing & Organization*

Other Departments
Private Banking
    Dionysios Kaperonis *Deputy General Manager* T **729 5387** F **729 5391**
Economic Research
    Georgios Valais *Manager* T **328 4903** F **331 1781**
    Haralambos Perrakis *Deputy General Manager*

Administration

Technology & Systems
Technical Consultants Division
    Dimitrios Kambanis *Manager* T **328 3210** F **324 2555**
Information & Production Systems
    Panayiotis Karahalios *Manager*
IT Operations
    Charalabos Perrakis T **328 2247** F **323 2854**

Legal / In-House Counsel
    Ioannis Spiridakis *Manager* T **328 3470** F **321 2509**

Public Relations
    Anastasios Floropoulos T **328 4306** F **325 4484**

Accounts / Audit
Accounting & Financial Division
    Georgios Meletis *Manager* T **328 4367** F **321 0733**
Audit Division
    Georgios Hatzis *Manager* T **328 3750** F **322 1086**

Other (Administration)
Training Division
    Nikolaos Malikoutis *Manager* T **328 43000** F **321 3416**
Security Services Division
    Chrysanthos Kostopoulos T **328 4454** F **321 3198**
Human Resources Division
    Georgios Gantzidis T **328 4960** F **321 0023**
Secretariat Division
    Grigorios Chryssikos *Manager* T **328 4403** F **322 4401**
Economic Research Division
    Georgios Valais *Manager* T **328 4903** F **331 1781**
Branches Networks Support Division
    Evagelos Fafalios *Manager* T **328 4632** F **321 5508**
Group Activities Division
    Athanasios Stamatiadis *Manager* T **328 2338** F **321 9334**

www.euromoneydirectory.com GREECE (+30)

Cyclos Securities SA
Head Office

39 Panepistimioy Street, GR-105 64 Athens
PO Box 8114, GR-105 64 Athens
Tel: (1) 321 2166; (1) 321 2167 **Fax:** (1) 323 9122 **Email:** kyclos@ote.net.gr

Senior Executive Officers
President | Panagiotis Stamatopoylos
Managing Director | Anastasios Stamatopoylos

Debt Capital Markets / Fixed Income
Domestic Government Bonds
Head of Sales; Head of Trading; Head of Research · | Demetrios Bizanos *Trader*

Equity Capital Markets
Domestic Equities
Head of Trading | Tassos Stomatopoulos *Deputy Managing Director*
Head of Research | Alexander Tavlaridis *Chief Analyst*

EFG Eurobank SA
Head Office

Formerly known as: Euromerchant Bank

8 Othonos Street, GR-105 57 Athens
Tel: (1) 333 7000; (1) 929 2100 **Fax:** (1) 323 3866; (1) 324 5916 **Telex:** 210975 **Reuters:** EMBA-EMBP

Senior Executive Officers
Chairman | George Gondicas ⊡ **333 7107**
Chief Executive Officer | Nicholas Nanopoulos ⊡ **333 7104**
Financial Director | Paula Hadjisotiriou ⊡ **333 7114**
Chief Operating Officer | Theodor Karakassis ⊡ **333 7172**
Treasurer | Yasmine Ralli ⊡ **333 7192**
General Manager | Vyron Ballis ⊡ **929 2250**
General Manager | Charalambos Kyrkos ⊡ **333 7275**
General Manager | Christos Sorotos ⊡ **333 7105**
Company Secretary | Pedro Carvalho ⊡ **333 7131**

Debt Capital Markets / Fixed Income
Head of Debt Capital Markets | Fokion Karavias

Equity Capital Markets
Head of Equity Capital Markets | Athina Dessypri ⊡ **333 7244**

Syndicated Lending
Head of Origination | Christos Komiopoulos ⊡ **333 7121**
Head of Syndication | Vassiliki Campbell ⊡ **333 7248**

Loan-Related Activities
Trade Finance | Christos Komiopoulos ⊡ **333 7121**
Shipping Finance | Lambros Theodorou *Head* ⊡ **333 7831**
Project Finance | Vassiliki Campbell ⊡ **333 7248**

Money Markets
Head of Money Markets | Nikos Andrianopoulos

Foreign Exchange
Head of Foreign Exchange | George Kyriacou

Risk Management
Head of Risk Management | Paula Hadjisotiriou ⊡ **333 7114**

Corporate Finance / M&A Advisory
Head of Corporate Finance | Nikos Aliprantis ⊡ **333 7246** ⌐ **324 7202**

Settlement / Clearing
Head of Settlement / Clearing; Back-Office | Dimitra Spyrou *Manager, Treasury Back Office* ⊡ **333 7233**

Global Custody
Head of Global Custody | Andreas Economides *Manager, Custody* ⊡ **333 7371**

Other Departments
Chief Credit Officer | Vassilios Floros *Head, Business Credit* ⊡ **333 7143**
Private Banking | Ballis Spandoni *Head, Domestic Private Banking* ⊡ **333 7331**
 | Ionna Makri *Head, International Private Banking* ⊡ **333 7280**
Correspondent Banking | Sotiria Massaveta ⊡ **929 2421**

GREECE (+30)   www.euromoneydirectory.com

EFG Eurobank SA (cont)
Administration
Head of Administration — Christina Karapatsa ☎ **929 2591**
Head of Marketing — Loucas Tamuakas ☎ **929 2286**
Technology & Systems
George Georgiou *Network Manager* ☎ **929 2275**
Petros Aggelakis ☎ **929 2552**
Legal / In-House Counsel
Rania Papavassiliou ☎ **929 2190**
Compliance
Christos Vagias *Compliance Officer* ☎ **333 7291**
Accounts / Audit
Despina Andreadou *Head, Internal Audit* ☎ **929 2499**
Other (Administration)
Human Resources — Theano Zambella *Head* ☎ **333 7261**

Egnatia Securities SA   Head Office

8 Dragatsaniou Street, GR-105 59 Athens
PO Box 30355, GR-105 59 Athens
Tel: (1) 331 1413; (1) 324 8608 **Fax:** (1) 331 1419 **Email:** egnasec@otenet.gr
Website: www.egnatiabank.gr

Senior Executive Officers
Chief Executive Officer — Dimitri Lekkas *General Manager*
Equity Capital Markets
Head of Equity Capital Markets — Dimitri Lekkas *General Manager*
Domestic Equities
Head of Sales — George Stratigos *Foreign Instutional, Equities Sales*
Head of Trading — Spyros Argyriou *International Instutional, Trading Desk*
Equity Research
Head of Equity Research — Costas Xenos *Head of Research*
Settlement / Clearing
Tel: 331 1413 **Fax:** 331 1419
Head of Settlement / Clearing — Kostas Souras *Equity Settlement, Clearing Officer* ☎ **331 1413**
Back-Office — John Mathioudakis *Head of Back-Office*
Administration
Technology & Systems
George Gialouris *EDP Manager*
Legal / In-House Counsel
Evanthia Tsiri ☎ **363 4262**
Compliance
Evi Tsgvreni *Head of Compliance*

Ergo Securities SA

40-44 Petroulaki Street, GR-105 61 Athens
Tel: (3) 324 2413; (3) 324 2414 **Fax:** (3) 321 4023

Senior Executive Officers
General Manager — Ageliki Petroulakis
Stock Exchange Representative — George Paganopoulos
Debt Capital Markets / Fixed Income
Head of Fixed Income — Nikos Nikolaides
Fixed-Income Repo
Head of Repo — Nikos Nikolaides
Equity Capital Markets
Domestic Equities
Head of Research — George Dimitriou *Analyst*
Settlement / Clearing
Head of Settlement / Clearing — Tasos Prekas
Other Departments
Cash Management — John Skianins *Accountant* ☎ **321 4023**

www.euromoneydirectory.com GREECE (+30)

Administration
Business Development

Technology & Systems

Legal / In-House Counsel

Public Relations

Corporate Communications

Ageliki Petroulakis *General Manager*

Manos Vernardos

Elina Perkeze *Legal Advisor*

Sissy Theoposopoulos

Alexandros Topaloglou *Accountant*

Ergobank SA

36 Panepistimiou Street, GR-106 79 Athens
Tel: (1) 323 8886 **Fax:** (1) 322 8906 **Telex:** 216140 **Swift:** ERGO GR AA

Senior Executive Officers
Chairman   X C Nickitas

Euroxx Securities SA   Head Office

5 Sophocleous Street, GR-105 59 Athens
Tel: (1) 331 3111 **Fax:** (1) 331 3103 **Email:** euroxx@techlink.gr

Senior Executive Officers
President   Giuseppe Giano
Managing Director   Pavlos Vranas
International Division   Nick Kontorozis

Debt Capital Markets / Fixed Income
Head of Fixed Income   Pavlos Vranas *Managing Director*

Equity Capital Markets
Head of Equity Capital Markets   Giuseppe Giano *President*

Money Markets
Head of Money Markets   Aristotelis Ninios

Settlement / Clearing
Head of Settlement / Clearing   Alexandros Billis

HypoVereinsbank   Full Branch Office

Heraklion 7, GR-106 73 Athens
Tel: (1) 645 0601 **Fax:** (1) 364 0063 **Swift:** BVBE GR AA

ING Bank   Full Branch Office

198 Synerou Avenue, GR-176 71 Athens
Tel: (1) 950 6122; (1) 950 6103 **Fax:** (1) 959 3380; (1) 959 0416 **Telex:** 222182 INGB GR **Swift:** INGB GR AA
Reuters: INGI
Treasury Tel: 950 6336

Senior Executive Officers
Chief Executive Officer   Periklis Dontas *General Manager*
                                     Frank Hawkes *Deputy General Manager*
Treasurer   Alexandra Vogiatzi ☏ **950 6336**

Risk Management
Head of Risk Management   Yiannis Patiniotis *Risk Manager* ☏ **950 6028**

Global Custody
Head of Global Custody   Eugenia Dimitrakopoulos *Head, Custody Services* ☏ **950 6123**

Administration
Accounts / Audit
                                     Yiannis Pantelidis *Manager, Internal Audit* ☏ **950 6866**

GREECE (+30)   www.euromoneydirectory.com

Ionian and Popular Bank of Greece SA   Head Office

Alternative trading name: Ionian Bank
45 Panepistimiou Street, GR-102 43 Athens
Tel: (1) 322 5501/9; (1) 323 0055/8 **Fax:** (1) 322 2882 **Telex:** 215269 IPAT GR **Swift:** IONP GR AA **Reuters:** IPBG
Telerate: 41924 **Cable:** IONPOPBANK
Website: www.kapatel.gr.ionian

Senior Executive Officers
Managing Director   Haris Stamatopoulos
General Manager   Dimitrios Frangetis
International Division   Nikolaos Zanaropoulos

General-Lending (DCM, SL)
Head of Corporate Banking   Dionyssios Bristoyannis

Administration
Head of Marketing   Constantine Lymberopoulos

Technology & Systems
       Titos Rendoumis

Legal / In-House Counsel
       Constantine Gontikas

Public Relations
       George Limberis

Kappa Securities SA

15 Valaoritou Street, GR-106 71 Athens
Tel: (1) 361 0371 **Fax:** (1) 364 1002 **Email:** kappa@netor.gr

Senior Executive Officers
President
Chief Executive Officer   Spiros Bellos
Financial Director   Dimitrios Paparistiois *Executive Manager*
Chief Operating Officer   Nikolaos Schizas *General Manager*
Company Secretary   Vasilios Vezerisis
       Vichy Ralli

Administration
Technology & Systems
       Kostantinos Georgopoulos

Karamanof Securities SA   Head Office

Pl Ag Theodoron 2, GR-105 61 Athens
Tel: (1) 321 2947 **Fax:** (1) 321 4355

Senior Executive Officers
Chairman   Metrios Papamichail
Managing Director   Anastassios Karamanof
Chief Executive Officer   Michael Karamanof
Financial Director   Vassilios Panagopoulos
Chief Operating Officer   Marios Karamanof
Treasurer   Maria Petriti
Managing Director   Anastassios Karamanof
General Manager   Vassilios Phocas
Company Secretary   Helen Galanopoulou

Syndicated Lending

Loan-Related Activities
Trade Finance   Diamantis Damiris

Administration
Business Development   Michael Karamanof
Head of Marketing   Marios Karamanof

Public Relations
       Marios Karamanof

www.euromoneydirectory.com GREECE (+30)

Merrill Lynch, Pierce, Fenner & Smith (Hellas) ELDE
Subsidiary Company

17 Valaoritou Street, GR-106 71 Athens
Tel: (1) 364 8040 **Fax:** (1) 364 8046 **Telex:** 222803
Website: www.ml.com

Midland Bank plc
Full Branch Office

1A Sekeri Street, GR-106 71 Athens
Tel: (1) 364 7410 **Fax:** (1) 364 4043; (1) 361 4495 **Telex:** 222318 MIDA GR **Swift:** MIDL GR AA
Reuters: MBGR-V, MBGX **Telerate:** 41916

Senior Executive Officers
Country Manager — Lefteris Hiliadakis

National Bank of Greece SA

86 Eolou Street, GR-102 32 Athens
Tel: (1) 334 1000 **Fax:** (1) 321 3119

Senior Executive Officers
Treasurer — Michael Antoniadis ☎ 334 3472

Debt Capital Markets / Fixed Income
Department: Treasury
Eolou 93, GR-102 32 Athens
Tel: +30 334 0801 **Fax:** +30 334 3318
Global Head — George Stamnos

Domestic Government Bonds
Head of Sales; Head of Trading — Vasilis Kavalos ☎ 334 0802
Head of Research — Gikas Manalis ☎ 334 3454

Eurobonds
Head of Trading; Head of Research — Rosa Polatou ☎ +44 (171) 623 1723

Libor-Based / Floating-Rate Products
FRN Origination; FRN Sales — Vasilis Kavalos ☎ 334 0802
Asset Swaps — Leonidas Fragiadanis ☎ 331 3760

Medium-Term Notes
Head of Origination — Nana Petrounakou ☎ 334 3465

Private Placements
Head of Origination — Nana Petrounakou ☎ 334 3465

Fixed-Income Repo
Head of Repo — Nana Petrounakou ☎ 334 3465

Eurobonds
Head of Trading; Head of Research — Rosa Polatou ☎ +44 (171) 623 1723

Money Markets
Global Head — Nana Petrounakou ☎ 334 3465

Wholesale Deposits
Head of Sales — Niky Soulopoulou ☎ 331 4750
Lily Pyrovolidou ☎ 331 0760

Foreign Exchange
Global Head — Anna Kousteni ☎ 331 4970

Risk Management

Fixed Income Derivatives / Risk Management
Global Head; IR Swaps Sales / Marketing; IR
Swaps Trading; IR Options Sales / Marketing — Leo Fragiadakis ☎ 331 3760

Foreign Exchange Derivatives / Risk Management
Cross-Currency Swaps, Sales / Marketing — Leo Fragiadakis ☎ 331 3760

GREECE (+30)   www.euromoneydirectory.com

National Securities Co

93 Eolou and Sophocleous Street, GR-10551 Athens
Tel: (1) 323 5155; (1) 325 0110 Fax: (1) 323 5155 Email: john@ndseco.gr

Senior Executive Officers
Chairman — Mr Karamouzis
Managing Director — Dimitrios Matsazanis

Debt Capital Markets / Fixed Income
Domestic Government Bonds
Head of Sales; Head of Trading — Liana Linardou

Equity Capital Markets
Head of Sales — Jannis Katsouridis *Head of Sales, Foreign Institutions*

Domestic Equities
Head of Trading — Athinodoros Diplas *Stock Exchange Representative* ☎ **(1) 323 5181**
Head of Research — George Tegopoulos *Analyst* ☎ **(1) 334 3347**

National Westminster Bank plc   Full Branch Office

5 Korai Street, GR-105 64 Athens
Tel: (1) 325 0924; (1) 324 1562 Fax: (1) 322 2951 Telex: 216346, 223987 Swift: NWBK GR AA Reuters: NWXA

Senior Executive Officers
Chief Executive Officer — Malcolm I Veale *Country Manager*
Financial Director — George Tzathas *Manager, Finance & Performance* ☎ **689 2007**
Chief Operating Officer — Christos Boules *Head of Administration*
Treasurer — George Mylonas *Deputy Chief Manager* ☎ **323 3877**

Debt Capital Markets / Fixed Income
Bonds - General

Marina Giannarou *Assistant Manager, Fixed Income*
Panagiotis Genakos *Assistant Manager, Fixed Income Sales*
Jack Canettis *Assistant Manager, Fixed Income Sales*

Money Markets
Country Head — Petros Koutsorrizos *Manager, Money Market*

Money Markets - General

Platon Haldeos *Assistant Manager, Money Market*
Konstandinos Fouskas *Assistant Manager, Money Market*
Chrysavgi Vassiliadou *Assistant Manager, Money Market*

Foreign Exchange
Country Head — Nikolaos Hinoporos *Manager, FX*

FX Traders / Sales People

Nikolaos Kontaroudis *Assistant Manager, FX*
John Kouletsis *Assistant Manager, FX*

Settlement / Clearing
Head of Settlement / Clearing — John Lovatt *Head of Settlements*

NedShip Financial Consultants E.P.E   Full Branch Office

Formerly known as: NedShip Bank
Alternative trading name: NedShip Greece

81 Akti Miaouli, GR-185 38 Piraeus
Tel: (1) 428 3515 Fax: (1) 428 0017 Telex: 211481

Senior Executive Officers
Manager — Martin L Hessels
Office Manager — Ellen Van da Schouw

Others (Senior Executives)
Account Manager — B Veldhuinen
A Roupas-Pautaleon

Nuntius Hellenic Securites   Head Office

6 Dragatsaniou Street, GR-105 59 Athens
Tel: (1) 331 3770 Fax: (1) 325 4846 Email: nuntius@netor.gr

Senior Executive Officers
Chairman — Alexander Moraitakis ☎ **325 4846** 📠 **325 4685**

570 Euromoney Directory 1999

www.euromoneydirectory.com GREECE (+30)

Omega Securities SA
Head Office

8 Dragatsaniou Street, GR-105 59 Athens
Tel: (1) 331 2650ext9 **Fax:** (1) 323 3781 **Email:** omega@netor.gr
Website: www.omegasec.gr

Senior Executive Officers
Chairman	Dimitpis Kouzionis
Vice Chairman	Hasdai Kapon
Managing Director & Stock Exchange Representative	Elias Tsotakos
General Manager International Division	Spyros Dimitras Christos Kavathas
Managing Director & Stock Exchange Representative	Elias Tsotakos

Equity Capital Markets
Head of Equity Capital Markets — Stefanos Noussias *Chief Trader*

Money Markets
Head of Money Markets — Caroula Manousaki

Corporate Finance / M&A Advisory
Head of Corporate Finance — Georgios Symiriotis

Settlement / Clearing
Head of Settlement / Clearing — Georgios Papoutsis *Head, Back Office*

P&K Securities SA
Head Office

5 Koubari Street, GR-106 74 Athens
Tel: (1) 338 6100 **Fax:** (1) 364 1666; (1) 338 6139 **Email:** pksec@ibm.net

Senior Executive Officers
Chairman	Lambros Papakinstantinou ☎ **338 6103**
Head of Sales	Achilleas Kontogouris ☎ **338 6106**

Debt Capital Markets / Fixed Income
Tel: 338 6133

Domestic Government Bonds
Head of Sales — Manos Drossatakis

Equity Capital Markets
Tel: 338 6130 **Fax:** 338 6139
Head of Sales — Achilleas Kontogouris *Head of Sales* ☎ **338 6106**
Head of Trading — Damianos Papakonstantinou ☎ **338 6130**

Equity Research
Head of Equity Research — Kostas Vrostopoulos ☎ **338 6170**

Settlement / Clearing
Head of Settlement / Clearing — Dimitris Kortesis ☎ **338 6115**

The Royal Bank of Scotland
Full Branch Office

61 Akti Miaouli, GR-185 10 Piraeus
Tel: (1) 459 6500 **Fax:** (1) 459 6600 **Telex:** 212055

Senior Executive Officers
General Manager — B W Martin

Sigma Securities
Head Office

10 Stadiou Street, GR-105 64 Athens
Tel: (1) 335 4100; (1) 331 1456 **Fax:** (1) 325 2241; (1) 323 3814 **Telex:** 210733 ATRA GR **Email:** info@sigma.gr
Reuters: ATGG-I **Telerate:** 17890-2
Website: www.sigma.gr

Senior Executive Officers
President	Iakerus Georganas ☎ **333 5551**
Chief Executive Officer	John Marcopoulos *Chief Executive Officer* ☎ **335 4103** 🖷 **335 4104**
Financial Director	George Nikiforakis *Finance Director* ☎ **335 4190**
Chief Executive Officer	John Marcopoulos ☎ **335 4103** 🖷 **335 4104**
General Manager	Anthony Athanassoglou ☎ **335 4118** 🖷 **335 4119**

Euromoney Directory 1999 571

GREECE (+30)   www.euromoneydirectory.com

Sigma Securities (cont)

Others (Senior Executives)
Head of Trading   Carina Pournara *Director, Sales & Trading*

General-Investment
Head of Investment   Iannis Apostolakos ☎ 335 4184

Debt Capital Markets / Fixed Income
Global Head   Anthony Athanassoglou *General Manager* ☎ 335 4118 📠 335 4119

Domestic Government Bonds
Head of Sales; Head of Trading   Anthony Athanassoglou *General Manager* ☎ 335 4118 📠 335 4119
Head of Research   Maria Kapetanaki

Equity Capital Markets
Head of Equity Capital Markets   Maria Douli *Director, Research & Sales*

Domestic Equities
Head of Trading   Carina Pournara *Director, Sales & Trading*
Head of Research   Maria Douli *Director, Research & Sales*

International Equities
Head of Trading   Carina Pournara *Director, Sales & Trading*
Head of Research   Maria Douli *Director, Research & Sales*

Warrants
Head of Sales   Iannis Apostolakos ☎ 335 4184

Syndicated Lending

Loan-Related Activities
Project Finance   George Nikolaidis ☎ 335 4112

Foreign Exchange
Department: Sigma Money Brokers
Head of Foreign Exchange   Andonis Katsaounis *General Manager* ☎ 331 1450

Corporate Finance / M&A Advisory
Global Head   Iannis Apostolakos ☎ 335 4184

Other Departments
Private Banking   Thanos Voglis ☎ 335 4228 📠 335 4229
     Kostas Papayannakopoulos

Administration
Compliance
     Vassilis Lazaris ☎ 335 4137

Public Relations
     Katerina Florou ☎ 335 4110

Société Générale

240-242 Kifissias Avenue, GR-152 31 Athens
Tel: (1) 679 0000 **Fax:** (1) 672 8796 **Telex:** 219055 **Swift:** SOGEGRAA **Email:** sgcust1@netor.gr
Website: www.socgen.com

Société Générale   Full Branch Office

11 Kountouriotou Street, GR-546 26 Thessaloniki
Tel: (31) 545 903; (31) 545 820 **Fax:** (31) 545 917; (31) 528 272

Senior Executive Officers
Chief Operating Officer   Paris Tsoukala *Manager, Operations* ☎ 545 977
Branch Manager   Dimitri Theodoridis

Others (Senior Executives)
     Anna Billis *Manager, Private Banking* ☎ 545 958

General-Lending (DCM, SL)
Head of Corporate Banking   Anthony Grammatikopoulos *Manager, Credit*

Settlement / Clearing
Operations   Paris Tsoukala *Manager, Operations* ☎ 545 977

Other Departments
Private Banking   Anna Billis *Manager, Private Banking* ☎ 545 958

Telesis Securities SA
Head Office

11 Voukourestiou Street, GR-106 71 Athens
Tel: (1) 338 6700 **Fax:** (1) 645 0743 **Email:** info@telesis.gr

Senior Executive Officers
Managing Director, Equities					Victor Asser
Managing Director, Fixed Income				Marina Efraimoglou

General-Investment
Head of Investment						Victor Pisante *Managing Director, Investment Banking*

Xiosbank SA
Head Office

11 Vas Sophias Avenue, GR-106 71 Athens
Tel: (1) 328 8888 **Fax:** (1) 324 4909 **Telex:** 220640 XIOS GR **Swift:** CHIO GR AA **Email:** xiosbank@netor.gr
Website: www.netor.gr/xiosbank

Senior Executive Officers
Chairman							Vardis Vardinoyannis
Vice Chairman							Yiannis Vardinoyannis
Managing Director						Panayiotis V Poulis

Others (Senior Executives)
Members of the Board						Georgios P Alexandridis *Director*
								Georgios A Georgiadis *Director*
								John B Goulandris *Director*
								Stavros P Triantaphillides *Director*
								Georgios V Vardinoyannis *Director*

General - Treasury
Head of Treasury						Likourgos Ladopoulos *Treasurer*

Risk Management
Head of Risk Management						Iordanis Aivazis *Risk & Corporate Manager*

Other Departments
Private Banking							John Siglas *Director of Private Banking*

Administration

Technology & Systems
Informastion System Manager					Vassilios Trapezanoglou

Legal / In-House Counsel
Legal Councel							Lambros Kotsiris

Compliance
Director Financial Control & Operations				Theodoros Gezepis

Accounts / Audit
Audit Director							Ireni Mavrommati

Other (Administration)
Human Resouces Director						Georgia Stergiopoulos

GUATEMALA
(+502)

Banco de Guatemala
Central Bank

7a Avenida 22-01, Guatemala Zona 1, 01001
Tel: (2) 306 222; (2) 306 232 **Fax:** (2) 328 509; (2) 534 035 **Telex:** 5231 GUABAN GU

Senior Executive Officers
President							Edin Velasquez
Chief Executive Officer						Giovanni Verbena *General Manager*

Others (Senior Executives)
Head, Economics & Statistics					Edwin Matul

GUATEMALA (+502)　　　www.euromoneydirectory.com

Banco de Occidente — Head Office

7a Avenida 7-33, Zona 9, Guatemala, 228
Tel: 361 1122 **Fax:** 361 1120 **Email:** occidente@occidente.com.gt
Website: www.occidente.com

Senior Executive Officers
President — Pedro Aguirre
Vice President — José Pivaral
Financial Director — Raymond Puccini *Finance Vice President*
Treasurer — Alvaro Monteros *Treasury Manager*
International Division — Elsie de Chávez *Manager, International Operations*

General-Lending (DCM, SL)
Head of Corporate Banking — Thomas Feurich *Manager, Corporate & Correspondent Banking*

Risk Management
Fax: 361 1155
Head of Risk Management — Rodney Tsuji *Manager of Risk & Credit*

Foreign Exchange Derivatives / Risk Management
Spot / Forwards Sales — Alvaro Monteros *Treasury Manager*

Corporate Finance / M&A Advisory
Head of Corporate Finance — Raymond Puccini *Finance Vice President*

Settlement / Clearing
Head of Settlement / Clearing — Samuel Espina *Head of Clearing* ☎ **530 5894**

Other Departments
Chief Credit Officer — Rodney Tsuji *Manager of Risk & Credit*
Correspondent Banking — Elsie de Chávez *Manager, International Operations*

Administration
Head of Administration — Gerald Brunelle
Business Development; Head of Marketing — Thomas Feurich *Manager, Corporate & Correspondent Banking*

Technology & Systems
— Carlos Lainfiesta *Vice President, Technology & Information* ☎ **230 5894**

Legal / In-House Counsel
— José Pivaral *Vice President*

Compliance
— Faustino Velásquez

Accounts / Audit
— Gilberto Batres *Corporate Auditor* ☎ **230 5894**

Banco Privado para el Desarrollo SA — Head Office

Alternative trading name: Bancasol
7 Avenida, 8-46, Guatemala Zona 9, 01009
Tel: 361 7777 **Fax:** 361 7217

Senior Executive Officers
President & Chief Executive Officer — José María Escamilla Valdés
International Division — Pablo Alexander Castellanos Rodríguez *International Division Director*

General-Lending (DCM, SL)
Head of Corporate Banking — Angel Mazariegos Rodas *Commercial & Corporate Banking Director*

Citibank NA — Full Branch Office

Avenida Reforma 15-45, Guatemala Zona 10, 01010
Tel: 333 6574 **Fax:** 333 6860 **Telex:** 6226 CITIBAN GU

Senior Executive Officers
Country Corporate Officer — Juan Miró
Financial Director — Mirella Juarez *Head, Financial Control*
Treasurer — Edwardo Oviedo
Company Secretary — Mara Pineda

General-Lending (DCM, SL)
Head of Corporate Banking — Enrique Umaña

Syndicated Lending
Project Finance — Luis Molina

GUINEA-BISSAU (+245)

Foreign Exchange
Head of Foreign Exchange — Rafael Kihm
Head of Institutional Sales — Jorge Palacios

Risk Management
Head of Risk Management — Karina Cabrera *Country Risk Manager*

Corporate Finance / M&A Advisory
Head of Corporate Finance — Maureen Riojas

Other Departments
Cash Management — Victor Arqueta

Administration
Head of Administration — Jose Miquel Bastias
Business Development — Marco Aragon

Technology & Systems
Maya Gonzales

Legal / In-House Counsel
Karin Herman

Compliance
Rebeca Castellanos

Public Relations
Claudia Morales

Accounts / Audit
Mayda Duarte

Other (Administration)
Human Resources — Yana Calderón

Ibero Platina Bank AG — Representative Office
Edif Centro Internaciones, Diagonal 6, 11-97, Zona 10, 5to Nivel, Office 501, Guatemala
Tel: 362 1752ext55 Fax: 362 1751 Email: ritapbg@infovia.com.gt Email: johanpbg@infovia.com.gt

Lloyds Bank plc — Full Branch Office
6 Avenida 9-51, Zona 9, Edificio Gran Via, Guatemala
Tel: 332 7580 Fax: 332 7641

Senior Executive Officers
General Manager — Nigel Hubbard

Others (Senior Executives)
Steven Robinson *Assistant Manager*

Global Custody
Regional Head — Nigel Hubbard *General Manager*

Société Générale — Representative Office
7a Av 1-2D, Zona 4, Edificio Torrecafe Oficina 101, Ciudad de Guatemala, Guatemala
Tel: 360 1472 Fax: 331 6264
Website: www.socgen.com

GUINEA-BISSAU (+245)

Banque Centrale des Etats de l'Afrique de l'Ouest — Central Bank
PO Box 38, Bissau
Tel: 215 548; 214 173 Fax: 201 305; 201 321 Telex: 289 BCGB 1

Senior Executive Officers
Country Director — Luis Candido Lopes Ribeiro

GUYANA (+592)

Bank of Guyana
Central Bank

1 Church Street & Avenue of the Republic, Georgetown
Tel: (2) 63250; (2) 63261 **Fax:** (2) 72965 **Telex:** 2267 CENBANK GY

Senior Executive Officers
Governor — Dolly S Singh ☎ **71535**
Legal Counsel & Company Secretary — Jennifer Branche

Others (Senior Executives)
Head, Banking — Lawrence Williams ☎ **71533**
Head, Banking Supervision — Ramnarine Lal *Director*
Head, Economics & Statistics — Gobind Ganga *Director*
Head, Operations Department — Leslie Glen *Director* ☎ **75179**

Money Markets
Head of Money Markets — Frank Tucker *Assistant Director*

Foreign Exchange
Head of Foreign Exchange — Vinod Sharma *Director*

Settlement / Clearing
Head of Settlement / Clearing — Joseph Lall *Assistant Director* ☎ **71532**

Administration
Head of Administration — Iris Prescott *Assistant Director*

Public Relations
Margaret Simpson *Communications Officer*

Accounts / Audit
Head, Accountancy — Linden Morrison *Chief Accountant*
Head, Internal Audit — Dudley Kirton *Assistant Director*

HAITI (+509)

Banque de la République d'Haiti
Central Bank

Rue du Magasin de l'Etat, Port-Au-Prince
PO Box 1570, Port-Au-Prince
Tel: 991 000; 991 012 **Fax:** 222 607; 991 145 **Telex:** 20076 **Swift:** BRHA HT PP

Senior Executive Officers
Governor — Fritz Jean ☎ **991 069**
Deputy Governor — Roland Pierre ☎ **991 071**
General Manager — Henry Cassion ☎ **991 067**

Others (Senior Executives)
Board of Governors — Venel Joseph *Member*
Max Etienne *Member*
Chief Cashier — Theodore Noel *Director* ☎ **991 046**
Head, Banking Supervision — Georgette Carisma *Assistant Director* ☎ **991 154**
Head, Economics — René Wiener Aubourg
Head, Public Debt — Ruddy Mentor *Chief of Service* ☎ **991 076**

Foreign Exchange
Head of Foreign Exchange — Richard Baptiste *Chief of Service* ☎ **991 076**

Settlement / Clearing
Head of Settlement / Clearing — Carmita Fievre *Chief of Service* ☎ **991 049**
Operations — Théodore Noel
Henry Lévêque

Other Departments
Chief Credit Officer — Ketleen Florestal *Assistant Director* ☎ **991 088**

Administration
Head of Administration — Jean-Baden Dubois *Director* ☎ **991 141**

Technology & Systems
Jean-Claude Pauwels *Chief of Service* ☎ **991 033**

www.euromoneydirectory.com   HONG KONG, CHINA (+852)

Legal / In-House Counsel
Legal Affairs   Charles Castel *Director* ☎ 991 100

Public Relations
    Margaret Desvarieux *Head* ☎ 991 068

Accounts / Audit
Head, Accountancy   Marie Laurence Boyer *Assistant Director* ☎ 991 169
Head, Internal Audit   Brigirre Prudent *Assistant Director* ☎ 991 108

Citibank NA   Full Branch Office

242 Delmas Road, Port-Au-Prince
Tel: 464 364 **Fax:** 993 227; 993 228

Senior Executive Officers
Treasurer   Alix Auguste ☎ 464 905

Others (Senior Executives)
Country Corporate Officer   Gladys Coupet

HONDURAS (+504)

Banco Mercantil SA   Head Office

Boulevard Suyapa, Cruce hacia el Boulevard, Juan Pablo II y las Lomas del Guijarro, Tegucigalpa, 116
Apartado Postal 116, Tegucigalpa
Tel: (23) 20006 **Fax:** (23) 23137

Senior Executive Officers
President   José Lamas Bezos
General Manager   Jacobo Atala Zablah
International Division   Gracia Maria Sierra *International Manager*

Others (Senior Executives)
    René Arturo Simón *Assistant General Manager*

Settlement / Clearing
Operations   Rufino Zelaya *Operation Manager*

Lloyds Bank plc   Full Branch Office

Edificio Europa, Colonia San Carlos, Calle República de México, Tegucigalpa
Tel: 236 6864 **Fax:** 236 6417

Senior Executive Officers
General Manager   Graham Johns

HONG KONG, CHINA (+852)

Hong Kong Monetary Authority   🏛 Central Bank

30th Floor, 3 Garden Road, Hong Kong
Tel: 2878 8196 **Fax:** 2878 8197 **Telex:** 74574 XFUND HX **Email:** hkma@hkma.gov.hk
Website: www.info.gov.hk/hkma

Senior Executive Officers
Chief Executive Officer   Joseph C K Yam ☎ 2878 8188 📠 2878 1690
    David T R Carse *Deputy Chief Executive* ☎ 2878 1688 📠 2878 1690
    Tony Latter *Deputy Chief Executive* ☎ 2878 8128 📠 2878 8130
    Norman T L Chan *Deputy Chief Executive* ☎ 2878 8138 📠 2878 8207

General - Treasury
Head of Treasury   Rose S M Luk *Head of Finance* ☎ 2878 8118 📠 2968 4531

Administration
Technology & Systems
Information Technology   Peter C K Hsueh *Head* ☎ 2878 8228 📠 2878 1670

Euromoney Directory 1999   **577**

HONG KONG, CHINA (+852) www.euromoneydirectory.com

Hong Kong Monetary Authority (cont)
Legal / In-House Counsel
  Stefan M Gannon *General Counsel, Legal Office* ☎ 2878 8123 ℻ 2878 1691
Other (Administration)
  Pont S K Chiu *Head of Support Services* ☎ 2878 8238 ℻ 2878 8213

Abbey National Treasury Services   Representative Office
Suite 3209-10, 32nd Floor, Dah Sing Financial Centre, 108 Gloucester Road, Wanchai, Hong Kong
Tel: 2923 1030 **Fax:** 2507 2333

Senior Executive Officers
Regional Director, Asia   Philip McDuell
Assistant General Manager   Anthony Haynes ☎ 2923 1037

ABN AMRO Asia Limited   Subsidiary Company
3rd Floor, Edinburgh Tower, The Landmark, 15 Queen's Road, Central, Hong Kong
Tel: 2868 0368 **Fax:** 2810 4932 **Telex:** 74111 HX
Website: www.hgasia.prx.net

Senior Executive Officers
Chief Executive Officer   Roger Sharp ☎ 2102 2403
Financial Director   Tony Dickel ☎ 2102 2333
Chief Operating Officer   Hans Steketee ☎ 2102 2356
Managing Director / General Manager David Roberts ☎ 2102 2100

Others (Senior Executives)
Asian Strategy & Economics   Eugene Galbraith *Head* ☎ 2102 2239

Equity Capital Markets
Tel: 2868 0368 **Fax:** 2523 2556
Head of Equity Capital Markets   Michiel Steenman ☎ 2102 2139
Head of Sales   Peter Bristowe ☎ 2102 2205
Head of Trading   Glenn Lesko ☎ 2102 2199

Equity Research
Head of Equity Research   Kalina Ip ☎ 2102 2263

Settlement / Clearing
Tel: 2868 0368 **Fax:** 2810 4932
Operations   Judy Au *Head of Operations* ☎ 2102 2283

ABSA Asia Limited   Subsidiary Company
13th Floor, Dah Sing Financial Centre, 108 Gloucester Road, Wanchai, Hong Kong
Tel: 2531 9388 **Fax:** 2802 1908 **Telex:** 64348 ABSA HX **Swift:** ABSA HK HH **Email:** absahk@absa.asia.com
Reuters: ABSK
Website: www.absaasia.com

Senior Executive Officers
Chief Executive Officer   Willouw Petrus Burger *Managing Director* ☎ 2531 9301
Financial Director   Winnie Au *Financial Controller* ☎ 2531 9320
Chief Operating Officer   Cejas Wong *Senior Manager, Operations* ☎ 2531 9313
Treasurer   Jimmy Lee *Senior Manager, Treasury* ☎ 2531 9319
GM, Business Development   Kenneth Michael Hughes ☎ 2531 9303

Syndicated Lending
Country Head   Kenneth Michael Hughes *GM, Business Development* ☎ 2531 9303

Loan-Related Activities
Trade Finance; Project Finance; Structured Trade Finance   Kenneth Michael Hughes *GM, Business Development* ☎ 2531 9303

Money Markets
Country Head   Jimmy Lee *Senior Manager, Treasury* ☎ 2531 9319

Foreign Exchange
Country Head   Jimmy Lee *Senior Manager, Treasury* ☎ 2531 9319

Corporate Finance / M&A Advisory
Country Head   Kenneth Michael Hughes *GM, Business Development* ☎ 2531 9303

Settlement / Clearing
Country Head   Alex Lam *Assistant Manager, Settlement & Treasury Admin.* ☎ 2531 9314

www.euromoneydirectory.com   HONG KONG, CHINA (+852)

Other Departments
Private Banking   Tony Fu *Officer* ☏ **2531 9354**
Correspondent Banking   Andrew Patrick Holliday *AGM, Financial Institutions* ☏ **2531 9310**
Administration
Compliance
                                             Gavin Cho *Manager, Compliance* ☏ **2531 9311**

AGIFEL International Limited   Head Office

Room 2606, 26th Floor, Bank of America Tower, 12 Harcourt Road, Hong Kong
PO Box 11442, General Post Office, Hong Kong
Tel: 2844 1661 Fax: 2810 0402 Telex: 65505 AGIFE HX

Senior Executive Officers
Managing Director   David Townsend
Company Secretary   Winnie Lau

Others (Senior Executives)
Director   Steve Leung

Equity Capital Markets
Head of Equity Capital Markets   David Townsend *Managing Director*

Foreign Exchange
Head of Foreign Exchange   Winnie Lau

Settlement / Clearing
Telex: 65505 AGIFE HX
Head of Settlement / Clearing   Winnie Lau

Administration
Head of Administration   Chris Siu *Office Manager*

Technology & Systems
                                                    Steve Leung

Accounts / Audit
Accounts Manager   Winnie Lau

AIG Financial Products Hong Kong Limited   Subsidiary Company

Suite 3408, One Exchange Square, 8 Connaught Place, Central, Hong Kong
Tel: 2526 2608 Fax: 2501 0710 Telex: 70743

Senior Executive Officers
Managing Director   Nigel Pentland

Settlement / Clearing
Department: AIG Financial Products Corp
100 Nyala Farm, Westport, CT 06880
Tel: +1 (203) 222 4700 Fax: +1 (203) 222 4780
Settlement (General)   Sabrina Jaques ☏ **+1 (203) 221 4805**
                                                    Carmine Paradiso ☏ **+1 (203) 221 4805**

AIG Investment Corp (Asia) Limited

14th Floor, AIA Building, 1 Stubbs Road, Hong Kong
Tel: 2832 1210 Fax: 2234 0637
Website: www.aiggig.com

Debt Capital Markets / Fixed Income
Fixed-Income Repo
Marketing & Product Development   Delyth Thomas *Director (Asia)* ☏ **2832 1210** ✉ **2234 0637**
                                                                 ✉ **delyth.thomas@aig.com**

Equity Capital Markets
Equity Repo / Securities Lending
Marketing & Product Development   Delyth Thomas *Director (Asia)* ☏ **2832 1210** ✉ **2234 0637**
                                                                 ✉ **delyth.thomas@aig.com**

Euromoney Directory 1999   **579**

Get the Latest Information Everyday with the PaineWebber Euromoney Directory ON-LINE

Euromoney Directory On-line is a unique electronic service providing access to the entire directory direct to your computer – continuously updated throughout the year. In addition the site contains:

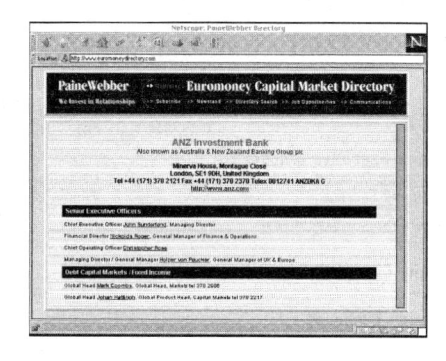

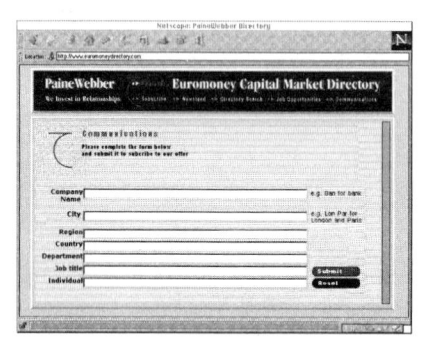

Daily News
New appointments, position/department changes, and the latest market gossip (updated every day).

Recruitment Services
Information and links on the very latest opportunities in the markets direct from the top recruitment consultancies.

PLUS – Sophisticated Search Facilities
Search by one or a combination of categories -- including country, region, job title, department, company, name and many more.

Launched in January 1999 this dedicated information service is only available to purchasers of the Directory.

Only £99/$160.

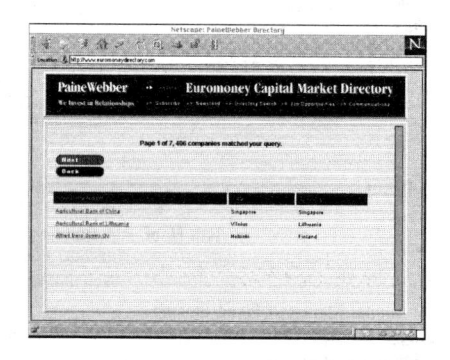

www.euromoneydirectory.com

To gain access to the PaineWebber Directory ON-LINE simply call our hotline on 44 171 779 8999 quoting ref. NSPW1

www.euromoneydirectory.com   HONG KONG, CHINA (+852)

Allied Capital Resources Limited
Head Office

1st/3rd Floors, Allied Capital Resources Building, 32/38 Ice House Street, Hong Kong
Tel: 2846 2288 **Fax**: 2810 0467; 2810 6388 **Telex**: 80790 ABANK HX

Senior Executive Officers
Chairman   Lucio Tan
Chief Executive Officer   Peter Ng
Chief Operating Officer   Benson Lam
Treasurer   Danny Lam

Other Departments
Private Banking   Andy Ko ☎ **2846 2251**

Administration
Technology & Systems
                                 Helmuth Lau ☎ **2846 2263**

Anglo Chinese Securities Limited
Head Office

Suite 4008, 40th Floor, Two Exchange Square, 8 Connaught Place, Central, Hong Kong
Tel: 2845 4400 **Fax**: 2523 3301

Senior Executive Officers
Director   Christopher Howe
Director   Steven Au ☎ **2845 8575**
Group General Manager   Joanna Busvine ☎ **2524 3130**

Arabian Gulf Investments (Far East) Limited
Head Office

Room 2606, 26th Floor, Bank of America Tower, 12 Harcourt Road, Hong Kong
Tel: 2844 1661 **Fax**: 2810 0402 **Telex**: 65505 AGIFE HX

Senior Executive Officers
Chairman   Morad Y Behbehani
General Manager   David Townsend
Company Secretary   Lau Winnie

Others (Senior Executives)
Deputy General Manager   Steve Leung

The Asahi Bank Limited
Full Branch Office

Level 32, One Pacific Place, 88 Queensway, Hong Kong
Tel: 2532 0500 **Fax**: 2868 4503 **Telex**: 86021 ASHHK **Swift**: SAIB HK HH **Reuters**: ASBH
Website: www.asahibank.co.jp

Senior Executive Officers
General Manager   Koichiro Mafune
Senior Deputy General Manager   Hiroyuki Miyashita

Equity Capital Markets
Equity Repo / Securities Lending
Marketing   Masayuki Shimizu *Manager, Loans & Securities*
                                 Hiroshi Saruyama *Manager, Loans & Securities*
                                 Theresa Chang *Assistant Manager, Loans & Securities*
                                 Amanda Leung *Assistant Manager, Loans & Securities*

Money Markets
Other (Wholesale Deposits)
Bills & Deposits   Stephen Lo *Manager*
Bills   Alice Chiu *Assistant Manager*
Deposit   Martin Sum *Assistant Manager*

Foreign Exchange
Global Head   Yoichi Okutani *Chief Dealer & Manager, FX & Treasury*
Regional Head   Shinichi Takizawa *Dealer & Manager, FX & Treasury*
                                 William Lee *Senior Dealer, FX & Treasury*

Settlement / Clearing
Settlement (General)   Hiroshi Saruyama *Manager*
                                 Ally Wong *Assistant Manager*

HONG KONG, CHINA (+852)   www.euromoneydirectory.com

Asahi Finance (Hong Kong) Limited   Subsidiary Company

Formerly known as: Kyowa Saitama Finance (Hong Kong) Limited
Level 32, One Pacific Place, 88 Queensway, Hong Kong
Tel: 2532 0660 **Fax:** 2918 0022 **Telex:** 74215 ASFHK **Email:** lisimon@bloomberg.net

Senior Executive Officers
Chairman   Yukio Yanase
Managing Director   Toru Kanamori

Debt Capital Markets / Fixed Income
Global Head   Masataka Tamaki *Executive Director*

Equity Capital Markets
Global Head   Kaoru Yunoki *Associate Director*

Syndicated Lending
Head of Syndication   Simon Li *Associate Director*

Risk Management
Global Head   Aaron Keung *Manager*

Corporate Finance / M&A Advisory
Global Head   Kaoru Yunoki *Associate Director*

Settlement / Clearing
Head of Settlement / Clearing   Iris Ho *Assistant Manager*

Administration
Head of Administration   Helen Ho *Assistant Manager*

Accounts / Audit
    Aaron Keung *Manager*

Asia Commercial Bank Limited   Head Office

Formerly known as: The Commercial Bank of Hong Kong Limited
Asia Financial Centre, 120 Des Voeux Road, Central, Hong Kong
Tel: 2541 9222 **Fax:** 2541 0009 **Telex:** 73085 HKACB **Swift:** CBHK HK HH
Website: www.afh.com.hk

Senior Executive Officers
Chairman, CEO & Chairman, Board, Executive Directo   Robin Y H Chan
Executive Director & General Manager   Richard W Chan
Executive Director & General Manager   Stephen Tan
Deputy General Manager   Wai Yin Siu
Executive Director & Senior DGM   Hinh-Ching Lam
Chief Credit Officer & DGM   Karen S Y Ko
Deputy General Manager   Pamela K F Ng

General-Lending (DCM, SL)
Head of Corporate Banking   Karen S Y Ko *Chief Credit Officer & DGM*
Calvin Y K Lam *AGM, Finance Division*
Desmond Y T Wu *AGM, Credit*

General - Treasury
Head of Treasury   Alfred K Y Lam *Chief Dealer, Treasury*

Relationship Manager
Financial Institutions   Pamela K F Ng *Deputy General Manager*

Money Markets
Money Markets - General
Bills   Chi Ming Kong *Senior Manager*

Settlement / Clearing
Operations   Sek Hong Yeung *Manager, Central Operations*
Peter K W Ng *Manager, Financial Control*
Peter S P Yeung *AGM, Operations*
Rolanda L K Lam *Manager, Shares Operations*
Disana L F Kwok *Assistant Manager, Loans Operations*

Other Departments
Private Banking   Pamela K F Ng *Deputy General Manager*

Administration
Head of Administration   Karen S Y Ko *Chief Credit Officer & DGM*

Technology & Systems
Information Technology   William C H Chan *Assistant General Manager*

www.euromoneydirectory.com   HONG KONG, CHINA (+852)

Accounts / Audit
Internal Audit   Kai Biu Chan *Chief Auditor*
Other (Administration)
Organization & Methods   Collin Y C Ma *Manager*
Personnel   Raymond K H Chui *Assistant General Manager*
General Affairs   Wong Mo Ho *Deputy Manager*

Australia & New Zealand Banking Group Limited Full Branch Office

27th Floor, One Exchange Square, 8 Connaught Place, Central, Hong Kong
Tel: 2843 7111 **Fax:** 2868 0089; 2525 2475 **Telex:** 86019 ANZBK HX **Swift:** ANZB HK HX **Reuters:** ANZH-I (Monitor)
Telerate: 9845/6
Reuters: ANZK (Dealing)

Senior Executive Officers
General Manager   David Morgan
Others (Senior Executives)
                                  Michael Tracey *Deputy General Manager*

General-Lending (DCM, SL)
Head of Corporate Banking   Ian Matheson *Manager, Credit*
                                  Adolphus Wan *Deputy General Manager*

General-Investment
Head of Investment   Richard Martin *Head of ANZ Investment Bank, North Asia*

General - Treasury
Head of Treasury   David Williams *Head of Treasury* ☏ **2843 7114**

Syndicated Lending
Loan-Related Activities
Trade Finance   Julia Kong *Senior Manager, Trade Finance*

Foreign Exchange
Global Head   David Williams *Head of Treasury* ☏ **2843 7114**

Settlement / Clearing
Operations   Teresa Wong *Chief Manager, Operations*

Administration
Head of Administration   Grace Chow *Manager Administration & Finance*

BA Asia Limited   Subsidiary Company

14th Floor, Bank of America Tower, 12 Harcourt Road, Hong Kong
Tel: 2847 6666 **Fax:** 2810 0821 **Telex:** 75679 HX

Senior Executive Officers
Group Executive Vice President   Robert Morrow III ☏ **2847 6083**
Chief Executive Officer   Ambi Venkateswaran *Senior Vice President* ☏ **2847 6090**
Financial Director   William Yiu *Senior Vice President* ☏ **2597 3773**
Chief Operating Officer   Edward Tse *Vice President* ☏ **2587 2268**
Treasurer   John Ellis *Senior Vice President* ☏ **2847 6710**
Others (Senior Executives)
Compliance Director   Timothy Hogan *Vice President* ☏ **2847 6475**

Debt Capital Markets / Fixed Income
Eurobonds
Head of Research   Andrew Freris *Vice President* ☏ **2847 6136**
Syndicated Lending
Head of Syndication   Peter Chan *Senior Vice President* ☏ **2847 6699**
Loan-Related Activities
Project Finance   Frank Packard *Vice President* ☏ **2847 6716**

Banca Nazionale del Lavoro SpA   Full Branch Office

Suite 4605-08, Two Exchange Square, 8 Connaught Place, Central, Hong Kong
Tel: 2101 0700 **Fax:** 2810 5243 **Telex:** 76403 BNLHK HX

Senior Executive Officers
Chief Manager   Claudio Franchi
Deputy Chief Manager   Yip Vincent

HONG KONG, CHINA (+852) www.euromoneydirectory.com

Banca di Roma SpA — Full Branch Office

16th Floor, The Hong Kong Club Building, 3A Chater Road, Central, Hong Kong
Tel: 2521 2221 **Fax:** 2868 0034 **Telex:** 60582 ROMHK HX **Swift:** BROM HK HH **Email:** bdrhk@hkstar.com
Reuters: BDRH
FX **Tel:** 2525 2252/4; Settlement **Tel:** 2533 0506/9

Senior Executive Officers
Chief Manager   Giovanni Orgrera

Others (Senior Executives)
Head of Business Division   Michele Cherenti *Deputy Chief Manager*
Head of Operations Division   Lisa Y Y Cheng *Assistant Chief Manager*

Banca San Paolo di Brescia — Representative Office

1119 Jardine House, 1 Connaught Place, Central, Hong Kong
Tel: 2523 5445 **Fax:** 2810 5228 **Telex:** 72414 BAV RP HX

Senior Executive Officers
Regional Representative   Augusto Scaglione

Banco di Napoli SpA — Full Branch Office

13th Floor, Two Exchange Square, 8 Connaught Place, Hong Kong
Tel: 2847 9800 **Fax:** 2845 2576 **Telex:** 66676 BANAP HX **Swift:** NAPB HK HH **Reuters:** NAPH

Senior Executive Officers
SVP & Regional GM, Asia Pacific   Antonio De Santis ☎ 2847 9812 📠 2845 0663

Bangkok Bank Public Company Limited — Full Branch Office

Bangkok Bank Building, 28 Des Voeux Road Central, Hong Kong
PO Box 4175, Hong Kong
Tel: 2801 6688 **Fax:** 2810 5679 **Telex:** 73679 BBANK HX (General) **Swift:** BKKB HK HH **Reuters:** BBLH
Treasury **Telex:** 64520BLFX HX

Senior Executive Officers
General Manager   Amnuey Lilaonitkul

Others (Senior Executives)
Overseas Treasury Centre   Goh Puay-Kiak *Senior Vice President & Manager*
                                           Patrick Wong S L *VP & Manager, Financial Institutions, OTC*

General - Treasury
Head of Treasury   Lau Pak-Ming *VP & Manager, Treasury*

Foreign Exchange
Department: Foreign Exchange & Money Market
Tel: 2801 6684
Head of Foreign Exchange   Alex Lau Pak-Ming *Vice President & Manager*

FX Traders / Sales People
HK$ Deposit, Swaps, Other Currencies   Serena Chan Siu-Fun *Assistant Manager*
ECP, CDs   Angela Chan Tsang-Fung *Assistant Manager*
Dealer   Tsui Lam *Dealer*
US$ Deposit   Louis Tam Wai-Kei *Dealer*
Baht / Asian Currencies   Clement Yeung Sin-Tsang *Senior Dealer*
                                           Eric Chan Wing-Leong *Dealer*
Yen   Matthew Chan Kai-Man *Dealer*
TT & Corporate   Pamela Goh York-Yun *Assistant Manager*
                                           Doris Ho Wai-I *Dealer*
                                           Daniel Lo Mun-Keung *Dealer*
Technical Analysis   Pamela Goh York-Yun *Assistant Manager*
                                           Elaine Chui Yin-Ling *Operations Officer*

Settlement / Clearing
Foreign Exchange Settlement   Lee Man-Tong *Deputy Manager, Back-Office Settlements*
Operations   Pramote Rojtanongchai *Vice President & Manager*

Administration
Head of Marketing   Lim Hau-Ting *Vice President & Manager*

www.euromoneydirectory.com   HONG KONG, CHINA (+852)

Bank of America NT & SA
Full Branch Office
1st Floor, Bank of America Tower, 12 Harcourt Road, Hong Kong
GPO Box 472, Hong Kong
Tel: 2847 6777 **Fax:** 2847 5232 **Telex:** 802 73373 **Swift:** BOFA HK HX **Reuters:** BAHK **Cable:** BNKAMERICA

Senior Executive Officers
Chief Operating Officer — John Leung Senior Vice President, Country Operations Officer ☏ 2597 2231
Treasurer — Anthony Yeun Country Treasurer ☏ 2847 6381

Others (Senior Executives)
Wholesale Division Manager — Terence Cuddyre Managing Director ☏ 2847 5868

Money Markets
Fax: 2868 5235
Head of Money Markets — Tony Ma VP & Head Money Trader ☏ 2847 6270

Foreign Exchange
Head of Foreign Exchange — Vincent Ho VP & Country Treasurer ☏ 2847 6302
Head of Institutional Sales — Geraldine Goh Vice President & Head of FX Sales ☏ 2847 6381
Corporate Sales — Emily Lao VP & Head Corp Advisor ☏ 2847 6393
Head of Trading — Philip Miao VP & FX Manager ☏ 2847 6390

Bank Austria Creditanstalt International AG
Full Branch Office
Formerly known as: Creditanstalt AG
41st Floor, Two Exchange Square, 8 Connaught Place, Central, Hong Kong
Tel: 2868 3111 **Fax:** 2868 5115

Senior Executive Officers
Regional Director, Asia — Brian Hobson
Chief Executive Officer — Manfred Puffer General Manager & Chief Executive Officer
General Manager & Deputy CEO — Paul Serfaty

Others (Senior Executives)
Commercial Banking — Francis Lui Deputy General Manager

General - Treasury
Head of Treasury — Andy Ng DGM, Treasury

Debt Capital Markets / Fixed Income
Head of Fixed Income — Peter Li Assistant General Manager, Institutional Banking

Libor-Based / Floating-Rate Products
FRN Sales; FRN Trading — Peter Li Assistant General Manager, Institutional Banking

Equity Capital Markets
Convertibles / Equity-Linked
Head of Sales — Michael Cheng Senior Manager

Syndicated Lending
Head of Syndication — Francis Lui Deputy General Manager

Loan-Related Activities
Structured Trade Finance — Winnie Li Senior Manager

Money Markets
Tel: 2526 7552 **Fax:** 2868 3287 **Reuters:** BAUH **Telex:** 69860
Head of Money Markets — Marco Foehn DGM, Treasury ☏ 2868 2929

Foreign Exchange
Tel: 2526 7552 **Fax:** 2971 0629 **Reuters:** BAUH **Telex:** 69860
Head of Foreign Exchange — Martin Ng Senior Manager, Treasury

Risk Management
Tel: 2868 3111 **Fax:** 2868 5115
Head of Risk Management — Michael Wolf Assistant General Manager, RMA

The Bank of Bermuda Limited
Full Branch Office
39th Floor, Edinburgh Tower, The Landmark, 15 Queen's Road, Central, Hong Kong
Tel: 2847 1100 **Fax:** 2523 1759 **Telex:** 81504 BDAFX HX **Reuters:** BBHK (Dealing)
Forex Tel: 2847 1135

Senior Executive Officers
SEVP, Asia Pacific — John A Hawkins ✉ hawkinja@bankofbermuda.com

General-Lending (DCM, SL)
Head of Corporate Banking — Glenn Trotman Director, Investment Services
✉ trotmag@bankofbermuda.com

Euromoney Directory 1999   **585**

HONG KONG, CHINA (+852)   www.euromoneydirectory.com

The Bank of Bermuda Limited (cont)

General - Treasury
Head of Treasury Anthony Gates *Director, Operations* E **gatesar@bankofbermuda.com**
                  Tim Lucas *Treasurer, Asia Pacific* E **lucastd@bankofbermuda.com**

Relationship Manager
Marketing & Client Servicing Shirley Lam *Director, Marketing & Client Servicing*
                               E **lamew@bankofbermuda.com**
Financial Institutions Rosemarie Kriesel *Director, Project Management*
                        E **krieserd@bankofbermuda.com**

Money Markets
Money Markets - General
Money Market Sherman Lung *Senior Dealer* E **lunght@bankofbermuda.com**

Foreign Exchange
Department: Foreign Exchange and Bullion
FX Traders / Sales People
Treasury Tim Lucas *Treasurer, Asia Pacific* E **lucastd@bankofbermuda.com**
FX Roger Chan *Senior Dealer* E **chanyz@bankofbermuda.com**
    Jude Ho *Senior Dealer* E **howe@bankofbermuda.com**
Money Market Sherman Lung *Senior Dealer* E **lunght@bankofbermuda.com**

Settlement / Clearing
Settlement (General) Sheron Yip *Senior Officer, Banking & Treasury Services*
                      E **yippz@bankofbermuda.com**
Operations Anthony Gates *Director, Operations* E **gatesar@bankofbermuda.com**
            Patrick Pun *Head, Operations, Banking & Treasury Services*
            E **puntw@bankofbermuda.com**

Bank Brussels Lambert SA — Full Branch Office

16th Floor, Entertainment Building, 30 Queen's Road, Central, Hong Kong
Tel: 2973 1300 **Fax:** 2845 9262 **Telex:** 86260 BBL HK **Swift:** BBRU HK HX **Email:** bblhkgm@netvigator.com
Reuters: BBLR
Website: www.bbl.be

Senior Executive Officers
General Manager Bruno Houdmount
Treasurer Tobi Yuen *Senior Manager*

Others (Senior Executives)
  Jan Van Wellen *Head of Credit Administration*
  Laurent Muguet *Head of HK / International Marketing*
  Benedicte Cocquyt *Head of China / Taiwan Marketing*
  K S Lee *Head of Operations & Administration*

Debt Capital Markets / Fixed Income
Head of Fixed Income Trading Toby Yuen *Senior Manager*

Fixed-Income Repo
Head of Repo Charles Terlinden *Head of Repo*

The Bank of NT Butterfield & Son Limited — Full Branch Office

26th Floor, Bank of China Tower, 1 Garden Road, Central, Hong Kong
Tel: 2868 1010 **Fax:** 2845 0336 **Telex:** 70793 BNTB HX **Reuters:** BNTB
Website: www.bankofbutterfield.com

Senior Executive Officers
Chief Executive Officer Alastair Murray *General Manager*
Treasurer Gary Lam *Senior Manager, Treasury*

Others (Senior Executives)
Compliance John Ham *Senior Manager*

General - Treasury
Head of Treasury Gary Lam *Senior Manager, Treasury*

Debt Capital Markets / Fixed Income
Eurobonds
Head of Trading Gary Lam *Senior Manager, Treasury*

Money Markets
Head of Money Markets William Cheung *Senior Dealer*

www.euromoneydirectory.com   HONG KONG, CHINA (+852)

Foreign Exchange
Head of Foreign Exchange   Dennis Shek *Manager, Treasury*
Head of Trading   Chris Tam *Senior Dealer*

Settlement / Clearing
Head of Settlement / Clearing   Annie Lee *Manager, Operations*

Administration

Technology & Systems
Information Technology   Agnes Chan *Manager*

Accounts / Audit
    Stanely Wong *Manager, Financial Control*

Bank of China   Full Branch Office

1 Garden Road, Central, Hong Kong
Tel: 2826 6888 **Fax:** 2810 5963 **Telex:** 73772 BKCHI HX **Cable:** CHUNGKUO HONG KO

Senior Executive Officers
General Manager   Mr Liujinbao
Deputy General Manager   Siao Ping Lian

General - Treasury
Head of Treasury   C W Yip *Senior Manager*
    Mao Cheng Liu *Deputy General Manager*

Settlement / Clearing
Head of Settlement / Clearing   N L Tang *General Manager*
    N A Or *Deputy General Manager*

PT Bank Dagang Negara (PERSERO)   Representative Office

6th Floor, Admiralty Centre, Tower II, Queensway, Hong Kong
Tel: 2529 4750 **Fax:** 2865 6372 **Telex:** 60322 BDN HX

Senior Executive Officers
Chief Representative   Sudirman Suwin

The Bank of East Asia Limited

10 Des Voeux Road, Central, Hong Kong
Tel: 2842 3244 **Fax:** 2845 8204; 2521 8204 **Telex:** HX 73017 **Swift:** BEAS HK HH **Reuters:** BEAH **Cable:** BEAKEASIA
Reuters: BEAK (Monitor)

Senior Executive Officers
Chairman   Li Fook-wo
Chief Executive Officer   Joseph Pang Yuk-wing
Managing Director / General Manager   Chan Kay-cheung

Global Custody
Tel: 2842 3244 **Fax:** 2521 8204
Regional Head   Siu Wing Law

Other (Global Custody)
    Shun Wo Leung

The Bank of Korea   Representative Office

Room 1208/9, Alexandra House, 20 Chater Road, Hong Kong
Tel: 2526 6508 **Fax:** 2868 5276 **Telex:** 71835 BOK HX

Senior Executive Officers
Chief Representative   B H Kang
Representative   Y S Lee
Representative   D H Kim
Representative   C M Jung

HONG KONG, CHINA (+852)   www.euromoneydirectory.com

Bank Melli Iran
Full Branch Office

4108 Gloucester Tower, The Landmark, 11 Pedder Street, Hong Kong
Tel: 2521 1127 Fax: 2868 4692 Telex: 75701 BANML HX Swift: BIC: MELI HK HH

Senior Executive Officers
Chief Executive Officer   Hossein Gholi Mobahat

Bank of New York - Inter Maritime Bank, Geneva
Representative Office

Room 1701, One Exchange Square, Central, Hong Kong
Tel: 2840 0878 Fax: 2840 0678 Telex: 68885 SPBAP

Senior Executive Officers
Chief Representative   Winston Yuen

Debt Capital Markets / Fixed Income
Fixed-Income Repo
Trading
Dickson Cheng *Trader*
Nobuyuki Honda *Trader*
Winnie Kwok *Head Trader*

The Bank of Nova Scotia
Full Branch Office

25th Floor, United Centre, 95 Queensway, Hong Kong
Tel: 2529 5511 Fax: 2527 2527 Telex: HX74224 (General), HX66601 Swift: NOSC HK HH Reuters: BNSH (Monitor)
Telerate: 2737
Dealing Tel: 2527 5023

Senior Executive Officers
VP, Hong Kong & China   P N Rooney
Assistant General Manager, China   C M Kwok

General-Lending (DCM, SL)
Head of Corporate Banking
Raymond Choo *Senior Manager & Unit Head*
Kitty Iu *Senior Manager & Unit Head*

General - Treasury
Head of Treasury   Karl Mak *Chief Dealer* ☎ 2527 5023

Syndicated Lending
Global Head   Matt Harris *VP, Structured Finance & Syndications*

Money Markets
Department: Capital Markets
Other (Wholesale Deposits)
Eurocurrency Deposits - Trading   Perry Cheng *Senior Money Dealer, Treasury* ☎ 2527 5023

Foreign Exchange
Global Head   Karl Mak *Chief Dealer* ☎ 2527 5023

Administration
Head of Administration   Daniel Chao *Senior Manager, Administration*

Bank of Scotland
Full Branch Office

11th Floor, Jardine House, 1 Connaught Place, Central, Hong Kong
Tel: 2521 2155; 2521 2159 Fax: 2845 9007 Telex: 73435 HK BOS Reuters: BOSH

Senior Executive Officers
Director, Hong Kong Branch   Ian A McKinney

Others (Senior Executives)
Loan Syndication   Brian R Allan *Associate Director*

Bank of Taiwan

4th Floor, 9 Queen's Road, Central, Hong Kong
Tel: 2521 0567 Fax: 2869 4957

Senior Executive Officers
General Manager   Kai Cheng Ho

www.euromoneydirectory.com　　HONG KONG, CHINA (+852)

The Bank of Yokohama Limited
Representative Office
Suites 2113-15, Jardine House, 1 Connaught Place, Central, Hong Kong
Tel: 2523 6041; 2523 6045 Fax: 2845 9022

Senior Executive Officers
Chief Representative　　Makoto Tamai

Bankboston NA
Full Branch Office
Formerly known as: The First National Bank of Boston
801-809 Jardine House, Central, Hong Kong
Tel: 2526 4361 Fax: 2845 9222 Telex: 75345 Swift: FNBB HK HX Reuters: FNBK

Senior Executive Officers
Managing Director, Greater China　　Frank K Y Moy

Syndicated Lending
Head of Syndicated Lending　　Loren J Romano *MD Syndications, Asia Region*
Head of Origination　　Zhiming Xu *Director & Head*

Other (Trade Finance)
Global Head of Trade　　Marina Luk *Vice President*

Money Markets
Head of Money Markets　　Randal Tiu *VP, Head of Treasury & Marketing*

Foreign Exchange
Head of Foreign Exchange　　Randal Tiu *VP, Head of Treasury & Marketing*

Bankers Trust Company
Full Branch Office
36th Floor, Two Pacific Place, 88 Queensway Central, Hong Kong
Tel: 2533 8000 Fax: 2845 1868; 2845 1882 Telex: HX73410 Email: www.bankerstrust.com
Website: btco.com/internet/index.htm

Senior Executive Officers
Managing Director, GM & Chief Executive　　Timothy S Rattray
Managing Director, GM & Chief Executive　　Edward Lo

Others (Senior Executives)
Head of Investment Banking　　Ki-Myung Hong *MD, Head of Regional Investment Banking*

Debt Capital Markets / Fixed Income
Bonds - General
Sales　　Howard Tong *Principal*
　　Crane Chen *Vice President*
Capital Markets　　Ki-Myung Hong *Managing Director*
　　Colin Geddes *Managing Director*
　　Andrew Millard *Managing Director*
　　Dean Knight *Principal*

Fixed-Income Repo
Marketing & Product Development; Sales　　Ramon Au Yeung *Marketing & Product Development* ☎ **2533 8472**
　　🖷 **2918 1877**

Equity Capital Markets
Equity Repo / Securities Lending
Head of Trading　　Maggie Fan *Vice President*
　　Vivienne Malneek *Assistant Treasurer*

Syndicated Lending
Other (Syndicated Lending)
Securities Lending　　Eleni Wang *Managing Director*

Other (Trade Finance)
Letters of Credit　　Raymond Lau *Vice President*

Money Markets
　　Kent Lai *VP, Money Market & Securities*

Corporate Finance / M&A Advisory
Department: Corporate Finance
Other (Corporate Finance)
　　Ambrose Lam *MD, Hong Kong / PRC Corporate Finance*

Settlement / Clearing
Operations　　Michael McFadden *MD, Regional Controllers*
　　Fatima Cheung *Principal*

Euromoney Directory 1999　**589**

HONG KONG, CHINA (+852)   www.euromoneydirectory.com

Bankers Trust Company (cont)

Global Custody
Regional Head   Eleni Wang *Managing Director*

Other Departments
Private Banking   Kenneth Toong *Managing Director*
Correspondent Banking   John Ball *Managing Director*
Global Trust   Gary Lew *MD, Corporate Trust & Agency Group*
Economic Research   Carson Cole *Principal*

Administration

Legal / In-House Counsel
    Kevin Wilkey *Managing Director*

Compliance
Regional Compliance   Daphne Doo *Managing Director*

Other (Administration)
Asia Human Resources   Michelle Li *Principal* ☎ **2533 8918** 🖷 **2522 7169**

Banque Générale du Luxembourg — Representative Office

Suite 2310, Jardine House, 1 Connaught Place, Central, Hong Kong
Tel: 2810 7266 **Fax:** 2845 0201 **Telex:** 82333 BGLHR HX

Senior Executive Officers
Chief Representative   Frank Veyder
Senior Manager   Knut Reinertz
Assistant Representative   Eleanor Woo

Banque Nationale de Paris — Full Branch Office

4-13 Floors, Central Tower, 28 Queen's Road, Central, Hong Kong
Tel: 2909 8888

Senior Executive Officers
Chief Executive Officer   Didier Balme *Chief Executive* ☎ **2909 8800**
Chief Operating Officer   Didier Martinez ☎ **2909 8803**
Treasurer   Bruno Boussard *Head, Treasury Division* ☎ **2909 8824**

Debt Capital Markets / Fixed Income
Head of Debt Capital Markets   Ian Adams *Head, Debt* ☎ **2909 8778**

Equity Capital Markets
Head of Equity Capital Markets   Jann Muzike *Head of Equities* ☎ **2909 8809**

Syndicated Lending
Head of Syndicated Lending   Ian Adams *Head, Debt* ☎ **2909 8778**

Money Markets
Head of Money Markets   Tony Fung *Head, Dealing Room* ☎ **2909 8832**

Foreign Exchange
Head of Foreign Exchange   Tony Fung *Head, Dealing Room* ☎ **2909 8832**

Risk Management
Head of Risk Management   Michel Limouzineau *Head of Risk* ☎ **2909 8606**

Corporate Finance / M&A Advisory
Head of Corporate Finance   Muriel Petit *Head, Corporate Finance* ☎ **2909 8779**

Settlement / Clearing
Head of Settlement / Clearing   Richard Gils *Head, Back Office* ☎ **2909 8138**

Banque Sudameris — Representative Office

Rooms 3302-3310 A, Edinburgh Tower, The Landmark, 15 Queen's Road, Central, Hong Kong
Tel: 2532 2700 **Fax:** 2845 0209 **Email:** bcihksys@hkstar.com

Senior Executive Officers
Representative   Clemente Benelli

www.euromoneydirectory.com   HONG KONG, CHINA (+852)

Banque Worms
Full Branch Office

3901 Central Plaza, 18 Harbour Road, Hong Kong
Tel: 2802 8382 **Fax:** 2802 8065 **Telex:** 60139 (General) **Swift:** BWOR HK KK **Email:** bwhk@vol.net **Reuters:** BWHK
Dealers Telex: 75295; Reuters: BWHL

Senior Executive Officers
Chief Executive Officer — Jean-Francois Ferrachat *GM & Branch Manager*
Treasurer — Michael Chan *Treasurer*
General-Lending (DCM, SL)
Head of Corporate Banking — Iris Ngo *Head, Corporate Banking*
Relationship Manager
 — Louis Yip *Relationship Manager*
Foreign Exchange
FX Traders / Sales People
 — Kenneth Cheung *Senior Dealer*
 — Michael Chan *Treasurer*
Risk Management
Other Currency Swap / FX Options Personnel
Currency Swaps — Ernst Fu *Dealer* ☏ 2827 1252
Settlement / Clearing
Foreign Exchange Settlement — Raymond Choi *Back-Office Settlements, Head of Operations*
Asset Management
Head — Bertrand Levavasseur *Sales & Marketing Manager* ☏ 2802 8373
Other Departments
Private Banking — Louis Yip *Relationship Manager*

Barclays Capital Asia Limited
Head Office

Formerly known as: Barclays de Zoete Wedd (Asia) Limited
42nd Floor, Citibank Tower, Citibank Plaza, 3 Garden Road, Hong Kong
PO Box 9716, General Post Office, Hong Kong
Tel: 2903 2000; 2903 2999 **Fax:** 2903 2839 **Telex:** 74077 BACLY HX
Website: www.barcapint.com

Senior Executive Officers
Chairman & CEO, Asia Pacific — Roger Davis ☏ 2903 2289
Debt Capital Markets / Fixed Income
Country Head — Stephen Diao *Head of Asian Debt Capital Markets*
Head of Fixed Income — Jackie Macaeode
Administration
Head of Administration — Jeff Deck *Chief Administrative Officer, Asia Pacific* ☏ +81 (3) 3276 1203
  ✉ +81 (3) 3276 1205
Corporate Communications
 — Nancy Lau ☏ 2903 2293 ✉ 2903 2599

Baring Brothers Limited
Subsidiary Company

8th Floor, Three Exchange Square, 8 Connaught Place, Central, Hong Kong
Tel: 2848 9600 **Fax:** 2868 5343; 2868 5397

Senior Executive Officers
Regional Head, Asia — David Hudson
Corporate Finance / M&A Advisory
Global Head — David Hudson *Regional Head, Asia*

Bayerische Landesbank
Full Branch Office

19th Floor, Standard Chartered Bank Building, 4A Des Voeux Road, Central, Hong Kong
Tel: 2978 8333 **Fax:** 2877 3817 **Telex:** 72501 BLB HK **Swift:** BYLA HK HH **Reuters:** BLHK

Senior Executive Officers
Others (Senior Executives)
Chief Executive Asia Pacific — Volker Stoeckel *Senior Executive Vice President, CEO Asia Pacific*
 — Paul C M Au *Executive Vice President & General Manager*

Euromoney Directory 1999   **591**

HONG KONG, CHINA (+852)　　　www.euromoneydirectory.com

Bayerische Landesbank (cont)
Debt Capital Markets / Fixed Income
Department: Debt Capital Markets - Corporate Banking
Bonds - General
SVP, Deputy General Manager　　　Oliver Molitor *Head of Corporate Banking*
Libor-Based / Floating-Rate Products
FRN Origination　　　Oliver Molitor *Head of Corporate Banking*
Syndicated Lending
Other (Syndicated Lending)
SVP, Deputy General Manager　　　Oliver Molitor *Head of Corporate Banking*
Money Markets
Money Markets - General
Vice President　　　Wallace Lam *Chief Dealer*
Wholesale Deposits
Marketing　　　Leo Leung *Treasurer*
Foreign Exchange
Department: Treasury
FX Traders / Sales People
SVP, Deputy General General　　　Leo Leung *Treasurer*
Risk Management
Other (FI Derivatives)
First Vice President　　　Edward Jessop *Financial Controller*
Corporate Finance / M&A Advisory
Global Head　　　Oliver Molitor *Head of Corporate Banking*
Settlement / Clearing
Regional Head　　　Iris Ng *Manager, Settlements*

BCA Finance Limited　　　Subsidiary Company

Formerly known as: Central Asia Capital Corporation Ltd
Room 2402 Worldwide House, 19 Des Voeux Road Central, Hong Kong
Tel: 2847 4388 Fax: 2810 6706 Telex: 83312 BCAHK.HX Swift: CENA HK HX Cable: CENTRACAP

Senior Executive Officers
Chief Executive Officer　　　Allen Tang *General Manager*
Financial Director　　　Andy Kwok *Financial Controller*
International Division　　　Katherine Tang *Senior Manager*
Money Markets
Head of Money Markets　　　Andy Kwok *Financial Controller*
Foreign Exchange
Head of Foreign Exchange　　　Andy Kwok *Financial Controller*
Risk Management
Head of Risk Management　　　Katherine Tang *Senior Manager*
Other Departments
Chief Credit Officer　　　Nancy Ho *Manager*
Administration
Head of Administration　　　Ching Chu *Assistant General Manager*
Accounts / Audit
　　　Stephen Wong *Accountant*
Other (Administration)
Marketing　　　Ringo Chan *Manager*

Bear Stearns Asia Limited　　　Subsidiary Company

26th Floor, Citibank Tower, Citibank Plaza, 3 Garden Road, Hong Kong
Tel: 2593 2700 Fax: 2593 2870
Website: www.bearstearn.com

Senior Executive Officers
Senior Managing Director　　　Donald Tang
Equity Capital Markets
Domestic Equities
Head of Trading　　　Craig Reilly
Head of Research　　　Daniel Widdicombe

www.euromoneydirectory.com   HONG KONG, CHINA (+852)

Equity Repo / Securities Lending
Head   John Lee Tin Jr *Vice President* ☎ **2593 2581** F **2593 2870**
Head of Trading   Florence Cheung *Securities lending sales representative*
                                  Florence Cheung *Securities lending sales representative*

Berliner Bank AG   Representative Office

26th Floor, Asia Pacific Centre, 8 Wyndham Street, Central, Hong Kong
Tel: 2523 9991 **Fax:** 2877 3739

Senior Executive Officers
Representative   Steffen Gunther

BGL Finance (Asia) Limited   Subsidiary Company

Suite 2310, Jardine House, 1 Connaught Place, Central, Hong Kong
Tel: 2810 7266 **Fax:** 2845 0201 **Telex:** 82333 BGLHR HX **Email:** bglhk@netvigator.com
Bloomberg: bang@bloomberg.net

Senior Executive Officers
Managing Director   Frank Veyder
Executive Director   Eleanor Woo ☎ **2525 0657**

Others (Senior Executives)
                                  Dickson Kwok *Senior Manager* ☎ **2525 3739**

General-Investment
Head of Investment   Knut Reinertz *Senior Investment Advisor* ☎ **2521 4046**
                                  Portia Wu *Senior Investment Advisor* ☎ **2810 7891**
                                  Raymond Tong *Senior Investment Advisor* ☎ **2147 3926**

Debt Capital Markets / Fixed Income
Country Head   Eleanor Woo *Executive Director* ☎ **2525 0657**

Syndicated Lending
Head of Syndication   Frank Veyder *Managing Director*

BHF-BANK AG   Full Branch Office

55th Floor, Central Plaza, 18 Harbour Road, Hong Kong
Tel: 2820 1428 **Fax:** 2802 9680

Senior Executive Officers
Chief Executive Officer   Patrick Chiu *CEO & General Manager*

Risk Management
Department: Credit Risk Management
Country Head   Bernie Poon

Settlement / Clearing
Operations   T H Lee

BII Finance Company Limited   Subsidiary Company

Suite 2208, St George's Building, 2 Ice House Street, Hong Kong
Tel: 2810 0318 **Fax:** 2810 6523 **Telex:** 75869 BII HX

Senior Executive Officers
Chairman   Kokaryadi Chandra
Chief Executive Officer   C K K Jung *Chief Executive & Managing Director*

General-Lending (DCM, SL)
Head of Corporate Banking   Juanna Lai *Senior Manager, Corporate & Commercial Banking*

General - Treasury
Head of Treasury   Vivian Lai *Assistant Manager*

Syndicated Lending

Other (Trade Finance)
Letters of Credit   Ketty Kwok *Assistant Manager*
Documentary Credits   Regina Lee *Assistant Manager*

Foreign Exchange
FX Traders / Sales People
                                  Anna Lo *Dealer*

HONG KONG, CHINA (+852)   www.euromoneydirectory.com

BII Finance Company Limited (cont)
Administration
Head of Administration   Cartys Wan *Manager Administration & Finance*

Other (Administration)
Human Resources   Cartys Wan *Manager Administration & Finance*

BNP Hong Kong   Full Branch Office

4-14th Floors, Central Tower, 28 Queen's Road, Central, Hong Kong
Tel: 2909 8888 **Fax:** 2865 2523 **Telex:** 73442HX **Swift:** BNPA HK HH
General Telex: 73786HX

Senior Executive Officers
Chief Executive Officer   Didier Balme *Chief Executive* T 2909 8802 F 2869 4960
Financial Director   Philippe Chan *Chief Financial Officer* T 2909 8805 F 2869 4960
Chief Operating Officer   Philippe Rioche *COO, Personnel & Banking Operations* T 2909 8805 F 2869 4960
Mignnonne Cheng *COO, Corporate & Commercial Banking* T 2909 8818 F 2530 2707

Others (Senior Executives)
Corporate & Commercial Banking Group   Jean Paul Ching *Head of Commercial Division* T 2909 8603 F 2845 1612
Dominique N Romain *Head of Corporate Division* T 2909 8701 F 2868 9421
Betty Chan *Head of Asset Restructuring Division* T 2909 8761 F 2524 5250

General - Treasury
Head of Treasury   Bruno Boussard *Head of Treasury Division* T 2909 8826 F 2868 3376

Debt Capital Markets / Fixed Income
Department: Debt Markets
Country Head   Patrick Thomas *Managing Director, Debt Markets* T 2909 8806 F 2525 7353
Ian Adams *Deputy Managing Director, Debt Markets* T 2909 8783 F 2525 7353

Syndicated Lending
Loan-Related Activities
Shipping Finance   Arnold K H Wu *Head of Asia Shipping Desk* T 2532 9300
Project Finance   Lina Zhang *Project Finance Manager* T 2909 8741 F 2525 7353

Corporate Finance / M&A Advisory
Country Head   Muriel Petit *Executive Director, Greater China Advisory Group* T 2909 8795 F 2525 7353

Other Departments
Private Banking   Bruno Mantorano *Head of Private Banking, Asia Hong Kong* T 2909 8232 F 2970 0283
Global Trust   Aurora Wong *Head of Trust Services* T 2909 8263 F 2530 1925

Administration
Other (Administration)
Financial Institutions   Barry Chung *Head of Financial Institutions & Commodities Desk* T 2909 8401 F 2868 9421

Boram Bank   Full Branch Office

Suite 3808, Jardine House, 1 Connaught Place, Central, Hong Kong
Tel: 2869 6715 **Fax:** 2869 6380 **Telex:** 87960 BRBHK HX **Swift:** BORB HK HH

Senior Executive Officers
General Manager   Ouan-Chul Chung

Syndicated Lending
Head of Syndication   Hyung-Joon Park *Deputy General Manager*

Money Markets
Head of Money Markets   Hyong-Jong Yio *Deputy General Manager*

BT Asia Limited
Subsidiary Company

36th Floor, Two Pacific Place, 88 Queensway, Hong Kong
Tel: 2533 8400 **Fax:** 2845 1868, 2845 1882 **Telex:** 73046 BTRUS HX **Swift:** BKTR HK HX XXX
Reuters: BTCF-G (Monitor) **Telerate:** 2721
Reuters: BTCH (Dealing)

Senior Executive Officers

Others (Senior Executives)

Edward Lo *Chief Executive, Director*
Timothy S Rattray *Director*
Ki Myung Hong *Director*
Ambrose Lam *Director*

BT Australia (Hong Kong) Limited
Subsidiary Company

Level 36, Two Pacific Place, 88 Queensway, Hong Kong
Tel: 2533 8000 **Fax:** 2533 8022 **Telex:** 65161

Senior Executive Officers

Others (Senior Executives)

Kent Lai *Vice President*
Charles Sim *Vice President*
David K Wong *Vice President*

BT Funds Management Asia Limited
Subsidiary Company

36th Floor, Two Pacific Place, 88 Queensway, Hong Kong
Tel: 2533 8111; 2533 8222 **Fax:** 2801 5690

Senior Executive Officers
Director
Senior Vice President
Vice President

Anthony Fasso
Grant Forster
Viola Cheung

Bumi Daya International Finance Limited
Subsidiary Company

7th Floor, Far East Finance Centre, 16 Harcourt Road, Central, Hong Kong
Tel: 2527 6611 **Fax:** 2529 8131 **Telex:** 84528 BEDE HX **Telex:** 84542 BDIF **Telex:** 80614 BDIF

Senior Executive Officers
Chief Executive Officer

Budi Utomo
Satyo Haryono *Deputy Chief Executive*

General - Treasury
Head of Treasury

Ratmoko Hadi *Manager, Treasury* ☎ **2861 3781/6**

Debt Capital Markets / Fixed Income
Country Head

Ratmoko Hadi *Manager, Treasury* ☎ **2861 3781/6**

Money Markets
Country Head

Ratmoko Hadi *Manager, Treasury* ☎ **2861 3781/6**

Foreign Exchange
Country Head

Ratmoko Hadi *Manager, Treasury* ☎ **2861 3781/6**

Settlement / Clearing
Operations

Henry Kan *Senior Manager, Operations*

Administration

Other (Administration)
Business Development

Satyo Haryono *Deputy Chief Executive*

HONG KONG, CHINA (+852) www.euromoneydirectory.com

Butterfield Trust (Hong Kong) Limited — Subsidiary Company

26th Floor, Bank of China Tower, 1 Garden Road, Hong Kong
Tel: 2868 1010 **Fax:** 2845 0390 **Telex:** 82370 BTHKL HX **Email:** butfldhk@netvigator.com
Website: www.bankofbutterfield.com

Senior Executive Officers
Chief Executive Officer — Alastair Murray *Managing Director* ☎ 2868 3860
Chief Operating Officer — Ian Leung *Operations Director* ☎ 2868 9752
Company Secretary — Rebecca Lee ☎ 2868 9784

Settlement / Clearing
Head of Settlement / Clearing — Greg Soares ☎ 2868 9731

Global Custody
Head of Global Custody — Greg Soares ☎ 2868 9731

Administration
Head of Administration — Grace Chan ☎ 2868 9788

Technology & Systems
Agnes Chan ☎ 2868 1426

Compliance
John Ham ☎ 2868 9783

Caisse Centrale des Banques Populaires — Representative Office

Unit C, 14th Floor, Entertainment Building, 30 Queen's Road, Central, Hong Kong
Tel: 2537 3581 **Fax:** 2530 1805

Senior Executive Officers
Representative — Claude Lesage

Canadian Eastern Finance Limited — Head Office

1st Floor, China Building, 29 Queen's Road, Central, Hong Kong
Tel: 2846 3788 **Fax:** 2845 1551

Senior Executive Officers
Financial Director — Joseph C L Wong *Executive Director*
Managing Director — Tony S S Leung

Others (Senior Executives)
P K Tang *Executive Director*

Canadian Imperial Bank of Commerce — Full Branch Office

10th Floor, China Building, 29 Queen's Road, Central, Hong Kong
Tel: 2841 6111 **Fax:** 2845 9218; 2524 7534

Senior Executive Officers
Managing Director, Asia — Peter Tulloch

Others (Senior Executives)
Head of Financial Products — Ming Wong *Managing Director*

Debt Capital Markets / Fixed Income
Department: Capital Markets
Head of Debt Capital Markets — Stephen Liu *Managing Director*

Syndicated Lending
Other (Syndicated Lending)
Head of Loan Products — Maureen Kwok *Executive Director*

Settlement / Clearing
Operations — Sankey Chu *Executive Director & Head of Operations*

Administration
Head of Administration
Technology & Systems

Legal / In-House Counsel

Sharia Leung *Associate*

George Hsu *Director*

Scott Wilson *Executive Director*

CARIPLO - Cassa di Risparmio delle Provincie Lombarde SpA
Full Branch Office

Suite 5207/8, 52nd Floor, Central Plaza, 18 Harbour Road, Wanchai, Hong Kong
Tel: 2820 6688 **Fax:** 2802 3822 **Telex:** 72575 CASHK HX **Swift:** CARI HK HH **Reuters:** CRPH
Dealing **Tel:** 2802 3754

Senior Executive Officers
General Manager
Deputy General Manager
Chief Executive Officer
Treasurer

Bruno Gamba
Alessandro Polacco
Stanley Luk *Senior Assistant General Manager*
Rosie Ong *Assistant General Manager*

WI Carr Indosuez Capital Asia Limited
Subsidiary Company

42-45th Floors, One Exchange Square, 8 Connaught Road, Central, Hong Kong
Tel: 2820 7373 **Fax:** 2868 1524 **Telex:** 78244 ISA HX

Senior Executive Officers
Chief Operating Officer

Régis Monfront ☏ **2820 7703** ✉ **2868 5257**

Casse di Risparmio Joint Representative Office

Suite 3102, Universal Trade Centre, 3-5A Arbuthnot Road, Central, Hong Kong
Tel: 2501 0338 **Fax:** 2501 0145 **Telex:** 70519 CASSE HX

CCIC Finance Limited

38th Floor, 'A' Bank of China Tower, 1 Garden Road, Hong Kong
Tel: 2820 0888 **Fax:** 2877 2105 **Telex:** 61931 CCICX HX **Swift:** CCIC HK HX

Senior Executive Officers
Chairman
Managing Director
Deputy Managing Director
Deputy Managing Director

Man-ah Or
Paul S Muther ☏ **2820 0806**
Satoshi Nakamura ☏ **2820 0809**
Christopher Chan ☏ **2820 0807**

Debt Capital Markets / Fixed Income
Head of Fixed Income Trading

Jane Ng *Dealer* ☏ **2820 0830**

Syndicated Lending
Loan-Related Activities
Trade Finance
Project Finance

Angus Yip *Manager* ☏ **2820 0842**
John Sung *Associate Director* ☏ **2820 0850**
Michael Wu *Associate Director* ☏ **2820 0857**

Money Markets
Head of Money Markets
Foreign Exchange
Head of Foreign Exchange

Jane Ng *Dealer* ☏ **2820 0830**

Jane Ng *Dealer* ☏ **2820 0830**

Cedel Bank
Representative Office

1106-7 Two Exchange Square, 8 Connaught Place, Central, Hong Kong
Tel: 2523 0728 **Fax:** 2523 7796 **Telex:** 2791 **Swift:** CEDELULL **Email:** marketing@cedelgroup.com
Website: www.cedelgroup.com

Senior Executive Officers
Director

Philippe Metoudi ✉ **pmetoudi@cedelgroup.com**

HONG KONG, CHINA (+852)   www.euromoneydirectory.com

Cedel Bank (cont)
Debt Capital Markets / Fixed Income
Fixed-Income Repo
Head of Repo Phillipe Metoudi *Senior Executive* ☎ 2523 7411 ☒ 2523 7796
Marketing & Product Development; Sales Paul Lo *Vice President* ✉ plo@cedelgroup.com

The CEF Group *Head Office*
Alternative trading name: CEF Holdings Limited
1st & 2nd Floors, China Building, 29 Queen's Road, Central, Hong Kong
Tel: 2846 3688 **Fax:** 2845 0173 **Telex:** 82658 CEFC HX

Senior Executive Officers
Group Managing Director Joseph Yu
Deputy Group Managing Director Tony Leung

Others (Senior Executives)
                                Dennis Hon *Chief Legal Counsel*
Group Finance & Administration Winston Chow *Head*
Department: CEF Capital Limited - Investment Banking (North Asia)
Chairman Joseph Yu
MD, North Asia Joseph Wong

Others (Senior Executives)
Equity Capital Markets & Corporate Finance Catherine Wong *Executive Director & Head*
Syndicated Credits & Project Finance Raymond Chui *Executive Director & Head*
                                Wesley Chan *Associate Director & Head*
CEF Beijing Representative Office; CEF Kai Kwai *Chief Representative*
Shanghai Representative Office

General-Lending (DCM, SL)
Head of Corporate Banking Alfred Lo *Executive Director*
Department: CEF (Singapore) Limited - Investment Banking (SE Asia)
Managing Director Yeo Siah Meng
Department: CEF New Asia Partners Limited - Direct Investment Management

General-Investment
Head of Investment Joseph Yu *Chairman*
                                Winnie Fok *Managing Director*
                                Yeo Siah Meng *MD, CEF New Asia Mgt Co Ltd*
Department: CIBC CEF Private Clients Investment Services Limited

Others (Senior Executives)
Private Clients Joseph Yu *Chief Executive Officer*
                                William Cheng *MD & Chief Operating Officer*
Department: CEF M B Investments Limited
Chief Executive Officer Joseph Yu *Chief Executive Officer*
Managing Director Winnie Fok
Department: Canadian Eastern Life Assurance Limited
Chief Executive Officer Terence Wu *Chief Executive Officer*
Department: CEF GC Brokerage Limited
Managing Director & Chief Operating Officer Perry Luk

Syndicated Lending
Department: Canadian Eastern Finance Limited

Other (Syndicated Lending)
Lending & Deposit Tony Leung *MD, Canadian Eastern Finance Ltd*

Asset Management
Department: CEF.TAL Investment Management Limited

Other (Asset Management)
Fund Management Peter Chau *Deputy Managing Director*
                                Shirley Chow *Deputy Managing Director*
Department: CEF.TAL Investment Management Australia

Other (Asset Management)
Fund Management Duncan Mount *Managing Director*

Administration
Head of Administration Winston Chow *Head*

Legal / In-House Counsel
                                Dennis Hon *Chief Legal Counsel*

www.euromoneydirectory.com   HONG KONG, CHINA (+852)

Chase Manhattan Asia Limited
39th Floor, One Exchange Square, Central, Hong Kong
Tel: 2843 1234 **Fax:** 2841 4396

Senior Executive Officers
Managing Director   Jonathan Weiss ☏ **2901 4031** F **2901 4035**

The Chase Manhattan Bank
35th Floor, One Exchange Square, 8 Connaught Place, Central, Hong Kong
Tel: 2841 4321 **Fax:** 2841 4396 **Telex:** 83830 CHASM HX

Senior Executive Officers
Others (Senior Executives)
Regional Manager, Greater China & the   Antony Leung *Managing Director*
Philippines

Chekiang First Bank Limited   Head Office
Chekiang First Bank Building, 60 Gloucester Road, Hong Kong
PO Box 691, Hong Kong
Tel: 2922 1222 **Fax:** 2866 3866; 2866 9133 **Telex:** 73686 **Swift:** CFHK HK HH

Senior Executive Officers
Chief Manager & CEO   James Kung ☏ **2921 8101** F **2869 6623**
Chief Executive Officer   Takaaki Chya *Vice Chairman & Deputy Chief Manager* ☏ **2921 8112**
                             F **2869 6623**
                             Yuzo Shibata *Vice Chairman & Deputy Chief Manager* ☏ **2922 1501**
                             F **2861 2138**
                             Yu-Yuan Wang *Director & Deputy Chief Manager* ☏ **2921 8118** F **2869 6623**
                             Leo Kung *Assistant Chief Manager* ☏ **2922 1218** F **2866 9007**
International Division   Chee-Chee Lam *General Manager, International Department* ☏ **2922 1388**
                             F **2865 5323**

Others (Senior Executives)
                             Billy So *Assistant Chief Manager* ☏ **2922 1333** F **2865 1015**
                             Katy Sin *Assistant Chief Manager* ☏ **29221 1282** F **2520 0746**
                             Wing-Yun Lam *Assistant Chief Manager* ☏ **2922 1571** F **2861 2138**

General-Lending (DCM, SL)
Head of Corporate Banking Tak-Keung Tse *Assistant Chief Manager* ☏ **2922 1503** F **2866 9007**

Debt Capital Markets / Fixed Income
Tel: 2922 1514 **Fax:** 2520 1882

Domestic Government Bonds
Head of Trading   Thomas Lai *Manager, Treasury* ☏ **2922 1510** F **2520 1882**

Eurobonds
Head of Trading   Thomas Lai *Manager, Treasury* ☏ **2922 1510** F **2520 1882**

Libor-Based / Floating-Rate Products
Asset Swaps   Thomas Lai *Manager, Treasury* ☏ **2922 1510** F **2520 1882**

Equity Capital Markets
Department: Treasury Department
Tel: 2922 1514 **Fax:** 2520 1882
Head of Trading   Kwai-Man Wong *GM, Central Head Office* ☏ **2921 8182** F **2810 0531**

International Equities
Head of Trading   Kwai-Man Wong *GM, Central Head Office* ☏ **2921 8182** F **2810 0531**

Syndicated Lending
Loan-Related Activities
Trade Finance   Chee-Chee Lam *General Manager, International Department* ☏ **2922 1388**
                             F **2865 5323**

Money Markets
Tel: 2922 1210 **Fax:** 2520 1882
Head of Money Markets   Thomas Lai *Manager, Treasury* ☏ **2922 1510** F **2520 1882**

Foreign Exchange
Tel: 2922 1514 **Fax:** 2520 1882
Head of Foreign Exchange   Eddie Chan *General Manager, Treasury*

HONG KONG, CHINA (+852)   www.euromoneydirectory.com

Chekiang First Bank Limited (cont)
Risk Management
Head of Risk Management
Tak-Keung Tse *Assistant Chief Manager* ☏ 2922 1503 🖷 2866 9007
Foreign Exchange Derivatives / Risk Management
Spot / Forwards Trading
Thomas Lai *Manager, Treasury* ☏ 2922 1510 🖷 2520 1882
Settlement / Clearing
Tel: 2922 1250 Fax: 2527 5570
Head of Settlement / Clearing
Shing-Tat Wong *Manager, Remittance Section* ☏ 2922 1250 🖷 2527 5570
Other Departments
Commodities / Bullion
Mea Chau *Dealer* ☏ 2921 8172 🖷 2810 0531
Correspondent Banking
Chee-Chee Lam *General Manager, International Department* ☏ 2922 1388 🖷 2865 5323
Administration
Head of Marketing
Tak-Keung Tse *Assistant Chief Manager* ☏ 2922 1503 🖷 2866 9007
Technology & Systems
Chun-Kong Lim *General Manager, EDP* ☏ 2922 1318 🖷 2528 4121
Legal / In-House Counsel
Gerami Cheng *Legal Advisor* ☏ 2922 1533 🖷 2845 4724
Public Relations
Tak-Keung Tse *Assistant Chief Manager* ☏ 2922 1503 🖷 2866 9007
Accounts / Audit
Accounts
Bing-Choi Cheung *General Manager* ☏ 2922 1262 🖷 2529 6616
Audit
Fanny Cheung *General Manager* ☏ 2922 1262 🖷 2866 1994

The Chiba Bank Limited   Full Branch Office
Unit 2510, 1 Pacific Place, 88 Queensway, Hong Kong
Tel: 2840 1222 Fax: 2840 0507 Telex: 62737 CHBK HX

Senior Executive Officers
General Manager
Yuji Watanabe
Syndicated Lending
Head of Syndication
Hiroyuki Toyama *Manager*
Money Markets
Domestic Commercial Paper
Head of Trading
Junichi Kuboshima *Manager*
Foreign Exchange
Country Head
Akihiro Yuki *Chief Dealer*

The Chuo Trust & Banking Co Limited   Full Branch Office
2303/8 Alexandra House, 16/20 Chater Road, Hong Kong
Tel: 2810 1461 Fax: 2845 1664 Telex: 72340 CTBRH HX

Senior Executive Officers
General Manager
Masanori Higuchi

Chuo Trust Asia Limited   Subsidiary Company
2303/8, Alexandra House, 16/20 Chater Road, Hong Kong
Tel: 2810 1461 Fax: 2845 1664 Telex: 72340 CTBRH HX

Citibank NA   Full Branch Office
40th & 44th-50th Floors, Citibank Tower, Citibank Plaza, 3 Garden Road, Hong Kong
Tel: 2868 8888; 2868 8213 Fax: 2868 8368; 2868 8866 Reuters: CIHK

Senior Executive Officers
Chief Executive Officer
Stephen H Long *Country Corporate Officer* ☏ 2868 8868
Ignatius T C Chan *Global Corporate Banking Head of HK* ☏ 2868 8899
Treasurer
Patrick Dewilde *Regional Treasurer* ☏ 2868 8870
General - Treasury
Head of Treasury
Jenny Mak *Treasury Marketing Head* ☏ 2868 8210
Debt Capital Markets / Fixed Income
Global Head
Avinder S Bindra *Vice President* ☏ 2868 6610

www.euromoneydirectory.com   HONG KONG, CHINA (+852)

Equity Capital Markets
Global Head   Avinder S Bindra *Vice President* ☎ 2868 6610
Equity Repo / Securities Lending
Head   James Coppola *Vice President, Regional Securities Lending* ☎ 2868 7347
Money Markets
Global Head   Chordio Chan *Vice President* ☎ 2868 8878
Foreign Exchange
Global Head   T H Suen *Vice President* ☎ 2868 8898

Citicorp International Limited   Head Office

47th/48th Floors, Citibank Tower, Citibank Plaza, 3 Garden Road, Hong Kong
Tel: 2868 6666; 2868 6611 **Fax:** 2521 8725

Senior Executive Officers
Chairman   Stephen H Long ☎ 2868 8868
Chief Executive Officer   Avinder S Bindra *Alternate Chief Executive* ☎ 2868 6610
                                     Catherine M Weir ☎ 2868 6637

Others (Senior Executives)
                                     Mark F Hart
                                     Alvin Mak Wing Sum
                                     Ignatius T C Chan
                                     Quentin K Hills

Debt Capital Markets / Fixed Income
Global Head   Avinder S Bindra *Alternate Chief Executive* ☎ 2868 6610
Asset-Backed Securities / Securitization
Global Head   Eric Alsberg *Managing Director* ☎ 2868 6600
Syndicated Lending
Loan-Related Activities
Project Finance; Structured Trade Finance   Joseph Casson *Managing Director* ☎ 2868 6690
Other (Trade Finance)
Structured Finance   David Pinkerton

Clariden Asset Management (Hong Kong) Limited
Subsidiary Company

Room 2309, 23rd Floor, Alexandra House, 16-20 Chater Road, Hong Kong
Tel: 2913 7678 **Fax:** 2845 5447

Senior Executive Officers
Managing Director   Michael F Galbraith

Commerzbank AG

21st Floor, Hong Kong Club Building, Central, Hong Kong
PO Box 11378, Hong Kong
Tel: 2842 9666 **Fax:** 2868 1414 **Telex:** 66400 CBK HX HK **Reuters:** CBKH

Senior Executive Officers
Managing Director   Michael J Oliver
Managing Director / General Manager Harald W A Vogy

Others (Senior Executives)
Treasurer   Bob Fotheringham
General-Lending (DCM, SL)
Head of Corporate Banking   Fu Johnson
Administration
Head of Administration   Cindy Chan

Commonwealth Bank of Australia   Full Branch Office

14th Floor, Two Exchange Square, 8 Connaught Place, Central, Hong Kong
Tel: 2844 7500 **Fax:** 2845 9194 **Telex:** 66802 CTB HX **Reuters:** CBAK

Senior Executive Officers
Chief Operating Officer   Gary Roach *Financial Controller* ☎ 2844 7589
Treasurer   Andrew Fung *Head of Financial Markets* ☎ 2844 7529

HONG KONG, CHINA (+852)   www.euromoneydirectory.com

Commonwealth Bank of Australia (cont)
Debt Capital Markets / Fixed Income
Tel: 2844 7533 Fax: 2845 8983
Head of Debt Capital Markets   Andrew Fung *Head of Financial Markets* ☎ **2844 7529**

Domestic Government Bonds
Head of Sales   Jimmy Jim *Senior Executive, Fixed Income Distribution* ☎ **2844 7531**
Head of Trading   Jenny Chau *Senior Executive, Capital Markets*

Eurobonds
Head of Origination   Jenny Chau *Senior Executive, Capital Markets*
Head of Syndication   Francis Wu ☎ **2844 7532**
Head of Sales   Jimmy Jim *Senior Executive, Fixed Income Distribution* ☎ **2844 7531**
Head of Trading   Karen Lo *Executive, Fixed Income Distribution* ☎ **2844 7538**

Libor-Based / Floating-Rate Products
FRN Origination   Jenny Chau *Senior Executive, Capital Markets*
FRN Sales   Jimmy Jim *Senior Executive, Fixed Income Distribution* ☎ **2844 7531**

Medium-Term Notes
Head of Origination   Jenny Chau *Senior Executive, Capital Markets*
Head of Sales   Jimmy Jim *Senior Executive, Fixed Income Distribution* ☎ **2844 7531**

Private Placements
Head of Origination   Jenny Chau *Senior Executive, Capital Markets*
Head of Sales   Jimmy Jim *Senior Executive, Fixed Income Distribution* ☎ **2844 7531**

Syndicated Lending
Head of Syndication   Maria Yeung *Chief Manager, Business Development* ☎ **2844 7502**

Money Markets
Tel: 2844 7535 Fax: 2844 8983
Head of Money Markets   Leo Au *Senior Executive, Interest Rate Trading* ☎ **2844 7535**

Domestic Commercial Paper
Head of Origination   Jenny Chau *Senior Executive, Capital Markets*
Head of Sales   Jimmy Jim *Senior Executive, Fixed-Income Distribution* ☎ **2844 7531**
Head of Trading   Raymond Fan *Executive, Interest Rate Trading* ☎ **2844 7536**

Eurocommercial Paper
Head of Sales   Karen Lo *Executive, Fixed Income Distribution* ☎ **2844 7538**

Wholesale Deposits
Marketing   Jimmy Jim *Senior Executive, Fixed Income Distribution* ☎ **2844 7531**

Foreign Exchange
Tel: 2844 7534 Fax: 2843 8983
Head of Institutional Sales   Clement Lam *Senior Executive, Foreign Exchange Products*
Head of Trading   Johnson Wong *Executive, Foreign Exchange Products* ☎ **2844 7539**

Risk Management
Country Head   Annie Leung *Credit Executive* ☎ **2844 7503**

Settlement / Clearing
Tel: 2844 7521 Fax: 2845 9294
Head of Settlement / Clearing   Gary Roach *Financial Controller* ☎ **2844 7589**
Fixed-Income Settlement; Foreign Exchange   Yee Man Mak *Settlement Manager*
Settlement

Other Departments
Private Banking   Gayle Gladhill *Regional Executive* ☎ **2844 7551**

Cooperatieve Centrale Raiffeisen-Boerenleenbank BA
Full Branch Office

Alternative trading name: Rabobank Hong Kong
42nd Floor, Two Exchange Square, 8 Connaught Place, Central, Hong Kong
Tel: 2103 2000 Fax: 2810 1327 Telex: 80556 RBHK HX Swift: RABO HK HH Email: rabohk@ims04.netvigator.com
Reuters: RABK
Financial Institutions & Governments Group Tel: 2103 2473, Fax: 2530 1728, Investment Banking Tel: 2103 2697;
Fax: 2501 5451; Settlement & Clearing Tel: 2103 2786; Fax: 2840 1993

Senior Executive Officers
General Manager   Dennis Ziengs ☎ **2103 2288**
Deputy General Manager   Cindy Kwong ☎ **2103 2303**

Others (Senior Executives)
Head of Financial Institutions & Government   Yuet Ming Chan *Assistant General Manager* ☎ **2103 2302**
Group

602 Euromoney Directory 1999

www.euromoneydirectory.com HONG KONG, CHINA (+852)

General-Investment
Head of Investment — Peter Yam *Managing Director & Head of Investment Banking* ☎ 2103 2699

Relationship Manager
Head of Food & Agribusiness — Clara Fung *Assistant General Manager* ☎ 2103 2424
Head of Local Corporates — Thomas Kwong *Senior Assistant General Manager* ☎ 2103 2391
Health Care, International Corporates & Euro Desk — Berry Marttin *Head* ☎ 2103 2871

Risk Management
Tel: 2103 2311 Fax: 2877 6439
Head of Risk Management — Stan Lee *Assistant General Manager* ☎ 2103 2319

Corporate Finance / M&A Advisory
Tel: 2103 2386
Head of Corporate Finance — May Tung *Managing Director* ☎ 2103 2866

Other Departments
Private Banking — Philippe Legrand *Director & Head* ☎ 2287 9888

Administration
Head of Administration — George Yau *AGM, Head of Financial Control & Administration* ☎ 2103 2882

Technology & Systems
Information Technology Service — Georgianna Tse *Assistant General Manager* ☎ 2103 2809

Legal / In-House Counsel
Legal — Anthony Trayhurn *AGM, Head of Legal, Tax & Compliance* ☎ 2103 2451

Compliance
Anthony Trayhurn *AGM, Head of Legal, Tax & Compliance* ☎ 2103 2451

Accounts / Audit
Financial Control — George Yau *AGM, Head of Financial Control & Administration* ☎ 2103 2882

Other (Administration)
Human Resources & Change Management — MIng Guo *Assistant General Manager* ☎ 2103 2428
Investment Banking Operations — Lucinda Wong *Assistant General Manager* ☎ 2103 2786

Coutts Bank
Full Branch Office

32nd Floor, One Exchange Square, 8 Connaught Place, Central, Hong Kong
Tel: 2525 6898 Fax: 2877 2183

Senior Executive Officers
Chief Executive Officer — Hans-Peter Brunner *Area Head, Asia* ☎ +65 223 3132 F +65 223 5098
Head of International Private Banking, North East — Dominic Li

Administration
Corporate Communications
Cheng-Han Tan *Manager, Regional Communications* ☎ 2847 8708 F 2801 6893

Crédit Agricole Indosuez
Full Branch Office

50th Floor, One Exchange Square, 8 Connaught Road, Central, Hong Kong
PO Box 16, Hong Kong
Tel: 2848 9000 Fax: 2868 1406 Telex: 73766 INDOC HX Swift: AGRI HK HH Reuters: CAHK-L

Senior Executive Officers
Senior Country Officer — François Beyler ☎ 2840 4188 F 2525 6537
Chief Operating Officer — John Fulker ☎ 2848 9849 F 2848 9711
International Division — Michel Demuynck *Corporate Banking* ☎ 2848 9855 F 2848 9722

General-Lending (DCM, SL)
Head of Corporate Banking — K K Wong *Corporate Banking, Greater China & HK* ☎ 2840 4226 F 2845 9284

Syndicated Lending
Head of Syndication — Frank Moy *Syndication & Distribution* ☎ 2848 9828 F 2848 9722

Loan-Related Activities
Commodities Financing — Gary Geller *First Vice President* ☎ 2848 9851 F 2848 9722
Project Finance — Arnaud Dornel *Project & Int'l Finance* ☎ 2848 9818 F 2848 9739

Other (Trade Finance)
Credit — John Shi ☎ 2848 9818 F 2848 9722

HONG KONG, CHINA (+852)   www.euromoneydirectory.com

Crédit Agricole Indosuez (cont)
Foreign Exchange
Department: Forex / Treasury
Global Head   Philippe Brenon *Forex / Treasury* T 2848 9838 F 2848 9713
Head of Institutional Sales; Corporate Sales   Miranda Tam *Senior Manager* T 2848 9834/5 F 2848 9737

FX Traders / Sales People
Treasury   Alan Lam T 2845 4888 F 2848 9737
Long-Term Products   Raymond Kong *Head of Investment Portfolio* T 2524 9220 F 2848 9737

Risk Management
Foreign Exchange Derivatives / Risk Management
Spot / Forwards Sales   Robert Smith *Chief Dealer* T 2848 9837 F 2848 9737
Vanilla FX option Sales   Laurent Combalot *Manager* T 2526 7721 F 2848 9738

Other Departments
Private Banking   François de Pelleport *Regional Head, North East Asia* T 2848 9098 F 2848 9727

Crédit Commercial de France   Full Branch Office
Room 3901-9, Jardine House, 1 Connaught Place, Central, Hong Kong
Tel: 2846 0200 **Fax:** 2868 1420 **Telex:** 61069 HKCCF **Swift:** CCFR HK HH **Reuters:** CCFK

Senior Executive Officers
General Manager   Alain Cany

Others (Senior Executives)
    Joseph Wong *Deputy General Manager*
    Alfred Leung *Deputy General Manager*
    Benoit Ober *Assistant General Manager*

Crédit Lyonnais
25th Floor, Three Exchange Square, 8 Connaught Place, Central, Hong Kong
PO Box 9757, Hong Kong
Tel: 2826 7333 **Fax:** 2810 1270 **Telex:** 76390 **Swift:** CRLY HK HH **Reuters:** CLHK-L **Cable:** CREDIONAIS HK

Senior Executive Officers
Chief Executive Officer   Bernard Mignucci *Chief Executive for Asia*
Head of North Asia   Pierre Finas

Others (Senior Executives)
Finance Control   Luc Auberger *Head of Finance for Asia*
Head of Merchant Banking   Hubert Vieille-Cessay *Deputy General Manager*

General-Lending (DCM, SL)
Head of Corporate Banking   Frankie Ng *Deputy General Manager*

General - Treasury
Head of Treasury   Patrick Gillot *Asia Regional Manager*

Relationship Manager
Bank Relationship   Jonathan Cheung *Regional Head*
Multinational Group- Asia   Michel Roy *Regional Head*

Debt Capital Markets / Fixed Income
Head of Debt Capital Markets   Patrick Gillot *Asia Regional Manager*

Equity Capital Markets
Head of Equity Capital Markets   Patrick Gillot *Asia Regional Manager*

Foreign Exchange
Head of Foreign Exchange   Patrick Gillot *Asia Regional Manager*

Other Departments
Chief Credit Officer   Kien Thanh Gia *Deputy General Manager, Credit Control*
Private Banking   Pascal Delvaque *Managing Director Asia*
Correspondent Banking   Frankie Ng *Deputy General Manager*

www.euromoneydirectory.com   HONG KONG, CHINA (+852)

Credit Suisse First Boston (Hong Kong) Limited

13th Floor, Three Exchange Square, 8 Connaught Place, Central, Hong Kong
22nd Floor, Exchange Square, Central, Hong Kong
Tel: 2101 6000 **Fax**: 2101 7990 **Telex**: 78297 CSFB HX **Swift**: CSFB H KHX
Website: www.csfb.com

Senior Executive Officers
Chairman   Stephen Stonefield

Debt Capital Markets / Fixed Income
Regional Head   William Battey *Managing Director*

Equity Capital Markets
Head of Equity Capital Markets   Julie Craddock *Managing Director*

Administration

Legal / In-House Counsel
    Neil Radey

Creditanstalt AG   Head Office

41st Floor, Two Exchange Square, 8 Connaught Place, Central, Hong Kong
Tel: 2868 3111 **Fax**: 2868 5115 **Telex**: 68220 CAHKB HX

Senior Executive Officers
Chairman   Erich Hampel
Chief Executive Officer   Brian W Hobson
Assistant General Manager & Regional Treasurer   Marco Foehn

Dah Sing Bank Limited   Head Office

36th Floor, Dah Sing Financial Centre, 108 Gloucester Road, Hong Kong
Tel: 2507 8866 **Fax**: 2598 5052 **Telex**: 74063 DSB HX **Swift**: DSBA HK HH **Reuters**: DSFX **Cable**: DAHSINGBANK
Website: www.dahsing.com.hk

Senior Executive Officers
Chairman   David S Y Wong
Chief Executive Officer   Ronald Carstairs *Managing Director*
Financial Director   Gary P L Wang *Financial Controller* ☎ **2507 8705**
Chief Operating Officer   Poon-Kien Ang ☎ **2507 8833**
Treasurer   Horace S Y Fan ☎ **2507 8878**
Managing Director   Ronald Carstairs
Company Secretary   Helen H L Soo ☎ **2507 8870**

Others (Senior Executives)
    Derek H H Wong *Senior Executive Director*
    Yiu-Ming Ng *Senior Executive Director* ☎ **2507 8782**
    John A Haddon *Executive Director*
    Lung-Man Chiu *Director & General Manager* ☎ **2507 8830**

General-Lending (DCM, SL)
Head of Corporate Banking   Teressa Lin *Senior Executive Director*

Corporate Finance / M&A Advisory
Head of Corporate Finance   David R Hinde *Executive Director*

Administration
Head of Administration   Cora Yu ☎ **2507 8935**
Head of Marketing   Shera Lee ☎ **2507 8916**

Technology & Systems
    Thomas Ng ☎ **2507 8520**

Accounts / Audit
Accounts   Renny Lie ☎ **2507 8963**

HONG KONG, CHINA (+852)   www.euromoneydirectory.com

The Dai-Ichi Kangyo Bank Limited
Full Branch Office

31st Floor, Gloucester Tower, 11 Pedder Street, Central, Hong Kong
Tel: 2526 6591 **Fax:** 2868 1421; 2869 1648 **Telex:** 60489 HKDKB HX
Website: www.dkb.co.jp

Senior Executive Officers
Managing Director / General Manager — Takeshi Tanimura

The Daiwa Bank Limited

12th Floor, The Hong Kong Club Building, 3A Chater Road, Central, Hong Kong
Tel: 2521 6433 **Fax:** 2868 1422 **Telex:** 61996 **Swift:** DIWAHKHHKG

Senior Executive Officers
General Manager — Nobuhiko Arai
Deputy General Manager — Shinichi Fujimaki

Debt Capital Markets / Fixed Income
Head of Debt Capital Markets — S Saito

Equity Capital Markets
Head of Equity Capital Markets — S Saito

Syndicated Lending
Head of Syndicated Lending — Koichi Morita

Money Markets
Head of Money Markets — Y Nakata

Foreign Exchange
Head of Foreign Exchange — Y Nakata

Corporate Finance / M&A Advisory
Head of Corporate Finance — S Saito

Administration
Other (Administration)
Operations — Ken Sasakawa *Head*
General Affairs — I Ota *Head* ☎ 2846 6116 📠 2522 5378

The Daiwa Bank

11th Floor, United Centre, 95 Queensway, Central, Hong Kong
Tel: 2862 6666 **Fax:** 2527 5651 **Telex:** 73637 **Swift:** DIWA HK HH **Cable:** DAIWA BK HK

Senior Executive Officers
SVP & General Manager — Kenneth Wong

Daiwa Overseas Finance Limited
Subsidiary Company

11th Floor, The Hong Kong Club Building, 3A Chater Road, Central, Hong Kong
Tel: 2526 1025 **Fax:** 2810 6731 **Telex:** 75286 DOFIN HX **Cable:** DAIWADOFIN HONG KONG **Telex:** 63539

Senior Executive Officers
Chairman — Nobuhiko Arai
MD & General Manager — Kenichi Nishimori

Settlement / Clearing
Settlement (General) — Ada Lem *Head of Operations*
Operations — Takayuki Ikuse

Daiwa Securities (Hong Kong) Limited
Subsidiary Company

Level 26, 1 Pacific Place, 88 Queensway, Hong Kong
Tel: 2525 0121 **Fax:** 2845 1621 **Telex:** 73325 DAIWA HX

Senior Executive Officers
Chairman — K Matsuba
Financial Director — H Kazahara
Managing Director / General Manager — T Nagano

General-Investment
Head of Investment — Richard Lamb *Head of Securitization*

www.euromoneydirectory.com   HONG KONG, CHINA (+852)

Debt Capital Markets / Fixed Income
Regional Head — S Kutsuma *Chief Dealer, Asia*

Asset-Backed Securities / Securitization
Global Head — Richard Lamb *Head of Securitization*

Equity Capital Markets
Department: Asian Equity Capital Markets
Regional Head — S Kutsuma *Chief Dealer, Asia*
John Fogerty *Joint Head*
David Russell *Joint Head*

Settlement / Clearing
Settlement (General) — Stephen Leung

Administration
Other (Administration)
Human Resources — Mr Lam *Head* ☎ 2848 4910 📠 2848 4077

Dao Heng Bank Limited

32nd Floor, Wu Chung House, 213 Queen's Road East, Hong Kong
Tel: 2831 5000 **Fax:** 2891 6683 **Telex:** HX 73345 **Swift:** DHBK HK HH **Reuters:** DHBH
Website: www.daoheng.com

Senior Executive Officers
Chairman — Quek Leng Chan ☎ 2831 7873
Chief Executive Officer — Kwek Leng Hai *Chief Executive* ☎ 2831 7873
Financial Director — Allan Tsang *Group Financial Controller* ☎ 2831 7789
Treasurer — Ping Shing Tam *General Manager* ☎ 2831 7728
Managing Director — Randolph Gordon Sullivan ☎ 2831 7709

Debt Capital Markets / Fixed Income
Tel: 2831 7835 **Fax:** 2891 2293

Domestic Government Bonds
Head of Trading — Joseph Chiu *Manager, Domestic Trading* ☎ 2831 5191

Eurobonds
Head of Trading — Ricky Choi *Manager, Secondary Market*

Private Placements
Head of Sales — Rainbow Cheung *Manager*

Asset-Backed Securities / Securitization
Head of Trading — Simon Lam *Senior Manager*

Money Markets
Tel: 2831 7839 **Fax:** 2831 2293
Country Head — Frank Li *Manager, Domestic Trading*

Foreign Exchange
Head of Institutional Sales — Cindy Kam *Senior Manager* ☎ 2831 7841
Corporate Sales — Henry S S Chan *Chief Dealer* ☎ 2831 7834

FX Traders / Sales People
Asian Currencies — Lawrence Chan *Senior Dealer* ☎ 2831 7830
Paul Yuen *Senior Dealer* ☎ 2831 7830
William Tsang *Dealer* ☎ 2831 7830
Sales — Franco Sze *Manager, Corporate FX* ☎ 2831 7841
Thomas Lee *Senior Dealer, Corporate FX* ☎ 2831 7841

Other Departments
Private Banking — Kim Chuan Tew *General Manager* ☎ 2831 2116
Correspondent Banking — Danny Cheung *Manager* ☎ 2831 2338

Administration

Technology & Systems — David Tsui *Chief Information Officer* ☎ 2831 5505

Legal / In-House Counsel — Anthony Somerset *Manager* ☎ 2831 7807

Public Relations — Helen Kwan *Manager* ☎ 2831 8710

Euromoney Directory 1999   607

HONG KONG, CHINA (+852)　　　www.euromoneydirectory.com

Den Danske Bank Aktieselskab — Full Branch Office

21st Floor, Two Exchange Square, 8 Connaught Place, Hong Kong
Tel: 2810 1871 Fax: 2810 4212 Telex: 80898 DABA HX Swift: DABA HK HH

Senior Executive Officers
Chief Executive Officer
Deputy General Manager

Thomas Dideriksen *General Manager*
Benedict Tse

Deutsche Bank AG — Full Branch Office

36th Floor, New World Tower, 16-18 Queen's Road, Central, Hong Kong
PO Box 3193, Hong Kong
Tel: 2971 5300; 2810 7879 Fax: 2810 5881; 2810 0903 Telex: 83907 DBHKGHX Swift: DEUT HKHC
Cable: DEUTBANK
Forex Tel: 2526 3060
Website: www.deutsche-bank.de

Senior Executive Officers
Chairman
Chief Executive Officer
Treasurer

Edson Mitchell
Chris Chi Keung Chan *Chief Country Officer*
Frank Cheung

Debt Capital Markets / Fixed Income
Fixed-Income Repo
Trading

Michael Yu *Repo Sales*

Money Markets
Head of Money Markets

Dominic Jones *Money Market & Repo Sales*

Money Markets - General

Michael Yu *Repo Sales*

Global Custody
Tel: 2971 5300 Fax: 2810 5881 Telex: 83907 DBHK GHX
Regional Head

Chow Keng *Head of Custody Services, Operations* ⓣ 2971 5320
ⓕ 2810 5881

Other (Global Custody)

Samuel Lau ⓣ 2971 8040 ⓕ 2525 8040

Administration
Other (Administration)
Operation
Human Resources

Leo Luk *Head* ⓣ 2843 0648 ⓕ 2973 6337
Kerrie Leung *Head* ⓣ 2843 0447 ⓕ 2525 9540

Deutsche Bank Capital Markets (Asia) Limited

36th Floor, New World Tower, 16/18 Queen's Road, Hong Kong
PO Box 9879, Hong Kong
Tel: 2525 5203 Fax: 2810 5881 Telex: 83907 DBHKG HX

Senior Executive Officers
Managing Director / General Manager　　Mehmet Dalman

Deutsche Capital Hong Kong Limited — Subsidiary Company

Formerly known as: Deutsche Morgan Grenfell Hong Kong Limited
28th Floor, One Pacific Place, 88 Queensway, Hong Kong
Tel: 2810 8686 Fax: 2845 9172

Senior Executive Officers
Managing Director　　Chris Chan ⓣ 2514 2788 ⓔ chris.chan@db.com

Deutsche Morgan Grenfell Capital Markets Limited — Head Office

20th Floor, Tower Two, 16-18 Queen's Road, Central, Hong Kong
Tel: 2971 5300 Fax: 2525 7990 Telex: 83907 dbhkg hx

www.euromoneydirectory.com			HONG KONG, CHINA (+852)

Deutsche Morgan Grenfell Securities Limited
28th Floor, One Pacific Place, 88 Queensway, Central, Hong Kong
Tel: 2868 0388 **Fax:** 2845 0228 **Telex:** 70719 MGASH HX

Senior Executive Officers
Financial Director				Eric Leung
Managing Director & GM			William Hamilton

Equity Capital Markets
Tel: 2514 4667 **Fax:** 2918 1459

Domestic Equities
Head of Trading					Noel McCulla
Head of Research				Lawrence Ang *China*
						Victor Kwok *Hong Kong*
						Brad West *Asian Equities*

Equity Repo / Securities Lending
Head						Tracey Taylor *Regional Manager*
						Tracey Taylor *Regional Manager* ⊤ 2514 4666/9 ⒡ 2918 1459
Marketing					Alan Lao
Head of Trading					Adrien Ong *Trader* ⊤ 2514 4667

Administration
Head of Administration				Lydia Kwok ⒡ 2526 3029

Deutsche Securities Limited
New World Tower, 16-18 Queen's Road, Central, Hong Kong
Tel: 2843 0040

Senior Executive Officers
Department: Senior Executives: Global Corporates & Institutions

Others (Senior Executives)
Head of Investment Banking			Josef Ackermann
Head of Global Markets				Edson Mitchell
Head of Equities				Michael Philipp
Head of Risk Management				Hugo Banziger
Head of Global Banking Services			Juergen Fitschen
Head of Structured Finance			Gavin Lickley
Head of IT / Operations				Marc Sternfeld

DG BANK
9th Floor, Admiralty Centre, Tower II, 18 Harcourt Road, Central, Hong Kong
Tel: 2864 3100 **Fax:** 2864 3160

Senior Executive Officers
General Manager					Clemens Wendland
General Manager					Peter van der Mespel
General Manager					Johannes Kux

# DKB Asia Limited					Subsidiary Company
31st Floor, Gloucester Tower, 11 Pedder Street, Central, Hong Kong
Tel: 2526 6591 **Fax:** 2810 1326 **Telex:** 65941 DKFHK HX **Swift:** DKBA LH KG
Website: www.dkb.co.jp

Senior Executive Officers
Chairman					Mr Toyota
Managing Director / General Manager		Yoshihiko Miyata

Debt Capital Markets / Fixed Income
Head of Fixed Income Sales			Toshiaki Toyama

Risk Management
Country Head					Katsuyoshi Matsuda *Risk Management*

Settlement / Clearing
Operations					Raymond Leung *Head of Operations*

HONG KONG, CHINA (+852)   www.euromoneydirectory.com

Dresdner Bank AG — Full Branch Office

6th Floor, Hutchison House, 10 Harcourt Road, Central, Hong Kong
PO Box 9910
Tel: 2826 2000 Fax: 2845 9071 Telex: 65550 DRES HX Swift: DRES HK HH Reuters: DRBK

Senior Executive Officers
General Manager — Stanley B C To ☏ 2877 9521
General Manager — Michael P Bornemann ☏ 2826 2000

General-Lending (DCM, SL)
Head of Corporate Banking — Felix von Joest *Head* ☏ 2826 2010

Debt Capital Markets / Fixed Income
Head of Fixed Income — Francis C W Li *Manager* ☏ 2524 6286
Head of Fixed Income Sales — Alex Woo *Senior Manager* ☏ 2521 0105

Syndicated Lending

Loan-Related Activities
Trade Finance — Peter S H Pang ☏ 2826 2920

Money Markets
Tel: 2521 0205 Fax: 2537 1834 Reuters: DRBK
Head of Money Markets; Country Head — Ronald P K Ng *Manager*

Risk Management
Tel: 2524 6286 Fax: 2523 8109
Head of Risk Management — Eric T P Cheung *Manager* ☏ 2524 6286

Other (FI Derivatives)
Head of Swaps — Jacky M F Tai *Deputy Manager* ☏ 2524 6286

Settlement / Clearing
Head of Settlement / Clearing — Peter Pang ☏ 2826 2070

Other Departments
Chief Credit Officer — Alexander Kan *Head of Credit & Loans* ☏ 2826 2022

Administration
Head of Administration — Claus Groeting ☏ 2826 2088

Technology & Systems
Carsten Paasch *Head* ☏ 2826 2069

Legal / In-House Counsel
Bronwen Sharp *Legal Advisor* ☏ 2826 2096

Accounts / Audit
Edmond Wong *Head* ☏ 2826 2068

East Asia Asset Management Company Limited — Head Office

8th Floor, Bank of East Asia Building, 10 Des Voeux Road, Central, Hong Kong
Tel: 2842 3531 Fax: 2845 2937; 2526 7992 Telex: 76785 EAFHX Swift: BEAS HK HH

Senior Executive Officers
Managing Director — Lau Ching Ching Stella ☏ 2842 3287

Settlement / Clearing
Head of Settlement / Clearing — Hon Yuet Wah Vionne ☏ 2842 3713

Asset Management
Head — Lau Ching Ching Stella *Managing Director* ☏ 2842 3287

Administration

Accounts / Audit
Man Oi Lan Givan *Deputy Manager* ☏ 2842 3299

Equitable Banking Corporation — Full Branch Office

7th Floor, Silver Fortune Plaza, 1 Wellington Street, Central, Hong Kong
Tel: 2524 6648 Fax: 2810 0050

Senior Executive Officers
Deputy Managing Director — P K Chan

www.euromoneydirectory.com   HONG KONG, CHINA (+852)

Euroclear Operations Centre
Representative Office

Morgan Guaranty Trust Company of New York, Edinburgh Tower, 15 Queen's Road, Central, Hong Kong
Tel: 2973 5636 Fax: 2841 1136

Senior Executive Officers
Representative for Asia-Pacific   Udo Jenner

The Export-Import Bank of Japan
Representative Office

Suite 3706, Level 37, One Pacific Place, 88 Queensway, Hong Kong
Tel: 2869 8505; 2869 8507 Fax: 2869 8712

Senior Executive Officers
Chief Representative   Hiroo Katsuta
Representative   Kazuaki Shirotsu

First National Bank of Chicago (The)
Full Branch Office

13th Floor, Jardine House, 1 Connaught Place, Central, Hong Kong
Tel: 2844 9222 Fax: 2844 9318; 2844 9313 Telex: 83536 FCHOP HX Swift: FNBC HK HX Reuters: FCHK
Website: www.fcnbd.com

Senior Executive Officers
Chief Executive Officer   Richard Kolehmainen *General Manager* T 2844 9213 F 2844 9318
Treasurer   Richard Siu T 2844 9231 F 2844 9318

Syndicated Lending
Head of Syndicated Lending   Veronique Lafon-Vinais *Head of Financial Markets, Asia-Pacific*
T 2844 9356 F 2844 9319

Loan-Related Activities
Trade Finance   James Schmelter T 2844 9265 F 2844 9318

Other Departments
Chief Credit Officer   Larry Cooper *Head of Credit, Greater China & South East Asia*
T 2844 9278 F 2844 9318
Cash Management   Alex Leung T 2844 9376 F 2844 9318

Administration
Technology & Systems
Carolyn Gourash *Head of Capital Markets Systems, Asia* T 2844 9390
F 2844 9318

First Pacific Bank Limited
Full Branch Office

22nd Floor, First Pacific Bank Centre, 56 Gloucester Road, Hong Kong
Tel: 2823 9823 Fax: 2865 5151 Telex: 83868 FPBHK HX Swift: FPBL HK HH Cable: FIRPACBANK

Senior Executive Officers
Chairman   Manuel V Pangilinan
Managing Director   James Ng

Others (Senior Executives)
Community Banking Group I   Alec Keung *Executive Vice President*
Community Banking Group II   Tony Tsui *Executive Vice President*
Community Banking Group III   Simon Lau *Senior Vice President*
Chief Financial Officer   Gladys Chen *Senior Vice President*

General - Treasury
Head of Treasury   Victor Yeung *Senior Vice President & Treasurer*

Syndicated Lending
Other (Trade Finance)
Asset Based Finance   Stephen Chung *Senior Vice President*

Risk Management
Department: Credit & Investment Risk Management Division
Head of Risk Management   Peter Choy *Senior Vice President*

Asset Management
Department: Asset Based Finance Division
Other (Asset Management)
Stephen Chung *Senior Vice President*

HONG KONG, CHINA (+852)   www.euromoneydirectory.com

First Pacific Bank Limited (cont)
Other Departments
Chief Credit Officer   Peter Choy *Senior Vice President*
Administration
Technology & Systems
Information & Technology   Egbert Chan *Vice President*
Accounts / Audit
Chief Auditor   Patrick Lo *Vice President*
Other (Administration)
Marketing & Product Management   Samuel Hui *Senior Vice President*

The Fuji Bank Limited

26th Floor, Gloucester Tower, The Landmark, 11 Pedder Street, Central, Hong Kong
Tel: 2521 4451 **Fax:** 2810 0243 **Telex:** 74604 FUJBK HX 6 **Reuters:** FJBK

Senior Executive Officers
GM & Regional Corporate Executive (Hong Kong)   Yasufumi Miyazaki

Fuji Capital Markets (HK) Limited

2502 Gloucester Tower, The Landmark, 11 Pedder Street, Central, Hong Kong
Tel: 2537 3810 **Fax:** 2826 4891

Senior Executive Officers
Managing Director / General Manager   Michio Tani

Fuji International Finance (Hong Kong) Limited   Subsidiary Company

3301 Gloucester Tower, 11 Pedder Street, Central, Hong Kong
Tel: 2521 7233 **Fax:** 2845 9177 **Telex:** 76884 FIFHK HX **Swift:** FUJI HK HF **Reuters:** FIFH

Senior Executive Officers
Chairman   Atsushi Takano ☎ **2521 7233**
Chief Executive Officer   Takehiro Sakurai *Managing Director & Chief Executive* ☎ **2913 9201**

Debt Capital Markets / Fixed Income
Head of Debt Capital Markets   Takehiro Sakurai *Managing Director & Chief Executive* ☎ **2913 9201**
Global Head   Koichiro Matsumoto *Director* ☎ **2913 9211**

Domestic Government Bonds
Head of Sales; Head of Trading   Koichiro Matsumoto *Director* ☎ **2913 9211**

Eurobonds
Head of Origination; Head of Syndication   Tsutomu Homma *Executive Director* ☎ **2913 9250**
Head of Sales; Head of Trading; Trading - Sovereigns, Corporates, High-yield   Koichiro Matsumoto *Director* ☎ **2913 9211**

Libor-Based / Floating-Rate Products
FRN Origination; FRN Sales; Asset Swaps; Asset Swaps (Sales)   Koichiro Matsumoto *Director* ☎ **2913 9211**

Medium-Term Notes
Head of Origination   Tsutomu Homma *Executive Director* ☎ **2913 9250**
Head of Structuring; Head of Sales   Koichiro Matsumoto *Director* ☎ **2913 9211**

Private Placements
Head of Origination   Tetsuya Kobayashi *Director* ☎ **2913 9260**
Head of Sales; Head of Structuring   Koichiro Matsumoto *Director* ☎ **2913 9211**

Asset-Backed Securities / Securitization
Head of Trading   Koichiro Matsumoto *Director* ☎ **2913 9211**

Mortgage-Backed Securities
Head of Trading   Koichiro Matsumoto *Director* ☎ **2913 9211**

Fixed-Income Repo
Head of Repo; Matched Book Manager; Sales   Koichiro Matsumoto *Director* ☎ **2913 9211**

Equity Capital Markets
Tel: 2845 9177
Country Head   Koichiro Matsumoto *Director* ☎ **2913 9211**

Domestic Equities
Head of Origination; Head of Syndication   Tsutomu Homma *Executive Director* ☎ **2913 9250**

www.euromoneydirectory.com   HONG KONG, CHINA (+852)

International Equities
Head of Origination; Head of Syndication   Tsutomu Homma *Executive Director* ☏ **2913 9250**
Head of Sales; Head of Trading   Koichiro Matsumoto *Director* ☏ **2913 9211**

Convertibles / Equity-Linked
Head of Origination; Head of Syndication   Tsutomu Homma *Executive Director* ☏ **2913 9250**
Head of Sales; Head of Trading   Koichiro Matsumoto *Director* ☏ **2913 9211**

Warrants
Head of Sales; Head of Trading   Koichiro Matsumoto *Director* ☏ **2913 9211**

Money Markets
Tel: 2845 9177

Domestic Commercial Paper
Head of Origination   Tsutomu Homma *Executive Director* ☏ **2913 9250**
Head of Sales; Head of Trading   Koichiro Matsumoto *Director* ☏ **2913 9211**

Eurocommercial Paper
Head of Origination   Tsutomu Homma *Executive Director* ☏ **2913 9250**
Head of Sales; Head of Trading   Koichiro Matsumoto *Director* ☏ **2913 9211**

Foreign Exchange
Head of Institutional Sales; Corporate Sales;   Koichiro Matsumoto *Director* ☏ **2913 9211**
Head of Trading

Risk Management
Head of Risk Management   Takehiro Sakurai *Managing Director & Chief Executive* ☏ **2913 9201**

Other Departments
Proprietary Trading   Koichiro Matsumoto *Director* ☏ **2913 9211**

Fukuoka Finance International Limited   Subsidiary Company
2201 Alexandra House, 16/20 Chater Road, Central, Hong Kong
Tel: 2524 2169 **Fax:** 2845 9250 **Telex:** 89497 FUKUB HX

Senior Executive Officers
General Manager   Mr Suzuki

Goldman Sachs (Asia) LLC
37th Floor, Asia Pacific Finance Tower, Citibank Plaza, 3 Garden Road, Central, Hong Kong
Tel: 2978 1000 **Fax:** 2978 0400

Senior Executive Officers
Chairman   John Thornton
President & Managing Director   Philip Murphy

Equity Capital Markets
Other (Domestic Equities)
Equities   Peter Mallinson
                                            Keith Baum

Guangdong Development Bank   Representative Office
Room 3202, 9 Queen's Road, Central, Hong Kong
Tel: 2851 6369; 2850 6738 **Fax:** 2850 4804

Senior Executive Officers
Chief Representative   Wang Xin

Hachijuni Asia Limited   Subsidiary Company
Suite 301/3, Three Exchange Square, 8 Connaught Place, Central, Hong Kong
Tel: 2845 4188 **Fax:** 2810 1706 **Telex:** 80709 HACHK HX

Senior Executive Officers
Vice Chairman   Masaru Sakamoto
Chairman   Minoru Chino
Chief Executive Officer   Katsuhiko Miyashita *Manager*
Chief Operating Officer   Masao Mizuya *Manager*
Director   Koichi Sato
Director   Kazuo Miyajima

HONG KONG, CHINA (+852)   www.euromoneydirectory.com

The Hachijuni Bank Limited
Full Branch Office

Suite 301/3, Three Exchange Square, 8 Connaught Place, Central, Hong Kong
Tel: 2845 4188 Fax: 2537 1757 Telex: 80709 HACHK HX

Senior Executive Officers
General Manager   Koichi Sato
Chief Executive Officer   Tomoo Kaneko *Manager*
Treasurer   Shigeru Ayabe *Manager*

Hamburgische Landesbank - Girozentrale
Full Branch Office

22nd Floor, Two Pacific Place, 88 Queensway, Hong Kong
Tel: 2843 2688 Fax: 2845 9018 Telex: 74539 HLGHK HX Swift: HALA HK HH

Senior Executive Officers
Chief Executive Officer   Juergen Niemann *General Manager, Banking*
                          Ewald Mueller *GM, International Finance*
Treasurer   Alan Chan *Treasury Manager*

Other Departments
Private Banking   A Joern Vosswinkel *Manager*
Correspondent Banking   Jaime Leung *Manager*

Administration
Technology & Systems
                          Frankie Ho *Senior Manager*

Hana Finance Asia Limited
Subsidiary Company

64A Bank of China Tower, 1 Garden Road, Central, Hong Kong
Tel: 2522 3646 Fax: 2526 2999 Telex: 87944 HNFH HK HX Swift: HNBN HK HH

Senior Executive Officers
Chief Executive Officer   Ju-Kyung Kim *Managing Director & Chief Executive*

Debt Capital Markets / Fixed Income
Regional Head   Kyu Tae Han *Director*

Libor-Based / Floating-Rate Products
FRN Origination   Hwan Ki Cho *Manager*

Syndicated Lending
Regional Head   Hwan Ki Cho *Manager*

Loan-Related Activities
Trade Finance; Structured Trade Finance   Hwan Ki Cho *Manager*

Money Markets
Regional Head   Kyu Tae Han *Director*

Foreign Exchange
Regional Head   Kyu Tae Han *Director*

Settlement / Clearing
Regional Head   Hwan Ki Cho *Manager*

Other Departments
Correspondent Banking   Hwan Ki Cho *Manager*

Hang Seng Bank Limited
Head Office

83 Des Voeux Road, Central, Hong Kong
Tel: 2825 5111 Fax: 2845 9301 Telex: 73311, 73323, 75225 Swift: HASE HK HH
Website: www.hangseng.com

Senior Executive Officers
Chairman   David G Eldon
Chief Executive Officer   Vincent Cheng *Vice Chairman & Acting Chief Executive*
                          Roger K H Luk *MD & Deputy Chief Executive*
General Manager   Peter M Sau
General Manager   W K Mok
General Manager   Anthony K K Wong

General - Treasury
Head of Treasury   Rita Chan *AGM, Head of Treasury*

www.euromoneydirectory.com   HONG KONG, CHINA (+852)

Other Departments
Private Banking
    Anthony K K Wong *General Manager*
Correspondent Banking
    Wing N Leung *AGM & Head of Financial Institutions*
Administration
Technology & Systems
    Paul To *AGM & Head of Technical Services*
Legal / In-House Counsel
    K W Ma *AGM & Company Secretary*
Public Relations
    Walter Cheung *AGM & Head of Corporate Communications*

Hani Securities Limited
Head Office

501 Henley Building, 5 Queen's Road, Central, Hong Kong
Tel: 2869 1318 **Fax:** 2868 0699 **Email:** haninet@haninet.com.hk
Website: www.haninet.com.hk

Senior Executive Officers
Chief Executive Officer
Financial Director
Chief Operating Officer
Executive Director
Executive Director

Daniel C M So *Director*
Livan K K Cheung *Director*
Kwan-Lung Yu *Director*
Anthony Y B Yeung
Leo H K Yeung

HG Asia Limited
Head Office

30th Floor, Edinburgh Tower, The Landmark, Central, Hong Kong
Tel: 2868 0368 **Fax:** 2810 4932 **Telex:** 74111 HX

Senior Executive Officers
Managing Director   David Roberts

The Hiroshima Bank Limited
Representative Office

15th Floor, The Hong Kong Club Building, 3A Chater Road, Central, Hong Kong
Tel: 2810 1636 **Fax:** 2810 0837

Senior Executive Officers
Chief Representative   K Wakamoto

Hoenig (Far East) Limited
Subsidiary Company

3404 Tower One, Lippo Centre, 89 Queensway, Central, Hong Kong
Tel: 2869 0788 **Fax:** 2525 7690; 2525 7726 **Telex:** 70456 HONIG HX **Email:** jfield@hoenig.com
Bloomberg: HOE <GO>
Freephone from USA Tel: 800 447 4154; **Freephone from UK Tel:** 0800 895 728; **Freephone from Japan Tel:** 00531 853 063; **Freephone from Australia Tel:** 800 504 342; **Freephone from Singapore Tel:** 800 852 3048

Senior Executive Officers
Chief Executive Officer
Financial Director
Company Secretary

Robin Green *Managing Director*
Stoney Chan *Financial Controller* [T] 2846 3515
Vivian Chan [T] 2846 3516

Others (Senior Executives)
Head of Trading
Head of Sales

Teresa Lee *Dealing Director* [T] 2846 3535 [F] 2826 9206
Ashley Dyer *Senior Vice President, Sales & Trading* [T] 2846 3540 [F] 2826 9206

Settlement / Clearing
Head of Settlement / Clearing   Thomas Lui *Settlements Manager* [T] 2846 3514 [F] 2530 4286

Other Departments
Economic Research   Jonathan Field *SVP, Sales & Marketing* [T] 2846 3589 [E] jfield@hoenig.com

Administration
Business Development   Kerry Ball *SVP, Sales & Marketing* [T] 2846 3588

Other (Administration)
Marketing & Product Development   Jonathan Field *SVP, Sales & Marketing* [T] 2846 3589 [E] jfield@hoenig.com

HONG KONG, CHINA (+852)   www.euromoneydirectory.com

The Hokuetsu Bank Limited
Representative Office

9th Floor, Far East Finance Centre, 16 Harcourt Road, Central, Hong Kong
Tel: 2529 3661 Telex: 70527 ETSBK HX

Senior Executive Officers
Chief Representative   Mr Enomodo

Hokuriku Finance (Hong Kong) Limited
Subsidiary Company

Suite 706/8, Two Exchange Square, 8 Connaught Place, Central, Hong Kong
Tel: 2755 8073; 2567 8497 Fax: 2845 3791 Telex: 81770 RIKBH HX

Senior Executive Officers
Manager   Y Tanaka
Managing Director & GM   J Takehara

The Hongkong & Shanghai Banking Corporation Limited
Head Office

Alternative trading name: HongkongBank

1 Queen's Road, Central, Hong Kong
PO Box 64, Hong Kong
Tel: 2822 1111 Fax: 2810 1112 Telex: 73201 HKBG HX Swift: HSBC HK HH
Website: www.hongkongbank.com

Senior Executive Officers
Chairman   John Strickland ☏ **2822 1200**
Chief Executive Officer   David Eldon ☏ **2822 1370**
Financial Director   Simon Penney *Chief Financial Officer* ☏ **2822 1255**
Treasurer   Stuart Gulliver *Treasurer, HongkongBank* ☏ **2822 3800**
International Division   Aman Mehta *Executive Director, International* ☏ **2822 1350**

Others (Senior Executives)
                                        Chris Langley *Executive Director* ☏ **2822 3600**
                                        Edwin Lau *Head, Personal Banking* ☏ **2822 3603**
                                        Eddie Wang *Head, China Business* ☏ **2822 2600**

General-Lending (DCM, SL)
Head of Corporate Banking   Raymond Or *Head, Corporate & Institutional Banking* ☏ **2822 3601**

Debt Capital Markets / Fixed Income
Department: HSBC Markets
Tel: 2822 1111 Fax: 2845 3703
Regional Head   Mark Bucknall *Head of Capital Markets* ☏ **2822 3076**

Domestic Government Bonds
Head of Sales   Anita Fung ☏ **2822 3018**
Head of Trading   Jack Cheung ☏ **2822 3008**
Head of Research   David Seto ☏ **2822 2025**

Non-Domestic Government Bonds
Asian Currency Bonds   Ken Yeadon ☏ **2822 3030**

Eurobonds
Head of Origination   Helen Wong ☏ **2822 3070**
Head of Syndication   Angel Chan ☏ **2822 3070**
Head of Sales   K C Chan ☏ **2822 3060**
Head of Trading   Ken Yeadon ☏ **2822 3030**
Head of Research   John Woods ☏ **2822 3070**

Fixed-Income Repo
Head of Repo   James Wong *Senior Manager, Securities Services* ☏ **2822 3121**
                                        ℻ **2845 5802**

Equity Capital Markets
Department: HSBC Investment Bank Asia / HSBC Securities Asia
Tel: 2841 8888 Fax: 2524 4961
Regional Head   Eamonn McManus *MD, Corporate Finance & Equity CM* ☏ **2841 8359**

Domestic Equities
Head of Origination   Eamonn McManus *MD, Corporate Finance & Equity CM* ☏ **2841 8359**
Head of Syndication   Tim Lambert *Head, Equity Syndication* ☏ **2996 6578**
Head of Sales; Head of Trading   Michael Bugel ☏ **2996 6555**
Head of Research   Guy Ashton ☏ **2996 6556**

www.euromoneydirectory.com   HONG KONG, CHINA (+852)

International Equities
Head of Origination — Eamonn McManus *MD, Corporate Finance & Equity CM* ☎ 2841 8359
Head of Syndication — Tim Lambert *Head, Equity Syndication* ☎ 2996 6578
Head of Sales; Head of Trading — Andrew Willner ☎ 2996 6600

Convertibles / Equity-Linked
Head of Origination — Eamonn McManus *MD, Corporate Finance & Equity CM* ☎ 2841 8359
Head of Syndication — Tim Lambert *Head, Equity Syndication* ☎ 2996 6578
Head of Sales — Christopher Lee *Head, Convertible Sales* ☎ 2996 6951

Warrants
Head of Sales; Head of Trading — Abdullah Rahail *Head, Asian Derivatives Trading* ☎ 2996 6726

Equity Repo / Securities Lending
Head — James Wong *Senior Manager, Securities Services* ☎ 2822 3121
F 2845 5802
Marketing & Product Development — Samuel Cheng *Manager, Stock Lending* ☎ 2822 3104 F 2537 9281
Head of Trading — Maria Chang *Trading Assistant*
Maria Chang *Assistant Trader*

Syndicated Lending
Department: HSBC Investment Bank Asia Limited
Tel: 2841 8888 **Fax:** 2524 4961
Regional Head — Paul Tay *Director, Syndications & Property Finance* ☎ 2841 8434

Loan-Related Activities
Trade Finance — Brian Allen *Director & Head, Project Finance / Syndications* ☎ 2841 8266
Chris Hothersall *Head, Trade Services Asia Pacific* ☎ 2822 2800
Project Finance; Structured Trade Finance — Brian Allen *Director & Head, Project Finance / Syndications* ☎ 2841 8266
Leasing & Asset Finance — Michael Caddy *Director & Head, Aircraft & Structured Finance*
☎ 2841 8289

Money Markets
Department: HSBC Markets
Fax: 2845 3703
Country Head — Jack Cheung ☎ 2822 3008

Foreign Exchange
Department: HSBC Markets
Fax: 2845 3703
Country Head — Mike Hillier *Head, FX & Institutional Sales* ☎ 2822 3838
Corporate Sales — Anna Leung *Head, Corporate Treasury Marketing* ☎ 2822 3896
C B Lim ☎ 2822 3896

Risk Management
Department: HSBC Markets
Fax: 2845 3703
Country Head — Anders Haagen *Risk Manager* ☎ 2822 3850

Fixed Income Derivatives / Risk Management
IR Swaps Sales / Marketing — Simon Cooke *Head, Financial Products Sales* ☎ 2822 3818
IR Swaps Trading — Ian Emmett *Head, N Asia Derivatives Trading* ☎ 2822 2176

Foreign Exchange Derivatives / Risk Management
Vanilla FX option Trading — Masatsugu Yoshida *Senior Currency & Interest Rate Trader* ☎ 2822 3899
Jimmy Ho ☎ 2822 3899

Exotic Options (Barriers, Range, Timers, Digitals, Faders etc)
Sales — Gordon Ho *Head, Specialised Derivatives Group* ☎ 2822 2148

Corporate Finance / M&A Advisory
Department: HSBC Investment Bank Asia Limited
Tel: 2841 8888 **Fax:** 2524 4961
Regional Head — Eamonn McManus *MD, Corporate Finance & Equity CM* ☎ 2841 8359

Global Custody
Department: Asia-Pacific Securities Services
Fax: 2822 2020
Country Head — Nicholas Bryan *Head, Securities Services* ☎ 2822 2020
Jeremy Davies *Head, Security Service* ☎ 2822 2021

Other Departments
Commodities / Bullion — Franue Lam ☎ 2822 2890
Private Banking — Monica Wong *MD, Private Banking* ☎ 2899 8777
Correspondent Banking — Geoff Armstrong *Head, Financial Institutions - Asia Pacific* ☎ 2822 3694
Martin Hale *Head, Financial Institutions - Asia Pacific* ☎ 2822 3694
Cash Management — David Tam *Senior Executive, Payments & Cash Management* ☎ 2822 1111

Administration
Technology & Systems
Y B Yeung *Head of Technical Services* ☎ 2822 1604

HONG KONG, CHINA (+852)   www.euromoneydirectory.com

The Hongkong & Shanghai Banking Corporation Limited (cont)
Legal / In-House Counsel
　　　　Richard Bennett *Head of Legal & Compliance* ☎ 2822 1232
Compliance
　　　　Richard Bennett *Head of Legal & Compliance* ☎ 2822 1232
Public Relations
　　　　Michael Broadbet *Head, Group Public Affairs - Asia* ☎ 2822 1133

The Hongkong Chinese Bank Limited

Lippo Centre, 89 Queensway, Hong Kong
PO Box 194, Hong Kong
Tel: 2867 6833 **Fax:** 2845 9221 **Telex:** 73749 HONCH HX **Swift:** HKCB HK HH **Reuters:** HCBB-E (Monitor)

Senior Executive Officers
Chairman	Mochtar Riady ☎ 2867 6888 ⌂ 2840 0408
Chief Executive Officer	David Pat Lam Chan *Managing Director & Chief Executive* ☎ 2867 6833 ⌂ 2522 6201
	Robert Kor *Deputy Managing Director* ☎ 2867 6833 ⌂ 2801 4305
Treasurer	Chi Hong Kwan ☎ 2522 0812 ⌂ 2868 3641
Senior General Manager	Peter Chan ☎ 2867 6833 ⌂ 2845 9221
General Manager	Norman Ho ☎ 2166 9288 ⌂ 2537 1000
General Manager	David Yau ☎ 2867 6833 ⌂ 2845 9221

Others (Senior Executives)
Executive Director	Jia Yan Fan ☎ 2867 6833 ⌂ 2234 9862
	Roger K M Yuen ☎ 2867 6833 ⌂ 2234 9862
Director	T C Chang ☎ 2867 6833 ⌂ 2522 6201
	Davy Lee *Corporate Secretary* ☎ 2867 6888
	Andrew Hau *Company Secretary* ☎ 2867 6888

Syndicated Lending
Loan-Related Activities
Trade Finance   Alex Lee *Senior Manager* ☎ 2166 9100 ⌂ 2530 1365

Money Markets
Tel: 2522 0812 **Fax:** 2868 3641 **Telex:** 89825
Head of Money Markets   Y C Au *Senior Dealer* ☎ 2522 0812 ⌂ 2868 3641

Foreign Exchange
Tel: 2522 0812 **Fax:** 2868 3641 **Telex:** 89825
Head of Foreign Exchange   K M Poon *Sub Manager* ☎ 2522 0812 ⌂ 2868 3641

Other Departments
Chief Credit Officer   Norman Ho *General Manager* ☎ 2166 9288 ⌂ 2537 1000
Administration
Head of Administration   Yau Man Chan *Manager* ☎ 2166 9328 ⌂ 2960 0217
Public Relations
　　　　Polly Ling *Manager*

Accounts / Audit
Accounts	Lawrence Tang *Assistant General Manager* ☎ 2166 9350 ⌂ 2801 4509
Audit	Lewis Lai *Assistant General Manager* ☎ 2166 9339 ⌂ 2960 0217

HSBC Investment Bank Asia Limited   Subsidiary Company

Formerly known as: Wardley Limited
Level 15, 1 Queen's Road, Central, Hong Kong
PO Box 8983, Hong Kong
Tel: 2841 8888 **Fax:** 2868 0065; 2524 4947 **Telex:** 75440 HIAHK HX **Swift:** WDLY HK HH **Telerate:** 2705, 9931

Senior Executive Officers
Chairman & Chief Executive	Kevin Anthony Westley
Financial Director	Walter Kam-Tong Au *Director of Finance*

Others (Senior Executives)
Member of the Board of Directors   Sabrina Mo-Fai Chan Or
　　　　　　　　　　　　　　　　Anrew Shiu-Keung Chu
　　　　　　　　　　　　　　　　Gavin Walker Edie
　　　　　　　　　　　　　　　　David Gordon Eldon
　　　　　　　　　　　　　　　　Kah Yeok Koh
　　　　　　　　　　　　　　　　Christopher Patrick Langley
　　　　　　　　　　　　　　　　William Kik Jeremiah Sheehan
　　　　　　　　　　　　　　　　Brian John Moss

www.euromoneydirectory.com   HONG KONG, CHINA (+852)

Others (Senior Executives) (cont)
Kenneth Yiu-Sun Sit
Paul Wing-Kit Tay
Murray Maxwell Ashdown
Peter Cheong-Yan Au-Yang

General-Lending (DCM, SL)
Head of Corporate Banking   Alexander Robert P Affleck *Director & Credit Controller*

Relationship Manager
Financial Brokerage   John Gin-Chung Seto *CEO, Wardley Financial Services Limited*

Equity Capital Markets
Head of Equity Capital Markets   Eamonn McManus *Director & Head*

Syndicated Lending

Loan-Related Activities
Shipping Finance   Chris Ohlson *MD, HSBC Shipbrokers Limited*

Other (Trade Finance)
Debt Finance   Michael John Caddy *Director & Head, Aircraft & Structured Finance*
Brian Jeffrey Allen *Director & Head, Project Finance / Syndications*

Corporate Finance / M&A Advisory
Head of Corporate Finance   Eamonn McManus *Director & Head*

Settlement / Clearing
Operations   K K Chin *Assistant Director, Finance*

Other Departments
Private Banking   Mimi Monica Wong *Managing Director*

Administration

Technology & Systems
ITS   Kwok-Bun Lo *Director & Head, Business Planning & Systems*

Legal / In-House Counsel
Jonathan Piers Latham *Director & Head, Legal & Compliance*

Corporate Communications
Saw Choo Dickson *Head*

Hua Chiao Commercial Bank Limited   Head Office

88-98 Des Voeux Road, Central, Hong Kong
Tel: 2542 9888 **Fax:** 2543 4035; 2543 5339 **Telex:** 83502 HCCB HX **Swift:** HCCB HK HH
Website: www.hccb.com

Senior Executive Officers
Chairman   Khoe Boen Tjoen
Chief Executive Officer   So Yuen Hing **2542 9842**
Treasurer   Chiu Man Ming **2542 9768**
Managing Director / General Manager   So Yuen Hing **2542 9842**

Debt Capital Markets / Fixed Income
Tel: 2543 8602 **Fax:** 2815 5731
Head of Debt Capital Markets   Lui Sai Mun **2542 8767**

Eurobonds
Head of Origination   Lui Sai Mun **2542 8767**

Libor-Based / Floating-Rate Products
FRN Origination; Asset Swaps   Lui Sai Mun **2542 8767**

Money Markets
Tel: 2543 8602 **Fax:** 2815 5731
Head of Money Markets   Lui Sai Mun **2542 8767**

Domestic Commercial Paper
Head of Origination   Lui Sai Mun **2542 8767**

Eurocommercial Paper
Head of Origination   Lui Sai Mun **2542 8767**

Foreign Exchange
Tel: 2543 9602 **Fax:** 2815 5731
Head of Foreign Exchange   Lui Sai Mun **2542 8767**

Other Departments
Correspondent Banking   Chiu Man Ming **2542 9768**

HONG KONG, CHINA (+852)   www.euromoneydirectory.com

Hua Nan Commercial Bank Limited
Full Branch Office

Suite 5601-5603, 56th Floor, Central Plaza, 18 Harbour Road, Wanchai, Hong Kong
Tel: 2824 0288 Fax: 2824 2515; 2824 2573 Telex: 87363 Swift: HNBK HK HH Reuters: HNAN

Senior Executive Officers
Chief Executive Officer; Financial Director; Shindar Chuang *SVP & General Manager* ☏ 2511 3861
Chief Operating Officer
Treasurer Jonathan Fang *Senior Officer* ☏ 2824 0350
SVP & General Manager Shindar Chuang ☏ 2511 3861

Debt Capital Markets / Fixed Income
Global Head Jonathan Fang *Senior Officer* ☏ 2824 0350

Government Bonds
Head of Syndication; Head of Origination Jonathan Fang *Senior Officer* ☏ 2824 0350

Eurobonds
Head of Sales; Head of Trading Jonathan Fang *Senior Officer* ☏ 2824 0350

Libor-Based / Floating-Rate Products
FRN Sales; FRN Trading; Asset Swaps; Asset Swaps (Sales) Jonathan Fang *Senior Officer* ☏ 2824 0350

Fixed-Income Repo
Head of Repo Jonathan Fang *Senior Officer* ☏ 2824 0350

Syndicated Lending
Head of Origination; Head of Syndication; Head of Trading Rudy Chang *Deputy Manager* ☏ 2824 0190

Loan-Related Activities
Trade Finance Janet Chang *Assistant General Manager* ☏ 2824 0362

Money Markets
Head of Money Markets Jonathan Fang *Senior Officer* ☏ 2824 0350

Domestic Commercial Paper
Head of Sales; Head of Trading Jonathan Fang *Senior Officer* ☏ 2824 0350

Eurocommercial Paper
Head of Sales; Head of Trading Jonathan Fang *Senior Officer* ☏ 2824 0350

Foreign Exchange
Head of Foreign Exchange; Head of Trading Jonathan Fang *Senior Officer* ☏ 2824 0350

FX Traders / Sales People
Dealer Frances Lin *Senior Officer* ☏ 2824 0288

Risk Management
Head of Risk Management Mei-Ying Shih *Manager* ☏ 2824 0227

Other Currency Swap / FX Options Personnel
Head of Swaps Jonathan Fang *Senior Officer* ☏ 2824 0350

Settlement / Clearing
Head of Settlement / Clearing Janet Chang *Assistant General Manager* ☏ 2824 0362
Fixed-Income Settlement Keith Pang *Assistant Manager* ☏ 2824 0288

Other Departments
Correspondent Banking Mei-Ying Shih *Manager* ☏ 2824 0227

Administration
Accounts / Audit Mark Liu *Deputy Manager* ☏ 2824 0288

HypoVereinsbank
Full Branch Office

Formerly known as: Bayerische Hypotheken-und Wechsel Bank AG
13th Floor, Citic Tower, 1 Tim Mei Avenue, Central, Hong Kong
Tel: 2533 4000 Fax: 2533 4700 Telex: 67774 HYPO HX Swift: HYPO HK HH

Senior Executive Officers
Treasurer Ross Atkinson
General Manager J Hetzler

General-Lending (DCM, SL)
Head of Corporate Banking Davina Au *Head*
Canny Lo *Associate Director*

Syndicated Lending
Head of Credit Committee Herbert Sheir *Head of Credit*

HONG KONG, CHINA (+852)

Global Custody
Other (Global Custody)
Fund Transfer   Mo Cheng *Head*

IBJ Asia Limited — Subsidiary Company
74-2 Pacific Place, 88 Queen's Way, Hong Kong
Tel: 2103 3838 **Fax:** 2103 3703 **Telex:** 75203 IBJAS HX

Senior Executive Officers
Chairman   N Izawa
Settlement / Clearing
Operations   E Yamanouchi *Head of Operations*
Administration
Compliance
                                  M Fukuda *Head, Compliance*

Indosuez WI Carr Securities Limited — Subsidiary Company
43rd Floor, One Exchange Square, 8 Connaught Road, Central, Hong Kong
Tel: 2820 7373 **Fax:** 2868 1524 **Telex:** 73036 WICAR HX

Senior Executive Officers
Chief Executive Officer   Nicholas Harbinson *Chief Executive* ☎ 2820 7386 📠 2524 2753

Others (Senior Executives)
Sales   David Williamson *Head of Sales, Hong Kong* ☎ 2820 7419

Debt Capital Markets / Fixed Income
Private Placements
Head of Origination   Erh-Fei Liu *Regional Head, Investment Banking* ☎ 2848 9069

Equity Capital Markets
Other (Domestic Equities)
Asian Equity Trading   Nakhle Zeidan *Head* ☎ 2820 7390 📠 2537 7402

International Equities
Head of Origination   Erh-Fei Liu *Regional Head, Investment Banking* ☎ 2848 9069
Head of Sales   Nicholas Harbinson *Chief Executive* ☎ 2820 7386 📠 2524 2753
Head of Trading   Nakhle Zeidan *Head* ☎ 2820 7390 📠 2537 7402
Head of Research   Malcolm Brown *Group Head, Research* ☎ +65 439 9557

Convertibles / Equity-Linked
Head of Origination   Erh-Fei Liu *Regional Head, Investment Banking* ☎ 2848 9069
Head of Sales   Nicholas Harbinson *Chief Executive* ☎ 2820 7386 📠 2524 2753
Head of Trading   Nakhle Zeidan *Head* ☎ 2820 7390 📠 2537 7402
Head of Research   Malcolm Brown *Group Head, Research* ☎ +65 439 9557

Corporate Finance / M&A Advisory
Global Head   Jean-Louis Vinciguerra *Regional Head, Corporate & Investment Services*
                                  ☎ +65 439 9903
Regional Head   Keisuke Kasagi *Director* ☎ 2820 7738

Indover Asia Limited — Subsidiary Company
13th Floor, Tower II, Admiralty Centre, Queensway, Hong Kong
PO Box 24, Hong Kong
Tel: 2528 5300 **Fax:** 2529 6914 **Telex:** 60317 INAS HX **Swift:** IOVE HK HH **Reuters:** IOAH

Senior Executive Officers
Chief Executive Officer   Permadi Gandapradja *Managing Director & Chief Executive*
                                  Lourdes A Salazar *Deputy MD & Chief Executive*
Treasurer   Eric C S Cheung *Senior Manager & Treasurer*

Debt Capital Markets / Fixed Income
Global Head   Eric C S Cheung *Senior Manager & Treasurer*

Administration
Business Development   Andres E C Pascual *General Manager*

HONG KONG, CHINA (+852)   www.euromoneydirectory.com

The Industrial Bank of Japan Limited

17th Floor, Two Pacific Place, 88 Queensway, Hong Kong
Tel: 2103 3000 Fax: 2845 9187 Telex: 63035 IBJBR HX

Senior Executive Officers
General Manager   Shinichi Watanabe

Industrial Bank of Korea
Full Branch Office

Suite 2401B, Bank of America Tower, 12 Harcourt Road, Hong Kong
Tel: 2521 1398 Fax: 2596 0920 Telex: 79177 IBKHKHX Swift: IBKO HK H1

Senior Executive Officers
General Manager   Young Chin Kim
Deputy General Manager   Hak Lim Dong

Others (Senior Executives)
    Yong Ho Ahn *Manager*
    Gyoon Ik Lee *Manager*
    Young Bae Park *Manager*

Syndicated Lending
Head of Syndicated Lending   Hak Lim Dong *Deputy General Manager*

Other (Syndicated Lending)
Commercial Loans   Yong Ho Ahn *Manager*

Loan-Related Activities
Trade Finance   Gyoon Ik Lee *Manager*

Administration
Accounts / Audit
Accounting   Young Bae Park *Manager*

ING Barings
Full Branch Office

Alternative trading name: ING Capital Markets (Hong Kong) Limited
8th/11th Floors, Alexandra House, 16 Chater Road, Central, Hong Kong
PO Box 2837, Hong Kong
Tel: 2846 3888 Fax: 2810 4412; 2526 8507 Telex: 76049 INGB HX Swift: INGB HK HH Reuters: INGB; NMBK

Senior Executive Officers
Country Manager   Peter Valks
General Manager   Willem R C Pijpers

Others (Senior Executives)
    K G Gong *Assistant General Manager*

Other Departments
Department: ING Baring Private Bank
Private Banking   Raymond Cheung *Manager*

Administration
Head of Administration   Simon Chu *Vice President*

ING Barings Asia

8th Floor, Three Exchange Square, 8 Connaught Place, Central, Hong Kong
Tel: 2848 8488 Fax: 2868 5192

Senior Executive Officers
Others (Senior Executives)
Regional Head, Asia   David Hudson

ING Barings Futures & Options Clearing Services
Subsidiary Company

8th Floor, Three Exchange Square, 8 Connaught Place, Central, Hong Kong
Tel: 2848 8590 Fax: 2801 4502

Senior Executive Officers
Director   Fred Hochberger ☎ **2848 8595**

www.euromoneydirectory.com   HONG KONG, CHINA (+852)

ING Trust (Hong Kong)

Room 905, 9th Floor, Alexandra House, 16 Chater Road, Central, Hong Kong
PO Box 12252, Hong Kong
Tel: 2521 2783 Fax: 2877 3515 Telex: 76049 INGB HK

Senior Executive Officers
Deputy General Manager   Queenie Ngai

International Bank of Asia Limited   Subsidiary Company

Formerly known as: Sun Hung Kai Bank
International Bank of Asia Building, 38 Des Voeux Road, Central, Hong Kong
GPO BOX 9878, Hong Kong
Tel: 2842 6222 Fax: 2810 1483 Telex: 63394 IBA HX Swift: IBAL HK HH Email: iba-info@iba.com.hk Reuters: IBAX
Cable: "IBAL HK" HONG KONG
Website: www.iba.com.hk

Senior Executive Officers
Chairman   Sheikh Ali Jarrah Al Sabah
Chief Executive Officer   Mike Murad
Financial Director   David Chan
Treasurer   Davy Kwan
Managing Director / General Manager   Mike Murad
Company Secretary   Ivan Young

Others (Senior Executives)
Head Of Consumer Banking   Bashar Samra *Executive Vice President*
Head of Credit Administration   James Leung *Senior Vice President*

General-Lending (DCM, SL)
Head of Corporate Banking   Michael Ipson *Executive Vice President*

General-Investment
Head of Investment   Betty Brow

Syndicated Lending
Head of Hire Purchase & Leasing   Francis Yeung *Senior Vice President*

Settlement / Clearing
Operations   Lana Lo *Head, Operations, SVP*

Other Departments
Private Banking   Jeffrey Li

Jardine Fleming Limited   Head Office

46th Floor, Jardine House, 1 Connaught Place, Central, Hong Kong
Tel: 2843 8888; 2840 6888 Fax: 2530 4698; 2522 9804 Telex: 75608 FLEDG HX Swift: JFCO HK HH
Reuters: JFHK, JFHD Telerate: 9525
Website: www.jfleming.com

Senior Executive Officers
Chairman   Henry Strutt ☏ **2843 8875**
Financial Director   Simon Heale *Group Finance Director* ☏ **2843 8453**
Managing Director / General Manager   Henry Strutt ☏ **2843 8875**
Group Company Secretary   Sarina Cassidy ☏ **2840 6870**

Debt Capital Markets / Fixed Income
Department: Capital Market
Fax: 2810 8819
Head of Fixed Income Sales   George De Tilly ☏ **2843 8733**
                                  Roger Wong ☏ **2978 7263**

Fixed-Income Research
Head of Fixed Income; Head of Credit   Daniel Leung ☏ **2840 6467**
Research

Equity Capital Markets
Department: Capital Markets
Fax: 2810 8819
Head of Equity Capital Markets   Russell Julius ☏ **2843 8792**

International Equities
Head of Sales   Colin Bradbury ☏ **2843 8885**
Head of Trading   Mark Graham ☏ **2978 7462**

HONG KONG, CHINA (+852)

www.euromoneydirectory.com

Jardine Fleming Limited (cont)

Equity Research
Head of Equity Research — Andrew Houston ☎ 2840 6131
Convertibles / Equity-Linked
Head of Trading — Matthew Bremner ☎ 2843 8510
Equity Repo / Securities Lending
Head — Jennifer Magarity *Manager* ✉ jennifer.magarity@jfleming.com
Syndicated Lending
Tel: 2843 8888 Fax: 2522 9804
Head of Origination; Head of Syndication — Joseph Chiu *Director* ☎ 2843 8878
Money Markets
Tel: 2843 8888 Fax: 2523 7746
Global Head — Stephen Cheung *Director* ☎ 2843 8846
Foreign Exchange
Tel: 2843 8888 Fax: 2523 7746
Head of Foreign Exchange — Eric Fu *Director* ☎ 2843 8463
FX Traders / Sales People
Assistant Director — Puay Khoon Saw ☎ 2843 8463
Risk Management
Department: Credit Department
Tel: 2843 8872 Fax: 2537 1662
Head of Risk Management — Vish Sowani *Head of Group Risk Management* ☎ 2843 8720
Settlement / Clearing
Head of Settlement / Clearing — William Fishman *Director* ☎ 2840 6859
Equity Settlement; Fixed-Income Settlement — Donald Barnfather *Assistant Director* ☎ 2199 3401
Administration
Head of Administration — Betty Law *Director* ☎ 2843 8294
Technology & Systems
Jeremy Mellors *Director of IT* ☎ 2978 7139
Legal / In-House Counsel
Mark Roberts *Group General Legal Counsel* ☎ 2843 8781
Compliance
David Robinson *Head of Group Compliance* ☎ 2978 7309
Public Relations
David Dodwell *Group Corporate Communications & Public Affairs Di*
☎ 2840 6776
Corporate Communications
David Dodwell *Group Corporate Communications & Public Affairs Di*
☎ 2840 6776
Accounts / Audit
Roy Kinnear *Group Financial Controller* ☎ 2843 8700

Jardine Fleming Securities Limited — Subsidiary Company

45th Floor, Jardine House, 1 Connaught Place, Central, Hong Kong
Tel: 2843 8888; 2843 8785 Fax: 2810 6028
Website: www.jfleming.com

Senior Executive Officers
Chief Executive Officer — Mark Dowie *Group Executive Director* ☎ 2843 8779 ✆ 2810 6558

Jian Sing Bank Limited — Head Office

Formerly known as: Hongkong Industrial & Commercial Bank Limited
99/105 Des Voeux Road, Central, Hong Kong
Tel: 2541 0088 Fax: 2544 7145 Telex: 65712 JISBK HX Swift: JSHK HKHH Email: admin@jsb.com.hk
Cable: JIANSINGBK

Senior Executive Officers
Chairman — David S Y Wong ☎ 2507 8866 ✆ 2598 7177
Chief Executive Officer — Patrick T Ho *General Manager* ☎ 2541 0088 ✆ 2543 9862
Chief Operating Officer — Jeffrey Lam *Division Head Operations* ☎ 2534 9383 ✆ 2543 4093
Treasurer — Zhong-Yun Lu *Deputy Division Head, FX & Treasury* ☎ 2534 9312
✆ 2544 3854

Others (Senior Executives)
Deputy Chief Executive — Joseph Yan ☎ 2534 9339 ✆ 2543 9862

www.euromoneydirectory.com　　　HONG KONG, CHINA (+852)

Syndicated Lending
Tel: 2534 9862
Regional Head　　　　　　　　　Philip Kan *Division Head Credit & Marketing* T 2534 9328 F 2543 9862

Loan-Related Activities
Trade Finance　　　　　　　　Louisa Lam T 2534 9381 F 2543 4093
Project Finance　　　　　　　Philip Kan *Division Head Credit & Marketing* T 2534 9328 F 2543 9862

Money Markets
Tel: 2544 3854
Regional Head　　　　　　　　　Zhong-Yun Lu *Deputy Division Head, FX & Treasury* T 2534 9312
　　　　　　　　　　　　　　　F 2544 3854

Domestic Commercial Paper
Head of Origination　　　　　Philip Kan *Division Head Credit & Marketing* T 2534 9328 F 2543 9862

Foreign Exchange
Tel: 2544 3854
Country Head　　　　　　　　　Zhong-Yun Lu *Deputy Division Head, FX & Treasury* T 2534 9312
　　　　　　　　　　　　　　　F 2544 3854

Settlement / Clearing
Tel: 2543 4093
Foreign Exchange Settlement　Steven Lau *Deputy Manager* T 2534 9411 F 2543 4093

Other Departments
Correspondent Banking　　　　Jeffrey Lam *Division Head Operations* T 2534 9383 F 2543 4093

The Joyo Bank Limited　　　　　　　　　　　　　　Representative Office
Suite 1302, The Hong Kong Club Building, 3A Chater Road, Central, Hong Kong
Tel: 2521 3228 **Fax:** 2521 3773

Senior Executive Officers
Chief Representative　　　　N Suzuki

JP Morgan (Hong Kong) Limited
24th Floor, Edinburgh Tower, 15 Queen's Road, Central, Hong Kong
Tel: 2841 1311 **Reuters:** MGTH-J **Cable:** JPMORGANHK

Debt Capital Markets / Fixed Income
Regional Head　　　　　　　　Mark Jones *Head of Capital Markets*

Administration
Corporate Communications
　　　　　　　　　　　　　　Benny Chan *Head* F 2841 1135

The Kagoshima Bank Limited　　　　　　　　　　Representative Office
3208 Jardine House, 1 Connaught Place, Central, Hong Kong
Tel: 2521 5419 **Fax:** 2868 0030

Senior Executive Officers
Chief Representative　　　　Takashi Tashiro
Senior Executive Officer　　Masahiro Shikishi

KBC Bank NV　　　　　　　　　　　　　　　　　　Full Branch Office
60th Floor, Central Plaza, 18 Harbour Road, Wanchai, Hong Kong
Tel: 2525 9231; 2879 3388 **Fax:** 2521 5893; 2879 3300 **Telex:** 61271 KBBRU HX **Swift:** KRED HK HX **Reuters:** KBIK
Telerate: 9527

Senior Executive Officers
Chief Executive Officer　　　Umberto Arts *General Manager*
Financial Director　　　　　Grace So *Financial Controller*
Chief Operating Officer　　　Keith Yum *Senior Operations Manager*
Treasurer　　　　　　　　　Elsa Lam *Treasurer*

General-Lending (DCM, SL)
Head of Corporate Banking　　Charles Ren *Head, Commercial Banking*

Syndicated Lending
Country Head　　　　　　　　Charles Ren *Head, Commercial Banking*
Head of Credit Committee　　Umberto Arts *General Manager*

Euromoney Directory 1999　**625**

HONG KONG, CHINA (+852)　　www.euromoneydirectory.com

KBC Bank NV (cont)
Loan-Related Activities
Trade Finance　　Charles Ren *Head, Commercial Banking*
　　Lilian Au *Senior Relationship Manager*
Project Finance　　Liam Donlon *Managing Director*
　　Jackie Surtani *Head, Project Finance - Asia Pacific*
Structured Trade Finance　　Ian Brigden *Managing Director*
Leasing & Asset Finance　　Charles Ren *Head, Commercial Banking*

Money Markets
Global Head
Country Head　　Willy Kestens *Global Treasurer*
　　Elsa Lam *Treasurer*

Wholesale Deposits
Marketing; Head of Sales　　Amy Leung *Corporate Dealer*

Foreign Exchange
Global Head
Country Head　　Willy Kestens *Global Treasurer*
　　Elsa Lam *Treasurer*
Corporate Sales　　Gordan Lam *Head, Corporate Dealing*

Settlement / Clearing
Country Head　　Keith Yum *Senior Operations Manager*
Operations　　Grace So *Financial Controller*

Other Departments
Chief Credit Officer　　Andy Fung *Head of Credit* ☎ **2879 3388**

Administration
Technology & Systems
　　Richard Wong *Senior Officer, IT*

Compliance
　　Chanel Mok *Compliance Officer*

Accounts / Audit
　　Teresa Fok *Internal Auditor*
　　Grace So *Financial Controller*

KDB Asia Limited　　Subsidiary Company
Suites 2101/3, 21st Floor, Two Exchange Square, 8 Connaught Place, Central, Hong Kong
Tel: 2524 7011　**Fax:** 2810 4447; 2537 3989　**Telex:** 65276 HX
General Telex: 80439 HX

Senior Executive Officers
Managing Director　　Jeong Soo Lee ☎ **2523 5482**

Debt Capital Markets / Fixed Income
Regional Head　　Byung-Ho Lee *Associate Director* ☎ **2526 3976**

Equity Capital Markets
Regional Head　　Byung-Ho Lee *Associate Director* ☎ **2526 3976**

Syndicated Lending
Regional Head　　Sam Hwan Oh *Deputy Managing Director* ☎ **2523 3588**

Money Markets
Regional Head　　Eun Young Jung *Associate Director* ☎ **2523 5778**

Foreign Exchange
Regional Head　　Eun Young Jung *Associate Director* ☎ **2523 5778**

Risk Management
Regional Head　　Byung-Ho Lee *Associate Director* ☎ **2526 3976**

Corporate Finance / M&A Advisory
Global Head　　Sam Hwan Oh *Deputy Managing Director* ☎ **2523 3588**

Settlement / Clearing
Regional Head　　Dong Ju Park *Executive Director* ☎ **2523 5770**

Keppel Bank of Singapore Limited　　Full Branch Office
17th Floor, 9 Queens Road, Central, Hong Kong
Tel: 2956 1878　**Fax:** 2956 3977　**Telex:** 85721 KBHK HX

Senior Executive Officers
Chief Executive Officer　　Daniel Ang Kok Thye *General Manager*
Chief Operating Officer　　Johnny Leong Tuck Kong *Deputy General Manager*

www.euromoneydirectory.com   HONG KONG, CHINA (+852)

Syndicated Lending
Head of Origination   Daniel Ang Kok Thye *General Manager*
Head of Syndication   Catherine Wong *Account Manager*
Loan-Related Activities
Project Finance   Catherine Wong *Account Manager*
Structured Trade Finance   Stephen Lam *Senior Bills Officer*
Money Markets
Head of Money Markets   Johnny Lee *Dealer*
Foreign Exchange
Head of Foreign Exchange   Johnny Lee *Dealer*
Other Departments
Correspondent Banking   Catherine Wong *Account Manager*

Kexim Asia Limited   Subsidiary Company

Suites 2017-22, 20th Floor, Two Pacific Place, 88 Queensway, Central, Hong Kong
Tel: 2810 0182 **Fax:** 2810 4460; 2801 7862 **Telex:** 63104 EXIMB HX
Senior Executive Officers
Chairman & Managing Director   Koo Moon-Ki ☏ **2810 0182**
Chief Executive Officer   Choi Jung-ha *Deputy Managing Director* ☏ **2810 0182**
Chief Operating Officer   Lee Young-Jae *Director*
Others (Senior Executives)
                                Hong Ki-Chul *Chief Accountant*
                                Han Gang-Han *Manager*
                                Yoon Hee-Sung *Manager*
                                Lee Sung-Joon *Manager*

Kincheng Banking Corporation   Head Office

Kincheng Bank Building, 55 Des Voeux Road, Central, Hong Kong
Tel: 2843 0222 **Fax:** 2845 0116 **Telex:** 73405 KCBK HX **Swift:** KBCO HK HH **Reuters:** KBCHK **Telerate:** 9889
Website: www.great-china.net/kincheng_bank
Senior Executive Officers
Chief Executive Officer   Hung-kay Sun *Managing Director & General Manager*
Financial Director; Treasurer   Wai Chung Wong *Assistant General Manager*
International Division   Man Sze Chan *Assistant General Manager*
Others (Senior Executives)
Deputy General Manager   Cheong Wah Chan
                                Hon Wen Lau
Sub Branches   Cho Chak Li *Assistant General Manager*
Finance   Man Kuen Ng *Assistant General Manager*
Credit Management   Man Wei Ko *Assistant General Manager*
Business   Chun Charm Lim *Assistant General Manager*
Debt Capital Markets / Fixed Income
Tel: 2843 0343 **Fax:** 2524 6698
Head of Debt Capital Markets   Jenie Tan *Manager* ☏ **2843 0383**
Syndicated Lending
Department: Kincheng Finance (HK) Limited
22nd Floor, Kincheng Bank Building, 55 Des Vouex Road, Central, Hong Kong
Head of Syndication   K C Leung *Senior Manager* ☏ **2912 3933**
Loan-Related Activities
Project Finance   K C Leung *Senior Manager* ☏ **2912 3933**
Tel: 2912 3988 **Fax:** 2869 4980
Head of Origination; Head of Syndication   K C Leung *Senior Manager* ☏ **2912 3933**
Loan-Related Activities
Trade Finance   Sik Wing Tang *Senior Manager* ☏ **2843 0202**
Money Markets
Tel: 2843 0343 **Fax:** 2524 6698
Head of Money Markets   Kent Tam *Manager*
Eurocommercial Paper
Head of Trading   Jenie Tan *Manager* ☏ **2843 0383**
Foreign Exchange
Tel: 2843 0343 **Fax:** 2524 6698
Head of Foreign Exchange   Andy Ho *Deputy Manager* ☏ **2843 0393**

HONG KONG, CHINA (+852)   www.euromoneydirectory.com

Kincheng Banking Corporation (cont)
Risk Management
Tel: 2843 0343 Fax: 2524 6698
Head of Risk Management   Derek Tse *Senior Manager* ☎ **2843 0750**
Settlement / Clearing
Tel: 2843 0770 Fax: 2530 4341
Head of Settlement / Clearing   Connie Lam *Manager*
Other Departments
Chief Credit Officer   Weng Tong Lam *Senior Manager* ☎ **2843 0267**
Correspondent Banking   Sik Wing Tang *Senior Manager* ☎ **2843 0202**
Administration
Head of Administration   Mun Yee Siu *Manager* ☎ **2843 0993**
Business Development; Head of Marketing   Kam Hang Chan *Senior Manager* ☎ **2843 0205**
Accounts / Audit
                             Shuk Han Shum *Senior Manager* ☎ **2843 0384**
Other (Administration)
China Business Department   Si Keung Li *Senior Manager* ☎ **2843 0369**
Customer Investment Services Department   Muk Yiu Wong *Senior Manager* ☎ **2843 0289**
Remittance Centre   Kam Fung Wong *Manager* ☎ **2843 0382**

Kookmin Finance Asia Limited   *Subsidiary Company*

Suite 308A-11, Jardine House, One Connaught Place, Central, Hong Kong
Tel: 2530 3633 Fax: 2869 6650 **Telex:** 68015 KOHA HX **Swift:** CZNB HK HH

Senior Executive Officers
Managing Director   Jue-som Roh
Debt Capital Markets / Fixed Income
Head of Debt Capital Markets   Hyo-naon Chon *Deputy Managing Director*
Equity Capital Markets
Head of Equity Capital Markets   Hyo-naon Chon *Deputy Managing Director*
Syndicated Lending
Head of Syndicated Lending   Do-hyun Lee *Manager*
Money Markets
Head of Money Markets   Do-hyun Lee *Manager*
Foreign Exchange
Head of Foreign Exchange   Do-hyun Lee *Manager*
Risk Management
Head of Risk Management   Do-hyun Lee *Manager*
Corporate Finance / M&A Advisory
Head of Corporate Finance   Do-hyun Lee *Manager*
Settlement / Clearing
Head of Settlement / Clearing   Do-hyun Lee *Manager*

Korea Commercial Finance Limited   *Subsidiary Company*

Formerly known as: Korea Commercial Finance Limited
Suite 4004, Jardine House, One Connaught Place, Central, Hong Kong
Tel: 2526 5339; 2526 5330 Fax: 2845 9129; 2523 0629 **Telex:** 85259 COBKH HX **Swift:** CBKOHKHH

Senior Executive Officers
Chairman of the Executive Committee &   Jee-Tae Chung
President
Managing Director   Won-Chul Hwang
Deputy Managing Director   Jong-Liep Lee
Debt Capital Markets / Fixed Income
Head of Fixed Income   Joo-Beom Kim *Manager* ☎ **2525 2196**
Equity Capital Markets
Head of Equity Capital Markets   Joo-Beom Kim *Manager* ☎ **2525 2196**
Syndicated Lending
Head of Syndication   Joo-Beom Kim *Manager* ☎ **2525 2196**
Loan-Related Activities
Trade Finance   Dae-Geun Lee *Manager* ☎ **2526 3307**
Money Markets
Head of Money Markets   Sang-Soon Hyun *Manager* ☎ **2525 2123**

www.euromoneydirectory.com   HONG KONG, CHINA (+852)

Foreign Exchange
Head of Foreign Exchange   Sang-Soon Hyun *Manager* ☎ **2525 2123**

Other Departments
Correspondent Banking   Sang-Soon Hyun *Manager* ☎ **2525 2123**

Korea Exchange Bank
32nd Floor, Far East Finance Centre, 16 Harcourt Road, Hong Kong
PO Box 2719
Tel: 2520 1221 **Fax:** 2861 2379 **Telex:** 73459 KOEXBK HX **Swift:** KOEX HK HH

Senior Executive Officers
General Manager   Jae-Kyu Ahn
Deputy General Manager   S M Min

Korea First Finance Limited   Subsidiary Company   H
Suite 2007, Jardine House, One Connaught Place, Central, Hong Kong
Tel: 2526 5025 **Fax:** 2845 9001 **Telex:** 85962 KOFST HX **Swift:** KOFR HK HH

Senior Executive Officers
Managing Director   Eung-Bok Park ☎ **2526 5025**
Deputy Managing Director   Chul-Wan Park ☎ **2526 5025**

Debt Capital Markets / Fixed Income
Tel: 2526 5025

Domestic Government Bonds
Head of Sales; Head of Trading   Wan-Sok Ahn *Senior Manager*

Eurobonds
Head of Sales; Head of Trading   Wan-Sok Ahn *Senior Manager*

Libor-Based / Floating-Rate Products
FRN Origination; FRN Sales   Wan-Sok Ahn *Senior Manager*

Fixed-Income Repo
Head of Repo   Wan-Sok Ahn *Senior Manager*

Equity Capital Markets
Head of Equity Capital Markets; Head of Sales;   Wan-Sok Ahn *Senior Manager*
Head of Trading

Domestic Equities
Head of Sales; Head of Trading   Wan-Sok Ahn *Senior Manager*

International Equities
Head of Sales; Head of Trading   Wan-Sok Ahn *Senior Manager*

Convertibles / Equity-Linked
Head of Sales; Head of Trading   Wan-Sok Ahn *Senior Manager*

Syndicated Lending
Head of Origination; Head of Syndication; Head   Wan-Sok Ahn *Senior Manager*
of Trading

Loan-Related Activities
Trade Finance   Tae-Sun Hong *Senior Manager*

Money Markets
Head of Money Markets   Yul-Wook Sung *Senior Manager*

Foreign Exchange
Head of Foreign Exchange   Yul-Wook Sung *Senior Manager*

Settlement / Clearing
Head of Settlement / Clearing; Equity   Wan-Sok Ahn *Senior Manager*
Settlement

Administration

Accounts / Audit
Manager   Ji-Hyuk Kim ☎ **2526 5025**

HONG KONG, CHINA (+852) www.euromoneydirectory.com

Kwangtung Provincial Bank Full Branch Office

Euro Trade Centre, 13-14 Connaught Road, Central, Hong Kong
PO Box 10011, Hong Kong
Tel: 2841 0410 Fax: 2845 9302 Telex: 83654 PROVL HX Swift: KWPB HK HH Reuters: KPBH Telerate: 9916, 9615
Cable: PROVINCIAL
Website: www.kpb-hk.com

Senior Executive Officers
General Manager Liru Qin ☏ 2841 0593
International Division Tat Cheung Mak *Deputy General Manager* ☏ 2841 0075
Others (Senior Executives)
Lic Ki Ho *Deputy General Manager* ☏ 2841 0661
Xiaolan Zhu *Deputy General Manager* ☏ 2841 0682
Siu Kwan Ng *Deputy General Manager* ☏ 2841 0528

Debt Capital Markets / Fixed Income
Department: Treasury Department
Tel: 2525 0489 Fax: 2521 7100 Reuters: KPBK Telex: 61414 KPBFX HX
Head of Fixed Income Pui Pui Wong *Senior Manager* ☏ 2525 5775

Money Markets
Tel: 2525 0489 Fax: 2521 7100 Reuters: KPBK Telex: 61414 KPBFX HX
Head of Money Markets Ming Sze Tang *Deputy Manager* ☏ 2841 0480

Foreign Exchange
Tel: 2841 0400 Fax: 2521 7100 Reuters: KPBK Telex: 61414 KPBFX HX
Head of Foreign Exchange Kam Fong Wong *Deputy Manager*

Kwong On Bank Limited Head Office

Asia Standard Tower, 59/65 Queen's Road, Central, Hong Kong
PO Box 9824, Hong Kong
Tel: 2815 3636 Fax: 2850 6129 Telex: 73359,73901 KOBFD HX
Website: www.kwongonbank.com.hk

Senior Executive Officers
Chairman Ronald Leung ☏ 2853 1300
Deputy Chairman Katsuma Ohara ☏ 2853 1222
Chief Executive Officer Kenneth Leung ☏ 2853 1100
Financial Director Stephen Lau *Chief Accountant* ☏ 2853 1183
Treasurer Allan Ling ☏ 2853 1141
Managing Director / General Manager Iwao Maruyama ☏ 2853 1333
Chief Accountant Stephen Lau ☏ 2853 1183
International Division Jun Kawaguchi *Director & Deputy General Manager* ☏ 2853 1202

Settlement / Clearing
Head of Settlement / Clearing Kam Cheun Wong *Manager* ☏ 2853 1126

Other Departments
Chief Credit Officer Chik Kau Chung *Senior Manager* ☏ 2853 1242
Correspondent Banking Hei Yu Ho *Assistant General Manager* ☏ 2853 1161

Administration
Head of Marketing Wing Lee Chan *Director & Deputy General Manager* ☏ 2853 1232

Technology & Systems
Xavier Ho *Corporate Technology Manager* ☏ 2979 8877

Legal / In-House Counsel
Wang Kung *Deputy General Manager* ☏ 2853 1323

Compliance
Wang Kung *Deputy General Manager* ☏ 2853 1323

Public Relations
Allen Cheng *Manager* ☏ 2853 1143

Accounts / Audit
Tak Wing Chan *Senior Manager* ☏ 2853 1262

Landesbank Hessen-Thüringen Girozentrale Representative Office

Alternative trading name: Helaba
19th Floor, Standard Chartered Bank Building, 4A Des Voeux Road, Central, Hong Kong
Tel: 2978 8371 Fax: 1868 3637

www.euromoneydirectory.com   HONG KONG, CHINA (+852)

LG Finance (Hong Kong) Subsidiary Company
Suite 1404, Two Exchange Square, 8 Connaught Place, Central, Hong Kong
Tel: 2826 9235 Fax: 2537 8537

Senior Executive Officers
Chairman   Kim Sung Tae
Chairman   Suh Kyung Suk
Managing Director   Kim Jung Seok
Manager   Ha Jae Wook

LG Securities (Hong Kong) Limited Subsidiary Company
Suites 1402-3, Two Exchange Square, 8 Connaught Place, Central, Hong Kong
Tel: 2532 6300 Fax: 2525 4204 Telex: 70300 LGS HX

Senior Executive Officers
Chief Executive Officer   Jong-An Kim *Managing Director* T 2532 6301
Director, Sales   Phillip Ham T 2532 6318 E pham@lgsec.com.hk

Debt Capital Markets / Fixed Income
Head of Debt Capital Markets   Phillip Ham *Director, Sales* T 2532 6318 E pham@lgsec.com.hk

Equity Capital Markets
Head of Equity Capital Markets   Phillip Ham *Director, Sales* T 2532 6318 E pham@lgsec.com.hk

Settlement / Clearing
Head of Settlement / Clearing; Country Head   K H Won T 2532 6304

LGT Bank in Liechtenstein AG Representative Office
11th Floor, Three Exchange Square, 8 Connaught Place, Hong Kong
PO Box 13398, Hong Kong
Tel: 2523 6180 Fax: 2868 0059

Senior Executive Officers
Chief Representative, Asia Pacific   Henri W Leimer
Senior Representative, Asia Pacific   Philip Jehle

Liu Chong Hing Bank Limited
24 Des Voeux Road, Central, Hong Kong
PO Box 2535, Central, Hong Kong
Tel: 2841 7417 Fax: 2845 9134 Telex: HX 75700 Swift: LCHB HK HH

Senior Executive Officers
Chairman & General Manager   Lit Mann Liu
Financial Director   Lee Yick Nam *Executive Director*
Director   Lit Man Lin
International Division   King Leung Chan *Senior Manager*

General-Lending (DCM, SL)
Head of Corporate Banking   Lee Yick Nam *Executive Director*

Lloyds Bank plc Full Branch Office
21st Floor, One Pacific Place, 88 Queensway, Hong Kong
Tel: 2847 3000 Fax: 2868 4733 Telex: 75150 HSHK HX Swift: HSAM HK HH

Senior Executive Officers
Chief Executive Officer   Geoffrey McEnery

London Forfaiting Hong Kong Limited Subsidiary Company
Formerly known as: LFC Far East Limited
Suite 3601, One Pacific Place, 88 Queensway, Hong Kong
Tel: 2525 4699 Fax: 2521 8679

Senior Executive Officers
Chief Executive Officer   Ooi Boon Aun
Financial Director   Johnny Quah

HONG KONG, CHINA (+852) www.euromoneydirectory.com

London Forfaiting Hong Kong Limited (cont)
Others (Senior Executives)
Wai Kin Wong *Director*
Michael Chye *Director*
Bock Kho Tan *Director*

The Long-Term Credit Bank of Japan Limited — Full Branch Office

9th Floor, One Pacific Place, 88 Queensway, Hong Kong
Tel: 2528 5670 Fax: 2865 6484 Telex: 76295 LTCBH HX

Senior Executive Officers
Director & General Manager Masao Fujimaki ☎ 2863 1401 📠 2865 6484

LTCB Asia Limited — Subsidiary Company

Suite 909, One Pacific Place, 88 Queensway, Hong Kong
Tel: 2528 5670 Fax: 2865 6484 Telex: 73321 LTCBA HX Reuters: LTBB

Senior Executive Officers
Chairman Kazuhide Koshiisho
Chief Executive Officer Norio Funayama *Executive Director*
Managing Director Makio Igarashi

Debt Capital Markets / Fixed Income
Department: International Securities Department - Asian Operations
Tel: 2863 1521 Fax: 2866 0047
Head of Fixed Income Norio Funayama *Executive Director*

Eurobonds
Head of Sales Norio Funayama *Executive Director*
Head of Trading Norio Funayama *Executive Director*

Risk Management
Head of Risk Management K Shintani *Senior Manager* ☎ 2863 1422

Settlement / Clearing
Head of Settlement / Clearing Wilson Chan *Senior Manager*

Luen Fat Securities Limited — Head Office

1st Floor, Chung Hing Communications Building, 62-63 Connaught Road, Central, Hong Kong
Tel: 2543 6086; 2541 4081 Fax: 2545 8348

Senior Executive Officers
Director Yue Wai Keung
Director So Kwan Ming
Chief Executive Officer Pang Kwok Leung *Director*

Malayan Banking Berhad — Full Branch Office

Alternative trading name: Maybank
18th & 19th Floors, Entertainment Building, 30 Queen's Road, Central, Hong Kong
Tel: 2522 7141; 2522 7312 Fax: 2810 6013; 2147 9959 Telex: 75287 Swift: MBBE HK HH Reuters: MBBH
Telerate: N114581

Senior Executive Officers
Chief Executive Officer Huan Woon Han *General Manager* ☎ 2522 5529
Chief Operating Officer Lew Taw Fong *Operations Manager* ☎ 2522 7312
Treasurer Wong Mun Nyun *Treasury Manager* ☎ 2521 1373

Syndicated Lending
Head of Syndicated Lending Tham Chin Choy *Credit Manager*

Money Markets
Head of Money Markets Wong Mun Nyun *Treasury Manager* ☎ 2521 1373

Foreign Exchange
Head of Foreign Exchange Wong Mun Nyun *Treasury Manager* ☎ 2521 1373

Risk Management
Head of Risk Management Chan Pui Ling *Deputy Manager*

Settlement / Clearing
Head of Settlement / Clearing Chan Pui Ling *Deputy Manager*

www.euromoneydirectory.com   HONG KONG, CHINA (+852)

Mansion House Securities (FE) Limited   Head Office

37A Bank of China Tower, One Garden Road, Central, Hong Kong
Tel: 2843 1431 Fax: 2845 9036 Telex: 83359 MHSEC HX

Senior Executive Officers
Chairman & Chief Executive Officer   Evans Carrera Lowe ☎ **2843 1438**
Chief Executive Officer   Evans Carrera Lowe *Chairman & Chief Executive Officer* ☎ **2843 1438**
                                           Irene Wai Yin So *Dealing Director* ☎ **2843 1411**
Financial Director   Danny Tak Tim Chan *Director* ☎ **2843 1430**
Treasurer   Kin Leung Chow *Financial Controller* ☎ **2843 1428**
International Division   Danny Tak Tim Chan *Director* ☎ **2843 1430**
Dealing Director   Irene Wai Yin So ☎ **2843 1411**

Equity Capital Markets
Domestic Equities
Head of Trading   Irene So
Head of Research   Stanley Ng

Settlement / Clearing
Head of Settlement / Clearing   Kitty Yip *Settlement Manager* ☎ **2843 1497**

Asset Management
Head   Eric Carrera Lowe *Director* ☎ **2843 1493**

Other Departments
Correspondent Banking   Kin Leung Chow *Financial Controller* ☎ **2843 1428**

Administration
Head of Administration   Timothy Ho *Personnel & Administration Manager* ☎ **2843 1463**

Legal / In-House Counsel
In-House Lawyer   Miranda Tse ☎ **2843 1459**

Compliance
                                           Cecilia Chow *Internal Auditor* ☎ **2843 1472**

Accounts / Audit
                                           Kin Leung Chow *Financial Controller* ☎ **2843 1428**
                                           Cecilia Chow *Internal Auditor* ☎ **2843 1472**

Merita Bank plc/Nordbanken AB (publ)   Representative Office

Suite 1502, Two Exchange Square, 8 Connaught Place, Central, Hong Kong
Tel: 2523 7505 Fax: 2526 7674

Senior Executive Officers
Representative   Peter Ostwald
Representative   Raymond Kwong

Merrill Lynch (Asia Pacific) Limited   Subsidiary Company

17th Floor, Asia Pacific Finance Tower, 3 Garden Road, Central, Hong Kong
Tel: 2536 3888 Fax: 2536 3789

Senior Executive Officers
Chairman   Peter Clarke

The Mitsubishi Trust & Banking Corporation   Full Branch Office

38th Floor, Gloucester Tower, 11 Pedder Street, Central, Hong Kong
Tel: 2844 8000 Fax: 2810 4123 Telex: 72496 MTBC HX Swift: MTBC HK HH Cable: MTBTRUST HG

Senior Executive Officers
General Manager   Akira Nakamura
Senior Deputy General Manager   Masahiro Kusaba
Deputy General Manager   Kazuo Sakamoto

Money Markets
Head of Money Markets   Akira Ozawa *Head of Foreign Exchange & Money Markets*

Foreign Exchange
Head of Foreign Exchange   Akira Ozawa *Head of Foreign Exchange & Money Markets*

Settlement / Clearing
Operations   Toshio Mitama *Head, Operations*

Euromoney Directory 1999 **633**

HONG KONG, CHINA (+852) www.euromoneydirectory.com

The Mitsubishi Trust & Banking Corporation (cont)
Administration
Business Development
          Kota Yamada *Head, Business Promotion*
          Takashi Sugita *Head, Business Promotion*
Compliance
          Steven Paul Wong *Compliance Officer*
Accounts / Audit
          Thomson F S Koon *Internal Auditor*

Mitsui Leasing & Development (Hong Kong) Co Limited
Room 509, 5th Floor, New East Ocean Centre, 9 Science Museum, Road, Tsimshatsui East, Kowloon, Hong Kong
Tel: 2528 4566 **Fax:** 2865 6533 **Telex:** 70330 MLDHK HX

Mitsui Trust Finance (Hong Kong) Limited   Subsidiary Company
Alternative trading name: Mitsui Trust & Banking Co Limited
9th Floor, Hong Kong Club Building, 3A Chater Road, Central, Hong Kong
Tel: 2521 1121 **Fax:** 2843 4198 **Telex:** 63413 MTBHK HX, 82718 MTRBG HX
Senior Executive Officers
General Manager   H Iwakami
Assistant Manager   Katsuyuki Hirai

Morgan Stanley Dean Witter Asia Limited   Full Branch Office
30th Floor, Three Exchange Square, Central, Hong Kong
Tel: 2848 8895 **Fax:** 2848 6633
Website: www.ms.com
Senior Executive Officers
Chairman - Asia   John S Wadsworth
President - Asia   Mario I Francescotti
Others (Senior Executives)
Chief Administrative Officer   Ali J Albers *CAO - Asia*
General-Investment
Head of Investment   Jon A Anda *Head, Investment Banking - Asia*
Debt Capital Markets / Fixed Income
Head of Debt Capital Markets   Michael Dee *Head, Debt CM Asia, MD, Morgan Stanley*
Head of Fixed Income   Victor Garber
High Yield / Junk Bonds
Head   Elizabeth Chandler
Equity Capital Markets
Head of Equity Capital Markets   John Crompton
Other (Domestic Equities)
Institutional Equity Division   Alastair W P Cooper *Head*
Foreign Exchange
Head of Foreign Exchange   Peter J Murray
Corporate Finance / M&A Advisory
Head of Corporate Finance   Michael J Berchtold
Head of Mergers & Acquisition   Harry van Dyke
Administration
Other (Administration)
Private Clients Services   E Michael Fung *Head*

The Nanto Bank Limited   Representative Office
Suite 2906/7, 29th Floor, Two Exchange Square, 8 Connaught Road, Hong Kong
Tel: 2868 9932 **Fax:** 2530 1583
Senior Executive Officers
Chief Representative   Mitsuo Kawata E hetian@hk.nttdata.net
Deputy Representative   Tomoya Nakaminami E **tomoyan@hk.nttdata.net**

www.euromoneydirectory.com HONG KONG, CHINA (+852)

Nanyang Commercial Bank Limited
Head Office

151 Des Voeux Road, Central, Hong Kong
Tel: 2852 0888 Fax: 2815 3333 Telex: 73412 NANHO HX Swift: NYCB HK HH Reuters: NYCB
Cable: NANYANGBANK
Website: www.nanyangbankhk.com

Senior Executive Officers
Honorary Chairman   Shih-ping Chuan
Chairman   Hong-yi Zhang
Vice Chairman   Ji-wen Li
Vice Chairman   Shui-ming Chung
Deputy General Manager   Man-wah Law

General - Treasury
Head of Treasury   Wing-chuen Lee *Assistant General Manager*

Relationship Manager
    Kiu-san Wong *Marketing Director*

Debt Capital Markets / Fixed Income
Head of Debt Capital Markets   Wing-chuen Lee *Assistant General Manager*

Equity Capital Markets
Head of Equity Capital Markets   Wing-chuen Lee *Assistant General Manager*

Syndicated Lending
Loan-Related Activities
Trade Finance   Ping-sheung Choy *Deputy General Manager*

Foreign Exchange
Head of Foreign Exchange   Wing-chuen Lee *Assistant General Manager*

Corporate Finance / M&A Advisory
Head of Corporate Finance   Wai-keung Yuen *Deputy General Manager*

Administration
Head of Administration   Shiu-chuen Ho *Deputy General Manager*

Technology & Systems
Information Technology Director   Man-wah Law *Deputy General Manager*

Natexis Banque BFCE

Alternative trading name: Groupe Crédit National BFCE
12th Floor, Citic Tower, 1 Tim Mei Avenue, Central, Hong Kong
Tel: 2828 0999 Fax: 2583 9801 Telex: 80186 BFCEX

Senior Executive Officers
Chief Executive Officer   Philippe Petitgas
Regional Director   Philippe Fricquegnon ☏ 2828 0906

Administration
Head of Administration   Gean Laurent ☏ 2828 0903 🖷 2583 9801

National Australia Bank Limited
Representative Office

Level 27, One Pacific Place, 88 Queensway, Hong Kong
Tel: 2826 8111 Fax: 2822 9704 Telex: 75315 NATHK Swift: NATA HK HH

Senior Executive Officers
Chief Representative   Paul F Y Law

National Australia Finance (Asia) Limited

Level 27, One Pacific Place, 88 Queensway, Hong Kong
Tel: 2826 8111 Fax: 2845 9251 Telex: 75315

Senior Executive Officers
Chief Executive Officer   Paul F Y Law *Managing Director*
    George Lo *Head of Operations*

HONG KONG, CHINA (+852) www.euromoneydirectory.com

The National Commercial Bank Limited — Head Office

Ground Floor, 1/3 Wyndham Street, Central, Hong Kong
Tel: 2843 2888 **Fax:** 2810 4634 **Telex:** 83491 NATEX HX **Swift:** NATB HK HH **Reuters:** NCBH **Cable:** NATCOMBANK

Senior Executive Officers
General Manager — M L Lam ☎ 2843 2828

Foreign Exchange
Tel: 2843 2871 **Fax:** 2596 0008
Country Head — G L Hung *Manager* ☎ 2843 2873

Settlement / Clearing
Country Head — S K Cheung *Senior Manager* ☎ 2843 2912

Other Departments
Correspondent Banking — W H Kan *Senior Manager* ☎ 2843 2857

National Westminster Bank — Full Branch Office

46th Floor, NatWest Tower, Times Square, Causeway Bay, Hong Kong
Tel: 2966 2800 **Fax:** 2506 0966 **Telex:** 61672 NAWES HX **Swift:** NWBK HK HH

Senior Executive Officers
Department: Group Head Office
Chief Executive Officer — David Edwards *Chief Corporate Officer, Asia Pacific* ☎ 2966 2692
F 2506 0802
Treasurer — Lawrence Lam *Director & Treasurer, North Asia*

Others (Senior Executives)
Group Financial Markets, Asia Pacific — Frank Wong *Regional Managing Director*
Greenwich Capital Markets — Jim Zhao *Vice President, Greenwich Proprietary Trading*

Nedcor Asia Limited — Subsidiary Company

Formerly known as: Nedfinance (Asia) Limited
50th Floor, Sun Hung Kai Centre, 30 Harbour Road, Wanchai, Hong Kong
PO Box 10090, Hong Kong
Tel: 2829 9111 **Fax:** 2802 0550 **Telex:** 86841 NDASA HX **Swift:** NEDS HK HH **Reuters:** NBHK

Senior Executive Officers
Chief Executive Officer — N W Burton *Managing Director* ☎ 2829 9100
Robin Lee *Director & General Manager* ☎ 2829 9102
Treasurer — Norman Li *Assistant General Manager* ☎ 2829 9128
Assistant General Manager — James Mok ☎ 2829 9237

General-Lending (DCM, SL)
Head of Corporate Banking — Jacky So *Manager* ☎ 2829 9113

Relationship Manager
General Manager — Gary Patterson ☎ 2829 9103
Johnson Li ☎ 2829 9126
Head of China Banking — Tam Moni *Manager* ☎ 2829 9119

Syndicated Lending
Head of Syndication — Dawen Chan *Manager* ☎ 2829 9282

Other (Trade Finance)
Export Finance — Christine Chung *Assistant Manager* ☎ 2829 9131
Import Finance — Winnie To *Assistant Manager* ☎ 2829 9132

Settlement / Clearing
Head of Settlement / Clearing — April Huang *Officer* ☎ 2829 9183

Other Departments
Chief Credit Officer — Theo Renard *Manager* ☎ 2829 9116
Private Banking — Helwina Slu *Manager* ☎ 2829 9115

Administration

Accounts / Audit
Ben Cheng *Manager* ☎ 2829 9160

www.euromoneydirectory.com   HONG KONG, CHINA (+852)

Nedship Bank
Representative Office
42nd Floor, Two Exchange Square, 8 Connaught Place, Hong Kong
Tel: 2103 2492 **Fax:** 2501 5592 **Telex:** 80556
Senior Executive Officers
Others (Senior Executives)
P Chang *Office Manager*

Niaga Finance Company Limited
Subsidiary Company
Room 3916/19, Jardine House, 1 Connaught Place, Central, Hong Kong
Tel: 2523 2145; 2523 2146 **Fax:** 2868 4963; 2810 4831 **Telex:** 72477 NIAGA HX **Email:** niagahk@hkstar.com
Senior Executive Officers
Chairman, Board of Directors — George S Tahija
Chief Executive Officer — Ananta Wiyogo *CEO / Managing Director*
Chief Operating Officer — Paul Lie *Senior Manager* ☏ **2523 6315**
Others (Senior Executives)
Mr Binhadi *Board of Directors*
Arwin Rasyid *Board of Directors*
Marketing & Credit — Ananta Wiyogo *CEO / Managing Director*
General-Lending (DCM, SL)
Head of Corporate Banking — Paul Lie *Senior Manager*
General - Treasury
Head of Treasury — Emirsyah Satar *CEO / Managing Director* ☏ **2526 0942**
Syndicated Lending
Other (Syndicated Lending)
Loans & Syndication — Ananta Wiyogo *CEO / Managing Director*
Loan-Related Activities
Trade Finance — Jety Teh *Manager*
Money Markets
Other (Wholesale Deposits)
Bills & Remittance — May Chau *Sub-Manager*
Settlement / Clearing
Settlement (General) — Florence Lee *Sub-Manager*
Operations — Paul Lie *Senior Manager*
Administration
Compliance
Credit & Compliance — Paul Lie *Senior Manager*
Accounts / Audit
Accounting — Kwok Sau Kuen *Sub-Manager*
Other (Administration)
Human Resources — Paul Lie *Senior Manager*

Nikko Securities Co (Asia) Limited
Subsidiary Company
19th Floor, One Pacific Place, 88 Queensway, Hong Kong
Tel: 2842 1111 **Fax:** 2840 0450
Senior Executive Officers
Chairman — Jun Okano
Chief Executive Officer — Yoshiro Katsuya *Managing Director & Chief Executive*
Director & General Manager — Tetsuo Nakagawa
Secretary to Managing Director — C Hui ☏ **2842 1187**
Others (Senior Executives)
Yoshiro Katsuya
Debt Capital Markets / Fixed Income
Head of Debt Capital Markets — G Rin
Global Head — Takeshi Sakuma *Managing Director, Capital Markets*
Regional Head — Taro Hayakawa *Managing Director, Fixed Income*
Equity Capital Markets
Head of Equity Capital Markets — Shu Fan Lee *Director*
Domestic Equities
Head of Trading — C Ogushi
Head of Research — U Matsushita

HONG KONG, CHINA (+852)   www.euromoneydirectory.com

Nikko Securities Co (Asia) Limited (cont)
Other (International Equity)
         Maria Lau *Assistant Manager*

Foreign Exchange
Head of Foreign Exchange   Benny Lam

Risk Management
Head of Risk Management   H Shigeura

The Nippon Credit Bank Limited   Representative Office

Suite 1012, Two Pacific Place, 88 Queensway, Hong Kong
Tel: 2820 9888 **Fax:** 2845 2724 **Telex:** 65744 NCIHK HX

Senior Executive Officers
Chief Representative   Junichi Hata

Administration
Head of Administration   Irene Wong *Manager*

Nippon Credit International (Hong Kong) Limited   Subsidiary Company

Suite 1012, Two Pacific Place, 88 Queensway, Hong Kong
Tel: 2820 9888 **Fax:** 2845 2724 **Telex:** 65744 NCIHK HX

Senior Executive Officers
Chairman   Masauasu Saki
Managing Director   Junichi Hata
Deputy Managing Director   Futaya Seiji
Deputy Managing Director   Watahiki Susumu

Nishi-Nippon Finance (Hong Kong) Limited   Head Office

19th Floor, The Hong Kong Club Building, 3A Chater Road, Central, Hong Kong
Tel: 2526 2259 **Fax:** 2845 9264 **Telex:** 89763 NNB HK **Email:** nnfhk@hk.nttdata.net

Senior Executive Officers
Chairman   Noritaka Inoue
President   Shiro Eguma
Chief Executive Officer   Ryuichi Tanaka
Chief Operating Officer   Eiji Taguma

Nittan Marshalls (Hong Kong) Limited   Subsidiary Company

29th Floor, Edinburgh Tower, 15 Queen's Road, Central, Hong Kong
Tel: 2521 2213; 2882 3889 **Fax:** 2848 5175 **Telex:** 74078 MARSH **Reuters:** MW HK

Senior Executive Officers
Managing Director   Denis Cheung ☎ **2848 5145**
General Manager   Joseph Lee ☎ **2848 5121**

Nomura International (Hong Kong) Limited

20th & 21st Floors, Asia Pacific Finance Tower, Citibank Plaza, 3 Garden Road, Central, Hong Kong
Tel: 2536 1111 **Fax:** 2536 1888; 2536 1396 **Telex:** 73299 NOMIN HX
Website: www.nomura.co.hk

Senior Executive Officers
Chairman   Taizo Kondo
President   Shigeru Fujinuma

Others (Senior Executives)
         K Azuma *President*

www.euromoneydirectory.com   HONG KONG, CHINA (+852)

Equity Capital Markets
Tel: 2536 1361 Fax: 2536 1287
Head of Trading   Derek Chan
Head of Research   Nicholas Pang

Equity Repo / Securities Lending
Marketing & Product Development   Mitch Redd *Regional Manager* ☎ **2536 1221**
                                            E hkgreddm@mail.nomura.com.hk
Head of Prime Brokerage   Mark Tidy *Head of Equity Finance* ☎ **+44 (171) 521 3928**
                                            F +44 (171) 521 2683 E mark.tidy@mail.nomura.com.hk
Head of Trading   Mary Woo *Trader*
                                            David Lai *Trader*

Nomura/JAFCO Investment (Hong Kong) Limited   Regional Head Office
Alternative trading name: NJI
    20th Floor, Asia Pacific Finance Tower, Citibank Plaza, 3 Garden Road, Central, Hong Kong
        Tel: 2536 1960 Fax: 2536 1979

Senior Executive Officers
President   Kazumasa Sakamoto
Senior Vice President & General Manager   Koichi Miyamoto

Administration
Head of Administration   Albert Leung *Administration Manager* ☎ **2536 1960**

OCBC Securities (Hong Kong) Limited   Subsidiary Company
    11th Floor, New World Tower Two, 18 Queen's Road, Central, Hong Kong
    Tel: 2249 8222 Fax: 2521 7531 Telex: 69657 OCBCS HX Email: khui@ocbcsec.com.hk

Senior Executive Officers
Chief Executive Officer   B K Gan ☎ **2249 8200**
Managing Director   Kinson Hui ☎ **2249 8262**

Oriental Patron Asia Limited   Head Office
    42nd Floor, Cosco Tower, 183 Queen's Road, Central, Hong Kong
    Tel: 2842 5888 Fax: 2842 5833; 2842 5811 Email: e-post@oriental-patron.com.hk

Senior Executive Officers
Managing Director   Gary Zhang

Corporate Finance / M&A Advisory
Head of Corporate Finance   Joseph Chan *Director*

ORIX Asia Limited   Subsidiary Company
    30th Floor, United Centre, 95 Queensway, Hong Kong
    Tel: 2862 9268 Fax: 2527 9688 Telex: 75680 ORIX HX Email: orix@orix.com.hk Cable: ORIXASIA
    Website: www.orix.com.hk

Senior Executive Officers
Chairman   Sato Takeshi ☎ **2862 9101**
Managing Director   Yuki Oshima ☎ **2862 9104**
Deputy MD, Domestic Business   Mitsuo Nishiumi ☎ **2862 9261**

Others (Senior Executives)
International Project   Hon Ching Yao *Executive Director* ☎ **2862 9110**
Domestic Business   John Leung *Associate Director* ☎ **2862 9242**
Asia Team   Oishi Yasuke *General Manager* ☎ **2862 9154**

General-Lending (DCM, SL)
Head of Corporate Banking   Dillon Tam *Senior Manager, Int'l, Planning & Development* ☎ **2862 9112**

General - Treasury
Head of Treasury   Hiroki Kamemoto *Director, Accounting, MIS, Treasury, Custody*
                                            ☎ **2862 9140**
                                            Annie Leung *Assistant General Manager, Treasury* ☎ **2862 9142**

Syndicated Lending
Loan-Related Activities
Shipping Finance   Masatoshi Yokota *Senior General Manager* ☎ **2862 9162**

Euromoney Directory 1999   **639**

HONG KONG, CHINA (+852)   www.euromoneydirectory.com

ORIX Asia Limited (cont)
Other (Trade Finance)
Consumer Finance   Donny Chan *Senior Manager* ☎ 2862 9262
Corporate Finance / M&A Advisory
Country Head   Jacky Ho *Senior Manager* ☎ 2862 9252
Settlement / Clearing
Settlement (General)   Charles Hui *General Manager* ☎ 2862 9181
Operations   Billy Kan *GM, Management Information Systems* ☎ 2862 9120
                                            Hiroki Kamemoto *Director, Accounting, MIS, Treasury, Custody*
                                            ☎ 2862 9140

Administration
Accounts / Audit
Accounting   Cooper Tam *Chief Accountant* ☎ 2862 9180
                                            Hiroki Kamemoto *Director, Accounting, MIS, Treasury, Custody*
                                            ☎ 2862 9140

Other (Administration)
Personnel & Administration, Custody; Document   Charles Hui *General Manager* ☎ 2862 9181
Checking

Overseas Union Bank Limited   Full Branch Office
5th Floor, Edinburgh Tower, 15 Queen's Road, Central, Hong Kong
Tel: 2521 1521 Fax: 2810 5506 Telex: 73258 Cable: OVERSUNION
Senior Executive Officers
Senior Vice President & General Manager   Kwik Sam Aik

Paribas
Level 27, Two Pacific Place, 88 Queensway, Hong Kong
Tel: 2108 5000 Fax: 2108 5200 Telex: 75418 PARHK HX
Website: www.paribas.com

Senior Executive Officers
GM, Head of Territory   Denis Antoine ☎ 2108 5001
Assistant General Manager   Raymond Chan ☎ 2108 5092
Others (Senior Executives)
Finance   David Lam
Debt Capital Markets / Fixed Income
Head of Fixed Income   Eddie Lee
Head of Fixed Income Sales   Alan Davies *Head, Asian Sales*
Head of Fixed Income Trading   Lloyd Smith
Equity Capital Markets
Head of Equity Capital Markets   Iain Donnachie *Head of Equity, Asia*
Head of Trading   Lloyd Smith
Other   Mark Coggins
Risk Management
Head of Risk Management   Edwin Har
Corporate Finance / M&A Advisory
Head of Corporate Finance   Christian de Charnacé
Settlement / Clearing
Operations   Raymond Chan *Assistant General Manager* ☎ 2108 5092
Other Departments
Economic Research   Mark Coggins
Other Departments
PPI   Philippe Aguignier
DBC   Patrick Lang
ALM   Eric Le Vernoy
PAM   Lawrence Lo
Administration
Head of Administration   Robby Pang *Manager* ☎ 2108 5925
Technology & Systems
Technology   Raymond Chan *Assistant General Manager* ☎ 2108 5092
Legal / In-House Counsel
                                            Derek Gobel

www.euromoneydirectory.com   HONG KONG, CHINA (+852)

Compliance
Felix Kwan
Corporate Communications
Virgina Hopes *Head* ☏ 2108 5165 ℻ 2108 5809
Other (Administration)
Human Resources   Jean-Hervé Monier *Head* ☏ 2108 5413 ℻ 2108 5840
Advisory   Steve Chu

Po Sang Bank Limited   Head Office

71 Des Voeux Road, Central, Hong Kong
Tel: 2843 6111 **Fax:** 2810 1126 **Swift:** SANG HK HH **Reuters:** PSBK

Senior Executive Officers
Chairman   Kwong Siu Lam
Chief Executive Officer   Ji-lu Gao
Money Markets
Head of Money Markets   Hung-yee Lam *Manager*
Foreign Exchange
Head of Foreign Exchange   Yim-chuen Wong *Senior Manager*

Polaris Securities (Hong Kong) Limited   Subsidiary Company

10th Floor, 19-20 Fung House, Connaught Road, Hong Kong
Tel: 2918 0799; 2918 0233 **Fax:** 2869 6916

Senior Executive Officers
Managing Director   Gary Chang
Debt Capital Markets / Fixed Income
Head of Debt Capital Markets   Teddy Yiu *Director*
Equity Capital Markets
Head of Equity Capital Markets   Fun Man Fu
Risk Management
Head of Risk Management   Vincent Tsai

Prebon Yamane (Hong Kong) Limited   Regional Head Office

15th Floor, Evergo House, 38 Gloucester Road, Wanchai, Hong Kong
Tel: 2527 8027 **Fax:** 2527 6125 **Telex:** 75161 PYHKHX **Reuters:** PYHK / PYHL
Website: www.prebon.com

Senior Executive Officers
Managing Director   Joseph Lam ☏ 2823 8288
Debt Capital Markets / Fixed Income
Tel: 2527 8027 **Fax:** 2527 6125 **Reuters:** PYHK/ PYHL
Head of Debt Capital Markets   Paul Mullin *Managing Director* ☏ 2823 8282
Head of Fixed Income   Jay Vitrella *Managing Director* ☏ 2823 8281
Other (Emerging Markets Bonds)
Head of Desk of Convertible Bonds   Geoff Snell *Manager* ☏ 2823 8342
Other (Libor-Based / Floating Rate Products)
Head of Desk of Bills of Exchange   Stephane Benayon *Manager, Asian Securities* ☏ 2823 8315
Fixed-Income Repo
Other   Adrian Dover *JGB Repo* ☏ 2823 8351
Ruairi Gogan *Credit Derivatives Broker* ☏ 2823 8361
Victoria Yuen *Credit Derivatives Broker* ☏ 2823 8361
Michael Poon *Associate Director, HKD Off Balance Sheet* ☏ 2823 8341
Anson Chow *Manager, International Off Balance Sheet* ☏ 2823 8336
Stephane Benayon *Manager, Asian Securities* ☏ 2823 8315

Equity Capital Markets
Other (Domestic Equities)
Hang Seng & Options   Dean Roberts *Manager* ☏ 2823 8360
Other (International Equity)
Nikkei Options   Sean Murphy *Director* ☏ 2861 1082
Money Markets
Tel: 2527 8027 **Fax:** 2527 6125 **Reuters:** PYHK / PYHL **Telex:** 75161 PYHKHX
Head of Money Markets   Peter Pao *Managing Director* ☏ 2823 8222

HONG KONG, CHINA (+852)　　　　www.euromoneydirectory.com

Prebon Yamane (Hong Kong) Limited (cont)
Other (Wholesale Deposits)
USD Deposit　　　　　　　　　　Alan Cheng *Associate Director* ☎ **2823 8323**
Currency Deposit　　　　　　　　Pedro Lau *Manager* ☎ **2823 8310**
Domestic Money Markets　　　　Alex Yu *Manager* ☎ **2823 8328**
Bills & Bonds　　　　　　　　　　Maggie Ng *Manager* ☎ **2823 8330**
Foreign Exchange
Tel: 2527 8027 **Fax:** 2527 6125 **Reuters:** PYHK/ PYHL **Telex:** 75161 PYHKHX
Spot / Forwards Sales　　　　　Tony Chan *Manager* ☎ **2823 8363**
FX Traders / Sales People
Contil Foward　　　　　　　　　　Steven Lo *Manager* ☎ **2823 8301**
Non- Deliverable Forward　　　　Charles Fong *Manager* ☎ **2823 8346**
Settlement / Clearing
Tel: 2527 8027 **Fax:** 2527 6125 **Reuters:** PYHK/ PYHL **Telex:** 75161 PYHKHX
Head of Settlement / Clearing　　Paula Yeung *Financial Controller* ☎ **2823 8212**
Operations　　　　　　　　　　　Cicy Lee *Settlement Supervisor* ☎ **2823 8202**
Administration
Head of Administration　　　　　Christina Mo *Personnel Manager* ☎ **2823 8207**
Head of Marketing　　　　　　　Sanda Ecimovic *Director Asian Marketing & Communication* ☎ **2823 8218**
Technology & Systems
　　　　　　　　　　　　　　　　　Jeff Love *Director, Information Technology* ☎ **2823 8290**
Legal / In-House Counsel
　　　　　　　　　　　　　　　　　Paul Kelly *General Counsel, Asia* ☎ **2527 8027**
Accounts / Audit
　　　　　　　　　　　　　　　　　Paula Yeung *Financial Controller* ☎ **2823 8212**

Republic National Bank of New York (Suisse) SA
Representative Office

6th Floor, Jardine House, One Connaught Place, Central, Hong Kong
Tel: 2524 8334 **Fax:** 2877 5376; 2877 5384

Senior Executive Officers
Chief Representative　　　　　　David Yau

Rolo Banca 1473 SpA
Representative Office

Formerly known as: Credito Romagnolo
c/o Credito Italiano SpA, 36th Floor, Bank of China Tower, 1 Garden Road, Hong Kong
Tel: 2820 7688 **Fax:** 2845 9511 **Telex:** 64949 CITHF HX **Swift:** CRIT HK HH **Reuters:** CRIH
Senior Executive Officers
Chief Representative　　　　　　Dante Pasqualini ☎ **2820 7688**

NM Rothschild & Sons (Hong Kong) Limited
Subsidiary Company

16th Floor, Alexandra House, 16-20 Chater Road, Central, Hong Kong
Tel: 2525 5333 **Fax:** 2868 1773 **Telex:** 74628

Senior Executive Officers
Chairman　　　　　　　　　　　　Paul M F Cheng
Chief Executive Officer　　　　　David Kiang *Managing Director*
Financial Director　　　　　　　　Frederick Chan *Director*
General-Investment
Head of Investment　　　　　　　Arthur Ng *Director, Investment Banking*
Debt Capital Markets / Fixed Income
Department: Debt Financial Markets
Head of Fixed Income　　　　　　John Lee *Director*
Equity Capital Markets
Head of Equity Capital Markets　　Michiel Steenman *Managing Director*
Foreign Exchange
Head of Foreign Exchange　　　　Fook Yuen Wong *Director*
Corporate Finance / M&A Advisory
Regional Head　　　　　　　　　Arthur Ng *Director, Investment Banking*

www.euromoneydirectory.com　　　HONG KONG, CHINA (+852)

Rothschild Bank AG
Representative Office
16th Floor, Alexandra House, 18 Chater Road, Central, Hong Kong
Tel: 2116 6300 Fax: 2877 0336
Senior Executive Officers
Vice President, Asia Pacific　　　Franco Cheng

The Royal Bank of Scotland
Full Branch Office
#701-704, Two Exchange Square, 8 Connaught Place, Central, Hong Kong
PO Box 10130, Hong Kong
Tel: 2532 6700 Fax: 2810 6157
Senior Executive Officers
Regional Manager　　　A G Willett

Sakura Bank Limited
Full Branch Office
Level 24, One Pacific Place, 88 Queensway, Hong Kong
Tel: 2825 0800 Fax: 2840 0535 Telex: 62432 Reuters: SAHKA-S
Senior Executive Officers
General Manager　　　Shigeru Sugano

Sakura Finance Asia Limited
Subsidiary Company
41st Floor, Far East Finance Centre, 16 Harcourt Road, Hong Kong
Tel: 2864 9300 Fax: 2861 2316 Telex: 83413 MTKAL HX Swift: MITK HK HF A Reuters: SAHKA-S
Senior Executive Officers
Managing Director　　　Seiji Tsutsumi
Deputy Managing Director　　　Tadashi Sasaki
Deputy Managing Director　　　Tetsuo Kawano

Debt Capital Markets / Fixed Income
Head of Debt Capital Markets　　　Katsunori Ono *Executive Director* 2864 9340

Domestic Government Bonds
Head of Sales　　　Wing-son Cheng *Senior Vice President* 2864 9315
Head of Trading　　　Hisae Ito *Associate Director* 2864 9316

Eurobonds
Head of Syndication　　　Koji Saito *Director* 2864 9323
Head of Sales　　　Wing-son Cheng *Senior Vice President* 2864 9315
Head of Trading　　　Hisae Ito *Associate Director* 2864 9316

Libor-Based / Floating-Rate Products
FRN Origination　　　Koji Saito *Director* 2864 9323
FRN Sales　　　Wing-son Cheng *Senior Vice President* 2864 9315
Asset Swaps　　　Hisae Ito *Associate Director* 2864 9316
Asset Swaps (Sales)　　　Wing-son Cheng *Senior Vice President* 2864 9315

Medium-Term Notes
Head of Origination　　　Koji Saito *Director* 2864 9323
Head of Sales　　　Wing-son Cheng *Senior Vice President* 2864 9315

Private Placements
Head of Origination　　　Koji Saito *Director* 2864 9323
Head of Sales　　　Wing-son Cheng *Senior Vice President* 2864 9315
Head of Structuring　　　Koji Saito *Director* 2864 9323

Asset-Backed Securities / Securitization
Regional Head　　　Shingo Kaname *Associate Director* 2864 9351

Mortgage-Backed Securities
Regional Head　　　Shingo Kaname *Associate Director* 2864 9351

Fixed-Income Repo
Head of Repo　　　Hisae Ito *Associate Director* 2864 9316
Sales　　　Wing-son Cheng *Senior Vice President* 2864 9315

Equity Capital Markets
Head of Equity Capital Markets　　　Masahisa Nyudo *Associate Director* 2864 9351

Domestic Equities
Head of Trading　　　Makoto Iizuka *Associate Director* 2864 9344

HONG KONG, CHINA (+852)   www.euromoneydirectory.com

Sakura Finance Asia Limited (cont)
International Equities
Head of Syndication — Masahisa Nyudo *Associate Director* ☎ 2864 9351
Head of Trading — Makoto Iizuka *Associate Director* ☎ 2864 9344
Other (International Equity)
Economist — David Leung ☎ 2864 9401
Syndicated Lending
Head of Syndicated Lending; Head of Origination — Kazuaki Karahi *Executive Director*
Head of Syndication; Head of Trading — Yukitoshi Miyata *Executive Director*
Head of Credit Committee — Michihiro Susa *Executive Director*
Loan-Related Activities
Project Finance — Atushi Abe *Director*
Money Markets
Head of Origination — Koji Saito *Director* ☎ 2864 9323
Head of Sales — Wing-son Cheng *Senior Vice President* ☎ 2864 9315
Head of Trading — Hisae Ito *Associate Director* ☎ 2864 9316
Risk Management
Department: Risk Management Team
Head of Risk Management — Hiromitsu Otsu *Associate Director* ☎ 2864 9342
Settlement / Clearing
Department: Business Operations Group
Head of Settlement / Clearing — Michael Choy *Executive Director*

Salomon Brothers Hong Kong Limited

Suite 2104, Three Exchange Square, Central, Hong Kong
Tel: 2501 2000 **Fax:** 2501 8146

Equity Capital Markets
Tel: 2501 2204 **Fax:** 2501 8109
Equity Repo / Securities Lending
Head of Prime Brokerage — Larry Komo *Director* ☎ 2501 2202
Head of Trading — Dennis Jackson *Vice President*
David Lane *Trader*
Judy Yip To *Trader* ☎ 2501 2204

The Sanwa Bank Limited   Full Branch Office

10th Floor, Fairmont House, 8 Cotton Tree Drive, Central, Hong Kong
Tel: 2843 3888 **Fax:** 2840 0730 **Telex:** 73423 SANWA HX **Swift:** SANWA HK HH **Cable:** SANWABANK HONGKO

Senior Executive Officers
Chief Executive Officer — Yoshihisa Asaumi *Managing Director*
Financial Director — Hiroto Makiyama *Financial Controller*
Chief Operating Officer — Keiichiro Kase *Chief Operating Officer*
Treasurer — Tatsuya Hyodo
General - Treasury
Head of Treasury — Tatsuya Hyodo
Money Markets
Head of Money Markets — Tatsuya Hyodo
Corporate Finance / M&A Advisory
Head of Corporate Finance — Rox Lam
Settlement / Clearing
Head of Settlement / Clearing — Oi Chun Lau
Other Departments
Chief Credit Officer — Yasushi Miki
Correspondent Banking — Caroline Chiu
Administration
Head of Administration — Po Chee Hui
Technology & Systems — Tomonobu Sato
Compliance — Raymond Li *Compliance Officer*

www.euromoneydirectory.com   HONG KONG, CHINA (+852)

Sanwa International Finance Limited — Subsidiary Company
2101 Edinburgh Tower, The Landmark, 15 Queen's Road, Central, Hong Kong
Tel: 2533 4300 **Fax:** 2845 3518 **Telex:** 64836 SIFL HX

Senior Executive Officers
Chairman   Nobuhiro Ito
Chief Executive Officer   Yoshihisa Asaumi *Managing Director & Chief Executive* ☎ **2533 4301**
                                      Fumio Kaneko *Joint Managing Director* ☎ **2533 4306**
                                      Takayuki Okamoto *Deputy Managing Director* ☎ **2533 4368**
Chief Operating Officer   Shigeki Enai *Executive Director* ☎ **2533 4304**

Debt Capital Markets / Fixed Income
Head of Debt Capital Markets   Fumio Kaneko *Joint Managing Director* ☎ **2533 4306**

Syndicated Lending
Head of Syndicated Lending   Fumio Kaneko *Joint Managing Director* ☎ **2533 4306**

Money Markets
Head of Money Markets   Takayuki Okamoto *Deputy Managing Director* ☎ **2533 4368**

Risk Management
Head of Risk Management   Shigeki Enai *Executive Director* ☎ **2533 4304**

Settlement / Clearing
Head of Settlement / Clearing   Shigeki Enai *Executive Director* ☎ **2533 4304**

Schiffshypotekenbank zu Lübeck — Representative Office
New World Tower, 16-18 Queen's Road, Central, Hong Kong
PO Box 3193, Central, Hong Kong
Tel: 2843 0584 **Fax:** 2973 6539 **Telex:** 73498 DBA HX

Schroders Asia Limited — Subsidiary Company
25th Floor, Two Exchange Square, 8 Connaught Place, Central, Hong Kong
PO Box 1379, Hong Kong
Tel: 2521 1633 **Fax:** 2868 1023 **Telex:** HX75682 **Reuters:** SCHH-N **Cable:** SCHROBANK

Senior Executive Officers
Chairman   Sidney Gordon
Chief Executive Officer   Mark Hopkinson *Managing Director*
Financial Director   Peter Smith *Director*
Treasurer   Tommy Lee *Director*
Company Secretary   Cindy Yau

General-Lending (DCM, SL)
Head of Corporate Banking   Philip Mallincrkodt *Head, Asia Pacific Corporate Finance*

General-Investment
Head of Investment   Mark Hopkinson *Managing Director*

Syndicated Lending
Head of Syndication   Kelvin Chow *Director*

Loan-Related Activities
Project Finance   Read Gomm *Director*

Money Markets
Head of Money Markets   Jennifer Kwong *Manager*

Foreign Exchange
Head of Foreign Exchange   Edward Wong *Director*
Corporate Sales   Albert Lam *Manager*

Settlement / Clearing
Head of Settlement / Clearing   Terence Tso *Assistant Director*
Equity Settlement   Richard Lin *Head, Investment Operations*

Asset Management
Head   Richard Haw *Director*

Administration
Head of Administration   Cindy Yau *Manager*

Technology & Systems
                                      Raymond Tse *Assistant Director*

Compliance
                                      Pang Teck Yong *Compliance Officer*

HONG KONG, CHINA (+852)　　　www.euromoneydirectory.com

Schroders Asia Limited (cont)
Accounts / Audit
　　　Alfred Wong *Assistant Director*

Other (Administration)
Business Development　　　Glenn Fok *Director*

Seapower Securities Limited　　　Head Office
32-34th Floor, Alexandra House, 16 Chater Road, Hong Kong
Tel: 2847 4888; 2521 1238 **Fax:** 2877 3410; 2810 4898

Senior Executive Officers
Director　　　　　　　　　　　　Shirley Choi
Chief Executive Officer　　　　　Wai-kit Lau
Financial Director　　　　　　　Patrick Chung
Chief Operating Officer　　　　　Tony Lueng
Managing Director / General Manager　　K C Ho

Settlement / Clearing
Head of Settlement / Clearing　　　Grace Chan

Seoulbank　　　Full Branch Office
Room 901/902, New World Tower, 16/18 Queen's Road, Central, Hong Kong
Tel: 2521 3451; 2526 6754 **Fax:** 2810 5691 **Telex:** 63514 BOSHK **Cable:** SEOUL BANK HONG
General **Tel:** 2521 3454; 2526 6755

Senior Executive Officers
Chief Executive Officer
　　　Kim Soo Young *General Manager*
　　　Chung Jin Sung *Deputy General Manager*

SG Securities (Hong Kong) Limited　　　Subsidiary Company
41st Floor, Edinburgh Tower, 15 Queen's Road, Central, Hong Kong
Tel: 2166 4988 **Fax:** 2166 4668 **Telex:** 86730 SOKHK HX

Senior Executive Officers
Chief Executive Officer
　　　Jean Peirre Mustier *Chief Executive* [T] **2166 4336** [F] **2166 4655**
　　　[E] **jean-pierre_mustier@socgen-crosby.com**
　　　Tim Boyce *Managing Director & Chief Executive* [T] **+65 423 2218**
　　　[F] **+65 423 2500** [E] **tim_boyce@socgen-crosby.com**

Others (Senior Executives)
　　　Manu Bhaskaran *Managing Director, Group Head of Research*
　　　[T] **+65 423 2348** [F] **+65 423 2501** [E] **manu_bhaskaran@socgen-crosby.com**
　　　Foo Fatt Kah *Managing Director,Group Head of Corporate Research*
　　　[T] **+65 423 2340** [F] **+65 423 2508** [E] **foo_fatt_kah@socgen-crosby.com**

Equity Capital Markets
Head of Sales　　　Michael Hanson-Lawson *Managing Director, Head of Equity Sales, Asia*
　　　[T] **2166 4375** [F] **2166 4663** [E] **michael_hanson-lawson@socgen-crosby.com**

International Equities
Head of Sales　　　Chris Thompson *President, North America, Head of US Sales*
　　　[T] **+1 (212) 278 2000** [F] **+1 (212) 278 4230**
　　　[E] **chris_thompson@socgen-crosby.com**

Equity Repo / Securities Lending
Marketing & Product Development　　　Alexandre de Vaivre *Head of Global Sales & Marketing (Paris Based)*
　　　[T] +33 (1) 4213 9113 [F] +33 (1) 4213 6985
　　　[E] **alexandre.de-vaivre@ota.fr.socgen.com**

Corporate Finance / M&A Advisory
Other (Corporate Finance)
　　　Stuart Mobray *MD, Co-Head of Equity Corporate Finance* [T] **2166 4727**
　　　[F] **2166 4649** [E] **stuart_mowbray@socgen-crosby.com**
　　　Joss Trout *MD, Co-Head of Equity Corporate Finance* [T] **2166 4701**
　　　[F] **2166 4649** [E] **joss_trout@soc-gen-crosby.com**

www.euromoneydirectory.com HONG KONG, CHINA (+852)

Shanghai Commercial Bank Limited
Head Office

12 Queen's Road, Central, Hong Kong
Tel: 2841 5415 **Fax:** 2810 4623 **Telex:** 73390, 73650 SCBK HX **Swift:** SCBK HK HH **Reuters:** SCBH

Senior Executive Officers
Chairman   Pao Chu Shih ☎ **2841 5231**
Managing Director & General Manager   John Kam-pak Yan ☎ **2841 5321**
Treasurer   Frank Kai-shu Lau ☎ **2841 5232**
Company Secretary   Edward Kawah Chu ☎ **2841 5333**
International Division   Frank Kai-shu Lau ☎ **2841 5232**

General-Investment
Head of Investment   John Yu-Kam Chow *Manager* ☎ **2841 5284**

Debt Capital Markets / Fixed Income
Head of Fixed Income   John Yu-Kam Chow *Manager* ☎ **2841 5284**

Syndicated Lending
Loan-Related Activities
Trade Finance   C Y Chan *Senior Manager* ☎ **2841 5243**

Money Markets
Head of Money Markets   Paul Wong *Manager* ☎ **2841 5283**

Foreign Exchange
Head of Foreign Exchange   Paul Wong *Manager* ☎ **2841 5283**

Settlement / Clearing
Head of Settlement / Clearing   Edmund Chan *Sub-Manager* ☎ **2841 5388**

Other Departments
Correspondent Banking   Elizabeth P S Ng *Sub-Manager* ☎ **2841 5290**

Administration
Head of Administration   Elizabeth P S Ng *Sub-Manager* ☎ **2841 5290**

Public Relations
                                          Peter Kwok *Assistant Manager* ☎ **2841 5383**

Shenyin Wanguo Securities (Hong Kong) Limited
Head Office

Formerly known as: Shanghai Hong Kong International Securities Limited
28th Floor, Citibank Tower, Citibank Plaza, 3 Garden Road, Central, Hong Kong
Tel: 2509 8333 **Fax:** 2509 0319 **Telex:** 83017 SWHK HX

Senior Executive Officers
Chairman   Jiang Guofang
Chief Executive Officer   Sok Un Chong
Financial Director   Man Chun Lee
Managing Director   Terence Howard

Corporate Finance / M&A Advisory
Country Head   Siu Ming Lee

Settlement / Clearing
Country Head   Kwok Kuen Kam

The Siam Commercial Bank Public Company Limited
Full Branch Office

703 Edinburgh Tower, The Landmark, 15 Queen's Road, Central, Hong Kong
Tel: 2524 4085 **Fax:** 2845 0293 **Telex:** 66150 SIAMB HX **Swift:** SICO HK HH

Senior Executive Officers
Chief Executive Officer   Santi Santikulanont *General Manager*
Treasurer   Tawatchai Chomrat *Treasury Manager*

Sin Hua Bank Limited
Full Branch Office

2A Des Voex Road, Central, Hong Kong
Tel: 2160 8888 **Fax:** 2854 2596 **Telex:** 73416 SINHU HX **Swift:** SINH HK HH **Reuters:** SHTK

Senior Executive Officers
Chairman   Zu Qi Jiang
Chief Executive Officer   Xiao Wei Mao *Executive Director*
General Manager, Executive Director   Jun Sheng Wu

HONG KONG, CHINA (+852)　　www.euromoneydirectory.com

Sin Hua Bank Limited (cont)
Others (Senior Executives)
　　　　　　　　　　　　　　　Mei Yung Yu *Deputy General Manager*
　　　　　　　　　　　　　　　Bing Kuen Leung *Deputy General Manager*
　　　　　　　　　　　　　　　Wai Choi Chow *Deputy General Manager*
　　　　　　　　　　　　　　　Kam Tong Chow *Deputy General Manager*
General - Treasury
Head of Treasury　　　　　　Herman Wong Wai Sang
Syndicated Lending
Loan-Related Activities
Trade Finance　　　　　　　Yip Hung Fat

Skandinaviska Enskilda Banken AB (publ)　　Full Branch Office
2201-10 Jardine House, One Connaught Place, Central, Hong Kong
Tel: 2822 6228 **Fax:** 2868 4367 **Telex:** 67341 ESSEB HX **Swift:** ESSE HK HH **Reuters:** SEBH
Senior Executive Officers
Managing Director / General Manager　Fredrik Boheman
General Manager　　　　　　Majnus Cavalli-Björkman
Syndicated Lending
Loan-Related Activities
Trade Finance; Project Finance　Marcel Ivison
Money Markets
Head of Money Markets　　　Thomson Cheung
Foreign Exchange
Head of Foreign Exchange　　Thomson Cheung
Corporate Sales　　　　　　Eric Fung
Risk Management
Head of Risk Management　　Sandra Leung *Head of Credit*
Settlement / Clearing
Operations　　　　　　　　Christina Chung *Head of Control, Finance & Operations*
Other Departments
Chief Credit Officer　　　　Sandra Leung *Head of Credit*
Administration
Other (Administration)
Trade Services　　　　　　Tendy Li *Head*

Société Génerale　　Full Branch Office
44th Floor, Edinburgh Tower, 15 Queen's Road, Central, Hong Kong
Tel: 2844 5388 **Fax:** 2868 2368; 2868 2388 **Telex:** 65023 SOGEN HX **Swift:** SOGE HK HH **Reuters:** SGHK-L (Monitor)
Senior Executive Officers
Chief Executive Officer　　　Alain Simon
Treasurer　　　　　　　　Stéphane Chretien *Executive Vice President*
Money Markets
Tel: 2844 5497 **Fax:** 2596 0625
Country Head　　　　　　Petrina Ho *SVP, Deputy Treasurer*
Other Departments
Private Banking　　　　　　Daniel Truchi *Managing Director* ☎ 2101 0128
Correspondent Banking　　　David Li ☎ 2844 5435
Administration
Public Relations
　　　　　　　　　　　　　　　Christine Rakusen *PA to CEO* ☎ 2844 5309

Société Générale Asia Limited　　Subsidiary Company
42nd Floor, Edinburgh Tower, 15 Queen's Road, Central, Hong Kong
Tel: 2583 8600 **Fax:** 2840 0738 **Telex:** 65023 SOGEN HX **Swift:** SOGE HK HH **Reuters:** SGHK (Monitor)
Senior Executive Officers
Chief Executive Officer　　　Tommy Chua ☎ 2583 8601

www.euromoneydirectory.com   HONG KONG, CHINA (+852)

Debt Capital Markets / Fixed Income
Regional Head   Stephen So *MD, Head of Debt Capital Markets* ☏ **2583 8638**
Domestic Government Bonds
Head of Sales   Jean Marc Croisy *Director, Head of Sales, Hong Kong* ☏ **2583 8730**
Head of Trading   Derek Ho *VP, Securities Trading* ☏ **2583 8711**
Eurobonds
Head of Sales   Jean Marc Croisy *Director, Head of Sales, Hong Kong* ☏ **2583 8730**
Trading (High-yield)   Gilbert Bourdon *Vice President* ☏ **2583 8731**
Emerging Market Bonds
Head of Sales   Jean Marc Croisy *Director, Head of Sales, Hong Kong* ☏ **2583 8730**
Libor-Based / Floating-Rate Products
FRN Origination   Tak Lap Leung *Director, Head of Primary Markets* ☏ **2583 8760**
FRN Sales   Jean Marc Croisy *Director, Head of Sales, Hong Kong* ☏ **2583 8730**
Syndicated Lending
Head of Origination   Michael Leemputte *MD, Head of Originations* ☏ **2583 8626**
Head of Syndication   Diana Cheung *MD, Head of Syndications* ☏ **2583 8611**
Loan-Related Activities
Project Finance   Ashley C Wilkins *Head, Project Finance & Advisory, Asia* ☏ **2583 8619**
                               Francis Favret *Vice President* ☏ **2583 8615**
                               David Gore *Vice President* ☏ **2583 8610**
                               Charles Law *Vice President* ☏ **2583 8674**
                               Clare Chan *Vice President* ☏ **2583 8696**
Other (Trade Finance)
Structured Finance   Jean-Francois Despoux *Director* ☏ **2583 8696**
Risk Management
Fixed Income Derivatives / Risk Management
Regional Head   Claude Piana *Managing Director* ☏ **2583 8780**
IR Swaps Sales / Marketing   Francis Luk ☏ **2583 8770**
IR Swaps Trading   Peter Yam ☏ **2583 8770**
IR Options Sales / Marketing Hanif Kanji ☏ **2583 8770**

The Standard Bank of South Africa Limited   Representative Office

36th Floor, Citibank Tower, Citibank Plaza, 3 Garden Road, Central, Hong Kong
Tel: 2822 7888; 2822 7977 **Fax:** 2822 7999; 2822 7998 **Telex:** 88055 STLA HX **Swift:** STLA HK HX
Senior Executive Officers
Regional Representative, Asia / Pacific   Roy Ross ☏ **2822 7977** 🖷 **2822 7998**

Standard Chartered Asia Limited   Subsidiary Company

10th Floor, Standard Chartered Bank Building, 4-4A Des Voeux Road, Central, Hong Kong
Tel: 2841 0333 **Fax:** 2810 0475
Senior Executive Officers
Managing Director / General Manager   Richard Winter ☏ **2841 0257** 🖷 **2868 5430**
Syndicated Lending
Global Head   Philip Cracknell
Corporate Finance / M&A Advisory
Head of Corporate Finance   Richard Winter ☏ **2841 0257** 🖷 **2868 5430**

Standard Chartered Bank   Full Branch Office

Standard Chartered Bank Building, 4-4A Des Voeux Road, Central, Hong Kong
PO Box 21, Hong Kong
Tel: 2820 3333 **Fax:** 2856 9129 **Telex:** 73430 SCHNK HX **Swift:** SCBL HK HH **Cable:** Stancharth
General Telex: 74750 SCHNK HX; **General Telex:** 66540 SCHNK HX
Senior Executive Officers
Others (Senior Executives)
Group Executive Director, Hong Kong, China & NEA   Mervyn Daines ☏ **2821 1881** 🖷 **2810 5781**
Consumer Banking, Hong Kong & China   Peter Wong *Head* ☏ **2804 8808** 🖷 **2560 2000**
Corporate & Institutional Bnkg, HK, Taiwan, China   Rafael Gil-Tienda *Head* ☏ **2821 1360** 🖷 **2877 0645**
Regional Treasurer, NEA   Stanley Wong ☏ **2820 3728** 🖷 **2521 4086**

Euromoney Directory 1999 **649**

HONG KONG, CHINA (+852) www.euromoneydirectory.com

State Street Bank & Trust Company   Full Branch Office

32nd Floor, Two Exchange Square, 8 Connaught Place, Central, Hong Kong
Tel: 2840 5388 **Telex:** 66694 SSASX HX **Swift:** SBOS HK HX **Reuters:** SSHK
General **Telex:** 62594 STATE HX; Global Investor Services **Fax:** 2868 1606; Global Trade Banking
Fax: 2845 9020; Global Treasury **Fax:** 2840 5412; State Street Global Advisors **Fax:** 2103 0190
Website: www.statestreet.com

Senior Executive Officers
Chief Executive Officer | Vincent Duhamel *Principal & CEO, State Street Global Advisors* 2103 0218
Managing Director, Global Trade Banking | Thomas Lynch 2840 5303
Managing Director, Global Investor Services Group | K K Tse 2978 9252
Managing Director, Global Treasury | Frederick Au 2840 5369

Others (Senior Executives)
Global Investor Services Group | Terese Choi *VP, Head of Marketing & Sales* 2840 5393
 | Margaret Quon *VP, Head of Client Accounts* 2840 5392
Global Trade Banking | Peter Lam *VP, Marketing* 2840 5328
 | Paul Li *VP, Marketing* 2840 5304
 | Patricia Chan *VP, Marketing* 2840 5470
 | Angela Arguelles *VP, Credit Administration Manager* 2840 5329
 | Esther Lam *VP, Bills Manager* 2840 5306
State Street Global Advisors | Hon Cheung *Director of Investments* 2103 0123 2103 0200
 | Cecilia Chin *Director of Marketing* 2103 0228

General - Treasury
Head of Treasury | Steven Chang *VP, Treasury Manager* 2840 5365 2840 5411
 | Lyle Pai *Vice President* 2840 5425
 | Linda Li *Operations Manager* 2840 5352 2830 5410

SüdwestLB   Representative Office

907 Two Exchange Square, 8 Connaught Place, Central, Hong Kong
Tel: 2525 5013 **Fax:** 2840 0474

Senior Executive Officers
SVP & Chief Representative | Thorsten K Amann
Deputy Representative | Meilan Gan

Sumitomo Finance (Asia) Limited   Subsidiary Company

32nd Floor, 3205 Edinburgh Tower, 15 Queen's Road, Central, Hong Kong
Tel: 2501 6600 **Fax:** 2868 1505; 2525 7188 **Telex:** 75300 SFALA HX
Dealing Tel: 2501 6740

Senior Executive Officers
Chief Executive Officer | Masaki Shimbo *Chief Executive*
Financial Director | Yoshihiro Imura *Deputy Chief Executive*
 | Joanna Law *Head, Administration & Accounts*
Chief Operating Officer | Lawrence Fu *Head of Settlements*
Treasurer | Frankie Li

Debt Capital Markets / Fixed Income

Eurobonds
Head of Syndication | Eric She *Executive Director*
Head of Research | John Kim *Executive Director*

Fixed-Income Repo
Sales | Hironori Hattori *Director*

Equity Capital Markets
Tel: 2521 0311

Equity Repo / Securities Lending
Head | Carolyn Lu *Executive Director*
Head of Trading | Hironori Hattori *Director*

650 Euromoney Directory 1999

www.euromoneydirectory.com   HONG KONG, CHINA (+852)

The Sumitomo Trust & Banking Company Limited Full Branch Office

18th Floor, Three Exchange Square, 8 Connaught Place, Central, Hong Kong
Tel: 2523 6026 **Fax:** 2840 0496; 2840 0502 **Telex:** 80541 SMTRB HX

Senior Executive Officers
General Manager — Ken Masunaga
Deputy General Manager — Tadashi Furue
Senior Manager — Akihiko Yasuda

Money Markets
Tel: 2524 5792 **Fax:** 2826 9163 **Reuters:** STBH
Head of Money Markets — Hironori Oizumi *Treasury Manager* ☎ 2801 8853

Foreign Exchange
Tel: 2524 5792 **Fax:** 2826 9163 **Reuters:** STBH
Head of Foreign Exchange — Hironori Oizumi *Treasury Manager* ☎ 2801 8853

FX Traders / Sales People
Ricky Wu *Chief Dealer* ☎ 2524 9945

Risk Management
Tel: 2523 6062 **Fax:** 2840 0496 **Telex:** 80541 SMTRB HX
Head of Risk Management — Frank Tsui *Assistant General Manager* ☎ 2801 8885

Settlement / Clearing
Tel: 2523 6062 **Fax:** 2801 8525
Head of Settlement / Clearing — Eric Tsoi *Settlement Manager* ☎ 2801 8812

Sun Hung Kai & Co Limited   Head Office

Level 12, One Pacific Place, 88 Queensway, Hong Kong
Tel: 2822 5678 **Fax:** 2822 5664 **Telex:** 74782 SHKSC HX **Email:** s78echan@netvigator.com
Website: www.irasia.com/listco/hk/shkco

Senior Executive Officers
Executive Chairman — Arthur Dew ☎ 2822 5506 🖷 2822 5332

Others (Senior Executives)
Executive Director — Tze Hien Chung ☎ 2822 5789 🖷 2520 6676
Gary Cheung ☎ 2822 5330 🖷 2822 5332

Equity Capital Markets
Department: Sun Hung Kai Investment Services Limited

Other (Domestic Equities)
Investment Holding & Share Broking — Gary Cheung *Director* ☎ 2822 5330 🖷 2822 5332
Patrick Wong *Director* ☎ 2822 5775 🖷 2528 5005
Gilbert Chu *Director* ☎ 2106 8830 🖷 2106 8800
Jimmy Fong *Director* ☎ 2822 5540 🖷 2528 6411

Department: Sun Hung Kai Investment Services Limited

Other (Domestic Equities)
Investment Holding & Share Broking — Bajun Zhou ☎ +86 (21) 6326 5030 🖷 +86 (21) 6323 3367
Bajun Zhou *Shenzhen* ☎ +86 (755) 217 1440 🖷 +86 (755) 217 1839

Department: Sun Hung Kai Securities (Phil.), Inc.
Tel: +63 (2) 810 3971 **Fax:** +63 (2) 817 5880
Regional Head — Tee Jin Ong *Director*
Gavin Ng *Director*

Foreign Exchange
Department: Sun Hung Kai Forex Limited

FX Traders / Sales People
Gary Cheung *Director* ☎ 2822 5330 🖷 2822 5332
Hop Chan *Director* ☎ 2822 5504 🖷 2822 5664
Jackco Chan *Director* ☎ 2822 5684 🖷 2822 5664
Henry Wong *Director* ☎ 2822 5684 🖷 2822 5664

Corporate Finance / M&A Advisory
Department: Sun Hung Kai International Limited

Other (Corporate Finance)
Corporate Finance Service — Daniel Ng *Director* ☎ 2106 8363 🖷 2106 8700

Asset Management
Department: Sun Hung Kai Fund Management Limited

Other (Asset Management)
SHK. Unit Trust Management Limited — Vincent Koo *Director* ☎ 2116 8205 🖷 2116 0196
Patrick Choo *Director* ☎ 2116 8203 🖷 2116 0196

HONG KONG, CHINA (+852)   www.euromoneydirectory.com

Sun Hung Kai & Co Limited (cont)
Department: SHK Financial Management Limited

Other (Asset Management)
Leverage FX & Gold Fund   Gary Cheung *Director* T 2822 5330 F 2822 5332
                                     Tony Chang *Director* T 2822 5738 F 2822 5664
                                     Stephen So *Director* T 2822 5868 F 2822 5664
                                     Jackco Chan *Director* T 2822 5684 F 2822 5664
Department: Tian An China Investments Company Ltd (Associated Company)

Other (Asset Management)
Investment Holding   David Hui *Managing Director* T 2533 3298 F 2533 3221

Other Departments
Department: Sun Hung Kai Commodities Limited
Commodities / Bullion   Gary Cheung *Director* T 2822 5330 F 2822 5332
                                     Hop Chan *Director* T 2822 5504 F 2822 5664
                                     Tony Chang *Director* T 2822 5738 F 2822 5664
                                     Jimmy Fong *Director* T 2822 5540 F 2528 6411
Department: Sun Hung Kai Research Limited
Economic Research   Gilbert Chu *Director* T 2106 8830 F 2106 8800
Department: Sun Hung Kai Insurance Consultants Limited

Other Departments
Insurance Broking   Stanley Ho *Director* T 2802 2515 F 2845 7743
Department: SHK Financial Data Limited

Other Departments
Financial Information Service   Victor Lo *Director* T 2591 1218 F 2520 0518
Department: Sun Hung Kai Bullion Company Limited
Commodities / Bullion   Gary Cheung *Director* T 2822 5330 F 2822 5332
                                     Hop Chan *Director* T 2822 5504 F 2822 5664
                                     Tony Chang *Director* T 2822 5738 F 2822 5664
Department: Sun Tai Cheung Credits Limited

Other Departments
Share Margin Financing   Tze Hien Chung *Director* T 2822 5789 F 2520 6676

Administration

Public Relations
Support   Elaine Chan *Assistant Public Relations Manager* T 2822 5787 F 2865 5877

Svenska Handelsbanken AB (publ)

2008 Hutchison House, 10 Harcourt Road, Central, Hong Kong
Tel: 2868 2131 **Fax:** 2868 4339 **Telex:** 64765 SHB HK **Reuters:** SHBO (Dealing)

Senior Executive Officers
Deputy General Manager   Matthew Chung

Taipei Business Bank   Representative Office

30th Floor, Unit 7210 Cosco Tower, 183 Queen's Road, Central, Hong Kong
Tel: 2541 9992 **Fax:** 2543 9243

Senior Executive Officers
General Manager   Ted Liao

The Toho Bank Limited   Representative Office

Suite 3006, Two Exchange Square, 8 Connaught Place, Central, Hong Kong
Tel: 2526 5900 **Fax:** 2526 9780

Senior Executive Officers
Chief Representative   Tadahiko Tomita

Tokai Asia Limited
Subsidiary Company

28th Floor, Alexandra House, 16/20 Chater Road, Central, Hong Kong
PO Box 13411, Hong Kong
Tel: 2978 6888 **Fax:** 2840 0069; 2526 8041 **Telex:** 85214 TOKHK HX **Swift:** TOAS HK HH
Website: www.tokaiasia.com.hk

Senior Executive Officers
Chief Executive Officer — Yoshimitsu Yamagata *Managing Director & Chief Executive* **2978 6100**
Brian Lippey *Joint Managing Director & Joint CEO* **2978 6102**
Financial Director — Craig Lindsay *Executive Vice President* **2978 6117**
Deputy Managing Director — Takahiro Takei **2978 6113**

General-Lending (DCM, SL)
Head of Corporate Banking — Drake Pike *Executive Vice President, Credit* **2978 6260**

Equity Capital Markets
International Equities
Head of Trading — Jeff Wallace *Executive Vice President* **2822 5100**
Eugene Lonergan *Executive Vice President* **2822 5100**

Convertibles / Equity-Linked
Head of Trading — James Dowd *Executive Vice President* **2822 5100**

Syndicated Lending
Other (Syndicated Lending)
Market Strategist — Philip Moffitt *Executive Vice President* **2822 5100**

Foreign Exchange
Head of Trading — David Hoe *Executive Vice President* **2822 5100**

Risk Management
Global Head — Sherif Sweillam *Executive Vice President* **2978 6188**

Settlement / Clearing
Settlement (General) — Freda Chan *Settlement Manager* **2978 6166**
Operations — William Keough *Operations Manager* **2978 6163**

Administration
Technology & Systems
Neil Mowbray *Executive Vice President* **2978 6190**

Tokai Maruman Securities (Asia) Limited
Subsidiary Company

Formerly known as: Maruman Securities (Asia) Limited
Suite 1704, One Exchange Square, 8 Connaught Place, Central, Hong Kong
Tel: 2810 0822 **Fax:** 2810 0394 **Telex:** 71905 MSCLH HX

Senior Executive Officers
Managing Director — Hideo Tomura

Tokyo-Mitsubishi International (Hong Kong) Limited
Subsidiary Company

Formerly known as: BOT International (HK) Limited & Mitsubishi Finance (HK) Limited
16th Floor, Tower I, Admiralty Centre, 18 Harcourt Road, Central, Hong Kong
Tel: 2520 2460 **Fax:** 2529 1550; 2529 1649 **Telex:** 62053 TMHKL HX **Swift:** MFHK HK HH **Reuters:** HK2795-001
Telerate: 001298

Senior Executive Officers
Managing Director — Toshiyuki Morioka **2860 1501**

Debt Capital Markets / Fixed Income
Global Head — Katsumi Hatao *Marketing Director* **2860 1430**

Domestic Government Bonds
Head of Sales — Tom Hsiao *Director* **2860 1583**
Head of Trading — Hisato Funase *Senior Manager* **2860 1570**
Head of Research — Daniel Tam *Manager* **2860 1590**

Eurobonds
Head of Origination — Katsumi Hatao *Marketing Director* **2860 1430**
Head of Trading — Hisato Funase *Senior Manager* **2860 1570**

Libor-Based / Floating-Rate Products
FRN Origination — Katsumi Hatao *Marketing Director* **2860 1430**

HONG KONG, CHINA (+852)　　　　　www.euromoneydirectory.com

Tokyo-Mitsubishi International (Hong Kong) Limited (cont)

Medium-Term Notes
Head of Origination　　　　　　　　Katsumi Hatao *Marketing Director* ☎ 2860 1430

Private Placements
Head of Origination　　　　　　　　Katsumi Hatao *Marketing Director* ☎ 2860 1430

Asset-Backed Securities / Securitization
Global Head　　　　　　　　　　　Katsumi Hatao *Marketing Director* ☎ 2860 1430

Mortgage-Backed Securities
Global Head　　　　　　　　　　　Katsumi Hatao *Marketing Director* ☎ 2860 1430

Syndicated Lending
Global Head　　　　　　　　　　　Katsumi Hatao *Marketing Director* ☎ 2860 1430

Loan-Related Activities
Trade Finance; Project Finance; Structured　　Kenichi Tabuchi *Associate Director* ☎ 2860 1530
Trade Finance

Risk Management
Country Head　　　　　　　　　　　Takeshi Ueno *Manager* ☎ 2860 1560

Fixed Income Derivatives / Risk Management
IR Swaps Sales / Marketing　　　　　Yuji Tokuhiro *Manager* ☎ 2860 1589
IR Swaps Trading　　　　　　　　　Tatsuyoshi Wada *Manager* ☎ 2860 1587
IR Options Sales / Marketing　　　　Yuji Tokuhiro *Manager* ☎ 2860 1589
IR Options Trading　　　　　　　　　Tatsuyoshi Wada *Manager* ☎ 2860 1587

Foreign Exchange Derivatives / Risk Management
Cross-Currency Swaps, Sales / Marketing　　Yuji Tokuhiro *Manager* ☎ 2860 1589
Cross-Currency Swaps, Trading　　　　Tatsuyoshi Wada *Manager* ☎ 2860 1587

Other Currency Swap / FX Options Personnel
IR Swaps / Options Trading　　　　　Simon Wong *Associate Director* ☎ 2860 1591
IR Swaps / Options Marketing　　　　Richard Wang *Manager* ☎ 2860 1588

Settlement / Clearing
Equity Settlement　　　　　　　　　Raymond Wong *Senior Manager* ☎ 2860 1420
Fixed-Income Settlement　　　　　　Fande Nam *Manager* ☎ 2860 1521

Global Custody
Other (Global Custody)
　　　　　　　　　　　　　　　　Raymond Wong *Senior Manager* ☎ 2860 1420

Other Departments
Proprietary Trading　　　　　　　　Hisato Funase *Senior Manager* ☎ 2860 1570
Private Banking　　　　　　　　　　Keisuke Kasai *Manager* ☎ 2860 1450

Administration
Technology & Systems
　　　　　　　　　　　　　　　　Y Y Chow *Manager* ☎ 2860 1540

Compliance
　　　　　　　　　　　　　　　　John Wu *Internal Auditor* ☎ 2860 1481

Public Relations
　　　　　　　　　　　　　　　　Lolly Chun *Manager* ☎ 2860 1510

Toronto-Dominion Bank　　　　　　　　　　　　　　Full Branch Office

Two Pacific Place, 88 Queensway, Hong Kong
Tel: 2846 4111 **Fax:** 2845 9191 **Telex:** 74356 TORDO HX **Swift:** TDOM HK HH AXXX
Dealing Tel: 2523 2933; **Treasury Fax:** 2523 5502

Senior Executive Officers
Managing Director　　　　　　　　　Ramon Yu

Debt Capital Markets / Fixed Income
Department: Treasury
Tel: 2523 2933 **Fax:** 2523 5502
Head of Fixed Income　　　　　　　Philip Ma *Vice President & Director*

Money Markets
Head of Money Markets　　　　　　Philip Ma *Vice President & Director*

www.euromoneydirectory.com   HONG KONG, CHINA (+852)

Toyo Trust & Banking Company Limited

Alternative trading name: Toyo Trust Asia Limited
15th Floor, Gloucester Tower, 11 Pedder Street, The Landmark, Hong Kong
Tel: 2526 5657 **Fax:** 2845 9247 **Telex:** 85198 TYTHK HX

Senior Executive Officers
General Manager   K Kuboyama
Managing Director / General Manager   Mikio Ito

Administration
Head of Marketing   Mr Fufawa

Public Relations
General Affairs   K F Yim *Head*

Tradition (Asia) Limited   Subsidiary Company

2608 Alexandra House, 16/20 Chater Road, Central, Hong Kong
Tel: 2525 2180; 2525 2189 **Fax:** 2868 1643 **Telex:** 75220 DTAHK **Reuters:** TRHK, TRFX

Senior Executive Officers
Managing Director   Francis Lai

Relationship Manager
ACU Deposit   Sapphire Hung *Senior Manager*
                                               Jimmy Lai *Manager*
Off-Shore Banking Unit   Kenny Moon *Manager*
Currency Deposit   Bin Chan *Manager*
OBS Products   Anthony Lee *Senior Manager*
Domestic Products   Andy Lau *Manager*
Exotic Currencies   Paul Chung *Manager*
Credit Derivatives   Jun Air Gara *Senior Manager*

Settlement / Clearing
Operations   Irene Lee *Financial Controller*

Tradition Financial Services (Hong Kong) Limited
Subsidiary Company

2610 Alexandra House, 16/20 Chater Road, Central, Hong Kong
Tel: 2521 5706 **Fax:** 2877 2719 **Telex:** 75220 DTAHK **Reuters:** TFSH

Senior Executive Officers
Managing Director   Dennis Trappitt

Settlement / Clearing
Operations   Irene Lee *Financial Controller*

Administration
Other (Administration)
Administrator   Lesley McLaren

UBAF (Hong Kong) Limited   Subsidiary Company

18th Floor, Far East Finance Centre, 16 Harcourt Road, Hong Kong
PO Box 9917, Hong Kong
Tel: 2520 1361 **Fax:** 2527 4256 **Telex:** 75386 HX **Swift:** UBAFHX **Reuters:** UBAK

Senior Executive Officers
Managing Director   Guy Thomas Alejandro
Company Secretary   Larry S S Yap

General-Lending (DCM, SL)
Head of Corporate Banking   Larry S S Yap *Senior Manager, Credit & Marketing*

General - Treasury
Head of Treasury   Benny Y K Cheng *Senior Dealer*

Settlement / Clearing
Operations   W L Chan *Manager*
                                               Raymond P C Cheng *Assistant Manager*

HONG KONG, CHINA (+852)   www.euromoneydirectory.com

UBAF (Hong Kong) Limited (cont)
Administration
Head of Administration   Grace S L Lynn *Assistant Manager*

Accounts / Audit
    Grace S L Lynn *Assistant Manager*

UBS AG

25th Floor, One Exchange Square, 8 Connaught Place, Central, Hong Kong
PO Box 506, Hong Kong
Tel: 2971 8888 **Fax:** 2868 1510 **Telex:** 64127 SBC HX **Swift:** SBCOHK HH **Cable:** HKSUIS

Senior Executive Officers

Others (Senior Executives)
Business Area Head, Asia	R Weil
Regional Market Manager, Greater China	K Shih
Regional Market Manager, Pacific	J Kamitsis
Head of Hong Kong Booking Centre	B Weber
Special Mandates	A Ludi
Portfolio Management	J McAteer
Active Advisory Team	P Amandini
Branded Investment Products	J Hong
Financial Planning & Wealth Management	E Lenyoun
Chief Operating Officer	P Liu

Unibank A/S   Full Branch Office

19th Floor, Jardine House, Central, Hong Kong
Tel: 2810 5610 **Fax:** 2810 1389 **Telex:** 76019 **Swift:** UNIB HK HH

Senior Executive Officers
General Manager   Vagn S Pedersen

UniCredito Italiano SpA   Full Branch Office

Formerly known as: Credito Italiano SpA
36th Floor, Bank of China Tower, 1 Garden Road, Hong Kong
Tel: 2820 7688 **Fax:** 2845 9511 **Telex:** 64949 CITHF XH **Swift:** CRIT HK HH **Reuters:** CRIH **Cable:** ITALCREDIT HONG
Dealing Tel: 2525 5331

Senior Executive Officers
Chief Manager   Dante Pasqualini

Union Bank of Hong Kong Limited   Head Office

Union Bank Tower, 122-126 Queen's Road, Central, Hong Kong
Tel: 2534 3333 **Fax:** 2805 1166 **Telex:** 73264 UNIBK HX **Swift:** UBHK HK HH **Email:** ubstd02@unionbank.com.hk
Website: www.unionbank.com.hk

Senior Executive Officers
Chairman   Yin Fei Li
Chief Executive Officer   David Man Tak Yau *Managing Director*

Union Européenne de CIC   Representative Office

Suite 1104, CITIC Tower, 1 Tim Mei Avenue, Central, Hong Kong
Tel: 2521 6151 **Fax:** 2810 6235 **Telex:** 62624BUEHK HX **Email:** cicbanks@asiaonline.net

Senior Executive Officers
Representative   Christopher Chen

656 Euromoney Directory 1999

www.euromoneydirectory.com HONG KONG, CHINA (+852)

United Chinese Bank Limited
Head Office

31 Des Voeux Road, Central, Hong Kong
GPO Box 80, Hong Kong
Tel: 2912 1818 **Fax:** 2868 4608 **Telex:** 74576 **Swift:** UNCH HK HH **Cable:** UCHINBANK
Website: www.hkbea.com

Senior Executive Officers
Chairman & Chief Executive — David K P Li ⓣ **2912 1818** ⓕ **2868 4608**
Financial Director — Simon K H Sham *Senior Deputy Manager* ⓣ **2912 1868** ⓕ **2521 8334**
Treasurer — Shu-Wing Cheung *Assistant Manager* ⓣ **2912 1748** ⓕ **2868 4608**
Executive Director & General Manager — Hon-Shing Tong ⓣ **2912 1800** ⓕ **2868 4608**

Syndicated Lending
Tel: 2912 1775 **Fax:** 2501 5605
Global Head of Syndication — Lisa W M Kwok *Manager* ⓣ **2912 1898** ⓕ **2501 5605**
Head of Credit Committee — Hon-Shing Tong *Executive Director & General Manager* ⓣ **2912 1800** ⓕ **2868 4608**

Loan-Related Activities
Trade Finance — Johnny W C Fung *Sub-Manager* ⓣ **2912 1705**
Structured Trade Finance — Johnny W C Fung *Deputy Manager* ⓣ **2912 1705** ⓕ **2525 0762**

Foreign Exchange
Tel: 2912 1781 **Fax:** 2521 8334
Global Head — Sander K C Tsang *Deputy Manager* ⓣ **2912 1788** ⓕ **2521 8334**

Settlement / Clearing
Tel: 2912 1781 **Fax:** 2521 8334
Head of Settlement / Clearing — Sander K C Tsang *Deputy Manager* ⓣ **2912 1788** ⓕ **2521 8334**

Other Departments
Chief Credit Officer — Bryan W K Lee *Senior Assistant Manager* ⓣ **2912 1793** ⓕ **2501 5605**
Correspondent Banking — Sander K C Tsang *Deputy Manager* ⓣ **2912 1788** ⓕ **2521 8334**
Cash Management — Shu-Wing Cheung *Assistant Manager* ⓣ **2912 1748** ⓕ **2868 4608**

Administration
Head of Administration — Annie Mimi Kam *Senior Manager* ⓣ **2912 1830**
Business Development — Eric K L Lau *Senior Deputy Manager* ⓣ **2912 1878**

Warburg Dillon Read

25th Floor, One Exchange Square, 8 Connaught Place, Central, Hong Kong
PO Box 506, Hong Kong
Tel: 2971 8888 **Fax:** 2868 1510 **Telex:** 64127 SBC HX **Swift:** SBCO HK HH **Cable:** HKSUIS

Senior Executive Officers
Country Head — H Jenkins

Debt Capital Markets / Fixed Income
Department: Rates
Bonds - General
P Jordan *Derivative & Structured Products, Asia*
S Kamlani *Head of Financing Asia*
S Williams *Head of Debt Capital Markets, Asia / Pacific*
R Berweger *Head of Global Trade Finance, Asia*

Equity Capital Markets
Other (Domestic Equities)
Peter Burnett *Head of ECMG, Asia*
David Paine *Head of Equity Syndicate*
Nicole Yuen *Product Marketing*
Equities — H Jenkins *Head of Asian Equities*
W McGrath *COO, Asian Equities*
J Wall *Head of Equity Trading, Asia & Japan*
H Cheuk-Yuet *Head of Equity Sales, HK / China*

Other (Equity Research)
B Orgill *Head of Asian Research*
S Rogers *Head of Hong Kong Research*
V Chan *Head of China Research*
Ti-sheng Young *Head of HK / China Research*
I McLennan *Head of Asian Equity Strategy*
E Chung *Chief Asian Equity Strategist*
T Williams *Head of Chemical Research*
M Mak *Head of Regional Infrastructure*

HONG KONG, CHINA (+852)   www.euromoneydirectory.com

Warburg Dillon Read (cont)
Other (Equity Research) (cont)
C Pennington *Head of Oil & Gas Asia*
J Lee *Asia Power & Infrastructure*
F Lam *Head of Regional Property*
J Billings *Telecoms*
S Ogus *Head of Asian Economics*

Syndicated Lending
Loan-Related Activities
Project Finance — J Thirsk *Head of Project Finance, Asia*
Department: Institutional Banking & Global Trade Finance
Regional Head — R Berweger *Regional Head, Asia / Pacific*

Foreign Exchange
Head of Foreign Exchange — S Wong
FX Traders / Sales People
A Cheung *Head of Precious Metal Trading*
N Delf *Precious Metal Sales*
A Cheng *Head of FX Spot Trading*
J Kremer *Alternative Asset Management*

Corporate Finance / M&A Advisory
Regional Head — T Kok Yew *Regional Head of Corporate Finance, Asia*
Other (Corporate Finance)
Head of Hong Kong — G Fung
Financial Institutions Group, Asia / Pacific — M Chiba
Head of China — H Di
Power & Pipelines — J Shaver
Senior Advisory — H Shih

Administration
Department: Logistics

Technology & Systems
Information Technology — M Hin Kwong

Legal / In-House Counsel
Legal Counsel, Hong Kong — V Wong

Compliance
Regional Compliance, Asia — N Clement-Jones

Corporate Communications
Corporate Communications, Asia / Pacific — M McGrath *Joint Head*
R Boerner *Joint Head*

Accounts / Audit
Corporate Audit — C Wan

Other (Administration)
C Woo *Head of Human Resources, Hong Kong*
J Schofield *Head of Operations, Asia / Pacific*
S Ip *Head of Financial Control*
C Ko *Corporate Services, Asia / Pacific*
K Lindsell *Senior Credit Officer, North Asia*
P Lofts *Chief Credit Officer, Asia / Pacific*

Westdeutsche Landesbank Girozentrale (WestLB) Full Branch Office

36th Floor, Bank of America Tower, 12 Harcourt Road, Central, Hong Kong
Tel: 2842 0288 Fax: 2842 0296 Telex: 75142 HX WSTLB Reuters: ASIA Telerate: 2732 Cable: WESTLB

Senior Executive Officers
Chief Executive Officer — Richard McDonald *SVP & General Manager* ☎ 2842 0271 📠 2842 0286
Chief Operating Officer — Esther Tang *Vice President & Assistant General Manager* ☎ 2842 0258 📠 2842 0261

Treasurer — Philip Chu *Vice President* ☎ 2842 0223 📠 2842 0286
Assistant Vice President — Priscilla Leung ☎ 2842 0407 📠 2842 0261

Equity Capital Markets
Fax: 2842 0438

International Equities
Head of Sales — Torsten Hinrichs *Vice President* ☎ 2842 0283 📠 2842 0286

Syndicated Lending
Head of Syndicated Lending — Johnny Lo *Vice President* ☎ 2842 0200 📠 2842 0438

www.euromoneydirectory.com HONG KONG, CHINA (+852)

Loan-Related Activities
Project Finance　　　　　　　　　　　Andrew Kinloch *Head of Structured Finance and Export Finance*
　　　　　　　　　　　　　　　　　　　Ⓣ 2842 0428 Ⓕ 2842 0298
Structured Trade Finance　　　　　　　Vereen Wong *Second Vice President* Ⓣ 2842 0236 Ⓕ 2842 0460
Money Markets
Fax: 2842 0286
Head of Money Markets　　　　　　　　Philip Chu *Vice President* Ⓣ 2842 0223 Ⓕ 2842 0286
Settlement / Clearing
Fax: 2842 0460
Head of Settlement / Clearing　　　　　Jason Wong *Vice President* Ⓣ 2842 0233 Ⓕ 2842 0460
Other Departments
Chief Credit Officer　　　　　　　　　 Kenneth Chan *Vice President, Credit* Ⓣ 2842 0205 Ⓕ 2842 0290
Administration
Head of Administration　　　　　　　　Esther Tang *VP & Assistant GM* Ⓣ 2842 0258 Ⓕ 2842 0261
Head of Marketing　　　　　　　　　　Thomas Wong *Vice President & Assistant General Manager* Ⓣ 2842 0216
　　　　　　　　　　　　　　　　　　　Ⓕ 2842 0411

Technology & Systems
　　　　　　　　　　　　　　　　　　　Esther Tang *Vice President & Assistant General Manager* Ⓣ 2842 0258
　　　　　　　　　　　　　　　　　　　Ⓕ 2842 0261

Compliance
　　　　　　　　　　　　　　　　　　　Alik Hertel *Internal Auditor* Ⓣ 2842 0407 Ⓕ 2842 0261

Accounts / Audit
Accounts　　　　　　　　　　　　　　Priscilla Leung *Assistant Vice President* Ⓣ 2842 0407 Ⓕ 2842 0261

Westpac Banking Corporation　　　　　　　　　　　　　　　　　　Full Branch Office
33rd Floor, Two Exchange Square, 8 Connaught Place, Hong Kong
Tel: 2842 9888 **Fax:** 2840 0591 **Telex:** HX75620 **Swift:** WPAC HK HX
Debt Securities Tel: 2842 9996; **Fax:** 2845 3982; **Money Markets Tel:** 2842 9989; **Fax:** 2845 2536; **Syndicated Lending Tel:** 2842 9982; **Fax:** 2845 2536; **Settlement/Clearing Tel:** 2842 9960; **Fax:** 2877 2022

Senior Executive Officers
Country Head　　　　　　　　　　　　Peter Chan Ⓣ 2842 9800
Chief Executive Officer　　　　　　　　Kenneth Wong *Deputy Country Head* Ⓣ 2842 9982
Financial Director　　　　　　　　　　Patsy So *Head of Operations & Finance* Ⓣ 2842 9823

Wing Hang Bank Limited　　　　　　　　　　　　　　　　　　　　Head Office
161 Queen's Road, Central, Hong Kong
PO Box 514, Hong Kong
Tel: 2852 5111 **Fax:** 2541 0036 **Telex:** HX 73268 **Swift:** WIHB HK HH **Cable:** WIHANGBA
Website: www.whbhk.com

Senior Executive Officers
Chairman & Chief Executive　　　　　　Patrick Y B Fung
Chief Executive Officer　　　　　　　　Raymond W H Lee *Director & Deputy CEO*
Director & General Manager　　　　　　Michael Y S Fung

Others (Senior Executives)
Loans & Securities Division　　　　　　Louis C W Ho *Director, DGM & Company Secretary*

General-Lending (DCM, SL)
Head of Corporate Banking　　　　　　Tsang Cheuk Lau *DGM, Corporate Banking*

Relationship Manager
Financial Management Division　　　　Stanley S C Yuen *Senior Manager*
Financial Institutes & Multinational　　Henry Y H Ng *Senior Manager*
Corporations

Syndicated Lending

Other (Trade Finance)
Import & Export　　　　　　　　　　　C K Mak *Senior Sub-Manager*
Auto & Equipment Finance　　　　　　Edward C F Chan *Senior Manager*

Foreign Exchange
Global Head　　　　　　　　　　　　 Liu Kwok Hing *Assistant General Manager, FX & Treasury*

Settlement / Clearing
Operations　　　　　　　　　　　　　Stephen C W Leung *Senior Manager*

Euromoney Directory 1999　659

HONG KONG, CHINA (+852)   www.euromoneydirectory.com

Wing Hang Bank Limited (cont)
Administration
Business Development — Lark Chan *Manager*
Technology & Systems
Information Technology — Fung Kin Wai *Assistant General Manager*
Other (Administration)
Branch & Internal Administration Division — Stephen C K Wong *Senior Manager*
Credit Administration — Ronnie H M Li *Manager*
Marketing — Danny Fung *Senior Manager*
Insurance & Trust Department — William Ng *Manager*

Wing Lung Bank Limited   Head Office

45 Des Voeux Road, Central, Hong Kong
PO Box 520, Hong Kong
Tel: 2826 8333 Fax: 2810 0592 Telex: HX73360 Swift: WUBA HK HH Email: wlb@winglungbank.com.hk
Reuters: WLBH
Website: www.winglungbank.com.hk

Senior Executive Officers
Chairman & Executive Director — Michael Po-ko Wu T 2826 8334 F 2525 6299
Vice Chairman & Executive Director — Patrick Po-kong Wu T 2826 8332 F 2525 6299
Executive Director — Philip Po-him Wu T 2826 8435 F 2525 6299
Executive Director & General Manager — Che-shum Chung T 2826 8235 F 2525 6299

Others (Senior Executives)
Pius Po-shung Wu *Assistant General Manager* T 2826 8224 F 2810 4873
Howard Li-chien Wu *Assistant General Manager* T 2826 8337 F 2810 4873
Alice Ngar-lai Wong *Assistant General Manager* T 2710 4388 F 2770 5159
Po-chiu Tam *Assistant General Manager* T 2826 8316 F 2810 4873
Shung-kwong Tsang *AGM & Secretary* T 2826 8237 F 2810 4873
Lai-him Chow *Manager* T 2541 3135 F 2544 2289

Securities / Futures Trading
Head of Lending — Ko-ming Ling *Manager, Loans* T 2826 8427 F 2801 4698
Head of Undertaking — Kei-yuen Pun *Senior Sub-Manager, Underwriting* T 2826 8228 F 2526 7045

Relationship Manager
Corporate Lending — Suen-kong Cheung *Sub-Manager* T 2826 8298 F 2526 7045

Equity Capital Markets
Department: Capital Markets
Head of Equity Capital Markets — Po-chiu Tam *Assistant General Manager* T 2826 8316 F 2810 4873

Syndicated Lending
Head of Syndication — Wai-man Eng *Sub-Manager* T 2826 8304 F 2868 4786

Loan-Related Activities
Trade Finance — Kam-wah Tsui *Manager* T 2826 8251 F 2521 7741

Other (Trade Finance)
Property Services — Wai-kit Yeung *Senior Assistant Manager* T 2826 8248 F 2537 2301

Foreign Exchange
Department: Treasury / Foreign Exchange
Head of Foreign Exchange — Po-chiu Tam *Assistant General Manager* T 2826 8316 F 2810 4873

Other Departments
Correspondent Banking — Howard Li-chien Wu *Assistant General Manager* T 2826 8337 F 2810 4873

Administration
Technology & Systems
Alice Ngar-lai Wong *Assistant General Manager* T 2710 4388 F 2770 5159

Public Relations
Yiu-leung Tang *Manager* T 2826 8336 F 2869 7713

Other (Administration)
Personnel — Kin-yiu Leung *Manager* T 2368 5811 F 2723 6763

The Yamaguchi Bank Limited   Full Branch Office

1706-7, 17th Floor, Two Exchange Square, 8 Connaught Place, Central, Hong Kong
Tel: 2521 7194 Fax: 2810 4902 Telex: 80806 YBKHK HX

Senior Executive Officers
General Manager — Tetsuhiko Takahashi
Assistant General Manager — M Miyahara

The Yamanashi Chuo Bank Limited
Representative Office
2020 Hutchison House, 10 Harcourt Road, Central, Hong Kong
Tel: 2801 7010 Fax: 2801 7026

Senior Executive Officers
Chief Representative   Fukuda Masuo

The Yasuda Trust & Banking Company Limited
Level 23, One Pacific Place, 88 Queensway, Hong Kong
Tel: 2810 1218 Fax: 2868 1612 Telex: 83397 YTBC HX

Senior Executive Officers
General Manager   Kimio Nagasaki

Yasuda Trust Asia Pacific Limited
Subsidiary Company
Level 23, One Pacific Place, 88 Queensway, Hong Kong
Tel: 2524 2664 Fax: 2877 0227 Telex: 68567 YTAP HX Swift: YTAP

Senior Executive Officers
Managing Director   Ichiro Arai ☎ 2918 8600

Equity Capital Markets
Equity Repo / Securities Lending
Head   Takashi Yamaguchi *Deputy General Manager* ☎ 2918 8601

The Yien Yieh Commercial Bank Limited
Full Branch Office
242/252 Des Voeux Road, Central, Hong Kong
Tel: 2541 1601 Fax: 2541 4037 Telex: 83542 YCB HX Swift: YYCB HK HH Cable: SALTBANK

Senior Executive Officers
Chairman   An Ge Zhao
General Manager   Wu Guo Rui

General-Lending (DCM, SL)
Head of Corporate Banking   Wong Muk Po *DGM, Credit & Loans*

General-Investment
Head of Investment   Tang Joe Kwok *DGM, Customer Investment Services*

General - Treasury
Head of Treasury   Chung Tsan Tong *AGM, Business & Treasury*

Syndicated Lending
Loan-Related Activities
Trade Finance   Li Siu Pang *Assistant General Manager*

Other Departments
Correspondent Banking   Li Siu Pang *Assistant General Manager*

Administration
Accounts / Audit
Accounting & Financial Analysis Luk Luen Fun *Assistant General Manager*

Other (Administration)
Business Promotion   Chu Pui Wai *Assistant General Manager*
Personnel   Liang Yue *Assistant General Manager*

HUNGARY (+36)

National Bank of Hungary
Central Bank
Szabadság tér 8/9, H-1850 Budapest
Tel: (1) 269 4760; (1) 302 3000 Fax: (1) 332 3913 Telex: 225755 Swift: MANE HU HB
Website: www.mnb.hu

Senior Executive Officers
President   Dr Gyorgy Suranyi

HUNGARY (+36)   www.euromoneydirectory.com

Allami Fejlesztési Intézet Részvénytársaság

Deák Ferenc utca 5, H-1052 Budapest
Pf 216, H-1909 Budapest, Pf 216, Budapest
Tel: (1) 266 3232; (1) 266 3232 **Fax:** (1) 266 3869 **Telex:** 225672

Senior Executive Officers
Chief Executive Officer — Dr Miklós Szöke
Financial Director — Gyuláné Molnár

Bank Austria Creditanstalt Hungary Rt — Subsidiary Company

Formerly known as: Creditanstalt Rt

Akadémia utca 17, H-1054 Budapest
Tel: (1) 269 0812 **Fax:** (1) 353 4959 **Telex:** 223546 CART H **Swift:** CART HU HB **Reuters:** CART

Senior Executive Officers
Chief Executive Officer — Matthias Kunsch *Chief Executive Officer* ☎ **301 1100**
Financial Director — Terézia Rózsa *General Manager* ☎ **301 1110**
Chief Operating Officer — Michael Vogt *General Manager* ☎ **301 1150**
Treasurer — Harald Edlinger-Zecher *Deputy Chief Executive* ☎ **301 1400**
Deputy Chief Executive — Agnes Doffek ☎ **301 1200**

Equity Capital Markets
Equity Repo / Securities Lending
Head of Trading — Eva Patzauer *Deputy Head of Division* ☎ **301 1295**

Syndicated Lending
Loan-Related Activities
Trade Finance — Peter Móger *Head of Department* ☎ **301 1358**
Project Finance — Monika Gogl *Deputy Head of Division* ☎ **301 1351**

Money Markets
Country Head — Sándor Szatmári *Chief Dealer* ☎ **301 1378**

Foreign Exchange
Country Head — Thomas Ruzek *Chief Dealer* ☎ **301 1375**

Corporate Finance / M&A Advisory
Country Head — Gábor Tamás *Head of Division* ☎ **301 1350**

Settlement / Clearing
Head of Settlement / Clearing — Ildikó Németh *Head of Department* ☎ **301 1230**
Foreign Exchange Settlement — Zsuzsanna Nagy *Head of Department* ☎ **301 1230**

Global Custody
Country Head — Gabriella Zelena *Head of Department* ☎ **301 1340**

Other Departments
Private Banking — Judit Kovács *Head of Division* ☎ **301 1330**
Correspondent Banking — Katalin Schukkert *Head of Division* ☎ **301 1290**

Administration
Technology & Systems
— József Kékuti *Head of Division* ☎ **301 1180**

Legal / In-House Counsel
— Judit Pettkó-Szandtner *Head of Department* ☎ **301 1393**

Banque Nationale de Paris — Representative Office

Honvéd utca 20, H-1055 Budapest
PO Box 66, H-1363 Budapest
Tel: (1) 332 4321 **Fax:** (1) 332 3360

Senior Executive Officers
Local Representative — Suzanne Soludi

Berliner Bank AG — Representative Office

Room 62, East West Business Center, Rákóczi út 1/3, H-1088 Budapest 70
Tel: (1) 317 3393 **Fax:** (1) 266 5010

Senior Executive Officers
Representative — Antal Molnár

www.euromoneydirectory.com   HUNGARY (+36)

BNP-Dresdner Bank (Hungaria) Rt
Subsidiary Company
Honvéd utca 20, H-1055 Budapest
Tel: (1) 269 3131 **Fax:** (1) 269 3967

Budapest Bank Limited
Head Office
Honvéd utca 10, H-1054 Budapest
PO Box 1852, H-1054 Budapest
Tel: (1) 269 2333; (1) 328 1700 **Fax:** (1) 269 2417 **Telex:** 226618 **Swift:** BUDA HU HB **Email:** szalai@bbrt.hu
Reuters: BUDA

Senior Executive Officers
Chairman — George Tappert
Chief Executive Officer — Béla Singlovics *Chief Executive Officer*
Financial Director — Zsolt Könye *CFO & Deputy Chief Executive Officer*
Chief Operating Officer — Grahame Howells *Deputy Chief Executive Officer*
Treasurer — Ágota Odry *Deputy Chief Executive Officer*

Debt Capital Markets / Fixed Income
Department: FX & Money Market Department
Tel: 269 2772 **Fax:** 269 2760
Country Head — Richard Makumi

Domestic Government Bonds
Head of Trading — Attila Vágó ☏ **269 2761**

Eurobonds
Head of Trading — Richard Makumi

Libor-Based / Floating-Rate Products
FRN Sales; Asset Swaps — Richard Makumi

Fixed-Income Repo
Head of Repo — Attila Vágó ☏ **269 2761**

Equity Capital Markets
Department: FX & Money Market Department
Tel: 269 2772 **Fax:** 269 2760
Country Head — Richard Makumi

International Equities
Head of Trading — Richard Makumi

Syndicated Lending
Department: Corporate Directorate
Tel: 328 1523 **Fax:** 269 2370
Head of Syndicated Lending — Tony Fekete *Deputy Chief Executive Officer* ☏ **328 1520**
Head of Origination — Gábor Horchler *Managing Director* ☏ **328 1523**

Loan-Related Activities
Project Finance — Klára Honos *Managing Director* ☏ **267 4114**
Leasing & Asset Finance — Mariann Rédey *Managing Director* ☏ **312 1821**

Money Markets
Department: FX & Money Market Department
Fax: 269 2760
Head of Money Markets — Gabriella Kutas ☏ **269 2763**

Foreign Exchange
Department: FX & Money Market Department
Fax: 269 2760
Head of Foreign Exchange — Gabriella Márkus ☏ **269 2771**

Risk Management
Department: Group Risk Management
Tel: 328 1904 **Fax:** 302 3013
Head of Risk Management — Karl Kieffer *Managing Director*

Fixed Income Derivatives / Risk Management
Global Head — Gary Prizzia ☏ **328 1243**

Foreign Exchange Derivatives / Risk Management
Cross-Currency Swaps, Sales / Marketing — Gary Prizzia ☏ **328 1243**

Settlement / Clearing
Department: Liquidity & Back Office Department
Tel: 328 1257 **Fax:** 269 2767
Head of Settlement / Clearing — Beatrix Tuboly

HUNGARY (+36)   www.euromoneydirectory.com

Budapest Bank Limited (cont)
Global Custody
Department: Department for Custody & Settlement Operations
Tel: 328 1543 Fax: 328 1542
Head of Global Custody   Attilla Szalay ☎ **328 1544**

Other Departments
Correspondent Banking   János Horváth General Manager ☎ **269 2377**
Administration
Technology & Systems
    André Weiner Managing Director ☎ **328 4582**
Legal / In-House Counsel
    Anna Halyustyik Managing Director ☎ **328 1614**

CA IB Securities Limited   Subsidiary Company
Formerly known as: Creditanstalt Securities Limited
Nagysándor József utca 10, H-1054 Budapest
PO Box 484, H-1372 Budapest
Tel: (1) 269 0711; (1) 269 0699 **Fax:** (1) 269 0712 **Telex:** 202530

Senior Executive Officers
Chief Executive Officer   Csaba Lantos Managing Director
Financial Director   László Geszti
Treasurer   Andrea Pásztor
Company Secretary   Márta Takács

Others (Senior Executives)
Global Head, Trading & Sales   Ákos Benke

General-Lending (DCM, SL)
Head of Corporate Banking   Gordon Bajnai

Debt Capital Markets / Fixed Income
Head of Fixed Income   Ákos Benke
Head of Fixed Income Sales   Szilvia Lovas
Head of Fixed Income Trading   János Szuda

Fixed-Income Research
Country Head   Csaba Ludányi

Equity Capital Markets
Country Head   Ákos Benke

Domestic Equities
Head of Sales; Head of Trading   Márton Oláh

Risk Management
OTC Credit Derivatives
Country Head   Anna Mészáros

Settlement / Clearing
Head of Settlement / Clearing   József Meizl
Back-Office   Attila Kovács Back Office Clerk

Asset Management
Head   Péter Holtzer

Other Departments
Global Trust   Katalin Szabó

Administration
Head of Administration   László Geszti
Head of Marketing   Mária Szalóky

Technology & Systems
    Sándor Pflanzner

Legal / In-House Counsel
    Márta Takács

Compliance
    Gábor Horváth

Public Relations
    Mária Szalóky

Accounts / Audit
    Marianna Kercsen

www.euromoneydirectory.com   HUNGARY (+36)

Central European International Bank Limited   Head Office

Alternative trading name: CIB Bank Rt
Medve utca 4-14, H-1027 Budapest
PO Box 394, H-1537 Budapest
Tel: (1) 212 1330 **Fax:** (1) 212 4200 **Telex:** 224759 CIBH **Swift:** CIBH HU HB **Email:** cib@cib.hu

Senior Executive Officers
Chairman   Luigi Vercellini
President & CEO   György Zdeborsky
Financial Director   Tibor Dóka *Deputy General Manager* ☏ **457 6803**
Chief Operating Officer   Pietro Gambino *General Manager*
Treasurer   Judit Teschler *Deputy General Manager* ☏ **212 1390**
Company Secretary   András Ráth ☏ **212 5810**

Others (Senior Executives)
                                        Frigyes Hárshegyi *Deputy Chief Executive Officer* ☏ **212 1380**
                                        Zoltán Bodnár *Deputy Chief Executive Officer* ☏ **457 6860**

General-Lending (DCM, SL)
Head of Corporate Banking   Béla Sándor *General Manager* ☏ **457 6819**

Debt Capital Markets / Fixed Income
Department: CIB Securities Trading and Investment Limited
Tel: 212 5552 **Fax:** 212 5162 **Reuters:** CIEB
Head of Fixed Income   Csaba Pásztor *Chief Executive*
Head of Fixed Income Trading   Nóra Konyáry *Head of Trading*

Government Bonds
Head of Sales   Egon Hajdú *Chief Trader*

Fixed-Income Research
Head of Fixed Income   István Győri *Head of Analysis*

Equity Capital Markets
Department: CIB Securities Trading and Investment Limited
Tel: 212 5552 **Fax:** 212 5162
Head of Equity Capital Markets   Csaba Pásztor *Chief Executive*
Head of Trading   Zoltán Pável *Head of Asset Management*

Other (Domestic Equities)
Head of Origination   István Győri *Head of New Issues*

Equity Research
Head of Equity Research   István Győri *Head of Analysis*

Syndicated Lending

Loan-Related Activities
Project Finance   Zsuzsa Borbély *Head of Department*

Money Markets
Tel: 212 1390 **Fax:** 212 5809 **Reuters:** CIBX
Head of Money Markets   Zita Pétery *Director*

Foreign Exchange
Tel: 212 1390 **Fax:** 212 5809 **Reuters:** CIBX **Telex:** 22 6101
Head of Foreign Exchange   Zoltán Tóth *Deputy Director & Chief Dealer*
Corporate Sales   János Töke *Deputy Chief Dealer*
Head of Trading   Csaba Radnóti *Deputy Chief Dealer*

Risk Management
Head of Risk Management   Zsuzsa Bartyik *Deputy General Manager* ☏ **212 4319**

Administration
Head of Marketing   Gábor dr. Aradi *Head of Department* ☏ **212 5563**

Legal / In-House Counsel
                                        Zoltán dr. Varga *Head of Department* ☏ **457 6833**

Public Relations
                                        Gábor dr. Aradi *Head of Department* ☏ **212 5563**

HUNGARY (+36) www.euromoneydirectory.com

Citibank Rt
Subsidiary Company

Szabadsag ter 7, H-1051 Budapest
PO Box 123, H-1367 Budapest
Tel: (1) 374 5000 **Fax:** (1) 374 5100 **Telex:** 227822 **Swift:** CITY HU HX
Website: www.citibank.hu

Senior Executive Officers
Chief Executive Officer	Richard D Jackson *CCO* ☎ **374 5136**
Financial Director	Edit Balogh *Vice President* ☎ **374 5186**
Chief Operating Officer	Kathryn Hornsby ☎ **374 5491**
Treasurer	Ilona Keleman ☎ **374 5497**
International Division	Agnes Kummer *Head, Fixed Income* ☎ **374 5177**
Public Relations Manager	Andrea Desics ☎ **374 5315**

General-Lending (DCM, SL)
Head of Corporate Banking — Mark Robinson ☎ **374 5250**

General-Investment
Head of Investment — Laszlo Jakab ☎ **328 4800**

Debt Capital Markets / Fixed Income
Department: CISH
Head of Fixed Income; Head of Fixed Income Sales; Head of Fixed Income Trading — Kriszta Ga'l *Chief Dealer* ☎ **374 5004**

Government Bonds
Head of Sales; Head of Trading — Kriszta Ga'l *Chief Dealer* ☎ **374 5004**
Head of Syndication; Head of Origination — Agnes Kummer *Head, Fixed Income* ☎ **374 5177**

Emerging Market Bonds
Head of Emerging Markets — Richard D Jackson *CCO* ☎ **374 5136**

Fixed-Income Research
Head of Fixed Income — Csaba Varga *Head of Research* ☎ **374 5015**

Equity Capital Markets
Department: CISH
Tel: 374 5080
Head of Equity Capital Markets; Head of Sales; Head of Trading — Laszlo Mago *Senior Dealer* ☎ **374 5009**

Domestic Equities
Head of Sales — Laszlo Mago *Senior Dealer* ☎ **374 5009**

International Equities
Head of Sales — Laszlo Mago *Senior Dealer* ☎ **374 5009**

Equity Research
Head of Equity Research — Csaba Varga *Head of Research* ☎ **374 5015**

Equity Repo / Securities Lending
Head; Marketing & Product Development — Gyula Bunna ☎ **374 5130**

Syndicated Lending
Tel: 374 5007 **Fax:** 374 5070
Head of Origination; Head of Syndication — Ga'bor Nagy *Assistant Vice President* ☎ **374 5011**

Loan-Related Activities
Trade Finance — Andrea Arvay *Department Head* ☎ **374 5389**
Project Finance — Ga'bor Nagy *Assistant Vice President* ☎ **374 5011**

Money Markets
Department: Treasury
Tel: 374 5335 **Fax:** 374 5090
Head of Money Markets — Gyorgy Bukta *Assistant Vice President* ☎ **374 5403**

Domestic Commercial Paper
Head of Sales — Kriszta Ga'l *Chief Dealer* ☎ **374 5004**

Eurocommercial Paper
Head of Sales — Peter Sziklai *Senior Broker* ☎ **374 5016**

Wholesale Deposits
Marketing — Gabriella Csanak *Marketing Director* ☎ **458 2234**
Head of Sales — Gabor Jakab ☎ **374 5345**

Foreign Exchange
Tel: 374 5335 **Fax:** 374 5090
Head of Foreign Exchange — Mihaly Donka ☎ **374 5344**
Head of Institutional Sales; Corporate Sales — Gabor Jakab ☎ **374 5345**
Head of Trading — Mihaly Donka ☎ **374 5344**

HUNGARY (+36)

Risk Management
Fax: 374 5445
Country Head David Costelloe *Country Risk Manager* ☏ **374 5095**

Corporate Finance / M&A Advisory
Head of Corporate Finance Edit Balogh *Vice President* ☏ **374 5186**

Settlement / Clearing
Fax: 374 5030
Head of Settlement / Clearing; Equity Settlement; Fixed-Income Settlement; Back-Office Andrea Halasi *Deputy Department Head* ☏ **374 5129**

Global Custody
Head of Global Custody Mark Kelley *Vice President* ☏ **374 5114**

Asset Management
Head Istuan Farkas *Deputy General Manager* ☏ **374 5001**

Other Departments
Chief Credit Officer David Costelloe *Country Risk Manager* ☏ **374 5095**
Private Banking Sanjeeb Chaudhuri *Consumer Banking Business Manager* ☏ **458 2147**
Correspondent Banking Agnes Kummer *Head, Fixed Income* ☏ **374 5177**
Cash Management Kevin Tissot *Vice President* ☏ **374 5026**

Administration
Head of Marketing Gabriella Csanak *Marketing Director* ☏ **458 2234**

Technology & Systems
Ervin Banyai *Technology Head* ☏ **374 5355**

Legal / In-House Counsel
Karoly Foti *Country Legal Counsel* ☏ **374 5291**

Compliance
Istvan Naszodi *Country Compliance Co-ordinator* ☏ **374 5064**

Public Relations
Andrea Desics *Public Relations Manager* ☏ **374 5315**

Accounts / Audit
Monika Schreiber ☏ **374 5079**

Citizens Bank Limited

1063 Budapest, Sziv utca 53, H-1063 Budapest
Tel: (1) 301 2100 **Fax:** (1) 301 2122 **Telex:** 223743 **Swift:** YBLB HU HB

Senior Executive Officers
Chairman of the Board of Directors Pàl Zoltàn Gàl
Chief Executive Officer Làszlò Dombòvàri *Chief Executive Officer*

Commerzbank (Budapest) Rt   Subsidiary Company

Széchenyi rkp 8, H-1054 Budapest
Tel: (1) 269 4510 **Fax:** (1) 269 4530

Senior Executive Officers
Chief Executive Officer Hans Herman von Rosenberg Lipinsky

Crédit Lyonnais Bank Hungary Rt   Subsidiary Company

József nádor tér 7, H-1051 Budapest
Tel: (1) 266 9000 **Fax:** (1) 266 9950 **Swift:** CRLY HU HB

Senior Executive Officers
Chief Executive Officer Mr Mulliez

Daewoo Bank (Hungary) Limited   Head Office

Formerly known as: MHB-Daewoo Bank
Bajcsy Zsilinszky 42-46, H-1054 Budapest
Tel: (1) 374 9900; (1) 374 9999 **Fax:** (1) 328 5218; (1) 329 5219 **Telex:** 222233, 225036 **Swift:** DAEW HU HB
Email: dwbhøø1@mail.datanet.hu **Reuters:** DWBB

Senior Executive Officers
Chairman Moon Han Kim ☏ **374 9901**
President & Vice Chairman Elemer Terta'k ☏ **374 9902**

Euromoney Directory 1999 **667**

HUNGARY (+36)   www.euromoneydirectory.com

Daewoo Bank (Hungary) Limited (cont)
Senior Executive Officers (cont)
Treasurer	Laszlo Havas *Treasurer* ☎ 374 9915
Director	Jae Chul ☎ 374 9955
General Manager	Kye Hoon Rhim ☎ 374 9977
General Manager	Tae Young Jung ☎ 374 9922

Debt Capital Markets / Fixed Income
Domestic Government Bonds
Head of Sales — Laszlo Havas *Treasurer* ☎ 374 9915

Equity Capital Markets
Department: Daewoo Securities (Hungary) Ltd
Apaczai Csere János u 11, H-1052 Budapest
Country Head — Myung Yul Choi *President*

Other (Domestic Equities)
Dealer — Akos Alegedj ☎ 374 9916 🖷 374 9912

Syndicated Lending
Department: Banking Relations & Syndications
Head of Syndication — János To'th *Associate Director*

Loan-Related Activities
Trade Finance; Project Finance; Structured Trade Finance — János To'th *Associate Director*
Leasing & Asset Finance — Tri Nguyen Duc *Manager* ☎ 266 0010

Money Markets
Domestic Commercial Paper
Head of Origination — Katalin Holicry *Senior Manager* ☎ 374 9962

Risk Management
Department: Credit Control
Country Head — Krisetina Makra *Senior Manager*

Settlement / Clearing
Country Head — Judit Osanyi *Manager* ☎ 374 9716
Foreign Exchange Settlement — Kinga Keresztesi *Manager* ☎ 374 9713

Other Departments
Correspondent Banking — János To'th *Associate Director*

Administration
Technology & Systems
Mr Son *Manager* ☎ 374 9939

Legal / In-House Counsel
Attila Jeviczky *Lawyer* ☎ 374 9906

Compliance
Andrea Jakas *Internal Auditor* ☎ 374 9985

Public Relations
Agnes Palos *Assistant Manager*

Deutsche Bank Rt   Subsidiary Company
Hold utca 27, H-1054 Budapest
PO Box 303, H-1393 Budapest
Tel: (1) 301 3700 **Fax:** (1) 269 3239 **Telex:** 202512
Auditing Department Tel: 301 3775; **Fax:** 301 3769; **Controlling Tel:** 301 3781; **Fax:** 269 3239; **Corporate Banking Tel:** 301 3710; **Fax:** 301 3719; **Credit Risk Management Tel:** 301 3725; **Fax:** 301 3719; **EDP Support Fax:** 301 3759; **EDP-Support Tel:** 301 3755; **Group Services Tel:** 301 3750; **Fax:** 301 3759; **Legal Department Fax:** 269 3239; **Legal Dept Tel:** 301 3726; **Management Tel:** 301 3704; **Fax:** 269 3239; **Payments Tel:** 301 3760; **Fax:** 301 3769; **Trade Finance Tel:** 301 3740; **Fax:** 301 3769; **Treasury Tel:** 301 3730; **Fax:** 301 3739

Senior Executive Officers
Chief Executive Officer	Imre Makai
Managing Director	Ludwig Blomeyer-Bartenstein

www.euromoneydirectory.com   HUNGARY (+36)

DG BANK
Pethényi köz 10, H-1122 Budapest
Tel: (1) 201 2612 Fax: (3) 155 3488

Senior Executive Officers
Representative   Laszlo Nadasdy

European Bank for Reconstruction & Development
Full Branch Office

Rákoczi utca 42, H-1072 Budapest
Tel: (1) 266 6000 Fax: (1) 266 6003

Senior Executive Officers
Others (Senior Executives)
    Hubert Warsmann *Principal*

The Export-Import Bank of the Republic of China
Representative Office

7th Floor, Károly Krt 11, H-1075 Budapest
Tel: (1) 269 7893; (1) 269 7894 Fax: (1) 269 7895 Email: eibbudapest@elender.hu

Senior Executive Officers
Chief Representative   Tzuu-Wang Hu

General Banking & Trust Co Limited   Head Office

Alternative trading name: Általános Értékforgalmi Bank Rt
Markó utca 9, H-1055 Budapest
PO Box 150, H-1991 Budapest
Tel: (1) 269 1473 Fax: (1) 269 1442; (1) 269 1443 Telex: 223578 VALOR H Swift: AEBB HU HB Reuters: GBTC
Cable: HUNGVALORBANK
Website: www.gtb.hu

Senior Executive Officers
Chairman & Chief Executive Officer   Megdet Rakhimkulov
Financial Director   Dmitry A Korachkov *Chief Financial Officer*
Chief Operating Officer   Balázs Vajda *COO, Finance*
Treasurer   András Pongrácz *Managing Director & Treasurer*
General Manager   Gábor Ralovich
International Division   Andrei F Kovalev

Others (Senior Executives)
Chief Accountant   Etelka Kirchner *Managing Director*
Head of Branch Network   Ferenc Márton *Managing Director, Branch Network*

Syndicated Lending

Loan-Related Activities
Trade Finance   Julianna Ferenczi *Head of International & Domestic Payments*

Money Markets
Other   Csaba Oravecz *Chief Dealer*

Other Departments
Chief Credit Officer   Benjamin Budai *Managing Director, Credit & Loans*

Administration

Technology & Systems
    Tibor Takács *Head of Information Technology*

Legal / In-House Counsel
    Miklós Havelda *Chief Legal Counsel*

Public Relations
    Sergei P Zhirnikhin *Managing Director, Media & Marketing*

Other (Administration)
SWIFT & Tested Telex   Árpád Sipos *Head of Department*

Euromoney Directory 1999   **669**

HUNGARY (+36)   www.euromoneydirectory.com

Hungarian Foreign Trade Bank Limited   Head Office

Alternative trading name: MKB (Magyar Külkereskedelmi Bank Rt)
Váci utca 38, H-1056 Budapest
Tel: (1) 269 0922; (1) 153 4211 **Fax:** (1) 269 0959 **Telex:** 226941 EXTR H **Swift:** MKKB HU HB **Reuters:** HFTB
Website: www.mkb.hu

Senior Executive Officers
Chairman & Chief Executive   Tamás Erdei T 268 8205 F 268 8209
Financial Director   Imre Balogh *Executive Director* T 268 8125 F 268 8039
Treasurer   István Szabolcs *Executive Director* T 268 7180 F 268 7189

Others (Senior Executives)
Corporate & Institutional Banking   Péter Stotz *Deputy Chief Executive* T 268 7701 F 268 7710

General-Investment
Head of Investment   Kárdly Szabó *Executive Director* T 268 7041 F 268 7046
     Gábor Miklós *Deputy Chief Executive* T 268 7288 F 268 7033

Debt Capital Markets / Fixed Income
Domestic Government Bonds
Head of Trading   Zsuzia Kelemen *Chief Dealer* T 268 7185

Syndicated Lending
Head of Syndication   Helga Kaiser *General Manager* T 268 7339 F 268 7366

Loan-Related Activities
Trade Finance   Sàndor Patyi *Executive Director* T 268 7610 F 268 7086
Project Finance   R Dimitrios Fokas *General Manager* T 268 7308 F 268 7239

Money Markets
Head of Money Markets   Zsuzsa Bereczhi *General Manager* T 268 7087 F 268 7019

Foreign Exchange
Head of Trading   Szilvia Kucsela *Chief Dealer* T 268 7076 F 268 7019

Risk Management
Fixed Income Derivatives / Risk Management
Trading   Zsuzsa Bereczhi *General Manager* T 268 7087 F 268 7019

Foreign Exchange Derivatives / Risk Management
Cross-Currency Swaps, Trading   János Mihalik *Chief Dealer* T 268 7079 F 268 7019

Corporate Finance / M&A Advisory
Tel: 268 7760 **Fax:** 268 7379
Global Head   Sàndor Patyi *Executive Director* T 268 7610 F 268 7086

Settlement / Clearing
Head of Settlement / Clearing   Csilla Bolla *Director* T 268 7760 F 268 7379

Global Custody
Head of Global Custody   Lászlo Koppel *Manager* T 268 7124 F 268 8431

Other Departments
Private Banking   Gábor Miklós *Deputy Chief Executive* T 268 7288 F 268 7033
     Gábor Aczél *Director* T 268 7686 F 268 7083
Correspondent Banking   György Rosta *General Manager* T 268 7249 F 268 7767

Administration
Business Development   Ferenc Müller *General Manager* T 268 8019 F 268 8293
Head of Marketing   Janos Müller *Director* T 327 8617 F 327 8727

Technology & Systems   Péter Póka *Director* T 268 7030 F 268 7037

Legal / In-House Counsel   Adrienne Kraudi *Executive Director* T 268 7406 F 268 7305

Compliance   Éva C László *Director* T 268 7722 F 268 7168

Accounts / Audit   Gyula Trenka *General Manager* T 268 8062 F 268 8049

Hungarian International Finance Limited   Representative Office

Szabadság Tér 7-9, H-1054 Budapest
Tel: (1) 301 3670; (30) 426 946 **Fax:** (1) 302 9507

Senior Executive Officers
Representative   Péter Gádor

www.euromoneydirectory.com　　　HUNGARY (+36)

HypoVereinsbank Hungaria Rt — Subsidiary Company

Formerly known as: HYPO-BANK Hungaria Rt
Nagymezö utca 44, H-1065 Budapest
PO Box 386, H-1242 Budapest
Tel: (1) 269 0400; (1) 269 0535 **Fax:** (1) 269 0398

ING Bank

Bathory ucta 12, H-1054 Budapest
Tel: (1) 452 2501 **Fax:** (1) 452 2884

Senior Executive Officers
General Manager　　　　　　　　Tibor E Rejt

Others (Senior Executives)
　　　　　　　　　　　　　　　　Peter Kraft *Deputy General Manager*

ING Bank Rt — Subsidiary Company

Andrássy ut 9, H-1061 Budapest
Tel: (1) 321 1320; (1) 321 0140 **Fax:** (1) 268 6447; (1) 268 0159 **Telex:** 22 2419 INGBH **Swift:** INGB HU HB
Email: ingbank@mail.matav.hu

Senior Executive Officers
Chairman　　　　　　　　　　　J P M Kemp ☎ **563 5000**
Chief Executive Officer　　　　　Tibor E Rejt *Managing Director* ☎ **342 7915** 📠 **322 2288**
Financial Director　　　　　　　Tamás Pál *Deputy Executive Director* ☎ **301 2600**
Chief Operating Officer　　　　　Robert Loggia *Assistant Managing Director* ☎ **322 2821**
Treasurer　　　　　　　　　　　György Takács *Executive Director* ☎ **235 8500**
Assistant Managing Director　　Peter Bombeld ☎ **322 2809**
Managing Director / General Manager　Martin Schouten

Syndicated Lending
Fax: 351 3305
Country Head　　　　　　　　　Béla Kolyenfalvy *Associate Senior Manager* ☎ **235 8762**

Money Markets
Tel: 235 8500
Country Head　　　　　　　　　Csaba Thaly *Manager* ☎ **235 8502**

Foreign Exchange
Tel: 235 8500
Country Head　　　　　　　　　Attila Behán *Manager* ☎ **235 8500**

Risk Management
Fax: 267 3738
Country Head　　　　　　　　　Gábor Wavrik *Deputy Executive Manager* ☎ **235 8713**

Corporate Finance / M&A Advisory
Tel: 322 2809 **Fax:** 322 2288
Country Head　　　　　　　　　Martin Schouten *Assistant Managing Director* ☎ **322 2809**

Settlement / Clearing
Country Head　　　　　　　　　András Czukor *Deputy Executive Director* ☎ **235 8726**

Global Custody
Fax: 267 3740
Country Head　　　　　　　　　Lilla Jurányi *Senior Manager* ☎ **235 8817**

Other Departments
Private Banking　　　　　　　　Anikó Kusztos *Manager*
Correspondent Banking　　　　Adrienn Nógrádi *Manager* ☎ **235 8827**

Administration

Technology & Systems
　　　　　　　　　　　　　　　　Zsolt Rasztouits *Deputy Executive Director* ☎ **235 8727**

Legal / In-House Counsel
　　　　　　　　　　　　　　　　Péter Dankó *Senior Manager* ☎ **235 8744**

HUNGARY (+36) www.euromoneydirectory.com

ING Baring Securities (Hungary)

Andra'ssy ucta 12, H-1061 Budapest
PO Box 320, H-1461 Budapest
Tel: (1) 351 3300 Fax: (1) 269 6447; (1) 268 0159

Senior Executive Officers
Country Manager   Tibor E Rejt

Inter-Európa Bank Rt   Head Office

Inter-Európa Bank Rt.
ASSOCIATED MEMBER OF THE SANPAOLO GROUP
Szabadság tér 15, H-1054 Budapest
Tel: (1) 373 6000 Fax: (1) 169 2526 Telex: 227879 INVES H Swift: INEB HU HB Email: ieb@ieb.hu Reuters: INTB
Website: www.ieb.hu

Senior Executive Officers
Tel: 269 2526
Chairman   László Bódy
Managing Director   Pier Franco Rubatto
Deputy Managing Director   Jeno Bardy

Others (Senior Executives)
IT & Back Office Operations   Tamas Foltanyi *Executive Director*
Controling Department   Ildiko Husz *Executive Director*
Finance   Sándor Sebók *Executive Director*
Credit Policy   Zsolt Gergely *Executive Director, Credit Policy*

Syndicated Lending
Head of Credit Committee   Zsolt Gergely *Executive Director, Credit Policy*

Settlement / Clearing
Operations   Tamás Foltányi *Executive Director*
Back-Office   Istvan Gombkoto *Senior Manager*

Administration

Technology & Systems
Technology Development   Istvan Gombkoto *Senior Manager*

Legal / In-House Counsel
                                 Erzsebet Radinko *Senior Manager*

Public Relations
                                 Krisztina Blazsek *Manager*

Accounts / Audit
Budget Control & Accountancy Division   Iaszlo Kiss *Senior Manager*
Internal Audit Division   Klara Mato *Senior Manager*

Other (Administration)
Marketing   Maria Novak *Senior Manager*
Arbitrage   Balazs Varga *Senior Manager*
Human Resource Division   Istvan Lampert *Deputy Senior Manager*
Strategy & Economic Division   Mihaly Buthl *Manager*

International Finance Corporation   Representative Office

Bank Center, 6th Floor, Gránit Tower, H-1944 Budapest
Tel: (1) 302 9593 Fax: (1) 269 9597
Website: www.ifc.org

Senior Executive Officers
Head of Mission   Borbála Czakó E **bczako@worldbank.org**

www.euromoneydirectory.com   HUNGARY (+36)

Konzumbank Limited
Head Office

Formerly known as: Konzumbank Commercial Bank
4 Tüköry Street, H-1369 Budapest
PO Box 300, H-1369 Budapest 114
Tel: (1) 374 7300 **Fax:** (1) 374 7460 **Telex:** 222525 **Swift:** KONZ HU HB **Reuters:** KOZB

Senior Executive Officers
Chairman — Gyula Pazmandi ☏ **374 7400**
Chief Executive Officer — Eva Pakozdi-Szabó ☏ **374 7301**
Financial Director — Marta Györi *Head of Finance* ☏ **374 7340**
Chief Operating Officer — Marta Markus *Deputy Chief Executive Officer* ☏ **374 7383**
Treasurer — Gabor Somlai *General Manager* ☏ **374 7388**
Head of Secretariat — Imre Varga ☏ **374 7304**
International Division — Katalin Jaczkovits *General Manager* ☏ **374 7412**

Other Departments
Correspondent Banking — Thomas Kenyeres *Head, Correspondent Banking* ☏ **374 7305**

Administration
Public Relations — Erika Bajko *Head of Department* ☏ **374 7328**

Landesbank Hessen-Thüringen Girozentrale
Representative Office

Alternative trading name: Helaba
Rákóczi utca 1-3, H-1088 Budapest VIII
Tel: (1) 266 6562 **Fax:** (1) 266 6762

National Savings & Commercial Bank Limited
Head Office

Nádor utca 16, H-1051 Budapest
Tel: (1) 353 1444 **Fax:** (1) 312 6858

Senior Executive Officers
Chairman & Chief Executive — Sándor Csányi
Managing Director — Olivia Dombovari

Nomura Investment Bank Hungary Limited
Subsidiary Company

Rákóczi utca 1/3, H-1088 Budapest
Tel: (1) 266 4723 **Fax:** (1) 235 5299 **Telex:** 222287 NOMUR H

Senior Executive Officers
President & Chief Executive Officer — Toshiro Kanome

Nova Ljubljanska banka dd
Representative Office

Alag Buda Centre, Hegyalja utca 11-13, H-1016 Budapest I
Tel: (1) 202 2416 **Fax:** (1) 202 2452 **Telex:** 222006 INABU H

Senior Executive Officers
Resident Representative — Nikola Geric

OTP Securities Limited
Full Branch Office

Mérleg utca 4, H-1051 Budapest
Tel: (1) 267 0504 **Fax:** (1) 267 0513; (1) 267 0514 **Reuters:** OTPSTU
Website: www.otpbroker.hu

Senior Executive Officers
Chief Executive Officer — Gyula Pleschinger
Ildikd Hidasine *Deputy Chief Executive Officer*
International Division — Robert Beck *Director, International Sales* ☏ **266 6362**

Debt Capital Markets / Fixed Income
Head of Fixed Income — Marton Kerekes
Head of Fixed Income Sales — Istvan Szigeti *Head of Trading*

HUNGARY (+36)

OTP Securities Limited (cont)
Debt Capital Markets / Fixed Income (cont)
Head of Fixed Income Trading — Zoltàn Egressy
Domestic Government Bonds
Head of Sales — Zoltàn Egressy
Head of Trading — Istvan Szigeti *Head of Trading*
Emerging Market Bonds
Head of Emerging Markets — Màrton Kerekes
Head of Sales — Csaba Nagy *Trader*
Libor-Based / Floating-Rate Products
FRN Sales — Csaba Nagy *Trader*
FRN Trading — Màrton Kerekes
Fixed-Income Research
Head of Fixed Income — Tomàs Köszeghy
Head of Credit Research — Pèter Bozso
Equity Capital Markets
Head of Sales — Robert Beck
Head of Trading — Zoltàn Egressy
Domestic Equities
Head of Sales — Zoltàn Egressy
Head of Trading — Istvan Szigeti *Head of Trading*
International Equities
Head of Sales — Robert Beck
Head of Trading — Levente Nandori
Equity Research
Head of Equity Research — Zoltan Nemeth
Risk Management
OTC Equity Derivatives
Sales — Zoltàn Egressy
Corporate Finance / M&A Advisory
Head of Corporate Finance — Peter Kiss *Director, Corporate Finance* ☎ 235 4236
Settlement / Clearing
Back-Office — Zsuzsa Tothne Szeibert

Postabank és Takarékpénztár Rt — Head Office

József Nádor tér 1, H-1920 Budapest V
Tel: (1) 318 0855; (1) 320 2081 Fax: (1) 317 1369; (1) 349 9351 Telex: 223294 PBANK Swift: POSB HU HB
Reuters: POSB

Senior Executive Officers
Chairman — Laszlo Madarasz
Chief Executive Officer — Henrik Auth
Chief Operating Officer — Laszlo Urban *Deputy Chief Executive Officer*
Treasurer — Katalin Igaz *Managing Director* ☎ 350 0275 F 349 5526

Raiffeisen Unicbank Rt

Formerly known as: Unicbank

Va'ci Utca 19-21, H-1052 Budapest
PO Box 173, H-1364 Budapest
Tel: (1) 266 2018 Fax: (1) 266 3140 Telex: 22-3172 Swift: UBRT HU HB
Telex: 22-3123

Senior Executive Officers
Chief Executive Officer — Péter Felcsuti *Managing Director*
Financial Director — Krisztina Kaposvárl ☎ 266 3135
Chief Operating Officer — Csaba Elbert ☎ 266 2542
Deputy Managing Director — Iván Gara ☎ 266 2824
Deputy Managing Director — R Hirst-Neckarsthal ☎ 266 2821
Deputy Managing Director — Krisztina Horvath ☎ 266 2411
Deputy Managing Director — Péter Verö ☎ 266 2018
Company Secretary — Eszter Görög ☎ 266 4469
International Division — Magdolna Czimer ☎ 266 2828

Others (Senior Executives)
Municipal Banking — Ildlkó Kemény-Koncz ☎ 266 2249

www.euromoneydirectory.com HUNGARY (+36)

General-Lending (DCM, SL)
Head of Corporate Banking   Róbert Huszár ☎ **266 2411**

General - Treasury
Head of Treasury   Ibolya Balint ☎ **266 4340**

Syndicated Lending
Head of Syndication   Magdolna Czimer ☎ **266 2828**

Other (Syndicated Lending)
Credit Risk   Imre Németh ☎ **266 4301**

Loan-Related Activities
Trade Finance   Éva Hancz-Mester ☎ **266 3550**

Settlement / Clearing
Operations   Csaba Elbert ☎ **266 2542**

Global Custody
Head of Global Custody   Marianna Sárvári ☎ **266 2018**

Other Departments
Commodities / Bullion   Éva Hancz-Hester ☎ **266 3550**
Private Banking   Judit Scharbert ☎ **266 3747**
Correspondent Banking   Magdolna Czimer ☎ **266 2828**
Cash Management   Peter Holczer

Administration
Head of Marketing   Zsofia Gonda-Fischer ☎ **266 2018**

Technology & Systems
Electronic Data Processing   Tamás Acs ☎ **266 4136**

Legal / In-House Counsel
                                        Attila Tajthy ☎ **266 4496**

Public Relations
                                        Zsofia Gonda-Fischer ☎ **266 2018**

Accounts / Audit
Accounting   Krisztina Kaposvárl ☎ **266 3135**
Internal Audit   Tamás Hortay *Head* ☎ **266 2018**

Other (Administration)
Human Resources   Szabolcs Budaházy ☎ **266 3278**
Technical Services   Pál Lakits ☎ **266 3749**
Organisation   Valéria Molnár ☎ **266 4136**
Controlling   Ágnes Tölgyes ☎ **266 4338**

Westdeutsche Landesbank (Hungaria) Rt   Subsidiary Company

Formerly known as: ÁVB Rt
Madách I utca 13/14, H-1075 Budapest
Tel: (1) 268 1680 **Fax:** (1) 268 1933 **Telex:** 61202681 **Swift:** WLBE HU HX

Senior Executive Officers
Chief Executive   Katalin Morgós ☎ **268 1650**
Chief Executive Officer   Katalin Morgós *Chief Executive* ☎ **268 1650**
Financial Director   Péter Legeza *Director*
Chief Operating Officer   Judit Kovács *Director*
Treasurer   Géza Egyed *Director*
Managing Director   Christian Bock ☎ **268 1651**

Syndicated Lending
Department: Syndicated Lending - Marketing Department
Global Head   W J Charles Weller *Director* ☎ **268 1520**

Risk Management
Department: Credit Department
Global Head   Zsuzsa Montvai Riedlné *Director* ☎ **268 1530**

Administration

Technology & Systems
                                        Robert Melli

Legal / In-House Counsel
                                        Ferenz Lenart

Public Relations
                                        Zoltán Salzmann *PR Manager*

Euromoney Directory 1999   **675**

HUNGARY (+36)

The World Bank
Representative Office

Szabád tér 5-7, H-1944 Budapest
Tel: (1) 302 9581 Fax: (1) 302 9586

Senior Executive Officers
Country Director .... Roger Grawe

ICELAND
(+354)

Sedlabanki Islands
🏛 *Central Bank*

Kalkofnsvegur 1, Reykjavik
Tel: 569 9600 Fax: 569 9605 Telex: 2020 CENTBK IS Swift: SISL IS REA Email: sedlabanki@sedlabanki.is
Reuters: ICES; ICET; ICEX
Website: www.sedlabanki.is

Senior Executive Officers
Governor .... Birgir Isleifur Gunnarsson

Bunadarbanki Islands

Austurstraeti 5, 155 Reykjavik
Tel: 525 6000 Fax: 525 6189 Telex: 2383 BUBANK IS Swift: BUIS IS RE Email: intdiv@bi.is
Website: www.bi.is

Senior Executive Officers
Chairman of the Board of Directors .... Palmi Jonsson
Senior Managing Director .... Stefan Palsson
Managing Director .... Solon R Sigurdsson
Managing Director .... Jon Adolf Gudjonsson

General - Treasury
Head of Treasury .... Thorsteinn Thorsteinsson *Deputy Managing Director*
Frederik S Halldorsson *Treasury*

Relationship Manager
Bank Relations .... Thorunn Sigurdardottirr *Senior Manager*

Debt Capital Markets / Fixed Income
Department: Markets
Bonds - General .... Arni Oddur Thordarson

Syndicated Lending
Other (Trade Finance)
Trade Finance & International Operations . Jana K Sigfusdottir *Senior Manager*
Documentary Collections .... Matthildur Agustsdottir
Documentary Credits & Guarantees .... Sigrun Fridgeirsdottir

Foreign Exchange
FX Traders / Sales People
Foreign Currency Lending .... Thordis Ulfarsdottir
Christian Staub *Chief Dealer*
Bolli Hedinsson *Dealer*

Risk Management
Head of Risk Management .... Gudmundur Gudmundsson

Corporate Finance / M&A Advisory
Head of Corporate Finance .... Gudmundur Gislason *Deputy Managing Director*

Settlement / Clearing
Operations .... Sigurjon Th. Arnason *Deputy Managing Director*
Maria Knudsen *Senior Manager*

Asset Management
Head .... Gudbjörn Maronsson

Other Departments
Chief Credit Officer .... Elin Sigfusdóttir
Correspondent Banking .... Thorunn Sigurdardottirr *Senior Manager*

www.euromoneydirectory.com　　　　　　　　　　　　　　INDIA (+91)

Administration
Head of Administration　　　　　　　Sigurjon Th. Arnason *Deputy Managing Director*
　　　　　　　　　　　　　　　　　　Arndis Björnsdottir *Branch Administration*
Head of Marketing　　　　　　　　　Edda Svavarsdottir
Technology & Systems
IT Services　　　　　　　　　　　　Ingi Örn Geirsson
Legal / In-House Counsel
Branches & Legal Services　　　　　Kristinn Zimsen *Deputy Managing Director*
Legal Services　　　　　　　　　　Arsaell Hafsteinsson
　　　　　　　　　　　　　　　　　　Thorvaldur G Einarsson

Accounts / Audit
Accounting & Budgeting　　　　　　Johannes Ingvarsson
Central Processing　　　　　　　　Sigurdur Kristjansson
Other (Administration)
Personnel　　　　　　　　　　　　Halldora Askelsdottir

Islandsbanki hf

Kirkjusandur, 155 Reykjavik
Tel: 560 8000 **Fax:** 560 8522 **Telex:** 2047 ISBA IS **Swift:** ISBA IS RE

Senior Executive Officers
Chairman　　　　　　　　　　　　Kristján Ragnarsson
Managing Director / General Manager　Valur Valsson

INDIA (+91)

Reserve Bank of India　　　　　　　　　　　　　　　　🏛 Central Bank

PO Box 10007, Central Office Building, Shahid Bhagatsingh Road, Mumbai 400 00
Tel: (22) 266 1602; (22) 266 1604 **Fax:** (22) 266 2105 **Telex:** 112318 **Swift:** RBIS IN BB
Email: rbiprd@giasbm#01.vsnl.net.in **Reuters:** RBIB **Cable:** RESERVBANK **Telex:** 112455 **Telex:** 114222
Website: www.rbi.org.in

Senior Executive Officers
Governor　　　　　　　　　　　　Bimal Jalan ☏ **266 0868**
Deputy Governor　　　　　　　　　S P Talwar ☏ **266 4069**
Deputy Governor　　　　　　　　　Y V Reddy ☏ **266 3155**
President　　　　　　　　　　　　Jagdish Capoor ☏ **266 0808**
Executive Director　　　　　　　　S A Hussain ☏ **266 0797**
Executive Director　　　　　　　　V Subrahmanyam ☏ **266 1630**
Executive Director　　　　　　　　A Vasudevan ☏ **266 2812**
Executive Director　　　　　　　　C Harikumar ☏ **266 3266**
Executive Director　　　　　　　　S Gurumurthy ☏ **266 0781**
Executive Director　　　　　　　　B S Sharma ☏ **266 1810**
Secretary & General Manager　　　I D Agarwal ☏ **266 1870**

Others (Senior Executives)
Head, Government & Bank Accounts　　　　　B A Patil *Chief General Manager* ☏ **644 1975**
Head, Banking Operations & Development　　Amalendu Ghosh *Chief General Manager* ☏ **218 6286**
Head, Banking Supervision　　　　　　　　　A Q Siddiqi *Chief General Manager* ☏ **218 2528**
Head, Non-Banking Supervision　　　　　　　V S N Murthy *Chief General Manager* ☏ **266 1841**
Head, Internal Debt Management　　　　　　K Kanagasabapathy *Chief General Manager* ☏ **266 1630**
Head, External Investments & Operations　　Smt Usha Thorat *Chief General Manager* ☏ **266 1859**
Head, Economic Analysis & Policy　　　　　　A L Verma *Chief General Manager* ☏ **266 3323**
Head, Statistical Analaysis　　　　　　　　　R B Barman *Chief General Manager* ☏ **640 4686**
Head, Exchange Control　　　　　　　　　　Khizer Ahmed *Chief General Manager* ☏ **266 3596**
Head, Industrial & Export Credit Department　A Chandramouliszwaran *Chief General Manager* ☏ **266 3750**

Administration
Head, Computer Services　　　　　　　　　　R B Barman *Chief General Manager* ☏ **640 4686**

Legal / In-House Counsel
　　　　　　　　　　　　　　　　　　　　　　N V Deshpande *Legal Advisor* ☏ **266 0819**

Public Relations
Press Relations Division　　　　　　　　　　Alpana Killawala *General Manager* ☏ **266 0502**

INDIA (+91)   www.euromoneydirectory.com

Bank of Baroda
Head Office

3 Walchand Hirachand Marg, Ballard Pier, Mumbai 400 001
Tel: (22) 261 0341; (22) 261 5779 **Fax:** (22) 262 0408 **Swift:** BARBIN BBA XXX **Email:** bob@bom2.vsnl.net.in
Cable: CENTODORAB

Senior Executive Officers
Chief Executive Officer — K Kannan ☎ **261 3939**
International Division — J K Satta *General Manager, International Operations* ☎ **262 5958**

Bank of India
Head Office

8th Floor, Express Towers, Nariman Point, Mumbai 400 021
Tel: (22) 202 3020 **Fax:** (22) 202 2831 **Telex:** 1182281 **Swift:** BKID IN BB **Reuters:** BOIB

Senior Executive Officers
Executive Director — S Gopalakrishnan

Others (Senior Executives)
Directors —
Gajendra Haldea
B A Patil
J S Bailur
K K Goel
Rashpal Malhotra
K S Khan
Kala Pant
A V Sadasiva
Y S Bhadauria

Bank Internasional Indonesia
Full Branch Office

Amerchand Mansions, Madame Cama Road, Colaba, Mumbai 400 039
Tel: (22) 288 6834; (22) 288 6835 **Fax:** (22) 288 5964; (22) 288 6837 **Telex:** 86326

Senior Executive Officers
Chief Executive Officer — Nurmala Damanik ☎ **285 1929**
Financial Director — Vivek Muley *Financial Controller* ☎ **288 6841**
Chief Operating Officer — Shakuntala Khosla *Deputy Head, Operations* ☎ **202 4402**
Treasurer — Narendra Bailkeri *Head of Money Markets* ☎ **288 6839/38**

General-Lending (DCM, SL)
Head of Corporate Banking — Zarina Engineer *Head of Corporate Banking* ☎ **285 1857**

Debt Capital Markets / Fixed Income
Country Head — Narendra Bailkeri *Head of Money Markets* ☎ **288 6839/38**

Syndicated Lending
Country Head — Hemant Vora *Relationship Manager* ☎ **202 4389**

Loan-Related Activities
Trade Finance — Erhard Rodrigues *Assistant Manager* ☎ **282 5743**

Money Markets
Head of Money Markets — Narendra Bailkeri *Head of Money Markets* ☎ **288 6839/38**

Wholesale Deposits
Marketing — Zarina Engineer *Head of Corporate Banking* ☎ **285 1857**
Head of Sales — Tushar Patankar *Relationship Manager* ☎ **202 4381**

Foreign Exchange
Country Head — Dhiren Khansaheb *Head of Forex* ☎ **288 6839**

Risk Management
Country Head — Zarina Engineer *Head of Corporate Banking* ☎ **285 1857**

Foreign Exchange Derivatives / Risk Management
Cross-Currency Swaps, Sales / Marketing; — Dhiren Khansaheb *Head of Forex* ☎ **288 6839**
Cross-Currency Swaps, Trading; Vanilla FX option Sales; Vanilla FX option Trading

Corporate Finance / M&A Advisory
Country Head — Kannan Ranganathan *Head, Merchant Banking* ☎ **288 5851**

Settlement / Clearing
Country Head — John Fernandes *Head, Settlement* ☎ **288 6230**

Administration
Head of Administration — Parizad Deboo *Executive Assistant* ☎ **288 6238**

Technology & Systems
S Rajshekharan *Senior Officer* ☎ **288 6841**

www.euromoneydirectory.com   INDIA (+91)

Legal / In-House Counsel
 Arvind Menon *Credit Controller* ☏ **202 4389**
Compliance
Concurrent Auditor Pandurang Hegde *Assistant Manager* ☏ **202 4386**
Public Relations
 Parizad Deboo *Executive Assistant* ☏ **288 6238**

Banque Sudameris   Representative Office
143 Maker Chambers VI, Nariman Point, Mumbai 400 021
Tel: (22) 287 1400 **Fax:** (22) 202 0333
Senior Executive Officers
Representative Pattabi K Raman

BHF-BANK   Representative Office
10th Floor, 107 Maker Chambers III, 223 Nariman Point, Mumbai 400 021
Tel: (22) 285 0079; (22) 285 0080 **Fax:** (22) 287 1423 **Telex:** 1184765
Senior Executive Officers
Chief Representative Vijay V Meghani

Canara Bank   Head Office
112 J C Road, Bangalore 2 560 002
PO Box 6648, Bangalore
Tel: (80) 222 1581; (80) 222 0490 **Fax:** (80) 222 2704 **Swift:** CNRBINBBBID **Email:** canbank@blr.vsnl.net.in
Reuters: CNFX **Cable:** CANARABANK, CANBANK
Website: www.canbankindia.com
Senior Executive Officers
Others (Senior Executives)
Corporate Credit A K S Rao *General Manager* ☏ **222 3166**
Treasury & International Operations V Aghoram *General Manager* ☏ **223 8406**
Personnel M V Kamath *General Manager* ☏ **223 7237**
Legal A K Mehta *General Manager* ☏ **222 3167**
Planning & Development P V Shenoy *General Manager* ☏ **222 1262**
Technology & Systems Sri Muralikrishna *Deputy General Manager* ☏ **558 4273**
International Division & Correspondent Banking B V Kamath *Deputy General Manager & Head* ☏ **(22) 285 2001**

Capital Trust Limited   Subsidiary Company
Corporate Office Capital Trust House 47, Community Centre, Friends Colony, New Delhi 110 065
Tel: (11) 682 0148; (11) 691 1010 **Fax:** (11) 691 4744 **Telex:** 03185090
Senior Executive Officers
Others (Senior Executives)
 Pradeep Khanna *Vice President*

Citibank NA   Full Branch Office
Tata Centre, Chowringhee Road, Calcutta 700 001
Tel: (33) 226 6551 **Fax:** (33) 400 375
Foreign Exchange
FX Traders / Sales People
 Malay Ghatek *Treasury Marketing* ☏ **298 186**

Citibank NA   Full Branch Office
Sakhar Bhavan, Nariman Point, Mumbai 400 021
Tel: (22) 202 8765 **Reuters:** CIBY
FX Tel: 2868 8892
Senior Executive Officers
Chief Executive Officer David Conner

Euromoney Directory 1999   **679**

INDIA (+91)   www.euromoneydirectory.com

Citibank NA (cont)
General-Lending (DCM, SL)
Head of Corporate Banking   Amal Bindra
General - Treasury
Head of Treasury   Jay Chakrabarty
Debt Capital Markets / Fixed Income
Global Head   Bramit Jhaveri ☎ 287 2680
Foreign Exchange
Head of Foreign Exchange   Jay Chakrabarty

Citibank NA   Full Branch Office
4th Floor, Jeevan Pharti Building, Tower 1, 124 Connaught Circus, New Delhi 1 10001
Tel: (11) 332 0136; (11) 371 4211 Fax: (11) 332 5912
Foreign Exchange
FX Traders / Sales People
    Anil Gudibande ☎ 332 6405

Commerzbank AG   Full Branch Office
13th Floor, 12B Free Press House, 215 Free Press Journal Road, Nariman Point, Mumbai 400 021
Tel: (22) 288 5510; (22) 288 5512 Fax: (22) 288 5524; (22) 288 5525 Telex: 1186859 COBO IN Telex: 1186889 CZBY IN
Senior Executive Officers
Manager   Peter Kenyon-Muir
Head of International Banking Relations   Robert von Olderhausen

Crédit Commercial de France   Representative Office
Harchandrai House, 6th Floor, 81 Queens Road, Marine Lines, Mumbai 400 002
Tel: (22) 208 8044; (22) 208 8045 Fax: (22) 205 1569 Email: ccfindia@bom2.vsnl.net.in
Senior Executive Officers
Representative   Anand Dalavi ☎ 208 8043

Deutsche Bank AG   Full Branch Office
Raheja Towers, 26/27 MG Road, Bangalore 560 001
PO Box 5002, Bangalore
Tel: (80) 559 4488 Fax: (80) 559 4388 Telex: 08453200;08453199;08458182 Cable: DEUTASIA BANGALO

Deutsche Bank AG   Full Branch Office
Brooke House, 9 Shakespeare Sarani, Calcutta 700 071
Tel: (33) 282 5050; (33) 282 6060 Fax: (33) 282 1716

Deutsche Bank AG   Full Branch Office
Hazarimal Somani Marg, Fort, Mumbai 400 001
PO Box 1142, Mumbai
Tel: (22) 207 4720 Fax: (22) 207 5047 Telex: 1184042 DEUT IN
Senior Executive Officers
Managing Director / General Manager   Harkirat Singh
Global Custody
Country Head   Thomas Sasse ☎ 207 3750 ✉ 207 5975

Deutsche Bank AG   Full Branch Office
Tolstoy House, 15/17 Tolstoy Marg, New Delhi 110 001
PO Box 33, New Delhi
Tel: (11) 331 3629 Fax: (11) 331 6237 Telex: 3165563 Cable: DEUTBANK

www.euromoneydirectory.com   INDIA (+91)

DSP Financial Consultants Limited
Subsidiary Company

11th Floor, West Wing, Tulsiani Chambers, 212 Backbay Reclamation, Mumbai 400 021
Tel: (22) 285 3801 Fax: (22) 204 8518 Telex: 86774 DSPF IN Reuters: DSPI-K

Senior Executive Officers
Chairman   Hemendra M Kothari [F] 287 5191
Financial Director   Kumar Shah
Vice Chairman & Managing Director   Shitin Desai

DSP Securities
Subsidiary Company

10th Floor, Chander Maklu, Nariman Road, Mumbai 400 021
Tel: (22) 288 2550 Fax: (22) 287 2093

The Export-Import Bank of Japan
Representative Office

Suite 250, The Oberoi, Dr Zakir Hussain Marg, New Delhi 110 003
Tel: (11) 439 5039; (11) 439 5040 Fax: (11) 439 5041 Email: jeximnd1@del2.vsnl.net.in
Website: www.japanexim.go.jp

Senior Executive Officers
Chief Representative   Kenichiro Mineta

The Fuji Bank Limited
Representative Office

5th Floor, World Trade Centre, Barakhamba Lane, New Delhi 110 001
Tel: (11) 371 1838; (11) 371 1808 Fax: (11) 371 1840

Senior Executive Officers
Business Area Head   Hiroyuki Sakurai

Generale Bank
Representative Office

13 Maker Chambers VI, 1st Floor, Nariman Point, Mumbai 400 021
Tel: (22) 287 2510; (22) 287 2511 Fax: (22) 204 5344

Senior Executive Officers
Chief Representative   Anil Gupte

The Hongkong & Shanghai Banking Corporation Limited
Full Branch Office

52/60 Mahatma Gandhi Road, Fort, Mumbai 400 001
Tel: (22) 267 4921; (22) 267 4924 Fax: (22) 265 8309; (22) 262 3890 Telex: 01182223 HSBC IN
Website: www.hongkongbank.com

Senior Executive Officers
Chief Executive Officer   John Dyfrig *CEO, India* [T] 261 9379

Others (Senior Executives)
                                            Zed Cama *Deputy Chief Executive Officer* [T] 261 9375
Banking Services   Ravin Narain *Senior Manager* [T] 267 6023
Personal Banking & Card Products   Richard Cromwell *Senior Manager* [T] 269 4048
General-Lending (DCM, SL)
Head of Corporate Banking   Sanjiv Bhasin *Senior Manager* [T] 261 9407
Syndicated Lending
Trade Finance   Kersi Patel *Manager Trade Services* [T] 267 5927
Project Finance   Rohit Johri *Manager Structured Finance* [T] 267 9407
Other Departments
Correspondent Banking   Ravi Rao *Senior Manager* [T] 262 3889
Cash Management   Swarup Choudhury *Head of Cash Management & Payments* [T] 262 5927
Administration
Technology & Systems
                                            Pat Dalton *Manager* [T] 204 1701

INDIA (+91)   www.euromoneydirectory.com

The Hongkong & Shanghai Banking Corporation Limited (cont)
Legal / In-House Counsel
                     Krish Krishnamurthy *Legal Advisor* ☏ **267 0511**
Compliance
                     Prem Panjwani *Manager* ☏ **267 6679**
Public Relations
                     Malini Thadani *Public Affairs Manager* ☏ **267 6505**
Accounts / Audit
Audit   Don Lansberry *Manager* ☏ **204 8203**

HypoVereinsbank   Representative Office
14, Mega Chambers VI, Nariman Point, Mumbai 400 021
Tel: (22) 288 2121 **Fax:** (22) 288 2121

IndusInd Bank Limited   Head Office
Indusind House, 425 D B Marg, Lamington Road, Mumbai 400 004
Tel: (22) 385 9901; (22) 385 9494 **Fax:** (22) 380 9931; (22) 385 6037 **Telex:** 11 71254 IIBL IN **Swift:** INDB IN BB
Reuters: IIBK
General Tel: (22) 385 7474; (22) 385 9909
Website: www.indusind.com

Senior Executive Officers
Chairman   P K Kaul
Managing Director   S Solomon Raj
Executive Director   S D Wadivkar
Executive Director   M Lau

ING Barings   Full Branch Office
7th Floor, Hoechst House, 193 Nariman Point, Mumbai 400 021
Tel: (22) 202 7082; (22) 202 9876 **Fax:** (22) 204 6134; (22) 287 0934 **Telex:** 85269/79 INGB IN **Swift:** INGB IN BB
Reuters: INBO (Dealing)

Senior Executive Officers
Others (Senior Executives)
Country Manager   Pradeep Saxena
Equity Capital Markets
Department: ING Barings India
Tel: +91 (22) 288 5922 **Fax:** +91 (22) 202 6197
Country Head   Pradeep Saxena
Asset Management
Department: ING Asset Management
Tel: 287 0962 **Fax:** 204 6134
Head   Sukhu D Nayyar *Co-Country Manager*

ING Barings   Full Branch Office
Upper Ground Floor, Gopal Das Bhavan, 28 Barakhambha Road, New Delhi 110 001
Tel: (11) 373 8841; (11) 373 8846 **Fax:** (11) 373 8849

Senior Executive Officers
Others (Senior Executives)
Area Head   Ranjit Mehta
Other Departments
Department: ING Bank
Private Banking   Kavita Hurry *General Manager*

Jardine Fleming India Broking Limited   Subsidiary Company
Amarchand Mansion, 16 Madame Cama Road, Mumbai 400 001
Tel: (22) 283 5841 **Fax:** (22) 287 2646

Senior Executive Officers
Managing Director   Robert Gibson

www.euromoneydirectory.com　　　　　　　INDIA (+91)

Jardine Fleming India Securities Limited
Full Branch Office

Amerchand Mansion, 16 Madame Cama Road, Mumbai 400 001
Tel: (22) 283 5841; (22) 283 5842 Fax: (22) 283 5846; (22) 282 6547 Email: india.jfelectra@jfleming.com

Senior Executive Officers
Managing Director　　　　　　　　　Robert Gibson
Company Secretary　　　　　　　　　Yarookh Bharucha

General-Investment
Head of Investment　　　　　　　　　Roddy Sale *Head of Investment Banking*

Equity Capital Markets
Head of Sales　　　　　　　　　　　Sam Tully
Head of Trading　　　　　　　　　　Robert Jackson

Equity Research
Head of Equity Research　　　　　　Nitin Anandkar

Settlement / Clearing
Head of Settlement / Clearing　　　　Kiran Shah

Asset Management
Head　　　　　　　　　　　　　　　U R Bhat [T] **284 6942/44**

Administration
Head of Administration　　　　　　　Anita Belani *Head of Human Resources*

Accounts / Audit
　　　　　　　　　　　　　　　　　Anand Kristina *Finance Director* [T] **283 5841** [F] **283 6746**

Lakshmi Vilas Bank Limited
Head Office

2nd Floor, International Division, 1 Bheemasena Garden II Street, Mylapore, Madras 600 004
Tel: (44) 499 3853; (44) 499 1815 Fax: (44) 499 1728 Telex: (41) 6126 FLEXIN; 5016

Senior Executive Officers
Chairman　　　　　　　　　　　　　K R Shenoy
General Manager　　　　　　　　　　R Muniswamy
International Division　　　　　　　　S Ravishanker *Assistant General Manager*

Foreign Exchange
Head of Foreign Exchange　　　　　　S Ravishanker *Assistant General Manager*

Lazard Creditcapital Limited
Subsidiary Company

Alternative trading name: Lazard Creditcapital India
Brady House, Veer Nariman Road, Fort, Mumbai 400 001
Tel: (22) 285 5926 Fax: (22) 283 5452 Telex: 83095 CASH IN Email: lazard@bom3.vsnl.net.in
Website: www.lccindia.com

Senior Executive Officers
Chairman & Chief Executive Officer　　Udayan Bose [T] **283 5559** [F] **283 5810**
Managing Director　　　　　　　　　Amitava Mukherjee [T] **283 5558**
Managing Director　　　　　　　　　Ashish Guha [T] **(11) 614 1901**
Vice President　　　　　　　　　　　Hiten Mehta [T] **285 5926**
International Division　　　　　　　　Somnath Roy *Director* [T] **283 6408**

General-Lending (DCM, SL)
Head of Corporate Banking　　　　　Mahinder Chugh *Director* [T] **283 7504**

General-Investment
Head of Investment　　　　　　　　　Sailesh Mukherjee *Director* [T] **283 5809**

Equity Capital Markets

Equity Research
Head of Equity Research　　　　　　Rajiv Sakena *President* [T] **283 9884**

Syndicated Lending

Loan-Related Activities
Project Finance　　　　　　　　　　Somnath Roy *Director* [T] **283 6408**

Corporate Finance / M&A Advisory
Head of Corporate Finance　　　　　Praween Napate *Director* [T] **282 1996**
　　　　　　　　　　　　　　　　　Rajiv Sakena *President* [T] **283 9884**
　　　　　　　　　　　　　　　　　Sreekant Javalgekar *President* [T] **284 4328**

INDIA (+91)　　　　　www.euromoneydirectory.com

Lazard Creditcapital Limited (cont)
Administration
Head of Administration　　　　　Jimi Dastur *Senior Manager* ☎ 285 5926
Technology & Systems
IT Services　　　　　Sudipto Pal *President* ☎ (11) 614 5369
Compliance
　　　　　R Subramaniam *Associate Vice President* ☎ 285 5926

London Forfaiting India Limited　　　　　Representative Office
97 Jolly Maker Chambers II, Nariman Point, Mumbai 400 021
Tel: (22) 285 3586 **Fax:** (22) 283 6804

Senior Executive Officers
Representative　　　　　Satish Gopinath
Others (Senior Executives)
　　　　　Himanshu Kohli *Manager*

Mecklai & Mecklai　　　　　Head Office
101 Mahatma Gandhi Road, Mumbai 400 023
Tel: (22) 267 1214; (22) 267 4024 **Fax:** (22) 265 2817 **Telex:** 82525 AMCO, 82011 MMBY
Email: mecklai@giasbmoi.vsnl.net.in **Reuters:** MMBY-Z

Senior Executive Officers
Chairman　　　　　Abdully Mecklai
Chief Executive Officer　　　　　Jamal Mecklai ☎ 264 2710
Chief Operating Officer　　　　　Zia Mecklai *Partner & Managing Director* ☎ 267 3419
Managing Director / General Manager　　　　　Amyn Mecklai
Foreign Exchange
Global Head　　　　　Zia Mecklai *Partner & Managing Director* ☎ 267 3419
Head of Trading　　　　　Freddie Castellino *Chief Dealer*
FX Traders / Sales People
　　　　　Shekhar Lolop
　　　　　Amyn Mecklai
　　　　　Manbir Bawa
　　　　　Mohan Mahadik
　　　　　Parag Parich
　　　　　Sushil Dalwi
　　　　　Rahul Aithal
　　　　　Sanjay Mistry
　　　　　Sunil Diwadkar
　　　　　Rashmin Parmar
　　　　　Sandeep Gonsalves
　　　　　Mangal Murthy
　　　　　Eric Almeida
　　　　　Amogh Moghe
　　　　　Jehangir Siddiquui

Risk Management
Department: Mecklai Financial & Commercial Services
19 Adi Marzban Path, Mumbai
Global Head　　　　　Jamal Mecklai ☎ 264 2710

DSP Merrill Lynch
Tulsiani Chambers, West Wing, 11th Floor, Nariman Point, Mumbai 400 021
Tel: (22) 284 5275; (22) 204 8653 **Fax:** (22) 204 8518 **Email:** crk_prasad@ml.com **Reuters:** DSPI; DSPJ; DSPK

Senior Executive Officers
Chairman　　　　　Hemandra Kothari ☎ 285 3801 F 2875191
Vice Chairman & Managing Director　　　　　Shitin Desai ☎ 285 3799 F 287 5191
Executive Vice President　　　　　Dhananjay Mungale ☎ 285 3796 F 287 5191
Financial Director　　　　　Kumar Shah *Chief Financial Officer* ☎ 284 6790 F 287 5191
First Vice President & Company Secretary　　　　　Raj Kataria ☎ 284 2080 F 204 8518
Others (Senior Executives)
Head of Capital Markets Group　　　　　Saurabh Sonthalia *First Vice President* ☎ 282 6853 F 204 8518
General-Investment
Head of Investment　　　　　Pradeep Dokania *Senior Vice President* ☎ 285 3793 F 204 8518

www.euromoneydirectory.com INDIA (+91)

Debt Capital Markets / Fixed Income
Tel: 288 1001/2/3/4/5 **Fax:** 283 1198
Head of Fixed Income Sales
Jayesh Mehta *First Vice President* T 285 4774
Premal Mehta *First Vice President* T 204 8774
Head of Fixed Income Trading
Deepak Jain *Debt Trader* T 204 8653 F 204 8518

Equity Capital Markets
Tel: 288 2533/4/5/6/7/8 **Fax:** 288 1732
Head of Sales
Nozer Shroff *Managing Director* T 284 1441 F 287 2093
Head of Trading
Raj Mehta T 288 2550

Domestic Equities
Head of Sales
Nozer Shroff *Managing Director* T 284 1441 F 287 2093
Head of Trading
Raj Mehta T 288 2550

International Equities
Head of Sales
Nozer Shroff *Managing Director* T 284 1441 F 287 2093
Head of Trading
Raj Mehta T 288 2550

Equity Research
Head of Equity Research
Andrew Holland *Senior Vice President & Head of Research* T 288 2539

Money Markets
Tel: 288 1001/2/3/4/5 **Fax:** 283 1198
Head of Money Markets
Premal Mehta *First Vice President* T 204 8774
Jayesh Mehta *First Vice President* T 285 4774

Risk Management
Head of Risk Management
R Jayakumar *First Vice President* T 284 1312 F 204 8518

Settlement / Clearing
Tel: 265 2404 **Fax:** 265 0196
Head of Settlement / Clearing
Uday Thakurdesai *Director* T 265 3715 F 265 6681
Back-Office
Jayesh Ghia *Vice President* T 284 6972 F 204 8518

Asset Management
Head
S Naganath *Chief Investment Officer* T 288 4827 F 288 4815

Administration
Head of Administration
Makarand Khatavkar *First Vice President* T 287 2565 F 282 1827

Technology & Systems
Arun Gupta *Vice President* T 284 0792 F 282 1827

Legal / In-House Counsel
Raj Kataria *First Vice President & Company Secretary* T 284 2080 F 204 8518

Compliance
Raj Kataria *First Vice President & Company Secretary* T 284 2080 F 204 8518

Morgan Stanley Trust Company
Subsidiary Company

4th Floor, Forbes Building, Charanjiit Rai Marg, Mumbai 400 001
Tel: (22) 209 6600 **Fax:** (22) 209 6601; (22) 209 6602

Global Custody
Regional Head
Anil Narang

Paribas
Representative Office

Intach Building, 71 Lodhi Estate, New Delhi 110 003
Tel: (11) 491 9460; (11) 491 9461 **Fax:** (11) 491 9463
General Tel: 461 9462

Senior Executive Officers
Group Regional Director — David Moleshead
Assistant Vice President — Tashi Zaidi
Assistant Vice President — Sandeep Aggarwal
Assistant Vice President — Sandeep Babbar
Financial Director — A R Singhal *Head, Corporate Banking*

INDIA (+91)　　　　　www.euromoneydirectory.com

The Sakura Bank Limited

2-B Mittal Court 224, Nariman Point, Mumbai 400 021
Tel: (22) 204 3931; (22) 282 6205 **Fax:** (22) 204 6754 **Telex:** 01182987

Senior Executive Officers
Managing Director / General Manager　　　Toshihiro Takiguchi

The Sakura Bank Limited

Ground Floor, Dr Gopal Das Bhawan, 28 Barakhamba Road, New Delhi 110 001
Tel: (11) 373 7637; (11) 373 7641 **Fax:** (11) 373 7642; (11) 332 2969 **Telex:** 65527 MITK

Senior Executive Officers
General Manager　　　Kazuo Hashimoto

Sakura Capital India Limited　　　Head Office

21 Mittal Chambers, 228 Nariman Point, Mumbai 400 021
Tel: (22) 288 4361 **Fax:** (22) 288 4367

Senior Executive Officers
Chairman　　　C H Mirani

Others (Senior Executives)
　　　Nayan Miriani *Deputy Managing Director*
　　　Masahiko Kuramura *Director*
　　　Madhav Mirani *Associate Director*
　　　V Ramachandran *Company Secretary & Financial Controller*

General-Investment
Head of Investment　　　Sunil Mirani *Associate Director*

Corporate Finance / M&A Advisory
Head of Corporate Finance　　　Nishit Sanghvi

SocGen-Crosby Securities India Private Limited Subsidiary Company

Maker Chamber IV, 13th Floor, Nariman Point, Mumbai 400 021
Tel: (22) 288 6055 **Fax:** (22) 288 6044

Equity Capital Markets
Tel: 288 6036

Equity Research
Regional Head　　　Ranjan Pai *Head of Research* E **ranjan_pai@socgen-crosby.com**

Other (Equity Research)
Strategy　　　Ranjan Pai *Head of Research* E **ranjan_pai@socgen-crosby.com**
Metals, Engineering　　　B Sashikanth *Associate Director* E **b_sashikanth@socgen-crosby.com**
Banks, Power　　　Prasanna Someshwar *Associate Director*
　　　E **prasanna_someshwar@socgen-crosby.com**
Telecom, Pharmaceuticals, IT　　　Prashant Vaishampayan *Associate Director*
　　　E **prashant_vaishampayan@socgen-crosby.com**
Cement, Conglomerates, Textiles　　　Nirjhar Gupta *Investment Analyst* E **nirhar_gupta@socgen-crosby.com**
Refineries, Petrochemicals, Packaging　　　Prakash Joshi *Investment Analyst* E **prakashi_joshi@socgen-crosby.com**
Consumer Goods　　　Gaurav Narain *Investment Analyst* E **gaurav@socgen-crosby.com**

Société Générale

13th Floor, Maker Chambers IV, PO Box 11534, Bajaj Marg, Nariman Point, Mumbai 400 021
Tel: (22) 287 0908; (22) 287 0909 **Fax:** (22) 204 5459

INDIA (+91)

SS Kantilal Ishwarlal Securities Limited — Full Branch Office

Alternative trading name: SSKI

701 Tulsiani Chamber, Nariman Point, Mumbai 400 021
3A Khatau Building, A D Modi Street, Mumbai 400 001
Tel: (22) 265 0120; (22) 284 3000 **Fax:** (22) 204 0282 **Email:** sski@sski.co.in **Bloomberg:** DEALERS SSKI
Website: www.sski.com

Senior Executive Officers
Chief Executive Officer — Shripal Morakhia **285 6000**
Financial Director — Shankar Vailaya **265 0120**

General-Investment
Head of Investment — Vikash Saraf *Director* **283 5424**

Equity Capital Markets
Tel: 285 6000 **Fax:** 282 5989
Head of Sales; Head of Trading — Dhiraj Agarwal *Director*

Domestic Equities
Head of Sales; Head of Trading — Dhiraj Agarwal *Director*

International Equities
Head of Sales; Head of Trading — Dhiraj Agarwal *Director*

Equity Research
Head of Equity Research — Sapna Malhotra *Head of Research* **284 3000**

Settlement / Clearing
Tel: 265 0120 **Fax:** 265 1358
Head of Settlement / Clearing; Equity Settlement; Back-Office — Shankar Vailaya **265 0120**

Administration
Head of Administration — Renuka Advani *Vice President, Corporate Affairs* **284 3000**
Business Development — Renuka Advani **284 3000**
Head of Marketing — Sapna Malhotra *Head of Research* **284 3000**

Technology & Systems
Shankar Vailaya **265 0120**

Compliance
Atul Doshi *Director* **265 0120**

Public Relations
Renuka Advani *Vice President, Corporate Affairs* **284 3000**

Accounts / Audit
Shankar Vailaya **265 0120**

Standard Chartered Bank — Full Branch Office

23-25 Mahatma Gandhi Road, Fort, Mumbai 400 001
PO Box 558, Mumbai 400 001
Tel: (22) 207 2550 **Fax:** (22) 204 8018; (22) 204 4703 **Telex:** 0118 2230 5142SCBY IN

Senior Executive Officers
Chief Executive Officer — Martin Fish *Chief Executive, India* **207 5567**
Financial Director — R Ganapathy *Chief Financial Officer* **207 1272**
Treasurer — Sharat Anand **285 3856**

General-Lending (DCM, SL)
Head of Corporate Banking — Jaspal Bindra *Head, Corporate Banking (India)* **285 5855**

Syndicated Lending
Trade Finance — Armeesh Sulati *Head, Trade Services* **204 4444**

Corporate Finance / M&A Advisory
Head of Corporate Finance — Sanjeev Nanauati **204 9909**

Global Custody
Other (Global Custody) — Mahesh Muzumder *Head of Custodial Services, India*

Other Departments
Chief Credit Officer — R S Mani *Senior Credit Officer* **287 5813**
Correspondent Banking — Raijit Baru *Head of Financial Institutions* **282 2099**
Cash Management — Nipum Bhatia **283 9661**

INDIA (+91) www.euromoneydirectory.com

Standard Chartered Bank (cont)
Administration
Head of Administration   Ajoy Kapoor *Head, Facilities Management* ☎ **207 2949**
Technology & Systems
                                  K S Nayak *Head, Global Technology Services* ☎ **287 4487**
Compliance
                                  Ramona Shenoy *Head* ☎ **204 4444**
Corporate Communications
                                  V Krishnan *Head, Corporate Affairs & Communication* ☎ **207 5816**
Accounts / Audit
                                  Sanjeer Agrawal

Syndicate Bank   Head Office
PO Box 1, Dakshina, Kannada District, Manipal 576 119, Karnataka
Tel: (8252) 71181 **Fax:** (8252) 70266 **Telex:** 0833 201, 0833 202, 0833 203 **Swift:** SYNBINBB
Email: sbid@syndicate.com **Reuters:** SYFX
Website: www.syndicatebank.com

Senior Executive Officers
Chairman & Managing Director   K V Krishnamurthy ☎ **70252** 📠 **70710**
Executive Director   J Y Divanji ☎ **70706** 📠 **70440**
International Division   B Samba Murthy *General Manager, Treasury & International Banking*
                                  ☎ **(22) 218 1276**

UBS AG
36, Maker Chambers VI, Nariman Point, Mumbai 400 021
Tel: (22) 282 1194 **Fax:** (22) 282 1348

Senior Executive Officers
Chairman, India   E R Macdonald
Country Head, India   A Sondhi
Syndicated Lending
Loan-Related Activities
Project Finance   S Balasubramanian
Other (Trade Finance)
Global Trade Finance   S Krishnamoorthy
Settlement / Clearing
Operations   A Phadnis *Logistics*
Other Departments
Economic Research   S Subramanian

Union Bank of India   Head Office
239 Vidhan Bhavan Marg, Nariman Point, Mumbai 21 400 021
Tel: (22) 202 4647 **Fax:** (22) 282 4689 **Telex:** 84208 UBID IN **Swift:** UBIN IN BB **Email:** union@bom3.vsnl.net.in
Reuters: UBCT
General Telex: 85156 UBID IN
Website: www.unionbankofindia.com

Senior Executive Officers
Chairman & Managing Director   Arokiasamy Pannir ☎ **202 3060**
Chairman & Managing Director   Thamarai Selvam ☎ **204 3319**
Executive Director   Dayanand Thimmappa Paj ☎ **204 3611**
International Division   Michael Bastian *General Manager* ☎ **202 4712** 📠 **202 6578**
Others (Senior Executives)
                                  G R Anande *General Manager*
                                  S P Roy *General Manager*
                                  A C Duggal *General Manager*
                                  T S Narayanasami *General Manager*
                                  Kum H A Daruwalla *General Manager*
                                  M S Kapur *General Manager*
                                  V Sridhar *General Manager*
                                  K V S Shyamsunder *General Manager*

688 Euromoney Directory 1999

Others (Senior Executives) (cont)
S P S Walia *General Manager*
Mr Rajadhyaksha *General Manager*
K S Rao *General Manager*
M S Mohan *General Manager*

United Bank of India

16 Old Court House Street, Calcutta 700 001
Tel: (33) 237 471 Telex: 0217387 UBIF IN

Senior Executive Officers
Chairman   N Gomathinayagam

Vijaya Bank

41/2 MG Road, Trinity Circle, Bangalore 560 001
Tel: (80) 558 4066 Fax: (80) 558 8853 Telex: 8452684 Email: vijbank@bgl.vsnl.net.in

Senior Executive Officers
Chairman   Vittaldas Leeladhar
Chief Executive Officer   N R Natarajan *Executive Director*
Financial Director   O S Ramamurthy *General Manager, Administration*
International Division   K Ratnakar Hedge *General Manager*

Others (Senior Executives)
B D Kakkar *General Manager*
K K Rai *General Manager, Credit*
Sridhar B Shetty *General Manager, Credit Recovery*
V P Shetty *General Manager*
Shanker K Shetty *General Manager*

Syndicated Lending
Head of Origination   K K Rai *General Manager, Credit*

Money Markets
Head of Money Markets   K Ratnakar Hedge *General Manager*

Foreign Exchange
Head of Foreign Exchange   K Ratnakar Hedge *General Manager*

Other Departments
Chief Credit Officer   K K Rai *General Manager, Credit*

INDONESIA
(+62)

Bank Indonesia   🏛 Central Bank

Jalan MH Thamrin 2, Jakarta 10010
Tel: (21) 231 1188 Email: bi@bi.go.id Bloomberg: DELEGASI
Treasury Fax: 301 3739
Website: www.bi.go.id

Senior Executive Officers
Governor   Syahril Sabirin ☏ **231 1188**

Others (Senior Executives)
Banking Regulations & Development   Erman Munzir *Director* ☏ **231 0787**

Foreign Exchange
Global Head   Mr Djakaria *Director* ☏ **231 0755**

Risk Management
Other (Equity Derivatives)
Economic Research   Burhanuddin Abdullah *Director* ☏ **231 0547**

Other Departments
Economic Research   Achjar Ilyas *Director*

Administration
Accounts / Audit
Bun Bunan Ej Hutapea *Director* ☏ **231 1438**

INDONESIA (+62)   www.euromoneydirectory.com

PT Bank Bali Tbk
Head Office

Bank Bali Tower, Jalan Jenderal, Sudirman Kav 27, Jakarta 12920
Tel: (21) 523 7788; (21) 523 7899 **Fax:** (21) 250 0708; (21) 250 0808 **Telex:** 60856 BALIFXIA **Swift:** BBBA ID JA
Email: bali@indoexchange.co.id **Reuters:** BALI, BNLI
Telex: 60863 BALIIA
Website: www.bankbali.com

Senior Executive Officers
Chairman — Sukanta Tanudjaja
Chief Executive Officer — Rudy Ramli *President / Director*
Investor Relations — Joys Djajanto ☏ **523 7914**
International Division — Hendra Firmansjah *Director* ☏ **523 7863**

Others (Senior Executives)
Liman Sandjaja *Commissioner*
Firmansjah Aluwi *Commissioner*
Engelsari Ramli *Commissioner*
Widjaja Kidarsa *Commissioner*
Firman Soetjahja *Deputy President Director*
I G M Mantera *Deputy President Director*
Agam P Napitupulu *Director*
Dino Ranti *Director*
Hendri Kurniawan *Director*

General-Lending (DCM, SL)
Head of Corporate Banking — Cecilia Laihad Wihardja *Director*

General-Investment
Head of Investment — Rusli Suryadi *Director* ☏ **523 7850**

Debt Capital Markets / Fixed Income
Medium-Term Notes
Head of Origination — Eddy Kurniawan *General Manager, Treasury* ☏ **745 3180**

Syndicated Lending
Fax: 250 0708
Global Head — Hendra Firmansjah *Director* ☏ **523 7863**
Head of Syndication — Soejanto Hadikoesoemo *Chief General Manager* ☏ **523 7774**

Loan-Related Activities
Trade Finance — Rufina Tinawati Marianto *General Manager* ☏ **523 7441**
Project Finance — Soejanto Hadikoesoemo *Chief General Manager* ☏ **523 7774**

Money Markets
Department: Treasury Department (Dealing Room)
Bank Bali Gedung Jaya II Bintaro, Jalan MH Thamtin 1, Kawasan Niaga Bintar, Tangerang, Jakarta 15224
Tel: +62 (21) 745 3311 **Fax:** +62 (21) 745 3170
Global Head — Rusli Suryadi *Director* ☏ **523 7850**
Regional Head — Eddy Kurniawan *General Manager, Treasury* ☏ **745 3180**
Country Head — Hanna Susiati *MM Dept Head* ☏ **745 3311**

Foreign Exchange
Department: Foreign Exchange
Bank Bali Gedung Jaya II, Bintaro, Jalan MH Thamrin 1, Kawasan Niaga, Bintaro, Jakarta 15224
Tel: +62 (21) 745 3311 **Fax:** +62 (21) 745 3170
Global Head — Rusli Suryadi *Director* ☏ **523 7850**
Regional Head — Eddy Kurniawan *General Manager, Treasury* ☏ **745 3180**

FX Traders / Sales People
IRBU — Krisnan Cahya *General Manager, IRBU* ☏ **745 2760**
IRBU Forex — Mr Yudi
Ms Merry
Mr Martono *Chief*
Ms Claudia
Mr Satya
MM Desk — Hanna Susiati *Chief*
Mr Luigi
Ms Fabiola
Ms Dina D
Forex Desk — Mr Hendra
Ms Megalani
Ms Yeally
Mr Mirza
Mr Surianto *Chief*

Risk Management
Tel: 523 7899
Global Head Firman Soetjahja *Deputy President Director*

Other (FI Derivatives)
Special Asset Management Dino Ranti *Director*
Department: Risk Management
Bank Bali Gedung Jaya II Bintaro, Jl. MH Thamrin I, Kawasan, Niaga Bintaro, Tangerang, Jakarta
Tel: +62 (21) 745 9888
Head of Risk Management T Lamuri *General Manager*

Other (FI Derivatives)
Risk Asset (Loan) Review Kasena Pandi *GM, Business Control Department* ☎ **745 9888**
Assets & Liabilities Committee Hadi Lesmono *Chief GM, Treasury Support*

Corporate Finance / M&A Advisory
Head of Corporate Finance Cecilia Laihad Wihardja *Director*

Settlement / Clearing
Department: Treasury Support
Bank Bali Gedung Jaya II Binaro, Jalan MH Thamrin 1, Kawasan Niaga Bintar, Tangerang, Jakarta 15224
Tel: +62 (21) 745 9888 **Fax:** +62 (21) 745 3170
Head of Settlement / Clearing; Foreign Budi Andriono *GM, Treasury Support* ☎ **745 5888**
Exchange Settlement

Global Custody
Head of Global Custody Daniek Tribuana *GM, Trust & Custody Services* ☎ **523 7561**
Country Head Hadi Lesmono *Chief GM, Treasury Support*

Other Departments
Chief Credit Officer Hendra Firmansjah *Director* ☎ **523 7863**
Private Banking Budi Tjahja Halim *Chief General Manager* ☎ **523 7775**
Correspondent Banking Hendra Firmansjah *Director* ☎ **523 7863**

Administration
Business Development Ganda Kusuma *Chief General Manager* ☎ **745 9888**
Head of Marketing Budi Tjahja Halim *Chief General Manager* ☎ **523 7775**

Technology & Systems
  Taryadi Supangkat *Chief GM, IT* ☎ **745 0668**

Legal / In-House Counsel
  Thomas Tan *General Manager* ☎ **523 7928**

Compliance
  Joys Djajanto *Investor Relations* ☎ **523 7914**

Public Relations
  Dian Syarif *Corporate Programs & Communications Mgr* ☎ **523 7935**

Accounts / Audit
  Kasena Pandi *GM, Business Control Department* ☎ **745 9888**

PT Bank BNP Lippo Indonesia Subsidiary Company

PO Box 1655/JKT, Jakarta 10016
Tel: (21) 572 2288 **Fax:** (21) 572 2280 **Telex:** 65405 **Swift:** BNPL ID JA **Email:** bnplippo@idola.net.id
General Telex: 65106 BNPLPB IA; **Foreign Exchange Telex:** 65089 BNPLPB IA

Senior Executive Officers
General Manager Henri Hunault
International Division Catherine Sirven *FVP, International Groups* ☎ **572 2305**

Others (Senior Executives)
Administration Olivier Charousset *Director, Operations & Administration*

General - Treasury
Head of Treasury Erling Hasan *Treasury*

Relationship Manager
Indonesian Groups Tan Swee Eng *Manager*
  Tjin Tjin Cindralela *Vice President*

Settlement / Clearing
Operations Tono Sunartono *Manager, Operations*

Administration
Head of Administration Olivier Charousset *Director, Operations & Administration*

INDONESIA (+62)　　　　　www.euromoneydirectory.com

PT Bank Buana Indonesia　　　　　Head Office

Bank Buana Building, Jalan Gajah Mada No 1A, Jakarta 10130
PO Box 4896, Jakarta 11048
Tel: (21) 231 2429; (21) 633 0585 **Fax:** (21) 632 4467; (21) 632 4478 **Telex:** 42042 **Swift:** BBIJ ID JA
Cable: Bank Buana Indonesia **Telex:** 42602 **Telex:** 42301 **Telex:** 42147

Senior Executive Officers
Chairman	Mr Rachmad [T] 631 2349
President	Hendra Suryadi
Chief Executive Officer	Ishak Sumarno Executive Vice President [F] 260 1011
	Pardi Kendy Head of Treasury [T] 231 4427
	Eddy Muljanto Executive Vice President [T] 692 2901 [F] 260 1033
	Karman Tandanu Executive Vice President [T] 260 1017 [F] 260 1013
Chief Operating Officer	Mr Antony [T] 260 1048 [F] 260 1033
Treasurer	Pardi Kendy Head of Treasury [T] 231 4427
Managing Director	Kamaruddin
Managing Director	Jimmy K Laihad
Managing Director	Aris Janasutanta Sutirto
Deputy President Director	Soetadi Limin [T] 260 1034 [F] 260 1013
General Manager	Mr Antony [T] 260 1048 [F] 260 1003
Company Secretary	Lany Martahadi
International Division	Mr Tedi Deputy Head [T] 260 1016 [F] 260 1013

General-Lending (DCM, SL)
Head of Corporate Banking	Mr Tedi Deputy Head [T] 260 1016 [F] 260 1013

Syndicated Lending
Head of Origination	Januar Tedjokusumo Head of Loan Department [F] 632 4941
Head of Syndication	Januar Tedjokusumo Head of Loan Department [F] 632 4941

Loan-Related Activities
Trade Finance	Mr Tedi [T] 260 1016 [F] 260 1013

Money Markets
Head of Money Markets	Pardi Kendy Head of Treasury [T] 231 4427

Foreign Exchange
Head of Foreign Exchange	Mr Danawira [T] 692 2045 [F] 260 1013

Settlement / Clearing
Head of Settlement / Clearing	Riki Iskandar [T] 692 2901 [F] 260 1013

Other Departments
Chief Credit Officer	Januar Tedjokusumo Head of Loan Department [F] 632 4941
Correspondent Banking	Mr Tedi [T] 260 1016 [F] 260 1013

Administration
Head of Administration	Winny Widya [F] 632 4942
Head of Marketing	Sukianto Sukagunas [T] 260 1051 [F] 632 4475

Technology & Systems

Basuki Tjahjono

Legal / In-House Counsel

Tristawati Widjaja [F] 632 4941

Accounts / Audit

Wimpie Wirjasurja Audit [F] 632 4475

Bank Credit Lyonnais Indonesia　　　　　Subsidiary Company

Suite 2501, Menara Mulia, Jalan Gatot Subroto Kav 9/11, Jakarta 12930
Tel: (21) 252 0234; (21) 252 0345 **Fax:** (21) 252 0123 **Telex:** 60975 CLI IA **Swift:** CRLY ID JA

Senior Executive Officers
President Director	Pierre-Alexandre Muyl

General-Lending (DCM, SL)
Head of Corporate Banking	Nuraida R Fatwana Credit Administration
	Jean François Balay Corporate Banking

General - Treasury
Head of Treasury	Laurence Kusuma Head of Treasury / Money Markets
	Sugihono Dealer, Treasury / Money Markets

Debt Capital Markets / Fixed Income
Global Head	Erwin Alamsyah Head

Equity Capital Markets
Global Head	Erwin Alamsyah Head

www.euromoneydirectory.com   INDONESIA (+62)

Syndicated Lending
Global Head
Head of Credit Committee
Erwin Alamsyah *Head*
Hermanus HM *Director, Credit & Head, Risk Management*

Money Markets
Global Head
Regional Head
Laurence Kusuma *Head of Treasury / Money Markets*
Sugihono *Dealer, Treasury / Money Markets*

Risk Management
Global Head
Regional Head
Hermanus HM *Director, Credit & Head, Risk Management*
Oliver De La Bernardie

Corporate Finance / M&A Advisory
Global Head
Erwin Alamsyah *Head*

Settlement / Clearing
Operations
François Bourg *Director, Operations & Administration*

Administration
Head of Administration
François Bourg *Director, Operations & Administration*

Legal / In-House Counsel
Lisa Andriana *Legal Counsel*

Other (Administration)
Human Resources
Marketing
Samuel Turangan *Director, Human Resources*
Tony Costa *Marketing Director*

PT Bank Dagang Negara (PERSERO)   Head Office

Jalan M H Thamrin 5, Jakarta 10340
PO Box 1338/JKT, Jakarta 10013
Tel: (21) 230 1107; (21) 230 0800 **Fax:** (21) 230 0618; (21) 230 0330 **Telex:** 61212 BDNKP IA **Swift:** BDNE ID JA
Email: upp1@bdn.co.id **Reuters:** BDNJ **Cable:** Stacopus
Treasury Fax: 301 3739; **General Tel:** 3902020; **Telex:** 61631 BDNKP IA
Website: www.bdn.co.id

Senior Executive Officers
Chairman, Board of Commissioners
President, Board of Directors
Managing Director
Managing Director
Managing Director
Managing Director
Managing Director
International Division

Mr Arifin ☎ 230 1568
Salahuddin N Kaoy ☎ 230 0341 🖷 230 0649
E C W Neloe ☎ 230 1569 🖷 230 1091
Lukman Nul Hakim ☎ 230 0350 🖷 230 0826
Bambang Hendrajatin ☎ 230 0985 🖷 230 2718
Mr Rudito ☎ 230 1092 🖷 230 0754
Bambang Sabariman ☎ 230 0828 🖷 230 0832
Mr Wirjono *Head* ☎ 230 3762 🖷 230 0618

Others (Senior Executives)
Marzuki Usman *Member, Board of Commissioners* ☎ 230 0476
J B Kristiadi Pudjosukanto *Member, Board of Commissioners* ☎ 230 1582

General-Lending (DCM, SL)
Head of Corporate Banking
Moerjanto Hargomoeljo *Head, Corporate I Division* ☎ 230 3874 🖷 230 3892
I Supomo *Head, Corporate II Division* ☎ 230 0530 🖷 230 2786

General - Treasury
Head of Treasury
Jonker Sihombing ☎ 230 3747 🖷 230 2595

Syndicated Lending
Recovery
Anny Andryani Hantarto ☎ 230 1129 🖷 230 0869

Other (Syndicated Lending)
Credit Examination & Control Division
M Machfudzs Samad *Head* ☎ 230 3460 🖷 230 3794

Other Departments
Correspondent Banking
Mr Wirjono ☎ 230 3762 🖷 230 0618

Administration
Technology & Systems
Information Technology
Kotrik Sudarno *Head* ☎ 230 1571 🖷 230 0314

Accounts / Audit
Accounting
Internal Audit
Atje Sasmita Hasan *Head* ☎ 230 3418
Hadi R Pane *Head* ☎ 230 0945 🖷 230 0326

Other (Administration)
Human Resources
Training Division
Logistics
Planning & Development
M Trahono *Head* ☎ 230 0626 🖷 230 2611
Mr Gunawan *Head* ☎ 390 7789 🖷 230 1088
Wahyono Surachmat *Head* ☎ 230 0807 🖷 230 3811
Ruhiat Wirasendjaja *Planning & Development Manager* ☎ 230 3746 🖷 230 3717

Euromoney Directory 1999 **693**

INDONESIA (+62)   www.euromoneydirectory.com

PT Bank Dai-Ichi Kangyo Indonesia — Subsidiary Company
3rd Floor, Wisma Rajawali Annex, Jalan Jenderal Sudirman Kav 35, Jakarta 10220
Tel: (21) 570 9270 Fax: (21) 570 9295 Telex: 65069 DKBJKT IA
Website: www.dkb.co.jp

Bank Duta — Head Office
12 Jalan Kebon Sirih, Jakarta 10110
Tel: (21) 380 0900; (21) 380 0901 Fax: (21) 380 1005 Telex: 46121, 45737, 46026, 46128, 4643 Swift: BADU ID JA
Cable: DUTABANK
Treasury Division Tel: 345 8290; 345 9137; Fax: 380 1380 Tel: 380 1412; 380 1420 Tel: 380 1448; Correspondent Banking Tel: 380 0900; 380 0901; Fax: 380 1324 Tel: 386 5352

Senior Executive Officers
Commissioner — Mr Hadjanto
Commissioner — Zahid Husein
Commissioner — Mung Parhadmulyo
President Director, Board of Directors — Muchtar Mandala
International Division — Sigit S Soalaiman *Head, Senior Assistant Vice President*

Others (Senior Executives)
Operational Division — Maharany Raza *Director*
Retail Banking — Musrizal Maszdi *Director*
Internal Control & Audit — Darman Rachman *Director*

General-Lending (DCM, SL)
Head of Corporate Banking — Mawan Cut Hasan *Director*

General - Treasury
Head of Treasury — Oebojo Gondosoebrata *Vice President & Head*

Relationship Manager
Credit Remedial 1 — Amsyler Slagian *Vice President & Head*
Credit Remedial II — Soiyan Edhar Harahap *Head, Senior Assistant Vice President*
Subsidiary Companies, Affiliated Supervision — Indriani A Haddy *Head, Senior Assistant Vice President*
Corporate Business 1 — Harun Rasyid Suhada *Head, Senior Assistant Vice President*
Corporate Business II — Thamrin Taher *Head, Senior Assistant Vice President*
Corpprate Business III — Ismet Yossoef *Vice President & Head*
Corporate Business IV — Muhamad Thamrin Taher *Head, Senior Assistant Vice President*
Credit Support — Gunawan Wibison *Head, Senior Assistant Vice President*
Special & Institutional Funding — Sagaputra C Syahrun
Operational Division — Mr Djajusman *Senior Vice President & Head*
Commercial Business Group — Saukani Hamid *Vice President & Head*
Consumer Business Group — Suryo Prasatyo *Vice President & Head*
Card Business Group — Endang Suhendi *Senior Vice President & Head*

Debt Capital Markets / Fixed Income
Global Head — Endi Pranadjaja *Assistant Vice President & Head* T 345 8290 F 380 1380

Equity Capital Markets
Global Head — Endi Pranadjaja *Assistant Vice President & Head* T 345 8290 F 380 1380

Syndicated Lending
Global Head — Mursid Lubis *Senior Manager & Head*

Money Markets
Global Head — Sri Budiasih *Assistant Vice President & Head* T 345 9137 F 380 1380

Foreign Exchange
Global Head — Endi Pranadjaja *Assistant Vice President & Head* T 345 8290 F 380 1380

Settlement / Clearing
Operations — Bambang Sri Sadhana *SAVP, Operational Service Unit*

Administration

Technology & Systems
— Mohammad Yasin Kara *Head, Senior Assistant Vice President*

Public Relations
Promotion & Public Relations — Agustian Partawjaya *Head, Senior Assistant Vice President*

Other (Administration)
Secretariat & General Affairs — Edyson Makmur *Vice President & Head*
Control — Mr Chaeruddin *Head, Senior Assistant Vice President*
Human Resources — Sri Indrawati Sukahar *Head, Senior Assistant Vice President*

www.euromoneydirectory.com INDONESIA (+62)

PT Bank Ekspor Impor Indonesia (PERSERO)   Head Office
Jalan Jenderal Gatot Subroto Kav 36-38, Jakarta 12190
PO Box 1032, Jakarta 12190
Tel: (21) 526 5045; (21) 526 5095 **Fax:** (21) 526 5008; (21) 526 5017 **Telex:** 60659 **Swift:** BEII ID JA
Cable: EXIMINDONESIA **Telex:** 60662 **Telex:** 60663 **Telex:** 60664 **Telex:** 60665 **Telex:** 60710

Senior Executive Officers
Chairman Mr Moersabdo T 524 5007 F 526 3517
President Director Mr Kodradi T 524 5256 F 526 3451
Treasurer J Bambang Kendarto Head of Treasury T 524 5504 F 526 3428
Managing Director Sutopo Djokotarbuko T 524 5003 F 526 3460
Managing Director M Sholeh Tasripan T 524 5005 F 526 3461
Managing Director Agus Marijanto Djojomartono T 524 5004 F 526 3453
Managing Director H A C Ratulangi T 524 5002 F 526 3452
Head of Office of the Board Division Winarso Tarupranoto T 524 5017 F 526 3621
International Division Hendarin Sukarmadji Executive GM, Foreign Dept T 526 3580 F 526 3581

General-Investment
Head of Investment J Bambang Kendarto Head of Treasury T 524 5504 F 526 3428

Syndicated Lending
Tel: 524 5139 **Fax:** 526 3441
Global Head Purwo Junianto General Manager T 524 5012 F 526 3441

Money Markets
Tel: 524 5506 **Fax:** 524 631ext32
Global Head Mr Sugiharto Treasury Manager

Foreign Exchange
Tel: 524 5506 **Fax:** 524 631ext32
Global Head Mr Sugiharto Treasury Manager

Risk Management
Tel: 524 5023 **Fax:** 526 3640
Global Head Heru Ratna Azimada Head of Research & Development Division

Settlement / Clearing
Tel: 524 5511 **Fax:** 526 3627
Regional Head Widowati Soemantri Treasury Back Office Manager

Other Departments
Correspondent Banking Nurizal Anwar Head of Financial Institutional Division T 524 5578
F 526 3583

Administration
Business Development Heru Ratna Azimada Head of Research & Development Division
Head of Marketing Aminuddin Ramli Division Head, Domestic Banking Services T 524 5666
F 526 3629

Technology & Systems
Edison Siahaan Head of Systems & Technology Division T 524 5018
F 526 3740

Public Relations
Winarso Tarupranoto Head of Office of the Board Division T 524 5017
F 526 3621

Accounts / Audit
M Saleh Sabana Head of Accounting T 524 5439 F 526 3625

Bank Indonesia Raya   Head Office
Alternative trading name: Bank Bira Tbk
Level 1-2 Wisma Metropolitan II, Kav 29-31, Jalan Jenderal Send Sudirman, Jakarta 12910
Tel: (21) 527 6888 **Fax:** (21) 251 2207; (21) 526 4129 **Telex:** 65728-228 BIRA IA **Swift:** BIRA IDJA
Email: brafgwsb@rad.net.id **Reuters:** BIRA **Cable:** BIRABANK

Senior Executive Officers
Chairman Atang Latief
President Director Bambang Panutomo
Corporate Financial Advisor Parveen Gandhi

General-Lending (DCM, SL)
Head of Corporate Banking Farman Gunawan Director

General-Investment
Head of Investment Farman Gunawan Director

Debt Capital Markets / Fixed Income
Head of Fixed Income Martono

INDONESIA (+62) www.euromoneydirectory.com

Bank Indonesia Raya (cont)

Equity Capital Markets
Head of Equity Capital Markets — Djumali Widjaja *Director* ☎ **526 1631**

Syndicated Lending
Head of Syndication — Ben Ramli

Loan-Related Activities
Trade Finance — Irawan

Money Markets
Head of Money Markets — Niniek Haryani

Corporate Finance / M&A Advisory
Head of Corporate Finance — Parveen Gandhi *Corporate Financial Advisor*

Asset Management
Head — Howard Chu ☎ **526 1631**

Other Departments
Correspondent Banking — Judi Sudjono

Administration
Head of Administration — Samksul
Business Development — David Burke *Advisor*

Technology & Systems — Indrahatna

Legal / In-House Counsel — Lucas

Public Relations — Parveen Gandhi *Corporate Financial Advisor*

Accounts / Audit — Willyson

PT Bank Internasional Indonesia Tbk — Head Office

Alternative trading name: BII

BII Plaza, Jalan MH Thamrin Kav 22, Jakarta 10350
PO Box 3445, Jakarta 10350
Tel: (21) 230 0888; (21) 230 0666 **Fax:** (21) 230 1412; (21) 230 2093 **Telex:** 61732 BII TH IA **Swift:** IBBK ID JA
Email: bii-info@idola.net.id **Cable:** INERNASBANK
Website: www.bii.co.id

Senior Executive Officers

Chairman — Eka Tjipta Widjaja
President Director — Indra Widjaja
Managing Director — H Ronnie Sujanjo
MD, Commercial Banking — Leo F Nagasaputra
International Division — A Taufik Rusdi

Others (Senior Executives)

Commercial Banking — Rosalina Dhanudimuljo
Consumer Banking — Dodi Susanto *Managing Director*
Banking Operations & System — Herman Soegiarto *Managing Director*
Corporate Secretary — H Syahvery Anwar ☎ **230 2107**
Foreign Business — Hiroshi Tadano

General-Lending (DCM, SL)
Head of Corporate Banking — Honggo Widjojo

General-Investment
Head of Investment — Yuli Soedargo *Managing Director*
Hengky Pangestu *Division Head*

Debt Capital Markets / Fixed Income
Head of Debt Capital Markets — Valentine V Veloo

Fixed-Income Repo
Head of Repo — Suzanna Irmawati

Syndicated Lending
Head of Origination — Margaret M Tang

Money Markets
Head of Money Markets — Melia Chandra ☎ **392 8282**

Settlement / Clearing
Head of Settlement / Clearing — Entin Rostini ☎ **392 8282**
Operations — Kairuddin Nur

www.euromoneydirectory.com INDONESIA (+62)

Global Custody
Head of Global Custody — Lies Asthama ☏ 392 8282
Other Departments
Correspondent Banking — Manuel T Sia *Financial Institutions*
Ratna M Santosa

Administration
Head of Marketing — Dodi Susando
Technology & Systems
Vijai K Jain
Electronic Banking — Ho Kwok Hoong ☏ 392 8282
Legal / In-House Counsel
Iswandari Yusuf ☏ 392 8282

Accounts / Audit
Board of Audit — Soengkowo Prijoredjo
Internal Audit Group — Antonius Halim ☏ 421 5885
Accounts & Finance — Kokaryadi Chandra
Other (Administration)
Human Resources — Gerard Gary Liwang ☏ 316 0977
Planning & Budgeting — Kokaryadi Chandra

PT Bank Mashill Utama Tbk Head Office

Plaza Mashill, Jalan Jenderal Sudirman Kav 25, Jakarta 12920
Tel: (21) 522 1995 **Fax:** (21) 522 1994; (21) 522 1985
General Fax **Fax:** 527 3227 **Fax:** 527 3228

Senior Executive Officers
President Commissioner — Karta Widjaja
Commissioner — Rasyim Wiraatmadja
Commissioner — Phillip Sandra Widjaja
Commissioner — Edwin Jaya Wiyanto
Commissioner — Dorodjatun Kuntjoro Jakti
President — Mr Moruba
Treasurer — Dradjat Bagus Prasetyo *Director, Treasury*

Others (Senior Executives)
Office of the Board Commisioner — Maruba Sihaloho *Head*
Anthon Widjaja

General-Lending (DCM, SL)
Head of Corporate Banking — Leo Yasin Satiadi *Director, Credit & Business Development*
Mr Harsono *Head, Commercial Banking*
Dara Wardhani *Head, Credit Review & Loan Administration*

General - Treasury
Head of Treasury — Dradjat Bagus Prasetyo *Director, Treasury*
Nilesh Bhatt *Treasury Adviser*
Mr Trisiladi *Head of Treasury*

Relationship Manager
Muliadi Hendri *Director, Corporate Management Development*
Financial Institutions — Dradjat Bagus Prasetyo *Director*
Ulina K *Head*
Branch Service Management — Yoseph Yudho *Head*
Risk Management
Global Head — Martinus Herman Tanoto *Head, Risk Management*
Corporate Finance / M&A Advisory
Global Head — Dradjat Bagus Prasetyo *Director*
Regional Head — Queenta Sylvia Gho *Head, Corporate Finance*
Settlement / Clearing
Operations — Anthon Widjaja
Karel Tjahjadi *Head, Domestic & International Operations*
Wibowo Suryadinata *Head, International Operations*
Jeanny Nurlitawati Djuhana *Head of Logistics*
Theresia Suhartaty *Operational Customer Services Authoriser*

Administration
Technology & Systems
Information Technology — Valens Tosin Kantawiria *Head*
Accounts / Audit
Internal Audit — Hendra Ginoto *Head*
Finance & Accounting — Hasmar Johni *Head*

Euromoney Directory 1999 **697**

INDONESIA (+62)   www.euromoneydirectory.com

PT Bank Mashill Utama Tbk (cont)
Other (Administration)
Human Resources Management   Trias W Redan *Head*

PT Bank Negara Indonesia (Persero) Tbk — Head Office
Jalan Jenderal Sudirman Kav 1, Jakarta
PO Box 2955, Jakarta 10001
Tel: (21) 251 1093; (21) 251 1102 **Fax:** (21) 251 1113; (21) 251 1103 **Telex:** 65185 BNI DLNIA **Swift:** BNIN ID JA
Cable: KANTOR BESAR **Tel:** 251 1104; **Telex:** 65215 BNI DLNIA

Senior Executive Officers
President Director   Widigdo Sukarman T 251 1945 F 251 1943
Managing Director   IG N G Antika T 251 1953 F 251 1944
Managing Director   Agus Daryanto T 251 1940 F 251 8914
Managing Director   Hasan Soeftendy T 251 1950 F 251 8941
Managing Director   Binsar Pangaribuan T 251 1942 F 251 8046
Managing Director   Sunardji Parto Adinoto T 251 1191 F 251 8941
Managing Director   Saiffudien Hasan T 251 1947 F 251 8044
International Division   Rachmat Wiriaatmadja *General Manager* T 251 1093 F 251 1113
                              Rudy R Subagio *Deputy General Manager* T 251 1234 F 251 1113
                              Bambang Wresniwiro *Deputy General Manager* T 251 1102 F 251 1103
                              Sri Astuti Kamarini *Deputy General Manager* T 251 1109 F 251 1103

Others (Senior Executives)
Office of the Board   Fauzi Azwar *General Manager* T 251 1959 F 251 1961
International Planning Group Head   Laliek Darliyanti *Group Manager* T 572 8474 F 251 1113
General - Treasury
Head of Treasury   Eko Budiwiyono *General Manager* T 572 8341 F 573 9913

Relationship Manager
Head, Investor Relations   Sudirman *General Manager* T 572 8387 F 872 8805
Investor Relations   Eddy Yusdaryono *Group Manager* T 572 8037 F 572 8805
Development of Int'l Trade Service   Syamsu *Group Manager* T 572 8458 F 251 1103
Head, Institutions Relationship   A Amien Mastur *General Manager* T 251 1114 F 251 1120

Debt Capital Markets / Fixed Income
Head of Debt Capital Markets Agus Warcoko *Group Manager* T 572 8366 F 573 9913
Head of Fixed Income   Ardi Nata Kesuma *Group Manager, International Division* T 572 8453 F 251 1113
Head of Fixed Income Sales   Eddy Junaedi Syahril *Sales Manager, Treasury Division* T 572 8366 F 573 9913

Other (Fixed Income)
FI Supporting Group   A Eddie Noegroho *Group Manager* T 572 8475 F 251 1113

Equity Capital Markets
Head of Equity Capital Markets   Agus Warcoko *Group Manager* T 572 8366 F 573 9913
Head of Sales   Eddy Junaedi Syahril *Sales Manager, Treasury Division* T 572 8366 F 573 9913

Syndicated Lending
Department: Syndication & Financial Services
Global Head   I Nyoman Sender *Group Manager* T 572 8201 F 574 6342
Head of Syndication   Suyitno Atmodihardjo *Group Manager* T 572 8203 F 251 1132
Other (Syndicated Lending)
Head, Legal & Documentation Group   Eddy N Soerjokoesoemo *Group Manager* T 572 8216 F 572 8068
Head, Credit Control   Boeditomo *General Manager* T 251 1147 F 251 1148

Money Markets
Global Head   Idris Rubian Sebayang *Group Manager* T 572 8247 F 573 9913
Other   Eddy Junaedi Syahril *Sales Manager, Treasury Division* T 572 8366 F 573 9913

Foreign Exchange
Global Head   F Sujatmoko *Group Manager* T 572 8347 F 573 9913

Corporate Finance / M&A Advisory
Department: Corporate Division 1
Fax: 251 1130
Global Head   Mohammad Arsjad *General Manager* T 572 8141

Other (Corporate Finance)
Senior Assistant Vice President   Arief Budiman *Group Manager* T 572 8144
Assistant Vice President   Hermin Setiyono *Group Manager* T 572 8145
                              Her Priantono *Group Manager* T 572 8146
                              Pandu Sasikirana *Group Manager* T 572 8147

698 Euromoney Directory 1999

Other (Corporate Finance) (cont)
Department: Corporate Division 2
Fax: +62 (21) 251 1135
Global Head
Other (Corporate Finance)
Head, Corporate Relationship Management

Head, Credit Documentation Management
Settlement / Clearing
Settlement (General)
Back-Office
Global Custody
Head of Global Custody
Fund Administration
Asset Management
Other (Asset Management)
Head, Investment Service Group
Head, Pension Fund Institution Group
Other Departments
Chief Credit Officer

Private Banking
Cash Management
Other Departments
Head, Financial Control Division
Head, Strategic Planning Division
Head, Corporate Remedial Division
Administration
Head of Marketing
Technology & Systems
Head, Information Technology
Legal / In-House Counsel
Head, Legal Division
Accounts / Audit
Head, Internal Audit
Other (Administration)
Head, General Affairs Division
Head, Human Resources
Head, Training & Development Division
Head, Personnel Supervision Division

Bambang Wiyono *Group Manager* T 572 8143

Masrokan Nasuha *General Manager* T 572 8264

Wewek Budiyanto *Group Manager* T 572 8237
Helmy M Zein *Group Manager* T 572 8274
Untari Arfan *Group Manager* T 572 8273
H B Wahyono *Group Manager* T 572 8259

Basmaridjal *Group Manager* T 572 8347 F 573 9913
Meriah Ate G *Support Function, Treasury Division* T 572 8347 F 573 9913

Suwaluyo *Group Manager* T 572 8211 F 251 1311
Imam Rusyamsi *Group Manager* T 572 8349 F 573 9913

Imam B Sarjito *Group Manager* T 572 8271 F 251 1311
Achmad Chusairi T 572 8211 F 2511 311

Boeditomo *General Manager, Credit Control Division* T 251 1147
F 251 1148
Bambang M Sardjono *Group Manager* T 572 8204 F 251 1259
Rudi Septian W *Group Manager* T 572 8349 F 573 9913

Moenir Rony *General Manager* T 251 1167 F 251 1139
I Dewa Gde Sutapha *General Manager* T 251 1181 F 572 8456
Marsahat Aritonang *General Manager* T 251 1163 F 251 1162

Djarot Ramelan *General Manager* T 251 1152 F 251 1158

Suryo Sutanto *General Manager* T 572 8602 F 251 1173

Soemarjoto *General Manager* T 251 1187 F 572 8036

Agoest Soebhektie *General Manager* T 251 1177 F 251 1179

Sediyono *General Manager* T 251 1212 F 251 1214
M Asrof *General Manager* T 251 1207 F 251 1209
Tjuk Suparman *General Manager* T 251 1270 F 251 1209
Soemadji *General Manager* T 251 1207 F 251 1209

PT Bank NISP
Head Office

Jalan Gunung Sahari 38, Jakarta 10720
Tel: (21) 600 9037/8; (21) 649 2262 **Fax:** (21) 649 2264; (21) 600 6507 **Telex:** 41467 NISPJKIA **Swift:** NISP ID JA
Reuters: NISP
Website: www.banknisp.com

Senior Executive Officers
Chairman
President & Chief Executive Officer
Financial Director
Chief Operating Officer
Managing Director
Others (Senior Executives)
Treasurer
Debt Capital Markets / Fixed Income
Department: Corporate Finance
Global Head
Government Bonds
Head of Sales
Head of Trading
Bonds - General
Research

Karmana Surjaudaja T +61 (22) 420 1600
Pramukti Surjaudaja E pramukti@banknisp.com
Kamsidin Wiradikusumah *Managing Director*
Hardi Juganda *Managing Director* T +61 (22) 420 1600
Ratna Dewitanti T +61 (22) 420 1600

Parwati Surjaudaja *Deputy President Director*

Wati T Chim E statang@ub.net.id

Wati T Chim E statang@ub.net.id
Edward Tambunan *Head, Dealing Room* T 600 6759

Vidi Vinandar

INDONESIA (+62) www.euromoneydirectory.com

PT Bank NISP (cont)

Fixed-Income Repo
Head of Repo — Wati T Chim statang@ub.net.id
Collateral Management — Nawati Senjoya

Syndicated Lending
Department: Corporate Finance
Head of Syndicated Lending — Wati T Chim statang@ub.net.id
Head of Syndication — Vidi Vinandar

Money Markets
Department: Dealing Room
Tel: 600 6757 **Fax:** 600 6758
Global Head — Edward Tambunan *Head, Dealing Room* 600 6759

Domestic Commercial Paper
Head of Origination — Wati T Chim statang@ub.net.id

Wholesale Deposits
Marketing — Edward Tambunan *Head, Dealing Room* 600 6759

Foreign Exchange
Department: Dealing Room
Tel: 600 6757 **Fax:** 600 6758
Global Head — Edward Tambunan *Head, Dealing Room* 600 6759

Risk Management
Foreign Exchange Derivatives / Risk Management
Cross-Currency Swaps, Sales / Marketing — Edward Tambunan *Head, Dealing Room* 600 6759

Corporate Finance / M&A Advisory
Department: Corporate Finance
Head of Corporate Finance — Wati T Chim statang@ub.net.id

Settlement / Clearing
Regional Head — Darmawati

Other Departments
Private Banking — Wati T Chim statang@ub.net.id
Correspondent Banking — Wati T Chim statang@ub.net.id

Administration

Technology & Systems — Yogadharma Ratnapalasari +61 (22) 420 1600

Legal / In-House Counsel — Levianty Austan +61 (22) 420 1600

Compliance — Wahyu Dewanti *Corporate Affairs Head* wahyu@banknisp.com

Public Relations — Wahyu Dewanti *Corporate Affairs Head* wahyu@banknisp.com

PT Bank Pembangunan Indonesia (PERSERO) — Head Office

Alternative trading name: Bapindo
2-14th Floor, Plaza Bapindo, Tower I, Jalan Jenderal Sudirman Kav 54-55, Jakarta 12190
PO Box 1140, Jakarta 12190
Tel: (21) 526 6566 **Fax:** (21) 526 6560; (21) 526 7379 **Telex:** 60892-4 BPINKB IA **Swift:** BPEI ID JA
Email: uinbond@idola.net.id **Reuters:** BPDO **Telerate:** Bapindo **Cable:** BAPINDO
Telex: 60899 BPINXM IA

Senior Executive Officers

President — Arbali Sukanal 526 7280 526 7350
Treasurer — Mr Apeppy
Managing Director / General Manager — F Bambang Kuntjoro
International Division — Agus Mertayasa 526 7282 526 7352

Others (Senior Executives)
Credit Dept — Adri S Prawira *Managing Director* 526 7283 526 7353
HRD & Technology — Siswanto *Managing Director* 526 7281 526 7354
Corporate Affairs & Legal — Soeryanto *Managing Director* 526 7281 526 7531

General - Treasury
Head of Treasury — Agus Mertayasa *Managing Director* 526 7282 526 7352

Syndicated Lending
Head of Credit Committee — Djoke Suyarso *General Manager* 526 7368 526 7351

www.euromoneydirectory.com INDONESIA (+62)

Other (Syndicated Lending)
Small & Medium Credit Dept. Trimono Santoso *General Manager* T 526 7315 F 526 7319
Special Debtors Dept. Basuki S Prawira *General Manager* T 526 7348 F 526 7356
Loan-Related Activities
Trade Finance Rosalin Maddolangeng *Manager* T 526 7415 F 526 7406
Money Markets
Money Markets - General
Treasury Eppy S Muhammad *General Manager* T 526 7321 F 526 7411
Ronggo Asmoro *Chief Dealer* T 526 8118 F 526 7411
Other Departments
Correspondent Banking Berkah Prasetya *Manager* T 526 7413 F 526 7406
Administration
Technology & Systems
Abdussalam *General Manager* T 526 7307 F 526 7293
Public Relations
Mr Kartomo
Accounts / Audit
Accounts Jusuf Subianto *General Manager* T 526 7311 F 526 7314
Internal Audit Budi Pranoto *General Manager* T 526 7340 F 526 7344
Other (Administration)
Information Jusuf Subianto *General Manager* T 526 7311 F 526 7314
Training & Productivity S Harismoyo *General Manager* T 526 7361 F 526 7408
Planning & Budgeting Nimrod Sitorus *General Manager* T 526 7291 F 526 7294
Human Resources Syahruddin Husein *General Manager* T 526 7345 F 526 7347
General Services & Logistics Zaitun Adisuseno *General Manager* T 526 7372 F 526 7376
International Banking Dept. Abdul Rachman *General Manager* T 526 7404 F 526 7379
Banking Services Rosalin Maddolangeng *Manager* T 526 7415 F 526 7406

Bank Prima Express   Head Office

Formerly known as: Bank Tani Nasional
6th & 7th Floors, Plaza Bapindo, Menara II, Jalan Jenderal Sudirman Kav 54/55, Jakarta 12190
Tel: (21) 526 6767; (21) 526 6777 **Fax:** (21) 526 6757; (21) 526 6787 **Telex:** 60690, 60691 TANIIDIA **Swift:** TANI ID JA
Email: primex@rad.net.id **Reuters:** TANI

Senior Executive Officers
Chairman   Arifin Oei
President   Wibowo Ngaserin
Chief Operating Officer   Darsuki Gani
Managing Director / General Manager   Trisno Husin
International Division   Rudy Dharma

General-Lending (DCM, SL)
Head of Corporate Banking   Hadi Irianto

Money Markets
Tel: 526 6770 **Fax:** 526 6775 **Reuters:** TANI
Global Head   Linda Atmadja

Foreign Exchange
Tel: 526 6770 **Fax:** 526 6775 **Reuters:** TANI
Global Head   Charisa Dini

FX Traders / Sales People
Erni Sucipto
Yvonne Maria

Settlement / Clearing
Tel: 526 6767 **Fax:** 526 6787 **Telex:** 60690 TANIIDIA
Country Head   Danial Sandin

Administration
Head of Administration   Rosmiati Chandra
Business Development; Head of Marketing   Hadi Irianto

Technology & Systems
Jacking Wijaya

Legal / In-House Counsel
Heryanto Lowardi

Accounts / Audit
Rudy Tanoto

INDONESIA (+62)　　　　www.euromoneydirectory.com

PT Bank Sakura Swadharma
Subsidiary Company

19th Floor, BNI Building, Jalan Jenderal Sudirman Kav 1, Jakarta 10220
Tel: (21) 570 1401 Fax: (21) 570 1398 Telex: 65179 SAKURA IA Swift: SAKUIDJA

Senior Executive Officers
President Director　　　　　　　　Yoshio Uchino
Managing Director　　　　　　　　Shinichiro Kushima
Managing Director　　　　　　　　Nobuyuki Shimoda
Managing Director　　　　　　　　Tjarsim Adisasmita

Money Markets
Global Head　　　　　　　　　　　Gaguk Fauzi Santosa *GM & Head, Money Markets*

PT Bank Société Générale

6th Floor, Bank Pacific Building, Jl Jend Sudirman Kav 7-8, Jakarta 10220
Tel: (21) 570 2020; (21) 570 6910 Fax: (21) 573 8855

PT Bank Sumitomo Niaga
Subsidiary Company

10th Floor, Summitmas Building II, Jalan Jenderal Sudirman Kav 61/2, Jakarta 12069
Tel: (21) 522 7011 Fax: (21) 522 7022 Telex: 62721 BKSUNI IA

Senior Executive Officers
President Director　　　　　　　　Ryoichi Hasegawa
Deputy President Director　　　　　Koesdarto Hadimoeljo
Deputy President Director　　　　　Takeaki Misumi

Others (Senior Executives)
　　　　　　　　　　　　　　　　Junichi Kohara *Director*
　　　　　　　　　　　　　　　　Soichiro Izumi *Director*

Debt Capital Markets / Fixed Income
Global Head　　　　　　　　　　　Takeaki Misumi *Deputy President Director*

Equity Capital Markets
Global Head　　　　　　　　　　　Takeaki Misumi *Deputy President Director*

Syndicated Lending
Global Head　　　　　　　　　　　Takeaki Misumi *Deputy President Director*

Money Markets
Global Head　　　　　　　　　　　Takeaki Misumi *Deputy President Director*

Foreign Exchange
Global Head　　　　　　　　　　　Takeaki Misumi *Deputy President Director*

Risk Management
Global Head　　　　　　　　　　　Takeaki Misumi *Deputy President Director*

Corporate Finance / M&A Advisory
Global Head　　　　　　　　　　　Soichiro Izumi *Director*

Settlement / Clearing
Regional Head　　　　　　　　　　Junichi Kohara *Director*

PT Bank Tiara Asia
Head Office

Wisma Bank Tiara, Jalan MT Haryono Kav 16, Jakarta 12810
Tel: (21) 831 0210; (21) 831 0220 Fax: (21) 831 0250; (21) 831 0201 Telex: 48618 TIARA IA Swift: TIAS ID JA

Senior Executive Officers
President Commissioner　　　　　　Ahmad Askander
Vice President Commissioner　　　　Mr Ekotjipto
Commissioner　　　　　　　　　　Amir Abadi Jusaf
Commissioner　　　　　　　　　　Tontowi Djauhari Lintang
Chief Executive Officer　　　　　　Eksir Mahfujana *President Director*
Financial Director　　　　　　　　Tony S Sechan *Vice President Director*
Chief Operating Officer　　　　　　Soesilo Basoeki *Director*
Treasurer　　　　　　　　　　　　Melly Kristanti *Managing Director*

Others (Senior Executives)
Head of Credit　　　　　　　　　　Gustiono Kustianto *Director*

General-Lending (DCM, SL)
Head of Corporate Banking　　　　　Benny Wennas *MD, Corporate Banking*
　　　　　　　　　　　　　　　　Tjandra Somali *Corporate Banking (Deposits)*

www.euromoneydirectory.com   INDONESIA (+62)

General-Lending (DCM, SL) (cont)
Fransiscus Chandra *MD, Commercial Banking*
Henry Koenaifi *MD, Commercial Banking*

General-Investment
Head of Investment   Dasa Sutantio *MD, Investment Banking*

Relationship Manager
International & Corporate Planning   K J Low *Foreign Treasurer*
Debt Finance   Santosa Suherman *Director*

Debt Capital Markets / Fixed Income
Global Head   Indra W Supriadi *Director, Debt Capital*
9th Floor, Plaza Bapindo Menara II, Jalan Jenderal Sudirman Kav 54/55, Jakarta 12190
Tel: +62 (21) 527 6226 **Fax:** +62 (21) 527 2220
Country Head   Dasa Sutantio *MD, Investment Banking*

Fixed-Income Repo
Head of Repo; Collateral Management;   Hananto Kristono *Treasury*
Matched Book Manager; Sales

Syndicated Lending
Loan-Related Activities
Trade Finance   Vonny Irawan *Director*
9th Floor, Plaza Bapindo Menara II, Jalan Jenderal Sudirman Kav 54/55, Jakarta 12190
Tel: +62 (21) 527 6226 **Fax:** +62 (21) 527 2220
Country Head   Dasa Sutantio *MD, Investment Banking*
Head of Origination; Head of Syndication   Santosa Suherman *Director*
Head of Credit Committee   Gustiono Kustianto *Director*

Loan-Related Activities
Project Finance   Vonny Irawan *Director*

Money Markets
Regional Head   Loeki S Putera *Vice President Director I*
Country Head   Melly Kristanti *Managing Director*

Domestic Commercial Paper
Head of Origination   Investment Banking Group
Head of Sales; Head of Trading   Widyastuti

Eurocommercial Paper
Head of Origination   Investment Banking Group
Head of Sales; Head of Trading   Widyastuti

Foreign Exchange
Country Head   Melly Kristanti *Managing Director*
Head of Institutional Sales; Corporate Sales;   Hananto Kristono *Treasury*
Head of Trading

Risk Management
Tel: 831 0210 **Fax:** 831 0250
Country Head   Gustiono Kustianto *Director*

Fixed Income Derivatives / Risk Management
Regional Head   Loeki S Putera *Vice President Director I*
Country Head   Melly Kristanti *Managing Director*
IR Swaps Sales / Marketing; IR Swaps Trading;   Hananto Kristono *Treasury*
IR Options Sales / Marketing; IR Options
Trading

Foreign Exchange Derivatives / Risk Management
Cross-Currency Swaps, Sales / Marketing;   Hananto Kristono *Treasury*
Cross-Currency Swaps, Trading

Settlement / Clearing
Regional Head   I Bambang Priambodo *Administration & Operations*
Country Head; Fixed-Income Settlement;   Sianny Widjaja *Director, Operations & Int'l Settlements*
Derivatives Settlement; Foreign Exchange
Settlement; Settlement (General); Operations
Operations   I Bambang Priambodo *Administration & Operations*

Other Departments
Private Banking   Harry Sasongko *Managing Director* 515 0848
Correspondent Banking   Vonny Irawan *Director*

Administration
Head of Administration   I Bambang Priambodo *Administration & Operations*

Technology & Systems
    Sugianto Nurteim *Director*

Legal / In-House Counsel
    Lana Anggraeni *Director, Legal & General Counsel*

INDONESIA (+62)

PT Bank Tiara Asia (cont)
Compliance
Financial Management Reports & Compliance Suryanty Lauan *Director*
Public Relations
  K J Low *Foreign Treasurer*
Accounts / Audit
Internal Audit & Control Djumharbey Anwar *Managing Director*
Other (Administration)
General Affairs (Capex) Louise Sucipto *Director*
Human Resources Development Margie Kristantie *Director*
Consumer Credit Suparman Kusuma *Director*

The Bank of Tokyo-Mitsubishi Limited — Full Branch Office
Formerly known as: The Bank of Tokyo Limited
Mid-Plaza Building 1, Floors 1-3, Jln Jend Sudirman Kav 10-11, Jakarta 10227 Jakarta
Tel: (21) 570 6185 Fax: (21) 573 6565 Telex: 65467, 65477 TOHBANK IA Swift: BOTKIDJX Reuters: TMJK
Senior Executive Officers
General Manager Tomoji Ikebata
Deputy General Manager Y Ashida
Deputy General Manager M Hirano
Foreign Exchange
Global Head S Kanazawa *Manager, FX & Treasury*
FX Traders / Sales People
  Y Ujihara *Manager, FX Sales*

Bank Universal — Head Office
Alternative trading name: PT Bank Universal Tbk
Plaza Setiabudi, Atrium Building, Jalan HR Rasuna Said Kav 62, Jakarta 12920
Tel: (21) 521 0550; (21) 521 0560 Fax: (21) 521 0588 Telex: 60668 BU HOAT IA Swift: BUNB ID JA
Email: bankuniversal@bu.astra.co.id
Website: www.bankuniversal.astra.co.id
Senior Executive Officers
Chairman Sumitro Djojohadikusumo
President Director Stephen Satyahadi
Deputy President Director Jerry Ng
Others (Senior Executives)
Business Segments; Corporate Services Hendradjaja Gunawan *Director*
Special Assets Management Lukito Dewandaya *Director*
Relationship Manager
Investor Relations Arief Harris *Assistant Vice President* [F] **521 0509**
Other Departments
Correspondent Banking Peter Suryadi *Assistant Vice President* [F] **521 0509**
Administration
Accounts / Audit
Audit Judo Djuwito *Director*

The Chase Manhattan Bank — Full Branch Office
4th Floor, Chase Plaza Podium, Jalan Jenderal Sudirman Kav 21, Jakarta 12920
Tel: (21) 571 2213 Fax: (21) 571 2445; (21) 578 0958 Telex: 62152 CMBCM IA, 44369 CHASE IA
Senior Executive Officers
MD & Senior Country Officer, Indonesia Edward T Nocco [T] **571 8400**
Money Markets
Head of Money Markets Ruth Setyabudi *Vice President* [T] **571 8433**
Foreign Exchange
Head of Foreign Exchange Ruth Setyabudi *Vice President* [T] **571 8433**
Corporate Finance / M&A Advisory
Head of Corporate Finance Dhalia Arioteojo *Vice President*
Settlement / Clearing
Head of Settlement / Clearing K T Theng *Vice President* [T] **571 8200**

www.euromoneydirectory.com   INDONESIA (+62)

Commerzbank AG
Representative Office
6th Floor, Summitas II, Jalan Jenderal Sudirman Kav 61/2, Jakarta 12069
Tel: (21) 252 6510 **Fax:** (21) 252 6514 **Telex:** 47773 CBKJKT IA **Email:** cobaja@idola.net.id

Senior Executive Officers
Representative   Udo Kissner

PT Daiwa Lippo Finance
5th Floor, Daiwa Perdania Bank Building, Jalan Jenderal Sudirman Kav 40-41, Jakarta
Tel: (21) 570 1956 **Fax:** (21) 570 1961

Senior Executive Officers
President Director   Shinichi Hatanaka

PT Daiwa Perdania Bank
Subsidiary Company
Jalan Jenderal Sudirman Kav 40-41, Jakarta
Tel: (21) 570 1958 **Fax:** (21) 570 1936; (21) 570 1939 **Telex:** 65658 **Swift:** BPIAIDJA **Cable:** JOINTBANK JAKARTA
Telex: 65074 **Telex:** 65195 **Telex:** 65075

Senior Executive Officers
President Director   Kiyoshige Ito

Others (Senior Executives)
                                  Yoshiyuki Shimadate *Director*
                                  Tsune Ueda *Director*

PT (Persero) Danareksa
Head Office
17th-19th Floor, Plaza Bapindo Tower II, Jalan Jenderal Sudirman Kav 54-55, Jakarta 12190
Tel: (21) 526 9777; (21) 526 9888 **Fax:** (21) 526 6893; (21) 526 6905 **Email:** cadana@cbn.net.id
Website: www.indoexchange.com/danareksa-holding/

Senior Executive Officers
Chairman   Sri Hadi
President   Glenn S Yusuf ☎ 526 9777 ext 1005
Chief Executive Officer   Glenn S Yusuf ☎ 526 9777 ext 1005
Financial Director   Susila Rahardja *Director* ☎ 526 9777 ext 5005
Treasurer   Evi Firmansyah ☎ 526 9777 ext 4103
Corporate Secretary   Ticke Soekrani ☎ 526 9777 ext 1200

Others (Senior Executives)
                                  Iwan P Pontjowinoto *President Director* ☎ 526 9777 ext 3005
                                  Edgar Sujanto *President Director*

Debt Capital Markets / Fixed Income

Fixed-Income Research
Head of Fixed Income   Robert Rerimassie *Head* ☎ 526 9777 ext 2305

Equity Capital Markets
Head of Sales   Edward Lee ☎ 526 9777 ext 2234
Head of Trading   Atty Abidin ☎ 526 9777 ext 2230

Domestic Equities
Head of Trading   Edward Lee ☎ 526 9777 ext 2234
Head of Research   Atty Lee ☎ 526 9777 ext 2234

International Equities
Head of Sales   Edward Lee ☎ 526 9777 ext 2234
Head of Trading   Atty Abidin ☎ 526 9777 ext 2230

Equity Research
Head of Equity Research   Irma Stamboel *Head* ☎ 526 9777 ext 2301

Risk Management
Head of Risk Management   Zas Ureawan ☎ 526 9777 ext 1300

Corporate Finance / M&A Advisory
Global Head   Agus Projosasmito *Managing Director*

Asset Management
Head   Amin Halim ☎ 526 9777 ext 3200

INDONESIA (+62) www.euromoneydirectory.com

PT (Persero) Danareksa (cont)
Administration
Head of Administration — Buddy Subagja ☎ 526 9777 ext 5200
Head of Marketing — Sjafrizal Kasim ☎ 526 9777 ext 3400

Technology & Systems
Alya Sabil ☎ 526 9777 ext 5500

Legal / In-House Counsel
Farida Helianti ☎ 526 9777 ext 1400

Compliance
Sahat Nainggolan ☎ 526 9777 ext 1500

Public Relations
Roditus Mangunsaputro ☎ 526 9777 ext 1222

Accounts / Audit
John Tibuludji ☎ 526 9777 ext 5300

Deutsche Bank AG — Full Branch Office
Deutsche Bank Building, Jalan Imam Bonjol 80, Jakarta 10310
PO Box 1135, Jakarta
Tel: (21) 331 092; (21) 390 4792 **Fax:** (21) 335 252 **Telex:** 61524 DBIA **Cable:** DEUTASIA
Forex Tel: 331502; 333035
Website: www.deutsche-bank.com

Development Capital Securities Indonesia — Head Office
Alternative trading name: Development Capital
Formerly known as: PT Peregrine Sewu Securities
Plaza Bapindo, Menara II, Lt 12, Jalan Jenderal Sudirman Kav 54/55, Jakarta 12190
Tel: (21) 524 6000 **Fax:** (21) 526 7511 **Telex:** 65654 PERGN IA
FX Tel: 333 035

Senior Executive Officers
President Director — Timothy S Gray ☎ 524 6010
Chief Operating Officer — Wawan Setiamihardja *MD, Operations* ☎ 524 6050

Debt Capital Markets / Fixed Income
Head of Fixed Income Trading — Devie Milayanti *Director, Fixed Income Sales & Trading* ☎ 524 6117 ℻ 526 7515

Equity Capital Markets
Domestic Equities
Head of Sales — Kris Wijoyo *Head of Equity Sales & Trading* ☎ 524 6139 ℻ 526 7514

Equity Research
Head of Equity Research — Eva Muis ☎ 524 6170 ℻ 526 7512

Corporate Finance / M&A Advisory
Global Head — Deswandhy Agusman *MD, Corporate Finance* ☎ 524 6020

Settlement / Clearing
Head of Settlement / Clearing — Enrico Djakman *General Manager, Operations* ☎ 524 6090 ℻ 526 7513
Equity Settlement — Tio Goban *Manager* ☎ 524 6089 ℻ 526 7517

Other Departments
Cash Management — Linda Surgani *Manager, Finance* ☎ 524 6067 ℻ 526 7513

Administration
Head of Administration — Jenny Salmon *Manager* ☎ 524 6052 ℻ 526 7513

Technology & Systems
Sejento Tresnohadi *Manager, IT* ☎ 524 6061 ℻ 526 7513

Compliance
Sharon Virojna *Assistant Director, Credit & Compliance* ☎ 524 6164 ℻ 524 6008

Accounts / Audit
Hanlim Supriunto *Manager, Financial Control* ☎ 524 6053 ℻ 526 7513

PT Dharmala Securities
Head Office

6th Floor, Wisma Dharmala Sakti, Jalan Jenderal Sudirman Kav 32, Jakarta 10220
Tel: (21) 570 1608; (21) 251 2851 **Fax:** (21) 570 6555; (21) 573 8995 **Email:** dharsec@uninet.net.id

Senior Executive Officers
Commissioner — Tjan Soen Eng
Commissioner — Suhargo Gondokusumo
Commissioner — Kenneth Lam

Others (Senior Executives)
Hendi Kariawan *Director of Corporate Finance Division*
Riki L Dago *Director, Stockbroking*

Debt Capital Markets / Fixed Income
Head of Fixed Income — Yulan Ragananta *Vice President*

Equity Capital Markets
Head of Sales — Johan Sunarwan *Head, Stockbroking* T 251 2851 F 570 6555
Head of Trading — Maryani *Head, Stockbroking* T 251 2851 F 570 6555

Corporate Finance / M&A Advisory
Head of Corporate Finance — Dyah A S Surowidjojo

Settlement / Clearing
Head of Settlement / Clearing — Nuraini Suharliman
Operations — Haryanto Leenardi *Head*

Administration
Technology & Systems — Trisiana

The Fuji Bank Limited
Representative Office

24th Floor, Plaza BII - Tower 2, Jalan MH Thamrin 51, Jakarta 10350
Tel: (21) 392 7061; (21) 392 5222 **Fax:** (21) 392 7064 **Telex:** 69172 FUJIBK IA

Senior Executive Officers
Chief Representative — Kimio Araki

Generale Bank
Representative Office

9th Floor, Panin Bank Centre, Jalan Jenderal Sudirman Senayan, Jakarta 10270
Tel: (21) 720 1292; (21) 720 5696 **Fax:** (21) 720 1293 **Telex:** 65032 GEBA IA

Senior Executive Officers
Representative — Elvia Sunityo

Haga Bank
Head Office

Jalan Abdul Muis No 28, Jakarta 10160
Tel: (21) 231 2021; (21) 231 2888 **Fax:** (21) 231 2250; (21) 231 2239 **Telex:** 46349 HAGA IA **Swift:** HAGA ID JA
Reuters: HAGA

Senior Executive Officers
Chairman — Aswar Sjarfi
President — Timoty E Marnandus
Financial Director — R M Sjariffudin *Executive Director*
Chief Operating Officer — Danny Hartono *Executive Director*

Syndicated Lending
Tel: 231 2021 **Fax:** 231 2250
Country Head — Daniel Satyawan *Vice President*
Head of Origination — Irene Lina K D *Manager*
Head of Credit Committee — Timoty E Marnandus *President*

Loan-Related Activities
Trade Finance — Jenny Santosa *Senior Manager*

Money Markets
Tel: 231 2062 **Fax:** 231 2250
Country Head — Endang Murwani *Senior Manager*

Foreign Exchange
Tel: 231 2062 **Fax:** 231 2250
Country Head — Endang Murwani *Senior Manager*

INDONESIA (+62)   www.euromoneydirectory.com

Haga Bank (cont)
Settlement / Clearing
Tel: 231 2021 Fax: 231 2250
Country Head   Hendra Wijaya *Senior Assistant Manager*

The Hongkong & Shanghai Banking Corporation Limited
Full Branch Office

1st/5th Floors, World Trade Center, Jalan Jenderal Sudirman Kav 29/31, Jakarta 12920
PO Box 2307, Jakarta 10023
Tel: (21) 524 6222 Fax: (21) 521 1103 Telex: 60137/8 HSBC IA Swift: HSBC ID JA Reuters: HBJA

Senior Executive Officers
Chief Executive Officer   Guy A Hamilton *Deputy Chief Executive*
                                   Eric W Gill

Others (Senior Executives)
                                   Alan Mitchell *Manager, Services*
General - Treasury
Head of Treasury   Hiran Cabraat *Manager, Treasury*
Relationship Manager
Corporate & Institutional Banking James C Hogan *Senior Manager*
Debt Capital Markets / Fixed Income
Asset-Backed Securities / Securitization
Global Head   Brian Stiles *Manager, Securities*
Syndicated Lending
Other (Trade Finance)
Trade Services   Dahlia Tarjoto *National Manager*
Money Markets
Country Head   Wil Ing Bolung *Head*
Foreign Exchange
Country Head   Chandru Sekhar *Head*
Settlement / Clearing
Regional Head   Alfons Linggar *Head*
Operations   Prem Kumar *Financial Controller*
                                   Tim Wuarring *Manager, Internal Control*
Administration
Other (Administration)
Human Resources   Fx Djoko Soedibjo *Director, Human Resources*
Technical Services   Bennet Chin *Manager*
Public Affairs   Leila Djafaar *Manager*

NV de Indonesische Overzeese Bank
Representative Office

Alternative trading name: Indover Bank
23rd Floor, Gedung Artha Graha, Jalan Jenderal Sudirman Kav 52-53, Jakarta 12190
Tel: (21) 515 2905 Fax: (21) 515 2906 Telex: 60376 IOBA IA Cable: Indover

Senior Executive Officers
Chief Representative   Sri Miyati Woeryanto
Senior Representative   Kharma Masjhur

PT Indosuez Indonesia Bank
Subsidiary Company

19th Floor, Summitmas II, Jalan Jenderal Sudirman Kav 61/2, Jakarta 12190
PO Box 6965, JKS Street, Jakarta
Tel: (21) 252 0981 Fax: (21) 252 0983

Senior Executive Officers
Chief Executive Officer   Bruce Fraser *Senior Executive Officer*
Chief Operating Officer   Philippe Dallée
Company Secretary   Djoko S Hoemardani
International Division   Christophe Michaud *International Projects*
Relationship Manager
International Projects Division   Christophe Michaud

708 Euromoney Directory 1999

www.euromoneydirectory.com   INDONESIA (+62)

PT ING Baring Securities (Indonesia)   Subsidiary Company

21st Floor, Gedung BEJ Menara II, Lantai 25, Jalan Jenderal Sudirman Kav 52-53, Jakarta 12190
Tel: (21) 551 1818 Fax: (21) 515 1212 Telex: 60372 INGB IA Swift: INGB ID JA

Senior Executive Officers
Others (Senior Executives)
ING Barings   Ian Clyne
                                        Darwin Sutanto *President Director*

PT ING Indonesia Bank   Subsidiary Company

Alternative trading name: ING Barings
14th Floor, New Summitmas II, Jalan Jenderal Sudirman 61/62, Jakarta 12190
PO Box 6928/JKSST, Jakarta 12069
Tel: (21) 520 5100 Fax: (21) 520 0238 Telex: 62990 INGB 1A Swift: INGB ID JA

Senior Executive Officers
President Director   Mark Wiessing ☎ 252 6680
Chief Operating Officer   Delilah Dijamco *Senior Vice President* ☎ 520 1909

Syndicated Lending
Country Head   Jan Overwater *Director, Structured Lending* ☎ 252 6680

Loan-Related Activities
Trade Finance   Bonar Panjaitan *SVP, Corporate Banking* ☎ 520 5103
Project Finance   Nancy Frohman *SVP, Project Finance* ☎ 252 6574
Structured Trade Finance   Paulus Irawan *Assistant Vice President* ☎ 520 5103

Money Markets
Country Head   Alexandra Tjendrawati *Assistant Vice President* ☎ 522 6385

Foreign Exchange
Country Head   Alexandra Tjendrawati *Assistant Vice President* ☎ 522 6385

Risk Management
Country Head   Arifin Haris *Director, Risk Management* ☎ 522 6502

Global Custody
Country Head   Restiana Linggadjaya *Vice President* ☎ 522 6581

Administration
Legal / In-House Counsel
                                        Marya Simamora *Vice President*

International Finance Corporation   Representative Office

Jakarta Stock Exchange Building, Tower II, 13th Floor, Jl. Jend Sudirman Kav 52-53, Jakarta 12190
Tel: (21) 5299 3001 Fax: (21) 5299 3002 Telex: 62141 Cable: CORINTFIN

Senior Executive Officers
Regional Representative   Amitava Banerjee

PT Jardine Fleming Nusantara Investment Management

Subsidiary Company

17th Floor, World Trade Centre, Jalan Jenderal Sudirman Kav 29-31, Jakarta 12920
PO Box 8388, Jakarta 12083
Tel: (21) 523 2221; (21) 523 2222 Fax: (21) 523 2188 Telex: 60172 FLEDG IA

The Long-Term Credit Bank of Japan Limited   Representative Office

9th Floor, Wisma BCA, Jalan Jenderal Sudirman Kav 22/3, Jakarta 12920
Tel: (21) 571 2225; (21) 571 2226 Fax: (21) 571 2237

INDONESIA (+62)

PT Merrill Lynch Indonesia
Full Branch Office

18th Floor, Jakarta Stock Exchange Building, Jalan Jenderal Sudirman Kav 52/3, Jakarta 12190
Tel: (21) 515 8790 Fax: (21) 515 8819

Senior Executive Officers
President Commissioner — Hashim Djotohadikusoim
President Director — Anthony Davies
Financial Director — Lily Widjaja *Director, Finance & Administration*

Natexis - BFCE
Representative Office

Formerly known as: Banque Française du Commerce Extérieur
8th Floor, Wisma Nusantara Building, Jalan MH Thamrin 59, Jakarta 10350
Tel: (21) 334 067; (21) 337 371 Fax: (21) 314 2271 Telex: 61202 IA Email: natocjkt@dnet.net.id

Senior Executive Officers
Chief Representative — François Monnier

National Australia Bank Limited
Representative Office

9th Floor, Bank Bali Tower, Jalan Jenderal Sudirman Kav 27, Jakarta 12920
Tel: (21) 250 0685; (21) 250 0687 Fax: (21) 250 0690

Senior Executive Officers
Chief Representative & Head of Emerging Markets — E John Mcleod

PT Nikko Securities Indonesia
Subsidiary Company

Wismaindosemen, 3rd Floor, Jl. Jend. Sudirman 1, Jakarta 12910
Tel: (21) 570 2474 Fax: (21) 251 0402 Telex: 65104

Senior Executive Officers
President — Akihide Hayashi
Vice President & Director — Harianto Solichin

Paribas

Suite 1211, 12th Floor Mehara Mulia Kav 9-11, Jalan Jenderal Gatot Subroto, Jakarta 12930
Tel: (21) 520 9874 Fax: (21) 520 9877

PT Rabobank Duta Indonesia
Subsidiary Company

9th Floor, Plaza 89, Jalan HR Rasuna Said Kav X-7/6, Jakarta 12940
Tel: (21) 252 0876 Fax: (21) 252 0875 Telex: 60633 RABO IA Swift: RABO ID JA Reuters: RABJ

Senior Executive Officers
President Director — Christian H A M Mol
Vice President Director — Basalamah Muhammad
Chief Operating Officer — Delilah Dijamzo *Director, Operations*

General-Lending (DCM, SL)
Head of Corporate Banking — Paul G Beiboer *Head, Corporate Banking*

Syndicated Lending

Other (Trade Finance)
Letters of Credit — Wagiantoro *Officer, Export / Import*

Foreign Exchange
FX Traders / Sales People — Setio Soejanto *Dealer*
Atma Sedjati *Dealer*

Risk Management
Country Head — Jeroen Nijsen *Head*

Settlement / Clearing
Operations — Rusli Yahya *Manager, Operations*

Other Departments
Correspondent Banking — Basalamah Muhammad *Vice President Director*

INDONESIA (+62)

Administration
Head of Administration — Tina Sugiro *Manager, General Administration*
Technology & Systems
Andy Onamg
Legal / In-House Counsel
Felix I Hartadi *Manager, Credit Control & Support*

PT Rabobank Finance Indonesia — Subsidiary Company

10th Floor, Plaza 89, Jalan HR Rasuna Said Kav X-7/6, Jakarta 12940
Tel: (21) 252 0876 **Fax:** (21) 252 0875 **Telex:** 60633 RABO IA **Swift:** RABO ID JA **Reuters:** RABJ

Settlement / Clearing
Operations — Wary Sumitro *Director, Operations*
Administration
Accounts / Audit
Accounts — Sani Effendy *Senior Account Manager*
Other (Administration)
Marketing — Tommy Chandra *Director*

The Sanwa Bank Limited — Representative Office

5th Floor, Bank Bali Tower, Jalan Jenderal Sudirman Kav 27, Jakarta 12920
Tel: (21) 250 0510; (21) 250 0511 **Fax:** (21) 250 0513 **Telex:** 60855 SANWA IA

Senior Executive Officers
Chief Representative — Mamoru Shibazaki

The Sumitomo Trust & Banking Company Limited
Representative Office

11th Floor, Summitmas Tower, Jalan Jenderal Sudirman Kav 61/2, Jakarta 12069
Tel: (21) 520 0057 **Fax:** (21) 520 0058 **Telex:** 60782 SMTRT IA

The Tokai Bank Limited — Representative Office

25th Level, Bapindo Plaza Tower II, Jalan Jenderal Sudirman Kav 54/55, Jakarta
Tel: (21) 526 6830 **Fax:** (21) 259 0141 **Telex:** 60898 TOKAIB IA

Senior Executive Officers
Chief Representative — Koichi Suzuki

PT Tokai Lippo Bank — Subsidiary Company

25th Floor, Bapindo Plaza Tower II, Jalan Jenderal Sudirman Kav 54-55, Jakarta
Tel: (21) 526 6820 **Fax:** (21) 526 6841 **Telex:** 60937 TOKAIL IA

Senior Executive Officers
President — Hajime Kato

Union Bank of California, NA — Representative Office

Formerly known as: The Bank of California, NA
11th Floor, Permata Plaza, Jalan MH Thamrin 57, Jakarta 10350
Tel: (21) 390 3222 **Fax:** (21) 390 3228; (21) 390 3455 **Telex:** 69252 **Telex:** 69253

Senior Executive Officers
VP & Regional Manager — John Hills
Assistant Representative — A M Fitrini Faisal
Assistant Representative — Yetty Harsono

INDONESIA (+62) www.euromoneydirectory.com

PT Vickers Ballas Tamara
Subsidiary Company

3rd Floor, Tamara Centre, Jalan Jenderal, Sudirman Kav 24, Jakarta 12430
Tel: (21) 520 6328; (21) 520 6336 **Fax:** (21) 520 3701; (21) 520 3702 **Email:** vickers@cbn.net.id
Bloomberg: Rumengan

Senior Executive Officers
President Director — Tariq Khan
Chief Executive Officer — Imamat Dalimunthe *Executive Director*
Santoso Walujo *Executive Director*

Equity Capital Markets
Head of Sales — Linawati Soenarso

Equity Research
Head of Equity Research — Noraya Soewarno

Risk Management
Head of Risk Management — Mirah Sumarti S
Danny Hartono

Corporate Finance / M&A Advisory
Head of Corporate Finance — Indra Sakti

Settlement / Clearing
Operations — Toni Setioko *Head*

Administration
Compliance
Mirah Sumarti S
Danny Hartono

MM Warburg Bank
Representative Office

Ground Floor, Ventura Building, Jalan RA Kartini 26 (outer Ring Road), Jakarta 12430
Tel: (21) 765 9134 **Fax:** (21) 765 9136

Senior Executive Officers
Representative for Indonesia — Helena van Unnik

PT Warburg Dillon Read Indonesia

Suite 1606, 16th Floor, Wisma GKBI, Jalan Jenderal Sudirman 28, Jakarta 10210
Tel: (21) 574 0111 **Fax:** (21) 251 1662

Senior Executive Officers
President Director — M Wong
Chief Operating Officer — C Tedjawidjaja

Equity Capital Markets
Domestic Equities
Head of Sales — R Macfarlane

Corporate Finance / M&A Advisory
Head of Corporate Finance — M Wong

Other Departments
Economic Research — S Hasjim *Research*

West Merchant Bank Limited
Representative Office

17th Floor Midpliga Building, Jalan Jenderal Sudirman Kav 10-11, Jakarta 12190
Tel: (21) 573 5908 **Fax:** (21) 573 5905 **Email:** richard.michael@westmerchant.co.

Senior Executive Officers
Chief Representative — Richard Michael

Westpac Banking Corporation
Representative Office

18th Floor, Standard Chartered Bank Building, Jalan Sudirman Kav 33a, Jakarta 10220
Tel: (21) 520 3903; (21) 574 3719 **Fax:** (21) 574 3720

Senior Executive Officers
Chief Representative — Steven J Orr

www.euromoneydirectory.com   IRAN (ISLAMIC REPUBLIC OF) (+98)

The World Bank — Full Branch Office

Alternative trading name: International Bank for Reconstruction & Development
12th & 13th Floors, Stock Exchange Building, Tower 2, Jalan Jenderal Sudirman, Kav 52, Jakarta 12190
Tel: (21) 5399 3000 **Fax:** (21) 5299 3111 **Telex:** 60086 IBRD IA **Cable:** INTBAFRAD JAKART

Senior Executive Officers
Country Director — Dennis de Tray

Administration
Head of Administration — Bakti Sudaryono *Manager, Administration*

IRAN (ISLAMIC REPUBLIC OF) (+98)

Bank Markazi Jomhouri Islami Iran — Central Bank

Alternative trading name: Central Bank of the Islamic Republic of Iran
213 Ferdowsi Avenue, Tehran
PO Box 11365/8551, Tehran
Tel: (21) 64461 **Fax:** (21) 390 323 **Telex:** 213965 MZBK IR **Swift:** BMJI IR TH **Reuters:** BMJI **Cable:** MARKAZBANK

Senior Executive Officers
Governor — Mohsen Nourbakhsh **311 1999**
Vice Governor — M Jafar Mojarrad **306 986**
Secretary General — Ebrahim Sheibani **311 2592**

Others (Senior Executives)
Head, Bank Licensing — Naser Yousefikia *Director* **833 435**
Head, Banking Supervision — Majid Haji Norooz *Director* **882 7516**
Head, Economics & Statistics — Assad-ollah Monajemi *Director* **832 8258**
Bahram Feiz-ZXarin Ghalam *Director* **879 8582**
Head, Public Debt — Bahereh Mirzaee Tehrani *Director* **311 3025**
Head, Reserves Management — Behrooz Nowbahar *Director* **311 2144**

Foreign Exchange
Head of Foreign Exchange — Freidoon Shirazi *Director* **311 2595**

Administration
Accounts / Audit
Head, Accountancy — M Es-hagh Lohrasbi *Director* **391 950**

Bank Melli Iran — Head Office

Ferdowsi Avenue, Tehran
PO Box 11365-171, Tehran
Tel: (21) 323 482; (21) 323 483 **Fax:** (21) 302 813 **Telex:** 214220 **Swift:** MWLIIRTH **Reuters:** BMIH
Telerate: BANKMELLI **Telex:** 213480 **Telex:** 214104

Senior Executive Officers
Managing Director & Chairman — Assadollah Amiraslani **311 1190**
Chief Executive Officer — Nasser Mansouri *Board Member* **311 1383**
Director General — Ghafour Memarzadeh
International Division — M Mouhammad Ahmadi Namin *Director* **302 811**

Syndicated Lending

Loan-Related Activities
Project Finance — Nasrin Jafari *Manager* **323 455**

Foreign Exchange

FX Traders / Sales People
Manager of FX and Money Market Section — Ali Amani **323 480**

Other Departments
Correspondent Banking — Mohammad Shadkami *Manager* **323 482**

Euromoney Directory 1999   **713**

IRAN (ISLAMIC REPUBLIC OF) (+98) www.euromoneydirectory.com

Bank Saderat Iran

Bank Saderat Tower, 43 Somayeh Avenue, Tehran
PO Box 15745-631, Tehran
Tel: (21) 883 6926; (21) 883 2699 Fax: (21) 883 9539 Telex: 226176 SABK IR Swift: BSIR IR TH

Senior Executive Officers
Chairman & Managing Director — M R Moghaddasi
Treasurer — Majidi *Manager*
Chairman & Managing Director
International Division — M R Moghaddasi
M R Salehpour *Manager Foreign Department*
M Dadashzadeh *Assistant Manager*

Others (Senior Executives)
Board Member — M A Vatani
Hamid Borhani
M Hashemi
M Paknejad

General-Investment
Head of Investment — Mr Davoudi *Investment Manager*

Foreign Exchange
FX Traders / Sales People
FX Accounting Department — M R Lebastchi *Manager*
FX Operation Department — H Salehi Shahrbabaki *Manager*
FX Operation Department, Finance — M Shamsaei *Assistant Manager*
FX Operation — M Mehdizadeh *Assistant Manager*
M Youssefi *Head of Dealing Room*

Administration
Legal / In-House Counsel
Rostami *Manager*

Public Relations
Rezagholi *Manager*

Commerzbank AG
Full Branch Office

35th Alley, No 9, Argentine Square, Alvand Street, Tehran 15166
PO Box 15745-757, Tehran
Tel: (21) 879 8664 Fax: (21) 879 8683

Senior Executive Officers
Representative — Rols Kretz

Deutsche Bank AG
Representative Office

35th Street, 25 Argentina Square, Alvand Avenue, Tehran
PO Box 15815-3378, Tehran
Tel: (21) 878 7943; (21) 878 8148 Fax: (21) 878 7943 Telex: 212428 DBAG IR Cable: DEUTSCHBANK

HypoVereinsbank
Representative Office

Avenue Dr Ali Shariati, Shahid Zokai Street 1, Tehran 16617
PO Box 11365-6516, Tehran
Tel: (21) 284 1844 Fax: (21) 284 1625

Inter-Alpha Group of Banks - Joint Representative Office
Representative Office

Alternative trading name: ING Bank
2nd Floor, No 14, 4th Alley, Shahid Ahmad Ghasir Avenue, Tehran 15146
Tel: (21) 873 3562; (21) 873 3565 Fax: (21) 873 3539 Telex: 2128321 IAGB IR

Senior Executive Officers
Joint Representative — Raoul Azizzadeh

Nordbanken AB (publ)
Representative Office

14, Fourth Alley, 2nd Floor, Shahid Ahmad Ghasir Avenue, Tehran
Tel: (21) 873 3562; (21) 873 3564 **Fax:** (21) 873 3539

Senior Executive Officers
Representative   Rasoul Azizzadeh

Société Générale
Representative Office

Vali Asr Esfandyar Avenue 56, PO Box 14155-4434, Tehran 19686
Tel: (21) 878 1020 **Fax:** (21) 878 1021
Website: www.socgen.com

Standard Chartered Bank
Representative Office

40 Apartment #2, Koushyar Building, Koushyar Street, Vali-Asr Avenue, Tehran
Tel: (21) 888 1918; (21) 888 1919 **Fax:** (21) 879 7983

Senior Executive Officers
Chief Representative   Mohammad Sarrafzadeh

The Sumitomo Bank Limited
Representative Office

4th Floor, Mellat Tower, 1 Vali-e-Asr Avenue, Tehran 19678
Tel: (21) 204 6480 **Fax:** (21) 205 4875 **Telex:** 213148 SMBK IR

Senior Executive Officers
Chief Representative   Mohammad Assadpour

The Tokai Bank Limited
Representative Office

34.1 4th Floor, Shahid Haqani, Express Way, Tehran
Tel: (21) 879 1105 **Fax:** (21) 879 1106 **Telex:** 215254 TOKB IR

Senior Executive Officers
Chief Representative   Kaoru Masuda

IRELAND (+353)

Central Bank of Ireland
Central Bank

PO Box 559, Dame Street, Dublin 2
Tel: (1) 671 6666 **Fax:** (1) 671 6561 **Telex:** 31041 **Swift:** IRCE IE 2D **Reuters:** CBII; CBIX

ABN AMRO Bank NV
Full Branch Office

ABN AMRO House, International Financial Services Centre, Dublin 1
Tel: (1) 609 3800 **Fax:** (1) 609 3838 **Telex:** 93566

Senior Executive Officers
Chief Executive Officer	Anton Dikken
Financial Director	Conor Walsh
Chief Operating Officer	Paul O'Grady
Treasurer	Patrick Fearon
Company Secretary	Laura Cullen

Debt Capital Markets / Fixed Income
Department: Treasury / Fixed Income
Head of Fixed Income	Jerry Kelly
Head of Fixed Income Sales	Enda Morgan
Head of Fixed Income Trading	Jim Ryan

Fixed-Income Repo
Head of Repo	Ross

IRELAND (+353)   www.euromoneydirectory.com

ABN AMRO Bank NV (cont)
Fixed-Income Research
Head of Fixed Income   Den McLaughnie
Equity Capital Markets
Department: ABN AMRO Stockbrokers
Head of Equity Capital Markets   Bob Aherne
Equity Research
Head of Equity Research   John Clarke
Syndicated Lending
Head of Origination   David Ward *Head of Loan Origination*
Head of Trading   John Bowe *Head*
Loan-Related Activities
Trade Finance   Mars McHuga
Project Finance   John Leenane *Head*
Foreign Exchange
Head of Foreign Exchange   Patrick Fearon
Head of Institutional Sales   John Neary
Corporate Sales   Donie Kerin
Risk Management
Head of Risk Management   Francis O' Niggem
Foreign Exchange Derivatives / Risk Management
Regional Head   John Neary *Head of Sales, OTC FX Derivatives*
Other Departments
Correspondent Banking   John Bowe *Head*

AIB Group   Head Office
PO Box 452, Bankcentre, Ballsbridge, Dublin 4
Tel: (1) 660 0311 Fax: (1) 660 9137 Reuters: AIBG; AIBI; AIBJ; AIBY; AIBZ
Website: www.aib.ie

Senior Executive Officers
Chairman   Lochlann Quinn
Chief Executive Officer   Tom Mulcahy
Financial Director   Gary Kennedy *Finance Director*
Treasurer   Pat Ryan *Group Treasurer*
MD, AIB Capital Markets   Michael Buckley
MD, AIB Bank   Kevin Kelly
MD, USA Division   Jerry Casey ☎ +1 (410) 244 3944
Department: Allied Irish Bank Group Treasury
Others (Senior Executives)
Treasury Relationships   Jim Costelloe *Senior Manager* ☎ 874 0222 F 679 9590
Global Head   Dermot O'Donoghue *General Manager, Treasury & International*
                                    ☎ 874 0222 F 679 5933
Country Head   John Kearney *Head of Treasury, Ireland* ☎ 874 0222 F 679 9590
                                    Nick Treble *Head of Treasury, Britain* ☎ +44 (171) 606 3070
                                    F +44 (171) 726 2456
                                    Gerry McGorman *Head of Treasury, New York* ☎ +1 (212) 339 8000
                                    F +1 (212) 339 8009
                                    George Yates *Head of Treasury, Singapore* ☎ +65 438 7333 F +65 438 1091
Funding / New Issues   Duncan Farquhar *Senior Dealer* ☎ 874 0222 F 679 9590
Department: Corporate & Commercial Treasury
General - Treasury
Head of Treasury   Donal Forde *Head, Corporate & Commercial Treasury* ☎ 874 0222
                                    Susan Kelly *Marketing Manager* ☎ 874 0222
                                    James Fitzpatrick *European Treasury* ☎ 874 0222
                                    Val McLoughlin *London Treasury* ☎ +44 (171) 606 2112
                                    Brendan O'Connor *New York Treasury* ☎ +1 (212) 339 8080
                                    Fergus Rohan *First Trust Treasury, Northern Ireland* ☎ + 44 (1232) 326118
Relationship Manager
Agribusiness   John Rice *Chief Dealer* ☎ 874 0222
                                    Niall Wallace ☎ 670 0450
International   John Rice *Chief Dealer* ☎ 874 0222
                                    Niamh Hurley ☎ 670 0170
Retail & Energy   John Rice *Chief Dealer* ☎ 874 0222
                                    Seoirse O'Reilly ☎ 670 0412
Institutional   Mick Purcell *Chief Dealer* ☎ 874 0222
                                    Brian Kelleher ☎ 670 0160

www.euromoneydirectory.com   IRELAND (+353)

Relationship Manager (cont)
IFSC / Financial Institutions   Mick Purcell *Chief Dealer* ☎ **874 0222**
                                          Con O'Toole ☎ **670 0137**
Commercial; Commercial - Southern Area John O'Donovan *Chief Dealer* ☎ **874 0222**
Commercial   Brian Colgan ☎ **670 0176**
Commercial - Southern Area   John Lacey ☎ **(21) 271 383**
Mobile Representative-Area East   Michael Kierans ☎ **086 243 4652**
Mobile Representative-Area West   Padraig Lee ☎ **086 2434654**

Money Markets
Department: Allied Irish Bank Group Treasury
Reuters: AIBJ, AIBY, AIBG
Country Head   Donal Murphy *Assistant Treasurer* ☎ **874 0222** F **679 9590**
                                          Eamon Hackett *Assistant Treasurer* ☎ **874 0222** F **679 9590**

Money Markets - General
Irish Pound / Euro   Finbar Douling *Chief Dealer* ☎ **679 8977** F **679 9590**
                                          Ray O'Neill *Senior Dealer* ☎ **679 8977** F **679 9590**
GBP   Jillian Mahon *Chief Dealer* ☎ **679 5770** F **679 9590**
US$ Peter Walsh *Chief Dealer* ☎ **679 4299** F **679 9590**
DM, Ffr, Ecu   Tom Maginn *Senior Dealer* ☎ **679 8977** F **679 9590**
Nlg, Esp, Itl   Tony Farrell *Senior Dealer* ☎ **679 8977** F **679 9590**
Aus, Can, Asia, Scandi / Eastern Euro   Tom Lynch *Senior Dealer* ☎ **679 4299** F **679 9590**

Foreign Exchange
Department: Allied Irish Bank Group Treasury
Reuters: AIBI, AIBJ

FX Traders / Sales People
Spot   Michael Cronin *Assistant Treasurer, FX* ☎ **679 2699** F **679 9590**
Forwards   Simone Phelan *Dealer* ☎ **679 4299** F **679 9590**
Options   Joe Naughton *Dealer* ☎ **670 1942** F **679 9590**

Risk Management
Tel: 874 0222 Fax: 670 1467
Country Head   Norbert Bannon *Head of Risk Management / Finance*
                                          E **nbannon@indigo.ie**
                                          Cyril Bennett *Head, Risk & Information* ☎ **874 0222** F **679 9590**

Settlement / Clearing
Settlement (General)   Michael Cullen ☎ **874 0222**

Other Departments
Private Banking   John Rockett *Head* ☎ **660 0311**

Administration
Technology & Systems
Technology & IT Systems   Michael Sweeney *GM, Information Technology* ☎ **660 0311**
Legal / In-House Counsel
                                          Bryan Sheridan *Group Law Agent* ☎ **660 0311**
Compliance
                                          Eddie Nugent *Grp Compliance Manager* ☎ **660 0311**
Public Relations
                                          Catherine Burke *Media Relations Manager* ☎ **660 0311**

AIB International Financial Services Limited — Subsidiary Company

AIB International Centre, International Financial Services Centre, Dublin 1
PO Box 2757, Dublin
Tel: (1) 874 0777 Fax: (1) 874 3050
Website: www.aibifs.ie

Senior Executive Officers
Financial Director   John Power
Managing Director   John O'Donnell ☎ **667 0233** F **667 0250**
Deputy Managing Director   Walter Brazil
Company Secretary   John Power

Others (Senior Executives)
Director   Liam Kelly
                                          Damian Warde
                                          John Power
                                          Pat Diamond
                                          Mon O'Driscoll
                                          Don McBrien

IRELAND (+353)   www.euromoneydirectory.com

AIB International Financial Services Limited (cont)
Others (Senior Executives) (cont)

Vernon Rushe
Tom Geary

Corporate Finance / M&A Advisory
Head of Corporate Finance   John O'Donnell *Managing Director* ☎ 667 0233 ⒻAX 667 0250
Administration
Technology & Systems
John Walsh *Manager, IT*

Accounts / Audit
Catherine Gardiner *Financial Controller*

Anglo Irish Bank Corporation plc
Stephen Court, 18/21 St Stephen's Green, Dublin 2
Tel: (1) 676 2000; (1) 676 3225 **Fax:** (1) 661 1981 **Telex:** 30264 ANGOEI **Reuters:** ANGL

Senior Executive Officers
Chief Executive Officer   S FitzPatrick

Others (Senior Executives)
Banking   W Barrett *Director*
Risk Asset Management   P Killen *Director*
Finance   W McAteer *Director*
Treasury   T O Mahoney *Director*
Area Offices   P Butler *Director*
Banking - Dublin   T Browne *Director*
Funding   B Daly *Director*
UK   J Rowan *Managing Director*
     D Murray *Deputy Managing Director*
Communications, Marketing & Personnel   J O'Keeffe *Director*
Lending   K Duggan *Associate Director*
Treasury   D Whyte *Associate Director*
     R Murphy *Secretary*

ANP International Finance Limited   Subsidiary Company
Formerly known as: IBWA Finance Company Limited
International House, 3 Harbourmaster Place, International Financial Services Centre, Dublin 1
Tel: (1) 670 0188 **Fax:** (1) 670 0195 **Telex:** 91841ANPI EI **Swift:** AFRN IE 2D

Senior Executive Officers
Chairman   John D Edozien
Deputy Chairman   Michael Madden
Chief Executive Officer   Jim Miller
GM & Company Secretary   Terry F Sadlier

Syndicated Lending
Other (Trade Finance)
Letters of Credit   Fintan Bannon *Deputy Manager*

Settlement / Clearing
Operations   Henry Arogundade *Manager*

Administration
Accounts / Audit
John Flynn *Manager*

Artesia Ireland   Subsidiary Company
Formerly known as: BACOB Ireland
International House, 3 Harbourmaster Place, International Financial Services Centre, Dublin 1
Tel: (1) 829 1566 **Fax:** (1) 829 1577 **Telex:** 91913 BACI EI

Senior Executive Officers
Chief Operating Officer   Eamonn Tuohy *Operations Manager*
Director   Ludo Schockaert
Assistant Manager   Conor Burns

www.euromoneydirectory.com   IRELAND (+353)

Debt Capital Markets / Fixed Income
Head of Fixed Income — Ludo Schockaert *Director*

Domestic Government Bonds
Head of Sales — Ludo Schockaert *Director*

Eurobonds
Head of Sales — Ludo Schockaert *Director*

Emerging Market Bonds
Head of Emerging Markets — Ludo Schockaert *Director*

Libor-Based / Floating-Rate Products
FRN Sales; FRN Trading; Asset Swaps; Asset Swaps (Sales) — Conor Burns *Assistant Manager*

Fixed-Income Research
Global Head — Eamonn Tuohy *Operations Manager*

Syndicated Lending
Head of Trading — Ludo Schockaert *Director*

Loan-Related Activities
Trade Finance; Project Finance; Leasing & Asset Finance — Ludo Schockaert *Director*

Settlement / Clearing
Regional Head — Deirdre Hickey *Assistant Manager*
Operations — Barry Ryan
Sinead Donohue

Administration
Head of Administration — Sinead Harty *PA to Director*

Technology & Systems
Eamonn Tuohy *Operations Manager*

Legal / In-House Counsel
Conor Burns *Assistant Manager*

Accounts / Audit
Amanda Greville *Financial Controller*

Banca Commerciale Italiana (Ireland) plc   Subsidiary Company

Formerly known as: Comit Finance (Ireland) Limited
AIB International Centre, International Financial Services Centre, Dublin 1
Tel: (1) 874 2713 **Fax:** (1) 679 5882 **Telex:** 32320 BCII EI **Email:** mail@bcidublin.ie

Senior Executive Officers
Chairman — Robert Burke
Chief Executive Officer — Richard Barkley *General Manager*
Financial Director — Gerard Flaherty *Chief Accountant*
Chief Operating Officer — Maureen Murphy *Manager*

Debt Capital Markets / Fixed Income
Global Head — Maureen Murphy *Manager*
Richard Barkley *General Manager*

Syndicated Lending
Global Head — Maureen Murphy *Manager*
Richard Barkley *General Manager*

Bank of America NT & SA   Full Branch Office

Russell Court, St Stephen's Green, Dublin 2
Tel: (1) 407 2100 **Fax:** (1) 407 2199 **Telex:** 93517 **Reuters:** BAEI **Cable:** BANKAMERICA

Senior Executive Officers
Country Manager — Adrian E Wrafter ☎ **407 2101**

Debt Capital Markets / Fixed Income
Country Head — Brendan Seaver *Country Treasurer* ☎ **407 2111**

Syndicated Lending
Country Head — Keld Mortensen *Country Credit Officer* ☎ **407 2137**

Money Markets
Country Head — Simon Gleeson *Assistant Vice President* ☎ **407 2111**

Foreign Exchange
Country Head — Brendan Seaver *Country Treasurer* ☎ **407 2111**

Euromoney Directory 1999   **719**

IRELAND (+353) www.euromoneydirectory.com

Bank of America NT & SA (cont)
Corporate Finance / M&A Advisory
Country Head Diarmuid Connaughton *Managing Director* ☎ **407 2152**
Settlement / Clearing
Country Head Catherine Meenaghan *Vice President* ☎ **407 2150**

Bank of Ireland Asset Management Limited   Head Office
Formerly known as: IBI Investment Services
26 Fitzwilliam Place, Dublin 2
Tel: (1) 661 6433 **Fax:** (1) 661 6688 **Telex:** 93811 **Swift:** BISSIE 2D
Website: www.biam.ie

Senior Executive Officers
Chief Executive Officer William R Cotter *Chief Executive Officer*
Financial Director Sean O'Dwyer *Head of Finance & Compliance*
Chief Operating Officer Denis Donavan
 Tom Finlay *Head of Investment Services*

Equity Capital Markets
Head of Equity Capital Markets Chris Reilly *Chief Investment Officer*
Money Markets
Head of Money Markets Chris Reilly *Chief Investment Officer*
Foreign Exchange
Head of Foreign Exchange Chris Reilly *Chief Investment Officer*

Bank of Ireland Group   Head Office
Head Office, Lower Baggot Street, Dublin 2
Tel: (1) 670 0600 **Fax:** (1) 661 5675 **Telex:** 91774 **Email:** boiss@boi.

Senior Executive Officers
Chief Executive Officer Maurice Keane *Group Chief Executive*
Financial Director Paul D'Alton *Group Chief Financial Officer*
Treasurer Brian Goggin
International Division Patty McGinley

Others (Senior Executives)
Head of Emerging Markets Tony O'Shea

General-Lending (DCM, SL)
Head of Corporate Banking Brian Goggin

General-Investment
Head of Investment Tony O'Shea

General - Treasury
Head of Treasury Tony O' Shea *BOI Group Treasury*

Debt Capital Markets / Fixed Income
Tel: 670 0244
Country Head Sean Crowe
Head of Fixed Income Sean Crowe *Director* ☎ **670 0600**

Domestic Government Bonds
Head of Trading Liam Whelan

Bonds - General
£ Bonds Dave Thompson ☎ **670 1644**
I£ Bonds Vincent Digby ☎ **670 1644**
$ Bonds Glen Miller ☎ **829 0111**

Emerging Market Bonds
Head of Emerging Markets Sean Crowe *Director* ☎ **670 0600**
Money Markets
Head of Money Markets Sean Crowe *Director* ☎ **670 0600**

Money Markets - General
I£ Money Market Paula Quinn ☎ **829 0099**

Foreign Exchange
Tel: 829 0166
Head of Foreign Exchange John Farrell *Associate Director*

FX Traders / Sales People
US$ Stuart Kirk
I£ John Farrell *Associate Director*
EMU Monty McKenzie

720 Euromoney Directory 1999

www.euromoneydirectory.com IRELAND (+353)

Risk Management
Head of Risk Management — Austin Jennings *Director*

Other Currency Swap / FX Options Personnel
£ Forward FX — James O'Dwyer ☎ **670 1644**
I£ Forward FX — John Barry ☎ **829 0111**

Settlement / Clearing
Head of Settlement / Clearing — Brandon Whelan
Settlement (General) — David Geraghty
Operations — Una Henry *Head of Operations*

Global Custody
Head of Global Custody — Tony O'Shea

Other Departments
Correspondent Banking — Patty McGinley

Administration
Business Development — Denis Hanrahan *Head of Group Corporate Developement*

Compliance
— John O'Sullivan *Head, Compliance*

Public Relations
— David Holden

Bank of Ireland Group Treasury Limited Head Office

La Touche House, International Financial Services Centre, Custom House Dock, Dublin 1
Tel: (1) 670 0600 **Fax:** (1) 829 0130 **Telex:** 91774
Website: www.treasury.boi.ie

Senior Executive Officers
Chief Executive Officer — Tony O'Shea *Head, Group Treasury*
Financial Director — Austin Jennings *Head, Finance & Risk*

Others (Senior Executives)
Trading — Michael Sweeney *Head of Trading*

Relationship Manager
Offshore Banking — Terry Hannaway *Head* ☎ **+44 (1624) 661 102**

Debt Capital Markets / Fixed Income
Domestic Government Bonds
Head of Sales — Séan E. Crowe *Head, Interest Rate Trading*

Non-Domestic Government Bonds
US$ Bonds — Philip Lenehan *Head, US Trading Desk*
ERM Bonds — Claire Timlin *Head, ERM Trading Desk*
GBP Bonds — Vincent Digby *Head, GBP Trading Desk*

Money Markets
Domestic Commercial Paper
Head of Origination — Stephen Whelan

Foreign Exchange
Head of Institutional Sales — Michael Geraghty
Corporate Sales — Joe Connolly
Head of Trading — John Farrell

Risk Management
Global Head — Austin Jennings *Head, Finance & Risk*

Fixed Income Derivatives / Risk Management
Global Head; IR Swaps Sales / Marketing — Catherine Keane *Head, Financial Engineering* ☎ **670 088**
IR Swaps Trading — Liam Whelan *Head, IEP Swaps Trading*

Settlement / Clearing
Operations — Una Henry *Head of Operations*

Administration
Other (Administration)
Human Resources — Phil O'Donnel

Bank of Ireland Securities Services

International Financial Services Centre, 1 Harbourmaster Place, Dublin 1
Tel: (1) 670 0300 **Fax:** (1) 829 0144 **Telex:** 90739 **Swift:** BISS IE 2D

Euromoney Directory 1999 721

IRELAND (+353) www.euromoneydirectory.com

Bank of Ireland Securities Services (cont)
Equity Capital Markets
Equity Repo / Securities Lending
Head   Mike Cosgrave *Head of Securities Lending & Product Development*
   michael.cosgrave@boi.ie
Marketing & Product Development   Mike Cosgrave
Head of Trading   Dave Hennessy *Trading Manager* T 605 4540
Global Custody
Other (Global Custody)
   Liam Manahan *Dublin*
   Trevor Lavin *Dublin*
   Stephen Baker *Jersey* T +44 (1534) 638 690 F +44 (1534) 617 815

Bankgesellschaft Berlin (Ireland) plc

5 George's Dock, International Financial Services Centre, Dublin 1
Tel: (1) 819 4400 Fax: (1) 819 4499 Swift: BEBE IE 2D

Senior Executive Officers
Managing Director / General Manager   David Allen
Others (Senior Executives)
Head of Banking   John O'Grady Walshe

Banque Nationale de Paris   Full Branch Office

5 George's Dock, Dublin 2
Tel: (1) 612 5000 Fax: (1) 612 5100 Telex: 90641 Swift: BNPA IE 2D Email: bnp@indigo.ie Reuters: BNPZ
Website: www.calvacom.fr/bnp

Senior Executive Officers
Chairman of Advisory Board   Gérard Lohier
General Manager-Country Manager   Michel de Vibraye
Deputy General Manager-Administration &   Christian Ménestrier
System

Others (Senior Executives)
Structured Finance   Tom Woulfe *Deputy General Manager*
Institutional Business   Denis Holland *Assistant General Manager*

General-Lending (DCM, SL)
Head of Corporate Banking   Frank M Carey *Deputy General Manager-Corporate Banking*

Corporate Finance / M&A Advisory
Global Head   John Coffey *Deputy General Manager-Treasury & Markets*

Other Departments
Cash Management   D Darcy *Officer*

Administration
Other (Administration)
Trust & Management Services   Denis Holland *Assistant General Manager*

Barclays Bank plc   Full Branch Office

Formerly known as: Barclays International Financial Services (Ireland) Ltd
47/48 St Stephens Green, Dublin 2
Tel: (1) 661 1777 Fax: (1) 662 3141

Senior Executive Officers
Ireland Director   Paul Shovlin

General-Lending (DCM, SL)
Head of Corporate Banking   Peter O'Toole *Head, Finance & Planning*
   Pat Brennan *Director*

General - Treasury
Head of Treasury   Sean Blake *Treasury Director*

Relationship Manager
Corporate Relationship   Valerie Mulhall *Director*

Settlement / Clearing
Operations   Donal Moore *Operations Director*

www.euromoneydirectory.com   IRELAND (+353)

Barings (Ireland) Limited
Subsidiary Company

IFSC House, International Financial Services Centre, Dublin 1
Tel: (1) 670 1190 **Fax:** (1) 670 1191 **Telex:** 91955 IFMI EI **Swift:** BIRL IE 2D

Senior Executive Officers
Managing Director — Paul Donnelly

BBL Ireland

BBL

Harcourt Centre, Harcourt Road, Dublin 2
Tel: (1) 603 9490 **Fax:** (1) 603 9400 **Telex:** 91809 BBLF EI **Swift:** BBRU IE 2D **Reuters:** BBLY

Senior Executive Officers
Managing Director — Robert L Fierens

General - Treasury
Head of Treasury — Laurence Gordon

Corporate Finance / M&A Advisory
Department: Corporate & Syndications

Other (Corporate Finance)
- Michael Headen *Head of Corporate / Syndications*
- Edmund Byrne *Regional Manager, Corporate Products*
- Norma McGrath *Regional Manager, Corporate Products*
- Patrick McGuire *Regional Manager, Corporate Products*

Settlement / Clearing
Operations — Noel Fahy *Head of Operations*

Bermuda Trust (Dublin) Limited
Subsidiary Company

Europa House, Harcourt Street, Dublin 2
Tel: (1) 407 2000 **Fax:** (1) 475 2466; (1) 475 2467 **Telex:** 32333

Senior Executive Officers
Chairman — Eldon Trimingham
President & Chief Executive Officer — Henry B Smith
Managing Director — Gerald J P Brady

Settlement / Clearing
Operations — Bill Roche *Manager, Finance & Administration*

Global Custody
Department: Funds Management & Administration
Fund Administration — Barry O'Rourke *Senior Manager, Corporate Trust Services*

Administration

Legal / In-House Counsel — Fionan Breathnach

Compliance — Paula Downey *Trustee*

Bikuben Dublin Limited
Subsidiary Company

La Touche House, International Financial Services Centre, Dublin 1
Tel: (1) 670 0611 **Fax:** (1) 670 0616

Senior Executive Officers
Managing Director — Henrik Vennike

Euromoney Directory 1999   **723**

IRELAND (+353) www.euromoneydirectory.com

Brown Brothers Harriman Fund Administration Services (Ireland) Limited
Subsidiary Company

80 Harcourt Street, Dublin 2
Tel: (1) 475 7840 Fax: (1) 475 7834 Email: brian.coughlin@bbh.com
Website: www.bbh.com

Senior Executive Officers
Managing Director — Brian A Coughlin T 475 7840 F 475 7834
Administration
Head of Administration — Brian A Coughlin *Managing Director* T 475 7840 F 475 7834

Brown Brothers Harriman Trustee Services (Ireland) Limited
Subsidiary Company

80 Harcourt Street, Dublin 2
Tel: (1) 475 7840 Fax: (1) 475 7834 Email: jeffrey.holland@bbh.com
Website: www.bbh.com

Senior Executive Officers
Managing Director — Jeffrey Holland
Global Custody
Head of Global Custody — Jeffrey Holland *Managing Director*

BT Trustee Company (Ireland) Limited

6 Georges Dock, International Financial Services Centre, Dublin 1
Tel: (1) 790 2400

Senior Executive Officers
General Manager — Michael Durcan
Others (Senior Executives)
Trustee Manager — Anne Deegan

BW Bank (Ireland) plc
Subsidiary Company

2 Harbourmaster, International Financial Services Centre, Dublin 1
PO Box 4566, Dublin 1
Tel: (1) 670 1812 Fax: (1) 670 1817; (1) 670 0587

Senior Executive Officers
Managing Director — Bryan Higgins

Caradas Ireland
Head Office

35 Dawson Street, Dublin 2
Tel: (1) 671 0522 Fax: (1) 671 0110

Senior Executive Officers
Chairman & Finance Director — Peter J Cosgrave
Chief Executive Officer — David O'Brian *Chief Executive Officer*
Financial Director — Peter J Cosgrave *Chairman & Finance Director*

Debt Capital Markets / Fixed Income
Department: Caradas Currency Brokers Ltd

Fixed-Income Repo
Head of Repo — Peter J Cosgrave *Chairman & Finance Director*
Trading — Peter J Cosgrave *Director*
John Sullivan *Broker*

Settlement / Clearing
Country Head — Shirley Kavanagh

www.euromoneydirectory.com   IRELAND (+353)

Chase Manhattan Bank (Ireland) plc   Subsidiary Company
International Financial Services Centre, Chase Manhattan House, Dublin 1
Tel: (1) 612 3000 **Fax:** (1) 612 3123 **Telex:** 93644 CHAS EI

Senior Executive Officers
Chief Executive Officer
Financial Director   Frank Gaynor *Managing Director*
                                                  Stephen Kirwan *Financial Controller*
Others (Senior Executives)
                                                  David Williams *Legal Counsel & Company Secretary*
Global Agency Treasury   Ian Talbot *Director*
Global Trust Services   Colm Holmes *Director*
Offshore Funds Services   Anthony Carey *Director*

Global Custody
Global Trust Services   Colm Holmes *Director, Global Trust Services*

Administration
Other (Administration)
Human Resources   Deborah Kelly *Manager*

CIBC Wood Gundy Ireland Limited   Subsidiary Company
Alternative trading name: CIBC World Markets
Ormonde House, 12 Lower Leeson Street, Dublin 2
Tel: (1) 662 4400 **Fax:** (1) 662 4371

Senior Executive Officers
Chair   Jill Denham ☏ **+44 (171) 234 6145**
Financial Director   Colette Yeates
Managing Director   Ian Letchfrord
Others (Senior Executives)
International Lending   Jim Barry *Head*

Settlement / Clearing
Operations   Ursula Baxter *Head of Operations, Banking Services*

CICM Fund Management Limited
AIB International Centre, International Financial Services Centre, Dublin 1
PO Box 2747, Dublin 1
Tel: (1) 874 2211 **Fax:** (1) 679 6399 **Telex:** 91865 CICMEI **Email:** hbeckmann@cicm.ie

Senior Executive Officers
General Manager   John Bowden
General Manager   Hans Beckmann
Company Secretary   Gerry Fahy

Global Custody
Fund Administration   Eoin Mangan *Head, Fund Administration* ✉ **eoinm@cicm.ie**

Asset Management
Portfolio Management   Tim O'Kerlihy

Administration
Accounts / Audit
Accounting   Gerry Fahy *Head*

CICM (Ireland) Limited   Subsidiary Company
AIB International Centre, International Financial Services Centre, Dublin 1
PO Box 2747, Dublin 1
Tel: (1) 874 2211 **Fax:** (1) 679 6499

Senior Executive Officers
General Manager   John Bowden
General Manager   Hans Beckmann ✉ **hbeckmann@cicm.ie**
Company Secretary   Gerry Fahy

Asset Management
Portfolio Management   Tim O'Herlihy

IRELAND (+353) www.euromoneydirectory.com

CICM (Ireland) Limited (cont)
Administration
Accounts / Audit
Accounting   Gerry Fahy *Head*

Citibank NA   Full Branch Office

IFSC House, Custom House Quay, Dublin 1
Tel: (1) 702 3500; (1) 670 0800 Fax: (1) 702 3550 Telex: 93721 CITI Swift: CITI IE 2X Reuters: CITI (Dealing)
Treasury Operations Tel: 574 7618; 574 7618

Senior Executive Officers
Chief Executive Officer   Aidan Brady ☏ **702 3501**
Treasurer   Steve O'Dwyer ☏ **702 3555**
General-Lending (DCM, SL)
Head of Corporate Banking   Conor O'Malley *Corporate* ☏ **702 3547**
General - Treasury
Head of Treasury   Brian Hayes *Customer Treasury* ☏ **702 3580**
Relationship Manager
IFSC   Sean Hayes ☏ **702 3531**
Financial Institutions   Brendan Crowe ☏ **702 3521**
Syndicated Lending
Other (Trade Finance)
Capital Structuring   Keith MacDonald ☏ **702 3542**

Commerzbank Europe (Ireland)

AIB International Centre, International Financial Services Centre, Dublin 1
Tel: (1) 670 0714 Fax: (1) 670 0186

Senior Executive Officers
Managing Director   John Bowden
Managing Director   Hans D Brammer
General - Treasury
Head of Treasury   Kevin Kilduff *Head of Treasury & Capital Markets*
Debt Capital Markets / Fixed Income
Department: Treasury & Capital Markets
Head of Debt Capital Markets   Kevin Kilduff *Head of Treasury & Capital Markets*
Bonds - General
                                                Pat Coleman *Senior Dealer*
                                                Colin Redmond *Dealer*
Equity Capital Markets
Head of Equity Capital Markets   Kevin Kilduff *Head of Treasury & Capital Markets*
Syndicated Lending
Other (Syndicated Lending)
Loans Dept   Wolf Delius
Settlement / Clearing
Head of Settlement / Clearing   Bernadette Brennan

Copex International Finance & Trading Limited

Offices 305/306, Shannon Airport House, Shannon Free Zone, Shannon, Co. Clare
Tel: (61) 474 200 Fax: (61) 474 060 Email: copex@iol.ie

Senior Executive Officers
Chairman   Gordon A Holmes
President & Deputy Chairman   James I Sexton
General Manager   Michael Markham
Debt Capital Markets / Fixed Income
Head of Debt Capital Markets   Michael Markham *General Manager*
Money Markets
Head of Money Markets   Michael Markham *General Manager*

www.euromoneydirectory.com   IRELAND (+353)

Administration
Head of Administration   Caitriona McMahon *Financial Controller*

Legal / In-House Counsel
Joseph O'Meara *Lawyer*

Davy Stockbrokers   Head Office

Davy House, 49 Dawson Street, Dublin 2
Tel: (1) 679 7788 **Fax:** (1) 671 2704 **Telex:** 93968 **Reuters:** DAVA **Telerate:** 17867/8
Website: www.davy.ie

Senior Executive Officers
Fax: 679 6423
Chairman   Brian Davy ☏ **614 8948**
Chief Executive Officer   Kyran McLaughlin *Joint Chief Executive* ☏ **614 8949**
    Tony Garry *Joint Chief Executive* ☏ **614 8948**
Financial Director   Brian Cahalin *Head of Finance*
Chief Operating Officer   Andrew Flynn *Head of Administration*

Debt Capital Markets / Fixed Income

Domestic Government Bonds
Head of Sales   Tony Garry *Joint Chief Executive* ☏ **614 8948**
    Anthony Childs ☏ **679 2800**
Head of Trading   Matt Fitzpatrick ☏ **679 2800**
Head of Research   Jim O'Leary

Libor-Based / Floating-Rate Products
FRN Origination   Chris Connaughton

Fixed-Income Repo
Head of Repo   Turlough Carolan ☏ **679 2800**

Equity Capital Markets
Global Head   Kyran McLaughlin *Joint Chief Executive* ☏ **614 8949**

Domestic Equities
Head of Origination   Kyran McLaughlin *Joint Chief Executive* ☏ **614 8949**
Head of Sales   Ronan Godfrey ☏ **679 2816**
Head of Trading   Roc Mehigan ☏ **679 2816**
Head of Research   Robbie Kelleher

Money Markets
Department: **Davy Money Brokers**
Tel: 679 2820 **Fax:** 679 6428

Domestic Commercial Paper
Head of Origination   Chris Connaughton

Eurocommercial Paper
Head of Sales   Tony O'Connor

Foreign Exchange
Department: **Davy Money Brokers**
Head of Institutional Sales   Tony O'Connor

Risk Management

Fixed Income Derivatives / Risk Management
IR Swaps Sales / Marketing   Chris Connaughton

Corporate Finance / M&A Advisory
Department: **Davy Corporate Finance**
Country Head   Tom Byrne ☏ **679 6363**

Settlement / Clearing
Equity Settlement   Andrew Flynn *Head of Administration*
Fixed-Income Settlement   Nuala McCormack

Administration

Technology & Systems
    Pat Phelan ☏ **614 8747** ℻ **617 2704**

Compliance
    Noirin McKeon

Euromoney Directory 1999   **727**

IRELAND (+353)   www.euromoneydirectory.com

DePfa-Bank Europe plc — Subsidiary Company

International House, International Financial Services Centre, 3 Harbourmaster Place, Dublin 1
Tel: (1) 607 1600 Fax: (1) 829 0213 Telex: 32311 DEFA EI

Senior Executive Officers
Chief Executive Officer — Dermot Cahillane *Managing Director*
Financial Director — Noel Reynolds

General - Treasury
Head of Treasury — Dermot Golden *Head of Treasury* ☎ **607 1516**

Debt Capital Markets / Fixed Income
Tel: 609 1518 Fax: 609 1555

Fixed-Income Repo
Marketing & Product Development — Jackie Hughes *Head of Financial Institutions & Investors* ☎ **607 1517**
📠 **829 0213**
Trading — Russell Waide *Dealer*
Gary Sheils *Dealer*

Deutsche Bank/DB Ireland plc — Subsidiary Company

George's Dock House, International Financial Services Centre, Dublin 1
Tel: (1) 607 6700; (1) 607 6701 Fax: (1) 607 6799 Swift: DEUT IE 2D
International Loans Tel: 6076 710; Money Market Tel: 6076 720

Deutsche Morgan Grenfell Corporate Services (Ireland) Limited — Subsidiary Company

International Financial Services Centre, George's Dock House, Dublin 1
Tel: (1) 661 9773 Fax: (1) 607 6579

Deutsche Morgan Grenfell (Ireland) Limited — Subsidiary Company

George's Dock House, International Financial Services Centre, Dublin 1
Tel: (1) 607 6300 Fax: (1) 607 6491 Telex: 91994 MGIL EI

Senior Executive Officers
Chief Executive Officer — Paul P McNaughton
Financial Director — John Donohoe

Dilmun Financial Services — Subsidiary Company

Custom House Docks, International Financial Services Centre, Harbourmaster Place 4, Dublin 1
Tel: (1) 670 0077 Fax: (1) 670 0181

Senior Executive Officers
Director — Ruth Eaton

Dresdner Bank (Ireland) plc — Subsidiary Company

Alternative trading name: Dresdner Asset Management Ireland Ltd & Dresdner International Management Services Limited
La Touche House, International Financial Services Centre, Dublin 1
Tel: (1) 818 1100 Fax: (1) 818 1199

Senior Executive Officers
General Manager — Thomas Kiefer
General Manager — Werner Schwanberg

Others (Senior Executives)
Head of Finance — Donal O'Sullivan *Manager*

General - Treasury
Head of Treasury — John Grehan *Senior Manager, Treasury & Investment*

Settlement / Clearing
Operations — Tadhg Young *Head*

Global Custody
Fund Administration — Markus Nilles *Manager*

728   Euromoney Directory 1999

www.euromoneydirectory.com IRELAND (+353)

Administration
Accounts / Audit
Accounting   Willie O'Gorman *Senior Manager*

FBD International Holdings   Subsidiary Company

2/3 Exchange Place, International Financial Services Centre, Dublin 1
Tel: (1) 670 1340 **Fax**: (1) 670 1342 **Email**: fbdint@iol.ie

Senior Executive Officers
Group Managing Director   Paul O'Callaghan ☎ **455 4292**
Deputy Group Managing Director   Philip Fitzsimons ☎ **455 4292**
Chief Executive Officer   John Prosser *General Manager* ☎ **670 1340**
Treasurer   Gerry Clifford *Group Treasurer* ☎ **455 4305**

Syndicated Lending
Loan-Related Activities
Trade Finance   John Prosser *General Manager* ☎ **670 1340**
                                        Gerry Clifford *Group Treasurer* ☎ **455 4305**
Project Finance   John Prosser *General Manager* ☎ **670 1340**
                                        Gerry Clifford *Group Treasurer* ☎ **455 4305**

Money Markets
Head of Origination   John Prosser *General Manager* ☎ **670 1340**

Foreign Exchange
Head of Institutional Sales; Corporate Sales;   Gavan Dunne *Floor Broker* ☎ **670 0512**
Head of Trading

Fimat International Banque

65/66 Lower Mount Street, Dublin 2
Tel: (1) 605 0400 **Fax**: (1) 662 2448

Senior Executive Officers
General Manager   Keith White ☎ **605 0402** 📠 **662 2448**
Relationship Manager
Custody Manager   Donal Duff

FINEX Europe   Financial Division of NY Cotton Exchange

FINEX provides a market for trading currency futures and options on a regulated open outcry futures Exchange. FINEX trades 10 Cross-rate currency contracts, 10 US dollar currency paired contracts and the US dollar Index. In addition, in late '98, FINEX launched EURO trading in 5 currency pairs. Additional currency contracts will be rolled out in 1999.

Parent: FINEX is the financial division of the New York Cotton Exchange (NYCE ®), whose parent is The Board of Trade of the City of New York, Inc.
Tel: +1 (212) 742 5021 Fax: +1 (212) 742 5026

Dublin Exchange Facility, International Financial Services Centre, Dublin 1
Tel: (1) 607 4000 **Fax**: (1) 607 4064 **Reuters**: FNXA
Website: www.nybot.com

Senior Executive Officers
Managing Director   Colman Candy ☎ **607 4001** 📧 colman.candy@finex.ie
Others (Senior Executives)
Director of Marketing   Pauline Leahy *Director of Marketing* ☎ **607 4004** 📧 pauline.leahy@finex.ie
Administration
Business Development   Eoin Smyth *Manager* ☎ **607 4005** 📧 eoin.smyth@finex.ie
Head of Marketing   Laura McLoughlin *Marketing Executive* ☎ **607 4003**
                                        📧 laura.mcloughlin@finex.ie

Other (Administration)
Membership Liaison   Gaye Moffat *Manager* ☎ **607 4006** 📧 gaye.moffat@finex.ie
Floor Manager   John McGarry *Operations Manager* ☎ **607 4040**

IRELAND (+353)   www.euromoneydirectory.com

FTI Finance
Head Office

International House, 3 Harbourmaster Place, International Financial Services Centre, Dublin 1
Tel: (1) 670 0200 **Fax:** (1) 670 0288 **Email:** post@fti.ie.

Senior Executive Officers
Managing Director	Aengus Murphy
Financial Director	Peter McDevitt *Financial Controller*
Managing Director	Aengus Murphy
Executive Director	Michael Delaney

Furman Selz Financial Services

3rd Floor, 12 Duke Lane, Dublin
Tel: (1) 679 7924 **Fax:** (1) 679 7928

Goodbody Stockbrokers
Head Office

122 Pembroke Road, Ballsbridge, Dublin 4
Tel: (1) 667 0400 **Fax:** (1) 667 0422; (1) 667 0334 **Telex:** 93519 **Email:** goodbody@goodbody.ie **Reuters:** GDA7
Bloomberg: GDSE

Senior Executive Officers
Chairman	Liam Jones
Managing Director	Roy Barrett ☏ **667 0400**

Debt Capital Markets / Fixed Income
Department: International Fixed Interest
Tel: 667 0444 **Fax:** 667 0334
Head of Fixed Income   Neil Carroll *Head* ☏ **667 0444**

Bonds - General
International Bonds   Martha Cordial *Sales & Trading*
Neil Carroll *Head* ☏ **667 0444**
Tommy Reilly *Sales & Trading*
Martin Tormey *Sales & Trading*

Equity Capital Markets
Department: Equities Department
Tel: 667 0222

Domestic Equities
Head of Sales   Bruce Ashmore *Head of Equities*

International Equities
Head of Sales   Eleanor Lanigan

Equity Research
Head of Equity Research   David Lowe

Settlement / Clearing
Tel: 667 0400 **Fax:** 667 0260
Head of Settlement / Clearing   Eileen Kelly

Administration

Technology & Systems
IT   Adrian Neville *Head*

Compliance
   Frank Robinson *Compliance Officer*

GPA Group plc
Head Office

GPA House, Shannon, Co. Clare
Tel: (61) 360 000 **Fax:** (61) 360 113

Senior Executive Officers
Chief Executive Officer	Patrick H Blaney *Chief Executive Officer, Executive Director*
Financial Director	Edward J Hansom *Chief Financial Officer*
Company Secretary	John Redmond

Others (Senior Executives)
Dennis Stevenson *Chairman, Non-Executive Director*
Michael Davies *Deputy Chairman, Non-Executive Director*
Maurice A Foley *Non-Executive Director*
Gerald B Scanlan *Non-Executive Director*

www.euromoneydirectory.com   IRELAND (+353)

Grand Metroplitan Finance Ireland
Subsidiary Company

La Touche House, International Financial Services Centre, Dublin 1
Tel: (1) 670 0722 **Fax:** (1) 670 0670

Senior Executive Officers
General Manager   Gerry Dempsey
Administration
Other (Administration)
Business Development   Pat Hannigan *Manager*

Helaba Dublin Landesbank Hessen-Thüringen International
Subsidiary Company

3 Georges Dock, International Financial Services Centre, Dublin 1
Tel: (1) 605 4900 **Fax:** (1) 829 1040 **Telex:** 32167 HELA **Reuters:** HEDU (Monitor)

Senior Executive Officers
Chairman   Frederick Roy Hopson
Chief Executive Officer   Alex Meyer *Managing Director*
                                                    Ernst Van Beek *Deputy Manager*
Financial Director   Paul Murray *Financial Controller*
Others (Senior Executives)
                                                    Val Diggin *Chief Dealer*
                                                    Conor Molloy *Head of Credit*

Helaba International Finance plc

AIB International Centre, Custom House Docks, Dublin 1
PO Box 3137, AIB International Centre, Dublin 1
Tel: (1) 679 7126 **Fax:** (1) 874 1945 **Reuters:** HEDU (Monitor)

Senior Executive Officers
Chairman   Frederick Roy Hopson
Others (Senior Executives)
Management   Alexandre G Meyer
                                                    Ulrich Gnath

HypoVereinsbank Ireland
Subsidiary Company

5 Exchange Square, International Financial Services Centre, Dublin 1
Tel: (1) 607 5930 **Fax:** (1) 670 2271

ICC Bank plc
Head Office

72/74 Harcourt Street, Dublin 2
Tel: (1) 475 5700 **Fax:** (1) 671 7797 **Telex:** 93220 EI **Swift:** ICCB IE 2D **Email:** info@icc.ie **Reuters:** ICCD
Telerate: 3928
Website: www.icc.ie

Senior Executive Officers
Chairman   P Flynn
Treasurer   John Staunton
Managing Director   M Quinn
Company Secretary   Pauline McLaughlin
Manager, Secretariat   Frank Treanor
General-Lending (DCM, SL)
Head of Corporate Banking   Charles Carroll *General Manager, Banking*
                                                    Tom Quirke *Divisional Manager, Corporate Banking*

General - Treasury
Head of Treasury   Martin Cahill *General Manager, Treasury*
                                                    Niall Duggan *Treasury Manager, ICC Investment Bank*
                                                    Imelda Malynn *Treasury Manager, Corporate Deposits*
                                                    John Rohan *Treasury Manager, ICC International Finance*

Relationship Manager
Group Financial Services   Martin Thornton *Divisional Manager*

IRELAND (+353)　　　　　　www.euromoneydirectory.com

ICC Bank plc (cont)
Syndicated Lending
Loan-Related Activities
Shipping Finance　　　　　　　　　　Stephen O'Neill *Manager*
Project Finance　　　　　　　　　　　John O'Malley *Manager*
Other (Trade Finance)
Syndicated Finance; Agribusiness　　Stephen O'Neill *Manager*
Finance　　　　　　　　　　　　　　Brendan Spierin *Manager*
Corporate Lending　　　　　　　　　Dennis O'Connell *Manager*
Risk Management
Global Head　　　　　　　　　　　　Henry Roche *Manager*
Corporate Finance / M&A Advisory
Global Head　　　　　　　　　　　　David Fassbender *MD, ICC Corporate Finance*
Other (Corporate Finance)
　　　　　　　　　　　　　　　　　　Ruairi O'Nuallain *Manager, Corporate Finance*
Department: ICC Venture Capital
Other (Corporate Finance)
　　　　　　　　　　　　　　　　　　Prisca Grady *Manager*
　　　　　　　　　　　　　　　　　　Tom Kirwan *Manager*
　　　　　　　　　　　　　　　　　　Maurice McHenry *Manager*
Settlement / Clearing
Operations　　　　　　　　　　　　　Paraig Conaghan *Manager, Operations*
　　　　　　　　　　　　　　　　　　Brendan Cahill *Manager, Operations & Support*
Other Departments
Economic Research　　　　　　　　　Mary Doyle *Group Economist*
Administration
Technology & Systems
Information Systems　　　　　　　　Colin Sharpe *Head*
Systems Development　　　　　　　Alan Kelly *Manager*
Accounts / Audit
Internal Audit　　　　　　　　　　　Alan Waterhouse *Divisional Manager*
　　　　　　　　　　　　　　　　　　Peter Crilly *Manager*
Other (Administration)
Personnel　　　　　　　　　　　　　Jim McGowan *Divisional Manager*
　　　　　　　　　　　　　　　　　　Roisin Quigley *Manager*

ING Barings　　　　　　　　　　　　　　　　　　　　　Full Branch Office
49 St Stephen's Green, Dublin 2
Tel: (1) 662 1911; (1) 662 1912 **Fax:** (1) 662 1916 **Telex:** 32308 INGB EI **Tel:** 662 1213
Senior Executive Officers
Chief Executive Officer　　　　　　　Peter D Nabney *Country Manager*
Chief Operating Officer　　　　　　　J Byrne
Risk Management
Global Head　　　　　　　　　　　　B Fehily
Corporate Finance / M&A Advisory
Global Head　　　　　　　　　　　　E Allen

Irish Intercontinental Bank Limited　　　　　　　Subsidiary Company
91 Merrion Square, Dublin 2
Tel: (1) 661 9744 **Fax:** (1) 678 5034 **Telex:** 33322
Senior Executive Officers
Chairman　　　　　　　　　　　　　Patrick McEvoy
Chief Executive Officer　　　　　　　Edward Marah

KBC Bank NV　　　　　　　　　　　　　　　　　　　Full Branch Office
Formerly known as: Kredietbank NV
Kredietbank House, International Financial Services Centre, Dublin 1
Tel: (1) 670 0888 **Fax:** (1) 670 0853 **Telex:** 39192 KBDEI **Swift:** KBDU IE 2D
Senior Executive Officers
General Manager　　　　　　　　　　Michael Monaghan ☏ **603 5405**

www.euromoneydirectory.com IRELAND (+353)

Others (Senior Executives)
　　　　　　　　　　　　　　　Luc Nouwen *Assistant General Manager* ☏ **603 5433**

Debt Capital Markets / Fixed Income
Department: Asset Swaps

Libor-Based / Floating-Rate Products
Asset Swaps　　　　　　　　　Peter Clarke *Manager* ☏ **670 1760**

Syndicated Lending
Country Head　　　　　　　　Luc Nouwen *Assistant General Manager* ☏ **603 5433**

Management International (Dublin) Limited　　Subsidiary Company
Europa House, Harcourt Centre, Harcourt Street, Dublin 2
Tel: (1) 407 2000 **Fax:** (1) 475 2466; (1) 475 2467 **Swift:** BBDA US 33

Senior Executive Officers
Chairman　　　　　　　　　　Eldon Trimingham
President　　　　　　　　　　Henry Smith
Managing Director　　　　　　Gerald Brady

Others (Senior Executives)
Corporate Trust　　　　　　　Barry O'Rourke *Senior Manager*
Client Relationship　　　　　　Peter Heaps *Senior Manager*
Financial Controller　　　　　Bill Roche

Global Custody
Regional Head　　　　　　　　Ruth Ward *Custody & Operations Manager*

Administration
Head of Administration　　　　Carmel McKenna *Accounting & Valuations Manager*

Legal / In-House Counsel
　　　　　　　　　　　　　　　Fionan Breathnach *Legal Counsel*

MeesPierson Fund Services (Dublin) Limited　　Subsidiary Company
Plaza 2, Custom House Plaza, International Financial Services Centre, Dublin 1
Tel: (1) 607 1800 **Fax:** (1) 829 1177 **Email:** funds@meespierson.ie

Senior Executive Officers
Director of Operations　　　　Brenda Buckley
Managing Director　　　　　　Brian Wilkinson ☏ **607 1801**
Company Secretary　　　　　　Damian Keane

Administration
Head of Administration　　　　Paul Drumm *Manager of Valuations*

Technology & Systems
Information Technology　　　　Paul Rooney *Manager*

Legal / In-House Counsel
　　　　　　　　　　　　　　　Richard Farrington *Legal Counsel*

Compliance
　　　　　　　　　　　　　　　Michael Maher *Compliance Officer*

Merrill Lynch Financial Services Limited　　Subsidiary Company
Alternative trading name: Merrill Lynch Capital Markets Bank Limited
The Treasury Building, Lower Grand Canal Street, Dublin 2
Tel: (1) 605 8500 **Fax:** (1) 605 8501

Senior Executive Officers
Chief Executive Officer　　　　Michael D'Souza
Chief Operating Officer　　　　Jane M Richardson

Settlement / Clearing
Operations　　　　　　　　　Steve Burton *Operations Manager*

IRELAND (+353) www.euromoneydirectory.com

Midland Bank plc / Midland International Financial Services (Ireland) Limited
Representative Office

Alternative trading name: Midland Life International / HSBC Insurance (Ireland) Limited & Midland Ireland Global Securities Services Limited

20-22 Lower Hatch Street, Dublin 2
Tel: (1) 662 5600 **Fax:** (1) 662 5145 **Telex:** 93459 MIDEK EI

Senior Executive Officers
Country Manager — James V Deeny

Mitsubishi Trust Finance (Ireland) plc
Subsidiary Company

Level 5, 4 Custom House Plaza, Harbourmaster Place, Dublin 1
Tel: (1) 829 1277 **Fax:** (1) 829 1280 **Telex:** 91927 MTIR EI

Senior Executive Officers
Managing Director — Yoichi Abe
Director & Company Secretary — Yoshihide Suzuki

Settlement / Clearing
Operations — Seamus Naughten *Operations Manager*

Administration
Accounts / Audit — Joe Hogon *Research Director*

Money Markets International Limited
Head Office

26 Lower Baggot Street, Dublin 2
Tel: (1) 676 6277 **Fax:** (1) 676 5250 **Telex:** 93485 **Reuters:** MMII

Senior Executive Officers
Managing Director — Oisín Fanning

Others (Senior Executives)
Peter O'Byrne *Financial Controller*
Paul Boucher *Director*
John Curran *Director*

Money Markets
Head of Money Markets — John Curran *Director*

Foreign Exchange
Head of Foreign Exchange — Paul Boucher *Director*

ORIX Ireland
Subsidiary Company

2nd Floor, IFSC House, International Financial Services Centre, Dublin 1
Tel: (1) 670 0622 **Fax:** (1) 670 0644

Senior Executive Officers
Chief Executive Officer — Akira Kashi *Managing Director*
Financial Director — Eoin Kelly *Financial Controller*

Asset Management
Head — Paul Egan *Manager, Assets*

Administration
Technology & Systems
Data Processing — Beryl Dunne *Manager*

Pfizer International Bank Europe

La Touche House, International Financial Services Centre, Dublin 1
Tel: (1) 670 0266 **Fax:** (1) 670 0466

Senior Executive Officers
Financial Director — William Roche
Chief Operating Officer — Paul Hillen
Treasurer — Brian Farrelly
Managing Director / General Manager — B Michael Senior

734 Euromoney Directory 1999

Rabobank Ireland Limited

George's Dock House, International Financial Services Centre, Dublin 1
Tel: (1) 607 6100 Fax: (1) 670 1724

Senior Executive Officers
General Manager   Ruurd Weulen Kranenberg
Others (Senior Executives)
Head of Banking   Jim Pender *Deputy General Manager*
General - Treasury
Head of Treasury   Fergus Murphy *Assistant General Manager*
Settlement / Clearing
Operations   Nigel McDonagh *Head*

SBN (Dublin) Limited
Subsidiary Company

Alternative trading name: Spar Nord Dublin
57c Harcourt Street, Dublin 2
Tel: (1) 475 0090 Fax: (1) 475 0164 Telex: 32182 SBND

Senior Executive Officers
Chairman   Jan Gerhardt
Managing Director   Soeren Jensen

SGZ-Bank Ireland plc
Head Office

West Block Building, PO Box 4720, International Financial Services Centre, Dublin 1
Tel: (1) 670 0715 Fax: (1) 829 0298 Email: sgz@iol.ie

Senior Executive Officers
Managing Director   Johannes Haas
Managing Director   Andreas Neugebauer
Others (Senior Executives)
Board of Directors   Ulrich Brixner
    Walter Brazil
    Martin Elsasser
    John McCloskey
    Wolfgang Müller
    Carl O'Sullivan
    Karl-Heinz Vollmer

Smurfit Paribas International
Subsidiary Company

4th Floor, IFSC House, Custom House Quay, Dublin 1
Tel: (1) 670 0568 Fax: (1) 670 0569

Senior Executive Officers
Senior Manager   Michael O'Sullivan
General Manager   Liam Miley

Société Générale Finance (Ireland) Limited

31-32 Morrison Chambers, Nassau Street, Dublin 2
Tel: (1) 670 4255 Fax: (1) 670 4262
Website: www.socgen.com

Sumitomo Finance (Dublin) Limited
Subsidiary Company

La Touche House, Custom House Docks, International Financial Services Centre, Dublin 1
Tel: (1) 670 0066; (1) 829 0188 Fax: (1) 670 0353 Telex: 91909

Senior Executive Officers
Managing Director   Shinichi Nishikiori
General Manager   Timothy O'Donovan
Others (Senior Executives)
    James Sheils *Joint Manager, Finance*
    Deirdre Collier *Buisness Promotion*

IRELAND (+353) www.euromoneydirectory.com

Trade Finance Limited
Head Office

17 Main Street, Blackrock, Dublin
Tel: (1) 288 6100 **Fax:** (1) 288 5481

Senior Executive Officers
Chief Executive Officer — David Murray *Managing Director*
Financial Director — Brian Keyes *Finance Manager*
Treasurer — Lorraine Murray *Secretary*

Debt Capital Markets / Fixed Income
Private Placements
Head of Origination — David Murray *Managing Director*
Head of Sales — Brian Keyes *Finance Manager*
Head of Structuring — Lorraine Murray *Secretary*

Asset-Backed Securities / Securitization
Global Head — David Murray *Managing Director*
Regional Head — Brian Keyes *Finance Manager*
Head of Trading — Lorraine Murray *Secretary*

Mortgage-Backed Securities
Global Head — David Murray *Managing Director*
Regional Head — Brian Keyes *Finance Manager*
Head of Trading — Lorraine Murray *Secretary*

Syndicated Lending
Global Head — David Murray *Managing Director*
Regional Head — Brian Keyes *Finance Manager*
Recovery — Lorraine Murray *Secretary*

Loan-Related Activities
Trade Finance — David Murray *Managing Director*
              Brian Keyes *Finance Manager*
Project Finance — David Murray *Managing Director*
                 Brian Keyes *Finance Manager*
Structured Trade Finance — David Murray *Managing Director*
                          Brian Keyes *Finance Manager*
Leasing & Asset Finance — David Murray *Managing Director*
                         James Norman *Finance Manager*

Corporate Finance / M&A Advisory
Tel: 288 5481
Global Head — David Murray *Managing Director*
Regional Head — Brian Keyes *Finance Manager*
Country Head — Lorraine Murray *Secretary*

Other (Corporate Finance)
County Head — James Norman *Leasing Executive*

TSB Bank
Head Office

TSB Corporate Centre, Blackrock, Co. Dublin
Tel: (1) 212 4000 **Fax:** (1) 212 4001 **Telex:** 93345 **Email:** info@tsbbank.ie
Website: www.tsbbank.ie

Senior Executive Officers
Chairman, Board of Trustees — Dermot P Whelan
Chief Executive Officer — H W Lorton *Chief Executive & Trustee*
                         J P Maher *Assistant Chief Executive & Trustee*

Others (Senior Executives)
F C Golden *Trustee*
D P Brazil *Trustee*
R M Greene *Trustee*
B D Uniacke *Trustee*
F M Sheehan *Trustee*

General-Lending (DCM, SL)
Head of Corporate Banking — T Dunleavy *General Manager, Finance*

General - Treasury
Head of Treasury — M Casey *Head of Treasury*

Relationship Manager
Advances — T O'Connell *General Manager*
Branch Banking — D O'Brien *General Manager*

Settlement / Clearing
Operations — D F Tippins *General Manager*

736 Euromoney Directory 1999

www.euromoneydirectory.com IRELAND (+353)

Administration
Other (Administration)
Marketing S Curtis *Head*
Personnel D M Conlon *Head*
Payment Systems S Scanlan *Head*
Business Development M McDermott *Head*

Ulster Bank Commercial Services Limited

Ulster Bank Group Centre, Georges Quay, Dublin 2
Tel: (1) 608 4000 **Fax:** (1) 608 4230

Senior Executive Officers
Chairman John Donnelly
Chief Executive Officer William Glynn
Financial Director Brendan Griffin

Ulster Bank Limited

33 College Green, Dublin 2
PO Box 3255, IFSC House, International Financial Services Centre, Dublin
Tel: (1) 670 0700 **Fax:** (1) 702 5656 **Telex:** 31525 **Reuters:** UBFX; UBFI; UIBI

Senior Executive Officers
Chairman W G H Quigley
Chief Executive Officer R D Kells
Financial Director I J Laird

Ulster Bank Markets   Subsidiary Company

IFSC House, International Financial Services Centre, Custom House Quay, Dublin 1
Tel: (1) 670 0700 **Fax:** (1) 702 5620 **Telex:** 30565 **Email:** treasury@ulsterbank.com **Reuters:** UBFI, UBFX, UIBI
Website: www.ulsterbank.com

Senior Executive Officers
Chief Executive Officer Paddy McMahon *Chief Executive, UB Markets*
Treasurer Declan J O'Neill *Group Treasurer*

Others (Senior Executives)
Bonds & Derivatives Jim Fox *Director*
Interbank Trading Michael Griffin *Director*
Corporate Treasury Brian Brady *Director*

General-Lending (DCM, SL)
Head of Corporate Banking Mike Nurse *Manager, Credit Risk*

General - Treasury
Head of Treasury Valerie Boyce *Associate Director, Corp Treasury (FX)*
  Brian Brady *Head, Corporate Treasury*
  Fionan MacDonagh *Head of FX, Corp Treasury*
  Kevin Mason *Associate Director, Corp Treasury (FX)*
  Bairbre Kean *Associate Director, Corp Treasury (FX)*
  Niamh Gilmore *Associate Director, Corp Treasury (FX)*
  Milton D'Rosario *Dealer*
  Orla Furey *Dealer, Options*
  Tommy Burke *Head of Deposits, Corp Treasury*
  Des Leavy *Associate Director, Corporate Treasury (Deposits)*
  Karen Sheppard *Senior Dealer, Corp Treasury (Deposits)*
  Barbara Tracey *Senior Dealer, Corp Treasury (Deposits)*
  Jim Mulligan *Senior Dealer, Corp Treasury (Deposits)*

Relationship Manager
Financial Institutions Paul Garrigan *Head*
  Richard Vaughan *Associate Director*

Debt Capital Markets / Fixed Income
Domestic Government Bonds
Head of Sales Aidan Clare *Head*
  Brian Lynch *Dealer & Senior Trader*

Fixed-Income Repo
Head of Repo Jim Fox *Head of Bonds & Derivatives* ☎ **670 0027**
Trading Brian Lynch *Senior Trader*

IRELAND (+353)　　　　　　www.euromoneydirectory.com

Ulster Bank Markets (cont)
Fixed-Income Repo (cont)
Sales　　　　　　　　　　　　　　Marguerite Gaffney *Senior Trader*
Group Treasury, IFSC House, International Financial Services Centre, Customs House Quay, Dublin 1
Tel: +353 (1) 670 0675 **Fax:** +353 (1) 702 5676
Marketing & Product Development; Trading　　Marguerite Gaffney *Dealer & Senior Trader* ☎ **670 0675**
Trading　　　　　　　　　　　　Brian Lynch *Dealer & Senior Trader*

Syndicated Lending
Department: International Trade Services
Ulster Bank Group Centre, Georges Quay, Dublin 2
Tel: +353 (1) 604 8000 **Fax:** +353 (1) 608 4711

Other (Trade Finance)
International Trade Services　　　　Joe Caulfield *Head*

Money Markets
Global Head　　　　　　　　　　Matt Cullen *Head*

Money Markets - General
US$　　　　　　　　　　　　　Peter Meehan *Associate Director*

Other (Wholesale Deposits)
Eurocurrencies　　　　　　　　　Peter Wilson *Head of Euros*
　　　　　　　　　　　　　　　Ciaran McArdle *Senior Dealer*
　　　　　　　　　　　　　　　David Lammas *Dealer*

Foreign Exchange
FX Traders / Sales People
Spot　　　　　　　　　　　　　Eamonn O'Connor *Head of FX*
　　　　　　　　　　　　　　　Michael McNelis *Associate Director*
　　　　　　　　　　　　　　　Paul Tancred *Associate Director*
　　　　　　　　　　　　　　　Liam Corbett *Associate Director*
　　　　　　　　　　　　　　　Pamela Moiselle *Assistant Manager*
　　　　　　　　　　　　　　　Ian McGuirk *Dealer*
　　　　　　　　　　　　　　　Aine McCleary *Dealer*
　　　　　　　　　　　　　　　Paul McEnroe *Dealer*
Forwards　　　　　　　　　　　Mary McCann *Associate Director*
　　　　　　　　　　　　　　　Michael Denvir *Associate Director*
Corporate Treasury　　　　　　　Brian Brady *Head, Corporate Treasury*
　　　　　　　　　　　　　　　Fionan MacDonagh *Head of FX, Corp Treasury*
　　　　　　　　　　　　　　　Kevin Mason *Associate Director, Corp Treasury (FX)*
　　　　　　　　　　　　　　　Bairbre Kean *Associate Director, Corp Treasury (FX)*
　　　　　　　　　　　　　　　Niamh Gilmore *Associate Director, Corp Treasury (FX)*
　　　　　　　　　　　　　　　Valerie Boyce *Associate Director, Corp Treasury (FX)*
　　　　　　　　　　　　　　　Milton D'Rosario *Dealer*
　　　　　　　　　　　　　　　Orla Furey *Dealer, Options*

Risk Management
Department: Capital Markets

Fixed Income Derivatives / Risk Management
IR Swaps Sales / Marketing　　　　John Reen *Dealer*
　　　　　　　　　　　　　　　Shane Hughes *Associate Director*

Foreign Exchange Derivatives / Risk Management
Cross-Currency Swaps, Sales / Marketing　　Shane Hughes *Associate Director*

Other Currency Swap / FX Options Personnel
Trading Risk　　　　　　　　　　Heather Gordon *Head*
Credit Risk　　　　　　　　　　　Mike Nurse *Manager, Credit Risk*

Settlement / Clearing
Settlement (General)　　　　　　Gerry Doyle
　　　　　　　　　　　　　　　Caroline Dunne
　　　　　　　　　　　　　　　Rus Carter
Operations　　　　　　　　　　　Gerry O'Neill *Head of Control*
　　　　　　　　　　　　　　　Philip Meers *Head, Operations & Administration*

Administration
Head of Administration　　　　　Philip Meers *Head, Operations & Administration*

Technology & Systems
Information Systems　　　　　　Ellvena Graham *Head*

738　Euromoney Directory 1999

www.euromoneydirectory.com   IRELAND (+353)

Ulster Bank Markets - Group Treasury   Subsidiary Company
IFSC House, International Financial Services Centre, Custom House Quay, Dublin 1
Tel: (1) 670 0700 Fax: (1) 702 5620 Telex: 30565 Email: treasury@ulsterbank.com Reuters: UBFI, UBFX, UIBI
Website: www.ulsterbank.com

Senior Executive Officers
Treasurer   Declan J O'Neill *Group Treasurer*
Managing Director / General Manager   Michael K Griffin

Others (Senior Executives)
Bonds & Derivatives   Jim Fox *Director*
Interbank Trading   Michael Griffin *Director*
Corporate Treasury   Brian Brady *Director*

General - Treasury
Head of Treasury   Brian Brady *Director, Corp Treasury*
                                             Fionan MacDonagh *Head of FX, Corp Treasury*
                                             Kevin Mason *Associate Director, Corp Treasury (FX)*
                                             Bairbre Kean *Associate Director, Corp Treasury (FX)*
                                             Niamh Gillmore *Associate Director, Corp Treasury (FX)*
                                             Valerie Boyce *Associate Director, Corp Treasury (FX)*
                                             Milton D'Rosario *Dealer*
                                             Orla Furey *Dealer*
                                             Tommy Burke *Head of Deposits, Corp Treasury*
                                             Des Leavy *Associate Director, Corporate Treasury (Deposits)*
                                             Karen Sheppard *Senior Dealer, Corp Treasury (Deposits)*
                                             Barbara Tracey *Senior Dealer, Corp Treasury (Deposits)*
                                             Jim Mulligan *Senior Dealer, Corp Treasury (Deposits)*
                                             Garreth Boyle *Dealer, Corp Treasury (Deposits)*

Relationship Manager
Interbank Trading   Michael Griffin *Director*
Financial Institutions   Paul Garrigan *Head*
                                             Richard Vaughan *Associate Director*

Debt Capital Markets / Fixed Income
Department: Capital Markets

Domestic Government Bonds
Head of Sales   Aidan Clare *Head*
                                             Brian Lynch *Dealer*

Non-Domestic Government Bonds
Government Securities & Trading   David Bradley *Director*
                                             Marguerite Gaffney *Dealer*

Bonds - General
Bonds & Derivatives   Jim Fox *Director*

Syndicated Lending
Department: International Trade Services
Ulster Bank Group Centre, Georges Quay, Dublin 2
Tel: +353 (1) 604 8000 Fax: +353 (1) 608 4711

Other (Trade Finance)
International Trade Services   Joe Caulfield *Head*

Money Markets
Global Head   Matt Cullen *Head*

Money Markets - General
                                             Peter Meehan *Associate Director*
                                             Michael Denvir *Associate Director*

Other (Wholesale Deposits)
US$ Peter Wilson *Head*
Eurocurrencies   Ciaran McArdle *Senior Dealer*
                                             David Lammas *Dealer*

Foreign Exchange
FX Traders / Sales People
Spot   Eamonn O'Connor *Head of FX*
                                             Michael McNeilis *Associate Director*
                                             Paul Tancred *Associate Director*
                                             Liam Corbett *Associate Director*
                                             Pamela Moiselle *Assistant Manager*
                                             Ian McGuirk *Dealer*
                                             Aine McCleary *Dealer*
                                             Paul McEnroe *Dealer*

IRELAND (+353)   www.euromoneydirectory.com

Ulster Bank Markets - Group Treasury (cont)
FX Traders / Sales People (cont)
Forwards   Michael Denvir *Associate Director*
                                    Mary McCann *Associate Director*
                                    John Reen *Dealer*

Risk Management
Department: Capital Markets
Other Currency Swap / FX Options Personnel
Interest Rate & Currency Swaps   David Bradley *Director*
                                    Shane Hughes *Associate Director*

Other (Exchange-Traded Derivatives)
Bonds & Derivatives   Jim Fox *Director*
Trading Risk   Heather Gordon *Head*
Credit Risk   Mike Nurse *Manager*

Settlement / Clearing
Derivatives Settlement   Gerry Doyle *Head*
Foreign Exchange Settlement   Caroline Dunne *Head, FX & MM Settlements*
Settlement (General)   Russ Carter *Head, Treasury Settlements*
Operations   Gerry O'Neill *Head of Control*
                                    Philip Meers *Head, Operations & Administration*

Administration
Head of Administration   Philip Meers *Head, Operations & Administration*

Technology & Systems
Information Systems   Ellvena Graham *Head*

VB International Finance Ireland   Subsidiary Company
Alternative trading name: VBIF
3, Harbourmaster Place, International Financial Services Centre, Dublin 1
Tel: (1) 605 4150 **Fax:** (1) 605 4105

Westdeutsche Landesbank (Ireland) plc   Subsidiary Company
2 Harbourmaster Place, International Financial Services Centre, Dublin 1
Tel: (1) 670 0100 **Fax:** (1) 670 0112 **Telex:** 93926 **Swift:** WELA IE 2D

Senior Executive Officers
Treasurer   Ken Maher
General Manager   Thomas Kaiser
Assistant General Manager   Sean Dunne

Others (Senior Executives)
                                    Margaret McGurk *Senior Dealer*

General-Lending (DCM, SL)
Head of Corporate Banking   Tom Rohan *Credit Manager*

General - Treasury
Head of Treasury   Peter Van Dessel

ISRAEL
(+972)

Bank of Israel   Central Bank
Qiryat Ben-Gurion, PO Box 780, Jerusalem 91007
Tel: (2) 655 2211 **Fax:** (2) 652 8805; (2) 651 9123 **Telex:** 25214 **Swift:** ISRA IL IJ **Reuters:** BOIJ
General **Telex:** 25215; International Affairs & External Relations **Tel:** 655 2728; **Fax:** 655 2778;
Reuters: BOFI (Dealing)
Website: www.bankisrael.gov.il

Senior Executive Officers
Governor   Jacob Frenkel ☎ **655 2701**
Senior Director   Odded Hezroni ☎ **655 2731** 🖷 **655 2756**

Others (Senior Executives)
Head, Banking Supervision   Itzhak Tal *Senior Director* ☎ **655 2401** 🖷 **655 2469**
Head, State Loans Administration Odded Hezroni *Senior Director* ☎ **655 2731** 🖷 **655 2756**

www.euromoneydirectory.com   ISRAEL (+972)

Others (Senior Executives) (cont)
Head, Monetary Operations
Monetary Department   David Klein *Senior Director* ☎ 655 2599 F 655 5984
                          Meir Sokoler *Director* ☎ 655 2557 F 655 2155

Foreign Exchange
Head of Foreign Exchange   David Klein *Senior Director* ☎ 655 2599 F 655 5984
                             Miki Eran *Director* ☎ 655 2510
                             Sylvia Piterman *Director* ☎ 655 2310 F 655 2457

Other Departments
Economic Research   Leonardo Leiderman *Senior Director* ☎ 655 2601 F 655 2615

Administration
Technology & Systems
Computer Services   Odded Hezroni *Senior Director* ☎ 655 2731 F 655 2756
                       Avram Jacoby *Director* ☎ 655 2987 F 655 2207

Legal / In-House Counsel
                       Eli Montag *General Counsel* ☎ 655 2706 F 655 2678

Astaire & Partners   Representative Office

Suite 324, 159 Yigal Alon Street, Tel Aviv 67443
Tel: (3) 696 3101 **Fax:** (3) 695 6389

Senior Executive Officers
Representative   Daniel Fuchs

Bank Hapoalim BM   Head Office

BANK HAPOALIM

50 Rothschild Boulevard, Tel Aviv 66883
PO Box 27, Tel Aviv 61000
Tel: (3) 567 3333 **Fax:** (3) 560 7028 **Swift:** POAL IL IT **Email:** international@bnhp.co.il
Website: www.bankhapoalim.co.il

Senior Executive Officers
Chairman of the Board of Directors   Shlomo Nehama
Chief Executive Officer   Amiram Sivan *Chairman, Board of Management & CEO*
Financial Director   Issac Behar *Chief Financial Officer*
Treasurer   Yehoshua Ginzburg ☎ 567 5234
Company Secretary   Yoram Weissbrem
International Division   Fuhrman Zvi ☎ 567 5909

General-Lending (DCM, SL)
Head of Corporate Banking   Moshe Amit

General-Investment
Head of Investment   Dan Yahas

Syndicated Lending
Loan-Related Activities
Trade Finance   Ehud Arnon *Senior Vice President* ☎ 567 3628
Project Finance   Dan Yahas

Money Markets
Regional Head   Zvi Nissim *Liquidity Manager* ☎ 567 4645
Country Head   David Humpfries *Treasurer* ☎ +44 (171) 872 9912
                                        Nachum Precel *Treasurer* ☎ +1 (212) 782 2000

Foreign Exchange
Tel: 567 3216 **Fax:** 567 3396
Head of Sales   Raya Jona *Head* ☎ 567 3216
Corporate Sales   Nachum Edelstein ☎ 567 3449
Head of Trading   Tal Vardi ☎ 567 3262

FX Traders / Sales People
Institutional Sales   Amos Fish *Head* ☎ 567 3442
FX Options   David Mermer ☎ 567 3549
FX Spot   Neil Corney ☎ 567 3549

Euromoney Directory 1999   **741**

ISRAEL (+972)　　　　　　　　www.euromoneydirectory.com

Bank Hapoalim BM (cont)

Risk Management
IR Swaps Sales / Marketing　　　　Raya Yong
IR Swaps Trading　　　　　　　　Didier Issimini

Foreign Exchange Derivatives / Risk Management
Global Head　　　　　　　　　　Schmulik Reuveni
Cross-Currency Swaps, Trading　　Raya Yong

OTC Credit Derivatives
Head　　　　　　　　　　　　　Tal Vardi

Exchange-Traded Derivatives
Head　　　　　　　　　　　　　Tal Vardi

Settlement / Clearing
Department: Securities Operations Department
Tel: 567 5792/3 Fax: 567 6318
Head of Settlement / Clearing　　Shalom Bitton *Manager*

Global Custody
Department: Securities Operations Department
Tel: 567 5792/3 Fax: 567 6318
Regional Head　　　　　　　　　Shalom Bitton *Manager*

Other (Global Custody)
Ruti Barzlai [T] **567 4476** [F] **567 6526**
Asher Windzberg [T] **567 5097**

Asset Management
Head　　　　　　　　　　　　　Menahem Zuta

Other Departments
Chief Credit Officer　　　　　　Dafna Pelli
Correspondent Banking　　　　　Francine Hope
Cash Management　　　　　　　Shouki Ginzburg

Administration
Head of Administration　　　　　Yoram Weissbrem
Head of Marketing　　　　　　　Noga Barak

Technology & Systems
　　　　　　　　　　　　　　　Itsak Rosenberk

Legal / In-House Counsel
　　　　　　　　　　　　　　　Channa Rosenberg

Compliance
　　　　　　　　　　　　　　　Yosef Yarom

Bank Leumi Le-Israel BM　　　　　　　　　　　　Head Office

19 Hertzel Street, Tel Aviv 61000
Tel: (3) 514 8111 Fax: (3) 566 1872 Telex: 33586 LEUMI IL Swift: LUMI IL IT Reuters: BLLTA
Treasury Operations Tel: 574 7618; Fax: 574 7618; Reuters: BLLI (Dealing)
Website: www.bankleumi.co.il

Senior Executive Officers
Chairman　　　　　　　　　　　Eitan Raff
Chief Executive Officer　　　　　Galia Maor *President & CEO*
Financial Director　　　　　　　Zeav Nahari [T] **514 8849**
International Division　　　　　Shlomo Hendel

Others (Senior Executives)
Head of Emerging Markets　　　　Yona Fogel [T] **514 9701**

Debt Capital Markets / Fixed Income
Head of Debt Capital Markets　　Chanoch Pearlman [T] **514 9443**

Equity Capital Markets
Head of Equity Capital Markets　Chanoch Pearlman [T] **514 9443**

Money Markets
Head of Money Markets　　　　　Zeav Nahari [T] **514 8849**

Administration
Head of Marketing　　　　　　　Chanoch Pearlman [T] **514 9443**

www.euromoneydirectory.com   ISRAEL (+972)

Bank Polska Kasa Opieki Tel-Aviv (Bank Pekao) Limited
Subsidiary Company

95 Allenby Street, PO Box 267, Tel Aviv 61001
Tel: (3) 564 2564; (3) 566 3641 **Fax:** (3) 566 3284; (3) 566 0840 **Telex:** 371471 **Swift:** PROKOP IL IT

Senior Executive Officers
Chairman of the Board of Directors   Henryk Pyrka ☎ **564 2566**
Chief Executive Officer   Tomasz Rydsy General Manager ☎ **564 2566**
Financial Director   Zeev Goldberg Deputy General Manager ☎ **564 2568**
Chief Operating Officer   Yosef Marco Deputy General Manager ☎ **564 2557**
Deputy General Manager   Zbigniew Magdziarz ☎ **564 2554**

Other Departments
Correspondent Banking   Benni Kobaivanov Head ☎ **564 2548**

Administration
Head of Administration   Shmuel Segal Head of Administration ☎ **564 2591**
Business Development   Alexander Woytynski ☎ **564 2581**

Banque Nationale de Paris
Representative Office

57 Rothschild Boulevard, Tel Aviv 65785
Tel: (3) 525 8686 **Fax:** (3) 525 8899

Senior Executive Officers
Directeur   Charles G Reisman

The First International Bank of Israel Limited
Head Office

Shalom Tower, 9 Ahad Ha'am Street, Tel Aviv 61290
PO Box 29036, Tel Aviv 61290
Tel: (3) 519 6111 **Fax:** (3) 510 0316 **Telex:** 341252 **Swift:** FIRB IL IT **Reuters:** FIBI **Telex:** 32373 **Telex:** 32365

Senior Executive Officers
Chairman   Yigal Arnon
Financial Director   Yehiel Mund DGM, Financial Controller
Managing Director   Shlomo Piotrkowsky
Corporate Secretary   Haim Dekez
International Division   Yehuda Levi Senior Assistant General Manager

General-Lending (DCM, SL)
Head of Corporate Banking   Leora R Meridor Senior AGM, Credit Division

General-Investment
Head of Investment   Shlomo Rothman Senior AGM

Syndicated Lending

Loan-Related Activities
Trade Finance   Eze Gahtan Senior General Manager's Assistant

Other (Trade Finance)
Documentary Credits   Gilda Schmukler Manager

Foreign Exchange
Head of Foreign Exchange   Yehuda Levi Senior Assistant General Manager
Regional Head   Vicky Douzly Manager

FX Traders / Sales People
    Arie Tokman Chief Dealer

Settlement / Clearing
Operations   David Ouziel Deputy General Manager

Other Departments
Correspondent Banking   Eze Gahtan Senior General Manager's Assistant

Administration
Head of Administration   David Ouziel Deputy General Manager
Head of Marketing   Shlomo Rothman Senior AGM

Technology & Systems
    David Ouziel Deputy General Manager

Legal / In-House Counsel
    Haim Dekez Corporate Secretary

Public Relations
    Marit Gilat

Euromoney Directory 1999   **743**

ISRAEL (+972) www.euromoneydirectory.com

The First International Bank of Israel Limited (cont)
Accounts / Audit
  Dov Goldfriend

IDB Holding Corporation Limited
Head Office

Formerly known as: IDB Bankholding Corporation Limited
'The Tower', 3 Daniel Frisch Street, Tel Aviv 64731
Tel: (3) 696 6766 Fax: (3) 695 2069
Website: www.idbh.co.il

Senior Executive Officers
Chairman & CEO	Raphael Recanati
Treasurer	Rina Cohen *Comptroller*
Joint Managing Director	Oudi Recanati
Joint Managing Director	Leon Recanati
Company Secretary	Arthur Caplin

Israel Continental Bank Limited
Head Office

65 Rothschild Boulevard, PO Box 37406, Tel Aviv 61373
Tel: (3) 564 1616 Fax: (3) 620 0399 Telex: 341447 Swift: ISCO IL IT Reuters: ICBI

Senior Executive Officers
Chairman	A Sivan
Treasurer	E Rosenberg
Managing Director	P Horev
Deputy Managing Director	Y Orbach [T] 564 1530
International Division	M Gozez *International Banking* [T] 564 1641

Foreign Exchange
Global Head
  L Lentzitsky *Manager* [T] 564 1601

Risk Management
Exchange-Traded Derivatives
FX Futures; FX Options
  L Lentzitsky *Manager* [T] 564 1601

Other Departments
Commodities / Bullion
  L Lentzitsky *Manager* [T] 564 1601

Administration
Legal / In-House Counsel
  Y Zohar [T] 564 1638
  Livigorel Apple

Israel Discount Bank Limited
Head Office

27 Yehuda Halevi Street, Tel Aviv 65136
Tel: (3) 514 5555 Fax: (3) 514 5346 Telex: 35611 Swift: IDBL IL IT Email: tqb@discountbank.net
Website: www.discountbank.net

Senior Executive Officers
Chairman	Arie Mientkavich
President & CEO	David Granot
Financial Director	Joseph Cohen *SEVP & Comptroller*
Company Secretary	Ruth Moshkovitz
International Division	Michael Fokschaner *EVP, International Banking*

Others (Senior Executives)
Deposits Savings & Capital Markets	Amnon Goldschmidt *Senior Executive Vice President*
Credit	Naaman Gur *Senior Executive Vice President*
Branches & Marketing	Ilan Segev *Senior Executive Vice President*
Computers & Operations	Menahem Gutterman *Senior Vice President*
Personnel & Property	Sasson Maron *Executive Vice President*
Executive Vice President	David Hermesh

Debt Capital Markets / Fixed Income
Department: Securities Division
Tel: 514 5575 Fax: 514 5719
Head of Debt Capital Markets
  Gadi Landau *Head of Securities Division* [T] 514 5575 [F] 514 5714
  Robert Aladjem *Head, Foreign Securities & Non-Residents* [T] 514 6504
  [F] 514 5799

Head of Fixed Income Trading
  Reuben Rashty *Head of Investment Counselling* [T] 514 5575 [F] 514 5719

www.euromoneydirectory.com ISRAEL (+972)

Government Bonds
Head of Sales Reuben Rashty *Head of Investment Counselling* T 514 5575 F 514 5719

Fixed-Income Research
Head of Fixed Income Tami Diamenstein

Equity Capital Markets
Department: Securities Division
Head of Equity Capital Markets Gadi Landau *Head of Securities Division* T 514 5575 F 514 5714
Head of Sales Reuben Rashty *Head of Investment Counselling* T 514 5575 F 514 5719

International Equities
Head of Sales Oren Shilony *Head of Foreign Securities Section* T 514 6514 F 514 5799
Head of Trading Oren Shilony *Head of Foreign Securities Section* T 514 6514 F 514 5799

Equity Research
Head of Equity Research Tami Diamenstein

Convertibles / Equity-Linked
Head of Sales Reuben Rashty *Head of Investment Counselling* T 514 5575 F 514 5719
Head of Trading Reuben Rashty *Head of Investment Counselling* T 514 5575 F 514 5719

Equity Repo / Securities Lending
Head Reuben Rashty *Head of Investment Counselling* T 514 5575 F 514 5719

Syndicated Lending
Tel: 514 5578 **Fax:** 514 5346
Head of Origination; Head of Syndication; Head of Trading Michal Alon *Head of International Banking Relations* T 514 5578
  F 514 5346

Loan-Related Activities
Trade Finance Michal Alon *Head of International Banking Relations* T 514 5578
  F 514 5346
Project Finance Naaman Gur *Senior Executive Vice President*

Money Markets
Tel: 514 5500 **Fax:** 514 5650 **Reuters:** IDBT
Head of Money Markets Ilan Raviv *Manager, Foreign Exchange & Money Markets Dept.*
  T 514 5508

Foreign Exchange
Head of Foreign Exchange Ilan Raviv *Manager, Foreign Exchange & Money Markets Dept.*
  T 514 5598
Head of Trading Ron Bedny *Chief Dealer* T 514 5500

FX Traders / Sales People
  Udi Sella *Senior Dealer* T 514 5500

Global Custody
Department: Securities & Capital Markets
Tel: 514 5695 **Fax:** 514 5799 **Telex:** 341126
Head of Global Custody Avi Kweller *Head of Foreign Investors Section* T 514 5695 F 514 5799

Other Departments
Correspondent Banking Michal Alon *Head of International Banking Relations* T 514 5578
  F 514 5346

Administration
Legal / In-House Counsel
  Lior Horer *Chief Legal Advisor*

Leumi Mortgage Bank Limited Subsidiary Company

31/37 Montefiore Street, Tel Aviv 65201
PO Box 69, Tel Aviv 61000
Tel: (3) 564 8444 Fax: (3) 564 8334

Senior Executive Officers
Chairman A Zeldman
General Manager R Zabag
Assistant General Manager H Wasserzog
Company Secretary M Ginsbourg

Euromoney Directory 1999 **745**

ISRAEL (+972)   www.euromoneydirectory.com

Tefahot Israel Mortgage Bank Limited   Head Office

9 Heleni Hamalka Street, Jerusalem 91902
PO Box 93, Jerusalem 91000
Tel: (2) 675 5222 Fax: (2) 675 5344

Senior Executive Officers
Chairman   David Brodet
Managing Director   Uri Würzburger
Deputy & Permanent Alternate to GM   Eliezer Wolf

Relationship Manager
Provident Funds   Zvi Greenwald *Manager*

Syndicated Lending

Other (Trade Finance)
Mortgage Division   Israel Segal *AGM & Manager, Bank Spokesman*

Settlement / Clearing
Operations   Doron Nachmani *AGM, Planning, Coordination & Control*

Administration
Head of Administration   Eli Tovel *AGM & Manager*

Technology & Systems
Information Systems Division   Daniel Eisenband *Manager*

Legal / In-House Counsel
Legal Adviser   Eliezer Wolf *Deputy & Permanent Alternate to GM*

Accounts / Audit
Internal Auditor   David Tal
Accounting Division   Menachem Steiner *Senior AGM, Comptroller & Manager*

Other (Administration)
Branch Administration   Yitzhak Meir *AGM & Head*

Union Bank of Israel Limited   Head Office

6/8 Ahuzat Bayit Street, Tel Aviv 65143
PO Box 2428, Tel Aviv 61024
Tel: (3) 519 1463 Fax: (3) 519 1606 Telex: 33493 Swift: UNBK IL IT Reuters: UBOI Cable: UNIONBANK
General Telex: 33494

Senior Executive Officers
Chairman of the Board   David Friedmann
Vice Chairman of the Board   Y Landau
Chief Executive Officer   Benjamin Oshman *CEO & General Manager*
Financial Director   Gil Kurtz *Head, Finance Division* ☎ **519 1235**
Chief Operating Officer   Aviram Shafrir *Head, Operational Division* ☎ **519 1435**
International Division   Zéev Gutman *Head, Capital Markets & International Division* ☎ **519 1231**
    Robert Zentler *Head, Risk Management & International Banking*
    ☎ **519 1246**

Others (Senior Executives)
Member of the Board   O Eliahu
    S Eliahu
    A Horev
    S Lahat
    I Manor
    M Reis
    M Shachal
    M Shavit
    M Steingart
    A Tiberg
    P Zackai
Ramat-Gan Diamond Branch   S Mosseri *Manager*

General-Lending (DCM, SL)
Head of Corporate Banking   S Eshel

Debt Capital Markets / Fixed Income
Global Head   Zéev Gutman *Head, Capital Markets & International Division* ☎ **519 1231**

Risk Management
Head of Risk Management   Robert Zentler *Head, Risk Management & International Banking*
    ☎ **519 1246**

www.euromoneydirectory.com ISRAEL (+972)

Administration
Technology & Systems
 Aviram Shafrir *Head, Operational Division* ☏ **519 1435**
Legal / In-House Counsel
 Amos Rosenzweig *Legal Counsel*
Public Relations
 Noam Pintor *Head, Human Resources & Branches Division* ☏ **519 1311**

United Mizrahi Bank Limited Head Office

MIZRAHI BANK

113 Allenby Road, Tel Aviv 61002
PO Box 309, Tel Aviv
Tel: (3) 567 9211 Fax: (3) 560 4780 Telex: 33625 MIZBKIL Swift: MIZB IL IT Email: umb-sec@mizrahi.co.il
Website: www.mizrahi.co.il

Senior Executive Officers
Chairman David Brodet ☏ **567 9278**
President & Chief Executive Officer Victor Medina ☏ **567 9207**
Financial Director Samuel Messenberg ☏ **567 9530**
Chief Operating Officer Arik Orlev ☏ **563 4434**
Treasurer Ruben Adler *Manager, Finance & Planning* ☏ **567 9364**

Debt Capital Markets / Fixed Income
Domestic Government Bonds
Head of Sales Itzchak Anielli ☏ **567 7962**
Head of Trading Ravit Moshe ☏ **567 7013**
Head of Research Ronen Algali ☏ **567 9572**
Eurobonds
Head of Sales Danny Frisch ☏ **525 3021**
Head of Trading Ella Gilboa ☏ **525 3020**
Head of Research Ezra Shayo ☏ **567 9157**
Libor-Based / Floating-Rate Products
FRN Origination Jacob Harpaz *Assistant Manager* ☏ **567 2103**

Equity Capital Markets
Domestic Equities
Head of Sales Tova Paz ☏ **567 9972**
Head of Trading Samuel Huper ☏ **567 9592**
Head of Research Ezra Shayo ☏ **567 9157**
International Equities
Head of Sales Ari Licht ☏ **525 2573**
Head of Trading Ella Gilboa ☏ **525 3020**
Head of Research David Kimche *Senior Vice President & Head* ☏ **567 9178**

Money Markets
Department: Trading in Financial Markets Sector
Global Head David Kimche *Senior Vice President & Head* ☏ **567 9178**
Domestic Commercial Paper
Head of Trading Jacob Harpaz *Assistant Manager* ☏ **567 2103**

Foreign Exchange
Department: Trading in Financial Markets Sector
Tel: 567 9666
Global Head David Kimche *Senior Vice President & Head* ☏ **567 9178**
Head of Trading Fin Kvitny *Chief Dealer* ☏ **567 9425**
FX Traders / Sales People
 Yehezkel Tubin *Dealer*
 Zippora Meir *Dealer*
 Ilan Zedaka *Dealer*
 Sandrin Finkelstein *Dealer*

Risk Management
Global Head Jacob Harpaz *Assistant Manager* ☏ **567 2103**
IR Swaps Trading Doron Levy *Manager* ☏ **567 9540**
IR Options Trading Jacob Harpaz *Assistant Manager* ☏ **567 2103**
Foreign Exchange Derivatives / Risk Management
Cross-Currency Swaps, Sales / Marketing; Jacob Harpaz *Assistant Manager* ☏ **567 2103**
Vanilla FX option Sales; Vanilla FX option Trading

ISRAEL (+972)

United Mizrahi Bank Limited (cont)
Other Currency Swap / FX Options Personnel

Shimon Vaknio ☎ **567 9425**
Avi Sharif ☎ **567 9425**

Exchange-Traded Derivatives
Global Head   Jacob Harpaz *Assistant Manager* ☎ **567 2103**

Settlement / Clearing
Regional Head   Japhet Tsedaka ☎ **567 9014**
Equity Settlement; Fixed-Income Settlement;   Shalom Cohen ☎ **567 9738**
Derivatives Settlement
Foreign Exchange Settlement   Japhet Tsedaka ☎ **567 9014**

Other Departments
Proprietary Trading   Jacob Harpaz *Assistant Manager* ☎ **567 2103**
Private Banking   Gad Arbel *Senior Manager* ☎ **567 9524**

ITALY
(+39)

Banca d'Italia   🏛 Central Bank

Via Nazionale 91, I-00184 Rome
Tel: (06) 479 21 **Fax:** (06) 479 22253

Senior Executive Officers
Governor   Antonio Fazio

Akros Finanziaria

Corso Italia 3, I-20122 Milan
Tel: (02) 8025 1 **Fax:** (02) 8025 376 **Swift:** AKRO IT MM

Debt Capital Markets / Fixed Income
Head of Debt Capital Markets   Mr Galletti ☎ **8025 243**

Government Bonds
Head of Trading   Enzo Chiesa ☎ **8025 240**

Eurobonds
Head of Trading   Vaifro Zullato ☎ **7200 0065**

Bonds - General
Domestic Fixed Income Trading   Cesare Pozzi ☎ **7200 0101**

Equity Capital Markets
Head of Equity Capital Markets   Mr Galletti ☎ **8025 243**
Head of Trading   Paolo Barbieri ☎ **8025 586**

Other (Equity Research)
Sales   James Kettner ☎ **8025 935**

Foreign Exchange
Reuters: AKMI
Head of Trading   Cesare Nuti ☎ **7200 0103**

Risk Management

Fixed Income Derivatives / Risk Management
IR Swaps Trading   Enzo Chiesa ☎ **8025 240**

Foreign Exchange Derivatives / Risk Management
Spot / Forwards Trading   Cesare Nuti ☎ **7200 0103**

Exotic Options (Barriers, Range, Timers, Digitals, Faders etc)
Trading   Mr Queirolo ☎ **7200 0103**
    Mr Scoccimaro ☎ **7200 0103**

Exchange-Traded Derivatives
Global Head   Paolo Barbieri ☎ **8025 586**

Other Departments
Private Banking   Francesco Cosmelli ☎ **8025 918**

Administration
Head of Administration   A Moscatelli *Director of Administration*

ITALY (+39)

Albertini & C SIM SpA
Head Office

Via Olona 2, I-20123 Milan
Tel: (02) 7245 1 **Fax:** (02) 8645 3653 **Telex:** 334079 **Email:** info@albertinisim.it

Senior Executive Officers
Chairman — Isidoro Albertini
Chief Executive Officer — Alberto Albertini *Managing Director*
Financial Director — Fabio Garlandini *Accounting Manager*
Treasurer — Angelo Drusiani
Managing Director — Alberto Albertini
International Division — Fabio Ferrando *Head of Sales*

Debt Capital Markets / Fixed Income
Head of Fixed Income — Stefano Maltese

Equity Capital Markets
Head of Equity Capital Markets — Robert Meier

Equity Repo / Securities Lending
Head — Sacques Torri

Settlement / Clearing
Head of Settlement / Clearing — Davide Vannisanti

Asset Management
Head — Marzio Zocca

Administration

Technology & Systems
— Davide Solbiati

Arab Banking Corporation (BSC)
Full Branch Office

Alternative trading name: ABC
Via Santa Maria, Fulcorina 6, I-20123 Milan
Tel: (02) 863 331; (02) 861 574 **Fax:** (02) 8645 0117 **Telex:** 322240 ABC MII **Reuters:** ABCX

Senior Executive Officers
General Manager — Jean Takchi
International Division — Sami Bengharsa *Deputy General Manager*

General-Lending (DCM, SL)
Head of Corporate Banking — Danilo Pavesi

Foreign Exchange
Telex: 322080 ABC FX I
Head of Foreign Exchange — Guido Bacci

Other Departments
Chief Credit Officer — Angelo Fossati

Administration
Head of Administration — Grace D'Ambros

ARCA Merchant SpA
Head Office

Via della Moscova 3, I-20121 Milan
Tel: (02) 636 121 **Fax:** (02) 2900 5511 **Telex:** 352132

ARCA SIM SpA
Head Office

Formerly known as: Arca Commissionaria SpA
Via della Moscova 3, I-20121 Milan
Tel: (02) 636 1253 **Fax:** (02) 2900 2213 **Telex:** 352132 ARCSIM I **Email:** info@arcasim.it **Reuters:** ARCSIM
Bloomberg: ARCA

Senior Executive Officers
Chairman — V Coda
President — Battini Fausto
Chief Executive Officer — Gianni Rossi
Managing Director / General Manager — Cesa Franco
International Division — Gianni Rossi

Euromoney Directory 1999 **749**

ITALY (+39)　　　www.euromoneydirectory.com

ARCA SIM SpA (cont)
Debt Capital Markets / Fixed Income
Department: Eurobond Desk
Head of Fixed Income	Gianni Rossi
Head of Fixed Income Sales	Carlo Franchini
Head of Fixed Income Trading	Gianni Rossi

Government Bonds
Head of Sales; Head of Trading	Claudio Ripamonti

Emerging Market Bonds
Head of Emerging Markets	Gianni Rossi

Fixed-Income Repo
Head of Repo	Claudio Ripamonti

Equity Capital Markets
Head of Equity Capital Markets; Head of Trading	Giorgio Pagani

Domestic Equities
Head of Sales	Giorgio Pagani
Head of Trading	Giorgio Pagani

International Equities
Head of Sales; Head of Trading	Giorgio Pagani

Equity Research
Head of Equity Research	Giovanni D'Amico

Money Markets
Domestic Commercial Paper
Head of Sales; Head of Trading	Claudio Ripamonti

Foreign Exchange
Head of Foreign Exchange	Gianni Rossi

Risk Management
Head of Risk Management	Aldo Furlani

Settlement / Clearing
Head of Settlement / Clearing	Cesare Ferrari

Administration
Head of Administration	Cesare Ferrari

Associazione Nazionale Banche Private — Head Office
Via Domenichino 5, I-20149 Milan
PO Box 1803, Milan
Tel: (02) 4801 0278 **Fax:** (02) 4801 0137 **Telex:** 334355 ASSBNK I

Senior Executive Officers
Chairman	Tancredi Bianchi
Chief Executive Officer	Lorenzo Frignati

Banca Agricola Mantovana SCaRL — Head Office
Corso Vittorio Emanuele 30, I-46100 Mantova
Tel: (0376) 331 1 **Fax:** (0376) 331 881; (0376) 331 261 **Telex:** 300435 BAM **Swift:** BAMN IT 22 **Reuters:** BAMM

Senior Executive Officers
Chairman	Piermaria Pacchioni
Chief Executive Officer	Mario Petroni
Financial Director	Leo Riveri *Risk Manager*
Treasurer	Fausto Fontanesi
International Division	Primo Brioni

Risk Management
Country Head	Leo Riveri *Risk Manager*

Other Departments
Correspondent Banking	Primo Brioni

Administration

Technology & Systems
	Maurizio Bonizzi

Legal / In-House Counsel
	Antonio Cerescioli

www.euromoneydirectory.com   ITALY (+39)

Public Relations
Graziano Mangoni

Banca Agricola Popolare di Ragusa SCaRL   Head Office

Viale Europa 65, Ragusa
Tel: (0932) 603 111 **Fax:** (0932) 603 286 **Telex:** 970256 BAPRGD

Senior Executive Officers
Chairman   Mario Scinina
Chief Executive Officer   Giovanni Cartia
Financial Director   Francesco DeStefano ☏ **603 416**
Treasurer   Anna Maria Puglisi ☏ **603 315**

Debt Capital Markets / Fixed Income
Domestic Government Bonds
Head of Sales   Anna Maria Puglisi ☏ **603 315**
Head of Trading   Felice Garozzo ☏ **603 219**

Eurobonds
Head of Sales   Francesco DeStefano ☏ **603 416**
Head of Trading   Anna Maria Puglisi ☏ **603 315**

Libor-Based / Floating-Rate Products
Asset Swaps   Felice Garozzo ☏ **603 219**
Asset Swaps (Sales)   Giuseppe Ini ☏ **603 212**

Fixed-Income Repo
Sales   Stefania Occhipinti ☏ **603 362**

Equity Capital Markets
Domestic Equities
Head of Sales   Giuseppina Fiorilla ☏ **603 326**
    Giovanna Occhipinti ☏ **603 366**
Head of Trading   Giuseppina Fiorilla ☏ **603 326**
    Giovanna Occhipinti ☏ **603 366**

Warrants
Head of Sales   Giuseppina Fiorilla ☏ **603 326**
    Giovanna Occhipinti ☏ **603 366**
Head of Trading   Giuseppina Fiorilla ☏ **603 326**
    Giovanna Occhipinti ☏ **603 366**

Money Markets
Wholesale Deposits
Marketing   Anna Maria Puglisi ☏ **603 315**
Head of Sales   Liliana Distefano ☏ **603 316**

Foreign Exchange
Head of Trading   G Battista Cartia ☏ **603 258**
FX Traders / Sales People
    Davide Nobile *Trader* ☏ **603 270**

Risk Management
Foreign Exchange Derivatives / Risk Management
Cross-Currency Swaps, Sales / Marketing   G Battista Cartia ☏ **603 258**
    Davide Nobile *Trader* ☏ **603 270**
Cross-Currency Swaps, Trading   G Battista Cartia ☏ **603 258**
    Davide Nobile *Trader* ☏ **603 270**
Vanilla FX option Sales   G Battista Cartia ☏ **603 258**
    Davide Nobile *Trader* ☏ **603 270**
Vanilla FX option Trading   G Battista Cartia ☏ **603 258**
    Davide Nobile *Trader* ☏ **603 270**

Banca Akros   Head Office

Corso Italia, 3, I-20122 Milan
Tel: (02) 8025 1 **Fax:** (02) 8025 300

Senior Executive Officers
Chairman   Oscar Zannoni
Chief Executive Officer   Marco Turrina
Treasurer   Carlo Portoni

Debt Capital Markets / Fixed Income
Global Head   Cesare Pozzi *Manager*

ITALY (+39)   www.euromoneydirectory.com

Banca Akros (cont)

Equity Capital Markets
Global Head   Pablo Barbieri *Manager*
Foreign Exchange
Global Head   Cesare Nuti *Manager*
Risk Management
Global Head   Luigi Lanzolo *Manager*
Corporate Finance / M&A Advisory
Global Head   Buccio Galletti *Manager*
Settlement / Clearing
Regional Head   Roberto Bozzi

Banca Antoniana-Popolare Veneta   Head Office

Alternative trading name: Banca Antonveneta
Via Verdi 13/15, I-35100 Padova
Tel: (049) 839 111 **Fax:** (049) 839 605; (049) 839 995 **Telex:** 432047 ANTEC **Swift:** ANTB IT **Reuters:** ANTX
Website: www.antonveneta.it

Senior Executive Officers
Chairman   Dino Marchiorello
Chief Executive Officer   Silvano Pontello
Financial Director   Natalino Oggiano
Chief Operating Officer   Franco Zorzi
Managing Director / General Manager Silvano Pontello

Debt Capital Markets / Fixed Income
Head of Debt Capital Markets   Natilino Oggiano
Foreign Exchange
Head of Foreign Exchange   Roberto Pagani
Corporate Finance / M&A Advisory
Head of Corporate Finance   Aldo Carosio

Banca Carige SpA   Head Office

Formerly known as: Cassa di Risparmio di Genova e Imperia
Via Caasa di Risparmio 15, I-16123 Genoa
PO Box 897, I-16100 Genoa
Tel: (010) 579 1 **Fax:** (010) 4000; (010) 2747 **Telex:** 270089 CARIGE I **Swift:** CRGE IT GG **Email:** carige@carige.it
Reuters: CRGE **Cable:** CARIGE BANK
Website: www.carige.it

Senior Executive Officers
Chairman   Fausto Cuocolo ☎ **579 2309**
Chief Executive Officer   Giovanni Berneschi *General Manager* ☎ **579 2306**
Financial Director   Achille Tori *Executive* ☎ **579 2576**
Chief Operating Officer   Renzo Oldrati *Assistant General Manager* ☎ **579 2521**
Treasurer   Alfredo Sanguinetto *Executive* ☎ **579 2398**
General Manager   Giovanni Berneschi ☎ **579 2306**
International Division   Amedeo Marchi *Senior Manager* ☎ **579 2412**

Debt Capital Markets / Fixed Income
Department: Direzione Finanza E Provvista
Tel: 579 2576 **Fax:** 579 4590
Government Bonds
Head of Trading   Enrico Viale *Manager* ☎ **579 2394**
Eurobonds
Head of Trading   Marco Capurro ☎ **579 4560**
Emerging Market Bonds
Head of Trading   Claudia Capelli ☎ **579 2749**
Libor-Based / Floating-Rate Products
FRN Trading   Maria Christina Rando ☎ **579 2598**
Fixed-Income Repo
Head of Repo; Head of Trading   Gino Guerisoli *Manager* ☎ **579 2247**

Equity Capital Markets
Tel: 579 2268 **Fax:** 579 2239
Head of Equity Capital Markets   Domenico Zuccarello

www.euromoneydirectory.com ITALY (+39)

Domestic Equities
Head of Trading Domenico Zuccarello
International Equities
Head of Trading Marco Capurro ☎ **579 4560**
Syndicated Lending
Tel: 579 4215 **Fax:** 579 2239
Head of Syndication Emilio Chiesi *Manager* ☎ **579 4215**
Loan-Related Activities
Trade Finance Angelo Balliana *Manager* ☎ **579 2361**
Project Finance Angelo Maura *Manager* ☎ **579 2825**
Money Markets
Tel: 579 4215 **Fax:** 579 4590
Head of Money Markets Maria Christina Rando ☎ **579 2598**
Foreign Exchange
Tel: 579 2567 **Fax:** 579 4590
Head of Foreign Exchange Giacomo Burro *Manager*
FX Traders / Sales People
 Paolo Palazzo ☎ **579 2594**
 Carla Cardarelli ☎ **579 2594**

Risk Management
Tel: 579 2576 **Fax:** 579 4904
Head of Risk Management Achille Tori *Executive* ☎ **579 2576**
OTC Equity Derivatives
Head Giambattista Pesce ☎ **579 2594**
Other (Equity Derivatives)
 Paolo Palazzo ☎ **579 2594**

Settlement / Clearing
Head of Settlement / Clearing Giuliano Centonze ☎ **579 2591**
Fixed-Income Settlement Luca Amelotti ☎ **579 2675**
Other Departments
Correspondent Banking Luigi Perigotti *Manager* ☎ **579 2340**
Administration
Business Development Ugo Galasso *Manager* ☎ **579 2663**
Head of Marketing Ugo Galasso *Manager* ☎ **579 2663**
Technology & Systems
 Giorgio Seronello *Senior Manager* ☎ **579 2322**
Legal / In-House Counsel
 Giancarlo Bach *Senior Manager* ☎ **579 2126**
Compliance
 Luca Sulpasso ☎ **579 2565**
Public Relations
 Emilio Pietro Molinari *Senior Manager* ☎ **579 2520**
Accounts / Audit
 Mario de Negri *Senior Manager* ☎ **579 2012**

Banca Cassa di Risparmio di Savigliano SpA Head Office

Formerly known as: Cassa di Risparmio di Savigliano
Piazza del Popolo 15, I-12038 Savigliano
Tel: (0172) 203 1 **Fax:** (0172) 203 203 **Telex:** 210511 CARSAV I **Swift:** SARC IT 2S
Senior Executive Officers
Chairman G Battista Rocca ☎ **203 281**
Managing Director / General Manager Giuseppe Allocco ☎ **203 201**
Foreign Exchange
Global Head Enrica Massimino ☎ **203 246**

Banca Cassa di Risparmio di Tortona SpA Head Office

Piazza Duomo 13, I-15057 Tortona
Tel: (0131) 819 1; (0131) 819 427 **Fax:** (0131) 815 781 **Telex:** 215040 **Swift:** TORC IT 22 **Email:** ctort@tor.it
Senior Executive Officers
Chairman Vittorio Moro
General Manager Luigi Cremonti
Deputy General Manager Dino Pastore

ITALY (+39)   www.euromoneydirectory.com

Banca Cassa di Risparmio di Tortona SpA (cont)
Money Markets
Global Head   Giovanni Vaccarella
Foreign Exchange
Global Head   Giovanni Vaccarella

Banca Commerciale Italiana   Head Office

Piazza della Scala, 6, I-20121 Milan
Tel: (02) 8850 1 Fax: (02) 8850 3026 Telex: 532465 BCI I Swift: BCIT IT MM
Website: www.bci.it

Senior Executive Officers
Chairman	Luigi Fausti
Vice Chairman	Gianfanco Gutty
Financial Director; Treasurer	Alberto Varisco
Managing Director	Alberto Abelli
Managing Director	Pier Francesco Saviotti
General Manager	Luigi Crippa
General Manager	Franco Riolo
General Manager	Enrico Meucci
General Manager	Giovanni Tedesco
General Manager, Corporate Lending	Riccardo Ferrari
Company Secretary	Gerardo Rizzi

Others (Senior Executives)

Guido Ainis *Deputy General Manager*
Vittorio Guerriero Conti *Deputy General Manager*
Alberto Geremia *Deputy General Director*
Marco Paolillo *Deputy General Manager*

General-Investment
Head of Investment   Dario Cossutta *Head, Investment Banking* ☏ **7601 2850**

Debt Capital Markets / Fixed Income
Head of Fixed Income	Luciano Steve ☏ **8850 2191**
Head of Fixed Income Sales	Rony Hamaui ☏ **8850 3059** ✉ **rhamaui@bci.it**
Head of Fixed Income Trading	Luciano Steve ☏ **8850 2191**

Government Bonds
Head of Sales	Fabio Matti ☏ **8540 9316**
Head of Trading	Giovanni Rossetti ☏ **8540 9102**
Head of Syndication; Head of Origination	Mario Arnaboldi ☏ **8850 2303**

Eurobonds
Head of Sales	Fabio Matti ☏ **8540 9316**
Head of Trading	Gabriele Fiorucci ☏ **8540 9030**

Libor-Based / Floating-Rate Products
FRN Sales	Fabio Matti ☏ **8540 9316**
FRN Trading	Luciano Steve ☏ **8850 2191**
Asset Swaps; Asset Swaps (Sales)	Gianni Movia ☏ **8540 9385**

Fixed-Income Repo
Head of Repo   Mario Proverbio ☏ **8540 9326**

Equity Capital Markets
Head of Equity Capital Markets   Marco Cerrina-Feroni ☏ **8850 3584**

Domestic Equities
Head of Sales	Pietro Battistella ☏ **8540 9275**
Head of Trading	Marco Bertolini ☏ **8540 9101**

International Equities
Head of Sales; Head of Trading   Orazio Ruggeri ☏ **8540 9004**

Convertibles / Equity-Linked
Head of Sales   Orazio Ruggeri ☏ **8540 9004**

Equity Repo / Securities Lending
Head	Giorgio Dainotto ☏ **8540 9318** ✉ **gdainotto@bci.it**
Marketing & Product Development	Vito Sgobba ☏ **8540 9314**
Head of Trading	Giorgio Dainotto ☏ **8540 9318** ✉ **gdainotto@bci.it**

Money Markets
Head of Money Markets   Giuseppe Attaná ☏ **8540 9305**

Domestic Commercial Paper
Head of Sales   Fabio Matti ☏ **8540 9316**

www.euromoneydirectory.com　　　　　　　ITALY (+39)

Foreign Exchange
Global Head　　　　　　　　　　Giuliano Vercesi ☏ **8540 9200**
Head of Institutional Sales　　　　Fabio Matti ☏ **8540 9316**
Corporate Sales　　　　　　　　 Giulio Sartirana ☏ **8540 9313**
Head of Trading　　　　　　　　 Giuliano Vercesi ☏ **8540 9200**

Risk Management

OTC Equity Derivatives
Sales; Trading　　　　　　　　　Orazio Ruggeri ☏ **8540 9004**

Global Custody
Head of Global Custody　　　　　Elisabetta Pellichero *Head of GSS Relationships & Network Management*
　　　　　　　　　　　　　　　☏ **8850 2466** ✉ epellichero@bci.it

Asset Management
Head　　　　　　　　　　　　　Giovanni Landi ☏ **8850 3828**

Banca Cooperativa Valsabbina　　　　　　　　　　　Head Office
Via Molino 4, I-25078 Vestone
Tel: (0365) 829 1 **Fax:** (0365) 820 647 **Telex:** 300492 VABANK I **Swift:** BCVA IT 2V **Cable:** BANCAVALSABBINA

Senior Executive Officers
President　　　　　　　　　　　Piero Caggioli
General Manager　　　　　　　　Ezio Soardi

Others (Senior Executives)
　　　　　　　　　　　　　　　Spartaco Gafforini *Vice General Manager*

Banca di Credito Cooperativo di Carrú e del Monregalese Scrl
Head Office

Formerly known as: Cassa Rurale ed Artigiana di Carrú e del Monregalese Scrl
Via Stazione 10, I-12061 Carrú
Tel: (0173) 757 111 **Fax:** (0173) 750 947; (0173) 759 283 **Telex:** 210175 CARUCA I **Swift:** CARU IT 2C

Senior Executive Officers
Chairman　　　　　　　　　　　Ermanno Lugua
Chief Executive Officer　　　　　　Sergio Nano
Financial Director　　　　　　　　Pellegrino D'Aquino ☏ **757 326**

Debt Capital Markets / Fixed Income
Global Head　　　　　　　　　　Pellegrino D'Aquino ☏ **757 326**

Domestic Government Bonds
Head of Trading　　　　　　　　 Claudio Pepino ☏ **757 302**

Eurobonds
Head of Trading　　　　　　　　 Mauro Menardi ☏ **757 111**

Fixed-Income Repo
Sales　　　　　　　　　　　　　Mauro Menardi ☏ **757 111**

Equity Capital Markets

Domestic Equities
Head of Trading　　　　　　　　 Claudio Pepino ☏ **757 302**

International Equities
Head of Trading　　　　　　　　 Claudio Pepino ☏ **757 302**

Foreign Exchange
Global Head　　　　　　　　　　Alessandro Magliano ☏ **757 378**

Risk Management

Fixed Income Derivatives / Risk Management
Global Head　　　　　　　　　　Pellegrino D'Aquino ☏ **757 326**

Foreign Exchange Derivatives / Risk Management
Cross-Currency Swaps, Sales / Marketing　　Alessandro Magliano ☏ **757 378**

ITALY (+39)   www.euromoneydirectory.com

Banca di Credito Popolare Torre del Greco — Head Office

Corso Vittorio Emanuele 92/100, Torre del Greco, I-80059 Naples
Tel: (081) 849 2077 Fax: (081) 849 1487; (081) 881 1878 Telex: 710265 Swift: BCPT IT NN Cable: BCPTORRE

Senior Executive Officers
President — Salvatore Gaglione
Managing Director / General Manager — Sebastiano Russo
Managing Director / General Manager — Manilo D'Aponte

Banca CRT SpA — Head Office

Alternative trading name: Cassa di Risparmio di Torino SpA
Via XX Settembre 31, I-10121 Turin
PO Box 444, I-10100 Turin
Tel: (011) 662 1 Fax: (011) 662 4377; (011) 663 9918 Telex: 221225 Swift: CRTO IT TT
Research Tel: 662 8855 Telex: 220350 Telex: 220351 Telex: 212278 Telex: 221615
Website: www.bancacrt.it

Senior Executive Officers
Chairman — Enrico Filippi
Deputy Chairman — Giuseppe Giordana
Deputy Chief General Manager — Sergio Morra ☏ 662 3320
Deputy Chief General Manager — Edoardo Massaglia ☏ 662 3320
Chief General Manager — Giorgio Giovando
International Division — Virgilio Olmo *GM, Domestic & International Division*
Claudio Ranghino *Chief Manager, Foreign Trade & Int'l Division*
Giuseppe Canuto *Chief Manager, Foreign Branches Division*

Others (Senior Executives)
Planning — Natale Secondino *Planning & Development Manager*

General-Lending (DCM, SL)
Head of Corporate Banking — Pietro Marcone *General Manager, Finance*
Franco Maia *General Manager, Credits & Loans*

General - Treasury
Head of Treasury — Franco Ariotti *Chief Manager*

Debt Capital Markets / Fixed Income
Head of Fixed Income Trading — Bruna Cerrato ☏ 662 8500

Equity Capital Markets
Head of Trading — Dario Castello ☏ 662 8340

Syndicated Lending
Head of Syndicated Lending — Carlo Bellati

Money Markets
Head of Money Markets — Luciano Malatesta ☏ 662 8610

Foreign Exchange
Department: Foreign Exchange & Treasury
Tel: 662 4619/4830
Global Head — Franco Alloggio *Chief Dealer* ☏ 662 8700

Risk Management
Head of Risk Management — Eraldo Petrignani
Global Head — Teresio Barioglio ☏ 662 8810

Other Departments
Correspondent Banking — Amelio Lombardi *Senior Vice President*

Administration
Head of Administration — Giovanni Cozzo *General Affairs Department*
Head of Marketing — Luciano Bovini

Technology & Systems
Head Systems & Technology — Piero Bertoglio
Head, Electronic Data Processing — Giuseppe Dovolich
Head, Technology Services — Alberto de Alessi

Legal / In-House Counsel
Head, Legal — Giorgio Spagarino

Accounts / Audit
Director, Audit & Inspection — Franco Grosso
Accounting & Tax Collection — Franco Leccacorvi *General Manager*
Head, Accountancy — Giorgio Prete

Other (Administration)
Head, Secretariat — Roberto Riganti
Human Resources Management — Alfonso Bruno
Human Resources Administration — Vladimino Rambaldi
Head, Organizational Development — Pietro Augusto Percio
Head, Financial Services — Olga Morello

Banca D'Intermediazions Mobiliare IMI SpA — Head Office

Formerly known as: IMI Sigeco SIM SpA
Corso Matteotti 6, I-20121 Milan
Tel: (02) 7751 1 **Fax:** (02) 7751 2030; (02) 7751 2426 **Telex:** 314326 SIGETOI **Swift:** IMIT IT MM **Reuters:** ISIG
General Telex: 321473 IMISIMI
Website: www.bimimin.it

Senior Executive Officers
Chairman of the Board — Vittorio Serafino ☏ **(06) 5959 3902**
Chief Executive Officer — Gianfranco Mattei *Executive Vice President* ☏ **7751 2599**
Managing Director, Investment Banking — Carlo Corradini ☏ **7751 2544**
Managing Director, Risk Management & Sales — Benedetto Marti ☏ **7751 2417**
Managing Director & CFO — Pasquale Casale ☏ **7751 2506**
Company Secretary — Giuseppe Catalano ☏ **7751 2250**

Debt Capital Markets / Fixed Income
Head of Fixed Income — Leonardo Bloch ☏ **7751 6051**

Emerging Market Bonds
Head of Emerging Markets — Domenica Lella Russo ☏ **7751 6037**

Fixed-Income Repo
Head of Repo — Barbara Ferri ☏ **7751 6032**

Equity Capital Markets
Head of Equity Capital Markets — Jürgen Dennert ☏ **7751 2560**

Equity Repo / Securities Lending
Head — Barbara Ferri ☏ **7751 6032**

Money Markets
Head of Money Markets — Giuseppe Di Stefano ☏ **7751 6000**

Foreign Exchange
Head of Foreign Exchange — Giuseppe Di Stefano ☏ **7751 6000**

Settlement / Clearing
Head of Settlement / Clearing — Aurelio Mustacciuoli ☏ **7751 6000**

Global Custody
Head of Global Custody — Aurelio Mustacciuoli ☏ **7751 6000**

Other Departments
Chief Credit Officer — Mauro Filacchione ☏ **7751 2531**
Correspondent Banking — France Valcarenghi ☏ **7751 2339**

Administration
Head of Administration — Aurelio Mustacciuoli ☏ **7751 6000**

Technology & Systems
Robert Grazioli *Chief Information Officer* ☏ **7751 2024**

Compliance
Maurizio Profeta ☏ **7751 2176**

Accounts / Audit
Giovanni Palacardo ☏ **7751 2730**

Banca Intermobiliare di Investimenti e Gestioni SpA — Head Office

Alternative trading name: Bito - Bim
Formerly known as: Intermobiliare SIM
via Gramsci 7, I-10121 Turin
Tel: (011) 516 2411 **Fax:** (011) 561 9359 **Telex:** 224125 IMTO I **Email:** fxfxbito@tin.it **Reuters:** BIM01

Senior Executive Officers
Chairman — Mario Scanferlin ☏ **5162 401**
President — Franca Bruna Segre ☏ **5162 565**
Treasurer — Alfredo Petruzzelli *Treasurer* ☏ **5162 450**
General Manager — Claudio Giovannone ☏ **5162 404**
Managing Director & General Manager — Pietro D'Aguí ☏ **5162 428**

ITALY (+39)   www.euromoneydirectory.com

Banca Intermobiliare di Investimenti e Gestioni SpA (cont)
Debt Capital Markets / Fixed Income
Country Head   Renato Ponzlo *Country Head* ☎ 5162 416
Domestic Government Bonds
Head of Trading   Renato Ponzlo *Country Head* ☎ 5162 416
Eurobonds
Head of Sales   Filippo Cornio ☎ 5162 421
Emerging Market Bonds
Head of Sales   Filippo Cornio ☎ 5162 421
Equity Capital Markets
Country Head   Marco Covelli *Head, Equities & Derivatives* ☎ 5162 430
Domestic Equities
Head of Sales   Fabio Grignolio *Domestic Equity Sales* ☎ 5162 433
Head of Trading   Andrea Dolsa *Domestic Equities Trader* ☎ 5162 431
Foreign Exchange
Country Head   Mauro Rivoltella *Head, Currencies & Eurobonds* ☎ 5162 415
FX Traders / Sales People
     Sandro Amandola *FX & Derivatives Trader*
Risk Management
Country Head   Stefano Ballarini *Compliance Officer* ☎ 5162 460
Corporate Finance / M&A Advisory
Country Head   Massimo Paparella *Head, Corporate Banking* ☎ 5162 586
Settlement / Clearing
Settlement (General)   Roberto Barbero *Head, Domestic Back Office* ☎ 5162 501
     Laura Giovannelli *Head, Foreign Back Office* ☎ 5162 520

Banca Intesa SpA

Alternative trading name: Banca Intesa SpA Cariplo SpA Banco Ambrosiano Veneto SpA
Piazza Paolo Ferrari 10, I-20121 Milan
PO Box 1235, I-20100 Milan
Tel: (02) 8844 1 **Telex:** 482663 BAV CT I **Swift:** CARI IT MF 009
General Telex: 313010 CARIPL I; **Foreign Bonds & Securities Settlement Tel:** 8866 2293; **Fax:** 8866 2357; **FX & Money Markets Settlement Tel:** 8866 3458; **Fax:** 8866 5561; **Derivatives Settlement Tel:** 8866 5572; **Fax:** 8866 5504; **Fixed Income Repo Settlement Tel:** 8866 3667; **Fax:** 8866 5404
Website: www.bancaintesa.it

Senior Executive Officers
Chairman   Giovanni Bazoli
Deputy Chairman   Lucien Douroux
Deputy Chairman   Sandro Molinari
MD, Chief Executive & GM   Carlo Salvatori
Deputy Chief Executive & GM   Christian Merle
International Division   Marzio Astarita *Head of International Business Development* F 7239 7326
     Gigliola Zecchi *Head of International Business Development* F 8866 2607

Others (Senior Executives)
Member of the Board of Directors   Giovanni Bazoli *Chairman*
     Lucien Douroux *Deputy Chairman*
     Carlo Salvatori *MD, Chief Executive & GM*
     Marc Antoine Autheman *Director*
     Alfonso Desiata *Director*
     Christian Merle *Deputy Chief Executive & GM*
     Luigi Amato Molinari *Director*
     Gian Giacomo Nardozzi *Director*
     Giampio Bracchi *Director*
     Franco Modigliani *Director*
     Jean Luc Perron *Director*
     Sandro Salvati *Director*
     Jean Simon *Director*
     Gino Trombi *Director*

General-Lending (DCM, SL)
Head of Corporate Banking   Alberto Mauri

General-Investment
Head of Investment   Christian Merle *Deputy Chief Executive & GM*
Department: Board of Statutory Auditors
Chairman   Felice Martinelli

www.euromoneydirectory.com ITALY (+39)

Others (Senior Executives)
Auditors   Francesco Paolo Beato
                                        Paolo Andrea Colombo
                                        Gianluca Ponzellini
                                        Bruno Rinaldi
Alternate Auditors   Enrico Cervellera
                                        Paolo Giolla

Debt Capital Markets / Fixed Income
Head of Debt Capital Markets   Sandro Cocco ☎ **8866 5402** 📠 **8866 5403**
Department: Foreign Bonds & Securities
Tel: +39 (02) 7235 3630 **Fax:** +39 (02) 8866 2101 **Reuters:** CRPN
Global Head   Renato Tarantola *Head, Banking Finance*
Department: Fixed Income Repo
Tel: +39 (02) 7235 2620 **Fax:** +39 (02) 8866 3909 **Telex:** 310268 CRP LFX I

Fixed-Income Repo
Head of Repo   Fernando Brenna ☎ **7235 2720**
Department: Italian Bonds & Securities
Tel: +39 (02) 7235 3660 **Fax:** +39 (02) 8866 2101
Global Head   Renato Tarantola *Head, Banking Finance*

Money Markets
Tel: 7235 2780 **Fax:** 8866 3909 **Reuters:** CRPL **Telex:** 310268 CRP LFX I
Global Head   Fernando Brenna ☎ **7235 2720**

Foreign Exchange
Tel: 7235 2740 **Fax:** 8866 3909 **Reuters:** CRPM **Telex:** 310268 CRP LFX I
Global Head   Patrizia de Horatiis

Risk Management
Tel: 7235 2780 **Fax:** 8866 3909 **Reuters:** CAPO **Telex:** 310268 CRP LFX I
Global Head   Gianluca Bolla ☎ **7235 2780**

Settlement / Clearing
Department: Italian Bonds & Securities Settlements
Tel: 8866 5319 **Fax:** 8866 5543
Head of Settlement / Clearing   Renato Tarantola *Head, Banking Finance*

Asset Management
Head   Christian Merle *Deputy Chief Executive & GM*
Portfolio Management   Roberto Ranieri ☎ **7235 2860**

Other Departments
Correspondent Banking   Gian Renato Banfi
Economic Research   Renzo Avesani *Risk Management & Research Division* ☎ **8866 5795**
                                        📠 **8866 3909** ✉ rga@opoipi.it

Administration
Legal / In-House Counsel
Head, Legal Affairs   Giovanni Baroni
Public Relations
Head, External Relations   Carlo Doneda
Accounts / Audit
Head, Planning & Control Area   Giampiero Auletta Armenise
Head, Internal Auditing   Renato Della Rivas
Other (Administration)
Head, Human Resources Area   Beniamino Anselmi

Banca delle Marche SpA
Head Office
Via Alessandro Ghislieri 6, I-60035 Jesi
Tel: (0731) 539 1 **Fax:** (0731) 539 695 **Telex:** 560053 CRMCDGI **Swift:** BAMA IT 3A **Reuters:** BCRM

Senior Executive Officers
President   Alfredo Cesarini
Director General   Camillo Piazza Spessa

Foreign Exchange
Global Head   Gerardo Bove

Risk Management
Global Head   Piero Giorgio *Risk Manager*

Other Departments
Proprietary Trading   Mauro Lancione
Private Banking   Marco Brisghelli
Correspondent Banking   Adriana Schiavoni

Euromoney Directory 1999   **759**

ITALY (+39)   www.euromoneydirectory.com

Banca delle Marche SpA (cont)
Administration
Public Relations
                            Giovanni Filosa

Banca Monte dei Paschi di Siena SpA — Head Office
Formerly known as: Monte dei Paschi di Siena
Piazza Salimbeni 3, I-53100 Siena
Tel: (0577) 294 111; (0577) 294 493 Fax: (0577) 294 313; (0577) 296 653 Telex: 313330 PAS WI TI Swift: PASC IT MM
Email: rel.estero.mps@agora.stm.it Reuters: MPSX Telerate: 8372 Cable: MONTE PASCHI
Reuters: MPSY; MPSM; MPSO; MPST
Website: www.mps.it

Senior Executive Officers
Chief Executive Officer — Divo Gronchi
                          Rinaldo Lascialfare *Deputy CEO*
Financial Director; Treasurer — Marco Mazzucchelli *General Manager, Finance* ☎ **(02) 6970 5728**
                          🖷 **(02) 6970 5428**
Head, General Secretariat — Alessandro Abbruzzese
International Division — Piergiorgio Primavera *General Manager*
                          Emanuele Marsiglia *Head*

Others (Senior Executives)
Group Co-Ordination — Felice Di Giulio *General Manager*
Tax Collection — Angelo Musco *General Manager*
Finance & Global Markets — Marco Mazzucchelli *General Manager, Finance* ☎ **(02) 6970 5728**
                          🖷 **(02) 6970 5428**
Strategic Planning & Market Research — Antonio Vigni *Head*
General Secretariat — Alessandro Abbruzzese *Head, General Secretariat*

Debt Capital Markets / Fixed Income
Head of Debt Capital Markets — Mauro Scalfi *Head, Securities, Bonds & Derivatives*

Equity Capital Markets
Other (Domestic Equities)
Domestic Shareholdings — Marco Antonio Bulletti *Head*
Other (International Equity)
Foreign Shareholdings — Emanuele Marsiglia *Head*

Syndicated Lending
Other (Syndicated Lending)
Credit Administration — Antonio Acampa *General Manager*
Credit & Lending — Mario Gastano Mazzarino *Head*
Credit & Lending (Large Corp Groups) — Roberto Menchetti *Head*

Loan-Related Activities
Leasing & Asset Finance — Alberto Quintiliani *Head*

Other (Trade Finance)
Factoring — Alberto Quintiliani *Head*

Risk Management
Fixed Income Derivatives / Risk Management
Global Head — Mauro Scalfi *Head, Securities, Bonds & Derivatives*

Settlement / Clearing
Operations — Omero Elmi *General Manager*
Back-Office — Giuseppe Inguanta *Head*

Global Custody
Head of Global Custody — Silvano Del Greco *Head*

Other Departments
Debt Recovery / Restructuring — Gianni Sampaolesi *General Manager*
                          Roberto Cofaool *Head*

Administration
Head of Administration — Giancarlo Brundi *General Manager*
Head of Marketing — Carlo Platania *General Manager*
                          Roberto Onniboni *Head*

Legal / In-House Counsel
Legal — Roberto Martinelli *General Manager*
                          Pasqualino Pauleau *Head*

Corporate Communications
                          Roberto Omniboni *Head*

www.euromoneydirectory.com ITALY (+39)

Accounts / Audit
Internal Audit   Graziano Barnini *Head*
Accounts   Ettore Biasi *Head*
Other (Administration)
Corporate Affairs   Roberto Martinelli *General Manager*
Organisation   Omero Elmi *General Manager*
                                        Giovanni Paglial *Head*
Human Resources   Alberto Cavalieri *General Manager*
Personnel Management   Roberto Orvleto *Head*

Banca Monte Parma SpA   Head Office
Piazzale J Sanvitale, 1, I-43100 Parma
Tel: (0521) 209 1 **Fax:** (0521) 209 302; (0521) 209 360 **Telex:** 539204 MONTE I **Swift:** BMPR IT 2P **Reuters:** BMPR
Senior Executive Officers
President   Franco Gorreri
Chief Executive Officer   Gianpaolo Martini
Financial Director   Roberto Mason
Chief Operating Officer   Maurizio Parisini
Managing Director / General Manager   Gianpaolo Martini

Banca Morgan Stanley SpA   Subsidiary Company
Palazzo Serbelloni, Corso Venezia 16, I-20121 Milan
Tel: (02) 760 351 **Fax:** (02) 783 057
Website: www.ms.com

Debt Capital Markets / Fixed Income
Bonds - General
Fixed-Income Sales & Trading   Paolo Moia *Executive Director*
                                        Paolo Borsani *Vice President*
                                        Raffaele Coriglione *Vice President*

Equity Capital Markets
Other (Domestic Equities)
Equity Sales   Giuseppina Minicucci *Executive Director*

Corporate Finance / M&A Advisory
Department: Investment Banking
Regional Head   Franco Gardella *Vice President*

Asset Management
Other (Asset Management)
Marketing   Stefano Russo *Executive Director*

Other Departments
Private Banking   Giovanni Luigi Grandi *Executive Director*

Banca Nazionale del Lavoro   Head Office
Via Vittorio Veneto 119, I-00187 Rome
PO Box 16121, I-00187 Rome
Tel: (06) 4702 1 **Fax:** (06) 4702 8345 **Telex:** 621030 BNLRM I **Swift:** BNLI IT RR **Email:** press.bnl@bnl.it
Website: www.bnl.it

Senior Executive Officers
Financial Director   Ugo Masini ☏ **4702 6088**

General - Treasury
Head of Treasury   Riccardo Lupi *Global Head*

Debt Capital Markets / Fixed Income
Head of Fixed Income   Paolo Tesoro ☏ **4702 6048**
Head of Fixed Income Sales   Alberto Egidi ☏ **4702 6039**
Head of Fixed Income Trading   Giorgio Bonsignore ☏ **4702 6380**

Government Bonds
Head of Sales   Vincenzo Scorza ☏ **4702 6085**
Head of Trading   Paolo Galasso ☏ **4702 6198**
Head of Syndication   Pietro Toso ☏ **4702 6111**
Head of Origination   Eugenio Cerione ☏ **4702 6528**

ITALY (+39)   www.euromoneydirectory.com

Banca Nazionale del Lavoro (cont)

Eurobonds
Head of Sales	Marina Lo Magro ☏ **4702 6438**
Head of Trading	Patrizia Passaretti ☏ **4702 6447**

Libor-Based / Floating-Rate Products
FRN Sales	Vincenzo Scorza ☏ **4702 6085**
FRN Trading	Paolo Galasso ☏ **4702 6198**
Asset Swaps	Roberto Antolini ☏ **4702 6849**
Asset Swaps (Sales)	M Grazia Ercolano ☏ **4702 6140**

Fixed-Income Repo
Head of Repo   Giorgio dell'Acqua ☏ **4702 6382**

Fixed-Income Research
Head of Fixed Income   Alessandra Mastrota ☏ **4702 6062**

Equity Capital Markets
Department: BNL Finance Division
Via Lombardia 31, I-00187 Rome
Head of Sales   Paolo Tesoro ☏ **4702 6048**

Domestic Equities
Head of Sales	Giovanni Rigamonti ☏ **(02) 8024 2129**
Head of Trading	Eduardo Palazzo ☏ **4702 6588**

International Equities
Head of Sales; Head of Trading   Federico Fabbri ☏ **4702 6446**

Convertibles / Equity-Linked
Head of Sales	Federico Fabbri ☏ **4702 6446**
Head of Trading	Salvatore Crescenti ☏ **4702 6833**

Syndicated Lending
Head of Origination   Leonardo Violet *Head of Loan Origination* ☏ **4702 6030**

Money Markets
Fax: 4702 6876 **Reuters:** BNLR **Telex:** 620030 - 610039
Head of Money Markets   Guido Grossi *Head, Money Market & FX Forwards* ☏ **4702 6894**

Domestic Commercial Paper
Head of Sales   Pierduilio Cocuccioni *Head of Sales* ☏ **4702 6991**

Wholesale Deposits
Head of Sales   Giuliana Luzi ☏ **4702 6893**

Foreign Exchange
Fax: 4702 6876 **Reuters:** BNLZ
Head of Foreign Exchange	Claudio Cornegliani ☏ **4702 6988**
Corporate Sales	Giorgio Grigolato *Head* ☏ **4702 6907**
Head of Trading	Alfredo Giuliani *Chief Dealer* ☏ **4702 6980**

Risk Management

Foreign Exchange Derivatives / Risk Management
Vanilla FX option Trading   Umberto Ferri *Chief Dealer* ☏ **4702 6901**

Exchange-Traded Derivatives
Head   Federico Fabbri ☏ **4702 6446**

Settlement / Clearing
Head of Settlement / Clearing	Augusto Correr ☏ **4702 6010**
Fixed-Income Settlement	Nella Ruggeri ☏ **4702 6003**
Operations	Piero Guarnieri ☏ **4702 6069**

Other Departments
Correspondent Banking   Alberto Berti *Head, Financial Institutions* ☏ **4702 6054**

Banca Nazionale dell'Agricoltura SpA   Head Office

Via Salaria 231, I-00199 Rome
PO Box 423, I-00100 Rome
Tel: (06) 8588 1 Telex: 625330 BNARM I Swift: NAGR IT RD
Treasury Operations Fax: (06) 574 7618

Senior Executive Officers
Chairman	Paolo Accorinti
Vice Chairman	Giuseppe Mormile
Chief Executive Officer	Massimo Bianconi *Managing Director & Chief Executive*
International Division	Paolo Mennini ☏ **8588 3201**

General - Treasury
Head of Treasury   Gianluca Baldassarri *Treasury* ☏ **8588 3410**

ITALY (+39)

Debt Capital Markets / Fixed Income
Head of Trading — Domenico Carbone *Chief Dealer, Futures, Italian Options, Govt Bonds* ☏ 8588 3014 [F] 8588 3780

Non-Domestic Government Bonds
Trading — Giuseppe Rocco *Dealer, Futures, Italian Options, Government Bonds* ☏ 8588 3014 [F] 8588 3780
Fabrizio Donnini *Dealer, Futures, Italian Options, Government Bonds* ☏ 8588 3014 [F] 8588 3780
Giovanni Valentino *Dealer, Futures, Italian Options, Government Bonds* ☏ 8588 3014 [F] 8588 3780

Bonds - General
Foreign Bonds & Stocks — Renato Kiikka *Dealer* ☏ 8588 3017 [F] 8588 3780
Enrico Vagnoni *Dealer* ☏ 8588 3017 [F] 8588 3780
Bruno Silvestri *Dealer* ☏ 8588 3017 [F] 8588 3780

Equity Capital Markets
Other (Domestic Equities) — Maurizio Nunnari ☏ 8588 3014 [F] 8588 3780
Alessandro Toccafondi ☏ 8588 3014 [F] 8588 3780

Syndicated Lending
Other (Trade Finance)
Credit Analysis & Documentation — Giancarlo Bonini *Head* ☏ 8588 3207

Money Markets
Department: Foreign Exchange & Money Market
Reuters: BNA-BANR -Dealer

Money Markets - General
Foreign Exchange & Money Markets — Gianluigi D'Amone *Chief Dealer & Treasurer* ☏ 8588 3880
Customer Desk — Patrizia Nardi *Senior Dealer* ☏ 8588 9589
Massimo Carducci *Senior Dealer* ☏ 8588 9589
Money Market — Renato Palmieri *Senior Dealer* ☏ 8588 9580
Domestic Money Market — Angela Marzeddu *Chief* ☏ 8588 3593
Alberto Semproni *Senior Dealer* ☏ 8588 3016, 8588 3505
Claudio Rossi *Dealer* ☏ 8588 3016, 8358 3505
Marco Fasulo *Dealer* ☏ 8588 3016, 8358 3505

Foreign Exchange
Department: Foreign Exchange & Money Market
Reuters: BNA-BANR -Dealer
Global Head — Gianluigi D'Amone *Chief Dealer & Treasurer* ☏ 8588 3880
Head of Trading — Marco Pirrottina *Senior Dealer* ☏ 8408 9586

Risk Management
Foreign Exchange Derivatives / Risk Management
Global Head — Federico Sieli *Senior Dealer* ☏ 8588 9583

Settlement / Clearing
Derivatives Settlement — Marina Figliolini *Officer* ☏ 8588 3389 [F] 8588 3820
Foreign Exchange Settlement — Philip Raymond Swayne *Officer, Forex & MM* ☏ 8588 3275 [F] 8588 3214
Giuseppe Giorgi *Head, Forex & MM* ☏ 8588 3643 [F] 8588 3214
Settlement (General) — Riccardo Mucci *Officer, Securities* ☏ 8588 3422 [F] 8588 3820
Maurizio Catafalmo *Head, Securities* ☏ 8588 3421 [F] 8588 3820

Other Departments
Correspondent Banking — Antonio Di Thiene *Head* ☏ 8588 3663 [F] 8588 3396
Franco Patacchiola *Central Europe & Americas* ☏ 8588 3519 [F] 8588 3396
Roberto D'Ascia *France & Africa* ☏ 8588 3493 [F] 8588 3396
Francesco Macioce *Iberia & Northern Europe* ☏ 8588 3210 [F] 8588 3396
Pietro Foti *Eastern Europe & former USSR* ☏ 8588 3559 [F] 8588 3396
Piero De Angelis *Greece, Turkey, Middle & Far East & Pacific* ☏ 8588 3263 [F] 8588 3396

Administration
Accounts / Audit
'Nostro' Accounts — Philip Raymond Swane *Officer* ☏ 8588 3275
Giuseppe Giorgi *Head* ☏ 8588 3643 [F] 8588 3214
'Vostro' / Ioro Accounts — Mario De Silvestris *Head* ☏ 8588 4763
Carlo Mione *Officer* ☏ 8588 4737

ITALY (+39) www.euromoneydirectory.com

Banca Popolare di Ancona SpA — Head Office

Via Don A Battistoni, I-60035 Jesi
Tel: (0731) 647 1 **Fax:** (0731) 208 288 **Telex:** 560109 BPAMES **Swift:** BPAM IT 3J **Reuters:** BPAJ
Foreign Division Fax: (0731) 647 740

Senior Executive Officers
Chairman	Riccardo Stecconi
Chief Executive Officer	Antonio Martinez
Financial Director	Claudio Rossi
Chief Operating Officer	Maurizio Frati
Treasurer	Maurizio Bocchini

Debt Capital Markets / Fixed Income
Country Head — Maurizio Frati

Equity Capital Markets
Country Head — Maurizio Frati

Foreign Exchange
Country Head — Maurizio Bocchini

Banca Popolare di Aprilia SCaRL — Head Office

Piazza Roma SNC, I-04011 Aprilia
Tel: (06) 928 6251 **Fax:** (06) 927 27551; (06) 927 5940 **Telex:** 680861 **Swift:** BAAR IT 21

Senior Executive Officers
President	Emilio Vescovi
Vice President	Mario Cavicchioli
Chief Executive Officer	Francesco Fornaro *Director General*

Banca Popolare Asolo e Montebelluna

BANCA POPOLARE ASOLO E MONTEBELLUNA

Piazza GB Dall'Armi 1, I-31044 Montebelluna
Tel: (0423) 283 1; (0423) 283 447 **Fax:** (0423) 301 997; (0423) 22072 **Telex:** 410317 **Swift:** AMBP IT 2M
Email: bpam@medianet.it
Website: www.bpam.it

Senior Executive Officers
Chairman	Flavio Trinca
Managing Director / General Manager	Vincenzo Consoli

Money Markets
Fax: 283 340
Head of Money Markets — Angelo Ceccato ☎ 283 323

Banca Popolare di Bergamo-Credito Varesino — Head Office

Piazza Vittorio Veneto 8, I-24122 Bergamo
Tel: (035) 392 111 **Fax:** (035) 392 480 **Telex:** 300410 BPBDIR I **Swift:** BEPO IT 22 **Email:** info@bpb.it
Reuters: PGPI.MI
Website: www.bpb.it

Senior Executive Officers
Chairman	Emilio Zanetti
Deputy Chairman	Antonio Parimbelli
Deputy Chairman	Giuseppe Calvi
Chief Executive Officer	Giorgio Frigeri *General Manager*
Financial Director	Riccardo Sora *Responsible for Finance*
General Manager	Giorgio Frigeri
Joint General Manager	Enzo Cattaneo
Deputy General Manager	Alfredo Gusmini
Deputy General Manager	Guido Lupini
Deputy General Manager	Antonio Martinez
Deputy General Manager	Marco Balzaretti

Foreign Exchange
Head of Foreign Exchange — Luciano Turba *Chief Dealer*

www.euromoneydirectory.com   ITALY (+39)

Corporate Finance / M&A Advisory
Head of Corporate Finance Fernando Forghieri *Director, Corporate Finance*

Other Departments
Correspondent Banking Maurizio Amaglio *International Relations*

Administration
Corporate Communications
    Cesare Combi ☏ **392 588**

Banca Popolare di Cividale ScaRL   Head Office
Piazza Duomo 8, Cividale del Friuli, I-33043 Udine
Tel: (0432) 7071 **Fax:** (0432) 73 0370 **Telex:** 450185 CIBANK I **Swift:** CIVI IT 2C
Website: www.sede.civibank.it

Senior Executive Officers
Chairman Lorenzo Pelizzo ✉ **sege@sede.civibank.it**
Chief Executive Officer Nereo Tereran
Financial Director Gianluca Picotti ✉ **picotti@sede.civibank.it**
Chief Operating Officer; Treasurer Lorenzo Cozzarolo ✉ **lcozzarolo@sede.civibank.it**
Managing Director / General Manager Silvano Chiappo ✉ **chiappo@sede.civibank.it**

Debt Capital Markets / Fixed Income
Global Head Bruno Pausa ✉ **pausa@sede.civibank.it**

Money Markets
Global Head Gianluca Picotti ✉ **picotti@sede.civibank.it**

Foreign Exchange
Global Head Gianfranco Nutrizio ✉ **nutrizio@sede.civibank.it**

Risk Management
Global Head Alberto Cudiz ✉ **acudiz@sede.civibank.it**

Corporate Finance / M&A Advisory
Global Head Gianluca Picotti ✉ **picotti@sede.civibank.it**

Banca Popolare Commercio e Industria   Head Office
Via della Moscova 33, I-20121 Milan
Tel: (02) 6275 1 **Fax:** (02) 6275 640 **Telex:** 310276 **Swift:** POCI IT MM **Reuters:** BPCX **Telex:** 320667

Senior Executive Officers
Chairman & Managing Director Giuseppe Vigorelli
Chief Executive Officer Carlo Garavaglia *Executive Vice Chairman*
Financial Director Giorgio Ricchebuono *Finance Director* ☏ **6275 563**
Treasurer Roberto Bini *Treasurer* ☏ **6275 393**
General Manager Carlo Porcari
International Division Federico Kerbaker

Debt Capital Markets / Fixed Income
Tel: 6275 318 **Fax:** 6275 598
Global Head Giorgio Ricchebuono *Finance Director* ☏ **6275 563**

Domestic Government Bonds
Head of Trading Diego Colciago *Chief Dealer-ITL* ☏ **6275 403**

Non-Domestic Government Bonds
    Massimo Villa *Eurobond Manager* ☏ **6275 318**

Eurobonds
Head of Trading Massimo Villa *Eurobond Manager* ☏ **6275 318**

Fixed-Income Repo
Sales Diego Colciago *Chief Dealer-ITL* ☏ **6275 403**

Equity Capital Markets
Tel: 6275 221 **Fax:** 6275 598
Global Head Giorgio Ricchebuono *Finance Director* ☏ **6275 563**

Domestic Equities
Head of Trading Luca Pavesi *Dealer* ☏ **6275 221**

International Equities
Head of Trading Massimo Villa *Chief Dealer* ☏ **6275 318**

Convertibles / Equity-Linked
Head of Trading Massimo Villa *Chief Dealer* ☏ **6275 318**

Warrants
Head of Trading Massimo Villa *Chief Dealer* ☏ **6275 318**

ITALY (+39)　　　　　　　www.euromoneydirectory.com

Banca Popolare Commercio e Industria (cont)
Money Markets
Tel: 6275 393 **Fax:** 6275 364
Global Head　　　　　　　　　Roberto Bini *Treasurer* ☏ **6275 393**
Foreign Exchange
Tel: 6275 393 **Fax:** 6275 364
Global Head　　　　　　　　　Roberto Bini *Treasurer* ☏ **6275 393**
Head of Institutional Sales; Head of Trading　Domenico Quartieri *Chief Dealer* ☏ **654 962**
FX Traders / Sales People
ITL / Majors　　　　　　　　Cesare Gheraldi *Dealer*
　　　　　　　　　　　　　　Sergio Pisaneschi *Dealer*
　　　　　　　　　　　　　　Marco Leoni *Dealer*
Forward Desk　　　　　　　Lorenzo Contardi *Dealer*
　　　　　　　　　　　　　　Manuele Cogni *Dealer*
Risk Management
Global Head　　　　　　　　Roberto Bini *Treasurer* ☏ **6275 393**
Fixed Income Derivatives / Risk Management
IR Swaps Sales / Marketing　　Fabio Ciut *Dealer* ☏ **6575 718**
Foreign Exchange Derivatives / Risk Management
Cross-Currency Swaps, Trading　Domenico Quartieri *Chief Dealer* ☏ **654 962**
Corporate Finance / M&A Advisory
Tel: 6275 263 **Fax:** 6275 718
Global Head　　　　　　　　Giorgio Rossin *Manager* ☏ **6275 263**
Settlement / Clearing
Equity Settlement; Fixed-Income Settlement　Giancarla Vaccher *Customer Desk-ITL* ☏ **6275 455**
Foreign Exchange Settlement　Renato Requiliani *Back-Office* ☏ **6275 352**
Other Departments
Correspondent Banking　　　Laura Ferraris ☏ **6275 528** 📠 **6275 640**

Banca Popolare di Crema　　　　　　　　　　　　Head Office
Via XX Settembre 18, I-26013 Crema
Tel: (0373) 891 1 **Fax:** (0373) 891 248 **Telex:** 320594 **Swift:** POCR IT 22 **Reuters:** BPCC **Cable:** BANCA POPOLARE
Senior Executive Officers
Chairman　　　　　　　　　Cesare Pasquali ☏ **891 223**
Chief Executive Officer　　　Claudio de Tuoni
　　　　　　　　　　　　　　Francesco Guerini Rocco ☏ **891 215**
Financial Director　　　　　Armando Soccini ☏ **891 217**
Treasurer　　　　　　　　　Aldo Buffele
Money Markets
Tel: 85105 **Fax:** 891 248
Global Head　　　　　　　　Aldo Buffele
Foreign Exchange
Tel: 85105 **Fax:** 891 606 **Reuters:** BPCC
Global Head　　　　　　　　Aldo Buffele
FX Traders / Sales People
　　　　　　　　　　　　　　Enrico Cremonesi
　　　　　　　　　　　　　　Paolo Cisarri
Settlement / Clearing
Tel: 85105 **Fax:** 891 606
Foreign Exchange Settlement　Paolo Cisarri

Banca Popolare di Cremona　　　　　　　　　　　Head Office
Via Cesare Battisti 14, I-26100 Cremona
Tel: (0372) 404 1 **Fax:** (0372) 404 362 **Telex:** 321099 POPCR **Swift:** CRBK IT 22 **Reuters:** BPCR
Senior Executive Officers
Chairman　　　　　　　　　Carlo Gosi ☏ **404 211**
Treasurer　　　　　　　　　Marino Ghilardi ☏ **404 311**
General Manager　　　　　Vincenzo Battarola ☏ **404 321**

www.euromoneydirectory.com ITALY (+39)

Banca Popolare dell'Adriatico SpA
Head Office

Via Gagarin 216, I-61100 Pesaro
Tel: (0721) 447 1 Fax: (0721) 447 325 Telex: 600044 POPADRI Swift: POAD IT 3P

Senior Executive Officers
President Giandomenico di Sante
Managing Director / General Manager Franco Ferri

Risk Management
Global Head Ivan Damiano

Banca Popolare dell'Alto Adige ScaRL
Head Office

Alternative trading name: Südtiroler Volksbank
Via Macello 55, I-39100 Bolzano
Tel: (0471) 996 111 Fax: (0471) 979 188 Telex: 400167 BZBANK I Swift: BPAA IT 2B Reuters: BPBZ
Website: www.popvoba.it

Senior Executive Officers
President Zeno Giaccomuzzi
Chief Executive Officer Arthur Walcher ☎ 996 441
Treasurer Stephan Dejaco *Manager, Treasury* ☎ 996 452
General Manager Klaus Mahlknecht ☎ 996 145
General Manager Paul Zanon ☎ 996 145

Foreign Exchange
Country Head Bruno Benedikter ☎ 996 465

Banca Popolare dell'Emilia Romagna
Head Office

Via San Carlo 8-20, I-41100 Modena
Tel: (059) 202111 Telex: 510031 EMIPOP I

Senior Executive Officers
Chairman Pier Luigi Colizzi
Managing Director / General Manager Guido Leoni

Banca Popolare dell'Etruria e del Lazio
Head Office

Corso Italia 179, I-52100 Arezzo
Tel: (0575) 307 1 Fax: (0575) 307 228 Telex: 574 047 POPERT I Swift: ARBA IT 33 Reuters: ETRU

Senior Executive Officers
Chairman Elio Faralli
Chief Executive Officer Alessandro Redi *General Manager*
Financial Director Giuseppe Amabile
Treasurer Pietro Bigazzi
General Manager Alessandro Redi

Debt Capital Markets / Fixed Income
Global Head Gianfranco Dabroni

Equity Capital Markets
Global Head Antonio Parnici

Syndicated Lending
Global Head Gianfranco Dabroni

Money Markets
Global Head Alfredo Landi

Foreign Exchange
Global Head Braldo Novembri

Corporate Finance / M&A Advisory
Global Head Plinio Pastonelli

Settlement / Clearing
Regional Head Fiorenzo Criurli

Euromoney Directory 1999 767

ITALY (+39) www.euromoneydirectory.com

Banca Popolare dell'Irpinia
Head Office

Centro Direzionale Località, Collina Liguorini, I-83100 Avellino
Tel: (0825) 651 **Fax:** (0825) 655 317 **Telex:** 722319 IRPBFX **Swift:** IRPB IT 3A

Senior Executive Officers
Chairman	Ernesto Valentino [T] 655 200 [F] 655 259
Chief Executive Officer	Antonio De Stefano [T] 655 202 [F] 655 281
Financial Director	Florindo Cirignano [T] 655 213 [F] 655 281
Chief Operating Officer	Vincenzo Penza [T] 655 207 [F] 655 264
Managing Director	Cosimo Lombardi [T] 655 203
Company Secretary	Antonio D'Amore [T] 655 229
International Division	Giuseppe Lepore [T] 655 220 [F] 655 317

Debt Capital Markets / Fixed Income
Head of Fixed Income   Alfonso Marra [T] 655 209 [F] 655 281

Foreign Exchange
Head of Foreign Exchange   Maurizio Ranaudo [T] 655 348

Other Departments
Correspondent Banking   Luigi Borrillo [T] 655 311

Administration
Head of Marketing   Carmelo Grimaldi [T] 655 248

Banca Popolare di Intra ScaRL
Head Office

Piazza Aldo Moro, 8, I-28921 Intra
Tel: (0323) 543 1 **Fax:** (0323) 403 445 **Telex:** 200594 **Swift:** BPIN IT 24

Senior Executive Officers
President   Sandro Saini
General Manager   Giovanni Brumana

Foreign Exchange
Global Head   Attilio Scotti *Head, International Department* [T] 543 371

Banca Popolare di Lodi
Head Office

Via Cavour 40/42, I-26900 Lodi
Tel: (0371) 5951 **Fax:** (0371) 67307 **Telex:** 340228 POPLOD I

Senior Executive Officers
Chairman   Giovanni Benevento
General Manager   Ambrogio Sfondrini

Banca Popolare di Luino e di Varese
Full Branch Office

Via Boccaccio 2, I-20123 Milan
Tel: (02) 480 85251 **Fax:** (02) 480 85299 **Telex:** 334831 LUINMI **Swift:** BPLV IT 22 **Reuters:** BPLV
Cable: LUINOBANK

Foreign Exchange
Regional Head   Pasquale Picarelli *Manager*

Banca Popolare di Milano SCaRL
Head Office

Piazza Meda 4, I-20121 Milan
Tel: (02) 7700 1 **Fax:** (02) 7700 2993 **Telex:** 324498 **Email:** bpm@ibm.net **Reuters:** BPMX
Website: www.bpm.it

Senior Executive Officers
Chairman	Paolo Bassi
Chief Executive Officer	Ernesto Paolillo
Financial Director	Oscar Cipelli
Treasurer	Pietro Panizzi
International Division	Enrico Bernasconi [T] 7700 2457

www.euromoneydirectory.com　　　　　　　　　ITALY (+39)

Debt Capital Markets / Fixed Income
Tel: 7700 2300 **Fax:** 7700 7499
Head of Debt Capital Markets　　　　　　Giuseppe Michelucci ☏ **7700 2228**

Domestic Government Bonds
Head of Sales　　　　　　　　　　　　　Silva Minora
　　　　　　　　　　　　　　　　　　　　Nadia Benatti
Head of Trading　　　　　　　　　　　　Massimo Piazzolla
　　　　　　　　　　　　　　　　　　　　Marco Ceva
　　　　　　　　　　　　　　　　　　　　Roberto Tronci

Eurobonds
Head of Trading　　　　　　　　　　　　Daniela Finocchio ☏ **7700 2773**

Libor-Based / Floating-Rate Products
Asset Swaps　　　　　　　　　　　　　　Gabriele Meroni ☏ **7700 2905**

Equity Capital Markets
Tel: 7700 2300 **Fax:** 7700 7499
Head of Equity Capital Markets　　　　　Giuseppe Michelucci ☏ **7700 2228**

Domestic Equities
Head of Trading　　　　　　　　　　　　Nunzio Patecchi ☏ **7700 7931**

International Equities
Head of Trading　　　　　　　　　　　　Giovanni Pollastri

Money Markets
Tel: 7700 7595 **Fax:** 7700 2690

Domestic Commercial Paper
Head of Origination; Head of Sales; Head of　Giuseppe Sangermani
Trading

Eurocommercial Paper
Head of Origination; Head of Sales; Head of　Luciano Battisti
Trading

Foreign Exchange
Head of Foreign Exchange　　　　　　　Sergio Sensalari
Global Head　　　　　　　　　　　　　　Luca Ferdori *Senior Dealer*
　　　　　　　　　　　　　　　　　　　　Aldo Bortolotti *Manager* ☏ **7700 2503** F **7700 2690**

Settlement / Clearing
Operations　　　　　　　　　　　　　　Paolo Colombi *Head of Operations*

Banca Popolare di Novara　　　　　　　　　　　　　　Head Office

Via Negroni 12, I-28100 Novara
Tel: (0321) 662 111 **Fax:** (0321) 662 546 **Telex:** 200212 **Swift:** NVRB IT 2N O1O **Email:** pronto?@bpn.it
Reuters: BPNX
Website: www.bpn.it

Senior Executive Officers
International Division　　　　　　　　　Enrico Agostoni ☏ **662 215** F **662 017** E **agostonie@bpn.it**

Others (Senior Executives)
　　　　　　　　　　　　　　　　　　　　Mauro Miglio *Head of Retail Banking* F **662 546** E **migliom@bpn.it**

General - Treasury
Head of Treasury　　　　　　　　　　　Angelo Monteverde ☏ **662 228** F **662 109**

Debt Capital Markets / Fixed Income
Fax: 662 019
Head of Debt Capital Markets　　　　　　Rachele Dell'Era ☏ **663 520**

Domestic Government Bonds
Head of Trading　　　　　　　　　　　　Alberto Amiotti ☏ **663 507**
　　　　　　　　　　　　　　　　　　　　Nicoletta Montagnoli ☏ **662 535**

Eurobonds
Head of Trading　　　　　　　　　　　　Paolo Tega ☏ **663 525**
　　　　　　　　　　　　　　　　　　　　Alessandro Bagiani ☏ **663 521**

Equity Capital Markets
Fax: 662 019
Head of Equity Capital Markets　　　　　Rachele Dell'Era ☏ **663 520**
Head of Trading　　　　　　　　　　　　Giorgio Consolini ☏ **662 040**

Money Markets
Domestic Commercial Paper
Head of Trading　　　　　　　　　　　　Ariotto Pacifico ☏ **662 550**

Euromoney Directory 1999　**769**

ITALY (+39) www.euromoneydirectory.com

Banca Popolare di Novara (cont)
Foreign Exchange
Head of Foreign Exchange
Andrea Dayan *Head of Dealing Room* ☎ 662 790 Ⓕ 662 106
Ugo Paves *Deputy Head of Dealing Room* ☎ 662 791 Ⓕ 662 106

Risk Management
Fixed Income Derivatives / Risk Management
Trading
Aldo Leo ☎ 662 064

Asset Management
Portfolio Management
Aldo Leo ☎ 662 064

Other Departments
Correspondent Banking
Enrico Silvio Zardo *Head* ☎ 662 745 Ⓕ 662 017 Ⓔ zardoes@bpn.it

Banca Popolare di San Felice Sul Panaro SCaRL — Head Office

Piazza Matteotti 23, I-41038 San Felice Sul Panaro
Tel: (0535) 898 11 Fax: (0535) 83112 Telex: 510863 BANFEL I

Senior Executive Officers
Chairman — Alberto Chelli ☎ 898 38
Chief Executive Officer — Anselmo Pizzi ☎ 898 12
Financial Director — Gabriele Bergamini ☎ 898 30
Chief Operating Officer — Marco Dotti
Treasurer — Gabreile Bergamini
Managing Director / General Manager — Anselmo Pizzi ☎ 898 12

Foreign Exchange
Global Head — Arrigo Bonetti ☎ 898 28

Risk Management
Fixed Income Derivatives / Risk Management
Global Head — Giuseppe Suffritti ☎ 898 51

Banca Popolare di Sondrio — Head Office

Via Lungo Mallero Cadorna 24, I-23100 Sondrio
Tel: (0342) 528 111; (0342) 528 220 Fax: (0342) 528 359; (0342) 528 622 Telex: 321347 Swift: POSO IT 22
Email: international.corbank@popso.it Reuters: BPSO
Website: www.popso.it

Senior Executive Officers
Chairman — Piero Melazzini
Managing Director / General Manager — A Dante

Banca Popolare Udinese ScaRL — Head Office

via Cavour, 24, I-33100 Udine
Tel: (0432) 516 311 Fax: (0432) 21113 Telex: 450194 BANCUD I
Website: www.xnet.it/bpu

Senior Executive Officers
President — Roberto Tonazzi
Chief Executive Officer — Alessandro M. Piozzi *Director General* ☎ 516 405
Financial Director — Arnaldo Antonini *Finance Director* ☎ 516 440 Ⓔ aantonini@bpu.xnet.it
Chief Operating Officer — Luigi Crepaldi ☎ 516 316
Treasurer — Umberto Bonazzi *Head of Treasury* ☎ 516 438
Director General — Stefano Semprini ☎ 516 400

Foreign Exchange
Global Head — Luigi Gerometta *Head of FX* ☎ 516 443

Banca Popolare di Verona San Giminiano e San Prospero — Head Office

Piazza Nogara 2, I-37100 Verona
Tel: (045) 8675 111 Fax: (045) 8675 474

Senior Executive Officers
President — Giorgio Zanotto
General Manager — Aldo Civaschi

www.euromoneydirectory.com　　　ITALY (+39)

Banca Popolare Vicentina scparl
Head Office

Via Btg Framarin 18, I-36100 Vicenza
Tel: (0444) 339 111 **Fax:** (0444) 329 364 **Telex:** 481194 BPVCON **Swift:** BPVI IT 22 **Email:** info@popvi.it
Reuters: BPVI **Cable:** POPOLARBANK VICE
Website: www.popvi.it

Senior Executive Officers
Chairman　　　　　　　　　　　　　Gianni Zonin
Chief Executive Officer　　　　　　　Piero Santelli
Financial Director; Treasurer　　　　　Gianni Gavagnin

Banca Profilo SpA
Head Office

Corso Italia 49, I-20122 Milan
Tel: (02) 584 081 **Fax:** (02) 5831 6057 **Email:** info@bancaprofilo.it
Website: www.bancaprofilo.it

Senior Executive Officers
Chairman　　　　　　　　　　　　　Sandro Capotosti
Vice Chairman　　　　　　　　　　　Marco Manara
Chief Executive Officer; Financial Director　Arnaldo Grimaldi *Managing Director & Finance Director*
International Division　　　　　　　　Gian Carlo Anduino

Other Departments
Private Banking　　　　　　　　　　Marco Manara *Vice Chairman*

Banca Regionale Europea SpA
Head Office

Via Monte de Pietà, 7, I-20121 Milan
PO Box 1898, I-20121 Milan
Tel: (02) 722 111 **Fax:** (02) 865 413 **Telex:** 310568 BMMDIR **Swift:** BREU IT M2

Senior Executive Officers
Chairman　　　　　　　　　　　　　Oscar Casnici
Acting Vice Chairman　　　　　　　　Lamberto Bellani
Vice Chairman　　　　　　　　　　　Stefano Caramelli
Vice Chairman　　　　　　　　　　　Mario Cera
Managing Director　　　　　　　　　Piero Bertolotto
General Manager　　　　　　　　　　Pierluigi Gardella

Others (Senior Executives)
　　　　　　　　　　　　　　　　　Ruggiero Cafari Panico *Director*
　　　　　　　　　　　　　　　　　Andrea Calleri *Director*
　　　　　　　　　　　　　　　　　Luigi Carosso *Director*
　　　　　　　　　　　　　　　　　Antonio Liserre *Director*
　　　　　　　　　　　　　　　　　Pietro Localetti *Director*
　　　　　　　　　　　　　　　　　Enrico Lusso *Director*
　　　　　　　　　　　　　　　　　Amilcare Merlo *Director*
　　　　　　　　　　　　　　　　　Maria Teresa Ragni *Director*
Finance Department　　　　　　　　　Silvio Giraudo *Senior Manager*

Syndicated Lending
Department: Credit Department
Global Head　　　　　　　　　　　　Sergio Martinengo *Senior Manager*

Administration
Other (Administration)
Commercial Department　　　　　　　Sergio Rabbia *Senior Manager*
Human Resources Department　　　　Alberto Mocchi *Senior Manager*

Banca di Roma
Head Office

Viale Umberto Tupini 180, I-00144 Rome
Tel: (06) 5445 1 **Fax:** (06) 5445 3572 **Telex:** 616184 BROMA I **Swift:** BROM IT RD **Reuters:** ROMR (FX);
ROMD (Deposits)
Website: www.bancaroma.it

Senior Executive Officers
International Division　　　　　　　　Massimiliano Maran *Chief Executive, Finance* ☏ **5445 3230**

Euromoney Directory 1999　**771**

ITALY (+39) www.euromoneydirectory.com

Banca di Roma (cont)
Debt Capital Markets / Fixed Income
Global Head — Angelo Brizi *Deputy Chief Executive* ☏ 5445 3701

Domestic Government Bonds
Head of Sales; Head of Trading — Franca Di Mario *Deputy Chief Manager* ☏ 5445 2240 F 5445 3595

Non-Domestic Government Bonds
Stefano Locatelli *Manager* ☏ 5445 2170 F 5445 3119
Giovanni Stocchi *Manager* ☏ 5445 2800

Eurobonds
Head of Syndication — Stefano Spina *Assistant Manager* ☏ 5445 2890
Head of Sales — Antonio Collinvitti *Manager* ☏ 5445 2170
Head of Trading — Stefano Locatelli *Manager* ☏ 5445 2170 F 5445 3119

Bonds - General
Head Global Sales — Luca Peviani *Joint Chief Manager* ☏ 5445 3704
Institutional Global Sales — Vincenzo Gonzalez *Manager* ☏ 5445 2948
Corporate Global Sales — Valerio Paoluci *Deputy Chief Manager* ☏ 5445 3705 F 5445 2706
Options & Futures (Foreign Securities) — Stefano Locatelli *Manager* ☏ 5445 2170 F 5445 3119

Libor-Based / Floating-Rate Products
Asset Swaps — Stefano Locatelli *Manager* ☏ 5445 2170 F 5445 3119

Private Placements
Head of Origination — Roberto Prato *Deputy Chief Manager* ☏ 5445 3205 F 5445 3542
Head of Sales — Luca Peviani *Joint Chief Manager* ☏ 5445 3704
Head of Structuring — Fabrizio Mennella *Manager* ☏ 5445 3754

Asset-Backed Securities / Securitization
Global Head — Roberto Prato *Deputy Chief Manager* ☏ 5445 3205 F 5445 3542

Mortgage-Backed Securities
Global Head — Roberto Prato *Deputy Chief Manager* ☏ 5445 3205 F 5445 3542

Equity Capital Markets
Global Head — Rodolfo Cimmino *Chief Manager & Department Head* ☏ 5445 2791 F 5445 3057

Domestic Equities
Head of Origination — Isabella Mastrofini *Manager* ☏ 5445 3583
Head of Syndication — Sandra Cecilia *Manager* ☏ 5445 2570 F 5445 2202
Head of Trading — Angela Del Re *Chief Manager* ☏ 5445 2619 F 5445 3595
Head of Research — Alberto Scolozzi *Manager* ☏ 5445 2226 F 5445 3143

International Equities
Head of Origination; Head of Syndication; Head of Sales; Head of Trading — Dominique Beauchat *Deputy Chief Manager* ☏ 5445 3510 F 5445 3119

Warrants
Head of Sales; Head of Trading; Head of Research — Dominique Beauchat *Deputy Chief Manager* ☏ 5445 3510 F 5445 3119

Syndicated Lending
Department: Finance Department of Securities & Treasury
Global Head — Rodolfo Cimmino *Chief Manager & Department Head* ☏ 5445 2791 F 5445 3057
Head of Origination — Roberto Prato *Deputy Chief Manager* ☏ 5445 3205 F 5445 3542
Head of Syndication — Cristina Graziosi *Manager* ☏ 5445 3215

Loan-Related Activities
Project Finance; Project Finance — Enrico Ceci *Deputy Chief Manager* ☏ 5445 2896 F 5445 3178
Structured Trade Finance — Luca Peviani *Joint Chief Manager* ☏ 5445 3704
Fabrizio Mennella *Manager* ☏ 5445 3754

Money Markets
Global Head — Augusto Aggio *Chief Manager & Department Head* ☏ 5445 2689 F 5445 3484
Country Head — Giovanni Minnucci *Senior Dealer* ☏ 5445 3725
Paola Roccia *Senior Dealer* ☏ 5445 3726
Stella Faninlo *Senior Dealer* ☏ 5445 3733
Quirino Di Manno *Deputy Chief Manager* ☏ 5445 3707

Money Markets - General
Medium Term Treasury: Origination — Giuseppe Drago *Deputy Chief Manager* ☏ 5445 2203
Michele Di Franco *Manager* ☏ 5445 3738
Alessandro D'Angelo *Manager* ☏ 5445 3737
Medium Term Treasury: Sales — Giuseppe Tassiello *Manager* ☏ 5445 3719
Medium Term Treasury: Trading — Paolo Cipriani *Manager* ☏ 5445 3718
Fabrizio Santarelli *Senior Dealer* ☏ 5445 3717

ITALY (+39)

Foreign Exchange
Tel: 5445 00
Global Head — Augusto Aggio *Chief Manager & Department Head* ☎ **5445 2689** 📠 **5445 3484**
Country Head — Quirino Di Manno *Deputy Chief Manager* ☎ **5445 3707**
Head of Trading — Loreta Palomba *Manager* ☎ **5445 3710** 📠 **5445 2397**

FX Traders / Sales People
$ / EURO — Marco Dioguardi *Senior Dealer* ☎ **5445 3712**
DM — Irene Gubernali *Junior Dealer* ☎ **5445 3711**
SME / ITL — Franco Di Menico *Senior Dealer* ☎ **5445 3764**
Exotic / ITL — Giulia Manciotti *Senior Dealer* ☎ **5445 3763**
Banknotes — Ugo Carlucci *Senior Dealer*

Risk Management
Global Head — Augusto Aggio *Chief Manager & Department Head* ☎ **5445 2689** 📠 **5445 3484**
Country Head — Davide Massatani *Deputy Chief Manager* ☎ **5445 3735**
IR Swaps Sales / Marketing — Valerio Paoluci *Deputy Chief Manager* ☎ **5445 3705** 📠 **5445 2706**
IR Swaps Trading — Agata Leccisotti *Senior Dealer* ☎ **5445 3736** 📠 **5445 3047**
IR Options Sales / Marketing; IR Options Trading — Fabio Massoli *Manager* ☎ **5445 3720**

Foreign Exchange Derivatives / Risk Management
Cross-Currency Swaps, Sales / Marketing; Cross-Currency Swaps, Trading — Davide Massatani *Deputy Chief Manager* ☎ **5445 3735**
Vanilla FX option Sales — Valerio Paoluci *Deputy Chief Manager* ☎ **5445 3705** 📠 **5445 2706**
Vanilla FX option Trading — Fabio Massoli *Manager* ☎ **5445 3720**

Other Currency Swap / FX Options Personnel
Massimiliano Scorpio *Senior Dealer* ☎ **5445 3734**
Agata Leccisotti *Senior Dealer* ☎ **5445 3736** 📠 **5445 3047**
Massimiliano Cabua *Senior Dealer* ☎ **5445 3731**

Exotic Options (Barriers, Range, Timers, Digitals, Faders etc)
Sales — Valerio Paoluci *Deputy Chief Manager* ☎ **5445 3705** 📠 **5445 2706**
Trading — Fabio Massoli *Manager* ☎ **5445 3720**

OTC Equity Derivatives
Sales — Valerio Paoluci *Deputy Chief Manager* ☎ **5445 3705** 📠 **5445 2706**
Trading — Fabio Massoli *Manager* ☎ **5445 3720**

OTC Credit Derivatives
Global Head — Augusto Aggio *Chief Manager & Department Head* ☎ **5445 2689** 📠 **5445 3484**
Regional Head — Davide Massatani *Deputy Chief Manager* ☎ **5445 3735**
Head of Sales — Valerio Paoluci *Deputy Chief Manager* ☎ **5445 3705** 📠 **5445 2706**
Head of Trading — Guido Contesso *Junior Dealer* ☎ **5445 3730**

Corporate Finance / M&A Advisory
Head of Corporate Finance — Rodolfo Cimmino *Chief Manager & Department Head* ☎ **5445 2791** 📠 **5445 3057**

Other (Corporate Finance)
Origination & Syndication — Roberto Prato *Deputy Chief Manager* ☎ **5445 3205** 📠 **5445 3542**

Asset Management
Head — Paolo Mallardo *Chief Manager & Department Head* ☎ **5445 2275** 📠 **5445 2411**

Banca di Romagna Spa
Head Office

Corso Garibaldi 1, I-48018 Faenza
Tel: (0546) 676 111 **Fax:** (0546) 661 707 **Telex:** 550374 **Swift:** BARO IT 2F

Senior Executive Officers
Chairman — Jean Luigi Facchini
General Manager — Giuseppe Xella

Others (Senior Executives)
Raffaele Clo *Deputy General Manager*

ITALY (+39) www.euromoneydirectory.com

Banca Sella SpA
Head Office

Via Italia 2, I-13900 Biella
Tel: (015) 350 1229 **Fax:** (015) 205 40; (015) 351 767 **Telex:** 223106 BANSEL I **Reuters:** SELB - SELLA

Senior Executive Officers
Chairman — Giorgio Sella
Managing Director / General Manager — Maurizio Sella

Settlement / Clearing
Operations — Cristina Allara *Head of Operations*

Banca Toscana SpA
Head Office

Via Leone Pancaldo 4, I-50127 Florence
PO Box 270, I-50127 Florence
Tel: (055) 4391 1 **Fax:** (055) 4391 227 **Telex:** 570083 BTCRE I **Swift:** TOSC IT 3F **Reuters:** TOSC; BTFF

Senior Executive Officers
Chairman — Fabio Merusi
Chief Executive Officer — Giuseppe Mazzini
Company Secretary — Luca Bonito

Debt Capital Markets / Fixed Income
Department: Titoli E Borsa
Tel: 4391 492 **Fax:** 437 9034
Head of Fixed Income — Silvio Bencini *Chief Manager* ☎ **4391 492**
Head of Fixed Income Trading — Ivan Ascari *Manager* ☎ **4391 269**

Government Bonds
Head of Trading — Roberto Capannoli *Manager* ☎ **4391 405**

Eurobonds
Head of Sales — Luca Picchi *Senior Dealer* ☎ **4391 405**

Equity Capital Markets
Department: Titoli E Borsa
Tel: 4391 492 **Fax:** 437 9034 **Telex:** 572186 TOBORS
Head of Equity Capital Markets — Silvio Bencini *Chief Manager* ☎ **4391 492**
Head of Trading — Alessandro Mugnai *Manager* ☎ **4391 243**

Money Markets
Tel: 4391 5104 **Fax:** 422 4332 **Reuters:** BTDE **Telex:** 570084 BTES
Head of Money Markets — Giancarlo Picchi *Chief Manager* ☎ **4391 360**

Foreign Exchange
Global Head — Moreno Cheli *Deputy Chief Manager* ☎ **4391 369**
Head of Trading — Paolo Livi *Senior Dealer* ☎ **4391 5343**

Other Departments
Correspondent Banking — Alessandro Vannini *SVP, Dept Head* ☎ **4391 370**

Banco Ambrosiano Veneto SpA

Piazza Paolo Ferrari 10, I-20121 Milan
PO Box 1235, 20100 Milan
Tel: (02) 8594 1; (02) 8646 8375 **Fax:** (02) 8646 1049 **Telex:** 482663 BAV CT I **Swift:** BAVE IT MM
Email: ambro@ambro.it
Website: www.ambro.it

Senior Executive Officers
Chairman — Francesco Cesarini
Deputy Chairman — Marc Antoine Autheman
Deputy Chairman — Angelo Caloia
Chief Executive Officer — Tommaso Cartone *CEO & General Manager*
Deputy Chief Executive & GM — Erminio Bevilacqua

Others (Senior Executives)
Marco Casu *Director*
Angelo Ferro *Director*
Franco Freddi *Director*
Marco Janni *Director*
Giovan Battista Limonta *Director*
Michel Maurau *Director*
Christian Merle *Director*
Jean Luc Perron *Director*

774 Euromoney Directory 1999

ITALY (+39)

Others (Senior Executives) (cont)

Carlo Salvatori *Director*
Alberto Valdembri *Director*
Paolo Vantellini *Director*
Franco Viezzoli *Director*

Director, Commercial Banking
General-Lending (DCM, SL)
Head of Corporate Banking
Department: Board of Statuory Auditors
Chairman

Victor Massiah

Flavio Venturini *Credit*

Giulio Castelli

Others (Senior Executives)

Antonio Cortellazzo *Auditor*
Giuseppe Levi *Auditor*
Nicola Bruni *Alternate Auditor*
Paolo Emilio Mariconda *Alternate Auditor*

Administration
Other (Administration)
Director, Human Resources

Omar Lodesani

Banco Bilbao Vizcaya
Full Branch Office

Via Cino del Duce 8, I-20122 Milan
Tel: (02) 76296 1 **Fax:** (02) 76296 234 **Reuters:** BBVM

Senior Executive Officers
Financial Director — Marco Malavasi ☏ **76296 299**
General Manager — Landolfo Caracciolo ☏ **76296 225**

Debt Capital Markets / Fixed Income
Libor-Based / Floating-Rate Products
Asset Swaps — Paola Caselli ☏ **76296 223**

Fixed-Income Repo
Sales — Riccardo Palvarini ☏ **76296 218**

Foreign Exchange
Head of Foreign Exchange — Gianni Minucci ☏ **76296 219**
FX Traders / Sales People
Damiano Del Tatto ☏ **76296 220**
Paolo Cavenago ☏ **76296 220**

Risk Management
Foreign Exchange Derivatives / Risk Management
Vanilla FX option Trading — Damiano Del Tatto ☏ **76296 220**
Exotic Options (Barriers, Range, Timers, Digitals, Faders etc)
Trading — Damiano Del Tatto ☏ **76296 220**

Settlement / Clearing
Head of Settlement / Clearing — Valeria Crivelli ☏ **76296 256**

Banco do Brasil SA
Full Branch Office

Via Baracchini 2, I-20123 Milan
PO Box 1495, Milan
Tel: (02) 8825 **Fax:** (02) 890 0265 **Telex:** 312085 SATELM I **Reuters:** BBIT

Senior Executive Officers
General Manager — Erninio Tadei

Others (Senior Executives)
Jose Eneas Bueno Junior *Deputy Manager*

Foreign Exchange
Head of Trading — Michele Sartori *Assistant Dealer*
Marina Cordini *Chief Dealer*

Banco Central Hispanoamericano
Full Branch Office

Via Dante 16, I-20121 Milan
Tel: (02) 806 7162 **Fax:** (02) 7200 1392 **Telex:** 313013

Senior Executive Officers
General Manager — Ernesto Palacios

ITALY (+39) www.euromoneydirectory.com

Banco Central Hispanoamericano (cont)
Others (Senior Executives)
　　　　　　　　　　　　　Caterina Sfondrini *Deputy General Manager*

Banco di Chiaveri e della Riviera Ligure SpA
Via Garibaldi 2, Genoa
Tel: (010) 2765 1 Fax: (010) 2765 238

Banco Espirito Santo
Representative Office

Formerly known as: Banco Espirito Santo e Comercial de Lisboa
Via Brera 19, I-20121 Milan
Tel: (02) 8901 2128 Fax: (02) 7201 4558

Senior Executive Officers
Representative　　　　　　　Luis Díniz Ferreira

Banco di Napoli
Head Office

Via Toledo 177-178, I-80132 Naples
Tel: (081) 791 1111 Fax: (081) 552 5020 Reuters: NAPE Telerate: 15188 Cable: DIRBANCO Telex: 15189
Telex: 15190

Senior Executive Officers
Chairman　　　　　　　Luigi Coccioli
Chief Executive Officer　　Ferdinando Ventriglia

Settlement / Clearing
Settlement (General)　　　Aniello Ardolino

Banco de la Provincia de Buenos Aires
Representative Office

Via Albricci 9, I-20122 Milan
Tel: (02) 867 661; (02) 875 525 Fax: (02) 869 2073 Telex: 322056 Email: baproit@iol.it

Senior Executive Officers
Representative　　　　　　　Juan Carlos Pérez Pannelli

Others (Senior Executives)
Assistant to the Representative　　Carla Giacalone

Banco di Sicilia
Representative Office

Via Santa Margarita 12, I-20121 Milan
Tel: (02) 88491 Fax: (02) 274 283 Telex: 311006 BSBT

Senior Executive Officers
Representative　　　　　　　Alberto Ranucci

Banco di Sicilia SpA
Head Office

Via Generale Magliocco 1, I-90141 Palermo
Tel: (091) 608 1111 Fax: (091) 608 5964; (091) 608 5185 Telex: 910059 Swift: BSIC IT RR RM3 Reuters: BSIR

Senior Executive Officers
Chief Executive Officer　　Giuseppe Spadafora
Financial Director　　　　Andrea Ragagni *Chief Financial Officer* ☎ **608 5966**
Treasurer　　　　　　　　Flavio Ottaviani *Treasurer* ☎ **608 3169**
Managing Director　　　　Cesare Caletti ☎ **608 3225**

Others (Senior Executives)
　　　　　　　　　　　　　Carlo Dominici *Deputy Chairman* ☎ **608 5628**
　　　　　　　　　　　　　Gian Franco Imperatori *Deputy Chairman* ☎ **608 5628**

776　Euromoney Directory 1999

ITALY (+39)

Banexi Italia

Via Dente 4, I-20121 Milan
Tel: (02) 7256 2050 Fax: (02) 7212 4454 Email: valebxi@tin.it

Senior Executive Officers
Chairman   Georges Chaudron de Courcel
Managing Director / General Manager   Giorgio E Dacome ☏ 7256 2052

Others (Senior Executives)
Senior Vice President   Pierfrancesco Puccio Senior Vice President ☏ 7256 2056

Bank Austria
Representative Office

Corso Venezia 5, I-20121 Milan
Tel: (02) 7601 4579 Fax: (02) 783 507 Email: bamirap@relay.comm2000.it

Senior Executive Officers
Chief Representative   Hans-Peter Tiefenbacher
Deputy Representative   Jürgen Mahler

Bank Brussels Lambert
Full Branch Office

Corso Garibaldi 86, I-20121 Milan
Tel: (02) 62520 1 Fax: (02) 62520 256; (02) 62520 254 Telex: 335364 BABRU I Swift: BBRU IT MX

Senior Executive Officers
Head   Albert Biebuyck

General-Lending (DCM, SL)
Head of Corporate Banking   Rodolfo Sertic Corporate Banking

General - Treasury
Head of Treasury   Beniamino Piccone

Foreign Exchange
Global Head   Beniamino Piccone

Settlement / Clearing
Operations   Giuseppe Perotti

The Bank of Tokyo-Mitsubishi Limited
Full Branch Office

Viale della Liberazione 18, I-20124 Milan
Tel: (02) 669 931 Fax: (02) 6671 3600 Telex: 32108 Swift: BOTK IT X

Senior Executive Officers
General Manager   Hiroshi Somoti

Bankers Trust Finanziaria SpA
Subsidiary Company

Via Turati 16/18, I-20121 Milan
Tel: (02) 6369 1 Fax: (02) 6369 334 Telex: 321350

Senior Executive Officers
Managing Director & President   Alberto Guazzi
Assistant Vice President   Stefano Agostoni

Bankers Trust International plc
Full Branch Office

Via Turati 16/18, I-20121 Milan
Tel: (02) 6369 1 Fax: (02) 6369 334 Telex: 321392

Debt Capital Markets / Fixed Income
Country Head   Andrea Zanotti Vice President

Equity Capital Markets
Head of Equity Capital Markets   Carlo Arsi Vice President
Country Head   Lorenzo Colucci MD & Head, Equities

Corporate Finance / M&A Advisory
Head of Corporate Finance; Head of Mergers &   Ricardo Sargiacomo Managing Director
Acquisition

Euromoney Directory 1999 777

ITALY (+39) www.euromoneydirectory.com

Banque Générale du Luxembourg SA
Representative Office

Via Larga 7, I-20122 Milan
Tel: (02) 5830 7563; (02) 5830 7565 Fax: (02) 5830 7564
Website: www.bgl.lu

Senior Executive Officers
Chief Representative   Christian Mognol

Banque Nationale de Paris
Full Branch Office

Via Meravigli 4, I-20123 Milan
PO Box 1269, Milan
Tel: (02) 72124 1 Fax: (02) 72124 465 Telex: 310641 NAPAR I Swift: BNPA IT MM

Senior Executive Officers
Managing Director / General Manager   Denot Gerad

Debt Capital Markets / Fixed Income
Domestic Government Bonds
Head of Trading   Renaud Labbee *Bonds*

Other Departments
Cash Management   M Rizzetto *Officer* [T] **72124 270**

Banque Paribas
Full Branch Office

Alternative trading name: Paribas Milan

Piazza San Fedele 2, I-20121 Milan
Tel: (02) 7247 1 Fax: (02) 866 388
Website: www.paribas.com

Senior Executive Officers
Financial Director   François Bugnon *Head of Finance* [T] **7247 2402** [F] **7247 2408**
General Manager & Legal Representative Robert Ricci [T] **7247 2256** [F] **7247 2408**
General Secretary   Graziano Ferrari [T] **7247 2219** [F] **7247 2408**

Others (Senior Executives)
Internal Control   Pierre Desbois *Head, Internal Control* [T] **7247 2203** [F] **7247 2060**
Institutional Banking   Gian Paolo Gamba *Head, Institutional Banking* [T] **7247 3535** [F] **7247 3598**
                                        Patrizio Rinaldi *Head* [T] **7247 3537** [F] **7247 3598**
                                        Alessandro Gioffreda *Head, Securities Services* [T] **7247 4365** [F] **7247 4444**
                                        Davide Grignani *Head of Advisory* [T] **7247 2258** [F] **7247 2041**
                                        Alberto Davoli *Sovereign & Financial Institutions* [T] **7247 2148** [F] **7247 2246**

General-Lending (DCM, SL)
Head of Corporate Banking   Alain Kaspereit [T] **7247 2404** [F] **7247 2246**

General-Investment
Head of Investment   Carlo Mammola *Head, Paribas Principles Investments* [T] **7247 2160**
                                        [F] **7247 2408**

Debt Capital Markets / Fixed Income
Head of Debt Capital Markets   Luca Falco [T] **7247 2830** [F] **7247 2030**

Asset-Backed Securities / Securitization
Regional Head   Antonella Tagliavini *Securitization* [T] **7247 2275** [F] **7247 2246**

Equity Capital Markets
Head of Equity Capital Markets   Andrew Shearn *Head of Equity* [T] **7247 3100** [F] **7247 3333**

Equity Repo / Securities Lending
Marketing & Product Development   Elisa Ori *Marketing Manager* [T] **7247 4405** [F] **7247 4444**

Risk Management
Head of Risk Management   Mathilde Jahan *Internal Control, Market Risk* [T] **7247 2230** [F] **7247 2060**

Settlement / Clearing
Operations   Carlo Faccio *Head of Operations* [T] **7247 4306** [F] **7247 4632**

Asset Management
Head   Giovanni Massaron *Head of Asset & Liability Management* [T] **7247 2800**
                                        [F] **7247 2030**

Other Departments
Chief Credit Officer   Silvia Gelfi *Head, Credit Risk Management* [T] **7247 2111** [F] **7247 2246**
Private Banking   Patrizio Rinaldi *Head* [T] **7247 3537** [F] **7247 3598**

www.euromoneydirectory.com ITALY (+39)

Administration
Technology & Systems
IT　　François Bugnon *Head of Finance* ☎ 7247 2402 📠 7247 2408
　　　Francesco Marchetti *Head of IT* ☎ 7247 4381 📠 7247 2350
Legal / In-House Counsel
　　　Graziano Ferrari *General Secretary* ☎ 7247 2219 📠 7247 2408
Compliance
　　　Fabrizio Mambretti *Compliance Officer* ☎ 7247 3257 📠 7247 2060
Other (Administration)
Human Resources　Graziano Ferrari *General Secretary* ☎ 7247 2219 📠 7247 2408

Barclays International Finanziaria SpA   Subsidiary Company
Via Moscova 18, I-20121 Milan
Tel: (02) 6372 1 **Fax:** (02) 6372 2045 **Telex:** 340487 BARFIN I
Senior Executive Officers
Director　　　　　　　　　Hugh Malim
Vice President　　　　　　Colin Vincent

Baring Brothers (Italia) Srl
Via Brera 3, I-20121 Milan
Tel: (02) 809 271 **Fax:** (02) 809 007
Senior Executive Officers
Chairman　　　　　　　　Renato Riverso
Managing Director　　　　Gherardo Barbini

BTM Finanziaria Italia   Representative Office
Formerly known as: BOT Finanziaria Italiana SpA
Viale Della Liberazione 18, I-20124 Milan
Tel: (02) 6698 5671 **Fax:** (02) 6699 3354 **Telex:** 321081

CAB SpA   Head Office
Via Cefalonia 62, I-25175 Brescia
Tel: (030) 2433 1 **Fax:** (030) 2433 242 **Telex:** 300403 BCABBT I **Swift:** BCAB IT 22 **Reuters:** CABS
Senior Executive Officers
President　　　　　　　　Alberto Folonari
Managing Director　　　　Corrado Faissola

Caboto Holding SIM SpA   Head Office
Piazzale Cadorna 5, I-20123 Milan
Tel: (02) 8021 1; (02) 8021 5943 **Fax:** (02) 8021 5701; (02) 8021 5232 **Telex:** 310430 Caboto I
Email: market.holding@caboto.it
Website: www.caboto.it

Senior Executive Officers
President　　　　　　　　　　Christian Merle
Chief Executive Officer　　　　Francesco De Vecchi
Financial Director　　　　　　Franco Ziborde ☎ 8021 5343
Director General　　　　　　　Fabio Arpe ☎ 8021 5515
General-Investment
Head of Investment　　　　　　Fabio Arpe *Director General* ☎ 8021 5515
Debt Capital Markets / Fixed Income
Head of Debt Capital Markets　　Carlo Sirtori ☎ 8021 5036
Head of Fixed Income　　　　　Fabio Arpe *Director General* ☎ 8021 5515
Head of Fixed Income Sales　　Claudio Lonardo *Head of Sales* ☎ 8021 5885
Head of Fixed Income Trading　Luca Zappa ☎ 8021 5749
Domestic Government Bonds
Head of Sales　　　　　　　　Claudio Lonardo *Head of Sales* ☎ 8021 5885
Head of Trading　　　　　　　Luca Zappa ☎ 8021 5749

Euromoney Directory 1999　779

ITALY (+39)

www.euromoneydirectory.com

Caboto Holding SIM SpA (cont)

Eurobonds
Head of Sales — Claudio Lonardo *Head of Sales* ☎ **8021 5885**
Head of Trading — Matteo Massardi ☎ **8021 5400**

Emerging Market Bonds
Head of Emerging Markets; Head of Trading — Claudia Segre ☎ **8021 5844**

Libor-Based / Floating-Rate Products
FRN Sales — Marco Regni *Sales* ☎ **8021 5801**
FRN Trading; Asset Swaps — Dario Cintioli ☎ **8021 5339**
Asset Swaps (Sales) — Marco Regni *Sales* ☎ **8021 5801**

Fixed-Income Repo
Head of Repo; Head of Trading — Dario Cintioli ☎ **8021 5339**
Other — Stephano Bernardinello ☎ **8021 5618**

Fixed-Income Research
Head of Fixed Income — Alessandro Fugnoli ☎ **8021 5544**
Head of Credit Research — Fabio Boninsegni ☎ **8021 5057**

Equity Capital Markets
Head of Equity Capital Markets — Daniele Recalcati ☎ **8021 5781**

Domestic Equities
Head of Trading — Daniele Recalcati ☎ **8021 5781**

International Equities
Head of Trading — Gabriele Andreotti ☎ **8021 5814**

Syndicated Lending
Head of Origination — Annibale Osti ☎ **8021 5041**

Money Markets
Country Head — Roberto Rossi *Head of Trading* ☎ **8021 5823**

Domestic Commercial Paper
Head of Sales — Rossella Marras ☎ **8021 5756**

Eurocommercial Paper
Head of Sales — Rossella Marras ☎ **8021 5756**

Money Markets - General
Settlements — Piera Velati

Foreign Exchange
Head of Foreign Exchange — Stefano Oneda ☎ **8021 5865**

Risk Management

Fixed Income Derivatives / Risk Management
Trading; IR Swaps Sales / Marketing — Dario Cintioli ☎ **8021 5339**

Foreign Exchange Derivatives / Risk Management
Spot / Forwards Sales; Spot / Forwards Trading — Stefano Oneda *Head of Trading*

Other Currency Swap / FX Options Personnel
Head of Swaps — Dario Cintioli ☎ **8021 5339**

OTC Equity Derivatives
Trading — Francesco Vercesi ☎ **8021 5856**

OTC Commodity Derivatives
Head — Dario Cintioli ☎ **8021 5339**

Settlement / Clearing
Head of Settlement / Clearing — Massimo Mazzocchi *International Bonds* ☎ **8633 5871**
Operations — Mario Begnini ☎ **8021 5057**

Other Departments
Chief Credit Officer — Fabio Boninsegni ☎ **8021 5057**

Administration
Head of Administration — Franco Ziborde ☎ **8021 5343**
Head of Marketing — Mauro Bussotti ☎ **8021 5443**

Technology & Systems
— Luigi Brambilla ☎ **8021 5775**

Legal / In-House Counsel
— Luciano Casiroli ☎ **8021 5334**

Public Relations
— Mauro Bussotti ☎ **8021 5443**

Accounts / Audit
— Paolo Marzocchini ☎ **8021 5847**

www.euromoneydirectory.com ITALY (+39)

Caisse Centrale des Banques Populaires
Representative Office

Piazza della Repubblica 7, I-20121 Milan
Tel: (02) 655 4704 **Fax:** (02) 655 2860 **Email:** ccbpmil@tin.it
Website: www.ccbp.fr

Senior Executive Officers
Representative — Philippe Arany

CARIPLO - Cassa di Risparmio delle Provincie Lombarde SpA
Head Office

Via Monte di Pietà 8, I-20121 Milan
PO Box 1784, Milan
Tel: (02) 8866 1; (02) 4142 1 **Fax:** (02) 8866 3250; (02) 8866 3240 **Telex:** 313010 CARIPL I **Swift:** CARI IT MF
Email: scrivici@cariplo.it **Reuters:** CRML **Telerate:** 59268-3684
Reuters: CRPL; CRPM
Website: www.cariplo.it

Senior Executive Officers
Chairman — Giovanni Ancarani [T] **8866 5691** [F] **8866 3419**
Deputy Chairman — Fabrizio Onida [T] **8866 2998** [F] **8866 5488**
Deputy Chairman — Gino Trombi [T] **8866 2658** [F] **8866 5488**
Managing Director — Gianfranco Denotte [T] **8866 3708** [F] **8866 3645**
Deputy Chief Executive & GM — Roberto Brambilla [T] **8866 3367** [F] **8866 2220**
Deputy Managing Director — Carlo Baraggia [T] **8866 7732** [F] **8866 2220**
Deputy Managing Director — Giovanni Bizzozero [T] **8866 3780** [F] **8866 2220**
Deputy Managing Director — Ernesto Tansini [T] **8866 2240** [F] **8866 3467**
International Division — Marzio Astarita *Head* [T] **8866 3620** [F] **8866 3250**

General - Treasury
Head of Treasury — Renato Tarantola *Head of Treasury Investments Division* [T] **8866 2626** [F] **8866 5446**

Debt Capital Markets / Fixed Income
Government Bonds
Head of Sales — Silvano Furlan [T] **7236 3740**
Head of Trading — Ivano Masiero [T] **7236 3660**

Eurobonds
Head of Sales — Silvano Furlan [T] **7236 3740**
Head of Trading — Ivano Masiero [T] **7236 3660**

Equity Capital Markets
Domestic Equities
Head of Sales — Silvano Furlan [T] **7236 3740**
Head of Trading — Carlo Iavazzo [T] **7236 3710**

Money Markets
Head of Money Markets — Fernando Brenna [T] **7236 2720**

Foreign Exchange
Head of Foreign Exchange — Massimo Mariani [T] **8866 3494**
Head of Institutional Sales; Corporate Sales — Gianpiero Enoch [T] **8866 2512**
Head of Trading — Patrizia De Horatiis [T] **7236 2740**

Risk Management
Head of Risk Management — Renzo Avesani [T] **8866 5795**

Fixed Income Derivatives / Risk Management
Head of Sales — Gianpiero Enoch [T] **8866 2512**
Trading — Gianluca Bolla [T] **7236 3850**

CARIPRATO Cassa di Risparmio di Prato SpA
Head Office

Via Degli Alberti 2, I-59100 Prato
Tel: (0574) 617 1 **Fax:** (0574) 617 507 **Telex:** 572382 PRATO E **Swift:** PRAT IT 3P **Reuters:** CRDP (Dealing)
Telex: 571562 CRDPFX

Senior Executive Officers
Chairman — Nilo Salvatici
Vice Chairman — Romano Lascialfari
Chief Executive Officer — Ettore Rondine *Deputy Chief Executive Officer*
Cesare Brogi

ITALY (+39)   www.euromoneydirectory.com

CARIPRATO Cassa di Risparmio di Prato SpA (cont)
Senior Executive Officers (cont)
Financial Director   Marcello Paladini *Manager*
Debt Capital Markets / Fixed Income
Department: Capital Markets
Global Head   Marcello Paladini *Manager*
Eurobonds
Head of Origination   Marco Lulli *Manager*
Equity Capital Markets
Equity Repo / Securities Lending
Marketing   Franco Colzi *Manager, Domestic Securities*
                                              Angelo Avenante *Dealer, Domestic Securities*
                                              Alberto Arrighi *Trader, Domestic Securities*
Syndicated Lending
Other (Trade Finance)
Documentary Credits; Letters of Credit   Fabrizio Gori *Manager*
Money Markets
Domestic Commercial Paper
Head of Origination   Angelo Avenante *Dealer, Domestic Securities*
Head of Sales   Cristina Ciulli
Foreign Exchange
Department: Foreign Exchange and Bullion
FX Traders / Sales People
                                              Marco Lulli *Manager*
                                              Massimiliano Marconi *Dealer*
Risk Management
Foreign Exchange Derivatives / Risk Management
Cross-Currency Swaps, Sales / Marketing   Massimiliano Marconi *Dealer*
                                              Marco Lulli *Manager*
Settlement / Clearing
Settlement (General)   Elisabetta Iandelli *Dealer, Back-Office Settlements*
                                              Renza Borgi *Trader*
Other Departments
Correspondent Banking   Marcello Paladini *Manager*

CARIT - Cassa di Risparmio di Terni e Narni SpA   Head Office

Formerly known as: Cassa di Risparmio di Terni
49 Corso Tacito, I-05100 Terni
Tel: (0744) 5481 **Fax:** (0744) 548 242; (0744) 421 248 **Telex:** 660197 CARIT **Cable:** CASSA RISPARMIO
Senior Executive Officers
Chairman   Mr Zurzolo
Vice Chairman   Mr Malvetani

Cariverona Banca SpA   Head Office

Via Garibaldi 1, I-37121 Verona
Tel: (045) 808 1111; (045) 808 8222 **Fax:** (045) 867 9769; (045) 867 9754 **Telex:** 482342 CRVER **Swift:** CRVR IT 2V
Reuters: CRVV
Website: www.cariverona.it

Senior Executive Officers
Chairman   Paolo Biasi ☎ **808 1104**
Chief Executive Officer   Giuseppe Mazzarello ☎ **808 1110**
Financial Director   Marco Carreri ☎ **808 1965**
Treasurer   Dario Valentino ☎ **808 1920**
Debt Capital Markets / Fixed Income
Country Head   Giacomo Carta ☎ **808 1818**
Equity Capital Markets
Country Head   Dario Valentino ☎ **808 1920**
Syndicated Lending
Country Head   Stefano Cacciani ☎ **808 8268**

www.euromoneydirectory.com ITALY (+39)

Money Markets
Country Head — Maurizio Vangelisti ☎ **808 1904**
Foreign Exchange
Country Head — Dario Valentino ☎ **808 1920**
Settlement / Clearing
Country Head — Alfonso Scipolo ☎ **808 1878**

Cassa di Risparmio di Alessandria — Head Office
Via Dante 2, I-15100 Alessandria
Tel: (0131) 203 111 **Fax:** (0131) 234 471 **Telex:** 212199 CRADIR **Swift:** RIAL IT 2A

Senior Executive Officers
President — Gianfranco Pittatore ☎ **203 151**
Managing Director / General Manager — Giuseppe Pernice ☎ **203 210**

Debt Capital Markets / Fixed Income
Department: Finanze Valori
Global Head — Corrado Rossi ☎ **203 350**

Equity Capital Markets
Department: Finanze Valori
Global Head — Corrado Rossi ☎ **203 350**

Syndicated Lending
Global Head — Corrado Rossi ☎ **203 350**

Cassa di Risparmio di Bolzano SpA — Head Office
Alternative trading name: Südtiroler Sparkasse AG
Formerly known as: Cassa Di Risparmio Della Privincia Di Bolzano
Via Cassa di Risparmio 12 B, I-39100 Bolzano
Tel: (0471) 231 111; (0471) 231 317 **Fax:** (0471) 231 300; (0471) 231 195 **Telex:** 400611 I CABZAU **Swift:** CRBZ IT 2B
Email: servizio_spe@spkbz.it **Reuters:** CRBZ **Bloomberg:** 29872
Website: www.spkbz.com

Senior Executive Officers
Chairman — Ander Amonn ☎ **231 227**
Chief Executive Officer — Erich Mayr *General Manager* ☎ **231 246**
Financial Director — Johann P P Hitthaler *Head of Division* ☎ **231 270**
General Manager — Erich Mayr ☎ **231 246**
Deputy General Manager — Richard Seebacher ☎ **231 247**
International Division — J Simon Weissenegger *Head of Division* ☎ **231 316**

Money Markets
Tel: 231 275 **Fax:** 231 219
Global Head — Johann P P Hitthaler *Head of Division* ☎ **231 270**

Domestic Commercial Paper
Head of Sales; Head of Trading — Manfred Klotz ☎ **231 276**

Foreign Exchange
Tel: 231 380
Global Head of Trading — Dario Bogni ☎ **231 380**

FX Traders / Sales People
Stefan Facchini *Trader* ☎ **231 310**
Maria Alexia Stricker *Trader* ☎ **231 309**

Risk Management
Tel: 231 136 **Fax:** 231 144
Global Head — Karl Mayr ☎ **231 134**

Other Departments
Correspondent Banking — Elmar Mahlknecht *Head of Correspondent Banking* ☎ **231 322**

Administration
Business Development; Head of Marketing — Markus Obermair *Head of Division* ☎ **231 376**

Technology & Systems
Andrea Brillo *Head of Division* ☎ **231 600**

Legal / In-House Counsel
Mario Dona *Head of Division* ☎ **231 359**

Public Relations
Hugo Daniel Stoffella ☎ **231 255**

Accounts / Audit
Sergio Broilo *Head of Division* ☎ **231 287**

ITALY (+39) www.euromoneydirectory.com

Cassa Risparmio Carpi SpA
Head Office

Formerly known as: Cassa Di Risparmio Di Carpi
Piazza Martiri 3, I-41012 Carpi
PO Box 345, I-41012 Carpi
Tel: (059) 648 111; (059) 642 300 **Fax:** (059) 640 204; (059) 690 078 **Telex:** 510233 **Swift:** CRCA IT 2C **Telex:** 511482

Senior Executive Officers
Chairman	Luigi Verrini ☎ **648 219**
Treasurer	Andrea Stermieri ☎ **648 619**
General Manager	Umberto Giacomelli ☎ **648 229**
Deputy General Manager	Giovanni Tavani ☎ **648 239**
Company Secretary	Mauro Federzoni ☎ **648 300**
International Division	Ottavio Coronati ☎ **648 300**

Debt Capital Markets / Fixed Income
Department: Treasury & Finance
Tel: 648 610 **Fax:** 648 625
Head of Fixed Income — Andrea Stermieri ☎ **648 619**

Government Bonds
Head of Sales — Andrea Stermieri ☎ **648 619**

Eurobonds
Head of Sales — Andrea Stermieri ☎ **648 619**

Libor-Based / Floating-Rate Products
FRN Sales — Stefano Slaviero ☎ **648 615**

Equity Capital Markets
Department: Treasury and Finance
Tel: 648 610 **Fax:** 648 625
Head of Equity Capital Markets — Andrea Stermieri ☎ **648 619**

Syndicated Lending
Department: Treasury & Finance
Tel: 648 610 **Fax:** 648 625
Head of Syndicated Lending — Andrea Stermieri ☎ **648 619**

Money Markets
Department: Treasury & Finance
Tel: 648 610 **Fax:** 648 625
Head of Money Markets — Andrea Stermieri ☎ **648 619**

Foreign Exchange
Tel: 648 615 **Fax:** 648 625
Head of Foreign Exchange — Stefano Slaviero ☎ **648 615**

FX Traders / Sales People
Daniela Lucchi Dealer ☎ **648 614**

Risk Management
Tel: 648 615 **Fax:** 648 625

Exchange-Traded Derivatives
Head — Stefano Slaviero ☎ **648 615**

Settlement / Clearing
Tel: 648 380 **Fax:** 648 385
Head of Settlement / Clearing — Loretta Lusette

Other Departments
Chief Credit Officer	Francesco Dalla Porta ☎ **648 315**
Correspondent Banking	Ottavio Coronati ☎ **648 300**

Administration
Head of Administration	Ermanno Vellani ☎ **648 265**
Head of Marketing	Manuela Rossi ☎ **648 351**

Technology & Systems
Paolo Pelloni ☎ **648 500**

Legal / In-House Counsel
Ferdinando Fiorcari ☎ **648 607**

Accounts / Audit
Salvatore Scivoletto ☎ **648 251**

www.euromoneydirectory.com   ITALY (+39)

Cassa di Risparmio di Cento SpA
Head Office

Via Matteotti 8b, I-44042 Cento
Tel: (051) 683 3111 **Fax:** (051) 683 3443 **Telex:** 510486 CRCEST I **Swift:** CRCE IT 2C **Cable:** RISPARCASSA

Senior Executive Officers
Chairman — Alberto Pivetti
General Manager — Alberto Cilloni
Others (Senior Executives)

Silvio Riboldazzi *Deputy General Manager*

Foreign Exchange
Tel: 683 3350 **Fax:** 901 911
Head of Foreign Exchange — Giuseppe Franciosi *Manager*

Administration
Head of Administration — Andrea Morini *Manager*

Cassa di Risparmio di Cesena SpA
Head Office

Corso Garibaldi 18, I-47023 Cesena
PO Box 161, I-47023 Cesena
Tel: (0547) 358 111 **Fax:** (0547) 358 215 **Telex:** 551032 CECARI I **Swift:** CECR IT 2C

Senior Executive Officers
Chairman, Board of Directors — Davide Trevisani
General Manager — Adriano Gentili

Foreign Exchange
Department: International Department
Tel: 358 265 **Fax:** 358 273
Head of Foreign Exchange — Rino Serra

FX Traders / Sales People

Paolo Maraldi *Dealer* ☎ **358 267**

Administration
Legal / In-House Counsel

Paolo Pizzoccheri *Executive Officer* ☎ **358 207**

Cassa di Risparmio di Firenze SpA
Head Office

Via Bufalini 4/6, I-50122 Florence
PO Box 271/2, Florence
Tel: (055) 261 21 **Fax:** (055) 261 2907 **Telex:** 572391 CRFIES I **Swift:** CRFI IT 3F **Reuters:** CRFF **Cable:** CARISFLOR

Senior Executive Officers
Chairman — Aureliano Benedetti
Chief Executive Officer — Paolo Campaioli *General Manager*
Financial Director — Giuseppe Manuelli *Financial Director*
Chief Operating Officer — Enio Marilli
Treasurer — Paolo Nardini

Debt Capital Markets / Fixed Income
Department: Financial Department
Global Head — Giuseppe Manuelli *Financial Director*

Domestic Government Bonds
Head of Sales — Giorgio Polara *Manager*
Head of Trading — Gianni Danti *Senior Bond Dealer*

Non-Domestic Government Bonds

Paolo Gambassini *Chief FX & MM Dealer*

Eurobonds
Head of Sales — Paolo Gambassini *Chief FX & MM Dealer*

Foreign Exchange
Department: Financial Department
Global Head — Paolo Gambassini *Chief FX & MM Dealer*

FX Traders / Sales People

Luciano Tortoli
Lorenzo Ronchi

Other Departments
Proprietary Trading — Paolo Nardini
Private Banking — Duilio Dei
Correspondent Banking — Romano Martini *Head, Foreign Dept*

ITALY (+39)   www.euromoneydirectory.com

Cassa di Risparmio di Firenze SpA (cont)
Administration
Technology & Systems
    Elvio Sonnino
Legal / In-House Counsel
    Giovanni Giglioli *Manager*
Public Relations
    Filippo Silvestri *Manager*

Cassa di Risparmio di Forli   Head Office

Corso della Republica 14, I-47100 Forli
Tel: (0543) 711 111 Fax: (0543) 711 448
Website: www.carispfo.it

Senior Executive Officers
President   Renato Ascari Raccagni ☎ **711 201**
Chief Executive Officer   Lucio Metri ☎ **711 202**
Syndicated Lending
Country Head   Vittorio Marcacci ☎ **711 381**
Money Markets
Country Head   Riccardo Fiumi ☎ **711 281**
Foreign Exchange
Country Head   Aldo Vialli ☎ **711 273**
Risk Management
Country Head   Franco Fiumi ☎ **711 203**
Corporate Finance / M&A Advisory
Country Head   Riccardo Fiumi ☎ **711 281**

Cassa di Risparmio di Fossano SpA   Head Office

Via Roma 122, I-12045 Fossano
Tel: (0172) 690 1 Fax: (0172) 60553 Telex: 210655 CARFOS I Swift: CRIF IT 2F

Senior Executive Officers
President   Giuseppe Ghisolfi
General Manager   Gianfranco Mondino
General - Treasury
Head of Treasury   Silvio Fissolo ☎ **690 407** 📠 **690 493**
Foreign Exchange
Global Head   Silvio Fissolo ☎ **690 407** 📠 **690 493**

Cassa di Risparmio di Imola SpA   Head Office

Via Cavour, 53, I-40026 Imola
Tel: (0542) 603 611; (0542) 603 981 Fax: (0542) 35936; (0542) 603 919 Telex: 510564 CRIMOL I Swift: CRIM IT 2I
Website: www.crimola.it

Senior Executive Officers
President   Paolo Casadio Pirazzoli
Managing Director / General Manager   Paolo Bianchi

Cassa di Risparmio in Bologna SpA   Head Office

Via Farini 22, I-40122 Bologna
Tel: (051) 645 4111 Fax: (051) 645 4366 Telex: 510282 Swift: CRBO IT 2B
Website: www.carisbo.it

Senior Executive Officers
Chairman   Gianguido Sacchi Morsiani ☎ **645 4462**
Chief Executive Officer   Leone Sibani ☎ **645 4226**
Managing Director / General Manager   Mr Lelli ☎ **645 5373**
International Division   Mr Rossi ☎ **645 6151**
General-Lending (DCM, SL)
Head of Corporate Banking   Mr Sibiani ☎ **645 4226**

Debt Capital Markets / Fixed Income
Tel: 643 6370 **Fax:** 643 6303
Head of Debt Capital Markets — Mr Civardi ☏ **266 936**
Head of Fixed Income Trading — Antonio Perini ☏ **643 6325**

Equity Capital Markets
Tel: 643 6370 **Fax:** 643 6303
Head of Trading — Atos Cavaza ☏ **643 6328**

Syndicated Lending
Head of Syndicated Lending — Mr Macchiavelli ☏ **261 384**

Money Markets
Tel: 643 6370 **Fax:** 643 6303
Head of Money Markets — Paolo Santini ☏ **643 6320**

Foreign Exchange
Tel: 643 6370 **Fax:** 643 6303
Head of Trading — Maurizio Pagani ☏ **643 6351**

Risk Management

Fixed Income Derivatives / Risk Management
Trading — Antonio Perini ☏ **643 6325**

Foreign Exchange Derivatives / Risk Management
Global Head — Maurizio Pagani ☏ **643 6351**

OTC Equity Derivatives
Trading — Atos Cavaza ☏ **643 6328**

Asset Management
Portfolio Management — Mariano Macchiavelli ☏ **645 6120** ℻ **26 1384**

Cassa di Risparmio di Padova e Rovigo SpA — Head Office

Via Trieste 57/59, I-35121 Padova
PO Box 1088, I-35121 Padova
Tel: (049) 822 8111 **Fax:** (049) 822 9240; (049) 822 9250 **Telex:** 430074 CREST I **Swift:** CRPD IT 2P
Email: internaz@cariparo.it
Website: www.cariparo.it

Senior Executive Officers
Chairman — Orazio Rossi
Chief Executive Officer — Pio Bussolotto *Managing Director*
Financial Director — Giulio Canazza *Chief Financial Officer*
General Manager — Alfredo Checchetto
International Division — Piero Zanettin

Cassa di Risparmio di Parma e Piacenza — Head Office

Formerly known as: Cassa di Risparmio di Parma
Via Universita 1, I-43100 Parma
Tel: (0521) 912 111 **Fax:** (0521) 912 665

Senior Executive Officers
President — Luciano Silingardi
Vice Director — Renzo Cesari
Financial Director — Emilio Bia
Director — Fabricio Ampollini
International Division — Franco Bellini

Others (Senior Executives)
Internal Financial Advisor — Fabio Sandrini *Vice Chairman*
Aquile Costamagna *Vice Chairman*

General-Lending (DCM, SL)
Head of Corporate Banking — Giuseppe Bertolini ☏ **(02) 8824 5330**

Other Departments
Correspondent Banking — Seroldi Fausto

ITALY (+39)   www.euromoneydirectory.com

Cassa di Risparmio di Pisa SpA
Head Office

Piazza Dante 1, I-56100 Pisa
Tel: (050) 591 111 Fax: (050) 591 496 Telex: 500281 Swift: CRPI IT 3P Reuters: CRPI
Website: www.caripisa.it

Senior Executive Officers
Chairman	Renato Buoncristiani
Chief Executive Officer	Aldo Sodi
Financial Director	Romano Carlesi

Cassa di Risparmio di Pistoia e Pescia SpA
Head Office

Via Roma, 3, I-51100 Pistoia
PO Box 81, Pistoia
Tel: (0573) 369 1 Telex: 571011 Swift: PIST IT 3P Email: caripit@tin.it Reuters: CRPT Telex: 572241
Website: www.caript.it

Senior Executive Officers
Chairman	Giorgio Rosi
Chief Executive Officer	Giovanni Tommasini
Financial Director	Adriano Tosi
Treasurer	Mario Giacomelli
International Division	Mauro Niccolai ☎ 369 374

Others (Senior Executives)
Deputy General Manager	Piero Lazzeri

Foreign Exchange
Fax: 369 572
Global Head	Mario Giacomelli

Cassa di Risparmio di Ravenna SpA
Head Office

Piazza Garibaldi 6, I-48100 Ravenna
Tel: (0544) 480 111 Fax: (0544) 480 535 Telex: 550665 CAREST I Swift: CRRA IT 2R
Cable: CASSARISPARMIO RAVENNA
International Division Tel: (0544) 480 464; Fax: (0544) 480 545

Senior Executive Officers
Chairman	Antonio Patuelli ☎ 480 411
Vice Chairman	Giorgio Sarti ☎ 480 411
Treasurer	Mirio Bargossi
Vice General Manager	Nicola Sbrizzi
General Manager	Mario Salerno
International Division	Andrea Valentini Manager ☎ 480 464

Syndicated Lending

Other (Trade Finance)
Documentary Credits	Aride Campanini

Foreign Exchange
Head of Foreign Exchange	Andrea Valentini Manager ☎ 480 464

Settlement / Clearing
Operations	Mauro Musacchi Dealer, Int'l Operations

Cassa di Risparmio di Reggio Emilia SpA
Head Office

Via Rivoluzione d'Ottobre 16, I-42100 Reggio Emilia
PO Box 214, I-42100 Reggio Emilia
Tel: (0522) 291 1 Fax: (0522) 322 985 Swift: CCRE IT 2R Email: info@carire.it
Website: www.carire.it

Senior Executive Officers
President	Vincenzo Morlini ☎ 291 201
Financial Director	Sandro de Berardis Director ☎ 291 704
General Manager	Claudio Manici ☎ 291 211
International Division	Ivan Margini Head, International Department ☎ 291 246

Money Markets
Global Head	Mario Franchi Head ☎ 291 314

788   Euromoney Directory 1999

www.euromoneydirectory.com   **ITALY (+39)**

Foreign Exchange
Global Head   Minari Silvana *Head* T **291 304**

Risk Management
Global Head   Canalini William *Head* T **291 254**

Cassa di Risparmio di San Miniato SpA   Head Office
Via IV Novembre 45, I-56027 San Miniato
Tel: (0571) 404 1 **Fax:** (0571) 404 310 **Telex:** 500142 CARISM I **Swift:** CRSM IT 3S **Reuters:** CRSM

Senior Executive Officers
Chairman   Crescenzaio Franci
Chief Executive Officer   Gian Carlo Marradi
Treasurer   Massimo Puccini

Equity Capital Markets

Domestic Equities
Head of Trading   Sergio Benvenuti *Head of Dealing* T **405 318** F **405 333**

Other Departments
Correspondent Banking   Lida Remorini *Head* T **404 579** F **404 346**
Cash Management   Andrea Berti *Head* T **405 381** F **405 337**

Cassa di Risparmio di Udine e Pordenone SpA
Via del Monte 1, I-33100 Udine
Tel: (0432) 599 211 **Fax:** (0432) 599 200

Senior Executive Officers
Chairman   Antonio Comelli
Financial Director   Mario Leonardi
General Manager   Giuseppe Zuccato

Debt Capital Markets / Fixed Income
Global Head   Claudio Deusciti T **599 776**

Domestic Government Bonds
Head of Trading   Maurizio Coseani T **599 794**
Head of Research   Loris Di Bernardo T **599 796**

Eurobonds
Head of Origination   Alberto Seno T **599 798**
Head of Sales   Paolo Dell'oste T **599 716**

Libor-Based / Floating-Rate Products
Asset Swaps   Maurizio Coseani T **599 794**

Fixed-Income Repo
Head of Repo   Maurizio Coseani T **599 794**

Equity Capital Markets
Global Head   Claudio Deusciti T **599 776**

Domestic Equities
Head of Trading   Andrea Fadini T **599 717**

Money Markets

Wholesale Deposits
Head of Sales   Bruno Nadalig T **599 795**

Foreign Exchange
Global Head   Claudio Deusciti T **599 776**
Head of Trading   Pasquale Cilento T **599 790**

FX Traders / Sales People   Concetta Esposito T **599 791**
    Paola Ferraro T **599 792**

ITALY (+39)

Cassa di Risparmio di Venezia SpA
Head Office

Alternative trading name: Carive

San Marco 4216, I-30124 Venice
Tel: (041) 529 1111 **Fax:** (041) 529 2336 **Telex:** 410660 RIVEDG **Swift:** CVCE IT 2V **Reuters:** RIVE
Website: www.carive.it

Senior Executive Officers
Chairman — Alfredo Guarini
Managing Director — Pio Bussolotto
General Manager — Emilio Crippa
Vice General Manager — Francesco Cervetti

Centrobanca
Head Office

Corso Europa 16, I-20122 Milan
Tel: (02) 7781 1; (02) 7781 40 **Fax:** (02) 7781 4474

Senior Executive Officers
Chairman — Emilio Zanetti
Chief Executive Officer — Gian Giacomo Faverio
Financial Director — Fabrizio Cornalba
Treasurer — Maurizio Motta

Money Markets
Global Head — Marco Chiesa ☏ **7781 40**

Risk Management
Global Head — Carlo Gabbi ☏ **7781 4421**

The Chase Manhattan Bank
Full Branch Office

Via Catena 4, I-20121 Milan
Tel: (02) 8895 1 **Fax:** (02) 8895 2218 **Telex:** 320223

Senior Executive Officers
Others (Senior Executives)
Senior Country Officer — Alessandro Mitrovich *Senior Country Officer*

The Chase Manhattan Bank
Full Branch Office

Via Bertoloni 26/B, I-00197 Rome
Tel: (06) 808 5655 **Fax:** (06) 808 5766

Senior Executive Officers
Others (Senior Executives)
Global Institutional Client Management — Francesco Rossi Ferrini *Client Executive*

Citibank NA
Full Branch Office

Foro Buonaparte 16, Casella Postale 10932, I-20121 Milan
Tel: (02) 86474 1; (02) 72001 161 **Fax:** (02) 72001 247; (02) 86474 697 **Telex:** 310027
Email: firstname.lastname@citicorp.com

Senior Executive Officers
Treasurer — Fabio Bolognini ☏ **86474 581**

General-Lending (DCM, SL)
Head of Corporate Banking — Alessandro Gumier ☏ **86474 507**

Relationship Manager
— Sergio Ungaro *Market Manager*

Debt Capital Markets / Fixed Income
Tel: 7200 1161
Global Head — Luigi Pigorini ☏ **86474 709**

Fixed-Income Repo
Trading — Alessandro Ravogli *Trader*
Ricardo Rama De Tisi *Trader*

790 Euromoney Directory 1999

www.euromoneydirectory.com						ITALY (+39)

Equity Capital Markets
Tel: 86474 424
Equity Repo / Securities Lending
Marketing & Product Development		Alessia Nanghetti
Money Markets
Country Head					Paolo Arnaldi *Head of Desk* ☎ **86474 374**
Foreign Exchange
Corporate Sales				Filippo Arena ☎ **86474 371**
Settlement / Clearing
Operations					Achille D'Antoni *Global Transaction Services* ☎ **86474 518**

# Commerzbank AG					Representative Office
Via Cordosio, I-20123 Milan
Tel: (02) 725 961 Fax: (02) 725 967; (02) 725 977
Senior Executive Officers
Direttore Generale				Antonio Marano
Direttore Generale				Franz Würzel

# CREDIOP SpA						Head Office
Via Venti Settembre 30, I-00187 Rome
Tel: (06) 4771 1 Fax: (06) 4771 5952 Telex: 611020 CRDPRO I Swift: CROP IT AR Reuters: CROP
Website: www.crediop.it
Senior Executive Officers
Chief of the Board				Antonio Pedone
Chief Executive Officer			Mauro Cicchiné *Managing Director*
Financial Director				Riccardo Massa *Central Manager*
Chief Operating Officer			Antonio de Lieto Vollaro *Central Manager*
Treasurer					Claudio Zecchi *Manager* ☎ **4771 3110**
Syndicated Lending
Loan-Related Activities
Project Finance				Sergio Zanfrisco *Manager* ☎ **4771 3240**
Money Markets
Global Head					Stefano Catalano *Head of Dealing* ☎ **4771 3900** F **4771 5954**
Foreign Exchange
Global Head					Paolo Gabriellini *Officer* ☎ **4771 3905**
Risk Management
Global Head					Alfredo Di Pasquale *Manager* ☎ **4771 3170**
Administration
Public Relations
						Alberto Mari *Manager*

# Crédit Agricole Indosuez				Full Branch Office
Formerly known as: Banque Indosuez SpA
Via Brera 21, I-20121 Milan
Tel: (02) 72303 1 Fax: (02) 72303 201; (02) 72303 316 Telex: 310581 SUEZIT I Swift: BSUI IT MM
Senior Executive Officers
Senior Country Officer			Ariberto Fassati ☎ **72303 300**
Chief Executive Officer			Olivier Toussaint *General Manager* ☎ **72303 250** F **72303 203**
Chief Operating Officer			Jean-Marie Paulou ☎ **72303 242** F **72303 203**
Treasurer					Francis Candylaftis ☎ **72303 332** F **72303 317**
General Secretary				Matteo Salvadori del Prato ☎ **72303 254**
General-Lending (DCM, SL)
Head of Corporate Banking			Antonio Cavallini ☎ **72303 243**
Debt Capital Markets / Fixed Income
Head of Fixed Income				Roberto Negroni *Head* ☎ **72303 333**
Government Bonds
Head of Sales					Andrea Cecchini ☎ **72303 333**
Eurobonds
Head of Origination				Marco Ragni *Primary Market* ☎ **7200 1915**
Head of Sales					Andrea Cecchini ☎ **72303 333**

Euromoney Directory 1999	**791**

ITALY (+39)   www.euromoneydirectory.com

Crédit Agricole Indosuez (cont)
Eurobonds (cont)
Head of Trading   Marco Ragni *Primary Market* ☏ **7200 1915**
Fixed-Income Repo
Head of Repo   Stefano Bertelli ☏ **72303 327**
Syndicated Lending
Head of Syndication   Antonio Cavallini ☏ **72303 243**
Head of Credit Committee   Claudio Clout *Chief Credit Officer* ☏ **72303 221** F **72303 205**
Loan-Related Activities
Project Finance   Guido Dubini ☏ **72303 249**
Money Markets
Global Head   Roberto Negroni *Head* ☏ **72303 333**
Money Markets - General
Marketing   Cristina Dallasera ☏ **72303 260**
Wholesale Deposits
Marketing   Cristina Dallasera ☏ **72303 260**
Foreign Exchange
Head of Institutional Sales   Francesco Antonini ☏ **72303 271**
Head of Trading   Andrea Dagrada ☏ **72303 271**
FX Traders / Sales People
Sales   Grazia Russo ☏ **72303 272**
    Patrizia de Ciutis ☏ **72303 273**
Risk Management
Head of Risk Management   Benedetto Habib ☏ **72303 329**
Fixed Income Derivatives / Risk Management
IR Swaps Sales / Marketing   Mario Prodi ☏ **72303 329**
IR Options Sales / Marketing   Fabio Castalli ☏ **72303 325**
Corporate Finance / M&A Advisory
Fax: 72303 436
Head of Mergers & Acquisition; Country Head   Giovanni Broggiato *Mergers & Acquisitions* ☏ **72303 434**
Other Departments
Private Banking   Saverio Perissinotto *Head* ☏ **72303 376** F **72303 380**
Administration
Compliance
    Matteo Salvadori del Prato *General Secretary* ☏ **72303 254**

Crédit Commercial de France   Full Branch Office

Piazzetta Bossi 1, I-20121 Milan
Tel: (02) 8553 1 **Fax:** (02) 878 829 **Telex:** 335332 CCFA **Swift:** CCFR IT MM MIL
Email: corpor.ccfitalia@interbusiness.it **Bloomberg:** CCF MI PB

Senior Executive Officers
General Manager   Enrico Marenco ☏ **8553 263**
General-Lending (DCM, SL)
Head of Corporate Banking   Alessandro Baroni *Manager* ☏ **8553 217**
Debt Capital Markets / Fixed Income
Head of Fixed Income Trading   Marco Calonghi *Deputy Manager* ☏ **7200 3250**
Domestic Government Bonds
Head of Trading   Paolo Frambrosi *Trader* ☏ **7200 3200**
Equity Capital Markets
Country Head   Fiancesco Dineri *Deputy Manager* ☏ **8553 353**
Syndicated Lending
Head of Credit Committee   Candido Vighi *Deputy Manager* ☏ **8553 218**
Money Markets
Country Head   Maurizio Galli *Deputy Manager* ☏ **7202 2755**
Foreign Exchange
Country Head   Mauro Giachero *Deputy Manager* ☏ **7200 3192**
Corporate Finance / M&A Advisory
Country Head   Allessandro Baroni *Manager* ☏ **8553 217**
Settlement / Clearing
Operations   Luciano Meroso *Officer* ☏ **8553 222**

www.euromoneydirectory.com　　　　　　　　ITALY (+39)

Asset Management
Head　　　　　　　　　　　　　Luca Pierazzi *Manager* ☎ 8553 339
Other Departments
Private Banking　　　　　　　Michele Savazzi *Manager* ☎ 8553 358
Administration
Head of Administration　　　Aristide Noro *Manager* ☎ 8553 216
Compliance
　　　　　　　　　　　　　　Luca Cremaschi *Officer* ☎ 8553 396

Credit Fiditalia   Head Office
Formerly known as: Sogen Fiditalia
　　　　　　　　　　　　Via Ciardi 9, I-20148 Milan
　　　　　　　　　　　　Tel: (02) 48797 1 **Fax:** (02) 48797 401
Senior Executive Officers
President　　　　　　　　Roberto Venturelli
Financial Director　　　Maurice Caulliez *Financial Director*
Treasurer　　　　　　　Gianfranco Restelli *Treasurer*
Managing Director　　　Pascal Serres

Creditanstalt Finanziaria SpA   Subsidiary Company
　　　　　　　　　　　　Via Cordusio 2, I-20123 Milan
　Tel: (02) 723 231 **Fax:** (02) 861 913 **Telex:** 321265 CAMI I **Email:** creditanstalt@creditanstalt.it
Senior Executive Officers
Managing Director　　　Antonio Lazzaroni
Syndicated Lending
Loan-Related Activities
Project Finance　　　　Stefano Cassella *Head of Structured Finance*
Administration
Head of Administration　Rosalba Amabile *Administrative Director*

Credito Bergamasco SpA   Head Office
　　　　　　　　　　　　Largo Porta Nuova 2, I-24122 Bergamo
Tel: (035) 393 111 **Fax:** (035) 393 457 **Telex:** 300147 CREBER **Swift:** CREB IT 22 **Reuters:** CREB **Telerate:** 3675-3676
Senior Executive Officers
Chairman　　　　　　　　　　Cesare Zonca
Vice Chairman　　　　　　　Carlo Fratta Pasini
Vice Chairman　　　　　　　Giorgio Zanotto
Financial Director　　　　Maurizio Faroni
Chief Operating Officer　Giancarlo Castelli *General Manager*
Treasurer　　　　　　　　　Romano Zanetti
Managing Director　　　　Franco Nale
General Manager　　　　　Alessandro Iori
General Manager　　　　　Giancarlo Castelli
General-Lending (DCM, SL)
Head of Corporate Banking　Giordano Simeoni
Debt Capital Markets / Fixed Income
Department: Mercati Obbligazionari E Derivati
Tel: 350 600 **Fax:** 393 037
Head of Fixed Income　　　　Mauro Nicoli
Head of Fixed Income Sales　Sara Carabella
Head of Fixed Income Trading　Giorgio Lella
Domestic Government Bonds
Head of Sales　　　　　　　　　Sara Carabella
Head of Trading　　　　　　　Mauro Nicoli
Head of Origination; Head of Syndication　Luca Pigolotti
Eurobonds
Head of Sales　　　　　　　　Nora Marchesi
Head of Trading　　　　　　Mauro Nicoli
Emerging Market Bonds
Head　　　　　　　　　　　　Mauro Nicoli
Head of Sales　　　　　　　　Nora Marchesi

Euromoney Directory 1999　**793**

ITALY (+39)	www.euromoneydirectory.com

Credito Bergamasco SpA (cont)

Libor-Based / Floating-Rate Products
FRN Sales	Sara Carabella
FRN Trading	Mauro Nicoli
Asset Swaps	Claudia Conti
Asset Swaps (Sales)	Sara Carabella

Fixed-Income Repo
Head of Repo	Franco Salini
Trading	Franco Salini

Fixed-Income Research
Country Head	Leopoldo Roviello
	Lorenzo Petrucci

Equity Capital Markets
Department: Mercati Azionari E Derivati
Tel: 350 700 **Fax:** 393 037
Head of Trading	Carlo Simeon

Domestic Equities
Head of Trading	Carlo Simeon

International Equities
Head of Sales	Massimo Vitali
Head of Trading	Giuseppe Mutti

Equity Research
Country Head	Leopoldo Roviello

Convertibles / Equity-Linked
Head of Trading	Davide Bendinelli

Equity Repo / Securities Lending
Head	Carlo Simeon

Money Markets
Tel: 350 400 **Fax:** 393 037
Global Head	Severino Legrenzi

Domestic Commercial Paper
Head of Sales	Luca Pigolotti
Head of Trading	Franco Salini

Foreign Exchange
Tel: 350 300 **Fax:** 393 037
Global Head	Romano Zanetti
Head of Institutional Sales	Sara Carabella
Corporate Sales	Salvatore Rendini
Head of Trading	Giorgio Cavallari

Risk Management
Tel: 350 500 **Fax:** 393 037
Country Head	Maurizio Faroni

Fixed Income Derivatives / Risk Management
IR Swaps Sales / Marketing	Sara Carabella
IR Swaps Trading	Mauro Nicoli

Foreign Exchange Derivatives / Risk Management
Spot / Forwards Sales	Sara Carabella
Spot / Forwards Trading	Romano Zanetti

OTC Equity Derivatives
Trading	Davide Bendinelli

Settlement / Clearing
Tel: 393 413
Regional Head	Alberto Visciglio
Operations	Giorgio Mister

Global Custody
Country Head	Alberto Visciglio

Other Departments
Private Banking	Giuseppe Decio

ITALY (+39)

Credito Emiliano SpA
Head Office

Via Emilia S Pietro 4, I-42100 Reggio Emilia
Tel: (0522) 4501 **Fax:** (0522) 433 969 **Telex:** 530658 BACDIR I **Swift:** BACR IT 22

Senior Executive Officers
Chairman   Giorgio Ferrari
Chief Executive Officer   Franco Bizzocchi
Financial Director   Nicolò Angileri
Chief Operating Officer   Giuliano Baroni
Treasurer   Rossano Zanichelli
Managing Director / General Manager   Adolfo Bizzocchi
International Division   Daniele Piccolo Manager

The Dai-Ichi Kangyo Bank Limited

Via dei Bossi 4, I-20121 Milan
Tel: (02) 7202 0152; (02) 8646 5084 **Fax:** (02) 7202 2792 **Telex:** 353095 DKBMIL I
Website: www.dkb.co.jp

Senior Executive Officers
Managing Director / General Manager   Tetsuro Fujinuma

Deutsche Bank SpA
Head Office

Via Borgogna 8, I-20122 Milan
Tel: (02) 4024 1; (02) 7795 1 **Fax:** (02) 4024 2636 **Telex:** 311350 BAIDIR I **Swift:** DEUT IT MM

Debt Capital Markets / Fixed Income
Tel: 7779 5023 **Fax:** 7779 5061

Fixed-Income Repo
Trading   Marco Cresti
                                                Guido Riviera

Equity Capital Markets
Tel: 4024 2532 **Fax:** 4049 443

Equity Repo / Securities Lending
Head   Nicola Meotti Director ☏ 4024 2532
Head of Trading   Marco Canton Trading ☏ 4024 3984

DG BANK
Representative Office

Piazza Castello 16, I-20121 Milan
Tel: (02) 7202 3406 **Fax:** (02) 7202 3574

Senior Executive Officers
Representative   Klaus-Dieter Reiter

Dresdner Bank AG
Full Branch Office

Piazza degli Affari 3, I-20123 Milan
Tel: (02) 724 021 **Fax:** (02) 805 7639

Senior Executive Officers
General Manager   Timothy M Brooks

EFIBANCA SpA
Head Office

Via Po 28/32, I-00198 Rome
Tel: (06) 8599 1 **Fax:** (06) 8599 250 **Telex:** 63033126 **Email:** efiagen@ntt.it

Senior Executive Officers
Chairman   Pietro Rastelli
Chief Executive Officer   Valerio Lattanzi

ITALY (+39)   www.euromoneydirectory.com

Eptasim SpA
Head Office

Via Camperio 9, I-20123 Milan
Tel: (02) 8827 1 **Fax:** (02) 8645 1880 **Telex:** 320141

Senior Executive Officers
Chief Executive Officer   Marco Bolgiani

Others (Senior Executives)
Principal Delegate   Alberto Pasqualone *Deputy Chief Executive*

Debt Capital Markets / Fixed Income
Head of Debt Capital Markets   Alberto Pasqualone *Deputy Chief Executive*

Domestic Government Bonds
Head of Trading   Michele Nani *Trader* ☎ **8827 332**
    Angelo Pensa *Trader* ☎ **8827 333**

Eurobonds
Head of Origination   Pietro Barrera *New Issues* ☎ **8827 409**
Head of Trading   Marco Civardi *Market Maker* ☎ **8827 412** F **8645 1980**
    Marie Christine Cuby *Market Maker* ☎ **8827 413** F **8645 1980**

Bonds - General
Italian Non-Government Bonds   Alfredo de Santis *Market Maker* ☎ **8827 409**
    Paolo Vismara *Market Maker* ☎ **8827 411**

Fixed-Income Repo
Trading   Fabio De Giorgi *Repo Trader* ☎ **8827 428**
    Marco Ermolli *Structured Products* ☎ **8827 362**

Settlement / Clearing
Fixed-Income Settlement   Adelio Colombo ☎ **8827 289**
    Sara Bianchi ☎ **8827 264**

Administration

Compliance
    Gianni Castiglioni *Head of Compliance*

Other (Administration)
    Claude Hassan *Head of Personnel*

Erste Bank der Österreichischen Sparkassen
Representative Office

Formerly known as: GiroCredit Bank AG der Sparkassen
Galleria Pattari 2, Piazza del Duomo 22, I-20122 Milan
Tel: (02) 7200 3520 **Fax:** (02) 8901 0300

Senior Executive Officers
Chairman   Maurizio Uggeri

Erste Bank Sparkassen Praha (CR) as
Representative Office

Formerly known as: GiroCredit Sparkassen Banka Praha as
Galleria Pattari 2, Piazza del Duomo 22, I-20122 Milan
Tel: (02) 7200 3520 **Fax:** (02) 8901 0300

Senior Executive Officers
Chairman   Maurizio Uggeri

European Investment Bank
Full Branch Office

Via Sardegna 38, I-00187 Rome
Tel: (06) 47191 **Fax:** (06) 4287 3438 **Telex:** 611130 BANKEU I

Senior Executive Officers

General-Investment
Head of Investment   Caroline Reid *Head*

www.euromoneydirectory.com   ITALY (+39)

Fiduciaria Indosuez SIM SpA
Subsidiary Company

Via Brera 21, I-20121 Milan
Tel: (02) 72303 1 Fax: (02) 72303 380 Telex: 321565

Senior Executive Officers
Chairman   Ariberto Fassati
Director   Gianni Angeletti
Director   Saverio Perissinotto

Asset Management
Portfolio Management   Fausto Artoni
                                  Grazia Pistone

Finanziaria Sumitomo (Italia) SpA
Subsidiary Company

Via Palestro 2, I-20121 Milan
Tel: (02) 760 81210 Fax: (02) 760 20921

Senior Executive Officers
President   Yoshihiro Nishigughi

Fineurop SpA
Head Office

Via Cerva 28, I-20122 Milan
Tel: (02) 7749 1 Fax: (02) 783 871; (02) 781 175 Telex: 332417 Email: fineurop@fineurop.it

Senior Executive Officers
Chairman   Solo M Dwek

Syndicated Lending
Loan-Related Activities
Trade Finance   Leonardo De Botton
                                  Bice Ceretti
                                  Enrico Seralvo
                                  Giovanni Cabrini
                                  Sergio Castelbolognesi
                                  Federico Manetti

Corporate Finance / M&A Advisory
Other (Corporate Finance)
                                  Eugenio Morpurgo
                                  Raymond Totah
                                  Matteo Carlotti
                                  Carlo Daveri
                                  Fabio Galli
                                  Gilberto Baj Macario

Gefina SpA - Generali Group
Head Office

Via Machiavelli 4, I-34132 Triest
Tel: (040) 671 466; (040) 671 468 Fax: (040) 671 422 Telex: 460190

Senior Executive Officers
Chairman   Gianfranco Gutty
Managing Director   Gesualdo Pianciamore
Company Secretary   Cinzia Ortolan ☏ 671 390

Settlement / Clearing
Regional Head   Cinzia Ortolan ☏ 671 390

Administration
Head of Administration   Patrizia Padovan ☏ 671 051

Generale Bank
Full Branch Office

Strada 4 - A8 - Milanofiori, I-20090 Assago
Tel: (02) 57532 1 Fax: (02) 5750 4242 Telex: 315472 GENMIL I Swift: GEBA IT MM

Senior Executive Officers
Chief Operating Officer   Raoul Carême ☏ 57532 308
Treasurer   Alberto Rago ☏ 825 7837
General Manager   Baudouin Gillon ☏ 57532 307

Euromoney Directory 1999   797

ITALY (+39)   www.euromoneydirectory.com

Giubergia Warburg SIM SpA

Via Santa Maria Segreta 6, I-20123 Milan
Tel: (02) 721 001

Equity Capital Markets
Department: Equities
Other (Domestic Equities)

P Basilico *Chief Executive Officer*

Goldman Sachs SIM SpA — Subsidiary Company

Passaggio Centrale 2, I-20123 Milan
Tel: (02) 8022 1000 Fax: (02) 8022 2130; (02) 8022 2209

Senior Executive Officers
President — Claudio Costamagna
Vice President & Managing Director — Paolo Zannoni
Managing Director — Massimo Paschetto
Managing Director — Ronald Marks

Others (Senior Executives)
John Chartres *Director*
Dante Roscini *Director*

HypoVereinsbank — Full Branch Office

Formerly known as: Bayerische Hypotheken-und Wechsel Bank AG
Via Durini 9, I-20122 Milan
Tel: (02) 7793 1 Fax: (02) 7793 272 Swift: BVBE IT MM

ICCREA SpA

Via Torino 146, I-00184 Rome
Tel: (06) 4716 1 Fax: (06) 474 7155

Senior Executive Officers
President — Giorgio Clementi ☏ **4716 5231**
Chief Executive Officer — Alfredo Neri *Managing Director* ☏ **4716 5576**

Others (Senior Executives)
International & Finance Area — Paolo Alessandro Carimini *Senior Manager* ☏ **4716 5431** ✉ **4716 5566**

General - Treasury
Head of Treasury — Eugenio Napoleoni *Head of International Treasury* ☏ **4716 5626** ✉ **4716 5566**
Salvatore Pilloni *Head of Domestic Treasury* ☏ **4716 5343** ✉ **4788 7721**
Conte Vittorio *Domestic Dealer* ☏ **4716 5381**
Silvio Vari *Domestic Dealer* ☏ **4716 5356**

Debt Capital Markets / Fixed Income
Department: Bonds Department
Country Head — Giorgio Della Tommasina ☏ **4716 5379** ✉ **4716 5288**

Domestic Government Bonds
Head of Sales — T Farcomeni *Head of Domestic Bonds & Equities* ☏ **4716 870**

Non-Domestic Government Bonds
International Bonds — G Marini *Head* ☏ **4716 824**

Bonds - General
Bonds Derivatives — F Polimeni ☏ **4716 874**

Equity Capital Markets
Domestic Equities
Head of Origination — T Farcomeni *Head of Domestic Bonds & Equities* ☏ **4716 870**

Other (International Equity)
International Equities — G Marini *Head* ☏ **4716 824**

Money Markets
Money Markets - General
International Money Markets — Luigi Coretti *Chief Dealer* ☏ **4716 5660** ✉ **4716 5566**
Antonio D'Alessandro *Senior Dealer* ☏ **4716 5659** ✉ **4716 5566**
Mario Ciccolella *Dealer* ☏ **4716 5661**
Roberto Lucci *Dealer* ☏ **4716 5484**

www.euromoneydirectory.com ITALY (+39)

Foreign Exchange
Country Head Eugenio Napoleoni ☎ 4716 5626 📠 4716 5566
FX Traders / Sales People
Luigi Coretti *Chief Dealer* ☎ 4716 5660 📠 4716 5566
Antonio D'Alessandro *Senior Dealer* ☎ 4716 5659 📠 4716 5566
Mario Ciccolella *Dealer* ☎ 4716 5661
Roberto Lucci *Dealer* ☎ 4716 5484

Settlement / Clearing
Settlement (General) Guido Renda ☎ 4716 5330
Alessandro Pellicano ☎ 4716 5779

Other Departments
Correspondent Banking Maurizio D'Ipoliti *Head of International Division* ☎ 4716 5583 📠 4716 5710
Viridiana De Nicola *Secretary*

ICCRI - Istituto di Credito delle Casse di Risparmio Italiane SpA
Head Office

Via Boncompagni 71/H, I-00187 Rome
Tel: (06) 4715 1; (06) 4715 3997 **Fax:** (06) 4715 3074 **Telex:** 626115 **Swift:** ICCRI IT RR **Reuters:** ICCR
Bloomberg: ICCRI

Senior Executive Officers
Chairman Edoardo Massaglia ☎ 4715 3912 📠 482 4508
Managing Director / General Manager Franco Pozzi ☎ 4715 3554 📠 482 4508
International Division Antonio Conforti ☎ 4715 3914 📠 4715 3966

Debt Capital Markets / Fixed Income
Domestic Government Bonds
Head of Trading Gino de Angelis ☎ 4715 3046 📠 4715 3936
Eurobonds
Head of Trading Guido de Conciliis ☎ 4715 3979 📠 4715 3936

Equity Capital Markets
Domestic Equities
Head of Trading Gino de Angelis ☎ 4715 3046 📠 4715 3936
International Equities
Head of Trading Guido de Conciliis ☎ 4715 3979 📠 4715 3936

Syndicated Lending
Head of Syndicated Lending Francesco de Sanctis ☎ 4715 3072 📠 4715 3074
✉ francesco_desanctis@iccri.it

Money Markets
Tel: 4715 3570 **Fax:** 4715 3579
Head of Money Markets Francesco Bottello ☎ 4715 3581

Foreign Exchange
Tel: 4715 3570 **Fax:** 4715 3579
Head of Foreign Exchange Francesco Bottello ☎ 4715 3581

Risk Management
Head of Risk Management Francesco de Sanctis ☎ 4715 3072 📠 4715 3074
✉ francesco_desanctis@iccri.it

Administration
Public Relations
Claudio Scaetta ☎ 4715 3081

IFP Intermoney Financial Products SIM SpA
Subsidiary Company

Via Cernaia 2, I-20121 Milan
Tel: (02) 2900 3383 **Fax:** (02) 2900 0638 **Telex:** 326022 **Reuters:** MONI (Dealing)
Corporate Unit Roma - German Desk Tel: 5848 3953; 5848 3953

Debt Capital Markets / Fixed Income
Libor-Based / Floating-Rate Products
Asset Swaps Umberto Mazzola
Riccardo Bianchi
Maurizio Santinelli
Elena Morgan de Coelho
Elisabetta Setari

Euromoney Directory 1999 **799**

ITALY (+39)   www.euromoneydirectory.com

IFP Intermoney Financial Products SIM SpA (cont)
Money Markets

Other (Wholesale Deposits)
Eurocurrency Deposits   Luigi Castello

Risk Management
Department: Capital Markets

Fixed Income Derivatives / Risk Management
IR Swaps Trading   Umberto Mazzola
         Riccardo Bianchi
         Maurizio Santinelli
         Elena Morgan de Coelho
         Elisabetta Setari
IR Options Trading   Umberto Mazzola
         Riccardo Bianchi
         Maurizio Santinelli
         Elena Morgan de Coelho
         Elisabetta Setari

Foreign Exchange Derivatives / Risk Management
Spot / Forwards Trading   Tommaso Setari
         Renato Malara
         Marco Turnbull
         Marco Cattini
         Francesca Rea
Cross-Currency Swaps, Trading   Umberto Mazzola
         Riccardo Bianchi
         Maurizio Santinelli
         Elena Morgan de Coelho
         Elisabetta Setari

Settlement / Clearing
Settlement (General)   Laura Cefali

Administration
Head of Administration   Eleonora Fratini

The Industrial Bank of Japan Limited   Full Branch Office

Via Senato 14/16, I-20121 Milan
Tel: (02) 760 8621 **Fax:** (02) 760 15311 **Telex:** 331541 IBJMIL

Senior Executive Officers
General Manager   Mr Imaoka

ING Bank   Full Branch Office

Via Tortona 33, I-20144 Milan
Tel: (02) 47780 1 **Fax:** (02) 47780 669 **Telex:** 321510 ING BAN

Senior Executive Officers
General Manager   Giovanni Lecchi

General-Lending (DCM, SL)
Head of Corporate Banking   Giorgio Minetti *Manager, Corporate Banking*

Asset Management
Department: ING Sviluppo Fiduciara SpA
Head   Giovanni Lecchi *General Manager*

Other (Asset Management)
Distribution, Investment Products   Giovanni Lecchi *General Manager*

Other Departments
Private Banking   Giovanni Lecchi *General Manager*
         Ferruccio Enrico Ferri *Manager*

www.euromoneydirectory.com ITALY (+39)

ING Investment Management Italia SGR — Subsidiary Company

Formerly known as: ING Sviluppo Gestioni SPA
Via Tortona 33, I-20144 Milan
Tel: (02) 47780 1 **Fax:** (02) 47780 696 **Telex:** 331045

Senior Executive Officers
Group Managing Director — Giovanni Lecchi ⊤ **47780 770** F **47780 771**
Financial Director — Pieter Louter *Financial Controller* ⊤ **47780 740** F **47780 686**
General Manager — Sandro Pierri ⊤ **47780 597** F **47780 429**

Other Departments
Private Banking — Ferruccio Enrico Ferrari *Manager*

Administration
Head of Administration — Luigi Russo ⊤ **47780 203** F **47780 513**

Interbanca SpA — Head Office

Alternative trading name: Banca per Finanziamenti a Medio e Lungo Termine SpA
Formerly known as: Interbanca
Corso Venezia 56, I-20121 Milan
Tel: (02) 77311 **Fax:** (02) 784 321; (02) 760 02758 **Telex:** 320458 **Email:** interban@tin.it **Reuters:** ITBX

Senior Executive Officers
Chairman — Antonio Ceola
Financial Director — Andrea Caraceni *Finance Director*
Managing Director — Giorgio Cirla
General Manager — Mario Gabriele
Deputy General Manager — Mauro Gambaro

Interfin SIM SpA — Head Office

Via Vittor Pisani 22, I-20124 Milan
Tel: (02) 669 6239; (02) 6671 2663 **Fax:** (02) 669 2108 **Telex:** 333847 **Email:** interfinmilano@ntt.it **Reuters:** INIT
General Telex: 333810

Senior Executive Officers
President — Renato Ingravalle
Chief Executive Officer — Pasquale Acquafredda
Financial Director — Vladimiro Sarzano
Chief Operating Officer; International Division — Stefano Feucori

International Capital Markets SIM SpA — Head Office

Alternative trading name: ICM SIM SpA
Via Vittorio Veneto 32, I-20124 Milan
Tel: (02) 2900 2948 **Fax:** (02) 2901 4088 **Telex:** 360395 **Reuters:** NIMH (Dealing); NIMH/ITLVIEW = ICMM;
ICM 01-02-03-04-05-06-07-08-09-10

Senior Executive Officers
Chairman of the Board — Sergio Zora ⊤ **2900 6260**

Others (Senior Executives)
Internal Auditing — Dario Sala Veni *Head* ⊤ **2900 7181**
Director of the Board — Bruno Seccardi ⊤ **2900 6260**
Claudio Santambrogio

Debt Capital Markets / Fixed Income
Fixed-Income Repo
Trading — Patrizia Alberti *Repos*
Philippe Brunaud *Repos*
Antonella De Santis *Repos*
Claudia Grassi *Repos*
Franco Ippoliti *Repos*

Money Markets
Wholesale Deposits
Head of Sales — Andrea Dametti *Deposits*
Barbara Martinelli *Deposits*

Euromoney Directory 1999 **801**

ITALY (+39) www.euromoneydirectory.com

International Capital Markets SIM SpA (cont)
Foreign Exchange
Spot / Forwards Trading Franco Alessandrin *Dealer*
  Roberto Cartoceti *Dealer*
  Paola Manenti *Dealer*
  Albertio Valtemara *Dealer*

Risk Management
Other (FI Derivatives)
  Silvio De Domenici *Forwards - FRAs*
  Pierino Tarolli *Forwards - FRAs*
  Domenico Di Bussolo *Forwards - FRAs, IRS*
  Massimo Bassi *IRS, FRAs, OIS*
  Cecilia Sala Veni *IRS, OIS*

Foreign Exchange Derivatives / Risk Management
Vanilla FX option Trading Luigi Uslenghi *Forwards - Currency Options - OIS*

Settlement / Clearing
Settlement (General) Debora Guamieri Rota *Back-Office*
  Monia Grossano *Back-Office*
  Antonella De Santis *Repos*

Administration
Technology & Systems
Information Technology Mirella Colombo *Back-Office*
Accounts / Audit
Accounting Elena Gregori
Internal Audit Dario Sala Veni *Head* ☏ **2900 7181**
Accounting Daniela Ponte

Istituto Bancario San Paolo di Torino SpA Head Office

Piazza San Carlo 156, I-10121 Turin
Tel: (011) 555 1 **Fax:** (011) 555 6198 **Telex:** 212040 ISPAOL I **Swift:** IBSP IT TM **Reuters:** ISTX
Investor Relations Tel: 555 2267; **Fax:** 555 2989; **Email:** investorrelation@sanpaolo.com; **Reuters:** SPBA-L
Website: www.sanpaolo.it

Senior Executive Officers
Chairman Luigi Arcuti ☏ **555 200**
Chief Executive Officer Rainer Masera *Managing Director* ☏ **555 2711**
  Luigi Maranzana *Managing Director* ☏ **555 2150**
Financial Director Bruno Picca ☏ **555 7411**
Chief Operating Officer Piero Gavazzi *Chief Business Officer* ☏ **555 2960**
  Amadio Lazzarini ☏ **555 2770**
Managing Director Luigi Maranzana ☏ **555 2150**
Managing Director Rainer Masera ☏ **555 2711**
Company Secretary Piero Luongo ☏ **555 2630**
International Division Rino Rocca ☏ **555 2457**

General-Lending (DCM, SL)
Head of Corporate Banking Roberto Civalleri ☏ **555 6562**

General-Investment
Head of Investment Antonio Pironti ☏ **555 2567**

Debt Capital Markets / Fixed Income
Department: Servizio Finanza Tesoreria & Titoli
Tel: 555 6482 **Fax:** 555 6660
Global Head Alessandro Frascarolo ☏ **555 6372**
Head of Fixed Income Sales Doriano Demi ☏ **554 7150**
Head of Fixed Income Trading Carlo Pittatore ☏ **+44 (171) 214 8000**

Government Bonds
Head of Sales Doriano Demi ☏ **554 7150**
Head of Trading Carlo Pittatore ☏ **+44 (171) 214 8000**
Head of Syndication Massimo Corsini ☏ **554 7123**

Eurobonds
Head of Sales Doriano Demi ☏ **554 7150**
Head of Trading Luigi SepEgno ☏ **554 7116**

Emerging Market Bonds
Head of Sales Doriano Demi ☏ **554 7150**

www.euromoneydirectory.com   ITALY (+39)

Libor-Based / Floating-Rate Products
FRN Sales   Doriano Demi ☏ **554 7150**
FRN Trading   Silva Lepore ☏ **554 7126**
Asset Swaps; Asset Swaps (Sales)   Aldo Allisiardi ☏ **554 7127**

Fixed-Income Repo
Head of Repo; Head of Trading   Renato Prelli ☏ **554 7172**
Other   Massimo Corsini ☏ **554 7123**

Fixed-Income Research
Head of Fixed Income   Andrea Dellitala ☏ **+44 (171) 214 8000**

Equity Capital Markets
Tel: 555 6482 **Fax:** 555 6660
Global Head   Alessandro Frascarolo ☏ **555 6372**
Head of Sales   Doriano Demi ☏ **554 7150**
Head of Trading   Carlo Pittatore ☏ **+44 (171) 214 8000**

Domestic Equities
Head of Sales   Emilio Foglia *Intersim SpA* ☏ **(02) 29099 311**
Head of Trading   Giuseppe Bonini *Intersim SpA* ☏ **(02) 29099 300**

International Equities
Head of Sales   Artemio Signorato ☏ **554 7171**

Equity Research
Head of Equity Research   Mauro Silva *Intersim SpA* ☏ **(02) 29099 0**

Convertibles / Equity-Linked
Head of Sales   Doriano Demi ☏ **554 7150**
Head of Trading   Carlo Pittatore ☏ **+44 (171) 214 8000**

Equity Repo / Securities Lending
Head   Giuseppe Bonini *Intersim SpA* ☏ **(02) 29099 300**

Syndicated Lending
Tel: 555 6482 **Fax:** 555 6660
Head of Origination   Raffaella Borghetti ☏ **554 7130**
Head of Syndication   Marco Graffigna ☏ **554 7131**
Head of Trading   Eugenio Nahor ☏ **+44 (171) 214 8000**

Money Markets
Tel: 555 6482 **Fax:** 555 6660
Global Head   Alessandro Frascarolo ☏ **555 6372**

Domestic Commercial Paper
Head of Sales   Doriano Demi ☏ **554 7150**

Eurocommercial Paper
Head of Sales   Doriano Demi ☏ **554 7150**

Wholesale Deposits
Marketing   Giovanni Mancuso ☏ **555 2854**
Head of Sales   Luciano Bollito ☏ **554 7160**

Foreign Exchange
Tel: 555 6482 **Fax:** 555 6660
Global Head   Alessandro Frascarolo ☏ **555 6372**
Head of Institutional Sales   Luciano Bollito ☏ **554 7160**
Corporate Sales   Doriano Demi ☏ **554 7150**
Head of Trading   Luciano Bollito ☏ **554 7160**

FX Traders / Sales People
                                            Franco Toscano ☏ **554 7118**
                                            Roberto Franco ☏ **554 7110**

Risk Management
Tel: 555 6482 **Fax:** 555 6660
Head of Risk Management   Alessandro Frascarolo ☏ **555 6372**

Fixed Income Derivatives / Risk Management
Head of Sales   Doriano Demi ☏ **554 7150**
Trading   Carlo Pittatore ☏ **+44 (171) 214 8000**

Foreign Exchange Derivatives / Risk Management
Spot / Forwards Sales   Doriano Demi ☏ **554 7150**
Spot / Forwards Trading   Carlo Pittatore ☏ **+44 (171) 214 8000**

OTC Equity Derivatives
Sales   Doriano Demi ☏ **554 7150**
Trading   Carlo Pittatore ☏ **+44 (171) 214 8000**

Corporate Finance / M&A Advisory
Department: Corporate Division
Tel: 555 6562 **Fax:** 555 2442
Global Head   Ezio Salvai ☏ **555 6742**

ITALY (+39)   www.euromoneydirectory.com

Istituto Bancario San Paolo di Torino SpA (cont)
Settlement / Clearing
Tel: 555 5436 Fax: 555 5850
Head of Settlement / Clearing; Equity   Ugo Primo *Head of Back Office* ☎ **555 3386**
Settlement; Fixed-Income Settlement; Back-
Office

Global Custody
Head of Global Custody   Gilberto Godino ☎ **555 3106**

Asset Management
Head   Giuseppe Passatore *Asset Management & Private Banking*
☎ **(02) 7238 3990**

Other Departments
Chief Credit Officer   Enrico Scotti ☎ **555 3452**
Private Banking   Giuseppe Passatore *Asset Management & Private Banking*
☎ **(02) 7238 3990**
Correspondent Banking   Rino Rocca ☎ **555 2457**

Administration
Business Development   Marina Tabacco ☎ **555 3745**
Head of Marketing   Ugo Marchesa Rossi ☎ **555 5545**

Technology & Systems
   Giovanni Guerci ☎ **555 3106**

Legal / In-House Counsel
   Franco Confortini ☎ **555 2195**

Public Relations
Press Office   Giorgio Alagliati ☎ **555 2884**

Accounts / Audit
   Paolo Chiumenti ☎ **555 6201**

Istituto Mobiliare Italiano SpA   Head Office

Alternative trading name: IMI SpA
Viale dell'Arte 25, I-00144 Rome
Tel: (06) 5959 1 Fax: (06) 5959 3888 Telex: 610256 IMIROM Swift: IMIT IT RR
Website: www.imispa.it

Senior Executive Officers
Chairman   Sandro Molinari
Chief Executive Officer   Luciano Martino *Deputy General Manager*
Financial Director   Vittorio Serafino *Deputy General Manager*
Chief Operating Officer   Massimo Mattera *Head of Credit*
Corporate Secretary   Enrico Fioravanti

General-Lending (DCM, SL)
Head of Corporate Banking   Massimo Mattera *Head of Credit*

Administration

Public Relations
Investor Relations   Lawrence Kay *Director*

JTB Forex SpA

Piazza Erculea 9, I-20122 Milan
Tel: (02) 722 051 Fax: (02) 805 6987 Telex: 312541 Reuters: JTB1; JTBX (Dealing); JTBCM (Monitor)

Senior Executive Officers
Sole Director   Dennis Jarvis

JTB Lira Services SIM SpA

Piazza Erculea 9, I-20122 Milan
Tel: (02) 722 051 Fax: (02) 805 6987 Telex: 312541 Reuters: JTB2; JTB3; JTBC; JTBX

Senior Executive Officers
President   Dennis Jarvis

ITALY (+39)

London Forfaiting Italia SpA
Subsidiary Company
Via F Petrarca 4, I-20123 Milan
Tel: (02) 467016 1 Fax: (02) 467016 37

Senior Executive Officers
Managing Director — Dario Ferrari

Syndicated Lending

Loan-Related Activities
Trade Finance
 — Angelo Dallocchio *Director*
 — Daniele Darsie *Director*
 — Dario Ferrari *Managing Director*
 — Stefano Cesari *Senior Manager*
 — Vittoria D'Addario *Manager*

Project Finance — Dario Ferrari *Managing Director*

Mediobanca - Banca di Credito Finanziario SpA
Via Filodrammatici 10, Milan
Tel: (02) 8829 1 Fax: (02) 8829 367; (02) 8829 411

Mediocredito Centrale SpA
Head Office
Via Piemonte 51, I-00187 Rome
Tel: (06) 4791 1 Fax: (06) 4791 550 Telex: 621699 MEDIOC C Swift: MCEN IT RR BIC
Website: www.mcc.it

Senior Executive Officers
Chairman — Gianfranco Imperatori
Chief Executive Officer — Giorgio Tellini

Others (Senior Executives)
Structured Finance Division — Alessandro Castellano
Domestic Banking & Finance Division — Paulo Alberto de Angelis
Administrative Division — Adgrado Anselmi

Mediocredito Lombardo SpA
Head Office
Via Broletto 20, I-20121 Milan
Tel: (02) 8870 1 Fax: (02) 878275 Telex: 335335 Swift: MLOM IT M1 Telex: 326526 MELOMB

Senior Executive Officers
Chairman — Giuseppe Vimercati
Chief Executive Officer — Pierluigi Novello
 — Carlo Pietrantoni *Deputy Chief Executive*
 — Manlio Appiotti *Deputy Chief Executive*
 — Mario Arfe *Deputy Chief Executive*

Equity Capital Markets
Global Head — Angelo Ghisalberti *Deputy Chief Executive*

Syndicated Lending

Loan-Related Activities
Trade Finance — Manlio Appiotti *Deputy Chief Executive*

Corporate Finance / M&A Advisory
Global Head — Paolo Grandi *General Manager*

Merrill Lynch Capital Markets Bank Limited
Full Branch Office
Via dei Giardini 4, I-20121 Milan
Tel: (02) 65530 1 Fax: (02) 65530 600

Senior Executive Officers
General Manager — Melanie Artem

ITALY (+39)   www.euromoneydirectory.com

Merrill Lynch International Bank Limited
Full Branch Office

Via Manzoni 31, I-20121 Milan
Tel: (02) 655 941 Fax: (02) 2900 0384

Senior Executive Officers
District Director   Anthony de Chellis
General Manager   Alessandro Albrighi
Branch Manager, Rome   Maurizio Cucchihara ☏ **(06) 683 931**

Asset Management
Portfolio Management   Gianluca Bussolati *Director*

Administration
Head of Administration   Alessandro Lorenzon *Administration Manager*

Compliance
                                   Laura Bernocchi *Compliance Officer*

Accounts / Audit
                                   Ivan Alippi *Finance Manager*

Merrill Lynch International Bank
Full Branch Office

Largo Fontanella di Borghese 19, I-00186 Rome
Tel: (06) 68393 1 Fax: (06) 68393 231
Website: www.ml.com

Midland Bank plc
Full Branch Office

Via Della Moscova 3, I-20121 Milan
Tel: (02) 6252 5200 Fax: (02) 6252 5333 Telex: 312580

Senior Executive Officers
Chief Executive Officer   C Wyss

Morgan Guaranty Trust Company of New York
Full Branch Office

Corso Venezia 54, I-20121 Milan
Tel: (02) 7744 1 Fax: (02) 7744 424 Telex: 334241 Cable: MORGANBANK MILAN

Senior Executive Officers
Managing Director   Enrico M Bombieri

Others (Senior Executives)
Senior Banker   Marco Morelli *Managing Director*
Head of Advisory, Italy   Francesco Silva *Vice President*
Head of Private Client Group   Paolo Moscovici *Managing Director*

Debt Capital Markets / Fixed Income
Head of Fixed Income   Paolo Chiaia *Vice President*

Foreign Exchange
Head of Foreign Exchange   Paolo Chiaia *Vice President*

Asset Management
Head   Massimo Greco *Vice President*

Nikko Italia Societa Di Intermediazione Mobiliare SpA
Subsidiary Company

Largo Augusto 7, I-20122 Milan
Tel: (02) 7601 2252 Fax: (02) 7601 3296 Telex: 353274

Senior Executive Officers
President   Andrea Orlandini

ITALY (+39)

Nomura Italia SIM SpA
Subsidiary Company

Via Turati 16/18, I-20121 Milan
Tel: (02) 62351 **Fax:** (02) 653 443 **Telex:** 332257 NOMITL
Website: www.nomura.co.uk

Senior Executive Officers
President	Yugo Ishida
Co-President	Alessandro M Cremona
Co-President	Koichi Koda
Financial Director	Mauro Coltorti *Chief FX & MM Dealer*
Chief Operating Officer	Atsuyoshi Aoyagi *Head of Equity Trading*

Equity Capital Markets
International Equities
Head of Sales	Atsuyoshi Aoyagi *Head of Equity Trading*

Convertibles / Equity-Linked
Head of Sales	Atsuyoshi Aoyagi *Head of Equity Trading*

Warrants
Head of Sales	Atsuyoshi Aoyagi *Head of Equity Trading*

Money Markets
Domestic Commercial Paper
Head of Sales	Koichi Koda *Co-President*

Risk Management
OTC Equity Derivatives
Sales	Atsuyoshi Aoyagi *Head of Equity Trading*

Corporate Finance / M&A Advisory
Tel: 623 5278 **Fax:** 655 1840
Global Head	Alessandro M Cremona *Co-President*

Settlement / Clearing
Equity Settlement	Claire Sedfawi

Administration
Head of Administration	Mauro Coltorti *Chief FX & MM Dealer*

Technology & Systems
	Diego Baragiola

The Nomura Securities Co Limited
Representative Office

Via Delle IV Fontane 16, I-00184 Rome
Tel: (06) 486 464 **Fax:** (06) 482 0797

Senior Executive Officers
Representative	Yugo Ishiga

Nova Ljubljanska banka dd
Full Branch Office

Piazza A Diaz 2, I-20123 Milan
Tel: (02) 806 9191 **Fax:** (02) 8646 5358 **Telex:** 360199 LJUBAM I **Swift:** LJBA IT MM

Senior Executive Officers
General Manager	Andrej Bratoz

Nova Ljubljanska banka dd
Representative Office

Via Valdirivo 26, I-34132 Triest
Tel: (040) 639 033 **Fax:** (040) 362 093 **Email:** nlbtrieste@spin.it

Senior Executive Officers
Resident Representative	Mitja Mocivnik

Paribas Finanziaria SpA
Subsidiary Company

Piazza San Fedele 2, I-20121 Milan
Tel: (02) 7247 2021 **Fax:** (02) 7247 2020 **Telex:** 322023 PARIBA I

Senior Executive Officers
Managing Director	Robert Ricci

ITALY (+39) www.euromoneydirectory.com

Paribas Finanziaria SpA (cont)
Corporate Finance / M&A Advisory
Acquistion Finance   Paolo Lisca *Mergers & Acquisitions*
Settlement / Clearing
Operations   Gabriella Beretta

Republic National Bank of New York — Full Branch Office
Via Santa Maria alla Porta, Nr 2, I-20123 Milan
Tel: (02) 72437 1; (02) 8646 1768 Fax: (02) 72437 402 Telex: BLICMI I 325403 Swift: BLIC IT MX Telex: 352142
Website: www.rnb.com.

Senior Executive Officers
Chief Executive Officer   Bruno Oriella *SVP & General Manager* ☎ **72437 351**
Financial Director   Daniel Shayo *First Vice President* ☎ **72437 417**
Chief Operating Officer   Brian Finnegan *Vice President* ☎ **72437 426**
SVP & General Manager   Bruno Oriella ☎ **72437 351**

Debt Capital Markets / Fixed Income
Country Head   Daniel Shayo *First Vice President* ☎ **72437 417**
Domestic Government Bonds
Head of Trading   Samuel Dwek *Associate Vice President* ☎ **72437 416**
Fixed-Income Repo
Head of Repo   Alessandro Cecchini ☎ **72437 416**

Equity Capital Markets
Country Head   Daniel Shayo *First Vice President* ☎ **72437 417**
Domestic Equities
Head of Trading   Luca Iannone ☎ **72437 387**

Syndicated Lending
Country Head   Giorgio Hassan *Vice President* ☎ **72437 368**

Money Markets
Country Head   Maria Panigone ☎ **72437 303**

Foreign Exchange
Country Head   Daniel Shayo *First Vice President* ☎ **72437 417**
Head of Institutional Sales   Alessandro Fumarola ☎ **72437 365**
Corporate Sales   Karim Skik *Associate Vice President* ☎ **72437 384**
FX Traders / Sales People
   Enrico Lorenzi ☎ **72437 301**

Risk Management
Country Head   Brian Finnegan *Vice President* ☎ **72437 426**
Foreign Exchange Derivatives / Risk Management
Vanilla FX option Trading   Alessandro Fumarola ☎ **72437 365**

Settlement / Clearing
Country Head   Giuseppe Pagano ☎ **72437 340**

Global Custody
Country Head   Giuseppe Pagano ☎ **72437 340**

Other Departments
Commodities / Bullion   Maria Panigone ☎ **72437 303**
Private Banking   David Hasbani *Senior Vice President* ☎ **72437 339**

Administration
Technology & Systems
   Claudia Cislaghi ☎ **72437 337**
Compliance
   Daniel Hallac ☎ **72437 325**

Rolo Banca 1473 SpA
Via Zamboni 20, I-40126 Bologna
PO Box 775, I-40100 Bologna
Tel: (051) 640 8111 Fax: (051) 640 8370 Telex: 510148 Swift: ROLO IT 2B Email: rolo.sysadm@alinet.it
Reuters: ROLX; ROLB; ROLC; ROLO

Senior Executive Officers
Chairman   Aristide Canosani
Chief Executive Officer   Franco Bellei
Managing Director / General Manager   Cesare Farsetti

www.euromoneydirectory.com ITALY (+39)

General-Lending (DCM, SL)
Head of Corporate Banking Enrico Montanari
General - Treasury
Head of Treasury Giuseppe Malerbi ☏ 640 8338/8339
Debt Capital Markets / Fixed Income
Tel: 643 4160 **Fax:** 640 8333
Head of Debt Capital Markets Gianluca Caniato ☏ 640 8362
Equity Capital Markets
Tel: 643 4140 **Fax:** 640 8333
Head of Equity Capital Markets Giuseppe Malerbi ☏ 640 8338/8339
Money Markets
Tel: 643 4130 **Fax:** 640 8333
Head of Money Markets Giuseppe Malerbi ☏ 640 8338/8339
 Andrea Gavioli ☏ 643 4362

Foreign Exchange
Tel: 643 4120 **Fax:** 640 8333
Head of Foreign Exchange Paolo Lodi
Corporate Finance / M&A Advisory
Head of Corporate Finance Andrea Camelli ☏ 640 7273 📠 640 7279

Rothschild Italia SpA

Corso Magenta 12, I-20123 Milan
Tel: (02) 72443 1 **Fax:** (02) 72443 300

Senior Executive Officers
Chairman Stefano Marsaglia
Financial Director Tomaso Barbini *Managing Director*
Managing Director Alessandro Daffina
Managing Director Eduardo Subert
Managing Director Robert H Berle

Equity Capital Markets
Head of Equity Capital Markets Tomaso Barbini *Managing Director*

Schroder Associati Spa Head Office

Corso Europa 12, I-20122 Milan
Tel: (02) 7600 4740 **Fax:** (02) 7600 4706

Senior Executive Officers
President Paolo Colonna
Chief Executive Officer Guido Paolo Gamucci *Administrative Delegate*

Others (Senior Executives)
 Giamluca Amdena *Director*
 Nicola Volpi *Director*

Corporate Finance / M&A Advisory
Private Equity Paolo Colonna *President*

Société Générale

Via Olona 2, I-20123 Milan
Tel: (02) 8549 1 **Fax:** (02) 8549 204
Website: www.socgen.com

The Tokai Bank Limited Representative Office

Via del Vecchio Politecnico 3, I-20121 Milan
Tel: (02) 7602 1234 **Fax:** (02) 794 439 **Telex:** 353208 TOKAI I

Senior Executive Officers
Chief Representative Hideo Hayashi

Euromoney Directory 1999 **809**

ITALY (+39) www.euromoneydirectory.com

Tradition Italia SIM SPA
Full Branch Office

Corso Matteotti 10, I-20121 Milan
Tel: (02) 7722 0210 **Fax:** (02) 7601 4091 **Telex:** 325491 **Reuters:** TRIT
Cash Tel: (02) 772 291; **Derivatives Tel:** (02) 772 293

Senior Executive Officers
Managing Director — Antonio Airaghi

Debt Capital Markets / Fixed Income
Tel: 772 294
Country Head — Gianmario Cattaneo

Money Markets
Other (Wholesale Deposits)
Interbank Deposits — Giuseppe Porta *Head*

Foreign Exchange
Tel: 772 292
Country Head — Pasquale Bruno *Head*

Risk Management
Department: Derivatives
Country Head — Alberto Schlauch *Head*

Unicredito Italiano SpA
Head Office

Formerly known as: Credito Italiano SpA

Piazza Cordusio, I-20123 Milan
Tel: (02) 8862 1 **Telex:** 312401, 310103 CRIT MM **Swift:** CRIT IT MM DIR **Email:** info@credit.it
Corporate Communication Fax: 8862 3034; **International Banking Relation Fax:** 8862 3524
Website: www.credit.it

Senior Executive Officers
Chairman — Lucio Rondelli
Chief Executive Officer — Alessandro Profumo
Financial Director; Treasurer — Pietro Modiano
International Division — Fausto Petteni

General-Lending (DCM, SL)
Head of Corporate Banking — Massimo Minolfi

General-Investment
Head of Investment — Pietro Modiano

Debt Capital Markets / Fixed Income
Head of Fixed Income Sales — Lorenzo Stanca
Head of Fixed Income Trading — Luigi Belluti

Government Bonds
Head of Trading — Stefano Inguscio
Head of Syndication — Niccoló Nuti
Head of Origination — Alessandro Gumier

Eurobonds
Head of Trading — Carla Tretto

Libor-Based / Floating-Rate Products
Asset Swaps — Marco Pavoni

Fixed-Income Repo
Head of Repo — Clarice Calderoni

Fixed-Income Research
Head of Fixed Income — Lorenzo Stanca

Equity Capital Markets
Head of Equity Capital Markets — Alessandro Gumier
Head of Sales — Kevin Compere
  Mark Tempestini
Head of Trading — Andrea Crouetto

Domestic Equities
Head of Sales — Kevin Compere
  Mark Tempestini

Other (Domestic Equities)
— Paolo Cigognani

International Equities
Head of Sales; Head of Trading — Marco Elli

Equity Research
Head of Equity Research								Claudia Vignati
											Vincenza Colucci
Convertibles / Equity-Linked
Head of Sales									Roberto Rati
Equity Repo / Securities Lending
Head										Luigi De Vito
Money Markets
Head of Money Markets								Luigi Parrilla
Foreign Exchange
Head of Foreign Exchange							Luca Fornoni
											Davide Mereghetti
Risk Management
Head of Risk Management							Paolo Pierri
Fixed Income Derivatives / Risk Management
Head of Sales; Trading								Ferdinando Samaria
Foreign Exchange Derivatives / Risk Management
Spot / Forwards Sales; Spot / Forwards Trading   Ferdinando Samaria
OTC Equity Derivatives
Sales; Trading									Ferdinando Samaria
Corporate Finance / M&A Advisory
Head of Corporate Finance							Pietro Modiano
Other Departments
Private Banking									Luca Majocchi *Global Head*
Administration
Legal / In-House Counsel
											Fabrizio Colonna
Accounts / Audit
											Giuseppe Aquaro

United Garanti Bank International NV   Full Branch Office
Via Senato 6, I-20121 Milan
Tel: (02) 76205 1 **Fax:** (02) 76205 800 **Telex:** 312558 UGBI MI **Swift:** UGBI IT MX
Senior Executive Officers
Country Manager								Gianni Bollea

Warburg Dillon Read Italia SIM SpA
Via Santa Maria Segreta 6, I-20123 Milan
Tel: (02) 72527 1 **Fax:** (02) 72527 770
Senior Executive Officers
Chairman									P Ottolenghi
Corporate Finance / M&A Advisory
Other (Corporate Finance)
											A Franzone *Head of Corporate Finance*
											D Pignatelli
											R Zippel

WestLB (Italia) SpA   Subsidiary Company
Casella Postale 1776, Via Canova 36-40, I-20145 Milan
Tel: (02) 345 0624 **Fax:** (02) 345 0360
Senior Executive Officers
Managing Director								Dario Segre
Managing Director								Giorgio Binda
General - Treasury
Head of Treasury								Clara Calabrese *Treasury / Institutional Investors*
											Alberto Carletti *Treasury / High Net Worth Individuals*
											Riccardo Leonardi *Treasury*
											Massimo Mattioli *Treasury / Institutional Investors*

ITALY (+39)

WestLB (Italia) SpA (cont)
Relationship Manager
Financial Institutions — Daniele Zanuso
Giorgio Ghiglieno

Syndicated Lending
Loan-Related Activities
Trade Finance — Henri Ninove
Laura Paternò

Corporate Finance / M&A Advisory
Department: Corporate Finance

Other (Corporate Finance) — Alberto Brazzelli
Marco Castiglione
Roberto Giacobone
Ludger Hahn
Alberto Lampertico
Mario Visioni

JAMAICA (+1 876)

Bank of Jamaica — Central Bank
Nethersole Place, Kingston
PO Box 621, Nethersole Place, Kingston
Tel: 922 0750; 922 0759 **Fax:** 922 0854; 922 0416 **Telex:** 2167 RESERVE **Email:** jmorgan@boj.org.jm
Telex: 2173 RESERVE
Website: www.boj.org.jm

Senior Executive Officers
Chief Executive Officer — Derick Latibeaudiere *Governor*

Others (Senior Executives)
Financial Institutions Supervisory Division — Audrey Anderson *Deputy Governor*
Finance and Technology — Frederick Manning *Deputy Governor*
Research and Economic Programming — Colin Bullock *Deputy Governor*
Banking and Market Operations — Brian Wynter *Deputy Governor*
Deposit Insurance — Winston Carr *Deputy Governor*

Citibank NA — Full Branch Office
63-67 Knutsford Boulevard, Kingston 5
Tel: 926 3270 **Fax:** 929 3745

Senior Executive Officers
Chief Executive Officer — Peter Moses *Country Corporate Officer* ☎ **926 4020**
Treasurer — Dennis Cohen *Country Treasurer* ☎ **926 7991**

Debt Capital Markets / Fixed Income
Head of Fixed Income — Eva Lewis ☎ **926 7090**

Equity Capital Markets
Head of Equity Capital Markets — Eva Lewis ☎ **926 7090**

Syndicated Lending
Loan-Related Activities
Structured Trade Finance — Sonia Wynter *Trade Coordinator* ☎ **926 3270**

Foreign Exchange
Head of Foreign Exchange — Dennis Cohen *Country Treasurer* ☎ **926 7991**

Risk Management
Head of Risk Management — Maureen Hayden-Cater ☎ **926 3260**

Other Departments
Cash Management — Marcia Woon Choy ☎ **929 6916**

JAPAN
(+81)

The Bank of Japan
🏛 Central Bank

1-1 Nihonbashi 2-chome, Hongoku-cho, Chuo-ku, Tokyo 103-8630
CPO Box 203, Tokyo
Tel: (3) 3279 1111 **Fax:** (3) 5200 2256; (3) 5201 5661 **Telex:** J22763 **Email:** qg7s-mttk@asahi-net.or.jp
Website: www.boj.go.jp/en/index.html

Senior Executive Officers
Governor & Chairman Policy Board   Masaru Hayame

Others (Senior Executives)
    Sakuya Fujiwara *Deputy Governor*
    Yutaka Yamaguchi *Deputy Governor*

ABN AMRO Bank NV
Full Branch Office

12th/13th Floors, Shiroyama JT Mori Building, 4-3-1 Toranomon, Minato-ku, Tokyo 105-6013
CPO Box 374, Tokyo 105-6013
Tel: (3) 5405 6500; (3) 5405 6501 **Fax:** (3) 5405 6900; (3) 5405 6903 **Telex:** 2222959 **Swift:** ABNA JP JT

Senior Executive Officers
Chief Executive Officer   Herman F Kesseler *Country Manager* ☎ **5405 6601** 📠 **5405 6901**
Treasurer   Shin Nagai *Treasurer* ☎ **5405 6506** 📠 **5405 6906**
Secretary to Country Manager   Kaori Masuda ☎ **5405 6601** 📠 **5405 6901**

Others (Senior Executives)
Transaction Services Division   Shigeo Aizawa *Division Manager* ☎ **5405 6650** 📠 **5405 6905**

Relationship Manager
Structured Finance Division   Michiel Schwartz *Manager* ☎ **5405 6561** 📠 **5405 6902**
Transaction Services Division   Shigeo Aizawa *Division Manager* ☎ **5405 6650** 📠 **5405 6905**

Syndicated Lending

Loan-Related Activities
Trade Finance   Machiko Murakami *Manager, Trade Services* ☎ **5405 6639** 📠 **5405 6905**
Structured Trade Finance   Michiel Schwartz *Manager* ☎ **5405 6561** 📠 **5405 6902**

Money Markets
Reuters: ABNQ
Country Head   Shin Nagai *Treasurer* ☎ **5405 6506** 📠 **5405 6906**

Foreign Exchange
Tel: 5405 6505 **Fax:** 5405 6906 **Reuters:** ABND **Telex:** 25714
Head of Foreign Exchange   Masatoshi Ishii *Manager, FX* ☎ **5405 6350**
Corporate Sales   Toshiyuki Takahashi *Manager, Forex Sales* ☎ **5405 6535**
Head of Trading   Yuichi Wada *Senior FX Trader* ☎ **5405 6531**

FX Traders / Sales People
FX Forward   Tsuyoshi Saiki *Senior FX Forward Trader* ☎ **5405 6534**
FX   Toshiyuki Takamatsu *Senior FX Trader* ☎ **5405 6532**

Risk Management
Fax: 5405 6906
Regional Head   Erinna Nash *Treasury Risk Control* ☎ **5405 6669**

Other (FI Derivatives)
Derivatives   Robert Perman *Trader* ☎ **5405 6555**
Derivatives Administration   Yoshinobu Takagi *Manager, Derivatives Administration* ☎ **5405 6513**

Settlement / Clearing
Tel: 5405 6512 **Fax:** 5405 6907
Operations   Atsuyoshi Murao *Manager, Treasury Administration* ☎ **5405 6621**

Asset Management
Head   Eric Buckens *Managing Director* ☎ **5405 6934** 📠 **5405 6903**

Other Departments
Chief Credit Officer   Yu Iguchi *Manager, Credit Loan Administration* ☎ **5405 6514** 📠 **5405 6903**

Administration
Head of Administration   Derrick King *Manager* ☎ **5405 6620** 📠 **5405 6905**

Technology & Systems
    Isao Takagi *Manager, Information Technology* ☎ **5401 6515** 📠 **5401 6909**

JAPAN (+81)　　　　　　　www.euromoneydirectory.com

ABN AMRO Bank NV (cont)
Accounts / Audit
　　　　　　　　　　　Kiyonobu Ueda *Manager Internal Audit* ⓣ **5405 6510** ⓕ **5405 6904**
Other (Administration)
Human Resources & General Affairs Division　Hiroshi Masui *Manager* ⓣ **5405 6516** ⓕ **5405 6904**
Accounting　　　　　　　　　　　　　　　Yasunobu Tanabe *Manager* ⓣ **5405 6518** ⓕ **5405 6908**

ABN AMRO Securities (Japan) Limited　　　　Full Branch Office

12th Floor, Shiroyama JT Mori Building, 4-3-1 Toranomon, Minato-ku, Tokyo 105-6012
Tel: (3) 5405 6700 **Fax:** (3) 5405 6710

Senior Executive Officers
President　　　　　　　　　　　Arthur Jesson
Chief Operating Officer　　　　　Tadashi Jitoku

The Aichi Bank Limited　　　　　　　　　　　　Head Office

14-12 Sakae 3-chome, Naka-ku, Nagoya 460-8678
Tel: (52) 251 3211 **Fax:** (52) 262 5793 **Telex:** J59687 AICHIBKA **Swift:** AICH JP JN **Cable:** AICHI BANK

Senior Executive Officers
President　　　　　　　　　　Shinichi Koide
Senior Managing Director　　　Tamotsu Hoshino
Managing Director　　　　　　Toshio Takabatake
Managing Director　　　　　　Takuo Fujii
Managing Director　　　　　　Susumu Ohashi
Managing Director　　　　　　Tadaaki Kurimoto
Managing Director　　　　　　Kunio Arai
Managing Director　　　　　　Gengo Sawada
International Division　　　　　Kazuma Tamiya *GM, International Department*

AIG Financial Products (Japan) Limited　　　Subsidiary Company

8th Floor, AIG Building, 1-3 Marunouchi, 1-chome, Chiyoda-ku, Tokyo 100
Tel: (3) 3214 1350 **Fax:** (3) 3214 1636

Senior Executive Officers
Managing Director　　　　　　Eiji Nakamura

Settlement / Clearing
Department: AIG Financial Products Corp
100 Nyala Farm, Westport, CT 06880
Tel: +1 (203) 222 4700 **Fax:** +1 (203) 222 4780
Settlement (General)　　　　　Sabrina Jaques ⓣ **+1 (203) 221 4805**
　　　　　　　　　　　　　　　Carmine Paradiso ⓣ **+1 (203) 221 4805**

Aizawa Securities Co Limited　　　　　　　　Head Office

1-20-3 Nihonbashi, Chuo-ku, Tokyo 103
Tel: (3) 5641 0802 **Fax:** (3) 5641 0804 **Telex:** 2227219 AIZAWA J

Senior Executive Officers
Chairman　　　　　　　　　　Motoya Aizawa

ANZ Securities (Asia) Limited　　　　　　　Representative Office

Formerly known as: ANZ McCaughan Limited
8th Floor, Yanmar Tokyo Building, 1-1 Yaesu 2-chome, Chuo-ku, Tokyo 104
Tel: (3) 5202 0731 **Fax:** (3) 5202 0730

Senior Executive Officers
Chief Representative　　　　　Shigehiro Matsuura

www.euromoneydirectory.com   JAPAN (+81)

The Ashikaga Bank Limited
Head Office

1-25 Sakura 4-chome, Utsunomiya, Tochigi 320-8610
International Division, PO Box 5329, Tokyo 100-31
Tel: (28) 622 0111 **Telex:** J28777 ASHIBK A/B **Swift:** ASIK JP JT
International Division **Tel:** (3) 3276 8686; **Fax:** (3) 3276 8666

Senior Executive Officers
President   Yoshio Yanagita
Senior Managing Director   Yasuo Yoshida
Managing Director   Shin Iizuka
Managing Director   Shigeru Nakayama
Managing Director   Noritoshi Hagawa
Managing Director   Takashi Tanaka
Managing Director   Tadashi Nagayasu
Managing Director   Hideyuki Obana
International Division   Kaneto Takayama *General Manager*
                                       Takashi Tomita *Deputy General Manager*

General-Lending (DCM, SL)
Head of Corporate Banking   Eiichi Kimura *Manager, Credit Analysis*

General-Investment
Head of Investment   Akinori Ito *Manager, International Investments & Loans*

Foreign Exchange
Department: Treasury Division
9-2 Nihonbashi 3-chome, Chuo-ku, Tokyo 103-0027
Tel: +81 (3) 3274 7671 **Fax:** +81 (3) 3274 7666
Head of Foreign Exchange   Kuniaki Arai

FX Traders / Sales People
International Funds & Forex   Takashi Mikami *Deputy General Manager*

Settlement / Clearing
Operations   Tutaka Horie *Deputy General Manager*
                                       Masayoshi Asou *Deputy General Manager*

Administration
Corporate Communications
Business Promotion   Takashi Tomita *Deputy General Manager*

Accounts / Audit
Accounting Administration   Kazuhiko Takano *Manager*

Australia & New Zealand Banking Group Limited
Full Branch Office

8th Floor, Yanmar Tokyo Building, 2-1-1 Yaesu, Chuo-ku, Tokyo 104-0028
Tel: (3) 3271 1151 **Fax:** (3) 3281 8417 **Telex:** J24157 **Swift:** ANZB JP JX **Reuters:** ANZQ; ANZR
Website: www.anz.co.jp

Senior Executive Officers
Country Head   Trevor Jordon
Treasurer   Peter Trumper *Head of Financial Markets*

Settlement / Clearing
Operations   Ove Weiseth *Chief Operations Manager*

Other Departments
Private Banking   Ken Torii *Head of Personal Banking*

The Awa Bank Limited
Head Office

24-1 Nishisemba-cho 2-chome, Tokushima 770-8601
Tel: (886) 233 131 **Fax:** (886) 526 629 **Telex:** 5862115 AWABKHJ **Swift:** AWAB JP JT

Senior Executive Officers
Chairman   Toshikazu Sumitomo
President   Tadaie Yamashita

Others (Senior Executives)
Deputy President   Takehiro Furukawa *Senior Managing Director*
                                       Naoto Sato *Senior Managing Director*
                                       Soichiro Wariishi
                                       Yoshikazu Fukunaga

Euromoney Directory 1999   **815**

JAPAN (+81)　　　www.euromoneydirectory.com

Banca Commerciale Italiana
Full Branch Office

Kishimoto Building, 2-1 Marunouchi 2-chome, Chiyoda-ku, Tokyo 100
Tel: (3) 5221 7800 Fax: (3) 5221 7850 Telex: 26493 COMIT J Swift: BCIT JP JT Reuters: BCIQ
Cable: COMITBANCA
Corporate Unit Roma - German Desk Tel: 5848 3953

Senior Executive Officers
Chief Manager　　　　　　　　　　　R Mazzi
Senior Manager　　　　　　　　　　S Sugimoto
Senior Manager　　　　　　　　　　M Santini
International Division　　　　　　　M Santini *Deputy Chief Manager*

Debt Capital Markets / Fixed Income
Head of Debt Capital Markets　　　Y Sakurai *Manager*

Domestic Government Bonds
Head of Trading　　　　　　　　　　S Yamamoto *Senior Manager & Chief Dealer*

Money Markets
Country Head　　　　　　　　　　　S Yamamoto *Senior Manager & Chief Dealer*

Foreign Exchange
Country Head　　　　　　　　　　　S Yamamoto *Senior Manager & Chief Dealer*

Settlement / Clearing
Country Head　　　　　　　　　　　M Noguchi *Assistant Manager*

Banca Nazionale del Lavoro SpA
Representative Office

510/511, 5th Floor, North Wing, Yurakucho Denki Building, 7-1 Yurakucho 1-chome, Chiyoda-ku, Tokyo 100-0004
Tel: (3) 3213 1591 Fax: (3) 3213 1594 Telex: 2223553 BNLTKJ Cable: LAVOROBANK

Senior Executive Officers
Chief Representative　　　　　　　Maurizio Accinni

Banco Bilbao Vizcaya
Representative Office

12th Floor, Fukoku Seimei Building, 2-2-2 Uchisaiwaicho, Chiyoda-ku, Tokyo 100-0011
Tel: (3) 3501 1076; (3) 3501 1061 Fax: (3) 3597 0249; (3) 3501 1064 Telex: J23542 BBV

Senior Executive Officers
Regional General Manager　　　　Javier Esparza

Others (Senior Executives)
Representative Office　　　　　　　Tetsuya Okubo *Manager* ☎ **3501 1069**
　　　　　　　　　　　　　　　　　　　　　Toshio Oishi *Representative*

Debt Capital Markets / Fixed Income
Department: Capital Markets & Securities
Country Head　　　　　　　　　　　Motoyoshi Ohta *Manager* ☎ **3501 1040**

Syndicated Lending
Loan-Related Activities
Trade Finance　　　　　　　　　　　Motoyoshi Ohta *Manager* ☎ **3501 1040**

Banco do Brasil SA
Full Branch Office

Shin-Kokusai Building, 4-1 Marunouchi 3-chome, Chiyoda-ku, Tokyo 100
Tel: (3) 3213 6511

Senior Executive Officers
Deputy General Manager　　　　　Alexandre Cardoso
Deputy General Manager　　　　　Mauro Cezar dos Santos
Deputy General Manager　　　　　Nilo José Panazzolo

Equity Capital Markets
Equity Repo / Securities Lending
Head of Trading　　　　　　　　　　Hatsuo Hosaka *Manager*

Syndicated Lending
Other (Trade Finance)
Loans & Foreign Trade　　　　　　Hatsuo Hosaka *Manager*

Foreign Exchange
Country Head　　　　　　　　　　　Masaru Horigome *Assistant Manager*

816　Euromoney Directory 1999

www.euromoneydirectory.com   JAPAN (+81)

Other Departments
Correspondent Banking
Administration
Technology & Systems

Accounts / Audit

Toshiharu Fujimoto *Assistant Manager*

Yukio Haraguchi *Systems Engineer*

Oscar J T Nagamine *Controller*

Banco Central Hispanoamericano SA   Full Branch Office

10th Floor, ATT Annex Building, 11-7 Akasaka 2-chome, Tokyo 107-0052
Tel: (3) 3582 4111 **Fax:** (3) 3505 3489 **Telex:** 2423463 BHATOK J **Swift:** HISP JP JT **Reuters:** BHAQ

Senior Executive Officers
General Manager, Japan   Gregory Testerman
Others (Senior Executives)
    Keisuke Terashima *Senior Adviser*
Syndicated Lending
Head of Syndicated Lending   Tomoyuki Oikawa *Manager*
Money Markets
Head of Money Markets   Noriaki Narita *Chief Dealer*
Foreign Exchange
Head of Foreign Exchange   Noriaki Narita *Chief Dealer*
Corporate Finance / M&A Advisory
Head of Corporate Finance   Tomoyuki Oikawa *Manager*

Banco do Estado de São Paulo SA (BANESPA)   Full Branch Office

Alternative trading name: BANESPA
Yurakucho Denki Building 'N' 16th, 7-1 Yurakucho 1-chome, Chiyoda-ku, Tokyo 100-0006
Tel: (3) 3214 0609 **Fax:** (3) 3214 7062 **Telex:** J26825 TOBESP **Swift:** BESP JP JT **Email:** banespa@gol.com
Website: www.banespa.com.br

Senior Executive Officers
General Manager   Jorge Massaro Okamura
Deputy General Manager   Tutomu Sakoda
General-Lending (DCM, SL)
Head of Corporate Banking   Yukio Shimada *Manager, Corporate Banking*
Syndicated Lending
Other (Trade Finance)
Documentary Credits; Letters of Credit   Yukie Kito *Assistant Manager*
Foreign Exchange
Head of Foreign Exchange   Shigeru Nagaoka *Assistant Manager*
Corporate Finance / M&A Advisory
Country Head   Takayoshi Goto *Senior Adviser*
Settlement / Clearing
Settlement (General)   Yasuji Yamazaki *Manager, Back-Office Settlements- FX*
Operations   Kuniyasu Bannai *Senior Manager & Controller*
Other Departments
Private Banking   Masao Kanaya *Assistant Manager*
Correspondent Banking   Tutomu Sakoda *Deputy General Manager*
Administration
Head of Administration   Nelson Kenji Taguchi *Manager Administration & Finance*

Banco Santander SA   Full Branch Office

8th Floor, Akasaka Twin Tower, Main Building, 2-17-22 Akasaka, Minato-ku, Tokyo 107-0052
Tel: (3) 5561 0591 **Fax:** (3) 5561 0580 **Telex:** 33649 **Swift:** BDER JP JT **Reuters:** BSTK

Senior Executive Officers
General Manager   Hideki Aihara
General-Lending (DCM, SL)
Head of Corporate Banking   Noriaki Hoshino *Manager, Credit*
Syndicated Lending
Trade Finance   Kurt Brunner *Director*

JAPAN (+81) www.euromoneydirectory.com

Banco Santander SA (cont)
Risk Management
Head of Risk Management Noriaki Hoshino *Manager*
Settlement / Clearing
Head of Settlement / Clearing Yoko Ikegami *Manager*
Other Departments
Chief Credit Officer Noriaki Hoshino *Head of Credit*
Administration
Business Development Seiichi Tamura *Senior Adviser*

Bangkok Bank Public Company Limited — Full Branch Office
Bangkok Bank Building, 8-10 Nishi-Shimbashi 2-chome, Minato-ku, Tokyo 105-0003
CPO Box 1602, Tokyo
Tel: (3) 3503 3333 **Fax:** (3) 3502 6420; (3) 3506 8503 **Telex:** J24373 BANKOK BK **Swift:** BKKB JP JT **Reuters:** BBTK
Senior Executive Officers
SVP & Branch Manager Thawee Phuangketkeow
Financial Director Masuo Ishikawa *AVP & Assistant Branch Manager*
Settlement / Clearing
Head of Settlement / Clearing Takao Ninomiya *Assistant Branch Manager*

Bank of America NT & SA — Full Branch Office
ARK Mori Building, 12-32 Akasaka 1-chome, Minato-ku, Tokyo 107
Tel: (3) 3587 3111 **Fax:** (3) 3587 1610 **Telex:** J22455 BANKOAM **Swift:** BOFA JP JX **Reuters:** BOAQ
Senior Executive Officers
SVP, Regional Manager, Japan, Australia, Korea Arun Duggal

Others (Senior Executives)
  Ikuo Kodama *VP & Country Administration Officer*

Other Departments
Department: Financial Markets
Other Departments
Financial Markets Mr Nakajima *Chief Dealer*

Bank Austria Creditanstalt AG — Representative Office
Room 6B, 6th Floor, Imperial Tower, 1-1 Uchisaiwaicho 1-chome, Chiyoda-ku, Tokyo 100
Tel: (3) 3501 8634 **Fax:** (3) 3592 0874 **Telex:** J36715
Senior Executive Officers
Chief Representative Michael Schifter

Bank Brussels Lambert — Representative Office
9th Floor, Landic Akasaka-Mitsuke Building, 3-9-18 Akasaka, Minato-ku, Tokyo 107-0052
Tel: (3) 3586 2791; (3) 3586 2792 **Fax:** (3) 3589 2436 **Email:** bbltokyo@sannet.ne.jp
Senior Executive Officers
Chief Representative Philippe Fonck

The Bank of Fukuoka Limited
International Division:, 8-7 Yaesu 2-chome, Chuo-ku, Tokyo 104
Tel: (3) 3242 6910 **Fax:** (3) 3242 6918 **Telex:** 2226508 **Swift:** FKBK JP JT **Cable:** FUKUOKAGINKO
Senior Executive Officers
Chairman Toyohiko Goto
President Ryoji Tsukuda
Managing Director / General Manager Kiyoto Watanabe

www.euromoneydirectory.com　　　JAPAN (+81)

The Bank of Ikeda Limited
Head Office

1-11 Jonan 2-chome, Ikeda 563-0025, Osaka Prefecture
Tel: (727) 513 521; (727) 533 737 **Fax:** (727) 512 716 **Telex:** 5242102 IKEBK J **Swift:** BIKE JP JS
Email: intl-div@ikedabank.co.jp **Reuters:** IKEJ
Website: www.ikedabank.co.jp

Senior Executive Officers
President　　　　　　　　　　　　Kazuya Kiyotaki
Chief Executive Officer　　　　　　Yoshitsugu Hara *Deputy President*
Financial Director　　　　　　　　Noboru Komiya *Managing Director*
International Division　　　　　　Toru Moriwaki *Director & General Manager* ☏ **(6) 251 3175**

Debt Capital Markets / Fixed Income
Department: International Division
Tel: (6) 251 3175 **Fax:** (6) 251 3421
Head of Fixed Income　　　　　　Koji Miyata *Manager* ☏ **(6) 251 0239**

Eurobonds
Head of Trading　　　　　　　　　Koji Miyata *Manager* ☏ **(6) 251 0239**

Syndicated Lending
Tel: (6) 251 3175 **Fax:** (6) 251 3421
Head of Syndication　　　　　　　Mamoru Kudo *Assistant Manager*

Money Markets
Tel: (6) 2514756 **Fax:** (6) 251 3421
Head of Money Markets　　　　　Yoshitaka Honda *Manager*

Foreign Exchange
Tel: (6) 251 4756 **Fax:** (6) 251 3421
Head of Foreign Exchange　　　　Yoshitaka Honda *Manager*

Risk Management
Tel: (6) 251 3175 **Fax:** (6) 251 3421
Head of Risk Management　　　　Kazuo Takai *Manager*

Settlement / Clearing
Tel: (6) 251 3175 **Fax:** (6) 251 3421
Head of Settlement / Clearing　　Kenji Kanda *Assistant Manager*

Bank Indonesia
Representative Office

310 Hibiya Park Building, 1-8-1 Yurakucho, Chiyoda-ku, Tokyo 100
Tel: (3) 3271 3415; (3) 3271 3417 **Fax:** (3) 3285 0783

Senior Executive Officers
Chief Representative　　　　　　Baridjussalam Hadi

Other Departments
Economic Research　　　　　　　Edy Setiadi *Economist*

Bank of Ireland
Representative Office

Level 16 Shiroyama JT Mori Building, 4-3-1 Toranomon, Minato-ku, Tokyo 105-6016
Tel: (3) 5403 4924 **Fax:** (3) 3341 5329

Senior Executive Officers
Senior Representative　　　　　　Dermot Killoran

The Bank of Kansai Limited
Head Office

7-21 Shinsaibashisuji 2-chome, Chuo-ku, Osaka 542-8654
PO Box Osaka Minami 294, Osaka 542-91
Tel: (6) 213 0213 **Fax:** (6) 213 2850 **Telex:** J65308 **Swift:** KSBJ JP JS

Senior Executive Officers
Chairman　　　　　　　　　　　Shoichi Taki
President　　　　　　　　　　　Kenichi Komatsu
Senior Managing Director　　　　Takao Iguchi
Managing Director　　　　　　　Nobuhiko Izutani
Managing Director　　　　　　　Hiroshi Yamazaki
Managing Director　　　　　　　Masakazu Tajima
International Division　　　　　　Motoi Tsuchiya *Director & General Manager*

Euromoney Directory 1999　**819**

JAPAN (+81)   www.euromoneydirectory.com

The Bank of Kansai Limited (cont)

General-Lending (DCM, SL)
Head of Corporate Banking   Shuji Babe *Director & General Manager*

General - Treasury
Head of Treasury   Takeshi Asano *General Manager*

Equity Capital Markets
Global Head   Takeshi Asano *General Manager*
Regional Head   Tomoyuki Fujita *Dealer*

Syndicated Lending
Department: Loan Syndication / Asset Sales
Head of Origination   Motoi Tsuchiya *Director & General Manager*

Other (Trade Finance)
Letters of Credit   Motoi Tsuchiya *Director & General Manager*

Foreign Exchange
Global Head   Motoi Tsuchiya *Director & General Manager*
Country Head   Kenji Ozaki *Head of Forex*
    Satoshi Tanaka *Dealer*

Risk Management

Fixed Income Derivatives / Risk Management
IR Swaps Trading   Motoi Tsuchiya *Director & General Manager*

Foreign Exchange Derivatives / Risk Management
Cross-Currency Swaps, Trading   Motoi Tsuchiya *Director & General Manager*
    Kenji Ozaki *Dealer*

Exchange-Traded Derivatives
FX Futures   Takeshi Asano *General Manager*
    Tomoyuki Fujita *Dealer*
FX Options   Motoi Tsuchiya *Director & General Manager*
    Kenji Ozaki *Dealer*

Settlement / Clearing
Settlement (General)   Motoi Tsuchiya *Director & General Manager*
    Kanji Miyagi *Head of Settlements*
Operations   Takuzo Miyauchi *General Manager*

Other Departments
Correspondent Banking   Motoi Tsuchiya *Director & General Manager*

Administration
Head of Administration   Shuji Babe *Director & General Manager*

The Bank of Kyoto Limited   Head Office

700 Yakushimae-cho, Karasuma-dori, Matsubara-Agaru, Shimogyo-ku, Kyoto 600-8652
Tel: (75) 361 2211 Fax: (75) 343 1276 Telex: J64770 BOKFD Swift: BOKF JP JZ

Senior Executive Officers
Chairman   Mitsuru Akimoto
President   Yasuo Kashihara
Deputy President   Tsuyoshi Koyama
Senior Managing Director   Takao Shiomi
Senior Managing Director   Yasuhiko Kumata
Managing Director   Hiroaki Ikeda
Managing Director   Yukitoshi Yasumura
International Division   Kenichi Nakagawa *General Manager*

Bank of Montreal   Representative Office

Kyobashi Dai-Ichi Seimei Building 805, 2-4-12 Kyobashi, Chuo-ku, Tokyo 104
Tel: (3) 3246 0103 Fax: (3) 3246 4215 Email: tkurisu@msn.com

Senior Executive Officers
VP & Senior Representative   Tokuo Kurisu

820 Euromoney Directory 1999

The Bank of Nagoya Limited
Head Office

19-17, Nishiki 3-chome, Naka-ku, Nagoya
Tel: (52) 962 9520 **Fax:** (52) 962 6043 **Telex:** J59651 NAGOBANK **Swift:** NAGO JP JN **Cable:** NAGOBANK
Corporate Unit Roma - German Desk **Tel:** 5848 3953; **Fax:** 5848 3953

Senior Executive Officers
President   Kazumaro Kato
Deputy President   Akihiro Aoi
Senior Managing Director   Hiroshi Sakai

The Bank of New York
Full Branch Office

2-2-2 Uchisaiwai-cho, Chiyoda-ku, Tokyo 100
PO Box 5246, Tokyo International, Tokyo
Tel: (3) 3595 1133 **Fax:** (3) 3595 0737 **Reuters:** BYNT
Corporate Unit Roma - German Desk **Tel:** 5848 3953; **Fax:** 5848 3953

Senior Executive Officers

Others (Senior Executives)
Global Foreign Exchange   C Ishii *Vice President*

General - Treasury
Head of Treasury   Don Rosini *Vice President*
  S Tomoda *Assistant Treasurer*
  R Yoshimatsu *Treasury*

Syndicated Lending
Head of Syndicated Lending   Shoji Sato *Vice President & Head*

Foreign Exchange
Department: Treasury
Tel: 3595 1139
Head of Foreign Exchange   Ghiaki Ishii *Vice President & Manager*

FX Traders / Sales People
Head, Currency Options   Don Rosini *Vice President*
Head of Spot   Kazuma Nagao *Vice President*
Spot Desk   Naruki Ito *Assistant Treasurer*
Assistant Dealer   Michael Herman *Assistant Vice President*
Forward Desk   Seiko Tomoda *Assistant Treasurer*
Assistant Dealer   Rieko Hirohata
  Yuriko Hagiya

Risk Management
Tel: 3595 1326
Global Head   Kazuma Yamashita *Vice President*

Other (FI Derivatives)
  Kazuhisa Shimbo *Assistant Vice President*
  Yoshiyuki Hino *Assistant Treasurer*
  Yoshio Nomura *Assistant Treasurer & Credit Risk Officer*

Corporate Finance / M&A Advisory
Head of Corporate Finance   Shoji Sato *Vice President & Head*

Bank of Okinawa Limited
Head Office

10-1 3-chome, Kumoji, Naha 900, Okinawa
Tel: (98) 867 2141; (98) 868 8357 **Fax:** (98) 863 8186; (98) 860 1891 **Telex:** J795248 **Swift:** BOKIJPJZ
Email: bank@ryukyu.ne.jp **Telex:** J79826
Website: www.ryukyu.ne.jp/bank

Senior Executive Officers
Chairman   Seizen Arasaki
President   Choshin Nakayoshi
Chief Executive Officer   Chuichi Uehara *Managing Director*
Managing Director   Tetsuo Chinen
Managing Director   Moritake Kudaka
Managing Director   Noriaki Nagamine
International Division   Isao Nakahara *General Manager*

The Bank of Osaka Limited — Head Office

4-1 Nishi-Hommachi 1-chome, Nishi-ku, Osaka 550-0005
Tel: (6) 538 1021 Fax: (6) 543 0589 Telex: J64538 OSAKABK Swift: OSAB JP JS Telex: 05254550 OSABKOJ

Senior Executive Officers
President	Yoneo Taniguchi
Deputy President	Michio Wakamei
Senior Managing Director	Tomoyoshi Kakihara
Managing Director	Takayoshi Matsumura
Managing Director	Yasutaka Oga
Managing Director	Michio Asogawa

The Bank of Saga Limited — Head Office

7-20 Tojin 2-chome, Saga City, Saga 840-0813
Tel: (952) 245 111 Fax: (952) 295 629 Telex: 746478 SAGABKJ

Senior Executive Officers
Chairman	Minoru Tanaka
President	Hiroyasu Sashiyama

Bank of Taiwan

7th Floor, Fukoku Seimei Building, 2-2 Uchisaiwaicho, 2-chome, Chiyoda-ku, Tokyo 100-0011
Tel: (3) 3504 8881 Fax: (3) 3504 8880

Senior Executive Officers
VP & General Manager	David H Lin

Bank of the Ryukyus Limited — Head Office

11-1, Kumoji 1-chome, Naha 900-0015, Okinawa
PO Box 310, Naha 900-8691, Okinawa
Tel: (98) 866 1212 Fax: (98) 860 1380 Telex: J79827 Swift: RYUB JP JZ
Website: www.ryucom.ne.jp/users/ryugin

Senior Executive Officers
Chairman	Akira Sakima
President	Yukio Matsumoto
Chief Executive Officer	Hiroshi Aguni *Senior Managing Director*
Managing Director	Takaaki Masaoka
Managing Director	Ryoji Nakayoshi
International Division	Hiroshi Miyazato *General Manager*

The Bank of Tokyo-Mitsubishi — Head Office

7-1 Marunouchi 2-chome, Chiyoda-ku, Tokyo 100-8388
Tel: (3) 3240 1111 Telex: J222220 Swift: BOTK JP JT SAD Telex: J222221
Website: www.btm.co.jp

Senior Executive Officers
Chairman	Tasuku Takagaki
President	Satoru Kishi
Deputy President	Kenji Yoshizawa
Deputy President	Shigemitsu Miki
Senior Managing Director	Takeshi Yano
Senior Managing Director	Tadashi Kurachi
Senior Managing Director	Shin Nakahara
Senior Managing Director	Akihiro Uno
Senior Managing Director	Yasuyuki Hirai
Senior Managing Director	Tetsuo Shimura

Others (Senior Executives)
Securities Investment	Yoshinobu Onishi *Director*
Corporate Advisory	Tsutomu Tanaka *General Manager*

General-Lending (DCM, SL)
Head of Corporate Banking	Moritoshi Hattori *GM, Credit Policy*
	Kuninori Kato *General Manager, Credit 1*

General-Lending (DCM, SL) (cont)

Katsunori Nagayasu *General Manager, Credit 2*
Ichiei Noguchi *GM, Credit Supervision 1*
Tsutomu Matsuo *GM, Credit Supervision 2*
Takeshi Yano *GM, Corporate Banking Group 1*
Noboru Takeuchi *GM, Corporate Banking Planning*
Hiizu Ichikawa *GM, Corporate Banking Credit*
Shuichi Takahashi *GM, Corporate Banking 1*
Shota Yasuda *GM, Corporate Banking 2*
Yasumasa Karaki *GM, Corporate Banking 3*
Yasuo Kezuka *GM, Corporate Banking 4*
Ryuichi Ono *GM, Corporate Banking Group 2*
Tetsuji Arita *GM, Corporate Banking 1*
Yoshikazu Kurokawa *GM, Corporate Banking 2*
Terufumi Hiroshima *GM, Corporate Banking 3*

General-Investment
Head of Investment
Kenichi Masuda *GM, Investment Banking Planning*

General - Treasury
Head of Treasury
Akira Okuhata *General Manager*
Tetsuo Iwata *GM, Treasury & Investment*
Hajime Asada *GM, Treasury Planning*
Masahiko Tanaka *GM, Treasury Operations*

Relationship Manager
Global Service Banking
Global Securities Services
National Banking Planning
Branch Banking
Department: Planning
Kiyoshi Morofushi *General Manager*
Toshio Obata *General Manager*
Masayuki Tanaka *General Manager*
Shunichi Tokuda *Director*

Others (Senior Executives)
Overseas Planning
Headquarters for the Americas
North American Planning
North American Credit
North American Investment Banking
European Planning
European Credit
European Investment Banking
Overseas
International Credit
Mutsuo Hatano *General Manager*
Hiroshi Watanabe *Managing Director*
Nobuyuki Hirano *General Manager*
Michio Koyama *General Manager*
Kenichi Shimada *General Manager*
Setsuo Yamada *General Manager*
Hajime Oda *General Manager*
Terutsugu Imanishi *General Manager*
Keiichi Kawakami *General Manager*
Katsuya Kumatani *General Manager*

Debt Capital Markets / Fixed Income
Head of Debt Capital Markets
Akira Kondo *General Manager*

Syndicated Lending
Other (Trade Finance)
Structured Finance
Kenichi Nakazato *General Manager*

Foreign Exchange
Regional Head
Akira Okuhata *General Manager*

Risk Management
Global Head
Seiji Naito *GM, Market Risk Management*

Other (FI Derivatives)
Derivative & Structured Products
Tetsuo Shimura *Senior Managing Director*

Corporate Finance / M&A Advisory
Head of Corporate Finance
Toshinkori Yagura *General Manager*

Settlement / Clearing
Operations
Yutaka Nishizawa *General Manager*

Asset Management
Other (Asset Management)
Asset Management Planning
Yoshihiro Watanabe *Director*

Other Departments
Economic Research
Hidefumi Yamagami *General Manager, Research*

Other Departments
Trust Business Planning
Financial Institutions
Public & Institutional Business
EC Banking
Credit Examination
Corporate Planning
Yoichi Kambara *General Manager*
Susumu Emori *General Manager*
Yoshikatsu Shibata *General Manager*
Hiroshi Egami *General Manager*
Akira Ishigami *General Manager*
Naotaka Obata *Director*

JAPAN (+81)   www.euromoneydirectory.com

The Bank of Tokyo-Mitsubishi (cont)
Administration
Systems   Kyota Omori *General Manager*
Legal / In-House Counsel
    Yoshiyuki Yanagida *General Manager*
Public Relations
    Ryoichi Kato *General Manager*
Accounts / Audit
Inspection   Kyozo Motoki *General Manager*
Other (Administration)
General Affairs   Toshiyuki Nishimura *Director*
Human Resources   Masaharu Hamakawa *Director*
Secretariat   Toru Takada *General Manager*
Affiliates & Subsidiaries Business   Noriyuki Mita *General Manager*

Bank von Ernst & Co Limited — Representative Office
Otemachi 1st Square Building, 1-5-1 Otemachi, Chiyoda-ku, Tokyo 100
Tel: (3) 3216 5801 Fax: (3) 3213 3790

The Bank of Yokohama Limited — Head Office
1-1 Minatomirai 3-chome, Nishi-ku, Yokohama 220-8611, Kanagawa
Tel: (45) 225 1111 Fax: (45) 225 1160 Telex: J24945 HAMABK Swift: HAMA JP JT Email: intldept@boy.co.jp
Cable: FOREXHAMA
Website: www.boy.co.jp

Senior Executive Officers
President   Sadaaki Hirasawa
Deputy President   Akira Yamagami
Managing Director   Nobuyuki Shimizu
Managing Director   Kazuhiko Nagasawa
Managing Director   Takao Kobayashi
Managing Director   Hiroshi Matsuzaki
International Division   Jiro Goto *Managing Director*
Others (Senior Executives)
Public Institutions Department   Isao Yamashita *Managing Director*
Directors   Motoya Hamada *General Manager*
    Kazumi Shimizu *General Manager*
    Teijiro Toyama *General Manager*
    Norito Ikeda *General Manager*
    Yasunaka Fujikawa *General Manager*
    Masahiro Hoshino *General Manager*
    Hiroshi Takahashi *General Manager*
    Hiroshi Hayakawa *General Manager*

General - Treasury
Head of Treasury   Jiro Goto *Managing Director*
Department: Treasury and Capital Markets Department
General Manager   Toshio Wakui
Deputy General Manager   Kazuo Ishida
Others (Senior Executives)
Planning   Kenji Yamada *Senior Deputy General Manager*
    Yasushi Ishiwa *Manager*
    Keisuke Sato *Manager*
    Shuji Isshiki *Manager*
    Manabu Hijikata *Manager*
    Hideaki Takeshiga *Manager*

Department: International Department
General Manager   Toshio Ishikawa
Deputy General Manager   Naoaki Ito
Others (Senior Executives)
International Planning   Yasuo Yamakawa *General Manager*
    Kentaro Nihei *Deputy General Manager*
    Hironori Nakajima *Manager*
    Hiroaki Yura *Manager*
Overseas Base Administration and General Affairs   Toshiya Amano *Deputy General Manager*
    Tomoko Amano *Manager*

824 Euromoney Directory 1999

Others (Senior Executives) (cont)

Shozo Yashiki *Manager*

Debt Capital Markets / Fixed Income
Department: Securities Investment Division
Country Head — Yutaka Kurorsuchi *Deputy General Manager*
Department: Trading First Division
Head of Fixed Income Trading — Mikihiko Sato *Deputy General Manager*
Kouichi Hirata *Manager*
Mineyuki Takahashi *Manager*

Equity Capital Markets
Department: Securities Investment Division
Country Head — Yutaka Kurorsuchi *Deputy General Manager*
Department: Trading First Division
Head of Trading — Mikihiko Sato *Deputy General Manager*
Kouichi Hirata *Manager*
Mineyuki Takahashi *Manager*

Syndicated Lending
Department: Credit Department
Global Head — Toshiyuki Nakamura *General Manager*
Country Head — Hiroshi Kono *Senior Deputy General Manager*
Toshiki Matsuo *Senior Deputy General Manager*

Other (Syndicated Lending)
Takayuki Moriyama *GM, International Credit*
Takeshi Suzuki *Manager, International Credit*

Department: Overseas Loan Group
Other (Syndicated Lending)
Shigeharu Kusano *Deputy General Manager*
Minoaki Tsushima *Deputy General Manager*

Money Markets
Department: Trading Division
Money Markets - General
First Division — Mikihiko Sato *Deputy General Manager*
Kouichi Hirata *Manager*
Mineyuki Takahashi *Manager*
Second Division — Mitsutoshi Hirano *Deputy General Manager*
Masaki Kimura *Manager*
Masayoshi Teshigawara *Manager*

Department: Money Desk
Country Head — Tetsuro Iwaki *Deputy General Manager*

Foreign Exchange
Department: Foreign Exchange Administration Planning
Global Head — Hiroshi Sodeyama *Senior Deputy General Manager*

FX Traders / Sales People
Takayuki Saruya *Deputy General Manager*
Ikuya Suhara *Manager*

Settlement / Clearing
Department: Market Operations Department
Head of Settlement / Clearing — Tomio Okuyama *General Manager*
Country Head — Satoshi Echigoya *Senior Deputy General Manager*
Operations — Teruo Shimuzu *Senior Deputy General Manager*
Kazuo Yamagishi *Deputy General Manager*
Tomoaki Kanno *Deputy General Manager*
Takashi Arai *Manager*
Kozo Fujikata *Manager*
Kaizou Kojima *Manager*
Kyoichi Masubuchi *Manager*
Back-Office — Akio Yamauchi *Deputy General Manager*
Toshikazu Moriya *Manager*
Minako Mizuhata *Manager*
Ryoichi Harada *Manager*
Yoshimi Maeda *Manager*

Asset Management
Department: Securities Portfolio Management
Portfolio Management — Soh Okada *Deputy General Manager*
Hirokazu Masuda *Manager*
Hitoshi Seo *Manager*

Other Departments
Private Banking — Isao Yamashita *Managing Director*

JAPAN (+81)　　　　　www.euromoneydirectory.com

The Bank of Yokohama Limited (cont)
Administration
Head of Administration　　　　Takao Kobayashi *Managing Director*
Business Development　　　　Masaharu Inaba *General Manager, Business Promotion*
Compliance
　　　　　　　　　　　　　　Takeshi Ishiura *General Manager*

BankBoston NA　　　　　　　　　　　　　　Full Branch Office

Formerly known as: The First National Bank of Boston
7th Floor, AIG Building, 1-3 Marunouchi 1-chome, Chiyoda-ku, Tokyo 100-0005
PO Box 643, Tokyo 100-8692
Tel: (3) 3211 2611; (3) 3211 2615 **Fax:** (3) 3201 6879 **Telex:** J26341 BOSTONBK **Swift:** FNBB JP JX
Senior Executive Officers
Country Manager - Japan　　　　Charles Vacher
General-Lending (DCM, SL)
Head of Corporate Banking　　　Sumimasa Fudaka *Manager, Corporate Banking*
Other Departments
Correspondent Banking　　　　　Hiroyasu Sato *Manager*

Bankers Trust Company　　　　　　　　　　Full Branch Office

Tokyo Ginko Kyokai Building, 1-3-1 Marunouchi, Chiyoda-ku, Tokyo 100-0005
Tel: (3) 3214 7171 **Fax:** (3) 3211 7875
Senior Executive Officers
Others (Senior Executives)
Sales & Trading　　　　　　　　Junsuke Motai *Senior Managing Director*
General-Investment
Head of Investment　　　　　　　Gary M Talarico *Managing Director*

Banque Sudameris　　　　　　　　　　　　Representative Office

c/o 1-2 Floor, Kishimoto Building, 2-1 Marunouchi 2-chome, Chiyoda-ku, Tokyo 100
PO Box 1613, Tokyo 100
Tel: (3) 5221 7820 **Fax:** (3) 5221 7855
Senior Executive Officers
Representative　　　　　　　　　Roberto Mazzi

Barclays Bank plc/Barclays Capital Group　　Full Branch Office

Formerly known as: BZW Securities (Japan) Limited
15th Floor, Urbannet Otemachi Building, 2-2 Otemachi 2-chome, Chiyoda-ku, Tokyo 100-0004
Tel: (3) 3276 1100 **Fax:** (3) 3276 1110
Senior Executive Officers
Chief Executive Officer　　　　　Patrick Lin *Chief Executive, Japan*
Debt Capital Markets / Fixed Income
Country Head　　　　　　　　　Yoshshiaichi Yamaguchi *Head of Sales*
Syndicated Lending
Other (Trade Finance)
Structured Finance　　　　　　　Satoaki Takahashi *Head*
Money Markets
Head of Money Markets　　　　　Stuart Baker *Head of Money Trading*
Foreign Exchange
Head of Foreign Exchange　　　　Makoto Kojima *Head of Forex*
Risk Management
Head of Risk Management　　　　Haruo Ebara *Head, Risk Management*
　　　　　　　　　　　　　　Henry Fajemirokun *Managing Director & Head of Derivatives*
Settlement / Clearing
Head of Settlement / Clearing　　　Yoshihori Shimada *Head of Settlements*

JAPAN (+81)

Barclays Global Investors
Ebisu Prime Square Tower, 1-1-39 Hiroo, Shibuya-ku, Tokyo 150-0012
Tel: (3) 5469 4300 Fax: (3) 5469 4301
Equity Capital Markets
Equity Repo / Securities Lending
Head   Masaru Yamazaki *Managing Director* 5469 4120 5469 4140

Barclays Trust & Banking Company (Japan) Limited
7-8 Floor, Ebisu Prime Square Tower, 1-39, Hiroo 1-chome, Shibuya-ku, Tokyo 150-0012
Tel: (3) 5469 4300 Fax: (3) 5469 4301
Senior Executive Officers
President   Kyogo Oda
Administration
Compliance
    Yuko Yamamoto 5469 4561 5469 4570
    yuko.yamamoto@barclaysglobal.com

Baring Brothers Limited
24th Floor, The New Otani Garden Court, 4-1 Kioi-cho, Chiyoda-ku, Tokyo 102
Tel: (3) 5210 0700 Fax: (3) 5210 0730
Senior Executive Officers
Manager   Kosaku Ujihara

Bayerische Hypo-und Vereinsbank AG   Full Branch Office
Formerly known as: Bayerische Vereinsbank AG
Alternative trading name: HypoVereinsbank
17th Floor, Otemachi First Square, 1-5-1 Otemachi, Chiyoda-ku, Tokyo 100-0004
PO Box 1379, Tokyo 100-8593
Tel: (3) 3284 1341 Fax: (3) 3284 1370; (3) 3284 1401 **Telex:** J26351 **Swift:** BVBE JP JT **Reuters:** HVTK
Senior Executive Officers
Executive Director, Japan   Peter Baron 3284 1342
Director & Deputy General Manager   Leonard Meyer zu Brickwedde 3284 1346
Treasurer   Kenji Akagi *Executive Director, Japan* 3284 1928
Syndicated Lending
Loan-Related Activities
Trade Finance   Nicolas Nakajima *Director* 3284 1344
Money Markets
Head of Money Markets   Takashi Nishiguchi *Manager* 3284 1928
Foreign Exchange
Head of Foreign Exchange   Yoshihiko Kobayahi *Director* 3284 1928
Settlement / Clearing
Operations   Wakako Konno *Manager* 3284 1478
Other Departments
Chief Credit Officer   Sandra von Miller *Manager* 3284 1424
Administration
Technology & Systems
    Fumio Sasaki *Manager* 3284 1416

Bayerische Landesbank   Representative Office
Yusen Building, 3-2 Marunouchi 2-chome, Chiyoda-ku, Tokyo 100-0005
Tel: (3) 3287 0135 Fax: (3) 3287 0136
Senior Executive Officers
Chief Representative   Franz-Hermann Hirlinger
Others (Senior Executives)
Senior Adviser   Eiichi Sugata

JAPAN (+81) www.euromoneydirectory.com

Bayerische Landesbank
Full Branch Office

Yusen Building, 3-2 Marunouchi 2-chome, Chiyoda-ku, Tokyo 100-0005
Tel: (3) 3201 5360; (3) 3201 5591 Fax: (3) 3201 5763; (3) 3201 5765 Telex: J22342 Swift: BYLA JP JT
Email: blbtokyo@al.mbn.or.jp

Senior Executive Officers
EVP & General Manager   Wolfgang Hühne
SVP & General Manager   Eiji Yamaguchi

General-Lending (DCM, SL)
Head of Corporate Banking
                                   Christoph Schmitz-Wenzel *AVP & Head of Credit*
                                   Hitoshi Kano *VP, Corporate Banking*
                                   Christoph Sattler *VP, Corporate Banking*
                                   Michimasa Minami *AVP, Corporate Banking*
                                   Tsutomu Ouchi *AVP, Corporate Banking*
                                   Markus Gfeller *AVP, Corporate Banking*

Money Markets
Department: Treasury Department
Tel: 3201 5591 Fax: 3201 5765
Country Head   Tatsuma Oinuma *FVP & Head of Treasury*

Other (Wholesale Deposits)
Chief Deposit Dealer   Mitsunori Maezawa *VP & Manager*

Foreign Exchange
FX Traders / Sales People
Chief FX Dealer   Masashi Imai *Assistant Vice President*

Settlement / Clearing
Operations   Urs W Schmid *Vice President & Head*

Bear Stearns (Japan) Limited
Full Branch Office

22nd Floor, Shiroyama Hills, 4-3-1 Toranomon, Minato-ku, Tokyo 105
Tel: (3) 3437 7800 Fax: (3) 3437 7880

Senior Executive Officers
President   Toshihiko Yamamoto
Branch Manager   Masaki Sato
Branch Manager   Tsutomu Nagazumi

BNP Securities (Japan) Limited
Full Branch Office

23rd Floor, Shiroyama JT Mori Building, 3-1 Toranomon 4-chome, Minato-ku, Tokyo 105
Tel: (3) 5473 3600 Fax: (3) 5473 3610 Telex: J33727 BNPSEJ

Senior Executive Officers
General Manager   Yasuo Takashima

Debt Capital Markets / Fixed Income
Head of Fixed Income Sales   Kazuhiro Andachi *Senior Sales Manager & Head*
Head of Fixed Income Trading   William Gibson *Senior Trader*

Other (Fixed Income)
Debt Origination   Mitsuo Fukuda *Marketing Manager*

Private Placements
Head of Sales   Yoshikazu Noda *Assistant General Manager*

Equity Capital Markets
Other (International Equity)
Foreign Equity Sales   Yasuki Umikawa *Senior Sales Manager & Head*

Syndicated Lending
Loan-Related Activities
Structured Trade Finance   Pascal Besson *Product Officer*

Risk Management
Exotic Options (Barriers, Range, Timers, Digitals, Faders etc)
Trading   Oren Amsellem *Senior Trader*

OTC Equity Derivatives
Sales   Nobuo Kabeyama *Assistant General Manager & Head*

Settlement / Clearing
Settlement (General)   Akiko Onishi *Senior Officer, Middle Office*
                                   Fujihiko Kanda *Assistant General Manager & Head*

www.euromoneydirectory.com   JAPAN (+81)

Administration
Compliance
Junko Miyamoto *Manager*

Accounts / Audit
Settlement Fujihiko Kanda *Assistant General Manager & Head*
Accounting Mitsugu Nozaki *Assistant Manager*

Brown Brothers Harriman & Co   Representative Office
4th Floor, Daimatsu Building, 8-14 Nihonbashi 3-chome, Chuo-ku, Tokyo 103-0027
Tel: (3) 3278 1411 **Fax:** (3) 3278 1610 **Telex:** 2224223 BBHTYOU **Swift:** BBH CUS 33
Website: www.bbh.com

Senior Executive Officers
Chief Representative & Partner Kyosuke Hashimoto
Manager Yutaka Hasegawa
Manager Masato Horino
Manager Yukinori Nagahisa

BT Asia Securities Limited   Full Branch Office
Tokyo Ginko Kyokai Building, 1-3-1 Marunouchi, Chiyoda-ku, Tokyo 100-0005
Tel: (3) 3286 0920 **Fax:** (3) 3216 2378 **Telex:** 2227214

Senior Executive Officers
Chief Executive Officer Kazuo Yamada *General Manager*

Canadian Imperial Bank of Commerce   Full Branch Office
8th Floor, Hibiya Kokusai Building, 2-3 Uchisaiwai-cho 2-chome, Chiyoda-ku, Tokyo 100-0011
Tel: (3) 5512 8888 **Fax:** (3) 3591 3169 **Telex:** J23391 CIBCTK **Swift:** CIBC JP JT
Corporate Finance Tel: 5512 8855; **Financial Products Tel:** 5512 8899; **FX & Money Markets Tel:** 3595 0451;
Management Tel: 5512 8900; **Operations Tel:** 5512 8933; **Risk Management Tel:** 5512 8911; **Securities Investment Tel:** 5512 8908

Senior Executive Officers
Managing Director Hiromichi Uehara

Debt Capital Markets / Fixed Income
Department: Financial Products
Head of Fixed Income Trading Ahihiro Oshima *Managing Director*

Bonds - General
Interest Rate Yasuhiko Kai *Executive Director*
Exotics Takahiro Yamanaka *Executive Director*
Credit Toru Sekimoto *Executive Director*
Equity Hiroyuki Takayama *Executive Director*
FX Yuki Saiki *Executive Director*
Quants Akihiko Tsuchiya *Executive Director*
Middle Office Koji Kontani *Executive Director*

Money Markets
Country Head Mami Yamaguchi *Director*

Foreign Exchange
Head of Trading Yasushi Takeishi *Executive Director*

FX Traders / Sales People
Trading Hiroshi Sudo *Director*
 Akio Takemoto *Director*
Sales Motohiko Uratani *Director*
 Gilbert Suzuki *Director*

Risk Management
Country Head Toshiyuki Shiohara *Managing Director*

Corporate Finance / M&A Advisory
Other (Corporate Finance)
 Yukihiro Hirasawa *Managing Director*
 Kazuyoshi Sakamoto *Director*

Administration
Other (Administration)
Infrastructure Akira Tokoyoda *Executive Director*

JAPAN (+81)　　　　　www.euromoneydirectory.com

Cantor Fitzgerald Shoken Kaisha Limited — Subsidiary Company
14th Floor, Toranomon Mitsui Building, Kasumigaseki 3-8-1, Chiyoda-ku, Tokyo 100-0013
Tel: (3) 3519 9100 Fax: (3) 3519 9157
Website: www.cantor.com

CARIPLO - Cassa di Risparmio delle Provincie Lombarde SpA — Representative Office
3rd Floor, Enokizaka Building, 1-12-12 Akasaka, Minato-ku, Tokyo 107
Tel: (3) 5562 9555 Fax: (3) 5562 9550

Senior Executive Officers
Chief Representative, Japan　　　T Isono

Cedel Bank — Representative Office
5th Floor, Sanbancho KB-6 Building, 6-1 Sanbancho, Chiyoda-ku, Tokyo 102-0075
Tel: (3) 5276 4391 Fax: (3) 5276 4393 Email: marketing@cedelgroup.com
Website: www.cedelgroup.com

Senior Executive Officers
Manager　　　Iwao Hidaka

Debt Capital Markets / Fixed Income
Fixed-Income Repo
Head of Repo　　　Iwao Hidaka *Manager*
Sales　　　Mitsuru Takeuchi *Vice President* [E] mtakeu@cedelgroup.com

The Chase Manhattan Bank — Full Branch Office
5-2-20 Akasaka, Minato-ku, Tokyo 100-8691
CPO Box 383, Tokyo 100-8691
Tel: (3) 5570 7500 Fax: (3) 5570 7960

Senior Executive Officers
Senior Country Officer　　　Kevin Kehoe

The Chiba Bank Limited — Head Office
1-2 Chiba-minato, Chuo-ku, Chiba 260-0026
International Division, 5-3 Nihombashi Muromachi 1-chome, Chuo-ku, Tokyo 103-0022
Tel: (43) 245 1111 Telex: J26666 Swift: CHBA JP JT
Website: www.chibabank.or.jp

Senior Executive Officers
Chairman　　　Takashi Tamaki
President　　　Tsuneo Hayakawa
Deputy President　　　Jiro Ishikawa
Deputy President　　　Toshiaki Ishii
Senior Managing Director　　　Yoshinori Ichihara
Managing Director　　　Toru Yoshimura
Managing Director　　　Toshio Shishido
Managing Director　　　Tadashi Takeyama
Managing Director　　　Ken Kataoka

Others (Senior Executives)
　　　Akihiro Ominato *Director*
　　　Toru Ishii *Director*
　　　Suketaka Ushioda *Director*
　　　Shinji Okamoto *Director*
　　　Akira Hasegawa *Director*
　　　Minoru Shingyouchi *Director*
　　　Masahiro Maki *Director*
　　　Tetsuo Suzuki *Director*

www.euromoneydirectory.com JAPAN (+81)

Department: International Division
5-3 Nihombashi Muromachi, 1-chome, Chuo-ku, Tokyo 103-0022
Tel: +81 (3) 3270 8351 Fax: +81 (3) 3242 1735/6
International Division Kuniomi Tomizuka *Managing Director*
  Masamichi Abe *General Manager*

General - Treasury
Head of Treasury Gaku Maeda *General Manager* ☏ (3) 3270 8357 ✉ (3) 3244 1227

The Chiba Kogyo Bank Limited Head Office

1-2 Saiwaicho 2-chome, Mihama-ku, Chiba 261-0001
Tel: (43) 243 2133 Fax: (43) 242 5320 Telex: 2522762 CHIKBK J Swift: CHIK JP JT

Senior Executive Officers
President Toshio Mende
Deputy President Akihiko Katsura
Senior Managing Director Kazuhiko Fukuda
Senior Managing Director Michihiko Ishimaru
General Manager, Finance Markets Division Shuntaro Namba

The Chugoku Bank Limited Head Office

1-15-20 Marunouchi, 1-chome, Okayama 700-8628
Tel: (86) 223 3111; (86) 234 6289 Fax: (86) 234 6593; (86) 227 5000 Telex: 592220 CHUGIN J Swift: CHGK JP JZ
Website: www.chugin.co.jp

Senior Executive Officers
Chairman & President Kanji Inaba
Deputy President Ryosuke Yamada
Senior Managing Director Shizuo Tani
Senior Managing Director Yoshiaki Yamamoto
Managing Director Michio Ishimura
Managing Director Katsutoshi Moriya
Managing Director Katsutoshi Sato
International Division Masaru Mushiake *GM, International Department*

The Chuo Trust & Banking Co Limited Head Office

7-1 Kyobashi 1-chome, Chuo-ku, Tokyo 104-8345
Tel: (3) 3567 1451 Fax: (3) 3562 6902 Telex: CTRUST J33568 Swift: CHUO JP JT Telex: J24789
Website: www.chuotrust.co.jp

Senior Executive Officers
Chairman of the Board Hisao Muramoto
President Shozo Endoh
Deputy President Kazuo Aoki
Senior Managing Director Akihiko Kitao
Senior Managing Director Hideie Hirakawa
Senior Managing Director Hiroshi Sugano
Managing Director Shuichi Ohnishi
Managing Director Toyozo Narita
Managing Director Kiyotsuga Murakami

Debt Capital Markets / Fixed Income
Department: International Treasury Department
Tel: 3562 6894 Fax: 3562 6898
Global Head Norihiko Tsuge *Director & General Manager*

Eurobonds
Head of Trading Norihiko Tsuge *Director & General Manager*
  Kaneaki Horiguchi *General Manager*
Trading (Sovereigns) Norihiko Tsuge *Director & General Manager*
  Kaneaki Horiguchi *General Manager*
Trading (Corporates) Norihiko Tsuge *Director & General Manager*
  Kaneaki Horiguchi *General Manager*
Trading (High-yield) Norihiko Tsuge *Director & General Manager*
  Kaneaki Horiguchi *General Manager*

Libor-Based / Floating-Rate Products
Asset Swaps Norihiko Tsuge *Director & General Manager*

Fixed-Income Repo
Head of Repo Norihiko Tsuge *Director & General Manager*

JAPAN (+81)   www.euromoneydirectory.com

The Chuo Trust & Banking Co Limited (cont)
Department: Treasury & Securities Department
Tel: 3562 6833 Fax: 3562 6840

Domestic Government Bonds
Head of Trading   Kaneaki Horiguchi *General Manager*

Eurobonds
Head of Trading   Kaneaki Horiguchi *General Manager*

Fixed-Income Repo
Head of Repo   Kaneaki Horiguchi *General Manager*
Department: Money & Capital Markets Department
Tel: 3562 6910 Fax: 3562 6904

Domestic Government Bonds
Head of Sales   Makoto Kojima *Managing Director*

Equity Capital Markets
Department: International Treasury Department
Tel: 3562 6894 Fax: 3562 6898

International Equities
Head of Trading   Norihiko Tsuge *Director & General Manager*
Department: Treasury & Securities Department
Tel: 3562 6833 Fax: 3562 6840
Global Head   Kaneaki Horiguchi *General Manager*

Domestic Equities
Head of Trading   Kaneaki Horiguchi *General Manager*

International Equities
Head of Trading   Kaneaki Horiguchi *General Manager*

Convertibles / Equity-Linked
Head of Trading   Kaneaki Horiguchi *General Manager*

Warrants
Head of Trading   Kaneaki Horiguchi *General Manager*

Syndicated Lending
Department: International Department
Tel: 3562 6900 Fax: 3562 6902
Global Head   Tomohiro Itoh *Managing Director*
Head of Credit Committee   Kazuo Aoki *Deputy President*

Money Markets
Department: International Treasury Department
Tel: 3562 6894 Fax: 3562 6898
Global Head   Norihiko Tsuge *Director & General Manager*

Domestic Commercial Paper
Head of Origination; Head of Sales; Head of   Makoto Kojima *Managing Director*
Trading

Foreign Exchange
Department: International Treasury Department
Tel: 3562 6894 Fax: 3562 6898
Global Head of Trading   Norihiko Tsuge *Director & General Manager*

Risk Management
Department: General Planning Department
Tel: 3562 6926 Fax: 3562 6928
Global Head   Sanpei Hamada *Director*

Fixed Income Derivatives / Risk Management
Global Head   Sanpei Hamada *Director*
IR Swaps Trading; IR Options Trading   Norihiko Tsuge *Director & General Manager*

Foreign Exchange Derivatives / Risk Management
Cross-Currency Swaps, Trading; Vanilla FX   Norihiko Tsuge *Director & General Manager*
option Trading

Settlement / Clearing
Department: International Operations Centre
Tel: 3562 6916 Fax: 3562 3852
Derivatives Settlement; Foreign Exchange   Mitsuyuki Yoshida *Director*
Settlement
Department: Securities Booking Department
2-19-6, Yanagibashi, Taito-ku, Tokyo
Tel: 3862 2441 Fax: 3862 2442
Equity Settlement; Fixed-Income Settlement   Souetsu Abe *General Manager*

www.euromoneydirectory.com　　　　　　　　JAPAN (+81)

Global Custody
Department: Securities Booking Department
2-19-6, Yanagibashi, Taito-ku, Tokyo
Tel: 3682 2441 Fax: 3682 2442
Other (Global Custody)
　　　　　Souetsu Abe *General Manager*

Other Departments
Correspondent Banking　　　Tomohiro Itoh *Managing Director*
Administration
Technology & Systems
　　　　　Mitsugu Masuda *Director*

Compliance
　　　　　Motomu Ueda *General Manager*

CIBC Wood Gundy Securities (Japan) Limited　Subsidiary Company

8th Floor, Hibiya Kokusai Building, 2-2-3 Uchisaiwai-cho, Chiyoda-ku, Tokyo 100
Tel: (3) 5512 8866 Fax: (3) 3591 0710 Telex: 2223524 WGUNDY J

Senior Executive Officers
Managing Director, Japan　　　Nobukatsu Nishimura

Debt Capital Markets / Fixed Income
Department: Global Capital Markets
Country Head　　　Tai Ishida *Managing Director*

Bonds - General
Fixed Income　　　Makoto Sasaki *Executive Director*
　　　　　Hiroaki Fujioka *Executive Director*
　　　　　Yukiko Kusaka *Executive Director*
　　　　　Toko Tanaka *Executive Director*
Equities　　　Masako Ando Schenck *Executive Director*

Corporate Finance / M&A Advisory
Other (Corporate Finance)
Corporate Finance　　　Jim Mori *Managing Director*
　　　　　Sei-Ichiro Komeda *Director*

Administration
Department: Financial Products
Head of Marketing　　　Soon-Il Lee *Managing Director*

Other (Administration)
Marketing　　　Hiroki Nara *Executive Director*
　　　　　Keiichi Suzuki *Executive Director*
　　　　　Takahiro Ishikawa *Executive Director*
　　　　　Toshifumi Horiba *Executive Director*
　　　　　Sususmu Nitta *Director*
　　　　　Hideharu Arai *Director*
　　　　　Kimiko Kambara *Director*
　　　　　Junko Arai *Associate*
Structuring　　　Yoshikuni Koga *Executive Director*
Advisory　　　Robert Ryan *Executive Director*
Legal / Compliance　　　Atsuyuki Ishihara *Executive Director*
Human Resources / Administration　　　Yuji Kasai *Executive Director*

Citibank NA　Full Branch Office

Citicorp Center, 2-3-14 Higashi Shinagawa, Shinagawa-ku, Tokyo 140-8639
Tel: (3) 5462 5000 Fax: (3) 5462 5055 Reuters: CITQ; CIMQ; CTTQ
Website: www.citicorp.com

Senior Executive Officers
Chief Executive Officer　　　Mike de Graffenried *Country Corporate Officer*

Others (Senior Executives)
Trading / Capital Markets　　　Sajeev Thomas [F] **5462 5148**
Corporate Finance　　　Robert Manning [F] **5462 5203**
Global Transaction Service　　　Akinaga Shimizu [F] **5462 6490**
Global Industry - Electronics　　　Jack Wood [F] **5462 5305**
Institutional Customers　　　Tsuneki Hara [F] **5462 5305**

Debt Capital Markets / Fixed Income
Head of Fixed Income Trading　　　Sajeev Thomas [F] **5462 5148**

Euromoney Directory 1999　833

JAPAN (+81) www.euromoneydirectory.com

Citibank NA (cont)
Equity Capital Markets
Head of Trading   Sajeev Thomas [F] **5462 5148**
Risk Management
Head of Risk Management   Bo Hammerich [F] **5462 5290**
Corporate Finance / M&A Advisory
Head of Corporate Finance   Robert Manning [F] **5462 5203**

Commerz Securities (Japan) Co Limited   Subsidiary Company

Tokyo Marine Building, Shinkan, 1-2-1 Marunoudi, Chiyoda-ku, Tokyo 100-0005
Tel: (3) 5293 9000 **Fax:** (3) 5793 9045 **Telex:** J24138

Senior Executive Officers
MD & General Manager   Nabil El-Arnaouty

Debt Capital Markets / Fixed Income
Department: **Fixed Income Department**
Tel: 5293 9337 **Fax:** 5293 9289
Head of Fixed Income   Norbert Wenninger *Managing Director* [T] **5293 9020** [F] **5293 9029**
Head of Fixed Income Sales   Kenji Mitani *General Manager* [T] **5293 9335** [F] **5293 9189**
Head of Fixed Income Trading   Thomas Gispert *Assistant General Manager* [T] **5293 9380** [F] **5293 9189**
Government Bonds
Head of Trading   Thomas Gispert *Assistant General Manager* [T] **5293 9380** [F] **5293 9189**
Eurobonds
Head of Sales   Kenji Mitani *General Manager* [T] **5293 9335** [F] **5293 9189**
Head of Trading   Thomas Gispert *Assistant General Manager* [T] **5293 9380** [F] **5293 9189**
Libor-Based / Floating-Rate Products
FRN Trading   Thomas Gispert *Assistant General Manager* [T] **5293 9380** [F] **5293 9189**
Fixed-Income Repo
Head of Repo   Thomas Gispert *Assistant General Manager* [T] **5293 9380** [F] **5293 9189**

Equity Capital Markets
Head of Trading   Ian Dhilo *Director* [T] **5293 9294**
Other (Domestic Equities)
Head of DIS   Yusuke Shibasaki *Managing Director* [T] **5293 9180**
Head of Corporate Sales   Kazuaki Tada *Managing Director* [T] **5293 9300**
                                          Takao Oku *Managing Director* [T] **5293 9390**
International Equities
Head of Sales   Yoshiyuki Katsuragi [T] **5293 9318**
Equity Research
Head of Equity Research   Lisa Oyama [T] **5293 9161**
Convertibles / Equity-Linked
Head of Sales   Yutaka Oba [T] **5293 9370**

Settlement / Clearing
Head of Settlement / Clearing   Mazakazu Ezure [T] **5293 9120** [F] **5293 9149**
Administration
Head of Administration   Katsuaki Umeda [T] **5293 9001** [F] **5293 9049**
Technology & Systems
                                          Peter Shima [T] **5293 9070** [F] **5293 9099**
Compliance
                                          Masao Gomi [T] **5293 9110** [F] **5293 9119**
Accounts / Audit
                                          Shin Sakamoto [T] **5293 9060** [F] **5293 9069**

Commerzbank AG   Full Branch Office

2nd Floor, Nippon Press Center Building, 2-2-1 Uchisaiwai-cho, Chiyoda-ku, Tokyo 100-0011
PO Box 1727, Central Post Office, Chiyoda-ku, Tokyo 100-8764
Tel: (3) 3502 4271 **Fax:** (3) 3508 7545 **Telex:** J25971 **Swift:** COBA JP JXXXX **Email:** cbkjapan@gol.com
Reuters: CMRQ
Website: www.commerzbank.com

Senior Executive Officers
General Manager   François de Belsunce
General Manager   Burkhardt Figge
International Division   Masayuki Nakamura *Assistant General Manager*

834 Euromoney Directory 1999

www.euromoneydirectory.com   JAPAN (+81)

General-Lending (DCM, SL)
Head of Corporate Banking   Norio Yatomi *Deputy Manager*
General - Treasury
Head of Treasury   Paul Goeldi *Assistant General Manager* F 3502 4463 E treasury@gol.com
Money Markets
Regional Head   Ryohei Muramatsu *Manager*
Foreign Exchange
Head of Sales   Toyomitsu Sakata *Senior Manager*
Head of Trading   Eizo Kishimune *Manager*
Administration
Head of Administration   Bernd Michel *Assistant General Manager*

Commonwealth Bank of Australia

Level 8, 12-1 Toranomon, 5-Chome, Minato-ku, Tokyo 105-0001
Tel: (3) 5400 7280 **Fax:** (3) 5400 7288 **Telex:** 7228510 COMBANK **Swift:** CTBA JP JT
Senior Executive Officers
Financial Director   Malcolm Potmore *Financial Controller*
Branch Manager   Deborah Hazelton
Others (Senior Executives)
                                       Ms. Saito *Project Manager*

Crédit Agricole Indosuez-Asian Aerospace Group Full Branch Office   J

Formerly known as: Indosuez Aifinance Asia Co. Limited
3-29-1 Kanda Jinbocho, Chiyoda-ku, Tokyo 101-0051
Tel: (3) 3261 2510 **Fax:** (3) 3261 2567; (3) 3261 2534 **Telex:** J24309 INDOCAB
Senior Executive Officers
Others (Senior Executives)
                                       Frederic Mireur *Vice President, Head of Aerospace Group Asia*
                                       T 3261 2197 F 3261 2567
                                       Yuji Igarashi *Vice President, Head of Aerospace Group Asia* T 3261 2529
                                       F 3261 2567

Crédit Lyonnais   Full Branch Office

7th Floor, Hibiya Kokusai Building, 2-3 Uchisaiwai-cho, Chiyoda-ku, Tokyo 100-0011
Tel: (3) 5512 5700 **Fax:** (3) 5512 5748 **Telex:** J26390 CLYTOK J **Swift:** CRLY JP JT **Reuters:** CLTQ; CLDQ
Senior Executive Officers
Chairman   Jean Peyrelevade
Managing Director   Allein Gilles
General-Investment
Head of Investment   Hironori Kikuchi *Head, Investment Banking* T 5510 8610 F 5512 5895
General - Treasury
Head of Treasury   Masaaki Yamakawa *Treasurer* T 5510 8807 F 5512 5679
                                       Yukio Yamakawa *Treasury, Yen* T 5510 8810 F 5512 5679
                                       Manabu Hirohashi *Treasury, FX* T 5510 8820 F 5512 5679
Relationship Manager
Financial Institutions   Masatoshi Yamada *Senior Manager* T 5512 5952 F 5512 5619
Debt Capital Markets / Fixed Income
Head of Debt Capital Markets   François Pagés *Head, Capital Markets Japan* T 5512 5870 F 5512 5869
Head of Fixed Income   Yun Yamada T 5510 8626 F 4412 5899
Other   Katsunori Nakazawa *Stock & CB Arbitrage* T 5510 8700 F 5512 5898
Equity Capital Markets
Head of Equity Capital Markets   François Pagés *Head, Capital Markets Japan* T 5512 5870 F 5512 5869
Other   Katsunori Nakazawa *Stock & CB Arbitrage* T 5510 8700 F 5512 5898
Domestic Equities
Head of Sales   Kazumi Takeuchi *Japanese Equities* T 5510 8690 F 3597 0102
Other (International Equity)
Asian Equities   Hideaki Nozawa T 5510 8650 F 5512 5896
Foreign Exchange
Head of Foreign Exchange   François Pagés *Head, Capital Markets Japan* T 5512 5870 F 5512 5869
                                       Marcel Bejjani *Head, FX & Interest Rate Products* T 5510 8616
                                       F 5512 5895

Euromoney Directory 1999   **835**

JAPAN (+81)   www.euromoneydirectory.com

Crédit Lyonnais (cont)
Foreign Exchange (cont)
                                               Manabu Hirohashi *Treasury, FX* ☎ **5510 8820** ℻ **5512 5679**
                                               Masayoshi Iwasaki ☎ **5510 8805** ℻ **5512 5679**
Risk Management
Head of Risk Management   François Pagés *Head, Capital Markets Japan* ☎ **5512 5870** ℻ **5512 5869**
                                               Marcel Bejjani *Head, FX & Interest Rate Products* ☎ **5510 8616**
                                               ℻ **5512 5895**
Fixed Income Derivatives / Risk Management
Country Head   Yves Ringler *Head, Interest Rate Derivatives* ☎ **5510 8620** ℻ **5512 5895**
Other Currency Swap / FX Options Personnel
Future Brokerage   Anthony Limbrick ☎ **5510 8830** ℻ **5512 5692**
OTC Equity Derivatives
Head   Stephane Decker *Head, Equity Derivatives* ☎ **5510 8660** ℻ **3597 8237**
Corporate Finance / M&A Advisory
Other (Corporate Finance)
Corporate Business   Mitsuru Tanida *Senior Executive Manager* ☎ **5512 5633** ℻ **5512 5619**
Financial Engineering   Tetsuro Miwa *Senior Manager* ☎ **5510 8795** ℻ **5512 5619**
Other Departments
Correspondent Banking   Reiichiro Yano *Senior Executive Manager* ☎ **5512 5628** ℻ **5512 5619**

Crédit Lyonnais Securities (Japan)   Full Branch Office
7th & 8th Floors, Hibiya Kokusai Building, 2-2-3, Uchisaiwai-cho, Chiyoda-ku, Tokyo 100-0011
Tel: (3) 5512 5900 Fax: (3) 5512 5961 Telex: J33110 CLSEC TOK

Senior Executive Officers
Director & Branch Manager   François Pagès
General-Investment
Head of Investment   Hironori Kikuchi *Senior Manager*
Debt Capital Markets / Fixed Income
Head of Fixed Income   Marcel Bejjani *Head of Fixed Income*
Equity Capital Markets
Domestic Equities
Head of Sales   Kazumi Takeuchi *Executive Senior Manager*
                                               Katunori Nakazawa *Senior Manager*
Other (Domestic Equities)
Equities Derivatives Trading   Stéphane Decker *Manager*
International Equities
Head of Sales   Hideaki Nozawa *Senior Manager, Asian Equities*
Settlement / Clearing
Tel: 5512 5910 Fax: 3597 8019
Head of Settlement / Clearing   Takao Hirano *Senior Manager*
Administration
Compliance
                                               Tasuku Ito *Assistant Branch Manager*
Other (Administration)
Human Resources   Yoshiharu Fujioka *Deputy General Manager*

Credit Suisse Financial Products   Full Branch Office
27th Floor, Shiroyama Hills, 4-3-1 Toranomon, Minato-ku, Tokyo 105-6027
Tel: (3) 5403 4000
Website: www.csfp.co.jp

Senior Executive Officers
Others (Senior Executives)
Business Planning & Branch Management   Hitomi Gambe ☎ **5403 4191** ℻ **5403 4177**
Administration
Business Development   Hitomi Gambe ☎ **5403 4191** ℻ **5403 4177**

836 Euromoney Directory 1999

www.euromoneydirectory.com　　　　　JAPAN (+81)

Credit Suisse First Boston Securities (Japan) Limited

Shiroyama Hills, 4-3-1 Toronomon, Minato-ku, Tokyo 105
Tel: (3) 5404 9490 Fax: (3) 5404 9831 Telex: J28559 Swift: CSFB JP JX
Website: www.csfb.com

Debt Capital Markets / Fixed Income
Tel: 5404 9440 Fax: 5404 9826

Fixed-Income Repo
Marketing & Product Development
Trading

Eigan Kaji *Vice President* E eigenkaji@csfb.com
Paul Jones *Vice President (Yen)*
Miki Yamazaki *Assistant Vice President*
Shingo Kasahara *Trader*

Equity Capital Markets

Equity Repo / Securities Lending
Marketing & Product Development; Head of Prime Brokerage

Toshi Kamitani *Vice President* T 5404 9490 F 5404 9831
E toshifumi.kamitani@csfb.com

Daewoo Securities Co Limited　　　　　Full Branch Office

6th Floor, Kyokuyo Building, 2-8-11 Nihonbashi, Chuo-ku, Tokyo 103
Tel: (3) 3242 2451 Fax: (3) 3243 0887 Reuters: DWSC-M

Senior Executive Officers
Branch Manager　　　　　Jang-Tae Kim

The Dai-Ichi Kangyo Bank Limited　　　　　Head Office

1-5 Uchisaiwaicho 1-chome, Chiyoda-ku, Tokyo 100-0011
Tel: (3) 3596 1111 Telex: J22315 Swift: DKBL JP JT Telex: J22379
Website: www.dkb.co.jp

Senior Executive Officers
President & Chief Executive Officer　　Katsuyuki Sugita
Deputy President　　　　　　　　　　Takasuke Kaneko
Deputy President　　　　　　　　　　Toshikuni Nishinohara
Senior Managing Director　　　　　　Takatsugu Murai
Senior Managing Director　　　　　　Tadashi Kudo
Senior Managing Director　　　　　　Nobuhiro Mori
Senior Managing Director　　　　　　Taira Hosaka

Others (Senior Executives)
International Banking Coordination Division　　Keiji Torii *GM, International Planning & Coordination Division*

General-Lending (DCM, SL)
Head of Corporate Banking

Tomomi Hiroi *GM, International Finance*
Makoto Sekino *GM, International Credit*

General-Investment
Head of Investment　　　　Masaharu Saito *AGM, International Investment Group*

General - Treasury
Head of Treasury　　　　　Toshio Sasaki *GM, Treasury & Securities Division*
　　　　　　　　　　　　　Tadashi Kawashima *GM, International Treasury*

Relationship Manager
Int'l Financial Institutions Division　　Noboru Takagi *General Manager*

Debt Capital Markets / Fixed Income
Head of Debt Capital Markets　　Seiichi Ishii *AGM, Capital Markets Trading Group*
　　　　　　　　　　　　　　　　Hayato Nishihara *AGM, Capital Markets Group*

Bonds - General
Bond Investment Group　　Yutaka Futamura *Assistant General Manager*

Asset-Backed Securities / Securitization
Global Head　　Shigeyoshi Nishiyama *Structured Finance and Derivatives Division*

Fixed-Income Research
Global Head　　Masaru Kusakawa *AGM, Capital Markets Research Group*

Equity Capital Markets

Other (Domestic Equities)
Equity Investment Group　　Shinichi Muramatsu *Assistant General Manager*

Syndicated Lending
Head of Syndication　　Yoshinori Yaso *AGM, Syndication Group*

Euromoney Directory 1999　837

JAPAN (+81)   www.euromoneydirectory.com

The Dai-Ichi Kangyo Bank Limited (cont)

Other (Syndicated Lending)
Loan Administration Group — Hiroshi Aono *Assistant General Manager*

Loan-Related Activities
Project Finance — Masahiko Furutani *AGM, Project Finance Group*

Other (Trade Finance)
Structured Finance & Derivatives — Shigeyoshi Nishiyama *General Manager*
Koichi Torihara *AGM, Planning Group*
Structured Finance Office — Shuichiro Hara *Assistant General Manager*

Money Markets
Money Markets Group — Hideaki Ikeuchi *Assistant General Manager*

Foreign Exchange

FX Traders / Sales People
FX Group
Foreign Currencies Financial Management Group
— Koichi Kubo *Assistant General Manager*
— Yoshiki Ihara *Assistant General Manager*

Risk Management
Head of Risk Management — Akira Sueda *GM, Market Risk Management Office*

Other (FI Derivatives)
— Zenpei Sasako *Assistant General Manager*

Other (Exchange-Traded Derivatives)
Derivative Products Group — Hirohisa Ishi *Assistant General Manager*

Settlement / Clearing
Operations — Syuji Yamada *Tokyo International Operations Center*

Global Custody

Other (Global Custody)
Custodian Group — Hitoshi Takemoto *Assistant General Manager* ☏ 3596 6110

Administration
Head of Administration — Itsuo Kodaka *General Manager*

The Daiwa Bank Limited — Head Office

2-1 Bingomachi 2-chome, Chuo-ku, Osaka 541
Tel: (6) 271 1221 Telex: J63284 Swift: DIWA JP JS

Senior Executive Officers
Chairman — Toru Abekawa
President — Akira Fujita
Managing Director / General Manager — Shigeyoshi Genjida
Department: International Division
1-1, Otemachi 2-Chome, Chiyoda-ku, Tokyo 100
Tel: +81 (3) 3231 1231 Telex: J22428
Senior Deputy General Manager — Yoshiaki Kawakami
Senior Deputy General Manager — Masaaki Kanda

Daiwa Securities Co Limited

6-4 Otemachi, 2-chome, Chiyoda-ku, Tokyo 100
Tel: (3) 3243 2111 Fax: (3) 3245 0797 Telex: J22411 Reuters: DWAA
Website: www.daiwa.co.jp

Senior Executive Officers
Chairman — Tomoaki Kusuda
President — Yoshinari Hara
Chief Executive Officer — Akira Kiyota *Deputy President*

Debt Capital Markets / Fixed Income

Fixed-Income Repo
Head of Repo — Mr. Matsushima *Trading*

Equity Capital Markets

Equity Repo / Securities Lending
Marketing & Product Development — Masanori Otsuka *Manager* ☏ 5620 7177

838   Euromoney Directory 1999

www.euromoneydirectory.com   JAPAN (+81)

Den Danske Bank Aktieselskab
Representative Office
Yusen Building, 2-3-2 Marunouchi, Chiyoda-ku, Tokyo 100-0005
Tel: (3) 3214 7070 Fax: (3) 3214 2425

Senior Executive Officers
Chief Representative   Anders Kjaer
Assistant Representative   Per Grönlund

Deutsche Bank AG
Full Branch Office
2nd Floor, Nagoya AT Building, 1-18-22 Nishiki, Naka-ku, Nagoya 460
CPO Box 132, Nagoya 450-91
Tel: (52) 203 5281 Fax: (52) 203 5280 Telex: 4424078 DEUTNA J Swift: DEUT JP JT 851

Deutsche Bank AG
Full Branch Office
8-12 Honmachi 1-chome, Chuo-ku, Osaka 541
PO Box 215, Osaka 540-91
Tel: (6) 266 1977 Fax: (6) 266 1985 Telex: 65696 DBOSAKAB J Swift: DEUT JP JT 850

Senior Executive Officers
Managing Director / General Manager   Erdmann R G Vogt

Deutsche Bank AG Tokyo
Full Branch Office
Deutsche Bank Building, 12-1 Toranomon 3-chome, Minato-ku, Tokyo 105
PO Box 1430, Tokyo 100-91
Tel: (3) 5401 1971 Fax: (3) 5401 6900; (3) 5401 6530 Telex: 24814 DEUTBKTK J Swift: DEUT JP JT
Administration Tel: 5401 7273; Fax: 5401 6529; Audit Tel: 5401 6790; Fax: 5401 6542; Corporate Banking
Tel: 5401 6669; Fax: 5401 6532; Corporate Communications Tel: 5401 6760; Fax: 5400 6533; Credit International
Tel: 5401 6681; Fax: 5401 6536; Custody Sales Tel: 5401 7267; Fax: 5401 7268; Customer Services Tel: 5401 6640;
Fax: 5401 6537; Financial Control Tel: 5401 6719; Fax: 5401 6538; Financial Institutions Tel: 5401 6617;
Fax: 5401 6540; Foreign Tel: 5401 6663; Fax: 5401 6531; Foreign Exchange Tel: 5401 6555; Fax: 5401 6535; Human
Resources Tel: 5401 7834; Fax: 5401 6539; IT/Operations Tel: 5401 6780; Fax: 5401 6541; Management -
Secretary Fax: 5401 6533; Management/Secretary Tel: 5401 6601; Management/Treasury - Secretary
Tel: 5401 7259; Fax: 5401 6535; Money Market/Repo Tel: 5401 6708; Fax: 5401 6535; Settlement Tel: 5401 6730;
Fax: 5401 6534; Structured Finance Tel: 5401 6634; Fax: 5401 6528; Treasury Tel: 5401 6710; Fax: 5401 6535
Website: www.deutsche-bank.com

Senior Executive Officers
Financial Director   Fumiya Aoki *Head of Financial Institutions* ☏ **5401 6617**
Managing Director / General Manager   Dr Thomas Duhnkrack

Others (Senior Executives)
Financial Control   Hiromi Nonaka *Head* ☏ **5401 6719**

General-Lending (DCM, SL)
Head of Corporate Banking   Mr Eisenach *Head, Corporate Banking* ☏ **5401 6669**

Relationship Manager
Credit International   Frank Kuhnke *Head* ☏ **5401 6681**
Management   Mrs Rampf ☏ **5401 6601**

Debt Capital Markets / Fixed Income
Tel: 5401 7993 Fax: 5401 2191

Fixed-Income Repo
Head of Repo; Trading   Warren Butler ☏ **5401 7992**
Trading   Makoto Tanaka
Trading; Sales   Yoshihiko Hada

Equity Capital Markets

Equity Repo / Securities Lending
Head of Trading   Yuko Obayashi *Trading*

Money Markets
Country Head   Junko Yoda *Head of Money Market / Repo* ☏ **5401 6708**

Foreign Exchange
Country Head   Tetsuo Seki *Head, Foreign Bills* ☏ **5401 6555**

JAPAN (+81)   www.euromoneydirectory.com

Deutsche Bank AG Tokyo (cont)

Settlement / Clearing
Country Head — Mr Sawada *Head* ☎ 5401 6730

Global Custody
Country Head — Kyoichi Murakawa *Regional Head of Sales* ☎ 5401 7267 F 5401 7268

Administration
Technology & Systems
Information Technology / Operations — Mr Makano *Head* ☎ 5401 6780
Accounts / Audit
— Mouri Naohiro *Head, Internal Audit* ☎ 5401 6790

Other (Administration)
Customer Service — Miss Miyashita *Senior Assistant Manager* ☎ 5401 6640
Mrs. Fukuma ☎ 5401 7273
Human Relations — Beatrice Meyer *Deputy Head* ☎ 5401 7834

Deutsche Bundesbank — Representative Office

6th Floor, Tokyo Kaijo Building, Shinkan, 1-2-1 Marunouchi, Chiyoda-ku, Tokyo 100
Tel: (3) 3211 1581 **Fax:** (3) 3211 1583

Senior Executive Officers
Representative — Wolfgang Mörke
Deputy Representative — Gerald Fey

Deutsche Morgan Grenfell Asset Management (Japan) Limited — Subsidiary Company

Otemachi First Square, East Tower, 16th Floor, 1-5-1 Otemachi, Chiyoda-ku, Tokyo 100-0004
Tel: (3) 5218 6300 **Fax:** (3) 5222 3550 **Telex:** 26868 DBMGAM
Website: www.morgan-grenfell.com

Senior Executive Officers
Chief Operating Officer — Dominic Delaforce
Group Representative — H Yamamoto
Asset Management
Head — Hitoshi Yamamoto *Group Representative* ☎ +81 (3)5218 6401

Deutsche Securities Limited

Deutsche Bank Building, 12-1, Toranomon, 3-chome, Minato-ku, Tokyo 105
Tel: (3) 5401 1986

Senior Executive Officers
Department: Senior Executives: Global Corporates & Institutions

Others (Senior Executives)
Head of Investment Banking — Josef Ackermann
Head of Global Markets — Edson Mitchell
Head of Equities — Michael Philipp
Head of Risk Management — Hugo Banziger
Head of Global Banking Services — Juergen Fitschen
Head of Structured Finance — Gavin Lickley
Head of IT / Operations — Marc Sternfeld

The Development Bank of Singapore Limited — Full Branch Office

606 Yurakucho Denki Building (North), 1-7-1 Yurakucho, Chiyoda-ku, Tokyo 100-0006
Tel: (3) 3213 4411 **Fax:** (3) 3213 4415 **Telex:** J25869 DBS TOKYO **Swift:** DBSS JP JT

Senior Executive Officers
Senior Vice President & General Manager — See Meng Wong
Vice President & General Manager — Stephen Lee
Syndicated Lending
Head of Syndication — Masaharu Miyaoka *AGM, Credit & Marketing*
Money Markets
Country Head — Tomoko Matsumoto *Assistant Manager - Treasury*

840   Euromoney Directory 1999

www.euromoneydirectory.com JAPAN (+81)

Foreign Exchange
Country Head — Tomoko Matsumoto *Assistant Manager - Treasury*
Settlement / Clearing
Country Head — Bunji Suzuki *Manager*
Other Departments
Correspondent Banking — Stephen Lee *Vice President & General Manager*

DG BANK — Representative Office
30th Floor East, ARK Mori Building, 1-12-32 Akasaka, Minato-ku, Tokyo 107
Tel: (3) 5570 0801 **Fax:** (3) 5570 0803
Senior Executive Officers
Representative — Alexander Bürkner

Dresdner Bank AG — Full Branch Office
1-8 Toranomon 4-chome, Minato-ku, Tokyo 105-0001
Tel: (3) 5403 9000 **Fax:** (3) 5403 9199 **Telex:** 2225295 DRESBK J **Swift:** DRES JP JX
Senior Executive Officers
General Manager — I Ogura
Others (Senior Executives)
Securities — Mr Shimada
Mr Toller
Settlement / Clearing
Head of Settlement / Clearing — Mr Takagi ☎ **5403 9170**

Dresdner Kleinwort Benson (Asia) Limited
Toranomon 4-chome Mori Building, 1-8 Toranomon 4-chome, Minato-ku, Tokyo 105-0001
Tel: (3) 5403 9500 **Fax:** (3) 5403 9090 **Telex:** 2226111 DRESEC J
Senior Executive Officers
Managing Director / General Manager — Simon Toller

Euroclear Operations Centre — Representative Office
Morgan Guaranty Trust Company of New York, Akasaka Park Building, 5-2-20 Akasaka, Minato-ku, Tokyo 107
Tel: (3) 5573 1546 **Fax:** (3) 5573 1550
Senior Executive Officers
Chief Representative — Yoshihisa Kanda

The Export-Import Bank of Japan — Head Office
4-1 Otemachi 1-chome, Chiyoda-ku, Tokyo 100
Tel: (3) 3287 9106; (3) 3287 9101 **Fax:** (3) 3287 9539
Website: www.japamexim.go.jp
Senior Executive Officers
Governor — Hiroshi Yasuda
Deputy Governor — Akira Nambara

The First Bank of Toyama Limited — Head Office
2-8 Sogawa 2-chome, Toyama City 930
Tel: (764) 24 1211 **Cable:** FIRST TOYAM
Senior Executive Officers
President — Junji Kanaoka
Managing Director — Koichi Sakamori
Managing Director — Hiroshi Wakabayashi
Managing Director — Minoru Shouzen
Managing Director — Koichiro Ishikawa
Managing Director — Isao Imai

JAPAN (+81)

The First Bank of Toyama Limited (cont)
Department: International Division
8th Floor, Nissay Sogawa Building, 7-15 Sogawa 1-chome, Toyama City
Tel: +81 (764) 420 002 Fax: +81 (764) 420 071 Telex: 5152140 FRTTYM J
International Division   Koichiro Ishikawa *MD & General Manager*

The First National Bank of Chicago   Full Branch Office
7th Floor, Hibiya Central Building, 2-9 Nishi-Shinbashi 1-chome, Minato-ku, Tokyo 105
Tel: (3) 3596 8700 Fax: (3) 3596 8744 Telex: 2224977
Senior Executive Officers
Others (Senior Executives)
Senior Vice President   Michael S Brown ☎ **3596 8732**

The Fuji Bank Limited   Head Office
1-5-5 Otemachi, Chiyoda-ku, Tokyo 100-0004
Tel: (3) 3216 2211 Fax: (3) 3532 7370 Telex: 22367 Swift: FUJI JP JT Telex: 22722 Telex: 22170
Website: www.fujibank.co.jp
Senior Executive Officers
Chairman   Toru Hashimoto
President & Chief Executive Officer   Yoshiro Yamamoto
International Division   Akio Takeuchi *General Manager, Overseas Business Division*
General-Lending (DCM, SL)
Head of Corporate Banking   Isao Hiraide *Managing Director*
General-Investment
Head of Investment   Atsushi Takano *Managing Director*
Corporate Finance / M&A Advisory
Head of Corporate Finance   Mitsuru Annen *Senior Managing Director*
Global Custody
Head of Global Custody   Hiroaki Shinoda *Managing Director*
Other Departments
Private Banking   Masaaki Sato *Managing Director*

Fujigin Factors Limited   Head Office
Togeki Building, 4-1-1 Tsukiji, Chuo-ku, Tokyo
Tel: (3) 3541 4145 Fax: (3) 3543 7406 Telex: 2523185 FUJIFA J
Senior Executive Officers
President   Kazushi Hara
Managing Director   Isamu Kato
Syndicated Lending
Other (Trade Finance)
Factoring   Seiichi Saito *Joint General Manager*
                            Iwao Saito *Joint General Manager*
                            Masato Shimizu *Joint General Manager*
                            Takane Imai *Joint General Manager*

The Fukutoku Bank Limited   Head Office
Higashi-Shinsaibashi 1-5-9, Chuo-ku, Osaka 542-91
Tel: (6) 252 1666 Fax: (6) 252 1913 Telex: J64866 FUKTOKBK Swift: FTOK JP JS Cable: FUKTOKBANK
Senior Executive Officers
President   Shinji Yoshida
Senior Managing Director   Katsuki Masawaki
Senior Managing Director   Kazuioshi Tomohiro
Managing Director   Yuji Iwase
Managing Director   Kazuyoshi Tomohiro
Managing Director   Junji Nishiza

www.euromoneydirectory.com JAPAN (+81)

Furman Selz

5th Floor Iwanami Shoten, 2-5-5 Hitosaibashi, Chiyoda-ku, Tokyo 101
Tel: (3) 5210 2462 Fax: (3) 5210 2461

Senior Executive Officers
Others (Senior Executives)
International Sales   Naotaka Fujimoto

Generale Bank
Representative Office

9th Floor, Imperial Tower, 1-1-1 Uchisaiwaicho, Chiyoda-ku, Tokyo 100
Tel: (3) 3503 4491 Fax: (3) 3503 4492

Senior Executive Officers
Chief Representative   Jean-Claude Delanghe

Goldman Sachs Asset Management Japan Limited
Subsidiary Company

10th Floor, ARK Mori Building, 1-12-32 Akasaka, Minato-ku, Tokyo 107-6010
Tel: (3) 5573 7800

Senior Executive Officers
President   Michiya Nagai
Representative   Shogo Maeda
Others (Senior Executives)
                                   Yasuyo Yamazaki *Manager, Marketing*

Goldman Sachs International Bank
Full Branch Office

5th Floor, ARK Mori Building, 1-12-32 Akasaka, Minato-ku, Tokyo 107-6005
Tel: (3) 3589 5320

Senior Executive Officers
Managing Director   Marc A Spilker
General Manager   Akihiko Usui

Goldman Sachs Investment Trust Management Limited
Subsidiary Company

10th Floor, ARK Mori Building, 1-12-32 Akasaka, Minato-ku, Tokyo 107-6010
Tel: (3) 5573 7800

Senior Executive Officers
President   Yasuyo Yamazaki
Others (Senior Executives)
Chief Investment   Shogo Maeda *Director & Senior Portfolio Manager*
                                   Michiya Nagai *Director*

Goldman Sachs (Japan) Limited
Full Branch Office

5th Floor, Ark Mori Building, 12-32 Akasaka, 1-chome, Minato-ku, Tokyo 107-6005
Tel: (3) 3589 7000 Fax: (3) 3589 9334 Telex: J23381 GOLSACHS Cable: GOLDSACHS TOKYO

Senior Executive Officers
Honorary Chairman   Hideo Suzuki
President   Mark Schwartz
General-Investment
Head of Investment   Richard Gnodde *Managing Director*
                                   Masanori Mochida *Managing Director*

Debt Capital Markets / Fixed Income
Tel: 3589 7317 Fax: 3589 9314
Regional Head   George Wellde Jr *Branch Manager & Managing Director*
                                   Oki Matsumoto *Managing Director*
                                   Tsutomu Sato *Managing Director*

Euromoney Directory 1999 843

JAPAN (+81)   www.euromoneydirectory.com

Goldman Sachs (Japan) Limited (cont)

Fixed-Income Repo
Head of Repo; Trading   Allen Arakel *Vice President* ☎ 3589 7317 F 3589 9314
Equity Capital Markets
Regional Head   Jun Makihara *Managing Director*
   David Heller *Managing Director*

The Gunma Bank Limited   Head Office

194 Motosojamachi, Maebashi, Gunma 371-8611
International Division, 2-3-21 Nihonbashi, Chuo-ku, Tokyo 103-8611
Tel: (27) 252 1111 **Telex:** J 28720 GUNMAGIN **Swift:** GUMA JP JT
Website: www.gunmabank.co.jp

Senior Executive Officers
Chairman   Takuji Tsuchikane
President   Kyozo Yoshida

The Hachijuni Bank Limited   Head Office

178-8 Okada, Nagano-City, Nagano 380-8682
Tel: (26) 227 1182 **Fax:** (26) 224 5077 **Telex:** J23763 HATINIBK **Swift:** HABK JP JT **Reuters:** HACQ
Website: www.82bank.co.jp

Senior Executive Officers
President   Minoru Chino
Chief Executive Officer   Yumitaro Takeshita *Deputy President*
Financial Director   Masaru Sakamoto *Managing Director*
International Division   Kazuo Miyajima *General Manager*

Debt Capital Markets / Fixed Income
Department: International Department
Tel: (3) 3242 0082 **Fax:** (3) 3277 0146
Head of Fixed Income   Fumiaki Nishikawa *Manager* ☎ **(26) 224 5690**

Eurobonds
Head of Trading   Akira Yamauchi *Manager* ☎ **(3) 3246 4651**

Syndicated Lending
Department: International Department
Tel: (3) 3242 0082 **Fax:** (3) 3277 0147
Head of Syndication   Makoto Nakamura *Assistant Manager* ☎ **(3) 3246 4650**
Head of Trading   Hidehiko Akanuma *Assistant Manager* ☎ **(3) 3277 0175**

Money Markets
Tel: (3) 3242 0082 **Fax:** (3) 3277 0147
Head of Money Markets   Satoshi Masuda *Assistant Manager* ☎ **(3) 3245 9887**

Foreign Exchange
Tel: (3) 3242 0082 **Fax:** (3) 3277 0147
Head of Foreign Exchange   Yoritaka Takayama *Deputy General Manager* ☎ **(3) 3246 4682**
FX Traders / Sales People
   Masaki Fujimori *Manager* ☎ **(3) 3246 4683**
   Tomohiko Takeuchi *Assistant Manager* ☎ **(3) 3277 0141**

Settlement / Clearing
Tel: (3) 3242 0082 **Fax:** (3) 3246 4825
Head of Settlement / Clearing   Atsushi Takahashi *Manager* ☎ **(3) 3277 0062**

The Hachijuni Bank Limited   Head Office

1-22 Nihonbashi Muromachi 4-chome, Chuo-ku, Tokyo 103
Tel: (3) 3242 0082 **Fax:** (3) 3277 0147 **Telex:** J23763 HATINIBK **Swift:** HABK JP JT **Reuters:** HACQ

Senior Executive Officers
President   Minoru Chino
Chief Executive Officer   Yumitaro Takeshita *Deputy President*
Financial Director   Masaru Sakamoto *Managing Director*
International Division   Kazuo Miyajima *General Manager, International Department*

Syndicated Lending
Department: International Department - International Finance Group
Global Head   Fumiaki Nishikawa *Manager*

www.euromoneydirectory.com   JAPAN (+81)

Other (Syndicated Lending)
Eurobonds   Dai Watanabe *Assistant Manager*
Syndicate Lending   Makoto Nakamura *Assistant Manager*

Money Markets
Department: International Department - Foreign Exchange & International
Global Head   Kenichi Ishii *Assistant Manager* ☎ **3277 0141**

Foreign Exchange
Department: International Department - Foreign Exchange & International
Global Head   Yoritaka Takayama *Manager* ☎ **3246 4682**

FX Traders / Sales People
                                               Tomohiko Takeuchi *Assistant Manager* ☎ **3246 4682**
                                               Masaki Fujimori *Manager* ☎ **3246 4682**
                                               Chiharu Yamazaki *Assistant Manager* ☎ **3246 4682**

Hanil Bank   Full Branch Office

1st Floor, Mitsui OSK Building, 2-1-1 Toranomun, Minato-ku, Tokyo 105-0001
Tel: (3) 3589 2351 Fax: (3) 3589 2359 Telex: J24911

Senior Executive Officers
General Manager   Sam Young Suh
Deputy General Manager   Hee Tae Kim
Deputy General Manager   Wan Ik Moon

The Hiroshima Bank Limited   Head Office

3-8 Kamiya-cho 1-chome, Naka-ku, Hiroshima 730
Tel: (82) 247 5151 Fax: (82) 240 7698 Telex: 653211 HIROBK J Swift: HIRO JP JT

Senior Executive Officers
Chairman   Shunsuke Kishida
President   Makoto Uda
Deputy President   Sho Takahashi
Senior Managing Director   Masao Tokunaga
Managing Director   Shigeru Tanii
Managing Director   Takehiko Muneyoshi
Managing Director   Isao Nairo
Managing Director   Shigeji Suzuki
Managing Director   Michifumi Yasashita

Hoenig & Co Inc   Full Branch Office

6th Floor, Diamond Plaza, 25 Ichibancho, Chiyoda-ku, Tokyo 102
Tel: (3) 3221 8860; (3) 3221 1805 Fax: (3) 3221 0471 Telex: 2324539 HOENIG J

Senior Executive Officers
Executive Vice President   Yuichi Okazaki
Managing Director   John F R Smilgin ✉ **jsmilgin@hoenig.com**
General Manager   Keiji Tadaki ✉ **keiji_tadaki@hoenig.com**

Equity Capital Markets
Department: Marketing and Trading Department

Domestic Equities
Head of Trading   Tsunehito Ikeda *Chief Trader* ☎ **3221 3464**

The Hokkaido Takushoku Bank Limited   Head Office

7 Odori-nishi 3, Chuo-ku, Sapporo 060-0042
International Division, 3-13, Nihombashi 1-chome, Chuo-ku, Tokyo 103
Tel: (11) 271 2111 Telex: J22804 Swift: HTAK JP JT Telex: J23241 Telex: J28485; International Division
Tel: (3) 3272 6611; Fax: (3) 3242 8725

Senior Executive Officers
Deputy President   Kenji Takamura
Deputy President   Hidemitsu Washida
Managing Director   Shinichi Aikawa
Managing Director   Okitsugu Takimoto
Managing Director   Manabu Ohura
Managing Director   Tatsuji Obara

Euromoney Directory 1999 **845**

JAPAN (+81)   www.euromoneydirectory.com

The Hokuriku Bank Limited
Head Office

2-26 Tsutsumicho-dori, 1-chome, Toyama City 930-8637
Tel: (764) 237 111 **Fax:** (764) 915 908 **Telex:** J23604 RIKBKJ **Swift:** RIKB JP JY **Telex:** J 28660 RIKBKJ
Telex: J 28649 RIKBKJ; **International Dept Tel:** (3) 3231 7354; (3) 3242 0541
Website: www.sphere.ad.jp/hokugin

Senior Executive Officers
President   Kenso Yashima
Senior Managing Director   Shinichiro Inushima
Senior Managing Director   Hisashi Tanaka
Managing Director   Tsuneharu Nakanishi
Managing Director   Motoichiro Hamatani
Managing Director   Masayuki Naruto
Managing Director   Kenichi Mizuno

HSBC Investment Bank Asia Limited
Representative Office

HSBC Building, 11-1, Nihonbashi 3-chome, Chuo-ku, Tokyo 103-0027
Tel: (3) 5203 3290 **Fax:** (3) 5203 3299 **Telex:** KDD 22372 HSBC TKYJ

Senior Executive Officers
Chief Representative   Haru Yamada

HSBC Securities Limited
Subsidiary Company

Formerly known as: HSBC James Capel Japan Limited
3-11-1 Nihombashi, Chuo-ku, Tokyo 103-0027
Tel: (3) 5203 3559 **Fax:** (3) 5203 3592 **Telex:** 2223489

Senior Executive Officers
Managing Director   David Kenny
Company Secretary   Ms Iizuka ☏ **5203 3556**

Administration
Other (Administration)
Public Affairs   Mariko Terazaki

HVB Capital Markets (Asia) Limited
Subsidiary Company

Otemachi 1st Square Ear Tower, 17F, 1-5-1 Otemachi, Chiyouda-ku, Tokyo 100-0004
CPO Box 1379, Tokyo 100-8693
Tel: (3) 3285 0055 **Fax:** (3) 3285 0058

The Hyakugo Bank Limited
Head Office

21-27 Iwata, Tsu, Mie 514-8666
Tel: (59) 227 2151 **Fax:** (59) 228 2010 **Telex:** J32424

Senior Executive Officers
President   Sadahisa Kawakita
Senior Managing Director   Hajimu Maeda
Senior Managing Director   Kikuji Iwasaki
Managing Director   Susumu Okamoto
Managing Director   Hisashi Isomura
Managing Director   Shunji Iida
Managing Director   Etsuo Mizutani

Others (Senior Executives)

                                        Masayuki Uchida *Director*
                                        Kouichi Murata *Director*
                                        Koei Kokawa *Director*
                                        Masataka Tanaka *Director*
                                        Toshihiko Yoshida *Director*
                                        Kenichi Yamada *Director*
                                        Kanji Yoneyama *Director*

www.euromoneydirectory.com　　　JAPAN (+81)

The Hyakujushi Bank Limited　　Head Office
5-1, Kamei-cho, Takamatsu-shi, Kagawa 760-0050
Tel: (87) 831 0114 **Telex:** J26151 HYAKBANK **Swift:** HYAK JP JT **Cable:** HYAKBANK

Senior Executive Officers
Chairman　　　　　　　　　　　Kyosuke Matsumoto
President　　　　　　　　　　　Shusaku Ayada
Senior Managing Director　　　Hiroshi Okawa
International Division　　　　Taichiro Sakuragawa

IBJ Securities Co Limited　　Head Office
5-1 Otemachi 1-chome, Chiyoda-ku, Tokyo 100
Tel: (3) 5252 3111 **Fax:** (3) 5252 4915
Website: www.ibjs.co.jp

Senior Executive Officers
Chairman　　　　　　　　　　　Atsuyoshi Yatsunami ☎ **5252 6800**
President & CEO　　　　　　　Hiroshi Nakamura ☎ **5200 7800**
Deputy President　　　　　　　Yoshio Ohsawa ☎ **5200 7811**

Debt Capital Markets / Fixed Income
Department: Sales & Trading Division
Tel: 5252 6801 **Fax:** 3212 1889
Head of Fixed Income　　　　Osamu Kuriharo Managing Director ☎ **5252 6801**
　　　　　　　　　　　　　　Kazuo Ichiki Director ☎ **5200 7802**
　　　　　　　　　　　　　　Naoyuki Inada Director ☎ **5252 6980**

Department: Capital Markets Division
Tel: +81 5252 6802 **Fax:** +81 3214 1251
Head of Debt Capital Markets　Manahu Okano Managing Director ☎ **5252 6802**
　　　　　　　　　　　　　　Kazuo Kawagoe Director ☎ **5252 6805**
　　　　　　　　　　　　　　Yoshiki Maribe Director ☎ **5200 2105**

Equity Capital Markets
Tel: 5252 6801 **Fax:** 3214 1887
Head of Equity Capital Markets　Shigeo Kobayashi Managing Director ☎ **5252 8903**

Syndicated Lending
Head of Syndication　　　　　Yojiro Shiba Director ☎ **5252 6900**

Risk Management
Tel: 5252 6841 **Fax:** 5252 4915
Head of Risk Management　　Yoshihisa Imada Director ☎ **5200 7803**

Settlement / Clearing
Tel: 5252 6829 **Fax:** 3211 6003
Head of Settlement / Clearing　Ikio Shinozaki Director ☎ **5252 6829**

Administration
Head of Administration　　　　Yoshihisa Imada Director ☎ **5200 7803**

Compliance
　　　　　　　　　　　　　　Jiro Tanaka Managing Director ☎ **5200 6803**

Accounts / Audit
Auditor　　　　　　　　　　　Kazyo Sasaki ☎ **5252 6804**
　　　　　　　　　　　　　　Shohzo Hayashi ☎ **5200 7804**
　　　　　　　　　　　　　　Kazuhide Kashiwabara ☎ **5200 7805**

Ichiyoshi Securities Co Limited　　Head Office
2-14-1 Hatchobori, Chuo-ku, Tokyo 104-0032
Tel: (3) 3555 6230 **Fax:** (3) 3555 6270 **Telex:** 2225572 IYST J

Senior Executive Officers
Chairman　　　　　　　　　　　Genji Ashiya
President　　　　　　　　　　　Masashi Takehi
Chief Executive Officer　　　　Akio Jokura Senior Managing Director
Financial Director　　　　　　　Shozo Yoritomi Senior Managing Director

Euromoney Directory 1999　**847**

JAPAN (+81)   www.euromoneydirectory.com

The Industrial Bank of Japan Limited
Head Office

3-3 Marunouchi, 1-chome, Chiyoda-ku, Tokyo 100-8210
Tel: (3) 3214 1111 Fax: (3) 3201 7643 Telex: J22325 Swift: IBJT JP JT Cable: KOGIN TOKYO
Telex: KOGIN J23215
Website: www.ibjbank.co.jp

Senior Executive Officers
Chairman, Board of Directors — Yoh Kurosawa
President & Chief Executive Officer — Yoshiyuki Fujisawa
President — Masao Nishimura
Chief Executive Officer — Masao Nishimura
International Division — Yuji Suzuki *Managing Director*

General-Investment
Head of Investment — Masayuki Yasuoka *Managing Director*

Debt Capital Markets / Fixed Income
Fixed-Income Repo
Trading — Takeshi Kawano

Syndicated Lending
Loan-Related Activities
Trade Finance — Yasuharu Ookawa
Project Finance — Noboru Fukutomi
Structured Trade Finance — Yasuharu Ookawa

Money Markets
Head of Money Markets — Nobushige Imai

Foreign Exchange
Head of Foreign Exchange — Nobushige Imai

Global Custody
Head of Global Custody — Toru Terashima

Other Departments
Chief Credit Officer — Sadayoshi Nakamura *Managing Director*
Correspondent Banking — Shizuhiro Yamauchi *Managing Director*

Administration
Head of Administration — Makoto Kiikkawa *Director*

Technology & Systems
— Yonezo Kobayashi

Legal / In-House Counsel
— Michio Furuta

Compliance
— Masanobu Naka

Public Relations
— Kazumasa Suezawa

Accounts / Audit
— Takeo Otsubo

Industrial Bank of Korea
Full Branch Office

9th Floor, Akasaka Twin Tower Main Building, 17-22 Akasaka 2-Chome, Minato-Ku, Tokyo 107
Tel: (3) 3586 7304; (3) 3586 7306 Fax: (3) 3586 7269 Telex: 2228350 IBK J

Senior Executive Officers
Managing Director / General Manager — Sung-Tae Jo

ING Bank NV
Full Branch Office

Alternative trading name: ING Barings
20th Floor, The New Otani Garden Court, 4-1 Kioicho, Chiyoda-ku, Tokyo 102-0094
PO Box 2191, Tokyo
Tel: (3) 5210 0100 Fax: (3) 5210 0760 Telex: 24985 INGB J Swift: INGB JP JT

Senior Executive Officers
General Manager, Japan — Donald H MacKenzie ☎ **5210 0100** 📠 **5210 0760**
Country Manager — Randolph S Koppa ☎ **5210 1500** 📠 **5210 1555**

Others (Senior Executives)
Yukio Rokuura *Assistant General Manager* ☎ **5210 0100** 📠 **5210 0760**

www.euromoneydirectory.com JAPAN (+81)

ING Baring Securities (Japan)
Full Branch Office
5th Floor, Fuso Doshomachi Building, 7-10, Doshomachi 1-chome, Chuo-ku, Osaka 541
Tel: (6) 208 6400 Fax: (6) 208 6421

Senior Executive Officers
Branch Manager Shigeki Iwahashi

ING Baring Securities (Japan) Limited
24th & 25th Floors, The New Otani Garden Court, 4-1 Kioi-cho, Chiyoda-ku, Tokyo 102
Tel: (3) 5210 1500 Fax: (3) 5210 1555 Telex: BSEFAJ 25791

Senior Executive Officers
Chief Executive Officer Rike Wootten *Branch Manager*
Financial Director Veryan Allen
Local Manager Mark Chmiel ⊤ 5210 1372 F 5210 1759

Debt Capital Markets / Fixed Income
Tel: 5210 1342

Eurobonds
Head of Sales Toshihiko Konishi ⊤ 5210 1211
Head of Trading Veryan Allen ⊤ 5210 1779

Fixed-Income Repo
Trading Steve Merritt *Desk Head*
  Sachiko Maeda *Sales Trader*

Equity Capital Markets
Tel: 5210 1351 Fax: 5210 1751
Country Head Rike Wootten *Branch Manager*

Equity Repo / Securities Lending
Marketing & Product Development Steve Hocking *Regional Manager-Asia, International Equity Financ*
  ⊤ 2848 8042 F 2530 5781 E steve.hocking@ing-baring.com
Head of Trading Steve Merritt *Desk Head*
  Sachiko Maeda *Sales Trader*

Risk Management

Other (FI Derivatives)
Futures & Options Mark Chmiel *Local Manager* ⊤ 5210 1372 F 5210 1759

Settlement / Clearing
Derivatives Settlement Mark Chmiel *Local Manager* ⊤ 5210 1372 F 5210 1759

ING Barings
Representative Office
6th Floor, Tokyo Marine Plaza, 2-53 Shiromi 2-chome, Cho-ku, Osaka 540
Tel: (6) 910 6500 Fax: (6) 910 6503 Telex: 24985 INGB J

Senior Executive Officers
Country Manager Randolph Koppa

ING Barings
5th Floor Kokusai Building, 1-1 Marunouchi 3-chrome, Chiyoda-ku, Tokyo 100
Tel: (3) 3212 6481 Fax: (3) 3214 5808; (3) 3212 5691 Telex: 24985 INGB J Swift: INGB JP JT

Senior Executive Officers
General Manager Donald H MacKenzie

The Iyo Bank Limited
Head Office
1 Minami-Horibata-cho, Matsuyama 790-8514
Tel: (89) 941 1141 Fax: (89) 946 9101 Telex: J28245 IYOGINKO Swift: IYOB JP JT
Website: www.iyobank.co.jp

Senior Executive Officers
President Shansuke Aso
International Division Kazuo Kikuchi *GM, International Division*

JAPAN (+81)   www.euromoneydirectory.com

Japan Leasing Corporation
Head Office
Ginza I Tower Building, 9-4 Ginza 2-chome, Chuo-ku, Tokyo 104-8129
Tel: (3) 3566 8175 Fax: (3) 3566 8186 Telex: J28419 JLC Email: katsushi_okamoto@jlc.co.jp

Japan Securities Finance Co Limited
Head Office
2-10 Nihonbashi-Kayaba-cho 1-chome, Chuo-ku, Tokyo 103
Tel: (3) 3666 0571 Fax: (3) 3666 1403

Jardine Fleming Securities (Asia) Limited
Full Branch Office
Yamato Seimei Building, 1-7 Uchisaiwai-cho 1-chome, Chiyoda-ku, Tokyo 100-0011
Tel: (3) 3508 0261 Fax: (3) 3503 0307 Telex: J28173 JFTKY

Senior Executive Officers
Director & General Manager   John Baldwin

The Joyo Bank Limited
Head Office
5-5 Minami-machi 2-chome, Mito 310-0021, Ibaraki
Tel: (29) 231 2151 Fax: (29) 231 2193

Senior Executive Officers
Chairman   Itaru Ishikawa
President   Toranosuke Nishino
Senior Managing Director   Genjiro Tanno
Senior Managing Director   Tohru Kawai
International Division   Shinichi Yamada *MD, International Banking*
                                 Yukihiko Watanabe *GM, International Division* F 231 2193
                                 Osamu Niida *DGM, International Division*

Others (Senior Executives)
Planning Group-Mito   Akira Tominaga *Chief Manager*

General-Investment
Head of Investment   Kaoru Miyata *DGM, Securities Investment Division*
Department: Planning Group
7-2 Yaesu 2-chome, Chuo-ku, Tokyo 104-0028
Tel: +81 (3) 3273 2631 Fax: +81 (3) 3274 1529
Manager   Kazushi Hashimoto
Department: International Division - Operations Office
3-3 Shinhara 1-chome, Mito 310-0045, Ibaraki
Tel: +81 (29) 255 6671 Fax: +81 (29) 255 6522 Reuters: 3632105 JOYOBK,
Deputy General Manager   Hiroshi Noguchi

Debt Capital Markets / Fixed Income
Department: Treasury & Securities Division
7-2 Yaesu 2-chome, Chuo-ku, Tokyo 104-0028
Tel: +81 (3) 3273 5245 Fax: +81 (3) 3242 3726

Domestic Government Bonds
Head of Trading   Ryouichi Yauchi

Eurobonds
Head of Trading   Ryouichi Yauchi

Asset-Backed Securities / Securitization
Head of Trading   Noboru Araki *Manager, Securities & Derivatives Trading*

Money Markets
Department: Treasury & Securities Division
7-2 Yaesu 2-chome, Chuo-ku, Tokyo 104-0028
Tel: +81 (3) 3273 5245 Fax: +81 (3) 3242 3726
Country Head   Osamu Midorikawa *Manager, Capital & MM Group*

Foreign Exchange
Department: Treasury & Securities Division
7-2 Ysesu 2-chome, Chuo-ku, Tokyo 104-0028
Tel: +81 (3) 3723 5245 Fax: +81 (2) 3242 3726
Head of Foreign Exchange   Yuichi Konno *Manager, FX*

www.euromoneydirectory.com　　　　　　　　　JAPAN (+81)

Risk Management
Department: Treasury & Securities Division
7-2 Yaesu 2-chome, Chuo-ku, Tokyo 104-0028
Tel: +81 (3) 3273 5245 **Fax:** +81 (3) 3242 3726

Fixed Income Derivatives / Risk Management
Trading　　　　　　　　Noboru Araki *Manager, Securities & Derivatives Trading*

Settlement / Clearing
Operations　　　　　　　Keno Ochiai *Chief Manager, Operations Group* ℻ **231 7519**
Department: Treasury & Securities Division
7-2 Yaesu 2-chome, Chuo-ku, Tokyo 104-0028
Tel: +81 (3) 3273 1741 **Fax:** +81 (3) 3242 3726
Operations　　　　　　　Shigeki Morita *Chief Manager, Planning Group* ☎ **(3) 3273 5245**
　　　　　　　　　　　　　Hironori Inoue *Manager, Treasury & Securities Admin Div*

Administration
Department: Treasury & Securities Administration
7-2 Yaesu 2-chome, Chuo-ku, Tokyo 104-0028
Tel: +81 (3) 3273 5245 **Fax:** +81 (3) 3242 3726
Head of Administration　　Tadashi Ebisawa *GM, Treasury & Securities Admin Div* ☎ **3273 1741**
　　　　　　　　　　　　　Takao Okoshi *DGM, Treasury & Securities Admin Div* ☎ **3273 1741**

Other (Administration)
Business Planning Group　　Masato Hasegawa *Manager*
Market Risk Supervision Group　Hirohiko Sato *Chief Manager, Treasury & Securities Admin* ☎ **3273 1741**
Group Planning & Administration　Hideto Kashimuka *Chief Manager, Treasury & Securities Admin*
　　　　　　　　　　　　　☎ **3273 1741**

Juroku Bank Limited　　　　　　　　　　　　　　　　　　　　　Head Office

8-26, Kandamachi, Gifu 500-91
Tel: (58) 265 2111 **Fax:** (58) 266 1698

Senior Executive Officers
President　　　　　　　　Yoshiyuki Shimizu
Chief Executive Officer　　Sadakazu Motoya

Debt Capital Markets / Fixed Income
Global Head　　　　　　　Takashi Kamichi

Domestic Government Bonds
Head of Sales　　　　　　Ryoichi Miyazaki

Eurobonds
Head of Syndication　　　Toru Daimon ☎ **(3) 3242 1621**

Money Markets
Department: Money Markets, International Division
Tel: (3) 3242 1621
Global Head　　　　　　　Toru Daimon ☎ **(3) 3242 1621**
Regional Head　　　　　　Kaoru Yokoyama

Foreign Exchange
Department: International Division
Global Head　　　　　　　Toru Daimon ☎ **(3) 3242 1621**

Risk Management
Department: Risk Management Office
Global Head　　　　　　　Satoshi Usui

The Kagoshima Bank Limited　　　　　　　　　　　　　　　　Head Office

6-6 Kinsei-cho, Kagoshima 892-0828
Tel: (99) 225 3111 **Fax:** (99) 227 2783 **Telex:** 2223590 KAGOBK J **Swift:** KAGO JP JT

Senior Executive Officers
President　　　　　　　　Yoshio Ohno
Chief Executive Officer　　Yatsutaka Tokuchi
Treasurer　　　　　　　　Yoshitaka Nomoto

Money Markets
Department: International Division
13-11 Nihonbashi 3-chome, Chuo-ku, Tokyo 103-0027
Tel: +81 (3) 3272 3196 **Fax:** +81 (3) 3272 3180
Global Head　　　　　　　Norio Nagi *Director & General Manager*

JAPAN (+81)   www.euromoneydirectory.com

The Kagoshima Bank Limited (cont)

Foreign Exchange
Department: International Division
13-11 Nihonbashi 3-chome, Chuo-ku, Tokyo 103
Tel: +81 (3) 3272 3196 **Fax:** +81 (3) 3272 3180
Global Head — Norio Nagi *Director & General Manager*

Other Departments
Correspondent Banking — Itaru Inoue *Senior Manager* ☏ 239 7380
Administration
Technology & Systems
— Norio Nakamura *General Manager*
Public Relations
— Kohzo Arimura *Director & General Manager* ☏ 239 9722

Kankaku Securities Co Limited   Head Office

Formerly known as: Nippon Kangyo Kakumaru Securities Co Limited
Sibusawa City Place, 13-16 Nihonbash-Kayaba-cho 1-chome, Chuo-ku, Tokyo 103-8658
Tel: (3) 5640 7805; (3) 5640 7808 **Fax:** (3) 5640 7976; (3) 5640 7977 **Telex:** J24930, J26358 KANKAKU
Swift: NKKSJPJT **Email:** kkskkg@mb.infoweb.or.jp
Website: www.infoweb.or.jp/kankaku/

Senior Executive Officers
President — Chuichi Numata
Financial Director — Keiichi Terada
International Division — Yo Haga

Debt Capital Markets / Fixed Income
Head of Fixed Income — Kunihiro Ishibashi ☏ 5640 2604

Eurobonds
Head of Sales — Mr Sakakibara ☏ 5640 7835

Fixed-Income Research
Head of Fixed Income — Mr Matsuyama ☏ 5640 2607

Equity Capital Markets
Head of Equity Capital Markets — Shuji Yasuma ☏ 5640 3021

International Equities
Head of Sales — Mikio Hayasaka ☏ 5640 3163

Equity Research
Head of Equity Research — Mr Kumai ☏ 5640 5001

Risk Management
Head of Risk Management — Mr Ninomine ☏ 5640 7832

Fixed Income Derivatives / Risk Management
Head of Sales — Mr Sakakibara ☏ 5640 7835

Corporate Finance / M&A Advisory
Head of Corporate Finance — Mr Eguchi

Settlement / Clearing
Head of Settlement / Clearing — Kayao Nemoto ☏ 5640 7860

Administration
Head of Administration — Mr Seki ☏ 5640 7650

The Kiyo Bank Limited   Head Office

35 Honmachi 1-chome, Wakayama 640-8656
Tel: (734) 239 111 **Fax:** (734) 315 100

Senior Executive Officers
President — Takao Nakahara

Others (Senior Executives)
Koi Ohta *Senior Managing Director*
Masayuki Ishihara *Managing Director*
Junzaburo Kusudo *Managing Director*
Yasuto Miyamoto *Managing Director*
Tomihisa Furuta *Managing Director*
Hirodhi Hayashi *Managing Director*

Others (Senior Executives) (cont)
International Department

Kunimasa Okamura *Director*
Hiroomi Katayama *Director*
Motomu Asai *Director*
Junzaburo Kusudo *Managing Director*

The Kofuku Bank Limited   Head Office
2-37 Tosabori 1-chome, Nishi-ku, Osaka
Tel: (6) 444 1551 **Fax:** (6) 444 2866 **Telex:** 65307 **Swift:** KOFK JP JS **Cable:** KOFUKUBANK

Senior Executive Officers
President
Deputy President
Senior Managing Director
Managing Director
Managing Director
Managing Director
Managing Director
Managing Director

Tokusuke Egawa
Benji Egawa
Tokuaki Egawa
Toshiaki Matsukura
Tadashi Yoshimatsu
Eitato Kimoto
Toru Ueki
Kimikazu Okamoto

Others (Senior Executives)

Hachiro Morigami *Director*
Ryoichi Iwamoto *Director*
Takuro Nakajima *Director*

Administration
Accounts / Audit
Auditor
Standing Auditor

Hideo Komatsu
Kazuyasu Satake
Chubei Watanabe
Tadahisa Seo

Kokusai Securities Co Limited   Head Office
Tokyo Sumitomo Twin Building East, 27-1 Shankawa, 2-chome, Chuo-ku, Tokyo 104-0033
Tel: (3) 3297 2111 **Fax:** (3) 3297 7474 **Telex:** J 24572 **Email:** info@kokusai.co.jp

Senior Executive Officers
Chairman
President & Chief Executive Officer
Financial Director
Chief Operating Officer

Yamato Ishii
Yoshitaka Matsutani
Yasuyuki Idotsuji *Chief Financial Officer*
Mario Kubo *Chief Operating Officer*

Debt Capital Markets / Fixed Income
Global Head

Tadao Yoshida *General Manager*

Domestic Government Bonds
Head of Sales
Head of Trading

Kimitaka Arisaka *General Manager*
Masao Kuboya *General Manager*

Eurobonds
Head of Trading

Toshihisa Ohno *Manager*

Fixed-Income Repo
Head of Repo

Keiji Ogita *Manager*

Fixed-Income Research
Head of Fixed Income

Kazuo Mizano *General Manager*

Equity Capital Markets
Global Head

Yu Takeda *Managing Director*

Domestic Equities
Head of Origination
Head of Syndication
Head of Sales
Head of Trading
Head of Research

Yoshihisa Ishikawa *General Manager*
Yoshio Harigaya *Manager*
Ikuo Kurosawa *General Manager*
Hidenori Kawasaki *General Manager*
Yoshiyuki Miyazawa *General Manager*

International Equities
Head of Origination
Head of Trading

Kazuya Higashida *General Manager*
Keiichi Urata *Manager*

Convertibles / Equity-Linked
Head of Trading

Keiichi Urata *Manager*

Warrants
Head of Trading

Keiichi Urata *Manager*

JAPAN (+81) www.euromoneydirectory.com

Kokusai Securities Co Limited (cont)
Money Markets
Global Head Tadao Yoshida *General Manager*
Domestic Commercial Paper
Head of Trading Keiji Ogita *Manager*
Eurocommercial Paper
Head of Trading Keiji Ogita *Manager*
Foreign Exchange
Global Head Seiichi Takeda
Risk Management
Global Head Hideyu Igarashi *Vice President*
Fixed Income Derivatives / Risk Management
Global Head Hideki Ishii *General Manager*
Corporate Finance / M&A Advisory
Global Head Toshihite Hayano *Managing Director*
Settlement / Clearing
Regional Head Tayoaki Kurimoto *General Manager*
Global Custody
Regional Head Yoshimitsu Twakawa *Manager*
Other Departments
Proprietary Trading Minoru Eda *General Manager*
Administration
Legal / In-House Counsel
 Katsuo Narukami *General Manager*
Compliance
 Hisao Saegusa *Executive Managing Director*
Public Relations
 Koichi Kinoshita *General Manager*

The Korea Development Bank Full Branch Office
305 Fuji Building, 2-3 Marunouchi 3-chome, Chiyoda-ku, Tokyo 100 - 0005
Tel: (3) 3214 4541 **Fax:** (3) 3214 6933 **Telex:** J26134 KODBANK **Swift:** KODB JP JT **Email:** kdbtk@ibm.net
Senior Executive Officers
General Manager Sung Ho Sohn
Senior Deputy General Manager Myung Ki Park
Deputy General Manager Hyun Zek Cho
Deputy General Manager Chul Hwan Kim
Senior Manager Kyung Hoon Jung
Senior Manager Kung Yub Lee

Kredietbank Luxembourg Representative Office
Suite 201, TBR Building, 10-2 Nagatacho 2-chome, Chiyoda-ku, Tokyo 100-0043
Tel: (3) 3581 3550 **Fax:** (3) 3593 0540
Senior Executive Officers
Chief Representative Marc Ulveling

Lazard Japan Asset Management KK Subsidiary Company
2nd Floor, AIG Building, 1-3 Marunouchi 1-chome, Chiyoda-ku, Tokyo 100-0005
Tel: (3) 3211 8600 **Fax:** (3) 3201 1395
Senior Executive Officers
Chairman & Chief Executive Officer Jeff Tanaka
President Max Kobayashi
Others (Senior Executives)
 Kazuhiro Hayashi *Vice President & Director*
 Yoshio Morita *Compliance Director*
 Julian McManus *Fund Manager*

www.euromoneydirectory.com JAPAN (+81)

Lehman Brothers Japan Inc
36th Floor, ARK Mori Building, 12-32 Akasaka 1-chome, Minato-ku, Tokyo 107
Tel: (3) 5571 7134 **Fax:** (3) 5571 7902
Debt Capital Markets / Fixed Income
Fixed-Income Repo
Trading   Fumiaki Tanaka
          Masao Okumura *Vice President*
Equity Capital Markets
Tel: 5571 7145 **Fax:** 5571 7962
Equity Repo / Securities Lending
Marketing   Naoko Matsuoka *Sales*
Head of Trading   Gareth Phillips *Trading*

Leonia Bank plc
Representative Office
Formerly known as: Postipankki Limited
5th Floor, Ogawanachi-Mitsui Building, 3 kanda, Ogawanachi 1-chome, Chiyoda-ku, Tokyo 101
Tel: (3) 3293 6211 **Fax:** (3) 3293 6217

The Long-Term Credit Bank of Japan Limited
Head Office
1-8 Uchisaiwaicho, 2-chome, Chiyoda-ku, Tokyo 100-8501
Tel: (3) 5511 5111 **Fax:** (3) 5511 5505 **Telex:** J24308 **Swift:** LTCB JP JT HED **Email:** webmaster@ltcb.co.jp
Website: www.ltcb.co.jp

Senior Executive Officers
President   Katsunobu Onogi
Deputy President   Tsuneo Suzuki
Deputy President   Kazuhide Koshiishi
Chief Executive Officer   Masami Suda *Director*
                            Takashi Uehara *Director*

Others (Senior Executives)
Senior Corporate Executive Officers   Masaru Ishii
Senior Corporate Executive Officer   Yusho Yamamoto
                                      Yasuyuki Ishii
                                      Kosaku Sakai
                                      Kozo Tabayashi
                                      Toshinari Takai
                                      Koji Terashima
                                      Kazuo Takano
Corporate Executive Officer   Tadao Nagashima
                                      Ryosuke Suzuki
                                      Rikuichi Yoshisue
                                      Tetsuo Makabe
                                      Ryuzo Nakanishi
Overseas Business Division   Satoru Otsubo *General Manager*
Corporate Planning Division   Kenji Seo *General Manager*
General-Investment
Head of Investment   Izumi Nishizaki *Chief Manager, Investment Bking Planning Dept*
General - Treasury
Head of Treasury   Masaki Yoshikawa *General Manager*
                                      Yasuo Miwa *GM, Trading Division*

Relationship Manager
International Banking Division   Koichiro Nakaya *Chief Manager*
International Financial Institutions Hiroyasu Masuno *Chief Manager*
International Finance Division   Kenichi Amano *General Manager*
The Americas Division   Akira Kagiichi *General Manager*
Department: Board of Statutory Auditors
Others (Senior Executives)
Standing Statutory Auditor   Michio Kishi
Statutory Auditor   Takayuki Itai
                                      Iwao Totsuka
                                      Michio Fukai

Syndicated Lending
International Credit Division   Toshiro Okada *General Manager*

JAPAN (+81)　　　　　www.euromoneydirectory.com

The Long-Term Credit Bank of Japan Limited (cont)
Risk Management
Head of Risk Management　　　　Yukinori Honma *General Manager*
Settlement / Clearing
Department: Trading & Securities Operations
Operations　　　　Shunichi Maruki *General Manager*

LTCB UBS Brinson

Landic Otemachi Building, 2-4 Otemachi 1-chome, Chiyoda-ku, Tokyo 100-0004
Tel: (3) 5223 4400 Fax: (3) 5223 4460

Senior Executive Officers
Chairman	Y Kage
President	H Kunita
Deputy President	G Olcott
Financial Director	D Fritz *Chief Investment Officer*
Chief Operating Officer	M Sugita

LTCB Warburg Securities Limited

Urbanet Otemachi Building, 2-2 Otemachi 2-chome, Chiyoda-ku, Tokyo 100-0004
Tel: (3) 5201 8004 Fax: (3) 5201 8010

Senior Executive Officers
Department: Tokyo Kamiyacho Branch
Kamiyacho Mori Building, 3-20 Toranomon 4-chome, Minato-ku, Tokyo 105-0001
Tel: +81 (3) 5402 9111 Fax: +81 (3) 5402 9000
Chairman	V Volpi
Chairman	S Katagiri
President	K Oiwa

Others (Senior Executives)
　　　　M Allen *Deputy President*

Debt Capital Markets / Fixed Income
Department: Interest Rates
Country Head
　　　　P Murphy *Head of Rates*
　　　　Y Kato *Debt Capital Markets*

Bonds - General
MTNs	P Morgan
Yen Primary Issues	K Oi
Yen Bond Trading	H Yasumoto
Repo	Y Kurono
US Treasuries / Corporates	B Scarfone
Euro Government Bonds	D Croll
Credit Trading	M Davis
	Lee Knight
Rates Derivatives	J Singh
Emerging Markets	F Kawasjee
Exchange Traded Derivatives	V Turcotte
Corporate Sales	E Kitahara
Foreign Bond Sales	M Yamazaki
Financial Institutions Yen Sales	N Akifuji
Regionals Yen Sales	M Onozuka
Public Corporations Sales	A Mori
International Yen Sales	R Freeman

Equity Capital Markets
Department: Equities
Country Head　　　　S Coombe *Head of Equities*

Other (Domestic Equities)

　　　　J West *Equity Chief Operating Officer*
Equity Distribution	G Barnard *Head*
Equities Trading - Japan	J Clark *Head*
Domestic Equity Distribution	H Nii
Sales / Trading & Execution	D Kerrigan *Head*
CB Sales	M Yoshizumi

Other (International Equity)
European Equity Sales	K Fujikawa
Asian Equity Sales	H Murphy

Other (International Equity) (cont)
Client Relationship Director   I Konishi
Equities Derivatives   M Lee

Equity Research
Head of Equity Research   J Wilson

Corporate Finance / M&A Advisory
Other (Corporate Finance)
Corporate Finance   M Wakasugi *Chairman*
    T Ito *Co-Head*
    T Yamazaki *Co-Head*

Settlement / Clearing
Operations   P Degnan *Chief Operating Officer*
    P Klaus
    M Kato *Financial Control*

Administration
Technology & Systems
Information Technology   S Lucocq

Legal / In-House Counsel
Legal   F Eshima

Other (Administration)
Human Resources, Asia / Pacific   K Nagata *Head*

The Marine & Fire Insurance Association of Japan Inc
Head Office

Non-Life Insurance Building, 9 Kanda Awajicho 2-chome, Chiyoda-ku, Tokyo 101-8335
Tel: (3) 3255 1437 **Fax:** (3) 3255 1234 **Email:** kokusai@sonpo.or.jp
Website: www.sonpo.or.jp

Senior Executive Officers
Chairman   Koukei Higuchi

Others (Senior Executives)
Executive Director   Noboru Araki
Managing Director   Tomotsu Mori
    Kazuo Kubota

Marusan Securities Co Limited
Head Office

Nihonbashi 2-5-2, Chuo-ku, Tokyo 103
Tel: (3) 3272 0145 **Fax:** (3) 3278 1187 **Telex:** J22851 MARSEC AIB
Website: www.marusan-sec.co.jp

Senior Executive Officers
President   Eijiro Nagao
Chief Executive Officer   Susumu Suzuki *Director & General Manager*
Chief Operating Officer   Yasuhiro Kandori *Deputy General Manager* ☏ **3271 5808**
Deputy General Manager   Hidenori Ogata ☏ **3274 3536**

Equity Capital Markets
Global Head   Zensiro Mizuno *Senior Managing Director*

Settlement / Clearing
Regional Head   Yasuhiro Kandori *Deputy General Manager* ☏ **3271 5808**

Meitan Tradition Co Limited

Sumitomo Fudosan Toyo Building, 29-17 Toyo 5-chome, Koto-ku, Tokyo 135
Tel: (3) 5634 3050 **Fax:** (3) 5634 3089 **Telex:** J33398 MEITAN **Reuters:** METK
Forward Tel: (3) 5634 3060; **Derivatives Tel:** (3) 3668 9781; **Dollar Money Tel:** (3) 5634 3065; **Yen Tel:** (3) 5634 3090; **Reuters:** MEIT

JAPAN (+81)   www.euromoneydirectory.com

Merita Bank Plc — Representative Office
4th Floor, SF Kayabacho Building, 10-5 Nihonbashi Kayabacho 1-chome, Chuo-ku, Tokyo 103
Tel: (3) 5641 2551 Fax: (3) 5641 2550 Email: merita@twics.com
Senior Executive Officers
Representative   Jukka Suomela

Merrill Lynch Capital Markets Bank Limited — Full Branch Office
10th Floor, Ote Center Building, 1-1-3 Otemachi, Chiyoda-ku, Tokyo 100
Tel: (3) 3213 7654 Fax: (3) 3213 7667
Website: www.ml.com
Senior Executive Officers
Managing Director / General Manager   Ryozo Suyama

Merrill Lynch Financial Services KK — Subsidiary Company
11th Floor, Ote Center Building, 1-1-3 Otemachi, Chiyoda-ku, Tokyo
Tel: (3) 3213 7090 Fax: (3) 3213 7290
Website: www.ml.com

Merrill Lynch Futures Japan Inc — Subsidiary Company
10th Floor, Ote Center Building, 1-1-3 Otemachi, Chiyoda-ku, Tokyo 100
Tel: (3) 3213 5301 Fax: (3) 3213 7620
Website: www.ml.com

Merrill Lynch International Bank Limited — Representative Office
11th Floor, Ote Center Building, 1-1-3 Otemachi, Chiyoda-ku, Tokyo 100
Tel: (3) 3213 8600 Fax: (3) 3213 7008
Website: www.ml.com

Merrill Lynch Japan Incorporated — Full Branch Office
12th Floor, Nagoya Mitsui Building, 1-24-30 Meieki Minami, Nakamura-ku, Nagoya 450
Tel: (52) 561 7940 Fax: (52) 561 7949
Website: www.ml.com

Merrill Lynch Japan Incorporated — Full Branch Office
6th Floor, Midosuji Diamond Building, 2-1-3 Nishi-Shinsaibashi, Chuo-ku, Osaka 542-0086
Tel: (6) 212 3850 Fax: (6) 212 3874
Website: www.ml.com

Merrill Lynch Japan Incorporated — Full Branch Office
OTE Center Building, 1-1-3 Otemachi, Chiyoda-ku, Tokyo 100-8180
Tel: (3) 3213 7000; (3) 3213 7747 Fax: (3) 3213 7001
Website: www.ml.com
Senior Executive Officers
President & COO
Chief Operating Officer   Hisashi Moriya
   John Sievwright
General-Investment
Head of Investment   Alfred Hurley *Managing Director*

www.euromoneydirectory.com　　　　　　　　JAPAN (+81)

Debt Capital Markets / Fixed Income
Department: Merrill Lynch Debt Markets
Tel: 3213 7821 Fax: 3213 7187

Fixed-Income Repo
Trading　　　　　　　　Dow Kim *Managing Director*
　　　　　　　　　　　　Curtis Baker *Managing Director*

Equity Capital Markets
Tel: 3213 7873 Fax: 3213 7006
Regional Head　　　　　David Lund *MD, Japan Equity Markets*

Other Departments
Economic Research　　　Hiroshi Nakagawa *Managing Director*

Administration
Legal / In-House Counsel
　　　　　　　　　　　　Masahito Amano *General Counsel*

Merrill Lynch Japan Securities Co Limited　　Full Branch Office
Otemachi First Square, 1-5-1 Otemachi, Chiyoda-ku, Tokyo 100-0004
Tel: (3) 5288 5500

Senior Executive Officers
President & Chief Executive Officer　　Ronald Strauss
Chief Executive Officer　　　　　　　Thomas Milton *Deputy President*
Financial Director　　　　　　　　　Kunihiko Kumagai *Deputy President*

Merrill Lynch Mercury Asset Management Japan Limited
Subsidiary Company

Ote Center Building, 1-1-3 Otemachi, Chiyoda-ku, Tokyo 100-8180
Tel: (3) 3213 7470 Fax: (3) 3213 8987

Senior Executive Officers
President　　　　　Clifford Shaw
Deputy President　　Hidemi Fukumura

Others (Senior Executives)
　　　　　　　　　　David Semaya *Chief Administrative Officer*
　　　　　　　　　　Ronald Pullen *Chief Investment Officer*

The Mitsui Trust & Banking Co Limited　　Head Office
2-1-1 Nihonbashi-Muromachi, Chuo-ku, Tokyo 103-8323
Tel: (3) 3270 9511 Fax: (3) 3243 1900 Telex: J26397 Swift: MTRBJPJT Reuters: MTBQ
Website: www.mitsuitrust.co.jp

Senior Executive Officers
President　　　　　　　Keiu Nishida
MD & General Manager　Tatsuo Maruyama

Foreign Exchange
Tel: 3277 7221 Fax: 3246 1688
Head of Foreign Exchange　Takeshi Nishi *General Manager* ☏ **3277 7560**
Corporate Sales　　　　　Katsunori Kitakura *Manager* ☏ **3277 7220**

Risk Management
Tel: 3277 7603 Fax: 3277 1024
Head of Risk Management　Yoshinobu Emi *General Manager* ☏ **3277 7603**

Morgan Stanley Japan Limited　　Subsidiary Company
Yebisu Garden Place Tower, 20-3 Ebisu 4-chome, Shibuya-ku, Tokyo 150-6008
Tel: (3) 5424 5000 Fax: (3) 5424 5099
Website: www.ms.com

Senior Executive Officers
MD, Chairman & General Manager　Takeo Kani
Managing Director & President　　Thierry Porté

JAPAN (+81)   www.euromoneydirectory.com

Morgan Stanley Japan Limited (cont)
Others (Senior Executives)
Vice-Chairman   Satoshi Kishimoto *MD, Vice-Chairman & GM*
Deputy Vice-Chairman   Barry M Davis *MD, Vice-Chairman & DGM*
   Jun Imanishi *MD, Vice-Chairman & DGM*
Equity Capital Markets
Country Head   Barry M Davis *MD, Vice-Chairman & DGM*
Settlement / Clearing
Operations   Michael C Bodson *Managing Director*
Administration
Department: Finance, Admin & Operations
Head of Administration   Michael C Bodson *Managing Director*

The Musashino Bank Limited — Full Branch Office

International Division, 15-9 Uchikanda 2-chome, Chiyoda-ku, Tokyo 101-0047
Tel: (3) 3254 4365 **Fax:** (3) 3254 4478 **Telex:** 2228493 MUSATK J **Swift:** MUBK JP JT
Email: jdh03656@niftyserve.or.jp **Cable:** MUSASHINOBANK
Head Office **Tel:** (48) 641 6111

Senior Executive Officers
Chairman   Hitoshi Yamada
President   Katsuaki Miwa
Chief Executive Officer   Kiyoshi Murata *Senior Managing Director*
Financial Director   Haruo Muraoka *Senior Managing Director*
Chief Operating Officer   Jinichi Mitani *Managing Director*
Treasurer   Koji Komazaki *Managing Director*
Managing Director   Shigeo Fukushima
International Division   Shiro Sameshima *General Manager & Director*

Nacional Financiera SNC — Representative Office

Room 841, Kokusai Building, 3-1-1 Marunouchi, Chiyoda-ku, Tokyo 100
Tel: (3) 3284 0331 **Fax:** (3) 3284 0330 **Email:** nafintok@il-net.or.jp

Senior Executive Officers
Chief Representative   Tito J Ayala
Others (Senior Executives)
   Isamu Ito *Advisor*

The Nanto Bank Limited — Head Office

16 Hashimoto-cho, Nara 630-8677
Tel: (742) 271 546 **Fax:** (742) 261 734 **Telex:** 5522119 **Swift:** NANTO JP JT
Website: www.nantobank.co.jp

Senior Executive Officers
Chairman   Michitaka Sakamoto
President   Hiromune Nishiguchi
General Manager   Eiji Hattori ☎ (3) 3214 1338
Debt Capital Markets / Fixed Income
Global Head   Norio Masuoka *Deputy General Manager* ☎ (3) 3214 1338
Equity Capital Markets
Global Head   Norio Masuoka *Deputy General Manager* ☎ (3) 3214 1338
Syndicated Lending
Global Head   Katsuhisa Tanaka *Senior Assistant Manager* ☎ (3) 3214 1338
Money Markets
Global Head   Mitsuhiko Asada *Assistant Manager* ☎ (3) 3214 1338
Foreign Exchange
Global Head   Mitsuhiko Asada *Assistant Manager* ☎ (3) 3214 1338
Risk Management
Global Head   Huneyoshi Sakaguchi ☎ 271 589
Settlement / Clearing
Regional Head   Hideaki Nishimoto *Assistant Manager* ☎ (3) 3214 1338

www.euromoneydirectory.com   JAPAN (+81)

National Australia Bank Limited

Mitsui Nigokan, 2-1-1 Nihonbashi Muromachi, Chuo-ku, Tokyo 103-0022
Tel: (3) 3241 8781 Fax: (3) 3241 5369 Telex: J22714NATAUS Swift: NATA JP JT Reuters: NABQ

Senior Executive Officers
GM & Head of North Asian Markets   Mark Fox
Deputy General Manager   Takashi Ouchi

Others (Senior Executives)
    Steve Lambert Head of Capital Markets & Derivatives Asia

Relationship Manager
Relationship Loans   Kan Shigematsu Relationship Manager ☎ **3241 1131**

Debt Capital Markets / Fixed Income
Tel: 3270 5691
Head of Debt Capital Markets   Steve Lambert Head of Capital Markets & Derivatives Asia
    Ryota Yashima Head of Capital Markets

Eurobonds
Head of Sales   Shigeki Hirano Manager

Other (Libor-Based / Floating Rate Products)
Swaps & Derivatives   Kazuhiro Tanase Senior Manager
    Shyuya Narasaki Manager

Money Markets
Money Markets - General
    Midori Koba Senior Dealer

Foreign Exchange
Tel: 3270 8381
Head of Foreign Exchange   Adrian Jones

FX Traders / Sales People
Yen   Shinjiro Kawakami Manager
    Adam Gazzoli Senior Dealer
FX Spot   Kent Unoki Dealer
Treasury Sales   Masahiro Kobori Head of Treasury Sales

Settlement / Clearing
Foreign Exchange Settlement; Settlement   Shigeru Kobayashi Manager, Operations ☎ **3241 1026**
(General)

Other Departments
Department: Customer Services
Tel: 3241 1026
Private Banking   Toru Tahara Head

National Bank of Hungary   Representative Office

1-7-1 Yurakucho, Chiyoda-ku, Tokyo 100-0006
Tel: (3) 3201 2811 Fax: (3) 3216 0430 Email: nbhtyo@gol.com

Senior Executive Officers
Director & Chief Representative   Bela Teremi

The National Commercial Bank   Representative Office

10-B-5, The Imperial Tower, 1-1-1 Uchisaiwaicho 1-Chome, Chiyoda-ku, Tokyo 100
Tel: (3) 3502 1228; (3) 3502 1229 Fax: (3) 3502 4998

Senior Executive Officers
Representative   Uichiro Kinoshita

National Westminster Bank plc   Full Branch Office

Riverside Yomiuri Building, 36-2 Nihonbashi-Hakozakicho, Chuo-ku, Tokyo 103-0015
Tel: (3) 5645 8000 Fax: (3) 5645 8010 Telex: J25420

Senior Executive Officers
Chief Executive Officer   Robert J Windsor Group General Manager & Branch Manager
Treasurer   Yukinobu Oguchi Head of Global Financial Markets, Japan

Euromoney Directory 1999   **861**

JAPAN (+81)   www.euromoneydirectory.com

National Westminster Bank plc (cont)
Risk Management
Head of Risk Management   David Charles *Assistant Director, Market Risk Asia*
Other (FI Derivatives)
Derivatives Products   Sandeep S Mand *Head of Marketing & Structuring*
   Allan L D Bedwick *Head of Trading*
Other (Exchange-Traded Derivatives)
Derivative Products   Sandeep S Mand *Head of Marketing & Structuring*

The New Japan Securities Co Limited   Head Office

3-11 Kanda Surugadai, Chiyoda-ku, Tokyo 101-8003
Tel: (3) 3219 1111 **Fax:** (3) 3292 6937 **Telex:** J22666 NEWSECURE

Senior Executive Officers
Chairman   Tadashi Iwase
President   Tadashi Kawaguchi
Financial Director   Tadaomi Tokunaga *Senior Managing Director*
Chief Operating Officer   Takeshi Kusakabe *Deputy President*
Treasurer   Koichi Fukushi
Managing Director   Kiyoei Miyazaki
International Division   Eitaro Tsunashima *Senior Managing Director*

General-Investment
Head of Investment   Hisamichi Kawada *Managing Director*

Debt Capital Markets / Fixed Income
Department: Capital Markets Department
Tel: 3219 3675 **Fax:** 3292 6926
Head of Fixed Income   Mikio Takano *Managing Director* ☎ 3219 4105
Head of Fixed Income Sales   Kinichi Murata *Deputy General Manager* ☎ 3219 3997
Head of Fixed Income Trading   Kazuharu Kawanouye *General Manager* ☎ 3219 3982

Government Bonds
Head of Sales   Mikio Takano *Managing Director* ☎ 3219 4105
Head of Trading   Kazuharu Kawanouye *General Manager* ☎ 3219 3982
Head of Syndication   Akio Nakano *General Manager* ☎ 3219 4660
Head of Origination   Koju Hozumi *Manager* ☎ 3259 8119

Eurobonds
Head of Sales   Akio Nakano *General Manager* ☎ 3219 4660
Head of Trading   Hiroshi Watanabe *Manager* ☎ 3219 4133

Emerging Market Bonds
Head of Emerging Markets   Kazuya Sudo *Manager* ☎ 3219 4551
Head of Trading   Toshihiro Ikejima *Manager* ☎ 3219 4549

Fixed-Income Repo
Head of Repo   Kazunori Hoshiya *Deputy General Manager* ☎ 3219 4624
Marketing & Product Development   Yoshiaki Akiyama *General Manager* ☎ 3219 3593
Head of Trading   Kazunori Hoshiya *Deputy General Manager* ☎ 3219 4624

Fixed-Income Research
Head of Fixed Income   Nasko Yamauchi ☎ 3219 1060
Head of Credit Research   Yeichi Sato ☎ 3219 4061

Equity Capital Markets
Department: Capital Markets Department
Tel: 3219 3696 **Fax:** 3292 6926
Head of Equity Capital Markets   Junichi Uchida *General Manager* ☎ 3219 3680
Head of Sales   Ryohei Morisawa *Manager* ☎ 3219 3688

Domestic Equities
Head of Sales   Shin Akamatsu *General Manager* ☎ 3219 3507
Head of Trading   Ichiro Honda *General Manager* ☎ 3219 4617

International Equities
Head of Sales   Junichi Shimizu *General Manager* ☎ 3219 3675
Head of Trading   Kumihiko Kawai *Deputy General Manager* ☎ 3219 3611

Equity Research
Head of Equity Research   Kumihiko Uchikoshi *General Manager* ☎ 3219 3601

Convertibles / Equity-Linked
Head of Sales   Shin Akamatsu *General Manager* ☎ 3219 3507

Money Markets
Tel: 3219 4624 **Fax:** 3219 4624
Head of Money Markets   Kazunori Hoshiya *Manager*

862   Euromoney Directory 1999

www.euromoneydirectory.com　　　　　　　JAPAN (+81)

Domestic Commercial Paper
Head of Sales　　　　　　　　　　　　Takashi Yamagata ☏ **3259 8138**
Head of Trading　　　　　　　　　　　Shigeki Hiramatsu ☏ **3259 8141**

Foreign Exchange
Tel: 3219 3579 **Fax:** 3292 6922
Head of Foreign Exchange; Head of Trading　Akira Kurane *General Manager* ☏ **3259 8147**

Risk Management
Tel: 3219 3600 **Fax:** 3292 6907
Head of Risk Management　　　　　　Masashi Takada *General Manager* ☏ **3219 3599**

Corporate Finance / M&A Advisory
Head of Corporate Finance　　　　　　Minotu Takeda *Managing Director*

Settlement / Clearing
Tel: 3277 1733 **Fax:** 3271 8316
Head of Settlement / Clearing　　　　Keiichino Ohata *General Manager* ☏ **3277 1730**
Equity Settlement; Fixed-Income Settlement　Kunio Kasai *Manager* ☏ **3277 1731**

Global Custody
Head of Global Custody　　　　　　　Tsutomu Katsu *Deputy General Manager* ☏ **3219 4613**

Administration
Head of Administration　　　　　　　Yasufumi Kudo ☏ **3219 3571** F **3219 4086**
Business Development　　　　　　　Mikio Aski ☏ **3219 3790** F **3219 3779**
Head of Marketing　　　　　　　　　Hkira Yashida ☏ **3219 3687** F **3292 6930**

Technology & Systems
　　　　　　　　　　　　　　　　　Chihiro Okamote ☏ **3219 3586** F **3292 6905**

Legal / In-House Counsel
　　　　　　　　　　　　　　　　　Toshihiko Fujimara ☏ **3219 3535** F **3219 5309**

Compliance
　　　　　　　　　　　　　　　　　Teruhiro Sumi ☏ **3219 3559** F **3292 6901**

Public Relations
　　　　　　　　　　　　　　　　　Kazuei Ito ☏ **3219 3569** F **3292 6902**

Accounts / Audit
　　　　　　　　　　　　　　　　　Norio Nosaka ☏ **3219 3801** F **3292 6901**

The Nikko Securities Co Limited　　　　　　　Head Office

3-1 Marunouchi 3-chome, Chiyoda-ku, Tokyo 100-8325
Tel: (3) 3283 2872 **Telex:** NIKOSE A J22410 **Email:** kabunushi@mail.nikko.co.jp
Website: www.nikko.co.jp

Senior Executive Officers
Chairman of the Board　　　　　　　Hajime Imada
President & Chief Executive Officer　　Masashi Kaneko
Financial Director　　　　　　　　　Takashi Yamamoto
International Division　　　　　　　Michel de Carvalho

Debt Capital Markets / Fixed Income
Head of Debt Capital Markets　　　　Osamu Yasaka

Equity Capital Markets
Head of Equity Capital Markets　　　Hiromasa Mizushima

Money Markets
Head of Money Markets　　　　　　Hideo Abe

Foreign Exchange
Head of Foreign Exchange　　　　　Hideo Abe

Risk Management
Head of Risk Management　　　　　Tomohike Ohori

Corporate Finance / M&A Advisory
Head of Corporate Finance　　　　　Osamu Yasaka

Settlement / Clearing
Head of Settlement / Clearing　　　　Junichi Kitamura

JAPAN (+81)   www.euromoneydirectory.com

The Nippon Credit Bank Limited
Head Office

Alternative trading name: NCBQ
13-10, Kudan-kita, 1-chome, Chiyoda-ku, Tokyo 102-8660
Tel: (3) 3263 1111 **Fax:** (3) 3239 8065 **Telex:** J26921 NCBTOK **Swift:** NCBT JP JT **Reuters:** NCBQ
Website: www.ncb.co.jp

Senior Executive Officers
Chairman — Hiroshi Kubota
President — Shigeoki Togo

Debt Capital Markets / Fixed Income
Domestic Government Bonds
Head of Sales — Akinori Aoki *Manager* ☎ **3222 4197**
Head of Trading — Toshiro Yanagiya *Manager* ☎ **3239 9584**
Head of Research — Soichi Okuda *Senior Economist* ☎ **3222 4079**

Asset-Backed Securities / Securitization
Global Head — Eiji Wada *General Manager* ☎ **3237 9651**

Fixed-Income Repo
Head of Repo; Matched Book Manager; Trading — Toshiro Yanagiya *Manager* ☎ **3239 9584**
Sales — Akinori Aoki *Manager* ☎ **3222 4197**

Syndicated Lending
Department: International Business Planning Division
Tel: 3264 8595 **Fax:** 3263 9872
Global Head — Yuji Inagaki *General Manager*

Money Markets
Domestic Commercial Paper
Head of Origination; Head of Sales; Head of Trading — Yukinobu Kaibe *Senior Manager* ☎ **3239 9503**

Foreign Exchange
Department: Foreign Markets Trading Division
Global Head — Ryoichi Kawai *General Manager* ☎ **3222 0787**
Head of Institutional Sales; Corporate Sales; Head of Trading — Hisanori Kuroda *Manager* ☎ **3239 9505**

Risk Management
Department: Financial Markets Trading Division
Tel: 3239 9582 **Fax:** 3221 1674
Global Head — Ryoichi Kawai *General Manager* ☎ **3222 0787**

Fixed Income Derivatives / Risk Management
Global Head; IR Swaps Sales / Marketing — Takanori Kondo *Manager* ☎ **3221 7282**
IR Swaps Trading — Takashi Ono *Manager* ☎ **3222 0865**
IR Options Sales / Marketing — Takanori Kondo *Manager* ☎ **3221 7282**
IR Options Trading — Takashi Ono *Manager* ☎ **3222 0865**

Foreign Exchange Derivatives / Risk Management
Cross-Currency Swaps, Sales / Marketing — Takanori Kondo *Manager* ☎ **3221 7282**
Cross-Currency Swaps, Trading — Takashi Ono *Manager* ☎ **3222 0865**
Vanilla FX option Sales; Vanilla FX option Trading — Hisanori Kuroda *Manager* ☎ **3239 9505**

Exotic Options (Barriers, Range, Timers, Digitals, Faders etc)
Sales — Takanori Kondo *Manager* ☎ **3221 7282**
Trading — Takashi Ono *Manager* ☎ **3222 0865**

Corporate Finance / M&A Advisory
Department: Investment Banking Division
Tel: 3261 2676 **Fax:** 3262 1584
Global Head — Osamu Aki *Joint General Manager* ☎ **3263 7680**

Settlement / Clearing
Department: Markets & International Administration Division
Tel: 3239 9561 **Fax:** 3262 1584
Fixed-Income Settlement — Yusuke Kashima *Manager* ☎ **3262 5836**
Derivatives Settlement — Hirofumi Yazawa *Manager* ☎ **3237 7406**
Foreign Exchange Settlement — Akira Shimogaki *Manager* ☎ **5276 2964**

Other Departments
Private Banking — Tomoyuki Mikami *General Manager* ☎ **3264 8563**

Administration
Technology & Systems
Systems Planning Division — Hiromasa Yamamoto *General Manager* ☎ **(0423) 717 135**

www.euromoneydirectory.com					JAPAN (+81)

Compliance
Operations Supervision	Toshiyuki Deura *General Manager* ☏ **3239 9527**
Public Relations
	Tsuneo Sakai *General Manager* ☏ **3263 1246**

## Nippon Trust Bank Limited							Head Office
1-8 Nihonbashi 3-chome, Chuo-ku, Tokyo 103-8266
Tel: (3) 3245 8329 **Fax:** (3) 3273 5387 **Telex:** J24197 NITRUST **Swift:** NITR JP JT **Cable:** NIPPONTRUST TOKYO
Senior Executive Officers
President	Tomoaki Hirano
Senior Managing Director	Yoshimitsu Moriya
Senior Managing Director	Yuzo Morio
Senior Managing Director	Isao Itoga
Department: Treasury and Investment
General - Treasury
Head of Treasury	Isao Itoga *Senior Managing Director*
	Masakazu Tanaari *General Manager*
	Hidenoroi Izao *Chief Manager*
	Kiyoshi Takahashi *Manager*
	Ikuo Nakamoto *Manager*

## The Nishi-Nippon Bank Limited						Head Office
3-6 Hakata-ekimae 1-chome, Hakata-ku, Fukuoka 812-8679
Tel: (92) 476 2481 **Fax:** (92) 476 2488 **Telex:** 724511 NISIBK J **Swift:** NISI JP JT **Telex:** 724512 NISIBK J
Website: www.nishigin.co.jp
Senior Executive Officers
Chairman	Tatsuta Goto
President	Seiji Koga
Deputy President	Tsuneo Shindo
Managing Director	Kiyoshi Noji
Managing Director	Kenichi Ryuno
Managing Director	Hideki Tokunhisa
Managing Director	Yoshiaki Migita
Managing Director	Hirotoshi Maeda
Managing Director	Osamu Fujimaru
Managing Director	Noritaka Inoue

## Nittan Exco Limited							Head Office
3-14, 3-chome, Nihonbashi Hongokucho, Chuo-ku, Tokyo 103
Tel: (3) 3271 8450; (3) 3242 7521 **Fax:** (3) 3242 8477; (3) 3246 1461
Senior Executive Officers
Chairman	Akio Sasaki
President	Kazuo Fujii
Senior Managing Director	Junichi Toyama

Nomura China Investment Co Limited
7-2, Nihonbashi-Honcho, 1-chome, Chuo-ku, Tokyo 103-0023
Tel: (3) 3274 4608 **Fax:** (3) 3274 6799
Senior Executive Officers
President	Hirohisa Suzuki

## The Nomura Securities Co Limited						Head Office
1-9-1 Nihonbashi, Chuo-ku, Tokyo 103
Tel: (3) 3211 1811 **Fax:** (3) 3278 0420
Website: www.nomura.co.jp
Senior Executive Officers
President & Chief Executive Officer	Junichi Wiie
Financial Director	Kenichi Watanabe *Director*
Treasurer	Mikihisa Fujiki *General Manager*

Euromoney Directory 1999   **865**

JAPAN (+81)   www.euromoneydirectory.com

The Nomura Securities Co Limited (cont)
Debt Capital Markets / Fixed Income
Country Head   Hiroshi Toda *Director*
Equity Capital Markets
Country Head   Takashi Tsutsui *Director*
Money Markets
Country Head   Hiroshi Toda *Director*
Risk Management
Country Head   Shunichi Ito *General Manager*
Corporate Finance / M&A Advisory
Country Head   Hiromi Yamaji *Director*
Settlement / Clearing
Country Head   Takao Ohtsubo *General Manager*

The Norinchukin Bank   Head Office
13-2, Yurakucho 1-chome, Chiyoda-ku, Tokyo 100-8420
Tel: (3) 3279 0111 **Fax:** (3) 3218 5176 **Telex:** J23918 **Swift:** NOCU JP JT **Telex:** J23919 **Telex:** J33573
Senior Executive Officers
President   Kenichi Kakudoh
Deputy President   Mitsuo Naito
Administration
Other (Administration)
International Business Management Division   Tsuyoshi Tomita *Senior Manager* Ⓕ **3218 5177**

The Ogaki Kyoritsu Bank Limited   Head Office
98 Kuruwamachi 3-chome, Ogaki City
Treasury Division: 6-1 Hatchobori 2-chom, Chuo-ku, Tokyo
Tel: (584) 742 111 **Fax:** (584) 742 130 **Telex:** 4793677 OGAKIB J **Swift:** OGAK JP JT

Oita Bank
4-1, Funaimachi 3-chome, Oita 870-0021
Tel: (97) 534 1111
International Division **Tel:** (97) 538 7535; **Fax:** (97) 532 3358
Senior Executive Officers
Chairman   Shozo Ando
President   Yasuchika Takahashi
Senior Managing Director   Nobumasa Araki
Others (Senior Executives)
   Yukoh Masuda *Managing Director*
   Masayoshi Kawamura *Managing Director*
   Tsutomu Kimoto *Managing Director*

Oversea-Chinese Banking Corporation Limited   Full Branch Office
15th Floor, Akasaka Twin Tower Main Building, 17-22 Akasaka 2-chome, Tokyo 107-0052
Tel: (3) 5570 3421 **Fax:** (3) 5570 3426 **Telex:** J 26186 OCHINBNK **Swift:** OCBC JP JT **Email:** ocbctokyo@msn.com
Senior Executive Officers
General Manager   Wee-Ghee Yeo Ⓣ **5570 3428**

Overseas Union Bank Limited   Full Branch Office
Shin Tokyo Building, 3-1 Marunouchi, 3-chome, Chiyoda-ku, Tokyo 100
Tel: (3) 3212 0958 **Fax:** (3) 3201 3369
Senior Executive Officers
Vice President & General Manager   Leow Min Siong

PaineWebber International (Asia) Limited

3rd Floor, Asahi Seimi Hibiya Building, 1-5-1 Yuraku-cho, Chiyoda-ku, Tokyo 100
Tel: (3) 3593 5200 Fax: (3) 3593 5225

Debt Capital Markets / Fixed Income
Department: Fixed Income
Bonds - General
        Jon Kathe
        Saladin Amery
        M Araki
        Brian Drew
        K Horiuchi
        T Ito
        T Katagiri
        M Koda
        T Moriya
        A Toyoda

Paribas   Full Branch Office

19th Floor - North, Yurakucho Denki Building, 1-7-1 Yurakucho, Chiyoda-ku, Tokyo 100-0006
Tel: (3) 5222 6500 Fax: (3) 5222 6139

Senior Executive Officers
General Manager   Gilles Pecriaux

Paribas Asset Management Japan Limited   Subsidiary Company

19th Floor, Yurakucho Denki Building North, 1-7-1 Yurakucho, Chiyoda-ku, Tokyo 100-0006
Tel: (3) 5222 6310 Fax: (3) 5222 6144 Telex: 2228241 BANPAR J

Senior Executive Officers
President & Chief Executive Officer   Clive Galliver

Paribas Capital Markets Limited   Full Branch Office

18th Floor, Yurakucho Denki Building North, 1-7-1 Yurakucho, Chiyoda-ku, Tokyo 100-0006
Tel: (3) 5222 6100 Fax: (3) 5222 6594 Telex: J32696

Senior Executive Officers
General Manager   Yusuke Yasuda
General Manager   Jacques d'Estais

Debt Capital Markets / Fixed Income
Fixed-Income Repo
Marketing & Product Development   Angela Osborne *Head of Marketing & Sales* [T] +44 (171) 595 8029
            [F] +44 (171) 595 5055 [E] a_osborne@paribas.com
Trading   Hiroshi Mochizuki *Trader*
          Takahiko Iwashi *Trader*

Paribas (Japan) Limited   Subsidiary Company

19th Floor, Yurakucho Denki Building North, 1-7-1 Yurakucho, Chiyoda-ku, Tokyo 100
Tel: (3) 5222 6714 Fax: (3) 5222 6587

Pictet Asset Management (Japan) Limited   Subsidiary Company

Formerly known as: Pictet (Japan) Limited
Kokusai Building, 3-1-1 Marunouchi, Chiyoda-ku, Tokyo 100
Tel: (3) 3212 3411 Fax: (3) 3211 6339

Senior Executive Officers
President   Yoshiharu Okazaki
Director   Yoshihiko Ozawa
Secretary   Akiko Jitsumatsu

JAPAN (+81) www.euromoneydirectory.com

Pictet Asset Management (Japan) Limited (cont)
Debt Capital Markets / Fixed Income
Country Head Shuji Kishita *Senior Portfolio Manager*
Bonds - General
US, Japan & Eurobonds Shuji Kishita *Senior Portfolio Manager*
Equity Capital Markets
Other (International Equity)
Global Equity Investment Shuji Kishita *Senior Portfolio Manager*
Administration
Head of Administration Yoshihiko Ozawa *Director*
Public Relations
  Yoshihiko Ozawa *Director*
Corporate Communications
  Yoshihiko Ozawa *Director*
Other (Administration)
Japanese Pension Marketing Midori Morita *Manager*

Rothschild Asset Management (Japan) Limited — Subsidiary Company
14th Floor, AIG Building, 1-1-3 Marunouchi, Chiyoda-ku, Tokyo 100-0005
Tel: (3) 3201 5682 **Fax:** (3) 3201 5690
Senior Executive Officers
Chairman Philippe de Nicolay
Managing Director Yasuhiro Ishii

Rothschild Japan KK — Subsidiary Company
14th Floor, AIG Building, 1-1-3 Marunouchi, Chiyoda-ku, Tokyo 100-0005
Tel: (3) 3201 8601 **Fax:** (3) 3201 8606
Senior Executive Officers
President Hideo Aomatsu

Salomon Smith Barney (Japan) Limited — Subsidiary Company
Formerly known as: Salomon Brothers Asia Limited
Akasaka Park Building 2-20, 5-chome, Minato-ku, Tokyo 107
Tel: (3) 5574 4111 **Fax:** (3) 5574 5551 **Telex:** 27938 **Email:** somoto@zip.sbi.com
Senior Executive Officers
Chief Executive Officer Toshiharu Kojima
Branch Manager Akio Kawamura

The San-in Godo Bank Limited — Head Office
10 Uo-Machi, Matsue 690-0062, Shimane
Tel: (852) 551 000; (3) 5623 2370 **Fax:** (852) 27 3398; (3) 3669 2127 **Telex:** 622230 (AAB:GODO BKJ)
Swift: SGBK JP JT **Email:** go-gin@sx.miracle.ne.jp. **Reuters:** 41/4 CI 53/3/1 **Telerate:** 40-026-10, 40-045-01
Cable: SANIN GODO
Wholesale Account Sales Tel: 5401 7850; **Fax:** 5401 7850
Website: www.web-sanin.co.jp/econo/gougin/
Senior Executive Officers
President Iwane Maru
Senior Managing Director Junnoshin Maeda
Senior Managing Director Akimi Kutuma
Managing Director Hisaki Okada
Managing Director Hiroyuki Wakasa
Managing Director Hirotaka Kobayashi
Managing Director Yasuhide Motoike

JAPAN (+81)

Debt Capital Markets / Fixed Income
Department: International Department, Capital Markets Trading Department
Tel: (3) 5623 2370 Fax: (3) 3669 2127

Bonds - General
General Manager — Hiroshi Hamabe *GM, International Department*
Takeshi Yamamoto *GM. Capital Markets Trading*
Assistant General Manager — Masayoshi Tsubokura *Assistant GM - International Department*
Keizou Kageyama *Assistant GM, Capital Markets Trading Dept.*

Syndicated Lending
Tel: (3) 5623 2370 Fax: (3) 3669 2127

Other (Syndicated Lending)
General Manager — Hiroshi Hamabe *GM, International Department*
Assistant General Manager — Masayoshi Tsubokura *Assistant GM - International Department*

Loan-Related Activities
Trade Finance — Hiroshi Hamabe *GM, International Department*
Project Finance — Yukio Nagai *General Manager, Loans*

Money Markets
Tel: (3) 5623 2370 Fax: (3) 3669 2127

Money Markets - General
General Manager — Hiroshi Hamabe *GM, International Department*
Takeshi Yamamoto *GM. Capital Markets Trading*
Assistant General Manager — Masayoshi Tsubokura *Assistant GM - International Department*
Hiroshi Nishimura *Assistant GM, Capital Markets Trading Dept.*

Foreign Exchange
Tel: (3) 5623 2370 Fax: (3) 3669 2127

FX Traders / Sales People
General Manager — Hiroshi Hamabe *GM, International Department*
Assistant General Manager — Masayoshi Tsubokura *Assistant GM - International Department*

Risk Management
Tel: (852) 551 000 Fax: (852) 248 131

Other (FI Derivatives)
General Manager — Yoshio Kotoku *GM, General Planning*
Assistant General Manager — Shuji Sota *Assistant GM, General Planning Dept. (ALM Section)*

Corporate Finance / M&A Advisory
Department: Loan Department, Business Information & Marketing Department
Tel: 327 123 Fax: 276 033

Global Head — Akihisa Kamo *Director & GM, Loan*
Makoto Furuse *GM, Business Information & Marketing*
Regional Head — Shigeo Ishikawa *AGM, Loan Planning Section*
Country Head — Junichi Konishi *AGM, Corporate Business Section*

Other Departments
Correspondent Banking — Hiroshi Hamabe *GM, International Department*

Administration

Technology & Systems
Takeshi Inoue *Director & GM Systems Department*

Compliance
Yoshio Kotoku *GM, General Planning*

Public Relations
Yoshio Kotoku *GM, General Planning*

Other (Administration)
Business Development; Marketing — Katsuomi Kakita *GM, Business Control Department*

The Sanwa Bank Limited — Head Office

1-1 Otemachi 1-chome, 1-chome, Chiyoda-ku, Tokyo
Tel: (3) 5252 1111 Fax: (3) 3215 1776 Telex: 23420 SANWAINA J Swift: SANW JP JY Reuters: SNWQ
Website: www.sanwabank.co.jp

Senior Executive Officers
Chairman — Hiroshi Watanabe
Deputy President — Mitsauki Naito
Deputy President — Minoru Eda
Deputy President — Isao Nakanishi
Senior Managing Director — Masahiro Maeda
Senior Managing Director — Kaneo Muromachi

JAPAN (+81) www.euromoneydirectory.com

The Sanwa Bank Limited (cont)
Senior Executive Officers (cont)
Senior Managing Director Shigetoshi Ando
Senior Managing Director Isao Matsuura
Senior Managing Director Hiroya Nobuhara
Senior Managing Director Hiroki Murao

Scotia Capital Markets
Full Branch Office

Alternative trading name: The Bank of Nova Scotia & ScotiaMcleod Inc
6th Floor, Toranomon Waiko Building, 5-12-1 Toranomon, Minato-ku, Tokyo 105
Tel: (3) 5408 0909 **Fax:** (3) 5408 0949 **Telex:** J33859
Senior Executive Officers
Managing Director J P Fairley

Seoulbank Limited
Full Branch Office

1st Floor, New Nisseki Building, 4-2 Marunouchi 3-chome, Chiyoda-ku, Tokyo 100-0005
Tel: (3) 3213 0901; (3) 3213 0902 **Fax:** (3) 3213 0975; (3) 3214 2929 **Telex:** J23985 **Swift:** BSEO JP JT **Reuters:** SELQ
Cable: SEOULBANK TOKYO
Senior Executive Officers
Managing Director / General Manager Keon-Su Han

SG (Société Générale) Tokyo

Ark Mori Building, 1-12-32 Akasaka, 1-Chome, Minato-ku, Tokyo 107-6014
Tel: (3) 5549 5966; (3) 5549 5354 **Fax:** (3) 5549 5207; (3)5549 5339
Website: www.socgen.com
Debt Capital Markets / Fixed Income
Fixed-Income Repo
Marketing & Product Development Lan Nguyen *Head of Repo & Interest Rate Arbitrage & Marketing*
 T 5549 5966
 Debbie Wloch-Vogt *Off-Shore Repo Market* T 44 (171) 256 6964
 F 44 (171) 571 2999
Trading Stephane Delacote *Repo & Interest Rate Arbitrage* T 5549 5966
Equity Capital Markets
Equity Repo / Securities Lending
Marketing & Product Development Alexandre de Vaivre *Global Head of Marketing & Sales*
 T +33 (1) 4213 9113 F +33 (1) 4213 6485
 E alexandre.de-vaivre@ota.fn.socgen.com

The Shiga Bank Limited
Head Office

1-38 Hamamachi, Otsu-City 520-8686, Shiga
Tel: (77) 521 2360; (77) 524 2141 **Fax:** (77) 521 2892; (77) 526 0454 **Telex:** 5464850 SHIGAB J **Swift:** SIGA JP JT
Cable: SHIGABANK
Website: www.mediagalaxy.co.jp/shigabank/
Senior Executive Officers
Chairman Sojiro Takahoshi
President Koichi Takata
Others (Senior Executives)
 Katsuji Hiiragi *Senior Managing Director*
 Toshikazu Araki *Managing Director*
 Nobuo Chikaraishi *Managing Director*
 Akitaka Yoshitake *Managing Director*
 Nagayasu Watanabe *Managing Director*
 Kunihko Kitamura *Managing Director*
Debt Capital Markets / Fixed Income
Department: Funds & Securities Operation Department
Tel: 521 2374 **Fax:** 521 2869
Head of Fixed Income Manabu Uematsu *Director & General Manager*

www.euromoneydirectory.com　　　　　　　　　　　　　　JAPAN (+81)

Government Bonds
Head of Sales　　　　　　　　　　Manabu Uematsu *Director & General Manager*
Head of Trading　　　　　　　　　Jiro Okada *Manager*

Eurobonds
Head of Sales　　　　　　　　　　Kazuo Nishida *Manager*

Libor-Based / Floating-Rate Products
FRN Sales　　　　　　　　　　　　Kazuo Nishida *Manager*

Equity Capital Markets
Department: Funds & Securities Operation Department
Tel: 521 2374 Fax: 521 2869
Head of Equity Capital Markets　　Masamichi Mizutani *Manager*

Domestic Equities
Head of Sales　　　　　　　　　　Masamichi Mizutani *Manager*

Equity Research
Head of Equity Research　　　　　Masamichi Mizutani *Manager*

Convertibles / Equity-Linked
Head of Sales　　　　　　　　　　Masamichi Mizutani *Manager*

Syndicated Lending
Tel: (3) 3661 1185 Fax: (3) 3662 0450
Head of Trading　　　　　　　　　Kazuo Nishida *Manager*

Money Markets
Tel: (3) 3661 1185 Fax: (3) 3662 0450
Head of Money Markets　　　　　　Kazuo Nishida *Manager*

Foreign Exchange
Department: International Division (FX, Monetary Section & Back-Office)
12-8 Kodenma-cho, Nihonbashi, Chuo-ku, Tokyo 103
Tel: +81 (3) 3661 1185 Fax: +81 (3) 3662 0450
Head of Foreign Exchange　　　　Kazuo Nishida *Manager*

Risk Management
Head of Risk Management　　　　Naotaka Torii *Director & General Manager*

Fixed Income Derivatives / Risk Management
Head of Sales　　　　　　　　　　Hideo Inoue *Assistant Manager*

Foreign Exchange Derivatives / Risk Management
Spot / Forwards Sales　　　　　　Kazuo Nishida *Manager*

Settlement / Clearing
Tel: (3) 3661 1185 Fax: (3) 3662 0450
Head of Settlement / Clearing　　Kikuji Hisada *Sub Manager*

Asset Management
Head　　　　　　　　　　　　　　Naotaka Torii *Director & General Manager*

Other Departments
Correspondent Banking　　　　　　Osamu Katayama *Director & General Manager*

Administration
Head of Administration　　　　　　Shigeru Tamura *Manager*
Business Development　　　　　　Kazuo Isobe *General Manager*

Technology & Systems
　　　　　　　　　　　　　　　　Akihiko Maegawa *General Manager*

Legal / In-House Counsel
　　　　　　　　　　　　　　　　Ichiro Kimura *Manager*

Compliance
　　　　　　　　　　　　　　　　Ichiro Kimura *Manager*

Public Relations
　　　　　　　　　　　　　　　　Katsuya Irie *Manager*

Accounts / Audit
　　　　　　　　　　　　　　　　Norio Fujiike *General Manager*

Shinhan Bank　　　　　　　　　　　　　　　　　　　　Full Branch Office

9th Floor, Shiroyama JT Mori Building, 3-1 Toranomon 4-chome, Minato-ku, Tokyo
Tel: (3) 3578 9321 Fax: (3) 3578 9355 Telex: J25776 SHBTKO

Senior Executive Officers
General Manager　　　　　　　　　Tae-myung Yum

JAPAN (+81)　　　　　　www.euromoneydirectory.com

The Shinwa Bank Limited
Head Office

10-12 Shimanose-cho, Sasebo, Nagasaki 857-0806
Tel: (956) 233 717 Fax: (956) 234 479 Swift: SHWA JP JT

Senior Executive Officers
President　　　　　　　　　　　　Hirokazu Matsuura

Foreign Exchange
Department: International Division
Tel: (3) 3535 5405 Fax: (3) 3564 5196
Global Head　　　　　　　　　　　Kunihiko Kodama *General Manager*
Head of Trading　　　　　　　　　Nobuyuki Watanabe *Assistant Manager*

The Shizuoka Bank Limited
Head Office

10 Gofukucho 1-chome, Shizuoka-shi, Shizuoka 420-8761
6-2 Otemachi 2-chome, Chiyoda-ku, Tokyo 100-0004
Tel: (3) 3246 4832 Fax: (3) 3279 6196 Telex: J28450 SHIZUBK Swift: SHIZ JP JT Reuters: SHIZ

Senior Executive Officers
President　　　　　　　　　　　　Soichiro Kamiya
Deputy President　　　　　　　　　Mutsuji Suzuki
Senior Managing Director　　　　　Hideo Tanaka
Managing Director　　　　　　　　Kazuyuki Hirao
Managing Director　　　　　　　　Nobuo Ikeda
Managing Director　　　　　　　　Yoshitaka Nishikawa
Managing Director　　　　　　　　Yasuo Matsuura
Managing Director　　　　　　　　Sadao Uehara
Managing Director　　　　　　　　Takashi Suzuki
Managing Director　　　　　　　　Yasuyoshi Ohno
International Division　　　　　　　Yoshinori Katayama *General Manager*
　　　　　　　　　　　　　　　　Setsuro Takahashi *Joint General Manager*
　　　　　　　　　　　　　　　　Akira Nakada *SDGM, International Department - Shizuoka Annex*
　　　　　　　　　　　　　　　　Kimihiko Asakawa *Assistant Manager, Int'l Dept, Shizuoka Annex*

Others (Senior Executives)
　　　　　　　　　　　　　　　　Eiichi Ito *Director*
　　　　　　　　　　　　　　　　Masakazu Oishi *Director*
　　　　　　　　　　　　　　　　Yasuaki Noda *Director*
　　　　　　　　　　　　　　　　Noboru Ikeda *Director*
　　　　　　　　　　　　　　　　Hiroyasu Sugiyama *Director*
　　　　　　　　　　　　　　　　Shigeru Masugi *Director*
　　　　　　　　　　　　　　　　Hiroyuki Kochi *Director*

General-Lending (DCM, SL)
Head of Corporate Banking　　　　Shinichi Kamio *AGM, International Finance*

General - Treasury
Head of Treasury　　　　　　　　Tomohiko Saito *DGM, Fund Trading & FX*
　　　　　　　　　　　　　　　　Naoto Oguri *AGM, Fund Trading & FX*
　　　　　　　　　　　　　　　　Masaru Sakamoto *DGM, Treasury & CM Operations*
　　　　　　　　　　　　　　　　Misao Nagakura *AGM, Treasury & CM Operations*
　　　　　　　　　　　　　　　　Atsushi Mizukami *Assistant Manager, Treasury & CM Operations*

Settlement / Clearing
Operations　　　　　　　　　　　Kazushi Serizawa *AGM, International Planning & Administration*
　　　　　　　　　　　　　　　　Masatoshi Konagaya *AGM, International Planning & Administration*
　　　　　　　　　　　　　　　　Minoru Mano *AGM, International Planning & Administration*
　　　　　　　　　　　　　　　　Ki Sugimura *AGM, International Planning & Administration*
　　　　　　　　　　　　　　　　Ichiro Unno *Assistant Manager, Int'l Planning & Administraion*
　　　　　　　　　　　　　　　　Shunichi Yamaguchi *Assistant Manager, Int'l Planning & Administraion*
　　　　　　　　　　　　　　　　Shinji Giga *Assistant Manager, Int'l Planning & Administraion*
　　　　　　　　　　　　　　　　Haruyoshi Yamamoto *Assistant Manager, Int'l Planning & Administraion*
　　　　　　　　　　　　　　　　Tadashi Nakamura *GM, Int'l Operations Center*
　　　　　　　　　　　　　　　　Koji Omura *AGM, International Operations Center*
　　　　　　　　　　　　　　　　Shigeru Abe *Assistant Manager, International Operations Center*

JAPAN (+81)

Société Générale
Full Branch Office

Ark Mori Building, 12-32 Akasaka 1-chome, Minato-ku, Tokyo 107-6014
Tel: (3) 5549 5800 Fax: (3) 5549 5729 Telex: J28611

Senior Executive Officers
Chief Executive Officer   Christian Gomez ☎ **5549 5801**
Treasurer   Akio Tagawa ☎ **5549 5933**

General-Lending (DCM, SL)
Head of Corporate Banking   Yuko Oyama ☎ **5549 5830**

Foreign Exchange
Global Head   Akio Tagawa ☎ **5549 5933**

Administration
Technology & Systems   Guy Dadillon ☎ **5549 5774**

Public Relations
Lize Araici ☎ **5549 5521**

Société Générale Securities (North Pacific) Limited
Full Branch Office

Ark Mori Building, 12-32 Akasaka 1-Chome, Minato-ku, Tokyo 107-6015
Tel: (3) 5549 5120 Fax: (3) 5549 5129

Senior Executive Officers
President   Toshihiko Nakane
Managing Director   Kim Ly

Debt Capital Markets / Fixed Income
Head of Fixed Income   Jean Frederic Desclaux ☎ **5549 5271**

Eurobonds
Head of Sales   Masahiro Ichikawa ☎ **5549 5451**

Equity Capital Markets
Country Head   Gregoire Varenne ☎ **5549 5331**

Domestic Equities
Head of Sales   Kiyoshi Noda *Head of Sales* ☎ **5549 5375**

International Equities
Head of Sales   Michael Hanson-Lawson ☎ **5549 5424**

Equity Research
Country Head   Kiyoshi Kimura ☎ **5549 5191**

Settlement / Clearing
Country Head   Shuji Takayanagi ☎ **5549 5151**

Administration
Head of Administration   Tim Coomber ☎ **5549 5133**

Technology & Systems
Korehisa Kuki ☎ **5549 5531**

Compliance
Kyohei Fukaya ☎ **5549 5180**

Public Relations
Lize Araki ☎ **5549 5521**

State Bank of India
Full Branch Office

6th Floor, Nomura Fudosan Osaka Building, Azuchimachi 1-chome, Chuo-ku, Osaka 541-0052
Tel: (6) 6271 3696; (6) 6271 3237 Fax: (6) 6271 3693 Email: sbios@gol.com

Senior Executive Officers
Chief Executive Officer   R Balaraman

Euromoney Directory 1999   **873**

JAPAN (+81)   www.euromoneydirectory.com

State Street Bank & Trust Company
Full Branch Office

2nd Floor, Fuji Building, 3-2-3 Marunouchi, Chiyoda-Ku, Tokyo 100-0005
Tel: (3) 3214 1771 Fax: (3) 3214 1774 Telex: J24921 STATE JP Swift: SBOS JP JX Reuters: STSQ
Website: www.statestreet.com

Senior Executive Officers
VP & General Manager   Christopher Picciotto

Debt Capital Markets / Fixed Income
Tel: 3213 2344

Fixed-Income Repo
Trading   Sakuaki Yasuda *Assistant Secretary, Trading* T 3216 3658 F 3213 2344
E syasuda@statestreet.com

Equity Capital Markets

Equity Repo / Securities Lending
Head   Sakuaki Yasuda *Assistant Secretary, Trading* T 3216 3658 F 3213 2344
E syasuda@statestreet.com
Marketing & Product Development   Edward Guillemette *Vice President (Australia)* T +61 (2) 9323 6531
F +61 (2) 9323 8540 E eguillemette@statestreet.com

Foreign Exchange
Head of Trading   Kazunari Kobayashi *VP & Treasury Manager* T 3214 1770 F 3214 5768

Settlement / Clearing
Tel: 3214 1771
Foreign Exchange Settlement   Taeko Aoki *VP & Operations Manager* T 3214 3586 F 3214 1774

Sumisho Lease Co Limited
Head Office

Sumitomo Chemical Engineering Center Building, 7-1 Nakase 1-chome, Mihama-ku, Chiba 261-8567
Tel: (43) 212 7122 Fax: (43) 212 7172 Telex: 3722153 SSLTKO J Email: y-hashiquchi@scl.co.jp
Website: www.iijnet.or.jp/scl

Senior Executive Officers
President   Toshihiko Morita
Financial Director   Eizaburo Morisada *Managing Director*
International Division   Munekazu Wakita *Managing Director*

Syndicated Lending

Loan-Related Activities
Aircraft / Aerospace Finance   Takamichi Abe *Manager*
Shipping Finance   Nobuhiro Yoneno *General Manager, Corporate Finance*

Other (Trade Finance)
Mortgage Finance & Leasing   Nobuhiro Yoneno *General Manager, Corporate Finance*

Corporate Finance / M&A Advisory
Head of Corporate Finance   Nobuhiro Yoneno *General Manager, Corporate Finance*

Settlement / Clearing
Tel: 212 7111 Fax: 212 7161
Head of Settlement / Clearing   Yutaka Ohashi *Manager, International Finance*

The Sumitomo Bank Limited

3-2 Marunouchi, 1-chome, Chiyoda-ku, Tokyo 100-0005
Tel: (3) 3282 8347; (3) 3282 8267 Fax: (3) 3282 8853 Telex: J22393SUMTBK Swift: SMIT JP JT

Debt Capital Markets / Fixed Income
Tel: 3282 8388

Fixed-Income Repo
Marketing & Product Development; Trading   Jun Iida *Assistant Manager* E iida569649@sumitomobank.co.jp

Equity Capital Markets

Equity Repo / Securities Lending
Marketing & Product Development   Akihito Ishikawa *Assistant General Manager*
E ishikawa495166@sumitomobank.co.jp
Jun Iida *Assistant Manager*

874 Euromoney Directory 1999

JAPAN (+81)

Svenska Handelsbanken
Representative Office

Toranomon Ishizaka Building 6F, 4-1-9 Toranomon, Minato-ku, Tokyo 105-0001
Tel: (3) 5401 3121 **Fax:** (3) 5401 3122

Senior Executive Officers
Chief Representative   Juan V Engström

Swedbank
Representative Office

Sweden Center, 6-11-9 Roppongi, Minato-ku, Tokyo 106
Tel: (3) 5474 6041 **Fax:** (3) 5474 6011 **Email:** swedbank@apo.co.jp

Senior Executive Officers
EVP & Representative   Robert Stenram

Taiheiyo Securities Co Limited

2-26-5 Nihonbashi-Ningyocho, Chuo-ku, Tokyo 103
Tel: (3) 5695 3211 **Fax:** (3) 5640 8460 **Telex:** J29613 PASC

Senior Executive Officers
President   Junichi Yoshino
International Division   Masayasu Ogura *Deputy General Manager*

The Toho Bank Limited
Head Office

3-16 Nihonbashi 1-chome, Chuo-ku, Tokyo
Tel: (3) 3281 7886 **Fax:** (3) 3271 5429 **Telex:** 2225241 THBKFJ J **Swift:** TOHO JP JT

Senior Executive Officers
President   Toshio Seya
Deputy President   Mitsuru Tarukawa
Managing Director   Tsuneo Mogami
Managing Director   Kanji Yamaki
Managing Director   Hirao Watanabe
Managing Director   Kazuya Noguchi
General Manager   Tsutomu Nakanishi
International Division   Masahiro Oriuchi *Manager*

General-Investment
Head of Investment   Kazuhide Otake *Officer, Loan & Investment*
Department: Internatinal Fund Section
3-25 Omachi, Fukushima
Tel: +81 (24) 523 3131

Others (Senior Executives)
Fumihiko Abe *Manager*
Hitoshi Nikaido *Dealer*

Other Departments
Correspondent Banking   Hiroki Sato *Officer, Correspondent Relations*

Administration
Other (Administration)
International Planning & Promotion   Yoshihiro Matsuno *Deputy General Manager*

The Tokai Bank Limited
Head Office

6-1 Otemachi 2-chome, Chiyoda-ku, Tokyo
Tel: (3) 3242 2111 **Fax:** (3) 3245 1487; (3) 3245 1489 **Telex:** J29234 TOKAITOK **Swift:** TKAU PJT
Cable: TOKAIBANK TOKYO **Telex:** J22577 TOKAIBK
Website: www.csweb.co.jp/tbk/

Senior Executive Officers
President   Satoru Nishigaki
Deputy President   Hideo Ogasawara
Deputy President   Yukio Nishiki
Senior Managing Director   Arata Murakami
Senior Managing Director   Shoji Tokumitsu

Euromoney Directory 1999   **875**

JAPAN (+81)   www.euromoneydirectory.com

The Tokai Bank Limited (cont)

General-Lending (DCM, SL)
Head of Corporate Banking — Yoshio Hirata *Director & GM, Investment Bnkg Planning*
Yoshiki Miyamoto *GM, International Credit*
Shinichiro Mizuno *GM, International Finance*

General-Investment
Head of Investment — Kenji Yamaoka *Manager, Int'l Securities Investment*

General - Treasury
Head of Treasury — Koji Nakano *GM, Int'l Treasury Division*
Takao Tashiro *Joint GM, Int'l Treasury Division*
Hitoshi Shimamura *AGM, International Treasury*

Relationship Manager
Investment Banking Headquarters — Arata Murakami *Senior MD & Head*
Investment Banking Business Development Group — Tateaki Ishida *Managing Director & Head*
Investment Banking Management — Tomio Tanaka *Managing Director & Head*

Debt Capital Markets / Fixed Income
Global Head — Satoshi Yamada *General Manager, Capital Markets*
Shinichi Ueda *Joint GM, Capital Markets*

Domestic Government Bonds
Head of Trading — Hideyasu Kobayashi *Chief*

Non-Domestic Government Bonds
International Trading — Hiroshi Iizumi *Chief*

Eurobonds
Head of Trading — Hideyasu Kobayashi *Chief*

Asset-Backed Securities / Securitization
Global Head — Junichi Shibano *AGM, Asset Securitization*
Regional Head — Kenji Yamaoka *Manager, Int'l Securities Investment*

Syndicated Lending

Loan-Related Activities
Trade Finance — Shinichiro Mizuno *General Manager*
Misao Osaki *Assistant General Manager*
Project Finance; Structured Trade Finance — Peter Higginbotham *Global Head*

Risk Management

Other Currency Swap / FX Options Personnel
Derivatives & Structured Products — Kenji Ishibe *General Manager*
Derivatives, Marketing — Haruo Yokio *Assistant General Manager*
Risk Advisory — Nobuaki Mizuno *Senior Manager*

Settlement / Clearing
Operations — Yuji Fujita *DGM, Chief Markets Operations*

Asset Management
Department: Mergers & Acquisitions
Head — Shunichi Onuki *General Manager*
Tsunehiro Tanaka *Joint General Manager*

Other Departments
Correspondent Banking — Shinichiro Mizuno *General Manager*
Misao Osaki *Assistant General Manager*
Economic Research — Katsunobu Katayama *AGM, Research & Development*

Administration

Other (Administration)
Business Information Development — Shunichi Onuki *General Manager*
Tsunehiro Tanaka *Joint General Manager*

Tokai Maruman Securities Co Limited   Head Office

Formerly known as: Maruman Securities Co Limited
4-21, Sakae 3-chome, Naka-ku, Nagoya 460
Tel: (52) 264 1111 **Fax:** (52) 264 1909

Senior Executive Officers
Chairman — Kaneo Takeda
President — Masao Okumura

876 Euromoney Directory 1999

www.euromoneydirectory.com   JAPAN (+81)

Debt Capital Markets / Fixed Income
Department: Planning Department
Tel: (52) 264 1788
Global Head   Yuzo Noda *Senior Managing Director*
Regional Head   Masaaki Takeda *General Manager*

Equity Capital Markets
Tel: (52) 264 1788
Global Head   Yuzo Noda *Senior Managing Director*
Regional Head   Masaaki Takeda *General Manager*

Tokyo Securities Co Limited   Head Office
7-3 Marunouchi 2-chome, Chiyoda-ku, Tokyo 100-0005
Tel: (3) 3214 3211 **Fax:** (3) 3214 3014 **Telex:** J32466

Senior Executive Officers
President   Tadao Soejima
Chief Executive Officer   Isao Ninomiya *Senior Managing Director*
Financial Director   Terukazu Hirooka *Senior Managing Director*
Managing Director   Osamu Kato
Managing Director   Haseo Mitsuishi
Managing Director   Ryosuke Suzuki

Debt Capital Markets / Fixed Income
10-5, Kayaba-cho, 2-chome, Nihonbashi, Chuo-ku, Tokyo
Tel: +81 (3) 5695 5641 **Fax:** +81 (3) 5605 5701

Domestic Government Bonds
Head of Sales   Tomoyoshi Abekawa ☎ **5695 5661**
Head of Trading   Kuniyasu Ohsawa *Manager* ☎ **5695 5661**

Eurobonds
Head of Sales   Takatoshi Yamazaki ☎ **5695 5662**
Head of Trading   Kaoru Nakayama ☎ **5695 5662**

Fixed-Income Repo
Head of Repo   Kunikazu Ino
Collateral Management   Shigeo Takenaka ☎ **5695 5762**

Equity Capital Markets
10-5, Kayaba-cho, 2-chome, Nihonbashi, Chuo-ku, Tokyo
Tel: +81 (3) 5695 5661 **Fax:** +81 (3) 5695 5730

Domestic Equities
Head of Sales   Tomoyoshi Abekawa ☎ **5695 5661**
Head of Trading   Tomoyoshi Hatae *Manager* ☎ **5695 5623**

International Equities
Head of Sales   Kotaro Satoh ☎ **5695 5632**
Head of Trading   Akira Ohmura ☎ **5695 5632**

Convertibles / Equity-Linked
Head of Sales   Sakae Fujishiro ☎ **5695 5671**
Head of Trading   Kazuya Miyazaki ☎ **5695 5671**

Warrants
Head of Trading   Sakae Fujishiro ☎ **5695 5671**
Head of Research   Kazuya Miyazaki ☎ **5695 5671**

Foreign Exchange
10-5, Kayaba-cho, 2-chome, Nihonbashi, Chuo-ku, Tokyo
Tel: +81 (3) 5695 5652 **Fax:** +81 (3) 5695 5650
Head of Trading   Kunikazu Ino

FX Traders / Sales People
                                 Youichi Shukuya
                                 Jack Lee

Risk Management
9-15, Futuba, 2-chome, Shinagawa-ku, Tokyo
Tel: +81 (3) 5702 0321 **Fax:** +81 (3) 5702 1023
Global Head   Yoshihiko Takizawa *Manager*

Corporate Finance / M&A Advisory
9-1, Nihonbashi, Kabuto-cho, Chuo-ku, Tokyo
Tel: +81 (3) 3666 3561 **Fax:** +81 (3) 3669 3555
Global Head   Tamaki Kawagishi *Manager*

JAPAN (+81)　　　　　　www.euromoneydirectory.com

Tokyo Securities Co Limited (cont)

Settlement / Clearing
9-1, Nihonbashi, Kabuto-cho, Chuo-ku, Tokyo
Tel: +81 (3) 3666 2501 Fax: +81 (3) 3667 2748
Equity Settlement — Tsunemi Matsumoto ☏ **3666 9231**
Fixed-Income Settlement — Mr Nakamura *Manager* ☏ **5702 0322**
Foreign Exchange Settlement — Atsuro Nishi

Global Custody
10-5, Kayaba-cho, 2-chom, Nihonbashi, Chuo-ku, Tokyo
Tel: +81 (3) 5695 5681 Fax: +81 (3) 5695 5680
Country Head — Yoshiaki Takeda *Manager*

Administration

Technology & Systems
　　Yoshio Nishida ☏ **5702 0151**

Legal / In-House Counsel
　　Masaru Ohgami *Manager* ☏ **5702 0151**

Compliance
　　Mr Nakamura *Manager* ☏ **5702 0322**

Public Relations
　　Noriko Nakajima ☏ **3214 3213**

The Toronto-Dominion Bank　　　　　Full Branch Office

16th Floor, Kamiyacho Mori Building, 4-3-20 Toranomon, Minato-ku, Tokyo 105
Tel: (3) 5473 1610 Fax: (3) 5473 6599 **Reuters:** TDBQ

Senior Executive Officers
VP & Managing Director — David Chang

General-Lending (DCM, SL)
Head of Corporate Banking — Ken Miyata *Manager, Credit*

Foreign Exchange

FX Traders / Sales People
FX — Masahiko Wakui *Senior Dealer*
　　　Hiroshi Ohtsu *Senior Dealer*
Currency Options — David Lu *Senior Dealer*
Institutional Sales — Jonathan Lin *Dealer*
Marketing — Tadatoshi Sato *Manager*

Risk Management
IR Swaps Trading — Hisaya Watanabe *Director*
　　　Munetaka Amemiya *Senior Dealer*
　　　Shinya Fukumoto *Marketing Officer*

Settlement / Clearing
Operations — Daniel Poon *Controller*

Towa Securities Co Limited　　　　　Head Office

1-16-7 Nihonbashi, Chuo-ku, Tokyo 103-0027
3-3, 1-Chome, Shinkawa, Chuo-Ku, Tokyo 104-0033
Tel: (3) 5566 9114 Fax: (3) 5566 9154 **Telex:** J33492

Senior Executive Officers
Chairman — Masahiko Inoue
President & Chief Executive Officer — Eisaku Tokuhiro
Senior Managing Director — Yukyo Kida

Others (Senior Executives)
　　Hitoshi Fujinami *Vice Chairman*
　　Shinzo Fujita *Senior Managing Director*
　　Hiroshi Kijima *Senior Managing Director*

Department: International Division
International Division — Naoto Shibata *Director & General Manager*

878　Euromoney Directory 1999

www.euromoneydirectory.com JAPAN (+81)

The Toyo Trust & Banking Company Limited   Head Office

4-3 Marunouchi 1-chome, Chiyoda-ku, Tokyo 100-0005
Tel: (3) 3287 2211 **Fax:** (3) 3214 0210 **Telex:** J22123 TYTBKI **Swift:** TOYO JP JT **Reuters:** TYTQ (Forex)
Cable: TOYOTRUCI TOKYO
Reuters: TYTR (Money)
Website: www.toyotrustbank.co.jp

Senior Executive Officers
General Manager   Nobuyoshi Takeuchi
International Division   Takao Shida *General Manager*

Others (Senior Executives)
Trading   Mikio Ito *General Manager*

General-Lending (DCM, SL)
Head of Corporate Banking   Kenshichi Hashimoto *General Manager*

General-Investment
Head of Investment   Haruo Matsuki *GM, Investment Strategy*

General - Treasury
Head of Treasury   Sumiyoshi Matsuzaki *General Manager*

Syndicated Lending

Other (Trade Finance)
Financial Engineering   Tetsuo Maeda *General Manager*
Real Estate   Masaharu Shigeta *General Manager*

Global Custody

Other (Global Custody)
Fund Management I   Kanji Nakatsuka *General Manager*
Fund Management II   Tashiyuki Watanabe *General Manager*

Asset Management
Securities Planning   Takayuki Inukai *General Manager*
International Securities Investment   Takashi Kume *General Manager*
Securities Administration   Saburo Kobayashi *General Manager*

Tradition Financial Services Japan Limited   Subsidiary Company

2-6 Toranomon 5-chome, Minato-ku, Tokyo 105
Tel: (3) 5401 7493; (3) 5401 7451 **Fax:** (3) 5401 7450 **Telex:** J33267 MEITRFIN **Reuters:** TFST

Senior Executive Officers

Others (Senior Executives)
Senior Officer   Larry Rosenshein

UBS AG   Full Branch Office

Urbannet Otemachi Building, 2-2 Otemachi 2-chome, Chiyoda-ku, Tokyo 100-0004
Tel: (3) 5201 8001

Senior Executive Officers
Branch Manager   T Sakoh

Syndicated Lending

Other (Trade Finance)
Global Trade Finance Japan   A Mattli *Head*
Operations   Y Fujii
Department: Loan Syndication / Leveraged Finance

Other (Syndicated Lending)
                                          T Sekiya *Associate Director*
Loan Portfolio Support   T Usuyama

Foreign Exchange
Head of Foreign Exchange   K Lee

FX Traders / Sales People
FX Option Sales   J Arachi *Deputy Head*
FX Sales   K Kwon
Senior Trader   G Lee
Senior Advisor   T Sakoh
                                          S Koike
                                          S Depp *Head of Risk Management Advisors - Asia*

Euromoney Directory 1999 **879**

JAPAN (+81)

UBS AG (cont)
Asset Management
Department: Asset Finance
Head   A Pizer

UBS AG
Representative Office

Urbannet Otemachi Building, 2-2 Otemachi 2-chome, Chiyoda-ku, Tokyo 100-0004
Tel: (3) 5201 8585 Fax: (3) 5201 8099
Senior Executive Officers
Others (Senior Executives)
                                  E Schuler *Executive Director and Senior Representative*
Department: Representative Office
Urbannet Otemachi Building, 2-2 Otemachi 2-chome, Chiyoda-ku, Tokyo 100-0004
Tel: +81 (3) 5473 5191 Fax: +81 (3) 5473 5171
Others (Senior Executives)
                                  M Kaitoh *Senior Representative*

UBS AG Osaka
Representative Office

Dokita Daibiru Building, 2-5, Dojima 1-chome, Kita-ku, Osaka 530-0003
Tel: (6) 442 6200 Fax: (6) 442 6217
Senior Executive Officers
Others (Senior Executives)
                                  H Matsushima *Senior Representative*
                                  R Jossi *Senior Representative*

UBS Fund Management (Japan) Co Limited

Urbannet Otemachi Building, 2-2 Otemachi 2-chome, Chiyoda-ku, Tokyo 100-0004
Tel: (3) 5201 8020 Fax: (3) 5201 8008
Senior Executive Officers
President   T P Itoh
Deputy President   G Marival
Others (Senior Executives)
                                  T Kasai *Head of Marketing*
                                  H Ishihara *Representative Director*

UBS (Trust and Banking) Limited

Urbannet Otemachi Building, 2-2 Otemachi 2-chome, Chiyoda-ku, Tokyo 100-0004
Tel: (3) 5201 8002 Fax: (3) 5201 8007
Senior Executive Officers
President   S Boote
Department: Private Banking
Urbannet Otemachi Building, 2-2 Otemachi 2-chome, Chiyoda-ku, Tokyo 100-0004
Tel: +81 (3) 5201 8383 Fax: +81 (3) 5201 8160
Chief Executive Officer   P Brutsche
Others (Senior Executives)
                                  K Fusa *President*

Unibank A/S
Representative Office

5th Floor, Sukuwaru Hibiya Building, 6-10 Yurakucho 1-chome, Chiyoda-ku, Tokyo 100-0006
Tel: (3) 3501 7421 Fax: (3) 3501 7425
Senior Executive Officers
Chief Representative   Jesper Bruun-Olsen

Union Bancaire Privée Japan KK
Fukoku Seimei Building, 5th Floor, 2-2-2, Uchisaiwaicho, Chiyoda-ku, Tokyo 100-8520
Tel: (3) 3506 3488 Fax: (3) 3506 1977
Senior Executive Officers
Managing Director / General Manager   Richard H Ahn

The Wakashio Bank Limited   Head Office
2-21 Kanda Jimbocho, Chiyoda-ku, Tokyo 101-0051
Tel: (3) 3230 8811 Fax: (3) 3239 4170
Senior Executive Officers
President   Hiroyasu Ichikawa
Managing Director   Hiroshi Nakasone
Managing Director   Mikio Sano

Wasserstein Perella & Co Japan Limited
Alternative trading name: Nomura Wasserstein Perella Co Limited
8th Floor, Dai-ichi Edobashi Building, 1-11-1 Nihonbashi, Chuo-ku, Tokyo 103-0027
Tel: (3) 3281 2031 Fax: (3) 3281 3304; (3) 3272 8993
Senior Executive Officers
Managing Director   Hiromasa Takakura

Westdeutsche Landesbank   Full Branch Office
Fukoku Seimei Building, 2-2-2 Uchisaiwaicho, Chiyoda-ku, Tokyo 100-0011
Tel: (3) 5510 6200 Fax: (3) 5510 6299 Telex: J23751 Swift: WELA JP JT
Senior Executive Officers
Others (Senior Executives)
Senior Vice President   Peter Clermont *General Manager, Japan*
                           Klaus Neuhaus *Regional GM, Credit - Asia Pacific*
                           Peter Clermont *Regional GM, Banks & Financial Institutions*
                           Yoshinobu Hashimoto *Head of Treasury*
                           Tobias Schmitt *Head of Operations*
                           Yoshinori Hirakawa *Head of Credit*

Westpac Banking Corporation   Full Branch Office
8th Floor, Imperial Tower, 1-1-1 Uchisaiwai-cho, Chiyoda-ku, Tokyo 100
Tel: (3) 3501 4101; (3) 3592 0886 Fax: (3) 3501 4100
Senior Executive Officers
Country Head, Japan   Harold A Rosario ⊤ **3592 0886** F **3592 1630**
Relationship Manager
Relationship Marketing   Shinji Fujigasaki *Manager, Corporate* ⊤ **3501 4105** F **3592 1630**
Debt Capital Markets / Fixed Income
Department: Fixed-Income Distribution
Tel: 3501 6737 Fax: 3503 5931
Global Head   Tom Carrick *Senior Manager*
Regional Head   Toru Kondo *Manager*
Foreign Exchange
Tel: 3501 4641 Fax: 3503 5931
FX Traders / Sales People
                           Yuzo Izumitani *Manager*
                           Ishida Toshiya *Senior Dealer*
                           Naruyoshi Haruki *Senior Dealer*
                           Susumu Sakairi *Senior Dealer*
Risk Management
Department: Swaps & Derivative Products
Tel: 3592 0791 Fax: 3592 0797
Other Currency Swap / FX Options Personnel
                           Takeo Yokemura *Senior Dealer*
                           James Mudie *Dealer*

JAPAN (+81) www.euromoneydirectory.com

Westpac Banking Corporation (cont)
Administration
Head of Administration Hidenori Nakase Head ☎ 3501 4110 F 3501 4100
Technology & Systems
  Andrew Bartaos
Public Relations
  Harumi Taguchi Supervisor, Admin Support Group ☎ 3501 6746
  F 3501 6744

Yagi Euro Corporation Head Office

Formerly known as: The Yagi Tanshi Co, Ltd
2-4-3 Nihonbashi-Muromachi, Chuo-ku, Tokyo 103-0022
Tel: (3) 3242 3441 Fax: (3) 3242 8055 Telerate: 6492 ($ Swaps)
Reuters: CAPZ (Caps & Floors); EBSW (US$ Swaps)

Senior Executive Officers
Chairman Shinji Mizuchi
Vice President Katsuhiko Hanashima
General Manager Motoji Emoto
General Manager Ian McKay ☎ 3578 4822

Foreign Exchange
Department: Broking Department 1
Tel: 3242 3443
Country Head Motoji Emoto General Manager
  Yutaka Kimoto Deputy General Manager

FX Traders / Sales People
US$ Deposit Takeshi Sano Manager
Euro yen Deposit Kohei Ando Manager

Risk Management
Department: Derivative Products - Broking Department
Tel: 3578 4855 Fax: 3578 4867

Fixed Income Derivatives / Risk Management
IR Options Trading Jeremy Vogler Manager ☎ 3578 4859

Other Currency Swap / FX Options Personnel
Yen IRS Ian McKay General Manager ☎ 3578 4822
  David Ashcroft Manager ☎ 3578 4822
$ IRS / FRAs Sachio Kobayashi Manager ☎ 3578 4842

Yamagata Bank Limited Head Office

1-2 Nanokamachi 3-chome, Yamagata 990-8642
Tel: (236) 231 221 Fax: (236) 314 636
International Division Fax: 257 185

Senior Executive Officers
Chairman Arata Miura
President Koetsu Niwa
Senior Managing Director Kichishige Hasegawa
Managing Director Tomiya Takahashi
Managing Director Hidetoshi Shirai

The Yamaguchi Bank Limited Head Office

2-36 Takezaki-cho 4-chome, Shimonoseki City, Yamaguchi Prefecture
PO Box 34, Shimonoseki City 750-91, Yamaguchi Prefecture
Tel: (832) 233 411 Fax: (832) 326 312 Telex: 0682331 YBK SM Swift: YMBK JP JT Telex: 0682333 YBK SM

Senior Executive Officers
President Kozo Tanaka
Senior Managing Director Satoshi Shiratsuchi
Managing Director Seiji Yoshimura
Managing Director Meiji Fujita
Managing Director Tetsunosuke Tabaru
Managing Director Kazuaki Katsuhara

General-Lending (DCM, SL)
Head of Corporate Banking Toshio Kato General Manager, Credit Supervision

www.euromoneydirectory.com JAPAN (+81)

Department: International Department
3-5, 3-chome Nihonbashi-Hongoku-cho, Chuo-ku, Tokyo
Tel: +81 (3) 3246 1264 Fax: +81 (3) 3231 8851
International Division   Sadamu Okura *General Manager, International Department*

Debt Capital Markets / Fixed Income
Asset-Backed Securities / Securitization
Global Head   Yoshio Nishimura *GM, Fund Management & Securities*

Administration
Other (Administration)
Inspection   Masakatsu Iwasaki *General Manager*
Personnel   Yutaka Uetani *General Manager*
Planning & Research   Katsunori Aoki *General Manager*
General Affairs   Kenji Kaji *General Manager*

Yasuda & Pama Limited   Subsidiary Company

5th Floor, Shinwa Building, 2-9-11 Toranomon, Minato-ku, Tokyo 105-0001
Tel: (3) 3597 0051; (3) 3597 0052 Fax: (3) 3597 0053

Senior Executive Officers
Chairman & Chief Executive   Makoto Yasuda

The Yasuda Trust & Banking Company Limited   Head Office   J

2-1 Yaesu, 1-chome, Chuo-ku, Tokyo 103-8670
Tel: (3) 3274 9419 Fax: (3) 3274 9314 Telex: J 23720 YSDTBT Swift: YTBC JP JT Reuters: YTBQ; YTBT
Website: www.ytb.co.jp

Senior Executive Officers
Chairman of the Board   Kazuhiko Kasai
President & Chief Executive Officer   Takahiko Kiminami
International Division   Isamu Kuwako *Managing Director*

Others (Senior Executives)
Transfer Agency   Makoto Ikegami *Senior Managing Director*
Real Estate Division   Kazuhiro Iguchi *Senior Managing Director*
Pension Division   Tadayoshi Ide *Senior Managing Director*
Securities Services   Hiroshi Nakajima *Managing Director*
Head Office   Hajime Hayasaka *Managing Director*
Business Planning   Tokio Ikehara *Managing Director & General Manager*
Branch Head, Osaka   Takao Fujino *Director & General Manager*
Branch Head, Kyoto   Toshiaki Kumada *Director & General Manager*
Branch Head, Nagoya   Yoshihiko Miyabe *Director & General Manager*
Branch Head, Sapporo   Yukio Okuni *Director & General Manager*

General-Investment
Head of Investment   Kazuo Asao *Director & General Manager*

General - Treasury
Head of Treasury   Isamu Kuwako *Managing Director*
                    Masahiro Watanabe *Director & General Manager*

Debt Capital Markets / Fixed Income
Head of Debt Capital Markets   Kazuo Asao *Director & General Manager*
                                 Isamu Kuwako *Managing Director*

Equity Capital Markets
Head of Equity Capital Markets   Kazuo Asao *Director & General Manager*

Money Markets
Head of Money Markets   Kazuo Ohashi *GM, Foreign Business*

Foreign Exchange
Head of Foreign Exchange   Isamu Kuwako *Managing Director*

Risk Management
Head of Risk Management   Eisuke Marumori *General Manager*

Global Custody
Country Head   Hideaki Namba *General Manager*

Asset Management
Head   Morikuni Souma *Managing Director*
         Masayuki Kodera *Director & General Manager*

Euromoney Directory 1999 **883**

JAPAN (+81)   www.euromoneydirectory.com

The Yasuda Trust & Banking Company Limited (cont)
Other Departments
Chief Credit Officer   Hirokazu Ishikawa *Director & GM, Domestic Credit*
Correspondent Banking   Yoshiyuki Ishikawa *General Manager*
Administration
Head of Administration   Yoshiki Kurusu *Senior Managing Director*
Legal / In-House Counsel
Counsellor   Masami Tachikawa *Director*
Other (Administration)
Personnel   Masami Kubota *Director & General Manager*
International Planning   Tsutomu Kameda *General Manager*

The Zenshinren Bank — Head Office
8-1 Kyobashi 3-chome, Chuo-ku, Tokyo 104-0031
Tel: (3) 3563 4111 Telex: 02524336 SKREN J Swift: ZENB JP JT
Secretary General's Office Fax: 3564 4766; International Business Division Fax: 3563 7554
Website: www.shinkin.co.jp/scb

Senior Executive Officers
Chairman   Keikichi Kato
President & Chief Executive Officer   Yasutaka Miyamoto
Vice President   Tsuneo Hatakeyama
Vice President   Hasakatsu Funayama
Managing Director   Hideo Kitajima ☎ **3563 8724**

Debt Capital Markets / Fixed Income
Department: Market Investment Division
Fax: 3563 8729
Global Head   Yuji Matsuoka *General Manager* ☎ **3563 8743**

Domestic Government Bonds
Head of Trading   Susumu Takemori *DGM & Head of Trading, $, DM* ☎ **3563 8732**

Eurobonds
Head of Trading   Susumu Takemori *DGM & Head of Trading, $, DM* ☎ **3563 8732**
                                            Hiroshi Kanesaka *DGM & Head of Trading, JPY & Banking* ☎ **3563 8737**
Trading (Sovereigns); Trading (Corporates) Masutoshi Shioyama *Assistant Manager, $, DM* ☎ **3563 8752**
Trading (Corporates)   Yoichi Tobizuka *Manager & Head of Trading, JPY* ☎ **3563 8737**

Libor-Based / Floating-Rate Products
Asset Swaps   Hiroshi Kanesaka *DGM & Head of Trading, JPY & Banking* ☎ **3563 8737**

Asset-Backed Securities / Securitization
Global Head   Yuji Matsuoka *General Manager* ☎ **3563 8743**

Mortgage-Backed Securities
Global Head   Yuji Matsuoka *General Manager* ☎ **3563 8743**

Fixed-Income Repo
Head of Repo   Hiroshi Kanesaka *DGM & Head of Trading, JPY & Banking* ☎ **3563 8737**
Collateral Management; Matched Book   Yoichi Tobizuka *Manager & Head of Trading, JPY* ☎ **3563 8737**
Manager

Equity Capital Markets
Global Head   Yuji Matsuoka *General Manager* ☎ **3563 8743**

International Equities
Head of Trading   Hiroshi Kanesaka *DGM & Head of Trading, JPY & Banking* ☎ **3563 8737**

Convertibles / Equity-Linked
Head of Trading   Hiroshi Kanesaka *DGM & Head of Trading, JPY & Banking* ☎ **3563 8737**

Syndicated Lending
Department: International Business Division
Tel: 3563 7550 Fax: 3563 7554
Global Head   Morihisa Hayakawa

Money Markets
Department: Market Investment Division
Global Head   Yuji Matsuoka *General Manager* ☎ **3563 8743**

Domestic Commercial Paper
Head of Trading   Hiroshi Kanesaka *DGM & Head of Trading, JPY & Banking* ☎ **3563 8737**

Foreign Exchange
Department: Market Business Division
Reuters: 3563 7550 Telex: 3563 7545
Global Head   Mitsuo Taya ☎ **3563 8724**
Head of Institutional Sales; Head of Trading   Kazuhisa Arai *Deputy General Manager* ☎ **3563 8724**

JORDAN (+962)

Risk Management
Department: Financial Management Division
Tel: 3563 7518 Fax: 3562 5965
Global Head   Mitsuo Tanabe *General Manager*

Fixed Income Derivatives / Risk Management
Global Head   Hideo Kitajima *Managing Director* ☎ **3563 8724**
IR Swaps Sales / Marketing; IR Swaps Trading; Masahiro Matsukura *Assistant Manager* ☎ **3563 8724**
IR Options Sales / Marketing; IR Options Trading

Settlement / Clearing
Regional Head   Tomosuke Shiota *General Manager* ☎ **3563 8720**
Equity Settlement; Fixed-Income Settlement Takatoshi Nakashima *Manager* ☎ **3563 8716**
Derivatives Settlement   Matsuo Sato *Advisory Officer* ☎ **3563 8727**

Administration

Public Relations
     Toshio Tanazawa *General Manager* ☎ **3563 7536** F **3562 5965**

JORDAN
(+962)

Arab Banking Corporation (Jordan)   Head Office
Al Malekah Noor Street, Shmeisani, Amman 11110
PO Box 926691, Amman 11110
Tel: (6) 562 1801/7; (6) 566 4183/5 **Fax:** (6) 568 6291 **Telex:** 22258 ABC JO **Swift:** ABCJJOAM
Email: asadi@go.com.jo **Reuters:** ABCJ **Cable:** ABC JO
Website: www.abc.com.jo

Senior Executive Officers
Chairman   Abdul Wahab Al-Tammar
Treasurer   Haya Khammash *Treasury Manager* ☎ **569 2713**
Deputy Chairman & General Manager   Jawad Hadid ☎ **569 1953**
Company Secretary   Ibrahim Al-Abadilah ☎ **562 2720**
International Division   Moh'd Disi *Assistant General Manager* ☎ **569 5084**

General-Lending (DCM, SL)
Head of Corporate Banking   Amer Salti *Deputy General Manager* ☎ **569 1954**

Syndicated Lending
Trade Finance   Naim Al-Najjar *Manager of Foreign Operations* ☎ **562 3680**

Money Markets
Tel: 569 2713 **Fax:** 568 6291 **Reuters:** ABCJ **Telex:** 23022 ABCFX JO
Head of Money Markets   Haya Khammash *Treasury Manager* ☎ **569 2713**

Foreign Exchange
Head of Foreign Exchange   Haya Khammash *Treasury Manager* ☎ **569 2713**

Corporate Finance / M&A Advisory
Head of Corporate Finance   Amer Salti *Deputy General Manager* ☎ **569 1954**

Other Departments
Chief Credit Officer   Faleh Al-Najjar *Manager of Credit Department*
Correspondent Banking   Shafik Dweik *FI Head* ☎ **568 9204**

Administration
Head of Administration   Ghadah Nazzal *Personnel & Administration Manager* ☎ **560 3608**
Business Development   Mahmoud Malkawi *Manager* ☎ **562 2726**

Technology & Systems
     Moh'd Asadi *Assistant General Manager, Finance & Admin.* ☎ **569 5083**

Public Relations
     Issa Al Shuaibi *Manager* ☎ **562 2723**

Accounts / Audit
Accounting & Finance   Issa Abu Mukkaddam *Manager* ☎ **562 2722**

JORDAN (+962) www.euromoneydirectory.com

Arab Jordan Investment Bank — Head Office

Ibn Hani Street, Shumeisani Commercial Area, Amman 11121
PO Box 8797, Amman 11121
Tel: (6) 560 7126; (6) 560 7138 **Fax:** (6) 568 1482 **Telex:** 22087 **Swift:** AJIB JO AX **Reuters:** AJIB
Website: www.ajib.com

Senior Executive Officers
Chairman & Chief Executive Officer Abdulkader Al-Qadi ☏ **566 8630**
General Manager & Chief Executive Officer Hani Al-Qadi ☏ **566 4120**
Financial Director Ibrahim Basbous *Head of Central Accounting*
Treasurer Rima Khoury

Debt Capital Markets / Fixed Income
Head of Debt Capital Markets Dia Mousa *Head of Investment Department* ☏ **568 1489**

Equity Capital Markets
Head of Equity Capital Markets Dia Mousa *Head of Investment Department* ☏ **568 1489**

Syndicated Lending
Head of Syndicated Lending Mohamad Zarka

Money Markets
Head of Money Markets Rima Khoury

Foreign Exchange
Head of Foreign Exchange Rima Khoury

Corporate Finance / M&A Advisory
Head of Corporate Finance Mohamad Zarka

Bank of Jordan plc — Head Office

Shmeisani Abdul Hamid Sharaf Street, Al-Zahawi Street, Amman
PO Box 2140, Amman 11181
Tel: (6) 569 6277 **Fax:** (6) 569 6291 **Telex:** 22033 BANJOR JO **Swift:** BJOR JO AX **Reuters:** BOJX
Wholesale Account Sales **Tel:** 5401 7850; **Fax:** 5401 7850

Senior Executive Officers
Chairman Tawfiq Fakhouri
Acting General Manager Moh'd Jum'a Al-Qassim
Deputy General Manager Shaker Fakhouri
Assistant General Manager Moh'd Anwar Hamdan
Assistant General Manager Nidal Al-Mikhi

Others (Senior Executives)
Palestine Branches Atiyeh Shananier *Assistant General Manager*
  Moh'd Subhi Saadeh *Manager, Commercial Credit*
Operations & Organization Fuad Jabre *Assistant General Manager*
  Walid Anabtawi *Executive Manager*

General-Lending (DCM, SL)
Head of Corporate Banking Hani Abdul Rub *Manager, Commercial Credit*
  Iman Al-Damen *Manager, Corporate Credit*
  Saleh Jarbou' *Manager, Finance*

General-Investment
Head of Investment Walid Fakhouri *Executive Manager*

General - Treasury
Head of Treasury Walid Fakhouri *Executive Manager*

Syndicated Lending
Other (Trade Finance)
Real Estate & General Services Hassan Haj Khalil *Manager*

Settlement / Clearing
Operations Fuad Jabre *Assistant General Manager*
  Walid Anabtawi *Executive Manager*

Administration
Head of Administration Hussein Kahoush *Manager*

Legal / In-House Counsel
  Osama Sukkari *Manager, Legal*

Accounts / Audit
Inspection & Audit Moh'd Abu Ziad *Executive Manager*

Other (Administration)
Credit Control and Follow up Abdullah Al Deiri *Manager*
Human Resources, Organization & Planning Mufeed Saqqa *Manager*

www.euromoneydirectory.com JORDAN (+962)

Cairo Amman Bank — Head Office

Wadi Saora Street, PO Box 950661, Amman 11195
Tel: (6) 461 6910/5 **Fax:** (6) 464 2860 **Telex:** 24049 CAIRGM JO **Swift:** CAAB JO AM **Reuters:** CABA

Senior Executive Officers
Chairman Khalil Talhouni 463 0260
General Manager Yazid Muftj 463 0912
Chief Executive Officer George Dallal *First Assistant General Manager* 464 0358
Financial Director Hani Abu Jbara *Assistant General Manager* 463 3490
Chief Operating Officer Salim Armali *Assistant General Manager* 464 2870
Treasurer Alida Orfali *Regional Manager* 464 8601
Executive Manager Mary Hana 461 6910
International Division Suha Tleel *Regional Manager* 469 3079

General-Lending (DCM, SL)
Head of Corporate Banking Kahlid Dajani *Assistant General Manager* 465 3074

General-Investment
Head of Investment Iyad Abu Maizar *Executive Manager* 464 2852

Debt Capital Markets / Fixed Income
Head of Fixed Income Hani Adu Jbarah *Assistant General Manager* 463 3490

Fixed-Income Repo
Head of Repo Hani Adu Jbarah *Assistant General Manager* 463 3490

Equity Capital Markets
Head of Equity Capital Markets Hani Adu Jbarah *Assistant General Manager* 463 3490

Syndicated Lending
Loan-Related Activities
Trade Finance Sahar Rabadi
Project Finance Hani Adu Jbarah *Assistant General Manager* 463 3490
Structured Trade Finance Sahar Rabadi

Money Markets
Head of Money Markets Alida Orfali *Regional Manager* 464 8601

Foreign Exchange
Head of Foreign Exchange Alida Orfali *Regional Manager* 464 8601

Corporate Finance / M&A Advisory
Head of Corporate Finance Kahlid Dajani *Assistant General Manager* 465 3074

Settlement / Clearing
Head of Settlement / Clearing Khalid Kassem *Regional Manager* 462 7295

Other Departments
Chief Credit Officer Simona Bishouty *Assistant General Manager*
Correspondent Banking Reem Khalidi *Assistant Manager* 465 3079

Administration
Head of Administration Moh'd Jamal *Assistant General Manager* 463 0837
Business Development Alice Hajara *Assistant General Manager* 464 5393

Technology & Systems
 Moh'd Kassem

Legal / In-House Counsel
 Zaher Jardanea 5683666

Public Relations
 Moh'd S Salah *Executive Manager*

Accounts / Audit
 Ibrahim Ghawi 461 8125

The Housing Bank — Head Office

PO Box 7693, Amman 11118
Tel: (6) 560 7315; (6) 566 7126 **Fax:** (6) 567 8121 **Telex:** 21693 ISKAN JO **Swift:** HBHO JO AX **Reuters:** HBHO

Senior Executive Officers
Chairman & Chief Executive Officer Zuhair M Khouri
Financial Director Mahmoud Khawaja *Executive Manager, Accounting Department*
Chief Operating Officer Ghassan Shahattit *Assistant General Manager*
Treasurer Awad Fadayel 568 8177
Treasurer A Rahman Dweik 567 3184

Euromoney Directory 1999 **887**

JORDAN (+962)   www.euromoneydirectory.com

The Housing Bank (cont)

Debt Capital Markets / Fixed Income
Tel: 567 3184 **Fax:** 567 8121

Head of Debt Capital Markets	Awad Fadayel ☏ **568 8177**

Domestic Government Bonds

Head of Sales; Head of Trading; Head of Research	A Rahman Dweik *Treasurer* ☏ **567 3184**

Non-Domestic Government Bonds

	Imad Salameh *Head of Capital Markets* ☏ **567 3185**
	Mahmoud Khaledy *Investment Officer* ☏ **567 3184**
	Faisal Azzazi *Investment Officer* ☏ **567 3185**

Eurobonds

Head of Origination; Head of Syndication; Head of Sales; Head of Trading; Head of Research; Trading - Sovereigns, Corporates, High-yield	Imad Salameh *Head of Capital Markets* ☏ **567 3185**

Libor-Based / Floating-Rate Products

FRN Origination	Imad Salameh *Head of Capital Markets* ☏ **567 3185**

Medium-Term Notes

Head of Origination; Head of Sales	Imad Salameh *Head of Capital Markets* ☏ **567 3185**

Private Placements

Head of Origination; Head of Sales; Head of Structuring	Imad Salameh *Head of Capital Markets* ☏ **567 3185**

Asset-Backed Securities / Securitization

Global Head; Regional Head of Trading	Imad Salameh *Head of Capital Markets* ☏ **567 3185**

Mortgage-Backed Securities

Global Head of Trading	Imad Salameh *Head of Capital Markets* ☏ **567 3185**

Fixed-Income Repo

Head of Repo	Imad Salameh *Head of Capital Markets* ☏ **567 3185**

Equity Capital Markets
Tel: 567 3184 **Fax:** 567 8121

Head of Equity Capital Markets	Awad Fadayel ☏ **568 8177**

Domestic Equities

Head of Origination; Head of Syndication	Awad Fadayel ☏ **568 8177**
Head of Sales; Head of Trading; Head of Research	Sager Falah *Manager, Stocks Investment* ☏ **567 0178**

International Equities

Head of Origination; Head of Syndication	Awad Fadayel ☏ **568 8177**
Head of Sales; Head of Trading; Head of Research	Imad Salameh *Head of Capital Markets* ☏ **567 3185**

Convertibles / Equity-Linked

Head of Origination; Head of Syndication	Awad Fadayel ☏ **568 8177**
Head of Sales; Head of Trading; Head of Research	Imad Salameh *Head of Capital Markets* ☏ **567 3185**

Syndicated Lending
Fax: 568 6345

Head of Syndicated Lending; Head of Origination; Head of Syndication	Nabeel Jebaru
Recovery	Ibrahim Daher
Head of Credit Committee	Ghassan Shahattit *Assistant General Manager*

Loan-Related Activities

Trade Finance; Project Finance; Leasing & Asset Finance	Nabeel Jebaru

Money Markets

Head of Origination	Awad Fadayel ☏ **568 8177**
Head of Sales	Imad Salameh *Head of Capital Markets* ☏ **567 3185**

Settlement / Clearing
Tel: 567 3184 **Fax:** 567 8121

Head of Settlement / Clearing	Awad Fadayel ☏ **568 8177**
Equity Settlement; Fixed-Income Settlement; Derivatives Settlement; Foreign Exchange Settlement	Mahmoud Khaledy *Investment Officer* ☏ **567 3184**
Foreign Exchange Settlement	Majeda Dajbes *Head of Settlements* ☏ **567 3184**

Global Custody

Head of Global Custody	Awad Fadayel ☏ **568 8177**

Other (Global Custody)

	Imad Salameh *Head of Capital Markets* ☏ **567 3185**

Other Departments
Private Banking
Correspondent Banking
Administration
Technology & Systems
Systems Department
Legal / In-House Counsel
Legal Office
Compliance

Public Relations

Jahid Jarrar *Executive Manager, Retail Banking*
Khaled Khdair *Head*

Salah Remawi *Executive Manager*

Salim Jarar *Manager*

Salah Remawi *Executive Manager*

Mohamed Abu Zeid *Executive Manager*

Islamic International Arab Bank plc — Head Office
Formerly known as: Amman Bank for Investments
ABI Building, Wasfi Al-Tal Street, Amman 11110
PO Box 925802, Amman
Tel: (6) 569 4901 **Fax:** (6) 569 4914 **Telex:** ISRA ' A JO 24013 **Swift:** IIBA JO AM **Reuters:** ABIX-Y, ABFI
Senior Executive Officers
Chairman   Khalid Shoman
General Manager   Jamil Al-Dasouki ☏ **569 2588**
General-Investment
Head of Investment   Faisal Ardah *Head of Finance & Investment*
Foreign Exchange
Head of Trading   Hani Masha'l *Dealer*
Settlement / Clearing
Operations   Nehad Maraqa *Head, Banking Operations & Organization*
Administration
Technology & Systems
Information Technology   Jamil Lafi *Head*
Legal / In-House Counsel
                                        Farouk Al-Mouhtadi *Head*
Accounts / Audit
Head of Inspection   Eid Tayeh
Other (Administration)
Human Resources   Emad Hudaib *Head*

Jordan Islamic Bank for Finance & Investment
Shmeisani, PO Box 926225, Amman 11110
Tel: (6) 567 7377 **Fax:** (6) 566 6326; (6) 568 4755 **Telex:** 21125 **Cable:** ISLAM BANK, AMMAN
Senior Executive Officers
Vice Chairman   Musa A Shihadeh
Deputy General Manager   Faisal M Rasheed
Others (Senior Executives)
Banking Relations Manager   Moh'd Allan

Jordan Kuwait Bank
Amman Abdali, Amman 11191
PO Box 9775, Amman 11191
Tel: (6) 568 8814 **Fax:** (6) 568 7452; (6) 569 5604 **Telex:** 21994 **Swift:** JKBA JO AM **Email:** jkbank@go.com.jo
Reuters: JKBA
Senior Executive Officers
Chairman & Chief Executive Officer   Abdul Karim Kabariti ☏ **566 3530**
Chief Executive Officer   Moh'd Yaser Al-Asmar *General Manager* ☏ **567 2617** ℻ **569 1796**
Financial Director   Lutfi Abu-Khadra *Deputy General Manager* ☏ **569 5207**
Chief Operating Officer   Majed Burjaq *Assistant General Manager* ☏ **566 2128**
Treasurer   William Dabaneii *Senior Manager, Treasury* ☏ **569 4397**
General-Lending (DCM, SL)
Head of Corporate Banking   Tawfiq Mukahal *Assistant General Manager* ☏ **569 5208**

JORDAN (+962) www.euromoneydirectory.com

Jordan Kuwait Bank (cont)
Other Departments
Correspondent Banking Hania Zawaneh *Manager, International Operations* ☏ **568 6829**
Administration
Legal / In-House Counsel
  Kamal Naser ☏ **568 6856**

Jordan National Bank plc Head Office
Jabal Amman, 3rd Circle, Amman
PO Box 1578, Amman 11181
Tel: (6) 464 2391; (6) 464 2393 **Fax:** (6) 462 8809 **Telex:** 21820 **Email:** JNB@go.com.jo **Reuters:** JNBC, JNBX
Website: www.qhli.com

Senior Executive Officers
Financial Director Sulaiman Dababneh *Financial Manager*
Treasurer Lina Bakhit *Deputy Assistant General Manager / Treasury & Fixed*

Foreign Exchange
FX Traders / Sales People
Jordan Khaldoon Al-Janini
  Sahab Shahateet
  Reema Hamceh
Lebanon Sameer Tutunji
Cyprus Yousef Sahlieh
  Shadi Al-Kayed

Other Departments
Commodities / Bullion Lina Bakhit *Deputy Assistant General Manager / Treasury & Fixed*
Private Banking Fuad Werr *Assistant General Manager* ☏ **562 2285**
Correspondent Banking Randa Toukan *Manager, Financial Institutions*

Administration
Legal / In-House Counsel
  Faris Al-Nabulsi *Legal Advisor*

Société Générale Representative Office
Shmeisani, 2nd Floor, Istiklal Bookshop Building, PO Box 35192, Amman
Tel: (6) 660 016 **Fax:** (6) 675 870
Website: www.socgen.com

Union Bank for Savings & Investment Head Office
Prince Shaker Ben Zeid Street, Amman 11180
PO Box 35104, Amman 11180
Tel: (6) 560 7011 **Fax:** (6) 566 6149 **Telex:** 21875 **Swift:** UBSIJOAX

Senior Executive Officers
Chairman Isam Salfiti
Financial Director Nabil Ramadan
Treasurer Hanna Khoury
Managing Director / General Manager Isam Salfiti
Company Secretary Ibrahim Faraj
International Division Rafiq Shuhaibar *Executive Manager & Advisor*

Others (Senior Executives)
  Ammar Haddadin *Deputy General Manager*
  Suhail Amin *Assistant General Manager*

Now you have the contacts –

Find out what they are saying by subscribing to *Euromoney*, the leading journal of the world's capital and money markets.

Call NOW on **+44 171 779 8999**

and order your one year subscription to *Euromoney* for £205 (UK only), $395 (Europe and North America), $420 (rest of world).

PW99

KAZAKHSTAN (+7)

ABN AMRO Bank Kazakhstan — Full Branch Office

45 Khadzhy Mukana Street, 480099 Almaty
Tel: (3272) 507 300 Fax: (3272) 507 303; (3272) 507 298 Telex: 251283 AABKA Swift: ABNA KZ KX
Email: abnamro@kaznet.kz

Senior Executive Officers
Chief Executive Officer — Otbert De Jong *General Manager*
Treasurer — Oleg Tsurkan *Head of Treasury* ☏ 507 302

Debt Capital Markets / Fixed Income
Government Bonds
Head of Trading — Andrei Nalov *Dealer* ☏ 507 302
Fixed-Income Repo
Head of Trading — Ludmila Poguliaeva *Dealer* ☏ 507 302

Syndicated Lending
Other (Trade Finance)
Trade & Commodity Finance — Maryanne Mauron

Foreign Exchange
Corporate Sales — Serik Zhukenov *Chief Dealer* ☏ 507 302
FX Traders / Sales People
Askbat Utegulov *Sales Person* ☏ 507 302
Zhanar Satpaeva *FX Trader* ☏ 507 302

Risk Management
Head of Risk Management — Saule Kishkimbaeva

Settlement / Clearing
Head of Settlement / Clearing — Amir Chagprov *Head of Trade Services*
Operations — Gauhar Nuskabaeva

Global Custody
Head of Global Custody — Yves Mauron *Head of Custody* ✉ yves.mauron@kz.abnamro.com

Asset Management
Head — Umut Shayahmetova *General Manager*

Other Departments
Chief Credit Officer — Saule Kishkimbaeva
Correspondent Banking — Aigul Urazbaeva *Relationship Manager, Banks & Fin. Institutions*
Cash Management — Rustem Rakpshev *Head of Cash*

Administration
Head of Administration — Rizwan Ali
Business Development — Elena Rubpnovichi
Head of Marketing — Una Grpbben

Technology & Systems
Felpx Avazbakpev *Head of EDP*

Legal / In-House Counsel
Elena Kerillovskaya *Legal Advisor*

Corporate Communications
Una Grpbben

Accounts / Audit
Rizwan Ali

Bank Caspiyskiy — Head Office

90 Adi Sharipova, 480012 Almaty
Tel: (3272) 675 767; (3272) 672 806 Fax: (3272) 509 596; (3272) 672 028 Email: postmaster@kcbank.almaty.kz
Website: www.kcbank.almaty.kz

Senior Executive Officers
Chairman — Nikolay Belyatsky
President — Raziya Atchibaeva
Chief Executive Officer — Natalya Pshenichnaya
Financial Director — Maksat Madzhinov ☏ 672 919
Chief Operating Officer — Tatyana Kasenova ☏ 674 939
Treasurer — Sergey Kolobov ☏ 673 870

892 Euromoney Directory 1999

www.euromoneydirectory.com   KAZAKHSTAN (+7)

Senior Executive Officers (cont)
Managing Director — Konstantin Kolpakov ☎ **672 806**
General Manager — Irina Grishina ☎ **675 767**
International Division — Tatyana Pupkova ☎ **673 464**

General-Lending (DCM, SL)
Head of Corporate Banking — Talgat Genispaev ☎ **671 428**

General-Investment
Head of Investment — Talgat Genispaev ☎ **671 428**

Debt Capital Markets / Fixed Income
Department: Dealing Department
Tel: 673 870 **Fax:** 509 596

Government Bonds
Head of Trading — Aleksey Lichman *Senior Trader* ☎ **673 870**

Emerging Market Bonds
Head of Emerging Markets — Aleksey Lichman *Senior Trader* ☎ **673 870**

Fixed-Income Repo
Head of Repo — Aleksey Lichman *Senior Trader* ☎ **673 870**

Money Markets
Tel: 673 870 **Fax:** 509 596
Head of Money Markets — Daulet Mamytov ☎ **671 963**

Foreign Exchange
Head of Foreign Exchange — Daulet Mamytov ☎ **671 963**

Corporate Finance / M&A Advisory
Head of Corporate Finance — Tolgat Zhanispayev ☎ **67 1428**

Asset Management
Head — Temir Tashenov ☎ **673 360**

Other Departments
Chief Credit Officer — Aliya Nurtasina ☎ **676 446**
Correspondent Banking — Marat Syzdikov ☎ **674 940**
Cash Management — Marina Shurhavets ☎ **677 428**

Administration
Head of Administration — Bota Mambetova ☎ **672 805**
Head of Marketing — Aliya Yegizbekova ☎ **675 976**

Technology & Systems
Vladimir Shahov ☎ **675 448**

Legal / In-House Counsel
Alfiya Safiatullina ☎ **675 966**

Accounts / Audit
Rufina Ibraeva ☎ **673 744**

Bank Turanalem   Head Office
Formerly known as: Alem Bank Kazakstan and Turan Bank
Alternative trading name: BTA
55 Aiteke Bi Street, 480091 Almaty
Tel: (3272) 500 100; (3272) 500 208 **Fax:** (3272) 500 224 **Telex:** 251393 ROSA KZ **Swift:** ABKZ KZ KX
Email: post@turanalem.almaty.kz **Reuters:** ALEM

Senior Executive Officers
Chairman of the Board — Yerzhan Tatishev
Chief Operating Officer — Victor Chajkovski ☎ **500 103**
Treasurer — Sadvakas Mameshtegi ☎ **500 112**
Company Secretary — Bertisbaeva Sholpan
International Division — Lebaeva Sholpan ☎ **500 165**

General-Investment
Head of Investment — Dunaer Arman *Head* ☎ **500 151**

Debt Capital Markets / Fixed Income
Tol: 500 124 **Fax:** 500 224

Domestic Government Bonds
Head of Sales — Nurian Muhametzhanov *Senior Dealer* ☎ **500 235**
Head of Trading — Timur Gabasov *Chief Dealer* ☎ **500 264**

Non-Domestic Government Bonds
Russia (RUR) — Askar Shinybaev *Dealer* ☎ **500 235**

Libor-Based / Floating-Rate Products
FRN Origination — Timur Gabasov *Chief Dealer* ☎ **500 264**

Euromoney Directory 1999   **893**

KAZAKHSTAN (+7)   www.euromoneydirectory.com

Bank Turanalem (cont)

Medium-Term Notes
Head of Sales — Askar Shinybaev *Dealer* ☎ **500 235**

Asset-Backed Securities / Securitization
Global Head — Sadvakas Meldybekov *Head of Department* ☎ **500 122**

Mortgage-Backed Securities
Global Head — Sadvakas Meldybekov *Head of Department* ☎ **500 122**

Equity Capital Markets
Tel: 500 122 **Fax:** 500 224
Head of Equity Capital Markets — Sadvakas Meldybekov *Head of Department* ☎ **500 122**

Domestic Equities
Head of Origination — Sadvakas Meldybekov *Head of Department* ☎ **500 122**

Equity Repo / Securities Lending
Head of Trading — Murat Altynbaev *Head of Division* ☎ **500 124**

Syndicated Lending
Loan-Related Activities
Trade Finance — Dunaer Arman *Head* ☎ **500 151**

Money Markets
Tel: 500 124 **Fax:** 500 224
Head of Money Markets — Murat Altynbaev *Head of Division* ☎ **500 124**

Wholesale Deposits
Head of Sales — Vladimir Zherebyatiev *Chief Specialist* ☎ **500 264**

Foreign Exchange
Tel: 500 264 **Fax:** 639 382
Head of Trading — Timur Gabasov *Chief Dealer* ☎ **500 264**

Risk Management
Tel: 621 774 **Fax:** 500 224
Head of Risk Management — Erlan Iyemberdiev *Head of Department*

Exotic Options (Barriers, Range, Timers, Digitals, Faders etc)
Trading — Timur Gabasov *Chief Dealer* ☎ **500 264**

Global Custody
Head of Global Custody — Ahmetova Rosa ☎ **635 939**

Asset Management
Head — Loginova Natali ☎ **500 871**

Other Departments
Commodities / Bullion; Proprietary Trading — Erik Balapanov *Director of Department* ☎ **500 164**
Chief Credit Officer — Saparov Arsen ☎ **500 115**
Private Banking — Erik Balapanov *Director of Department* ☎ **500 164**
Correspondent Banking — Aljanova Botagoz *Head* ☎ **500 208**

Administration
Head of Marketing — Zazrov Marat ☎ **500 115**

Technology & Systems
Satarov Tursun *Head* ☎ **500 163**

Legal / In-House Counsel
Gaddulin Niyazbek *Head* ☎ **637 397**

Accounts / Audit
Ablyazova Armarel *Head of Accounts* ☎ **500 119**

Open Joint-Stock Society Bank "Centercredit"   Head Office

Formerly known as: Kazakh Central Joint-Stock Bank "Centerbank"
100, Shevchenko Street, 480072 Almaty
Tel: 692 929; 622 814 **Fax:** 692 924; 507 813 **Telex:** 613856 CENTB KZ **Swift:** KCJB KZ KX **Email:** mail@cbank.kz
Reuters: CNKZ

Senior Executive Officers
Board Chairman — Vladislav Lee ☎ **692 929**
Supervisory Council Chairman — Bakhytbek Baiseitov ☎ **630 493**
Financial Director — Kambar Shalgimbaev *Director of Planning and Financial Control* ☎ **608 246**
Treasurer — Tolegen Muldashev *Director of Treasury Department* ☎ **622 024**
Company Secretary — Alibek Nigmatulin ☎ **692 903**
International Division — Natalia Kolesnik *Head of International Division* ☎ **622 814**

Others (Senior Executives)
Maksat Aljanov *Global Head of Branches Network* ☎ **692 798**
Maiko Sagindykova *Global Head of Mortgage Lending* ☎ **692 991**

Syndicated Lending
Loan-Related Activities
Trade Finance   Natalia Kolesnik *Head of International Division* ☏ **622 814**
Project Finance   Alimzhan Abdrakhmanov *Director of Credit* ☏ **621 133**

Money Markets
Tel: 634 531 **Fax:** 608 018 **Reuters:** CNKZ **Telex:** 613856 CENTB KZ
Head of Money Markets   Valery Lee *Manager* ☏ **634 531**

Foreign Exchange
Tel: 634 531 **Fax:** 634 531
Global Head   Valery Lee *Manager* ☏ **634 531**

FX Traders / Sales People
    Darkhan Dusenov *Chief Dealer* ☏ **634 531**
    Vadim Kim *Dealer* ☏ **634 531**

Risk Management
Tel: 630 929 **Fax:** 507 813
Head of Risk Management   Beibut Olzhabaév ☏ **608 018**

Settlement / Clearing
Tel: 628 908 **Fax:** 608 018 **Telex:** 613856 CENTB KZ
Head of Settlement / Clearing   Svetlana Amanzholova ☏ **628 908**

Other Departments
Chief Credit Officer   Alimzhan Abdrakhmanov *Director of Credit* ☏ **621 133**
Correspondent Banking   Natalia Kolesnik *Head of International Division* ☏ **622 814**

Administration
Head of Administration   Bulan Adilkhanov *Director of Administration* ☏ **692 905**
Head of Marketing   Zhanargul Rakhmadieva *Head of Marketing* ☏ **608 014**

Technology & Systems
    Medet Rakhimbaev *Director of IT* ☏ **634 644**

Public Relations
    Zhanargul Rakhmadieva *Head of Marketing* ☏ **608 014**

Commerzbank AG   Representative Office
155 Prospekt Abaja, 7 Stock, 480009 Almaty
Tel: (3272) 409 900; (3272) 403 915 **Fax:** (3272) 509 578 **Telex:** 612484 CBALM SU

Senior Executive Officers
Representative   Dr. Marco Graff

Deutsche Bank AG   Representative Office
10a Prospect Abai, 480013 Almaty
Tel: (3272) 638 550; (3272) 638 584 **Fax:** (3272) 630 950

European Bank for Reconstruction & Development
Representative Office
8th Floor, 10a Prospect Abaya, 480013 Almaty
Tel: (3272) 581 424; (3272) 581 476 **Fax:** (3272) 581 422

Senior Executive Officers
Resident Representative   Martyn Nicholls
Deputy Resident Representative   Paul Burton

The Export Import Bank of the Republic of Kazakstan
118 Pushkin Street, 480021 Almaty
Tel: (3272) 622 815; (3272) 634 300 **Fax:** (3272) 631 985 **Telex:** 251768 EXIM KZ
Website: www.eximbank.kz

Senior Executive Officers
Chairman   Beisembay I Izteleuov
Deputy Chairman   Almat K Turtayev

KAZAKHSTAN (+7) www.euromoneydirectory.com

The Export Import Bank of the Republic of Kazakstan (cont)
Senior Executive Officers (cont)
Deputy Chairman Timur E Zhakselekov
Chief Executive Officer Kuat Zhandosov
  Natalya Akentyeva
Financial Director Galina Moskalcva

OJSC Halyk Savings Bank of Kasakstan
Head Office

97 Rozybakiev Street, 480046 Almaty
Tel: (3272) 509 991 Fax: (3272) 679 738 Telex: 251531 KRONA KZ Swift: HSBKKZKX Email: aiguln@resp.narbank.kz
Reuters: SVKZ

Senior Executive Officers
Chairman Karim Massimov
Vice Chairman Erserik Siyrbaev

Others (Senior Executives)
Macroeconomic Research Leonid Ivanov *Vice Chairman*
Project Management Saule Joldybaeva *Vice Chairman & Director*

General - Treasury
Head of Treasury Irina Sindonis *Vice Chairman, Operations & Treasury*
  Olzhas Asylbekov

Relationship Manager
Correspondent Relations Nurgul Zhapparova *Director*

Syndicated Lending
Other (Syndicated Lending)
Commercial Lending Anuar Buranbaev *Director*

Loan-Related Activities
Structured Trade Finance Aigul Nurieva *Director*

Settlement / Clearing
Operations Irina Sindonis *Vice Chairman, Operations & Treasury*
  Almaz Jamanbckov *Director, Logisitics*
Back-Office Irina Soboleva *Director*

Other Departments
Chief Credit Officer Rausham Sagdieva *First Vice Chairman, Credit policy*
Cash Management Tatyana Maryasova *Deputy Director*
Economic Research Leonid Ivanov *Vice Chairman*
  Galina Raiko *Director of Research*

Other Departments
Cash Collection Sayat Tolymbekov *Director*

Administration
Information Technology Askar Idrjsov *First Vice Chairman, IT*
  Altynai Eleuova *Director*

Legal / In-House Counsel
Legal Department Elena Molchanova *Vice Chairman & Director*

Public Relations
Public Relations & Marketing Julia Khobot *Head*

Accounts / Audit
Accounting & Financial Control Kanat Orynbekov *Vice Chairman & Director*

Other (Administration)
Human Resources Valeriy Maly *Director*

ING Barings
Representative Office

85a Dostyk, 480100 Almaty
Tel: (3272) 534 334 Fax: (3272) 534 455

Senior Executive Officers
Representative Timur Issatayev

www.euromoneydirectory.com   KAZAKHSTAN (+7)

Kazkommerts Securites
Head Office

65 Furmanov Street, 5th Floor, 480005 Almaty
Tel: (3272) 509 060 Fax: (3272) 509 162; (3275) 811 498 Telex: 251304 TIMUR KZ Swift: KZKO KZ KX
Email: enquiry@kazks.kz Reuters: KAZK
Website: kozcombank.almaty.kz

Senior Executive Officers
Chief Executive Officer
Financial Director

Aidan Karibzhanov *Chief Executive Officer*
Iskander Erimbetov

Corporate Finance / M&A Advisory
Head of Corporate Finance

Nicolay Varenco *Director, Corporate Finance*

Administration
Legal / In-House Counsel

Lyazzat Dauenbekova *Director*

Public Relations

Vitaly Kuchura *Deputy Chief Executive Officer*

Kazkommertsbank
Head Office

49 Baiseyitova Street, 480013 Almaty
Tel: (3272) 505 101; (3272) 505 106 Fax: (3272) 505 100; (3272) 501 002 Telex: 251304 TIMUR KZ Swift: KXKO KZ KX
Email: mailbox@kazcombank.almaty.kz Reuters: KAZK
Website: www.kazcombank.almaty.kz

Senior Executive Officers
Chairman
Chief Executive Officer; Financial Director
Chief Operating Officer
Treasurer
International Division

Nurzhan Subkhanbordin
Nina Zhussupova *First Deputy Chairman* ☎ **505 301**
Elvira Kamalitdinova *Managing Director* ☎ **505 321**
Aidar Akhmetov *Managing Director* ☎ **505 374**
Meirambek Karazhigitor ☎ **505 110**
Oleg Kononenko *Managing Director* ☎ **505 105**

Others (Senior Executives)
Emerging Market

Aidan Karibzhanov *Managing Director* ☎ **509 060**

General-Lending (DCM, SL)
Head of Corporate Banking

Vladimir Kim

General-Investment
Head of Investment

Askar Alshinbaev *Managing Director* ☎ **505 107**
Yergeni Feld *Managing Director* ☎ **505 107**
Yuri Shpakov *Managing Director*

Debt Capital Markets / Fixed Income
Department: Dealing
Fax: 509 507

Government Bonds
Head of Sales

Sergey Vagilyiev ☎ **505 270**

Eurobonds
Head of Sales

Andrei Tolochenko ☎ **505 119**

Libor-Based / Floating-Rate Products
FRN Sales

Lev Kim ☎ **505 270**

Fixed-Income Repo
Head of Repo

Sophia Seidalina ☎ **505 270**

Equity Capital Markets
Head of Equity Capital Markets

Aidan Karibzhanov *Managing Director* ☎ **509 060**

Syndicated Lending
Tel: 505 112 Fax: 501 002
Head of Origination

Yeldar Abdrazakov ☎ **505 119**

Loan-Related Activities
Trade Finance

Mrs Belotserkovskaya *Head* ☎ **505 193**

Foreign Exchange
Head of Foreign Exchange
Corporate Sales
Head of Trading

Talgat Biskenov ☎ **505 270**
Mr Shokan ☎ **505 270**
Lev Kim ☎ **505 270**

Risk Management
Head of Risk Management

Aidar Dautov ☎ **505 247**

KAZAKHSTAN (+7)   www.euromoneydirectory.com

Kazkommertsbank (cont)

Corporate Finance / M&A Advisory
Head of Corporate Finance — Mr Iskakov

Settlement / Clearing
Tel: 505 321
Head of Settlement / Clearing — Elvira Kamalitdinova *Managing Director* ☎ 505 321

Asset Management
Head — Ludmila Vozlublennaya *Managing Director* ☎ 505 202

Other Departments
Chief Credit Officer — Mr Dautov
Private Banking — E Shamuratou *Managing Director*
Correspondent Banking — Mr Iskakov ☎ 505 280
Cash Management — Daniar Shariffulin

Administration
Head of Administration — Georgii Gukasov ☎ 505 171
Nickolay Rizhov *Director* ☎ 505 172
Head of Marketing — Tatyana Eiyodorova ☎ 505 253

Technology & Systems
Yuri Lim *Head*

Legal / In-House Counsel
Mrs Mikhaylovskaya *Attorney* ☎ 505 192

Public Relations
Mr Mulikov *Head* ☎ 505 126

Accounts / Audit
Mrs Zhumataeva *Head*

KZI Bank - Kazkommerts-Ziraat International Bank   Head Office

143 A Tole Bi Street, 480096 Almaty
PO Box 34, 480096 Almaty
Tel: (3272) 506 080/1; (3272) 501 014/5 Fax: (3272) 506 082 Telex: 251277 KAZIB KZ Swift: KZIB KZ KA
Email: kzibank@sovam.com
Website: www.kzibank.com

Senior Executive Officers
Chairman — Nina Zhusupova ☎ 505 301 ℻ 505 162
Treasurer — Evgeniy Onichko ☎ 507 768 ℻ 506 082
General Manager — Hasan Ferit Yice Yilmaz ☎ 501 013 ℻ 507 769
International Division — Cem Berik *Head of Correspondent Banking* ☎ 501 015 ℻ 506 082

Others (Senior Executives)
M Naci Piskin *Assistant General Manager* ☎ 501 064
Arlen Dautov *Assistant General Manager* ☎ 506 081

Foreign Exchange
Head of Foreign Exchange — Evgeniy Onichko ☎ 507 768 ℻ 506 082

Other Departments
Correspondent Banking — Cem Berik *Head of Correspondent Banking* ☎ 501 015 ℻ 506 082
Cash Management — Atalay Altundas *Head of Cash Management* ☎ 682 778

Administration

Technology & Systems
Michael Drachuk ☎ 501 065 ℻ 506 082

Accounts / Audit
Aysulu Mukazhanova ☎ 501 014

Other (Administration)
Marketing — Yilmaz Gungor ☎ 680 174 ℻ 506 082

Société Générale   Representative Office

Kazak Business Center, 85A, Pr Dostyk, Room 307, 480021 Almaty
Tel: (3272) 506 214; (3272) 811 523 Fax: (3272) 506 206
Website: www.socgen.com

Senior Executive Officers
Chairman — Jean-Claude Valentin

www.euromoneydirectory.com KENYA (+254)

Open Joint Stock Company 'TemirBank'
Head Office

Formerly known as: Joint Stock Railway Bank 'TemirBank'
80 Shevchenco Street, 480091 Almaty
Tel: (3272) 630 222; (3272) 633 393 **Fax:** (3272) 506 241 **Telex:** 251855 TEMIR **Swift:** JSRB KZ KA
Email: board@temirbank.kz
Website: www.temirbank.kz

Senior Executive Officers
Chairman — Saodat Tashpulatova
Treasurer — Kairat Bektanov *Head of Treasury* 621 120
International Division — Bauyrzhan Akhmetzhanov 624 902

Others (Senior Executives)
Andrey Butukhanov *Deputy Chairman* 632 915
Serikzhan Ramazanov *Deputy Chairman* 622 176
Moryam Mirayeva *Deputy Chairman* 630 372
Berik Sarin *Deputy Chairman* 633 393

Syndicated Lending
Loan-Related Activities
Trade Finance — Irina Kushnareva 624 901

Foreign Exchange
Tel: 605 742 **Fax:** 507 785 **Telex:** 251855 TEMIR
Head of Foreign Exchange — Sergey Tromin *Head of Dealing* 60 5742

Settlement / Clearing
Tel: 604 988 **Fax:** 506 241 **Telex:** 251855 TEMIR
Settlement (General) — Nurlun Bikhozhayev *Head of Settlements* 605 041

Other Departments
Correspondent Banking — Nina Velichko *Head* 605 041

Administration
Technology & Systems — Vladimir Frolov *Head* 638 466

Legal / In-House Counsel
Alexandr Bratus *Head* 694 700

Accounts / Audit
Khalicha Abdeayeva *Chief Accountant* 604 869

KENYA
(+254)

Central Bank of Kenya
Central Bank

PO Box 60000, Nairobi
Tel: (2) 226 431; (2) 330 500 **Fax:** (2) 340 192 **Telex:** 22324 **Swift:** CBKE KE NX **Email:** benkikuu@arcc-or.ke
Reuters: BOKM

Senior Executive Officers
Governor — Micah Cheserem
Deputy Group Chief Executive — Nzioki Kibua
Bank Secretary — James Gikonyo

Others (Senior Executives)
Head, Banking Supervision — Simon Anzangi *Director*
Head, Economics & Staistics — Maurice Kanga *Director*
Head, Public Debt — Samuel Kimani *Deputy Director*
Head, Banking — Reuben Marambi *Chief Manager*

Foreign Exchange
Head of Foreign Exchange — Edwin Ogola *Deputy Director*

Administration
Head of Administration — Peter Rottich *Deputy Director*

Technology & Systems
Daniel Kiangura *Director*

Legal / In-House Counsel
Kakai Cheloti *Deputy Director*

Public Relations
Mark Lesiit *PA to Governor*

KENYA (+254) www.euromoneydirectory.com

Central Bank of Kenya (cont)
Accounts / Audit
Head, Accountancy Jones Nzomo *Finance Director*
Audit Matilda Onyango *Chief Internal Auditor*
Other (Administration)
Training Lawamba Binett *Senior Manager*

The Bank of Tokyo-Mitsubishi Limited — Representative Office

3rd Floor, International Life House, Mama Ngina Street, Nairobi
PO Box 30441, Nairobi
Tel: (2) 220 951 **Fax:** (2) 230 841 **Telex:** 22169

Senior Executive Officers
Chief Representative Masato Uchiba

Citibank NA — Full Branch Office

Fedha Towers, Muindi Mbingu Street, PO Box 30711, Nairobi
Tel: (2) 333 524 **Fax:** (2) 714 811 **Telex:** 22051 22161 **Reuters:** CTIN

Senior Executive Officers
Financial Director Peter Harris *General Manager*

Debt Capital Markets / Fixed Income
Global Head Kitili Mbethi

Syndicated Lending
Country Head Richard Kimani *Head, Commercial Loans*

Foreign Exchange
Country Head Paul Fletcher

FX Traders / Sales People
Customer FX Head & Treasury Marketing Head Kitili Mbathi

Settlement / Clearing
Operations Abdulla Abdulahalik *Transaction Services Head*

Commercial Bank of Africa Limited — Head Office

Standard/Wabera Streets, PO Box 30437, Nairobi
Tel: (2) 228 881 **Fax:** (2) 335 827; (2) 340 157 **Telex:** 23205 **Swift:** CBAF KE NX **Reuters:** CBAN
Website: www.africaonline.co.ke

Senior Executive Officers
Chairman Mirabeau de Gama-Rose
Chief Executive Officer John Docherty *Managing Director*
  Isaac Awuondo *Executive Director*
Financial Director Douglas Pinto *AGM, Finance & Operations*
Treasurer Hasudi Ramprasad *Head of Treasury*
GM, Credit Management Nelson Mainnah
Corporate Secretary, Legal Counsel Rosemin Bhanji
International Division George Mashashi *Manager*

Others (Senior Executives)
Coast Region Arun Mathur *General Manager*

General-Lending (DCM, SL)
Head of Corporate Banking Madabushi Soundarajan *Executive Director*

Syndicated Lending
Tel: 228 802 **Fax:** 340 217
Head of Trading Madabushi Soundarajan *Executive Director*

Loan-Related Activities
Trade Finance Madabushi Soundarajan *Executive Director*

Other (Trade Finance)
Corporate and Trade Finance Mr Echaria *Assistant General Manager*

Money Markets
Tel: 228 881 **Fax:** 213 038 **Reuters:** 330261
Head of Money Markets Hasudi Ramprasad *Head of Treasury*

KENYA (+254)

Foreign Exchange
Tel: 228 881 Fax: 213 038
Head of Foreign Exchange
Head of Trading
Hasudi Ramprasad *Head of Treasury*
Dheerendrath *Chief Dealer*

Risk Management
Tel: 228 881 Fax: 340 157
Head of Risk Management
Nelson Mainnah *GM, Credit Management*

Corporate Finance / M&A Advisory
Head of Corporate Finance
Madabushi Soundarajan *Executive Director*

Other Departments
Private Banking
Correspondent Banking
Catherine M Njoroge *Head of Personal Banking*
Hasudi Ramprasad *Head of Treasury*

Administration
Technology & Systems
Siraj Siddiqui *Manager*

Legal / In-House Counsel
Rosemin Bhanji *Corporate Secretary, Legal Counsel*

Accounts / Audit
Derrick Ouma *Chief Accountant*
Peter Njenga *Chief Auditor*

HSBC Equator Bank plc
Representative Office
Lonrho House, 14th Floor, Standard Street, Nairobi
PO Box 62360, Nairobi
Tel: (2) 217 778 Fax: (2) 217 147

Senior Executive Officers
Senior Vice President
Vice President
Thomas F Wescott
Peter A Panciera

Shah, Munge & Partners Limited
PO Box 14686, 14th Floor, Nation Centre, Kimathi Street, Nairobi
Tel: (2) 219 782; (2) 225 811 Fax: (2) 213 024 Email: shamunge@iconnect.co.ke

Senior Executive Officers
Others (Senior Executives)
Director
John P Munge
Paul A Spence
Franklin K Kirigia
Amish Gupta *Associate Director*

Debt Capital Markets / Fixed Income
Head of Debt Capital Markets
Ben Nyamweya *Senior Manager, Debt*
Brian Muchiri

Domestic Government Bonds
Head of Sales
Joel Mittlestadt *Senior Manager, Debt*
Ben Nyamweya *Senior Manager, Debt*
Head of Trading
Joel Mittlestadt *Senior Manager, Debt*
Ben Nyamweya *Senior Manager, Debt*
Head of Research
Joel Mittlestadt *Senior Manager, Debt*
Ben Nyamweya *Senior Manager, Debt*

Equity Capital Markets
Domestic Equities
Head of Trading
Susan Kimanzi *Foreign Relations* [F] **225 811**
Lucas Otieno *Equity Research / Equity Dealer*
Amish Gupta *Associate Director*
Head of Research
Susan Kimanzi *Foreign Relations* [F] **225 811**
Lucas Otieno *Equity Research / Equity Dealer*
Amish Gupta *Associate Director*

International Equities
Head of Sales
Susan Kimanzi *Foreign Relations* [F] **225 811**
Amish Gupta *Associate Director*
Lucas Otieno *Equity Research / Equity Dealer*
Head of Trading
Susan Kimanzi *Foreign Relations* [F] **225 811**
Lucas Otieno *Equity Research / Equity Dealer*
Amish Gupta *Associate Director*

KENYA (+254)   www.euromoneydirectory.com

Shah, Munge & Partners Limited (cont)
International Equities (cont)
Head of Research   Susan Kimanzi *Foreign Relations* ☏ **225 811**
                                      Lucas Otieno *Equity Research / Equity Dealer*
                                      Amish Gupta *Associate Director*

Stanbic Bank Kenya Limited
Stanbic Bank Building, Kenyatta Avenue, PO Box 30550, Nairobi
Tel: (2) 335 888 **Fax:** (2) 229 287 **Telex:** 25207
Senior Executive Officers
General Manager   P J W Lewis-Jones

Trust Bank Limited   Head Office
PO Box 46342, Nairobi
Tel: (2) 226 413; (2) 226 415 **Fax:** (2) 216 255; (2) 244 528 **Telex:** 25143 **Swift:** TRBAKENA **Tel:** 216 264; 216 267
Senior Executive Officers
Executive Chairman   Ajay Shah
Financial Director   Renuka Shah *Financial Controller* ☏ **330 605**
Debt Capital Markets / Fixed Income
Private Placements
Head of Origination   Darshna Bhatt *Manager*
Money Markets
Country Head   Darshna Bhatt *Manager*
Corporate Finance / M&A Advisory
Country Head   Vinod Agrawal *Senior Manager*
Settlement / Clearing
Country Head   Renuka Shah *Financial Controller* ☏ **330 605**
Other Departments
Correspondent Banking   Vinod Patel *Manager*

KOREA, DEM. PEOPLE'S REP OF
(+850)

ING-North East Asia Bank   Representative Office
Room 418, Potonggang Hotel, Ansandong, Pyongchon Kuyok, Pyongyang, Pyongchon District
Tel: (2) 381 4373 **Fax:** (2) 381 4703
Senior Executive Officers
Representative   Tony Holmes

KOREA, SOUTH
(+82)

The Bank of Korea   🏛 Central Bank
110 3-ga Namdaemun-ro, Jung-Gu, Seoul 100-794
Tel: (2) 759 4114 **Fax:** (2) 759 5826 **Email:** bokdina@bok.or.kr
Website: www.bok.or.kr
Senior Executive Officers
Governor   Chol-Hwan Chon ☏ **759 4001**
Deputy Governor   Hoon Shin ☏ **759 4003**
Assistant Governor   Kwi-Sup Yoon ☏ **759 4006**
International Division   Hyunchul Shin *Director* ☏ **759 5801**
Others (Senior Executives)
Head of International Relations   Johng-In Ha ☏ **759 5695**

www.euromoneydirectory.com   KOREA, SOUTH (+82)

ABN AMRO Bank NV
Full Branch Office

15th Floor, Young Poong Building, 33 Seorin-dong,Chongro-ku, Seoul 110-110
Tel: (2) 399 6600 **Fax:** (2) 399 6665 **Telex:** K24624 **Swift:** ABNA KR SE **Email:** hye.kyung.kim@ap.adnamro.com
Reuters: ABSH **Bloomberg:** EUGENEHONG

Senior Executive Officers
Others (Senior Executives)
Country Manager — Dick A Van den Ham *Senior Vice President* T 399 6666 F 399 6665
Deputy GM / CFO — Duck-Mo Chung *Vice President* T 399 6667 F 399 6665
Head of Transactional Banking — Hong-Soo Kim *Vice President* T 399 6655 F 399 6647
Head of Relation Management / Local — Jia-Ha Shin *Vice President* T 399 6622 F 399 6647
Head of Relation Management / Global — Hyun-Jae Choi *Vice President* T 399 6617 F 399 6612
Structured Finance — George L Schaafsma *Vice President* T 399 6614 F 399 6612

General - Treasury
Head of Treasury — Seung-Hoon Baek *Vice President* T 399 6511 F 399 6558

Debt Capital Markets / Fixed Income
Department: Treasury
Tel: 399 6511 **Fax:** 399 6558
Head of Fixed Income — Seung-Hoon Baek *Vice President* T 399 6511 F 399 6558

Syndicated Lending
Loan-Related Activities
Trade Finance — Dahl-Soon Lee *Assistant Vice President* T 399 6633 F 399 6647

Foreign Exchange
Tel: 399 6611 **Fax:** 399 6558
Head of Foreign Exchange — In-Woo Jung *Assistant Vice President* T 399 6608
Head of Institutional Sales — Seok-Hoon Yoon *Assistant Vice President* T 399 6610
Corporate Sales — Young-Min Cho *Assistant Vice President* T 399 6606

Risk Management
Tel: 399 6656 **Fax:** 399 6612
Head of Risk Management — Young-Joo Sone *Assistant Vice President* T 399 6656

Fixed Income Derivatives / Risk Management
Head of Sales — Eugene Hong *Assistant Vice President* T 339 6611 F 399 6558

Global Custody
Head of Global Custody — Sue-Kyung Oh *Associate* T 399 6669 F 399 6612

Other Departments
Chief Credit Officer — Jeong-Hee Kim *Associate* T 399 6615 F 399 6612
Correspondent Banking — Kyu-Chan Kwon *Assistant Associate* T 399 6614 F 399 6647
Cash Management — Hee-Young Cha *Assistant Vice President* T 399 6616 F 399 6647

Administration
Compliance
Dong-Han Bae *Assistant Vice President* T 399 6652 F 399 6612

The Asahi Bank Limited

18th Floor, Kyobo Life Insurance Building, 1 Chongro 1-ka, Chongro-ku, Seoul
Tel: (2) 738 5183 **Fax:** (2) 736 1242 **Telex:** K23356 ASHSLA
Website: www.asahibank.co.jp

Senior Executive Officers
General Manager — Yoshimi Maeda

Asian Banking Corporation
Head Office

33 Seorin-dong, Chongro-ku, Seoul
PO Box 7004, Seoul
Tel: (2) 399 5500; (2) 399 5452 **Fax:** (2) 399 5400; (2) 399 5519 **Telex:** ABCORP K 23449 **Swift:** ASBC KR SE

Senior Executive Officers
Chairman — Won Shik Sull T 399 5410
Chief Executive Officer — Kwan Haeng Cho T 399 5407
                        Kwan Haeng Cho *Chief Executive Officer* T 399 5407
Financial Director — Byung-Tae Min *Domestic Financial Director* T 399 5412
                    John Limb *International Financial Director* T 399 5413
Chief Operating Officer — Taeyoung Kang *Chief Operating Officer* T 399 5421
Treasurer — Hyun-Ki Sull *Treasurer* T 399 5457

KOREA, SOUTH (+82) www.euromoneydirectory.com

Asian Banking Corporation (cont)

Debt Capital Markets / Fixed Income
Department: International Finance Department
Tel: 399 5452 Fax: 399 5400
Global Head Dong-Ki Kang *Treasurer* 399 5452

Eurobonds
Head of Trading Jung Keun Lee 399 5489

Libor-Based / Floating-Rate Products
FRN Origination Jin-Ho Choi 399 5512

Equity Capital Markets

Domestic Equities
Head of Trading Nam Hoon Kim 399 5463

Syndicated Lending
Department: International Finance Department
Tel: 399 5452 Fax: 399 5400
Global Head Dong-Ki Kang *Treasurer* 399 5452

Money Markets
Department: Treasury Department
Tel: 399 5513 Fax: 399 5420
Global Head Hyun-Ki Sull *Treasurer* 399 5457

Domestic Commercial Paper
Head of Trading Nam Hoon Kim 399 5463

Foreign Exchange
Department: International Finance Department
Tel: 399 5512 Fax: 399 5420
Global Head Dong-Ki Kang *Treasurer* 399 5452
Head of Trading Jin-Ho Choi 399 5512

Settlement / Clearing
Department: Operations Department
Tel: 399 5492 Fax: 399 5548
Regional Head Duk Jin Shim 399 5449
Fixed-Income Settlement Jae Ryong Park 399 5472

Australia & New Zealand Banking Group Limited Full Branch Office

18th Floor, Kyobo Building 1, 1-ka, Chongro-ku, Seoul 110-714
PO Box 1065, Seoul
Tel: (2) 730 3151 Fax: (2) 737 6325 Telex: K27338 Email: maf1@anz.com Cable: ANZBANK

Senior Executive Officers
Chief Executive Officer Michael Frowen *General Manager* 737 6323
Chief Operating Officer J S Rhee
Treasurer K H Kim *Treasury Manager*

General-Lending (DCM, SL)
Head of Corporate Banking C S Yoon *Deputy General Manager* 736 5174

Bank Brussels Lambert Representative Office

Alternative trading name: BBL
14th Floor, KorAm Building, 39 Da-dong, Chung-ku, Seoul 100-180
Tel: (2) 775 8371; (2) 775 8372 Fax: (2) 775 8373

Senior Executive Officers
Representative O S Seo

The Bank of Nova Scotia Full Branch Office

9th Floor, KCCI Building, 45, 4-ka, Namdaemun-ro, Chung-ku, Seoul 100-094
Tel: (2) 757 7171 Fax: (2) 752 7189 Telex: 29245 SCOTIAX Swift: NOSC KR SE

Senior Executive Officers
Vice President & Manager Henry Yong 756 0755

www.euromoneydirectory.com KOREA, SOUTH (+82)

Syndicated Lending
Regional Head Matt Harris *Managing Director* ☎ +852 2861 4804
Country Head of Origination; Head of E S Park *Senior Account Manager* ☎ 757 7178
Syndication
Loan-Related Activities
Trade Finance Gary Gorton *Vice President* ☎ +852 2861 4802
  E S Park *Senior Account Manager* ☎ 757 7178
Project Finance Matt Harris *Managing Director* ☎ +852 2861 4804
  Y K Rim *Commercial Secretary* ☎ 778 8356
Money Markets
Country Head S Y Oh *Senior Dealer* ☎ 757 7186
Foreign Exchange
Country Head of Trading S Y Oh *Senior Dealer* ☎ 757 7186
FX Traders / Sales People
  M H Lee *Dealer* ☎ 778 8355
Risk Management
Regional Head Adil Chaudry *Director, Derivatives* ☎ +65 539 4693
Foreign Exchange Derivatives / Risk Management
Cross-Currency Swaps, Sales / Marketing Adil Chaudry *Director, Derivatives* ☎ +65 539 4693
Other Currency Swap / FX Options Personnel
  Adil Chaudry *Director, Derivatives* ☎ +65 539 4693
Exotic Options (Barriers, Range, Timers, Digitals, Faders etc)
Sales Adil Chaudry *Director, Derivatives* ☎ +65 539 4693
Other Departments
Private Banking C H Bae *Senior International Marketing Offic*

Bayerische Landesbank
Representative Office

12th Floor, Nae Wei Building, 6, Eulji-ro 2-ka, Chung-ku, Seoul
Tel: (2) 778 1263 **Fax:** (2) 778 1269

Senior Executive Officers
Chief Representative K B Kim
Chief Representative Franz-Herman Hirlinger
Representative J H Jun

Boram Bank
Head Office

9-10, 2-ga, Ulchi-ro, Chung-gu, Seoul 100-720
Tel: (2) 3788 5000 **Fax:** (2) 775 7472; (2) 754 8263 **Telex:** K33555 BORAMBK **Swift:** BORB KR SE
Email: bfc@boram.co.kr **Reuters:** BORH
General Telex: K33556 BORAMBK
Website: www.boram.co.kr

Senior Executive Officers
Chairman of the Executive Committee & Ja-Jung Koo ☎ 3788 5001
President
Chief Executive Officer Chul-Soo Lee ☎ 3788 5001
Financial Director Dal-Yong Lee *Chief Financial Director & Senior Vice President*
  ☎ 3788 5008
Chief Operating Officer Chul-Soo Lee *Director & Deputy President* ☎ 3788 5001
Director & Executive Vice President Sang-Heun Lee ☎ 3788 5005
General Manager Tae-Oh Kim ☎ 3788 5021
International Division Sang-Koul Lee *General Manager* ☎ 3788 5441

Others (Senior Executives)
Director & Senior Vice President Sung-Ho Choi *Director & SVP* ☎ 3788 5007
  Yong-Ho Rim *Standing Auditor* ☎ 3788 5003

General-Lending (DCM, SL)
Head of Corporate Banking Hoon-Kyu Kim *Director & Executive Vice President* ☎ 3788 5004

Debt Capital Markets / Fixed Income
Department: International Banking Unit
Tel: 754 7545 **Fax:** 775 7472
Head of Fixed Income Seok-Ku Kim *Head* ☎ 3788 5442
Head of Fixed Income Sales Je-Bong Yoo *Manager* ☎ 3788 5461

Government Bonds
Head of Sales Seok-Ku Kim *Head* ☎ 3788 5442

KOREA, SOUTH (+82)   www.euromoneydirectory.com

Boram Bank (cont)

Eurobonds
Head of Origination; Head of Syndication   Seok-Ku Kim Head ☎ 3788 5442
Head of Sales   Seok-Ku Kim Head ☎ 3788 5442

Emerging Market Bonds
Head of Emerging Markets   Seok-Ku Kim Head ☎ 3788 5442
Head of Sales   Sang-Joon Yoon Manager ☎ 3788 5462

Libor-Based / Floating-Rate Products
FRN Origination   Seok-Ku Kim Head ☎ 3788 5442
FRN Sales   Sang-Joon Yoon Manager ☎ 3788 5462

Fixed-Income Repo
Head of Repo   Seok-Ku Kim Head ☎ 3788 5442
Head of Trading   Je-Bong Yoo Manager ☎ 3788 5461

Fixed-Income Research
Head of Fixed Income   Seok-Ku Kim Head ☎ 3788 5442

Equity Capital Markets
Department: Trust Fund Management Department
Tel: 3788 5243 **Fax:** 776 3268
Head of Equity Capital Markets   Jim-Hee Kim General Manager ☎ 3788 5211

Domestic Equities
Head of Sales   Jim-Hyoung Lee Head ☎ 3788 5212
Head of Trading   Hyoung-Joo Kim Manager ☎ 3788 5241

International Equities
Head of Sales   Sang-Joon Yoon Manager ☎ 3788 5462

Equity Research
Head of Equity Research   Kyoo-Chan Lee Manager ☎ 3788 5243

Syndicated Lending
Department: International Banking Unit
Tel: 3788 5461 **Fax:** 775 7472
Head of Origination   Je-Bong Yoo Manager ☎ 3788 5461
Head of Syndication   Je-Bong Yoo Manager ☎ 754 7545
Head of Trading   Seok-Ku Kim Head ☎ 3788 5442

Loan-Related Activities
Trade Finance   Seo-Ki Lee ☎ 3788 5481
Project Finance   Seok-Ku Kim Head ☎ 3788 5442

Money Markets
Department: International Banking Unit
Tel: 757 0058 **Fax:** 775 7472
Head of Money Markets   Young-Seok Cho Head ☎ 3788 5451

Domestic Commercial Paper
Head of Sales   Jae-Ho Choo Head ☎ 3788 5214

Eurocommercial Paper
Head of Sales   Je-Bong Yoo Manager ☎ 3788 5461

Wholesale Deposits
Marketing   Yong-Sik Nho Head ☎ 3788 5101

Foreign Exchange
Department: International Banking Unit
Tel: 757 0058 **Fax:** 775 7472 **Reuters:** BORH **Telex:** K33557 BORAMFX
Head of Foreign Exchange   Young-Seok Cho Head ☎ 3788 5451
Head of Institutional Sales; Corporate Sales In-Hwan Jung Manager ☎ 3788 5452

Risk Management
Department: International Banking Unit
Tel: 778 0316 **Fax:** 771 5378
Head of Risk Management   Young-Seok Cho Head ☎ 3788 5451

Foreign Exchange Derivatives / Risk Management
Cross-Currency Swaps, Sales / Marketing;   Young-Seok Cho Head ☎ 3788 5451
Cross-Currency Swaps, Trading

Settlement / Clearing
Head of Settlement / Clearing   Seung-Keon Oh Manager ☎ 3788 5457

Other Departments
Chief Credit Officer   Kyoo-Hwan Lee General Manager ☎ 3788 5161
Private Banking   Chul-Soo Song Director & SVP ☎ 3788 5006
Cash Management   Yong-Seon Kim General Manager ☎ 3788 5141

www.euromoneydirectory.com　　　KOREA, SOUTH (+82)

Administration
Head of Marketing
　　　Yong-Sik Nho *General Manager* ☎ **3788 5101**
Technology & Systems
　　　In-Sung Kang *General Manager* ☎ **3457 8601**
Public Relations
　　　Moon-Hwan Bae *Deputy General Manager* ☎ **3788 5022**
Accounts / Audit
　　　In-Seok Park *General Manager* ☎ **3788 5381**
　　　Yong-Ho Rim *Standing Auditor* ☎ **3788 5003**

The Chase Manhattan Bank　　Full Branch Office

Chase Plaza Building, 34/35 Chung-dong, Chung-ku, Seoul 100-622
PO Box 2249, Seoul 100-622
Tel: (2) 758 5114 **Fax:** (2) 758 5423 **Telex:** K23249 CHASBANK **Swift:** CHAS KR SX

Senior Executive Officers
Managing Director & Senior Country Officer　　Michael Taylor ☎ **758 5211**
Managing Director, Corporate　　Dong Jin Kim ☎ **758 5273**
Others (Senior Executives)
　　　Bang Ho Shin *Vice President, MNC & Trade* ☎ **758 5260**
　　　Jae Yoo Kim *Vice President, Finance* ☎ **758 5283**

General - Treasury
Head of Treasury
　　　Chang Nam Sohn *Vice President & Treasurer* ☎ **758 5240**
Settlement / Clearing
Operations
　　　Sang Won Lee *Vice President, Operations* ☎ **758 5300**
Other Departments
Chief Credit Officer
　　　William Agee *Vice President, Country Credit Officer* ☎ **758 5467**

Cho Hung Bank　　Head Office

14 1-ka, Namdaemun-ro, Chung-ku, Seoul 100-752
Tel: (2) 733 2000 **Fax:** (2) 3700 4910; (2) 3700 4911 **Telex:** CHOBANK K23321 **Swift:** CHOH KR SE **Reuters:** CHOH
Telex: 23325
Website: www.chohungbank.co.kr

Senior Executive Officers
Chairman　　Chull-Hoon Jang ☎ **734 2200**
Chief Executive Officer　　Byung Joo Byun ☎ **733 2811**
General Manager　　Ki Nam Chung ☎ **3700 4017**
General Manager　　Myong Hyun Kyong ☎ **3700 4016**

Debt Capital Markets / Fixed Income
Mortgage-Backed Securities
Global Head　　Yong Kil Kim *Deputy General Manager* ☎ **3700 4203**
Regional Head　　Kong Hyun Cho *Manager* ☎ **3700 4219**
Fixed-Income Repo
Head of Repo　　Jung Ki Min *Manager* ☎ **3700 4217**

Equity Capital Markets
Department: International Finance Division
Tel: 3700 4214 **Fax:** 3700 4908
Global Head　　Yong Kil Kim *Deputy General Manager* ☎ **3700 4203**
Regional Head　　Myung Kyu Choi *Assistant Manager* ☎ **3700 4229**

Syndicated Lending
Department: International Finance Division
Tel: 3700 4214 **Fax:** 3700 4908
Global Head　　Young Hoon Ham *Deputy General Manager* ☎ **3700 4204**
Regional Head　　Kang Hyun Koo *Assistant Manager* ☎ **3700 4210**
Country Head　　Seong Won Kim *Assistant Manager* ☎ **3700 4211**

Money Markets
Department: International Treasury Office
Tel: 3700 4732 **Fax:** 3700 4923
Global Head　　Chan Il Park *General Manager* ☎ **3700 4018**
Country Head　　Chang Eul Jun *Deputy General Manager* ☎ **3700 4202**

Eurocommercial Paper
Head of Sales　　Yee Yong Jo *Manager* ☎ **3700 4731**
Head of Trading　　Joong Gwi Lee *Manager* ☎ **3700 4733**

KOREA, SOUTH (+82) www.euromoneydirectory.com

Cho Hung Bank (cont)
Foreign Exchange
Department: International Treasury Office
Tel: 3700 4724 Fax: 3700 4923

Country Head	Sang Sik Choo *Senior Deputy General Manager* ☏ **3700 4200**
Head of Trading	Min Ki Jang *Manager* ☏ **3700 4728**

FX Traders / Sales People
US$ / KRW	Byung Don Kim *Assistant Manager* ☏ **3700 4722**
Corporate Sales	Yong Bum Kim *Assistant Manager* ☏ **3700 4724**
	Myung Sun Kim *Assistant Manager* ☏ **3700 4725**
Other Currency	Yong O Lee *Assistant Manager* ☏ **3700 4748**

Risk Management
Department: International Treasury Office
Tel: 3700 4231 Fax: 3700 4912

Country Head	Jae Kyung Yang *Assistant Manager* ☏ **3700 4231**

Foreign Exchange Derivatives / Risk Management
Cross-Currency Swaps, Sales / Marketing	Gun Bae Kim *Assistant Manager* ☏ **3700 4232**
Vanilla FX option Sales	Tae Kyung Jin *Assistant Manager* ☏ **3700 4276**

OTC Credit Derivatives
Global Head	Yong Kil Kim *Deputy General Manager* ☏ **3700 4203**
Regional Head	Myong Kyu Choi *Manager* ☏ **3700 4229**
Head of Sales	Dong Hyun Hwang *Manager* ☏ **3700 4208**
Head of Trading	Keun Sik Lim *Manager* ☏ **3700 4234**

Settlement / Clearing
Department: International Treasury Office
Tel: 3700 4236 Fax: 3700 4913

Country Head	Jae Joon Lee *Deputy General Manager* ☏ **3700 4205**
Fixed-Income Settlement	Tea Yon Eim *Assistant Manager* ☏ **3700 4228**
Derivatives Settlement	Nam Soo Baek *Assistant Manager* ☏ **3700 4245**
Foreign Exchange Settlement	Myung Sook Jang *Assistant Manager* ☏ **3700 4237**

Other Departments
Correspondent Banking	Yang Won Yoon *Deputy General Manager* ☏ **3700 4241**

Cho Hung Securities Co Limited Head Office

44-5 Youido-dong, Youngdeungpo-gu, Seoul
Tel: (2) 3770 9000 Fax: (2) 786 2925 Telex: K24159

Senior Executive Officers
President & Chief Executive Officer	Syng Cho Paik
Chief Executive Officer	Il Bum Song *Senior Managing Director*
Financial Director	Dungil Cho *Managing Director*

Citibank NA Full Branch Office

Citicorp Center Building, 89-29, 2-ka, Sinmum-Ro, Chongro-ku, Seoul 110-062
PO Box 749, Seoul
Tel: (2) 731 1114 Fax: (2) 738 0095 Reuters: CISH

Senior Executive Officers
Chief Executive Officer	Sajjad Razvi ☏ **731 1200**
Treasurer	Jin Hei Park *Country Treasurer* ☏ **731 1620**
Public Affairs Officer	Hoi Seung Chung ☏ **731 1214** ✉ **hoi-seung.chan@citicorp.com**

General-Lending (DCM, SL)
Head of Corporate Banking	Dabney Carr ☏ **731 1600**

General - Treasury
Head of Treasury	B Y Lee *Treasury Marketing Head* ☏ **731 1601**

Settlement / Clearing
Operations	Mike O'Donnell *Transaction Services & Cash Head*

908 Euromoney Directory 1999

www.euromoneydirectory.com KOREA, SOUTH (+82)

The Commercial Bank of Korea Limited
Head Office
111-1, 2-ka, Namdaemun-ro, Chung-gu, Seoul 100-792
PO Box 126, Seoul
Tel: (2) 754 3920; (2) 775 0050 **Fax:** (2) 318 5225; (2) 773 6779 **Telex:** K 24611/6 **Swift:** CBKO KA SE **Reuters:** COMH
Telex: 24616
Website: www.cbk.co.kr

Senior Executive Officers
Chairman   Chan Byung Bae
Chief Executive Officer   Chan Byung Bae
Financial Director   Ja-Yong Ku *Director & Deputy President*
Director & Executive Vice President   Dong-Hoon Park
General Manager   Kichul Ham ☎ **756 1848**
Chief Secretary   Young-Dae Kim
International Division   Kichul Ham *General Manager* ☎ **756 1848**

Others (Senior Executives)
Head of Foreign Promotion   Seoung-Heam Kim *General Manager* ☎ **775 5129**

General-Lending (DCM, SL)
Head of Corporate Banking   Kichul Ham *General Manager* ☎ **756 1848**

General-Investment
Head of Investment   Kichul Ham *General Manager* ☎ **756 1848**

Debt Capital Markets / Fixed Income
Head of Debt Capital Markets   Kyoung-Wam Kim *General Manager* ☎ **756 9424**

Emerging Market Bonds
Head of Emerging Markets   Kyoung-Wam Kim *General Manager* ☎ **756 9424**

Fixed-Income Repo
Head of Repo   Kyoung-Wam Kim *General Manager* ☎ **756 9424**

Equity Capital Markets
Head of Equity Capital Markets   Kyoung-Wam Kim *General Manager* ☎ **756 9424**

Equity Repo / Securities Lending
Head   Kyoung-Wam Kim *General Manager* ☎ **756 9424**

Syndicated Lending
Head of Origination   Jae-Nam Kim *Deputy General Manager* ☎ **777 1788**
Head of Syndication   Dang-Sun Seo *Deputy General Manager* ☎ **777 7746**

Loan-Related Activities
Trade Finance   Dong-Young Park *Deputy General Manager* ☎ **755 0165**
Project Finance   Dang-Sun Seo *Deputy General Manager* ☎ **777 7746**

Money Markets
Head of Money Markets   Sang-Chul Woo *Deputy General Manager* ☎ **7565 8736**

Foreign Exchange
Head of Foreign Exchange   Sang-Chul Woo *Deputy General Manager* ☎ **7565 8736**

Corporate Finance / M&A Advisory
Head of Corporate Finance   Kichul Ham *General Manager* ☎ **756 1848**

Settlement / Clearing
Head of Settlement / Clearing   Jae-Sun Oh *Deputy General Manager* ☎ **754 4360**

Global Custody
Head of Global Custody   Jae-Sun Oh *Deputy General Manager* ☎ **754 4360**

Other Departments
Correspondent Banking   Sung-Il Lee *Deputy General Manager* ☎ **774 4780**
Cash Management   Dong-Young Park *Deputy General Manager* ☎ **755 0165**

Administration
Head of Administration   Sung-Ho Doh *Senior Deputy General Manager*

Technology & Systems
                                            Jong-Taik Park *General Manager* ☎ **416 7811**

Legal / In-House Counsel
                                            Bang-Woo Song *Deputy General Manager* ☎ **775 3870**

Public Relations
                                            Yong-Jim Kim *Relationship Manager* ☎ **775 0098**

KOREA, SOUTH (+82)   www.euromoneydirectory.com

Commerzbank AG
Representative Office

8th Floor, Hanway Building, 70 Da-dong, Chung-gu, Seoul 100-180
PO Box 4558, Seoul
Tel: (2) 776 6200 Fax: (2) 776 6806 Email: cbseoul@ppp.kornet.nm.kr

Senior Executive Officers
Representative   Peter Born

Crédit Lyonnais
Full Branch Office

8/10th Floors, Youone Building, 75/95 Seosomun-dong, Chung-ku, Seoul 100-110
Tel: (2) 772 8000 Fax: (2) 755 5379 Telex: K23484 CREDIKO Swift: CRLY KR SE Reuters: CLSH
Telex: K32901 CREDIKO

Senior Executive Officers
Country Manager   Jacques Beyssade ☎ 772 8111

General-Lending (DCM, SL)
Head of Corporate Banking   C W Park *Assistant General Manager* ☎ 772 8118

General - Treasury
Head of Treasury   J A Enrile *Assistant General Manager* ☎ 772 8501

Debt Capital Markets / Fixed Income
Global Head   J A Enrile *Assistant General Manager* ☎ 772 8501
Regional Head   M H Cho *Senior Manager* ☎ 772 8505

Syndicated Lending
Head of Syndication   C W Park *Assistant General Manager* ☎ 772 8118

Loan-Related Activities
Trade Finance; Project Finance   W T Park *Assistant General Manager* ☎ 772 8181

Foreign Exchange
Global Head   J A Enrile *Assistant General Manager* ☎ 772 8501

Corporate Finance / M&A Advisory
Head of Corporate Finance   C W Park *Assistant General Manager* ☎ 772 8118

Settlement / Clearing
Settlement (General)   H C Chung *Senior Manager* ☎ 772 8301

Other Departments
Chief Credit Officer   P H Jo *Assistant General Manager* ☎ 772 8113
Correspondent Banking   N W Kang *Senior Manager*

Administration
Head of Administration   Claude Pescheux *Assistant General Manager* ☎ 772 8117

Legal / In-House Counsel
   P H Jo *Assistant General Manager* ☎ 772 8113

The Daegu Bank Limited

118 2-ga, Susong-dong, Susong-gu, Taegu 706-600
CPO Box 1, Tacgu, CPO Box 1, Taegu
Tel: (53) 756 2001 Fax: (53) 756 2095 Telex: K54634 Swift: DAEB KR 22

Senior Executive Officers
Chairman   Suh Duk-kyu
President   Kim Kuk-nyun

Daewoo Securities Co Limited
Head Office

34-3 Youido-dong, Yongdungpo-gu, Seoul 150-716
Tel: (2) 768 3355; (2) 768 3992 Telex: K26332 DWSEC
Website: www.securities.co.kr

Senior Executive Officers
Chairman   Joon Huh ☎ 768 2050
President   Chang Hee Kim ☎ 768 2001
Chief Executive Officer   Kun-Ho Hwang *Managing Director* ☎ 768 2023
Chief Operating Officer   Jong-Gui Park *Deputy General Manager* ☎ 768 3992 ℱ 786 4496
International Division   Kun-Ho Hwang *Managing Director* ☎ 768 2023

910   Euromoney Directory 1999

www.euromoneydirectory.com					KOREA, SOUTH (+82)

Debt Capital Markets / Fixed Income
Head of Fixed Income					Phil-Hyun Oh *General Manager* ☏ **768 3500**

Emerging Market Bonds
Head of Emerging Markets				Hoon-Kyo Jeong *General Manager* ☏ **768 3822**

Fixed-Income Repo
Head of Repo						Phil-Hyun Oh *General Manager* ☏ **768 3500**

Equity Capital Markets
Head of Equity Capital Markets			Jun-Ho Chung *General Manager* ☏ **768 3950**

Corporate Finance / M&A Advisory
Head of Corporate Finance				Kyung-Ho Yeo *General Manager* ☏ **768 3810**

Settlement / Clearing
Head of Settlement / Clearing			Joun-Shik Shin *Deputy General Manager* ☏ **768 3992** F **786 4496**

Administration
Head of Administration					Mu-Yul Park *General Manager* ☏ **768 3830**

Public Relations
								Mu-Yul Park *General Manager* ☏ **768 3830**

The Dai-Ichi Kangyo Bank Limited

Nae Wei Building 6, 2-ka, Eulji-ro, Chung-ku, Seoul 100
Tel: (2) 756 8181 **Fax**: (2) 754 6844 **Telex**: K27387 DKBANK
Website: www.dkb.co.jp

Senior Executive Officers
Managing Director / General Manager		Hiroyuki Tameda

# Daishin Securities Co Limited					Head Office

34-8 Yoido-dong, Youngdungpo-gu, Seoul 150-010
Tel: (2) 769 2000; (2) 769 2161 **Fax**: (2) 769 2772; (2) 769 2810 **Telex**: K29471 DAISHIN
Email: intlteam@www.daishin.co.kr
Website: www.daishin.co.kr

Senior Executive Officers
Chairman						Jae-Bong Yang
President						Kyoung-Kook Choi
Managing Director / General Manager		Tae Song Kim
International Division				Kyung Keum Park

Others (Senior Executives)
								In-Soo Kim *Head of International Team* ☏ **769 2173**
								Chung-Nam Ro *Head of International Division* ☏ **769 2170**

Debt Capital Markets / Fixed Income
Tel: 769 2160

Domestic Government Bonds
Head of Sales						Tae-Geun Joo *Manager* ☏ **769 2421**

Equity Capital Markets
Tel: 769 2290/2289

Domestic Equities
Head of Origination					Sang-Hyuck Lee *New Issues* ☏ **769 2187**
								Yong-Soo An *New Issues* ☏ **769 2197**
Head of Sales						Tae-Sub Song *Sales & Trading*
								In-Soo Kim ☏ **769 2173**
								Kee-Young Lee *General Manager* ☏ **769 3049**
								Hyung-Keun Park *Head of Sales*
Head of Research					Kee-Young Lee *General Manager* ☏ **769 3049**

International Equities
Head of Sales						Hong-Nam Kim *Manager* ☏ **769 2181**

Settlement / Clearing
Country Head						Dong-Gook Kim *Head of Settlements* ☏ **769 2165**
Operations						Han Kim *Head of Operations*

Administration
Compliance
								Young-Chung Yang *Head, Compliance*

Euromoney Directory 1999 **911**

KOREA, SOUTH (+82)　　　www.euromoneydirectory.com

The Daiwa Bank Limited
Full Branch Office

8th Floor, Shinhan Bank Building 120, 2-ka, Taepyung-ro, Chung-ku, Seoul 100-102
PO Box 8594, Seoul 100-102
Tel: (2) 752 0831 Fax: (2) 756 2830 Telex: K27114

Senior Executive Officers
Managing Director / General Manager　　　Shinichi Inoue
Deputy General Manager　　　Toshiaki Yamada
Company Secretary　　　Young Hee Park

Deutsche Bank
Full Branch Office

7th Floor, Sei An Building, 116 Shinmoonro 1-ka, Chongro-ku, Seoul 110-061
PO Box 512, Seoul 110-605
Tel: (2) 724 4590 Fax: (2) 736 3872 Telex: K 26353 DBASL Swift: DEUT KR SE
Corporate Banking Fax: 736 3871; Credit Fax: 736 3871; Dealing Room Tel: 734 3501; Financial Institutions Fax: 736 3871; International Trade Finance/Controllers Fax: 736 3870; Management Fax: 736 3871; Operations Fax: 736 3871; Securities & Custody Services Fax: 736 3872; Treasury/FX Settlement Fax: 736 3872
Website: www.deutsche-bank.de

Senior Executive Officers
Managing Director / General Manager　　　Axel-Peter C Ohse

Deutsche Morgan Grenfell Capital Markets (Asia) Limited

Sei An Building, 7th Floor, 116 Shinmoonro 1-ka, Chongro-ku, Seoul 110-700
Tel: (2) 724 4650 Fax: (2) 736 6701/3

Deutsche Morgan Grenfell Capital Markets Limited
Representative Office

7th Floor, Sei An Building, 116 Shinmoonro-1, ka, Chongro-ku, Seoul 110-061
Tel: (2) 724 4650 Fax: (2) 736 6701

The Development Bank of Singapore Limited
Full Branch Office

20th Floor, Kwanghwamoon Building, 64-8 Taepyungro 1-ka, Chung-ku, Seoul
Tel: (2) 399 2660; (2) 399 2661 Fax: (2) 732 7953 Telex: K22764 DBSEOUL Swift: DBSSKRSE

Senior Executive Officers
General Manager　　　Yin Chong Boey ☏ 399 2663

DG BANK
Representative Office

Suite 400-5, Leema Building, #146-1 Susong-Dong, Chongro-ku, Seoul 110-140
Tel: (2) 736 4877 Fax: (2) 736 4878

Senior Executive Officers
Representative　　　Semin Lee

Dresdner Bank AG
Representative Office

KorAm Building, 12th Floor, 39 Da-Dong, Chung-ku, Seoul 100-180
PO Box 4466, Seoul 100-644
Tel: (2) 311 3490; (2) 311 3492 Fax: (2) 756 8919

Senior Executive Officers
Chief Representative　　　Johannes von Ballestrem ✉ johannes.ballestrem@dresdner-bank.com

The Fuji Bank Limited
Full Branch Office

15th Floor, Doosan Building 101-1, Uljiro-1ka, Choong-ku, Seoul 100-191
Tel: (2) 311 2000; (2) 311 2171 Fax: (2) 754 8177; (2) 779 1052 Telex: K27216 Swift: FUJI KR SE Reuters: FJSH

912　Euromoney Directory 1999

www.euromoneydirectory.com KOREA, SOUTH (+82)

Debt Capital Markets / Fixed Income
Country Head Hiroshi Akino *Manager* ☎ **311 2180**
Syndicated Lending
Country Head Soo Hyun Kim *Manager* ☎ **311 2166**
Money Markets
Country Head Chang Sub Ahn *Manager* ☎ **311 2130**
Foreign Exchange
Country Head Young Keun Lee *Manager* ☎ **311 2150**
Risk Management
Country Head Tatsuyuki Mitsuda *Manager* ☎ **311 2140**
Corporate Finance / M&A Advisory
Country Head Junji Sakurai *Manager* ☎ **311 2164**

Housing & Commercial Bank   Head Office

Formerly known as: Korea Housing Bank
36-3, Yoido-dong, Youngdeungpo-gu, Seoul 150-758
Tel: (2) 769 8358; (2) 769 8373 **Fax:** (2) 784 8324; (2) 769 8350 **Telex:** K27879 **Swift:** KHBA KR SE
Email: corres@hcb.co.kr **Reuters:** KHBH
Website: www.hcb.co.kr

Senior Executive Officers
Chairman, President & CEO Jungtae Kim ☎ **769 7052**
International Division Wook Hur *GM, International Banking Division* ☎ **769 8373**
Debt Capital Markets / Fixed Income
Head of Debt Capital Markets Hyungjae Park *Senior Deputy Manager* ☎ **769 8356**
Equity Capital Markets
Head of Equity Capital Markets Hyungjae Park *Senior Deputy Manager* ☎ **769 8356**
Syndicated Lending
Loan-Related Activities
Trade Finance Bonjune Koo ☎ **769 8251**
Money Markets
Head of Money Markets Choongwon Cho *Senior Deputy General Manager* ☎ **769 8353**
Foreign Exchange
Head of Foreign Exchange Choongwon Cho *Senior Deputy General Manager* ☎ **769 8353**

HSBC Forfaiting Asia Seoul   Representative Office

Formerly known as: HSBC Investment Banking Seoul
6th Floor, Kyobo Building, 1, Jongro-1ka, Chongro-ku, Seoul 110-714
PO Box 942, Seoul 110-714
Tel: (2) 723 1446; (2) 723 1447 **Fax:** (2) 723 1448; (2) 723 1008 **Telex:** K22022 HSBCSEL

Senior Executive Officers
Associate Director Jung Chul Lee ☎ **3700 9690**

HypoVereinsbank   Representative Office

15th Floor, Daekyung Building, 120 2-ga, Taepyung-ro, Chung-gu, Seoul
Tel: (2) 318 3330 **Fax:** (2) 318 3078

Hyundai International Merchant Bank   Head Office

Hyundai Building, 77 Mugyo-Dong, Chung-gu, Seoul 100-170
Tel: (2) 259 9114; (2) 755 1625 **Fax:** (2) 259 9005; (2) 259 9216 **Telex:** K24335 HIMBANK **Swift:** HIMB KR SE
Reuters: HIMI
Hyundai International Merchant Bank Tel: (2) 755 4200; **Fax:** (2) 755 1378; **Telex:** K34314 HIMBANK
Website: www.himb.co.kr

Senior Executive Officers
Chairman M I Chung ☎ **259 9101**
President J J Suh ☎ **259 9103**

KOREA, SOUTH (+82)

www.euromoneydirectory.com

Hyundai International Merchant Bank (cont)

Others (Senior Executives)
Executive Director	B O Choi ☏ 259 9170
Associate Director	A S Kwon ☏ 259 9201
	C S Moon ☏ 259 9470
International Finance Division	K N Kim *General Manager* ☏ 259 9262
Capital Market Division	S J Lee *General Manager* ☏ 259 9450
Personnel & GA Team	M G Song *General Manager* ☏ 259 9120
Information System Division	J R Soh *General Manager* ☏ 259 9011
Credit Analysis	H O Kim *General Manager* ☏ 259 9061
Corporate Finance Division I	D D Cho *General Manager* ☏ 259 9300
Corporate Finance Division II	K R Kim *Assistant General Manager* ☏ 259 8461
Leasing Division	T K Yoon *Assistant General Manager* ☏ 259 9402
Business Division	N K Kwak *Assistant General Manager* ☏ 259 9351
Planning & IR Division	Hyun S Kim *Assistant General Manager* ☏ 259 9171
Securities Dealing Team	D N Lee *Assistant Manager* ☏ 259 9471

Debt Capital Markets / Fixed Income
Department: International Finance Division, Corporate Finance Division
Tel: 319 5045 **Fax:** 259 9005

Global Head	K N Kim *General Manager* ☏ 259 9262
Country Head	S J Lee *General Manager* ☏ 259 9450

Domestic Government Bonds
Head of Sales; Head of Trading	S J Lee *General Manager* ☏ 259 9450
Head of Research	J G Song *Manager* ☏ 259 9451

Non-Domestic Government Bonds
	D Y Jung *Assistant General Manager* ☏ 259 9202

Eurobonds
Head of Origination; Head of Syndication; Head of Sales; Head of Trading	D Y Jung *Assistant General Manager* ☏ 259 9202
Head of Research; Trading - Sovereigns, Corporates, High-yield	S H Lee *Assistant Manager* ☏ 259 9254

Libor-Based / Floating-Rate Products
FRN Origination; FRN Sales; FRN Trading	S H Lee *Assistant Manager* ☏ 259 9254
Asset Swaps; Asset Swaps (Sales)	S B Shim *Manager* ☏ 259 9252

Medium-Term Notes
Head of Origination; Head of Structuring; Head of Sales	S B Shim *Manager* ☏ 259 9252

Equity Capital Markets
Department: Securities Dealing Team, Capital Market Division
Tel: 318 6658 **Fax:** 259 9004

Country Head	S J Lee *General Manager* ☏ 259 9450

Domestic Equities
Head of Origination; Head of Syndication; Head of Sales	S J Lee *General Manager* ☏ 259 9450
Head of Trading; Head of Research	D N Lee *Assistant Manager* ☏ 259 9471

Convertibles / Equity-Linked
Head of Origination; Head of Syndication; Head of Sales; Head of Trading; Head of Research	S J Lee *General Manager* ☏ 259 9450

Syndicated Lending
Department: International Investment Division
Tel: 318 5045 **Fax:** 259 9005

Global Head	D Y Jung *Assistant General Manager* ☏ 259 9202
Head of Origination; Head of Syndication; Head of Trading; Recovery	S B Sim *Manager* ☏ 259 9252

Loan-Related Activities
Trade Finance; Project Finance; Structured Trade Finance	S B Sim *Manager* ☏ 259 9252
Leasing & Asset Finance	T K Yoon *Assistant General Manager* ☏ 259 9402

Money Markets
Department: International Finance Division, Corporate Finance Division
Tel: 319 5045 **Fax:** 259 9005

Global Head	A S Kwon ☏ 259 9201
Country Head	D D Cho *General Manager* ☏ 259 9300

Domestic Commercial Paper
Head of Origination; Head of Sales; Head of Trading	Bonik Koo *Assistant General Manager* ☏ 259 9301

KOREA, SOUTH (+82)

Eurocommercial Paper
Head of Origination; Head of Sales; Head of Trading   S H Lee *Assistant Manager* ☎ 259 9254

Wholesale Deposits
Marketing   H S Chung *Manager* ☎ 259 9302
Head of Sales   Y T Park *Assistant Manager* ☎ 259 9463

Foreign Exchange
Department: International Finance Division
Tel: 755 1625 **Fax:** 259 9005
Global Head   A S Kwon ☎ 259 9201
Head of Institutional Sales; Corporate Sales; Head of Trading   H W Kim *Manager* ☎ 259 9203

FX Traders / Sales People
    J C Lee *Assistant Manager* ☎ 259 9209
    Hyun Choi *Assistant Manager* ☎ 259 9206

Risk Management
Department: International Finance Division, International Investment Div
Tel: 755 1625 **Fax:** 259 9005
Global Head   A S Kwon ☎ 259 9201

Fixed Income Derivatives / Risk Management
Global Head; Trading; IR Swaps Sales / Marketing; IR Swaps Trading; IR Options Sales / Marketing; IR Options Trading   S B Shim *Manager* ☎ 259 9252

Foreign Exchange Derivatives / Risk Management
Cross-Currency Swaps, Sales / Marketing; Cross-Currency Swaps, Trading; Vanilla FX option Sales; Vanilla FX option Trading   Hyun Choi *Assistant Manager* ☎ 259 9206

Exotic Options (Barriers, Range, Timers, Digitals, Faders etc)
Sales; Trading   Hyun Choi *Assistant Manager* ☎ 259 9206

Corporate Finance / M&A Advisory
Department: International Finance Division, Corporate Finance Division
Tel: 319 5045 **Fax:** 259 9005
Head of Corporate Finance   A S Kwon ☎ 259 9201
Country Head   D D Cho *General Manager* ☎ 259 9300

Other (Corporate Finance)
Corporate Finance Division II   K R Kim *Assistant General Manager* ☎ 259 9461

Settlement / Clearing
Department: International Finance Division
Tel: 755 1625 **Fax:** 259 9005
Country Head   A S Kwon ☎ 259 9201
Equity Settlement; Fixed-Income Settlement; Derivatives Settlement; Foreign Exchange Settlement; Operations   D N Lee *Assistant Manager* ☎ 259 9471

Global Custody
Department: International Investment Division
Tel: 319 5045 **Fax:** 259 9005
Regional Head; Fund Administration   S H Lee *Assistant Manager* ☎ 259 9254

Administration

Technology & Systems
    J R Soh *General Manager* ☎ 259 9011

Public Relations
    Hyun S Kim *Assistant General Manager* ☎ 259 9171

Accounts / Audit
Auditor   D J Suh ☎ 259 9400

The Industrial Bank of Japan Limited   Representative Office

10th Floor, Press Center Building, 25 Taepyung-Ro 1-ga, Chung-ku, Seoul 100-101
Tel: (2) 736 2684; (2) 736 2685 **Fax:** (2) 736 2686

Senior Executive Officers
Chief Representative   T Yoshida

KOREA, SOUTH (+82)   www.euromoneydirectory.com

Industrial Bank of Korea
Head Office

Formerly known as: Small and Medium Industry Bank
Alternative trading name: IBK
50, Ulchiro 2-ga, Chung-gu, Seoul 100-758
Tel: (2) 729 7076; (2) 729 7956 **Fax:** (2) 729 7095; (2) 729 7003 **Telex:** K26108 **Swift:** IBKO KR SE **Reuters:** IBKH
Website: www.ibk.co.kr

Senior Executive Officers
Chairman of the Board & President	Kyung-Jae Lee T 729 6211 F 729 6260
Financial Director	Chul-Soo Han *Director & Deputy President* T 729 6217 F 729 6260
Treasurer	Yong Kang *Director & Executive Vice President* T 729 6229 F 729 6260
Director & Executive Vice President	Il-Cheak Park T 729 6219 F 729 6260
International Division	Kyung-Jun Lee *GM, International Banking Division* T 729 7060 F 729 7904

Debt Capital Markets / Fixed Income
Head of Debt Capital Markets   Jin-Soo Son *DGM, International Banking Department* T 729 7949

Emerging Market Bonds
Head of Emerging Markets   Jin-Soo Son *DGM, International Banking Department* T 729 7949

Fixed-Income Repo
Head of Repo   Hyung-Gu Jeon *DGM, International Banking Department* T 729 7930

Equity Capital Markets
Head of Equity Capital Markets   Jin-Soo Son *DGM, International Banking Department* T 729 7949

Equity Repo / Securities Lending
Head   Jin-Soo Son *DGM, International Banking Department* T 729 7949

Syndicated Lending
Head of Origination; Head of Syndication   Choong-Won Lee *DGM, International Banking Department* T 729 7090

Loan-Related Activities
Project Finance   Young-Chin Kim *GM, Foreign Operations Department* T 729 7210
F 729 7204

Money Markets
Country Head   In-Soo Lee *DGM, International Banking Department* T 729 7062 F 729 7944

Foreign Exchange
Head of Foreign Exchange   In-Soo Lee *DGM, International Banking Department* T 729 7062 F 729 7944

Settlement / Clearing
Head of Settlement / Clearing   Kyo-Sung Kim *DGM, International Banking Department* T 729 7058
F 729 7943

Global Custody
Head of Global Custody   Jin-Soo Son *DGM, International Banking Department* T 729 7949

Other Departments
Correspondent Banking   Hyung-Gu Jeon *DGM, International Banking Department* T 729 7930

Administration
Head of Administration   Sung-Tae Jo *General Manager* T 729 7410

Technology & Systems
Informations Systems Department   Nam-Ryul Yoon *General Manager* T 729 6150 F 729 6695

Public Relations
    Jae-Kyung Kim *General Manager* T 729 6350 F 729 6375

Accounts / Audit
Audit   Young-Ho Bae *Auditor* T 729 6231 F 729 6260

ING Baring Securities
Full Branch Office

Alternative trading name: Baring Brothers
14th Floor, Samdo Building, 1-170 Soonhwa-dong, Chung-ku, Seoul 100-130
Tel: (2) 317 1500 **Fax:** (2) 317 1600 **Email:** kyung.hu.yoon@ing-barings.com

Senior Executive Officers
Country Manager   Kyung Hee Yoon

Equity Capital Markets

Equity Research
Country Head   Kyung Hee Yoon *Manager*

www.euromoneydirectory.com   KOREA, SOUTH (+82)

ING Baring Securities (Korea)
Subsidiary Company

Alternative trading name: Baring Brothers
14th Floor, Samdo Building, 1-170 Soonhwa-dong, Chung-ku, Seoul 100-130
Tel: (2) 317 1500 **Fax:** (2) 317 1600

Senior Executive Officers
Country Manager — Kyung Yoon Yoon

ING Barings
Full Branch Office

7th Floor, Kwanghwamun Building, 211 Sejong Ro, Chung-ku, Seoul 110-050
PO Box 81, Seoul 110-600
Tel: (2) 399 3250; (2) 399 3254 **Fax:** (2) 399 3313 **Telex:** 22073 INGB K **Swift:** INGB KR SE

Senior Executive Officers
Country Manager — Kyung Hee Yoon

Others (Senior Executives)
G H Nam *Assistant General Manager*
Won Lak Choi *Manager*

Jardine Fleming Securities Limited
Head Office

10th Floor Hanwha Building, 111-5 Sokong-dong, Chung-ku, Seoul 110-070
Tel: (2) 3706 4700 **Fax:** (2) 779 0553

Senior Executive Officers
Branch Manager — Edward Campbell-Harris ☎ **3706 4701**

Others (Senior Executives)
Research — Stephen Marvin *Head* ☎ **3706 4710**
Broking — Toby S H Cha *Head* ☎ **3706 4800**

General-Investment
Head of Investment — Y B Chang *Head, Investment Banking* ☎ **3706 4770**

The Kangwon Bank Limited
Head Office

140-2 Gye-dong, Chongro-gu, Seoul 110-270
Tel: (2) 746 4461; (2) 746 4448 **Fax:** (2) 746 4410; (2) 746 4404 **Telex:** K24556 **Swift:** KWBA KR SE **Reuters:** KWBH
Telex: K29322

Senior Executive Officers
Chairman — Jong-Moon Choi ☎ **240 3311**
Standing Auditor — Bong-Kyun Hahn ☎ **240 3308**
Chief Executive Officer — Soo-Hyo Lee *Director & Executive Vice President* ☎ **240 3308**
Financial Director — Jun-Ho Ham *Director & Executive Vice President* ☎ **240 3308**

Debt Capital Markets / Fixed Income
Department: International Department
Tel: 746 4474 **Fax:** 746 4410
Global Head — Sung-Hak Youn *General Manager* ☎ **746 4444**

Libor-Based / Floating-Rate Products
FRN Origination — Hung-Soo Lee *Deputy General Manager* ☎ **746 4447**

Medium-Term Notes
Head of Origination — Hung-Soo Lee *Deputy General Manager* ☎ **746 4447**

Asset-Backed Securities / Securitization
Global Head — Hung-Soo Lee *Deputy General Manager* ☎ **746 4447**

Fixed-Income Repo
Head of Repo — Hung-Soo Lee *Deputy General Manager* ☎ **746 4447**

Equity Capital Markets
Department: Funds Operations Department
Global Head — Kyung-Jun Whang *General Manager* ☎ **240 3350**

International Equities
Head of Origination — Sung-Hak Youn *General Manager* ☎ **746 4444**

Foreign Exchange
Department: International Department
Global Head — Sung-Hak Youn *General Manager* ☎ **746 4444**
Head of Trading — Sung-Chon Hahn *Manager* ☎ **746 4471**

KOREA, SOUTH (+82)   www.euromoneydirectory.com

The Kangwon Bank Limited (cont)

FX Traders / Sales People
Sung-Yong Choi *Dealer* ☏ **746 8078**
In-Sun Kang *Dealer* ☏ **746 4459**

Risk Management
Global Head — Sung-Hak Youn *General Manager* ☏ **746 4444**
Regional Head — Sung-Roik Hong *Deputy General Manager* ☏ **746 4448**

Fixed Income Derivatives / Risk Management
Global Head — Sung-Hak Youn *General Manager* ☏ **746 4444**
IR Swaps Sales / Marketing; IR Swaps Trading; — Hung-Soo Lee *Deputy General Manager* ☏ **746 4447**
IR Options Sales / Marketing; IR Options Trading

Foreign Exchange Derivatives / Risk Management
Cross-Currency Swaps, Sales / Marketing; — Sung-Chon Hahn *Manager* ☏ **746 4471**
Cross-Currency Swaps, Trading; Vanilla FX option Sales; Vanilla FX option Trading

Exchange-Traded Derivatives
Global Head — Sung-Chon Hahn *Manager* ☏ **746 4471**

Settlement / Clearing
Department: International Department
Country Head — Sang-Gil Jung *Assistant Manager* ☏ **746 4464**

Administration
Technology & Systems
Sung-Roik Hong *Deputy General Manager* ☏ **746 4448**

Kookmin Bank

9-1, 2-ka, Namdaemoon-ro, Choong-ku, Seoul 100-203
PO Box 815, Seoul
Tel: (2) 317 2460 **Fax:** (2) 257 3679 **Telex:** K23481 **Swift:** CZNB KR SE **Telex:** K26109
Website: www.kookmin-bank.com

Senior Executive Officers
Chairman, President & CEO — Dal-Ho Song
General Manager — Duk-Hyun Kim

Debt Capital Markets / Fixed Income
Department: International Finance Department
Tel: 317 6169 **Fax:** 317 2246
Global Head — Chang-Hwan Kim *General Manager* ☏ **317 2047**

Eurobonds
Head of Trading — Heung-Kee Baek *Manager* ☏ **317 2908**

Libor-Based / Floating-Rate Products
FRN Origination — Hong Lee *Manager* ☏ **728 6127**

Medium-Term Notes
Head of Origination — Hong Lee *Manager* ☏ **728 6127**

Private Placements
Head of Origination — Hong Lee *Manager* ☏ **728 6127**

Asset-Backed Securities / Securitization
Head of Trading — Hwang-Soo Song *Deputy General Manager* ☏ **317 2162**

Fixed-Income Repo
Head of Repo — Hwang-Soo Song *Deputy General Manager* ☏ **317 2162**

Equity Capital Markets
Convertibles / Equity-Linked
Head of Trading — Heung-Kee Baek *Manager* ☏ **317 2908**

Syndicated Lending
Department: International Finance Department
Tel: 728 6127 **Fax:** 728 6079
Global Head — Chang-Hwan Kim *General Manager* ☏ **317 2047**
Head of Origination — Hwang-Soo Song *Deputy General Manager* ☏ **317 2162**

Money Markets
Department: International Finance Department
Tel: 728 6177 **Fax:** 319 2884
Global Head — Chang-Hwan Kim *General Manager* ☏ **317 2047**

KOREA, SOUTH (+82)

Eurocommercial Paper
Head of Origination — Jae-Kyun Choi *Manager* ☏ **728 6177**
Head of Trading — Heung-Kee Baek *Manager* ☏ **317 2908**

Foreign Exchange
Department: International Finance Department
Tel: 317 2505 **Fax**: 317 2884
Global Head — Chang-Hwan Kim *General Manager* ☏ **317 2047**
Head of Trading — Chang-Hoon Jung *Deputy General Manager* ☏ **317 2085**
FX Traders / Sales People
FX Dealer — Chang-Young Lee *Assistant Manager* ☏ **728 6119**
Young-Song Chung *Senior Clerk* ☏ **317 2505**

Risk Management
Department: International Finance Department
Tel: 728 6325 **Fax**: 773 2363
Global Head — Byung-Keun Lee *Deputy General Manager* ☏ **317 2548**
Fixed Income Derivatives / Risk Management
IR Swaps Trading — Heung-Kee Baek *Manager* ☏ **317 2908**
Foreign Exchange Derivatives / Risk Management
Cross-Currency Swaps, Sales / Marketing — Kwang-Keun Yoo *Manager* ☏ **728 6375**
Cross-Currency Swaps, Trading — Jai-Un Shim *Deputy General Manager* ☏ **728 6499**
Vanilla FX option Sales — Seung-Sik Lee *Manager* ☏ **317 2778**
Vanilla FX option Trading — Kwang-Keun Yoo *Manager* ☏ **728 6375**
Exotic Options (Barriers, Range, Timers, Digitals, Faders etc)
Sales — Seung-Sik Lee *Manager* ☏ **317 2778**
Trading — Kwang-Keun Yoo *Manager* ☏ **728 6375**

Settlement / Clearing
Fixed-Income Settlement — Hun-Chul Lee *Assistant Manager* ☏ **728 6169**

Other Departments
Correspondent Banking — Ki-Youl Suh *Deputy General Manager* ☏ **317 2094**

KorAm Bank
Head Office

39, Da-dong, Chung-gu, Seoul 100-639
PO Box 1084, Seoul
Tel: (2) 3455 2114 **Telex**: K27814 **Swift**: KOAM KR SE

Senior Executive Officers
Chairman — Jin Man Kim ☏ **3455 2001**
Vice Chairman — Zareh M Misserlian ☏ **3455 2003**

Debt Capital Markets / Fixed Income
Department: International Banking Department
Tel: 3455 2537 **Fax**: 3455 2966
Domestic Government Bonds
Head of Sales — Hwan Min Park ☏ **3455 2537**
Eurobonds
Head of Origination; Head of Syndication — Myung Rul Song ☏ **3455 2533**
Head of Trading — Hwan Min Park ☏ **3455 2537**
Libor-Based / Floating-Rate Products
FRN Origination; FRN Sales — Myung Rul Song ☏ **3455 2533**
Asset Swaps; Asset Swaps (Sales) — Hwan Min Park ☏ **3455 2537**
Fixed-Income Repo
Head of Repo — Hwan Min Park ☏ **3455 2537**

Syndicated Lending
Department: International Banking Department
Fax: 3455 2966
Global Head — Myung Rul Song ☏ **3455 2533**

Loan-Related Activities
Trade Finance — Sang Eun Lee ☏ **3455 2541**
Project Finance — Kun Ho Jung ☏ **3455 2564**
Structured Trade Finance; Leasing & Asset Finance — Jae Beom Kim ☏ **3455 2547**

Money Markets
Department: International Banking Department
Tel: 3455 2550 **Fax**: 3455 2976
Global Head — Kyung Mo Park ☏ **3455 2570**
Domestic Commercial Paper
Head of Origination — Hwan Min Park ☏ **3455 2537**

KOREA, SOUTH (+82) www.euromoneydirectory.com

KorAm Bank (cont)

Eurocommercial Paper
Head of Origination   Hwan Min Park ☏ 3455 2537
Foreign Exchange
Department: International Banking Department
Fax: 3455 2976
Global Head   Jae Yi Kim ☏ 3455 2550
Corporate Finance / M&A Advisory
Department: International Banking Department
Fax: 3455 2966
Global Head   Jung Hee Kim ☏ 3455 2530
Settlement / Clearing
Department: Foreign Exchange Operations Team
Tel: 3455 2580 Fax: 3455 2967
Regional Head   Young Chang Kwak ☏ 3445 2580
Other Departments
Correspondent Banking   Dong Hwun Song ☏ 3455 2534
Administration
Technology & Systems
                                                      Ho Geun Min ☏ 731 8710

The Korea Development Bank
10-2 Kwanchol-dong, Chongno-gu, Seoul 110-11
Tel: (2) 398 6114 Fax: (2) 733 4722 Telex: 33147/33155

Korea Exchange Bank   Head Office
181, 2-Ga, Eulji-ro, Chung-gu, Seoul 100-793
Tel: (2) 729 8000 Telex: 23141 Swift: KOEX KR SE Email: chan@koexbank.co.kr Reuters: KEBPTW1
Telerate: 711000801 Bloomberg: KEBITRD
Website: www.koexbank.co.kr

Senior Executive Officers
Chairman of the Board & President   Se Pyo Hong ☏ 729 0055 F 775 9811
Treasurer   Young Rae Kim General Manager ☏ 729 0351 F 771 2414
General Manager   Un chul Bek ☏ 729 0041 F 775 9811
International Division   Do Jae Cho General Manager ☏ 729 8911 F 754 9817
Others (Senior Executives)
Head of Emerging Markets   Yoon Soo Kim General Manager ☏ 729 0531 F 775 9813
General-Lending (DCM, SL)
Head of Corporate Banking   Bog Gyu Ahn General Manager ☏ 729 0261 F 771 9216
General-Investment
Head of Investment   Yoon Soo Kim General Manager ☏ 729 0531 F 775 9813
Debt Capital Markets / Fixed Income
Head of Fixed Income   Chun Ryang Chung General Manager ☏ 729 0471 F 771 9355
Fixed-Income Repo
Head of Repo   Chun Ryang Chung General Manager ☏ 729 0471 F 771 9355
Equity Capital Markets
Head of Equity Capital Markets   Yoon Soo Kim General Manager ☏ 729 0531 F 775 9813
Equity Repo / Securities Lending
Head   Chun Ryang Chung General Manager ☏ 729 0471 F 771 9355
Syndicated Lending
Head of Origination; Head of Syndication   Mak Jung Hwang General Manager ☏ 729 8191 F 771 2897
Loan-Related Activities
Trade Finance   Do Jae Cho General Manager ☏ 729 8911 F 754 9817
Project Finance   Yoon Soo Kim General Manager ☏ 729 0531 F 775 9813
Money Markets
Head of Money Markets   Young Rae Kim General Manager ☏ 729 0351 F 771 2414
Foreign Exchange
Head of Foreign Exchange   Chun Ryang Chung General Manager ☏ 729 0471 F 771 9355
Corporate Finance / M&A Advisory
Head of Corporate Finance   Kyung Song General Manager ☏ 729 0261 F 771 9216

www.euromoneydirectory.com　　　　　　KOREA, SOUTH (+82)

Settlement / Clearing
Head of Settlement / Clearing
　　Chun Ryang Chung *General Manager* ☎ 729 0471 ℻ 771 9355

Global Custody
Head of Global Custody
　　Yoon Soo Kim *General Manager* ☎ 729 0531 ℻ 775 9813

Asset Management
Head
　　Byung-Koo Chang *General Manager* ☎ 729 0071 ℻ 775 9812

Other Departments
Commodities / Bullion　　Sang Q Lee *General Manager* ☎ 729 0191 ℻ 771 9242
Private Banking　　Kwan Byung Chai *General Manager* ☎ 729 0131 ℻ 776 2046
Correspondent Banking　　Do Jae Cho *General Manager* ☎ 729 8911 ℻ 754 9817
Global Trust　　Kyung Song *General Manager* ☎ 729 0261 ℻ 771 9216
Cash Management　　Young Rae Kim *General Manager* ☎ 729 0351 ℻ 771 2414

Administration
Head of Administration　　Woo Jin Kwon *General Manager*
Business Development; Head of Marketing　　Sang Q Lee *General Manager* ☎ 729 0191 ℻ 771 9242

Technology & Systems
　　Hyung-Hyun Cho *General Manager* ☎ 729 0661 ℻ 771 9214

Legal / In-House Counsel
　　Seung-Il Kim *General Manager* ☎ 3705 5454 ℻ 3705 5460

Compliance
　　Won-Tai Soh *General Manager* ☎ 729 8131 ℻ 774 8705

Public Relations
　　Koo Soon Jung *General Manager* ☎ 729 0161 ℻ 754 9080

Accounts / Audit
　　Byung-Koo Chang *General Manager* ☎ 729 0071 ℻ 775 9812

Korea First Bank　　　　　　　　　　　　　　　　　　Head Office

100 Kongpyung-Dong, Chongro-ku, Seoul 110-702
PO Box 2242, Seoul 110-702
Tel: (2) 3702 3114; (2) 3702 3838 **Fax:** (2) 3702 4941; (2) 3702 4942 **Telex:** K23685 FIRSTBK **Swift:** KOFB KR SE
Email: kfbk@soback.kornet.nm.kr **Reuters:** KFBH **Cable:** FIRSTBANK SEOUL

Senior Executive Officers
Chairman & President　　Shee Yul Ryoo ☎ 3702 3100
Senior MD & Deputy President　　Kyu Shin Yoon ☎ 3702 3110
Financial Director　　Kwang Woo Chong *Managing Director & EVP* ☎ 3702 3131
Chief Operating Officer　　Kya Shin Yoon ☎ 3702 3110
Company Secretary　　Chang Hwan Cho ☎ 3702 3202
International Division　　Kwang Woo Chong *Managing Director & EVP* ☎ 3702 3131

General-Lending (DCM, SL)
Head of Corporate Banking　　Kwang Woo Chong *Managing Director & EVP* ☎ 3702 3131

General-Investment
Head of Investment　　Kwang Woo Chong *Managing Director & EVP* ☎ 3702 3131

Debt Capital Markets / Fixed Income
Head of Fixed Income　　Kwang Woo Chong *Managing Director & EVP* ☎ 3702 3131

Emerging Market Bonds
Head of Emerging Markets　　Kwang Woo Chong *Managing Director & EVP* ☎ 3702 3131

Fixed-Income Repo
Head of Repo　　Kwang Woo Chong *Managing Director & EVP* ☎ 3702 3131

Equity Capital Markets
Head of Equity Capital Markets　　Jai Heung Shim ☎ 3702 3123

Equity Repo / Securities Lending
Head　　Jai Heung Shim ☎ 3702 3123

Syndicated Lending
Head of Origination　　Ho Keun Lee *Managing Director & EVP* ☎ 3702 3120
Head of Syndication　　Kwang Woo Chong *Managing Director & EVP* ☎ 3702 3131

Loan-Related Activities
Trade Finance　　Kwang Woo Chong *Managing Director & EVP* ☎ 3702 3131
Project Finance　　Kwang Woo Chong *Managing Director & EVP* ☎ 3702 3131

Money Markets
Head of Money Markets　　Kwang Woo Chong *Managing Director & EVP* ☎ 3702 3131

Foreign Exchange
Head of Foreign Exchange　　Kwang Woo Chong *Managing Director & EVP* ☎ 3702 3131

Korea First Bank (cont)

Corporate Finance / M&A Advisory
Head of Corporate Finance — Kwang Woo Chong *Managing Director & EVP* ☏ 3702 3131

Settlement / Clearing
Head of Settlement / Clearing — Kwang Woo Chong *Managing Director & EVP* ☏ 3702 3131

Global Custody
Head of Global Custody — Kwang Woo Chong *Managing Director & EVP* ☏ 3702 3131

Asset Management
Head — Kwang Woo Chong *Managing Director & EVP* ☏ 3702 3131

Other Departments
Commodities / Bullion — Lark Won Kahng *Managing Director & EVP* ☏ 3702 3118
Chief Credit Officer — Ho Keun Lee *Managing Director & EVP* ☏ 3702 3120
Private Banking — Kwang Woo Chong *Managing Director & EVP* ☏ 3702 3131
Correspondent Banking — Kwang Woo Chong *Managing Director & EVP* ☏ 3702 3131
Cash Management — Lark Won Kahng *Managing Director & EVP* ☏ 3702 3118

Administration
Head of Administration — Kyu Shin Yoon *Senior MD & Deputy President* ☏ 3702 3110
Business Development
Head of Marketing — Lark Won Kahng *Managing Director & EVP* ☏ 3702 3118
Jai Heung Shim ☏ 3702 3123

Technology & Systems
Myung Ahm Cho *Managing Director & EVP* ☏ 3702 3122

Legal / In-House Counsel
Jun Keun Lee ☏ 3702 3128

Public Relations
Lark Won Kahng *Managing Director & EVP* ☏ 3702 3118

Korea First Bank Securities Co Limited — Head Office

Alternative trading name: KFB Securities Co Limited
198 Euljiro 2-Ka, Chung-ku, Seoul 100-192
Tel: (2) 771 0900; (2) 777 8497 **Fax:** (2) 778 4659 **Telex:** K33158K FBFC

Senior Executive Officers
President & Chief Executive Officer — Sae-Sun Lee
Treasurer — Juny-Goo Kong *Standing Auditor*
Executive Managing Director — Pyung-Yeal Ryou

Debt Capital Markets / Fixed Income
Global Head — In-Sung Moon

Equity Capital Markets
Global Head — Kwon-Il Yong

Money Markets
Global Head — Sung-Bo Shin

Foreign Exchange
Global Head — In-Sung Moon

Risk Management
Global Head — Song Whom Lee

Korea International Merchant Bank — Head Office

Hanway Building 70, Da-dong, Chung-ku, Seoul 100-180
PO Box 5265, Seoul
Tel: (2) 728 6500; (2) 728 6608 **Fax:** (2) 728 6700; (2) 728 6718 **Telex:** K26676 **Swift:** KIMB KR SE
Email: cypark@kimb.co.kr **Reuters:** KIMH **Cable:** hanway **Telex:** K26370
Website: www.kimb.co.kr

Senior Executive Officers
President — Jim-Bohm Kim ☏ 728 6511 F 728 6707
Treasurer — Myung-Jae Lee *Deputy General Manager* F 728 6716
Managing Director — Joo-Sun Yeom ☏ 728 6519 F 728 6707
Deputy General Manager — Soon-Ki Kwon ☏ 728 6643 F 728 6703
International Division — Han-Ki Chang *Managing Director* ☏ 728 6606 F 728 6707

General-Investment
Head of Investment — Boo-Shik Hong *Director* ☏ 728 6551 F 728 6701

Equity Capital Markets
Head of Equity Capital Markets — Suk-Sun Hong *General Manager* ☏ 728 6566 F 728 6701

www.euromoneydirectory.com   KOREA, SOUTH (+82)

Syndicated Lending
Head of Syndication   Yoon-Gil Ahn *Deputy General Manager* ☏ **728 6623**
Money Markets
Head of Money Markets   Kang-Kon Lee *Manager* ☏ **728 6612** F **728 6716**
Foreign Exchange
Head of Foreign Exchange   Chul-Yong Park *Manager* ☏ **728 6612** F **728 6716**
Other Departments
Cash Management   Sang-Won Lee *Director* ☏ **728 6531** F **728 6712**
Administration
Head of Administration   Hee-Wan Kang *Managing Director* ☏ **728 6655**
Public Relations
    Duk-Yoon Kim *Manager* ☏ **728 6645** F **728 6703**
Accounts / Audit
    Yoon-Soo Kang *Manager* ☏ **728 6645** F **728 6703**

Korea Long-Term Credit Bank

15-22 Yoido-dong, Yongdeungpo-ku, Seoul 150-759
Tel: (2) 3779 8611; (2) 3779 8613 **Fax:** (2) 3779 8628; (2) 3779 8685 **Telex:** K26342 KLBANK **Reuters:** KLBH
Website: www.klbank.co.kr

Senior Executive Officers
President & Chief Executive Officer   Sei Jong Oh ☏ **728 0089**
General Manager   Dong Hwan Moon ☏ **3779 8610**
Debt Capital Markets / Fixed Income
Department: International Treasury Department
Tel: 3779 8610 **Fax:** 3779 8629
Global Head   Dong Hwan Moon *General Manager* ☏ **3779 8610**
Domestic Government Bonds
Head of Trading; Head of Research   S W Nam *Team Head* ☏ **3779 8119**
Eurobonds
Head of Origination; Head of Syndication   S J Park *Team Head* ☏ **3779 8587**
Trading - Sovereigns, Corporates, High-yield   Min Choi *Team Head* ☏ **3779 8630**
Libor-Based / Floating-Rate Products
FRN Origination   S J Park *Team Head* ☏ **3779 8587**
Asset Swaps   S H Cho *Team Head* ☏ **3779 8954**
Medium-Term Notes
Head of Origination   S J Park *Team Head* ☏ **3779 8587**
Private Placements
Head of Origination   S J Park *Team Head* ☏ **3779 8587**
Asset-Backed Securities / Securitization
Global Head   Min Choi *Team Head* ☏ **3779 8630**
Fixed-Income Repo
Head of Repo   Min Choi *Team Head* ☏ **3779 8630**
Equity Capital Markets
Domestic Equities
Head of Origination   H H Kwon *Team Head* ☏ **3779 8476**
Head of Trading   S H Nam *Team Head* ☏ **3779 8640**
International Equities
Head of Origination; Head of Syndication   H J Bae *Team Head* ☏ **3779 8524**
Head of Trading; Head of Research   Min Choi *Team Head* ☏ **3779 8630**
Convertibles / Equity-Linked
Head of Trading   Min Choi *Team Head* ☏ **3779 8630**
Money Markets
Department: International Treasury Department
Tel: 3779 8610 **Fax:** 3779 8628
Global Head   W H Hong *Money Market Dealer* ☏ **3779 8638**
Domestic Commercial Paper
Head of Origination   W H Hong *Money Market Dealer* ☏ **3779 8638**
Eurocommercial Paper
Head of Origination   W H Hong *Money Market Dealer* ☏ **3779 8638**
Foreign Exchange
Department: International Treasury Department
Tel: 3779 8636 **Fax:** 3779 8628
Global Head   T S Yoon ☏ **3779 8636**

Euromoney Directory 1999   **923**

KOREA, SOUTH (+82) www.euromoneydirectory.com

Korea Long-Term Credit Bank (cont)
Risk Management
Department: Financial Engineering Team
Tel: 3779 8954 Fax: 3779 8649
Global Head   S H Cho *Team Head* ☎ **3779 8954**
Fixed Income Derivatives / Risk Management
Global Head   S H Cho *Team Head* ☎ **3779 8954**
Foreign Exchange Derivatives / Risk Management
Cross-Currency Swaps, Trading   S H Cho *Team Head* ☎ **3779 8954**

Korea Merchant Banking Corporation — Head Office

Daewoo Centre Building 541, 5-ka, Namdaemun-Ro, Chung-ku, Seoul 100-714
PO Box 3869, Seoul
Tel: (2) 3788 0114 Fax: (2) 753 9740 Telex: K28579 KOMBANK Swift: KMBC KR SE Email: webmaster@kmbc.co.kr
Reuters: KMBH Cable: MERCHANTBANK
Website: www.kmbe.co.kr

Senior Executive Officers
Representative Director & President   In Ju Kim
Others (Senior Executives)
Administration Division Head   Soo Kil Lee *Director & Executive Vice President*
                                            Christopher Hodges *Director & Executive Vice President*
Domestic Business Division   Kun Jong Kim *Executive Director*
International Business Division   Kyung Yang Min *Associate Director, FX & Funding Team*
General-Lending (DCM, SL)
Head of Corporate Banking   Choong Hee Lee *Head, Planning & Credit Analysis*
Debt Capital Markets / Fixed Income
Department: Capital Markets
Global Head   Gab Joong Yim *Head, Capital Markets*
Foreign Exchange
Head of Foreign Exchange   Kyung Yang Min *Associate Director, FX & Funding Team*
Corporate Finance / M&A Advisory
Head of Mergers & Acquisition   Daivid Timblick
Administration
Head of Administration   Soo Kil Lee *Director & Executive Vice President*
Business Development   Ig Seong Kang *Associate Director*
Accounts / Audit
Standing Auditor   Chong Koo Han
Other (Administration)
General Affairs   Hyung Jin Yoon *Associate Director*
Head, Kangnam Branch   Kie Yong Chang
Head, Business Team II   Young Mhan Roh

Kumho Merchant Bank — Head Office

11th Floor, Hanway Building, 70 Da-dong, Joong-ku, Seoul 100-180
Tel: (2) 775 2591; (2) 775 0181 Fax: (2) 775 7590; (2) 775 0180 Telex: K35058 KHMBA Swift: KHMB KR SE
Reuters: KHMH
Website: www.kumho.co.kr

Senior Executive Officers
President & Chief Executive Officer   Rok H Yoon ☎ **775 2141**
Financial Director   Byung W Park *Executive Managing Director* ☎ **775 2142**
Chief Operating Officer   Bong H Kim *Executive Director* ☎ **223 5520**
General Manager   Hyun K Lee ☎ **775 2143** ✉ **mblhkl@ksc.kumho.co.kr**
Debt Capital Markets / Fixed Income
Global Head   Yong C Kim *Vice General Manager* ☎ **775 2597**
Equity Capital Markets
Global Head   Dae H Hwang *Vice General Manager* ☎ **775 2591**
Syndicated Lending
Global Head   Yong C Kim *Vice General Manager* ☎ **775 2597**
Money Markets
Global Head   Kyung Y Kim *Vice General Manager* ☎ **775 2144**

www.euromoneydirectory.com　　　　　KOREA, SOUTH (+82)

Foreign Exchange
Global Head — Kyung Y Kim *Vice General Manager* ☎ 775 2144
Risk Management
Global Head — Yong C Kim *Vice General Manager* ☎ 775 2597
Corporate Finance / M&A Advisory
Global Head — Yong C Kim *Vice General Manager* ☎ 775 2597
Settlement / Clearing
Regional Head — Kyung S Kim *Manager* ☎ 775 2594

The Kwangju Bank Limited　　　　　Head Office

43-2, Yoido-dong, Youngdeungpo-gu, Seoul 150-010
Tel: (2) 767 3463; (2) 767 3471 **Fax:** (2) 780 4622; (2) 784 4944 **Telex:** 25853 KANUBKS **Swift:** KWAB KR SE
Reuters: KJUH **Telex:** 29176 KANUBKS

Senior Executive Officers
General Manager — Kim Ok Sam
Deputy General Manager — Kang Dae Chum

General-Investment
Head of Investment — Park Yeon Seo *Assistant Manager, Overseas Investment* ☎ 767 3473

Foreign Exchange
FX Traders / Sales People
FX Chip Dealer — Han Byung Hoon *Assistant Manager* ☎ 767 3471

Other Departments
Correspondent Banking — Heo Yun Nam *Assistant Manager* ☎ 767 3463

Kyongnam Bank　　　　　Head Office

246-1, Sokchon-dong, Hoewon-gu, Masan 630-010, Kyong Sang Nam Do
Tel: (551) 908 000; (551) 908 453 **Fax:** (551) 949 426; (551) 940 369 **Telex:** 53351 **Swift:** KTNA KR 22 **Reuters:** KNBH

Senior Executive Officers
Chairman & President — Lee Choon Yung
Director & Deputy President — Lee Sang Won
International Division — Kim Ha Doo *Director & Executive Vice President*
Hur Moon Young *General Manager* ☎ (2) 3455 1964

Others (Senior Executives)
Kim Seong Kyoun *Director & Executive Vice President*
Yoon Hyung Deuk *Director & Executive Vice President*
Lee Kee Yong *Director & Executive Vice President*
Standing Auditor — Cho Chun Rai *Director & Executive Vice President*
International Business Promotion — Kim Kong Yang *General Manager* ☎ 908 451

Equity Capital Markets
Department: International Equity Markets
Global Head — Hur Moon Young *General Manager* ☎ (2) 3455 1964
Syndicated Lending
Global Head — Hur Moon Young *General Manager* ☎ (2) 3455 1964
Money Markets
Global Head — Hur Moon Young *General Manager* ☎ (2) 3455 1964
Foreign Exchange
Global Head — Hur Moon Young *General Manager* ☎ (2) 3455 1964
Risk Management
Global Head — Hur Moon Young *General Manager* ☎ (2) 3455 1964
Settlement / Clearing
Regional Head — Hur Moon Young *General Manager* ☎ (2) 3455 1964
Kim Kong Yang *General Manager* ☎ 908 451

LG Merchant Banking Corp　　　　　Head Office

9th Floor, LG Building, Da-dong, Chung-ku, Seoul 100-180
Tel: (2) 757 6000 **Fax:** (2) 757 6220 **Telex:** 35016 **Swift:** LGMB KR SE **Reuters:** LGMH

Senior Executive Officers
President & Chief Executive Officer — Kyung-Suk Suh ☎ 310 1801
Chief Executive Officer — Dong-Ryool Lee *Managing Director* ☎ 310 1802

KOREA, SOUTH (+82) www.euromoneydirectory.com

LG Merchant Banking Corp (cont)
Senior Executive Officers (cont)
Chief Operating Officer — Jong-Whan Oh *Managing Director* ☏ **310 1802**
Treasurer — Kun-Jung Chang *General Manager* ☏ **310 1841**

Debt Capital Markets / Fixed Income
Department: International Finance Team
Global Head — J H Yoo *Team Head* ☏ **310 1890**

Eurobonds
Head of Trading — C J Lee *Manager* ☏ **310 1889**
Trading (Sovereigns) — W H Lee *Manager* ☏ **310 1819**

Libor-Based / Floating-Rate Products
Asset Swaps — C K Jo *Deputy General Manager* ☏ **310 1828**

Asset-Backed Securities / Securitization
Global Head — J H Yoo *Team Head* ☏ **310 1890**

Fixed-Income Repo
Head of Repo — H N Maeng *Manager* ☏ **310 1819**

Equity Capital Markets
Domestic Equities
Head of Sales — A K Kim *Deputy General Manager* ☏ **310 1830**

Syndicated Lending
Loan-Related Activities
Leasing & Asset Finance — S J Lee *General Manager* ☏ **310 1861**

Money Markets
Department: International Finance Department
Tel: 310 1823 **Fax:** 759 8059
Global Head — H S Lee *Deputy General Manager* ☏ **310 1822**
Regional Head — J H Jung *Manager* ☏ **310 1823**

Domestic Commercial Paper
Head of Origination — K J Chang *General Manager* ☏ **310 1841**
Head of Sales — J Y Kim *Deputy General Manager* ☏ **310 1842**
Head of Trading — S S Kim *Deputy General Manager* ☏ **310 1888**

Foreign Exchange
Department: International Finance Department
Tel: 759 6211 **Fax:** 759 6211
Corporate Sales — W S Kim *Deputy General Manager* ☏ **310 8718**

FX Traders / Sales People
KRW — W S Kim *Deputy General Manager* ☏ **310 8718**

Risk Management
Department: International Operations Department
Global Head — D S Lee *General Manager* ☏ **310 1871**

Fixed Income Derivatives / Risk Management
Regional Head — C K Jo *Deputy General Manager* ☏ **310 1828**

Foreign Exchange Derivatives / Risk Management
Global Head — W S Kim *Deputy General Manager* ☏ **310 8718**

Other Currency Swap / FX Options Personnel
Structured Products — S W Moon *Manager* ☏ **310 1825**

Settlement / Clearing
Department: International Operations Department
Tel: 759 6211 **Fax:** 759 8058
Regional Head — D S Lee *General Manager* ☏ **310 1871**
Fixed-Income Settlement — H N Maeng *Manager* ☏ **310 1819**
Derivatives Settlement — T S Kim *Assistant Manager* ☏ **310 1829**
Foreign Exchange Settlement — C W Chung *Assistant Manager* ☏ **310 1826**

Administration
Technology & Systems
T W Kim *Deputy General Manager* ☏ **810 0180**

Legal / In-House Counsel
S R Seo *General Manager* ☏ **810 0200**

Compliance
S R Seo *General Manager* ☏ **810 0200**

Public Relations
H K Lee *Manager* ☏ **310 1892**

www.euromoneydirectory.com	KOREA, SOUTH (+82)

LG Securities Co Limited　Head Office
34-6 Yeoido-dong, Yeoungdeungpo-ku, Seoul 150-010
PO Box 378, Yeoido Yeongdeungpo-ku, Seoul 150-010
Tel: (2) 768 7376; (2) 768 7056 **Fax**: (2) 768 7956; (2) 768 7958 **Telex**: LGSEC K29771
Email: smhwang@lgsmail.lg.co.kr
Website: www.lgsec.co.kr

Senior Executive Officers
Chairman　　　　　　　　　　　　　　Yung-Euy Chung ☎ **768 7001**
President & Chief Executive Officer　　Ho-Soo Oh ☎ **768 7002**
Chief Executive Officer　　　　　　　Cha-Yol Koo *Executive Vice President* ☎ **768 7014**
Financial Director　　　　　　　　　Seung-Hyun Yoon *Vice President* ☎ **768 7006**
Treasurer　　　　　　　　　　　　　Byung-Hwa Suh *Domestic Finance* ☎ **768 7200**
International Division　　　　　　　Suk-Ryang Lee *Senior Vice President* ☎ **784 6963**

General-Lending (DCM, SL)
Head of Corporate Banking　　　　　Suk-Ryang Lee *Senior Vice President* ☎ **784 6963**

General-Investment
Head of Investment　　　　　　　　Suk-Kyun Mok *International Finance* ☎ **768 7480**

Debt Capital Markets / Fixed Income
Head of Fixed Income　　　　　　　Jung-Ki Kim *Equity Sales* ☎ **768 7460**

Fixed-Income Repo
Head of Repo　　　　　　　　　　　Jung-Ki Kim *Equity Sales* ☎ **768 7460**

Equity Capital Markets
Head of Equity Capital Markets　　　Jung-Ki Kim *Equity Sales* ☎ **768 7460**

Equity Repo / Securities Lending
Head　　　　　　　　　　　　　　　Hong-Kook Kim ☎ **768 7310**

Money Markets
Head of Money Markets　　　　　　Suk-Kyun Mok *International Finance* ☎ **768 7480**

Foreign Exchange
Head of Foreign Exchange　　　　　Byung-Chol Sung *International Operations* ☎ **768 2030**

Corporate Finance / M&A Advisory
Head of Corporate Finance　　　　　Suk-Kyun Mok *International Finance* ☎ **768 7480**

Settlement / Clearing
Head of Settlement / Clearing　　　　Byung-Chol Sung *International Operations* ☎ **768 2030**

Global Custody
Head of Global Custody　　　　　　Byung-Chol Sung *International Operations* ☎ **768 2030**

Asset Management
Head　　　　　　　　　　　　　　　Sung-Hoon Lee *Vice President* ☎ **784 6981**

Other Departments
Cash Management　　　　　　　　Byung-Hwa Suh *Domestic Finance* ☎ **768 7200**

Administration
Head of Administration　　　　　　Seung-Hwa Nam *General Affairs Department* ☎ **768 7107**
Business Development　　　　　　Dae-Soo Lee *Planning* ☎ **768 7340**
Head of Marketing　　　　　　　　Ki-Hwan Kim ☎ **768 7400**

Technology & Systems
　　　　　　　　　　　　　　　　　Hong-Sup Song *Information Systems* ☎ **413 3948**

Legal / In-House Counsel
　　　　　　　　　　　　　　　　　Dae-Soo Lee *Planning* ☎ **768 7340**

Compliance
　　　　　　　　　　　　　　　　　Hyun-Woo Lee *Auditor* ☎ **768 7580**

Public Relations
　　　　　　　　　　　　　　　　　Kwang-Sig Min *Vice President* ☎ **768 7030**

Accounts / Audit
Accounting　　　　　　　　　　　Byung-Kwan Lee ☎ **768 7320**

The Long-Term Credit Bank of Japan Limited　Full Branch Office
14th Floor, Kwanghwamoon Building 64-8, 1-ga, Taepyung-ro, Chung-gu, Seoul
Tel: (2) 399 2450 **Fax**: (2) 399 2480

KOREA, SOUTH (+82)　　　www.euromoneydirectory.com

Merrill Lynch International Inc
Full Branch Office
17th Floor Dong-Ah Life Insurance Building, 33 Da-dong, Chung-ku, Seoul 100-180
Tel: (2) 3707 0400 Fax: (2) 3707 0401
Website: www.ml.com

The National Commercial Bank
Representative Office
Unit 1504, Jangkyo Building, 1 Jangkyo-dong, Chung-ku, Seoul 100-760
Tel: (2) 778 5011 Fax: (2) 778 9304

Senior Executive Officers
Representative　　　　　　　　　Y Andrew Ghim

Overseas Union Bank Limited
Full Branch Office
8th Floor, Kyobo Building, Suite 806, #1-1 Chongro, 1-ka Chongro-ku, Seoul
Tel: (2) 739 3441 Fax: (2) 732 9004

Senior Executive Officers
Vice President & General Manager　　　Ooi Kooi Keat

Paribas
21st Floor, Kyobo Building, 1 Chongro 1-ka, Chongro-ku, Seoul 110-714
Tel: (2) 721 6600; (2) 721 6612 Fax: (2) 739 5378 Telex: K24144 Swift: PARB KR SE XXXX Reuters: BPSH

Senior Executive Officers
Managing Director / General Manager　　　Ullrich-Gunther Schubert

Peace Bank of Korea
Head Office
4th Floor, 823-21 Peace Bank Building, Yeoksan-dong, Kangnam-ku, Seoul 135-080
Tel: (2) 222 2228; (2) 222 2217 Fax: (2) 564 8464; (2) 222 2234 Telex: K32777 Swift: PBOK KR SE Reuters: PCEH
Bloomberg: 87665 Telex: K32778

Senior Executive Officers
Chairman of the Executive Committee &　　Kyng Woo Kin ☏ 222 2121
President
Director & Deputy President　　　　　　　Ki Young Han ☏ 222 2123
Financial Director　　　　　　　　　　　Ki Hack Nam Director & Executive Vice President ☏ 222 2126
International Division　　　　　　　　　So Nam Jon General Manager & Head ☏ 222 2211

Administration
Accounts / Audit
Auditor　　　　　　　　　　　　　　　Duck Moon Park ☏ 222 2124

Pusan Bank
Head Office
830-38, Pomil-dong, Tong-ku, Pusan 601-060
Tel: (51) 642 3300 Fax: (2) 774 7077 Telex: K27605 PUSANBK Swift: PUSB KR 2P
Website: www.pusanbank.co.kr

Senior Executive Officers
Chairman & President　　　　　　　　Yon-Hyong Lee
Director & Deputy President　　　　　Ki-Yoon Kim

Others (Senior Executives)
　　　　　　　　　　　　　　　　　　Joon-soo An *Director & Executive Vice President*
　　　　　　　　　　　　　　　　　　Yee-Tay Kim *Director & Executive Vice President*
　　　　　　　　　　　　　　　　　　Seung-Woong Chang *Director & Executive Vice President*
　　　　　　　　　　　　　　　　　　Ke-Ho Son *Director & Executive Vice President*
　　　　　　　　　　　　　　　　　　Kun-Je Park *Director & Executive Vice President*
　　　　　　　　　　　　　　　　　　Sea-Gun Lim *Director & Executive Vice President*
　　　　　　　　　　　　　　　　　　Seak-Jae Song *Director & SVP*
　　　　　　　　　　　　　　　　　　Byung-Geun Shin *Director & SVP*

Debt Capital Markets / Fixed Income
Global Head　　　　　　　　　　　　Ho-Shick Joo ☏ (2) 777 6295

www.euromoneydirectory.com　　　　　　KOREA, SOUTH (+82)

Equity Capital Markets
Global Head　　　　　　　　　　　Ho-Shick Joo ☎ **(2) 777 6295**
Syndicated Lending
Global Head　　　　　　　　　　　Ho-Shick Joo ☎ **(2) 777 6295**
Money Markets
Global Head　　　　　　　　　　　Ho-Shick Joo ☎ **(2) 777 6295**
Foreign Exchange
Global Head　　　　　　　　　　　Ho-Shick Joo ☎ **(2) 777 6295**
Risk Management
Global Head　　　　　　　　　　　Ho-Shick Joo ☎ **(2) 777 6295**
Corporate Finance / M&A Advisory
Global Head　　　　　　　　　　　Ho-Shick Joo ☎ **(2) 777 6295**
Settlement / Clearing
Regional Head　　　　　　　　　　Ho-Shick Joo ☎ **(2) 777 6295**
Administration
Accounts / Audit
Auditor　　　　　　　　　　　　　Yee-Tay Kim *Director & Executive Vice President*

The Sakura Bank Limited　　　　　　　　　　　　　　　Full Branch Office

7th Floor, Young Poong Building, 33 Sorin-dong, Chongro-ku, Seoul 110-752
Tel: (2) 399 6311 **Fax:** (2) 399 6322 **Telex:** 26303 MITKBK **Email:** sakurabk@soback.konnet.nm.kr
Senior Executive Officers
General Manager　　　　　　　　Satoshi Murayama

Seoulbank　　　　　　　　　　　　　　　　　　　　　　　　Head Office

10-1 Namdaemun-ro 2-ga, Chung-gu, Seoul 100-746
PO Box 276, Seoul
Tel: (2) 3709 5114 **Fax:** (2) 3709 6439; (2) 3709 6449 **Telex:** K23311 **Swift:** BSEO KR SE
Email: com1208@chollian.net **Reuters:** SELH
Website: seoulbank.co.kr

Senior Executive Officers
Chairman, President & CEO　　　　Bok Young Shim ☎ **3709 6001**
Treasurer　　　　　　　　　　　　Sang Sung Oh *General Manager, Treasury & Securities*
Debt Capital Markets / Fixed Income
Global Head　　　　　　　　　　　Jo Young Son *Senior Deputy General Manager* ☎ **3709 5639**
Syndicated Lending
Global Head　　　　　　　　　　　Jo Young Son *Senior Deputy General Manager* ☎ **3709 5639**
Money Markets
Global Head　　　　　　　　　　　Won Kyu Lee *Senior Deputy General Manager* ☎ **3709 5652**
Foreign Exchange
Global Head　　　　　　　　　　　Won Kyu Lee *Senior Deputy General Manager* ☎ **3709 5652**
Risk Management
Global Head　　　　　　　　　　　Young Yuon Park *Senior Deputy General Manager* ☎ **3709 5635**
Corporate Finance / M&A Advisory
Global Head　　　　　　　　　　　Jo Young Son *Senior Deputy General Manager* ☎ **3709 5639**
Settlement / Clearing
Regional Head　　　　　　　　　　Young Yuon Park *Senior Deputy General Manager* ☎ **3709 5635**

Shinhan Bank　　　　　　　　　　　　　　　　　　　　　Head Office

120, 2 Ka, Taepyung-ro, Chung-ku, Seoul 100-102
Tel: (2) 774 7674; (2) 756 0505 **Fax:** (2) 774 7013; (2) 771 6834 **Telex:** K29590 **Swift:** SHBK KR SE
Website: www.shinhanbank.co.kr

Senior Executive Officers
Chairman　　　　　　　　　　　　Heui-Keon Lee ☎ **757 2761**
Non-Executive Chairman　　　　　Jong Park
President　　　　　　　　　　　　Eung-Chan Ra ☎ **757 3767**
Director & Deputy President　　　In-Ho Lee ☎ **756 8477**
Financial Director　　　　　　　　Young-Sun Koh *Director & Deputy President* ☎ **757 2770**
International Division　　　　　　Hae-Sung Jung *Director & Executive Vice President* ☎ **757 2765**

Euromoney Directory 1999　**929**

KOREA, SOUTH (+82)

www.euromoneydirectory.com

Shinhan Bank (cont)
Senior Executive Officers (cont)

Young-Han Kim *General Manager* ☎ 771 2588 🖷 774 7013

Others (Senior Executives)

Dong-Woo Han *Director & Executive Vice President* ☎ 756 7494
Young-Hwi Choi *Director & Executive Vice President* ☎ 771 2566
Joon Park *Director & Executive Vice President* ☎ 757 2768
Woo-Keun Lee *Director* ☎ 752 4062
Sung-Kyun Hong *Director* ☎ 318 0831
Yung-Jim Kwon *Standing Auditor* ☎ 757 2769

General-Lending (DCM, SL)
Head of Corporate Banking

Seo-Kyu Chang *General Manager, Corporate Planning* ☎ 757 2766 🖷 777 1883
Young-Sang Kweon *General Manager, Corporate Banking* ☎ 756 5404 🖷 756 9599
Bo-Kil Baek *General Manager, Credit Administration* ☎ 757 9487 🖷 778 4980

General-Investment
Head of Investment

Jung-Ok Huh *General Manager, Trust & Investment* ☎ 771 4635 🖷 774 7014

General - Treasury
Head of Treasury

Chang-Hong Hong *General Manager, Treasury* ☎ 756 7057 🖷 754 9619

Debt Capital Markets / Fixed Income
Country Head

Kee-Rae Chang *Deputy General Manager* ☎ 754 0339 🖷 771 6834

Libor-Based / Floating-Rate Products
FRN Trading

Kee-Rae Chang *Deputy General Manager* ☎ 754 0339 🖷 771 6834

Medium-Term Notes
Head of Origination

Kee-Rae Chang *Deputy General Manager* ☎ 754 0339 🖷 771 6834

Asset-Backed Securities / Securitization
Regional Head

Kee-Rae Chang *Deputy General Manager* ☎ 754 0339 🖷 771 6834

Fixed-Income Repo
Head of Repo

Kee-Rae Chang *Deputy General Manager* ☎ 754 0339 🖷 771 6834

Syndicated Lending
Loan-Related Activities
Trade Finance

Sung-In Kim *General Manager* ☎ 774 7672 🖷 773 6552

Money Markets
Country Head

Suk-Jim Koh *Deputy General Manager* ☎ 779 7324 🖷 754 6443

Foreign Exchange
Country Head

Suk-Jim Koh *Deputy General Manager* ☎ 779 7324 🖷 754 6443

Risk Management
Head of Risk Management

Suk-Jim Koh *Deputy General Manager* ☎ 779 7324 🖷 754 6443

Settlement / Clearing
Regional Head

Young-Moo Kim *Deputy General Manager* ☎ 756 0505 ext 4250

Global Custody
Regional Head

Yong-Kyun Park *Deputy General Manager* ☎ 771 4837 🖷 779 7323

Administration
Technology & Systems

Jin-Won Seo *General Manager* ☎ 756 5130 🖷 318 7240

Public Relations

Eun-Sik Kim *General Manager* ☎ 771 0297 🖷 771 2564

Accounts / Audit
Audit & Examination

Hyun-Soo Kim *General Manager* ☎ 774 3174 🖷 774 2958

Other (Administration)
Customer Services
Human Resources
General Affairs

Je-Kweon Lee *General Manager* ☎ 318 7344 🖷 773 4785
Dong-Girl Lee *General Manager* ☎ 771 2567 🖷 776 8198
Sang-Ho Kim *General Manager* ☎ 779 2170 🖷 776 0569

Société Générale — Full Branch Office

12th Floor, Kwanghwamoon Building, 211 Sejongro-ro, Chongro-ku, Seoul 8518
PO Box 8518, Seoul
Tel: (2) 399 2159 **Fax:** (2) 399 2151 **Telex:** K22666 **Swift:** SOGE KR SE

Senior Executive Officers
Chief Executive Officer — E Berthelemy
Deputy Chief Executive Officer — A Viry

www.euromoneydirectory.com KOREA, SOUTH (+82)

General-Investment
Head of Investment K J Lee *Head of Investment Banking*
Debt Capital Markets / Fixed Income
Head of Debt Capital Markets S M Koh *Head of Dealing Room*
Settlement / Clearing
Operations J B Kim *Head of Operations*

Ssangyong Investment & Securities Co Limited

4th Floor, Ssangyong Tower, 23-2 Yoido-dong, Yongdungpo-ku, Seoul 150-010
Tel: (2) 3772 1000 **Fax:** (2) 780 3372 **Telex:** K33957 **Email:** jhpark@ssyisc.co.kr
General Telex: K29179

Senior Executive Officers
Chief Executive Officer Milton S Kim ☎ **3772 1234** 🗎 **3772 1390**
Financial Director Yong Jin Kwon
Managing Director Jae-Hong Kim ☎ **3772 1500** 🗎 **3772 1580**
General-Lending (DCM, SL)
Head of Corporate Banking Jong Sop Yom *Director* ☎ **3772 2500** 🗎 **769 1232**
Debt Capital Markets / Fixed Income
Head of Fixed Income Je Young Sung *Director* ☎ **3772 2300** 🗎 **3772 1580**
Fixed-Income Repo
Head of Repo Je Young Sung *Director* ☎ **3772 2300** 🗎 **3772 1580**
Equity Capital Markets
Head of Equity Capital Markets Jung Sam Park *Director* ☎ **3772 2020** 🗎 **783 7958**
Money Markets
Head of Money Markets Je Young Sung *Director* ☎ **3772 2300** 🗎 **3772 1580**
Foreign Exchange
Head of Foreign Exchange Young Jin Kwon *Director* ☎ **3772 1080** 🗎 **769 1231**
Corporate Finance / M&A Advisory
Head of Corporate Finance Jong Sop Yom *Director* ☎ **3772 2500** 🗎 **769 1232**
Settlement / Clearing
Head of Settlement / Clearing Byung Ho Yi *Director* ☎ **3772 3200** 🗎 **783 3799**
Global Custody
Head of Global Custody Byung Ho Yi *Director* ☎ **3772 3200** 🗎 **783 3799**
Asset Management
Head Jung Sam Park *Director* ☎ **3772 2020** 🗎 **783 7958**
Other Departments
Private Banking Jong Sop Yom *Director* ☎ **3772 2500** 🗎 **769 1232**
Cash Management Young Jin Kwon *Director* ☎ **3772 1080** 🗎 **769 1231**
Administration
Business Development Byung Ho Yi *Director* ☎ **3772 3200** 🗎 **783 3799**
Technology & Systems
  Byung Ho Yi *Director* ☎ **3772 3200** 🗎 **783 3799**
Accounts / Audit
Accounts Jung Sam Park *Director* ☎ **3772 2020** 🗎 **783 7958**

Standard Chartered Bank   Full Branch Office

13th Floor, Nae Wei Building 6, 2-ka Ulchi-ro, Chung-ku, Seoul 100-8192
Tel: (2) 750 6114 **Fax:** (2) 757 7444; (2) 757 0818 **Telex:** K24242 SCBSEO **Swift:** SCBL KR SE **Cable:** Stanchart
Senior Executive Officers
Chief Executive Officer Matt Wake ☎ **750 6008** 🗎 **750 6129**
Financial Director Jane Kwak *Head* ☎ **750 6084**
Treasurer H J Park ☎ **750 6121**

Relationship Manager
Head of Coporate Sales Sung Bae Park ☎ **750 6010**
Institutional Banking K Y Sul ☎ **750 6052**
Head of Institutional Sales J W Park ☎ **750 6020**
Foreign Exchange
Tel: 750 6121 **Fax:** 757 0818
Corporate Sales M S Hong
Head of Trading W J Hong

Euromoney Directory 1999 **931**

KOREA, SOUTH (+82)   www.euromoneydirectory.com

Standard Chartered Bank (cont)
Settlement / Clearing
Operations   D K Seo *Head* ☏ 750 6041
Administration
Compliance
   Christine Lee ☏ 750 6069

The Tokai Bank Limited   Full Branch Office
   17th Floor, Kyobo Building 1, 1-ka Chongro, Chongro-ku, Seoul
   Tel: (2) 739 9810 **Fax:** (2) 739 9814 **Telex:** 25716 TOKAISL K
Senior Executive Officers
General Manager   Takashi Yoshida

UBS AG
   19th Floor, Young Poong Building, 33 Seorin-dong, Chongro-ku, Seoul 110-752
   Tel: (2) 399 5566 **Fax:** (2) 399 5577
Senior Executive Officers
Chairman   Chan-Keun Lee
Chief Operating Officer   Joong-On Chang
Debt Capital Markets / Fixed Income
Department: Debt Capital Markets / Fixed-Income / Eurobonds
Country Head   Joon-Kee Hong *Head of Rates*
Equity Capital Markets
Department: International / Domestic Equities
Head of Equity Capital Markets   R Samuelson *Head of Equity*
Corporate Finance / M&A Advisory
Head of Corporate Finance   Chan-Keun Lee

KUWAIT
(+965)

Central Bank of Kuwait   🏛 Central Bank
   PO Box 526, Abdulla Alsalem Street, 13006 Safat
   Tel: 244 9200 **Fax:** 240 2715 **Telex:** KUMBANK **Swift:** CBKU KW KW **Email:** cbk@cbk.gov.kw **Reuters:** CBKX
   Website: www.cbk.gov.kw
Senior Executive Officers
Governor   Salem Abdulaziz Al-Sabah
Deputy Governor   Ali Mousa Al-Mousa

Others (Senior Executives)
Head, Monetary Policy   Nabeel Al-Manahee *Executive Director*
Head, Organization & Administration   Hameed Al-Rasheed *Executive Director*
Head, Banking Supervision   Ibrahim Al-Qhadi *Manager*
Head, Banking Operations   Jalil Al-Jasim *Manager*

Foreign Exchange
Head of Foreign Exchange   Fawzi Al-Thunayan *Manager, Foreign Relations*

Other Departments
Economic Research   Sami Al-Anbaee *Deputy Manager*

Administration
Head of Administration   Essa Al-Attal *Manager*

www.euromoneydirectory.com   KUWAIT (+965)

Alahli Bank of Kuwait

Safat Square, Kuwait City, 13014 Safat
PO Box 1387, 13014 Safat
Tel: 240 0900/19; 241 1100/19 **Fax:** 242 4557; 2417284 **Telex:** 22067 **Swift:** ABKKKWKW **Reuters:** AHLIBANK - KT
Cable: HLIBANK KT

Senior Executive Officers
Chairman of the Board of Directors — Morad Behbehani ☎ **244 3443** 🖷 **244 1130**
Deputy Chairman & MD — Sheikh Ahmed Al-Sabah ☎ **244 3443** 🖷 **244 1130**
Chief Executive Officer — Redha Behbehani *Deputy Chief GM & Deputy Chief Exec.Officer* ☎ **244 1144** 🖷 **241 6356**
Naser Malek *Deputy Chief GM & Deputy Chief Exec.Officer* ☎ **244 1199** 🖷 **241 6356**
Financial Director — Jagmohan Chopra *Assistant GM, Financial Control* ☎ **244 3366** 🖷 **245 7854**
Chief Operating Officer — Jamal Abdul Raheem ☎ **244 1122** 🖷 **244 1441**
Treasurer — Willem Dubelaar *Acting Assistant General Manager - Treasury* ☎ **242 1265** 🖷 **242 8547**
General Manager — Mohammad Ahmed Al-Ali ☎ **245 3346** 🖷 **243 3090**
International Division — Bader Al-Awadi *Assistant GM, International & Investment* ☎ **244 1188** 🖷 **243 3995**

Others (Senior Executives)
Automation Services — Hamed Abbas *Senior Manager* ☎ **246 7965** 🖷 **241 6356**
Organisation & Methods — Venkatesh Partbasarathy *Senior Manager* ☎ **243 3084** 🖷 **243 3090**
Legal Division — Soliman Abdul Meguid *General Counsel Head of Legal Division* ☎ **242 4270** 🖷 **243 3995**

General-Lending (DCM, SL)
Head of Corporate Banking — Stephen McClintic *Assistant General Manager, Credit* ☎ **240 1916** 🖷 **240 2349**

General-Investment
Head of Investment — Bader Al-Awadi *Assistant GM, International & Investment* ☎ **244 1188** 🖷 **243 3995**

Debt Capital Markets / Fixed Income
Department: International & Investment Division
Tel: 243 3106 **Fax:** 243 3999
Government Bonds
Head of Syndication — Bader Al-Awadi *Assistant GM, International & Investment* ☎ **244 1188** 🖷 **243 3995**

Eurobonds
Head of Trading — Bader Al-Awadi *Assistant GM, International & Investment* ☎ **244 1188** 🖷 **243 3995**

Equity Capital Markets
Department: International & Investment Division
Tel: 243 3106 **Fax:** 243 3999
Head of Equity Capital Markets — Bader Al-Awadi *Assistant GM, International & Investment* ☎ **244 1188** 🖷 **243 3995**

Domestic Equities
Head of Sales; Head of Trading — Bader Al-Awadi *Assistant GM, International & Investment* ☎ **244 1188** 🖷 **243 3995**

Other (Domestic Equities)
Investment (Heads) — Bader Al-Awadi *Assistant GM, International & Investment* ☎ **244 1188** 🖷 **243 3995**

International Equities
Head of Sales; Head of Trading — Bader Al-Awadi *Assistant GM, International & Investment* ☎ **244 1188** 🖷 **243 3995**

Syndicated Lending
Tel: 243 3106 **Fax:** 243 3999
Head of Syndicated Lending; Head of Origination; Head of Syndication — Bader Al-Awadi *Assistant GM, International & Investment* ☎ **244 1188** 🖷 **243 3995**

Loan-Related Activities
Structured Trade Finance — Naeem Chaudhry *Trade Finance Manager* ☎ **241 7359** 🖷 **243 3074**

Money Markets
Tel: 240 4522 **Fax:** 242 8547 **Reuters:** AHLK **Telex:** 44429/ 44430
Head of Money Markets — Willem Dubelaar *Acting Assistant General Manager - Treasury* ☎ **242 1265** 🖷 **242 8547**

Wholesale Deposits
Marketing — Abdul Azim Jassim *Manager, Corporate Service Department* ☎ **244 1136** 🖷 **242 8547**

Euromoney Directory 1999   **933**

KUWAIT (+965) www.euromoneydirectory.com

Alahli Bank of Kuwait (cont)
Other (Wholesale Deposits)
Head of International Sales — Guy Rottiers *Chief Dealer, Money Markets* ☏ 240 4522 🖷 242 8547

Foreign Exchange
Head of Foreign Exchange — Willem Dubelaar *Acting Assistant General Manager - Treasury* ☏ 242 1265 🖷 242 8547
Head of Institutional Sales — Guy Rottiers *Chief Dealer, Money Markets* ☏ 240 4522 🖷 242 8547
Corporate Sales — Abdul Azim Jassim *Manager Corporate Services Department* ☏ 244 1136 🖷 242 8547

FX Traders / Sales People
Hamed Al- Wazzan *Assistant Chief Dealer, FX* ☏ 240 4521 🖷 242 8547

Settlement / Clearing
Fax: 2453063
Head of Settlement / Clearing — Ismaeel Al- Mousavi *Sr. Supervisor General Ser.* ☏ 240 1730 🖷 245 3036
Fixed-Income Settlement — Aziza Al- Qabndi *Sr. Supervisor Clearing* ☏ 240 1730 🖷 245 3036
Operations — Maamoon Anabtawi *Supervisor* ☏ 240 1730 🖷 245 3063

Other Departments
Chief Credit Officer — Stephen McClintic *Assistant General Manager, Credit* ☏ 240 1916 🖷 240 2349
Correspondent Banking — Bader Al-Awadi *Assistant GM, International & Investment* ☏ 244 1188 🖷 243 3995
Cash Management — Ibrahim Safer *Supervisor Central Cash* ☏ 244 2222

Administration
Head of Administration — Jamal Abdul Raheem ☏ 244 1122 🖷 244 1441
Head of Marketing — Caroline Rosinski *Services Quality & Sales Administrator* ☏ 242 5706 🖷 241 4870

Technology & Systems

Legal / In-House Counsel
Soliman Abdul Meguid *General Counsel Head of Legal Division* ☏ 242 4270 🖷 243 3995

Public Relations
Human Resources Division — Hamed Abbas *Senior Manager* ☏ 246 7965 🖷 241 6356
Public Relations — Salwa Al-Sharqawi *Senior Manager* ☏ 244 3322 🖷 240 1334
Caroline Rosinski *Services Quality & Sales Administrator* ☏ 242 5706 🖷 241 4870

Accounts / Audit
Auditor — Mansour Shashtari *General Auditor* ☏ 245 3351 🖷 245 3351

Bank of Bahrain and Kuwait BSC Full Branch Office
Ahmed Al Jaber Street, Sharq, 13104 Safat
PO Box 24396, 13104 Safat
Tel: 241 7140; 241 7180 Fax: 244 0937 Telex: 23220 a/b KUWBBK KT Swift: BBKU KW KW
Cable: BAHKUBANK KUWAIT

Senior Executive Officers
Chief Executive Officer — Michel Khazen *General Manager* ☏ 246 2192 🖷 244 5285
Treasurer — Thunayan Alghanim *Treasurer* ☏ 243 4670 🖷 241 9521
International Division — Firoze Hansotia *Senior Operations Manager* ☏ 244 0239

Others (Senior Executives)
Credit & Marketing — Saleh Al-Ateeqi *Senior Manager* ☏ 241 8979
Customer Services — Mona Al-Hunayan *Manager* ☏ 246 2191
Commercial Services — A. Nabi Al-Jazzaf *Manager* ☏ 242 0926
General Services — Mahmood Zainaldeen *Manager* ☏ 242 7914
Personnel Services — Afaf Al-Essa *Manager* ☏ 243 0914

The Bank of Kuwait & the Middle East, KSC Head Office
East Tower, Joint Banking Centre, Darwazat Abdul Razzak, 13001 Safat
PO Box 71, 13001 Safat
Tel: 802 000 Fax: 246 1430 Telex: 22405 BKME KT Email: bkmekw@mcc.moc.kw Cable: BANKUWAIT
Website: www.bkme.com

Senior Executive Officers
Chairman & Managing Director — Saleh Mubarak Al-Falah ☏ 244 0630, 241 7347
Deputy Chairman — Ali Mohammed Al-Otaibi ☏ 246 2920, 241 6082

934 Euromoney Directory 1999

KUWAIT (+965)

Others (Senior Executives)
Board Member
　　　　　　　　　　Anwar Shaker Al-Kazemi
　　　　　　　　　　Barrak Abdul Mohsen Al-Tukhaim
　　　　　　　　　　Mahmoud Adbul Khaleq Al-Nouri
　　　　　　　　　　Saleh Ali Al-Qadi
　　　　　　　　　　Mishaal Mohammed Al-Hammad
Adviser to the Board
Acting General Manager
　　　　　　　　　　Saud Abdel Aziz Al Gharabally ☏ **246 2921**
　　　　　　　　　　Issam Abdul Aziz Al-Usaimi ☏ **246 1428**

General-Lending (DCM, SL)
Head of Corporate Banking
　　　　　　　　　　Nasser Abdul Aziz Al-Jallal *AGM, Corporate Banking* ☏ **246 2971**
　　　　　　　　　　Salah Abdul Aziz Al-Humaidhi *AGM, Finance & Planning* ☏ **246 2926**
　　　　　　　　　　Issam Eisa Al-Assousi *Head, Banking Services Group* ☏ **246 2923, 245 3757**
　　　　　　　　　　Abdullah Fahad Al-Zouman *Domestic Corporate Banking, Division Head*
　　　　　　　　　　☏ **240 8514**
　　　　　　　　　　Basel Jassem Al-Obaid *International Corporate Banking Division Head*
　　　　　　　　　　☏ **246 0659**

General - Treasury
Head of Treasury　　　　　Anthony Thornicroft *Head of Treasury* ☏ **246 2523, 246 2554**

Settlement / Clearing
Settlement (General)
　　　　　　　　　　Tareq Khaled Al-Sabeeh *Assistant General Manager, Support* ☏ **245 7233**
　　　　　　　　　　🖷 **240 0635**
Operations　　　　　　Saeed Eisa Al-Nawfal *Head* ☏ **246 2976** 🖷 **240 5831**

Other Departments
Private Banking
　　　　　　　　　　Mohammed Sadek Al-Rasheed *AGM, Retail & Private Banking Services*
　　　　　　　　　　☏ **246 2972** 🖷 **246 2804**

Administration
Head of Administration
　　　　　　　　　　Abdal Mustapha Abdal *Head, Administration & Technical* ☏ **246 1420**
　　　　　　　　　　🖷 **246 6309**

Technology & Systems
　　　　　　　　　　John Stevenson *Head of EDP* ☏ **243 7005** 🖷 **243 2925**

Legal / In-House Counsel
　　　　　　　　　　Suad Abdulla Al-Jassem *Counselor & Head* ☏ **243 4554** 🖷 **242 2983**

Accounts / Audit
　　　　　　　　　　Kayomerd J Cooper *Chief Auditor* ☏ **246 1422** 🖷 **242 6683**

Other (Administration)
Branches Division　　　　Ahmad Shehab Al-Qaderi *Head* ☏ **246 2960** 🖷 **245 3675**
Human Resources Division　Hani Suod Al-Meer *Head* ☏ **243 7001**

Burgan Bank SAK

PO Box 5389, 13054 Safat
Tel: 243 9000 **Fax:** 246 1148 **Telex:** 22767 **Reuters:** BBFK

Senior Executive Officers
Chairman　　　　　　　　Sheikh Ahmed Al Abdu Al-Sabah
Treasurer　　　　　　　　Dick Bjornemark
Managing Director / General Manager　Mohammed Aqeel Tawfiqi

The Commercial Bank of Kuwait SAK

Mubarak Al-Kabir Street, 13029 Safat
PO Box 2861, Safat
Tel: 241 1001 **Fax:** 245 0150 **Telex:** 22004 **Swift:** COMB KW KW **Reuters:** COMK (Money Dealers) **Cable:** Banktijari

Senior Executive Officers
Chairman　　　　　　　　Hamad A Abdul Latif Hamad
Financial Director　　　　Bakhtiar Liaqat
Managing Director / General Manager　Ghassan Dimitri

General-Lending (DCM, SL)
Head of Corporate Banking　Yousef Al Obaid *Executive Manager, Credits* ☏ **246 8753** 🖷 **241 7885**

Euromoney Directory 1999　**935**

KUWAIT (+965)   www.euromoneydirectory.com

The Gulf Bank KSC

Mubarak Al Kabir Street, 13032 Safat
PO Box 3200, 13032 Safat
Tel: 244 9501 Fax: 244 5212 Telex: 22001 GULFBK KT Swift: GULB KW KW Reuters: GBKK (Dealing)
Cable: GULFBANK

Senior Executive Officers
Chairman   Ali Al Hilal Al Mutairi
Deputy Chairman   Mohammed Ibrahim Maarafi
Deputy Chief General Manager   Ziad F Sarawan
General Manager   Jassem Zainal
International Division   Ibrahim Ibrahim *Head, International Banking*

Others (Senior Executives)
Commercial Banking Group   Abdulla Al Sumeit *General Manager*
Consumer Banking Group   Ali Al-Bader *General Manager*
Finance & Planning Group   Daniel Brown

General-Investment
Head of Investment   Jassem Zainal *General Manager*

General - Treasury
Head of Treasury   Ziad F Sarawan *Deputy Chief General Manager*

Risk Management
Head of Risk Management   Adnan Al Ibrahim *Head, Credit Risk Management*

Administration
Legal / In-House Counsel
General Counsel   Adnan Ibrahim

Accounts / Audit
Internal Auditor   Khaled Khuraibit

Other (Administration)
Support Services Group   Nazem Al-Qanae

Gulf Investment Corporation (GIC)   Subsidiary Company

Joint Banking Centre, KREB Building, Safat
PO Box 3402, 13035 Safat
Tel: 243 1911 Fax: 244 8894; 240 8006 Telex: 44002 GICORP KT Swift: GCOR KW KW Reuters: GICK
Cable: GICORP KT Telex: 23146 GICORP KT
Website: www.gic.com.kw

Senior Executive Officers
Chairman   Ahmed Al-Tayer ☎ 723 162
Chief Executive Officer   Khaled Al-Fayez ☎ 244 8823
Financial Director   Nabil Guirgis *SVP, Financial Control*
General Manager   Hisham Abdulrazzak Razzuqi ☎ 244 8890

Others (Senior Executives)
Global Markets Group   Michael Zeller *Executive Vice President*

General-Investment
Head of Investment   Khaled Al Awadi *SVP, Merchant Banking Division*
   Abdalla H Nour *EVP, Investment Banking*
   Hamza Behbehani *SVP, Investment Banking*

General - Treasury
Head of Treasury   Tawfiq Al Fraih *SVP, Treasury*
   Martin Joy *VP & Chief Dealer*

Debt Capital Markets / Fixed Income
Global Head   William Clarke *Vice President*
Other   Harold Davis *VP, Global Markets Strategy*

Equity Capital Markets
Global Head   Paul Kennedy *Vice President*
Other   Harold Davis *VP, Global Markets Strategy*

Syndicated Lending
Loan-Related Activities
Project Finance   Abdulrahman Al Ali *SVP, Projects Division*
   Mohammed Al Sanie *SVP, Projects Division*

Risk Management
Global Head   Fouad J Masrieh *Vice President*

Corporate Finance / M&A Advisory
Global Head — Mahmoud Rateb *SVP, Corporate Finance Division*

Settlement / Clearing
Operations — Shawki Khalaf *Vice President*
Kazem Hayat *VP, Investment Support*

Asset Management
Head — Jamal Al Saeed *Senior Vice President*

Other Departments
Economic Research — Sharif Ghalib

Administration
Head of Administration — Fouad Al Sinan *Executive Vice President*

Technology & Systems
Hani Al Shakhs *Vice President*

Compliance
Compliance & Control — Ahmed Al Mehza *Vice President*

Corporate Communications
S M Nadeem Mujtaba *Second Vice President*

Accounts / Audit
Audit — Anthony W Ede *Senior Vice President*

Other (Administration)
Human Resource & Training — Yousef Al Ghanim *Vice President*
Administrative Services — Hisham Al Hossayan *Vice President*

Industrial Bank of Kuwait — Head Office

PO Box 3146, 13032 Safat
Tel: 245 7661 **Fax:** 246 2057 **Telex:** 2246946313 **Swift:** IBKU KW KW **Reuters:** IBKK

Senior Executive Officers
Chairman — Saleh M Al-Yousef
Chief Executive Officer — Ali A Khajah

Inter-Arab Investment Guarantee Corporation (IAIGC) — Head Office

The Arab Organizations Headquarters Building, Juncture of Aiirport Road &, Jamal Abdulnasser, Al Shuwaikh
PO Box 23568, 13096 Safat
Tel: 484 4500 **Fax:** 481 5741/2 **Telex:** 46312 **Email:** iaigc@iai.org.kw

Senior Executive Officers
Director — Mamoun Hassan ☏ **483 8009**
Deputy Director — Gium Giuma ☏ **481 5709**

Settlement / Clearing
Operations — Abdul Issa *Director* ☏ **483 2960**

Other Departments
Economic Research — Khobali Abubaker *Director* ☏ **483 9670**

Administration
Legal / In-House Counsel
Al Fadil Hassan *Director* ☏ **483 8241**

Kuwait Finance House KSC

Alternative trading name: KFH
Abdullah Al Mubarak Street, Safat Square, Safat
PO Box 24989, 13110 Safat
Tel: 244 5050 **Fax:** 245 5135 **Telex:** 23381 **Swift:** KFHO KW KW **Email:** kfh@kfh.com.kw **Reuters:** KFHK
Cable: BAITMAL KUWAIT
International Tel: 243 5534; 240 9693; **Fax:** 246 1397; **Treasury/FX Tel:** 244 9967
Website: www.kfh.com

Senior Executive Officers
Chairman & Managing Director — Bader Abdul Mohsen Al-Mukaizeem
Vice Chairman — Mohmmad Yousuf Al-Roumi
Deputy General Director — Jassar Al-Jasser
Deputy General Manager — Nabeel Ameen

KUWAIT (+965)   www.euromoneydirectory.com

Kuwait Finance House KSC (cont)
Others (Senior Executives)
Trading Sector   Barrak F Al-Sabeeh *Assistant General Manager*
                              Fawaz S Al Othman *Deputy Assistant General Manager*

General-Lending (DCM, SL)
Head of Corporate Banking   Essa M Al-Asfoor *Assistant General Manager, Banking*
                              Yousuf A Al-Mailam *Deputy AGM, Finance*

General-Investment
Head of Investment   Sami Nada *International Investment Manager*
                              Jassar D Al-Jassar *AGM, International Investment*

General - Treasury
Head of Treasury   Mohammad Al Kandari *Departmental Manager*

Settlement / Clearing
Settlement (General)   Talal A Al-Houti *Deputy AGM, Support Services*

Other Departments
Correspondent Banking   Matloob A Khan *Senior Manager*

Administration
Business Development   Sulaiman A Al-Braikan *Assistant General Manager*

Other (Administration)
Board of Directors' Office   Ibrahim A Al-Khamees *Deputy Assistant General Manager*
Chairman's Office   Fahad M Al-Othman *Deputy Assistant General Manager*
Support Services   Talal A Al-Houti *Deputy AGM, Support Services*

Kuwait Fund for Arab Economic Development — Head Office

Al-Murqab, Al-Shohda & Mubarak Al-Kabeer Street, PO Box 2921, 13050 Safat
Tel: 243 8430 Fax: 243 6196 Telex: 22025 ALSUNDOUK Email: info@kuwait-fund.org
Website: www.kuwait-fund.org

Senior Executive Officers
Director General   Bader Al-Humaidhi
Chief Executive Officer   Abdulwahab Al-Bader *Deputy Director General*
Financial Director   Hamad Al-Omar *Deputy Director General, Admin & Finance*
Chief Operating Officer   Hesham Al-Waqayan *Deputy Director General, Ops & Disbursement*

Others (Senior Executives)
Disbursement Dept   Ossama M Al-Attal *Director*

General-Investment
Head of Investment   Fadhel D Al-Oun *Director*

Settlement / Clearing
Operations   Fawzi Y Al-Hunaif *Director*

Administration
Head of Administration   Abdullah S Al-Oun *Director*

Technology & Systems
Informations Systems   Esmael S Ebrahim *Director*

Accounts / Audit
Internal Audit   Ahmad S Shaheen Al-Ghanim *Director*
Accounts   Faiza H Al-Roumi *Director*

Other (Administration)
Technical Office   Fahad A Al-Dakheel *Director*
Information Center   Abdullah A I Al-Ansari *Director*

Kuwait Real Estate Bank

West Tower, Joint Banking Centre, Darwazat Abdul Razak, Safat
PO Box 22822, 13089 Safat
Tel: 245 8177 Fax: 246 2516 Telex: 22321 AKARI Swift: KREB KW KW

Senior Executive Officers
Chairman & Managing Director   Ali Khalifa Al-Sabah ☎ 244 0172
Deputy Chairman   Emad Jawad BU-Khamseen ☎ 246 2109
Financial Director   Mohamed Munir Mirza *Financial Controller* ☎ 246 2357
Managing Director / General Manager   Fajhan Roumi Al-Fahad

General - Treasury
Head of Treasury   Waleed Al-Asfoor *Head* ☎ 246 2274

www.euromoneydirectory.com   KUWAIT (+965)

Relationship Manager
Appraisal Department
Housing Loans Dept.   Jawad Maqseed *Executive Manager* ☏ 246 2242
Real Estate Loans Dept.   Adel Al-Roumi *Head* ☏ 246 2515
Property Management Section   Fahad Al-Fouzan *Head* ☏ 246 2217
Current & Savings Account Section   Abdulrahman Al-Jean *Head* ☏ 246 2423
Remittances & Private Deposits Section   Ahmed Abdulzahar *Head* ☏ 246 2420
Cash Section   Raja Al-Marzouk *Head* ☏ 246 2337
Loans Servicing Section   Seif Al-Shihab *Head* ☏ 246 2507
Letters of Credit Section   Ibtihal Al-Rifai *Head* ☏ 246 2238
    Dia'a Al-Khawari *Head* ☏ 246 2267

Syndicated Lending
Other (Syndicated Lending)
Syndicated Loans & Correspondent Banking   Talal Mishan Al-Khudair *Executive Manager* ☏ 246 2272

Settlement / Clearing
Settlement (General)   Omar Al-Hasawi *Purchased Debts Settlement / Re-Scheduling Dept.*
    ☏ 243 9406
Operations   Waleed Al-Ayyadhi *Executive Manager* ☏ 246 2334
    Essam Abdullah Al-Madhaf *Manager* ☏ 246 2506

Administration
Head of Administration   Jassem Yousef Hamada *Executive Manager* ☏ 246 2240
    Adnan Al-Ibrahim *Head* ☏ 246 2236

Technology & Systems
Electronic Data Process Dept.   Mohammed Sharawy *Head* ☏ 245 8608

Legal / In-House Counsel
General Legal Advisor   Medhat Zaki *Manager* ☏ 244 0155

Accounts / Audit
Auditor   Robert Montgomery *Chief Auditor* ☏ 246 2276
Accounts Section   Majed Al-Ali *Head* ☏ 246 2421
Internal Audit Section   Ijaz Minhas *Head* ☏ 246 2235

Other (Administration)
Facilities Department   Lamia Al-Qattami *Manager* ☏ 243 9406
Human Resources   Sami Al-Saleh *Head* ☏ 243 5975
Training Section   Abdul Rahman Al-Qahtani *Head* ☏ 246 2239

National Bank of Kuwait SAK   Head Office

Abdullah Al-Ahmad Street, PO Box 95, 13001 Safat
Tel: 242 2011 **Fax:** 243 1888 **Telex:** 44653/4 NATBANK **Swift:** NBOK KWKW **Reuters:** NBKX **Telerate:** 8350
Cable: NATIONAL
Website: www.nbk.com

Senior Executive Officers
Chairman   Mohamed Al-Bahar ☏ 242 2011 F 243 1888
Deputy Chairman   Nasser Al Sayer ☏ 242 2011 F 243 1888
Chief Executive Officer   Ibrahim Sh Dabdoub ☏ 243 1625 F 246 2469
Financial Director   Peter Moir *Assistant General Manager* ☏ 241 4288 F 242 2730
Treasurer   Salah Al Fulaij ☏ 246 3533 F 246 7627
Deputy Chief Executive Officer   Isam Al Sager ☏ 244 3974 F 246 2469
International Division   Robert Eid *General Manager* ☏ +44 (171) 317 5500 F +44 (171) 487 5544

Others (Senior Executives)
Controls & Support   Hanafi Hussien ☏ 241 7653 F 246 4162
Head of Domestic Retail Banking   Adel Al Majed *General Manager* ☏ 246 5838 F 246 7929
Head of Domestic Branches   Aly Shalaby *Assistant General Manager* ☏ 246 7625 F 246 7929
Head of Consumer Banking   Louis Scotto *Assistant General Manager* ☏ 244 3971 F 246 7929

General-Lending (DCM, SL)
Head of Corporate Banking   Shaikah Al Bahar *General Manager* ☏ 244 0761 F 245 9032

General-Investment
Head of Investment   George Nasra *General Manager* ☏ 246 4158 F 241 9528

Equity Capital Markets
Head of Sales   Shaikah Al Bahar *General Manager* ☏ 244 0761 F 245 9032

Domestic Equities
Head of Sales   Shaikah Al Bahar *General Manager* ☏ 244 0761 F 245 9032

International Equities
Head of Sales   George Nasra *General Manager* ☏ 246 4158 F 241 9528

KUWAIT (+965) www.euromoneydirectory.com

National Bank of Kuwait SAK (cont)
Syndicated Lending
Loan-Related Activities
Project Finance   Shaikah Al Bahar *General Manager, Domestic Division*
                                            George Nasra *International*
Money Markets
Tel: 246 7086 **Fax:** 246 7627 **Reuters:** NBKK NBKX **Telex:** 47811/ 12
Head of Money Markets   Sebastian D'Cunha *Chief Dealer* ☎ **246 7086** 🅵 **246 7627**
Wholesale Deposits
Marketing   Mohammed Dimachkie *Manager* ☎ **246 2054** 🅵 **246 7627**
Head of Sales   Mazen Al Nahedh *Senior Dealer* ☎ **246 2054** 🅵 **246 7627**
Foreign Exchange
Tel: 246 5186 **Fax:** 246 7627 **Reuters:** NBK NBKX **Telex:** 47811/ 12
Head of Foreign Exchange   Mammen Varkey *Chief Dealer* ☎ **246 5186** 🅵 **246 7627**
Corporate Sales   Yusra Al Qatami *Manager* ☎ **246 2052** 🅵 **246 7627**
FX Traders / Sales People
                                            Rai Rangel
                                            Hanan Al Gharabally
                                            Hussien Al Aryan
                                            Tareq Al Samaraie
Risk Management
Head of Risk Management   Rick Mckenzie *General Manager* ☎ **246 3532** 🅵 **246 7627**
Corporate Finance / M&A Advisory
Other (Corporate Finance)
Domestic   Shaikah Al Bahar *General Manager* ☎ **244 0761** 🅵 **245 9032**
Asset Management
Head   George Nasra *General Manager* ☎ **246 4158** 🅵 **241 9528**
Other Departments
Private Banking   Adel Al Majed *General Manager* ☎ **246 5838** 🅵 **246 7929**
Correspondent Banking   Malek Al Ajeel *Executive Manager* ☎ **246 8031** 🅵 **246 4156**
Administration
Head of Administration   Waleed Al Yaquot *Deputy General Manager* ☎ **241 1644** 🅵 **246 6864**
Business Development   Patrick Miranda *Retail Banking Manager* ☎ **242 2011** 🅵 **246 7929**
Head of Marketing   Faten Abu Ghazaleh *Marketing Manager* ☎ **242 2011** 🅵 **246 7929**
Technology & Systems
Info Technology   Simon Clements *General Manager* ☎ **246 3803** 🅵 **245 9233**
Legal / In-House Counsel
                                            Osma Al Naquib *Legal Advisor* ☎ **244 8755** 🅵 **244 5098**
Public Relations
                                            Iqbal Al Haddad *Advertising & PR Manager* ☎ **242 2276** 🅵 **246 5190**
Accounts / Audit
                                            Jasim Al Hasawi *Assistant General Manager* ☎ **571 1526** 🅵 **571 1785**
Other (Administration)
Economics   Randa Azaar *Chief Economist* ☎ **244 5095** 🅵 **246 5098**

KYRGYZ REPUBLIC
(+996)

The National Bank of the Kyrgyz Republic   🏛 Central Bank
101 Umetalieva Street, Bishkek, 720040
Tel: (3312) 215 852; (3312) 217 237 **Fax:** (3312) 610 724; (3312) 610 730 **Telex:** 245127 RAHAT KH
Email: mail@nbk.bishkek.su

Senior Executive Officers
Chairman   Marat A Sultanov ☎ **217 593**
Deputy Chairman   Emil Abdumanapov ☎ **214 427**
Deputy Chairman   Mariya Taranchieva
Deputy Chairman   Jamilya Esenalieva ☎ **217 592**
Others (Senior Executives)
Board Member   Azamat Tokbaev ☎ **211 996**
                                Victor Chebyshev ☎ **223 590**
                                Abdybaly tegin Souerkoul ☎ **222 976**
                                Ulan Sarbanov ☎ **217 754**

LATVIA (+371)

Others (Senior Executives) (cont)
Head, Economic Department
Head, Banking Supervision
Head, Currency / Cash
Head, Financial Division

Larisa Tsyplakova ☎ 217 353
Saltanat Despayeva ☎ 217 754
Gulnara Abdyldaeva ☎ 222 976
Chmara Imankulova ☎ 227 253
Ruslan Akmatbekov ☎ 212 835

General-Investment
Head of Investment

Marles Duyshegulov *Director* ☎ 215 854

Foreign Exchange
Head of Foreign Exchange

Gennadi Lim ☎ 217 662

Settlement / Clearing
Department: Payment Systems
Head of Settlement / Clearing

Alexander Tsybizov *Head* ☎ 213 588

Administration
Head of Administration

Evgenia Cholakidi *Head, Service Department* ☎ 215 646

Technology & Systems
Head, Information Systems

Roman Khan ☎ 213 675

Legal / In-House Counsel
Head, Legal Division

Elena Bit-Abragim ☎ 215 995

Accounts / Audit
Head, Accounting & Reporting
Head, Internal Audit

Irina Aramiyan *Chief Accountant* ☎ 217 595
Tatiana Aidjigitova ☎ 210 995

Other (Administration)
Head, Personnel
Head, General Issues
Head, Security Service

Aichurek Jakypova ☎ 212 632
Gulnara Nazaraliyeva ☎ 213 244
Abdumalik Myrzayev ☎ 220 495

European Bank for Reconstruction & Development
Representative Office

26 Geologicheskaya Street, Bishkek, 720031
Tel: (3312) 530 017 **Fax:** (3312) 530 016 **Email:** hadjiysn@Bsk.ebrd.com

Senior Executive Officers
Resident Banker
Deputy Representative

Nikolay Hadjiyski
Jyldyz Galieva ✉ galievaj@Bsk.ebrd.com

LATVIA
(+371)

Bank of Latvia
🏛 Central Bank

Alternative trading name: Latvijas Banka
2a, Kr Valdemara Street, LV-1050 Riga
Tel: 702 2300; 702 2260 **Fax:** 702 2420; 702 2404 **Telex:** 161146 BNK LV **Swift:** LACB LV 2X **Email:** info@bank.lv
Website: www.bank.lv

Senior Executive Officers
Governor
Chief Executive Officer
Financial Director
Chief Operating Officer
Treasurer
International Division

Einars Repše
Ilmars Rimševics *Deputy Governor* ☎ 702 2238
Helmuts Ancans *Head, Monetary Policy* ☎ 702 2408 🖷 702 2119
Anttonija Sileniece *Chief Accountant* ☎ 702 2285 🖷 702 2406
Uldis Klauss *Head, Cash Operations* ☎ 702 2365 🖷 702 2216
Guntis Valujevs *Head of Foreign Relations* ☎ 702 2275 🖷 702 2404

LATVIA (+371) www.euromoneydirectory.com

Baltic International Bank
Head Office

43 Kaleju Street, LV-1050 Riga
Tel: 722 2789; 721 0172 Fax: 721 6870; 722 0330 Telex: 161334 BIB LV Swift: BLIB LV 22 Email: info@www.bib.lv
Reuters: BIBX
Website: www.bib.lv

Senior Executive Officers
Chairperson of the Board — Alla Tkachenko ☎ **722 1856**
Chairman, Shareholders Council — Valeri Belokon ☎ **722 2824**
Chief Executive Officer — Oleg Gerasimov *Vice President & Executive Director*
Financial Director — Elena Brinskih *Chief Accountant* ☎ **722 1866**
Treasurer — Vilori Belokon *Chairman of Resource Supervision Committee*
Manager, Secretariat — Inese Rotkaja
International Division — Maxim Ignatyev *Manager, Correspondent Banking* ☎ **721 3911**

General-Investment
Head of Investment — Vadim Pcholkin *Chairman, Investment Credit Committee*

Debt Capital Markets / Fixed Income
Head of Fixed Income — Vadim Pcholkin *Chairman, Investment Credit Committee*
Head of Fixed Income Sales; Head of Fixed Income Trading — Irina Graubina *Manager, Loans & Deposits* ☎ **722 1856**

Government Bonds
Head of Sales — Vita Japina *Manager, Personal Banking* ☎ **722 2508**
Head of Trading — Zana Vorobjova *Personal Banker* ☎ **722 2508**

Equity Capital Markets
Head of Equity Capital Markets — Vadim Pcholkin *Chairman, Investment Credit Committee*

Domestic Equities
Head of Sales; Head of Trading — Maris Cheichs *Manager, Trust Operations*

International Equities
Head of Sales; Head of Trading — Maris Cheichs *Manager, Trust Operations*

Equity Research
Head of Equity Research — Maris Cheichs *Manager, Trust Operations*

Convertibles / Equity-Linked
Head of Sales; Head of Trading — Nataliya Kartashova *Manager, Soft Currency Conversion* ☎ **721 0172**

Syndicated Lending
Head of Origination — Irina Graubina *Manager, Loans & Deposits* ☎ **722 1856**

Loan-Related Activities
Trade Finance — Galina Ushakova *Chief Financial Officer* ☎ **722 1426**

Money Markets
Head of Money Markets — Oleg Matavkin *Manager, Foreign Exchange Division* ☎ **722 2947**

Domestic Commercial Paper
Head of Trading — Oleg Matavkin *Manager, Foreign Exchange Division* ☎ **722 2947**

Wholesale Deposits
Marketing — Irina Graubina *Manager, Loans & Deposits* ☎ **722 1856**

Foreign Exchange
Head of Institutional Sales — Nataliya Kartashova *Manager, Soft Currency Conversion* ☎ **721 0172**

FX Traders / Sales People
— Oleg Matavkin *Manager, Foreign Exchange Division* ☎ **722 2947**

Risk Management

Foreign Exchange Derivatives / Risk Management
Spot / Forwards Sales — Oleg Matavkin *Manager, Foreign Exchange Division* ☎ **722 2947**
Spot / Forwards Trading — Nataliya Kartashova *Manager, Soft Currency Conversion* ☎ **721 0172**

Exchange-Traded Derivatives
Head — Vilori Belokon *Chairman of Resource Supervision Committee*

Global Custody
Head of Global Custody — Leonid Kramnoy *Manager, Securities* ☎ **722 9257**

Other Departments
Chief Credit Officer — Vadim Pcholkin *Chairman, Investment Credit Committee*
Private Banking — Vita Japina *Manager, Personal Banking* ☎ **722 2508**
Correspondent Banking — Maxim Ignatyev *Manager, Correspondent Banking* ☎ **721 3911**
Cash Management — Liana Salmane

www.euromoneydirectory.com   LATVIA (+371)

Administration
Head of Administration   Oleg Gerasimov *Vice President & Executive Director*
Business Development   Vilori Belokon *Chairman of Resource Supervision Committee*

Technology & Systems
Hardware, Software & Telecommunication   Albert Reznik

Legal / In-House Counsel
Legal Department   Inga Durite-Petrone *Manager* ☏ **722 1426**

Compliance
                                            Iveta Kerpe ☏ **722 1426**

Public Relations
                                            Lolita Roze *Manager, Advertising Division*

Accounts / Audit
Internal Audit Department   Ludmila Rozgina *Manager*

Baltijas Tranzitu   Full Branch Office
Alternative trading name: Baltic Transit Bank
3, 13 Janvara Street, LV-1050 Riga
Tel: 702 4747 **Fax:** 721 1985 **Telex:** 161353 TRBANK LV **Swift:** BATR LV 2X **Email:** btblv@majl.bkc.lv **Reuters:** BTBC

Senior Executive Officers
Chairman of the Council   Ojars Kehris
President   Galina Alijeva ☏ **702 4701**
Chief Executive Officer   Vitalijs Kokalis *First Vice President* ☏ **702 4701**
Financial Director   Alexandrs Panchuks *Chief Accountant* ☏ **702 4701**
Chief Operating Officer   Svetlana Vaiculevicha ☏ **702 4744**
Treasurer   Galina Borisenko *Head, Cash Department* ☏ **721 3560**
Head, General Service Department   Vladimirs Belko ☏ **702 4720**
Counsellor   Edmunds Johanson ☏ **702 4701**
Secretary   Irena Kovalevska ☏ **702 4701**
International Division   Dmitrijs Latishevs *Head, Correspondent Department* ☏ **702 4790**

Others (Senior Executives)
                                            Aldis Duntavs *Vice President* ☏ **702 4701**
Emerging Markets   Ekirijs Pupchenoks *Vice President* ☏ **702 4701**

General-Lending (DCM, SL)
Head of Corporate Banking   Kaspars Krauze *Vice President* ☏ **702 4788**

General-Investment
Head of Investment   Leonids Mandels ☏ **731 3010**

Equity Capital Markets
Head of Equity Capital Markets   Kaspars Krauze *Vice President* ☏ **702 4788**

Syndicated Lending
Head of Origination; Head of Syndication Ludmila Danilova *Head, Credit Dept* ☏ **702 4712**

Loan-Related Activities
Trade Finance   Alexandrs Ivanous *Head, Transit Business Development Department*
                                            ☏ **731 3010**

Money Markets
Head of Money Markets   Vitalijs Leshchenko *Head, Securities Dept* ☏ **702 4763**

Foreign Exchange
Head of Foreign Exchange   Dmitrijs Pupchenoks *Head, Dealing Department* ☏ **702 4758**

Corporate Finance / M&A Advisory
Head of Corporate Finance   Kaspars Krauze *Vice President* ☏ **702 4788**

Settlement / Clearing
Head of Settlement / Clearing   Inna Ardasheva ☏ **702 4739**

Global Custody
Head of Global Custody   Svetlana Vaiculevicha ☏ **702 4744**

Asset Management
Head   Sofija Vilberga *Head of Asset & Liability Management* ☏ **702 4743**

Other Departments
Commodities / Bullion   Gelija Serga ☏ **731 3010**
Chief Credit Officer   Ludmila Danilova *Head, Credit Dept* ☏ **702 4712**
Correspondent Banking   Dmitrijs Latishevs *Head, Correspondent Department* ☏ **702 4790**
Cash Management   Galina Borisenko *Head, Cash Department* ☏ **721 3560**

LATVIA (+371)   www.euromoneydirectory.com

Baltijas Tranzitu (cont)
Administration
Business Development   Alexandrs Ivanous *Head, Transit Business Development Department*
                                          ☏ 731 3010
Head of Marketing   Inese Shevchenko ☏ 702 4716
Technology & Systems
Information Systems Department   Armands Krauze *Head* ☏ 702 4711
Legal / In-House Counsel
Law Department   Furijs Zlakomanovs *Head* ☏ 702 4778
Public Relations
                                          Valdis Freidenfelds ☏ 702 4750
Accounts / Audit
Audit Department   Fanina Berzina *Head* ☏ 731 3010

Banka Land
Head Office

54/15 Vidus prospekts, LV-2010 Jurmala
Tel: 775 2232; 775 2286 **Fax:** 789 2711; 775 2183 **Telex:** 161293 LAND LV **Swift:** BANL LV 22
Email: land@mail.neonet.l **Tel:** 775 2591; 775 2183 **Tel:** 789 2712
Website: www.land.lv

Senior Executive Officers
Chairman   Edgars Zuza
Chairman   Didzis Ziraps

Others (Senior Executives)
                                          Viktors Ozolins *First Vice President*
                                          Aleksandr Chernavsky *Vice President*
                                          Nina Jubele *Customer Service*

General - Treasury
Head of Treasury   Valdis Apalka *Head, Dealing*
Other Departments
Correspondent Banking   Edmunds Stalgis
Administration
Accounts / Audit
                                          Elita Ramute *Chief Accountant* ☏ 768 6329
                                          Aleksandra Greza *Head of Internal Audit*

Dresdner Bank AG
Representative Office

1 Vilandes Street, LV-1010 Riga
Tel: 783 0405; 732 1355 **Fax:** 783 0406; 732 1367

Senior Executive Officers
Representative   Lothar Krieger

Others (Senior Executives)
                                          Irena Bagdonaite *Assistant Representative*
                                          Aira Magone *Assistant Representative*
                                          Rom Vool *Assistant Representative*

European Bank for Reconstruction & Development
Full Branch Office

4th Floor, 15 Kalku Street, LV-1050 Riga
Tel: 783 0300 **Fax:** 783 0301 **Email:** zaliteb@rig.ebrd.com
Website: www.ebrd.com

Senior Executive Officers
Others (Senior Executives)
Co-Head of Riga Office   Jonathan Harfield
                                          Urmas Paavel
Associate Banker   Guntars Levans

944 Euromoney Directory 1999

www.euromoneydirectory.com　　　LATVIA (+371)

Hansa Investments Latvia
Full Branch Office

11 Elizabetes Street, LV-1010 Riga
Tel: 732 2011; 732 1998 Fax: 732 2291
Website: www.hansa.ee/invest

Senior Executive Officers
Chief Executive Officer — Ben Wilson *Executive Director*

Debt Capital Markets / Fixed Income
Private Placements
Head of Origination — Ben Wilson *Executive Director*
Head of Sales — John Wilson *Director, Sales & Trading* ☎ **+372 640 0415**
Head of Structuring — Harry Rozenstein *Associate Director*

Asset-Backed Securities / Securitization
Global Head — Ben Wilson *Executive Director*
Head of Trading — John Wilson *Director, Sales & Trading* ☎ **+372 640 0415**

Equity Capital Markets
Head of Equity Capital Markets — Ben Wilson *Executive Director*

Domestic Equities
Head of Origination — Ben Wilson *Executive Director*
Head of Sales — John Wilson *Director, Sales & Trading* ☎ **+372 640 0415**
Head of Trading — Paul-Endel Luedig *Director* ☎ **+372 640 0416**
Head of Research — Ben Wilson *Executive Director*

Other (Domestic Equities)
Indra Wilson *Associate*
Vladimir Loginov *Associate*

Syndicated Lending
Head of Syndicated Lending — Ben Wilson *Executive Director*

Loan-Related Activities
Trade Finance — John Wilson *Director, Sales & Trading* ☎ **+372 640 0415**
Project Finance — Ben Wilson *Executive Director*

Corporate Finance / M&A Advisory
Head of Corporate Finance — Ben Wilson *Executive Director*
Country Head — Harry Rozenstein *Associate Director*

Settlement / Clearing
Head of Settlement / Clearing — Ben Wilson *Executive Director*
Equity Settlement — John Wilson *Director, Sales & Trading* ☎ **+372 640 0415**

Hansabank-Latvija
Head Office

26 Kalku Street, LV-1050 Riga
Tel: 702 4444 Fax: 702 4400 Swift: DLBR LV 2X Reuters: HABL
Website: www.hbl.lv

Senior Executive Officers
Chairperson of the Council — Hannes Tamjarv
Chairperson of the Board — Ingrīda Blūma

Others (Senior Executives)
Head of Adminstration — Valdis Purvinskis *Member of the Board*
Head of Retail Banking — Ugis Zemturis *Member of the Board*

General-Lending (DCM, SL)
Head of Corporate Banking — Viesturs Kulikovskis *Member of the Board*

General-Investment
Head of Investment — Sergey Sergejev *Associate*

Relationship Manager
Securities Services — Anrijs Cheksters *Client Relations Manager*

Debt Capital Markets / Fixed Income
Department: Fixed Income & Currency
Head of Fixed Income Trading — Māris Vinklers

Bonds - General
Liquidity Manager — Mâtins Jaunarâjs

Equity Capital Markets
Domestic Equities
Head of Sales — Andreta Petersone *Private Client Sales*

Euromoney Directory 1999　**945**

LATVIA (+371)   www.euromoneydirectory.com

Hansabank-Latvija (cont)
Foreign Exchange
Corporate Sales   Druvis Múrmanis
FX Traders / Sales People
    Egons Strazdins *Dealer, Spot FX*
    Sandris Pavlous *Dealer, Spot FX*

Asset Management
Head   Raimonds Vessers *Associate*

Other Departments
Private Banking   Adis Liepiöd *Senior Managing Director*
Correspondent Banking   Mari Saraskin *Head*

A/S HypoVereinsbank   Full Branch Office
63 Eliabetes Iela, LV-1050 Riga
Tel: 708 5500 Fax: 708 5509 Swift: VBRI LV 2X

Industrial Bank of Latvia   Head Office
Alternative trading name: Lainbank
6 Grecinieku Street, LV-1587 Riga
Tel: 721 6406; 721 6528 Fax: 722 1135 Telex: 161267 EMMA LV Swift: IBLA LV 2X Email: lain@lain.bkc.lv
Website: www.lain.bkc.lv

Senior Executive Officers
Chairman of the Board   Dzintars Pelcbergs
President   Vilis Dambins
Chief Executive Officer   Valts Vigants *Vice President*
Financial Director   Dace Usherovska *Head, Economics Division* ☎ **721 6528**
Treasurer   Edmunds Zivtins
Vice President   Valts Vigants
International Division   Inga Klavina *Head, International Division*

Debt Capital Markets / Fixed Income
Head of Fixed Income   Valts Vigants *Vice President*

Equity Capital Markets
Head of Equity Capital Markets   Valts Vigants *Vice President*

Syndicated Lending
Head of Origination; Head of Syndication   Valts Vigants *Vice President*

Loan-Related Activities
Trade Finance; Project Finance   Dzintars Pelcbergs *Chairman of the Board*

Foreign Exchange
Head of Foreign Exchange   Dace Usherovska *Head, Economics Division* ☎ **721 6528**

Other Departments
Correspondent Banking   Dace Usherovska *Head, Economics Division* ☎ **721 6528**

Investment Bank of Latvia
Kalku Street 15, LV-1050 Riga
Tel: 782 0323 Fax: 782 0325 Telex: 161337 LATIB LV Email: latib@latib.org.lv

Senior Executive Officers
Manager   Aivars Jurcans

Latvijas Krajbanka   Head Office
Formerly known as: Latvian Savings Bank
1 Palasta Street, LV-1954 Riga
Tel: 722 2871; 732 2121 Fax: 721 2083; 721 0807 Telex: 614462 BANK RU Swift: UBAL LV 2X Email: info@lkb.lv
Reuters: SAVS
Ilze Arklina Email: ilzea@sfs.lkb.bkc.lv

Senior Executive Officers
Supervisory Council Chairman   Ivars Godmanis ☎ **721 1419**
President   Arnolds Laksa ☎ **722 2871**

LATVIA (+371)

Senior Executive Officers (cont)
Financial Director
Treasurer
Member of the Board
Company Secretary
International Division
Manager, Marketing

Christer Sjöberg *Finance Director* ☎ **722 8285**
Janis Donins *Head of Treasury* ☎ **733 8086**
Gundars Sturis ☎ **721 3121**
Solvita Vilmane ☎ **722 2871**
Andris Rigerts *President's advisor on international affairs* ☎ **721 0585**
Olafs Zvejnieks ☎ **732 3281**

Debt Capital Markets / Fixed Income
Department: Treasury
Tel: 733 1198 **Fax:** 783 0229
Head of Fixed Income Sales

Ervins Jonass *Chief Dealer* ☎ **733 1198**

Government Bonds
Head of Sales

Ervins Jonass *Chief Dealer* ☎ **733 1198**

Domestic Government Bonds
Head of Sales

Maris Avotins *Dealer, Money Markets* ☎ **733 1198**

Eurobonds
Head of Sales

Maksims Koluskins *Dealer, FX* ☎ **733 1198**

Emerging Market Bonds
Head of Sales

Maksims Koluskins *Dealer, FX* ☎ **733 1198**

Libor-Based / Floating-Rate Products
FRN Origination

Maksims Koluskins *Dealer, FX* ☎ **733 1198**

Fixed-Income Repo
Head of Repo

Ervins Jonass *Chief Dealer* ☎ **733 1198**

Fixed-Income Research
Head of Fixed Income

Ervins Jonass *Chief Dealer* ☎ **733 1198**

Syndicated Lending
Department: Credit
Tel: 722 3921 **Fax:** 722 5392
Head of Origination

Uldis Zorgenfreijs *Manager, Credit* ☎ **722 3921**

Money Markets
Tel: 733 1198 **Fax:** 783 0229
Head of Money Markets

Ervins Jonass *Chief Dealer* ☎ **733 1198**

Domestic Commercial Paper
Head of Sales

Ervins Jonass *Chief Dealer* ☎ **733 1198**

Eurocommercial Paper
Head of Sales

Ervins Jonass *Chief Dealer* ☎ **733 1198**

Wholesale Deposits
Head of Sales

Ervins Jonass *Chief Dealer* ☎ **733 1198**

Foreign Exchange
Head of Foreign Exchange

Ervins Jonass *Chief Dealer* ☎ **733 1198**

Risk Management
Tel: 733 1737
Head of Risk Management

Veneta Cuntonova *Manager* ☎ **733 1198**

Settlement / Clearing
Department: Settlement Department
Tel: 721 0609
Head of Settlement / Clearing

Irena Valdmane *Manager* ☎ **721 0609**

Other Departments
Chief Credit Officer
Private Banking
Correspondent Banking
Cash Management

Uldis Zorgenfreijs *Manager, Credit* ☎ **722 3921**
Ilga Tiknuse *Head of Branch Department, Board Member* ☎ **722 8277**
Signe Reuta *Manager* ☎ **733 1198**
Guntis Bruners *Manager* ☎ **721 3121**

Administration
Head of Administration
Business Development
Head of Marketing

Juris Sprogis *Administration Director* ☎ **722 5367**
Gundars Sturis *Member of the Board* ☎ **721 3121**
Ugis Erins *Manager* ☎ **733 8083**

Technology & Systems

Gatis Porietis *Manager, IS* ☎ **722 9237**

Legal / In-House Counsel

Vladimirs Potanins *Manager* ☎ **722 9604**

Public Relations

Ilze Arklina *Manager, Public Relations* ☎ **733 8083**

Accounts / Audit

Olga Lomass *Board Member* ☎ **721 2298**

LATVIA (+371)　　　　www.euromoneydirectory.com

Latvijas Unibanka
Head Office

23 Pils Iela, LV-1050 Riga
PO Box 380, LV-1047 Riga
Tel: 721 2808; 721 5535 **Fax:** 721 5335 **Telex:** 161361 UNIBN LV **Swift:** UNLA LV 2X **Email:** contact@unibanka.lv
Website: www.unibanka.lv

Senior Executive Officers
President, Executive Management
Financial Director
　　　　Andris Berzins
　　　　Ivars Kirsons ☎ **722 5151**

General-Lending (DCM, SL)
Head of Corporate Banking
　　　　Kazimirs Slakota Vice President ☎ **721 5410**

General - Treasury
Head of Treasury
　　　　Viesturs Neimanis Vice President, Treasury ☎ **721 5375**
　　　　Dainis Senbergs Treasury ☎ **721 5585**

Debt Capital Markets / Fixed Income
Asset-Backed Securities / Securitization
Head of Trading
　　　　Viesturs Sterns Head, Treasury Securities ☎ **721 5641**

Syndicated Lending
Other (Syndicated Lending)
Corporate Lending
　　　　Roberts Bernis ☎ **721 5635**

Risk Management
Head of Risk Management
　　　　Aivars Spilbergs ☎ **721 5527**

Settlement / Clearing
Country Head
Settlement (General)
Operations
　　　　Inese Blekte Head, Settlements & Clearing ☎ **721 5524**
　　　　Ugis Birka Head, Back Office ☎ **721 5655**
　　　　Ivars Kirsons VP, Planning & Finance ☎ **722 5151**
　　　　Ingrida Garoza Head, Planning & Finance ☎ **721 5510**
　　　　Andris Lazdins Bank Operations ☎ **721 5592**
　　　　Valters Kaze Head, Stategy and Analysis ☎ **721 5501**
　　　　Juris Aizezers VP, Banking Operations ☎ **721 5583**

Other Departments
Economic Research
　　　　Valters Kaze Head, Stategy and Analysis ☎ **721 5501**

Administration
Business Development
　　　　Zigurds Jeromanovs Vice President ☎ **721 5397**

Technology & Systems
Information Systems
　　　　Maija Treija Head ☎ **721 5590**
　　　　Juris Aizezers VP, Banking Operations ☎ **721 5583**

Programming
Computer Network
　　　　Janis Linde ☎ **721 5568**
　　　　Janis Cevers Head ☎ **721 5511**

Legal / In-House Counsel
　　　　Armands Grinbergs Head ☎ **721 5507**

Accounts / Audit
　　　　Daina Lazdina Chief Accountant ☎ **721 5606**
Internal Audit
　　　　Andris Ikvilds ☎ **721 5440**

Other (Administration)
Marketing
Personnel
Corporate Customer Services
　　　　Zigurds Strigelis Head ☎ **721 5539**
　　　　Arnolds Kardels Head ☎ **721 5360**
　　　　Zigurds Cirulis ☎ **721 5641**

Multibanka Joint Stock Company
Head Office

57 Elizabetes Street, LV-1772 Riga
Tel: 728 9546; 728 3445 **Fax:** 782 8232; 728 1505 **Telex:** 161128 BANK LV **Swift:** MULT LV 2X
Email: info@multibanka.com
Website: www.multibanka.com

Senior Executive Officers
Chairman of the Council
Chairman of the Board
Chief Executive Officer
Financial Director
Chief Operating Officer
Treasurer
Secretary
International Division
　　　　Guido Senkans ☎ **728 9546**
　　　　Svetlana Dzene ☎ **728 8950**
　　　　Oskars Gulans First Vice President ☎ **728 3445**
　　　　Natalija Prohorova Trade & Distribution ☎ **728 9666**
　　　　Tamara Assane Head of Department ☎ **728 2752**
　　　　Aleksandrs Margolis Vice President ☎ **728 7461**
　　　　Ruta Liepa ☎ **728 9546**
　　　　Sergejs Golubchikovs Vice President ☎ **728 4374**

LATVIA (+371)

Debt Capital Markets / Fixed Income
Head of Debt Capital Markets — Aleksandrs Margolis *Head of Department* ☏ **728 7461**
Government Bonds
Head of Sales; Head of Trading — Inese Shmite *Dealer* ☏ **728 0329**
Non-Domestic Government Bonds
Moldova; Russia; Ukraine — Gints Melnalksivis *Dealer* ☏ **728 0329**
Eurobonds
Head of Sales; Head of Trading — Inese Shmite *Dealer* ☏ **728 0329**
Emerging Market Bonds
Head of Emerging Markets; Head of Sales — Inese Shmite *Dealer* ☏ **728 0329**

Equity Capital Markets
Head of Equity Capital Markets — Aleksandrs Margolis *Head of Department* ☏ **728 7461**
Head of Sales; Head of Trading — Inese Shmite *Dealer* ☏ **728 0329**
Domestic Equities
Head of Sales; Head of Trading — Inese Shmite *Dealer* ☏ **728 0329**
International Equities
Head of Sales; Head of Trading — Inese Shmite *Dealer* ☏ **728 0329**

Money Markets
Tel: 728 7461 **Fax:** 728 1505
Head of Money Markets — Aleksandrs Margolis *Head of Department* ☏ **728 7461**
Domestic Commercial Paper
Head of Sales; Head of Trading — Lidija Tabakerina *Head of Department* ☏ **728 7975**
Eurocommercial Paper
Head of Sales; Head of Trading — Lidija Tabakerina *Head of Department* ☏ **728 7975**
Wholesale Deposits
Marketing; Head of Sales — Lidija Tabakerina *Head of Department* ☏ **728 7975**

Foreign Exchange
Tel: 728 7461 **Fax:** 728 1505
Head of Foreign Exchange — Aleksandrs Margolis *Head of Department* ☏ **728 7461**
Head of Institutional Sales; Corporate Sales — Dmitrijs Skomorohovs *Dealer* ☏ **728 0547**
Head of Trading — Jurijs Shmagins *Dealer* ☏ **728 0547**

Settlement / Clearing
Tel: 728 4374 **Fax:** 782 8232
Head of Settlement / Clearing — Sergejs Golubchikovs *Vice President* ☏ **728 4374**

Asset Management
Head — Aleksandrs Margolis *Head of Department* ☏ **728 7461**

Other Departments
Chief Credit Officer — Ivars Lapinsh *Head of Department* ☏ **728 6840**
Private Banking — Tamara Assane *Manager* ☏ **728 8308**
Correspondent Banking — Sergejs Golubchikovs *Vice President* ☏ **728 4374**
Cash Management — Marite Melniece *Manager* ☏ **728 2752**

Administration
Head of Marketing — Dainis Zelmenis *Head of Department* ☏ **728 2487**

Technology & Systems
Sergejs Shantarins *Manager* ☏ **728 2618**

Legal / In-House Counsel
Guntars Senkans *Legal Counsel* ☏ **728 7166**

Public Relations
Normuds Jirgensons *Press Attache* ☏ **728 2487**

Accounts / Audit
Dmitrijs Kozlovs *Internal Auditor* ☏ **728 3408**

Parekss-banka
Head Office

Alternative trading name: Parex

3 Smilshy, LV-1522 Riga
Tel: 701 0000 **Fax:** 701 0001

Senior Executive Officers
Chairman — Victor Krasovidsky
President — Valery Kargim
Treasurer — Andrew Zadornov *Head, Capital Markets*

Debt Capital Markets / Fixed Income
Head of Debt Capital Markets — Andrew Zadornov *Head, Capital Markets*

Euromoney Directory 1999 **949**

LATVIA (+371)   www.euromoneydirectory.com

Parekss-banka (cont)
Equity Capital Markets
Head of Equity Capital Markets — Andrew Zadornov *Head, Capital Markets*
Foreign Exchange
Head of Foreign Exchange — Kirill Yurzdsky ☎ **701 0199**
Settlement / Clearing
Foreign Exchange Settlement — Marina Bessalaja *Head, Foreign Payments* ☎ **701 0208**

Rietumu Banka   Full Branch Office

54 Brivibas Street, LV-1011 Riga
Tel: 702 5555; 702 5220 **Fax:** 702 5588 **Telex:** 161234 RIET LV **Swift:** RTMB LV 2X **Email:** info@rietumu.lv
Reuters: RIET
Foreign Exchange **Tel:** 702 5284; **Fax:** 702 5284
Website: www.rietumu.lv

Senior Executive Officers
Chairman, President & CEO — Michael Bourke ☎ **702 5222**
Financial Director — Rolf Fuls *Chief Financial Officer* ☎ **702 5224**
Chief Operating Officer — Yelena Popova *Director, Banking Operations* ☎ **702 5590**
Treasurer — Alexander Kalinovski *Executive Vice President* ☎ **702 5284**
First Vice President — Natalia Fetosiva ☎ **702 5284**
Company Secretary — Vita Lokomete
International Division — Ludmila Alasheyeva *Head, Correspondent Relations* ☎ **702 5574**
Others (Senior Executives)
  Olga Esterkina *Director, IT* ☎ **702 55990**

General-Lending (DCM, SL)
Head of Corporate Banking — Evgeny Shikhman *VP & Director, Corporate Banking & Lending* ☎ **702 5240**
Debt Capital Markets / Fixed Income
Department: Investment Management Department
Tel: 702 5284 **Fax:** 702 5284
Head of Fixed Income — Alexei Generalov *Assistant Treasurer*
Head of Fixed Income Sales — Vadim Burcev *Head, Customer Relations*
Head of Fixed Income Trading — Dmitry Kroutik
Equity Capital Markets
Tel: 702 5284
Head of Equity Capital Markets — Leonid Kil
Head of Sales — Vadim Burcev *Head, Customer Relations*
Head of Trading — Dmitry Kroutik
International Equities
Head of Trading — Dmitry Kroutik
Syndicated Lending
Tel: 702 5240
Loan-Related Activities
Project Finance — Evgeny Shikhman *VP & Director, Corporate Banking & Lending* ☎ **702 5240**
Money Markets
Tel: 702 5284 **Fax:** 702 5284
Head of Money Markets — Irena Zharova *Head, Dealing Department* ☎ **702 5284**
Foreign Exchange
Head of Foreign Exchange — Irene Zharova *Dealing Department*
Risk Management
Head of Risk Management — Natalia Fetosiva *First Vice President* ☎ **702 5284**
Other Departments
Chief Credit Officer — Svetlana Chinchenko
Correspondent Banking — Lidia Maliouskiene
Cash Management — Irena Zharova *Head, Dealing Department* ☎ **702 5284**
Administration
Head of Marketing — Vadim Alekseyev *Head, Sales & Marketing* ☎ **702 5282**
Technology & Systems
  Olga Esterkina *Director, IT* ☎ **702 55990**
  Misha Vaynshenker *Chief Information Officer* ☎ **702 55990**
Legal / In-House Counsel
  Irina Grzhibovskaja *Head, Legal Department*
Compliance
  Silvija Lejniece *Director, Risk Management & Compliance* ☎ **702 5590**

www.euromoneydirectory.com   LATVIA (+371)

Public Relations
Vadim Alekseyev *Head, Sales & Marketing* ☏ **702 5282**

Accounts / Audit
Internal Audit   Eduards Gribovoda *Head* ☏ **702 5540**

Rigas Komercbanka plc   Head Office

6 Smilshu, LV-1803 Riga
Tel: 701 5237; 701 5214 **Fax:** 732 3449; 782 0080 **Telex:** 161112 BARK LV **Swift:** RIKO LV 2X **Email:** president@rkb.lv
Reuters: RIGX **Telerate:** RIGX
Website: www.rkb.lv

Senior Executive Officers
Chairman of the Supervisory Board   Janis Aboltinsh ☏ **701 5200**
President & Chief Executive Officer   Vladimir Kulik ☏ **701 5202**
Financial Director   Tatyana Ratnikova *Head of Financial Division* ☏ **701 5246**
Treasurer   Andrei Sergeyev *Head of Treasury* ☏ **701 5218**
Head   Arnis Jakobsons ☏ **701 5317**
International Division   Elena Ignatieff *Director, Financial Institutions* ☏ **701 5234**

General-Lending (DCM, SL)
Head of Corporate Banking   Elga Zeize *Vice President & Head* ☏ **701 5238**

General-Investment
Head of Investment   Maris Lazdinsh *Head of Corporate Finance Unit* ☏ **701 5355**

Debt Capital Markets / Fixed Income
Department: Securities Department
Tel: 701 5294 **Fax:** 701 5391
Head of Fixed Income; Head of Fixed Income Andris Rudzitis *Head, West* ☏ **701 5437**
Trading

Domestic Government Bonds
Head of Trading   Alexander Kulikov *Deputy Director, Securities Dept* ☏ **707 7157**

Eurobonds
Head of Sales; Head of Trading   Andris Rudzitis *Head, West* ☏ **701 5437**

Emerging Market Bonds
Head of Emerging Markets; Head of Trading   Andris Rudzitis *Head, West* ☏ **701 5437**

Fixed-Income Repo
Head of Repo   Galina Beketova *Director, Resources Department* ☏ **701 5293**
Head of Trading   Andris Rudzitis *Head, West* ☏ **701 5437**

Fixed-Income Research
Head of Fixed Income; Head of Credit   Oleg Karas *Sector Head* ☏ **701 5391**
Research

Equity Capital Markets
Department: Securities Department
Tel: 701 5294 **Fax:** 701 5391
Head of Equity Capital Markets   Serghejs Shepovalov *Head Broker* ☏ **701 5295**
Head of Sales   Arturs Stikuts *Customer Sector Head* ☏ **701 5925**
Head of Trading   Serghejs Shepovalov *Head Broker* ☏ **701 5295**

Domestic Equities
Head of Sales   Arturs Stikuts *Customer Sector Head* ☏ **701 5925**
Head of Trading   Serghejs Shepovalov *Head Broker* ☏ **701 5295**

International Equities
Head of Sales   Janis Neimanis *Specialist* ☏ **707 7160**

Equity Research
Head of Equity Research   Oleg Karas *Sector Head* ☏ **701 5391**

Equity Repo / Securities Lending
Head   Andris Rudzitis *Head, West* ☏ **701 5437**

Syndicated Lending
Head of Origination   Elena Ignatieff *Director, Financial Institutions* ☏ **701 5234**
Head of Syndication   Elena Ignatieff *Director, Financial Institutions* ☏ **701 5234**
Head of Trading   Galina Beketova *Director, Resources Department* ☏ **701 5293**

Loan-Related Activities
Trade Finance   Anita Sele *Chief Manager, Trade Finance Unit* ☏ **701 5210**
Project Finance   Raimo Smukais *Head, Large Co & Firm Loans Unit* ☏ **701 5260**

Money Markets
Head of Money Markets   Roman Caiko ☏ **701 5382**

Euromoney Directory 1999   **951**

LATVIA (+371)   www.euromoneydirectory.com

Rigas Komercbanka plc (cont)

Eurocommercial Paper
Head of Sales — Elena Ignatieff *Director, Financial Institutions* ☏ **701 5234**
Head of Trading — Andris Rudzitis *Head, West* ☏ **701 5437**

Foreign Exchange
Global Head — Uldis Bush *Director of Dealing* ☏ **701 5230**
Head of Institutional Sales — Andris Savickis *Deputy Director, Dealing* ☏ **701 5247**
Corporate Sales — Vents Udris *Dealer* ☏ **701 5247**
Head of Trading — Andris Savickis *Deputy Director, Dealing* ☏ **701 5247**

Risk Management
Head of Risk Management — Irena Skobeleva *Head of Lending Division* ☏ **701 5231**

Fixed Income Derivatives / Risk Management
Trading — Serghei Grigoryev *Head of Investment Unit* ☏ **701 5437**

Foreign Exchange Derivatives / Risk Management
Spot / Forwards Trading — Serghei Grigoryev *Head of Investment Unit* ☏ **701 5437**

Corporate Finance / M&A Advisory
Head of Corporate Finance — Maris Lazdinsh *Head of Corporate Finance Unit* ☏ **701 5355**

Settlement / Clearing
Head of Settlement / Clearing — Kaspars Kravchuns *Director, Settlement Dept.* ☏ **701 5386**
Equity Settlement; Fixed-Income Settlement; Operations — Alexander Kulikov *Deputy Director, Securities Dept* ☏ **707 7157**

Global Custody
Department: Securities Department
Head of Global Custody — Harijs Zulgis *Trade Sector Head* ☏ **701 5457**

Asset Management
Head — Andrei Korp *Head, Trust Unit* ☏ **701 5340**

Other Departments
Chief Credit Officer — Irena Skobeleva *Head of Lending Division* ☏ **701 5231**
Correspondent Banking — Elena Ignatieff *Director, Financial Institutions* ☏ **701 5234**
Cash Management — Mark Moskvin *Acting Head* ☏ **701 5226**

Administration
Head of Administration — Vyacheslav Derkach *Head of Administration* ☏ **701 5250**
Business Development — Vyacheslav Mishin *Director, Strategic Development Dept.* ☏ **701 5224**
Head of Marketing — Valdis Jalinskis *Head of Marketing* ☏ **701 5395**

Technology & Systems
Alexander Teplykh *Head of IT* ☏ **701 5290**

Legal / In-House Counsel
Aivars Kruminsh *Head of Legal Dept* ☏ **701 5264**

Public Relations
Mikhail Sulsky *Press Secretary* ☏ **701 5215**

Accounts / Audit
Valentina Voskresenskaya *Chief Auditor* ☏ **701 5236**

Saules Banka Inc   Head Office

16 Smilshu Street, LV-1873 Riga
Tel: 702 0500 **Fax:** 702 0505 **Telex:** 161348 SLBNK LV **Swift:** SAUL LV 2X **Email:** wolf@saules.com **Reuters:** SAFX

Senior Executive Officers
Chairman of the Council — Youri Schetinin
Chairman of the Board — Natalia Klendere
Treasurer — Dmitry Rabinovich

Syndicated Lending
Department: Project Finance & Syndications
Tel: 702 0559 Fax: 702 0505
Global Head — Dimitry Pyshkin

Loan-Related Activities
Trade Finance — Natalia Shavliuk *Head of Documentary Credits*

Money Markets
Global Head — Dmitry Rabinovich

Risk Management
Global Head — Edgar Dubra *Vice President*

Other Departments
Correspondent Banking — Andrew Stolbushkin

952   Euromoney Directory 1999

www.euromoneydirectory.com LEBANON (+961)

Administration
Technology & Systems
  Alexander Smelov
Legal / In-House Counsel
  Didzis Azando

Société Générale
Full Branch Office
55 Brivibas Street, LV-1010 Riga
Tel: 731 0051; 731 0053 **Fax:** 731 0060 **Telex:** 709680 SGRIGRU **Swift:** SOGE LV 2X **Reuters:** SOCX
Website: www.socgen.com

Senior Executive Officers
General Manager Philippe Chasse ☎ 731 0055 🖷 731 0061

Others (Senior Executives)
Marketing Division Lija Makare *Deputy General Manager* ☎ 731 2120 🖷 731 0061
Commercial Division Jean-Michel Renard *Deputy General Manager*

General - Treasury
Head of Treasury David Field *Treasury Manager* ☎ 724 0084

LEBANON
(+961)

Arab African International Bank
Riad El Sohl Street, PO Box 11-6066, Beirut
Tel: (1) 980 162; (1) 980 163 **Fax:** (1) 980 910 **Telex:** ARAFRO 22285 LE
General Tel: 980 264; 980 265; **General Telex:** ARAFRO 20507 LE

Bank of Beirut & the Arab Countries SAL
Head Office
250 Clemenceau Street, Beirut
PO Box 11-1536, Beirut
Tel: (1) 602 401; (1) 369 835 **Fax:** (1) 602 401; (1) 369 835 **Telex:** 21422, 40031 BBACFX LE **Swift:** BBAC LB BX
Email: bbac@inco.com.lb **Cable:** ARABCONTRIBANK
General Tel: 602 402; 369 836; **Fax:** 602 402; **General Tel:** 602 403; **Fax:** 602 403; **General Tel:** 602 404;
Fax: 602 404; **General Fax:** 369 836

Senior Executive Officers
Chairman & General Manager Ghassan Assaf
Vice Chairman Fawzi Ghandour
Member, Secretary of the Board Abbas El-Halabi
International Division Samira Farha *Manager*

Others (Senior Executives)
  Jean Mehanna *Senior Regional Manager - Bekaa Region*
  Abdulsalam Abulhosn *Senior Regional Manager - Aley Region*
  Omar Saab *Senior Regional Manager - Beirut Western Region*
  Munir Abu Ayash *Senior Regional Manager - Chouf Region*
  Ali Nabouche *Senior Regional Manager - North Region*
  Hassan Fayad *Regional Manager - South Region*
  Michel Kazan' *Regional Manager - Kessrouan Area*
  Ali El-Khalil *Member*
  Habib Maamari *Member*
  Walid Assaf *Member*

Syndicated Lending
Head of Credit Committee Feryal Asseh *Senior Manager, Credit*

Foreign Exchange
Global Head Talal Abou Zeki *Manager, FX*

Risk Management
Global Head Georges Mirza *Assistant General Manager*

Settlement / Clearing
Operations Berge Daw *Manager, Operations*

Other Departments
Correspondent Banking Walid Haddad *Manager*

Euromoney Directory 1999 **953**

LEBANON (+961)   www.euromoneydirectory.com

Bank of Beirut & the Arab Countries SAL (cont)
Administration
Head of Administration — Samir Abi Khouzam *Assistant General Manager*
Technology & Systems
Dames El Ghali *Manager, Technology & Software*
Legal / In-House Counsel
Abbas El-Halabi *AGM, Legal Counsel*
Accounts / Audit
Inspection & Audit — Soufian Asseh *Senior Manager, Inspection & Credit*
Other (Administration)
Human Resources — Adnan Aridi *Manager*
Marketing — Elie Francis *Manager*
Credit Information Department — Adel Hamden *Manager*
Equipment & Maintenance Department — Sabah Khatounian *Manager*

Banque Audi SAL — Head Office

Charles Malek Avenue, St Nicolas Area, Sofil Centre, Beirut
PO Box 11-2560, Beirut
Tel: (1) 200 250; (1) 331 600 **Fax:** (1) 200 955 **Telex:** DIRODI 42291 **Swift:** AUDB LB BX **Cable:** BANAUDI
General Telex: 42292 DIRODI LE; **General Telex:** 42393 DIRODI LE; **General Telex:** 43012 DIRODI LE; **General Telex:** 43014 DIRODI LE

Senior Executive Officers
Chairman & General Manager — Raymond W Audi
Director & General Manager — Samir N Hanna
Deputy General Manager — Gaby G Kassis
Assistant General Manager — Jean A Karam
International Division — Marc J Audi *Deputy General Manager & Head*

Debt Capital Markets / Fixed Income
Department: Treasury & Capital Markets
Tel: 200 951/3 **Fax:** 200 288
Domestic Government Bonds
Head of Sales — Nabil E Chaya *Local Currency Desk*
Mirielle Yared *Sales*
Non-Domestic Government Bonds
Dollar Desk — Michel E Aramouni
Foreign Exchange
Global Head — Stephan E Awaida *Senior Manager* ☏ **871 427**
Other Departments
Correspondent Banking — Salah K Labaki *Manager, Correspondent Banking & Operations* ☏ **871 424**

Banque d'Affaires du Liban et d'Outre-Mer — Head Office

Alternative trading name: BALOM
Blom Building, 2nd Floor, Rachid Karameh Street, Verdun, Beirut
PO Box 11-1912, Beirut
Tel: (1) 743 300; (1) 348 246 **Fax:** (1) 738 916 **Swift:** BLOM LB BX
Website: www.blom.com.lb

Senior Executive Officers
Chairman — Naaman Azhari
Chief Executive Officer — Fadi Osseiran *General Manager*

Banque du Liban et d'Outre-Mer SAL — Head Office

Formerly known as: BLOM
BLOM Building, Rachid Karameh Street, Beirut
PO Box 11-1912, Beirut
Tel: (1) 743 300; (1) 738 938 **Fax:** (1) 738 946 **Telex:** 214535 (France), 20740 (FX) **Swift:** BLOM LB BX
Email: blommail@inco.com.lb **Reuters:** BLOM
Website: www.blom.com.lb

Senior Executive Officers
Chairman, President & CEO — Naaman Azhari
General Manager — Habib Rahal

Senior Executive Officers (cont)
Managing Director / General Manager — Samer Azhari
Assistant General Manager — Fawaz Kayal

Others (Senior Executives)
Board of Directors — Philippe Takla
Sheikh Ghassan Shaker
Mohamed Jaroudi
Ghazi Shaker
Fouad El Bizri
Salim Boutros El-Khoury
Me. Jean Asfar
Joseph Emile Kharrat
Nicolas Saade
Samer Azhari
Saad Azhari *Group General Secretary*

Administration
Head of Administration — Samih Zeineddine *Senior Manager*
Head of Marketing — Khalil Abou-Assaly *Senior Manager*

Technology & Systems
Information Technology & Development — Antoine Lawandos *Senior Manager*
Computer Department — Mohamed Soubra *Senior Manager*

Accounts / Audit
— Riad Tabbara *Senior Manager, Accounting*
Group Inspection Department — Naoum Raphael *Senior Manager*

Other (Administration)
Group Inspection — Naoum Raphael *Senior Manager*
Inspection — Sélim Mouawad *Senior Manager*
Human Resources — Pierre Abou-Ezze *Senior Manager*
Georges Sayegh *Senior Manager*

Banque Misr-Liban SAL
Head Office

Riad El-Sohl Street, Beirut
PO Box 11-7, Beirut
Tel: (1) 867 397; (1) 787 864 **Fax:** (1) 868 490; (1) 787 863 **Telex:** 22783-40449-21468-20538 BAMISL L
Swift: BIMS LB B BIC **Email:** mail@blm.com.lb
Website: www.blm.com.lb

Senior Executive Officers
Chairman & General Manager — Ibrahim Nour El-Dine ☎ **868 492**
Treasurer — Anas Zantout *Deputy General Manager* ☎ **868 491**
Deputy General Manager — Nizar Sultani ☎ **787 862**

Debt Capital Markets / Fixed Income
Tel: 787 397 **Fax:** 787 7863
Global Head — Ibrahim Nour El-Dine *Chairman & General Manager* ☎ **868 492**
Regional Head — Nizar Sultani *Deputy General Manager* ☎ **787 862**
Country Head — Anas Zantout *Deputy General Manager* ☎ **868 491**

Equity Capital Markets
Global Head — Ibrahim Nour El-Dine *Chairman & General Manager* ☎ **868 492**
Regional Head — Nizar Sultani *Deputy General Manager* ☎ **787 862**
Country Head — Anas Zantout *Deputy General Manager* ☎ **868 491**

Banque Paribas
Representative Office

Sabbagh Center, Hamra, PO Box 11-5262, Beirut
Tel: (1) 340 480/1; (1) 349 427/8 **Fax:** (1) 347 235; (1) 349 098 **Email:** paribas@nethopper.inco.com.lb

Senior Executive Officers
Head Representative — Nicolas Constantinesco ☎ **248 525**

LEBANON (+961)   www.euromoneydirectory.com

Banque Saradar SAL
Head Office

Saradar Building, 31st Street, Rabyé
PO Box 11-1121 & 11-3312, Beirut
Tel: (4) 404 493; (4) 410 048 **Fax:** (4) 404 490 **Telex:** 41803/4 MARSAR LE **Swift:** BSAR LB BX
Email: saradar@saradar.com.lb **Reuters:** SARL **Cable:** MARSAR BEIRUT
Foreign Exchange Tel: 220 226/7; 334 134; **Fax:** 200 268; **Telex:** 40268 MARSAR LE; **Private Banking Tel:** 218 866; 330 726; **Fax:** 218 433
Website: www.saradar.com.lb

Senior Executive Officers
Chairman   Mario Saradar ⓣ **404 493** ⓕ **404 490**
Deputy Chairman   Abdo Jeffi ⓣ **404 493** ⓕ **404 490**
Managing Director   Fady Amatoury ⓣ **404 493** ⓕ **404 490**
Assistant General Manager   Charles Harfouche ⓣ **404 493** ⓕ **404 490**
International Division   Joseph Nader *Deputy Manager, International Dept* ⓣ **404 493** ⓕ **404 490**

Others (Senior Executives)
Member   Marielle Saradar
                                           Henriette Saradar
                                           Salim El Meouchy
                                           Carl Azar
Main Branch Manager   Toufic Aouad ⓣ **200 260** ⓕ **200 265**

General - Treasury
Head of Treasury   Pierre Gaspard *Executive Manager, Treasury & Financial Markets*
                                           ⓣ **200 266** ⓕ **200 268**

Syndicated Lending
Other (Trade Finance)
Real Estate Finance   Pierre Naggear *Executive Manager* ⓣ **257 788** ⓕ **259 076**

Corporate Finance / M&A Advisory
Head of Corporate Finance   Pierre Naggear *Executive Manager* ⓣ **257 788** ⓕ **259 076**

Settlement / Clearing
Operations   Rodolphe Attallah *Executive Manager, Operations Manager* ⓣ **200 260**
                                           ⓕ **218 431**

Administration
Legal / In-House Counsel
                                           Etude Badri
                                           Salim Badri El Meouchy

Public Relations
                                           Samir El-Tawilé *Manager* ⓣ **404 493** ⓕ **404 490**
Other (Administration)
Commercial Manager   Izzat El-Hage *Commercial Manager* ⓣ **200 260** ⓕ **200 265**

British Arab Commercial Bank Limited
Representative Office

Beirut Representative Office, Aresco Center, 13th Floor, Banque Duliban Street, Beirut
Tel: (1) 343 998; (1) 602 437 **Fax:** (1) 602 438

Senior Executive Officers
Others (Senior Executives)
                                           Meguerditch Bouldoukian *Representative*

The British Bank of the Middle East

SNA Building, Tabaris Square, Ashrafich, PO Box 11-1380, Beirut
Tel: (1) 203 156/7; (1) 203 158/9 **Fax:** (1) 203 155 **Telex:** 48043 BBME LB **Swift:** BBME LB BX
Email: bbmelbm@dm.net.lb **Cable:** BACTRIA
Website: www.britishbank.com

Senior Executive Officers
Chief Executive Officer   Youssef Bakri
                                           Gordon V Jones *Deputy Chief Executive Officer*

Others (Senior Executives)
Personal Banking   Anthony Ussher *Manager*
Securities Services   Ahmad Takkoush ⓣ **742 641** ⓕ **349 483** ⓔ **lbmscc@inco.com.lb**

956 Euromoney Directory 1999

www.euromoneydirectory.com   LEBANON (+961)

Administration
Other (Administration)
Human Resources   Sanaa Chami *Manager*

CCF Finance M-O SAL   Subsidiary Company
10th Floor, SNA Building, Tabaris Square, Ashrafieh, Beirut
Tel: (1) 203 267 **Fax:** (1) 333 636

The Chase Manhattan Bank   Representative Office
16th Floor, Block B, Gefinor Center, Clemenceau Street, Beirut
Tel: (1) 361 065 **Fax:** (1) 739 581 **Telex:** 20357 LE

Senior Executive Officers
Others (Senior Executives)
Senior Country Officer   Mohamad Yasser Mortada *Senior Country Officer* 739 583 739 581

Citibank NA   Full Branch Office
Gefinor Centre, Bloc E, 6th Floor, Clemenceau Street, PO Box 113-5794, Beirut
Tel: (1) 738 400 **Fax:** (1) 738 993; (1) 738 406 **Telex:** 48635 CITILE **Swift:** CITI LB BE **Reuters:** CTLB (DEALING); CTLB01-10 (Pages)

Senior Executive Officers
Chief Executive Officer   Walid Alamuddin *Country General Manager*
                               Elia Samaha *Deputy General Manager*
Chief Operating Officer   George Galiounghi *Senior Country Operations Officer*
Treasurer   Yousuf Sandeela *Country Treasurer* 738 410
Others (Senior Executives)
Head of Financial Instituitions   Antoine Raphael *Head of Financial Institutions*
Head of Retail Marketing   Najat Abi-Nader

Debt Capital Markets / Fixed Income
Department: Treasury
Tel: 738 411 **Fax:** 738 993 **Reuters:** CTLB **Telex:** 48635 CITILE
Head of Fixed Income   Yousuf Sandeela *Country Treasurer* 738 410
Head of Fixed Income Trading   Adel Jabre *Assistant Treasurer* 738 988

Syndicated Lending
Loan-Related Activities
Trade Finance   Elia Samaha *Deputy General Manager*

Foreign Exchange
Tel: 738 411 **Fax:** 738 993 **Reuters:** CTLB **Telex:** 48635 CITILE
Head of Foreign Exchange   Yousuf Sandeela *Country Treasurer* 738 410
Head of Trading   Adel Jabre *Assistant Treasurer* 738 988

Settlement / Clearing
Head of Settlement / Clearing   George Galiounghi *Senior Country Operations Officer*
Fixed-Income Settlement   Bassem Kantari *Head of Operations*
Operations   Jean Paul Wannous *Operations Assistant*

Asset Management
Head   Yousuf Sandeela *Country Treasurer* 738 410

Other Departments
Chief Credit Officer   Elia Samaha *Deputy General Manager*
Correspondent Banking   Antoine Raphael *Head of Financial Institutions*
Cash Management   Khalil Geagea

Administration
Business Development   Walid Alamuddin *Country General Manager*

Technology & Systems
        Sami Bou-Habib *Head of Data Centre*

Compliance
        George Galiounghi *Senior Country Operations Officer*

Accounts / Audit
        Afif Ramadan *Financial Controller*

LEBANON (+961) www.euromoneydirectory.com

Commerzbank AG
Representative Office

7th Floor, Liberty Tower, Hamra, Beirut
PO Box 113-6440, Beirut
Tel: (1) 744 246; (1) 602 482 Fax: (1) 744 245

Senior Executive Officers
Chief Representative Hans G Pirner

Federal Bank of Lebanon SAL
Head Office

Dora Circus, Federal Bank Building, PO Box 11-2209, Beirut
Tel: (1) 255 255 Fax: (1) 268 711 Telex: 42307 FBDRAN LE Swift: FBLE LB BX Email: fedliban@cyberia.net.lb
General Telex: 20267 FBDRAN LE

Senior Executive Officers
Chairman & President Fadi Saab
Vice Chairman & EVP Fadi Michel Saab
Chief Executive Officer Riyad Hassan Kaidbey *General Manager & Chief Executive*
Treasurer Phrem Kamal *Manager, Treasury* ☎ **262 174**
International Division Khalil Safi *Manager, International Banking*
  Abdo Zeidan *General Manager, International Banking*

Others (Senior Executives)
Member of the Board Antranik Bedros Atamian *Director*

Settlement / Clearing
Operations Azzam Bechara *Manager & Head of Operations*

Administration

Technology & Systems
Information Technology Antoinette Al-Tayar *Manager*

Corporate Communications
Information Micheline Nahas *Manager*

Accounts / Audit
  George Rawady *Manager*

Other (Administration)
Human Resources Azzam Bechara *Manager & Head of Operations*
Internal Control Fadi Abou Diab *Manager*

Robert Fleming Holdings Limited
Subsidiary Company

Office 202, Bloc C, Gefinor Centre, Beirut
Tel: (1) 738 694; (1) 738 695 Fax: (1) 738 694; (1) 738 695 Email: flemmings@dm.net.lb
Website: www.flemings.com

Fransabank SAL
Head Office

Sabbag Center, 1st Floor, Hamra Street, Hamra, Beirut
Tel: (1) 340 180/8; (1) 738 711/3 Fax: (1) 354 572 Telex: FRANSA 20631 LE Swift: FSAB LB BX
Email: fsb@fransabank.com.lb Reuters: FRBK
Website: www.fransabank.com.lb

Senior Executive Officers
Chairman & General Manager Adnan Kassar
Deputy Chairman & General Manager Adel Kassar
Deputy General Manager Hanna El Khal
Deputy General Manager Ibrahim Fouad Koleilat
Deputy General Manager Faouzi Moussa
Deputy General Manager Mansour Bteish
Secretary General Wajdi Abi Chacra

Others (Senior Executives)
  Youssef Hadathi *Head of Inspection*

Gulf International Bank BSC
Representative Office

Gefinor Centre, Block B, Office Number 1401, PO Box 113/6793, Beirut
Tel: (1) 739 505/7 **Fax:** (1) 739 503

Senior Executive Officers
Chief Representative   Hassan A Yaseen

ING Barings
Full Branch Office

Fouad Boutros Building, Sursock Street, PO Box 11-4096, Beirut Achrafieh, 4096
Tel: (1) 325 020 **Fax:** (1) 325 022 **Telex:** 48632 INGBEY LE **Swift:** INGB LB BE

Senior Executive Officers
Country Manager   Konrad L Petersen

Merrill Lynch, Pierce, Fenner & Smith (Middle East) SAL
Subsidiary Company

15th Floor, Sabbagh Centre, Hamra Street, Beirut
PO Box 11-5316, Beirut
Tel: (1) 348 175 **Fax:** (1) 602 123
Website: www.ml.com

Metropolitan Bank SAL
Head Office

Nihako Building, Antelias Highway, Antelias, PO Box 70216, Beirut
Tel: (1) 415 824; (1) 406 862 **Fax:** (1) 406 861; (1) 649 726 **Telex:** METRON 42130LE **Swift:** MNBK LB BE
Email: metro@metrob.com **Reuters:** MTRP **Cable:** METROBANK

Senior Executive Officers
Chairman & General Manager   Mershed Baaklini [T] **406 862** [F] **406 861**
Chief Executive Officer   Rafic Menhem *Director & General Manager* [T] **415 822**
Chief Operating Officer   Ghassan Tohme *Manager of Operations* [T] **415 824**
Treasurer   Antoine Gharby *Head* [T] **417 511**
Company Secretary   Layla Chammas [T] **415 862**
International Division   Rafic Menhem *Director & General Manager* [T] **415 822**

Others (Senior Executives)
Marketing   Maroun Baaklini *Manager*
Administration   Georges Khoury *Manager* [T] **415 826**
Credits & Facilities   Jack Samaha *Credit Manager* [T] **415 826**
IT   Mrad Mrad *Manager* [T] **415 822**
Import / Export   Elie Nasser *Manager* [T] **415 826**

General-Investment
Head of Investment   Rafic Menhem *Director & General Manager* [T] **415 822**

Relationship Manager
Import / Export   Elie Nasser *Manager* [T] **415 826**
Credit Officer   Jack Samaha *Credit Manager* [T] **415 826**
Trade Finance   Elie Nasser *Manager* [T] **415 824**
Project Finance   Elias Rashed *Assistant Manager* [T] **415 824**

Debt Capital Markets / Fixed Income
Department: Securities Department
Tel: 406 862 **Fax:** 406 861 **Reuters:** MTRP **Telex:** METRON 42130 LE
Head of Fixed Income   Rafic Menhem *Director & General Manager* [T] **415 822**

Emerging Market Bonds
Head of Emerging Markets   Rafic Menhem *Director & General Manager* [T] **415 822**

Equity Capital Markets
Department: Securities Department
Tel: 415 824 **Fax:** 406 861 **Reuters:** MTRP **Telex:** METRON 42130 LE
Head of Equity Capital Markets   Rafic Menhem *Director & General Manager* [T] **415 822**

Syndicated Lending

Loan-Related Activities
Trade Finance   Elie Nasser *Manager* [T] **415 824**
Project Finance   Elias Rashed *Assistant Manager* [T] **415 824**

LEBANON (+961)

www.euromoneydirectory.com

Metropolitan Bank SAL (cont)

Money Markets
Department: Treasury Department
Head of Money Markets — Antoine Gharby *Head* ☎ **417 511**

Domestic Commercial Paper
Head of Sales — Jack Samaha *Credit Manager* ☎ **415 826**

Eurocommercial Paper
Head of Sales — Jack Samaha *Credit Manager* ☎ **415 826**

Wholesale Deposits
Marketing — Antoine Gharby *Head* ☎ **417 511**

Foreign Exchange
Head of Foreign Exchange — Antoine Gharby *Head* ☎ **417 511**

Risk Management
Tel: 406 862 Fax: 406 861
Head of Risk Management — Antoine Gharby *Head* ☎ **417 511**

Fixed Income Derivatives / Risk Management
Head of Sales; Trading — Antoine Gharby *Head* ☎ **417 511**

Other Currency Swap / FX Options Personnel
Antoine Gharby *Head* ☎ **417 511**

Settlement / Clearing
Tel: 415 824 Fax: 406 861
Head of Settlement / Clearing; Regional Head Operations — Jeanette Arbid *Deputy Manager* ☎ **415 824**
Mary Abboud *Dealer* ☎ **411 751**

Global Custody
Head of Global Custody — George Khoury *Manager* ☎ **415 822**

Other Departments
Commodities / Bullion — Antoine Gharby *Head* ☎ **417 511**
Chief Credit Officer — Jack Samaha *Credit Manager* ☎ **415 826**
Private Banking; Correspondent Banking — Rafic Menhem *Director & General Manager* ☎ **415 822**
Cash Management — Antoine Gharby *Head* ☎ **417 511**

Administration
Head of Administration — Georges Khoury *Manager* ☎ **415 826**
Head of Marketing — Marwan Baaklini *General Manager*

Technology & Systems
Mrad Mrad *Manager* ☎ **415 822**

Compliance
Raouf Matar *Head* ☎ **415 824**

Public Relations
Marwan Baaklini *General Manager*

Accounts / Audit
Accounts Department — Lubnan Zeidouni *Manager* ☎ **406 862**

Other (Administration)
Credits & Facilities — Jack Samaha *Credit Manager* ☎ **415 826**

National Bank of Kuwait (Lebanon) — Subsidiary Company

Sanayeh Square, Justinian Street, BAC Building, Beirut
PO Box 11-5727, Beirut
Tel: (1) 741 111; (1) 742 222 Fax: (1) 602 328 Telex: 20742 Swift: NBOK LB BE

Senior Executive Officers
Chairman — Ibrahim Dabdoub
General Manager — Basil Karam ☎ **747 872**

Paribas Limited — Full Branch Office

Sabbagh Center, 5th Floor, PO Box 11-5262, Hamra, Beirut
Tel: (1) 340 480/1; (1) 349 427/3 Fax: (1) 347 235; (1) 349 098 Email: paribas@nethopper.inco.com.lb

Senior Executive Officers
Managing Director — Nicolas Constantinesco ☎ **248 525**

The Saudi National Commercial Bank
Full Branch Office

Verdun Plaza Centre, Corniche Al Mazaa, Beirut
PO Box 11-2355, Beirut
Tel: (1) 860 863; (1) 787 381/2/3/4 **Fax:** (1) 867 728 **Telex:** 20642 LE - 43619 LE **Swift:** SNCBLBBE

Senior Executive Officers
Chief Executive Officer
Treasurer

Houssami Hani *General Manager*
Antoine Gebran ☎ **865 059**

Société Générale Libano Europeene de Banque

Sin El Fil Rond-Point Saloume, Immeuble Sehnaoui, PO Box 112955, Beirut
Tel: (1) 499 813 **Fax:** (1) 500 836
Website: www.socgen.com

Transorient Bank SAL

Bauchrieh, Serail Street, Transorient Bank SAL Building, Beirut
PO Box 11-6260, Beirut
Tel: (1) 888 630; (1) 897 706 **Fax:** (1) 897 705 **Telex:** 44925-43947 LE TOBank **Swift:** TRAN LB BX **Reuters:** TOBX

Senior Executive Officers
Chairman
Financial Director
Treasurer
Managing Director / General Manager
International Division

Adib Millet
Jean Honein *Central Manager*
Nabil Issa *Assistant General Manager*
Adib Millet
Nabil Issa *Assistant General Manager*

Foreign Exchange
Head of Foreign Exchange

Nabil Issa *Assistant General Manager*

LESOTHO
(+266)

Central Bank of Lesotho
Central Bank

Alternative trading name: Banka e Kholo ea Lesotho
PO Box 1184, Corner Airport and Mushoeshoe Roads, Maseru, 100
Tel: 314 281 **Fax:** 310 051; 310 557 **Telex:** 4367 **Swift:** CBLE LS MX

Senior Executive Officers
Governor
Deputy Governor

Anthony Maruping
Felix Burciho

Others (Senior Executives)
Head, Bank Licensing
Head, Economics & Statistics
Head, Reserves Management

Lerato Mukhesi
Motlais Matekane *Chief Economist*
Gail Makenete *Manager* ☎ **315 770**

Foreign Exchange
Head of Foreign Exchange

Gail Makenete *Manager* ☎ **315 770**

Administration
Head of Administration

Thabu Makara *Director*

Technology & Systems

Sam Mahouana *Manager*

Accounts / Audit
Head, Accountancy

Francina Monasca *Manager*

LIBYA
(+218)

Libyan Arab Foreign Bank
Head Office

Dat El Imad Administrative Complex, Tower 2, Tripoli
PO Box 2542, Tripoli
Tel: (21) 335 0155; (21) 335 0160 **Fax:** (21) 335 0164; (21) 335 0168 **Telex:** 20200 **Swift:** LAFB LY LT BIC
Telerate: LABL

Senior Executive Officers
Chairman   Mohamed Layas ☎ **335 0086**
Chief Executive Officer   Abdullatif Elkib *Deputy Chairman*
Financial Director   Saddik Abu Hellala *Manager* ☎ **335 0023**
Chief Operating Officer   Bashir Zoghni *Manager* ☎ **335 0024**
Treasurer   Mohamed Riany *Manager* ☎ **335 0170**

Equity Capital Markets
Head of Equity Capital Markets   Mohamed Riany *Manager* ☎ **335 0170**

Syndicated Lending
Head of Syndicated Lending   Najib Eljamel *Manager* ☎ **335 0025**

Money Markets
Head of Money Markets   Mohamed Riany *Manager* ☎ **335 0170**

Foreign Exchange
Head of Foreign Exchange   Mohamed Riany *Manager* ☎ **335 0170**

Corporate Finance / M&A Advisory
Head of Corporate Finance   Najib Eljamel *Manager* ☎ **335 0025**

Settlement / Clearing
Head of Settlement / Clearing   Saddit Abuhelala *Manager* ☎ **335 0023**

LIECHTENSTEIN
(+41 75)

Bank Wegelin (Liechtenstein) AG

Heiligkreuz 49, Postfach, FL-9490 Vaduz
Tel: 237 4800 **Fax:** 237 4801 **Swift:** WEGELI 21 **Email:** wegelin@bwl.li
Website: www.wegelin.li

Senior Executive Officers
Chairman   Richard Negele
Vice Chairman   Otto Bruderer
Chief Executive Officer   Cyrill Escher
Managing Director / General Manager   Michael Frommelt

Centrum Bank AG
Independent Fund Management Company

Heiligkreuz 8, FL-9490 Vaduz
PO Box 1168, 9490 Vaduz
Tel: (75) 235 8585 **Fax:** (75) 235 8686 **Telex:** 889203 CENT FL **Swift:** CBK LI 2X

Senior Executive Officers
Chairman & President   Peter Marxer
Chief Executive Officer   Jochen Hadermann
Managing Director / General Manager   Matthias Trösch
Managing Director / General Manager   Jochen Hadermann

Debt Capital Markets / Fixed Income
Department: Trading
Tel: 235 8586 **Fax:** 235 8687
Regional Head   Matthias Trosch *Director*
                                               Herman Neusüss *Holder of Procuration*

Other Departments
Private Banking   Aribert Schurte *Director*
Correspondent Banking   Matthias Trosch *Director*

www.euromoneydirectory.com　　　LIECHTENSTEIN (+41 75)

Administration
Head of Administration　　　Matthias Trosch *Director* ☏ 235 8586
Technology & Systems
　　　　　　　　　　　　　　Arno Gerrier *Director*
Public Relations
　　　　　　　　　　　　　　Jochen Hadermann

LGT Bank in Liechtenstein AG　　　　　　　　　　　Head Office
Herrengasse 12, FL-9490 Vaduz
Tel: 235 1122 Fax: 235 1522 **Swift:** BLFL LI 2X **Email:** info@lgt.com **Reuters:** BILU
Website: www.lgt.com

Senior Executive Officers
Board of Directors　　　　　　Philipp von und zu Liechtenstein
Chief Executive Officer　　　　Heinz Nipp *Chief Executive Officer*
Others (Senior Executives)
Production Area　　　　　　　Walter G Marxer
Distribution Area　　　　　　　Thomas Piske
Finance / IT Area　　　　　　　Bruno B Pfister
Debt Capital Markets / Fixed Income
Head of Fixed Income　　　　　Joseph Ruettimnn *Head of Fixed Income* ☏ 375 3588 F 375 3122
Head of Fixed Income Sales　　Joseph Ruettimnn *Head of Fixed Income* ☏ 375 3588 F 375 3122
Administration
Head of Administration　　　　Werner Ospelt ☏ 235 1670

Liechtensteinische Landesbank AG　　　　　　Full Branch Office
Städtle 44, FL-9490 Vaduz
PO Box 384, FL-9490 Vaduz
Tel: 236 8811 Fax: 236 8822 Telex: 889401
Website: www.llb.li

Senior Executive Officers
Chairman　　　　　　　　　　Karlheiuz Heeb
President　　　　　　　　　　　René Kzistli
Others (Senior Executives)
　　　　　　　　　　　　　　　Peter Marxer

Verwaltungs-und Privat-Bank AG　　　　　　　　Head Office
Im Zentrum, FL-9490 Vaduz
Tel: 235 6655 Fax: 235 6500 **Telex:** 889200 VPB FL **Swift:** VPBV LI 2X **Email:** info@vpbank.li **Cable:** Privatbank
Website: www.vp.bank.li

Senior Executive Officers
Chairman　　　　　　　　　　Hans Brunhart
Honorary Chairman　　　　　　Heinz Batliner
Chief Executive Officer　　　　Adolf E Real *Chief Executive Officer*
Others (Senior Executives)
Board of Directors　　　　　　Olaf Walser
　　　　　　　　　　　　　　　Emil Kuster
　　　　　　　　　　　　　　　Rudolf Staub
　　　　　　　　　　　　　　　Gerard Batliner
　　　　　　　　　　　　　　　Matthias Donhauser
　　　　　　　　　　　　　　　Markus Thomas Hilti
　　　　　　　　　　　　　　　Guido Meier
Dealing　　　　　　　　　　　Walter Seger
Regional Clients　　　　　　　Viktor Büchel
International Clients　　　　　Rolf Ehlers
Relationship Manager
Individual Clients　　　　　　　Walter Forrer
Private Clients　　　　　　　　Fredy Wolfinger
Corporate Clients　　　　　　Anton Caviezel
Client Services　　　　　　　　Bruno Büchel

LIECHTENSTEIN (+41 75)   www.euromoneydirectory.com

Verwaltungs-und Privat-Bank AG (cont)
Debt Capital Markets / Fixed Income
Bonds - General
Securities Dealing   Lydia Hilti
Securities Administration   Walter Dünser
Money Markets
Country Head   Anton Kindle
Foreign Exchange
Head of Trading   Anton Kindle
Risk Management
Country Head   Helmut Quaderer
Other (FI Derivatives)
Banks & Derivatives   Helmut Quaderer
Corporate Finance / M&A Advisory
Other (Corporate Finance)
Corporate Planning   Fredy Vogt
Settlement / Clearing
Operations   Christoph Baumgartner *Front Office*
Asset Management
Other (Asset Management)
Professional Clients / Asset Management   Adelgunde Sengthaler
Administration
Head of Marketing   Rainer Gassner
Legal / In-House Counsel
Legal Services   Beat Peter
Accounts / Audit
Accounting / Controlling   Adrian Hasler
Other (Administration)
Personnel   Karl Walch
Organization   Georg Wohlwend
Internal Services   Josef Niedhart

LITHUANIA
(+370)

Bank of Lithuania   🏛 Central Bank

Gedimino Avenue 6, 2001 Vilnius
Totoriu Street, 4, 2629 Vilnius
Tel: (2) 224 008; (2) 629 042 **Fax:** (2) 620 430; (2) 221 501 **Telex:** 261090 LTBID **Swift:** LIAB LT 2X
Email: bank.of.lithuania@mail.lbank.lt **Reuters:** LITH-I
Website: www.lbank.lt

Senior Executive Officers
Governor   Reinoldijus Sarkinas
Financial Director   Stase Strickaite *Director of Accounting and Information Technologie*
                                            ☎ 225 721 📠 226 005
International Division   Stasys Kropas *Director of International Relations Department* ☎ 617 813
                                            📠 226 909

Others (Senior Executives)
Head, Bank Policy Department   Gitanas Naliseda *Director* ☎ 224 423 📠 224 423
Head, Banking Supervision   Kazimieras Ramonas *Director* ☎ 623 001 📠 615 665
Head, Market Operations Department   Arvydas Kregzde *Director* ☎ 224 836 📠 224 843
Head, Information & Statistics   Vladimiras Truksinas *Director* ☎ 227 209 📠 227 209
Head, General Division   Ramune Grazulyte *Head* ☎ 629 862 📠 221 501
Settlement / Clearing
Tel: 700 120 **Fax:** 721 011
Head of Settlement / Clearing   Alis Zaramaitis *Director*
Other Departments
Cash Management   Arunas Dulkys *Director of Cash Department* ☎ 626 047
Administration
Technology & Systems
Information System Implementation   Marijonas Pulkauninkas *Head* ☎ 225 786

964 Euromoney Directory 1999

www.euromoneydirectory.com　　　　　　　LITHUANIA (+370)

Public Relations
　　　　Viktoras Parulskis *Head of Public Relations* ☏ **629 042**

Accounts / Audit
Internal Audit Division　　　　Jurgis Balaisis *Head* ☏ **700 175**

Agricultural Bank of Lithuania　　　　　　　Head Office

Alternative trading name: AB Lietuvos Zemes Ukio Bankas
J Basanaviciaus 26, 2600 Vilnius
Tel: (2) 239 060; (2) 239 070 **Fax:** (2) 238 886 **Telex:** 261097 VOD LT **Swift:** AGBL LT 2X

Senior Executive Officers
Chairman & Chief Executive Officer　　　Jonas Dieninis
Financial Director　　　Stanislovas Vaiciukevicius *Director of Finance* ☏ **239 095**
Treasurer　　　Robert Anuskevic *Member of the Board* ☏ **239 094**

Debt Capital Markets / Fixed Income
Tel: 629 764 **Fax:** 627 762
Global Head　　　Vytautus Kupliauskas *Director*

Equity Capital Markets
Tel: 629 764 **Fax:** 627 762
Global Head　　　Vytautus Kupliauskas *Director*

Warrants
Head of Sales　　　Dzeralda Kondratiene *Head of Corporate Finance* ☏ **238 891**

Syndicated Lending
Tel: 239 071 **Fax:** 238 613
Global Head　　　Modestas Keliauskas *Director of Credit*

Loan-Related Activities
Trade Finance　　　Dzeralda Kondratiene *Head of Corporate Finance* ☏ **238 891**

Money Markets
Tel: 239 044 **Fax:** 263 433
Global Head　　　Mindaugas Vaiciulis *Director*

Wholesale Deposits
Marketing　　　Vilma Ceplinskaite *Dealer, Money Markets* ☏ **263 433**

Foreign Exchange
Tel: 239 074 **Fax:** 263 433
Global Head　　　Mindaugas Vaiciulis *Director*

FX Traders / Sales People
　　　Remigijus Petruseviciusa *Dealer, FX*
　　　Vilma Ceplinskaite *Dealer, Money Markets* ☏ **263 433**
　　　Saulius Tamosiunias *Dealer, FX*
　　　Romas Grigalis *Corporate Dealer*

Risk Management
Other Currency Swap / FX Options Personnel
　　　Remigijus Petruseviciusa *Dealer, FX*
　　　Vilma Ceplinskaite *Dealer, Money Markets* ☏ **263 433**

Corporate Finance / M&A Advisory
Tel: 238 891 **Fax:** 239 058
Global Head　　　Dzeralda Kondratiene *Head of Corporate Finance* ☏ **238 891**

Settlement / Clearing
Tel: 238 602 **Fax:** 239 058
Regional Head　　　Zydrunas Burvys *Head of International Payments*

Other Departments
Proprietary Trading　　　Sarunas Benediktavicius *Director* ☏ **238 889**
Private Banking　　　Gintaus Piragius *Director* ☏ **239 073**
Correspondent Banking　　　Vita Morkunaite *Head, Correspondent Banking* ☏ **238 892**

Administration
Technology & Systems
　　　Romas Remeika *Director* ☏ **239 077**

Legal / In-House Counsel
　　　Vadimas Tolocko *Director* ☏ **238 616**

Public Relations
　　　Imandra Dauksiene *Public Relations Officer* ☏ **239 000**

Euromoney Directory 1999　**965**

LITHUANIA (+370) www.euromoneydirectory.com

AB Bankas Hermis

Head Office

Jogailos Street 9/1, 2001 Vilnius
Tel: (2) 226 165; (2) 224 757 **Fax:** (2) 224 477 **Telex:** 261210 HERMI LT **Swift:** COBH LT 2X
Email: bankas@hermis.ot.lt **Reuters:** HERM
Website: www.hermis.lt

Senior Executive Officers
Chairwoman & CEO Nadiezda Novickiene
Chairman of Council Jonas Karciauskas ☏ **627 477**
Financial Director Vytautass Jurna *Deputy Chairman of the Board & CFO* ☏ **226 745**
Treasurer Vytautas Polujanskas *Deputy Chairman & Head of Treasury* ☏ **627 634**
Chancellor Algimantas Kundrotas ☏ **626 657**
International Division Rima Larionovaite ☏ **226 335**
Chief Representative Antanas Petrauskas ☏ **628 809**

General-Lending (DCM, SL)
Head of Corporate Banking Danuta Ryntevic *Head of Operations* ☏ **225 734**

General-Investment
Head of Investment Ivo Gueorguiev *Deputy Chairman* ☏ **628 754**

Debt Capital Markets / Fixed Income
Department: Treasury Department
Tel: 619 770
Head of Fixed Income Trading Edmundas Makaravicuis *Dealer*

Government Bonds
Head of Sales Arvydas Kvietkauskas *Acting Director, Financial Brokerage Dept* ☏ **229 470**

Eurobonds
Head of Trading Edmundas Makaravicuis *Dealer*

Emerging Market Bonds
Head of Trading Edmundas Makaravicuis *Dealer*

Fixed-Income Repo
Head of Repo Vytautas Polujanskas *Deputy Chairman & Head of Treasury* ☏ **627 634**

Syndicated Lending
Department: International & Relations Department
Tel: 226 335
Head of Origination Judita Ramonaite *Head of Credit Department* ☏ **618 279**
Head of Trading Rima Larionovaite ☏ **226 335**

Money Markets
Department: Treasury Department
Tel: 619 770
Head of Money Markets Vytautas Polujanskas *Deputy Chairman & Head of Treasury* ☏ **627 634**

Domestic Commercial Paper
Head of Trading Jonas Irzikevicius *Deputy Director & Chief Dealer* ☏ **619 770**

Foreign Exchange
Tel: 619 770
Head of Foreign Exchange Vytautas Polujanskas *Deputy Chairman & Head of Treasury* ☏ **627 634**
Head of Trading Jonas Irzikevicius *Deputy Director & Chief Dealer* ☏ **619 770**

Risk Management
Tel: 626 783
Head of Risk Management Danguole Zinyté *Head* ☏ **626 783**

Corporate Finance / M&A Advisory
Head of Corporate Finance Ivo Gueorguiev *Deputy Chairman* ☏ **628 754**

Global Custody
Tel: 627 537
Head of Global Custody Alvydas Kunavicuis ☏ **226 718**

Other Departments
Chief Credit Officer Judita Ramonaite *Head of Credit Department* ☏ **618 279**
Correspondent Banking Rima Larionovaite ☏ **226 335**
Cash Management Gerardas Jurkonis *Head* ☏ **627 652**

Administration
Head of Marketing Viktoras Radusis ☏ **627 170**

Legal / In-House Counsel
  Andrius Ignotas *Head* ☏ **226 273**

Public Relations
  Laima Grybauskaite ☏ **627 837**

Accounts / Audit
Audit Irena Ungailiene ☏ **626 631**

LITHUANIA (+370)

European Bank for Reconstruction & Development
Representative Office

3rd Floor, Jaksto 5, 2600 Vilnius
Tel: (2) 227 258 Fax: (2) 224 666

Senior Executive Officers
Others (Senior Executives)
Head of Office — Urmas Paavel

Hansa Investments
Full Branch Office

K. Kalinausko 9/7-12, Vilnius
Tel: (2) 626 766; (2) 611 766 Fax: (2) 627 892
Website: www.hansa.ee/invest

Senior Executive Officers
Managing Director — Linas Sasnauskas

Debt Capital Markets / Fixed Income
Private Placements
Head of Origination — Linas Sasnauskas *Managing Director*
Head of Structuring — Nerijus Eidukevicius *Associate Director*

Equity Capital Markets
Country Head — Linas Sasnauskas *Managing Director*

Domestic Equities
Head of Origination — Linas Sasnauskas *Managing Director*
Head of Research — Nerijus Eidukevicius *Associate Director*

Corporate Finance / M&A Advisory
Country Head — Linas Sasnauskas *Managing Director*

Lietuvos Taupomasis bankas
Head Office

Savanoriu Avenue 19, 2009 Vilnius
Tel: (2) 232 370; (2) 232 379 Fax: (2) 232 431; (2) 232 433 Telex: 261840 TAUP LT Swift: TAUP LT 2X
Email: info@ltb.tdd.lt Reuters: TBVL; TAUP, (Dealing)
Website: www.ltb.tdd.lt

Senior Executive Officers
Chairman — Romualdas Visokavicius T 232 371 F 232 432
Financial Director — Rene Mecinskiene T 232 375
Treasurer — Stanislovas Dzinozeleta *Director, Treasury* T 250 559
International Division — Vytenis Jurkus *Director, International Division* T 232 379 F 232 433

Equity Capital Markets
Head of Equity Capital Markets — Daiva Rackauskiene T 232 434

Syndicated Lending
Loan-Related Activities
Trade Finance — Ramune Sauleviciene T 232 964 F 251 760

Foreign Exchange
Head of Foreign Exchange — Skirmantas Jareckas T 232 847

Settlement / Clearing
Head of Settlement / Clearing — Dalia Adomaviciene *Director, Payments & Clearing* T 251 787 F 251 760

Asset Management
Head — Povilas Milasauskas T 232 372

Other Departments
Correspondent Banking — Jonas Juskevicius T 251 793 F 232 433

Administration
Head of Marketing — Loreta Ramanauskiene T 481 304

Technology & Systems
Robertas Urbonavicius *Director, IT* T 633 711 F 236 541

Legal / In-House Counsel
Saulius Jakstas *Director, Legal* T 232 377 F 232 527

Public Relations
Ceslovas Iskauskas *Director, Public Relations* T 251 797 F 251 603

Euromoney Directory 1999 967

LITHUANIA (+370)　　www.euromoneydirectory.com

Lietuvos Taupomasis bankas (cont)
Accounts / Audit
Internal Audit Dept.　　Algis Sasnauskas *Director* ℡ 705 150 🖷 705 147

Lithuanian Development Bank　　Head Office
Stulginskio 4/7, 2600 Vilnius
Tel: (2) 617 031; (2) 623 012 **Fax:** (2) 225 259 **Email:** 83536@ldb.omnitel.net

Senior Executive Officers
President　　Juozas Aliukonis ℡ 227 360
Financial Director　　Giedrius Vegys *VP & Head of Finance* ℡ 625 886

Relationship Manager
Project Department　　Aidas Mackevicius ℡ 624 123

Other Departments
Economic Research　　Olga Stavinskiene *Chief Economist*

Administration

Technology & Systems
　　Virginijus Zemaitis *EDP Manager* ℡ 624 476

Legal / In-House Counsel
　　Jurga Novikiene *Legal Counsel* ℡ 623 012

The State Commercial Bank of Lithuania　　Head Office
Alternative trading name: Bank Vytis
Basanaviciaus Street 7, LV-2631 Vilnius
Tel: (2) 626 872; (2) 615 428 **Fax:** (2) 615 428 **Telex:** 261346 OPERA LT **Swift:** BARU LT 2X **Reuters:** SBTX
Website: www.lvkb.lt

Senior Executive Officers
Governor　　Alvydas Mackevicius
Financial Director　　Milda Zalkauskiene *Head* ℡ 225 925
Treasurer　　Audrone Vaitkiene *Director* ℡ 628 400
Director　　Kazys Ratkevicius ℡ 227 682

Debt Capital Markets / Fixed Income
Department: Securities Brokerage Department
Tel: 227 598 **Fax:** 615 649
Global Head　　Grazina Niauriene *Head* ℡ 227 598 ✉ graz@lvkb.lt

Domestic Government Bonds
Head of Sales　　Grazina Niauriene *Head* ℡ 227 598 ✉ graz@lvkb.lt
Head of Trading　　Vladimiras Jurkevicius *Head* ℡ 615 649

Equity Capital Markets
Department: Securities Brokerage Department
Tel: 227 598 **Fax:** 615 649
Global Head　　Grazina Niauriene *Head* ℡ 227 598 ✉ graz@lvkb.lt

Domestic Equities
Head of Sales　　Grazina Niauriene *Head* ℡ 227 598 ✉ graz@lvkb.lt
Head of Trading　　Vladimiras Jurkevicius *Head* ℡ 615 649

Warrants
Head of Sales　　Dzeralda Kondratiene *Head* ℡ 614 933

Syndicated Lending
Department: Credit Department
Tel: 615 162
Global Head　　Sergejus Ignatjevas *Head*
Head of Credit Committee　　Alvydas Mackevicius *Governor*

Loan-Related Activities
Trade Finance　　Dzeralda Kondratiene *Head* ℡ 614 933
Project Finance　　Sergejus Ignatjevas *Head*

Money Markets
Tel: 225 171 **Fax:** 225 726
Global Head　　Igorius Pancerevas *Head* ✉ pancerevas@lvkb.lt

www.euromoneydirectory.com LITHUANIA (+370)

Foreign Exchange
Tel: 225 171 Fax: 225 726
Global Head Igorius Pancerevas *Head* E pancerevas@lvkb.lt
FX Traders / Sales People
 Rytis Maliukevicius *Trader*
 Rimas Markevicius *Trader* T **614 924**

Corporate Finance / M&A Advisory
Tel: 226 846 Fax: 225 726
Global Head Dzeralda Kondratiene *Head* T **614 933**

Settlement / Clearing
Tel: 226 846 Fax: 225 921
Regional Head Ramute Pilkiene *Global Head* E rpil@lvkb.lt
Equity Settlement; Fixed-Income Settlement Grazina Niauriene *Head* T **227 598** E graz@lvkb.lt

Global Custody
Department: Securities Brokerage Department
Tel: 227 598 Fax: 615 679
Regional Head Grazina Niauriene *Head* T **227 598** E graz@lvkb.lt

Other Departments
Correspondent Banking Justinas Vanagas *Manager* T **619 483**

Administration
Technology & Systems
 Pranas Slusnys *Director* T **724 768**

Legal / In-House Counsel
 Paulius Koverovas *Head* T **619 830**

Public Relations
 Gediminas Koncius *Head* T **225 946**

Ukio Bankas Head Office **L**

J Gruodzio Street 9, 3000 Kaunas
Tel: (7) 203 651 Fax: (7) 323 188 Telex: 269897 UKIS LT Swift: UKIO LT 2X Email: ub@ub.lt Telerate: 56771
Website: www.ukiobankas.online.lt

Senior Executive Officers
Chairman of the Board Juozas Lukauskas
Deputy Chairman of the Board Jonas Saulenas T **204 296**
Financial Director Gintaras Rasavicius *Deputy Chairman of the Board* T **203 591**
Treasurer Romualdas-Jonas Rutkauskas *Head of Treasury* T **205 369**
International Division Edita Navickaite *Head of International Division* T **204 209**

Other Departments
Chief Credit Officer Saulius Zostautas *Head of Credit Division* T **204 615**
Correspondent Banking Edita Navickaite *Head of International Division* T **204 209**

Vilniaus Bankas AB Head Office

Gedimino pr 12, 2600 Vilnius
Tel: (2) 610 723; (2) 227 590 Fax: (2) 626 557; (2) 225 906 Telex: 261601 VILBK LT Swift: CBVI LT 2X Reuters: VIBX
Website: www.vb.lt

Senior Executive Officers
Chairman of the Board Julius Niedvaras
Financial Director Vladas Andrijauskas *Director, Book-keeping & Reporting Department*
  T **626 022**
Investor Relations Officer Erlendas Grigorovic T **610 910**
Others (Senior Executives)
 Gintautas Bareika *Head of Credit Division* T **227 590**
 Virginija Skuncikiene *Head of Operations & Information Systems* T **613 716**
 Marijonas Misiukonis *Head of Administration & Legal Division* T **226 172**

General-Lending (DCM, SL)
Head of Corporate Banking Raimondas Kutra *Director, Commercial Development Division* T **226 744**

General-Investment
Head of Investment Raimondas Kvedaras *Director, Treasury & International Finance* T **227 465**

General - Treasury
Head of Treasury Raimondas Kvedaras *Director, Treasury & International Finance* T **227 465**

Euromoney Directory 1999 **969**

LITHUANIA (+370) www.euromoneydirectory.com

Vilniaus Bankas AB (cont)
Debt Capital Markets / Fixed Income
Department: Treasury Department / Financial Brokerage Department
Tel: 313 287 **Fax:** 618 407
Head of Fixed Income   Romas Cesnavicius *Director of Treasury & Brokerage Department* ☎ **625 043**

Government Bonds
Head of Sales   Rita Lodiene *Director of Money Market Unit* ☎ **313 287**

Eurobonds
Head of Sales   Rita Lodiene *Director of Money Market Unit* ☎ **313 287**

Emerging Market Bonds
Head of Emerging Markets   Rita Lodiene *Director of Money Market Unit* ☎ **313 287**

Fixed-Income Repo
Head of Repo   Rita Lodiene *Director of Money Market Unit* ☎ **313 287**

Fixed-Income Research
Head of Fixed Income; Head of Credit Research   Saulius Racevicius *Director of Brokerage Department* ☎ **721 559**

Equity Capital Markets
Department: VB Vilfima UAB
Tel: (2) 390 400 **Fax:** (2) 390 499
Head of Equity Capital Markets   Vidas Jelinskas *Director*
Alvydas Zabolis *Director*

Syndicated Lending
Tel: 226 370 **Fax:** 612 629
Head of Origination; Head of Syndication   Rimantas Purtulis *Director, Investment & Structured Finance* ☎ **226 393**

Loan-Related Activities
Trade Finance   Linas Staniulis *Director, International Finance* ☎ **626 980**
Project Finance   Jonas Brazdzionis *Director of Credit* ☎ **220 358**

Money Markets
Tel: 626 043 **Fax:** 618 407
Head of Money Markets   Romas Cesnavicius *Director of Treasury & Brokerage Department* ☎ **625 043**

Domestic Commercial Paper
Head of Sales   Rita Lodiene *Director of Money Market Unit* ☎ **313 287**

Eurocommercial Paper
Head of Sales   Rita Lodiene *Director of Money Market Unit* ☎ **313 287**

Wholesale Deposits
Marketing   Rita Lodiene *Director of Money Market Unit* ☎ **313 287**

Foreign Exchange
Head of Foreign Exchange; Head of Institutional Sales; Corporate Sales; Head of Trading   Paulius Tarbūnas *Manager, Foreign Exchange Unit* ☎ **223 409** 📠 **618 407**

FX Traders / Sales People
Aidas Molis *Dealer* ☎ **223 409**

Risk Management
Tel: 313 287 **Fax:** 618 407
Head of Risk Management   Romas Cesnavicius *Director of Treasury & Brokerage Department* ☎ **625 043**

Fixed Income Derivatives / Risk Management
Head of Sales   Rita Lodiene *Director of Money Market Unit* ☎ **313 287**

Foreign Exchange Derivatives / Risk Management
Spot / Forwards Sales   Paulius Tarbūnas *Manager, Foreign Exchange Unit* ☎ **223 409** 📠 **618 407**

OTC Equity Derivatives
Sales   Rita Lodiene *Director of Money Market Unit* ☎ **313 287**

Corporate Finance / M&A Advisory
Head of Corporate Finance   Raimondas Kvedaras *Director, Treasury & International Finance* ☎ **227 465**

Settlement / Clearing
Tel: 620 451 **Fax:** 227 510
Head of Settlement / Clearing   Dalia Poteliunaite ☎ **620 451**
Equity Settlement   Mindaugas Rizgelis
Back-Office   Dalia Poteliunaite ☎ **620 451**

Global Custody
Head of Global Custody   Saulius Racevicius *Director of Brokerage Department* ☎ **721 559**

Asset Management
Head   Bronius Zibaitis *Director* ☎ **753 920**

www.euromoneydirectory.com LUXEMBOURG (+352)

Other Departments
Commodities / Bullion
Chief Credit Officer
Private Banking
Correspondent Banking

Linas Staniulis *Director, International Finance* ☎ **626 980**
Gintautas Bareika *Head of Credit Division* ☎ **227 590**
Raimondas Kutra *Director, Commercial Development Division* ☎ **226 744**
Audrius Ziligzda *Head, Financial Institutions* ☎ **22 6370**

Administration
Head of Administration
Head of Marketing

Marijonas Misiukonis *Head of Administration & Legal Division* ☎ **226 172**
Alexander Federas *Director of Marketing* ☎ **791 092**

Technology & Systems
Technology & Systems Department

Arunas Baraliskas *Head* ☎ **22 6180**
Virginija Skuncikiene *Head of Operations & Information Systems* ☎ **613 716**

Legal / In-House Counsel

Juozas Kunca ☎ **227 147**
Marijonas Misiukonis *Head of Administration & Legal Division* ☎ **226 172**

Public Relations

Sigitas Krivickas ☎ **614 732**

Accounts / Audit

Arturas Feiferas *Director* ☎ **223 428**

LUXEMBOURG
(+352)

Banque Centrale du Luxembourg   🏛 Central Bank

Formerly known as: Institut Monetaire Luxembourgeois
63 Avenue de la Liberté, L-2983, Luxembourg
Tel: 402 929 203; 402 929 250 **Fax:** 492 180 **Telex:** 2766

Senior Executive Officers
President & General Manager — Y Mersch
Manager — Jean-Nicolas Schaus
Manager — Arthur Philippe

ABN AMRO Bank (Luxembourg) SA   Subsidiary Company

4 rue Jean Monnet, L-2180, Luxembourg Kirchberg
PO Box 581, L-2015, Luxembourg
Tel: 424 949 42 **Fax:** 424 949 499 **Telex:** 60816

Senior Executive Officers
Managing Director — F B Deiters
Secretary to Managing Director — Marleen Demuynck ☎ **424 949 301** 📠 **424 949 399**

Others (Senior Executives)
ABN AMRO Investment Management — B Renner *Managing Director*

General-Lending (DCM, SL)
Head of Corporate Banking — J C Thoma *Manager, Finance*

General - Treasury
Head of Treasury — Piet Huyjgen *Manager, Treasury & Securities*

Debt Capital Markets / Fixed Income
Head of Fixed Income — Piet Huyjgen *Manager, Treasury & Securities*

Equity Capital Markets
Head of Equity Capital Markets — Piet Huyjgen *Manager, Treasury & Securities*

Syndicated Lending
Loan-Related Activities
Structured Trade Finance — C Spaan *Manager*

Corporate Finance / M&A Advisory
Other (Corporate Finance)
Corporate & Structured Finance — C Spaan *Manager*

Other Departments
Private Banking — Peter H M Aelbers *Manager, Private Banking*

Administration
Head of Administration — S H Behm *Manager*

Euromoney Directory 1999   **971**

LUXEMBOURG (+352)　　　　www.euromoneydirectory.com

American Express Bank (Luxembourg) SA — Subsidiary Company

34 Avenue de la Porte Neuve, L-2227, Luxembourg
PO Box 919, L-2019, Luxembourg
Tel: 241 891 **Fax:** 472 419 **Telex:** 2621 AEB LU **Swift:** AEIB LU LX **Reuters:** AELU

Senior Executive Officers
General Manager　　　　　　　　　　　　Irteza Shah
Deputy General Manager　　　　　　　　Edouard Karaguilla
International Division　　　　　　　　　Irteza Shah *General Manager, International & Treasury*

General-Lending (DCM, SL)
Head of Corporate Banking　　　　　　Jutta Laupichler *Credit Manager*

General - Treasury
Head of Treasury　　　　　　　　　　　Eli Aubertin *Manager, Treasury*

Debt Capital Markets / Fixed Income

Other (Fixed Income)
　　　　　　　　　　　　　　　　　　　Irteza Shah *Manager, Buying & Distribution*
　　　　　　　　　　　　　　　　　　　Eli Aubertin *Dealer, Buying & Distribution*
　　　　　　　　　　　　　　　　　　　Isabell Belot *Dealer, Buying & Distribution*

Eurobonds
Head of Trading　　　　　　　　　　　Irteza Shah
　　　　　　　　　　　　　　　　　　　Eli Aubertin *Trader*

Bonds - General
　　　　　　　　　　　　　　　　　　　Isabell Belot *Trader*
　　　　　　　　　　　　　　　　　　　Udo Leuca *Trader*

Libor-Based / Floating-Rate Products
FRN Trading　　　　　　　　　　　　　Irteza Shah
　　　　　　　　　　　　　　　　　　　Eli Aubertin *Trader*

Other (Libor-Based / Floating Rate Products)
　　　　　　　　　　　　　　　　　　　Isabell Belot *Trader*
　　　　　　　　　　　　　　　　　　　Olivier Lang *Trader*

Medium-Term Notes
Head of Origination　　　　　　　　　Eli Aubertin *Trader*
　　　　　　　　　　　　　　　　　　　Isabell Belot *Trader*

Equity Capital Markets

International Equities
Head of Syndication　　　　　　　　　Irteza Shah
Head of Sales　　　　　　　　　　　　Eli Aubertin *Trader*

Convertibles / Equity-Linked
Head of Trading　　　　　　　　　　　Irteza Shah
　　　　　　　　　　　　　　　　　　　Eli Aubertin *Trader*
　　　　　　　　　　　　　　　　　　　Isabell Belot *Trader*

Warrants
Head of Trading　　　　　　　　　　　Irteza Shah
　　　　　　　　　　　　　　　　　　　Eli Aubertin *Trader*
　　　　　　　　　　　　　　　　　　　Isabell Belot *Trader*

Syndicated Lending

Other (Trade Finance)
Documentary Credits　　　　　　　　　Jutta Laupichler *Credit Manager*

Money Markets

Eurocommercial Paper
Head of Origination　　　　　　　　　Eli Aubertin *Trader*
　　　　　　　　　　　　　　　　　　　Isabell Belot *Trader*

Other (Wholesale Deposits)
Eurocurrency Deposits & CDs　　　　Eli Aubertin *Trader*
　　　　　　　　　　　　　　　　　　　Isabell Belot *Trader*

Foreign Exchange
Head of Foreign Exchange　　　　　　Irteza Shah *Manager*
　　　　　　　　　　　　　　　　　　　Eli Aubertin *Manager*

FX Traders / Sales People
　　　　　　　　　　　　　　　　　　　Isabell Belot *Trader*
　　　　　　　　　　　　　　　　　　　Olivier Lang *Trader*

www.euromoneydirectory.com   LUXEMBOURG (+352)

Risk Management
IR Swaps Trading
Irteza Shah *Manager, Buying & Distribution*
Eli Aubertin *Dealer, Buying & Distribution*

Foreign Exchange Derivatives / Risk Management
Cross-Currency Swaps, Trading
Irteza Shah *Manager, Buying & Distribution*
Eli Aubertin *Dealer, Buying & Distribution*

Other (Exchange-Traded Derivatives)
Equity & Commodity Derivatives
Irteza Shah *Manager, Buying & Distribution*
Eli Aubertin *Dealer, Buying & Distribution*

Settlement / Clearing
Settlement (General)
Pascal Moris *Manager, Back-Office Settlements*
Operations
Zia Amanullah

Asset Management
Portfolio Management
Irteza Shah *General Manager*
Arduine Lonazzi

Other Departments
Correspondent Banking
Irteza Shah *General Manager*

Administration
Compliance
Zia Amanullah

Artesia Bank Luxembourg SA   Subsidiary Company

Formerly known as: BACOB Bank Luxembourg SA
47 Boulevard Prince Henri, L-1724, Luxembourg
PO Box 11, L-2010, Luxembourg
Tel: 461 341 1 **Fax:** 226 318 **Telex:** 1270 ARTE LU **Swift:** ARTE LU LL
Website: www.artesia.lu

Senior Executive Officers
Chairman   Dirk Bruneel
Managing Director   Maureen Ford
General Manager   Stephen Graham

Debt Capital Markets / Fixed Income
Department: Capital Markets
Country Head   Marc Troch

Foreign Exchange
Head of Foreign Exchange   Kurt Ibendahl

Risk Management
Head of Risk Management   Jan Mertens *Risk Management Officer*

Settlement / Clearing
Head of Settlement / Clearing   Hugo Mertens

Other Departments
Private Banking   Fred Matyn *General Manager*

Administration
Compliance
Stephen Graham *General Manager*

Accounts / Audit
Reeba Nachtegaele

ASLK-CGER

12-16 Avenue Monterez, L-2163, Luxembourg
Tel: 46 800 1 **Fax:** 46 800 222

Senior Executive Officers
President   Pierre De Tournay [T] 46 800 253 [F] 46 800 666

Aurea Finance Company   Head Office

50 rue Basse, L-7307, Steinsel
Tel: 333 301 1 **Fax:** 333 301 30 **Email:** aurea@pt.lu

Senior Executive Officers
Managing Director   Henri de Crouy-Chanel
General Manager   Gererd de Ganay

Euromoney Directory 1999   **973**

LUXEMBOURG (+352) www.euromoneydirectory.com

Aurea Finance Company (cont)
Senior Executive Officers (cont)
General Manager   Eriik Droemer
Equity Capital Markets
Equity Research
Head of Equity Research   Yvonne Nagel
Settlement / Clearing
Back-Office   Stephanie Weisse

Banca Popolare di Novara   Full Branch Office
9A Boulevard Prince Henri, L-1724, Luxembourg
Tel: 477 601 1; 474 255 **Fax:** 474 558; 221 630 **Telex:** 3671, 3664 NOVBA LU **Swift:** NVRB LU LL **Email:** bpnlux@pt.lu
Senior Executive Officers
Branch Manager   Gianfranco Barp
Debt Capital Markets / Fixed Income
Country Head   Stephan Hacker
Equity Capital Markets
Country Head   Stephan Hacker
Syndicated Lending
Country Head   Dario Ercolini
Money Markets
Country Head   Steve Tonizzo
Foreign Exchange
Country Head   Steve Tonizzo
Risk Management
Country Head   Dario Ercolini
Corporate Finance / M&A Advisory
Country Head   Nicola Pegoraro
Settlement / Clearing
Country Head   Gilbert Denell

Banco Itaú Europa Luxembourg SA   Subsidiary Company
Formerly known as: Banco Bamerindus do Brasil à Luxembourg SA
29 Avenue de la Porte-Neuve, L-2227, Luxembourg
PO Box 572, L-2015, Luxembourg
Tel: 223 377 1 **Fax:** 223 377 210 **Telex:** 60511 BIELULU **Swift:** ITAU LU LL **Email:** george.crosby@itau.com.br
Website: www.itau.com.br
Senior Executive Officers
Chief Executive Officer   George Crosby *Managing Director* ☏ **223 377 200**
Financial Director   Guilherme Bezerril *Director* ☏ **223 377 202**
Treasurer   Stephan Gottlieb *Treasury* ☏ **223 377 450**
Relationship Manager
Private Banking   Didier H Buffard *Director* ☏ **223 377 201**
Administration
Head of Administration   Guilherme Bezerril *Director* ☏ **223 377 202**

Banco Mello (Luxembourg) SA   Subsidiary Company
10 rue de la Grève, L-1643, Luxembourg
PO Box 365, L-2013, Luxembourg
Tel: 402 112; 402 121 **Fax:** 405 834; 402 111 **Telex:** 2898 UNIBA LU **Swift:** BMEC LU LL **Email:** bmellolu@p.t.lu
Reuters: BMEU
Senior Executive Officers
Chairman   Francisco Lacerda
Others (Senior Executives)
    Luís Pereira-Coutinho *Director*
    Manuel Ortigano-Ramos *Director*

974   Euromoney Directory 1999

www.euromoneydirectory.com   LUXEMBOURG (+352)

Others (Senior Executives) (cont)

António Fernandes-Tato *Director*
António Sousa-Mota *Director*
Eliane Fuchs *Manager*
Manuel Félix *Manager*

Banco Mercantil de São Paulo International SA   Subsidiary Company

5 Boulevard Joseph II, L-1840, Luxembourg
PO Box 921, L-2019, Luxembourg
Tel: 254 131 **Fax:** 254 139 **Telex:** 3528 BMSPI **Swift:** BMSP LU LL

Senior Executive Officers
Chairman of the Board   Gastão Eduardo de Bueno Vidigal

Others (Senior Executives)
Management   Peter Gerrard *Directeur Général*
                                               Robert Duncan *Directeur*

General - Treasury
Head of Treasury   Romain Lenz *Arbitrage / Treasury* ☎ 254 142 222

Syndicated Lending
Loan-Related Activities
Trade Finance   Florencio Muñoz Perez ☎ 254 142 217

Other Departments
Private Banking   Søren Møller ☎ 254 142 241

Administration
Head of Administration   Richard Prommenschenkel ☎ 254 142 224

Accounts / Audit
Accounting   Robertine Vanetti-Hanff ☎ 254 142 223
Internal Audit   Emmanuelle Wathier-Viart ☎ 254 142 240

Other (Administration)
Electronic Data Processing / Personnel   Richard Prommenschenkel ☎ 254 142 224

Banco di Napoli International SA   Subsidiary Company

10/12 Avenue Pasteur, L-2310, Luxembourg
PO Box 1301, L-1013, Luxembourg
Tel: 475 959 1; 47 4284 **Fax:** 22 7614; 47 4117 **Telex:** 1533 DIRNAP LU (Management) **Swift:** NAPB LU LL
Reuters: NALU, NALT, ITFX **Telerate:** 3708 **Cable:** NAPINTER LUXEMBOURG
Reuters: ITFX-Y

Senior Executive Officers
Chairman   Sabino Fortunato
Deputy Chairman   Marco Zanzi
Managing Director   Oliviero Pesce
General Manager   Lorenzo Ranzini
Chief Manager   Quirico Piras

Corporate Finance / M&A Advisory
Other (Corporate Finance)
                              Gabriele Nemi *Deputy Manager, Financial Division*

Other Departments
Chief Credit Officer   Robin Alder *Assistant Manager, Credit*
Private Banking   Benedetto Rosetti *Deputy Chief Manager*

Administration
Other (Administration)
Administration & Personnel Quirico Piras *Chief Manager*

Banco Popolare di Verona Luxembourg   Head Office

Formerly known as: Gemina Europe Bank SA
26 Boulevard Royal, L-2449, Luxembourg
PO Box 822, L-2018, Luxembourg
Tel: 465 7571 **Fax:** 470 170; 472 590 **Telex:** 60749 GEMIN LU **Swift:** GEMI LU LL **Reuters:** GEMI

LUXEMBOURG (+352)   www.euromoneydirectory.com

Banco di Sicilia International SA   Subsidiary Company

14 Avenue Marie Thérèse, L-2132, Luxembourg
Tel: 454 040 1 Fax: 454 040 22 Telex: 60563

Senior Executive Officers
Director & General Manager   Antonino Federico
Deputy General Manager   Giovanni Motta

Bank Anhyp Luxembourg

8 rue de la Greze, L-1643, Luxembourg
Tel: 403 8081 Fax: 40 38 07

Bank of Bermuda (Luxembourg) SA   Subsidiary Company

13 rue Goethe, L-1637, Luxembourg
PO Box 413, L-2014, Luxembourg
Tel: 404 646 1 Fax: 404 674 Telex: 60864 Swift: BBDA LU LX

Senior Executive Officers
Chief Executive Officer   Christopher J Wilcockson *Managing Director*
Financial Director   Dan Rasmussen *Manager, Accounting & Operations*

Others (Senior Executives)
Corporate Trust   Christopher J Wilcockson *Managing Director*

General - Treasury
Head of Treasury   Claude Noesen *Treasury Manager*

Relationship Manager
Corporate Trust   Christopher J Wilcockson *Head*
                                 Neil Millward *General Manager*

Money Markets
Global Head   Claude Noesen *Manager*

Money Markets - General
                                 Eric Rubay *Senior Dealer*
                                 Claude Quintus *Dealer*
                                 Marco Manieri *Dealer*

Foreign Exchange
Global Head   Claude Noesen *Manager*

FX Traders / Sales People
                                 Eric Rubay *Senior Dealer*
                                 Claude Quintus *Dealer*
                                 Marco Manieri *Dealer*

Settlement / Clearing
Operations   Dan Rasmussen *Head*

Global Custody
Regional Head   Audray Lewis

Administration

Accounts / Audit
Financial Accounting & Operation   Claude Noesen *Head*
Accounting & Valuations   Rosie Scott *Manager*

Other (Administration)
Shareholder Services   Susan S Lee *Manager*

Bank of China Luxembourg   Full Branch Office

37/39 Boulevard Prince Henri, L-1724, Luxembourg
PO Box 114, L-2011, Luxembourg
Tel: 466 791 1; 221 791 Fax: 221 795 Telex: 3546 Swift: BKCH LU LL Reuters: BOCU

Senior Executive Officers
General Manager   Liu Daguo ☏ **466 791 1**
Deputy General Manager   Shi Yingru ☏ **466 791 265**
Assistant General Manager   Li Guangying ☏ **466 791 257**
Assistant General Manager   Xu Xiaofeng ☏ **466 791 250**

Money Markets
Country Head   J Z Wu *Chief Dealer* ☏ **226 934**

976 Euromoney Directory 1999

www.euromoneydirectory.com LUXEMBOURG (+352)

Foreign Exchange
Country Head   J Z Wu *Chief Dealer* 226 934
Settlement / Clearing
Country Head; Foreign Exchange Settlement   Li Zhiqiang *Deputy Manager* 466 791 238
Other Departments
Private Banking   Wee Wongyin *Manager* 466 791 223

Bank Leumi

6D rue Treves, Stnningerverg, L-2633, Luxembourg
Tel: 346 390 Fax: 346 396

Senior Executive Officers
President   Michael Ginsburg
Financial Director   Arlette Koresh
Other Departments
Private Banking   Moshe Yardeni *Head*
Administration
Head of Marketing   Herve Lanini

Bank of Tokyo-Mitsubishi (Luxembourg) SA   Subsidiary Company

Formerly known as: The Bank of Tokyo (Luxembourg) SA
287-289 Route d'Arlon, L-1150, Luxembourg
PO Box 364, L-1150, Luxembourg
Tel: 445 180 1 **Fax:** 446 091 **Telex:** 1341 **Swift:** BOTK LU LX **Reuters:** BTLU
FX Tel: 472 065/7

Senior Executive Officers
Managing Director   Tamio Kobayakawa
Executive Vice President   Mr Takase

General - Treasury
Head of Treasury   Hiroshi Yamada *Manager, Capital Markets & Treasury*
    Alain Schanen *Officer, Capital Markets & Treasury*

Relationship Manager
Corporate Actions & Dividends   Mr Dries
Financial Services & Promotion   Patrick Loutsch *Officer*
    André Weicker *Supervisor*

Debt Capital Markets / Fixed Income
Country Head   Hiroshi Yamada *Manager, Capital Markets & Treasury*
    Alain Schanen *Officer, Capital Markets & Treasury*

Asset-Backed Securities / Securitization
Head of Trading   Hiroshi Tomita *Manager, Securities Administration*
Settlement / Clearing
Settlement (General)   Patrick Glodt
    Toshiko Igarashi *Manager, Back-Office Nostro*
    Xavier Guehl *Officer, Back-Office Nostro*

Global Custody
Regional Head   Mario Mantrisi *Supervisor*
Asset Management
Investment Funds   Mr Daoud
Administration
Technology & Systems
Electronic Data Processing / Organization   Hiroshi Tomita *Manager, Securities Administration*
    Roland Van Mulders *Supervisor*
    Franck Asztalos

Compliance
Compliance Matters   Mr André
Other (Administration)
Fees & Administration   Robert Gaia

LUXEMBOURG (+352)   www.euromoneydirectory.com

Bankers Trust Luxembourg SA
Subsidiary Company

14 Boulevard FD Roosevelt, L-2450, Luxembourg
PO Box 807, L-2018, Luxembourg
Tel: 460 241 **Fax**: 473 136 **Telex**: 3392

Senior Executive Officers
Managing Director — Barry Wilkinson

Administration
Head of Administration — Pascale Navette *Manager*

Other (Administration)
Paying Agency — Sarah Bridge *Supervisor*
Cedel Depository — Peter Dickinson *Supervisor*

Bankgesellschaft Berlin International SA
Subsidiary Company

30 Boulevard Royal, L-2449, Luxembourg
PO Box 163, L-2011, Luxembourg
Tel: 468 969 1; 4778 1 **Fax**: 468 969 2009; 468 969 2029 **Telex**: 60805 LBB NL **Swift**: BEBE LU LL
Reuters: BBGU (Dealing)
General Telex: 1803 BBI CR

Senior Executive Officers
Chairman of the Board — Leopold Tröbinger
MD & Spokesman — Horst-Dieter Hochstetter
Managing Director — Klaus A Heiliger
General Manager — Michael Renner
Secretary & Managing Director — Dagmar Schanen

Equity Capital Markets
Head of Equity Capital Markets — Stefan Bungarten

Syndicated Lending
Head of Origination; Head of Syndication — Werner Streitz

Money Markets
Head of Money Markets — Gustav Maerten

Foreign Exchange
Head of Foreign Exchange — Gustav Maerten

Settlement / Clearing
Head of Settlement / Clearing — Dirk Vollkommer

Asset Management
Head — Uwe Jungerwirth

Other Departments
Private Banking — Uwe Jungerwirth

Administration
Head of Administration — Erwin Lütge *Administration & Personnel*
Head of Marketing — Markus Postler

Technology & Systems
Roland Bauler
Patricia Muller

Compliance
Erwin Lütge *Administration & Personnel*

Public Relations
Markus Postler

Accounts / Audit
Accounts — Alain Schmit
Colette Hurt-Migliosi
Audit — Wolfgang Schulze

Other (Administration)
Organisation — Helmut Haag

www.euromoneydirectory.com   LUXEMBOURG (+352)

Banque Audi (Luxembourg) SA
Head Office

22 Avenue Marie-Thérèse, L-2132, Luxembourg
Tel: 457 777 Fax: 450 192 Telex: 60450 AUDI LU

Senior Executive Officers
Chairman   Raymond Audi
Treasurer   Helene Hanna *Assistant Manager*
Managing Director   Bechara Issa

Banque Banespa International SA
Subsidiary Company

3B Boulevard du Prince Henri, L-1724, Luxembourg
Tel: 225 055 Fax: 225 060 Telex: 60821BBI LU Swift: BESP LU LL Email: banespa@innet.lu
Capital Markets Tel: 223 508
Website: www.uunet.lu

Senior Executive Officers
Chairman of the Board   Antonio Barreto de Paiva
Managing Director   Elcio Luiz Romão
Director   Hélvio Rocholli

Syndicated Lending

Loan-Related Activities
Trade Finance   Hélvio Rocholli *Director*

Other Departments
Correspondent Banking   Hélvio Rocholli *Director*

Administration
Head of Administration   Chantal Godard *Personnel & Administration Officer*

Technology & Systems
                                      Laurent Lefevre

Accounts / Audit
                                      Patrick Javel *Head of Accounting*

Banque Baumann & Cie SA
Head Office

36 rue Marie-Adelaïde, L-2128, Luxembourg
PO Box 2214, L-1022, Luxembourg
Tel: 454 311 Fax: 452 740

Senior Executive Officers
Chief Executive Officer   Hans Gerner *Chief Executive & Managing Director*
Financial Director   Hans Gerner *CFO & Treasurer*
Chief Operating Officer   Roger Kayser *Chief Executive, MD & COO*

Debt Capital Markets / Fixed Income

Eurobonds
Head of Origination   Pol Kenens *Manager*
Head of Trading   Marc de Windt *Dealer*
                                      Jean-Paul Krier *Dealer*
                                      Bart van den Wijngaert *Dealer*

Money Markets

Other (Wholesale Deposits)
Eurocurrency Deposits   Jean-Paul Krier *Trading*

Foreign Exchange

FX Traders / Sales People
                                      Jean-Paul Krier *Dealer*

Euromoney Directory 1999   **979**

LUXEMBOURG (+352)   www.euromoneydirectory.com

Banque Carnegie Luxembourg SA
Subsidiary Company

Formerly known as: Nordbanken Luxembourg SA
5 Place de la Gare, L-1616, Luxembourg
PO Box 1141, L-1011, Luxembourg
Tel: 404 030 1 Fax: 491 802; 491 806 Telex: 1556 CARNE LU Swift: CARN LU LL Email: general@carnegie.lu
Reuters: NBLU

Senior Executive Officers
Chairman of the Board of Directors — Bertil Hult
Managing Director — Carl Uggla

Others (Senior Executives)
Front Office — Niels-Eiler Nystroem *General Manager*
Administration — Bruno Frèrejean *General Manager*

General - Treasury
Head of Treasury — Kim Kromand

Debt Capital Markets / Fixed Income
Head of Fixed Income Trading — Peter Brondum-Nielsen *Securities Trading*

Money Markets
Money Markets - General
Dealing — Henrik Sjoestroem

Foreign Exchange
FX Traders / Sales People
Dealing — Henrik Sjoestroem

Risk Management
Country Head — Danillo Linosa *Senior Manager*

Settlement / Clearing
Country Head — Karen Hopson

Global Custody
Fund Administration — Michael Hughes

Other Departments
Private Banking — Anders Lindbergh *Private Banking*

Administration
Technology & Systems — Philippe Braquet *EDP Manager*

Compliance
— Danillo Linosa *Senior Manager*

Accounts / Audit
Internal Audit — Danillo Linosa *Senior Manager*

Other (Administration)
Securities Administration — Marie Perfetto

Banque Colbert (Luxembourg) SA
Subsidiary Company

1 rue Thomas Edison, L-1445, Luxembourg
PO Box 736, L-2017, Luxembourg
Tel: 254 243 1 Fax: 254 257 Telex: 2931 IBI LU Swift: COLB LU LL

Senior Executive Officers
Managing Director — Michel E Raffoul
General Manager — Georges Mahnen
General Manager — Aad N D Spaan

General-Lending (DCM, SL)
Head of Corporate Banking — Yves Bayle ☎ 254 243 268

Syndicated Lending
Head of Syndication — Aad N D Spaan *General Manager*

Money Markets
Head of Money Markets — Jean Steffen ☎ 254 243 207

Foreign Exchange
Head of Foreign Exchange — Jean Steffen ☎ 254 243 207

Settlement / Clearing
Head of Settlement / Clearing; Back-Office — Fernande Flesch ☎ 254 243 200

Asset Management
Head — Jean Steffen ☎ 254 243 207

Other Departments
Private Banking — Jean Steffen ☎ 254 243 207
Administration
Head of Marketing — Aad N D Spaan *General Manager*
Technology & Systems
Organization & Electronic Data Processing — Michael Bisset ☎ 254 243 236
Accounts / Audit
Lorna Cassidy *Financial Control & Internal Audit* ☎ 254 243 200
Other (Administration)
Company Management Services — Thierry Schmit ☎ 254 243 208

Banque de Commerce et de Placements SA — Full Branch Office

140 Boulevard de la Pétrusse, L-2330, Luxembourg
Tel: 404 022 1 Fax: 404 202 Telex: 60120 BCP LU

Senior Executive Officers
Others (Senior Executives)
Heiner Richters *Branch Manager*
Tayfun Bayazit *Branch Manager*
Foreign Exchange
Country Head — Heiner Richters *Branch Manager*
Global Custody
Other (Global Custody)
Custodian Banking — Heiner Richters *Branch Manager*
Asset Management
Head — Heiner Richters *Branch Manager*
Other Departments
Correspondent Banking — Heiner Richters *Branch Manager*

Banque Continentale du Luxembourg SA — Head Office

2 Boulevard Emmanuel Servais, L-2535, Luxembourg
PO Box 1405, L-1014, Luxembourg
Tel: 474 491; 477 688 1 Fax: 477 688 529 Telex: 2656; 2657; 3797
FX Fax: 472 065/7

Senior Executive Officers
Chairman — Damien Wigny
Managing Director — Marc Hubert Henry
General Manager — Jean-Maris Henricot
Other Departments
Private Banking — Claude Belva

Banque Degroof Luxembourg SA — Subsidiary Company

7 Boulevard Joseph II, L-1840, Luxembourg
PO Box 902, L-2019, Luxembourg
Tel: 453 545 1 Fax: 250 721 Telex: 60653 Swift: DEGR LU LL Reuters: DELW-Z

Senior Executive Officers
Chairman — Jacques Planchard ☎ 453 545 2103
President — Alain Philippson
Chief Executive Officer — Fernand de Jamblinne ☎ 453 545 2102 F 250 721 2102
Financial Director — Vincent Scarfo ☎ 453 545 2142 F 250 721 2142
Chief Operating Officer — Christopher Misson ☎ 453 545 2126 F 250 721 2126
Treasurer — Hervé Rodier ☎ 453 545 2201 F 250 721 2201
Managing Director — Gérald Everaert ☎ 453 545 2104
General Manager — Viviane Glavic ☎ 453 545 2222
International Division — Fernand de Jamblinne ☎ 453 545 2102 F 250 721 2102
General-Lending (DCM, SL)
Head of Corporate Banking — Gérald Everaert *Managing Director* ☎ 453 545 2104
Debt Capital Markets / Fixed Income
Head of Fixed Income; Head of Fixed Income Sales; Head of Fixed Income Trading — Hervé Rodier ☎ 453 545 2201 F 250 721 2201

LUXEMBOURG (+352)   www.euromoneydirectory.com

Banque Degroof Luxembourg SA (cont)

Government Bonds
Head of Sales   Luc Paindavoine [T] 453 545 2218 [F] 250 721 2218
Head of Trading   Roland Bache [T] 453 545 2212 [F] 250 721 2212

Eurobonds
Head of Sales   Luc Paindavoine [T] 453 545 2218 [F] 250 721 2218
Head of Trading   Johan Cok [T] 453 545 2206 [F] 250 721 2206

Libor-Based / Floating-Rate Products
FRN Trading   Robert Kieffer [T] 453 545 2202 [F] 250 721 2202

Equity Capital Markets
Head of Equity Capital Markets   Hervé Rodier [T] 453 545 2201 [F] 250 721 2201
Head of Trading   Jean De Winter [T] 453 545 2204

Domestic Equities
Head of Trading   Jean De Winter [T] 453 545 2204

International Equities
Head of Trading   Jean De Winter [T] 453 545 2204

Money Markets
Head of Money Markets   Hervé Rodier [T] 453 545 2201 [F] 250 721 2201

Domestic Commercial Paper
Head of Trading   Robert Kieffer [T] 453 545 2202 [F] 250 721 2202

Wholesale Deposits
Head of Sales   Patrick Dubray [T] 453 545 2203 [F] 250 721 2203

Foreign Exchange
Department: Foreign Exchange and Bullion
Head of Foreign Exchange   Hervé Rodier [T] 453 545 2201 [F] 250 721 2201
Head of Institutional Sales Robert Kieffer [T] 453 545 2202 [F] 250 721 2202
Corporate Sales   Patrick Dubray [T] 453 545 2203 [F] 250 721 2203

Risk Management
Tel: 453 545 2236 Fax: 250 721 2236
Head of Risk Management Thierry Lopez

Corporate Finance / M&A Advisory
Head of Corporate Finance   Hervé Rodier [T] 453 545 2201 [F] 250 721 2201

Settlement / Clearing
Head of Settlement / Clearing   Maria-Pia Lardenais [T] 453 545 2220 [F] 250 721 2220

Global Custody
Head of Global Custody   Christopher Misson [T] 453 545 2126 [F] 250 721 2126

Asset Management
Head   Geert De Bruyne [T] 453 545 2012 [F] 250 721 2012

Other Departments
Chief Credit Officer   Gérald Everaert *Managing Director* [T] 453 545 2104
Private Banking   Geert De Bruyne [T] 453 545 2012 [F] 250 721 2012
Correspondent Banking   Hervé Rodier [T] 453 545 2201 [F] 250 721 2201

Administration
Head of Administration   Christopher Misson [T] 453 545 2126 [F] 250 721 2126
Business Development; Head of Marketing   Fernand de Jamblinne [T] 453 545 2102 [F] 250 721 2102

Technology & Systems
                         Marcelle Goffart [T] 453 545 2146 [F] 250 721 2146

Legal / In-House Counsel
                         Jean-Francois Leidner [T] 453 545 2112 [F] 250 721 2112

Compliance
                         Jean-Francois Leidner [T] 453 545 2112 [F] 250 721 2112

Public Relations
                         Hans Schütz [T] 453 545 2132 [F] 250 721 2132

Accounts / Audit
                         Vincent Scarfo [T] 453 545 2142 [F] 250 721 2142

Banque Dewaay SA Succursale de Luxembourg Full Branch Office

Formerly known as: Dewaay Luxembourg SA
18 Boulevard Royal, L-2018, Luxembourg
PO Box 843, L-2449, Luxembourg
Tel: 229 391 Fax: 221 304 Telex: 2503 Reuters: DEWA/DEWAAY11-19

Senior Executive Officers
President   Henri Servais

www.euromoneydirectory.com   **LUXEMBOURG (+352)**

Others (Senior Executives)
     Monique Engel
     Richard Schneider

Debt Capital Markets / Fixed Income
Department: Fixed Income
Country Head   Marc Lambot
     Christophe De L'Arbre

Equity Capital Markets
Department: Equities
Country Head   Monique Engel
     Michel Frank

Administration
Head of Administration   Alain Weicker

Banque et Caisse d'Epargne de l'Etat, Luxembourg   Head Office

Formerly known as: Caisse d'Epargne de l'Etat du Grande-Duche de Luxembourg, Banque de l'Etat
1 & 2 Place de Metz, L-1930, Luxembourg
L-2954, L-2954, Luxembourg
Tel: 4015 1 **Fax:** 4015 2099 **Telex:** 3417 EPPDA LU **Swift:** BCEE LU LL **Reuters:** BCEE (FID)
Website: www.bcee.lu

Senior Executive Officers
Chairman   Victor Rod [T] **4015 3000** [F] **485 986**
President & Chief Executive Officer   Raymond Kirsch [T] **4015 2000**
Treasurer   Michel Birel *Senior Vice President* [T] **4015 5100** [F] **480 989**
Others (Senior Executives)
     Henri Germeaux *Deputy Chief Executive Officer* [T] **4015 2005** [F] **4015 2007**
     Jean-Paul Kraus *Executive Vice President* [T] **4015 2015** [F] **4015 2007**
     Gilbert Ernst *Executive Vice President* [T] **4015 5500** [F] **4015 5507**
     Jean-Claude Finck *Executive Vice President* [T] **4015 5000** [F] **4015 5080**

Relationship Manager
     Paul Huberty *Head of Relationship Management* [T] **4015 4123** [F] **4015 4142**

Debt Capital Markets / Fixed Income
Department: Capital Markets
Tel: 4015 5203 **Fax:** 403 240
Head of Fixed Income   Paul Waringo *Senior Vice President* [T] **4015 5200**

Government Bonds
Head of Sales   Pierre Cames *Division Head* [T] **4015 5256** [F] **403 240**
Head of Trading   Marco Huberty *Division Head* [T] **4015 5257** [F] **403 240**

Domestic Government Bonds
Head of Sales   Pierre Cames *Division Head* [T] **4015 5256** [F] **403 240**
Head of Trading   Marco Huberty *Division Head* [T] **4015 5257** [F] **403 240**
Head of Origination; Head of Syndication   Julien Schroeder [T] **4015 5254** [F] **403 240**

Libor-Based / Floating-Rate Products
FRN Trading; Asset Swaps   François Simon *Chief Dealer* [T] **4015 5108** [F] **480 989**

Fixed-Income Repo
Head of Repo   François Kill *Dealer* [T] **4015 5240** [F] **480 989**

Equity Capital Markets
Department: Capital Markets
Tel: 4015 5203 **Fax:** 403 240 **Telex:** 3417 eppda lu
Head of Equity Capital Markets   Paul Waringo *Senior Vice President* [T] **4015 5200**
Head of Sales   Monique Verweft [T] **4015 5258**
Head of Trading   Ferdinand Kutten [T] **4015 5258**

Equity Repo / Securities Lending
Head   François Kill *Dealer* [T] **4015 5240** [F] **480 989**

Syndicated Lending
Department: International Loans & Securitized Assets
Head of Syndicated Lending   John Dhur *Head of Syndicated Loans & Securitized Assets* [T] **4015 4296** [F] **4015 4284**

Loan-Related Activities
Trade Finance; Project Finance   John Dhur *Head of Syndicated Loans & Securitized Assets* [T] **4015 4296** [F] **4015 4284**

Money Markets
Tel: 4015 5102 **Fax:** 480 989 **Reuters:** CELU **Telex:** 3417 eppda lu
Global Head   Michel Birel *Senior Vice President* [T] **4015 5100** [F] **480 989**

LUXEMBOURG (+352) — www.euromoneydirectory.com

Banque et Caisse d'Epargne de l'Etat, Luxembourg (cont)

Domestic Commercial Paper
Head of Trading — Romain Gleis *Assistant Chief Dealer* ☎ 4015 5240

Foreign Exchange
Tel: 498 611 Fax: 480 989 Reuters: CEPU Telex: 3417 eppda lu
Head of Foreign Exchange — Arno Forman *Chief Dealer* ☎ 498 611
Head of Institutional Sales; Corporate Sales — Yvon Streff *Chief Dealer* ☎ 4015 5220
Head of Trading — Arno Forman *Chief Dealer* ☎ 498 611

FX Traders / Sales People
Forex Trader — Marc Baily *Dealer* ☎ 498 611

Risk Management
Department: Risk Control
Fax: 480 989
Head of Risk Management — Paul Peckels ☎ 4015 5110

Fixed Income Derivatives / Risk Management
Trading — François Kill *Dealer* ☎ 4015 5240 F 480 989

Other Currency Swap / FX Options Personnel
François Kill *Dealer* ☎ 4015 5240 F 480 989

Settlement / Clearing
Tel: 4015 5303 Fax: 4015 5306 Telex: 3417 eppda lu
Country Head — Pierre Meyers *Head of Settlements* ☎ 4015 5300 F 4015 5306
Equity Settlement — Jean Laux *Deputy Head of Settlements* ☎ 4015 5302
Fixed-Income Settlement — Mike Feiereisen *Head of Division* ☎ 4015 5342
Derivatives Settlement — Gilles Feiereisen *Head of Division* ☎ 4015 5346
Foreign Exchange Settlement — Robert Weiss *Head of Division* ☎ 4015 5325
Other — Joseph Ewen *Head of International Payments* ☎ 4015 3596 F 491 297

Global Custody
Head of Global Custody — Camille Thommes *Head of Securities* ☎ 4015 4437 F 4015 4487

Asset Management
Head — Roland Werdel *Head of Institutional Asset Management* ☎ 4015 5008 F 480 882
Investment Funds — Jean Fell ☎ 4015 3200 F 480 882

Other Departments
Chief Credit Officer — Guy Rosseljong *Senior VP, Head of Domestic Loans* ☎ 4015 4162 F 4015 4172
Private Banking — Georges Gudenburg *Head of Private Banking* ☎ 4015 5005 F 480 882
Correspondent Banking — Guy Queudeville *Head of Financial Institutions* ☎ 4015 4300 F 4015 4283

Administration
Head of Marketing — Lucien Peter *Head of Marketing* ☎ 4015 2110 F 404 322

Technology & Systems
Jean Hilger *Head of Organization and IT Development* ☎ 4015 5411 F 4015 5504

Legal / In-House Counsel
Joseph Delhaye *Head of Legal Department* ☎ 4015 3018 F 402 449

Public Relations
Alix Wagner *Head of Communications* ☎ 4015 2150 F 404 625

Accounts / Audit
Audit — Paul Gaspar *Head of Internal Audit* ☎ 4015 8211 F 491 322
Book-Keeping and Budgeting — Doris Engel *Head* ☎ 4015 3066 F 485 079

Other (Administration)
Management Support and Control — Frank Mosar *Head* ☎ 4015 2213 F 4015 2223
Financial Policy and Sovereign Risk — Guy Seyler *Head* ☎ 4015 2260 F 4015 2261
Data Processing — Pierre Reuter *Head* ☎ 4015 5513 F 4015 5545
Electronic Banking and Transmissions — Lysiane Hames *Head* ☎ 4015 4378 F 4015 4377

Banque Générale du Luxembourg SA — Head Office

50 Avenue John F Kennedy, L-2951, Luxembourg
Tel: 4242 1; 4799 1 Fax: 4242 2579 Telex: 3401 BGL LU, 2742 BGL LU (FX) Swift: BGLL LU LL
Reuters: BGLA, BGLX (FX) Telerate: 21010/9, 3721 (FX)
Reuters: BGLA-O (Eurobond Trading)
Website: www.bgl.lu

Senior Executive Officers
Chairman, Management Board — Alain Georges

BANQUE EUROPÈENE D'INVESTISSEMENT/EUROPEAN INVESTMENT BANK

Address: 100, Boulevard Konrad Adenauer L-2950 Luxembourg-Kirchberg

Telephone:	4379-1 (General); 43 77 07 (Liquidity Management); 43 77 10 (Portfolio Management, Operational ALM);
Facsimile:	4377-04 (General); 4379-4288, 4379 4290 (Capital Markets); 4379-4282 (Issue Monitoring); 4379-5153 (Asset Liability Management); 4379-5155 (Portofolio Management); 4379-5162 (Liquidity Management);
Telex:	3530 BNKEU LU (General); 3532 EIBPOLU (Portfolio Management, Repurchase Operations, Back-Offices) 3535 EIBFILU (Treasury, Liquidity Management, Loan Disbursements); 3537 EIBONDLU (Capital Markets);
Swift:	BEIL LU LL
Reuter Monitor:	EIBU (Dealing)
Other electronic mail:	H320 Videoconference : 439367

Finance Directorate
Facsimile: 4379-5262
Ren Karsenti, Director General, 4379-5269

Capital Markets Department
Ulrich Damm, Deputy Director General, 4379-5270; Jean-Claude Bresson, Deputy Director, 4379-4270; Aldo Romani, Officer, 4379-4253

New Issues (Borrowings)
Facsimile: 4379-4288 / 4379-4290
Telex: 3537 EIBOND LU
Greece, France, Italy, Portugal:
Carlo Sartorelli, Head, 4379-4246; Carlos Ferreira da Silva, Senior Officer, 4379-4243; Giancarlo Sardelli, Officer, 4379-4251; Yolande Hicks, Assistant, 4379-4247;

ECU, Spain, Ireland, UK, Australia, Canada, USA, South East Asia:
Bresson, Deputy Director, 4379-4270; Carlos Guille, Managerial Adviser, 4379-4266; David O. Clark, Assistant, 4379-4269; Lydia Thiry, Assistant, 4379-4263; Zurine Aguirre, Assistant, 4379-4259

Germany, Austria, Switzerland, Central & Eastern Europe:
Barbara Steuer, Head, 4379-4234; Eila Kreivi, Officer, 4379-4227; Richard Teichmeister, Officer, 4379-4223

Belgium, Denmark, Luxembourg, Netherlands, Finland, Sweden, Norway, Japan:
Joseph Vogten, Head, 4379-4238; Bjorn Lygum, Deputy Head, 4379-4235; Hendrik Van Ommen; Officer, 4379-4231; Tina Doughty, Assistant; 4379-4239;

Treasury Department
Anneli PESHKOFF, Director, 4379-5118

Portfolio Management
Facsimile: 4379-5155
Telex: 3532 EIBPO LU
Dealing Telephone: 43 77 10
Anneli PESHKOFF, Director; James Ranaivoson, Senior Officer; Carlos De Nicola; Officer; Nicole Henin; Assistant;
Liquidity Management
Facsimile: 4379-5162
Telex : 3541 BEIFXLU

Dealing Telephone: 43 77 07
Money Markets Transactions: 4379-5111; 4379-5115
Swaps, Repo & Forex Transactions: 4379-5109; 4379-5113; 4379-5117
Reuter Monitor: EIBU (Dealing)
Francis Zeghers, Head; Tim O'Connell, Dealer; Lucia Cook, Dealer; Frederic Eggen, Dealer; Dino Fabbro, Dealer;

Operational Asset Liability Management
Facsimile: 4379-5153
Dealing Telephone: 43 77 10
Jean-Dominique Potocki, Senior Officer; Guido Bichisao, Officer, Nicola Santini, Officer; Mirella Schmitz, Assistant;

Planning and Settlement of Operations
Eberhard Uhlmann, Director, 4379-5203;

Planning, Loan Cashflows, Disbursements:
Francisco De Paula Coelho, Head, 4379-5215;

Interest Rate: Jean-Claude Minne, Officer, 4379-5231;
Loan Disbursements and Planning: 4379-5223;
Administration: Yvan Grard, Senior Officer, 4379-5219;
Disbursements Execution: Denise Bour, Assistant, 4379-5102;
Loans Service: Giuseppe Gianotti, Assistant, 4379-5227;

Administration of Accounts, Back-Offices, Transfers, Teletransmissions:
Erling Cronqvist, Head, 4379-5142;

Accounts: Irne Peiffer, Assistant, 4379-5134;
Back-Offices:
Telex: 3535 EIBFILU
Swift: BEIL LU LL
Settlement Money Market: Gwen Jack, Officer, 4379-5138
Settlement Portfolio: Anny Caas, Assistant, 4379-5126

Issue Monitoring
Facsimile: 4379-4282
Telex: 3537 EIBOND LU
Yves Kirpach, Senior Officer, 4379-4211; Antonio Vieira, Officer, 4379-4205; Franca Cardillo, Officer, 4379-4215; Eve Walter, Assistant, 4379-4211;

LUXEMBOURG (+352)　　　　　www.euromoneydirectory.com

Banque Générale du Luxembourg SA (cont)

Others (Senior Executives)

	Jean Meyer *Management Board*
	Paul Meyers *Management Board*
	Christian Schaack *Management Board*
	Michel Waringo *Management Board*
	Ernest Cravatte *Management Board*

General-Lending (DCM, SL)
Head of Corporate Banking　　　　Marc Hentgen *Corporate Banking*
　　　　　　　　　　　　　　　　　Fernand Schweitzer *Lending*

General - Treasury
Head of Treasury　　　　　　　　 Jean Thill *Treasury*
　　　　　　　　　　　　　　　　　Guy Rommes *Treasury & Capital Markets*

Relationship Manager
Financial Engineering　　　　　　 André Birget *Capital Markets*
Domestic Branch Network　　　　 Thierry Schuman
Small & Medium Sized Businesses　 Marc Hentgen
International Banking Relations　　 Sverre Schaanning
International Payments　　　　　　Pierre Weins
Holding Companies & Fiduciary Operations　Dirk van Reeth

Debt Capital Markets / Fixed Income
Department: Listing, Paying Agency, Common Depository
Global Head　　　　　　　　　　 Guy Rommes *Treasury & Capital Markets*

Domestic Government Bonds
Head of Sales; Head of Trading　　 Norbert Friedrich

Non-Domestic Government Bonds
　　　　　　　　　　　　　　　　　André Birget *Capital Markets*

Eurobonds
Head of Sales; Head of Trading　　 Norbert Friedrich

Asset-Backed Securities / Securitization
Global Head　　　　　　　　　　 Georges Gaasch *Securities*

Equity Capital Markets
Domestic Equities
Head of Trading　　　　　　　　　Nicholas Ogden
International Equities
Head of Trading　　　　　　　　　Nicholas Ogden

Syndicated Lending
Other (Syndicated Lending)
Syndicated Loans　　　　　　　　 Claude Ludovicy
Primary Markets & Syndication　　 Paul Wagner

Other (Trade Finance)
Documentary Credits　　　　　　 Robert Schroeder
Leasing & Factoring　　　　　　　 Jean Darche

Money Markets
Global Head　　　　　　　　　　 Alain Ries

Foreign Exchange
Global Head　　　　　　　　　　 Marc Calmes

Risk Management
Global Head　　　　　　　　　　 Yves Wagner

Corporate Finance / M&A Advisory
Department: International Corporate Finance
Global Head　　　　　　　　　　 Marc Olinger

Settlement / Clearing
Settlement (General)　　　　　　　Marc Reiser
Operations　　　　　　　　　　　 Gérard Dupont *Organization*
Electronic Banking　　　　　　　　Gilbert Kolbach

Asset Management
Head　　　　　　　　　　　　　　Yves Wagner

Other Departments
Private Banking　　　　　　　　　Robert Scharfe
Global Trust　　　　　　　　　　 Jacques Prost *Trust & Investment Funds*

Administration
Head of Administration　　　　　　Jeannot Sauber

Technology & Systems
Electronic Data Processing　　　　 Pascale Massard

www.euromoneydirectory.com   LUXEMBOURG (+352)

Legal / In-House Counsel
André Hoffmann

Accounts / Audit
Carlo Lessel *Accounting*
Jean Koepfler *Internal Auditor*

Other (Administration)
Marketing   Yves Stein
Customer Desk   Gabriel di Letizia
Personnel & Social Affairs   Carlo Thill
                                             Nadine Schweyen
Company Secretariat   Kik Schneider

Banque Hapoalim (Luxembourg) SA   Subsidiary Company

Formerly known as: Bank Hapoalim BM
18 Boulevard Royal, L-2017, Luxembourg
PO Box 703, L-2017, Luxembourg
Tel: 475 256 1 **Fax:** 229 847 **Swift:** POAL LU LL **Cable:** BANKPOALIM
FX Tel: 22 9846

Senior Executive Officers
Managing Director   Bernard Biever
Managing Director   Dalia Kaizerman
International Division   Dalia Kaizerman *Managing Director*

Relationship Manager
Financial Services   Jean-Jacques Gallet
                                             Dalia Kaizerman *Managing Director*

Debt Capital Markets / Fixed Income
Global Head   Dalia Kaizerman *Managing Director*

Syndicated Lending
Other (Syndicated Lending)
Loans & Administration   Dalia Kaizerman *Managing Director*

Foreign Exchange
Global Head   Dalia Kaizerman *Managing Director*

Asset Management
Portfolio Management   Dalia Kaizerman *Managing Director*

Other Departments
Commodities / Bullion; Private Banking   Dalia Kaizerman *Managing Director*
Correspondent Banking   Karin Gales

Banque Hapoalim (Suisse) SA Luxembourg   Full Branch Office

18 Boulevard Royal, PO Box 703, L-2017, Luxembourg
Tel: 475 256 1 **Fax:** 229 847 **Swift:** POAL LU LL
FX Tel: 22 9846

Senior Executive Officers
International Division   Bernard Biever *Deputy Manager*

General-Investment
Head of Investment   Dalia Kaizerman *Manager, Private Banking & Capital Markets*

Relationship Manager
Financial Services   Jean-Jacques Gallet *Dealer*

Debt Capital Markets / Fixed Income
Global Head   Dalia Kaizerman *Manager, Private Banking & Capital Markets*

Syndicated Lending
Other (Syndicated Lending)
                                             Dalia Kaizerman *Manager, Private Banking & Capital Markets*

Foreign Exchange
Global Head   Bernard Biever *Deputy Manager*

Asset Management
Portfolio Management   Dalia Kaizerman *Manager, Private Banking & Capital Markets*

Other Departments
Commodities / Bullion; Private Banking   Dalia Kaizerman *Manager, Private Banking & Capital Markets*
Correspondent Banking   Karin Gales

LUXEMBOURG (+352)   www.euromoneydirectory.com

Banque Internationale à Luxembourg SA — Head Office
69 route d'Esch, L-2953, Luxembourg
Tel: 4590 1 Fax: 4530 2010 Telex: 3626 BIL LU Swift: BILL LU LL Email: contact@bil.lu Reuters: BILA-H
Website: www.bil.lu

Senior Executive Officers
Treasurer — Claude Schon *Senior Vice President* T **4590 2398** F **4590 3840**
E **schon@bil.lu**
Managing Director — André Roelants T **4590 3498**

Debt Capital Markets / Fixed Income
Department: Capital Markets Department
Tel: 4590 1 Fax: 4590 4227 Telex: 3626 BIL LU
Head of Fixed Income — Gilles Reiter *First Vice President* T **4590 4226** F **4590 4227**
Head of Fixed Income Sales — Frank Reinert *Senior Manager* T **4590 2585** F **4590 4227**
Head of Fixed Income Trading — Sakari Saro *Head of Trading* T **4590 2030** F **4590 4227**

Government Bonds
Head of Sales — Frank Reinert *Senior Manager* T **4590 2585** F **4590 4227**
Head of Trading — Sakari Saro *Head of Trading* T **4590 2030** F **4590 4227**
Head of Syndication; Head of Origination — Frank Reinert *Senior Manager* T **4590 2585** F **4590 4227**

Fixed-Income Repo
Head of Repo — Romain Grethen *Assistant Vice President* T **4590 2594** F **4590 3446**

Equity Capital Markets
Tel: 4590 1 Fax: 4590 3447 Telex: 3626 BIL LU
Head of Equity Capital Markets; Head of Sales — Claude Schettgen *Assistant Vice President* T **457 052**
Head of Trading — Roland Schaus *Manager* T **457 052**

Domestic Equities
Head of Origination; Head of Syndication — Claude Schettgen *Assistant Vice President* T **457 052**
Head of Trading — Charles Franz *Manager* T **4590 2722**

Other (Domestic Equities)
Paying Agencies; Listings; Common Depositary — Marc Schammo *Head, Documentation, Listing & Fiscal Agencies* T **4590 4229**

International Equities
Head of Origination; Head of Syndication; Head of Trading — Claude Schettgen *Assistant Vice President* T **457 052**

Warrants
Head of Trading — Claude Schettgen *Assistant Vice President* T **457 052**

Equity Repo / Securities Lending
Marketing — Romain Grethen *Assistant Vice President* T **4590 2594** F **4590 3446**

Money Markets
Tel: 457 074 Fax: 4590 3446
Head of Money Markets — Henry Munster *Vice President* T **4590 3468** F **4590 2164**

Wholesale Deposits
Marketing; Head of Sales — Jean-Marc Steines *Assistant Vice President* T **4590 3547** F **4590 3446**

Foreign Exchange
Tel: 457 038 Fax: 4590 3446 Reuters: CODE BILU
Head of Foreign Exchange — Joseph Hensen *Vice President* T **4590 3420**
Head of Institutional Sales — Fernando Pascolini *Assistant Vice President* T **457 045**
Head of Trading — Jean-Charles Grézault *Assistant Vice President* T **457 038**

FX Traders / Sales People
FX Trading — Nello Monacelli T **457 038**
Sales — Alex Hornung T **457 045**

Risk Management
Head of Risk Management — Jacques De Joux *Global Risk Manager* T **4590 2672** F **4590 2164**

Banque Leu (Luxembourg) SA — Subsidiary Company
16 rue Jean-Pierre Brasseur, L-1258, Luxembourg
PO Box 718, L-2017, Luxembourg
Tel: 453 222 1 Fax: 453 177 Telex: 3582 (Dealing), 2492 (General) Swift: LEUZ LU LS BIC Reuters: LEU U
Dealing Tel: 45 3161

Senior Executive Officers
Chairman — Reto Donatsch
Managing Director — Albert J Ulrich
General - Treasury
Head of Treasury — Marc Kuborn *Member, Senior Management* T **453 161**

988 Euromoney Directory 1999

www.euromoneydirectory.com LUXEMBOURG (+352)

Foreign Exchange
Department: Foreign Exchange and Bullion
Global Head Marc Kuborn *Member, Senior Management* 🕾 **453 161**

FX Traders / Sales People
Futures Jacques Prange *Member, Senior Management* 🕾 **453 161**

Risk Management
Department: Capital Markets

Other Currency Swap / FX Options Personnel
Interest & Currency Swaps Jacques Prange *Member, Senior Management* 🕾 **453 161**

Settlement / Clearing
Foreign Exchange Settlement Antoine Buda *Authorized Signatory*

Other Departments
Private Banking Heiner Hartwich *Member, Senior Management* 🕾 **446 488**

Banque de Luxembourg SA Head Office

14 Boulevard Royal, L-2449, Luxembourg
Tel: 499 241 **Fax:** 472 665; 221 139 **Telex:** 3465 BLA LU (Dealing) **Swift:** BLUX LU LL **Email:** bllux@pt.lu
Reuters: BDLU (Dealing)

Senior Executive Officers

Relationship Manager
Client Services Claudine Muller 🕾 **49924 2543** 📠 **462 668**
  Pierre Ahlborn 🕾 **49924 3102** 📠 **462 668**
  Laurence Vandewalle 🕾 **49924 3064** 📠 **462 668**

Debt Capital Markets / Fixed Income
Department: Capital Markets, Tresury: Bonds, Equity & Money Markets
Fax: 221 139
Global Head Théo Meder *Head, Dealing Room* 🕾 **220 116**

Bonds - General
Dealers Claudio Tommasini 🕾 **49924 3221**
  Patrick Hansen 🕾 **49924 3222**
  René Schroeter 🕾 **49924 3710**
  Hélène Duchatellier 🕾 **49924 3226**
  Luc Bauler 🕾 **49924 3229**
  Jos Kettels
  Stefano Torres
  Roger Diedenhofen 🕾 **461 045**
  Thésy Frank 🕾 **461 045**
Client Services Alain Biren 🕾 **49924 3044**
  Guy Mertens 🕾 **220 007**
  Paul Slunecko 🕾 **220 007**
  Nicole Mersch 🕾 **49924 3045**
Middle Office Securities Jeff Rosen 🕾 **49924 2451** 📠 **492 384**
  Laurent Hertzog 🕾 **49924 2049** 📠 **492 384**
Middle Office Treasury Fernand Weimerskirsch 🕾 **49924 2460**
  Claude Dionysius 🕾 **49924 2410**

Foreign Exchange

FX Traders / Sales People
  Astrid Moll 🕾 **220 272**
  Guy Gierenz 🕾 **220 272**
  Georges Mootz 🕾 **220 272**

Risk Management
Fax: 49924 3227
Country Head Quan Kha Gia 🕾 **49924 2512**
  Fernand Reiners 🕾 **49924 2518**

Other Departments
Correspondent Banking Marc Ketter 🕾 **49924 3068** 📠 **462 668**
  Thierry Feis 🕾 **49924 3062** 📠 **462 668**

Euromoney Directory 1999 **989**

LUXEMBOURG (+352)   www.euromoneydirectory.com

Banque Nationale de Belgique
Full Branch Office

37A Boulevard du Prince Henri, L-1724, Luxembourg
PO Box 628, L-2016, Luxembourg
Tel: 475 251 **Fax:** 220 171 **Telex:** 3473 **Swift:** NBBE LU LX

Senior Executive Officers
Chief Executive Officer
Chief Operating Officer

A Billon *Deputy Chief Executive*
F Yasse
P Mathey *Operating Officer*

Others (Senior Executives)
Adviser

L Rode

Banque Nationale de Paris (Luxembourg) SA
Subsidiary Company

24 Boulevard Royal, L-2952, Luxembourg
Tel: 4764 1 **Fax:** 226 480 **Telex:** 3447 **Swift:** BNPA LU LL **Cable:** NATIOLUX

Senior Executive Officers
Chairman of the Board
General Manager
Managing Director
General Secretary

Vivien Levy-Garboua
Bertrand du Passage
Paul-François Gauvin
Béatrice Duhamel

Others (Senior Executives)

Théo Braun *Deputy Manager*
Jean Leómant *Administration Manager* ☎ 4764 369
Guy Reding *Deputy Manager* ☎ 4764 323
Maurice Haag *Deputy Manager* ☎ 4764 302

General-Lending (DCM, SL)
Head of Corporate Banking

Maurice Haag *Deputy Manager* ☎ 4764 302 ℻ 4764 341
Claude Hoffmann *Corporate Banking*

General - Treasury
Head of Treasury

Samia Toumi *Treasury & FX* ☎ 4764 296

Debt Capital Markets / Fixed Income
Tel: 4764 302 **Fax:** 46 3930
Country Head

Maurice Haag *Deputy Manager* ☎ 4764 302

Foreign Exchange
Country Head

Samia Toumi *Treasury & FX* ☎ 4764 296

Risk Management
Country Head

Agnès Charbonnel ☎ 4764 223

Settlement / Clearing
Department: Holding Companies & Fiduciary Operations
Operations

Marina Lespagnard
Théo Braun *Deputy Manager*

Global Custody
Country Head

André Angelsberg ☎ 4764 282
Jean Leómant *Administration Manager* ☎ 4764 369

Asset Management
Head
Investment Funds

Jean-Marc De Volder *Investment Manager* ☎ 4764 300
Jean Leómant *Administration Manager* ☎ 4764 369

Other Departments
Private Banking

Lucien Dalscheid *Assistant Manager* ☎ 4764 267
Stéphane Wilmot ☎ 4764 866
Jean-Marc De Volder *Investment Manager* ☎ 4764 300
Bertrand du Passage *General Manager*

Administration
Head of Administration

Guy Reding *Deputy Manager* ☎ 4764 323

Legal / In-House Counsel

Anne Kayser-Neuss ☎ 4764 843

www.euromoneydirectory.com   LUXEMBOURG (+352)

Banque Paribas Luxembourg
Subsidiary Company

10A Boulevard Royal, L-2093, Luxembourg
PO Box 51, L-2449, Luxembourg
Tel: 4646 4323 Fax: 4646 4492 Telex: 2332 PARIB LU Swift: PARBLU

Senior Executive Officers
Chief Executive Officer   Charles Hamer

General-Lending (DCM, SL)
Head of Corporate Banking   Luc-Henri Jamar *International Credits*
                                                    Patrick Lefebvre *Management Committee - Corporate*
                                                    Christian Issanchou *International Credits*

General-Investment
Head of Investment   Pierre Corbiau *Investment Funds - Marketing*
                                                    Jean-Michel Loehr *Investment Funds - Administration*

Relationship Manager
Financial Engineering   Jean-Charles Cathenoz *Management Committee*
International Banking Relations   Marie-Paule Weides-Schaeffer *Management Committee*
                                                    Jean-Louis Masson
International Payments & Cashiers   Jean-Paul Lecarme
Trust Dept, Holding Companies   Noël Didier

Debt Capital Markets / Fixed Income
Country Head   Marie-Paule Weides-Schaeffer *Management Committee*

Bonds - General
Capital Markets - New Issues   Cecilia Ibarra

Syndicated Lending
Department: Syndication, Corporate Trust, Agencies & Listings
Country Head   Philippe van Looy

Other (Syndicated Lending)
                                                    François Valeri

Money Markets
Money Markets - General
Foreign Currencies   Dominique Goulem
Francs   Jean Quintus

Foreign Exchange
Country Head   René Bonetti

FX Traders / Sales People
Treasury & Forex Administration   Arlette Amiel

Risk Management
Other Currency Swap / FX Options Personnel
Risk Monitoring   François Garnier

Settlement / Clearing
Operations   Yvan Juchem *Financial Control*
                                                    Alain Gregond *Banking & Securities Operations*

Global Custody
Other (Global Custody)
Securities - Custody, Corporate   Claude Bihain

Asset Management
Head   Charles Hamer *General Management & Management Committee*

Other Departments
Private Banking   Freddy Durinck
                                                    Georges Lescure
                                                    Jean-Cl. Boutet
                                                    Charles Hamer *General Management & Management Committee*
                                                    Guy Kieffer
                                                    Raimondo Buscemi *Fund Management*

Administration
Technology & Systems
IT   Jean-Michel Marq
IT & Global Support   Michel Messeca *Management Committee*

Legal / In-House Counsel
                                                    Mado Wictor

Compliance
General Control & Compliance   Bernard Caby *Management Committee*

Euromoney Directory 1999   **991**

LUXEMBOURG (+352)   www.euromoneydirectory.com

Banque Paribas Luxembourg (cont)

Public Relations
Press & Public Relations — Charles Hamer *General Management & Management Committee*
Corporate Communications
Communications — Liliane Peiffer
Accounts / Audit
Institutional Accounts — Pierre-Yves Augsburger
Accounting & General Services — Joseph Winandy *Management Committee*
Accounting — Eric Berg
Daniel Gratiot
Internal Audit — Jean-Marc Noel
Other (Administration)
Human Resources — Michel Valleix *Management Committee*
Norbert Lan
Customer Administration — Sylvie Regnicoli
General Services — Gerd Lentz

Banque Pictet (Luxembourg) SA

1 Boulevard Royal, L-2449, Luxembourg
Tel: 467 1711

Banque Privée Edmond de Rothschild SA — Subsidiary Company

20 Boulevard Emmanuel Servais, L-2535, Luxembourg
PO Box 474, L-2014, Luxembourg
Tel: 479 346 1 **Fax:** 479 346 222 **Telex:** 3232 **Swift:** PRIB LU LL

Senior Executive Officers
SVP & Chairman, Branch Management Committee — Mr Otto
SVP & Vice Chairman, Branch Management Committee — Geoffroy Linard de Guertechin
Senior Vice President — Benoît de Hults
Settlement / Clearing
Operations — Linard de Guertechin *Senior Vice President*
Other Departments
Private Banking — Benoît de Hults *Senior Vice President*

Bayerische Landesbank International SA — Subsidiary Company

3 rue Jean Monnet, L-2180, Luxembourg
PO Box 602, L-2016, Luxembourg
Tel: 42434 1 **Fax:** 42434 5099 **Swift:** BYLA LU LL **Email:** bank@bayernlux.lu **Reuters:** BALU
Dealing Fax: 42434 3099; **General Email:** bililux@pt/lu; **Operations Telex:** 1229; **Treasury Telex:** 1249
Website: www.bayernlux.lu

Senior Executive Officers
Chief Executive Officer — Henri Stoffel
Treasurer — Robert Spliid
Managing Director — Romain Wohl
Debt Capital Markets / Fixed Income
Department: Capital Markets
Country Head — Peter Fritsch
Eurobonds
Head of Trading — Wilhelm Boenner
Libor-Based / Floating-Rate Products
Asset Swaps — Harald Krauss
Equity Capital Markets
Department: Capital Markets
Head of Equity Capital Markets — Colette Schifferling
Head of Trading — Klaus Michaelsen
Syndicated Lending
Head of Origination; Head of Syndication; Head of Trading — Hans-Peter Radermacher

www.euromoneydirectory.com LUXEMBOURG (+352)

Money Markets
Head of Money Markets Wolfgang Müller

Foreign Exchange
Corporate Sales Wolfgang Koettner
Head of Trading Eric Hewitt

Settlement / Clearing
Head of Settlement / Clearing Brigitte Duprel

Other Departments
Private Banking Guy Schmit

Administration
Head of Administration; Head of Marketing Alain Weber

Technology & Systems
  Claude Roeltgen

Legal / In-House Counsel
  Bernd-Dieter Buetzow

Compliance
  Bernd-Dieter Buetzow

Public Relations
  Alain Weber

Accounts / Audit
Internal Audit Hannelore Otto
Accounting & Control Alain Weber

Other (Administration)
Organisation Klaus-Peter Holz-Westhoff

Berenberg Bank   Full Branch Office
8/12 rue Henri VII, L-1725, Luxembourg
Tel: 466 380 **Fax:** 466 386

Senior Executive Officers
Senior Manager Michael Schröder-Castendyck

BfG Bank Luxembourg SA   Head Office
2 rue Jean Bertholet, L-1233, Luxembourg
PO Box 1123, L-1011, Luxembourg
Tel: 452 255 1 **Fax:** 452 2255 309; 452 2555 77

Senior Executive Officers
Chairman Dr Paul Wieandt
Managing Director / General Manager Bernard Müller

BG Bank International SA   Subsidiary Company
18-20 Avenue Marie-Thérèse, L-2132, Luxembourg
PO Box 594, L-2015, Luxembourg
Tel: 457 868 1 **Fax:** 457 860 **Telex:** 60346 **Swift:** BIKU LU LL **Reuters:** BIBU

Senior Executive Officers
Chairman Gert Kristensen
Deputy Managing Director Finn Ancker
Managing Director Jens Kristian Andersen
International Division Jens Kristian Andersen *Managing Director*

Debt Capital Markets / Fixed Income
Department: Capital Markets
Global Head Finn Ancker *Deputy Managing Director*

Syndicated Lending
Department: Loan Syndication / Asset Sales
Head of Origination Per Henrik Jensen *Deputy General Manager*

Foreign Exchange
Global Head Ole Hartmann Christensen *Deputy General Manager*

Corporate Finance / M&A Advisory
Global Head Per Henrik Jensen *Deputy General Manager*

LUXEMBOURG (+352)   www.euromoneydirectory.com

BG Bank International SA (cont)
Other Departments
Private Banking   Peter Andersen *Deputy General Manager*
Correspondent Banking   Finn Ancker *Deputy Managing Director*
Administration
Head of Administration   Finn Ancker *Deputy Managing Director*

BHF-BANK International SA   Subsidiary Company
283 route d'Arlon, L-1150, Luxembourg
PO Box 258, L-2012, Luxembourg
Tel: 457 676 1 **Fax:** 458 320 **Telex:** 2661, 2891 BHFLU (FX) **Reuters:** Recipient **Telerate:** Recipient
Bloomberg: Recipient
FX Tel: 457 658; **Fax:** 458 321

Senior Executive Officers
Managing Director   Heinrich S Wintzer
Managing Director   Hartmut Rothacker
General - Treasury
Head of Treasury   Hartmut Rothacker *Managing Director*
Money Markets
Other (Wholesale Deposits)
Eurocurrency Credit   Heinrich S Wintzer *Managing Director*
                       Klaus Bodenröder *Vice President*
Deposits   Hartmut Rothacker *Managing Director*
             Claude Peffer *Vice President*
             Danielle Ivesic
             Holger Rech
             Claude Wollner
             Gerhard Röller

Risk Management
Exchange-Traded Derivatives
FX Futures   Claude Peffer *Vice President*
Corporate Finance / M&A Advisory
Global Head   Heinrich S Wintzer *Managing Director*
Regional Head   Klaus Bodenröder *Vice President*

Caisse Centrale Raiffeisen   Head Office
28, Boulevard Royal, L-2449, Luxembourg
Tel: 462 151 **Fax:** 471 469 **Telex:** 3249 CCR LU **Swift:** CCRA LU LL **Email:** info@raiffeisen.lu

Debt Capital Markets / Fixed Income
Head of Debt Capital Markets   René Kinnen
Domestic Government Bonds
Head of Sales   Patrick Haupert
Eurobonds
Head of Origination; Head of Sales; Head of Trading   René Kinnen
Private Placements
Head of Origination   René Kinnen
Money Markets
Head of Money Markets   René Kinnen
Foreign Exchange
Head of Foreign Exchange   René Kinnen
Head of Trading   Jacques Kohner
Other Departments
Commodities / Bullion   Jacques Kohner
Private Banking   Jeannine Alff
Correspondent Banking   René Kinnen
Administration
Public Relations
                  Alphonse Sinnes

www.euromoneydirectory.com LUXEMBOURG (+352)

Cariplo Bank International SA
Subsidiary Company

12 rue Goethe, L-1637, Luxembourg
PO Box 2032, L-1020, Luxembourg
Tel: 405 504 1 **Fax:** 405 543 **Telex:** 60191 CRPLG **Swift:** CARI LU LL AXXX **Reuters:** CALU

Senior Executive Officers
Chairman — Mario Talamona
Vice Chairman — Mario Boselli
Managing Director — Bruno Agostini

Others (Senior Executives)
Mario Iacopini *Executive Manager*

Debt Capital Markets / Fixed Income
Eurobonds
Head of Trading — Giacomo Ferraro *Chief Dealer*
Stefano Ciccarello *Dealer*

Equity Capital Markets
International Equities
Head of Syndication — Giacomo Ferraro *Chief Dealer*
Stefano Ciccarello *Dealer*

Money Markets
Other (Wholesale Deposits)
Eurocurrency Deposits — Guy Wandivinit *Chief Dealer*
Franco Malerba *Dealer*

Foreign Exchange
FX Traders / Sales People
Peter Dahllof *Dealer*
Guy Wandivinit *Chief Dealer*

Risk Management
IR Swaps Trading — Guy Wandivinit *Chief Dealer*

Foreign Exchange Derivatives / Risk Management
Cross-Currency Swaps, Trading — Guy Wandivinit *Chief Dealer*

Settlement / Clearing
Settlement (General) — Jean Lisarelli *Back-Office Settlements*

Asset Management
Head — Christian Unsen

Other Departments
Correspondent Banking — Tarantino Antonio

Administration
Technology & Systems
Joël Danhyer

Legal / In-House Counsel
Legal Counsel — Philippe Pasquasy

Public Relations
Marie-Franco Spano

Other (Administration)
Human Resources — Anna-Vera Ceccacci

Cedel Bank
Head Office

67 Boulevard Grande Duchesse Charlotte, L-1331, Luxembourg
Tel: 44992 1 **Fax:** 44992 8210 **Telex:** 2791 **Swift:** CEDE LU LL **Email:** marketing@cedel.sprint.com
Website: www.cedelgroup.com

Senior Executive Officers
Chairman — Robert R Douglass
Chief Executive Officer — André Lussi
Financial Director — Raymond Soudah *Chief Financial & Investment Officer* 44992 6164
General Counsel & Secretary General's Office — Henri Marquenie 44992 550

Others (Senior Executives)
Group Information Systems — Gerard Donlin *Executive Director* 44992 585
Customer Services & Marketing — Carlos Salvatori *Executive Director* 44992 580
Products, Network & Strategy — Antonio Riera *Executive Director* 44992 6034
Human Resources — Simon Oostra *Director*

Euromoney Directory 1999 **995**

LUXEMBOURG (+352)

www.euromoneydirectory.com

Cedel Bank (cont)

General-Lending (DCM, SL)
Head of Corporate Banking — Stewart Wright *Financial Markets & Credit* ☎ 44992 6635

Relationship Manager
Worldwide Sales — Thomas Connaghan ☎ 44992 6189
Netherlands & Scandinavia — Alain Myers ☎ 44992 6099
Europe — Martin Brennan ☎ 44992 6013
Network Relationship Management — Craig Dudsak ☎ 44992 6023

Debt Capital Markets / Fixed Income

Fixed-Income Repo
Marketing & Product Development — Jean-Robert Wilkin *Vice President* ☎ 44992 595 F 44992 9595
📧 jwilki@cedelgroup.com

Equity Capital Markets
Tel: 44992 595 Fax: 44992 8221

Equity Repo / Securities Lending
Head — Martin Brennan *Director* ☎ 44992 6013 F 44992 9013
📧 mbrenn@cedelgroup.com
Marketing & Product Development — Jean-Robert Wilkin *Vice President* ☎ 44992 595 F 44992 9595
📧 jwilki@cedelgroup.com

Settlement / Clearing
Operations — Douglas Reeve ☎ 44992 6610
Michel Peeters *Group Financial Control* ☎ 44992 6125

Administration

Technology & Systems
Group Information Systems — Gerard Donlin *Executive Director* ☎ 44992 585
Information Processing & Communion — Jan Stevens ☎ 44992 415

Compliance
Corporate Audit & Compliance — Robert Massol ☎ 44992 239

Corporate Communications
John Gilchrist ☎ 44992 529

Accounts / Audit
Corporate Audit — Robert Massol ☎ 44992 239

Other (Administration)
Customer Service & Marketing — Carlos Salvatori *Executive Director* ☎ 44992 580
Products, Network & Strategy — Antonio Riera *Executive Director* ☎ 44992 6034
Human Resources — Simon Oostra *Director*
Marketing — Thomas Connaghan ☎ 44992 6189

CERABANK Luxembourg SA *Subsidiary Company*

7 Boulevard Royal, L-2449, Luxembourg
PO Box 47, L-2010, Luxembourg
Tel: 475 060 1 Fax: 220 460 Telex: 60830

Senior Executive Officers
Chairman, Executive Committee — Jean-Pierre Vandendorpe
Vice Chairman, Executive Committee — Jean-Francois Caeymaex

Debt Capital Markets / Fixed Income
Department: Financial Markets

Bonds - General
Rudi Mauquoi *Manager, Financial Markets* ☎ 475 060 330

Asset Management
Investment Funds — René Van den Bosch *Manager* ☎ 475 060 210

Other Departments
Private Banking — Eddy Raes *Manager* ☎ 475 060 209

Administration

Accounts / Audit
Accounting, EDP — Jean-Luc Debry *Manager* ☎ 475 060 350

Other (Administration)
Loans, Holding Companies, Legal Counsel — Piere Dochen *Manager* ☎ 475 060 207

Chase Manhattan Bank Luxembourg SA
Subsidiary Company

5 rue Plaetis, L-2012, Luxembourg
PO Box 240, L-2012, Luxembourg
Tel: 462 685 1 **Fax:** 224 590 **Telex:** 1233 CHASE LU **Swift:** CHAS LU LX

Senior Executive Officers
Others (Senior Executives)
Senior Country Officer Chris Edge *Senior Country Officer*

CIM Société de Bourse SA
Head Office

10 Avenue de la Liberté, L-1930, Luxembourg
Tel: 407 010 1 **Fax:** 490 944 **Reuters:** CFML-M

Senior Executive Officers
President Francesco Signorio
Managing Director / General Manager Jean-Luc Jourdan

Citibank (Luxembourg)
Subsidiary Company

58 Boulevard Grande-Duchesse Charlotte, Grand Duchy of Luxembourg, L-1330, Luxembourg
PO Box 1373, Luxembourg
Tel: 451 414 1 **Fax:** 451 414 74; 451 414 75 **Telex:** 3798 CICMG LU **Swift:** CITI LU LX

Senior Executive Officers
Chief Executive Officer Steven Fee ☎ **451 414 298**
Financial Director Myriam Wolny
Chief Operating Officer David Ruckert ☎ **451 414 227**
Treasurer Shyan Chaudhri ☎ **451 414 207**

General-Investment
Head of Investment Josie Altmann *Global Head* ☎ **451 414 220**

General - Treasury
Head of Treasury Shyan Chaudhri ☎ **451 414 207**

Debt Capital Markets / Fixed Income
Country Head David Ruckert ☎ **451 414 227**

Equity Capital Markets
Country Head David Ruckert ☎ **451 414 227**

Risk Management
Head of Risk Management Ulich Wuitt

Administration
Head of Marketing Lonny Schlessel *Head*

Other (Administration)
Operations Patrick Watelet *Head*
Human Resources Joelle Heydel *Head* ☎ **451 414 379** ℻ **451 414 436**

Commerzbank International SA Luxembourg
Subsidiary Company

11 rue Notre-Dame, L-2240, Luxembourg
PO Box 303, L-2013, Luxembourg
Tel: 477 911 1 **Fax:** 477 911 270 **Telex:** 1292 **Swift:** COBA DE FX LUX **Reuters:** CBLU, CBLX **Telerate:** 3742

Senior Executive Officers
Chairman Martin Kohlhaussen
Managing Director Klaus Tjaden ☎ **477 911 203** ℻ **477 911 410**
Managing Director Gérard Ferret ℻ **477 911 410**
Managing Director Adrien Ney ☎ **477 911 201** ℻ **477 911 410**

General - Treasury
Head of Treasury Jean-Marie Scholler *Senior Vice President* ☎ **477 911 320** ℻ **477 911 355**

Relationship Manager
International Banking Relations Helmut Keuten *Senior Vice President* ☎ **477 911 260** ℻ **477 911 419**

Debt Capital Markets / Fixed Income
Country Head Jean-Marie Scholler *Senior Vice President* ☎ **477 911 320** ℻ **477 911 355**

Syndicated Lending
Country Head Helmut Keuten *Senior Vice President* ☎ **477 911 260** ℻ **477 911 419**

LUXEMBOURG (+352)   www.euromoneydirectory.com

Commerzbank International SA Luxembourg (cont)

Risk Management
Country Head   Peter Gradl *Assistant Vice President* ☏ 477 911 638 ℻ 477 911 630

Settlement / Clearing
Settlement (General)   Thomas Vogelbusch *Vice President* ☏ 477 911 244 ℻ 477 911 350
Operations   Steve Arent *Vice President* ☏ 477 911 900 ℻ 477 911 960

Other Departments
Commodities / Bullion   John Patisas *Senior Vice President* ☏ 477 911 497 ℻ 477 911 355
Private Banking   Gerd Bauer *Senior Vice President* ☏ 477 911 313 ℻ 477 911 293

Administration

Technology & Systems
Electronic Data Processing   Steve Arent *Vice President* ☏ 477 911 900 ℻ 477 911 960

Legal / In-House Counsel
                                  Elmar Winter *Legal Advisor* ☏ 477 911 407 ℻ 477 911 807

Accounts / Audit
Internal Audit   Hans-Jörg Obertreis *Assistant Vice President* ☏ 477 911 473 ℻ 477 911 844
Accounting   Herbert Watermann *Vice President* ☏ 477 911 233 ℻ 477 911 470

Other (Administration)
Personnel   Elmar Winter *Legal Advisor* ☏ 477 911 407 ℻ 477 911 807

Crédit Agricole Indosuez SA   Subsidiary Company

Formerly known as: Banque Indosuez Luxembourg SA
39 Allée Scheffer, L-2520, Luxembourg
Tel: 4767 1 **Fax:** 462 442 **Telex:** 1254 INSU LU **Swift:** BSUI LU LL

Senior Executive Officers
Chairman   Philippe Guiral
Chief Executive Officer   Patrick Zurstrassen *President of the Executive Committee* ☏ 4767 2301
Chief Operating Officer   Eugène Serste *Member, Executive Committee* ☏ 4767 2350
Treasurer   Gilles Normand *Member, Executive Committee* ☏ 4767 2316

Debt Capital Markets / Fixed Income
Telex: 474 061

Government Bonds
Head of Sales; Head of Syndication   Maxine Bianconi ☏ 4767 2367

Fixed-Income Repo
Head of Repo   Maxine Bianconi ☏ 4767 2367

Equity Capital Markets
Head of Equity Capital Markets Gilles Normand *Member, Executive Committee* ☏ 4767 2316

Domestic Equities
Head of Sales   Yan Le Vernoy ☏ 4767 2374

Money Markets
Head of Money Markets   Gilles Normand *Member, Executive Committee* ☏ 4767 2316

Foreign Exchange
Head of Foreign Exchange   Gilles Normand *Member, Executive Committee* ☏ 4767 2316
Head of Trading   Walter Fontan ☏ 4767 2376

Settlement / Clearing
Back-Office   Olivier Thomas ☏ 4767 2663

Other Departments
Private Banking   Hugh Russell *Member, Executive Committee* ☏ 4767 2572

Administration

Technology & Systems
                                  Guy Peiffer ☏ 4767 2360

Legal / In-House Counsel
                                  Jacques Mahaux *Member, Executive Committee* ☏ 4767 2305

Compliance
                                  Jean-Marie Legendre ☏ 4767 2607

www.euromoneydirectory.com   LUXEMBOURG (+352)

Crédit Commercial de France (Luxembourg) SA Subsidiary Company

8 Avenue Marie-Thérèse, L-2132, Luxembourg
PO Box 358, L-2013, Luxembourg
Tel: 463 649 1 Fax: 463 539 Telex: 60797 CCFSA LU

Senior Executive Officers
Chairman
International Division

Daniel de Laender
Daniel de Laender MD, International Bank Relations

General-Investment
Head of Investment

André Jovet AVP, Undertakings-Collective Investments

General - Treasury
Head of Treasury

Jean-Marie Bondioli SVP, Treasury & Capital Markets

Relationship Manager
Holding Companies

Nicole Pollefort Senior Vice President
Giancarlo Cervino

Settlement / Clearing
Settlement (General)
Operations

Francine Belluccci Back-Office Money & Precious Metals
Daniel Hussin SVP, Operational Management

Global Custody
Other (Global Custody)
Custodian Services

Francine Marting

Other Departments
Private Banking

Jean Souillard Executive Vice President
Guy Genin Assistant Vice President
Daniel Burgués Assistant Vice President
Didier Closset Assistant Vice President

Administration
Technology & Systems
Electronic Data Processing

Antonio Spagnuolo

Public Relations
Press, Public Relations & Marketing

Daniel de Laender Chairman
Jean-Marie Bondioli SVP, Treasury & Capital Markets

Accounts / Audit
Accounting

Philippe Zune

Other (Administration)
Human Resources

Daniel de Laender Chairman

Crédit Européen SA Head Office

52 Route d'Esch, L-2965, Luxembourg
Tel: 44991 1; 406 540 1 Fax: 44991 231; 406 540 231 Telex: 2524 CBANK LU Swift: CELL LU
Email: newproducts@crediteurop.lu

Senior Executive Officers
Chairman of the Board
Managing Director
Senior General Manager

Daniel Cardon de Lichtbuer
Elmar Baert
Bernard Trempont

Others (Senior Executives)

Christian Molitor Senior Manager
Jean Paul Cames Senior Manager
Denis Truyens Senior Manager

Debt Capital Markets / Fixed Income
Head of Fixed Income
Head of Fixed Income Sales
Head of Fixed Income Trading

Denis Truyens Senior Manager
Caroline Angé ☏ 455 705
Marc Krier Deputy Assistant Manager ☏ 455 705

Government Bonds
Head of Sales
Head of Trading

Caroline Angé ☏ 455 705
Marc Krier Deputy Assistant Manager

Eurobonds
Head of Sales
Head of Trading

Caroline Angé ☏ 455 705
Marc Krier Deputy Assistant Manager

Equity Capital Markets
Head of Equity Capital Markets

Denis Truyens Senior Manager

LUXEMBOURG (+352)   www.euromoneydirectory.com

Crédit Européen SA (cont)

Money Markets
Head of Money Markets — Pierre Dumont *Deputy Manager*

Domestic Commercial Paper
Head of Sales — Pierre Dumont *Deputy Manager*

Eurocommercial Paper
Head of Sales — Pierre Dumont *Deputy Manager*

Wholesale Deposits
Head of Sales — Pierre Dumont *Deputy Manager*

Foreign Exchange
Department: Foreign Exchange & Money Markets
Head of Foreign Exchange — Pierre Dumont *Deputy Manager*

Risk Management
Head of Risk Management — Alain Bastin *Deputy Assistant Manager*

Settlement / Clearing
Head of Settlement / Clearing — Franz Kouijzer *Deputy Manager*
Equity Settlement — Fabien Heilbronn

Global Custody
Head of Global Custody — Claude Marichal

Asset Management
Head — Bernard Coucke *Deputy Manager*

Other Departments
Chief Credit Officer — Alain De Winter *Deputy Assistant Manager*
Private Banking — Bernard Coucke *Deputy Manager*
Correspondent Banking — Philippe Hermans *Deputy Manager*
Cash Management — Alain Schifflers

Administration
Head of Administration — Bernard Trempont *Senior General Manager*
Head of Marketing — Jean Paul Cames *Deputy Manager*
Jean Grosges *Deputy Manager*

Technology & Systems
Christian Molitor *Senior Manager*

Legal / In-House Counsel
Patrick Chillett *Deputy Assistant Manager*

Compliance
Monica Fischer

Public Relations
Press & Public Relations — Jean Grosges *Deputy Manager*

Accounts / Audit
MIS, Accounting — Murad Ihktiar
Internal Audit — Alain Chantrenne *Deputy Manager*

Other (Administration)
Domestic Branches — Pierre Voos
Human Resources — Lilette Domken

Crédit Suisse (Luxembourg) SA

56 Grand'Rue, L-1660, Luxembourg
PO Box 40, L-2010, Luxembourg
Tel: 460 0111 Fax: 475 541 Telex: 1356 CSLUX LU Swift: CRES LU LL

Senior Executive Officers
Financial Director — Pierre Hoesly
Managing Director — Hansulrich Hugli

Others (Senior Executives)
Senior Manager — Vivian Leurin

Debt Capital Markets / Fixed Income
Head of Fixed Income — Pierre Hoesly

Asset Management
Head — Melchers Raymond

Other Departments
Private Banking — Hansulrich Hugli *Managing Director*

Administration
Other (Administration)
General Affairs — Vincent Cusce *Head* ☏ 460 0111 680

LUXEMBOURG (+352)

Dai-Ichi Kangyo Bank (Luxembourg) SA
Subsidiary Company

Place de l'Etoile, 2 Boulevard de la Foire, L-1528, Luxembourg
PO Box 43, L-2010, Luxembourg
Tel: 451 755 1 Fax: 453 337 Telex: 60534 DKB LU Swift: DAIK LU LL Email: dkbluxbo@pt.lu
Website: www.dkb.co.jp

Senior Executive Officers
Managing Director / General Manager — Tadashi Katono

Den Danske Bank International SA
Full Branch Office

2 rue du Fossé, L-2011, Luxembourg
PO Box 173, Luxembourg
Tel: 461 275 1; 473 841 Fax: 473 078 Telex: 1891 DDB LU Swift: DABA LU LL Reuters: DDBI-J, DDBU

Senior Executive Officers
Chief Executive Officer — Søren Rose *Deputy General Manager*
Peer Kierstein Nielsen *Managing Director*
Treasurer — Mogens Dalhoff Pedersen

Foreign Exchange
Global Head — Kim Dengler Jensen *Chief Dealer*

FX Traders / Sales People
Carlo Steuer *Senior Dealer*

Settlement / Clearing
Operations — John Kristian Jørgensen *Senior Manager*

Other Departments
Private Banking — Thomas Mitchell *Assistant General Manager*

Deutsche Bank Luxembourg SA
Subsidiary Company

2 Boulevard Konrad Adenauer, L-1115, Luxembourg
PO Box 586, Luxembourg, L-2015, Luxembourg
Tel: 42122 1 Fax: 42122 449 Telex: 60109 Reuters: DEUU
Credit Department Tel: 42122 330; Fax: 42122 287; Private Banking Tel: 42122 324; Fax: 42122 346; Treasury Tel: 42122 500; Fax: 42122 535

Senior Executive Officers
Treasurer — Klaus Michael Vogel ☎ **42122 500**
Managing Director — Ernst Wilhelm Contzen ☎ **42122 220**

Debt Capital Markets / Fixed Income
Head of Fixed Income — Klaus Michael Vogel ☎ **42122 500**

Syndicated Lending
Other (Syndicated Lending)
International Loans — Klaus Michael Vogel ☎ **42122 500**

Other Departments
Private Banking — Reinhold Weisenfeld ☎ **42122 324**

Administration
Other (Administration)
Resources & Controlling — Wolfgang Stroeher

Deutsche Girozentrale - Deutsche Kommunalbank
Full Branch Office

16 Boulevard Royal, L-2449, Luxembourg
PO Box 848, L-2018, Luxembourg
Tel: 474 360 Fax: 462 477 Telex: 3101 DGZ LU Swift: DGZF LU LL Reuters: DGZB

Senior Executive Officers
Chief Executive Officer — Bruno Stuckenbroeker *General Manager*
Horst Weber *Senior Manager*
Treasurer — Werner Symolka *Manager* ☎ **475 022**

Settlement / Clearing
Regional Head — Marie-Thérèse Lanser *Assistant Manager* ☎ **462 4711**

LUXEMBOURG (+352)   www.euromoneydirectory.com

Deutsche Girozentrale International SA   Subsidiary Company

16 Boulevard Royal, L-2449, Luxembourg
PO Box 19, L-2010, Luxembourg
Tel: 462 471 1; 474 360 **Fax:** 462 477 **Telex:** 2841DGZIN LU **Swift:** DGZF LU LI **Reuters:** DGZX, DGZU

Senior Executive Officers
Chairman   Ernst-Otto Sandvoss
Treasurer   Werner Symolka *Manager* ☎ **475 022**
     Johann-Matthias Blomeyer *Deputy Director & Treasurer* ☎ **220 911**
MD, Management Board   Bruno Stuckenbroeker

Others (Senior Executives)
Management Board   Horst Weber *Director*
     Luc Croize-Pourcelet *Director*

General-Lending (DCM, SL)
Head of Corporate Banking   Eric Lamarcq *Assistant Manager, Credit*
     Joseph Vallendar *Assistant Manager, Credit*

Debt Capital Markets / Fixed Income
Eurobonds
Head of Origination   Frank Grunow *Assistant Manager* ☎ **2209 1450**

Foreign Exchange
FX Traders / Sales People
Foreign Exchange & Eurodeposits   Tom Megyimori *Manager* ☎ **220 911**

Settlement / Clearing
Regional Head   Marie-Thérèse Lanser *Assistant Manager*

Deutsche Postbank International SA   Subsidiary Company

2 route de Trèves, Senningerberg, Luxembourg
Tel: 349 531 1; 349 534 **Fax:** 346 206; 341 120 **Telex:** 60705 PBI LU **Swift:** PBNKLULL **Reuters:** POST (Dealing)
Bloomberg: ANDRÉ SCHUMACHER

Senior Executive Officers
Chairman   Joachim Sperbel
Treasurer   Winfried Mittné ☎ **349 534**
General Manager   Christoph Schmitz ☎ **349 531 200**
General Manager   Yochen Begos ☎ **349 531 202**

Others (Senior Executives)
Portfolio Management   Helmut Peuser ☎ **349 531 400**
Private Banking   Ralf Schermully ☎ **359 531 360**

General-Lending (DCM, SL)
Head of Corporate Banking   Mathious Ringler ☎ **349 531 211**

Debt Capital Markets / Fixed Income
Department: Money Markets, Foreign Exchange Securities
Tel: 349 534 **Fax:** 346 206
Head of Fixed Income; Head of Fixed Income Sales; Head of Fixed Income Trading   Winfried Mittné ☎ **349 534**

Government Bonds
Head of Sales; Head of Trading   André Schumacher ☎ **349 534**

Eurobonds
Head of Sales; Head of Trading   André Schumacher ☎ **349 534**

Libor-Based / Floating-Rate Products
FRN Sales; FRN Trading; Asset Swaps; Asset Swaps (Sales)   Winfried Mittné ☎ **349 534**

Fixed-Income Repo
Head of Repo; Marketing & Product Development; Head of Trading   Winfried Mittné ☎ **349 534**

Syndicated Lending
Tel: 341 390 **Fax:** 346 206 **Reuters:** POST
Head of Trading   Mathious Ringler ☎ **349 531 211**

Money Markets
Tel: 349 534 **Fax:** 346 206
Head of Money Markets   Winfried Mittné ☎ **349 534**

www.euromoneydirectory.com LUXEMBOURG (+352)

Foreign Exchange
Tel: 349 534 Fax: 346 206
Head of Foreign Exchange; Head of Institutional Winfried Mittné ☏ 349 534
Sales; Corporate Sales; Head of Trading

Settlement / Clearing
Tel: 349 531 1 Fax: 346 206
Head of Settlement / Clearing	Adolf Schares ☏ 349 531 280
Fixed-Income Settlement	Holger Nahlke ☏ 349 531 284
Back-Office	Maurizio Guerrieri ☏ 349 531 240

Global Custody
Head of Global Custody Adolf Schares ☏ 349 531 280

Asset Management
Portfolio Management Helmut Peuser ☏ 349 531 400

Other Departments
Private Banking Ralf Schermully ☏ 359 531 360

Administration
Head of Administration Jo Geraets ☏ 349 531 236

Technology & Systems
Bernd Ysinnwell ☏ 349 531 300

Legal / In-House Counsel
Yochen Begos *General Manager* ☏ 349 531 202

DG Bank Luxembourg SA

4 rue Thomas Edison, L-1445, Luxembourg
PO Box 661, L-2016, Luxembourg
Tel: 44903 1 Fax: 44903 2001 Telex: 3757 DGBK LU Swift: GENO LU LL

Senior Executive Officers
Chairman	Bernd Thiemann
Treasurer	John Stefen *Treasurer* ☏ 44903 8010 ℻ 44903 8001

Others (Senior Executives)
Hans-Peter Sättele *Managing Director*
Bernhard Singer *Managing Director*
Franz Schulz *Managing Director*
Rainer Stegmann *Managing Director*

Debt Capital Markets / Fixed Income
Head of Fixed Income	John Stefen *Treasurer* ☏ 44903 8010 ℻ 44903 8001
Head of Fixed Income Sales	Gerd Schwickerath ☏ 44903 8093 ℻ 44903 8001

Money Markets
Head of Money Markets John Stefen *Treasurer* ☏ 44903 8010 ℻ 44903 8001

Foreign Exchange
Head of Foreign Exchange John Stefen *Treasurer* ☏ 44903 8010 ℻ 44903 8001

Risk Management
Head of Risk Management John Stefen *Treasurer* ☏ 44903 8010 ℻ 44903 8001

Settlement / Clearing
Head of Settlement / Clearing Volker Lehmann ☏ 44903 4110 ℻ 44903 4101

Asset Management
Department: Funds

Other (Asset Management)
Funds Thomas Amendd

Other Departments
Chief Credit Officer Klaus-Peter Bräuer ☏ 44903 5110 ℻ 457 393

Administration
Head of Administration	Wilfried Ehrhard ☏ 44903 2810 ℻ 44903 2801
Head of Marketing	Ulrich Freund ☏ 44903 2210 ℻ 44903 2201

Technology & Systems
Wilfried Ehrhard ☏ 44903 2810 ℻ 44903 2801

Legal / In-House Counsel
Klaus-Peter Bräuer ☏ 44903 5110 ℻ 457 393

Compliance
Axel Rau ☏ 44903 2410 ℻ 44903 2401

Public Relations
Ulrich Freund ☏ 44903 2210 ℻ 44903 2201

Euromoney Directory 1999 **1003**

LUXEMBOURG (+352)   www.euromoneydirectory.com

DG Bank Luxembourg SA (cont)
Accounts / Audit
Accounts   Erwin Thömmes ☎ 44903 2310 ☒ 44903 2301
Audit   Axel Rau ☎ 44903 2410 ☒ 44903 2401

Dresdner Bank Luxembourg SA   Subsidiary Company
26 rue du Marché-aux-Herbes, PO Box 355, L-2097, Luxembourg
Tel: 4760 1 **Fax:** 4760 562 **Telex:** 2558 DRES LU, 2308 DREFX LU (FX) **Swift:** DRES LU LL **Reuters:** DRBU (Dealing)
Telerate: 3716
Corporate Banking Tel: 4745 46; **Eurocurrency Tel:** 4612 12; **Forex & Precious Metals Tel:** 4616 16; **Private Banking Tel:** 4707 03; **Private Investors' Advisory Tel:** 4760 718; **Securities Tel:** 4628 28

Senior Executive Officers
Managing Director   Wolfgang A Baertz
Managing Director   Walter H Draisbach
Managing Director   F Otto Wendt

General-Investment
Head of Investment   Bernd Ehinger *AGM, Private Investors' Advisory*

Debt Capital Markets / Fixed Income
Tel: 4612 12 **Fax:** 4760 562
Non-Domestic Government Bonds
                                Ernst Krause *AGM & Chief Dealer*
                                Harald Stieler *Senior Manager*

Asset-Backed Securities / Securitization
Head of Trading   René Jean *Manager*
                                Michael Daniel *Assistant Manager, Securities*

Fixed-Income Repo
Trading   Manuel Hoffman *Assistant Manager*
                                Michael Burg *Officer Euromoney*

Equity Capital Markets
Tel: 4628 28 **Fax:** 4760 562
Equity Repo / Securities Lending
Head
Head of Trading   Manuel Hoffman *Assistant Manager*
                                René Jean *Manager*
                                Michael Burg *Officer Euromoney*

Money Markets
Other (Wholesale Deposits)
Eurocurrency   Bernd Birkenstock *Manager*
                                Manuel Hoffmann *Assistant Manager*

Foreign Exchange
Department: Foreign Exchange & Precious Metals
Global Head   Wolfgang Tischer *Assistant Manager*

Corporate Finance / M&A Advisory
Department: Global Finance
Global Head   Chlodwig M Reuter *General Manager*

Other (Corporate Finance)
Loans   John Schlim *Senior Manager*
Syndications   Dietmar Stuhrmann *Senior Manager*
Corporate Banking & New Issues Peter Kaul *Senior Manager*
                                Marita Kraemer *Senior Manager*
                                Wolfgang Hormesch *Manager*

Other Departments
Private Banking   Dieter Berodt *Manager, Private Banking*

DSL Bank Luxembourg SA   Subsidiary Company
5 rue Höhenhof, L-1736, Luxembourg Senningerberg
PO Box 1921, L-1019, Luxembourg
Tel: 349 494 1 **Fax:** 349 494 222; 349 494 555 **Telex:** 60860 DSLUX **Swift:** BIC DSL BLU LI **Reuters:** DSLU

Senior Executive Officers
Chairman   Ernst Seulen
Managing Director   Hubertus Brandt
Managing Director   Wolfgang Matthey

www.euromoneydirectory.com LUXEMBOURG (+352)

Debt Capital Markets / Fixed Income
Tel: 349 494 300
Global Head Marc Lamesch *Chief Dealer*
Regional Head Elisabeth Tarento *Senior Dealer*

Eurobonds
Head of Trading Marc Lamesch *Chief Dealer*

Libor-Based / Floating-Rate Products
Asset Swaps Thomas Pfleger *Vice President*
Asset Swaps (Sales) Irene Eppers *Assistant Vice President*

Syndicated Lending
Tel: 349 494 410 Fax: 349 494 555
Global Head Irene Eppers *Assistant Vice President*
 Thomas Pfleger *Vice President*

Foreign Exchange
Tel: 349 494 300
Global Head Marc Lamesch *Chief Dealer*

FX Traders / Sales People
 Elisabeth Tarento *Senior Dealer*

Settlement / Clearing
Tel: 394 494 240
Regional Head Nathalie Dell *Assistant Manager*

East-West United Bank SA   Subsidiary Company
10 Boulevard Joseph II, L-1840, Luxembourg
PO Box 34, L-2010, Luxembourg
Tel: 253 153 1 Fax: 450 412 Telex: 1373 EOBANK, Email: eastwestlux@hermes.net.com Reuters: EWUU

Senior Executive Officers
Chairman Serguei Rodionov
Deputy Chairman & MD Serguei Pavlov
Deputy Chairman & MD Tatiana de Planta-Peltzer
Member of the Board Serguei Ilioukhine
International Division Serguei Pavlov

General-Lending (DCM, SL)
Head of Corporate Banking S Pavlov

General - Treasury
Head of Treasury Pierre-Paul Boegen *Head, International Business Relations*

Debt Capital Markets / Fixed Income
Department: Capital Markets
Tel: 452 151
Global Head Pierre-Paul Boegen *Head, International Business Relations*

Eurobonds
Head of Trading Konstantin Mikhailov *Dealer*
 Dimitri Vaneev *Dealer*

Bonds - General
Buying Dimitri Vaneev *Dealer*

Private Placements
Head of Origination Pierre-Paul Boegen *Head, International Business Relations*

Syndicated Lending
Department: Loan Syndication / Asset Sales

Other (Syndicated Lending)
Syndication Reinald Moreau
Origination Serguei Pavlov *Deputy Chairman & MD*
Asset Sales Régine Petit

Other (Trade Finance)
Letters of Credit; Forfaiting; Documentary Credits Serguei Pavlov

Money Markets
Department: Capital Markets

Other (Wholesale Deposits)
Eurocurrency Deposits - Origination Konstantin Mikhailov *Dealer*
 Dimitri Vaneev *Dealer*

Euromoney Directory 1999 1005

LUXEMBOURG (+352)   www.euromoneydirectory.com

East-West United Bank SA (cont)
Foreign Exchange
Tel: 452 151
FX Traders / Sales People
    Konstantin Mikhailov *Dealer*
    Dimitri Vaneev *Dealer*

Risk Management
Tel: 452 151
IR Swaps Trading
    Konstantin Mikhailov *Dealer*
    Dimitri Vaneev *Dealer*

Foreign Exchange Derivatives / Risk Management
Cross-Currency Swaps, Trading
    Konstantin Mikhailov *Dealer*
    Dimitri Vaneev *Dealer*

Settlement / Clearing
Settlement (General)
    René Weis *Back-Office*

Other Departments
Correspondent Banking
    Francine van Zeeland *General Secretary*

Administration
Head of Administration
    Francine van Zeeland *General Secretary*

EFG Private Bank (Luxembourg) SA   Head Office

Formerly known as: Banque de Dépôts (Luxembourg) SA
5 rue Jean Monnet, L-2180, Luxembourg
PO Box 897, L-2018, Luxembourg
Tel: 420 724 1   Telex: 60570 EFGBLU

Senior Executive Officers
Chairman   Jean-Marc Wagener
Managing Director   François Ries
General Manager   Antoines Karayannis

Others (Senior Executives)
    Fouad Edmond Rathle *Senior Vice President*
    Ava C Baker *First Vice President*

Debt Capital Markets / Fixed Income
Department: Treasury
Global Head   Martin Shapiro *Deputy Vice President* ☎ **420 724 304**
Head of Fixed Income Trading   Spyridon Politis *Head* ☎ **420 724 310**

Risk Management
Head of Risk Management   Luc Tougis *Head of Accounting* ☎ **420 724 229**

Settlement / Clearing
Head of Settlement / Clearing; Equity Settlement   Marco Girardi *Head of Back Office* ☎ **420 724 228**
Fixed-Income Settlement; Back-Office   Marco Giradi ☎ **420 724 228**

Global Custody
Head of Global Custody   Ana Baker *First Vice President* ☎ **420 724 231**

Asset Management
Head   Leonidas Nauthopoulos *Head of Private Banking* ☎ **420 724 201**

Other Departments
Chief Credit Officer   Fouad Edmond Rathle *Senior Vice President*
Private Banking   Leonidas Nauthopoulos *Head of Private Banking* ☎ **420 724 201**
Correspondent Banking   Ana Baker *First Vice President* ☎ **420 724 231**
Cash Management   Spyros Routis ☎ **420 724 310**

Administration
Head of Administration   Ana Baker ☎ **420 724 231**
Business Development   Antoines Karayannis *General Manager*
Head of Marketing   Leonidas Nauthopoulos *Head of Private Banking* ☎ **420 724 201**

Technology & Systems
Operations & Information Technology   Ana Baker *First Vice President* ☎ **420 724 231**

Compliance
    Fouad Rathle *Director* ☎ **420 724 1**

Public Relations
    Francais Ries ☎ **420 724 1**

Accounts / Audit
    Luc Tougis *Head of Accounting* ☎ **420 724 229**

www.euromoneydirectory.com LUXEMBOURG (+352)

Europa Bank AG
Subsidiary Company

Alternative trading name: Banque pour l'Europe SA & Bank for Europe Limited
13 rue Beaumont, L-1219, Luxembourg
PO Box 734, L-2017, Luxembourg
Tel: 470 830 1 **Fax:** 470 830 39 **Telex:** 2566 EURBK LU **Swift:** BEUR LU LL **Reuters:** EUBK

Senior Executive Officers
Chairman
Treasurer
General Manager
General Manager
Managing Director

Jürgen Sarrazin
Torsten Ottens *Chief Dealer* ☎ 470 830 20
Klaus Désor
Armin Kürzinger
Wolfgang A. Baertz

Others (Senior Executives)
Treasury

Ansgar Kettern *Dealer*

General-Lending (DCM, SL)
Head of Corporate Banking

Clemens Beer *Assistant Manager* ☎ 470 830 28
Jürgen Lohmüller ☎ 470 830 32
Marion Reher ☎ 470 830 34

Syndicated Lending

Other (Syndicated Lending)
Head of Loans & Syndication

Uwe Eichhorn ☎ 470 830 38
Jens Fischer ☎ 470 830 25

Europäische HypothekenBank SA
Subsidiary Company

2 Boulevard Konrad Adenauer, L-1115, Luxembourg
PO Box 911, L-2019, Luxembourg
Tel: 426 626 1 **Fax:** 426 626 749

Robert Fleming & Co Limited
Full Branch Office

European Bank & Business Centre, 2633 Route de Trèves Senningerberg, L-2888, Luxembourg
Tel: 341 01 **Fax:** 340 873 **Telex:** 60338 **Email:** info@flemings.lu
Website: www.flemings.lu

Senior Executive Officers
DGM, Robert Fleming & Co.
General Manager

Gerd Gebhard
Richard Goddard

Settlement / Clearing
Operations

Richard Goddard *General Manager*

Fleming Asset Management (Luxembourg) SA
Subsidiary Company

European Bank & Business Centre, 6 Route de Trèves, Senningerberg, L-2888, Luxembourg
Tel: 341 01 **Fax:** 340 873 **Telex:** 60338 **Email:** info@flemings.lu
Website: www.flemings.lu

Senior Executive Officers
Managing Director

Veit Schuhen

Others (Senior Executives)
Sales
Finance

Campbell Fleming
Henry Kelly *Director*

Relationship Manager
Register & Transfer Agency Services

Henry Kelly *Director*

Administration
Head of Administration

Richard Goddard *Director*

Technology & Systems
Business Systems

Didier Tredan *Director*

Legal / In-House Counsel

Henry Kelly *Director*

Compliance

Henry Kelly *Director*

Euromoney Directory 1999 **1007**

LUXEMBOURG (+352)   www.euromoneydirectory.com

Fortis Bank Luxembourg — Subsidiary Company

Formerly known as: Banque Universelle et Commerciale du Luxembourg
12/16 Monterey, L-2163, Luxembourg
Tel: 46 800 1 Fax: 46 800 222 Telex: FORTIS LU 2395 Swift: FBLX LU LL Email: info@fortisbank.lu
Website: www.fortisbank.lu

Senior Executive Officers
President & CEO — Pierre Detournay
Financial Director — Claude Jeitz *Director* T 46 800 321 F 46 800 312
Managing Director — Georges Logelin

Others (Senior Executives)
Commercial Director — Alain Demeur

General - Treasury
Head of Treasury — Claude Jeitz *Director* T 46 800 321 F 46 800 312

Debt Capital Markets / Fixed Income
Head of Debt Capital Markets — Claude Jeitz *Director* T 46 800 321 F 46 800 312

Equity Capital Markets
Head of Equity Capital Markets — Claude Jeitz *Director* T 46 800 321 F 46 800 312

Foreign Exchange
Head of Foreign Exchange — Claude Jeitz *Director* T 46 800 321 F 46 800 312

Administration
Head of Marketing — Philippe Piette T 46 800 248 F 46 800 417

Fuji Bank (Luxembourg) SA — Subsidiary Company

29 Avenue de la Port-Neuve, L-2227, Luxembourg
PO Box 894, L-2018, Luxembourg
Tel: 474 681 Fax: 474 688 Telex: 3213 Swift: FUJI LU LL Reuters: FUJU

Senior Executive Officers
Managing Director — Tadashi Omiya

Debt Capital Markets / Fixed Income
Head of Fixed Income — Odette Wagner *Senior Manager* T 473 933 503

Syndicated Lending
Head of Syndicated Lending — Hiroyuki Obata *Senior Manager* T 473 933 602

Foreign Exchange
Head of Foreign Exchange — Tadashi Omiya *Managing Director*

Settlement / Clearing
Head of Settlement / Clearing — Odette Wagner *Senior Manager* T 473 933 503

Administration
Head of Administration — Norihiro Nakajima *Senior Manager* T 473 933 202

Hauck & Aufhäuser Banquiers Luxembourg SA — Subsidiary Company

Formerly known as: Hauk Banquiers Luxembourg S.A.
6 Boulevard Joseph II, L-2014, Luxembourg
PO Box 414, L-1840, Luxembourg
Tel: 451 3141 Fax: 451 714 Telex: 1381 hauckblu Swift: HAUK LUL Email: haucklux@pt.lu

Senior Executive Officers
Chairman — J E Cramer
Managing Director — Armin Wollert

Others (Senior Executives)
Matthias Meyer *Director*
Lothar Ratalski *Director*

Debt Capital Markets / Fixed Income
Bonds - General
Eurobonds — Kirsten Meibner-Lange

Money Markets
Other (Wholesale Deposits) — Kirsten Meibner-Lange

Asset Management
Other (Asset Management)
Asset Management — Matthias Schirpke

www.euromoneydirectory.com LUXEMBOURG (+352)

Helaba Luxembourg

Alternative trading name: Landsbank Hessen Thüringen International SA
2 Place de Paris, L-2314, Luxembourg
PO Box 1702, L-1017, Luxembourg
Tel: 499 401 1 **Fax:** 499 401 277 **Telex:** 3295 HELA LU (General) **Swift:** HELA LU LL **Cable:** HELA LU
Treasury Tel: 49 9401 5001/6

Senior Executive Officers
President, Board of Directors	Günther Merl
Vice President, Board of Directors	Walter Schäfer
Managing Director	Alex Meyer
Managing Director	Jürgen Völzer
Deputy Managing Director	Raymond Goebbels

General - Treasury
Head of Treasury — Francesco Fumarola

Money Markets
Head of Money Markets — Francesco Fumarola

Foreign Exchange
Head of Foreign Exchange — Francesco Fumarola

Risk Management
Head of Risk Management — Norbert Kohn

Settlement / Clearing
Head of Settlement / Clearing — Stefan Speicher

Other Departments
Private Banking — Joachim Planta

Administration
Accounts / Audit
Accounting — Gabriele Schmitt

HypoVereinsbank Luxembourg Société Anonyme   Head Office

4 rue Alphonse Weicker, L-2721, Luxembourg
PO Box 453, L-2099, Luxembourg
Tel: 4272 1 **Fax:** 4272 4500 **Telex:** 1570 HYPOB LU **Swift:** HYVE LU LL **Email:** contact@hypovereinsbank.lu
Reuters: HVLU
Bond Trading Tel: 4272 5400; **Forex Tel:** 4272 5200; 4272 5300; **Fax:** 4272 4579
Website: www.hypovereinsbank.lu

Senior Executive Officers
President	Martin Schütte
Vice President	Norbert Juchem

Others (Senior Executives)
Members — Rolf Kirchfeld
Martin Kölsch
Wolfgang Prißler
Josef F Wertschulte
Gunnar Homann
Bernd Janietz
Ernst-Dieter Wiesner

Management — Ernst-Dieter Wiesner *Managing Director & Speaker*
Gunnar Homann *Managing Director*
Bernd Janietz *Managing Director*

General-Lending (DCM, SL)
Head of Corporate Banking — Holger Möller *Corporate Banking & Credit Department*

General - Treasury
Head of Treasury — Jean-Claude Wirthor

Debt Capital Markets / Fixed Income
Bonds - General
Bond Trading — Wolfgang Krammel

Foreign Exchange
Country Head — Dirk Kockler *FX / MM Operations*

Risk Management
Other (FI Derivatives)
Risk Control — Bernd Biermann

Euromoney Directory 1999 **1009**

LUXEMBOURG (+352) www.euromoneydirectory.com

HypoVereinsbank Luxembourg Société Anonyme (cont)

Settlement / Clearing
Back-Office — Michael Borelbach

Global Custody
Other (Global Custody)
Custodian Service — Gerd Plaßmann

Other Departments
Private Banking — Wolfgang Przybyl
Jürgen Kühn
Nicholas Illgen
Renée Keipes *Private Banking Operations*
Economic Research — Jörg Hahn

Other Departments
Coordination — Joachim Beckert

Administration
Head of Administration — Peter Mertens

Technology & Systems
Electronic Data Processing — Friedrich Giebler

Legal / In-House Counsel
Legal Counsel — Jost Löschner

Corporate Communications
— Barbara Fischer Fürwentsches

Accounts / Audit
Accounting — Herbert Emminger

Other (Administration)
Personel Department — Roland Lindner
Internal Control — Jean Wirtz

IKB Deutsche Industriebank AG Full Branch Office

2 rue Jean Monnet, L-2180, Luxembourg
PO Box 771, L-2017, Luxembourg
Tel: 423 777 1; 423 790 (FX) **Fax:** 420 603 **Telex:** 3571 INBANK LU **Reuters:** IKBU

Senior Executive Officers
Senior Vice President — Jean-Paul Frisch
Senior Vice President — Winfried Reinke
VP, International Credits — Sylviane Lizambri
Senior Vice President — Alfons Schmid

General-Lending (DCM, SL)
Head of Corporate Banking — Sylviane Lizambri *VP, International Credits*

Debt Capital Markets / Fixed Income
Global Head — Jean-Paul Frisch *Senior Vice President*

Money Markets
Department: Eurocurrency Deposits, Swaps & FRS's

Other (Wholesale Deposits)
— Jean-Paul Frisch *Senior Vice President*
Stefan Eckermann *Dealer*
Henrik Boyander *Dealer*
Ferdinand Kordel *Dealer*
Markus Thesen *Dealer*

Settlement / Clearing
Settlement (General); Operations — Klaus Elsen *Manager, Int'l Payments & Transfers*

Administration

Technology & Systems
— Rolf Heinemann *Manager*

Accounts / Audit
— Frank Kählke *Manager*

Other (Administration)
Marketing — Jean-Paul Frisch *Senior Vice President*

www.euromoneydirectory.com LUXEMBOURG (+352)

IKB International
Subsidiary Company

2 rue Jean Monnet, L-2180, Luxembourg
Tel: 424 111 1 Fax: 420 603 Telex: 3571 INBANK LU

Senior Executive Officers
Senior Vice President   Alfons Schmid
Senior Vice President   Michael Braun
Senior Vice President   Jean-Paul Frisch

The Industrial Bank of Japan (Luxembourg) SA
Subsidiary Company

6 rue Jean Monnet, L-2180, Luxembourg
PO BOX 68, L-2010, Luxembourg
Tel: 421 617 1 Fax: 421 617 489 Telex: IBJLX LU Email: flamion.ibj@luxembourg.com

Senior Executive Officers
Chairman   Haruhiko Takenaka
Managing Director   Akira Imai
General Manager   Bertrand Klein

Others (Senior Executives)
                        Atobe Ken *Deputy General Manager*

Money Markets
Head of Money Markets   Geoffroy Glenisson *Chief Dealer*

Risk Management
Head of Risk Management Ciaran McKay *Deputy General Manager*

Settlement / Clearing
Head of Settlement / Clearing; Equity   Guy Dratwicki *Deputy General Manager*
Settlement; Fixed-Income Settlement;
Operations

Other Departments
Global Trust   Jean-Claude Simon *Manager*

Administration
Head of Administration Ciaran McKay *Deputy General Manager*

Accounts / Audit
Audit   Valerie Remy-Tomas *Chief Auditor*

Other (Administration)
Marketing   Atobe Ken *Deputy General Manager*

ING Bank (Luxembourg) SA
Subsidiary Company

224 route d'Arlon, L-8010, Strassen
PO Box 1961, L-1019, Strassen
Tel: 316 6111 Fax: 316 868

Senior Executive Officers
Managing Director   Aernout Goldberg

General-Investment
Head of Investment   G Pieters *GM, Investment Management*

Settlement / Clearing
Operations   D L Walker *General Manager, Operations*

Other Departments
Private Banking   John Kerckhoffs *Head, Private Banking*

ING Trust (Luxembourg)

8 Boulevard Joseph II, PO Box 2383, L-1019, Luxembourg
Tel: 250 440 Fax: 250 448

Senior Executive Officers
General Manager   Herman Moors

Euromoney Directory 1999 **1011**

LUXEMBOURG (+352)   www.euromoneydirectory.com

Kredietbank SA Luxembourg
Head Office

43 Boulevard Royal, L-2955, Luxembourg
Tel: 4797 1 **Fax:** 472 667 **Telex:** 3418 KBLUX LU **Swift:** KBLX LU LL
Website: www.kbl.lu

Senior Executive Officers
Chairman   Jan Huyghebaert
President   Damien Wigny

Others (Senior Executives)
Executive Directors
    Etienne Verwilghen
    Charles Ruppert
    Jean-Marie Barthel
    Antoine D'Hondt

Debt Capital Markets / Fixed Income
Marketing   Guy Knepper *Head of International Securities Lending* ☎ **4797 2951** 🖷 **4797 3909**
Head of Fixed Income Trading   Luc Caytan ☎ **4797 2951** 🖷 **4797 2822**

Equity Capital Markets
Fax: 472 667
Marketing   Rafik Fischer *International Securities Lending* ☎ **4797 2644** 🖷 **4797 3910**
    Guy Knepper *Head of International Securities Lending* ☎ **4797 2951** 🖷 **4797 3909**
Head of Sales   John Jentges ☎ **4797 2273**
Head of Trading   Luc Caytan ☎ **4797 2951** 🖷 **4797 2822**

Money Markets
Regional Head   Pierre Dantinne ☎ **4797 2739**

Foreign Exchange
Tel: 473 671 **Fax:** 4797 2822
Regional Head   Jean Kayser ☎ **4797 2734**
Corporate Sales   Raymond Schaeffer ☎ **4797 2547**

Risk Management

Other (Exchange-Traded Derivatives)
Derivatives Trading   Luc Caytan ☎ **4797 2951** 🖷 **4797 2822**

Corporate Finance / M&A Advisory
Department: Corporate
Tel: 4797 3898 **Fax:** 4797 73 3952
Head of Corporate Finance   Jacques Worré *Head of Corporate / Syndications* ☎ **4797 3885** 🖷 **460 019**

Other (Corporate Finance)
Corporate Finance & Syndication
    Eric Bonte ☎ **4797 3885**
    Jean-Paul Dekerk ☎ **4797 3905**
    Christian Springuel ☎ **4797 2657**
    Guy Regnier ☎ **4797 2289**
    Jean-Yves Dourte ☎ **4797 2964**
    Candido Romero ☎ **4797 2767**
    Benoit van Oldeneel ☎ **4797 2941**
Mergers & Acquisitions   Jean-Louis de Potesta ☎ **4797 2978**

Global Custody
Fax: 4797 73 910
    Serge D'Orazio ☎ **4797 2474**
    Christine Schmit ☎ **4797 2477** 🖷 **4797 3326**

Other Departments
Private Banking   Michel Hubert ☎ **4797 3919**
Correspondent Banking   Raymond Gleis ☎ **4797 2628**
Economic Research   Marc Demey *Risk Management & Research Division* ☎ **4797 3970**

Administration

Technology & Systems
    Philippe Paquay ☎ **46819 2932**

Legal / In-House Counsel
    Philippe Bourin ☎ **4797 3110**

www.euromoneydirectory.com LUXEMBOURG (+352)

Lampebank International SA
Subsidiary Company

2 rue de l'Eau, L-1449, Luxembourg
PO Box 164, L-2011, Luxembourg
Tel: 462 626 1 Fax: 462 201 34 Telex: 3361/2 Swift: LAMI LU LL

Senior Executive Officers
President   Hans-Jens Trelde
Chief Executive Officer   Thomas Köhler *Chief Executive & Vice President* ☏ **462 626 241**
Financial Director   Brigitte Hary *General Manager* ☏ **462 626 242**
Chief Operating Officer   Jean Kaiser *Assistant General Manager* ☏ **462 626 223**
Treasurer   Ronald Dunker *Vice President* ☏ **462 626 274**

Debt Capital Markets / Fixed Income
Global Head   Brigitte Hary *General Manager* ☏ **462 626 242**

Eurobonds
Head of Trading   Helene Braun *Authorized Officer* ☏ **462 626 275**

Equity Capital Markets
Global Head   Brigitte Hary *General Manager* ☏ **462 626 242**

International Equities
Head of Trading   Helene Braun *Authorized Officer* ☏ **462 626 275**

Syndicated Lending
Loan-Related Activities
Trade Finance   Daniel Bardina *Authorized Officer* ☏ **462 626 246**

Foreign Exchange
Global Head   Ronald Dunker *Vice President* ☏ **462 626 274**

FX Traders / Sales People
                                           Volker Schmoll ☏ **462 626 279**

Settlement / Clearing
Fixed-Income Settlement   Antoine Clement *Assistant Vice President* ☏ **462 626 236**
Foreign Exchange Settlement   Guy Muller *Assistant Vice President* ☏ **462 626 262**

Other Departments
Private Banking   Ralf Meinerzag *Assistant Vice.President* ☏ **462 626 244**

Landesbank Rheinland-Pfalz International SA
Subsidiary Company

10-12 Boulevard Roosevelt, L-2450, Luxembourg
PO Box 84, L-2010, Luxembourg
Tel: 475 9211 Fax: 475 921 314

Senior Executive Officers
Others (Senior Executives)
Director   Alain Baustert

Landesbank Schleswig-Holstein International SA
Subsidiary Company

2 rue Jean Monnet, L-2180, Luxembourg
Tel: 424 1411 Fax: 427 040 Telex: 3120 LSHI

Senior Executive Officers
Others (Senior Executives)
                                           Hanns Grad *Head of Trading*

Settlement / Clearing
Operations   Françoise Arnould *Head of Operations*

F van Lanschot Bankiers (Luxembourg) SA
Subsidiary Company

106 route d' Arlon, Mamer, L-8210, Luxembourg
PO Box 673, L-2016, Luxembourg
Tel: 319 911 1 Fax: 319 911 222 Telex: 60843

Senior Executive Officers
Chairman   H J Baeten
Chief Operating Officer   Henri Schong *Director & Manager* ☏ **319 911 400**
Managing Director   Henk Ester ☏ **319 911 401**

Euromoney Directory 1999 **1013**

LUXEMBOURG (+352) www.euromoneydirectory.com

F van Lanschot Bankiers (Luxembourg) SA (cont)
Other Departments
Private Banking — Donald Dijkstal
Administration
Head of Administration — Richard De Bruijn
Technology & Systems
— Pierre Boever

Accounts / Audit
Accounts — Marco Gillen
Other (Administration)
Marketing — Jup Van Crugten

MeesPierson (Luxembourg) SA — Subsidiary Company
Formerly known as: Bank Oppenheim Pierson International SA
10 rue Antoine Jans, L-1820, Luxembourg
PO Box 239, L-2012, Luxembourg
Tel: 476 867 1 Fax: 476 867 229 Telex: 1220 MPSA LU
Trust Fax: 476867ext275

Senior Executive Officers
Chairman — Bart F A de Haas
Chief Executive Officer — Helga T Zult *Chief Executive & Managing Director*
Managing Director — Bas L M Schreuders

Others (Senior Executives)
— Joseph R Goergen *Deputy Manager*

Settlement / Clearing
Regional Head — Jérome Reyter

Other Departments
Private Banking — Walter R Kieboom
— Astrid Ceelen

Administration
Technology & Systems
— Gerhard Kopp

Merita Bank Luxembourg SA — Subsidiary Company
189 Avenue de la Faiencerie, L-1511, Luxembourg
PO Box 569, L-2015, Luxembourg
Tel: 477 6111 Fax: 477 611 251 Telex: 1575 UBFIN LU Swift: MRIT LU LL Email: meritalux.innet.lu
Website: www.merita.fi/luxembourg

Senior Executive Officers
Managing Director — Kjell Westermark

General-Investment
Head of Investment — Jørgen Jakobsen ☎ 477 611 384

Risk Management
Global Head — Jürgen Ebel *Manager* ☎ 477 611 311

Settlement / Clearing
Tel: 477 611 340
Regional Head — Gilbert Grethen *Manager & Head*

Global Custody
Fund Administration — Jackie Legille *Senior Officer* ☎ 477 611 401

Asset Management
Portfolio Management — Tarja Eskelinen *Deputy General Manager* ☎ 477 611 360
— Neil Adams ☎ 477 611 300

Administration
Head of Administration — Gilbert Grethen
Legal / In-House Counsel
— Jeroen van der Rolen *Legal Advisor* ☎ 477 611 312

Public Relations
— Kjell Westermark *Managing Director*

LUXEMBOURG (+352)

Merrill Lynch (Luxembourg) SarL
Subsidiary Company

68/70 Boulevard de la Petrusse, L-2320, Luxembourg
Tel: 494 911 1 Fax: 481 271 Telex: 1380

Senior Executive Officers
Manager — Marc Van de Pol
Deputy General Manager — William Meersman

Administration
Head of Administration — Muammer Kardelen *Administrative Manager*
Accounts / Audit
Jeannine Walschaerts *Account Manager*

Other (Administration)
Tania Solfa *Service Manager*

Mutuel Bank Luxembourg
Subsidiary Company

Alternative trading name: MBL

17 Côte d'Eich, L-1450, Luxembourg
PO Box 884, L-2018, Luxembourg
Tel: 469 989 1 Fax: 469 989 222 Telex: 60522 MBLUX LU

Senior Executive Officers
President of the Executive Committee — Jean Decker
Managing Director & Administrative Delegate — Pierre Font ☐ 469 989 201
Director — Jean-Jacques Greff ☐ 469 989 202

Other Departments
Private Banking — Pierre Font *Managing Director & Administrative Delegate* ☐ 469 989 201

Administration
Head of Administration — Jean Kehren *Assistant Director* ☐ 469 989 203
Accounts / Audit
Jean Kehren *Assistant Director* ☐ 469 989 203

Natexis Banque (Luxembourg) SA
Subsidiary Company

Formerly known as: Credit National (Luxembourg) SA

28 Avenue Marie-Therese, L-2132, Luxembourg
PO Box 541, L-2015, Luxembourg
Tel: 25 3418 1 Fax: 25 3418 341 Telex: 3650 NBL

Senior Executive Officers
Managing Director — Patrick Lavbry

Asset Management
Head — Evelyne Etienne

Other Departments
Private Banking — Guy Hennico

Nikko Bank (Luxembourg) SA
Bank Subsidiary

16 Boulevard Royal, PO Box 14, L-2010, Luxembourg
Tel: 462 384 1 Fax: 462 384 221 Telex: 1348 NIKKO LU Swift: NIKO LU LL Reuters: NKLU (Dealing)

Senior Executive Officers
Managing Director — Yoichi Ueno
Deputy Managing Director — John Pierre Hettinger
Director & General Manager — Koji Mashima

Money Markets
Head of Money Markets — Hajime Mizuno

Foreign Exchange
Head of Foreign Exchange — Hajime Mizuno

Global Custody
Head of Global Custody — Michele Stern

Administration
Head of Administration — Christiane Neuman *Assistant Manager*

Technology & Systems
Francois Bourdon

LUXEMBOURG (+352)   www.euromoneydirectory.com

Nikko Bank (Luxembourg) SA (cont)
Legal / In-House Counsel
                                       Laurent Pichonnier
Accounts / Audit
                                       Laurent Belloco

NOBIS Société des Banques Privées   Head Office
2 rue Jean Monnet, L-2180, Luxembourg
PO Box 183, L-2011, Luxembourg
Tel: 424 121 1 **Fax:** 424 109 **Telex:** 60264 NOBIS LU

Senior Executive Officers
Managing Director   Hans Georg Andlauer ☎ **424 121 500**
Managing Director   Alfons Schmid ☎ **424 121 200**

Debt Capital Markets / Fixed Income
Eurobonds
Head of Trading   Heidi Amendt *Assistant Manager* ☎ **424 121 542**
Bonds - General
                                       Marion Riewer ☎ **424 121 543**
                                       Carlo Tompers ☎ **424 121 540**

Money Markets
Global Head   Heidi Amendt *Assistant Manager* ☎ **424 121 542**

Foreign Exchange
Global Head   Heidi Amendt *Assistant Manager* ☎ **424 121 542**
FX Traders / Sales People
                                       Marion Riewer ☎ **424 121 543**

Settlement / Clearing
Regional Head   Marianne Magar ☎ **424 221 512**

Other Departments
Private Banking   Ruth Weiss *Senior Manager* ☎ **424 121 530**

Administration
Technology & Systems
                                       Christiane Schmit ☎ **424 121 520**
                                       Michael Kopf ☎ **424 121 525**

Nomura Bank (Luxembourg) SA   Subsidiary Company
6 Avenue Emile Reuter, L-2420, Luxembourg
PO Box 289, L-2012, Luxembourg
Tel: 463 888 8 **Fax:** 463 333; 463 888 450 **Telex:** 60856 NOM LU **Swift:** NBLX LU LL **Reuters:** 475151400

Senior Executive Officers
Non-Resident Chairman   Seiichi Takeda
President & Managing Director   Shiro Fujitsu ☎ **463 888 340**
Director & General Manager   Yasuhiro Bansho ☎ **463 888 236** F **463 333**
Director & General Manager, Investment Fund Johny de Smet ☎ **463 888 307** F **463 888 450**

General - Treasury
Head of Treasury   Denis Cronin *Senior Manager, Treasury* ☎ **463 888 218** F **463 333**

Global Custody
Regional Head   Nikae Awano *Senior Manager* ☎ **463 888 261** F **463 333**

Administration
Technology & Systems
                                       Kimiyoshi Sano *Senior Manager* ☎ **463 888 324** F **463 888 450**

Compliance
                                       Ajmal Perwaz *Senior Manager* ☎ **463 888 369** F **463 888 450**

Other (Administration)
Marketing & New Product Developer   Yuko Matsuoka ☎ **463 888 388** F **463 888 450**
Project & Planning   Mr Nakano *Manager* ☎ **463 888 265** F **463 333**
Client Service Department   Nari Shiraishi *Manager* ☎ **463 888 296** F **463 888 461**

LUXEMBOURG (+352)

Norddeutsche Landesbank Luxembourg SA   Subsidiary Company
26 route d'Arlon, L-1140, Luxembourg
PO Box 121, L-2011, Luxembourg
Tel: 452 211 1 Fax: 452 211 319 Telex: 2485 NLB LU (General), 2885 NLB Swift: NOLA LU LL
Reuters: NLBU (Dealing), Cable: NORDLUX
Reuters: NOLL (Monitor)

Senior Executive Officers
General Manager   Jochen Petermann

Others (Senior Executives)
Treasury Manager   Heinz Kühne

General - Treasury
Head of Treasury   Heinz Kühne

Debt Capital Markets / Fixed Income
Department: Capital Markets
Country Head   Wolf-Thilo von Trotha *Assistant Manager, Capital Markets*

Syndicated Lending
Other (Syndicated Lending)
Credit & Syndicated Loans   Franz-Josef Glauben *Assistant Manager, Credits & Syndicated Loans*

Money Markets
Money Markets - General
Money Markets   Dirk Vormberge *Deputy Manager*
                              Thorsten Schmidt *Assistant Manager*
                              Heike Hemmerling *Dealer*
                              Oliver Mazur *Dealer*
                              Kerstin Meyer *Dealer*
                              Dorothea Paffhausen *Dealer*
                              Carsten Schliephake *Dealer*
                              Monika Weis *Dealer*

Foreign Exchange
FX Traders / Sales People
                              Dirk Vormberge *Deputy Manager*
                              Thorsten Schmidt *Assistant Manager*
                              Heike Hemmerling *Dealer*
                              Oliver Mazur *Dealer*
                              Kerstin Meyer *Dealer*
                              Dorothea Paffhausen *Dealer*
                              Carsten Schliephake *Dealer*
                              Monika Weis *Dealer*

Other Departments
Commodities / Bullion   Wolf-Thilo von Trotha *Assistant Manager, Capital Markets*
                              Søren Jagd Nielsen *Dealer*
Private Banking   Wolfgang Georg *Assistant Manager*

Administration
Head of Administration   Karl-Fritz Bewig *Manager Administration*

Prebon Yamane (Luxembourg) SA   Subsidiary Company
2 rue Henri Schnadt, L-2530, Luxembourg
Tel: 291 911; 2928 1818 Fax: 291 929 Telex: 3691 Reuters: FULT

Senior Executive Officers
Managing Director   Peter Svensson
Managing Director   Ian A Johnston

Others (Senior Executives)
                              Gerd Recht *Director*
                              Mike Leighton *Director*

Money Markets
Tel: 2729 1818 Fax: 291 929

Money Markets - General
                              Gerd Recht *Director*
                              Fonsi Grethen *Associate Director*
                              Raymond Behm *Associate Director*

LUXEMBOURG (+352) www.euromoneydirectory.com

Prebon Yamane (Luxembourg) SA (cont)
Foreign Exchange
Tel: 291 801 **Fax:** 291 929
Country Head   Mike Leighton *Director*
                                    Neil Underwood *Associate Director*

Rabobank Luxembourg SA

PO Box 1408, L-1014, Luxembourg
Tel: 457 8801 **Fax:** 452 396

Senior Executive Officers
Managing Director   J P Van Keymeulen
Deputy General Manager   G Berben
Deputy General Manager   A Whiteman
Operations Manager   T Collet

Republic National Bank of New York (Luxembourg) SA
Subsidiary Company

32 Boulevard Royal, L-2449, Luxembourg
PO Box 733, L-2017, Luxembourg
Tel: 47 0711 **Fax:** 479 331 226 **Telex:** 3320 RNBNY LU **Swift:** BLIC LU LX

Senior Executive Officers
Treasurer   Selim Kindy *Manager*
Managing Director   Leigh Robertson

Others (Senior Executives)
                                    Philippe de Chaumont Quitry *Manager*

General-Lending (DCM, SL)
Head of Corporate Banking   Dirk Heimann *Manager*

Debt Capital Markets / Fixed Income
Head of Fixed Income   Jean-Pierre Jaume *Assistant Manager*

Settlement / Clearing
Head of Settlement / Clearing   Nicola Gilij *Back-Office Settlements*

Other Departments
Private Banking   David Levy *General Manager*

Administration
Head of Administration   Julien Tanson *Manager*

Legal / In-House Counsel
                                    Claude Marx *Legal Counsel*

Rolo Banca 1473 SpA
Full Branch Office

16 rue des Bains, L-1212, Luxembourg
PO Box 770, L-2017, Luxembourg
Tel: 220 8421 **Fax:** 469 026 **Telex:** 60730 ROLOL LU **Swift:** ROLO LU LL

Senior Executive Officers
Head, Fixed-Income Trading   E Polito
Deputy Manager   Giovanni Giallombardo

Debt Capital Markets / Fixed Income
Country Head   E Polito *Arbitrage & Capital Markets*

Asset-Backed Securities / Securitization
Global Head   Tiziano Arcangeli *Securities*

Other Departments
Private Banking   C Gastaldi

1018 Euromoney Directory 1999

www.euromoneydirectory.com   LUXEMBOURG (+352)

Roussin (Luxembourg) SA
Subsidiary Company

25 Boulevard Prince Henri, L-1724, Luxembourg
Tel: 460 512
Website: www.roussin.com

Senior Executive Officers

Others (Senior Executives)
                                    Jacques Chopin *Manager*

Sakura Bank (Luxembourg) SA
Subsidiary Company

33 Boulevard Prince Henri, L-1724, Luxembourg
PO Box 30, L-2010, Luxembourg
Tel: 225 455; 462 436 **Fax:** 462 439; 475 781 **Telex:** 60792, 2466 **Swift:** MITK LU LL **Reuters:** MTLU (Dealing)

Senior Executive Officers
Chairman   Tsuyoshi Kuriyama
Vice Chairman   Tsugumasa Kojima
Managing Director   Koji Irisawa
Deputy Managing Director   Yukio Ohmichi
International Division   Kazuhiro Kondo *Manager*

General - Treasury
Head of Treasury   Kazuhiro Kondo *Manager*

Debt Capital Markets / Fixed Income

Eurobonds
Head of Syndication   Kazuhiro Kondo *Manager*

Bonds - General
Underwriting   Kazuhiro Kondo *Manager*

Foreign Exchange
Global Head   Kazuhiro Kondo *Manager*
Regional Head   Eric Verleyen

Risk Management

Fixed Income Derivatives / Risk Management
IR Swaps Trading   Kazuhiro Kondo *Manager*

Foreign Exchange Derivatives / Risk Management
Cross-Currency Swaps, Trading   Kazuhiro Kondo *Manager*

Global Custody

Other (Global Custody)
Custodian Banking   Kyoji Yamazaki *Manager*

Asset Management
Portfolio Management   Kazuhiro Kondo *Manager*

Other Departments
Correspondent Banking   Seiji Higashimura *Manager*

Administration
Head of Administration   Seiji Higashimura *Manager*

Schroder Investment Management (Luxembourg) SA
Subsidiary Company

5 rue Höhenhof, L-1736, Senningerberg
Tel: 341 342 202 **Fax:** 341 342 342 **Email:** schroders@pt.lu
Website: www.schroders.lu

Senior Executive Officers
Chairman   Josiane Pain
Managing Director   John Hall

LUXEMBOURG (+352)   www.euromoneydirectory.com

S-E-Banken Luxembourg SA
Subsidiary Company

16 Boulevard Royal, L-2449, Luxembourg
PO Box 487, L-2014, Luxembourg
Tel: 461 717 1 Fax: 461 710 Telex: 3753 BSL LU

Senior Executive Officers
Vice Chairman — Per Anders Fast
Managing Director — Tore Samuelsson
First Deputy Managing Director — Andreas Economides
Deputy Managing Director — Jos Hemmer

Others (Senior Executives)
Jos Hellers *Senior Manager*
Johan Kuylenstierna *Senior Manager*
Tomas Ljungkvist *Senior Manager*
Alain Meulemans *Senior Manager*

General-Lending (DCM, SL)
Head of Corporate Banking — Ann-Kathrine Björnsen *Credits Manager*

General - Treasury
Head of Treasury — Stefan Renno *Treasury / Trading*

Asset Management
Investment Funds — Jos Hemmer *Deputy Managing Director*
Emile Kremer
Portfolio Management — Tomas Ljungkvist *Senior Manager*

Other Departments
Private Banking — Johan Kuylenstierna *Senior Manager*

Administration
Head of Marketing — Mats Olsson

Technology & Systems
Information Technology — Alain Meulemans *Senior Manager*

Accounts / Audit
Accounting & Reporting — Liliane Minsart
Internal Audit — Hugues Chambon

Other (Administration)
Business Support — Jos Hellers *Senior Manager*
Johan Lindberg
Customer Support Services — Lotte Hedman
Business Processing — Olivier Scholtes
Business Control — Johan Lindberg

SGZ-Bank International SA
Head Office

26B rue des Muguets, 2167, Luxembourg
PO Box 785, L-2167, Luxembourg
Tel: 421 752 1 Fax: 421 752 255; 421 752 3277 Telex: 60640 Reuters: SGZL
Website: www.sgz-bank.lut

Senior Executive Officers
Chairman — Ulrich Brixner ☎ 697 139 1
Treasurer — Jacques Barthel *Sous-directeur* ☎ 426 185
Administrateur Déléguée — Otto L Quadbeck
Directeur — Kai Benniss

Skandinaviska Enskilda Banken Group

Alternative trading name: SEB Luxembourg SA
16 Boulevard Royal, L-2449, Luxembourg
PO Box 487, L-2014, Luxembourg
Tel: 461 717 1 Fax: 461 711 0 Telex: 3753 BSL LU Swift: ESSE LU LL

Senior Executive Officers
Managing Director — Tore Samuelsson
Deputy Managing Director — Andreas Econoides

Asset Management
Head — Tomas Ljungkvist

Other Departments
Private Banking — Johan Kuylenstierna *Head*

LUXEMBOURG (+352)

Administration
Head of Marketing — Mats Olsson

Société Européenne de Banque SA
Head Office

19/21 Boulevard du Prince Henri, L-1724, Luxembourg
PO Box 21, L-2010, Luxembourg
Tel: 461 4111 Fax: 462 140 Telex: 1274 SEB LU Swift: SEBK LU LL

Senior Executive Officers
President — Claude Deschenaux
Managing Director — Arnaldo Lanteri

General-Lending (DCM, SL)
Head of Corporate Banking — Patrick Ehrhardt *Assistant Manager, Financial Markets*

General - Treasury
Head of Treasury — Gerd Fricke *Treasury Sales*

Relationship Manager
Private Clientele — Ermanno Barbini *Conseiller*

Debt Capital Markets / Fixed Income
Country Head — Andrew Simms *Sub-Manager*

Domestic Government Bonds
Head of Sales — Nico Hansen *Sub-Manager*

Eurobonds
Head of Sales — Nico Hansen *Sub-Manager*

Syndicated Lending
Country Head — Andrew Simms *Sub-Manager*

Money Markets
Country Head — Rita Theisen *Principal Proxy Holder*

Money Markets - General
Franz Ulrich *Proxy Holder*

Foreign Exchange
FX Traders / Sales People
Patrick Picco
Antonio Beneduci

Settlement / Clearing
Operations — Richard Marck *Assistant Manager*
Georges Chamagne *Proxy Holder*

Asset Management
Investment Funds — Germain Birgen *Principal Proxy Holder*
Portfolio Management — Sabine Schiettinger *Proxy Holder*

Administration
Head of Administration — Richard Marck *Assistant Manager*

Technology & Systems
Data Processing — François Diderich *General Manager*
Antoine De Haeck *Project Manager*

Legal / In-House Counsel
General Secretariat & Legal — Dirk Raeymaekers *Sub-Manager*

Other (Administration)
Personal — Bruno D'Handrea

Société Générale Bank & Trust
Subsidiary Company

11-13 Avenue Emile Reuter, L-1021, Luxembourg
PO Box 1271, L-1021, Luxembourg
Tel: 479 311 1 Fax: 228 859 Telex: 3516 SGBT LU Swift: SGAB LU LL

Senior Executive Officers
Chairman — Henri Lassalle
Managing Director — Bernard Caussignac
Company Secretary — Guy Launay

Others (Senior Executives)
Jacques E Bouhet *Director*
Bernard David
Xavier de Bonneuil
Pierre Mathe *Director*

LUXEMBOURG (+352)   www.euromoneydirectory.com

Société Générale Bank & Trust (cont)

Others (Senior Executives) (cont)
Private Banking & Asset Engineering   Christian Zerry *Manager*
CM, Corporate Banking & Logistics   Vincent Decalf *Manager*
Swiss Branches   Antoine Larue de Charlus *Manager*

General-Lending (DCM, SL)
Head of Corporate Banking   Roland Hamen *Corporate & Commercial Banking*

General - Treasury
Head of Treasury   Philippe Baboulin *Treasury*

Debt Capital Markets / Fixed Income
Department: Capital Markets
Global Head   Philippe Baboulin *Senior Officer / Manager*

Bonds - General
New Issue Syndication   Gerard Muller *Dealer*
    Jean-Michel Righi *Manager*

Asset-Backed Securities / Securitization
Global Head   Michel Becker *Manager*

Syndicated Lending

Other (Trade Finance)
Letters of Credit, Documentary Credits   Dora Ferronato

Money Markets

Eurocommercial Paper
Head of Origination   Bertrand Kauffmann

Money Markets - General
Trader   Najib El Bassri
    Olivier Bremont
    Laurent Mabila
    Volker von Debschitz
    Gzégoire Glotin
    Pierre-Jean Palayis

Foreign Exchange
Global Head   Ralf Kray *Manager*

FX Traders / Sales People
    John Korter *Dealer*
    Didier Charlier *Dealer*

Risk Management

Other Currency Swap / FX Options Personnel
Risk & Credit Risk Management   Andre Rehlinger

Settlement / Clearing
Settlement (General)   Jean-Patrick Tran-Phat *Back-Office Settlements*
Operations   Michel Becker *Manager*

Global Custody

Other (Global Custody)
Custodian Banking   Michel Becker *Manager*

Asset Management
Investment Funds   Michel Becker

Other (Asset Management)
Asset Management   Herve Plista

Other Departments
Private Banking   Georges Popinat
Correspondent Banking   Roland Hamen *Corporate & Commercial Banking*

Administration
Head of Administration   Philippe Thibaut

Other (Administration)
Human Resources   Rene Dalvit

www.euromoneydirectory.com LUXEMBOURG (+352)

Société Nationale de Crédit et d'Investissement Head Office

Alternative trading name: SNCI
7 rue du St Esprit, L-1475, Luxembourg
PO Box 1207, L-1012, Luxembourg
Tel: 461 971 1 Fax: 461 979 Telex: 60664 SNCI LU

Senior Executive Officers
President   Georges Schmit ☎ **461 971 21**
Chief Executive Officer   Georges Bollig General Manager ☎ **461 971 23**
Financial Director   Lucien Bechtold Attaché Financier ☎ **461 971 28**

State Street Bank Luxembourg SA Subsidiary Company

PO Box 275, L-2012, Luxembourg
Tel: 464 010 1 Fax: 463 631

Senior Executive Officers
Senior Vice President   Timothy J Caverly

General-Lending (DCM, SL)
Head of Corporate Banking   Shane Ah-Piang Assistant Vice President

General - Treasury
Head of Treasury   Claude F Lang VP & General Manager, Global Treasury

Debt Capital Markets / Fixed Income
Marketing   Michael M Vareika Vice President

Settlement / Clearing
Operations   Hartmut Gunther Vice President
                                    Guy Becker Assistant Vice President
                                    Guy Albrecht Assistant Secretary
                                    Luis Perez Assistant Secretary

Global Custody
Fund Administration   Julian J H Presber VP, DMD & Head, Fund Admin & Transfer Agency
                                    Raphael Remond VP & Deputy Head, Fund Admin
                                    Sonia Biraschi Assistant Vice President
                                    Conlon Chen Assistant Vice President
                                    Megan Faust Assistant Vice President
                                    Marcel Guibout Assistant Secretary
                                    Keith Durrant Assistant Secretary
                                    Ralf Reinig Assistant Vice President
                                    Eileen O Connell Assistant Vice President

Other (Global Custody)
Transfer Agency   Michel Donckel Assistant Vice President

Administration
IT / IA   Lawrence P Heim Assistant Vice President

Accounts / Audit
Audit   Jean-Pierre Aventin Assistant Vice President

Other (Administration)
Human Resources   Hartmut Gunther Vice President
                                    Dirk Leistico Assistant Secretary

Sumitomo Trust & Banking (Luxembourg) SA

18 Boulevard Royal, L-2449, Luxembourg
PO Box 882, L-2018, Luxembourg
Tel: 477 9851 Fax: 47 4608 Telex: 60232/3 SMITB LU Swift: STBC LU LL Email: stblux@pt.lu

Senior Executive Officers
MD & General Manager   Junji Watanabe

General - Treasury
Head of Treasury   Kiyotaka Sato Deputy General Manager
                                    Dominique Lefevre Dealer

Debt Capital Markets / Fixed Income
Department: Capital Markets

Libor-Based / Floating-Rate Products
Asset Swaps (Sales)   Kiyotaka Sato Deputy General Manager

Syndicated Lending
Country Head   Yujiro Kishimoto Deputy General Manager

Euromoney Directory 1999 **1023**

LUXEMBOURG (+352) www.euromoneydirectory.com

Sumitomo Trust & Banking (Luxembourg) SA (cont)
Risk Management
Department: Capital Markets
Other Currency Swap / FX Options Personnel
Interest Swaps   Kiyotaka Sato *Deputy General Manager*
                                        Dominique Lefevre *Dealer*

Settlement / Clearing
Head of Settlement / Clearing   Hirotsuga Suguri
Regional Head   Hirotsugu Suguri *Manager*
Back-Office   Hirotsuga Suguri

Global Custody
Head of Global Custody   Hirotsuga Suguri

Other Departments
Correspondent Banking   Hirotsugu Suguri *Manager*

Administration
Technology & Systems
                                        Thierry Koch *Manager*

Svenska Handelsbanken SA   Subsidiary Company
146 Boulevard de la Pétrusse, L-2016, Luxembourg
PO Box 678, Luxembourg
Tel: 499 811 1 Fax: 490 004 Telex: 2405 Swift: HAND LU LL Reuters: SHBU
Website: www.handelsbanken.se

Senior Executive Officers
Executive Vice President   Bjorn C Andersson ☎ +46 (8) 701 1000
Managing Director   Thord Mellström ☎ 498 1111

Others (Senior Executives)
Global Head of Private Banking   Leo Tolstoy *Senior Manager*
Investment Funds   Marie-Therese Schanus-Legrand *Senior Manager*
Accounting & Administration   Annick Nelissen *Senior Manager*
IT Department   Robert Martin *Senior Manager*

General-Lending (DCM, SL)
Head of Corporate Banking   Thomas Goldschmidt *Deputy Managing Director* ☎ 498 1111

Equity Capital Markets
International Equities
Head of Sales; Head of Trading   Jan Danesjö *Group Head*

Money Markets
Tel: 494 111 Fax: 402 881 Telex: 2404
Global Head   Christiane Junio *Department Head*

Wholesale Deposits
Head of Sales   Theresa Chiarello *Dealer*
                                        Enrico Betti *Dealer*

Foreign Exchange
Tel: 494 111 Fax: 402 881
Global Head   Christiane Junio *Department Head*

FX Traders / Sales People
                                        Anton di Lorenzo *Dealer*
                                        Anne Finmark *Dealer*

Settlement / Clearing
Regional Head   Serge Grandjean *Manager*

Asset Management
Investment Funds   Marie-Therese Schanus-Legrand *Senior Manager*

Other Departments
Private Banking   Leo Tolstoy *Senior Manager*

Administration
Head of Administration   Annick Nelissen *Senior Manager*

Technology & Systems
                                        Robert Martin *Senior Manager*

Legal / In-House Counsel
                                        Jan Selin *Legal Advisor*

Accounts / Audit
                                        Annick Nelissen *Senior Manager*

Swedbank (Luxembourg) SA
Subsidiary Company

8/10 Avenue de la Gare, L-1610, Luxembourg
PO Box 1305, L-1013, Luxembourg
Tel: 404 940 1 **Fax**: 404 908 **Telex**: 1771 SWEDG **Swift**: BNEX LU LL

Senior Executive Officers
Chairman — Lars-Olof Ödlund
President — Göran Rylander

Others (Senior Executives)
Board — Per Axelson *Senior Vice President*
Lars Idermark *Deputy President*
Management — Göran Rylander
Michael Ekelund *Private Banking*
Ole Stenersen *Credit Control*
Rudolf Bolen *Operations*

Settlement / Clearing
Operations — Rudolf Bolen *Operations*

Other Departments
Private Banking — Michael Ekelund *Private Banking*

Tradition Eurobond SA

68-70 Boulevard de la Pétrusse, L-2320, Luxembourg
Tel: 492 001 **Fax**: 492 004

Senior Executive Officers
Managing Director — Christian Weitzmann

Tradition SA Succursale de Luxembourg
Full Branch Office

Centre Neuberg, 30 Grand-Rue, L-1660, Luxembourg
PO Box 69, L-2010, Luxembourg
Tel: 465 601; 465 6029 **Fax**: 461 912 **Telex**: 60661/2 TRAD LU **Reuters**: TRLU

Senior Executive Officers
Others (Senior Executives)
Bernd R Bachhausen *Manager*
Victor Troch *Manager*

Trinkaus & Burkhardt (International) SA
Subsidiary Company

1/7 rue Nina et Julien Lefèvre, PO Box 579, L-2015, Luxembourg
Tel: 471 847 1 **Fax**: 471 847 641; 471 847 642 **Telex**: 1747 TUBILU LU **Telex**: 1748 TUBILU LU

Senior Executive Officers
Chairman — Sieghardt Rometsch
Vice Chairman — Harold Hörauf
Managing Director — Hans-Joachim Rosteck ☏ **471 847 751**
Managing Director — Jürgen Berg
Director — Jörg Meier
International Division — Hans-Joachim Rosteck *Managing Director* ☏ **471 847 751**

General-Lending (DCM, SL)
Head of Corporate Banking — Georges Weyer *Credit Manager* ☏ **471 847 401**

General - Treasury
Head of Treasury — Alwin Schneider *Treasury Manager* ☏ **471 847 200**

Debt Capital Markets / Fixed Income
Department: Capital Markets
Tel: 471 847 350
Country Head — Gerhard Philipps *Manager*

Domestic Government Bonds
Head of Sales; Head of Trading — Gerhard Philipps *Manager*

Eurobonds
Head of Sales; Head of Trading — Gerhard Philipps *Manager*

Other (Libor-Based / Floating Rate Products)
Fixed Rate / Straights — Mathilde Rosar-Ladendorff *Trading*

LUXEMBOURG (+352)   www.euromoneydirectory.com

Trinkaus & Burkhardt (International) SA (cont)
Equity Capital Markets
Department: Capital Markets
Tel: 471 847 350
Domestic Equities
Head of Trading   Heike Recken-De Roy *Trading*
International Equities
Head of Trading   Heike Recken-De Roy *Trading*
Foreign Exchange
Tel: 471 847 200
Country Head
                                    Alwin Schneider *Manager* ☎ 471 847 200
FX Traders / Sales People
                                    Marion Metzen *Dealer*
                                    Monique Mahowald *Dealer*
                                    Mechthild Servatius *Dealer*
                                    Myriam Kerschen *Dealer*
Settlement / Clearing
Foreign Exchange Settlement   Marinette Jungers *Manager* ☎ 471 847 501
Operations   Jürgen Berg *Managing Director*
Asset Management
Investment Funds   Heike Recken-De Roy *Trading*
Other Departments
Commodities / Bullion   Alwin Schneider *Manager* ☎ 471 847 200
Correspondent Banking   Georges Weyer *Credit Manager* ☎ 471 847 401
Administration
Head of Administration   Jürgen Berg *Managing Director*
Technology & Systems
                                    Jürgen Berg *Managing Director*
Other (Administration)
Marketing   Hans-Joachim Rosteck *Managing Director* ☎ 471 847 751

Turkiye Garanti Bankasi AS   Full Branch Office

Alternative trading name: Garanti Bank
22/24 Boulevard Royal, L-2449, Luxembourg
PO Box 213, L-2072 Luxembourg, Luxembourg
Tel: 223 321 221 Fax: 223 321 288 Telex: GABW 60370 Swift: TGBA LU LL
Senior Executive Officers
Branch Manager   Murat Agabeyoglu ☎ 223 321 210
Local Manager   Jean Lemaire
Debt Capital Markets / Fixed Income
Non-Domestic Government Bonds
                                    Ahmet Koteane *Treasurer* ☎ 213 321 231
Syndicated Lending
Global Head   Tuncer Mutwcan *Treasurer* ☎ 223 321 274
Foreign Exchange
Head of Trading   Ahmet Koteane *Treasurer* ☎ 213 321 231
Settlement / Clearing
Country Head   Ozlem Cagdas *Assistant Treasurer* ☎ 223 321 282

UBS (Luxembourg) SA
36-38 Grand-rue, L-2010, Luxembourg
P.O Box 2, L-2010, Luxembourg
Tel: 451 212 001 Fax: 451 212 800
Senior Executive Officers
Others (Senior Executives)
Head of Private Banking UBSL & Head   Roy Darphin *Managing Director*
Subsidiary
Head of Country Desk Germany   Thomas Steiger *Deputy Managing Director, Executive Director*
Head of Credit Products   Markus Vollenweider *Director*
Information Technology   Hermann Kranz *Head*

1026 Euromoney Directory 1999

www.euromoneydirectory.com   LUXEMBOURG (+352)

Unibank SA
Subsidiary Company

672 rue de Neudorf, L-2220, Luxembourg
PO Box 562, L-2015, Luxembourg
Tel: 43887 1 Fax: 439 352 Telex: 1590 UBLUX LU Swift: UNIB LU LL Reuters: UNIU

Senior Executive Officers
Chairman   Peter Schütze
Managing Director   Jhon Mortensen
Deputy Managing Director   Peter Green Lauridsen
Deputy General Manager   Lars Højberg

General - Treasury
Head of Treasury   Jens Høgh *Executive Director* ☏ **ext204**

Debt Capital Markets / Fixed Income
Head of Debt Capital Markets   Jens Høgh *Executive Director* ☏ **ext204**

Money Markets
Other (Wholesale Deposits)
Eurocurrency Deposits   Jens Høgh *Executive Director* ☏ **ext204**

Foreign Exchange
Country Head   Jens Høgh *Executive Director* ☏ **ext204**
FX Traders / Sales People
                                        Lars Jensen *Dealer* ☏ **ext210**
                                        Kristian Berg *Dealer* ☏ **ext206**
                                        Kaj Riisberg *Dealer* ☏ **ext205**

Risk Management
IR Swaps Trading   Kaj Riisberg *Dealer* ☏ **ext205**
                                        Jens Høgh *Executive Director* ☏ **ext204**

Foreign Exchange Derivatives / Risk Management
Cross-Currency Swaps, Trading   Jens Høgh *Executive Director* ☏ **ext204**

Exchange-Traded Derivatives
FX Futures   Kaj Riisberg *Dealer* ☏ **ext205**
                                        Jens Høgh *Executive Director* ☏ **ext204**
FX Options   Kaj Riisberg *Dealer* ☏ **ext205**
                                        Jens Høgh *Executive Director* ☏ **ext204**

Settlement / Clearing
Settlement (General); Operations   Joël Lequeux *Senior Manager* ☏ **ext339**

Asset Management
Head   Peter Green Lauridsen *Deputy Managing Director*

Other Departments
Economic Research   Kim Asger Olsen *Executive Director, Economics*

Administration
Head of Administration   Lars Højberg *Deputy General Manager*
Head of Marketing   Susanne Anderson

Technology & Systems
                                        Morten Nielsen *Executive Director*

Other (Administration)
Finance   Jan Hansen *Executive Director*

Union Bank of Norway International SA
Subsidiary Company

22 rue Jean-Pierre Brasseur, L-1258, Luxembourg
PO Box 867, L-2018, Luxembourg
Tel: 454 945 1 Fax: 454 945 200 Telex: 60164 UBNG LU

Senior Executive Officers
General-Lending (DCM, SL)
Head of Corporate Banking   Alf Muhlig *AGM, Credit*

Foreign Exchange
Global Head   François Scheffen *General Manager*

Settlement / Clearing
Operations   Patrick Laurent *Assistant General Manager*

Other Departments
Private Banking   Per Holm *General Manager*

Euromoney Directory 1999   **1027**

LUXEMBOURG (+352)   www.euromoneydirectory.com

United European Bank (Luxembourg) SA
Full Branch Office

Formerly known as: Groupe Banque Nationale de Paris
3b, Boulevard du Prince Henri, L-1724, Luxembourg
PO Box 830, L-2018, Luxembourg
Tel: 475 476 **Fax:** 228 428 **Telex:** 3159 **Swift:** UEBG LU LL

Senior Executive Officers
Chairman   Bernard Fleury
Managing Director   Jean Pierre Bourdet
Secretary General   Wolfang Spittra

Asset Management
Portfolio Management   Guy Levieux *Senior Vice President*
                                  Peter Vanneste *Vice President*

VP Bank (Luxembourg) SA
Subsidiary Company

23 Avenue de la Liberté, L-2019, Luxembourg
PO Box 923, L-2019, Luxembourg
Tel: 404 777 1 **Fax:** 481 117 **Telex:** 0402 60861 **Swift:** VPBV LU LL **Reuters:** VPLU

Senior Executive Officers
Chairman   Rolf Kormann
Chief Executive Officer   Anton Engler
Treasurer   Alfred Pletschet ☎ 404 788

Debt Capital Markets / Fixed Income
Global Head   Frank Tüffers ☎ 404 788

Equity Capital Markets
Global Head   Frank Tüffers ☎ 404 788

Syndicated Lending
Global Head   Ute Permesang ☎ 404 777 202

Money Markets
Global Head   Romain Deister ☎ 404 788

Foreign Exchange
Global Head   Alfred Pletschet ☎ 404 788

Settlement / Clearing
Regional Head   Vera Steilen ☎ 404 777 262

Global Custody
Regional Head   Vera Steilen ☎ 404 777 262

Other Departments
Private Banking   Hans-Werner Peter ☎ 404 777 270
Correspondent Banking   Alfred Pletschet ☎ 404 788

Administration
Legal / In-House Counsel
                                  Yves de Vos

Public Relations
                                  Anton Engler

MM Warburg & Co Luxembourg SA
Head Office

Alternative trading name: MM Warburg Bank Luxembourg
2 Place Dargent, L-1413, Luxembourg
PO Box 16, L-2010, Luxembourg
Tel: 424 545 1 **Fax:** 424 569 **Telex:** 2887 MMWBLU **Swift:** WBWC LU LL **Email:** info@mmwarburg.lu
Reuters: WMAA; WMAB; WMAC; WMAD
Website: www.mmwarburg.lu

Senior Executive Officers
Chairman   Christian Olearius
Director   Jürgen Förster

Debt Capital Markets / Fixed Income
Tel: 424 626

Eurobonds
Head of Trading   Rüdiger Tepke *Fondé de Pouvoirs*

www.euromoneydirectory.com MACAU (+853)

Settlement / Clearing
Head of Settlement / Clearing — Eckard Lang *Vice President*
Equity Settlement — Joachim Block
Administration
Accounts / Audit — Peter Johannsen *Vice President*

WestLB International SA
Subsidiary Company

32/34 Boulevard Grande-Duchesse Charlotte, L-1330, Luxembourg
Boîte Postale 420, L-2014, Luxembourg
Tel: 447 411 **Fax:** 4474 1627 **Telex:** 2209 **Cable:** WESTLB

Senior Executive Officers
Chairman — Gerhard Roggemann
Managing Director — Georg Bissen
Managing Director — Franz Ruf

General - Treasury
Head of Treasury — Günter Pfarrer *Deputy Manager*

Debt Capital Markets / Fixed Income
Global Head — Günter Pfarrer *Deputy Manager*

Equity Capital Markets
Global Head — Günter Pfarrer *Deputy Manager*

Syndicated Lending
Global Head — Johannes Scheel *Deputy Manager*

Risk Management
Global Head — Ralf Kwiedor *Head*

Corporate Finance / M&A Advisory
Global Head — Johannes Scheel *Deputy Manager*

Settlement / Clearing
Regional Head — Klaus-Dieter Brand *Deputy Manager*

WGZ-Bank Luxemberg SA
Head Office

Alternative trading name: Westdeutsche Genossenschafts-Zentralbank eG
5 rue Jean Monnet, L-2180, Luxembourg
Tel: 428 328 1 **Fax:** 428 328 333 **Telex:** 60395 WGZLU **Swift:** WGZL LU LX
Website: www.wgz-bank.lu

MACAU
(+853)

AMCM - Autoridade Monetária e Cambial de Macau
🏛 Central Bank

45 Rua Pedro Nolasco da Silva, Macau
Tel: 325 416 **Fax:** 325 433; 353 253 **Telex:** 88480 **Swift:** MFAM MO MX **Reuters:** AMCM **Telerate:** 9540

Senior Executive Officers
Chairman & Chief Executive — Morgado
Financial Director — Antonio Pontes *Executive Director*
Chief Operating Officer — Antonio Ramos *Executive Director*
Treasurer — Stanley Tang ✉ tktang@macau.ctm.net

Debt Capital Markets / Fixed Income
Head of Debt Capital Markets — Rogerio Celerio *Manager*

Money Markets
Global Head — Cesar I *Manager*

Foreign Exchange
Global Head — Cesar I *Manager*

Settlement / Clearing
Head of Settlement / Clearing — Manuel Fong *Officer*

Euromoney Directory 1999 **1029**

MACAU (+853) www.euromoneydirectory.com

AMCM - Autoridade Monetária e Cambial de Macau (cont)
Administration
Legal / In-House Counsel
                                    Antonio Jonet Manager
Public Relations
                                    Berta Lei Officer

Banco Totta & Açores SA Full Branch Office
21st Floor, Centro Comercial da Praia Grande, 429 Avenida Praia Grande, Macau
PO Box 912, Macau
Tel: 573 251; 573 531 Fax: 563 852 Telex: 88517 TOTAM, 88727 TOTTA Swift: TOTA MO MX
Email: totta@macau.ctm.net Reuters: BTAM

Senior Executive Officers
General Manager   Carlos Castro
Deputy General Manager   Rodrigo Nascimento
General-Lending (DCM, SL)
Head of Corporate Banking   Stephen Ku Manager, Credit
                                    Mafalda Silva Branch Manager, Commercial Banking
General - Treasury
Head of Treasury   Tony Tan Chief Dealer
Debt Capital Markets / Fixed Income
Department: Capital Markets & Bonds
Global Head   Stephen Ku Manager, Credit
Syndicated Lending
Other (Trade Finance)
Export & Import Finance; Documentary Credits Joyce Cheong Assistant Operations Manager
Foreign Exchange
Head of Foreign Exchange   Tony Tan Chief Dealer
Settlement / Clearing
Back-Office   Albert Chao Back-Office, Manager
Other Departments
Correspondent Banking   Joyce Cheong Assistant Operations Manager
Administration
Technology & Systems
                                    Steve Chau Officer, EDP
Accounts / Audit
                                    Joaquim Ribas da Silva Manager, Administration & Accounts

Deutsche Bank AG Full Branch Office
7th Floor, Nam Wah Commercial Edificio, 1L/1LB, 99 Avenida Almeida Ribeiro, Macau
Tel: 356 200 Fax: 304 939 Telex: 88550 DBA OM

International Bank of Taipei Macau Branch Full Branch Office
Formerly known as: International Bank of Taipei
52-58 Avenida do Infante D. Henrique, Macau
Tel: 715 175 Fax: 715 035; 715 186 Telex: 88249 TPBBM Swift: TPBB MO MX
Senior Executive Officers
General Manager   Cliff Chang ☎ 715 138

Luso International Banking Limited Subsidiary Company
Avenida Dr Mario Soares 47, Macau
Tel: 378 977 Fax: 578 517 Telex: 88220 LIBLM OM Swift: LUSO MO MX Email: lusobank@lusobank.com.mo
Reuters: LIBM
Website: www.lusobank.com.mo

Senior Executive Officers
Chairman   Eugene Ho
Treasurer   Philip Ieong Head of Treasury Division ☎ 515 712

1030 Euromoney Directory 1999

www.euromoneydirectory.com   MACEDONIA (+389)

Senior Executive Officers (cont)
General Manager   Kai Ming Ip
Settlement / Clearing
Settlement (General)   Richard Ho *Department Head* ☏ **779 4144**
Administration
Head of Marketing   Thomson Lo *Assistant Manager* ☏ **779 4109**
Public Relations
                                                Elly Long *Public Relations Officer* ☏ **799 4207**
Accounts / Audit
                                                Amy Tsoi *Head of Accounts* ☏ **562 349**

Standard Chartered Bank   Full Branch Office
8th Floor, Office Tower, Macau Landmark, Anevinda Amizade, Z A P E, Macau
Tel: 786 111 **Fax:** 786 222 **Telex:** 88518 SCBMAC OM **Swift:** SCBL HK HH MAC **Cable:** STANCHART

Tai Fung Bank Limited   Head Office
Tai Fung Bank Headquarter Building, 418 Alameda Dr. Carlos, d'Assumpcao, Macau
Tel: 322 323 **Fax:** 570 737 **Telex:** 88212 TFUNG OM **Swift:** TFBL MO MX **Reuters:** TAIK **Telerate:** 3234
Website: www.taifungbank.com

Senior Executive Officers
Chairman   Ka York Fung
Vice Chairman   Hau Hung Ho
Executive Director & General Manager   Hau Wah Ho
Executive Director & DGM   Ng Kan Sio
Director & Deputy General Manager   Chi Cheng Cheong
Deputy General Manager   Sao Lap Ma
Deputy General Manager   Jiequn Wang

MACEDONIA
(+389)

The National Bank of the Republic of Macedonia   Central Bank
PO Box 401, Skopje, 91000
Tel: (91) 112 177; (91) 233 358 **Fax:** (91) 111 161
Governor's Office Tel: (91) 239 015; (91) 229 105; **Fax:** (91) 234 916

Senior Executive Officers
Governor   Ljube Trpeski
Deputy Governor   Gligor Bishev

Others (Senior Executives)
Head, Governor's Office   Antoneta Manova
Head, Banking Supervision   Gazmend Kadriu
Head, Central Banking Operations   Zorica Bukleska
Head, Foreign Reserves   Vlado Ristic
Head, Foreign Exchange Documentation   Carka Nakova

General - Treasury
Head of Treasury   Dobri Mickovski

Foreign Exchange
Head of Foreign Exchange   Dušanka Hristova *Vice Governor*

Other Departments
Economic Research   Zoran Stavreski

Administration
Head of Administration   Šaban Prevala *Vice Governor*
                                                Blagoja Tomovski

Technology & Systems
Data Processing   Lihnida Sajkova Dzukleska

Legal / In-House Counsel
                                                Snezana Bundalevska

Corporate Communications
Publications   Snezana Bundalevska

Euromoney Directory 1999 **1031**

MACEDONIA (+389) www.euromoneydirectory.com

The National Bank of the Republic of Macedonia (cont)
Accounts / Audit
Internal Audit
Head, Financial Accounting
Other (Administration)
Personnel

Ilija Graorkovski *Auditor*
Cvetanka Gecheva

Snezana Bundalevska

European Bank for Reconstruction & Development
Full Branch Office

2nd Floor, Dame Gruev 14, Skopje, 91000
Tel: (91) 134 394; (91) 211 050 **Fax:** (91) 126 047

Senior Executive Officers
Mission Advisor   Bilyana Miloshevska

Komercijalna Bank AD
Head Office

Formerly known as: Stopanska Banka & Osnovna Banka
Kej Dimitar Vlahov 4, Skopje, 91000
PO Box 563, Skopje
Tel: (91) 107 107 **Fax:** (91) 113 494; (91) 111 780 **Telex:** 51162 KB SK MB **Swift:** KOBS MK 2X
Email: international@kb.com.mk **Reuters:** KOSK
General Telex: 51794 KB SK MB
Website: www.kb.com.mk

Senior Executive Officers
General Manager   Hari Kostov ☎ **125 273** 🖷 **125 274**
Deputy General Manager   Lazar Cvotkovski ☎ **126 099**

Others (Senior Executives)
Business Policy Division   Risto Stamenov *Manager* ☎ **211 132**

General-Investment
Head of Investment   Sasko Manakovski *Manager* ☎ **225 543**

General - Treasury
Head of Treasury   Jadranka Mrsic *Manager* ☎ **233 273**

Syndicated Lending
Other (Syndicated Lending)
Corporate Lending   Sterio Dimov *Manager* ☎ **211 566**
Manufacturing Sector   Vera Bibanovska *Manager* ☎ **211 599**
Agricultural & Private Sector   Afrodita Gavrilovska *Manager* ☎ **234 275**
Trade & Tourism Sector   Voskresija Anevska *Manager* ☎ **231 966**
Construction & Transport Sector   Danica Jonovska *Manager* ☎ **234 915**

Foreign Exchange
Head of Foreign Exchange   Jadranka Mrsic *Manager* ☎ **233 273**

Corporate Finance / M&A Advisory
Head of Corporate Finance   Jagoda Kuzmanovska *Manager, Finance Department* ☎ **233 051**

Settlement / Clearing
Operations   Risto Prentovski *Manager, International Operations* ☎ **137 031**
Other   Violeta Markovska *Manager, International Payments* ☎ **211 577**

Other Departments
Chief Credit Officer   Margarita Zdravkovska *Manager, Control & Credit Guarantee Department* ☎ **225 155**

Correspondent Banking   Mihajlo Nauncevski *Communications & Correspondent Banking* ☎ **113 228**
Cash Management   Jadranka Mrsic *Manager* ☎ **233 273**
Economic Research   Vora Stanoeva Atanasova *Manager, Planning & Analysis* ☎ **211 325**
Debt Recovery / Restructuring   Agis Sajnoski *Manager, Problem Loan & Workout Department* ☎ **235 040**

Administration
Technology & Systems
Organisation & Technical Operations   Jovan Gjokeski *Manager* ☎ **229 200**
EDP Department   Ljupco Todevski *Manager* ☎ **122 436**

Legal / In-House Counsel
Legal Operations   Aleksander Salevic *Manager* ☎ **211 360**

Public Relations
Management & Information   Tomislav Velkovski *Manager* ☎ **211 744**

Other (Administration)
General Affairs   Slavko Razmilic *Manager* ☏ **213 035**

Stopanska Banka AD

7-11 Oktomvri Street, Skopje, 91000
PO Box 164, Skopje, 91000
Tel: (91) 115 322 **Fax:** (91) 114 503 **Telex:** 51140 MBSBANK **Swift:** STOP MK 2X **Reuters:** SBRM
Cable: STOPBANKA **Telex:** 51 226 **Telex:** 51 472

Senior Executive Officers
General Manager   Ljubomir Popovski ☏ **231 744**
Deputy General Manager   Spase Lazarevsko ☏ **231 317**

General - Treasury
Head of Treasury   Ilinka Mitovska *Manager* ☏ **236 575**
Department: International Division
15, Dimitar Vlahov Street, PO Box 164, Skopje, 91000
Tel: +389 (91) 115 322 **Fax:** +389 (91) 113 263
International Division   Kostadin Dimkov *Manager* ☏ **244 555**

Syndicated Lending
Other (Syndicated Lending)
Foreign Loans Department   Simo Dobrevski *Manager* ☏ **236 364**

Other (Trade Finance)
Payment Orders, Letters of Credit & Collection   Gjorgji Licenovski *Manager* ☏ **236 106**
Foreign Guarantees Department   Dragica Atanasova *Manager* ☏ **119 202**

Foreign Exchange
Head of Foreign Exchange   Ilinka Mitovska *Manager* ☏ **236 575**

Settlement / Clearing
Operations   Blagoja Nestorovski *Investment Operations* ☏ **221 155**
    Kiro Zrmanovski *Manager* ☏ **237 566**

Other Departments
Correspondent Banking   Ilinka Mitovska *Manager* ☏ **236 575**

MADAGASCAR
(+261)

Banque Centrale de Madagascar   🏛 Central Bank

Rue de la Révolution Socialiste, Antananarivo, 101
PO Box 550, Antananarivo, 101
Tel: (20) 222 1751; (20) 222 1752 **Fax:** (20) 222 3465; (20) 222 7596 **Telex:** 22468 **Swift:** REPU MG MG **Telex:** 22329

Senior Executive Officers
Governor   Gaston Edouard Ravelojaona
General Manager   Ferdinand Velomita

Others (Senior Executives)
Head, Supervision   Solofosoa Andrianalijaona *Manager*
Head, Foreign Relations & External Debt   André Rajaonali-Ratsimisetra *Manager*
Head, Financial Operations   Lala Andriamampionona *Manager*
Head, Credit   Henri Bernard Razakariasa *Manager*

Other Departments
Economic Research   Clotilde Razana Ramiandrisoa Rabenja *Manager*

Administration
Head of Administration   Andriamanohisoa Rajaona *Manager*

Technology & Systems
Head, Data Processing   Benjamin Razafinanja *Manager*

Legal / In-House Counsel
Head, Legal Affairs Department   Daniel Rakotonirina *Manager*

Accounts / Audit
Head, Accountancy   Fetra Rakotomalala *Manager*

Other (Administration)
Human Resources   Louisette Rahajarivony *Manager*

MALAWI (+265)   www.euromoneydirectory.com

MALAWI
(+265)

Reserve Bank of Malawi   🏛 Central Bank

PO Box 30063, Capital City, Lilongwe 3
Tel: 780 600 Fax: 782 289; 782 752 Telex: 44788 Swift: RBMA MW MW Reuters: RBML Telex: 44843

Senior Executive Officers
Governor   Mathews Chikaonda ☎ 784 707

Others (Senior Executives)
Economic Services   Charles Chuka *General Manager* ☎ 780 401
   Tobias Chinkwangwa *Deputy General Manager* ☎ 782 157
Head, Bank Licensing; Head, Banking Supervision   Wilson Milonde *Director* ☎ 780 506
Head, Economics & Statistics   Paul Mamba *Director* ☎ 780 593
Head, Public Debt   Neil Nyirongo *Director, Financial Markets* ☎ 782 301
Head, Reserves Management   Nedson Somanje *Director, International* ☎ 783 042

Foreign Exchange
Head of Foreign Exchange   Nedson Somanje *Director, International* ☎ 783 042

Settlement / Clearing
Head of Settlement / Clearing Operations   John Biziwick *Director* ☎ 780 561
   Ellias Kambalame *General Manager* ☎ 780 767
   Peter Mitachi *Deputy General Manager* ☎ 780 929

Administration
Head of Administration   Rick Malamulo *Deputy General Manager* ☎ 784 116
   Lenia Banda *Director* ☎ 782 802

Technology & Systems
Information Technology   Douglas Phoya *Director* ☎ 780 600

Accounts / Audit
Head, Accountancy   James Banda *Director* ☎ 782 703
Internal Audit   Sauko Chiliango *Director* ☎ 782 856

Other (Administration)
Human Resources   Mozo Zeleza *Director* ☎ 781 529

MALAYSIA
(+60)

Bank Negara Malaysia   🏛 Central Bank

Jalan Dato' Onn, 50480 Kuala Lumpur
PO Box 10922, Peti Surat, 50929 Kuala Lumpur
Tel: (3) 298 8044 Fax: (3) 291 2990 Telex: MA30201 Swift: BNMA MY KL Cable: BANKMALAYSIA

Senior Executive Officers
Governor   Tan Fri Ali Abul
Deputy Governor   Zeti Akhtar Aziz
Assistant Governor   Abdul Murad Khalid
Assistant Governor   Mohamad Daud Dol Moin

Others (Senior Executives)
Board of Directors   Muhamad Ali Hashim
   Bujang Mohd Nor
   Kishu Tirathrai
   Mohd Noordin Md Sopiee

www.euromoneydirectory.com MALAYSIA (+60)

Affin Discount Berhad
Head Office

Formerly known as: Antara Discount Berhad
12th Floor, Menara Boustead, Jalan Raja Chulan, 50200 Kuala Lumpur
Tel: (3) 201 2366; (3) 201 3688 **Fax:** (3) 244 2325; (3) 202 2826 **Telex:** MA 33510 ANTARA
Email: antara@po.jaring.my

Senior Executive Officers
Chairman   Haji Mohd Yunus bin Mohd Tasi
Chief Executive Officer   Mohd Mokhtar bin Ghazali
General Manager   Wan Kamarul Zaman bin Wan Yaacob

Money Markets
Department: Treasury & Money Markets

Money Markets - General

Mariam bt Bahaman *Senior Manager*
Mohd Yusof bin Ishak *Manager*
Noormala bt Mohd Dahlan *Assistant Manager*
Adnan bin Osman *Senior Dealer*
Marziah bt Bahaman *Senior Dealer*
Ahmad Rubil bin Ahmad *Dealer*
Hafizan bin Sulaiman *Dealer*
Sarida bt Mohd Shariff @ Hassan *Dealer*

Corporate Finance / M&A Advisory
Department: Corporate Finance, Capital Markets Department

Other (Corporate Finance)

Samsul Bahri bin Alias *Senior Manager*
Rashidah bt Rahmat *Assistant Manager*
Khairuddin bin Md Zin *Officer*
Wan Badroel Hisham bin Wan Mohamed *Officer*
Tajul Aznam bin Mohd Taib *Officer*
Amylia bt Mustapha *Officer*
Chong Mee Leng *Officer*

Administration
Head of Administration   Chek Bi bt Abu Bakar *Officer*
                                        Albert Mah Kai Leong *Manager, Finance & Administration*
                                        Nor Hisham bin Shafii *Officer*

Technology & Systems

Shahbudin bin Osman *Senior Manager*
Rosalina bt Ramlan *Officer*
Mohamed Harun bin Noor Mohamed *Officer*

Other (Administration)
Personnel   Nor Hayati bt Ramlan *Senior Officer*

Amanah Finance Malaysia Berhad
Subsidiary Company

11th Floor, Bangunan Amanah Capital, 82 Jalan Raja Chulan, 50200 Kuala Lumpur
Tel: (3) 261 4155 **Fax:** (3) 261 7748

Senior Executive Officers
Chief Executive Officer   Haron Kassim *Acting Chief Executive Officer*
Group Managing Director   Seri Syed Anwar Jamilullail
Acting General Manager   Abdul Rauf Abdul Kadir

Others (Senior Executives)
Islamic Banking   Haji Norisam Selamat *Senior Manager*
Retail Hire Purchase   Clayton Teo *Senior Manager*
Hire Purchase Centre   Peter Chong *Senior Manager*

General - Treasury
Head of Treasury   Mohd Hakim Abd Hamid *Manager, Treasury*

Syndicated Lending
Head of Credit Committee   Fakhriah Hanim Mahfudz *Assistant GM, Credit Supervision*

Settlement / Clearing
Operations   Zainodin Johar *Assistant GM, Finance & Operations*

Other Departments
Debt Recovery / Restructuring   Abdullah Saat *Manager, Credit Recovery & Rehabilitation*
                                        Mohd Sharif Mohd Nasir *Manager, Credit Recovery & Rehabilitation*
                                        Ismail Mohamed *Manager*

Euromoney Directory 1999   **1035**

MALAYSIA (+60) www.euromoneydirectory.com

Amanah Finance Malaysia Berhad (cont)

Administration
Head of Administration — Lim Jid Leong *Manager Administration & Finance*

Technology & Systems
Information Technology — Yau Wee Liam *Manager*

Other (Administration)
Human Resources — Hiruddin Hashim *Senior Manager*

Amanah Merchant Bank Berhad — Head Office

19th Floor, Bangunan Amanah Capital, 82 Jalan Raja Chulan, 50200 Kuala Lumpur
PO Box 12492, 50200 Kuala Lumpur
Tel: (3) 261 0155 **Fax:** (3) 261 5770 **Telex:** MA30602 **Email:** amanah@amanahb.po.my **Cable:** AMANAH

Senior Executive Officers
Chairman — Abdul Khalid Ibrahim ☏ 255 3707
Chief Executive Officer — T Jeyaratnam
Deputy General Manager — Ee Kok Sin

Others (Senior Executives)
Head of Operations & Finance — Eugene Hon *Deputy General Manager*

General-Lending (DCM, SL)
Head of Corporate Banking — Mohamed Adnan Zain *Deputy General Manager* ☏ 263 3838

General-Investment
Head of Investment — Iskander Ismail

General - Treasury
Head of Treasury — Megat Hisham Megat Mahmud *Deputy General Manager*

Debt Capital Markets / Fixed Income
Department: Corporate Finance
Head of Debt Capital Markets — Abdul Rahim Mohamed Zin *General Manager*

Equity Capital Markets
Head of Equity Capital Markets — Abdul Rahim Mohamed Zin *General Manager*

Syndicated Lending
Department: Structured & Project Finance Department
Fax: 263 3368
Head of Syndicated Lending — Chua Bee Chin *Assistant General Manager*

Other (Trade Finance)
Structured & Project Finance — Chua Bee Chin *Assistant General Manager*

Money Markets
Department: Treasury
Fax: 263 4455
Head of Money Markets — Megat Hisham Megat Mahmud *Deputy General Manager*

Risk Management
Department: Risk Management Unit
Fax: 263 3838
Head of Risk Management — Poon Kar Kwee *Senior Manager*

Corporate Finance / M&A Advisory
Department: Corporate Finance Department
Fax: 263 2828
Head of Corporate Finance — Abdil Rahim Mohamed Zin *General Manager*

Settlement / Clearing
Operations — Eugene Hon *Deputy General Manager*

Asset Management
Head — Iskander Ismail ☏ 262 0080

Administration
Head of Administration — Eugene Hon *Deputy General Manager*

Legal / In-House Counsel
Legal — Geetha Sivapathasundram *Senior Manager*

Compliance
— Geetha Sivapathasundram *Senior Manager*

Other (Administration)
Business Development Unit — Shariffudin Khalid *Deputy General Manager*
Human Resources — Faridah Hashim *Senior Manager*

www.euromoneydirectory.com MALAYSIA (+60)

AMMB International Limited
Subsidiary Company

Level 12 (B), Block 4 Office Tower, Financial Park Labuan Complex, Jalan Merdeka, 87000 Labuan
Tel: (87) 413 133; (87) 439 399 Fax: (87) 425 211; (87) 439 395 Telex: MA85075 AMMB
Email: paulong@ammb.com.my Reuters: AMIL
Website: www.ammb.com.my

Senior Executive Officers
Chairman — Azman Hashim (3) 238 2633
Deputy Chairman — Haji Azlan Hashim (3) 238 2633
Director — Tek Kuang Cheah (3) 238 2816
Director — Azlan Zainol (3) 206 3939
Director — Tuck Cheong Kok (3) 238 3072
General Manager — Paul Ong (3) 201 9080
Resident Secretary — Chin Fah Tan 413 524

Others (Senior Executives)
Gopikrishnan Menon *Senior Manager, Credit* (3) 201 9070

General - Treasury
Head of Treasury; Head of Treasury — Timothy Chong *Senior Manager, Operations & Treasury* 439 398
Head of Treasury — Chye Peng Lim *Manager, Treasury* 439 338

Debt Capital Markets / Fixed Income
Department: Credit and Marketing
Tel: (3) 201 7899 Fax: (3) 201 7909
Head of Fixed Income — Chye Peng Lim *Manager, Treasury* 439 338

Libor-Based / Floating-Rate Products
Asset Swaps — Chye Peng Lim *Manager, Treasury* 439 338

Fixed-Income Repo
Head of Repo — Chye Peng Lim *Manager, Treasury* 439 338

Syndicated Lending
Tel: (3) 201 7899 Fax: (3) 201 7909 Telex: MA 021593
Head of Origination; Head of Syndication — Gopikrishnan Menon *Senior Manager, Credit* (3) 201 9070

Loan-Related Activities
Project Finance — Gopikrishnan Menon *Senior Manager, Credit* (3) 201 9070

Money Markets
Tel: 425 213 Fax: 425 211 Reuters: AMIL Telex: MA 85075 AMMB
Head of Money Markets — Stephanie Huang 425 213

Domestic Commercial Paper
Head of Trading — Chye Peng Lim *Manager, Treasury* 439 338

Eurocommercial Paper
Head of Trading — Chye Peng Lim *Manager, Treasury* 439 338

Wholesale Deposits
Marketing — Chye Peng Lim *Manager, Treasury* 439 338

Foreign Exchange
Tel: 425 213 Reuters: AMIL
Head of Foreign Exchange; Head of Trading — Chye Peng Lim *Manager, Treasury* 439 338

FX Traders / Sales People
Stephanie Huang 425 213
Fang Yih Lim *Assistant Dealer* 424 150

Risk Management
Tel: 425 213 Reuters: AMIL
Head of Risk Management — Chye Peng Lim *Manager, Treasury* 439 338

Settlement / Clearing
Tel: 413 133 Fax: 439 399 Telex: MA 87075 AMMB
Head of Settlement / Clearing; Equity Settlement; Fixed-Income Settlement Back-Office — Timothy Chong *Senior Manager, Operations & Treasury* 439 398
Susie Simon Gonsilou *Settlements Officer* 413 313 ext 18

Other Departments
Chief Credit Officer — Gopikrishnan Menon *Senior Manager, Credit* (3) 201 9070
Correspondent Banking — Timothy Chong *Senior Manager, Operations & Treasury* 439 398
Cash Management — Timothy Chong *Senior Manager, Operations & Treasury*

Administration
Head of Administration — Timothy Chong *Senior Manager, Operations & Treasury*
Business Development; Head of Marketing — Gopikrishnan Menon *Senior Manager, Credit* (3) 201 9070

Technology & Systems
Timothy Chong *Senior Manager, Operations & Treasury* 439 398

MALAYSIA (+60)   www.euromoneydirectory.com

AMMB International Limited (cont)

Legal / In-House Counsel
Phyllis Moe *Senior Manager, Legal* ☎ (3) 234 6287

Compliance
Timothy Chong *Senior Manager, Operations & Treasury*

Public Relations
Timothy Chong *Senior Manager, Operations & Treasury* ☎ 439 398

Accounts / Audit
Timothy Chong *Senior Manager, Operations & Treasury*

Arab-Malaysian Bank Berhad — Head Office

Level 18, Menara Dion, Jalan Sultan Ismail, 50250 Kuala Lumpur
PO Box 10424, 50732 Kuala Lumpur
Tel: (3) 206 3939 **Fax:** (3) 206 6855 **Telex:** MA30424 **Swift:** ARBK MY KL **Reuters:** AMBB **Cable:** AMBANK MAL

Senior Executive Officers
Chairman — Azman Hashim
Deputy Chairman — Azlan Hashim
Managing Director — Azlan Zainol
Senior General Manager — Sim How Chuah
General Manager — Ahmad Zaini Othman

General-Lending (DCM, SL)
Head of Corporate Banking
Michael Lim Tung Kean *Senior Manager, Corporate Banking*
Man Fuk Lim *Senior Manager, Corporate Banking*
Goh Hean Peen *Senior Manager, Corporate Banking*
Abdul Rahman Mohd Sharif *Senior Manager, Corporate Banking*
Katsuo Arakawa *Senior Manager, Corporate Banking*

General - Treasury
Head of Treasury
Mohd Iqbal b.Mohd Iqbal *AGM, Treasury & Correspondent Banking*
Wong Moo Chai *Manager, Treasury & Correspondent Banking*
Chan Tuck Yew *Manager, Treasury & Correspondent Banking*

Relationship Manager
Small Medium Enterprises — Looi See Chiong *Assistant General Manager*
Islamic Banking & Institutional Banking — Zulkiflee Ahmad *Manager*

Syndicated Lending

Loan-Related Activities
Trade Finance
Lawrence Nonis *Assistant General Manager*
Jaafar Abu *Assistant General Manager*
Zaleha Mahmood *Senior Manager*

Settlement / Clearing
Operations
Yew Teik Jin *Manager*
Hizwani Hassan *Manager, Quality Assurance, Organization & Methods*

Other Departments
Correspondent Banking — Ali Yasak Ishak *Manager*

Administration

Legal / In-House Counsel
Noraini Abdullah *Manager*

Corporate Communications
Information Services — Albert Ang Chai Kiat *Senior Manager*

Accounts / Audit
Accounts & Administration — Peter Chan Kim Hui *Manager*

Other (Administration)
Information Services — Albert Ang Chai Kiat *Senior Manager*
Branches Supervision — Hasim Dau *Assistant General Manager*
Information Services — Michael Chin Chan Hwee *Manager*
Human Resources & Training — Salmah Abdul Karim *Senior Manager*

1038 Euromoney Directory 1999

MALAYSIA (+60)

Arab-Malaysian Merchant Bank Berhad

22nd Floor, Bangunan Arab-Malaysian, 55 Jalan Raja Chulan, 50200 Kuala Lumpur
PO Box 10233, 50708 Kuala Lumpur
Tel: (3) 238 2633; (3) 238 2644 Fax: (3) 238 2842 Telex: MA 31167 Swift: AMMB MY KL
Email: sasa@ammb.com.my Cable: ARABMAL KUALA LUMPUR
General Telex: 31169 ABMAL
Website: www.ambg.com.my

Senior Executive Officers
Deputy Chairman — Azlan Hashim
Financial Director — Arunasalam Muthusamy *Head of Finance*
Treasurer — Chean Choy Teng *Group Treasurer*
Managing Director — Tek Kuang Cheah
Senior General Manager — Tuck Cheong Kok
Senior General Manager — Kwee Bee Chok
Group Company Secretary — Ravindra Kumar Thambimuthu

Others (Senior Executives)
Banking — Alice Dora Boucher *General Manager*
Wan Seong Chan *General Manager*
Toh Ching Goh *Assistant General Manager*
Interest Free Banking — Mohd Effendi Abdullah *Assistant General Manager*
Commercial Services — Kim Heng Quek *General Manager*
Group Systems Services — Chee Thim Ooi *Head*

General-Lending (DCM, SL)
Head of Corporate Banking — Wan Marina Tunku Mohd Jamil *Assistant General Manager*

General - Treasury
Head of Treasury — Freddy Khoo *Senior Manager, Treasury Operations* 234 6322 201 1314
Gregory John Mackay *General Manager, Treasury Derivatives*
Philip Shane Jorgenson *Head, Treasury Structured Products*

Debt Capital Markets / Fixed Income
Department: Fixed Income Desk
Fax: 201 4821
Head of Fixed Income Sales — Farah Fazrina 238 2077
Head of Fixed Income Trading — Voon Pin Liew 238 2077

Equity Capital Markets
Equity Repo / Securities Lending
Marketing & Product Development — Eugene Khoo *Senior Manager, Equity Structured Products*

Syndicated Lending
Head of Credit Committee — Ponnampalam Seenivasagam *Head, Credit Administration*

Loan-Related Activities
Project Finance — Adrian Long *Assistant General Manager*
Ismael Fariz Ali *GM, Privatisation & Project Advisory*
Soo Nam Ooi *AGM, Privatisation & Project Advisory*
Nor Badll Munawir *AGM, Privatisation & Project Advisory*
Structured Trade Finance — Eddie Fong *Assistant General Manager*
Eng Hooi Gan *Assistant General Manager*

Money Markets
Tel: 238 2033 Fax: 201 4821 Reuters: AMMB
Head of Money Markets — Kevin Chan *Manager* 238 2033

Foreign Exchange
Tel: 238 2044 Fax: 201 4821
Head of Foreign Exchange — Frances Siew Luan Wong 238 2044
Mohd Fauzi Lebai Talib *AGM, FX Islamic Treasury*

Risk Management
Tel: 206 5673 Fax: 201 1314
Head of Risk Management — Henry Tan Koon Seng *Senior Manager* 206 4439

Corporate Finance / M&A Advisory
Head of Corporate Finance — Murugiah Singham *General Manager*
Pushparani Moothathamby *General Manager*

Global Custody
Head of Global Custody — Jaspal Singh *AGM, Custodian Services*

Asset Management
Portfolio Management — Christine Lee *General Manager*

Other Departments
Chief Credit Officer — Ponnampalam Seenivasagam *Head, Credit Administration*

MALAYSIA (+60) www.euromoneydirectory.com

Arab-Malaysian Merchant Bank Berhad (cont)
Administration
Public Relations
Group Public Affairs Syed Anuar Syed Ali *Head*
Group Information Services Sau Leong Lum *General Manager*
Corporate Communications
Corporate Services Amarjeet Kaur *Assistant General Manager*
Accounts / Audit
 Kok Cheeng Tan *Group Internal Auditor*
Other (Administration)
Group Human Resources Fauziah Yacob *General Manager*

The Asahi Bank Limited
12th Floor, Pernas International, Jalan Sultan Ismail, 50250 Kuala Lumpur
Tel: (3) 262 2902; (3) 262 2896 **Fax:** (3) 262 1875 **Telex:** 33608 ASHKL
Senior Executive Officers
Chief Representative Toshiyasu Nagura

AseamBankers Malaysia Berhad — Subsidiary Company
Formerly known as: Asian & Euro American Merchant Bankers Berhad
33rd Floor, Menara Maybank, 100 Jalan Tun Perak, 50050 Kuala Lumpur
PO Box 11057, 50936 Kuala Lumpur
Tel: (3) 238 4211; (3) 238 4233 **Fax:** (3) 238 4194; (3) 201 2037 **Telex:** MA20227 ASEAMB **Swift:** MBEA MY KI
Email: faudziah@aseam.com.my **Cable:** ASEAMBANK, KUALA LUMPUR

Senior Executive Officers
Chairman Mohammed Basir Ahmad ☏ **230 8833**
Managing Director Mohammed Hussein ☏ **238 4211**
General Manager, Corporate Finance Wong Yoke Nyen ☏ **238 4237**
General Manager, Banking Services Rozidin Masari ☏ **238 4213**
Company Secretary, Head of Corporate Services Faudziah Ismail ☏ **238 4203**

Others (Senior Executives)
Head of Corporate Services Faudziah Ismail *Company Secretary, Head of Corporate Services* ☏ **238 4203**
Head of Northern Regional Office Mohd Daniel Mat Noh ☏ **(4) 263 4014**

General-Lending (DCM, SL)
Head of Corporate Banking Tracy Ong *Head, Corporate Banking* ☏ **238 4214**

General - Treasury
Head of Treasury Abdul Hadi Ali *Head of Treasury* ☏ **238 4223**

Debt Capital Markets / Fixed Income
Head of Sales Abdul Hadi Ali *Head of Treasury* ☏ **238 4223**

Fixed-Income Repo
Head of Repo Abdul Hadi Ali *Head of Treasury* ☏ **238 4223**

Syndicated Lending
Tel: 238 4214 **Fax:** 202 1571
Head of Syndication Tracy Ong *Head, Corporate Banking* ☏ **238 4214**
Recovery Mohd Mazlan Baba *Head of Credit Restructuring* ☏ **238 4236**

Other (Syndicated Lending)
Head of Loan Administration Raudzah Mohd Majzub ☏ **236 4204**

Loan-Related Activities
Project Finance Rohaya Mohd Yusuf *Joint Head, Corporate Finance* ☏ **232 3431**

Money Markets
Tel: 238 4205 **Fax:** 202 2502 **Telex:** MA 20228 ASEAM
Head of Money Markets Abdul Hadi Ali *Head of Treasury* ☏ **238 4223**

Domestic Commercial Paper
Head of Sales Abdul Hadi Ali *Head of Treasury* ☏ **238 4223**

Wholesale Deposits
Marketing Abdul Hadi Ali *Head of Treasury* ☏ **238 4223**

Foreign Exchange
Tel: 238 4205 **Fax:** 202 2502 **Telex:** MA 20228 ASEAM
Head of Foreign Exchange; Country Head Abdul Hadi Ali *Head of Treasury* ☏ **238 4223**

1040 Euromoney Directory 1999

www.euromoneydirectory.com MALAYSIA (+60)

Risk Management
Tel: 236 2710 Fax: 238 6720
Head of Risk Management Rozidin Masari *General Manager, Banking Services* ☏ **238 4213**

Corporate Finance / M&A Advisory
Head of Corporate Finance Rohaya Mohd Yusuf *Joint Head, Corporate Finance* ☏ **232 3431**
Yong Lee Mei *Joint Head, Corporate Finance*

Settlement / Clearing
Tel: 238 4223 Fax: 201 2037
Head of Settlement / Clearing; Operations Afidah Mohd Ghazali *Head of Operations* ☏ **236 4204**

Administration
Head of Administration Afidah Mohd Ghazali *Head of Operations* ☏ **236 4204**

Technology & Systems
Information Systems Mohd Amir Abdullah *Head* ☏ **236 2738**

Public Relations
Faudziah Ismail *Company Secretary, Head of Corporate Services*
☏ **238 4203**

Corporate Communications
Head of Information System Mohd Amir Baba *Head, ISD* ☏ **238 4236**

Accounts / Audit
Afidah Mohd Ghazali *Head of Operations*
Internal Audit Mohd Ghazali Abbas *Head* ☏ **236 2709**

Australia & New Zealand Banking Group Limited
Representative Office

Alternative trading name: ANZ Grindlays Bank Ltd
4th Floor, Wisma Genting, Jalan Sultan Ismail, 50250 Kuala Lumpur
Tel: (3) 261 6088; (3) 261 6790 Fax: (3) 261 3210

Senior Executive Officers
Group Representative Murray J Bordignon

Ban Hin Lee Bank Berhad
Head Office

BHL BANK

51 Jalan Sultan, Ahmad Shah, 10500 Pulau Pinang
PO Box 232, 10720 Pulau Pinang
Tel: (4) 227 7882 Fax: (4) 262 3601 Telex: BHLB MA40087 Swift: BHLB MY KLA 001 Email: ccd@bhlbank.com.my
Cable: BANHINBANK Telex: BHLB MA 40225
Website: www.bhlbank.com.my

Senior Executive Officers
Chairman Goh Eng Toon
Deputy Chairman Yeap Leong Huat
Chief Executive Officer Neoh Choo Kean

General-Lending (DCM, SL)
Head of Corporate Banking Lynda Goh Phaik Lynn *Assistant General Manager* ☏ **(3) 206 6882**
🖷 **(3) 206 2632**

General - Treasury
Head of Treasury Ng Joon Chee *Treasury, International Division*

Syndicated Lending
Other (Syndicated Lending)
Commercial & Retail Lending Tan Leng Hock *Senior Manager*

Risk Management
Department: Treasury & Risk Control
Country Head Alex Por Peng Seong *Senior Manager*

Euromoney Directory 1999 **1041**

MALAYSIA (+60)   www.euromoneydirectory.com

Ban Hin Lee Bank Berhad (cont)
Settlement / Clearing
Department: Financial Control Division
Other (Settlement & Clearing)
Financial Control   Michael Lim Hock Aun *Senior Manager*
Administration
Head of Administration   Koay Beng Tin *Senior Manager*
Technology & Systems
Information Technology Division   En Abdul Rahim bin Abdul Razak *Assistant General Manager*
Legal / In-House Counsel
Corporate, Legal Division   Tuan Haji Idrus bin Ismail *Assistant General Manager*
Accounts / Audit
Internal Audit   Lee Tai Nee *Senior Manager*
Other (Administration)
Human Resource Division   Au Yeong Wan Yoke *Senior Manager*

Bangkok Bank Berhad   Subsidiary Company
105 Jalan Tun HS Lee, 50000 Kuala Lumpur
PO Box 10734, 50923 Kuala Lumpur
Tel: (3) 232 4555 **Fax:** (3) 238 8569 **Telex:** MA 30509 **Swift:** BKKB MY KL **Email:** bbb@tm.net.my
Cable: BANGKOK BANK

Senior Executive Officers
Chairman   Albert Cheok Saychuan ⊤ 201 7905 F 230 4028
Chief Executive Officer   Chalit Tayjasanant ⊤ 232 8677 F 201 4260
International Division   Yam Seck Hong *Senior Manager* ⊤ 232 1042
General-Lending (DCM, SL)
Head of Corporate Banking   Choo Peng Sum *Senior Manager* ⊤ 2019008
Syndicated Lending
Trade Finance   Zamran Ghazali *Manager*

Bank Brussels Lambert   Full Branch Office
Level 4H, Main Office Tower, Financial Park Labuan Complex, Jalan Merdeka, 87000 Labuan
Tel: (87) 453 133 **Fax:** (87) 452 122 **Email:** bblmsia@po,jaring.my

Senior Executive Officers
General Manager   Tan Swee Ho
Others (Senior Executives)
                                                 Jean-Francois Gillard *Senior Manager*

Bank Bumiputra Malaysia Berhad   Head Office
Menara Bumiputra, Jalan Melaka, 50100 Kuala Lumpur
PO Box 10407, 50913 Kuala Lumpur
Tel: (3) 298 1011; (3) 298 8011 **Fax:** (3) 293 4667; (3) 298 7264 **Telex:** PUTRA MA30445 **Swift:** BBMB MY KL
Email: webmaster@bbmb.com.my **Reuters:** BUMI **Telerate:** 3571
General Telex: PUTRA MA31619
Website: www.bank.bumiputra.net

Senior Executive Officers
Chairman   Abdul Khalid Sahan
Chief Executive Officer   Abdul Aziz Haji Othman *CEO & Chairman, Executive Committee*
Financial Director   Chan Jit Loon *General Manager*
Chief Operating Officer   Halim Muhamat E **dhalim@bbmb.com.my**
Chief GM & Member, Executive Committee   Halim Muhamat
Chief GM & Member, Executive Committee   Haji Arsam Damis
Secretary   Norhayati Hashimi
Company Secretary   Zauyah Wan Chik
General-Lending (DCM, SL)
Head of Corporate Banking   Fazlur Rahman Ebrahim *DGM, Corporate Banking*
General - Treasury
Head of Treasury   Abdul Aziz Mokhtar *Head of Treasury & Investment Banking*
Relationship Manager
                                                 Kamaralzaman Arshad *GM, Branch Operations*

1042 Euromoney Directory 1999

www.euromoneydirectory.com   MALAYSIA (+60)

Debt Capital Markets / Fixed Income
Global Head   Abdul Aziz Mokhtar *Head of Treasury & Investment Banking*
Domestic Government Bonds
Head of Sales   Abdul Aziz Mokhtar *Head of Treasury & Investment Banking*
Foreign Exchange
Department: Foreign Exchange & Treasury Management
Global Head   Tajuddin Atan *Deputy General Manager, Treasury*
Risk Management
Head of Risk Management   Ishak Mohd Yussof *Senior General Manager*
Corporate Finance / M&A Advisory
Other (Corporate Finance)
M & A, Venture Capital   Nik Hassan Nik Mohd Amin *Chief Executive Officer*
Settlement / Clearing
Operations   Kamaralzaman Arshad *GM, Branch Operations*
Administration
Technology & Systems
Information Technology   Azharuddin Ibrahim *Deputy General Manager*
Legal / In-House Counsel
                                       Noryahati Hashim *Head of Legal*
Public Relations
Public Affairs   Badruddin Haji Othman *Deputy General Manager*
Other (Administration)
Personnel   Abdul Malek Abdul Majid *Senior General Manager*
Librarian   Halilah Abu Bakar *Head*
Corporate Resources   Haji Arsam Damis *Chief GM & Member, Executive Committee*

Bank of Commerce (L) Berhad   Subsidiary Company

Floor 13A, Main Office Tower, Financial Park, Jalan Merdeka, 87000 Labuan
Tel: (87) 410 305; (87) 410 302 **Fax:** (87) 410 313; (87) 451 007 **Telex:** MA 85053 **Swift:** BOCM MY KA

Senior Executive Officers
Chairman   Radin Soenarno Al-Haj ☏ **(3) 293 1722**
General Manager   Hari Prasad
Others (Senior Executives)
                                       G K Rama Iyer *Director*
                                       Md Nor Md Yusof *Director*
                                       Robert Cheim Dau Meng *Director*
                                       Naveen Chander *Director*

Corporate Finance / M&A Advisory
Head of Corporate Finance   Rahiyah Yahya *Assistant Vice President*
Settlement / Clearing
Head of Settlement / Clearing   Nanda Kumar *Assistant Vice President*

Bank of Commerce (M) Berhad   Head Office

6 Jalan Tun Perak, 50050 Kuala Lumpur
PO Box 10753, 50724 Kuala Lumpur
Tel: (3) 293 1722 **Fax:** (3) 291 2030 **Telex:** MA31710 BOCM CU **Swift:** BOCM MY KL **Reuters:** BOCM; BCKL

Senior Executive Officers
Chairman   Radin Soenarno Al-Haj
President & Chief Executive Officer Md Nor Md Yusof
Others (Senior Executives)
                                       Azmi bin Abdullah *Executive Vice President*
                                       Hashimim Albakri *Executive Vice President*
                                       Ikuma Hosokawa *Executive Adviser*
Company Secretary   Jamil Hajar Abdul Muttalib
General - Treasury
Head of Treasury   Naveen Chander *Senior Vice President* ☏ **292 0540**
Syndicated Lending
Department: International Banking
Loan-Related Activities
Trade Finance   Zakaria Merican *Senior Vice President* ☏ **293 5411**

Euromoney Directory 1999   **1043**

MALAYSIA (+60)   www.euromoneydirectory.com

Bank of Commerce (M) Berhad (cont)
Money Markets
Department: Treasury
Head of Money Markets   Mas'od bin Mazlan *Chief Dealer* ☏ 293 4433
Money Markets - General
Treasury Corporate Services   S Sivalingam *Chief Dealer* ☏ 298 1166
Treasury Processing Department   Mak Sook Yin *Vice President* ☏ 298 1722
Foreign Exchange
Department: Treasury
Head of Foreign Exchange   Jason Teh Chor Kooi *Chief Dealer* ☏ 298 1166

The Bank of East Asia Limited   Representative Office
17th Floor, MUI Plaza, Jalan P Ramlee, 50250 Kuala Lumpur
Tel: (3) 206 6210 **Fax:** (3) 206 6212
Senior Executive Officers
Chief Representative   Eric Koh Thong-hau

The Bank of Nova Scotia Berhad   Subsidiary Company
Menara Boustead, 69 Jalan Raja Chulan, 50200 Kuala Lumpur
Tel: (3) 241 0766 **Fax:** (3) 241 2160 **Telex:** MA21124 **Swift:** NOSC MY KL **Reuters:** BNSK
Senior Executive Officers
Managing Director   Rasool Khan
General-Lending (DCM, SL)
Head of Corporate Banking   Mr Muthupalaniappan *Snr Account Mgr, Credit-Admin & Marketing*
Syndicated Lending
Other (Trade Finance)
Mortgage Finance   Leela Davei *Manager*
Foreign Exchange
Tel: 241 0908
Country Head   John Koh *Chief Dealer*
FX Traders / Sales People
     Azhani Wahab *Dealer*
Other Departments
Correspondent Banking   Mohd Rusli *Senior Account Manager*
Administration
Head of Administration   Elaine Wong *Manager Administration & Finance*
Other (Administration)
Corporate Marketing   Sivadas Menon *Senior Deputy MD*
Customer Services   Steven Narendran

Bank of Tokyo-Mitsubishi (Malaysia) Berhad   Subsidiary Company
1 Leboh Ampang, 50100 Kuala Lumpur
PO Box 10959, 50931 Kuala Lumpur
Tel: (3) 238 9100; (3) 238 5855 **Fax:** (3) 230 8340; (3) 232 1024 **Telex:** MA30306, MA30616 **Swift:** BOTKMYKX
Telerate: TMKL **Cable:** BTMKLP
Senior Executive Officers
Chief Executive Officer & President   Chiharu Ishikuri
Executive Vice President   Yukio Kumatani
Executive Vice President   Tee Kock Beng
Executive Vice President   Karomdad Padzoldad
Others (Senior Executives)
     Mazlan Mohamad *SVP, Int'l Trade & Inv Information Services*
General-Lending (DCM, SL)
Head of Corporate Banking   Isao Murakami *Executive Adviser*
General-Investment
Head of Investment   Hideki Yamafuku *Executive Adviser*
General - Treasury
Head of Treasury   Masatoshi Nakai *Executive Adviser*
Relationship Manager
Foreign Remittances   Yong Poi Fook *Senior Vice President*

Syndicated Lending
Other (Trade Finance)
Mazlan Mohamad *SVP, Int'l Trade & Inv Information Services*
Administration
Technology & Systems
Information Technology
Jo Fujii *Executive Adviser*

Bank Utama (Malaysia) Berhad   Head Office
Lot 363, Jalan Kulas, 93400 Kuching, Sarawak
PO Box 2049, 93740 Kuching, Sarawak
Tel: (82) 419 294 **Fax**: (82) 424 954 **Telex**: MA70101 **Swift**: UTMA MY KL **Email**: utamab@tm.net.my
Reuters: UTMA **Telerate**: 3573
Website: www.cmsb.com.my

Senior Executive Officers
Chairman — Amar Mohammed J B Serjan
Chief Executive Officer — Nik Hashim Bin Nik Yusoff *President & Chief Executive Officer*
Financial Director — Peter Ng Chong Joo *SVP, Finance*
Company Secretary — Norazzah Sulaiman

General-Lending (DCM, SL)
Head of Corporate Banking
Rajaretnam Soloman Daniel *VP, Credit Evaluation*
Haji Julhi bin Ahmad *VP, Interest Free Banking*

General - Treasury
Head of Treasury
Loke Kok Pong *VP, Treasury & Int'l Banking*

Relationship Manager
Regional Office (East) — Philip Lu Nam Ann *Vice President*
Regional Office (West) — Hanif Yeop Mohd Rose *Vice President*

Settlement / Clearing
Operations
Haji Iskandar Haji Razali *Senior Vice President*

Administration
Technology & Systems
Group Information Technology
Lawrence Anthony McDonald *Senior Vice President*

Other (Administration)
Human Resources — Drahman Jaladin *Vice President*
Special Functions — Cheong Yuen Hong *Vice President*

Banque Nationale de Paris   Representative Office
6th Floor, MUI Plaza, Jalan P Ramlee, 50250 Kuala Lumpur
Tel: (3) 248 4377; (3) 248 4489 **Fax**: (3) 248 5408 **Telex**: MA31128 BNPKL **Cable**: NATIOPAR
Dealers Tel: 457 278

Senior Executive Officers
Chief Representative & FVP — Daniel Gillen
Assistant — Abu Bakar Majid

BSN Commercial Bank (Malaysia) Berhad   Head Office
27th Floor, Putra Place, 100 Jalan Putra, Wilayah Persekutuan, 50350 Kuala Lumpur
Tel: (3) 443 6466 **Fax**: (3) 441 3703; (3) 442 7880 **Telex**: BSNC MA 31269 **Swift**: BSNC MY KL **Reuters**: BSNB
Website: www.bsncom.com.my

Senior Executive Officers
Chairman — Abd Aziz Raja Salim ☎ **443 1534**
Chief Executive Officer — Nik Mohd Amin Nik Abd Majid ☎ **443 1626**
General Manager, Treasury — En Zaulkifli Mohamed ☎ **441 4910**
General Manager, Banking — En Jamal Mohd Aris ☎ **443 1767**
General Manager, Corporate Services — Zaulkifli Mohamed ☎ **441 4910**
General Manager, Finance — Chua Eng Kee ☎ **443 5582**

General - Treasury
Head of Treasury
Asri Awang *General Manager* ☎ **443 2034**

Debt Capital Markets / Fixed Income
Department: Money Market Department
Fax: 442 7880
Country Head
Omar Dali *Head* ☎ **443 2387**

MALAYSIA (+60)

BSN Commercial Bank (Malaysia) Berhad (cont)
Domestic Government Bonds
Head of Sales; Head of Trading — Omar Dali *Head* ☎ **443 2387**
Private Placements
Head of Sales — Abd Hadi Ismail *Head* ☎ **443 1871**

Equity Capital Markets
Department: Equity Investment Department
Fax: 442 7880
Head of Equity Capital Markets — Azhar Othman *Head* ☎ **441 4659**
Domestic Equities
Head of Origination — Azhar Othman *Head* ☎ **441 4659**

Money Markets
Fax: 443 2387
Head of Money Markets — Omar Dali *Head* ☎ **443 2387**
Wholesale Deposits
Marketing — Abd Hadi Ismail *Head* ☎ **443 1871**

Foreign Exchange
Fax: 442 7880
Head of Trading — Omar Dali *Chief Dealer* ☎ **443 2387**

Risk Management
Fax: 441 3703
Head of Risk Management — Chiang Khai Chong *Head* ☎ **444 9223**
Fixed Income Derivatives / Risk Management
Global Head — Raymond Yeow *Head* ☎ **443 6466**
IR Swaps Sales / Marketing — Kamaruddin Baharom *Manager* ☎ **443 6466**
IR Swaps Trading — Raymond Yeow *Head* ☎ **443 6466**
Foreign Exchange Derivatives / Risk Management
Vanilla FX option Sales — Omar Dali *Chief Dealer* ☎ **443 5050**
Vanilla FX option Trading — Raymond Yeow *Head* ☎ **443 6466**

Settlement / Clearing
Department: Treasury Processing Centre
Fax: 443 0750
Head of Settlement / Clearing — Oon Hoon San *Manager* ☎ **443 4762**
Foreign Exchange Settlement — Alvin Tan *Assistant Manager* ☎ **443 6466**

Other Departments
Correspondent Banking — Mark Ong *Head* ☎ **443 2402**

Other Departments
Financial Institutions — Shaharin Abu Hashim *Head* ☎ **443 2402**

Administration

K Uthayasoorian *Head* ☎ **469 2111**

Legal / In-House Counsel

Puan Bizura Hj Mustapha *Company Secretary* ☎ **443 2473**

Compliance

Nor Azly Mohd Nor *Chief Auditor* ☎ **443 2864**

Public Relations

Mohd Uzir Sulaiman *Head* ☎ **441 1446**

The Chase Manhattan Bank (Malaysia) Berhad Subsidiary Company

Menara Dion, Level 26, Jalan Sultan Ismail, 50250 Kuala Lumpur
PO Box 11090, 50734 Kuala Lumpur
Tel: (3) 270 4111 Fax: (3) 270 4110 Telex: MA 30224 CHAMAN Swift: CHAS MY KX Cable: CHAMANBANK

Senior Executive Officers
Chief Executive Officer — Windsor Newton Hall, Jr. *CEO / Managing Director* ☎ **270 4101**
Financial Director — Souk Huan Lau *Vice President* ☎ **270 4270**

Foreign Exchange
Department: Treasury / Foreign Exchange
Head of Foreign Exchange — Su Ming Tham *VP & Treasurer* ☎ **270 4338**

Corporate Finance / M&A Advisory
Department: Corporate Finance
Other (Corporate Finance)
Corporate & Investment Banking — Khuan Eoi Lee *VP & Manager* ☎ **270 4128**
Abdul Mutalib Alias *VP & Manager* ☎ **270 4129**
Lily Maznah Lokman Hakim *VP & Manager* ☎ **270 4126**

www.euromoneydirectory.com MALAYSIA (+60)

Global Custody
Global Investor Services Wei Chin Chia *Vice President & Manager* ☎ **270 4210**

Other Departments
Chief Credit Officer Fauziah Hisham *Country Credit Officer* ☎ **270 4127**
Correspondent Banking Mee Yoon Choong *VP & Manager, Financial Institutions* ☎ **270 4130**

Administration
Technology & Systems
Technology & Operations Tulu UI Islam *Manager* ☎ **270 4200**

Citibank Berhad
Full Branch Office

Formerly known as: Citibank NA
28 Medan Pasar, 50050 Kuala Lumpur
PO Box 10112, 50904 Kuala Lumpur
Tel: (3) 232 8585 **Fax:** (3) 232 8763 **Telex:** MA 31165 CITIBANK **Swift:** CITY MY KL **Reuters:** CTKL
Website: www.citibank.com.my

Senior Executive Officers
Chief Executive Officer Robert Matthew ☎ **209 2000** 📠 **232 7932**
Treasurer Noorazman Abdul Aziz *Country Treasurer* ☎ **209 2100**

Others (Senior Executives)
Citicorp Capital Eillen Tan ☎ **209 2060**

General-Lending (DCM, SL)
Head of Corporate Banking Andrew Duff ☎ **209 2101**

Money Markets
Head of Money Markets Philip Tan ☎ **209 2108**

Foreign Exchange
Head of Foreign Exchange Robert Kwan ☎ **209 2102**
Head of Institutional Sales Stephen Li ☎ **209 2103**

Corporate Finance / M&A Advisory
Head of Corporate Finance Arnold Kwan ☎ **209 2012**

Other (Corporate Finance)
Corporate Finance Analysis & Strategies Hsiu-Yi Lin *Head* ☎ **209 2231**

Settlement / Clearing
Operations Sunil Garg *Global Transaction Services Head* ☎ **236 6400** 📠 **298 8375**

Commerce International Merchant Bankers Berhad
Head Office

12th Floor, Commerce Square, Jalan Semantan, Damansara Heights, 50490 Kuala Lumpur
Tel: (3) 253 6688 **Fax:** (3) 253 5522 **Telex:** MA30903 PEBSAM

Senior Executive Officers
Chairman Md Nor Bin Md Yusof
Chief Executive Officer Robert Cheim *Managing Director*
Deputy Chief Executive Nazir Razak
Deputy General Manager Kok Kwan Lee
International Division Robert Cheim *Managing Director*

Debt Capital Markets / Fixed Income
Head of Debt Capital Markets Shai Weng Loh *Deputy General Manager*

Equity Capital Markets
Head of Equity Capital Markets Choon Thye Tan *General Manager*

Syndicated Lending
Head of Syndicated Lending Shai Weng Loh *Deputy General Manager*

Money Markets
Head of Money Markets Kok Kwan Lee *Deputy General Manager*

Foreign Exchange
Head of Foreign Exchange Kok Kwan Lee *Deputy General Manager*

Risk Management
Head of Risk Management Yuet Peng Lee *Deputy General Manager*

Corporate Finance / M&A Advisory
Head of Corporate Finance; Global Head Choon Thye Tan *General Manager*

MALAYSIA (+60)   www.euromoneydirectory.com

Commerzbank AG
Full Branch Office

Level 6 (E), Main Office Tower, Financial Park Labuan Complex, Jalan Merdeka, 87000 Labuan
Tel: (87) 416 953; (87) 417 153 Fax: (87) 413 542

Senior Executive Officers
General Manager — Geoff Ho
General-Lending (DCM, SL)
Head of Corporate Banking — Norman Lee *Assistant General Manager*

The Dai-Ichi Kangyo Bank Limited
Representative Office

5th Floor, Mui Plaza, Jalan P Ramlee, 50784 Kuala Lumpur
PO Box 12613, Kuala Lumpur
Tel: (3) 241 5635 Fax: (3) 242 2760 Telex: 32147 DKBKL

Senior Executive Officers
Representative — Yuki Chikamoto

The Dai-Ichi Kangyo Bank Limited
Branch, Marketing Office

5th Floor, Mui Plaza, Jalan P Ramlee, 50784 Kuala Lumpur
PO Box 12613, Kuala Lumpur
Tel: (3) 245 9331 Fax: (3) 245 9323 Telex: 20104 DKBKL MA

Senior Executive Officers
General Manager — Ryoichi Shimizu

The Dai-Ichi Kangyo Bank Limited
Full Branch Office

Level 9 (B) & (C), Main Office Tower, Financial Park Labuan, Jalan Merdeka, 87000 Labuan
Tel: (87) 419 418 Fax: (87) 419 424 Telex: 85015 DKBLAB MA

Senior Executive Officers
General Manager — Ryoichi Shimizu

Delta Finance Berhad
Head Office

85/89 Jalan Kampong Nyabor, Sibu, 96000 Sarawak
PO Box 704, Sibu, 96007 Sarawak
Tel: (84) 333 070 Fax: (84) 342 848; (84) 316 312 Email: deltafin@tm.net.my

Senior Executive Officers
Chairman — Jack Sung Ding
Chief Executive Officer — Sui Cheng Hii ☏ 316 313
Executive Director — Tuan Haji Sallen B Abdullah
Company Secretary — Tien Fuang Luk

Other Departments
Chief Credit Officer — Kho Chan Lee *Senior Manager, Credit*

Administration
Head of Administration — Chin Hian Ho *Manager, Finance & Administration*
Business Development — Kie Yong Wong *SM, Business Development & Branch Operations*

Deutsche Bank (Malaysia) Berhad
Subsidiary Company

Level 18/20, Menara IMC, 8 Jalan Sultan Ismail, 50250 Kuala Lumpur
PO Box 12211, 50770 Kuala Lumpur
Tel: (3) 202 1163 Fax: (3) 201 8710 Telex: 0084 20367 DBA Swift: DEUT MY KL
Forex Tel: 201 7798

Senior Executive Officers
Managing Director / General Manager — Thomas A Verlohr

www.euromoneydirectory.com   MALAYSIA (+60)

Dresdner Bank AG — Representative Office

5th Floor, Wisma Genting, Jalan Sultan Ismail, 50250 Kuala Lumpur
PO Box 10221, 50704 Kuala Lumpur
Tel: (3) 201 5088 Fax: (3) 201 5061

Senior Executive Officers
Chief Representative   Albrechtl Langelueddeke

Dresdner Bank AG

Level 13C, Financial Park, 87000 Labuan
Tel: (87) 419 271

The Fuji Bank Limited — Offshore Banking Unit

Level 10A, Main Office Tower, Financial Park Complex, Jalan Merdeka, 87000 Labuan
Tel: (87) 417 766 Fax: (87) 419 766 Swift: MA 85062 FUJLAB

Senior Executive Officers
General Manager   Ken Ueda
Department: Marketing Office
Letter Box 138, 30th Floor, UBN Tower, 10 Jalan P Ramlee, 50250 Kuala Lumpur
Tel: +60 (3) 201 5020 Fax: +60 (3) 201 5030 Telex: MA30920 FUJLAK
General Manager   Ken Ueda

Hock Hua Bank Berhad — Head Office

15 Jalan Pulau, 96000 Sibu, 96000 Sarawak
PO Box 11, Sibu, 96007 Sarawak
Tel: (84) 333 888 Fax: (84) 337 888 Telex: HOKHUA 72042 MA Swift: HHBB MY KL SBH Reuters: HHMB
Website: www.hhb.com.my

Senior Executive Officers
Chairman   Amar Ling Beng Siew
Chief Executive Officer   Ting Sik Kang
                                                   Lau Hieng Ing *Deputy Chief Executive and Company Secretary*
Regional Manager for West Malaysia   Michael Wei Hsiao Kuang
Deputy Regional Manager for West Malaysia   Ko Wai Khion
Company Secretary   Augustine Siaw Meng Kun
International Division   Yong Yen Seng *Manager*

General - Treasury
Head of Treasury   Ting Chek Ping *Manager*

Other Departments
Chief Credit Officer   Lau Sie Hui *Manager*
Economic Research   Ting Ka Hua *Manager*

Administration

Legal / In-House Counsel
                                                   Teh Saw Lan *Manager*

Accounts / Audit
Internal Audit   Tiong Nieng Chiong *Manager*
Finance & Accounts   Matthew Wong Bak Tiong *Manager*

Other (Administration)
Human Resources   Patrick Kiew Chiong Yiing *Manager*
Branch Banking & Supervision   Loi Pui Khim *Manager*
Executive Office   Mary Hii Chiu Hung *Manager*
Electronic Data Processing   Chew Sii Men *Manager*
Interest Free Banking   Shahrul Bariah bt. A. Ghani *Manager*
Organization & Methods   Lee Meng Hee *Manager*
Property & General Services   Wong Tek Kong *Manager*
Statistics   Toh Lee Cheng *Manager*

MALAYSIA (+60)   www.euromoneydirectory.com

Hong Leong Bank Berhad
Head Office

Formerly known as: Mui Bank Berhad
Level 3, Wisma Hong Leong, 18 Jalan Perak, 50450 Kuala Lumpur
PO Box 12372, 50776 Kuala Lumpur
Tel: (3) 264 2828; (3) 269 2749 **Fax:** (3) 264 3240; (3) 264 1514 **Telex:** MA 33654 HLBCBL **Swift:** HLBB MY KL
Email: gohaiying@hlbb.hongleong.com.my **Reuters:** HLBB **Cable:** HLBBCBL
Website: www.hlb.hongleong.com.my

Senior Executive Officers
Executive Chairman	Quek Leng Chan
Chief Executive Officer	James Lim Cheng Poh *Senior Group Managing Director*
Financial Director	Soon Leh Hong *Group Financial Controller* T 264 3021 F 264 1519
Executive Director	Zulkiflee Hashim T 925 8928 F 264 8181
International Division	Kim Brix Andersen *General Manager, Treasury*

Others (Senior Executives)
Credit Management	Peter Choo Eng Kong *General Manager* T 262 8513 F 264 1517
Human Resources	Stephen Wong Tuck Kan *General Manager* T 264 2935 F 925 8623
Economic Services	Aminah Pit Abdul Rahman *GM, Economic Services & Islamic Banking Division* T 284 3259 F 284 4368
Internal Audit	Hazimi Bin Kassim *General Manager, Internal Audit Division* T 925 7901 F 925 7902
Information Services	Chin Wai Fong *General Manager* T 264 3212 F 264 1588
Singapore Operations	Evelyn Ow *General Manager, Singapore Branch* T 535 9788

General-Lending (DCM, SL)
Head of Corporate Banking	Teo Tong Kooi *Senior GM, Corporate Banking* T 264 2996 F 264 2997

Syndicated Lending
Trade Finance	Chang Wing Hoh *Senior Manager, Trade Finance & Correspondent Bank* T 269 2750 F 264 3240

Money Markets
Tel: 264 3070 **Fax:** 264 9305 **Reuters:** HLBB **Telex:** MA 30714 HLBFX

Head of Money Markets	Fadhlan Thoo Lip Bong *Assistant Manager*

Foreign Exchange
Tel: 264 3070 **Fax:** 264 9305 **Reuters:** HLBB **Telex:** MA 30714 HLBFX

Head of Foreign Exchange	Thong Kok Kee *Head, Spot Interbank & Currency Options Desk*
Corporate Sales	Chee Pok Kang *Manager, Treasury*
Head of Trading	Kim Brix Andersen *General Manager, Treasury*

FX Traders / Sales People
Dealing	Tan Sim Lim *Senior Manager, Treasury*

Risk Management
Tel: 269 2741 **Fax:** 925 8718 **Reuters:** HLBB

Head of Risk Management	Soon Leh Hong *Group Financial Controller* T 264 3021 F 264 1519

Settlement / Clearing
Tel: 264 2904 **Fax:** 925 7817 **Telex:** MA 30470

Head of Settlement / Clearing	Soon Leh Hong *Group Financial Controller* T 264 3021 F 264 1519
Operations	Lee Ai Ngoh *Acting Manager* T 264 2904 F 925 8718

Other Departments
Private Banking	Chin Yuen Yin *General Manager, Personal Banking Division* T 264 2998 F 264 1516
Correspondent Banking	Chang Wing Hoh *Senior Manager, Trade Finance & Correspondent Bank* T 269 2750 F 264 3240
Economic Research	Aminah Pit Abdul Rahman *GM, Economic Services & Islamic Banking Division* T 284 3259 F 284 4368

Administration

Legal / In-House Counsel

	Ng Choi Foong *Senior Manager, Legal & Secretariat* T 264 2507 F 264 2503

Other (Administration)

Human Resources	Stephen Wong Tuck Kan *General Manager* T 264 2935 F 925 8623
Banking Services	Hazimi Bin Kassim *General Manager, Internal Audit Division* T 925 7901 F 925 7902
Information Services	Chin Wai Fong *General Manager* T 264 3212 F 264 1588
Singapore Operations	Evelyn Ow *General Manager, Singapore Branch* T 535 9788

www.euromoneydirectory.com   MALAYSIA (+60)

Hongkongbank Malaysia Berhad
Subsidiary Company

No 2 Leboh Ampang, 50100 Kuala Lumpur
PO Box 10244, 50912 Kuala Lumpur
Tel: (3) 230 0744 Fax: (3) 230 1146 Telex: 30381 HSBCKL MA Swift: HBMB MYKL
Email: hbmmpa@hkbank-msia.com.my
Website: www.hkbank-msia.com

Senior Executive Officers
Chairman — J E Strickland
Chief Executive Officer — T W O'Brien *Deputy Chairman & CEO*
Financial Director — Baldev Singh *Chief Financial Officer*
Chief Operating Officer — P W Boyles *Executive Director & Deputy CEO*
Treasurer — Neil Foster
Legal Counsel & Company Secretary — Patricia Khaw

Others (Senior Executives)
Sulaiman Sujak *Executive Director & Adviser*
Ramli Ibrahim *Non-Executive Director*
Abdullah bin Mohd Salleh *Non-Executive Director*
Augustine Ong Soon Hock *Non-Executive Director*
H E Barlow *Non-Executive Director*
Francis McWilliams *Non-Executive Director*
J R H Bond *Non-Executive Director*

General-Lending (DCM, SL)
Head of Corporate Banking — U Chen Hock *Manager, CBA Services & Marketing*

The Industrial Bank of Japan Limited
Representative Office

Suite 1403, 14th Floor, Pernas International, Jalan Sultan Ismail, 50250 Kuala Lumpur
Tel: (3) 261 5111 Fax: (3) 261 5620 Telex: 32298 IBJKL MA

Senior Executive Officers
Representative — Takahiko Matsushita

The Industrial Bank of Japan Limited
Full Branch Office

Level 11 (A), Main Office Tower, Financial Park Labuan, Jalan Merdeka, 87000 Labuan
Tel: (87) 419 115 Fax: (87) 419 121 Telex: MA85061 IBJLB

Senior Executive Officers
General Manager — Hiroshi Kitagawa

ING Baring Research (Malaysia) Sendirian Berhad
Subsidiary Company

Suite No 22.3, Level 22, Menara IMC, 8 Jalan Sultan Ismail, 50250 Kuala Lumpur
PO Box 39, 50250 Kuala Lumpur
Tel: (3) 230 2100 Fax: (3) 230 4682

Senior Executive Officers
Country Manager — Phoebe Yap

ING Barings
Full Branch Office

Level 8 (B2), Main Office Tower, Financial Park Labuan, Jalan Merdeka, 87000 Labuan
Tel: (87) 425 733 Fax: (87) 425 734

Senior Executive Officers
Manager — Milly Tan

Interfinance Berhad

Lot 4.08/4.10, Level 4, Wisma Satok, Jalan Satok, 93600 Kuching, Sarawak
Tel: (82) 251 323; (82) 258 511 Fax: (82) 415 340 Email: ifb@po.jaring.my

Senior Executive Officers
Chairman — Liang Kim Bang

MALAYSIA (+60)   www.euromoneydirectory.com

Interfinance Berhad (cont)
Others (Senior Executives)
                        Abang Haji Abdul Karim Bin Tun Abang Hj Openg *Executive Director*
General-Lending (DCM, SL)
Head of Corporate Banking   Fung Yee Kwok *AGM, Credit & Business Development*
Settlement / Clearing
Operations   Jong Yiak Kong *Snr Manager, Operations & Finance*
Administration
Other (Administration)
Corporate Affairs   Edward Minggu Nyantau *Manager & Head*

KAF-Astley & Pearce Sdn Berhad   Head Office

18th Floor, Menara Boustead, Jalan Raja Chulan, 50200 Kuala Lumpur
Tel: (3) 242 9954; (3) 248 0057 **Fax:** (3) 244 3486 **Telex:** MA 0494

Senior Executive Officers
Director & Head   Khatijah Ahmad
Others (Senior Executives)
Director   Zulkifli Ishak *Director*

Debt Capital Markets / Fixed Income
Tel: 248 0195 **Fax:** 244 3486
Head of Debt Capital Markets Raymond Yap *Assistant General Manager* ☎ 466 8220
Domestic Government Bonds
Head of Trading   Zulkifli Mohd Tahir *Senior Manager* ☎ 248 0039

Money Markets
Tel: 248 0039 **Fax:** 244 3486
Head of Money Markets   Zulkifli Ishak *Chief Executive* ☎ 248 0039/243 1134
Domestic Commercial Paper
Head of Trading   Elina Choy *Manager* ☎ 248 0039
Wholesale Deposits
Head of Sales   Zulkifli Mohd Tahir *Senior Manager* ☎ 248 0039

Foreign Exchange
Department: Spot / Forward, MYR / US$, Sing$
Head of Foreign Exchange   Zulkifli Ishak *Chief Executive* ☎ 248 0039/243 1134
Head of Trading   Royston Pinto *Manager* ☎ 243 1134

Risk Management
Fixed Income Derivatives / Risk Management
IR Swaps Trading   Raymond Yap *Assistant General Manager* ☎ 466 8220
Foreign Exchange Derivatives / Risk Management
Cross-Currency Swaps, Trading Raymond Yap *Assistant General Manager* ☎ 466 8220
Other Currency Swap / FX Options Personnel
                                Cynthia Tay *Assistant Manager* ☎ 248 0039

Malaysian Industrial Development Finance Berhad (MIDF)
Head Office

195A Jalan Tun Razak, 50400 Kuala Lumpur
PO Box 12110, Kuala Lumpur
Tel: (3) 261 1166; (3) 261 0066 **Fax:** (3) 261 5973 **Cable:** MALINDEV

Senior Executive Officers
Chairman   Seri Ahmad Sarji Abdul Hamid ✆ 261 4227 ✉ sarji@pnb.com.my
Chief Executive Officer   Haji Darwis Mohd Daek *Group Chief Executive* ✆ 261 1952
                                ✉ darwis@midf.po.my
Financial Director   Allen N Lopez *Group Finance Director* ✆ 262 9531 ✉ allen@midf.po.my
General Manager, Services   Khoo Chin Guan ✆ 262 9531 ✉ khoo@midf.po.my
General Manager, Corporate Affairs Jamaludin Hassan ✆ 262 9531 ✉ jamal@midf.po.my
General Manager, Operations   Abdul Muis Hassan ✆ 262 9531 ✉ muis@midf.po.my
Administration
Legal / In-House Counsel
Legal & Secretarial   Hj Shamsiah Ibrahim *Senior Manager* ✆ 261 3908 ✉ shamsiah@midf.po.my
Other (Administration)
Business Development   Ahmad Radzi Abd Majid *Senior Manager* ✆ 261 3906 ✉ radzi@midf.po.my
Projects   Wang Leong Heng *Senior Manager* ✆ 261 3906 ✉ wang@midf.po.my

1052 Euromoney Directory 1999

www.euromoneydirectory.com   MALAYSIA (+60)

Malaysian International Merchant Bankers Berhad — Head Office

4th Floor, Bangunan MIDF, 195A Jalan Tun Razak, 50400 Kuala Lumpur
PO Box 12250, 50772 Kuala Lumpur
Tel: (3) 261 1200 **Fax:** (3) 263 5022; (3) 264 7593 **Telex:** MA30299

Senior Executive Officers
Chairman — Wan A Rahman Yaacob
Chief Executive Officer — Yang Shu-Yin Lai *Chief Executive Officer & Executive Director*
Financial Director — Tan Boh Seng *General Manager & Head, Finance*

General-Lending (DCM, SL)
Head of Corporate Banking — Noordin Abdullah *Senior GM & Head, Corporate Banking*

General-Investment
Head of Investment — Ahkter Abdul Manan *GM & Head, Investment & Securities*

General - Treasury
Head of Treasury — Cheah Chor Chuan *General Manager & Head, Treasury*

Relationship Manager
Privatization & Project Consultancy — Aminah Mohamed Nawi *Assistant General Manager & Head*

Debt Capital Markets / Fixed Income
Global Head — Hasleen Isnin *Manager & Head, CMBD*

Risk Management
Global Head — Hock Ghee Heng *General Manager & Head, Risk Asset Management*

Administration
Head of Administration — Mohd Ridzwan Tay Abdullah *Manager & Head, HR*

Technology & Systems
Information Technology — Steve Tan Kim Yong *Manager & Head, ITD*

Accounts / Audit
Internal Audit — Jennifer Yip Tsui Yoke *Assistant General Manager & Head, IAD*

Other (Administration)
Business Development — Hasleen Isnin *Manager & Head, CMBD*
Corporate Advisory — Lim Siew Eng *Senior General Manager & Head, IAD*
Human Resources — Mohd Ridzwan Tay Abdullah *Manager & Head, HR*

Mayban Finance Berhad — Subsidiary Company

1 Medan Tuanku Satu, Kuala Lumpur
Tel: (3) 293 1255 **Fax:** (3) 291 1121

Senior Executive Officers
Chairman — Richard Ho Ung Hun
Chief Executive Officer — Wan Ismail Abdul Rahman
Treasurer — Haron Kassim
Managing Director / General Manager — Muhamed Naim Abullah

Maybank — Head Office

Alternative trading name: Malayan Banking Berhad
Custody Services Department, 3rd Floor, Menara Maybank, 100 Jalan Tun Perak, 50050 Kuala Lumpur
PO Box 12010, 50936 Kuala Lumpur
Tel: (3) 230 8833 **Fax:** (3) 230 4027; (3) 238 1464 **Telex:** MA 30438 **Swift:** MBBE MY KL A
Email: maybank@po.jaring.my **Cable:** maybank
Website: www.maybank.com.my/maybank

Senior Executive Officers
Chairman of the Board — Mohamed Basir bin Ahmad
Vice Chairman — Richard Ho Ung Hun
Managing Director — Amirsham A Aziz
Executive Director — Mohd Salleh bin Hj Harun
Executive Director — Ismail Shahudin

Others (Senior Executives)
Board of Directors —
Raja Mohammad Alias bin Raja Muhd Ali *Director*
Mohammad bin Abdullah *Director*
Hj Mohd Hilmey bin Mohd Taib *Director*
Teh Soon Poh *Director*
Md Yusof bin Hussin *Director*
Tuan Hj Mohd Hashir Haji Abdullah *Director*

MALAYSIA (+60)

www.euromoneydirectory.com

Maybank (cont)

Others (Senior Executives) (cont)

Singapore Operations
Corporate Banking Division — Spencer Lee Tien Chye *Senior General Manager*
Branch Operations Division — Md Agil Mohd Natt *Senior General Manager*
Consumer Banking — Abdul Aziz Peru Mohamed *General Manager*
Information Systems Division — Ashraf Ali bin Abdul Kadir *General Manager*
Commercial Banking Division — Tong Hon Keong *General Manager*
Human Resources — Johar Che 'Mat *General Manager*
Commercial Retail Banking Division, Singapore — Azizan Ahmad *General Manager*
Lee Hong Kim *Assistant General Manager*

General - Treasury
Head of Treasury — Hooi Lai Hoong *Senior General Manager*

Money Markets
Head of Money Markets — Syed Mahadzir Syed Ismail *Assistant General Manager*

Foreign Exchange
Head of Foreign Exchange — Syed Mahadzir Syed Ismail *Assistant General Manager*

Settlement / Clearing
Operations — Spencer Lee Tien Chye *Senior GM, Singapore Operations*
Ismail Shahudin *Senior GM, Malaysian Operations*

Other Departments
Chief Credit Officer — Choo Yee Kwan *General Manager, Credit Control Division*

Administration

Technology & Systems
Information Systems Division — Tong Hon Keong *General Manager*

Accounts / Audit
Audit Division — Mohd Zaini Kamaruddin *Head, Audit*

Other (Administration)
Human Resource & Corporate Planning, Singapore — Loh Oun Hean
Human Resource Division — Azizan Ahmad *General Manager*

MBf Finance Berhad — Head Office

8, Plaza MBf, Jalan Yapap Kwan Seng, 50450 Kuala Lumpur
PO Box 10027, 50901 Kuala Lumpur
Tel: (3) 261 1177 Fax: (3) 262 4780 Telex: MA 30154 MBF
Forex Tel: 201 7798

Senior Executive Officers
Chief Executive Officer — Dada Loy Teik Ngan
Chief Operating Officer — Tan Loon Hoon *COO & Executive Vice President*

General-Lending (DCM, SL)
Head of Corporate Banking — Catherine Lip Ah Chun *Senior Vice President, Credit*

General - Treasury
Head of Treasury — Chang Yew Khoon *VP, Treasury & Capital Markets*

Relationship Manager
Branches Operations — Ho Seng Yee *Vice President*

Debt Capital Markets / Fixed Income
Global Head — Chang Yew Khoon *VP, Treasury & Capital Markets*

Administration
Other (Administration)
Marketing — Patrick Nadhan

Multi-Purpose Bank Berhad

5th Floor, Menara Multi-Purpose, Capital Square, 8 Jalan Munshi Abdullah, 50100 Kuala Lumpur
PO Box 10069, 50704 Kuala Lumpur
Tel: (3) 294 8800 Fax: (3) 294 6727 Telex: MA30251 Swift: MFBBMYKL Email: csloh@pc.jaring.my
Cable: MAFBANK KUALA LUMPUR

Senior Executive Officers
Chairman — Abu Talib bin Othman ☎ 296 4911
Chief Executive Officer — Ng Siek Chuan ☎ 296 4921
Treasurer — Leow Bock Lim *SVP, Treasury & International Banking* ☎ 296 4641
First Vice President — Ginny Lee Sew Thai ☎ 296 4719

www.euromoneydirectory.com　　　　　　　　　MALAYSIA (+60)

Senior Executive Officers (cont)
International Division　　　　　　　　　Leow Bock Lim *SVP, Treasury & International Banking* ☏ 296 4641
Others (Senior Executives)
Corporate Services　　　　　　　　　　George Chong You Peng *Senior Vice President* ☏ 296 4931
General-Lending (DCM, SL)
Head of Corporate Banking　　　　　　Wong Kon Fook *SVP, Corporate Banking & Capital Markets* ☏ 296 4811
Relationship Manager
Regional Manager (Northern Area)　　Foo Lai Hoon *First Vice President* ☏ 331 4863
Regional Manager (Southern Area)　　Chair Pot Kong *First Vice President* ☏ 386 2502
Money Markets
Head of Money Markets　　　　　　　Eddie Lim Eng Cheng *First Vice President*
Foreign Exchange
Head of Foreign Exchange　　　　　　Eddie Lim Eng Cheng *First Vice President*
Risk Management
Head of Risk Management　　　　　　Wen Yey Leong *Senior Vice President* ☏ 296 4711
Other Departments
Correspondent Banking　　　　　　　Noysius Wee Toh Beng *Vice President*
Administration
Head of Administration　　　　　　　Tee Joo Teik
Technology & Systems
Information Systems　　　　　　　　Goh Tee Khiong *First Vice President* ☏ 230 1322
Legal / In-House Counsel
Legal & Recoveries　　　　　　　　Ginny Lee Sew Thai *First Vice President* ☏ 296 4719
Corporate Communications
　　　　　　　　　　　　　　　　　Yeoh Lin Lin
Accounts / Audit
Internal Audit　　　　　　　　　　　Alfred Fernando *Vice President* ☏ 230 1322
Other (Administration)
Human Resources　　　　　　　　　Hajar bin Ahmad *Senior Vice President* ☏ 230 1322

National Westminster Bank plc　　　　　　　　　　　Full Branch Office
Lot 2A, Level 5, Wisma Lazenda, Jalan Kemajuan, 87007 Labuan
Tel: (87) 423 667; (87) 423 659 **Fax:** (87) 423 669
Senior Executive Officers
Branch Manager　　　　　　　　　Len Pong Liew ☏ 423 667 ✉ lpliew@tm.net.my

OCBC Bank (Malaysia) Berhad　　　　　　　　　　Subsidiary Company
Wisma Lee Rubber, Jalan Melaka, Wilayah Persekutuan, 50100 Kuala Lumpur
PO Box 10197, 50911 Kuala Lumpur
Tel: (3) 292 0344; (3) 292 0177 **Fax:** (3) 298 4363; (3) 292 6518 **Telex:** OCBC MA30507, 30358, 31502
Swift: OCBCMYKLNSD **Cable:** OCBC KUALA LU
Senior Executive Officers
Chairman　　　　　　　　　　　　Ton Sri Dato Nasaruddin Bahari ☏ 292 0344
Chief Executive Officer　　　　　　Ng Tat Pun ☏ 292 2523
Senior Vice President　　　　　　　Helen Lim ☏ 291 1146
Vice President　　　　　　　　　　Zuraidah Atan ☏ 292 0344 ✉ zuraida@pc.jaring.my
Debt Capital Markets / Fixed Income
Fax: 291 6616
Country Head　　　　　　　　　　Zuraidah Atan *Vice President* ☏ 292 0344 ✉ zuraida@pc.jaring.my
Domestic Government Bonds
Head of Sales　　　　　　　　　　Su Kuang Teo *VP & Senior Manager* ☏ 291 4629
Head of Trading　　　　　　　　　Ley Ley Tan *Vice President* ☏ 291 4629
Eurobonds
Head of Origination　　　　　　　　Zuraidah Atan *Vice President* ☏ 292 0344 ✉ zuraida@pc.jaring.my
Libor-Based / Floating-Rate Products
FRN Origination　　　　　　　　　Zuraidah Atan *Vice President* ☏ 292 0344 ✉ zuraida@pc.jaring.my
Medium-Term Notes
Head of Origination　　　　　　　　Zuraidah Atan *Vice President* ☏ 292 0344 ✉ zuraida@pc.jaring.my
Private Placements
Head of Origination　　　　　　　　Zuraidah Atan *Vice President* ☏ 292 0344 ✉ zuraida@pc.jaring.my

MALAYSIA (+60)　　　　　　www.euromoneydirectory.com

OCBC Bank (Malaysia) Berhad (cont)

Asset-Backed Securities / Securitization
Global Head　　　　　　　　　　　　Zuraidah Atan *Vice President* ☎ 292 0344 ✉ zuraida@pc.jaring.my

Fixed-Income Repo
Head of Repo　　　　　　　　　　　　Su Kuang Teo *VP & Senior Manager* ☎ 291 4629

Syndicated Lending
Department: Corporate Finance & Capital Markets
Country Head of Origination; Head of　　Zuraidah Atan *Vice President* ☎ 292 0344 ✉ zuraida@pc.jaring.my
Syndication

Loan-Related Activities
Trade Finance　　　　　　　　　　　Cheong Choi Mun *Vice President* ☎ 298 1019

Money Markets
Department: Treasury & Dealing Room
Country Head　　　　　　　　　　　Su Kuang Teo *VP & Senior Manager* ☎ 291 4629

Domestic Commercial Paper
Head of Origination　　　　　　　　　Zuraidah Atan *Vice President* ☎ 292 0344 ✉ zuraida@pc.jaring.my
Head of Sales　　　　　　　　　　　Su Kuang Teo *VP & Senior Manager* ☎ 291 4629
Head of Trading　　　　　　　　　　Ley Ley Tan *Vice President* ☎ 291 4629

Wholesale Deposits
Marketing　　　　　　　　　　　　Su Kuang Teo *VP & Senior Manager* ☎ 291 4629
Head of Sales　　　　　　　　　　　Ley Ley Tan *Vice President* ☎ 291 4629

Foreign Exchange
Country Head　　　　　　　　　　　Su Kuang Teo *VP & Senior Manager* ☎ 291 4629
Head of Institutional Sales　　　　　　Ley Ley Tan *Vice President* ☎ 291 4629
Corporate Sales　　　　　　　　　　Ummi Kalthom Shaharuddin *Assistant Vice President* ☎ 292 4869
Head of Trading　　　　　　　　　　Daniel Kum Chuen Choy *Assistant Vice President* ☎ 298 1482

Risk Management
Country Head　　　　　　　　　　　Stephen Louis *VP & Senior Manager* ☎ 292 0260

Corporate Finance / M&A Advisory
Department: Corporate Finance & Capital Markets
Country Head　　　　　　　　　　　Zuraidah Atan *Vice President* ☎ 292 0344 ✉ zuraida@pc.jaring.my

Settlement / Clearing
Department: Nominee Services
Country Head　　　　　　　　　　　Jit Toong Lim *Vice President* ☎ 298 7282

Global Custody
Department: Nominee Services
Country Head　　　　　　　　　　　Jit Toong Lim *Vice President* ☎ 298 7282

Other Departments
Private Banking　　　　　　　　　　Bee Gaik Teh *Vice President* ☎ 298 5418
Correspondent Banking　　　　　　　Cheong Choi Mun *Vice President* ☎ 298 1019

Administration

Technology & Systems
　　　　　　　　　　　　　　　　Chee On Lum *VP & Senior Manager* ☎ 291 1558

Legal / In-House Counsel
　　　　　　　　　　　　　　　　Grace Tong *Vice President* ☎ 298 9539

Compliance
　　　　　　　　　　　　　　　　Grace Tong *Vice President* ☎ 298 9539

Oriental Bank Berhad　　　　　　　　　　　　　　　　　　　　　Head Office

Bangunan Oriental Bank, 1 Jalan Hang Lekiu, 50100 Kuala Lumpur
PO Box 10243, 50708 Kuala Lumpur
Tel: (3) 202 4600 **Fax:** (3) 202 4267 **Telex:** MA31382 **Cable:** OrientBank

Senior Executive Officers
Chairman　　　　　　　　　　　　Mohd Abu Bakar bin Mohd Noor
Chief Executive Officer　　　　　　　Datuk Ramly bin Ahmad *Executive Director & CEO*
GM, Commercial Bnkg & Mgt Services　Ch'ng Soo Keong
International Division　　　　　　　Edham bin Abdul Ghani *AGM, International Treasury*

Others (Senior Executives)
Corporate Services　　　　　　　　Farida Abdul Hamid *General Manager*

General-Lending (DCM, SL)
Head of Corporate Banking　　　　　Razmi bin Alias *AGM, Corporate Banking*

General - Treasury
Head of Treasury　　　　　　　　　Edham bin Abdul Ghani *AGM, Treasury*

www.euromoneydirectory.com   MALAYSIA (+60)

Syndicated Lending
Loan-Related Activities
Trade Finance   Wong Souh Chng *Trade Finance Officer*

Other (Trade Finance)
Letters of Credit & Documentary Credits   Wong Souh Chng *Trade Finance Officer*

Money Markets
Country Head   Sharifah Bintl Haji Sidek *Senior Dealer*

Money Markets - General
FX & Money Market   Mohd Yazid bin Diah *Chief Dealer*
Money Market   Norazman bin Mohamed *Dealer*
                                     Mohd Saat bin Yahya *Dealer*

Foreign Exchange
FX Traders / Sales People
FX & Money Market   Mohd Yazid bin Diah *Chief Dealer*
Spot Desk, FX   Awalluddin bin Hj Sharif *Head*
Foreign Exchange   Hasnah Binti Kader *Senior Dealer*
                                     S. Siva Shankar *Dealer*

Risk Management
Head of Risk Management   David Quah Ti Hui

Settlement / Clearing
Head of Settlement / Clearing   Abdul Razak bin Abdul Rahman *Head, Treasury Operations*

Administration
Legal / In-House Counsel
                                     Jasvinder Kaur *Head*

Public Relations
                                     Adrian Peh *Public Affairs Officer*

Other (Administration)
General Services   Mohamad Sapian bin Ayub *Senior Manager*
Human Resources   Abdullah bin Hassan *Senior Manager*

Overseas Union Bank (Malaysia) Berhad   Head Office

OUB Building, Leboh Pasar Besar, 50050 Kuala Lumpur
Tel: (3) 230 5005 **Fax:** (3) 230 9696 **Telex:** 30356 **Swift:** OUBK MY KL **Reuters:** OUBX **Cable:** OVERSUNION

Senior Executive Officers
Chairman   Hee Seng Lee ☏ **533 8758**
President   Peter Lim Huat Seah ☏ **533 8620**
Chief Executive Officer   Beng Hong Kung *Director & Chief Execurtive* ☏ **230 4182**
Chief Operating Officer   Mun Kei Cheong *Director & SVP* ☏ **230 0612**
Treasurer   Kim Huat Soh *VP & Head of Treasury* ☏ **204 1617**
Assistant Vice President   Siew Choo Lee ☏ **230 5651**

General-Lending (DCM, SL)
Head of Corporate Banking   Marina Abdul Rahman *VP & Head of Corporate Banking* ☏ **230 4980**

Debt Capital Markets / Fixed Income
Department: Treasury Department
Tel: 230 5005 **Fax:** 204 1784

Domestic Government Bonds
Head of Trading   Keam Mun Thong *Assistant Vice President* ☏ **230 5719**

Foreign Exchange
Tel: 230 5005 **Fax:** 204 1784
Head of Foreign Exchange   Poh Keong Leong *VP & Chief Dealer* ☏ **204 1615**
Corporate Sales   Chau Hing Oon *Assistant Vice President* ☏ **232 6867**

Risk Management
Tel: 232 8642 **Fax:** 230 7540 **Telex:** 30356
Head of Risk Management   Swee Yuen Chia *VP & Head* ☏ **232 7209**

Settlement / Clearing
Head of Settlement / Clearing   Ahmad Azhar HJ Aminudin *Assistant Vice President* ☏ **230 8990**

Other Departments
Private Banking   Kan Hing Chan *VP & Head of Commercial Banking* ☏ **230 4991**

Euromoney Directory 1999   **1057**

MALAYSIA (+60) www.euromoneydirectory.com

The Pacific Bank Berhad
Head Office

2nd Floor, Wisma Genting, Jalan Sultan Ismail, 50250 Kuala Lumpur
PO Box 10930, 50250 Kuala Lumpur
Tel: (3) 261 4822; (3) 262 6746 **Fax:** (3) 232 1549; (3) 230 8648 **Telex:** MA30075, 30824 PBBKL **Swift:** PABB MY KL

Senior Executive Officers
Chairman
Siew Hong Choi
Chief Executive Officer
Lai Wan *Acting Chief Executive Officer, SEVP*
Treasurer
Chau Oh Ong *Senior Vice President* ☎ **232 0470**
FVP, Group Legal Affairs
Hayati Majid

Syndicated Lending

Loan-Related Activities
Trade Finance
Jenny Hwang *Assistant Vice President*
Leasing & Asset Finance
Yoke Soon Lim *GM, PAC Lease Sdn Bhd*

Money Markets
Global Head
Alan Yee *First Vice President* ☎ **232 0470**

Foreign Exchange
Head of Foreign Exchange
Alan Yee *First Vice President* ☎ **232 0470**
Global Head
Chau Oh Ong *Senior Vice President* ☎ **232 0470**
Corporate Sales
Kelvin Low *Manager* ☎ **232 0470**
Head of Trading
Min Onn Chien *Manager* ☎ **232 0470**

Risk Management
Tel: 232 0470 **Fax:** 230 8648 **Reuters:** Dealing - PACB **Telex:** MA 20244, MA 30075

Exchange-Traded Derivatives
Global Head
Beo Lin Ng *Senior Vice President*

Settlement / Clearing
Tel: 261 4822 **Fax:** 232 1549 **Telex:** MA 30075, 30824 PBBKL
Back-Office
Theresa Siow

Asset Management

Other (Asset Management)
Asset & Liability Management
Beo Lin Ng *Senior Vice President*

Other Departments
Correspondent Banking
Ching Choon Wu *Manager*

Administration

Technology & Systems
IT Support & Development System
Yun Sin Yap

Legal / In-House Counsel
Hayati Majid *FVP, Group Legal Affairs*

Other (Administration)
Zalina Ghazali *Manager, Public Affairs*

Paribas

17th Floor, MUI Plaza, Jalan P Ramlee, 50250 Kuala Lumpur
Tel: (3) 248 8095; (3) 248 8095 **Fax:** (3) 241 3041 **Telex:** MA30693 PARIBA

Senior Executive Officers
General Manager
Yap Siew Ying

Perdana Merchant Bankers Berhad
Head Office

11th Floor, Wisma Genting, Jalan Sultan Ismail, 50250 Kuala Lumpur
PO Box 10491, 50714 Kuala Lumpur
Tel: (3) 232 4188 **Fax:** (3) 232 2964 **Telex:** MA 30694

Senior Executive Officers
Chairman
Nik Ibrahim Kamil
Chief Executive Officer
Hugh Loh Siew Hooi

1058 Euromoney Directory 1999

www.euromoneydirectory.com MALAYSIA (+60)

Permodalan Nasional Berhad　　　　　　　　　　Head Office

3rd Floor, Balai PNB, 201-A, Jalan Tun Razak, 50400 Kuala Lumpur
Tel: (3) 261 0588 **Fax:** (3) 261 8259 **Telex:** MA 21373 **Email:** pnb_corp@pnb.com.my
Website: www.pnb.com.my

Senior Executive Officers
Chairman — Seri Ahmad Sarji bin Abdul Hamid
Chief Executive Officer — Hamad Kama Piah bin Che Othman *Group Chief Executive Officer*
Financial Director — Siti Ramelah binti Yahya *GM, Finance & Investment Processing*
Group Company Secretary — Meriam binti Haji Yaacob

Others (Senior Executives)
Human Resources & Corporate Affairs — Nik Mustapha bin Nik Mohamed *General Manager*
Corporate Services — Jamiah binti Abdul Hamid *General Manager*
Unit Trust — Syed Agel bin Syed Salim *General Manager*

General-Investment
Head of Investment — Idris bin Kechot *GM, Investment Operations*
Ong Euwan George *Senior Manager, Investment*

Department: PNB Senior Managers
Chief Executive Officer — Abdul Rahim Bidin *Senior Manager I*
Financial Director — Mohm. Nizam Zainordin *Senior Manager II*

Others (Senior Executives)
Aida Daud *Senior Manager I*
Kartini Abdul Manaf *Investment Development Unit, Senior Manager II*
Kamarul Baharain Mohd. Daud *Investment Operation, Senior Manager II*
Pengurusan Pelaburan ASW 2020 Berhad — Normah Hashim *Senior Manager II*
Amanah Saham Nasional Berhad — Haji Fauzi Mustapha *Senior Manager, Operations*
PNB Property Management Sdn. Berhad — Ayub Abdul Aziz *Senior Manager I*
PNB Equity Resources Corperation Sdn. Berhad — Mior Abd. Rahmaan Mior Mohd. Khan *Senior Manager I*
Pengurusan Pelaburan ASN Berhad — Mohamed Ishak Hamidun *Senior Manager II*
Pelaburan Hartanah Nasional Berhad — Ibrahim Awang *Senior Manager II*
Amanah Saham Nasional Berhad — Md. Nor Mat Zain *Services Dept. Senior Manager II*
Tajul Razi Abdul Aziz *Marketing, Senior Manager II*
Corporate Services — Wan Roshdi Wan Musa *Senior Manager II*

Debt Capital Markets / Fixed Income
Global Head — Idris bin Kechot *AGM, Local Investment-Equity / Fixed-Income*
Ong Euwan George *Senior Manager, Investment*

Corporate Finance / M&A Advisory
Other (Corporate Finance)
PNB-NJI Holdings Sdn. Berhad — Takeshi Sugii *Senior Manager I*

Settlement / Clearing
Operations — Kamarul Baharin bin Mohd Daud *Senior Manager, Investment*
Paisol Ahmad *Senior Manager II*

Asset Management
Other (Asset Management)
Fund Management — Ong Euwan George *Senior Manager, Investment*

Administration
Business Development — Norhapizah Ahmad *Senior Manager II*

Accounts / Audit
Audit — Osman Ismail *Senior Manager II*

Other (Administration)
Human Resources — Rosna Mahmud *Senior Manager I*
Corporate Affairs — Azizah Mohamed *Senior Manager II*

Perwira Affin Merchant Bank Berhad　　　　　　Head Office

PO Box 11424, 50744 Kuala Lumpur
Tel: (3) 242 3700 **Fax:** (3) 241 7701; (3) 241 7120

Senior Executive Officers
Chairman — Tan Sri Yacob Bin Mohamed Zain
Chief Executive Officer — Hassan Hussain

Others (Senior Executives)
Arshad Bin Ayub *Director*
Abdul Jamil Bin Haji Ahmad *Director*
Ahmad Fakhrizzaki Bin Abdullah *Director*
Tunku Dato'Jaafar Laksmana Bin Tunku Nong Jiwa *Director*

MALAYSIA (+60) www.euromoneydirectory.com

Perwira Affin Merchant Bank Berhad (cont)
General-Lending (DCM, SL)
Head of Corporate Banking
Prasad Rathinasamy *Senior GM, Corporate Banking*
Jamil Haroun *AGM, Corporate Banking*
Tracy Chen Wee Keng *AGM, Corporate Banking*
Fong Chee Wai *AGM, Corporate Finance*

General - Treasury
Head of Treasury
Ali Aspar Amat Diron *Senior General Manager, Treasury*
Noraiza Bte Mohd Shariff *Senior Manager, Treasury*
Sivanesan Muthusamy *Manager, Treasury*

Debt Capital Markets / Fixed Income
Department: Financial Markets
Other
Mohamed Ayob Bin Abu Hassan *Head of Trading* ☏ 242 3700 ext 279

Corporate Finance / M&A Advisory
Head of Corporate Finance
Wan Hashimah Bte Ahmad Merican *General Manager, Corporate Finance*

Other (Corporate Finance)
Corporate Finance
Allen Cheong *Assistant General Manager*
Francine Goonting *Assistant General Manager*
Julian Cheah *Senior Manager*
Saridah Bte Ismail *Manager*
Yee Yit Yang *Manager*
Thang Siew Loong *Manager*
Joseph Soo *Assistant Manager*
Teh Sew Hong *Assistant Manager*

Settlement / Clearing
Settlement (General)
Lim Swee Kee *Assistant Manager, Processing & Settlement*

Administration
Head of Administration
Peter Chan Kok Weng *Senior Manager* ☏ 242 3700 ext 330

Pesaka Jardine Fleming Sdn Bhd — Subsidiary Company
31st Floor, Menara Keck Seng, 203 Jalan Bukit Bintang, 55100 Kuala Lumpur
Tel: (3) 241 7388 **Fax:** (3) 241 0008 **Telex:** 31094

PhileoAllied Berhad (PhileoAllied Group) — Head Office
Level 22 Menara Phileo, 189 Jalan Tun Razak, 50400 Kuala Lumpur
PO Box 1, Kuala Lumpur
Tel: (3) 266 3388; (3) 460 3388 **Fax:** (3) 266 2266; (3) 266 3500 **Email:** enquiry@phileo.com.my
General - Bank Fax: 266 3500; **General - Group Fax:** 266 2266
Website: www.phileo.com.my

Senior Executive Officers
Chairman
Md Taib Abdul Hamid
Chief Executive Officer
Kooi Ong Tong *Chief Executive Officer*
Financial Director
Seng Hin Ng *Executive Director*
Company Secretary
Thian Hwa Teh

Others (Senior Executives)
PhileoAllied Bank
Meng Seong Lean *Executive Director*
Retail Banking
May Wan Chan *General Manager*
Credit Management
Tat Meng Cheah *General Manager*
Network Operations
Sulaiman Zulkifly *General Manager*
PhileoAllied Bank
Peng Kei Leong *Chief Finance Officer*

General-Lending (DCM, SL)
Head of Corporate Banking
Mee Chen Chong *General Manager, Corporate Banking*

General - Treasury
Head of Treasury
Peggy Tan *General Manager, Treasury*

Debt Capital Markets / Fixed Income
Head of Fixed Income; Head of Fixed Income Sales
Peggy Tan *General Manager, Treasury*
Head of Fixed Income Trading
Edward Toh *Chief Dealer, Money Markets*

Government Bonds
Head of Trading
Edward Toh *Chief Dealer, Money Markets*

Eurobonds
Head of Trading
Peggy Tan *General Manager, Treasury*

MALAYSIA (+60)

Emerging Market Bonds
Head of Emerging Markets; Head of Trading — Peggy Tan *General Manager, Treasury*
Libor-Based / Floating-Rate Products
FRN Trading — Peggy Tan *General Manager, Treasury*
Fixed-Income Repo
Head of Repo; Head of Trading — Edward Toh *Chief Dealer, Money Markets*
Equity Capital Markets
Department: PhileoAllied Securities Sdn Berhad
Tel: (5) 255 1518 Fax: (5) 241 8863 Telex: MA 044151
Head of Equity Capital Markets — Kooi Ong Tong *Chief Executive Officer*
Head of Sales; Head of Trading — Andrew C S Lim *Head of Dealing*
Domestic Equities
Head of Sales; Head of Trading — Andrew C S Lim *Head of Dealing*
International Equities
Head of Sales; Head of Trading — Andrew C S Lim *Head of Dealing*
Equity Research
Head of Equity Research — Benjamin Paul
Convertibles / Equity-Linked
Head of Sales; Head of Trading — Shaun Chan *Executive Director*
Syndicated Lending
Fax: 266 3518
Head of Origination; Head of Syndication — Mee Chen Chong *General Manager, Corporate Banking*
Loan-Related Activities
Trade Finance — Boon Hoe Shue *Manager*
Money Markets
Tel: 266 3311 Fax: 266 3501 Reuters: ALLB
Head of Money Markets — Edward Toh *Chief Dealer, Money Markets*
Domestic Commercial Paper
Head of Sales — Peggy Tan *General Manager, Treasury*
Head of Trading — Edward Toh *Chief Dealer, Money Markets*
Eurocommercial Paper
Head of Trading — Peggy Tan *General Manager, Treasury*
Wholesale Deposits
Marketing — Edward Toh *Chief Dealer, Money Markets*
Foreign Exchange
Tel: 266 3311 Fax: 266 3501 Reuters: ALLB Telex: ALIED MA 28279
Head of Foreign Exchange; Head of Institutional Sales — Thim Loong Lye *Chief Dealer, Foreign Exchange*
Corporate Sales — Kevin Chin *Senior Dealer, Foreign Exchange*
Head of Trading — Thim Loong Lye *Chief Dealer, Foreign Exchange*
Risk Management
Tel: 266 3311 Fax: 266 3501 Reuters: ALLB Telex: ALIED MA 28279
Head of Risk Management — Peggy Tan *General Manager, Treasury*
Fixed Income Derivatives / Risk Management
Trading — Peggy Tan *General Manager, Treasury*
Foreign Exchange Derivatives / Risk Management
Spot / Forwards Trading — Peggy Tan *General Manager, Treasury*
OTC Equity Derivatives
Sales; Trading — Shaun Chan *Executive Director*
Exchange-Traded Derivatives
Head — Richard Kooi Keong Tong *Executive Director*
Corporate Finance / M&A Advisory
Head of Corporate Finance — Michael Ting *Head*
Settlement / Clearing
Head of Settlement / Clearing; Fixed-Income Settlement — Sook Yee Lau *Manager, Treasury Processing*
Asset Management
Head — Shaun Chan *Executive Director*
Other Departments
Correspondent Banking — Annie Peck Neo Ng
Administration
Head of Administration — Sally Wai Peng Lim *Manager, Group Administration*
Head of Marketing — Fung Chiaw Law *General Manager, Group Marketing*
Technology & Systems
— Kim Yihe Kong *General Manager, Group IT*

MALAYSIA (+60)   www.euromoneydirectory.com

PhileoAllied Berhad (PhileoAllied Group) (cont)

Legal / In-House Counsel
Philip T N Koh *Head, Group Legal*

Public Relations
Julius Evanson *Head, Group Communications*

Accounts / Audit
Seng Hin Ng *Executive Director*

Other (Administration)
Group Human Resource Development — Philip Karuppiah

Public Bank Berhad — Head Office

Menara Public Bank, 146 Jalan Ampang, 50450 Kuala Lumpur
PO Box 12542, 50947 Kuala Lumpur
Tel: (3) 263 8888; (3) 263 8899 **Fax:** (3) 263 9517 **Telex:** MA28290 **Swift:** PBBE MY KL
Cable: PBBKLCITY KUALA LUMPUR
General Telex: MA 28291

Senior Executive Officers
President & Chief Executive Officer — Teh Hong Piow
Chief Executive Officer — Tay Ah Lek *Executive Director*

Others (Senior Executives)
Property and Banking Operations — Lee Kong Lam *Senior General Manager*
Corporate Services — Patricia Teoh Kim Seing *Senior General Manager*
PB Card Services — Abu Huraira Abu Yazid *General Manager*
Information Services — Joseph Anthony Peter Heathcote *Information Services Controller*
Overseas Operations — Lai Kim Leong *General Manager*
Credit Operations — Ismail Ibrahim *General Manager*
Treasury Division — Leong Kwok Nyem *Treasurer*
Finance Division — Daniel Yeoh Beng Teong *Director, Finance Division*
Internal Audit Division — Soong Hoe Seng *Chief Internal Auditor*
Retail Credit Division — Chang Kat Kiam *Director*
Branch Administration Division — Sam Chak Ming *Director*
Corporate Planning Division — Zulkifli Mohd Ali *Director*
Public Affairs Division — Razak Dali *Director*
Corporate Banking & Trade Finance Division — Chan Chew Fung *Director*
Business Processes & Procedures Division — Chan Heng Sing *Director*
Credit Administration & Supervision Division — Eddie Chan Kok Kwai *Director*
Human Resource Division — Jenny Cheng Siew Ngoh *Director*
Secretariat Division — Chia Lee Kee *Director*
Property Division — Goh Ah Bah *Director*
Information Technology Division — Leong Kwok Hung *Director*
Computerised Banking Liaison & Support Division — Meor Danial Meor Muhamad *Director*
Economics Division — Nasaruddin Arshad *Director*
Legal Division — Satwant Kaur *Director*
Security Division — Nizam Zainal Abidin *Senior Manager*

Debt Capital Markets / Fixed Income
Department: Treasury Division
Tel: 263 8081 **Fax:** 263 9923 **Reuters:** PUBX **Telex:** MA 28290
Head of Fixed Income — Leong Kwok Nyem *Treasurer*

Government Bonds
Head of Sales — Chee Chiew Har *Manager* ☎ 263 8262
Head of Trading — Tang Hong Keat *Manager* ☎ 263 8081

Syndicated Lending
Department: Corporate Banking
Tel: 247 6261 **Fax:** 263 9916
Head of Origination; Head of Syndication — Chan Chew Fung *Director*

Money Markets
Tel: 263 8081 **Fax:** 263 9923
Head of Money Markets — Leong Kwok Nyem *Treasurer*

Domestic Commercial Paper
Head of Sales — Chee Chiew Har *Manager* ☎ 263 8262
Head of Trading — Tang Hong Keat *Manager* ☎ 263 8081

Wholesale Deposits
Marketing; Head of Sales — Chee Chiew Har *Manager* ☎ 263 8262

www.euromoneydirectory.com MALAYSIA (+60)

Foreign Exchange
Tel: 263 8081 Fax: 263 9923 Reuters: PUBX Telex: MA 28290
Head of Foreign Exchange   Leong Kwok Nyem *Treasurer*
Head of Institutional Sales   Stephanie Chan *Head* T **263 9033**
Corporate Sales   Chee Chiew Har *Manager* T **263 8262**
Head of Trading   Yee Ling Soong *Manager* T **263 8081**

FX Traders / Sales People
                                 Gan Eng Thiam *Senior Dealer* T **263 8081**
                                 Kevin Yam *Senior Dealer* T **263 8081**

Risk Management
Tel: 263 8033 Fax: 263 9919 Reuters: PUBX Telex: MA 28290
Head of Risk Management   Leong Kwok Nyem *Treasurer*

Settlement / Clearing
Tel: 263 0223 Fax: 263 9920 Telex: MA 28291
Head of Settlement / Clearing   Chew Nam Hing *Manager* T **263 0223**
Fixed-Income Settlement   Chew Nam Hing *Manager* T **263 0223**
Operations   Chew Nam Hing *Manager* T **263 0223**

Other Departments
Correspondent Banking; Cash Management   Stephanie Chan *Head* T **263 9033**

Rashid Hussain Securities

Level 9, Tower One, RHB Centre, Jalan Tun Razak, 50400 Kuala Lumpur
Tel: (3) 985 2233 Fax: (3) 985 5522 Telex: RHSSB MA 31790 Reuters: RHBS KL

Senior Executive Officers
Chairman   Abdul Rashid Hussain
Financial Director   Chong Kin Leong
Senior General Manager   Rosley Ahmad

RHB Bank Berhad   Head Office

Formerly known as: DCB Bank Berhad
Tower Two and Three RHB Centre, Jalan Tun Razak, 50400 Kuala Lumpur
Tel: (3) 987 8888 Fax: (3) 987 9000 Telex: MA 31032 DCB BANK Swift: DCBB MY KL

Senior Executive Officers
Chairman   Geh Ik Cheong T **987 4335** F **987 7155**
Chief Executive Officer   Yvonne Chia T **981 2323** F **981 7155**
Treasurer   Khor Sim Lee *General Manager, Treasury & International Banking*
                                 T **987 4178** F **987 2514**
General Manager, Internal Audit Division   Wan Heng Wah T **987 4305** F **987 4307**
Company Secretary   Ong Suan Sim T **987 4257** F **980 6507**

General-Lending (DCM, SL)
Head of Corporate Banking   Rossana Anizah Mohd Rashidi *General Manager, Corporate Banking*

Relationship Manager
Finance, HR & Services Divsion   A. Ismail *Senior General Manager* T **985 1321** F **987 4307**
Transaction Banking Divsion   Raja Shaharul Niza *Senior General Manager* T **985 3250** F **987 4307**
Channel Management Division   Brian Aw *Senior General Manager* T **981 3663** F **987 4307**
Islamic Banking   Raja Shaharul Niza *Senior General Manager* T **985 3250** F **987 4307**
Commercial Banking   Lee Chaing Hunt *General Manager* T **986 2232** F **987 4307**

Debt Capital Markets / Fixed Income
Fax: 987 4607
Head of Debt Capital Markets   Ng Eng Whye T **980 6158**

Money Markets
Fax: 987 4607
Head of Money Markets   Ng Eng Whye T **980 6158**

Foreign Exchange
Head of Foreign Exchange   Goh Beow Hock *Head of Foreign Exchange & Money Markets* T **980 6160**

Risk Management
Head of Risk Management   Christopher Chan T **980 6153**

Settlement / Clearing
Tel: 987 4216
Head of Settlement / Clearing   Looi Moon Kwan *Head of Treasury, Processing & Control* T **980 6255**

MALAYSIA (+60)   www.euromoneydirectory.com

RHB Bank Berhad (cont)

Other Departments
Correspondent Banking — Wong Sow Chee *AGM, Correspondent Banking & Fund Transfer* T 987 4180 F 987 2514
Cash Management — Victor Khor *Senior Manager*

Administration
Head of Administration — Azizah Abdul Aziz *Manager* T 980 6300 F 980 6299

Technology & Systems
Information Technology — Abdul Razak bin Mohamed Ismail *Assistant General Manager* T 260 5165

Public Relations
— Chan Wai Ying *Assistant Manager* T 980 6390 F 980 6395

Accounts / Audit
Finance & Accounts — Rupert Koh *General Manager*

Other (Administration)
Deposit Marketing — Mohd Razif Mohd Nor *Manager*

RHB Sakura Merchant Bankers Berhad — Subsidiary Company

Formerly known as: DCB Sakura Merchant Bankers Berhad
Level 9, Tower Three, RHB Centre, Jalan Tun Razak, 50400 Kuala Lumpur
Tel: (3) 987 3888 **Fax:** (3) 987 8000 **Telex:** DCNOMU MA30913 **Email:** rhbscf@tm.net.my **Reuters:** RHBS
Telerate: 50669 **Bloomberg:** RSMB MK **Cable:** DACMITSUI KUALA LUMPUR
Accounts Fax: 987 3300; **Corporate Banking Fax:** 987 3322; **Corporate Finance Fax:** 987 2233; **Privatisation Fax:** 987 3344; **Treasury Fax:** 987 4888

Senior Executive Officers
Chairman — Abdul Rashid Hussain
Managing Director — George Ratilal T 980 5005 F 987 0888
Company Secretary — Suan Sim Ong T 980 6508 F 980 6507
International Division — Axa Hamzah *Senior General Manager* T 980 5500 F 987 4888

Others (Senior Executives)
— Haruo Kawamoto *Executive Director* T 980 5002 F 987 3399
Head of Privatisation — Mohd Jamil Omar *General Manager* T 980 5200 F 987 3300
Head of Finance & Accounts — Mahathir Ismail *General Manager* T 980 5400 F 987 3300

General-Lending (DCM, SL)
Head of Corporate Banking — Theow Hiang Goh *Senior General Manager* T 982 5008 F 981 5000

General - Treasury
Head of Treasury — Axa Hamzah *Senior General Manager* T 980 5500 F 987 4888

Relationship Manager
Privatization — Azman Alias *Manager*
— Mohd Jamil Omar *General Manager* T 980 5200 F 987 3300

Debt Capital Markets / Fixed Income
Department: Treasury Capital Markets
Tel: 981 1000 **Fax:** 987 4888 **Telex:** DCSRA MA 30465
Head of Fixed Income; Head of Fixed Income Trading — Hamdan Abd Manaf *Assistant General Manager* T 980 5512 F 987 4888

Government Bonds
Head of Sales; Head of Trading — Hamdan Abd Manaf *Assistant General Manager* T 980 5512 F 987 4888

Syndicated Lending
Fax: 987 3322
Head of Origination — Peter Kia Woh Choong *General Manager* T 980 5300 F 987 3322
Head of Syndication — Kim Seng Tan *Assistant General Manager* T 980 5308 F 987 3322

Money Markets
Tel: 981 1000 **Fax:** 987 4888 **Telex:** DCSRA MA 30465
Head of Money Markets — Aza Hamzah *Senior General Manager* T 980 5500 F 987 4888

Domestic Commercial Paper
Head of Sales; Head of Trading — Hamdan Abd Manaf *Assistant General Manager* T 980 5512 F 987 4888

Wholesale Deposits
Marketing — Angie Kat Wei Ng *Manager* T 980 5507 F 987 4888

Foreign Exchange
Tel: 981 1000 **Fax:** 987 4888 **Telex:** DCSRA MA 30465
Head of Foreign Exchange — Abd Malik Mohd Idris *Manager* T 980 5509 F 987 4888

FX Traders / Sales People
— Roszali Ramlee *Senior Officer* T 980 5504 F 987 4888

www.euromoneydirectory.com							MALAYSIA (+60)

Risk Management
Tel: 981 1000 **Fax:** 987 4888 **Telex:** DCSRA MA 30465
Head of Risk Management				Patrick Kwong Hoong Ho *General Manager* 980 5502 987 4888

Fixed Income Derivatives / Risk Management
Head of Sales; Trading				Patrick Kwong Hoong Ho *General Manager* 980 5502 987 4888

Foreign Exchange Derivatives / Risk Management
Spot / Forwards Sales				Patrick Kwong Hoong Ho *General Manager* 980 5502 987 4888

Exchange-Traded Derivatives
Head						Patrick Kwong Hoong Ho *General Manager* 980 5502 987 4888

Corporate Finance / M&A Advisory
Head of Corporate Finance			Kong Han Tan *General Manager* 980 5102 987 2233

Settlement / Clearing
Fax: 987 3300 **Telex:** DCBS MA 30830
*Head of Settlement / Clearing; Fixed-Income	Kim Leng Teh *Senior Manager* 980 5403 987 3300
Settlement; Back-Office*

Administration
Head of Administration				Jamilah Abdul Sallam *Senior Manager* 980 5600

Technology & Systems
Information Technology				Catherine Lam *Manager* 980 5405 987 3300

Accounts / Audit
Finance & Accounts				Mahathir Ismail *General Manager* 980 5400 987 3300

## Sabah Development Bank Berhad						Subsidiary Company

SDB Tower, Wisma Tun Fuad Stephens, Km 2.4 Jalan Tuaran, Karamunsing, Kota Kinabalu, 88300 Sabah
PO Box 12172, 88824 Kota Kinabalu Kota Kinabalu, Sabah
Tel: (88) 232 177 **Fax:** (88) 222 852 **Telex:** MA80214 SABANK **Email:** sdbank@p.ojaring.my **Cable:** SABDEVBANK
Website: www.borneo-online.com.my/sdb

Senior Executive Officers
Chairman					Haji Hassan Ibrahim
Chief Executive Officer			Jimmy Duis *Managing Director*
General Manager				Francis Lu
Company Secretary				Awang Ismail Saimin

Others (Senior Executives)
Executvie Director				D R Fowzi Razi
						Abdul Razak Sidek *Senior Manager*
						Francis Dayah *Senior Manager*
						Mohd Akbal Nasir Ahmad *Senior Manager*
						Kuldeep K Gill *Acting Senior Manager*

General - Treasury
Head of Treasury				Chang Sui Loong *DGM, Treasury & Investment Banking*
						Yong Nget Chin *Senior Manager, Accounting & Treasury*

Syndicated Lending

Other (Trade Finance)
Loans						George Ukang *Deputy General Manager*
Corporate Loans				Robert Liau *Group Senior Manager*

## Sabah Finance Berhad								Subsidiary Company

84 Jalan Gaya, 88000 Kota Kinabalu, Sabah
PO Box 13425, 88838 Kota Kinabalu, Sabah
Tel: (88) 216 663; (88) 216 770 **Fax:** (88) 215 724; (88) 215 761

Senior Executive Officers
Chairman					Datuk Richard Thien Soong Ngui **431361**
Managing Director / General Manager		Jamalul Kiram Bin Datuk Haji Mohd Zakaria
Manager					Sharifah Seri Lailah Bte Tuanku Sh-Hamid

Others (Senior Executives)
Loans / Branch Operations			Francis Thien Kui Shim *Manager*
Finace					Judy Lee *Department Head*

General-Lending (DCM, SL)
Head of Corporate Banking			Judy Lee *Department Head*

MALAYSIA (+60)   www.euromoneydirectory.com

Sabah Finance Berhad (cont)

Syndicated Lending

Other (Trade Finance)
Loans / Branch Operations — Francis Thien Kui Shim *Manager*
New Buisness — Fui Ming Choo *Department Head*
Loans Supervision I — Jennifer Daut *Department Head*
Loans Supervision II — George Sipuji *Department Head*

Settlement / Clearing
Operations — Francis Shim Thien Kui *Manager, Operations*

Administration
Head of Administration — Sharifah Seri Lailah Bte Tuanku Sh-Hamid *Manager*

Technology & Systems
Electronic Data Processing — Margaret Thau Lam Liew *Department Head*

Accounts / Audit
Internal Audit — Stephen Kwan Ngee Sim *Manager* ☎ 435905

Other (Administration)
Human Resources — Sharifah Seri Lailah Bte Tuanku Sh-Hamid *Manager*
Administration & Training — Richard A Gontusan *Department Head*

The Sakura Bank Limited — Representative Office

Letter Box No. 25, 29th Floor, UBN Tower, 10 Jalan P Ramlee, 50250 Kuala Lumpur
Tel: (3) 206 8544 **Fax:** (3) 206 8303

Senior Executive Officers
Chief & General Representative (Malaysia) — Akira Miyama

The Sakura Bank Limited — Full Branch Office

Level 15A, (1) Main Office Tower, Financial Park Labuan, Jalan Merdeka, 87000 Labuan
Tel: (87) 419 451 **Fax:** (87) 419 455

Senior Executive Officers
Department: Kuala Lumpur Marketing Office
Letter Box No. 25, 29th Floor, UBN Tower, 10 Jalan P. Ramlee, 50250 Kuala Lumpur
Tel: +60 (3) 206 8392 **Fax:** +60 (3) 206 8395
General Manager — Motohiko Asanuma

The Sanwa Bank Limited — Representative Office

Level 16, Menara IMC, 8 Jalan Sultan Ismail, 50250 Kuala Lumpur
Tel: (3) 202 4722 **Fax:** (3) 202 4711

Senior Executive Officers
Chief Representative — Koshi Akagi

Sime Merchant Merchant Bankers Berhad — Head Office

Formerly known as: Asian International Merchant Bankers Berhad
10th Floor, Bangunan Sime Bank Annexe, Jalan Sultan Sulaiman, 50000 Kuala Lumpur
PO Box 10988, 50732 Kuala Lumpur
Tel: (3) 201 2022 **Fax:** (3) 201 7967 **Telex:** MA30205 SIMEMB

Senior Executive Officers
Acting Chief, GM — Chan Soon Lee

General-Lending (DCM, SL)
Head of Corporate Banking — Jane Ch'ng Hui Leng *Assistant General Manager* ☎ 272 1257

General - Treasury
Head of Treasury — En Dzulkifli Mohamed *Senior Manager*

Debt Capital Markets / Fixed Income
Head of Debt Capital Markets — Ng Chee Tut *Senior Manager*

Corporate Finance / M&A Advisory
Head of Corporate Finance — Yap Chee Leong *Assistant General Manager*

www.euromoneydirectory.com				MALAYSIA (+60)

Administration
Head of Administration			Hon Wei Ming *Senior Manager*
Technology & Systems
					Steven Se Tho Hong Fai *Senior Manager*
Accounts / Audit
					Connie Yap Meng Chin *Senior Manager*

## Société Générale					Representative Office
Suite 23-03, 23rd Floor, Menara Tan & Tan, 207 Jalan Tun Razak, 50400 Kuala Lumpur
PO Box 6157 Pudu, 55700 Kuala Lumpur
Tel: (3) 264 4882 **Fax:** (3) 264 0360

## Southern Bank Berhad					Head Office
20th Floor, Wisma Genting, 28 Jalan Sultan Ismail, 50250 Kuala Lumpur
Tel: (3) 263 7000 **Fax:** (3) 232 0651 **Telex:** MA31023, 30174 SOBANK **Email:** info@sbbgroup.com.my
Website: www.sbbgroup.com.my

Senior Executive Officers
Chairman					Osman S Cassim T **209 3777**
Chief Executive Officer				Teong Hean Tan *Chief Executive Director* T **209 3800**
Financial Director				Rahim Zin *General Manager, Group Finance* T **209 3160**
Company Secretary & General Counsel		Ghee Kay Tan T **209 3253**
International Division				Philip Low *Manager, International & Treasury* T **209 3991**

Others (Senior Executives)
Payment Systems					Pin Siong Wong *General Manager* T **209 3633**
Retail Banking					Tengku Zaitum *General Manager* T **200 5251**
Direct Banking					Pete Collins *Senior Manager* T **794 6897**
Enterprise Banking				Constance Goh *Manager* T **209 3338**

General-Lending (DCM, SL)
Head of Corporate Banking			Hon Thiam Chan *Senior Manager, Corporate Banking* T **209 3181**

Equity Capital Markets
Head of Equity Capital Markets

Other (Domestic Equities)
Head of Dealing					James Lau *Chief Executive Officer* T **253 2877**
						Seang Seng Lee *Dealing Director* T **253 2433** F **253 7666**

Equity Research
Analyst						How Weng Chang *Senior Analyst* T **253 2877** F **254 6103**

Syndicated Lending
Tel: 263 7000 **Fax:** 263 6310
Head of Syndication				Tak Kong Lai *Manager, National Banking Division* T **209 3286** F **263 6310**

Money Markets
Tel: 263 6300 **Fax:** 201 1364 **Reuters:** SBKL **Telex:** SOBANK MA30182
Head of Money Markets				Kwok Wah Philip Low *Manager International Banking Group (IBG)*
						T **232 2921** F **201 1364**

Wholesale Deposits
Marketing					Kam Wah Lam *Chief Dealer, Money Market - IBG(T)* T **209 3393**
						F **201 1364**

Foreign Exchange
Tel: 263 6303 **Fax:** 201 1364 **Reuters:** SBKL **Telex:** SPBANK MA 30182
Head of Foreign Exchange			Kwok Wah Philip Low *Manager International Banking Group (IBG)*
						T **232 2921** F **201 1364**
Corporate Sales					Chee Wai Lim *Chief Dealer, Forex - IBG(T)* T **209 3591** F **201 1364**

FX Traders / Sales People
Forex - IBG (T)					Min Wah Jeffery Yap *Senior Dealer*
						Cheng Sun Ross Saw *Senior Dealer*
						Ahmad Nazir Bin Che Yen *Senior Dealer*
						Siew May Khoo *Dealer*

Settlement / Clearing
Tel: 263 7000 **Fax:** 263 6311 **Telex:** SOBANK MA 30174
Head of Settlement / Clearing			Charmaine Low *Manager - IBG (Treasury Processing)* T **201 1954**
						F **263 6311**

Asset Management
Head						Pearl Wong *Head of Asset Management* T **209 3235** F **201 6881**

MALAYSIA (+60) www.euromoneydirectory.com

Southern Bank Berhad (cont)

Other Departments
Correspondent Banking

Kwok Wah Philip Low *Manager International Banking Group (IBG)*
T 232 2921 F 201 1364

Administration
Head of Administration

Bee Suan Lee *Manager* T 238 9000 F 232 9702

Technology & Systems

Tan Hui Khim *Senior Manager - Group Information Technology* T 264 9173
F 262 6928

Legal / In-House Counsel

Ghee Kay Tan *Company Secretary & General Counsel* T 209 3253
F 232 0651

Compliance

Ghee Kay Tan *Company Secretary & General Counsel* T 209 3253
Tan Ghee Kay

Accounts / Audit

Gek Sui Ng *Chief Accountant* T 200 5350 F 238 9379

The Sumitomo Bank Limited   Full Branch Office

3rd Floor, MUI Plaza, Jalan P Ramlee, 50250 Kuala Lumpur
Tel: (3) 245 7271 **Fax:** (3) 245 7289 **Cable:** SUMITBANK KUALA LUMPUR

Senior Executive Officers
General Manager   Takaya Iida

Telenas (Malaysia) Sdn Berhad   Head Office

12th Floor, Menara Boustead, Jalan Raja Chulan, 50200 Kuala Lumpur
Tel: (3) 248 9222 **Fax:** (3) 248 9019 **Telex:** TELNAS MA 30895 **Reuters:** TNAS

Senior Executive Officers
Chairman   Nasrudin Bahari
Chief Executive Officer   Wan Kamaruzaman Wan Ahmad

Money Markets

Other (Wholesale Deposits)
CDs - Origination   Wahed Sarpin
Eurocurrency Deposits - Origination Rashid Diron

Foreign Exchange
Country Head   Richard Oh *Manager*
                                     Chandra Nair *Manager*

FX Traders / Sales People
                                     Clinton Ch'ng *Dealer*
                                     Ted Lee *Dealer*
                                     Faridah *Dealer*
                                     Sonia *Dealer*
                                     Mohd Zin *Dealer*

Risk Management

Foreign Exchange Derivatives / Risk Management
Cross-Currency Swaps, Trading   Lim Soon Kim *Manager*
                                     Zainun *Manager*
                                     Mohd Noor *Dealer*
                                     Jeannie Tham *Dealer*

The Tokai Bank Limited   Branch, Marketing Office

18th Floor, Arab-Malaysian Building, Letter Box 18A, 55 Jalan Raja Chulan, 50200 Kuala Lumpur
Tel: (3) 201 5234 **Fax:** (3) 201 5239 **Telex:** MA 031782 TOKLMO

Senior Executive Officers
General Manager   Susumu Araki

www.euromoneydirectory.com MALAYSIA (+60)

The Tokai Bank Limited
Representative Office
18th Floor, Arab-Malaysian Building, Letter Box 18, 55 Jalan Raja Chulan, 50200 Kuala Lumpur
Tel: (3) 238 0933 **Fax:** (3) 230 1059 **Telex:** MA 31244

Senior Executive Officers
Chief Representative — Tsuneo Horita

The Tokai Bank Limited
Level 7D, Main Office Tower, Financial Park Labuan, Jalan Merdeka, Labuan
Tel: (87) 408 025 **Fax:** (87) 419 193

Senior Executive Officers
General Manager — Susumu Araki

United Overseas Bank (Malaysia) Bhd
Subsidiary Company
Menara UOB, Jalan Raja Laut, 50350 Kuala Lumpur
PO Box 11212, 50738 Kuala Lumpur
Tel: (3) 292 7722; (3) 292 4511 **Fax:** (3) 291 0281 **Telex:** MA 31877 UOBMMP **Swift:** UOVBMYKL
Email: headcus@uobgrp.po.my **Reuters:** UOBM **Cable:** BANKUOBM

Senior Executive Officers
Chairman — Cho-Yaw Wee T +65 533 9898 F +65 534 2334
President — Ernest Yuen-Weng Wong T +65 533 9898 F +65 534 2334
Deputy President — Ee-Cheong Wee T +65 533 9898 F +65 534 2334
Chief Executive Officer — Samuel Hon-Thang Poon *EVP, Commercial Banking* T +65 533 9898 F +65 534 2334
Francis Chin-Yong Lee *Executive Vice President & Chief Executive Officer*

Others (Senior Executives)
Commercial Banking — Kim-Choong Wong *First Vice President*
International Trade Services & Remitances — Lawrence Yeo *First Vice President* T 232 3288 F 466 3885
Branch Support — Kok-Hoi Lin *Vice President* T 202 4210 F 201 6481

General-Lending (DCM, SL)
Head of Corporate Banking — Steven Ling-Tee Ng *First Vice President*

General - Treasury
Head of Treasury — Kee-Yee Foo *First Vice President*

Money Markets
Tel: 291 8215 **Fax:** 291 1608 **Telex:** MA30265
Head of Money Markets — Wah-Kok Yee *First Vice President*

Foreign Exchange
Tel: 291 0376 **Fax:** 291 1608
Head of Foreign Exchange — Kee-Yee Foo *First Vice President*
Corporate Sales — Michael Beh *Assistant Vice President*
Head of Trading — Eric Choong *Assistant Vice President* T 291 0376

Risk Management
Fax: 291 1608
Head of Risk Management — Kok-Seong Chan *First Vice President* T 292 4529

Settlement / Clearing
Head of Settlement / Clearing — Keen-Siew Wong *Assistant Vice President* T 292 5357

Other Departments
Correspondent Banking — Kee-Yee Foo *First Vice President*

Administration

Technology & Systems
Information Technology — Sin-Kheong Ho *Senior Vice President*

Accounts / Audit
Internal Audit — Tuck-Wah Goh *Senior Vice President* T 230 3755 F 232 8795

Other (Administration)
Corporate Services — Shiau-Sun Chong *First Vice President*
Human Resources — Voon-Seng Lee *First Vice President* T 230 3744 F 230 8020

MALAYSIA (+60) www.euromoneydirectory.com

Wah Tat Bank Berhad

15 Jalan Bank, Sibu, 96000 Sarawak
PO Box 87, 96007, Sibu, 96007 Sarawak
Tel: (84) 336 733; (84) 337 922 **Fax:** (84) 332 803; (84) 311 548 **Telex:** MA72102 WAHTAT **Cable:** DRAGON
General **Telex:** 72024 WAHTAT; **Forex Tel:** 201 7798

Senior Executive Officers
Chairman Chew Peng Hong
Managing Director Chew Peng Cheng
General Manager Yii Liong Chai

General-Lending (DCM, SL)
Head of Corporate Banking Wee Geok Leng *Head of Credit*

Syndicated Lending
Global Head Chris Tan Kheng Leong *Head, Business Dev / Syndicated Lending*

Money Markets
Global Head Victor Goh Tong *Head, MM & Forex Dept*

Foreign Exchange
Global Head Victor Goh Tong *Head, MM & Forex Dept*

Settlement / Clearing
Regional Head Chieng Chai Ling *Head*

Administration
Accounts / Audit
Accounts Chieng Chai Ling *Head*

Warburg Dillon Read (Malaysia) Sdn Berhad

Level 7, Wisma Hong Leong, 18 Jalan Perak, 50450 Kuala Lumpur
Tel: (3) 261 7850 **Fax:** (3) 261 7981; (3) 263 7285

Senior Executive Officers
Country Head L Fee Yee

Equity Capital Markets
Equity Research
Country Head L Fee Yee *Country Head*

Corporate Finance / M&A Advisory
Head of Corporate Finance N Tham

MALDIVES (+960)

Maldives Monetary Authority   🏛 Central Bank

Umar shopping Arcade, 3rd Floor, Chaandhanee Magu, Male, 20-02
Tel: 323 783; 312 343 **Fax:** 323 862; 337 035 **Telex:** 66055 BOLI MF **Email:** mma@dhivehinet.net.mv

Senior Executive Officers
Governor Maumoom Abdul Gayyoom
Vice Governor Arif Hilmy ☎ **326 894**
Company Secretary Khadeeja Hassan ☎ **322 990**

Others (Senior Executives)
Head, Banking Supervision Fathmath Shafeega *Deputy Manager* ☎ **310 372**
Head, Economics & Statistics Mohamed Jaleel *Deputy General Manager* ☎ **314 940**

Foreign Exchange
Head of Foreign Exchange Khadeeja Hassan ☎ **322 990**

Settlement / Clearing
Operations Mohamed Thaufeeq *Deputy Manager* ☎ **323 896**

Administration
Head of Administration Ali Maniku *Deputy General Manager* ☎ **322 992**

Public Relations
  Neeza Imad *Public Relations Officer* ☎ **312 343**

Accounts / Audit
Head, Accountancy Aishath Zahira *Assistant Manager* ☎ **325 057**

1070 Euromoney Directory 1999

MALI (+223)

Banque Centrale des Etats de l'Afrique de l'Ouest — Central Bank
PO Box 206, Bamako
Tel: 223 756; 223 757 Fax: 224 786 Telex: 2574 BCEAO BAMAKO

Senior Executive Officers
Country Director   Idrissa Traore
Branch Director   Métanga Sanogo

MALTA (+356)

Central Bank of Malta — Central Bank
Castille Place, Valletta CMR01
Tel: 247 480 Fax: 243 051 Telex: MW 1262

Senior Executive Officers
Governor   Emanuel Ellul
General Manager   Joseph B Laspina

Others (Senior Executives)
Head, Banking Supervision   Herbert Zammit Lafezla *Deputy General Manager*
Head, International Markets   David A pulliano *Deputy General Manager*
HEad, Domestic Markets   Rene G Saliba *Deputy General Manager*

Other Departments
Economic Research   Alfred Demarco *Deputy General Manager*

Administration
Head of Administration   John Agius *Deputy General Manager*

Public Relations
                                Jospeh R Guma *Manager*

Accounts / Audit
Head, Accountancy   Godfrey huber *Financial Controller*

Bank of Valletta International Limited — Subsidiary Company
86 South Street, Valletta VLT 11
PO Box 203, Valletta CMR 01
Tel: 249 970 Fax: 222 132; 236 725 Telex: MW 1297 Swift: BOVI MT MT Email: bovi@waldonet.net.ml
Website: www.bov.com

Senior Executive Officers
Chairman   Reno Borg
General Manager   Anthony Paris ☎ **231 019**
Assistant General Manager   Mark Castillo ☎ **249 979**
Company Secretary   Victor Cardona

Others (Senior Executives)
Board of Directors   Tom Anastasi Pace
                                Frederick E Amato-Gauci
                                John Cassar White
                                Joseph V Gatt
                                Frank Xerri de Caro

General - Treasury
Head of Treasury   John Pace *Manager, Treasury* ☎ **24 9970**

Foreign Exchange
Head of Foreign Exchange   Charles Alamango ☎ **249 970**

Settlement / Clearing
Operations   Aaron Tanu *Manager* ☎ **243 162**
Back-Office   Alfred Spiteri *Head* ☎ **249 570**

MALTA (+356)   www.euromoneydirectory.com

Bank of Valletta International Limited (cont)
Other Departments
Private Banking   Victor Zammit *Manager* ☏ **249 970**

Other Departments
Banking Hall   Noel Lewis *Manager* ☏ **249 970**

Administration
Head of Marketing   Lucianne Vassallo ☏ **222 177**

Technology & Systems
    Norbert Galdes *Manager, IT* ☏ **249 970**

Accounts / Audit
    Steven Schranz *Manager, Finance* ☏ **249 970**

Bank of Valletta plc
BOV Centre, High Street, Sliema SIM 16
Tel: 333 084 **Fax:** 333 279 **Telex:** MW1459 **Swift:** VALL MT MT **Email:** helpdesk@bov.com
Website: www.bov.com

Senior Executive Officers
Chairman	Reno Borg
Director	John Falzon
Director	Mario Grima
Director	Joan M Haber
Director	Mariene Mizzi
Director	George Portanier
Director	Norman Rossignaud
Director	Francesco Vermiglio
Director	Joseph M Zrinzo
Secretary to the Board	Victor J Cardona

Others (Senior Executives)
Finance & Support Services   John White *General Manager*
Special Duties   Joseph M Formosa *General Manager*
Corporate Affairs & Strategy   Joseph V Gatt *General Manager*
Operations   Frank Xerri de Caro *General Manager*
International Division   Thomas Anastasi Pace *Deputy General Manager*
Banking Operations   Anthony Darmanin *Deputy General Manager*
Advances   Noel L Radmilli *Deputy General Manager*

First International Merchant Bank Limited   Head Office
Alternative trading name: FIMBank
7th Floor, Plaza Commercial Centre, Bisazza Street, Sliema SLM 15
Tel: 322 100; 322 101 **Fax:** 322 122; 322 123 **Telex:** 1775 FIMBNK **Swift:** FIMB MT M3
Email: fimbank@kemmunet.net.mt

Senior Executive Officers
Chairman	Najeeb H M Al Saleh
General Manager	Claude L Roy
Company Secretary	Max Ganado

General - Treasury
Head of Treasury   Martin Chetcuti

Relationship Manager
Advances Control   Rennie Azzopardi
Trader Services   Renald Theuma
Finance   Doreen Saliba
London Representative   Arun Chauhan

Settlement / Clearing
Operations   Raymond Busuttil

Administration
Head of Marketing   Josephine Grima

Technology & Systems
IT   Silvio Mifsud

1072 Euromoney Directory 1999

www.euromoneydirectory.com	MALTA (+356)

Lombard Bank Malta plc
Head Office

Formerly known as: Lombard Bank (Malta) Limited
Lombard House, 67 Republic Street, Valletta VLT 05
PO Box 584, Valletta CMR 01
Tel: 248 411; 248 412 **Fax:** 246 600; 247 442 **Telex:** 1379 MW **Swift:** LBMA MT MT **Email:** lombard@maltanet.net
Reuters: LBMA; LOMB (Dealing)

Senior Executive Officers
Chairman — Albert Muscat ☏ 240 442 ℻ 247 442
General Manager, Finance & International — Marcel Cassar ☏ 240 442 ℻ 247 442
General Manager, Credit & Operations — Graham Fairclough ☏ 240 442 ℻ 247 442

Others (Senior Executives)
Branch Operations — Paul Baldacchino *Assistant General Manager*
Head of Advances — George Gusman *Assistant General Manager*
Financial Controller — Aurelio Theuma *Assistant General Manager*

Administration
Head of Administration — Victor Rizzogiusti *Assistant General Manager*

Technology & Systems
Head of Information Technology — Eugenio Farrugia *Assistant General Manager*

Accounts / Audit
Chief Internal Auditor — Carmel Vassallo *Assistant General Manager*

Other (Administration)
Human Resources — Victor Rizzogiusti *Assistant General Manager*

Midland Bank plc
Full Branch Office

5th Floor, 114 The Strand, Gzira GZR 03
Tel: 333 993 **Fax:** 333 767

Senior Executive Officers
Chief Executive Officer — T Mahoney

Mid-Med Bank Limited

233 Republic Street, Valletta VLT 05
PO Box 428, Valletta
Tel: 245 281 **Fax:** 485 857 **Telex:** MW1215 **Swift:** MMEB MT MT

Senior Executive Officers
Chairman — Norman P Mifsud
Managing Director / General Manager — Joseph C Caruana

Türkiye Garanti Bankasi AS
Full Branch Office

Alternative trading name: Garanti Bank
11/12 St Barbara Bastion, Valletta VLT 06
Tel: 234 913 **Fax:** 234 914 **Telex:** MW TGBMLT 1024

Senior Executive Officers
Chief Executive Officer — Ahmet Fesci *Branch Manager* ☏ 234 900
Financial Director — Michael Vella *Financial Institutions* ☏ 224 588
Chief Operating Officer — Nuray Hayal *Operations Officer* ☏ 224 544
Treasurer — Erkan Ergüngör *Operations Officer* ☏ 224 570

Euromoney Directory 1999 **1073**

MAURITIUS (+230)

Bank of Mauritius
Central Bank

Sir William Newton Street, Port Louis
Tel: 208 4164 **Fax:** 208 9204 **Telex:** 4803 IW
Website: www.bankofmauritius.co.uk

Senior Executive Officers
Governor — Maraye Mitrajeet D ☎ 212 6127
Managing Director — Gujadhur Budeshwar
Secretary — Prithipaul Anil Kumar ☎ 208 6164

Others (Senior Executives)
Head, Banking Supervision — Gujadhur Baboo Rajendranatsing *Director* ☎ 208 6164
Head, Economics & Stastics — Basant Roi Rameshwurlall *Director*
Head, Public Debt; Head, Reserves Management — Googoolye Yandraduth *Director*

Foreign Exchange
Head of Foreign Exchange — Googoolye Yandraduth *Director*

Settlement / Clearing
Head of Settlement / Clearing — Googoolye Yandraduth *Director*

Administration
Technology & Systems
Information Technology — Nagawa Praveen *Director*

Cavell Securities

18 Edith Cavell Street, Port Louis
Tel: 208 0807; 208 0808 **Fax:** 208 8798 **Email:** alh@bow.intnet.mu

Senior Executive Officers
Chairman & Stock Broker — Guy Raffray
Director & Stock Broker — Antoine L Harel ☎ 208 4802
Dealer's Representative — Lucus Denis Koernig

Mauritius Commercial Bank Limited
Head Office

Sir William Newton Street, Port Louis
Tel: 202 5000 **Fax:** 208 7054 **Swift:** MCBL, MUMU **Email:** mcb@bow.internet.mu **Reuters:** MCBD

Senior Executive Officers
President — Jacques Harel
Chief Executive Officer — Pierre Guy Noel *General Manager* ☎ 202 5112
Financial Director — Jean Francois Desvaux de Marigny *Group Finance & International* ☎ 202 5161
Treasurer — Andre Wong Ting Fook *Accounting & Finance* ☎ 202 5220
Assistant General Manager — Philippe A Forget ☎ 202 5113

Equity Capital Markets
Department: MCB Stockbrokers Limited
Country Head — Thierry Sauzier *Manager* ☎ 202 5247

Syndicated Lending
Loan-Related Activities
Trade Finance — Ramapatee Gujadhur *Manager, Import Financing* ☎ 202 5377
Project Finance — Alain Law Min *Manager* ☎ 202 5198
Leasing & Asset Finance — Jocelyn Thomasse *Manager, Finlease Co. Ltd* ☎ 202 5508

Money Markets
Country Head — Robert Lesage *Chief Manager, Resource Management & Institutions* ☎ 202 5189

Foreign Exchange
Head of Foreign Exchange — Philippe Lesage *Manager, FX* ☎ 202 5166

Risk Management
Country Head — Cyril Nicole *Assistant Manager, International Division* ☎ 202 5569

Foreign Exchange Derivatives / Risk Management
Cross-Currency Swaps, Sales / Marketing — Philippe Lesage *Manager, FX* ☎ 202 5166

Corporate Finance / M&A Advisory
Head of Corporate Finance   Hassam M Vayid *Chief Manager* ☏ **202 5205**
Other Departments
Private Banking   Beatrice Espitalier Noel ☏ **202 5588**
Correspondent Banking   Cyril Provencal *Manager, International Division* ☏ **202 5455**
Administration
Technology & Systems
Information Technology   Vincent Annibal *Chief Manager* ☏ **202 5406**
Legal / In-House Counsel
Legal Department   Maurice Lesage *Manager* ☏ **202 5173**
Compliance
Inspection Department   Denys Martineau *Manager* ☏ **202 5146**
Public Relations
                              Therese Pilot *Manager* ☏ **202 5104**

State Bank of Mauritius Limited — Head Office

1 Queen Elizabeth II Avenue, Port Louis
Tel: 202 1111 Fax: 202 1234 Swift: STCB MU MU Email: sbm@sbm.internet.mu
Website: www.mauritius-island.com/sbm

Senior Executive Officers
Chairman   Regis Yat Sin
Chief Executive Officer   Muni Krishna T Reddy ☏ **202 1545**
International Division   Mary Ng Thow Hing ☏ **202 1454**

General-Lending (DCM, SL)
Head of Corporate Banking   Chaitlall Gunness *Corporate Banking* ☏ **202 1509**
                              Soopaya Parianen *Retail Banking Manager* ☏ **202 1454**

Syndicated Lending
Department: International Banking Division
Global Head   Mary Ng Thow Hing ☏ **202 1454**

Money Markets
Department: International Banking Division
Global Head   Mary Ng Thow Hing ☏ **202 1454**

Foreign Exchange
Department: International Banking Division
Global Head   Mary Ng Thow Hing ☏ **202 1454**

MEXICO (+52)

Banco de Mexico — Central Bank

Avenida 5 de Mayo 2, Centro, 06059 Mexico DF
Tel: (5) 237 2010 Fax: (5) 237 2070
Website: www.banxico.org.mx

Senior Executive Officers
Governor   Guillermo Ortiz
Sub Governor   José J Sidaoui
Sub Governor   Everardo Elizondo

Administration
Public Relations
Public Relations   Elena Horz
Press Office   Eduardo Turrent

ABN AMRO Bank NV — Representative Office

Prolongación Paseo de la reforma, no. 600-320, Col Santa Fé Penã Balnaca, Delegación Alavaro Obregón, Mexico DF
Tel: (5) 257 7800 Fax: (5) 257 7829 Telex: 1771887

Senior Executive Officers
Representative   K G A M Van Laack

MEXICO (+52)   www.euromoneydirectory.com

ACCIVAL
Subsidiary Company

Alternative trading name: Acciones y Valores de Mexico SA de CV
4th Floor, Paseo de la Reforma 398, Colonia Juárez, Delegación Cuauhtemoc, 06600 Mexico DF
Tel: (5) 326 4848; (5) 208 0011 **Fax:** (5) 208 5048 **Telex:** 1777383 ACCIME **Email:** jfuentes@banamex.com
Website: www.banamex.com

Senior Executive Officers
Chairman — Roberto Hernandez ☎ 225 3191
President — Carlos Levy ☎ 225 0610

Corporate Finance / M&A Advisory
Head of Corporate Finance — Nadia Kadise *Deputy President* ☎ 225 0661

Other Departments
Economic Research — Alfredo Loera *Deputy President* ☎ 225 0633

Administration
Head of Administration — Luis M Canal *Deputy President, Administration & Control* ☎ 225 0843
Head of Marketing — Ernesto J Fuentes *Deputy President, International Promotion* ☎ 225 0734

BANACCI
Head Office

Formerly known as: Grupo Financiero Banamex Accival SA de CV
Isabel la Católica 44, Centro Histórico, 06089 Mexico DF
Agencia de Correos 229, 06089 Mexico DF
Tel: (5) 225 5136; (5) 225 4498
Website: www.banamex.com

Senior Executive Officers
Chairman — Alfredo Harp ☎ 225 5178
President — Manuel Medina Mora ☎ 225 4526

Others (Senior Executives)
Strategic Planning — Fernando Quiroz *Deputy President* ☎ 225 5525
Financial Planning — Jorge Hierro *Deputy President* ☎ 225 6751
Risk Control — Carlos Vallebueno *Deputy President* ☎ 225 4075
Economic & Social Research — Pablo Aveleyra *Executive Vice President* ☎ 225 6616

BANAMEX
Head Office

Formerly known as: Banco Nacional de Mexico
Roberto Medellín 800, Colonia Santa Fe, 01210 Mexico DF
Agencia de Correos 229, 06089 Mexico DF
Tel: (5) 725 0000 **Fax:** (5) 720 4060 **Telex:** 1773871 **Swift:** BNMX MX MM **Reuters:** BNMX
Cable: BANAMEX MEXICO
Website: www.banamex.com

Senior Executive Officers
Chairman — Roberto Hernandez ☎ 225 3191
Treasurer; International Division — Luis Peña *Deputy President* ☎ 225 3183

Others (Senior Executives)
Deposits & Services — Enrique Zorrilla *Deputy President* ☎ 225 3185
Commercial Credits — Javier de la Calle *Deputy President* ☎ 720 7360
Retail Credits — Augusto Escalante *Deputy President* ☎ 225 3189
Credit Control — Jose Arce *Deputy President* ☎ 225 3186
Mortgage Loans — Lorenzo Peon *Deputy President* ☎ 720 7723

Banca Confia SA
Head Office

Paseo de la Reforma 450, Colonia Juárez, 06600 Mexico DF
Tel: (5) 209 3900 **Fax:** (5) 208 5821; (5) 208 5881

Senior Executive Officers
President — Alexander Mettehaimer
International Division — Juan Carlos Ansause *Director*

1076   Euromoney Directory 1999

MEXICO (+52)

Banco Atlántico (España) SA
Representative Office

Andrés Bello 10, Colonia Polanco, Edificio Fórum, 11560 Mexico DF
Tel: (5) 282 9063 Fax: (5) 282 9069

Senior Executive Officers
Representative — Francisco J Colás

Banco Exterior de España - Argentaria
Representative Office

Aristóteles 110 PH, Colonia Polanco, Moliere 80, piso 4°, 11560 Mexico DF
Tel: (5) 280 2624; (5) 280 2418 Fax: (5) 281 1804

Senior Executive Officers
Representative — Antonio Sacido Martin

Banco de Iberoamérica (Panamá) SA
Representative Office

Andrés Bello 10, Colonia Polanco, Edificio Fórum 402, 11560 Mexico DF
Tel: (5) 282 9063 Fax: (5) 282 9069 Telex: 1773346

Senior Executive Officers
Representative — Francisco Colás

Banco Inbursa
Head Office

Paseo de las Palmas, 736 Col. Lomas de Chapultec, 11000 Mexico DF
Tel: (5) 625 4900; (5) 625 4925 Fax: (5) 259 2542; (5) 596 8603 Swift: INBUMXMX
Website: www.binbursa.com.mx

Senior Executive Officers
Chairman of the Board — Eduardo Valdes Acra
Chief Executive Officer — Marco Antonio Slim Domit
Chief Operating Officer — Javier Foncerrada *Credit Manager*
Treasurer — Juan Carrizales *Local Currency Treasurer*
Jose Heredia Breton *Foreign Currencies Treasury*
Administrative Manager — Mario Bermudez

Debt Capital Markets / Fixed Income
Head of Debt Capital Markets — Eduardo Valdes

Equity Capital Markets
Head of Equity Capital Markets — Eduardo Valdes

Syndicated Lending
Loan-Related Activities
Trade Finance — Luis Frias

Other (Trade Finance)
Documentary Credit — Luis Frias

Foreign Exchange
Head of Foreign Exchange — Jose Luis Morales

Risk Management
Head of Risk Management — Javier Cervantes

Corporate Finance / M&A Advisory
Head of Corporate Finance — Jose Heredia Breton *Foreign Currencies Treasury*

Settlement / Clearing
Back-Office — Federico Vera *Back-Office*

Other Departments
Correspondent Banking — Luis Frias

Banco Inverlat SA

Boulevard Manuel Avila Camacho 1, Colonia Chapultepec Polanc, Delegacion Miguel Hidalgo, 11560 Mexico DF
Tel: (5) 229 2929 Fax: (5) 229 2491 Telex: 1775837 IVEME Swift: MBCO MX MM

Senior Executive Officers
Chairman of the Board — Xavier Autrey Maza
Vice Chairman of the Board — Carlos Muriel Vázquez

MEXICO (+52)   www.euromoneydirectory.com

Banco Inverlat SA (cont)
Senior Executive Officers (cont)
President of the Senior Management Committee — William P Sutton
President of the Senior Management Financial Director — Peter Cardinal
General Director — José I del Águila Ferrer *Assistant Managing Director*
International Division — William Sutton
Alexandro Rocha

Others (Senior Executives)
Geographic Divisions — Rómulo Figueiras González *Assistant Managing Director*
Metro Division — Pablo Aspe Poniatowski *Director*
North Division — León Teutli Ficachi *Director*
Central Division — Gonzálo Rojas Ramos *Director*

General-Lending (DCM, SL)
Head of Corporate Banking — Francisco J Gómez Fernández *Assistant Managing Director*
Randi Boris Crath

General-Investment
Head of Investment — Juan Carlos Rosales

Settlement / Clearing
Operations — Timothy Hayward *Executive Director*

Other Departments
Chief Credit Officer — Luis Ivandic Vesel *Assistant Managing Director*

Administration
Technology & Systems
Systems — Timothy Hayward *Executive Director*
Tomás G Guillén Cienfuegos *Assistant Managing Director*

Legal / In-House Counsel
Legal Department — Luis Ivandic Vesel *Assistant Managing Director*

Other (Administration)
Human Resources & Organisation — Carlos G Verduzco Igartúa *Assistant Managing Director*
Material Resources — Sergio Olivera Diaz *Assistant Managing Director*

Banco Nacional de Comercio Exterior SNC   Head Office

Alternative trading name: BANCOMEXT
Camino a Sta. Teresa 1679, Colonia Jardines del Pedregal, Delegación Alvaro Obregón, 01900 Mexico DF
Tel: (5) 327 6000; (5) 227 9007/9 **Fax:** (5) 227 9030; (5) 227 9028 **Telex:** 1764394
Website: www.mexico.businessline.gob.mx

Senior Executive Officers
Chief Executive Officer — Enrique Vilatela Riba *Director General*
Financial Director — Julio César Méndez Rubio *Deputy Director General, Finance* ☎ 327 6017
Chief Operating Officer — Gabriel Leyva Lara *Deputy Director General, Administration*
Treasurer — Luis Alfredo López Candiani *Executive Director, Financial Mgt & Treasury* ☎ 327 6155

Debt Capital Markets / Fixed Income
Global Head — Miguel Siliceo *MD, International Finance* ☎ 327 6064
Regional Head — Ruben Calderon *Senior Vice President* ☎ 327 6136
Country Head — Enrique Caamaño *VP, Money & Capital Markets* ☎ 327 6061

Domestic Government Bonds
Head of Sales — Guillermo Albo *Financial Management & Treasury* ☎ 327 6256
José Luis Patiño *Financial Management & Treasury* ☎ 327 6160
Head of Trading — Nicolas Traschikoff *Financial Management & Treasury* ☎ 327 6216

Bonds - General
Trading — José Luis Patiño *Financial Management & Treasury* ☎ 327 6160
Guillermo Albo *Financial Management & Treasury* ☎ 327 6256

Fixed-Income Repo
Head of Repo — Enrique Caamaño *VP, Money & Capital Markets* ☎ 327 6061

Syndicated Lending
Global Head — Gustavo Castillo *Investment Banking* ☎ 327 6237
Head of Origination — Luis Martinez *Investment Banking* ☎ 327 6068
Head of Syndication — Luis Acosta *Investment Banker* ☎ 327 6080

Loan-Related Activities
Structured Trade Finance — Gustavo Castillo *Investment Banking* ☎ 327 6237
Leasing & Asset Finance — Luis Martinez *Investment Banking* ☎ 327 6068
Luis Acosta *Investment Banker* ☎ 327 6080

www.euromoneydirectory.com　　　　　　　　　　　　　　　　MEXICO (+52)

Money Markets
Global Head　　　　　　　　　　　Arturo Basurto *Financial Management & Treasury* ☎ **327 6163**
Country Head　　　　　　　　　　Guillermo Albo *Financial Management & Treasury* ☎ **327 6256**
Domestic Commercial Paper
Head of Origination　　　　　　　Arturo Basurto *Financial Management & Treasury* ☎ **327 6163**
Head of Trading　　　　　　　　　Carlos Guerrero *Financial Management & Treasury* ☎ **327 6158**
Eurocommercial Paper
Head of Origination　　　　　　　Enrique Caamaño *VP, Money & Capital Markets* ☎ **327 6061**
Head of Trading　　　　　　　　　Carlos Guerrero *Financial Management & Treasury* ☎ **327 6158**
Wholesale Deposits
Marketing; Head of Sales　　　　 Arturo Basurto *Financial Management & Treasury* ☎ **327 6163**
Foreign Exchange
Head of Trading　　　　　　　　　Arturo Basurto *Financial Management & Treasury* ☎ **327 6163**
FX Traders / Sales People
Trader 1　　　　　　　　　　　　 Miguel Angel Menendez *Financial Management & Treasury* ☎ **327 6039**
Trader 2　　　　　　　　　　　　 Rose Martha Acevedo *Financial Management & Treasury* ☎ **327 6164**
Risk Management
IR Swaps Sales / Marketing　　　 Luis Alfredo López Candiani *Executive Director, Financial Mgt & Treasury*
　　　　　　　　　　　　　　　　 ☎ **327 6155**
IR Swaps Trading　　　　　　　　 Arturo Basurto *Financial Management & Treasury* ☎ **327 6163**
IR Options Sales / Marketing　　 Miguel Angel Menendez *Financial Management & Treasury* ☎ **327 6039**
Foreign Exchange Derivatives / Risk Management
Cross-Currency Swaps, Sales / Marketing　Arturo Basurto *Financial Management & Treasury* ☎ **327 6163**
Cross-Currency Swaps, Trading　　 Miguel Angel Menendez *Financial Management & Treasury* ☎ **327 6039**
Exchange-Traded Derivatives
Global Head　　　　　　　　　　　Arturo Basurto *Financial Management & Treasury* ☎ **327 6163**
Regional Head　　　　　　　　　　Miguel Angel Menendez *Financial Management & Treasury* ☎ **327 6039**
Corporate Finance / M&A Advisory
Global Head　　　　　　　　　　　Gustavo Castillo *Investment Banking* ☎ **327 6237**
Regional Head　　　　　　　　　　Luis Martinez *Investment Banking* ☎ **327 6068**
Country Head　　　　　　　　　　 Luis Acosta *Investment Banker* ☎ **327 6080**
Settlement / Clearing
Regional Head　　　　　　　　　　Fabian Carmona *Financial Management & Treasury* ☎ **327 6225**
Global Custody
Regional Head　　　　　　　　　　Carlos Guerrero *Financial Management & Treasury* ☎ **327 6158**
Administration
Public Relations
　　　　　　　　　　　　　　　　Luis Miguel Fernández *Director* ☎ **327 6215**

Banco de Oriente　　　　　　　　　　　　　　　　　　　　　　　　　　Head Office

Avenida 2 Oriente 6, 72000 Puebla
Tel: (22) 46 1099 **Fax:** (22) 46 1099 ext 2612

Bancomer SA　　　　　　　　　　　　　　　　　　　　　　　　　　　　Head Office

Avenida Universidad 1200, col. Xoco, 03339 Mexico DF
Tel: (5) 621 3434 **Telex:** 1775781 1764041 **Swift:** BCMR MX MM
Website: www.bancomer.com.mx

Senior Executive Officers
Chairman　　　　　　　　　　　　Eugenio Garza Laguera ☎ **621 3301**
Vice Chairman　　　　　　　　　　Jose Antonio Fernandez ☎ **328 6028**
Chief Executive Officer　　　　　Ricardo Guajardo ☎ **621 3301**
Financial Director　　　　　　　　Javier Fernandez *Chief Financial Officer* ☎ **621 3375**
Treasurer　　　　　　　　　　　　Jose Luis Acuna *Director* ☎ **621 9934**
Secretary　　　　　　　　　　　　Javier Lozano ☎ **621 7714**
International Division　　　　　　Rodolfo Rosado *Director* ☎ **621 6698**

Others (Senior Executives)
Specialized Banking　　　　　　　Mario Laborin *Deputy Chief Executive Officer* ☎ **621 3351**
Retail Banking　　　　　　　　　　Juan Carlos Braniff *Deputy Chief Executive Officer* ☎ **621 3319**
Consumer Banking　　　　　　　　Guillermo Acedo *Deputy Chief Executive Officer* ☎ **621 6681**
Commercial Banking　　　　　　　Victor Borras *Deputy Chief Executive Officer* ☎ **621 3381**
Institutional Banking　　　　　　　Hector Rangel *Deputy Chief Executive Officer* ☎ **621 3023**
General-Lending (DCM, SL)
Head of Corporate Banking　　　　Jose Antonio Palacios *Director* ☎ **226 9050**

MEXICO (+52) www.euromoneydirectory.com

Bancomer SA (cont)

Debt Capital Markets / Fixed Income
Head of Fixed Income Carranza Eduardo *Head of International Treasury* ☎ **621 9594**

Emerging Market Bonds
Head of Emerging Markets Cristina Perez Gil *Vice President* ☎ **621 9693**
Head of Sales Mauricio Muriel *Vice President* ☎ **621 9687**

Libor-Based / Floating-Rate Products
Asset Swaps Mauricio Llaguno *Vice President* ☎ **621 9848**

Fixed-Income Repo
Head of Repo Cristina Perez Gil *Vice President* ☎ **621 9693**

Fixed-Income Research
Head of Credit Research Gerardo Ferrando *Vice President* ☎ **621 9767**

Equity Capital Markets
Head of Equity Capital Markets Hugo Najera *Director* ☎ **621 9871**

Syndicated Lending
Head of Syndication Jesus Tueme *Director* ☎ **226 9168**

Money Markets
Head of Money Markets Antonio Lopez *Director* ☎ **621 9731**

Domestic Commercial Paper
Head of Trading Jorge Arboleya *Director* ☎ **621 9700**

Foreign Exchange
Head of Foreign Exchange Fernando Garcia *Director* ☎ **621 9909**
Head of Trading Cecilia Maquinay *Director* ☎ **621 9744**

Risk Management
Head of Risk Management Pedro Arguelles *Director* ☎ **621 9919**

Fixed Income Derivatives / Risk Management
Global Head Francisco Shelley *Director* ☎ **621 9851**

Foreign Exchange Derivatives / Risk Management
Global Head Francisco Shelley *Director* ☎ **621 9851**

OTC Equity Derivatives
Sales Francisco Shelley *Director* ☎ **621 9851**

OTC Commodity Derivatives
Head Juan Icaza *Director* ☎ **621 9738**

OTC Credit Derivatives
Head Juan Icaza *Director* ☎ **621 9738**

Exchange-Traded Derivatives
Head Juan Icaza *Director* ☎ **621 9738**

Corporate Finance / M&A Advisory
Head of Corporate Finance Gerardo Estrada *Director* ☎ **621 6909**

Settlement / Clearing
Head of Settlement / Clearing Jose Cal y Mayor *Director* ☎ **621 3464**
Back-Office Alberto Campos *Vice President* ☎ **621 5877**

Global Custody
Head of Global Custody Roberto Reyna ☎ **621 9656**

Other Departments
Chief Credit Officer Guillermo Chavez *Deputy Chief Executive Officer* ☎ **321 3333**
Private Banking Agustin De La Barra *Director* ☎ **621 9609**
Cash Management Jorge Monge *Director* ☎ **621 4688**

Administration
Head of Administration Steven Saide *Deputy Chief Executive Officer* ☎ **621 3329**

Technology & Systems
 Jorge Laborin *Deputy Chief Executive Officer* ☎ **621 5946**

Legal / In-House Counsel
 Miguel Garcia *Director* ☎ **621 3331**

Compliance
 Carlos Aguilar *Comptroller* ☎ **621 6518**

Public Relations
 Enrique Bay *Director* ☎ **621 6518**

www.euromoneydirectory.com   MEXICO (+52)

Bank of America NT & SA
Representative Office

Avenida Lázaro Cárdenas 329, Edificio Bank of America, Col, Valle Oriente, 66260 Garza Garcia, Avevo Leon
Tel: (8) 319 0479 Fax: (8) 319 0481 Email: rodrigo.jimenez@bankamerica.com
Website: www.bankamerica.com

Senior Executive Officers
Vice President   Rodrigo Jiménez

Bank Hapoalim BM
Representative Office

Homero 109, Oficina 1603, Esquina Mariano Escobedo 375, Colonia Polanco, 11560 Mexico DF
Tel: (5) 254 3841 Fax: (5) 545 5346

Senior Executive Officers
Representative   Alexandre Klein

Others (Senior Executives)
                                                Rony Schneider *Deputy Director*

Banorte

Zaragoza Sur 920, Centro, 64000 Monterrey Nuevo Leon
Tel: (8) 319 5200 Fax: (8) 319 6243 Swift: MENO MX MT
Trading Department Tel: 319 6381; 319 6382 Tel: 319 6383; 319 6384 Tel: 319 6385; 319 6386 Tel: 319 6387;
319 6388 Tel: 319 6389; 319 6390

Senior Executive Officers
Chairman   Roberto Gonzalez
Chief Executive Officer   Otonruiz Montemajor
Treasurer   Adriana Salinas Garza *Treasurer*

Debt Capital Markets / Fixed Income
Tel: 319 6381 till 90
Head of Debt Capital Markets   Adriana Salinas Garza *Treasurer*

Eurobonds
Head of Trading   Ignacio Soldaña

Money Markets
Tel: 319 6381 till 90
Head of Money Markets   Adriana Salinas Garza *Treasurer*

Money Markets - General
Trading   Ignacio Soldaña

Foreign Exchange
Tel: 319 6381 till 90
Head of Foreign Exchange   Ubaldo Cervantes *Chief Dealer, Foreign Exchange*
Spot / Forwards Trading   Mauricio Mesa *Spot & Forwards*

Banque Nationale de Paris
Representative Office

Bosque de Alisos 47B, piso 2°, Colonia Bosques de las Lomas, 05120 Mexico DF
Apartado Postal 5-521, 06500 Mexico DF
Tel: (5) 258 2900 Fax: (5) 258 2977; (5) 258 2978 Email: 103144.2770@compuserve.com

Senior Executive Officers
Representative   Etienne Vincent-Peralta ☏ **258 2992**

Banque Sudameris
Representative Office

Torre Chapultepec, Ruben Dario 281, piso 17°, Colonia Bosque de Chapultepec, Mexico DF
PO Box 11580, Mexico DF
Tel: (5) 280 3590 Fax: (5) 280 9006

Senior Executive Officers
Representative   Ettore Franceschi

MEXICO (+52) www.euromoneydirectory.com

Bolsa Mexicana de Valores SA de CV
Head Office

Avenida Paseo de la Reforma 255, Colonia Cuauhtémoc, CP 06500 Mexico DF
Tel: (5) 726 6600; (5) 726 6940 Fax: (5) 726 6805; (5) 726 6836 Email: cinforma@bmv.com.mx

Senior Executive Officers
Chairman   Manuel Robleda ☎ 726 6724
Chief Operating Officer   Gerardo Flores ☎ 726 6973

Debt Capital Markets / Fixed Income
Department: Trading Division
Head of Debt Capital Markets   Antonio Villarruel Director ☎ 726 6729

Equity Capital Markets
Department: Trading Division
Head of Equity Capital Markets   Antonio Villarruel Director ☎ 726 6729

Money Markets
Department: Trading Division
Head of Money Markets   Antonio Villarruel Director ☎ 726 6729

Corporate Finance / M&A Advisory
Department: Financial Resources Division
Head of Corporate Finance   Marco A Hernández Director ☎ 726 6736

Settlement / Clearing
Department: SD Indeval
Country Head   Héctor Pérez Galindo Director ☎ 726 6600 (ext 6670)

Global Custody
Department: SD Indeval
Head of Global Custody   Héctor Pérez Galindo Director ☎ 726 6600 (ext 6670)

Administration
Technology & Systems
    Carlos Ramírez Director

Legal / In-House Counsel
    Alma R Murillo Director

Compliance
    Alma R Murillo Director

Public Relations
    Alvaro Mancera Director ✉ amancera@bmv.com.mx

Bursamex, Casa de Bolsa SA de CV
Head Office

Blas Pascal 205, Colonia Morales Polanco, Delegación Miguel Hidalgo, 11510 Mexico DF
Tel: (5) 282 6000 Fax: (5) 282 6549

Senior Executive Officers
General Director   Miguel Cano

Others (Senior Executives)
    Humberto Gómez García
    Miguel Angel Castañeda Labra
    Pedro Dominguez Ramírez

Casa de Bolsa Arka SA de CV
Head Office

Emilio Castelar 75, Colonia Chapultepec Polanco, Delegación Miguel Hidalgo, 11560 Mexico DF
Tel: (5) 625 1500; (5) 280 1022 Fax: (5) 280 3280

Senior Executive Officers
Managing Director   Carlos Villagómez Castro
International Division   Javier López

Equity Capital Markets
Domestic Equities
Head of Trading
    Fernando Guerrero Guerrero
    Enrique Valencia Espinosa
    Pablo Javier Garza Roche
    Francisco Martínez y Zambrano

1082 Euromoney Directory 1999

The Chase Manhattan Bank — Representative Office

Prolongación Paseo de la Reforma 600, Planta Baja, 01210 Mexico DF
Tel: (5) 257 9700 Fax: (5) 257 9798 Telex: 1771370 CHBME

Senior Executive Officers
Representative — John Donnelly

Citibank Mexico SA — Subsidiary Company

Alternative trading name: Grupo Financiero Citibank

Paseo de la Reforma 390, 06695 Mexico DF
Tel: (5) 229 7100 Fax: (5) 229 7395 Reuters: CBMX
Corporate Dealers Tel: 229 7324; 229 7191

Senior Executive Officers
General Director — Julio A de Quesada

Money Markets
Country Head — Guillermo Vega 229 7151

Risk Management
Foreign Exchange Derivatives / Risk Management
Global Head — Alke Ortiz 229 7318
Vanilla FX option Sales — Gilbert Ojeda

Commerzbank AG — Representative Office

Ruben Dario 281, 1301, Colonia Bosques de Chapultepec, 11580 Mexico DF
Tel: (5) 282 2914 Fax: (5) 282 2260 Telex: 1772334 EUCOME

Senior Executive Officers
Representative — Rainer Goischke

Crédit Lyonnais — Representative Office

Monte Sinai 120, Lomas de Chapultepec, 11000 Mexico DF
Tel: (5) 202 0727 Fax: (5) 202 0966

Senior Executive Officers
Representative — Michel Anastassiades

Credit Suisse — Representative Office

345 Campos Eliseos, piso 9°, Edificio Omega, Colonia Chapultepec, Polanco, 11560 Mexico DF
Apartado Postal 105-81, 11560 Mexico DF
Tel: (5) 202 5525 Fax: (5) 202 4223

Senior Executive Officers
Representative — Hans Gysin

Deutsche Bank AG — Representative Office

Boulevard Manuel Avila Camacho 40, piso 17°, Torre Esmeralda, Colonia Lomas, Chapultepec, 11000 Mexico DF
Tel: (5) 201 8000 Fax: (5) 201 8097; (5) 201 8098

Senior Executive Officers
Representative — Dr. Giselher Foeth

Dresdner Bank Latinoamérica — Representative Office

Formerly known as: Deutsch-Südamerikanische Bank AG & Dresdner Bank AG

Bosque de Alisos 47A, piso 4°, Bosques de las Lomas, 05120 Mexico DF
Tel: (5) 258 3170 Fax: (5) 258 3199

Senior Executive Officers
Representative — Nicolas Rodolfo Bergengruen

MEXICO (+52)　　　　　　　www.euromoneydirectory.com

Generale Bank — Representative Office

Florencia 39, Despacho 601/2, Colonia Juárez, 06600 Mexico DF
Tel: (5) 533 0865 Fax: (5) 525 7295

Senior Executive Officers
Representative — Juan-Carlos Goyenechea

Groupo Financiero Serfin — Head Office

Paseo De La Reforma #500, Santa Fe, 01219 Mexico DF
Tel: (5) 257 8000 Telex: 1771891 / 1771130 Swift: SERFMXMM Email: jantonovj@dfl.telmex.net.mx Reuters: SERX
Website: www.serfin.com.mx

Senior Executive Officers
Chief Executive Officer — Adrian Sada T **399 9936**
Adolfo Lagos T **259 9036** F **257 8387**
Financial Director — Guillermo Quiroz *Chief Financial Officer*
Treasurer — Antonio Sanchez T **257 8011ext 46003**
International Division — Jose Carasso *Senior Vice President* T **257 8012**

Debt Capital Markets / Fixed Income
Head of Debt Capital Markets — Oscar Correa T **ext42857** F **ext42879**

Eurobonds
Head of Sales — Gustavo Lopez-Paniaga *Director* T **ext43099** F **ext41303**

Emerging Market Bonds
Head of Emerging Markets — Oscar Correa T **ext42857** F **ext42879**

Fixed-Income Repo
Head of Repo — Oscar Correa T **ext42857** F **ext42879**

Fixed-Income Research
Head of Fixed Income — Hector Lara T **ext40697**

Equity Capital Markets
Department: Capital Markets
Head of Equity Capital Markets — Santiago Saldivar *Senior Vice President* T **ext41600** F **ext41136**

Syndicated Lending
Head of Trading — Pedro Jorge Villareal T **ext41600** F **ext41736**

Loan-Related Activities
Trade Finance; Project Finance — Jose Carasso *Senior Vice President* T **257 8012**

Money Markets
Tel: 528 399 9906 Fax: 528 151 0914
Head of Money Markets — Lorena Caso *Senior Vice President* T **ext42882** F **ext42879**

Domestic Commercial Paper
Head of Sales — Antionio Ordaz

Foreign Exchange
Head of Foreign Exchange — Pedro Sanchez *Senior Vice President* T **ext48001**
Corporate Sales — José Bomerza

FX Traders / Sales People
FX Traders — Fernando Hurtado T **ext43001**
Raul Bonilla T **ext4305**

Risk Management
Head of Risk Management — Antonio Sanchez T **ext46003**

Other (FI Derivatives)
Demetrio Bolanos *Director* T **ext43001** F **ext43006**

Foreign Exchange Derivatives / Risk Management
Global Head — Antonio Ordaz T **ext46311** F **257 8203**

Other Currency Swap / FX Options Personnel
Demetrio Bolanos *Director* T **ext43001** F **ext43006**

OTC Equity Derivatives
Sales — Luis Perezcand *Director* T **ext46417** F **ext47479**

Settlement / Clearing
Head of Settlement / Clearing — Mario Saenz

Global Custody
Head of Global Custody — Mario Saenz

Other Departments
Chief Credit Officer — Carlos Gonzalez T **ext46120** F **ext47399**
Private Banking — Antonio Ordaz T **ext46311** F **257 8203**

www.euromoneydirectory.com MEXICO (+52)

Other Departments (cont)
Correspondent Banking
Cash Management
Administration
Head of Administration
Business Development
Legal / In-House Counsel

Accounts / Audit

Jose Carasso *Senior Vice President* [T] **257 8012**
Javier Reynoso *Senior Vice President* [T] **ext10622 / 3** [F] **10645**

Javier Lorenzo
Antonio Solano [T] **ext46014** [F] **ext47407**

Juan Carlos Garcia Cuellar *Senior Vice President* [T] **ext46882** [F] **ext40087**

Fernando Calvillo [T] **ext46078** [F] **ext47079**

Grupo Financiero Banorte
Representative Office

Formerly known as: Banco del Centro
Venustiano Carranza 235, 78000 San Luis Potosí SLP
Tel: (48) 121 316 ext 53110 **Fax:** (48) 121 316 ext 53090
Senior Executive Officers
Chairman   Roberto González Barrera

Harlow Butler Mexico SA de CV
Subsidiary Company

Plaza Inverlat, piso 12a°, Boulevard MA Camacho #1, CP-11000 Mexico DF
Tel: (5) 283 5600 **Fax:** (5) 283 5650 **Reuters:** HBMX
Currency Options **Tel:** 221 0331
Senior Executive Officers
Chief Executive Officer   Robert I McCully *New York*
General Manager & Chief Dealer   Javier Mateo [T] **283 5601**
Foreign Exchange
Head of Foreign Exchange   Javier Mateo *General Manager & Chief Dealer* [T] **283 5601**
Spot / Forwards Sales   Ma De Lourdes Alfaro *Manager, Spot* [T] **283 5619**
                                        Denis Ramos *Spot* [T] **283 5620**
Spot / Forwards Trading   Jesus Ruiz Belasco *Forwards* [T] **283 5625**
Other Departments
Other Departments
Cash   Silvia Chavez *Manager* [T] **283 5605**

HypoVereinsbank
Representative Office

Apartado Postal 10-1030, Llomas de Chapultepec, 11002 Mexico DF
Tel: (5) 520 9082 **Fax:** (5) 520 6715

Indosuez Mexico SA de CV
Subsidiary Company

Rubén Darío 281-21, 11580 Mexico DF
Tel: (5) 282 1623 **Fax:** (5) 282 1015
Senior Executive Officers
Director   Luís Gerardo Martínez
Corporate Finance / M&A Advisory
Country Head   Luís Gerardo Martínez *Director*
Other Departments
Correspondent Banking   Alfonso Del Valle *Vice President*
Administration
Head of Administration   Jorge Sandoval *Manager*

The Industrial Bank of Japan Limited
Representative Office

Edificio Omega, Campos Eliseos 345, piso 11°, Colonia Chapultepec Polanco, Deleg. Miguel Hidalgo, 11580 Mexico DF
Tel: (5) 281 5037; (5) 281 3206 **Fax:** (5) 281 5374
Senior Executive Officers
Chief Representative   Yoishi Enomoto

Euromoney Directory 1999 **1085**

MEXICO (+52)   www.euromoneydirectory.com

ING Baring México SA de CV

Casa de Bolsa, pisos 3,4 & 5°, Bosque de Alios 45-B, Bosques de las Lomas, 05120 Mexico DF
Tel: (5) 258 2000 Fax: (5) 259 2756

Senior Executive Officers
Country Manager
Director General

Carlos Muriel
R Butler

Debt Capital Markets / Fixed Income
Fixed-Income Research
Analyst

Sergio Martin *Analyst, Sovereign* 258 2147
E sergio.martin@ing-barings.com

Equity Capital Markets
Domestic Equities
Head of Origination

Carlos Muriel *Head of Equity, Broking & Trading* 258 2210
E carlos.muriel@ing-barings.com

Other (Domestic Equities)
Sales / Trading

Mario Carias-Borjas *Analyst* 258 2167
E mario.cariasborjas@ing-barings.com

International Equities
Head of Origination

Carlos Muriel *Head of Equity, Broking & Trading* 258 2210
E carlos.muriel@ing-barings.com

Other (International Equity)
Sales / Trading

Mario Carias-Borjas *Analyst* 258 2167
E mario.cariasborjas@ing-barings.com

Other (Equity Research)
Financials
Retail

Consumer Products, Construction

Felix Boni *Head of Research* 258 2142 E felix.boni@ing-barings.com
Sebastian Barry-Taylor *Analyst* 258 2167
E sebastian.barrytaylor@ing-barings.com
Ana Maria Mendez *Analyst* 258 2160
E annamaria.mendez@ing-barings.com

Other Departments
Economic Research

Sergio Martin *Senior Economist* 258 2147
E sergio.martin@ing-barings.com

Inserf SA de CV   Head Office

Paseo de la Reforma 383, piso 12°, Colonia Cuauhtemoc, 06500 Mexico DF
Tel: (5) 326 8631; (5) 326 8600 Fax: (5) 326 8642; (5) 326 8674

Senior Executive Officers
Managing Director

Raúl Solis Wolfowitz

Merrill Lynch Mexico   Full Branch Office

Paseo de las Palmas 405, piso 8°, Colonia Lomas de Chapultepec, 11000 Mexico DF
Tel: (5) 201 3200 Fax: (5) 201 3222
Website: www.ml.com

Midland Bank plc   Representative Office

Avenida Insurgentes Sur No 1605, piso 18°, Edificio Centro Insurgentes, 03900 Mexico DF
Tel: (5) 663 4060 Fax: (5) 663 5007 Telex: 1763351

Senior Executive Officers
Group Representative

L M Vitatela

Morgan Grenfell & Co Limited   Representative Office

Torre Esmeralda, piso 17°, Blvd Manuel Avila, Camacho No. 40, Col. Lomas de Chapultepec, 11000 Mexico DF
Tel: (5) 201 8000 Fax: (5) 201 8001

Senior Executive Officers
Senior Representative

Felipe de Yturve

www.euromoneydirectory.com   MEXICO (+52)

Nacional Financiera SNC
Head Office

Insurgentes sur 1971, Guadalupe Inn, 01020 Mexico DF
Tel: (5) 325 6000 **Reuters:** NFAX-Y
Website: www.nafin.gob.mx

Senior Executive Officers
Chairman	Jose Angel Gurria ☏ **228 1023**
President & Chief Executive Officer	Carlos Sales ☏ **325 6700**
Financial Director	Marcos Ramirez ☏ **325 6070**
Chief Operating Officer	Hector Montes ☏ **325 7710**
Treasurer	Marcos Ramirez ☏ **325 6070**

Debt Capital Markets / Fixed Income
Head of Debt Capital Markets — Roberto Casillas ☏ **325 7050**

Equity Capital Markets
Head of Equity Capital Markets — Hector Montes ☏ **325 7710**

Syndicated Lending

Other (Syndicated Lending)
Lending — Federico Patiño ☏ **325 6722**

Money Markets
Head of Money Markets — Sergio Milla ☏ **325 7016**

Foreign Exchange
Head of Foreign Exchange — Marco Arvizu ☏ **325 7632**

Risk Management
Head of Risk Management — Rodolfo Alcantara ☏ **325 6350**

Corporate Finance / M&A Advisory
Head of Corporate Finance — Antonio Castaño ☏ **325 7706**

Settlement / Clearing
Head of Settlement / Clearing — Javier Quiroz ☏ **325 7660**

Rabobank Nederland
Representative Office

Bosque de Alisos 47 B, piso 2°, Col Bosques de las Lomas, 05120 Mexico DF
Tel: (5) 261 0000 **Fax:** (5) 261 0061; (5) 261 0060

Senior Executive Officers
Representative — Frits P M Mönking

Republic National Bank of New York (Mexico) SA
Subsidiary Company

Campos Eliseos 1A, Chapultepec Polanco, 11560 Mexico DF
Tel: (5) 327 5100; (5) 327 4700 **Fax:** (5) 327 5114 **Swift:** BLIC MX MM
Website: www.rnb.com

Senior Executive Officers
General Manager	John Gorman ☏ **327 5102**
Deputy General Manager	Mark Aledda ☏ **327 5101**

Others (Senior Executives)
Armando Dunn ☏ **327 5144**

NM Rothschild & Sons Limited
Representative Office

Edificio Omega, Campos Eliseos 345, piso 8°, Colonia Polanco, 11550 Mexico DF
Tel: (5) 327 1450 **Fax:** (5) 327 1485 **Telex:** 1771906 NMR MME

Senior Executive Officers
Representative — Rubén Goldberg

Euromoney Directory 1999 **1087**

MEXICO (+52)   www.euromoneydirectory.com

The Sakura Bank Limited
Representative Office

Paseo de la Reforma 382-301, Colonia Juárez, 06600 Mexico DF
Tel: (5) 514 3158; (5) 525 2989 Fax: (5) 525 0699 Telex: WU1773587 MITKME

Senior Executive Officers
Chief Representative   Yoshinori Takahashi

Société Générale Mexico

Edificio Arcos Oriente 47-A, Bosques de Alisos no 47, Bosques de Las Lomas, 05120 Mexico DF
Tel: (5) 258 5800 Fax: (5) 259 7045
Website: www.socgen.com

The Sumitomo Bank Limited
Representative Office

Campos Elíseos 345, piso 11°, Colonia Chapultepec Polanco, 11560 Mexico DF
Tel: (5) 281 4662; (5) 281 4787 Fax: (5) 280 8859 Telex: 1773145 SMTBME

Senior Executive Officers
Chief Representative   Toshiro Kubota

The Tokai Bank Limited
Representative Office

Paseo de la Reforma No. 199, Despacho 503, Col. Cuauhtemoc, 06500 Mexico DF
Tel: (5) 566 2966 Fax: (5) 592 6538 Telex: 1777596 TOKBME

Senior Executive Officers
Chief Representative   Akira Tsunekawa

Valores Mexicanos Casa de Bolsa SA de CV
Head Office

Avenida Reforma No. 144-1, Colonia Juarez, 06600 Mexico DF
Tel: (5) 703 3433; (5) 566 5800 Fax: (5) 705 3067; (5) 703 3433 Email: iscab@valmex.com.mx
Website: www.valmex.com.mx

Senior Executive Officers
President   Raul Obregon ☏ 546 7214
Chief Executive Officer   Rafael MacGregor Director General
Financial Director   Juan Gonzalez Director
Chief Operating Officer   Luis Murillo Director
Treasurer   Gerardo Garcia Sub Director, Treasury
Director   Miguel Nieto

Others (Senior Executives)
Money Market   Eligio Esquivel Director, Money Markets
Analysis   Ismael Capistran Director, Analysis
Promotion   Agustin Rubio Director

Equity Capital Markets
Department: Capital Markets
Tel: 566 5800 Fax: 705 3067ext1858
Head of Equity Capital Markets   Luis Murillo Director
Head of Sales   Agustin Rubio Director
Head of Trading   Francisco Otero Director, Operations

Domestic Equities
Head of Sales   Agustin Rubio Director
Head of Trading   Francisco Otero Director, Operations

International Equities
Head of Sales   Jean Terrein Sub Director, International Operations

Equity Research
Head of Equity Research   Ismael Capistran Director, Analysis

Convertibles / Equity-Linked
Head of Sales   Agustin Rubio Director
Head of Trading   Francisco Otero Director, Operations

Syndicated Lending
Head of Origination; Head of Syndication   Omar Campusano Sub Director, Finance

Loan-Related Activities
Trade Finance   Eligio Esquivel Director, Money Markets

www.euromoneydirectory.com MOLDOVA, REPUBLIC OF (+373)

Money Markets
Head of Money Markets — Eligio Esquivel *Director, Money Markets*
Domestic Commercial Paper
Head of Trading — Jose Declementi *Sub Director*
Risk Management
Head of Risk Management — Adriana Flores *Risk Administration*
Fixed Income Derivatives / Risk Management
Trading — Eligio Esquivel *Director, Money Markets*
Other Currency Swap / FX Options Personnel
OTC Foreign Exchange Derivatives — Joaquin Alducin *Manager, Derivatives*
OTC Equity Derivatives
Trading — Joaquin Alducin *Manager, Derivatives*
Settlement / Clearing
Head of Settlement / Clearing Operations — Gerardo Garcia *Sub Director, Treasury*
Irma Hernandez *Sub Director, Control*
Asset Management
Head — Miguel Nieto *Director*
Other Departments
Cash Management — Gerardo Garcia *Sub Director, Treasury*
Administration
Head of Administration — Miguel Nieto *Director*
Business Development — Ana Escalante *Director, New Products*
Technology & Systems
System — Raul Gonzalez *Director*
Legal / In-House Counsel
Legal — Susanne Daberkow *Manager*
Compliance
Enrique Santa Anna
Accounts / Audit
Juan Gonzalez *Director*

The World Bank
Representative Office

Alternative trading name: International Bank for Reconstruction & Development
Torre Mural, Centro Insurgentes 1605, piso 24°, Colonia Sanjose, 03900 Mexico DF
Tel: (5) 480 4200 **Fax:** (5) 480 4271 **Telex:** 1772809 **Cable:** INTBAFRAD
Senior Executive Officers
Resident Representative — Olivier Lafourcade

MOLDOVA, REPUBLIC OF
(+373)

National Bank of Moldova
Central Bank

7 Renasterii Avenue, MD-2006 Chisinau
Tel: (2) 221 679; (2) 229 472 **Fax:** (2) 229 591; (2) 243 049 **Telex:** 163123 CONT **Swift:** NBMD MD 2X
Senior Executive Officers
Governor — Leonid Talmaci
Deputy Governor — Dumitru Ursu 225 052
Treasurer — Anatol Tonconog 229 788
Secretary — Pavel Uluc 227 448
Others (Senior Executives)
Chief Cashier — Elena Chipcalo 229 788
Head, Bank Licensing — Valentina Radautan 228 600
Head, Banking Supervision — Radu Musteata 221 415
Head, Economics & Statistics — Elena Dobanda 228 694
Aurel Margineanu 247 351
Head, Public Debt — Lucia Calpagiu 229 386
Head, Reserves Management — Sorin Hadarca 246 872
Foreign Exchange
Head of Foreign Exchange — Sorin Hadarca 246 872
Settlement / Clearing
Head of Settlement / Clearing — Anatolie Sitari 227 361

MOLDOVA, REPUBLIC OF (+373)   www.euromoneydirectory.com

National Bank of Moldova (cont)
Administration
Head of Administration   Nicolae Percium ☏ **228 359**

Technology & Systems
   Veaceslav Stavila ☏ **226 053**

Public Relations
   Nicolae Mosoi ☏ **226 374**

Accounts / Audit
Head, Accountancy   Olga Osadciuc ☏ **227 679**

CB Moldova-Agroindbank SA   Head Office
9 Cosmonautilor Street, MD-2006 Chisinau
Tel: (2) 222 770 Fax: (2) 232 706; (2) 242 454 Telex: 163363 AGRO MD Swift: AGRN MD 2X
Website: www.cios.ken.pubs.co.uk

Senior Executive Officers
Chairwoman   Natalia Vrabie ☏ **222 770** F **232 706**
Financial Director   Raisa Safaler *Chief Accountant* ☏ **232 569**
Treasurer   Larisa Rudeva *Deputy Chairman* ☏ **241 588**

Debt Capital Markets / Fixed Income
Department: Treasury Department
Tel: 241 588 Fax: 222 440
Global Head   Larisa Rudeva *Deputy Chairman* ☏ **241 588**

Domestic Government Bonds
Head of Sales   Marcel Teleuca *Head, Dealing* ☏ **222 440**

Equity Capital Markets
Department: Corporate Finance Division
Tel: 226 162 Fax: 226 162
Global Head   Sergiu Cebotari *Deputy Chairman* ☏ **232 716**

Domestic Equities
Head of Origination; Head of Sales; Head of Trading   Sergiu Cebotari *Deputy Chairman* ☏ **232 716**

Syndicated Lending
Department: Credit Department
Tel: 227 522 Fax: 221 104
Global Head   Sergiu Cebotari *Deputy Chairman* ☏ **232 716**
Regional Head   Tatiana Groza *Head, Credit Dept* ☏ **227 522**
Head of Credit Committee   Vrabii *Chairman of the Management Board*

Loan-Related Activities
Trade Finance   Galina Grecu *Deputy Head, Treasury Operations* ☏ **244 474**
Project Finance   Tatiana Groza *Head, Credit Dept* ☏ **227 522**

Money Markets
Department: Treasury Department
Tel: 241 588 Fax: 242 781
Global Head   Larisa Rudeva *Deputy Chairman* ☏ **241 588**

Domestic Commercial Paper
Head of Origination   Larisa Rudeva *Deputy Chairman* ☏ **241 588**

Wholesale Deposits
Marketing   Nina Djandjgava *Head, Marketing Customer Relations* ☏ **243 263**

Foreign Exchange
Department: Treasury Operations Division
Tel: 244 769 Fax: 227 440
Global Head   Dumitru Midrigan *Head of Forex* ☏ **244 769**

Risk Management
Department: Treasury Deprtment
Tel: 248 292 Fax: 244 266
Global Head   Larisa Rudeva *Deputy Chairman* ☏ **241 588**
Regional Head   Ala Tabarcea *Head, Risk Management* ☏ **248 292**

Settlement / Clearing
Department: Treasury Department
Tel: 244 471 Fax: 242 781
Regional Head   Larisa Rudeva *Deputy Chairman* ☏ **241 588**
Country Head   Galina Grecu *Deputy Head, Treasury Operations* ☏ **244 474**

www.euromoneydirectory.com   MOLDOVA, REPUBLIC OF (+373)

Global Custody
Department: Personal Marketing, Customer Relations & Branch Development
Tel: 245 072 **Fax:** 245 072
Regional Head
Country Head   Dumitru Ionascu *Deputy Chairman* ☏ **228 025**
                              Nina Djandjgava *Head, Marketing Customer Relations* ☏ **243 263**
Other Departments
Correspondent Banking   Nina Pcelintfevea *Head of Correspondent Banking* ☏ **225 379**
Administration
Head of Administration   Nicolae Dobinda *Deputy Chairman* ☏ **229 656**
Technology & Systems
                              Ion Iuras *Deputy Chairman* ☏ **229 671**
Legal / In-House Counsel
                              Xenofont Fetescu *Head of Legal Department* ☏ **241 459**
Public Relations
                              Mihai Bacical *Head of Marketing* ☏ **232 729**

European Bank for Reconstruction & Development
Full Branch Office

309, 31 August 1989 Street, MD-2012 Chisinau
Tel: (2) 249 810 **Fax:** (2) 249 363

Senior Executive Officers
Mission Advisor   Marina Cotruta
Mission Advisor   Maxim Kakareka

Joint Stock Commercial Bank "Export-Import"
Head Office

Alternative trading name: Exim Bank of Moldova
6 Stefan cel Mare Avenue, MD-2001 Chisinau
Tel: (2) 260 748; (2) 262 583 **Fax:** (2) 263 531; (2) 260 480 **Telex:** 163111 BANAN **Swift:** EXMM MD 22
Website: www.eximbank.moldova.net

Senior Executive Officers
President   Vladimir Stratulat
Financial Director   Marcel Chirca *Vice President* ☏ **541 482**
Chief Operating Officer   Veaceslav Burcouschii *Vice President* ✉ **slava@eximbank.moldova.net**

Moldindconbank SA

38 Armeneasca Street, Kishinev, MD-2012 Chisinau
Tel: (2) 225 521 **Fax:** (2) 229 382 **Telex:** 163228 INCON MD **Swift:** MOLD MD 2X

Senior Executive Officers
Chairman of the Board of Directors   Ana Gheorghil
Financial Director   Peter Berdila *Director of Accounting* ☏ **220 448**
Chief Operating Officer   Nadejda Cuharski ☏ **546 373**
Treasurer   Victor Cibotarli ☏ **222 549**
Company Secretary   Angela Poia
International Division   Octavian Turcan *Head of International Division* ☏ **221 026**

Debt Capital Markets / Fixed Income
Head of Fixed Income Sales   Ruslan Dobos *Economist* ☏ **546 388**

Government Bonds
Head of Sales   Andrei Munteanu *Economist* ☏ **546 388**

Eurobonds
Head of Sales   Anatol Mereuta *Economist*

Equity Capital Markets
Head of Equity Capital Markets   Victor Cibotarli ☏ **222 549**
Head of Sales   Renata Morari *Economist* ☏ **546 403**

Domestic Equities
Head of Sales   Ruslan Dobos *Economist* ☏ **546 388**

International Equities
Head of Sales   Victor Cibotarli ☏ **222 549**

Equity Research
Head of Equity Research   Renata Morari *Economist* ☏ **546 403**

Euromoney Directory 1999 **1091**

MOLDOVA, REPUBLIC OF (+373) www.euromoneydirectory.com

Moldindconbank SA (cont)

Equity Repo / Securities Lending
Head
Head of Prime Brokerage

Alexander Misov *Head of Credit Department* ☎ **212 106**
Ruslan Dobos *Economist* ☎ **546 388**

Syndicated Lending
Tel: 223 317
Head of Trading

Boris Urzica *Economist*

Money Markets
Tel: 540 337
Head of Money Markets

Angela Bahneanli *Economist*

Foreign Exchange
Head of Foreign Exchange

Nina Gurali ☎ **226 665**

Risk Management
Head of Risk Management

Ion Stratan ☎ **546 384**

Other Departments
Chief Credit Officer

Alexander Misov *Head of Credit Department* ☎ **212 106**

Administration
Head of Administration
Head of Marketing

Dumitrli Agapi ☎ **546 404**
Eugen Cramarenco *Head of Marketing & Communications* ☎ **546 403**

Technology & Systems

Vladimir Pupazan *Director, Technology & Infrastructure System* ☎ **546 405**

Compliance

Victor Cibotarli ☎ **222 549**

Public Relations

Eugen Cramarenco *Head of Marketing & Communications* ☎ **546 403**

Accounts / Audit

Peter Berdila *Director of Accounting* ☎ **220 448**
Sergili Brinzila ☎ **546 380**

Victoriabank

141, 31 August Street, MD-2004 Chisinau
Tel: (2) 233 065; (2) 232 319 **Fax:** (2) 233 933; (2) 233 561 **Telex:** 163188 BCAV SU **Swift:** VICB MD 2X
Email: visa@vbank.euro-apriori.com
Extra Tel: 234 203; **Fax:** 233 089

Senior Executive Officers
Chairman of the Board
Vice Chairman

Victor Turcanu
Galina Proidisvet

Syndicated Lending
Other (Syndicated Lending)
Credit Resources Coordination Unit
Hard Currency Loans
National Currency Loans

Natalya Kalasnik *Head* ☎ **232 730**
Valentina Volcinscaia *Head* ☎ **249 145**
Vlad Girbu *Head* ☎ **249 125**

Settlement / Clearing
Operations

Lidia Perjaru *Head* ☎ **232 270**
Tatiana Prodan *Head, Currency Operations*
Lilia Ciobanu *Head, Hard Currency Operations*
Jana Cucu *Head, Soft Currency Operations* ☎ **234 292**

Other Departments
Cash Management
Economic Research

Lilia Borodina *Head* ☎ **232 754**
Parascovia Grabco *Vice General Director, Credit & Economic Analysis* ☎ **232 730**
Maria Virtosu *Head, Economic Analysis* ☎ **249 125**

Administration
Head of Administration

Valeriu Zabolotnii *Vice General Director* ☎ **232 758**

Technology & Systems
Banking Technology
IT Division & Development

Igor Gaidarji *Head* ☎ **234 819**
Vitalie Tataru *Head* ☎ **232 735**

Legal / In-House Counsel
Legal

Valerian Bordeianu *Head* ☎ **234 850**

Accounts / Audit

Valentina Lebada *Chief Accountant* ☎ **232 270**
Internal Audit   Pavel Cusnir *Head*

Other (Administration)
Political, Personnel & Security Problems — Alexander Ghiduleanov *Vice General Director* ☏ **234 178**
Construction & Development — Nicolai Pavelescu *Vice General Director* ☏ **234 804**
Accounting & Reports — Maria Iova *Head* ☏ **232 270**
Securities — Igor Spoialo *Head* ☏ **233 089**
External Economic Relations — Tatiana Prodan *Head, Currency Operations*
Organisation — Feodora Virlan *Head* ☏ **233 949**

MONACO
(+377)

ABN AMRO Bank
Full Branch Office

7 Boulevard des Moulins, MC-98000, Monaco Cedex
Tel: 92 16 88 32 **Fax**: 93 50 34 77 **Telex**: 469960 AABMC
Private Banking **Fax**: 92 16 88 49

Senior Executive Officers
General Manager — C P S Noyon

Banque Edouard Constant
Representative Office

Formerly known as: Banque Scandinave en Suisse
Les Caravelles, 25 Boulevard Albert 1er, MC-98000, Monaco
Tel: 93 50 84 61 **Fax**: 93 50 03 97

Senior Executive Officers
Chief Representative — Thomas Werup

Banque Française de l'Orient
Full Branch Office

Formerly known as: Banque Libano-Française
Le Bahia, 39 Avenue Princesse Grace, MC-98000, Monaco Cedex
Tel: 97 97 75 75 **Fax**: 93 25 42 86 **Telex**: 469126 BFOMON MC

Senior Executive Officers
Manager — Mr Zovighian

Banque Sudameris

2 Boulevard des Moulins, MC 98000, Monte Carlo
Tel: 92 16 51 00 **Fax**: 92 16 51 13

Senior Executive Officers
Assistant Director — Alberto Zago

CCF (Monaco) SAM
Full Branch Office

2 bis Boulevard des Moulins, MC-98000, Monaco
Tel: 93 30 97 00 **Fax**: 93 25 67 69 **Telex**: 479428 MC

Senior Executive Officers
General Manager — Jean-François Cullieyrier

Citibank NA
Full Branch Office

Les Terrasses, 2 Avenue de Monte Carlo, MC-98000, Monaco
PO Box 165, MC-98000, Monte Carlo
Tel: 93 15 75 00 **Fax**: 93 15 75 99

Debt Capital Markets / Fixed Income
Global Head — Guy-Michel Crozet

Administration
Compliance — Rose Roumian

Euromoney Directory 1999 **1093**

MONACO (+377)　　　www.euromoneydirectory.com

Citibank NA (cont)
Public Relations
　　　　　　　　　　Edouard Baudoin

Compagnie Monégasque de Banque SAM — Head Office

23 Avenue de la Costa, MC-98000, Monaco
PO Box 140, MC-98000, Monte Carlo
Tel: 93 15 77 77 **Fax:** 93 25 08 69 **Telex:** 479269 MC **Swift:** CMB MC MX **Email:** cmb@imcn.mc

Senior Executive Officers
Chairman — Enrico Braggiotti
Vice Chairman — Raoul Biancheri
Vice Chairman — Luigi Fausti
Managing Director — Francesco Morabito
General Manager — Etienne Franzi
Deputy General Manager — Giorgio Muratorio

Crédit du Nord — Full Branch Office

27 Avenue de la Costa, MC-98000, Monaco Cedex
PO Box 57, MC-98001, Monte Carlo Cedex
Tel: 92 16 59 60 **Fax:** 93 50 55 89

Senior Executive Officers
General Manager — René Nave

Crédit Foncier de Monaco — Head Office

11 Boulevard Albert 1er, MC-98000, Monaco
PO Box 499, MC-98012, Monaco
Tel: 93 10 20 00; 93 10 20 52 **Fax:** 93 10 23 50 **Telex:** 469738 **Swift:** CFMO MC MX **Reuters:** CFMM

Senior Executive Officers
President — Bernard Egloff ☏ 93 10 20 20
Chief Operating Officer — Jean Paul Piotrowski *Director* ☏ 93 10 21 65
Treasurer — Francis Herbin *Treasurer* ☏ 93 10 22 53
General Director, Administration — Alain Massiera ☏ 93 10 20 22
General Secretary — Michel Le Cornet ☏ 93 10 24 01

Others (Senior Executives)
　　　　　　　　　　Dominique Henry *Director* ☏ 93 10 20 27

Debt Capital Markets / Fixed Income
Department: Direction des Investissements
Tel: 93 10 23 23 **Fax:** 93 10 23 60
Head of Fixed Income Sales — Gilbert Buzzi *Director of Investments*

Equity Capital Markets
Department: Direction des Investissements
Tel: 93 10 23 23 **Fax:** 93 10 23 60
Head of Sales — Gilbert Buzzi *Director of Investments*

Money Markets
Tel: 93 10 22 33 **Fax:** 93 10 23 56
Head of Money Markets — Francis Herbin *Treasurer* ☏ 93 10 22 53

Foreign Exchange
Tel: 93 10 22 33
FX Traders / Sales People
　　　　　　　　　　Ruffo Paolini *Trader*

Risk Management
Tel: 93 10 24 03 **Fax:** 93 10 24 41
Head of Risk Management — Marie-Odele Joris ☏ 93 10 24 03

Settlement / Clearing
Head of Settlement / Clearing Operations — Bernard Bolzoni ☏ 93 10 21 11
　　　　　　　　　　Bruno Renzini ☏ 93 10 21 24

Other Departments
Correspondent Banking — Francis Herbin *Treasurer* ☏ 93 10 22 53

Administration
Technology & Systems
    Charles Mula ☎ 93 10 24 71

Legal / In-House Counsel
    Marie-Odile Joris ☎ 93 10 24 03

Compliance
    Michel Le Cornet *General Secretary* ☎ 93 10 24 01

Credit Suisse (France) SA
Subsidiary Company

27 Avenue de la Costa, MC-98003, Monaco Cedex
PO Box 155, Monte Carlo
Tel: 93 15 27 27 **Fax:** 93 25 27 99

Senior Executive Officers
General Manager   Marius Wetzel

ING Societe de Gestion

1 Avenue des Citronniers, Monte Carlo, MC-98000, Monaco
Tel: 93 10 50 00 **Fax:** 93 10 50 05

Senior Executive Officers
Senior Manager   Varga Bartalini

KB Luxembourg (Monaco)
Subsidiary Company

8 Avenue de Grande Bretagne, MC-98000, Monaco
Tel: 92 16 55 55 **Fax:** 92 16 55 99 **Telex:** 489 859 **Swift:** KBLX MC MC

Senior Executive Officers
Managing Director   Paul-Marie Jacques ☎ 92 16 55 79
General Manager   Georges Damiano ☎ 92 16 55 52
Secretary General   Jacqueline Bassignana ☎ 92 16 55 68

Relationship Manager
Private Banking   Gabriele Marotta *Head* ☎ 92 16 55 55

Administration
Head of Administration   Fabien Lafitte *Head* ☎ 92 16 55 59

Lloyds Bank plc
Full Branch Office

11, Boulevard des Moulins, MC-98000, Monaco
PO Box 239, MC-98000, Monaco
Tel: 92 16 58 58 **Fax:** 92 16 58 69 **Swift:** LOYD MC X

Senior Executive Officers
Senior Manager   Martin Peake

Risk Management
Head of Risk Management   André Caspar *Head of Department* ☎ 92 16 52 84 📠 92 16 58 65

Other Departments
Cash Management   Marc Jurlina *Treasurer* ☎ 92 16 58 54

Administration
Head of Administration   Guy Stanoyevitch *Administrative Manager* ☎ 92 16 58 43 📠 92 16 58 69

Merrill Lynch SAM
Representative Office

Le Prince de Galles, 3/5 Avenue des Citronniers, Monte Carlo, MC-98003, Monaco Cedex
PO Box 163, Monte Carlo
Tel: 92 16 67 67 **Fax:** 93 25 53 82 **Telex:** 469553
Website: www.ml.com

MONACO (+377)   www.euromoneydirectory.com

Société Générale Bank & Trust (Monaco)
Le Régina, 13/15 Boulevard des Moulins, MC-98007, Monte Carlo Cedex
Tel: 93 15 57 00 **Fax:** 93 15 57 70 **Telex:** 469919 MC **Swift:** SGBT MC MC
Senior Executive Officers
Chairman   Henri Lassalle
Chief Executive Officer   Joseph-Alain Sauzier

MONGOLIA
(+976)

Bank of Mongolia   🏛 Central Bank
Alternative trading name: The Central Bank of Mongolia
Commerce Street 6, Ulan Bator 11
Tel: (1) 311 019; (1) 372 858 **Fax:** (1) 311 471 **Telex:** 79333 BOMCB MH **Swift:** BOMU MN UB
Senior Executive Officers
Governor   Jigjid Unenbat ☎ **322 166**
Deputy Governor   Magvan Bold ☎ **327 090**
Treasurer   Gaasuren Tumurbaatar *Head of Treasury* ☎ **327 087**
Secretary   Munkhtuya ☎ **322 166**
Others (Senior Executives)
Chief Cashier   T Khaltar *Chief*
Head, Bank Licensing; Head, Banking   Byadran Ukhagvasuren *Director* ☎ **328 482**
Supervision
Head, Economics & Statistics   Luvsandagua Chimgee *Director* ☎ **329 164**
Head, Monetary Policy   Dagvadorj Boldbaatar ☎ **323 391**
Head, Reserves Management   Yansanjay Ochirsukh *Director* ☎ **327 088**
Foreign Exchange
Head of Foreign Exchange   Yansanjay Ochirsukh *Director* ☎ **327 088**
Settlement / Clearing
Head of Settlement / Clearing   Ganzerig Togtokhbaatar *Acting Director* ☎ **324 340**
Administration
Head of Administration   Dashpuntsag Ganbold ☎ **320 847**
Legal / In-House Counsel
Head, Legal Division   Gombo Erdenebayar ☎ **322 847**
Accounts / Audit
Head, Accountancy   Ganzorig Togtokhbaatar *Acting Director* ☎ **324 340**
Head, Internal Audit   Genen Tomorkhuyag ☎ **322 850**

MOROCCO
(+212)

Bank Al-Maghrib   🏛 Central Bank
Alternative trading name: Banque du Maroc
277 Avenue Mohammed V, Rabat
Tel: (7) 702 626 **Fax:** (7) 706 677 **Telex:** 31612 **Swift:** BKAM MA MR **Reuters:** BKDH
Senior Executive Officers
Governor   Mohamed Seqat
General Manager   Abdelhamid Benamour
Others (Senior Executives)
Head, Banking Supervision   Ahmed Essaid El Feydi *Central Director*
Head, Economics & Statistics   Roukia Boutales *Central Director*
Head, Reserves Management   Abdelmalek Ouenniche *Central Director*
Foreign Exchange
Head of Foreign Exchange   Idriss Bennani Smires *Assistant Director*
Administration
Head of Administration   Abdelouahab Kissi *Central Director*
Technology & Systems
                                        Mohamed Lafqie *Director*

1096 Euromoney Directory 1999

www.euromoneydirectory.com MOROCCO (+212)

Accounts / Audit
Head, Accountancy   Brahim Benmouama *Deputy Director*

Banque Commerciale du Maroc
Head Office

2 Boulevard Moulay Youssef, Casablanca 20000
Tel: (2) 224 169; (2) 298 888 **Fax:** (2) 294 125; (2) 223 825 **Telex:** 22863; 21014 **Swift:** BCMA MAMC
Email: cap@attijari.com **Reuters:** BCMD
General Tel: 476 439; 275 774; **International Email:** dgai@attijari.com; **Communications Email:** com@attijari.com
Website: www.attijari.com

Senior Executive Officers
Chairman & Chief Executive Officer   Abdelaziz Alami E **275 774**
Chief Executive Officer   Ali Iben Mansour *Director & General Manager* E **202 476**
                                         Omar Benider *Director & General Manager* E **202 476**
Financial Director   Mohamed Moussatef *Comptroller General* E **268 931**
Managing Director   Mohamed Salmi E **293 465**
Company Secretary   Wafaa Guessous E **294 125**
International Division   Mohamed Cherkani *Assistant General Manager* E **294 123**

General-Lending (DCM, SL)
Head of Corporate Banking   Mohamed Kettani *Assistant General Manager* E **202 476**

General-Investment
Head of Investment   Mohamed Kettani *Assistant General Manager* E **202 476**

Debt Capital Markets / Fixed Income
Head of Fixed Income   Mohamed Ghallab *Auditor General* E **200 094**

Fixed-Income Repo
Head of Repo   Boubker Jai *Assistant General Manager* E **203 379**

Equity Capital Markets
Head of Equity Capital Markets   Abdesslam Ouali *Assistant General Manager* E **274 926**

Equity Repo / Securities Lending
Head   Hamza Tahiri *Executive Director* E **491 488** E cap@attijari.com

Syndicated Lending
Head of Origination   Abdelkrim Chlyah *Assistant General Manager*
                                         Mohamed Lasry *Assistant General Manager*

Corporate Finance / M&A Advisory
Head of Corporate Finance   Mohamed Kettani *Assistant General Manager* E **202 476**

Global Custody
Regional Head   Tahiri Hamza
                                         Reda Fathmi Mehdi

Other Departments
Private Banking   Rachid Tlencani T **476 432**

Banque Nationale pour le Développement Economique - BNDE
Head Office

12 Place des Alaouites, PO Box 407, Rabat 10000
Tel: (7) 706 040; (7) 708 844 **Fax:** (7) 703 706 **Telex:** BDMAROC 31942M, 32758M **Swift:** BDEC MA MR
Corporate Dealers Fax: 229 7324/7191

Senior Executive Officers
Chairman & President   Farid Dellero
Secretary General   A Berkia
Assistant   F Jazouli

General-Lending (DCM, SL)
Head of Corporate Banking   R Frej *Deputy Director, Finance*
                                         A Chafik *Assistant, Finance*
                                         M Amraoui *Managing Director, Investment Banking*

General-Investment
Head of Investment   M Aissaoui *Assistant MD, Investments Financing Directorate*
                                         M Hafsi *Assistant, Investments Financing Directorate*

General - Treasury
Head of Treasury   L Mellouki

Euromoney Directory 1999 **1097**

MOROCCO (+212) www.euromoneydirectory.com

British Arab Commercial Bank Limited
Representative Office

Espace Porte D'Anfa, Immeuble A, 1st Etage, Angle Rua Bab Mansour et Blvd My. Rachid, Casablanca
Tel: (2) 950 002 **Fax:** (2) 950 035

Senior Executive Officers
General Manager   Farid Arfaoui

Citibank Maghreb
Full Branch Office

52 Avenue Hassan II, Casablanca
PO Box 13 362, Casablanca
Tel: (2) 224 168 **Fax:** (2) 205 724 **Reuters:** CBNX

Senior Executive Officers
Chief Executive Officer   Eric Stoclet
Treasurer   Chakib Erquizi ☎ **203 2046**
General - Treasury
Head of Treasury   Amine Berraoui *Head of Desk*

Crédit du Maroc
Head Office

48/58 Boulevard Mohammed V, Casablanca 20000
PO Box 13579, Casablanca 20000
Tel: (2) 477 866; (2) 477 867 **Fax:** (2) 440 311; (2) 310 267 **Telex:** 46677 **Swift:** CDMA MA MC
Email: jlemridi@atlasnet.net.ma **Reuters:** CDMB
Website: www.creditdumaroc.co.ma

Senior Executive Officers
Chairman & Chief Executive   Jawad Ben Brahim ☎ **477 000** ℻ **277 127**
Foreign Exchange
Head of Foreign Exchange   Abdulmajid Berrada ☎ **477 070** ℻ **476 247**
Other Departments
Correspondent Banking   Mohammadine Menjra *Head, Correspondent Banking* ☎ **440 309** ℻ **440 311**

Crédit Populaire du Maroc
Head Office

Alternative trading name: Banque Centrale Populaire & CPM
101 Boulevard Zerktouni, Casablanca 21100
Tel: (2) 202 533; (2) 224 111 **Fax:** (2) 201 931 **Telex:** BANCEPO 21723, 23078 **Swift:** BCPO MA MC
Website: www.morocco.web.com/gdp

Senior Executive Officers
President & General Director   Abdallah El Naaroufi
Chief Executive Officer   Fayçal Zemmama *Director General*
Treasurer   Chafika Raghib *Capital Markets*
International Division   Ahmed Slamyi
General-Lending (DCM, SL)
Head of Corporate Banking   Abdellatif El Morjani *Head, Capital Markets Division*
General-Investment
Head of Investment   Abdeslam Tahiri
Debt Capital Markets / Fixed Income
Department: Direction Centrale des Finances
Tel: 202 533 **Fax:** 203 263
Global Head   Mohamed Chamcham *Chargé de Mission* ☎ **222 589**
Regional Head   Abdellatif El Morjani *Head, Capital Markets Division*
Domestic Government Bonds
Head of Sales   Abdellatif El Morjani *Head, Capital Markets Division*
Libor-Based / Floating-Rate Products
FRN Origination   Mohamed Chamcham *Chargé de Mission* ☎ **222 589**
FRN Sales   Raghib Chafika *Treasurer* ☎ **222 589**
Equity Capital Markets
Department: Direction Centrale des Finances
Tel: 202 533 **Fax:** 203 263
Global Head   Abdellatif El Morjani *Head, Capital Markets Division*

www.euromoneydirectory.com　　　　　　　　　MOROCCO (+212)

Domestic Equities
Head of Origination　　　　　　　　　　Nouredine Baroudi ☎ **220 151**

Syndicated Lending
Head of Syndication　　　　　　　　　　Abdelhafid Tazi

Money Markets
Head of Money Markets　　　　　　　　　Abdellatif El Morjani *Head, Capital Markets Division*

Settlement / Clearing
Department: Direction Centrale des Finances
Tel: 202 533 **Fax:** 203 263
Head of Settlement / Clearing　　　　　　Nouredine Baroudi ☎ **220 151**

Global Custody
Department: Direction Centrale des Finance
Head of Global Custody　　　　　　　　　Nouredine Baroudi ☎ **220 151**

Administration
Business Development; Head of Marketing　Brahim Maghrabi

Technology & Systems
　　　　　　　　　　　　　　　　　　　Abdelfattah Belemlih *Directeur Central* ☎ **310 363**

Legal / In-House Counsel
　　　　　　　　　　　　　　　　　　　Mustapha Khadir *Directeur*

Compliance
　　　　　　　　　　　　　　　　　　　Mustapha Khadir *Directeur*

Public Relations
　　　　　　　　　　　　　　　　　　　Arbi Ouazzani

Accounts / Audit
Accounts　　　　　　　　　　　　　　　Abdellah Alaoui

International Finance Corporation　　　　　　　　　Representative Office
8 Rue Kamal Mohamed, Casablanca
Tel: (2) 484 686/7; (2) 312 278 **Fax:** (2) 484 690

Senior Executive Officers
Regional Representative, North Africa　　Andre Leude

Wafabank　　　　　　　　　　　　　　　　　　　　　　Head Office
163 Avenue Hassan II, Casablanca
Tel: (2) 224 105; (2) 200 200 **Fax:** (2) 266 202; (2) 470 398 **Telex:** 21051 **Swift:** WAFA MA MC
Email: wafadcie@mail.cbi.net.ma

Senior Executive Officers
Chairman	Abdelhak Bennani
Chief Executive Officer	Abdellatif Ghazouani
	Hassan Elkouhene
Financial Director	Mohamed Abbad
Chief Operating Officer	Labbès Mtioui
Treasurer	Mohamed Agouzoul
Managing Director / General Manager	Labbès Mtioui
International Division	Ahmed Layine

Debt Capital Markets / Fixed Income
Head of Fixed Income　　　　　　　　　Mohamed Agouzoul

Equity Capital Markets
Head of Equity Capital Markets　　　　　Abdelhak Bennani

Syndicated Lending
Loan-Related Activities
Trade Finance　　　　　　　　　　　　Azeddine El Hilali
Project Finance　　　　　　　　　　　Mohamed Mikou

Money Markets
Head of Money Markets　　　　　　　　Ali Bennani

Foreign Exchange
Head of Foreign Exchange　　　　　　　Ali Bennani

MOZAMBIQUE
(+258)

HSBC Equator Bank plc
Representative Office

256 Rua da Impresna, 5° andar, Suite 522/523, Predio 33, Maputo
Tel: (1) 431 919 **Fax:** (1) 431 918

Senior Executive Officers
Vice President   Lisa M Audet

MYANMAR
(+95)

Central Bank of Myanmar
Central Bank

Formerly known as: Union of Myanmar Bank

26(A) Settmu Road, Yankin Township, Yangon
PO Box 184, Yangon
Tel: (1) 543 751; (1) 543 757 **Fax:** (1) 543 677; (1) 543 743 **Telex:** 21211 CENTBK BM

Senior Executive Officers
Governor	U Kyaw Kyaw Maung **543 657**
Deputy Governor	U Than Lwin **543 668**
Chief Executive Officer	U Tin Maung Gyi *Director* **543 751**

Others (Senior Executives)
Head, Bank Licensing; Head, Banking Supervision   U Nyi Aung *Director* **543 753**
Head, Currency   U Than Tun **543 752**

Foreign Exchange
Head of Foreign Exchange   U Soe Tin *Deputy Director* **286 269**

Other Departments
Economic Research   Ommar Sein *Deputy Director* **543 761**

Administration
Head of Administration   U Tin Maung Gyi *Director* **543 751**

Accounts / Audit
Head, Accountancy   Daw Mi Mi *Deputy Director* **543 757**

Other (Administration)
Head, Security   U Win Naing *Director* **543 756**

NAMIBIA
(+264)

Bank of Namibia
Central Bank

PO Box 2882, Windhoek
Tel: (61) 226 401; (61) 227 673 **Fax:** (61) 227 649; (61) 239 760 **Telex:** 0908710 **Swift:** CBKN NA NX
Email: capital5@iwwn.com.na

Senior Executive Officers
Governor	Tom Alweendo
Deputy Governor	Lazarus Ipangelwa
Financial Director	Ubaidullah Davids *Senior Manager, Operations*

Bank Windhoek Limited
Head Office

PO Box 15, Windhoek
Tel: (61) 299 1122 **Fax:** (61) 299 1283 **Telex:** 908-660 WK **Swift:** BWLINANX **Reuters:** BWNA

Senior Executive Officers
Chairman	J C Brandt **299 1122**
Financial Director	H W Lens **299 1531**

www.euromoneydirectory.com   NAMIBIA (+264)

Senior Executive Officers (cont)
Treasurer   T B Liebenberg *Treasurer* ☎ **299 1248**
Managing Director   J L J Van Vuuren ☎ **299 1122**

Debt Capital Markets / Fixed Income
Domestic Government Bonds
Head of Trading   T B Liebenberg *Treasurer* ☎ **299 1248**

Money Markets
Tel: 299 1531 Fax: 299 1283
Head of Money Markets   T B Liebenberg *Treasurer* ☎ **299 1248**

Wholesale Deposits
Head of Sales   T B Liebenberg *Treasurer* ☎ **299 1248**

Foreign Exchange
Tel: 299 1248 Fax: 299 1283
Head of Trading   T B Liebenberg *Treasurer* ☎ **299 1248**

Settlement / Clearing
Department: International Business Department
Head of Settlement / Clearing   S V D Westhuizen *Manager* ☎ **299 1260**

The Commercial Bank of Namibia Limited   Head Office

12-20 Bülow Street, PO Box 1, Windhoek
Tel: (61) 295 9111 **Fax:** (61) 224 417 **Telex:** 50908 898 **Email:** cbon@iwwn.com.na

Senior Executive Officers
Managing Director   Udo H Reinhold
Deputy Managing Director   Stephanus C du Plessis

Others (Senior Executives)
Financial Planning & Controlling   Johannes C Jurgens

General-Lending (DCM, SL)
Head of Corporate Banking   Lindsay P Crawford *General Manager, Corporate Banking*
Van Zyl Kruger *Corporate Banking*
Martin A Moeller *Corporate Banking*
Werner Thesen *Corporate Banking*

General - Treasury
Head of Treasury   Anthony J Edmunds *Treasury*

Risk Management
Other (FI Derivatives)
Risk Management   Annette Struchtemeier
Theo Swaak
Ian Stevenson
Piet van der Wath

Settlement / Clearing
Operations   Peter de Meersseman *Operations*

Administration
Other (Administration)
Human Resources   Joern Wiedow

First National Bank of Namibia Limited   Head Office

207-209 Independence Avenue, PO Box 195, Windhoek
Tel: (61) 299 2222; (61) 299 2178 **Fax:** (61) 220 979 **Swift:** FIRN NA NX

Senior Executive Officers
Chairman   Dieter Voigts
Financial Director   Johan Thirion *Head, Finance & Administration*
Treasurer   C H R Green
Managing Director   Stuart Moir

Others (Senior Executives)
   Christine Thompson *Manager, International Operations* ☎ **299 2178**

Other Departments
Correspondent Banking   Christine Thompson *Manager, International Operations* ☎ **299 2178**

Euromoney Directory 1999   **1101**

NAMIBIA (+264)

Fleming Martin Securities Limited
Subsidiary Company
1st Floor Frins, Indongo Gardens, 19 Bulow Street, Windhoek
PO Box 3970, Windhoek
Tel: (61) 254 194 Fax: (61) 254 193

Standard Bank Namibia
3rd Floor, Mutual Platz, Post Street Mall, PO Box 3327, Windhoek
Tel: (61) 294 9111 Fax: (61) 294 2369; (61) 294 2495 Telex: 0908679 Swift: SBNM NANX

Senior Executive Officers
Managing Director — V B Moll

NAURU (+674)

Bank of Nauru
Central Bank
PO Box 289, Nauru
Tel: 444 3238 Fax: 444 3203 Telex: 33085 Cable: BANK NAURU

Senior Executive Officers
Chairman — Amos Cook ☎ **444 3152**
General Manager — Nagendra Goswami ☎ **444 3241**

NEPAL (+977)

Nepal Rastra Bank
Central Bank
PO Box 73, Baluwatar, Kathmandu
Tel: (1) 419 805; (1) 419 806 Fax: (1) 414 553 Telex: 2207 RABA NP Email: nrb@mos.com.np

Senior Executive Officers
Chairman & Governor — Satyendra P Shrestha ☎ **410 386**
Deputy Governor — Prafulla K Kafle ☎ **412 963**
Deputy Governor — Bharat K Sharma ☎ **412 262**
Secretary to the Board — Bhola R Shrestha ☎ **410 203**

Others (Senior Executives)
Kathmandu Banking Office — Bhaskar P Risal *Chief Manager* ☎ **226 832**
Head, Issue Department — Achyut P Bajgain *Chief Currency Officer* ☎ **227 283**
Head, Banking Operation (Policy) Department — Ram B Pant *Chief Manager* ☎ **414 552**
Head, Bank Inspection & Supervision — Jayaram S Bohra *Chief Manager* ☎ **412 306**
Head, Public Debt — Dibya N Bista *Chief Manager* ☎ **213 732**
Head, Mint — Damodar P Sharma *Chief Manager* ☎ **226 965**

Foreign Exchange
Head of Foreign Exchange — Bijaya B Bhattarai *Chief Controller* ☎ **412 204**

Other Departments
Economic Research — Mukunda P Sharma *Chief Economic Advisor* ☎ **411 638**

Administration
Head of Administration — Manohar L Shrestha *Chief Manager* ☎ **414 014**

Technology & Systems
Computer Manager — Sudarshan R Poudyal ☎ **413 584**

Public Relations
Chief Public Relations Officer — Chandika Amatya ☎ **410 211**

Accounts / Audit
— Ganesh P Adhikari *Chief Accountant* ☎ **411 622**

Sow and thou shalt reap

BNG is the principal Dutch public sector agency and market leader in public sector finance. On an annual basis, BNG raises approximately Euro 8 billion by issuing both large and liquid bonds and offering tailor-made private placements. Due to its excellent ratings - BNG bonds and notes are rated Triple-A by the leading rating agencies - BNG offers an alternative to Dutch State Loans for yield-conscious, risk-averse investors. Moreover, BNG bonds and notes are available across the curve and in all major currencies. **BNG - plant now for a flourishing investment.**

Sole Office The Hague, employees - 340, balance sheet total 1997 - NLG 116 billion. BNG, the Dutch public sector agency. BNG provides public authorities and related entities, utilities, housing associations, health and educational institutions, public transport boards and communication services with short and long-term loans, deposits, medium and long-term investments, payment processing services, electronic banking, consultancy services, and cash and treasury management **nv Bank Nederlandse Gemeenten,** *Koninginnegracht 2, 2514 AA The Hague, The Netherlands. Telephone +31-70-30 81 730, fax +31-70-36 51 596.*

DUTCH PUBLIC SECTOR FINANCE

By Bert de Kock, Managing Director Capital Markets, BNG

The Way to EMU
The Netherlands have successfully shed the "Dutch disease" in an unprecedented concerted action of politicians, employers and employees, the famous poldermodel. Nowadays, they are among the most prosperous EMU members, as is illustrated by the following indicators (June 1998 forecast):

- With 4.00%, GDP growth is significantly above EMU initiators Germany (2.70%) and France (3.00%)
- Compared to France (11.9%) and Germany (11.4%), Dutch unemployment is less than half (4.7%)
- The debt over GDP ratio (69.4%, down from over 80%) is well in line with France (65.7%) and Germany (64.5%)

How has this transformation of a Welfare State affected the Dutch public sector? A closer look at the organisation of the local authority system may be helpful.

Organisation
The Netherlands look small, but they are populated by nearly 16 million inhabitants on 42'000 square kilometres. Politically, the Netherlands are a constitutional monarchy in the form of a decentralised unitary state. Its local authority system has two tiers, 12 provinces (provincies) and approximately 550 municipalities (gemeenten). The size of municipalities is variable, ranging from rural communities to cities, the largest of which, Amsterdam, has about 700.000 inhabitants. The creation, merger and abolition of authorities and the relationship between the two tiers of local authorities are governed by the Provincial and the Municipal Law. The constitution limits municipal activities, as the highest officials are centrally appointed, the budgets and other major financial decisions of authorities must be referred for higher approval, and central government may overrule any act of local government that runs against the general interest.

The Agency System
The Dutch system functions as an agency system, in which local authorities carry out the tasks set by central government. The broad range of tasks is the result of a process of accumulation initiated at the beginning of the twentieth century. Then, the transfer of education and utilities to local authorities was prompted by a need for their quality and reliability. A more recent trend towards decentralisation is motivated by the belief that better efficiency is attained at local levels. This resulted in a gradual transfer and/or a

gradual liberalisation of municipal functions over the past few years. Nowadays, all new legislation carries a statutory requirement to consider whether provincial or municipal authorities might be the best bodies to be given responsibility for implementing it. The VNG (Association of Dutch Municipalities) must be consulted as well.

The Public Sector At Large
Two more key players need to be mentioned - the housing associations and the utilities. The 800 non-profit housing associations provide about 40% of all Dutch housing. Founded and run as municipal enterprises, they nowadays are liberalised in that they act independently and must respond to break-even criteria. As their function is still deemed to be a governmental function, their liabilities are ultimately state-guaranteed. Their debt is not included in the EU Maastricht Treaty arithmetic.

The 55 monopolistic utilities are government-owned enterprises, which, legally, are organised as private corporations. Their main shareholders are municipalities, whereas pricing policies are decided by central government. Their liabilities are not included under Maastricht criteria either.

Financials
In 1997, the Dutch GDP amounted to approximately EUR 290 billion. The combined budgets of the local authorities accounted for 12% of the 1998 GDP.

Close to 85% of municipal revenues stem from state transfers, as local tax authority is restricted. Specific transfers destined for particular uses made up close to 50% of municipalities in 1998, declining from 70% in 1986. This is due to substantial cuts in social security and social housing, and to the increasing liberalisation of the 800 housing associations.

The use of general transfers is unrestricted. Local economic and social factors co-determine their allocation. Since 1986, general transfers increased from 22% to 37% of total municipal revenues, thereby lessening the impact of declining specific transfers.

The steady decrease of state transfers, from 92% of total revenues in 1986 to 84% in 1998 has led to the municipalities' increasing their own sources of income to NLG 9.5 billion in 1998, i.e. 16% of total revenue. This stems mainly from local taxes, duties and levies.

Housing Associations no longer receive state transfers. Projects that exceed their immediate means are financed via the domestic capital market and protected by the Guarantee Fund and the ultimate state guarantee. Total market size is approximately EUR 69 billion (yearly turnover: 10%).

Utilities do not benefit from state transfers either. Their total borrowings amount to approximately one fifth of the housing associations'.

The Dutch Public Sector in the Capital Markets

Total market size in municipal debt is about EUR 35 billion (yearly turnover: 10%). Even Amsterdam and Rotterdam have needed to borrow at most EUR 45 million in one go. Municipalities are free to approach all lenders, but BNG, their jointly-owned agency, is the market leader.

While the law permits the Dutch municipalities tap the (domestic) capital markets, bond issuance has been scarce. Unlike comparable European issuers, Dutch municipalities may not incur foreign currency debt. They are required by law to balance their budgets and to classify debt service as a mandatory expenditure, under the Municipal Government Act of 1994. The Local Government Finance Act ensures sound financial fundamentals. The legal framework provides additional funding and strict supervision for any municipality running into financial difficulties - basically, the other municipalities have to bail it out under Article 12 of the Allocation of Finance Act. Municipal loans are zero per cent. risk-weighted by the Dutch Central Bank, and there has never been a bankruptcy, rescheduling or default.

Next To No Bond Issuance

As municipal demand is very fragmented and does not correspond to a classic Eurobond profile, there have only ever been one bond issue by Rotterdam and two by Amsterdam since the 1960s. Local authorities with relatively small infrastructure projects have next to no access to international investors. The classic funding instrument has been the onderhandse lening which is comparable to German Schuldschein. But, whereas the latter can be used as Pfandbrief-collateral, no Dutch Pfandbrief permits bundling municipal demand and surmounting the volume threshold for successful bond issuance. The same goes for the entire public sector.

BNG - The Joint Borrowing Agency

Therefore, the Dutch municipalities set up a joint funding agency in 1914. Entirely owned by the Dutch municipalities and central government, BNG has a market share of over 30% in public sector. Due to the strength of its assets, BNG bonds are Triple A rated by the three major rating agencies and BNG raises about EUR 8 billion per annum on the international capital markets. By transforming fragmented demand into liquid, state-of-the-art offers, BNG fulfills its statutory role as the Dutch Public Sector Agency.

NETHERLANDS
(+31)

De Nederlandsche Bank NV
🏛 Central Bank

Westeinde 1, 1017 ZN Amsterdam
PO Box 98, 1000 AB Amsterdam
Tel: (20) 524 9111 Fax: (20) 524 2500

Senior Executive Officers
President — A H E M Wellink

Others (Senior Executives)
Head, Monetary Affairs
Monetary Affairs
 — H J Brouwer *Executive Director*
 — A F P Bakker *Deputy Director*
 — M M G Fase *Deputy Director*
 — M van Nieuwkerk *Deputy Division Head*

Head, Banking Supervision
Banking Supervision
 — A Schilder *Executive Director*
 — J W Brockmeijer *Deputy Director*
 — P A A M Cornet *Deputy Director*
 — A L Touw *Deputy Director*

Head, Payments & Internal Operations
Secretariat & Services
Personnel & Automation
Payments
 — J Koning *Executive Director*
 — W L Benard *Deputy Director*
 — J T G Uttien *Deputy Director*
 — H C J van der Wielen *Deputy Director*

ABN AMRO Bank NV
Head Office

Foppingadreef 22, 1000 EA Amsterdam
PO Box 283, 1000 EA Amsterdam
Tel: (20) 628 9393 Fax: (20) 628 2363 Telex: 74957 ABAM NL Swift: ABNANL
Website: www.abnamro.com

Senior Executive Officers
Chairman — P J Kalff ☎ 628 1020

Others (Senior Executives)
Division Investment Banking
 — R W F van Tets *Member of the Management Board* ☎ 628 3681
 — W G Jiskoot *Member of the Management Board* ☎ 628 2221

Department: Investment Banking

Others (Senior Executives)
Corporate & Structured Finance — G Kuyper *Senior Executive Vice President* ☎ 628 3682
Global Equities — N W Bannister *Senior Executive Vice President* ☎ +44 (171) 374 1365
Treasury & Fixed Income — J Ch L Kuiper *Senior Executive Vice President* ☎ 628 3103
Finance & Operations — A C Tupker *Senior Executive Vice President* ☎ 628 0001

Equity Capital Markets
Global Head
 — G Kuyper *Senior Executive Vice President* ☎ 628 3682
 — N W Bannister *Senior Executive Vice President* ☎ +44 (171) 374 1365

Other (International Equity)
ABN AMRO Rothschild
 — C J F van Schelle ☎ +1 (212) 314 1198
 — M de Jager ☎ +44 (171) 374 1740

Equity Research
Global Head — N Hugh-Smith ☎ +44 (171) 374 1632

Risk Management
Regional Head
 — A J Deknatal *Regional Head, Europe* ☎ 628 2646
 — H Mulder *Regional Head, Asia & Americas* ☎ 628 4889

Other (FI Derivatives)
Market Risk — J Sijbrand ☎ 628 1603

Corporate Finance / M&A Advisory
Global Head — G Kuyper *Senior Executive Vice President* ☎ 628 3682

Other Departments
Private Banking; Correspondent Banking — P A Casey *Senior Executive Vice President* ☎ 628 0982

Administration
Technology & Systems
Information Technology Solutions — F I A Lion *Senior Executive Vice President* ☎ 629 5501

Compliance
Planning & Control — W M ten Berg *Senior Executive Vice President* ☎ 629 2675

NETHERLANDS (+31) www.euromoneydirectory.com

ABN AMRO Bank NV (cont)
Other (Administration)
Personnel & Central Services   R A Kleyn *Senior Executive Vice President* ☎ **629 3431**

AKBANK TAS
Representative Office

Westblaak 12, 3012 KL Rotterdam
Tel: (10) 414 5200 **Fax:** (10) 412 0517

Senior Executive Officers
Senior Representative   I Koksal

Amstel Securities NV
Head Office

Museum Plaza, Wetering Schans 87E, 1017 RZ Amsterdam
Tel: (20) 620 7606; (20) 620 6906 **Fax:** (20) 620 8903; (20) 620 1075 **Telex:** 15010 AMSEC NL
Email: mail@amstelsec.A2000.nl

Senior Executive Officers
Director   Joost Pielage

Equity Capital Markets
International Equities
Head of Sales   Joost Pielage *Director*
Head of Research   Hans Groenewegen

Other (International Equity)
Sales   Jan Chris Heupers
          Fred Buining

Convertibles / Equity-Linked
Head of Sales   Joost Pielage *Director*
Head of Research   Hans Groenewegen

Other (Convertibles)
Sales   Jan Chris Heupers
          Fred Buining

Warrants
Head of Sales   Joost Pielage *Director*
Head of Research   Hans Groenewegen

Settlement / Clearing
Tel: 620 6906
Regional Head   Ellen den Dekker *Financial Director*
Equity Settlement   Karen Sassen

Administration
Compliance   Karen Sassen

Amstgeld NV

Paleisstraat 1, 1012 RB Amsterdam
Tel: (20) 623 6438 **Fax:** (20) 624 3358 **Telex:** 15489 AGELD **Reuters:** AMGE, RRRC, AMLA

Senior Executive Officers
Chairman   M B Bolle
Chief Executive Officer   A G M Enthoven
Chief Operating Officer   N Heystek

Artesia Bank Nederland NV

Formerly known as: Bacob Bank

Herengracht 539-543, 1017 BW Amsterdam
Tel: (20) 520 4911 **Fax:** (20) 624 7502

Senior Executive Officers
General Manager   Vanock Hoven
Secretary to Managing Director   A Schulien ☎ **520 4509** 📠 **520 4585**

NETHERLANDS (+31)

Banco do Brasil SA
Full Branch Office

Herengracht 457, BS 1017 Amsterdam
Tel: (20) 625 5942 **Fax:** (20) 625 3241 **Swift:** BRAS NL 2A **Email:** info@bancobrasil-nl.com
Website: www.bancobrasil-nl.com

Senior Executive Officers
General Manager — Joao Alberto Bührer

Bank of America NT & SA
Full Branch Office

Herengracht 469, 1017 BS Amsterdam
PO Box 1638, 1000 BP Amsterdam
Tel: (20) 557 1888 **Fax:** (20) 557 1600 **Telex:** 14054 **Swift:** BOFA NL NX

Senior Executive Officers
Treasurer — A J Lensvelt
Managing Director — W Nijboer

Bank Brussels Lambert
Full Branch Office

4G-4H Prinsenkade (Constantijn Office), 4811 NL Breda
Tel: (76) 530 1800 **Fax:** (76) 521 4043

Senior Executive Officers
Others (Senior Executives)
Philippe Bergez *Head*

Bank Insinger de Beaufort NV
Head Office

Herengracht 504, 1017 CB Amsterdam
PO Box 10820, 1001 EV Amsterdam
Tel: (20) 626 3011 **Fax:** (20) 622 9222 **Telex:** 15288

Senior Executive Officers
Others (Senior Executives)
F M A Kee *Director*
R J M De Beaufort *Director*
K H Swierenga *Director*
P G Sieradzki *Director*

Debt Capital Markets / Fixed Income
Global Head — F M A Kee *Director*

Bonds - General
Bonds — J J Sekrève

Equity Capital Markets
Global Head — F M A Kee *Director*

Other (Domestic Equities)
Trading & Sales — F Monnik
P van Leur
H Scheper
B van Keimpema
P L A T Coomans
W B Loggere
G Th Wouters
N Wouters
C A M Heemskerk
F Kerkhof
W A D Hooghwinkel

Money Markets
Global Head — E H Boddéus *Head*

Foreign Exchange
Global Head — E H Boddéus *Head*

Risk Management
Global Head — R Mooij *Head*

Other Currency Swap / FX Options Personnel
Derivatives — M D de Lange

Euromoney Directory 1999 **1109**

NETHERLANDS (+31)   www.euromoneydirectory.com

Bank Insinger de Beaufort NV (cont)
Corporate Finance / M&A Advisory
Other (Corporate Finance)
Corporate Finance   R Mooij *Head*

Settlement / Clearing
Regional Head; Settlement (General)   M G Boessenkool *Head*
Settlement (General)   H F J Heidstra
                                                H W Westerhoud

Asset Management
Portfolio Management   N Wijburg *Deputy Managing Director*
                                                J P van der Ent
                                                J B J Snijders *Deputy Managing Director*
                                                J J Human
                                                V Polak

Bank Labouchere NV   Head Office

Keizersgracht 617, 1017 DS Amsterdam
PO Box 808, 1000 AV Amsterdam
Tel: (20) 520 9300 **Fax:** (20) 620 5239 **Telex:** 13080 **Swift:** BVHL NL 2A

Senior Executive Officers
Chairman   C J M Bierman
Vice Executive Chairman   W J C Brouwer
Financial Director   R M de Louw
Chief Operating Officer   W J J Mooijer
Treasurer   W R Dekker
Company Secretary   B M Hendrilise Abeln

General-Investment
Head of Investment   P D Borst *Head of Investment Banking*

Debt Capital Markets / Fixed Income
Head of Fixed Income   P D Borst *Head of Investment Banking*
Head of Fixed Income Trading   P Roethof

Private Placements
Head of Origination   A J Mak van Waay

Corporate Finance / M&A Advisory
Head of Corporate Finance   R van der Heide

Settlement / Clearing
Head of Settlement / Clearing   H W van Arem

Other Departments
Private Banking   A J Mak van Waay
Correspondent Banking   William Mooyer

Administration
Head of Marketing   A M Ham

Compliance
                                                G Roggen

Public Relations
                                                A M Ham

Bank Nederlandse Gemeenten NV

Koninginnegracht 2, 2155 GH The Hague
PO Box 30305, 2500 GH The Hague
Tel: (70) 375 0730 **Telex:** 31046 BNG NL **Email:** www.bng.ne **Bloomberg:** BNG

Senior Executive Officers
President of the Executive Board   P P J J M van Besouw ☎ 375 0503 📠 375 0926
Company Secretary   G J Thomas ☎ 375 0521 📠 345 4743

Debt Capital Markets / Fixed Income
Head of Fixed Income   Bert de Kock *Managing Director, Capital Markets* ☎ 308 1730 📠 365 7093

Government Bonds
Head of Trading   Piet Hein Verloop *Deputy Managing Director, Treasury* ☎ 308 1710
                                                📠 365 1596

Eurobonds
Head of Sales   Henk van Hemert *Head of Domestic Capital Markets* ☎ 356 0516
                                                📠 365 1596

1110   Euromoney Directory 1999

www.euromoneydirectory.com   NETHERLANDS (+31)

Libor-Based / Floating-Rate Products
Asset Swaps   Henk van Hemert *Head of Domestic Capital Markets* ☏ 356 0516
                               ⓕ 365 1596

Fixed-Income Repo
Head of Trading   Piet Hein Verloop *Deputy Managing Director, Treasury* ☏ 308 1710
                               ⓕ 365 1596

Fixed-Income Research
Head of Fixed Income   Bert de Kock *Managing Director, Capital Markets* ☏ 308 1730 ⓕ 365 7093

Syndicated Lending
Head of Syndication   Sjerp Martin *MD, Customers Account Management* ☏ 375 0517 ⓕ 363 6703

Money Markets
Head of Money Markets   Piet Hein Verloop *Deputy Managing Director, Treasury* ☏ 308 1710
                               ⓕ 365 1596

Domestic Commercial Paper
Head of Sales   Piet Hein Verloop *Deputy Managing Director, Treasury* ☏ 308 1710
                               ⓕ 365 1596

Eurocommercial Paper
Head of Sales   Piet Hein Verloop *Deputy Managing Director, Treasury* ☏ 308 1710
                               ⓕ 365 1596

Risk Management
Head of Risk Management   Piet Hein Verloop *Deputy Managing Director, Treasury* ☏ 308 1710
                               ⓕ 365 1596

Settlement / Clearing
Head of Settlement / Clearing Ad Noordermeer *Manager, Loan & Derivatives* ☏ 375 0747 ⓕ 375 0927

Other Departments
Chief Credit Officer   Sjerp Martin *MD, Customers Account Management* ☏ 375 0517 ⓕ 363 6703
Cash Management   Piet Hein Verloop *Deputy Managing Director, Treasury* ☏ 308 1710
                               ⓕ 365 1596

Administration
Head of Administration   Jean Schneiders *MD, Reporting & Control* ☏ 375 0510
Head of Marketing   Mat Meijs *Head, Public Relations* ☏ 375 0837 ⓕ 365 5178
Technology & Systems
                               Leo Velthoven *MD, Information Technology* ☏ 375 0590 ⓕ 375 0947

Legal / In-House Counsel
                               Jos Hillen *Head, Legal Department* ☏ 375 0674 ⓕ 375 0928

Compliance
                               Cees van Kalleveen *Compliance Officer* ☏ 375 0720 ⓕ 375 0960

Public Relations
                               Mat Meijs *Head, Public Relations* ☏ 375 0837 ⓕ 365 5178

Accounts / Audit
                               Cees van Kalleveen *Compliance Officer* ☏ 375 0720 ⓕ 375 0960

The Bank of Tokyo-Mitsubishi (Holland) NV   Subsidiary Company

World Trade Centre, Strawinskylaan 565, 5th Floor, Tower D, 1077 XX Amsterdam
Tel: (20) 573 7737 **Fax:** (20) 679 1016 **Telex:** 14497 BTMAM NL **Swift:** BOTK NL 2X **Reuters:** TMHL **Telerate:** 2988

Senior Executive Officers
Chief Operating Officer   Masami Uchida *Managing Director & GM* ☏ 573 7737
                               Shun Kakuno *Managing Director & DGM* ☏ 573 7872
Treasurer   Ton van der Veldt *Managing Director & DGM* ☏ 573 7914

Debt Capital Markets / Fixed Income
Domestic Government Bonds
Head of Trading   Tetsuya Yamada *Manager* ☏ 573 7915
Eurobonds
Head of Syndication   Tetsuya Yamada *Manager* ☏ 573 7915
Head of Sales; Head of Trading Yuichi Sawa *Manager* ☏ 573 7829
Private Placements
Head of Origination   Tetsuya Yamada *Manager* ☏ 573 7915

Syndicated Lending
Head of Origination; Head of Syndication   Shigeshi Mori *Assistant General Manager* ☏ 573 7843

Money Markets
Domestic Commercial Paper
Head of Origination   Simon Karregat ☏ 573 7863

➡

Euromoney Directory 1999   **1111**

NETHERLANDS (+31)   www.euromoneydirectory.com

The Bank of Tokyo-Mitsubishi (Holland) NV (cont)

Eurocommercial Paper
Head of Origination — Simon Karregat ☎ 573 7863

Foreign Exchange
Head of Trading — Yuichi Sawa *Manager* ☎ 573 7829

Risk Management
Foreign Exchange Derivatives / Risk Management
Cross-Currency Swaps, Sales / Marketing; — Tetsuya Yamada *Manager* ☎ 573 7915
Cross-Currency Swaps, Trading

Corporate Finance / M&A Advisory
Head of Corporate Finance — Shigeshi Mori *Assistant General Manager* ☎ 573 7843

Other Departments
Correspondent Banking — Bert Giebel *Assistant General Manager* ☎ 573 7862

Administration
Technology & Systems
— Koos van der Zel *Manager* ☎ 573 7889

Compliance
— Bert Giebel *Assistant General Manager* ☎ 573 7862

Public Relations
— Ton van der Veldt *Managing Director & DGM* ☎ 573 7914

Bank voor Zeeland NV — Head Office

Grote Markt 21, 4461 AH Goes
PO Box 7, 4460 Goes
Tel: (113) 247 211 **Fax:** (113) 232 062 **Telex:** 55448 BAVOZ NL **Swift:** MEES NL 2R

Senior Executive Officers
General Manager — M C I M den Exter

General-Lending (DCM, SL)
Head of Corporate Banking — T A Van de Bilt *Manager, Corporate Banking*

Other Departments
Private Banking — F Stobbelaar *Head of Private Banking*

Banque Artesia Nederland NV

Formerly known as: Bank Paribas Nederland NV

Herengracht 539-543, 1017 BW Amsterdam
PO Box 274, 1000 AG Amsterdam
Tel: (20) 520 4911; (20) 520 4202 **Fax:** (20) 624 7502; (20) 520 4500 **Swift:** PARB NL 2A

Senior Executive Officers
Chairman of the Board of Supervisory Directors — Philippe Romagnoli
Chief Executive Officer — Jan Van Broeckhoven *Chairman of the Board of Managing Directors*
Treasurer — Henk Jan van Leeuwen *Treasurer*

General-Lending (DCM, SL)
Head of Corporate Banking — Daniel Waebens *Managing Director*

Settlement / Clearing
Head of Settlement / Clearing — Bram Hartzema

Other Departments
Private Banking — Jan Snippe *Managing Director*

Administration
Compliance
— Frans Visser

Banque Nationale de Paris — Full Branch Office

Herengracht 477, 1017 BS Amsterdam
Tel: (20) 550 1212 **Fax:** (20) 625 3921 **Telex:** 14217 NAPAR NL **Swift:** BNPA NL 2A **Email:** bnpinfo@bnp.nl

Senior Executive Officers
Chief Executive Officer — Guy Sancerres *General Manager*
Treasurer — Peter van der Velden *Treasurer* ☎ 550 1304 📠 550 1373

Others (Senior Executives)
Commercial — Joot Niessen *Commercial Manager*

NETHERLANDS (+31)

Debt Capital Markets / Fixed Income
Head of Debt Capital Markets   Peter van der Velden *Treasurer* 550 1304 550 1373
Administration
Head of Administration   Philippe Sirgant *Secretary General* 550 1274 550 1373

Banque Nationale de Paris
Full Branch Office
Oranjesingel 12, 6511 NT Nijmegen
Tel: (24) 360 3277 Fax: (24) 360 4412
Senior Executive Officers
Directeur   Peter Hendrickx

Banque Nationale de Paris
Full Branch Office
4th Floor, Westblaak 190, 3012 KN Rotterdam
Tel: (10) 411 2880 Fax: (10) 411 0720 Telex: 25001 BNPRO NL
Senior Executive Officers
Chief Executive Officer   Jeroen Blok *Senior Executive Officer*

Bayernhypo Finance NV
Subsidiary Company
Strawinskylaan 3105, 7th Floor, 1077 Amsterdam ZX
Tel: (20) 442 0294 Fax: (20) 406 4555

BHF-Finance (Netherlands) BV
Representative Office
Haaksbergweg 27, 1101 BP Amsterdam
Tel: (20) 691 9611 Fax: (20) 691 9811
Senior Executive Officers
Managing Director   Maurits Regenboog regenboog@bhf.nl
Managing Director   Onno Folkers ofolkers@bhf.nl
Company Secretary   Ita Paat itapaat@bhf.nl
Company Secretary   Sabrina Tersi sabrina@bhf.nl

Cen E Bankiers NV
Head Office
Formerly known as: Credit-en Effectenbank NV
Herculesplein 5, 3584 AA Utrecht
PO Box 85100, 3508 AC Utrecht
Tel: (30) 256 0911 Fax: (30) 256 0566 Email: info@cene.nl
Website: www.cene.nl

Senior Executive Officers
Chairman   Peter Lindeboom
Chief Executive Officer   Pieter Jan v.d. Brink
Treasurer   Jos Gerards
General-Lending (DCM, SL)
Head of Corporate Banking   Stefan Antonissen
Debt Capital Markets / Fixed Income
Head of Fixed Income   Erik Tak
Equity Capital Markets
Head of Equity Capital Markets   Erik Tak
Money Markets
Head of Money Markets   Jan Hoogendoorn
Foreign Exchange
Head of Foreign Exchange   Ronald Geel
Corporate Finance / M&A Advisory
Head of Corporate Finance   Stefan Antonissen
Settlement / Clearing
Head of Settlement / Clearing   Rob Rÿkenberg
Global Custody
Head of Global Custody   Rob Rÿkenberg

NETHERLANDS (+31)

Cen E Bankiers NV (cont)

Asset Management
Head — Maarten Kneepkens

Other Departments
Chief Credit Officer — Wim v.d. Mark
Private Banking — Robert Doornbos
Correspondent Banking — Hans Eland

Administration
Head of Marketing — Frank Bouman

Technology & Systems — Henk Quispel

Legal / In-House Counsel — Henk Maas

Compliance — Harry Vredendaal

Public Relations — Frank Bouman

Accounts / Audit — Henk de Vries

The Chase Manhattan Bank — Full Branch Office

4th Floor, Atrium, Strawinskylaan 3077, 1077 ZX Amsterdam
Tel: (20) 546 9700 **Fax:** (20) 546 9707

Senior Executive Officers
Others (Senior Executives)
Senior Officer — Holly M Johnson *Senior Officer*

CITCO Bank Nederland NV — Head Office

16th Floor, Tower B, World Trade Centre, Strawinskylaan 1629, 1077 XX Amsterdam
PO Box 7241, 1007 JE Amsterdam
Tel: (20) 572 2200 **Fax:** (20) 662 8167 **Telex:** 11960 CBNNLL **Swift:** CITC NL 2A

Senior Executive Officers
Managing Director — H C Beers
Managing Director — W Holst
Managing Director — S Hadjali
International Division — H C Beers *MD, International & Treasury*

General-Lending (DCM, SL)
Head of Corporate Banking — S Hadjali *MD, International Finance*
R J Boonstra *Credit & Guarantees*

General-Investment
Head of Investment — W Holst *Investment Management*

Debt Capital Markets / Fixed Income
Global Head — W Holst *Managing Director*

Domestic Government Bonds
Head of Trading — W Holst *Managing Director*

Asset-Backed Securities / Securitization
Global Head — W Holst *Managing Director*

Equity Capital Markets
Other (Domestic Equities)
Domestic Securities — W Holst *Managing Director*

Syndicated Lending
Project Finance — R J Boonstra *Credit & Guarantees*

Foreign Exchange
Global Head — Rene Gartner *Officer, Corporate FX Services* ☎ **572 2229**

Risk Management
Fixed Income Derivatives / Risk Management
IR Options Trading — W Holst *Managing Director*

Foreign Exchange Derivatives / Risk Management
Vanilla FX option Trading — W Holst *Managing Director*

Exotic Options (Barriers, Range, Timers, Digitals, Faders etc)
Trading — W Holst *Managing Director*

Exchange-Traded Derivatives
FX Options; IR Options   W Holst *Managing Director*
Settlement / Clearing
Operations   M Thiel
Other Departments
Commodities / Bullion   W Holst *Managing Director*
Correspondent Banking   R Steketee

Citibank NA
Full Branch Office

Hoogoorddreef 54B, 1101 BE Amsterdam 20
PO Box 23445, 1100 DX Amsterdam 20
Tel: (20) 651 4211 **Fax:** (20) 651 4272 **Telex:** 12261 **Reuters:** CIAM, CITA **Reuters:** CITA

Senior Executive Officers
Chief Executive Officer   Chris Devries ☏ **651 4287**
Treasurer   Martha Harel ☏ **651 4496**
Secretary to Managing Director   Jolande van den Haak ☏ **651 4287**

General - Treasury
Head of Treasury   Jan Bak *Head of Treasury and Capital Markets* ☏ **651 4325**

Debt Capital Markets / Fixed Income
Head of Fixed Income   Jan Bak *Head of Treasury and Capital Markets* ☏ **651 4325**

Equity Capital Markets
Equity Repo / Securities Lending
Head   Peter Verduin ☏ **651 4276**

Money Markets
Head of Money Markets   Martha Harel ☏ **651 4496**

Foreign Exchange
Head of Foreign Exchange   Jan Bak *Head of Treasury and Capital Markets* ☏ **651 4325**

Corporate Finance / M&A Advisory
Head of Corporate Finance   Jeroen Leffelaar ☏ **651 4261**

Global Custody
Head of Global Custody   Peter Verduin ☏ **651 4276**

Other Departments
Cash Management   Tim Flemming ☏ **651 4398**

Commerzbank (Nederland) NV
Subsidiary Company

Herengracht 571-579, 1017 CD Amsterdam
PO Box 140, 1000 AC Amsterdam
Tel: (20) 557 4911 **Fax:** (20) 627 2446 **Telex:** 18076 **Swift:** COBA NL 2X **Email:** mailbox@commerzbank.nl
Reuters: CBKA

Senior Executive Officers
Financial Director   Rob v.d. Heijden *Head, Corporate Banking* ☏ **557 4629**
Chief Operating Officer   Dirk Fischer *Head of Administration* ☏ **557 4630**
Treasurer   Ruud Meijer *Head of Treasury* ☏ **557 4760**
Managing Director   Herman P Weij ☏ **557 4600**
Managing Director   Manfred Breuer ☏ **557 4700**

Credit Suisse First Boston

Atrium, Strawinskilaan 3053, 1077 ZX Amsterdam
PO Box 160, 1000 AZ Amsterdam
Tel: (20) 504 5145 **Fax:** (20) 504 5199

Senior Executive Officers
Financial Director   A C Smith
Managing Director   J C Teerhuim
General Manager   D Vanmarle ☏ **575 4444** 📠 **575 4455**

General-Investment
Head of Investment   D Vanmarle *General Manager* ☏ **575 4444** 📠 **575 4455**

Administration
Other (Administration)
Operations   J C Teerhuim *Managing Director*

NETHERLANDS (+31) www.euromoneydirectory.com

Credit Suisse First Boston (Internationale) AG — Representative Office
Formerly known as: CS First Boston (Nederland) NV
Johannes Vermearstraat 9, 1071 DK Amsterdam
Tel: (20) 575 4444 Fax: (20) 575 4455

Senior Executive Officers
Managing Director   Tÿo van Marle

Dai-Ichi Kangyo Bank Nederland NV — Subsidiary Company
Alternative trading name: DKB NL
Apollolaan 171, 1077 AS Amsterdam
PO Box 7075, 1007 JB Amsterdam
Tel: (20) 574 0200 Fax: (20) 676 0301 Telex: 15717 DKB NL Swift: DKBN NL 2A
Website: www.dkb.co.jp

Senior Executive Officers
Managing Director & General Manager   Toshihiko Kai
Managing Director & Deputy General Manager   Katsuyoshi Fukuda

General - Treasury
Head of Treasury   Shinya Mamezuka *Manager, Treasury* ☏ **574 0292**

Corporate Finance / M&A Advisory
Head of Corporate Finance   Luc Reynders *Senior Manager, Corporate Finance I* ☏ **574 0258**
                                             Marilyn Blancaflor *Manager* ☏ **574 0275**

Other (Corporate Finance)
Corporate Finance Administration   Marilyn Blancaflor *Manager* ☏ **574 0275**

Administration
Information Technology   Paul Koenders *Manager* ☏ **574 0217**

Accounts / Audit
Accounting Department   Victoria Twist *Manager* ☏ **574 0234**

Other (Administration)
International Operations Department   Hong Lok Njio *Senior Manager* ☏ **574 0371**
General Affairs Department   Ton Raaymakers *Manager* ☏ **574 0331**

Delta Lloyd Bank NV — Head Office
Joan Muyskenweg 4, 1000 AE Amsterdam
PO Box 231, 1000 AE Amsterdam
Tel: (20) 560 8208 Fax: (20) 560 8328 Telex: 16561 DLBK NL Swift: DLBK NL 2A Reuters: DLBA

Senior Executive Officers
Chairman   Mr Prop
Vice Chairman & General Manager   Mr Stalenhoef

Debt Capital Markets / Fixed Income
Head of Debt Capital Markets   Bert Mets *General Manager, Securities Dept* ☏ **560 8254**

Equity Capital Markets
Head of Equity Capital Markets   Bert Mets *General Manager, Securities Dept* ☏ **560 8254**
Head of Sales   Lex C G Bouwmeester *Sales & Trading* ☏ **560 8292**
                                             Bianca Kelatow-Pot *Sales & Trading* ☏ **560 8295**
                                             Marvin J Lambert *Sales & Trading* ☏ **560 8895**
                                             Hans J H Sibeijn *Sales & Trading* ☏ **560 8256**
Head of Trading   Lex C G Bouwmeester *Sales & Trading* ☏ **560 8292**
                                             Bianca Kelatow-Pot *Sales & Trading* ☏ **560 8295**
                                             Marvin J Lambert *Sales & Trading* ☏ **560 8895**
                                             Hans J H Sibeijn *Sales & Trading* ☏ **560 8256**

Settlement / Clearing
Settlement (General)   Joop Weel ☏ **560 8224**

www.euromoneydirectory.com NETHERLANDS (+31)

Deutsche Bank AG
Full Branch Office

Formerly known as: Deutsche Bank de Bary NV
Herengracht 450, 1017 CA Amsterdam
PO Box 268, NL 1000 AG Amsterdam
Tel: (20) 555 4911 **Fax:** (20) 555 4428 **Swift:** DEUT NL ZA
Website: www.deutsche-bank.de

Senior Executive Officers
Others (Senior Executives)
       Leonhard N Degle *Senior Managing Director* ☏ **555 4262**
       Ronald A H Lemke *Senior Managing Director* ☏ **555 4264**
       Elisabeth M Mulder-Mosman *Senior Managing Director* ☏ **555 4450**

Deutsche Bank de Bary NV
Full Branch Office

Westplein 12, 3016 BM Rotterdam
PO Box 1711, 3000 BS Rotterdam
Tel: (10) 436 6400 **Fax:** (10) 436 8017; (10) 436 4330 **Telex:** 22608 **Swift:** BARY NL 2A RTD

DG BANK
Representative Office

Herengracht 386, NL 1016 CJ Amsterdam
Tel: (20) 520 7333 **Fax:** (20) 638 1849

Senior Executive Officers
Representative   Bjørn C W Jonker

Discount Bank & Trust Company
Full Branch Office

Weteringschans 26, 1017 SG Amsterdam
PO Box 3241, 1001 AA Amsterdam
Tel: (20) 623 7682 **Fax:** (20) 622 8564 **Telex:** 16381 DBTCA NL **Swift:** DBTC NL 2X **Reuters:** DBTH

Senior Executive Officers
Director   J A van Essen

Dutch State Treasury Agency
Agency

Formerly known as: Ageny of the Ministry of Finance
Orlyplein 32, 1043 DP Amsterdam
PO Box 345, Amsterdam
Tel: (20) 581 0700 **Fax:** (20) 581 0701; (20) 581 0702 **Email:** agent@dutchstate.nl **Reuters:** AGFB - AGFZ
Telerate: 39211-39229 **Bloomberg:** DSTA
Website: www.dutchstate.nl

Senior Executive Officers
Agent   Leo H Uerwoerd ☏ **581 0730**
Others (Senior Executives)
      Jan Th. M Hamers *Deputy Agent* ☏ **581 0731**
      Patrick B G van der Wansem *Head of Capital Markets* ☏ **581 0788**

Friesland Bank Securities

Formerly known as: Banger Bangert Pontier NV
Herengracht 500, 1017 CB Amsterdam
PO Box 11788, 1001 GT Amsterdam
Tel: (20) 520 6520 **Fax:** (20) 623 1736 **Telex:** 16102 **Email:** info@fbs.nl
Website: www.fbs.nl

Senior Executive Officers
Managing Director   J A J Koster
Managing Director   B Tishauser
Others (Senior Executives)
Head of Trading   B Tishauser *Managing Director*
Head of Sales   R M J Habets

NETHERLANDS (+31)   www.euromoneydirectory.com

Friesland Bank Securities (cont)
Others (Senior Executives) (cont)
Head of Research   D H M Muusers
Debt Capital Markets / Fixed Income
Bonds - General
New Issues   D H van der Schagt
Equity Capital Markets
Domestic Equities
Head of Sales   F Berens
                                M van Bruggen

Risk Management
Other (FI Derivatives)
Sales Derivatives   T Hoefakker
                                R J Schulein

Settlement / Clearing
Settlement (General)   M van Cleef
                                R J Houtkamp
                                H Weij
Operations   C A J Bastiaenen *Head of Operations*
Asset Management
Head   O V Strubbe
Administration
Head of Administration   Kees Bastiaenen *Head of Back Office*
Compliance
                                E M Beck

Other (Administration)
Head of Personnel   J A J Koster *Managing Director*

Fuji Bank Nederland NV   Subsidiary Company

166 Amsteldijk, 1079 LH Amsterdam
PO Box 70103, 1007 KC Amsterdam
Tel: (20) 661 0049 **Fax:** (20) 661 0201 **Telex:** 10395
Senior Executive Officers
Managing Director   Y Ono
Deputy Managing Director   Y Fujii
Administration
Head of Administration   J de Vries *Manager*
Accounts / Audit
                                J de Vries *Manager*

Other (Administration)
Data Processing   E B Borghaerts *Manager*

Garanti Bank   Full Branch Office

Westblaak 34, 3012 KM Rotterdam
Tel: (10) 411 0591 **Fax:** (10) 404 8705 **Swift:** UGBI NL 2R
Senior Executive Officers
Managing Director   Jan de Grout

Gilde Investment Management   Head Office

Newtonlaan 91, 3584 BP Utrecht
PO Box 85067, 3508 AB Utrecht
Tel: (30) 219 2525 **Fax:** (30) 254 0004 **Email:** info@gilde.nl
Website: www.gilde.nl
Senior Executive Officers
Executive Director   Leendert J van Driel
Corporate Secretary   Annemiek Van Den Ham
Others (Senior Executives)
                                Albert C Steketee *Executive Director*
                                Diederik W Heyning *Executive Director*

www.euromoneydirectory.com　　　NETHERLANDS (+31)

General-Investment
Head of Investment　　　　　　　　Boudewijn Molenaar *Investment Director*
　　　　　　　　　　　　　　　　Toon den Heijer *Investment Director*
　　　　　　　　　　　　　　　　Ton A J M Gardeniers *Investment Director*

Eduard de Graaff & Co BV　　　　　　　　　　　　　　Head Office

Dam 27, 1012 JS Amsterdam
Tel: (20) 550 6550; (20) 627 3311 **Fax:** (20) 624 9435 **Telex:** 15196 **Email:** edgco@xsyall.nl **Bloomberg:** edg
Senior Executive Officers
Managing Director　　　　　　　　Robert R Th. Heezius ☏ **550 6418**
Settlement / Clearing
Operations　　　　　　　　　　　Zaid T Guman *Manager of Operations* ☏ **550 6430**
Administration
Compliance
　　　　　　　　　　　　　　　　Zaid T Guman *Manager of Operations* ☏ **550 6430**

Helaba Finance BV　　　　　　　　　　　　　　　Subsidiary Company

Herengracht 442, 1017 BZ Amsterdam
Tel: (20) 638 2246 **Fax:** (20) 638 2226
Senior Executive Officers
Chairman　　　　　　　　　　　　Frederick Roy Hopson
Others (Senior Executives)
Management　　　　　　　　　　　Alexandre G Meyer *Managing Director*
　　　　　　　　　　　　　　　　Klaus Schreiner *Managing Director*
　　　　　　　　　　　　　　　　Pierre L A M Schroeder *Managing Director*
　　　　　　　　　　　　　　　　W C B van Wettum *Managing Director*

van der Hoop Effektenbank NV　　　　　　　　　　　　Head Office

Herengracht 469, PO Box 741, 1000 AS Amsterdam
Tel: (20) 522 6000 **Fax:** (20) 522 6999 **Email:** effektenbank@vanderhoop.nl
Senior Executive Officers
Chairman, Board, Executive Directors　　Peter van Hooijdonk ☏ **522 6010**
Chief Executive Officer　　　　　　Dirk J. Nienhuis *Member of the Board*
Managing Director　　　　　　　　Adrian Kavelaars ☏ **522 6621**
Managing Director　　　　　　　　Nick Mouthaan ☏ **522 6501**
Managing Director　　　　　　　　Geurt Szabang
Managing Director　　　　　　　　Hein de Vries
Debt Capital Markets / Fixed Income
Tel: 522 6600 **Fax:** 522 6960
Global Head　　　　　　　　　　　Adrian Kavelaars *Managing Director* ☏ **522 6621**
Equity Capital Markets
Tel: 522 6600 **Fax:** 522 6960
Global Head　　　　　　　　　　　Adrian Kavelaars *Managing Director* ☏ **522 6621**
Settlement / Clearing
Tel: 522 6600 **Fax:** 522 6910
Regional Head　　　　　　　　　　Jan Hendriks *Head of Settlements* ☏ **522 6120**
Other Departments
Private Banking　　　　　　　　　Nick Mouthaan *Managing Director* ☏ **522 6501**

HSBC Investment Bank NV　　　　　　　　　　　　　Head Office

Herengracht 466, 1017 CA Amsterdam
Tel: (20) 550 2502 **Fax:** (20) 550 2550 **Telex:** 15071 VMEER NIL
Senior Executive Officers
Chairman, MD & Head of Trading　　Dirk De Jong
Chief Executive Officer　　　　　　Dirk De Jong *Chairman, MD & Head of Trading*
Financial Director　　　　　　　　R Korinth *Chief Financial Officer*
Chief Operating Officer　　　　　　Dirk De Jong *Chairman, MD & Head of Trading*
Treasurer　　　　　　　　　　　　R Korinth *Chief Financial Officer*
Chairman, MD & Head of Trading　　Dirk De Jong

Euromoney Directory 1999　**1119**

NETHERLANDS (+31) www.euromoneydirectory.com

HSBC Investment Bank NV (cont)
Equity Capital Markets
Country Head Dirk De Jong *Chairman, MD & Head of Trading*
Settlement / Clearing
Country Head K Van Der Hoek

Indover Bank
Head Office

Alternative trading name: NV De Indonesische Overzeese Bank
Stadhouderskade 84, 1073 AT Amsterdam
PO Box 526, 1000, 1000 AM Amsterdam
Tel: (20) 570 0700 **Fax:** (20) 662 6119 **Telex:** 11327/18452 ioba nl **Swift:** IOVE NL 2A **Email:** info@indover.nl
Reuters: D:IOBA / M: IOBA **Telerate:** 2976 **Cable:** INDOVER
Back Office Treasury Department Tel: 570 0860; **Fax:** 570 0869; **Board of Managing Directors Tel:** 570 0606;
Fax: 664 7729; **Corrspondent Banking/ Treasury Fax:** 662 3886; **Credit Administration Dept. Tel:** 570 0800;
Fax: 570 0809; **Credit Supervision Tel:** 570 0730; **Fax:** 570 0739

Senior Executive Officers
President Muhamad Muchtar ☏ **570 0606**
Treasurer R A Schara ☏ **570 0831**
Managing Director / General Manager Bambang Trianto ☏ **570 0606**

Syndicated Lending
Tel: (20) 570 0840 **Fax:** (20) 570 0849
Global Head A S Pamudji *Head of Syndication* ☏ **570 0841ext941**

Money Markets
Tel: (20) 570 0701/ 9 **Fax:** (20) 662 2546 **Telex:** 18345 iofx nl
Head of Money Markets R A Schara ☏ **570 0831**

Other (Wholesale Deposits)
Bills / Payments A J de Bell *Head* ☏ **570 0761**

Foreign Exchange
Tel: (20) 570 0701/ 9 **Fax:** (20) 662 2546 **Telex:** 18345 iofx nl
Head of Foreign Exchange R A Schara ☏ **570 0831**

Risk Management
Head of Risk Management J P L van Straalen *Head* ☏ **570 0821**

Settlement / Clearing
Operations D van Lesuwen *Head of Operations* ☏ **570 0811**
Back-Office P H L The *Head of Back Office Treasury* ☏ **570 0701** F **570 0869**

Other Departments
Chief Credit Officer F de Groot *Head of Credit Supervision* ☏ **570 0731**
Correspondent Banking B Gandasoebrata *Head* ☏ **570 0721**

Administration
Head of Administration R A van Rees Vellinga *Head of Credit Administration* ☏ **570 0801**

Technology & Systems
A. Schmitz du Moulin *Head of EDP* ☏ **570 0771**

Compliance
J M L M van der Weiden *Head of Internal Audit* ☏ **570 0671**

Accounts / Audit
Accounting & Reporting J L M de Goede *Head* ☏ **570 0681**

Other (Administration)
General Affairs R F A Blommestijn *Head* ☏ **570 0641**
J M Lim *Deputy Head* ☏ **570 0645**

ING Bank NV
Treasury Centre

Treasury Centre, Foppingadreef 7, 1102 BD Amsterdam
PO Box 1800, 1000 BV Amsterdam
Tel: (20) 563 8012; (20) 563 8019 **Fax:** (20) 563 8013
Website: www.ing-barings.com

Senior Executive Officers
Chairman Ted de Vries ☏ **563 8000** F **563 8002**
General Manager Ben M Th Kok ☏ **563 8003** F **563 8005**

www.euromoneydirectory.com　　　　　　　NETHERLANDS (+31)

Others (Senior Executives)
Cash Management / International Money　　Jan W Menger ⓣ 563 8008 ⓕ 563 8013
Market Trading
Trading & Sales Interest Rate Derivatives　　Ben J J Hakfoort ⓣ 563 8022 ⓕ 563 8013
Investments & Funding　　　　　　　　　　Anton C Sonneveldt ⓣ 563 8034 ⓕ 563 8013
Proprietary Trading Foreign Exchange　　　Ernst K Moritz ⓣ 563 8007 ⓕ 563 8005
Treasury Advisory / Customer Desk　　　　Yeb Sj van Dijk ⓣ 563 8020 ⓕ 563 8013
Special Products & Commercial Support　　Peter J H Kühne ⓣ 563 8006 ⓕ 563 8013
Market Making Equity Derivatives　　　　　Rob H Staalstra ⓣ 520 7080 ⓕ 520 7081
Futures & Options Clearing Services　　　　Jap A Kaptein ⓣ 501 3401 ⓕ 501 3402
Trading & Sales Fixed Income (Eurobonds)　Lau Veldink ⓣ 563 8011 ⓕ 563 8013
Debt Capital Markets Origination　　　　　Michel A B Harmsen ⓣ 501 3033 ⓕ 563 8546
Trading & Sales Equities　　　　　　　　　Charles L de Kock ⓣ 563 8084 ⓕ 563 8018
　　　　　　　　　　　　　　　　　　　　Ted C de Vries ⓣ 563 8000 ⓕ 563 8002
Equities Strategic Portfolios　　　　　　　Jan C M Kager ⓣ 563 8016 ⓕ 563 8018
　　　　　　　　　　　　　　　　　　　　Aart Veerman ⓣ 563 8089 ⓕ 563 8018
COO Treasury　　　　　　　　　　　　　　Geurt van Thuyl ⓣ 563 8250 ⓕ 563 8251
Treasury - London　　　　　　　　　　　　Mark van Rijswijk ⓣ +44 (171) 767 6747 ⓕ +44 (171) 767 7310
Treasury - Asia　　　　　　　　　　　　　Leo Janssen ⓣ +852 2913 8130 ⓕ +852 2537 3167
Treasury - Americas　　　　　　　　　　　Don Taggart ⓣ +1 (212) 409 6428

ING Bank NV　　　　　　　　　　　　　　　　　　　　　　　　　　　　　　Head Office

Strawinskylaan 2631, 1077 ZZ Amsterdam
PO Box 1800, 1000 BV Amsterdam
Tel: (20) 541 5411; (20) 563 9111 **Fax:** (20) 541 5444; (20) 563 5700 **Telex:** 11888/12010 **Swift:** INGB NL 2A
Reuters: INGX
Website: www.ingbank.com

Senior Executive Officers
Department: Executive Board - ING Groep NV
Chairman　　　　　　　　　　　　　　　　G J A van der Lugt
Financial Director　　　　　　　　　　　　C Maas *Chief Financial Officer*

Others (Senior Executives)
　　　　　　　　　　　　　　　　　　　　E Kist
　　　　　　　　　　　　　　　　　　　　J H Holsboer
　　　　　　　　　　　　　　　　　　　　J H M Lindenbergh
　　　　　　　　　　　　　　　　　　　　M Minderhoud
　　　　　　　　　　　　　　　　　　　　A H G Rinnooy Kan
　　　　　　　　　　　　　　　　　　　　M Tilmant
Department: ING Nederland
Chairman　　　　　　　　　　　　　　　　E Kist

Others (Senior Executives)
　　　　　　　　　　　　　　　　　　　　J H M Lindenbergh
　　　　　　　　　　　　　　　　　　　　D Brands
　　　　　　　　　　　　　　　　　　　　J A Nijssen
　　　　　　　　　　　　　　　　　　　　A H van Tooren
Department: ING Financial Services International
Chairman　　　　　　　　　　　　　　　　J H Holsboer

Others (Senior Executives)
Atlanta　　　　　　　　　　　　　　　　　R G Hilliard
Sydney　　　　　　　　　　　　　　　　　P R Shirriff
Amsterdam　　　　　　　　　　　　　　　H K Verkoren
Department: ING Corporate & Investment Banking
Chairman　　　　　　　　　　　　　　　　M Minderhoud
Chief Executive Officer　　　　　　　　　D Robins

Others (Senior Executives)
Chief Operating Officer - London　　　　　P Bennett
CEO Americas - New York　　　　　　　　F Gentil
Global Head Risk Management - Amsterdam　H Idzerda
CEO Europe, Middle East & Africa - Amsterdam　J Kemp
Global Head Equities / Investment Banking -　J Palmer
London
CEO Asia - Hong Kong　　　　　　　　　　D Hudson
CEO Western Europe - London　　　　　　W Douin
Global Head Treasury - Amsterdam　　　　T de Vries
Department: ING Belgium
24 Avenue Marnix, 1000 Brussels
Tel: +32 (2) 547 2111 **Fax:** +32 (2) 547 3844
Chairman　　　　　　　　　　　　　　　　M Tilmant

Euromoney Directory 1999　**1121**

NETHERLANDS (+31)   www.euromoneydirectory.com

ING Bank NV (cont)
Syndicated Lending
Department: ING Barings - Export Finance
Global Head   B L Wijnen *Global Head Export & Project Finance* ☎ 563 5362 ℻ 563 5164

Loan-Related Activities
Project Finance   B L Wijnen *Global Head Export & Project Finance* ☎ 563 5362 ℻ 563 5164
                                                W A A R Hansen *Head, Export & ECA-Related Project Finance* ☎ 563 5309
                                                ℻ 563 5164

Other (Trade Finance)
Mid-Corporate Export Finance   W A J van der Have *Manager* ☎ 563 5605 ℻ 563 5164
Export Finance International Network   C J J Wientjes *Manager* ☎ 563 5514 ℻ 563 5164
Structured Export Finance   J B Klapwijk *Manager* ☎ 563 5298 ℻ 563 5164
Energy Finance   J J Prins *Head* ☎ 563 5433 ℻ 563 5164
Power Finance   P H M Staal *Head* ☎ 563 5513 ℻ 563 5164
Metals & Mining Finance   R A Schouten *Head* ☎ 563 5355 ℻ 563 5164
Media Finance   S Schach von Wittenau *Head* ☎ 576 8828 ℻ 563 5505
Telecommunications Finance   J Katz *Head* ☎ 563 5084 ℻ 563 5505
Loans Syndications   J Boardman *Head* ☎ 563 5214 ℻ 565 1020
Project Advisory   F W J Mansveldt Beck *Head* ☎ 563 4911 ℻ 563 5164
Structured Finance   S E N Ng *Manager* ☎ 563 5606 ℻ 563 5164
Structured Leasing   G Kiers *Manager* ☎ 565 1042 ℻ 563 5164
Tax-Based Lending & Leasing   A J M Roozen *Global Manager, Financial Engineering* ☎ 563 5405
                                                ℻ 563 5164

Asset Management
Department: ING Asset Management
Head   A H G Rinnooy Kan

Other (Asset Management)
                                                G H Heida

Istituto Bancario San Paolo di Torino SpA   Full Branch Office
Herengracht 446, 1017 CA Amsterdam
PO Box 15490, 1000 ND Amsterdam
Tel: (20) 521 6100 Fax: (20) 521 6161 Telex: 15690
Senior Executive Officers
General Manager   A Mellano

JP Morgan Nederland NV   Representative Office
Apollolaan 171, 1077 AS Amsterdam
Tel: (20) 676 7766 Fax: (20) 676 9641 Telex: 12220 Reuters: MBSA-E
Senior Executive Officers
Managing Director   John Trip
Office Manager   Patricia Oschatz

KAS-Associatie NV   Head Office
Spuistraat 172, 1012 VT Amsterdam
Tel: (20) 557 5911 Fax: (20) 622 4917 Telex: 12286 Swift: KASA NL 2A Email: sec-lending@kas-associatie.com
Website: www.kas-associate.com
Senior Executive Officers
Chairman of the Board of Managing Directors   Mr Von Balluseck ☎ 557 5295
Financial Director   Mr Van Heese *Managing Director* ☎ 557 5279

Relationship Manager
Structured Products   Yuo van Rynsoever *Trader*
                                                Marc Hamel *Trader*

Debt Capital Markets / Fixed Income
Fax: 638 1969

Fixed-Income Repo
Trading   Yuo van Rynsoever *Trader*

www.euromoneydirectory.com NETHERLANDS (+31)

Equity Capital Markets
Fax: 638 1969
Equity Repo / Securities Lending
Head   Robero Lobo ☏ **557 5521**
Head of Trading   Thausrine Theyes *Trader*
                                          Ruud van de Putte *Trader*
                                          Yvo van Rynooever *Trader*

Money Markets
Country Head   John Van Scheijndel *Head of Treasury* ☏ **557 5393**
Settlement / Clearing
Country Head   Henk Brink *Head, Administrative Account Mgmt & Product Dev.*
                                          ☏ **557 5327**

Kempen & Co NV   Head Office

Herengracht 182, 1016 BR Amsterdam
PO Box 11363, 1001 GJ Amsterdam
Tel: (20) 557 1571 **Fax:** (20) 557 1414

Senior Executive Officers
Chairman   J Krant
Financial Director   H C van't Hoff
Company Secretary   C Hovstra
Others (Senior Executives)
Board of Management   R J Meuter
                                          W O Wentges

Debt Capital Markets / Fixed Income
Fax: 557 1488
Fixed-Income Repo
Head of Repo   Hans de Haan *Director* ☏ **557 1430** ✉ **hhaa@kempen.nl**
Marketing & Product Development; Trading Andre Licht ☏ **557 1432** ✉ **alic@kempen.nl**
Trading   Remco Wesselius *Trading*
                                          Hans Grundeken *Trading*
Sales   Andre Licht ☏ **557 1432** ✉ **alic@kempen.nl**

Equity Capital Markets
Department: Securities & Brokerage
Fax: 557 1519 **Telex:** 15689 KEMC NL
Global Head   J Krant
Country Head   M C M Groot *Director of Equities*
                                          C P J Vlek

Domestic Equities
Head of Research   H J van Everdingen ✉ **557 1415**
Other (Domestic Equities)
Fixed-Income   H de Haan
Equity Repo / Securities Lending
Marketing   C van Herwaarden *Securities Administration*

Corporate Finance / M&A Advisory
Department: Corporate Finance
Fax: 557 1410
Global Head   R J Meuter
Regional Head   J L A Lycklama
Country Head   J A F van Zwieteren

Asset Management
Fax: 557 1584
Head   W O Wentges

F van Lanschot Bankiers NV   Head Office

Hooge Steenweg 29, 5211 JN 's-Hertogenbosch
PO Box 1021, 5211 JN 's-Hertogenbosch
Tel: (73) 615 3911 **Fax:** (73) 615 3066 **Telex:** 50641 FVLI NL **Swift:** FVLB NL 22 **Reuters:** FVLH
Website: www.vanlanschot.nl

Senior Executive Officers
Chairman   Hubertus Heemskerk
International Division   Peter van Raak ☏ **615 3318**

Euromoney Directory 1999 **1123**

NETHERLANDS (+31)

www.euromoneydirectory.com

F van Lanschot Bankiers NV (cont)

Others (Senior Executives)
Management Board — Carél van der Spek
Harry Baeten
Peter Zwart

Debt Capital Markets / Fixed Income
Head of Debt Capital Markets — Berry Debrauwer ☎ 615 3586

Domestic Government Bonds
Head of Sales — Wim van Bokhoven ☎ 615 3598
Head of Trading — Irving van Dijk ☎ 615 3184
Head of Research — Arno Barens ☎ 615 3177

Eurobonds
Head of Origination — Caroline Huyskes
Head of Syndication — Berry Debrauwer ☎ 615 3586
Head of Sales — Wim van Bokhoven ☎ 615 3598
Head of Trading — Irving van Dijk ☎ 615 3184
Head of Research — Arno Barens ☎ 615 3177

Private Placements
Head of Sales — Wim van Bokhoven ☎ 615 3598

Equity Capital Markets
Head of Equity Capital Markets — Berry Debrauwer ☎ 615 3586

Domestic Equities
Head of Origination — Caroline Huyskes
Head of Syndication — Berry Debrauwer ☎ 615 3586
Head of Research — Ruurd Verdam ☎ 614 3935

International Equities
Head of Trading — Hennie Veugelers ☎ 615 3564
Frank Kamsteeg ☎ 613 9285

Syndicated Lending
Department: International Division
Tel: 615 3318
Head of Syndicated Lending — Peter van Raak ☎ 615 3318

Loan-Related Activities
Trade Finance — Walther Kops ☎ 615 3317
Mario De Stefani ☎ 615 3323
Marion von Bannisseht ☎ 615 3400

Money Markets
Department: Treasury / Money Markets
Tel: 612 2322 **Fax:** 615 3077
Head of Money Markets — Piet van Schijndel *General Manager, Treasury* ☎ 615 3310

Money Markets - General
Piet Swartjes *Head of Money Market* ☎ 615 3145
Anita Reijnders *Money Market Dealer* ☎ 615 3479
Mario de Haan *Money Market Dealer* ☎ 615 3313

Foreign Exchange
Department: Treasury / Foreign Exchange
Tel: 612 4331 **Fax:** 615 3077
Global Head — Robbie Meezen *Deputy General Manager* ☎ 615 3312

FX Traders / Sales People
All Currencies — Paul Koopal *Dealer, FX & Money Market* ☎ 615 3129
Frits Vortman *Dealer, FX & Money Market* ☎ 615 3314
Maarten Boutkan *Dealer, FX & Money Market* ☎ 615 3311
Joost Derks *Dealer, FX & Money Market* ☎ 615 3308

Global Custody
Head of Global Custody — Cees van Iersel ☎ 615 3199

Other Departments
Correspondent Banking — Rudolph Jurgens ☎ 615 3207

Other Departments
International Division — Peter van Raak ☎ 615 3318

Administration
Legal / In-House Counsel
Bert Jansen ☎ 615 3447

Compliance
Jan Remijn ☎ 615 3210

1124 Euromoney Directory 1999

www.euromoneydirectory.com   NETHERLANDS (+31)

Lloyds Bank plc
Full Branch Office
Gatwickstraat 17/19, 1001 AH Amsterdam
PO Box 3518, 1001 AH Amsterdam
Tel: (20) 581 5900; (20) 581 5902 Fax: (20) 688 9265 Telex: 15333 LBFX NL Swift: LOYD NL 2A
Email: treasury@lloydsbank.nl Reuters: LBNA-D
Website: www.lloydsbank.nl

Senior Executive Officers
Principal Manager — James Lewin ☎ **581 5901**
Chief Executive Officer — Bart Ijssel de Schepper *Senior Manager, Corporate Banking* ☎ **581 5907**
Financial Director — Bert Knoppert *Financial Controller* ☎ **581 5940**
Treasurer — Matthijs Roverts *Manager, Treasury* ☎ **581 5975**

Debt Capital Markets / Fixed Income
Tel: 581 5975 Fax: 688 9265
Head of Debt Capital Markets — Matthijs Roverts *Manager, Treasury* ☎ **581 5975**

Domestic Government Bonds
Head of Trading — Matthijs Roverts *Manager, Treasury* ☎ **581 5975**

Non-Domestic Government Bonds
Matthijs Roverts *Manager, Treasury* ☎ **581 5975**

Eurobonds
Head of Trading — Matthijs Roverts *Manager, Treasury* ☎ **581 5975**

Libor-Based / Floating-Rate Products
Asset Swaps — Matthijs Roverts *Manager, Treasury* ☎ **581 5975**

Private Placements
Head of Sales — Jeremy Perl *Senior Account Manager* ☎ **581 5911**

Syndicated Lending
Loan-Related Activities
Trade Finance; Project Finance — Jeremy Perl *Senior Account Manager* ☎ **581 5911**

Money Markets
Tel: 688 7066 Fax: 688 9265
Head of Money Markets — Matthijs Roverts *Manager, Treasury* ☎ **581 5975**

Money Markets - General
Fanchette Geerlings *Dealer* ☎ **688 7066**
Klarien Moojaart *Dealer* ☎ **688 7066**

Foreign Exchange
Tel: 688 6616 Fax: 688 9268
Head of Foreign Exchange — Matthijs Roverts *Manager, Treasury* ☎ **581 5975**
Regional Head — Ron van der Does *Deputy Manager, Treasury* ☎ **688 6616**
Corporate Sales — Rene Rieder *Senior Dealer* ☎ **688 5732**
Head of Trading — Chris Gane *Senior Dealer* ☎ **688 6616**

FX Traders / Sales People
Corporate Institutional — Lex Grannetia *Senior Dealer* ☎ **688 5732**

Risk Management
Tel: 581 5950 Fax: 688 9265
Head of Risk Management — Bert Knoppert *Financial Controller* ☎ **581 5940**

Fixed Income Derivatives / Risk Management
Global Head — Matthijs Roverts *Manager, Treasury* ☎ **581 5975**

Foreign Exchange Derivatives / Risk Management
Vanilla FX option Sales — Rene Rieder *Senior Dealer* ☎ **688 5732**

Other Currency Swap / FX Options Personnel
Option Sales — Lex Grannetia *Senior Dealer* ☎ **688 5732**

Corporate Finance / M&A Advisory
Tel: 581 5900 Fax: 688 9265
Head of Corporate Finance — Bart Ijssel de Schepper *Senior Manager, Corporate Banking* ☎ **581 5907**

Settlement / Clearing
Fax: 688 9265
Head of Settlement / Clearing; Fixed-Income Settlement — Leo Dirven *Treasury Administration Manager* ☎ **581 5932**
Derivatives Settlement — Jacqueline van Duuren *Chef Positie Behandeling* ☎ **581 5968**
Foreign Exchange Settlement — Odette van Woerkom *Section Head, Treasury* ☎ **581 5937**

Other Departments
Proprietary Trading — Matthijs Roverts *Manager, Treasury* ☎ **581 5975**
Correspondent Banking — John Baly *Commercial Secretary* ☎ **581 5906**

NETHERLANDS (+31)　　　www.euromoneydirectory.com

Lloyds Bank plc (cont)
Administration
Technology & Systems

　　　Marcel Schippers *Facilities Manager* ☎ 581 5927

Compliance

　　　Peter Grooters *Internal Auditor* ☎ 581 5956

MeesPierson NV　　　Head Office
Rokin 55, PO Box 243, 1000 AE Amsterdam
Tel: (20) 527 1489; (20) 527 9111 **Fax:** (20) 527 4994; (20) 625 8164 **Telex:** 21231 BMH **Swift:** MEES NL 2A
Email: global.custody@meespierson.com
Website: www.meespierson.nl

Senior Executive Officers
Member of the Board　　　Eric van de Merwe

Others (Senior Executives)
Information Bank　　　Sjoerd van Keulen *Director*
Private Bank & Trust　　　Chris Van Boetzelaar *Director*

General-Lending (DCM, SL)
Head of Corporate Banking　　　Joop Feilzer *Director*

General-Investment
Head of Investment　　　Maarten van Berckel *Head of Corporate Finance*

General - Treasury
Head of Treasury　　　Folkert van Zinderen Bakker *Director*

Debt Capital Markets / Fixed Income
Fixed-Income Repo
Head of Repo　　　Doug Lindsay *Senior Executive* ☎ 527 1271 F 527 1923
　　　Jaap Hoff *Senior Executive*
　　　Wesley Pritchett *Senior Executive*
Trading　　　Wouter S van der Ploeg *Manager* ☎ 527 1637 F 527 1835
　　　Frank Vogel *Trader*
Sales　　　Bert Sanders ☎ 527 1638 F 527 1969

Equity Capital Markets
Warrants
Head of Sales　　　Philip Stork ☎ 527 1310 F 527 2053

Equity Repo / Securities Lending
Head　　　Nico Zwikker *Director* ☎ 527 1589 F 527 1665
　　　Doug Lindsay *Senior Executive* ☎ 527 1271 F 527 1923
　　　Jaap Hoff *Senior Executive*
　　　Wesley Pritchett *Senior Executive*
Marketing　　　Wouter S van der Ploeg *Manager* ☎ 527 1637 F 527 1835
　　　Frank Vogel *Trader*
Head of Trading　　　Edward Lea *Manager* ☎ 527 2625 F 527 1835
　　　Ruud Fernhout *Senior Representative*
　　　Cornelius van Oosterhout *Senior Representative*
　　　Kees Schouten *Collateral Management* ☎ 527 2133 F 527 1835
　　　Bert Sanders *Manager, Repo Trading*

Corporate Finance / M&A Advisory
Regional Head　　　Maarten van Berckel *Head of Corporate Finance*

Settlement / Clearing
Regional Head　　　Frans Demmenig *Head, Derivatives Clearing* ☎ 527 1758 F 527 2020

Global Custody
Other (Global Custody)
Head of Sales & Marketing　　　Fred Dellemijn *Director of Global Custody Management / Sales & Mark*
　　　☎ 527 1543 F 527 4994

Other Departments
Private Banking　　　Chris Van Boetzelaar *Director*

Administration
Public Relations

　　　Ronald de Wilde *Director, Corporate Communications* ☎ 527 1225
　　　F 527 1883

1126　Euromoney Directory 1999

Merrill Lynch NV
Subsidiary Company

27th Floor, Rembrandt Tower, Amstelplein 1, 1096 HA Amsterdam
PO Box 95232, 1090 HE Amsterdam
Tel: (20) 592 5777 Fax: (20) 692 5200 Telex: 14231

Senior Executive Officers
Managing Director | Eric Dale ☎ 592 2603
Deputy Manager | Nicholas Stonestreet ☎ 592 5605
Administration
Head of Administration | Meindert Leloux Administrative Manager ☎ 592 5601

Morgan Stanley Asset Management Limited
Full Branch Office

11th Floor, Rembrandt Tower, Amstelplein 1, 1096 HA Amsterdam
Tel: (20) 462 1300 Fax: (20) 462 1310
Website: www.ms.com

Senior Executive Officers
Executive Director | Frits Fiene ☎ 462 1320 ✉ fienef@ms.com

De Nationale Investeringsbank NV
Head Office

Carnegieplein 4, PO Box 380, 2501 BH The Hague
Tel: (70) 342 5425 Fax: (70) 365 1071 Telex: 31368 INVES NL Email: dnib_thehague@dnib.com
Website: www.dnib.com

Senior Executive Officers
Chairman | M J L Jonkhart ☎ 342 5200
Deputy Chairman | J de Vroe ☎ 342 5240
Treasurer | J W Van der Made
Managing Director | J F Ariëns
Managing Director | R van der Borch
Director | E J van der Burg
Director | P N S Luttjehuizen
Company Secretary | A G Oerlemons

Others (Senior Executives)
Equity Holdings Investment | E J van der Burg Director
Corporate & Institutional Finance | Marius C Meurs Director ☎ 342 5222

Debt Capital Markets / Fixed Income
Asset-Backed Securities / Securitization
Global Head | Rob van den Berg ☎ 342 5363
Mortgage-Backed Securities
Global Head | Rob van den Berg ☎ 342 5363

Equity Capital Markets
Department: NIB Financial Markets
Herengracht 600, 1017 CJ Amsterdam
Domestic Equities
Head of Trading | André Willemsen ☎ (20) 556 7600

Syndicated Lending
Global Head | Theo Huizing ☎ 342 5228

Loan-Related Activities
Project Finance | Paul Jinek ☎ 342 5270
Structured Trade Finance | Rob van den Berg ☎ 342 5363
Leasing & Asset Finance | Jos Schodmeesters ☎ 342 5248

Money Markets
Tel: 342 5485
Global Head | J W Van der Made

Risk Management
Global Head | Paul Buyze ☎ 342 5346
Fixed Income Derivatives / Risk Management
Global Head | Paul Buyze ☎ 342 5346
Foreign Exchange Derivatives / Risk Management
Cross-Currency Swaps, Sales / Marketing | Paul Buyze ☎ 342 5346

Corporate Finance / M&A Advisory
Global Head | Marius C Meurs Director ☎ 342 5222

NETHERLANDS (+31)　　　　www.euromoneydirectory.com

De Nationale Investeringsbank NV (cont)
Settlement / Clearing
Regional Head　　　　　　Paul Buyze ☎ **342 5346**

Nederlandse Waterschapsbank

Rooseveltplantsoen 3, 2517 KR The Hague
PO Box 580, 2501 CN The Hague
Tel: (70) 416 6266 **Fax:** (70) 416 6262 **Email:** tmeuwissen@nwb.nl **Bloomberg:** meuwissen
Website: www.nwb.nl

Senior Executive Officers
Chief Executive Officer　　　　Fon Koemas ☎ **416 6266**
General - Treasury
Head of Treasury　　　　　　Tom Meuwissen ☎ **416 6270** F **416 6279**

Nedship Bank　　　　　　　　　　　　　　　　　Head Office

Parklaan 2, 3016 BB Rotterdam
PO Box 307, 3000 AH Rotterdam
Tel: (10) 436 0841 **Fax:** (10) 436 2957; (10) 436 2883 **Telex:** 4421038

Senior Executive Officers
Chairman of the Supervisory Board　　J van Rijn
Managing Director / General Manager　S H Arnesen
Managing Director / General Manager　R M L Krijthe
Managing Director / General Manager　B H M Rosenmöller
Deputy Managing Director　　　　　　G A Gommers

Others (Senior Executives)
　　　　　　　　　　　　　　　　G A Gommers *Deputy Managing Director*
　　　　　　　　　　　　　　　　A R van Herwijnen *Deputy Managing Director*
　　　　　　　　　　　　　　　　W J Kolff *Member, Supervisory Board*
　　　　　　　　　　　　　　　　G J Swart *Deputy Managing Director*
　　　　　　　　　　　　　　　　M J Muller *Member, Supervisory Board*
　　　　　　　　　　　　　　　　J Verschoor *Deputy Managing Director*
　　　　　　　　　　　　　　　　D J M G von Slingelandt *Secretary*
　　　　　　　　　　　　　　　　P Stephansen *Member, Supervisory Board*

Nikko Europe plc　　　　　　　　　　　　　　　Full Branch Office

12th Floor, Parnassustoren, Locatellikade 1, 1076 AZ Amsterdam
Tel: (20) 662 3296 **Fax:** (20) 675 1236 **Telex:** 11306

Senior Executive Officers
Branch Manager　　　　　　Chieko Higashidani

Nomura Bank Nederland NV

Rembrandt Tower, Amstelplein 1, 1096 HA Amsterdam
Tel: (20) 599 9000 **Fax:** (20) 468 4682 **Telex:** 16408 **Swift:** NOMANL2A **Reuters:** NOMA **Cable:** NOMURASHIN

Senior Executive Officers
President　　　　　　　　　Masafumi Nakada ☎ **599 9017**
Managing Director　　　　　Daisuke Fujita ☎ **599 9011**

Nyenburgh　　　　　　　　　　　　　　　　　　Head Office

Rokin 92-96, 1012 KZ Amsterdam
Tel: (20) 556 3131 **Fax:** (20) 638 2779 **Email:** info@nyenburgh.com

Senior Executive Officers
Chief Executive Officer　　　　Jan van de Water ☎ **556 3131**
　　　　　　　　　　　　　　　Peek Emmelot ☎ **556 3131**

Debt Capital Markets / Fixed Income
Domestic Government Bonds
Head of Sales　　　　　　　Cor Soethout *Senior Sales* ☎ **556 3726**

1128　Euromoney Directory 1999

www.euromoneydirectory.com NETHERLANDS (+31)

Equity Capital Markets
Domestic Equities
Head of Sales   Fred Van der Scheer *Director* ☏ 556 3145
Head of Trading   Bekt Mullek *Vice President* ☏ 556 3134
Head of Research   Duco Frie *Investment Research* ☏ 556 3125
International Equities
Head of Sales   Fred Van der Scheer *Director* ☏ 556 3145
Convertibles / Equity-Linked
Head of Sales   Fred Van der Scheer *Director* ☏ 556 3145
Warrants
Head of Sales   Fred Van der Scheer *Director* ☏ 556 3145
Settlement / Clearing
Operations   Wilma Grootemah *Head of Back Office* ☏ 556 3114

Omni Finance & Investment Group BV   Head Office
Van Stolkweg 3, 2585 JL The Hague
Tel: (70) 352 1104 Fax: (70) 352 3469 Email: info@omni.nl
Website: www.omni.nl

Senior Executive Officers
Chief Executive Officer   Edward de Jager *Managing Director*
Financial Director   Hans Peddemors *Finance Director*
Chief Operating Officer   Jan Mekenkamp *Director, Business Development*
Managing Director of Legal Affairs   Walter Remmerswaal
Director, Buisness Intelligence   Onno Van Veldhuizen

Prebon Yamane (Nederland) BV   Subsidiary Company
Herengracht 545-549, 1017 BW Amsterdam
PO Box 3590, 1001 Amsterdam AJ
Tel: (20) 625 6877 Fax: (20) 620 9716 Telex: 15421 Reuters: PYFM-N
Corporate Dealers Tel: 229 7324; 229 7191; Reuters: PYFL; PYNL (Dealing)

Senior Executive Officers
Managing Director   Ben Siersema
Managing Director / General Manager   Garry Pithers
Relationship Manager
Prebon Financial Consulting   Peter Krom *Manager*
Debt Capital Markets / Fixed Income
Private Placements
Head of Origination   Jaap Overeem *Private Placements / Long Loans Broker*
Head of Sales   Marten Tiddens *Private Placements / Long Loans Broker*
Head of Structuring   Ruurd Prins *Private Placements / Long Loans Broker*
Money Markets
Money Markets - General
Currency Deposit Division   Ruud Nijveld *Manager*
  Ric Hageman *Deputy Manager*
  Hans Juffermans *Deputy Manager*
  Jim Boeljon *Broker*
  André Velder *Broker*
  Mark-Jan Martens *Broker*
  Lara Helsloot *Broker*
  Michael van Rijsdam *Broker*
Guilder Division   Rob Rijswijk *Manager*
  Bryan Schokking *Money Market Broker*
  Alex van Dijck *Money Market Broker*
  Mario van de Veerdonk *Money Market Broker*

Risk Management
Other Currency Swap / FX Options Personnel
FRAs / Short-Term Swaps Division   Peter van der Laan *Manager*
  Erik-Jan Kusters *Broker*
  Norbert Albstmeijer *Broker*
  Herbert Adam *Broker*

OTC Equity Derivatives
Sales   Bert van Ijssel *Manager, OTC Division*

NETHERLANDS (+31) www.euromoneydirectory.com

Rabo Securities NV
Subsidiary Company

Amstelplein 1, 1096 HA Amsterdam
PO Box 94640, 1090 GP Amsterdam
Tel: (20) 460 4747 **Fax:** (20) 460 4954 **Telex:** 11386 **Reuters:** RABC

Senior Executive Officers
General Manager — Andries Mak van Waay ☎ **460 4844**

Others (Senior Executives)
Administration — Dennis Patrikios *Managing Director* ☎ **460 4845**

Equity Capital Markets
Country Head — Dominique Bech *Managing Director* ☎ **460 4912**

Domestic Equities
Head of Origination — Dominique Bech *Managing Director* ☎ **460 4912**
Head of Syndication — Amin Mansour *Head of Syndication* ☎ **460 4904**
Head of Sales — Gerbrand ter Brugge ☎ **460 4703**
Head of Trading — Huib Boissevain *Managing Director* ☎ **460 4843**
Head of Research — Bert van den Broek ☎ **460 4819**

International Equities
Head of Origination — Jan Quist ☎ **460 4914**

Warrants
Head of Sales — Cees Smit ☎ **460 4723**
Head of Trading — Geert Toebast ☎ **460 4787**

Money Markets
Country Head — Rob Schot *Market Risk Control* ☎ **460 4738**

Settlement / Clearing
Country Head — Dennis Patrikios *Managing Director, Administration* ☎ **460 4845**
Equity Settlement; Derivatives Settlement — Maurice Mulders *Head of Operations* ☎ **460 4874**

Rabobank Group
Head Office

Cvoeselaan 18, 3521 CB Utrecht
PO Box 17100, 3500 HG Utrecht
Tel: (30) 216 0000 **Swift:** RABO NL 2U
Website: www.rabobank.nl

Senior Executive Officers
Chief Executive Officer — H H F Wijffels *Chairman Executive Board*

Robeco Group
Head Office

Coolsingel 120, 973 / 3011 AG Rotterdam
Tel: (10) 224 1224 **Fax:** (10) 411 5288
Website: www.robeco.nl

Senior Executive Officers
President & Chief Executive Officer — Pieter Korteweg
Financial Director — Jacob Van Duijn *Chief Investment Officer*
Chief Operating Officer — Géry Daeninck *Chief Finance Officer*
Treasurer — Peter Bruin ☎ **224 2420**
Company Secretary — Dave Cross ☎ **224 2250**

Others (Senior Executives)
Jan de Kreij *Executive Vice Chairman*
Willem van der Schoot *Chief Marketing Officer, Institutional*
Hans Leenaars *Chief Marketing Officer, Retail*

Debt Capital Markets / Fixed Income
Department: Fixed Income Department
Tel: 224 2289
Head of Fixed Income — Bas Vliegenthart ☎ **224 2253**

Emerging Market Bonds
Head of Emerging Markets — Leendert Meijaard ☎ **224 2305**

Fixed-Income Repo
Head of Repo — Michiel de Beauvesier-Watson *Repo Manager* ☎ **224 2203**

Fixed-Income Research
Head of Fixed Income — Martijn Tans ☎ **224 2529**
Head of Credit Research — Peter Ferket ☎ **224 2437**

1130 Euromoney Directory 1999

Equity Capital Markets
Tel: 224 2271 Fax: 224 1224
Head of Equity Capital Markets — Angelien Kemna ☏ **224 2457**
Equity Research
Head of Equity Research — Jaap van der Hart ☏ **224 2556**
Equity Repo / Securities Lending
Head — Nico Gouderjaan *Manager of International Securities Lending* ☏ **224 2483**
Money Markets
Tel: 224 1224
Head of Money Markets — Bas Vliegenthart ☏ **224 2253**
Foreign Exchange
Tel: 224 1777
Head of Foreign Exchange — Peter Bruin ☏ **224 2420**
Risk Management
Tel: 224 2208
Head of Risk Management — Pim Poppe
Settlement / Clearing
Tel: 224 2481
Head of Settlement / Clearing — Susan van der Linden ☏ **224 2481**
Equity Settlement — Onno Hoekstra ☏ **224 2003**
Simone Mennink ☏ **224 3189**
Fixed-Income Settlement — Carl Meiracker ☏ **224 2421**
Global Custody
Head of Global Custody — Frans van Dongen ☏ **224 2485**
Administration
Head of Administration — Bert Mekes *Head* ☏ **224 2495**
Business Development — Peter Hans Budde *Head of RIAM business developement* ☏ **224 3216**
Head of Marketing — Hans Leenaars *Chief Marketing Officer, Retail*
Technology & Systems
Géry Daeninck *Chief Finance Officer*
Legal / In-House Counsel
Hans Janssen Daalen *Head of Legal Dept* ☏ **224 2367**
Compliance
Cees Frohn *Compliance Officer* ☏ **224 2024**
Public Relations
Hans de Klerk *Head* ☏ **224 2810**
Accounts / Audit
Cees Frohn *Compliance Officer* ☏ **224 2024**

The Sanwa Bank Limited — Representative Office
World Trade Centre, Strawinskylaan 1447, 1077 XX Amsterdam
Tel: (20) 675 3111 Fax: (20) 675 4731
Senior Executive Officers
Chief Representative — Yutaha Kitamura
Others (Senior Executives)
Senior Representative — Pim B Kodde
Satoshi Ito

Schroders International Property Fund NV — Head Office
Herengracht 469, 1017 BS Amsterdam
Tel: (20) 530 6030 Fax: (20) 530 6040
Senior Executive Officers
General Manager — Jeremy Lewis

SNS Bank Nederland NV — Head Office
Pettelaarpark 120, 5216 PT 's-Hertogenbosch
PO Box 70053, 5201 DZ 's-Hertogenbosch
Tel: (73) 683 3333 Fax: (73) 683 3600 Swift: BBSN NL 2A Email: info@snsbank.nl Reuters: SNSN
Senior Executive Officers
Chairman, Management Board — W G J M Blind
Financial Director — T G Korver

NETHERLANDS (+31) www.euromoneydirectory.com

SNS Bank Nederland NV (cont)
Senior Executive Officers (cont)

Treasurer	P van der Harst
Debt Capital Markets / Fixed Income	
Global Head	F R Spaan
Equity Capital Markets	
Global Head	G T van Wakeren
Syndicated Lending	
Global Head	P van der Harst
Money Markets	
Global Head	F R Spaan
Foreign Exchange	
Global Head	P van der Harst
Risk Management	
Global Head	M Damm
Corporate Finance / M&A Advisory	
Global Head	R A H Soedjak
Settlement / Clearing	
Regional Head	L Brand

SNS Securities NV
Full Branch Office

Formerly known as: Suez Nederland Securities NV
Nieuwezijds Voorburgwal 162, 1000 AE Amsterdam
PO Box 235, 1000 AE Amsterdam
Tel: (20) 550 8500 **Fax:** (20) 420 4186 **Telex:** 16643 **Swift:** SUEZ NL 2A **Reuters:** SNS
Website: www.snsams.nl

Senior Executive Officers
Chief Operating Officer — Erik Böttcher *Managing Director* ☎ 550 8535 ✉ erik.böttcher@snsams.nl
Managing Director — Joltier Gerritse ☎ 550 8522
Company Secretary — Marly Hoftijzer ✉ marly.hoftijzer@snsams.nl

Debt Capital Markets / Fixed Income
Head of Fixed Income — Rob Hogenhuis ☎ 620 8456

Government Bonds
Head of Sales — Rob Hogenhuis ☎ 620 8456

Eurobonds
Head of Sales — Rob Hogenhuis ☎ 620 8456

Emerging Market Bonds
Head of Emerging Markets — Rob Hogenhuis ☎ 620 8456

Equity Capital Markets
Tel: 550 8522 **Fax:** 420 4186

Domestic Equities
Head of Sales — Reinart van Zessen ☎ 550 8522
Head of Trading — Paul Brouwer ☎ 550 8440

International Equities
Head of Trading — Paul Brouwer ☎ 550 8440

Equity Research
Head of Equity Research — Nico van Geest ☎ 550 8482 ✉ nico.vangeest@snsams.nl

Foreign Exchange
Head of Foreign Exchange — Chris Suiter

Settlement / Clearing
Head of Settlement / Clearing; Equity Settlement; Fixed-Income Settlement; Operations — Egbert Tillema ☎ 550 8541

Asset Management
Head — Paul Loos ☎ 550 8512

Other Departments
Private Banking — Robert Ter Braake ☎ 550 8510

Administration
Compliance — Andre Bakker ☎ 550 8537 ✉ andre.bakker@snsams.nl

www.euromoneydirectory.com   NETHERLANDS (+31)

Société Générale
13th Floor, Rembrandt Tower, Amstelplein 1, 1096 HA Amsterdam
Tel: (20) 462 2822 **Fax:** (20) 465 3361; (20) 463 5324 **Telex:** 13124 SGAM NL **Reuters:** SOGA
Website: www.socgen.com

Senior Executive Officers
General Manager   C Garsen

Staal Bank NV
Alternative trading name: Staal Bankiers
8 Lange Houtstraat, 2511 CW The Hague
PO Box 327, 2501 CH The Hague
Tel: (70) 310 1510 **Fax:** (70) 364 4508 **Telex:** 31460 STAL NL **Swift:** STAL NL 26
Website: www.staalbankiers.nl

Senior Executive Officers
Chairman   Mr Van Hal ☏ **310 1422**
Financial Director   Mr Van Hal ☏ **310 1422**
Treasurer   Mr Vos ☏ **310 1740**

General-Lending (DCM, SL)
Head of Corporate Banking   Mr De Jonge ☏ **310 1497**

Debt Capital Markets / Fixed Income
Head of Debt Capital Markets   Mr Van Gameren ☏ **310 1734**

Equity Capital Markets
Head of Equity Capital Markets   Mr Massaar

Syndicated Lending
Head of Syndicated Lending   Mr Glasius ☏ **310 1461**

Money Markets
Head of Money Markets   Mr Peerenboom ☏ **310 1555**

Foreign Exchange
Head of Foreign Exchange   Mr Vos ☏ **310 1740**

Risk Management
Head of Risk Management   Mr Van Zanten ☏ **310 1434**

Corporate Finance / M&A Advisory
Head of Corporate Finance   Mr Somberg ☏ **310 1404**

Administration
Head of Marketing   Mr Keesom ☏ **310 1614**

Tokai Bank Nederland NV   Subsidiary Company
Keizersgracht 452, 1016 GD Amsterdam
Tel: (20) 627 1616 **Fax:** (20) 624 1872; (20) 638 5669 **Telex:** 15626 **Swift:** TKAI NL 2A BIC **Reuters:** TOKA
Cable: TOKAIBK NL AMSTE

Senior Executive Officers
Chairman   Satoru Nishigaki
Chief Operating Officer   Akihiro Wakao
Managing Director / General Manager   Yukitoshi Harayama

Debt Capital Markets / Fixed Income
Domestic Government Bonds
Head of Sales   Bob Burlage *Assistant Manager*
Head of Trading   Hiroyuki Hayashi *Manager*
Head of Research   Bob Burlage *Assistant Manager*

Eurobonds
Head of Origination   Hiroyuki Hayashi *Manager*
Head of Trading   Bob Burlage *Assistant Manager*

Libor-Based / Floating-Rate Products
FRN Origination; FRN Sales; Asset Swaps;   Hiroyuki Hayashi *Manager*
Asset Swaps (Sales)

Money Markets
Global Head   Hiroyuki Hayashi *Manager*

Domestic Commercial Paper
Head of Origination   Hiroyuki Hayashi *Manager*

NETHERLANDS (+31)   www.euromoneydirectory.com

Tokai Bank Nederland NV (cont)

Eurocommercial Paper
Head of Origination   Hiroyuki Hayashi *Manager*

Foreign Exchange
Global Head   Hiroyuki Hayashi *Manager*

FX Traders / Sales People
All currencies   Mathias Vinandy *Assistant*
                           Hideo Saburi *Assistant*
                           Berthil Bosch *Assistant*

Risk Management
Global Head   Hiroyuki Hayashi *Manager*

Foreign Exchange Derivatives / Risk Management
Cross-Currency Swaps, Sales / Marketing   Hiroyuki Hayashi *Manager*

Corporate Finance / M&A Advisory
Global Head   Atsushi Murakami *Senior Manager*

Other Departments
Commodities / Bullion   Hiroyuki Hayashi *Manager*
Private Banking; Correspondent Banking   Atsushi Murakami *Senior Manager*

Administration

Technology & Systems
                           Anthony Jager *Manager*

Compliance
                           Hendrikus Dekker *Manager*

Public Relations
                           Johnny Wessels *Manager*

Turkiye Garanti Bankasi AS   Full Branch Office

Westblaak 34, 3012 KM Rotterdam
Tel: (10) 411 0591 **Fax:** (10) 404 8705 **Swift:** VGBI NL 2R

Senior Executive Officers
Branch Manager   Jan de Groot

Others (Senior Executives)
                           Murat Bayburtcuoglu *EVP, Amsterdam Branch*

UBS (Nederland) BV

Herengracht 564, 1017 CH Amsterdam
Tel: (20) 551 0100 **Fax:** (20) 551 0155

Senior Executive Officers

Others (Senior Executives)
Senior Executive Officer   S E Beelaerts van Blokland

Equity Capital Markets
Department: Equities

Other (Domestic Equities)
                           J-D Bronkhorst *Chief Operating Officer*
                           N Holtby *Head of Dutch Trading*
                           L Jonkman *Dutch Sales / Trading*
                           J D G Morris *Head of Dutch Sales*
                           G R M Steens *Head of Dutch Research*

Corporate Finance / M&A Advisory

Other (Corporate Finance)
                           S E Beelaerts van Blokland *Managing Director, Corporate Finance Department*

www.euromoneydirectory.com   NETHERLANDS (+31)

Unico Banking Group

Herengracht 386, 1016 CJ Amsterdam
Tel: (20) 530 1212 **Fax:** (20) 626 7846 **Email:** unicobnk@euronet.nl
Website: www.unico.nl

Senior Executive Officers
Chairman   Walter Rothensteiner ☎ +43 (1) 717 070
Managing Director / General Manager   Remy Lasne

Unico Banking Institute   Representative Office

Herengracht 386, 1016 CJ Amsterdam
Tel: (20) 620 4070 **Fax:** (20) 624 5723 **Email:** unicobnk@euronet.nl
Website: www.unico.nl

Senior Executive Officers
Chairman   Walter Rothensteiner ☎ +43 (1) 717 070
Managing Director / General Manager   Rémy Lasne ☎ 530 1212

United Garanti Bank International NV   Head Office

Alternative trading name: UGBI Bank
Herengracht 478, 1001 JN Amsterdam
PO Box 17650, Amsterdam
Tel: (20) 553 9700 **Fax:** (20) 624 2466 **Telex:** 12709 UGBI NL **Swift:** UGBI NL 2A **Reuters:** UGBI

Senior Executive Officers
Chief Executive Officer   Turgay Gönensin *Senior GM / Senior Managing Director* ☎ 553 9715
Treasurer   H Fehmi Çubukcu *Executive Vice President* ☎ 553 9709
                            ✉ fcubukcu@ugbi.nl
GM / Managing Director   Marc P Padberg ☎ 553 9711

Debt Capital Markets / Fixed Income
Department: Treasury Department
Tel: 638 8581 Fax: 638 8731
Global Head   Machiel L van Breen *Executive Vice President* ☎ 553 9771 F 420 1046
                            ✉ mvbreen@ugbi.nl

Domestic Government Bonds
Head of Trading   Özgen Etker *Senior Vice President* ☎ 638 8581

Non-Domestic Government Bonds
TRL   Özgen Etker *Senior Vice President* ☎ 638 8581

Fixed-Income Repo
Head of Repo   Özgen Etker *Senior Vice President* ☎ 638 8581

Syndicated Lending
Department: Correspondent Banking Department
Global Head   Aytac Yuksel *Senior Vice President* ☎ 553 9722
Head of Credit Committee Turgay Gönensin *Senior GM / Senior Managing Director* ☎ 553 9715

Loan-Related Activities
Trade Finance   Sinan Sahinbas *Executive Vice President* ☎ 553 9721 ✉ ssahinba@ugbi.nl
Project Finance   Oral Draman *Senior Vice President* ☎ 553 9724

Money Markets
Department: Treasury Department
Global Head   H Fehmi Çubukcu *Executive Vice President* ☎ 553 9709
                            ✉ fcubukcu@ugbi.nl

Wholesale Deposits
Marketing   Bert Verkerk *Assistant Vice President* ☎ 553 9774

Foreign Exchange
Department: Treasury Department
Corporate Sales   Bert Verkerk *Assistant Vice President* ☎ 553 9774
Head of Trading   Dilek Basara *Assistant Vice President*

Risk Management
Department: Management
Global Head   Machiel L van Breen *Executive Vice President* ☎ 553 9771 F 420 1046
                            ✉ mvbreen@ugbi.nl

Other Departments
Proprietary Trading   Sema Zeyneloglu *Senior Vice President* ☎ 553 9804 ✉ szeynelo@ugbi.nl
Correspondent Banking   Aytac Yuksel *Senior Vice President* ☎ 553 9722

NETHERLANDS (+31) www.euromoneydirectory.com

United Garanti Bank International NV (cont)
Administration
Technology & Systems
Ronald Smit *Senior Vice President* ☎ 553 9792
Compliance
Ton Gorissen *Senior Vice President* ☎ 553 9733

NETHERLANDS ANTILLES
(+599)

Bank van de Nederlandse Antillen — Central Bank
Breedestraat 1 (P), Willemstad, Curaçao
Tel: (9) 434 5500 **Fax:** (9) 461 5004 **Telex:** 1155 BNACU NA **Swift:** NEAN AN CU **Email:** info@centralbank.an
Website: www.centralbank.an

Senior Executive Officers
President — Emsley Tromp
Executive President — Robert Reijnart
Treasurer — Lawrence Bennett *Head, Financial Markets* ☎ 434 5529

Others (Senior Executives)
Carlos Vanderpool *Chief Cashier* ☎ 434 5510
Bank Licensing & Supervision — Ulrich Dalnoot *Head* ☎ 434 5620
Alberto Romero *Executive Director*
Economics & Statistics — Eric Matto *Head* ☎ 434 5643
Reserves Management — Lawrence Bennett *Head, Financial Markets* ☎ 434 5529
Supervision, Institutional Investors — Raynold Nivillac ☎ 434 5602
Publication Department — Nancy Van der Wall *Head* ☎ 434 5572

Foreign Exchange
Head of Foreign Exchange — Kenneth Pietersz ☎ 434 5642

Settlement / Clearing
Head of Settlement / Clearing — Claudette Suydon ☎ 434 5532

Administration
Head of Administration — Glensher Maduro ☎ 434 5550

Technology & Systems
Information, Organization & Planning — Roy Everts ☎ 434 5670

Legal / In-House Counsel
Roselle Garcia ☎ 434 5608

Public Relations
Jerrald Hasselmeyer *Assistant to the President* ☎ 434 5517

Accounts / Audit
Accountancy — Marco La Cruz *Deputy Director, Finance Affairs* ☎ 434 5549
Henri Gerrets *Internal Auditor* ☎ 434 5663

Deutsche Bank Finance NV — Subsidiary Company
Pietermaai 17, Willemstad, Curaçao
PO Box 4905, Curaçao
Tel: (9) 461 2369 **Fax:** (9) 465 2212 **Telex:** 1157 GENTR

Exprinter International Bank NV — Head Office
Emancipatie Boulevard 31C, Willemstad, Curaçao
Tel: (9) 734 1122 **Fax:** (9) 734 1133 **Swift:** EINB AN C1 **Email:** info@exprinter.an

Senior Executive Officers
Board of Managing Directors — Enrique Jorge Carrier
Board of Managing Directors — Malcolm Hood MacCormack
Board of Managing Directors — Herman John Behr

Others (Senior Executives)
Board of Supervisory Directors — Jean Marie Louis Fano

NEW ZEALAND (+64)

ING Barings
Full Branch Office

Zeelandia Commercial Centre, Kaya WFG (Jombi), Mensing 14, Curaçao
PO Box 3895, Willemstad, Curaçao
Tel: (9) 432 7000 Fax: (9) 432 7502; (9) 432 7503 Telex: 1074 INGB NA Swift: INGB AN CU
Extra Telex: 1116 INGB NA

Senior Executive Officers
General Manager   Jos de Wit

Others (Senior Executives)
                            Willhem Redemecter Deputy General Manager

Other Departments
Department: ING Baring Private Bank
Private Banking   Jan D Elings ☎ 432 7320 📠 432 7507

ING Trust (Antilles)

Zeelandia Commercial Centre, Kaya WFG (Jombi), Mensing 14, Curaçao
PO Box 3895, Curaçao
Tel: (9) 432 7400 Fax: (9) 432 7590

Senior Executive Officers
General Manager   Ronald Jacobs

Nedship Bank (America) NV

Formerly known as: Nedship Finance Antillen NV
Scharlooweg 55, Willemstad, Curaçao
PO Box 3107, Willemstad, Curaçao
Tel: (9) 465 2311 Fax: (9) 465 2366

Senior Executive Officers
Relationship Manager
Office Manager   R J L van Heel

Netherlands Caribbean Bank

Kaya WFG (Jombi), Mensing 14, Curaçao
PO Box 3895, Curaçao
Tel: (9) 432 7000 Fax: (9) 432 7512 Telex: 1074 INGB NA

Senior Executive Officers
Managing Director   Arthur Rosaria

NEW ZEALAND
(+64)

Reserve Bank of New Zealand
🏛 Central Bank

2 The Terrace, Wellington, 6001
PO Box 2498, Wellington, 6015
Tel: (4) 472 2029 Fax: (4) 473 8554 Telex: NZ 3568 Email: rbnz-info@rbnz.govt.nz
Website: www.rbnz.govt.nz

Senior Executive Officers
Governor   D T Brash
Deputy Governor   M A Sherwin
Deputy Governor   R Carr

Others (Senior Executives)
Financial Markets   D Archer *Chief Manager*
Economics   A Orr *Chief Manager*
Banking System   P J Ledingham *Chief Manager*
Accounting Services   S J Anderson *Chief Manager*
Registry   J S R Woodhouse *Chief Manager*
Corporate Services   K Sullivan *Chief Manager*

Euromoney Directory 1999 **1137**

NEW ZEALAND (+64)	www.euromoneydirectory.com

Reserve Bank of New Zealand (cont)
Others (Senior Executives) (cont)
Currency	B J Lang *Chief Manager*
Internal Audit	J Galt *Manager*
Overseas Investment Commission Secretariat	S Dawe

ABN AMRO New Zealand Limited

Level 10, 45 Queen Street, Auckland
Tel: (9) 358 7500 **Fax:** (9) 377 9797

Senior Executive Officers
Managing Director	Simon Allen

## ASB Bank Limited	Head Office

135 Albert Street, Auckland, 1015
PO Box 35, Auckland, 1015
Tel: (9) 377 8930 **Fax:** (9) 358 3511 **Telex:** NZ60881 **Swift:** ASBB NZ 2A **Reuters:** ASBX
Website: www.asbbank.co.nz

Senior Executive Officers
Chairman	G J Judd
Chief Executive Officer	Ralph Norris *Managing Director*
Treasurer	Kerry Francis *Treasurer* ☎ **306 0067**
General Manager, Corporate & Institutional	Peter Hall
Banking

Money Markets
Tel: 309 2072 **Fax:** 302 0992
Head of Money Markets	Kerry Francis *Treasurer* ☎ **306 0067**

Domestic Commercial Paper
Head of Trading	Brent Cook ☎ **309 2072**

Foreign Exchange
Tel: 302 3055 **Fax:** 302 0992
Head of Foreign Exchange	Kerry Francis *Treasurer* ☎ **306 0067**
Head of Trading	Richard Turner ☎ **302 3055**

## Bank of New Zealand	Head Office

1 Willis Street, Wellington
PO Box 2392, Wellington
Tel: (4) 474 6999 **Fax:** (4) 474 6563 **Telex:** NZ3344 **Swift:** BKNZ NZ 22 **Reuters:** BNZW **Telerate:** 2460
Website: www.bnz.co.nz

Senior Executive Officers
Chairman	T K McDonald
Managing Director	M Pratt

Others (Senior Executives)
Risk Management	B G Donhardt *General Manager*
Wholesale Banking	C Campbell *General Manager*
Personal Financial Services	A J J Casey *National Sales Manager*
Business Financial Services	P L Thodey *General Manager*
Customer Services	D McDonald *General Manager*
Marketing	G Campbell *General Manager*
Direct Banking	M Laing *General Manager*
Financial Services Group	D C Jones *General Manager*
Finance	G Devonport *General Manager*
Chief Economist	T A Alexander *Chief Economist*
Corporate Relations	R McArthur *Head*

General-Lending (DCM, SL)
Head of Corporate Banking	Sarah Vrede *Manager, Financial Engineering* ☎ **473 1890**

General - Treasury
Head of Treasury	A J Cakebread *Head of Treasury*

Debt Capital Markets / Fixed Income
Country Head	Graeme Liddell *Manager, Interest Rate Risk* ☎ **473 9864**

Domestic Government Bonds
Head of Sales	Sue Brake *National Manager, Sales & Service* ☎ **474 6742**

1138 Euromoney Directory 1999

www.euromoneydirectory.com NEW ZEALAND (+64)

Non-Domestic Government Bonds
Domestic Securities Origination; Domestic Securities Syndication B A Stockwell *Senior Manager* ☏ **474 6923**
Domestic Securities Origination Phillippe Blin *Senior Manager* ☏ **474 6701**
Private Placements
Head of Origination Phillippe Blin *Senior Manager* ☏ **474 6701**
Department: **NZ$ Denominated Securities**
Bonds - General
Treasury Bills, Promissory Notes & Bank Bills Mark Lowler *Senior Dealer* ☏ **473 6160**
New Zealand Government Bonds & SOE Bonds Lloyd Cartwright *Manager, Long-Term Securities* ☏ **437 4616**
Syndicated Lending
Department: **Loan Syndication / Asset Sales**
Head of Origination; Head of Syndication B A Stockwell *Senior Manager* ☏ **474 6923**
Money Markets
Money Markets - General
CDs - Trading Graeme Liddell *Manager, Interest Rate Risk* ☏ **473 9864**
 Mark Lowler *Senior Dealer* ☏ **473 6160**
Other (Wholesale Deposits)
Interbank Deposits - All Major Currencies Charles Roberts *Manager, Funding* ☏ **474 6160**
 Dean Spicer *Dealer* ☏ **474 6160**
Foreign Exchange
Global Head Michael Symonds *Manager, Spot* ☏ **474 9722**
FX Traders / Sales People
NZ$, A$, DM, Yen, Sterling O / N to 1 year Mark Perry *Senior Dealer Spot FX* ☏ **474 6160**
NZ$, A$, DM, Yen, Sterling O / N to 1 year; Mark Lower *Senior Dealer Spot FX* ☏ **474 6160**
NZ$, A$, DM, Yen, Sterling 1-5 years
NZ$, A$, DM, Yen, Sterling 1-5 years Mark Perry *Senior Dealer Spot FX* ☏ **474 6160**
Majors / US$ & NZ$ Mark Lower *Senior Dealer Spot FX* ☏ **474 6160**
 Mark Perry *Senior Dealer Spot FX* ☏ **474 6160**
All Major Currency / NZ$ Peter Dunn *Dealer, Currency Option* ☏ **474 6160**
Risk Management
Global Head B G Donhardt *General Manager*
Other Currency Swap / FX Options Personnel
Interest Swaps Mark Perry *Assistant Chief Dealer* ☏ **474 6161**
Other (Exchange-Traded Derivatives)
NZ$ Interest Rate Derivatives Mark Perry *Dealer* ☏ **474 6160**
Settlement / Clearing
Settlement (General) Chris Bransgove *Manager, Treasury Support* ☏ **474 6868**
Other Departments
Correspondent Banking Jason Clinton *Manager*
Economic Research T A Alexander *Chief Economist*

Banque Nationale de Paris

Level 16, Phillips Fox Tower, National Bank Centre, 209 Queen Street, Auckland
PO Box 7342, Wellesley Street, Auckland
Tel: (9) 912 2622 **Fax:** (9) 912 2620 **Swift:** BNPA NZ 2A
Senior Executive Officers
General Manager Michaël Sanders ✉ **msanders@bnp.com.au**
Deputy General Manager Mark Davison ✉ **mdavison@bnp.com.au**

BT Alex.Brown NZ Limited   Full Branch Office

Formerly known as: BT Securities & Doyle Paterson Brown Limited

BT Alex.Brown NZ Ltd
A Member of the New Zealand Stock Exchange
Level 18, IBM Centre, 171 Featherston Street, Wellington
Tel: (4) 471 0470 **Fax:** (4) 471 0439 **Email:** doyle.paterson.brown@dpb.co.nz **Bloomberg:** BT ALEXBROWN NZ LTD
Senior Executive Officers
Managing Director Murray Doyle
Financial Controller Neil Brydyes

Euromoney Directory 1999 **1139**

NEW ZEALAND (+64) www.euromoneydirectory.com

BT Alex.Brown NZ Limited (cont)
Others (Senior Executives)
Institutional Advisor
Head of Research
Senior Equities Analyst
Economist / Strategist
Equity Capital Markets
Head of Sales
Equity Research
Country Head
Settlement / Clearing
Head of Settlement / Clearing

Darren Manning *Vice President*
Andrew Bascand *Vice President*
Kevin Bennett *Vice President*
Stephen Toplis *Vice President*

Murray Doyle *Managing Director*

Andrew Bascand *Vice President*

Elaine Jackson *Settlement Manager*

Cavill White Securities Limited
Head Office

18th Floor, Westpac Tower, 120 Albert Street, Auckland, 1000
Tel: (9) 377 1201 **Fax:** (9) 377 1975 **Telex:** NZ63034

Senior Executive Officers
Financial Director
Managing Director
Debt Capital Markets / Fixed Income
Tel: 373 3586
Head of Debt Capital Markets
Equity Capital Markets
Head of Equity Capital Markets
Domestic Equities
Head of Sales
Head of Trading
Head of Research
International Equities
Head of Sales
Settlement / Clearing
Head of Settlement / Clearing
Equity Settlement

Robert Poulter *Financial Controller* ☏ **300 5252**
Don Turkington

Tim Kronfeld *Bond Dealer*

Don Turkington *Managing Director*

Richard Burton ☏ **377 7630**
Wayne Schuler ☏ **377 7629**
John Cairns ☏ **300 5256**

Don Turkington *Managing Director*

Robert Poulter *Financial Controller* ☏ **300 5252**
Kelly Beehre ☏ **300 5251**

Citibank NA
Full Branch Office

Citibank Centre, 23 Customs Street East, Auckland 1
PO Box 3429, Auckland
Tel: (9) 302 3128 **Fax:** (9) 308 9928 **Telex:** 64 60890 **Reuters:** CIAK
Website: www.citibank.com

Senior Executive Officers
Chief Executive Officer
Treasurer
General-Lending (DCM, SL)
Head of Corporate Banking
General - Treasury
Head of Treasury
Foreign Exchange
Head of Foreign Exchange
Corporate Sales
Settlement / Clearing
Head of Settlement / Clearing

Brad Nowland
Roy Savage *Treasurer, Foreign Exchange and Capital Markets*

Ken Camble *Head, Corporate & GRB Banking*

Paul Duncan *Manager, Money Market*

Lindsay Diggelmann ☏ **302 3118**
Dean Sheridan ☏ **302 3116**

Ross Hedges *Transaction Services Head*

Credit Suisse First Boston
Subsidiary Company

Level 10 Caltex Tower, 282-292 Lambton Quay, Wellington
PO Box 3394, Wellington
Tel: (4) 474 4400 **Fax:** (4) 474 4051 **Email:** info@csfb.co.nz **Telerate:** 8993
Website: www.csfb.com

Senior Executive Officers
Chairman
Chief Executive Officer

Bryan Johnson ☏ **474 4004**
Bill Trotter ☏ **474 4083**

1140   Euromoney Directory 1999

www.euromoneydirectory.com   NEW ZEALAND (+64)

Senior Executive Officers (cont)
Chief Operating Officer   Tony Broad ☎ **474 4460**
General-Investment
Head of Investment   David Smith *Managing Director, Investment Banking* ☎ **474 4472**
Debt Capital Markets / Fixed Income
Department: Fixed Income, Sales & Trading
Fax: 474 4432
Head of Fixed Income   Scott Dewar *Director* ☎ **474 4495**
Fixed-Income Repo
Head of Repo   Michael Warrington *Vice President* ☎ **474 4491**
Equity Capital Markets
Department: Equity Sales & Trading
Fax: 474 4060
Head of Equity Capital Markets   Peter Keenan *Managing Director, Sales & Trading* ☎ **474 4463**
Head of Sales   Scott St. John *Director* ☎ **474 4095**
Other (Domestic Equities)
Investor Services   Philip Hunter *Associate Director* ☎ **474 4036**
Equity Research
Head of Equity Research   Guy Hallwright *Director* ☎ **474 4464**
Settlement / Clearing
Fax: 474 4051
Head of Settlement / Clearing   Helen Stevens *Head of NZ Operations*
Other Departments
Private Banking   Peter Keenan *Managing Director, Sales & Trading* ☎ **474 4463**

Deutsche Bank AG - NZ   Full Branch Office

Formerly known as: Deusche Morgan Grenfell New Zealand Limited & Bain & Company NZ Limited
Level 11, ASB Tower, 135 Albert Street, Auckland, 1001
PO Box 5642, Wellesley Street, Auckland
Tel: (9) 373 8520; (9) 373 8550 **Fax:** (9) 379 4352 **Reuters:** DMGAA; DMGAB
Debt Capital Markets / Fixed Income
Domestic Government Bonds
Head of Sales   Kevin Stirrat ☎ **373 8530**
Head of Trading   Alastair Wait ☎ **373 8540**
Head of Research   Ulf Schoefisch ☎ **373 8510**

FR Partners Limited   Full Branch Office

PO Box 6440, Auckland
Tel: (9) 355 9100 **Fax:** (9) 355 9199
Senior Executive Officers
Managing Director   William Birnie
Financial Director   Simpson Wayne *Executive Director, Operations*

FRP Securities

PO Box 10-085, Wellington
Tel: (4) 498 7000 **Fax:** (4) 498 7064
Senior Executive Officers
Managing Director / General Manager   Chris Lambert ☎ **498 7064**

Garlick & Co Limited   Head Office

PO Box 2098, Wellington
Tel: (4) 473 4620
Senior Executive Officers
Managing Director   Bill Garlick ☎ **470 0200**
General Manager   Peter Marshall ☎ **495 2035**
Director   John Andrews ☎ **470 0208**

Euromoney Directory 1999   **1141**

NEW ZEALAND (+64)   www.euromoneydirectory.com

Garlick & Co Limited (cont)
Equity Capital Markets
Tel: 473 4529
Domestic Equities
Head of Origination   John Andrews *Director* ☏ 470 0208
Warrants
Head of Sales   Shane Gavegon *Operator* ☏ 470 0210
Corporate Finance / M&A Advisory
Tel: 473 4061
Global Head   Bill Garlick *Managing Director* ☏ 470 0200
Settlement / Clearing
Tel: 473 4620
Regional Head   Glen Phillips *Settlement Manager* ☏ 470 0218
Global Custody
Tel: 471 0974
Regional Head   Raewyn Senior *Custody Manager* ☏ 470 0219

Merrill Lynch (New Zealand) Limited   Subsidiary Company

Level 39, Coopers & Lybrand Building, 23-29 Albert Street, Auckland, 1000
Tel: (9) 356 2929 Fax: (9) 356 2931; (9) 356 2933
Website: www.ml.com

Ord Minnett Securities Group

Level 14, City Tower, 95 Custom House Quay, Wellington
Tel: (4) 495 0333 Fax: (4) 495 0369
Website: www.ords.co.nz

Equity Capital Markets
Tel: 495 0347
Equity Repo / Securities Lending
Head   Julian A Smith *Manager, Securities Lending* ☏ +61 (2) 9220 1413
                                ⌨ +61 (2) 9220 1379 ✉ jsmith@ords.com.au
Head of Trading   Rob Spittal *Securities Lending Agent*

TSB Bank Limited

Devon Street East, New Plymouth, Taranaki
PO Box 240, New Plymouth, Taranaki
Tel: (6) 757 9159 Fax: (6) 759 9208

Senior Executive Officers
Chairperson   E Gill
Chief Executive Officer   J McConachy
Managing Director / General Manager   K W Rimmington
Others (Senior Executives)
Deputy Chair   B C Richards
Financial Services   K J Murphy *Manager*
Branch Services   G Sheehan *Manager*
Syndicated Lending
Lending Services   R Main *Manager*
Administration
Head of Marketing   R Grant *Manager*
Other (Administration)
Information Services   J A Hollins *Manager*

Warburg Dillon Read New Zealand Limited

Level 23, 191 Queen Street, Auckland
PO Box 45, Auckland
Tel: (9) 913 4800 Fax: (9) 913 4888

Senior Executive Officers
Chairman   J Cimino

www.euromoneydirectory.com NEW ZEALAND (+64)

Equity Capital Markets
Department: Equities
Country Head   C Stuart *Head of Equities*
Other (Domestic Equities)
Equity Capital Markets   A Coupe
Corporate Finance / M&A Advisory
Head of Corporate Finance   S Wills

Warburg Dillon Read New Zealand Limited
Level 14, 1-3 Willeston Street, Wellington
PO Box 2681, Wellington
Tel: (4) 496 5500 Fax: (4) 496 5566

Westpac Banking Corporation   Full Branch Office
Alternative trading name: Westpac Trust
318 Lambton Quay, Wellington
PO Box 691, Wellington
Tel: (4) 498 1583 Fax: (4) 472 9715 Telex: 30038 Swift: WPAC NZ 2W Reuters: WBCW

Senior Executive Officers
Chief Executive Officer   Harry Price *Chief Executive for New Zealand* T **498 1150**
Financial Director   John Frechtling *General Manager, Finance* T **494 7753** E **john_frechtling@westpactrust.co.nz**
Treasurer   Catherine Joice *Treasurer for New Zealand* T **498 1312**
     E **catherine_joice@westpactrust.co.nz**
GM, New Zealand Financial Markets   Stephen Moir T **498 1534** E **stephen_moir@westpactrust.co.nz**

Debt Capital Markets / Fixed Income
Marketing   Mark Butcher *Chief Dealer, Fixed-Income & Derivatives* T **471 1658**
     E **mark_butcher@westpactrust.co.nz**

Syndicated Lending
Other (Syndicated Lending)
Debt & Securities   Melissa Cameron *Senior Manager* T **498 1430**
     E **melissa_cameron@westpactrust.co.nz**

Money Markets
Country Head   Graeme Edie *Chief Dealer, STIRR* T **473 0202**
     E **graeme_edie@westpactrust.co.nz**

Domestic Commercial Paper
Head of Sales; Head of Trading   Joanne Freeman *Dealer, Risk Management* T **498 1269**
     E **joanne_freeman@westpactrust.coo.nz**

Money Markets - General
Head of Liquidity   Mike Pearce *Senior Manager, NZ Financial Markets* T **498 1269**

Foreign Exchange
Head of Foreign Exchange   Stuart Nattrass *Senior Manager, Foreign Exchange* T **471 1631**
Head of Institutional Sales   Mike Burns *Senior Manager, CID* T **471 1631**
     E **mike_burns@westpactrust.co.nz**
Head of Trading   Basil Payn *Chief Dealer* T **471 1631** E **basil_payn@westpactrust.co.nz**
FX Traders / Sales People
     Daren Manks *Senior Dealer, Fwd NZ$ Trader* T **498 1237**
     E **daren_manks@westpactrust.co.nz**
     David Brook *Senior Dealer* T **498 1261**
     E **david_brook@westpactrust.co.nzq**

Risk Management
Head of Risk Management   Michael Parrott *Senior Manager, Trading & Risk Management* T **498 1094**
Fixed Income Derivatives / Risk Management
IR Swaps Sales / Marketing   Peter Adams *Senior Manager, Derivative Products* T **473 7842**
     E **peter_adams@westpactrust.co.nz**

Corporate Finance / M&A Advisory
Department: Corporate Finance / M&A Advisory
Level 19, Westpac Tower, 120 Albert Street, Auckland
Tel: +64 (9) 309 8464 Fax: +64 (9) 367 3833
Head of Corporate Finance   Mike Allen *Chief Manager* T **(9) 367 3819** F **(9) 367 3733**
     Jarrod Smith *Senior Manager* T **(9) 367 3757** F **(9) 367 3757**

NEW ZEALAND (+64) www.euromoneydirectory.com

Westpac Banking Corporation (cont)
Settlement / Clearing
Head of Settlement / Clearing   Peter Thomas Manager, Settlements ☏ 498 1292
                                 ✉ peter_thomas@westpactrust.co.nz

NICARAGUA
(+505)

Banco Central de Nicaragua   🏛 Central Bank

Km 7 Carretera Sur, Managua
Tel: 265 0500; 265 2272 **Fax:** 265 0562; 265 2272 **Telex:** 2460 **Swift:** BCNI NI MA
Website: www.bcn.gob.ni

Senior Executive Officers
President   Noel Ramirez ☏ 265 3316
Treasurer   Manuel Picón Treasury Manager ☏ ext 531
Others (Senior Executives)
                                 Mario Flores Executive Director ☏ ext 562
Banking Supervision   Carlos Cerda Finance Manager ☏ ext 589
Economics & Statistics   José Solis Manager, Economic Studies ☏ ext 560
Reserves Management   Róger Sobalvarro Sub Manager ☏ ext 590
Foreign Exchange
Head of Foreign Exchange   Noel Picado Sub Manager ☏ ext 583
Administration
Head of Administration   Roger Etienne Manager ☏ ext 504
Technology & Systems
                                 Maximillano Muñoz ☏ ext 513
Public Relations
                                 Carlos Maturana Director, Public Relations ☏ 265 0495
Other (Administration)
Personnel   Roger Etienne Manager ☏ ext 504

NIGER
(+227)

Banque Centrale des Etats de l'Afrique de l'Ouest 🏛 Central Bank

PO Box 487, Niamey
Tel: 722 491; 722 492 **Fax:** 734 743 **Telex:** BCEAO 5218 NI

Senior Executive Officers
Country Director   Abdoulaye Soumana
Branch Director   Moulicatou Agalheir

NIGERIA
(+234)

First Bank of Nigeria   Head Office

35 Marina Street, Samuel Asabia House, Lagos Island
PO Box 5216, Lagos Island
Tel: (1) 266 5900; (1) 266 5900ext20 **Fax:** (1) 266 5934 **Swift:** FBNI NG LA **Email:** qmm.obi@fbn.com.ng
Website: fbn.com.ng

Senior Executive Officers
Chairman   Mahmoud Atta ☏ 266 3890
Chief Executive Officer   Christian Adimorah Managing Director & Chief Executive ☏ 266 1300
Financial Director   C F Awosika ☏ 266 0077
Company Secretary   Tijani M Borodo ☏ 266 0759
International Division   Chief A K Akinlade Head of International Banking ☏ 266 3880

1144   Euromoney Directory 1999

NIGERIA (+234)

Others (Senior Executives)
Commercial & Consumer Banking
Corporate Banking
Strategic Resources & Management Comp.

D T Iordaah *Executive Director* ☏ **266 1054**
Alhaji Aod Y Wanka *Executive Director* ☏ **266 4041**
Alhaji Umar Yahaya *Executive Director* ☏ **266 9248**

General-Lending (DCM, SL)
Head of Corporate Banking

A O O Odunmbaku *Head of Corporate Banking (SBU)* ☏ **266 0817**
P O Sideso *Head of Corporate Banking* ☏ **266 5930**

General-Investment
Head of Investment

F B Abiola-Cudjoe *Head of Domestic Banking Operations* ☏ **266 1037**

Equity Capital Markets
Head of Equity Capital Markets

Chief C C Offiah *Managing Director & Chief Executive* ☏ **263 6354**

Money Markets
Head of Money Markets

A I Atta *Head of Treasury* ☏ **266 9675**

Foreign Exchange
Head of Foreign Exchange

Chief A K Akinlade *Head of International Banking* ☏ **266 3880**

Corporate Finance / M&A Advisory
Head of Corporate Finance

A O O Odunmbaku *Head of Corporate Banking (SBU)* ☏ **266 0817**

Asset Management
Head

B A Bakare *Head of Risk Assets Management* ☏ **266 3562**

Other Departments
Correspondent Banking
Cash Management

Chief A K Akinlade *Head of International Banking* ☏ **266 3880**
F B Abiolu-Kudjoe *Head of Domestic Banking Operations* ☏ **266 1037**

Administration
Head of Administration
Business Development

B B Oshadiya ☏ **266 9523**
D O Abass *Head of Corporate Planning & Developement* ☏ **266 8826**

Technology & Systems

G M M Obi *Head of Information Technology* ☏ **266 3606**

Legal / In-House Counsel

A O Ajibade *Head of Legal* ☏ **266 2721**

Public Relations

T Abayomi-Banjo *Head of Corporate Affairs* ☏ **266 1057**

NAL Merchant Bank plc   Head Office

NAL Towers, 20 Murina, Lagos, 12735
Tel: (1) 260 0420; (1) 260 0850 **Fax:** (1) 263 3294; (1) 263 7527 **Telex:** 23677 **Swift:** NAME NG LA
Email: cpbranch@nalbank.com.ng **Cable:** NAL NG
Website: www.nalbank.com.ng

Senior Executive Officers
Chairman
Managing Director & Chief Executive
Executive Director
General Manager
Company Secretary

Alhaji I Yerima Abdullahi
Shamsuddeen Usman
Sam C Uka
J M Odetola-Odeleye
Ronke Savage

General-Investment
Head of Investment

A Fabunmi *Head of Investments*

General - Treasury
Head of Treasury

F O Onabowale *Head of Treasury Operations*

Relationship Manager
Conglomerates & Food Group
Energy & Chemicals Group
Corporate Planning & Branches

J M Odetola-Odeleye *Head*
O K Danjuma *Head*
Kehinde Simpson *Head*

Settlement / Clearing
Operations

H Usman *Financial Control*

Administration

Technology & Systems
Information Systems

O A Akingbade *Head, Information Systems*

Accounts / Audit
Internal Audit

M G Shuaibu *Head of Internal Audit*

Other (Administration)
Human Resources
Port Harcourt Area Office

G Ahmed *Assistant General Manager*
S K Bandi *Head*

Euromoney Directory 1999   **1145**

NIGERIA (+234)   www.euromoneydirectory.com

Stanbic Merchant Bank Nigeria Limited
188 Awolowo Road, Ikoyi, Lagos
Tel: (1) 269 0402 Fax: (1) 269 2469 Swift: SBIC NGLX

United Bank for Africa plc
Head Office
Uba House, 57, Marina, Lagos
PO Box 2406, Lagos
Tel: (1) 264 4651 Fax: (1) 264 4722 Telex: 28492 MIBANK Swift: UNAF NG LA Email: uba@linkserve.com.ng
Reuters: UBA FMNG Cable: MINDOBANK Telex: 28497 Telex: 28498 MIBAN

Senior Executive Officers
Chairman	Hakeem Belo-Osagie ☏ 264 4651 ✉ beloosagie@jewel.uba
Managing Director & Chief Executive	Abba Kyari ☏ 264 4652 ✉ kyari@jewel.uba
General Manager	S S Osobase
Company Secretary	Isabella Okagbue

General-Lending (DCM, SL)
Head of Corporate Banking — Mike Ajukwu

General-Investment
Head of Investment — Mahmud Isa-Dutse

General - Treasury
Head of Treasury — Nana Mensah *DGM & Head of Treasury*

Debt Capital Markets / Fixed Income

Emerging Market Bonds
Head of Emerging Markets — Nigel Lardner

Money Markets
Head of Money Markets — Nana Mensah *DGM & Head of Treasury*

Corporate Finance / M&A Advisory
Head of Corporate Finance — Toni Phido

Settlement / Clearing
Head of Settlement / Clearing — Dennis Eborieme
Operations — Peter Longe

Other Departments
Chief Credit Officer — Gaston Hoyami
Private Banking — Reginald Ihejiahi
Cash Management — Solola Hughes

Administration
Head of Administration — Olufemi Lijadu

Technology & Systems
John Ayoh

Legal / In-House Counsel
Amina Oyagbola

Compliance
Sam Oniovosa

Public Relations
Ogie Eboigbe

Accounts / Audit
I O Shongotola

NORWAY (+47)

Norges Bank
Central Bank

Bankplassen 2, N-0107 Oslo
PO Box 1179 Sentrum, N-0107 Oslo
Tel: 2231 6000 **Fax:** 2241 3105 **Telex:** 71369 NBANK N **Swift:** NBHK NO KK **Email:** central.bank@norges-bank.no
Reuters: CBON **Telerate:** 9289/94
Reuters: CBOS
Website: www.norges-bank.no

Senior Executive Officers
Chairman & Governor — Kjell Storvik
Deputy Chairman & Governor — Jarle Bergo
General Manager — Kari Gjesteby
International Division — Audun Grønn *Director*

Others (Senior Executives)
Esther Kostøl *Member of the Executive Board*
Dagfinn Høybråten *Member of the Executive Board*
Marianne Andreassen *Member of the Executive Board*
Torgeir Høien *Member of the Executive Board*
Lars Velsand *Member of the Executive Board*
Bernt Nyhagen *Executive Director*

Head, Monetary Policy — Jan F Qviqstad *Executive Director*
Financial Markets & Payment Systems — Jon Solheim *Executive Director*
Asbjørn Fidjestøl *Deputy Executive Director*
Central Bank Administration — Inger-Johanne Sletner *Executive Director*
Head, Market Operations — Harald Bøhn *Director*
Economics Department — Jon Nicolaisen *Director*
Chief Cashier's Department — Sylvi Johansen *Chief Cashier*

Asset Management
Department: Norges Bank Investment Management
Head — Knut N Kjær *Executive Director*
Sigbjørn Atle Berg *Director*

Other Departments
Economic Research — Eilev S Jansen *Director*

Administration
Technology & Systems
Bjørn Helge Vatne *Director*

Legal / In-House Counsel
Legal Department — Bernt Nyhagen *Executive Director*

Accounts / Audit
Budget & Accounting Department — Harald Haare *Director*

Other (Administration)
Personnel Department — Anne-Britt Nilsen *Director*

Alfred Berg Norway
Full Branch Office

Stortorvet 10, N-0105 Oslo
PO Box 483 Sentrum, N-0105 Oslo
Tel: 2200 5000 **Fax:** 2241 7480 **Telex:** 71287 BERG
Website: www.sto.alfredberg.se

Senior Executive Officers
Chief Executive Officer — Arne Vaagen *Managing Director* 2200 5319
Financial Director — Gunleir Berget 2200 5024
Chief Operating Officer — Christer Berger 2200 5306

Equity Capital Markets
Head of Equity Capital Markets — Arne Vaagen *Managing Director* 2200 5319

Domestic Equities
Head of Sales — Dag Arne Wivelstad *Head of Sales* 2200 5304
Head of Trading — Morten Groven *Head of Trading* 2200 5317
Head of Research — Rune Kaland *Head of Research* 2200 5070

NORWAY (+47) www.euromoneydirectory.com

Alfred Berg Norway (cont)
Corporate Finance / M&A Advisory
Head of Corporate Finance — Christen Heiberg *Head, Corporate* ☎ 2200 5033
Settlement / Clearing
Head of Settlement / Clearing — Gunleir Berget ☎ 2200 5024
Equity Settlement — Arne Brokhaug ☎ 2200 5027

Banque Nationale de Paris — Full Branch Office

Biskop Gunnerus' Gate 2, N-0155 Oslo
PO Box 106 Sentrum, N-0102 Oslo
Tel: 2282 9500 **Fax:** 2282 9510; 2282 9512 **Telex:** 77145 BNP N **Swift:** BNPA NO KK **Reuters:** BNPO

Senior Executive Officers
Managing Director — Jean-Claude Helle
Administration
Head of Administration — Jean Pierre Harris

Chase Manhattan International Limited — Subsidiary Company

4th Floor, Fridtjof Nansens Plass 2, Oslo 1
Tel: 2294 1919 **Fax:** 2242 5861 **Telex:** 19950

Senior Executive Officers
Others (Senior Executives)
Senior Country Officer — Finn H Enger *Senior Country Officer*

Christiania Bank og Kreditkasse ASA — Head Office

Middelthuns Gate 17, N-0368 Oslo 3
PO Box 1166 Sentrum, N-0107 Oslo
Tel: 2248 5000 **Fax:** 2248 4749 **Telex:** 71043 XIAB N

Senior Executive Officers
Chairman — Harald Arnkvaern
Vice Chairman — Martin Maeland
President & Chief Executive Officer — Tom Ruud
SVP, Secretariat to Board of Directors — Thor Johnsrud

Others (Senior Executives)
Barro Syrrist *Group Executive Vice President*
Christiania Bank Retail & Commercial Division — Thorstein Øverland *Group Executive Vice President*
Large Corps, Subsidiaries & Asset Management — Stein Wessel-Aas *Group Executive Vice President*
Head of Christiania Markets — Tom Knoff *Director*

Relationship Manager
Int't Cash Management / Financial Institutions — Claudine Smith *Executive Vice President*

Debt Capital Markets / Fixed Income
Department: Fixed Income
Country Head — Mark Wingate

Bonds - General
Capital Market Clients — Jan Pollestad *Senior Dealer & Head of Capital Market Clients*
Jon Birger Tysnes *Senior Dealer*
May Munkvold *Dealer*
Fixed Income — Knut Halden *Chief Dealer*
Jan Ekeberg *Dealer*
Gunnar Krogh *Dealer*
Morten Madsen *Dealer*
Ole Christian Schjørn *Senior Dealer*
New Issues — Ole Andreas Bjerke *Chief Dealer*
Pål Solberg *Dealer*
Kristian Sørensen *Dealer*
Fixed-Income / Bonds — Tor Boye *Chief Dealer*
Eivind Solheim *Dealer*

Department: Capital Market Debt
Global Head — Jan B Kjærvik *Head of Structured Debt*
Bonds - General
Syndication — Ronny Andersen
Mari Hjemdal

NORWAY (+47)

Fixed-Income Research
Analyst — Tron Østby *Structured Debt, Analysis*

Equity Capital Markets
Global Head — Ketil Arvesen *Head, Equity Sales & Research*

Other (Domestic Equities)
Equities - General — Arnt Bakken *Senior Broker*
Thor Bihli *Senior Broker*
Jan Petter Skjensvold *Senior Broker*
Rune Husby *Broker*
Monica Santiago *Broker*
Helge Knudsen *Broker*
Einar Wisth *Broker*
Torgeir Thorn *Broker*
Lars Vinnem *Broker*
Kari Ween Sundby *Broker*
Hans Christian Henriksen *Broker*
Stig Sørland *Broker*
Ivar Heggem *Broker*
Linda Johannessen *Broker*
Glenn Kristiansen *Financial Analyst*

Other (International Equity)
International Equities — Eigil Thorp *First Vice President*
Lawrence Keeler *Vice President*
Einar Odd Bruusgaard *Vice President*

Equity Research
Head of Equity Research — Bjørn Haugen Morstad *Head, Equity Research*
Analyst — Mitra Hagen *Financial Analyst*
Bjørn Knutsen *Financial Analyst*
Nicolai Hansteen *Financial Analyst*
Stig Andersen *Financial Analyst*
Stig Heggertvedt *Financial Analyst*
Erik Gyula Kovacs *Financial Analyst*
Glenn Kristiansen *Financial Analyst*
Kjell Erik Eilertsen *Financial Analyst*
Morten Normann *Analyst*

Equity Repo / Securities Lending
Head — John Sagegg *Manager, Securities Lending* ☎ 484 936

Syndicated Lending
Loan-Related Activities
Trade Finance — Jens Chr Løvic *Senior Vice President*

Money Markets
Department: Money Market / Fixed Income
Country Head — Mark Wingate

Foreign Exchange
Department: Foreign Exchange, Fixed-Income, Sales & Trading
Global Head — Mark Wingate
Country Head — Jan Pollestad *Head*
Corporate Sales — Jan Pollestad *Senior Dealer & Head of Capital Market Clients*

FX Traders / Sales People
FX — Steen Jakobsen *Chief Dealer*
Spot — Njål Os *Chief Dealer*
Mikael Scherman *Senior Dealer*
Eirik Bergersen *Dealer*
Mona G Andersen *Dealer*
Tone Bettum *Dealer*
Stein Korterud *Dealer*
Lars Nørgaard *Dealer*
Ingrid Mamen *Dealer*

Risk Management
Country Head — Tor Braathen *Dealer*
Sjur Espen Hansen *Dealer*
Snorre Roaas *Dealer*

Fixed Income Derivatives / Risk Management
Trading — Tor Boye *Chief Dealer*
Ottar Strompdal *Chief Dealer*
Svein Ove Sandvik *Dealer*
Eivind Solheim *Dealer*
Per Inge Heggem *Dealer*

NORWAY (+47)

Christiania Bank og Kreditkasse ASA (cont)

Foreign Exchange Derivatives / Risk Management
Spot / Forwards Trading Arve Tegander *Chief Dealer*
  Magnus Larsson *Head, Forwards*

Other Currency Swap / FX Options Personnel
Interest / Fixed-Income Trading Arve Tegander *Chief Dealer*
Interest / Fixed-Income - Interest Morten Tysnes *Chief Dealer*
Interests Lars Walvig *Dealer*
  Webjørn Saur *Dealer*
Analysis / Currency Interest Marius Lomo *Head*
Analysis / Currency Interest - Macro Karl Johan Haarberg
Analysis / Currency Interest - Micro Guttorm Egge
  Einar Olsen

Other (Exchange-Traded Derivatives)
Exchange Traded Derivatives Janicke Førde *Broker*
  Jean Jordan *Broker*
  Bjørn Bekk *Broker*
Derivatives Ottar Strompdal *Chief Dealer*
  Christelle T Seem *Dealer*
  Magnus Larsson *Dealer*
  Nils Alexander Torsen *Dealer*
  Espen Østlyngen *Dealer*

Exchange-Traded Derivatives
FX Options Pia T Næss *Junior Dealer*

Corporate Finance / M&A Advisory
Department: Corporate Finance - Equities
Global Head Christian Holst *Head*

Other (Corporate Finance)
  Ketil Arvesen *Head, Equity Sales & Research*
  Erik Valen
  Roy Halvorsen
  Einar Kirkbø
  Per Ivar Vik

Department: Strategic Trading
Other (Corporate Finance)
  Ragnhild Heim *Dealer*
  Tor Larsen *Dealer*
  Hans Møvik *Dealer*
  Kjell Tertnes *Dealer*
  Stein Tombra *Dealer*
  Morten Tønjum *Dealer*

Settlement / Clearing
Operations Per Berg *SVP, Operations & Sales Support*
  Ola Forberg *Group EVP & Head, Operations, Products & Systems*
  Ludvik Sandnes *Deposit Products*

Asset Management
Department: Large Companies, Subsidiaries & Asset Management
Head Stein Wessel-Aas *Group Executive Vice President*
  Torkild Varran *Head, Active Asset Management*

Other (Asset Management)
Capital Markets Customers Arnfinn Hafsteen *Executive Vice President*
  Morten Grønn *Executive Vice President*
  Eva Holm *Executive Vice President*
Shipping, Energy, Transportation Carl E Steen *Executive Vice President*
Corporate Clients Terje Nygaard *Executive Vice President*
Financial Institutions Claudine Smith *Executive Vice President*
Credit & Analysis Stein H. Offenberg *Executive Vice President*

Other Departments
Cash Management Ola Forberg *Group EVP & Head, Operations, Products & Systems*
Economic Research Audun Gleinsvik *Chief Economist*

Administration
Technology & Systems
Information Technology Jan M Melandsø *Senior Vice President*

Legal / In-House Counsel
  Ivar Sagbakken Jr. *General Counsel*

Public Relations
Strategy, Equity & Investor Relations Sigurd Carlsen
  Kjell Flø

www.euromoneydirectory.com   NORWAY (+47)

Accounts / Audit
Vegard Østlien *General Auditor*

Other (Administration)
Product Development
Marketing
Security
Real Estate
Operations & Sales Support

Mathias Martinsen *Senior Vice President*
Arne Lambech *Director*
Randolf Hammer *First Vice President*
Olav E Sæbøe *Senior Vice President*
Per E Berg *Senior Vice President*

Citibank International plc   Full Branch Office
Tordenskioldsgt 8/10, PO Box 1481 Vika, N-0116 Oslo
Tel: 2200 9600; 2200 9696 **Fax:** 2200 9622; 2200 9623 **Telex:** 19570 CITAS

Senior Executive Officers
Chief Executive Officer
Chief Operating Officer

Per Kumle *Managing Director*
Helge Strømme *Senior Chief Operating Officer*

General - Treasury
Head of Treasury

Øystein Aannerud *Head, Treasury Customer Unit*

Foreign Exchange
Corporate Sales

Øystein Aannerud

Crédit Agricole Indosuez   Representative Office
Formerly known as: Banque Indosuez
Ruseløkkveien 6, N-0251 Oslo
PO Box 1675 Vika, N-0120 Oslo 1
Tel: 2283 3050 **Fax:** 2283 3055 **Email:** credit.agricole.indosuez@os.telia.no

Senior Executive Officers
Managing Director & Representative,
Representative, Corporate

Bjorn Hundevadt Gulbrandsen
Eli Valheim

Den Danske Bank Aktieselskab   Full Branch Office
Stortingsgaten 8, N-0125 Oslo
PO Box 1934, Oslo
Tel: 2313 9000 **Fax:** 2313 9090 **Swift:** DABA NO KX

Senior Executive Officers
Chief Executive Officer
Deputy General Manager

Johnny Johnsen *General Manager*
Torben With

Den norske Bank AS   Head Office
Formerly known as: Bergen Bank/Den norske Creditbank
Stranden 21, N-0107 Oslo
PO Box 1171 Sentrum, N-0107 Oslo
Tel: 2248 1050 **Fax:** 2248 1170; 2248 1870 **Telex:** 78175 **Swift:** DNBA NO KK **Email:** dnb@dnb.no **Reuters:** DNOP-T
Telerate: 3311/5
Website: www.dnb.no

Senior Executive Officers
Chairman
Chief Executive Officer
Deputy Managing Director
Deputy Managing Director

Gerhard Heiberg
Svein Aaser *Group Managing Director & CEO*
Eskil Vogt
John Giverholt

Others (Senior Executives)
Shipping Division
Corporate Division
Product Developement
Asset Management Division
Retail Banking Division
DnB Markets
Commercial Banking Division

Anne Øian *Deputy Managing Director*
Erik Borgen *Deputy Managing Director*
Knut Holmen *Deputy Managing Director*
Leif Teksum *Deputy Managing Director*
Geir Andersen *Deputy Managing Director*
Audun Bø *Deputy Managing Director*
Gisèle Marchand *Deputy MD, Commercial Banking Division*

Debt Capital Markets / Fixed Income
Global Head

Tor Sydnes ☏ **2294 8032**

NORWAY (+47)

www.euromoneydirectory.com

Den norske Bank AS (cont)

Domestic Government Bonds
Head of Sales — Tor Sydnes ☏ **2294 8032**
Head of Trading — Arne Mjelde ☏ **2294 8059**
Head of Research — Svein Åge Aanes ☏ **2294 9288**

Eurobonds
Head of Sales — Bjørn Karlsen ☏ **5521 1807**
Head of Trading — Jon Vonheim ☏ **5521 1358**

Libor-Based / Floating-Rate Products
FRN Origination — Tor Sydnes ☏ **2294 8032**
Asset Swaps — Ole Gunnar Jonsrud ☏ **2294 8030**

Medium-Term Notes
Head of Origination — Tor Sydnes ☏ **2294 8032**

Private Placements
Head of Origination — Tor Sydnes ☏ **2294 8032**

Asset-Backed Securities / Securitization
Global Head — Ole Gunnar Jonsrud ☏ **2294 8030**

Mortgage-Backed Securities
Global Head — Tor Sydnes ☏ **2294 8032**

Fixed-Income Repo
Head of Repo — Tor Sydnes ☏ **2294 8032**
Collateral Management — Ole Gunnar Jonsrud ☏ **2294 8030**
Sales — Tor Sydnes ☏ **2294 8032**

Equity Capital Markets
Department: DnB Markets, Nordic Equities
Tel: 2294 8850 **Fax:** 2283 0627
Global Head — Sigmund Ellingbø *General Manager* ☏ **2294 8920**
Country Head — Sveinung Hartvedt ☏ **2294 8927**

Other (Domestic Equities)
Nordic Equities - Syndication — Rolf Straume ☏ **2294 8893**
Nordic Equities - Origination — Sveinung Hartvedt ☏ **2294 8927**
Nordic Equities - Sales — Gunnar Laksesvela ☏ **2294 8917**
Nordic Equities - Trading — Mark Carey ☏ **2294 8923**
Nordic Equities - Research — Viktor Jakobsen ☏ **2294 8878**

Syndicated Lending
Department: DnB Markets (a Division of Den norske Bank ASA)
Tel: 2294 9946 **Fax:** 2248 2983
Global Head of Origination; Head of Syndication — Andrew Sayer *GM & Head, Loan Syndication* ☏ **2248 1167**
Recovery; Head of Credit Committee — Trygve Young ☏ **2248 1828**

Loan-Related Activities
Trade Finance — Nelvin Farstad ☏ **2294 8656**
Shipping Finance — Anne Øian *Deputy Managing Director*
Project Finance — Per Aage Jacobsen ☏ **2248 3609**
Leasing & Asset Finance — Morten Guldhaug ☏ **2257 4303**

Money Markets

Domestic Commercial Paper
Head of Origination; Head of Sales; Head of Trading — Tor Sydnes ☏ **2294 8032**

Foreign Exchange
Tel: 2294 8300 **Fax:** 2294 8290
Global Head — Audun Bø ☏ **2294 9247** [F] **2248 2983**
Head of Institutional Sales; Corporate Sales — Gunnar Gullaksen ☏ **2248 3798**
Head of Trading — Jørn Pedersen ☏ **2248 1958**

Risk Management

Fixed Income Derivatives / Risk Management
Global Head — Harald de Lange ☏ **2294 8054**
IR Swaps Trading — Kjell Arne Trondsen ☏ **2294 8057**
IR Options Trading — Atle Belsnes ☏ **2294 8056**

Foreign Exchange Derivatives / Risk Management
Cross-Currency Swaps, Trading — Helge Arnesen ☏ **2294 8080**
Vanilla FX option Sales — Ole Christian Presterud ☏ **2294 8043**

Other Currency Swap / FX Options Personnel
$ Swaps — Jon Andresen ☏ **2294 8078**

www.euromoneydirectory.com　　　　　　　　　　NORWAY (+47)

Corporate Finance / M&A Advisory
Department: DnB Corporate Finance
Tel: 2294 8889/91 Fax: 2283 2000
Global Head　　　　　　　　　　Rolf Straume ☎ **2294 8893**

Settlement / Clearing
Equity Settlement　　　　　　　　Rolv Fosse ☎ **2294 8968**
Derivatives Settlement　　　　　　Janne Nordeide ☎ **2294 8974**
Foreign Exchange Settlement　　　Kåre Larsen ☎ **5521 9601**

Global Custody
Country Head　　　　　　　　　　Jørgen Krager *General Manager* ☎ **2248 1252**
Other (Global Custody)
　　　　　　　　　　　　　　　　　Erik O. Slette ☎ **2248 2568**

Asset Management
Head　　　　　　　　　　　　　　Leif Teksum *Deputy Managing Director*

Other Departments
Proprietary Trading　　　　　　　Einar Johansen ☎ **5521 9510**
Private Banking　　　　　　　　　Halgeir Isdahl ☎ **2248 2910**
Correspondent Banking　　　　　　Henrik Åsland ☎ **2248 3566**

Administration
Technology & Systems
　　　　　　　　　　　　　　　　　Knut Holmen ☎ **2248 2730**

Legal / In-House Counsel
　　　　　　　　　　　　　　　　　Olav Hendal ☎ **2294 9312**

Compliance
　　　　　　　　　　　　　　　　　Ottar Ertzeid ☎ **2248 1979**

Public Relations
　　　　　　　　　　　　　　　　　Jarl Veggan ☎ **2248 1691**

Eksportfinans ASA　　　　　　　　　　　　　　Head Office

Formerly known as: AS Eksportfinans
Dronning Maudsgate 15, N-0250 Oslo
PO Box 1601 Vika, N-0119 Oslo
Tel: 2201 2201 **Fax:** 2201 2202 **Telex:** 78213 EXFIN N
Website: www.eksportfinans.com

Senior Executive Officers
President & Chief Executive Officer　　Tor F Johansen
Financial Director　　　　　　　　　　Mai-Lill Ibsen *Executive Vice President*
Chief Operating Officer　　　　　　　Ole-Jacob Lund *Executive Vice President*
Treasurer　　　　　　　　　　　　　　Olav T Breilid *Senior Vice President*

Others (Senior Executives)
Legal Director　　　　　　　　　　　Jens O Feiring *Executive Vice President*
Controller　　　　　　　　　　　　　Kjell Danielsen *Executive Vice President*
Head of Strategy　　　　　　　　　　Arnulf Arnøy *Senior Vice President*
Head of Information　　　　　　　　Ellen C Tonseth *Senior Vice President*

Enskilda Securities　　　　　　　　　　　　Subsidiary Company

Rosenkrantzgate 22, PO Box 1843, Vika, N-0123 Oslo
Tel: 2282 7000 **Fax:** 2282 7111

Senior Executive Officers
Director　　　　　　　　　　　　　Tore Rynninng Nielson

Fokus Bank ASA　　　　　　　　　　　　　　Head Office

Vestre Rosten 77, N-7005 Trondheim
Tel: 7288 2011 **Fax:** 7288 2061 **Telex:** 55050 FOKUS N **Swift:** FOKB NO 22 **Reuters:** FOBE, FOBR-T **Telerate:** 3325/6

Senior Executive Officers
Chairman　　　　　　　　　　　　　Stein H Annexstad
Chief Executive Officer　　　　　　Bjarne Borgersen *Managing Director* ☎ **7288 2111**
Financial Director　　　　　　　　　Terje Svendsen ☎ **7288 2115**
Chief Operating Officer　　　　　　Bernt Pettersen

Others (Senior Executives)
Capital Markets　　　　　　　　　　Erik Franck *Director* ☎ **7288 2247**

Euromoney Directory 1999　**1153**

NORWAY (+47) www.euromoneydirectory.com

Fokus Bank ASA (cont)
Debt Capital Markets / Fixed Income
Tel: 7288 2011 **Fax:** 7288 2290
Head of Debt Capital Markets Erik Franck *Director* ☏ **7288 2247**
  Rolf Geving *Manager* ☏ **7288 2296**

Domestic Government Bonds
Head of Sales Kjell Johansen ☏ **7288 2546**
Head of Trading Berg Jenskristian ☏ **7288 2578**

Equity Capital Markets
Tel: 7288 2577 **Fax:** 7288 2660
Head of Equity Capital Markets Alf K Karoliussen *Head* ☏ **7288 2577**
Regional Head Håvard Cartfjord *Manager*

Domestic Equities
Head of Research Morten Aarnseth ☏ **7288 2474**

International Equities
Head of Trading Per Iversen ☏ **7288 2180**

Equity Repo / Securities Lending
Marketing Alf K Karoliussen *Head* ☏ **7288 2577**

Syndicated Lending
Head of Syndicated Lending Einar Kaasen ☏ **7288 2250**

Money Markets
Fax: 7288 2290
Head of Money Markets Rolf Geving *Manager* ☏ **7288 2296**

Money Markets - General
  Anita Stiemen *Dealer* ☏ **7288 2291**

Foreign Exchange
Fax: 7288 2290
Global Head Ståle Nerland ☏ **7288 2552**

FX Traders / Sales People
  Asgeir Koteng ☏ **7288 2553**
  Erik Møller ☏ **7288 2557**
  Olve Rydning ☏ **7288 2298**

Risk Management
Head of Risk Management Kjetil Malvik ☏ **7288 2270**
Regional Head Terje Olsen ☏ **7288 2507**

Fixed Income Derivatives / Risk Management
IR Swaps Trading; IR Options Trading Helge Moe ☏ **7288 2297**

Other Currency Swap / FX Options Personnel
  Rune Vist ☏ **72 88 2556**

Corporate Finance / M&A Advisory
Fax: 7288 2063
Head of Corporate Finance Espen Müller ☏ **7288 2215**

Other (Corporate Finance)
  Pál Kristian Moe ☏ **7288 2522**

Settlement / Clearing
Tel: 7288 2211 **Fax:** 7288 2155
Regional Head Kjetil Malvik ☏ **7288 2270**
Equity Settlement Ove Grötheim ☏ **7288 2665**
Fixed-Income Settlement Oddveig Tangen ☏ **7288 2237**
Foreign Exchange Settlement Tove B Johansen ☏ **7288 2201**

Global Custody
Fax: 7288 2079
Regional Head Inge Five *Director* ☏ **7288 3415**
Country Head Gerd I Digre ☏ **7288 2466**

Other (Global Custody)
  Stig Weigner ☏ **7288 2463**

Other Departments
Correspondent Banking Steinar Robertsen ☏ **7288 2240**

Administration
Technology & Systems
  Alf Engdal ☏ **7288 2311**

Legal / In-House Counsel
  Ken Barnholdt ☏ **7288 4209**

Public Relations
  Harald Lynum ☏ **7288 2148**

www.euromoneydirectory.com NORWAY (+47)

Gjensidige Bank AS
Head Office

Strandveien 18, N-1324 Lysaker
PO Box 02, N-1324 Lysaker
Tel: 2296 9000 Fax: 2296 8920 Telex: 79303 GBGE N Swift: GJENNOKK Reuters: GJEN

Senior Executive Officers
Chairman of the Board   Sverre Høegh Krohn ☎ 2296 8820
Financial Director   Terje Ulriksen ☎ 7358 7102
Managing Director   Bente Rathe ☎ 7358 7388
International Division   Kåre Sandvik Deputy General Manager ☎ 2296 7592

Relationship Manager
Head of Business & Trade   Erik Kongelf Division Director ☎ 2296 7502

Settlement / Clearing
Tel: 2296 9000 Fax: 2296 7602
Head of Settlement / Clearing   Lars Tell Deputy General Manager ☎ 2296 7602

Other Departments
Private Banking   Tormod Peterson Deputy Managing Director ☎ 2296 9630
Correspondent Banking   Kåre Sandvik Deputy General Manager ☎ 2296 7592

Administration
Other (Administration)
Business Development   Tormod Peterson Deputy Managing Director ☎ 2296 9630

TJ Heggeli & Co AS
Head Office

Harbitzalléen 2A, N-0212 Oslo
PO Box 7, Skøyen, N-0212 Oslo
Tel: 2250 8310 Fax: 2250 8381

Senior Executive Officers
Chairman & Chief Executive   Tore Heggeli
Managing Director   Øivind Andersen

Corporate Finance / M&A Advisory
Department: Maritime Corporate Finance
Global Head   Tore Heggeli Chairman & Chief Executive
Country Head   Øivind Andersen Managing Director

Nedship Bank (Nordic)
Subsidiary Company

Christian Michelsens Gate 2A, N-5000 Bergen
PO Box 701, N-5001 Bergen
Tel: 5530 9400 Fax: 5530 9450 Telex: 40966

Senior Executive Officers
Managing Director   J Hjellestad

Nordlandsbanken ASA
Head Office

Storgaten 38, N-8002 Bodø
Tel: 7554 1100 Fax: 7554 1490

Senior Executive Officers
Chairman   Harald Mellerud
Managing Director   Nils Moe
Deputy Managing Director   Finn Strøm-Gundersen ☎ 2247 3600
Senior General Manager   Morten Støver

Syndicated Lending
Global Head   Odd Eben Senior General Manager

Money Markets
Global Head   Morten Støver Senior General Manager

Domestic Commercial Paper
Head of Origination   Morten Støver Senior General Manager

Euromoney Directory 1999 **1155**

NORWAY (+47) www.euromoneydirectory.com

Nordlandsbanken ASA
Full Branch Office

Rosenkrantzgaten 21, N-0110 Oslo 1
PO Box 1213 Vika, N-0110 Oslo 1
Tel: 2247 3600 Fax: 2233 6710 Telex: 77386 NORBKN Swift: NOBA NO 22 OSL

Senior Executive Officers
Director
Chief Executive Officer
Treasurer
General Manager
Deputy General Manager

Gunnar Viken ☏ **2245 0100**
Finn Strøm-Gundersen *Deputy Managing Director*
Esben Jensrúd *Manager*
Geir Lars Sagen
Ole Jacob Skeie

Syndicated Lending
Global Head

Geir Lars Sagen *General Manager*

Loan-Related Activities
Trade Finance

Per Arne Larsen *Manager*

Money Markets
Global Head

Ingrid Aga *Manager, International Division*

Foreign Exchange
Global Head

Esben Jensrúd *Manager*

Corporate Finance / M&A Advisory
Regional Head

Geir Lars Sagen *General Manager*

Settlement / Clearing
Derivatives Settlement

Finn Quande

Other Departments
Private Banking
Correspondent Banking

Paal Riise *Manager*
Ingrid Aga *Manager, International Division*

Administration
Technology & Systems

Ole Jacob Skeie *Deputy General Manager*

Norges Kommunalbank
Head Office

Nedre Vollgate 11, N-0102 Oslo 1
PO Box 382 Sentrum, N-0102 Oslo 1
Tel: 2220 2553 Fax: 2233 6613; 2233 3490 Reuters: NKBA; NKAZ

Senior Executive Officers
Chairman
Managing Director
Financial Director
Treasurer

Odvar Nordli
Petter Skouen
Petter Skouen *Chief Financial Officer*
Thomas Moeller *Treasurer*

Debt Capital Markets / Fixed Income
Global Head

Thomas Moeller *Treasurer*

Domestic Government Bonds
Head of Sales

Siv Galligani *Assistant Treasurer*

Fixed-Income Repo
Head of Repo

Cato Gaustad *Assistant Treasurer*

Money Markets
Domestic Commercial Paper
Head of Origination
Head of Sales
Head of Trading

Thomas Moeller *Treasurer*
Siv Galligani *Assistant Treasurer*
Cato Gaustad *Assistant Treasurer*

Postbanken

Biskop Gunnerusgate 14, N-0021 Oslo
Tel: 2297 6000 Fax: 2217 6459
Website: www.postbanken.no

Senior Executive Officers
Chairman
Managing Director
Company Secretary

Tormod Hermansen
Olav Fjell ☏ **2297 9020**
Sigrid Melsom ☏ **2297 9037**

1156 Euromoney Directory 1999

Others (Senior Executives)
Director
Insurance & Financial Products

Knut Utvik *Director*
Bjørn Eggen

General - Treasury
Head of Treasury

Bjørn Eggen

Debt Capital Markets / Fixed Income
Bonds - General

Jo Teslo *Head of Trading*
Rolf Palmer *Head of Short Term Trading*

Equity Capital Markets
Other

Jon Stinessen *Head*

Other (Domestic Equities)
Equity Instruments

Jon Stinessen *Head*

Money Markets
Head of Money Markets

Jørgen Lønø *Head of Trading* ☐ 2297 6195

Money Markets - General
Corporate Market
Household Markets

Tom Rønning *Deputy Managing Director*
Petter Jansen *Deputy Managing Director*

Foreign Exchange
Department: Finance & Foreign Exchange
Head of Foreign Exchange

Geir Owe Skogø *Deputy General Manager*

Settlement / Clearing
Head of Settlement / Clearing
Settlement (General)
Operations

Lena Scharp
Arnt S Eilertsen *Head*
Bard Brække *Middle Office*

Other Departments
Proprietary Trading

Rolf Palmer *Head of Short Term Trading*

Administration
Technology & Systems
Internettbank & Analysis

Charles Granquist *Head*

Corporate Communications

Tore Dyrdahl

Accounts / Audit
Accounts

Arnt S Eilertsen *Head*

Other (Administration)
Personnel
Service & Production

Rolv Økland *Deputy Managing Director*
Evlyn Raknerud *Deputy Managing Director*

Schiffshypotekenbank zu Lübeck
Representative Office

Nils Chr. Green, Aker Brygge, Stranden 1, Oppg. B, 7.etj, N-0250 Oslo
Tel: 2283 6810 **Fax:** 2283 6811

Société Générale
Representative Office

Kongensgate 9, PO Box 17 Sentrum, Oslo 1
Tel: 2220 5130 **Fax:** 2220 5405
Website: www.socgen.com

Sparebank 1 Vest
Head Office

Formerly known as: Sparebanken Vest
PO Box 854, Kaigaten 4, N-5002 Bergen
Tel: 5521 7000 **Fax:** 5521 7410 **Telex:** 42249 SPAV N **Swift:** SPAV NO BB **Reuters:** SPVS (Dealing); SPVT (Monitor)

Senior Executive Officers
Chairman
Managing Director
International Division

Haldor Høyte
Knut Ravnå
Egil Mokleiv *International*

Foreign Exchange
FX Traders / Sales People

Torleif Berg

NORWAY (+47) www.euromoneydirectory.com

Sparebanken Midt-Norge

Sondregate 4, 7005 Trondheim
Tel: 7358 5111 **Fax:** 7358 5384

Senior Executive Officers
Chairman   Stein Atle Andersen
Chief Executive Officer   Fill Haugan

Sparebanken Møre   Head Office

Kipervikgaten 4/6, PO Box 121, N-6001 Ålesund
Tel: 7011 3000

Senior Executive Officers
Chairman   Lief-Arne Langøy
Treasurer   Runar Sandanger *Deputy General Manager* ☎ **7011 3172**
International Division   Per Bakken *Manager* ☎ **7011 3282**
Foreign Exchange
Head of Foreign Exchange   Aud-Janne Myklebust *Foreign Exchange Manager* ☎ **7011 3175**
FX Traders / Sales People
                                      Knut-Ove Bostrand *Dealer* ☎ **7011 3176**
Corporate Finance / M&A Advisory
Head of Corporate Finance   Fan-Eric Dale *General Manager* ☎ **7011 3211**
Country Head   Willy Bjørge *General Manager*

Sparebanken Nord Norge   Head Office

Storgaten 65, N-9005 Tromsø
Tel: 7762 2000 **Fax:** 7762 2571; 7762 2399 **Telex:** 64170 NORDB N **Swift:** SNOW NO 22 **Reuters:** TROM;
                                            SNOW (Dealing)
Website: www.snn.no

Senior Executive Officers
Chairman   Kurt Mosbakk ☎ **6911 7000** 📠 **6911 7118**
Vice Chairman   Harald Overvaag
Chief Executive Officer   Hans Olav Karde *Chief Executive Officer*
                                      Oddmund Åsen *Deputy Chief Executive Officer*
Financial Director   Rolf Eigil Bygdnes *Group Manager*
Chief Operating Officer   Geir Andreassen *Group Manager*
International Division   Merete Tøllofsen *Manager, Treasury & Int'l*

General-Lending (DCM, SL)
Head of Corporate Banking   Rolf Eigil Bygdnes *Group Manager*
General - Treasury
Head of Treasury   Merete Tøllofsen *Manager, Treasury & Int'l*
Debt Capital Markets / Fixed Income
Global Head   Rolf Eigil Bygdnes *Head*
Equity Capital Markets
Global Head   Rolf Eigil Bygdnes *Head*
Syndicated Lending
Global Head   Oddmund Åsen *Head*
Money Markets
Global Head   Rolf Eigil Bygdnes *Head*
Foreign Exchange
Global Head   Bjørn Kristiansen *Head*
FX Traders / Sales People
                                      Geir Arntzen *Chief Dealer* ☎ **7762 2480**
                                      Trond Ewold *Dealer* ☎ **7762 2481**
                                      Jan Hestad *Dealer* ☎ **7762 2479**
                                      Per Arne Austlid *Dealer* ☎ **7762 2483**

Risk Management
Global Head   Rolf Eigil Bygdnes *Head*
Corporate Finance / M&A Advisory
Global Head   Rolf Eigil Bygdnes *Head*

www.euromoneydirectory.com NORWAY (+47)

Settlement / Clearing
Regional Head Bente Noreng *Head*
Operations Geir Andreassen *Group Manager*

Sparebanken Sør
Head Office

Vesterveien 1A, N-4800 Arendal
PO Box 310, N-4801 Arendal
Tel: 3702 5000 **Fax:** 3702 4150 **Telex:** 21164 **Swift:** AASP NO 22 **Email:** mail@sparesor.no
Website: www.sparesor.no

Senior Executive Officers
Managing Director Hans A Iversen ☏ 3705 7090 F 3702 1936
Deputy Managing Director Olav Karlsen ☏ 3705 7092 F 3702 1936

Others *(Senior Executives)*
Foreign Hans Petter Mortensen *Manager* ☏ 3705 7199 F 3702 4150

General-Lending *(DCM, SL)*
Head of Corporate Banking Jan Oscar Kvist *AGM, Corporate Banking* ☏ 3705 7153 F 3702 7240

General - Treasury
Head of Treasury Kåre Oveland *Assistant General Manager* ☏ 3705 7130 F 3702 4150

Administration
Head of Administration Morten Kraft *General Manager* ☏ 3705 7093 F 3702 1936

Sundal Collier & Co ASA

Munkedamsveien 45, N-0250 Oslo
PO Box 1444 Vika, N-0115 Oslo
Tel: 2201 6000 **Fax:** 2201 6060 **Telex:** 74490

Senior Executive Officers
Chairman Jan Petter Collier
Managing Director / General Manager Leiv Askvig

Svenska Handelsbanken AB (publ)
Full Branch Office

Alternative trading name: Svenska Handelsbanken Markets
Rådhusgatan 27, N-0101 Oslo
Tel: 2294 0700; 2294 0922 **Fax:** 2233 6915 **Telex:** 11237 HAFO N

Debt Capital Markets / Fixed Income
Domestic Government Bonds
Head of Sales Bente Haugan ☏ 820 885
Head of Trading Peter Weis ☏ 823 037
Head of Research Knut Anton Mork ☏ 820 881

TFS Nordisk Energi AS

Radhusgaten 7, PO Box 301, N-3201 Sandefjord
Tel: 3348 4343 **Fax:** 3347 2745

Senior Executive Officers
Managing Director Jarle Grytten

Unibank A/S
Full Branch Office

7th Floor, Stortingsgata 8, N-0161 Oslo
PO Box 1392, N-0114 Oslo
Tel: 2200 1900 **Fax:** 2200 1910 **Swift:** UNIB NO KK

Senior Executive Officers
General Manager Steffen Johansen

Euromoney Directory 1999 **1159**

NORWAY (+47)   www.euromoneydirectory.com

Union Bank of Norway — Head Office

NOR
union bank of norway

Kirkegaten 18, N-0107 Oslo
PO Box 1172, Sentrum, Oslo
Tel: 2231 9050 **Fax:** 2231 9985 **Telex:** 19470 UBNOR **Swift:** UBNO NO KK **Email:** norinfo@online.no
Reuters: UBNF/Y **Cable:** UBN OSLO
Reuters: UBNX; UBNO
Website: www.internett.nor.no/nvestor/nor-eng

Senior Executive Officers
Chairman — Hans Bø
President & Chief Executive Officer — Kjell O Kran ☎ **2231 8821**
Deputy President & CEO — Olav Hytta ☎ **2231 8821** F **2231 9260**
Chief Executive Officer — Geir Bergvoll *Senior General Manager* ☎ **2231 9980**
Treasurer — Jon E Skajem *Head of Markets* ☎ **2231 9854**
Director — Stein Rohde Hanssen ☎ **2231 8586** F **2231 8333**

Debt Capital Markets / Fixed Income

Bonds - General
Market Head — John E Skajem *General Manager* ☎ **2231 9854**
Group Finance — Geir Bergvoll *Senior General Manager* ☎ **2231 9980**
Long Term Funding — Helge Stray *General Manager* ☎ **2231 9368**
Trading — John E Skajem *Deputy General Manager* ☎ **2231 9854**

Syndicated Lending

Loan-Related Activities
Shipping Finance — Hans Christer Elowsson ☎ **2231 9250**

Risk Management
Group Market Risk Management — Jan Otto Lahn *General Manager* ☎ **2231 8777**

Other (OTC Credit Derivatives)
Group Credit Risk Management — Steinar Ouren *General Manager*

Settlement / Clearing
Operations — Bente Lansnes *General Manager* ☎ **2231 8938**
Lasse S Nikolaisen

Other Departments

Other Departments
Corporate Customer Division — Øyvind Birkeland *Group Director* ☎ **2231 9700**
Stategic Group Functions — Karl-Olav Hovden *Group Director* ☎ **2231 9893**

Administration
Head of Administration — Tore V Knudsen *Group Director* ☎ **2231 8350**
Business Development — Nils Terje Furunes *Chief Economist* ☎ **2231 8791**
Head of Marketing — Einar Hvidsten *Development Director* ☎ **2231 9009**

Technology & Systems
Einar Hvidsten *Development Director* ☎ **2231 9009**

Legal / In-House Counsel
Arild Harsson *Group Attorney-at-law* ☎ **2231 9342**

Corporate Communications
Frode Helgerud *Director, Corporate Communications* ☎ **2231 8794** F **2231 8764**

Accounts / Audit
Roar Lie *Accounting Director* ☎ **2231 9330**
Auditor — Thomas Winsnes *Group Internal Auditor* ☎ **2231 9564**

Other (Administration)
Management Developement; Management Development — Erik Blekeli *Organisations Director* ☎ **2231 9034**
Personnel Director — Geir Nagel *Personnel Director* ☎ **2231 8826**

1160   Euromoney Directory 1999

www.euromoneydirectory.com OMAN (+968)

VAR BANK AS
Head Office

Formerly known as: Landsbanken A/S
Henrik Ibsen's Gate 9, N-0106 Oslo 1
PO Box 778, N-0106 Oslo
Tel: 2306 6666 **Fax:** 2306 6200 **Telex:** 76034 LBANK N **Swift:** LABA NO KK

Senior Executive Officers
Chairman   Bente N Halvorsen
Vice Chairman   Roar Flåthen
Group President & Chief Executive Officer   Jan Tore Berg-Knutsen
Senior Executive Vice President   Ottar Karbøl
Executive Vice President   Øyvind Engen
International Division   Thomas G Engelsen *First Vice President*

Syndicated Lending
Other (Trade Finance)
Letters of Credit   Knut Rydning *Assistant Area Manager*

Money Markets
Global Head   Knut Lysdahl *Assistant Vice President*

Foreign Exchange
Country Head   Eva V Rahman *Assistant Vice President*

Corporate Finance / M&A Advisory
Global Head   Nils Svendsøy *First Vice President*

Other Departments
Correspondent Banking   Eva V Rahman *Assistant Vice President*
Cash Management   Knut Lysdahl *Assistant Vice President*

Administration
Technology & Systems
                                             Ole Harald Slemdal *Assistant Vice President*

Legal / In-House Counsel
                                             Lars Engen *First Vice President*

Public Relations
                                             Erik Kikut *First Vice President*

OMAN (+968)

Central Bank of Oman
Central Bank

44 Mutrah Commercial Centre Street, PO Box 1161, 112 Muscat
Tel: 702 222 **Fax:** 702 253; 789 265 **Cable:** MARKAZI
President's Office Telex: 3554 MRKZI ON; **Accounts Telex:** 3794 MARKZI ON; **Clearing House Telex:** 3070 MARKZI ON; **Treasury, Investment & Settlement Telex:** 3288 MARKFX ON

Senior Executive Officers
Deputy Chairman   Ali Mohamed Moosa
Executive President   Hamood Sangour Al Zadjali
Executive Vice President   Mohd Abdulaziz Kalmoor
Treasurer   Mohd Nasser Al Jahadhmy *Senior Vice President*

Others (Senior Executives)
Currency, Accounts & Branches   Iqbal Ali Khamis *Vice President*
Banking Affairs   Hamoud Saleh Ali Al Anbori *Senior Manager*
Banking Supervision Department   Moosa Abdulrehman Khamis *Senior Manager*
Market Operations Department   Rashi Abdulla Al Kittany *Manager*
Currency   Khalid Moosa Darwish *Manager*

General-Investment
Head of Investment   Mohd Nasser Al Jahadhmy *Senior Vice President*
                                             Mahboob Moosa Mohd Al Moosa *Manager*

General - Treasury
Head of Treasury   Mahboob Moosa Mohd Al Moosa *Manager*

Settlement / Clearing
Fax: 707 913 **Telex:** 3493 MRKZI
Settlement (General)   Mohd Nasser Al Jahadhmy *Senior Vice President*
                                             Hilal Ali Soud Al Barwany *Manager*
Operations   Seif Said Seif Al Busaidy *Senior Manager*

Euromoney Directory 1999 **1161**

OMAN (+968)　　　　　　　www.euromoneydirectory.com

Central Bank of Oman (cont)
Other Departments
Economic Research　　　　　　　　Ali Hamdan Al Raisi *Manager*
Administration
Head of Administration　　　　　　Haythem Ali Al Kadi *Senior Manager*
　　　　　　　　　　　　　　　　Khalfan Mohd Al Harthy *Manager*
Business Development　　　　　　Hamoud Saleh Ali Al Anbori *Senior Manager*
Technology & Systems
Computer Dept　　　　　　　　　Iqbal Ali Khamis *Vice President*
　　　　　　　　　　　　　　　　Abdul Qahar Ibrahim Al Khanjari *Manager*

Accounts / Audit
Audit & Inspection Department　　Abdulla Sha'aban Ballan *Senior Manager*
Accounts Dept　　　　　　　　　Aysha Zahir Nasser Al Maully *Senior Manager*
Other (Administration)
Personnel & Human Resources Development　　Fuad Jaffer Moh'd *Vice President*
　　　　　　　　　　　　　　　　Ghaya Ahmed Al Riyami *Manager*

Bank Muscat Al Ahli Al Omani SAOG

1073 Muttrah, Commercial District, PO Box 134, Muscat 112, Ruwi
Tel: 703 044; 703 137 **Fax:** 707 806; 210 115 **Telex:** 3450 BK AHLAN ON

Senior Executive Officers
Chief Executive Officer　　　　　　Abdul Razak Ali Issa
Managing Director / General Manager　　JS George

Citibank NA　　　　　　　　　　　　　　　　　　　　Full Branch Office

Beit Al Falaj Street, MBD Area, Salalah Building, Way 2706, Building 346, CBD Ruwi, 114 Muscat
PO Box 1994, 114 Muscat
Tel: 795 705; 789 050 **Fax:** 789 051; 794 568 **Telex:** 3444 CITIBK ON

Senior Executive Officers
Chief Executive Officer　　　　　　Ravi Bhatia *Country Corporate Officer* ☎ **798 728**
General - Treasury
Head of Treasury　　　　　　　　Anwer Iqbal *Manager* ☎ **707 572**
Settlement / Clearing
Operations　　　　　　　　　　　Muneer Khan *Manager* ☎ **795 723**
Administration
Other (Administration)
Sales / Marketing / CSR　　　　　Mohammed Abbas Noorani *Manager* ☎ **701 600**

Commercial Bank of Oman　　　　　　　　　　　　　　Head Office

105 Al Burj Street, 112 Ruwi
PO Box 1696, Ruwi
Tel: 701 528 **Fax:** 705 607 **Telex:** 3275 COM BNK HO **Swift:** BOBK OM RX **Reuters:** BOBK

Senior Executive Officers
Chief Executive Officer　　　　　　Steven Pinto ☎ **793 475** 🖷 **785 547**
Chief Operating Officer　　　　　　Lanka Nesiah *Manager, Operations* ☎ **703 727**
Others (Senior Executives)
Corporate Affairs　　　　　　　　Saad Al Jenaiby *Deputy General Manager & EVP* ☎ **707 725** 🖷 **793 136**
Management Services　　　　　　R Seetharaman *Assistant General Manager* ☎ **797 471** 🖷 **795 616**
General-Lending (DCM, SL)
Head of Corporate Banking　　　　P Balasubramaniam *Deputy General Manager & SVP* ☎ **706 008** 🖷 **706 911**
General-Investment
Head of Investment　　　　　　　P Balasubramaniam *Deputy General Manager & SVP* ☎ **706 008** 🖷 **706 911**
General - Treasury
Head of Treasury　　　　　　　　Frederick Colaco *Manager, Treasury* ☎ **702 439**
Money Markets
Country Head　　　　　　　　　Frederick Colaco *Manager, Treasury* ☎ **702 439**
Foreign Exchange
Head of Trading　　　　　　　　Frederick Colaco *Manager, Treasury* ☎ **702 439**
Risk Management
Head of Risk Management　　　　Yaseen Abdullatif *Assistant General Manager* ☎ **700 181** 🖷 **702 429**

www.euromoneydirectory.com　　　　　　　　　　　　OMAN (+968)

Settlement / Clearing
Tel: 706 601 **Fax:** 705 607
*Fixed-Income Settlement; Derivatives　　　　*Fawziya Mohammed Amin *Supervisor, Treasury Back-Office*
Settlement; Foreign Exchange Settlement*
Other Departments
*Correspondent Banking　　　　　　　　　　*Lanka Nesiah *Manager, Operations* ☏ **703 727**
Administration
*Head of Administration　　　　　　　　　　*Hussain Mohd. Ali *Acting AGM & RVP* ☏ **797 384** F **790 166**
Technology & Systems
　　　　　　　　　　　　　　　　　　　　James Campbell *Manager, IT* ☏ **700 184**
Accounts / Audit
*Chief Internal Auditor　　　　　　　　　　*Ashikrao ☏ **771 3462** F **771 1934**

Oman Development Bank (SAOG)
PO Box 309, Muscat 113
Tel: 738 021; 738 025 **Fax:** 738 026 **Telex:** 5179 ODEBE ON
Senior Executive Officers
*General Manager　　　　　　　　　　　　*Murtadha M Fadhil

Oman International Bank (SAOG)　　　　　　　　　　　Head Office
PO Box 1727, 111 Seeb
Tel: 682 500 **Fax:** 682 800; 682 886 **Telex:** 5406 OMINBNK ON **Swift:** OIBA OM MX **Email:** omintbnk@gto.net.om
Reuters: OIBO **Telerate:** 17287
Senior Executive Officers
*Chairman　　　　　　　　　　　　　　　　*Noor Mohd Abdulrahman
*Financial Director　　　　　　　　　　　　*Khalfan Al Taley *Assistant General Manager* ☏ **682 772**
*Chief Operating Officer　　　　　　　　　*Mohsin Ebrahim Ali Al Lawaita *Assistant General Manager* ☏ **682 562**
*Treasurer　　　　　　　　　　　　　　　　*Vasanth Shetty *Chief Manager, Treasury* ☏ **693 240**
*General Manager　　　　　　　　　　　　*Yahya Said Abdullah Al Jabry ☏ **682 541**
Deputy General Manager, Credit & Marketing　Amitabha Banerjee
Acting Deputy General Manager, Banking　　Suleiman Al Kindy
Debt Capital Markets / Fixed Income
Department: Investment Management - Oman
Domestic Government Bonds
*Head of Sales　　　　　　　　　　　　　　*Hamid Al Bahry *Manager* ☏ **682 649**
*Head of Trading　　　　　　　　　　　　　*R Y Kamat *Senior Dealer* ☏ **682 570**
Equity Capital Markets
Domestic Equities
*Head of Sales　　　　　　　　　　　　　　*Hamid Al Bahry *Manager* ☏ **682 649**
*Head of Trading　　　　　　　　　　　　　*Mohd Dohadwala *Assistant Manager* ☏ **682 647**
Syndicated Lending
Department: Corporate Credit (Oman)
*Global Head　　　　　　　　　　　　　　*Arthur Fernandes *Manager* ☏ **682 865**
*Recovery　　　　　　　　　　　　　　　　*Zuleika Al Jadjali *Manager* ☏ **682 756**
Loan-Related Activities
*Trade Finance　　　　　　　　　　　　　*Anthony Sequeira *Manager, International* ☏ **682 661**
　　　　　　　　　　　　　　　　　　　　Mustafa Mukhthar *Head* ☏ **682 622**
*Project Finance　　　　　　　　　　　　　*Arthur Fernandes *Manager* ☏ **682 865**
Structured Trade Finance; Leasing & Asset　Anthony Sequeira *Manager, International* ☏ **682 661**
Finance
Money Markets
Department: Head Office - Treasury (Oman)
*Global Head　　　　　　　　　　　　　　*Vasanth Shetty *Chief Manager, Treasury* ☏ **693 240**
*Regional Head　　　　　　　　　　　　　*R Y Kamat *Senior Dealer* ☏ **682 570**
Wholesale Deposits
*Marketing　　　　　　　　　　　　　　　　*Vasanth Shetty *Chief Manager, Treasury* ☏ **693 240**
*Head of Sales　　　　　　　　　　　　　　*R Y Kamat *Senior Dealer* ☏ **682 570**
Foreign Exchange
Department: Head Office - Treasury (Oman)
*Global Head　　　　　　　　　　　　　　*Vasanth Shetty *Chief Manager, Treasury* ☏ **693 240**
*Country Head of Institutional Sales　　　　*Kalatharan Nadarajah *Senior Dealer* ☏ **693 240**
*Corporate Sales; Head of Trading　　　　　*Basheer Al Subhy *Senior Dealer* ☏ **693 240**

OMAN (+968)   www.euromoneydirectory.com

Oman International Bank (SAOG) (cont)

Risk Management
Department: Head Office - Treasury (Oman)
Global Head   Khalfan Al Taley *Assistant General Manager* ☏ **682 772**

Fixed Income Derivatives / Risk Management
Global Head   Vasanth Shetty *Chief Manager, Treasury* ☏ **693 240**
Country Head; IR Swaps Sales / Marketing; IR   R Y Kamat *Senior Dealer* ☏ **682 570**
Options Sales / Marketing

Foreign Exchange Derivatives / Risk Management
Cross-Currency Swaps, Sales / Marketing   R Y Kamat *Senior Dealer* ☏ **682 570**
Cross-Currency Swaps, Trading   Suhail Al Shamsi *Dealer* ☏ **69 3240**
Vanilla FX option Sales   Kalatharan Nadarajah *Senior Dealer* ☏ **693 240**

OTC Credit Derivatives
Head of Sales   Arthur Fernandes *Manager* ☏ **682 865**

Corporate Finance / M&A Advisory
Department: Corporate Credit (Oman)
Global Head   Arthur Fernandes *Manager* ☏ **682 865**

Settlement / Clearing
Department: Treasury Operations (Oman)
Tel: 682 823 Fax: 682 821
Country Head   Anthony Sequeira *Manager, International* ☏ **682 661**
Equity Settlement   Hamid Al Bahry *Manager* ☏ **682 649**
Derivatives Settlement; Foreign Exchange   Mohd Harmary *Head of Division* ☏ **682 823**
Settlement

Global Custody
Department: Investment Management (Oman)
Country Head   Hamid Al Bahry *Manager* ☏ **682 649**

Other (Global Custody)
   Mohd Dohadwala *Assistant Manager* ☏ **682 647**

Other Departments
Correspondent Banking   Anthony Sequeira *Manager, International* ☏ **682 661**

Administration

Technology & Systems
   Peter Woodford *Chief Manager, Computer Systems Development* ☏ **682 848**

Legal / In-House Counsel
Legal Adviser   Mohammed Z Sheiha ☏ **682 729**

Compliance
   Suleiman Al Kindy *Acting Deputy General Manager, Banking*

Public Relations
   Khalfan Al Taley *Assistant General Manager* ☏ **682 772**

Standard Chartered Bank   Full Branch Office

PO Box 2353, Bait Al Falaj Street, 112 Ruwi
Tel: 703 999 Fax: 796 864; 701 451 Telex: 3217 SCBMUS OM Cable: STANCHART

Senior Executive Officers
Manager   Murray Sims ☏ **704 434**

General-Lending (DCM, SL)
Head of Corporate Banking   Rod Sampson *Head of Corporate & Commercial Banking* ☏ **796 865**

Relationship Manager
   Shan Sultan *Senior Relationship Manager* ☏ **704 434**

Settlement / Clearing
Operations   Saleh Thabit Al Awaidy *Manager* ☏ **786 095**

1164   Euromoney Directory 1999

www.euromoneydirectory.com   PAKISTAN (+92)

PAKISTAN
(+92)

State Bank of Pakistan
🏛 Central Bank

PO Box 4456, II Chundrigar Road, Karachi 74600, Sindh
Tel: (21) 241 4140; (21) 241 4149 **Fax:** (21) 241 6608 **Telex:** 21774 SBPK **Telex:** 20730 SBPK **Telex:** 20054 SBPK

Senior Executive Officers
Governor — Muhammad Yaqub ☎ **241 7864**
Deputy Governor — Mukhtar Nabi Qureshi ☎ **241 5266**
Deputy Governor — Rashid Akhtar Chughtai ☎ **243 0205**
Chief Executive Officer — Ali Akbar Dhakan *Executive Director* ☎ **241 4165**
Khalid Mahmud Salim *Executive Director* ☎ **241 7871**
Imtiaz Ahmed *Executive Director* ☎ **241 7872**
Muhammad Ainuddim *Executive Director* ☎ **242 2197**
Tasadduq Hussain *Executive Director* ☎ **241 3548**

Others (Senior Executives)
Head, Banking Supervision — Shahdar Ali *Director* ☎ **262 9161**
Tassawar Hussain Shah *Director* ☎ **262 9162**
Muhammad Altaf *Director* ☎ **241 0046**
Head, Banking Policy & Regulation — Mansur-ur-Rehman Khan *Director* ☎ **241 2064**
Head, Corporate Affairs — Ch. Rashid Ahmed Javed *Director* ☎ **241 3036**
Head, Credit Information Bureau — Munir Ahmed *Director* ☎ **242 4492**
Head, Monetary & Fiscal Research — Abdul Naseer *Director* ☎ **241 1897**
Head, Securities — Riaz Riazuddin *Director* ☎ **242 8943**
Head, Statistics — Muhammad Hanif *Director* ☎ **241 1094**

Foreign Exchange
Head of Foreign Exchange — Inam Ahmed *Director* ☎ **241 1544**
Shah Abul Hasan *Director* ☎ **293 3463**

Other Departments
Economic Research — Aftab Ahmed Nadeem *Director* ☎ **241 7391**
Muhammad Ahmed *Director, International* ☎ **241 2185**

Administration
Head of Administration — Rukhsar Ahmed *Director* ☎ **241 0181**

Public Relations
Syed Wasimuddin *Director* ☎ **241 3257**

Accounts / Audit
Head, Accounting — Farhat Saeed *Director* ☎ **243 2657**
Head, Audit — Mukhtar Ahmed *Director* ☎ **242 7349**

Other (Administration)
Personnel — Riaz Ahmed *Director* ☎ **241 7873**

Bank of America NT & SA
Full Branch Office

4/5 Floors, Jubilee Insurance House, II Chundrigar Road, Karachi 74400, Sindh
Tel: (21) 241 2520 **Fax:** (21) 241 5371; (21) 240 0842 **Swift:** 21081 BOA PK

Senior Executive Officers
Senior Vice President — S Ali Raza

Others (Senior Executives)
Country Credit & Marketing — Nauman Dar

Chase Manhattan Overseas Corporation
Subsidiary Company

13th Floor, C Tower, Sidco Avenue Centre, 264 R A Lines, Karachi, Sindh
Tel: (21) 568 4238 **Fax:** (21) 568 1467 **Telex:** 29554 CHASE PK

Senior Executive Officers

Others (Senior Executives)
Manochere Alamgir *Senior Country Officer*

Euromoney Directory 1999   **1165**

PAKISTAN (+92) www.euromoneydirectory.com

Citibank NA
Full Branch Office

AWT Plaza, II Chundrigar Road, Karachi 74200, Sindh
PO Box 4889, Karachi 74200, Sindh
Tel: (21) 111 999 999 **Fax:** (21) 263 8200 **Telex:** 20745 CITI PK **Swift:** CITI PK KK **Email:** snaqvi@citicorp.com
Reuters: CIPK; CIKA (Dealing)
Website: www.citicorp.com, www.citibank.com

Senior Executive Officers

Chief Executive Officer	Shahzad Naqvi *Chief Executive Officer* ☎ **263 8222** ✉ **snaqvi@citicorp.com**
Financial Director	Akbar Abdul Aziz *Financial Controller* ☎ **263 8224**
Chief Operating Officer	Kamal Akbar *Country Corporate Officer* ☎ **263 8306**
Treasurer	Risha Mohyeddin *Treasurer* ☎ **263 8215** ✉ **risha.mohyeddin@citicorp.com**

Deutsche Bank
Full Branch Office

Unicentre - Unitowers, II Chundrigar Road, Karachi 74000, Sindh
PO Box 4925, Karachi, Sindh
Tel: (21) 241 9611 **Fax:** (21) 241 1134 **Telex:** 20295 DBA PK **Swift:** DEUT PKKA **Cable:** DEUTBANK
Website: www.deutsche-bank.de

Senior Executive Officers

Managing Director / General Manager	Mohammad Younus Khan

Deutsche Bank AG
Full Branch Office

40-E Jang Plaza, Ataturk Avenue, Blue Area, Islamabad
Tel: (51) 1115 55777 **Fax:** (51) 823 522 **Telex:** 54739 DBAIB PK

Deutsche Bank AG
Full Branch Office

Escorts House, 26 Davis Road, Sir Agha Khan Road, Lahore
Tel: (42) 636 4713; (42) 636 4714 **Fax:** (42) 636 4424 **Telex:** 47057 DBAL PK **Cable:** DEUTBANK **Tel:** 636 4715; 636 4716 **Tel:** 636 4440; 636 4441 **Tel:** 636 4442; 636 4443
Website: www.deutsche-bank.com

Jahangir Siddiqui & Co Limited
Head Office

Alternative trading name: JSCL
Formerly known as: Bear Stearns Jahangir Siddiqui Limited
14th Floor, Chapal Plaza, Hasrat Mohani Road, Karachi 75000, Sindh
Tel: (21) 243 1181; (21) 242 9206 **Fax:** (21) 243 1178; (21) 241 2426 **Telex:** 20133 BSJSL PK
Email: jscl@jahangirsiddiqui.com **Reuters:** BSJS.KA
Website: www.jahangirsiddiqui.com

Senior Executive Officers

Chairman	Jahangir Siddiqui ☎ **241 9491**
Chief Executive Officer	Jahangir Siddiqui *Chairman* ☎ **241 9491**
Financial Director	Suleman Lalani *Company Secretary / Finance Manager* ☎ **241 9491**
Chief Operating Officer	Munaf Ibrahim *Executive Director*
Company Secretary / Finance Manager	Suleman Lalani ☎ **241 9491**

Debt Capital Markets / Fixed Income
Tel: 243 1167 **Fax:** 243 1151

Head of Fixed Income	Tariq Bhatti *EVP & Money Market Controller*
Head of Fixed Income Sales	Hafeezur Rehman *Assistant Vice President & Money Markets Dealer*
Head of Fixed Income Trading	Basir Shamsie *Assistant Vice President & Money Markets Dealer*

Government Bonds

Head of Sales	Hafeezur Rehman *Assistant Vice President & Money Markets Dealer*
Head of Trading	Basir Shamsie *Assistant Vice President & Money Markets Dealer*
Head of Origination	Basir Shamsie *Assistant Vice President & Money Markets Dealer*

Domestic Government Bonds

Head of Sales	Basir Shamsie *Assistant Vice President & Money Markets Dealer*

www.euromoneydirectory.com PAKISTAN (+92)

Eurobonds
Head of Origination; Head of Trading; Trading - Basir Shamsie *Assistant Vice President & Money Markets Dealer*
Sovereigns, Corporates, High-yield

Emerging Market Bonds
Head of Emerging Markets; Head of Sales Safdar Akbari *Associate Director, Money Market*
Head of Trading Basir Shamsie *Assistant Vice President & Money Markets Dealer*

Libor-Based / Floating-Rate Products
FRN Origination; FRN Sales Basir Shamsie *Assistant Vice President & Money Markets Dealer*

Private Placements
Head of Origination Basir Shamsie *Assistant Vice President & Money Markets Dealer*
Head of Structuring Mohammad Sajid

Fixed-Income Repo
Head of Repo Hafizur Rehman *Assistant Vice President & Money Markets Dealer*
Head of Trading Basir Shamsie *Assistant Vice President & Money Markets Dealer*

Fixed-Income Research
Head of Fixed Income Mansoor Ali *Chief Economist* ☎ **242 7460**

Equity Capital Markets
Tel: 242 5505 **Fax:** 241 8106
Head of Equity Capital Markets; Regional Head Adil Matcheswala ☎ **242 7460**
of Sales; Head of Trading

Domestic Equities
Head of Origination; Head of Syndication Mohammad Sajid
Head of Sales; Head of Trading Adil Matcheswala ☎ **242 7460**

International Equities
Head of Sales; Head of Trading Adil Matcheswala ☎ **242 7460**

Equity Research
Head of Equity Research Mansoor Ali *Chief Economist* ☎ **242 7460**

Convertibles / Equity-Linked
Head of Origination; Head of Syndication Mohammad Sajid
Head of Sales; Head of Trading Basir Shamsie *Assistant Vice President & Money Markets Dealer*

Equity Repo / Securities Lending
Head Munaf Ibrahim *Executive Director*

Syndicated Lending
Head of Trading Munaf Ibrahim *Executive Director*

Loan-Related Activities
Leasing & Asset Finance Mohammad Sajid

Money Markets
Tel: 243 1167 **Fax:** 243 1151
Head of Money Markets Tariq Usman *EVP & Money Market Controller*

Domestic Commercial Paper
Head of Origination Mohammad Sajid
Head of Sales; Head of Trading Basir Shamsie *Assistant Vice President & Money Markets Dealer*

Wholesale Deposits
Marketing Aman Meher Khan

Foreign Exchange
Tel: 243 1175 **Fax:** 243 1151
Head of Foreign Exchange; Country Head Munaf Usman

FX Traders / Sales People
  Safdar Akbari *Associate* ☎ **243 1167**

Risk Management
Tel: 243 1181 **Fax:** 241 2426
Head of Risk Management Suleman Lalani *Company Secretary / Finance Manager* ☎ **241 9491**
Country Head Suleman Lalani *Finance Manager*

Settlement / Clearing
Tel: 243 1167 **Fax:** 243 1151
Head of Settlement / Clearing Aftab Munshi ☎ **243 1181**
Equity Settlement Farooq Habib *Operations Manager* ☎ **242 5590**
Fixed-Income Settlement Abdul Samad *Settlement Officer*
Back-Office Abdul Samad *Settlement Officer*

Administration
Head of Administration Suleman Lalani *Company Secretary / Finance Manager* ☎ **241 9491**

Technology & Systems
IT Sohail Ahmed *Senior Manager*

Compliance
  Asif Hameed Abdullah *Manager, Legal & Compliance*

Euromoney Directory 1999 **1167**

PAKISTAN (+92)   www.euromoneydirectory.com

Jardine Fleming Pakistan (Pvt) Limited
Subsidiary Company

2nd Floor, Bahria Complex II, M T Khan Road, Karachi 74000, Sindh
Tel: (21) 561 0861; (21) 561 0862 **Fax:** (21) 561 0875 **Email:** jahanzeb.naseer@jfleming.com

Senior Executive Officers
Chief Executive Officer   Charles Blackmore *Chief Executive Officer* [T] 561 0867 [F] 561 0261
Financial Director   Fazal Gaffoor *Finance Director* [T] 561 0197 [F] 561 0170

Equity Capital Markets
Country Head   Jahanzeb Naseer *Head of Broking* [T] 561 0866 [F] 561 0875
                               [E] jahanzeb.nasser@jfleming.com

Corporate Finance / M&A Advisory
Head of Corporate Finance   Reza Rahim *Head of Corporate Finance* [T] 561 0868 [F] 561 0175
                               [E] reza.rahim@jfeming.com

Settlement / Clearing
Head of Settlement / Clearing Shahid Khan *Head of Settlements* [T] 242 6203 [F] 242 6436
                               [E] shahid.khan@jfleming.com

Administration
Head of Administration   Zillehasnain Rizya *Head* [T] 561 0861

Compliance
                               Fazal Gaffoor [T] 561 0861

Société Générale
Full Branch Office

3rd Floor, PNSC Building, Moulvie Janrizuddin Khan Road, Karachi, Sindh
PO Box 6766, Karachi, Sindh
Tel: (21) 561 1846; (21) 561 1847 **Fax:** (21) 561 0679; (21) 561 1672 **Telex:** 29605 SGKAR PK

Senior Executive Officers
Chief Executive Officer   Paul Henri Rusch *Chief Executive Officer* [T] 561 0677
Chief Operating Officer   Lakeria Noorani *Head Account Administration*
Treasurer   Hanif Akhai *Assistant General Manager*
Managing Director   Jacques Faucheux [T] 561 0366

Others (Senior Executives)
Branch Manager, Islamabad   Ishrat Abid *Branch Manager* [T] (51) 824 127
Branch Manager, Lahore   Kamaluddin Khan *Branch Manager* [T] (42) 631 4201

General-Lending (DCM, SL)
Head of Corporate Banking   Shahid Fakhruddin *Country Corporate Officer* [T] 561 0680

General-Investment
Head of Investment   Iqbal Ashraf *Country Head of Investment Banking*

Syndicated Lending

Loan-Related Activities
Trade Finance   Ahsanullah Khan *Manager, Trade Finance* [T] 561 1846

Money Markets
Head of Money Markets   Ovais Ismail *Money Market* [T] 5611 8469

Foreign Exchange
Head of Foreign Exchange   Raza Hussain *Foreign Exchange* [T] 561 1846
Corporate Sales   Marcia Rawalpiniwala *Corporate* [T] 5611 8469

Settlement / Clearing
Head of Settlement / Clearing Saleem Lalani *Head of Money Markets, FX & Settlements* [T] 561 1846

Other Departments
Chief Credit Officer   Zain Majidulla *Country Head of Credit* [T] 561 0683
Private Banking   Amer Siddiqui *Head, Private Banking*
Correspondent Banking   Iqbal Ashraf *Head, Investment Banking* [T] 561 0592

Administration

Technology & Systems
                               Faiz Siddiqui *EDP Manager* [T] 561 1846

Public Relations
                               Jehmima Bux *Manager, Communications* [T] 568 2925

Accounts / Audit
                               Naveen Namazi *Head of Internal Audit* [T] 561 1846

www.euromoneydirectory.com   PAKISTAN (+92)

Soneri Bank Limited
Head Office

87 Shahrah-e-Quaid-e-Azam, Lahore
PO Box 49, Lahore
Tel: (42) 636 8142; (42) 636 8143 **Fax**: (42) 636 8138 **Telex**: 47694 SONRI PK

Senior Executive Officers
Chairman	Jaffer Ali Feerasta ☏ **571 3101**
President	Safar Ali K Lakhani ☏ **243 9582**
Chief Executive Officer	Qamar Wahab *Senior Executive Vice President* ☏ **243 9586**
	✉ soneri@khi.fascom.com
	Farrukh Hussain Rizvi *SEVP & General Manager - North* ☏ **636 8139**
	Karim Naseeruddin *SEVP & General Manager - South* ☏ **243 9583**
Treasurer	Ali Nayyer *Vice President* ☏ **242 7967**
Company Secretary	Abdul Hayee
International Division	Nemat Ali *Executive Vice President* ☏ **243 9584**

Debt Capital Markets / Fixed Income

Domestic Government Bonds
Head of Trading   Ali Nayyer *VP, Forex / Treasury* ☏ **242 7967**

Equity Capital Markets

Domestic Equities
Head of Sales   Qamar Wahab *Senior Executive Vice President* ☏ **243 9586**
✉ soneri@khi.fascom.com

Syndicated Lending
Tel: 243 9562/7 **Fax**: 243 9561 **Telex**: 21262 SONRI PK
Head of Syndication   Qamar Wahab *Senior Executive Vice President* ☏ **243 9586**
✉ soneri@khi.fascom.com

Money Markets
Tel: 243 9562/7 **Fax**: 243 9561
Head of Money Markets   Qamar Wahab *Senior Executive Vice President* ☏ **243 9586**
✉ soneri@khi.fascom.com

Foreign Exchange
Head of Institutional Sales   Nemat Ali *Executive Vice President* ☏ **243 9584**
Head of Trading   Ali Nayyer *VP, Forex / Treasury* ☏ **242 7967**

Settlement / Clearing
Head of Settlement / Clearing   Ali Nayyer *Vice President* ☏ **242 7967**

Other Departments
Correspondent Banking   Nemat Ali *Executive Vice President* ☏ **243 9584**

Administration

Technology & Systems
   Haider Devjianie *Vice President, EDP Manager* ☏ **240 0919**

Legal / In-House Counsel
Legal Counsel   Tahir Ali Tayebi *Legal Advisor* ☏ **581 209**

The World Bank
Full Branch Office

20-A Shahrah-e-Jamhuriat, G5-1, Islamabad
PO Box 1025, Islamabad
Tel: (51) 819 781; (51) 819 786 **Fax**: (51) 279 648; (51) 279 649 **Telex**: 5827 **Cable**: INTBAFRAD

Senior Executive Officers

Others (Senior Executives)
   Sadiq Ahmed *Country Director, Pakistan & Afghanistan*

PANAMA
(+507)

Banco Nacional de Panamá 🏛 Central Bank

Banconal Tower, Vía España, Panama City
PO Box 5220, Panama City 5
Tel: 263 5151; 263 7527 **Fax:** 269 0091 **Telex:** 3194 **Swift:** NAPA PA PA **Telex:** 2773

Senior Executive Officers
President
Chief Executive Officer
Financial Director
Chief Operating Officer
Treasurer
Executive Legal Secretary
International Division

Roosevelt Thayer T 269 0060 F 264 7155
Eduardo C Urriola *General Manager* T 269 2955 F 264 7155
Virgilio Castillo *Deputy General Manager* T 263 8025 F 223 3842
Galileo Ferrabone *Deputy General Manager* T 263 7396 F 269 0001
Rodrigo O Perea *Executive Treasury Manager* T 269 3397 F 269 0091
Francisco Vásquez T 269 0060 F 264 7155
Querube de Alvarado T 263 8292 F 263 6466

Money Markets
Head of Money Markets

Gladys Perez *Chief Dealer* T 263 7422 F 269 0091

Other Departments
Correspondent Banking

Aminta de Portugal *Head* T 269 3397 F 269 0091

Administration
Head of Administration

Miguel Lee *Deputy General Manager* T 269 6106 F 269 5645

Technology & Systems

Osvaldo Gallardo *Executive Manager* T 261 8467 F 229 3952

Public Relations

Raúl Cedeño *Executive Manager* T 269 5764 F 264 6834

Accounts / Audit

Ernesto Aparicio *Executive Manager* T 226 4875 F 226 3990

ABN AMRO Bank NV Full Branch Office

Edificio 4, Calle Manuel María Icaza, Panama City 4
Tel: 263 6200 **Fax:** 269 0526

Senior Executive Officers
Country Manager

José Luis Peláez Pérez

General-Lending (DCM, SL)
Head of Corporate Banking

Aleida De Bello *Commercial & Corporate Banking Director*

Administration
Other (Administration)
Commercial Banking

Aleida De Bello *Commercial & Corporate Banking Director*

Banco Confederado de América Latina Head Office

Alternative trading name: COLABANCO
Calle 50 y 56 Victoriano Lorenzo, Panama City
PO Box 7547, Panama City 5
Tel: 269 9888 **Fax:** 263 3518 **Telex:** 2608 COLA. BCO.

Senior Executive Officers
President
First Vice President
Financial Director
Chief Operating Officer
Treasurer
VPE and General Manager
Company Secretary
International Division

Manuel Rabines
Sincrito Cifuentes
Eduardo Pazmiño *VP, Finance & Planning*
David Plata *Vice President, Operations*
Ana Maria de Lachman *Treasury Manager*
Juan Antino Niño
Marco A Alcerro
Marisín de Ávila *Manager, International Division*

General-Lending (DCM, SL)
Head of Corporate Banking

Betzaida de Delgadeo *AVP Corporate Credit*

General-Investment
Head of Investment

María Isabel Fraser *Investment Banking Officer*

www.euromoneydirectory.com PANAMA (+507)

Debt Capital Markets / Fixed Income
Department: Banca de Inversions
Tel: 263 1628 Fax: 263 3506
Head of Fixed Income María Isabel Fraser *Investment Banking Officer*

Emerging Market Bonds
Head of Emerging Markets María Isabel Fraser *Investment Banking Officer*

Syndicated Lending
Loan-Related Activities
Trade Finance Marisín de Ávila *Manager, International Division*

Money Markets
Tel: 263 1628
Head of Money Markets Ana María de Lacham *Treasury Manager*

Other Departments
Chief Credit Officer Betzaida Delgado *AVP Corporte Credit*
Private Banking Sonia Pardo *Private Banking Officer*
Correspondent Banking Ana María de Lacham *Treasury Manager*

Administration
Head of Administration Domingo de Odaldía *Administrative Manager*
Business Development Eduardo Grimaldo *AVP, Business Development*

Technology & Systems
Information System José Domínguez *Manager*

Legal / In-House Counsel
  Rogelio Biendicho

Compliance
  Marisín de Ávila *Manager, International Division*

Public Relations
  Miren de Barbero *Manager, Public Relations*

Accounts / Audit
  Enrique Jaén *Internal Auditor*

Banco del Istmo SA Full Branch Office

Banco del ISTMO

Calle 55 y 77 Este, San Francisco, Panama City
PO Box 6-3823, El Dorado
Tel: 269 0015 Fax: 270 1952 Telex: 2146 BANISTMO PG Swift: BIST PA PA BIC Email: ckirkland@banistmo.com
Website: www.banistmo.com

Senior Executive Officers
President Samuel Lewis Galindo
Chief Executive Officer Alberto Vallarino *Executive Vice President*
General Manager L J Montague Belanger

Others (Senior Executives)
Banco Mercantil del ISTMO SA Manuel Barredo *General Manager* ☎ **263 6262**
Compañía de Seguros Chagres Raul Novey *General Manager* ☎ **263 7455**
  Juan Carlos Fabrega *Executive Manager, International Banking*

General-Lending (DCM, SL)
Head of Corporate Banking Javier Carrizo *Executive Manager, Commercial Banking*
  David Múnoz *Executive Manager, Credit*

Corporate Finance / M&A Advisory
Head of Corporate Finance Hans Kupfer *Executive Manager, Finance*

Settlement / Clearing
Operations Horacio Montenegro *Executive Manager, Operations*

Administration
Head of Administration Gianfranco Mazzeo *Administrative Manager* ☎ **269 5555**

Technology & Systems
Credit Cards & Electronic Banking Raul Jiminez *Executive Manager*
Technology Hernando Pang *Manager*

Legal / In-House Counsel
  Lidia De Aizpurua *Manager*

PANAMA (+507)   www.euromoneydirectory.com

Banco del Istmo SA (cont)
Compliance
Rafael Moreno *Compliance Officer*
Public Relations
Marketing & Public Relations   Victoria Zarak *Manager*
Accounts / Audit
Audit   Lilia Cambra *Manager*
Other (Administration)
Human Resources   Edgardo Quintero *Executive Manager* ☏ **269 5555**

Banco Disa SA   Head Office

Calle 51 Este, Campo Alegre, Panama City 5
PO Box 7201, Panama City
Tel: 263 5933; 263 9950 **Fax:** 264 1084; 223 5147 **Telex:** 3713 DISA BANK PG **Swift:** CHAS US 33
Website: www.bdisa.com

Senior Executive Officers
Chairman   Joaquín J Vallarino ☏ **263 5833**
Chief Executive Officer   Rafael Endara *EVP & General Manager* ✉ **rendara@bdisa.com**
Chief Operating Officer   Roberto Thomas *Credit Manager* ✉ **rthomas@bdisa.com**
Treasurer   Lisette Gronchi ✉ **lgronchi@bdisa.com**
Debt Capital Markets / Fixed Income
Department: Disa Securities, Inc
Global Head   Rafael Endara *EVP & General Manager* ✉ **rendara@bdisa.com**
Domestic Government Bonds
Head of Sales   Dulcidio de la Guardia *Manager, Private Banking* ✉ **dulcidio@bdisa.com**
Head of Trading   Gustavo Chacin *Trader* ✉ **gchacin@bdisa.com**
Head of Research   Abey Saied *Analyst & Financial Advisor* ✉ **asaied@bdisa.com**
Non-Domestic Government Bonds
Trading   Gustavo Chacin *Trader* ✉ **gchacin@bdisa.com**
Eurobonds
Head of Origination   Roberto Brenes *Head, Corporate Finance* ✉ **rbrenes@bdisa.com**
Head of Trading; Trading (Sovereigns); Trading   Gustavo Chacin *Trader* ✉ **gchacin@bdisa.com**
(Corporates)
Trading (High-yield)   Lisette de Gronchi *Chief Trader* ✉ **lgronchi@bdisa.com**
Medium-Term Notes
Head of Origination   Roberto Brenes *Head, Corporate Finance* ✉ **rbrenes@bdisa.com**
Head of Sales   Gustavo Chacin *Trader* ✉ **gchacin@bdisa.com**
Private Placements
Head of Origination   Roberto Brenes *Head, Corporate Finance* ✉ **rbrenes@bdisa.com**
Head of Sales   Dulcidio de la Guardia *Manager, Private Banking* ✉ **dulcidio@bdisa.com**
Head of Structuring   Abey Saied *Analyst & Financial Advisor* ✉ **asaied@bdisa.com**
Asset-Backed Securities / Securitization
Global Head   Roberto Thomas *Credit Manager* ✉ **rthomas@bdisa.com**
Regional Head   Roberto Brenes *Head, Corporate Finance* ✉ **rbrenes@bdisa.com**
Head of Trading   Gustavo Chacin *Trader* ✉ **gchacin@bdisa.com**
Mortgage-Backed Securities
Global Head; Regional Head   Roberto Brenes *Head, Corporate Finance* ✉ **rbrenes@bdisa.com**
Head of Trading   Lisette de Gronchi *Chief Trader* ✉ **lgronchi@bdisa.com**
Equity Capital Markets
Department: Disa Securities, Inc
Global Head; Regional Head   Federico Roa *Head of International Equities* ✉ **froa@bdisa.com**
Domestic Equities
Head of Origination   Roberto Brenes *Head, Corporate Finance* ✉ **rbrenes@bdisa.com**
Head of Syndication   Dulcidio de la Guardia *Manager, Private Banking* ✉ **dulcidio@bdisa.com**
Head of Sales   Federico Roa *Head of International Equities* ✉ **froa@bdisa.com**
Head of Trading   Carlos Ledezma *Trader* ✉ **cledezma@bdisa.com**
Head of Research   Abey Saied *Analyst & Financial Advisor* ✉ **asaied@bdisa.com**
International Equities
Head of Origination   Roberto Brenes *Head, Corporate Finance* ✉ **rbrenes@bdisa.com**
Head of Sales   Federico Roa *Head of International Equities* ✉ **froa@bdisa.com**
Head of Trading; Head of Research   Carlos Ledezma *Trader* ✉ **cledezma@bdisa.com**
Syndicated Lending
Tel: 263 5933 **Fax:** 264 1084
Global Head   Roberto Thomas *Credit Manager* ✉ **rthomas@bdisa.com**
Head of Origination   Roberto Brenes *Head, Corporate Finance* ✉ **rbrenes@bdisa.com**

www.euromoneydirectory.com   PANAMA (+507)

Syndicated Lending (cont)
Head of Trading   Dulcidio de la Guardia *Manager, Private Banking* E **dulcidio@bdisa.com**

Loan-Related Activities
Trade Finance; Project Finance; Structured   Roberto Thomas *Credit Manager* E **rthomas@bdisa.com**
Trade Finance; Leasing & Asset Finance

Money Markets
Global Head   Lisette de Gronchi *Chief Trader* E **lgronchi@bdisa.com**

Domestic Commercial Paper
Head of Origination   Roberto Brenes *Head, Corporate Finance* E **rbrenes@bdisa.com**
Head of Sales   Lisette de Gronchi *Chief Trader* E **lgronchi@bdisa.com**
Head of Trading   Gustavo Chacin *Trader* E **gchacin@bdisa.com**

Eurocommercial Paper
Head of Sales   Gustavo Chacin *Trader* E **gchacin@bdisa.com**
Head of Trading   Lisette de Gronchi *Chief Trader* E **lgronchi@bdisa.com**

Wholesale Deposits
Marketing   Lisette de Gronchi *Chief Trader* E **lgronchi@bdisa.com**

Foreign Exchange
Global Head   Lisette de Gronchi *Chief Trader* E **lgronchi@bdisa.com**
Corporate Sales   Mayra Bogantes *Officer* E **mbogantes@bdisa.com**
Head of Trading   Sally Loo *Assistant Treasurer* E **sloo@bdisa.com**

Risk Management
Global Head   Roberto Thomas *Credit Manager* E **rthomas@bdisa.com**
Regional Head   Federico Albert *Planning Manager* E **falbert@bdisa.com**

Fixed Income Derivatives / Risk Management
Regional Head; Country Head   Gustavo Chacin *Trader* E **gchacin@bdisa.com**

Corporate Finance / M&A Advisory
Department: Disa Securities, Inc
Tel: 263 5933 **Fax**: 223 5147
Global Head   Roberto Brenes *Head, Corporate Finance* E **rbrenes@bdisa.com**
Country Head   Dulcidio de la Guardia *Manager, Private Banking* E **dulcidio@bdisa.com**

Settlement / Clearing
Regional Head   Guillermo Willis *Operations Manager* E **gwillis@bdisa.com**
Country Head   Jilma de Abadia *Operations Manager* E **jdeabadia@bdisa.com**

Other Departments
Proprietary Trading   Lisette de Gronchi *Chief Trader* E **lgronchi@bdisa.com**
Private Banking   Dulcidio de la Guardia *Manager, Private Banking* E **dulcidio@bdisa.com**
Correspondent Banking   Mayra Bogantes *Officer* E **mbogantes@bdisa.com**

Administration
Technology & Systems
   Domingo Latorraca *Officer* E **dlatorraca@bdisa.com**

Legal / In-House Counsel
   Nadiuska Lopez *Officer* E **nlopez@bdisa.com**

Compliance
   Gisela Lombardo *Officer* E **glombardo@bdisa.com**

Public Relations
   Malena de Obarrio *Officer* E **mdeobarrio@bdisa.com**

Banco Latinoamericano de Exportaciones SA - BLADEX
Head Office

Alternative trading name: BLADEX
Calle 50 & Aquilino de la Guardia, Panama City
PO Box 6-1497, El Dorado, Panama City
Tel: 263 6766 **Fax**: 269 6333 **Telex**: 2356

Senior Executive Officers
President, Board of Directors   Gonzalo Menendez Duque
Chief Executive Officer   José Castaneda
Financial Director   Daniel Casal *VP, Credit & Marketing*
Chief Operating Officer   Hydee De Cano *VP, Administration*

Euromoney Directory 1999   **1173**

PANAMA (+507)　　　　　　　www.euromoneydirectory.com

Banco de la Provincia de Buenos Aires — Full Branch Office

22nd Floor, Banco Exterior Building, 42/43 Avenida Balboa, Panama City
Box 6-4592, El Dorado, Panama City
Tel: 227 2167 Fax: 225 0431

Senior Executive Officers
Manager　　　　　　　　　　　　　Juan C Sturlesi

Bank of China — Full Branch Office

Calle Manuel Maria Icaza 14, Panama City
PO Box 871056, Panama City 7
Tel: 263 5522 Fax: 269 1079

Senior Executive Officers
General Manager　　　　　　　　　He Qui Ren

Banque Nationale de Paris Panamá SA — Subsidiary Company

Edificio Omanco, Via España n°200, Apartado Aereo 1774, Panama City 1
Tel: 263 6600 Fax: 263 6970 Telex: PATCO 2128, 2270, 2219 Swift: BNPA PA PA

Senior Executive Officers
Vice President & General Director　　Pierre Thomé ☏ 223 6923

Others (Senior Executives)
　　　　　　　　　　　　　　　　Jorge Dixon *Branch Manager* ☏ 223 9235

Banque Sudameris — Full Branch Office

Avenida Balboa y Calle 41, Panama City 9A
PO Box 1847, Panama City
Tel: 227 2777 Fax: 227 5828

Senior Executive Officers
General Manager　　　　　　　　　Julio-Alberto Cortés García

The Dai-Ichi Kangyo Bank Limited — Full Branch Office

Via España, Condiminio Plaza Internacional, Planta Baja, Panama City 9A
PO Box 2637, Panama City 9A
Tel: 269 6111 Fax: 269 6815 Telex: 2030 DKB PA
Website: www.dkb.co.jp

Senior Executive Officers
General Manager　　　　　　　　　Yutaka Koyama
Joint General Manager　　　　　　　Gakuo Fukutomi
International Division　　　　　　　Marisol Barreto *Assistant General Manager*

Others (Senior Executives)
　　　　　　　　　　　　　　　　Kenichi Yamada *Assistant General*

Syndicated Lending
Head of Credit Committee　　　　　Inés Ruiz *Assistant General Manager*

Other (Trade Finance)
Documentary Credits　　　　　　　Marisol Barreto *Assistant General Manager*

Other Departments
Correspondent Banking　　　　　　Marisol Barreto *Assistant General Manager*

Administration
Head of Administration　　　　　　Angela T Broussard *Assistant General Manager*

1174　Euromoney Directory 1999

PANAMA (+507)

Groupe BNP Panama
Subsidiary Company

Edificio Omanco, Via España 200, piso 4°, Panama City 1
PO Box 201, Panama City 1
Tel: 264 8555 Fax: 263 6970 Telex: 2128 PANAMA
General Telex: 2681 PANAMA

Senior Executive Officers
General Manager   Pierre Thome
Assistant General Manager   Julien Samit Solas

Syndicated Lending
Loan-Related Activities
Trade Finance   Julien Samit Solas *Assistant General Manager*

The Industrial Bank of Japan Limited
Representative Office

13th Floor, Swiss Bank Tower, 53rd Street East, Urbanizacion Obarrio, Panama City
PO Box 55-1587, Paitilla, Panama City
Tel: 263 8233 Fax: 264 0685

Senior Executive Officers
Chief Representative   Shuhei Sakuma

The International Commercial Bank of China Co Limited
Full Branch Office

Calle 50 y Esquina Margarita A. de Vallarino, Planta Baja, Edificio ICBC 74, Panama City
PO Box 4453, Panama City 5
Tel: 263 8108; 264 9022 Fax: 263 8392; 223 9162 Telex: 2294 ICBC PA

Senior Executive Officers
Vice President & General Manager   Show Loong Hwang

Merrill Lynch International
Full Branch Office

Calle Aquilinio de la Guardia 18, Panama City 7
PO Box 8065, Panama City
Tel: 263 9911 Fax: 264 7284
Website: www.ml.com

Senior Executive Officers
General Manager   John Garrett

Midland Bank plc
Full Branch Office

Rodolfo Chiari Avenue, Aguadulce Cocle, Aguadulce
PO Box 075, Aguadulce
Tel: 997 0608; 997 0618 Fax: 997 0658 Telex: 9749 MDBK PAG

Senior Executive Officers
General Manager   Israel Reed

Société Générale
Full Branch Office

Torre World Trade Center, piso 10°, Oficina 1001, Calle 53 Urb Marbella, Panama City
PO Box 832-0039, Torre World Trade Center, Panama City
Tel: 264 9611 Fax: 264 0295 Telex: 3563 Swift: SOGE PA PA

Senior Executive Officers
General Manager   Celestin Cuq
International Division   Diana de Silvera *Deputy General Manager*

Administration
Other (Administration)
Commercial Banking   Rogelio Wong *Commercial Banking Director*

PAPUA NEW GUINEA (+675)   www.euromoneydirectory.com

PAPUA NEW GUINEA
(+675)

Westpac Bank-PNG-Limited — Subsidiary Company
5th Floor, Mogoru Moto Building, Champion Parade, Port Moresby
PO Box 706, Port Moresby
Tel: 322 0800 **Fax:** 321 4068 **Telex:** NE 23243 WBANK C **Reuters:** WBPG **Cable:** WBANK

Senior Executive Officers
Chairman — Bruce Alexander T 322 0800
Financial Director — Bradley Danes *Financial Control* T 322 0847
Treasurer — Daryl Jarrett T 322 0845
Managing Director / General Manager — Simon Millett T 322 0830
Company Secretary — David Browne T 322 0836

PARAGUAY
(+595)

Banco Central del Paraguay — Central Bank
Avenida Federacion Rusa y Sargento Marecos, Barrio Santo Domingo, Asunción
PO Box 861, Asunción
Tel: (21) 608 011 **Fax:** (21) 608 119; (21) 600 437 **Telex:** 46000 CENBANK PY **Email:** bcp@uninet.com.py
Cable: BANCOCENTRAL **Telex:** 46002 CENBANK PY

Senior Executive Officers
President — Hermes A Gomez Ginard T 609 131/2 F 608 136
Treasurer — Roberto Caballero T 608 128
Managing Director / General Manager — Edgar Caceres T 608 127 F 610 407
Company Secretary — Jorge Augusto Sanchez T 608 119
International Division — Rolando Arrellaga *Manager* T 608 141 F 660 437

Others (Senior Executives)
Member of the Board — Dionisio Coronel Benitez T 608 165 F 610 611
Alvaro Caballero Carrizosa T 608 125 F 610 408
Jorge Gullino Ferrari T 608 121 F 608 167
Jorge Schreiner Marengo T 608 123 F 608 169
Banking Superintendent — Edgar Luguizamon Carmona T 608 148 F 608 149
Insurance Superintendent — Guatavo Alexi Osorio T 608 145

Relationship Manager
Development & Institutional Management — Julio Gonzalez Ugarte T 608 130
Secretary to the Board — Luis Brunn Zucolillo T 608 118
Private Secretariat Presidents office — Luis Oritz Acosta T 608 132 F 608 136

Foreign Exchange
Head of Foreign Exchange — Rolando Arrellaga *Manager* T 608 141 F 660 437

Other Departments
Economic Research — Paul Jose Vera Bogado *Manager* T 608 158 F 608 150

Administration
Head of Administration — Gregorio Blaires *Manager* T 608 117 F 610 403

Technology & Systems
Data Processing — Oscar Milciades Saldivar *Director* T 608 122 F 608 101
Foreign Technical Assistance Office — Jorge Humberto Gini T 608 116

Legal / In-House Counsel
Legal Department — Abogado Benigno Lopez T 608 126

Public Relations
Public Relations & Protocol — Sandra Saldivar T 611 118 F 610 088
Press — Andres Bentez T 610 088

Accounts / Audit
Accountancy & Budget — Carlos Gonzales Escobar *Manager* T 608 154 F 608 155
Internal Audit — Gilberto Rodriguez *Manager* T 608 137 F 661 596

Other (Administration)
Human Resources / Personnel — Mario Becker *Director* T 608 120 F 610 409

www.euromoneydirectory.com   PARAGUAY (+595)

ABN AMRO Bank NV Asunción
Subsidiary Company

Eduardo Victor Haedo 128, Esquina Independencia Nacional, Asunción
Casilla de Correo 1180, Asunción
Tel: (21) 490 001; (21) 490 008 Fax: (21) 491 734

Senior Executive Officers
Country Manager   Herman G Klaassen
Others (Senior Executives)
                               María Clotilde de Silva *Deputy Manager*

Banco Nacional de Fomento
Head Office

Independencia Nacional y Cerro Corá, Asunción, 134
Tel: (21) 444 440; (21) 444 441 Fax: (21) 446 053 Telex: 44019 BNFASN PY Tel: 444 442; 444 443;
Telex: 44022 BNFASN PY

Senior Executive Officers
President   Victor María Chamorro Abadie ☎ **444 502**
Chief Executive Officer   Vidal Francisco Capurro Mendieta *Executive Director* ☎ **448 895**
Financial Director   Oscar Ignacio Franco Villalba *Director* ☎ **444 571**
Chief Operating Officer   Juan Fernando Ortíz Monges *Chief* ☎ **490 699**
Treasurer   Bernardo Urdapilleta *Chief* ☎ **494 645**

Banco Sudameris Paraguay SA

Independencia Nacional, Esquina Cerro Corá, Asunción
PO Box 1433, Asunción
Tel: (21) 494 542 Fax: (21) 448 670 Telex: SUDAS PY 44015 Swift: BSUD PY PX Email: sudameris@infonet.com.py

Senior Executive Officers
Chief Executive Officer   Giuseppe Di Francesco

Citibank NA
Full Branch Office

Estrelle 345 y Chile, Asunción
Tel: (21) 494 951; (21) 494 959 Fax: (21) 444 820

Senior Executive Officers
President   Antonio Uvive ☎ **492 000** 📠 **444 820**
Treasurer   Oscar Biesel
Managing Director / General Manager   Antonio Uvive ☎ **492 000** 📠 **444 820**
General-Lending (DCM, SL)
Head of Corporate Banking   Daniel Saa

Dresdner Bank Lateinamerika AG
Representative Office

Formerly known as: Deutsch-Südamerikanische Bank AG/Dresdner Bank AG
14 de Mayo 337, Edificio AsuBank, piso 10°, Asunción
Casilla de Correo 196, Asunción
Tel: (21) 445 039; (21) 494 710 Fax: (21) 441 268

Senior Executive Officers
Representative   Juan Carlos Borchert

ING Barings
Full Branch Office

Avenida España y San Rafael, PO Box 10007, Asunción
Tel: (21) 606 423; (21) 606 427 Fax: (21) 606 437 Telex: 46059 INGB PY Swift: INGB PY PX

Senior Executive Officers
Country Manager   Peter A J A Boot
Others (Senior Executives)
                               R de Palacios *Deputy General Manager*

Euromoney Directory 1999   **1177**

PARAGUAY (+595)   www.euromoneydirectory.com

Lloyds Bank plc
Full Branch Office

Palma y O' Leary, Asunción
PO Box 696, Asunción
Tel: (21) 491 090; (21) 491 099 **Fax:** (21) 443 569 **Telex:** 44014 LONDONBANK **Swift:** LOYD PY PX

Senior Executive Officers
General-Lending (DCM, SL)
Head of Corporate Banking — Jorge Solis
Foreign Exchange
Head of Trading — Santiago Vega *Dealer*
Administration
Head of Administration — Ricardo Sales
Other (Administration)
Human Resources — Rubén Decoud *Manager*

PERU (+51)

Banco Central de Reserva del Perú
Central Bank

Jirón Antonio Miró Quesada 441, Lima 1
PO Box 1958, Lima 1
Tel: (1) 427 6250; (1) 427 9582 **Fax:** (1) 426 1229; (1) 426 0520 **Telex:** 20169 **Swift:** CRPE PR PL

Senior Executive Officers
Chairman — Germám Suárez
Chief Executive Officer — Javier de la Rocha *General Manager*
Treasurer — Jorge Patrón *Head*
International Division — Carlos Ballón *Manager*
Others (Senior Executives)
Mario Tovar Velarde *Director & Senior Vice President*

General-Lending (DCM, SL)
Head of Corporate Banking — Jorge Patrón *Head*
General - Treasury
Head of Treasury — Carlos Ballón *Manager*
Money Markets
Head of Money Markets — Juan Miguel Cayo ☎ 426 1229
Foreign Exchange
Tel: 428 1830 **Telex:** BRPE
Head of Foreign Exchange — Juan Miguel Cayo ☎ 426 1229
Head of Trading — Alberto Zapata *Head*
FX Traders / Sales People
Ricardo Alvarado *Dealer*
Ella Zamudio *Dealer*

Settlement / Clearing
Country Head — Gonzalo Iparraguirre
Global Custody
Head of Global Custody — Gonzalo Iparraguirre
Other Departments
Commodities / Bullion — Sandra Mansilla
Correspondent Banking — Javier Olivera

Argenta
Head Office

Arias Aragüez 133, Lima 18
Tel: (1) 444 0014; (1) 241 1717 **Fax:** (1) 446 8911 **Email:** Agt_001@hermes.bvl.com.pe
Website: www.agt.bvl.com.pe

Senior Executive Officers
Chairman, President & Manager — Juan Miguel Bakula-Budge
Chief Operating Officer — Monica de Ycaza-Clerc *Vice Chairman & COO*
Treasurer — Susana Kam *Treasurer*

1178 Euromoney Directory 1999

www.euromoneydirectory.com PERU (+51)

Others (Senior Executives)
Monica de Ycaza-Clerc *Vice Chairman & COO*
Risk Management
Trading Fernando Sanchez *Trader*
Foreign Exchange Derivatives / Risk Management
Country Head Susana Kam *Treasurer*
Settlement / Clearing
Operations Juan Miguel Bakula-Budge *Chairman, President & Manager*
Other Departments
Economic Research Claudio Brignetti *Research Manager*
Administration
Head of Administration Ana Villegas *Assistant Manager*
Technology & Systems
Carol Bartra *Systems Manager*
Legal / In-House Counsel
Enrique Ferrari *Attorney*

Banco de Comercio   Head Office

Jirón Lampa 560, Lima 1
Casilla de Correo 4195, Lima
Tel: (14) 289 400 Fax: (14) 269 075

Senior Executive Officers
President Percy Tabory Andrade ☏ **267 859**
General Manager Hector Quezada Macchiavello ☏ **278 102**
International Division Luis Chang Escobedo *Director* ☏ **282 064**
Administration
Other (Administration)
Commercial Banking Luis de la Cruz Yauri *Director* ☏ **280 027**

Banco Continental SA   Head Office

Avenida República de Panamá 3055, San Isidro, Lima 27
Tel: (1) 211 1000 Fax: (1) 211 1788; (1) 211 2406 Telex: 21282 Swift: BCON PE PL Reuters: BCLP

Senior Executive Officers
Chairman of the Board Pedro Brescia Cafferata ☏ **211 1005**
Chief Executive Officer José Carlos Pla Royo *Director General Manager* ☏ **211 1006**
Financial Director José Manuel Baños Santos *Joint General Manager* ☏ **211 1013**
Chief Operating Officer Juan Gonzalez Lucas *Joint General Manager* ☏ **211 1008**
Treasurer Giorgio Bernasconi Carozzi *Manager* ☏ **211 2365**

Equity Capital Markets
Department: Continental Bolsa SAB

Domestic Equities
Head of Origination; Head of Syndication; Head Rafael Carranza Jahnsen *General Manager* ☏ **211 2380**
of Sales; Head of Trading; Head of Research

Syndicated Lending
Global Head Javier Marin Estevez *Joint General Manager* ☏ **211 1023**
Head of Origination Daniel Oblitas *Officer* ☏ **211 1094**

Loan-Related Activities
Trade Finance Javier Marin Estevez *Joint General Manager* ☏ **211 1023**
  Karina Bruce de Ramsey *Manager* ☏ **211 2070**
Project Finance Daniel Oblitas *Officer* ☏ **211 1094**
Structured Trade Finance Karina Bruce de Ramsey *Manager* ☏ **211 2070**
Leasing & Asset Finance Daniel Oblitas *Officer* ☏ **211 1094**

Money Markets
Global Head Giorgio Bernasconi Carozzi *Manager* ☏ **211 2365**
Domestic Commercial Paper
Head of Trading Elio Soto ☏ **211 2366**
Wholesale Deposits
Marketing Irma Dawson ☏ **211 2369**
Foreign Exchange
Head of Trading Luis Gamero Savastano *Head of Forex* ☏ **211 2370**

Euromoney Directory 1999 **1179**

PERU (+51) www.euromoneydirectory.com

Banco Continental SA (cont)
Risk Management
Foreign Exchange Derivatives / Risk Management
Cross-Currency Swaps, Trading — Saul Vasquez Nassi *Trader* ☏ 211 2367
Corporate Finance / M&A Advisory
Global Head — Alfonso Zarate Rivas *Manager* ☏ 211 1860
Regional Head — Enrique Hermosa Hoyle *Joint Manager* ☏ 211 1878
Other Departments
Private Banking — Marco Danuser Wepf *Manager* ☏ 211 1622
Correspondent Banking — Karina Bruce de Ramsey *Manager* ☏ 211 2070
Administration
Technology & Systems — Juan Gonzalez Lucas *Joint General Manager* ☏ 211 1008
Legal / In-House Counsel — Dominga Sota Nadal *Manager* ☏ 211 1018
Compliance — José Manuel Baños Santos *Joint General Manager* ☏ 211 1013
Public Relations — Elsa Camino B. *Manager* ☏ 211 1260

Banco de Crédito del Perú
Head Office

Calle Centenario 156, Santa Patricia, La Molina, Lima 12
PO Box 12-067, Lima 12
Tel: (1) 349 0808; (1) 349 0606 **Fax:** (1) 426 5644 **Telex:** 20158 **Swift:** BCPL PE PL

Senior Executive Officers
President & Chief Executive Officer — Dionisio Romero ☏ 349 0566
Financial Director — Benedicto Cigueñas *Chief Financial Officer*
General Manager — Raimundo Morales ☏ 394 0563
International Division — Alcides Portocarrero *International Operations Director* ☏ 349 0491

Others (Senior Executives)
Luis Nicolini *Vice Chairman*
Pedro Rubio

General-Lending (DCM, SL)
Head of Corporate Banking — Jesús Zamora *Corporate Banking Director* ☏ 349 0800
General - Treasury
Head of Treasury — Andrés Figuerola *Assistant Vice President*
Syndicated Lending
Other (Syndicated Lending)
Documentary Credits — Tomás Kanashiro *Assistant Vice President*
Other Departments
Correspondent Banking — Gonzalo Alvarez Calderón *Vice President*
Administration
Other (Administration) — Walter Bayly *Commercial Banking Director* ☏ 349 0309

Banco del Nuevo Mundo SAEMA
Head Office

Avenida Paseo de la República 3033, Lima 27
Tel: (1) 442 9649; (1) 442 1800 **Fax:** (1) 442 6731; (1) 442 4529 **Telex:** 21093 PE NOVOBANC **Swift:** BDNMPEPL
Email: telemark@nuevomundo.com.pe **Telex:** 21094
Website: www.nuevomundo.com.pe

Senior Executive Officers
Chairman of the Board — Jacques Levy Calvo ☏ 471 6329 F 440 2940 E jlevy@nuevomundo.com.pe
Vice President — Vitaly Franco Varón ☏ 442 6508 F 440 2940
E vfranco@nuevomundo.com.pe
Chief Executive Officer — Juan Chau Elias ☏ 422 1508 E jchau@nuevomundo.com.pe
Treasurer — Arturo Náquira ☏ 471 6386 F 442 4529 E anaquira@nuevomundo.com.pe
International Division — Marco A Hurtado ☏ 442 9649 F 442 6731
E mhurtado@nuevomundo.com.pe

Others (Senior Executives)
Business Manager — Edgardo Alvarez ☏ 471 6269 F 442 6731 E ealvarez@nuevomundo.com.pe

www.euromoneydirectory.com   PERU (+51)

Syndicated Lending
Loan-Related Activities
Trade Finance   Jorge Palma ☎ **442 1800** 🖷 **441 6675** ✉ **jpalma@nuevomundo.com.pe**

Settlement / Clearing
Operations   Franklin Alarco *Manager* ☎ **442 1800** 🖷 **441 6675**
✉ **falarco@nuevomundo.com.pe**

Banco de Lima-Sudameris

Jiron Augusto Wiese, 698, Lima 1
Tel: (1) 426 9002 **Fax:** (1) 426 2505

Senior Executive Officers
General Manager   Eugenio Bertini Vinci

Banco de la Nación   Head Office

Avenida Nicolás de Piérola 1065, Lima
PO Box 1835, Lima
Tel: (1) 426 2000; (1) 426 1133 **Fax:** (1) 426 8099 **Telex:** 20003 PE NACBANK **Swift:** BANC PE PL **Reuters:** PEBN
Cable: NACIONBANC LIMA

Senior Executive Officers
President   Alfredo Jalilie Awapara
Financial Director   Armando Ganoza Lizarzaburu *Finance Manager*
Treasurer   Mario Odria *Finance Manager*
General Manager   José Luis Miguel de Priego Palomino

Others (Senior Executives)
Director   Rosario Almenara de Pezo
Reynaldo Bringas Delgado
Jaime Iberico

Foreign Exchange
Department: Treasury
Tel: 426 9539 **Fax:** 427 0318
Head of Foreign Exchange   Wilfredo Borja

Settlement / Clearing
Head of Settlement / Clearing   Adolfo Indacochea *Chief of External Operations*
Operations   Carlos Díaz Mariños *External Operations Manager*

Administration

Public Relations
    Miguel Angel Risco Esquén *Manager*

Banco Santander   Regional Head Office

Formerly known as: Banco InterAndino SAEMA
Augusto Tomajo 120, San Isidro, Lima 27
Tel: (1) 221 5000 **Fax:** (1) 221 5000 ext 2810

Senior Executive Officers
Chief Executive Officer   Jaime Chocano *General Manager* ☎ **221 1517**
Financial Director   Javier Arroyo
International Division   Javier Camareno *International Division Director*

General-Lending (DCM, SL)
Head of Corporate Banking   Alberto Ridaura *Corporate Banking Director*
Carlos Cano *Commercial Banking Director*

Administration
Head of Marketing   Jorge Risco *Director*

Euromoney Directory 1999 **1181**

PERU (+51)　　　www.euromoneydirectory.com

Banco Wiese Ltdo
Head Office

Jirón Cusco 245, Lima 1
PO Box 1235, Lima 1
Tel: (1) 427 6000 **Fax:** (1) 426 3977 **Telex:** 20164 BANK WIE **Swift:** BWLT PE PL **Cable:** BANCOWIESE
Website: www.wiese.com.pe

Senior Executive Officers
Chairman　　　　　　　　　　　　　　　　Guillermo Wiese de Osma
Financial Director　　　　　　　　　　　Manuel Custodio Poémape *Finance Manager*
General Manager & Director　　　　　Víctor Miró Quesada G
International Division　　　　　　　　　Héctor Grisolle *International Division Manager*

Others (Senior Executives)
　　　　　　　　　　　　　　　　　　　　Alfredo Llosa Barber *Joint General Manager*
　　　　　　　　　　　　　　　　　　　　Antonio Moreno Ortiz *International Division Adviser*
　　　　　　　　　　　　　　　　　　　　Augusto Felipe Wiese de Osma *Vice Chairman*

General-Lending (DCM, SL)
Head of Corporate Banking　　　　　　Manuel Pinzas Domingo *Corporate Banking Manager*

Settlement / Clearing
Operations　　　　　　　　　　　　　　　Humberto Callirgos Camones *Central Manager*

Global Custody
Regional Head　　　　　　　　　　　　　Maria Amelia Lazarte *Assistant Manager* ☎ **427 1131** 📠 **426 9414**
　　　　　　　　　　　　　　　　　　　　✉ **mlazarte@wiese.com.pe**

Administration
Head of Administration　　　　　　　　Oscar Furuya Hirose *Central Manager*

Legal / In-House Counsel
General Counsel　　　　　　　　　　　　Gino Sangalli Ratti *Central Manager*

Other (Administration)
Middle Market Banking　　　　　　　　Alberto Ugarteche *Manager*

Banque Sudameris
Representative Office

Pardo y Aliaga, 540, San Isidro, Lima 27
PO Box 270176, Lima
Tel: (1) 422 3875 **Fax:** (1) 422 4185

Senior Executive Officers
Representative　　　　　　　　　　　　Robert Marcuse

Banque Worms
Representative Office

Avenida la Republica 150, San Isidro, Lima 27
Tel: (1) 221 1575 **Fax:** (1) 221 1722 **Telex:** 21049 TAM

Senior Executive Officers
Representative　　　　　　　　　　　　José Miguel Raffo-Rodrigo

Citibank NA
Full Branch Office

Avenida Camino Real 456, piso 5°, San Isidro, Lima 27
Tel: (1) 421 4000 **Fax:** (1) 440 9044 **Telex:** 21227 CITIBNK

Senior Executive Officers
Treasurer　　　　　　　　　　　　　　　Eduardo de las Casas

Deutsche Bank Securities
Subsidiary Company

Formerly known as: Deutsche Morgan Grenfell
Torre Real 1701, Avenida Camino Real 456, Lima 27
Tel: (1) 421 1900 **Fax:** (1) 421 1980

Senior Executive Officers
General-Lending (DCM, SL)
Head of Corporate Banking　　　　　　Pyers S Griffith *Director General* ✉ **pyers@mail.cosapidata.com.pr**

1182　Euromoney Directory 1999

www.euromoneydirectory.com　　　　　　　　　　　　PERU (+51)

Equity Capital Markets
Emerging Markets　　　　　　　　　　Carlos Rojas *Trader*
International Equities
Head of Syndication　　　　　　　　Pyers S Griffith *Director General* E pyers@mail.cosapidata.com.pr
Equity Research
Country Head　　　　　　　　　　　　Georgette Montalvan
　　　　　　　　　　　　　　　　　　　　Guillermo Arbe

Corporate Finance / M&A Advisory
Head of Corporate Finance　　　　Pyers S Griffith *Director General* E pyers@mail.cosapidata.com.pr
Administration
Head of Administration　　　　　　Cecilia Salinas *Manager*

Fleming Latin Pacific Peru SA　　　　　　　　　Subsidiary Company
Torre Central, Camino Real 390, piso 13°, San Isidro
Tel: (1) 442 3394 **Fax:** (1) 442 0531

Ibero Platina Bank AG　　　　　　　　　　　　Representative Office
Avenue Los Talladores 353, Alt - Vitarte, Lima
Tel: (1) 437 5326 **Fax:** (1) 437 5326 **Email:** pschreier@esan.edu.pe

ING Barings　　　　　　　　　　　　　　　　　Representative Office
Avenida Victor Andres Belaunde 147, Via Principal 110, piso 10°, Edificio Real Cinco, Lima 27
Tel: (1) 422 8565 **Fax:** (1) 422 8745

Senior Executive Officers
Country Manager　　　　　　　　　　Maria Jesus Hume

Merrill Lynch　　　　　　　　　　　　　　　　　Full Branch Office
Canaval y Moreyra 452, piso 15°, San Isidro, Lima 27
Tel: (1) 421 0710 **Fax:** (1) 422 1701 **Email:** miguel.palomino@ml.com
Website: www.ml.com

Norbank　　　　　　　　　　　　　　　　　　　　　Head Office
Formerly known as: Banco Regional del Norte
Avenida República de Panamá 3655, San Isidro, Lima 27
Tel: (1) 215 3000; (1) 221 7707 **Fax:** (1) 222 7670; (1) 422 1155
Website: www.norbank.com.pe

Senior Executive Officers
President　　　　　　　　　　　　　　Francisco González
Chief Executive Officer　　　　　　Andy Altena
Chief Operating Officer　　　　　　Renzo Lucioni
Treasurer　　　　　　　　　　　　　　Marco Lucioni
Managing Director　　　　　　　　　Fernando Parodi

Prisma SAB　　　　　　　　　　　　　　　　　　　Head Office
Avenida Republica de Panama 3680, piso 3°, San Isidro, Lima 27
Tel: (14) 210 330 **Fax:** (14) 440 0595

Settlement / Clearing
Operations　　　　　　　　　　　　　Magally Martínez Díaz *Custody Officer*

PERU (+51)

Santander Investment
Subsidiary Company

Centro Impresarial Pardo y Aliaga, Avenida Pardo y Aliaga 699, piso 8°, Esquina Camino Real, San Isidro, Lima
Tel: (1) 221 9033; (1) 221 8914 **Fax:** (1) 221 8384

Senior Executive Officers
Managing Director — Antonio Villa Mardón

Other Departments
Department: Financial Markets
Tel: 221 8918 **Fax:** 221 0577

Other Departments
Financial Markets — Jose Luis Cueto *Chief Dealer*

Standard Chartered Bank
Full Branch Office

Pardo Ilaga 699, piso 3°, San Isidro, Lima 27
Tel: (1) 222 7575 **Fax:** (1) 222 7580

Senior Executive Officers
Senior Regional Manager — Luis Jose Giove

PHILIPPINES (+63)

Bangko Sentral ng Pilipinas
Central Bank

Alternative trading name: Central Bank of the Philippines

A Mabini corner Pablo Ocampo Sr Streets, Malate, Manila, 1004
Tel: (2) 524 7011; (2) 524 7051 **Fax:** (2) 522 3987; (2) 521 5224 **Telex:** 27550 CBPPH **Swift:** PHCB PH MM
Email: bsp@mnl.sequel.net

Senior Executive Officers
Governor — Gabriel C Singson **593 380**

Others (Senior Executives)
Head, Banking Services — Edgardo P Zialcita *Deputy Governor* **523 2608**
Head, Supervision & Examination — Alberto V Reyes *Deputy Governor* **521 1662**
Supervision & Examination — Ricardo P Lirio *Managing Director* **521 1683**
Fe B Barin *Company Secretary* **523 3820**

Department: Monetary Board
Governor — Gabriel C Singson **593 380**

Others (Senior Executives)
Cayetano W Paderanga *Member* **523 3251**
Andre Navato *Member* **525 5817**
Guillermo R Suarez *Member* **524 5993**
Vicente B Valdepenas *Member* **523 3983**
Teodoro B Montecillo *Member* **525 0342**
Cesar B Bautista *Secretary* **521 3365**

Foreign Exchange
Head of Foreign Exchange — Gregorio R Suarez *Managing Director* **521 1658**

www.euromoneydirectory.com　　　　PHILIPPINES (+63)

Other Departments
Economic Research　　　　　　　　Amando M Tetangco Jr *Managing Director* ☎ **521 1663**
Administration
Technology & Systems
Information Technology　　　　　Teresita O Hatta ☎ **525 5991**
Legal / In-House Counsel
General Counsel　　　　　　　　　Armando L Suratos ☎ **521 0280**
Public Relations
Pubic Relations　　　　　　　　　Fe B Barin *Company Secretary* ☎ **523 3820**
Accounts / Audit
Accounting　　　　　　　　　　　Teresita O Hatta ☎ **525 5991**
Other (Administration)
Human Resources　　　　　　　　Armando L Suratos ☎ **521 0280**

All Asia Capital & Trust Corporation　　　　Head Office

All AsiaCapital Center, 105 Paseo de Roxas, Makati City, Manila, 1200
Tel: (2) 818 3211; (2) 813 0188 **Fax:** (2) 817 1728; (2) 893 4382 **Telex:** 14814 **Telerate:** 816-2436

Senior Executive Officers
Chairman & Chief Executive Officer　　Roland Young ☎ **818 2543** ✉ rolyoung@mnl.allasiacapital.com.ph
President & Chief Operating Officer　　Eleuterio Coronel ☎ **817 1620** ✉ ecoronel@mnl.allasiacapital.com.ph
Financial Director　　　　　　　　　　Joycelyn Tañada *Executive Vice President* ☎ **817 1735**
　　　　　　　　　　　　　　　　　　　✉ jktanada@mnl.allasiacapital.com.ph
Treasurer　　　　　　　　　　　　　　José Ramiscal ☎ **911 8218**

Debt Capital Markets / Fixed Income
Department: Financial Markets Division
Head of Fixed Income　　　　　　　　Joycelyn Tañada *Executive Vice President* ☎ **817 1735**
　　　　　　　　　　　　　　　　　　　✉ jktanada@mnl.allasiacapital.com.ph
Head of Fixed Income Sales; Head of Fixed　Alice Ann Parlan *Vice President* ☎ **817 1672**
Income Trading

Government Bonds
Head of Sales　　　　　　　　　　　Alice Ann Parlan *Vice President* ☎ **817 1672**
Head of Trading　　　　　　　　　　Philip Panlilio *Assistant Manager* ☎ **813 3294**

Libor-Based / Floating-Rate Products
FRN Sales　　　　　　　　　　　　Alice Ann Parlan *Vice President* ☎ **817 1672**
Asset Swaps　　　　　　　　　　　Joycelyn Tañada *Executive Vice President* ☎ **817 1735**
　　　　　　　　　　　　　　　　　　✉ jktanada@mnl.allasiacapital.com.ph
Asset Swaps (Sales)　　　　　　　　Alice Ann Parlan *Vice President* ☎ **817 1672**

Fixed-Income Repo
Head of Repo　　　　　　　　　　　Alice Ann Parlan *Vice President* ☎ **817 1672**
Marketing & Product Development　　Emilio Gancayco Jr *Executive Vice President* ☎ **848 2205**
　　　　　　　　　　　　　　　　　　✉ gancayco@mnl.allasiacapital.com.ph
Head of Trading　　　　　　　　　　Bettina Gordon *Senior Manager* ☎ **893 2373**

Fixed-Income Research
Head of Fixed Income; Head of Credit　Helen Alvarez *Vice President* ☎ **848 2096**
Research　　　　　　　　　　　　　✉ halvarez@mnl.allasiacapital.com.ph

Equity Capital Markets
Department: Capital Markets Division
Head of Equity Capital Markets　　　Emilio Gancayco Jr *Executive Vice President* ☎ **848 2205**
　　　　　　　　　　　　　　　　　　✉ gancayco@mnl.allasiacapital.com.ph
Head of Sales; Head of Trading　　　Don Calderon *Senior Vice President* ☎ **818 3211**

Domestic Equities
Head of Origination　　　　　　　　Emilio Gancayco Jr *Executive Vice President* ☎ **848 2205**
　　　　　　　　　　　　　　　　　　✉ gancayco@mnl.allasiacapital.com.ph
Head of Trading　　　　　　　　　　Don Calderon *Senior Vice President* ☎ **818 3211**

Equity Research
Head of Equity Research　　　　　　Helen Alvarez *Vice President* ☎ **848 2096**
　　　　　　　　　　　　　　　　　　✉ halvarez@mnl.allasiacapital.com.ph

Convertibles / Equity-Linked
Head of Origination　　　　　　　　Emilio Gancayco Jr *Executive Vice President* ☎ **848 2205**
　　　　　　　　　　　　　　　　　　✉ gancayco@mnl.allasiacapital.com.ph
Head of Trading　　　　　　　　　　Don Calderon *Senior Vice President* ☎ **818 3211**

Warrants
Head of Sales; Head of Trading　　　Don Calderon *Senior Vice President* ☎ **818 3211**

PHILIPPINES (+63)   www.euromoneydirectory.com

All Asia Capital & Trust Corporation (cont)
Syndicated Lending
Head of Origination   Emilio Gancayco Jr *Executive Vice President* ☏ 848 2205
    ✉ gancayco@mnl.allasiacapital.com.ph
Head of Syndication   Michael Calingo *Vice President* ☏ 893 3819
Loan-Related Activities
Project Finance   Michael Calingo *Vice President* ☏ 893 3819
Money Markets
Global Head   Joycelyn Tañada *Executive Vice President* ☏ 817 1735
    ✉ jktanada@mnl.allasiacapital.com.ph
Domestic Commercial Paper
Head of Sales   Alice Ann Parlan *Vice President* ☏ 817 1672
Head of Trading   Bettina Gordon *Senior Manager* ☏ 893 2373
Risk Management
Head of Risk Management   Joycelyn Tañada *Executive Vice President* ☏ 817 1735
    ✉ jktanada@mnl.allasiacapital.com.ph
Settlement / Clearing
Fixed-Income Settlement; Operations   Renato Villar *First Vice President* ☏ 818 3211
Other Departments
Cash Management   Josephine Agregado *Senior Manager* ☏ 818 3211
Administration
Head of Administration   Renato Villar *First Vice President* ☏ 818 3211
Technology & Systems
    Andrew Ong *Senior Vice President* ☏ 818 3211
Legal / In-House Counsel
    Leah Lao-Cabrera ☏ 818 3211
Accounts / Audit
    Susan Grio-Gutierrez *Senior Assistant Vice President* ☏ 818 3211

Asia Pacific Inc   Subsidiary Company
G/F Ferros Building (52), 176 Salcedo Street, Legaspi Vlg Makati, Metro, Manila
Tel: (2) 800 9999

Asian Development Bank
6 ADB Avenue, 0401 Mandaluyong City, Metro Manila, Manila
PO Box 789, Manila, 0980
Tel: (2) 632 4444 Fax: (2) 636 2444 Swift: ASDB PH MM Email: adbhq@mail.asiandevbank.org
Treasury Fax: 636 2611
Website: www.asiandevbank.org

Senior Executive Officers
President   Mitsuo Sato
Others (Senior Executives)
Region West   Bong-Suh Lee *Vice President*
Region East   P H Sullivan *Vice President*
Finance & Administration   Pierre Uhel *Vice President*
Department: The Presidents Group
Others (Senior Executives)
Office of the General Auditor   Louis Wong *General Auditor*
Post Evaluation Office   A T Paterson *Chief*
Strategy & Policy Office   Yoshihiro Iwasaki *Chief*
Environment & Social Development   Kazi F Jalal *Chief*
Debt Capital Markets / Fixed Income
Department: Treasury Department
Global Head   Shinji Ichishima *Treasurer*
    Erkki K Jappinen *Deputy Treasurer*
Bonds - General
Capital Markets - Funding   Peter M Balon *Assistant Treasurer*
Funding & Swaps   Juanito Limandibrata *Senior Treasury Officer*
Market Research, Bond Admin & Liability   Ju-Hyung Lee *Treasury Officer*
Management
Settlement / Clearing
Back-Office   David R Parker *Assistant Treasurer*

www.euromoneydirectory.com				PHILIPPINES (+63)

Asset Management
Department: Investments

Other (Asset Management)

Portfolio Management & Trading, Asia Pacific
North America

Europe

Portfolio Mgmt & Pension Investment Support

Other Departments
Cash Management

Department: Operations Group West

Other Departments
Programs Department
Agriculture & Social Sectors
Infrastructure, Energy & Financial Sectors;
Private Sector Group
Economics & Development Resources
Department: Operations Group East

Other Departments
Programs Department
Agriculture & Social Sectors
Infrastructure, Energy & Financial Sectors
Office of Pacific Operations
Office of Cofinancing Operations
Central Operations Services Office

Administration
Head of Administration

Technology & Systems
Computer Services

Legal / In-House Counsel
General Counsel

Accounts / Audit
Office of the General Auditor

Other (Administration)
Personnel & Management Systems
Controllers Department
Information Office

Jelle Mann *Assistant Treasurer*
Philip Erquiaga *Senior Treasury Officer*
Tania Toivanen *Treasury Officer*
Makoto Kubota *Treasury Officer*
Isabel Haley *Senior Treasury Officer*
Garwood Weatherhead *Treasury Officer*
Aurapin Sipper *Senior Treasury Officer*

Yong Cheng *Senior Treasury Officer*
Gee Wha Moon *Senior Treasury Officer*

G H P B van der Linden *Director*
Eustace A Nonis *Director*
John D Taylor *Director*

Jungsoo Lee *Chief Economist*

Shoji Nishimoto *Director*
Wiemin Yang *Director*
Paul M Dickie *Director*
Basudev Dehal *Director*
Jeremy Hovland *Acting Chief*
Vladimir Bohun *Chief*

Guo Xianzhi *Chief*

John W Thorp *Chief*

Barry Metzgar

Louis Wong *General Auditor*

Mamoru Umemoto *Director*
Magdi Morcos *Controller*
Robert H Salamon *Chief*

# Banque Nationale de Paris						Full Branch Office

14th Floor, PCIB Tower 2, Makati Avenue corner HV de la Costa St, Makati City, Manila
Tel: (2) 815 8821; (2) 815 8827 **Fax:** (2) 817 9321 **Telex:** 63707 BNP PN **Swift:** BNPA PH MM
Email: bnpmnlpi@philonline.com

Senior Executive Officers
Senior Vice President

General-Lending (DCM, SL)
Head of Corporate Banking

General-Investment
Head of Investment

General - Treasury
Head of Treasury

Other Departments
Private Banking

Correspondent Banking

Administration
Head of Administration

Other (Administration)
Marketing

Peter M Green

Richard B Lee *Assistant Vice President*

Manuel Luis Velasco *Senior Manager, Investment Banking* ☏ **812 5405**

Joselito Jacob *Assistant Vice President, Treasury & FX* ☏ **817 3750**
Jacques Jouve *Assistant Vice President* ☏ **812 5406**

Shirley Santiago-Chua *Vice President, Private Banking* ☏ **819 2005**
℻ **817 9231**
Elisa Miranda-Cua *Vice President* ☏ **812 5407**

Adriano S Pantino III *VP, Administration* ☏ **812 5403**

Elisa Miranda-Cua *Vice President* ☏ **812 5407**

Euromoney Directory 1999   **1187**

PHILIPPINES (+63)   www.euromoneydirectory.com

China Banking Corporation

8745 Paseo de Roxas Corner, Villar Street, Makati City, Manila, 1200
Tel: (2) 817 7981; (2) 819 1476 Fax: (2) 817 3169 Telex: 63695
General Tel: (2) 817 7995; (2) 819 1479

Senior Executive Officers
Chairman — Gilbert U Dee
President — Peter S Dee
Financial Director — Ricardo R Chua
Treasurer — Danilo A Alcoseba

Citibank NA
Full Branch Office

8741 Paseo de Roxas, Makati City, Manila
Tel: (2) 813 9388 Fax: (2) 817 0142 Reuters: CIPH

Senior Executive Officers
Chief Executive Officer — Suresh Maharaj *Country Corporate Officer*
Treasurer — Patrick Dewilde

General-Lending (DCM, SL)
Head of Corporate Banking — Monique Manalo

General - Treasury
Head of Treasury — Geocel Olanday *Treasury Marketing Head*

Debt Capital Markets / Fixed Income
Global Head — Andy Alcid *Head, Capital Markets*

Equity Capital Markets
Global Head — Andy Alcid *Head, Capital Markets*

Foreign Exchange
Global Head — Bong Arjonillo

Risk Management
Foreign Exchange Derivatives / Risk Management
Global Head — Ceasar Santos

Settlement / Clearing
Operations — Mr Itchon *Transaction Services Head*

Equitable Banking Corporation
Head Office

262 Juan Luna Street, 1006 Binondo, Makati City, Manila
PO Box 3616, Makati City, Manila
Tel: (2) 242 7101; (2) 243 0311 Fax: (2) 241 5984 Telex: Eastern:63286 EQUIBK PN Swift: EQUI PH MM

Senior Executive Officers
Chairman — George L Go
President & Chief Financial Officer — Wilfrido V Vergara
International Division — Bernard C Uy *SVP, International Operations*

Others (Senior Executives)
Corporate Planning — Edilberto V Javier *Executive Vice President*

General-Lending (DCM, SL)
Head of Corporate Banking — Antonio Y Tee *SVP, Corporate Banking*
Oscar Lopez-Dee *SVP, Corporate Banking*
Merlita B Ng *First Vice President*

General - Treasury
Head of Treasury — Romuald U Dy Tang *SVP, Treasury & International Banking*

Relationship Manager
Office of the President — Arthur E Soberano *Senior Vice President*
Juana Gavino *First Vice President*

Settlement / Clearing
Operations — Miraflor R Bangco *FVP, Comptrollership Group*

Other Departments
Global Trust — Rolando D Esguerra *FVP, Trust Service Group*

Administration
Head of Administration — Virgilio Indiongco *First Vice President*

Technology & Systems
Technology Management — Deanna S Tacardon *First Vice President*

1188 Euromoney Directory 1999

www.euromoneydirectory.com PHILIPPINES (+63)

Legal / In-House Counsel
    Manuel B Curato *First Vice President*
Corporate Communications
    Fredeswinda P Cruz *Manager*
Other (Administration)
Human Resources   Vivian Lee-Tiu *Vice President*
Facilities Division   Jonathan C Go *Vice President*
Resources & Services   Edilberto V Javier *Executive Vice President*

ING Baring Securities (Philippines)
Subsidiary Company

20th Floor, Tower I, Ayala Triangle, Makati City, Manila, 1200
Tel: (2) 840 8400 **Fax:** (2) 891 9838; (2) 891 9727

Senior Executive Officers
Country Manager   Renato de Guzman

ING Barings
Full Branch Office

21st Floor, Tower 1, Ayala Triangle, Makati City, Manila, 1200
Tel: (2) 840 8888 **Fax:** (2) 815 1116 **Telex:** 62571 ING PN **Email:** ingbphmm@usinc.net

Senior Executive Officers
Country Manager   Renato T Guzman

Others (Senior Executives)
    Consuelo D García *Deputy General Manager*

Other Departments
Department: ING Baring Private Bank
Fax: 848 5223
Private Banking   Maria Teresa P Gallego *Head of Private Banking*

Jardine Fleming Exchange Capital Securities Inc
Subsidiary Company

22nd Floor, Tower One, Exchange Plaza, Ayala Avenue, Makati City, Manila, 1200
Tel: (2) 841 9800 **Fax:** (2) 841 9802

Land Bank of the Philippines
Head Office

319 Sen Gil Puyat Avenue Ext, Makati City, Manila
PO Box 1108, Makati City, Manila
Tel: (2) 818 9411; (2) 818 9429 **Fax:** (2) 840 3067 **Email:** lbppag@hotmail.com
Website: www.landbank.com

Senior Executive Officers
Chairman   Edgardo B Espiritu
President & Chief Executive Officer   Florido P Casuela

Others (Senior Executives)
Institutional Banking Sector   Jeronimo U Kilayko *Executive Vice President*
LBPCCC   Reynaldo J Gregorio *Executive Vice President*
Operation & Support Sector   Gilda E Pico *Executive Vice President*
Agrarian & Domestic Banking Sector   Jesus F Diaz *Executive Vice President*
Treasury Group   Corazon S delos Santos *Senior Vice President*
Legal Service Group   Miguel M Gonzales *Senior Vice President*
Domestic Banking Group - I   Antonio T Hernandez *Senior Vice President*
Domestic Banking Group - II   Rodrigo B Supena *Senior Vice President*
Investment Banking Group   Jose Carmelo C Nograles *SVP, Investment Banking*
Landowners Compensation Assistance Group   Roberto C A Ong *Senior Vice President*

General-Lending (DCM, SL)
Head of Corporate Banking   Edgardo C Amistad *AVP, Cooperative Loans*
    Yolanda D Velasco *VP, Global Banking*
    Jose Carmelo C Nograles *SVP, Investment Banking*
    Nenita H Veran *VP, Program Lending Group*
    Daisy Macalino *AVP, Wholesale Lending*
    Renato M Chico *AVP, Credit & Central Liability*

Euromoney Directory 1999 **1189**

PHILIPPINES (+63)   www.euromoneydirectory.com

Land Bank of the Philippines (cont)

General - Treasury
Head of Treasury   Corazon S delos Santos *Senior Vice President*
    Jeniffer A Tantan *AVP, Treasury Operations Department*

Relationship Manager
Countryside Financial Institutions   Teresita S Garcia *Vice President*
Farmers Livelihood & Assistance   Harold J. Dacumos *Vice President*
Commercial Credit Management   Cecilia C Borromeo *Vice President*
Financial Institutions   Udela C Salvo *Assistant Vice President*
Budget Office   Thelma O Ramirez *Assistant Vice President*

Syndicated Lending
Other (Syndicated Lending)
Loan Syndication   Gabriel M Jayme *Vice President*

Loan-Related Activities
Project Finance   Gabriel M Jayme *Vice President*

Other (Trade Finance)
Investment Trading   Zenaida A Dayao *Assistant Vice President*

Corporate Finance / M&A Advisory
Head of Corporate Finance   Omar T Salvo *Vice President*

Settlement / Clearing
Operations   Carmencita A Bayot *AVP, Cash Operations*
    Conrado B Roxas *Vice President*
    Luz C Generoso *AVP, Dealership Development & Management*
    Fe Nieva S J Sandoval *VP, Banking Operations*

Asset Management
Other (Asset Management)
Special Assets   Carmeline J Reyes *Assistant Vice President*

Administration
Technology Management Group   Vergel O David *Vice President*
Technical Support   Conrado B Roxas *Vice President*
Data Center & Network Operations   Alan V Bomas *Assistant Vice President*
Branch Automation Department   Ana S Santos *Assistant Department Manager*

Legal / In-House Counsel
Legal Services Group   Miguel M Gonzales *Senior Vice President*

Public Relations
Public Affairs Group   Amylyn S de Quiros *Vice President*

Accounts / Audit
Audit Group   Andres C Sarmiento *Vice President*
Accounting   Rosario D Gabutero *Assistant Vice President*
Branch Automation   Santos S Ana *Acting Head*

Other (Administration)
Corporate Planning   Julio D Climaco Jr *Vice President*
Administrative Support   Julieta A Silva *Vice President*
Human Resources Development   Luisa Antero *Assistant Vice President*
Personnel   Ethel C Balaaldia *Assistant Vice President*
Administrative Services   Generoso R Espinosa *Vice President*
General Services   Carmelita L Uy *Assistant Vice President*
Marketing Research & Product Development   Bueno B Castillo *Vice President*

Overseas Union Bank Limited   Full Branch Office

7th Floor, Corinthian Plaza, Paseo de Roxas, Makati City, Manila
Tel: (2) 817 9951 **Fax:** (2) 811 3168

Senior Executive Officers
Assistant Vice President & Manager   Tan Lye Oon

PCI Capital Corporation   Head Office

Alternative trading name: PCI Capital
20th Floor, PCI Bank Tower 1, Makati Avenue, Corner HV de la Costa Street, Makati City, Metro Manila, 0520
Tel: (2) 891 2033; (2) 818 4287 **Fax:** (2) 817 1833; (2) 891 2034 **Email:** pcicapit@skyinet.net

Senior Executive Officers
Chairman   Eugenio Lopez Sr ☎ **631 3102**
President & CEO   Roberto Panlilio ☎ **892 0191**

www.euromoneydirectory.com   PHILIPPINES (+63)

Senior Executive Officers (cont)
Treasurer   Esperanza Osmeña ☏ **818 1426**

Debt Capital Markets / Fixed Income
Fixed Income (Trading)
Commercial Paper / Term Loans   Erlaster Sotto *Head, Origination & Syndication* ☏ **817 4529**

Equity Capital Markets
Domestic Equities
Head of Origination   Gabriel Lim *Head, Corfin - PCI Capital* ☏ **891 2056**
Head of Syndication   Erlaster Sotto *Head, Origination & Syndication* ☏ **817 4529**

Convertibles / Equity-Linked
Head of Origination   Gabriel Lim *Head, Corfin - PCI Capital* ☏ **891 2056**
Head of Syndication   Erlaster Sotto *Head, Origination & Syndication* ☏ **817 4529**

Syndicated Lending
Head of Origination; Head of Syndication   Erlaster Sotto *Head, Origination & Syndication* ☏ **817 4529**

Loan-Related Activities
Project Finance   Gabriel Lim *Head, Corfin - PCI Capital* ☏ **891 2056**

Money Markets
Domestic Commercial Paper
Head of Trading   John Escolin *Fund Management Group* ☏ **750 6274**

Corporate Finance / M&A Advisory
Head of Corporate Finance   Roberto Panlilio *President & CEO* ☏ **892 0191**

Other (Corporate Finance)
Private Equity Placements, Origination   Gabriel Lim *Head, Corfin - PCI Capital* ☏ **891 2056**
Private Equity Placements, Syndication   Erlaster Sotto *Head, Origination & Syndication* ☏ **817 4529**

PCIBank - Philippine Commercial International Bank Head Office

Formerly known as: Philippine Commercial & Industrial Bank
Makati Avenue, Corner HV de la Costa Street, Makati City, Metro Manila, 0726
Tel: (2) 840 7000; (2) 812 5101 **Fax:** (2) 817 6984 **Telex:** 63265 PCIBANK PN **Swift:** PCIB PH MM
Email: webmaster@pcib.com

Senior Executive Officers
Chairman   Eugenio Lopez, Jr ☏ **631 3102**
President & Chief Executive Officer   Rafael Buenaventura ☏ **817 2424**
Chief Operating Officer   Edward Sy *Senior Executive Vice President* ☏ **840 7608**
Treasurer   Esperanza Osmeña *Segment Head, Treasury & Funding* ☏ **818 1426**

General-Lending (DCM, SL)
Head of Corporate Banking   Isidoro Alcantara *Segment Head, Corp. Banking & Corp. Finance* ☏ **818 1553**

General-Investment
Head of Investment   Roberto Panlilio *Segment Head, Investment Banking* ☏ **892 0191**

Debt Capital Markets / Fixed Income
Global Head   Esperanza Osmeña *Segment Head, Treasury & Funding* ☏ **818 1426**

Domestic Government Bonds
Head of Trading   Roland Avante *Head, Domestic Funds Management* ☏ **817 2350**

Eurobonds
Head of Syndication   Leslie Limsico *Head, FX Management* ☏ **813 5611**

Libor-Based / Floating-Rate Products
FRN Sales   Pier-Angela Caguioa *Head, Treasury Distribution* ☏ **813 3938**

Medium-Term Notes
Head of Origination; Head of Structuring; Head of Sales   Pier-Angela Caguioa *Head, Treasury Distribution* ☏ **813 3938**

Private Placements
Head of Origination; Head of Sales; Head of Structuring   Pier-Angela Caguioa *Head, Treasury Distribution* ☏ **813 3938**

Fixed-Income Repo
Head of Repo; Collateral Management; Matched Book Manager; Sales   Leslie Limsico *Head, FX Management* ☏ **813 5611**

Syndicated Lending
Head of Syndication   Aristotle Villaraza *Head, Corporate Finance* ☏ **817 3892**

Loan-Related Activities
Trade Finance   Isidro Alcantara *Segment Head, Corporate Banking* ☏ **818 1553**
Project Finance   Aristotle Villaraza *Head, Corporate Finance* ☏ **817 3892**
    Gabriel Lim *Head, Corfin - PCI Capital* ☏ **891 2056**

PHILIPPINES (+63)　　　　www.euromoneydirectory.com

PCIBank - Philippine Commercial International Bank (cont)

Money Markets
Domestic Commercial Paper
Head of Trading　　　　　　　　　　Roland Avante *Head, Domestic Funds Management* ☎ 817 2350
Other (Wholesale Deposits)
Domestic; Foreign　　　　　　　　　Pier-Angela Caguioa *Head, Treasury Distribution* ☎ 813 3938

Foreign Exchange
Global Head　　　　　　　　　　　　Esperanza Osmeña *Segment Head, Treasury & Funding* ☎ 818 1426
Head of Institutional Sales　　　　　　Leslie Limsico *Head, FX Management* ☎ 813 5611
Corporate Sales　　　　　　　　　　Pier-Angela Caguioa *Head, Treasury Distribution* ☎ 813 3938
Head of Trading　　　　　　　　　　Leslie Limsico *Head, FX Management* ☎ 813 5611

Risk Management
Global Head　　　　　　　　　　　　Edward Zshornack *Head, Risk Management* ☎ 891 2060
　　　　　　　　　　　　　　　　　　Angeles Lorayes *Head, Credit Policy* ☎ 817 0039

Fixed Income Derivatives / Risk Management
Global Head　　　　　　　　　　　　Esperanza Osmeña *Segment Head, Treasury & Funding* ☎ 818 1426
IR Swaps Sales / Marketing　　　　　Pier-Angela Caguioa *Head, Treasury Distribution* ☎ 813 3938
IR Swaps Trading　　　　　　　　　Leslie Limsico *Head, FX Management* ☎ 813 5611
IR Options Sales / Marketing　　　　Pier-Angela Caguioa *Head, Treasury Distribution* ☎ 813 3938
IR Options Trading　　　　　　　　　Leslie Limsico *Head, FX Management* ☎ 813 5611

Foreign Exchange Derivatives / Risk Management
Cross-Currency Swaps, Sales / Marketing　Pier-Angela Caguioa *Head, Treasury Distribution* ☎ 813 3938
Cross-Currency Swaps, Trading　　　Leslie Limsico *Head, FX Management* ☎ 813 5611
Vanilla FX option Sales　　　　　　　Pier-Angela Caguioa *Head, Treasury Distribution* ☎ 813 3938
Vanilla FX option Trading　　　　　　Leslie Limsico *Head, FX Management* ☎ 813 5611

Exotic Options (Barriers, Range, Timers, Digitals, Faders etc)
Sales; Trading　　　　　　　　　　Leslie Limsico *Head, FX Management* ☎ 813 5611

Corporate Finance / M&A Advisory
Head of Corporate Finance　　　　　Isidro Alcantara *Segment Head, Corporate Banking* ☎ 818 1553

Settlement / Clearing
Head of Settlement / Clearing　　　　Evelyna Avila *Segment Head, Operations & Admin* ☎ 818 1247
Fixed-Income Settlement; Derivatives　Danilo Palugod *Division Head, Treasury Support & Ops* ☎ 813 5999
Settlement; Foreign Exchange Settlement

Other Departments
Correspondent Banking　　　　　　Bernadette Inguito *Head, Financial Institutions* ☎ 894 1866

Other Departments
Anvil Center　　　　　　　　　　　Helen Fargas ☎ 751 1803

Administration
　　　　　　　　　　　　　　　　　Rebecca Torres *Head* ☎ 817 6926

Legal / In-House Counsel
　　　　　　　　　　　　　　　　　Nestor Romulo *Head* ☎ 817 7422

Compliance
　　　　　　　　　　　　　　　　　Edgardo Herrera *Head, Audit* ☎ 815 3487

Public Relations
　　　　　　　　　　　　　　　　　Mary Ann Morales *Head* ☎ 818 1339

Corporate Communications
　　　　　　　　　　　　　　　　　Mary Ann Morales *Head* ☎ 818 1339

Rizal Commercial Banking Corporation　　　　　　　　　　　Head Office

333 Sen Gil J Puyat Avenue, Makati City, Manila, 1200
PO Box 1005, MCPO/ ADC 7575, Makati City, Manila, 1200
Tel: (2) 894 9000 **Fax:** (2) 894 9958 **Telex:** 22207 RCL PH, 23557 RCL PH **Swift:** RCBCPHMMA **Reuters:** RCBC
Bloomberg: RCBC PM
General Telex: 4857 RCBC PS
Website: www.rcbc.com

Senior Executive Officers
Chairman　　　　　　　　　　　　　Cesar Virata ☎ 891 0777
President & Chief Executive Officer　　Francisco Dizon ☎ 891 0900
Treasurer　　　　　　　　　　　　　Rosauro Zaragoza *Head of Investment Banking* ☎ 891 0700
Corporate Secretary　　　　　　　　Marcelo Dy ☎ 844 1675

General-Lending (DCM, SL)
Head of Corporate Banking　　　　　Chun Bing Uy *EVP, Instutional* ☎ 891 0803

www.euromoneydirectory.com   PHILIPPINES (+63)

General-Investment
Head of Investment   Rosauro Zaragoza *Head of Investment Banking* ☎ **891 0700**

Debt Capital Markets / Fixed Income
Department: Buisness Developement Department - Treasury Division
Tel: 891 0750 **Fax:** 891 0748
Head of Fixed Income   Carlos Gotauco Jr *FVP / Deputy Head of Treasury* ☎ **894 9021**
Head of Fixed Income Trading   Winona Mayuga *Assistant Vice President* ☎ **894 9030**

Equity Capital Markets
Department: Investment Services Department -Trust & Investments Division
Tel: 891 0722 **Fax:** 891 0711
Head of Equity Capital Markets   Cristina Rosales *FVP / Head of Investment Services Dept.* ☎ **894 9012**
    ☎ **894 9080**

Equity Research
Head of Equity Research   Christina Sotelo *Head Manager, Investment Research Section* ☎ **891 0723**

Syndicated Lending
Department: Project Finance Department
Tel: 894 9802
Head of Syndicated Lending   Renato Carpio *VP / Head, Project Finance* ☎ **894 9802**

Money Markets
Tel: 891 0754 /59 **Fax:** 891 0748
Head of Money Markets   Arturo Corpus *VP / Head, Liquidity & Domest.* ☎ **894 9028**

Foreign Exchange
Department: FX & Foreign Currency Money Markets
Tel: 891 0750 **Fax:** 891 0748 **Reuters:** RCBC **Telex:** 23557 or 22207
Head of Foreign Exchange   Ernesto Leynes *VP / Head, FX Management Dept.* ☎ **894 9023**
Head of Trading   Florentina Recio *Assistant Vice President* ☎ **894 9024**

FX Traders / Sales People
    Teresa Nuguid *Assistant Vice President* ☎ **894 9025**
    Rosemarie Roca *Manager* ☎ **894 9027**

Risk Management
Tel: 894 9880 **Fax:** 891 0939
Head of Risk Management   Joseph Monzon *VP / Head, Risk Management Unit* ☎ **894 9880**

Settlement / Clearing
Tel: 894 9035 **Fax:** 891 0766
Head of Settlement / Clearing   Liwayway Tan *FVP / Head, Operations Division* ☎ **894 9035**
Operations   Florenda Noche *AVP, Treasury Operations Department* ☎ **894 9036**

Other Departments
Private Banking   Rosauro Zaragoza *Head of Investment Banking* ☎ **891 0700**

Administration
Head of Administration   Winston Obidos *SVP, Head of Corporate Affairs* ☎ **891 0811**

Technology & Systems
    Al Jan Yao *FVP* ☎ **891 0851**

Legal / In-House Counsel
    Merlyn Dueñas *VP / Head of Legal* ☎ **894 9961**

Public Relations
    Virgilio Pantaleon *Head* ☎ **894 9983** ☎ **818 6669**

Accounts / Audit
    Rogelio Cabrera *FVP, Internal Audit* ☎ **840 3694**

Security Bank Corporation   Head Office

Formerly known as: Security Bank and Trust Company
Security Bank Centre, 6776 Ayala Avenue, Makati City, Manila, 0719
PO Box 2026, Makati, Manila, 1200
Tel: (2) 867 6788 **Fax:** (2) 813 2069 **Telex:** 63534 SECBNK PN **Swift:** SETC PH MM **Email:** secb@mnl.sequel.net
Reuters: SECB.PS **Telerate:** SBCO **Bloomberg:** SEB PM **Cable:** SECBANK

Senior Executive Officers
Chairman   Frederick Dy ☎ **817 1880**
President   Rafael Simpao Jr ☎ **893 2591**
Treasurer   Anastasia Dy *Corporate Treasurer* ☎ **891 1044**
Corporate Secretary   Antonio Pacis
International Division   Belen Au *FVP, International Banking / Options*

Others (Senior Executives)
    Melissa Aquino *FVP, Corporate Planning* ☎ **894 5288**
    Fabian Dee *FVP, Treasury & Funds Management* ☎ **893 7943**

Euromoney Directory 1999   **1193**

PHILIPPINES (+63) www.euromoneydirectory.com

Security Bank Corporation (cont)
Others (Senior Executives) (cont)

Reynold Gerongay *President, Security Finance* ☏ **891 1021**
Virgilio Katigbak *FVP, Branch Banking* ☏ **893 2572**
Belen Lim *FVP, General Services* ☏ **894 5259**
Maximo Madridejos Jr *FVP, Corporate Business Relations* ☏ **810 1084**
Eutropio Mercado *FVP, Retail Lending* ☏ **867 6761**
Myra Sevilla *FVP, Account Management* ☏ **893 4920**
Daniel Yu *President, SEC Info. Technology* ☏ **891 1053**

General-Lending (DCM, SL)
Head of Corporate Banking — Oscar Cajipe *SVP, Business Development* ☏ **892 1062**

General-Investment
Head of Investment — Remy Tigulo *President, SB Capital Investment Corp* ☏ **840 3740**

Debt Capital Markets / Fixed Income
Tel: 888 7000 **Fax:** 893 7840
Head of Fixed Income; Head of Fixed Income Sales; Head of Fixed Income Trading — Fabian Dee *FVP, Treasury & Funds Management* ☏ **893 7943**

Government Bonds
Head of Sales; Head of Trading — Mina Figueroa *VP, Domestic Treasury* ☏ **893 2592**

Domestic Government Bonds
Head of Sales; Head of Trading — Mina Figueroa *VP, Domestic Treasury* ☏ **893 2592**

Non-Domestic Government Bonds
Natividad Gutierrez *VP, International Treasury* ☏ **894 5283**

Eurobonds
Head of Sales; Head of Trading — Natividad Gutierrez *VP, International Treasury* ☏ **894 5283**

Emerging Market Bonds
Head of Sales; Head of Trading — Natividad Gutierrez *VP, International Treasury* ☏ **894 5283**

Libor-Based / Floating-Rate Products
FRN Sales; FRN Trading — Natividad Gutierrez *VP, International Treasury* ☏ **894 5283**

Fixed-Income Repo
Head of Repo; Marketing & Product Development; Head of Trading — Mina Figueroa *VP, Domestic Treasury* ☏ **893 2592**

Fixed-Income Research
Head of Fixed Income — Fabian Dee *FVP, Treasury & Funds Management* ☏ **893 7943**
Head of Credit Research — Fabian Dee *FVP, Treasury & Funds Management* ☏ **893 7943**

Equity Capital Markets
Department: SB Capital Investment Corporation
Tel: 867 6788 **Fax:** 891 1089
Head of Equity Capital Markets; Head of Sales; Head of Trading — Remy Tigulo *President, SB Capital Investment Corp* ☏ **840 3740**

Domestic Equities
Head of Sales; Head of Trading — Conrado Gloria *Managing Director* ☏ **888 7353**

Equity Research
Head of Equity Research — Roque Fortu *Head, Corporate Planning & Research* ☏ **888 7353**

Syndicated Lending
Tel: 867 6788 **Fax:** 812 1660
Head of Syndicated Lending; Head of Origination; Head of Syndication; Head of Trading — Oscar Cajipe *SVP, Business Development* ☏ **892 1062**

Loan-Related Activities
Trade Finance — Oscar Cajipe *SVP, Business Development* ☏ **892 1062**
Project Finance — Remy Tigulo *President, SB Capital Investment Corp* ☏ **840 3740**
Leasing & Asset Finance — Reynold Gerongay *President, Security Finance, Inc* ☏ **891 1036**

Money Markets
Tel: 888 7000 **Fax:** 893 7840
Head of Money Markets — Fabian Dee *FVP, Treasury & Funds Management* ☏ **893 7943**

Domestic Commercial Paper
Head of Sales; Head of Trading — Mina Figueroa *VP, Domestic Treasury* ☏ **893 2592**

Foreign Exchange
Tel: 888 7000 **Fax:** 893 7840
Head of Foreign Exchange — Fabian Dee *FVP, Treasury & Funds Management* ☏ **893 7943**
Head of Institutional Sales; Corporate Sales; Head of Trading — Natividad Gutierrez *VP, International Treasury* ☏ **894 5283**

FX Traders / Sales People
Raul Aurellano *Assistant Vice President* ☏ **888 7382**

www.euromoneydirectory.com　　　　　　　　PHILIPPINES (+63)

Risk Management
Tel: 888 7000 **Fax:** 893 7840
Head of Risk Management　　　　　　　　Fabian Dee *FVP, Treasury & Funds Management* ☎ **893 7943**

Corporate Finance / M&A Advisory
Department: SB Capital Investment Corporation
Head of Corporate Finance　　　　　　　　Remy Tigulo *President, SB Capital Investment Corp* ☎ **840 3740**

Other Departments
Chief Credit Officer　　　　　　　　　　　Jeanette Keh *Vice President* ☎ **891 1043**
Private Banking　　　　　　　　　　　　　Rafael Ayuste Jr. *VP, Trust* ☎ **894 5494**
Correspondent Banking　　　　　　　　　Maximo Madridejos Jr *FVP, Corporate Business Relations* ☎ **810 1084**

Administration
Business Development　　　　　　　　　Oscar Cajipe *SVP, Business Development* ☎ **892 1062**
Head of Marketing　　　　　　　　　　　Emma Yuhico *Vice President, Marketing* ☎ **893 2563**

Technology & Systems
　　　　　　　　　　　　　　　　　　　　Daniel Yu *President, SEC Info. Technology* ☎ **891 1053**
　　　　　　　　　　　　　　　　　　　　Raymundo Serafica III *AVP, Systems* ☎ **891 1368**

Legal / In-House Counsel
　　　　　　　　　　　　　　　　　　　　Eduardo Plana *Vice President, Legal* ☎ **812 8015**

Compliance
　　　　　　　　　　　　　　　　　　　　Eduardo Plana *Vice President, Legal* ☎ **812 8015**

Public Relations
　　　　　　　　　　　　　　　　　　　　Emma Yuhico *Vice President, Marketing* ☎ **893 2563**

Accounts / Audit
　　　　　　　　　　　　　　　　　　　　Angelita Esguerra *VP, Audit & Financial Control* ☎ **894 5295**

SG Securities (Phils) Inc　　　　　　　　　　　　　　Subsidiary Company

21/F, Antel Corporate Centre, 139 Valero Street, Salcedo Village, Makati City, Manila
Tel: (2) 841 0777 **Fax:** (2) 849 2900

Equity Capital Markets
Equity Research
Regional Head　　　　　　　　　　　　　Neel Sinha *Acting Head of Research* ☎ **849 2823**
　　　　　　　　　　　　　　　　　　　　✉ neel_sinha@socgen-crosby.com

Other (Equity Research)
Telecoms, Utilities, Ports　　　　　　　　Neel Sinha *Acting Head of Research* ☎ **849 2823**
　　　　　　　　　　　　　　　　　　　　✉ neel_sinha@socgen-crosby.com
F&B, Consumer　　　　　　　　　　　　Damian Kestel *Investment Analyst* ☎ **849 2822**
　　　　　　　　　　　　　　　　　　　　✉ damian_kestel@socgen-crosby.com
Banking　　　　　　　　　　　　　　　　Paul J Garcia *Investment Analyst* ☎ **849 2821**
　　　　　　　　　　　　　　　　　　　　✉ paul-garcia@socgen-crosby.com
Cement　　　　　　　　　　　　　　　　Jennifer Luy *Investment Analyst* ☎ **849 2824**
　　　　　　　　　　　　　　　　　　　　✉ jennifer_luy@socgen-crosby.com

Société Générale Manila

17th Floor, Solidbank Building, 777 Paseo De Roxas, 1226 Makati City - Metro, Manila
Tel: (2) 894 8839; (2) 894 8841 **Fax:** (2) 751 2283

Standard Chartered Bank　　　　　　　　　　　　　　Full Branch Office

Bankmer Building, 6756 Ayala Avenue, Makati City, Manila
Tel: (2) 878 2855 **Fax:** (2) 892 4457 **Telex:** 22434 SCB MNL PH **Swift:** SCBL PH MM

Senior Executive Officers
Chief Executive Officer　　　　　　　　　Eirvin B Knox ☎ **817 2680** 📠 **878 2855**
　　　　　　　　　　　　　　　　　　　　✉ ebknox@scbphilp.mhs.compuserve.com
Financial Director　　　　　　　　　　　Julie D Pua *Head of Finance* ☎ **878 2998** 📠 **812 8063**
　　　　　　　　　　　　　　　　　　　　✉ jdpua@scbphilp.mhs.compuserve.com

General - Treasury
Head of Treasury　　　　　　　　　　　Michel Angelo Aguilar *Head, Treasury Division* ☎ **878 2875** 📠 **812 4163**
　　　　　　　　　　　　　　　　　　　　✉ maguilar@scbphilp.mhs.compuserve.com

Administration
Other (Administration)
Human Resources　　　　　　　　　　　Belinda Morales-Galang *Head* ☎ **812 5711** 📠 **813 6214**
　　　　　　　　　　　　　　　　　　　　✉ bgalang@scbphilp.mhs.compuserve.com

PHILIPPINES (+63)   www.euromoneydirectory.com

Standard Chartered Bank Australia Limited — Bank Subsidiary
6th Floor, Bankmer Building, 6756 Ayala Avenue, Makati City, Manila, 1200
PO Box 3088, Makati Central Post Office, Makati City, Manila
Tel: (2) 815 9241 **Fax:** (2) 810 3554; (2) 893 4464 **Telex:** 63741 SCBAUS PN **Swift:** SCBL PHM2
Email: aangeles@scbphilp.mhs.compuserve.com

The Tokai Bank Limited — Representative Office
9th Floor, Metrobank Plaza Building, Senator Gil Puyat Avenue, Makati City, Manila
Tel: (2) 818 8616 **Fax:** (2) 818 3082 **Telex:** 66172 TOKAI PN

Senior Executive Officers
Chief Representative   Hitoshi Matsushita

Traders Royal Bank — Head Office
TRB Tower, Roxas Boulevard, Pasay City, Metro Manila
Tel: (2) 831 2821; (2) 831 2860 **Fax:** (2) 831 2494 **Telex:** 63254 TRABNK PN **Email:** tnbm@mnl.sequel.net
Telex: 14718 TRABNK PS
Website: www.sequel.net/trbm

Senior Executive Officers
Chairman   Roberto Benedicto
President & Chief Executive Officer Renato Peronilla

Money Markets
Department: Fund Management & Investment Department
Tel: 831 1320 **Fax:** 831 0181
Head of Money Markets   Cristina Atienza *Vice President*

Foreign Exchange
Department: International Department
Tel: 831 4844
Head of Foreign Exchange   Monserrat Palugod *Senior Manager*

United Coconut Planters Bank — Head Office
Alternative trading name: UCPB
UCPB Building, Makati Avenue, Makati City, Manila, 1200
Tel: (2) 811 9000 **Fax:** (2) 811 9706 **Telex:** 63332, 14805 **Swift:** UCPB PH MM
Email: ucpb.customercenter@philonline.com.ph **Reuters:** UCPB
Website: www.ucpb.com

Senior Executive Officers
Chairman & Chief Executive Officer   Jeronimo Kilayco
President & Chief Operating Officer   Lorenzo Tan
Chief Executive Officer   Jeronimo Kilayco *Chairman & Chief Executive Officer*
Chief Operating Officer   Lorenzo Tan *President & Chief Operating Officer*
Treasurer   Corazon de Guzman *First Vice President* ☏ **811 9600/61**
Assistant Vice President   Delfin Catapang Jnr
International Division   Ismael Deveza *First Vice President* ☏ **811 9300**

General-Lending (DCM, SL)
Head of Corporate Banking   Angelo Manahan *Senior Vice President*

General-Investment
Head of Investment   Angelo Manahan *Senior Vice President* ☏ **811 9400**

Debt Capital Markets / Fixed Income
Global Head   Corazon de Guzman *First Vice President* ☏ **811 9600/61**
Head of Fixed Income   Raul Tan *Vice President* ☏ **811 9626**
                                        Olivia Cruz *Vice President* ☏ **811 9659**
Head of Fixed Income Sales   Raul Tan *Vice President* ☏ **811 9626**
Head of Fixed Income Trading   Olivia Cruz *Vice President* ☏ **811 9659**

Government Bonds
Head of Sales   Raul Tan *Vice President* ☏ **811 9626**
Head of Trading   Olivia Cruz *Vice President* ☏ **811 9659**

Eurobonds
Head of Sales; Head of Trading   Raul Tan *Vice President* ☏ **811 9626**

www.euromoneydirectory.com PHILIPPINES (+63)

Emerging Market Bonds
Head of Emerging Markets   Raul Tan *Vice President* ☏ **811 9626**

Libor-Based / Floating-Rate Products
FRN Sales; Asset Swaps   Raul Tan *Vice President* ☏ **811 9626**

Fixed-Income Repo
Head of Repo   Olivia Cruz *Vice President* ☏ **811 9659**
Marketing & Product Development; Head of Trading   Raul Tan *Vice President* ☏ **811 9626**

Equity Capital Markets
Department: Investment Banking
Tel: 818 6763 **Fax:** 814 2923
Global Head   Angelo Manahan *Senior Vice President* ☏ **811 9400**

Domestic Equities
Head of Origination   Pamela Detabali *Vice President* ☏ **811 9832**

Syndicated Lending
Department: Investment Banking
Global Head   Angelo Manahan *Senior Vice President* ☏ **811 9400**
Head of Origination; Head of Syndication   Pamela Detabali *Vice President* ☏ **811 9832**

Loan-Related Activities
Project Finance   Isagani Bisnar Jr *Manager* ☏ **811 9468**

Money Markets
Department: Treasury Division
Head of Money Markets   Oscar Hipolito *Assistant Vice President* ☏ **811 9635**

Domestic Commercial Paper
Head of Sales   Oscar Hipolito *Assistant Vice President* ☏ **811 9635**

Eurocommercial Paper
Head of Sales   Raul Tan *Vice President* ☏ **811 9626**

Wholesale Deposits
Marketing   Olivia Cruz *Vice President* ☏ **811 9659**

Foreign Exchange
Department: Foreign Exchange Management Department
Tel: 817 2497 **Fax:** 817 4549
Head of Foreign Exchange; Head of Trading   Raul Tan *Vice President* ☏ **811 9626**

FX Traders / Sales People
                                  Arwin Guste *Manager* ☏ **811 9629**
                                  Edna Castrudes *Manager*

Corporate Finance / M&A Advisory
Department: Investment Banking
Tel: 818 6763 **Fax:** 814 2923
Global Head   Angelo Manahan *Senior Vice President* ☏ **811 9400**

Settlement / Clearing
Department: Treasury Operations
Regional Head   Liza Lucas *Assistant Vice President* ☏ **811 9634**
Fixed-Income Settlement; Foreign Exchange Settlement   Liza Salazar *Manager* ☏ **811 9652**

Other Departments
Private Banking; Correspondent Banking   Angelo Manahan *Senior Vice President* ☏ **811 9400**
Correspondent Banking   Ismael Deveza *First Vice President* ☏ **811 9300**

Administration
Head of Administration   Carolina Diangco *First Vice President*
Head of Marketing   Ronald G Tumao *First Vice President* ☏ **811 9250**

Technology & Systems
                                  Salvador Aque *First Vice President* ☏ **811 9011**

Legal / In-House Counsel
                                  Mervyn Encanto *Senior Vice President* ☏ **811 9850**

Compliance
                                  Frank Capalongan *Assistant Vice President* ☏ **811 9469**

Public Relations
                                  Ronald G Tumao *First Vice President* ☏ **811 9250**

Accounts / Audit
                                  Francisco Josef *First Vice President*

Euromoney Directory 1999   **1197**

PHILIPPINES (+63)   www.euromoneydirectory.com

Warburg Dillon Read Securities (Philippines) Inc

19th Floor, Tower One Ayala Triangle, Ayala Avenue, Makati City, Manila, 1254
Tel: (2) 754 8888 **Fax:** (2) 754 8899

Senior Executive Officers
MD Country Head   R Gerber
Others *(Senior Executives)*
      Seet Lip Teng *Chief Operating Officer*
Equity Capital Markets
Department: Equities
Head of Equity Capital Markets   R Loo *Head of Equities*

POLAND
(+48)

National Bank of Poland   🏛 Central Bank

11/21 ul Swietokrzyska, 00-919 Warsaw
PO Box 1011, 00-049 Warsaw
Tel: (22) 653 1000 **Fax:** (22) 620 8518 **Telex:** 814681 NBP PL **Swift:** NBPL PL PW **Email:** nbpgpno@telbank.pl
Reuters: NBPQ **Telerate:** 38268 **Cable:** NARBANK **Telex:** 38269; **Reuters:** NBPP; NBPR; NBPS; NBPT

Senior Executive Officers
President   Hanna Gronkiewicz-Waltz ☎ **826 9955** 📠 **653 2473**
First Deputy President   Jerzy Stopyra ☎ **826 5515** 📠 **620 5749**
Deputy President   Ryszard Kokoszozynski ☎ **826 8335** 📠 **653 2575**
Financial Director   Ewa Popowska *Director & Member of the Board* ☎ **826 6307** 📠 **826 4123**
Treasurer   Barbara Kamienska *Director* ☎ **826 9319** 📠 **826 3853**
International Division   Michal Krakowiak *Director* ☎ **826 7903** 📠 **826 9683**
Others *(Senior Executives)*
Management Board   Andrzej Jakubiak *Director* ☎ **826 6295** 📠 **826 9330**
                                     Krzysztof Majczuk *Director* ☎ **620 4477** 📠 **826 6848**
                                     Waldemar Szostak *Director* ☎ **(61) 852 9306** 📠 **(61) 852 3788**
Relationship Manager
Office of the President   Piotr Szuksrta *Director* ☎ **826 9758** 📠 **653 2475**
Department of Statistics   Jozef Sobota *Director* ☎ **826 5641** 📠 **826 5645**
Department of Monetary & Credit Policy Anna Trzecinska *Director* ☎ **826 5556** 📠 **826 6750**
Payment Systems Department   Adam Tochmanski *Director* ☎ **620 8338** 📠 **620 8338**
Foreign Exchange
Global Head   Krzysztof Majczuk *Director* ☎ **620 4477** 📠 **826 6848**
Other Departments
Economic Research   Pawel Durjasz ☎ **826 3760** 📠 **826 9935**
Administration
Head of Administration   Henryk Jan Sokolnicki *Director* ☎ **826 3566** 📠 **653 2366**
Technology & Systems
IT   Lech Szuksrta *Director* ☎ **826 8365** 📠 **826 9799**
Legal / In-House Counsel
                                     Andrzej Jakubiak *Director* ☎ **826 6295** 📠 **826 9330**
Accounts / Audit
Accounting & Operations Departtment   Ewa Popowska *Director & Member of the Board* ☎ **826 6307** 📠 **826 4123**
Internal Audit Department   Dariusz Lewandowski *Director* ☎ **826 9104** 📠 **826 4187**
Other *(Administration)*
Personnel Department   Jerzy Kerszke *Director* ☎ **827 3589** 📠 **653 1163**

ABN AMRO Securities (Polska) SA   Subsidiary Company

Formerly known as: ABN AMRO Hoare Govett (Polska) Sp zoo
Plac Trzech Krzyzy 16A, 00-499 Warsaw
Tel: (22) 621 0370 **Fax:** (22) 622 3453

Senior Executive Officers
President of the Board   Michal Otto
Financial Director   Arkadivsa Klos *Chief Accountant*
Chief Operating Officer   Waldemar Dolezek *Chief Operations Officer*

1198 Euromoney Directory 1999

www.euromoneydirectory.com				POLAND (+48)

Debt Capital Markets / Fixed Income
Government Bonds
Head of Sales				Zbigniew Urban ☎ 621 0370 ext 121 ℻ 622 3452
Equity Capital Markets
Domestic Equities
Head of Trading				Pawel Wisniewski *Trader* ☎ 621 0370 ext 158
International Equities
Head of Sales				Mariusz Koziowski ☎ 621 0370 ext 145
Equity Research
Head of Equity Research			Andreas Madej ☎ +44 (171) 678 5611
Settlement / Clearing
Head of Settlement / Clearing			Katarzyna Lopaciuk ☎ 621 0370 ext 138 ℻ 622 0781
Administration
Technology & Systems
					Lesdek Kramarski *IT Specialist* ☎ 621 0370 ext 128
Legal / In-House Counsel
					Jan Habrat *Compliance Officer & Lawyer* ☎ 621 0370 ext 120
Compliance
					Jan Habrat *Compliance Officer & Lawyer* ☎ 621 0370 ext 120

## American Bank in Poland Inc				Head Office
Marszaekowska 115, 00-102 Warsaw
Tel: (22) 624 8505; (391) 20360 **Fax:** (22) 624 9981; (391) 20354 **Telex:** 816284 **Swift:** AMER PL PW **Reuters:** AMER
Senior Executive Officers
Chairperson					Katherina von Fraunhofer Kosinski
President					Marek Gadomski
Financial Director				Dorota Mliczewska *Finance Director*
Treasurer					Jaroslaw Mikolazozyk
Others (Senior Executives)
					Wlodzinierz Paszkowski *Vice President*

## Banca Nazionale del Lavoro SpA			Representative Office
Al Jerozolimskie 65/79, 00-697 Warsaw
Tel: (22) 630 6780 **Fax:** (22) 630 6781
Senior Executive Officers
Chief Representative				Avati Domeniro

## Bank of America (Polska) SA				Full Branch Office
7th Floor, Atrium Tower, Al Jana Pawla II 25, 00-854 Warsaw
Tel: (22) 654 2500 **Fax:** (22) 654 2515 **Telex:** 816141 **Reuters:** BOAW
Senior Executive Officers
Chairman, Supervisory Board			Ralph Schauss ☎ +44 (171) 634 4897
Chairman, Management Board & MD		Stan Popow
Treasurer					Olivier Kintgen *Capital Markets & Treasury Director* ☎ 654 2490
Others (Senior Executives)
Country Credit Manager			Abbas Hasan *Credit Director*
General-Investment
Head of Investment				Maciej Wolanski *Head of Corporate Banking & Finance*
						Eric Fay *Director, Multinational Corporates & Financial Ins*
Debt Capital Markets / Fixed Income
Country Head					Olivier Kintgen *Capital Markets & Treasury Director* ☎ 654 2490
Domestic Government Bonds
Head of Sales					Danuta Wolniak ☎ 654 2491
Head of Trading				Rafal Petsch ☎ 654 2495
Syndicated Lending
Country Head					Maciej Wolanski *Head of Corporate Banking & Finance*
Loan-Related Activities
Trade Finance; Project Finance; Structured	Maciej Wolanski *Head of Corporate Banking & Finance*
Trade Finance

POLAND (+48) www.euromoneydirectory.com

Bank of America (Polska) SA (cont)
Money Markets
Domestic Commercial Paper
Head of Trading — Rafal Petsch ☎ 654 2495
Wholesale Deposits
Marketing — Jaroslaw Goreki *Sales Manager, Treasury Division*
Foreign Exchange
Country Head — Olivier Kintgen *Capital Markets & Treasury Director* ☎ 654 2490
Risk Management
Country Head — Olivier Kintgen *Capital Markets & Treasury Director* ☎ 654 2490
Fixed Income Derivatives / Risk Management
Country Head — Olivier Kintgen *Capital Markets & Treasury Director* ☎ 654 2490
Corporate Finance / M&A Advisory
Country Head — Maciej Wolanski *Head of Corporate Banking & Finance*
Settlement / Clearing
Country Head — Anthony Theodore *Operations Director*
Equity Settlement; Fixed-Income Settlement; Derivatives Settlement; Foreign Exchange Settlement — Bozena Lonc *Middle Office Manager*
Operations — Anthony Theodore *Operations Director*
Administration
Head of Marketing — Mr Wolansky *Vice President*
Compliance
— Maciej Opoka *Country Audit & Compliance Manager*

Bank Austria Creditanstalt Poland SA   Subsidiary Company
ul Porsta 69, 00-838 Warsaw
Tel: (22) 637 9000 **Fax:** (22) 637 9099 **Telex:** 816575 BCA WA **Swift:** CABV PL PW
Website: www.creditanstalt.co.at

Senior Executive Officers
Chairman — Jacek Mosàcki
Financial Director — Justyma Strus
Treasurer — Piotr Limke

Others (Senior Executives)
— Mirostaw Bieszki *Member of the Board*
— Krzysztof Foremniak *Member of the Board*

General-Lending (DCM, SL)
Head of Corporate Banking — Mathias Goergen
Debt Capital Markets / Fixed Income
Head of Trading — Piotr Broda ☎ 637 9424
Syndicated Lending
Trade Finance — Tomasz Mazurkiewiuz
Money Markets
Head of Money Markets — Pawel Kowalski ☎ 637 9400
Foreign Exchange
Head of Foreign Exchange — Marek Cherubin ☎ 697 9400
Head of Institutional Sales — Monika Grochowska ☎ 637 9426
Corporate Sales — Monika Kucinska ☎ 637 9426
Head of Trading — Artur Pilewicz ☎ 637 9400
Risk Management
Foreign Exchange Derivatives / Risk Management
Spot / Forwards Sales; Spot / Forwards Trading — Jacek Kukowski ☎ 637 9424
Settlement / Clearing
Head of Settlement / Clearing — Piotr Kasznik
Other Departments
Chief Credit Officer — Carl Norman Vökt *Credit Risk Manager*
Private Banking — Anna Slepak
Correspondent Banking — Robert Budzinski
Administration
Head of Administration — Urszula Balcerak
Head of Marketing — Maigorzata Anuzewska
Technology & Systems
— Grazyna Brzezinska

www.euromoneydirectory.com   POLAND (+48)

Legal / In-House Counsel
Artur Jesdrych

Public Relations
Andrzej Voigt

Accounts / Audit
Cezery Dudziak

Bank Creditanstalt SA   Subsidiary Company
Prosta 69, 00-838 Warsaw
Tel: (22) 637 9000 **Fax:** (22) 637 9099 **Telex:** 816575 BCA WA **Cable:** CABVPLPW

Senior Executive Officers
Chief Executive Officer   Jacek Moscicki Managing Director & Chief Executive
Managing Director   Miroslaw Bieszki
Managing Director   Foremniak Krzyszfok

Bank Handlowy w Warszawie SA   Head Office
ul Chalubinskiego 8, PO Box 129, 00-950 Warsaw
Tel: (22) 690 1000; (22) 690 2000 **Fax:** (22) 830 0113; (22) 690 4835 **Telex:** 814811 BHWPL **Swift:** BHWA PL PW
Email: listy@bh.com.pl **Reuters:** BHWP (FX) **Cable:** Handlobank Warszawa
Reuters: BHWW (Money Market); BHWK (Fixed Income)
Website: www.bh.com.pl

Senior Executive Officers
Chairman of the Supervisory Board   Andrzej Olechowski [T] **690 3435** [F] **826 1601**
President of the Bank   Cezary Stypulkowski [T] **830 0100** [F] **690 3749**
Financial Director   Witold Walkowiak Finance Director [T] **830 0148** [F] **690 3124**
Treasurer   Grzegorz Bialek Director of the Treasury Department [T] **830 0137**
                                       [F] **690 4121**
Managing Director Administration & Support   Slawomir Cytrycki [T] **830 0231** [F] **690 3833**
International Division   Antoni Sala Executive Vice President of the Bank [T] **830 0101** [F] **690 3749**

Others (Senior Executives)
Head of Technology & Systems   Marek Oles Member of the Management Board [T] **830 0104** [F] **690 3833**
Head of Retail Banking   Maciej Lebkowski Managing Director, Retail Banking [T] **690 1700**
                                       [F] **690 2482**

General-Lending (DCM, SL)
Head of Corporate Banking   Wieslaw Kalinowski Executive Vice President of the Bank [T] **830 0102**
                                       [F] **690 3740**

General-Investment
Head of Investment   Przemyslaw Krych Managing Director [T] **830 0324** [F] **690 4440**

Debt Capital Markets / Fixed Income
Department: Fixed Income Department
Tel: 830 0001/16 **Fax:** 830 0942/0018 **Telex:** 812-531/813-411
Head of Fixed Income   Wojciech Kowalczyk Fixed Income Department Director
Head of Fixed Income Sales   Elwir Swietochowski

Emerging Market Bonds
Head of Emerging Markets   Artur Nieradko Member of the Management Board [T] **830 0105** [F] **690 4440**

Equity Capital Markets
Department: Capital Markets Centre
Tel: 625 0625 **Fax:** 625 6949
Head of Equity Capital Markets   Piotr Habiera Capital Markets Centre, Director [T] **661 7506**

Equity Research
Head of Equity Research   Wlodzimierz Parzydlo Head of Research Department, Director [T] **627 3493**
                                       [F] **627 3475**

Syndicated Lending
Loan-Related Activities
Trade Finance   Krzysztof Michalski Director, Foreign Settlement Centre [T] **372 208**
                                       [F] **690 2031**
Project Finance   Tomasz Klukowski Director, Corporate Banking [T] **830 0325** [F] **690 3413**

Money Markets
Tel: 830 0001/16 **Fax:** 830 0018/0942 **Telex:** 812-531/813-411
Head of Money Markets   Andrzej Ladko FX & Money Market Department, Director

Foreign Exchange
Tel: 830 0001/16 **Fax:** 830 0018/0942 **Telex:** 812-531/813-411
Head of Foreign Exchange   Mateusz Bieniek Foreign Exchange, Director [T] **690 4463** [F] **690 4121**

Euromoney Directory 1999   **1201**

POLAND (+48)　　　　　　　www.euromoneydirectory.com

Bank Handlowy w Warszawie SA (cont)
Risk Management
Tel: 830 0001/16 Fax: 830 0018/0942 Telex: 812531/813411
Fixed Income Derivatives / Risk Management
Global Head　　　　　　　　　Marcin Burda *Head of Derivatives* ☏ 690 4459
Settlement / Clearing
Tel: 690 4412 Fax: 690 4384
Head of Settlement / Clearing　　Malgorzata Zawada *Director* ☏ 830 0242
Global Custody
Head of Global Custody　　　　Elzbieta Iwonin *Deputy Director, Custody Department* ☏ 690 4316
　　　　　　　　　　　　　　🖷 830 0222　📧 eiwonin@bh.com.pl

Other Departments
Correspondent Banking　　　　Jerzy Dzierzynski *Director, International Correspondent Banking Depa*
　　　　　　　　　　　　　　☏ 830 0122　🖷 690 4660
Administration
Head of Administration　　　　Tadeusz Czerwinski *Director, Administration & Security Department*
　　　　　　　　　　　　　　☏ 372 120　🖷 690 2005
Business Development　　　　Rafal Grodzicki *Director, Sales & Product Development Department*
　　　　　　　　　　　　　　☏ 690 3850　🖷 690 3723
Technology & Systems
　　　　　　　　　　　　　　Jerzy Moraczewski *Director, IT Department* ☏ 690 1114　🖷 690 2012
Legal / In-House Counsel
　　　　　　　　　　　　　　Wojciech Góralczyck *Director, Legal Department* ☏ 830 0117　🖷 690 4138
Public Relations
　　　　　　　　　　　　　　Iwona Ryniewicz *Director, Public Relations* ☏ 690 3940　🖷 690 4835
Accounts / Audit
　　　　　　　　　　　　　　Wanda Sieminska *Director, Internal Audit* ☏ 690 1108　🖷 690 2007

Bank Polska Kasa Opieki - Grupa Pekao SA　　　　Head Office
Alternative trading name: Pekao SA - Grupa Pekao SA
　　　　　　　　Grzybowska Street 53/57, 00-950 Warsaw
　　　　　　　　PO Box 1008, 00-950 Warsaw
Tel: (22) 656 0000 Fax: (22) 656 0004; (22) 656 0005 Telex: 816582 Swift: PKO PL PW Reuters: PKOD
　　　　　　　　Cable: BANKPEKAO
　　　　　　　　Website: www.pekao.com.pl

Senior Executive Officers
Department: Board of Directors
Chairman　　　　　　　　　　Alicja Kornasiewicz
Vice Chairman　　　　　　　　Pawel Samecki
Company Secretary　　　　　　Elzbieta Piechocka
Others (Senior Executives)
　　　　　　　　　　　　　　Zbigniew Radwanski *Director*
　　　　　　　　　　　　　　Jaroslaw Stypa *Director*
　　　　　　　　　　　　　　Wieslaw Federowicz *Director*
　　　　　　　　　　　　　　Jacek Ambroziak *Director*
　　　　　　　　　　　　　　Leszek Pawlowick *Director*

Department: General Management
President of the Management Board　Maria Wisniewska ☏ 656 0223
Others (Senior Executives)
Deputy President　　　　　　　Janusz Dedo
　　　　　　　　　　　　　　Witold Grzeskoiak
　　　　　　　　　　　　　　Sabina Olton *Chief Accountant*
　　　　　　　　　　　　　　Henryk Pyrka
　　　　　　　　　　　　　　Jerzy Zdrzalka
Member of the General Management　Andrzej Bujarski *Managing Director*
　　　　　　　　　　　　　　Igor Chalupec *Managing Director*
　　　　　　　　　　　　　　Mieczyslaw Skolozynski *Managing Director*
International Division　　　　　Zbigniew Lichocki *Director, International Banking*
Others (Senior Executives)
　　　　　　　　　　　　　　Teresa Klusek *Director, President's Office*
Domestic Branches　　　　　　Anna Przybysz *Managing Director*
General-Lending (DCM, SL)
Head of Corporate Banking　　　Robert Kozinski *Director*

1202　Euromoney Directory 1999

www.euromoneydirectory.com   POLAND (+48)

General - Treasury
Head of Treasury   Piotr Epsztein *Director*
Debt Capital Markets / Fixed Income
Head of Debt Capital Markets   Piotr Robak *Director*
Global Head   Cezary Smorszczewski *Director* ☎ **656 0702**
Equity Capital Markets
Head of Equity Capital Markets   Cezary Smorszczewski *Director* ☎ **656 0702**
Syndicated Lending
Loan-Related Activities
Trade Finance   Andrzej Szymanski *Director*
Project Finance   Kazimierz Sender *Director*
                                              Krystyna Tymosiewicz *Director, Central Branch of Project Financing*

Risk Management
Head of Risk Management   Józef Wdowiak *Director*
Settlement / Clearing
Settlement (General)   Maria Bucyk *Director, Financial Settlement*
Operations   Bozena Jarzyna *Director*
Global Custody
Country Head   Pavel Muszalski *Head of Custody*
Other Departments
Private Banking   Pawel Suszcynski *Director*
Cash Management   Urszula Tempska *Director, Cash & Currency Dept*
Debt Recovery / Restructuring   Henryka Kobas *Director*
Other Departments
Financial Policy & Analysis   Alfred Brodzki *Managing Director*
Administration
Head of Administration   Michal Krechowiecki *Director*
Head of Marketing   Jerzy Borowski *Director*
Technology & Systems
EDP Dept   Tadeusz Kuranowski *Director*
IT Development Dept   Jerzy Stremlau *Director*
Legal / In-House Counsel
Legislative Legal Dept   Jerzy Kotarski *Director*
Public Relations
                                              Jacek Kozlowski *Director*

Accounts / Audit
Accounting   Elzbieta Kifner *Managing Director*
                                              Hanna Maziejuk *Director*
Internal Audit   Janusz Minski *Director*
Other (Administration)
Personnel   Marian Karolczak *Director*
Organisation   Janusz Chajecki *Director*
Bank Security Bureau   Marek Paradowski *Director*

Bank Przemyslowo-Handlowy SA   Head Office

Alternative trading name: Bank BPH & BPH SA
11Na Zjezdzie Street, 30-527 Krakow
Tel: (12) 618 7888; (12) 422 3333 **Fax:** (12) 618 7803; (12) 618 7543 **Telex:** 326426 BPH PL **Swift:** BPHK PL PK
Email: h.pieronkiewicz@bph.krakow.pl **Reuters:** PRHK

Senior Executive Officers
Chairman of the Supervisory Board   Pawek Gizbert-Studnicki ☎ **618 7805**
President, Management Board   Henryka Pieronkiewicz ☎ **618 7805**
Financial Director   Krzysztof Bredjak *VP, Management Board & First Deputy President*
                                              ☎ **618 7815**
Chief Operating Officer   Kazimierz Dolny *Director of Operations* ☎ **618 7425**
Treasurer   Danuta Kuras *Director, Treasury Division* ☎ **618 7565**
Director, Board Office   Janusz Stopa ☎ **618 7845/96**
Relationship Manager
Dir of Corp. Customer Dept.   Alina Szloch
Debt Capital Markets / Fixed Income
Department: Capital Investment Department / Money Market Department
Tel: 618 7832 **Fax:** 618 7226
Government Bonds
Head of Trading   Wojuech Kaciak *Senior Dealer* ☎ **618 7615**

Euromoney Directory 1999   **1203**

POLAND (+48)   www.euromoneydirectory.com

Bank Przemyslowo-Handlowy SA (cont)

Domestic Government Bonds
Head of Trading — Wojciech Kaciak *Senior Dealer* ☎ **618 7615**

Eurobonds
Head of Origination — Beata Urbanczyk-Komonska *Director, Capital Investment Dept* ☎ **618 7113**
Head of Trading — Skawomir Soroczynski *Senior Dealer* ☎ **618 7656**

Equity Capital Markets
Department: Capital Investment Department
Tel: 618 7113 **Fax:** 618 7254
Head of Equity Capital Markets — Beata Urbanczyk-Komonska *Director, Capital Investment Dept* ☎ **618 7113**
Grzegorz Piwowar

Domestic Equities
Head of Origination — Adam Weglarz *Consultant* ☎ **618 7171**
Head of Syndication — Ireneusz Koziok *Officer* ☎ **632 9389**
Head of Research — Adam Weglarz *Consultant* ☎ **618 7171**

Syndicated Lending
Department: Credit Risk Management Department / Investment Project Finance
Tel: 618 7185 **Fax:** 618 7224
Global Head — Irena Folta *Member, Management Board*
Recovery — Barbara Sobala *Director, Work-Out Dept* ☎ **618 7166**
Head of Credit Committee — Irena Folta *Member, Management Board*

Loan-Related Activities
Trade Finance — Halina Dudkiewicz *Director, Credit Risk Management* ☎ **618 7124**
Project Finance — Alina Szwedyk-Kozlowska *Director, Investment Project Financing*
☎ **618 7485**

Money Markets
Tel: 618 7832 **Fax:** 618 7826
Global Head — Robert Dabek *Director, Money Markets*

Domestic Commercial Paper
Head of Origination — Witold Rusinek *Officer* ☎ **618 7256**
Head of Trading — Wojciech Kaciak *Senior Dealer* ☎ **618 7615**

Money Markets - General
Dir of the Capital Invest. Dept. — Beata Urbanczyk-Komonska *Director, Capital Investment Dept* ☎ **618 7113**

Wholesale Deposits
Head of Sales — Piotr Karnkowski *Dealer* ☎ **618 7613**

Foreign Exchange
Department: Money Market Department
Tel: 618 7832 **Fax:** 618 7826
Global Head — Robert Dabek *Director, Money Markets*
Country Head — Miroskaw Witek *Chief Dealer* ☎ **618 7655**
Head of Sales — Malgorzata Czerska *Director Foreign Division*
Head of Trading — Leszek Pawkowicz *Dealer* ☎ **618 7573**

FX Traders / Sales People
All currencies — Piotr Nowak *Dealer* ☎ **618 7575**
Marek Gackowski *Dealer* ☎ **618 7574**

Risk Management
Department: Treasury Department
Tel: 618 7565 **Fax:** 618 7563
Global Head — Danuta Kuras *Director, Treasury Division* ☎ **618 7565**

Corporate Finance / M&A Advisory
Department: Capital Invesment Department
Global Head — Beata Urbanczyk-Komonska *Director, Capital Investment Dept* ☎ **618 7113**

Other Departments
Private Banking — Barbara Kochanska-Ducek *Director, Corporate Customer* ☎ **618 7106**
Correspondent Banking — Makgorzata Czerska *Director, Foreign Department* ☎ **618 7525**

Administration
Head of Administration — Norbert Dzierwa *Director* ☎ **618 6180**
Head of Marketing — Tomas Grabouski *Director, Marketing & Promotion* ☎ **618 6188**

Technology & Systems
Henryk Baniowski *Director, IT* ☎ **618 7705**

Legal / In-House Counsel
Marek Rutkowicz *Director, Legal* ☎ **618 7405**

Compliance
Jan Dkugosz *Director, Internal Audit* ☎ **618 7109**

Public Relations
Janusz Stopa *Director, Board Office* ☎ **618 7845**

www.euromoneydirectory.com POLAND (+48)

Accounts / Audit
Krystyna Ukasynowicz *Chief Accountant* ☎ 618 7505

Bank Rozwoju Eksportu SA
Alternative trading name: BRE Bank SA
ul Senatorska 18, PO Box 728, 00-950 Warsaw
Tel: (22) 829 0000 Fax: (22) 829 0033 Telex: 825070 BREX PL Swift: BREX PL PW Reuters: BREP
Website: www.bresa.com.pl

Senior Executive Officers
Chairman Krzysztof Szwarc ☎ 829 0100 F 829 0118
President & CEO Wojciech Kostrzewa ☎ 829 0104 F 829 0010
Managing Director Janusz Maciewicz ☎ 829 0114 F 829 0119

Others (Senior Executives)
Anton M Burghardt *Deputy President*
Henryk Okrzeja *Deputy President*
Jan Zielinski *Deputy President*
Mieczystaw Groszek *Deputy President*
Krzysztof Kokot *Member of the Board*

General-Lending (DCM, SL)
Head of Corporate Banking Anna Winiarska ☎ 829 1563 F 829 1560

General - Treasury
Head of Treasury Miroslaw Boniecki ☎ 829 0202 F 829 0201

Debt Capital Markets / Fixed Income
Head of Debt Capital Markets Agnieszka Czuba ☎ 829 0250 F 829 0245

Syndicated Lending
Other (Syndicated Lending)
Credit Administration Jerzy Chojna ☎ 829 1616 F 829 1637

Loan-Related Activities
Trade Finance Anna Bartnicka-Jodko ☎ 829 0150 F 829 0160

Corporate Finance / M&A Advisory
Other (Corporate Finance)
Small & Medium Enterprises Elzbieta Urbanska ☎ 829 1540 F 829 1541

Settlement / Clearing
Head of Settlement / Clearing Beata Mossakowska ☎ 829 0402 F 829 0403
Operations Elzbieta Trzcianko *Head, Banking Operations* ☎ 829 0450 F 829 0460
Roland Pac *Controlling* ☎ 829 0450 F 829 0460

Global Custody
Head of Global Custody Beata Mossakowska ☎ 829 0402 F 829 0403

Asset Management
Head Ewa Bryx-Soltysik ☎ 829 1597 F 829 1598

Other Departments
Chief Credit Officer Wieslaw Thor *Credit* ☎ 829 0305 F 829 0333
Private Banking Jacek Wiecek ☎ 829 0265 F 829 0280
Correspondent Banking Jerzy Bujnowski ☎ 829 0122 F 829 0120

Administration
Head of Administration Wieslaw Staniszewski ☎ 829 1770 F 829 1777
Business Development Hans-Ascan Wieck *Head, Strategy & Development* ☎ 829 1515 F 829 1519

Technology & Systems
Information Technology Jacek Markowski ☎ 829 1711 F 829 1707
Banking Systems Maria Bujnowska ☎ 829 1656 F 829 1655

Legal / In-House Counsel
Legal Ewa Butkiewicz ☎ 829 0730 F 829 0743

Public Relations
Alicja Kos ☎ 829 0300 F 829 0303

Accounts / Audit
Accounting & Tax Anna Kacprowska ☎ 829 1701 F 829 1703
Internal Audit Teresa Heger ☎ 829 1640 F 829 1642

Other (Administration)
Human Resources & Organization Anna Kozinska ☎ 829 0050 F 829 0065
Quality & Safety Piotr Cegiella ☎ 829 1970 F 829 1971

Euromoney Directory 1999 **1205**

POLAND (+48) www.euromoneydirectory.com

Bank Slaski SA
Head Office

ul Warszawska 14, 40-950 Katowice
PO Box 137, Katowice
Tel: (32) 253 8906; (32) 253 7284 **Fax:** (32) 253 9944; (32) 253 7734 **Telex:** 0312809 **Swift:** SKAT PL PK
Senior Executive Officers
President Bruno Bartkiewicz [T] **253 9944**

Bank Wstopracy-Europejskej SA
Head Office

Alternative trading name: BWE SA
ul Senatorska 14, 00-954 Warsaw
Tel: (22) 829 9800; (22) 829 9934 **Fax:** (22) 826 0261; (22) 828 0932 **Telex:** 815059 BWE PL **Swift:** BWEU PL PW
Senior Executive Officers
President Ryszard Pidek [T] **829 9801** [F] **827 0949**
Vice President Alicja Franiewsk-Gujska [T] **829 9803** [F] **827 0949**
Vice President Przemyslaw Seczkowski [T] **829 9825** [F] **827 0949**
Others (Senior Executives)
Marian Ducki *Member of the Board* [T] **829 9804** [F] **827 0949**
General - Treasury
Head of Treasury Andrzej Hirsz *Director* [T] **829 9820** [F] **828 0939**
Settlement / Clearing
Operations Konrad Topolewski *Manager, Foreign Operations* [T] **829 9905** [F] **828 0932**
Other Departments
Chief Credit Officer Anna Milewska *Director* [T] **829 9813** [F] **826 6879**
Private Banking Tomasz Tokarski *Director* [T] **829 9815** [F] **828 0939**
Correspondent Banking Barbara Adamska *Manager* [T] **829 9904** [F] **828 0932**
Administration
Business Development Jerzy Swiderski *Director* [T] **829 9811**
Technology & Systems
IT & Telecommunications Department Konrad Kobylecki *Director* [T] **829 9809** [F] **828 0930**

Bank Zachodni SA Wroclaw
Head Office

Rynek 9/11, 50-950 Wroclaw
Tel: (71) 723 138; (71) 445 411 **Fax:** (71) 441 982; (71) 723 138 **Swift:** BANZ PL PR
Senior Executive Officers
Chairman Tadeusz Gluszczuk [T] **370 1103**

Bankers Trust Company
Representative Office

ul Emilii Plater 28, 00-688 Warsaw
Tel: (22) 630 3366 **Fax:** (22) 630 3377
Senior Executive Officers
Managing Director Hubert Janiszewski

Berliner Bank AG
Representative Office

ul Niepodleglosci 27, 61-714 Poznan
Tel: (61) 851 7787 **Fax:** (61) 851 7771
Senior Executive Officers
Representative Piotre Klebar

BNP-Dresdner Bank (Polska) SA
Subsidiary Company

ul Zielna 41/43, 00-108 Warsaw
Tel: (22) 654 6263 **Fax:** (22) 697 2309 **Telex:** 825155 MARGU PL **Swift:** BNDB PL PX
Senior Executive Officers
General Manager Pierre Gauthier [T] **697 2321** [F] **697 2329**
Deputy General Manager Rolf Michel [T] **697 2325** [F] **697 2329**
International Division Mirostaw Bartoszewski [T] **697 2360** [F] **697 2398**

www.euromoneydirectory.com   POLAND (+48)

General-Lending (DCM, SL)
Head of Corporate Banking   Thierry Marottine ☎ 697 2461 F 697 2479
                                     Klaus Meissner ☎ 697 2460 F 697 2479
Other Departments
Chief Credit Officer   Jochen von Kameke *Head of Credit* ☎ 697 2500 F 697 2519

CA IB Financial Advisers SA   Head Office

Formerly known as: Creditanstalt Financial Advisers SA
Al Jerozolimskie 56C, 00-803 Warsaw
Tel: (22) 630 6055 **Fax:** (22) 630 6003

Senior Executive Officers
Managing Director, Corporate Finance   Richard Golden
Managing Director, Fund Administration   Jaroslaw Orlikowski
Service

Syndicated Lending
Head of Syndicated Lending   Piotr Samojlik *Assistant Director, Corporate Finance*

Loan-Related Activities
Project Finance   Gregory Karachuk *AD, Capital Raising & Project Finance*

Corporate Finance / M&A Advisory
Head of Corporate Finance   Richard Golden *Managing Director, Corporate Finance*

Administration
Corporate Communications
                                             Anna Wolek *Corporate Communications Manager*

CA IB Securities SA   Head Office

Formerly known as: Creditanstalt Securities SA
Al Jerozolimskie 56C, 00-803 Warsaw
Tel: (22) 630 6272 **Fax:** (22) 630 6268

Senior Executive Officers
Chairman & CEO   Wolfgang Bauer
Financial Director   Marciu Modzelewski *Chief Financial Officer*

Debt Capital Markets / Fixed Income
Department: Fixed Income
Head of Fixed Income Trading   Matqorzata Nowak

Equity Capital Markets
Head of Equity Capital Markets   Wojciech Sadowski *Head of Brokerage & Trading*

Equity Repo / Securities Lending
Head   Pawel Tamborski *Director, Head of New Issues*

Asset Management
Head   Maciej Kwiatkowski *President, Investment Management*

Administration
Head of Marketing   Anna Wolek *Corporate Communications Manager*
Corporate Communications
                                             Anna Wolek *Corporate Communications Manager*

Caisse Centrale des Banques Populaires   Representative Office

Al Jerozolimskie 56C, 00-803 Warsaw
Tel: (22) 630 2682 **Fax:** (22) 630 2684

Senior Executive Officers
Representative   Margaret Zamojska-Sabater

CDM Pekao SA Securities   Head Office

18 Woloska Street, 02-675 Warsaw
Tel: (22) 640 2840; (22) 640 2841 **Fax:** (22) 640 2800
Website: www.cdmpekao.com.pl

Senior Executive Officers
President & CEO   Tomasz Adamski
Executive Vice President   Jan Kuzma ☎ 640 2838

Euromoney Directory 1999   **1207**

POLAND (+48) www.euromoneydirectory.com

CDM Pekao SA Securities (cont)
Senior Executive Officers (cont)

Executive Vice President	Wojciech Kolenda ☎ **625 4359**
Financial Director	Krystyna Pulit *Executive Vice President* ☎ **640 2841**
Chief Operating Officer	Krzysztof Trojanowski *Managing Director* ☎ **625 5906**
Managing Director	Maciej Trybuchowski ☎ **640 2832**

Debt Capital Markets / Fixed Income
Department: Prime Market
Tel: 640 2832 Fax: 640 2806

Domestic Government Bonds
Head of Sales — Makgorzata Jabkonska *Head of Bond Sales* ☎ **640 2802**
Department: Secondary Market Department
Tel: 661 7481 Fax: 661 7997
Global Head — Krzysztof Trojanowski *Managing Director* ☎ **625 5906**
Regional Head — Michak Kowalczewski *Deputy Department Head* ☎ **661 7476**
Country Head — Agata Gawin *Deputy Department Head* ☎ **661 7581**

Domestic Government Bonds
Head of Sales — Magdalena Raszdorf *Manager, Institutional Client Division* ☎ **661 7767**
Head of Trading — Anita Borowska *Trade & Settlement* ☎ **625 5693**
Head of Research — Iwona Pugacewicz *Analyst* ☎ **856 1706**

Equity Capital Markets
Department: Prime Market
Tel: 640 2832 Fax: 640 2806
Global Head — Maciej Trybuchowski *Managing Director* ☎ **640 2832**

Domestic Equities
Head of Origination — Agnieszka Buyalska *Deputy Director* ☎ **640 2848**
Head of Syndication — Katarzyna Nichalczuk *Head of Syndication* ☎ **640 2780**
Head of Sales — Tomasz Obredlzarek *Head of Sales* ☎ **640 2834**

Other (Domestic Equities)
Mutual Funds Units Distribution — Ewa Krupinska *Head of Distribution* ☎ **640 2796**
Department: Secondary Market Department
Tel: 661 7481 Fax: 661 7991
Global Head — Krzysztof Trojanowski *Managing Director* ☎ **625 5906**
Regional Head — Michak Kowalczewski *Deputy Department Head* ☎ **661 7476**
Country Head — Agata Gawin *Deputy Department Head* ☎ **661 7581**

Domestic Equities
Head of Sales — Magdalena Raszdorf *Manager, Institutional Client Division* ☎ **661 7767**
Head of Trading — Tomasz Ilczyszyn *Trader* ☎ **625 5575**
Head of Research — Jacek Stefanski *Head of Research* ☎ **640 2835** F **640 2803**

Corporate Finance / M&A Advisory
Department: Prime Market
Tel: 640 2832 Fax: 640 2806
Global Head — Maciej Trybuchowski *Managing Director* ☎ **640 2832**
Country Head — Agnieska Bogaj *Head of Corporate Finance* ☎ **640 2844**

Settlement / Clearing
Department: Secondary Market Department
Tel: 661 7481 Fax: 661 7991
Equity Settlement; Fixed-Income Settlement — Anita Borowska *Trade & Settlement* ☎ **625 5693**

Administration

Technology & Systems
Roman Weinfeld *Director* ☎ **640 2793**

Compliance
Pawek Gkadysz *Director* ☎ **856 1829**

Public Relations
Wojciech Grzybowski *Manager* ☎ **640 2797**

Centro Internationale Handelsbank AG Representative Office

ul Szpitana 1, 00-020 Warsaw
Tel: (22) 827 2824 Fax: (22) 625 6654

Senior Executive Officers
Representative — Marcin Wloch

www.euromoneydirectory.com POLAND (+48)

The Chase Manhattan Bank
Representative Office

18th Floor, FIM Tower, Al Jerozolimske 81, 02 001 Warsaw
Tel: (22) 695 0850 Fax: (22) 695 0840

Senior Executive Officers
Others (Senior Executives)
Senior Country Officer Kenneth Foretek *Senior Country Officer*

Citibank (Poland) SA

Senatorska 16, 00-923 Warsaw 55
Tel: (22) 657 7200 Fax: (22) 657 7580 Telex: 815014 CITI PL Swift: CITI PL PX Reuters: CITW; CIPN; CTPO

Senior Executive Officers
President of the Management Board Shirish Apte
Vice President of the Management Board Kenneth J Lewis
Vice President of the Management Board Harit Talwar
Financial Director Julian Clarke *Financial Controller*
General Director Maciej Bardan

General-Lending (DCM, SL)
Head of Corporate Banking Robert Litwin *Corporate Banking Director*
 Gian Paolo Potsios *Corporate Banking Director*

General - Treasury
Head of Treasury Ted Dabrowski *Treasury Head*

Relationship Manager
Investor Relationship Management Jacek Fotek *Group Head*

Risk Management
Global Head Edward B Ward *Vice President of the Management Board*

Corporate Finance / M&A Advisory
Head of Corporate Finance Albert May *Corporate Finance Director*

Administration
Head of Marketing Vivek Vig *Country Marketing Director*

Legal / In-House Counsel
 Aneta M Poplawska *Country Legal Counsel*

Other (Administration)
Human Resources Stanistaw Wojnicki *Director*

Commerzbank AG
Representative Office

ul Jasna 24, 00-054 Warsaw
Tel: (22) 826 8489; (22) 826 8591 Fax: (22) 826 8678

Senior Executive Officers
Representative Alfred W Neuhaus

Crédit Lyonnais Bank Polska SA
Regional Head Office

Al Jerozolimskie 65-79, Lim Center, 00-697 Warsaw
PO Box 50, 00-950 Warsaw
Tel: (22) 630 6888 Fax: (22) 635 4500

Senior Executive Officers
President Bernard Szlachetka

Den Danske Bank
Representative Office

Warsaw Corporation Center, ul Emilii Plater 28, 00- 688 Warsaw
Tel: (22) 630 3170 Fax: (22) 620 3171

Senior Executive Officers
Chief Representative Lars Møller-Christensen

POLAND (+48)   www.euromoneydirectory.com

Deutsche Bank
Subsidiary Company

Pl Grzybowski 12/14/16, 00-104 Warsaw
Tel: (22) 652 5000 Fax: (22) 652 5159 Swift: DEUT PL PX
Website: www.deutsche-bank.de

Deutsche Morgan Grenfell
Representative Office

Formerly known as: Morgan Grenfell & Co Limited
Pl Grzybowski 12/16, 00-104 Warsaw
Tel: (22) 652 5400 Fax: (22) 652 5432

Senior Executive Officers
Director — Michael Rummel

DG BANK
Representative Office

Al Jerozolimskie 51/3, 00-697 Warsaw
Tel: (22) 628 0205 Fax: (22) 628 5825

Senior Executive Officers
Representative — Waldemar Wrobel

Erste Finance (Warsaw) Limited
Representative Office

Formerly known as: Girocredit Finance (Warsaw) Limited
LIM Centre, Suite 1816, Al Jerozolimskie 65/79, 00-657 Warsaw
Tel: (22) 630 6772 Fax: (22) 630 6774

Senior Executive Officers
Managing Director — Sophie Pols

Erste Securities Polska SA
Subsidiary Company

Formerly known as: IB Austria Securities (Warsaw) SA
Al Jana Pawta 11 23, 00-854 Warsaw
Tel: (22) 653 9333; (22) 653 9330 Fax: (22) 653 9334 Email: erste.securities@erste.ikp.pl

Senior Executive Officers
Financial Director — Padraic Coll *Chief Finance Officer*

Equity Capital Markets
Head of Sales; Head of Trading — Hieczystaw Tazor *Head of Sales & Trading*

Equity Research
Head of Equity Research — Pawet Lubecki

Settlement / Clearing
Head of Settlement / Clearing — Artur Michatowski *Head of Back-Office*

Administration
Business Development — Bozena Dewiszek *Compliance Officer*

Legal / In-House Counsel — Jan Magrel

Compliance — Bozena Dewiszek *Compliance Officer*

European Bank for Reconstruction & Development
Representative Office

Alternative trading name: EBRD
15-10 LIM Centre-Marriott, Al Jerozolimskie 65/79, 02-697 Warsaw
Tel: (22) 630 7275; (22) 630 7273 Fax: (22) 630 6651
Website: www.ebrd.com

Senior Executive Officers
Head — Irene Grzybowski

Robert Fleming (Polska) SA
Subsidiary Company

Ist Floor, Atrium Building, Al Jana Pawla 23, 00-854 Warsaw
Tel: (22) 653 9380 Fax: (22) 653 9383

HypoVereinsbank Polska SA
Subsidiary Company

Al Jana Pawla II, 23 Atrium, 00-854 Warsaw
Tel: (22) 652 4100 Fax: (22) 652 4222

ING Baring Securities (Poland)
Subsidiary Company

Plac Trzech Krzyzy 10/14, 3 Crosses Square, 00-499 Warsaw
PO Box 29, 00-950 Warsaw
Tel: (22) 820 4000; (22) 820 4008 Fax: (22) 820 4009; (22) 820 4010

Senior Executive Officers
General Manager   Jerzy Filip

ING Barings
Representative Office

4th Floor, ul Dlugi Targ 39/40, 80-830 Gdansk
Tel: (58) 346 2374 Fax: (58) 301 1591

Senior Executive Officers
Representative   Andrzej Dzuryk

ING Barings
Full Branch Office

Plac Trzech Krzyzy 10/14, 00-499 Warsaw
PO Box 29, 00-950 Warsaw
Tel: (22) 820 4000; (22) 820 4008 Fax: (22) 820 4009; (22) 820 4010 Telex: 824141 INGB PL Swift: INGB PL PW
Reuters: INGW
Website: www.ing.com.pl

Senior Executive Officers
Chief Executive Officer   Eli Leenaars *Country Manager*
Chief Operating Officer   Patrick Mackay *Deputy Country Manager*

Others (Senior Executives)
Head of Markets & Treasury   Maciek Wegrzynski *Deputy Country Manager*

General-Investment
Head of Investment   George Storozynski *Deputy Country Head*

Corporate Finance / M&A Advisory
Head of Corporate Finance   Maciek Wegrzynski *Deputy Country Manager*

Other Departments
Department: ING Baring Private Bank
Private Banking   Ryszard Jach *Head of Private Banking*

International Finance Corporation
Representative Office

Alternative trading name: IFC

ul Emilii Plater 28, 00-688 Warsaw
Tel: (22) 630 3444 Fax: (22) 630 3445 Email: ttelma@ifc.org
Website: www.ifc.org

Senior Executive Officers
Manager   Tomasz Telma

POLAND (+48)   www.euromoneydirectory.com

KBC Bank NV
Representative Office

Formerly known as: Kredietbank NV
ul Kasprzaka 2/8, 01-211 Warsaw
Tel: (22) 634 5460 **Fax:** (22) 634 5895 **Email:** toczekg@kredytbank.com.pl

Senior Executive Officers
Chief Representative   Jozef M Toczek

Kredyt Bank PBI SA
Head Office

ul Kasprzaka 2/8, 01-211 Warsaw
Tel: (22) 634 5400 **Fax:** (22) 634 5335 **Telex:** 824129 KBSA PL **Swift:** KRDB PL PW **Email:** bp@kredybank.com.pl
Website: www.kredytbank.com.pl

Senior Executive Officers
Chairman   Andrzej Witkowski
President, Board of Management   Stanislaw Pacuk [T] **634 5401**

Others (Senior Executives)
Management Board   Dariusz Wilczewski *Deputy President* [T] **634 5470**
                                            Malgorzata Kroker-Jachiewicz *Deputy President* [T] **634 5478**
                                            Marek Królak *Deputy President* [T] **634 5405**
                                            Dariusz Sokolowski *Deputy President* [T] **634 5402**
                                            Izabela Sewerynik [T] **634 5416**
                                            Bronislawa Trzeszkowska *Chief Accountant* [T] **634 5479**
                                            Bogdan Bronowski *Director* [T] **634 5492** [F] **634 5898**

General-Lending (DCM, SL)
Head of Corporate Banking   Ewa Milaszewicz *Director, Corporate Banking* [T] **634 5439** [F] **634 5649**
General-Investment
Head of Investment   Marek Gurdziel *Director, Investment Banking* [T] **634 5428**
General - Treasury
Head of Treasury   Bogdam Adamowicz *Director, Treasury* [T] **634 5408** [F] **634 5340**

Debt Capital Markets / Fixed Income
Bonds - General
Own Issues Office   Michal Dwurzynski *Director* [T] **634 5010** [F] **634 5677**

Risk Management
Head of Risk Management   Andrzej Stopczywski *Director* [T] **634 5458** [F] **634 5333**

Settlement / Clearing
Operations   Grazyna Szczesna *Director, Foreign Operations Department* [T] **634 5484**
                                            [F] **634 5865**
                                            Malgorzata Rosiecka *Director, Organisation & Network Management*
                                            [T] **634 5410** [F] **634 5662**

Asset Management
Other (Asset Management)
Pension Fund Organisation Office   Boguslaw Hadyniak *Director* [T] **634 5810** [F] **634 5801**

Other Departments
Chief Credit Officer   Ewa Chojecka *Director, Credit Department* [T] **634 5474** [F] **634 5277**
                                            Janusz Markowski *Director, Credit System Department* [T] **634 5009**
                                            [F] **634 5920**
Private Banking   Albert Kucharski *Director* [T] **634 5030**
Economic Research   Iwona Kozlowska *Director, Reporting & Analysis Department* [T] **634 5412**
                                            [F] **634 5334**

Administration
Head of Administration   Jan Tylkowski *Director* [T] **634 5472**
Business Development   Pawel Karpinski *Director, Development Office* [T] **634 5011** [F] **634 5970**
Head of Marketing   Maria Kudelska *Director, Marketing* [T] **634 5005** [F] **634 5230**

Technology & Systems
Computer System Implementation Department Janusz Golab *Director* [T] **634 5482** [F] **634 5799**
Telecommunications & IT Department   Dariusz Adamowski *Director* [T] **634 5444** [F] **634 5522**

Legal / In-House Counsel
                                            Krystyna Skolkowska *Director, Legal Department* [T] **634 5432** [F] **634 5519**

Public Relations
                                            Marcin Olkowicz *Director, Press Office* [T] **634 5462**

Accounts / Audit
Internal Audit Department   Bronislawa Trzeszkowska *Chief Accountant* [T] **634 5479**
                                            Wladyslaw Godlewski *Director* [T] **634 5480** [F] **634 5820**

www.euromoneydirectory.com   POLAND (+48)

Accounts / Audit (cont)
Tax Planning Department
Operational & Accounting Standards Department
Other (Administration)
Personnel & Training Department
Synergy Department
Separate Projects Department

Hanna Maczyk *Director* ☏ **634 5412** 🖷 **634 5334**
Miroslawa Respondek *Director* ☏ **634 5430** 🖷 **634 5545**

Janusz Nowak *Director* ☏ **634 5431** 🖷 **634 5632**
Andrzej Pawelczyk *Director* ☏ **634 5009** 🖷 **634 5089**
Witold Sowilski *Director* ☏ **634 5451** 🖷 **634 5508**

Landesbank Hessen-Thüringen Girozentrale   Representative Office
Alternative trading name: Helaba
ul Emilii Plater 28 - IX p, 00-688 Warsaw
Tel: (22) 630 3930; (22) 630 3931 **Fax:** (22) 630 3933; (22) 630 3934

LG Petro Bank SA   Subsidiary Company
ul Rzgowska 34/36, 93-172 Lodz
Tel: (42) 681 9060; (42) 684 9060 **Fax:** (42) 684 6192 **Swift:** LGPB PL DW **Reuters:** PTRO **Telerate:** 884199

Senior Executive Officers
Chairman   Chong Suk Lee
President & CEO   Dong Chang Park
Financial Director   Halina Walczau *Vice Director* ☏ **684 4471**
Treasurer   Anna Skzepankowska *Vice Director of Treasury & Risk Management*
                                            ☏ **654 8484**
President & CEO   Dong Chang Park
Secretary   A Kocik ☏ **684 9060**
International Division   Aldona Sierzputowska-Lejman *Vice Director, Foreign Banking Department*
                                            ☏ **654 2403 ext 181**

General-Lending (DCM, SL)
Head of Corporate Banking   Mieczyskaw Muszunski *Vice Director* ☏ **654 2406**

General-Investment
Head of Investment   Anna Skzepankowska *Vice Director of Treasury & Risk Management*
                                            ☏ **654 8484**

Equity Capital Markets
Head of Equity Capital Markets   Gabriel Kielak *Vice Director, Capital Market Department* ☏ **654 2400 ext 219**

Money Markets
Head of Money Markets   Gabriel Kielak *Vice Director, Capital Market Department* ☏ **654 2400 ext 219**

Risk Management
Head of Risk Management   Anna Skzepankowska *Vice Director of Treasury & Risk Management*
                                            ☏ **654 8484**

Other Departments
Correspondent Banking   Aldona Sierzputowska-Lejman *Vice Director, Foreign Banking Department*
                                            ☏ **654 2403 ext 181**

Administration
Head of Administration   Krzysztof Gerlach *Vice Director* ☏ **684 4570**
Head of Marketing   Barbara Szozomicka *Vice Director* ☏ **654 2409**

Technology & Systems
Information Technology Department   Anrezej Banasiak *Director*

Public Relations
                                            Barbara Szozomicka *Vice Director* ☏ **654 2409**

Accounts / Audit
                                            Jin Young Yang *Bank Director* ☏ **684 1800**

London Forfaiting Polska Sp zoo   Full Branch Office
11th Floor, Ilmet Building, ul Jana Pawla II 15, 00-828 Warsaw
Tel: (22) 697 7277 **Fax:** (22) 697 7279

Senior Executive Officers
Others (Senior Executives)
                                            Darek Sobieraj *Director*
                                            Joanna Stogowska *Manager*
                                            Rafal Kozlowski *Manager*

POLAND (+48) www.euromoneydirectory.com

Malopolski Bank Regionalam SA — Head Office
Alternative trading name: MBR SA
ul Bozego Ciala 23, 31-059 Krakow
Tel: (12) 423 5676; (12) 423 5721 **Fax:** (12) 656 2772; (12) 656 2809 **Reuters:** PD02284

Senior Executive Officers
President   Stanislav Osak
Vice President   Ewa Rytel-Wasilewska
Vice President   Zdzislaw Wolos
Financial Director   Mieczyslaw Bil
Treasurer   Danuta Latala *Director*

Administration
Technology & Systems
    Bozena Kozlowska *Director*

Legal / In-House Counsel
    Grazyna Krawczyk *Co-ordinator*

Compliance
    Stanislaw Knaga *Director*

Public Relations
    Boleslaw Budzicz *Specialist*

Merita Bank plc — Representative Office
25, Jana Pawla II, 6th Floor, 00-854 Warsaw
Tel: (22) 653 4770 **Fax:** (22) 653 4771

Senior Executive Officers
Representative   Sami Loukkola

Merrill Lynch Polska sp zoo
Llm Centre, Marriott Hotel, Al Jerozolimskie 65/79, 00-697 Warsaw
Tel: (22) 630 6219 **Fax:** (22) 630 6218
Website: www.ml.com

Pierwszy Polsko-Amerykanski Bank SA — Head Office
Formerly known as: Pierwszy Polsko-Ameryknasi Bank w Krakowie SA
Kordylewskiego 11, 31-547 Krakow
Krakow 53, 31-075 Krakow
Tel: (12) 618 3333 **Fax:** (12) 618 3344 **Telex:** 0325739 **Swift:** PPAB PL KA **Reuters:** PPAB

Senior Executive Officers
Chairman & President   Marek Kulczycki
Financial Director   Thomas C Cianfrani *Chief Financial Officer*
Chief Operating Officer   Benjamin H Turnbull

Relationship Manager
Branches   Dorota Pietrow

Money Markets
Global Head   Artur Wolak

Foreign Exchange
Global Head   Artur Wolak

Administration
Head of Administration   Jacek Klimkowicz

Technology & Systems
    Jaromir Pelczarski

Legal / In-House Counsel
    Boguslawa Wladzielczyk

Compliance
    Boguslawa Wladzielczyk

Other (Administration)
Human Resources   Marta Oracz

www.euromoneydirectory.com   POLAND (+48)

Powszechna Kasa Oszczednosci-Bank Panstwowy   Head Office

Alternative trading name: PKO bp & State Savings Bank
ul Nowy Swiat 6/12, 00-497 Warsaw
Tel: (22) 635 4000 **Fax:** (22) 635 5855 **Swift:** BPKO PL PW **Email:** pkomail@pkopb.pl **Reuters:** KASA; KASE
Website: www.pkobp.pl

Senior Executive Officers
Deputy Chairman — Izabela Dudzin
President — Andrzej Topinski ☏ **625 6129**
Financial Director — Andrzej Jakubaszek *Director, Financial Policy Department* ☏ **625 6083**
Treasurer — Konrad Greszta *Director, Treasury* ☏ **636 5504**
Managing Director — Wladyslaw Binkowski ☏ **625 7132**

Debt Capital Markets / Fixed Income
Department: Treasury Department
Pl Bankowy 2, 00-095 Warsaw
Tel: 636 5505 **Fax:** 531 1589
Country Head — Ilona Witkowska *Dealer* ☏ **636 5515**

Non-Domestic Government Bonds
US$ — Wojciech Dunaj *Dealer* ☏ **636 5515**

Equity Capital Markets
Department: Capital Investments Department
ul Sienkieqicza 12, 11-010 Warsaw
Tel: 826 0870 **Fax:** 826 4983
Country Head — Edward Szczytowski *Director* ☏ **622 7419**
Department: Bank Brokerage House of PKO bp (Secondary Market Division)
ul Mysia 5, 00-950 Warsaw
Tel: +48 661 7886 **Fax:** +48 661 7880
Country Head — Grzegorz Klepacki *Head of Secondary Market* ☏ **622 7419**

Syndicated Lending
Department: Corporate Banking Department
ul Mysia 5, 00-950 Warsaw
Tel: 661 7876 **Fax:** 629 2752
Global Head — Malgorzata Kakol *Director* ☏ **629 5356**
Head of Credit Committee — Krzysztof Markowski *Deputy President*

Money Markets
Department: Treasury Department
Pl Bankowy 2, 00-950 Warsaw
Tel: 636 5505 **Fax:** 531 1589
Country Head — Jacek Tomaszewicz *Chief Dealer* ☏ **636 5509**

Foreign Exchange
Department: Treasury Department
Pl Bankowy 2, 00-950 Warsaw
Tel: 636 5505 **Fax:** 531 1589
Country Head — Jacek Tomaszewicz *Chief Dealer* ☏ **636 5509**

Settlement / Clearing
Department: Treasury Department
Pl Bankowy 2, 00-950 Warsaw
Tel: 636 5505 **Fax:** 531 1589
Country Head — Krystyna Slaszynska *Manager, Back Office* ☏ **636 6668**

Global Custody
Department: Bank Brokerage House of PKO bp (Secondary Market Department)
ul Mysia 5, 00-496 Warsaw
Tel: 661 7886 **Fax:** 661 7880
Regional Head — Grzegorz Klepacki *Head of Secondary Market* ☏ **622 7419**

Other Departments
Correspondent Banking — Andrzej Szczepanski *Director, Financial Institutions* ☏ **635 4000**

Administration

Technology & Systems
Information Technology Department — Jacek Pulwarski *Director* ☏ **826 6291**

Legal / In-House Counsel
Legal Department — Jerzy Jackiewucz *Director* ☏ **625 6097**

Public Relations — Malgorzata Wyznikiewicz *Director, Public Relations* ☏ **826 0991**

POLAND (+48)	www.euromoneydirectory.com

Schroder Polska Sp zoo — Subsidiary Company

Warsaw Corporate Center, 3/F, ul Emilii Platter 28, 00-688 Warsaw
Tel: (22) 630 3565 Fax: (22) 630 3599

Senior Executive Officers
Chief Executive Officer
Financial Director
Chief Operating Officer

Krzysztof Opawski *Managing Director*
Peter Smart *Deputy Managing Director*
Andrzez Micinski *Deputy Managing Director*

Société Générale

ul Zlota 44/46, 00-950 Warsaw
PO Box 54, 00-950 Warsaw
Tel: (22) 652 4500; (22) 652 4600 Fax: (22) 625 7156
Website: www.socgen.com

Staropolski Dom Maklerski Spólka Akeyjna — Head Office

Formerly known as: Biuro Maklerski Banku Staropolskiego SA
ul Szkolna 1, 61-832 Poznan
Tel: (61) 854 4580 Fax: (61) 852 0204 Email: office@sdm.com.pl
Website: www.sdm.com.pl

Senior Executive Officers
President
Vice President
Assistant to the President

Miroslaw Kwiatkowski
Zbiguiew Puybylczak
Barbara Sikora

General-Investment
Head of Investment

Pawei Zawachki *Director* [T] **854 4535**

Debt Capital Markets / Fixed Income
Domestic Government Bonds
Head of Sales
Head of Trading
Head of Research

Andriej Jarocha *Vice Director* [T] **854 4580** [F] **852 0204**
Magda Marsziaykiewicz *Stock Market Specialist* [T] **854 4546** [F] **852 9349**
Pavel Zawadzki *Investment Advisor* [T] **854 4595** [F] **852 0204**

Corporate Finance / M&A Advisory
Head of Corporate Finance

Marek Laziewski *Director* [T] **854 4546**

Asset Management
Head

Anduej Kosiúski *Director* [T] **854 4508**

Administration
Head of Administration

Joanna Sokolowska *Director* [T] **854 4595**

Technology & Systems

Preingislaw Piotrowski *Director* [T] **854 4582**

Accounts / Audit

Avtur Kuch [T] **854 4559**

Westdeutsche Landesbank Polska SA — Subsidiary Company

Warsaw Corporate Centre, ul Emilii Plater 28, 00-688 Warsaw
Tel: (22) 653 0500 Fax: (22) 653 0501

Senior Executive Officers
Others (Senior Executives)
Management

Baudouin van Caubergh [T] **653 0601**
Maciej Stanczuk [T] **653 0601**

Wielkopolski Bank Kredytowy SA — Head Office

Plac Wolnosci 16, 60-967 Poznan
Tel: (61) 856 4900 Fax: (61) 852 1113 Swift: WBKP PL PP Cable: WUBEKA
International Division Tel: 856 4785; Fax: 856 4828

Senior Executive Officers
President
First Vice President
Treasurer

Jacek Ksen
Cornelius Osullivan
Mr Moyney [T] **856 5805**

1216 Euromoney Directory 1999

www.euromoneydirectory.com   PORTUGAL (+351)

Debt Capital Markets / Fixed Income
Tel: 856 5835 **Fax:** 856 4822
Head of Debt Capital Markets   Mr Uminski *Chief Dealer*
Other (Fixed Income)
Trading   Mr Ponanski *Trading*
                                      Mr Kusik *Trading*

Equity Capital Markets
Tel: 856 5835 **Fax:** 856 4822
Head of Equity Capital Markets   Mr Uminski *Chief Dealer*
Head of Trading   Mr Ponanski *Trading*
                                      Mr Kusik *Trading*

Money Markets
Tel: 856 5835 **Fax:** 856 4822
Head of Money Markets   Mr Uminski *Chief Dealer*
Money Markets - General
Trading   Mr Ponanski *Trading*
                                      Mr Kusik *Trading*

Foreign Exchange
Tel: 856 5835 **Fax:** 856 4822
Head of Foreign Exchange   Mr Uminski *Chief Dealer*
Head of Trading   Mr Seroka
Spot / Forwards Trading   Lopuazynski *Swaps & Forwards*

Risk Management
Tel: 856 5835 **Fax:** 856 4822
Head of Risk Management   Mr Uminski *Chief Dealer*
Country Head   Mr Ponanski *Trading*
                                      Mr Kusik *Trading*

The World Bank   Representative Office

Alternative trading name: International Bank for Reconstruction & Development
17th Floor, 2 Stawki Street, 00-193 Warsaw
Tel: (22) 635 0553 **Fax:** (22) 635 9857

Senior Executive Officers
Country Director, Poland & Baltics   Basil Kavalsky

PORTUGAL
(+351)

Banco de Portugal   Central Bank

Rua do Comércio 148, P-1100 Lisbon
Tel: (1) 321 5300; (1) 313 0000 **Fax:** (1) 346 4543 **Telex:** 65832 BPADM
Website: www.bportugal.pt

Senior Executive Officers
Governor   Antonio de Sousa
Vice Governor   Antonio Marto
Vice Governor   Wis Campos e Cunha
Others (Senior Executives)
Head, Bank Licensing; Head, Banking   Carlos Santos
Supervision
Head, Economics & Statisitcs   Vitor Gaspar
Head, Public Debt   Silvino Paive Lopes
Head, Reserves Management   José Ramalho

Foreign Exchange
Head of Foreign Exchange   José Ramalho

Settlement / Clearing
Head of Settlement / Clearing   Silvino Paive Lopes

Administration
Head of Administration   Henrique Moiller Miranda

Technology & Systems
                                      Paulino Magalhaé Correia

PORTUGAL (+351)   www.euromoneydirectory.com

Banco de Portugal (cont)
Accounts / Audit
Head, Accountancy   Americo Sequeira

Argentaria - Banco Exterior de España
Rua Castilho 39, Edificio Castil, P-1250 Lisbon
Tel: (1) 386 2101 **Fax:** (1) 386 3208 **Telex:** 66299 **Swift:** EXTE PT PL

Banco Bilbao Vizcaya (Portugal) SA   Head Office
Alternative trading name: BBV (Portugal) SA
Avenida da Liberdade 222, P-1250 Lisbon
Tel: (1) 311 7200; (1) 311 7201 **Fax:** (1) 311 7500 **Telex:** 62635 **Swift:** BBVI PT PL **Email:** bbvinfo@mail.telepac.pt
Reuters: BBVL

Senior Executive Officers
Chief Executive Officer	José Luis Jolo
President	Julio Castrocaldas
Financial Director	José Ponte daSilva
Treasurer	Javier Judel

Debt Capital Markets / Fixed Income
Head of Debt Capital Markets   Carlos Tiesgnita

Equity Capital Markets
Head of Equity Capital Markets   Carlos Bastardo

Syndicated Lending
Head of Syndicated Lending   Ana Claudino

Money Markets
Head of Money Markets   Alice Toreira

Foreign Exchange
Head of Foreign Exchange   Celia Faustino

Risk Management
Head of Risk Management   Jose J Poute de Silva

Corporate Finance / M&A Advisory
Head of Corporate Finance   Carlos Tiesgnita

Settlement / Clearing
Head of Settlement / Clearing   Ana Carno

Banco BPI SA
Formerly known as: BPI Group & BPI - SGPS (Holding Company)
Rua Sá da Bandeira 20, P-4000 Oporto
Tel: (2) 207 5000 **Fax:** (2) 208 4432 **Telex:** 12557 SANVISP **Swift:** BFYB PT PL

Senior Executive Officers
Chairman	Artur Santos Silva
Deputy Chairman	Fernando Ulrich

Others (Senior Executives)
Members of the Board
    António Domingues *Director*
    António Seruca Salgado *Director*
    António Viana Baptista *Director*
    Carlos Mascarenhas de Almeida *Director*
    Jorge Holtreman Roquette *Director*
    José Pena do Amaral *Director*
    Luis Braz Teixeira *Director*
    Paulo Rodrigues da Silva *Director*
    Rui de Faria Lélis *Director*
    Sérgio Augusto Sawaya *Director*
    Vitor Constancio *Director*

www.euromoneydirectory.com   PORTUGAL (+351)

Banco Comercial dos Açores
Head Office

Rua Dr Bruno Tavares Carreiro, P-9503 Ponta Delgada, Azores
Apartado 1379, P-9503 Ponta Delgada, Azores
Tel: (96) 629 070 Fax: (96) 629 657 Swift: CDAC PT PA Email: bca@mail.telepac.pt

Senior Executive Officers
Chairman   Horácio Roque
Chief Executive Officer   José Castro Rocha
Financial Director   Luís Anselmo *Finance Director* ☎ 200 2930
Company Secretary   Vanda Melo
International Division   Lauriano Reis *Manager*

Foreign Exchange
Head of Foreign Exchange   Nuno Mendes *Chief Dealer* ☎ (1) 721 1575

Other Departments
Correspondent Banking   Lauriano Reis *Manager*

Administration
Technology & Systems
                                      José Resendes *Director*

Banco Comercial Português SA
Full Branch Office

Rua Augusta 62/96, P-1100 Lisbon
Tel: (1) 321 1000 Fax: (1) 321 1729 Telex: 64059 Swift: BCOM PT PL DIF Email: bcp@bcp.pt

Senior Executive Officers
Chairman   Jorge Jardim Gonçalves
Financial Director   Pedro Libano Monteiro ☎ 422 4000
Treasurer   Pedro Turras ☎ 721 8080
Representative   José Pinto Bastos ☎ 422 4000

General-Lending (DCM, SL)
Head of Corporate Banking   José Prata

Debt Capital Markets / Fixed Income
Head of Debt Capital Markets   Luis Feria ☎ 721 8400

Equity Capital Markets
Head of Equity Capital Markets   Luis Feria ☎ 721 8400

Syndicated Lending
Head of Syndicated Lending   Nuno Alves ☎ 721 800

Money Markets
Head of Money Markets   Carlos Ribeiro ☎ 721 8080

Foreign Exchange
Head of Foreign Exchange   Carlos Ribeiro ☎ 721 8080

Risk Management
Head of Risk Management   Carlos Ribeiro ☎ 721 8080

Settlement / Clearing
Head of Settlement / Clearing   João Esteves Oliveira ☎ 321 1751

Banco Comercial Português SA
Head Office

Alternative trading name: BCP
Rua Júlio Dinis 705-719, P-4000 Oporto
Tel: (2) 607 1100 Fax: (2) 607 1209 Telex: 27415 BCOMPO P Swift: BCOM PT PL Email: bcp@bcp.pt
Website: www.bcp.pt

Senior Executive Officers
Chairman & CEO   Jorge Jardim Gonçalves
Financial Director   Pedro Turras
Chief Operating Officer   Augusto Rodrigues Lopes
Company Secretary   José Pinto Bastos
International Division   João Esteves Oliveira

General-Lending (DCM, SL)
Head of Corporate Banking   José Almeida ☎ 721 3020
                                      José Prata

General-Investment
Head of Investment   Alexandre Magalhães

Euromoney Directory 1999   **1219**

PORTUGAL (+351)

www.euromoneydirectory.com

Banco Comercial Português SA (cont)
Debt Capital Markets / Fixed Income
Head of Fixed Income — João Pereiri Pinto *Manager* ☎ 721 8661 📠 721 3192
Head of Fixed Income Sales — João Gufrasio ☎ 721 8657 📠 721 3192

Equity Capital Markets
Head of Equity Capital Markets — Nuno Santos ☎ 721 8654 📠 727 0845
Head of Sales — Gonçalo Rocha ☎ 721 8680

Equity Research
Head of Equity Research — Gonçalo Rocha ☎ 721 8680

Money Markets
Tel: 721 3190 Fax: 721 3199 Reuters: BPAZ
Head of Money Markets — Carlos Ribeiro *Director* ☎ 721 3000

Domestic Commercial Paper
Head of Trading — António Pinheiro *Chief Dealer* ☎ 721 3080

Wholesale Deposits
Marketing — António Marques *Chief Dealer* ☎ 721 3100
Head of Sales — Ana Batista *Chief Dealer* ☎ 721 3100

Foreign Exchange
Tel: 721 3080 Fax: 721 3199 Reuters: BPAX
Head of Foreign Exchange — Carlos Ribeiro *Director* ☎ 721 3000
Head of Trading — Joaquim Pires *Chief Dealer* ☎ 721 3020

Risk Management
Tel: 721 3000 Fax: 721 3199 Reuters: BPAZ
Head of Risk Management — Carlos Ribeiro *Director* ☎ 721 3000

Fixed Income Derivatives / Risk Management
Head of Sales — Ana Carvalho *Assistant Director* ☎ 721 3090
Trading — José Silva *Chief Dealer* ☎ 721 3070

Foreign Exchange Derivatives / Risk Management
Spot / Forwards Sales — Ana Carvalho *Assistant Director* ☎ 721 3090
Spot / Forwards Trading — José Almeida ☎ 721 3020

Banco EFISA SA — Head Office

Avenida Fontes Pereira de Melo 51, piso 9°, P-1050 Lisbon
Tel: (1) 311 7800 Fax: (1) 353 0634 Telex: 66133 EFISAL P Swift: EFIS PT PL Email: banco.efisa@telepac.pt

Senior Executive Officers
Chairman, Supervisory Board — Pedro Pires de Miranda
Chief Executive Officer — Abdool Magid A Karim Vakil *Chairman & Chief Executive*
José Manuel Baptista *Vice Chairman & Deputy CEO*

Others (Senior Executives)
Carlos Medeiros *Executive Director*
Isalita Falcao *Executive Director*
Hugo de Jesus *Executive Director*
Roger Reynolds *Executive Director*

General-Lending (DCM, SL)
Head of Corporate Banking — Mahomed Iqbal *Senior Manager, Corporate Banking*

Relationship Manager
Merchant Banking — Abdool Magid A Karim Vakil *Chairman & Chief Executive*

Rua da Paz 66-6°, P-4000 Oporto
Tel: +351 (2) 607 9050 Fax: +351 (2) 606 5305 Telex: 29835 EFISA P

Others (Senior Executives)
Administration — Prazeres Pereira *Chief Manager*
Department: Operations - Managers & Executives

Others (Senior Executives)
Chief Executive Officer — Abdool Magid A Karim Vakil *Chairman & Chief Executive*
Foreign Exchange and Money Market — José Manuel Baptista *Vice Chairman*
Domestic Market — Ernesto Teixeira *General Manager*
Treasury & Finance — José Manuel Melo da Silva *General Manager*
Human Resources — José Manuel Baptista *Vice Chairman*
Leasing & Retail — Carlos Medeiros *Executive Director*

Equity Capital Markets
Department: Capital Markets

Other (Domestic Equities)
Securities & Settlement — Ana Maria Bras *Head of Back Office*

www.euromoneydirectory.com   PORTUGAL (+351)

Syndicated Lending
Other (Syndicated Lending)
International Syndication
Portuguese Asset Syndication   Ana Almeida *Assistant Manager, Corporate Banking*
                                Nuno Cardoso *Senior Manager*
Loan-Related Activities
Trade Finance   Ana Almeida *Assistant Manager, Corporate Banking*
Project Finance   Nuno Cardoso *Senior Manager, Corporate Finance I*
                                Paula Guerra *Assistant Manager*
Other (Trade Finance)
Leasing   Carlos Medeiros *Executive Director*
Leasing (Oporto)   Ricardo Pinto Leite
Local Credits   Mahomed Iqbal *Senior Manager*

Money Markets
Global Head   José Manuel Baptista *Vice Chairman & Deputy CEO*
Money Markets - General
                                José Manuel Melo da Silva *General Manager*
                                Augusto de Carvalho *Manager*

Foreign Exchange
Global Head   José Manuel Baptista *Vice Chairman & Deputy CEO*
FX Traders / Sales People
Treasury & Finance   José Manuel Melo da Silva *General Manager*
                                Augusto de Carvalho *Manager*

Risk Management
Other (FI Derivatives)
Derivatives   Luis F Rebelo *Associate*

Corporate Finance / M&A Advisory
Country Head   Nuno Cardoso *Senior Manager, Corporate Finance I*
Other (Corporate Finance)
Mergers & Acquisitions   Jorge Freire Cardoso *Deputy Manager*

Settlement / Clearing
Settlement (General)   Jorge Cunha *Senior Manager*

Other Departments
Private Banking   Ernesto Teixeira *General Manager*
                                Nidia Caetano *Account Manager*
Correspondent Banking   Mahomed Iqbal *Senior Manager*

Administration
Other (Administration)
Human Resources   José Manuel Baptista *Vice Chairman & Deputy CEO*
Corporate Advisory   Jorge Freire Cardoso *Deputy Manager*
Head of Administration   Prazeres Pereira *Chief Manager*

Banco Espirito Santo e Comercial de Lisboa SA   Head Office

195 Avenida da Liberdade, P-1250 Lisbon
Tel: (1) 315 8331 **Fax:** (1) 350 1180; (1) 350 8972 **Telex:** BESCLP 12191 **Swift:** BESC PT PL
Website: www.bes.pt

Senior Executive Officers
Chairman   António Luis Roquett Ricciardi
President   Ricardo Espirito San Salgado
International Division   André Navarro

Debt Capital Markets / Fixed Income
Fax: 350 1179
Head of Debt Capital Markets   Amilcar Morais Pires *General Manager* T 350 8817 F 350 8972
Head of Fixed Income   Antonio Soars *Chief Dealer* T 314 6171
Head of Fixed Income Trading   Pedro Amaral *Dealer* T 314 6171

Equity Capital Markets
Fax: 350 1179
Head of Equity Capital Markets Amilcar Morais Pires *General Manager* T 350 8817 F 350 8972
Head of Trading   Antonio Soars *Chief Dealer* T 314 6171
                                Pedro Amaral *Dealer* T 314 6171

Equity Repo / Securities Lending
Marketing & Product Development Ana Rita Gomes Barosa *Senior Manager* T 350 8983 F 350 8972
                                E arbarosa@bes.pt
Head of Prime Brokerage   Rogério Simões *Manager* T 350 1160 F 350 8972

PORTUGAL (+351) www.euromoneydirectory.com

Banco Espirito Santo e Comercial de Lisboa SA (cont)

Money Markets
Fax: 350 1179
Head of Money Markets — Rogeiro Simões *Manager* ⊤ 350 1160 F 350 8972
Global Head — Pedro Santos *Chief Dealer* ⊤ 357 6906

Foreign Exchange
Fax: 350 1179
Head of Foreign Exchange — Joaquim Soares *Manager* ⊤ 350 1158 F 350 8972
Head of Trading — Jose Martins *Chief Dealer* ⊤ 355 7429

Risk Management
Head of Risk Management — João Moita *Manager* ⊤ 350 8842 F 350 8972
Global Head — Joao Poppe *Chief Dealer* ⊤ 355 7758

Corporate Finance / M&A Advisory
Head of Corporate Finance — Conceição Lucas *General Manager* ⊤ 350 1153 F 350 1189

Settlement / Clearing
Operations — Acélia Vilela *Head* ⊤ 350 8840 F 350 1005

Global Custody
Head of Global Custody — Maria Celeste Costa ⊤ 350 8843 F 350 1005

Banco ESSI SA — Head Office
Torre 3-14° andar, Rua Tierno Galvan, P-1070 Lisbon
Tel: (1) 380 8500 **Fax:** (1) 388 8259 **Telex:** 63595 ESSI P **Reuters:** ESLP-Q

Senior Executive Officers
Chairman — Manuel Serzedelo de Almeida

Debt Capital Markets / Fixed Income

Eurobonds
Head of Origination — Cristina Frazão
Alexandre Viçoso
Head of Sales — Leonardo Mathias ⊤ 387 0101
Martim A. Neto ⊤ 387 0101
Luis Pina ⊤ 387 0101
Frederico Alegria ⊤ 387 0101
Carlos Pinto ⊤ 387 0101
Head of Trading — Leonardo Mathias ⊤ 387 0101
Martim A. Neto ⊤ 387 0101
Luis Pina ⊤ 387 0101
Frederico Alegria ⊤ 387 0101
Carlos Pinto ⊤ 387 0101

Equity Capital Markets

Domestic Equities
Head of Origination — Diogo Abreu *Head* ⊤ 380 3550
Isabel Lima ⊤ 380 3550
Silvia Costa ⊤ 380 3550
Head of Sales — Antonio Ramos ⊤ 380 8624
José Freire ⊤ 380 8624
Diogo Abreu *Head* ⊤ 380 3550
Head of Trading — Antonio Ramos ⊤ 380 8624
José Freire ⊤ 380 8624
Diogo Abreu *Head* ⊤ 380 3550

Settlement / Clearing
Tel: 380 8561/2
Settlement (General) — João Bolila
Raul Silva
Operations — João Pereira da Silva *Head of Operations*

Administration

Compliance
Alexandre Jardim *Head, Compliance*

1222 Euromoney Directory 1999

www.euromoneydirectory.com   PORTUGAL (+351)

Banco Finantia SA
Head Office

Formerly known as: Finantia-Sociedade de Investimentos SA
1st Floor, 5 Rua General Firmino Miguel, P-51600 Lisbon
Tel: (1) 720 2000 **Fax:** (1) 726 5310 **Telex:** 65829 **Swift:** BFIA PT PL **Email:** finantia@finantia.com **Reuters:** FNT 1
Website: www.finantia.pt

Senior Executive Officers
President   António Guerreiro
Treasurer   Duarte Correia de Sá *Executive Director* F **726 3366** E **duarte.sá@finanatia.com**
International Division   Luis Nogueira *Executive Director* F **726 6984** E **luis.nogueira@finantia.com**

Debt Capital Markets / Fixed Income
Head of Debt Capital Markets   Paulo Marta *Executive Director* E **paulo.marta@finantia.com**

Domestic Government Bonds
Head of Research   Walter Palma *Director* E **walter.palma@finantia.com**

Eurobonds
Head of Origination; Head of Syndication   Nuno Teixeira *Director* F **726 7722** E **nuno.teixeira@finantia.com**

Private Placements
Head of Origination   Nuno Teixeira *Director* F **726 7722** E **nuno.teixeira@finantia.com**

Other (Fixed Income Research)
Research, Medium Term Notes   Carmo Cal *Associate Director* E **carmo.cal@finantia.com**

Equity Capital Markets
Head of Equity Capital Markets   José Salgado *Executive Director* E **josé.salgado@finantia.com**

Domestic Equities
Head of Origination   Paulo Marta *Executive Director* E **paulo.marta@finantia.com**

Syndicated Lending
Head of Syndicated Lending   Paulo Marta *Executive Director* E **paulo.marta@finantia.com**

Loan-Related Activities
Project Finance   Luis Asconcelos *Executive Director* F **726 9503** E **luis.asconcelos@finantia.com**

Money Markets
Head of Money Markets   Pedro Benites *Director* E **pedro.benites@finantia.com**

Domestic Commercial Paper
Head of Origination   Paulo Marta *Executive Director* E **paulo.marta@finantia.com**
Head of Sales   Miguel Guiomar *Director* E **miguel.guiomar@finantia.com**

Eurocommercial Paper
Head of Origination   Paulo Marta *Executive Director* E **paulo.marta@finantia.com**
Head of Sales   Miguel Guiomar *Director* E **miguel.guiomar@finantia.com**

Foreign Exchange
Head of Foreign Exchange   Pedro Benites *Director* E **pedro.benites@finantia.com**

Risk Management
Head of Risk Management   Luis Nogueira *Executive Director* F **726 6984** E **luis.nogueira@finantia.com**

Corporate Finance / M&A Advisory
Head of Corporate Finance   Filipe Silva *Executive Director* F **726 8563** E **filipe.silva@finantia.com**

Settlement / Clearing
Head of Settlement / Clearing   António Azevedo *Director* E **antónio.azevedo@finantia.com**

Global Custody
Head of Global Custody   Susana Branco *Associate Director* E **susana.c.branco@finantia.com**

Other Departments
Private Banking   Paula Moniz *Executive Director* F **720 2099** E **paula.moniz@finantia.com**

Administration

Legal / In-House Counsel
    Artur Ferreira *Senior Counsel* F **726 9820** E **artur.ferreira@finantia.com**

Public Relations
    Carlota Martins F **720 1050** E **carlota.martins@finantia.com**

PORTUGAL (+351)   www.euromoneydirectory.com

Banco Internacional do Funchal
Head Office

Alternative trading name: Banif
José Malhoa Avenue, 1792, P-1070 Lisbon
Tel: (1) 721 1200; (1) 721 1300 **Fax:** (1) 721 1201 **Telex:** 42640 BANIF P **Swift:** BNIF PT PL **Reuters:** BNFL
General Telex: 64534 BANIF P

Senior Executive Officers
Chairman of the Executive Board — José Manuel Castro Rocha ☏ **721 1273**
Chief Executive Officer — José Manuel Castro Rocha *Chairman of the Executive Board* ☏ **721 1273**
Financial Director — Carlos David Duarte de Almeida *Executive Director* ☏ **721 1272**
Treasurer — João Paulo Marques de Almeida *General Manager* ☏ **721 1223**

Debt Capital Markets / Fixed Income
Head of Fixed Income — Wilson Pereira Camilo *Head, International Division* ☏ **721 1236**

Equity Capital Markets
Head of Equity Capital Markets — João Paulo Marques de Almeida *General Manager* ☏ **721 1223**

Syndicated Lending

Loan-Related Activities
Trade Finance — Wilson Pereira Camilo *Head, International Division* ☏ **721 1236**

Money Markets
Head of Money Markets — João Paulo Marques de Almeida *General Manager* ☏ **721 1223**

Foreign Exchange
Head of Foreign Exchange — João Paulo Marques de Almeida *General Manager* ☏ **721 1223**

Banco de Investimento Imobiliário
Head Office

Avenida da Liberdade 108/112, P-1250 Lisbon
Tel: (1) 321 5050 **Fax:** (1) 321 5078
Website: www.embital.pt

Senior Executive Officers
Chairman & CEO — Jorge Manuel Jardim Gonçalves
Deputy Chairman — Filipe De Jesus Pinhal
Chief Executive Officer — Joaquim Miguel Ribeirinho Dos Santos Paupéro *Member of the Executive Board*

Others (Senior Executives)
Fernando Nogueira *Member of the Executive Board*
Romano Pesci *Member of the Executive Board*
Giuseppe Vimercati *Member of the Executive Board*
Alberto Mauri *Member of the Executive Board*
Maurizio Radici *Assistant to the Board of Directors*

Banco Itaú Europa SA
Head Office

Rua Tierno Galvan, Amoreiras - Torre 3, piso 11°, P-1070 Lisbon
Tel: (1) 381 1020; (1) 381 1030 **Fax:** (1) 388 7219; (1) 388 7256 **Telex:** 60476 **Swift:** ITAUPTPL **Reuters:** EURI

Senior Executive Officers
Chairman — Roberto Setubal
Vice Chairman — Carlos C Pestana ☏ **381 1001**
President & CEO — Alberto D Barretto ☏ **381 1002**
Financial Director — Almir Vienoto ☏ **381 1004**
Chief Operating Officer — José Francisco Claro ☏ **381 1003**

Others (Senior Executives)
International & Finance — Alberto C de Mendonca *Managing Director* ☏ **381 1007**

1224   Euromoney Directory 1999

PORTUGAL (+351)

Banco Mello de Investimento SA
Head Office
Rua Alexandre Herculano 50, Piso 5, P-1250 Lisbon
Tel: (1) 312 5000 **Fax:** (1) 312 5003; (1) 312 5001 **Telex:** 65952 MELLOP **Swift:** BMEL PT PL
Email: investor@bancomello.pt **Reuters:** BMEL **Cable:** MEL PL
Corporate & Risk Management Email: np87dm@mail.telepac.pt **Market Risk Management (Middle Office)**
Email: drm.bancomello@mail.telepac.pt
Website: www.bancomello.pt

Senior Executive Officers
Chief Executive Officer — Francisco José Queiróz de Barros De Lacerda *Chief Executive*
António Carlos de Magalhães Fernandes Tato *Deputy Chief Executive*
Luis Maria França de Castro Pereira Coutinho *Deputy Chief Executive*
Financial Director — Fernando Bicho *Chief Financial Officer* ☎ **312 5221**
Chief Operating Officer — Luis Gomes dos Santos ☎ **720 1888**
Treasurer — José Carlos Mateus ☎ **311 7641**
Corporate Secretary — Joaquim Pereira Durão ☎ **312 5178**
International Division — José Sequeira *Foreign Operations* ☎ **720 1700**

Others (Senior Executives)
Rui Afonso Galvão Mexia de Almeida Fernandes
Francisco José Anjos Salema Garção
Manuel Coutinho de Oritgão Ramos

General-Lending (DCM, SL)
Head of Corporate Banking — Diogo Querós de Barros de Lacerda ☎ **312 76064**
Relationship Manager
Investor Relations — Fernando Bicho *Chief Financial Officer* ☎ **312 5221**
Financial Institutions Group — Pedro M Casquinho ☎ **312 5170**
Department: Board of Directors
Chairman — Vasco Maria Guimarães José de Mello
Chief Executive — Francisco José Queiróz de Barros De Lacerda

Others (Senior Executives)
José da Cunha Guimarães
Jaime Roque de Pinho d'Almeida
João Pedro Stilwell Rocha e Melo
António Carlos de Magalhães Fernandes Tato *Deputy Chief Executive*
Luis Maria França de Castro Pereira Coutinho *Deputy Chief Executive*
Francisco José Anjos Salema Garção
Manuel Coutinho de Oritgão Ramos
Luis Filipe da Conceiçã Pereira

Debt Capital Markets / Fixed Income
Fax: 312 5017
Head of Debt Capital Markets — Pedro F Pinto ☎ **311 7674**
Bonds - General
Sales & Trading — Gonçalo Conceiçao ☎ **311 7675**
Bernardo Collaço ☎ **311 7675**
Noé Oliveira ☎ **311 7671**
João Pinhao ☎ **311 7673**
João Zorro ☎ **311 7681**
João Vinagre ☎ **311 7682**
Francisco Carvalho ☎ **311 7676**
Miguel Rasteiro ☎ **311 7675**
Marta Valle ☎ **312 5313**

Equity Capital Markets
Fax: 312 5501
Head of Equity Capital Markets — João B Jorge ☎ **312 5516** F **312 5502**
Head of Sales — Paulo Guerreiro *Head, Equity Sales* ☎ **312 5521**
Alexander Ferguson *Equity Sales* ☎ **312 5520**
Helena J Silva *Equity Sales* ☎ **312 5534**
Head of Trading — Francisco D'Orey *Head, Equity Trading* ☎ **312 5533**
Eduardo Cunha *Equity Trader* ☎ **312 5554**
Hugo Pinto *Equity Trader* ☎ **312 5553**
Sérgio Geraldes *Equity Trader* ☎ **312 5552**
Manuel Raposo *Equity Trader* ☎ **312 5532**
Richard Jones *Equity Trader* ☎ **312 5531**

Equity Research
Head of Equity Research — João Leandro *Head* ☎ **312 5528** F **312 5014** E jml@mello-valores.pt
Other (Equity Research)
Retail, Electric Utilit., Cement — João Leandro *Head* ☎ **312 5528** F **312 5014** E jml@mello-valores.pt
Bank, Insurance — Sofia Raposo ☎ **312 5121** F **312 5014** E snr@mello-valores.pt

PORTUGAL (+351)   www.euromoneydirectory.com

Banco Mello de Investimento SA (cont)
Other (Equity Research) (cont)

Forestry, Ceramics, Holdings   Carim Jafair ☎ **312 5527** 🖷 **312 5014** ✉ **caj@mello-valores.pt**
Construction, Oil, Gas, Motorways   José Soares ☎ **312 5526** 🖷 **312 5014** ✉ **jms@mallo-valores.pt**
Food, Beverage, Tourism, Real Estate   José Alves ☎ **312 5522** 🖷 **312 5014** ✉ **jaa@mello-valores.pt**
Telecom, Media, Package   Rui Pereira ☎ **312 5523** 🖷 **312 5014** ✉ **rcp@mello-valores.pt**

Foreign Exchange
Fax: 312 5041
Head of Foreign Exchange   Miguel Pardal *Chief Dealer, Foreign Exchange* ☎ **311 7615**
Head of Sales   Pedro Matona ☎ **311 7610**
    António Vaz ☎ **311 7654**
    Martim de Lima Mayer ☎ **311 7614**
    Tiago Pereira ☎ **311 7613**
Corporate Sales   Gonçalo Oliveira ☎ **311 7653**
    Margarida Rosa ☎ **311 7652**
    António Vaz ☎ **311 7654**
    Marta Martins

Risk Management
Department: Corporate & Risk Management
Fax: 312 5009
Head of Risk Management   Vítor Pereira *Corporate* ☎ **312 5296**

OTC Equity Derivatives
Head   João Martins *Head, Equity Derivatives* ☎ **312 5519**
Trading   Manuel Matos ☎ **312 5266**
    Carlos Veiga ☎ **312 5539**

Other (Exchange-Traded Derivatives)
    Filipa Bragança ☎ **312 5297**
    Rui Santos ☎ **312 5251**
    Frederico Pratas ☎ **312 5311**
Corporate Unit   Gonçalo Oliveira ☎ **311 7653**
    António Vaz ☎ **311 7654**
    Margarida Rosa ☎ **311 7652**
    Marta Correia ☎ **311 7651**
Volatility Desk; Foreign Branches Desk   Miguel Borges ☎ **311 7665**
Department: Market Risk Management (Middle Office)
Fax: +351 (1) 312 5009
Global Head   Luis Gomes da Costa ☎ **312 5442**

Other (Exchange-Traded Derivatives)
    Luis Mendonca ☎ **312 5454**
    Carmo Duarte Ferreira ☎ **312 5204**
    António Chorâo ☎ **311 7672**

Administration
Business Development   Filipe Ravara *Corporate Planning & Development* ☎ **312 5476**
Technology & Systems
    Joaquim Frade ☎ **720 1380**
Legal / In-House Counsel
    Leonor Torres ☎ **720 1830**
Corporate Communications
    Luis d'Eça Pinheiro ☎ **312 5154**
Other (Administration)
Management Information   Duarte Costa ☎ **720 1403**

Banco Nacional Ultramarino SA   Head Office

Avenida 5 de Outubro 175, P-1050 Lisbon
PO Box 10139, P-1017 Lisbon Codex
Tel: (1) 791 8000 **Telex:** 13305 **Swift:** BNUL PT PL **Email:** sandro.guilherme@cgd.pt **Reuters:** BULX
Treasury Fax: 7012 1301; **Reuters:** BULM (Macao)
Website: www.bnu.pt

Senior Executive Officers
Chairman   João M F Salgueiro
Chief Executive Officer   António J S V Monteiro
International Division   Margarida Robin de Andrade Barros Gomes *General Manager*

Others (Senior Executives)
    António Luís Neto
    José J G Rosa

www.euromoneydirectory.com   PORTUGAL (+351)

Others (Senior Executives) (cont)
                                José Alberto Santos da Costa Bastos
                                Fernando Miguel Sequeira
                                Alexandre Manuel de Pinho Sobral Torres
General - Treasury
Head of Treasury   António Pontes *General Manager, Treasury*
                                João Oliveira *AGM, Treasury* ☎ **795 0175** 🖷 **797 8502**
Debt Capital Markets / Fixed Income
Department: Treasury & Capital Markets
Global Head   António Pontes *General Manager*
Country Head   António Malheiro *Deputy General Manager*
                                Marta Magalhães *Manager*

Domestic Government Bonds
Head of Sales   Nuno Dâmaso *Equity Desk*
                                Manuela Quintal *Bond Desk*
Head of Trading   Nuno Dâmaso *Equity Desk*
                                Manuela Quintal *Bond Desk*

Money Markets
Tel: 793 6139 **Reuters:** BULZ (Monitor), **Telex:** 43525
Money Markets - General
Forward & Swap Desk   José Ramos *Senior Dealer*
                                Mário Rui *Dealer*
                                Teresa Alho *Dealer*
                                Armando Oliveira *Dealer*

Foreign Exchange
Tel: 793 3514 **Reuters:** BNUL **Telex:** 43525
FX Traders / Sales People
Spot Desk   António Félix *Senior Dealer*
                                Sónia Lopes *Dealer*

Corporate Finance / M&A Advisory
Global Head   Jorge Matos *General Manager*
Settlement / Clearing
Settlement (General)   Luís Páris *Operations - Foreign Currency* ☎ **797 8595**
Operations   Arnaldo Veiga *AGM, Operations*
                                Nuno Jacinto *Operations - Domestic Currency* ☎ **797 8595** 🖷 **793 6338**
                                Luís Páris *Operations - Foreign Currency* ☎ **797 8595**

Global Custody
Regional Head   Maria Alice Nunes *GM, Custodian Banking*
Other Departments
Economic Research   Zolá Simões *General Manager*
Administration
Technology & Systems
                                Rui Taborda *General Manager*
Legal / In-House Counsel
                                Marta Cochat-Osório *General Manager*

Banco Pinto & Sotto Mayor   Head Office
Rua Do Ouro, 28, P-1103 Lisbon
P.O.Box 2148, P-1103 Lisbon Cedex
Tel: (1) 347 6261 **Fax:** (1) 342 7078 **Telex:** 12516 **Swift:** BPSM PT PL **Reuters:** PSML **Cable:** OTTOS
Senior Executive Officers
Chairman & CEO   Luis Champalimaud ☎ **340 2929** 🖷 **321 1580**
Financial Director   Carlos Rodrigues *Vice Chairman* ☎ **340 2929** 🖷 **321 1642**
Treasurer   Predro Lameira *Executive Vice President* ☎ **313 7300**
International Division   Joao Filipe De Lima Mayer *Executive Vice President* ☎ **350 5182**
                                🖷 **357 3973**
Money Markets
Head of Money Markets   Julio Campos ☎ **313 7300** 🖷 **313 7493**
Foreign Exchange
Head of Foreign Exchange   Julio Campos ☎ **313 7300** 🖷 **313 7493**
Asset Management
Head   Joao Martins ☎ **727 1005** 🖷 **727 1383**

Euromoney Directory 1999 **1227**

PORTUGAL (+351)   www.euromoneydirectory.com

Banco Português do Atlântico
Head Office

Avenido José Malhoa, lote 1686, P-1070 Lisbon, www.bpatlantico.pt
Tel: (1) 392 5600 **Fax:** (1) 422 4459
Public Relations Department **Tel:** 422 4253; 422 4459; **Fax:** 422 4459

Senior Executive Officers
Chairman   Jorge Jardim Gonçalves [T] 322 1100 [F] 321 1119
Financial Director   Pedro Libano Monteiro *Member of the Board & Managing Director*
                            [T] 422 4121 [F] 322 4169

Relationship Manager
Head, Investors Relations   Miguel Rosa [T] 422 4360

Other Departments
Other Departments
Investor relations   Miguel Almeida [T] 422 4084 [F] 422 4359

Banco Português do Atlântico SA
Head Office

Praça dom João I 28, P-4000 Oporto
Tel: (2) 207 2000
Website: www.bpatlantico.pt

Senior Executive Officers
Chairman   Jorge Jardim Gonçalves

Banco Português de Investimento SA
Head Office

Formerly known as: BPI Group & BPI - SGPS SA (Holding Company)
Rua Tenente Valadim 284, P-4100 Oporto
Tel: (2) 607 3100 **Fax:** (2) 609 8787 **Telex:** 29884 BPIDF P **Swift:** BPIP PT PL OPR **Reuters:** BPI-O-E-F

Senior Executive Officers
Chairman   Artur Santos Silva
Chief Executive Officer   Fernando Ulrich *Deputy Chairman* [T] (1) 310 1000 [F] (1) 352 5228
Financial Director   Antònio Domingues *Managing Director & Head, Financial Department*
                            [T] (1) 310 1000 [F] (1) 310 1282

Treasurer   Maria João Reis *Head of Treasury* [T] (1) 310 1000 [F] (1) 310 1286
International Division   José Toscano *Head* [T] (1) 310 1000 [F] (1) 310 1281

General-Investment
Head of Investment   Fernando Ulrich *Deputy Chairman* [T] (1) 310 1000 [F] (1) 352 5228

Debt Capital Markets / Fixed Income
Head of Fixed Income   Antònio Domingues *Managing Director & Head, Financial Department*
                            [T] (1) 310 1000 [F] (1) 310 1282

Equity Capital Markets
Head of Equity Capital Markets   Manuel Ferreira da Silva *Managing Director & Head of Equity*

Syndicated Lending
Head of Origination; Head of Syndication   Antònio Lobo Ferreira *Manager* [T] (1) 310 1000 [F] (1) 3153 9027

Loan-Related Activities
Trade Finance   José Toscano *Head* [T] (1) 310 1000 [F] (1) 310 1281

Money Markets
Head of Money Markets   Maria João Reis *Head of Treasury* [T] (1) 310 1000 [F] (1) 310 1286

Foreign Exchange
Head of Foreign Exchange   Maria João Reis *Head of Treasury* [T] (1) 310 1000 [F] (1) 310 1286

Corporate Finance / M&A Advisory
Head of Corporate Finance   Fernando Ulrich *Deputy Chairman* [T] (1) 310 1000 [F] (1) 352 5228

Settlement / Clearing
Head of Settlement / Clearing   Luis Carlos Silva [T] (1) 310 1000 [F] (1) 3153 9027

Global Custody
Head of Global Custody   Luis Carlos Silva [T] (1) 310 1000 [F] (1) 3153 9027

Asset Management
Department: BPI Fundos
Head   Isabel Castelo Branco *Managing Director* [T] (1) 311 1025 [F] (1) 350 3073

Other Departments
Private Banking   José Carlos Agrelios *Managing Director & Head of Private Banking*
Correspondent Banking   José Toscano *Head* [T] (1) 310 1000 [F] (1) 310 1281

www.euromoneydirectory.com PORTUGAL (+351)

Administration
Head of Marketing João Oliveira e Costa *Marketing Manager* ☏ (1) 310 1000 ℻ (1) 315 3793
Technology & Systems
  Manuel Peres de Sousa *Head*
Legal / In-House Counsel
  Rui Lélis *Managing Director*
Public Relations
  Ana Rita Laurenço *Head* ☏ (1) 310 1000 ℻ (1) 310 1298
Accounts / Audit
  Maria da Conciçao Monteiro *Head*

Banco Totta & Açores SA
Head Office

Rua do Ouro 88, P-1100 Lisbon
Tel: (1) 321 1500 **Fax:** (1) 321 1591 **Telex:** 12266 **Swift:** TOTA PT PL **Reuters:** BTAX

Senior Executive Officers
Chairman & Chief Executive Luis Champalimaud ☏ 340 2929 ℻ 321 1580
Financial Director Carlos Rodrigues *Vice Chairman* ☏ 340 2929 ℻ 321 1642
Treasurer Pedro Lameira *Executive Vice President* ☏ 313 7300
International Division Joao Filipe De Lima Mayer *Executive Vice President* ☏ 350 5182
  ℻ 357 3973

Others (Senior Executives)
Africa & Asia Agostinho de Oliveira *Regional General Manager*
Europe & Americas Caetano de Lancastre *Regional General Manager*
Money Markets
Head of Money Markets Julio Campos ☏ 313 7300 ℻ 313 7493
Foreign Exchange
Head of Foreign Exchange Julio Campos ☏ 313 7300 ℻ 313 7493
Asset Management
Head Joao Martins ☏ 727 1005 ℻ 727 1383

The Bank of Tokyo-Mitsubishi Limited
Full Branch Office

Rua Castilho 165, piso 2°, P-1070 Lisbon
Tel: (1) 383 1300 **Fax:** (1) 383 2363; (1) 383 2058 **Telex:** 43673 BOTLIS P **Swift:** BOTK PT PX

Senior Executive Officers
General Manager Naoki Ito
Assistant General Manager Kunio Igarashi

Banque Nationale de Paris
Full Branch Office

Avenida 5 de Outubro 206, P-1050 Lisbon
Tel: (1) 791 0200 **Fax:** (1) 795 5616 **Telex:** 60717 BNPSUC P **Swift:** BNPA PT PL

Senior Executive Officers
Chief Executive Officer Patrick Du Saint *General Manager*

Others (Senior Executives)
Business Clients Antonio Ladeira *Manager*

Relationship Manager
Regional Manager North Serafim Fernandez

Other Departments
Cash Management Luciano Salgueiro *Officer*
  Carlos Leiria Pinto ☏ 791 0273

Banque Sudameris
Representative Office

Campo Grande, 28-9D, P-1700 Lisbon
Tel: (1) 797 5454 **Fax:** (1) 793 4927

Senior Executive Officers
Representative Carla Cavallotti

Euromoney Directory 1999 **1229**

PORTUGAL (+351)   www.euromoneydirectory.com

Barclays Bank plc
Full Branch Office
Avenida da República 50, P-1050 Lisbon
Tel: (1) 791 1100 **Fax:** (1) 791 1123
Website: www.barclays.pt

Senior Executive Officers
General Manager   João Freixa

BNC - Banco Nacional de Crédito Imobiliário SA
Head Office
Rua do Comércio 85, P-1100 Lisbon
Tel: (1) 323 8500 **Fax:** (1) 323 8695 **Telex:** 42561 BANCRE **Swift:** CRBN PT PL **Email:** bncdfi@comnexo.pt
Reuters: BNCL

Senior Executive Officers
Chairman   Alberto Oliveira Pinto ☎ **323 8511**
Financial Director   José Manuel Piriquito Costa *Co-ordination Manager* ☎ **323 8565**
Chief Operating Officer   Rui Nunes *Co-ordination Manager* ☎ **323 8643**
Treasurer   José Manuel Piriquito Costa *Co-ordination Manager* ☎ **323 8565**

Equity Capital Markets
Domestic Equities
Head of Trading   Paula Dias *Analyst* ☎ **323 8664**

Money Markets
Head of Money Markets   Luis Romao *Dealer* ☎ **323 8568**

Foreign Exchange
Fax: 323 8695
Head of Foreign Exchange; Head of Trading   Luis Romao *Dealer* ☎ **323 8568**
FX Traders / Sales People
Traders   José Carvalho *Dealer* ☎ **323 8567**
    Pedro Almeida *Dealer* ☎ **323 8572**

Settlement / Clearing
Fax: 323 8692
Head of Settlement / Clearing   Rui Nunes *Co-ordination Manager* ☎ **323 8643**
Foreign Exchange Settlement   Abilio Fonseca *Head of Department* ☎ **323 8599**

Global Custody
Other (Global Custody)
    Rui Nunes *Co-ordination Manager* ☎ **323 8643**

Other Departments
Correspondent Banking   José Manuel Piriquito Costa *Co-ordination Manager* ☎ **323 8565**

Administration
Technology & Systems
    Manuel Oliveira Faztudo *Co-ordination Manager* ☎ **318 5000**

Public Relations
    Antonio Dias Antunes *Manager* ☎ **323 8663**

BSN - Banco Santander de Negócios Portugal SA
Subsidiary Company

Formerly known as: Banco Santander de Negócios Portugal
Avenida Eng Duarte Pacheco, Amoreiras Torre 1, piso 6°, P-1070 Lisbon
Tel: (1) 380 1500 **Fax:** (1) 385 9133

Senior Executive Officers
President of the Executive Committee   Antonio Osorio
Chief Executive Officer   Eduardo Cunha *VP, Executive Committee*
Financial Director; Chief Operating Officer   Angel Sanz
Treasurer   João C Silva

Debt Capital Markets / Fixed Income
Global Head   Pedro Fialho
Domestic Government Bonds
Head of Sales   Pedro Fialho
Eurobonds
Head of Origination; Head of Syndication; Head of Sales   Pedro Fialho

1230   Euromoney Directory 1999

www.euromoneydirectory.com PORTUGAL (+351)

Private Placements
Head of Origination; Head of Sales — Pedro Fialho
Money Markets
Global Head — João C Silva
Domestic Commercial Paper
Head of Origination — José Costa
Head of Sales; Head of Trading — João C Silva
Foreign Exchange
Global Head — João C Silva
Global Custody
Regional Head — Pedro Fialho
Other (Global Custody) — Hugo Rocha

Caixa Central de Crédito Agrícola Mútuo CRL — Head Office

Rua Castilho 233-233 A, P-1070 Lisbon
Tel: (1) 386 0006; (1) 380 5530 **Fax:** (1) 387 0840 **Swift:** CCCM PT PL **Telerate:** CCCM
Website: www.credito-agricola.pt

Senior Executive Officers
Chief Executive Officer — Joao Costa Pinto
José Lemos *Deputy Chief Executive Officer*
International Division — José Vareda *General Manager* ⓣ 380 5562 Ⓕ 387 4586
Debt Capital Markets / Fixed Income
Head of Fixed Income Trading — Alexandra Rebelo ⓣ 381 0444 Ⓕ 387 4586
Equity Capital Markets
Head of Equity Capital Markets — José Vareda *General Manager* ⓣ 380 5562 Ⓕ 387 4586
Syndicated Lending
Head of Trading — Ofelia Gomez ⓣ 381 0444 Ⓕ 387 4586
Money Markets
Money Markets - General
Dealer — Luis Marques ⓣ 381 0450 Ⓕ 387 4586
Foreign Exchange
Head of Trading — Alipio Santos ⓣ 381 0450 Ⓕ 387 4586
Risk Management
Head of Risk Management — Helena Aparicio *Deputy Manager* ⓣ 380 5562 Ⓕ 387 4586

Caixa Economica Montepio Geral — Head Office

Alternative trading name: Montepio Geral
Rua de Santa Justa, 109, P-1200 Lisbon
Tel: (1) 347 6361 **Fax:** (1) 342 6466 **Telex:** 60752 INTRCE P **Swift:** MPIO PT PL
Website: www.montepiogeral.com

Senior Executive Officers
Chairman — António de Seixas da Costa Leal
International Division — Carlos A Pereira Martins ⓣ 342 5674 Ⓕ 347 1814
Ⓔ cpmartins@montepiogeral.pt

Others (Senior Executives)
Executive Directors — Alberto José dos Santos Ramalheira
António Manuel Maldonado Gonelha
José Joaquim Fragoso
Ludovico Morgado Candido

Debt Capital Markets / Fixed Income
Department: Capital Market / Trasury (Bond & Equity)
Bonds - General
Head, Capital Market — Francico Simeòes ⓣ 347 3889
Treasury, Bond & Equity Trading Manager — Luis Lourenço ⓣ ext 3347
Chief Dealer — Fernando Baptista ⓣ ext 3203
Dealer — André Lopes ⓣ 347 3889 Ⓕ 342 5258
Research & Financial Advising — Carlos Castro ⓣ ext 3345
Domestic Market International Operations Promotion — Manuel Alexandre ⓣ ext 3247
Pedro Martins ⓣ ext 3210
Back Office — João Barradinhas ⓣ ext 3340

Euromoney Directory 1999 **1231**

PORTUGAL (+351)   www.euromoneydirectory.com

Caixa Economica Montepio Geral (cont)
Syndicated Lending
Head of Syndicated Lending   Artur Gama ☎ 347 3308
Money Markets
Head of Money Markets   Filomena Costa ☎ 342 8450
Foreign Exchange
Head of Foreign Exchange   Francisco Gomes ☎ 342 8450
Risk Management
Head of Risk Management   Francico Simeòes ☎ 347 3889
Administration
Department: International Division

Other (Administration)
Financial Institutions   Vasco Carvalho ☎ 346 4654 ext 3211 ✉ vacarvalho@montepiogeral.pt
   Hugo Mendes ☎ ext 3230
Operational Department   Fernando Rosa *Manager* ☎ ext 3200
Payment Orders & Cheques   Mário Marques ☎ ext 3218
Documentary Collections & Credit Guarantees   Fernanda Galvào ☎ ext 3223
& Aval

Caixa Geral de Depositos — Offshore Banking Unit
Avenida Arriaga 17/19, 3rd Floor, P-9000 Funchal, Madeira
Tel: (91) 231 020 **Fax:** (91) 233 092 **Telex:** 72621 CASSFE P **Swift:** CGDI PT PL AOFF
Email: offbranch@mail.selepac.pt

Senior Executive Officers
General Manager   Albino Martins

Others (Senior Executives)
   José Mata *Assistant Manager*

Caixa Geral de Depositos SA — Head Office
Alternative trading name: CGD
Avenida João XXI 63, Apartado 1795, P-1017 Lisbon Codex
Tel: (1) 795 3000 **Fax:** (1) 790 5063; (1) 790 5263 **Telex:** 42621 CASCRE **Swift:** CDGI PT PL **Email:** dtm@cgd.pt
Reuters: CGDL
Website: www.cgd.pt

Senior Executive Officers
Chairman   João Salgueiro
Chief Executive Officer   Vitor Martins *Chief Executive & COO* ☎ 848 1231
Financial Director   José Brito *Finance Director & Treasurer*
Managing Director / General Manager   Manuel Sousa

Debt Capital Markets / Fixed Income
Global Head   Paulo Lopes

Equity Capital Markets
Tel: 848 1231 **Fax:** 790 5258
Global Head   Vitor Martins *Chief Executive & COO* ☎ 848 1231

Equity Repo / Securities Lending
Marketing & Product Development   Fernando Marques Pereira *Manager* ☎ 790 5379 ✉ 790 5063

Money Markets
Global Head   Ondina Oliveira

Foreign Exchange
Global Head   Siragusa Leal

Risk Management
Global Head   Paulo Lopes

Corporate Finance / M&A Advisory
Global Head   Fernando M Pereira

Settlement / Clearing
Regional Head   Paulo Lopes

www.euromoneydirectory.com   PORTUGAL (+351)

Central Banco de Investimento
Head Office

233 Rua Castilho, piso 4°, P-1070 Lisbon
Tel: (1) 386 4097 Fax: (1) 380 5567 Email: bcdi@mail.eunet.pt

Senior Executive Officers
Chairman   J Tavares Moreira
Chief Executive Officer   José Lemos Vice Chairman & Acting CEO
Chief Operating Officer   Miguel Azevedo
Treasurer   Carlos Gonçalves

Others (Senior Executives)
Head of Sales   Joáo Vermelmo ☏ **380 5568**
Head of Trading   Joaquim Reis ☏ **381 0400**
Head of Research   Inés Osório ☏ **386 4097**
Senior Manager - Sales   Juan Simon ☏ **380 5569**
Senior Manager - Asset Mgt.   Pedro Assunsáo ☏ **386 4097**

Equity Capital Markets
Tel: 386 4097
Head of Equity Capital Markets; Head of Sales   Joáo Vermelmo ☏ **380 5568**
Head of Trading   Joaquim Reis ☏ **381 0400**

Domestic Equities
Head of Sales   Joáo Vermelmo ☏ **380 5568**
Head of Trading   Joaquim Reis ☏ **381 0400**

International Equities
Head of Sales   Joáo Vermelmo ☏ **380 5568**
Head of Trading   Joaquim Reis ☏ **381 0400**

Other (International Equity)
Senior Manager   Juan Simon ☏ **380 5569**

Equity Research
Head of Equity Research   Inés Osório ☏ **386 4097**

Risk Management
Head of Risk Management   Carlos Gonçalves

Corporate Finance / M&A Advisory
Head of Corporate Finance   Miguel Azevedo

The Chase Manhattan Bank
Representative Office

Rua Barata Salgueiro 30, 3° Dto, P-1250 Lisbon
Tel: (1) 314 1195 Fax: (1) 352 6302

Senior Executive Officers
Others (Senior Executives)
Senior Country Officer   Fernando Pereira Coutinho Senior Country Officer

CISF Dealer SA
Head Office

Avenue José Malhoa 1686, P-1070 Lisbon
Tel: (1) 721 8700 Fax: (1) 721 8709

Senior Executive Officers
Chairman   Carlos Oliveira
Managing Director   Emanuel Santos

Debt Capital Markets / Fixed Income
Domestic Government Bonds
Head of Trading   Vitor Almeida Chief Trader ☏ **727 0455**

Equity Capital Markets
Domestic Equities
Head of Trading   Paolo Cruz Chief Trader ☏ **727 0455**
Head of Research   Goncalo Rocha ☏ **721 8685**

Risk Management
Other (Equity Derivatives)
                                      Antonio Aranha Chief Trader ☏ **721 8714**

Settlement / Clearing
Settlement (General)   Jose Santos ☏ **721 8443**

Euromoney Directory 1999 **1233**

PORTUGAL (+351)　　　　　www.euromoneydirectory.com

Citibank Portugal SA
Full Branch Office

Piso 4, Rua Barata Salgueiro 30, P-1250 Lisbon
Tel: (1) 311 6300; (1) 315 4181 **Fax:** (1) 311 6392; (1) 311 6399 **Telex:** 15316 **Swift:** CITI PT PX
Treasury Tel: 7012 1301

Senior Executive Officers
President   Alexander Van Tinhoven ☎ 311 6312 📠 311 6391
Treasurer   Antonio Cacorino ☎ 311 6328

Debt Capital Markets / Fixed Income
Global Head   Paulo Gray *Head of Capital Markets & Derivatives* ☎ 311 6322

Fixed-Income Repo
Head of Repo   Paulo Gray *Head of Capital Markets & Derivatives* ☎ 311 6322
Trading   Jorge Oliveira *Trader*

Equity Capital Markets
Global Head   Paulo Gray *Head of Capital Markets & Derivatives* ☎ 311 6322

Syndicated Lending
Global Head   Paulo Gray ☎ 311 6323

Money Markets
Global Head   Catarina Cardoso ☎ 311 6306

Foreign Exchange
Corporate Sales   Vasco Duarte-Silva ☎ 311 6302

Crédit Commercial de France
Representative Office

Torres das Amoreiras, Torre 2, 10° andar 12, P-1070 Lisbon
Tel: (1) 383 0303 **Fax:** (1) 387 0220

Senior Executive Officers
Representative   Luis Patricio

Credito Predial Português
Head Office

Rua Augusta 237, P-1101 Lisbon
PO Box 2002, P-1101 Lisbon Codex
Tel: (1) 321 4200; (1) 321 3600 **Fax:** (1) 312 3699; (1) 790 8824 **Telex:** 12264 CREDAL P **Swift:** BCPP PT PL
Reuters: CPPX **Cable:** CREDITO LISBON

Senior Executive Officers
Chairman & CEO   Luis Champalimaud ☎ 340 2920 📠 321 1580
Financial Director   Carlos Rodrigues *Vice Chairman* ☎ 340 2929 📠 321 1642
Treasurer   Pedro Lameira *Executive Vice President* ☎ 313 7300
International Division   Joao Filipe De Lima Mayer *Executive Vice President* ☎ 350 5182 📠 357 3973

Money Markets
Head of Money Markets   Julio Campos ☎ 313 7300 📠 313 7493

Foreign Exchange
Head of Foreign Exchange   Julio Campos ☎ 313 7300 📠 313 7493

Asset Management
Head   Joao Martins ☎ 727 1005 📠 727 1383

Deutsche Bank de Investimento SA
Subsidiary Company

Rua Castilho 20, P-1250 Lisbon
Tel: (1) 311 1200 **Fax:** (1) 353 5241

European Investment Bank
Representative Office

Avenida da Liberdade 144/156, piso 8°, P-1250 Lisbon
Tel: (1) 342 8989 **Fax:** (1) 347 0687

Senior Executive Officers
Representative   Manuel A Rocha Fontes

Fincor - Mediação Financiera SA

9 Rue Braamcamp, piso 7°, P-1250 Lisbon
Tel: (1) 312 7000 **Fax:** (1) 354 4949 **Telex:** 13043 FINCO P **Reuters:** FINN

Debt Capital Markets / Fixed Income

Domestic Government Bonds
Head of Trading   Joao Lontrao
                                   Maria Jésus Abreu
                                   Paula Rodrigues

Non-Domestic Government Bonds
                                   Joao Lontrao
                                   Maria Jésus Abreu
                                   Paula Rodrigues

Bonds - General
Margin Trading   Paulo Lima
                                   Ana Lucia Vaz
                                   Teresa Moreira

Fixed-Income Repo
Head of Repo   Carlos Dores ☎ 312 7031
                                   Joao P Pinto

Fixed-Income Research
Country Head   Isabel Cabral ☎ 312 7002

Equity Capital Markets

Domestic Equities
Head of Sales   Fernando Manuel Abreu *Sales*
                                   Carlos Alberto Rodrigues *Sales*
Head of Trading   Pierre Boulle
                                   Jorge Neves
                                   Ulugbek Suyumov
                                   Miguel Cabral
                                   Ana Vanessa
                                   Ricardo Contino
                                   Pedro Andrada

Money Markets

Money Markets - General
Off-Balance Sheet Products   Francisco Cadete
                                   José Garcia
                                   Antonio Agante
                                   Oliveira Cardoso

Risk Management

Spot / Forwards Trading   Juan Carlos Jara *MMK / Fwds*
                                   Sergio Oliveira *MMK / Fwds*
                                   Edouardo Rodrigues *MMK / Fwds*
                                   Paula Baptista *MMK / Fwds*
                                   Nuno Machado *MMK / Fwds*
                                   Rui Miguel Abreu *MMK / Fwds*
                                   Francisco Silva *MMK / Fwds*
                                   Nigel Williams *Spot*
                                   Neil Goodale *Spot*

Exchange-Traded Derivatives
FX Futures; FX Options; IR Futures; IR Options   Filipe Worsdell

Settlement / Clearing

Settlement (General)   Ana Silva *Administration / Back-Office*
                                   Cristina Castelhano *Administration / Back-Office*
                                   Ana Bela Abreu *Administration / Back-Office*
                                   Elisete Dos Santos *Administration / Back-Office*
                                   Maria Manuela Caeiro *Back-Office*
                                   Paulo Agostinho *Back-Office*
                                   Vanda Nascimento *Back-Office*
                                   Carlos Mello *Back-Office*
                                   Joao Esteves

Administration

Technology & Systems
Systems   Helder Martins
                                   Antonio Palma

PORTUGAL (+351) www.euromoneydirectory.com

Fincor - Mediação Financiera SA (cont)
Accounts / Audit
Finance / Accounting Adelaide Bico
  Luisa Reis
  Nathalia Sardinha

Other (Administration)
Human Resources / Secretarial Mauro Vicente
  Sandra Nunes
  Fatima Alves
  Sofia De Braganca
  Aldina Rolo
  Miguel Abrantes

Fincor Sociedade Corretora SA
Rua Braamcamp 9, piso 7°, P-1250 Lisbon
Tel: (1) 312 7000; (1) 352 3780 **Fax:** (1) 354 4949 **Email:** resfinn@mail.telepac.pt

Debt Capital Markets / Fixed Income
Domestic Government Bonds
Head of Sales John Lontrao ☎ **312 7031** F **315 6126**
Head of Trading John Lontrao
Head of Research Isabel Cabral ☎ **312 7002** F **315 6126**

Eurobonds
Head of Sales Joël Pinto *Head* ☎ **312 7031** F **315 6126**
Head of Trading Joël Pinto ☎ **312 7031**

Equity Capital Markets
Domestic Equities
Head of Trading Jorge Neves
Head of Research Isabel Cabral ☎ **312 7002** F **315 6126** E **resfinn@mail.telepac.pt**

International Equities
Head of Sales Pierre Boule

Generale Bank
Full Branch Office
Rua Alexandre Herculano 50, piso 6°, P-1250 Lisbon
Tel: (1) 313 9300 **Fax:** (1) 313 9350 **Telex:** 42996 GEBAPT P **Swift:** GEBA PT PL **Reuters:** GBPX

Senior Executive Officers
Chief Executive Officer Yves De Clerck ☎ **313 9301**
Financial Director Rui Lopes ☎ **313 9303**
Chief Operating Officer Américo Vaz ☎ **313 9309**

Interbanco SA
Head Office
Rua Castilho 2, P-1050 Lisbon
Tel: (1) 317 6500; (1) 350 6000 **Fax:** (1) 317 6666 **Telex:** 42419 INTERB P **Reuters:** ITBP

Senior Executive Officers
Chairman & President João Coutinho
Financial Director João Bugalho *Finance Director* ☎ **317 6622**
Chief Operating Officer Domingos Ferreira *Director, Operations* ☎ **317 6622**

Money Markets
Tel: 314 1161 **Fax:** 317 6502
Global Head João Bruno *Chief Dealer*

Foreign Exchange
Global Head João Bruno *Chief Dealer*

Risk Management
Fixed Income Derivatives / Risk Management
IR Swaps Sales / Marketing Pedro Dias *Junior Dealer* ☎ **314 1161**
IR Swaps Trading João Bruno *Chief Dealer*

Settlement / Clearing
Derivatives Settlement; Foreign Exchange Settlement Álvaro Santos *Responsável GMP* ☎ **317 6585**

www.euromoneydirectory.com   PORTUGAL (+351)

Midas Investimentos
Head Office

Formerly known as: Midas Corretora-Sociedade Corretora de Valores Mobiliários SA
Rua Mouzinho da Silveira, 15, P-1250 Lisbon
Tel: (1) 318 8800 **Fax:** (1) 343 3665

Senior Executive Officers
Financial Director Daniel Santos
Debt Capital Markets / Fixed Income
Head of Fixed Income Jorge Botelho
Equity Capital Markets
Other (Domestic Equities)
International Sales Elizabeth Rothfield
  Graca P Carvalho
  Cidália Morgado
  Luis C Almeida
  Luis Melo
Domestic Sales José Pinto Basto
  Miguel Lemos
Trading Francisco M Pereira
  Rita Borges
  Patricia Garrett

Equity Research
Head of Equity Research Diego Hernando *Head*
Other (Equity Research)
Equity Research James Harrison
  Alexandre Simões
  John Dos Santos

Risk Management
Head of Risk Management Aires Amaral
Settlement / Clearing
Head of Settlement / Clearing Jose Marques
Operations Nelio Esteves

Montepio Geral

Rua de Santa Justa 109, piso 3°, P-1100 Lisbon
Tel: (1) 347 6361 **Fax:** (1) 342 6766 **Telex:** 60752 INTRCE P **Swift:** MPIO PT PL

Senior Executive Officers
Chairman of the Board Antonio de Seixas da Costa Leal
Others (Senior Executives)
  Alberto José dos Santos Ramalheira *Executive Director*
  Antonio Manuel Maldonado Gonelha *Executive Director*
  José Joaquim Fragoso *Executive Director*
  Ludovico Morgado Candido *Executive Director*

Department: International Division
Rua de Santa Justa 109, piso 2°, Lisbon
Tel: +351 (1) 347 6361 **Fax:** +351 (1) 342 6766
International Division Carlos A Pereira Martins *Head* ☏ **342 5674** 🖷 **347 1814**
  ✉ **cpmartins@montepiogeral.pt**

Debt Capital Markets / Fixed Income
Department: Capital Market / Treasury
Head of Debt Capital Markets Francisco Simões ☏ **347 3889**
Global Head Luis Lourengo *Treasury, Bond & Equity Trading Manager*
  ☏ **347 6361 ext 3347**
Head of Fixed Income Trading Fernando Baptista *Chief Dealer* ☏ **347 6361 ext 3203**
Bonds - General
Research & Financial Advising Carlos Castro ☏ **347 6361 ext 3345**
Equity Capital Markets
Head of Equity Capital Markets Francisco Simões ☏ **347 3889**
Head of Trading Luis Lourengo *Treasury, Bond & Equity Trading Manager*
  ☏ **347 6361 ext 3347**
  Fernando Baptista *Chief Dealer* ☏ **347 6361 ext 3203**

Domestic Equities
Head of Research Carlos Castro ☏ **347 6361 ext 3345**
Syndicated Lending
Head of Syndicated Lending Artur Gama ☏ **347 6361 ext 3308**

Euromoney Directory 1999   **1237**

PORTUGAL (+351)   www.euromoneydirectory.com

Montepio Geral (cont)
Money Markets
Head of Money Markets   Filomena Costa ☏ 342 8450
Foreign Exchange
Head of Foreign Exchange   Francisco Gomes ☏ 342 8450
Risk Management
Head of Risk Management   Francisco Simões ☏ 347 3889
Settlement / Clearing
Operations   Fernando Rosa Manager ☏ 347 6361 ext 3200
Back-Office   João Barradinhas ☏ 347 6361 ext 3340
Other (Settlement & Clearing)
Payment Orders & Cheques   Mario Marques ☏ 347 6361 ext 3218
Documentary Collections & Credits Guarantee   Fernanda Galvão ☏ 347 6361 ext 3223
& Avai
Domestic Market International Operations   Manuel Alexandre ☏ 347 6361 ext 3247
Promotion
Domestic Market International Operations   Pedro Martins ☏ 347 6361 ext 3210
Other Departments
Financial Institutions   Vasco Carvalho ☏ 346 4654 ext 3211 ✉ vacarvalho@montepiogeral.pt
   Hugo Mendes ☏ 346 4654 ext 3230

Servimédia Sociedade Corretora SA
Rua Artilharia Um 103b, P-1070 Lisbon
Tel: (1) 387 8108 **Fax:** (1) 383 1993 **Telex:** 66098 **Email:** servimedia@mail.telepac.pt
Equity Capital Markets
*Equity Repo / Securities Lending
Marketing & Product Development*   Juan Carlos Jara *Head of International Department*

Société Générale   Representative Office
Empreendimento Amoreiras, Avenida Eng Duarte Pacheco, Torre 2, 9th Andar Sala 9, P-1070 Lisbon
Tel: (1) 383 3473 **Fax:** (1) 385 4903
Website: www.socgen.com

SOSERFIN - Serviços Financeiros SA   Head Office
Avenida da Boavista 1180, piso 7°, P-4100 Oporto
Tel: (2) 609 4190 **Fax:** (2) 609 4253 **Email:** sose@mail.telepac.pt **Reuters:** SOSERFIN
Senior Executive Officers
Chairman   José Santo
Chief Executive Officer   Gabriel Rothes *Director*
Director   Rui Cunha
Money Markets
Head of Money Markets   Rui Cunha *Director*
Foreign Exchange
Head of Foreign Exchange   Rui Cunha *Director*
FX Traders / Sales People
   Julia Duarte
   Isabel Machado
Risk Management
Head of Risk Management   Rui Cunha *Director*

UBS AG
Rua Barata Salgueiro 30, piso 7°, P-1250 Lisbon
Tel: (1) 355 9955 **Fax:** (1) 355 9933
Senior Executive Officers
Managing Director   R Costa-Santos
Corporate Finance / M&A Advisory
Other (Corporate Finance)
Corporate Finance   A Pinho

… PUERTO RICO (+1 787)

PUERTO RICO
(+1 787)

Banco Bilbao Vizcaya Puerto Rico — Full Branch Office

BBV Plaza, Avenue FD Roosevelt 1510, Corner San Patricio, Hato Rey, San Juan 00768
PO Box 4745, Hato Rey, San Juan 00936
Tel: 782 3717 Fax: 277 3780

Senior Executive Officers
President — Jorge A Colomer
International Division — Arlene Izquierdo Officer, Int'l Div
Others (Senior Executives)
Angel Carrasco Executive Vice President

Banco Santander — Full Branch Office

Formerly known as: Caguas Central
Avenida Ponce de León 207, Hato Rey, San Juan 00917
PO Box 362589, Hato Rey, San Juan 00936-2589
Tel: 759 7070 Fax: 250 2573; 250 3048
Corporate Communications Tel: 250 3042; 250 3043

Senior Executive Officers
President — Benito Cantalapiedra
Debt Capital Markets / Fixed Income
Department: Investors Department
Other — Carlos Santos Director, Investments & Treasury ☎ **250 3059**
Department: Santander Securities
Tel: +1 787 759 5330 Fax: +1 787 759 5366
Other — Carlos Pou Vice President ☎ **759 5335**
Carmen Vallecillo Trader ☎ **759 5382**

Citibank NA

Citibank Centre, 1 Citibank Drive, Hato Rey, San Juan 00926
PO Box 364106, Hato Rey, San Juan 00936-4106
Tel: 753 5555 Fax: 766 3697

Senior Executive Officers
Country Corporate Officer — Arthur Zeller ☎ **766 3700**
Treasurer — Felix Vega ☎ **766 3970**
Debt Capital Markets / Fixed Income
Head of Debt Capital Markets — Stuart Lasson ☎ **776 1174**
Foreign Exchange
Global Head — Joanna Arias ☎ **766 1414**

Merrill Lynch & Co Inc — Full Branch Office

One Banco Popular Center, Munoz Rivera Avenue, Hato Rey, San Juan 00918
Tel: 754 5454 Fax: 753 1401

Senior Executive Officers
Vice President — Anador Rodriguez
Associate Vice President — Sergio Santana

Paine Webber Incorporated of Puerto Rico — Full Branch Office

American International Plaza, Avenida Muñoz Rivera #250, Penthouse Floors, Hato Rey, San Juan 00918
Tel: 250 3600 Fax: 250 3691

Senior Executive Officers
Chairman — Mark B Sutton
President — Miguel A Ferrer
Executive Vice President — Eugenio S Belaval
Executive Vice President — Carlos V Ubinas

PUERTO RICO (+1 787)   www.euromoneydirectory.com

Samuel A Ramirez & Company
Head Office

Formerly known as: Clark Melvin Securities Corporation
Ponce de León 207, Hato Rey, San Juan 00918
PO Box 36289, San Juan, 00936-2589
Tel: 759 7070 **Fax:** 767 7913

Senior Executive Officers
Vice President, Public Relations   Iris Rivera

QATAR
(+974)

Qatar Central Bank
Central Bank

Alternative trading name: Qatar Monetary Agency
PO Box 1234, Doha
Tel: 456 456 **Swift:** QMAG QA QA

Senior Executive Officers
Governor   Abdulla Al-Attiya
Deputy Governor   Abdulla Al-Thani
Treasurer   Hassan Al-Khal
Secretary   Eissa Al-Mannai

Others (Senior Executives)
Chief Cashier   Ali Kumbar
Head, Bank Licensing; Head, Banking   Moajab Al-Khal
Supervision
Head, Economics & Statistics   Abdulla Al-Mulla
Head, Reserves Management   Hassan Al-Khal

Foreign Exchange
Head of Foreign Exchange   Hassan Al-Baker

Settlement / Clearing
Head of Settlement / Clearing   Ahmed Al-Obaidaly

Administration
Head of Administration   Ahmed Abdul Rab

Technology & Systems
                                        Hashim Al-Sada

Public Relations
                                        Ahmed Khalaf

ANZ Grindlays Bank Limited
Full Branch Office

Rayyan Road, Doha
PO Box 2001, Doha
Tel: 418 222 **Fax:** 428 077 **Telex:** 4209 GRNDLY DH **Swift:** GRND QA QX

Senior Executive Officers
Chief Operating Officer   G F Fernandes ☏ **362 541**
Treasurer   B M Sidhique ☏ **420 521**
General Manager   J F Murray ☏ **425 466**
International Division   G J Twitcher ☏ **426 356**

Others (Senior Executives)
Private Bank Middle East   Mohd Al Okar *General Manager* ☏ **410 515**

The British Bank of the Middle East

810 Abdulla Bin Jassim Street, Doha
PO Box 57, Doha
Tel: 335 271 **Fax:** 416 353; 416 593 **Telex:** 4204 BBME DH **Swift:** BBME QA QX **Reuters:** BBMQ

Senior Executive Officers
Chief Executive Officer   C M Meares ☏ **422 646** ✉ **436 794**

1240   Euromoney Directory 1999

www.euromoneydirectory.com					QATAR (+974)

The Commercial Bank Of Qatar Limited (QSC)   Head Office

Grand Hamad Avenue, PO Box 3232, Doha
Tel: 490 222 Fax: 438 182 Telex: 4351 TEJARI DH Swift: CBQA QA QA Email: cbqitech@qatar.net.qa
Reuters: CBQQ Cable: BANKTEJARI
Website: www.cbqbank.com

Senior Executive Officers
Chairman   Ali Bin Jabor Al Thani
Deputy Chairman   Abdullah bin Khaufa Al Attiyah
Managing Director   Hussain Alfardan
General Manager   Timothy Nunan ☎ **490 253**

Others (Senior Executives)
Deputy General Manager   Mohammed Mandani ☎ **490 256**
Corporate Banking   Salah Jaidah *Assistant General Manager* ☎ **490 231**

General-Lending (DCM, SL)
Head of Corporate Banking   Salah Jaidah *Assistant General Manager* ☎ **490 231**

General-Investment
Head of Investment   Mazin Shakarchi *Assistant General Manager* ☎ **490 254**

General - Treasury
Head of Treasury   Mazin Shakarchi *Assistant General Manager* ☎ **490 254**

Settlement / Clearing
Operations   Alan Rea *Senior Manager* ☎ **490 261**

Doha Bank Limited

Grand Hamad Avenue, PO Box 3818, Doha
Tel: 456 600 Fax: 416 631; 410 625 Telex: 4534 DOHBNK DH Swift: DOHB QA QA Reuters: DBDQ
Cable: DOHABANK
Website: www.dohabank.com

Senior Executive Officers
Chairman   Fahd Bin Mohd Bin Jabor Al Thani
Managing Director   Abdul Rahman Bin Moh Al-Thani
General Manager   Mohammad M Jamjourn
International Division   Mohamed Atiq *Deputy General Manager*

Others (Senior Executives)
Financial Controller   Emad Zubi

Settlement / Clearing
Operations   Ahmed Karrar Karrar *Assistant General Manager*

Asset Management
Other (Asset Management)
Domestic Investment   Ismail Mousa *Senior Executive Manager*
    Maher Al Duwiek *Assistant General Manager*
International Investment   Abdul Latif Al Meer *Assistant General Manager*
Invest. Analysts & Control   Abdul Rahman Mustafa *Senior Executive Manager*

Other Departments
Correspondent Banking   Osman Sharaf

Administration
Public Relations
    Ibrahim AhmedHussain Al Sada

Accounts / Audit
Internal Audit   Choudhry Wasi *Executive Manager*

Other (Administration)
Domestic Investment & Marketing   Maher Al Duwiek *Assistant General Manager*
Foreign Relations   Abdul Latif Al Meer *Assistant General Manager*
Finance & Administration   Ahmed Karrar Karrar *Assistant General Manager*
Banking Services   Ali Al-Zubaid *Assistant General Manager*
Domestic Investment & Marketing   Ismail Mousa *Senior Executive Manager*
Marketing Bank Services   Mohamed Al Ansari *Senior Executive Manager*
Dubai Office Manager   Nabil Osman *Senior Executive Manager*
Administration & Training   Hussain Al Fadalla *Executive Manager*
Real Estate Dept.   Sabah Bader *Executive Manager*

QATAR (+974)　　　　　　　　www.euromoneydirectory.com

Qatar Islamic Bank

Grand Hamad Avenue, PO Box 559, Doha
Tel: 409 409; 409 205 Fax: 412 700; 409 509 Telex: 5177 ISAMB DH Swift: QISB QA QAA

Senior Executive Officers
Chairman & President — Khalid Al Sowaidi ☎ 424 234 🖷 409 305
Chief Executive Officer — Marwan Awad *General Manager* ☎ 439 498 🖷 409 307
Financial Director — Ahmed Karrar *Finance Director & COO* ☎ 409 330 🖷 412 700
Treasurer — Ismail Umlai ☎ 409 393 🖷 350 306
International Division — Abdul Latif Al Meer

Others (Senior Executives)
Vice Chairman — Abdulla Al Mirre
Board Member — Saad Al Sabah
Mohammad Al Mana
Abdul Rahman Abdul Ghani
Abdulla Emadi
Abdullatif Al-Mahmoud
Mohamed Al Mohanadi
Abdul Rahman Abdul Ghani

Qatar National Bank SAQ — Head Office

PO Box 1000, Doha
Tel: 407 407 Fax: 413 753 Telex: 4064 QATBK DH Swift: QNBA QA QA Reuters: QNBQ Telex: 4212 QATBK DH
Telex: 4357 QATBK DH
Website: www.qatarbank.com

Senior Executive Officers
Chairman — Yousef Hussain Kamal
Vice Chairman — Saleh M Abu Dawood Al Muhanadi
Chief Executive Officer — John P Finigan *General Manager & Chief Executive Officer* ☎ 430 240 🖷 438 349
Deputy General Manager — Saeed Bin Abdullah Al Misnad ☎ 414 529 🖷 415 019
International Division — Mohamed Al Sheeb *Senior Manager* ☎ 407 329 🖷 410 418

General-Lending (DCM, SL)
Head of Corporate Banking — Ihsan Rashid *Corporate Banking* ☎ 407 321 🖷 431 036
Ali Ahmed Al Kuwari *AGM, Retail Banking* ☎ 413 790 🖷 413 889

General-Investment
Head of Investment — Waleed Al Mosallam *Manager, Capital Markets* ☎ 432 402 🖷 414 943

General - Treasury
Head of Treasury — Peter Clarke *Assistant General Manager* ☎ 432 444 🖷 414 943

Debt Capital Markets / Fixed Income
Head of Debt Capital Markets — Waleed Al Mosallam *Manager, Capital Markets* ☎ 432 402 🖷 414 943

Equity Capital Markets
Domestic Equities
Head of Trading — Yousef Sulaiti *Equity Trader* ☎ 355 220 🖷 355 330
Abdul Majid Lari *Equity Trader* ☎ 355 220 🖷 355 330
Abdullah-Sadek Suwaila *Equity Trader* ☎ 355 220 🖷 355 330

Money Markets
Money Markets - General
David Axtell *Head, Dealing Room* ☎ 407 295 🖷 414 744
Wafa Kassab *Senior Dealer* ☎ 432 402 🖷 414 943
Mariamma Thomas *Dealer* ☎ 432 402 🖷 414 943

Foreign Exchange
Regional Head — Vijay Valabhdas *FX Dealer* ☎ 432 407 🖷 414 943
Head of Institutional Sales — Adel Mustafawi *Manager* ☎ 432 444 🖷 414 943
Corporate Sales — Khaleel Abdul-Malik *Corporate* ☎ 432 444 🖷 414 943
Sadek Awouda *Corporate* ☎ 432 444

Risk Management
Fixed Income Derivatives / Risk Management
Country Head — David Axtell *Head, Dealing Room* ☎ 407 295 🖷 414 744

Settlement / Clearing
Operations — Krishna Ranganathan *Senior Manager, Operations* ☎ 413 126 🖷 439 727
Keith Warden *AGM, Financial Control* ☎ 434 957 🖷 438 983

Other Departments
Private Banking
Economic Research
Administration
Head of Administration

Technology & Systems
Information Systems
Legal / In-House Counsel
Legal Department
Accounts / Audit
Internal Audit

Khaled Bin Ahmed Al Thani *AGM, Private Banking*
Mohamed F Moabi *Economics & Planning* [T] **434 685**

Nasser Mohamed Al Naemi *Assistant General Manager* [T] **410 139**
[F] **439 727**

Marwan Marouf Mahmoud [T] **414 092** [F] **433 943**

Mussab El Hadi Babiker *Senior Manager* [T] **418 194** [F] **430 792**

Mustafa Mohamed Osman *Senior Manager* [T] **413 876** [F] **438 612**

Standard Chartered Bank   Full Branch Office
Box 29, Abdullah Bin Jasim Street, Doha
Tel: 414 252 **Fax:** 413 739

Senior Executive Officers
Managing Director / General Manager   Nick Ellison [T] **414 248**
Relationship Manager

Rehan Riaz [T] **415 679**

ROMANIA
(+40)

The National Bank of Romania   🏛 Central Bank
25 Lipscani Street, 70421 Bucharest 3
Tel: (1) 313 0410 **Fax:** (1) 312 3831 **Telex:** 11136 BNBUCR

Banca Agricola SA
3 Smârdan Street, 70006 Bucharest
Tel: (1) 613 5520; (1) 312 6900 **Fax:** (1) 312 6306; (1) 310 4680 **Telex:** 11622 BANAG R **Swift:** BKAG RO BU
Reuters: BABR
General **Telex:** 11709 BANAG R; **Capital Markets Division Tel:** 614 3001

Senior Executive Officers
President
Financial Director
Treasurer
International Division
Others (Senior Executives)

Liviu Adrian Istrate [T] **614 4260**
Marin Ilie *Managing Director* [T] **315 1014** [F] **323 8449**
Teodor Stanescu *Managing Director* [T] **312 6833** [F] **614 7347**
Alexandru Zaharia *Managing Director* [T] **312 6309**

Gheorghe Mateescu *First Vice President* [T] **312 6300**
Liviu Marica *Vice President* [T] **615 5303**
Gheorghe Muresam *Vice President* [T] **614 4412**
Iulius Cezar Petredeanu *Vice President* [T] **614 4562**
Vasile Tánásoiu *Vice President* [T] **613 9041**

General-Investment
Head of Investment
Foreign Exchange
Head of Foreign Exchange
Risk Management
Tel: 315 1666 **Fax:** 315 1672
Head of Risk Management
Other Departments
Correspondent Banking
Administration
Legal / In-House Counsel

Public Relations

Gheorghe Matei *Managing Director* [T] **614 5884**

Alexandru Bica *Managing Director* [T] **312 6801**

Marius Matache *Managing Director* [T] **315 1666**

Yolanda Oncescu *Executive Director* [T] **312 6801** [F] **312 6304**

Mihai Ene *Managing Director* [T] **613 9124** [F] **315 3610**

Lucian Groza *Managing Director* [T] **312 6835** [F] **310 4680**

ROMANIA (+40)   www.euromoneydirectory.com

Banca Bucuresti SA
Head Office

Piata Gh, Cantacuzino 6, 70203 Bucharest
PO Box 13-128, Bucharest
Tel: (1) 210 9042; (1) 210 9043 **Fax:** (1) 210 8284 **Telex:** 12648 BBRU R **Swift:** BUCU RO BU **Reuters:** BUCB

Senior Executive Officers
President   Panagis Vourloumis
First Vice President   Radu Gratian Ghetea
Chief Executive Officer   Ioannis Brintakis *Vice President*
Financial Director   Andreas Marangoudakis *Vice President* ☏ **210 9692**

Syndicated Lending
Global Head   Andreas Marangoudakis *Vice President* ☏ **210 9692**

Loan-Related Activities
Trade Finance   Andreas Marangoudakis *Vice President* ☏ **210 9692**

Money Markets
Global Head   Bogdan Mihai *Head of Treasury* ☏ **210 2667**

Foreign Exchange
Global Head   Bogdan Mihai *Head of Treasury* ☏ **210 2667**

Administration
Technology & Systems
    Elena Vlaicu *Manager* ☏ **210 8794**

Banca Comerciala Romana
Full Branch Office

Alternative trading name: Romanian Commercial Bank SA
5 Regina Elisabeta, 70348 Bucharest
Tel: (1) 312 6185; (1) 312 4104 **Fax:** (1) 312 1463 **Telex:** 10893 BCROM **Swift:** RNCB RO BU **Reuters:** RCBB
Telex: 10903 **Telex:** 10983 **Telex:** 111124

Senior Executive Officers
President   Ion Ghica ☏ **312 1678**
Vice President   Stanel Ghencea
Vice President   Gheorghe Irimiea
Vice President   Valeriu Mosoeanu
Vice President   Ion Nitu
International Division   Emilian Radau

General-Lending (DCM, SL)
Head of Corporate Banking   Ilie Mihai *Credit Policies & Risk*
    Elvira Moise *Credit I*
    Niculae Balan *Credit II*

General - Treasury
Head of Treasury   Marian Miclea

Debt Capital Markets / Fixed Income
Global Head   Rasvan Radu

Foreign Exchange
FX Traders / Sales People
Foreign Currency Credits   Elena Dinu

Settlement / Clearing
Settlement (General)   Ion Matei *Non-Commercial Settlements*
    Sonia Ghica *Commercial Settlements*
Operations   Victor Juganaru *Workout Division*
    Ionel Mihail Cetateanu *Strategy & Studies*

Other Departments
Cash Management   Marin Treapat *Cash Transactions*

Administration
Head of Administration   Gheorghe Vládoi

Technology & Systems
Information Technology   Antoaneta Petrescu

Legal / In-House Counsel
    Elisabeta Burdus

Accounts / Audit
General Accounting   Nerina Petrescu
Foreign Transaction Accounting   Mariuca Vasile

www.euromoneydirectory.com   ROMANIA (+40)

Other (Administration)
Marketing   Mariean Busca
Organization & Human Resources   Mihai Alexe
Branch Management   Petru Popescu
Premises & Investments   Ion Laiu
Control   Dan Mogos

Banca de Credit si Dezvoltare Romexterra SA   Head Office

21 Piata Trandafirilor, 4300 Targu Mures
Tel: (65) 166 640; (65) 166 641 **Fax:** (65) 166 047; (65) 166 648 **Telex:** 65304 ROMEXT R **Email:** rext@teddy.netsoft.ro
Reuters: REXT

Senior Executive Officers
Chairman   Ioan Albu
Chief Executive Officer   Vasile Rosca *Deputy Chairman*
Financial Director   Viorica Lörinczi *Executive Manager* **166 643**
Chief Operating Officer   Elena Ionita *Executive Manager* **166 642**
Treasurer   Vasile Rosca *Deputy Chairman*
Senior Manager   Nicolae Pastor **166 646**
General Secretary   Sabin Popoviciu
International Division   Emilian Tepelus *Senior Officer* **166 644**

Debt Capital Markets / Fixed Income
Head of Fixed Income   Nicolae Pastor *Senior Manager* **166 646**

Government Bonds
Head of Trading   Vasile Rosca *Deputy Chairman* **166 640**

Libor-Based / Floating-Rate Products
FRN Sales   Viorica Lörinczi *Executive Manager* **166 643**

Equity Capital Markets
Tel: 166 642
Head of Equity Capital Markets   Elena Ionita *Executive Manager* **166 642**

Domestic Equities
Head of Trading   Maria Titiu *Officer* **166 644**

Syndicated Lending
Tel: 166 646
Head of Syndication   Nicolae Pastor *Senior Manager* **166 646**

Money Markets
Tel: 166 644
Head of Money Markets   Adriana Prunea *Senior Officer* **166 644**

Wholesale Deposits
Marketing   Cornelia Serb *Officer* **166 644**

Foreign Exchange
Tel: 166 644
Head of Foreign Exchange   Emilian Tepelus *Senior Officer* **166 644**

Risk Management
Head of Risk Management   Ioan Albu *Chairman*

Settlement / Clearing
Head of Settlement / Clearing   Veronica Ioja *Senior Officer* **166 641**

Other Departments
Chief Credit Officer   Ioan Sampalean *Officer* **166 646**
Correspondent Banking   Emilian Tepelus *Senior Officer* **166 644**

Administration
Head of Marketing   Cornelia Serb *Officer* **166 644**

Technology & Systems
    Aurel Munteanu *Senior Officer* **166 979**

Legal / In-House Counsel
    Andronic Alb *Legal Counsellor*

Public Relations
    Iuliana Stefanescu *Officer*

ROMANIA (+40)

Banca de Export-Import a României
Head Office

Alternative trading name: Eximbank of Romania
15 Splaiul Independentei Street, Sector 5, 761042 Bucharest
Tel: (1) 336 6162 **Fax:** (1) 336 6163 **Telex:** 12575 EXIMTR **Swift:** EXIM RO BU **Email:** stragcom@snmail.softnet.ro

Senior Executive Officers
Chairman of the Board & CEO   Mihai Bogza [T] 336 0743 [F] 336 6176
Financial Director   Dan Gabriel Mihut *Director* [T] 336 1885 [F] 336 6169
International Division   Cezar Moldoveanu *Head of Department* [T] 336 4187

Others (Senior Executives)
Director Foreign Loans   Elena Ionescu *Director* [T] 336 4181 [F] 336 6171
Director Strategy & Banking Communications   Adrian Burinaru [T] 336 4187 [F] 336 6380

Syndicated Lending
Loan-Related Activities
Trade Finance   Ioana Pantelimon *Deputy Manager* [T] 336 1985
Project Finance   Silvia Tanasie *Director* [T] 336 4171 [F] 336 6180

Money Markets
Head of Money Markets   Octav Scridon [T] 336 1985 [F] 336 6179

Foreign Exchange
Head of Foreign Exchange   Octav Scridon [T] 336 1985 [F] 336 6179

Settlement / Clearing
Head of Settlement / Clearing   Elena Ionescu *Director* [T] 336 4181 [F] 336 6171
Operations   Cornelia Hotaranci [T] 336 1985 [F] 336 6171

Asset Management
Head   Claudia Alicus *Deputy Manager* [T] 336 1985 [F] 336 6171

Other Departments
Correspondent Banking   Emilia Aioanei [T] 336 1985 [F] 336 6171
Cash Management   Cristina Rada [T] 336 1985 [F] 336 6171

Administration
Technology & Systems
                                  Nicoleta Macovei [T] 336 4170 [F] 336 6167

Legal / In-House Counsel
                                  Jana Popovici *Director* [T] 336 1883 [F] 336 6186

Accounts / Audit
                                  Doina Matei *Director* [T] 336 1987 [F] 336 6188

Banca Romana Pentru Dezvoltare

Alternative trading name: Romanian Bank for Development
4 Doamnei Street, Sector 3, 70016 Bucharest
Tel: (1) 313 3200 **Fax:** (1) 313 7384; (1) 313 9600 **Telex:** 11289 BRDSA **Swift:** BRDE RO BU **Reuters:** RBDB

Senior Executive Officers
Chairman   Bogdan Baltazar [T] 315 8909 [F] 312 1562
Financial Director   Ion Petre *Director* [T] 314 9589
Treasurer   Ioan Marzac *Director* [T] 613 6891

Others (Senior Executives)
                                  Petre Bunescu *Vice President* [T] 613 0378 [F] 312 1563
                                  Ioan Niculescu *Vice President* [T] 312 3424 [F] 310 3268
                                  Nicolae Boeti *Vice President* [T] 312 3204 [F] 312 3411
                                  Marcela Trandafir *Vice President* [T] 311 1639 [F] 3103268

Banca Turco Romana

Alternative trading name: BTR
16 Ion Canpineanu Street, Sector 1, Bucharest
Tel: (1) 312 3143; (1) 314 0040 **Fax:** (1) 311 1732; (1) 315 1783 **Telex:** 12400 **Swift:** BTRC RO BU **Reuters:** TRBR
Telex: 12404

Senior Executive Officers
Chairman & CEO   Levent Yurukoglu

General - Treasury
Head of Treasury   Cristian Dumitrescu *EVP, Treasury & Correspondent Banking*

www.euromoneydirectory.com　　　　　　　　　　　ROMANIA (+40)

Debt Capital Markets / Fixed Income
Department: Capital Markets
Bonds - General
　　　　　　　　　Simona Constantinescu *Head of Department*

Money Markets
Money Markets - General
　　　　　　　　　Bogdan Gherghe *Chief Dealer*

Foreign Exchange
FX Traders / Sales People
　　　　　　　　　Bogdan Gherghe *Chief Dealer*

Settlement / Clearing
Operations
　　　　　　　　　Figen Yalcinkaya Cetin *EVP, International Operations*

Other Departments
Correspondent Banking
　　　　　　　　　Sorina Aioanei *Director, Correspondent Banking*

Administration
Head of Marketing
　　　　　　　　　Murat Koncavar *EVP, Marketing & Credits*

Accounts / Audit
　　　　　　　　　Sinan Culha *EVP, Accounting & Internal Audit*

The Chase Manhattan Bank　　　　　　　　　　Full Branch Office
42-44 Vasile Lascar Street, 70212 Bucharest II
PO Box 13-109, Bucharest
Tel: (1) 210 7646 **Fax:** (1) 210 3137; (1) 211 3176 **Telex:** 11572

Senior Executive Officers
Chief Executive Officer　　　　Miray Muminoglu *Senior Country Officer*
Financial Director　　　　　　Sorin Anghel *Senior Finance Officer*
Chief Operating Officer　　　　Murat Kavurga *Senior Operations Officer*
Executive Secretary　　　　　　Mirela Stanciulescu

Citibank Romania SA　　　　　　　　　　　　Full Branch Office
8, Iancu de Hunedoara Blvd, BL H3, 2 & 3 Floors, 712042 Bucharest
Tel: (1) 210 1850; (1) 311 0061 **Fax:** (1) 210 1854; (1) 210 0659 **Telex:** 111 61 CITIB R

Senior Executive Officers
President　　　　　　　　　　Z Turek ☎ **311 0088** 🖷 **210 0659**
Financial Director　　　　　　Janet Heckman ☎ **230 0567**
Chief Operating Officer　　　　Lucky Jayaratne ☎ **230 0565**

Risk Management
Country Head　　　　　　　　Z Turek *President* ☎ **311 0088** 🖷 **210 0659**

Other Departments
Correspondent Banking　　　　Janet Heckman ☎ **230 0567**

Administration
Technology & Systems
　　　　　　　　　Pierre Olaru *IT Manager* ☎ **210 1850**

Compliance
　　　　　　　　　Anca Bocanici ☎ **210 1850**

Daewoo Bank (Romania) SA　　　　　　　　　Head Office
International Business Center, Bv Carol I, 34-36, I Floor, Bucharest Sector 2
Tel: (1) 250 5711 **Fax:** (1) 250 5831; (1) 250 5832 **Telex:** 11375 DWBFX R **Swift:** DARO RO BU **Reuters:** DAEW

Senior Executive Officers
President　　　　　　　　　　Yong-Il Ma ☎ **250 5755**
Vice President　　　　　　　　Bum-Shik Bae ☎ **250 5758**
Vice President　　　　　　　　Gheorghe Cristescu ☎ **250 5761**
Senior Director　　　　　　　Yong-Woon Kook ☎ **250 5756**
Administration Manager　　　　Jae-Bok Ahn ☎ **250 5754**

Syndicated Lending
Head of Origination　　　　　Diana Bonciu *Loan Inspector* ☎ **250 6745**
Head of Trading　　　　　　　Bum-Shik Bae *Vice President* ☎ **250 5758**

ROMANIA (+40)   www.euromoneydirectory.com

Daewoo Bank (Romania) SA (cont)
Money Markets
Head of Money Markets   Bum-Shik Bae *Vice President* ☏ 250 5758
Domestic Commercial Paper
Head of Sales   Augustin Razasanu *Chief Dealer* ☏ 250 6704
Foreign Exchange
Head of Foreign Exchange   Bum-Shik Bae *Vice President* ☏ 250 5758
Head of Institutional Sales   Augustin Razasanu *Chief Dealer* ☏ 250 6704
Corporate Sales   Yong-Woon Kook *Senior Director* ☏ 250 5756
FX Traders / Sales People
    Lucian Dode *Dealer* ☏ 250 6704
Settlement / Clearing
Head of Settlement / Clearing   Mihaela Piciorus *Manager* ☏ 250 6744
Country Head   Petre Ionescu *Country Manager*
Operations   Diana Istrate ☏ 250 2775
Other Departments
Correspondent Banking   Laura Costache *Officer*
Administration
Technology & Systems
    Razvan Ghetea *Manager*
Legal / In-House Counsel
    Matei Giugariu *Legal Advisor*
Public Relations
    Camelia Adam *Marketing Officer*

Eco-Invest Brd SA   Subsidiary Company

13/17 Boulevard Corneliu Coposu, Bloc 104, 3rd District, 70091 Bucharest
Tel: (1) 322 4941; (1) 321 0072 **Fax:** (1) 321 0068
Senior Executive Officers
Financial Director   Anca Fadi *Deputy General Manager* ☏ 321 2129
Treasurer   Maria Zamfiroiu *Head of Economics Division*

European Bank for Reconstruction & Development

Representative Office

38, Jean Louis Calderon Street, Sector 2, Bucharest 2
Tel: (1) 312 2232 **Fax:** (1) 312 2233
Senior Executive Officers
Resident Representative   Salvadore Candido

ING Barings   Full Branch Office

11-13 Kiseleff Sos, 71268 Bucharest 1
PO Box 2-208, 71268 Bucharest
Tel: (1) 222 1600 **Fax:** (1) 222 1401 **Telex:** 10299 INGRO R **Swift:** ING BRO BU
Senior Executive Officers
Chief Executive Officer   Anthony J J M van der Heijden *Country Manager*
Chief Operating Officer   Hans M Abma *AGM & Manager, Operations*
Debt Capital Markets / Fixed Income
Country Head   Misu Negritoiu *Manager, Investment Banking*
Equity Capital Markets
Country Head   Misu Negritoiu *Manager, Investment Banking*
Syndicated Lending
Head of Origination; Head of Syndication   Mihaela Burtoiu *Manager, Capital Markets*
Money Markets
Domestic Commercial Paper
Head of Origination   Mihaela Burtoiu *Manager, Capital Markets*
Risk Management
Country Head   John Rietbergen *Risk Manager*

www.euromoneydirectory.com RUSSIA (+7)

Corporate Finance / M&A Advisory
Country Head Misu Negritoiu *Manager, Investment Banking*
Global Custody
Country Head Hendrik Moorrees *Manager, Custody Services*
Administration
Technology & Systems
  Gabriel Diamandopol *EDP Manager*
Legal / In-House Counsel
  Luminita Anghel *Legal & Loan Documentation Officer*
Public Relations
  Ioana Biro *Executive Secretary*
Other (Administration)
Human Resources Daniela Gămulescu *Manager*

London Forfaiting Company plc
Representative Office
World Trade Centre Bucharest, Unit 2.02, 2 Boulevard Expozitiei, Bucharest 1
Tel: (1) 224 2429 **Fax:** (1) 224 2421
Senior Executive Officers
Representative Chris Rogers
Others (Senior Executives)
  Cristina Dumitrescu *Manager*
  Dana Buriman *Assistant Manager*

Société Générale
11 Strada Ion Cîmpineanu, Sector 1, Bucharest
Tel: (1) 311 1640; (1) 311 1730 **Fax:** (1) 312 0026 **Telex:** 10651 SOGEBR **Swift:** SOGE RO BU **Reuters:** SOBU
Senior Executive Officers
Managing Director / General Manager Caude Soule

RUSSIA
(+7)

Central Bank of the Russian Federation
Central Bank
Formerly known as: State Bank of the USSR
ul Neglinnaya 12, 103016 Moscow
Tel: (095) 928 6676 **Fax:** (095) 921 6890 **Telex:** 411283 GB SU **Email:** webmaster@cbr.ru
Website: www.cbr.ru

Senior Executive Officers
Chairman	Sergey K Dubinin **924 0321**
First Deputy Chairman	Sergey V Alexashenko **923 1641**
First Deputy Chairman	Andrey A Kozlov **923 0416**
First Deputy Chairman	Arnold V Voilukov **923 0908**
Deputy Chairman	Denis A Kiseliov **921 6836**
Deputy Chairman	Nikolai V Egorov
Deputy Chairman	Alexander V Turbanov **921 7439**
Deputy Chairman	Alexander A Khandruev **928 8328**
Deputy Chairman	Konstantin D Lubenchenko **921 8091**
Deputy Chairman	Alexander I Potemkin **921 7763**
Deputy Chairman	Tatyana K Artiomova **925 8545**

Others (Senior Executives)
Head, General Economic Department	Nadezhda Yu Ivanova
Head, Foreign operations	Alexander I Potemkin *Deputy Chairman* **921 7763**
Head, Cash Issuance	Alexander V Yurov **747 4180**
Head, Bank Licensing	Olga K Prokofieva **921 5600**
Head, Banking Supervision	Alexey Yu Simanovsky **929 4774**
Head, Budget & Extra Budgetary Funds	Natalia A Pavlova **929 4554**
Head, Credit Institutions Supervision	Dmitry Yu Budakov **925 3231**
Head, Open Market Operations	Konstantion N Korishenko **928 5417**
Head, Foreign Relations	Alexander E Korshunov **921 7995**

RUSSIA (+7)   www.euromoneydirectory.com

Central Bank of the Russian Federation (cont)
Settlement / Clearing
Settlement (General)   Yury V Maltsev *Head, Settlement* ☎ **921 2876**
Other Departments
Economic Research   Vladimir N Smenkovsky *Head, Research, Information & Statistics*
☎ **921 8879**
Administration
Head of Administration   Valery B Bogdanov ☎ **924 6850**
Technology & Systems
Information & Technology Department   Tatyana S Matveeva ☎ **237 3185**
Head, Telecommunications   Mikhail Yu Senatorov ☎ **237 5684**
Accounts / Audit
Head, Accounting   Ludmila I Gudenko ☎ **924 3126**

Aljba Alliance   Head Office

3rd Frunzenskaya Street, 12, 119146 Moscow
Tel: (095) 252 0000 **Fax:** (095) 252 6868 **Telex:** (64) 911068 ALAL RU **Swift:** ALAL RU MM **Email:** webmaster@alal.ru
Reuters: ALAL; ALAM
Website: www.alal.ru

Senior Executive Officers
President   Igor Annenski
Financial Director   Olga Anokhina *Chief Accounting Officer*
Treasurer   Alexei Kozlov *Vice President*
Others (Senior Executives)
Head of Emerging Markets   Andrei Kareyev *Vice President*
General-Investment
Head of Investment   Andrei Kareyev *Vice President*
Debt Capital Markets / Fixed Income
Head of Fixed Income   Andrei Kareyev *Vice President*
Emerging Market Bonds
Head of Emerging Markets   Andrei Kareyev *Vice President*
Equity Capital Markets
Department: Aljba Alliance Capital Markets Limited Co
1/9 Kremlyovskaya Nab., Moscow
Head of Equity Capital Markets   Andrei Kareyev *Director General*
Money Markets
Head of Money Markets; Global Head   Alexei Kozlov *Vice President*
Foreign Exchange
Head of Foreign Exchange; Global Head   Alexei Kozlov *Vice President*
Settlement / Clearing
Head of Settlement / Clearing   Alexander Gorshkov *Head, International Settlements*
Other Departments
Correspondent Banking   Andrei Shalashnikoff *Head of Correspondent Banking*
Administration
Accounts / Audit
    Alexander Yakimov *Manager, Internal Audit & Tax Planning*

Avtobank   Head Office

Alternative trading name: Bank of Automobile Industry Development (The)
41 Lesnaya Street, 101514 Moscow
Tel: (095) 723 7733; (095) 956 1616 **Fax:** (095) 978 9214; (095) 978 6623 **Telex:** 412245 BOND RU
Swift: AVTB RU MM **Email:** kuznecop@avtobank.ru **Reuters:** AVBK **Bloomberg:** DEREZA **Cable:** 207796 VERSEL
Reuters: AVBM
Website: www.avtobank.ru

Senior Executive Officers
Chairman   Natalia Raevskaya ☎ **978 9412**
Treasurer   Vladimir Rashevsky *Head*
Others (Senior Executives)
Deputy Chairman   Irina Busheva
    Vera Kalashnikona

Others (Senior Executives) (cont)

Natalia Artemieva
Andrei Astakhov
Yury Koval *Deputy Chairman*

General-Lending (DCM, SL)
Head of Corporate Banking   Natalia Kovovalova *General Manager* ☎ **723 7810**

Debt Capital Markets / Fixed Income
Tel: 723 7655 **Fax:** 978 2925
Head of Fixed Income   Konstantin Slavtsov

Government Bonds
Head of Sales   Igor Panin *Chief Trader* ☎ **723 7805**

Eurobonds
Head of Sales   Leonid Arkhipkin ☎ **723 7025**

Fixed-Income Repo
Head of Repo   Natalia Starikova ☎ **723 7636**

Fixed-Income Research
Head of Fixed Income   Konstantin Slavtsov

Equity Capital Markets
Tel: 723 7655 **Fax:** 978 2925
Head of Equity Capital Markets   Konstantin Slavtsov

Domestic Equities
Head of Sales   Konstantin Slavtsov

Equity Research
Head of Equity Research   Konstantin Slavtsov

Equity Repo / Securities Lending
Head   Konstantin Slavtsov

Syndicated Lending
Tel: 723 7025 **Fax:** 234 9766
Head of Origination   Leonid Arkhipkin ☎ **723 7025**

Loan-Related Activities
Trade Finance; Project Finance   Valery Ratorznov *General Manager* ☎ **723 7672**

Money Markets
Fax: 978 5069

Wholesale Deposits
Head of Sales   Gleb Yusufovich

Foreign Exchange
Fax: 978 5069
Head of Foreign Exchange   Vladimir Rashevsky *Head*

Risk Management
Tel: 723 7015 **Fax:** 978 6927
Head of Risk Management   Oleg Samohvalov

Fixed Income Derivatives / Risk Management
Head of Sales   Victoria Dereza *Chief Trader* ☎ **723 7997**

Foreign Exchange Derivatives / Risk Management
Spot / Forwards Sales   Victoria Dereza *Chief Trader* ☎ **723 7997**

OTC Equity Derivatives
Sales   Victoria Dereza *Chief Trader* ☎ **723 7997**

OTC Commodity Derivatives
Head   Victoria Dereza

OTC Credit Derivatives
Head   Victoria Dereza *Chief Trader* ☎ **723 7997**

Exchange-Traded Derivatives
Head   Victoria Dereza *Chief Trader* ☎ **723 7997**

Settlement / Clearing
Tel: 723 7652 **Fax:** 956 1512
Head of Settlement / Clearing   Olga Skorobogatoka *General Manager*
Equity Settlement; Fixed-Income Settlement   Tatiana Lelechenko ☎ **723 7826**
Back-Office   Alexander Potadov *Deputy Head* ☎ **723 7669**

Other Departments
Chief Credit Officer   Michail Vinogradov *Head* ☎ **723 7960**
Correspondent Banking   Sergey Kovalyov *General Manager* ☎ **723 7673**

RUSSIA (+7)   www.euromoneydirectory.com

Avtobank (cont)
Administration
Head of Administration — Nokolai Antonov ☎ 723 7906
Technology & Systems
Vladimir Maskatov *Head* ☎ 723 7838
Legal / In-House Counsel
Maina Zaslavskaya *Head* ☎ 723 7823
Public Relations
Nikolai Popov *Head of Public Relations* ☎ 723 7865
Accounts / Audit
Audit — Artem Korolev ☎ 723 7811
Accounts — Eugenia Inyazeva *General Manager* ☎ 723 7082

Bank Austria (Moscow) LLC
Subsidiary Company

Bank Austria House, 1-st Kazachy per 9/1, 109017 Moscow
Tel: (095) 956 3000 **Fax:** (095) 956 3030 **Telex:** 413 700 BKAUM RU **Swift:** BKAU RU MM **Reuters:** BAUR

Senior Executive Officers
Chairman — Alejandro Eduardoff
Deputy Chairman — Elena I Sorochan

Others (Senior Executives)
Member of the Board — Alexander S Zhitnik
Commercial Banking — Charlotte Lechnitzky *Head*

General-Lending (DCM, SL)
Head of Corporate Banking — Garrett Pettinggell

General - Treasury
Head of Treasury — Peter Gabriel *Head of Treasury Division*

Risk Management
Head of Risk Management — Pierre Girault

Settlement / Clearing
Operations — Arnold Krassnitzer *Head of Controlling Division*

Other Departments
Private Banking — Alla Y Taratorina

Administration
Accounts / Audit
Chief Accountant — Tatyana F Tertishnikova

Other (Administration)
Human Resources — Svetlana Y Philippovich
Banking Operations Division — Alexander S Semyonov *Head*

Bank for Foreign Economic Affairs (Vnesheconombank)
Head Office

Alternative trading name: Vnesheconombank
9 Academic Sakharov Ave, 103810 Moscow B-78
Tel: (095) 207 1037 **Fax:** (095) 975 2143 **Telex:** 64, 412232 VEBX RU **Swift:** BFEA RU MM **Email:** postmaster@veb.ru
Press Service **Tel:** 208 4693

Senior Executive Officers
Chairman — A L Kostin
First Deputy Chairman — V A Dmitriev
First Deputy Chairman — N N Kosov

Bank for Foreign Trade
Head Office

Alternative trading name: Vneshtorgbank
16 Kuznetsky Most, 103031 Moscow
Tel: (095) 204 6441; (095) 929 8900 **Fax:** (095) 258 4781 **Telex:** 412362 BFTR RU **Swift:** VTB RU MM **Reuters:** VTBA; VTBG; VTBE; VTBR; VTBX
Website: www.vtb.ru

Senior Executive Officers
Chairman — Demitri V Tulin ☏ 234 0475
Deputy Chairman — Leonid A Anikeev

RUSSIA (+7)

Senior Executive Officers (cont)
Deputy Chairman — Alexander I Kozin
Deputy Chairman & CFO — Serguei I Kolotoukhine
Deputy Chairman — Alexander V Osiptsev
Deputy Chairman — Alexander G Rychenkov
Deputy Chairman — Mikhail A Sarafanov
Deputy Chairman — Sergei G Tatsi
Deputy Chairman — Boris I Sergeev
Deputy Chairman — Boris I Boulatov
Financial Director — Serguei I Kolotoukhine *Deputy Chairman & CFO*

Others (Senior Executives)
Member of the Board — Igor D Aksenov

General-Lending (DCM, SL)
Head of Corporate Banking — Maksim Y Balod
Richard Hopewell
Elena A Krasavtseva
Andrey G Shipilov

General-Investment
Head of Investment — Dmitri K Novikov
Elena N Serikova

General - Treasury
Head of Treasury — Yuri V Mityuk

Debt Capital Markets / Fixed Income
Head of Debt Capital Markets — Valery I Novikov

Equity Capital Markets
Head of Equity Capital Markets — Valery I Novikov

Settlement / Clearing
Head of Settlement / Clearing Operations — Galina E Ivanova *Head, International Settlements*
Andrey A Plionkin

Global Custody
Head of Global Custody — Dmitri L Mozgin *Senior General Manager* T 234 3488 F 956 6811

Other Departments
Proprietary Trading — Victor Y Ustinov
Correspondent Banking — Gavril N Agadzhanov
Economic Research — Sergey V Mytarev

Administration
Head of Marketing — Demitri V Tulin F **234 0475**

Legal / In-House Counsel
Legal — Nikolai M Chernyshov

Compliance
Natalia A Trubenkova *Head*

Public Relations
Ludmila S Khoudiakova

Accounts / Audit
Internal Audit — Alexander V Sobolev
Chief Accountant — Igor D Aksenov

Other (Administration)
Personnel — Nina V Slepniova
Research & Information — Ludmila S Khoudiakova
Regional Development Dept. — Dmitri A Chernev
Office of Financial Controller — Sergey D Sizov
Strategic & Financial Planning Dept — Alexander L Grzymalski
Denis L Mikhailov
Olga N Ignatieva

Bank Imperial
Head Office
40 Bolshaya Yakimanka Street, 117049 Moscow
Tel: (095) 737 3825 **Fax:** (095) 230 0200 **Telex:** 412093 IMPB SU **Swift:** IMPJ RU MM **Email:** common@imperial.ru

Senior Executive Officers
Chairman — Vladimir Forosenko

Euromoney Directory 1999 **1253**

RUSSIA (+7) www.euromoneydirectory.com

Bank of New York - Inter Maritime Bank, Geneva
Representative Office

Ul Tverskaya 9, Entrance 1, Suite 4, 103009 Moscow
Tel: (095) 956 1540 Fax: (095) 956 1542

Senior Executive Officers
Vice President   Vladimir Barsoukov

Banque Société Générale Vostok

9th Floor, Nikitski Pereoulok 5, 103009 Moscow
Tel: (095) 940 0815 Fax: (501) 994 0809 Swift: SOGE RU
Website: www.socgen.com

Bashcreditbank
Head Office

3/1 Ya Gashek Street, 150004 Ufa, Bashkortostan
Tel: (3472) 238 612 Fax: (3472) 235 835

Senior Executive Officers
Chairman   Rim Bakiev
President   Azat Kourmanaev

Debt Capital Markets / Fixed Income
Domestic Government Bonds
Head of Trading   Rustem Khazipov

Equity Capital Markets
Domestic Equities
Head of Sales   Oleg Chalov

Foreign Exchange
Head of Trading   Oleg Masutin

Risk Management
Global Head   Ivan Lebedev

Other Departments
Commodities / Bullion   Amir Afanasiev *Head of Bullion*
Private Banking   Alexander Kapustin
Correspondent Banking   Mikhail Smirnov

Administration
Legal / In-House Counsel
Advisor   Faizi Ghizatullin

Public Relations
                                      Sergei Lobanov

Berliner Bank AG
Representative Office

1 Kasatschij Per 5, 109017 Moscow
Tel: (503) 956 9802 Fax: (503) 956 9803

Senior Executive Officers
Representative   Rolf Steinert

BNP-Dresdner Bank (ZAO)
Full Branch Office

30, Podsosensky per, 103062 Moscow
Tel: (095) 737 3450 Fax: (095) 737 3451 Telex: 412033 BNDBRU Swift: BNDB RU 2X MDS Reuters: BDMO

Senior Executive Officers
General Manager   Michel Sadarnac ⓣ **737 3452** Ⓕ **737 3461**
Deputy General Manager   Matthias Warnig ⓣ **737 3460** Ⓕ **737 3461**
International Division   Dany Barth *Head of International Division* ⓣ **737 3445** Ⓕ **737 3455**

General-Lending (DCM, SL)
Head of Corporate Banking   Volker den Duder *Head of Corporate Customers Division* ⓣ **737 3440**
                                      Ⓕ **737 3441**

General - Treasury
Head of Treasury   Ton van Kasteren ⓣ **737 3456** Ⓕ **737 3462**

Syndicated Lending
Other (Trade Finance)
Commodity Trade Finance		Florentin Trachsel *Head of Commodity, Trade Finance* ⬜ **737 3454**
		F **737 3441**

Risk Management
Head of Risk Management		Johannes Hack *Head of Credit* ⬜ **737 3443** F **737 3458**

BNP-Dresdner Bank (ZAO) — Subsidiary Company
Formerly known as: BNP-Dresdner Bank (ROSSIJA)
11 St Isaac Square, 190000 St Petersburg
PO Box 124, SF-53501 Lapeenranta Finland
Tel: (812) 325 9191 **Fax:** (812) 325 8870 **Telex:** 121086 BNPDB RU **Swift:** BNDB RU 2X **Reuters:** BDMO

Senior Executive Officers
President		Hans-Jurgen Stricker
Chief Executive Officer		Gilbert Caignan *Vice President*
Financial Director		Sergei Draganov
Chief Operating Officer		Werner Klinkmann *Head of Operations*
Treasurer		Ton Van Kasteren ⬜ **(095) 737 3450**
International Division		Alexander Konyshkov

Others (Senior Executives)
Chief Accountant		Dmitry Tyanutov *Chief Accountant*

General-Lending (DCM, SL)
Head of Corporate Banking		Felix Strehober *Head of Corporate Customers Division*

Relationship Manager
Corporate Customers		Volker Den Duden ⬜ **(095) 737 3450**

Syndicated Lending
Loan-Related Activities
Commodities Financing		Florentin Trachsel ⬜ **(095) 737 3450**

Settlement / Clearing
Back-Office		Irina Soboleva *Head*

Other Departments
Chief Credit Officer		Jens Schuker *Head of Credit*
Private Banking		Evgeny Lukyanov *Head of Customer Services*
Correspondent Banking		Tatiana Samoilova ⬜ **(095) 737 3450**

Administration
Technology & Systems
		Vladimir Martynov *Head*

Legal / In-House Counsel
		Natalia Rasskazova *Head of Legal Department*

Public Relations
		Irena Sotina

Accounts / Audit
		Dmitry Tyanutov *Chief Accountant*

Chase Manhattan Bank International — Subsidiary Company
1st Tverskaya-Yamskaya Street 23, 125047 Moscow
Tel: (095) 956 9393; (095) 956 9399 **Fax:** (095) 956 9366 **Telex:** 413912 CHASE SU

Senior Executive Officers
Others (Senior Executives)
Senior Country Officer		Murad Megalli *Senior Country Officer*

Citibank T/O — Full Branch Office
8-10 Gasheka Street, 125047 Moscow
Tel: (095) 258 6999 **Fax:** (095) 725 6600

Senior Executive Officers
President		David Amsell

The **WORLD'S LEADING** law magazine
dedicated to the business of international finance

IFLR

INTERNATIONAL FINANCIAL LAW REVIEW

Launched in 1982 as a specialist publication for lawyers serving the financial markets, IFLR provides unrivalled coverage of developments in international banking, commerce and finance. Every month, our team of journalists and international correspondents report on legal changes and innovations in banking, securities, project finance and M&A. IFLR now incorporates Asialaw, a sister publication, and gives subscribers enhanced Asian coverage from our Hong Kong desk.

Every issue of IFLR contains:
- World News
- Deals
- Features
- Surveys
- Country Reports
- Profiles
- International Briefings

Don't take our word for it:

"IFLR is clearly for practitioners. I like the way there are always articles on new subjects, so it remains fresh. I also like the in-house profiles in IFLR about the organisation of legal departments."
**Jean-Pierre Mattout, General Counsel
Banque Paribas**

"Essential reading for all financial lawyers, absolutely indispensable."
**Philip Wood, Head of Banking
Allen & Overy, London**

For a
free trial subscription
contact:
**Kate Colchester
Subscriptions Manager**
Tel: +44 171 779 8337 — Fax: +44 171 779 8790

www.euromoneydirectory.com   RUSSIA (+7)

Commerzbank AG
Representative Office
Office 9, 4 Mamonovski Pereulok, 103001 Moscow
Tel: (095) 209 6440; (095) 209 2866 Fax: (095) 200 0246 Telex: 413274 CBK SU

Senior Executive Officers
Representative   Wolfgang Haring

Dalrybbank
Head Office
51A Svetlansraya Street, 690600 Vladivostok
Tel: (4232) 228 550; (4232) 510 325 Fax: (4232) 516 180; (4232) 516 170 Telex: 213122 MRH RU Swift: CBFI RU 8V
Email: rybbank@online.ru Reuters: DALB

Senior Executive Officers
Chairman   Yuri Moskaltsov ☏ 224 640
General Director   Galina Belyaeva ☏ 228 550
Financial Director   Svetlana Fokina ☏ 225 525
Treasurer   Eugene Khromchenko *Head of Division* ☏ 516 171
International Division   Victor Varlamov *Deputy General Director* ☏ 510 625

Debt Capital Markets / Fixed Income
Tel: 510 620 Fax: 266 409
Head of Fixed Income   Valery Ovechkin *Senior Dealer* ☏ 510 620 ✉ andy@dalrybbank.ru

Domestic Government Bonds
Head of Sales   Alexander Gorelov ☏ 510 620
Head of Trading   Andrew Makhov

Fixed-Income Repo
Head of Repo   Vitaly Souslov

Equity Capital Markets
Department: Securities Department
Tel: 510 620 Fax: 516 171
Country Head   Andrew Sirenko *Trader*

Domestic Equities
Head of Sales   Vitaly Souslov
Head of Trading   Andrew Sirenko *Trader*

Money Markets
Department: Securities Division
Tel: 510 527 Fax: 266 409 Reuters: DALB
Head of Money Markets   Eugene Khromchenko *Head of Division* ☏ 516 171

Foreign Exchange
Tel: 510 620 Fax: 266 409 Reuters: DALB
Head of Foreign Exchange   Andrew Olejnik *Senior Dealer* ✉ andy@dalrybbank.ru
Head of Institutional Sales   Vladimir Potapov *Senior Dealer* ☏ 510 521

Settlement / Clearing
Department: Financial Division
Tel: 510 512 Fax: 510 512
Head of Settlement / Clearing   Yelena Shatokhina *Head of Division* ☏ 510 512
Fixed-Income Settlement   Eugene Belozerov *Head of Department* ☏ 516 176
Back-Office   Natalja Rogova *Head of Department* ☏ 510 512

Global Custody
Head of Global Custody   Eugene Khromchenko *Head of Division* ☏ 516 171

Other Departments
Chief Credit Officer   Eugenia Solomonova *Head of Division* ☏ 516 182
Correspondent Banking   Mikhail Neskoromniouk *Head of Department* ☏ 516 170
Cash Management   Galina Koslova *Chief Cashier* ☏ 265 618

Administration

Technology & Systems
    Aleksei Drobyshevsky *Department Director* ☏ 264 436

Legal / In-House Counsel
    Victor Borisenko ☏ 516 188

Accounts / Audit
    Valentina Krivosheeva *Chief Accountant* ☏ 516 175

RUSSIA (+7)

Deutsche Bank AG
Representative Office
ul Ostoshenka 23, 119034 Moscow
Tel: (095) 201 2988; (095) 201 4675 **Fax:** (095) 200 1227 **Telex:** 413073 DB SU

Deutsche Bank AG
Representative Office
101 Kanal Gribojedowa, 190000 St Petersburg
Tel: (812) 315 0216; (812) 315 0600 **Fax:** (812) 315 0655 **Telex:** 121607 DBSTP SU

DG BANK
Representative Office
ul Mytnaja 3, 117049 Moscow
Tel: (095) 230 2322 **Fax:** (095) 230 6303

Senior Executive Officers
Representative — Dieter Pinnow

East-West Investment Bank
Head Office
10 Povarskaya Street, 121069 Moscow
Tel: (501) 721 1000; (501) 721 1100 **Fax:** (501) 721 1020 **Telex:** 612396 **Swift:** EWIB RU MM
Email: marketing@ewib.com **Reuters:** EWIB
Website: www.ewib.com

Senior Executive Officers
Chairman, Board of Directors — Boris Fedorov ☎ 721 1155
Chairman, Executive Board — Alexander Doumnov ☎ 721 1010
Deputy Chairman, Executive Board — Gennady Zaitsev ☎ 721 1156
Deputy Chairman, Executive Board — Alexei Parfenenko ☎ 721 1021
Deputy Chairman, Executive Board — Alexander Shevelyov ☎ 721 1002
President & First Deputy Chairman, Executive Board — Vladimir Raevsky ☎ 721 1003
Financial Director — Anatoly Konyaev *Chief Accountant & Member, Executive Board* ☎ 721 1058

General-Lending (DCM, SL)
Head of Corporate Banking — Mark Shirokov *DGM, Financial Markets* ☎ 721 1022
Debt Capital Markets / Fixed Income
Asset-Backed Securities / Securitization
Global Head — Erlan Imanbaev *Manager, Securities Trading* ☎ 721 1027
Foreign Exchange
Global Head — Sergey Bobkov *Manager* ☎ 721 1023
Corporate Finance / M&A Advisory
Global Head — Dmitri Vlasov *DGM, Corporate Finance* ☎ 721 1035
Other Departments
Private Banking — Alexander Dobychin *Director, Retail & Private Banking* ☎ 721 1053
Correspondent Banking — Ivan Zotov *Manager* ☎ 721 1032
Economic Research — Vladimir Pozdniakov *Manager, Financial Analysis & Strategic Planning* ☎ 721 1075

Administration
Technology & Systems
Data Processing & Technology — Boris Suslov *General Manager* ☎ 721 1041
Public Relations — Anna Borzilova *Senior Expert* ☎ 721 1083

Energobank
Head Office
Karl Marx Street 43/10, 420015 Kazan
Tel: (8432) 384 422; (8432) 388 811 **Fax:** (8432) 384 422; (8432) 387 202 **Telex:** 224637 KREZ RU **Swift:** TRCB RU 2K
Email: post@energobank.ru
Website: www.energobank.ru

Senior Executive Officers
President — Vladimir Zaikin
Chief Executive Officer — Dmitriy Vagizov *Senior Vice President* ☎ 388 605

Senior Executive Officers (cont)
Chief Operating Officer　　　　　　　Nina Paranina *Chief Accountant* ☎ **389 907**
Treasurer　　　　　　　　　　　　　Irek Shamsiev ☎ **389 105**
International Division　　　　　　　Ildar Minnibayev ☎ **384 432**

Debt Capital Markets / Fixed Income
Government Bonds
Head of Sales; Head of Trading　　　Edward Vagizov ☎ **387 202**

Money Markets
Domestic Commercial Paper
Head of Sales　　　　　　　　　　　Edward Vagizov ☎ **387 202**
Head of Trading　　　　　　　　　　Albert Kildeev ☎ **385 606**

Foreign Exchange
Head of Foreign Exchange　　　　　Ildar Minnibayev ☎ **384 432**

FX Traders / Sales People
　　　　　　　　　　　　　　　　　Rustem Ismagilov *Dealer* ☎ **384 422**

Risk Management
Head of Risk Management　　　　　Dmitriy Vagizov *Senior Vice President* ☎ **388 605**

Settlement / Clearing
Head of Settlement / Clearing　　　Nina Paranina *Chief Accountant* ☎ **389 907**
Back-Office　　　　　　　　　　　　Ludmila Shlupkina *Head* ☎ **384 472**

Other Departments
Chief Credit Officer　　　　　　　　Oleg Gorokhov *Head, Credit Dept* ☎ **387 202**
Correspondent Banking　　　　　　Ildar Daminov ☎ **384 402**

Administration
Technology & Systems
　　　　　　　　　　　　　　　　　Alexey Mikhailik *Head, Information Technology* ☎ **387 393**

Public Relations
　　　　　　　　　　　　　　　　　Boris Leushin *Vice President* ☎ **318 173**

Accounts / Audit
　　　　　　　　　　　　　　　　　Rashid Mukhametrakhimov *Chief Auditor* ☎ **387 202**

European Bank for Reconstruction & Development
Representative Office

6th Floor, 8/10 Gasheka Street, 125047 Moscow
Tel: (503) 956 1111 **Fax:** (503) 956 1122

Senior Executive Officers
Resident Representative　　　　　　Neil Barison

European Bank for Reconstruction & Development
Representative Office

25 Nevsky-Prospekt, 191186 St Petersburg
Tel: (812) 326 2525 **Fax:** (812) 326 2526

Senior Executive Officers
Regional Representative　　　　　　Grigory Glazkov

European Bank for Reconstruction & Development
Representative Office

Room 404, 46 Verkhneportovaya Street, 690003 Vladivostok
Tel: (4232) 517 766 **Fax:** (4232) 517 767

Senior Executive Officers
Regional Representative　　　　　　Elena Danysh

RUSSIA (+7)   www.euromoneydirectory.com

European Bank for Reconstruction & Development
Representative Office

15A Gogolia Street, 620151 Yekaterinburg
Tel: (3432) 592 980; (3432) 569 212 **Fax:** (3432) 592 980

Senior Executive Officers
Regional Representative   Tatyana Yemboulaeva

The Export-Import Bank of Japan
Representative Office

Office No. 905, World Trade Center, Krasnopresnenskaya Nab 12, 123610 Moscow
Tel: (095) 258 1832; (095) 258 1835 **Fax:** (095) 258 1858

Senior Executive Officers
Chief Representative   Kensaku Kumabe

Garanti Bank Moscow
Subsidiary Company

5th Floor, Kosmodameanskaya nab 52, Buliding 1, 113054 Moscow
Tel: (095) 961 2500 **Fax:** (095) 961 2503; (095) 961 2502 **Telex:** 485370 GBMW RU **Swift:** GABM RU MM
Email: postmaster@garantim.ru **Reuters:** GBMR

Senior Executive Officers
Chairman   Y Akin Öngör ☎ **+90 (212) 285 4040**
President & CEO   Hülagü Özcan ☎ **961 2504**
Chief Operating Officer   Svat Albayrak *SVP, Operations* ☎ **961 2515**
Treasurer   Semih Tavli *SVP, Treasury* ☎ **961 2510**
International Division   Filiz Süyür *SVP, Financial Institutions* ☎ **961 2506**

General-Lending (DCM, SL)
Head of Corporate Banking   Derya Okutan *Senior Vice President* ☎ **961 2509**

Debt Capital Markets / Fixed Income
Department: Treasury Department
Head of Fixed Income   Semih Tavli *SVP, Treasury* ☎ **961 2510**

Government Bonds
Head of Sales   Semih Tavli *SVP, Treasury* ☎ **961 2510**

Domestic Government Bonds
Head of Sales   Semih Tavli *SVP, Treasury* ☎ **961 2510**

Eurobonds
Head of Sales   Semih Tavli *SVP, Treasury* ☎ **961 2510**

Fixed-Income Repo
Head of Repo   Semih Tavli *SVP, Treasury* ☎ **961 2510**

Equity Capital Markets
Department: Treasury Department
Country Head   Semih Tavli *SVP, Treasury* ☎ **961 2510**

Syndicated Lending
Tel: 961 2506
Head of Syndication   Filiz Süyür *SVP, Financial Institutions* ☎ **961 2506**

Money Markets
Department: Treasury Department
Head of Money Markets   Semih Tavli *SVP, Treasury* ☎ **961 2510**

Foreign Exchange
Department: Treasury Department
Head of Foreign Exchange   Semih Tavli *SVP, Treasury* ☎ **961 2510**

Settlement / Clearing
Tel: 961 2515
Head of Settlement / Clearing   Suat Albayrak *Senior Vice President*

Other Departments
Correspondent Banking   Filiz Süyür *SVP, Financial Institutions* ☎ **961 2506**

www.euromoneydirectory.com   RUSSIA (+7)

Hansa Financial Services
Full Branch Office

Shpalernaya 36, 191194 St Petersburg
Tel: (812) 329 5730; (812) 329 5729 Fax: (812) 279 8500
Website: www.hansa.ee/invest

Senior Executive Officers
Chairman of the Board   Joakim Helenius ⏹ +372 509 1282
Chief Executive Officer   Ben Wilson ⏹ +371 732 2011
Director, Corporate Finance   Viktor Mahhov ⏹ 329 5730

Others (Senior Executives)
Sales & Trading   Sergei Bayov *Director* ⏹ 329 5730

Debt Capital Markets / Fixed Income

Bonds - General
Corporate Finance   Gleb Ogniannikov *Associate* ⏹ 329 5730
                               Denis Askinadze *Analyst* ⏹ 329 5730

Private Placements
Head of Origination   Viktor Mahhov *Director, Corporate Finance* ⏹ 329 5730
Head of Sales   Sergei Bayov *Director* ⏹ 329 5730

Asset-Backed Securities / Securitization
Regional Head   Viktor Mahhov *Director, Corporate Finance* ⏹ 329 5730
Head of Trading   Sergei Bayov *Director* ⏹ 329 5730

Mortgage-Backed Securities
Regional Head   Viktor Mahhov *Director, Corporate Finance* ⏹ 329 5730
                               Sergei Bayov *Director* ⏹ 329 5730

Equity Capital Markets
Tel: 329 5730 Fax: 279 8500
Global Head   Ben Wilson ⏹ +371 732 2011
Country Head   Viktor Mahhov *Director, Corporate Finance* ⏹ 329 5730

Domestic Equities
Head of Origination   Viktor Mahhov *Director, Corporate Finance* ⏹ 329 5730
Head of Sales   Sergei Bayov *Director* ⏹ 329 5730
Head of Research   Viktor Mahhov *Director, Corporate Finance* ⏹ 329 5730

Corporate Finance / M&A Advisory
Global Head   Ben Wilson ⏹ +371 732 2011
Country Head   Viktor Mahhov *Director, Corporate Finance* ⏹ 329 5730

Settlement / Clearing
Regional Head   Ben Wilson ⏹ +371 732 2011
Country Head   Viktor Mahhov *Director, Corporate Finance* ⏹ 329 5730
Equity Settlement   John Wilson *Director, Sales & Trading* ⏹ 640 0415

HypoVereinsbank
Representative Office

Gazetny Per, 17/9, 103009 Moscow
Tel: (095) 940 2966 Fax: (095) 940 2969

IFP Intermoney Financial Products Limited
Subsidiary Company

3 Krasina Ul, 123056 Moscow
Tel: (095) 232 5656 Fax: (095) 792 5870 Reuters: IFPM
Website: www.ifpmoscow.co.ru

Senior Executive Officers

Others (Senior Executives)
                               Marina Sitnina
                               Sylvain Naggar

RUSSIA (+7) www.euromoneydirectory.com

Industry & Construction Bank
Head Office

Formerly known as: Promstoybank
38 Nevsky Prospect, 191014 St Petersburg
17/18 Kovensky, 191014 St Petersburg
Tel: (812) 329 8456; (812) 329 8451 **Fax:** (812) 310 6173; (812) 329 8451 **Telex:** 121612 ICBNK RU **Swift:** ICSP RU 2P
Email: lider@icb.spb.su **Reuters:** ICSP

Senior Executive Officers
Acting Chairman of the Managing Board
International Division
Alexander Emdim ☎ **329 8417**
Valery Drouzhinin *Head of Financial Institutions Division* ☎ **329 8451**

Others (Senior Executives)
Processing Center
SWIFT
Dmitri Andreev ☎ **329 8229**
Sergei Shipovski ☎ **324 2080**

Syndicated Lending
Loan-Related Activities
Trade Finance
Boris Djeriev ☎ **329 8392**

Other Departments
Proprietary Trading
Correspondent Banking
Sergei Borisov ☎ **326 1540**
Irina Ivanova ☎ **329 8456**

Administration
Accounts / Audit
Nelly Petrunenko *Chief Accountant*

ING Barings
Representative Office

11 Svetlanskaya Street, 690 000 Vladivostok
Tel: (4232) 264 403 **Fax:** (4232) 260 751

Senior Executive Officers
Representative
Victor Tumanov

ING Barings Eurasia ZAO
Full Branch Office

31 Krasnaya Presnya, Building 31, 123 022 Moscow
Tel: (095) 755 5400 **Fax:** (095) 755 5499 **Email:** nadezhda.ushakova@ingbank.com **Reuters:** INGR (Dealing)

Senior Executive Officers
Country Manager
Dick H W ten Bosch

Others (Senior Executives)
P L T van der Krogt *Deputy General Manager*

Inkom Capital

69 Prospekt Mira, 129110 Moscow
Tel: (095) 755 6852 **Fax:** (095) 755 6859 **Email:** info@inkomcap.com.ru
Website: www.inkomcap.com.ru

Senior Executive Officers
President
Financial Director
Vice President
Igor Gryaznov ☎ **208 1225**
Vadim Mikhan ☎ **975 1191**
Vladimir Pleshkov ☎ **208 2051**

Others (Senior Executives)
Zimortsev Igor *Vice President* ☎ **208 1962**

Debt Capital Markets / Fixed Income
Head of Fixed Income
Head of Fixed Income Sales
Head of Fixed Income Trading
Vladimir Romanov ☎ **755 6852**
Irina Filatova ☎ **755 6852**
Vladimir Pleshkov *Vice President* ☎ **208 2051**

Equity Capital Markets
Head of Sales
Head of Trading
Irina Filatova ☎ **755 6852**
Alexei Tzaruk ☎ **288 9713**

Domestic Equities
Head of Sales
Head of Trading
Irina Filatova ☎ **755 6852**
Alexei Tzaruk ☎ **288 9713**
Ury Komarov *Trader* ☎ **755 6852**

www.euromoneydirectory.com RUSSIA (+7)

Equity Research
Head of Equity Research Peter Grebenshikov ☏ 755 6852
Money Markets
Domestic Commercial Paper
Head of Trading Vladimir Makashov ☏ 281 1843
Risk Management
Head of Risk Management Valeri Tolkachov ☏ 755 6852
Asset Management
Head Evgeni Vishiakov ☏ 755 6852
Administration
Technology & Systems
 Sergey Streltzov ☏ 755 6852

International Bank for Economic Co-operation
11 Masha Poryvaeva Street, 107815 GSP Moscow B-78
Tel: (095) 975 3851; (095) 975 2089 **Fax:** (095) 975 2202 **Telex:** 411391 MZBK RU **Swift:** IBEC RU MM **Reuters:** IBEC
Senior Executive Officers
Chairman V Khokhlov

International Company for Finance & Investments   Head Office
Alternative trading name: ICFI
USADBA- CENTRE, 22/13 Voznesensky Pereylok, 103009 Moscow
Tel: (095) 258 7777 **Fax:** (095) 258 7778; (095) 725 5590 **Telex:** 911653 ICFI RU **Swift:** ICFI RU MM **Reuters:** IFCM
Cable: INCOFIN **Telex:** 911656 ICFI RU; **Reuters:** IFCI
Website: www.icfi.ru

Senior Executive Officers
Chairman Dmitry Bobakov
Chief Executive Officer Mikhail Zaitsev *First Deputy Chairman* ☏ 725 5797
Financial Director Andrey Samsonov ☏ 725 5738
Treasurer Alexey Borzunov *Deputy Chairman* ☏ 725 5701
First Deputy Chairman Sergey Vassiliev ☏ 725 5577
Company Secretary Leonid Pomerantsev ☏ 725 5583
International Division Elena Izotova *Head* ☏ 725 5742

General-Lending (DCM, SL)
Head of Corporate Banking Maxim Finsky *Head, Commercial Banking* ☏ 725 5838
Debt Capital Markets / Fixed Income
Head of Fixed Income Sergey Ivanov ☏ 725 5826
Fixed-Income Repo
Head of Repo Konstantin Beirit
Syndicated Lending
Head of Origination; Head of Syndication Alexey Borzunov *Deputy Chairman* ☏ 725 5701
Loan-Related Activities
Trade Finance Vadim Serebriannikov ☏ 725 5589
Project Finance Maxim Finsky *Head, Commercial Banking* ☏ 725 5838
Money Markets
Head of Money Markets Alexey Borzunov *Deputy Chairman* ☏ 725 5701
Foreign Exchange
Head of Foreign Exchange Alexey Borzunov *Deputy Chairman* ☏ 725 5701
Settlement / Clearing
Head of Settlement / Clearing Dmitry Matsenov ☏ 725 5678
Other Departments
Chief Credit Officer Denis Morozov ☏ 725 5839
Private Banking Sergey Tatarinov ☏ 725 5660
Correspondent Banking Elena Izotova *Head* ☏ 725 5742
Cash Management Natalia Kurbatova *Head* ☏ 725 5727
Administration
Head of Administration Leonid Pomerantsev ☏ 725 5583
Business Development; Head of Marketing Sergey Vassiliev *First Deputy Chairman* ☏ 725 5577
Technology & Systems
 Dmitry Petropavlovsky ☏ 725 5622

Euromoney Directory 1999 **1263**

RUSSIA (+7)   www.euromoneydirectory.com

International Company for Finance & Investments (cont)

Legal / In-House Counsel
　　　　Vadim Kondakov

Compliance
　　　　Sergey Soukhinin *Deputy Chairman* ☎ **725 5601**

Public Relations
　　　　Michail Zaitsev *First Deputy Chairman*

Accounts / Audit
　　　　Sergey Soukhinin *Deputy Chairman* ☎ **725 5601**

International Moscow Bank — Head Office

9 Prechistenskaya Naberezhnaya, 119034 Moscow
Tel: (095) 258 7258 **Fax:** (095) 258 7772 **Telex:** 412284 IMBA RU **Swift:** IMBK RU MM **Email:** imbank@imbank.ru
Reuters: IMBM **Telex:** 412285 IMB RU

Senior Executive Officers
Chairman — Ilkka Salonen ☎ **258 7201** 📠 **258 7303**
Financial Director — Alex Popov ☎ **258 6505** 📠 **258 7272**
Treasurer — Sergey Troshin ☎ **258 7270**
International Division — Vladimir Vasyatkin ☎ **258 7267**

General-Lending (DCM, SL)
Head of Corporate Banking — Yuriy Tverskoy ☎ **258 7205**

Debt Capital Markets / Fixed Income
Head of Fixed Income — Valeriy Chicherin ☎ **258 7392**

Emerging Market Bonds
Head of Emerging Markets — Valeriy Chicherin ☎ **258 7392**

Equity Capital Markets
Head of Equity Capital Markets — Valeriy Chicherin ☎ **258 7392**

Syndicated Lending

Loan-Related Activities
Trade Finance — Inna Tsymalina ☎ **258 7343**
Project Finance — Alexander Myagkov ☎ **258 7268**

Money Markets
Head of Money Markets — Sergey Troshin ☎ **258 7270**

Foreign Exchange
Head of Foreign Exchange — Sergey Troshin ☎ **258 7270**

Settlement / Clearing
Head of Settlement / Clearing — Nina Bakanova

Asset Management
Head — Alexander Myagkov ☎ **258 7268**

Other Departments
Correspondent Banking — Vladimir Vasyatkin ☎ **258 7267**

Administration
Head of Administration — Inessa Karlova ☎ **258 7223** 📠 **258 7272**
Head of Marketing — Sergy Tropin ☎ **258 7209**

Legal / In-House Counsel
　　　　Genadiy Lukyanenko ☎ **258 7216**

Public Relations
　　　　Sergey Levskoy ☎ **258 6528**

London Forfaiting Syndications Limited — Representative Office

Krasnopresnenskaya Naberezhaya 6, 123100 Moscow
Tel: (095) 247 2122 **Fax:** (095) 247 2123 **Email:** lfc@aha.ru

Senior Executive Officers
Representative — Vladislav Poshmorga

www.euromoneydirectory.com RUSSIA (+7)

London Forfaiting Vostok Limited
Representative Office

Krasnopresnenskaya Naderezhaya 6, 123100 Moscow
Tel: (095) 247 2120 Fax: (095) 247 2121

Senior Executive Officers
Representative Nikolai Ivashkovsky

Menatep
Head Office

Alternative trading name: Bank Menatep

Ulamsky Lane 24, 103045 Moscow
Tel: (095) 956 7524; (095) 928 9970

Senior Executive Officers
Chairman Alexander Zourabov
Treasurer Ilia Yurov
International Division Constantine Kagalovsky

General-Lending (DCM, SL)
Head of Corporate Banking Alex Okum

General-Investment
Head of Investment Alexander Chiastyakov

Debt Capital Markets / Fixed Income
Head of Debt Capital Markets Ilia Yurov
Head of Fixed Income Sales Sergei Khimich

Government Bonds
Head of Sales Sergei Khimich

Eurobonds
Head of Sales Sergei Khimich

Equity Capital Markets
Head of Equity Capital Markets Alexander Chiastyakov
Head of Sales Sergei Khimich

Syndicated Lending
Head of Syndicated Lending Sergei Loginov

Loan-Related Activities
Trade Finance Sergei Loginov
Project Finance Alexander Chiastyakov

Money Markets
Head of Money Markets Ilia Yurov

Foreign Exchange
Head of Foreign Exchange Ilia Yurov

Risk Management
Head of Risk Management Vladimir Metuegev

Corporate Finance / M&A Advisory
Head of Corporate Finance Alan Sepols

Settlement / Clearing
Head of Settlement / Clearing Eduarg Kravchenko

Global Custody
Head of Global Custody Natalia Galenko

Asset Management
Head Sergei Khimich

Other Departments
Correspondent Banking Helen Melnikova

Administration
Head of Administration Sergei Zhdanov

Public Relations
  Irene Nelson

Merita Bank plc
Representative Office

20 Ulitsa Chaplygina, 103062 Moscow
Tel: (095) 721 1646 Fax: (095) 721 1647

Senior Executive Officers
Representative Sirpa Sara-aho

Euromoney Directory 1999 **1265**

RUSSIA (+7) www.euromoneydirectory.com

Merita Bank plc
Representative Office

Ulitsa Malaya Konjushennaya 1/3, Sweden House, Office B42, 191186 St Petersburg
Tel: (812) 329 2500 Fax: (812) 329 2501

Senior Executive Officers
Representative Hanna Loikkanen

MFK Renaissance
Head Office

USADBA Centre, 22/13 Vosnesensky Per, 103009 Moscow
Tel: (501) 258 7777 Fax: (501) 258 7778
Website: www.mfkren.com

Senior Executive Officers
Chairman, President & CEO Boris Jordan
Financial Director Bruce Gardner
Chief Operating Officer Stephen Jennings
Equity Capital Markets
Other (Equity Research)
Energy Analyst Irina Liskoverts

Midland Bank plc
Representative Office

Room 1305, 13th Floor Sovincentre, Entrance 3, Krasnopresnenskaya Naberezhnaya 12, Moscow
Tel: (502) 253 0113 Fax: (502) 253 0056

Senior Executive Officers
Representative S J Davies

Morgan Stanley (Europe) Limited
Representative Office

Ducat Plaza II, 7 Gasheka Street, 123056 Moscow
Tel: (095) 785 2200; (501) 785 2200 Fax: (095) 785 2229; (501) 785 2229
Website: www.ms.com

Senior Executive Officers
Managing Director Rair Simonyan
Executive Director Andrew Balgarnie
General-Investment
Head of Investment Gregory Stoupnitzky *Executive Director, Investment Banking*
 Craig Kennedy *Vice President, Investment Banking*

Mosbusinessbank
Head Office

Kuznetsky Most Street,15, 103780 Moscow
Tel: (095) 924 3038; (095) 925 0740 Fax: (095) 924 0490 Telex: 412368 VALTSU Swift: MOSB RU MM
Email: lii@mosbb.com Reuters: MBGT; MIAM; MGBM; MBGR

Senior Executive Officers
Chairman of the Management Board Victor Bukato ☏ **928 1701**
Treasurer Anatoly Milukov *Head of Treasury* ☏ **924 1060**
International Division Alexei Obozintsev *Deputy Chairman of the Board* ☏ **921 8335**
Debt Capital Markets / Fixed Income
Tel: 924 1060 Fax: 924 7238
Head of Fixed Income Pavel Navolokin ☏ **924 1060**
Syndicated Lending
Loan-Related Activities
Trade Finance Vladimir Merzlov ☏ **960 2479**
Project Finance Igor Konuhov ☏ **973 2447**
Money Markets
Tel: 924 1060 Fax: 924 7238
Head of Money Markets Roman Kystov
Foreign Exchange
Head of Foreign Exchange Oleg Pyatakov

www.euromoneydirectory.com   RUSSIA (+7)

Risk Management
Tel: 921 7923 **Fax:** 960 2482
Head of Risk Management   Konstantin Zyryanov
Other Departments
Correspondent Banking   Oleg Kuznetsov ☏ **924 0237**

Moscow Narodny Bank Limited   Representative Office
13, 1-IJ Kadashevskij Per., Building 1, 113035 Moscow
Tel: (095) 792 3060; (095) 792 3059 **Fax:** (095) 792 3062 **Telex:** 413121 MNBRO SU
Senior Executive Officers
Representative   Kuzmin Gennady Alekseevich

Nordbanken AB (publ)   Representative Office
Ulansky Per 4, 5th Floor, 101000 Moscow
Tel: (095) 792 3544 **Fax:** (095) 792 3548
Senior Executive Officers
Representative   Joel Cachet

Nova Ljubljanska banka dd   Representative Office
Office 608, Mashi Porirayevoy 7, 107078 Moscow
Tel: (095) 975 2191 **Fax:** (095) 956 3196 **Email:** nlbmos@dol.ru
Senior Executive Officers
Chief Representative   Pavel Savli

OLMA Investment Company   Head Office
7/1 Malyi Karetnyi per, 103051 Moscow
Tel: (095) 299 5772; (095) 960 3121 **Fax:** (095) 299 4062; (095) 960 3130 **Email:** info@olma.co.ru
Website: www.olma.co.ru
Senior Executive Officers
Chairman   Alexandr Chulkov ☏ **299 9989**
President   Oleg Yachnik
Chief Executive Officer   Yuri Mishin ☏ **299 4151**
Financial Director   Olga Lapina ☏ **299 2738**
Chief Operating Officer   Polina Pankratova ☏ **960 3123**
Managing Director   Vladimir Lezhnin ☏ **960 3121**
Company Secretary   Anastasiya Milyaeva
Syndicated Lending
Loan-Related Activities
Project Finance   Genadiy Zalko
Settlement / Clearing
Head of Settlement / Clearing   Polina Pankratova ☏ **960 3123**

Open Joint-Stock Company Alfa Bank   Head Office
Formerly known as: Commercial Innovation Bank Alfa Bank
11 Mashy Poryvaevoy Street, 107078 Moscow
Tel: (095) 207 6001; (095) 974 2515 **Fax:** (095) 207 6136; (095) 913 7182 **Telex:** 412089 ALFA RU **Swift:** ALFA RU MM
Reuters: ALFM
Website: www.alfabank.ru
Senior Executive Officers
Chairman   Leonard Vid
President   Peter Aven
Chief Executive Officer   Alexander Knaster ☏ **923 5673**
Financial Director   Ildar Karimov
Treasurer   Tejo Pankko ☏ **745 5786**
International Division   Maxim Topper
General-Lending (DCM, SL)
Head of Corporate Banking   Andrey Sokolov

Euromoney Directory 1999 **1267**

RUSSIA (+7)   www.euromoneydirectory.com

Open Joint-Stock Company Alfa Bank (cont)

Debt Capital Markets / Fixed Income
Head of Fixed Income   Simon Vein ☏ 755 5830
Head of Fixed Income Trading   Ilya Savkin
Eurobonds
Head of Trading   Alexey Petrov

Equity Capital Markets
Equity Research
Head of Equity Research   Stuart Thomas ☏ 755 5830

Syndicated Lending
Loan-Related Activities
Trade Finance   Victoria Ermakova
Project Finance   Vsevolod Antonovsky

Foreign Exchange
Head of Foreign Exchange   Igor Vasiliev

Corporate Finance / M&A Advisory
Head of Corporate Finance   Alexander Tolchinsky ☏ 755 5830

Settlement / Clearing
Head of Settlement / Clearing   Mikhail Panfilov
Operations   Oleg Gubin

Other Departments
Chief Credit Officer   Alexander Lukanov
Correspondent Banking   Maxim Topper

Administration
Technology & Systems
                                      Boris Bukin

Legal / In-House Counsel
                                      Rushan Hvesuk *Chief Lawyer*

Public Relations
                                      Andrey Nasonovsky

Promradtekhbank   Head Office

35 Myasnitskaya, 101959 Moscow
Tel: (095) 967 1529; (095) 967 1428 **Fax:** (095) 204 1338; (095) 204 1512 **Telex:** 911077 PRTB RU **Swift:** PRAD RU MM

Senior Executive Officers
Financial Director   Michael Belinev *Chief Accountant* ☏ 967 1450
Treasurer   Alexey Solodukha ✉ solodukha@prtb.com.ru
General Manager   Konstantin Kouzmine ☏ 967 1424 ⓕ 208 9757

Debt Capital Markets / Fixed Income
Domestic Government Bonds
Head of Research   Valdimir Pavlov *Vice Head, Fixed-Income* ☏ 258 2579
                                      ✉ rw3vp@prtb.com.ru

Money Markets
Fax: 967 1542
Global Head   Alexander Korablev *Head* ☏ 255 2689 ✉ korablev@prtb.com.ru

Foreign Exchange
Fax: 967 1542
Global Head   Sergey Fabizhevskiy *Head* ☏ 207 9160
Head of Trading   Yaroslav Melikhov *Chief Dealer, FX* ☏ 967 1574

FX Traders / Sales People
$ / RUR   Sergey Lazorenko *Dealer* ☏ 967 1535 ✉ lazo@prtb.com.ru
                                      Sergey Menzhinsky *Dealer* ☏ 258 2674
$ / RUR Spot   Sergey Kocherov *Dealer* ☏ 967 1541
$ / DM, Cable   Alexey Novikov *Dealer* ☏ 967 1539 ✉ lesha-i@prtb.com.ru

Settlement / Clearing
Fax: 967 1571
Regional Head   Sergey Fabizhevskiy *Head* ☏ 207 9160
Foreign Exchange Settlement   Yaroslav Melikhov *Chief Dealer, FX* ☏ 967 1574

Other Departments
Proprietary Trading   Margarita Gudz ☏ 967 1471
Correspondent Banking   Oxana Trefilova *Head* ☏ 258 2549 ✉ oxana@prtb.com.ru

www.euromoneydirectory.com   RUSSIA (+7)

Administration
Technology & Systems
                                Pavel Boltrukevich *Head* ☏ **967 1454**
Legal / In-House Counsel
                                Boris Puginsky *Head* ☏ **258 2555**
Compliance
                                Irina Seregina *Head, Internal Audit* ☏ **967 1491**

Promstroybank of Russia   Head Office
13 Tverskoy Boulevard, 103867 Moscow
Tel: (095) 200 7028; (095) 200 7287 **Fax:** (095) 200 7816; (095) 200 6507 **Telex:** 411943 PSB RU **Swift:** PRST RU MM
Reuters: PSBR
General Tel: 200 7945

Senior Executive Officers
Chairman of the Council   Ram I Viakhirev
Others (Senior Executives)
Member of the Board   Yakov N Dubenetsky *Chairman of the Board*
                                    Mikhail N Novikov *First Deputy Chairman*
                                    Andrey G Dubiniak *Deputy Chairman*
                                    Alexander P Zubkov *Deputy Chairman*
                                    Artur V Zhuravlev *Deputy Chairman*
                                    Yury V Uvarov *Deputy Chairman*
                                    Andrey N Kudinov *MD, Economic Planning Division*
                                    Sergey A Moissev *Chief Accountant & MD, Book-Keeping & Settlements*
                                    Sergey I Liashenko *MD, Information Technologies Div*
                                    Alexander M Masterkov *MD, Administration*

General - Treasury
Head of Treasury   Vladimir A Orlov *Managing Director, Treasury*
Syndicated Lending
Loan-Related Activities
Trade Finance   Tatiana S Boussygina *Head of Trade Finance Department*
Money Markets
Other   Natalia I Kukhtarova *Managing Director, Investment & Commercial Credit*
Foreign Exchange
Global Head   Alexander V Vassilevsky *Chief Dealer*
Settlement / Clearing
Regional Head   Sergey A Moissev *Chief Accountant & MD, Book-Keeping & Settlements*
Other Departments
Correspondent Banking   Mikhail K Zharov *MD, Foreign Currency Finance & Correspondent Banki*
                                    Marina V Krupina *Head of Correspondent Banking*

Administration
Technology & Systems
                                    Sergey I Liashenko *MD, Information Technologies Div*
Legal / In-House Counsel
                                    Mikhail Paniakin *Head of Legal Department*
Other (Administration)
                                    Natalia A Klekovkina *Manager, Telecommuncations*

Regiobank   Head Office
18 Amursky Boulevard, 680000 Khabarovsk
Tel: (4212) 324 794; (4212) 329 684 **Fax:** (4212) 338 708; (4212) 324 066 **Telex:** 614433 REGIO RU **Swift:** REGK RU 8K
Email: admin@regio.ru **Reuters:** REGI

Senior Executive Officers
General Director   Vyacheslav Vasilenko ☏ **(272) 46113**
President & CEO   Sergey Grebenyuk
Financial Director   Antonina Borets ☏ **327 424**
Chief Operating Officer   Tamara Ilina ☏ **324 952**
Senior Vice President   Zinaida Romashkina ☏ **324 407**
International Division   Tatianna Starikova ☏ **714 240**

General-Lending (DCM, SL)
Head of Corporate Banking   Tamara Ilina ☏ **324 952**

Euromoney Directory 1999   **1269**

RUSSIA (+7)   www.euromoneydirectory.com

Regiobank (cont)

General-Investment
Head of Investment   Vyacheslav Gritsaenko *Head, Securities* ☎ **324 066**

Relationship Manager
Management & Settlements   Andrey Yelfimov *Vice President* ☎ **714 282**
Technology & Systems   Vitaly Khabarov *Vice President* ☎ **235 141**

Debt Capital Markets / Fixed Income
Department: Securities & F / X Operations Division
Tel: 327 153 Fax: 324 066 Reuters: REGI Telex: 614433 REGIO RU
Head of Fixed Income   Irina Morozova *Chief Specialist - Stock Emission* ☎ **327 153**

Domestic Government Bonds
Head of Sales   Vyacheslav Gritsaenko *Head, Securities* ☎ **324 066**

Libor-Based / Floating-Rate Products
FRN Origination   Vyacheslav Gritsaenko *Head, Securities* ☎ **324 066**

Fixed-Income Repo
Head of Repo   Vyacheslav Gritsaenko *Head, Securities* ☎ **324 066**

Equity Capital Markets
Head of Equity Capital Markets   Irina Morozova *Chief Specialist - Stock Emission* ☎ **327 153**

Syndicated Lending

Loan-Related Activities
Trade Finance   Yuri Kovalev *Head, Credit Operations* ☎ **328 623**

Money Markets
Head of Money Markets   Andrey Stoyakin *Head, FX Operations* ☎ **324 066**

Domestic Commercial Paper
Head of Origination   Vyacheslav Gritsaenko *Head, Securities* ☎ **324 066**

Wholesale Deposits
Marketing   Andrey Stoyakin *Head, FX Operations* ☎ **324 066**

Foreign Exchange
Head of Foreign Exchange   Andrey Stoyakin *Head, FX Operations* ☎ **324 066**

FX Traders / Sales People
                                   Dimtry Gridnev *FX Dealer*

Risk Management
Head of Risk Management   Sergey Grebenyuk *President & CEO*

Other Currency Swap / FX Options Personnel
FX Derivatives Sales   Andrey Stoyakin *Head, FX Operations* ☎ **324 066**

Corporate Finance / M&A Advisory
Head of Corporate Finance   Yuri Kovalev *Head, Credit Operations* ☎ **328 623**

Settlement / Clearing
Tel: 337 871 Fax: 338 708
Head of Settlement / Clearing   Tatianna Kalugina *Head, RUR Operations*

Global Custody
Head of Global Custody   Oleg Olejnik *Head, Security Service* ☎ **326 030**

Asset Management
Head   Tamara Tumashova ☎ **327 863**

Other Departments
Private Banking   Yuri Kovalev *Head, Credit Operations* ☎ **328 623**
Correspondent Banking   Elena Chumakova *Head, Correspondent Banking* ☎ **329 684**
Cash Management   Valentina Yudina ☎ **326 321**

Administration
Business Development   Galina Danilenko ☎ **327 424**
Head of Marketing   Sergey Semirichev ☎ **326 952**

Technology & Systems
                                   Vitaly Khabarov *Vice President* ☎ **235 141**

Legal / In-House Counsel
                                   Gennady Proschaev *Head of Legal Department* ☎ **327 272**

Compliance
                                   Nina Borodavko *Chief Accountant* ☎ **326 867**

Accounts / Audit
Internal Audit   Tatianna Brandt *Head* ☎ **326 905**

Republic National Bank of New York (RR)
Subsidiary Company

Dmintrovsky pereulok, 9, 103031 Moscow
Tel: (501) 721 1515 Fax: (501) 258 3154; (501) 721 1576 Telex: 414317 RNB RU Swift: BLIC RU MM Reuters: RNBW
Website: www.rnb.com

Senior Executive Officers
President & CEO — Urs Haener ☐ 721 1500
Chief Executive Officer — Urs Haener *President & CEO* ☐ 721 1500
Financial Director — Roberto Avondon *Financial Controller* ☐ 721 1512
Treasurer — Guy Bouaziz *SVP & Director of Treasury* ☐ 721 1577

Rossiyskiy Kredit Bank
Head Office

26/9 Smolensky Boulevard, 121002 Moscow
Tel: (095) 258 0710 Fax: (095) 913 5736 Swift: BKRC RU MM
International Department Tel: 258 0710; Fax: 913 5736; Secretary of the Board of Management Tel: 247 3846;
Reception (No English spoken) Tel: 967 3443
Website: www.roscredit.ru

Senior Executive Officers
Chairman — Mr Lubimim
Financial Director — Mr Lysenko
Treasurer — Mrs Tichoneyheva
International Division — Mr Yrodkin

Debt Capital Markets / Fixed Income
Head of Fixed Income — Mr Sychev ☐ 755 8737

Equity Capital Markets
Head of Equity Capital Markets — Demitry Shulgenko ☐ 755 8797

Money Markets
Head of Money Markets — Kirill Lubemsky ☐ 755 8737

Foreign Exchange
Head of Foreign Exchange — Dimitry Yakovlev ☐ 755 8753

Settlement / Clearing
Settlement (General) — Vadim Majushkym *International Settlements*

Other Departments
Correspondent Banking — Dimtry Malisko

Administration
Head of Marketing — Alla Kotlyar

Public Relations
Galina Subjena *Head, Public Relations* ☐ 785 0688 ☐ 785 0688

Russky Slaviansky Bank
Head Office

Building 2, 14 Donskaya Street, 117049 Moscow
Tel: (095) 237 1941 Fax: (503) 232 0295 Telex: 112233 BAGUS RU Swift: RSLB RU MM Reuters: RSLB
Website: www.russlavbank.com

Senior Executive Officers
Chairman of the Board — Nikolai Gousman
International Division — Alexander Povalyaev ☐ (503) 232 0296

Debt Capital Markets / Fixed Income
Tel: (095) 236 4154 Fax: (095) 236 2153
Global Head — Pavel Shmarov

Money Markets
Global Head — Sergey Bludov

Foreign Exchange
Tel: 236 4272 Fax: (095) 237 0768
Global Head — Sergey Bludov

RUSSIA (+7)   www.euromoneydirectory.com

Société Générale
Representative Office

9th Floor, 5 Nikitski Pereoulok, (ex ulitsa Belinskogo), 103009 Moscow
Tel: (095) 940 4520; (502) 225 2100 **Fax:** (095) 940 4525; (502) 225 2101 **Telex:** 413190 SOGE RU
Senior Executive Officers
Representative   Serge Kniazeff

Svenska Handelsbanken
Representative Office

2nd Floor, Khlebny per 19A, 121069 Moscow
Tel: (095) 291 6811; (502) 220 4200 **Fax:** (095) 230 6256; (502) 230 6256 **Cable:** HANDELSBANK
Senior Executive Officers
Chief Representative   Per Lundberg
Others (Senior Executives)
     Natalya Grishuenkova *Company Secretary*

T Garanti Bankasi AS
Representative Office

Formerly known as: Garanti Bank
52 Kosmodaneanskaya Naberezhnaya, Building 1, Block A, 113054 Moscow
Tel: (095) 961 2500 **Fax:** (095) 961 2503 **Telex:** 485370 **Swift:** GABM RU MM
Senior Executive Officers
Representative   Erkan Korc

Tradition CIS LLC
Representative Office

Business Centre 'Stoleshniki', 14 Stoleshnikov Perulok, 103031 Moscow
Tel: (517) 733 9250 **Fax:** (517) 733 9248 **Reuters:** TMOW
Senior Executive Officers
Chief Representative   Jonathan Perree ☎ **733 9246**

Union Européenne de CIC
Representative Office

23/10, Petrovka Street, 103031 Moscow
Tel: (095) 924 5201; (095) 923 9373 **Fax:** (095) 924 7526
Senior Executive Officers
Head Representative   Jean-Jacques Vrignaud

United Export Import Bank of Russia

Alternative trading name: Unexim Bank of Russia
11 Masha Poryvaeva Street, PO Box 207, 107078 Moscow
Tel: (095) 204 7461; (095) 232 3727 **Fax:** (095) 975 2205 **Telex:** 411277 UNEI SU **Swift:** UNEI RU MM **Reuters:** UNEX; UNEM

Senior Executive Officers
Chairman   Mikhail Brokhorov
Treasurer   Alton Popov
Others (Senior Executives)
1st Deputy Chairman   Vladimir Wiyskim
Debt Capital Markets / Fixed Income
Head of Debt Capital Markets; Head of Fixed Income Trading   Alton Popov
Government Bonds
Head of Trading   Alton Popov
Domestic Government Bonds
Head of Trading   Alton Popov
Equity Capital Markets
Head of Equity Capital Markets   Alton Popov

www.euromoneydirectory.com RUSSIA (+7)

Syndicated Lending
Head of Syndicated Lending — Julia Basova
Loan-Related Activities
Structured Trade Finance — Alexander Ozhegov
Money Markets
Head of Money Markets — Alton Popov
Foreign Exchange
Head of Foreign Exchange — Alton Popov
Risk Management
Head of Risk Management — Vladimir Wiyskim
Corporate Finance / M&A Advisory
Head of Corporate Finance — Julia Basova
Global Custody
Head of Global Custody — Mikhail Alekseez
Other Departments
Correspondent Banking — Eugemil Yarovikov
Administration
Public Relations
Modest Kolerov

Closed Joint Stock Company Yapi Toko Bank   Head Office

Alternative trading name: Yapi Toko Bank
1/2, Goncharnaya Naberezhnaya, 109172 Moscow Moscow
Tel: (095) 915 3182; (095) 234 9889 **Fax:** (095) 956 1972 **Telex:** 414150 YATO RU **Swift:** YTOB RU MM
Email: yap@online.ru **Reuters:** YPTO

Senior Executive Officers
Chairman of the Council of Directors — Cemil Koksal
President — Dmitry Dubensky
Chief Operating Officer — Bayram Yalin *Manager of Operations*
Treasurer — Adnan Anacali *EVP, Head of Treasury*
Managing Director — Erhan Ozcelik
Secretary to the Board — Sofia Roschina

Others (Senior Executives)
Head of Documentary Business — Ludmila Akishina
General-Lending (DCM, SL)
Head of Corporate Banking — Natalya Matveyeva *Head of Correspondent Banking & Accounting*
Corporate Finance / M&A Advisory
Head of Corporate Finance — Pavel Savkin *Head of Credit*
Settlement / Clearing
Head of Settlement / Clearing — Natalya Matveyeva *Head of Correspondent Banking & Accounting*
Back-Office — Irina Bgantseva *Back Office Specialist*
Other Departments
Chief Credit Officer — Pavel Savkin *Head of Credit*
Correspondent Banking — Natalya Matveyeva *Head of Correspondent Banking & Accounting*
Administration
Head of Administration — Sergey Yemilianov *Head of Administration*
Technology & Systems
Victor Burioukov *Head of IT*
Public Relations
Dmitry Belyakov *Secretary General*
Accounts / Audit
Bozkurt Kaplangi *EVP, Head of Audit Department*

Yugbank

52 Krasnaya Street, 350016 Krasnodar
Tel: (8612) 622 146; (8612) 621 121; (8612) 623 738 **Fax:** (8612) 622 146 **Telex:** 612831 YUGBK RU
Email: yugbank@sovcust.sprint.com **Reuters:** YUGB
General Telex: 211153 SOUTH SU; **Email:** gene@yugb.kuban.ru

Senior Executive Officers
Chairman — Gennadiy Vasilievich Pimenov
General Director — Vladimir Petrovich Guryanov

Euromoney Directory 1999   **1273**

RUSSIA (+7) www.euromoneydirectory.com

Yugbank (cont)
Senior Executive Officers (cont)
International Division Aleftina A Manzharova *Deputy Director*
Others (Senior Executives)
Domestic Markets, Assets Viktor M Kurbatov *Deputy Director*
General-Investment
Head of Investment Galina S Frankova *Deputy Director*
Debt Capital Markets / Fixed Income
Head of Debt Capital Markets Aleftina A Manzharova *Deputy Director*
Government Bonds
Head of Sales Antonina V Ivanova *Chief Manager*
Domestic Government Bonds
Head of Sales Antonina V Ivanova *Chief Manager*
Equity Capital Markets
Head of Equity Capital Markets Aleftina A Manzharova *Deputy Director*
Syndicated Lending
Other (Syndicated Lending)
Credit Administration Valentina N Pogorelaya *Chief Manager*
Foreign Exchange
Head of Foreign Exchange Galina F Ravilova *Chief Manager*
  Eugene A Balchansky *Senior Manager*
Corporate Finance / M&A Advisory
Head of Corporate Finance Galina S Frankova *Deputy Director*
Settlement / Clearing
Head of Settlement / Clearing Igor V Goncharov *Chief Manager*
Other Tatyana V Dorofeyeva *Manager, International Payments & Investigations*
Other Departments
Correspondent Banking Eugene A Balchansky *Senior Manager*
Administration
Accounts / Audit
  Alla N Kukharenko *Chief Accountant*

RWANDA (+250)

Banque Nationale du Rwanda 🏛 Central Bank
Avenue Paul VI, PO Box 531, Kigali
Tel: 74282; 75319 **Fax:** 72551; 72961 **Telex:** 22508 **Swift:** BNRW RW RW **Telex:** 22589

Senior Executive Officers
Governor François Mutemberezi
Deputy Governor Laurien Rutayisire
Vice Governor J Damascène Munyarukiko
General Secretary François Ntagara

Others (Senior Executives)
Chief Cashier Apolinaire Muyango
Head, Bank Licensing Gregory Muramira
Head, Banking Supervision Angélique Kantengwa
Head, Economics & Statistics Olivier Munyaneza
Head, Public Debt Jean Nkurunziza
Head, Reserves Management Canisius Gatsinzi

Foreign Exchange
Head of Foreign Exchange Gakuba Kabati

Settlement / Clearing
Head of Settlement / Clearing François Hajabakiga

Administration
Head of Administration François Ntagara *General Secretary*

Technology & Systems
  Gaston Bushayija

Public Relations
  Appolinaire Murasira

Accounts / Audit
Head, Accountancy   Vianney Kagabo

SAINT KITTS AND NEVIS
(+1 809)

Eastern Caribbean Central Bank — Central Bank
PO Box 89, Birdrock, Basseterre
Tel: 465 2537 Fax: 465 1051 Email: eccberu@carib.surf.com

Senior Executive Officers
Governor   K Dwight Venner
Deputy Governor   Errol N Allen
Bank Secretary   Wentworth Harris

Others (Senior Executives)
Head, Banking Supervision   Mignon Wade *Senior Director*
Head, Economics & Statistics   Wendell Samuel *Senior Director*
Head, Reserves Management   Robertine Chaderton *Director*

Administration

Public Relations
Communications   Cheryl Fletcher

SAMOA (WESTERN)
(+685)

Central Bank of Samoa — Central Bank
PO Box Private Mail Bag, Apia
Tel: 34100; 34237 Fax: 20293; 24058 Telex: 64200 CENBANK SX

Senior Executive Officers
Chairman   Afoa Kolone Vaai
Governor   Papli'i Tommy Scanlan ☎ **22318**
Chief Executive Officer   Philip Penn *Deputy Chief Executive, Policy* ☎ **24014**
                                      Ray Ah Liki *Deputy Chief Executive, Administration* ☎ **26500**
Governor's Secretary   Fogatia Mau ☎ **34204**

Others (Senior Executives)
Chief Cashier   Mika Leo *Cashier* ☎ **34258**
Head, Bank Licensing; Head, Banking   Gilbert Wongsin *Manager, Financial Institutions* ☎ **34222**
Supervision
Head, Economics & Statistics   Iosefo Bourne *Manager, Research & Statistics* ☎ **34228**
Head, Reserves Management   Ray Ah Liki *Deputy Chief Executive, Administration* ☎ **26500**

Foreign Exchange
Head of Foreign Exchange   Sootala Pua *Manager, International* ☎ **34250**

Settlement / Clearing
Head of Settlement / Clearing   Sanele Afoa *Manager, Banking & Administration* ☎ **23367**

Administration
Head of Administration   Puipui Teneri *Manager, Administration & Personnel* ☎ **34251**

Technology & Systems
                                      Harry Porter *Manager, Building & Services* ☎ **34236**

Accounts / Audit
Head, Accountancy   Sanele Afoa *Manager, Banking & Administration* ☎ **23367**

SAO TOMÉ AND PRINCIPE (+239)   www.euromoneydirectory.com

SAO TOMÉ AND PRINCIPE
(+239)

Banco Central de São Tomé e Príncipe — Central Bank

Alternative trading name: Central bank of Sao Tomé and Principe
São Tomé
Tel: (12) 21300; (12) 21269 **Fax:** (12) 22501; (12) 22777 **Telex:** 264 TOPBANK ST
Email: bcentral@sol.stome.telepac.net **Telex:** 219 TOPBANK ST

Senior Executive Officers
Governor — Carlos Quaresma Batista de Sousa

Others (Senior Executives)
Head, Economic Policy & Financial Programming — Eugénio Lourenço Soares *Executive Director*
Head, General Operations — Maria Madre Deus Santiago Lima *Executive Director*
Head, Administration — José dos Ramos Lucens e Silva *Executive Director*
General Operations — Edite Diogo Afonso Soares
Monetary Statistics & Balance of Payments — Ângela Maria da Graça Viegas Santiago
Head, External Debt & Reserves Management — Maria de Fátima Fortes
Head, Banking Supervision — Alcino Costa Batista de Sousa
Governor's Office — Luís da Conceição

General - Treasury
Head of Treasury — Fernando Trovoada da Costa

Other Departments
Economic Research — Maria do Carmo Trovoada Pires Carvalho *Head*

Administration
Head of Administration — José dos Ramos Lucens e Silva *Executive Director*
Amadeu de Jesus *Head*

Technology & Systems
Data Processing — Manuel Argentino Madre de Deus

Accounts / Audit
Head, Internal Auditing — Maria Irene Ferreira

SAUDI ARABIA
(+966)

Al Rajhi Banking & Investment Corporation — Head Office

Formerly known as: Al Rajhi Company for Currency Exchange Commerce
Olalya Main Street, New Akariyah Building, Riyadh 11411
PO Box 28, Riyadh 11411
Tel: (1) 460 1000 **Fax:** (1) 460 0922 **Telex:** 403538 **Swift:** RJHI SA RI **Reuters:** RAJR **Telerate:** AL RAJHI

Senior Executive Officers
Chairman — Sheikh Saleh Bin Abdulaziz Al Rajhi
Financial Director — Ahmed Al Hossan *Deputy Managing Director* ☎ **460 1501**
Treasurer — Colin Willis *Treasurer* ☎ **460 1996**
Managing Director — Sheikh Sulaiman Bin Abdulaziz Al Rajhi ☎ **460 1418**
General Manager — Abdullah Sulaiman Al Rajhi ☎ **460 2015**
International Division — Fahad Abdullah Al Rajhi *Deputy General Manager* ☎ **460 1485**

Others (Senior Executives)
Global Head of Trading Group — Sulaiman Saleh Al Rajhi *Deputy General Manager* ☎ **460 1544**

Other Departments
Private Banking — David Gibson Moore *Executive Manager* ☎ **461 0127**

Administration
Head of Administration — Ibrahim Al Gofaily

Technology & Systems
Mansoor Al Ghulaiga *Deputy General Manager* ☎ **460 1358**

Compliance
Tony Davies

Public Relations
Mohd Saad Thaqib *Manager* ☎ **460 1407**

1276 Euromoney Directory 1999

www.euromoneydirectory.com　　　SAUDI ARABIA (+966)

Al-Bank Al-Saudi Al Fransi
Head Office

Maather Road, Riyadh 11554
PO Box 56006, Riyadh 11554
Tel: (1) 404 2222 **Fax:** (1) 404 2311 **Telex:** 407666 SFGM SJ **Swift:** BSFR SA RI **GEM Reuters:** BSFX
Website: www.saudifransi.com

Senior Executive Officers
Chairman — Ibrahim Al-Touq
Chief Executive Officer — Bertrand Viriot *Managing Director*
Aboulrahman Jawa *Deputy Managing Director*
Financial Director — Abdulqadir Mirza *Finance & Accounting Manager*
Treasurer — Osamah Bakhit *Treasurer*

Others (Senior Executives)
Brokerage — Samer Alrayyan *Manager*
Credit Banking — Francois Rivier *Manager*

General-Lending (DCM, SL)
Head of Corporate Banking — Robin Demouxy *Manager, Corporate Banking I*

General-Investment
Head of Investment — Tareq Mashouk *Investment Manager*

Arab National Bank
Head Office

King Faisal Street, North Murabaa, Riyadh 11564
PO Box 56921, Riyadh
Tel: (1) 402 9000 **Fax:** (1) 402 7747 **Telex:** 402660 ARNA SJ **Swift:** ARNB SA RI **Reuters:** ANBR-S **Telerate:** 17274
Website: www.anb.com.sa

Senior Executive Officers
Chairman — Abdul Aziz S Al-Saghyir
Treasurer — Roy Garnham *Acting General Manager*

General-Lending (DCM, SL)
Head of Corporate Banking — Maurice Horan *General Manager, Corporate Banking*
Khalid Al-Qwais *General Manager, Credit Group*

General - Treasury
Head of Treasury — Tareq Bin Taleb *DGM, Treasury & International Relations Group*

Settlement / Clearing
Operations — Mohammed I Al-Mansour *GM, Operations & Services*
Marwan Abiad *Deputy General Manager, Comptroller*

Other Departments
Chief Credit Officer — Khalid Al-Qwais *General Manager*
Private Banking — Alain L Field *General Manager*

Arab Petroleum Investments Corporation (APICORP)
Head Office

Alternative trading name: APICORP
PO Box 448, Dhahran Airport 31932
Tel: (3) 864 7400 **Fax:** (3) 894 5076; (3) 864 0061 **Telex:** 870068 APIC SJ **Email:** apicorp@arabia.com

Senior Executive Officers
Chairman & BO Director — Abdullah Al-Zaid
Chief Executive Officer — Nureddin Farrag *General Manager & Chief Executive*
Financial Director — Edward Lutley *Financial Controller*
Treasurer — Dino Moretto *Head of Treasury and Capital Markets* ☏ **894 4057**

Debt Capital Markets / Fixed Income
Eurobonds
Head of Trading — Hesham M Farid *Assistant Portfolio Manager, Fixed-Income* ☏ **894 4057**
Mohamed Assaad *Portfolio Manager, Fixed-Income* ☏ **894 4057**

Equity Capital Markets
International Equities
Head of Trading — Mark Coombe-Tennant *Portfolio Manager, Equities* ☏ **896 0737**
Head of Research — Mirza Saeed Arshad *Assistant Analyst* ☏ **894 4057**

Convertibles / Equity-Linked
Head of Trading — Zafar Raja *Manager, Money Market* ☏ **894 4057**

Money Markets
Head of Money Markets — Zafar Raja *Manager, Money Market* ☏ **894 4057**

Euromoney Directory 1999　**1277**

SAUDI ARABIA (+966) www.euromoneydirectory.com

Arab Petroleum Investments Corporation (APICORP) (cont)
Money Markets - General
  Fadhel Mansoor *Money Market Officer* ☏ **896 0737**
Foreign Exchange
Head of Trading
  Gary Moyse *Senior Dealer, Forex* ☏ **896 0737**
Administration
Technology & Systems
  Galal Osman *Manager, ISC*
Legal / In-House Counsel
  Mohamed Omar *General Legal Counsel*
Public Relations
  Mahdi Al-Mahdi *Public Affairs Officer*

Bank Al-Jazira

Khalid Bin Walid Street, PO Box 6277, Jeddah 21442
Tel: (2) 651 8070 **Fax:** (2) 653 2478 **Telex:** 601574 HJAZSJ **Swift:** BJAZ SA JE **Reuters:** BAJJ

Senior Executive Officers
Chairman
  Adel Fakheih
Chief Executive Officer
  Mishari Al-Mishari *General Manager & Chief Executive Officer*
Financial Director
  John Evans *AGM, Finance & Human Resources*
Treasurer
  Clive Reed
General Manager & Chief Executive Officer
  Mishari Al-Mishari
Manager
  Hassan Ibrahim
International Division
  Mazen Abdul Majeed *Division Head*

Others (Senior Executives)
Support Services
  Saleh El-Remahi *Assistant General Manager*
General-Lending (DCM, SL)
Head of Corporate Banking
  Nabil Abdel Ghani *Assistant General Manager, Corporate Banking*
General-Investment
Head of Investment
  Tawfik Khanifani *Assistant General Manager* ☏ **651 8080**
Syndicated Lending
Loan-Related Activities
Trade Finance
  Ziad Aba Al-Khail *Division Head*
Corporate Finance / M&A Advisory
Head of Corporate Finance
  Nabil Abdel Ghani *Assistant General Manager, Corporate Banking*
Settlement / Clearing
Operations
  Ziad Aba Al-Khail *Division Head*
Other Departments
Chief Credit Officer
  Nabil Abdel Ghani *Assistant General Manager, Corporate Banking*
Private Banking
  Hisham Abul'ola *Assistant General Manager, Branches Systems*
Correspondent Banking
  Mazen Abdul Majeed *Division Head*
Administration
Head of Administration
  Sami Abu'al Faraj *Division Head*
Head of Marketing
  Badr Suwaidan *Senior Manager*
Technology & Systems
  Robert Tranter *Assistant General Manager, Operations & Technology*
  Tawfik Khanifani *Assistant General Manager* ☏ **651 8080**
Legal / In-House Counsel
  Souheil Hasbini *Division Head*
Accounts / Audit
  Joel Abraham *Division Head*
Other (Administration)
Human Resource Division
  Sami Abu'al Faraj *Division Head*

The National Commercial Bank   Head Office

NCB Building, King Abdul-Aziz Street, Jeddah 21481
PO Box 3555, Jeddah 21481
Tel: (2) 644 6644 **Fax:** (2) 644 6644 **Telex:** 605571 NCB SJ **Swift:** NCBK SA JE

Senior Executive Officers
Chairman
  Khalid bin Salim bin Mahfouz
Chief Operating Officer
  Saleh Kaki

SAUDI ARABIA (+966)

Senior Executive Officers (cont)
Treasurer Don Hill
International Division Ala'a Al Jabri

Others (Senior Executives)
Management Committee Abdulrahman Khalid Bin Mahfouz
 Abdulhadi Shayif *Deputy Chairman*
Retail Banking Bilal Hakim ☎ **643 8427**
Investment Services Frederick Crawford ☎ **669 7378**
Corporate Banking Jawdag Halebi ☎ **644 8488**
Islamic Banking Abdulrazzak Elkhereiji ☎ **644 6490**

Corporate Finance / M&A Advisory
Global Head Tariq Ali ☎ **(1) 477 1525**

Other Departments
Private Banking Abdul Kareem Abu Al Nasr ☎ **660 7868**
Correspondent Banking Hany Faidy ☎ **644 6908**

Administration
Public Relations
Head Farouk Eid ☎ **644 7979**

Riyad Bank   Head Office
King Abdulaziz Road, PO Box 22622, Riyadh 11416
Tel: (1) 401 3030 **Fax:** (1) 404 2707 **Telex:** 407490 **Reuters:** RYBJ **Telex:** 407500

Senior Executive Officers
Chairman Omran Muhammed Al-Omran
Vice Chairman Rashed Abdulaziz Al-Rashed
General Manager Alan Thompson
Deputy General Manager Talal I Al-Qudaibi
Associate DGM Abdulrahman Al-Amoudi
AGM, Domestic Banking Sulliman A Al-Gwaiz
AGM, International Banking Riyad M Al-Dughaither
AGM, Financial Control Thalib A Al-Shamrani

Others (Senior Executives)
International & Investment Banking
 Riyad M Al-Dughaither *AGM, International Banking*
 Basel Al-Gadhib *Executive Manager, Investment Banking*
 Said Hashim *Assistant Executive Manager, Overseas Banking*
 Ousep Matten *Senior Manager, Investment Services Department*

Debt Capital Markets / Fixed Income
Department: Treasury

Bonds - General
 Jack R Shar *Treasurer*
 Ghassan Saqallah *Chief Dealer*
 Abdul Aziz Al-Malki *Chief Dealer, Sales*
Saudi Riyad Desk Sanjay Behuria *Senior Dealer*

Money Markets
Department: Treasury

Money Markets - General
International Money Market Chris Wilmot *Chief Dealer*
 Mark Abrahams *Senior Dealer*

Foreign Exchange
Department: Treasury

FX Traders / Sales People
 Frank Johansen *Assistant Chief Dealer*
 Hossam Gawdat *Senior Dealer*
 Jamaan Al-Ghamdi *Senior Dealer*
 Sayid Ali *Senior Dealer*
Corporate Sales Tariq Rahmat *Senior Dealer*
 Batel Al-Batel *Senior Dealer*
 Samir Sweidan *Senior Dealer*
 Mukesh Punjabi *Senior Dealer*

Risk Management
Head of Risk Management James Stewart

Corporate Finance / M&A Advisory
Department: Loan Syndications
Head of Corporate Finance Colin Edwards *Senior Manager*

SAUDI ARABIA (+966)   www.euromoneydirectory.com

Riyad Bank (cont)
Other Departments
Chief Credit Officer   Geoffrey E Rimmer *Senior Executive Manager, Credit Control*
Administration
Technology & Systems
   John Hoinicki *Executive Manager, Information Technology*
Compliance
   Gary Coia *Compliance Officer*
Public Relations
   Atiah Al-Zahrani *Manager*
Other (Administration)
   John Hackwood *Manager, Marketing*

Saudi American Bank — Head Office
Old Airport Road, PO Box 833, Riyadh 11421
Tel: (1) 477 4770 **Fax:** (1) 479 9317; (1) 479 9410 **Telex:** 400195 **Swift:** SAMB SA RI **Reuters:** SABR; SAFX; SAGB

Senior Executive Officers
Chairman   Abdulaziz Bin Hamad Al-Gosaibi
Chief Executive Officer   Robert Eichfeld *Managing Director & Chief Executive*
Treasurer   Misbah Shah *General Manager & Corporate Treasurer*
GM, Head & Corporate Secretary   Abdulrahman Sadhan

Others (Senior Executives)
Services Management   Naveed Sultan *General Manager*
Private & Investment Banking Group   Eisa Al-Eisa *General Manager*
Credit Policy   Stephen McClintock *General Manager*
Senior Credit Officer - Corporate Bank   Steve Venter *General Manager*
Senior Credit Officer - Treasury & Private Bank   Jared Dornburg *General Manager*
Senior Credit Officer - Western Region   Ron De Angelis *General Manager* ☎ **(2) 653 3555 ext 344**
Senior Credit Officer - Eastern Region   Mousa Al-Mousa *General Manager* ☎ **(3) 857 5503 ext 508**
Public Sector & FI Head   Abdulaziz Al-Barakat *General Manager*
Financial Controller   Mazhar Ul-Latif *Assistant General Manager*
Chief Internal Auditor   Barry Belbin *Assistant General Manager*
Technology Group   Dimitrios Tsiridakis *Assistant General Manager*
Economist   Kevin Taecker *Assistant General Manager*
London Branch   Tom Mulvihill *General Manager* ☎ **+44 (171) 355 4411**
SAMBA Finance   Fadi Elkhoury *General Manager* ☎ **+33 (1) 43 80 00 80**
SAMBA Capital Management International   Richard Keigher *General Manager* ☎ **+44 (171) 355 4411**

General-Lending (DCM, SL)
Head of Corporate Banking   Augusto Felix Jr *General Manager*

Debt Capital Markets / Fixed Income
Department: Treasury Group / Money Market
Fax: 477 0608 **Telex:** 401072
Head of Fixed Income   Mehdi Shirazee *Assistant General Manager*

Government Bonds
Head of Sales   Mehdi Shirazee *Assistant General Manager*

Eurobonds
Head of Sales   Mehdi Shirazee *Assistant General Manager*

Emerging Market Bonds
Head of Sales   Deepak Benegal *Assistant General Manager*

Libor-Based / Floating-Rate Products
FRN Sales   Mehdi Shirazee *Assistant General Manager*

Fixed-Income Repo
Head of Repo   Mehdi Shirazee *Assistant General Manager*

Fixed-Income Research
Head of Fixed Income   Mehdi Shirazee *Assistant General Manager*

Syndicated Lending
Tel: 477 4770 ext 1357 **Fax:** 479 9317 **Telex:** 400195 SAMBA SJ
Head of Syndication   Enrico Grino *Assistant General Manager*

Loan-Related Activities
Trade Finance   Enrico Grino *Assistant General Manager*
Project Finance   Michael Austin *Assistant General Manager*
Structured Trade Finance   Thomas Cotton *Assistant General Manager*

Other (Trade Finance)
Structured Finance & Leasing   Thomas Cotton *Assistant General Manager*
Merchant Banking   Michael Baker *Assistant General Manager*

www.euromoneydirectory.com   SAUDI ARABIA (+966)

Money Markets
Fax: 477 0608 **Telex:** 401072
Head of Money Markets   Mehdi Shirazee *Assistant General Manager*

Eurocommercial Paper
Head of Sales   Abdul Qadir Khanani *Assistant General Manager*

Foreign Exchange
Fax: 477 0608 **Telex:** 401072
Head of Foreign Exchange   Deepak Benegal *Assistant General Manager*

Risk Management
Fax: 477 0608 **Telex:** 401072
Head of Risk Management   Ajaz Ahmed *AGM, Treasury Risk Management*

Settlement / Clearing
Fax: 477 0608 **Telex:** 401072
Operations   Muhammed Al-Ruwais *Assistant General Manager*

Other Departments
Chief Credit Officer   Stephen McClintock *General Manager*
Private Banking   Eisa Al-Eisa *General Manager*
Correspondent Banking   Enrico Grino *Assistant General Manager*
Cash Management   Hany Sherif *Assistant General Manager*

Administration
Head of Marketing   Suren Khirwadker *Assistant General Manager*

Technology & Systems
                                 Dimitrios Tsiridakis *Assistant General Manager*

Legal / In-House Counsel
                                 Chadhan Jebeyli *Assistant General Manager*

Compliance
                                 Chadhan Jebeyli *Assistant General Manager*

Accounts / Audit
Accounting   Mazhar Ul-Latif *Assistant General Manager*
Internal Audit   Barry Belbin *Assistant General Manager*

The Saudi British Bank

Dabab Street, Riyadh 11413
PO Box 9084, Riyadh 11413
Tel: (1) 405 0677 **Fax:** (1) 405 8652

Senior Executive Officers
Chairman   Sheikh Abdullah Moha Hugail
Financial Director   Robert White
Treasurer   Steve Eggelhoessr *Treasurer*
Managing Director / General Manager Alexander Flockhart

Debt Capital Markets / Fixed Income
Department: Treasury
Tel: 405 0020
Head of Debt Capital Markets   Mutsher Almarshad *Deputy Treasurer*
Other   Abdul Alkhrayji *Head, Corporate Desk*

Money Markets
Department: Treasury
Tel: 405 0020
Head of Money Markets   Mutsher Almarshad *Deputy Treasurer*
Other   Abdul Alkhrayji *Head, Corporate Desk*

Foreign Exchange
Department: Treasury
Tel: 405 0020
Head of Foreign Exchange   Mutsher Almarshad *Deputy Treasurer*
                                 Khalid Alrayes *Head, Foreign Exchange*
Corporate Sales   Abdul Alkhrayji *Head, Corporate Desk*

SAUDI ARABIA (+966)   www.euromoneydirectory.com

Saudi Hollandi Bank
Head Office

Formerly known as: AlBank AlSaudi AlHollandi
Al Rashid Building, Al Dhabab Street, PO Box 1467, Riyadh 11431
Tel: (1) 406 7888; (1) 401 0288 **Fax:** (1) 405 8820; (1) 403 1104 **Telex:** 401488 BSHR SJ **Swift:** AAAL SA RI
Reuters: BSHR **Fax:** 405 0973

Senior Executive Officers
Chairman	Sulaiman Alsuhaimi ☎ **401 1020** 📠 **401 0968**
Managing Director	Herman Erbe ☎ **405 0898** 📠 **401 0968**
Treasurer	Richard Bruens *AGM & Treasurer* ☎ **406 6665** 📠 **405 0968**
Managing Director	Herman Erbe ☎ **405 0898** 📠 **401 0968**
Deputy Managing Director	Mohamad Abdulhadi ☎ **405 4746** 📠 **405 8820**
Company Secretary	Farid Zaouk ☎ **401 1020** 📠 **401 0968**
International Division	Syed Ziaudding ☎ **ext 517** 📠 **401 0736**

General-Lending (DCM, SL)
Head of Corporate Banking — Mohamad Abdulhadi *Deputy Managing Director* ☎ **405 4746** 📠 **405 8820**

General-Investment
Head of Investment — Abdulrahman Al Yahya *Assistant General Manager* ☎ **456 1320** 📠 **453 1777**

Debt Capital Markets / Fixed Income
Head of Fixed Income — Richard Bruens *AGM & Treasurer* ☎ **406 6665** 📠 **405 0968**
Head of Fixed Income Trading — Bo Hansson *Chief Dealer* ☎ **406 6665** 📠 **405 0968**

Syndicated Lending

Other (Trade Finance)
Structured Finance — Jim Rose *Manager* ☎ **ext 538** 📠 **401 0968**

Money Markets
Head of Money Markets — Richard Bruens *AGM & Treasurer* ☎ **406 6665** 📠 **405 0968**

Foreign Exchange
Head of Foreign Exchange — Richard Bruens *AGM & Treasurer* ☎ **406 6665** 📠 **405 0968**

FX Traders / Sales People
Edward Thorig *Chief Dealer* ☎ **402 9840** 📠 **405 0968**
Paul Denys *Senior Manager* ☎ **402 9840** 📠 **405 0968**

Corporate Finance / M&A Advisory
Head of Corporate Finance — Jim Rose *Manager* ☎ **ext 538** 📠 **401 0968**

Settlement / Clearing
Operations — Abdulaziz Al-Oraifi *Assistant General Manager* ☎ **ext 690** 📠 **ext 277**

Other Departments
Chief Credit Officer — Grant Scroggie *AGM* ☎ **ext 515** 📠 **401 0730**
Private Banking — Mohamad Abdulhadi *Deputy Managing Director* ☎ **405 4746** 📠 **405 8820**
Correspondent Banking — Syed Ziaudding ☎ **ext 517** 📠 **401 0736**

Administration
Head of Administration — Abdulaziz Al-Oraifi *Assistant General Manager* ☎ **ext 690** 📠 **ext 277**
Business Development — Mohamed Fahim ☎ **ext 553** 📠 **ext 625**
Head of Marketing — Khaled Al-Dughaither *Assistant General Manager* ☎ **ext 553** 📠 **ext 625**

Technology & Systems
Information Services — Mohamed Fahim ☎ **ext 553** 📠 **ext 625**

Legal / In-House Counsel
Farid Zaouk ☎ **401 1020** 📠 **401 0968**

Accounts / Audit
Internal Audit — Bas Van Veelen *Manager* ☎ **ext 540**

Other (Administration)
Information — Mohamed Fahim ☎ **ext 553** 📠 **ext 625**

The Saudi Investment Bank
Head Office

PO Box 3533, Riyadh 1 11481
Tel: (1) 477 8433 **Fax:** (1) 477 6781 **Telex:** 401170 SAIB RH SJ **Swift:** SIBC SA RI **Email:** saud@saibank.com

Senior Executive Officers
Chairman	Abdulaziz O Hali
Chief Executive Officer	Saud Al-Saleh *General Manager*
Financial Director	Musaed Al-Mineefi *Group Head*
Treasurer	Jerry McCabe *Group Head*
International Division	Ramzi Al-Nassar *Head, Institutional & Retail*

General-Lending (DCM, SL)
Head of Corporate Banking — Elias Haddad *Group Head*

www.euromoneydirectory.com　　　　　　　　**SAUDI ARABIA (+966)**

Syndicated Lending
Head of Syndication　　　　　　　　Ivan Hopkins *Head of Corporate Banking* ☏ **ext 1700**

Money Markets
Department: Treasury & Investment Banking
Head of Money Markets　　　　　　Jerome McCabe *Group Head* ☏ **476 1976**

Foreign Exchange
Tel: 476 1580 **Fax:** 476 1976
Head of Foreign Exchange　　　　Bassam Jarrar *Head of Treasury*

Other Departments
Chief Credit Officer　　　　　　　　Abdul Malek Al-Sanea *Head, Credit Administration*
Private Banking　　　　　　　　　　Jerome McCabe *Group Head* ☏ **476 1976**

Administration
Technology & Systems
　　　　　　　　　　　　　　　　　　Michael Carpenter *Head*

Accounts / Audit
Audit　　　　　　　　　　　　　　Charles Barry James *Group Head*

United Saudi Bank　　　　　　　　　　　　　　　　Head Office

Formerly known as: United Saudi Commercial Bank
Sitteen Street, Malaz, PO Box 25895, Riyadh 11476
Tel: (1) 478 4200 **Fax:** (1) 478 3197 **Telex:** 405461 SAUCOM SJ **Swift:** USCB SA RI XXX **Reuters:** USCR

Senior Executive Officers
Chairman　　　　　　　　　　　　Prince Alwaleed Bin Abdulaziz Al Saud
Chief Executive Officer　　　　　　Maher Al-Aujan *Managing Director*
Treasurer　　　　　　　　　　　　Vijay Khanna *Treasurer* ☏ **473 0684**
Corporate Secretary　　　　　　　Khalid Althukair

Others (Senior Executives)
Human Resources　　　　　　　　Jamal Al-Guwafli *Head*
　　　　　　　　　　　　　　　　　　Tariq Amjad *Risk Manager*
　　　　　　　　　　　　　　　　　　Saleem Jangda *Head, Capital Markets*

General-Lending (DCM, SL)
Head of Corporate Banking　　　　Mohammed Ghanameh

Debt Capital Markets / Fixed Income
Department: Capital Markets
Tel: 478 4074 **Fax:** 479 3731
Head of Debt Capital Markets; Head of Fixed Income　　Saleem Jangda *Head, Capital Markets*
Head of Fixed Income Sales; Head of Fixed Income Trading　　Gary McGraw *Senior Dealer*

Government Bonds
Head of Sales; Head of Trading　　Gary McGraw *Senior Dealer*

Eurobonds
Head of Sales; Head of Trading　　Gary McGraw *Senior Dealer*

Emerging Market Bonds
Head of Emerging Markets　　　　Vijay Khanna *Treasurer* ☏ **473 0684**
Head of Sales; Head of Trading　　Nadir Al Koraya *Senior Dealer*

Syndicated Lending
Tel: 478 4570
Head of Syndication　　　　　　　Mohammed Ghanameh *Head, Corporate Banking*

Money Markets
Tel: 473 0684 **Fax:** 479 3731
Head of Money Markets　　　　　Ahmed Al-Aey *Senior Dealer*

Foreign Exchange
Tel: 473 0684 **Fax:** 479 3731
Head of Foreign Exchange　　　　Samer Farhoud *Head, Corporate Treasury*

Risk Management
Tel: 478 4200 **Fax:** 479 3731
Head of Risk Management　　　　Tariq Amjad *Risk Manager*

OTC Commodity Derivatives
Head　　　　　　　　　　　　　　Samer Farhoud *Head, Corporate Treasury*

Exchange-Traded Derivatives
Head　　　　　　　　　　　　　　Bakr Al Khudairy *Derivatives Trading*

SAUDI ARABIA (+966)

www.euromoneydirectory.com

United Saudi Bank (cont)
Settlement / Clearing
Head of Settlement / Clearing; Equity Settlement; Fixed-Income Settlement; Operations
Ibrahim Al Hazza *Treasury Operation*

Asset Management
Head
Bakr Al Khudairy

Other Departments
Commodities / Bullion
Samer Farhoud *Head, Corporate Treasury*
Chief Credit Officer
Tariq Amjad *Head of Financial Institutions* ☎ **478 4575**
Private Banking
Habib Faris *Head of Private Banking*
Correspondent Banking
Tariq Amjad *Head of Financial Institutions* ☎ **478 4575**

Administration
Head of Administration
Mazin Al-Khudairy *Financial Controller*

Technology & Systems
Ghassan Kutbi *Head of IT* ☎ **479 1515**

Legal / In-House Counsel
Yusuf Jadaan *Head of Legal Department*

Accounts / Audit
Auditor
Asad Kanaan

Other (Administration)
Human Resources
Jamal Al-Guwafli *Head*

SENEGAL (+221)

Banque Centrale des Etats de l'Afrique de l'Ouest 🏛 Central Bank
PO Box 3108, Avenue Abdoulaye Fadiga, Dakar
Tel: 839 0500 **Fax:** 839 9335 **Telex:** 21833 SG
General Telex: 21530 SG **Telex:** 21597 SG **Telex:** 21815 SG

Senior Executive Officers
Governor
Charles Konan Banny
Vice Governor
Boukary Adji
Vice Governor
Damo Justin Baro
General Secretary
Michel Komlanvi Klousseh
General Secretary
Mbaye Diop Sarr

Citibank NA
Full Branch Office

2 Place de L'Independence, PO Box 3391, Dakar
Tel: 823 2981 **Fax:** 823 8817 **Telex:** 21 662 **Reuters:** CIDK

Senior Executive Officers
Chief Executive Officer
Kandolo Kasongo *Country Corporate Officer* ☎ **823 3369**
Treasurer
Oulimata Ndiaye *Treasurer* ☎ **823 7006**

General-Lending (DCM, SL)
Head of Corporate Banking
Asif Zaidi ☎ **823 4948**

Debt Capital Markets / Fixed Income
Head of Debt Capital Markets
Oulimata Ndiaye *Treasurer* ☎ **823 7006**

Equity Capital Markets
Head of Equity Capital Markets
Oulimata Ndiaye *Treasurer* ☎ **823 7006**

Money Markets
Head of Money Markets
Oulimata Ndiaye *Treasurer* ☎ **823 7006**

Foreign Exchange
Head of Foreign Exchange
Oulimata Ndiaye *Treasurer* ☎ **823 7006**

FX Traders / Sales People
FX Trader
Abdoulaye Dieng ☎ **823 7006**

Risk Management
Head of Risk Management
Ahmed Iyane Dia *Risk Manager* ☎ **823 2981**

Settlement / Clearing
Head of Settlement / Clearing
Oulimata Ndiaye *Treasurer* ☎ **823 7006**
Back-Office
Saiba Fainke *Head* ☎ **823 2981**

SINGAPORE (+65)

Other Departments
Cash Management

Aicha Pouye ☎ **823 2981**

Administration

Technology & Systems

Macoumba Fall ☎ **823 8609**

Legal / In-House Counsel

Ahmed Iyane Dia *Risk Manager* ☎ **823 2981**

Compliance

Bachir Camara ☎ **823 2981**

Public Relations

Ahme D Iyane Dia *Risk Manager* ☎ **823 2981**

SEYCHELLES
(+248)

Central Bank of Seychelles — 🏛 Central Bank

PO Box 701, Victoria
Tel: 225 200 **Fax:** 224 958 **Telex:** 2301 SZ CENBNK **Email:** cbs@seychelles.net

Senior Executive Officers
Governor — Norman Weber ☎ **225 252**
Director — Erol Dias ☎ **383 000**
Director — Francis Chang-Sam ☎ **383 000**
Treasurer — Jacques Berlouis
General Manager — Francis Chang-Leng
Director General, Banking Services — Patrick Stravens

Others (Senior Executives)
Head, Bank Licensing; Head, Banking Supervision — Jennifer Morel *Director General, Bank Supervision*
Head, Economics & Statistics — Pierre Laporte *Director, Research*
Head, Public Debt; Head, Reserves Management — Patrick Stravens *Director General, Banking Services*

Foreign Exchange
Head of Foreign Exchange — Patrick Stravens *Director General, Banking Services*

Settlement / Clearing
Head of Settlement / Clearing — Patrick Stravens *Director General, Banking Services*

Administration
Head of Administration — Lorna Renaud *Manager*

Accounts / Audit
Head, Accountancy — Patrick Stravens *Director General, Banking Services*

SINGAPORE
(+65)

The Monetary Authority of Singapore — 🏛 Central Bank

MAS Building, 10 Shenton Way, Singapore, 079117
Tel: 225 5577 **Telex:** RS28174 ORCHID **Swift:** MASG SG SG **Email:** webmaster@mas.gov.sg **Reuters:** MAST
Marketing & Investment Department **Fax:** 229 9491
Website: www.mas.gov.sg.

Senior Executive Officers
Deputy Prime Minister — Lee Hsien-Loong
Deputy Chairman — Lee Ek Tieng

SINGAPORE (+65)   www.euromoneydirectory.com

ABN AMRO Asia Merchant Bank (Singapore) Limited
Subsidiary Company

Formerly known as: ABN AMRO Hoare Govett Merchant Bank (Singapore) Ltd
63 Chulia Street, #11-01, Singapore, 049514
Tel: 231 8088 **Fax:** 532 6637 **Telex:** RS29114 AMRASI

Senior Executive Officers
Chairman — Ray Rajan
Managing Director — Charles Lew

Others *(Senior Executives)*
Ronald Low *Executive Director*
Corporate Finance — Chai Boon Lim *Director, Corporate Finance*

Corporate Finance / M&A Advisory
Head of Corporate Finance — Chai Boon Lim *Director, Corporate Finance*

Settlement / Clearing
Operations — Koh Kok Eng *Senior Manager*

ABN AMRO Bank NV, Global Trading Unit
Regional Head Office

Global Trading Unit, Level 9, 63 Chulia Street, Singapore, 049514
Tel: 231 8888; 231 7786 **Fax:** 536 9371; 535 8775 **Telex:** 24430 ABNEXCH **Swift:** ABNA SG SG **Telerate:** 2839
General Telex: 20874 ABNEXCH; **Reuters:** ABNS, ABNT, ABSS, DCDB (Monitor); ABSS, ABNS, AABO (Dealing)

Senior Executive Officers

Others *(Senior Executives)*
Investment Banking, Treasury & Debt Capital Market — Nils Lorenzen *Managing Director* T 231 7834 F 533 3358
Derivatives Markets Asia — Arjen van der Linden *Derivative Markets, Asia* T 231 7838 F 536 9371
Regional Treasury Support Manager — Steven Sng *Senior Vice President* T 231 7835 F 535 7790
Treasury & Fixed Income, Asia — Robert Hadley *Chief Operating Officer* T 231 7803 F 536 9371
Regional Treasurer Asia Pacific — Egge de Vries *Senior Vice President* T 231 7840 F 535 7790
Credit Trading & Fixed Income Sales, Asia Pacific — Zafar Alam *Regional Head & SVP* T 231 7836 F 536 6627

Debt Capital Markets / Fixed Income
Fax: 536 6627

Bonds - General
Head of Trading & Sales, Asian Fixed Income — Zafar Alam *Regional Head & SVP* T 231 7836 F 536 6627
Head of Sales — Nicholas R H Langman *SVP, Regional Head of Fixed Income Sales* T 231 7886

Credit Trading — Brian Piening T 231 7886
Local Currency Trader — Tow Wee Chiam T 231 7887
Roy Gwee T 231 7887
Floating Rate Trader — Jeff Sia T 231 7887
Sales & Distribution Head — Nick Langman *SVP, Regional Head of Fixed Income Sales* T 231 7890
Asian Fixed Income Sales — Soo Meng Chia T 231 7886
Giorgio Pilla T 231 7886
Beng Wah Tan T 231 7886
G7 Sales — Lydia Kew T 231 7890 F 438 4932
Patrick Yeo T 231 7886 F 438 4932
Head of Fixed Income Origination / Syndication Asia — Roland Plan *Senior Vice President* T 231 7891 F 438 5049

Money Markets
Fax: 535 8775
Head of Money Markets — Sow Chun Lim *VP & Regional Depo Head* T 532 2330

Money Markets - General
Kok Kuan Kang *VP & Forwards Head* T 536 3687

Foreign Exchange
Head of Foreign Exchange — Richard Lim *Vice President, Head of Foreign Exchange Trading* T 231 7845
Head of Institutional Sales — David Chong *Vice President, Institutional Sales* T 231 7865
Corporate Sales — Donald Thio *Vice President, Corporate Sales* T 231 7851

FX Traders / Sales People
Philip Phang *Sales*
Ashley Tan *Sales*
Chitin Ben-David *Sales*
Alain Tan *Sales*
Jacqueline Tay *Sales*

1286 Euromoney Directory 1999

Risk Management
Global Head — Jeroen P M M Thijs *Head, Risk Management* ☎ 231 7842 🖷 535 2108

Fixed Income Derivatives / Risk Management
Regional Head — Arjen van der Linden *Derivative Markets, Asia* ☎ 231 7838 🖷 536 9371
IR Swaps Sales / Marketing — Peter Colvin *Regional Head, Marketing - DMA* ☎ 231 7881 🖷 536 2071
IR Swaps Trading — Gary Hawkins *Regional Head, Trading - DMA* ☎ 231 7881 🖷 536 2071

Foreign Exchange Derivatives / Risk Management
Cross-Currency Swaps, Sales / Marketing — Peter Colvin *Regional Head, Marketing - DMA* ☎ 231 7881 🖷 536 2071
Cross-Currency Swaps, Trading — Gary Hawkins *Regional Head, Trading - DMA* ☎ 231 7881 🖷 536 2071

Settlement / Clearing
Fixed-Income Settlement — Tee-Meng Tan *VP & Head, Fixed-Income Operations* ☎ 231 7784
Derivatives Settlement — Yvan Trifilieff *AVP & Head, DMA Back-Office* ☎ 231 7802
Operations — Janice Chua *VP, Head of Treasury Operations* ☎ 231 7933

AFC Merchant Bank
Head Office

Alternative trading name: ASEAN Finance Corporation Limited
#17-00, Bangkok Bank Building, 180 Cecil Street, Singapore, 069546
Tel: 224 7155 **Fax:** 225 0727
Website: www.signet.com.sg/-asean

Senior Executive Officers
Chairman — Piti Sithi-Amnuai
President & CEO — Kah Chye Tay
Financial Director — Choon Hong Hun *SVP, Admin & Treasury, Investment Div Head*

Debt Capital Markets / Fixed Income
Department: Business Development
Global Head — See Tong Tan *SVP & Head, Business Development*
Regional Head — Jeffrey Song *VP, Business Development*
Country Head — Alex Tan *AVP, Business Development*
Daniel Chin *AVP, Business Development*
Peter Loh *Assistant Manager, Business Development*
See Keat Tan *Assistant Manager, Business Development*

Bonds - General
Credit Head — Wai Ming Mok *Vice President, Business Development*

Syndicated Lending
Department: Business Development
Global Head — See Tong Tan *SVP & Head, Business Development*
Regional Head — Jeffrey Song *VP, Business Development*
Country Head — Alex Tan *AVP, Business Development*
Daniel Chin *AVP, Business Development*
Peter Loh *Assistant Manager, Business Development*
See Keat Tan *Assistant Manager, Business Development*
Head of Credit Committee — Wai Ming Mok *Vice President, Business Development*

Money Markets
Department: Money Market, Treasury
Global Head — Choon Hong Hun *SVP, Admin & Treasury, Investment Div Head*
Regional Head — Kee Ching Ho *Dealer*

Foreign Exchange
Global Head — Choon Hong Hun *SVP, Admin & Treasury, Investment Div Head*
Regional Head — Kee Ching Ho *Dealer*

Risk Management
Department: Compliance Division
Global Head — Kian Meng Lim *VP & Head, Compliance*

Foreign Exchange Derivatives / Risk Management
Global Head; Cross-Currency Swaps, Trading — Kee Ching Ho *Dealer*

Corporate Finance / M&A Advisory
Department: Business Development
Global Head — See Tong Tan *SVP & Head, Business Development*

Settlement / Clearing
Foreign Exchange Settlement — Jane Yeo *Assistant Manager, Settlements*

SINGAPORE (+65)   www.euromoneydirectory.com

Agricultural Bank of China
Full Branch Office

#27-20 UOB Plaza 2, 80 Raffles Place, Singapore, 048624
Tel: 535 5255 **Fax:** 538 7960 **Telex:** RS 24990 ABOCSB **Swift:** ABOCSGSG

Senior Executive Officers
Chief Executive Officer — Tang Qingbao *General Manager* ☎ **535 5255**
Treasurer — Frankie Chia *Manager* ☎ **230 5806**

Debt Capital Markets / Fixed Income
Tel: 536 5055 **Fax:** 536 7255

Domestic Government Bonds
Head of Sales; Head of Trading; Head of Research — Frankie Chia *Manager* ☎ **230 5806**

Eurobonds
Head of Origination; Head of Syndication; Head of Sales; Head of Trading; Head of Research; Trading - Sovereigns, Corporates, High-yield — Frankie Chia *Manager* ☎ **230 5806**

Libor-Based / Floating-Rate Products
FRN Origination; FRN Sales; FRN Trading; Asset Swaps; Asset Swaps (Sales) — Frankie Chia *Manager* ☎ **230 5806**

Medium-Term Notes
Head of Origination; Head of Structuring; Head of Sales; Head of Trading — Frankie Chia *Manager* ☎ **230 5806**

Fixed-Income Repo
Head of Repo; Collateral Management; Matched Book Manager; Trading; Sales — Frankie Chia *Manager* ☎ **230 5806**

Syndicated Lending
Tel: 535 5255 **Fax:** 536 3575
Country Head of Origination; Head of Syndication; Head of Trading; Recovery — Peh Eng Thong *Manager* ☎ **230 5807**
Head of Credit Committee — Tang Qingbao *General Manager* ☎ **535 5255**

Loan-Related Activities
Trade Finance; Project Finance; Structured Trade Finance; Leasing & Asset Finance — Michael Kong ☎ **230 5804**

Money Markets
Tel: 536 5055 **Fax:** 536 7255
Country Head — Frankie Chia *Manager* ☎ **230 5806**

Domestic Commercial Paper
Head of Origination; Head of Sales; Head of Trading — Frankie Chia *Manager* ☎ **230 5806**

Eurocommercial Paper
Head of Origination; Head of Sales; Head of Trading — Frankie Chia *Manager* ☎ **230 5806**

Wholesale Deposits
Marketing; Head of Sales — Frankie Chia *Manager* ☎ **230 5806**

Foreign Exchange
Country Head of Institutional Sales; Corporate Sales; Head of Trading — Frankie Chia *Manager* ☎ **230 5806**

FX Traders / Sales People
Mario Soon *Senior Dealer* ☎ **230 5851**
Alvin Chu *Dealer* ☎ **230 5852**

Risk Management
Country Head; Trading; IR Swaps Sales / Marketing; IR Swaps Trading; IR Options Sales / Marketing; IR Options Trading — Frankie Chia *Manager* ☎ **230 5806**

Foreign Exchange Derivatives / Risk Management
Country Head; Cross-Currency Swaps, Sales / Marketing; Cross-Currency Swaps, Trading; Vanilla FX option Sales; Vanilla FX option Trading — Frankie Chia *Manager* ☎ **230 5806**

Other Currency Swap / FX Options Personnel
Money Market — Matthew Poh *Senior Dealer* ☎ **230 5858**
Jenny Koh *Dealer* ☎ **230 5857**

www.euromoneydirectory.com SINGAPORE (+65)

Settlement / Clearing
Fax: 538 7960
Country Head; Equity Settlement; Fixed-Income Lim Cheng Kee *Manager* ☎ 230 5805
Settlement; Derivatives Settlement; Foreign Exchange Settlement

Allied Irish Bank Group Treasury   Full Branch Office

#13-01 Robinson Point, 39 Robinson Road, Singapore, 068911
Tel: 438 7333 **Fax:** 438 1091 **Reuters:** AIBS
Website: www.aib.ie/capitalmarkets/singapore

Senior Executive Officers
General - Treasury
Head of Treasury   George Yates *Head of Treasury* ☎ 438 6996 ⓕ 438 1097
Debt Capital Markets / Fixed Income
Head of Debt Capital Markets   David Fallon
Money Markets
Head of Money Markets   Lawrence Foo
Foreign Exchange
Head of Foreign Exchange   Peter Carpenter

Allied Irish Bank plc   Full Branch Office

#13-01 Robinson Point, 39 Robinson Road, Singapore, 068911
Tel: 438 7333 **Fax:** 438 1091 **Telex:** RS25421 **Swift:** AIBK SG SG **Reuters:** AIBS **Telerate:** 2816

Senior Executive Officers
General Manager, Singapore Branch   John Canniffe
Regional General Manager, Asia Pacific   Seamus Doherty
General - Treasury
Head of Treasury   George Yates *Head of Treasury*
Relationship Manager
Regional Markets   David Fallon *Head*
Syndicated Lending
Head of Syndication   Jansen Lim *Manager*
Loan-Related Activities
Trade Finance   Jansen Lim *Manager*
Foreign Exchange
FX Traders / Sales People
Spot FX   Peter Carpenter *Head*
Settlement / Clearing
Operations   Mei Heng Kwok *Manager, Financial Control*

American Express Bank Limited   Full Branch Office

16 Collyer Quay, Singapore, 049318
PO Box 3083, Robinson Road, Singapore, 905083
Tel: 538 4833 **Fax:** 534 3022 **Telex:** 21172 **Swift:** AEIB SG SG **Reuters:** AMXS (Dealing)
Capital Markets Fax: 536 8254; **Dealers Tel:** 532 3122; **Telex:** 20273; **Treasury Fax:** 538 5431; **Reuters:** AEFX; AEFY; AEFZ (Monitor)

Senior Executive Officers
Chief Executive Officer   Andrew Grant *Executive Director & Regional Treasurer*
Treasurer   Philip Chua *Senior Director & Head, Treasury Singapore*
Senior Director & COO   Edward Sadler
International Division   Lynn Skelly *Snr Director, Regional Head of Capital Markets*
Others (Senior Executives)
Treasury & Marketing   Simon Chng *Senior Director*
                                            Sherrilyn Koh *Director, Treasury Marketing*
                                            Pheabe Chau *Director, Treasury Marketing*
                                            Freddy Lee *Manager, Treasury Marketing*
                                            Geraldine Goh *Manager, Treasury Marketing*
General - Treasury
Head of Treasury   Simon Chng *Director & Head, Treasury Marketing*
                                            Sherrilyn Koh *Manager, Treasury Marketing*

Euromoney Directory 1999   **1289**

SINGAPORE (+65)   www.euromoneydirectory.com

American Express Bank Limited (cont)
General - Treasury (cont)

Freddy Lee *Manager, Treasury Marketing*
Pheabe Chau *Director, Treasury Marketing*
Geraldine Goh *Manager, Treasury Marketing*

Debt Capital Markets / Fixed Income
Head of Fixed Income   Steve Howell *Senior Director & Senior Trader*

Fixed-Income Repo
Marketing & Product Development   Jessica Chang *Director & Marketing Officer*

Fixed-Income Research
Head of Fixed Income   Babar Mufti *Director & Trader, Fixed-Income & IR*
Head of Credit Research   Biswaroop Barua *Manager*

Money Markets
Head of Money Markets   Liana Ho *Director*
Global Head   Mun Keat Kong *Director*

Foreign Exchange
Head of Foreign Exchange   Anthony Yeong *Director & Head*

FX Traders / Sales People
Ronnie Soh *Director*
Douglas Wong *Director*
Siang Kend Loh *Director*

Risk Management
Head of Risk Management   Michael Tham *SRN Director* ☏ **439 3138**

Foreign Exchange Derivatives / Risk Management
Spot / Forwards Sales   Johnny Bhatkar *Structuring & Derivatives Director*
Spot / Forwards Trading   Jeffrey Lim *Structured Products Director*

Other Currency Swap / FX Options Personnel
Dennis Harhalakis *Director & Trader*
Harold Shorrock *Director & Trader*
Betty Wee *Manager*

Arab Bank plc

#32-20 UOB Plaza 2, 80 Raffles Place, Singapore, 048624
Tel: 533 0055 **Fax:** 532 2150 **Telex:** RS 22955 ARABNK **Swift:** ARAB SG SG **Telex:** RS 22956 ARABNK

Senior Executive Officers
Executive Vice President & Chief Executive- Asia Pacific   James J Liu
VP & General Manager-Singapore   Poh Lam Loke

General - Treasury
Head of Treasury   John Tan *VP & Manager*

Settlement / Clearing
Operations   Peng Hock Ng *VP & Manager, Operations & International Trade*

Asset Management

Other (Asset Management)
Investment Management Group   Gladys Lau *Assistant Vice President & Manager*

Other Departments
Chief Credit Officer   Raphael von Reding *VP & Area Manager, Credit*

Administration
Head of Administration   Evelyn Goh *VP & Area Manager*

Technology & Systems
Information Technology   Chong Kiet Ling *Assistant VP & Head*

Accounts / Audit
Audit & Quality Management-Asia Pacific   Bernard Kai Luen Chan *Assistant VP & Regional Auditor*

Other (Administration)
Human Resources-Asia Pacific   Evelyn Goh *VP & Area Manager*
Control   Say Pean Lim *VP & Regional Controller*

The Asahi Bank Limited

#40-01 Millenia Tower, 1 Temasek Avenue, Singapore, 039192
Tel: 333 0378 Fax: 333 0797 Telex: 22059 ASHSP
Website: www.asahibank.co.jp

Senior Executive Officers
General Manager						Yoshihiro Mizutani

## ASC Capital Pte Limited											Head Office

#17-04 Clifford Centre, 24 Raffles Place, Singapore, 048621
Tel: 535 8066 Fax: 535 6629 Telex: RS23295 ASCSIN

Senior Executive Officers
Managing Director					Cheong Seng Lee

Others (Senior Executives)
						David Tian Bin Chia
						Victor Mong Yang Yeo
						John Yew Kong Lim
						Mei Chean Hong
						Peng Seng Ang
						Thomas Liang Huat Teo
						Sheau Lan Cheah

Australia & New Zealand Banking Group Limited Full Branch Office

#17-01/07 Ocean Building, 10 Collyer Quay, Singapore, 049315
Tel: 535 8355 Fax: 539 6111 Telex: RS33930 Swift: ANZB SG SX Reuters: ANZS

Senior Executive Officers
Head of ANZ Investment Bank, SEA		Philip Forrest

## Ban Hin Lee Bank Berhad										Full Branch Office

#01-02 Robinson Point, 39 Robinson Road, Singapore, 068911
Tel: 532 1318 Fax: 535 5366 Telex: RS24191 A/B BHLBSIN Swift: BHLB SG SG

Senior Executive Officers
Chief Executive Officer				Yeap Lam Yang *Resident Director & CEO*
Senior Country Manager				Philip Hong

## Banca Commerciale Italiana										Full Branch Office

#51-02 Republic Plaza, 9 Raffles Place, Singapore, 048619
Tel: 220 1333; 220 2583 Fax: 227 1619; 225 2004 Telex: RS24545 Swift: BCIT SG SG
Email: bcisgsys@pacific.net.sg Reuters: BCIS Telex: RS 23453

Senior Executive Officers
SVP & Chief Manager				Giorgio Porcu

Money Markets
Head of Money Markets				Nora Chong *Chief Dealer, Money Markets*

Wholesale Deposits
Head of Sales					Agnes Mah *Chief Dealer, Corporate*

Foreign Exchange
Head of Foreign Exchange				Jit Ting Lim *Chief Dealer, FX*
Corporate Sales					Agnes Mah *Chief Dealer, Corporate*

FX Traders / Sales People
Regionals / LIT Swaps				Peter Quah *Dealer*
DM, LIT, EMS					Goh Chiang Looi *Dealer*
Sing$ (Local)					John Teo *Dealer, Money Markets*
Euro / Asian					Leonard Lee *Dealer, Money Markets*

Settlement / Clearing
Operations					Margaret Lim *Assistant Head of Department* ☎ 231 3631

SINGAPORE (+65)   www.euromoneydirectory.com

Banca Monte dei Paschi di Siena SpA — Full Branch Office

Formerly known as: Monte dei Paschi di Siena
#13-01 Ocean Building, 10 Collyer Quay, Singapore, 049315
Tel: 535 2533 **Fax:** 532 7996 **Telex:** RS24617 MPASCHI **Reuters:** MPSS **Cable:** PASCHIBANK
Dealers Tel: 532 6820; 532 6829

Senior Executive Officers
Deputy General Manager   Giorgio Marchetti
General Manager   Giuseppe De Giosa

General-Lending (DCM, SL)
Head of Corporate Banking   George Kong Meng Yeo *Head, Credit & Lending*

General - Treasury
Head of Treasury   Mahammad Rofik *Treasury Manager*

Settlement / Clearing
Operations   Shou Shian Foo *Head*

Banca Nazionale del Lavoro SpA — Full Branch Office

#50-01 Republic Plaza, 9 Raffles Place, Singapore, 048619
Tel: 536 6063 **Fax:** 536 5213 **Telex:** RS28351 **Swift:** BNLI SG SG **Reuters:** BNLA

Senior Executive Officers
Chief Executive Officer   Guido Del Panta *Regional General Manager*

Others (Senior Executives)
Vice President   Mauro Simonato *Deputy General Manager*
                                      Luigi Tirelli *Head, Treasury & Forex Division*

Money Markets
Money Markets - General
                                      Foo Meng Ho *Chief Dealer* ☎ **536 1182**
                                      Ooi Teck Chua *Senior Dealer* ☎ **536 1182**
                                      Vivien Tan *Senior Dealer* ☎ **536 1182**
                                      Chai Hong Tong *Dealer* ☎ **536 1182**

Foreign Exchange
Head of Trading   Hai Yong Tay *Chief Dealer* ☎ **536 1182**

FX Traders / Sales People
                                      Soon Joon Foo *Senior Dealer* ☎ **536 1182**
                                      Sally Chua *Senior Dealer* ☎ **536 1182**
                                      Alex Lim *Dealer* ☎ **536 1182**
                                      Richard Wong *Dealer, Forwards* ☎ **536 1182**

Settlement / Clearing
Operations   Carlo Passino *Head*
                                      Lucy Lim *Manager, Operations*

Administration
Head of Administration   Gianfranco Mosca *VP, Administration*
Business Development   Sokhbir Kaur *Assistant Vice President*

Banca di Roma SpA — Full Branch Office

#20-20/21 Republic Plaza II, 9 Raffles Place, Singapore, 048619
Tel: 438 7509 **Fax:** 535 2267 **Telex:** RS21497 BROMA **Swift:** BROM SG SG **Email:** bdrsi@mbox5.signet.com.sg
Reuters: ROMS **Cable:** BANCROMA SINGAPORE

Senior Executive Officers
General Manager   Giovanni Rio
Deputy General Manager   Mario Fattorusso
Assistant General Manager   David Mok

General-Lending (DCM, SL)
Head of Corporate Banking   Orazio Coco *Credit Manager*

Debt Capital Markets / Fixed Income
Department: Credit
Head of Fixed Income   Antonio D'Angio *Credit Manager*

Syndicated Lending
Other (Syndicated Lending)
Loan Syndication   Orazio Coco *Marketing Manager*

1292 Euromoney Directory 1999

www.euromoneydirectory.com   SINGAPORE (+65)

Money Markets
Head of Money Markets   Stefano Falconi *Chief Dealer*

Foreign Exchange
Head of Foreign Exchange   Stefano Falconi *Chief Dealer*

Risk Management
Head of Risk Management   Stefano Falconi *Chief Dealer*

Settlement / Clearing
Head of Settlement / Clearing   Susanna Yu *Accounting Manager*

Banco do Brasil SA   Full Branch Office

#09-00 One Phillip Street, Singapore, 048692
Tel: 535 1177 **Fax:** 535 4138 **Telex:** RS25668 BBCING **Swift:** BRAS SG SG

Senior Executive Officers
Treasurer   Manoel A Santos *General Manager*
    Carlos R Z Fonseca *Deputy General Manager, Treasury*

Syndicated Lending
Loan-Related Activities
Trade Finance   George Heng *Manager*

Foreign Exchange
Department: Foreign Exchange and Bullion
Head of Foreign Exchange   Carlos R Z Fonseca *Deputy General Manager*

Risk Management
Department: Capital Markets

Other Currency Swap / FX Options Personnel
Currency Swaps   Carlos R Z Fonseca *Deputy General Manager*

Settlement / Clearing
Head of Settlement / Clearing   Michelle Wong *Officer*

Other Departments
Correspondent Banking   Kiat Seng Lim *Manager*

Administration
Head of Administration   George Heng *Manager*
Head of Marketing   Kiat Seng Lim *Manager*
    Stephanie Lim *Officer*

Technology & Systems
    Ganti Vijaya Lakshmiward *IT Executive*

Accounts / Audit
Accounts   Dorothy Tan *Officer*

Bangkok Bank Public Company Limited   Full Branch Office

180 Cecil Street, Singapore, 069546
PO Box 941, Singapore, 901841
Tel: 221 9400 **Fax:** 225 5852 **Telex:** RS21359 BKBANK **Swift:** BKKB SG SG **Reuters:** BBLS **Telerate:** 2808
Telex: RS 25639 BKBANK

Senior Executive Officers
SVP & General Manager   Rushda Theeratharathorn

Others (Senior Executives)
Head of Operations   Yaovaluk Suksathit *VP & Operations Manager*
Head of Control   Parnsak Pruksakit *VP & Manager, Control*

General-Lending (DCM, SL)
Head of Corporate Banking   Kan Ah Chye *VP & Corporate Banking Manager*

General - Treasury
Head of Treasury   Wong Cheong Boou *VP & Treasury Manager*

Syndicated Lending
Loan-Related Activities
Trade Finance   Yaovaluk Suksathit *VP & Operations Manager*

Money Markets
Reuters: BBSS **Telex:** RS 34159, RS25639 BKBANK
Head of Money Markets   Jessie Cheong Poh Lim *Head of Money Markets*

SINGAPORE (+65)   www.euromoneydirectory.com

Bangkok Bank Public Company Limited (cont)
Foreign Exchange
Reuters: BBSS
Head of Foreign Exchange Corporate Sales
FX Traders / Sales People
Chief Dealer
Settlement / Clearing
Head of Settlement / Clearing
Other Departments
Correspondent Banking
Administration
Head of Administration
Technology & Systems

Accounts / Audit

Christopher Koh Guan Tat *Head of Foreign Exchange*
Terry Chai Fook Sin *Head, Treasury Marketing*

Seah Chong Khoi *AVP & Assistant Manager*

Yaovaluk Suksathit *VP & Operations Manager*

Wong Cheong Boou *VP & Treasury Manager*

Emily Tan Chay Hwan *Head of Human Resources*

Lydia Heng Mui Foon *AVP & Assistant Manager*

Parnsak Pruksakit *VP`& Manager, Control*

Bank of America NT & SA   Full Branch Office
#18-00, 9 Raffles Place, Republic Plaza Tower 1, Singapore, 048619
PO Box 97, Robinson Road, Singapore
Tel: 239 3888 Fax: 239 3068 Telex: RS 24570 Swift: BOFA SG 2X

Senior Executive Officers
Chief Executive Officer
Chief Operating Officer
Treasurer

Others (Senior Executives)
Country Credit Officer
Finance Manager
Marketing
Human Resources

Debt Capital Markets / Fixed Income
Department: Global Capital Markets Group
Tel: 239 3249 Fax: 438 5278
Head of Fixed Income
Head of Fixed Income Sales

Domestic Government Bonds
Head of Trading

Syndicated Lending
Tel: 239 3452 Fax: 239 3214
Head of Origination

Money Markets
Tel: 239 3276 Fax: 438 5428 Reuters: BAMS
Head of Money Markets

Foreign Exchange
Fax: 438 5428 Reuters: BAFS
Head of Foreign Exchange
Head of Institutional Sales
Corporate Sales

FX Traders / Sales People
Spot Trading
Forward Trading

Risk Management
Tel: 239 3257 Fax: 438 5428 Reuters: BASO

Other Currency Swap / FX Options Personnel
Currency Options Trading

Settlement / Clearing
Regional Head

Administration
Public Relations
Human Resources

Other (Administration)
Marketing

Colm M McCarthy *Managing Director & Regional Head - SEA*
Eugene C H Heng *VP & Country Operations Officer*
Gary K Ryder *Managing Director & Country Treasurer*

James D Baddams *VP & Country Credit Officer*
Mei Leng Fong *Vice President*
Alan T H Koh *Managing Director & Marketing Head*
Hoon Kee Low *Vice President*

Michael Hyde *Vice President*
Angus Amran *Vice President*

Gary K Ryder *Managing Director & Country Treasurer*

Jagathesan Radhakrishnan *Vice President* ☎ **239 3174**

Gary K Ryder *Managing Director & Country Treasurer*

Pang Liang Ong *Managing Director* ☎ **239 3288**
Matthew K T Sim *Vice President* ☎ **239 3288**
Janet B C Lam *Vice President* ☎ **239 3280**

James T J Phoen *Vice President* ☎ **239 3288**
Chee Pin Lee *Vice President* ☎ **239 3288**

Chi Ban Huynh *Vice President* ☎ **239 3257**

Joanne P L Teo *Vice President* ☎ **239 3220**

Hoon Kee Low *Vice President*

Alan T H Koh *Managing Director & Marketing Head*

www.euromoneydirectory.com　　　　SINGAPORE (+65)

Bank Austria Creditanstalt International
Full Branch Office

#12-20 UOB Plaza 2, 80 Raffles Place, Singapore, 048624
Tel: 438 4800 **Fax:** 438 4900 **Telex:** RS20385 BKAU **Swift:** BKAU SG SG

Senior Executive Officers
General Manager　　　　　　　　　　Thomas Eidenberger
General Manager　　　　　　　　　　Douglas Wright

General-Lending (DCM, SL)
Head of Corporate Banking　　　　　Wong Kook Fei *Head, Commercial Banking*

General - Treasury
Head of Treasury　　　　　　　　　　Peter Foo *Head of Treasury*

Risk Management
Head of Risk Management　　　　　Hubert Ladstaetter *Head, Risk Management*

Settlement / Clearing
Operations　　　　　　　　　　　　Wong Song Heng *Head of Operations*

Bank Brussels Lambert
Full Branch Office

#42-00 OUB Centre, 1 Raffles Place, Singapore, 048616
PO Box 360, Robinson Road, Singapore, 900710
Tel: 532 4088 **Fax:** 530 5750 **Telex:** RS20294 BBLSIN **Swift:** BBRU SG SG **Reuters:** BBLZ **Cable:** BRUXELAMBT
ACU Tel: 532 6588; **Bonds Tel:** 532 5488; **Forex Tel:** 532 5688; **Telex:** RS 20295 BBLFX; **Reuters:** BBLS (Dealing)

Senior Executive Officers
Chief Executive Officer　　　　　　Steven Braekeveldt *General Manager*
Treasurer　　　　　　　　　　　　Ryan Padgett

Debt Capital Markets / Fixed Income
Country Head　　　　　　　　　　Bernard De Becker *Senior Dealer*

Eurobonds
Head of Origination　　　　　　　Ryan Padgett

Syndicated Lending

Other (Syndicated Lending)
Commercial Banking / Loan Syndication　　Richard Choy *Manager*
　　　　　　　　　　　　　　　　Yoon Phooi Leng *Senior Manager*
　　　　　　　　　　　　　　　　Vincent Liow *Senior Manager*
　　　　　　　　　　　　　　　　Richard Choy *Manager*
　　　　　　　　　　　　　　　　Raymond Tan *Manager*

Money Markets

Money Markets - General
Eurocurrency Deposits　　　　　　Patricia Sim *Deputy Manager*
　　　　　　　　　　　　　　　　May Ong *Dealer*
　　　　　　　　　　　　　　　　Catherine Tan *Assistant Dealer*

Risk Management

Fixed Income Derivatives / Risk Management
IR Swaps Trading; IR Options Trading　　Bernard De Becker *Senior Dealer*

Bank of China
Full Branch Office

4 Battery Road, Singapore, 049908
Tel: 535 2411 **Fax:** 534 3401 **Telex:** RS23046 BKCHINA **Swift:** BKCH SG SG **Reuters:** BOCS
Dealers Tel: 535 2933; **Fax:** 538 4517; **Telex:** RS36298 FRXBOC

Senior Executive Officers
General Manager　　　　　　　　Hua Zhu
Deputy General Manager　　　　　Zhongqian Chen
Deputy General Manager　　　　　Hung Pheng Tan
Deputy General Manager　　　　　Juzheng Lin
Deputy General Manager　　　　　Zhang Lianli
Deputy General Manager　　　　　Kuangyu Cao
Deputy General Manager　　　　　Yuebao Jiang

Syndicated Lending
Country Head　　　　　　　　　　Kok Leong Tay *AGM, Loans Syndication*

Money Markets
Department: Treasury Department
Country Head　　　　　　　　　　Eng Khim Ng *Assistant General Manager*

Euromoney Directory 1999　　**1295**

SINGAPORE (+65) www.euromoneydirectory.com

Bank of China (cont)
Other (Wholesale Deposits)
Asian Currency Unit
Local Money Markets
Foreign Exchange
Department: Treasury Department
Country Head
FX Traders / Sales People

Geraldine Ong *Senior Manager*
Pin Koon Lim *Manager*

Eng Khim Ng *Assistant General Manager*

Winston Ong *Deputy Manager*
Kelvin Ang *Dealer*
Anna Ang *Dealer*
Lai Siem Lee *Dealer*
Hock Lee Tan *Dealer*
Joseph Lee *Dealer*
Ted Chan *Dealer*
Jun Cai *Dealer*

Settlement / Clearing
Settlement (General)
Other Departments
Correspondent Banking

Chuh Meng Chin *Manager, Treasury Settlements*

Kim Hoo Chong *Assistant General Manager*

Bank of Communications
Offshore Banking Unit

#49-01, 9 Raffles Place, Republic Plaza, Singapore, 048619
Tel: 532 0335 **Fax:** 532 0339 **Telex:** RS 20335 BOCOMS **Swift:** COMM SG SG

Senior Executive Officers
Managing Director / General Manager
Senior Secretary
Others (Senior Executives)
Assistant GM; Assistant General Manager
Manager Accounts
Manager Operations
Deputy Manager Treasury
Assistant Manager Trade Finance
Syndicated Lending
Head of Syndication
Money Markets
Telex: RS 20339 COMMFX
Head of Money Markets
Foreign Exchange
Telex: RS 20339 COMMFX
Head of Foreign Exchange
Settlement / Clearing
Head of Settlement / Clearing Operations

Ma Hui Ping
Lee Foong Oi

Gu Wei Wei
Yin Hong Liang
Chen Hong Jun
Meng Jun *Deputy Manager*
Esther Ng Bee Kian

Gu Wei Wei

Meng Jun *Deputy Manager*

Meng Jun *Deputy Manager*

Chen Hong Jun
Steven So Shun Piao *Senior Operations Officer*

The Bank of East Asia Limited
Full Branch Office

137 Market Street, Singapore, 048943
Tel: 224 1334 **Fax:** 225 1805

Senior Executive Officers
General Manager

Khoo Kee-cheok

Bank of Hawaii
Full Branch Office

#10-03 SIA Building, 77 Robinson Road, Singapore, 068769
Tel: 538 5248; 538 5249 **Fax:** 536 9430 **Telex:** RS21925 BKOHSPR **Swift:** BOHI SG SG

Senior Executive Officers
Vice President & General Manager, Regional Manager
Others (Senior Executives)
Trade Banking; Institutional Banking
General-Lending (DCM, SL)
Head of Corporate Banking

Donald J Huse ☏ **538 1817**

John Liu *Assistant Vice President & Manager*

Craig Dimmick *Assistant Vice President & Manager*

1296 Euromoney Directory 1999

www.euromoneydirectory.com SINGAPORE (+65)

General - Treasury
Head of Treasury Victor Seng *AVP & Manager of Treasury*

Foreign Exchange
Tel: 538 5248 **Fax:** 536 9430
Country Head Victor Seng *AVP & Manager of Treasury* ☏ **536 1125**

FX Traders / Sales People
  Stephanie Lim *Assistant Manager* ☏ **536 1127**
  Stella Ng *Dealer* ☏ **536 1127**

Settlement / Clearing
Operations Terry Soo *Assistant Vice President & Manager*

Bank of India
Full Branch Office

#01/03-01 Hong Leong Centre, 138 Robinson Road, Singapore, 068906
PO Box 488, Robinson Road, Singapore, 9009
Tel: 222 0011 **Fax:** 225 4407; 225 2976 **Telex:** RS22520 BOISING **Email:** boisgi@asiaconnect.com
Cable: STRINGENT SINGAPORE

Senior Executive Officers
Chief Executive Officer N S Nayak *Chief Executive* ☏ **320 4694**
Chief Manager G Sreedhar ☏ **320 4104**

General-Lending (DCM, SL)
Head of Corporate Banking N S Surti *Manager, Credit* ☏ **320 4676**
  M M Prabhu *Manager, Credit* ☏ **320 4682**
  S Venkateswarlu *Manager, Credit* ☏ **320 4681**

General-Investment
Head of Investment R C Khurana *Manager, Investments & India Desk*

Syndicated Lending
Head of Syndication R C Khurana *Manager, Credit* ☏ **320 4669**

Loan-Related Activities
Structured Trade Finance R Seshadri *Manager* ☏ **320 4654**

Money Markets
Head of Money Markets G Sreedhar *Chief Manager* ☏ **320 4104**

Foreign Exchange
Head of Foreign Exchange P K Bajaj *Chief Dealer* ☏ **320 4103**

The Bank of Korea
Representative Office

#20-02A Clifford Centre, 24 Raffles Place, Singapore, 048621
Tel: 532 3522; 532 3523 **Fax:** 535 5127 **Cable:** KOREA BANK

Senior Executive Officers
Chief Representative Tae-Bong Park
Deputy Representative Yoon Yong Jin

Bank Leu Limited
Representative Office

#10-03, 80 Robinson Road, Singapore, 068898
Tel: 221 7400 **Fax:** 221 7443

Senior Executive Officers
Representative Peter Wirth

Bank of Montreal Asia Limited
Subsidiary Company

#26-01 Gateway West, 150 Beach Road, Singapore, 189720
Tel: 296 3233 **Fax:** 296 5044 **Telex:** RS20660 MONTBK

Senior Executive Officers
Managing Director Marc Vandal

SINGAPORE (+65)   www.euromoneydirectory.com

PT Bank Negara Indonesia (Persero) Tbk
Full Branch Office

#01/04-00 Dapenso Building, 158 Cecil Street, Singapore, 069545
PO Box 2260, Robinson Road, Singapore, 904260
Tel: 225 7755; 222 1933 (Dealers) Fax: 225 4757 Telex: RS21749 Swift: BNIN SG SG
Email: ptbni@cyberway.com.sg Reuters: BNIS Telex: RS 26253 Telex: RS 28040; Dealers Tel: 225 3552; 222 1933

Senior Executive Officers
SVP, Int'l & General Manager
International Division
  Toni Indartono
  Berlin Sembiring *FVP, Int'l & Deputy General Manager*
  Khatijah M Rosli *FVP, Int'l & DGM, Credit & Marketing*

General-Lending (DCM, SL)
Head of Corporate Banking
  Khatijah M Rosli *FVP, Int'l & DGM, Credit & Marketing*
  Eddy Junaidi Syahril *VP, International Treasury*
  Saswira Ismail *VP, International & Corporate Banking*
  Suraya Salleh *VP, Int'l, Credit Admin & Control*

Relationship Manager
Financial Institutions Syndications
  Wendy Siew *AVP, International*

Syndicated Lending

Loan-Related Activities
Structured Trade Finance
  Mark Liu *AVP, International*

Settlement / Clearing
Settlement (General)
Operations
  Dorothy Chua
  Berlin Sembiring *FVP, Int'l & Deputy General Manager*
  Suraya Salleh *VP, Int'l, Credit Admin & Control*
  Huzaifah Madjedi *VP, Int'l, Business Operations*

Other Departments
Correspondent Banking
  Mark Liu *AVP, International*

Administration

Accounts / Audit
Accounting & Financial Control
  Boon Huat Lee *Vice President, International*

Other (Administration)
Marketing
Customer Service
  Khatijah M Rosli *FVP, Int'l & DGM, Credit & Marketing*
  Hermani Abdurrachman *VP, International*

Bank of New Zealand
Full Branch Office

#15-01 Suntec City Tower, 5 Temasek Boulevard, Singapore, 038985
PO Box 2431, Robinson Road, Singapore, 904431
Tel: 332 2990 Fax: 332 2991 Telex: RS22149 BANKNZ Swift: BKNZ SG SG

Senior Executive Officers
Treasurer
General Manager
Executive Secretary
International Division
  Brian Lavelle ☎ 433 6799
  Neil Frost ☎ 433 6688
  Rose Zee ☎ 433 6610
  Robert Rigg *Head of Markets, South Asia* ☎ 433 6788

General-Lending (DCM, SL)
Head of Corporate Banking
  Craig Manning *Head of Corporate Banking, South Asia* ☎ 433 6601

Foreign Exchange
Head of Foreign Exchange
  Henry Quek *Head of Treasury* ☎ 433 6888

Other Departments
Chief Credit Officer
  Estella Koh *Head of Credit* ☎ 433 6603

The Bank of Nova Scotia Asia Limited
Full Branch Office

#15-01/04 Ocean Building, 10 Collyer Quay, Singapore, 049315
Tel: 535 8688 Fax: 532 7554 Telex: RS23848 BNSAL

Senior Executive Officers
Managing Director
  W S Seong Koon

1298 Euromoney Directory 1999

Bank of Singapore Limited
Subsidiary Company

#01-02 Tong Eng Building, 101 Cecil Street, Singapore, 069533
OCBC Centre, 65 Chulia Street, Singapore, 049513
Tel: 223 9266 **Fax:** 224 7731; 535 3768 **Telex:** RS27149 **Swift:** BSLI SG SG

Senior Executive Officers
Chairman & Chief Executive — Lee Seng Wee ☎ **530 1505**
Treasurer — Wong Yew Kuen *Head, Global Treasury* ☎ **530 1619**

Debt Capital Markets / Fixed Income
Fax: 533 3768
Country Head — Chee Kian Seng ☎ **530 6014**

Domestic Government Bonds
Head of Trading — Chee Kian Seng ☎ **530 6014**

Money Markets
Fax: 535 3768
Country Head — Chee Kian Seng ☎ **530 6014**

Foreign Exchange
Fax: 535 3768
Country Head — Chee Kian Seng ☎ **530 6014**

Settlement / Clearing
Fax: 438 2613
Country Head — Tan Peng Chew ☎ **530 6693**

The Bank of Yokohama Limited
Full Branch Office

#30-03/05 Singapore Land Tower, 50 Raffles Place, Singapore, 048623
Tel: 221 7733 **Fax:** 224 6410 **Telex:** RS20224 HAMAGI **Cable:** FOREXHAMA

Senior Executive Officers
General Manager — Toru Chiba

Others (Senior Executives)
Katsunori Yatsuhashi *Assistant General Manager*
Masahiro Shimada *Assistant General Manager*
Takeshi Iwanaga *Assistant General Manager*

Bankers Trust Company

#08-00 Suntec City Tower, 5 Temasek Boulevard, Singapore, 038985
Tel: 336 2838 **Fax:** 331 4868; 331 4828 **Telex:** RS 28626 BANKERS

Senior Executive Officers
Managing Director / General Manager — Jose Isidro N Camacho

Bankers Trust International (Asia) Limited

#08-00 Suntec City Tower, 5 Temasek Boulevard, Singapore, 038985
Tel: 336 2838 **Fax:** 331 4828 **Telex:** RS28626 BANKERS

Senior Executive Officers

Others (Senior Executives)
Jose Isidro N Camacho *Director*
David R Dredge *Director*
Peter Cardosa *Director*

Banque et Caisse d'Epargne de l'Etat Luxembourg
Representative Office

#38-06 Singapore Land Tower, 50 Raffles Place, Singapore, 048623
Tel: 438 4033; 438 5005 **Fax:** 536 0155

Senior Executive Officers
Regional Representative, SE Asia — Claude Wagner

SINGAPORE (+65)   www.euromoneydirectory.com

Banque Internationale à Luxembourg BIL (Asia) Limited
Subsidiary Company

#22-01 Republic Plaza, 9 Raffles Place, Singapore, 048619
PO Box 1804, Robinson Road, Singapore, 903604
Tel: 222 7622 **Fax:** 536 0201 **Telex:** RS 21396 BILASI **Swift:** BILL SG SG A

Senior Executive Officers
Managing Director — Han Eng Juan

Debt Capital Markets / Fixed Income
Bonds - General

Ou-Yang Hiok Tong *Deputy Manager* ☎ **435 3398**
Chan Geok Chye *Deputy General Manager* ☎ **435 3388**

Syndicated Lending
Country Head — Chan Geok Chye *Deputy General Manager* ☎ **435 3388**

Money Markets
Country Head — Goh Poh Seah *Assistant General Manager* ☎ **435 3323**

Foreign Exchange
Country Head — Goh Poh Seah *Assistant General Manager* ☎ **435 3323**

Risk Management
Foreign Exchange Derivatives / Risk Management
Country Head — Goh Poh Seah *Assistant General Manager* ☎ **435 3323**

Corporate Finance / M&A Advisory
Country Head — Lim Cheng Ghim *Manager* ☎ **435 3387**

Settlement / Clearing
Country Head — Kwa Leh Chu *Assistant General Manager* ☎ **435 3350**

Other Departments
Private Banking — Lee Kong Eng *Assistant General Manager* ☎ **435 3320**

Administration
Head of Administration — Kwa Leh Chu *Assistant General Manager* ☎ **435 3350**

Banque Nationale de Paris
Full Branch Office

Tung Centre, 20 Collyer Quay, Singapore, 049319
Tel: 224 0211 **Fax:** 224 3459 **Telex:** RS24315 **Swift:** BNPA SG SGA **Reuters:** BNPS **Telerate:** 7268
Reuters: BNPD; BNPT; BNPS (FX); SBNP (MM); GBNP (Regional)

Senior Executive Officers
Chief Executive Officer — Alain Bailly *Chief Executive & General Manager* ☎ **224 0211**
Peter Labrie *Deputy General Manager* ☎ **224 3891**
Treasurer — Eric Raynaud *Regional Treasurer, Asia* ☎ **536 5727** F **532 2025**
Beatrice Hiriart *Singapore* ☎ **224 3892**

Others (Senior Executives)
Secretary General — Yves Drieux *Administration Manager* ☎ **223 5643**

Debt Capital Markets / Fixed Income
Tel: 536 4991 **Fax:** 222 7997

Government Bonds
Head of Sales

Kanol Pal
Anthony Tan
Jackie Lee

Eurobonds
Head of Trading

Kanol Pal
Anthony Tan
Jackie Lee

Bonds - General
Asian Bonds Trading

Kanol Pal
Anthony Tan
Jackie Lee

IRS Trading — John Geranda ☎ **221 5802** F **222 7997**
Steve Kim ☎ **221 5802** F **222 7997**
Currency Options Trading — Ronald Tam ☎ **224 7329** F **222 7997**

Money Markets
Department: Foreign Exchange G7 / Money Market G7 / Regional
Fax: 222 7997
Head of Money Markets — Janice Ng *Chief Dealer* ☎ **223 7156**

1300 Euromoney Directory 1999

www.euromoneydirectory.com SINGAPORE (+65)

Money Markets - General
Traders
    Henry Chiang
    Kheng Chwee Yeo
    Francis Loh
    Wen Huey Lee

Department: Treasury Sales
Regional Head
    Kenneth Tan *Head of Desk* ☏ **224 0311**

Money Markets - General
Treasury Sales
    Kok Chee Tan
    Patrick Yeo
    Swee Khim Sam
    Poh Puay Awyong
    A P Guillon
    Raymond Goh
    Wendy Ang
    Susan Chew
    Raymond Guan *Night Desk*
    Albert Fong *Night Desk*

Foreign Exchange
Fax: 222 7997
Head of Trading
    Jason Sie *Chief Dealer* ☏ **223 7014**

FX Traders / Sales People
Regional Currency Sales
    Seng Leng Chia *Head of Desk* ☏ **221 9680/1**
    Yet Har Chai
    Chin Hong Wong
FX Spot
    Henry Yee
    Eddie Yeo
    Fred Chee
Forwards
    Joyce Tan
    Boon Tiong Tan
Foreign Exchange
    Jason Sie *Chief Dealer* ☏ **223 7014**
EMS, FRF, Crosses, Scandies
    Ngee Tee Lim *Trader*
GBP, AUD, NZD, CAD
    Ivan Ng *Trader*
USD, CHF, DEM
    Willie Sim *Trader*
JPY, DEM / JPY
    Ju Huat Kuek *Trader*

Barclays Bank plc   Offshore Banking Unit

#23-01 Singapore Land Tower, 50 Raffles Place, Singapore, 048623
Tel: 224 8555; 220 3774 **Fax:** 224 4717 **Telex:** RS 26877 **Swift:** BARC SG SG **Reuters:** BBSI
Dealers Telex: RS 23240

Senior Executive Officers
Chief Executive Officer
    Suan Kiat Quek *Country Manager* ☏ **322 3102** F **323 7151**
Financial Director
    Robert Cranmer *Financial Controller, Finance & Accounts* ☏ **322 3109**
    F **532 0365**
Chief Operating Officer
    Suan Kiat Quek *Country Manager* ☏ **322 3102** F **323 7151**
Treasurer
    Ivan Ferraroni *Head, Global Forex, Asia / Pacific* ☏ **535 5673** F **536 5231**

Debt Capital Markets / Fixed Income
Bonds - General
Fixed Income Sales
    Lin Fee Chiu *Head of Sales* ☏ **323 6747** F **538 3802**

Money Markets
Tel: 224 8555 **Fax:** 224 1080 **Reuters:** BBSI **Telex:** RS23240
Head of Money Markets
    Be Be Quek *Associate Director* ☏ **322 3963/4** F **224 4180**

Foreign Exchange
Tel: 220 3774 **Fax:** 538 3802 **Reuters:** BBIS
Head of Foreign Exchange
    Ivan Ferraroni *Head, Global Forex, Asia / Pacific* ☏ **535 5673** F **536 5231**
Head of Sales
    Lin Fee Chiu *Head of Sales* ☏ **323 6747** F **538 3802**
Head of Trading
    Fred Belak *Head of GFX, Singapore* ☏ **225 8940** F **538 3802**

FX Traders / Sales People
Chief Dealer
    Pasquale Litterio *Chief Dealer* ☏ **220 3774** F **538 3802**
Options Desk
    Justin Gan *Associate Director* ☏ **323 5153** F **538 3802**

Risk Management
Other Currency Swap / FX Options Personnel
Head of FX Forwards
    Kee Seng Lee

Settlement / Clearing
Equity Settlement
    Meng Eng Yeow *Associate Director, Global Treasury Operations*
    ☏ **322 3111**

SINGAPORE (+65) www.euromoneydirectory.com

Barclays Bank plc (cont)
Other Departments
Chief Credit Officer — David Williams *Director & Head of Credit Risk Mgt S.E. Asia* ☎ **322 3174**
📠 **536 2248**
Private Banking — Poh Hoon Tiang *CEO, Singapore & COO, Asia* ☎ **322 3147**
Lick Ho *Head of Marketing, ASEAN* ☎ **322 3758**

Administration
Head of Administration — Theresa Ng *Manager* ☎ **322 3139** 📠 **224 4717**

Technology & Systems
Chin Hock Loh *Head of Dept, RUP* ☎ **322 3105** 📠 **536 1553**

Compliance
Julie Chan *Compliance Executive* ☎ **322 3113** 📠 **438 3520**

Accounts / Audit
Robert Cranmer *Financial Controller, Finance & Accounts* ☎ **322 3109**
📠 **532 0365**

Bayerische Hypo-und Vereinsbank AG   Full Branch Office
Formerly known as: Bayerische Vereinsbank AG
#17-01 No 1 Finlayson Green, Singapore, 049246
Tel: 536 8583 **Fax:** 230 0715
Senior Executive Officers
Chief Executive Officer — Phillip Seet *CEO Asia / Pacific*

Bayerische Landesbank   Full Branch Office
#37-01 The Concourse, 300 Beach Road, Singapore, 199555
Tel: 293 3822 **Fax:** 293 2151 **Telex:** RS21445 **Swift:** BYLA SG SG **Reuters:** BLBS **Telex:** RS 25461
Senior Executive Officers
Chief Executive Officer — Peter H H Gleue *Executive Vice President, General Manager & CEO*
☎ **390 6610** 📠 **292 8505**
Executive Vice President & General Manager — Heinz Anton Hoffmann ☎ **390 6682** 📠 **292 8505**
Executive Vice President & General Manager — Chandrashekhar Gupta ☎ **390 6630** 📠 **292 8505**

Syndicated Lending
Department: Institutional & Corporate Banking (ICB)
Regional Head — Kai Preugschat *SVP, ICB* ☎ **390 6640**
Head of Syndication — Aveline Fong *VP, Syndication Unit* ☎ **390 6635**

Loan-Related Activities
Trade Finance — Michael Giang *Assistant Vice President* ☎ **390 6642**
Project Finance — Rod Spencer *Vice President* ☎ **390 6633**

Other (Trade Finance)
Property Finance — Patricia Sum *Senior Assistant Vice President* ☎ **390 6636**
Eur MNCs — Stefan Hattenkofer *AVP, ICB* ☎ **390 6618**
Non Eur MNCs — Chong Inn Ng *AVP, ICB* ☎ **390 6637**

Money Markets
Department: Treasury & Securities
Regional Head — Yin Leng Tan *SVP, Treasury & Securities* ☎ **390 6620**

Money Markets - General
Securites — Eric Tang *VP, Securities* ☎ **390 6624**
Wendy Wee *VP, Securities* ☎ **390 6624**
James Lim *AVP, Securities* ☎ **390 6627**
Foreign Exchange — Gary Teng *VP, Forex* ☎ **390 6625**
Victor Whang *AVP, Forex* ☎ **390 6625**
James Lim *AVP, Securities* ☎ **390 6627**
Money Market — Kevin Koh *VP, MM* ☎ **390 6626**
Tien Wah Koh *VP, MM* ☎ **390 6626**
Meng Yam Pang *Trainee Dealer* ☎ **390 6626**
Treasury Sales — Farn Wah Cheng *VP, Treasury Sales* ☎ **390 6623**
Janet Chua *AVP, Treasury Sales* ☎ **390 6623**

Risk Management
Department: Credit & Risk Management
Head of Risk Management — Jimmy Chin *VP, Credit* ☎ **390 6646**

Settlement / Clearing
Settlement (General) — Pak Ling Yip *VP, Back-Office Settlement* ☎ **390 6670**

www.euromoneydirectory.com SINGAPORE (+65)

Administration
Technology & Systems
                        Chrisopher Lim *Vice President* ☏ **390 6652**
Accounts / Audit
Accounts   Chay Joo Teo *Vice President* ☏ **390 6666**
Internal Audit   Yvonne Aw *Vice President* ☏ **390 6608**

BHF-BANK AG
Full Branch Office

Formerly known as: Berliner Handels- und Frankfurter Bank
#03-00 Gateway West, 150 Beach Road, Singapore, 189720
Tel: 291 2177 **Fax:** 291 2755; 392 6209 **Telex:** 28484 BHF SI **Swift:** BHFB SG SG **Reuters:** BHFS
General Telex: 29363; Financial Markets **Tel:** 291 8677

Senior Executive Officers
DGM & Head, Corporate Banking   Ho Chai Seng
SVP & General Manager   Klaus Borig
SVP & General Manager   Frank Behrends

General-Lending (DCM, SL)
Head of Corporate Banking   Ho Chai Seng *DGM & Head, Corporate Banking*

Debt Capital Markets / Fixed Income
Department: Financial Markets
Global Head; Regional Head   Percy Rueber *Senior Manager & Head, Financial Markets*

Non-Domestic Government Bonds
Dealer   Peter Tay
                                       Allan Foo
                                       Belinda Teo
                                       Alex Seah
                                       Tan See Han
                                       Boey Kok Kit
                                       Derek Lim
                                       Nicholas Sparrow

Syndicated Lending

Other (Trade Finance)
Documentary Credits   Jimmy Ong *Senior Manager & Head*

Money Markets

Other (Wholesale Deposits)
Bills   Jimmy Ong *Senior Manager & Head*

Canadian Imperial Bank of Commerce
Full Branch Office

#04-02 Hitachi Tower, 16 Collyer Quay, Singapore, 049318
Tel: 535 2323 **Fax:** 535 7565 **Telex:** RS24005 CANIMP **Swift:** CIBC SG SG **Reuters:** CBSC (Global CM)
Cable: CANIMPEAST
Financial Products Group **Tel:** 536 8113; **Fax:** 536 6286; Global Capital Markets **Tel:** 535 8080; **Fax:** 538 0578;
Reuters: CIBS (Foreign Exchange); CIBM (Asian Currencies & Interest Rates); CIFP (Financial Products Group)

Senior Executive Officers
EVP, Asia Pacific   Y J Mirza

Debt Capital Markets / Fixed Income
Department: Financial Products Group
Head of Debt Capital Markets   Susan Hall *Executive Director, Regional Head, Asia (ex-Japan)*

Bonds - General
                                       Christopher J Iley *Managing Director, Asia Pacific*
Asian Currency & Interest Rates Trading   Water C W Cheung *Managing Director*
Credit Products   Eugene Philalithis *Director*
Research   Chiang Yao Chye *Executive Director, Asia Pacific*
Loan Underwriting & Distribution   Anna Chu *Managing Director Asia*

Asset-Backed Securities / Securitization
Regional Head   Fazel Ahmed *Managing Director, Asia Pacific*

Syndicated Lending
Department: Origination & Structuring

Other (Syndicated Lending)
Loan Products   Randall P Quinn *Executive Director, Asia Pacific*

SINGAPORE (+65)   www.euromoneydirectory.com

Canadian Imperial Bank of Commerce (cont)
Loan-Related Activities
Structured Trade Finance   Rodney Ballard *Executive Director, Asia Pacific*
                                    Yew May Lee *Executive Director, Asia Pacific*
Other (Trade Finance)
Aerospace, Airlines & Defence   Nicholas Forget *Executive Director, Asia Pacific*
Public Services & Infrastructure Finance   William K B Goh *Managing Director, Asia Pacific*
Foreign Exchange
Department: Global Capital Markets
Head of Foreign Exchange   Kenneth Lai *Managing Director*
FX Traders / Sales People
Asian Currencies   Kenneth Lai *Managing Director*
Forward Desk   Bernard Gauvin *Executive Director*
Spot Desk   Howard N Sarkar *Managing Director*
Sales, Marketing & Distribution   Maurice Lam *Executive Director*
Risk Management
Head of Risk Management   Anand P Srinivasan *Managing Director*
                                    Douglas Paterson *Managing Director*
Corporate Finance / M&A Advisory
Department: Origination & Structuring
Other (Corporate Finance)
                                    Russell A Cranwell *Managing Director, Asia Pacific*
Asset Securitisation   Fazel Ahmed *Managing Director, Asia Pacific*
Country Executives   Devdatt Shah *Managing Director - India*
                                    Eri Reksopuodjo *Executive Director, Indonesia*
                                    Vilas Suvidejkosol *Executive Director - Thailand*
Forestry   Sean Sailes *Executive Director, Asia Pacific*
Multimedia & Technology   Chin Foo Chun *Managing Director, Asia Pacific*
Oil & Gas   Cosmas T Kapsanis *Executive Director*
Power   David B Krett *Managing Director, Asia Pacific*
Settlement / Clearing
Operations   Robert Verity *MD, Asia Pacific*
Other Departments
Liquidity Management   Norman Sim *MD, Funding & Liquidity Management*
Other Departments
Financial Control   Veronica J McCann *Managing Director, Asia Pacific*
Administration
Head of Marketing   Cynara Tan *Executive Director*
Technology & Systems
Global Technology   T Rajah *Head, Asia Pacific*
Legal / In-House Counsel
                                    Ralph J Lutes *MD & Counsel, Asia Pacific*
Compliance
                                    Ralph J Lutes *MD & Counsel, Asia Pacific*
Corporate Communications
                                    Cynara Tan *Executive Director*
Accounts / Audit
Audit Services, Internal Audit & Corp. Security   Vijaykumar Rajagopalan *Regional Director*
Other (Administration)
Human Resources   Terence Lim *MD, Asia Pacific*

CEF (Singapore) Limited   Subsidiary Company

#25-05 Ocean Building, 10 Collyer Quay, Singapore, 049315
Tel: 533 1889 **Fax:** 533 1127

Senior Executive Officers
Managing Director   Siah Meng Yeo ☏ **533 1839**
Syndicated Lending
Loan-Related Activities
Project Finance   Kuan Hung Tan *Executive Director*
Corporate Finance / M&A Advisory
Head of Corporate Finance   Kuan Hung Tan *Executive Director*
Asset Management
Head   Ken Tan *Executive Director*

1304   Euromoney Directory 1999

www.euromoneydirectory.com				SINGAPORE (+65)

Other Departments
Private Banking				George So *Executive Director*
Administration
Head of Administration			Pin Kim Lai *Associate Director*
Accounts / Audit
					Pin Kim Lai *Associate Director*
Other (Administration)
Financial Controller				Paul Ng *Chief Financial Officer*

# The Chase Manhattan Bank					Full Branch Office

150 Beach Road, Gateway West, Singapore, 189720
Tel: 291 1298 **Fax:** 290 1756 **Telex:** RS21370 CHASMAN **Swift:** CHAS SG SGA **Telex:** RS23022 CHASMAN;
Reuters: CHAE (FX Spot Regional); CHMS (FX Spot G10); CHBS (FX Sales & Options Sales);
CMSD (Structured Derivatives); CHCO (FX Corp Sales); CHDS (IRMG Regional & Non Deliverables);
CHAE (IRMG NDF); CHSG (IRMG G3); CMOQ, CMBR (Options Trading); CBMM (International Treasury)

Senior Executive Officers
Country Manager, Managing Director		Morgan T McGrath ☎ 391 7135 📠 392 7375
Others (Senior Executives)
Global Trading Division			Fraser Partridge *Managing Director* ☎ 290 1633 📠 290 1750
General-Lending (DCM, SL)
Head of Corporate Banking			Nicholas de Boursac *MD, Corporate Banking / MNC* ☎ 391 7392
						📠 392 7350

General - Treasury
Head of Treasury				Judy Ang *VP, International Treasury Division* ☎ 290 1406 📠 290 1420
Relationship Manager
Special Industry Group-Chemical		Terence Robinson *Managing Director* ☎ 290 1342 📠 290 1427
Special Industry Group-Telecommunication	Windsor Hall *Managing Director* ☎ 290 1343 📠 290 1627

Syndicated Lending
Loan-Related Activities
Trade Finance					Amita Jhangiani *MD, Trade Finance* ☎ 391 7459 📠 392 7361
Project Finance				Douglas McMurrey *MD, Project Finance* ☎ 290 1602 📠 290 1637

Foreign Exchange
FX Traders / Sales People
Trading - Regional Spot FX			C K Lam *Vice President & Manager* ☎ 299 4877 📠 290 1798
Trading - G10 Spot FX				Peter Newman *Vice President & Manager* ☎ 291 7929 📠 290 1798
Sales - Singapore Corporates			Su Ming Tham *Vice President & Manager* ☎ 290 1600 📠 392 7239
Sales - US Funds				Vincent Faust *Vice President & Manager* ☎ 291 7989 📠 290 1701
Sales - Options				Leigh Winton *Vice President* ☎ 291 7989 📠 290 1701
Sales - Structured Derivatives		Andrew Best *Vice President* ☎ 297 9353 📠 290 1692

Risk Management
Department: Interest Rate Management
Country Head					Kumi Fujii *Managing Director* ☎ 291 9018 📠 290 1755

Other (FI Derivatives)
IRMG - Regional				David Bailey *Vice President & Manager* ☎ 291 9018 📠 290 1755
IRMG - G7					Guy Rowcliffe *Vice President & Manager* ☎ 291 9018 📠 290 1755
Restructuring					Stuarte Dagg *Vice President* ☎ 291 9018 📠 290 1755

Other Currency Swap / FX Options Personnel
Head of Option Trading			Richard Leighton *Managing Director*
Exchange-Traded Derivatives
FX Options					Richard Leighton *Managing Director*

Other Departments
Private Banking				Chew-Mee Kirtland *MD, Private Banking* ☎ 391 7147 📠 392 7419
Correspondent Banking				Florence Gan *VP, Correspondent Banking* ☎ 391 7266 📠 392 7362
Cash Management				S Natarajan *Vice President* ☎ 391 7109 📠 392 7269

# Cho Hung Bank					Full Branch Office

#40-02/03 Singapore Land Tower, 50 Raffles Place, Singapore, 048623
Tel: 536 1144 **Fax:** 533 1244 **Telex:** RS25049 **Swift:** CHOH SG SG **Telex:** RS26521

Senior Executive Officers
General Manager				Kyung Sup Song
General - Treasury
Head of Treasury				I Hyun Kim *Manager*

Euromoney Directory 1999 **1305**

SINGAPORE (+65) www.euromoneydirectory.com

Cho Hung Bank (cont)

Syndicated Lending
Head of Syndication I Hyun Kim *Manager*

Money Markets
Money Markets - General
Loans & Bills Soon Cheol Kim *Deputy General Manager*

Administration
Head of Administration Sung Woo Park *Manager*

Accounts / Audit
Account Sung Woo Park *Manager*

Christiania Bank   Offshore Banking Unit

#21-01 Odeon Towers, 331 North Bridge Road, Singapore, 188720
Tel: 338 2728 **Fax:** 338 2729 **Telex:** RS 42888 XIABS **Swift:** XIAN SG SG

Senior Executive Officers
Branch Manager & EVP Bjorn Ostrom

General-Lending (DCM, SL)
Head of Corporate Banking Limm Mee Fong *Manager, Corporate Banking*

Syndicated Lending
Project Finance Finn A Norbye *FVP, Shipping / Project Finance*
  Gro E Lundevik *VP, Shipping / Project Finance*

Foreign Exchange
Department: Foreign Exchange / Treasury
Global Head Antonello Di Lorenzo *Vice President*

FX Traders / Sales People
Treasury Jacqueline Chuang *Senior Dealer*
Foreign Exchange Samantha Wong *Senior Dealer*

Administration
Other (Administration)
Administration / Operations Irene Tham *Senior Vice President*

CIBC Asia Limited   Subsidiary Company

#04-02 Hitachi Tower, 16 Collyer Quay, Singapore, 049318
Tel: 535 2323 **Fax:** 535 7565 **Telex:** RS24005 CANIMP **Swift:** CIBC SG SG **Cable:** CANIMPEAST
Financial Products Group Tel: 536 8113; **Fax:** 536 6286; **Global Capital Markets Tel:** 535 8080; **Fax:** 538 0578;
Telex: RS28305 CANIMP; **Reuters:** Monitor: CBCS (Global Capital Markets); Dealing: CIBS (FX);
CIBM (Asian Currencies & Interest Rates); CIFP (Financial Products Group)

Senior Executive Officers
Managing Director Y J Mirza
Deputy Managing Director Ralph Lutes

Others (Senior Executives)
  Anand P Srinivasan *Director*
  Veronica McCann *Director*

Citicorp Investment Bank (Singapore) Limited   Subsidiary Company

#38-0304 UIC Building, 5 Shenton Way, Singapore, 068808
Tel: 225 5533 **Fax:** 224 7801 **Telex:** RS 22891 **Reuters:** CIAQ-Z

Senior Executive Officers
Managing Director Tit Koon Soon ☎ **320 5505**

Others (Senior Executives)
Operations Hock Lan Tan *Deputy Senior Country Manager*

Administration
Compliance
  Seng Jin Sim *Head* ☎ **320 5420**

Other (Administration)
Operations Grace Seah *Head* ☎ **426 8203** 📠 **426 8056**

1306 Euromoney Directory 1999

www.euromoneydirectory.com   SINGAPORE (+65)

Clariden Asset Management (Singapore) Pte Limited   Subsidiary Company

#45-01, 80 Raffles Place, UOB Plaza 1, Singapore, 048624
Tel: 532 5325 Fax: 534 5551

Senior Executive Officers
Managing Director   Roland Knecht

Commerzbank (South East Asia) Limited   Subsidiary Company

#41-01 Temasek Tower, 8 Shenton Way, Singapore, 068811
Tel: 223 4855 Fax: 225 3943 Telex: RS27189 Swift: COBA SG SX XXX Reuters: CBSI
Dealing Tel: 220 9989; 223 6002; Fax: 323 9197; Telex: RS27190; Reuters: CBST; CBSC

Senior Executive Officers
Managing Director   Gerhard Held
Managing Director   Wolfgang Rohde

General-Lending (DCM, SL)
Head of Corporate Banking   Antony Withers *AGM, Corporate Banking*

General - Treasury
Head of Treasury   Karen Teo *Manager, Treasury Settlements*
                                             Patrice Keck *AGM, Treasury*

Relationship Manager
Regional Banks   Vivien Kuah *Assistant Manager*
Margin Accounts   Thomas Walliser *Senior Dealer*
                                             Michael Ho *Dealer*

Debt Capital Markets / Fixed Income
Bonds - General
Sales   Lim Jit Yeow *Manager*
Securities & Bonds   Nigel Blowers *Assistant General Manager*
Sales   Philip Wen *Assistant Manager*
                                             Jeremy Lee *Dealer*
                                             Sonia Lai *Assistant Dealer*

Syndicated Lending
Department: Corporate Banking
Head of Syndication   Wong Sow Fook *Manager*
                                             Dominic Hernon *Senior Manager*

Loan-Related Activities
Trade Finance   Carol Cheong *Senior Manager*

Money Markets
Head of Money Markets   Foo Soo Liang *Senior Manager*

Money Markets - General
                                             Chan Chong San *Manager*
                                             Chow Chin Lin *Dealer*
                                             Wan Li Chin *Dealer*
                                             Chris Khoo *Assistant Manager, Corporate Desk*
                                             Wan Chuan Chee *Senior Dealer*
                                             Karen Wee *Senior Dealer, Corporate Desk*

Foreign Exchange
Country Head   Victor Lam *Senior Manager, FX Spot*

FX Traders / Sales People
FX Spot   Ng Kok Leong *Assistant Manager*
                                             Sujit Kumar Hazra *Assistant Manager*
                                             Patrick Saczawa *Assistant Manager*
                                             Jerry Gee *Dealer*

Risk Management
Head of Risk Management   Peter-Joerge Lauschke *Assistant General Manager*
Country Head   Julian Sandt *Manager*
                                             Philip Ong *Manager*

Foreign Exchange Derivatives / Risk Management
Country Head   Chng Yeow Teck *Manager*
                                             Randy Brummette *Assistant Manager*

Settlement / Clearing
Settlement (General)   Karen Teo *Manager, Treasury Settlements*
Operations   Heino Geick *Assistant General Manager*

SINGAPORE (+65)　　　　　www.euromoneydirectory.com

Commerzbank (South East Asia) Limited (cont)
Other Departments
Proprietary Trading　　　　　　　　Janet Tan *Manager*
　　　　　　　　　　　　　　　　　Yeung Sze Chung *Assistant Manager*
Private Banking　　　　　　　　　Rolf Mueller-Glodde *Assistant General Manager*
Administration
Head of Administration　　　　　　Heino Geick *Assistant General Manager*
Other (Administration)
Marketing　　　　　　　　　　　　Gilbert Lim *Senior Manager*
　　　　　　　　　　　　　　　　　Roy Lim *Senior Manager*
　　　　　　　　　　　　　　　　　Soh Chee Yong *Senior Manager*
　　　　　　　　　　　　　　　　　Martin Ruecker *Manager*

Commonwealth Bank of Australia
#22-04 Singapore Land Tower, 50 Raffles Place, Singapore, 048623
Tel: 224 5132 **Fax:** 224 5812 **Telex:** RS20920 CTBSIN **Swift:** CTBA SG SG **Reuters:** CBAS; CBAR; CBSG
Senior Executive Officers
Financial Director　　　　　　　　Gary Roach
Managing Director / General Manager　Gavin Forte E **forteg@cba.com.au**

Compagnie Financière de CIC et de l'Union Européenne
Offshore Banking Unit

Alternative trading name: Union Européenne de CIC
#23-01/02, Republic Plaza, 9 Raffles Place, Singapore, 048619
Tel: 536 6008 **Fax:** 536 7008 **Telex:** 29070 CICSGP

Senior Executive Officers
Treasurer　　　　　　　　　　　　Vincent Joulia *Head of Treasury* T **231 9830**
General Manager　　　　　　　　　Jean-Luc Anglada T **231 9800**
Syndicated Lending
Fax: 438 0625
Head of Syndication　　　　　　　Wui Ming Low *Assistant General Manager* T **231 9880**
Loan-Related Activities
Project Finance　　　　　　　　　Julia Tan *Head, International Banking* T **231 9828**
Money Markets
Fax: 438 0626
Country Head　　　　　　　　　　Christopher Ouvrard *VP & Head, Money Markets* T **438 0619**
Wholesale Deposits
Marketing　　　　　　　　　　　　Willem Nabarro *VP & Head, Treasury Sales* T **438 0612**
Foreign Exchange
Fax: 438 0626
Country Head　　　　　　　　　　Philippe Chen *VP & Head, Forex Options & Spot Group* T **438 0609**
Head of Institutional Sales　　　　Willem Nabarro *VP & Head, Treasury Sales* T **438 0612**
Corporate Sales　　　　　　　　　Kin Wah Yew *VP, Treasury Sales* T **438 0612**
Risk Management
Country Head　　　　　　　　　　Chew Shiuan Tang *Head, Credit & Risk* T **231 9801**
Foreign Exchange Derivatives / Risk Management
Country Head　　　　　　　　　　Philippe Chen *VP & Head, Forex Options & Spot Group* T **438 0609**
Settlement / Clearing
Country Head　　　　　　　　　　Jason Soh *AVP, Settlements* T **231 9730**
Administration
Head of Administration　　　　　　Thierry Croiset *Administration & Organization Manager* T **231 9860**
Technology & Systems
　　　　　　　　　　　　　　　　　Nicolas Arbogast *Vice President* T **231 9750**
Compliance
　　　　　　　　　　　　　　　　　Cecilia Goh *VP, Audit & Financial Control* T **231 9863**
Accounts / Audit
　　　　　　　　　　　　　　　　　Valerie Ho *Vice President, Accounts & Finance* T **231 9740**

www.euromoneydirectory.com SINGAPORE (+65)

Coutts Bank (Singapore) AG
Full Branch Office

Formerly known as: Coutts & Co AG
#06-01 Land Tower, 50 Raffles Place, Singapore, 048623
Tel: 223 3132 **Fax:** 223 5098 **Telex:** RS24881 COUTTS **Swift:** COUT SG SG

Senior Executive Officers
Financial Director — Keith A D Harrison *CFO & Deputy General Manager* ☎ 326 1340
 F 536 6796
Chief Operating Officer — Hans-Peter Brunner *GM & Area Head, Asia* ☎ 326 1311 F 536 6796

Other Departments
Private Banking — Hans-Peter Brunner *GM & Area Head, Asia* ☎ 326 1311 F 536 6796

Administration
Head of Administration — Belinda Jeow *Administration Officer* ☎ 326 1318 F 536 6796

Other (Administration)
Human Resources — Bee Tin Lim *Human Resources Administrator* ☎ 326 1308 F 536 6796

Crédit Agricole Indosuez
Full Branch Office

Formerly known as: Banque Indosuez
Level 17, 6 Raffles Quay, Singapore, 048580
Tel: 535 4988 **Fax:** 532 2422 **Telex:** RS24435 INDOCAB **Reuters:** INDS (Monitor) **Cable:** INDOSUEZ SINGAPORE
Commodities Finance Fax: 439 9755; **Corporate Banking Fax:** 439 9754; **Corporate Sales Tel:** 535 3177;
Fax: 439 9887; **Derivatives Sales Tel:** 439 9800; **Fax:** 439 9887; **Derivatives Trading Tel:** 535 1913; **Fax:** 439 9887;
Financial Institutions Sales Tel: 535 7525; **Fax:** 439 9887; **Private Banking Fax:** 439 9285; **Proprietary Trading
Tel:** 439 9802; **Fax:** 439 9887; **Regional Treasury Tel:** 439 9894; **Fax:** 439 9899; **Spot Tel:** 535 5377; **Fax:** 439 9887

Senior Executive Officers
Chief Executive Officer — James Foo *Senior Country Officer*
Chief Operating Officer — Francis Moracchini
Treasurer — Hérve Martin

General-Lending (DCM, SL)
Head of Corporate Banking — Patrice Couvegnes
 Philippe Pellegrin *Head, Corporate Banking*

General-Investment
Head of Investment — Vivian Kan
 Donna Kng

Relationship Manager
Corporate Sales — Swee Huat Seah
Financial Institutions Sales — Marc Wenda

Debt Capital Markets / Fixed Income
Head of Fixed Income — Sheau Fen Phua

Syndicated Lending
Head of Credit Committee — Ann Cheong

Loan-Related Activities
Trade Finance — Kim Fui Liew
Commodities Financing — Gilles Sayer
Project Finance — Patrick Blanchard

Money Markets
Tel: 535 3977 **Fax:** 439 9887
Country Head — Kum Thin Lai

Foreign Exchange
Tel: 535 5177 **Fax:** 439 9887
Head of Trading — Derek Kwok

Risk Management
Foreign Exchange Derivatives / Risk Management
Country Head — Frederic Lamotte

Other (Exchange-Traded Derivatives)
Derivatives Trading — Pascal Petri
Derivatives Sales — Harry Bronn
 Melisa Lee

Settlement / Clearing
Operations — Edmund Lee

Other Departments
Proprietary Trading — Kim Seng Chang
Private Banking — Gilles Martinengo *Int'l Private Banking*

Euromoney Directory 1999 **1309**

SINGAPORE (+65) www.euromoneydirectory.com

Crédit Agricole Indosuez (cont)
Administration
Technology & Systems
                            Eric Wong
Other (Administration)
Human Resources   Gek Kee Lim
Accounting & Administration Beng See Lee

Crédit Lyonnais   Full Branch Office
#11-01, Centennial Tower, 3 Temasek Avenue, Singapore, 039190
PO Box 1839, Robinson Road, Singapore, 903639
Tel: 333 6331 **Fax:** 333 6332 **Telex:** RS 27225 CLSING **Swift:** CRLY SG SG **Reuters:** CLSS (Spot FX)
Cable: CREDIONAIS
Dealing Tel: 333 8108; 333 8109; **Fax:** 333 8119; **Telex:** RS 27223 CLSING; **Reuters:** CLOS (FX Options); CLSX; CHCK; CHCL; CHCM

Senior Executive Officers
General Manager & Regional Manager   Henri Laumet
Deputy General Manager   Eric Bogros

Others (Senior Executives)
Head of Administration - Asia   Christian Lapie
Merchant Banking   Dominique Blanchard *Deputy General Manager*
Head of Regional Service Centre - Asia Youm Sung Soo
Oil & Commodities Trade Finance   Charles Maulino *Regional Manager*
Private Banking, Asia   Pascal Delvaque *Managing Director*
Credit & Loan Administration   Roland Tan *Assistant General Manager*
Head of Treasury & Foreign Exchange   Jean d'Orival *Assistant General Manager*
Head of Project Finance, Asia   Pierre Philippe Martin *Director*
Asian Aviation Group   Christophe Bernardini *Managing Director*
Head of Information Systems Projects, Asia Fabrice Garambois

General-Lending (DCM, SL)
Head of Corporate Banking   Jeffrey Low *Assistant General Manager*

Debt Capital Markets / Fixed Income
Department: Capital Markets, Syndication, Origination & Participation
Bonds - General
Merchant Banking   Dominique Blanchard *Deputy General Manager*
                                       Quah Siew Hock *Assistant General Manager*

Syndicated Lending
Loan-Related Activities
Project Finance   Pierre Philippe Martin *Director*

Other (Trade Finance)
Oil & Commodities Trade Finance   Charles Maulino *Regional Manager*

Foreign Exchange
Head of Foreign Exchange   Jean d'Orival *Assistant General Manager*
Regional Head   Samuel Hung *Asia Head of Foreign Exchange*

FX Traders / Sales People
FX Spot   Tan Teck Huat *Chief Dealer*
                                       Yuji Kojima *Deputy Chief Dealer*
FX Options (Asia)   Hossein Zaimi *Head*
Interest Rate Group   Lucy Toh *Head*
                                       Thierry Delrieu *Senior Dealer*
                                       Tan Siam Keng *Senior Dealer*
Treasury Sales   Desmond Tan *Asia Head, FX Marketing*
                                       Angkana Sapcharoen *Vice President*
                                       Jessline Ang *Vice President*
                                       Abdullah Yusoff *Vice President*
                                       Marc Dray *Dealer*
Derivative Sales   Rosalind Teo *VP, Interest Rates Derivatives Marketing*

Other Departments
Private Banking   Pascal Delvaque *Managing Director*
Correspondent Banking   Low Whee Hoon *Manager*

Other Departments
Commercial Banking   Eric Bogros *Deputy General Manager*

Administration
Head of Administration   Christian Lapie

www.euromoneydirectory.com　　　　　　　　SINGAPORE (+65)

Technology & Systems
Information Systmes Projects　　　　Fabrice Garambois

The Dai-Ichi Kangyo Bank Limited　　　　　　Full Branch Office
#47-00 OUB Centre, 1 Raffles Place, Singapore, 048616
Tel: 533 2626; 533 2525 (Dealers) **Fax:** 536 0647; 533 2190 **Telex:** RS21622 DKBSP **Reuters:** DKBS (FX)
Cable: BANKDAIKAN
Reuters: DKBR (Money & Forwards)
Website: www.dkb.co.jp

Senior Executive Officers
General Manager	Ken-Ichi Satomura
Joint General Manager	Masaki Kato
Joint General Manager	Kohei Hosoya
Assistant General Manager	Guan Yeow Kwang
Assistant General Manager	Tan Yee Hoon
Assistant General Manager	Ang Boon Kiat

General - Treasury
Head of Treasury　　　　　　　　Jimmy Koh *Treasury Control*
　　　　　　　　　　　　　　　Naoki Wada *Treasury Settlement*

Syndicated Lending
Other (Syndicated Lending)
Loan Administration　　　　　　Steven Ang *Senior Manager*

Money Markets
Department: Foreign Exchange, ACU & Local Money Market

Money Markets - General
Market Dealing　　　　　　　　Eiji Yokoyama *Senior Manager*
　　　　　　　　　　　　　　　Selva Raj Sinnan *Dealer*
　　　　　　　　　　　　　　　Lim Sock Wee *Dealer*
　　　　　　　　　　　　　　　Mee Nah Fong *Dealer*
　　　　　　　　　　　　　　　Yoshitsugu Okumura *Dealer*
　　　　　　　　　　　　　　　Yuki Nakamori *Dealer*
　　　　　　　　　　　　　　　Naoto Takahashi *Dealer*

Foreign Exchange
Department: Foreign Exchange, ACU & Local Money Market
Corporate Sales　　　　　　　　Yoshiharu Yamadori *Senior Manager*
　　　　　　　　　　　　　　　David Chua *Dealer*

FX Traders / Sales People
Market Dealing　　　　　　　　Eiji Yokoyama *Senior Manager*
　　　　　　　　　　　　　　　Selva Raj Sinnan *Dealer*
　　　　　　　　　　　　　　　Lim Sock Wee *Dealer*
　　　　　　　　　　　　　　　Mee Nah Fong *Dealer*
　　　　　　　　　　　　　　　Yoshitsugu Okumura *Dealer*
　　　　　　　　　　　　　　　Yuki Nakamori *Dealer*
　　　　　　　　　　　　　　　Naoto Takahashi *Dealer*

Corporate Finance / M&A Advisory
Corporate Finance & Syndication I　　　Koju Okano *Senior Manager*
Corporate Finance & Syndication II　　　Edwin Toh *Senior Manager*
Corporate Finance & Syndication III　　　Khoe Poo Loen *Senior Manager*
Corporate Finance & Syndication IV　　　Ling Kok Dung *Senior Manager*

Settlement / Clearing
Operations　　　　　　　　　　Teresa Kwan *Senior Manager, Bills & Operations*

Administration
Business Development　　　　　Osamu Ukegawa *Department Head, Business Planning & Co-ordination*

Technology & Systems
Information Technology　　　　　Kikuichi Tanimoto *Senior Manager*

Accounts / Audit
Internal Audit　　　　　　　　　Fong Mei Lan *Manager*
Accounting　　　　　　　　　　Connie Yan

Other (Administration)
General Affairs　　　　　　　　Leong Mui Leng *Senior Manager*
　　　　　　　　　　　　　　　Isao Takaishi *Manager*

SINGAPORE (+65) www.euromoneydirectory.com

The Daiwa Bank Limited
Full Branch Office

#30-01 Temasek Tower, 8 Shenton Way, Singapore, 068811
Tel: 220 1791; 220 1792 **Fax:** 224 6840; 223 3712 **Telex:** RS22123 **Swift:** DIWA SG SG

Senior Executive Officers
Treasurer — Yutaka Nakamura *Manager*
General Manager — Yutaka Ueda
Deputy General Manager — Masanori Matsui

Syndicated Lending
Other (Trade Finance)
Letters of Credit — Yoshikatsu Tamiya *Manager*

Foreign Exchange
Global Head — Yutaka Nakamura *Manager*
FX Traders / Sales People
Credit — A Tahara *Senior Manager*

Corporate Finance / M&A Advisory
Global Head — A Tahara *Senior Manager*

Other Departments
Correspondent Banking — Yoshikatsu Tamiya *Manager*

Administration
Head of Administration — A Tahara *Senior Manager*

Technology & Systems — Yoshikatsu Tamiya *Manager*

Daiwa Merchant Bank (Singapore) Limited
Subsidiary Company

#30-01 Temasek Tower, 8 Shenton Way, Singapore, 068811
Tel: 220 1791 **Fax:** 224 6840 **Telex:** RS22123 **Cable:** SINGDAIWA SINGAPORE

Senior Executive Officers
Managing Director — Yutaka Ueda
Director — Masanori Matsui

Daiwa Securities
Subsidiary Company

#26-08 DBS Tower Two, 6 Shenton Way, Singapore, 068809
Tel: 220 3666 **Fax:** 225 3797 **Telex:** RS 21126 DAIWA

Senior Executive Officers
Chairman — Kiyoshi Matsuba

Debt Capital Markets / Fixed Income
Department: Securities
Regional Head — Mr Terashima *Chief Dealer, Securities Trading & Distribution*

Daiwa Singapore Limited
Subsidiary Company

#26-08 DBS Tower Two, 6 Shenton Way, Singapore, 068809
Tel: 220 3666 **Fax:** 225 3797 **Telex:** RS 21126 DAIWA

Senior Executive Officers
President — Kiyoshi Matsuba

Settlement / Clearing
Operations — Soh Liam Kiat *Head of Operations*

DBS Bank
Head Office

Alternative trading name: Development Bank of Singapore Limited
DBS Building, 6 Shenton Way, Singapore, 068809
Tel: 220 1111 **Fax:** 221 1306 **Telex:** RS 24455 **Swift:** DBSS SG SG **Email:** dbspr@dbs.com.sg
Website: www.dbs.com.sg

Senior Executive Officers
Chairman — S Dhanafalan ☎ **321 5802**
President — Kee Choe Ng ☎ **321 5806**
Chief Executive Officer — John T Olds *Deputy Chairman & CEO*
Chief Operating Officer — Kee Choe Ng *President* ☎ **321 5806**

1312 Euromoney Directory 1999

www.euromoneydirectory.com SINGAPORE (+65)

Debt Capital Markets / Fixed Income
Head of Fixed Income — Mun Seng Chau ☎ 321 5131 F 225 6783
Libor-Based / Floating-Rate Products
FRN Sales; Asset Swaps (Sales) — Donne Lee *Vice President* ☎ 224 5433

Equity Capital Markets
Department: Capital Markets
Tel: 321 6381 **Fax:** 221 8847
Head of Equity Capital Markets — Shik Lum Kan *Senior Vice President* ☎ 321 6382
Head of Sales — Chee Kong Choo *Vice President* ☎ 321 5353

Syndicated Lending
Head of Origination — Joan Ting Wong *Senior Vice President* ☎ 321 5243
Lim Sok Hia *Senior Vice President* ☎ 321 5205
Cheo Chai Hong *Senior Vice President* ☎ 321 5210
Andrew Chua *Senior Vice President* ☎ 321 5652

Head of Syndication — Joan Ting Wong *Senior Vice President* ☎ 321 5243
Lim Sok Hia *Senior Vice President* ☎ 321 5205
Cheo Chai Hong *Senior Vice President* ☎ 321 5210
Andrew Chua *Senior Vice President* ☎ 321 5652

Head of Trading — Joan Ting Wong *Senior Vice President* ☎ 321 5243
Lim Sok Hia *Senior Vice President* ☎ 321 5205
Cheo Chai Hong *Senior Vice President* ☎ 321 5210
Andrew Chua *Senior Vice President* ☎ 321 5652

Money Markets
Domestic Commercial Paper
Head of Trading — Tiong Sang Ho *Vice President* ☎ 220 5272

Foreign Exchange
Head of Institutional Sales; Corporate Sales — Donne Lee *Vice President* ☎ 224 5433
Head of Trading — Peter Soh *Vice President* ☎ 223 2137

FX Traders / Sales People
Woei Kyet Kwa *Assistant Vice President* ☎ 223 2137
Nicholas Yap *Assistant Vice President* ☎ 223 2137
Jimmy Au-Eong *Assistant Vice President* ☎ 223 2137

Risk Management
IR Swaps Sales / Marketing — Donne Lee *Vice President* ☎ 224 5433
IR Swaps Trading — Tan Siew Kheng *Senior Vice President* ☎ 223 3153
IR Options Sales / Marketing — Donne Lee *Vice President* ☎ 224 5433
IR Options Trading — Tan Siew Kheng *Senior Vice President* ☎ 223 3153

Foreign Exchange Derivatives / Risk Management
Vanilla FX option Sales — Donne Lee *Vice President* ☎ 224 5433
Vanilla FX option Trading — Peter Soh *Vice President* ☎ 223 2137

Other Currency Swap / FX Options Personnel
Arivara Hagan *Vice President*
Bernard Goh *Vice President*

Corporate Finance / M&A Advisory
Global Head — Eric Ang *Executive Vice President* ☎ 321 5238
Regional Head — Kan Shik Lum *Senior Vice President* ☎ 321 6382

Settlement / Clearing
Department: Settlements
Tel: 220 1111 **Fax:** 224 5490
Head of Settlement / Clearing — Siew Mooi Ong *Senior Vice President* ☎ 321 5279
Fixed-Income Settlement — Cheong Ghee Chua *Assistant Vice President* ☎ 321 5834

Global Custody
Department: Investment Banking Investor Services
Head of Global Custody — M N J Vilcassin *Senior Vice President* ☎ 321 5156 F 533 9271

Administration
Head of Administration — Seh Boo Yeo *Vice President* ☎ 780 2701

Technology & Systems
Fong Lian Ho *Senior Vice President* ☎ 321 5860

Legal / In-House Counsel
Lee Cheng Heng *Vice President* ☎ 321 5311

Compliance
Kim How Khoo ☎ 321 5816

Public Relations
Lee Cheng Heng *Vice President* ☎ 321 5311

Accounts / Audit
Peng Khian Ng *Senior Vice President* ☎ 780 2601

SINGAPORE (+65)   www.euromoneydirectory.com

DBS Finance Limited
Subsidiary Company

DBS Finance Building, 112 Robinson Road, Singapore, 068902
Tel: 223 0355 **Fax:** 223 5066 **Telex:** RS43427 **Cable:** DBSBANK
Website: www.dbsf.com.sg

Senior Executive Officers
Chairman & CEO — Kim Soon Soh ☎ **321 5829**

Others (Senior Executives)
— Peter Tan *Executive Director* ☎ **320 3803**

Syndicated Lending
Loan-Related Activities
Leasing & Asset Finance — Ting Hoe Shu *AGM, Credit & Marketing* ☎ **320 3803**

Money Markets
Country Head — Jina Lee *Senior Manager, Funds & Investment* ☎ **320 3980**

Wholesale Deposits
Marketing; Head of Sales — Jina Lee *Senior Manager, Funds & Investment* ☎ **320 3980**

Administration
Technology & Systems
Information Technology — Anthony Tan *Assistant General Manager* ☎ **320 3810**

Public Relations
Human Resources & Corporate Affairs — Peggy Quah *Assistant General Manager* ☎ **320 3907**

Other (Administration)
Business Develpment & Corporate Planning — Kong Hwa Gui *Assistant General Manager* ☎ **320 3810**

Den Danske Bank Aktieselskab
Full Branch Office

#24-01 Singapore Land Tower, 50 Raffles Place, Singapore, 048623
Tel: 323 5589 **Fax:** 224 3320 **Telex:** 28030 DDBSIN **Swift:** DABA SG SG **Reuters:** DDBS

Senior Executive Officers
Chief Executive Officer — Mogens Syndergaard
 — Thomas Tan *Deputy General Manager*
Treasurer — Ole Bremholm Jorgensen

Others (Senior Executives)
— Jørgen Fonøe *Manager, Credit & Risk Management*

General-Lending (DCM, SL)
Head of Corporate Banking — Eunice Warren *Assistant General Manager*

Risk Management
Regional Head — Jørgen Fonøe *Manager, Credit & Risk Management*

Den norske Bank ASA
Full Branch Office

#48-02 Temasak Tower, 8 Shenton Way, Singapore, 068811
PO Box 1769, Robinson Road, Singapore, 903519
Tel: 220 6144; 220 6147 **Fax:** 224 9743 **Telex:** RS21737 DNBSIN **Swift:** DNBA SG SG **Reuters:** DNBS-T
Dealers Tel: 224 8022; **Fax:** 224 7305

Senior Executive Officers
General Manager — Pal Skoe

Others (Senior Executives)
DnB Markets — Jeff Ang Kim Hai *Deputy General Manager*

General-Lending (DCM, SL)
Head of Corporate Banking — Kee Song Wei *Snr Manager, Corp Banking-Shipping*
 — Bjørnar Lund *Senior Manager, Corporate Banking*

Relationship Manager
Product Support — Tan Ooh Chye *Manager*

Syndicated Lending
Other (Trade Finance)
Trade & Industry — Bjørnar Lund *Senior Manager, Corporate Banking*

Risk Management
Country Head — Ann Marit Fjaerli *Senior Manager, Risk Management*

Other Departments
Cash Management — Bjørnar Lund *Senior Manager, Corporate Banking*

www.euromoneydirectory.com SINGAPORE (+65)

Administration
Technology & Systems
Information Technology Daniel Pang *Manager*

Accounts / Audit
Finance & Accounts Nio Yee Ling *Manager*

Deutsche Bank AG Regional Head Office
#20-01 Temasek Tower, 8 Shenton Way, Singapore, 068811
PO Box 7, Robinson Road, Post Office, Singapore, 900007
Tel: 423 8001 **Fax:** 225 4911 **Telex:** RS24499 **Swift:** DEUT SG SG
Controllers Fax: 226 0637; Corporate & Institutional Banking Fax: 226 1252; Corporate Banking Fax: 227 1301; Corporate Communications Fax: 222 0565; Credit Risk Management Fax: 225 9039; Human Resources Fax: 223 3295; Organization Fax: 225 4911; RHOIT Fax: 225 8271

Senior Executive Officers
Chief Executive Officer Simon Murray

Deutsche Bank AG Full Branch Office
#15-08 Tower 2, DBS Building, 6 Shenton Way, Singapore, 068809
Tel: 224 4677 **Fax:** 225 9442; 222 3589 **Telex:** RS 21189 DBA **Swift:** DEUT SG SG
Bills & Customer Service Fax: 226 2006; Corporate Banking Fax: 226 2007; Dev.Hdl./FX Tel: 225 6955; FX/Money Market Fax: 224 0897; Institutional Investment Fax: 224 1949; Management Fax: 226 1910; Portfolio Management Fax: 224 5002; Private Banking Fax: 221 9245; Securities & Custody Services Fax: 220 6707

Senior Executive Officers
Managing Director / General Manager U Norbert Wanninger

Debt Capital Markets / Fixed Income
Tel: 224 4665

Fixed-Income Repo
Trading Nick Fowle *Senior Associate Director*
  Andrew Smoler *Senior Associate Director*

Equity Capital Markets
Tel: 423 6012 Fax: 220 6707

Equity Repo / Securities Lending
Marketing & Product Development Louise H Neville *First VP & Head of Securities Lending, Asia* ☏ 423 6041
  ⌂ 324 8311
Head of Trading Winston Lee Chian Yen *Senior Securities Lending Officer*

Deutsche Capital (Singapore) Limited Subsidiary Company
20th Floor, Temasek Tower, 8 Shenton Way, Singapore, 068811
Tel: 533 2828 **Fax:** 538 2672 **Telex:** RS23102 MGASIA
Asia Project & Export Finance Fax: 538 2621; Asia Project & Export Finance Fax: 538 0528; Asset-Backed Securitization, Leasing & Asset-Backed Finance Fax: 538 2656; Investment Banking Fax: 538 2629; Investment Banking Fax: 538 2632; Operations Fax: 538 2673; Syndications Fax: 538 2917

Senior Executive Officers
Managing Director / General Manager Michael Desa

Debt Capital Markets / Fixed Income

Asset-Backed Securities / Securitization
Global Head Gary Watmore *Head of Securitization*

Syndicated Lending
Head of Syndication Ray Ho *Director, Syndications*

Loan-Related Activities
Project Finance Pradeep Mathur *Director, Asian Project & Export Finance*
  Philip Crotty *Director, Asian Project & Export Finance*

Euromoney Directory 1999 **1315**

SINGAPORE (+65)   www.euromoneydirectory.com

Deutsche Morgan Grenfell & Partners Securities Pte Ltd

Formerly known as: Morgan Grenfell & Partners Securities Pte Ltd
#20-01 Ocean Towers, 20 Raffles Place, Singapore, 048620
Tel: 533 1818 **Fax:** 532 6211 **Telex:** RS263

Senior Executive Officers
Chairman   E-Min Su
Chief Operating Officer   Pauline Lim
Managing Director   Soo Liat Ooi

Equity Capital Markets
Domestic Equities
Head of Research   Tim Buckley
International Equities
Head of Sales   Tsjen Po Kiang

Deutsche Securities Limited

#20-01 Treasury Building, 8 Shenton Way, Singapore, 068811
Tel: 321 6600

Senior Executive Officers
Department: Senior Executives: Global Corporates & Institutions
Others (Senior Executives)
Head of Investment Banking   Josef Ackermann
Head of Global Markets   Edson Mitchell
Head of Equities   Michael Philipp
Head of Risk Management   Hugo Banziger
Head of Global Banking Services Juergen Fitschen
Head of Structured Finance   Gavin Lickley
Head of IT / Operations   Marc Sternfeld

The DKB Futures (Singapore) Pte Limited   Subsidiary Company

#47-00 OUB Centre, 1 Raffles Place, Singapore, 048616
Tel: 533 2626 **Fax:** 533 2790 **Telex:** RS21622 DKBSP **Swift:** DKBL SG SG

Senior Executive Officers
Managing Director   Ken-Ichi Satomura
Others (Senior Executives)
                                 Kazutaka Hosoda *Director*
                                 Masaki Kato *Director*

DKB Merchant Bank (Singapore) Limited   Subsidiary Company

#51-00 OUB Centre, 1 Raffles Place, Singapore, 048616
Tel: 538 2330 **Fax:** 538 7713 **Telex:** RS25866 DKBMB
Website: www.dkb.co.jp

Senior Executive Officers
Managing Director   Hosoya Kohei
Administration
Head of Administration   Koiichiro Yano *Director, Administration*
Other (Administration)
International Marketing Division Boon Kiat Ang *Director*

Dresdner (South East Asia) Limited   Subsidiary Company

#22-00 Tung Centre, 20 Collyer Quay, Singapore, 049319
PO Box 3699, Robinson Road, Singapore, 905699
Tel: 222 8080 **Fax:** 224 4008 **Telex:** RS29355 DREASIA **Swift:** DRES SG SD SEA
Dealers Tel: 220 9251; **Money & FX Dealers Tel:** 220 9333

Senior Executive Officers
Managing Director   Manfred Barth
Managing Director   Raymond B T Koh

1316 Euromoney Directory 1999

www.euromoneydirectory.com　　　　　　　SINGAPORE (+65)

Senior Executive Officers (cont)
Managing Director　　　　　　　　　G B Low
Managing Director　　　　　　　　　Tan Eng Huat
Managing Director　　　　　　　　　Robert S Lette

Relationship Manager
Investment Advisory　　　　　　　　Andre Ruppli *Senior Manager*

Debt Capital Markets / Fixed Income
Head of Fixed Income Sales　　　　Jan-Hendrik Bornemann *Manager*

Syndicated Lending
Other (Syndicated Lending)
Syndications　　　　　　　　　　　Gerald A K Yeo *Assistant General Manager*

Loan-Related Activities
Project Finance　　　　　　　　　　Hans-Jürgen Schniewind *Assistant General Manager*

Other (Trade Finance)
Structured Finance　　　　　　　　Oliver Drews *Senior Manager*

Foreign Exchange
FX Traders / Sales People
FX Trading / Treasury　　　　　　　Lee Siew Chiang *Assistant General Manager*

Settlement / Clearing
Settlement (General)　　　　　　　Liang Chooi Kuan *Deputy Manager, Back-Office Settlements*
Operations　　　　　　　　　　　　Tommy Tay *Deputy Manager*

Other Departments
Chief Credit Officer　　　　　　　　H Michael Blum *Senior Manager, Credit*

The Export-Import Bank of India
Representative

#15-06 Ocean Building, 10 Collyer Quay, Singapore, 049315
Tel: 532 6464 **Fax:** 535 2131 **Telex:** RS64101 EXIM RS **Email:** eximbank@singnet.com.sg
Cable: INDIAEXIM SINGAP

Senior Executive Officers
Resident Representative　　　　　　R Venkateswaran

Fimat Futures Asia Pte Limited
Subsidiary Company

#27-00, 80 Robinson Road, Singapore, 068898
Tel: 323 5711 **Fax:** 323 5722

Senior Executive Officers
Chief Executive Officer　　　　　　Stephen Hawksworth *CEO*

Financial Security Assurance Inc

6 Temasek Boulevard, Suntec Tower Four, Singapore, 038986
Tel: 333 6968 **Fax:** 430 5601

Senior Executive Officers
Managing Director, Asia Pacific　　　Richard G Holzinger
Managing Director & Chief Underwriting Officer　Geoffrey H Durno
Director　　　　　　　　　　　　　　Nils Dahl

Others (Senior Executives)
　　　　　　　　　　　　　　　　　Raymond Lee *Assistant Vice President*
　　　　　　　　　　　　　　　　　Cecilia Xie *Assistant Vice President*

Finanz AG Zürich
Representative Office

#48-01, UOB Plaza 1, 80 Raffles Place, Singapore, 048624
PO Box 776, Singapore, 901526
Tel: 531 2814 **Fax:** 533 0420

Senior Executive Officers
Chief Representative, Asia Pacific　　Mateos Atamyan

Euromoney Directory 1999　**1317**

SINGAPORE (+65)   www.euromoneydirectory.com

First Commercial Bank
Full Branch Office

#01-02, 76 Shenton Way, Singapore, 079119
Tel: 221 5755 Fax: 225 1905 Telex: 25667

Senior Executive Officers

General-Lending (DCM, SL)
Head of Corporate Banking
  Duang Shaw-Ging
  Yap Kiok Eng *Manager, Commercial Banking*

General - Treasury
Head of Treasury
  Wang Liang Chin *AVP & Manager of Treasury*

Debt Capital Markets / Fixed Income
Department: Capital Markets
Global Head
  Lin Hann-Chyi *VP & General Manager*

Syndicated Lending
Head of Syndication
  Hwang Shiuh Jyh *Manager, Syndication*

Risk Management

Fixed Income Derivatives / Risk Management
IR Swaps Trading
  Wang Liang Chin *Manager* ☎ **222 1462**
  Wu Lon Chek *Dealer* ☎ **222 1462**

Foreign Exchange Derivatives / Risk Management
Cross-Currency Swaps, Trading
  Wang Liang Chin *Manager* ☎ **222 1462**
  Wu Lon Chek *Dealer* ☎ **222 1462**

Exchange-Traded Derivatives
FX Futures
  Wang Liang Chin *Manager* ☎ **222 1462**
  Wu Lon Chek *Dealer* ☎ **222 1462**

Other Departments
Correspondent Banking
  Hoh Hai Sin *Manager*

Four Seas Bank Limited
Subsidiary Company

110 Robinson Road, Singapore
OCBC Centre, 65 Chulia Street, Singapore
Tel: 224 9898 Fax: 224 4936; 535 3768 Telex: RS22133 Swift: FSEA SG SG

Senior Executive Officers
Chairman   Tan Puay Yong
Chief Executive Officer   Lee Seng Wee ☎ **503 1505**
Treasurer   Wong Yew Kuen *Head, Global Treasury* ☎ **530 1616**

Debt Capital Markets / Fixed Income
Fax: 535 3768
Country Head
  Chee Kian Seng ☎ **530 6012**

Domestic Government Bonds
Head of Trading
  Chee Kian Seng ☎ **530 6012**

Money Markets
Country Head
  Chee Kian Seng ☎ **530 6012**

Foreign Exchange
Fax: 535 3768
Country Head
  Chee Kian Seng ☎ **530 6012**

Settlement / Clearing
Fax: 438 1491
Country Head
  Ang Ee Mui ☎ **530 1784**

The Fuji Bank Limited

1 Raffles Place, 20-00 OUB Centre, Singapore
Tel: 534 3500 Fax: 532 7310 Telex: RS24610 FUJIGTN Swift: FUJI SG SG Reuters: FBKS

Senior Executive Officers

Others (Senior Executives)
Member of the Board
  Toru Ishihara *Regional Corporate Executive (Southeast Asia)*

www.euromoneydirectory.com　　　　　　　　　　　　　　　　　　SINGAPORE (+65)

The Fuji Futures (Singapore) Pte Limited

#13-06, Six Battery Road, Singapore, 049909
Tel: 221 3633 Fax: 227 3038

Senior Executive Officers
Managing Director　　　　　　　　　　　　Kahgee Tan [T] 227 7933 [F] 227 3038
Others (Senior Executives)
Senior Vice President　　　　　　　　　　　Wilson Koh *Head, Business Development & Sales* [T] 438 1303 [F] 227 3038
　　　　　　　　　　　　　　　　　　　　　　Nancy Lam *Head, Operations & Compliance* [T] 227 6233 [F] 227 3038

Goldman Sachs (Singapore) Pte

29-01 Singapore Land Tower, 50 Raffles Place, Singapore, 048623
Tel: 228 8100 Fax: 228 8128

Senior Executive Officers
Managing Director, Principal Investment　　Steven Shafran [T] 228 8611 [F] 228 8308
Managing Director, Investment Banking　　Richard Ong [T] 228 8623 [F] 228 8308
Managing Director, Equities　　　　　　　　Thomas Ryan [T] 228 8102 [F] 228 8128
Managing Director, Futures Services　　　　Robert Cox [T] 228 8150 [F] 228 8148
Others (Senior Executives)
Regional Director　　　　　　　　　　　　　Gilbert Young *Energy Trading* [T] 228 8426 [F] 228 8185
　　　　　　　　　　　　　　　　　　　　　　Stefan Van Riet *Energy Trading* [T] 228 8171 [F] 228 8185
General-Investment
Head of Investment　　　　　　　　　　　　Richard Seow *Vice President, Investment Banking* [T] 228 8637 [F] 228 8308

Gulf International Bank BSC

#11-06, Shell Tower, 50 Raffles Place, Singapore, 048623
Tel: 224 8771 Fax: 224 8743 Telex: 28096 GIBSIN

Senior Executive Officers
Others (Senior Executives)
Senior Representative, Asia　　　　　　　　Peter Smith *Senior Vice President*

The Hachijuni Bank Limited　　　　　　　　　　　　　　　　Representative Office

#11-05, 6 Battery Road, Singapore, 049909
Tel: 221 1182 Fax: 221 0556

Senior Executive Officers
Chief Representative　　　　　　　　　　　Akira Kaneko

Hanil Bank　　　　　　　　　　　　　　　　　　　　　　　　　Full Branch Office

#23-02 OUB Centre, 1 Raffles Place, Singapore, 048616
Tel: 538 6696 Fax: 538 0056 Telex: RS26857 Swift: HANI SG SG Reuters: HIBS

Senior Executive Officers
General Manager　　　　　　　　　　　　　Tae Woong Chung
Others (Senior Executives)
Reconciliazion & Import　　　　　　　　　　Yoon Jung Il *Deputy General Manager*
Accounting / Export / Reimbursement　　　Park Nam Sun *Manager*
Treasury / Planning / Dealing / Investment / 　Kim Jong Kyoo *Manager*
Marketing
Administration
Head of Administration　　　　　　　　　　Nak Jin Hwang *Manager*

Hong Leong Finance Limited　　　　　　　　　　　　　　　Head Office

#01-05 Hong Leong Building, 16 Raffles Quay, Singapore, 048581
Tel: 220 9433 Fax: 224 6773

Senior Executive Officers
Chairman & Managing Director　　　　　　Leng Beng Kwek
General Manager　　　　　　　　　　　　　Peng Boon Lim
Financial Director　　　　　　　　　　　　　Soon Yee Christie *AGM, Finance*

Euromoney Directory 1999　**1319**

SINGAPORE (+65)　　　　www.euromoneydirectory.com

Hong Leong Finance Limited (cont)
Others (Senior Executives)
Marketing　　　　　　　　　　Linda Quek *AGM, Credit & Marketing*

The Hongkong & Shanghai Banking Corporation Limited
Full Branch Office

Alternative trading name: HSBC Markets
#02-00 HongkongBank Building, 21 Collyer Quay, Singapore, 049320
Tel: 530 5000 **Fax:** 225 0663 **Telex:** RS21259 HSBC **Cable:** HONGBANK **Telex:** RS29052; **Dealers Fax:** 225 8824; **Money Market Dealers Tel:** 224 7677; **Capital Markets - Dealers Tel:** 538 0201; **FX Dealers - G7 Tel:** 224 7977; **Regional Currency Dealers Tel:** 221 5308; **Corporate FX Sales Dealers Tel:** 224 6869; 224 9578; **Reuters:** HKSC (Capital Markets); HKMS (Money Markets); HKBS (FX - G7); HKRS (FX - Regional Currency); HKST (Corporate FX Sales)

Senior Executive Officers
Chief Executive Officer　　　　J C S Rankin *General Manager & Chief Executive*
　　　　　　　　　　　　　　　D Dew *Deputy Chief Executive*

General - Treasury
Head of Treasury　　　　　　Alan R Bird *Head, Treasury & Debt Capital Markets*

Debt Capital Markets / Fixed Income
Department: Treasury & Capital Markets - HSBC Markets
Regional Head　　　　　　　Alan R Bird *Head, Treasury & Debt Capital Markets*
　　　　　　　　　　　　　　Michael Chan *Deputy Head*

Non-Domestic Government Bonds
Debt Product Sales　　　　　Martin F T Taylor *Head*

Foreign Exchange
Department: Treasury & Capital Markets - HSBC Markets
Head of Foreign Exchange　　Daniel Foo *Head*

FX Traders / Sales People
Major Currency FX Trading　　Annie Tee *Chief Dealer*
　　　　　　　　　　　　　　Maurice Low *Chief Dealer*
Corporate FX Sales　　　　　John Chung *Manager*

Risk Management
Regional Head　　　　　　　Mark T Beckwith *Risk Manager*

Other Currency Swap / FX Options Personnel
SGD Derivative Trading; SGS Primary　　Chua Ghee Kiat *Chief Dealer*
Dealership; Regional Currency Debt Securities
Derivatives Marketing　　　　Azam Mistry *Head*

HSBC Investment Bank plc
Full Branch Office

#09-00, HongkongBank Building, 21 Collyer Quay, Singapore, 049320
Tel: 224 8080 **Fax:** 223 7146 **Telex:** RS24520 HIBS **Swift:** HIBL SG SG **Reuters:** HKIS **Cable:** HSBCHIBS

Senior Executive Officers
Chief Executive Officer　　　　Kah Yeok Koh *Chief Executive*
Financial Director　　　　　　Lucy Teo *Financial Controller*

Others (Senior Executives)
　　　　　　　　　　　　　　Suh-Ting Sim *Corporate / Legal Adviser*

Equity Capital Markets
Department: Corporate Finance and Equity Capital Markets
Global Head　　　　　　　　Harry Naysmith *Head, SE Asia*
Regional Head　　　　　　　Say Teik Shih *Associate Director*
　　　　　　　　　　　　　　Simon Cooper *Associate Director*

Other (Domestic Equities)
Broking　　　　　　　　　　Simon Pang *Head of Securities*
　　　　　　　　　　　　　　Lennard Ho *Senior Manager, Securities*

Syndicated Lending
Regional Head　　　　　　　Poo Swee Gan *Loan Syndication Director Head, South East Asia*
Country Head　　　　　　　Benedict Tan *Senior Vice President*
　　　　　　　　　　　　　　Hock Thye Tan *Senior Vice President*

Other (Syndicated Lending)
Vice President　　　　　　　Harrison Ong
　　　　　　　　　　　　　　Eugene Szeto

www.euromoneydirectory.com   SINGAPORE (+65)

Other (Syndicated Lending) (cont)
                                   Jek Sen Sim
                                   Mark Yeo
Loan-Related Activities
Project Finance   Murray M Ashdown *Head, Project Finance*
                                   Peter Fraser *Director, Project Finance*
                                   Kok-Chen Lim *Director, Project Finance*
                                   Ram Iyer *Assistant Director*

Foreign Exchange
Department: Treasury
FX Traders / Sales People
                                   Kok Ping Lim *Head of Treasury*
                                   Jeffrey Foo *Senior Dealer, Forex*
                                   Jerry Tan *Senior Dealer, Forex*
                                   Stanley Heng *Senior Dealer, MM*

Settlement / Clearing
Operations   Eddie Wong *Head*
                                   Jonathan Wong *Vice President*

Other Departments
Private Banking   Jimmy So *Head*
                                   Yuen Peng Mok *Senior VP, Head of Investment Advisory*
                                   Michael Lim *Senior VP, Investment Advisory*
                                   Mike Hue *VP, Investment Advisory - Fixed Income*
                                   Gareth Sung *VP, Investment Advisory*
                                   Yew Kiang Lim *VP, Investment Advisory*

Administration
Technology & Systems
Information Technology & Systems   Puay Cheng Ng *Head*
Legal / In-House Counsel
Corporate / Legal Adviser   Suh-Ting Sim
Accounts / Audit
Accounts   Denise Tay *Head*
Other (Administration)
Marketing Team   Jonathan Watson *Head, Marketing*
                                   Andrew Saxton *Senior VP, Area Head*
                                   Charles Ng *Senior VP, Area Head*
                                   Felicia Fu *VP, Team Head*
                                   Jimmy Goh *VP, Team Head*
                                   Victor Lim *VP, Team Head*
                                   Yan Han Wee *VP, Team Head*
                                   Timothy Yu *Vice President*
                                   Bernard Kan *Vice President*

IBJ Merchant Bank (Singapore) Limited   Subsidiary Company

#14-00 Hitachi Tower, 16 Collyer Quay, Singapore, 049318
Tel: 538 7500 **Fax:** 538 7779 **Telex:** RS 21880 **Swift:** IMBS SG SG

Senior Executive Officers
Chairman   Yasunori Nagai
Chief Executive Officer   Hidetaka Tanaka *Managing Director & Chief Executive*
Chief Operating Officer   Manabu Yamamoto *Director* ☎ **437 6110**

Debt Capital Markets / Fixed Income
Global Head   Manabu Yamamoto *Director* ☎ **437 6110**
Regional Head   Takashi Kobanawa *Vice President* ☎ **437 6135**

Libor-Based / Floating-Rate Products
FRN Origination   Manabu Yamamoto *Director* ☎ **437 6110**
FRN Sales   Takashi Kobanawa *Vice President* ☎ **437 6135**

Medium-Term Notes
Head of Origination   Takashi Kobanawa *Vice President* ☎ **437 6135**

Equity Capital Markets
Global Head   Manabu Yamamoto *Director* ☎ **437 6110**

Money Markets
Global Head   Manabu Yamamoto *Director* ☎ **437 6110**

Settlement / Clearing
Regional Head   Han Tuan Juan *Vice President* ☎ **437 6113**

SINGAPORE (+65) www.euromoneydirectory.com

IBJ Merchant Bank (Singapore) Limited (cont)
Global Custody
Regional Head   Han Tuan Juan *Vice President* ☎ **437 6113**
                                       Mieko Nakajima *Senior Officer* ☎ **437 6147**
Other Departments
Private Banking   Manabu Yamamoto *Director* ☎ **437 6110**

The Industrial & Commercial Bank of China

#12-01 John Hancock Tower, 6 Raffles Quay, Singapore, 048580
Tel: 538 1066 **Fax:** 538 1370; 538 4392 **Telex:** 24421 ICBCSB **Swift:** ICBK SG SG **Reuters:** ICBX
Telex: 20130 ICBCSB

Senior Executive Officers
Treasurer   Lee Wee Sum
General Manager   Wang Dewen
Syndicated Lending
Tel: 538 1066 **Fax:** 538 1370
Head of Syndication   Chong Wun Hin
Loan-Related Activities
Trade Finance   Fung Kwok Ying
Project Finance   Chong Wun Hin

The Industrial Bank of Japan Limited   Offshore Banking Unit

#14-00 Hitachi Tower, 16 Collyer Quay, Singapore, 049318
Tel: 538 7366 **Fax:** 538 7779 **Telex:** RS21880 KOGINPO **Swift:** IBJT SG SG **Reuters:** IBJS (Dealing)
Cable: KOGYOGINKO
Dealers Tel: 538 7771; 538 7773; **Telex:** RS25102 KOGINPO

Senior Executive Officers
General Manager   Yasunori Nagai
Joint General Manager   Hidetaka Tanaka
Joint General Manager   Tomoyuki Urabe
General-Lending (DCM, SL)
Head of Corporate Banking   Y Miyazaki *Senior Manager, Corporate Banking I*
                                       Y Yonezawa *Manager, Corporate Banking I*
                                       T Higaki *Manager, Corporate Banking I*
                                       M Nakayama *Assistant Manager, Corporate Banking I*
                                       H Takayama *Assistant Manager, Corporate Banking I*
                                       Wong Chwee Khim *Assistant Manager, Corporate Banking I*
                                       S Ota *Senior Manager, Corporate Banking II*
                                       Yap Nget Wah *Manager, Corporate Banking II*
                                       Teo Kok Liang *Manager, Corporate Banking II*
                                       Ng Hock Boon *Assistant Manager, Corporate Banking II*
Relationship Manager
International Business   H Omote *Manager*
                                       Christina Liew *Assistant Manager*
Syndicated Lending
Other (Syndicated Lending)
Loans Dept - Credit Administration   Ng Poh Sun *Manager*
Money Markets
Department: Foreign Exchange, ACU, Local Money Market, Bullion
Global Head   N Iwami *Head of Treasury, Senior Manager*
Other   Y Ishida *Chief Dealer*
Foreign Exchange
Department: Foreign Exchange, ACU, Local Money Market, Bullion
Global Head   N Iwami *Head of Treasury, Senior Manager*
FX Traders / Sales People
Derivatives & Sales   H Yamauchi *Manager*
Foreign Exchange & FX Forward   Patrick Tan *Assistant Manager & Chief Dealer*
FX Forward   T Kabe *Assistant Manager*
                                       N Suzuki *Senior Dealer*
Risk Management
Department: Risks Control Department
Other (FI Derivatives)
                                       Yeun Chee Meng *Senior Manager*

SINGAPORE (+65)

Foreign Exchange Derivatives / Risk Management
Vanilla FX option Trading   T Kabe *Assistant Manager*

Settlement / Clearing
Settlement (General)   Martin Chong *Manager, Settlements*
                                             Doris Loh *Assistant Manager, Settlements*

Other Departments
Economic Research   Y Sakamoto *Senior Manager, Research & Credit*

Administration
Head of Administration   Francis Chua *Manager Administration & Finance*

Technology & Systems
                                             Roland Chew *Manager, Systems*
Systems Planning   F Hirata *Manager*

Compliance
                                             Yeun Chee Meng *Senior Manager*

Accounts / Audit
Accounting   Mok May Kin *Manager*
Internal Auditor   Yip Sai Leng

Other (Administration)
General Service   Jessie Chng *Assistant Manager*
Personnel   Joanne Quek *Manager*
Telecommunications   Albert Tay *Assistant Manager*

ING Baring Securities (Singapore) Pte Limited — Subsidiary Company

#19-01 Republic Plaza, 9 Raffles Place, Singapore, 048619
Tel: 535 3688 **Fax:** 535 3233 **Telex:** RS26881

Senior Executive Officers
Managing Director   Richard Jones

Risk Management

Other (FI Derivatives)
Futures & Options   A Lim *Managing Director*

ING Barings — Full Branch Office

#19-02 Republic Plaza, 9 Raffles Place, Singapore, 048619
Tel: 535 3688 **Fax:** 533 8329 **Telex:** RS21178 INGB **Swift:** INGB SG SG **Reuters:** INGS **Telerate:** 2815
Cable: ING BANK

Senior Executive Officers
General Manager   Peter Teo

ING Barings Futures & Options Clearing Services

Subsidiary Company

#19-08 Republic Plaza, 9 Raffles Place, Singapore, 048619
Tel: 536 8283 **Fax:** 536 1998

Senior Executive Officers
Managing Director   Amy Lim

ING Barings Regional Office-Asia Pacific — Regional Head Office

53-00 Republic Plaza, 9 Raffles Place, Singapore, 048619
Tel: 535 3688 **Fax:** 535 0288

Senior Executive Officers
Country Manager   Graham Willis

Others (Senior Executives)
Regional Head, Asia (based in Hong Kong)   David Hudson
Deputy Regional Head, Asia   Jaap Manse

SINGAPORE (+65)   www.euromoneydirectory.com

ING Merchant Bank (Singapore) Limited
Subsidiary Company

#19-02 Republic Plaza, 9 Raffles Place, Singapore, 048619
Tel: 533 4182 **Fax:** 533 8329 **Telex:** RS21178 INGB **Swift:** INGB SG SG **Reuters:** INGS **Telerate:** 2815

Senior Executive Officers
General Manager   Peter Teo
General-Lending (DCM, SL)
Head of Corporate Banking   Toh Kai Leong *SVP, Corporate Banking*
General - Treasury
Head of Treasury   Jimmy Lim *SVP, Treasury*
Syndicated Lending
Other (Trade Finance)
Trade & Commodity Finance   Wong Chin Aun *SVP, Trade & Commodity Finance*
Risk Management
Head of Risk Management   Harold Quay *SVP, Risk Management*
Settlement / Clearing
Operations   Seng Cheow Kiang *Vice President*
Other Departments
Private Banking   Tan Hin Huat *SVP, International Private Banking*

Istituto Bancario San Paolo di Torino SpA
Full Branch Office

#42-04/05, Suntec Tower Four, 6 Temasek Boulevard, Singapore, 038456
Tel: 333 8270 **Fax:** 333 8252 **Telex:** RS 29317 **Swift:** IBSP SG SG **Reuters:** ISTS
Treasury Tel: 225 1344

Senior Executive Officers
General Manager   Dante Campioni
Debt Capital Markets / Fixed Income
Department: Treasury & Financial Markets
Tel: 333 8230 **Fax:** 333 8252
Head of Fixed Income   Guido Imbimbo *Deputy General Manager*
Syndicated Lending
Tel: 333 8270 **Fax:** 333 8252 **Reuters:** ISTS **Telex:** RS 22656 ISPAOL
Head of Syndication   Chwee Pheng Lim *Deputy General Manager*
Money Markets
Tel: 333 8230 **Fax:** 333 8252 **Telex:** RS 29318 / RS 29319 IBSPFX
Head of Money Markets   Wei Ming Cheong *Vice President*
Foreign Exchange
Tel: 333 8230 **Fax:** 333 8252 **Reuters:** ISTS **Telex:** RS 29318 / RS 29319 IBSPFX
Head of Foreign Exchange   Eddie Cheng *Assistant Vice President*
FX Traders / Sales People
                                                   Ng Chong Heng *Senior Dealer*
Settlement / Clearing
Department: Operations
Head of Settlement / Clearing; Operations   Kong Leong Chan *Vice President*
Other Departments
Chief Credit Officer   Siew Lan Gwee *Vice President*
Administration
Business Development; Head of Marketing   Chwee Pheng Lim *Deputy General Manager*
Technology & Systems
                                                   Khai Seng Lim *Deputy General Manager*
Compliance
                                                   Kahi Seng Lim *Deputy General Manager*

Jardine Fleming Singapore Securities Pte Limited
Full Branch Office

Formerly known as: Jardine Fleming International Securities Limited
#42-01 Republic Plaza, 9 Raffles Place, Singapore, 048619
Tel: 532 1933 **Fax:** 532 1922; 532 1309

Senior Executive Officers
Country Head   Philip Smiley

1324   Euromoney Directory 1999

www.euromoneydirectory.com				SINGAPORE (+65)

Equity Capital Markets
Head of Sales					Olivier Stocker *Head of Brokerage*
Head of Trading				Ron Tan *Head of Dealing*

Domestic Equities
Head of Trading				Ron Tan *Head of Dealing*

International Equities
Head of Sales					Olivier Stocker *Head of Brokerage*
Head of Trading				Ron Tan *Head of Dealing*

Equity Research
Head of Equity Research			Anthony Wilkinson *Head of Research*

Settlement / Clearing
Operations					Chiew Meng Lye *Head of Operations*

JM Sassoon & Co Pte Limited

#44-00 OUB Centre, 1 Raffles Place, Singapore, 048616
Tel: 532 7880 **Fax**: 534 5072

Equity Capital Markets
Domestic Equities
Head of Trading				Lim Kiat Seng *Executive Director* ☏ **535 2888**
Head of Research				Lim Eng Hai *Director, Research* ☏ **532 7880**

JP Morgan Securities Asia Limited

Alternative trading name: Morgan Guaranty Trust Co & JP Morgan Securities Inc
#32-08 DBS Building, Tower Two, 6 Shenton Way, Singapore, 068809
Tel: 220 8144 **Fax**: 222 8831 **Telex**: RS23640

Senior Executive Officers
MD, Capital Markets				Adam Howard

Keppel Bank of Singapore Limited   Head Office

Keppel Towers, 10 Hoe Chiang Road, Singapore, 089315
Tel: 222 8222 **Fax**: 225 2256
Website: www.keppelbank.com.sg

Senior Executive Officers
Chairman					Kee Boon Sim
President & CEO				Benedict Kwek ☏ **321 7902**
Financial Director				Victor Ow *Executive Vice President* ☏ **321 7005**

Others (Senior Executives)
Commercial Business				Eric Tham *Senior Vice President* ☏ **321 7045**
Head of Trade Finance				Daniel Wong *First Vice President* ☏ **321 7979**
Head of International Banking			Kok Chai Teo *First Vice President* ☏ **321 7030**
Company Secretary				Lynette Tan *Vice President* ☏ **321 7949**

General-Lending (DCM, SL)
Head of Corporate Banking			Jit Seng Lim *First Vice President* ☏ **321 7026**
						Chee Yong Foo *First Vice President* ☏ **329 6718**

General-Investment
Head of Investment				Ping Siong Kwak *Vice President* ☏ **321 7027**

General - Treasury
Head of Treasury				Kenneth Koh *Senior Vice President* ☏ **422 7836**

Syndicated Lending
Loan-Related Activities
Trade Finance					Daniel Wong *First Vice President* ☏ **321 7979**

Money Markets
Money Markets - General
Local Curency Desk				Hau Loong Kok *Vice President* ☏ **225 3363**

Other (Wholesale Deposits)
Commercial Business				Richard Chua *Vice President* ☏ **225 3363**
Eurocurrency					Wood On Tang *Assistant Vice President* ☏ **225 3363**

Euromoney Directory 1999   **1325**

SINGAPORE (+65)   www.euromoneydirectory.com

Keppel Bank of Singapore Limited (cont)

Foreign Exchange
Department: Foreign Exchange / Futures Trading
Tel: 225 3233
Global Head   Wan Cheng Neo *Senior Vice President*

FX Traders / Sales People
                                       Raymond Tay *Vice President*
                                       Kim Yam Tay *Vice President*

Settlement / Clearing
Settlement (General)   Michael Yuen *Vice President* ☎ **422 7728**
Operations   Susan Hwee *Executive Vice President* ☎ **329 4288**
                                       Quee Choo Lee *VP, Finance* ☎ **329 4101**

Asset Management
Department: Keppel Investment Management Limited

Other (Asset Management)
Investment Management   Victor Ow *Director* ☎ **321 7005**

Other Departments
Correspondent Banking   Freddie Siow *Vice President* ☎ **321 7967**

Administration

Technology & Systems
Technology & Operations   Susan Hwee *Executive Vice President* ☎ **329 4288**

Legal / In-House Counsel
Legal & Secretariat   Lynette Tan *Vice President* ☎ **321 7949**

Public Relations
                                       Joan Tan *Vice President* ☎ **329 7822**

Accounts / Audit
Audit   Sai Choong Loo *First Vice President* ☎ **223 5081**

Other (Administration)
Human Resources   King Khoong Kuang *First Vice President* ☎ **321 8600**

Kexim International (Singapore) Limited — Subsidiary Company

#16-20 UOB Plaza 2, 80 Raffles Place, Singapore, 048624
Tel: 536 0717; 536 0718 **Fax:** 536 0653; 536 0654 **Telex:** RS 23886 EXIMSP

Senior Executive Officers
Managing Director   Yunhee Cho

Debt Capital Markets / Fixed Income

Libor-Based / Floating-Rate Products
FRN Sales   Sung Keun Yoon *Senior Manager*

Syndicated Lending
Global Head   Wahn Kil Chung *Deputy Managing Director*

Money Markets
Global Head   Hee Sung Yoon *Manager*

Risk Management

Fixed Income Derivatives / Risk Management
Global Head   Hee Sung Yoon *Manager*

Settlement / Clearing
Fixed-Income Settlement   Janet Tay *Assistant Manager*

Korea Exchange Bank — Full Branch Office

#01-00 2 Finlayson Green, Asia Insurance Building, Singapore, 049257
PO Box 2861, Singapore, 904861
Tel: 224 1633; 224 7680 **Fax:** 224 3701 **Telex:** RS21956 **Swift:** KOEX SG SG **Cable:** KOEXBANK

Senior Executive Officers
Chief Executive Officer   Sang Ki Park *General Manager*

www.euromoneydirectory.com   SINGAPORE (+65)

Korea Leasing (Singapore) Pte Limited
Full Branch Office

#14-02 Chartered Bank Building, 6 Battery Road, Singapore, 049909
Tel: 532 1020 Fax: 532 1030 Telex: RS24345 KLOSIN

Senior Executive Officers
Managing Director   Cheong Ju Hwan

Korea Long-Term Credit Bank
Full Branch Office

#39-01 Suntec Tower one, 7 Temasek Boulevard, Singapore, 038987
Tel: 337 6100; 337 9855 Fax: 337 6100; 337 0766 Telex: RS20687 KLBSIN Reuters: KLBS

Senior Executive Officers
General Manager   Song Young Guk ☏ **337 5900**
Senior Manager   Kang Eui Joong ☏ **337 9855**
Manager   Jang Yong ☏ **337 3266**

Lehman Brothers Inc
Full Branch Office

#11-01 Suntec City Tower, 5 Temasek Boulevard, Singapore, 038985
Tel: 433 6288 Fax: 433 6188 Telex: RS36246 LBSING

Senior Executive Officers
Managing Director   Wai Kwong Seck ☏ **433 6002**

General-Investment
Head of Investment   Stephen Bonebrake *Senior Vice President, Investment Banking* ☏ **433 6358**

Debt Capital Markets / Fixed Income
Department: Fixed-Income
Head of Fixed Income Sales   Jiun In Lim *SVP, Fixed-Income Sales* ☏ **433 6432**

Bonds - General
                           Arianto Subagio *SVP, Derivatives Products* ☏ **433 6412**

Risk Management
Other Currency Swap / FX Options Personnel
SIMEX   K C Tan *Senior Vice President* ☏ **538 8680**

Settlement / Clearing
Operations   Pauline Lee *Vice President, Finance & Operations* ☏ **433 6318**

Administration
Head of Administration   Pauline Lee *Vice President, Finance & Operations* ☏ **433 6318**

Other (Administration)
Finance & Operations   Pauline Lee *Vice President, Finance & Operations* ☏ **433 6318**

Leu Asset Management Services (Asia) Pte Limited
Subsidiary Company

#10-03, 80 Robinson Road, Singapore, 068898
Tel: 221 7400 Fax: 221 7443

Senior Executive Officers
Managing Director / General Manager   Peter Wirth

The Long-Term Credit Bank of Japan Limited
Full Branch Office

#27-01 UOB Plaza 1, 80 Raffles Place, Singapore, 048624
Tel: 535 9633 Fax: 532 6048; 532 6759 Telex: RS23813 Reuters: LTJS
General Telex: RS20147; General Telex: RS20148; Dealers Tel: 534 1977; 534 1978; Fax: 534 5543

Senior Executive Officers
General Manager   Yukio Koba
Deputy General Manager   Tetsuya Fujisaki
Deputy General Manager   Hirotaka Ikeda

General - Treasury
Head of Treasury   Lee Wai Ching *Treasury Manager*
                             Kotaro Aoki *Deputy General Manager, Treasury*
                             Katsuhiko Fujimoto *Manager*

SINGAPORE (+65) www.euromoneydirectory.com

The Long-Term Credit Bank of Japan Limited (cont)
Money Markets
Country Head
Francis Seow *Manager*
Jennifer Tay *Dealer*
Foreign Exchange
FX Traders / Sales People
Dealer
Vincent Ho
Mah Sook Cheng

LTCB Merchant Bank (Singapore) Limited   Subsidiary Company
#26-01 UOB Plaza 1, 80 Raffles Place, Singapore, 048624
Tel: 533 8111 Fax: 533 0392

MW Marshall (Singapore) Pte Limited
#37-01, 6 Battery Road, Singapore, 049909
Tel: 535 5155 Fax: 535 6818 Telex: RS26669
Senior Executive Officers
Managing Director   Richard Low

Maybank
Alternative trading name: Malayan Banking Berhad
#01-00 Singapore Land Tower, 50 Raffles Street, Singapore, 048 623
Tel: 535 2266 Fax: 532 7909 Telex: RS21036 Swift: MBBE SG SG Reuters: MBBS
Senior Executive Officers
Chairman   Mohamed Basir bin Ahmad
Managing Director   Amirsham A Aziz
Senior General Manager   Spencer Lee
Administration
Corporate Communications
                                    Priscilla Luk *Head*
Other (Administration)
Services Quality   W S Fong *Officer* [F] 535 3397

MeesPierson Asia Limited   Subsidiary Company
#18-00 Caltex House, 30 Raffles Place, Singapore, 048622
Tel: 539 4788 Fax: 538 2205
Senior Executive Officers
Chief Executive Officer   Peter de Ruijter *Managing Director*
Financial Director   Julia Teo *CFO*
Chief Operating Officer   Kees Stoute *Deputy Managing Director*
Legal & Compliance Officer   Conrad Lim
Others (Senior Executives)
                                    Hock Chye Ong *Managing Director, Private Banking & Trust*
                                    Danny Chia *Head of Credit*
                                    Maarten Levering *Risk Manager*
Debt Capital Markets / Fixed Income
Department: Investment Management Group
Tel: 539 4723 Fax: 539 4913
Head of Fixed Income   Robert Alboher *Chief Investment Officer (Fixed Income)*
Other Departments
Private Banking   Hock Chye Ong *Managing Director, Private Banking & Trust*
Administration
Head of Administration   Hilda Tunstill *Manager Administration*
Technology & Systems
                                    Peter Hepworth *Head, IT*
Legal / In-House Counsel
                                    David Tan *Legal Counsel*
Compliance
                                    Conrad Lim *Legal & Compliance Officer*

Accounts / Audit
Internal Audit Janet Luk *Manager*
Other (Administration)
Human Resources Hoon Lee *Manager*

MeritaNordbanken Merchant Bank Singapore Limited
Subsidiary Company

Formerly known as: Merita Merchant Bank Singapore Limited
#15-01 Singapore Land Tower, 50 Raffles Place, Singapore, 048623
Tel: 225 8211 **Fax**: 225 5469 **Telex**: RS34253 **Swift**: MRIT SG S1 **Reuters**: MBSI **Telex**: RS34254
Senior Executive Officers
Tel: 225 8211 **Fax**: 225 5469
Chairman of the Board K G Lindvall
Managing Director Jonny Beckman
Asst. General Manager, Admin / Operations Y S Ng
General-Lending (DCM, SL)
Head of Corporate Banking Heikki Pero *Senior Manager, Corporate Banking*
Debt Capital Markets / Fixed Income
Emerging Market Bonds
Head of Emerging Markets Adrian Chew *Senior Manager, Treasury*
Equity Capital Markets
Head of Equity Capital Markets Adrian Chew *Senior Manager, Treasury*
Domestic Equities
Head of Origination; Head of Syndication Terence Chee *Snr Mgr, Structured Expo & Trade Finance*
Syndicated Lending
Loan-Related Activities
Project Finance; Structured Trade Finance Terence Chee *Snr Mgr, Structured Expo & Trade Finance*
Money Markets
Head of Money Markets Adrian Chew *Senior Manager, Treasury*
Foreign Exchange
Head of Foreign Exchange Adrian Chew *Senior Manager, Treasury*
Corporate Finance / M&A Advisory
Head of Corporate Finance Heikki Pero *Senior Manager, Corporate Banking*
Settlement / Clearing
Head of Settlement / Clearing Martina Heng *Assistant Manager, Settlements*
Other Departments
Chief Credit Officer Jacqueline Cheng *Senior Manager, Credit*
Cash Management Martin Kallerman *Senior Manager, Nordic Corp. Banking*
Administration
Head of Administration Y S Ng *Asst. General Manager, Admin / Operations*
Technology & Systems
 Y S Ng *Asst. General Manager, Admin / Operations*
Compliance
 Y S Ng *Asst. General Manager, Admin / Operations*
Accounts / Audit
 Ngoh Kiong Kirk *Manager, Accounting*

Merrill Lynch International Bank Limited
Subsidiary Company

2 Raffles Link, Marina Bayfront, Singapore, 039392
Tel: 331 3888 **Fax**: 331 3207 **Telex**: RS22846 MLIBSN **Reuters**: MLBS
FX Sales Tel: 330 7888; **Fax**: 330 7600; **Institutional Clients Sales Tel**: 330 7888; **Fax**: 330 7600; **Local Currency Trading/Treasury Tel**: 330 7888; **Fax**: 330 7600
Senior Executive Officers
Managing Director Raymundo A Yu Jr [T] **331 3001** [F] **331 3200**
Others (Senior Executives)
Executive Director Thai-Fong Wong *Chief Administrative Officer* [T] **331 3024** [F] **331 3203**
Relationship Manager
Private Clients Eng Huat Kong *Manager* [T] **331 3010** [F] **331 3500**
 Cheong Soon Tan *Manager* [T] **331 3113** [F] **331 3500**
 Simon Ho *Operation Manager* [T] **331 3700** [F] **331 3203**

Euromoney Directory 1999 **1329**

SINGAPORE (+65)   www.euromoneydirectory.com

Merrill Lynch International Bank Limited (cont)
Debt Capital Markets / Fixed Income
Head of Fixed Income   Richard Huston *Treasury Manager* T 330 7300 F 330 7309
Fixed-Income Research
Head of Fixed Income   William Belchere *First Vice President* T 330 7300 F 330 7309
Foreign Exchange
Head of Foreign Exchange   Richard Huston *Treasury Manager* T 330 7300 F 330 7309
Head of Institutional Sales   Frank Topedino *FX Sales Manager* T 330 7381 F 330 7600
FX Traders / Sales People
FX Trading   Adam Reynolds *Chief Dealer* T 330 7602 F 330 7600
Risk Management
Other (FI Derivatives)
                                    Richard Huston *Treasury Manager* T 330 7300 F 330 7309
Settlement / Clearing
Operations   Debbie Chin *Manager, Operations*
Other Departments
Commodities / Bullion   Pradipto Mazumder *Manager, Commodity Linked Finance* T 330 7677
                                    F 330 7684
Private Banking   Wendy Wong *Manager* T 331 3086 F 331 3209
                                    Dennis Tan *Manager* T 331 3005 F 331 3201
                                    Eng Heng Goh *Manager* T 331 3087 F 331 3207
                                    Cheng Swee Ong *Treasury Manager* T 331 3067 F 331 3205
                                    Joyce Woo *Admin & Control Manager* T 331 3085 F 331 3203
                                    Ambrose Law *Finance Manager* T 331 3200 F 331 3203

The Mitsubishi Trust & Banking Corporation   Full Branch Office

#42-01 Singapore Land Tower, 50 Raffles Place, Singapore, 048623
Tel: 225 9155 Fax: 225 0370 Telex: RS20184 MTBCSP

Senior Executive Officers
General Manager   Shigeo Matsueda
General-Lending (DCM, SL)
Head of Corporate Banking   Yutaka Hamabe *Chief Manager*
Syndicated Lending
Tel: 322 5630
Head of Origination; Head of Syndication; Head   Yutaka Hamabe *Chief Manager*
of Trading
Money Markets
Head of Money Markets   Ichiro Kumakiri *Deputy General Manager* T 322 5601

Morgan Grenfell Investment Management (Asia) Limited

Subsidiary Company

#23-08 Ocean Towers, 20 Raffles Place, Singapore, 048620
Tel: 538 7011 Fax: 538 3171

Senior Executive Officers
Chief Operating Officer   Nancy Boehm T 423 5628
Managing Director   James Goulding T 423 5632
Debt Capital Markets / Fixed Income
Department: Asian Fixed Income
Head of Fixed Income   Gerard Lee *Head of Asian Fixed Income* T 423 5615
Equity Capital Markets
Department: Asian Equities
Head of Equity Capital Markets   James Goulding *Chief Investment Officer* T 423 5632
Settlement / Clearing
Head of Settlement / Clearing   Karen Ng *Associate Director, Fund Administration* T 423 5653
Administration
Business Development   Yuit Chieng Lee *Director, Business Development* T 423 5639
Head of Marketing   Philip Hsin *Director, Sales & Marketing* T 423 5430
Technology & Systems
                                    Alex Jong *Associate Director, Information Technology* T 423 5438
Compliance
                                    Jennifer Davies *Associate Director, Compliance* T 423 5664

www.euromoneydirectory.com   SINGAPORE (+65)

Accounts / Audit
Accounts & Administration   Annie Low *Associate Director, Accounts & Administration* ☎ 423 5639

Morgan Stanley Asia (Singapore) Pte
#16-01, 23 Church Street, Capital Square, Singapore, 049481
Tel: 834 6888 **Fax:** 834 6817; 834 6815

Moscow Narodny Bank Limited
MNB Building, 50 Robinson Road, Singapore, 068882
Tel: 220 9422 **Fax:** 225 0140 **Telex:** RS27126 NARODNY **Swift:** MNBL SG SG **Reuters:** MNBS
Website: www.moscownarodny.com

Senior Executive Officers
Managing Director   A P Semikoz
Deputy General Manager   Evgueni M Grevtsev
Deputy General Manager   H G Bobby Teo

Others (Senior Executives)
                                         Siok Eng Ng *Assistant General Manager*
                                         Tony Tan *Assistant General Manager*
                                         David Yee *Senior Manager*

General - Treasury
Head of Treasury   Tony Tan *Assistant General Manager*

Syndicated Lending
Other (Trade Finance)
Forfaiting & Countertrade   David Yee *Senior Manager*
                                         Allan Teo *Deputy Manager*
                                         Allan Lee *Assistant Manager*
Letters of Credit; Documentary Credits   Tian Jui Kien *Deputy Manager*

Money Markets
Department: Money Market & Bullion
Global Head   Michael Tay *Assistant Manager*
Regional Head   Bee Yan Tan *Senior Dealer*
Other   Hui Thor Chua *Senior Dealer*

Money Markets - General
                                         Michael Tay *Assistant Manager*
                                         Bee Yan Tan *Senior Dealer*
Treasury Services   Hui Thor Chua *Senior Dealer*

Asset Management
Other (Asset Management)
Capital Markets   Chumnan Suddee *Senior Dealer*
Asset Trading   Andrei Tcharouchine

Other Departments
Proprietary Trading   Hong Eng Wong *Deputy Manager*
                                         Michael Su *Senior Dealer*
                                         Peggy Wong *Dealer*

Natexis Banque - BFCE   Subsidiary Company
Formerly known as: Banque Francaise Du Commerce Exterieur
#41-01 Singapore Land Tower, 50 Raffles Place, Singapore, 048623
Tel: 224 1455 **Fax:** 224 8651 **Telex:** RS28277 BFCESG **Swift:** BFCE SG SG **Cable:** EXTECOMEXE

Senior Executive Officers
Deputy General Manager   Philippe L Sirand
General Manager   Bernard Huberdeau

General-Investment
Head of Investment   Clara Hang *First Vice President*

Syndicated Lending
Global Head   Karen Lim *First Vice President*

Foreign Exchange
Department: Foreign Exchange and Treasury Management
Global Head   Lucy Tam *First Vice President*

SINGAPORE (+65)   www.euromoneydirectory.com

Natexis Banque - BFCE (cont)
Settlement / Clearing
Operations   Lee Tian Mong *VP, Assistant Head, Operations*
    Goy Joey Poh *First Vice President & Head*
Other Departments
Commodities / Bullion   Guillaume De Parscau *First Vice President*

National Australia Bank Limited   Full Branch Office
#15-01 Suntec City, 5 Temasek Boulevard, Singapore, 038985
Tel: 338 0038 Fax: 338 0039 Reuters: CRAB

Senior Executive Officers
Chief Executive Officer   Neil Frost *General Manager*
Treasurer   Robert Rigg *Head of Treasury* ☎ **338 0019**
Debt Capital Markets / Fixed Income
Libor-Based / Floating-Rate Products
Asset Swaps   Louise Doig *Manager, Fixed-Income* ☎ **388 0019**
Money Markets
Regional Head   Sophie Tay *Chief Dealer* ☎ **338 0019**
Foreign Exchange
Regional Head   Mike Moran *Head of Forex* ☎ **338 0019**
Head of Institutional Sales   Henry Quek ☎ **338 0019**
Risk Management
Fixed Income Derivatives / Risk Management
IR Swaps Trading   Chris Howlett ☎ **338 0019**
Other Departments
Private Banking   Ronnie Goh ☎ **338 0019**

National Bank of Canada (Asia) Limited
#25-01 Clifford Centre, 24 Raffles Place, Singapore, 048721
Tel: 538 7581 Fax: 538 7582 Reuters: NBCS

Senior Executive Officers
Managing Director   Jean Kin

National Bank of Kuwait SAK   Full Branch Office
#20-00 Tung Centre, 20 Collyer Quay, Singapore, 049319
Tel: 222 5348 Telex: RS20538 KUBANK
Treasury Tel: 225 6377; Telex: RS35533 NBK FX

Senior Executive Officers
General Manager & Chief Rep   R J McKegney
General - Treasury
Head of Treasury   T L Jones *Manager, Treasury*
Settlement / Clearing
Operations   Peter Ho *Manager*
Administration
Head of Administration   Mary Soo *Manager*
Other (Administration)
Marketing, Asia Pacific   K N Furnish *Manager*
Marketing, South East Asia   Lan Tan *Manager*

The National Commercial Bank   Representative Office
#14-01, 6 Battery Road, Singapore, 0104
Tel: 222 8496 Fax: 222 8396 Telex: 27196 NCBSIN

Senior Executive Officers
Representative   Mustaza Bin Kassim

1332   Euromoney Directory 1999

www.euromoneydirectory.com			SINGAPORE (+65)

National Westminster Bank plc
Offshore Banking Unit

#08-00 Singapore Land Tower, 50 Raffles Place, Singapore, 048623
Tel: 530 1000; 220 4144 **Fax:** 225 9827 **Telex:** 28491 **Swift:** NWBK SG SG **Reuters:** NWSX **Cable:** NATWESBAN **Capital Markets Telex:** RS23049 NATWEST; **Dealers Fax:** 225 8843; **Telex:** RS21989 NATWEST; **Derivatives Fax:** 531 2991; **Derivatives Marketing Tel:** 438 1778; **Global Debt Markets Tel:** 532 2427; **Fax:** 220 3637; **Interest Rate Management Tel:** 222 2029; **Sales Tel:** 220 2177; **Spot Forex Tel:** 222 1009; **Reuters:** NWSD

Senior Executive Officers

Others (Senior Executives)
Regional Chief Admin. Officer, Asia Pacific   Wendy Tan *General Manager*
Regional Head of Compliance, Asia Pacific   William Thomson
CFO, South & South East Asia   Gary Wilson
Regional Head of IT, Asia Pacific   Jim Cass

Debt Capital Markets / Fixed Income
Department: Global Financial Markets
Regional Head   David Lau *MD & Regional Head*
Head of Fixed Income Sales   Indrajit Advani *Director, Fixed Income Sales*
                                                 Jonathan Tiu *Director, Fixed Income Sales*
                                                 Lily Tan *Director, Fixed Income Sales*

Foreign Exchange
Head of Foreign Exchange   Charlton Mui *Director & Regional Head, FX*
Regional Head   Henry Tan *Director & Manager*
Head of Sales   Jonathan Prince *Associate Director*

Risk Management

Other (FI Derivatives)
Head, Interest Rate Management   Bill Tae *Director*
Derivatives Marketing   Veronica Pang *Director & Head*
Derivatives Marketing, Central Banks   Yap Teck Yong *Associate Director & Head*

Asset Management
Portfolio Management   Damien Tan *Director & Head*

Other Departments

Other Departments
Off Balance Sheet   Alvin Tham *Director & Head*

Administration
                                                 Jim Cass

Compliance
                                                 William Thomson

NDC Merchant Bank Limited
Subsidiary Company

#41-00 DBS Building, Tower One, 6 Shenton Way, Singapore, 068809
Tel: 220 8133 **Fax:** 224 4532 **Telex:** RS22553 NDCMFX **Swift:** NDME SG SG **Email:** NDCX

Senior Executive Officers
Chairman   Chan Sin Lau
Chief Executive Officer   Heng Keng Liau *General Manager*
Financial Director; Chief Operating Officer   Nyuk Yin Wong *Director, Operations Finance*
Treasurer   Carina Lee *Director, Treasury*

Money Markets
Head of Money Markets   Lynn Wong *Manager*

Foreign Exchange
Head of Foreign Exchange   Choong Fatt Leong *Associate Director*

Corporate Finance / M&A Advisory
Head of Corporate Finance   Quee Yin Foo *Director, Corporate Finance & Capital Markets*

Other (Corporate Finance)
                                                 Jeffrey Ling *Associate Director, Corporate Finance*

Settlement / Clearing
Settlement (General)   Mui Lan Tan *Manager*

Euromoney Directory 1999   **1333**

SINGAPORE (+65)   www.euromoneydirectory.com

Nedship Merchant Bank (Asia) Limited — Subsidiary Company
#57-00 Republic Plaza, 9 Raffles Place, Singapore, 048619
Tel: 230 6708 Fax: 536 3066 Telex: RS42479

Senior Executive Officers

Others (Senior Executives)
Office Manager   L E Hogestol

The Nikko Bank (UK) plc — Representative Office
#31-02 SIA Building, 77 Robinson Road, Singapore, 068796
Tel: 533 3373 Fax: 535 2355 Email: nikkobk@mbox4.signet.com.sg

Senior Executive Officers

Others (Senior Executives)
Chief Representative - Asia   J A N Dinger ☏ 535 8522 / 239 4113
Assistant Representative   Lim Liang ☏ 239 4164

The Nikko Merchant Bank (Singapore) Limited — Subsidiary Company
#31-01 SIA Building, 77 Robinson Road, Singapore, 068796
Tel: 533 5775 Fax: 438 1155 Telex: RS35089 Swift: NKMB SG SG Telex: RS42562

Senior Executive Officers
Chairman & Managing Director   Kozo Ishikawa
Chairman & Managing Director   Okachi Yoshihiro ☏ 239 4114

General-Lending (DCM, SL)
Head of Corporate Banking   Goh Kee Teong *Vice President* ☏ 239 4176

General - Treasury
Head of Treasury   Chua Darren *Vice President* ☏ 239 4145

Equity Capital Markets
Head of Equity Capital Markets   Fujiki Yoshitsune *Director* ☏ 239 4104

Settlement / Clearing
Head of Settlement / Clearing   Tan (DereK) Koon Thiam *Manager* ☏ 239 4144

Administration
Head of Administration   Iwahori Yoshio *Director* ☏ 239 4103

Compliance
Compliance / Audit & Accounts   Chua Sing Wee *Manager* ☏ 239 4137

The Nippon Credit Bank Limited — Representative Office
#23 -02 Suntec Tower 4, 6 Temasek Boulevard, Singapore, 038 986
Tel: 333 6781 Fax: 333 6807 Telex: CXL

Senior Executive Officers
Chief Representative   Seiichiro Isoda

Others (Senior Executives)
Representative   Isao Tamamoto
                                        Hisae Suzuki

Administration
Head of Administration   Tina Soo-Tho *Secretary*

Nomura Asset Management (Singapore) Limited — Subsidiary Company
#40-02, 6 Battery Road, Singapore, 049909
Tel: 225 5108 Fax: 420 1799

Senior Executive Officers
Chairman   H Kobayahi

1334   Euromoney Directory 1999

www.euromoneydirectory.com SINGAPORE (+65)

Nomura Futures (Singapore) PTE Limited
Subsidiary Company

#34-01, 6 Battery Road, Singapore, 049909
Tel: 420 1811 Fax: 420 1888 Telex: RS 21198 Swift: SNOM SG SG Cable: SINGNOM

Senior Executive Officers
President — Yamada Hiroshi

Others (Senior Executives)
Tan Pius *Director*
Takiyanagi Masaaki *Director*

Nomura Securities Singapore PTE Limited
Subsidiary Company

#34-01, 6 Battery Road, Singapore, 049909
Tel: 420 1811 Fax: 420 1888 Telex: RS 21198 Swift: SNOM SG SG Cable: SINGNOM

Senior Executive Officers
Chairman — Yamada Hiroshi
Managing Director — Hayashi Daijiro

Nomura Singapore Limited
Subsidiary Company

#34-01, 6 Battery Road, Singapore, 049909
Tel: 420 1811 Fax: 420 1888 Telex: RS 21198 Swift: SNOM SG SG Cable: SINGNOM

Senior Executive Officers
Chairman — Wong Kok Siew
President — Yamada Hiroshi

Others (Senior Executives)
Takiyanagi Masaaki *Deputy President*

NORD/LB Norddeutsche Landesbank Girozentrale
Offshore Banking Unit

#16-08 DBS Building Tower 2, 6 Shenton Way, Singapore, 068809
Tel: 323 1223 Fax: 323 0223; 323 7804 Telex: RS24272 Email: nordlb@pacific.net.sg

Senior Executive Officers
Chief Executive Officer — Juergen Langmaack *General Manager & Chief Executive*
Heinz Werner Frings *General Manager & Regional Head Asia / Pacific*
Juergen Langmaack *General Manager & Chief Executive*
Treasurer — Bernd Hartwig *Treasury Manager* ☎ 420 3130 📠 221 3160

Others (Senior Executives)
Head of Operations — Wolfgang Kamp *Assistant General Manager* ☎ 420 3170 📠 323 7804
Head of Credit — Ee San Sim *Credit Manager* ☎ 420 3111 📠 323 7090
Head of Capital Markets — David Read *Manager Capital Markets / Swaps* ☎ 420 3150 📠 323 4414

General-Lending (DCM, SL)
Head of Corporate Banking — Simon Seah *Assistant General Manager* ☎ 420 3110 📠 323 7090
Sim Ee San *Deputy Manager, Corporate Banking*

Debt Capital Markets / Fixed Income
Head of Debt Capital Markets — David Read *Manager Capital Markets / Swaps* ☎ 323 4414 📠 221 3160
David Read *Manager Capital Markets / Swaps* ☎ 420 3150 📠 323 4414
Country Head — Petra Elanger *Officer* ☎ 323 4414 📠 221 3160
Chong Wee Kee *Assistant Manager*

Bonds - General
Alice Loh *Assistant Manager* ☎ 323 4414 📠 221 3160
Petra Elanger *Officer* ☎ 323 4414 📠 221 3160

Private Placements
Head of Origination — Bernd Hartwig *Treasury Manager* ☎ 323 4414 📠 221 3160
David Read *Manager Capital Markets / Swaps* ☎ 420 3150 📠 323 4414
Head of Origination; Head of Origination — Petra Elanger *Officer* ☎ 323 4414 📠 221 3160
Head of Origination — Alice Loh *Assistant Manager* ☎ 323 4414 📠 221 3160

Foreign Exchange
Head of Foreign Exchange — Bernd Hartwig *Treasury Manager* ☎ 323 4414 📠 221 3160
Bernd Hartwig *Treasury Manager* ☎ 420 3130 📠 221 3160

FX Traders / Sales People
Alice Loh *Assistant Manager* ☎ 323 4414 📠 221 3160

SINGAPORE (+65) www.euromoneydirectory.com

NORD/LB Norddeutsche Landesbank Girozentrale (cont)
Risk Management
IR Swaps Trading   David Read *Manager Capital Markets / Swaps* ☎ **323 4414** ℱ **221 3160**
Petra Elanger *Officer* ☎ **323 4414** ℱ **221 3160**
Chong Wee Kee *Assistant Manager*

Foreign Exchange Derivatives / Risk Management
Cross-Currency Swaps, Trading   Petra Elanger *Officer* ☎ **323 4414** ℱ **221 3160**
Chong Wee Kee *Assistant Manager*

Other (Exchange-Traded Derivatives)
Derivatives - Short Term   Bernd Hartwig *Treasury Manager* ☎ **323 4414** ℱ **221 3160**
Derivatives - Long Term   Chong Wee Kee *Assistant Manager*
Petra Elanger *Officer* ☎ **323 4414** ℱ **221 3160**
Derivatives - Short Term   Alice Loh *Assistant Manager* ☎ **323 4414** ℱ **221 3160**
Derivatives - Long Term   Petra Elanger *Officer* ☎ **323 4414** ℱ **221 3160**
Derivatives - Short Term   Alice Loh *Assistant Manager* ☎ **323 4414** ℱ **221 3160**

Settlement / Clearing
Operations   Wolfgang Kamp *Assistant General Manager* ☎ **420 3170** ℱ **323 7804**

The Norinchukin Bank
Full Branch Office

#53-01 UOB Plaza 1, 80 Raffles Place, Singapore, 048624
Tel: 535 1011 **Fax:** 535 2883 **Telex:** RS 21461 NOCHU **Reuters:** NORS

Senior Executive Officers
Treasurer   Wataru Ariga *Senior Manager, Head of Treasury* ☎ **439 0151**
General Manager   Mitsuhiro Kubo

Others (Senior Executives)
Chief Dealer / Manager   Marc Teo ☎ **439 0152**

OCBC Finance Singapore Limited
Subsidiary Company

#01-01 Tong Eng Building, 101 Cecil Street, Singapore, 069533
Tel: 223 9733 **Fax:** 225 0580

Senior Executive Officers
Director & General Manager   Teo Sok Nguang

General-Lending (DCM, SL)
Head of Corporate Banking   Sharon Lee *AGM, Credit*

Syndicated Lending

Other (Trade Finance)
Real Estate & Property Finance   Sharon Lee *AGM, Credit*
Factoring   Jorene Kwan *Assistant Manager*
Mortgage Finance   Sharon Lee *AGM, Credit*
Hire Purchase Financing   Victor Liaw *Assistant Manager*

Other Departments
Cash Management   Kua Heng *Manager*

Ong Tradition Singapore (Pte) Limited
Subsidiary Company

#07-01 Clifford Centre, 24 Raffles Place, Singapore, 048721
Tel: 533 1615 **Fax:** 533 5517 **Telex:** RS26660 OTRADS **Reuters:** ONGT
Conti/Forward/Local Tel: 533 2130; **US$ Deposit Tel:** 533 2131

Senior Executive Officers
Managing Director   Chew Kheng Cheong

Others (Senior Executives)
Business Development   Andrew Lim *Director*
Associate Director   Denis E Nicklin

Money Markets
Global Head   Thomas Ho *Money Market Director*

Money Markets - General
Dollar Deposit   Dominic Tan *Senior Manager*
Jean Tseng *Manager*
Julian Tan *Manager*
Paul Hoo *Manager*
Masataka Terada *Manager*
Currency Deposit   Victor Yeong *Senior Manager*

www.euromoneydirectory.com SINGAPORE (+65)

Money Markets - General (cont)

Local Deposit

Lun Chang Lin *Manager*
Walter Tay *Linker*
Nancy Koh *Local Money Market Director*
Shann Tan *Senior Manager*
David Lim *Manager*
Ronald Mak *Manager*

Risk Management
Other Currency Swap / FX Options Personnel
FX Forwards

Mohd Hanafiah Bin Tumin *Senior Manager*
William Lim *Senior Manager*
Alfred Tan *Senior Manager*
Laurence Boey *Manager*
Jeffrey Lim *Manager*

Oversea-Chinese Banking Corporation Limited   Head Office
Alternative trading name: OCBC Bank
OCBC Centre, 65 Chulia Street, Singapore, 049513
Tel: 535 7222 **Fax:** 535 7955 **Telex:** RS21209 OVERSEA **Swift:** OCBC SG SG **Email:** info@ocbc.com.sg
Website: www.ocbc.com.sg

Senior Executive Officers
Chairman of the Board — Seng Wee Lee ☏ **530 1505**
Deputy President — Nang Jang Wong
Deputy President — Elizabeth Sam ☏ **530 1567**
Chief Executive Officer — Alex Au *Vice Chairman & CEO*
Financial Director — Winston Tan *Group Chief Accountant* ☏ **530 1247**
Treasurer — Yew Kuen Wong *Head, Global Treasury* ☏ **530 1619**
Head, Group Legal & Secretarial — Aung Than ☏ **530 1510**

Debt Capital Markets / Fixed Income
Department: Capital Markets
Tel: 535 1616 **Fax:** 535 4256
Global Head — Sai Fan Pei *Head* ☏ **530 1688**
Head of Fixed Income Sales — Daniel Kong *Vice President* ☏ **530 1268**
Head of Fixed Income Trading — Daniel Kong *Vice President* ☏ **530 1268**

Libor-Based / Floating-Rate Products
FRN Sales — Sai Fan Pei *Head* ☏ **530 1688**
Asset Swaps — Daniel Kong *Vice President* ☏ **530 1268**
Asset Swaps (Sales) — Amy Lim *Assistant Vice President* ☏ **530 6821**

Fixed-Income Repo
Head of Repo — Daniel Kong *Vice President* ☏ **530 1268**

Syndicated Lending
Tel: 530 1616 **Fax:** 535 4256
Head of Trading — Daniel Kong *Vice President* ☏ **530 1268**

Loan-Related Activities
Trade Finance — Ngiap Joo Tan *Executive Vice President* ☏ **530 6877**
Project Finance — Sai Fan Pei *Head*

Money Markets
Head of Money Markets — Tiong Kian Tan *VP & Head of Trading* ☏ **530 1336**

Domestic Commercial Paper
Head of Sales; Head of Trading — Amy Lim *Assistant Vice President* ☏ **530 6821**

Eurocommercial Paper
Head of Trading — Chuang Hwak Chia *AVP & Trading Head* ☏ **530 1336**

Wholesale Deposits
Marketing — Ngiap Joo Tan *Executive Vice President* ☏ **530 6877**

Foreign Exchange
Head of Foreign Exchange — Chwee Kiat Ang *Vice President* ☏ **530 1333**
Chuang Hwak Chia *AVP & Trading Head* ☏ **530 1336**
Corporate Sales — Swee Wan Koh *Vice President* ☏ **530 1333**
Head of Trading — Chwee Kiat Ang *Vice President* ☏ **530 1333**

Corporate Finance / M&A Advisory
Head of Corporate Finance — Lye Mun Mak *Head, Corporate Finance* ☏ **530 1267**

Asset Management
Head — Boon Kuan Tay

Euromoney Directory 1999   **1337**

SINGAPORE (+65)   www.euromoneydirectory.com

Oversea-Chinese Banking Corporation Limited (cont)
Other Departments
Commodities / Bullion
Private Banking
Correspondent Banking

Dennis Seet *General Manager*
Diana Quek *Head* ☏ **530 6307**
Vivian Lye *Head* ☏ **530 1329**

Administration
Head of Administration
Head of Marketing

Vivian Lee *Vice President, Administration* ☏ **530 1329**
Michelle Yap *Vice President* ☏ **530 6365**

Technology & Systems

Soon Lang Teng *Head, Group IT* ☏ **530 1201**

Legal / In-House Counsel

Aung Than *Head, Group Legal & Secretarial* ☏ **530 1510**

Public Relations

David Cheam *VP, Corporate Communications* ☏ **530 1531**

Accounts / Audit

Winston Tan *Group Chief Accountant* ☏ **530 1247**
Betty Koh *Head, Group Audit*

Overseas Union Bank Limited
Head Office

OUB Centre, 1 Raffles Place, Singapore, 048616
Tel: 533 8686 **Fax:** 533 2293; 533 8686 **Telex:** RS24475 OVERSBK **Swift:** OUBK SG SG **Reuters:** OUBB
Cable: OVERSUNION SINGA
Reuters: OUBC; OUBD; OUBS; OUBT; OUBU
Website: www.oub.com.sg

Senior Executive Officers
Chairman   Lee Hee Seng
President   Peter Seah Lim Hunt
Senior Vice President   Chew Eng Hwa
Senior Vice President   Koh Chye Seng
Senior Vice President   Kwik Sam Alk
Senior Vice President   Tan Liang Hwe
Senior Vice President   Glen Yuen Yuet Fai
Chief Operating Officer   Gracy Choo *Director & CEO*
Treasurer   Victor Liew Cheng San *Executive Vice President*
Group Corporate Secretary   Jeannie Tng
International Division   Tan Ng Chee *Executive Vice President*

Others (Senior Executives)
Board of Directors   Tan Puay Hee
                                        Peter Seah Lim Hunt
                                        Lim Boon Kheng
                                        Tan Sri Dato Tan Teck Khim
                                        Teo Soo Chuan
                                        Cheong Siew Keong
                                        Tan Kok Quan
                                        Lim Pin
                                        Andrew Chew Guan Khuan
Executive Committee of the Board   Lee Hee Seng
                                        Peter Seah Lim Hunt
                                        Cheong Slew Keong
                                        Tan Puay Hee
Audit Committee   Tan Kok Quan
                                        Lee Hee Seng
                                        Lim PIn
                                        Andrew Chew Guan Khuan
National Banking Division   Kuo How Nam *Executive Vice President*
Group Audit & Inspection Division   Alfred Shee Ping Fatt *Senior Vice President*

General-Lending (DCM, SL)
Head of Corporate Banking   Wee Joo Yeow *Executive Vice President*
                                        Richard Tan Tew Han *Investment Banking*

Administration
Technology & Systems

Nicholas Chong Tjee Teng *Executive Vice President*

Other (Administration)
Human Resources   Philip Tan Yuen Fah *Executive Vice President*

1338 Euromoney Directory 1999

www.euromoneydirectory.com SINGAPORE (+65)

PaineWebber International (Singapore) Pte Limited
#13-20 UOB Plaza 2, 80 Raffles Place, Singapore, 0104
Tel: 323 0188 **Fax:** 536 0188 **Telex:** RS 23685 KISS

Debt Capital Markets / Fixed Income
Department: Fixed Income
Bonds - General

    Rafat Rizvi
    Paul Devlin
    Eunice Khoo
    Glen Lau
    Chris Mersey
    Joseph Walsh

Paribas
Full Branch Office
#43-01 UOB Plaza 1, 80 Raffles Place, Singapore, 048624
Tel: 439 5000 **Fax:** 538 4300 **Telex:** RS20414 PARSIN **Swift:** PARB SG SG **Reuters:** BAPS **Telerate:** 7261

Senior Executive Officers
Area Manager — Alain Kokocinski

Others (Senior Executives)
Asia Pacific Member, Executive Committee — Ho Kah Leong *Regional Head*
Senior Banker — Heng Yeow Khing
Thomas Pascarella *Media & Telecommunication Sector*
M G Balachandar

General-Lending (DCM, SL)
Head of Corporate Banking
Philippe Reynieix *Regional Head, Corporate Banking, SE Asia & India*
Wee Chye Kin *Joint Head, Large Corporate & Syndication Groups*
Jimmy Teo *Joint Head, Large Corporate & Syndication Groups*
Pascal Notte *Senior Credit Officer, Corp. Bking, SE Asia & Indi*
Veronica Leong *Head, Credit Administration*
Diana Tan *Credit Administration*
Thuy Doan *Credit Risk*

Relationship Manager
Financial Institutions Group
Multinationals
Media Finance
Sovereign & Financial Institutions Group
Whee Kong Lim *Senior Manager*
Frederic Amoudru *Head*
James Christian
Lim Whee Kong *Senior Manager*

Debt Capital Markets / Fixed Income
Head of Fixed Income
Ho Kah Leong *Head, Asia Pacific*
Eric Nicholas *Deputy Head, Asia Pacific*
Other — Barry Cohen *Head, Hedge Funds*

Government Bonds
Head of Sales — Eric Delaunay
Head of Trading — Gary Hopkins

Non-Domestic Government Bonds
International Bond Sales — Josiah Chan *Head*

Bonds - General
Financing Desk, Asia Pacific — Patricia McKean *Head*

Fixed-Income Research
Analyst — Warren Mar *Research Bonds Credit*

Equity Capital Markets
Country Head — Victor Leong *Marketing Director*
Head of Sales — James Spence

Domestic Equities
Head of Trading — Anthony Lloyd Smith

Other (Domestic Equities)
Primary Equity — Victor Leong *Marketing Director*

Equity Research
Head of Equity Research — James Spence

Convertibles / Equity-Linked
Head of Sales — Rebecca Sim

Warrants
Head of Sales — Rebecca Sim

SINGAPORE (+65) www.euromoneydirectory.com

Paribas (cont)
Syndicated Lending
Other (Syndicated Lending)
Bills & Loans Ronnie Lim *Head*
Loan-Related Activities
Trade Finance Han Yong Guan *Head of Commodities & Trade Finance*
Project Finance Christophe Rousseau *Head*
Other (Trade Finance)
Multinationals & Structured Finance Frederic Amoudru *Head*

Money Markets
Eurocommercial Paper
Head of Trading Patrick Wong *Assets / Liabilities Management*
  Lee Gek Seng *Assets / Liabilities Management*

Other (Wholesale Deposits)
Euronotes Patrick Wong *Assets / Liabilities Management*
  Lee Gek Seng *Assets / Liabilities Management*

Foreign Exchange
Head of Sales Timothy Potter *Head*
Head of Trading Guy Piserchia *Head*
FX Traders / Sales People
Asian Regional Currencies Salu Manzoor

Risk Management
Other (FI Derivatives)
Interest Rate Derivatives Cheah Teik Seng *Head*
Derivatives Marketing Eugene Park *Co-Head*
Other Currency Swap / FX Options Personnel
Currency Options Catherine Blaikblock *Trading*
OTC Equity Derivatives
Trading Eugene Lonergan
Exchange-Traded Derivatives
FX Options Catherine Blaikblock *Trading*
  Christian Baudoin *Trading*

Settlement / Clearing
Operations Patrice Kouyoumdjian *Treasury Operations, Administration*

Administration
Department: Business Development Department
Head of Administration Bernard Pittie *Regional Head, Administration - Asia*
Technology & Systems
  Philippe Laniesse

Legal / In-House Counsel
  Benoit Faure *International Finance & Legal*

Compliance
  Devaki Vaithianathan

Accounts / Audit
Financial Accounting Wong Hian Seong *Head*
Management Accounting Subh Gursahani
Other (Administration)
Facilities Mok Kwong Hay
Internal Control Cyrille Parant
Human Resources Theresa Ho

Philippine National Bank Offshore Banking Unit
#10-01/02 Bangkok Bank Building, 180 Cecil Street, Singapore, 069546
Tel: 222 8261 Fax: 225 5704 Telex: RS21792 Email: pnbsing@mbox2.singnet.com.sg Reuters: PNBS
Dealers Tel: 222 5624

Senior Executive Officers
VP & General Manager Celestino G Marquez Jr ☏ **223 0127**
Syndicated Lending
Loan-Related Activities
Trade Finance Farida Syedx Mohamed *Trade Finance Officer* ☏ **222 8261 ext 17**
Foreign Exchange
Head of Foreign Exchange Rosanna P Sarmiento *Chief Dealer* ☏ **222 8261 ext 25**

1340 Euromoney Directory 1999

www.euromoneydirectory.com					SINGAPORE (+65)

Other Departments
Chief Credit Officer			Rosa L. Lansangan *Credit Officer* ☎ **222 8261 ext 16**
Administration
Head of Administration		Samantha C L Lee *Secretary* ☎ **222 8261 ext 13**
Technology & Systems
					Jocelyn F Aclan *IT Analyst* ☎ **222 8261 ext 31**
Accounts / Audit
					Marie Jane G Manigque *Account Officer* ☎ **222 8261 ext 15**
Other (Administration)
Marketing				Lee Hock Chua *Senior Assistant Manager* ☎ **222 8261 ext 12**

## POSBank					Head Office
#06-00 POSB Centre, 73 Bras Basah Road, Singapore, 189556
Tel: 339 3333 **Fax:** 336 4153

Senior Executive Officers
Chairman				Moses Lee ☎ **330 9229**
Chief Executive Officer		Dileep Nair ☎ **330 9109**
Corporate Finance / M&A Advisory
Country Head				Poh Gek Goh *Vice President, Financial Division* ☎ **330 9130**
Asset Management
Head					Wai Seng Low *Senior Vice President* ☎ **330 9536**

## Prebon Yamane (Singapore) Limited			Regional Head Office
#39-00 Singapore Land Tower, 50 Raffles Place, Singapore, 048623
Tel: 535 0777 **Fax:** 535 7266 **Reuters:** PYSG
Website: www.prebon.com

Senior Executive Officers
Chairman				John Ng ☎ **535 5011**
Managing Director			Linda Neo ☎ **535 5600**
Debt Capital Markets / Fixed Income
Department: Capital Markets
Tel: 536 4877 **Fax:** 535 0611 **Telex:** RS 23182 PYSG
Head of Debt Capital Markets		Mark Spring *Managing Director* ☎ **535 7622**

Other (Fixed Income)
Fixed Income & New Products		Craig Bannister *Associate Director* ☎ **536 4877**
Credit Derivatives			Kevin Spencer *Associate Director* ☎ **536 4877**
Regional Off Balance Sheet		Craig Smyth *Manager* ☎ **536 5077**
Money Markets
Department: Money Market & Foreign Exchange
Tel: 538 4933 **Fax:** 535 7266 **Reuters:** PYSG
Head of Money Markets			Seng Jin Ong *Managing Director, Foreign Exchange & Money Market*
					☎ **536 0233**

Other (Wholesale Deposits)
Dollar Deposit			Richard Teo *Associate Director* ☎ **535 1866**
Conti Deposit				Simon Chua *Manager* ☎ **535 1866**
Domestic Deposit			Kok Beng Tan *Deputy Manager* ☎ **536 4933**
Foreign Exchange
Tel: 536 4933 **Fax:** 535 7066 **Reuters:** PYSG **Telex:** RS 42707 PYSG
Head of Foreign Exchange		Seng Jin Ong *Managing Director, Foreign Exchange & Money Market*
					☎ **536 0233**

FX Traders / Sales People
Regional Forward			Benson Lim *Associate Director, Regional FX & Money Market* ☎ **536 4933**
Sing Forward				Kok Beng Tan *Deputy Manager* ☎ **536 4933**
Non-Deliverable Forward		Kelly Chua *Manager* ☎ **536 4577**
Settlement / Clearing
Tel: 535 0777 **Fax:** 535 8978
Head of Settlement / Clearing		Tiew Soon Heng *Settlement Officer* ☎ **536 8978**
Administration
Head of Administration		Sharon Koh *Office Manager* ☎ **535 4133**
Technology & Systems
					Matthew Johnson *Manager, Information Systems* ☎ **534 2871**

SINGAPORE (+65)   www.euromoneydirectory.com

Prebon Yamane (Singapore) Limited (cont)
Legal / In-House Counsel
                                Paul Kelly *General Counsel, Asia* ☏ **534 2871**
Accounts / Audit
                                Stephen Tan *Finance & Operations Director* ☏ **535 0155**

Rabobank   Full Branch Office
Alternative trading name: Cooperatieve Centrale Raiffeisen-Boerenleenbank BA
#58-00 Republic Plaza, 9 Raffles Place, Singapore, 048619
Tel: 536 3363 **Fax:** 536 3236 **Telex:** RS42479 **Swift:** RABO SG SG **Reuters:** RABS-U (Monitor) **Cable:** RABOBANK
Dealers Tel: 536 3368; **Fax:** 536 2868; **Telex:** RS28480

Senior Executive Officers
Regional General Manager   Roelf Hagoort
Deputy General Manager, Operations   Song Cheng Miang

General-Investment
Head of Investment   Lee Mon Sun *Managing Director, Asia Pacific Investment Banking*
                                    Gibert Ee *Head of Trading, Investment Banking*
                                    Loong Soo Yong *Head of Sales, Investment Banking*

Relationship Manager
Senior Account Managers   How Seen Tiat *Senior Account Manager*
                                    Peter Tang *Senior Account Manager*
                                    Marcus Lee *Senior Account Manager*
                                    Alvin Cheng *Senior Account Manager*
                                    Jacqueline Chang *Senior Account Manager*
                                    Chow Kok Weng *Senior Account Manager*
                                    Sunil Kumar *Senior Account Manager*
                                    Yeo Woei Kuen *Senior Account Manager*
                                    Ong Poon Lee *Senior Account Manager*

Syndicated Lending
Other (Trade Finance)
Agri Project Finance   Hans van De Weerd Jr. *Senior Project Manager*
                                    Hidzer K de Jonge *Senior Project Manager*
                                    Vivek Gupta *Senior Project Manager*
                                    Lee Peck Leng *Senior Project Manager*

Risk Management
Other (FI Derivatives)
Investment Banking   Harrison Kim *Head of Derivatives / Arbitrage Trading*

Corporate Finance / M&A Advisory
Head of Corporate Finance   Koh Ban Aik *Senior Assistant General Manager*

Asset Management
Portfolio Management   Carl Walsh *Head of Portfolio Management, Investment Banking*

Administration
Accounts / Audit
Corporate Audit Services   Kristine Chen *Senior Manager*
Other (Administration)
Human Resources   Neville Kiang

Republic National Bank of New York   Full Branch Office
#01-00, GB Building, 143 Cecil Street, Singapore, 069542
Tel: 224 0077 **Fax:** 225 5769 **Telex:** RS 20237 RNBSIN **Swift:** BLIC SG SG **Reuters:** REPN

Senior Executive Officers
Fax: 229 0282
Vice Chairman & Managing Director   Kurt Andersen ☏ **229 0838**
Managing Director & Country Head   John C Hanson ☏ **229 0808**
Managing Director & Deputy Country Head Ian Pollock ☏ **229 0837**

Debt Capital Markets / Fixed Income
Department: Treasury
Tel: 227 1686 **Fax:** 223 4131
Regional Head   Yong Meng Quek *Senior Vice President* ☏ **229 0885**
                                       Chong Teck Giam *Deputy Head & Senior Vice President* ☏ **229 0327**

1342   Euromoney Directory 1999

www.euromoneydirectory.com   SINGAPORE (+65)

Equity Capital Markets
Other (Domestic Equities)
Capital Market   Mark Chan *Vice President & Head* ☎ **227 1678**

Money Markets
Tel: 227 1678 **Fax:** 223 4131
Regional Head   Yong Meng Quek *Senior Vice President* ☎ **229 0885**
Country Head   Chong Teck Giam *Deputy Head & Senior Vice President* ☎ **229 0327**

Money Markets - General
                                    Yong Pin Koh *VP & Manager, Money Market Desk* ☎ **227 1678**

Other (Wholesale Deposits)
Banknotes Trading   Victor Mills *First Vice President & Manager* ☎ **229 0806** F **225 5765**
Wealth Management   Paul Kwek *Regional Head & FVP, Wealth Management* ☎ **229 0833**
                                    F **229 0281**

Foreign Exchange
Tel: 227 1686 **Fax:** 223 4131
Regional Head   Yong Meng Quek *Senior Vice President* ☎ **229 0885**
Country Head   Chong Teck Giam *Deputy Head & Senior Vice President* ☎ **229 0327**
Head of Trading   Annie Ler *VP & FX Manager* ☎ **227 1678**

FX Traders / Sales People
Treasury Marketing Unit   Eng-Seng Lim *VP & Manager* ☎ **227 7848**
Treasury Marketing, Financial Institutions Kamal Muthalib *Vice President & Head* ☎ **227 7848**
Treasury Advisory Unit, Corporate Benjamin Lee *Vice President & Head* ☎ **227 7848**

Risk Management
Foreign Exchange Derivatives / Risk Management
Spot / Forwards Trading   Philip Lim *VP & Chief Dealer* ☎ **227 1686**
                                    Haresh Chandirmani *VP, FX Forward Desk* ☎ **227 1678**
Vanilla FX option Sales   Laura Day *VP & Sales Manager, Republic Financial Products* ☎ **224 7679**

Settlement / Clearing
Tel: 224 0077 **Fax:** 225 5769
Regional Head   Robert Pavone *Deputy Regional Operations Manager & FVP* ☎ **229 0836**
                                    F **229 0282**
Country Head   Daniel Teo *Manager & FVP, Customer Services, Options, Settl's*
                                    ☎ **229 0831** F **229 0285**

Other Departments
Commodities / Bullion   Cheng-Thye Ng *FVP & Head, Precious Metals* ☎ **224 2251** F **223 4131**
Private Banking   Gerald Goh *SVP & Head, Private Banking* ☎ **229 0805** F **225 1330**

Administration
Tel: 224 0077 **Fax:** 225 5769

Technology & Systems
                                    Chor-Kheng Tan *VP & Manager, IT* ☎ **229 0856** F **225 5769**
Regional   Adrian Chow *VP, Regional IT* ☎ **229 0810** F **225 5769**

Compliance
                                    Robert Pavone *Deputy Regional Operations Manager & FVP* ☎ **229 0836**
                                    F **229 0282**

Other (Administration)
Financial Control   Lay-Choo Tan *Manager & FVP, Financial Control* ☎ **229 0820** F **225 5769**
Credit Administration & Treasury Control Wing-kin Chan *First Vice President & Manager* ☎ **229 0864** F **225 5769**

NM Rothschild & Sons (Singapore) Limited   Subsidiary Company
#09-00 The Exchange, 20 Cecil Street, Singapore, 049705
Tel: 535 8311 **Fax:** 535 8326 **Telex:** RS36549 **Cable:** ROTHSCHILD
Banking Fax: 534 2407; **Corporate Finance Fax:** 534 2124; **Dealers Tel:** 535 9677; **Dealing Fax:** 535 8713; **Project Finance Fax:** 535 9109; **Treasury Operations Fax:** 538 8120

Senior Executive Officers
Chairman   Goh Keng Swee
Managing Director   Mark Greaves

Others (Senior Executives)
                                    Eric Ang Chong Lim *Director*

Euromoney Directory 1999   **1343**

SINGAPORE (+65)   www.euromoneydirectory.com

The Royal Bank of Scotland
Full Branch Office
#27-01, 6 Battery Road, Singapore, 049909
Tel: 225 1233 Fax: 225 1254

Senior Executive Officers
Treasurer   Alan Colven *Regional Treasurer, Asia Pacific*
Regional Manager   G A Leslie

RZB-Singapore
Offshore Banking Unit
#38-04 Singapore Land Tower, 50 Raffles Place, Singapore, 048623
Tel: 225 9578 Fax: 225 3973 Telex: RS42524 RZBSIN Swift: RZBA SG SG Email: rzbsin@singnet.com.sg

Senior Executive Officers
General Manager   Rainer Silhavy 225 9578 225 3973
General Manager   Douglas Chew

Others (Senior Executives)
Head of Commercial Banking   Kah Eng Leaw *Assistant General Manager*
Head of Structured Trade Finance   Jimmy Lee *Assistant General Manager*
Risk Control Manager   Michael Meyer *Assistant General Manager*
Asset Sales   Wolfgang Beckmann *Head of Syndication*
Treasurer   Chun Kay Chua
Head of Operations   Linnet Koh

The Sakura Bank Limited
Full Branch Office
#01-04 Hong Leong Building, 16 Raffles Quay, Singapore, 048 581
Tel: 220 9761 Fax: 225 0962 Telex: RS21319 MITKBK

Senior Executive Officers
Managing Director   Kazuhiro Kosuge

The Sanwa Bank Limited
#24-01 John Hancock Tower, 6 Raffles Quay, Singapore
Tel: 538 4838 Fax: 538 4636 Telex: RS28573 Reuters: SNWS (Monitor)

Senior Executive Officers
General Manager   Takashi Miura

Schroder International Merchant Bankers Limited
#36-01 OCBC Centre, 65 Chulia Street, Singapore, 049513
Tel: 535 3411 Fax: 534 3917 Telex: RS28146 SIMBL

Senior Executive Officers
Chairman   Chee Ken Thai
Managing Director / General Manager   Andrew Brandler

Administration

Other (Administration)
Human Resources   Jane Tan *Manager*

Scotia Capital Markets
Full Branch Office
Alternative trading name: The Bank of Nova Scotia
#15-01 Ocean Building, 10 Collyer Quay, Singapore, 049315
Tel: 535 8688 Fax: 536 3325 Telex: RS22177 SCOSING Swift: NOSC SG SG

Senior Executive Officers
MD & Head, Asian Operations   I A Berry
Managing Director, Global Trading   G W D Martin

Others (Senior Executives)
Branch Manager   Y K Heng *Manager*

Relationship Manager
Integrated Support Services   K L A Choi *Assistant General Manager*

www.euromoneydirectory.com SINGAPORE (+65)

Debt Capital Markets / Fixed Income
Bonds - General
Debt Products   A A Chaudhry *Director*
Foreign Exchange
Global Head   P A Harrison *Managing Director*
Risk Management
Country Head   H B Woodhouse *Senior Manager, Middle Office*
Other (Exchange-Traded Derivatives)
Derivative Products   A A Chaudhry *Director*

SG Securities (Singapore) Pte Limited
Subsidiary Company

#21-00, 80 Robinson Road, Singapore, 068898
Tel: 423 2288 **Fax:** 423 2002 **Telex:** RS 430000 SG SIN

Equity Capital Markets
Department: Equity Research / Economic / Strategy
Equity Research
Global Head   Manu Bhaskaran *MD, Global Head of Research* **423 2348** **423 2501**
Other (Equity Research)
     Jou Min Foo *Head of Singapore Research* **423 2342**
Regional Corporate   Foo Fatt Kah *MD, Group Head of Corporate Research* **423 2340**
     423 2508
Regional Telecoms   Michael Millar *Vice President* **423 2334**
Conglomerates   Jou Min Foo *Head of Singapore Research* **423 2342**
Marine, Property, Consumer Goods   Michael Ong *Vice President* **423 2346**
Defence, Bank, Finance   Michael Sia *Vice President* **423 2231**
Electronics, Hotel   Pearly Yap *Vice President* **423 2283**
Property   Gregory Lui *Vice President* **423 2431**

Other Departments
Department: Regional Macro Research
Economic Research   Arjuna Mahendran *Director, Economic Research (South Asia)*
     Neil Saker *Director, Economic Research (East & SE Asia)* **423 2280**
     Nilesh Jasani *Vice President* **423 2347**

Shinhan Bank
Representative Office

#44-01 Suntec Tower One, 7 Temasek Boulevard, Singapore, 038987
Tel: 333 0771 **Fax:** 333 0772

Senior Executive Officers
Chief Representative   Seong-Yung Park

Skandinaviska Enskilda Banken (South East Asia) Limited
Subsidiary Company

S

#36-01 Singapore Land Tower, 50 Raffles Place, Singapore, 048623
Tel: 223 5644 **Fax:** 225 3047 **Telex:** RS25188 ESSEBK **Swift:** ESSE SG SA **Reuters:** SEBS (Dealing)
Dealers Tel: 223 9292; **Treasury Fax:** 538 3826; **Reuters:** SEBX (Monitor)

Senior Executive Officers
Chairman   Rutger Blennow
Managing Director   Göran Bronner
Others (Senior Executives)
     Hanse Ringström *Director*
     Fredrik Boheman *Director*

General-Lending (DCM, SL)
Head of Corporate Banking   Philip Winckle *Head*
     Lars Bjerrek *Head, Commercial Banking*

General - Treasury
Head of Treasury   Athanase Pispas *Head, Treasury & Derivatives*
     Jaimi Tan *Junior Dealer, Treasury & Derivatives*

Debt Capital Markets / Fixed Income
Country Head   Fredrik Ektander *Head, Trading & Capital Markets*

SINGAPORE (+65)   www.euromoneydirectory.com

Skandinaviska Enskilda Banken (South East Asia) Limited (cont)
Syndicated Lending
Loan-Related Activities
Project Finance   Anders Lindström *Manager, Project & Structured Finance*

Foreign Exchange
Country Head   Fredrik Ektander *Head, Trading & Capital Markets*

FX Traders / Sales People

    Sim Yew Pin *Chief Dealer*
    Lawrence Lim *Senior Dealer*
    Eugene Tay *Senior Dealer*
    Alan Seah *Dealer*
    Jolene Loh *Trainee Dealer*
FX & Treasury Sales   Eddie Amin *Head*
    Clarence Tsang *Deputy Head*
    Frederick Ng *Senior Dealer*
    Wee Liang Tong *Senior Dealer*
    Ho Soo Mui *Senior Dealer*

Risk Management
Department: Credit & Counterparty Risk Management
Head of Risk Management   Philip Winckle *Head*

Settlement / Clearing
Operations   Kee Chin Fah *Regional Head, Operations & Finance*

Administration
Head of Administration   Maureen Koh *Regional Head, Personnel*

Société Générale   Full Branch Office
#25-00, 80 Robinson Road, Singapore, 068898
Tel: 222 7122 Fax: 225 2609 Telex: RS27213 SOGESI Reuters: SOGS (Monitor) Cable: SOGESI
Corporate Marketing Tel: 326 7310; Currency Options Tel: 221 6001; MNCs Tel: 326 7372; Treasury Tel: 222 2866; Fax: 222 0865; Treasury Sales Tel: 222 4956

Senior Executive Officers
Chief Executive Officer   Daniep Moffé ☎ **326 7887**
Managing Director   Philippe Mathé ☎ **326 7890**

General-Lending (DCM, SL)
Head of Corporate Banking   Raymond Koh *Executive Vice President* ☎ **326 7310**

General - Treasury
Head of Treasury   Franck du Plessix *Executive Vice President, Treasury* ☎ **326 7817**

Relationship Manager
Regional Sales   Vincent Lauwick *Executive Vice President* ☎ **326 7830**
MNC   Frederic Sem *Senior Vice President & Head* ☎ **326 7372**
Financial Institutions Group   Low Wai Choong *Senior Vice President* ☎ **326 7356**

Syndicated Lending
Other (Trade Finance)
    Philippe Fournier *GM (Asia) & Head, Commodity & Trade* ☎ **326 7324**

Money Markets
Head of Money Markets   Herman Lee *SVP, Money Market & Forward* ☎ **326 7821**

Foreign Exchange
Head of Foreign Exchange   Frederic Mersch *GM (Asia) & Head, FX Product Line* ☎ **326 7817**

Risk Management
Foreign Exchange Derivatives / Risk Management
Regional Head   Craig Jones *Senior Vice President* ☎ **326 7835**
Spot / Forwards Sales   Kyle Paige *Vice President, Spot FX* ☎ **222 2866**

Other Currency Swap / FX Options Personnel
Currency Options Product Line   Rich Giftner *Vice President & Head* ☎ **221 6001**

Settlement / Clearing
Operations   Andy Yap *Vice President* ☎ **326 7690**

Other Departments
Commodities / Bullion   Philippe Fournier *GM (Asia) & Head, Commodity & Trade* ☎ **326 7324**
Private Banking   Soh Chye Guan *Senior Vice President* ☎ **326 7902**

Administration
Head of Administration   Mabel Sim *EVP, Operations & Administration* ☎ **326 7120**

1346 Euromoney Directory 1999

www.euromoneydirectory.com SINGAPORE (+65)

Société Générale Asia (Singapore) Limited
Subsidiary Company

#13-01/2, 80 Robinson Road, Singapore, 068898
Tel: 222 7122 Fax: 225 2609 Telex: RS 27213 SOGESI Cable: SOGESI

Senior Executive Officers
Chief Executive Officer					Yves Le Port ☎ 326 7894 F 324 3633
Debt Capital Markets / Fixed Income
Department: Capital Markets
Global Head					Dennis Seah Managing Director ☎ 326 7071 F 225 742
Bonds - General
Syndications					Jimmy Chan Managing Director ☎ 326 7081

Société Générale Asset Management (Asia) Pte Limited
Subsidiary Company

#13-03, 80 Robinson Road, Singapore, 068898
Tel: 326 7979 Fax: 224 2752 Telex: RS24434 SGAMA

Senior Executive Officers
Chief Executive Officer					Laurent Bertiau ☎ 326 7980
Others (Senior Executives)
Head of Investment					Marco Wong Chief Investment Officer ☎ 223 8004 F 224 5118
					Ho Sing Ming VP & Fund Manager ☎ 326 7972
					Sabiha Sultan VP & Fund Manager ☎ 326 7961
					Winson Fong Senior Vice President ☎ 324 2583
					Lee Geok Eng Vice President ☎ 223 8002
					Lawrence Lee Vice President ☎ 211 2896

Standard Chartered Bank
Full Branch Office

6 Battery Road, Singapore, 049909
Robinson Road, PO Box 1901, Singapore, 903801
Tel: 225 8888 Fax: 789 3756 Telex: RS 24290 SCB COM Swift: SCBL SG SG Reuters: SCMS Cable: STAN CHART
Reuters: STAN; SCRS; EYES
Website: www.stanchart.com

Senior Executive Officers
Group Executive Director			David Moir ☎ 331 5901 F 338 4243
Group Executive Director			Fred Enlow ☎ 331 2798 F 334 8271
Chief Executive Officer			Theresa Foo Chief Executive Officer ☎ 530 3007 F 534 1554
Financial Director			Vincent Kwong Head of Finance ☎ 780 7350 F 789 6984
Others (Senior Executives)
Corporate & Institutional Banking			Euleen Goh Head ☎ 530 3017 F 227 3558
General-Lending (DCM, SL)
Head of Corporate Banking			Euleen Goh Head ☎ 530 3017 F 227 3558
General - Treasury
Head of Treasury			Mike Rees Group Head, Treasury ☎ 530 3003 F 536 5726
			Boon Huat Lee Regional Treasurer, SEA ☎ 530 3471 F 225 6132

Syndicated Lending
Tel: 225 2000 Fax: 222 1990
Head of Syndication			Chester Dee Head, Syndications & Asset Sales, SEA ☎ 228 3835
			F 222 1990

Loan-Related Activities
Structured Trade Finance			Tim Utama Head of Trade Services ☎ 780 7358 F 260 8731
Other (Trade Finance)
Structured Finance			Iris Fang Head, Network Corporates, Structured Finance ☎ 530 3393
			F 538 9363

Money Markets
Tel: 530 3111 Fax: 225 6132 Reuters: SCMS
Head of Money Markets			Nicholas Tan Manager, Money Market
Domestic Commercial Paper
Head of Sales			Trent Beacroft Head, Institutional Sales
Head of Trading			Nicholas Tan Manager, Money Market
Wholesale Deposits
Marketing; Head of Sales			Kiam Kong Ho Global Head of Treasury, Sales & Marketing

SINGAPORE (+65) www.euromoneydirectory.com

Standard Chartered Bank (cont)

Foreign Exchange
Tel: 530 3111 Fax: 225 6132 Reuters: SCBS
Regional Head — Boon Huat Lee *Regional Treasurer, SEA* ☎ **530 3471** 🖷 **225 6132**
Head of Institutional Sales — Trent Beacroft *Head, Institutional Sales*
Corporate Sales — Hardy Saat *Head, Network-Treasury Financial Services*
Head of Trading — Patrick Lim *Manager, FX*

FX Traders / Sales People
Spot Forex Majors — Paul Wong *Head of Spot Trading*
Spot, Regional Currencies — Percy Tham *Chief Dealer*
Forward, Regional Currencies — Frank Ng *Chief Dealer*

Risk Management
Department: Global Products
Tel: 530 0212 Fax: 535 2660 Reuters: STAN
Global Head — James Adam *Global Head*
Regional Head — Lee Guan Liu *Market Risk Manager, SEA & Global Products* ☎ **530 3060** 🖷 **223 0213**

Other (FI Derivatives)
— David Worth *Global Head, Financial Engineering*

Foreign Exchange Derivatives / Risk Management
Spot / Forwards Sales — Kang Heng Teo *Senior Manager, Global FX Sales & Marketing*
Spot / Forwards Trading — Richard Davidson *Global Head, FX Options*

Corporate Finance / M&A Advisory
Head of Corporate Finance — Daniel Ee ☎ **228 3403** 🖷 **225 2022**

Settlement / Clearing
Head of Settlement / Clearing — Khuay Guan Lee *Head, Treasury Operations* ☎ **780 7236** 🖷 **783 3115**

Global Custody
Head of Global Custody — Daniel Tan *Head, Customer Services* ☎ **530 3034** 🖷 **225 5623**

Other Departments
Chief Credit Officer — Philip Yeo *Head of Credit* ☎ **530 3175** 🖷 **227 3558**
Correspondent Banking — David Chew *Head, Institutional Banking* ☎ **530 3304** 🖷 **534 5410**
Cash Management — Tom McCabe *Head, Cash Management Sales, C&IB* ☎ **530 3410** 🖷 **438 2432**
Economic Research — Wong Yit Fan *Chief Economist* ☎ **530 3250** 🖷 **438 6311**

Other Departments
External Affairs, Banking & Treasury — Paul E Dowling *Head* ☎ **331 5933** 🖷 **334 2736**

Administration
— Andrew Goh *Service Manager, Group Technology* ☎ **331 5089** 🖷 **338 5202**

Legal / In-House Counsel
— Edward Lee-Smith *Director, Compliance* ☎ **228 3433** 🖷 **220 0605**

Compliance
— Edward Lee-Smith *Director, Compliance* ☎ **228 3433** 🖷 **220 0605**

Public Relations
External Affairs — Andrew Goldsmith *Regional Head, External Affairs, SEA* ☎ **331 2984** 🖷 **334 2736**

Accounts / Audit
Accounts — Vincent Kwong *Head of Finance* ☎ **780 7350** 🖷 **789 6984**

Standard Chartered Merchant Bank Asia Limited

Subsidiary Company

#06-08, 6 Battery Road, Singapore, 049909
Tel: 225 2000 Fax: 227 7028

Senior Executive Officers
Chief Executive Officer — Daniel Ee ☎ **228 3403** 🖷 **225 2022**
MD, Corporate Finance — Rupert Ponsonby ☎ **228 3406** 🖷 **227 7028**

Equity Capital Markets
Global Head — Daniel Ee ☎ **228 3403** 🖷 **225 2022**
Country Head — Rupert Ponsonby *MD, Corporate Finance* ☎ **228 3406** 🖷 **227 7028**

Corporate Finance / M&A Advisory
Tel: 225 2000 Fax: 227 7028
Global Head — Daniel Ee ☎ **228 3403** 🖷 **225 2022**
Country Head — Rupert Ponsonby *MD, Corporate Finance* ☎ **228 3406** 🖷 **227 7028**

1348 Euromoney Directory 1999

www.euromoneydirectory.com SINGAPORE (+65)

Administration
Legal / In-House Counsel
　　　　　　　　　　　Edward Lee-Smith *Director - Compliance / Legal Affairs* ☎ **228 3435**
Compliance
　　　　　　　　　　　Edward Lee-Smith *Director - Compliance / Legal Affairs* ☎ **228 3435**
Accounts / Audit
　　　　　　　　　　　Pheck Swee Tan *Assistant Manager* ☎ **228 3434** 🖷 **327 5191**

State Bank of India   Offshore Banking Unit

#22-08 DBS Building, Tower II, 6 Shenton Way, Singapore, 068809
Tel: 222 2033 **Fax:** 225 3348 **Telex:** RS23184 SBISING **Swift:** SBIN SG SG **Email:** sbinsgsg@pacific.net.sg
Cable: THISTLE

Senior Executive Officers
Chief Executive Officer
　　　　　　　　　　　R C Sharma *Chief Executive Officer*
Syndicated Lending
Other (Syndicated Lending)
Credit Administration
　　　　　　　　　　　T A Padmanabhan *Manager*
Money Markets
Money Markets - General
　　　　　　　　　　　P K Das *Manager*

Foreign Exchange
FX Traders / Sales People
　　　　　　　　　　　P K Das *Manager*

Settlement / Clearing
Operations
　　　　　　　　　　　S L F Fernandes *Manager, Operations & Services*
Administration
Technology & Systems
Systems
　　　　　　　　　　　B Sriram *Manager*
Accounts / Audit
Internal Audit
　　　　　　　　　　　F Blazey *Manager*
Other (Administration)
Business Development
　　　　　　　　　　　Mr Jaikaran *Manager*

Südwestdeutsche Landesbank (Singapore)   Offshore Banking Unit

#01-70 Gerwan Centre, 25 International Business Park, Singapore, 609916
Tel: 562 7722 **Fax:** 562 7729 **Telex:** RS 20173 **Swift:** SOLA SG SG **Email:** swibsgp@mbox3.singnet **Reuters:** SWSG

Senior Executive Officers
Chief Executive Officer　　　　　　　Peter Kaemmerer *Regional Head, Asia / Pacific*
General Manager　　　　　　　　　　Guido Paris
Executive Assistant　　　　　　　　　Monika Stohr
Executive Secretary　　　　　　　　　Karen Goh
Syndicated Lending
Department: Corporate & Institutional Banking
Other (Trade Finance)
Financial Institutions & Trade Finance　Patrick Lam
　　　　　　　　　　　　　　　　　　Nellie Tan
　　　　　　　　　　　　　　　　　　Wai Quen Lam
Corporate Customers & Credit Support　Hartmut Dongus
　　　　　　　　　　　　　　　　　　Magdalene Tan

Money Markets
Department: Treasury
Money Markets - General
　　　　　　　　　　　Karl Broecker *Head of Treasury*
　　　　　　　　　　　Kenneth Tai
　　　　　　　　　　　Samantha Wong
　　　　　　　　　　　Cathrerine Koh
　　　　　　　　　　　Michael Brodback
　　　　　　　　　　　Nobert Strozynski

Settlement / Clearing
Operations
　　　　　　　　　　　K V Miyapan *Head of Operations*
　　　　　　　　　　　Ivy Liu

SINGAPORE (+65)　　　　www.euromoneydirectory.com

Südwestdeutsche Landesbank (Singapore) (cont)
Administration
Technology & Systems
　　　　　　　　　　　P J Karthik
　　　　　　　　　　　Alfonso Poh

Accounts / Audit
　　　　　　　　　　　Lynette Lee
　　　　　　　　　　　Doreen Tan
Internal Audit Division　Mahesh D Kotai
Other (Administration)
　　　　　　　　　　　Theresa Lee
　　　　　　　　　　　Fazilah Awang
　　　　　　　　　　　Stephen Ng
　　　　　　　　　　　Keok Mei Kei
　　　　　　　　　　　Aw Poh Sing
　　　　　　　　　　　Nordin Kadir *Support*

The Sumitomo Bank Limited
Full Branch Office

#27-08 DBS Building, Tower 2, 6 Shenton Way, Singapore, 068809
Tel: 220 1611; 220 0610 (Dealers) **Fax:** 225 9647 **Telex:** RS 21656 **Swift:** SUMIT SG SX
Email: sumi8806@mbox4.singnet.com.sg
Dealers Telex: RS 20830

Senior Executive Officers
General Manager　　　　　　　　Yasuji Sumitomo
Joint General Manager　　　　　Naoto Ishizuka
Joint General Manager　　　　　Koichi Inagaki
Joint General Manager　　　　　Danny Teo
Deputy General Manager　　　　Hiroshi Okamoto
Deputy General Manager　　　　Chee Soon Hock

General-Lending (DCM, SL)
Head of Corporate Banking　　　Hiroaki Sumino *Manager & Head of Customer Dealing*
　　　　　　　　　　　　　　　　　Yoshio Taku *AGM & Head of Credit*

Relationship Manager
Business Promotion 1　　　　　Osamu Nakano *Assistant General Manager & Head*
Business Promotion 2　　　　　Kazushige Goto *Assistant General Manager & Head*
Business Promotion 3　　　　　Takashi Shimahara *Assistant General Manager & Head*

Syndicated Lending
Other (Syndicated Lending)
Loan Administration　　　　　　Catherine Lai *Deputy Manager*

Loan-Related Activities
Project Finance　　　　　　　　Toshilhide Orita *Joint General Manager & Head*
　　　　　　　　　　　　　　　　　Masaaki Sasai *Assistant General Manager*
　　　　　　　　　　　　　　　　　David Gardner *Assistant General Manager*
Structured Trade Finance　　　Chong Paw Zen *Assistant General Manager & Head*

Money Markets
Department: Treasury Department
Country Head　　　　　　　　　Yoshio Tanaka *Joint General Manager*

Money Markets - General
Forex　　　　　　　　　　　　　Oliver Cheung *Chief Dealer & Head*
Money　　　　　　　　　　　　　Simon Ito *Assistant General Manager & Head*
Planning　　　　　　　　　　　　Yasuhiro Otani *Assistant General Manager & Head*

The Sumitomo Trust & Banking Company Limited
Offshore Banking Unit

#45-01 Temasek Tower, 8 Shenton Way, Singapore, 068811
Tel: 224 9055 **Fax:** 224 2873 **Telex:** RS20717 SMTRST

Senior Executive Officers
General Manager　　　　　　　Yutaka Inoue
Deputy General Manager　　　Masakazu Okamoto
Deputy General Manager　　　Phoon Yew Kwok

www.euromoneydirectory.com   SINGAPORE (+65)

Syndicated Lending
Other (Syndicated Lending)
Singapore, Malaysia, Thailand   Seow Boon Ann *Senior Vice President*
Indonesia, India   Barry Lee *First Vice President*
Japanese Accounts   Tetsuya Kodama *First Vice President*
Loan-Related Activities
Project Finance   Yukio Iwasaki *Vice President*
Money Markets
Head of Money Markets   Jiro Kumazawa *Vice President*
Foreign Exchange
Head of Foreign Exchange   Jiro Kumazawa *Vice President*
Risk Management
Head of Risk Management   Serene Chew *Assistant Vice President*
Settlement / Clearing
Head of Settlement / Clearing   Phoon Yew Kwok *Senior Vice President & Deputy General Manager*

Svenska Handelsbanken   Full Branch Office
#21-00 OCBC Centre, 65 Chulia Street, Singapore, 049513
Tel: 532 3800; 534 2127 **Fax:** 534 4909; 536 4778 **Telex:** RS29012 **Swift:** HAND SG SG
Email: hmtsin@singnet.com.sg **Reuters:** SHBS

Senior Executive Officers
Chief Executive Officer   Aoran Johnsson *General Manager* ☏ **532 3800**
Treasurer   Peter Altefelt *Head of Trading* ☏ **534 2127**
Syndicated Lending
Loan-Related Activities
Trade Finance   Celia Kwek *Manager* ☏ **532 3800**
Foreign Exchange
Department: Treasury
Tel: 534 2127 **Fax:** 536 9778
Head of Trading   Peter Altefelt *Head of Trading* ☏ **534 2127**
Administration
Technology & Systems
    Bernard Siu *Manager*

TFS Currencies Pte Limited Singapore   Subsidiary Company
#23-02 Shenton House, 3 Shenton Way, Singapore, 068805
Tel: 226 5616 **Fax:** 226 2812 **Reuters:** TFSS
Currency Options **Tel:** 221 0331

Senior Executive Officers
Others (Senior Executives)
    Dennis Trappitt *Director*

TFS Energy (S) Limited (Singapore)   Subsidiary Company
#23-02 Shenton House, 3 Shenton Way, Singapore, 068805
Tel: 226 5616 **Fax:** 226 2812 **Telex:** RS26192 TFSEN
Oil Desk **Tel:** 221 9790

Senior Executive Officers
Others (Senior Executives)
    Dennis Trappitt *Director*
    Richard Yap *Director*

The Tokai Bank Limited   Full Branch Office
#16-01 UOB Plaza 1, 80 Raffles Place, Singapore, 048624
Tel: 535 8222 **Fax:** 535 5972 **Telex:** 21848 TOKAIBK RS

Senior Executive Officers
Others (Senior Executives)
Director, Head of South East Asia   Hiroshi Aoki *General Manager*

SINGAPORE (+65)　　　　www.euromoneydirectory.com

Tokai Financial Futures (Singapore) Pte Limited
Offshore Banking Unit
#16-01 UOB Plaza 1, 80 Raffles Place, Singapore, 048624
Tel: 535 8222 Fax: 532 5453 Telex: 21848 TOKAIBK RS
Senior Executive Officers
General Manager　　　　　　　　　H Aoki

The Toyo Trust & Banking Co Limited
#24-01, 6 Battery Road, Singapore, 049909
Tel: 225 0177 Fax: 224 7367 Telex: RS20091 TYTSP
Senior Executive Officers
General Manager　　　　　　　　　Toshihiko Nakahashi

UBS AG
Full Branch Office
#18-00 Suntec City Tower, 5 Temasek Boulevard, Singapore, 038985
Tel: 431 8000 Fax: 431 8188 Telex: RS 24140 SINSUIS Cable: SINPORSUIS
Senior Executive Officers
Chairman Asia　　　　　　　　　　L Ho Kee
Managing Director & Head of Singapore　R Gerber
Branch
Other Departments
Private Banking　　　　　　　　　L Teo Ping

UBS Brinson Pte Limited
#18-20/21 Republic Plaza 2, 9 Raffles Place, Singapore, 048619
Tel: 531 7912 Fax: 531 7975
Senior Executive Officers
Others (Senior Executives)
Global Institutional Asset Management　R Tallboys

UBS CAPITAL
Alternative trading name: UBS Capital Asia (S) Limited
#18-20/21 Republic Plaza 2, 9 Raffles Place, Singapore, 048619
Tel: 532 2888 Fax: 531 7982
Senior Executive Officers
Others (Senior Executives)
　　　　　　　　　　　　　　　　D Lai *Partner, Regional Head Asia*

UCO Bank
Formerly known as: United Commercial Bank
Bharat Building, 3 Raffles Place, Singapore, 048617
PO Box 1611, Singapore
Tel: 532 5944 Fax: 532 5044 Telex: RS21682 Swift: UCBA SG SG Email: ucobank@mbox5.singnetcom.sg
Reuters: UCOS Cable: UCO BANK Telex: RS43339
Senior Executive Officers
Chief Executive Officer　　　　　　Sunanda Lahiri ☎ **532 5054**
Others (Senior Executives)
Senior Manager　　　　　　　　　Ravi Chatterjee ☎ **532 6404**
　　　　　　　　　　　　　　　　Pritam Lal Angural ☎ **532 4849**
　　　　　　　　　　　　　　　　Srinivasan Sankaran ☎ **532 7540**
　　　　　　　　　　　　　　　　Surojeet Chandra Dhole ☎ **532 6404**

Syndicated Lending
Loan-Related Activities
Trade Finance　　　　　　　　　Srinivasan Sankaran ☎ **532 7540**

1352　Euromoney Directory 1999

www.euromoneydirectory.com　　　　　SINGAPORE (+65)

Foreign Exchange
Head of Foreign Exchange
　　Radhakrishnan Kupleri *Dealer* ☏ **532 4890**
FX Traders / Sales People
　　Shanti Ramanathan *Dealer* ☏ **532 4890**
Settlement / Clearing
Head of Settlement / Clearing
　　S Rajesvari *Joint Manager* ☏ **532 4014**
Administration
Head of Administration
　　Ravi Chatterjee ☏ **532 6404**

UniCredito Italiano SpA　　　　　　　　　　　　Head Office

Formerly known as: Credito Italiano SpA
#50-01 UOB Plaza 1, 80 Raffles PLace, Singapore, 048624
Tel: 532 4811 **Fax:** 534 4300 **Telex:** RS 23783 CRJTSG **Swift:** CRIT SG SG **Email:** treasury@ci-sg.com.sg
Telerate: CRIS **Cable:** CRITSPORE

Senior Executive Officers
Tel: 532 4811 **Fax:** 534 4300
Chief Executive Officer　　　　Frederico Ghizzoni *Chief Manager*
Financial Director　　　　　　Gianni Papa *Deputy Chief Manager*
Chief Operating Officer　　　　Patrizia Chiozza *Operations Manager*
Treasurer　　　　　　　　　Wing Kee Lee *Treasury Manager*

Others (Senior Executives)
Credit Department　　　　　Janice Lim *Manager, Head of Credit & Marketing*
Settlement Dept　　　　　　Patricia Tan *Manager, Settlement / Trade Finance*

Syndicated Lending
Loan-Related Activities
Structured Trade Finance　　Janice Leong *Junior Officer*

Money Markets
Tel: 532 3055 **Fax:** 532 4748 **Reuters:** CRIS **Telex:** RS 24030 CRISSG
Head of Money Markets　　　Sinil Gupta *MM Senior Dealer* ☏ **532 3055** ℻ **532 4748**

Foreign Exchange
Tel: 532 3055 **Fax:** 532 4748 **Reuters:** CRIS **Telex:** RS 24030 CRISSG
Head of Foreign Exchange　　Andrew Pearce *FX Senior Dealer* ☏ **532 3055** ℻ **532 4748**

Settlement / Clearing
Operations　　　　　　　　Leg Lian Chia *Settlements Officer* ☏ **532 4811**

Administration
Tel: 532 4811
Head of Administration　　　Sue Ismail *Administrative Officer*

Technology & Systems
　　　　　　　　　　　　　Clarence Ng *Head of IT*

Accounts / Audit
　　　　　　　　　　　　　Josephine Lee *Head of Accounts*

Union de Banques Arabes et Françaises - UBAF　　Full Branch Office

#25-04/05 Suntec Tower Four, 6 Temasek Boulevard, Singapore, 038726
Tel: 333 6188 **Fax:** 333 6789 **Telex:** RS 28000 UBAFSX **Swift:** UBAF SG SX **Cable:** UNIBANQUE
Forex Tel: 333 8133; **Telex:** RS280001 UBAF SX; **Trade Finance Tel:** 333 6733

Senior Executive Officers
General Manager　　　　　Antoine R Homsy

General-Lending (DCM, SL)
Head of Corporate Banking　Andrew Lim *Manager, Credit & Marketing* ☏ **333 8022**

General - Treasury
Head of Treasury　　　　　A Sabry El-Zawahry *Head of Treasury*

Syndicated Lending
Loan-Related Activities
Trade Finance　　　　　　Laura Mok *Manager* ☏ **333 8022**

Money Markets
Country Head　　　　　　Ginny Tan *Deputy Manager, Money Markets*

Settlement / Clearing
Settlement (General)　　　Hoon Ping Teo *Manager, Settlements*

SINGAPORE (+65)   www.euromoneydirectory.com

Union de Banques Arabes et Françaises - UBAF (cont)
Administration
Accounts / Audit
Accounts   Florence Tham *Manager*

United Overseas Bank Limited   Head Office

UOB Plaza, 80 Raffles Place, Singapore, 048624
Tel: 533 9898 **Fax:** 534 2334 **Telex:** RS 21539 TYEHUA **Swift:** UOVB SG SG **Cable:** TYEHUABANK
Website: www.uob.com.sg

Senior Executive Officers
Chairman & Chief Executive Officer   Cho-Yaw Wee
President   Ernest Yuen-Weng Wong
Deputy President   Ee-Cheong Wee

Others (Senior Executives)
Corporate Services / Risk Management /   Francis Teng-Yang Yeo *Senior Executive Vice President*
Stockbroking
Investment Banking   Hiang-Meng Gn *Executive Vice President*
Corporate Services   Bin-Thun Lam *Executive Vice President*
Commercial Banking   Samuel Hon-Thang Poon *Executive Vice President*
International Banking   Terence Sea-Eng Ong *Executive Vice President*
Commercial Banking   Eng-Cheong Yeo *Executive Vice President*
                                                    Khay-Pin Neo *Executive Vice President*
Information Technology   Bak-Wee Lim *Executive Vice President*
United Overseas Bank (Malaysia) Bhd   Francis Chin-Yong Lee *Executive Vice President & Chief Executive Officer*
                                                    T +60 (3) 292 7722 F +60 (3) 294 0617

Debt Capital Markets / Fixed Income
Department: Money & Bond Markets Division
Tel: 533 9898 **Fax:** 534 3028/4698 **Reuters:** UOBT, UOBY **Telex:** RS 21539 TYEHUA
Head of Fixed Income   Joseph Chen *Senior Vice President & Head, Money & Bond Markets*
                                                    T 539 2931 F 534 3028
Head of Fixed Income Trading   Dorothy Geok-Sim Tan *Vice President* T 539 2975 F 534 4698

Government Bonds
Head of Trading   Leonard Keok-Poh Ng *Vice President* T 539 2997 F 534 4698

Eurobonds
Head of Trading   Dorothy Geok-Sim Tan *Vice President* T 539 2975 F 534 4698

Libor-Based / Floating-Rate Products
FRN Trading; Asset Swaps   Dorothy Geok-Sim Tan *Vice President* T 539 2975 F 534 4698

Money Markets
Tel: 533 9898 **Fax:** 534 3028/4698 **Reuters:** UOBT,UOBY **Telex:** RS 21539 TYEHUA

Money Markets - General
Money & Bond Markets   Joseph Chen *Senior Vice President & Head, Money & Bond Markets*
                                                    T 539 2931 F 534 3028

Wholesale Deposits
Head of Sales   Dorothy Geok-Sim Tan *Vice President* T 539 2975 F 534 4698

Foreign Exchange
Department: FX / Treasury Services Division
Tel: 533 9898 **Fax:** 533 1570/534 3028 **Reuters:** UOBT, UOBX, UOBY **Telex:** RS 21539 TYEHUA
Head of Foreign Exchange   Kim-Soon Lee *First Vice President, FX / Treasury Services* T 539 2901
                                                    F 533 1570
Head of Institutional Sales   Jeffrey Chin-Heng Tan *Assistant Vice President* T 539 2907 F 534 3028
Corporate Sales   Susan Siew-San Ng *Vice President* T 539 2907 F 534 3028
Head of Trading   Eng-Lee Chua *First Vice President* T 539 2973 F 534 3028

FX Traders / Sales People
Head of Commercial Sales   Kwee-Ming Ng *Vice President* T 539 2902 F 534 3028

Risk Management

Other (Exchange-Traded Derivatives)
Head of Derivatives   James Kou *First Vice President, Derivatives Trading* T 539 2870
                                                    F 538 6013

Settlement / Clearing
Tel: 533 9898 **Fax:** 538 6617 **Telex:** RS 21539 TYEHUA
Head of Settlement / Clearing   Say-Tai Lim *First Vice President, Settlements* T 539 2990 F 538 6617

www.euromoneydirectory.com SINGAPORE (+65)

Other Departments
Commodities / Bullion Hock-Bee Soon *Vice President & Head, Gold / Bullion & Futures*
 ☎ 539 2983 Ⓕ 538 3990
Correspondent Banking Frank Chin-Kok Choo *Senior Vice President & Head,Correspondent Banking* ☎ 539 2933 Ⓕ 536 4043
Administration
Department: Other Departments
Other (Administration)
Head of International Branches John Thian-Hock Sng *Senior Vice President, International Branches*
 ☎ 539 3003 Ⓕ 533 1570
Head of Currency Management Ghee-Soon Chan *First Vice President, Currency Management* ☎ 539 2899
 Ⓕ 534 3028

Warburg Dillon Read

#18-00 Suntec City Tower, 5 Temasek Boulevard, Singapore, 038985
Tel: 431 8000 **Fax:** 431 8188 **Telex:** RS24140 SINSUIS **Cable:** SINPORSUIS

Senior Executive Officers
Chief Executive Officer C Standish *CEO Asia / Pacific*
Head, Singapore Branch R Gerber

Debt Capital Markets / Fixed Income
Department: Interest Rates
Bonds - General
 J Loh *Rates Asia*

Equity Capital Markets
Other (Domestic Equities)
Asian Equities Chia Kum Ho

Syndicated Lending
Other (Trade Finance)
Global Trade Finance A Applegarth

Risk Management
Other (FI Derivatives)
Credit Risk Management J Mitchell
Market Risk Management P Wilkinson

Corporate Finance / M&A Advisory
Head of Corporate Finance C West

Settlement / Clearing
Operations J Ang *Regional Financial Control*
  S Hirt

Asset Management
Other (Asset Management)
Loan Portfolio Management M Groeflin

Administration
Regional Information Technology Management D Bull
Accounts / Audit
Corporate Audit N Khokhar

West Merchant Bank Limited

Full Branch Office

#33-00 Centennial Tower, 3 Temasek Avenue, Singapore, 039190
Tel: 333 2100 **Fax:** 333 2188 **Telex:** RS 23754 WMBSIN

Senior Executive Officers
General Manager Peter Edmondson ☎ 333 2003

Debt Capital Markets / Fixed Income
Eurobonds
Head of Sales Jonathan Grosvenor *Head, Capital Markets Sales*
Bonds - General
Distressed Debt Mark Askew *Assistant Director*

Equity Capital Markets
International Equities
Head of Trading Yi Loh *Manager* ☎ 439 6567

SINGAPORE (+65)   www.euromoneydirectory.com

West Merchant Bank Limited (cont)

Settlement / Clearing
Tel: 538 0980 Fax: 538 0672
Country Head
Equity Settlement; Fixed-Income Settlement;
Derivatives Settlement; Foreign Exchange
Settlement

Gek-Whang Tan *Head of Operations*
Priscilla Guam *Manager*

Administration

Compliance

Gek-Whang Tan *Head of Operations*

Westdeutsche Landesbank Girozentrale   Full Branch Office

#33-00 Centennial Tower, 3 Temasek Avenue, Singapore, 039790
Tel: 333 2388 Fax: 333 2399 Telex: RS25255 Swift: WELA SG SX Reuters: WDLB (Dealing)
General Telex: RS26177; General Telex: RS25262; Equity Research Tel: 333 2868; FX Sales Tel: 333 2378;
Interest Rate Derivatives Tel: 333 2338; Reuters: WDOS (Regional FX Options); WDLC (Treasury Sales)

Senior Executive Officers
Senior Vice President
Vice President

Klaus R Gerritzen
Wolfhart Von Auer

Others (Senior Executives)
Clients Business Unit
Clients Business Unit (Banking & Fin. Institution)
Corporate Finance / Bond Coverage
Head of Credit

Matthew Tan *Vice President*
Susan Kelly *Vice President*

Willi Schnell *Vice President*
Too Swee Lua *Senior Vice President*

General - Treasury
Head of Treasury

Gregor Huesgen *Vice President*

Relationship Manager
Banks & Financial Institutions
Clients Business Unit

Susan Kelly *Vice President*
Matthew Tan *Vice President*

Debt Capital Markets / Fixed Income
Head of Fixed Income

Sheng Mong Ee *Vice President* ☏ 333 2368

Syndicated Lending
Head of Origination
Head of Syndication

Matthew Tan *VP* ☏ 333 2510
Matthew Tan *Vice President*

Money Markets
Department: Treasury
Regional Head

Gregor Huesgen *Vice President*

Domestic Commercial Paper
Head of Origination

Albert Boudville *VP & Chief Dealer*

Eurocommercial Paper
Head of Origination

Albert Boudville *VP & Chief Dealer*

Foreign Exchange

FX Traders / Sales People
Treasury Sales
Chief dealer (FX)

Stephen Yolland *Vice President* ☏ 333 2398
Ronny Chow *Vice President* ☏ 333 2318

Risk Management
Head of Risk Management

Perumal Ramanathan *VP, Risk Management & Control* ☏ 333 2388

Other Currency Swap / FX Options Personnel
Regional FX Options

John Arvanitis *Vice President Regional FX Options* ☏ 333 2818

Corporate Finance / M&A Advisory

Other (Corporate Finance)
Corporate Fin / Bond Coverage

Willi Schnell *Vice President*

Settlement / Clearing
Operations

Ee Ngoh Teo *Vice President*

Other Departments
Chief Credit Officer

Too Swee Lua *Senior Vice President*

1356   Euromoney Directory 1999

www.euromoneydirectory.com   SLOVAK REPUBLIC (+421)

Westpac Banking Corporation   Full Branch Office

Formerly known as: Bank of New South Wales
#19-00 SIA Building, 77 Robinson Road, Singapore, 068896
Tel: 530 9898; 533 8673 **Fax:** 532 6781 **Telex:** RS21763 **Swift:** WPAC SG SG **Reuters:** WBCS
Website: www.westpac.com.au

Senior Executive Officers
Chief Executive Officer   Tony Mathers *General Manager, Asia* T 530 9520 F 535 7509
Financial Director   Yogan Rasanayakam *Financial Controller, Asia* T 530 9531 F 535 7509
Deputy Country Head & Branch Mgr   Lee Yew Huat T 530 9530 F 530 9889

Others (Senior Executives)
Corporate Relations   Magdalene Low-Chan *Senior Manager, Sales & Marketing* T 530 9527
Financial Markets   Russell Burton *Manager, Sales* T 530 9845
Human Resources   Chan Siong Yu *Manager* T 530 9568

Money Markets
Fax: 538 3481 **Reuters:** WBCS
Country Head   Tan Phet Lah *Chief Dealer, Treasury* T 530 9843

Corporate Finance / M&A Advisory
Country Head   Richard Ng *Head of Corporate Finance, Asia* T 530 9524 F 534 0244

Settlement / Clearing
Head of Settlement / Clearing   Michael Yap *Manager, Operations & Personal Banking* T 530 9529
                                     F 530 9558

Administration
Technology & Systems
Info & Technology   Zarul Amar *Manager* T 530 9543 F 532 6781

The Yasuda Trust & Banking Company Limited   Representative

#16-02 Singapore Land Tower, 50 Raffles Place, Singapore, 048623
Tel: 223 7266 **Fax:** 224 1613 **Telex:** RS33285 YTBC SI

Senior Executive Officers
General Manager   Yutaka Kitamura

The Zenshinren Bank   Representative Office

#29-02 UOB Plaza 1, 80 Raffles Place, Singapore, 048624
Tel: 532 7066 **Fax:** 532 6134

Senior Executive Officers
Chief Representative   Takeo Sato

Zürcher Kantonalbank   Representative Office

#38-03 Singapore Land Tower, 50 Raffles Place, Singapore, 048623
Tel: 534 4700 **Fax:** 534 4711 **Telex:** RS24333 ZKBSIN **Email:** zkbsinph@mbox5.signet.com.sg

Senior Executive Officers
Chief Representative   Patrick Hörler

SLOVAK REPUBLIC
(+421)

Národná banka Slovenska   Central Bank

Alternative trading name: National Bank of Slovakia
Stúrova 2, 818 54 Bratislava
Tel: (7) 513 1111 **Fax:** (7) 364 721 **Swift:** NBSB FK BX **Reuters:** NBSB **Telerate:** 39624 **Telex:** 38267
Website: www.nbs.sk

Senior Executive Officers
Governor   Vladimír Masár
Vice Governor   Marián Jusko

SLOVAK REPUBLIC (+421) www.euromoneydirectory.com

Národná banka Slovenska (cont)
Senior Executive Officers (cont)
Chief Executive Officer
Director, Foreign
Spokesman

Jozef Mudrík *Vice Governor*
Stefan Pavúk ☎ 513 2174 🖷 394 979
Ján Onda ☎ 513 2825 🖷 513 2882

General - Treasury
Head of Treasury

Frantisek Szulényi *Director, Treasury* ☎ 513 2556 🖷 513 2876

Money Markets
Department: Banking Transactions Department
Head of Money Markets

Juraj Jánosik *Director* ☎ 513 2535 🖷 321 898

Bank Austria Creditanstalt Slovakia as   Head Office
Mostova 6, 811 02 Bratislava
Tel: (7) 539 9111; (7) 359 1111 **Fax:** (7) 539 9406; (7) 394 923 **Telex:** 92161 BKAU **Swift:** BKAU SK BX

Senior Executive Officers
Chairman   Regina Ovesny-Straka
Treasurer   Viktor Štrauch

Citibank (Slovakia) AS   Subsidiary Company
Viedenska cesta 5, 852 51 Bratislava
Tel: (7) 6827 8111; (7) 6827 8323 **Fax:** (7) 6827 8499; (7) 6827 8210 **Telex:** 92155 **Swift:** CITI SK BA BIC
Reuters: CISR **Telex:** 92156

Senior Executive Officers
Chief Executive Officer   David Francis *Country Corporate Officer* ☎ 6827 8222 🖷 6727 2689
Financial Director   Naji Amini *Financial Controller* ☎ 6827 8538
Treasurer   Roman Kovac *Country Treasurer* ☎ 6827 8422

Debt Capital Markets / Fixed Income
Regional Head; Country Head   Steve Fisher *Head, Corporate Finance* ☎ +420 (2) 2430 4352

Domestic Government Bonds
Head of Sales   Peter Kostka *Treasury Marketing Head* ☎ 6827 8425
Head of Trading   Peter Kostka *Treasury Marketing Head* ☎ 6827 8425

Eurobonds
Head of Origination   Steve Fisher *Head, Corporate Finance* ☎ +420 (2) 2430 4352
Trading (Sovereigns)   Peter Kostka *Treasury Marketing Head* ☎ 6827 8425
                                     Roman Kovac *Country Treasurer* ☎ 6827 8422
Trading (Corporates)   Peter Kostka *Treasury Marketing Head* ☎ 6827 8425
                                     Roman Kovac *Country Treasurer* ☎ 6827 8422
Trading (High-yield)   Peter Kostka *Treasury Marketing Head* ☎ 6827 8425
                                     Roman Kovac *Country Treasurer* ☎ 6827 8422

Libor-Based / Floating-Rate Products
FRN Origination   Steve Fisher *Head, Corporate Finance* ☎ +420 (2) 2430 4352

Medium-Term Notes
Head of Origination; Head of Structuring   Steve Fisher *Head, Corporate Finance* ☎ +420 (2) 2430 4352

Private Placements
Head of Origination; Head of Structuring   Steve Fisher *Head, Corporate Finance* ☎ +420 (2) 2430 4352

Mortgage-Backed Securities
Regional Head   Steve Fisher *Head, Corporate Finance* ☎ +420 (2) 2430 4352

Fixed-Income Repo
Head of Repo   Roman Kovac *Country Treasurer* ☎ 6827 8422
Collateral Management   Roman Kovac *Country Treasurer* ☎ 6827 8422
Matched Book Manager   Peter Kostka *Treasury Marketing Head* ☎ 6827 8425
                                     Roman Kovac *Country Treasurer* ☎ 6827 8422
Sales   Peter Kostka *Treasury Marketing Head* ☎ 6827 8425

Equity Capital Markets
Regional Head   Mike Slattery *Regional Head, Sales & Trading* ☎ +44 (171) 500 1693

Convertibles / Equity-Linked
Head of Sales   Mike Slattery *Regional Head, Sales & Trading* ☎ +44 (171) 500 1693

Warrants
Head of Sales   Mike Slattery *Regional Head, Sales & Trading* ☎ +44 (171) 500 1693

SLOVAK REPUBLIC (+421)

Syndicated Lending
Regional Head; Country Head of Origination; Steve Fisher *Head, Corporate Finance* ☏ +420 (2) 2430 4352
Head of Syndication
Head of Trading Peter Kostka *Treasury Marketing Head* ☏ 6827 8425
 Roman Kovac *Country Treasurer* ☏ 6827 8422
Head of Credit Committee David Francis *GM, Senior Credit Officer* ☏ 6827 8222

Money Markets
Country Head Peter Kostka *Treasury Marketing Head* ☏ 6827 8425
 Roman Kovac *Country Treasurer* ☏ 6827 8422

Domestic Commercial Paper
Head of Origination Steve Fisher *Head, Corporate Finance* ☏ +420 (2) 2430 4352
Head of Sales Peter Kostka *Treasury Marketing Head* ☏ 6827 8425
Head of Trading Roman Kovac *Country Treasurer* ☏ 6827 8422

Eurocommercial Paper
Head of Origination Steve Fisher *Head, Corporate Finance* ☏ +420 (2) 2430 4352

Wholesale Deposits
Marketing; Head of Sales Peter Kostka *Treasury Marketing Head* ☏ 6827 8425

Other (Wholesale Deposits)
MM Traders / Sales People Jaroslav Hora *MM Dealer* ☏ 6827 8424

Foreign Exchange
Country Head Peter Kostka *Treasury Marketing Head* ☏ 6827 8425
 Roman Kovac *Country Treasurer* ☏ 6827 8422
Head of Institutional Sales; Corporate Sales Peter Kostka *Treasury Marketing Head* ☏ 6827 8425
Head of Trading Roman Kovac *Country Treasurer* ☏ 6827 8422

FX Traders / Sales People
 Martin Luptak *Senior Dealer* ☏ 6827 8426
 Oto Mohnansky *FX Dealer* ☏ 6827 8429
 Iva Surorova *Treasury Marketing* ☏ 6827 8421

Risk Management
Country Head Terrance Kyle *Country Risk Manager* ☏ +420 (2) 2430 4332

Fixed Income Derivatives / Risk Management
Country Head Hayden Owen-Thomas *Regional Head, Sales & Trading* ☏ 6827 8370
Trading Roman Kovac *Country Treasurer* ☏ 6827 8422
IR Swaps Sales / Marketing; IR Swaps Trading; Jaro Daniska ☏ +44 (171) 500 0530
IR Options Sales / Marketing; IR Options Trading

Foreign Exchange Derivatives / Risk Management
Cross-Currency Swaps, Sales / Marketing Peter Kostka *Treasury Marketing Head* ☏ 6827 8425
Cross-Currency Swaps, Trading Jaro Daniska ☏ +44 (171) 500 0530
Vanilla FX option Sales Peter Kostka *Treasury Marketing Head* ☏ 6827 8425
Vanilla FX option Trading Jaro Daniska ☏ +44 (171) 500 0530

OTC Equity Derivatives
Sales Peter Kostka *Treasury Marketing Head* ☏ 6827 8425
Trading Jaro Daniska ☏ +44 (171) 500 0530

OTC Commodity Derivatives
Sales Peter Kostka *Treasury Marketing Head* ☏ 6827 8425
Trading Jaro Daniska ☏ +44 (171) 500 0530

Exchange-Traded Derivatives
Regional Head Mike Slattery *Regional Head, Sales & Trading* ☏ +44 (171) 500 1693

Corporate Finance / M&A Advisory
Country Head Steve Fisher *Head, Corporate Finance* ☏ +420 (2) 2430 4352

Settlement / Clearing
Country Head; Equity Settlement; Fixed-Income Ian Burbury *Senior Country Operations Officer* ☏ 6827 8522
Settlement; Derivatives Settlement; Foreign Exchange Settlement

Global Custody
Regional Head Ranjit Chatterji *Regional Custody Head* ☏ +44 (171) 508 1336

Other Departments
Proprietary Trading Roman Kovac *Country Treasurer* ☏ 6827 8422
Correspondent Banking Martin Sebesta *Head, Financial Institutions* ☏ 6827 8329

Administration
Technology & Systems
 Peter Harmady *Technology Head* ☏ 6827 8566

Legal / In-House Counsel
 Tomas Borec *Legal Counsel* ☏ 6827 8240

SLOVAK REPUBLIC (+421)   www.euromoneydirectory.com

Citibank (Slovakia) AS (cont)
Compliance
　　Ian Burbury *Senior Country Operations Officer* ☏ **6827 8522**
Public Relations
　　Denisa Kralikova *Head, Human Resources* ☏ **6827 8223**

Commerzbank AG   Representative Office

Pribinova 25, 810 11 Bratislava
PO Box 129, 810 11 Bratislava
Tel: (7) 563 4522; (7) 563 4524 **Fax:** (7) 563 4518 **Email:** coba_bratislava@gaston.sk
Corporate Dealers **Tel:** 576 2403

Senior Executive Officers
Representative　　　　　　　　　　Guy De Roeck

Credit Lyonnais Bank Slovakia AS   Full Branch Office

Medená 22, 811 02 Bratislava
PO Box 70, 811 02 Bratislava
Tel: (7) 325 320; (7) 361 919 **Fax:** (7) 326 209; (7) 361 093 **Telex:** 92539 **Swift:** CRLY SK BX **Reuters:** CLBL

Senior Executive Officers
Chief Executive Officer　　　　　J-Michel Giovannetti *General Director* ✉ **giovannetti@creditlyonnais.sk**
Treasurer　　　　　　　　　　　　Martin Hrozány *Treasury Manager* ✉ **hrozany@creditlyonnais.sk**
Deputy General Manager　　　　Jaroslav Zubák ✉ **zubak@creditlyonnnais.sk**

Devin Banka JSC   Head Office

Františkánske námestie 8, 813 10 Bratislava
Gundulicova 3
Tel: (7) 530 6111; (7) 530 6102 **Fax:** (7) 533 2311 **Telex:** 92659 DEVN SK **Swift:** DEVB SK BA
Email: vjanci@devinbanka.sk **Reuters:** DEBA

Senior Executive Officers
Chairman　　　　　　　　　　　　Sergej G Gorodkov
President　　　　　　　　　　　　Lubomir Kanis
Chief Executive Officer　　　　　Pavel Rusnák
Financial Director　　　　　　　　Ida Pálešová
Treasurer　　　　　　　　　　　　Vladimir Janci
International Division　　　　　　Eva Klemanová

Syndicated Lending
Head of Origination　　　　　　　Dáša Lisá

Money Markets
Head of Money Markets　　　　　Miroslav Bertovic

Foreign Exchange
Head of Foreign Exchange　　　Nidal Fakhouri

Administration
Head of Marketing　　　　　　　　Mária Venceliková
Accounts / Audit
　　　　　　　　　　　　　　　　　　Viera Kostrošová

European Bank for Reconstruction & Development
                                                                 Representative Office

Grösslingova 4, 814 18 Bratislava
Tel: (7) 324 143 **Fax:** (7) 321 459

Senior Executive Officers
Resident Representative　　　　Tomis Sibos

HypoVereinsbank Slovakia A/S   Subsidiary Company

Lazaretská ulicas 24, 811 08 Bratislava
Tel: (7) 535 8111 **Fax:** (7) 535 8600

www.euromoneydirectory.com SLOVAK REPUBLIC (+421)

ING Baring Securities (Slovakia)
Full Branch Office

Kolárska 6, 811 06 Bratislava
PO Box 123, 814 99 Bratislava
Tel: (7) 5934 6111 Fax: (7) 5936 1235

Senior Executive Officers
Branch Manager   Vladimir Valach

ING Barings
Full Branch Office

Kolárska 6, 811 06 Bratislava
PO Box 123, 814 99 Bratislava
Tel: (7) 534 6111 Fax: (7) 536 1222 Telex: 92658 INGB SK Swift: INGB SK BX

Senior Executive Officers
Chief Executive Officer   Jan Hillered Country Manager
                                   Marta Hollá Co-Country Manager
Financial Director   Darina Gallasova Manager
Chief Operating Officer   Stanislav Hodeck Operations Manager
Treasurer   Vladimut Valach Manager, Treasury
Senior Executive Secretary   Jana Cechova

General-Lending (DCM, SL)
Head of Corporate Banking   Oskar Sotak Manager, Corporate Finance

ING Barings

Komenského 3, 042 05 Kosice
PO Box D25, Kosice
Tel: (95) 622 7094 Fax: (95) 623 4692 Telex: 92658 INGB SK

Senior Executive Officers
Manager   Alexander Hudak

Investicna a Rozvojová banka as
Head Office

Stúrova 5, 813 54 Bratislava
Tel: (7) 389 1111 Fax: (7) 363 484 Telex: 92309 INRB SK Swift: INRB SK BX Reuters: IRBB

Senior Executive Officers
Chairman   Dusan Krkoska ☎ 389 2500
Financial Director   Julius Chovanec General Director ☎ 389 2524
Chief Operating Officer   Miloslav Klus General Director ☎ 389 2504
Treasurer   Julius Chovanec General Director ☎ 389 2524

Debt Capital Markets / Fixed Income
Head of Debt Capital Markets   Miroslav Fecko Director ☎ 589 2506

Equity Capital Markets
Head of Equity Capital Markets   Julius Chovanec General Director ☎ 389 2524

Syndicated Lending
Head of Syndicated Lending   Miroslav Fecko Director ☎ 589 2506

Money Markets
Head of Money Markets   Julius Chovanec General Director ☎ 389 2524

Foreign Exchange
Head of Foreign Exchange   Miloslav Klus General Director ☎ 389 2504

Risk Management
Head of Risk Management   Julius Chovanec General Director ☎ 389 2524

Corporate Finance / M&A Advisory
Head of Corporate Finance   Julius Chovanec General Director ☎ 389 2524

Settlement / Clearing
Head of Settlement / Clearing   Julius Chovanec General Director ☎ 389 2524

SLOVAK REPUBLIC (+421)   www.euromoneydirectory.com

Istrobanka AS
Head Office

Laurinská 1, 811 01 Bratislava 1
PO Box 109, 810 00 Bratislava 1
Tel: (7) 539 7111; (7) 533 1742 **Fax:** (7) 533 1744 **Telex:** 92194 ISTR SK **Swift:** ISTR SK BA
Email: horska@istrobanka.et.sk **Reuters:** ISTR
Istrobanka as **Telex:** 92172 ISTRSK
Website: www.istrobanka.sk

Senior Executive Officers
Chairman	Edita Bukovská ☎ **539 7343** 📠 **533 1744**
Financial Director	Miroslav Paulen ☎ **539 7501** 📠 **539 7547**
Chief Operating Officer	Ladislav Holubanský ☎ **539 7472** 📠 **539 7559**
Treasurer	Stanislav Štit ☎ **539 7514** 📠 **539 7561**
General Manager	Edita Bukovská ☎ **539 7343** 📠 **533 1744**
Company Secretary	Viera Bobriková ☎ **539 7225** 📠 **533 1744**
International Division	Brigita Horská ☎ **539 7240** 📠 **539 7524**

Others (Senior Executives)
Operational Division	Miroslav Zatovic *Deputy General Manager* ☎ **531 8270** 📠 **539 7418**
Commercial Division	Peter Procka *Deputy General Manager* ☎ **539 7344** 📠 **533 1738**
Financial Management Division	Vladimir Zervan *Deputy General Manager* ☎ **539 7419** 📠 **539 7294**

General-Lending (DCM, SL)
Head of Corporate Banking   Miroslav Paulen ☎ **539 7501** 📠 **539 7547**

General-Investment
Head of Investment   Miroslav Paulen ☎ **539 7501** 📠 **539 7547**

Debt Capital Markets / Fixed Income
Department: Department of Securities Secondary Market
Tel: 539 7530 **Fax:** 539 7549

Emerging Market Bonds
Head of Emerging Markets   Ján Bukoven ☎ **539 7530** 📠 **539 7549**

Equity Capital Markets
Department: Department of Liquidity and Treasury
Tel: 539 7514 **Fax:** 539 7561
Head of Equity Capital Markets   Stanislav Štit ☎ **539 7514** 📠 **539 7561**

Syndicated Lending
Tel: 539 7514 **Fax:** 539 7561
Head of Trading   Lubomír Mráz ☎ **539 7536** 📠 **539 7561**

Loan-Related Activities
Trade Finance; Project Finance   Terézia Mikulová ☎ **539 7280** 📠 **533 1738**

Money Markets
Tel: 539 7514 **Fax:** 539 7561
Head of Money Markets   Vladmir Kubricky ☎ **539 7552** 📠 **539 7561**

Foreign Exchange
Tel: 539 7514 **Fax:** 539 7561
Head of Foreign Exchange   Stanislav Štit ☎ **539 7514** 📠 **539 7561**

Risk Management
Tel: 539 7514 **Fax:** 539 7561
Head of Risk Management   Ján Bukoven ☎ **539 7530** 📠 **539 7549**

Corporate Finance / M&A Advisory
Head of Corporate Finance   Miroslav Paulen ☎ **539 7501** 📠 **539 7547**

Settlement / Clearing
Operations   Miroslav Zatovic *Deputy General Manager* ☎ **531 8270** 📠 **539 7418**

Global Custody
Head of Global Custody   Pavel Vladovic ☎ **539 7301** 📠 **533 1738**

Other Departments
Chief Credit Officer	Terézia Mikulová ☎ **539 7280** 📠 **533 1738**
Private Banking	Peter Procka *Deputy General Manager* ☎ **539 7344** 📠 **533 1738**
Correspondent Banking	Brigita Horská ☎ **539 7240** 📠 **539 7524**

Administration
Head of Marketing   Milan Jezo ☎ **539 7238** 📠 **539 7248**

Technology & Systems
    Ladislav Holubanský ☎ **539 7472** 📠 **539 7559**

Legal / In-House Counsel
    Lubica Licková ☎ **539 7275** 📠 **539 7357**

www.euromoneydirectory.com SLOVAK REPUBLIC (+421)

Public Relations
Milan Jezo ☏ 539 7238 ℻ 539 7248

Accounts / Audit
Oto Breštanský ☏ 539 7314 ℻ 539 7261

Ludová banka AS
Head Office

Formerly known as: Ludová banka Bratislava AS
Vysoká 9, PO Box 81, 810 00 Bratislava
Tel: (7) 435 1111 **Fax:** (7) 531 2444 **Telex:** 66692649 LBBA SK **Swift:** LUBA SK BX **Reuters:** LUBA; LUBB
Website: www.luba.sk

Senior Executive Officers
Director, Chairman of the Board — Karl Mayr-Kern ☏ 435 1100
Chief Executive Officer — Jozef Kollár *Director* ☏ 453 1510
Treasurer — Jana Kudláčová *Head of Treasury* ☏ 435 1200

Debt Capital Markets / Fixed Income
Tel: 435 1200 **Fax:** 435 1542

Fixed-Income Repo
Head of Repo — Peter Kníz *Head* ☏ 435 1210

Money Markets
Tel: 435 1200 **Fax:** 435 1542
Head of Money Markets — Peter Kníz *Head* ☏ 435 1210

Foreign Exchange
Head of Foreign Exchange — Peter Kníz *Head* ☏ 435 1210

Risk Management
Fixed Income Derivatives / Risk Management
Global Head — Jana Kudláčová *Head of Treasury* ☏ 435 1200

Other Departments
Correspondent Banking — Miloš Ihnat *Area Manager*

Pol'nobanka AS
Head Office

Formerly known as: Slovenská pol'nohospodárska banka
Vajnorská 21, 832 65 Bratislava
Tel: (7) 420 2112; (7) 420 2211 **Fax:** (7) 273 975 **Telex:** 92731 SPB C **Swift:** SLPO SK BX **Email:** mail@polnobanka.sk
Reuters: SLPO
Website: www.polnobanka.sk

Senior Executive Officers
Chairman of the Board — Františck Palic ☏ 273 964
Deputy Chairman — Clifford W Evans ☏ 420 2306
Financial Director — Jaroslav Šinák ☏ 542 3108
Treasurer — Daniel Bytoánek *Director, Treasury* ☏ 273 955
Company Secretary — Rudolf Hanuljak ☏ 420 2275
International Division — Ivica Bachledová ☏ 272 196

Others (Senior Executives)
Business Division — Anna Pilkova *Senior Manager* ☏ 272 147
Banking Services Division — Ivan Lamoš *Senior Manager* ☏ 420 3203
Legal & Property Division — Jozef Theis *Senior Manager* ☏ 273 961
Information Systems Division — Jozef Gubka *Senior Manager* ☏ 556 4102

General-Investment
Head of Investment — Eva Štrbová *Head, Investment Banking* ☏ 420 2281

Debt Capital Markets / Fixed Income
Department: Primary Issuances, Brokerage
Head of Fixed Income — Miroslav Cibul'a *Commercial Officer* ☏ 420 2392
Head of Fixed Income Sales — Eva Markovicová *Supervisor, Custody Services* ☏ 420 2274

Fixed-Income Repo
Head of Repo — Mário Schrenkel *Commercial Officer* ☏ 420 2390

Fixed-Income Research
Head of Fixed Income — Miroslav Gudába *Commercial Officer* ☏ 420 2356

Equity Capital Markets
Department: Primary Issuances, Brokerage
Head of Equity Capital Markets — Miroslav Cibul'a *Commercial Officer* ☏ 420 2392
Head of Sales — Eva Markovicová *Supervisor, Custody Services* ☏ 420 2274

SLOVAK REPUBLIC (+421)   www.euromoneydirectory.com

Pol'nobanka AS (cont)

Equity Research
Head of Equity Research — Miroslav Gudába *Commercial Officer* ☎ **420 2356**

Money Markets
Head of Money Markets — Miroslav Baca *Supervisor, Dealing Room Dept.* ☎ **420 2325**

Foreign Exchange
Head of Foreign Exchange — Martin Viest *Commercial Officer* ☎ **420 2336**

Risk Management
Head of Risk Management — Alexander Bartovic *Head, Risk Management* ☎ **420 2373**

Settlement / Clearing
Head of Settlement / Clearing; Equity Settlement; Fixed-Income Settlement; Operations — Miroslav Mucha *Supervisor* ☎ **420 2340**

Global Custody
Head of Global Custody — Eva Markovicová *Supervisor, Custody Services* ☎ **420 2274**

Other Departments
Correspondent Banking — Marian Guckýý *Supervisor* ☎ **420 2319**

Administration
Head of Marketing — Rudolf Gálik *Director, Strategy & Marketing Dept.* ☎ **429 2295**

Technology & Systems
— Jozef Gubka *Senior Manager* ☎ **556 4102**

Legal / In-House Counsel
— Jozef Theis *Senior Manager* ☎ **273 961**

Public Relations
— Michal Štefánek *Press Officer* ☎ **420 2207**

Accounts / Audit
— Milan Kuco *Director, Internal Audit* ☎ **420 3234**

Postová banka as   Head Office

Gorkého 3, 814 99 Bratislava
PO Box 149, Bratislava
Tel: (7) 430 3333; (7) 430 3373 **Fax:** (7) 430 3344 **Telex:** PBNK 666/92779 **Swift:** POBN SK BA
Email: marketing@pabk.sk **Reuters:** PABK
Telex: PBNK 666
Website: www.pabk.sk

Senior Executive Officers
President — Milan Loncik

Others (Senior Executives)
Consultant to President — Jozef Knizat ☎ **430 3304**
Secretary to President — Zlata Treichelova ☎ **430 3330**
Business Network Management — Stanislav Zeman ☎ **430 3421**
Bank Trading Division — Adam Celusak *VP & General Director* ☎ **430 3137**
Banking Consultancy — Frantisek Parovsky ☎ **430 3142**

General - Treasury
Head of Treasury — Vaclav Haluza ☎ **430 3143**

Syndicated Lending
Department: Bank Trading Division

Other (Syndicated Lending)
Bank Trading — Adam Celusak *VP & General Director* ☎ **430 3137**
Loans Department — Vladimira Skutletyova ☎ **430 3119**
Credit Analysis & Administration — Emilia Sedlakova ☎ **430 3141**
Capital Investments — Stanislav Brecka ☎ **430 3248**
Int'l Relations & Trading — Ilja Ilit ☎ **430 3247**
Banking Consultancy — Frantisek Parovsky ☎ **430 3142**

Settlement / Clearing
Department: Payments & Services Division

Other (Settlement & Clearing)
Payment & Services Division — Jaroslav Masek *General Director* ☎ **6060 2168**
Domestic Currency Services — Anna Stanova ☎ **6060 2160**
Foreign Currency Services — Katarina Pavlakova ☎ **6060 2160**
Payment Operations — Pavel Hordac ☎ **6060 2116**
Cooperations with Post Office — Zoltan Kovacs ☎ **6060 2164**

1364 Euromoney Directory 1999

SLOVAK REPUBLIC (+421)

Other Departments
Economic Research Maria Gresnerova ☏ **430 3218**
Other Departments
Financial Management Division Zdenko Kovac *General Director* ☏ **430 3249**
Administration
Head of Administration Juraj Schramm ☏ **430 3418**
Head of Marketing Dusan Valo *Director, Business Policy, Strategy & Marketing* ☏ **430 3337**
Technology & Systems
Automated Information Systems Division Anna Badurova *VP & General Director* ☏ **6060 2134**
Bank System Development Frantisek Psenko *Director* ☏ **6060 2169**
Automated Information System Gabriel Fedorko *Director* ☏ **6060 2395**
Technical Development Marian Cvecko *Director* ☏ **6060 2268**
Legal / In-House Counsel
Ludovit Sajgal ☏ **430 3406**
Public Relations
Jozef Knizat ☏ **430 3304**
Accounts / Audit
Accounts Lubica Strakova *Director* ☏ **430 3336**
Other (Administration)
Personnel Peter Sevcik ☏ **430 3422**
Advertising & Promotion Iveta Pavlisova ☏ **430 3415**
Supervisory Department Jaroslav Magal ☏ **430 3137**
Investments & Property Administration Ladislav Benedik ☏ **430 3009**

Priemyselná banka AS

Stúrova 27, 040 01 Kosice
Tel: (95) 680 4411; (95) 680 4420 **Fax:** (95) 680 4555 **Telex:** 77315 PBKO **Swift:** PBKO SS K2X
Email: magda@pbko.sk
Website: www.pbko.sk

Senior Executive Officers
President Jaroslav Maricák
Financial Director Július Seman ☏ **680 4457**
Treasurer Marian Paholok ☏ **680 4430**
Syndicated Lending
Head of Origination Viera Dubikova ☏ **680 4266**
Other Departments
Correspondent Banking Pavel Hric ☏ **680 4487**
Administration
Head of Marketing Miroslav Lukac ☏ **680 4381**

Prvá komunálna banka AS — Head Office

Formerly known as: PKB

Hodzova 11, 010 11 Zilina
Tel: (89) 624 093; (89) 622 091 **Fax:** (89) 624 129; (89) 621 901 **Telex:** 75245 **Swift:** KOMA SK 2X
Email: pecko@pkb.sk
Website: www.pkb.sk

Senior Executive Officers
Chairman & President Jozef Mihalik ☏ **624 093**
Vice Chairman & VP Eugen Mistrík ☏ **622 091**
Financial Director Demeter Markulcek *GM, Economies & Services Division* ☏ **623 306**
Treasurer Jaroslav Durman *Head of Treasury* ☏ **624 710**
General Manager, Commercial Division Pavol Durinik ☏ **621 394**
Debt Capital Markets / Fixed Income
Tel: 624 816 **Fax:** 624 788
Head of Debt Capital Markets Helena Stepová *Head, Capital Markets* ☏ **622 674**
Domestic Government Bonds
Head of Sales Roman Hedera ☏ **622 674**
Libor-Based / Floating-Rate Products
FRN Origination Jaroslav Durman *Head of Treasury* ☏ **624 710**
Mortgage-Backed Securities
Global Head Ján Trajcik *Head, Housing Finance* ☏ **621 394**

SLOVAK REPUBLIC (+421) www.euromoneydirectory.com

Prvá komunálna banka AS (cont)
Syndicated Lending
Loan-Related Activities
Project Finance — Ladislav Keltos *Commercial Specialist* ☏ **621 394**

Money Markets
Tel: 624 710 Fax: 624 742
Head of Money Markets — Jaroslav Durman *Head of Treasury* ☏ **624 710**

Money Markets - General
MM Traders — Jozef Króko *Dealer* ☏ **624 709**
Customer Desk — Maria Kovalikova *Dealer*

Foreign Exchange
Fax: 621 901
Head of Foreign Exchange — Peter Gazdik *Head, International* ☏ **623 306**

Risk Management
Tel: 624 710 Fax: 624 742
OTC Credit Derivatives
Global Head — Jaroslav Durman *Head of Treasury* ☏ **624 710**
Exchange-Traded Derivatives
Global Head — Jaroslav Durman *Head of Treasury* ☏ **624 710**

Corporate Finance / M&A Advisory
Global Head — Anton Durana *Head of Corporate Loans* ☏ **621 394**

Settlement / Clearing
Tel: 623 306 Fax: 621 901
Head of Settlement / Clearing — Iveta Varadová ☏ **623 306**

Other Departments
Proprietary Trading — Ján Trajcik *Head, Housing Finance* ☏ **621 394**
Private Banking — Anton Durana *Head of Corporate Loans* ☏ **621 394**
Correspondent Banking — Markéta Kubiková *Head* ☏ **623 306**

Administration
Technology & Systems
 — Jozef Kaniok *Head of IT* ☏ **620 585**

Legal / In-House Counsel
 — Vladimir Hrtko *Head of Legal Department* ☏ **622 091**

Compliance
 — Helena Stepová *Head, Capital Markets* ☏ **622 674**

Public Relations
 — Jarmila Kremenová *Manager, Public Relations* ☏ **621 394**

Prvà stavebná sporitel'na as — Head Office
Bajkalska 30, 820 05 Bratislava
PO Box 48, Bratislava
Tel: (7) 523 1111 **Fax:** (7) 521 5082 **Email:** webmaster@pss.sk
Website: www.pss.sk

Senior Executive Officers
Chairman of the Board — Ján Roland Burger
Others (Senior Executives)
 — Herbert G Pfeiffer *Member of the Board*
 — Wolfgang Riemann *Member of the Board*

Slovenská Kreditná Banka AS — Head Office
Na'mestie SNP 13, 814 99 Bratislava
PO Box 97
Tel: (7) 306 5111; (7) 306 5400 **Fax:** (7) 321 233; (7) 321 021 **Telex:** 92735 SKB SK **Swift:** SLKB SK BA

Senior Executive Officers
Chairman & President — Norbert Tenczer
Chief Executive Officer — Roman Hascik *VP, Marketing & Strategy Division* ☏ **306 5126**
Financial Director — Emil Burák ☏ **306 5225** 🖷 **323 447**
Treasurer — Ján Szalay *Vice President* ☏ **306 5223** 🖷 **323 447**
Head of Administration — Katarína Luknárová ☏ **306 5417**
International Division — Viliam Pešta *Director, Banking Services Division* ☏ **306 5508** 🖷 **362 691**

1366 Euromoney Directory 1999

www.euromoneydirectory.com SLOVAK REPUBLIC (+421)

Debt Capital Markets / Fixed Income
Head of Debt Capital Markets Ladislav Jakab ☎ 306 5323

Fixed-Income Repo
Head of Repo Ladislav Jakab ☎ 306 5323

Equity Capital Markets
Head of Equity Capital Markets Jan Szalay *Vice President* ☎ 306 5223 F 323 447

Equity Repo / Securities Lending
Head Ladislav Jakab ☎ 306 5323

Money Markets
Head of Money Markets Ladislav Jakab ☎ 306 5323

Foreign Exchange
Head of Foreign Exchange Ladislav Jakab ☎ 306 5323

Corporate Finance / M&A Advisory
Global Head Martha Jankovicová *Global Head* ☎ 306 5121 F 368 548

Other Departments
Chief Credit Officer Sylvie Puskásová *Director, Loans Administration Division* ☎ 306 5409 F 323 447
Private Banking Martha Jankovicová *Global Head* ☎ 306 5121 F 368 548
Correspondent Banking Jana Tesarová ☎ 306 5503 F 362 691

Administration
Head of Administration Katarína Luknárová *Head of Administration* ☎ 306 5417
Head of Marketing Marian Pucek ☎ 306 5227 F 321 021

Technology & Systems
Branislav Sábriš ☎ 306 5208 F 362 692

Legal / In-House Counsel
Karol Kocsis ☎ 306 5407

Public Relations
Marian Pucek ☎ 306 5227 F 321 021

Accounts / Audit
Zuzana Glogeiová ☎ 306 5404

Slovenská Sporitel'na AS
Head Office

Na'mestie SNP 23, 974 01 Banská Bystrica
Tel: (88) 432 5111; (88) 432 5638 **Fax:** (88) 432 5512; (88) 432 5513 **Swift:** SLSP SK BX **Email:** postmaster@slsp.sk
Reuters: SBVR Telerate: 39634
Reuters: SVBS
Website: www.slsp.sk

Senior Executive Officers
Chairman of the Board & President Ivan Kino ☎ 432 5602
Treasurer Ivan Benda *General Director* ☎ (7) 520 6588
Director, President's Office Roman Polakovic ☎ 432 5602
International Division Albin Mraz *Director, Financial Institutions* ☎ (7) 520 6580

General-Investment
Head of Investment Jozef Švenk *Director, Investment Banking* ☎ (7) 520 6583

Foreign Exchange
Head of Foreign Exchange Anna Glasova ☎ (7) 520 6665

Société Générale
Representative Office

Spitálska 2, PO Box 150, 814 99 Bratislava
PO Box 278, Bratislava
Tel: (7) 361 071; (7) 366 461 **Fax:** (7) 366 462

Senior Executive Officers
Representative Viera Svecová

SLOVAK REPUBLIC (+421) www.euromoneydirectory.com

Tatra Banka AS
Head Office

Vajahskéno nábrezie 5, 810 11 Bratislava
PO Box 50, 810 11 Bratislava
Tel: (7) 5931 6111 Fax: (7) 324 760 Telex: 92644 TATR SK Swift: TATR SK BX
Website: www.tatrabanka.sk

Senior Executive Officers
Chairman of the Board of Directors & GM — Rainer Franz ☎ **431 6202**
Deputy Chairman of the Board of Directors & DGM — Miroslav Ulicny ☎ **431 6204**

Others (Senior Executives)
Member of the Board of Directors — Philippe M Moreels ☎ **431 6232**
Igor Vida ☎ **431 6370**
Procurist — Ivan Sramko ☎ **431 6947**

General-Investment
Head of Investment — Vladimir Jurik *Head of Institutional Client Sales Department* ☎ **431 6440**
Miroslav Mlynar *Head of Capital Markets Products Department* ☎ **431 7215**
Michal Kustra *Head of Research* ☎ **431 6243**

General - Treasury
Head of Treasury — Jozef Bozek ☎ **431 6373**

Relationship Manager
Financial Institutions Department — Maria Markusova *Head* ☎ **533 4369**
Stefania Rakovska *Deputy Head* ☎ **533 4369**
SWIFT & Telex Keys Officer — Michaela Turcanova ☎ **533 4369**
Bank Analyst — Adriana Beladicova ☎ **533 4369**

Corporate Finance / M&A Advisory
Department: Corporate Banking Division

Other (Corporate Finance)
Corporate Banking — Christian Masser *Head of Corporate Banking Division* ☎ **431 6260**
Corporate Finance Department I — Zuzana Kostialova *Head* ☎ **431 6504**
Corporate Finance Department II — Anton Slavkovsky *Head* ☎ **431 6276**
Project Finance — Marcel Kascak *Head* ☎ **431 6274**
Special Products — Dusan Krizko *Head* ☎ **431 6278**
Corporate & Financial Analysis — Lubica Cakova ☎ **431 6406**
International Finance Department — Monika Molnarova *Head* ☎ **533 0098**
Credit Administration & Control — Jaroslav Packa ☎ **431 6263**

Settlement / Clearing
Head of Settlement / Clearing — Natalia Major *Head of Settlements* ☎ **431 6326**
Electronic Banking — Marcela Grausova ☎ **431 6293**

Other (Settlement & Clearing)
Foreign Payments — Marcela Grausova ☎ **431 6293**
Domestic Payments — Andrea Strasiftakova ☎ **431 6310**

Other Departments
Chief Credit Officer — Jaroslav Packa ☎ **431 6263**

Administration
Head of Marketing — Ivan Bednar ☎ **431 6610**

Technology & Systems
Pavel Karel *Head, EDP* ☎ **431 6700**

Legal / In-House Counsel
Legal Department — Lubica Adamcova *Head* ☎ **533 5931**

Public Relations
Adela Laktisova *Head* ☎ **431 6608**

Accounts / Audit
Accounting Division — Maria Paldanova *Director* ☎ **431 6900**

Vseobecná Úverová Banka AS
Head Office

Mlynské Nivy 1, 82005 Bratislava
Tel: (7) 5055 2477; (7) 5055 1111 Fax: (7) 5556 6677; (7) 5556 6656 Swift: SUBA SK BX Reuters: VUBB

Senior Executive Officers
Chairman of the Board & President — Ján Gabriel ☎ **5055 2101**
Financial Director — Dusan Paulík *Member of the Board, VP, GM* ☎ **5055 2300**
Treasurer — Jozef Paměticky *Member of the Board, VP, GM* ☎ **5055 2200**
International Division — Jozef Gális *General Manager, International Banking*

1368 Euromoney Directory 1999

www.euromoneydirectory.com   SLOVAK REPUBLIC (+421)

Others (Senior Executives)
Investment Banking Division   Lubos Vrazda *General Manager* ☏ **5441 0529**
Strategic Planning & Liquidity Department Frantisek Szikhart *General Manager*
Bank Logistics Division   Ludovít Hudek *Member of the Board, VP, GM* ☏ **5055 2500**
General-Lending (DCM, SL)
Head of Corporate Banking   Frantisek Palic *Member of the Board, VP, GM* ☏ **5055 2400**
General-Investment
Head of Investment   Frantisek Palic *Member of the Board, VP, GM* ☏ **5055 2400**

Debt Capital Markets / Fixed Income
Department: Investment Banking Division
Tel: 5055 2450 **Fax:** 5441 0583
Global Head   Înbos Vrazda *General Manager*
Domestic Government Bonds
Head of Sales   Mr Vavrus
Head of Trading   Frantisek Kurucz *Head of Trading* ☏ **5055 2473** F **5556 6678**
Head of Research   Marian Matusovic ☏ **5055 2292**
Non-Domestic Government Bonds
CZK   Stanislav Figlár *Dealer* ☏ **5055 2474**
Eurobonds
Trading (Sovereigns); Trading (Corporates) Silvia Abelovská *Portfolio Manager* ☏ **5055 2295**
Private Placements
Head of Origination   Juraj Lazový *Director* ☏ **5055 2470**
Head of Sales   Mr Vavrus
                                           Juraj Lazový *Director* ☏ **5055 2470**
Asset-Backed Securities / Securitization
Global Head   Zita Zemková *Director* ☏ **5055 2480**
Regional Head   Juraj Lazový *Director* ☏ **5055 2470**
Mortgage-Backed Securities
Global Head   Sevcik
Head of Trading   Judita Bischofová *Deputy General Manager* ☏ **5441 0559**
Fixed-Income Repo
Head of Repo   Betrik
Fixed-Income Research
Analyst   Peter Senk ☏ **5055 2293**

Equity Capital Markets
Department: Investment Banking Division
Tel: 5055 2450 **Fax:** 5441 0583
Global Head   Lubos Vrazda *General Manager* ☏ **5441 0529**
Domestic Equities
Head of Origination   Zita Zemková *Director* ☏ **5055 2480**
Head of Origination; Head of Syndication   Juraj Lazový *Director* ☏ **5055 2470**
Head of Sales   Mr Vavrus
Head of Trading   Frantisek Kurucz *Head of Trading* ☏ **5055 2473** F **5556 6678**
Head of Research   Marian Matusovic ☏ **5055 2292**
Convertibles / Equity-Linked
Head of Origination   Zita Zemková *Director* ☏ **5055 2480**
Head of Syndication   Juraj Lazový *Director* ☏ **5055 2470**
Head of Sales   Mr Vavrus
Head of Trading   Frantisek Kurucz *Head of Trading* ☏ **5055 2473** F **5556 6678**
Head of Research   Marian Matusovic ☏ **5055 2292**
Equity Repo / Securities Lending
Marketing   Mr Vavrus
Head of Trading   Frantisek Kurucz *Head of Trading* ☏ **5055 2473** F **5556 6678**

Syndicated Lending
Department: International Banking Division
Tel: 5955 8100 **Fax:** 5441 7914
Global Head   Juraj Baxa *Director* ☏ **5055 8181**
Head of Syndication   Tibor Hodosy *Manager* ☏ **5955 8233**
                                           Jaroslav Jakuk *Manager* ☏ **5955 8240**

Loan-Related Activities
Trade Finance; Project Finance; Structured Lukác Cervenák *Director* ☏ **5441 7320**
Trade Finance
Department: Corporate Banking Division Domestic Market
Tel: 5055 2400/1 **Fax:** 5441 0598
Global Head   Dana Hlozníková *Director* ☏ **5055 2560**
Regional Head of Syndication   Beata Hrbácková *Head* ☏ **5055 2466**
Head of Credit Committee   Vaskovis

SLOVAK REPUBLIC (+421)

www.euromoneydirectory.com

Vseobecná Úverová Banka AS (cont)

Loan-Related Activities
Trade Finance — Dana Hlozníková *Director* ☏ 5055 2560

Money Markets
Department: Strategic Planning & Liquidity Division
Tel: 5055 2210 Fax: 5441 0584
Global Head — Frantisek Szikhart *General Manager*

Domestic Commercial Paper
Head of Trading — Frantisek Kurucz *Head of Trading* ☏ 5055 2473 ✉ 5556 6678

Foreign Exchange
Department: Strategic Planning and Liquidity Division
Tel: 5055 2240 Fax: 5441 0581
Global Head — Frantisek Szikhart *General Manager*
Head of Trading — Paksi

FX Traders / Sales People
Customer Dealer — Jozefina Juríková ☏ 5055 2527
Mariana Hubíková *Chief Dealer* ☏ 5055 2212

Risk Management
Department: Strategic Planning and Liquidity Division
Tel: 5055 2240 Fax: 5441 0581
Global Head — Pavol Ralbovský *Risk Manager* ☏ 5055 2533

Foreign Exchange Derivatives / Risk Management
Cross-Currency Swaps, Sales / Marketing — Mariana Hubíková *Chief Dealer* ☏ 5055 2212
Cross-Currency Swaps, Trading — Elena Hindická *Dealer* ☏ 5055 2526

OTC Equity Derivatives
Sales — Mr Vavrus
Trading — Frantisek Kurucz *Head of Trading* ☏ 5055 2473 ✉ 5556 6678

Corporate Finance / M&A Advisory
Department: Investment Banking Division
Tel: 5055 2450 Fax: 5441 0583
Global Head — Lubos Vrazda *General Manager*
Bozena Janaková *Head* ☏ 5055 2279
Zita Zemková *Director* ☏ 5055 2480

Settlement / Clearing
Department: Strategic Planning and Liquidity Division
Tel: 5055 2240 Fax: 5441 0581
Equity Settlement; Fixed-Income Settlement; Derivatives Settlement — Mária Sisková *Head* ☏ 5055 2478
Foreign Exchange Settlement — Mária Pavlíková *Head* ☏ 5055 2529

SLOVENIA (+386)

Bank of Slovenia — Central Bank

Slovenska 35, SLO-1505, Ljubljana
Tel: (61) 171 9000 Fax: (61) 215 516 Telex: 31214 BS LJB SI Swift: BSLJ SI 2X

Senior Executive Officers
Governor — France Arhar

Administration

Public Relations
Marjeta Sketa *Head, Governor's Office* ☏ 171 9103 ✉ marjeta.sketa@bsi.si

Abanka dd Ljubljana — Head Office

Slovenska 58, SLO-1000, Ljubljana
PO Box 1517, Ljubljana
Tel: (61) 171 8100 Fax: (61) 132 5165; (61) 132 9322 Telex: 31228 ABANKA SI Swift: ABAN SI 2X
Email: info@abanka.si Reuters: ABAS
Website: www.abanka.si

Senior Executive Officers
Chairman, Supervisory Board
President & Chief Executive Officer — Branko Drobnak
Aljoša Tomaz ☏ 133 7260

1370 Euromoney Directory 1999

SLOVENIA (+386)

Senior Executive Officers (cont)
Financial Director — Bogomir Kos *Deputy President & CEO* ☎ **133 4257**
Chief Operating Officer — Vito Verstovsek *Deputy President & CEO* ☎ **133 4086**
Treasurer — Majda Klemencic *General Manager, Treasury* ☎ **302 075**
Secretariat Head — Mira Babic ☎ **171 8138**
International Division — Anica Vehovar-Znidaršic *Executive Director* ☎ **131 2092**

Others (Senior Executives)
Managaement Services — Lidija Simenko-Ozura *Executive Director* ☎ **132 5216**
Finance — Nada Mertik *Executive Director* ☎ **132 9026**
Albin Hojnik *Chief Executive Officer, Branch Network* ☎ **(62) 27157**
Beno Bajda *Head, Koper Subsidiary* ☎ **(66) 38010**

General-Lending (DCM, SL)
Head of Corporate Banking — Vanja Jeraj Markoja ☎ **132 5159**

General-Investment
Head of Investment — Vera Dolinar *General Manager* ☎ **300 1530**

Debt Capital Markets / Fixed Income
Department: ABH (Abanka's Brokerage House)
Slovenska 50, Ljubljana
Tel: +386 (61) 133 3121 **Fax:** +386 (61) 310 985
Global Head — Vera Dolinar *General Manager* ☎ **300 1530**

Eurobonds
Head of Trading — Suzana Lenarcic *Head of Trading* ☎ **171 8213**
Department: ABH (Abanka Brokerage House)
Tel: 300 1500 **Fax:** 310 985
Head of Fixed Income — Mateja Gubanec ☎ **300 1520**
Head of Fixed Income Sales; Head of Fixed Income Trading — Tomislav Apollonio ☎ **300 1522**

Government Bonds
Head of Sales; Head of Trading — Tomislav Apollonio ☎ **300 1522**

Eurobonds
Head of Trading — Tina Rovsek *Head of Trading* ☎ **171 8213**

Equity Capital Markets
Department: ABH (Abanka's Brokerage House)
Slovenska 50, Ljubljana
Tel: +386 (61) 133 3121 **Fax:** +386 (61) 310 985
Global Head — Vera Dolinar *General Manager* ☎ **300 1530**

Domestic Equities
Head of Sales — Vera Dolinar *General Manager* ☎ **300 1530**
Department: ABH
Tel: 300 1500 **Fax:** 310 985
Head of Equity Capital Markets — Mateja Gubanec ☎ **300 1520**
Head of Sales; Head of Trading — Andrej Obed *Head* ☎ **300 1524**

Domestic Equities
Head of Sales; Head of Trading — Andrej Obed *Head* ☎ **300 1524**

Equity Research
Head of Equity Research — Tadej Tufek ☎ **300 1540**

Convertibles / Equity-Linked
Head of Sales; Head of Trading — Mateja Gubanec ☎ **300 1520**

Syndicated Lending
Head of Syndication — Marko Flisek *General Manager, International Interbank Relations* ☎ **302 473**

Money Markets
Tel: 133 4257 **Fax:** 302 430
Global Head — Bogomir Kos *Deputy President & CEO* ☎ **133 4257**
Regional Head — Majda Klemencic *General Manager, Treasury* ☎ **302 075**
Country Head — Suzana Lenarcic *Head of Trading* ☎ **171 8213**

Domestic Commercial Paper
Head of Sales; Head of Trading — Tomislav Apollonio ☎ **300 1522**

Wholesale Deposits
Marketing — Bogomir Kos *Deputy President & CEO* ☎ **133 4257**
Head of Sales — Majda Klemencic *General Manager, Treasury* ☎ **302 075**

Foreign Exchange
Tel: 133 4257 **Fax:** 302 430
Global Head — Bogomir Kos *Deputy President & CEO* ☎ **133 4257**
Regional Head — Majda Klemencic *General Manager, Treasury* ☎ **302 075**
Head of Trading — Suzana Lenarcic *Head of Trading* ☎ **171 8213**

SLOVENIA (+386)

www.euromoneydirectory.com

Abanka dd Ljubljana (cont)
FX Traders / Sales People
Tina Rovsek *Head of Trading* ☏ 171 8213
Klemen Ahac *FX & Money Market* ☏ 171 8203

Risk Management
Head of Risk Management
Vida Krzan *Manager, Strategic Planning and Risk Management* ☏ 133 4257

Foreign Exchange Derivatives / Risk Management
Cross-Currency Swaps, Sales / Marketing
Majda Klemencic *General Manager, Treasury* ☏ 302 075

Corporate Finance / M&A Advisory
Head of Corporate Finance
Milena Zrnec ☏ 171 8458

Settlement / Clearing
Head of Settlement / Clearing
Vera Dolinar *General Manager* ☏ 300 1530
Operations
Desanka Gersak *General Manager, Int'l Operations & Documentary Bu* ☏ 302 330

Other Departments
Correspondent Banking
Marco Flisek *General Manager, International Interbank Relations* ☏ 302 473

Administration
Technology & Systems
Simona Kogovšek *Manager, Information Technology* ☏ 302 411

Legal / In-House Counsel
Tomaz Marincek *Manager, Legal* ☏ 132 5216

Public Relations
Mira Babic *Secretariat Head* ☏ 171 8138

Accounts / Audit
Boris Sesek *Manager Internal Audit* ☏ 132 9014

Banka Celje dd   Head Office

Vodnikova 2, SLO-3000, Celje
PO Box 431, Celje
Tel: (63) 431 000 **Fax:** (63) 483 510 **Telex:** 36537 BA CE SI **Swift:** SBCE SI 2X **Email:** info@banka.-celje.si
Erna Vrabic **Email:** erna.vrabic@banka-celje.si
Website: www.banka-celje.si

Senior Executive Officers
Department: Board of Directors
Chairman — Boris Završnik
Deputy Chairman — Zdravilišče Atomske Toplice
Deputy Chairman — Tone Turnšek
Financial Director — Viktoria Svet
International Division — Erna Vrabic *General Manager* ☏ 431 309 ℻ 442 039
✉ erna.vrabic@banka-celje.si

Others (Senior Executives)
Pivovarna Laško
Stantislava Cesenj
Vekoslav Marzidošek
Ivan Mirnik
Zavaravalnica Triglav
Alenka Novak
Hmezad Tovarna Krmil
Karla Kajba
Rudi Cizej
Brigita Hrncic

General - Treasury
Head of Treasury
Andreja Mackovšek *Head* ☏ 431 308 ℻ 442 039

Department: Supervisory Board
Chairman — Angela Decman
Deputy Chairman — Marina Sencar-Boric
Deputy Chairman — Vili Brence
Treasurer — Bertold Hartman
Managing Director — Niko Kac
Assistant Managing Director — Dušan Drofenik
Assistant Managing Director — Viktorija Svet

1372 Euromoney Directory 1999

SLOVENIA (+386)

Supervisory Board (cont)
Deputy Managing Director — Miloš Pešec
Others (Senior Executives)
International Banking — Erna Vrabic *General Manager* ☎ 431 309 ℱ 442 039
✉ erna.vrabic@banka-celje.si

General-Lending (DCM, SL)
Head of Corporate Banking — Slavko Mezner

Syndicated Lending
Other (Syndicated Lending)
Credit Analysis — Cveta Urleb Kovacic
Credit & Guarantee Dept — Andreja Mackovšek *Head* ☎ 431 308 ℱ 442 039
Nataša Hostnik *Senior Officer* ☎ 431 307 ℱ 442 039
Credit & Loan Dept — Davorin Leskovar *Chief Dealer* ☎ 431 337 ℱ 442 039
✉ davorin.leskovar@banka-celje.si

Settlement / Clearing
Other — Mihaela Planinšek *Head of International Payments* ☎ 431 311 ℱ 442 039
Breda Senicar *Assistant Head, International Payments* ☎ 431 314 ℱ 483 504
Stanislava Krajnc *Officer, International Payments* ☎ 431 314 ℱ 483 504
Mateja Vrhovsek *Officer, International Payments* ☎ 431 315 ℱ 483 504
Aleš Ograjensek *SWIFT Operations Supervisor* ☎ 431 319 ℱ 483 504
✉ ales.ograjensek@banka-celje.si

Other Departments
Correspondent Banking — Sabina Koleša *Head* ☎ 431 338 ℱ 483 504 ✉ sabina.kolesa@banka-celje.si
Alenka Vajgl ☎ 431 323 ℱ 483 504 ✉ alenka.vajgl@banka-celje.si

Administration
Head of Marketing — Irena Muzic
Technology & Systems
Information Technology — Bojan Rucigaj
Legal / In-House Counsel
Legal — Bojan Salobir
Accounts / Audit
Internal Audit — Terezija Kac
Accounting — Ida Ratej
Other (Administration)
Non-Resident Accounts — Marija Pipan *Senior Officer* ☎ 431 312 ℱ 483 504

Banka Koper   Head Office
Pristaniška 14, SLO-6502, Koper
Tel: (66) 451 100 **Fax:** (66) 37451 **Telex:** 6634187 BA KO SI **Swift:** BAKO SI 2X **Email:** info@banka-koper.si
Website: www.banka-koper.si

Senior Executive Officers
President & Chief Executive Officer — Vojko Cok ☎ 451 470
Others (Senior Executives)
Franc Ohnjec *Executive Director*
Darjo Valentic *Executive Director*
Dušan Hocevar *Executive Director*
Tatjana Faust *Executive Division Manager*

Banka Société Générale dd
Trg republike 3, SLO-1000, Ljubljana
Tel: (61) 126 2214; (61) 126 2268 **Fax:** (61) 126 2158

Banka Vipa dd   Head Office
Kidriceva 7, SLO-5000, Nova Gorica
PO Box 52, Nova Gorica
Tel: (65) 12850; (65) 28507 **Fax:** (65) 28506; (65) 28516 **Telex:** 38107 VIPA SI **Swift:** VIPA SI 2X
Email: int@banka-vipa.si **Reuters:** VIPA

Senior Executive Officers
Managing Director — Egidij Birsa

SLOVENIA (+386)   www.euromoneydirectory.com

Banka Vipa dd (cont)
Syndicated Lending
Department: Banking Operations
Head of Trading — Zvonka Cermelj *Director*

Money Markets
Domestic Commercial Paper
Head of Sales — Jasmin Furlan *Director of Dept*

Foreign Exchange
Head of Foreign Exchange — Radovan Jereb *Director of International Division*

Other Departments
Correspondent Banking — Radovan Jereb *Director of International Division*

Administration
Technology & Systems
— Edi Cijan *Director*

Legal / In-House Counsel
— Vesna Colja *Director*

Dolenjska Banka dd   Head Office

Seidlova 3, SLO-8000, Novo Mesto
PO Box 206, Novo Mesto
Tel: (68) 316 500; (68) 321 130 **Fax:** (68) 321 019 **Telex:** 35736 DBNMSI **Swift:** DBNM SI 2X **Email:** jhj.db@eunet.sl

Senior Executive Officers
Managing Director — Franci Borsan
Deputy Managing Director — Josip Škoberne
Assistant Managing Director — Joze Jevnikar
International Division — Andrej Blazon *Assistant Managing Director*

Others (Senior Executives)
Corporate Service Division — Miroslav Doltar *Assistant Managing Director*
Accounting Division — Milena Dular *Assistant Managing Director*

Department: Management Board
President — Viktor Kozjan
Deputy President — Stanislav Plavec

Others (Senior Executives)
Milan Dragišic *Member of the Board*
Peter Gerbec *Member of the Board*
Marjan Hutar *Member of the Board*
Stanislav Hribar *Member of the Board*
Joze Pravne *Member of the Board*

Department: Supervisory Board
President — Anton Tomc

Others (Senior Executives)
Milivoj Papez *Member of the Board*
Adolf Zupan *Member of the Board*

European Bank for Reconstruction & Development
Representative Office

9th Floor, Trg Republika 3, SLO-61000, Ljubljana
Tel: (61) 126 3600 **Fax:** (61) 126 3636

Senior Executive Officers
Resident Representative — Agneta Hallman

Factor banka dd   Head Office

Zelezna C 16, PP 2626, SLO-1001, Ljubljana
Tel: (61) 131 1136; (61) 131 4380 **Fax:** (61) 132 8066; (61) 137 6044 **Telex:** 39193 FACTOR SL **Swift:** FCTB SL 2X
Website: www.factorb.sl

Senior Executive Officers
General Manager — Fabio Skopac
Deputy General Manager — Boris Pesjak
Assistant General Manager — Ciril Dragonja

www.euromoneydirectory.com   SLOVENIA (+386)

Equity Capital Markets
Department: Stock Exchange
Tel: 131 6370
Global Head   Polona Cec *Executive Director* ☏ **137 7613**

Money Markets
Department: Treasury
Tel: 173 5247
Domestic Commercial Paper
Head of Origination   Dusan Varencic ☏ **173 5247**

Foreign Exchange
Department: International Department
Tel: 137 7383 Fax: 137 6044
Global Head   Elvira Zvipey *Executive Director* ☏ **131 4404**
FX Traders / Sales People
                                 Breda Kuzelj *FX Dealer* ☏ **137 7383**
                                 Natasa Samar *FX Dealer* ☏ **173 5247**

Corporate Finance / M&A Advisory
Department: Corporate Services & Loan Department
Tel: 131 6370
Global Head   Mojca Lampret-Kricoy *Executive Director* ☏ **131 6370**

Other Departments
Correspondent Banking   Breda Kuzelj *FX Dealer* ☏ **137 7383**

Administration
Technology & Systems
                                 Bojan Kenda ☏ **173 5241**

Gorenjska banka dd Kranj

Bleiweisova Cesta 1, SLO-4000, Kranj
PO Box 147, SLO-4001, Kranj
Tel: (64) 284 0 Fax: (64) 221 503; (64) 221 718 Telex: 37108 GORBAN SI Swift: GORE SI 2X Email: info@gbkr.si

Senior Executive Officers
Chairman   Miro Pinteric
Chief Executive Officer   Zlatko Kavcic *Managing Director & Chief Operating Officer* ☏ **284 0201**
Financial Director   Tatjana Kavcic *General Manager* ☏ **284 0329**
Treasurer   Gregor Hudobivnik *General Manager* ☏ **284 0330**
International Division   Kristina Dolenc ☏ **284 0309**

General-Lending (DCM, SL)
Head of Corporate Banking   Edvard Košnjek ☏ **284 0429**

General-Investment
Head of Investment   Edvard Košnjek ☏ **284 0429**

Debt Capital Markets / Fixed Income
Fax: 22 1613
Head of Fixed Income Sales   Mira Dragonia *Manager, Investment Banking* ☏ **284 0328**

Equity Capital Markets
Fax: 22 1613
Head of Trading   Mira Dragonia *Manager, Investment Banking* ☏ **284 0328**

Domestic Equities
Head of Trading   Brane Care *Securities Broker* ☏ **384 0294**

Syndicated Lending
Fax: 22 1625
Head of Syndication   Bojan Mandic *Assistant General Manager* ☏ **284 0314**

Money Markets
Fax: 22 1613
Head of Money Markets   Meta Drinovec *Deputy General Manager, Treasury* ☏ **284 0327**

Wholesale Deposits
Head of Sales   Gorazd Marcun *Senior Officer* ☏ **284 0302**

Foreign Exchange
Head of Foreign Exchange; Head of Trading Jozica Vavpotic-Srakar ☏ **284 0414**
FX Traders / Sales People
                                 Darja Pirec *Dealer* ☏ **284 0425**

Corporate Finance / M&A Advisory
Head of Corporate Finance   Edvard Košnjek ☏ **284 0429**

SLOVENIA (+386)   www.euromoneydirectory.com

Gorenjska banka dd Kranj (cont)
Settlement / Clearing
Head of Settlement / Clearing — Gorazd Marcun *Senior Officer* ☎ 284 0302

Other Departments
Private Banking — Igor Poljšak ☎ 284 0439
Correspondent Banking — Ana Kralj *Assistant General Manager* ☎ 284 0426
Cash Management — Jozica Vavpotic-Srakar ☎ 284 0414

Administration
Head of Marketing — Bojan Likar ☎ 284 0329

Technology & Systems
Janez Prešern *General Manager* ☎ 284 0300

Legal / In-House Counsel
Chief Legal Counsellor — Senka Sifkovic-Vrbida ☎ 284 0473

Public Relations
Marija Murnik *General Manager* ☎ 284 0482

Accounts / Audit
Sonja Kerec *General Manager* ☎ 284 0465

Other (Administration)
Personnel — Marija Murnik *General Manager* ☎ 284 0482

Mariborska Borznoposredniska

Alternative trading name: MBH d.o.o.
Vita Kraigherja 5, SLO-2000, Maribor
Tel: (62) 229 2081; (62) 229 2328 **Fax:** (62) 229 2329 **Email:** mbht@si@nkbm.si

Senior Executive Officers
Executive Director — Stanko Brglez ☎ 229 2335
Chief Executive Officer; Financial Director — Stanko Brglez ☎ 229 2335
Chief Operating Officer — Srecko Judar ☎ 229 2336
Company Secretary — Draga Cipot ☎ 229 2309

Debt Capital Markets / Fixed Income
Tel: 229 2081 **Fax:** 229 2329
Head of Fixed Income — Srecko Judar ☎ 229 2336
Head of Fixed Income Sales — Tomaz Ivanic ☎ 229 2385
Head of Fixed Income Trading — Gvido Jemensek ☎ 229 2328

Government Bonds
Head of Sales — Srecko Judar ☎ 229 2336
Head of Trading — Gvido Jemensek ☎ 229 2328
Head of Origination — Sasa Cernel ☎ 229 2328

Fixed-Income Research
Head of Fixed Income — Gvido Jemensek ☎ 229 2328
Head of Credit Research — Tomaz Ivanic ☎ 229 2385

Equity Capital Markets
Tel: 229 2081 **Fax:** 229 2329
Head of Equity Capital Markets — Srecko Judar ☎ 229 2336
Head of Sales — Mojca Pahor ☎ (65) 131 450
Head of Trading — Gvido Jemensek ☎ 229 2328

Domestic Equities
Head of Sales — Primoz Ladava ☎ (65) 131 450
Head of Trading — Gvido Jemensek ☎ 229 2328

Equity Research
Head of Equity Research — Tomaz Ivanic ☎ 229 2385

Convertibles / Equity-Linked
Head of Sales — Sasa Cernel ☎ 229 2328

Equity Repo / Securities Lending
Head — Draga Cipot ☎ 229 2309
Head of Trading — Marica Fras ☎ 229 2330

Syndicated Lending
Tel: 229 2081 **Fax:** 229 2329
Head of Origination — Draga Cipot ☎ 229 2309

Money Markets
Tel: 229 2081 **Fax:** 229 2329
Head of Money Markets — Dragica Ilersic ☎ 229 2344

www.euromoneydirectory.com　　　　SLOVENIA (+386)

Foreign Exchange
Tel: 229 2081 Fax: 229 2329
Head of Foreign Exchange　　　　Stanko Brglez ☎ 229 2335
Settlement / Clearing
Tel: 229 2081 Fax: 229 2329
Head of Settlement / Clearing　　　　Tatjana Zunko ☎ 229 2386
Administration
Head of Administration　　　　Draga Cipot ☎ 229 2309

Nova Kreditna Banka Maribor dd
Head Office

Alternative trading name: Nova KBM
Formerly known as: Kreditna Banka Maribor dd
Vita Kraigherja 4, SLO-2505, Maribor
Tel: (62) 229 229 Fax: (62) 224 333; (62) 224 371 Telex: 33167 Swift: KBMA SI 2X Email: info@nkbm.si
Reuters: KBMS
Website: www.nkbm.si

Senior Executive Officers
President & CEO　　　　Joze Glogovsek ☎ 229 2022
Deputy President　　　　Matjaz Kovacic ☎ 229 2027
Chief Executive Officer　　　　Joze Glogovsek *President & CEO* ☎ 229 2022
Financial Director　　　　Drago Pisek *Executive Director, Finance Management* ☎ 229 2029
Company Secretary　　　　Ervin Hlede ☎ 229 2500
International Division　　　　Irena Znidarsic *GM, FX Treasury & Financial Institutions* ☎ 229 2210
Others (Senior Executives)
　　　　Andrej Riedl *Executive Director, Accounting* ☎ 229 2705
　　　　Zoran Nemec *Executive Director, Retail Banking* ☎ 229 2025
　　　　Bojan Lovric *GM, International Division*

General-Lending (DCM, SL)
Head of Corporate Banking　　　　Manja Skernisak *General Manager, Corporate Lending* ☎ 229 2527
　　　　Alojz Jarc *Executive Director, Corporate Banking* ☎ 229 2400

Equity Capital Markets
Equity Repo / Securities Lending
Head of Prime Brokerage　　　　Stane Brglez ☎ 229 2335
Syndicated Lending
Loan-Related Activities
Trade Finance　　　　Vera Deticek-Frkovic *General Manager*
Project Finance　　　　Anita Okretic *Manager, Credit & Guarantees* ☎ 229 2530
Money Markets
Head of Money Markets　　　　Irena Znidarsic *GM, FX Treasury & Financial Institutions* ☎ 229 2210
Foreign Exchange
Country Head　　　　Janja Pusnik *Head of FX* ☎ 229 2206
Risk Management
Global Head　　　　Irena Znidarsic *GM, FX Treasury & Financial Institutions* ☎ 229 2210
Settlement / Clearing
Regional Head　　　　Vera Deticek-Frkovic *General Manager*
Asset Management
Head　　　　Veronika Korosec *General Manager, SIT Treasury* ☎ 229 2350
Other Departments
Chief Credit Officer　　　　Manja Skernisak *General Manager, Corporate Lending* ☎ 229 2527
Correspondent Banking　　　　Marko Podlipnik *Head, Correspondent Banking* ☎ 229 2284
Administration
Head of Marketing　　　　Nadja Jerman *Public Relations Officer* ☎ 229 2502
Technology & Systems
　　　　Benjamin Kravina *Manager, Data Processing* ☎ 229 2310
Legal / In-House Counsel
　　　　Bojan Zadravec *Head of Legal Department* ☎ 229 2854
Compliance
　　　　Danilo Kline *Manager, Personnel & Org.* ☎ 229 2886
Public Relations
　　　　Mija Mise-Srajlehner *Marketing* ☎ 229 2591
Accounts / Audit
　　　　Boza Lesnik-Korbar *Head, Audit* ☎ 229 2879

Euromoney Directory 1999　**1377**

SLOVENIA (+386)   www.euromoneydirectory.com

Nova Ljubljanska banka dd
Head Office

Šubiceva 2, SLO-1520, Ljubljana
Tel: (61) 125 5333 **Fax:** (61) 125 6339 **Telex:** (38661) 31256 **Swift:** LJBA SI 2X **Email:** info@n-lb.si **Reuters:** LBLJ
Cable: L-BANKA
Forex Tel: 333 2544; **Fax:** 333 2544
Website: www.n-lb.si

Senior Executive Officers
President & CEO, Managing Board   Marko Voljc
Deputy President & CEO, Managing Board   Boris Zakrajsek
Deputy President & CEO, Managing Board   Alojz Jamnik
International Division   Jurij Deticek *Exec Director, Financial Institutions & Int'l Div*

General-Lending (DCM, SL)
Head of Corporate Banking   Peter Velkavrh *GM, Investment Banking*
    Marjana Konstantin *Deputy Executive Director, Corporate Banking*

General - Treasury
Head of Treasury   Janez Saje *Executive Director, Treasury*

Relationship Manager
Financial Institutions   Doroteja Zerjal *General Manager*
Group Management   Milan Marinic *Executive Director*

Risk Management
Global Head   Janez Maksimiljan Sencar *Senior Executive*

Corporate Finance / M&A Advisory
Other (Corporate Finance)
Corporate Finance   Miran Vicic *Assistant Executive Director & General Manager*

Settlement / Clearing
Settlement (General)   Danijel Omahen *Executive Director, Support Services*

Other Departments
Economic Research   Franjo Stiblar *Chief Economist*
Debt Recovery / Restructuring   Janez Potocnik *Senior Executive, Intensive Care & Recovery*

Post Bank of Slovenia Limited
Head Office

Vita Kraigherja 5, SLO-2000, Maribor
Tel: (62) 228 800; (62) 228 8202 **Fax:** (62) 228 8203 **Email:** info@pbs.si

Senior Executive Officers
Chairman   Albin Hojnik
President   Romana Fišer
Chief Executive Officer   Viktor Lence ☏ **(61) 174 1230**
Financial Director   Tanja Lešnik
Chief Operating Officer   Natalija Tomazic ☏ **228 8222**
Company Secretary   Branka Merhar
Chief Representative   Jozica Grden ☏ **(61) 174 1231**

Debt Capital Markets / Fixed Income
Head of Fixed Income; Head of Fixed Income Sales   Natalija Tomazic ☏ **228 8222**

Government Bonds
Head of Sales; Head of Trading   Mojca Gornjak ☏ **228 8226**

Fixed-Income Repo
Head of Trading   Davorin Mejal ☏ **228 8205**

Fixed-Income Research
Head of Fixed Income   Natalija Tomazic ☏ **228 8222**
Head of Credit Research   Petra Bogadi ☏ **228 8233**

Equity Capital Markets
Tel: 228 8226
Head of Equity Capital Markets   Mojca Gornjak ☏ **228 8226**

Domestic Equities
Head of Sales   Mojca Gornjak ☏ **228 8226**

Syndicated Lending
Head of Trading   Ivica Poderzaj ☏ **(61) 174 1211**

Money Markets
Tel: 228 8222
Head of Money Markets   Natalija Tomazic ☏ **228 8222**

www.euromoneydirectory.com SLOVENIA (+386)

Risk Management
Head of Risk Management Davorin Mejal ☎ 228 8205

Fixed Income Derivatives / Risk Management
Head of Sales; Trading Boris Bobek ☎ 228 8206

Foreign Exchange Derivatives / Risk Management
Spot / Forwards Sales; Spot / Forwards Trading Boris Bobek ☎ 228 8206

OTC Equity Derivatives
Sales; Trading Mojca Gornjak ☎ 228 8226

Administration
Head of Administration Branka Merhar

Probanka dd
Head Office

Gospoka Street 23, SLO-2000, Maribor
Tel: (62) 220 500 **Fax:** (62) 224 817; (62) 225 844 **Telex:** 33245 proban si **Swift:** PROB SI 2X
Email: info@afna.probanka.si
Website: www.probanka.si

Senior Executive Officers
Chairman of the Board Peter Grujic
Managing Director Romana Pajenk ☎ 220 501
Company Secretary Danica Zizek ☎ 229 4975
International Division Tanja Murn Lah General Manager ☎ 220 530

Others (Senior Executives)
Janez Senica Assistant Managing Director ☎ 220 502

General-Lending (DCM, SL)
Head of Corporate Banking Peter Lobnik Branch Manager ☎ 220 506

Money Markets
Tel: 220 555 **Fax:** 225 844

Money Markets - General
Andrej Svejda Dealer

Foreign Exchange
Tel: 220 547 **Fax:** 220 555

FX Traders / Sales People
Andrej Svejda Dealer

Corporate Finance / M&A Advisory
Head of Corporate Finance Milana Lah ☎ 220 577

Publikum dd
Head Office

Miklosiceva 38, SLO-1000, Ljubljana
Tel: (61) 133 4114 **Fax:** (61) 133 1050 **Email:** info@publikum.si
Website: www.publikum.si

Senior Executive Officers
Chairman Zvone Taljat
President & Chief Executive Officer Dean Cendak
Financial Director Zineta Kikels

Others (Senior Executives)
Member of the Board Damjan Belic
  Janez Klobcar

Debt Capital Markets / Fixed Income
Head of Fixed Income Sales Boris Antolic
Head of Fixed Income Trading Boris Antolic

Fixed-Income Research
Head of Fixed Income Tomaz Bizjak

Equity Capital Markets
Head of Sales Boris Antolic
Head of Trading Boris Antolic

Equity Research
Head of Equity Research Tomaz Bizjak

Euromoney Directory 1999 **1379**

SLOVENIA (+386)   www.euromoneydirectory.com

SKB banka dd
Head Office

Ajdovščina 4, SLO-1000, Ljubljana
Tel: (61) 312 396 Fax: (61) 171 5757; (61) 30 2808 Telex: 39144 SKB DP SI Swift: SKBA SI 2X Email: info@skb.si
Reuters: SKBS
Website: www.skb.si

Senior Executive Officers
President of the Management Board & CEO   Ivan Nerad
Treasurer   Polona Bevc *DGM Treasury International* ☏ **171 5062**
International Division   Cvetka Selsek *Executive Director, International Banking* ☏ **302 027**

Others (Senior Executives)
Head of Trade Finance   Vlado Sodin *Adviser to Executive Committee* ☏ **319 560**
Head of Project Finance   Janez Krevs *Adviser to Executive Committee* ☏ **319 560**

General-Lending (DCM, SL)
Head of Corporate Banking   Joze Setnikar *Executive Director, Commercial Banking* ☏ **171 5014**

Debt Capital Markets / Fixed Income
Department: Investment Banking Division
Head of Debt Capital Markets   Alenka Markic *General Manager, Investment Banking* ☏ **171 5049**
Global Head   Igor Krizman *Executive Director, Capital Investments*

Domestic Government Bonds
Head of Sales   Alenka Markic *General Manager, Investment Banking* ☏ **171 5049**

Fixed-Income Repo
Head of Repo   Alenka Markic *General Manager, Investment Banking* ☏ **171 5049**

Equity Capital Markets
Global Head   Alenka Markic *General Manager, Investment Banking* ☏ **171 5049**

Domestic Equities
Head of Origination; Head of Syndication; Head   Alenka Markic *General Manager, Investment Banking* ☏ **171 5049**
of Sales; Head of Trading; Head of Research

Syndicated Lending
Global Head   Cvetka Selsek *Executive Director, International Banking* ☏ **302 027**
Regional Head   Janez Krevs *Head Foreign Department* ☏ **131 9560**
Country Head   Alesa Korencic *Senior Officer* ☏ **171 5603**

Loan-Related Activities
Trade Finance   Ida Berlocnik-Urbas *AGM, International* ☏ **131 2123**
Project Finance   Janez Krevs *Head Foreign Department* ☏ **131 9560**

Money Markets
Head of Money Markets   Polona Bevc *DGM Treasury International* ☏ **171 5062**

Domestic Commercial Paper
Head of Origination   Zeljka Beg *Head Foreign Department* ☏ **171 5061**

Money Markets - General
Trader / Sales   Dušanka Vodopivec *Money Market Dealer* ☏ **171 5913**

Foreign Exchange
Head of Foreign Exchange   Polona Bevc *DGM Treasury International* ☏ **171 5062**
Head of Trading   Bojan Merlak *Chief Dealer* ☏ **171 5914**

FX Traders / Sales People
   Tanja Popovic *Senior Dealer* ☏ **171 5912**
   Dušanka Vodopivec *Money Market Dealer* ☏ **171 5913**

Risk Management
Global Head   Joze Setnikar *Executive Director, Commercial Banking* ☏ **171 5014**

Other Currency Swap / FX Options Personnel
Trader / Sales   Igor Javorsek ☏ **171 5910**

Corporate Finance / M&A Advisory
Global Head   Joze Setnikar *Executive Director, Commercial Banking* ☏ **171 5014**

Settlement / Clearing
Regional Head   Ida Berlocnik-Urbas *AGM, International* ☏ **131 2123**

Global Custody
Head of Global Custody   Alenka Markic *General Manager, Investment Banking* ☏ **171 5049**

Asset Management
Head   Polona Bevc *DGM Treasury International* ☏ **171 5062**

Other Departments
Proprietary Trading   Polona Bevc *DGM Treasury International* ☏ **171 5062**
Private Banking   Bozo Tisel *Manager* ☏ **171 5142**
Correspondent Banking   Nevenka Lovše ☏ **312 396**
Cash Management   Polona Bevc *DGM Treasury International* ☏ **171 5062**

www.euromoneydirectory.com   SOUTH AFRICA (+27)

Administration
Head of Marketing

Milojka Aleksic *Manager* ☎ **171 5100**

Technology & Systems

Andrej Cetinski *Deputy CEO & Member of the Management Board*

Legal / In-House Counsel

Igor Zemljaric *Press Secretary* ☎ **171 5497**

Compliance

Igor Zemljaric *Press Secretary* ☎ **171 5497**

Public Relations

Milojka Aleksic *Manager* ☎ **171 5100**

Slovenska Zadruzna

Miklosiceva 4, 1000, Ljubljana
Tel: (61) 172 7100 **Fax:** (61) 217 057 **Email:** info@szkbanka.si
Website: www.szbanka.si

Senior Executive Officers
Chairman
Financial Director
International Division

Milan Knezevic
Robert Sega *Executive Manager*
Maria Jordan

SOLOMON ISLANDS (+677)

Central Bank of Solomon Islands   🏛 Central Bank

PO Box 634, Honiara
Tel: 21791 **Fax:** 23513 **Telex:** 42320

Senior Executive Officers
Governor
Deputy Governor
Manager, Corporate Services

Rick Houo
John Kaitu
Jerry Pitasoda

Others (Senior Executives)
Chief Cashier
Head, Bank Licensing; Head, Banking Supervision
Head, Economics & Statistics
Head, Public Debt
Head, Reserves Management

Raynick Aquila *Manager, Currency & Banking Operations*
Katalulu Maepio *Manager, Banking Services*

Denton Rarawa *Manager, Economics*
Raynick Aquila *Manager, Currency & Banking Operations*
Gane Simbe *Manager*

Foreign Exchange
Head of Foreign Exchange

Gane Simbe *Manager*

Administration
Head of Administration

Jerry Pitasoda *Manager, Corporate Services*

Technology & Systems

Anthony Ghona *Manager*

Public Relations

Jerry Pitasoda *Manager, Corporate Services*

Accounts / Audit
Head, Accountancy

Rodney Ivupitu *Accountant*

SOUTH AFRICA (+27)

South African Reserve Bank   🏛 Central Bank

370 Church Street, Pretoria 0002
PO Box 427, Pretoria 0001
Tel: (12) 313 3911 **Fax:** (12) 313 3197 **Telex:** 322136/7 **Cable:** RESBANK

Senior Executive Officers
Governor
Deputy Governor

C L Stals
C J de Swardt

SOUTH AFRICA (+27)　　　　www.euromoneydirectory.com

South African Reserve Bank (cont)
Senior Executive Officers (cont)
Deputy Governor　　　　　　　　T T Thahane
Deputy Governor　　　　　　　　J H Cross
Secretary　　　　　　　　　　　J J Rossouw

ABSA Bank Limited　　　　　　　　　　　　　　　　　　Head Office

3rd Floor, ABSA Towers East, 170 Main Street, Johannesburg 2001
PO Box 260596, Johannesburg 2000
Tel: (11) 350 4000 **Fax:** (11) 350 4928 **Swift:** ABSA ZA JJ
Website: www.absa.co.za

Senior Executive Officers
Chairman　　　　　　　　　　　Danie Cronje ☎ **350 4337**
Group Managing Director　　　　Nallie Bosman ☎ **350 6855**
Group General Manager　　　　　Friedel Meisenholl ☎ **350 3870**
Others (Senior Executives)
ABSA Direct　　　　　　　　　　Ben Solomon ☎ **350 7010**
ABSA Offshore　　　　　　　　　G G Ciucci
　　　　　　　　　　　　　　　　Frans Du Toit *Group Executive Director* ☎ **350 4211**

Risk Management
Head of Risk Management　　　　Friedel Meisenholl *Group General Manager* ☎ **350 3870**
Settlement / Clearing
Operations　　　　　　　　　　　Eugene Smith ☎ **350 5601**
Other Departments
Private Banking　　　　　　　　A S Swart ☎ **480 5000**
Economic Research　　　　　　　Hans Falkena *Chief Economist* ☎ **330 4721**
Administration
Technology & Systems
Business Systems Division　　　 Maarten Venter ☎ **350 4249**
Corporate Communications
Group Communications & Corporate Affairs　　Thys McLean *Deputy Operating Executive* ☎ **350 6834**

Bank of America NT & SA　　　　　　　　　　　　　　Representative Office

2 Merchant Place, 1 Fredman Drive, Sandown, Benmore 2010
PO Box 653144, Benmore
Tel: (11) 784 9292 **Fax:** (11) 784 8180

Senior Executive Officers
Chief Representative　　　　　　John E Osborne ✉ john.e.osborne@bankamerica.com
Others (Senior Executives)
Credit Products　　　　　　　　Roger Keighley *Manager*
Administration
Head of Administration　　　　　Amanda Louise Renwick *Office Manager*
　　　　　　　　　　　　　　　　✉ amanda.renwick@bankamerica.com

Bank of Taiwan (South Africa) Limited　　　　　　　Subsidiary Company

11 Cradock Avenue, Rosebank, Johannesburg 2196
PO Box 1999, Parklands, Johannesburg 2121
Tel: (11) 880 8008 **Fax:** (11) 477 1868 **Telex:** 420092 **Swift:** BKTW ZA JJ **Email:** botsa@global.co.za

Senior Executive Officers
Chairman　　　　　　　　　　　Chang-Hua Yeh
Managing Director　　　　　　　Louis Y H Hu
General Manager　　　　　　　　Kevin H H Hsieh
Company Secretary　　　　　　　Vincent Blaauw
International Division　　　　　Kevin H H Hsieh *General Manager*
Others (Senior Executives)
　　　　　　　　　　　　　　　　Wade W Y Sheu *IT Manager*
　　　　　　　　　　　　　　　　Forest H W Liao *Treasury Manager & Forex Manager*
　　　　　　　　　　　　　　　　Raymond J L Sun *Accounting Manager*

www.euromoneydirectory.com SOUTH AFRICA (+27)

Debt Capital Markets / Fixed Income
Domestic Government Bonds
Head of Trading
Head of Syndication
Forest H W Liao *Treasury Manager & Forex Manager*
Kevin H H Hsieh
Syndicated Lending
Head of Syndication
Kevin H H Hsieh *Executive Director* ☏ **880 8008**
Money Markets
Head of Money Markets
Forest H W Liao *Treasury Manager & Forex Manager*
Foreign Exchange
Head of Foreign Exchange
Forest H W Liao *Treasury Manager & Forex Manager*
FX Traders / Sales People
Anna C H Chen *Supervisor*
Risk Management
Head of Risk Management
Kevin H H Hsieh *Executive Director* ☏ **880 8008**
Settlement / Clearing
Head of Settlement / Clearing
Forest H W Liao *Treasury Manager & Forex Manager*
Other Departments
Correspondent Banking
Forest H W Liao *Treasury Manager & Forex Manager*
Administration
Head of Administration
Business Development
Raymond J L Sun *Accounting Manager*
Vincent Blaauw
Technology & Systems
Wade W Y Sheu *IT Manager*

Banque Nationale de Paris
Representative Office

13 Fredman Drive, 6th Floor, Norwich Life Towers, Saridton, Benmore 2010
Tel: (11) 884 8032; (11) 884 8033 **Fax:** (11) 884 4574 **Email:** bnp2@pixie.co.za

Senior Executive Officers
Regional Executive
Gérard Raffaud

Others (Senior Executives)
Commodities
Eddy Verbruggen *Vice President*

Barclays Bank of South Africa Limited
Full Branch Office

261 Oxford Road, Illovo, Johannesburg 2196
PO Box 1542, Saxonwold 2132, Johannesburg
Tel: (11) 441 6300 **Fax:** (11) 447 4837 **Telex:** 421305

Senior Executive Officers
Chief Executive Officer
Financial Director
Treasurer
Philip Howell
Christina Tay ☏ **441 6349**
Tracey Vardy *Chief Dealer* ☏ **441 6336**

Others (Senior Executives)
Senior Corporate Manager
Stephen Clarke

BHF-BANK
Representative Office

1st Floor Cradock Heights, 21 Cradock Avenue, Rosebank, Johannesburg 2196
PO Box 1933, Saxonwood, Johannesburg 2132
Tel: (11) 447 6748 **Fax:** (11) 442 4386

Senior Executive Officers
Representative
R Alexander Camerer

Cape of Good Hope Bank Limited
Head Office

117 St George's Mall, Cape Town 8000
PO Box 2125, Cape Town 8000
Tel: (21) 480 5000; (21) 480 5050 **Fax:** (21) 424 2710; (21) 426 1453 **Email:** hfoat@coghb.co.za

Senior Executive Officers
Chairman
Chief Executive Officer
Richard Laubscher ☏ **(11) 630 7111**
Michael Thompson *Managing Director & Chief Executive* ☏ **480 5050**

SOUTH AFRICA (+27)   www.euromoneydirectory.com

Cape of Good Hope Bank Limited (cont)
Senior Executive Officers (cont)
Financial Director   Shirley Ridler *Chief Accountant* ☎ **480 5750**
General Manager, Operations   Angus Thompson ☎ **480 5090**
Company Secretary   Penny Steeds ☎ **480 5990**

Others (Senior Executives)
Asset Management   Chris Vietri *General Manager* ☎ **480 5060**
Funding   Pieter Raubenheimer *General Manager* ☎ **480 5080**
Retail Banking   Michael Walters *Assistant General Manager* ☎ **480 5500**
Instalment Credit   Ernie Van Heerden *Assistant General Manager* ☎ **480 5550**
Strategic Alignment   Peter Smith *Assistant General Manager* ☎ **480 5950**
Commercial Property Lending & Development Casey Vid Vlucat *Assistant General Manager* ☎ **480 5450**

General-Investment
Head of Investment   J C Vid Westhuizen ☎ **480 5652**

General - Treasury
Head of Treasury   Lex Kriel *Assistant General Manager, Treasury* ☎ **480 5520**

Money Markets
Tel: 480 5531 Fax: 423 6270
Head of Money Markets   Lex Kriel *Assistant General Manager, Treasury* ☎ **480 5520**

Wholesale Deposits
Marketing   Bradley Anthony *Senior Dealer* ☎ **480 5532**

Foreign Exchange
Tel: 480 5130 Fax: 423 1386
Head of Foreign Exchange   Fay De Waal ☎ **480 5130**

Risk Management
Tel: 480 5995 Fax: 424 2710
Head of Risk Management   Chris Vietri *General Manager* ☎ **480 5060**

Corporate Finance / M&A Advisory
Head of Corporate Finance   J C Vid Westhuizen ☎ **480 5652**

Settlement / Clearing
Tel: 480 5511 Fax: 423 6270
Head of Settlement / Clearing   Debbie Olivier ☎ **480 5511**

Asset Management
Head   Chris Vietri *General Manager* ☎ **480 5060**

Other Departments
Chief Credit Officer   Richard Edwards ☎ **480 5970**

Administration
Head of Administration   Thandi Kwane *Support Manager* ☎ **480 5770**
Business Development   Rojie Kisten Smith ☎ **480 5960**
Head of Marketing   Peter Smith *Assistant General Manager* ☎ **480 5950**

Technology & Systems
                                           Sally Fisher *Assistant General Manager - IT* ☎ **480 5600**

Legal / In-House Counsel
                                           Gerda Duprez *Assistant General Manager* ☎ **480 3550**

Compliance
                                           Ginniy Johnson *Assistant General Manager* ☎ **480 5970**

Public Relations
                                           Ulrich Fobian *PR Manager* ☎ **480 5955**

Accounts / Audit
                                           Robert Humphreys *Accountant* ☎ **480 5760**

Cedef Capital Markets (Pty) Limited

3rd Floor Norwich Towers, 13 Fredman Drive, Sandown, Johannesburg
Tel: (11) 884 2787
Administration Tel: 305 3700; Rand Gilts Tel: 884 2787; Rand Fra's Tel: 305 3000

Senior Executive Officers
Managing Director / General Manager   David Humphreys

1384 Euromoney Directory 1999

www.euromoneydirectory.com　　　SOUTH AFRICA (+27)

The Chase Manhattan Bank
Representative Office

Formerly known as: The Chase Manhattan Overseas Corporation
PO Box 651996, Benmore 2010
Tel: (11) 444 1266 Fax: (11) 444 8989

Senior Executive Officers
Others (Senior Executives)
Senior Officer　　　　　　　　　　David Adomakoh *Senior Officer*

Commerzbank AG
Full Branch Office

5 Keyes Avenue, Rosebank, Johannesburg 2196
PO Box 860, Parklands, Johannesburg 2121
Tel: (11) 328 7600 Fax: (11) 328 7635 Telex: 485718

Senior Executive Officers
Chief Executive Officer　　　　　　Götz Hagemann *General Manager, Branch* ☎ **328 7601**
General Manager, Branch　　　　　Clive Kellow ☎ **328 7604**

Crédit Agricole Indosuez
Full Branch Office

Formerly known as: French Bank of Southern Africa Ltd
4 Ferreira Street, Johannesburg 2007
PO Box 61523, Marshalltown 2107, Gauteng
Tel: (11) 240 0400 Fax: (11) 240 0555 Swift: BSUI ZA JJ Email: caisa@icon.co.za Reuters: BIJB

Senior Executive Officers
Chief Executive Officer　　　　　　Jean Marion ☎ **240 0428**
Chief Operating Officer　　　　　　Hayley McKenna ☎ **240 0421**
Manager, Forex & Treasury　　　　Jacques-Alban Callies ☎ **240 0434**

Crédit Agricole Indosuez
Full Branch Office

Marshaltown Street, Johannesburg 2107
PO Box 61523, Johannesburg
Tel: (11) 240 0400 Fax: (11) 240 0555; (11) 240 0506 Telex: 4-82896 Swift: PSUI ZA JJ

Senior Executive Officers
Financial Director; Chief Operating Officer　Hayley McKenna
Treasurer　　　　　　　　　　　　Jackes Alban Callies
General Manager　　　　　　　　John Marion

Deutsche Bank AG
Representative Office

3rd Floor, 25 Fredman Drive, Sandton 2196
PO Box 781948, Sandton 2146
Tel: (11) 883 4812; (11) 883 4813 Fax: (11) 883 4815

Dresdner Bank AG
Representative Office

PO Box 9722, Johannesburg 2000
Tel: (11) 834 5872 Fax: (11) 838 7652

Senior Executive Officers
Representative for Southern Africa　Guenter Z Steffens

Others (Senior Executives)
　　　　　　　　　　　　　　　　Andreas Scheer *Assistant Representative*

Euromoney Directory 1999　**1385**

SOUTH AFRICA (+27)   www.euromoneydirectory.com

First National Bank of Southern Africa Limited

6th Floor, 1 First Place, Bankcity, Johannesburg 2001
PO Box 1153, Johannesburg 2000
Tel: (11) 371 2111; (11) 371 6116 **Fax:** (11) 371 2402 **Swift:** FIRN ZA JJ **Reuters:** BBJX
Cable: BANKHOUDER JOHAN
Website: www.fnb.co.za

Senior Executive Officers
Chairman   Nent Chapman
Managing Director   V W Bartlett

First National Bank of Southern Africa Limited   Head Office

3 First Place, BankCity, Johannesburg 2000
PO Box 7713, Johannesburg 2000
Tel: (11) 371 3938; (11) 371 3956 **Fax:** (11) 371 3887 **Telex:** 489592 **Swift:** FIRN ZA JJ 896
Email: renee.theron@fnbinvest.co.za
Website: www.fne.co.za

Equity Capital Markets

Equity Repo / Securities Lending
Head   Chris van den Heever *Head of Securities Lending* ☏ **371 3671**

Settlement / Clearing
Head of Settlement / Clearing   Alice Wax ☏ **371 3946**

Administration
Head of Marketing   Renee Theron ☏ **371 3942**

Firstcorp Merchant Bank Limited

6th Floor, 4 First Place, BankCity, Johannesburg 2001
PO Box 9773, Johannesburg 2000
Tel: (11) 371 8336 **Fax:** (11) 371 8350; (11) 371 8351 **Telex:** 48-7092 **Swift:** FICO ZA JJ

Senior Executive Officers
Chairman   V W Bartlett
Managing Director   A Roux

Others (Senior Executives)
                                        J A Arnott *Director*
                                        P M Jackson *Director*
                                        J B Meiring *Director*
                                        J Moses *Alternate Director*

Fleming Martin Securities Limited   Subsidiary Company

10th Floor, The Stock Exchange, 17 Diagonal Street, Johannesburg 2001
Tel: (11) 240 2400 **Fax:** (11) 838 2344

Senior Executive Officers
Chairman   Winston Floquet
Financial Director   Kevin Penwarden

Debt Capital Markets / Fixed Income

Domestic Government Bonds
Head of Sales   Colin Stewart *Head of Bond Sales* ☏ **240 2462**

Equity Capital Markets

Domestic Equities
Head of Trading   Brian D Phillips *Head of Dealing*
Head of Research   Jerome B O'Ryan *Head of Research* ☏ **240 2479**

1386   Euromoney Directory 1999

www.euromoneydirectory.com SOUTH AFRICA (+27)

Genbel Securities Limited
Head Office

3a Summit Road, Dunkeld West, Johannesburg 2196
PO Box 411420, Craighall, Johannesburg 2024
Tel: (11) 280 1000 **Fax:** (11) 280 1093 **Email:** moreinfo@gensec.com
Website: www.gensec.com

Senior Executive Officers
Chairman — Marinus Daling
Managing Director — Anton Botha ☎ 280 1066 ✉ antonb@gensec.com
Company Secretary — Liezl Byliefeldt ☎ 280 1026

Others (Senior Executives)
Wyrand Hurnan *Financial Manager* ☎ 280 1016

General-Lending (DCM, SL)
Head of Corporate Banking — Peter Cook *Executive Director* ☎ 280 1067 ✉ peterc@gensec.com

General - Treasury
Head of Treasury — Marius Ferreira *Executive Director, Banking & Treasury* ☎ 280 1068 ✉ mariusf@gensec.com
Rob McJanet ☎ 280 6802

Debt Capital Markets / Fixed Income
Head of Fixed Income — George Herman *Manager* ☎ 280 6808 ✉ georgeh@gensec.com

Asset-Backed Securities / Securitization
Global Head — Machiel Reyneke ☎ 280 6847 ✉ machielr@gensec.com
Mark Murning *Executive Director* ☎ 280 1078 ✉ markm@gensec.com

Equity Capital Markets
Head of Equity Capital Markets — Rob May *Executive Director, Equities* ☎ 280 1021 ✉ robm@gensec.com
Country Head — Steve Müller *Chief Executive Officer* ☎ 280 1044
Head of Sales — Robert Fihrer *Senior Manager* ☎ 280 1017
Head of Trading — Daron Walker ☎ 280 1011
Other — Danie Herbst *Dealer* ☎ 280 1022
Bruce Simpson *Dealer* ☎ 280 1022
Vaughn Webber *Dealer* ☎ 280 1011
Byron Cunningham-Scott *Dealer* ☎ 280 1011
Derek Saely *Dealer*

Domestic Equities
Head of Origination — Neil Gardyne *General Manager* ☎ 280 1013

Equity Research
Analyst — Gus Louw *Quantitative Analyst* ☎ 280 1033

Equity Repo / Securities Lending
Head — Alta van Loggerenberg *Dealer* ☎ 280 1022

Syndicated Lending
Other (Syndicated Lending)
Credit Analyst — Christina van der Merwe ☎ 280 1076
Juliette Bester

Money Markets
Head of Money Markets — Mike Sandler *Manager* ☎ 280 1022 ✉ mikes@gensec.com

Money Markets - General
Dealer — Caty Sacca ☎ 280 1022
Marc Menealaou ☎ 280 1022

Foreign Exchange
Head of Foreign Exchange — Greg Thomas *Manager* ☎ 280 1022 ✉ gregt@gensec.com

Risk Management
Head of Risk Management — Tony Gouveia ☎ 280 1043 ✉ tonyg@gensec.com

Fixed Income Derivatives / Risk Management
IR Swaps Sales / Marketing — George Herman *Manager* ☎ 280 6808 ✉ georgeh@gensec.com
IR Options Trading — Mark Hendrikz *Options Trader*

Other (FI Derivatives)
Interest Rate Derivatives — Pieter van der Merwe *Trader* ☎ 280 1022

OTC Equity Derivatives
Head — Mark Murning *Executive Director* ☎ 280 1078 ✉ markm@gensec.com
Tony Evans *Manager* ☎ 280 6824 ✉ tonye@gensec.com
Klaus Göbel *Manager* ☎ 280 6823
Trading — Michael Grobler *Dealer* ☎ 280 1011
Joshua Mohan *Dealer* ☎ 280 1011

Corporate Finance / M&A Advisory
Private Equity — Christoff Botha *General Manager* ☎ 280 6819

SOUTH AFRICA (+27) www.euromoneydirectory.com

Genbel Securities Limited (cont)
Asset Management
Head Johan Van Reehen *Executive Director* ☎ 280 1069 ✉ johanvr@gensec.com

Other (Asset Management)
  Dries du Toit *General Manager*

Other Departments
Economic Research Nico le Roux *Senior Analyst* ☎ 280 1024
  Chris Visser *Senior Analyst* ☎ 280 1055
  Loyiso Jiya *Economist* ☎ 280 1035

Administration
Head of Administration Nelis Bezuidenhout *Manager* ☎ 280 1019
Head of Marketing Lydia Du Plessis *Marketing Manager* ☎ 280 1080 ✉ lydiadp@gensec.com
  Audrey Erasmus *Client Liaison Officer* ☎ 280 1031

Technology & Systems
IT Manager Sabir Munshi ☎ 280 1048

Legal / In-House Counsel
Legal Advisor Francien Meyer ☎ 280 6813
  Sophia Steyn

Public Relations
  Glyn Kruger *Public Relations Officer* ☎ 280 1054

Other (Administration)
Human Resources Natalie May *Consultant*
  Hennie de Wet *Senior Manager* ☎ 280 6840
Personnel Administration Jackie van Loggerenberg *Manager* ☎ 280 6840

Gensec Bank Limited

PO Box 411420, Craighall, Johannesburg 2024
Tel: (11) 280 1022 **Fax:** (11) 280 1087 **Email:** altavl@gensec.com
Website: www.genbel.co.za

Debt Capital Markets / Fixed Income

Fixed-Income Repo
Marketing & Product Development M Murning *General Manager* ☎ 280 1078 📠 280 1085
  ✉ markm@gensec.com
Trading A van Loggerenberg *Securities Lending Trader*
  M Sandler *Manager*
  C Sacca *Securities Lending Trader*

Equity Capital Markets

Equity Repo / Securities Lending
Marketing & Product Development M Murning *General Manager* ☎ 280 1078 📠 280 1085
  ✉ markm@gensec.com

HSBC Equator Bank plc   Representative Office

1st Floor Block A Rosebank Office Park, 181-185 Jan Smuts Avenue, Parktown North, Johannesburg 2193
Tel: (11) 442 8600 **Fax:** (11) 442 2938

Senior Executive Officers
Chief Executive Officer Franklin H Kennedy
  Richard M Bouma *Executive Officer*

HypoVereinsbank   Representative Office

Formerly known as: Bayerische Vereinsbank AG
St Margaret's, 3 Rockridge Road, Parktown, Johannesburg 2193
PO Box 1483, Parklands, Johannesburg 2121
Tel: (11) 482 2022 **Fax:** (11) 482 4350

www.euromoneydirectory.com SOUTH AFRICA (+27)

ING Barings Southern Africa (Pty) Limited
Subsidiary Company

3rd Floor, 2 Merchant Place, Fredman Drive, Sandton 2146
PO Box 782080, Sandton 21446
Tel: (11) 302 3000 Fax: (11) 302 3131

Senior Executive Officers
Chief Executive Officer
Chief Operating Officer
Treasurer

Simon Hollis *Managing Director & CEO* T 302 3052
Kevin McKenna T 302 3070
Kobus Fick T 302 3393

General-Lending (DCM, SL)
Head of Corporate Banking

Lars Vriens *Director* T 302 3251

Debt Capital Markets / Fixed Income
Domestic Government Bonds
Head of Sales; Head of Trading
Head of Research

Klaus Göbel T 302 3433 F 302 3151
Dana Becker T 302 3020

Equity Capital Markets
Head of Equity Capital Markets

Johann Blersch *Director* T 302 3026

Domestic Equities
Head of Trading
Head of Research

Craig Kimber *Head of Equity Trading* T 302 3434 F 302 3151
Dana Becker *Head of Equity Research* T 302 3020 F 302 3151

Other (Domestic Equities)

Leslie Nagan *Head of Equity Risk Management* T 302 3247 F 302 3131
Klaus Göbel *Head of Equity Derivatives Sales & Trading* T 302 3433
F 302 3151

Settlement / Clearing
Head of Settlement / Clearing

Simon Krool *Assistant Director* T 302 3071

Other Departments
Chief Credit Officer

Leslie Nagan *Director* T 302 3247 F 302 3131

International Bank of Southern Africa Limited
Head Office

3rd Floor, Sunnyside Ridge Building, 32 Princess of Wales Terrace, Johannesburg 2193
PO Box 8771, Johannesburg 2000
Tel: (11) 644 3300 Fax: (11) 643 1122 Telex: 420616 Swift: IBSL ZA JJ Email: ibsaltd@iafrica.com Reuters: SFOM

Senior Executive Officers
Chairman
Financial Director
Chief Operating Officer
Treasurer
Managing Director
General Manager & Director
International Division

Hans-Heinrich Matthias
Wolfgang Meyer *Divisional Manager, Finance*
James Brent *Divisional Manager, Operations*
Rob Wade
Nigel Palmer
Stéphane Bourdel
Michael Niemann *Divisional Manager, International Finance*

Others (Senior Executives)

Hermann Brincker *Divisional Manager, Risk* E ibsaltd@iafrica.com

Relationship Manager

Johan van der Berg *Divisional Manager, Corporate Relationship Banking*

Syndicated Lending
Loan-Related Activities
Trade Finance

Peter Higgins *Divisional Manager, Trade Finance*

Other (Trade Finance)

Jonathan Mortimer *Divisional Manager, Structured Finance*

Investec Bank Limited

55 Fox Street, Johannesburg 2001
PO Box 11177, Johannesburg 2000
Tel: (11) 286 7600; (11) 838 1300 Fax: (11) 498 2699 Telex: 488381 Swift: IVES ZA JJ
Email: mvermeulen@investec.co.za Reuters: INHX
Website: www.investec.co.za

Senior Executive Officers
Chairman
Chief Executive Officer

Hugh Herman
Stephen Koseff

Euromoney Directory 1999 **1389**

SOUTH AFRICA (+27)   www.euromoneydirectory.com

Investec Bank Limited (cont)
Senior Executive Officers (cont)
Financial Director — Bradley Tapnack
Chief Operating Officer — Bernard Kantor
Debt Capital Markets / Fixed Income
Fixed-Income Repo
Head of Repo — Eric Wood *Head, Bond Trading* ☏ 286 7000 F 286 777
E ewood@investec.co.za
Trading — Nancy Myburgh *Dealer*
Sales — Michael Vermeulen *Head, Repo Trading* E mvermeulen@investec.co.za
Equity Capital Markets
Equity Repo / Securities Lending
Head — Trevor Amoils *Head of Securities Lending Activities*
E tamoils@investec.co.za
Head of Trading — Tracey Hendriks *Securities Lending*

Lawfin Financial Services (Pty) Limited   Head Office
26th Floor, Trust Bank Centre, Heerengracht, Cape Town 8001
PO Box 2300, Cape Town 8000
Tel: (21) 419 8260 **Fax:** (21) 217 419
Senior Executive Officers
Chairman — Lawrence N Miller

Mercantile Bank Limited   Head Office
Mercantile Lisbon House, 142 West Street, Sundown, Johannesburg 2196
Tel: (11) 302 0300 **Fax:** (11) 302 0700 **Telex:** 4-85076 SA **Swift:** LISA ZA JJ **Email:** feed@mercantile.co.za
Reuters: MBLJ
Website: www.mercantile.co.za

Senior Executive Officers
Chairman — Henry Vorster ☏ 884 7170
Chief Executive Officer — Derek Cohen *Managing Director* ☏ 302 0301
Financial Director — Piet Van Deventer *Executive Director* ☏ 302 0305
Chief Operating Officer — Alan Greenstein *Executive Director* ☏ 302 0401
Treasurer — Graham Lund *Executive Director* ☏ 302 0465
Group Secretary — Francisco Coelho ☏ 302 0407
International Division — Graham Lund *Executive Director* ☏ 302 0465
General-Investment
Head of Investment — Peter Du Toit *General Manager* ☏ 302 0481
Debt Capital Markets / Fixed Income
Tel: 302 0445 **Fax:** 302 0739
Head of Fixed Income Trading — Robert Eikenboom *Assistant General Manager* ☏ 302 0503
Syndicated Lending
Tel: 302 0482 **Fax:** 302 0743
Head of Trading — Estienne Du Toit *General Manager* ☏ 302 0481
Loan-Related Activities
Trade Finance — Greg Miller *Manager* ☏ 302 0462
Money Markets
Tel: 302 0445 **Fax:** 302 0739
Head of Money Markets — Robert Eikenboom *Assistant General Manager* ☏ 302 0503
Foreign Exchange
Tel: 302 0445 **Fax:** 302 0739
Head of Foreign Exchange — Craig Thompson *Chief Dealer* ☏ 302 0481
Corporate Sales — Peter Nock *Head of Corporate Dealing* ☏ 302 0501
FX Traders / Sales People
All Currencies — Craig Thompson *Chief Dealer* ☏ 302 0481
Kate Forbes *FX Dealer* ☏ 302 0501
Risk Management
Tel: 302 0300 **Fax:** 302 0700
Head of Risk Management — Malcom Brown *General Manager* ☏ 302 0339
Corporate Finance / M&A Advisory
Tel: 302 0494 **Fax:** 302 0744
Head of Corporate Finance — Peter Oosthuizen *General Manager* ☏ 302 0496

www.euromoneydirectory.com   SOUTH AFRICA (+27)

Settlement / Clearing
Tel: 302 0445 **Fax:** 302 0739
Foreign Exchange Settlement   Jill Murtagh *Assistant General Manager* ☎ **302 0464**
Asset Management
Head   Howard Rabins *General Manager* ☎ **302 0623**
Other Departments
Proprietary Trading   Mike McHardy *Assistant General Manager* ☎ **302 0474**
Chief Credit Officer   Iann Mann *Assistant General Manager* ☎ **302 0320**
Private Banking   Alan Greenstein *Executive Director* ☎ **302 0401**
Correspondent Banking   Fred Costa E Silva *Assistant General Manager* ☎ **302 0473**
Administration
Head of Marketing   Fayelizabeth Foster *Manager* ☎ **302 0408**
Technology & Systems
                                       Sean Colson *Assistant General Manager* ☎ **302 0355**
Legal / In-House Counsel
                                       Fred Schutte *Legal Advisor* ☎ **302 0322**
Public Relations
                                       Nicolene Venter *Public Relations Officer* ☎ **302 0613**
Accounts / Audit
                                       Joao Real Pereira *Executive Director* ☎ **302 0310**

Nedcor Bank   Head Office
Formerly known as: Nedcor Limited (Holding Company)
100 Main Street, Johannesburg 2001
PO Box 1144, Johannesburg 2001
Tel: (11) 630 7111 **Fax:** (11) 630 7958 **Telex:** 482765 NEDIT SA
Website: www.nedcor.co.za

Senior Executive Officers
Chairman   C F Liebenberg ☎ **630 7680**
Chief Executive Officer   R C M Laubscher ☎ **630 7690**
Financial Director   A A Routledge *Group Finance Director* ☎ **630 7568**
Chief Operating Officer   M J Leeming ☎ **630 7557**
Group Company Secretary   G S Nienaber ☎ **630 7328**
Others (Senior Executives)
Nedcor Bank (Commercial Bank)   D G Muller *Divisional Director*
Nedcor Investment Bank   I J Botha *Group Managing Director*
Cape of Good Hope Bank   M A Thompson *Managing Director*
General - Treasury
Head of Treasury   M S Parker *Executive General Manager*
Debt Capital Markets / Fixed Income
Department: Trading Room (Commercial Bank)
Head of Debt Capital Markets   Dog Haynes *Head of Trading*
Head of Fixed Income Trading   Nick Chalmers
Money Markets
Department: Trading Room (Commercial Bank)
Head of Money Markets   Dog Haynes *Head of Trading*
Money Markets - General
Trading   Bruce Stuart
Foreign Exchange
Department: Trading Room (Commercial Bank)
Head of Foreign Exchange   Dog Haynes *Head of Trading*
Head of Trading   Moss Brikman
Other Departments
Economic Research   D M Dykes *Chief Economist* ☎ **480 1048**

Nedcor Investment Bank   Full Branch Office
24 Wale Street, Cape Town 8001
Tel: (21) 488 2911 **Fax:** (21) 24 4432
Website: www.nedcor.co.za

Senior Executive Officers
General - Treasury
Head of Treasury   Stephan Rogers

SOUTH AFRICA (+27) www.euromoneydirectory.com

Nedcor Investment Bank (cont)

Equity Capital Markets
Other   Ivan Palframan

Money Markets
Department: Treasury
Tel: 488 2774
Global Head   Stephen Rogers

Money Markets - General
Treading   Saleem Gamza
                                     Adel Van Emmens

Foreign Exchange
Department: Treasury
Tel: 488 2774
Head of Foreign Exchange   Stephen Rogers
Head of Trading   Saleem Gamza
                                     Adel Van Emmens

Nedcor Investment Bank   Head Office

Formerly known as: Nedcor Limited (Holding Company)
1 Newtown Avenue, Killarndy, Johannesburg 2193
PO Box 582, Johannesburg
Tel: (11) 480 1000 **Fax:** (11) 480 1525
Website: www.nedcor.co.za

Senior Executive Officers
Managing Director   I J Botha

Debt Capital Markets / Fixed Income
Global Head   Peter Lane
Head of Fixed Income Trading   Andre Mostert ☎ **486 3939**

Equity Capital Markets
Global Head   Peter Lane
Head of Trading   Eben Mare ☎ **480 1246**

Money Markets
Global Head   Peter Lane

Money Markets - General
Trading   Chris Doyle *Trading* ☎ **480 1247**

Foreign Exchange
Global Head   Peter Lane
Head of Trading   David Gracey ☎ **486 3491**

Risk Management
Global Head   Peter Lane
Country Head   Chris Doyle *Trading* ☎ **480 1247**

NIB International   Subsidiary Company

1 Newtown Avenue, Killarney 2193
Tel: (11) 480 3838 **Fax:** (11) 480 3833

Senior Executive Officers

Others (Senior Executives)
Senior Officer   Debbie Sunasky *Marketing Manager*

Pangaea Partners Limited   Representative Office

102 William Road, Norwood, Johannesburg 2192
Tel: (11) 483 2930 **Fax:** (11) 483 2157

Senior Executive Officers
Representative   Benjamin Duchen

www.euromoneydirectory.com   SOUTH AFRICA (+27)

Rand Merchant Bank Limited
1 Merchant place, cnr Fredman Drive & Rivonia Road, Sandton, Johannesburg 2199
PO Box 786273, Sandton 2146
Tel: (11) 883 3650; (11) 883 3622 **Fax:** (11) 783 8651 **Telex:** 427796 SA **Swift:** RMBK ZA JJ

Securities Investment Bank Limited
21 Eastwold Way, corner Oxford & Eastwold Way, Saxonwold, Johannesburg 2196
PO Box 1499, Saxonwold, Johannesburg 2132
Tel: (11) 328 9200 **Fax:** (11) 486 3218; (11) 486 3219 **Telex:** 431101 SDH SA

Senior Executive Officers
Chairman   S Koseff
Financial Director   A de Net *Financial Manager*
Managing Director / General Manager   D B Gouws

Smith Borkum Hare & Co Inc   Subsidiary Company
10th Floor, 27 Diagonal Street, Johannesburg
Tel: (11) 498 6000 **Fax:** (11) 832 1967

Société Générale   Full Branch Office
2nd Floor, Societe Generale House, 30 Wellington Road, Parktown, Johannesburg 2193
Tel: (11) 488 1400 **Fax:** (11) 488 1401 **Telex:** 489818 **Swift:** SOGE ZA JJ **Reuters:** SGJX
Website: www.socgen.com

Senior Executive Officers
Chief Executive Officer   Jean-Philippe Coulier ☏ **488 1500**
Treasurer   Peter Wylie *General Manager, Treasury* ☏ **488 1530**
Managing Director   Peter Gray ☏ **488 1550**

Debt Capital Markets / Fixed Income
Country Head   Peter Wylie *General Manager, Treasury* ☏ **488 1530**

Domestic Government Bonds
Head of Sales   Johan Wessels *Assistant General Manager* ☏ **488 1527**
Head of Trading   Hannes Combrinck *Chief Dealer* ☏ **488 1565**

Private Placements
Head of Origination   Johan Wessels *Assistant General Manager* ☏ **488 1527**
Head of Sales   Robert Aspeling *Chief Dealer* ☏ **488 1563**

Fixed-Income Repo
Head of Repo   Johan Wessels *Assistant General Manager* ☏ **488 1527**
Matched Book Manager   Robert Aspeling *Chief Dealer* ☏ **488 1563**

Equity Capital Markets
Telex: 484552

Equity Repo / Securities Lending
Head   Ray Kopke *GM, Financial Institutions* ☏ **488 1567**
Head of Trading   Margaret Goncalves *Client Securities Services*
                                             Sharmayne Danielsen *Client Securities Services*

Syndicated Lending
Loan-Related Activities
Trade Finance   Roy Van Rooyen *General Manager* ☏ **488 1505**
Project Finance   Justin Moore *Senior Vice President* ☏ **488 1410**
Structured Trade Finance   Roy Van Rooyen *General Manager* ☏ **488 1505**
Leasing & Asset Finance   Philippe Chapat *Senior Manager* ☏ **488 2621**

Money Markets
Country Head   Johan Wessels *Assistant General Manager* ☏ **488 1527**

Domestic Commercial Paper
Head of Origination   Robert Aspeling *Chief Dealer* ☏ **488 1563**

Wholesale Deposits
Marketing   Ria Chapman *Dealer* ☏ **488 1555**

Foreign Exchange
Country Head   Peter Wylie *General Manager, Treasury* ☏ **488 1530**
Corporate Sales   Bossie Boshoff *Chief Dealer* ☏ **488 1533**

SOUTH AFRICA (+27)   www.euromoneydirectory.com

Société Générale (cont)

FX Traders / Sales People
Forward Trader   David Hancock ☏ **488 1541**
Spot Trader   Grant Harris ☏ **488 1546**
Sales   Roger Hewson ☏ **488 1544**
     Brent Ceotzee ☏ **488 1542**

Risk Management
Regional Head   Hennie Coertse *General Manager* ☏ **488 1494**

Fixed Income Derivatives / Risk Management
Country Head   Johan Wessels *Assistant General Manager* ☏ **488 1527**
IR Swaps Sales / Marketing; IR Swaps Trading   Hannes Combrinck *Chief Dealer* ☏ **488 1565**

Foreign Exchange Derivatives / Risk Management
Spot / Forwards Trading   James Holland *Chief Dealer, Spot* ☏ **488 1545**
     Nelson P Ponnen *Chief Dealer, Forwards* ☏ **488 1545**

Corporate Finance / M&A Advisory
Department: Societe Generale Corporate Finance South Africa (Pty) Ltd
Regional Head   Melvyn Antonie *Director* ☏ **488 2642**

Settlement / Clearing
Equity Settlement   Kevin Rogers *Assistant General Manager & Head* ☏ **488 1421**
Foreign Exchange Settlement   Yveline Piller *Operations Head* ☏ **488 1405**

Global Custody
Regional Head   Kevin Rogers *Assistant General Manager & Head* ☏ **488 1421**

Other Departments
Correspondent Banking   Ray Kopke *GM, Financial Institutions* ☏ **488 1567**

Standard Bank Investment Corporation Limited   Head Office

9th Floor, Standard Bank Centre, 5 Simmonds Street, Johannesburg 2001
PO Box 7725, Johannesburg 2000
Tel: (11) 636 9111 **Fax:** (11) 636 4975

Senior Executive Officers
Joint Deputy Chairman   W A M Clewlow ☏ **801 2014**
Chairman   C B Strauss ☏ **636 3422**
Joint Deputy Chairman   D Gordon
Chief Executive Officer   M H Vosloo *Group Chief Executive* ☏ **636 5481**
Managing Director / General Manager   N T Webb

Others (Senior Executives)
Standard Bank of South Africa   D R Busse *Executive Director* ☏ **636 6065**
International Representation   P C Prinsloo *Chairman*
Africa Banking Group   R J Rossouw *Managing Director* ☏ **636 3184**

The Standard Bank of South Africa Limited   Head Office

Financial Asset Services Division, 5th Floor, Standard Bank Centre, 3 Simmonds Street, Johannesburg 2001
PO Box 6075, Johannesburg 2000
Tel: (11) 636 9111 **Fax:** (11) 636 5117 **Telex:** 484191(Int'l), 484065/6-Treasury **Swift:** SBZA ZA JJ
Email: fasd@scmb.co.za
Forex Tel: 333 2544; **Fax:** 333 2544
Website: www.sbic.co.za/scmb

Senior Executive Officers
Chairman   C B Strauss ☏ **636 3422**
Deputy Chairman   W A M Clewlow ☏ **801 2014**
Deputy Chairman   D Gordon
Director   J N Leggett
Director   R E Norval
Chief Executive Officer   M H Vosloo *Group Chief Executive* ☏ **636 5481**
Managing Director   R J Rossouw
Deputy Managing Director   A B D Wright
Group Secretary   K D Curr ☏ **636 5082**

Others (Senior Executives)
Group Financial Services   A F van Biljon *Senior General Manager* ☏ **636 3756**
Credit   S J Caley *Senior Manager*
Regional Banking   C Lombard *Managing Director* ☏ **636 5215**
Retail Banking   N T Webb *Managing Director* ☏ **636 2126**

www.euromoneydirectory.com   SOUTH AFRICA (+27)

Others (Senior Executives) (cont)
Commercial Banking   H L Hofman *Managing Director* ☎ **636 5539**
Merchant Banking   M J D Ruck *Managing Director* ☎ **636 3039**

Relationship Manager
Standard Bank Financial Services   W Meiring *Managing Director* ☎ **636 2042**
Standard Bank Insurance Brokers   D S T Tunbridge *Managing Director* ☎ **636 5203**

Debt Capital Markets / Fixed Income
Department: Domestic Money & Capital Markets
Global Head   J Cruickshank *Director, Domestic Treasury* ☎ **636 6458**

Bonds - General
                                      J Payne *Chief Dealer* ☎ **636 5433**

Equity Capital Markets
Tel: 636 0524/0551 **Fax:** 636 1929 **Telex:** 4 87620/4 87629

Equity Repo / Securities Lending
Marketing & Product Development   Carol Ford *Head of Securities Lending*

Foreign Exchange
Global Head   W J Potgieter *Director, Treasury (FX)* ☎ **636 6775**

FX Traders / Sales People
                                      D G W Collett *Head, Forex Systems & Admin* ☎ **636 4892**
                                      S L Gill *Head, Commercial & Retail Sales* ☎ **636 9580**
                                      L R Shearer *Director, Offshore Forex Sales* ☎ **636 5709**

Risk Management
Global Head   P J Smith *Director* ☎ **636 1904**

Settlement / Clearing
Operations   N P Simpson *Manager, Financial Control*
                                      W R Hyde *Senior General Manager* ☎ **636 4124**

Other Departments
Economic Research   A Hammersma *Group Economist* ☎ **636 2900**

Administration

Technology & Systems
                                      C S Gibb *Director*
Information Technology   R T Holtshousen *General Manager* ☎ **636 4356**

Legal / In-House Counsel
                                      A V Pienaar *Group Legal Adviser* ☎ **636 6061**

Compliance
Corporate Governance & Secretariat Services   G R Bartlett *Manager*

Corporate Communications
                                      R S Steyn *General Manager* ☎ **636 3826**

Accounts / Audit
Internal Audit Division   A N D Toms *General Manager* ☎ **636 4677**

Other (Administration)
Group Human Resources   J M Verster *General Manager* ☎ **636 3509**
Human Resources Development   W M Lewis *Head* ☎ **636 4179**
Compensation & Benefits   G P Stapley *Head* ☎ **636 5725**
Public Affairs   A Hamersma *General Manager* ☎ **636 2900**
Management Services / Admin.   N J Gericke *Senior Manager*
Personnel Manager   J M Cresswell
Projects Manager   A Van Den Heuwel
Credit   N D Robertson *General Manager* ☎ **636 3947**

Standard Chartered Bank   Representative Office
31 Princess of Wales Terrace, Parktown, Johannesburg
Tel: (11) 484 7556 **Fax:** (11) 484 6100

Senior Executive Officers
Representative   Bill Owens

Euromoney Directory 1999   **1395**

SOUTH AFRICA (+27) www.euromoneydirectory.com

Standard Corporate & Merchant Bank Subsidiary Company

Standard Bank Centre, 3 Simmonds Street, Johannesburg 2001
Tel: (11) 636 9115 **Fax:** (11) 636 2242 **Telex:** 487620/487629 **Swift:** SBZA ZAJJ **Email:** fornoe@scmb.co.za
Website: www.sbic.co.za/scmb

Senior Executive Officers
Managing Director — M J D Ruck ☏ **636 2441** F **636 7754**
Deputy Managing Director — B J Kruger ☏ **636 5524**

General-Lending (DCM, SL)
Head of Corporate Banking
- A Gain *Director, Corporate Banking* ☏ **636 2424**
- D Finlayson *Director, Client Relationships - Corporate Banking* ☏ **636 5013**
- C J Newson *Director, Corporate Banking* ☏ **636 3945**

General - Treasury
Head of Treasury
- B J Koen *Director, IR Products - Treasury* ☏ **636 2400**
- B J Kruger *Deputy Managing Director* ☏ **636 5524**
- M P Lamont *Director, Fixed Interest - Treasury* ☏ **636 1872**

Equity Capital Markets
5th Floor, Financial Asset Services Division, 3 Simmons Stret, Johannesburg 2001
Tel: +27 (11) 636 0524 **Fax:** +27 (11) 636 1929 **Telex:** 487620/487629

Equity Repo / Securities Lending
Marketing & Product Development — Carol Ford *Head of Securities Lending Activities* ☏ **636 0565** F **636 1929** E forde@scmbjhbm.scmb.co.az

Syndicated Lending
Other (Trade Finance)
International Division — Gerard Nolan *Head of International Finance* ☏ **636 5062**

Foreign Exchange
Global Head — M S Cohen *Director, Corporate FX Sales* ☏ **636 2420**

Corporate Finance / M&A Advisory
Global Head
- B Hemphill *Director, Corporate Finance* ☏ **636 3037**
- R Shuter *Director, Corporate Finance* ☏ **636 7096**
Regional Head — B H Katz *Director, Corporate Finance* ☏ **636 2813**

Settlement / Clearing
Operations — A C Mendes *Director, Operations - Financial Asset Services* ☏ **240 3007**

Asset Management
Head — J Liackman *Director, Asset Management* ☏ **636 0658**

TEC South Africa Full Branch Office

PO Box 605 (52), Northlands, Johannesburg 2116
Tel: (11) 902 9252

Unibank Limited Head Office

37 Homestead Lane, Rivonia 2128
PO Box 5490, Rivonia 2128
Tel: (11) 806 700 **Fax:** (11) 803 4494 **Email:** unibank@icon.co.za

Senior Executive Officers
Chairman — Johnny Copelyn
Chief Executive Officer — Gerrit Van Der Merwe *Chief Executive & Managing Director* ☏ **806 7600**
Financial Director — Willem Nel *General Manager Finance* ☏ **806 7603**
Treasurer — Johan Van Rooyen *General Manager, Risk* ☏ **806 7600**
Chief Executive & Managing Director — Gerrit Van Der Merwe ☏ **806 7600**
General Manager, Operations — Llewellyn Walters ☏ **806 7600**
General Manager Finance — Willem Nel ☏ **806 7603**

Others (Senior Executives)
Central Recoveries — Eugene Van Der Mervlie *General Manager* ☏ **806 7600**
Savings & Loans Limited — Vanessa Van Der Merwe *General Manager* ☏ **806 7600**
Human Resources — Jackie Van Zyl *Manager* ☏ **806 7600**

Corporate Finance / M&A Advisory
Head of Corporate Finance — Llewellyn Walters *General Manager, Operations* ☏ **806 7600**

Administration
Tel: 806 7600
Head of Administration — Leoni Myburgh *Manager*
Business Development — Allan Phillips *Manager*

1396 Euromoney Directory 1999

Administration (cont)
Head of Marketing

Technology & Systems

Compliance

Public Relations

Accounts / Audit

Ronel Lundell *Manager*

Chris Parrish *Manager, IT*

Johan Van Rooyen *General Manager, Risk* ☎ 806 7600

Rouel Luudell *Manager, Marketing*

Cuan Helen *Manager, Finance*

Warburg Dillon Read (South Africa) (Pty) Limited

Alternative trading name: Warburg Dillon Read Securities (South Africa) (Pty) Limited
64 Wierda Road East, Wierda Valley, Sandton ZA 2196
PO Box 652863, Benmore ZA 2010
Tel: (11) 322 7000 **Fax:** (11) 784 8280; (11) 784 8260

Senior Executive Officers
Country Head South Africa

W Lawson-Turnbull

Others (Senior Executives)

J Graham *Head of Equities*
I Gladman *Head of Corporate Finance*
D Du Toit *Head of Rates*

SPAIN (+34)

Banco de España
🏛 Central Bank

Alcalá 50, E-28014 Madrid
Tel: (91) 338 5000 **Fax:** (91) 531 0059 **Telex:** 27642 **Swift:** ESPB ES MM

Senior Executive Officers
Governor

Luis Angel Rojo

Others (Senior Executives)

Julio Segura *Counsellor*
José Manuel Gonzalez *Counsellor*
Miguel Martín *Deputy Governor*
Luis M Linde *General Director*
Gonzalo Gil *General Director*
Raimundo Poveda *General Director*
Manuel Zamanillo *General Director*
José Luis Malo de Molina *General Director*

3i Europe plc
Full Branch Office

Ruiz de Alarcón 12, piso 2°, E-28014 Madrid
Tel: (91) 521 4419 **Fax:** (91) 521 9819 **Email:** madrid@3igroup.com

Senior Executive Officers
Managing Director

Gabriel Gutierrez Ugalde

AB Asesores
Head Office

Formerly known as: Asesores Bursátiles
2nd Floor, Plaza de la Leatlad 3, E-28014 Madrid
Tel: (91) 580 1100; (91) 580 1200 **Fax:** (91) 521 8884; (91) 580 7342
Website: www.abasesores.es

Senior Executive Officers
President
Financial Director
Vice President

Salvador Garcia-Atance
Angel Luis Rodriguez
Pedro Guerrero

SPAIN (+34) www.euromoneydirectory.com

AB Asesores (cont)

Debt Capital Markets / Fixed Income
Tel: 580 1120
Head of Debt Capital Markets — Ana Núñez

Domestic Government Bonds
Head of Sales; Head of Trading — Carlos De La Peña

Eurobonds
Head of Origination — Ana Núñez
Head of Sales — Rafael Valera
Head of Trading — Alberto González

Private Placements
Head of Origination — Ana Núñez
Head of Sales — Rafael Valera
Head of Structuring — Alberto González

Equity Capital Markets
Tel: 580 1110
Global Head — Juan Antonio Bertran *Director of Equities* 580 1100

Domestic Equities
Head of Origination — Manuel Gil
Head of Syndication — Cristobal Rodriguez Aguirre
Head of Sales — Cesar González
Head of Trading — Natalia Duñabitia
Head of Research — Juan Luis Pérez

Foreign Exchange
Tel: 580 1110
Head of Foreign Exchange — Alvaro Martinez

Risk Management

OTC Equity Derivatives
Head — Gregorio Urdiroz

Corporate Finance / M&A Advisory
Global Head — José Antonio Abad *Strategic Consultancy and Privatization*

ABN AMRO Bank NV — Full Branch Office

José Ortega y Gasset 29, 5th Floor, E-28006 Madrid
Tel: (91) 423 6900 **Fax:** (91) 423 6903 **Telex:** 4236917 **Swift:** ABMA ES MM **Cable:** BANCOLANDA

Senior Executive Officers
General Manager, Spain — Ignacio Muñoz Pidal

Debt Capital Markets / Fixed Income
Head of Debt Capital Markets — Ignacio Mataix

Equity Capital Markets
Head of Equity Capital Markets — Ignacio Mataix

Domestic Equities
Head of Trading — Antolin Gonzalez *Dealer*

Foreign Exchange
Head of Trading — Antolin Gonzalez *Dealer*

AIAF Mercado de Renta Fija SA — Head Office

Torre Picasso, Planta 43, E 20020 Madrid
Tel: (91) 597 4402; (91) 597 2744 **Fax:** (91) 597 4403; (91) 597 1833
Website: www.aiaf.es

Senior Executive Officers
President — Francisco Oña
Chief Executive Officer — Julio Alcantara
Financial Director — Gonzalo Gomez
Chief Operating Officer — Rodriguo Navia-Osorio

www.euromoneydirectory.com SPAIN (+34)

All Trading Brokers Europe
Head Office

Fortuny 18, E-28010 Madrid
Tel: (91) 592 8118 Fax: (91) 592 8170 Email: alltrading@alltrading.es Reuters: ALLT

Senior Executive Officers
Chairman   Santos Abascal
Managing Director   Antonio Marti

Debt Capital Markets / Fixed Income
Head of Fixed Income   Enrique Nuñez ☏ 592 8100

Fixed-Income Repo
Head of Repo   José Luis Moreno

Equity Capital Markets
Head of Equity Capital Markets   Jaime Krahe ☏ 592 8111

Money Markets
Head of Money Markets   Manuel Monsalvo ☏ 592 8181

Foreign Exchange
Head of Foreign Exchange   Francisco Muñoz ☏ 592 8222

American Express Bank Limited
Representative Office

Francisco Gervás 10, E-28020 Madrid
Tel: (91) 322 5189 Fax: (91) 570 4106

Senior Executive Officers
Chief Representative   Hector Cuéllar

Argentaria Banco de Negocios
Head Office

Paseo de Recoletos 10, E-28001 Madrid
Tel: (91) 537 7000 Fax: (91) 537 8423 Swift: BNAR ES MM
Website: www.argentaria.es

Senior Executive Officers
Chairman   Gregorio Villa la Beitia
Chief Executive Officer   Miguel Zorita ☏ 537 6931

Debt Capital Markets / Fixed Income
Head of Debt Capital Markets   Javier Alarcó ☏ 537 8340 ✉ 537 9388

Eurobonds
Head of Trading   Vicente Ortueta ☏ 537 6773

Libor-Based / Floating-Rate Products
FRN Origination   Vicente Ortueta ☏ 537 6773

Equity Capital Markets
Head of Equity Capital Markets   Ignacio Moliner ☏ 537 8023

International Equities
Head of Origination   Carlos González ☏ 537 8996

Equity Repo / Securities Lending
Marketing & Product Development   Francisco Pascual ☏ 537 6904

Syndicated Lending
Head of Origination; Head of Syndication   Francisco F de Trocóniz ☏ 537 8479

Money Markets
Head of Money Markets   Javier Alarcó ☏ 537 8340 ✉ 537 9388

Risk Management
Head of Risk Management   Jaime Azcoiti ☏ 537 8568

Fixed Income Derivatives / Risk Management
Trading   José Luis Diaz ☏ 537 4966

Corporate Finance / M&A Advisory
Head of Corporate Finance   Francisco Esteve ☏ 537 8424

Other Departments
Economic Research   Jaime Azcoiti ☏ 537 8568

Administration
Legal / In-House Counsel
                                       Antonio Truan ☏ 537 8593

Euromoney Directory 1999   **1399**

SPAIN (+34) www.euromoneydirectory.com

Argentaria Caja Postal Banco Hipotecario SA   Head Office

Alternative trading name: Argentaria
Formerly known as: Corporacion Bancaria de España
Paseo de Recoletos 10, E-28001 Madrid
Tel: (91) 537 7000 **Fax:** (91) 537 7855 **Telex:** 48739 **Swift:** EXTE ES MM **Cable:** EXTBA E
Website: www.argentaria.es

Senior Executive Officers
Chairman	Francisco González Rodríguez
Chief Executive Officer	Francisco Gómez Roldán
Treasurer	Didac Artes
Managing Director	Federico Outón
Managing Director	Gregorio Villalabeitia
Managing Director	Manuel Méndez
Managing Director	José Antonio Fernández Rivero
Company Secretary	José Maldonado Ramos
International Division	José Ignacio Leyún

Corporate Finance / M&A Advisory
Head of Corporate Finance   Miguel Zorita

Asset Management
Head   Manuel Galatas

Administration
Technology & Systems
   Joseph Montero

Compliance
   Soledad Duro

Accounts / Audit
   José Luis de los Santos

Banca Catalana SA   Head Office

Avinguda Diagonal 662-664, E-08034 Barcelona
Tel: (93) 404 4000 **Telex:** 51764 BICK E **Swift:** CATA ES BB **Email:** bcacat01@cinet.fcr.es

Senior Executive Officers
Chairman	Pedro Fontana
Financial Director	Jaume Adam
Chief Operating Officer	Abilio Ferreruela *Head of Department* ☎ 404 3836
Treasurer	Luis Piñana
Managing Director / General Manager	Jaume Guardiola
International Division	Angel Apesteguia

Debt Capital Markets / Fixed Income
Tel: 404 4835 **Fax:** 404 3738
Global Head   Abilio Ferreruela *Head of Department* ☎ 404 3836

Fixed-Income Repo
Trading   Joan Nomtañez *Head of Sales*
Santi Latorre *Currencies Chief Dealer*
Abili Ferreruela *Domestic Chief Dealer*
Daniel Oliver *Money Market*
Maneul Alvarez *Money Market*
Josep M Verdaguer *FRAS / SWAPS*
Miquel Pardo *Bonds / Futures / Options*
Carlos Galofre *Bonds / Repo*
Jordt Sans *Money Market*
Elisa Nueno *Sales*
Xavier Caminal *Sales*
Jordi Escarmis *Sales*
Albert Marca *Sales*
Manuel Garcia *Sales*
Begoña Ponce *Sales*

Equity Capital Markets
Global Head   Abilio Ferreruela *Head of Department* ☎ 404 3836

Syndicated Lending
Global Head   Joaquin Silvestre

Foreign Exchange
Global Head   Santi Latorre *Currencies Chief Dealer*

www.euromoneydirectory.com   SPAIN (+34)

Risk Management
Global Head   Jordina Mensa

Fixed Income Derivatives / Risk Management
Trading   Miquel Pardo *Bonds / Futures / Options*

Settlement / Clearing
Country Head   Albert Casabón

Administration

Technology & Systems
                                           Montse Jiménez *Systems Manager*

Banca Commerciale Italiana   Full Branch Office

Calle Serrano 67, E-28006 Madrid
Tel: (91) 426 4000 **Fax:** (91) 426 4063 **Telex:** 27561 BCIE **Swift:** BCIT ES MM

Senior Executive Officers
Senior Manager   Giacomo Ghillani

General-Lending (DCM, SL)
Head of Corporate Banking   Fausto Corvini *Credit*
                                           M Soledad Milán *Credit*

General - Treasury
Head of Treasury   Jesús García
                                           Miguel Angel Arnes

Settlement / Clearing
Operations   Ignacio Escribano

Banca March SA   Head Office

Avenida Alejandro Rosselló 8, E-07002 Palma de Mallorca, Baleares
Tel: (971) 779 100; (971) 779 325 **Fax:** (971) 779 187; (971) 779 400 **Telex:** 68661 BMPEX E **Swift:** BMAR ES 2M
Email: internacional@banca.march.es **Reuters:** BMPM

Senior Executive Officers
Chairman   Carlos March
Vice Chairman   Pablo Vallbona
Chief Executive Officer   Francisco Verdu *Managing Director*

Others (Senior Executives)
                                           Gabriel Cortes *Head, International* ☏ 779 197

Money Markets
Tel: 779 377 **Fax:** 779 397
Global Head   Manuel Busom

Foreign Exchange
Tel: 779 377 **Fax:** 779 400
Global Head   Jesus Peña

FX Traders / Sales People
                                           Margarita Catany ☏ 779 219
                                           Antonia Pujol ☏ 779 219
                                           Carlos Poole ☏ 779 279
                                           Romulo Palou ☏ 779 279
                                           Ricardo Peraza ☏ 779 279

Other Departments
Correspondent Banking   Janet Chilton ☏ 779 325 ☏ 779 400

Banca Popolare di Novara   Representative Office

Plaza Marqués de Salamanca 7, E-28006 Madrid
Tel: (91) 431 1779 **Fax:** (91) 575 4448 **Telex:** 44675 NOVB E

Senior Executive Officers
Representative   Andrés Trabanco y Trabanco

SPAIN (+34)　　　　　www.euromoneydirectory.com

Banco Bilbao Vizcaya
Head Office

Paseo de la Castellana 8, piso 4°, E-28046 Madrid
Tel: (91) 374 6000 **Fax:** (91) 374 6969 **Telex:** 22236 45938 **Swift:** BBVIES MM **Email:** jose.crespo@grupobbv.com
Website: www.bbv.es

Senior Executive Officers
Chairman	Emilio Ybarra ☎ **374 6350** 🖷 **556 6372**
Chief Executive Officer	Pedro Luis Uriarte ☎ **374 6320** 🖷 **556 3778**
Financial Director	Luis Javier Bastida ☎ **374 6265** 🖷 **374 7327**
Treasurer	Juan Luis Mayordomo *Head, Treasury & Capital Markets Div* ☎ **374 3877** 🖷 **374 4512**
Managing Director	Javier Ecehenique ☎ **374 6252**
International Division	Gonzalo Terreros ☎ **374 6156** 🖷 **374 6965**

Debt Capital Markets / Fixed Income
Head of Fixed Income	Alvaro Aresti ☎ **374 3498**

Equity Capital Markets
Head of Equity Capital Markets	Luis Iturbe ☎ **374 6209**

Syndicated Lending
Head of Origination	Antonio Uguina ☎ **374 4193**
Head of Syndication	Juan Ortueta ☎ **374 3947**

Loan-Related Activities
Trade Finance	Timothy Bradbury ☎ **374 7740**
Project Finance	Pedro Michelena ☎ **374 4178**

Money Markets
Head of Money Markets	Tomas Antona ☎ **374 5115**

Foreign Exchange
Head of Foreign Exchange	Tomas Antona ☎ **374 5115**

Risk Management

Fixed Income Derivatives / Risk Management
Trading	Miguel Angel Cestero *Derivatives Trader*

OTC Equity Derivatives
Trading	Juan Pablo JImeno

Other (Exchange-Traded Derivatives)
Derivatives Analysis	Gilbert Mateu

Exchange-Traded Derivatives
IR Options	Marta Déniz *OTC Derivatives Options Trader*

Settlement / Clearing
Operations	Sebastian Ubiria *Head of Operations*

Administration

Compliance
	Vicente Sánchez *Head, Compliance*

Banco do Brasil SA
Full Branch Office

Calle Serrano 73, E-28006 Madrid
Apartado 50041, Madrid
Tel: (91) 431 1872 **Fax:** (91) 575 2607 **Telex:** 45795 **Swift:** BRAS ES MM **Email:** bbespana@tsai.es

Senior Executive Officers
General Manager	Claudinel Perez
Manager	Paulo Raimundo Martiningui
Deputy General Manager	Elenelson Honorato Marquez

Banco Central Hispano
Head Office

Plaza de Canalejas 1, E-28014 Madrid
Tel: (91) 558 1111 **Fax:** (91) 532 7659; (91) 531 4094 **Telex:** 45473/45157 **Swift:** CENT ES MM
Website: www.bch.es

Senior Executive Officers
Chairman	José María Amusategui de la Cierva
Chief Executive Officer	Angel Corcostegui Guraya
International Division	Antonio Escamez Torres *General Manager* ☎ **558 2004**

1402　Euromoney Directory 1999

SPAIN (+34)

Debt Capital Markets / Fixed Income
Fax: 558 1029 **Reuters:** BHAC
Head of Debt Capital Markets   Ramon Barajas ☎ **558 1090**

Equity Capital Markets
Fax: 558 1029
Head of Equity Capital Markets   Antonino Ubieta Bravo ☎ **558 1217**

Syndicated Lending
Head of Syndicated Lending   Iñigo Sanchez-Asiain Mardones ☎ **558 1979**

Money Markets
Fax: 558 1029 **Reuters:** BHAM
Head of Money Markets   Manuel Barranco ☎ **558 1382**

Foreign Exchange
Fax: 558 1029 **Reuters:** BCHS
Head of Foreign Exchange   Juan Martinez ☎ **558 2651**

Corporate Finance / M&A Advisory
Head of Corporate Finance   Iñigo Sanchez-Asiain Mardones ☎ **558 1979**

Settlement / Clearing
Settlement (General)   Marcos Santo ☎ **558 5685**
Operations   Enrique Sobrevila *Head of Operations*
    Mariano Pérez *Head of Operations*

Administration
Compliance
    Marcos Santos *Head, Compliance*

Banco Cooperativo Español SA

Virgen de los Peligros 6, E-28013 Madrid
Tel: (91) 595 6700 **Fax:** (91) 595 6780

Senior Executive Officers
Chairman   Juan del Aguila Molina ☎ **(950) 210 100** F **(950) 210 266**
Chairman   Friedbert Malt ☎ **+49 (69) 744 701** F **+49 (69) 7447 6369**
General Manager   Javier Petit Asumendi ☎ **595 6702** F **595 6845**
Company Secretary   Gloria Garcia
International Division   Gustavo Riveros Spring ☎ **595 6707** F **595 6845**

Others (Senior Executives)
Vice Chairman   Friedbert Malt ☎ **+49 (69) 744 701** F **+49 (69) 7447 6369**
Commercial Manager   Juan Luis Coghen ☎ **595 6774** F **595 6721**

General - Treasury
Head of Treasury   Francisco de Pablos Gómez ☎ **595 6735** F **595 6781**

Debt Capital Markets / Fixed Income
Head of Debt Capital Markets   Ignacio Benlloch Fernández-Cuesta *Manager* ☎ **595 6703** F **595 6721**
Head of Fixed Income   Javier Moreno Rumbao ☎ **595 6807** F **595 6845**

Risk Management
Head of Risk Management   Angel Espinosa *Risk Manager* ☎ **595 6725** F **595 6780**

Settlement / Clearing
Operations   Ignacio de Castro Sanchez *Manager* ☎ **595 6704** F **595 6845**
    Joaquín Carrilo *Head* ☎ **595 6711** F **595 6780**

Administration
Head of Marketing   Alejandro Castilla *Manager* ☎ **595 6774** F **595 6721**

Other (Administration)
Personnel & Legal   Moisés Menéndez Andrés *Manager* ☎ **595 6701** F **595 6845**

Banco Español de Credito SA   Head Office

Alternative trading name: Banesto
C/ Alcalá 14, E-28014 Madrid
Tel: (91) 338 3100; (91) 338 1000 **Fax:** (91) 338 1405 **Telex:** 27644, 27645 **Swift:** ESPC ES MM **Cable:** BANESTO
Website: www.banesto.es

Senior Executive Officers
Chairman   Alfredo Saenz
Chief Executive Officer   Victor Menéndez
Secretary to the Board   Juan Carlos R Cantarero

SPAIN (+34) www.euromoneydirectory.com

Banco Español de Credito SA (cont)
Others (Senior Executives)
    Matias Rodriguez Inciarte *Director*
    José Corral *Director*
    José Angel Merodio *Director*
    David Arce *Director*
    Juan Delibes *Director*

Wholesale Banking — José Luis Roselló *Director & General Manager*

General-Investment
Head of Investment — José Angel Merodio *Director & GM, Domestic Banking*

General - Treasury
Head of Treasury — Fernando Gutierrez Ojanguren *GM, Treasury & Capital Markets*

Debt Capital Markets / Fixed Income
Department: Treasury - Financial Markets
Tel: 338 1000 Fax: 338 1707
Global Head — Fernando Gutierrez Ojanguren *GM, Treasury & Capital Markets*
Other — Ricardo Castresana *Director, Trading*
    Fernando Utrera *Director, Trading*
    Felipe Jimene *FX Dealer*

Syndicated Lending
Other (Trade Finance)
Real Estate — Pedro Pablo Arechabaleta *Assistant General Manager*
Loans & Recoveries — José Corral *Director & General Manager*
Lending — José Maria Nus *Assistant General Manager*

Administration
Business Development — Miguel Angel Lorente *General Manager*

Legal / In-House Counsel
Legal & Tax Advice — Juan Carlos R Cantarero *Secretary to the Board*

Accounts / Audit
Internal Auditing
Financial, Planning & Control — David Arce *Director*
Juan Delibes *Director & General Manager*

Other (Administration)
Human Resources — Timoteo Patricio *General Manager*
Resources — José Antonio Aróstegui *General Manager*
Corporate Office — Luis Abril *General Manager*

Banco Espirito Santo e Comercial de Lisboa — Full Branch Office
c/ Velázquez 108/110, E-28006 Madrid
Tel: (91) 566 7150 Fax: (91) 566 7160

Senior Executive Officers
General Manager — Aureliano Neves

Others (Senior Executives)
Mariano De Carvalho *Deputy General Manager*

General - Treasury
Head of Treasury — Henrique Sánchez *Chief Dealer*

Debt Capital Markets / Fixed Income
Head of Trading — Henrique Sánchez *Chief Dealer*

Equity Capital Markets
Domestic Equities
Head of Trading — Henrique Sánchez *Chief Dealer*

Risk Management
Head of Risk Management — Pedro Sarabia *Risk Manager*

Settlement / Clearing
Operations — Francisco Guardeño *Operations Manager*

Banco do Estado de São Paulo — Representative Office
Plaza Manuel Gómez Moreno 2, Planta 7a, Zona Azca, Edificio Alfredo Mahou, E-28020 Madrid
Tel: (91) 597 1728; (91) 597 2455 Fax: (91) 597 2553 Telex: 45093 Swift: BESPESMM
Email: banespa_madrid@net64.es

Senior Executive Officers
General Manager — Rogerio De Castro Favero

www.euromoneydirectory.com   SPAIN (+34)

Banco de Extremadura SA — Head Office
Calle Pintores 8, E-10003 Cáceres
Tel: (927) 62 6102 Fax: (927) 62 6103; (927) 62 6104 Swift: CGDI ES 2C

Senior Executive Officers
Chairman   Alfredo Antas Teles
President   Antonio Tomás Corria
Managing Director / General Manager   José Manuel Bagorro

Banco de Fomento & Exterior - Portugal — Full Branch Office
Basiocastillana 40B, E-28046 Madrid
Tel: (91) 577 8974 Fax: (91) 575 7352 Telex: 41153 FOBAN E

Senior Executive Officers
General Director   Gaspar Prata Dias

Banco Guipuzcoano SA — Head Office
Avenida de la Libertad 21, E-20004 San Sebastian
Tel: (943) 418 273; (943) 418 100 Fax: (943) 418 337; (943) 416 828 Telex: 36369 COGUI E Swift: BGUI ES 22
Email: info@bancogui.es Reuters: BGSP
Website: www.bancogui.es

Senior Executive Officers
Chairman   José María Aguirre González
Chief Operating Officer   Juan Luis Arrieta
Treasurer   José Antonio González *Treasurer* ☎ **418 336**
International Division   Xabier Larrañaga ☎ **418 234**

General-Lending (DCM, SL)
Head of Corporate Banking   Agustín Ibarguren ☎ **418 165**

Debt Capital Markets / Fixed Income
Fax: 214 372
Head of Fixed Income   José Antonio González *Treasurer* ☎ **418 336**

Domestic Government Bonds
Head of Trading   Jone Aguirre ☎ **418 173**

Syndicated Lending
Tel: 418 109 Fax: 418 337
Head of Trading   Xabier Larrañaga ☎ **418 234**

Money Markets
Fax: 214 372
Head of Money Markets   José Antonio González *Treasurer* ☎ **418 336**

Foreign Exchange
Fax: 214 372
Global Head   José Antonio González *Treasurer* ☎ **418 336**

FX Traders / Sales People
                                          María Angeles Elizondo ☎ **418 236**
                                          Juan Castillo ☎ **418 236**

Risk Management
Head of Risk Management   Francisco Javier Rapún ☎ **418 192**

Settlement / Clearing
Head of Settlement / Clearing   Jesús López ☎ **418 237**
Operations   Malen Zuloaga ☎ **418 275**

Other Departments
Correspondent Banking   Xabier Larrañaga ☎ **418 234**

Administration

Technology & Systems
                                          Pedro Ibáñez ☎ **418 356**

Legal / In-House Counsel
                                          Francisco López de Tejada ☎ **418 163**

SPAIN (+34)   www.euromoneydirectory.com

Banco Herrero SA
Head Office

Fruela 11, E-33003 Oviedo
Tel: (985) 968 080 **Fax:** (985) 968 221 **Telex:** 83340 **Swift:** BHRO ES M2 **Reuters:** BHOE **Cable:** BANCHERRERO

Senior Executive Officers
Chairman   Ignacio Herrero Alvarez
Chief Executive Officer   Marcelino Armenter Vidal *Executive Director*
Treasurer   A Isabel Ferandez
Managing Director   J Antonio Menendez
International Division   Joaquin Orejas

Syndicated Lending
Head of Syndicated Lending   David Corte

Loan-Related Activities
Trade Finance   Javier Breton

Foreign Exchange
Head of Foreign Exchange   Manuel Rodriguez

Banco Hipotecario de España

Paseo de Recoletos 10, E-28001 Madrid
Tel: (91) 537 4000

Senior Executive Officers
President   Francesco Gonzales
Financial Director   Jose Antonia Alvarez *Chief Financial Officer*

Administration

Corporate Communications
                                            Belen Montero ☎ **537 7486**

Other (Administration)
Translation Department   Berta Chaves ☎ **537 7271**

Banco Inversion SA
Head Office

Felipe IV 7, E-28014 Madrid
Tel: (91) 531 0157; (91) 531 0593 **Fax:** (91) 522 3133; (91) 522 6821 **Telex:** 47321 GPSV E **Reuters:** BISX; BIRZ

Senior Executive Officers
Chairman   José Luis Várez Fisa

Debt Capital Markets / Fixed Income
Tel: 532 9748

Domestic Government Bonds
Head of Trading   Miguel Forteza

Settlement / Clearing
Settlement (General)   Michele Goyet *International Settlements* ☎ **531 0157 ext 362**
                                            Alexander Henrich *Domestic Settlements* ☎ **531 0157 ext 378**

Banco Luso Español SA
Subsidiary Company

María de Molina 39, E-28006 Madrid
Tel: (91) 309 9000 **Fax:** (91) 562 2856 **Swift:** CGDI ES MM

Senior Executive Officers
Chairman   António Tomás Correia
Chief Executive Officer   Mateo Ruiz Oriol
General Manager   Alberto Umbelino Gonçalves
General Manager   Carlos Coelho Alves
Company Secretary   Manuel Fernández Neira

Banco de la Nación Argentina
Full Branch Office

José Ortega y Gasset 26, E-28006 Madrid
Tel: (91) 576 3703 Fax: (91) 576 6142 Telex: 23749 BNRA E Swift: NACNESMM

Senior Executive Officers
Chief Operating Officer
Treasurer
General Manager

Antonio Daura *Operation Manager*
Alberto Hick *Treasury Manager*
Jorge Luis Volpini

Banco Pastor SA

Cantón Pequeño No.1, E-15003 A Coruña
Tel: (981) 227 800 Fax: (981) 207 288 Telex: 82095

Senior Executive Officers
Chairman
Executive Vice President
Executive Vice President
Managing Director / General Manager
Company Secretary

Carmela Arias y Diaz de Rabago
Vicente Arias Mosquera
José Maria Arias Mosquera
Alfonso Porras del Corral
Miguel Sanmartin Losada

Others (Senior Executives)
Member, Executive Committee
Head, Commercial Banking

Guillermo de la Dehesa Romero ☎ **(91) 522 6111**
Jaime Crespo Varela ☎ **227 800 ext 305**

General-Investment
Head of Investment

Francisco José Mañas López ☎ **(91) 522 6111 ext 296**
Alvaro Garcia de la Rasilla y Pineda *Head, Financial Markets*
☎ **(91) 522 6111**

General - Treasury
Head of Treasury

Alvaro de Torres Gestal *Head, Capital Markets* ☎ **(91) 522 6111 ext 256**

Debt Capital Markets / Fixed Income
Head of Fixed Income Trading

Jürgen R Bollack ☎ **(91) 522 6111 ext 456**
José Luis Castro ☎ **(91) 522 6111 ext 456**

Equity Capital Markets
Head of Equity Capital Markets

Alvaro Garcia de la Rasilla y Pineda *Head, Financial Markets*
☎ **(91) 522 6111**

Head of Trading

Isabel Sánchez Vallejo ☎ **(91) 522 6111 ext 419**

Money Markets
Domestic Commercial Paper
Head of Trading

Nieves Bianco ☎ **(91) 522 6111 ext 265**

Eurocommercial Paper
Head of Trading

Juan Carlos Colinas ☎ **(91) 522 6111 ext 392**

Foreign Exchange
Head of Trading

Arturo Burgaz ☎ **(91) 522 6111 ext 265**

Risk Management
Country Head

José Angel Naya Rodriguez *Head of Finance* ☎ **207288 294**

Settlement / Clearing
Operations

Ignacio de Sopeña Sainz *Head* ☎ **227 800 ext 509**

Asset Management
Portfolio Management

Manuel Durán

Other Departments
Private Banking

Enrique Saez Ponte *Head* ☎ **227 800 ext 399**

Administration
Head of Administration

Manuel Lopez Perez ☎ **227 800 ext 591**

Other (Administration)
Head, Human Resources

Marcelino Pernas Sabio ☎ **227 800 ext 438**

Banco Popular Español SA
Head Office

Velázquez, 34, E-28001 Madrid
Tel: (91) 520 7000 Fax: (91) 577 9208 Telex: 44351 BPE SC Email: usu16@medusa.as

Senior Executive Officers
Chairman
Chairman
Deputy Chairman
Chief Executive Officer

Luis Valls
Javier Valls
Gabreil Gancedo
Ricardo Lacasa

SPAIN (+34)

Banco Popular Español SA (cont)
Senior Executive Officers (cont)

Company Secretary — Amable Gonzales

General - Treasury
Head of Treasury — Miguel Perez Somalo *Treasury*

Relationship Manager
Investor Relations — Juan Echanojauregui

Debt Capital Markets / Fixed Income
Tel: 577 9736 Fax: 576 3684
Head of Debt Capital Markets — Julio Coto ☎ 576 3684

Eurobonds
Head of Origination — Yolanda de la Morena ☎ 520 7292 F 435 8922

Equity Capital Markets
Tel: 577 9763 Fax: 576 3684
Head of Equity Capital Markets — Julio Coto ☎ 576 3684
Global Head — Rodolfo Velarde *Equity & Stock Markets*
Head of Trading — Vicente Baquero *Trader*

Domestic Equities
Head of Origination — Yolanda de la Morena ☎ 520 7292 F 435 8922

Syndicated Lending
Tel: 577 9763 Fax: 576 3684
Head of Syndication — Vicente Martinez
Julio Coto ☎ 576 3684

Money Markets
Tel: 577 9763 Fax: 576 3684
Head of Money Markets — Doroteo Polo

Foreign Exchange
Head of Sales — José Fernandez
Head of Trading — Rafael Ruiz de Luna ☎ 520 7405

FX Traders / Sales People
Foreign Trade Promotion — José Fernandez
Foreign Transactions Accounting — Antonio Romero

Risk Management
Head of Risk Management — Alfredo Herrero *Risk Assessment*

Fixed Income Derivatives / Risk Management
Trading — Angel Gonzalez

Settlement / Clearing
Operations — Rafael Bermejo *Controller*

Asset Management
Portfolio Management — Yolanda de la Morena ☎ 520 7292 F 435 8922

Other Departments
Correspondent Banking — Luis Pintado
Economic Research — Manuel Martin *Economics & MIS*

Administration
Head of Marketing — Angel Pesquera

Technology & Systems
Systems & EDP — Isaac Botija

Legal / In-House Counsel
Legal Advisory — Pedro Huerta

Accounts / Audit
Auditing — Jesús Arellano
Resource Management & Auditing — Angel Gomez

Other (Administration)
Human Resources — Eulimio Morales
Euro Office — Alfonso Jordan
International Activities — José Sartorius
Corporate Affairs — Fernando de Soto

www.euromoneydirectory.com　　　　　　　SPAIN (+34)

Banco Sabadell
Head Office

Plaza de Catalunya 1, E-08201 Sabadell
Tel: (93) 728 9289 **Fax:** (93) 725 9733 **Telex:** 94400 BANSA E **Swift:** BSAB ES BB **Email:** info@mail.bancsabadell.es
Reuters: PTSX, BSAB
Website: www.bancsabadell.es

Senior Executive Officers
Chairman — Juan Corominas Vila ☎ **728 9331**
Chief Executive Officer — Josep Oliu *Chief Executive Officer* ☎ **728 9339**
International Division — Joan Saborido *Senior Manager* ☎ **728 9452**
Eugeni Vilardell Talló *Corporate Finance & International Operations* ☎ **728 9234**
Joan Saborido *Senior Manager* ☎ **728 9452**

Others (Senior Executives)
IT Systems — Manuel Dueñas ☎ **728 9137**
Organization — Ramón Subirana ☎ **728 9461**
Communications & External Relations — Juan Mateu ☎ **728 9332**

General-Lending (DCM, SL)
Head of Corporate Banking — Lluis Buil *Senior Manager* ☎ **728 9797**
Josep Tarrés *Commercial Banking Manager* ☎ **728 9054**

General-Investment
Head of Investment — Jaime Ventura *Senior Executive Officer* ☎ **728 9052**
Ignacio Cami *Investments & Insurance Institutions* ☎ **728 9414**

General - Treasury
Head of Treasury — Joan M Grumé Sierra ☎ **728 9629** 📠 **725 5175**
✉ **grume@mail.bancsabadell.es**

Relationship Manager
Operational Services — Antonio López *Senior Manager* ☎ **728 9216**

Debt Capital Markets / Fixed Income
Head of Fixed Income Trading — Joaquim Pascual Cañero *Director of Capital Markets* ☎ **728 9709**
📠 **726 1955** ✉ **pascualj@mail.bancsabadell.es**

Money Markets
Head of Money Markets — Manuel Garcia Hidalgo ☎ **728 9513** 📠 **725 5376**
✉ **garciahi@mail.bancsabadell.es**

Foreign Exchange
Head of Trading — Ramon Navalon Lafuente ☎ **728 9545** 📠 **725 5376**
✉ **navalon@mail.bancsabadell.es**

Corporate Finance / M&A Advisory
Global Head — Eugeni Vilardell Talló *Corporate Finance & International Operations* ☎ **728 9234**

Settlement / Clearing
Head of Settlement / Clearing — Antoni Abella Ulldemolins ☎ **728 9705** 📠 **726 2559**
✉ **abellaant@mail.bancsabadell.es**
Other — Jaume Viladrosa Cutrina *Head, Middle Office* ☎ **728 96 71** 📠 **726 1955**
✉ **viladrosaj@mail.bancsabadell.es**

Administration
Technology & Systems
IT System — Manuel Dueñas ☎ **728 9137**
Legal / In-House Counsel
Head, Investment Legal Department — Francisco R Romagosa Torres
Public Relations — Juan Mateu ☎ **728 9332**

Accounts / Audit
Head, Internal Audit — Tomás Varela Muiña
Other (Administration)
Organization — Ramón Subirana ☎ **728 9461**
Department: International Division
Other (Administration)
Foreign Network — Rosa Solench ☎ **728 9503**
International Financial Institutions — Antoni Torruella ☎ **728 9478**
Area Manager — Pere Serra ☎ **728 9659**
Ian Hiscock ☎ **728 9808**
Jaume Ferrer ☎ **728 9502**
Credit Analysis — Juan Gutiérrez ☎ **728 9077**
Financial Services — Luciano Méndez ☎ **728 9640**
International Products — Antònia Bosch ☎ **728 9474**

Euromoney Directory 1999　**1409**

SPAIN (+34)　　www.euromoneydirectory.com

Banco Sanpaolo SA
Subsidiary Company

Pasaje Mercader 7-9, E-08008 Barcelona
Tel: (93) 227 5380; (93) 215 9731 **Fax:** (93) 215 6576 **Swift:** CATCESBB

Senior Executive Officers
President　　　　　　　　　　　　　Abel Matutes Tur ☎ **227 5380**
Managing Director / General Manager　Joaquin Meseguer

Banco Santander
Head Office

Paseo de la Castellana 24, E-28046 Madrid
Tel: (91) 342 3266 **Fax:** (91) 342 3371 **Telex:** 46382 **Swift:** BDER ES MM
Investor Relations **Tel:** 342 4887; 342 4892; **Fax:** 342 4894
Website: www.bancosantander.es

Senior Executive Officers
Chairman & Chief Executive	Emilio Botín-Sanz de Sautuola
First Vice Chairman	Jaime Botín-Sanz de Sautuola
Second Vice Chairman	Matías Rodríguez Inciarte
Executive Vice President	Ignacio Benjumea
Senior Vice President	José Manuel Maceda

Others (Senior Executives)
Commercial Banking, Spain	Casto de la Mora *Executive Vice President*
Commercial Banking, International	Javier Torres *Senior Vice President*
Commercial Banking, Latin America	Ignacio Rasero *Senior Vice President*
Finance	Juan Rodríguez Inciarte *Executive Vice President*
Financial Institutions	Rafael G Abolafio *Senior Vice President*
Institutional Banking	Francisco J Ibarrola *Senior Vice President*
	José María Espí *Executive Vice President*
Global Banking	Francisco Martín *Executive Vice President*
Global Markets	Didac Artés *Senior Vice President*
	José Barreiro
	Robert Harding
Strategic Advisor	José Juan Ruiz

General-Lending (DCM, SL)
Head of Corporate Banking	José Illana *Senior Vice President*
	Antonio Bernardo *Senior Vice President*

General-Investment
Head of Investment	Ana Patricia Botín *Executive Vice President*

General - Treasury
Head of Treasury	Ravinder Mehra
	Javier Pazos *Senior Vice President*
	Miguel Villanueva *Senior Vice President*

Relationship Manager
Institutional Relations	José Manuel Reyero *Senior Vice President*
	Francisco Luzón *Executive Vice President*
Investor Relations	Victor Barallat

Debt Capital Markets / Fixed Income
Head of Fixed Income	Emilio Osana
Head of Fixed Income Trading	José Rodríguez

Equity Capital Markets
Head of Equity Capital Markets	José Maria F Castañera
Head of Trading	José Rodríguez

Syndicated Lending
Other (Syndicated Lending)
Global Banking, Credit	Teodoro Bragado *Executive Vice President*
	Francisco Calleja *Senior Vice President*
Credit, Spain	Javier Peralta *Executive Vice President*
	José Ramón Rodrigo *Senior Vice President*

Loan-Related Activities
Trade Finance	Antonio G del Riego
Leasing & Asset Finance	Francisco Pérez Mansilla

Other (Trade Finance)
International Credits	Belén Aguilera
Vehicle Finance	Genaro Llampayas

Settlement / Clearing
Operations	Ricardo Alonso *Executive Vice President*

www.euromoneydirectory.com   SPAIN (+34)

Asset Management
Investment Funds   Carmen Cavero
                                            Encarna Dávila
Portfolio Management   Prosper Lamote
Other (Asset Management)
Asset Management, Spain   Eduardo Suárez *Senior Vice President*
Equity Investments   Gonzalo Milans
Other Departments
Economic Research   Jacobo Moreno
                                            Ignacio Rupérez
Debt Recovery / Restructuring   José Manuel Pena
Administration
Head of Administration   Antonio Aparicio *Senior Vice President*
Technology & Systems
Systems   Francisco Navamuel *Senior Vice President*
                                            Eduardo G Arroyo

Legal / In-House Counsel
Legal Counsel, International   Pablo Castilla
Legal Counsel, Spain   José Ignacio Uclés *Senior Vice President*
Corporate Communications
                                            Federico Ysart
                                            Ana Rodríguez Moreira

Accounts / Audit
Internal Audit   José Manuel Hernández Beneyto *Senior Vice President*
                                            David Arce *Executive Vice President*
Internal Audit, Commercial Banking   Miguel García Izquierdo
Cost Control   Reyes Artiñano
                                            José R Jiménez *Executive Vice President*
Tax Counsel   Junio Banacloche
Mangement Accounting   Imara Barrera
                                            Jesús Cepeda
Financial Accounting   Susana Clemente
Financial Standards   José María G Tubío
Comptroller   José Tejón *Executive Vice President*
Other (Administration)
Human Resources, Corporate Policy   Francisco González Robatto *Executive Vice President*
                                            Basillio Colmenero
                                            Carlos G de Juana
                                            José Luis G Alciturri
Planning & Research   Pedro Chicharro *Executive Vice President*

Banco Santander   Head Office

Paseo de Pereda 9/12, E-39004 Santander
PO Box 45, E-39080 Santander
Tel: (942) 206 100 **Fax:** (942) 206 302 **Telex:** 35833 **Reuters:** BSMX
Senior Executive Officers
Chairman   Emilio Botín-Sanz de Ríos

Banco Simeon SA   Head Office

Policarpo Sanz 5, E-36202 Vigo
Tel: (986) 810 700 **Fax:** (986) 810 762 **Telex:** 83288 **Swift:** CGDIES2V **Cable:** SIMEON
Senior Executive Officers
President   Dr Antonio Tomás Correia
Managing Director   José H Cerqueira Gonçalves
Secretary   Manuel Mendoza Villar
International Division   Onorat Perez *Head*
Others (Senior Executives)
                                            José Simöes Correia *Director*
                                            Alfredo Manuel Antas Teles *Director*
                                            José Rodrigues Rito *Director*
                                            Mateo Ruiz Oriol Castera *Director*
                                            Jacinto Rey González *Director*
                                            Olegario Vázquez Raña *Director*

SPAIN (+34)   www.euromoneydirectory.com

Banco Simeon SA (cont)
Other Departments
Head, Financial Markets (Madrid)   Mario de Oliveira

Banco Urquijo SA   Head Office
Príncipe de Vergara 131, E-28002 Madrid
Tel: (91) 337 2000 **Fax:** (91) 337 2096 **Telex:** 27854 BUKMDE **Swift:** UIJO ES MM
Email: j_fdezrubies@bancourquijo.es **Reuters:** URQX **Cable:** URQUIJO

Senior Executive Officers
Chief Executive Officer   Alfonso Alvárez Tolcheff ☎ 337 2178
Financial Director   Luis Gabarda Duran Head of Capital Markets ☎ 337 2264
Chief Operating Officer   Francisco Claveria ☎ 337 2094
Treasurer   Milagros Méndez ☎ 337 2066
International Division   José Ramon Fernández-Rubíes ☎ 337 2105

Debt Capital Markets / Fixed Income
Global Head   Santiago Arpon ☎ 337 2050

Domestic Government Bonds
Head of Sales   Alfonso Oliva ☎ 337 2230
Head of Trading   Consuelo Curia ☎ 337 2220

Eurobonds
Head of Origination; Head of Syndication   Juan Quiroga ☎ 337 2111
Head of Sales   Francisco Lara ☎ 337 2220
Head of Trading   Jesus Mendoza ☎ 337 2220

Medium-Term Notes
Head of Origination; Head of Structuring   Juan Quiroga ☎ 337 2111
Head of Sales   Francisco Lara ☎ 337 2220

Fixed-Income Repo
Head of Repo   Paz Arribas ☎ 337 2210
Matched Book Manager   Guadalupe Pallares ☎ 337 2210
Sales   Alfonso Oliva ☎ 337 2230

Equity Capital Markets
International Equities
Head of Sales   Raquel Cuesta ☎ 337 2220

Syndicated Lending
Global Head   Luis Gabarda Duran Head of Capital Markets ☎ 337 2264
Head of Origination; Head of Syndication   Juan Quiroga ☎ 337 2111

Loan-Related Activities
Trade Finance   Luz Maria Ecclefield ☎ 337 2103

Money Markets
Global Head   Paz Arribas ☎ 337 2210

Domestic Commercial Paper
Head of Origination   Juan Quiroga ☎ 337 2111

Foreign Exchange
Global Head   Javier Torres ☎ 337 2200
Head of Institutional Sales   Enrique Kaibel
Head of Trading   José Manuel Lesmes ☎ 337 2200

Risk Management
Global Head   Santiago Arpon ☎ 337 2050

Fixed Income Derivatives / Risk Management
Global Head   Santiago Arpon ☎ 337 2050

Foreign Exchange Derivatives / Risk Management
Cross-Currency Swaps, Trading   Enrique Cebas ☎ 337 2200

Corporate Finance / M&A Advisory
Global Head   Jaime Lacalle ☎ 337 2144

Settlement / Clearing
Regional Head   José Ramon Fernández Rubies ☎ 337 2105

Global Custody
Regional Head   José Ramon Fernández Rubies ☎ 337 2105

Other (Global Custody)
    Esther Dannert International Custody ☎ 337 2102
    E e_gudrun@bancourquijo.es
    Belén Saavedra International Custody ☎ 337 2097 F 337 2096
    E b_saavedra@bancourquijo.es

1412 Euromoney Directory 1999

www.euromoneydirectory.com　　　　　　　　　　SPAIN (+34)

Other Departments
Private Banking　　　　　　　　　Alfonso Rodriguez ☏ 337 2167
Correspondent Banking　　　　　 Luis Rosales ☏ 337 2524

Banco de Valencia SA　　　　　　　　　　　　　　　　　　Head Office

Pintor Sorolla 2/4, E-46002 Valencia
Tel: (96) 398 4640 **Fax:** (96) 398 4642 **Telex:** 62741 VALCA E **Swift:** VALE ES VV

Senior Executive Officers
Chairman & President　　　　　　　　　　　Julio de Miguel ☏ 398 4506
Chief Executive Officer　　　　　　　　　　 Domingo Parra ☏ 398 4503
Financial Director; Chief Operating Officer;　Juan Hernández *Manager, International* ☏ 398 4640
Treasurer
Manager　　　　　　　　　　　　　　　　　 Bartolome Diaz ☏ **(91) 398 4503**

Syndicated Lending
Department: International Division
Avenida del Puerto 31, 2nd Floor, E-46021 Valencia
Tel: 398 4640 **Fax:** 398 4642
Head of Syndicated Lending　　　　　　　　Víctor Beristain *Assistant General Manager* ☏ 398 4503
Head of Syndication　　　　　　　　　　　　Juan Hernández *Manager, International* ☏ 398 4640

Foreign Exchange
Department: International Division
Avenida del Puerto 31, 2nd Floor, E-46021 Valencia
Tel: 398 4633 **Fax:** 398 4640
Head of Foreign Exchange　　　　　　　　　Juan Hernández *Manager, International* ☏ 398 4640

Other Departments
Correspondent Banking　　　　　　　　　　 Juan Hernández *Manager, International* ☏ 398 4640

Banco Zaragozano SA

Coso 47, E-50003 Zaragoza, Aragon
Tel: (976) 470 303 **Fax:** (976) 296 941 **Telex:** 58044 BANZA E **Email:** info@bancozaragozano.es
Website: www.bancozaragozano.es

Senior Executive Officers
President　　　　　　　　　　　　　　　　　Alberto Dealcocer Torra
President　　　　　　　　　　　　　　　　　Alberto Cortina De Alcocer
Chief Executive Officer　　　　　　　　　　 Felipe Echevarria Herrerias *Chief Executive*

Bank of America SA

Capitán Haya 1, E-28020 Madrid
Tel: (91) 396 5000 **Fax:** (91) 396 5123 **Telex:** 27574 **Reuters:** BOAZ, BMRA

Senior Executive Officers
Financial Director　　　　　　　　　　　　　Miguel Fernández Tardío
Chief Operating Officer　　　　　　　　　　 Benito Roncero
Treasurer　　　　　　　　　　　　　　　　　Inigo Trincado
Managing Director / General Manager　　　 Prudencio Pedrosa

Bank Austria Creditanstalt　　　　　　　　　　　　　　Representative Office

Fernando El Santo 3/3, E-28010 Madrid
Tel: (91) 319 3900 **Fax:** (91) 319 3458

Senior Executive Officers
Representative　　　　　　　　　　　　　　Johannes-Peter Spalek

Bank Brussels Lambert　　　　　　　　　　　　　　　　Full Branch Office

Avenida Diagonal 605-8°, piso 5°, Edificio Herón Barcelona, E-08028 Barcelona
Tel: (93) 439 0303 **Fax:** (93) 439 5118 **Telex:** 97582 BBLB E

Settlement / Clearing
Operations　　　　　　　　　　　　　　　　Antonio Lázaro *Operation Manager*

Euromoney Directory 1999　**1413**

SPAIN (+34) www.euromoneydirectory.com

Bank Brussels Lambert (cont)
Administration
Other (Administration)
Commercial Banking — Antonio Ollé *Commercial Director*

Bank Brussels Lambert — Full Branch Office
Paseo de la Castellana 95, piso 14°, E-28046 Madrid
Tel: (91) 598 4000 Fax: (91) 598 4001 Telex: 49548 Swift: BBRU ES M
Senior Executive Officers
General Manager — Andrés Trujillo Rios

The Bank of New York — Representative Office
Torre de Colón 1, piso 13a°, Plaza de Colón 2, E-28046 Madrid
Tel: (91) 319 2213 Fax: (91) 319 2247 Telex: 49087
Senior Executive Officers
Representative — Javier I de Ussel

Bankers Trust Company — Full Branch Office
Paseo de la Castellana 31, piso 4°, E-28046 Madrid
Tel: (91) 538 7500 Fax: (91) 538 7588; (91) 538 7599 Telex: 27261 BTCO E
Senior Executive Officers
Managing Director — Julio A García García

BANKINTER SA — Head Office
Formerly known as: Banco Intercontinental Espanol SA
Paseo de la Castellana 29, E-28046 Madrid
Tel: (91) 339 7500 Fax: (91) 339 7540 Telex: 42760 BANKI E Swift: BKBK ES MM
Email: international@bankinter.es
Website: www.bankinter.es

Senior Executive Officers
Chairman — Jaime Botin
Chief Executive Officer — Juan Arelia
Chief Operating Officer — Fernando Azcona ✉ acubeiro@bankinter.es
Treasurer — Pablo de Diego *Head, Treasury & Capital Markets Div*
Managing Director / General Manager — Jaime Echegoyen

Debt Capital Markets / Fixed Income
Tel: 339 7801 Fax: 339 7625
Head of Debt Capital Markets — Lazaro De Lazaro ☏ 339 7842

Domestic Government Bonds
Head of Sales — Maria Mtz-Verdu ☏ 339 7839 ✉ mmverdu@bankinter.es

Eurobonds
Head of Origination — David Perez ☏ 339 7811 ✉ dperez@bankinter.es

Medium-Term Notes
Head of Origination — David Perez ☏ 339 7811 ✉ dperez@bankinter.es

Fixed-Income Repo
Head of Repo — Rosendo Brenes ☏ 339 7822 ✉ rbrenes@bankinter.es

Equity Capital Markets
Domestic Equities
Head of Sales — Maria Mtz-Verdu ☏ 339 7839 ✉ mmverdu@bankinter.es
Head of Trading — Francisco Rgez-Acosta ☏ 339 7602

International Equities
Head of Trading — Alonso Madariaga ☏ 339 7839

Warrants
Head of Trading — Estanislao Urquijo *Head, Financial Products* ✉ eurquijo@bankinter.es

Money Markets
Head of Money Markets — Lazaro De Lazaro ☏ 339 7842

Domestic Commercial Paper
Head of Trading — Rosendo Brenes ☏ 339 7822 ✉ rbrenes@bankinter.es

SPAIN (+34)

Foreign Exchange
Head of Foreign Exchange — Kiko Lopez T 339 7823
Risk Management
Fixed Income Derivatives / Risk Management
IR Swaps Trading — Estanislao Urquijo *Head, Financial Products* E **eurquijo@bankinter.es**
Foreign Exchange Derivatives / Risk Management
Vanilla FX option Trading — Luis Munoz T 339 7611
Exotic Options (Barriers, Range, Timers, Digitals, Faders etc)
Trading — Carlos Encinas E **cencinas@bankinter.es**
OTC Equity Derivatives
Trading — Estanislao Urquijo *Head, Financial Products* E **eurquijo@bankinter.es**
Settlement / Clearing
Head of Settlement / Clearing — Jose Luis Sanchez T 339 8175 E **jlschez@bankinter.es**
Global Custody
Head of Global Custody — Antonio Timon T 339 8175 E **atimon@bankinter.es**
Other Departments
Proprietary Trading — Lazaro De Lazaro T 339 7842
Private Banking — Gonzalo Nebreda
Correspondent Banking — Javier Martin-Casado T 339 7530 E **jmartinc@bankinter.es**
Administration
Technology & Systems

Jesus Marquina

Legal / In-House Counsel

Francisco Pala

Compliance

Fernando Azcona E **acubeiro@bankinter.es**

Public Relations

Angeles Cubeiro

Banque Sudameris
Representative Office
Serrano 67, E-28006 Madrid
Tel: (91) 426 4000 **Fax:** (91) 426 4063 **Telex:** 23091
Senior Executive Officers
Representative — Giacomo Ghillani

Barclays Bank SA
Subsidiary Company
Plaza de Colón 1, E-28046 Madrid
Tel: (91) 336 1000; (91) 336 1318/1420 **Fax:** (91) 336 1134; (91) 336 1925 **Telex:** 27385 BRCLA-E **Swift:** BARC ES MM
Cable: BARSPAIN
Senior Executive Officers
Chairman — Carlos Martínez de Campos
Vice Chairman — Manuel V López Figueroa
Financial Director — Jacobo González-Robatto *Finance Director*
Country Manager, Managing Director — Eduardo Arbizu
Others (Senior Executives)
IT & Resources — Francisco Elias
Corporate Banking — Francisco Lana
Treasurer — Enrique Titos
Debt Capital Markets / Fixed Income
Tel: 336 1211 **Fax:** 336 1695
Country Head — Luis Rodriguez de Guzmán *Manager* T 336 1387 F 336 1429
Fixed-Income Repo
Trading — Pilar Soler *Dealer*
Money Markets
Country Head — Luis Rodriguez de Guzman *Manager* T 336 1387 F 336 1429
Foreign Exchange
Country Head — Alfonso Melon T 336 1246 F 336 1429
Risk Management
Country Head — José Maria Martínez González T 336 1848 F 336 1756

Euromoney Directory 1999 **1415**

SPAIN (+34)　　　　　www.euromoneydirectory.com

Baring Brothers (España) SA
Subsidiary Company

Montalbán 7, piso 6°, E-28014 Madrid
Tel: (91) 524 9024 **Fax:** (91) 531 3336

Senior Executive Officers
Managing Director　　　　　　　　Iñigo Churruca
Corporate Finance / M&A Advisory
Country Head　　　　　　　　　　Iñigo Churruca *Managing Director*

Bayerische Hypo-und Vereinsbank AG
Representative Office

Alternative trading name: Hypovereinsbank
Formerly known as: Bayerische Vereinsbank
Plaza de Colon 2, E-28046 Madrid
Tel: (91) 308 3051 **Fax:** (91) 319 8671 **Email:** hypover@accessneet.es

Senior Executive Officers
Senior Relationship Manager　　　　Franz Arnold

Beta Capital SA
Head Office

Claudio Coello 78, E-28001 Madrid
Tel: (91) 436 5600 **Telex:** 41194

Senior Executive Officers
Chairman　　　　　　　　　　　　Alfonso Ferrari
Managing Director / General Manager　Fernando Ortesa

BHF-BANK
Representative Office

Marqués de Cubas 21, piso 4°, E-28014 Madrid
Tel: (91) 429 0072 **Fax:** (91) 429 0341 **Telex:** 46206

Senior Executive Officers
Representative　　　　　　　　　Torsten-Detlef Halenke

Bilbao Bizkaia Kutxa

Gran Vía 23, piso 3°, E-48001 Bilbao
Tel: (94) 487 7775 **Fax:** (94) 487 7208; (94) 487 7212 **Telex:** 31873 **Swift:** BASK ES 2B **Email:** bbk0007@bbk.es

Senior Executive Officers
Fax: 487 7660
Chairman & Chief Executive Officer　　José Ignacio Berroeta ☎ **487 7152**
General Manager　　　　　　　　　 Manfred Nolte ☎ **487 7108**

Others (Senior Executives)
　　　　　　　　　　　　　　　　Guillermo Ibañez *General Controller* ☎ **487 7170**

General-Lending (DCM, SL)
Head of Corporate Banking　　　　　Gabril Astiz *General Manager* ☎ **487 7109** 🅕 **487 7211**
General - Treasury
Head of Treasury　　　　　　　　　José M Escribano *Treasury* ☎ **487 7583** 🅕 **487 7211**
Debt Capital Markets / Fixed Income
Head of Debt Capital Markets　　　　Ricardo Gabilondo *Capital Markets* ☎ **487 7570**
Equity Capital Markets
Head of Equity Capital Markets　　　 Ricardo Gabilondo *Capital Markets* ☎ **487 7570**
Syndicated Lending
Loan-Related Activities
Trade Finance　　　　　　　　　　Gabril Astiz *General Manager* ☎ **487 7109** 🅕 **487 7211**
Project Finance　　　　　　　　　 Javier Egaña *Deputy General Manager* ☎ **487 7124**
Foreign Exchange
Head of Foreign Exchange　　　　　José M Escribano *Treasury* ☎ **487 7583** 🅕 **487 7211**
Asset Management
Investment Funds　　　　　　　　 José Luis Lorenzo ☎ **487 7918**

www.euromoneydirectory.com					SPAIN (+34)

Administration
Public Relations
    Juan M Saenz de Buruaga *Deputy General Manager* ☏ **487 7118**
Accounts / Audit
    Gillermo Ibañez *General Controller* ☏ **487 7159**
Other (Administration)
International Division   Agustin Lacambra *Head* ☏ **487 7749**

BNP-España   Subsidiary Company

Genova 27, E-28004 Madrid
Tel: (91) 349 1100 **Fax:** (91) 349 1282 **Telex:** 22653

Senior Executive Officers
Chairman   Jean-Louis Hautcoeur
Chief Executive Officer   Jean-Claude Tremosa *Vice Chairman & Executive Officer*
General Director   Christian Giraudon.
Administration
Head of Administration   Serge Nicolaou *General Director*
Public Relations
     Danielle Flamant *Director of Communications*

Caisse Centrale des Banques Populaires   Representative Office

Paseo de la Castellana 18, piso 4°, E-28046 Madrid
Tel: (91) 431 9760 **Fax:** (91) 577 4562

Senior Executive Officers
Representative   Patrick Lara

Caixa d'Estalvis de Catalunya   Full Branch Office

Formerly known as: Caixa de Catalunya
Alternative trading name: Caixa Catalunya

Plaza Antonio Maura 6, E-08003 Barcelona
Tel: (93) 484 5000 **Fax:** (93) 484 5141 **Telex:** 50209 CADC **Swift:** CESC ES BB
Email: secretaria.general@caixacat.es
Website: www.caixacat.es

Senior Executive Officers
Chairman   Antoni Serra
Chief Executive Officer   Francesc Costabella
     Josep M Loza *Deputy Chief Executive*
     Carles Monreal *Deputy Chief Executive*
Treasurer   Isidre Blanch ☏ **484 5323**
Company Secretary   Jordi Monreal
International Division   Francesc X Fornt
Others (Senior Executives)
Assistant General Manager   Lluis Gasull
     Alfons-Joan Aran
     Francesc Sàez
Assistant Manager   Josep Codorniu ☏ **484 5556**
     Joan Arnau

General-Lending (DCM, SL)
Head of Corporate Banking   Isidre Blanch ☏ **484 5323**
Debt Capital Markets / Fixed Income
Head of Fixed Income   Santiago Mora ☏ **306 9404**
Head of Fixed Income Sales   Joan Carles Cebrián ☏ **306 9401**
Government Bonds
Head of Sales   Joan Carles Cebrián ☏ **306 9401**
Head of Trading   Santiago Mora ☏ **306 9404**
Eurobonds
Head of Sales   Joan Carles Cebrián ☏ **306 9401**
Head of Trading   Santiago Mora ☏ **306 9404**
Libor-Based / Floating-Rate Products
FRN Sales   Joan Carles Cebrián ☏ **306 9401**

SPAIN (+34)

www.euromoneydirectory.com

Caixa d'Estalvis de Catalunya (cont)

Fixed-Income Repo
Head of Repo — Ricard Ibarra ☏ 306 9412
Head of Trading — Mar Gallego ☏ 306 9403

Equity Capital Markets
Head of Equity Capital Markets — Isidre Blanch ☏ 484 5323

Domestic Equities
Head of Trading — Isidre Blanch ☏ 484 5323

Convertibles / Equity-Linked
Head of Trading — Santiago Mora ☏ 306 9404

Syndicated Lending
Loan-Related Activities
Trade Finance — Aagusti Faus ☏ 484 5175

Money Markets
Head of Money Markets — Ricard Ibarra ☏ 306 9412

Domestic Commercial Paper
Head of Trading — Mar Gallego ☏ 306 9403

Eurocommercial Paper
Head of Trading — Mar Gallego ☏ 306 9403

Wholesale Deposits
Head of Sales — Mar Gallego ☏ 306 9403

Foreign Exchange
Head of Foreign Exchange — Ricard Ibarra ☏ 306 9412
Head of Trading — Josep Garcia ☏ 306 9411

Risk Management
Head of Risk Management — Santiago Mora ☏ 306 9404

Fixed Income Derivatives / Risk Management
Head of Sales — Joan Carles Cebrián ☏ 306 9401
Trading — Santiago Mora ☏ 306 9404

Foreign Exchange Derivatives / Risk Management
Spot / Forwards Trading — Victor Urós ☏ 306 4913

OTC Equity Derivatives
Sales — Joan Carles Cebrián ☏ 306 9401
Trading — Victor Urós ☏ 306 4913

OTC Commodity Derivatives
Head — Victor Urós ☏ 306 4913

OTC Credit Derivatives
Head — Isidre Blanch ☏ 484 5323

Exchange-Traded Derivatives
Head — Isidre Blanch ☏ 484 5323

Settlement / Clearing
Head of Settlement / Clearing; Equity Settlement; Fixed-Income Settlement; Operations — Isabel Castells ☏ 484 5932

Global Custody
Head of Global Custody — Luis Gutierrez ☏ 484 5316

Other Departments
Chief Credit Officer — Lluis Àangel Palacios ☏ 484 5035
Correspondent Banking — Francesc X Fornt ☏ 484 5183

Administration
Head of Administration — Josep Codorniu ☏ 484 5556
Business Development — Àngels Balsells
Head of Marketing — Miquel Perdiguer

Technology & Systems
Ignacio Alegre ☏ 484 5489

Legal / In-House Counsel
Manuel Ledesma ☏ 484 5025

Public Relations
Josep M Montseny ☏ 484 5085

Accounts / Audit
Accounts — Antoni Hernandez
Audit — Alexandre Subirats

www.euromoneydirectory.com   SPAIN (+34)

La Caixa   Head Office

Alternative trading name: Caja de Ahorros y Pensiones de Barcelona
Avenida Diagonal 621/629, E-08028 Barcelona
Tel: (93) 404 6000 **Fax:** (93) 339 5703

Senior Executive Officers
President & Chief Executive Officer	José Vilarasau
Senior Executive Vice President	Isidro Fainé
Senior Executive Vice President	Antonio Brufau
Executive Vice President	Antonio Massanell
Executive Vice President	Tomás Muniesa
Executive Vice President	Rosa Maria Cullell
Senior Vice President	Joan Sogues
Senior Vice President	Fernando Ramirez
Senior Vice President	Antoni Vila
International Division	Alfonso Maristany
	Félix Alegre *Head, Foreign Dept*

General - Treasury
Head of Treasury — Fernando Cánovas *Head, Treasury & Financial Markets*

Debt Capital Markets / Fixed Income
Head of Debt Capital Markets — Asunción Ortega *Head*

Risk Management
Head of Risk Management — Jesús Escolano *GM, Risk & Foreign*

Other (FI Derivatives)
Special Risks Management — José Antonio Ruiz-Garma *General Manager*

Settlement / Clearing
Electronic Banking — Maria Victòria Matia *Head, Services Mgt & Electronic Banking*

Other Departments
Economic Research — Josep M Carrau *Head of Research*

Administration
Head of Marketing — Ricardo Agramunt *Head*

Technology & Systems
DP Technology / Telecommunications — Ramón José Rius *Head*
Organization & Information — Luis Furnells *General Manager*

Legal / In-House Counsel
Legal Services — Sebastià Sastre *General Manager*

Corporate Communications
Communications & External Relations — Javier Zuloaga *Head*

Accounts / Audit
Internal Audit — Joan Llopis *Head*
Accounting & Management Control — Joaquim Vilar *Head*

Other (Administration)
Human Resources	Andrés Pita *General Manager*
Quality	Luis Rullán *General Manager*
General Services Management	Julián Cabanillas *Head*
Applied Strategy Management	Pere Huguet *Head*
Taxation Services	Javier José Paso *Head*

Caixa Manresa   Head Office

Alternative trading name: Caixa d'Estalvis de Manresa
Passeig de Pere III 24, Manresa, E-08240 Barcelona
Tel: (93) 878 2700 **Fax:** (93) 878 2725; (93) 878 2756 **Telex:** 94605 CMAN E **Swift:** CECA ES MM 041
Email: bustia@caixamanresa.com

Senior Executive Officers
President	Valentí Roqueta
President	Ramon Busquet
Chief Executive Officer	Adolf Todó
Financial Director	Jaume Masana
Technical General Secretary	Feliu Formosa

Syndicated Lending
Other (Syndicated Lending)

Ferran Viladomat *Loans Director*

Administration
Head of Administration — Manuel Ferrer *Organization Director*

Euromoney Directory 1999 **1419**

SPAIN (+34) www.euromoneydirectory.com

Caixa Manresa (cont)
Technology & Systems
Rossend Vergé *Systems Director*
Other (Administration)
Josep Vives *Customers Director*

Caja de Ahorros del Mediterraneo — Head Office

San Fernando 40, E-03001 Alicante
Tel: (96) 590 5000; (96) 590 6101 **Fax:** (96) 590 6901; (96) 590 5276 **Swift:** CAAM ES 2A
Website: www.cam.es

Senior Executive Officers
President	Roman Bono
Financial Director	Roberto López
Chief Operating Officer	Jorge Abad
Treasurer	José Pina
Managing Director / General Manager	Juan Antonio Gisbert

Debt Capital Markets / Fixed Income
Head of Debt Capital Markets — José Pina

Equity Capital Markets
Head of Equity Capital Markets — José Pina

Syndicated Lending
Head of Syndicated Lending — José Pina

Money Markets
Head of Money Markets — José Pina

Foreign Exchange
Head of Foreign Exchange — José Pina

Risk Management
Head of Risk Management — José Pina

Corporate Finance / M&A Advisory
Head of Corporate Finance — José Pina

Settlement / Clearing
Head of Settlement / Clearing — José Pina

Caja de Ahorros de Galicia — Head Office

Alternative trading name: Caixa Galicia
Rua Nueva 30, E-15003 A Coruña
Tel: (981) 187 000 **Fax:** (981) 188 001 **Telex:** 82123 CAGC E **Swift:** CAGL ES MM
Website: www.caixagalicia.es

Senior Executive Officers
President	José Ramón Docal Labaen
Financial Director	Juan Dapena Traseira *Financial & Int'l Director* 🗈 **(91) 586 6007**
Treasurer	José De la Morena Rello 🗈 **(91) 586 6077**
Director General	José Luis Méndez López

Debt Capital Markets / Fixed Income
Department: Financial Markets Division
Serrano 45, E-28001 Madrid
Tel: +34 (91) 586 6000 **Fax:** +34 (91) 586 6006
Head of Debt Capital Markets — José De la Morena Rello 🗈 **(91) 586 6077**

Domestic Government Bonds
Head of Sales — Ramón Gómez 🗈 **(91) 577 7794**
Head of Trading — Manuel Sánchez 🗈 **(91) 586 6020**

Non-Domestic Government Bonds
— Carlos De la Torre 🗈 **(91) 586 6079**

Eurobonds
Head of Sales — José de Pablo 🗈 **(91) 586 6021**
Head of Trading — Arturo Bermúdez 🗈 **(91) 586 6349**

Libor-Based / Floating-Rate Products
FRN Origination — José de Pablo 🗈 **(91) 586 6021**
FRN Sales — Arturo Bermúdez 🗈 **(91) 586 6349**

www.euromoneydirectory.com   SPAIN (+34)

Equity Capital Markets
Department: Financial Markets Division
Serrano 45, E-28001 Madrid
Tel: +34 (91) 586 6000 **Fax:** +34 (91) 586 6006
Head of Equity Capital Markets   José De la Morena Rello ☏ **(91) 586 6077**

Domestic Equities
Head of Sales   José de Pablo ☏ **(91) 586 6021**
Head of Trading   Arturo Bermúdez ☏ **(91) 586 6349**

International Equities
Head of Sales   José de Pablo ☏ **(91) 586 6021**
Head of Trading   Arturo Bermúdez ☏ **(91) 586 6349**

Syndicated Lending
Department: Financial Markets Division
Serrano 45, E-28001 Madrid
Tel: +34 (91) 586 6000 **Fax:** +34 (91) 586 6006
Head of Syndicated Lending   José De la Morena Rello ☏ **(91) 586 6077**
Head of Syndication   José de Pablo ☏ **(91) 586 6021**
Head of Trading   Arturo Bermúdez ☏ **(91) 586 6349**

Money Markets
Department: Financial Markets Division
Serrano 45, E-28001 Madrid
Tel: +34 (91) 586 6000 **Fax:** +34 (91) 586 6006
Head of Money Markets   Moisés Rodríguez ☏ **(91) 431 7222**

Wholesale Deposits
Head of Sales   Carlos De la Torre ☏ **(91) 586 6079**

Foreign Exchange
Department: Financial Markets Division
Serrano 45, E-28001 Madrid
Tel: +34 (91) 586 6000 **Fax:** +34 (91) 586 6006
Head of Foreign Exchange   Moisés Rodríguez ☏ **(91) 431 7222**

FX Traders / Sales People
                                        Angel Cancela
                                        Miguel A Mestres
                                        Fernando Pedreira
                                        Javier Ayuso

Risk Management
Global Head   José de Pablo ☏ **(91) 586 6021**

Foreign Exchange Derivatives / Risk Management
Cross-Currency Swaps, Sales / Marketing José de Pablo ☏ **(91) 586 6021**
Cross-Currency Swaps, Trading   Arturo Bermúdez ☏ **(91) 586 6349**

Corporate Finance / M&A Advisory
Department: Financial Markets Division
Serrano 45, E-28001 Madrid
Tel: +34 (91) 586 6000 **Fax:** +34 (91) 586 6006
Head of Corporate Finance   Francisco Zamorano ☏ **586 6012**

Settlement / Clearing
Department: Financial Markets division
Serrano 45, E-28001 Madrid
Tel: +34 (91) 586 6000 **Fax:** +34 (91) 586 6006
Head of Settlement / Clearing   David Estany ☏ **586 6065**

Other Departments
Correspondent Banking   Angel L Rojo ☏ **(91) 586 6055** ✉ **arojo@caixagalicia.es**

Caja de Ahorros de la Inmaculada de Aragón   Head Office

Independencia 10, E-50004 Zaragoza, Aragon
Tel: (976) 718 100 **Fax:** (976) 718 306 **Telex:** 58480 CAIC E **Swift:** CECA ES MM
Website: www.cai.es

Senior Executive Officers
President   José Maria Sas ☏ **718 116**
Chief Executive Officer   Juan José Gravalos *General Manager* ☏ **718 109**
Financial Director   Luis Calvera *Deputy General Manager* ☏ **718 113**
Treasurer   Raimundo Garcia ☏ **718 122**

General-Lending (DCM, SL)
Head of Corporate Banking   Adolfo Duque ☏ **718 105**

Euromoney Directory 1999   **1421**

SPAIN (+34)
www.euromoneydirectory.com

Caja de Ahorros de la Inmaculada de Aragón (cont)

General-Investment
Head of Investment — Antonio Hernandez ☎ 718 131

Debt Capital Markets / Fixed Income
Head of Debt Capital Markets — Raimundo Garcia ☎ 718 122

Domestic Government Bonds
Head of Sales — Raimundo Garcia ☎ 718 122

Eurobonds
Head of Origination — Raimundo Garcia ☎ 718 122

Medium-Term Notes
Head of Origination — Raimundo Garcia ☎ 718 122

Private Placements
Head of Origination — Raimundo Garcia ☎ 718 122

Asset-Backed Securities / Securitization
Global Head — Raimundo Garcia ☎ 718 122

Mortgage-Backed Securities
Global Head — Raimundo Garcia ☎ 718 122

Fixed-Income Repo
Head of Repo — Raimundo Garcia ☎ 718 122

Equity Capital Markets
Head of Equity Capital Markets — Raimundo Garcia ☎ 718 122

Domestic Equities
Head of Origination — Raimundo Garcia ☎ 718 122

International Equities
Head of Origination — Raimundo Garcia ☎ 718 122

Convertibles / Equity-Linked
Head of Origination — Raimundo Garcia ☎ 718 122

Warrants
Head of Sales — Raimundo Garcia ☎ 718 122

Equity Repo / Securities Lending
Marketing — Raimundo Garcia ☎ 718 122

Syndicated Lending
Head of Syndicated Lending — Raimundo Garcia ☎ 718 122

Money Markets
Head of Money Markets — Raimundo Garcia ☎ 718 122

Foreign Exchange
Head of Foreign Exchange — Raimundo Garcia ☎ 718 122

Risk Management
Head of Risk Management — Elena Vivas ☎ 718 499

Corporate Finance / M&A Advisory
Head of Corporate Finance — Elena Vivas ☎ 718 499

Global Custody
Head of Global Custody — Miguel A Serrano ☎ 718 488

Asset Management
Head — Jesus Rubio ☎ 718 290

Other Departments
Proprietary Trading — Francisco Egido ☎ 718 101
Private Banking — Juan Zubizarreta ☎ 718 642

Administration
Business Development; Head of Marketing — Martin Hermo ☎ 718 118

Technology & Systems
Javier Perez ☎ 718 118

Public Relations
José A Fando ☎ 718 489

www.euromoneydirectory.com   SPAIN (+34)

Caja de Ahorros de Manlleu
Head Office

Plaza Fra Bernadi 24-25, E-08560 Manlleu, Barcelona
Apartado de Correos 5, Manlleu, Barcelona
Tel: (93) 851 0800 **Fax:** (93) 850 6343 **Telex:** 50973 CECME **Email:** bdgbe@caixamanlleu.es
Website: www.caixamanlleu.es

Senior Executive Officers
Chairman   Pedro Rifa Ferrer
General Manager   Didac Herrero Autet

Caja de Ahorros Municipal de Vigo - CAIXAVIGO
Head Office

Alternative trading name: Caixavigo
Avenida García Barbón 1/3, E-36201 Vigo
Apartado de Correos 1512, Vigo
Tel: (986) 431 133 **Fax:** (986) 430 980 **Telex:** 83079 **Cable:** CAJAHORROS

Senior Executive Officers
President   Ramón Cornejo Molíns
Financial Director   Angel López-Corona Davila *Financial Director*
Managing Director   Julio Fernández Gayoso
Secretary   Fernando García del Valle Gutiérrez
International Division   Dolores Montero Vilariño *Director*

Others (Senior Executives)
Santiago González-Babé Ozores *Second Vice President*
Guillermo Alonso Jáudenes *First Vice President*

Debt Capital Markets / Fixed Income
Head of Debt Capital Markets   Maria Victoria Vázquez Sacristán *Director*

Equity Capital Markets
Head of Equity Capital Markets   Maria Victoria Vázquez Sacristán *Director*

Syndicated Lending
Head of Credit Committee   Gonzalo Lamas González *Director*

Settlement / Clearing
Operations   José Luis Pego Alonso *Director*

Administration
Head of Administration   Carlos Vázquez García *Director*

Technology & Systems
Technology Counsel   José María Carro Martín *Director*
Computers   Oscar N. Rodríguez Estrada *Director*

Legal / In-House Counsel
José Luis Franco Grande *Legal Counsel*

Accounts / Audit
Accounts   Manuel González Franco *Area Director*
Audit   Miguel Angel Echarren Chasco *Aœa Director*

Other (Administration)
Commercial Banking   Gregorio Gorriarán Laza *Commercial Director*
Human Resources   Juan José González Portas *Director*

Caja de Ahorros de Murcia
Head Office

Gran Via Escultor Salzillo 23, E-30005 Murcia
Tel: (968) 361 600 **Fax:** (968) 242 214 **Telex:** 67684 CAHM

Senior Executive Officers
President   Ramón Ojeda Valcárcel
General Manager   Carlos Egea Krauel

Euromoney Directory 1999   **1423**

SPAIN (+34)   www.euromoneydirectory.com

Caja de Ahorros de Navarra   Head Office
Alternative trading name: CAN
Avenida de Carlos III 8, E-31002 Pamplona, Navarra
Tel: (948) 208 208; (948) 208 416 **Fax:** (948) 208 227; (948) 211 333 **Telex:** 37826, 37827 **Swift:** CECA ES MM 054
Email: gabinete@can.es
Website: www.can.es

Senior Executive Officers
President	Miguel Sanz Sesma
Vice Chairman	Ramón Bultó Llevat
Financial Director	José Manuel Arlabán Esparza *Assistant Manager, Finance*
Chief Operating Officer	José Antonio Remírez Prados *Director, Administration*
	José Luis Antúnez Riezu *Commercial Director*
Treasurer	José Manuel Aldaz Díaz de Rada
Managing Director	Lorenzo Riezu Artieda
International Division	Joaquin Arbeloa Alvarez *Director, International Division*

Administration
Legal / In-House Counsel
F Javier Arrequi Celaya

Other (Administration)
Human Resources   Rodolfo López Hernández

Caja de Ahorros de Pollença   Head Office
Plaça Major 7, Pollença, Balearic Islands
Tel: (971) 530 162 **Fax:** (971) 530 500; (971) 530 409

Senior Executive Officers
Chairman	Martín Torrandell Orell
General Manager	Gabriel Mestre Far
International Division	Gabriel Bauza Manresa *Foreign Manager*

Others (Senior Executives)
Jaime Amengual Llompart *Assistant General Manager*

Caja de Ahorros Provincial de Guadalajara   Full Branch Office
Juan Bautista Topete 1 & 3, E-19001 Guadalajara
Apartado de Correos 54, E-19001 Guadalajara
Tel: (949) 888 137 **Fax:** (949) 888 134; (949) 888 135 **Telex:** 47968

Senior Executive Officers
President	Juan Pablo Sánchez Sánchez-Seco
General Manager	Félix Pérez Rodriguez

Caja de Ahorros de Santander y Cantabria   Head Office
Formerly known as: Caja de Ahorros de Santander
Plaza de Velarde 3, E-39001 Santander
Apartado de Correos 230, Santander
Tel: (942) 204 500 **Fax:** (942) 361 717 **Telex:** 35835 CADER

Senior Executive Officers
Chairman	Carlos Saas Martinez
General Manager	José María Pérez Alvarez

Caja de Ahorros de Valencia, Castellón y Alicante   Head Office
Alternative trading name: BANCAJA
Caballeros 2, Castellón de la Plana, E-12001 Valencia
Tel: (96) 387 5500; (96) 435 6400 **Fax:** (96) 352 7550; (96) 423 2488 **Telex:** 62609 **Swift:** CVAL ES VV

Senior Executive Officers
Chairman	Julio de Miguel Aynat
First Vice Chairman	Antonio José Tirado Jiménez
Second Vice Chairman	Ana Isabel Zarzuela Luna
Third Vice Chairman	José María Mas Millet

www.euromoneydirectory.com **SPAIN (+34)**

Senior Executive Officers (cont)
Fourth Vice Chairman — José María Cataluña Oliver
Fifth Vice Chairman — Enrique Roig Olmos
Chief Executive Officer — José Fernando García Checa *General Manager & Chief Executive*
Financial Director — Aurelio Izquierdo Gómez *Chief Financial Officer*
Secretary — Angel Daniel Villanueva Pareja
Vice Secretary — Vicente Montesinos Vernetta
Secretary General — Josep Vicent Palacios Bellver

Debt Capital Markets / Fixed Income
Department: Treasury and Capital Markets
Global Head — Benito Castillo Navarro ☎ 387 5551
Head of Fixed Income Sales; Head of Fixed Income Trading — Santiago de Santos ☎ 387 5543

Fixed-Income Repo
Head of Repo — Antonio España ☎ 352 6693

Fixed-Income Research
Head of Fixed Income — Jorge Salavert ☎ 387 5500
Head of Credit Research — Jose Antonio Algarra ☎ 387 5732

Equity Capital Markets
Department: Treasury and Capital Markets
Head of Equity Capital Markets — Santiago de Santos ☎ 387 5543

Money Markets
Head of Money Markets — Antonio España ☎ 352 6693

Foreign Exchange
Head of Foreign Exchange — Pierre Porcher ☎ 387 5500

FX Traders / Sales People — Jaime Villarroya ☎ 387 5500

Risk Management
Head of Sales — Alvaro Cano ☎ 352 9462

Settlement / Clearing
Head of Settlement / Clearing — Juana Estrada ☎ 387 5523

Administration
Technology & Systems
Technical Resources — Pedro Vázquez Fernández

Legal / In-House Counsel
Legal Counseling — Adolfo Porcar Rodilla

Other (Administration)
Human Resources — José C Cañero Rojano

Caja de Ahorros de Vitoria y Alava
Head Office

Alternative trading name: Caja Vital Kutxa
Calle Postas 13-15, E-01004 Vitoria
Tel: (945) 162 000 **Fax:** (945) 162 028

Senior Executive Officers
President — Urdangarin Berritxoa
Chief Executive Officer — Barrend Llorente *Director General*
Financial Director — Iglesias Lezaula *Finance Director*
Chief Operating Officer — Caudepon Gurria *Commercial Director*
Director General — Arriba Urrutia

Caja de Ahorros y Monte de Piedad del Círculo Católico de Obreros de Burgos
Head Office

Avenida de los Reyes Católicos 1, E-09005 Burgos
Apartado de Correos 38, E-09005 Burgos
Tel: (947) 288 200 **Fax:** (947) 288 210 **Telex:** 39511 CACCO **Swift:** CECA ES MM 017

Senior Executive Officers
Honorary Chairman — Santiago Martinez
Chairman — Juan Manuel Velázquez Ruiz
Vice Chairman — José Ignacio Mijangos Linaza
Vice Chairman — Juan Francisco A de la Iglesia
Company Secretary — José María Manero Frías

Euromoney Directory 1999 **1425**

SPAIN (+34)   www.euromoneydirectory.com

Caja de Ahorros y Monte de Piedad del Círculo Católico de Obreros de Burgos (cont)
Others (Senior Executives)
Advisor   Carlos Conde Díaz *Advisor*
Department: Senior Executives
General Manager   José Ortega González
Assistant General Manager   José Antonio Rodríguez Temiño
International Division   Vicente Barcenilla Gil
Foreign Exchange
Head of Foreign Exchange   Vicente Barcenilla Gil

Caja de Ahorros y Monte de Piedad de Extremadura Head Office
Alternative trading name: Caja de Ahorros de Extremadura & Caja de Extremadura
San Pedro 15, E-10003 Cáceres
Tel: (927) 255 100 Fax: (927) 211 600
Senior Executive Officers
Chairman   Jesús Medina Ocaña
General Manager   Daniel Santos Jorge

Caja de Ahorros y Monte de Piedad de Guipuzkoa y San Sebastián Head Office
Alternative trading name: Caja Gipuzkoa San Sebastián - Gipuzkoa Donostia Kutxa & Kuxta
Garibay Street 13/15, E-20004 San Sebastian
Tel: (943) 411 000; (943) 412 032 Fax: (943) 426 006; (943) 423 679 Telex: 36706 KUTXA E Swift: CGGK ES 22
Reuters: CGGK
Website: www.kutxa.es
Senior Executive Officers
Chairman   Fernando Spagnolo
President   Xabier Alkorta
President   Luis Allaflor
Financial Director   José Ignacio Juaristi *Financial Manager*
Chief Operating Officer   Tomás Gallastegui *Planning & Control Manager*
Treasurer   Carlos Tamayo *Foreign Exchange Manager*
International Division   Daniel Bernáldez *International Manager*

Caja de Ahorros y Monte de Piedad Municipal de Pamplona Head Office
Alternative trading name: Caja Pamplona
Avenida del Ejército 2, E-31002 Pamplona, Navarra 31002 Pamplona, Navarra
Tel: (948) 425 262 Fax: (948) 224 448 Telex: 37843 CAMU Swift: CECA ES MM 053
Email: administrador@cajapamplona.es
Senior Executive Officers
President   Javier Chourraut
Chief Executive Officer   Manuel Lopez Merino ☏ **425 185**
Financial Director   Luis Lopez Ozcariz ☏ **425 135**
Treasurer   Francisco Arraiza ☏ **425 193**
Debt Capital Markets / Fixed Income
Tel: 425 135 Fax: 425 223
Head of Fixed Income   Luis Lopez Ozcariz ☏ **425 135**
Domestic Government Bonds
Head of Sales; Head of Trading   Luis Lopez Ozcariz ☏ **425 135**
Syndicated Lending
Tel: 425 184
Head of Syndication   Miguel Angel Tantos ☏ **425 148**
Money Markets
Tel: 425 193 Fax: 425 223
Global Head   Francisco Arraiza ☏ **425 193**
Domestic Commercial Paper
Head of Origination   Ramon Oloriz ☏ **425 165**

www.euromoneydirectory.com   SPAIN (+34)

Wholesale Deposits
Marketing   Damaso Munarriz ☎ **425 133**
Administration
Technology & Systems
                                         Jose Manuel Gil ☎ **425 109**
Legal / In-House Counsel
                                         Jose Manuel Ruiz Ganuza ☎ **425 125**

Caja de Ahorros y Monte de Piedad de Ontinyent   Head Office

Alternative trading name: Caixaontinyent
                    Avenida del Dextil 43, E-46870 Ontinyent, Valencia
                    Tel: (96) 291 9100 **Fax:** (96) 291 9160
                    Website: www.caixaontinyen.es

Senior Executive Officers
President   Ricardo García Bayo ☎ **291 9119**
Financial Director   Rafael Beneyto Cabanes ☎ **291 9113**
Treasurer   Ricardo Cucart Tolsá ☎ **291 9151**
Managing Director / General Manager   Francisco Sanchís Penadés ☎ **291 9129**

Others (Senior Executives)
                                         Vicente Penadés Torre *Second Manager* ☎ **291 9111**
                                         José Francisco Sanfélix Gandía *Branch Manager* ☎ **291 9135**

Debt Capital Markets / Fixed Income
Tel: 291 9151 **Fax:** 291 9159
Global Head   José Ureña Sanz ☎ **291 9151**

Syndicated Lending
Tel: 291 9109 **Fax:** 291 9159
Global Head   Francesc Tortosa Llin
Head of Syndication   Daniel García Silvaje ☎ **291 9122**

Money Markets
Tel: 291 9112 **Fax:** 291 7159
Global Head   Conrado Miralles Alberola

Domestic Commercial Paper
Head of Origination   Vicente Galbís Mora ☎ **291 9173**

Foreign Exchange
Avenida Textil 43, Ontinyent, Valencia
Tel: +34 (96) 291 9163 **Fax:** +34 (96) 291 9160
Global Head   Javier Mollá Pascual

Risk Management
Tel: 291 9114 **Fax:** 291 9159
Global Head   Carlos Graullera Escrig

Corporate Finance / M&A Advisory
Avenida Textil 43, Ontinyent, Valencia
Tel: +34 (96) 291 9161 **Fax:** +34 (96) 291 9160
Global Head   Francisco Nadal Gil

Administration

Technology & Systems
                                         Vicente Sanchís Penadés ☎ **291 9197**

Legal / In-House Counsel
                                         Antonio Penadés Torró ☎ **291 2640**

Public Relations
                                         Rafael Reig Tortosa ☎ **291 9133**

Accounts / Audit
Audit   Miguel Espí Carbonell ☎ **291 9152**

Other (Administration)
Human Resources   José Manuel Gramage García ☎ **291 2644**

Euromoney Directory 1999 **1427**

SPAIN (+34)　　　　　　　www.euromoneydirectory.com

Caja de Ahorros y Monte de Piedad de Segovia　Full Branch Office

Avenida Fernández Ladreda 8, E-40001 Segovia
Tel: (921) 415 000 **Fax:** (921) 415 160 **Telex:** 25403 CASG E **Swift:** CECAES MM 069
Website: www.cajasagovia.es

Senior Executive Officers
President　　　　　　　　　　　　Atilano Soto Rábanos [T] **415 005** [F] **415 160**
Vice President　　　　　　　　　　Francisco Javier Reguera García
Vice President　　　　　　　　　　Antonio Alfredo Bautista García
Chief Executive Officer　　　　　　Manuel Escribano Soto [T] **415 006** [F] **415 164**
Company Secretary　　　　　　　　Antonio Luis Tapias Domínguez [T] **415 003**
International Division　　　　　　　José María Gonzalo Corredor *Head, Financial Markets* [T] **415 032**
　　　　　　　　　　　　　　　　　　[F] **415 164** [E] **jmgonzal@cajasegovia.es**

Others (Senior Executives)
Head, Finance　　　　　　　　　　Miguel Angel Sánchez Plaza *Deputy Director* [T] **415 097** [F] **415 171**
Head, Planning & Research　　　　Juan Antonio Folgado Pascual [T] **415 023** [F] **415 163**
　　　　　　　　　　　　　　　　　　[E] **jafolgado@cajasegovia.es**
Head, Financial Markets　　　　　　José María Gonzalo Corredor *Head, Financial Markets* [T] **415 032**
　　　　　　　　　　　　　　　　　　[F] **415 164** [E] **jmgonzal@cajasegovia.es**

General-Lending (DCM, SL)
Head of Corporate Banking　　　　Luis Miguel Gómez Fraile *Deputy Director* [T] **415 029** [F] **415 166**

Debt Capital Markets / Fixed Income
Head of Debt Capital Markets　　　José María Gonzalo Corredor *Head, Financial Markets* [T] **415 032**
　　　　　　　　　　　　　　　　　　[F] **415 164** [E] **jmgonzal@cajasegovia.es**

Equity Capital Markets
Head of Equity Capital Markets　　　José María Gonzalo Corredor *Head, Financial Markets* [T] **415 032**
　　　　　　　　　　　　　　　　　　[F] **415 164** [E] **jmgonzal@cajasegovia.es**

Money Markets
Head of Money Markets　　　　　　José María Gonzalo Corredor *Head, Financial Markets* [T] **415 032**
　　　　　　　　　　　　　　　　　　[F] **415 164** [E] **jmgonzal@cajasegovia.es**

Foreign Exchange
Head of Foreign Exchange　　　　　José María Gonzalo Corredor *Head, Financial Markets* [T] **415 032**
　　　　　　　　　　　　　　　　　　[F] **415 164** [E] **jmgonzal@cajasegovia.es**

Risk Management
Head of Risk Management　　　　　José María Gonzalo Corredor *Head, Financial Markets* [T] **415 032**
　　　　　　　　　　　　　　　　　　[F] **415 164** [E] **jmgonzal@cajasegovia.es**

Administration
Technology & Systems
Organization & Systems　　　　　　Juan Bautista Magaña Busutil *Head* [T] **415 107** [F] **415 171**

Public Relations
　　　　　　　　　　　　　　　　　　Malaquías del Pozo de Frutos *Head* [T] **415 089** [F] **415 166**

Corporate Communications
　　　　　　　　　　　　　　　　　　Malaquías del Pozo de Frutos *Head* [T] **415 089** [F] **415 166**

Other (Administration)
Head, Human Resources　　　　　　Enrique Quintanilla Herrero *Head* [T] **415 141** [F] **415 175**

Caja de Burgos　Head Office

Alternative trading name: Caja de Ahorros Municipal de Burgos
Plaza de Calvo Sotelo, 'Casa del Cordón', E-09004 Burgos
Tel: (947) 258 100 **Fax:** (947) 258 115
Website: www.cajadeburgos.es

Senior Executive Officers
Director General
President　　　　　　　　　　　　Francisco José Isasi Martinez
Financial Director　　　　　　　　Francisco Javier Quintanilla Fernández
Chief Operating Officer　　　　　　José Maria Achirica Martin *Finance Director*
　　　　　　　　　　　　　　　　　　Leonicio Garcia Nuñez *Commercial Director*

Risk Management
Head of Risk Management　　　　　Horacio Mesonero Morales *Head, Risk Management*

SPAIN (+34)

Caja General de Ahorros de Canarias
Head Office

Plaza del Patriotismo 1, E-38002 Santa Cruz de Tenerife
Tel: (922) 471 000; (922) 471 040 Fax: (922) 471 045; (922) 471 035 Telex: 91099 Email: admin@cajacanarias.es
Website: www.cajacanarias.es

Senior Executive Officers
Chairman   Rodolfo Núñez Ruano
General Manager   Alvaro Arvelo Hernández

Others (Senior Executives)
                                 Rafael Daranas Hernández *First Vice Chairman*
                                 Juan Ramón Oreja Rodríguez *Second Vice Chairman*
                                 Alfonso Gómez Marrero *Assistant General Manager*
                                 Alfredo Orán Cury *Manager*

Caja General de Granada
Head Office

Formerly known as: Caja Provincial de Ahorros de Granada
Plaza de Villamena 1, E-18001 Granada
Tel: (958) 244 500 Fax: (958) 278 419

Senior Executive Officers
Chairman   Julio Rodriguez López
General Manager   José Maria Moreno Molina

Caja Insular de Ahorros de Canarias
Head Office

Triana 110, E-35002 Las Palmas de Gran Canaria, Canary Islands
Apartado de Correos 854, Las Palmas de Gran Canaria, Canary Islands
Tel: (928) 442 244 Fax: (928) 442 599; (928) 442 672 Telex: 95043 CIAGCE Swift: CECA ES MM 052
Email: marketing@lacajadecanarias.es
Website: www.lacajadecanarias.es

Senior Executive Officers
Chairman   Manuel Lezcano González
Director General   Juan Francisco García González
Legal Advisor & General Secretary   José Antonio Rodríquez Quevedo

Others (Senior Executives)
Cost Management
                                 Manuel Alemán Quintana *Director*
                                 José A Guerra Martín *Director*
                                 Francisco J Ramos Déniz *Commercial Director*
Management Control   Luiz Déniz Naranjo *Director*
Institutional Relations   Tomás Pérez Santana *Director*
                                 Miguel Ramírez Cruz *Director*
                                 Habib Victor William Haddad *Director*

General-Investment
Head of Investment   Francisco Rodríguez González *Director*

General - Treasury
Head of Treasury   Jesús Galván García *Director*

Debt Capital Markets / Fixed Income
Head of Debt Capital Markets   Jesús Galván García *Director*

Equity Capital Markets
Head of Equity Capital Markets   Jesús Galván García *Director*

Syndicated Lending
Recovery   Francisco Rodríguez González *Director*

Money Markets
Head of Money Markets   Jesús Galván García *Director*

Risk Management
Head of Risk Management   José A Guerra Martín *Director*

Settlement / Clearing
Operations   Habib Victor William Haddad *Director*

Administration
Business Development; Head of Marketing   Miguel Ramírez Cruz *Director*

Technology & Systems
                                 Habib Victor William Haddad *Director*

SPAIN (+34)   www.euromoneydirectory.com

Caja Insular de Ahorros de Canarias (cont)
Legal / In-House Counsel
                                   José Antonio Rodríquez Quevedo *Legal Advisor & General Secretary*

Accounts / Audit
Audit   José A Guerra Martín *Director*

Other (Administration)
Human Resources   Manuel Alemán Quintana *Director*

Caja Laboral Popular

Paseo José M Arizmendiarreta S/N, E-20500 Mondragon
Tel: (943) 719 500 **Fax:** (943) 719 781; (943) 719 778 **Swift:** CLPE ES 2M **Email:** mjesus.uribarren@cajalaboral.es
Reuters: D:CLPM

Senior Executive Officers
Chairman   Mario Adornato
Managing Director / General Manager   Giorgio Magnoni

Debt Capital Markets / Fixed Income
Head of Debt Capital Markets   Javier Gorroñogoitia **T 719 729** **F 719 775**

Equity Capital Markets
Head of Equity Capital Markets   Javier Gorroñogoitia **T 719 729** **F 719 775**

Syndicated Lending
Head of Syndicated Lending   Julio Gallastegui **T 719 536** **F 719 786**

Money Markets
Head of Money Markets   Javier Gorroñogoitia **T 719 729** **F 719 775**

Foreign Exchange
Head of Foreign Exchange   Pedro Arambarri **T 719 551** **F 719 777**

Corporate Finance / M&A Advisory
Head of Corporate Finance   Julio Gallastegui **T 719 536** **F 719 786**

Caja Madrid   Head Office

Formerly known as: Caja de Madrid
Paseo de la Castellana 189, E-28046 Madrid
Tel: (91) 423 5059; (91) 423 5058 **Fax:** (91) 423 5606 **Telex:** 46655 ECAM E **Swift:** CAHM ES MM
Email: pbarrabb@cajamadrid.es **Reuters:** CAJA; CAJF

Senior Executive Officers
Chairman & CEO   Miguel Blesa
Financial Director   Matias Amat
Treasurer   Juan-Manuel Maze
Managing Director   Carlos Vela
Company Secretary   Enrique de la Torre
International Division   Enrique Tierno **T 423 9268**

General-Lending (DCM, SL)
Head of Corporate Banking   Peoro Larena **T 423 5159**

General-Investment
Head of Investment   Carlos Contreras *Head of Capital Markets* **T 423 9424**

Syndicated Lending
Head of Origination; Head of Syndication   Jose Lius Garcia

Loan-Related Activities
Trade Finance   Carlos Alonso **T 423 9569**
Project Finance   Jesus Puy **T 423 9581**

Foreign Exchange
Head of Foreign Exchange   Borja Murube **T 433 9286**

Corporate Finance / M&A Advisory
Head of Corporate Finance   Ignacio Soria **T 423 5154**

Other Departments
Correspondent Banking   Caulos Alonjo **T 423 9569**

SPAIN (+34)

CARIPLO - Cassa di Risparmio delle Provincie Lombarde
Full Branch Office

Calle Alcalà 44, piso 2b°, E-28014 Madrid
Tel: (91) 522 9901 Fax: (91) 523 3981; (91) 523 4425 Telex: 49870 CARIP E Swift: CARI ES MM
Email: cariplo@globalnet.es

Senior Executive Officers
General Manager Renato Bassi
Others (Senior Executives)
José Luis Martín Robledo *Deputy General Manager*

The Chase Manhattan Bank
Full Branch Office

Paseo de la Castellana 51, piso 5°, E-28046 Madrid
Tel: (91) 349 2800 Fax: (91) 319 7323 Telex: 46587

Senior Executive Officers
Others (Senior Executives)
Senior Country Officer José A Garay *Senior Country Officer*

Citibank España SA
Subsidiary Company

Avenida de Europa 19, Parque Empresarial la Moraleja, Alcobendas, E-28108 Madrid
Tel: (91) 663 1000 Fax: (91) 663 1430 Telex: 43869 Reuters: CITE
Website: www.citibank.com

Senior Executive Officers
Business Manager Charles del Porto
Others (Senior Executives)
Global Head Francesco Vani

Citibank NA

29 José Y Ortega Gasset, E-28006 Madrid
Tel: (91) 538 4100; (91) 538 4238 Fax: (91) 577 9300
Website: www.citicorp.com

Equity Capital Markets
Fax: 577 9300
Equity Repo / Securities Lending
Marketing & Product Development Francisco de Ascanio *Resident Vice President* ☎ 538 4395
✉ francisco.deascanio@citicorp.com

CM Capital Markets Brokerage SA AV
Head Office

Calle Ochandiano, 2, Centro Empresarial El Plantio, E-28023 Madrid
Tel: (91) 509 6200 Fax: (91) 509 6216 Telex: 47692 Email: cmarkets@serenet.es Reuters: CMBM Bloomberg: CAPI
Reuters: CMBB

Senior Executive Officers
Fax: 509 6214
Chairman Tomas Saldaña
Financial Director Jose Antonio Cordero
Managing Director / General Manager Miguel Angel Albero
Debt Capital Markets / Fixed Income
Head of Fixed Income Ramiro Cuenllas ☎ 509 6203 ✉ 509 6211
Fixed-Income Repo
Head of Repo Javier Bru ☎ 509 6202 ✉ 509 6211
Money Markets
Head of Money Markets Federico de la Vega ☎ 509 6202 ✉ 509 6211
Foreign Exchange
Head of Foreign Exchange Jorge Ortega ☎ 509 6208 ✉ 509 6211

Euromoney Directory 1999 **1431**

SPAIN (+34) www.euromoneydirectory.com

CM Capital Markets Futures SA AV
Head Office
Calle Ochandiano, 2, Centro Empresarial el Plantio, E-28023 Madrid
Tel: (91) 509 6200 **Fax:** (91) 509 6216 **Telex:** 47692 **Email:** cmarkets@saramet.es **Reuters:** CMBE **Bloomberg:** CAPI
Senior Executive Officers
Fax: 509 6214
Chairman Miguel Abel Albero
Financial Director Jose Antonio Cordero

Commerzbank AG
Full Branch Office
Consejo de Ciento 357/359, 5a Planta, E-08007 Barcelona
Tel: (93) 496 1010 **Fax:** (93) 487 6633 **Telex:** 45135 CBKE E (via Madrid)
Senior Executive Officers
Manager Alois Brüggemann

Commerzbank AG
Full Branch Office
Paseo de la Castellana 110, E-28046 Madrid
Apartado 50612, Madrid
Tel: (91) 572 4700 **Fax:** (91) 572 4850; (91) 572 4830 **Telex:** 45135 CBKE E
Forex Fax: 333 2544
Senior Executive Officers
Manager Dieter Joswig
Manager Mariano Riestra

Confederación Española de Cajas de Ahorros
Alcalá 27, E-28014 Madrid
Tel: (91) 596 5000 **Fax:** (91) 596 5742 **Telex:** 23413 **Swift:** CECA ES MM **Reuters:** CECA (Monitor); CECA (Dealing)
Website: www.ceca.es
Senior Executive Officers
Chairman Manuel Pozouro ☎ **596 5621**
Chief Executive Officer Juan Ramon Quintas *General Manager* ☎ **596 5615**
Financial Director Juan Antonio Olavarrieta *Joint General Manager* ☎ **596 5616**
Chief Operating Officer Juan de Dios Gomez *Manager, Operations & Control* ☎ **596 5642**
Treasurer Jose Maria Verdugo *Manager, International Treasury* ☎ **596 5638**
Manager, Capital Markets Roberto Aleu ☎ **596 5652**
International Division Jose Maria Maranon *Manager, Int'l Products & Services* ☎ **596 5652**
General-Lending (DCM, SL)
Head of Corporate Banking Idoya Armendi ☎ **596 5362**
Debt Capital Markets / Fixed Income
Domestic Government Bonds
Head of Sales Jose Ignacio Navas *Manager, Domestic Treasury* ☎ **596 5671**
Non-Domestic Government Bonds
 Eusebio Morales *Chief Officer, Capital Markets* ☎ **596 5651**
Eurobonds
Head of Origination Eusebio Morales *Chief Officer, Capital Markets* ☎ **596 5651**
Libor-Based / Floating-Rate Products
FRN Origination Jose Manuel Villaverde *Chief Dealer* ☎ **596 5691**
Fixed-Income Repo
Head of Repo Jose Ignacio Navas *Manager, Domestic Treasury* ☎ **596 5671**
Equity Capital Markets
Domestic Equities
Head of Origination Jose Ramon Fernandez *Manager, Domestic Equities* ☎ **596 5686**
International Equities
Head of Origination Eusebio Morales *Chief Officer, Capital Markets* ☎ **596 5651**
Syndicated Lending
Head of Syndication Robert Bauer *Manager* ☎ **+44 (171) 925 2560**
Money Markets
Domestic Commercial Paper
Head of Origination Jose Ramon Fernandez *Manager, Domestic Equities* ☎ **596 5686**

SPAIN (+34)

Wholesale Deposits
Marketing Jose Manuel Villaverde *Chief Dealer* ☎ **596 5691**
Foreign Exchange
Global Head Jose Manuel Villaverde *Chief Dealer* ☎ **596 5691**
Risk Management
Global Head Enrique Hernandez *Risk Manager* ☎ **596 5647**
Exotic Options (Barriers, Range, Timers, Digitals, Faders etc)
Sales Jose Maria Verdugo *Manager, International Treasury* ☎ **596 5638**
OTC Credit Derivatives
Global Head Jose Maria Verdugo *Manager, International Treasury* ☎ **596 5638**
Exchange-Traded Derivatives
Global Head Jose Maria Verdugo *Manager, International Treasury* ☎ **596 5638**
Corporate Finance / M&A Advisory
Global Head Carlos Bartolome *Commercial Manager* ☎ **596 5726**
Other Departments
Correspondent Banking Jose Maria Maranon *Manager, Int'l Products & Services* ☎ **596 5652**

Crédit Agricole Indosuez   Full Branch Office

Formerly known as: Banque Indosuez
Paseo de la Castellana 1, E-28046 Madrid
Tel: (91) 432 7200 **Fax:** (91) 432 7506; (91) 432 7507 **Telex:** 23161 EBSUM E

Crédit du Nord   Representative Office

Calle Principe de Vergara 131, E-28002 Madrid
Tel: (91) 337 2136 **Fax:** (91) 337 2130

Senior Executive Officers
Representative Jean-Michel Ayello

The Dai-Ichi Kangyo Bank Limited   Full Branch Office

Maria de Molina 4, piso 5a°, E-28006 Madrid
Tel: (91) 564 2221 **Fax:** (91) 564 4388 **Telex:** 44916
Website: www.dkb.co.jp

Senior Executive Officers
Managing Director / General Manager Keiyu Kitagawa

Den Danske Bank International SA   Representative Office

Centro Idea, Ctra de Mijas km 3.6, E-29650 Málaga
Tel: (952) 463 336; (952) 473 873 **Fax:** (952) 479 983

Senior Executive Officers
Representative John Lundskov Larsen
Assistant Representative Niels Hansen

Deutsche Bank SA   Full Branch Office

Paseo de la Castellana 18, E-28046 Madrid
Apartado 221, E-28080 Madrid
Tel: (91) 335 5800; (91) 335 5505 **Fax:** (91) 335 5868; (91) 335 5520 **Telex:** 27778 **Swift:** DEUT ES BB 030

Senior Executive Officers
Chief Executive Officer Juan Carlos Garay Ibargaray
Debt Capital Markets / Fixed Income
Tel: 431 2484 **Fax:** 335 5763

Fixed-Income Repo
Trading Rafael Verdasco Bravo *Senior Trader*
Other Departments
Cash Management Jim Horth *Manager of Product Development & Cash Management*

SPAIN (+34) www.euromoneydirectory.com

Deutsche Bank SA Española
Head Office
Avenida Diagonal 446, E-08006 Barcelona
Apartado 416, E-08080 Barcelona
Tel: (93) 404 2102 Fax: (93) 404 2170 Telex: 53031 Swift: DEUT ES BB

Deutsche Bank Securities SA
Subsidiary Company
Paseo de la Castellana 18, E-28046 Madrid
Tel: (91) 335 5544 Fax: (91) 335 5593

Other Departments
Other Departments
Financial Markets Manager   Costantino Gomes

Dexia Banco Local
Subsidiary Company
Formerly known as: Crédit Local de France - España SA
Fortuny 6, E-28010 Madrid
Tel: (91) 308 3588 Fax: (91) 319 9538

Senior Executive Officers
President   Roland Hecht
Chief Executive Officer   José Luis Castillo
Financial Director   Francisco Javier Herraez *Director of Operations*
Treasurer   Juan Cuadrado *Treasurer*

Risk Management
Head of Risk Management   Joaquin Diaz-Reganon *Head of Risk*

DG BANK
Representative Office
Virgen de los Peligros 4, piso 5°, E-28013 Madrid
Tel: (91) 595 6817 Fax: (91) 595 6819

Senior Executive Officers
Representative   Alfred E Mallmann

Dresdner Kleinwort Benson
Subsidiary Company
Formerly known as: Kleinwort Benson Iberfomento
Paseo de la Castellana 151 bis, E-28708 Madrid
Tel: (91) 567 2238 Fax: (91) 570 7442

Senior Executive Officers
Chairman   Jaime Carvajal
Managing Director   Francisco Paradinas

Fimat International Banque, Sucursal en España
Full Branch Office
Alternative trading name: FIMAT
Plaza de Colon 2, pisos 17/18°, Torre de Colon, E-28046 Madrid
Tel: (91) 557 8911 Fax: (91) 557 8951

Senior Executive Officers
General Manager   Nicolas Bouët ☎ 557 8911 📠 557 8951

Financial Security Assurance (UK) Limited
Representative Office
Paseo de la Castellana 36/38, Edificio Castellana, E-28046 Madrid
Tel: (91) 431 3597 Fax: (91) 431 8899

Senior Executive Officers
Chief Representative   Jorge Edwards

SPAIN (+34)

Robert Fleming Spain AV SA
Subsidiary Company
Paseo de la Castellana 21, piso 4°, E-28046 Madrid
Tel: (91) 310 5050 Fax: (91) 308 4446

Senior Executive Officers
Managing Director   George Katzaros

Generale Bank - Banco Belga
Full Branch Office
Paseo de Gracia 85, piso 6a°, E-08008 Barcelona
Tel: (93) 467 7328 Fax: (93) 215 9394 Telex: 97311 GBBB E Swift: GEBA ES MM BAR

Senior Executive Officers
Director   Sergio Vila

Settlement / Clearing
Operations   Rafel Marti

Administration

Accounts / Audit
Accounts   Joaquin Gual

Generale Bank - Banco Belga
Full Branch Office
C/ Ibáñez de Bilbao 28, piso 4°, E-48009 Bilbao
Tel: (94) 423 6318 Fax: (94) 423 0614 Telex: 34046 GBBB E Swift: GEBA ES MM BIL

Senior Executive Officers
Director   Cesáreo Rey-Baltar

Settlement / Clearing
Operations   Mariario De Leonardo

Generale Bank - Banco Belga
Full Branch Office
José Ortega y Gasset 29, piso 6°, E-28006 Madrid
Tel: (91) 432 6767; (91) 432 6738 Fax: (91) 432 6740; (91) 432 6714 Telex: 46174 GBB E Swift: GEBA ES MM

Senior Executive Officers
Managing Director & CEO   Alvaro Elio

Others (Senior Executives)
Commercial Manager   Jaime A Hap

Money Markets
Head of Money Markets   José Bravo

Foreign Exchange
Department: Foreign Exchange & Treasury
Tel: 432 6738 Fax: 432 6714 Telex: 47681 GBB E
Head of Foreign Exchange   José Bravo

Other Departments
Correspondent Banking   Andrés Sola

Administration
Head of Administration   Claude Vanbaelen

Generale Bank - Banco Belga
Full Branch Office
Calle Pérez Pújol 4, piso 3°, E-46002 Valencia
Tel: (96) 353 4080 Fax: (96) 394 2457 Telex: 63249 GBBB E Swift: GEBA ES MMVAL

Senior Executive Officers
Director   Michael Branson

Settlement / Clearing
Operations   Inmaculada Garcia

SPAIN (+34)	www.euromoneydirectory.com

Goldman Sachs International
Representative Office

Paseo de la Castellana 21, piso 2°, E-28046 Madrid
Tel: (91) 319 1000 **Fax:** (91) 319 1543

Senior Executive Officers
Others (Senior Executives)
Senior Manager — Melanie L Stickland *Administrator*

Ibercaja
Head Office

Formerly known as: Caja de Ahorros de Zaragoza, Aragón y Rioja
Plaza Basilio Paraiso, E-50008 Zaragoza, Aragon
Tel: (976) 767 676; (976) 220 913 **Fax:** (976) 211 847; (976) 214 417 **Telex:** 58743 & 58744 **Swift:** CAZR ES 2Z
Cable: CAJAMONTE

Senior Executive Officers
Chairman — Manuel Pizarro
Chief Executive Officer — Amado Franco
Financial Director — Fernando Galdamez
Chief Operating Officer — José Luis Aguirre
Treasurer — Victor Iglesias ☎ **767 420**

Debt Capital Markets / Fixed Income
Head of Debt Capital Markets — Victor Iglesias ☎ **767 420**

Domestic Government Bonds
Head of Sales — Victor Iglesias ☎ **767 420**

Eurobonds
Head of Origination — Victor Iglesias ☎ **767 420**

Libor-Based / Floating-Rate Products
FRN Origination — Victor Iglesias ☎ **767 420**

Equity Capital Markets
International Equities
Head of Origination — José Palma

Syndicated Lending
Head of Syndicated Lending — Javier Palomar

Money Markets
Head of Money Markets — Victor Iglesias ☎ **767 420**

Domestic Commercial Paper
Head of Origination — Victor Iglesias ☎ **767 420**

Foreign Exchange
Head of Foreign Exchange — Pablo Olive

Risk Management
Head of Risk Management — Valero Penon

Other Departments
Correspondent Banking — Miguel Artazos ☎ **220 913**

Administration
Technology & Systems — Fernando Martinez ☎ **767 777**

Public Relations — Miguel Artazos ☎ **220 913**

IBJ-Sucursal en España
Branch, Marketing Office

Plaza Pablo Ruiz Picasso s/n, Torre Picasso, piso 9°, E-28020 Madrid
Tel: (91) 597 2612 **Fax:** (91) 597 4697

ING Barings
Representative Office

Montalbán 7, piso 5°, E-28014 Madrid
Tel: (91) 532 1118; (91) 532 3492 **Fax:** (91) 522 0183

Senior Executive Officers
Representative — Ton Rouwenhorst

www.euromoneydirectory.com SPAIN (+34)

Jyske Bank (España) SA
Representative Office

Edificio Maria Teresa, Avenida de Suel 8, Puebla Lucía, Fuengirola, E-29640 Málaga
PO Box 134, Fuengirola, E-29640 Málaga
Tel: (952) 460 112 Fax: (952) 460 162

Senior Executive Officers
Senior Representative   Arne Skjaerris

KBC Bank NV
Representative Office

Formerly known as: Kredietbank NV
Paseo de la Castellana 95, piso 5°, E-28046 Madrid
Tel: (91) 598 3680 Fax: (91) 598 3590 Email: jan.roos@kb.be

Senior Executive Officers
Representative   Jan Roos ☎ **598 3305**

Landesbank Hessen-Thüringen Girozentrale
Representative Office

Alternative trading name: Helaba
General Castaños, 4, E-28004 Madrid
Tel: (91) 391 1004 Fax: (91) 391 1132

London Forfaiting à Paris SA
Representative Office

Avenida Diagonal 611, 6-B, E-08028 Barcelona
Tel: (93) 494 8870 Fax: (93) 494 8871 Email: forfaiting@logiccontrol.es

Senior Executive Officers
Representative   Jaume Pujol Benet

Merrill Lynch Capital Markets España
Subsidiary Company

Torre Picasso 40, Plaza Ruiz Picasso, E-28020 Madrid
Tel: (91) 514 3000 Fax: (91) 514 3001 Reuters: MERN

Senior Executive Officers
Managing Director & Country Head   Claudio Aguirre
Vice President   Sainz de Vicúna Ana
Chief Executive Officer   Robert W Pease
Financial Director   José María Martin *Group Manager, Operations & Finance*

General-Investment
Head of Investment   Moises Israel

Debt Capital Markets / Fixed Income
Fixed-Income Research
Head of Fixed Income   Cesar Mounas *Research*

Equity Capital Markets
Head of Equity Capital Markets   Ignacio Gomez Montep *Research*

Corporate Finance / M&A Advisory
Head of Corporate Finance   Francisco Sanchez-Asiain

Other Departments
Private Banking   Miguel Matossian *President* ☎ **432 9900**
Correspondent Banking   José Luis De Mora *Research*

Administration
Corporate Communications
     Silvia Albert *Manager*

Merrill Lynch Española Agencia de Valores SA
Subsidiary Company

Paseo de la Castellas 31, piso 7°, E-28046 Madrid
Tel: (91) 432 9900 Fax: (91) 310 2619

Administration
Head of Administration   Miguel Matossian *Office Manager*

SPAIN (+34)   www.euromoneydirectory.com

Midland Bank plc — Full Branch Office
Offices 3 & 4, Edificio Heron Barcelona, piso 6°, Avenida Diagonal 605, E-08028 Barcelona
Tel: (93) 322 2223 Fax: (93) 439 4259

Senior Executive Officers
Manager — Jordi Riera

Midland Bank plc — Full Branch Office
Torre Picasso, piso 33°, Plaza Pablo Ruiz Picasso s/n, E-28020 Madrid
Tel: (91) 456 6200 Fax: (91) 456 6205 Telex: 48015

Senior Executive Officers
Chief Executive Officer — John Wheeler *Chief Executive Officer*
Jaime Galobart *Deputy Chief Executive*
Financial Director — Alain Baillez
Chief Operating Officer — David Ridgway
Treasurer — Luis Antoñanzas

General-Lending (DCM, SL)
Head of Corporate Banking — Jesus Apraiz

Debt Capital Markets / Fixed Income
Head of Fixed Income — Jose Blazquez

Money Markets
Head of Money Markets — Juan Carlos Sanmartin

Foreign Exchange
Head of Foreign Exchange — Emilio Lefort

Global Custody
Head of Global Custody — Francisco Huertas

Morgan Guaranty Trust Company of New York — Full Branch Office
2nd Floor, José Ortega y Gasset 29, E-28006 Madrid
Tel: (91) 435 6041 Fax: (91) 516 1616 Telex: 45523 MGT E Cable: MORGANBANK

Senior Executive Officers
Treasurer — Juan Manuel García Maestro *Vice President*
Managing Director & GM — Emilio Saracho

Debt Capital Markets / Fixed Income
Country Head — José Maria Jerez *Vice President*
Manuel Delgado *Vice President*

Equity Capital Markets
Equity Repo / Securities Lending
Head of Trading — Guillermo Monroy *Trading*
Hermiño Crespo *Trading*

Foreign Exchange
FX Traders / Sales People
FX Sales — José Olivé *Vice President*

Settlement / Clearing
Country Head — Susan Richards *Vice President*

Asset Management
Head — Daniel de Fernando *Co-Head*
José Maria Gamazo *Co-Head*

Morgan Stanley Dean Witter (España) SA — Full Branch Office
Fortuny 6, piso 5a°, E-28010 Madrid
Tel: (91) 700 7200 Fax: (91) 700 7299
Website: www.ms.com

Senior Executive Officers
Managing Director — Luis Isasi

www.euromoneydirectory.com   SPAIN (+34)

Corporate Finance / M&A Advisory
Regional Head   Luis Isasi *Managing Director*
Other (Corporate Finance)
                                          Jorge Lucaya *Managing Director*
                                          Gonzalo Gortazar *Vice President*
                                          Andres Esteban *Vice President*

Mutuactivos SA SGIIC

Calle Almagro 9, E-28010 Madrid
Tel: (91) 319 1113 **Fax:** (91) 308 4090 **Email:** fondos@mutuactivos.com
Website: www.mutuactivos.com

Senior Executive Officers
Chief Executive Officer   Jose Ignacio Comenge
Managing Director / General Manager   Miguel Ángel Taús Rodriguez
International Division   Javier Mira
General - Treasury
Head of Treasury   Pedro Martinez Roda
Debt Capital Markets / Fixed Income
Tel: 319 1417 **Fax:** 319 3065
Head of Debt Capital Markets   José Manuel Pérez Jofre
Equity Capital Markets
Tel: 319 1417 **Fax:** 319 3065
Head of Equity Capital Markets   Javier Mira
Money Markets
Tel: 319 1417 **Fax:** 319 3065
Head of Money Markets   Pedro Martinez Roda
Foreign Exchange
Tel: 319 1330 **Fax:** 319 3065
Head of Foreign Exchange   Javier Mira
                                          María Otaegui

Nikko España Sociedad de Valores SA   Subsidiary Company

Paseo de la Castellana 31/7, E-28046 Madrid
Tel: (91) 319 9977 **Fax:** (91) 310 2658; (91) 319 0812 **Telex:** 42280 NKSEC E **Email:** jose.nestola@nikko-spain.com
Bloomberg: NKMO2@bloomberg.net

Senior Executive Officers
President   José C Néstola

Nomura España Sociedad de Valores SA   Subsidiary Company

Calle Alcala 44, piso 3aº, E-28014 Madrid
Tel: (91) 532 0920 **Fax:** (91) 521 6010 **Telex:** 27542 NOMU E

Senior Executive Officers
Chief Executive Officer   Yutaka Morimoto

SA Nostra   Head Office

Alternative trading name: Caja de Ahorros y Monte de Piedad de las Baleares
Calle Ter 16, E-07009 Palma de Mallorca, Baleares
Tel: (971) 171 717 **Fax:** (971) 171 788 **Telex:** 68681 **Swift:** CECA ES MM 051
Website: www.sanostra.es

Senior Executive Officers
President   Antonio L Marí Ramón ☎ **171 900**
Financial Director   Pablo Dois Bover ☎ **171 822**
Chief Operating Officer   Carlos Loshuertos Tous ☎ **171 822**
Treasurer   Sebastian Ambros Alberti ☎ **171 853**
Managing Director / General Manager   Pedro Batle Mayol ☎ **171 900**
International Division   Javier Brotons Galan ☎ **171 929**

Euromoney Directory 1999   **1439**

SPAIN (+34)

www.euromoneydirectory.com

SA Nostra (cont)

Debt Capital Markets / Fixed Income
Head of Debt Capital Markets — Sebastian Ambros Alberti ☎ 171 853

Domestic Government Bonds
Head of Sales — Jose Luis Vivo Alonso

Non-Domestic Government Bonds — Isabel Lucio Parla

Eurobonds
Head of Origination — Sebastian Ambros Alberti ☎ 171 853

Libor-Based / Floating-Rate Products
Asset Swaps — Sebastian Ambros Alberti ☎ 171 853
Asset Swaps (Sales) — Isabel Lucio Parla

Medium-Term Notes
Head of Origination — Isabel Lucio Parla

Private Placements
Head of Origination — Sebastian Ambros Alberti ☎ 171 853

Mortgage-Backed Securities
Global Head — Sebastian Ambros Alberti ☎ 171 853

Fixed-Income Repo
Head of Repo — Sebastian Ambros Alberti ☎ 171 853

Equity Capital Markets
Head of Equity Capital Markets — Sebastian Ambros Alberti ☎ 171 853

Domestic Equities
Head of Origination — Sebastian Ambros Alberti ☎ 171 853

International Equities
Head of Origination — Sebastian Ambros Alberti ☎ 171 853

Convertibles / Equity-Linked
Head of Origination — Sebastian Ambros Alberti ☎ 171 853

Warrants
Head of Sales — Sebastian Ambros Alberti ☎ 171 853

Equity Repo / Securities Lending
Marketing — Sebastian Ambros Alberti ☎ 171 853

Syndicated Lending
Head of Syndicated Lending — Carlos Loshuertos Tous ☎ 171 822

Loan-Related Activities
Trade Finance — Carlos Loshuertos Tous ☎ 171 822

Money Markets
Head of Money Markets — Sebastian Ambros Alberti ☎ 171 853

Domestic Commercial Paper
Head of Origination — Antonio Jordi Miro

Eurocommercial Paper
Head of Origination — Janice Watson

Wholesale Deposits
Marketing — Isabel Lucio Parla

Foreign Exchange
Head of Foreign Exchange — Sebastian Ambros Alberti ☎ 171 853

Risk Management
Head of Risk Management — Carlos G Saenz

Foreign Exchange Derivatives / Risk Management
Global Head; Cross-Currency Swaps, Sales / Marketing — Sebastian Ambros Alberti ☎ 171 853

Exotic Options (Barriers, Range, Timers, Digitals, Faders etc)
Sales — Sebastian Ambros Alberti ☎ 171 853

OTC Equity Derivatives
Sales — Sebastian Ambros Alberti ☎ 171 853

OTC Commodity Derivatives
Sales — Sebastian Ambros Alberti ☎ 171 853

OTC Credit Derivatives
Global Head — Sebastian Ambros Alberti ☎ 171 853

Exchange-Traded Derivatives
Global Head — Sebastian Ambros Alberti ☎ 171 853

Corporate Finance / M&A Advisory
Head of Corporate Finance — Carlos Loshuertos Tous ☎ 171 822

www.euromoneydirectory.com SPAIN (+34)

Settlement / Clearing
Head of Settlement / Clearing
Antonio Mateu Rossello
Global Custody
Head of Global Custody
Carlos Loshuertos Tous ☏ **171 822**
Administration
Public Relations
Carlo Grignano ☏ **171 924**

Paribas SA
Full Branch Office

Calle Hermanos Becquer 3, E-28006 Madrid
Tel: (91) 745 9000; (91) 432 8704 **Fax:** (91) 745 8888; (91) 432 8792 **Telex:** 46439 PARB E **Swift:** PARB ES MX

Senior Executive Officers
Financial Director — Claude Gatte ☏ **745 8903**
Treasurer — Ana del Mar Serrano ☏ **745 8895**
General Manager — Ramiro Mato ☏ **745 8901**

General-Lending (DCM, SL)
Head of Corporate Banking — Dominique Sandrei ☏ **745 8980**

Equity Capital Markets
Equity Repo / Securities Lending
Head — Christophe Vallée *Head of Securities Services* ☏ **432 8756** 🖷 **432 8792**
✉ christophe_vallee@paribas.com

Marketing & Product Development — Javier Lasso *Co-Head, Product Development*
Jose A Fernandez *Co-Head, Product Development*
Marketing — Alvaro Camunas *Head of Sales & Relationship Management* ☏ **432 8770**
✉ alvaro_camunas@paribas.com

Syndicated Lending
Loan-Related Activities
Project Finance — Jose Maria Arana ☏ **745 8987**

Corporate Finance / M&A Advisory
Head of Corporate Finance — Ramiro Mato *General Manager* ☏ **745 8901**

Settlement / Clearing
Head of Settlement / Clearing — Philippe Ricard ☏ **432 8786**

Asset Management
Head — Jaime Gil Delgado ☏ **745 8921**

Other Departments
Chief Credit Officer — Carmen Rurio ☏ **745 8977**
Correspondent Banking — Manuel Cadenas ☏ **745 8905**
Cash Management — Cristina Mañueco ☏ **432 8743**

Administration
Technology & Systems
Danny Bernfield ☏ **745 8947**

Legal / In-House Counsel
Carlos Gardeazabal ☏ **745 8963**

Compliance
Carlos Gardeazabal ☏ **745 8963**

Public Relations
Julio Carlavilla ☏ **745 8975**

Accounts / Audit
Jose Gefaell ☏ **745 8925**

Probanca Servicios Financieros
Head Office

Paseo Castellana 95, piso 7°, Edificio Torre Europa, E-28046 Madrid
Tel: (91) 597 4222 **Fax:** (91) 597 0275 **Telex:** 27535 PROBA E **Swift:** PROA ES MM
Website: www.probanca.com

Senior Executive Officers
President — Rodolfo Frigeri
Chief Executive Officer — Alfonso Navio
Financial Director — Juan Carlos García-Cordero *Deputy General Manager*
Treasurer — Karl Klobuznik *Head, Treasury & Capital Markets Div*
Head, Corporate Finance — Kevin Begg

Euromoney Directory 1999 **1441**

SPAIN (+34) www.euromoneydirectory.com

Probanca Servicios Financieros (cont)
Debt Capital Markets / Fixed Income
Tel: 555 7930 **Fax:** 597 0275
Head of Debt Capital Markets Karl Klobuznik *Head, Treasury & Capital Markets Div*
Syndicated Lending
Tel: 597 4222 **Fax:** 597 0275
Head of Syndicated Lending Kevin Begg *Head, Corporate Finance*
Corporate Finance / M&A Advisory
Head of Corporate Finance Kevin Begg *Head, Corporate Finance*

Prudential-Bache Securities AV SA Full Branch Office

Principe de Vergara 132, piso 11°, E-28002 Madrid
Tel: (91) 590 8500 **Fax:** (91) 563 9519

Senior Executive Officers
Branch Office Manager Claude Benzaquen

Rothschild España SA Subsidiary Company

Fortuny Bajo, piso 6°, E-28010 Madrid
Tel: (91) 319 3062 **Fax:** (91) 319 5050

Senior Executive Officers
Chairman Stefano Marsaglia
Chief Executive Officer Jorge Delclaux *Managing Director*

Santander Investment Head Office

Alternative trading name: Banco Santander de Negocios SA
Paseo de la Castellana 32, E-28046 Madrid
Tel: (91) 520 9000 **Fax:** (91) 575 4463 **Swift:** BDER ES MM
Trade Finance Tel: 418 7175; 418 7175; **Renta Fija Tel:** 342 3101; **Derivados Tel:** 597 4261; **Money Markets Tel:** 342 3550
Website: www.bancosantander.com

Senior Executive Officers
Chairman Emilio Botín-Sanz de Sautuola
Chief Executive Officer Ana Patricia Botín *Executive Vice President*
Company Secretary Juan Guitard
General-Lending (DCM, SL)
Head of Corporate Banking José Manuel Araluce *Investment Banking*
Debt Capital Markets / Fixed Income
Head of Debt Capital Markets Ana Bolado
Equity Capital Markets
Head of Equity Capital Markets Francisco de Lera
Global Custody
Other (Global Custody)
Custodial Services Nicolás Fernández
Administration
Accounts / Audit
Comptroller Marta Elorza
Other (Administration)
Human Resources Anthony Beale

SBS-Agro Representative Office

Alternative trading name: Stalichny Bank of Saving-Agro
Calle Fernando el Santo, 15, E-28010 Madrid
Tel: (91) 319 9878 **Fax:** (91) 319 3387

Senior Executive Officers
Director Iouri Timofeev
Others (Senior Executives)
Deputy Representative Alexei Yakovlev *Deputy Director*

1442 Euromoney Directory 1999

www.euromoneydirectory.com				SPAIN (+34)

Sindicato de Banqueros de Barcelona SA
Head Office

Alternative trading name: Sindibank SB
Roger de Lluria 48, E-08009 Barcelona
Tel: (93) 290 2219; (93) 290 2100 **Fax:** (93) 290 2288 **Telex:** 50239 banq e **Swift:** SIBB ES BB **Reuters:** SBSB

Senior Executive Officers
Chairman — Mario Sposi ☎ 290 2100
General Manager — Paolo Punchina

Others (Senior Executives)
Financial Markets — Juan Josi Foz *Head* ☎ 290 2216
Francisco Rodriguez *Manager - Treasury* ☎ 290 2340

Other Departments
Correspondent Banking — Antoni Milian

Société Générale
Full Branch Office

Calle Genova 26, E-28004 Madrid
Tel: (91) 589 8060 **Fax:** (91) 589 3805 **Telex:** 44175 SGBE **Swift:** SOGE ES AGM **Email:** jcrebollar@socgen.es
Reuters: SOGE, SGBD

Senior Executive Officers
General Manager — Claude Schaeffer ☎ 589 3780
Deputy General Manager — Mariano Pérez ☎ 589 8091
Chief Executive Officer — Philipe Aymerich *Assistant General Manager* ☎ 589 3782
Financial Director — Vicent Decalp *Financial Manager* ☎ 589 8095
Chief Operating Officer — Joel Jarry *Head Corporate Finance* ☎ 589 3881

Debt Capital Markets / Fixed Income
Tel: 589 5000 **Fax:** 589 3720
Global Head — Antonio Carranceja *Director* ☎ 589 8084

Private Placements
Head of Origination — Demetrio Salorio *Director* ☎ 589 3666

Fixed-Income Repo
Head of Repo — Pablo Romagosa
Sales — Pedro Rodriguez

Equity Capital Markets
Global Head — Donato González *Director* ☎ 589 50 60

Syndicated Lending
Global Head — Carlos Lavilla *Director* ☎ 589 3784

Loan-Related Activities
Trade Finance — Iñigo Imedio *Director* ☎ 589 3876
Project Finance — Alberto Diaz *Director* ☎ 589 3082
Leasing & Asset Finance — Dominique Allbin *Director* ☎ (93) 304 7409

Money Markets
Global Head — Antonio Gómez *Director* ☎ 589 38 00

Foreign Exchange
Global Head — Antonio Gómez *Director* ☎ 589 38 00

Risk Management
Global Head — Patrick Charneau *Director* ☎ 589 3901

Fixed Income Derivatives / Risk Management
Global Head — Juan José Macias *Director* ☎ 589 3802

Foreign Exchange Derivatives / Risk Management
Vanilla FX option Sales — Victor Fernández *Director* ☎ 589 3800

OTC Equity Derivatives
Sales — Olivier Potart *Director* ☎ 589 8050

Corporate Finance / M&A Advisory
Global Head — José Couret *Director* ☎ 589 8057

Settlement / Clearing
Regional Head — Guy Tamby *Director* ☎ 589 3840

Global Custody
Regional Head — Guy Tamby *Director* ☎ 589 3840

Other Departments
Private Banking — Marilena Orfanides *Director* ☎ 589 3641
Correspondent Banking — Javier Pons *Director* ☎ (93) 304 7464

Euromoney Directory 1999   **1443**

SPAIN (+34)　　　　　　　　www.euromoneydirectory.com

Société Générale (cont)
Administration
Legal / In-House Counsel
　　　　　　　　　　　　　　Ramón Larraya Director ⊤ 589 3966
Other (Administration)
　　　　　　　　　　　　　　Jorge Harmat Regional Head ⊤ (93) 304 7401

Unicaja　　　　　　　　　　　　　　　　　　　　　　　　　　　Head Office

Formerly known as: Montes de Piedad y Cajas de Ahorros de Ronda, Cádiz, Almería, Malaga y Antequera
　　　　　　　　　Avenida Andalucía, 10-12, E-29007 Málaga
　　　　　　　Tel: (95) 213 8000 Fax: (95) 213 8081 Swift: CECA ES MM
　　　　　　　　　　　　　Website: www.unicaja.es

Senior Executive Officers
President　　　　　　　　　　　Braulio Medel
Chief Executive Officer　　　　　Pedro Costa Managing Director
Financial Director　　　　　　　Antonio Lopez Finance Director
Chief Operating Officer　　　　　Angel Rodriguez Director of Operations
Treasurer　　　　　　　　　　　Rafael Pozo Director
Director General　　　　　　　　Miguel Angel Cabello

Debt Capital Markets / Fixed Income
Head of Debt Capital Markets　　Cristina Roquero Associate Director, Treasury & Capital Markets

Equity Capital Markets
Head of Equity Capital Markets　Jose Maria Garrido Director, Marketing

Foreign Exchange
Head of Foreign Exchange　　　Jose Antonio Barrera Director, Foreign Department

Risk Management
Head of Risk Management　　　Jose Miguel Fernandez Associate Director

Warburg Dillon Read España SA

　　　　　　　　　　　C/ Fortuny 18, piso 2°, E-28010 Madrid
　　　　　　　　　　　Tel: (91) 436 9000 Fax: (91) 436 9040

Senior Executive Officers
Unit Head　　　　　　　　　　　J Calvet

Equity Capital Markets
Other (Domestic Equities)
Equities　　　　　　　　　　　　J Echanove
　　　　　　　　　　　　　　　　P Castela
　　　　　　　　　　　　　　　　P Díaz
　　　　　　　　　　　　　　　　J Márquez

Corporate Finance / M&A Advisory
Other (Corporate Finance)
Corporate Finance　　　　　　　M Gómez del Rio
　　　　　　　　　　　　　　　　P Pasquín
　　　　　　　　　　　　　　　　J Gich

Westdeutsche Landesbank Madrid　　　　　　　　　　　　Full Branch Office

　　　　　　　　　　　　c/ Velazquez 123, E-28006 Madrid
　　　　Tel: (91) 432 8000 Fax: (91) 432 8051 Telex: 48779 Swift: WLBE ES MX

Senior Executive Officers
General Manager　　　　　　　Kevin J Birch ⊤ 432 8001 F 432 8054

General-Lending (DCM, SL)
Head of Corporate Banking　　Berto Nuvoloni Director, Corporate Banking ⊤ 432 8056 F 432 8054
　　　　　　　　　　　　　　　Manuel López Director, Corporate Banking ⊤ 432 8012 F 432 8054
　　　　　　　　　　　　　　　Jorge Rosón Director, Corporate Banking ⊤ 432 8013 F 432 8054
　　　　　　　　　　　　　　　Sergio Casado Marketing Manager ⊤ 432 8015 F 432 8054

General - Treasury
Head of Treasury　　　　　　　Hugo Narrillos Manager, Treasury Sales ⊤ 432 8045 F 432 8062

Syndicated Lending
Loan-Related Activities
Trade Finance　　　　　　　　José Ignacio Echevarriá Manager ⊤ 432 8049 F 432 8054

1444　Euromoney Directory 1999

Other (Trade Finance)
Trade Finance — Rafael Llanos ☎ 432 8048 ℻ 432 8054
Settlement / Clearing
Settlement (General) — José Ignacio Rodriguez *Manager, Back Office* ☎ 432 8027 ℻ 432 8055
Stephan Szirmai *Manager, Operations* ☎ 432 8005 ℻ 432 8051
Other Departments
Chief Credit Officer — Francisco Serrat *Director* ☎ 432 8018 ℻ 432 8051

SRI LANKA (+94)

Central Bank of Sri Lanka
🏛 Central Bank

World Trade Centre, Echelon Square, Colombo 1
PO Box 590, Colombo 1
Tel: (1) 346 251 **Fax:** (1) 346 284; (1) 346 308 **Telex:** 21176 CENBANK CE **Swift:** CECB LK LX
Email: cbslgen@sri.lanka.net **Cable:** CENTRABANK **Telex:** 21627 CENBANK CE **Telex:** 21290 CENBANK CE
Website: www.centralbanklanka.org

Senior Executive Officers
Governor & Chairman of the Monetary Board — A S Jayawardena
Deputy Governor — S Easparathasan ☎ 346 265
Deputy Governor — P Amarasinghe ☎ 346 254
Treasurer — M B Dissanayake *Chief Accountant* ☎ 422 980
Secretary — T G Savundranayagam ☎ 346 308

Others (Senior Executives)
Chief Cashier — R G Jayaratne ☎ 436 541
Head, Bank Licensing — C Abeynaike *Director, Banking Development* ☎ 323 850
Head, Banking Supervision — Y A Piyatissa *Director* ☎ 423 918
Head, Public Debt — T S N Fernando ☎ 346 291
Head, Reserves Management — M B Dissanayake *Chief Accountant* ☎ 422 980

Foreign Exchange
Head of Foreign Exchange — M R Fernando *Controller* ☎ 321 059

Settlement / Clearing
Head of Settlement / Clearing — S N Fernando *Director* ☎ 346 297

Other Departments
Economic Research — R A Jayatissa *Director, Economic Research* ☎ 346 275
S S Colombage *Director, Statistics* ☎ 46278

Administration
Head of Administration — T G Savundranayagam *Secretary* ☎ 346 308

Technology & Systems
Data Processing — S N Fernando *Director* ☎ 346 297

Public Relations
Information Dept — M A R C Cooray

Accounts / Audit
M B Dissanayake *Chief Accountant* ☎ 422 980

Bank of Ceylon
Head Office

4 Bank of Ceylon, Mawatha, Colombo 1
PO Box 241, Colombo
Tel: (1) 446 790 **Fax:** (1) 447 171 **Telex:** 21331 LANKBK CE **Email:** agmint@boc.lanka.net **Reuters:** BCSL

Senior Executive Officers
Chairman — Dayani de Silva ☎ 348 877
Chief Executive Officer — Savithri Jayasinghe *General Manager* ☎ 348 878
Chief Operating Officer — A Sarath de Silva *Deputy General Manager, Operations* ☎ 446 826
Treasurer — R Nadarajah *Deputy General Manager, Treasury* ☎ 445 790

Debt Capital Markets / Fixed Income
Head of Debt Capital Markets — Mano Alles *Senior Deputy General Manager* ☎ 445 793

Domestic Government Bonds
Head of Sales; Head of Trading; Head of Research — R Nadarajah *Deputy General Manager, Treasury* ☎ 445 790

Libor-Based / Floating-Rate Products
FRN Sales — R Nadarajah *Deputy General Manager, Treasury* ☎ 445 790

SRI LANKA (+94)

Bank of Ceylon (cont)

Fixed-Income Repo
Head of Repo — R M P Ratnayake *Chief Dealer* ☎ **445 785**
Sales — S Palihawadana *Chief Dealer* ☎ **445 785**

Syndicated Lending
Head of Syndicated Lending — Mano Alles *Senior Deputy General Manager* ☎ **445 793**
Head of Credit Committee — Savithri Jayasinghe *General Manager* ☎ **348 878**

Loan-Related Activities
Trade Finance — Mano Alles *Senior Deputy General Manager* ☎ **445 793**

Money Markets
Head of Money Markets — R Nadarajah *Deputy General Manager, Treasury* ☎ **445 790**

Domestic Commercial Paper
Head of Origination — S N P Palihena *Assistant General Manager, Treasury* ☎ **34 7645**
Head of Sales — S Palihawadana *Chief Dealer* ☎ **445 785**

Foreign Exchange
Department: Treasury Division
Head of Foreign Exchange — R Nadarajah *Deputy General Manager, Treasury* ☎ **445 790**
Head of Trading — R M P Ratnayake *Chief Dealer* ☎ **445 785**

Risk Management
Head of Risk Management — R Nadarajah *Deputy General Manager, Treasury* ☎ **445 790**

Foreign Exchange Derivatives / Risk Management
Cross-Currency Swaps, Trading — R M P Ratnayake *Chief Dealer* ☎ **445 785**

OTC Equity Derivatives
Sales — S Palihawadana *Chief Dealer* ☎ **445 785**

Corporate Finance / M&A Advisory
Department: Corporate Branch
Tel: 323 479 **Fax:** 323 479
Head of Corporate Finance — Rohana Ranaweera *Deputy General Manager*

Other Departments
Correspondent Banking — K B Senanyake *Manager, Correspondent Banking* ☎ **445 791**

Administration
Business Development — V Wijenathan *Deputy General Manager* ☎ **544 345**

Technology & Systems — V Wijenathan *Deputy General Manager* ☎ **544 345**

Legal / In-House Counsel — V S Marapana *Chief Legal Officer* ☎ **445 813**

Public Relations — H P G J Kulasinghe *Public Relations Officer* ☎ **544 302**

Citibank NA
Full Branch Office

67 Dharmapala Mawatha, Colombo 7
Tel: (1) 447 316; (1) 447 318 **Fax:** (1) 445 487 **Telex:** 21824 **Swift:** CITI LK LX **Reuters:** CISL

Senior Executive Officers
Country Corporate Officer — Kapica Jayawardena ☎ **449 062**
Treasurer — Kapica Jayawardena *Country Corporate Officer* ☎ **449 062**

General-Investment
Head of Investment — Usman Hassan ☎ **436 278**

Debt Capital Markets / Fixed Income
Global Head — Kapica Jayawardena *Country Corporate Officer* ☎ **449 062**

Equity Capital Markets
Global Head — Kapica Jayawardena *Country Corporate Officer* ☎ **449 062**

Money Markets
Global Head — Romesh Elapata ☎ **326 086**

Foreign Exchange
Global Head — Romesh Elapata ☎ **326 086**

Deutsche Bank
Full Branch Office

86 Galle Road, PO Box 314, Colombo 7
Tel: (1) 447 062 **Fax:** (1) 447 067 **Telex:** 21506 DB ACE **Swift:** DEUTLKLX
Forex Fax: 54 8060
Website: www.deutsche-bank.de

www.euromoneydirectory.com   SRI LANKA (+94)

Indian Overseas Bank   Full Branch Office
114 Main Street, Colombo 11
PO Box 671, Colombo
Tel: (1) 324 422; (1) 324 423 Fax: (1) 447 900 Telex: 21515 IOBEE CE Email: iob.cm@sri.lanka.net.

Senior Executive Officers
Country Head   V R Veerasekaran ⊡ **320 515**
Senior Manager   Ramachandran Kalyanaraman ⊡ **445 390**
Chief Executive Officer   Ajay Kumar Raizada Manager, FCBU ⊡ **448 301**

Syndicated Lending
Tel: 448 302 Fax: 447 900 Telex: 21515 IOBEE CE
Head of Syndication   V N S Lakshminarayanan Credits Manager ⊡ **448 302**

Administration
Head of Administration   Ramachandran Kalyanaraman Senior Manager ⊡ **445 390**

Jardine Fleming HNB Securities (Pvt) Limited   Subsidiary Company
Formerly known as: HDF Securities (PVT) Limited
#10-01 East Tower, World Trade Centre, Echelon Square, Colombo 1
Tel: (1) 331 075; (1) 331 082 Fax: (1) 431 848; (1) 431 849 Email: securities@jf-hnb.com

Senior Executive Officers
Managing Director & Chief Executive   Anura Wickremasinghe ⊡ **331 083**

Equity Capital Markets
Tel: 346 014
Head of Equity Capital Markets   Ravi Abeysuriya Head of Corporate Finance

Domestic Equities
Head of Sales   Deva Ellepola DGM & Head of Domestic Sales ⊡ **331 085**
Head of Trading   Harsha Fernando Manager, International Dealing ⊡ **346 011**

Equity Research
Head of Equity Research   Panduka Ambanpola Head of Research ⊡ **346 010**

National Development Bank of Sri Lanka   Head Office
Alternative trading name: NDB
40 Navam Mawatha, Colombo 2
PO Box 1825, 40 Navam Mawatha, Colombo
Tel: (1) 437 701; (1) 437 350 Fax: (1) 440 262; (1) 341 044 Telex: 21399 NDB CE Email: info@ndb.org Tel: 437 702;
437 703 Tel: 437 704; 437 705 Tel: 437 706; 437 707 Tel: 437 708; 437 409 Tel: 437 710
Website: www.ndb.org

Senior Executive Officers
Chairman   Nimal Sanderatne ⊡ **447 474** F **440 262**
Chief Executive Officer   Ranjit Fernando Director & General Manager ⊡ **448 889** F **440 262**
Financial Director   Ranjit Gunasekara Assistant General Manager ⊡ **440 263** F **440 262**
Chief Operating Officer   Faizal Salieh COO-Retail Banking ⊡ **321 129** F **341 049**
Treasurer   Nilam Jayasinghe AGM, Treasury & Research Mobilisation ⊡ **341 050**
                                          F **440 193**
Manager - Legal Services   Chrishanthi Jayawardena ⊡ **440 194** F **341 044**

Others (Senior Executives)
Head of Marketing   Shehara de Silva Assistant General Manager ⊡ **321 130**
Head of Small Industries & Branches; Head of   Lionel Somaratne Assistant General Manager ⊡ **440 175** F **341 046**
Business Consultancy; Privatisation &
Underwriting

General-Investment
Head of Investment   Lionel Somaratne Assistant General Manager ⊡ **440 175** F **341 046**

Equity Capital Markets
Department: Merchant Banking
Head of Equity Capital Markets   Faizal Salieh COO-Retail Banking ⊡ **321 129** F **341 049**

Domestic Equities
Head of Sales   Don Barnabas Senior Manager ⊡ **347 913**

Other (Domestic Equities)
Head of Venture Capital Investment   Steven Enderby COO-Ayojana Fund Management (PVT) Limited
                                          ⊡ **(74) 510 505**

Equity Research
Head of Equity Research   Kishan Vairavanatham Assistant General Manager ⊡ **695 683**

SRI LANKA (+94)

www.euromoneydirectory.com

National Development Bank of Sri Lanka (cont)

Convertibles / Equity-Linked
Head of Sales — Usman Hassan *CEO-Citi National Investment Bank (Subsidiary)* ☏ 300 392 F 300 393

Syndicated Lending
Fax: 341 045
Head of Origination; Head of Syndication — Amaralal Peiris *Assistant GM, Corporate Finance* ☏ 436 270 F 341 045

Loan-Related Activities
Trade Finance — Nimal Ratnayake *Senior Manager, Trade Finance* ☏ 341 051
Project Finance — Amaralal Peiris *Assistant GM, Corporate Finance* ☏ 436 270 F 341 045

Money Markets
Fax: 440 193
Head of Money Markets — Nilam Jayasinghe *AGM, Treasury & Research Mobilisation* ☏ 341 050 F 440 193

Domestic Commercial Paper
Head of Sales — Nilam Jayasinghe *AGM, Treasury & Research Mobilisation* ☏ 341 050 F 440 193

Foreign Exchange
Fax: 440 193
Head of Foreign Exchange — Nilam Jayasinghe *AGM, Treasury & Research Mobilisation* ☏ 341 050 F 440 193

FX Traders / Sales People
Nimal Ratnayake *Senior Manager, Trade Finance* ☏ 341 051

Risk Management
Department: Risk Services
Fax: 341 047
Head of Risk Management — Champa Weerasinghe *Manager* ☏ 347 914

Corporate Finance / M&A Advisory
Head of Corporate Finance — Amaralal Peiris *Assistant GM, Corporate Finance* ☏ 436 270 F 341 045

Asset Management
Department: Eagle NDB Fund Management Co
Head — Manjula de Silva *General Manager* ☏ 337 644 F 436 522

Administration
Head of Administration — Henry Perera *Manager* ☏ 440 195 F 341 044
Head of Marketing — Shehara de Silva *Assistant General Manager* ☏ 321 130

Legal / In-House Counsel
Chrishanthi Jayawardena *Manager - Legal Services* ☏ 440 194 F 341 044

Compliance
Finance & IT — Ranjit Gunasekara *Assistant General Manager* ☏ 440 263 F 440 262

Public Relations
Marketing & Strategic Planning — Shehara de Silva *Assistant General Manager* ☏ 321 130

People's Bank — Head Office

75, Sir Chittampalam A Gardnier Mw, Colombo 2
Tel: (1) 327 841ext9; (1) 446 316 **Fax:** (1) 433 127 **Telex:** 21143 **Swift:** PSBK LK LX **Email:** info@peoples.is.lk
Reuters: PBCL
Website: www.is.lk/ispeoples

Senior Executive Officers
Department: Board of Directors
Chairman — Gamini Fernando ☏ 329 822

Others (Senior Executives)
S S Sahabandu *Director*
A S Ihalagama *Director*
G Hettiarachchi *Director*
A P Weerasinghe *Director*
A N Subasinghe *Director*
N M Perera *Director*
A Alfred *Director*
K Guruge *Director*
S Jayaweera *Director*
M A S Fernando *Secretary to the Board* ☏ 436 562 F 434 550

Department: Management
Chairman — Gamini Fernando ☏ 329 822
General Manager — K A Wijesekara ☏ 324 188 F 447 671

www.euromoneydirectory.com　　　　　　　　**SRI LANKA (+94)**

Management (cont)
Additional General Manager　　　　　　Chandra Sahabandu ☎ 334 040 ℱ 334 040
International Division　　　　　　　　　T Karunasena *Deputy General Manager*
General-Lending (DCM, SL)
Head of Corporate Banking　　　　　　T Karunasena *Deputy General Manager*
Syndicated Lending
Head of Credit Committee　　　　　　　Y Galagedera *Deputy General Manager, Credit*
Other (Syndicated Lending)
Development Credit　　　　　　　　　　S N Warnakulasooriya *Deputy General Manager*
Commercial Credit　　　　　　　　　　　W J M Fernando *Deputy General Manager*
Settlement / Clearing
Operations　　　　　　　　　　　　　　　S Gunaratne *Deputy General Manager*
Other Departments
Economic Research　　　　　　　　　　S L Siriwardena *Director*
Administration
Head of Administration　　　　　　　　Asoka de Silva *Deputy General Manager*
Head of Marketing　　　　　　　　　　　K B Kumarapathirana *General Manager*
Technology & Systems
　　　　　　　　　　　　　　　　　　　　　K B Kumarapathirana *General Manager*
Legal / In-House Counsel
　　　　　　　　　　　　　　　　　　　　　Palitha Gunasekera *Chief Legal Officer*
Other (Administration)
Human Resources　　　　　　　　　　　Asoka de Silva *Deputy General Manager*

People's Merchant Bank Limited　　　　　　　　　　　　Head Office
Level 4, Hemas House, 75 Braybrooke Place, Colombo 3
Tel: (1) 300 191; (1) 300 193 **Fax:** (1) 300 190

Senior Executive Officers
Chief Executive Officer　　　　　　　　Ananda Wehalle *Director & General Manager* ☎ 300 192
Financial Director　　　　　　　　　　　Senaka Blok *Manager, Finance & Administration* ☎ 300 191
Debt Capital Markets / Fixed Income
Private Placements
Head of Origination　　　　　　　　　　Gamini Sarath *Senior Manager, Corporate Finance* ☎ 300 194
Syndicated Lending
Head of Syndication　　　　　　　　　　Gamini Sarath *Senior Manager, Corporate Finance* ☎ 300 194
Other (Trade Finance)
Leasing & Trade Finance　　　　　　　Ajith Medis *Manager* ☎ 300 194
Corporate Finance / M&A Advisory
Country Head　　　　　　　　　　　　　Gamini Sarath *Senior Manager, Corporate Finance* ☎ 300 194

Sampath Bank Limited　　　　　　　　　　　　　　　　　Head Office
110 Sin James Peinis Mawatha, Colombo 2
PO Box 997, Colombo 2
Tel: (75) 331 441; (1) 300 260 **Fax:** (1) 300 143 **Telex:** 22780 ICBANK CE **Swift:** BSAM LK LX **Reuters:** SAML

Senior Executive Officers
Chairman　　　　　　　　　　　　　　　　Dunstan De Alwis
Chief Executive Officer　　　　　　　　Kumar Abayanayaka *General Manager & Chief Executive* ☎ 300 152
Financial Director; Treasurer　　　　　W Bandaranayake *Deputy General Manager, Treasury* ☎ 300 151
General Manager & Chief Executive　Kumar Abayanayaka ☎ 300 152
International Division　　　　　　　　　N Patrick S De Siva *DGM, International Division* ☎ 300 153

Others (Senior Executives)
International　　　　　　　　　　　　　　Parama Dharmawardene *Assistant General Manager* ☎ (75) 331 456
Operations　　　　　　　　　　　　　　　Shanthi Gooneratne *Assistant General Manager* ☎ (75) 331 460
Credit　　　　　　　　　　　　　　　　　　Aravinda Perena *Assistant General Manager* ☎ (75) 331 459
Information Technology　　　　　　　　Jayantha Alwis *Assistant General Manager* ☎ 300 140
Card Centre　　　　　　　　　　　　　　　Palitha Kannangara *Assistant General Manager* ☎ (74) 712 009
General-Lending (DCM, SL)
Head of Corporate Banking　　　　　　Anil Amarasuniya *Deputy General Manager, Credit* ☎ 300 150
Debt Capital Markets / Fixed Income
Head of Fixed Income　　　　　　　　　W Bandaranayake *Deputy General Manager, Treasury* ☎ 300 151

SRI LANKA (+94)   www.euromoneydirectory.com

Sampath Bank Limited (cont)

Domestic Government Bonds
Head of Sales; Head of Trading — W Bandaranayake *Deputy General Manager, Treasury* ☏ **300 151**

Eurobonds
Head of Trading — W Bandaranayake *Deputy General Manager, Treasury* ☏ **300 151**

Syndicated Lending
Fax: 300 144
Head of Origination; Head of Syndication; Head of Trading — Anil Amarasuniya *Deputy General Manager, Credit* ☏ **300 150**

Loan-Related Activities
Trade Finance — Anil Amarasuniya *Deputy General Manager, Credit* ☏ **300 150**

Money Markets
Head of Money Markets — W Bandaranayake *Deputy General Manager, Treasury* ☏ **300 151**

Foreign Exchange
Fax: 300 144 Telex: 22761 SAMBK CE
Head of Foreign Exchange; Global Head — Ruwan Coonay *Assistant General Manager, FX* ☏ **331 567**

Risk Management
Head of Risk Management — W Bandaranayake *Deputy General Manager, Treasury* ☏ **300 151**

Other Departments
Chief Credit Officer — Anil Amarasuniya *Deputy General Manager, Credit* ☏ **300 150**
Correspondent Banking — N Patrick S De Silva *Deputy General Manager* ☏ **300 153**

Administration
Business Development; Head of Marketing — N Patrick S De Siva *DGM, International Division* ☏ **300 153**

Technology & Systems — Jayantha Alwis *Assistant General Manager* ☏ **300 140**

Legal / In-House Counsel — Mahinda Jayawardene *Manager, Legal* ☏ **(74) 712 010**

Accounts / Audit — L Piyasena *Senior Manager, Finance & Planning* ☏ **327 860**

SG Securities Asia Limited - Sri Lanka Liaison Office
Subsidiary Company

Formerly known as: SocGen-Crosby Securities Limited
6th Floor, Samnath Centre, 110 Sir James Pieris Mawatha, Colombo 2
Tel: (74) 710 071 **Fax:** (74) 300 052

Equity Capital Markets
Equity Research
Regional Head — Anush Amarasinghe *Head of Research*
✉ anush_amarasinghe@socgen-crosby.com

Other (Equity Research)
Banking, Finance — Anush Amarasinghe *Head of Research*
✉ anush_amarasinghe@socgen-crosby.com
Hotel, Manufacturing — Gunendra Sellahewa *Investment Analyst*
✉ gunendra_sellahewa@socgen-crosby.com

Société Générale

6th Floor, Samnath Center, 110 Sir James Pieris Mawatha, 2 Colombo
Tel: (74) 711 000 **Fax:** (74) 711 010

Standard Chartered Bank
Full Branch Office

17 Janadhipathi Mawatha, Colombo 11
PO Box 27, Colombo 11
Tel: (1) 326 671; (1) 433 302 **Fax:** (1) 432 522 **Telex:** 21117 **Swift:** SCBL LK LX **Cable:** STANDCHART COLOMBO

Senior Executive Officers
Chief Executive Officer — Carey Leonard ☏ **(74) 797 500** ✉ **(74) 334 186**
Financial Director — Bertal Pinto-Jayawardene *Head of Finance* ☏ **(74) 797 550**

Others (Senior Executives)
Consumer Banking — Sabry Ghouse ☏ **(74) 797 700** ✉ **(74) 432 522**

www.euromoneydirectory.com SWAZILAND (+268)

General-Lending (DCM, SL)
Head of Corporate Banking   Shivan De Silva ☏ **(74) 797 600** 🖷 **(74) 348 959**

General - Treasury
Head of Treasury   Yashwanth Kumar ☏ **(74) 797 790** 🖷 **(75) 330 135**

Syndicated Lending

Loan-Related Activities
Trade Finance   Kumar Mayadunne *Head* ☏ **(74) 797 625** 🖷 **(74) 332 595**

Settlement / Clearing
Operations   David McCreath *Head of Operations* ☏ **(74) 797 675** 🖷 **(74) 432 522**

Administration
Business Development   Godfrey Wijetilleke *Manager* ☏ **(74) 797 505**
Head of Marketing   Nayana Godamunne ☏ **(74) 797 702** 🖷 **(74) 432 522**

SUDAN
(+249)

Tadamon Islamic Bank   Head Office

PO Box 3154, Khartoum
Tel: (11) 771 210; (11) 771 505 **Fax:** (11) 773 840 **Telex:** 22158 **Email:** tadamon@sudanet.com **Cable:** BANKDAMAN

Senior Executive Officers
General Manager   Salah Eldeen Ali Abu Alnaja ☏ **781 709**
Deputy General Manager   Abd Alla Nogd Alla Ahmaidi ☏ **773 819**
Deputy General Manager   Suliman Hashim Mohammed ☏ **774 297**
Assistant General Manager   Ahamed Mohammed Ahmed Almustafa ☏ **773 640**
Assistant General Manager   Musaad Mohammed Ahmed ☏ **785 480**
Assistant General Manager   Babiker Sheikh Idris Manaa ☏ **782 961**

General-Investment
Head of Investment   Ahmed Albadawi Abdel Alazeem *Manager Investment Division* ☏ **785 484**

Settlement / Clearing
Operations   Huseen Tag Elasfia *Manager, Foreign Operations* ☏ **785 482**

Other Departments
Economic Research   Mukhawi Mudawi Mukhawi *Manager* ☏ **784 832**

Administration
Head of Administration   Abdelmoneim Abdel Rahman *Manager, Administration Affairs* ☏ **774 878**

Technology & Systems
                                     Elmudasir Ali Elrashid *Manager* ☏ **782 943**

Accounts / Audit
                                     Mohammed Bakheet Mabrook *Manager, Internal Audit & Inspection*
                                     ☏ **784 777**

Other (Administration)
Personnel   Faisal Saeed Fadlalla *Manager* ☏ **773 629**
Training   Adil Altigani *Manager* ☏ **781 711**

SWAZILAND
(+268)

Central Bank of Swaziland   🏛 Central Bank

PO Box 546, Mbabane
Tel: 43221; 43225 **Fax:** 40038 **Telex:** 2029 WD **Swift:** SWAZ SZ MB **Reuters:** SWAZ

Senior Executive Officers
Governor   Martin Dlamini ☏ **42197**
Deputy Governor   Sibongile Mdluli ☏ **43194**
Secretary to the Board   Sydney Kumalo ☏ **40029**

Euromoney Directory 1999 **1451**

SWAZILAND (+268)　　　　www.euromoneydirectory.com

Central Bank of Swaziland (cont)

Others (Senior Executives)
Chief Cashier
Executive Director
Head, Bank Licensing; Head, Banking Suprevision
Head, Economics & Statistics
Head, Public Debt; Head, Reserves Management

Foreign Exchange
Head of Foreign Exchange

Settlement / Clearing
Head of Settlement / Clearing

Administration
Head of Administration

Technology & Systems
Information Technology

Public Relations

Accounts / Audit
Head, Accountancy

Beauty Hlope *Director, Operations*
Vinah Nkambule *Senior Director, Operations* ☏ **40336**
Stephen Simelane *Director* ☏ **45547**

Busi Dlamini *Research Manager* ☏ **43221/5**
Cleopas Dlamini *Director* ☏ **43009**

Cleopas Dlamini *Director* ☏ **43009**

Albert Mhlanga *Manager* ☏ **43221**

Bakhombisile Mkhwanazi *Director, Administration* ☏ **40034**

Arie van Beusekom *Advisor* ☏ **43221**

Sydney Kumalo *Secretary to the Board* ☏ **40029**

Ephraim Mntungwe *Director, Internal Finance* ☏ **43221**

Stanbic Bank Swaziland Limited
PO Box A294, Swazi Plaza, Mbabane
Tel: 46587; 46589 **Fax:** 45899 **Telex:** STBIC 2216 WD **Swift:** SBIC SZ MX

SWEDEN
(+46)

Sveriges Riksbank　　　　　　　　　　　　　🏛 Central Bank
Brunkebergsborg 11, S-103 37 Stockholm
Tel: (8) 787 0000 **Fax:** (8) 210 531 **Telex:** 19150 RIKSBK S **Swift:** RIKS SE SS **Email:** info@riksbank.se
Reuters: RIKA-Z
Website: www.riksbank.se

Senior Executive Officers
Chairman, Governing Board
Governor
Deputy Governor
Deputy Governor

Kjell-Olof Feldt
Urban Bäckström
Lars Heikensten
Stefan Ingves

Aragon Fondkommission AB　　　　　　　　　Head Office
Mäster Samuelsgatan 6, S-103 96 Stockholm
PO Box 7794, Stockholm
Tel: (8) 791 3500 **Fax:** (8) 611 8861 **Reuters:** ARAG **Bloomberg:** ARAG

Senior Executive Officers
Managing Director / General Manager

Administration
Compliance

Christer Billard

Anders Råge

Aros Securities AB　　　　　　　　　　　　Head Office
Birger Jarlsgatan 57B, S-113 96 Stockholm
Tel: (8) 458 5600 **Fax:** (8) 458 5699

Senior Executive Officers
President

Others (Senior Executives)
Head of Sales / Traders

Nils Bengtsson

Mikael Malmquist

1452 Euromoney Directory 1999

www.euromoneydirectory.com　　　　　　　　SWEDEN (+46)

Corporate Finance / M&A Advisory
Head of Corporate Finance　　　　　Ulf Hjalmarsson *Head, Corporate Finance*

Settlement / Clearing
Settlement (General)　　　　　　　Anders Carlsson *Head of Settlements*

Administration
Other (Administration)
Marketing　　　　　　　　　　　Richard Montgomery *Head of Marketing* ☎ 458 5600 📠 458 5699

Carnegie Fondkommission

Gustav Adolfs Torg 18, S-103 38 Stockholm
Tel: (8) 676 8800 **Fax:** (8) 676 8895
Website: www.carnegie.se

Senior Executive Officers
Managing Director　　　　　　　Matti Kinnunen

Corporate Finance / M&A Advisory
Head of Corporate Finance　　　　　Anders Muttin

Other Departments
Economic Research　　　　　　　Lars Petterson *Chief Economist*

Citibank International plc　　　　　　　　　　　　　　Full Branch Office

Norrlandsgatan 15 9C, Stockholm
Box 1422, S-111 84 Stockholm
Tel: (8) 723 3400 **Fax:** (8) 611 4843 **Telex:** 17542
Forex Tel: 54 8060

Senior Executive Officers
Managing Director　　　　　　　James Morrow

Relationship Manager
Financial Institutions　　　　　　　Eric Gelfgren *Head*
　　　　　　　　　　　　　　　Catarina Bygge
　　　　　　　　　　　　　　　Jan Esseen
　　　　　　　　　　　　　　　Anders Johansson
Corporate　　　　　　　　　　　Joachim Eriksson
　　　　　　　　　　　　　　　Filip Gustafson
　　　　　　　　　　　　　　　Donald G. Brett
　　　　　　　　　　　　　　　Cathrine Sandgren
　　　　　　　　　　　　　　　Clas Ronnlov
　　　　　　　　　　　　　　　Par Svensson
　　　　　　　　　　　　　　　Christian Nordstrom
　　　　　　　　　　　　　　　Anders Wilner
　　　　　　　　　　　　　　　Pontus Kiil
　　　　　　　　　　　　　　　Ann-Christine Hagelin

Foreign Exchange
Corporate Sales　　　　　　　　　Ulf Rydebark *Head, Treasury Customer Unit*

FX Traders / Sales People
　　　　　　　　　　　　　　　Johan Karlsved
　　　　　　　　　　　　　　　Patrik Lunning
　　　　　　　　　　　　　　　Martin Hessle
　　　　　　　　　　　　　　　Gustat Ljungdahl
　　　　　　　　　　　　　　　Morten Tinggaard

Crédit Agricole Indosuez

Regeringsgatan 38, S-111 56 Stockholm
PO Box 7734, S-103 95 Stockholm
Tel: (8) 796 6900; (8) 454 5800 (Forex) **Fax:** (8) 10 1040; (8) 796 6959 **Telex:** 16646 **Swift:** BSUISESS

Senior Executive Officers
Senior Country Officer　　　　　　Jean-Claude Bergadaa

Others (Senior Executives)
　　　　　　　　　　　　　　　Nick Luijteh *Chief Operating Officer*

Euromoney Directory 1999　**1453**

SWEDEN (+46)   www.euromoneydirectory.com

Danske Bank Consensus
Full Branch Office

Alternative trading name: Den Danske Bank
Formerly known as: Consensus Fondkommission AB

Stureplan 13, S-111 44 Stockholm
PO Box 5375, S-102 49 Stockholm
Tel: (8) 5688 0800 **Fax:** (8) 5688 0740 **Telex:** 16590 CONSENS S **Reuters:** PMCO-N **Bloomberg:** CSUS
Future Desk **Tel:** (8) 5688 0899; Sales **Tel:** (8) 5688 0988; Trading **Tel:** (8) 5688 0844

Senior Executive Officers
General Manager   Bengi Svelander

Debt Capital Markets / Fixed Income
Department: Bonds, Money Markets & Futures

Bonds - General
Money & Bond Markets - Sales   Fredrik Wilkens ☏ **5688 0988**
    Marcus Cederberg ☏ **5688 0988**
    Joakim Anjou ☏ **5688 0988**
    Michael Claezon ☏ **5688 0988**
    Bengt Svelander ☏ **5688 0988**
    Ann-Christin Thorsell ☏ **5688 0988**
Money & Bond Markets - Trading   Johny Engberg ☏ **5688 0844**
    Stefan Eriksson ☏ **5688 0844**
    Jan Hansson ☏ **5688 0844**
    Tommy Olsson ☏ **5688 0844**
Market Analysis   Michael Boström
    Tomas Niemelä

Den norske Bank ASA

Biblioteksgatan 29, PO Box 5550, S-114 85 Stockholm
Tel: (8) 440 5800 **Fax:** (8) 440 5840

Senior Executive Officers
Director   Börje Thelin

Deutsche Morgan Grenfell
Full Branch Office

Stureplan 4A, 4th Floor, S-114 87 Stockholm
PO Box 5781, S-114 87 Stockholm
Tel: (8) 463 5500 **Fax:** (8) 463 5550

Other Departments

Other Departments
Financial Markets   Mats Andersson *Head of Trading*

Enskilda Securities
Subsidiary Company

Nybrokajen 5, S-103 36 Stockholm
Tel: (8) 5222 9500 **Fax:** (8) 5222 9760

Senior Executive Officers

Others (Senior Executives)
    Lars Linder-Aronson
    John Abrahamson
    Arvid O Carlsen
    Thomas Åkerman
    Urban Rönnerdahl
    Martin Brandt
    Carl Helge Josefsson
    Peter Rabe

www.euromoneydirectory.com   SWEDEN (+46)

Fischer Partners Fondkommission AB
Hovslagargatan 5, S-103 21 Stockholm
Box 16027, Stockholm
Tel: (8) 5061 8940 **Fax:** (8) 611 6405; (8) 5061 8582
Website: www.fip.se

Senior Executive Officers
President   Olos Hedengren ☏ 463 8500
Financial Director   Bo Svensson

Debt Capital Markets / Fixed Income
Head of Debt Capital Markets   Martin Abrahamsson *Deputy Managing Director* ☏ 5061 8600
                                    ✉ martin.abrahamsson@fip.se

Equity Capital Markets
Head of Trading   Claes Osterlin ☏ 5061 8640 ✉ claes.osterlin@fip.se

Corporate Finance / M&A Advisory
Head of Corporate Finance   Stefan Lundftron ☏ 5601 8500 ✉ stefan.lundftron@fip.se

FöreningsSparbanken - SwedBank   Head Office
Brunkebergstorg 8, S-105 34 Stockholm
Tel: (8) 5859 1000 **Fax:** (8) 796 8092 **Telex:** 12826 SWED BNK S **Swift:** SWED SE SS
Email: info@foreningssparbanken.se
Website: www.foreningssparbanken.se

Senior Executive Officers
Executive Chairman   Goran Collert
President & CEO   Reinhold Geijer
Acting President & CEO   Lars Idermark
Financial Director   Nils-Fredrik Nybleaus *Executive Manager, Group Finance*

Others (Senior Executives)
Human Resources   Lena Ahlström
Strategy Development & Planning   Sören Andersson
CIO, IT Strategy & Development   Roger Gulqvist
Independent Saving Banks & Local Markets Gunnar Gunnarsson
Local Bank Coordination   Tomas Johansson
Credit, Legal & Environmental Affairs   Lars-Erik Källqvist
Swedbank Markets   Håkan Källåker
Payments & Lending   Jan Liden
Accounting, Control, Admin. & Internal Services Nils-Fredrik Nybleaus *Executive Manager, Group Finance*
Trade & Government Contacts   Eva Srejber
Marketing Communications   Elisabeth Ström
International Banking Services   Annika Wijkstrom
Financial Institutions   Claes-Johan Geijer
Department: Swedbank Markets
Executive Vice President   Håkan Källåker

Others (Senior Executives)
Finance   Robert Charpentier

Relationship Manager
Large Corporates   Måns Höglund
Financial Institutions   Claes-Johan Geijer

Debt Capital Markets / Fixed Income
Department: Swedbank Markets - Securities

Other (Fixed Income)
Retail Market   Ronny Jacobson
Net Trade   Annika Fagerlund
Department: Swedbank Markets
Head of Fixed Income   Per Aspegren

Syndicated Lending
Department: Swedbank Markets

Other (Trade Finance)
Trade & Banking Services   Annika Wijkstrom

Foreign Exchange
Department: Swedbank Markets
Head of Foreign Exchange   Per Aspegren

Euromoney Directory 1999   **1455**

SWEDEN (+46) www.euromoneydirectory.com

FöreningsSparbanken - SwedBank (cont)

Risk Management
Department: Swedbank Markets
Head of Risk Management — Fredrik Thulin

Other (FI Derivatives)
Credit & Country Risks — Lars Lundqvist

Corporate Finance / M&A Advisory
Department: Swedbank Markets
Head of Corporate Finance — Alf Blomqvist

Other Departments
Department: Swedbank Markets
Economic Research — Hubert Fromlet *Chief Economist*

Other Departments
Global Bank Market — Elisabeth Mattisson

Administration
Department: Swedbank Markets
Head of Administration — Agneta W Kåremar
Business Development — Magnus Franke
Head of Marketing — Birgitta Lerström

Technology & Systems
Head of Information Technology — Jens Oregard

Legal / In-House Counsel
Legal Matters, Capital Markets — Johan Stenberg

Compliance
— Johan Stenberg

Accounts / Audit
Head of Accounting — Agneta W Kåremar

Other (Administration)
Business Controller — Per Åman

JP Bank AB   Head Office

Klarabergsviadukten 70, S-107 81 Stockholm
Tel: (8) 700 4700 **Fax:** (8) 411 0686 **Email:** jpb@jpbank.se **Reuters:** PMJP **Telerate:** 3330
Website: www.jpbank.se

Senior Executive Officers
Chairman — Lennart Mansson
President — Ante Nilsson ☏ **700 4870**
Financial Director — Roland Nilsson *Head, Finance & Control* ☏ **700 4861**
Treasurer — Lars Krook *Head of Treasury* ☏ **700 4864**

Debt Capital Markets / Fixed Income
Tel: 700 4720 **Fax:** 105 883
Global Head — Anders Hellström

Domestic Government Bonds
Head of Sales — Mats Wallander
Head of Research — Jonas Mohlin

Bonds - General
Fixed Income Finance — Fredrik Dahlström

Medium-Term Notes
Head of Origination; Head of Structuring; Head of Sales — Lan Ling Wolff *Assistant Vice President* ☏ **700 4753**

Private Placements
Head of Origination; Head of Sales; Head of Structuring — Lan Ling Wolff *Assistant Vice President* ☏ **700 4753**

Asset-Backed Securities / Securitization
Global Head; Regional Head of Trading — Lan Ling Wolff *Assistant Vice President* ☏ **700 4753**

Mortgage-Backed Securities
Head of Trading — Jens Vahlquist ☏ **440 1573**

Fixed-Income Repo
Head of Repo — Helena Forsell *Assistant Vice President* ☏ **440 1575**
Sales — Gurli Jarsjö *Manager* ☏ **440 1576**

Equity Capital Markets
Head of Equity Capital Markets — Helena Holmgrene *Head, Swedish Equities*

1456 Euromoney Directory 1999

www.euromoneydirectory.com   SWEDEN (+46)

Money Markets
Regional Head   Martin Noren *Manager* ☏ **440 1410**

Other Departments
Private Banking   Stig Jogsten

Administration
Technology & Systems
    Anders Ivarsson *Manager, IT* ☏ **700 4782**

Legal / In-House Counsel
    Nils Wedborn *Executive Vice President* ☏ **700 4874**

Compliance
    Göran Nilsson *Head* ☏ **700 4877**

Public Relations
    Lars Krook *Head of Treasury* ☏ **700 4864**

Landesbank Schleswig-Holstein Girozentrale   Representative Office

Alternative trading name: LB-Kiel
Birger Jarisgatan 13, S-111 45 Stockholm
Tel: (8) 5450 1070 **Fax:** (8) 5450 1089 **Email:** cb@lbkiel.dk
Website: lbkiel.dk

Senior Executive Officers
Chief Representative   Ove Juven ☏ **5450 1071**

Lendtech AB   Head Office

Norrlandsgatan 31, S-105 78 Stockholm
PO Box 16077, S-103 22 Stockholm
Tel: (8) 405 6340 **Fax:** (8) 405 6331
Website: www.omgroup.com

Senior Executive Officers
Managing Director   Bo Hedenssö
Managing Director   Eric Sandström

Debt Capital Markets / Fixed Income
Bonds - General
    Pia Ekman *Trader*
    Albert Hammar *Trader*

Equity Capital Markets
Equity Repo / Securities Lending
Head; Marketing   Eric Sandström *President* ✉ **eric.sandstrom@omgroup.com**
Head of Trading   Albert Hammar *Trader*
    Pia Ekman *Trader*

London Forfaiting Company plc   Representative Office

Stortorget 18/20, S-111 29 Stockholm
Tel: (8) 230 450 **Fax:** (8) 230 523 **Email:** klas.henrikson@forfaiting.se

Senior Executive Officers
Representative   Klas Henrikson

Others (Senior Executives)
    Eva Espmark *Senior Manager*
    Patrick Achtman *Manager*

Maizels, Westerberg & Co AB   Subsidiary Company

Västra Trädgårdsgatan 11A, S-111 53 Stockholm
Tel: (8) 791 7900 **Fax:** (8) 791 7904

Senior Executive Officers
Chairman   Sten Westerberg

Corporate Finance / M&A Advisory
Other (Corporate Finance)
    Sten Westerberg *Chairman*
    Jonas de Verdier *Director*

SWEDEN (+46)   www.euromoneydirectory.com

Maizels, Westerberg & Co AB (cont)
Other (Corporate Finance) (cont)
Peter Wikström
Jonas Mårtensson
Kenneth Westlund
Per Hesselmark
Caroline Söderlund

Midland Bank plc   Full Branch Office
Alternative trading name: HSBC Group
Vastra Tradgardsgatan 17, S-103 94 Stockholm
Box 7615, Stockholm
Tel: (8) 454 5400 **Fax:** (8) 454 5454 **Telex:** 15917 MDBK S **Swift:** MIDLSESX
Senior Executive Officers
Managing Director / General Manager   Kevin Smorthwaite
Secretary, Management   Jeanette Lewald [T] **454 5404** [F] **545 5454**
Secretary, Corporate Banking   Ellen Kirkevold [T] **454 5417** [F] **454 5454**

Nordbanken AB (publ)   Head Office
Hamngatan 10, S-105 71 Stockholm
Tel: (8) 614 7000 **Fax:** (8) 614 9610 **Telex:** 12399 NBBANK S **Swift:** NBBK SE SS **Reuters:** NBSS; NBSF; NBSD
Website: www.nb.se

Senior Executive Officers
Chairman   Vesa Vainio
Vice Chairman   Jacob Palmstierna
President & CEO   Hans Dalborg
Treasurer   Jakob Grinbaum *Executive Vice President*
    Sven-Åke Johansson *Executive Vice President*
International Division   K G Lindvall *Head*

Others (Senior Executives)
Head of Retail Banking   Lars G Nordström *Executive Vice President*
Group Staff & Industry Issues   Pertti Voutilainen *Group Staff & Industry Issues*
International Products   Sylve Svensson *First Vice President*
Head of Trading   Christer Serennov *Senior Vice President*
Deputy Head of Retail Banking   Markku Pohjola *Executive Vice President*
Markets   Jussi Laitinen *Executive Vice President*

General-Lending (DCM, SL)
Head of Corporate Banking   Carl-Johan Granvik *Executive Vice President*

General - Treasury
Head of Treasury   Jakob Grinbaum *Executive Vice President*

Relationship Manager
Investor Relations   Björn Westberg *Senior Vice President*

Debt Capital Markets / Fixed Income
Telex: 10889 NB BONDS
Head of Debt Capital Markets   Jussi Laitinen *Executive Vice President*

Fixed-Income Repo
Head of Repo   Annica Sjöberg [T] **723 0797**
Head of Trading   Christer Serenhov *Head of Trading*
Trading   Johan Boberg *Repo Trader*
    Mikael Gustavsson *Repo Trader*
    Björn Suurwee *Head of Money Markets*

Equity Capital Markets
Equity Repo / Securities Lending
Head   Lars Jonasson *Senior Vice President*

Syndicated Lending
Head of Credit Committee   Claes Östberg *Executive Vice President, Credit Policy & Control*

Other (Syndicated Lending)
International Payment Services   Rune Olofsson *First Vice President*

Foreign Exchange
Foreign Exchange Administration   Lars Jonasson *Head*

Global Custody
Regional Head   Lars Jonasson *Head*

SWEDEN (+46)

Asset Management
Head   Karl-Olof Hammarkvist *Executive Vice President*

Administration

Technology & Systems
Information Technology & Strategic Analysis   Kalevi Kontinen *Executive Vice President*

Public Relations
    Björn Westberg *Senior Vice President*

Accounts / Audit
Accounting & Control   Arne Lijedahl *Executive Vice President*

Other (Administration)
International Administration   Bo Westerberg ☎ **614 8362**
Information Department   Carina Danielsson ✉ **614 7030**

Nordbanken Finans AB (publ)   Subsidiary Company

Regeringsgatan 29, S-103 92 Stockholm
PO Box 7455, S-103 92 Stockholm
Tel: (8) 787 6500 **Fax:** (8) 21 7506

Senior Executive Officers
General Manager   Stefan Källström

Okobank-Filial

NorrmaLmstorg 2, S-103 91 Stockholm
PO Box 7432, S-103 91 Stockholm
Tel: (8) 614 3200 **Fax:** (8) 611 8012 **Telex:** 11236 OKOSS **Swift:** OKOY SE

Senior Executive Officers
President   Stefan Silfver ☎ **614 3204**

OM Gruppen AB   Head Office

Norrlandsgatan 31, S-105 78 Stockholm
Tel: (8) 405 6000 **Fax:** (8) 405 6001
Website: www.omgroup.com

Senior Executive Officers
Chairman   Olof Stenhammar
President & Chief Executive Officer   Per E Larsson
Executive Vice President   Magnus Karlsson

Debt Capital Markets / Fixed Income

Fixed-Income Repo
Head of Repo   Anders Bygren *Manager, Repos*
Trading   Peder Wilhelmsson
Sales   Gunilla Oscarsson *Business Development* ☎ **405 6788**

Equity Capital Markets
Tel: 220 130 **Fax:** 791 8555

Equity Repo / Securities Lending
Head   Lennart Sodergren *Manager, Bond Options*
Marketing & Product Development; Marketing   Craig Fairbrother *Broker*
Head of Prime Brokerage; Head of Trading   Joakim Primen *Broker*

Administration

Technology & Systems
    Magnus Karlsson *Executive Vice President*

Legal / In-House Counsel
    Hans Berggren

Public Relations
    Gustaf Sahlman

SWEDEN (+46)   www.euromoneydirectory.com

Erik Penser Fondkommission AB
Head Office

Biblioteksgatan 9, S-103 91 Stockholm
Box 7405, Stockholm
Tel: (8) 463 8000 **Fax:** (8) 611 2705 **Reuters:** PMEP-Q

Senior Executive Officers
Chairman of the Board — Erik Penser
President, CEO & MD — Fredrik Gottlieb
Chief Operating Officer — Anders Lund *Vice Managing Director*
Treasurer — Hakan Stridh

Debt Capital Markets / Fixed Income
Tel: 468 8300 **Fax:** 611 2715
Global Head — Anders Lund *Vice Managing Director*

Domestic Government Bonds
Head of Research — Lars Engstrom *Head of Research* ☎ **463 8302**

Mortgage-Backed Securities
Global Head — Per Storfalt *Head of Sales* ☎ **463 8340**
Head of Trading — Lars Engstrom *Head of Research* ☎ **463 8302**

Equity Capital Markets
Global Head — Fredrik Gottlieb *President, CEO & MD*

Domestic Equities
Head of Sales — Magnus Oscarsson *Head of Sales* ☎ **463 8103**
Head of Research — Anders Sandberg *Head, Equity Research* ☎ **463 8041**

Settlement / Clearing
Department: Fixed-Income & Equity
Regional Head — Ingela Malmas *Co-Head, Back-Office* ☎ **463 8038**
Ulrika Eklund *Co-Head, Back-Office* ☎ **463 8037**
Fixed-Income Settlement — Ingela Malmas *Co-Head, Back-Office* ☎ **463 8038**
Ulrika Eklund *Co-Head, Back-Office* ☎ **463 8037**

S-E-Banken BoLån AB
Subsidiary Company

Regeringsgatan 65, S-103 91 Stockholm
PO Box 7370, S-130 91 Stockholm
Tel: (8) 723 7500 **Fax:** (8) 105 296

Senior Executive Officers
Chairman — Monica Caneman
Managing Director — Carl Sundvik

General-Lending (DCM, SL)
Head of Corporate Banking — Thomas Sjöström *Manager, Credit*
Charles Hillgren *Deputy MD, Private Credit*
Staffan Olsson *Chief Financial Officer*

Debt Capital Markets / Fixed Income
Department: Capital Markets
Country Head — Mikael Angervall

Settlement / Clearing
Operations — Pontus Sardal *Financial Controller*

Administration
Legal / In-House Counsel — Catrine Ellweñ *Manager*

Skandinaviska Enskilda Banken
Head Office

Kungsträdgårdsgatan 8, S-103 22 Stockholm
PO Box 16067, Stockholm
Tel: (8) 763 8000 **Fax:** (8) 679 8444; (8) 611 5196 **Telex:** 17620 ESSEDS
Website: www.sebank.se

Senior Executive Officers
Chairman — Jacob Wallenberg
President & Chief Executive Officer — Lars H Thunell
Financial Director — Lars Isacsson *Chief Financial Officer*

General-Investment
Head of Investment — Lars Linder-Aronson *Global Head of Investment Banking*

www.euromoneydirectory.com SWEDEN (+46)

Debt Capital Markets / Fixed Income
Head of Fixed Income — Annika Bolin
Head of Fixed Income Trading — Annika Bolin *Global Head of Trading*

Fixed-Income Repo
Head of Repo — Katinka Elfström ☎ 5062 3049 ℻ 5062 3249

Equity Capital Markets
Head of Equity Capital Markets — Per Elcar *Global Head*

Foreign Exchange
Head of Foreign Exchange; Head of Trading — Annika Bolin *Global Head of Trading*

Risk Management
Country Head — Annika Bolin

Fixed Income Derivatives / Risk Management
IR Options Trading — Annika Bolin

Foreign Exchange Derivatives / Risk Management
Vanilla FX option Trading — Annika Bolin

Global Custody
Head of Global Custody — Einar Thodal-Ness

Asset Management
Head — Lars Lundquist *Executive Vice President*

Other Departments
Chief Credit Officer — Liselotte Hjort

Administration
Head of Marketing — Olle Söderberg

Public Relations
Gunilla Wikman *Head of Group Communications*

Société Générale
Representative Office

8th Floor, Nybrokajen 7, S-111 48 Stockholm
Tel: (8) 611 7730 **Fax:** (8) 678 1112

Senior Executive Officers
Representative — Lars Söderberg

AB Svensk Exportkredit (publ)
Head Office

Alternative trading name: Swedish Export Credit Corporation
Västra Trädgårdsgatan 11B, S-103 27 Stockholm
PO Box 16368, S-103 27 Stockholm
Tel: (8) 613 8300 **Fax:** (8) 20 3894; (8) 20 3918 **Telex:** 12166 SEK S

Senior Executive Officers
Chairman of the Board — Anders Sahlén ☎ 405 4877
President — Peter Yngwe ☎ 613 8370

Others (Senior Executives)
Bo Leander *Executive Vice President* ☎ 613 8355
Per Åkerlind *Executive Director & Treasurer* ☎ 613 8367
Trading & Capital Markets — Richard Anund *Manager, Capital Markets* ☎ 613 8351
Ulrika Bohlin *Manager, Capital Markets* ☎ 613 8390
Jan Hernqvist *Manager, Capital Markets* ☎ 613 8399

Debt Capital Markets / Fixed Income
Emerging Market Bonds
Head of Emerging Markets — Miriam Forss-Bratt ☎ 613 8408

Asset Management
Head — Johanna Clason *Head of Trading & Capital Markets* ☎ 613 8372

Other (Asset Management)
Ann-Sofi Reichhuber *Asset Manager* ☎ 613 8348
Jan Törnstrand *Asset Manager* ☎ 613 8379
Ulrika Johansson *Asset Manager* ☎ 613 8371

Euromoney Directory 1999 **1461**

SWEDEN (+46) www.euromoneydirectory.com

Svenska Handelsbanken

Östra Hamngatan 23, S-405 40 Gothenburg
Tel: (31) 774 8000 **Fax:** (31) 774 8301 **Telex:** 27500 HANDGB S **Swift:** HAND SE SG **Reuters:** SVEG
Cable: HANDELSBANK

Senior Executive Officers
International Division — Else-Britt Jarfelt *SVP & Manager*

Others (Senior Executives)
Credits — Bengt K G Gustafasson *Vice President*
Payments — Linnéa Bystrom *Vice President*

Equity Capital Markets
Head of Equity Capital Markets — Linnéa Bystrom *Vice President*

Syndicated Lending
Loan-Related Activities
Trade Finance — Torsten Wickström *Vice President*

Other Departments
Private Banking — Christina Backman *Vice President*

Svenska Handelsbanken — Head Office

Kalendegatan 13, S-202 11 Malmö
PO Box 50104, S-202 11 Malmö
Tel: (40) 245 000; (40) 245 401 **Fax:** (40) 245 405 **Swift:** HAND SE SM **Reuters:** SVEM (Dealing)
Sales Desk Tel: 234 740; 236 930; **Sales Desk Tel:** 245 420; **Reuters:** SYDX (Monitor)

Debt Capital Markets / Fixed Income
Head of Fixed Income Trading — Mananne Nilsen *Head of Trading* T 245 404

Equity Capital Markets
Head of Trading — Mananne Nilsen *Head of Trading* T 245 404

Asset Management
Department: Portfolio Management, Equities
Portfolio Management — Jonas Rosengren *Head* T 245 017

Svenska Handelsbanken — Head Office

Alternative trading name: Handelsbanken Markets
Kungstradgårdsgatan 2, S-106 70 Stockholm
Tel: (8) 701 1000 **Fax:** (8) 701 2103; (8) 611 3022 **Telex:** 10510 HANSEC S **Swift:** HAND SE SS **Reuters:** SVES
Cable: HANDELSBANK
Forex Tel: 54 8060; **Reuters:** SHBT

Senior Executive Officers
Chairman — Tom Hedelius
President & Chief Executive Officer — Arné Mårtensson
Financial Director — Pehr Wissen *Executive Vice President* T 701 1870
Secretary & SVP — Agnetta Ahlbeck T 701 1159

Others (Senior Executives)
Pertti Hiltunen *Head of Global Trading* T 701 2286 F 701 2608

General-Investment
Head of Investment — Goran Bjorling *Executive Vice President* T 701 3925

Debt Capital Markets / Fixed Income
Department: Handelsbanken Markets
Head of Debt Capital Markets — Anders Arozin *Head, Debt Capital Markets* T 701 2146 F 701 2058
Head of Fixed Income — Fredrik Behring T 463 4515 F 701 1643
Head of Fixed Income Sales — Glenn Söderholm T 463 4556 F 701 1643

Government Bonds
Head of Sales — Glenn Söderholm T 463 4556 F 701 1643

Eurobonds
Head of Sales — Glenn Söderholm T 463 4556 F 701 1643

Emerging Market Bonds
Head of Emerging Markets; Head of Sales; — Rairno Valo T 463 4510 F 701 1781
Head of Trading

1462 Euromoney Directory 1999

www.euromoneydirectory.com SWEDEN (+46)

Equity Capital Markets
Equity Repo / Securities Lending
Head — Gösta Patzelt *Assistant Vice President* T 701 1075 F 701 3990
Marketing — Karin Vikner
Monica Algstedt Johansson
Arne Zippis

Syndicated Lending
Loan-Related Activities
Trade Finance — Agneta Freyschuss *Senior Vice President* T 701 3688

Money Markets
Domestic Commercial Paper
Head of Origination — Anders Arozin *Head, Debt Capital Markets* T 701 2146 F 701 2058
Eurocommercial Paper
Head of Sales — Anders Arozin *Head, Debt Capital Markets* T 701 2146 F 701 2058

Foreign Exchange
Head of Foreign Exchange — Niklas Karlsson *Head, FX Trading* T 463 4511 F 701 2831
Head of Institutional Sales — Glenn Söderholm T 463 4556 F 701 1643
Corporate Sales — Esa Pernu *Head of Treasury Sales, London* T +44 (171) 578 8621 F +44 (171) 578 8093

Risk Management
Head of Risk Management — Jeffrey Pritchard T +44 (171) 578 8637 F +44 (171) 578 8094

Corporate Finance / M&A Advisory
Head of Corporate Finance — Kjell Ormegaro *Senior Vice President*

Settlement / Clearing
Head of Settlement / Clearing — Lisciana Pacor Hygrill *Senior Vice President* T 701 1738
Equity Settlement — Niclas Waldenstrout *Manager* T 701 1558
Fixed-Income Settlement — Michael Danielsson T 701 2298 F 701 1643
Operations; Back-Office — Lise-Lotte Jakobsson T 701 4304 F 701 3734

Asset Management
Head — Bjorn Anderson *Executive Vice President* T 701 1021

Other Departments
Chief Credit Officer — Lendart Franke T 701 4360
Correspondent Banking; Cash Management — Agneta Freyschuss *Senior Vice President* T 701 3688

Administration
Head of Administration — Janita Thorner-Lehrmark *Senior Vice President* T 701 1219
Business Development — Lars O Gronstedt *Executive Vice President* T 701 1633

Technology & Systems
Goran Elvanez *Executive Vice President* T 701 1649

Legal / In-House Counsel
Larse Kinander *Senior Vice President* T 701 1362

Public Relations
Lars Lindmark *Head of Public Relations* T 701 1036

Accounts / Audit
Tord Jonerot *Senior Vice President* T 701 3887

United Securities Hagströmer & Qviberg Fondkommission AB

Norrlandsqatan 15, S-103 71 Stockholm
Tel: (8) 696 2010 **Fax:** (8) 696 2001 **Telex:** 15117 UBROK S **Reuters:** PMUS

Senior Executive Officers
President — Stefan Dahlbo
Managing Director / General Manager — Rose Marie Westman

Debt Capital Markets / Fixed Income
Head of Fixed Income Trading — Mats Thufvesson T 696 1755

Equity Capital Markets
Head of Trading — Mats Thufvesson T 696 1755

Foreign Exchange
Head of Trading — Mats Thufvesson T 696 1755

Administration
Head of Marketing — Jacob Lannerl F 696 2001

Public Relations
Bibi Sandqvist T 696 1883

The financial magazine for the global insurance market.

Reactions

A few years ago, the securitization of insurance risk seemed inconceivable.

Now, hardly a month goes by without a new insurance-bond issue.

For the latest in financial risk solutions, read **Reactions**, the financial magazine for the global insurance market.

For a **FREE** trial subscription to **Reactions** call +1 212 224 3570 in New York
+44 (0)171 779 8199 in London

www.euromoneydirectory.com SWITZERLAND (+41)

Warburg Dillon Read
Regeringsgatan 38, 7th Floor, S-111 87 Stockholm
PO Box 1722, S-111 87 Stockholm
Tel: (8) 453 7300 **Fax:** (8) 289 130

Senior Executive Officers
Country Head & Head of Nordic Equities — R Silander

Equity Capital Markets
Domestic Equities
Head of Sales — A Palmqvist *Head of Nordic Sales*
Head of Trading — J Siljestrom *Head of Trading*
Head of Research — P Afrell *Head of Nordic Research*

Settlement / Clearing
Operations — H Soderstrom *Head of Logistics*

Administration
Compliance
A Ramel *Compliance Officer*

West Merchant Bank Limited
Representative Office
Formerly known as: WestLB Group
Birger Jarlsgatan 13, S-111 45 Stockholm
Tel: (8) 5450 1070; (8) 5450 1080 **Fax:** (8) 5450 1089

Senior Executive Officers
Chief Representative — Joachim Claesson ☏ **5450 1081**

SWITZERLAND
(+41)

Banque Nationale Suisse
🏛 Central Bank
Alternative trading name: Schweizerische Nationalbank & Banca Nazionale Svizzera
Börsenstrasse 15, CH-8022 Zürich
PO Box 4388, CH-8022 Zürich
Tel: (1) 631 3111 **Fax:** (1) 631 3910; (1) 631 3911 **Telex:** 812600 SNB CH **Email:** snb@snb.ch
Website: www.snb.ch

Senior Executive Officers
Chairman — Hans Meyer
Vice Chairman — Jean-Pierre Roth
Member of the Governing Board — Bruno Gehrig
Director — Peter Schöpf
Assistant Director — Hans-Ueli Hunziker

Others (Senior Executives)
Head, Economic Division — Georg Rich *Director*
Head, Economic Studies — Michel Peytrignet *Deputy Director*
Head, International Monetary Relations — Werner Hermann *Deputy Director*
Head, Banking Studies — Urs W Birchler *Director*
Head, Statistics — Christoph Menzel *Director*
Head, Monetary Statistics — Robert Fluri *Assistant Director*
Head, Balance of Payments — Thomas Schlup *Assistant Director*
Head, Banking Division — Theodor Scherer *Director*
Head, Securities — Hans-Christoph Kesselring *Deputy Director*
Head, Monetary Operations — Erich Spörndli *Director*

Foreign Exchange
Head of Foreign Exchange — Karl Hug *Deputy Director*

Settlement / Clearing
Head of Settlement / Clearing — Daniel Wettstein *Deputy Director*

Administration
Head of Administration — Peter Klauser *Director*

Technology & Systems
General Processing & Informatics — Erwin Sigrist *Director*

Euromoney Directory 1999 **1465**

SWITZERLAND (+41)   www.euromoneydirectory.com

Banque Nationale Suisse (cont)
Legal / In-House Counsel
Legal Service   Peter Merz *Director*
Public Relations
Press Relations   Werner Abegg *Assistant Director*
Accounts / Audit
Internal Auditor   Ulrich W Gilgen *Director*
Head, Accounting   Peter Bechtiger *Assistant Director*
Other (Administration)
Personnel   Christine Breining-Kaufmann *Director*

A & A Actienbank   Head Office

Bahnhofstrasse 92, CH-8023 Zürich
Tel: (1) 229 5555 **Fax:** (1) 229 5557

Senior Executive Officers
Chairman   Andreas Schweizer
Vice Chairman   Ernst Müller-Möhl
Chief Executive Officer   Peter Zuppinger
Others (Senior Executives)
Head of Asset Management   Mark Dangel
Head of Research   Peter Wick
Head of Logistics   Frank Müller Erkelenz
Head of Institutional   Alessandro Parenti

Aargauische Kantonalbank   Head Office

Bahnhofstrasse 58, CH-5001 Aarau
Tel: (62) 835 7777 **Fax:** (62) 835 7925 **Telex:** 981200 **Swift:** KBAG CH 22

Senior Executive Officers
President   Wendolin Stutz
Chief Executive Officer   Urs Grätzer
Others (Senior Executives)
     Walter Berchtold
     Rudolf Hochreutener
     Peter Steiner
     Walter Bolleter

ABN AMRO Bank NV Amsterdam   Full Branch Office

Beethovenstrasse 33, PO Box 52239, CH-8022 Zürich
Tel: (1) 631 4111 **Fax:** (1) 631 4181

Senior Executive Officers
Chief Executive Officer   Erich Noskes
General - Treasury
Head of Treasury   Ramon Koss *Head of Treasury* ☎ **631 6262**
Debt Capital Markets / Fixed Income
Eurobonds
Head of Origination; Head of Syndication   Bruno Niederberger ☎ **631 6430**
Head of Sales   Marc Eberle ☎ **631 6475**
Head of Trading   Victor Senn ☎ **631 6420**
Libor-Based / Floating-Rate Products
FRN Origination   Bruno Niederberger ☎ **631 6430**
FRN Sales   Marc Eberle ☎ **631 6475**
Equity Capital Markets
Regional Head   Toni Jacober ☎ **631 5485**
Domestic Equities
Head of Origination; Head of Syndication   Bruno Niederberger ☎ **631 6430**
Head of Sales   Fritz Keller ☎ **631 6430**
Head of Research   Thomas Kalbermatten ☎ **631 6330**
Convertibles / Equity-Linked
Head of Origination; Head of Syndication   Bruno Niederberger ☎ **631 6430**

SWITZERLAND (+41)

Corporate Finance / M&A Advisory
Department: Corporate Banking
Head of Corporate Finance   Walter Fritz Head of Department ☏ 631 4210

ABN AMRO Bank (Switzerland) — Full Branch Office
Aeschengraben 9, CH-4002 Basle
PO Box 2143, Basle
Tel: (61) 272 3200 Fax: (61) 272 1913 Telex: 963786
Senior Executive Officers
Branch Manager   Peter Ettlin

ABN AMRO Bank (Switzerland) — Full Branch Office
Waisenhausplatz 25, CH-3001 Berne
PO Box 5362, Berne
Tel: (31) 329 9292 Fax: (31) 329 9280 Telex: 911 775 ABF CH Cable: BANKFINANZ BERN
Senior Executive Officers
Branch Manager   Kurt Röthlisberger

ABN AMRO Bank (Switzerland) — Full Branch Office
12 Quai Général-Guisan, CH-1211 Geneva 3
PO Box 3026, Geneva
Tel: (22) 819 7777 Fax: (22) 819 7755 Telex: 412626 ABN CH Cable: GARDONA
Senior Executive Officers
Branch Manager   B J de Hoop Scheffer

ABN AMRO Bank (Switzerland) — Full Branch Office
Via Balestra 11, CH-6900 Lugano
PO Box 2802, Lugano
Tel: (91) 910 0101 Fax: (91) 910 0191 Telex: 842060 ABN CH
Senior Executive Officers
Managing Director / General Manager   Hans E Buck

ABN AMRO Bank (Switzerland) — Full Branch Office
Beethovenstrasse 33, CH-8022 Zürich
PO Box 5239, Zürich
Tel: (1) 631 4111 Fax: (1) 631 4185 Telex: 813136 ABN CH
Senior Executive Officers
Managing Director / General Manager   Kurt Rothlisberger

Adler & Co AG — Head Office
Claridenstrasse 22, CH-8022 Zürich
Tel: (1) 202 7811 Fax: (1) 201 3652 Telex: 815967
Senior Executive Officers
President   Gian G Klainguti
Managing Director / General Manager   Christoph Hegglin
Settlement / Clearing
Settlement (General)   Jürg Büchi

Alpha Securities AG — Head Office
Churerstrasse 82, PO Box, CH-8808 Pfäffikon SZ
Tel: (55) 415 1251 Fax: (55) 415 1277 Reuters: ALPHAA-B
Senior Executive Officers
Chief Executive Officer   Ernst Schoenbaechler Managing Director

SWITZERLAND (+41)   www.euromoneydirectory.com

Alpha Securities AG (cont)
Debt Capital Markets / Fixed Income
Head of Debt Capital Markets   Ernst Schoenbaechler *Managing Director*
Private Placements
Head of Origination   Ernst Schoenbaechler *Managing Director*
Equity Capital Markets
Head of Equity Capital Markets   Ernst Schoenbaechler *Managing Director*
Convertibles / Equity-Linked
Head of Syndication   Ernst Schoenbaechler *Managing Director*
Corporate Finance / M&A Advisory
Head of Corporate Finance   Ernst Schoenbaechler *Managing Director*

American Express Bank (Switzerland) SA   Subsidiary Company

50 rue de Rhône, CH-1204 Geneva 3
PO Box 3072, CH-1211 Geneva 3
Tel: (22) 319 0808 **Fax:** (22) 311 2288 **Telex:** 418131 EXBKPL G

Anker Bank

19 rue de la Croix-D'Or, CH-1211 Geneva 3
PO Box 3017, CH-1211 Geneva 3
Tel: (22) 312 0312 **Fax:** (22) 312 0357 **Swift:** ANKBCH2L

Senior Executive Officers
Senior Vice President   Jacques Rochat
Asset Management
Head   Marc Tissot *Vice President*

Anker Bank

Avenue de la Gare 50, CH-1001 Lausanne
PO Box 159, CH-1001 Lausanne
Tel: (21) 321 0707 **Fax:** (21) 323 9767 **Swift:** ANKBCH2L

Senior Executive Officers
Senior Vice President   Philippe Rithner
Asset Management
Head   Jean-Marc Del Custode *First Vice President*

Anker Bank

Riva Caccia 1A, CH-6900 Lugano
Tel: (91) 985 9050 **Fax:** (91) 985 9059 **Swift:** ANKBCH2L

Senior Executive Officers
Senior Vice President   Fabio Pelegrini
Asset Management
Head   Matteo Celio *Assistant Vice President*

Anker Bank

Talstrasse 82, CH-8001 Zürich
PO Box 4923, CH-8022 Zürich
Tel: (1) 224 6565 **Fax:** (1) 211 9954 **Telex:** 812565 **Swift:** ANKBCH2L

Senior Executive Officers
Chairman   Dominique Ducret
Vice Chairman   Raymond Flücklger
Chief Executive Vice President   Bertrand Germond

Others (Senior Executives)

Jean Buhler *Director*
Marc Fues *Director*
Markus Hugelshofer *Director*
Jean-Pierre Strebel *Director*

www.euromoneydirectory.com SWITZERLAND (+41)

Debt Capital Markets / Fixed Income
Head of Debt Capital Markets Jean-Claude Hofstetter *Senior Vice President*
Asset Management
Head Félix Rattin *Vice President*
Administration
Business Development Patrik Loertscher *Senior Vice President*
Accounts / Audit
Accounts Jean-Bernard Morel *First Vice President*
Other (Administration)
Human Resources Jean-Bernard Morel *First Vice President*

Anlage-und Kreditbank   Head Office

Falkenstrasse 28, CH-8008 Zürich
PO Box 4372, CH-8022 Zürich
Tel: (1) 268 1616 **Fax**: (1) 251 7689 **Telex**: 817109 **Swift**: AKRA CH ZZ **Email**: akb@access.ch **Cable**: 8692
Website: www.akb.ch

Senior Executive Officers
Chairman Martin Kólsch
Chief Executive Officer Bruno Merki *Chairman of the Executive Committee* ☎ **268 1602**
Financial Director Paul Ammann *Vice President* ☎ **268 1760**
Chief Operating Officer Martin Spring *Vice President*
Chairman of the Executive Committee Bruno Merki ☎ **268 1602**
Assistant to the Executive Committee Peter Graf ☎ **268 1646**
International Division Michael Widmer *Vice President* ☎ **268 1680**

General-Investment
Head of Investment Marc Keller *Vice President* ☎ **268 1670**

Debt Capital Markets / Fixed Income
Tel: 268 1661 **Fax**: 261 7913
Head of Fixed Income Trading Philippe Wagner *Assistant Treasurer*

Government Bonds
Head of Trading Philippe Wagner *Assistant Treasurer*

Eurobonds
Head of Trading Philippe Wagner *Assistant Treasurer*

Emerging Market Bonds
Head of Trading Philippe Wagner *Assistant Treasurer*

Fixed-Income Research
Head of Fixed Income Philippe Wagner *Assistant Treasurer*

Equity Capital Markets
Department: Trading
Head of Equity Capital Markets; Head of Trading Pascal Hotz *Vice President* ☎ **268 1660**

Domestic Equities
Head of Trading Pascal Hotz *Vice President* ☎ **268 1660**

International Equities
Head of Trading Pascal Hotz *Vice President* ☎ **268 1660**

Equity Research
Head of Equity Research Marc Keller *Vice President* ☎ **268 1670**

Money Markets
Tel: 268 1650 **Fax**: 261 7913
Head of Money Markets Rolf Bolleter *Vice President* ☎ **268 1650**

Foreign Exchange
Tel: 268 1650 **Fax**: 261 7913
Head of Foreign Exchange; Head of Trading Rolf Bolleter *Vice President* ☎ **268 1650**
Head of Trading Pascal Hotz *Vice President* ☎ **268 1660**

Corporate Finance / M&A Advisory
Head of Corporate Finance Andrea Meinde *Assistant Vice President* ☎ **268 1750**

Asset Management
Head Marc Keller *Vice President* ☎ **268 1670**

Other Departments
Chief Credit Officer Andrea Meinde *Assistant Vice President* ☎ **268 1750**
Private Banking Bruno Merki *Chairman of the Executive Committee* ☎ **268 1602**
 Edmond Violand *Vice President & Head of Private Banking CH* ☎ **268 1691**

Euromoney Directory 1999 **1469**

SWITZERLAND (+41)   www.euromoneydirectory.com

Anlage-und KreditBank (cont)
Administration
Head of Administration   Martin Spring Vice President
Head of Marketing   Christina Hammer
Technology & Systems
   Wolfgang Müllner Assistant Vice President
Compliance
   Peter Graf Assistant to the Executive Committee ☎ 268 1646
Public Relations
   Christina Hammer
Accounts / Audit
   Paul Ammann Vice President ☎ 268 1760

ANZ Grindlays Bank Limited   Subsidiary Company
7 Quai du Mont-Blanc, CH-1211 Geneva 1
PO Box 1560, Geneva
Tel: (22) 906 0111 **Fax:** (22) 906 0122 **Telex:** 412521 ANZCH **Swift:** GRND CH GG
Senior Executive Officers
Chief Operating Officer   Pierre-Yves Roten ☎ 906 0227 F 906 0127
General Manager   Timothy Fraser-Smith ☎ 906 0345 F 906 0129
Other Departments
Private Banking   Timothy Fraser-Smith General Manager ☎ 906 0345 F 906 0129
Administration
Business Development   Roland Woerandli Director ☎ 906 0301 F 906 0129

Appenzell-Innerrhodische Kantonalbank   Head Office
Bankgasse 2, CH-9050 Appenzell
Tel: (71) 788 8888 **Fax:** (71) 788 8889; (71) 788 8833 **Telex:** 883727 **Cable:** KANTONALBANK APP
Senior Executive Officers
Präs Bankrat   Josef Sutter
Others (Senior Executives)
   Bruno Doerig Direktor
Debt Capital Markets / Fixed Income
Tel: 788 8817
Head of Debt Capital Markets   Alfred J Langenegger ☎ 788 8816
Foreign Exchange
Tel: 788 8854
Head of Foreign Exchange   Emil Ulmann
Corporate Finance / M&A Advisory
Tel: 788 8809 **Fax:** 788 8833
Head of Corporate Finance   Albert Doerig ☎ 788 8807

Arab Bank (Switzerland)   Head Office
Limmatquai 92, CH-8022 Zürich
PO Box 5281, CH-8022 Zürich
Tel: (1) 265 7111 **Fax:** (1) 265 7330 **Telex:** 812279 ARB CH **Swift:** ARBS CH ZZ **Email:** arabbank@csi.com
Reuters: ABLZ **Cable:** ARABIBANK
Website: www.arabbank.com
Senior Executive Officers
Chairman   Abdul Majeed Shoman
Chief Executive Officer   Josef Müller General Manager
Chief Operating Officer   Placi Caduff Manager
Treasurer   Richard Wiesli Manager
Others (Senior Executives)
Geneva Branch   Said Al-Habal Manager
Foreign Exchange
Head of Foreign Exchange   Jean-François Binnendijk Deputy Manager
Asset Management
Head   Rudolf Müller Deputy Manager

1470   Euromoney Directory 1999

www.euromoneydirectory.com **SWITZERLAND (+41)**

Other Departments
Private Banking Matthias Oettli *Deputy Manager*
Administration
Technology & Systems
Holder of Procuration Remo Segalla

Armand von Ernst & Cie AG

Bundesgasse 30, CH-3011 Berne
Tel: (31) 311 1321 **Fax:** (31) 312 0342 **Telex:** 911801 **Cable:** AVECO

Senior Executive Officers
Chairman Georges Gagnebin
Board of Directors Freddy W Schwab
Board of Directors Arno Curty
Board of Directors Oskar Hunziker

Asahi Bank (Schweiz) AG   Subsidiary Company

Talacker 41, CH-8001 Zürich
Tel: (1) 217 8484 **Fax:** (1) 217 8485 **Telex:** 815484 ASZH CH **Reuters:** ASZA

Senior Executive Officers
General Manager Akihiro Matsuyama
Debt Capital Markets / Fixed Income
Head of Fixed Income Trading Shinkhi Tamura
Settlement / Clearing
Head of Settlement / Clearing Hanspeter Willi

Banca Commerciale Italiana (Suisse)   Subsidiary Company

Ramistrasse 31, CH-8001 Zürich
Tel: (1) 269 8211 **Fax:** (1) 269 8209 **Telex:** 814100 BCI CH

Equity Capital Markets
Equity Repo / Securities Lending
Head of Trading Alan Traversi *Securities Trader*
Settlement / Clearing
Tel: 220 8290
Settlement (General) Slaveo Peneta
Evonne Tlebeata
Gianpiero Marangio

Administration
Public Relations
Elvio Gasparin *Head* ☏ 220 8210 ℻ 211 7793

Banca del Ceresio   Head Office

Via Pretorio 13, CH-6900 Lugano
PO Box 2860, CH-6900 Lugano
Tel: (91) 923 8422 **Fax:** (91) 923 5508 **Telex:** 841256 **Swift:** BACE CH 22

Senior Executive Officers
Chairman Peter Alther
Chief Executive Officer Vihorio Sbarbaro
Others (Senior Executives)
Giambattista Foglia *Manager*
Alberto Foglia *Manager*
Antonio Ronconi *Deputy Manager*
Antonio Foglia *Assistant Manager*

Euromoney Directory 1999 **1471**

SWITZERLAND (+41) www.euromoneydirectory.com

Banca del Ceresio (cont)
Others (Senior Executives) (cont)
 Maurizio Solaro del Borgo *Assistant Manager*
 Mario Calcagno *Assistant Manager*
 Giacomo Foglia *Assistant Manager*

Banca del Gottardo Head Office
Alternative trading name: Gotthard Bank
 Viale Franscini 8, CH-6900 Lugano
 PO Box 2811, CH-6901 Lugano
Tel: (91) 808 1111 **Fax:** (91) 923 9487 **Telex:** 841 051 **Swift:** BDGLCH22 **Email:** gottardo@gottardo.ch
Reuters: BDGC **Telerate:** 85 GOTT **Bloomberg:** GOT SW **Cable:** gottardbank.lugano
 Reuters: BDGO, BDGT
 Website: www.gottardo.ch

Senior Executive Officers
Chairman   Claudio Generali
President   Marco Netzer
Financial Director   Sirio Bassi *Head of Financial Division*

Others (Senior Executives)
Head of Logistics   Loris Biaggio
Credits and Risks   Tiziano Pellandini
Corporate Clients   Philippe Tron-Lozai

General - Treasury
Head of Treasury   Claudio Camplani *Member of Management*

Debt Capital Markets / Fixed Income
Head of Debt Capital Markets   Fabio Testori
                                       Claudio Pisoni *Member of Management*
Head of Fixed Income Trading   Erminio Brocchi

Equity Capital Markets
Country Head   Fabio Testori *Head of Markets*

Foreign Exchange
Head of Foreign Exchange   Franco Charrey *Head, Global Treasury*
Head of Trading   Paolo Patelli

FX Traders / Sales People
Banking Relations   Mariangelo Sandoli *Member of Management*
Trading Options   Jean-Luc Cracco *Member of Management*

Risk Management
Department: Credits and Risks Department
Head of Risk Management   Mauro Guerra

Settlement / Clearing
Operations   Loris Biaggio

Asset Management
Head   Enzo Fassora

Other Departments
Private Banking   Luca Soncini *Senior Executive Officer*

Administration
Head of Marketing   Mario Maccanelli

Technology & Systems
IT   Giuseppe Bollini

Legal / In-House Counsel
                                       Massimo Antonini

Public Relations
                                       Mario Maccanelli

Accounts / Audit
Audit   Mario Riva *Head*
Accounts   Raimondo Casanova

Other (Administration)
Organisation   Vincenzo Manzoni
Customers Area   Nicola Mordasini *Head*
Personnel   Paolo Felix
Controlling   Loris Biaggio

www.euromoneydirectory.com SWITZERLAND (+41)

Banca del Sempione
Head Office
Via Peri 5, CH-6900 Lugano
Tel: (91) 910 7111 **Fax:** (91) 922 6040 **Telex:** 841168 SEM CH **Swift:** BASE CH 22 **Email:** banca@bancasempione.ch
Cable: SIMPLONBANK

Senior Executive Officers
Chairman   Fiorenzo Perucchi
Managing Director / General Manager   Sergio Barutta

Banca dello Stato del Cantone Ticino
Head Office
Viale Guisan 5, CH-6501 Bellinzona
Tel: (91) 803 7111 **Fax:** (91) 826 1364; (91) 803 7488 **Telex:** 846481

Senior Executive Officers
President   Franco Gianoni
Managing Director / General Manager   Romano Mellini

Banca Monte Paschi (Suisse) SA

Alternative trading name: Banca Monte dei Paschi di Siena
11 Avenue Henri Dunant, CH-1205 Geneva
PO Box 352, Geneva 4
Tel: (22) 809 0300 **Fax:** (22) 809 0399 **Telex:** 428 383 MPS CH **Swift:** BMPS CH GG **Email:** montep@worldcom.ch
Website: www.montepaschi.ch

Senior Executive Officers
Chairman & General Manager   Edio Delcò

Banca Privata Solari & Blum SA
Head Office
Via Ginevera 2, CH-6901 Lugano
Tel: (91) 921 4500; (91) 923 6833 **Fax:** (91) 923 4501; (91) 922 8972 **Telex:** 844200 **Swift:** SOLB CH 22

Settlement / Clearing
Fax: 921 3225 **Telex:** 841171
Settlement (General)   Renzo Ricci
                                      Heidi Schuetz

Banca Unione di Credito Ginevra
Full Branch Office
3 rue du Mont-Blanc, CH-1211 Geneva 1
PO Box 1176, CH-1211 Geneva 1
Tel: (22) 732 7939 **Fax:** (22) 732 5089 **Telex:** 412689

Senior Executive Officers
Branch Manager   Camille R Perusset

Banca Unione di Credito Lugano
Head Office
Piazza Dante 7, CH-6900 Lugano
PO Box 2861, CH-6901 Lugano
Tel: (91) 806 3111 **Fax:** (91) 922 7009 **Telex:** 841188 **Swift:** BUCL CH 22

Senior Executive Officers
Chairman   Carlo Sganzini
Vice Chairman   Fausto Boffi
Vice Chairman   Giulio Merlani
General Manager   Piero Raimondo
Joint GM, Administrative   Ernesto Pozzoli
Deputy General Manager   Gianfilippo Maiga
International Division   Gianfilippo Maiga *Deputy General Manager*

Debt Capital Markets / Fixed Income
Asset-Backed Securities / Securitization
Head of Trading   Fiorenzo Bernasconi *SVP, Securities*

Foreign Exchange
Head of Foreign Exchange   Gianfilippo Maiga *Deputy General Manager*

SWITZERLAND (+41)   www.euromoneydirectory.com

Banca Unione di Credito Lugano (cont)
FX Traders / Sales People
                                            Jean Jacques Ringier *Vice President*
Settlement / Clearing
Operations   Osvaldo Guggiari *Vice President*
Other Departments
Correspondent Banking   Angelo Lanfranconi *First Vice President*
Administration
Head of Administration   Ernesto Pozzoli *Joint GM, Administrative*
Other (Administration)
Commercial   Piergiorgio Rezzonico *Senior Vice President*

Banca Unione di Credito Zurigo   Full Branch Office
Tödistrasse 5, CH-8002 Zürich
PO Box 5022, CH-8022 Zürich
Tel: (1) 206 6611 **Fax:** (1) 206 6688 **Telex:** 815973

Senior Executive Officers
Senior Vice President   Piergiorgio Martinetti
First Vice President   Rudolf Infanger

Banco Central Hispanoamericano SA   Representative Office
Brandschenkestrasse 10, CH-8002 Zürich
Tel: (1) 202 8662 **Fax:** (1) 202 8663 **Telex:** 816117

Senior Executive Officers
Chief Representative   Adolfo Fernández

Banco Exterior (Suiza) SA   Subsidiary Company
Zeltweg 63, CH-8021 Zürich
PO Box 3930, CH-8021 Zürich
Tel: (1) 265 9511 **Fax:** (1) 251 9014 **Telex:** 814600 BEX CH **Swift:** EXTE CH ZZ

Senior Executive Officers
Chairman   Ignacio Figaredo
Chief Executive Officer   Alberto Ramirez
Chief Operating Officer   Hans Kaiser [E] **hans.kaiser@argentaria.ch**
Settlement / Clearing
Settlement (General)   Ramon Sala
Operations   Hans Kaiser [E] **hans.kaiser@argentaria.ch**
Administration
Compliance   Hans Kaiser [E] **hans.kaiser@argentaria.ch**

Banco Popular Español   Representative Office
64/66 rue de Lausanne, CH-1202 Geneva
Tel: (22) 731 7610 **Fax:** (22) 738 3765

Senior Executive Officers
Deputy Representative, Geneva   José Prieto López

Banco Popular Español   Representative Office
Badenerstrasse 255, CH-8003 Zürich
Tel: (1) 451 0535; (1) 451 0536 **Fax:** (1) 451 1610

Senior Executive Officers
Representative   Manuel Montoya Rico

www.euromoneydirectory.com　　　　　　　　SWITZERLAND (+41)

Banco Santander (Suisse) SA
Subsidiary Company

2-4, Place des Alpes, CH-1201 Geneva 1
PO Box 1256, CH-1211 Geneva 1
Tel: (22) 909 2222 **Fax:** (22) 738 6728 **Telex:** 412265 BCO CH **Swift:** BDERCHGG

Senior Executive Officers
Financial Director　　　　　　　　　　Francois Garcia
Chief Operating Officer　　　　　　　　Luis Lopez Bregel
Managing Director / General Manager　Paul Saurel

Asset Management
Head　　　　　　　　　　　　　　　　Manuel Echeverria

Other Departments
Correspondent Banking　　　　　　　Maria Vazquez

Banco Urquijo SA
Representative Office

6 rue Céard, CH-1204 Geneva
Tel: (22) 311 5030 **Fax:** (22) 310 6480 **Telex:** 428430 MARC CH

Senior Executive Officers
Chief Representative　　　　　　　　Norbert Danville ☏ **310 8922**

Bank Adamas AG
Full Branch Office

Formerly known as: Bank Albis

Gerbergasse 6, CH-8023 Zürich
Tel: (1) 221 0668 **Fax:** (1) 211 9849 **Telex:** 813991

Senior Executive Officers
Chairman　　　　　　　　　　　　　Fabio Conti
Managing Director　　　　　　　　　Fabrizio Donati

Others (Senior Executives)
　　　　　　　　　　　　　　　　　　Niculin à Porta *Director, Zurich Office*

Settlement / Clearing
Operations　　　　　　　　　　　　　J Giezendanner *Head of Operations*

Bank of America NT & SA
Full Branch Office

40 rue du Marché, CH-1204 Geneva
Tel: (22) 318 6911; (22) 318 6938 **Fax:** (22) 318 6900; (22) 318 6939 **Telex:** 421135A BOA CH
Bloomberg: francis1@bloomberg.net
General Telex: 421 542 BAGE CH

Senior Executive Officers
Vice President & Country Manager　　Fred Schut ☏ **318 6960**

Others (Senior Executives)
Senior Account Officer　　　　　　　Christoph T KaderlI *Vice President* ☏ **318 6962**
Account Officer　　　　　　　　　　Philippe Garcelon *Assistant Vice President* ☏ **318 6963**
　　　　　　　　　　　　　　　　　　Edmond Viedma *Assistant Vice President* ☏ **318 6990**
Customer Service　　　　　　　　　Adrian Streit *Senior Authorized Officer* ☏ **318 6933** 📠 **318 6939**
Country Relationship Manager　　　Linda Richards *Vice President* ☏ **318 6930** 📠 **318 6939**

Syndicated Lending
Department: Accounting / Finance & Control Services

Other (Trade Finance)
Finance Officer　　　　　　　　　　Jean-Louis Ingold *Assistant Vice President* ☏ **318 6992**

Settlement / Clearing
Department: Settlement / Clearing - Private Banking
Operations　　　　　　　　　　　　　Henrik Kjellqvist *Vice President* ☏ **318 6970** 📠 **318 6979**

Other Departments
Private Banking　　　　　　　　　　Fred Schut *Vice President & Country Manager* ☏ **318 6960**

Administration
Compliance
Compliance Officer　　　　　　　　Marie-France Tschachtli *Assistant Vice President* ☏ **318 6995**

SWITZERLAND (+41)   www.euromoneydirectory.com

Bank of America NT & SA (cont)
Public Relations
Personnel Office   Linda Wolf *Senior Authorized Officer* ☎ 318 6953
                       ✉ linda.e.richards@bankamerica.com

Bank Clariden Heusser
Head Office

St Alban-Vorstadt 58, CH-4052 Basle
PO Box 132, CH-4010 Basle
Tel: (61) 287 8787 **Fax:** (61) 287 8272 **Telex:** 962108

Senior Executive Officers
Chairman   Robert L Genillird
Chief Executive Officer   Max Cotting

Asset Management
Portfolio Management   Markus Allemann *Analyst*

Other Departments
Private Banking   Marco Benziger
                                 Peter Diemand
                                 Christoph Etter
                                 Hans-Rudolf Fischer
                                 Thomas Herzig
                                 Peter Greinemann
                                 Kurt Himmelsbach
                                 Rolf Horstmann
                                 Patrick Huurdeman
                                 Rolf Maurer
                                 Markus Spielmann
                                 Franz Spirig
                                 André Thalmann
                                 Karl Würz

Bank für Handel & Effekten
Head Office

Talacker 50, PO Box, CH-8039 Zürich
Tel: (1) 226 3100 **Fax:** (1) 226 3120 **Swift:** BHEF CH ZZ **Cable:** HANDEFFEKT

Senior Executive Officers
Chairman   Oswald J Gruebel
Chief Executive Officer   Cristoph Schaerer
Treasurer   Ulrich Frei *Executive Vice President*

Syndicated Lending
Loan-Related Activities
Trade Finance   Heinz Brechbühl *Assistant Vice President*

Money Markets
Head of Money Markets   Thomas A Heuberger *First Vice President*

Foreign Exchange
Global Head   Edith Buri *First Vice President*

Other Departments
Private Banking   Thomaz C Burckhardt *First Vice President*

Bank Guinness Mahon Flight AG
Head Office

Talacker 41, CH-8001 Zürich
PO Box 8039, CH-8039 Zürich
Tel: (1) 226 1000 **Fax:** (1) 226 1010 **Telex:** 817128 GMZ CH

Senior Executive Officers
Chairman   Stuart Wells ☎ +44 (171) 772 7400
General Manager   Richard Raynar

Foreign Exchange
Head of Foreign Exchange   Roger Kernbach

Settlement / Clearing
Head of Settlement / Clearing André Hügli

Other Departments
Private Banking   Reto Kuoni *Manager*

www.euromoneydirectory.com				SWITZERLAND (+41)

Administration
Business Development; Head of Marketing	Teja von Holzschuher *Manager*
Accounts / Audit
					Rolf Vogel *Assistant Manager*

Bank Hapoalim (Switzerland) Limited
Head Office

33 Stockerstrasse, CH-8039 Zürich
PO Box 870, CH-8039 Zürich
Tel: (1) 283 8181 **Fax:** (1) 202 7740 **Telex:** 813762 **Swift:** POAL CH ZZA **Reuters:** Recipient
Cable: BANKPOALIM ZURIC

Senior Executive Officers
Chairman					Shimon Ravid
Chief Executive Officer			U Meir *General Manager*
Financial Director; Chief Operating Officer	H Gareus
Treasurer					M Beasley
Secretary of the General Manager		A Brunner Dragsnes
General-Lending (DCM, SL)
Head of Corporate Banking			R Haenni
Money Markets
Head of Money Markets				M Beasley
Foreign Exchange
Head of Foreign Exchange			M Beasley
Other Departments
Private Banking				M Lahav
Administration
Technology & Systems
						R Wymann
Public Relations
						A Brunner Dragsnes *Secretary of the General Manager*

Bank Hofmann AG

PO Box 5445, CH-1211 Geneva
Tel: (22) 818 5600 **Fax:** (22) 818 5610

Senior Executive Officers
Others (Senior Executives)
Business Unit Heads				J Younes
						B Von Below

Bank Hofmann AG
Head Office

Talstrasse 27, CH-8022 Zürich
Tel: (1) 217 5111 **Fax:** (1) 211 7368 **Telex:** 813485 **Swift:** HOFM CH ZZ **Email:** bank@hofmann.ch
Cable: HOFMANNBANK ZURI
Website: www.hofmann.ch

Senior Executive Officers
Chairman					William Wirth
Vice Chairman					Oswald J Grübel
Chief Executive Officer			Markus R Tödtli ☎ **217 5501**
Financial Director				Bruno Riethmann *Head, Controlling & Accounting* ☎ **217 5400**
Others (Senior Executives)
Member of the Executive Board			Hugo Renz
						Frank Ramsperger *Chief Investment Officer*
General-Investment
Head of Investment				Frank Ramsperger *Chief Investment Officer*
General - Treasury
Head of Treasury				Thomas Schaad *Head, Treasury & Trading Division*
Relationship Manager
International Private Clients			Egidio Parigi *Head*
Equity Capital Markets
Department: Stock Exchanges
Head of Equity Capital Markets		Heinz Leibbrand *Head*

SWITZERLAND (+41)   www.euromoneydirectory.com

Bank Hofmann AG (cont)

Foreign Exchange
Head of Foreign Exchange   Bernhard Wismer *Senior Vice President*

Asset Management
Portfolio Management   Andres Rüfli *Head*

Other Departments
Private Banking   Roman Ziegler *Head*
Economic Research   Andres Rüfli *Head*

Administration
Technology & Systems
     Hans Christen *Head of IT*

Legal / In-House Counsel
     Roland Vetterli *Head*

Compliance
     Roland Vetterli *Head*

Other (Administration)
Human Resources   Daniel Fahrni

Bank Hugo Kahn & Co AG   Head Office

Stockerstrasse 38, CH-8002 Zürich
PO Box 663, CH-8027 Zürich
Tel: (1) 201 1060 **Fax:** (1) 201 4233 **Telex:** 815340 **Email:** bank@hugokahn.ch
Website: www.hugokahn.ch

Senior Executive Officers
Chairman   Claude H Kahn
Chief Executive Officer   Urs P Jost

Others (Senior Executives)
First Vice President   Daniel Schlauri
     Hans Schuppisser
Vice President   Severino Zollinger
     Werner Teuber

Bank J Vontobel & Co AG   Head Office

Bahnhofstrasse 3, CH-8022 Zürich
Tel: (1) 283 7111 **Fax:** (1) 283 7650 **Telex:** 812306 **Swift:** VONT CH ZZ **Reuters:** BVZD
Website: www.vontobel.ch

Senior Executive Officers
Chairman   Hans-Dieter Vontobel
Chief Executive Officer   Jörg Fischer

Bank Julius Baer & Co Limited   Head Office

Bahnhofstrasse 36, CH-8010 Zürich
PO Box 8010, CH-8010 Zürich
Tel: (1) 228 5111 **Fax:** (1) 211 2560 **Email:** postoffice@juliusbaer.com
Website: www.juliusbaer.com

Senior Executive Officers
Chairman   Rudolf E Baer
President   Ruetch Franz
Company Secretary   Harry Bopp

Others (Senior Executives)
Private Banking   Heinrich Looser *Deputy President, Member of Mgmt Committee*
Money Market & Forex   Michael Baer *Deputy President, Member of Mgmt Committee*
Brokerage & Capital Markets   Martin Eberhard *Deputy President, Member of Mgmt Committee*
Banking Operations   Alexander Hartmann *Deputy President, Member of Mgmt Committee*
International Systems   Markus Schildknecht *Deputy President, Member of Mgmt Committee*
Securities   Michel Vukotic *Deputy President, Member of Mgmt Committee*

Debt Capital Markets / Fixed Income
Head of Debt Capital Markets   Michel Vukotic *Deputy President, Member of Mgmt Committee*

www.euromoneydirectory.com SWITZERLAND (+41)

Equity Capital Markets
Head of Equity Capital Markets — Michel Vukotic *Deputy President, Member of Mgmt Committee*
Head of Sales — Roger Hochener

Other (International Equity)
New Issues — Jueg Sturzenegger

Equity Research
Head of Equity Research — Otto Waser

Equity Repo / Securities Lending
Head — Peter Schönenberger *Vice President* ☎ 437 4184 F 431 8116

Money Markets
Head of Money Markets — Fredy Lutz
Michael Baer *Deputy President, Member of Mgmt Committee*

Foreign Exchange
Head of Foreign Exchange — Fredy Lutz
Michael Baer *Deputy President, Member of Mgmt Committee*

Risk Management
Head of Risk Management — Michel Vukotic

Global Custody
Other (Global Custody)
Jürg Ryffel *Senior Vice President*
Margrit Koch *Assistant Vice President*
Daniel Waeber *Assistant Vice President*

Administration
Head of Administration — Markus Schildknecht *Deputy President, Member of Mgmt Committee*
Public Relations
Juerg Stachelin

Bank Leu Limited
Head Office

Bahnhofstrasse 32, PO Box, CH-8022 Zürich
Tel: (1) 219 1111 **Fax:** (1) 219 3197 **Telex:** 812 174 **Swift:** LEUZ CH ZZ **Email:** webmaster@leu.com **Reuters:** LEUD; LEUG; LEUZ
Website: www.leu.com

Senior Executive Officers
Chairman — Oswald Grübel
President — Reto Donatsch

Administration
Public Relations
Angelika Beretta *Member of Senior Management*

Bank Leumi Le-Israel (Schweiz)
Subsidiary Company

Claridenstrasse 34, CH-8022 Zürich
Tel: (1) 207 9111 **Fax:** (1) 207 9100 **Telex:** 815441 BLIZH **Swift:** LUMI CH ZZ **Reuters:** BLIZ

Senior Executive Officers
Chairman — Galia Maor
Treasurer — Roland Wyss *Manager* ☎ 207 9222
General Manager — Meir Grosz ☎ 207 9202

Debt Capital Markets / Fixed Income
Head of Debt Capital Markets — Otto Wolf *Deputy Manager* ☎ 207 9255

Non-Domestic Government Bonds
Guy Klement *Assistant Manager* ☎ 207 9250

Eurobonds
Head of Origination — Guy Klement *Assistant Manager* ☎ 207 9250

Bonds - General
Guy Klement *Assistant Manager* ☎ 207 9250

Medium-Term Notes
Head of Sales — Guy Klement *Assistant Manager* ☎ 207 9250

Private Placements
Head of Sales — Guy Klement *Assistant Manager* ☎ 207 9250

Equity Capital Markets
Tel: 207 9100
Head of Equity Capital Markets — Guy Klement *Assistant Manager* ☎ 207 9250

SWITZERLAND (+41)   www.euromoneydirectory.com

Bank Leumi Le-Israel (Schweiz) (cont)

Domestic Equities
Head of Trading — P Scalisi *Holder of Procuration* ☎ 207 9610

International Equities
Head of Trading; Head of Research — Guy Klement *Assistant Manager* ☎ 207 9250

Convertibles / Equity-Linked
Head of Trading; Head of Research — Guy Klement *Assistant Manager* ☎ 207 9250

Warrants
Head of Trading — Guy Klement *Assistant Manager* ☎ 207 9250

Syndicated Lending
Tel: 207 9100
Head of Syndicated Lending — Stefan Pilet *Assistant Manager* ☎ 207 9230

Money Markets
Tel: 207 9100
Head of Money Markets — Roland Wyss *Manager* ☎ 207 9222

Foreign Exchange
Tel: 207 9100
Global Head — Claude Guggenheim *Assistant Manager* ☎ 207 9224

FX Traders / Sales People
All Currencies — N Liuzzi *Mandatory* ☎ 207 9225
M L Geering *Holder of Procuration* ☎ 207 9227
Zolt Zalotay *Dealer* ☎ 207 9223

Risk Management
Tel: 207 9100
Head of Risk Management — Roland Wyss *Manager* ☎ 207 9222

Fixed Income Derivatives / Risk Management
Global Head; IR Swaps Sales / Marketing; IR Swaps Trading; IR Options Sales / Marketing; IR Options Trading — Claude Guggenheim *Assistant Manager* ☎ 207 9224

Foreign Exchange Derivatives / Risk Management
Cross-Currency Swaps, Sales / Marketing; Cross-Currency Swaps, Trading; Vanilla FX option Sales; Vanilla FX option Trading — Claude Guggenheim *Assistant Manager* ☎ 207 9224

OTC Equity Derivatives
Sales; Trading — Guy Klement *Assistant Manager* ☎ 207 9250

OTC Credit Derivatives
Global Head of Sales; Head of Trading — Claude Guggenheim *Assistant Manager* ☎ 207 9224

Exchange-Traded Derivatives
Global Head — Claude Guggenheim *Assistant Manager* ☎ 207 9224

Settlement / Clearing
Tel: 207 9100
Regional Head — Benno Mechner *Assistant Manager* ☎ 207 9277
Equity Settlement; Fixed-Income Settlement — Th Fink *Assistant Manager* ☎ 207 9261
Foreign Exchange Settlement — Kavindra Bakshi *Holder of Procuration* ☎ 207 9204

Global Custody
Tel: 207 9100
Other (Global Custody)
All — Th Fink *Assistant Manager* ☎ 207 9261

Other Departments
Commodities / Bullion — Claude Guggenheim *Assistant Manager* ☎ 207 9224
Private Banking — Ernst Imfeld *Manager* ☎ 207 9299
Correspondent Banking — Roland Wyss *Manager* ☎ 207 9222

Administration
Technology & Systems — Martin Häberli *EDP Manager* ☎ 207 9283

Compliance — Roland Wyss *Manager* ☎ 207 9222

Public Relations — Roland Wyss *Manager* ☎ 207 9222

Bank Lips AG   Head Office

Mittelstrasse 6, CH-8034 Zürich
Tel: (1) 382 1700; (1) 388 6464 **Fax:** (1) 382 1513 **Telex:** 816079

www.euromoneydirectory.com   SWITZERLAND (+41)

Bank Morgan Stanley AG
Subsidiary Company

Bahnhofstrasse 92, CH-8023 Zürich
Tel: (1) 220 9111 Fax: (1) 220 9800
Website: www.ms.com

Senior Executive Officers
Managing Director — Adolf Bründler

Equity Capital Markets
Other (International Equity)
Equity Sales — Daniele Hendry *Executive Director*

Other Departments
Private Banking — Adolf Bründler *Managing Director*
Willi Leimer *Managing Director*
Luis Palacios *Vice President*

Bank of New York - Inter Maritime Bank, Geneva
Head Office

5 Quai du Mont-Blanc, CH-1201 Geneva 1
PO Box 1683, CH-1211 Geneva
Tel: (22) 906 8888 Fax: (22) 906 8989 Telex: 412577 IMB CH Swift: BNYI CH GG Bloomberg: 733492-0, 733527-1
Website: www.bny-imb.com

Senior Executive Officers
Chairman — Bruce Rappaport
Vice Chairman — Deno D Papageorge

Others (Senior Executives)
Board of Directors — Guido Condrau *Director*
Geoffrey W Bennet *Director*
Paul Lachausse *Director*
Hans Rudolf Voegeli *Director*

Management — Matthew Stevenson *General Manager & Chief Executive*
Lars J Cullert *General Manager & COO*

Private Banking — Stephen Beekman *Director*
Jean-Pierre Ernst *Director*

Operations & Systems — Bernard Dufour *Director*
Corporate Banking — Jean Goutchkoff *Director*
Investment Strategy — Gerry Wand *Director*
Advisor to the Executive Management — Serge Belleli

Syndicated Lending
Other (Trade Finance)
Letters of Credit / Documentary Credits — Monika Pfister
Adriano Conceprio

Money Markets
Department: Stock Exchange & Investment Analysis

Money Markets - General — Gerry Wand *Director*
Serge Laedermann *Deputy Manager*
André Buhler *Assistant Manager*
Michele Cottarelli

Foreign Exchange
Department: Foreign Exchange & Bullion

FX Traders / Sales People
Foreign Exchange & MM — Gerry Wand *Director*
Adrian Schönauer *Deputy Manager*
Christophe Gayère
Marc Lang
Xavier Mugnier

Risk Management
Country Head — David Hättenschwiller *Assistant Manager*

Settlement / Clearing
Settlement (General) — Franca Taddei *Securities Clearing / Custody*
Operations — Bernard Dufour *Director*

Global Custody
Country Head — Franca Taddei *Securities Clearing / Custody*

SWITZERLAND (+41)   www.euromoneydirectory.com

Bank of New York - Inter Maritime Bank, Geneva (cont)
Other Departments
Private Banking   Stephen Beekman *Director*
    Jean-Pierre Ernst *Director*
    Serge Belleli
    Eric Brüderlein
    John Cannock *Deputy Manager*
    Michele Cottarelli
    Hugette Luginbuhl
    Vincent Payot
Correspondent Banking   Nurullah Kurum
Administration
Technology & Systems
Technology & Software   Didier Pluss
Administration, Operations & Systems   Bernard Dufour *Director*
Accounts / Audit
Accounting / Financial Control   Pascal Rohrer
Other (Administration)
Human Resources   Nicole Molleyres

Bank Sal Oppenheim jr & Cie (Schweiz) AG   Subsidiary Company

Uraniastrasse 28, CH-8001 Zürich
PO Box 4439, CH-8022 Zürich
Tel: (1) 214 2214 **Fax:** (1) 211 1085 **Telex:** 813532 **Swift:** BOPS CH ZZ
Website: www.oppenheim.ch

Senior Executive Officers
Chairman   Alfred von Oppenheim
General Manager   Georg von Richter ☎ **214 2358**

Equity Capital Markets
Domestic Equities
Head of Sales   René Braginsky *Manager* ☎ **214 2347**
Head of Trading   Bruno Tambini *Deputy Manager* ☎ **214 2374**
International Equities
Head of Trading   Alex Weiss *Assistant Vice President* ☎ **214 2354**
Convertibles / Equity-Linked
Head of Trading   Alex Weiss *Assistant Vice President* ☎ **214 2354**
Foreign Exchange
Head of Trading   Alex Weiss *Assistant Vice President* ☎ **214 2354**
Settlement / Clearing
Equity Settlement   Werner Singer *Vice President* ☎ **214 2322**
Other Departments
Private Banking   Georg von Richter *General Manager* ☎ **214 2358**
Administration
Technology & Systems
    Guido Vollenweider *Manager* ☎ **214 2336**
Legal / In-House Counsel
    Maurizio Genoni *Manager* ☎ **214 2299**
Compliance
    Guido Vollenweider *Manager* ☎ **214 2336**

Bank Sarasin & Cie

Elisabethenstrasse 62, CH-4002 Basle
Tel: (61) 277 7777 **Fax:** (61) 272 0205 **Telex:** 964 567 **Swift:** SARA CH BB **Email:** marketing@sarasin.ch
Website: www.sarasin.ch

Senior Executive Officers
Partner   Georg F Krayer ☎ **277 7216**
Chief Executive Officer   Peter Merian *Partner* ☎ **277 7565**
Financial Director   Ernst Spichiger *First Vice President* ☎ **277 7628**
Company Secretary   Madeleine Regli
Company Secretary   Eva Schmidlin

www.euromoneydirectory.com			SWITZERLAND (+41)

General-Lending (DCM, SL)
Head of Corporate Banking			Ernst Spichiger *Finance*

Relationship Manager
Institutional Banking			Hans-Rudolf Hufschmid *Partner*
Private Clients - Basle			Philip R Baumann
Sales & Brokerage			Thomas Vonaesch
Private Clients - Zürich			Conrad P Schwyzer *VP, Executive Committee, Partner*
Institutional Zürich			Urs Chicherio

Money Markets
Department: Securities Trading
Global Head			Heinz Feldmann *Securities Trading*

Money Markets - General
FFOP			Markus Pfäffli
Swiss Stock Exchange			Hans Keist
Foreign Stock Exchange			Leonhard Roth
Own Trading, Basle			Josef Stadler
Underwriting			Hans Weber
SIS London			Tomas N M Service

Foreign Exchange
FX Traders / Sales People
Cash & Foreign Exchange - Basle			Max Schwarz
Cash & Foreign Exchange - Zurich			Walter Zech
Payment Transactions / Loans - Basle			Walter Good
Payment Transactions - Basle			Rainer Keller

Corporate Finance / M&A Advisory
Acquisition & Marketing			Eric G Sarasin *Institutional Banking, Partner*
Acquisition & Financial Planning			Wendelin Vischer *Basle & Zürich*

Settlement / Clearing
Operations			Andreas R Sarasin *Logistics, Partner*

Global Custody
Fund Administration			Philipp Mohler

Asset Management
Department: Sarasin Asset Management Limited
Head			Paul Cooper
Investment Funds			Rolf Wittendorfer
				Christoph Fuchs *Investment Funds - Marketing*
Portfolio Management			Matthias Preiswerk

Other Departments
Private Banking			Conrad P Schwyzer *VP, Executive Committee, Partner*
Economic Research			Markus Furler *Brokerage Research*
				Andreas Knörzer *Investment Research*
				Daniel Scheibler *Economics*

Administration
Head of Administration			Andreas R Sarasin *Partner* ☎ **277 7296**

Technology & Systems
EDP			Peter Streule

Legal / In-House Counsel
				Samuel Jenzer

Accounts / Audit
Auditing			Paul Hagmann

Other (Administration)
Secretariat			Madeleine Regli
Advertising			Felix Rudolf von Rohr
Secretariat			Eva Schmidlin
Personnel			Walter Frech
Securities Administration			Peter Wirth

Bank of Tokyo-Mitsubishi (Switzerland) Limited   Full Branch Office
67 rue du Rhône, CH-1207 Geneva
PO Box 3827, CH-1211 Geneva 3
Tel: (22) 718 6600 **Fax:** (22) 718 6666 **Telex:** 413147 CH

Senior Executive Officers
Others (Senior Executives)
Management			Fumihiko Tateno *Deputy President*

SWITZERLAND (+41)   www.euromoneydirectory.com

Bank of Tokyo-Mitsubishi (Switzerland) Limited Full Branch Office

Stockerstrasse 23, CH-8002 Zürich
PO Box 4188, CH-8022 Zürich
Tel: (1) 289 1111 **Fax:** (1) 289-1199 **Telex:** 812167 BTMZ CH

Senior Executive Officers

Others (Senior Executives)
Management   Yasafumi Imaki ☎ **289 1111**
                                         Masato Takei *Deputy President* ☎ **289 1105**
Capital Markets   John Martin *Director* ☎ **289 1350**
Administration   André Neiger *Director* ☎ **289 1510** 🖷 **289 1191**

General-Lending (DCM, SL)
Head of Corporate Banking   Saburo Yao *Manager, Corporate* ☎ **289 1150**

Debt Capital Markets / Fixed Income
Department: Capital Markets
Global Head   John Martin *Director* ☎ **289 1350**

Bonds - General
Primary   Yoshiya Kikokoro ☎ **289 1253**
                                         Toyu Kawamura ☎ **289 1252**
Secondary   Philip Faulkner ☎ **289 1352**
                                         Peter Howe ☎ **289 1312**
                                         Morgan Murphy ☎ **289 1250**
                                         John M O'Donnell ☎ **289 1353**
                                         Eleonara Rajmann ☎ **289 1354**
                                         Keizo Yamada ☎ **289 1356**

Money Markets
Global Head   Yasushi Banno *Manager, Treasury* ☎ **289 1450**

Money Markets - General
                                         Sumiko Yamaguchi ☎ **289 1452**

Foreign Exchange
Global Head   Yasushi Banno *Manager, Treasury* ☎ **289 1450**
Country Head   Roman Mock ☎ **289 1453**

Settlement / Clearing
Head of Settlement / Clearing   André Neiger *Director* ☎ **289 1510** 🖷 **289 1191**
Foreign Exchange Settlement   Sandra Marcellino ☎ **289 1542** 🖷 **289 1191**
Settlement (General)   Roland Munz *Securities Settlement* ☎ **289 1520** 🖷 **289 1191**
Other   Alain Kuhn *Money Transfer / Cashier* ☎ **289 1541** 🖷 **289 1191**

Administration
Head of Administration   André Neiger *Director* ☎ **289 1510** 🖷 **289 1191**

Bank von Ernst & Cie AG

Marktgasse 63/65, CH-3001 Berne
Tel: (31) 329 1111 **Fax:** (31) 311 6391 **Telex:** 912206 BVE CH **Swift:** BVER CH 2230A

Bank von Ernst & Cie AG Head Office

Stauffacherplatz 6, CH-8049 Zürich
Tel: (1) 245 6111 **Fax:** (1) 245 6611 **Telex:** 812083 BVE CH **Swift:** BVER CH ZZ **Reuters:** BVEA

Debt Capital Markets / Fixed Income
Head of Debt Capital Markets   Ulrich M Studer *Senior Vice President* ☎ **245 6273**

Money Markets
Head of Money Markets   Marco Chinni *First Vice President* ☎ **245 6710**

Foreign Exchange
Head of Foreign Exchange   Marco Chinni *First Vice President* ☎ **245 6710**

Settlement / Clearing
Head of Settlement / Clearing   Markus Angst *Associate Vice President* ☎ **245 6290**

1484   Euromoney Directory 1999

www.euromoneydirectory.com   SWITZERLAND (+41)

Bankers Trust AG

Stauffacherquai 42, PO Box 1024, CH-8039 Zürich
Tel: (1) 639 2500 **Fax:** (1) 639 2900 **Telex:** 815606 BTAG CH **Cable:** BANKERSTRUST

Senior Executive Officers
Chairman   Philippe Souviron
Financial Director   Walter Frauchiger *Head of Control* ☏ **639 2310**
Chief Operating Officer   Veli Zimmermann ☏ **639 2242**
Treasurer   Stefano Schirru ☏ **(22) 716 2552**
Managing Director / General Manager   Robert Martinez ☏ **(22) 716 2560**

Debt Capital Markets / Fixed Income
Head of Debt Capital Markets   Eduard Kauffmann ☏ **639 2230**

Money Markets
Head of Money Markets   Stefano Schirru ☏ **(22) 716 2552**

Foreign Exchange
Head of Foreign Exchange   Stefano Schirru ☏ **(22) 716 2552**

Settlement / Clearing
Head of Settlement / Clearing   Marcel Stöckli ☏ **639 2380**
    Federico Franzell ☏ **639 2360**

Banque Audi (Suisse) SA   Head Office

2 rue F Massot, CH-1211 Geneva 12
PO Box 384, Geneva 12
Tel: (22) 704 1111 **Fax:** (22) 704 1100 **Telex:** 429298 AUD CH **Swift:** AUDS CH GG

Senior Executive Officers
Chairman   Raymond Audi
General Manager   Joe Debbane
International Division   Christine Audi *Principal Manager*

Others (Senior Executives)
    Michel Audi *Manager*
    Fouad Hakim *Manager*

Debt Capital Markets / Fixed Income
Eurobonds
Head of Trading   Yaël Cohen *Mandatory*

Emerging Market Bonds
Head of Emerging Markets   Isabelle Gemes

Equity Capital Markets
International Equities
Head of Trading   Jordi Guillo

Convertibles / Equity-Linked
Head of Sales   Yaël Cohen *Mandatory*

Money Markets
Head of Money Markets   Xuan Ho *Holder of Procuration*

Foreign Exchange
Head of Foreign Exchange   Elie Baz *Assistant Manager*

FX Traders / Sales People
    Marc Vuillermet *Mandatory*

Settlement / Clearing
Head of Settlement / Clearing   Fabienne Audi-Sikiardis *Assistant Manager*
Equity Settlement   Lydia Deom *Holder of Procuration*

Other Departments
Correspondent Banking   Christine Audi *Principal Manager*

Administration
Accounts / Audit
    Michel Audi *Manager*

SWITZERLAND (+41) www.euromoneydirectory.com

Banque Banorient (Suisse)

1 rue de la Rôtisserie, Geneva
PO Box 3040, CH-1211 Geneva 3
Tel: (22) 311 3922 **Fax:** (22) 311 6664 **Telex:** 427378 BANO CH **Swift:** BANO CH GG

Senior Executive Officers
General Manager   Saad Azhari

Banque Baring Brothers (Suisse) SA Full Branch Office

112 rue du Rhône, CH-1211 Geneva 3
PO Box 3024, Geneva
Tel: (22) 317 9811 **Fax:** (22) 310 3880 **Telex:** 422824 BBSCH **Swift:** BABR CH GG

Senior Executive Officers
Chairman   Johannes M Yntema
President of the Executive Board   Eric I Sturdza
Financial Director   Marcel Kramer *Deputy General Manager*
Chief Operating Officer   Marc Boryszewski *Member of Management*
Treasurer   Claudia Nater *Member of Management*

Debt Capital Markets / Fixed Income
Head of Debt Capital Markets   Luis Ortola *Deputy Member, Board of Managing Directors*

Equity Capital Markets
Head of Equity Capital Markets   Marcel Kramer *Deputy General Manager*

Money Markets
Head of Money Markets   Claudia Nater *Member of Management*

Foreign Exchange
Head of Foreign Exchange   Claudia Nater *Member of Management*

Risk Management
Head of Risk Management   Günter Woernle *Member of Management*

Settlement / Clearing
Head of Settlement / Clearing   Marc Boryszewski *Member of Management*

Banque Bonhôte & Cie SA Head Office

1 rue Pury, CH-2001 Neuchâtel
Tel: (32) 722 1000 **Fax:** (32) 721 4342

Senior Executive Officers
Managing Director   Jean Berthoud

Banque Bruxelles Lambert (Suisse) SA Subsidiary Company

Avenue de Frontenex 30, CH-1211 Geneva 6
PO Box 6405, Geneva 6
Tel: (22) 787 1111; (22) 735 6104 **Fax:** (22) 736 6602; (22) 787 1551 **Telex:** 413600 BBLCH **Swift:** BBRU CH GG
Reuters: BBLG **Bloomberg:** Hostipi:1034292/Bloombbl **Cable:** BBLSUISSE

Senior Executive Officers
Chairman   Eric Andersen
Financial Director   Yvan Rion *Director & General Secretary* [T] 787 1334 [F] 735 7218
                                         [E] yvan.rion@bbls.ch
Managing Director / General Manager   Guy de Marnix [T] 787 1300 [F] 735 1840 [E] guy.demarnix@bbls.ch

Syndicated Lending
Other (Trade Finance)
Commodities & Trade Finance   Paul Baszanger [T] 787 1438 [F] 786 3002 [E] paul.baszanger@bbls.ch

Other Departments
Private Banking   Gianluigi Monti *Deputy General Manager* [T] 787 1476 [F] 735 1840
                                         [E] gianluigi.monti@bbls.ch
Correspondent Banking   Michel Requet *Deputy Manager* [T] 787 1255 [F] 736 6602

Administration
Technology & Systems
                                         Jacques Taberlet *Manager* [T] 787 1275 [F] 736 6602
                                         [E] jacques.taberlet@bbls.ch

www.euromoneydirectory.com SWITZERLAND (+41)

Banque Cantonale du Valais
Head Office

8 rue des Cèdres, CH-1950 Sion
Tel: (27) 324 6111 Fax: (27) 324 6666
Website: www.bcvs.ch & www.wkb.ch

Senior Executive Officers
Managing Director — Jean-Daniel Papilloud

Others (Senior Executives)
Pierre-André Roux *Manager*
Michel Délèze *Manager*
Georges Luggen *Manager*
André Premand *Manager*

Banque Cantonale de Genève
Head Office

17 quai de l'Ile, PO Box 2251, CH-1204 Geneva 2
PO Box 2251, CH-1211 Geneva 2
Tel: (22) 317 2727 Fax: (22) 793 5960 Telex: 422182 BCGE Swift: BCGE CH GG

Senior Executive Officers
Chairman — Dominique Ducret
Chief Executive Officer — Marc Fues *Executive Vice President*
Financial Director — Jean Buhler *Deputy Executive Vice President*
Vice President — Daniel Burkhardt ☎ 809 2544 📠 310 8879
International Division — Pierre Iseli *Deputy Executive Vice President*

General-Investment
Head of Investment — Jean Buhler *Deputy Executive Vice President*

Debt Capital Markets / Fixed Income
Head of Fixed Income — Neil Carnegie *First Vice President* ☎ 809 3530 📠 809 3535

Government Bonds
Head of Sales — Reto Frei *Deputy Vice President* ☎ 809 3524 📠 312 3022
Head of Trading; Head of Syndication — Reto Frei

Eurobonds
Head of Sales — Reto Frei

Fixed-Income Repo
Head of Repo — Reto Frei *Deputy Vice President* ☎ 809 3524 📠 312 3022

Fixed-Income Research
Head of Fixed Income — Jean-Luc Lederrey *Vice President* ☎ 805 2128 📠 809 2122

Equity Capital Markets
Head of Sales — Neil Carnegie *First Vice President* ☎ 809 3530 📠 809 3535

Domestic Equities
Head of Sales; Head of Trading — Antoine Betran *Assistant Vice President* ☎ 809 3537 📠 809 3567

International Equities
Head of Sales — Antoine Betran *Assistant Vice President* ☎ 809 3537 📠 809 3567

Equity Research
Head of Equity Research — Marc Visian *Assistant Treasurer* ☎ 809 2107 📠 809 2122

Convertibles / Equity-Linked
Head of Sales — Carole Babel *Assistant Treasurer* ☎ 809 3534 📠 809 3567

Syndicated Lending
Head of Trading — Neil Carnegie *First Vice President* ☎ 809 3530 📠 809 3535

Money Markets
Head of Money Markets — Marc Hollistein *Assistant Vice President* ☎ 809 3538 📠 312 3021

Domestic Commercial Paper
Head of Sales — Marc Hollistein *Assistant Vice President* ☎ 809 3538 📠 312 3021

Eurocommercial Paper
Head of Sales — Marc Hollistein *Assistant Vice President* ☎ 809 3538 📠 312 3021

Wholesale Deposits
Marketing — Marc Hollistein *Assistant Vice President* ☎ 809 3538 📠 312 3021

Foreign Exchange
Head of Foreign Exchange — Neil Carnegie *First Vice President* ☎ 809 3530 📠 809 3535
Head of Institutional Sales; Corporate Sales — Hugo Odermatt *Vice President* ☎ 809 3518 📠 809 3476
Head of Trading — Hugo Odermatt *Vice President* ☎ 809 3518 📠 809 3476

Risk Management
Head of Risk Management — René Curti *Deputy Executive Vice President*

SWITZERLAND (+41)   www.euromoneydirectory.com

Banque Cantonale Vaudoise   Head Office

Place Saint-François 14, CH-1003 Lausanne
PO Box 300, CH-1001 Lausanne
Tel: (21) 212 1212 **Fax:** (21) 212 1222 **Telex:** 454304 BCVL CH **Swift:** BCVL CH 2L 10A **Email:** webmaster@bcv.ch
Website: www.bcv.ch

Senior Executive Officers
Chairman of the Board   Jacques Treyvaud
Chief Executive Officer   Gilbert Duchoud *President of the Executive Board*
Financial Director   Jean-Pierre Schrepfer *Head of Controlling*
Chief Operating Officer   Jean-Claude Grangier *Head of Logistics*
Treasurer   Max Weber *Head of Forex*
General Secretary   Jean-Pierre Launaz
International Division   Ralph Ziegler

Others (Senior Executives)
Network   Jean-Marie Brandt *Head of Banking Network*
Trading   Pierre Fischer *Head of Trading*

Debt Capital Markets / Fixed Income
Department: Securities Exchange Department
Tel: 212 4024 **Fax:** 212 1361
Head of Fixed Income; Head of Fixed Income   Pierre Grandjean
Sales; Head of Fixed Income Trading

Government Bonds
Head of Sales   Bernard Ravussin
Head of Trading   Pierre Munier
Head of Syndication; Head of Origination   Ingo Christl

Eurobonds
Head of Sales   Jean-Luc Maillard
Head of Trading   Pierre Munier

Emerging Market Bonds
Head of Emerging Markets   Jean-Luc Maillard
Head of Trading   Pierre Munier

Libor-Based / Floating-Rate Products
FRN Sales   Jean-Luc Maillard
FRN Trading   Pierre Munier

Fixed-Income Research
Head of Fixed Income   René-Pierre Giavina

Equity Capital Markets
Department: Securities Exchange Department
Tel: 212 4024 **Fax:** 212 1361
Head of Equity Capital Markets; Head of Sales;   Pierre Grandjean
Head of Trading

Domestic Equities
Head of Sales   Yvan Cochard
Head of Trading   Jean-Pierre Favre

International Equities
Head of Sales; Head of Trading   Jean-Nicolas Muff

Equity Research
Head of Equity Research   José Fernando Martins da Silva

Convertibles / Equity-Linked
Head of Sales; Head of Trading   Bernard Ravussin

Syndicated Lending
Tel: 212 2899 **Fax:** 212 2583
Head of Origination   Ingo Christl
Head of Syndication   Georges Suri

Loan-Related Activities
Trade Finance   Christian Bless
Project Finance   Alexandre Poltier

Money Markets
Tel: 212 4246 **Fax:** 212 1357
Head of Money Markets   Christian Melet

Wholesale Deposits
Head of Sales   Christian Melet

www.euromoneydirectory.com SWITZERLAND (+41)

Foreign Exchange
Avenue de la Vallombreuse 100, CH-1008 Prilly
Tel: +41 (21) 212 4242 Fax: +41 (21) 212 1330
Global Head   Max Weber *Head of Forex*
Corporate Sales   François Spicher
Head of Trading   Eric Vauthey

Risk Management
Fixed Income Derivatives / Risk Management
IR Swaps Trading   Christian Melet

Foreign Exchange Derivatives / Risk Management
Spot / Forwards Trading   Stéphane Melly

OTC Equity Derivatives
Trading   André Zumwald

Exchange-Traded Derivatives
Global Head   André Zumwald

Corporate Finance / M&A Advisory
Head of Corporate Finance   Alexandre Poltier

Settlement / Clearing
Tel: 212 1421 Fax: 212 1357
Head of Settlement / Clearing   Philippe Sautier
Equity Settlement; Fixed-Income Settlement;   Hans-Joerg Wolfer
Operations

Asset Management
Head   Jacques Brossard

Other Departments
Chief Credit Officer   Daniel Crausaz *Head, Commercial Division*
Private Banking   Claude Courvoisier *Head of Financial Division*
Correspondent Banking   Vincent Perrier
Cash Management   François Seydoux

Administration
Head of Administration   Jean-Claude Grangier *Head of Logistics*
Business Development   Charly Denervaud
Head of Marketing   Jean-Philippe Gétaz

Legal / In-House Counsel
   Christian Pella *First Legal Advisor*

Compliance
   Rose-Marie Sewer *Compliance Officer*

Public Relations
   Jean-Bernard Ponci

Accounts / Audit
Internal Audit   Jean Gravina *Head*

Banque de Commerce et de Placements SA — Head Office

25 rue de Chantepoulet, CH-1211 Geneva 1
PO Box 1331, CH-1211 Geneva
Tel: (22) 909 1919 Fax: (22) 909 1900 Telex: 412391 BCP CH Swift: BPCP CH GG Reuters: BCPG

Senior Executive Officers
Chairman   Mehmet Emin Karamehmet
President & Chief Executive Officer   Tayfun Bayazit
Financial Director   Mete Karamemis *SVP, Finance & Operations*
International Division   HansUlrich Wäfler *SVP, International Division*

General-Lending (DCM, SL)
Head of Corporate Banking   Ernst Schlatter *SVP, Commercial Banking*

Syndicated Lending
Other (Trade Finance)
Trade Finance & Marketing   Nil Danisman *Senior Vice President*
   Maryse Napoli *Vice President*

Money Markets
Head of Money Markets   Doris Jäger *Vice President*

Foreign Exchange
Head of Foreign Exchange   Doris Jäger *Vice President*

Other Departments
Private Banking   Franz Maissen *Senior Vice President*
   Jacqueline Piguet *Vice President*

Euromoney Directory 1999 **1489**

SWITZERLAND (+41)   www.euromoneydirectory.com

Banque du Crédit Agricole (Suisse)

Place de la Fusterie 12, CH-1211 Geneva 11
PO Box 5529, CH-1211 Geneva 11
Tel: (22) 819 4555 Fax: (22) 819 4599

Senior Executive Officers
Chairman   Michael Marks
Chief Executive Officer   Paul Roy

Banque Edouard Constant SA   Head Office

Formerly known as: Banque Scandinave en Suisse
11 Cours de Rive, CH-1204 Geneva
PO Box 1211, CH-1211 Geneva 3
Tel: (22) 787 3111 Fax: (22) 735 3370 Telex: 413500 Swift: BECW CH GG Email: info@bec.ch Reuters: EDGE
Website: www.bec.ch

Senior Executive Officers
Chairman   Oskar Holenweger
Vice Chairman   Marc-Edouard Landolt
Chief Executive Officer   Jean-Bernard Mettraux

Others (Senior Executives)
Board of Directors   Jacob Zgraggen *Director*
                                   Pierre Landolt *Director*
                                   Heinz Zimmermann *Director*
                                   Pierre-Olivier Zingg *Director*
Executive Committee   Fritz Amstutz *Senior Vice President*
                                   Emile Crombez
                                   Grégoire Dinichert *Senior Vice President*
                                   Bernard Labouchère *Senior Vice President*
                                   Michel Terrier *Senior Vice President*

Relationship Manager
Banking Services   Fritz Amstutz *Senior Vice President*

Debt Capital Markets / Fixed Income
Department: Trading
Global Head   Christian Meier *Department Head*

Domestic Government Bonds
Head of Sales   André Fischbacher
                                   Sylvie Weibel
                                   Benjamin Kuehnis

Equity Capital Markets
Domestic Equities
Head of Sales   Pablo Guerrero
                                   Thomas Veillet
                                   Thierry Kammerer

Money Markets
Country Head   Patrick Terrier

Foreign Exchange
Head of Foreign Exchange   Christian Meier *Senior Vice President*
                                   Michel Terrier *Senior Vice President*
Head of Sales   Mamadou M'Baye
                                   Christian Mangold
                                   Roger Sammerhalder
                                   Hans Peter Zbinden
Head of Trading   Serge Dupraz
                                   Sangh Fiore Donno

Risk Management
Foreign Exchange Derivatives / Risk Management
Spot / Forwards Sales   Lorenzo Ricca

Settlement / Clearing
Operations   Fritz Amstutz *Senior Vice President*

Other Departments
Private Banking   Daoud Al-Hayderi *Senior Vice President*
                                   Marc-André Bacuzzi *Senior Vice President*
                                   Emile Crombez *Senior Vice President*
                                   Bernard Labouchère *Senior Vice President*

www.euromoneydirectory.com SWITZERLAND (+41)

Other Departments (cont)
Economic Research Michel Girardin *Investment Research, Senior Vice President*
Administration
Head of Administration Jean Luc L'Eplatenier
Legal / In-House Counsel
General Consuel / Legal Grégoire Dinichert *Senior Vice President*
Other (Administration)
External Manager & Institutions Emile Crombez
Human Resources Marco A Torti *Senior Vice President*

Banque Franck SA   Bank Subsidiary
1 rue Toepffer, CH-1206 Geneva
PO Box 3254, CH-1211 Geneva 3
Tel: (22) 839 4646 **Fax:** (22) 839 4650 **Telex:** 422360 FRA **Swift:** BAFR CH GG **Cable:** FRANCKANDCO

Senior Executive Officers
President Luc Hafner
Chief Executive Officer Patrick Gigon *Managing Director*
Financial Director Jean Claude Mermoud
Chief Operating Officer Daniel Balmer
Debt Capital Markets / Fixed Income
Head of Debt Capital Markets Guy Damond *AVP, Fixed-Income Investments & Recommendations*
Equity Capital Markets
Head of Equity Capital Markets Jean-Claude Héritier *VP, Equity Recommendations & Investments*
Asset Management
Department: Portfolio Management
Other (Asset Management)
Senior Portfolio Manager Mason de Chochor *Senior Vice President*
  Patrick Gigon *Managing Director*
  Arlette Tiger *Senior Vice President*
Portfolio Manager Pierre Brandt *Assistant Vice President*
  Cinzia Paragin *Vice President*
Fund Selections & Comparative Fund Tracking Ross Evans *Third Party Manager*
Other Departments
Private Banking Mason de Chochor
Administration
Head of Administration Jacques Bourger *Vice President*

Banque Générale du Luxembourg (Suisse) SA
Rennweg 57, CH-8023 Zürich
Tel: (1) 225 6767 **Fax:** (1) 225 6868 **Telex:** 813003 BGL

Senior Executive Officers
President Hans Peter Rahm
Managing Director / General Manager Walter Arnold

Banque Julius Baer (Geneve) SA   Subsidiary Company
Formerly known as: Société Bancaire Julius Baer SA
2 Boulevard du Théâtre, CH-1204 Geneva 11
PO Box, CH-1211 Geneva 11
Tel: (22) 317 6000 **Fax:** (22) 312 2342

Senior Executive Officers
Chief Executive Officer Istvan Nagy *Chairman, Management Committee*
Financial Director François Pesenti *Assistant Manager*
Equity Capital Markets
International Equities
Head of Trading Michel Fatton *Sub-Manager*
Money Markets
Global Head Jose Balague *Assistant Manager*
Foreign Exchange
Global Head Jose Balague *Assistant Manager*

Euromoney Directory 1999 **1491**

SWITZERLAND (+41)   www.euromoneydirectory.com

Banque Julius Baer (Geneve) SA (cont)

Risk Management
Global Head   Robert Vodoz *Assistant Manager*

Settlement / Clearing
Regional Head   Roman Kessler *Sub-Manager*

Global Custody
Regional Head   Robert Flammand *Assistant Manager*

Other Departments
Private Banking   Gerard Bagnoud *Manager*

Banque Nationale de Paris (Switzerland) Limited   Head Office

Alternative trading name: BNP Switzerland
Aeschengraben 26, CH-4002 Basle
PO Box, CH-4002 Basle
Tel: (61) 276 5600 **Fax:** (61) 276 5500 **Telex:** 962286, 962245, 412158 **Swift:** BNPA CH BB **Reuters:** BNPD

Senior Executive Officers
Chief Executive Officer   André Kessler *Managing Director & GM*
Treasurer   Stefan Knoepfel *Head of Markets Division*
General Secretary   Aime Archard
International Division   Pierre Delmaise *Deputy Managing Director*

General-Lending (DCM, SL)
Head of Corporate Banking   Pierre Delmaise *Deputy Managing Director*

Debt Capital Markets / Fixed Income
Head of Fixed Income   Paul Rudin *Capital Markets*

Fixed-Income Repo
Head of Repo   Paul Rudin *Capital Markets*

Equity Capital Markets
Head of Equity Capital Markets   Paul Rudin *Capital Markets*

Equity Repo / Securities Lending
Head   Paul Rudin *Capital Markets*

Syndicated Lending
Head of Origination; Head of Syndication   Albert Veidie *Risk Controller*

Loan-Related Activities
Trade Finance   Simon Charles Heyer *First Vice President*

Money Markets
Head of Money Markets   Peter Mosimann *Head of Dealing Room*

Foreign Exchange
Head of Foreign Exchange   Peter Mosimann *Head of Dealing Room*

Settlement / Clearing
Head of Settlement / Clearing   Andre Schnepf *Head of Transfer Department*

Global Custody
Head of Global Custody   Theodor Kassuba *Head of Operations*

Other Departments
Chief Credit Officer   Wolfgang Ewen *Head of Credit Department*
Private Banking   Hans-Rudolpm Schaub *Deputy Managing Director*
Correspondent Banking   Bertrand Meyer *Banking Relations* T 276 5316 F 276 5505

Administration
Head of Administration   Jean Jacques Meyer *Vice President*
Head of Marketing   Joseph Unold *Vice President*

Technology & Systems
                                                    Adrien Munch *Vice President*

Legal / In-House Counsel
                                                    Beat Eisner *Legal Operations, Vice President*

Compliance
                                                    Beat Eisner *Legal Operations, Vice President*

Banque Paribas (Suisse) SA
Subsidiary Company

2 Place de Hollande, CH-1204 Geneva
Tel: (22) 787 2111 Fax: (22) 787 8000 Telex: 422165 Swift: PARB CH GG 12A Reuters: PBHA
Website: www.paribas.com

Senior Executive Officers
Chairman of the Supervisory Board — Michel François-Poncet
President — François de Rancourt
Chief Executive Officer — Claude Alain Burnand *Secretary General*
Financial Director — Philippe Nierlé *Financial Management*

Others (Senior Executives)
Internal Audit — Pierre Yves Despland

Banque Pasche SA
Head Office

10 rue de Hollande, CH-1204 Geneva
Tel: (22) 818 8222 Fax: (22) 818 8225 Telex: 422776 PSA Swift: BPGE CH GG Cable: PASCHECO

Senior Executive Officers
Directeur — Richard Kamm

Banque Tardy, de Watteville & Cie SA

6 Place de l'Université, CH-1205 Geneva
PO Box 268, CH-1211 Geneva 4
Tel: (22) 320 9255 Fax: (22) 781 0313 Telex: 422737 TEB

Senior Executive Officers
Chairman — Hans-Dieter Vontobel
Managing Director / General Manager — Wolfhard Graetz

Barclays Bank (Suisse) SA
Subsidiary Company

8/10 rue d'Italie, CH-1211 Geneva 3
PO Box 3941, Geneva 3
Tel: (22) 819 5111 Fax: (22) 310 6460 Telex: 423247 BB CH Swift: BARC CH GG

Senior Executive Officers
Chief Executive Officer — Paul A Brown
Chief Operating Officer — Marcel Kengelbacher

Others (Senior Executives)
Finance Director — Beat Scheibli

General-Investment
Head of Investment — Werner Wolfer *Chief Investment Officer*

Other Departments
Private Banking — Robert du Plessis *Head of Private Banking*

Basellandschaftliche Kantonalbank
Head Office

Rheinstrasse 7, CH-4410 Liestal
Tel: (61) 925 9111 Fax: (61) 925 9411 Telex: 966166 Swift: BLKB CH 22

Senior Executive Officers
Chairman — Werner Degen
Chief Executive Officer — Paul Nyffeler
Financial Director — Meinrad Geering *Head, Investment Banking* T 925 9201
Treasurer — Bruno Imsand
Head, Loans, Lendings & Credits — Lukas Spiess
Head, Retail Banking — Hans Rudolf Matter
International Division — Bruno Imsand

Debt Capital Markets / Fixed Income
Head of Debt Capital Markets — Roland Hofstetter T 925 9440 F 925 9446

Equity Capital Markets
Head of Equity Capital Markets — Werners Eger T 925 9310 F 925 9407

Syndicated Lending
Head of Syndicated Lending — Roland Hofstetter T 925 9440 F 925 9446

SWITZERLAND (+41) www.euromoneydirectory.com

Basellandschaftliche Kantonalbank (cont)
Money Markets
Head of Money Markets Dieter Wundrak ☎ 925 9220 ℻ 925 9411
Foreign Exchange
Head of Foreign Exchange Christopher Merckx ☎ 925 9410 ℻ 925 9411
Risk Management
Head of Risk Management Jean-Pierre Hunzikes ☎ 925 9413 ℻ 925 9208

Basler Kantonalbank Head Office
Spiegelgasse 2, CH-4002 Basle
PO Box 4002, CH-4002 Basle
Tel: (61) 266 2121 **Fax:** (61) 261 8434 **Telex:** BKB CH 965959 **Reuters:** KABE, BKBD
Senior Executive Officers
Chief Executive Officer Werner Sigg

Baumann & Cie Banquiers Head Office
St Jakobs-Strasse 46, CH-4002 Basle
PO Box 2282, Basle
Tel: (61) 279 4141 **Fax:** (61) 279 4114 **Telex:** 962235
Senior Executive Officers
Others (Senior Executives)
Niklaus C Baumann *Partner*
Wolfgang Baumann *Partner*
Wilhelm Hansen *Partner*

Bayerische Landesbank (Schweiz) AG
Münsterstrasse 2, CH-8001 Zürich
Tel: (1) 265 4444 **Fax:** (1) 252 9614 **Telex:** 817 127 BUR CH **Swift:** BYL ACH ZZ
Settlement / Clearing
Operations Johannes Mazzolini *Head*
Other Departments
Private Banking M Moser *Associate*

BBV Privanza Bank (Switzerland) Limited
Formerly known as: Banco Bilbao Vizcaya
Neumühlequai 6, CH-8001 Zürich
PO Box 7530, CH-8023 Zürich
Tel: (1) 268 9111 **Fax:** (1) 268 9191 **Telex:** 817615 **Swift:** BBVI CH ZZ **Email:** bbv.ch@cyberlink.ch
Senior Executive Officers
Chief Executive Officer Alfredo Rosello *General Manager* ℡ a.rosello@bbvprivanza.ch
Financial Director Richard Magermans *Deputy General Manager* ☎ 268 9108
 ℡ r.magermans@bbvprivanza.ch
Money Markets
Head of Money Markets Richard Magermans *Deputy General Manager* ☎ 268 9108
 ℡ r.magermans@bbvprivanza.ch
Foreign Exchange
Head of Foreign Exchange Enrique Jiménez *Holder of Procuration* ☎ 268 9160
Asset Management
Head Rodolfo H Ibáñez *First Vice President* ☎ 268 9150
Other Departments
Private Banking J Antonio Redondo *Director* ☎ 268 9152
Administration
Head of Administration Jose Ángel Martinez *Director*

1494 Euromoney Directory 1999

www.euromoneydirectory.com SWITZERLAND (+41)

BDL Banco di Lugano
Head Office

Piazzetta San Carlo 1, CH-6901 Lugano
PO Box 2810, CH-6901 Lugano
Tel: (91) 910 8111 Fax: (91) 923 2631 Telex: 841080 LUG CH Swift: BLUG CH 22 69A Cable: LUGABANCO Lugano
Foreign Exchange Telex: 841088 LUG CH; Stock Exchange Telex: 841085 LUG CH

Senior Executive Officers
Chairman   Karl Janjöri
Executive President   Bernard Keller
Executive Vice President   Piergiorgio Ballerini
First Vice President, Finance   Beda Krähenmann

Others (Senior Executives)
Staff Executive Board   Gianni Quadri *First Vice President*
Commerce   Florindo Brazzola *Senior Vice President*
Trading & Sales   Enrico Pedrazzini *Assistant Vice President*
Logistics   Renato Arrigoni *Senior Vice President, Logistics*

General-Lending (DCM, SL)
Head of Corporate Banking   Beda Krähenmann *First Vice President, Finance*

Debt Capital Markets / Fixed Income
Head of Sales   Mauro Bunkofer *Vice President*

Syndicated Lending
Other (Syndicated Lending)
Real Estate, Property & Export / Import Finance Silla Giovanni Trezzini *Vice President*

Money Markets
Head of Origination   Mauro Bunkofer *Vice President*

Risk Management
Country Head   Enrico Berardo *Vice President*

Settlement / Clearing
Electronic Banking   Renato Arrigoni *Senior Vice President, Logistics*

Other Departments
Economic Research   Robert Nalbach *VP, Economic Analysis*

Berenberg Finance Limited
Subsidiary Company

Gartenstrasse 19, CH-8039 Zürich
Tel: (1) 284 2020 Fax: (1) 284 2022 Telex: 817534 BFLZ CH

Senior Executive Officers
Managing Director   Michael A P Sager
Managing Director   Juergen Hepp

Berner Kantonalbank
Head Office

Alternative trading name: Banque Cantonale Bernoise & Cantonal Bank of Berne
Bundesplatz 8, PO Box, CH-3001 Berne
Tel: (31) 666 1111 Fax: (31) 666 6040 Telex: 31 911122 Swift: KKBE CH 22 Reuters: KTBB
Website: www.bekb.ch

Senior Executive Officers
President   Max Kopp
Chief Executive Officer   Peter Kappeler *President of the Board*
Financial Director   Albert Keller *Executive Vice President*
Chief Operating Officer   André Suter *Executive Vice President*
International Division   Fritz Frey *Senior Vice President*

General-Lending (DCM, SL)
Head of Corporate Banking   Hans Furthmueller

Debt Capital Markets / Fixed Income
Head of Debt Capital Markets   Beat Flueckiger

Government Bonds
Head of Sales   Peter Heller
Head of Trading   Ulrich Schuppli

Domestic Government Bonds
Head of Sales   Peter Heller
Head of Trading   Ulrich Schuppli

Euromoney Directory 1999 **1495**

SWITZERLAND (+41) www.euromoneydirectory.com

Berner Kantonalbank (cont)
Eurobonds
Head of Sales   Ulrich Schuppli
Emerging Market Bonds
Head of Emerging Markets   Ulrich Schuppli
Equity Capital Markets
Head of Equity Capital Markets   Beat Flueckiger
Domestic Equities
Head of Sales; Head of Trading   Beat Flueckiger
Syndicated Lending
Head of Syndicated Lending   Fritz Frey *Senior Vice President*
Loan-Related Activities
Trade Finance   Urs Grunder
Money Markets
Head of Money Markets   Ulrich Schuppli
Foreign Exchange
Head of Foreign Exchange   Ulrich Schuppli
Risk Management
Head of Risk Management   Erhard Gyger
Corporate Finance / M&A Advisory
Head of Corporate Finance   Beat Flueckiger
Settlement / Clearing
Head of Settlement / Clearing   Beat Burkhalter
Global Custody
Head of Global Custody   Beat Burkhalter
Administration
Head of Administration   Markus Minder
Head of Marketing   Roland Leuenberger

BFC Banque Financière de la Cité   Head Office

1 rue des Moulins, CH-1204 Geneva
PO Box 5030, CH-1211 Geneva 11
Tel: (22) 818 2525 **Fax:** (22) 818 2626 **Telex:** 423923 BFC CH **Swift:** BFCG CH GG

Senior Executive Officers
Chairman   André Hintermann
Chief Operating Officer   Pierre Baumgartner
Debt Capital Markets / Fixed Income
Global Head   Hervé Tauxe ☏ **818 2530**
Equity Capital Markets
Global Head   Hervé Tauxe ☏ **818 2530**
Foreign Exchange
Global Head   Alain Christen ☏ **818 2540**
Settlement / Clearing
Regional Head   Thomas Sussli *Global Head* ☏ **818 2550**
Other Departments
Correspondent Banking   Pierre Baumgartner
Administration
Technology & Systems
                                                    Pierre Baumgartner

BFI - Banque de Financement et d'Investissement SA

2 rue Jean-Petiôt, CH-1204 Geneva 11
PO Box 5710, CH-1211 Geneva 11
Tel: (22) 807 2800 **Fax:** (22) 310 6024; (22) 311 0754 **Telex:** 527573 BFI **Swift:** BFIN CH GG **Email:** bfibw@iprolink.ch
Reuters: BFIG

Senior Executive Officers
Chairman of the Board   Marc Vuillermet
Chief Executive Officer   Patrick Bernard ☏ **807 2825**
                                                    Pierre E Michel ☏ **807 2811**
Financial Director; Chief Operating Officer   Yves Dherbécourt *Senior Manager* ☏ **807 2831**

1496   Euromoney Directory 1999

www.euromoneydirectory.com SWITZERLAND (+41)

Senior Executive Officers (cont)
Treasurer
Assistant Vice President
Chief Representative

Erik Sommer *Assistant Vice President* ☏ **807 2807**
Christina Tournier ☏ **807 2822**
Patrick Bernard ☏ **807 2825**

General-Lending (DCM, SL)
Head of Corporate Banking

Pierre E Michel ☏ **807 2811**

Administration
Head of Administration
Business Development
Head of Marketing

Yves Dherbécourt *Senior Manager* ☏ **807 2831**
Antoine Vivant *Senior Vice President* ☏ **807 2813**
Pierre E Michel ☏ **807 2811**

Technology & Systems

Yves Dherbécourt *Senior Manager* ☏ **807 2831**

Legal / In-House Counsel

Thierry Cochand ☏ **807 2826**

Compliance

Thierry Cochand ☏ **807 2826**

Public Relations

Christina Tournier *Assistant Vice President* ☏ **807 2822**

Accounts / Audit

Patrice Baumgartner *Chief Accountant* ☏ **807 2840**

BHF-BANK (Schweiz) AG

Schulhausstrasse 6, CH-8002 Zürich
PO Box 25, CH-8027 Zürich
Tel: (1) 209 7511 **Fax:** (1) 202 5606 **Telex:** 815519 BHFCH **Swift:** BHFB CH ZZ

Senior Executive Officers
Managing Director / General Manager
Managing Director / General Manager
Managing Director / General Manager

Dr Eckhart Koch
Michael Eggensperger
Markus Zwyssig

Bondpartners SA   Head Office

24 Avenue de l'Elysée, CH-1006 Lausanne
PO Box 174, CH-1001 Lausanne
Tel: (21) 613 4343 **Fax:** (21) 617 9715 **Telex:** 454207 **Reuters:** BPLA-S
Website: www.bpl-bondpartners.ch

Senior Executive Officers
Chairman & Chief Executive
Treasurer
Executive Manager; International Division

Henri Plomb
Didier Fürbringer *Assistant Vice President*
Christian Plomb *Executive Manager*

Debt Capital Markets / Fixed Income
Head of Fixed Income
Head of Fixed Income Sales

Ruedi Ulrich *Senior Vice President*
Daniel Felder *Senior Vice President*

Eurobonds
Head of Origination

Ruedi Ulrich *Senior Vice President*

Bonds - General
Eurobonds - Trading

R Maiolatesi *Assistant Vice President*
T Friedmann *Authorized Officer*
J-L Marion *Authorized Officer*
P Kaeslin *Authorized Officer*
S Hack *Dealer*
S Fauquex *Dealer*
M Berger *Dealer*
A Berger *Dealer*
A Geissmann *Dealer*

Equity Capital Markets
Department: Stocks & Shares
Head of Sales

Daniel Felder *Senior Vice President*

Other (Domestic Equities)
Brokerage

R Maiolatesi *Assistant Vice President*
J Bodevin *Assistant Vice President*
M-N La Ngoc *Authorized Officer*
S Fauquex *Dealer*

Euromoney Directory 1999 **1497**

SWITZERLAND (+41)   www.euromoneydirectory.com

Bondpartners SA (cont)
Other (Domestic Equities) (cont)
Helvetica   P Kaeslin *Authorized Officer*
                                           M Berger *Dealer*
Settlement / Clearing
Head of Settlement / Clearing   Olivier Perroud *Assistant Vice President*
Asset Management
Head; Portfolio Management   Henri Plomb *Chairman & Chief Executive*
Administration
Head of Administration   Robert Heppel *Vice President*
Technology & Systems
Computers   Luc Mettraux *Assistant Vice President*
Legal / In-House Counsel
                                           Christian Plomb *Executive Manager*
Compliance
                                           Olivier Perroud *Assistant Vice President*
Corporate Communications
Communications   Luc Mettraux *Assistant Vice President*
Other (Administration)
Staff   A Zuercher *Authorized Officer*

Bridport & Cie SA
Head Office

1 Place Longmalle, CH-1204 Geneva
Tel: (22) 312 2000 **Fax:** (22) 312 2190 **Telex:** 425007 BRI CH

Senior Executive Officers
Chief Executive Officer   Alexander Bridport
Chief Operating Officer   Thomas Bartholdi
Managing Director / General Manager   Enrico Chincarini

The British Bank of the Middle East
Full Branch Office

2 quai Général Guisan, CH-1204 Geneva
PO Box 5526, CH-1211 Geneva
Tel: (22) 818 0511 **Fax:** (22) 818 0512 **Telex:** 423780 BBME CH **Swift:** BBME CH GX **Reuters:** BBMG (Monitor)

Senior Executive Officers
Chief Executive Officer   Charles P De Boissezon ☎ **818 0688**
Chief Operating Officer   Jean-Paul De Beco ☎ **818 0525**
Treasurer   François Chenevard *Manager, Treasury & Securities* ☎ **818 0521**
Settlement / Clearing
Operations   Pascal Friess ☎ **818 0541**
Administration
Head of Administration   Graziano Balestra ☎ **818 0506**
Compliance
                                           Georges Durand *Compliance & Risk Manager* ☎ **818 0533**
Accounts / Audit
                                           Patrick Bulliard *Financial Controller* ☎ **818 0518**

Brown Brothers Harriman Services AG

Bärengasse 25, CH-8001 Zürich
Tel: (1) 227 1818 **Fax:** (1) 227 1890 **Telex:** 815113

Senior Executive Officers
Managing Director   Nicolas K Wyss

BSI-Banca della Svizzera Italiana
Full Branch Office

Via Magatti 2, CH-6900 Lugano
Tel: (91) 809 3111 **Fax:** (91) 809 3678 **Telex:** 841021 **Swift:** BSIL CH 22 **Reuters:** BSIZ

Senior Executive Officers
President   Alfredo Gysi
General Director   Luigi Butti

www.euromoneydirectory.com   SWITZERLAND (+41)

Canadian Imperial Bank of Commerce (Switzerland) SA
Subsidiary Company

Route de Florissant 13, CH-1206 Geneva
PO Box 400, CH-1211 Geneva 12
Tel: (22) 839 6800 **Fax:** (22) 839 6868 **Telex:** 423036 CIBC **Swift:** CIBC CH GG

Senior Executive Officers
President Robert Hain
Vice President H U Vetsch
General Manager M Cartillier

Others (Senior Executives)
Member of the Board B W Boesch
 R P Briner
 G Colomb
 G De Cnop
 C Gebhard
 A M Minard

Department: Management Board
President, Management Board M M Cartillier

Others (Senior Executives)
Member of Management Board M M P Carrad
 G J Forsyth
 A Wiederkehr

Canadian Imperial Bank of Commerce
Full Branch Office

Lintheschergasse 15, CH-8001 Zürich
PO Box 7476, CH-8023 Zürich
Tel: (1) 215 6070 **Fax:** (1) 215 6098

Senior Executive Officers
General Manager M A Wiederkehr

Others (Senior Executives)
Member of Management Board M M Eigenmann
 E Frei
 B Hefti
 P de Maertrlaere
 M M W Moser
 E Rohrer
 E Schneider
 R Eisenring
 M W Schwarz
Executive D Davenport

Settlement / Clearing
Operations D Davenport *Control*

Canto Consulting
Head Office

Zugerstrasse 50, CH-6302 Zug
PO Box 2288, Zug
Tel: (41) 760 4848 **Fax:** (41) 760 4949 **Telex:** 862133
Website: www.canto.ch

Senior Executive Officers
Chairman Jürg Schwarz
Chief Executive Officer Roland E Staehli *Head*
Financial Director Stefan Tobler *Head, Mergers & Acquisitions*

Syndicated Lending
Head of Syndicated Lending Rainer Senn *Head of Lending*

Corporate Finance / M&A Advisory
Head of Mergers & Acquisition Stefan Tobler *Head, Mergers & Acquisitions*

Other Departments
Private Banking Roland E Staehli *Head*

Euromoney Directory 1999 **1499**

SWITZERLAND (+41)　　　　www.euromoneydirectory.com

Cantonal Bank of Berne
Head Office

Alternative trading name: Berner Kantonalbankbank (German)/Banque Cantonal Bernoise (French)

BEKB | BCBE

Bundesplatz 8, CH-3011 Berne
Tel: (31) 666 1111 **Fax:** (31) 666 6040 **Telex:** 911122 **Swift:** KKBE CH 22 **Email:** bekb@bekb **Reuters:** KTBB
Bloomberg: bekb@bloomberg.net
Website: www.bekb.ch

Senior Executive Officers
President	Dr Max Kopp
Chief Executive Officer	Peter Kappeler
Financial Director	Albert Keller
Chief Operating Officer	André Suter
Treasurer	Erhard Gyger
Company Secretary	Hanspeter Merz
International Division	Fritz Frey

Others (Senior Executives)
Head of Trading	Ulrich Shuppli
Head of Sales	Peter L Heller

Debt Capital Markets / Fixed Income
Head of Fixed Income Sales	Beat Flückiger

Government Bonds
Head of Sales	Valentin Huwiler
Head of Trading	Stefan Bachofner
Head of Syndication	Beat Flückiger

Eurobonds
Head of Trading	Marc Remund

Fixed-Income Repo
Head of Repo; Head of Trading	Fritz Iseli

Equity Capital Markets
Head of Sales	Remo Kunz
Head of Trading	Rolf Bigler

Domestic Equities
Head of Sales	Remo Kunz
Head of Trading	Rolf Bigler

International Equities
Head of Sales	Markus Hegetscheweiler

Equity Repo / Securities Lending
Head	Beat Burkhalter

Syndicated Lending
Head of Syndication	Fritz Frey

Money Markets
Tel: 666 6505 **Fax:** 666 6035 **Reuters:** KTBB
Head of Money Markets	Fritz Iseli

Foreign Exchange
Tel: 666 6580 **Fax:** 666 6033
Head of Foreign Exchange	Markus Blaser
Head of Trading	Oliver Ritter

Risk Management
Tel: 666 1040 **Fax:** 666 6033
Head of Risk Management	Fritz Frey

Exchange-Traded Derivatives
Head	Urs Grunder ☎ **666 6362**

Settlement / Clearing
Head of Settlement / Clearing	Christoph Marti ☎ **666 6494**

Global Custody
Head of Global Custody	Beat Burkhalter

Other Departments
Chief Credit Officer	Norbert Eisenring
Cash Management	Fritz Iseli

Administration
Head of Administration	Hans Rudolf Gysin
Business Development	Jean Claude Nobili

Administration (cont)
Head of Marketing — Roland Leuenberger
Technology & Systems — Gerhard Schindler
Legal / In-House Counsel — Philipp Abegg
Compliance — Renato Paratore
Public Relations — Hanspeter Merz
Accounts / Audit — Robert Thommen

Cantonal Bank of Saint Gall
Head Office

Alternative trading name: St Gallische Kantonalbank
St Leonhardstrasse 25, CH-9001 St Gallen
Tel: (71) 231 3131 **Fax:** (71) 231 3232 **Telex:** 881188 **Swift:** KBSG CH 22 **Reuters:** KBSG (Dealing)

Senior Executive Officers
Chairman — F P Oesch
Vice Chairman — Brigitte Braendlin-Menzl
President of the Executive Board — G E Meyer

Others (Senior Executives)
J C Müller *Member of the Executive Board, Finance*
M Zoller *Member of the Executive Board, Retail Banking*
G Sutter *Member of the Executive Board, Credits*
Bonds, Stocks, Soffex, Derivatives — B Sonderegger *Member of Senior Management*

Debt Capital Markets / Fixed Income
Department: Capital Markets
Head of Debt Capital Markets — J Geel *Member of Management*

Money Markets
Head of Money Markets — A Zünd *Member of Senior Managment*

Foreign Exchange
Tel: 220 8520 **Fax:** 231 3349
Head of Foreign Exchange — A Zünd *Member of Senior Managment*

Asset Management
Portfolio Management — R Rupprechter *Member of Management*

Other Departments
Private Banking — J Brauchli *Member of Senior Managment*
Correspondent Banking — A Mauchle *Member of Management*

Administration
Public Relations — W Erni *Member of Senior Management*

Cantonalbank of Fribourg
Head Office

Alternative trading name: Banque Cantonale de Fribourg
Boulevard de Pérolles 1, CH-1701 Fribourg
Tel: (26) 350 7111 **Fax:** (26) 350 7700
Website: www.bcf.ch

Senior Executive Officers
General Manager — Albert Michel
Chief Executive Officer; Financial Director — Bernhard Aeby *Director*
Chief Operating Officer — Roger Gehrig *Assistant Vice President*
Treasurer — Bernhard Aeby *Director*

General-Lending (DCM, SL)
Head of Corporate Banking — Bernhard Aeby *Director*

Debt Capital Markets / Fixed Income
Head of Debt Capital Markets — Roger Gehrig *Assistant Vice President*

Equity Capital Markets
Head of Equity Capital Markets — Roger Gehrig *Assistant Vice President*

Money Markets
Head of Money Markets — Francois Python *Assistant Vice President*

SWITZERLAND (+41) www.euromoneydirectory.com

Cantonalbank of Fribourg (cont)

Foreign Exchange
Head of Foreign Exchange — Francois Python *Assistant Vice President*

Risk Management
Head of Risk Management — Francois Python *Assistant Vice President*

Settlement / Clearing
Head of Settlement / Clearing — Francois Python *Assistant Vice President*

Administration
Head of Administration — Francois Python *Assistant Vice President*
Head of Marketing — Andre Helbling *Assistant Vice President*

Legal / In-House Counsel
Olivier Carrel

Public Relations
Andre Helbling *Assistant Vice President*

CEDEF SA

8 Chemin du Midi, CH-1260 Nyon
Tel: (22) 361 6668; (22) 361 5151 **Fax:** (22) 361 4675 **Reuters:** CDEF-L CDEF-J, Z
Belgian Cash/Fra's/Forwards **Tel:** 363 1255; European Euro Currencies-Options & Swaps **Tel:** 994 1300;
Government Bonds **Tel:** 994 1736; Scandinavian Bonds **Tel:** 994 1600; Scandinavian Swaps **Tel:** 363 1263;
Asset Swaps & Credit Derivatives **Tel:** 994 1710; Administration **Tel:** 361 5151

Senior Executive Officers
Managing Director / General Manager — G Cartiglia

CFC Securities SA — Head Office

Avenue C-F Ramuz 60, Pully, CH-1009 Lausanne
PO Box 616, CH-1009 Lausanne
Tel: (21) 721 5141 **Fax:** (21) 721 5215 **Telex:** 454009 CFC CH **Email:** www.cfc@worldcom.ch
Dealing **Tel:** 721 5121; **Fax:** 721 5140; Settlements **Tel:** 721 5200; **Fax:** 721 5205

Senior Executive Officers
Chairman & Chief Executive — Boris Merkenich
President — Jacques Baumgartner
Chief Operating Officer — Cossette Guignard

Debt Capital Markets / Fixed Income
Head of Fixed Income — Martin Perfect *Head*

Bonds - General
Fixed Income
Emile Borrer
Jan Breiter
Claudio Cecchet
Frank Huebscher
Marco Gazzola
Oliver Gester
Markus Lex
Stefan Keller
Olivier Nahas
Michael Pisler
Patrick Rewcastle
Jean-François Simzac

Equity Capital Markets
Department: Equity Related Products
Head of Equity Capital Markets — Simon Pettitt *Head*

Other (Domestic Equities)
Joel de Blois
Ha Sung Park

Settlement / Clearing
Tel: 721 5200 **Fax:** 721 5205
Settlement (General) — Kim Noronha
Irma Mauron

SWITZERLAND (+41)

The Chase Manhattan Bank
Full Branch Office
Gartenstrasse 33, CH-8002 Zürich
Tel: (1) 206 6211 **Fax:** (1) 206 6289

Senior Executive Officers
Others (Senior Executives)
Senior Officer   Josiane Fleming *Vice President*

The Chase Manhattan Private Bank (Switzerland)
Subsidiary Company
63 rue du Rhône, CH-1204 Geneva
PO Box 476, Geneva
Tel: (22) 787 9111 **Fax:** (22) 736 2430

Senior Executive Officers
Others (Senior Executives)
                    Federico Imbert *Private Banking Executive*

Citibank NA
Full Branch Office
16 Quai Général Guisan, CH-1211 Geneva 3
PO Box 3946, CH-1211 Geneva 3
Tel: (22) 317 5111 **Fax:** (22) 317 5574 **Telex:** 823920

Senior Executive Officers
Others (Senior Executives)
Officer-in-Charge   Ernst Bartlome *Vice President* ☎ **317 5455**

Citibank NA
Full Branch Office
Seestrasse 25, PO Box 5081, CH-8022 Zürich
Tel: (1) 205 7111 **Fax:** (1) 205 7899 **Telex:** 823920
Fund Management Tel: 205 7151

Senior Executive Officers
Managing Director / General Manager   Thomas Huertas ☎ **205 7347**
Debt Capital Markets / Fixed Income
Global Head   Thomas Huertas *Market Manager*

Citibank (Switzerland)
Subsidiary Company
Seestrasse 25, CH-8021 Zürich
PO Box 244, Zürich
Tel: (1) 205 7171 **Fax:** (1) 205 7768 **Telex:** 817159 **Email:** lorenzo.martino@citicorp.com
Forex Tel: 54 8060; 54 8060

Senior Executive Officers
Financial Director   Bob Fox ☎ **205 7062**
Chief Operating Officer   Philippe Gibert *Vice President* ☎ **205 8745**
Others (Senior Executives)
Capital Markets   Lorenzo Martino *Vice President* ☎ **205 7888**
Equity Capital Markets
Regional Head   Lorenzo Martino *Vice President* ☎ **205 7888**
Warrants
Head of Sales; Head of Trading   Lorenzo Martino *Vice President* ☎ **205 7888**
Foreign Exchange
Department: Citibank, NA
Global Head   Guy Whittaker *Global FX Manager* ☎ **+44 (171) 500 1830**
Regional Head   Martin Dyer *Head, Global FX Sales* ☎ **+44 (171) 500 1517**
FX Traders / Sales People
Head of FX Sales   Christian M Schild *VP & FX Sales Manager* ☎ **205 7746**

Euromoney Directory 1999 **1503**

SWITZERLAND (+41)   www.euromoneydirectory.com

Citibank (Switzerland) (cont)
Risk Management
OTC Equity Derivatives
Head   Lorenzo Martino *Vice President* ☏ 205 7888
Other Departments
Correspondent Banking   Ted Pitt *Vice President* ☏ 205 7460
Administration
Legal / In-House Counsel
   Livia Müller-Fembeck *Vice President* ☏ 205 7894
Compliance
   Walter Glanemann *Vice President* ☏ 205 7923

Clariden Bank   Full Branch Office
1 Quai du Mont-Blanc, CH-1201 Geneva 1
PO Box 1304, CH-1211 Geneva 1
Tel: (22) 908 1611 Fax: (22) 908 1649

Senior Executive Officers
EVP, Member of Executive Board of Management   Max Cotting
Others (Senior Executives)
Senior Managers   Ernst Klossner *Executive Vice President*
   Daniel Kropf *Executive Vice President*
   Arnold Meier *Executive Vice President*
   René Wagner *Executive Vice President*
   Ghassan El Saleh *Senior Vice President*
   Antonio Garcia del Rio *Senior Vice President*
   Marc Paulic *Senior Vice President*
   Peter H White *Senior Vice President*

Clariden Bank   Head Office
Claridenstrasse 26, CH-8002 Zürich
PO Box 5080, CH-8022 Zürich
Tel: (1) 205 6262 Fax: (1) 205 6209 Telex: 816919 CBZH Reuters: CLARIFUNDS Bloomberg: Equity TK CLARIDEN
Cable: CLARBANK

Senior Executive Officers
Chairman   Robert L Genillard
Vice Chairman   Oswald J Grübel
Chief Executive Officer   Alex Hoffmann
Others (Senior Executives)
   Markus A Frey *Director*
   Alexandere Jetzer *Director*
General-Lending (DCM, SL)
Head of Corporate Banking   Hans Ammann *Senior Vice President, Credit*
General - Treasury
Head of Treasury   Bruno Gisler *EVP, Finance & Treasury*
Debt Capital Markets / Fixed Income
Asset-Backed Securities / Securitization
Global Head   Rudolf Dingetschweiler *SVP, Securities*
Risk Management
Fixed Income Derivatives / Risk Management
Country Head   Andreas Roca *Vice President, Derivatives*
Settlement / Clearing
Operations   Markus Nussbaumer *VP, Operations*
   Hans-Jürg Diem *SVP, Planning & Controlling*
Asset Management
Head   Bernard Stalder *Executive Vice President*
Administration
Head of Administration   Peter Gubler *Executive Vice President*
Technology & Systems
Information Technology   Manuel Keller *Vice President*
   Peter Morf *Senior Vice President*

www.euromoneydirectory.com SWITZERLAND (+41)

Compliance

Jean-Pierre Colombara *Senior Vice President*

Accounts / Audit
Internal Audit Jean-Pierre Colombara *Senior Vice President*

Other (Administration)
Human Resources Othmar Locher *Senior Vice President*

Cofep SA

Via Balestra 27, CH-6901 Lugano
PO Box 3477, Lugano
Tel: (91) 922 8901 **Fax:** (91) 922 8904

Senior Executive Officers
Managing Director / General Manager Francesco C Nessi

Commercial & Investment Credit Corp SA Head Office

Alternative trading name: CICC

59 rue du Rhône, CH-1204 Geneva
Tel: (22) 310 2360 **Fax:** (22) 781 0783

Senior Executive Officers
Chairman Jean-Pierre Imhoos
Managing Director A Latif Benani
Chief Executive Officer A Latif Benani *Managing Director*

Others (Senior Executives)

Nathan Anastasiou *Executive Vice President*

Commerzbank (Schweiz) AG Subsidiary Company

Lintheschergasse 7, CH-8001 Zürich
PO Box 7383, CH-8023 Zürich 1
Tel: (1) 219 7111 **Fax:** (1) 219 7240 **Telex:** 814321
Forex Tel: 54 8060; 54 8060

Senior Executive Officers
General Manager Wolfgang Perlwitz
General Manager Horst Engel

Debt Capital Markets / Fixed Income
Department: Securities

Eurobonds
Head of Trading Charles Monard *FVP, Bond, Stock & Shares* ☏ 219 7255 ℻ 219 7292

Bonds - General
Trading Jacqueline Burkart *Assistant Vice President*
John P Elben *Assistant Treasurer*

Libor-Based / Floating-Rate Products
FRN Trading Charles Monard *FVP, Bond, Stock & Shares* ☏ 219 7255 ℻ 219 7292

Money Markets

Other (Wholesale Deposits)
Eurocurrency Deposits Bruno Rieser *FVP, Money Markets*
Heinz Weyermann *Assistant Treasurer*

Foreign Exchange
FX Traders / Sales People
Swaps Ulrich Wild *First Vice President*
Markus Schnider *Vice President*
Erlinda Haug *Assistant Treasurer*

Asset Management
Portfolio Management François B Devaud *Senior Vice President*

Other Departments
Economic Research Christoph Riniker *Assistant Vice President*

Administration
Head of Administration Peter Semder *First Vice President*

SWITZERLAND (+41)   www.euromoneydirectory.com

Compagnie Financière Espirito Santo SA — Subsidiary Company

15 Avenue de Montchoisi, CH-1006 Lausanne
Tel: (21) 619 5555 Fax: (21) 619 5556; (21) 619 5557 Telex: 454510 Swift: CFES CH 22

Senior Executive Officers
President   José Manuel Espírito Santo Silva
Chief Executive Officer   José Pedro Caldeira da Silva *General Manager*

Debt Capital Markets / Fixed Income
Tel: 619 5300 Fax: 619 5444
Global Head   Pierre-Antoine Trezzini *Senior Manager*

Money Markets
Tel: 619 5316
Global Head   Daniel Ryssl *Assistant Manager*

Foreign Exchange
Tel: 619 5314
Global Head   Michel Eggmann *Deputy Manager*

Settlement / Clearing
Regional Head   Mariana Devaud *Deputy Manager*

Other Departments
Private Banking   Fernando Espírito Santo Silva *Senior Manager*

Administration
Technology & Systems
   Philippe Schmutz *Manager*

Compagnie Financière Tradition

11 rue de Langallerie, CH-1003 Lausanne
Tel: (21) 343 5252 Fax: (21) 343 5570 Telex: 454601 TRAD

Senior Executive Officers
Chairman   Patrick Combes
TFS Group Managing Director   Julian Harding
TFS Group Managing Director   David Pinchin
TSH Group Managing Director   Guido Boehi

Compagnie de Gestion et de Banque Gonet SA — Full Branch Office

8 Place de l'Université, CH-1211 Geneva 4
Tel: (22) 322 0322 Fax: (22) 328 4527; (22) 322 0435 Telex: 422967 Swift: CGBG CH GG 3X

Senior Executive Officers
Chairman   Marc Yves Blanpain
General Manager   Louk de Wilde

Compagnie de Gestion et de Banque Gonet SA — Head Office

9 Place Bel-Air, CH-1260 Nyon
Tel: (22) 322 0322 Fax: (22) 328 4527 Telex: 422967 Swift: CGBG CH GG 3X

Senior Executive Officers
Chairman   Marc Yves Blanpain
General Manager   Louk de Wilde

Conseil Alain Aboudaram SA

38 Chemin de Mornex, CH-1001 Lausanne
Tel: (21) 312 7764 Fax: (21) 312 3302 Telex: 455417 ABU CH

Senior Executive Officers
Chief Executive Officer   Alain Aboudaram

Others (Senior Executives)
New York   Fillippo Valli *Managing Director*
   Luca Cantelli *Senior Manager*
Asia   Francis Vincent *Director*

www.euromoneydirectory.com SWITZERLAND (+41)

Coop Bank
Head Office

Formerly known as: CCB Cooperative Central Bank Limited
Aeschenplatz 3, CH-4002 Basle
Tel: (61) 286 2121 **Fax:** (61) 271 4595 **Telex:** 962290 **Swift:** COOP CH BB **Email:** netteam@coopbank.ch
Reuters: COPB
Website: www.coopbank.ch

Senior Executive Officers
Chairman of the Board of Directors	Gerhard Metz
President of the General Management	Heinz Wälti
General Manager	Paul Huber
General Manager	Fritz Leuenberger

Debt Capital Markets / Fixed Income
Tel: 286 2413 **Fax:** 272 8494

Head of Fixed Income	Marco Prétôt *Senior Manager* 286 2325
Head of Fixed Income Sales; Head of Fixed Income Trading	Martin Rychen *Executive* 286 2343

Government Bonds
Head of Sales; Head of Trading; Head of Syndication; Head of Origination	Martin Rychen *Executive* 286 2343

Eurobonds
Head of Sales; Head of Trading	Martin Rychen *Executive* 286 2343

Emerging Market Bonds
Head of Sales; Head of Trading	Martin Rychen *Executive* 286 2343

Libor-Based / Floating-Rate Products
FRN Sales; FRN Trading	Martin Rychen *Executive* 286 2343
Asset Swaps; Asset Swaps (Sales)	Jürg Gutzwiller *Executive* 286 2336

Fixed-Income Repo
Head of Repo; Marketing & Product Development; Head of Trading	Martin Manz *Senior Manager* 286 2720

Fixed-Income Research
Head of Fixed Income; Head of Credit Research	Alfred Binggeli *Senior Manager* 286 2415

Equity Capital Markets
Fax: 272 8494

Head of Equity Capital Markets; Head of Sales; Head of Trading	Marco Prétôt *Senior Manager* 286 2325

Domestic Equities
Head of Sales; Head of Trading	Marco Prétôt *Senior Manager* 286 2325

International Equities
Head of Sales; Head of Trading	Martin Rychen *Executive* 286 2343

Equity Research
Head of Equity Research	Alfred Binggeli *Senior Manager* 286 2415

Convertibles / Equity-Linked
Head of Sales; Head of Trading	Martin Rychen *Executive* 286 2343

Syndicated Lending
Head of Trading	Werner Schneider *Senior Manager* 286 2395

Loan-Related Activities
Trade Finance	Karlheinz Lässer *Executive* 286 2602
Project Finance	Werner Schneider *Senior Manager* 286 2395

Money Markets
Tel: 286 2720 **Fax:** 272 8418

Head of Money Markets	Martin Manz *Senior Manager* 286 2720

Domestic Commercial Paper
Head of Sales; Head of Trading	Martin Manz *Senior Manager* 286 2720

Eurocommercial Paper
Head of Sales; Head of Trading	Martin Manz *Senior Manager* 286 2720

Wholesale Deposits
Marketing; Head of Sales	Martin Manz *Senior Manager* 286 2720

Foreign Exchange
Tel: 268 2250 **Fax:** 272 8414

Head of Foreign Exchange	Otmar Thaler *Senior Manager* 286 2255
Head of Institutional Sales; Corporate Sales	Richard Bloch *Executive* 286 2740
Head of Trading	Rolf Boss *Executive* 286 2250

SWITZERLAND (+41)   www.euromoneydirectory.com

Coop Bank (cont)
Risk Management
Fixed Income Derivatives / Risk Management
Head of Sales; Trading   Martin Manz *Senior Manager* ☏ 286 2720
Foreign Exchange Derivatives / Risk Management
Spot / Forwards Sales; Spot / Forwards Trading   Peter Lütolf *Executive* ☏ 286 2268
OTC Equity Derivatives
Sales; Trading   Jürg Gutzwiller *Executive* ☏ 286 2336
OTC Commodity Derivatives
Head   Jürg Gutzwiller *Executive* ☏ 286 2336
OTC Credit Derivatives
Head   Jürg Gutzwiller *Executive* ☏ 286 2336
Exchange-Traded Derivatives
Head   Jürg Gutzwiller *Executive* ☏ 286 2336
Settlement / Clearing
Head of Settlement / Clearing   Ulrich Soltermann *Senior Manager* ☏ 286 2622
Equity Settlement   Paul Berndt *Senior Manager* ☏ 286 2763
Fixed-Income Settlement; Operations   Jolanda Sigg-Voss *Executive* ☏ 286 2550
Global Custody
Regional Head   Paul Berndt *Senior Manager* ☏ 286 2763
Asset Management
Head   Alfred Binggeli *Senior Manager* ☏ 286 2415
Other Departments
Commodities / Bullion   Otmar Thaler *Senior Manager* ☏ 286 2255
Correspondent Banking   Konrad Bretscher *Senior Manager* ☏ 286 2407
Administration
Head of Marketing   Dirk Metzger *Senior Manager* ☏ 286 2402
Technology & Systems
                                      Willi Harr *Senior Manager* ☏ 286 2420
Legal / In-House Counsel
                                      Martin Wicki *Senior Manager* ☏ 286 2509
Compliance
                                      Urs Luginbühl *Senior Manager* ☏ 286 2790
Public Relations
                                      Dirk Metzger *Senior Manager* ☏ 286 2402

Cornèr Bank Limited   Head Office
Via Canova 16, CH-6901 Lugano
PO Box 2835, CH-6901 Lugano
Tel: (91) 800 5111 **Fax:** (91) 800 5349 **Telex:** 841041 **Swift:** CBLU CH 22 **Email:** infobank@corner.ch **Reuters:** CBLF
Forex Telex: 841042 CBL CH; **Management Telex:** 841041 CBL CH; **Security Department Telex:** 841240 CBL CH;
Reuters: CBLM

Senior Executive Officers
Chairman   Giancarlo Viscardi
Vice Chairman   Alfred Hirs
Vice Chairman   Fabia Dell'Acqua Cornaro
General Manager   Paolo Cornaro
General Manager   Luigi Dell'Acqua
General - Treasury
Head of Treasury   Nicola Lafranchi *Manager*
Syndicated Lending
Other (Syndicated Lending)
Loans & Credit   Mario Alberti *Manager*
Money Markets
Department: Stock Exchange
Head of Money Markets   Claudio Molo *Manager*
Foreign Exchange
Department: Stock Exchange
Head of Foreign Exchange   Claudio Molo *Manager*
Settlement / Clearing
Operations   Giancarlo Martinelli *Manager*
Other   Isidor Wittmer *Manager, Payment Traffic*

www.euromoneydirectory.com　　　　　　　　**SWITZERLAND (+41)**

Asset Management
Portfolio Management　　　　　　　　　Claudio Genasci Manager

Other Departments
Private Banking　　　　　　　　　　　　Gianni Berto Manager
Economic Research　　　　　　　　　　Iris Canonica Manager

Administration
Business Development　　　　　　　　Piercarlo Lissi Manager

Technology & Systems

　　　　　　　　　　　　　　　　　　Roberto Pezzoli Manager, EDP

Accounts / Audit

　　　　　　　　　　　　　　　　　　Alberto Cameroni Manager, Accounting

Other (Administration)
Bank Relations　　　　　　　　　　　　Gianluigi Bianchi Manager

Cosmorex Zürich AG　　　　　　　　　　　　　　　　　　　　Head Office

Schützengasse 4, CH-8001 Zürich
PO Box, CH-8021 Zürich
Tel: (1) 224 3434; (1) 211 0950 **Fax:** (1) 211 3025 **Telex:** 813391 CRX CH **Reuters:** Recipient
Forex Tel: 54 8060

Senior Executive Officers
President　　　　　　　　　　　　　　Heinz Kost

Risk Management

Foreign Exchange Derivatives / Risk Management
Spot / Forwards Trading　　　　　　　Spartaco Becuzzi Manager & Chief Dealer, Spot
　　　　　　　　　　　　　　　　　　Patrik Epstein Deputy Manager, Spot
　　　　　　　　　　　　　　　　　　Daniel Bradovka Holder of Procuration, Spot
　　　　　　　　　　　　　　　　　　Markus Flaschmann Holder of Procuration, Spot
　　　　　　　　　　　　　　　　　　Eric Santschi Holder of Procuration, Spot
　　　　　　　　　　　　　　　　　　Lawrence Gage Spot
　　　　　　　　　　　　　　　　　　David Hamilton Spot
　　　　　　　　　　　　　　　　　　Patrick Maier Spot
　　　　　　　　　　　　　　　　　　Cyrill Kiefer Spot
　　　　　　　　　　　　　　　　　　Ferenc Mailath Assistant Manager & Chief Dealer, Forwards
　　　　　　　　　　　　　　　　　　Erika Schneider Holder of Procuration, Forwards
　　　　　　　　　　　　　　　　　　Werner Will Holder of Procuration, Forwards
Cross-Currency Swaps, Trading　　　 Mark Scott Assistant Manager & Chief Dealer
　　　　　　　　　　　　　　　　　　Christian Flory Crosses

Other Currency Swap / FX Options Personnel
FRAs　　　　　　　　　　　　　　　　Roland Hegglin Assistant Manager
　　　　　　　　　　　　　　　　　　Ralph Enderes
　　　　　　　　　　　　　　　　　　Jörg Zangger

Administration
Head of Administration　　　　　　　　Wolfgang Hofer Assistant Manager

Coutts Bank (Switzerland) Limited

Talstrasse 59, CH-8022 Zürich
Tel: (1) 214 5111 **Fax:** (1) 214 5396 **Telex:** 815486

Senior Executive Officers
Chairman & Chief Executive Officer　　Hugh Matthews

Others (Senior Executives)
Members of the General Management　Werner H Peyer
Committee
　　　　　　　　　　　　　　　　　　Paul I Davies
　　　　　　　　　　　　　　　　　　Alain Diriberry
　　　　　　　　　　　　　　　　　　Michael Tintelnot

Administration

Corporate Communications

　　　　　　　　　　　　　　　　　　Sabina Korfmann-Bodenmann Head ☎ 214 5504 ⌕ 214 5514

Other (Administration)
Human Resources　　　　　　　　　　Walter Hiltbrunner Head ☎ 214 5657 ⌕ 214 5654

Euromoney Directory 1999　**1509**

SWITZERLAND (+41)   www.euromoneydirectory.com

Crédit Commercial de France (Suisse) SA

1 Place Longemalle, CH-1204 Geneva
PO Box 3216, CH-1211 Geneva 3
Tel: (22) 819 1212 Fax: (22) 310 6702 Telex: 428694 CCF CH Cable: FRANCIALGE

Senior Executive Officers
Managing Director / General Manager   Claude Le Ber

Crédit Commercial de France (Suisse) SA

12 Theaterstrasse, CH-8022 Zürich
Tel: (1) 254 6565 Fax: (1) 251 3787 Telex: 817763 CCZ CH Cable: FRANCIALZH

Senior Executive Officers
President   T Stohler

Crédit Lyonnais Securities (Switzerland) AG   Subsidiary Company

Zollikerstrasse 4, CH-8032 Zürich
PO Box 1873, Zürich
Tel: (1) 383 0077 Fax: (1) 383 9572 Telex: 812157 Reuters: CLSI/H/B/C, CLFG; CLSG

Senior Executive Officers
Chairman   Jean Paul Le Roy
Chief Executive Officer   Gérard Bouvet

Debt Capital Markets / Fixed Income
Domestic Government Bonds
Head of Sales; Head of Trading   Jacques Cohen *Senior Officer*

Eurobonds
Head of Sales; Head of Trading   Jacques Cohen *Senior Officer*

Private Placements
Head of Sales   Jacques Cohen *Senior Officer*

Equity Capital Markets
International Equities
Head of Sales   Paul S Larue *Senior Officer & Head, Sales*

Risk Management
Country Head   Laurent Oudin *Risk Manager*

Other (Equity Derivatives)
Domestic Equity Derivatives   Francis Biron *Senior Officer*

Settlement / Clearing
Settlement (General)   Walter Bohnenberger *Senior Officer*

Administration
Head of Administration   Walter Bohnenberger *Senior Officer*

Crédit Lyonnais (Suisse) SA   Subsidiary Company

Place Bel-Air, CH-1211 Geneva 11
PO Box 5260, Geneva
Tel: (22) 705 6666 Fax: (22) 705 6240 Telex: 422449 CLG CH Reuters: CLGY

Senior Executive Officers
Chairman, Board of Directors   Serge Boutissou
Financial Director   Alain Joly *Financial Controller* ☎ 705 6401
Chief Operating Officer   Jean-Pierre Delavouet *Operations* ☎ 705 6602
Treasurer   Christopher Blease ☎ 705 6000
General Manager   Maurice Monbaron ☎ 705 6206

Debt Capital Markets / Fixed Income
64 rue du Stand, CH-1204 Geneva
Tel: +41 (22) 705 6000 Fax: +41 (22) 705 6387
Head of Debt Capital Markets   Michel Bassi ☎ 705 6038

Money Markets
64 rue du Stand, CH-1204 Geneva
Tel: +41 (22) 705 6000 Fax: +41 (22) 705 6387
Global Head   Armand Jost *Head, Treasury & Money Markets* ☎ 705 6039

SWITZERLAND (+41)

Foreign Exchange
64 rue du Stand, CH-1204 Geneva
Tel: +41 (22) 705 6000 **Fax:** +41 (22) 705 6387
Head of Foreign Exchange — François Oesch *FX Trading* ☎ **705 6033**

Risk Management
64 rue du Stand, CH-1204 Geneva
Tel: +41 (22) 705 6211 **Fax:** +41 (22) 705 6234
Head of Risk Management — Denis Foltzer *Secretary General, Logistics & Risk Mgt* ☎ **705 6211**

Exchange-Traded Derivatives
Global Head — Roberto Falzoni ☎ **705 6000**

Other Departments
Commodities / Bullion — Pierre Fah *International Trading* ☎ **705 6778**
Private Banking — Jean Brandenburg ☎ **705 6527**
Correspondent Banking — Richard Palazzetti ☎ **705 6788**

Administration

Technology & Systems
Electronic Data Processing — Didier Bruneau ☎ **705 6804**

Legal / In-House Counsel
Jean-Philippe Babel *Legal Advisor* ☎ **705 6232**

Compliance
Chantal Dremer *Compliance Officer* ☎ **705 6232**

Public Relations
Denis Foltzer *Secretary General, Logistics & Risk Mgt* ☎ **705 6211**

Credit Suisse First Boston

PO Box 900, Uetlibergstrasse 231, CH-8070 Zürich
Tel: (1) 335 4444; (1) 335 5555 **Fax:** (1) 335 7812 **Telex:** 812412 CSCH **Swift:** CRES CHZZ 80A
Website: www.csfb.com

Debt Capital Markets / Fixed Income

Fixed-Income Repo
Trading — Ralf Lehnis *Vice President*

Equity Capital Markets
Tel: 335 4444 **Fax:** 333 7812

Equity Repo / Securities Lending
Head — Greg Scarffe *Vice President* ✉ **gscarffe@csfbg.csfb.com**
Marketing & Product Development; Marketing — Hans-Andrea Disch *Associate* ✉ **hans-andrea.disch@ska.com**
Head of Trading — Chris Zimmermann *Trader, Asia*
Carmen Beck *Vice President*
Mike von Orelli *Trader, Europe*
Jeremy Baker *Head of Trading*

Global Custody

Other (Global Custody)
Securities Operator / Credit Suisse Private Banking — Burkhard H Gutzeit *Member of Senior Managment*
✉ **burkhard.gutzeit@csfb.com**

Credit Suisse Group

Head Office

Paradeplatz 8, CH-8070 Zürich
PO Box 1, CH-8070 Zürich
Tel: (1) 212 1616 **Fax:** (1) 333 2587
Website: www.csg.ch

Senior Executive Officers
Chairman — Rainer E Gut
Chief Executive Officer — Lukas Mühlemann
Financial Director — Richard E Thornburgh
Company Secretary — Philip Hess

Others (Senior Executives)
Chief Risk Officer — Hans-Ulrich Dörig
CEO Credit Suisse — Paul Meier
CEO Credit Suisse Private Banking — Oswald J Grübel
CEO Credit Suisse First Boston — Allen D Wheat
CEO Credit Suisse Asset Management — Phillip M Colebatch
CEO Winterthur — Thomas Wellauer

Euromoney Directory 1999 **1511**

SWITZERLAND (+41)   www.euromoneydirectory.com

Credit Suisse Group (cont)
Debt Capital Markets / Fixed Income
Head of Fixed Income — Marc Hotimsky ☏ +44 (171) 888 3127
Equity Capital Markets
Head of Equity Capital Markets — Bradly W Dougan ☏ +1 (212) 325 3865
Other Departments
Chief Credit Officer — Robert C O'Brien ☏ +1 (212) 325 9166
Other Departments
Head of Credit Suisse Private Banking Asia-Pacific — Alex W Widmer *Managing Director*
Administration
Business Development — Holger Demuth
Head of Marketing — Beat Buchmann
Technology & Systems
  Ahmad Abu El-Ata
Legal / In-House Counsel
  Peter Derendinger
Compliance
  Christian Schmid
Public Relations
  Karin Rhomberg
Corporate Communications
  Rolf Dörig *Chief of Staff & Chief Communications Officer*
Accounts / Audit
  Peter Bachmann
Other (Administration)
Advisory — Alfred Gremli
Investor Relations — Gerhard Beindorff
Audit — Urs Hänni
Security — Jean-Pierre Huwyler
Human Resources — Eugen Schmid

Credit Suisse Leasing

Formerly known as: CS Leasing Group
Thurgauerstrasse 56, CH-8070 Zürich
Tel: (1) 334 2800 **Fax:** (1) 334 2813
Senior Executive Officers
Chairman — U Linsi
President — M Vollenwyder
Financial Director — T Gulich

Dai-Ichi Kangyo Bank (Schweiz) AG   Subsidiary Company

Löwenstrasse 32, CH-8023 Zürich
Tel: (1) 216 9111 **Fax:** (1) 216 9222 **Telex:** 813886
Senior Executive Officers
Chairman — Mr Sugita
Managing Director / General Manager — Hiroshu Ando
Settlement / Clearing
Operations — Bruno Marty *Head of Operations*

Daiwa Cosmo Bank (Schweiz) AG   Subsidiary Company

Bahnhofstrasse 69, PO Box 8023, Zürich
Tel: (1) 211 0311 **Fax:** (1) 211 2427 **Telex:** 814284 **Cable:** DAIBA ZURICH
Senior Executive Officers
Chairman — Satoshi Maeshima
General Manager — Shoichi Masuda

www.euromoneydirectory.com   SWITZERLAND (+41)

Daiwa Securities Bank (Switzerland)

Rennweg 38, CH-8001 Zürich
PO Box 5088, CH-8022 Zürich
Tel: (1) 217 7111 **Fax:** (1) 217 7370 **Telex:** 815141 DWA CH **Email:** daiwa@access.ch **Reuters:** DACH-K

Senior Executive Officers
Chairman   Nagayoshi Miyata
President   Kaji Takeuchi
Chief Operating Officer   Bo Dahlgren *Deputy General Manager*

Darier Hentsch & Cie   Head Office

Formerly known as: Hentsch & Cie/Darier & Cie
4 rue de Saussure, CH-1204 Geneva
Tel: (22) 708 6000 **Fax:** (22) 708 6945 **Telex:** 422237 DAR CH **Swift:** DACO CH GG
Website: www.darierhentsch.ch

Senior Executive Officers

Others (Senior Executives)
Partners   Bénédict Hentsch
                            Pierre Darier
                            Bertrand Darier
                            Eric Demole
                            Thierry Kern
                            Jacques Rossier
Managers   Yves-Michel Baechler
                            Eric Jaques
                            Renaldo Moreschi
                            Rudolph Schwegler
                            Roberto Seiler
                            Germain Steiner

Deutsche Bank Securities Inc   Subsidiary Company

Place des Bergues 3, CH-1211 Geneva 1
PO Box 1416, Geneva
Tel: (22) 739 0606 **Fax:** (22) 739 0600

Deutsche Bank (Suisse) AG   Bank Subsidiary

Place des Bergues 3, CH-1211 Geneva 1
PO Box 1416, CH-1211 Geneva 1
Tel: (22) 739 0111 **Fax:** (22) 739 0700 **Telex:** 412240 DBS CH **Swift:** DEUT CH GG **Cable:** DEUTBANK GENEVE

Senior Executive Officers
Chief Operating Officer   Christian Reckmann *MD & Chief Operating Officer*
Head, Private Banking   Herbert J Scheidt

Other Departments
Private Banking   Herbert J Scheidt *Head, Private Banking*

Deutsche Bank (Suisse) AG   Full Branch Office

Via Ferruccio Pelli 1, CH-6901 Lugano
PO Box 2783, Lugano
Tel: (91) 910 3838 **Fax:** (91) 910 3939 **Telex:** 844014 DBL CH **Cable:** DEUTBANK LUGANO

Senior Executive Officers
Managing Director / General Manager   Giorgio Lupi

SWITZERLAND (+41)   www.euromoneydirectory.com

Deutsche Bank Switzerland AG   Full Branch Office

Bahnhofquai 9/11, CH-8023 Zürich 23
PO Box 7381, Zürich
Tel: (1) 224 5000; (1) 224 7979 Fax: (1) 224 5050; (1) 224 7989 Telex: 815638; 815775 Cable: DEUTBANK ZUERICH

Senior Executive Officers
GM, Investment Management   Karl Ludwig Göldner

Debt Capital Markets / Fixed Income
Tel: 224 5222
Country Head   Mike Neumann ⊤ 224 5220 F 224 5270
Marketing   Claudio Schivoni ⊤ 224 5185 F 224 5160

Bonds - General
Bond Sales   Jean-Pierre Bourkuin ⊤ 224 5361 F 224 5353
Chris Buchser ⊤ 224 5382
Pierre Degiorgi ⊤ 224 5388
Sales Convertible / Bonds   Tony Blaser ⊤ 224 5200
Sales Group   Claudio Schivoni ⊤ 224 5185 F 224 5160
Maroan Maizar ⊤ 224 5186
Tanya Hodge ⊤ 224 5333

Equity Capital Markets
Tel: 224 5366
Head of Equity Capital Markets   Andreas Zehnder
Marketing   Mr Reimer
Head of Sales   Peter Ellenbergen *Institutional Equity Sale*

Domestic Equities
Head of Trading   Mr Minnig *Trader*
Mr Eindiguer *Trader*
Mirian Matt *Trader*

Foreign Exchange
Tel: 224 5150
Head of Foreign Exchange   Patrick Schneider
Mr Seiler

Other Departments
Private Banking   Rolf Wirth *Head, Private Banking*
Beat Schaerer *Private Investment Orders* ⊤ 224 5484 F 224 5450

DG Bank (Schweiz) AG   Head Office

Münsterhof 12, CH-8022 Zürich
PO Box 5178, CH-8022 Zürich
Tel: (1) 214 9111 Fax: (1) 214 9285 Telex: 814330 DG CH Swift: GENO CH ZZ

Senior Executive Officers
Chairman   Bernd Thiemann ⊤ +49 (69) 7447 1010
Financial Director   Urs Leuenberger *Finance Director* ⊤ 214 9265
Managing Director   Michael Zemmer ⊤ 214 9205
General Manager   Daniela Schwaiger ⊤ 214 9205
Chief Representative   Jacqueline Maser ⊤ 214 9214

Syndicated Lending
Head of Trading   Wolfgang Müller ⊤ 214 9260

Money Markets
Head of Money Markets   Wolfgang Müller ⊤ 214 9260

Foreign Exchange
Head of Foreign Exchange   Wolfgang Müller ⊤ 214 9260

Risk Management
Head of Risk Management   Urs Leuenberger *Finance Director* ⊤ 214 9265

Settlement / Clearing
Head of Settlement / Clearing   Luca De Blasio ⊤ 214 9273

Other Departments
Chief Credit Officer   Felix Kirscher ⊤ 214 9226
Private Banking   Elisabeth Baumann ⊤ 214 9384
Correspondent Banking   Marianne Vonwyl ⊤ 214 9275

Administration
Head of Administration   Louis Metiler ⊤ 214 9422

Technology & Systems
Louis Metiler ⊤ 214 9422

www.euromoneydirectory.com   SWITZERLAND (+41)

Legal / In-House Counsel
Urs Galli ☎ **214 9454**

Accounts / Audit
Urs Galli ☎ **214 9454**

Other (Administration)
EDVI Organisation   Roland Gasser ☎ **214 9224**

Discount Bank & Trust Company   Head Office

3 quai de l'Ile, CH-1204 Geneva
PO Box 5430, CH-1211 Geneva
Tel: (22) 705 3111 **Fax:** (22) 310 1703 **Telex:** 422566 **Swift:** DBTC CH GG **Email:** s.post@dbtc.ch
Website: www.dbtc.ch

Senior Executive Officers
Chairman & President   Raphael Recanati
Chief Executive Officer   Joseph Assaraf *General Manager*
Financial Director   Jean-François Charrey *Deputy General Manager*
Chief Operating Officer   Ronald G Strauss *Deputy General Manager*
Treasurer   Jean-François Charrey *Deputy General Manager*

Debt Capital Markets / Fixed Income
25 rue du Stand, CH-1204 Geneva
Tel: +41 (22) 705 3170
Head of Debt Capital Markets   Laurent Elkrief ☎ **705 3133**

Government Bonds
Head of Sales   Alexandre Agret *Trader* ☎ **328 8283**

Eurobonds
Head of Sales; Head of Trading   Alexandre Agret *Trader* ☎ **328 8283**

Medium-Term Notes
Head of Origination; Head of Structuring; Head of Sales   Laurent Elkrief ☎ **705 3133**

Private Placements
Head of Origination; Head of Sales; Head of Structuring   Laurent Elkrief ☎ **705 3133**

Equity Capital Markets

Domestic Equities
Head of Trading   Roberto Mozzetti *Trader* ☎ **320 6689**

International Equities
Head of Trading   Reto Jaeggli *Trader* ☎ **320 5993**

Equity Research
Head of Equity Research   Stephane Theus *Manager* ☎ **705 3875**

Money Markets
25 rue du Stand, CH-1204 Geneva
Tel: +41 (22) 705 3105 **Fax:** +41 (22) 705 3137
Head of Money Markets   Gabriel Kahana ☎ **705 3101**

Domestic Commercial Paper
Head of Trading   Maurice Munoz *Chief Dealer* ☎ **705 3105**

Eurocommercial Paper
Head of Trading   Maurice Munoz *Chief Dealer* ☎ **705 3105**

Wholesale Deposits
Marketing   Maurice Munoz *Chief Dealer* ☎ **705 3105**

Foreign Exchange
25 rue du Stand, CH-1204 Geneva
Tel: +41 (22) 705 3115
Head of Foreign Exchange   Gabriel Kahana ☎ **705 3101**
Head of Institutional Sales; Corporate Sales   Marc Sieber *Chief Dealer* ☎ **705 3115**
Head of Trading   Jean-Pascal Spagnol *Chief Dealer* ☎ **705 3115**

Risk Management
Head of Risk Management   Marc Evequoz ☎ **705 3132**

Fixed Income Derivatives / Risk Management
IR Swaps Trading; IR Options Sales / Marketing; IR Options Trading   Maurice Munoz *Chief Dealer* ☎ **705 3105**

Other (FI Derivatives)
Dealer   Bruno Lehnis *Dealer* ☎ **705 3115**
     Olivier Poulet *Dealer* ☎ **705 3115**

SWITZERLAND (+41)   www.euromoneydirectory.com

Discount Bank & Trust Company (cont)
Foreign Exchange Derivatives / Risk Management
Spot / Forwards Sales Maurice Munoz *Chief Dealer* ☎ **705 3105**
Exotic Options (Barriers, Range, Timers, Digitals, Faders etc)
Sales Olivier Poulet *Dealer* ☎ **705 3115**
  Bruno Lehnis *Dealer* ☎ **705 3115**

Settlement / Clearing
25 rue du Stand, CH-1204 Geneva
Tel: +41 705 3395
Head of Settlement / Clearing; Operations Claude Corbet *Sub Manager* ☎ **705 3395**

Global Custody
Head of Global Custody Rudolf Kunz ☎ **705 3061**

Other Departments
Commodities / Bullion Marc Sieber *Chief Dealer* ☎ **705 3115**
Proprietary Trading Jean-Pascal Spagnol *Chief Dealer* ☎ **705 3115**
Chief Credit Officer J-P Delerce *Manager*
Private Banking Henri Klein *Deputy General Manager*
Correspondent Banking Jean-Louis Jacquinod *Group Manager* ☎ **705 3060**

Administration
Head of Marketing Shalom Bendayan *Manager*

Technology & Systems
  David Benaïch *Manager*

Compliance
  Horst Looke *Manager*

Public Relations
  Stephan Post

Dresdner Bank (Switzerland) Limited   Subsidiary Company
Utoquai 55, CH-8034 Zürich
PO Box 264, CH-8034 Zürich
Tel: (1) 258 5111 **Fax:** (1) 258 5352 **Telex:** 815797 DRB CH **Swift:** DRES CH ZZ **Cable:** DRESDBANK ZURICH

Senior Executive Officers
Chairman Jürgen Sarrazin
President Enrico Clerici ☎ **258 5111**

Others (Senior Executives)
  Jacques Bour *General Manager*
  Arno Horn *General Manager* ☎ **258 5111**

Dresdner Suisse   Subsidiary Company
Formerly known as: Banque Kleinwort Benson SA
2 Place du Rhône, CH-1211 Geneva 11
PO Box 5525, CH-1211 Geneva
Tel: (22) 318 9494 **Fax:** (22) 318 9595 **Swift:** DBKB CH GG

Senior Executive Officers
Chairman Jürgen Sarrazin
President Jacques Bour

Les Fils Dreyfus & Cie SA, Banquiers   Head Office
Aeschenvorstadt 14-16, PO Box 2656, CH-4002 Basle
Tel: (61) 286 6666 **Fax:** (61) 272 2438 **Telex:** 962391 LFD **Swift:** DREY CH BB

Senior Executive Officers
Chairman Hans Guth
Chief Executive Officer Andreas Guth *Manager*
Financial Director Paul Dubey *Manager*
Chief Operating Officer Otto E Bargezi *Manager*
Treasurer Bruno Baumann *Treasurer & Head of Dealing* ☎ **286 6259**
Assistant Manager Bernard Blum ☎ **286 6304**

Debt Capital Markets / Fixed Income
Government Bonds
Head of Trading Werner Meyer *Deputy Manager* ☎ **286 6255**

www.euromoneydirectory.com SWITZERLAND (+41)

Eurobonds
Head of Trading Werner Meyer *Deputy Manager* ☎ 286 6355
Equity Capital Markets
Domestic Equities
Head of Trading Fred Dankner *Manager* ☎ 286 6253
Other (Domestic Equities)
 Claude Kiener *Assistant Manager* ☎ 286 6392

International Equities
Head of Trading David Waldmann *Deputy Manager* ☎ 286 6270
Other (International Equity)
 Urs Kaufmann *Dealer* ☎ 286 6208

Convertibles / Equity-Linked
Head of Trading Werner Meyer *Deputy Manager* ☎ 286 6355
Foreign Exchange
Tel: 286 6565 **Fax:** 272 6187
Head of Trading Heinrich Ihr *Deputy Manager* ☎ 286 6273
FX Traders / Sales People
 Jürg Stalder *Assistant Manager* ☎ 286 6261
 Christoph Güdemann *Holder of Procuration* ☎ 286 6357

Settlement / Clearing
Fixed-Income Settlement Jean-Pierre Wyss *Holder of Procuration* ☎ 286 6301
Other Departments
Correspondent Banking Bruno Baumann *Treasurer & Head of Dealing* ☎ 286 6259
Administration
Technology & Systems
 Peter Lehmann *Manager* ☎ 286 6287

Legal / In-House Counsel
 Bernard Blum *Assistant Manager* ☎ 286 6304

Compliance
 Bernard Blum *Assistant Manager* ☎ 286 6304

EFG Bank European Financial Group
Head Office

Formerly known as: Banque de Dépôts SA
94 rue du Rhône, CH-1204 Geneva 3
PO Box 3200, CH-1211 Geneva 3
Tel: (22) 319 1333 **Fax:** (22) 319 1300 **Swift:** EFGB CH GG

Senior Executive Officers
Chairman Spiro J Latsis
Chief Executive Officer Périclès-Paul Petalas
Financial Director Emmanuel L Bussetil *Group Finance Executive*
Senior Vice President Richard Francis
Company Secretary Périclès-Paul Petalas

Others (Senior Executives)
Group Credit & Risk Executive Patrick de Figueredo *Senior Vice President*
Risk Management
Department: Group Credit & Risk
Head of Risk Management Patrick de Figueredo *Senior Vice President*
Other Departments
Chief Credit Officer Patrick de Figueredo *Senior Vice President*
Correspondent Banking Patrick Arnoux
Administration
Head of Marketing Richard Francis

Public Relations
 Richard Francis

Accounts / Audit
 Roland Furer

Euromoney Directory 1999 **1517**

SWITZERLAND (+41)   www.euromoneydirectory.com

EFG Private Bank SA
Head Office

Formerly known as: Royal Bank of Scotland AG
Bahnhofstrasse 16, CH-8001 Zürich
PO Box 5216, CH-8001 Zürich
Tel: (1) 226 1717 **Fax:** (1) 226 1726 **Telex:** 422351 **Swift:** EFGB CH ZZ

Senior Executive Officers
Chairman — Jean-Pierre Cuoni
Chief Executive Officer — Lawrence D Howell *Chief Executive Officer*
Chief Operating Officer — Ian R Cookson *Chief Operating Officer*
International Division — Nigel Paul *Head of Private Banking, Geneva*

General-Investment
Head of Investment — Marcus Caduff *Head of Private Banking, Zurich*

EPS Finance Limited
Full Branch Office

Alternative trading name: EPS
Bahnhofstrasse 46, CH-8021 Zürich
Tel: (1) 212 7474 **Fax:** (1) 212 7484 **Telex:** 812846 **Email:** info@eps-finance.int.ch

Senior Executive Officers
President & Chief Executive Officer — Rolf Wägli
Financial Director — Yannick Lelen *Chief Financial Officer* ☎ **(22) 849 0150**

General-Investment
Head of Investment — Michael Eicher *Vice President* ☎ **212 7481**

Relationship Manager
Small & Medium Sized Companies — Rolf Wägli *President & Chief Executive Officer*

Debt Capital Markets / Fixed Income

Private Placements
Head of Origination; Head of Sales; Head of Structuring — Rolf Wägli *President & Chief Executive Officer*

Foreign Exchange
Global Head — Rolf Wägli *President & Chief Executive Officer*
Head of Trading — Oswaldo Barbieri *Assistant Vice President* ☎ **212 7485**

Corporate Finance / M&A Advisory
Head of Corporate Finance — Peter Letter *Vice President* ☎ **212 7478**

Other Departments
Private Banking — Michael Eicher *Vice President* ☎ **212 7481**
Economic Research — Christoph Loudan *VP, Economic Efficiency Dept* ☎ **212 7482**

Administration
Business Development; Head of Marketing — Rolf Wägli *President & Chief Executive Officer*

Public Relations
Rolf Wägli *President & Chief Executive Officer*

Accounts / Audit
Yannick Lelen *Chief Financial Officer* ☎ **(22) 849 0150**

EUFINGEST - Compagnia di Gestione e Finanza
Head Office

Via San Gottardo 10, CH-6900 Lugano
PO Box 356, CH-6908 Lugano
Tel: (91) 923 2307 **Fax:** (91) 923 9087

Senior Executive Officers
Chairman — Alfredo Lo Monaco
Managing Director — Marco Coppini

EUFINTRADE SA
Head Office

Via San Gottardo 10, CH-6900 Lugano
Tel: (91) 923 2307 **Fax:** (91) 923 9087 **Telex:** 844398 EUFI CH

Senior Executive Officers
President — Alfredo Lo Monaco
Managing Director / General Manager — Raffaele D'Aló

www.euromoneydirectory.com   SWITZERLAND (+41)

Syndicated Lending
Other (Trade Finance)
 Kurt Abrate *Forfaiting Manager*
 Lanfranco Casartelli *Forfaiting Manager*
Administration
Head of Administration Mari Paolini
Business Development Barbara Lo Monaco

Euroclear Clearance System plc
Head Office

Bleicherweg 33, CH-8002 Zürich
PO Box 656, CH-8027 Zürich
Tel: (1) 249 2910; (1) 202 5649 **Fax:** (1) 202 8258 **Email:** haljankson@compusewe.com
Senior Executive Officers
Chairman Andrew Large
Director G Hal Jackson

Faisal Finance (Switzerland) SA
Head Office

Formerly known as: Shari' a Investment Services Limited
84 Avenue Louis-Casai, Cointrin, CH-1216 Geneva
PO Box 42, CH-1216 Geneva
Tel: (22) 929 5300; (22) 791 7111 **Fax:** (22) 929 5399 **Telex:** 415 354 FFS CH **Email:** info@ffs.dmitrust.com
Administration Department **Fax:** 791 7299; Equity Capital Markets **Fax:** 929 5398; Senior Executive Officers
Fax: 929 5398; Syndicated Lending **Fax:** 929 5398
Website: www.ffs.dmitrust.com

Senior Executive Officers
Chairman HRH Prince Mohamed F Saud
President & Chief Executive Officer Mahmoud El Helw [T] **929 5340** [F] **929 5397**
Chief Executive Officer Mahmoud El Helw *President & Chief Executive Officer* [T] **929 5340**
 [F] **929 5397**
Financial Director Jamal Heiniger *Director* [T] **929 5332** [F] **929 5397**
Treasurer Frank Perlwitz *Vice President* [T] **929 5309** [F] **929 5397**
SVP & Deputy General Manager Rachid Teymour [T] **929 5316** [F] **929 5399**
Equity Capital Markets
Head of Equity Capital Markets Frank Perlwitz *Vice President* [T] **929 5309** [F] **929 5397**
Syndicated Lending
Loan-Related Activities
Trade Finance Sabri Hassanein *Director* [T] **929 5303** [F] **929 5397**
Asset Management
Head Suleiman Dualeh *Director* [T] **929 5326**
Administration
Head of Administration Daniel Huber *Group Vice President* [T] **791 7137** [F] **791 7298**
Head of Marketing Mohamed Ali Eid *Manager* [T] **929 5320** [F] **929 5399**
Technology & Systems
 Daniel Jol*Senior Manager* [T] **791 7148** [F] **791 7298**
Legal / In-House Counsel
 Osama Mohamed Ali *Legal Counsel* [T] **791 7110** [F] **791 7298**
Compliance
 Jean-Jacques Dur *Manager* [T] **929 5353** [F] **929 5399**
Public Relations
 Mouaouia Mokhtar *Director* [T] **791 7135** [F] **791 7298**
Accounts / Audit
 Mohamed Ali *Director* [T] **791 7161** [F] **791 7298**

Ferrier Lullin & Cie SA
Head Office

46 rue du Stand, CH-1204 Geneva
Tel: (22) 708 3838; (22) 781 1201 **Fax:** (22) 708 3812; (22) 708 3826 **Telex:** 422186 **Swift:** FERL CH GG
Email: ferrierlullin@iprolink.ch **Cable:** FERULIN
Senior Executive Officers
Chairman Walter Infanger

Euromoney Directory 1999   **1519**

SWITZERLAND (+41) www.euromoneydirectory.com

Ferrier Lullin & Cie SA (cont)
Others (Senior Executives)
Pierre Deage *Head of Trading*

Fibi Bank (Switzerland) Limited
Head Office

Seestrasse 61, CH-8027 Zürich
PO Box, CH-8027 Zürich
Tel: (1) 201 6969 **Fax:** (1) 201 1441 **Telex:** 814132 FIB CH **Swift:** FIRB CH ZZ **Email:** fibich@ibm.net **Reuters:** FBSW
Website: www.fibi.ch

Senior Executive Officers
Chairman of the Board — F Peter von Muralt
Vice Chairman — Shlomo Piotrkowsky
General Manager — David Nochimowski
Deputy Manager — Shraga Grabinsky
Deputy Manager — Mario Rizzo

Finansbank (Suisse) SA
Subsidiary Company

Formerly known as: FB Finansbank (Suisse) SA
13 route de Florissant, CH-1211 Geneva 12
Tel: (22) 839 1919 **Fax:** (22) 839 1903 **Telex:** 413133 FBS **Swift:** FSUI CH GG

Senior Executive Officers
Chairman — Hüsnü M Özyegin
Chief Executive Officer — Haluk Dürust *General Manager* ☏ **839 1920**
Chief Operating Officer — Aykut Gimir *Vice President* ☏ **839 1979**
Treasurer — Unal Aksit *Vice President* ☏ **839 1941**

Debt Capital Markets / Fixed Income
Non-Domestic Government Bonds
All Currencies — Unal Aksit *Vice President* ☏ **839 1941**

Syndicated Lending
Loan-Related Activities
Trade Finance — Placide Machoud *Assistant General Manager* ☏ **839 1923**

Other (Trade Finance)
Forfaiting — Philippe Balle *Vice President* ☏ **839 1922**

Money Markets
Head of Money Markets — Martial Ballaman *Dealer* ☏ **839 1948**

Foreign Exchange
Head of Foreign Exchange — Ayka Akin *Chief Dealer* ☏ **839 1945**

Risk Management
OTC Credit Derivatives
Global Head — Placide Machoud *Assistant General Manager* ☏ **839 1923**

Finanz AG Zürich
Head Office

Bliechervig 10, CH-8070 Zürich
PO Box 900, Zürich
Tel: (1) 211 2830 **Fax:** (1) 211 3854 **Telex:** 812498

Senior Executive Officers
Managing Director / General Manager — Jörg Hübner

FINARBIT AG
Head Office

Kohlrainstrasse 10, CH-8700 Küsnacht/Zürich
Tel: (1) 913 8000 **Fax:** (1) 913 8010 **Telex:** 815945 **Reuters:** FNAR **Telerate:** 353/3432

Senior Executive Officers
Senior Officer — Robert Keller

Money Markets
Money Markets - General
International & Forwards — Mikael Duvaker
Francisco José Alvarez

www.euromoneydirectory.com   SWITZERLAND (+41)

Money Markets - General (cont)

Fiduciaries
Helga Wagner
Philippe Mouchart
Barbara Blaettler
Marco Schirinzi

Domestic
Cécile Eberhard Baur *Head*
Robert Schorer
José F Ruiz
Antonio Di Maio
Remo Jegi

Administration
Head of Administration   Mary Fay

FINARBIT SA   Subsidiary Company

9 rue Mauborget, CH-1003 Lausanne
Tel: (21) 319 9900 **Fax:** (21) 319 9910 **Reuters:** FNAL **Telerate:** 353/3432

Senior Executive Officers
Senior Officer   Robert Keller

Money Markets
Department: Money Markets & Forwards
Head of Money Markets   Felix Lenzinger

Money Markets - General
Ernst Lengweiler
Jean-Marc Dalmadi
Yves R Gasser
Thierry Weber
Paul Marchetti

Finex Swiss Money Broker AG   Subsidiary Company

Formerly known as: Premex AG

Dufourstrasse 101, CH-8034 Zürich
Tel: (1) 384 9700; (1) 383 2569 **Fax:** (1) 384 9899; (1) 383 1708 **Telex:** 817151 FNEX CH
Email: premex.admin@bluewin.ch **Reuters:** (Dealing) FNEX **Telerate:** 3468

Senior Executive Officers
Managing Director & Chief Executive   Jürg P Angehrn 🖃 **jpa.premex@bluewin.ch**

Money Markets
Tel: 383 1850 **Reuters:** FNEX

Money Markets - General
Cash
Enzo Jandolo *Department Head* 🖃 **finex1@blomberg.net**
Plus Schmaiz *Vice President*
Peter Schmid *Vice President*
Robert Reinhard *Vice President*
Peter Martin *Senior Director*
Kenny W Chandler *Senior Director*
Marco Barecca *Director*

OBS
Beat Cavegn *Department Head* 🖃 **cavegn@finex.ch**
Stefan Bollinger *Senior Director* 🖃 **bollinger@finex.ch**
René Krebs *Vice President*
Daniel Ferri *Senior Director*
Corinne Pestana *Director*

Finter Bank Zürich   Head Office

Claridenstrasse 35, 8032 Zürich
Tel: (1) 289 5500 **Fax:** (1) 289 5600 **Telex:** 815326 FBZZ CH **Swift:** FBZU CH ZZ **Email:** zh@finter.ch
Cable: FINTERBANK ZURIC
Website: www.finter.ch

Senior Executive Officers
Chief Executive Officer   Martin A Murbach ☎ **289 5501**

Euromoney Directory 1999   **1521**

SWITZERLAND (+41)

Robert Fleming (Switzerland) AG
Full Branch Office

Röschibachstrasse 22, CH-8032 Zürich
Tel: (1) 276 1511 Fax: (1) 272 9441

Senior Executive Officers
Chairman — J G Archibald
Vice Chairman — H W Niederer
Chief Operating Officer — P Gyger *First Vice President*
General Manager — G Valsecchi

FTI - Banque Fiduciary Trust

World Trade Center 2, 29 route de Pré-Bois, CH-1215 Geneva 15
PO Box 156, Geneva
Tel: (22) 710 6070 Fax: (22) 710 6080 Telex: 428540

Senior Executive Officers

Others (Senior Executives)
Pierre Weiss

Settlement / Clearing
Operations — David Georsa *Head of Operations*

Administration

Compliance
Brian Cox *Head, Compliance*

Fuji Bank (Schweiz) AG
Subsidiary Company

Tiefenhöfe/ Parapeplatz 6, CH-8022 Zürich
Tel: (1) 211 3313 Fax: (1) 211 6629 Telex: 812138 FUJCH Swift: FUJI CH ZZ Reuters: FUJZ

Senior Executive Officers
President
Chief Executive Officer — Minoru Egashira
— Takashi Torii *Executive Vice President*

Debt Capital Markets / Fixed Income

Bonds - General
Head of Securities Trading — Eiichiro Kozuka *Vice President*
Head of Securities Underwriting — Takaaki Fukami *Vice President*

Equity Capital Markets
Head of Equity Capital Markets — Nobuhiro Abiko *First Vice President*

Money Markets
Head of Money Markets — Goichi Usami *Vice President*

Foreign Exchange
Head of Foreign Exchange — Goichi Usami *Vice President*

Settlement / Clearing
Head of Settlement / Clearing — Karl Stocker *Vice President*

Other Departments
Correspondent Banking — Andre Naville *Vice President*

Administration

Compliance
Brigitte Fotsch *Vice President*

Garanti Bank
Representative Office

80 rue de Rhone, CH-1204 Geneva
Tel: (22) 318 0030 Fax: (22) 311 3262

Senior Executive Officers
Representative — Yucel Arat

1522 Euromoney Directory 1999

www.euromoneydirectory.com SWITZERLAND (+41)

Girofin SA
Head Office

2 Chemin de Valerie, CH-1292 Geneva
Tel: (22) 346 4446 **Fax:** (22) 346 5401 **Telex:** 458 071 **Reuters:** GIRG (Dealing)

Senior Executive Officers
Chairman Michel Sudan
Secretary Werner Strohmeier

Girofin SA
Full Branch Office

15 rue de la Gare, CH-1110 Morges
BO Box 273, CH-1110 Morges
Tel: (21) 802 2055 **Fax:** (21) 802 2155 **Telex:** 458071 **Reuters:** (Dealing) GIRG **Telerate:** RECIPIENT

Senior Executive Officers
Chairman Michel Sudan
Secretary Werner Strohmeier

Goldman Sachs & Co
Subsidiary Company

Münsterhof 4, CH-8022 Zürich
Tel: (1) 224 1000 **Fax:** (1) 224 1050

Senior Executive Officers
Managing Director W Thomas York Jr.

Gottex Brokers SA
Head Office

Formerly known as: Gottex SA - Financial Services

48 Avenue de Rhodanie, CH-1007 Lausanne
PO Box 132, CH-1000 Lausanne 6
Tel: (21) 617 1017; (21) 617 1540 **Fax:** (21) 617 7155 **Telex:** 455103 GTX CH **Reuters:** GOTX **Telerate:** 25270/280
Bloomberg: GOTX - GOTY
Reuters: GOTY (dealing)
Website: www.gottex.com

Senior Executive Officers
President Maurice Von der Mühll
Company Secretary Patrick Schneider

Others (Senior Executives)

Charles Dupont *Deputy Chairman*

Groupement des Banquiers Prives Genevois
Head Office

Rue Bovy-Lysberg, CH-1211 Geneva 11
PO Box 5639, Geneva
Tel: (22) 807 0380 **Fax:** (22) 320 1289 **Email:** gbpg@bluewin.ch

Senior Executive Officers
President Charles Pictet
Chief Executive Officer Michel Dérobert
Company Secretary Denis Mathieu

GTC Globo Trading & Consulting AG
Head Office

Alternative trading name: GTC

Samstagernstrasse 45, CH-8832 Wollerau
Tel: (1) 786 2525 **Fax:** (1) 786 1818

Senior Executive Officers
Chairman, President & MD Daniel Eggenberger
Chief Operating Officer Christopher Widman *Vice President*
Vice President Stefan Hurzcler

Money Markets
Country Head Peter Stelznen *Vice President & Head*

Euromoney Directory 1999 **1523**

SWITZERLAND (+41)   www.euromoneydirectory.com

GTC Globo Trading & Consulting AG (cont)
Foreign Exchange
Country Head — Peter Stelznen *Vice President & Head*
Risk Management
Country Head — Chris Widman *Vice President & Head*

Guyerzeller Bank AG — Head Office

Genferstrasse 8, CH-8027 Zürich
Tel: (1) 206 7111 Fax: (1) 206 7397 Telex: 815364

Senior Executive Officers
Chairman, Executive Committee — K W Preisig

Handelsfinanz-CCF Bank — Head Office

3 bis, Place de la Fusterie, CH-1204 Geneva 11
PO Box 5054, CH-1211 Geneva 11
Tel: (22) 310 5444 Fax: (22) 310 1344 Swift: HFBK CH GG Reuters: HFBG

Senior Executive Officers
Chairman — Henri Danguy des Déserts
Chief Executive Officer — Gennaro Persico

Others (Senior Executives)
International Banking — Fritz Barmettler *Executive Vice President*

Relationship Manager
Corporate Clients — Berthold Hoffman *First Vice President*
Eric Deslex

Debt Capital Markets / Fixed Income
Eurobonds
Head of Origination — Victor Cesana *Vice President*
Bonds - General
Eurobonds — Roland Batt
Luigi Mondati

Equity Capital Markets
Other (Domestic Equities) — Victor Cesana *Vice President*
Luigi Mondati
Roland Batt

Equity Repo / Securities Lending
Marketing — Victor Cesana *Vice President*
Luigi Mondati
Roland Batt

Syndicated Lending
Loan-Related Activities
Trade Finance — Berthold Hoffman *First Vice President*
Eric Deslex

Foreign Exchange
Department: Treasury & Foreign Exchange
FX Traders / Sales People — Serge Pellanda *Vice President*
Albert Raven
Joakim Bunzli

Settlement / Clearing
Operations — Laurent Dunkel *Executive Vice President*
Henri Imholz *Vice President*

Other Departments
Private Banking — Francesco Cavicchi *Executive Vice President*
Fritz Barmettler *Executive Vice President*

Administration
Head of Administration — Laurent Dunkel *Executive Vice President*
Henri Imholz *Vice President*

www.euromoneydirectory.com　　　　SWITZERLAND (+41)

Handelsfinanz-CCF Bank

Tödistrasse 44, CH-8027 Zürich
Tel: (1) 287 2525 Fax: (1) 201 4283 Telex: 815847

Senior Executive Officers
Others (Senior Executives)
　　　　Christian Lemmerich *Manager*

Helaba Investment AG
Subsidiary Company

Froumüsterstraße 25 14, CH-8001 Zürich
Tel: (1) 225 3790 Fax: (1) 225 3791

Senior Executive Officers
Managing Director　　　　Bernhard Steng

Helaba (Schweiz) Landesbank Hessen Thüringen
Subsidiary Company

Börsenstrasse 16, CH-8022 Zürich
Tel: (1) 225 3636 Fax: (1) 225 3600 Telex: 813303 Reuters: HISFUNDS

Senior Executive Officers
Chairman　　　　Günther Merl
Treasurer　　　　Manfred Weiss *First Vice President*
Executive Vice President　　　　Rainer Erdmann
Executive Vice President　　　　Walter Nötzli

Debt Capital Markets / Fixed Income
Tel: 225 3751 Fax: 225 3660 Telex: 813 303
Head of Fixed Income Trading　　　　Marco Di Fante *Assistant Vice President*

Equity Capital Markets
Tel: 225 3751 Fax: 225 3660 Reuters: HISFUNDS Telex: 813 303
Country Head　　　　Marco Di Fante *Assistant Vice President*

Money Markets
Tel: 225 3751 Fax: 225 3660 Telex: 813 303
Head of Money Markets　　　　Manfred Weiss *First Vice President*

Foreign Exchange
Tel: 225 3751 Fax: 225 3660 Telex: 813 303
Head of Foreign Exchange　　　　Manfred Weiss *First Vice President*

Settlement / Clearing
Fax: 225 3660 Telex: 813 303
Head of Settlement / Clearing　　　　Elena Doukakis *Authorized Officer* ☏ **225 3711**

Asset Management
Head　　　　Christian Elsener *Assistant Vice President* ☏ **225 3675**

Other Departments
Private Banking　　　　Hans Lötscher *First Vice President*

Administration
Head of Administration　　　　Bernhard Gross ☏ **225 3700** ☒ **225 3660**

Helarb Management SA
Head Office

30 Avenue Ruchonnet, CH-1001 Lausanne
PO Box 864, CH-1001 Lausanne
Tel: (21) 341 0303 Fax: (21) 341 0329

Senior Executive Officers
Chief Executive Officer　　　　Christian Wildmoser *Chief Executive & General Manager*

Others (Senior Executives)
Executive Director　　　　Matthias Graeper
　　　　Thierry Lainé

SWITZERLAND (+41)   www.euromoneydirectory.com

Hottinger & Cie — Full Branch Office

Place des Bergues 3, CH-1211 Geneva 1
Tel: (22) 908 1200 **Fax:** (22) 908 1299 **Telex:** 412279 HOTCH

Senior Executive Officers
Branch Manager — Willy Vogelsang

Hottinger & Cie — Head Office

Dreikoenigstrasse 55, CH-8027 Zürich
Tel: (1) 284 1200 **Fax:** (1) 284 1299 **Telex:** 815651 HOZH CH **Swift:** HOTT CH ZZ

Senior Executive Officers
Partner — Henri G Hottinger
Partner — Paul B Hottinger
Partner — Rodolphe E Hottinger
Partner — Frédéric G Hottinger
Senior Vice President — Alain B Fischer
Senior Vice President — Hans Lauxmann
Senior Vice President — Henri Stalder
International Division — Alain B Fischer *Senior Vice President*

General-Lending (DCM, SL)
Head of Corporate Banking — George Isliker *Vice President*

General - Treasury
Head of Treasury — Hans Lauxmann *Senior Vice President*

Debt Capital Markets / Fixed Income
Tel: 284 1260
Global Head — Marcel Monsch *Vice President* 284 1265

Syndicated Lending

Other (Trade Finance)
Credit; Letters of Credit; Documentary Credits — George Isliker *Vice President*

Money Markets

Domestic Commercial Paper
Head of Origination — Marcel Monsch *Vice President* 284 1265

Eurocommercial Paper
Head of Origination — Marcel Monsch *Vice President* 284 1265

Other (Wholesale Deposits)
Eurocurrency Deposits — Vincent Tesoro *Assistant Vice President* 284 1204

Foreign Exchange
Global Head — Vincent Tesoro *Assistant Vice President* 284 1204

Corporate Finance / M&A Advisory
Global Head — George Isliker *Vice President*
Private Equity — Alain B Fischer *Senior Vice President, LBOs & MBOs*

Other (Corporate Finance)
Corporate Finance — George Isliker *Vice President*

Settlement / Clearing
Operations; Electronic Banking — Hans Lauxmann *Senior Vice President*

Asset Management
Portfolio Management — Henri Stalder *Senior Vice President*

Other Departments
Correspondent Banking — Hans Lauxmann *Senior Vice President*

Other Departments
Commercial Banking — George Isliker *Vice President*

Administration
Head of Administration — Hans Lauxmann *Senior Vice President*

Legal / In-House Counsel
— Alain B Fischer *Senior Vice President*

www.euromoneydirectory.com   SWITZERLAND (+41)

HYPOSWISS

Schutzengasse 4, CH-8001 Zürich
PO Box, CH-8023 Zürich
Tel: (1) 214 3111 **Fax:** (1) 211 5223

Senior Executive Officers
Chairman Dr Andreas Henrici
Managing Director Theodor Horat
Asset Management
Portfolio Management A Schaad *Head*
Administration
Head of Administration Urs Eggenberger *Head* ☎ 214 3316 📠 214 3375

IFP Intermoney Financial Products SA   Head Office

36 route de Lavaux, CH-1095 Lutry
PO Box 341, Lutry
Tel: (21) 796 6627; (21) 796 6611 **Fax:** (21) 796 6633 **Telex:** 450230 IFP CH **Email:** ifp.intermoney@urbanet.ch
Reuters: IFSL
Website: www.ifp.ch

Senior Executive Officers
Others (Senior Executives)
 Sylvain Naggar *Senior Executive Officer*
 Pamela Zell-Naggar *Senior Executive Officer*
 Eric Weder *Senior Executive Officer*
Debt Capital Markets / Fixed Income
Head of Debt Capital Markets Eric Weder *Senior Executive Officer*
Non-Domestic Government Bonds
Italian Government Bonds Pamela Zell-Naggar *Senior Executive Officer*
Eurobonds
Head of Origination Eric Weder *Senior Executive Officer*
Fixed-Income Repo
Head of Repo Pamela Zell-Naggar *Senior Executive Officer*
Equity Capital Markets
Other (Domestic Equities)
Swfr Market Maker on Primary (grey); Equity & Eric Weder *Senior Executive Officer*
Related Products
Money Markets
Head of Money Markets Sylvain Naggar *Senior Executive Officer*
Other (Wholesale Deposits)
Eurocurrency Deposits; Short / Long-Term Sylvain Naggar *Senior Executive Officer*
Forwards
Foreign Exchange
Head of Foreign Exchange André George
Risk Management
Fixed Income Derivatives / Risk Management
IR Swaps Trading; IR Options Trading Sylvain Naggar *Senior Executive Officer*
Foreign Exchange Derivatives / Risk Management
Cross-Currency Swaps, Trading Sylvain Naggar *Senior Executive Officer*
Other Currency Swap / FX Options Personnel
Asset Swaps & Special Structures Sylvain Naggar *Senior Executive Officer*
Administration
Head of Administration George Anagnostaras

Ihag Handelsbank Zürich

Bleicherweg 18, PO Box 4880, CH-8022 Zürich
Tel: (1) 205 1111 **Fax:** (1) 205 1285 **Telex:** 815323 IHA CH

Senior Executive Officers
Chairman Dr Dieter Bührle
Managing Director / General Manager Hans Grunder

Euromoney Directory 1999   **1527**

SWITZERLAND (+41) www.euromoneydirectory.com

Index Securities SA — Head Office

2 rue de Jargonnant, CH-1207 Geneva
Tel: (22) 737 0000 Fax: (22) 737 0099
Website: www.index.ch

Senior Executive Officers
Senior Partner — Gerald Rimer
Chief Executive Officer — Neil Rimer *Managing Partner*
Financial Director — Giuseppe Zocco *Partner*
Chief Operating Officer — David Rimer *Partner*

Debt Capital Markets / Fixed Income

Private Placements
Head of Origination — Giuseppe Zocco *Partner*
Head of Sales — David Rimer *Partner*

The Industrial Bank of Japan Limited — Subsidiary Company

Bahnhofstrasse 82A, CH-8023 Zürich
Tel: (1) 218 9878 Fax: (1) 218 9860 Telex: 814468 Swift: IBJT CH ZH

Senior Executive Officers
Regional Manager — Yusuke Sakaue
Branch Manager — Keiichiro Okuda
First Vice President — Daniel Renner
Vice President — Thomas Michel
Senior Vice President — Walter Mazenauer

The Industrial Bank of Japan NJ (Switzerland) Limited

Bahnhofstrasse 82A, CH-8023 Zürich
Tel: (1) 218 9595 Fax: (1) 218 9945 Telex: 812298 Swift: IBJT CH ZZ

Senior Executive Officers
President — Yusuke Sakaue
Executive Vice President — Jun Kumazaki

Debt Capital Markets / Fixed Income

Bonds - General
Capital Markets & Swfr Bonds Issuing — Ken Yokohama *Senior Vice President*
Hiroki Yasuda *Vice President*
M T Fattorini *Vice President*

Fixed-Income Repo
Trading — Jean-Pierre Mottl *VP, Fixed-Income Trading*

Equity Capital Markets

Equity Repo / Securities Lending
Head of Trading — Stefan van der Sluijs *VP, Equity Trading*
Makoto Hirose *VP, Equity Brokerage*

Risk Management
Head of Risk Management — Rei Tasaki *First Vice President*

Asset Management
Portfolio Management — Jun Kumazaki *Executive Vice President*
Osamu Honda *Senior Vice President*
David Tye *First Vice President*
Roberto Cyprian *Senior Vice President*
Naobumi Kikuchi *VP, Securities Trading*

Administration

Other (Administration)
Administration / Finances — Lobsang Gangshontsang *Senior Vice President*

ING Bank Suisse

6 rue Petitot, CH-1204 Geneva
PO Box 5026, CH-1211 Geneva 11
Tel: (22) 817 6111 **Fax:** (22) 817 6575 **Telex:** 422299 INGB CH **Swift:** INGB CH ZZ GVA

Senior Executive Officers
General Manager, Private Banking   Jan H W Beunderman
Country General Manager   Jean-Christophe Ganz

General-Lending (DCM, SL)
Head of Corporate Banking   Dominique Schramm *Manager*

Other Departments
Department: ING Bank Suisse
Riva Antionio Caccia 1a, CH-6900 Lugano
Tel: +41 (91) 985 0811 **Fax:** +41 (91) 985 0833
Private Banking   Renze Keegstra *Manager*

ING Bank (Switzerland)   Subsidiary Company

Glärnischstrasse 36, CH-8002 Zürich
PO Box 4623, CH-8002 Zürich
Tel: (1) 207 4111 **Fax:** (1) 207 4260 **Telex:** 815490 ING CH **Swift:** INGB CH ZZ

Senior Executive Officers
Chairman   J M A Yntema
Vice Chairman & Secretary   P Widmer

Others (Senior Executives)
                                           J H W Beunderman *Director*
                                           G J A van der Lugt *Director*
                                           F Lütolf *Director*
                                           A Richoz *Director*
                                           H Secretan *Director*
                                           A Seiler *Director*
                                           E Simonius *Director*
                                           Jan B A A Huisman *General Manager*
                                           J C Ganz *General Manager*

ING Baring Securities Limited   Full Branch Office

7 rue du Commerce, CH-1204 Geneva
Tel: (22) 818 7777 **Fax:** (22) 818 7676

Senior Executive Officers
Branch Manager   Daniel Fust

Equity Capital Markets
Other (International Equity)
Equity Brokerage & Trading   Daniel Fust *Branch Manager*
                                           T Renz

ING Trust (Suisse)

Anstrasse 1, CH-6304 Zug
PO Box 4027, CH-6304 Zug
Tel: (41) 712 0893 **Fax:** (41) 712 0904

Senior Executive Officers
General Manager   Stefan Amgwerd

Interacor AG   Head Office

Wehntalerstrasse 639, CH-8046 Zürich
Tel: (1) 377 9411 **Fax:** (1) 371 9492 **Telex:** 815603 INA CH **Reuters:** INTZ
Website: www.access.ch/interz/

Senior Executive Officers
Senior Officer   Urs Schweizer

SWITZERLAND (+41)   www.euromoneydirectory.com

Interacor AG (cont)
Debt Capital Markets / Fixed Income
Department: International & Domestic Treasury
Global Head   Urs Schweizer *Senior Officer*

Bonds - General
International & Domestic Treasury   Markus Farner
Sylvia Beck
Roberto Umiker
Hans Johner

Intercapital plc
Badenerstrasse 170, CH-8004 Zürich
Tel: (1) 299 9150 **Fax:** (1) 291 6464
Senior Executive Officers
Others (Senior Executives)
Marc Kipfer

Interchange SA   Head Office
15 rue de la Gare, PO Box 239, CH-1110 Morges
Tel: (21) 802 3041 **Fax:** (21) 802 2597 **Telex:** 458270 **Swift:** ICHM CH 21 **Reuters:** ICHM **Telerate:** 3436
Senior Executive Officers
President   Jean-René Zobrist
Manager   Johanne Robert Pantanella
Manager   Mike Homanski

Money Markets
Head of Money Markets   Jean-René Zobrist
Regional Head   Johanne Robert Pantanella *Manager*
Mike Homanski *Manager*

Foreign Exchange
Head of Foreign Exchange   Jean-René Zobrist
Regional Head   Johanne Robert Pantanella *Manager*
Mike Homanski *Manager*

Risk Management
Fixed Income Derivatives / Risk Management
Trading   Mike Homanski *Manager*
Jean-René Zobrist

INTERSETTLE - Swiss Corporation for International Securities Settlements
Thurgauerstrasse 54, CH-8050 Zürich
Tel: (1) 308 7248 **Fax:** (1) 308 7222 **Swift:** INSE CHZZ

Debt Capital Markets / Fixed Income

Fixed-Income Repo
Head of Repo   Wolfgang Michaelis *Chief Executive Officer* ☏ **308 7201**
Marketing & Product Development   René Eberhard *Head of Securities Borrowing & Lending* ☏ **308 7244**
🖷 **308 7250** 🖃 **rene.eberhard@intersettle.ccom**
Trading   René Eberhard
Sales   René Eberhard *Head of Securities Borrowing & Lending* ☏ **308 7244**
🖷 **308 7250** 🖃 **rene.eberhard@intersettle.ccom**

Equity Capital Markets

Equity Repo / Securities Lending
Marketing & Product Development   René Eberhard *Head of Securities Borrowing & Lending* ☏ **308 7244**
🖷 **308 7250** 🖃 **rene.eberhard@intersettle.ccom**

JP Morgan (Suisse) SA
Subsidiary Company

3 Place des Bergues, CH-1201 Geneva
Tel: (22) 731 5800 Fax: (22) 732 2655 Telex: 412896 JPMCH Cable: MORGANSUIS

Senior Executive Officers
Managing Director / General Manager — William L Oullin

Debt Capital Markets / Fixed Income
Head of Fixed Income — Jim Manansala

Equity Capital Markets
Head of Equity Capital Markets — Reto Bodenmann

Settlement / Clearing
Settlement (General) — Robert Chardon
Operations — Marc-Henri Balma

Administration

Compliance
Jürg Egli Head, Compliance

Jyske Bank (Schweiz)
Subsidiary Company

Wasserwerkstrasse 12, CH-8035 Zürich
Tel: (1) 368 7373 Fax: (1) 368 7379 Telex: 816288 JBA CH

Senior Executive Officers
Managing Director — Konrad Meier
Deputy Managing Director — Börge Sörensen
Deputy Managing Director — Niels Hansen

Kredietbank (Suisse) SA
Head Office

7 Boulevard Georges-Favon, CH-1211 Geneva 11
PO Box 5510, CH-1211 Geneva 11
Tel: (22) 311 6322 Fax: (22) 311 5443; (22) 310 6446 Telex: 427603 KBSCH Swift: KSUI CH GG

Senior Executive Officers
Chairman — Etienne Verwilghen
Chief Executive Officer — Bernard Serre Managing Director
Chief Operating Officer — Pierre Jone Director
Assistant-Managing Director — Roland Matthys

General-Investment
Head of Investment — Ahmet Eren Director

Other Departments
Private Banking — Ahmet Eren Director

F van Lanschot Bankiers (Schweiz) AG
Subsidiary Company

Mittelstrasse 10, CH-8008 Zürich
Tel: (1) 381 9009 Fax: (1) 383 1787

Senior Executive Officers
General Manager — Guido Grossman

Lehman Brothers Finance SA

Genferstrasse 24, CH-8002 Zürich
PO Box 311, CH-8002 Zürich
Tel: (1) 287 8842 Fax: (1) 287 8825 Telex: 812096 LBFS CH Reuters: LMAN

Senior Executive Officers
General Manager — Jim Staricco

SWITZERLAND (+41)　　　　www.euromoneydirectory.com

LGT Bank in Liechtenstein AG

Gladbachstrasse 105, CH-8044 Zürich
PO Box 832, CH-8044 Zürich
Tel: (1) 250 8181 **Fax:** (1) 252 5178 **Swift:** BLFL CH 22

Senior Executive Officers
Managing Director　　　　　　　　Heinz Luterbacher

Liechtensteinische Landesbank AG

Utoquai 29, CH-8008 Zürich
PO Box 4678, CH-8008 Zürich
Tel: (1) 269 9111 **Fax:** (1) 269 9122 **Telex:** 816621

Senior Executive Officers
President of the Board of Directors　　René Kästle
Vice President, Board of Directors　　Theodor Stäuble
Others (Senior Executives)

　　　　　　　　　　　　Karlheinz Heeb *Member, Board of Directors*
　　　　　　　　　　　　Franz Jaeger *Member, Board of Directors*
　　　　　　　　　　　　Hans Rudolf Steiner *Member, Board of Directors*

Department: Executive Board
President of the Executive Board　　Hans Jürg Niederer
Others (Senior Executives)

　　　　　　　　　　　　Franco Taisch *Director*

Lloyds Bank plc　　　　　　　　　　　　　　　　　　　Full Branch Office

1 Place Bel-Air, CH-1204 Geneva
PO Box 5145, CH-1211 Geneva 11
Tel: (22) 307 3333 **Fax:** (22) 307 3424 **Telex:** 422242 LBI CH (General) **Swift:** LLOYD CH GG XXX **Reuters:** LBGA-I
Cable: INTERLLOYD GENEVA

Senior Executive Officers
Senior General Manager　　　　　　Nigel Simpson ⓣ 307 3274 ⓕ 307 3724
Others (Senior Executives)
Private Banking　　　　　　　　　René Keller *General Manager* ⓣ 307 3310 ⓕ 307 3080
Treasury & Advisory Services　　　Cliff Marr *Senior Manager* ⓣ 307 3672 ⓕ 307 3710
Investment Management Services　Michael Ferguson *Senior Manager* ⓣ 307 3489 ⓕ 307 3711
Other Departments
Private Banking　　　　　　　　　René Keller *General Manager* ⓣ 307 3310 ⓕ 307 3080

Lloyds Bank plc　　　　　　　　　　　　　　　　　　　Full Branch Office

Goethestrasse 18, CH-8001 Zürich
PO Box 4722, CH-8022 Zürich
Tel: (1) 265 2111 **Fax:** (1) 265 2222 **Telex:** 422242 LBI CH **Swift:** LOYD CH GG XXX **Reuters:** LBGA-F
Cable: INTERLOYD ZURICH

Other Departments
Private Banking　　　　　　　　　P Leuenberger *GM, Americas, Middle East, Asia & Africa*
　　　　　　　　　　　　　　　　　E Maurer *Senior Manager, Europe*

Lombard Odier & Cie　　　　　　　　　　　　　　　　　Head Office

11 rue de la Corraterie, CH-1204 Geneva
Tel: (22) 709 2111 **Fax:** (22) 709 2911 **Telex:** 422148 LOC CH **Swift:** LOCY CH GG **Reuters:** LOCG

Senior Executive Officers
Others (Senior Executives)
Partners　　　　　　　　　　　Thierry Lombard *Senior Partner*
　　　　　　　　　　　　　　　Jean A Bonna *Partner*
　　　　　　　　　　　　　　　Hans R Spillmann *Partner*
　　　　　　　　　　　　　　　Patrick Odier *Partner*
　　　　　　　　　　　　　　　Richard de Tscharner *Partner*
　　　　　　　　　　　　　　　Philippe A Sarasin *Partner*

www.euromoneydirectory.com　　　　　　　　　　SWITZERLAND (+41)

Others (Senior Executives) (cont)
　　　　　　　　　　　　　　　　　Jean Pastré *Partner*
　　　　　　　　　　　　　　　　　Anton Affentranger *Partner*
Head, Securities Trading & Underwriting　Bernard Droux *First Executive VP* T 709 2209 F 709 3209
　　　　　　　　　　　　　　　　　E bernard.droux@lombardodier.ch

General - Treasury
Head of Treasury　　　　　　　　Rudolf Leutwiler *Chairman of the Board of Management* T 709 2213
　　　　　　　　　　　　　　　　　F 709 3604

Debt Capital Markets / Fixed Income
Global Head　　　　　　　　　　Bernard Droux *First Executive VP* T 709 2209 F 709 3209
　　　　　　　　　　　　　　　　　E bernard.droux@lombardodier.ch

Domestic Government Bonds
Head of Trading　　　　　　　　Guy Steinegger *Vice President* T 709 2060 F 709 2577
　　　　　　　　　　　　　　　　　E guy.steinegger@lombardodier.ch

Eurobonds
Head of Syndication; Head of Trading　Guy Barbey *Vice President* T 709 2080 F 709 2916
　　　　　　　　　　　　　　　　　E guy.barbey@lombardodier.ch

Equity Capital Markets
Department: Swiss Research & Advisory Services (SWAS)
Domestic Equities
Head of Syndication　　　　　　Guy Barbey *Vice President* T 709 2080 F 709 2916
　　　　　　　　　　　　　　　　　E guy.barbey@lombardodier.ch
Head of Sales　　　　　　　　　Yves Delaporte *SVP & Global Head, SWAS* T 709 2052 F 709 2996
　　　　　　　　　　　　　　　　　E yves.delaporte@lombardodier.ch
Head of Research　　　　　　　Jochen Gutbrod *VP & Head, SWAS Research* T 709 2048 F 709 2996
　　　　　　　　　　　　　　　　　E jochen.gutbrod@lombardodier.ch

International Equities
Head of Sales　　　　　　　　　Stéphane Trezzini *VP, Europe-USA* T 709 2073 F 709 2916
　　　　　　　　　　　　　　　　　E stephane.trezzini@lombardodier.ch
　　　　　　　　　　　　　　　　　Marcel Romer *VP, Europe-USA* T 709 2400 F 709 2916
　　　　　　　　　　　　　　　　　E marcel.romer@lombardodier.ch
　　　　　　　　　　　　　　　　　Oscar Robadey *VP, Japan-South East Asia* T 709 2133 F 709 2916
　　　　　　　　　　　　　　　　　E oscar.robadey@lombardodier.ch
Head of Trading　　　　　　　　Stéphane Trezzini *VP, Europe-USA* T 709 2073 F 709 2916
　　　　　　　　　　　　　　　　　E stephane.trezzini@lombardodier.ch
　　　　　　　　　　　　　　　　　Marcel Romer *VP, Europe-USA* T 709 2400 F 709 2916
　　　　　　　　　　　　　　　　　E marcel.romer@lombardodier.ch
　　　　　　　　　　　　　　　　　Oscar Robadey *VP, Japan-South East Asia* T 709 2133 F 709 2916
　　　　　　　　　　　　　　　　　E oscar.robadey@lombardodier.ch

Convertibles / Equity-Linked
Head of Syndication　　　　　　Oscar Robadey *VP, Japan-South East Asia* T 709 2133 F 709 2916
　　　　　　　　　　　　　　　　　E oscar.robadey@lombardodier.ch
Head of Syndication; Head of Sales　Giuliano Mazzoni *Assistant Vice President* T 709 2316 F 709 2916
　　　　　　　　　　　　　　　　　E giulian.mazzoni@lombardodier.ch
Head of Trading　　　　　　　　Stéphane Trezzini *VP, Europe-USA* T 709 2073 F 709 2916
　　　　　　　　　　　　　　　　　E stephane.trezzini@lombardodier.ch
　　　　　　　　　　　　　　　　　Oscar Robadey *VP, Japan-South East Asia* T 709 2133 F 709 2916
　　　　　　　　　　　　　　　　　E oscar.robadey@lombardodier.ch

Warrants
Head of Trading　　　　　　　　Oscar Robadey *VP, Japan-South East Asia* T 709 2133 F 709 2916
　　　　　　　　　　　　　　　　　E oscar.robadey@lombardodier.ch
　　　　　　　　　　　　　　　　　Sandrine Bon *Assistant Vice President, Europe-USA* T 709 2087
　　　　　　　　　　　　　　　　　F 709 2916 E sandrine.bon@lombardodier.ch

Equity Repo / Securities Lending
Head　　　　　　　　　　　　　Paul André Pittard *Assistant Manager* T 709 2332 F 709 3216

Money Markets
Fax: 709 2925
Global Head　　　　　　　　　　Charles Heutschi *Senior Vice President* T 709 2535
　　　　　　　　　　　　　　　　　E charles.heutschi@lombardodier.ch

Eurocommercial Paper
Head of Trading　　　　　　　　Kinh-Duong Pham *Assistant Vice President* T 709 2367
　　　　　　　　　　　　　　　　　E kinghuduong.pham@lombardodier.ch

Foreign Exchange
Tel: 709 2535 **Fax:** 709 2925
Global Head of Trading　　　　　Charles Heutschi *Senior Vice President* T 709 2535
　　　　　　　　　　　　　　　　　E charles.heutschi@lombardodier.ch

SWITZERLAND (+41)   www.euromoneydirectory.com

Lombard Odier & Cie (cont)
Risk Management
Tel: 709 2363 **Fax:** 709 3931
Head of Risk Management — James Tadion *Assistant Vice President* T 709 2714
 E james.tadion@lombardodier.ch

Corporate Finance / M&A Advisory
Tel: 709 2283 **Fax:** 709 2899
Head of Mergers & Acquisition — Frank Guemara *Senior Vice President* T 709 2088 F 709 3899

Settlement / Clearing
Tel: 709 2836 **Fax:** 709 2912
Head of Settlement / Clearing — Alain Plattet *Vice President* T 709 2836 F 709 3755
Foreign Exchange Settlement — Didier Ménétrey *Assistant Manager* T 709 2447 F 709 2915
Operations — Christophe Gabriel *Senior Vice President* T 709 2850 F 709 3755

Global Custody
Tel: 709 2390 **Fax:** 709 2913
Regional Head — Laurent Bachmann *Vice President* T 709 2390 F 709 3755

Asset Management
Head — Jean de Haller *Executive Vice President* T 709 2484 F 709 2971
Investment Funds — Yvar Mentha *Executive Vice President* T 709 2272 F 709 2933
Portfolio Management — Jean de Haller *Executive Vice President* T 709 2484 F 709 2971

Other (Asset Management)
Institutional Asset Management — Jean-Michel Mivelaz *Executive Vice President* T 709 2678 F 709 2934

Other Departments
Economic Research — Serge Robin *EVP, Investment Research* T 709 2406 F 702 2918

Administration
Technology & Systems
Information Technology — Ernst Messmer *Executive Vice President* T 709 2679 F 709 3782

Legal / In-House Counsel
Legal & Fiscal — Anne-Marie de Weck *Executive Vice President* T 709 2177 F 709 2969

Other (Administration)
Human Resources — Laurence Berkovits-Ody *Senior Vice President* T 709 2230 F 709 2974

Luzerner Kantonalbank   Subsidiary Company
Pilatusstrasse 12, CH-6002 Lucerne
Tel: (41) 206 2222 **Fax:** (41) 206 2200 **Telex:** 862860, 868239, 862855 **Swift:** LUKB CH 22 60A **Email:** info@lukb.ch
Website: www.lukb.ch

Senior Executive Officers
President — Fritz Studer

Others (Senior Executives)
Executive Vice President — Franz Grüter
 Rudolf Freimann
 Rudolf Stäger

Securities Dealing — Roland Schürmann *Assistant Vice President*
 Othmar Som *Vice President*

General-Lending (DCM, SL)
Head of Corporate Banking — Peter Bieri *FVP, Corporate Banking*

Relationship Manager
Institutional Banking — Oskar Heini *Senior Vice President*
 Robert Lustenberger *Vice President*

Money Markets
Head of Money Markets — Marcel Birrfelder *Vice President*

Money Markets - General
 Peter Achermann *Assistant Vice President*

Foreign Exchange
Head of Foreign Exchange — Marcel Birrfelder *Vice President*

FX Traders / Sales People
 Sergio Sigrist *Assistant Vice President*

Settlement / Clearing
Settlement (General) — Claude Fracheboud *Vice President*

Other Departments
Private Banking — Angelo Elsener *AVP, Private Banking International*
 Bruno Jenny *First VP, Private Banking International*

www.euromoneydirectory.com					SWITZERLAND (+41)

Other Departments (cont)

Economic Research
Administration
Public Relations

Beatrice Ulrich *Vice President, Private Banking International*
Werner Hunkeler *Vice President, Private Banking International*
Werner Mauerhofer *Vice President, Private Banking International*
Daniel Bieri *AVP, Investment Research*

Daniel von Arx *Vice President*

## Merrill Lynch Bank (Suisse) SA					Subsidiary Company

7 rue Munier-Romilly, CH-1211 Geneva 3
PO Box 3070, CH-1211 Geneva 3
Tel: (22) 703 1717 **Fax:** (22) 703 1727
Forex **Tel:** 54 8060; 54 8060; **Fax:** 54 8060
Website: www.ml.com

## Merrill Lynch Capital Markets AG					Full Branch Office

Stauffacherstrasse 5, CH-8039 Zürich
Tel: (1) 297 7400 **Fax:** (1) 291 4460 **Telex:** 817530 MCM CH

## Merrill Lynch International					Full Branch Office

13 route de Florissant, CH-1206 Geneva
Tel: (22) 703 1212 **Fax:** (22) 703 1300

Other Departments
Private Banking

Kathleen Wiltshire *Head of Private Banking*

## Merrill Lynch International Inc					Subsidiary Company

Stockerhof, Stockerstrasse 23, CH-8022 Zürich
Tel: (1) 289 4800 **Fax:** (1) 289 4802
Website: www.ml.com

## MFC Merchant Bank					Head Office

Formerly known as: Lehman Brothers Bank (Switzerland)
6 Cours de Rive, CH-1206 Geneva 3
PO Box 3540, CH-1211 Geneva 3
Tel: (22) 818 2929 **Fax:** (22) 818 2930 **Swift:** MFCM CH GG **Email:** mfc@mfcbank.ch

Senior Executive Officers
Chairman
Chief Executive Officer
Treasurer

Jimmy S H Lee
Claudio Morandi *General Manager*
Jean-Christophe Claude

General-Investment
Head of Investment

Michael J Smith

Other Departments
Private Banking

Urs W Brauder

MIGROSBANK

Seidengasse 12, CH-8023 Zürich
PO Box 6640, Zürich
Tel: (1) 229 8111 **Fax:** (1) 211 1244 **Telex:** 813464 MBZS

Senior Executive Officers
Financial Director
Managing Director / General Manager

Alfred Achermann
Erich Hort

General-Lending (DCM, SL)
Head of Corporate Banking

Alfred Achermann

Euromoney Directory 1999 **1535**

SWITZERLAND (+41)   www.euromoneydirectory.com

MIGROSBANK (cont)
General-Investment
Head of Investment — Alfred Achermann
Risk Management
Head of Risk Management — Thomas Straubinger
Settlement / Clearing
Operations — Fritz Reich
Administration
Head of Administration — Fritz Reich
Head of Marketing — Arnold Bohl
Legal / In-House Counsel
— Monika Hunkeler

Mirabaud & Cie — Head Office

3 Boulevard du Théâtre, CH-1204 Geneva
PO Box 5815, CH-1211 Geneva 11
Tel: (22) 818 2222 **Fax:** (22) 311 6402 **Telex:** 423136 MIRAB CH **Swift:** MIRA CH GG

Senior Executive Officers
Others (Senior Executives)
Pierre Mirabaud *Partner*
Thierry Fauchier-Magnan *Partner*
Yves Mirabaud *Partner*
Antoine Boissier *Partner*
Thierry De Marignac *Partner*
Eric Schaerer *Senior Vice President*

Debt Capital Markets / Fixed Income
Head of Fixed Income — Daniel Debonneville *Vice President*
Equity Capital Markets
Head of Equity Capital Markets — Martial Devaud *Vice President*
Foreign Exchange
Head of Foreign Exchange — René Fiaux *Officer*
Settlement / Clearing
Head of Settlement / Clearing — Marc Ledermann *Vice President*
Other Departments
Correspondent Banking — Eric Schaerer *Senior Vice President*
Administration
Head of Marketing — Eric Schaerer *Senior Vice President*
Technology & Systems
— Jean-Claude Schneider *First Vice President*
Accounts / Audit
— Stefano Granieri *Vice President*
Other (Administration)
Administration & Logistics — Antonio Palma *Senior Vice President*

Mitsubishi Trust & Banking Corporation (Switzerland) Limited

Talacker 41, CH-8001 Zürich
PO Box 774, CH-8039 Zürich
Tel: (1) 212 1515 **Fax:** (1) 212 1061 **Telex:** 816162 MTF CH

Senior Executive Officers
Chairman — Yuji Ohashi
President — Mineo Yamamoto
Chief Operating Officer — Toru Komura

Multi Securities SA — Head Office

7 Avenue, Pictet-de-Rochemont, CH-1211 Geneva 6
Tel: (22) 700 7151 **Fax:** (22) 700 7157 **Reuters:** DEAE

Debt Capital Markets / Fixed Income
Country Head — Jean-Pierre Giroud *Head of Trading*

1536 Euromoney Directory 1999

SWITZERLAND (+41)

Domestic Government Bonds
Head of Trading   Jean-Pierre Giroud *Head of Trading*
Eurobonds
Head of Sales   Christian Hecquet
                                       Barry Harris *Head of Sales*
Head of Trading   Christian Hecquet
Bonds - General
Straight Bonds   Jean-Pierre Giroud *Head of Trading*

Nesbitt Burns Inc   Full Branch Office

17 Boulevard Helvétique, CH-1211 Geneva
PO Box 3093, Geneva
Tel: (22) 735 7688 **Fax:** (22) 735 7674; (22) 700 2378

Senior Executive Officers
Branch Manager   Tiziano Romagnoli

Nesbitt Burns Inc   Full Branch Office

Via Pioda 4, CH-6900 Lugano
Tel: (91) 922 6344 **Fax:** (91) 922 8190

Senior Executive Officers
Vice President   Paolo Bernasconi

Nesbitt Burns Inc   Full Branch Office

Zürcherstrasse 6a, CH-8142 Zürich
Tel: (1) 493 1955 **Fax:** (1) 493 2441

Senior Executive Officers
Vice President & Director   France Iseli-Crevier

Nikko Bank (Switzerland) Limited   Full Branch Office

65 rue de Rhone, 1204 Geneva
Tel: (22) 718 8888 **Fax:** (22) 718 8800

Senior Executive Officers
Managing Director & General Manager   Christopher Graves
General-Investment
Head of Investment   Christopher Graves *Managing Director & General Manager*

Nikko Bank (Switzerland) Limited   Head Office

Utoquai 55, CH-8008 Zürich
Tel: (1) 259 9111 **Fax:** (1) 261 6518 **Telex:** 817222 NZ **Reuters:** NSFR

Senior Executive Officers
Chairman   Tadao Osada
President   Reto A Cavelti
Financial Director   Toshio Koba *General Manager*
Chief Operating Officer   Andreas Engel *General Manager*
Treasurer   Toshio Koba *General Manager*
Debt Capital Markets / Fixed Income
Head of Debt Capital Markets   Alfred Rüttimann *First Vice President*
Foreign Exchange
Head of Foreign Exchange   Andreas Engel *General Manager*
Risk Management
Head of Risk Management   Toshio Koba *General Manager*
Other Departments
Private Banking   Alfred Rüttimann *First Vice President*
Administration
Legal / In-House Counsel
                                       Michael Loretan *Vice President*

Euromoney Directory 1999 **1537**

SWITZERLAND (+41) www.euromoneydirectory.com

Nikko Bank (Switzerland) Limited (cont)
Compliance
                                Michael Loretan *Vice President*
Public Relations
                                Michael Loretan *Vice President*

Nomura Bank (Switzerland) Limited
Kasermenstrasse 1, CH-8021 Zürich
PO Box, CH-8021 Zürich
Tel: (1) 295 7111 **Fax:** (1) 242 2141 **Telex:** 813782

Senior Executive Officers
President   Nobuo Ando ☏ **295 7201**
Others (Senior Executives)
EVP, Head, Support Services Division   N Ueda ☏ **295 7301**
EVP, Head, Securities Division   Kunio Watanabe ☏ **295 7212**
SVP, Head, Administration   Alexander Baldinger ☏ **295 7333**
Equity Capital Markets
Head of Trading   H Matoba ☏ **295 7446**

Nordfinanz Bank Zürich   Head Office
Bahnhofstrasse 1, CH-8001 Zürich
Tel: (1) 228 7111; (1) 211 2272 **Fax:** (1) 228 7447 **Telex:** 812547 NFZ CH **Swift:** NFZB CH ZZ **Cable:** NORDFINANZ

Senior Executive Officers
Chairman   Maurice De Preux
Chief Executive Officer   Peter Haber
Chief Operating Officer   John Varghese
Company Secretary   Judith Weber
Foreign Exchange
Head of Foreign Exchange   Andy Schuemperli
Administration
Head of Administration   Charles Zürrer
Legal / In-House Counsel
                                Dorothea Gleich
Accounts / Audit
                                Karim Dahinden

Norfinsud Partners SA   Head Office
Formerly known as: Finorsud SA
1 Place du Port, CH-1204 Geneva
Tel: (22) 781 1666 **Fax:** (22) 310 5750 **Telex:** 427146 FINO CH

Senior Executive Officers
President & General Manager   François-Xavier Nicoletti
International Division   François-Xavier Nicoletti *President & General Manager*
Others (Senior Executives)
Merchant Banking   François-Xavier Nicoletti *President & General Manager*
Relationship Manager
Oil & Energy Finance   Christian Weyer *Member of the Board*
Syndicated Lending
Loan-Related Activities
Project Finance   François-Xavier Nicoletti *President & General Manager*
Corporate Finance / M&A Advisory
Other (Corporate Finance)
Mergers & Acquisitions   François-Xavier Nicoletti *President & General Manager*
Asset Management
Portfolio Management   Jérôme Joliat *Member of the Board*
Other Departments
Commodities / Bullion   Christian Weyer *Commodities & Countertrade*
Administration
Head of Administration   Marie-Christine Paley *Secretary*

www.euromoneydirectory.com　　　SWITZERLAND (+41)

Obwaldner Kantonalbank
Head Office

Bahnofstrasse 2, CH-6061 Sarnen
Tel: (41) 666 2211 Fax: (41) 666 2260

Senior Executive Officers
President　　　　　　　　　　Markus Villiger
General Manager　　　　　　　Beat Naegeli

PaineWebber International (UK) Limited

13 Cours de Rive, CH-1211 Geneva 3

Debt Capital Markets / Fixed Income
Department: Fixed Income
Tel: (22) 849 0749 Fax: (22) 849 0793

Bonds - General

　　　　　　　　　　Jules Weinberger
　　　　　　　　　　Bruno Buzzi
　　　　　　　　　　Michele Boulade
　　　　　　　　　　Patrick König
　　　　　　　　　　Christine Rohrbach

Equity Capital Markets
Department: Equity Sales
Tel: (22) 849 0707 Fax: (22) 849 0714

Domestic Equities
Head of Sales　　　　　　　　Michael McFadden

PaineWebber International (UK) Limited

41 Talacker, CH-8001 Zürich

Debt Capital Markets / Fixed Income
Department: Fixed Income
Tel: (1) 226 3366 Fax: (1) 226 3399

Bonds - General

　　　　　　　　　　Thomas Stumm
　　　　　　　　　　Uwe Günther
　　　　　　　　　　Michael Mikyska
　　　　　　　　　　Marit Zwahlen

Equity Capital Markets
Department: Equity Sales
Tel: (1) 221 3344 Fax: (1) 221 0790

Other (Domestic Equities)

　　　　　　　　　　Dino Andreani
　　　　　　　　　　Paolo Cerri

Pictet & Cie
Head Office

29 Boulevard Georges-Favon, CH-1211 Geneva
PO Box 5130, CH-1204 Geneva
Tel: (22) 318 2211 Fax: (22) 781 3131 Telex: 422209 pic ch Swift: PICT CH GG Email: mail@pictet.com
Reuters: PICT-V Cable: PICTETCO GENEVA
Website: www.pictet.com

Senior Executive Officers
Senior Partner　　　　　　　　Pictet
Principal Manager　　　　　　Pierre Cogne

Others (Senior Executives)

　　　　　　　　　　Philippe Bertherat *Partner*
　　　　　　　　　　Renaud De Planta *Partner*
　　　　　　　　　　Jacques de Saussure *Partner*
　　　　　　　　　　Claude Demole *Partner*
　　　　　　　　　　Ivan Pictet *Partner*
　　　　　　　　　　Nicolas Pictet *Partner*
　　　　　　　　　　Charles Pictet *Partner*
　　　　　　　　　　René Bruderlin *Director*

SWITZERLAND (+41)   www.euromoneydirectory.com

Pictet & Cie (cont)
Others (Senior Executives) (cont)

	Léo Muller *Director*
	Henri-Christophe Oppenheim *Director*
	Jean Pilloud *Director*
	Michel Rosset *Director*
	Daniel Pineau *Director*
Institutional Banking	Rolf Banz *Senior Manager*
	Patrick Bedat *Senior Manager*
	Kurt Feller *Senior Manager*
	Daniel Wydler *Senior Manager*
	Jean-François Demole *Senior Manager*
	Alain Freymond
	Gérard Huber
	Peter Stolz
Relationship Manager	
Assistant Director	Raymond Bianchi
	Jean-Pierre Gaudet
	Kurt Gautschi
	Richard Joller
	Philippe Lamuniere
	Daniel Wanner

Debt Capital Markets / Fixed Income
Domestic Government Bonds

Head of Sales	Guy Rivoir *Deputy Manager*
	Philippe Treyvaud *Senior Manager*
Head of Trading	Guy Rivoir *Deputy Manager*
	Christian Sculati *Trader*
	Carine Stoffel *Trader*
	Serge Delaude *Trader*

Eurobonds

Head of Syndication	Philippe Treyvaud *Senior Manager*
Head of Syndication; Head of Sales; Head of Trading	Michel Arnold *Manager*

Bonds - General

Ffr, A$	Cédric Maillard *Trader*
US$, C$	Andrea Cristofari *Trader*
DM, Fls	Walter Egli *Trader*
£, Lire, Pta	Alexandre Friederich *Trader*

Libor-Based / Floating-Rate Products

FRN Trading	Andrea Cristofari *Trader*

Fixed-Income Repo

Sales	Salvatore Di Secli *Manager*
	Werner Stich

Equity Capital Markets

Country Head	Patrick Rosenberg *Senior Management*

Domestic Equities

Head of Syndication	Philippe Treyvaud *Senior Manager*

Other (Domestic Equities)

Swiss Stock Exchange	Mirko Sangiorgio *Manager*
	Salvatore Di Secli *Manager*
	Werner Stich *Manager*

International Equities

Head of Trading	Michel Arnold *Manager*

Convertibles / Equity-Linked

Head of Trading	Patrick Serafini

Other (Convertibles)

Convertibles	Michel Arnold *Manager*

Warrants

Head of Sales	Martin Binggeli *Assistant Manager*
Head of Trading	Frederic Borgnand *Trader*
	Xavier Delfini *Trader*
	Martin Binggeli *Assistant Manager*

Equity Repo / Securities Lending

Head	Maurus Wüst *Manager*
Marketing	Christian Dirac *Deputy Manager*

www.euromoneydirectory.com   SWITZERLAND (+41)

Money Markets
Country Head   Jean Vogt *Payments / Settlements*
                                            Michel Conus

Foreign Exchange
Head of Trading   Michel Conus

Risk Management
Country Head   Christophe Oppenheim *Head of Operations*

Corporate Finance / M&A Advisory
Head of Corporate Finance   Daniel Pineau *Director*
Private Equity   Jean Pilloud *Director*

Other (Corporate Finance)
Mergers & Acquisitions   Jean Pilloud *Director*

Settlement / Clearing
Country Head   Kurt Gautschi
                                            Yolanda Baer
Settlement (General)   Jean Vogt *Payments / Settlements*
Operations   Yves Aufranc *Securities Operations*
                                            Maurus Wust
                                            Christophe Oppenheim *Head of Operations*

Global Custody
Regional Head   Richard Humes *Manager*
Fund Administration   Yves Aufranc *Securities Operations*

Other (Global Custody)
                                            Judith Webster *Deputy Manager*
                                            François Babel *Deputy Manager*

Asset Management
Department: Pictet Fund Management SA
Head   Michel Petitpierre *Senior Manager, Fund Management*
                                            Raoul-Philippe Bachmann *Senior Manager, Fund Management*

Other Departments
Commodities / Bullion   Paul Ettlin
Private Banking   Pierre Brunner *Senior Manager*
                                            Heinz Christen *Senior Manager*
                                            Michel Brunner *Senior Manager*
                                            Thomas Egger *Senior Manager*
                                            Christian Mallet *Senior Manager*
                                            Norbert Riesen *Senior Manager*
                                            Jean-Pierre Tobler *Senior Manager*
                                            Antoine Wavre *Senior Manager*
Correspondent Banking   Christophe Oppenheim *Head of Operations*
Economic Research   Jean-Pierre Beguelin *Financial Analyst*
                                            Philippe Treyvaud *Senior Manager*
                                            Mirko Sangiorgio *Manager*
                                            Pierre-Yves Bacchetta *Financial Analyst*

Administration
Technology & Systems
                                            Egon Dettwiler *Manager*
                                            Kurt Dierauer *Senior Manager*
                                            Andrej Volckov *Manager*

Legal / In-House Counsel
Legal   Yves Martignier *Manager*
                                            Philippe Liniger *Manager*
                                            Sylvain Matthey *Manager*

Public Relations
                                            Ricardo Payro *Manager*

Accounts / Audit
Internal Audit   Maurice Bernet *Deputy Manager*
                                            Bernard Jolliet
Accounting Department   Beat Rieder *Deputy Manager*

Other (Administration)
Support Front   Bernard Lutz
Personnel Department   François Conne *Deputy Manager*
General Services   Jean-Pascal Senglet
Support Services   Daniel Pineau *Director*

Euromoney Directory 1999 **1541**

SWITZERLAND (+41)   www.euromoneydirectory.com

PKB Privatbank AG — Full Branch Office

Formerly known as: Privat Kredit Bank

12 rue Charles-Galland, CH-1211 Geneva 6
PO Box 391, Geneva
Tel: (22) 346 9155 **Fax:** (22) 346 4256 **Telex:** 841035 PRIL CH

Senior Executive Officers
Senior Vice President	Marc Roth
Senior Vice President	Pierre-Alain Patry

PKB Privatbank AG — Head Office

Formerly known as: Privat Kredit Bank

Via Pretorio 22, CH-6901 Lugano
Tel: (91) 910 5252 **Fax:** (91) 923 3522; (91) 922 2521 **Telex:** 841035 PRIL CH (General) **Swift:** PKBS CH 22 69A
Cable: PRIKRED

Senior Executive Officers
Chairman	Jean Patry
President	Fernando M Zari

General-Lending (DCM, SL)
Head of Corporate Banking	Giovanni Borsetti *SVP, Corporate Banking*
	Luciano Pasqualini *FVP, Corporate Banking*
	Guglielmo Vaucher de la Croix *FVP, Corporate Banking*
	Anthony Graves *Vice President*

General - Treasury
Head of Treasury	Pierluigi Croce *SVP, Treasury / Foreign Exchange*
	René Grassi *FVP, Treasury / Foreign Exchange*

Asset Management
Portfolio Management	Roberto Berti *FVP, Finance, Portfolio Management*
	Christoph Benz *VP, Finance, Portfolio Management*

Other Departments
Private Banking	Umberto Trabaldo Togna *Senior Vice President*
	Benedetto Fontana *Senior Vice President*
	Gabriella Facchinotti *First Vice President*
	Marco Osella *First Vice President*
	Florio Bernasconi *First Vice President*
	Ferdinando Coda Nunziante *Vice President*
	Raffaella Jaquet *Vice President*

Administration
Head of Administration	Enrico Tonella *Senior Vice President*
	Ermanno Bianchi *Senior Vice President*

Technology & Systems
Organization & Automation	Luigi Rodriguez *Senior Vice President*
	Roberto Algisi *Vice President*

Accounts / Audit
Internal Audit	Sancho Prosperi

Other (Administration)
Personnel	Eveline Obrist *First Vice President*

PKB Privatbank AG — Full Branch Office

Formerly known as: Privat Kredit Bank

Tödistrasse 47, CH-8002 Zürich
Tel: (1) 201 3982 **Fax:** (1) 201 3988 **Telex:** 841035 PRIL CH

Senior Executive Officers
Senior Vice President	Michele Moor
First Vice President	Felix Arnold
Vice President	René Koufmam

www.euromoneydirectory.com SWITZERLAND (+41)

Premex AG
Head Office

Dufourstrasse 101, PO Box, CH-8034 Zürich
Tel: (1) 389 8100 Fax: (1) 389 8105 Reuters: PREZ

Senior Executive Officers
Managing Director   Jürg P Angehrn jpa@bluewin.ch

Risk Management
Other Currency Swap / FX Options Personnel
Bullion - Spot / Swaps   Rolf Siebenmann *First Vice President* trading@bluewin.ch
                            Clive Stepham *Vice President* 389 8111
                            Martin Schletti *Vice President* 389 8111

Other (Exchange-Traded Derivatives)
Bullion - Options   Rolf Straub *Vice President* 389 8181

Privredna banka Zagreb dd / PB Invest u Finanz AG

Lowenstrasse 22, CH-8001 Zürich
Tel: (411) 211 5425 Fax: (411) 211 5424

Rahn & Bodmer

Talstrasse 15, Zürich
Tel: (1) 211 3939

RBC Dominion Securities Inc

20 Avenue de Rumine, CH-1005 Lausanne
Tel: (21) 310 2424 Fax: (21) 310 2414 Telex: 454300 Reuters: Recipient

Senior Executive Officers
President   Jean-Claude Blanc

Renault Finance SA
Head Office

Avenue de Rhodanie 48, CH-1002 Lausanne
PO Box 3720, CH-1002 Lausanne
Tel: (21) 612 0600 Fax: (21) 617 0530 Telex: 454437 REN CH Swift: RENO CH 22 Reuters: RENO

Senior Executive Officers
Chief Executive Officer   Christian Polin

Money Markets
Department: Eurocurrency Division
Global Head   Georges-Albert Despland *Senior Vice President*

Other (Wholesale Deposits)
Eurocurrency Deposits   Patrick Brunet *Assistant Vice President*
                           Dominique Girard Soppet *Assistant Vice President*
                           Philippe Goll

Foreign Exchange
Global Head   Didier Landry *Vice President*

FX Traders / Sales People
                 Guy Voegeli *Assistant Vice President*
                 Raphaël Jäggi *Dealer*

Settlement / Clearing
Settlement (General)   Due Doan *Assistant Vice President*
                          Bernadette Steulet *Clearing Accounts Officer*

Republic National Bank of New York (Suisse) SA

2 Place du Lac, CH-1211 Geneva
PO Box 3580, Geneva
Tel: (22) 705 5555 Fax: (22) 311 9960 Telex: 427153 RNB CH

Senior Executive Officers
Chairman   Edmond J Safra
President   Sem Almaleh

Euromoney Directory 1999 **1543**

SWITZERLAND (+41) www.euromoneydirectory.com

Republic National Bank of New York (Suisse) SA (cont)
Senior Executive Officers (cont)
Financial Director Clauge Frossarg
General Manager Joseph Benhamou
Secretary to the President Van Hoorn ☏ 705 5323/5530
Administration
Corporate Communications
  Alex Bruggmann *Head* ☏ 705 5246 ℻ 705 5617
Other (Administration)
Personnel Roland Freudigvr *Head*

Royal Bank of Canada (Suisse)   Subsidiary Company
Rue Diday 6, CH-1204 Geneva
PO Box 5696, CH-1211 Geneva 11
Tel: (22) 819 4242 **Fax:** (22) 819 4343 **Telex:** 422147 **Swift:** ROYC CH GG **Email:** rbcgeneva@ibm.net **Reuters:** RBCG
Website: www.royalbank.com

Senior Executive Officers
VP & General Manager Thomas (Tom) Emch ☏ 819 4243
Financial Director Antonello Francescato *Senior Manager, Administration & Operations* ☏ 819 4326
Treasurer René Schaller *Senior Manager, Forex & Money Market* ☏ 819 4281
Other Departments
Private Banking Jürg Hofer *Senior Manager* ☏ 819 4267
Administration
Technology & Systems
EDP José Alvarez *Senior Manager* ☏ 819 4329
Legal / In-House Counsel
Legal & Trust Jérôme Cosandier *Senior Manager* ☏ 819 4308
Compliance
  Jacques Berra *Manager* ☏ 819 4312

Rüd, Blass & Cie AG Bankgeschäft   Subsidiary Company
Selnaustrasse 32, PO Box, CH-8039 Zürich
Tel: (1) 217 2111 **Fax:** (1) 211 7057 **Telex:** 814211

Senior Executive Officers
Chairman of the Board Rolf Hänggi
Chief Executive Officer Reto Kuhl *Managing Director*
Others (Senior Executives)
Trading Hansruedi Hardmeier *Head of Trading*
Debt Capital Markets / Fixed Income
Tel: 211 3710 **Fax:** 211 8586
Head of Debt Capital Markets Rolf Studer
Equity Capital Markets
Tel: 211 3710 **Fax:** 211 8586
Head of Equity Capital Markets Paul Loepfe
Money Markets
Head of Money Markets Markus Probst
Foreign Exchange
Head of Foreign Exchange Markus Probst
Risk Management
Head of Risk Management Roger Leu
Settlement / Clearing
Head of Settlement / Clearing Robert Diener
Other Departments
Private Banking Daniel Wittmer *Head*
  Reto Kuhl *Managing Director*

Rüegg Bank AG

Talstrasse 66, CH-8039 Zürich
Tel: (1) 218 5611 Fax: (1) 211 6416 Telex: 812972 Swift: RUEG CH ZZ

Senior Executive Officers

Others (Senior Executives)
R Cudkowicz *Manager*

Russian Commercial Bank Limited   Subsidiary Company

Alternative trading name: Russische Kommerzial Bank AG
Schützengasse 1, CH-8023 Zürich
PO Box 6039, CH-8023 Zürich
Tel: (1) 218 1111 Fax: (1) 221 0779 Telex: 812644 RKBZ CH Swift: RKBZ CH ZZ Reuters: RKBZ
Website: www.rkb.ch

Senior Executive Officers
Financial Director   Walter Meier *Managing Director*
Treasurer   Andrei B Balashov *Managing Director*
General Manager   Ildar K Nigmetzanov

Sakura Bank (Schweiz) AG   Subsidiary Company

Lintheschergasse 10, CH-8001 Zürich
PO Box 2029, CH-8021 Zürich
Tel: (1) 212 3066 Fax: (1) 212 3270 Telex: 813826 MITK CH Reuters: MFSA-J

Senior Executive Officers
Chairman   Tsugumasa Kojima
President   Kazuo Suga
Executive Vice President Macao Sujimoto
Senior Vice President   Heinz Weidmann

Others (Senior Executives)
Masami Hagiwara *Vice President*
Yasushi Morikawa *Vice President*
Masahiro Abe *Vice President*
Samu Ikegami *Vice President*

Debt Capital Markets / Fixed Income
Head of Debt Capital Markets   Yasushi Morikawa *Vice President*

Asset-Backed Securities / Securitization
Regional Head   Masami Hagiwara *VP, Securities Trading*

Equity Capital Markets
Head of Equity Capital Markets Yasushi Morikawa *Vice President*

Money Markets
Head of Money Markets   Masami Hagiwara *Vice President*

Foreign Exchange
Head of Foreign Exchange   Masami Hagiwara *Vice President*

Settlement / Clearing
Head of Settlement / Clearing   Samu Ikegami *Vice President*

Other Departments
Private Banking   Masahiro Abe *Vice President*

Administration

Other (Administration)
General Affairs   Heinz Weidmann *Senior Vice President*

SWITZERLAND (+41)   www.euromoneydirectory.com

Salomon Brothers International Limited
Full Branch Office

Alternative trading name: Salomon Brothers Finanz AG
Schipfe 2, CH-8001 Zürich
PO Box 4406, CH-8022 Zürich
Tel: (1) 215 4500 **Fax:** (1) 215 4590; (1) 215 4591 **Telex:** 815259 **Reuters:** SAZA
OTC Equity Derivatives Sales Tel: 215 4525; European Equity Sales Tel: 215 4554; Financial Futures & Commodities Tel: 215 4666; US Equity Sales Tel: 215 4545

Senior Executive Officers
Managing Director — David Turnbull

Others (Senior Executives)
Branch Manager — Reto Leibacher *Director*
Office Manager — Denise de Vries-Münger *Vice President*

Equity Capital Markets
Other (International Equity)
US Equities — Reto Leibacher *Director*
European Equities — Beat Schädler *Vice President*

Risk Management
Country Head — Pierre Schaub *Vice President*

OTC Equity Derivatives
Head — Jan Auspurg *Vice President*

Settlement / Clearing
Department: Commodities
Head of Settlement / Clearing — Giovanni Russo

Sanwa Bank (Schweiz) AG
Subsidiary Company

Badenerstrasse 6, CH-8004 Zürich
Tel: (1) 296 1400 **Fax:** (1) 296 1496 **Telex:** 813989 SBCH **Reuters:** SAWA

Senior Executive Officers
President — Yoshikazu Yabe

Equity Capital Markets
Head of Equity Capital Markets — Kentaro Akiyama *Vice President*
Head of Sales — Anne Brägger *Vice President*

Other Departments
Private Banking — Naoto Kawahara *First Vice President*

Administration
Head of Administration — Hans-Peter Schück *Senior Vice President*

Schweizer Verband der RaiffeisenBanken
Full Branch Office

Alternative trading name: Union Suisse des Banques Raiffeisen
Vadianstrasse 17, CH-9001 St Gallen
Tel: (71) 225 8888 **Fax:** (71) 225 8887 **Telex:** 881350 (General), 881432 RAI CH **Swift:** RAIF CH 22
Forex Fax: 54 8060

Senior Executive Officers
Senior Vice President — Felix Walker
Senior Vice President — René Bentele
Senior Vice President — Pierin Vincenz
Senior Vice President — Kurt Zobrist
Senior Vice President — Thomas Scherrer

Others (Senior Executives)
Marcel Kesseli *VP, Logistics*
Management — Pierin Vincenz *Senior Vice President*

General-Lending (DCM, SL)
Head of Corporate Banking — Thomas Scherrer *SVP, Credit*
Heinz Hedinger *SVP, Investment Banking*

General - Treasury
Head of Treasury — Heinz Hedinger *Treasury*

Relationship Manager
Stock Exchange — Claude Brasey *Head*

Debt Capital Markets / Fixed Income
Country Head — Heinz Hedinger *SVP, Government & Domestic Securities*

www.euromoneydirectory.com   SWITZERLAND (+41)

Syndicated Lending

Other (Syndicated Lending)
Syndicated Loans and Bonds   Alberto Gelpi *Head*

Loan-Related Activities
Trade Finance; Project Finance   Thomas Scherrer *Senior Vice President*

Other (Trade Finance)
Export / Import Finance; Mortgage Finance   Thomas Scherrer *Senior Vice President*

Foreign Exchange
Head of Foreign Exchange   René Lüthi *Head*

Corporate Finance / M&A Advisory
Country Head   Thomas Scherrer *Senior Vice President*

Settlement / Clearing
Operations   Urs Bleichenbacher *Vice President*
                                   Marcel Kesseli *VP, Logistics*

Other Departments
Private Banking   Thomas Scherrer *Senior Vice President*
Correspondent Banking   Heinz Hedinger *Senior Vice President*

Administration

Technology & Systems
                                   Urs Bleichenbacher *Vice President*

Legal / In-House Counsel
                                   Walo Bauer *First Vice President*

Other (Administration)
Personnel & Librarian   Franz Würth *Vice President*

Schwyzer Kantonalbank (SKB)

PO Box 6431, Bahnhofstrasse, Schwyz
Tel: (41) 819 4111 **Fax:** (41) 811 7355

Senior Executive Officers
Chief Executive Officer   Hansjorg Koller
Financial Director   Franz Steiner
Treasurer   Paul Laimbacher
International Division   Konrad Ochlin

General-Lending (DCM, SL)
Head of Corporate Banking   Eugene Diegheln

General-Investment
Head of Investment   Thomas Amstutz

Debt Capital Markets / Fixed Income
Head of Debt Capital Markets   Werner Sehibig

Government Bonds
Head of Sales   Bruno Hickin
Head of Trading   Thomas Amstutz

Eurobonds
Head of Sales   Bruno Hickin
Head of Trading   Thomas Amstutz

Syndicated Lending

Loan-Related Activities
Trade Finance   Paul Laimbacher

Money Markets
Head of Money Markets   Thomas Amstutz

Foreign Exchange
Head of Foreign Exchange   Konrad Ochlin

Risk Management
Head of Risk Management   Andrew Scegubarth

Asset Management
Head   Paul Laimbacher

Euromoney Directory 1999   **1547**

SWITZERLAND (+41)   www.euromoneydirectory.com

Société Générale Bank & Trust
Full Branch Office
Bleicherweg 1, PO Box, CH-8022 Zürich
Tel: (1) 220 7111 **Fax:** (1) 211 9941; (1) 220 7409 **Telex:** 823789 **Swift:** SGAB CH ZZ

Senior Executive Officers
Chief Executive Officer	Antoine Larue de Charlus ☎ **220 7224**
Financial Director	Jost Baumgartner ☎ **220 7224**
Chief Operating Officer	Bruno Lèbre ☎ **220 7660**
Treasurer	Marc Maria Van Roessel ☎ **445 5865**

Debt Capital Markets / Fixed Income
Tel: 445 5874 **Fax:** 220 7369

Global Head	Jost Baumgartner ☎ **220 7224**

Domestic Government Bonds
Head of Sales; Head of Trading	Fritz Voegeli ☎ **445 5827**

Non-Domestic Government Bonds
	Martin Sauser ☎ **445 5896**
	Doris Hofer ☎ **445 5826**
	Urs Schneider ☎ **445 5898**
	Alexander Stadelmann ☎ **445 5897**

Eurobonds
Head of Sales	Fritz Voegeli ☎ **445 5827**

Equity Capital Markets
Tel: 220 7872 **Fax:** 220 7710

Global Head	Werner Bernhard ☎ **220 7851**

Domestic Equities
Head of Origination; Head of Sales	Werner Bernhard ☎ **220 7851**
Head of Trading	Peter Schoedler ☎ **220 7810**
Head of Research	Beat Kaeser ☎ **220 7384**

Other (Domestic Equities)
SOFFEX (Financial Futures & Traded Options)	Narkus Keller ☎ **220 7816**

Other (International Equity)
Pan-European Equities	Douglas Bennett ☎ **220 7863**

Other (Convertibles)
International Convertibles	Douglas Bennett ☎ **220 7863**
Swfrs	Fritz Voegeli ☎ **445 5827**

Syndicated Lending
Tel: 220 7223 **Fax:** 220 7254

Global Head of Origination; Head of Syndication; Head of Trading; Recovery	Giampaolo Fabris
Head of Credit Committee	Franck Wilhelm ☎ **220 7132**

Loan-Related Activities
Trade Finance; Project Finance	Giampaolo Fabris

Money Markets
Tel: 445 5875 **Fax:** 220 7369

Global Head	Jost Baumgartner ☎ **220 7224**

Domestic Commercial Paper
Head of Sales; Head of Trading	Marc Maria Van Roessel ☎ **445 5865**

Eurocommercial Paper
Head of Sales; Head of Trading	Marc Maria Van Roessel ☎ **445 5865**

Wholesale Deposits
Marketing	Alex Glowacki ☎ **220 7398**
Head of Sales	Jürg Schlittler ☎ **220 7867**

Foreign Exchange
Tel: 220 7868 **Fax:** 220 7494

Global Head	Jost Baumgartner ☎ **220 7224**
Head of Institutional Sales; Corporate Sales	Jürg Schlittler ☎ **220 7867**
Head of Trading	André Fuerbringer ☎ **220 7868**

FX Traders / Sales People
US$ / DM	Peter Schmid ☎ **220 7846**
DM / Swfr	Robert Luetolf ☎ **220 7847**
US$ / Swfr	Martin Grolimund ☎ **220 7868**
Cross	Roland Studer
	Ariane Bassat
	Daniel Staehli ☎ **220 7867**

www.euromoneydirectory.com　　　　　　　　　**SWITZERLAND (+41)**

Risk Management
Tel: 220 7592 **Fax:** 220 7494
Global Head　　　　　　　　　　　　　Jost Baumgartner ☎ **220 7224**

Fixed Income Derivatives / Risk Management
Global Head　　　　　　　　　　　　　Marc Maria Van Roessel ☎ **445 5865**
IR Swaps Sales / Marketing　　　　　　Sylvie Chassard ☎ **220 7866**
IR Swaps Trading　　　　　　　　　　Marc Maria Van Roessel ☎ **445 5865**
IR Options Sales / Marketing; IR Options　Sylvie Chassard ☎ **220 7866**
Trading

Foreign Exchange Derivatives / Risk Management
Cross-Currency Swaps, Sales / Marketing　Marc Maria Van Roessel ☎ **445 5865**
Vanilla FX option Sales; Vanilla FX option　Roberto Pegoraro ☎ **220 7866**
Trading

Exotic Options (Barriers, Range, Timers, Digitals, Faders etc)
Sales　　　　　　　　　　　　　　　Roberto Pegoraro *Forex* ☎ **220 7866**
Trading　　　　　　　　　　　　　　Sylvie Chassard *IR* ☎ **220 7866**

Settlement / Clearing
Tel: 220 7422 **Fax:** 220 7549
Regional Head　　　　　　　　　　　Verena Roth ☎ **220 7422**
Equity Settlement; Fixed-Income Settlement　Rosa-Maria Marchini ☎ **220 7520**
Derivatives Settlement　　　　　　　　René Untersander ☎ **220 7515**
Foreign Exchange Settlement　　　　　Walter Soell ☎ **220 7471**

Other Departments
Private Banking　　　　　　　　　　Regis De Reilhac ☎ **220 7270**
Correspondent Banking　　　　　　　Josef Kornmann ☎ **220 7418**

Administration
Technology & Systems
　　　　　　　　　　　　　　　　　André Helfer ☎ **220 7680**

Legal / In-House Counsel
　　　　　　　　　　　　　　　　　Matthias Ley ☎ **220 7236**

Compliance
　　　　　　　　　　　　　　　　　Matthias Ley ☎ **220 7236**

Svenska Handelsbanken　　　　　　　　　Representative Office
Gotthard Strasse 21, CH-8002 Zürich
PO Box 4387, CH-8022 Zürich
Tel: (1) 287 1020 **Fax:** (1) 287 1029

Senior Executive Officers
Chief Representative　　　　　　　　Gösta Bergholtz

Thurgauer KantonalBank　　　　　　　　　Head Office
Bankplatz 1, CH-8570 Weinfelden
Tel: (71) 626 6111 **Fax:** (71) 626 6368

Senior Executive Officers
Tel: 626 6111
Chairman　　　　　　　　　　　　　Peter Lindt
Chief Executive Officer　　　　　　　Theo Prinz *President of the Executive Board*
Financial Director　　　　　　　　　Hans-Peter Vogt *Member of the Executive Board*

Debt Capital Markets / Fixed Income
Head of Debt Capital Markets　　　　Adrian Stadler *Member of Management* ☎ **626 6280**

Money Markets
Head of Money Markets　　　　　　　Willy Müller *Member of Management* ☎ **626 6315**

Foreign Exchange
Head of Foreign Exchange　　　　　　Ralph Maissen *Member of Management* ☎ **626 6333**

Other Departments
Tel: 626 6111
Proprietary Trading　　　　　　　　　Ernst Albrecht *Member of Senior Management*
Private Banking; Correspondent Banking　Hans-Peter Vogt *Member of the Executive Board*

Administration
Tel: 626 6111
Technology & Systems
　　　　　　　　　　　　　　　　　Kurt Bill *Member of Executive*

Euromoney Directory 1999　**1549**

SWITZERLAND (+41)   www.euromoneydirectory.com

Thurgauer KantonalBank (cont)
Legal / In-House Counsel
                                Detlev Basse *Legal Counsellor*
Compliance
                                Detlev Basse *Legal Counsellor*
Public Relations
                                Martin Briner *Member of Senior Management*

Tokai Bank (Schweiz) AG   Subsidiary Company
Formerly known as: Tokai Finanz (Schweiz) AG
                    Nüschelerstrasse 30, CH-8001 Zürich
                    PO Box 4189, CH-8022 Zürich
          Tel: (1) 212 6464 **Fax:** (1) 212 6550 **Telex:** 822244 **Reuters:** TFZA-J
Senior Executive Officers
President   Fusayoshi Nakanishi
Deputy President   Masahiro Masui
Chief Operating Officer   Rolf Kriech *Senior Vice President*
Others (Senior Executives)
                                Koichi Tajima *First Vice President*
Debt Capital Markets / Fixed Income
Head of Debt Capital Markets; Country Head Koichi Tajima *First Vice President*
Equity Capital Markets
Head of Equity Capital Markets   Koichi Tajima *First Vice President*
Administration
Head of Administration   Rolf Kriech *Senior Vice President*
Accounts / Audit
                                Rolf Kriech *Senior Vice President*

Toyo Trust & Banking (Schweiz) AG
                    Falkenstrasse 23, CH-8008 Zürich
                    Tel: (1) 252 7511 **Fax:** (1) 252 2587 **Telex:** 814645
Senior Executive Officers
General Manager   Yuichi Sakuma
Deputy General Manager   Hidetsugu Ogawa
Others (Senior Executives)
                                Hans Peter Haltinner *Director*
Debt Capital Markets / Fixed Income
Head of Debt Capital Markets Mikako Yoshioka *Assistant Vice President*
Equity Capital Markets
Head of Equity Capital Markets Mikako Yoshioka *Assistant Vice President*

Tradition SA
                    11 rue de Langallerie, CH-1003 Lausanne
                    PO Box 2400, CH-1002 Lausanne
          Tel: (21) 343 5252 **Fax:** (21) 343 5550 **Telex:** 454501 TRAD **Reuters:** TRDL **Cable:** TRADITION LAUSANNE
          Capital Markets Tel: 343 5350; **Eurocurrency Deposits, FRAs Tel:** 343 5400; **Forex Forwards Tel:** 343 5300
Senior Executive Officers
Chairman   Guido Boehi

UBS Securities Limited
                    Gartenstrasse 9, CH-4052 Basle
                    PO Box, CH-4002 Basle
                    Tel: (61) 205 1515 **Fax:** (61) 205 1555
Senior Executive Officers
Others (Senior Executives)
Rates Distribution   Stephan Voegelin

1550   Euromoney Directory 1999

www.euromoneydirectory.com   SWITZERLAND (+41)

UBS Securities Limited
35 rue des Noirettes, CH-1227 Geneva
PO Box 2600, CH-1211 Geneva 2
Tel: (22) 389 5222 **Fax:** (22) 388 8240

Senior Executive Officers
Others (Senior Executives)
Rates Distribution   Olivier Schmid

UBS Securities Limited
Palazzo Suglio, Via Cantonale 18, CH-6928 Lugano
PO Box 2837, CH-6901 Lugano
Tel: (91) 801 8500 **Fax:** (91) 801 8455

Senior Executive Officers
Others (Senior Executives)
Rates Distribution   Ueli Gnos

UBS Securities Limited
Warburg Dillon Read Center, Europastrasse 1, CH-8152 Zürich
PO Box, CH-8098 Zürich
Tel: (1) 874 1111 **Fax:** (1) 874 1200

Senior Executive Officers
Others (Senior Executives)
Rates Distribution   Robert Bertschinger

Union Bancaire Privée   Head Office
96/98 rue du Rhône, PO Box 1320, CH-1211 Geneva 1
Tel: (22) 819 2111 **Fax:** (22) 819 2200 **Telex:** 415 423 **Email:** ubp@ubp.ch

Senior Executive Officers
Chairman   Edgar de Picciotto
Vice Chairman   Jean Zwahlen
President   Guy de Picciotto

Others (Senior Executives)
Private Banking & Lugano Branch   Ilan Hayim
Asset Management   Daniel de Picciotto
Financial Markets, London Branch Michael de Picciotto
Zurich Branch & Nordfinanz Bank Zurich   Maurice de Preux
Management Development   Maxime Morand
Risk Control & Administration   Pierre Pissaloux
Secretary General   Jean-Claude Manghardt

Debt Capital Markets / Fixed Income
Bonds - General
Securities   Urs Ruppli

Foreign Exchange
FX Traders / Sales People
Forex   Paul-Marie Dacorogna
Stock Exchange   Pascal Traber

Settlement / Clearing
Operations   Rudolf Trachsel
Back-Office   Denis Bollut

Other Departments
Economic Research   Marc Polydor *Financial Analysis and Research*

Administration
Technology & Systems
Information Management   Olivier Barraud
Computer   Jean-Louis Amez-Droz

Legal / In-House Counsel
                                  Georges Pittet

SWITZERLAND (+41)   www.euromoneydirectory.com

Union Bancaire Privée (cont)
Other (Administration)
Bank Relations   Hans Kurman
Administration Change & Investment   Jean-Claude Maegerli
Human Resources   Evelyne Gouzes

United Bank AG (Zürich)

Feldeggstrasse 55, CH-8008 Zürich
PO Box 1176, CH-8034 Zürich
Tel: (1) 422 9449 **Fax:** (1) 422 9444 **Telex:** 816305

Senior Executive Officers
Chairman   Zubyr I Soomro
Manager   Peter E J Singer

United European Bank   Head Office

Formerly known as: United Overseas Bank
11 Quai des Bergues, CH-1201 Geneva
PO Box 2280, CH-1211 Geneva 11
Tel: (22) 906 2111 **Fax:** (22) 732 3002 **Telex:** 412100 UOB CH **Swift:** UOBG CH GG **Cable:** UTRAFBANK GENEVA

Senior Executive Officers
General Manager   Bernard Fleury
Director & General Secretary   Philippe Vion

Others (Senior Executives)
Commercial Division   Raymond Liefooghe *Deputy General Manager*
Adviser to General Manager   Robert Equery *Executive Vice President*

Money Markets

Money Markets - General
                                        Pierre Apruzzese

Foreign Exchange

FX Traders / Sales People
                                        Pierre Apruzzese

Other Departments
Private Banking   Patrick Sulliger *Executive Vice President*
                                        Marcel Gaillard *Deputy General Manager*
Correspondent Banking   Cinzia Maurer-Tatti

Administration

Legal / In-House Counsel
                                        Asma Benelmouffok *Chief Legal Counsel*

Valcourt SA

2 rue Jean Petitot, CH-1211 Geneva 11
PO Box 5620, Geneva
Tel: (22) 312 1120 **Fax:** (22) 312 0948 **Email:** valcourt@bluewin.ch **Bloomberg:** Valcourtici@Bloomberg.Net

Senior Executive Officers
Chairman   Anthony Conway-Fell

Debt Capital Markets / Fixed Income

Eurobonds
Head of Sales   Mike Conway
                                        Robert Wellhauser

Settlement / Clearing
Fixed-Income Settlement   Rene-Pierre Balet
Settlement (General)   Sylvie Coquoz

1552 Euromoney Directory 1999

www.euromoneydirectory.com   SWITZERLAND (+41)

Viking Ship Finance Limited
Head Office

Formerly known as: Finance Company Viking
Claridenstrasse 40, CH-8002 Zürich
PO Box 645, CH-8021 Zürich
Tel: (1) 201 4344 **Fax:** (1) 234 4066 **Email:** shipfinance@viking.ch

Senior Executive Officers
Chairman	Robert A Sutz
President & Chief Executive Officer	Erwin J Zehnder
Treasurer	Werner Isenring
Company Secretary	Sonja Oesch

Vontobel Holding AG

Tödistrasse 27, CH-8022 Zürich
Tel: (1) 283 5900 **Fax:** (1) 283 7500
Website: www.vontobel.ch

Senior Executive Officers
Chairman	Hans-Dieter Vontobel
Financial Director	Walter Kaeser *Chief Financial Officer*

Wako Bank (Switzerland) Limited
Head Office

Schuetzengasse 4, CH-8023 Zürich
Tel: (1) 211 0011 **Fax:** (1) 221 3366; (1) 221 3377 **Telex:** 814590 WAK CH

Senior Executive Officers
Chairman	Shigeo Sekita
President	Hiromichi Tomiyama
President	Noboru Iwakura
Chief Operating Officer	Daniel Brunner

Equity Capital Markets
Country Head	Hiromichi Tomiyama

Syndicated Lending
Country Head	Hiromichi Tomiyama

Risk Management
Country Head	Daniel Brunner

Corporate Finance / M&A Advisory
Country Head	Paul Thurig ☏ **211 0528**

Warburg Dillon Read

Gartenstrasse 9, CH-4052 Basle
PO Box, CH-4002 Basle
Tel: (61) 288 2020 **Fax:** (61) 288 9630

Senior Executive Officers
Unit Head	Walter Bommer

Others (Senior Executives)
Rates Distribution CHF	Urs Gfeller

Equity Capital Markets
Other (Domestic Equities)
Equities & Derivatives Distribution	Daniel Wehrli

Syndicated Lending
Other (Trade Finance)
Trade Finance CH	Franz Gutzwiller

Foreign Exchange
FX Traders / Sales People
FX Sales	Marcel Imbach
FX Bank Notes Trading	Armin Weisskopf
FX Precious Metals	Anton Kleiber

Euromoney Directory 1999 **1553**

SWITZERLAND (+41)　　　　　www.euromoneydirectory.com

Warburg Dillon Read

35 rue des Noirettes, CH-1227 Geneva
PO Box 2600, CH-1211 Geneva 2
Tel: (22) 388 1111 Fax: (22) 388 4883

Senior Executive Officers
Others (Senior Executives)
Unit Head   Jean-Marie Martin

Equity Capital Markets
Other (Domestic Equities)
Equities   Jean-Marie Martin

Syndicated Lending
Other (Trade Finance)
Trade Finance Origination   Francis Piccand
Trade Finance Document. Prod.   Daniel Nuesch
Trade Finance Guarantees   Corinne Morgenthaler
Structured Trade & Commodity Finance   Yves LeHur

Foreign Exchange
FX Traders / Sales People
Bank Notes Trading   Yves Bourquin
FX Precious Metals   Andeas Maag
FX Sales   Yves Bergin
Rates Distribution CHF   Thierry Spicher

Warburg Dillon Read

Palazzo Suglio, Via Cantonale 18, CH-6928 Lugano
PO Box 2837, CH-6901 Lugano
Tel: (91) 801 7111 Fax: (91) 801 8569

Senior Executive Officers
Others (Senior Executives)
Unit Head   Philipp Baerlocher

Equity Capital Markets
Other (Domestic Equities)
Equities   Rolf Winkelmann

Syndicated Lending
Trade Finance   Bruno Butti
Other (Trade Finance)
Structured Trade & Commodity Finance   Leonardo Monopoli

Foreign Exchange
FX Traders / Sales People
FX Precious Metals & Banknotes   Mauro Rossi
FX Sales   Andrea Bertoglio

Warburg Dillon Read

Warburg Dillon Read Center, Europastrasse 1, CH-8152 Zürich
PO Box, CH-8098 Zürich
Tel: (1) 239 1111 Fax: (1) 239 2075

Senior Executive Officers
Others (Senior Executives)
Unit Head   Martin Bachem

Debt Capital Markets / Fixed Income
Non-Domestic Government Bonds
Fixed Income Switzerland   Felix Ronner
Fixed Income Trading   Marcus Guhl
                                        Armin Bischofberger
Fixed Income Execution   Hans Schuler
Debt Capital Markets Origination   Theo Felix

Bonds - General
Convertible Bond Sales   Zeno Dürr
Rates Distribution   Marcel Strobel

SWITZERLAND (+41)

Bonds - General (cont)
Rates Syndication — Ronald Hinterkircher
Rates Management — Andreas Amschwand
Rates STIR — Stephan Schibli
Rates MM, Fwds & Fiduciaries — Juerg Eberle

Equity Capital Markets
Head of Equity Capital Markets — Tino Tratschin

Other (Domestic Equities)
Equities Management — Daniel Schweizer
Swiss Equities Trading — Andreas Walder
 — Andi Haeberli
Swiss Equities Salestrading — Willi Bucher
Swiss Equities Sales — Thomas Wyler
Equities Structured Products — Vito Schiro

Other (International Equity)
International Equities Trading — Simon Aeschbacher
International Equities Sales — Helmut Fleischmann

Equity Research
Head of Equity Research — Andreas Vogler

Equity Repo / Securities Lending
Head — Felix Oegerli

Syndicated Lending
Other (Trade Finance)
Global Trade Finance — Dieter Kiefer
Trade Finance — Peter Furrer
Structured Trade & Commodity Finance — Patricia Horgan Hertig

Foreign Exchange
FX Traders / Sales People
FX Trading — Christoph Meier
FX Sales — Martin Wiedmann
FX Bank Notes Trading — Werner Stalder
FX Precious Metals Sales — Martin Gauch

Risk Management
Other (Exchange-Traded Derivatives)
Asset Derivatives Marketing — André Imhoff

Exchange-Traded Derivatives
Head — Willi Isenring

Corporate Finance / M&A Advisory
Country Head — Chris Tanner
 — Dieter Probst

Other (Corporate Finance)
Global Advisory Group — Carsten ten Brink
Leveraged Finance Group — Marie-Louise Faering

Wegelin & Co, General Partners Bruderer, Hummler & Co

Bohl 17, CH-9000 St Gallen
PO Box, CH-9004 St Gallen
Tel: (71) 242 6464 **Fax:** (71) 242 6465 **Telex:** 883622 **Swift:** WEGE CH ZG **Email:** wegelin@wegelin.ch

Senior Executive Officers
Chief Executive Officer — O Bruderer *Partner*
 — Konrad Hummler *Partner*
Manager — Gallus Mayer

Westdeutsche Landesbank (Schweiz) AG — Subsidiary Company

Bleicherweg 50, CH-8002 Zürich
PO Box, CH-8039 Zürich
Tel: (1) 285 7411 **Fax:** (1) 201 2652 **Telex:** 815386 **Swift:** WELA CH ZZ **Reuters:** WLSD-H

Senior Executive Officers
President — Gerhard Roggemann
Chief Executive Officer — Wolfgang Spehr

SWITZERLAND (+41) www.euromoneydirectory.com

Zürcher Kantonalbank Head Office

Bahnhofstrasse 9, CH-8001 Zürich
PO Box 715, CH-8010 Zürich
Tel: (1) 220 1111 **Fax:** (1) 211 1525 **Telex:** 812140 ZKB CH **Swift:** ZKBK CH ZZ **Reuters:** ZKBX, ZKBZ
Website: www.zkb.ch

Senior Executive Officers
Chairman of the Board — Hermann Weigold
Vice Chairman of the Board — Martin Zollinger
Vice Chairman of the Board — Rolf Krämer
President of the Executive Board — Paul Hasenfratz

Others (Senior Executives)
Private Banking, Trading Operations Int'l — Jürg Schwarz *Member, Executive Board*
Banking
Retail Banking — Gottfried Weber *Member, Executive Board*
Corporate Banking — Ulrich Naef *Member, Executive Board*
Logistics — Hans F Vögeli *Member, Executive Board*
Credit Management — Charles Stettler *Member, Senior Management*
Corporate Customers, Corporate Center — Bruno Meier *Member, Senior Management*
International Banking — Peter Huwyler *Head, International Banking*

General - Treasury
Head of Treasury — Marco Stadler *Member, Senior Management*

Relationship Manager
Central Services — Walter Meyer *Member, Senior Management*
Department: Germany, Austria, USA, Canada, Middle East, North Europe

Others (Senior Executives)
International Banking — Jürg Reichen *Head of Region 1*
Department: Middle / East Europe, Asia, Japan, China, Australia, N Zealand

Others (Senior Executives)
International Banking — Jürg Reichen *Head of Region 1*
Department: S Europe, Turkey, Benelux, France, GB, L America, Africa

Others (Senior Executives)
International Banking — Markus Stoll *Head of Region 2*
Department: Switzerland & Liechtenstein

Others (Senior Executives)
International Banking — Markus Stoll *Head of Region 2*

Syndicated Lending

Other (Trade Finance)
Documentary Credits — Edwin Schmuki
Real Estate Services — Kurt Rebmann
Export Financing — Edwin Schmuki

Risk Management
Head of Risk Management — Edwin Schmuki

Settlement / Clearing
Operations — Eugen Brenner *Trading Operations*

Asset Management
Head — Christoph Lanter *Member, Senior Management*

Other Departments
Private Banking — Heinz Waech *Member, Senior Management*
Economic Research — Marco Curti *Investment Research*
Philipp Halbherr *Economic Research & Risk Controlling*

Administration

Technology & Systems
Information Technology — Walter F Widmer

Legal / In-House Counsel
Legal Services — Othmar Strasser

Corporate Communications
Marketing & Corporate Communications — Fritz Lienhard

Accounts / Audit
Accounting — Paul Borschberg

Other (Administration)
Corporate Staffs & Co-operations — Fritz Treichler
Human Resources — Alex Eggli

1556 Euromoney Directory 1999

SYRIAN ARAB REPUBLIC
(+963)

Central Bank of Syria

Al Tajrida Al Maghrabia Square, Damascus
PO Box 2254, Damascus
Tel: (11) 221 2642; (11) 221 2438 **Fax:** (11) 221 3076; (11) 222 7109

Senior Executive Officers
Governor — Mohammad Bashar Kabbarah
Deputy Governor — Hicham Mutewalli
Treasurer — Adnan Attar
Company Secretary — Ali Arafat

Others (Senior Executives)
Head, Banking Supervision — Ismail Sarayji
Head, Economics & Statistics — Mouaffak Nahas

Foreign Exchange
Country Head — Mahmoud Haj Saeed

Administration

Accounts / Audit
Head, Accountancy — Tyseer Irbeeni

TAIWAN, REPUBLIC OF CHINA
(+886)

The Central Bank of China

🏛 Central Bank

2 Roosevelt Road, Section 1, Taipei 10757
Tel: (2) 393 6161 **Fax:** (2) 357 1973 **Telex:** 21532

Senior Executive Officers
Governor — Fai-Nan Perng T 357 1601 F 322 3223
Deputy Governor — Jia-Dong Shea T 357 1602 F 341 3296
Deputy Governor — Yi-Hsiung Hsu T 357 1603 F 397 2618
Treasurer — Chin-Tsair Tsai *Director General* T 357 1001 F 357 1969
Director General, Secretariat — Spencer S W Chang T 357 1501 F 357 1974

Others (Senior Executives)
K S Chung *Director General, Issue* T 357 1901 F 357 1958
Sheng-Yann Lii *Director General, Banking* T 357 1301 F 357 1950
Fred S C Chen *Director General, Bank Examination* T 357 1401 F 357 1971

Foreign Exchange
Department: Foreign Exchange and Bullion
Global Head — A-Ting Chou *Director General, FX* T 357 1101 F 357 1966

Other Departments
Economic Research — Yen Chrystal Shih *Director General* T 357 1701 F 357 1973

Administration

Technology & Systems
Information Systems — Cheng-Hong Hsieh *Director* T 357 1848 F 357 1979

Legal / In-House Counsel
Peter M F Sheu *Director* T 357 1861 F 357 1980

Accounts / Audit
Carol T Chu *Director General* T 357 1801 F 357 1977

Other (Administration)
Personnel — Yi-Shin Wei *Director* T 357 1850 F 357 1978

TAIWAN, REPUBLIC OF CHINA (+886) www.euromoneydirectory.com

American Express Bank Limited

2nd & 3rd Floors, 214 Tun Hwa North Road, Taipei
PO Box 1753, Taipei
Tel: (2) 2715 1581 **Fax:** (2) 2713 0263 **Telex:** 11349 **Swift:** AEIB TW TX

Senior Executive Officers
Managing Director / General Manager   Howard A Law

The Asahi Bank Limited   Representative Office

9th Floor-H, Hung-Tai Centre, 168 Tun Hwa North Road, Taipei
Tel: (2) 545 9777 **Fax:** (2) 545 9776
Website: www.asahibank.co.jp

Senior Executive Officers
Chief Representative   Toshikazu Ishibashi

The Bank of Nova Scotia   Full Branch Office

Alternative trading name: Scotiabank
8th Floor, 109 Ming Sheng East Road, Section 3, Taipei 105
Tel: (2) 713 2792; (2) 514 7338 **Fax:** (2) 712 6183 **Telex:** 13022 BNSTP **Swift:** NOSC TW TP

Senior Executive Officers
VP & Manager   Benny Cheong ☎ 713 2792 ✉ bnstp@topz.ficnet.net.tw

Bank of Overseas Chinese   Full Branch Office

6th Floor, Heng Yang Road 102, Taipei 100
PO Box 1636, Taipei 100
Tel: (2) 2311 3348 **Fax:** (2) 2331 2347; (2) 2389 3102 **Telex:** 12380 OCCBHO **Swift:** OCCB TW TP
Email: b03348@ms17.hinet.net **Reuters:** OCBT **Bloomberg:** 755429
Website: www.booc.com.tw

Senior Executive Officers
Chairman & Chief Executive Officer   Linin Day ☎ 2371 5181
President & Chief Operating Officer   Richard L C Chern ☎ 2371 5181
Treasurer   Alan Wang *SVP & General Manager* ☎ 2311 3348
International Division   Yen Feng Lee *General Manager* ☎ 2311 3348

General-Lending (DCM, SL)
Head of Corporate Banking   Sheng Shey Tai *SVP & General Manager* ☎ 2371 5181

General-Investment
Head of Investment   H T Chen *SVP & General Manager* ☎ 2311 3348

Debt Capital Markets / Fixed Income
Head of Fixed Income   Alan Wang *SVP & General Manager* ☎ 2311 3348

Fixed-Income Repo
Head of Repo   H T Chen *SVP & General Manager* ☎ 2311 3348

Equity Capital Markets
Head of Equity Capital Markets   H T Chen *SVP & General Manager* ☎ 2311 3348

Equity Repo / Securities Lending
Head   H T Chen *SVP & General Manager* ☎ 2311 3348

Syndicated Lending
Head of Syndication   Jimmy C S Huang *SVP & General Manager* ☎ 2311 3348

Money Markets
Head of Money Markets   Alan Wang *SVP & General Manager* ☎ 2311 3348

Foreign Exchange
Head of Foreign Exchange   Alan Wang *SVP & General Manager* ☎ 2311 3348

Settlement / Clearing
Head of Settlement / Clearing   Yen Feng Lee *General Manager* ☎ 2311 3348

Asset Management
Head   Alan Wang *SVP & General Manager* ☎ 2311 3348

Other Departments
Chief Credit Officer   Marsas C S Chen *General Manager* ☎ 2371 5181
Correspondent Banking   Yen Feng Lee *General Manager* ☎ 2311 3348
Cash Management   Alan Wang *SVP & General Manager* ☎ 2311 3348

www.euromoneydirectory.com   TAIWAN, REPUBLIC OF CHINA (+886)

Administration
Head of Administration; Business Development   Jey F N Lee *General Manager* ☏ **2371 5181**

Technology & Systems
C L Chen *SVP & General Manager* ☏ **2371 5181**

Legal / In-House Counsel
Far East Law Office
Ya Wen Chiu ☏ **2392 8811**

Compliance
Jey F N Lee *General Manager* ☏ **2371 5181**

Public Relations
H C Chen *VP & General Manager* ☏ **2371 5181**

Accounts / Audit
General Auditor
W C Huang *Executive Vice President* ☏ **2371 5181**

Bank of Taiwan   Head Office

120 Chungking South Road, Section 1, Taipei 100
PO Box 305, Taipei 100
Tel: (2) 2349 3456 **Fax:** (2) 2388 4315 **Telex:** 11201 TAIWANBK **Swift:** BKTW TW TP
Email: bot076@mail.bot.com.tw **Reuters:** BTTW **Cable:** TAIWAN BANK, TAIPEI
Website: www.bot.com.tw

Senior Executive Officers
Chairman   James C T Lo
President   K H Ho
Chief Executive Officer   William J W Teng *Executive Vice President*
Financial Director   Kao Chin Wang *Executive Vice President*

Central Trust of China   Head Office

49 Wu Chang Street, Section 1, Taipei 10006
Tel: (2) 2311 1511 **Fax:** (2) 2311 8107 **Telex:** 21154 TRUSTEX/23579 TRUSTEX **Swift:** CTOC TW TP **Reuters:** CTOC

Senior Executive Officers
Chairman   Chia Sheng Wu
President   Edward Y T Lee

Syndicated Lending
Department: Offshore Banking Branch
Tel: 2381 7196 **Fax:** 2371 1944
Head of Trading   L P Shu *SVP & General Manager*

Money Markets
Department: Offshore Banking Branch
Tel: 2371 1940 **Fax:** 2371 1944
Global Head   L P Shu *SVP & General Manager*

Foreign Exchange
Department: Offshore Banking Branch
Tel: 2371 1940 **Fax:** 2371 1944
Global Head   L P Shu *SVP & General Manager*

Other Departments
Commodities / Bullion   Chen Han Ho *SVP & General Manager* ☏ **2331 3695**
Correspondent Banking   Stuart T F Li *SVP & General Manager* ☏ **2331 9801**

Chang Hwa Commercial Bank Limited   Head Office

7th Floor, 57 Chung-Shan North Road, Section 2, Taipei 104
PO Box 672, Taipei 104
Tel: (2) 2536 2951; (2) 2562 1919 **Fax:** (2) 2511 4735; (2) 2523 9935 **Telex:** 11323 **Swift:** CCBC TW TP
Cable: CHBANK

Senior Executive Officers
Chairman   M H Tsai
President   C S Wu

Others (Senior Executives)
Head of Offshore Banking Branch   William Lin *General Manager*

TAIWAN, REPUBLIC OF CHINA (+886) www.euromoneydirectory.com

Chiao Tung Bank
Head Office

91 Heng Yang Road, Taipei 100
Tel: (2) 2361 3000 **Fax:** (2) 2361 2046; (2) 2311 3263 **Telex:** 11341 CHIAOTUNG **Swift:** BKCM TW TP
Email: dp092@ctnbank.com.tw
Website: www.ctnbank.com.tw

Senior Executive Officers
Chairman — Patrick C J Liang
President — Chieh-Chien Chao
International Division — Feng-yi Huang *SVP & General Manager*

Debt Capital Markets / Fixed Income
Department: Offshore Banking Branch
Tel: 2361 2058
Global Head — Feng-yi Huang *SVP & General Manager*

Domestic Government Bonds
Head of Trading — Jennifer Tsai ☎ **2331 8101**

Non-Domestic Government Bonds
Euro-DM — Jennifer Tsai ☎ **2331 8101**
Euro-Yen — Jennifer Tsai ☎ **2331 8101**

Eurobonds
Head of Syndication — Shel S G Liao *VP & Deputy Manager* ☎ **2361 3000**
Head of Trading — Jennifer Tsai ☎ **2331 8101**

Bonds - General
Emerging Countries — Jessie Chen *Banking Officer* ☎ **2361 3000**

Libor-Based / Floating-Rate Products
Asset Swaps — Jennifer Tsai ☎ **2331 8101**

Other (Libor-Based / Floating Rate Products)
FRN Trading — Jessie Chen *Banking Officer* ☎ **2361 3000**

Syndicated Lending
Head of Origination; Head of Syndication — Jin-Schong Sheu *SVP & General Manager*

Loan-Related Activities
Trade Finance — Maria D H Lu *SVP & General Manager*

Money Markets
Department: Offshore Banking Branch
Fax: 361 2058
Head of Money Markets — Maria D H Lu *SVP & General Manager*
Global Head — Feng-yi Huang *SVP & General Manager*

Domestic Commercial Paper
Head of Trading — Jennifer Tsai ☎ **2331 8101**

Foreign Exchange
Department: Offshore Banking Branch
Fax: 361 2058
Global Head — Feng-yi Huang *SVP & General Manager*
Head of Trading — Jennifer Tsai ☎ **2331 8101**

FX Traders / Sales People
All major currencies — Andy Chen *AGM, Europe* ☎ **2361 3000**
Jessie Chen *Banking Officer* ☎ **2361 3000**
Wendy Yeh *Dealer* ☎ **2361 3000**
Evelyn Li *Dealer* ☎ **2361 3000**
Lauren Hsieh *Dealer* ☎ **2361 3000**

Risk Management
IR Swaps Trading; IR Options Trading — Jennifer Tsai ☎ **2331 8101**

Foreign Exchange Derivatives / Risk Management
Cross-Currency Swaps, Trading — Jennifer Tsai ☎ **2331 8101**
Vanilla FX option Trading — Andy Chen *AGM, Europe* ☎ **2361 3000**

Other Currency Swap / FX Options Personnel
FX options — Jessie Chen *Banking Officer* ☎ **2361 3000**

Settlement / Clearing
Department: Offshore Banking Branch
Fax: 361 2058
Regional Head — Jennifer Tsai *Manager* ☎ **2361 3000**

Other Departments
Correspondent Banking — Feng-yi Huang *SVP & General Manager*
Cash Management — Maria D H Lu *SVP & General Manager*

www.euromoneydirectory.com TAIWAN, REPUBLIC OF CHINA (+886)

Administration
Head of Administration — Chung-Cherng Kau *SVP & General Manager*

Public Relations — Chung-Cherng Kau *SVP & General Manager*

Accounts / Audit — Y S Teng *SVP & General Manager*

China Development Corporation   Head Office

CDC Tower, 125 Nanking East Road, Section 5, Taipei 10654
Tel: (2) 763 8800 **Fax:** (2) 768 6060; (2) 276 0047 **Telex:** 23147 CHIDELCO
Website: www.cdcdpbnk.com

Senior Executive Officers
Chairman & Chief Executive Officer — Tai-Ying Liu
President — Benny T Hu
Senior Executive Vice President — Kung-Yung Chen
Senior Vice President & Manager — J H Chen
Senior Vice President & Manager — Ben C B Chang

Others (Senior Executives)
Direct Investment Department — River T K Yang *Senior Vice President & Manager*
Investment Banking & Trust Department — Kate M Wu *First Vice President & Manager*
Credit & Research Department — Vivien H Hsich *First Vice President & Manager*

General-Lending (DCM, SL)
Head of Corporate Banking — Ethen Hsu *First Vice President & Manager*

General - Treasury
Head of Treasury — Shu-Kuang Jen *First Vice President & Manager*

Relationship Manager
Overseas Business Department — Brian C Keng *First Vice President & Manager*
Corporate Planning Department — Chiang Sung *First Vice President & Manager*

Syndicated Lending
Global Head — Ethan Hsu *First Vice President & Manager*

Loan-Related Activities
Project Finance — Gearge K So *First Vice President & Manager*

Money Markets
Domestic Commercial Paper
Head of Origination — Shu-Kuang Jen *First Vice President & Manager*

Wholesale Deposits
Marketing — Ethan Hsu *First Vice President & Manager*

Corporate Finance / M&A Advisory
Global Head — Kate M Wu *First Vice President & Manager*

Administration
Technology & Systems —
John C Yu *First Vice President & Manager*
Ricky Liu *First Vice President & Manager*

Legal / In-House Counsel — Lai-Tsun Tsai *First Vice President & Manager*

Public Relations — Grace Fang *Vice President*

Accounts / Audit — Jack J L Chou *First Vice President & Controller*

Other (Administration)
General Administration — Victor Ho *First Vice President & Manager*
Personnel Department — James H Su *Vice President & General Manager*

China Securities Co Limited   Head Office

11th Floor, 96 Cheung Shan North Road, Section 2, Taipei
Tel: (2) 2521 5001; (2) 2521 7162 **Fax:** (2) 2537 7606 **Email:** chinasec@top2.ficnet.tw

Senior Executive Officers
Chairman — Chang-chong Wang
President — Angela Koo

TAIWAN, REPUBLIC OF CHINA (+886)   www.euromoneydirectory.com

Chinatrust Commercial Bank
Head Office

3 Sung Shou Road, Taipei
Tel: (2) 2722 2002 Fax: (2) 2723 9775 Telex: 24654 CTCBK Swift: CTCB TW TP

Senior Executive Officers
Chairman   Jeffrey L.S. Koo
Chief Executive Officer   Jeffrey L.S. Koo

Debt Capital Markets / Fixed Income
Department: Dealing Room
Other   Jeson Hsu Manager, Dealing

The Chinese Bank
Head Office

68 Nan-King East Road, Section 3, Taipei
Tel: (2) 2516 8686 Fax: (2) 2517 7727; (2) 2517 0797 Telex: 26641 CHEB TW TP Swift: CHEB TW TP Reuters: CHEB
Website: www.chinesebank.com.tw

Senior Executive Officers
Chairman   You-Theng Wang ☏ 2517 0788
President   Fen Chen ☏ 2517 0778
Chief Executive Officer   Fan-Hsiung Kao Senior Executive Vice President ☏ 2517 0779
                                        Lun-Hung Wei Senior Executive Vice President ☏ 2517 0777
                                        Wen-Sun Liu Chief Executive Officer ☏ 2517 0798
Managing Director   Sung-Chiu Chu
Managing Director   Lin-Tai Wang
Managing Director   Chin She-Ying Wang
Company Secretary   Jiao-Jeng Lo ☏ 2517 0789
International Division   Paul Leu Senior Vice President ☏ 2516 8211

Others (Senior Executives)
Planning & Development Department   Edward Tao Executive Vice President & General Manager ☏ 2517 3632
Marketing Department   Sheng-Yu Lai Executive Vice President & General Manager ☏ 2517 0790

Other Departments
Chief Credit Officer   Sheng-Yu Lai Executive Vice President & General Manager ☏ 2517 0790

Administration
Head of Marketing   Edward Tao Executive Vice President & General Manager ☏ 2517 3632

Accounts / Audit
Auditing Department   Chueh-Sen Kang General Auditor ☏ 2517 0783

Chinfon Commercial Bank
Head Office

Formerly known as: Cathay Investment & Trust Co

1 Nanyang Street, Taipei
3rd Floor, 180 Chunghsiao, E Road, Section 4, Taipei
Tel: (2) 2311 4881; (2) 2731 6177 Fax: (2) 2331 3271; (2) 2778 8663 Reuters: CFBK

Senior Executive Officers
Chairman   Shi H Huang ☏ 2311 4881 ext 566
President   Howard Lin ☏ 2311 4881 ext 533
Treasurer   Chen-Chuan Liang Vice President ☏ 2311 4881 ext 582
Managing Director   Wu-Tien Chiang
Company Secretary   H F Mai ☏ 2311 4881 ext 588
International Division   Michael Hsieh Vice President ☏ 2731 6177 ext 600

Equity Capital Markets
Equity Repo / Securities Lending
Head   C F Hsieh Vice President ☏ 2311 4881 ext 591

Syndicated Lending
Loan-Related Activities
Trade Finance   Michael Hsieh Vice President ☏ 2731 6177 ext 600

Money Markets
Head of Money Markets   Chen-Chuan Liang Vice President ☏ 2311 4881 ext 582

Foreign Exchange
Head of Foreign Exchange   Chen-Chuan Liang Vice President ☏ 2311 4881 ext 582

Other Departments
Correspondent Banking   Susan Chang Manager ☏ 2731 6177 ext 506

www.euromoneydirectory.com TAIWAN, REPUBLIC OF CHINA (+886)

Administration
Technology & Systems
　　　　　　　　　　　　　M L Chien *Vice President* ☎ **2311 4881 ext 560**

Chung Shing Bank   Head Office
230 Sung-Chiang Road, Taipei 104
Tel: (2) 2561 6601 **Fax:** (2) 2511 4389; (2) 2523 8743 **Telex:** 26441 or 26052 CHUNSHIN **Swift:** CSBK TW TP
Email: csb022@ms15.hinet.net **Reuters:** CSTP
Website: www.scbank.com.tw

Senior Executive Officers
Chairman　　　　　　　　　　　Yu-Yun Wang ☎ **2561 0599**
President　　　　　　　　　　　Abel S Wang ☎ **2511 5268**
Financial Director　　　　　　　Chen-Chung Pai *General Manager* ☎ **2511 6125**
Treasurer　　　　　　　　　　　Vincent Yeh *Assistant Vice President* ☎ **2521 4641**
Managing Director　　　　　　　Ching-Lien Wang ☎ **2511 5431**
General Secretary　　　　　　　Chin-Yi Chen
International Division　　　　　Stephen J C Shen *SVP & General Manager* ☎ **2511 8160**

General-Lending (DCM, SL)
Head of Corporate Banking　　　Wang-San Chien *Executive Vice President* ☎ **2511 6139**

General-Investment
Head of Investment　　　　　　　Tung-Lin King *Executive Vice President* ☎ **2511 5426**

Debt Capital Markets / Fixed Income
Department: Offshore Banking Branch
Tel: 2521 4641 **Fax:** 2523 8743
Head of Fixed Income　　　　　　Stephen J C Shen *SVP & General Manager* ☎ **2511 8160**
Head of Fixed Income Trading　　Richard Cheng *Assistant Manager* ☎ **2511 5286**

Government Bonds
Head of Sales; Head of Trading; Head of　　Vincent Yeh *Assistant Vice President* ☎ **2521 4641**
Syndication; Head of Origination

Eurobonds
Head of Sales; Head of Trading　　Apple Wang *Assistant Manager* ☎ **2521 4641**

Emerging Market Bonds
Head of Emerging Markets; Head of Sales;　　Peggy Lee *Officer* ☎ **2521 4641**
Head of Trading

Libor-Based / Floating-Rate Products
FRN Sales; FRN Trading; Asset Swaps; Asset　　Vincent Yeh *Assistant Vice President* ☎ **2521 4641**
Swaps (Sales)

Fixed-Income Repo
Head of Repo; Marketing & Product　　Apple Wang *Assistant Manager* ☎ **2521 4641**
Development; Head of Trading

Fixed-Income Research
Head of Fixed Income; Head of Credit　　Peggy Lee *Officer* ☎ **2521 4641**
Research

Equity Capital Markets
Head of Equity Capital Markets　　Tung-Ling King *Executive Vice President* ☎ **2511 5426**
Head of Trading　　　　　　　　Chian-Yang Liu *Vice President* ☎ **2511 5493**

Domestic Equities
Head of Trading　　　　　　　　Chian-Yang Liu *Vice President* ☎ **2511 5493**

International Equities
Head of Sales; Head of Trading　　Chian-Yang Liu *Vice President* ☎ **2511 5493**

Equity Research
Head of Equity Research　　　　Chian-Yang Liu *Vice President* ☎ **2511 5493**

Convertibles / Equity-Linked
Head of Sales; Head of Trading　　Chian-Yang Liu *Vice President* ☎ **2511 5493**

Equity Repo / Securities Lending
Head; Marketing & Product Development; Head　　Chian-Yang Liu *Vice President* ☎ **2511 5493**
of Prime Brokerage; Head of Trading

Syndicated Lending
Head of Syndicated Lending; Head of　　Vincent Yeh *Assistant Vice President* ☎ **2521 4641**
Origination; Head of Syndication

Loan-Related Activities
Structured Trade Finance　　　　Stephen J C Shen *SVP & General Manager* ☎ **2511 8160**
Leasing & Asset Finance　　　　Vincent Yeh *Assistant Vice President* ☎ **2521 4641**

Euromoney Directory 1999 **1563**

TAIWAN, REPUBLIC OF CHINA (+886)   www.euromoneydirectory.com

Chung Shing Bank (cont)

Money Markets
Head of Money Markets — Stephen J C Shen *SVP & General Manager* ☎ 2511 8160
Domestic Commercial Paper
Head of Sales; Head of Trading — Joseph Chiang *Assistant Vice President* ☎ 2511 5477
Eurocommercial Paper
Head of Sales; Head of Trading — Vincent Yeh *Assistant Vice President* ☎ 2521 4641
Wholesale Deposits
Marketing; Head of Sales — Vincent Yeh *Assistant Vice President* ☎ 2521 4641
Foreign Exchange
Head of Foreign Exchange; Head of Institutional Sales; Corporate Sales — Vincent Yeh *Assistant Vice President* ☎ 2521 4641
Head of Trading — Richard Cheng *Assistant Manager* ☎ 2511 5286
FX Traders / Sales People
— Apple Wang *Assistant Manager* ☎ 2521 4641
— Jonathon Huang *Officer* ☎ 2511 5286
Risk Management
Head of Risk Management — Wang-San Chien *Executive Vice President* ☎ 2511 6139
Fixed Income Derivatives / Risk Management
Head of Sales; Trading — Vincent Yeh *Assistant Vice President* ☎ 2521 4641
Foreign Exchange Derivatives / Risk Management
Spot / Forwards Sales; Spot / Forwards Trading — Vincent Yeh *Assistant Vice President* ☎ 2521 4641
Corporate Finance / M&A Advisory
Head of Corporate Finance — Wang-San Chien *Executive Vice President* ☎ 2511 6139
Settlement / Clearing
Head of Settlement / Clearing; Equity Settlement; Fixed-Income Settlement; Operations; Back-Office — Fanny Huang *Deputy Manager* ☎ 2522 4999
Asset Management
Head — Chen-Chung Pai *General Manager* ☎ 2511 6125
Other Departments
Chief Credit Officer — Wang-San Chien *Executive Vice President* ☎ 2511 6139
Correspondent Banking — Stephen J C Shen *SVP & General Manager* ☎ 2511 8160
Cash Management — Chen-Chung Pai *General Manager* ☎ 2511 6125
Administration
Head of Administration — Chen-Chung Pai *General Manager* ☎ 2511 6125
Business Development; Head of Marketing — Daniel Chu *Vice President* ☎ 2511 5427
Technology & Systems
— James A Lu *Vice President & General Manager* ☎ 2521 9323
Legal / In-House Counsel
— Shih-Yang Yu *Assistant Vice President* ☎ 2511 5490
Compliance
— Shih-Yang Yu *Assistant Vice President* ☎ 2511 5490
Public Relations
— Tung-Lin King *Executive Vice President* ☎ 2511 5426
Accounts / Audit
— S S Hsu *Executive Vice President* ☎ 2511 5445

Commerzbank AG   Representative Office

Suite E, 14th Floor, 207 Tun Hwa Road, Section 2, Taipei
Tel: (2) 2378 9688 **Fax:** (2) 2378 7801

Senior Executive Officers
Chief Representative — Rachel Chou

Cosmos Bank   Head Office

39 Tunhwa S Road, Section 2, Taipei
Tel: (2) 2701 1777 **Fax:** (2) 2784 9842 **Telex:** 26505 CSMB **Swift:** CSMB TW TP **Email:** bbb@cosmosbank.com.tw

Senior Executive Officers
Chairman — Sheng-Fa Hsui
President — C C Hu
Managing Director — Ken S J Hsui
Director & General Manager — Chin-Tsai Lee

www.euromoneydirectory.com TAIWAN, REPUBLIC OF CHINA (+886)

Others (Senior Executives)

Yin-Lien Lin *Senior Executive Vice President*
William M C Lin *General Auditor*

Administration
Head of Administration

Shang-Chang Wu *EVP & General Manager, Credit Administration*

Technology & Systems

Mark D Yang *SVP & General Manager*

Accounts / Audit
Accounting

C S Yang *SVP & General Manager*
William M C Lin *General Auditor*

Auditing

James Wu *EVP & General Manager*

Other (Administration)
International Banking
Human Resources
Business Development

Alex W S Wang *SVP & General Manager*
Lung-Mao Chen *EVP & General Manager*
Kung-Liang Shih *EVP & General Manager*

Crédit Lyonnais   Full Branch Office

16th Floor, Hung Kuo Building, 167 Tun Hua North Road, Taipei 105
Tel: (2) 2717 5252 **Fax:** (2) 2718 8292 **Telex:** 10304 CREDTPE **Email:** crlytpe@email.gcn.net.tw

Senior Executive Officers
Country Manager
Financial Director; Chief Operating Officer
Treasurer

Real Deamarais
Allan Benche *Assistant General Manager*
Rosy Tsorng *VP & Treasurer*

Dah An Commercial Bank   Head Office

117 Ming Sheng East Road, Section 3, Taipei 104
Tel: (2) 2712 6666 **Fax:** (2) 2719 7415 **Telex:** 26487 DACBTWA **Swift:** DACB TW TP
International Banking Department **Tel:** 2516 6699; 2517 0539
Website: www.dab.com.tw

Senior Executive Officers
Chairman
President
Financial Director
Chief Operating Officer
Treasurer
International Division
Senior Executive Vice President

J K Loh
Ping Keng
Dolly Yang *Senior Executive Vice President*
Rong-chuen Pan *Executive Vice President & General Manager*
Elisa Chang *SVP & General Manager*
Charles C C Wang *Executive Vice President & General Manager*
C H Chen

The Dai-Ichi Kangyo Bank Limited   Full Branch Office

167 Hung Kuo Building, 167 Tun Hua North Road, Taipei 105
Tel: (2) 2715 3911 **Fax:** (2) 2715 3780 **Cable:** BANKDAIKAN
Website: www.dkb.co.jp

Senior Executive Officers
Managing Director / General Manager

Tsuneo Yanagida

The Development Bank of Singapore Limited   Full Branch Office

5th Floor, 117 Min Sheng East Road, Section 3, Taipei
Tel: (2) 713 7711 **Fax:** (2) 713 7774 **Telex:** 13066 DBS TPE **Swift:** DBSS TW TP

Senior Executive Officers
General Manager

Soon Ghee Soh ☏ **ext 201**

TAIWAN, REPUBLIC OF CHINA (+886) www.euromoneydirectory.com

The Farmers Bank of China

85 Nanking East Road, Section 2, Taipei 104
Tel: (2) 2100 3456 Fax: (2) 2562 2161 Telex: 11841 FARMERBK Swift: FBOC TW TP Reuters: FBOC
Cable: FARMERBANK
Website: www.farmerbank.com.tw

Senior Executive Officers
Chairman   Mu-Tsai Chen ☏ **2100 3000**
President   Ching-Chi Huang ☏ **2100 3010**
Executive Vice President   Henry K C Chen ☏ **2100 3011**
Executive Vice President   Jen-Poo Chen ☏ **2100 3012**
Managing Director / General Manager   You-Tsao Wang

Others (Senior Executives)
CR Funding   Ming-Chen Leu *SVP & General Manager* ☏ **2100 3311**
Planning   S K Ho *SVP & General Manager* ☏ **2100 3346**
Banking   Hank. C Cheng *SVP & General Manager* ☏ **2100 3021**
International Banking   James Y T Lin *SVP & General Manager* ☏ **2100 3117**
Agriculture   Shen-Hsiung Huang *SVP & General Manager* ☏ **2311 0681**
Savings   Francis Y T Lin *SVP & General Manager* ☏ **2563 1487**
Investigation   William L Chen *SVP & General Manager* ☏ **2100 3416**
Offshore Banking   James Y T Lin *SVP & General Manager* ☏ **2100 3117**
Documentary Credits / International Operations   Hung-Yuan Su *SVP & General Manager* ☏ **2100 3128**
Correspondent Services   Jean Feng Mei Liu *SVP & General Manager* ☏ **2100 3118**
Wire Transactions (Forex)   Pao-Hwa Tung *SVP & General Manager* ☏ **2100 3156**

First Commercial Bank   Head Office

30 Chungking South Road, Section 1, Taipei
PO Box 395, Taipei 100-56
Tel: (2) 2348 1111 Fax: (2) 2361 0036; (2) 2375 2616 Telex: 11310 Swift: FCBK TW TP Cable: FIRSTBANK TAIPEI

Senior Executive Officers
Chairman   T L Huang
President & Chief Executive Officer   An-Chyr Chen
Managing Director   Yau-Fong Wu
Managing Director   Tez-Fu Chang
Managing Director   Feng-Shih Cheng

Debt Capital Markets / Fixed Income
Department: Offshore Banking Branch
Fax: 23118976
Country Head   Ming-Ren Chien *VP & General Manager* ☏ **2348 1410**

Fubon Commercial Bank   Head Office

2nd Floor, 169 Jen Ai Road, Section 4, Taipei 106
Tel: (2) 2771 6699 Fax: (2) 2773 0763 Telex: 26277 FUBA Swift: FBTW Reuters: FBTW
Website: www.fubon.com.tw

Senior Executive Officers
Chairman   Wan-Tsai Tsai
President   Chuan-Hsi Wang
Assistant Manager   Shu-Fen Ku ☏ **2771 6699ext8245**

Debt Capital Markets / Fixed Income
Global Head   Chao Yang Kao *Senior Vice President* ☏ **2775 8009** 🖷 **2773 0763**

Syndicated Lending
Department: Offshsore Banking Branch
Global Head   Chao Yang Kao *Senior Vice President* ☏ **2775 8009** 🖷 **2773 0763**

Loan-Related Activities
Trade Finance   Chao Yang Kao *Senior Vice President* ☏ **2775 8009** 🖷 **2773 0763**

Money Markets
Global Head   Paul Wang *Manager* ☏ **2775 8075** 🖷 **2773 0763**

Foreign Exchange
Global Head   Paul Wang *Manager* ☏ **2775 8075** 🖷 **2773 0763**

www.euromoneydirectory.com TAIWAN, REPUBLIC OF CHINA (+886)

Risk Management
Foreign Exchange Derivatives / Risk Management
Cross-Currency Swaps, Trading; Vanilla FX Paul Wang *Manager* T 2775 8075 F 2773 0763
option Trading
Exotic Options (Barriers, Range, Timers, Digitals, Faders etc)
Trading Paul Wang *Manager* T 2775 8075 F 2773 0763

Settlement / Clearing
Tel: 2771 6699 **Fax:** 2773 0763
Regional Head Wan-Chen Hwang *Manager* T 2775 8065
Fixed-Income Settlement; Foreign Exchange Jennifer Wu *Assistant Manager* T 2775 8065 F 2773 0763
Settlement

Other Departments
Correspondent Banking Chao Yang Kao T 2775 8009 F 2773 0763

Administration
Technology & Systems
  Kuo-Tai Hwang *Senior Vice President* T 2717 9982 F 2715 1504

Fubon Securities Co Limited   Head Office
5th Floor, 237 Chien Kuo S Road, Section 1, Taipei 106
Tel: (2) 2754 2866 **Fax:** (2) 2707 3854; (2) 2706 0311 **Telex:** 60130 **Email:** rbellau@fbs.com.tw **Bloomberg:** Fubonsec
Website: www.fubon.com.tw

Senior Executive Officers
Chairman Kung Liang Yeh T 2754 2866 ext 700 F 2755 7448
Financial Director Shiaw Shyong Chen *Assistant Vice President* T 2754 2866 ext 705
  F 2755 7448
Treasurer Yu Yuan Chiu *Manager*
International Division Eric Chou *Director*
  Caroline Hsieh *Manager* T 2754 2866 ext 825

Debt Capital Markets / Fixed Income
Head of Fixed Income Shwu-Huey Goh *Manager* T 2754 2866 ext 717

Syndicated Lending
Loan-Related Activities
Project Finance Ying-Ying Liao *Project Manager* T 2754 2866 ext 812

Foreign Exchange
Head of Foreign Exchange Chao Yang Goh *Manager*

Asset Management
Head Shiang Gon Chen *Director* T 2754 2866 ext 790

Administration
Head of Administration Shyue Jiann Lu *Manager* T 2754 2866 ext 168
Head of Marketing Richard M Bellau *Marketing Manager* T 2704 0911
Technology & Systems
  Yeong Shiah Chuang *Manager* T 2754 2866 ext 757
Accounts / Audit
  I-Chorng Ho *Chief Auditor* T 2754 2866 ext 780

Grand Cathay Securities Corporation   Head Office
14th Floor, #2 Chung Ching South Road, Section 1, Taipei 100
Tel: (2) 2314 8800 **Fax:** (2) 2381 9161; (2) 2314 2206 **Reuters:** GCTA **Telerate:** 26556
Website: www.gcsc.com.tw

Senior Executive Officers
Chairman H A Lee T 2375 3231
President Lee I C Chang
Chief Executive Officer J R Tsai *Senior Executive Vice President*
  Shirley Shen Wang *Senior Executive Vice President*

Debt Capital Markets / Fixed Income
Tel: 2388 5325 **Fax:** 2388 5419
Global Head Albert Ding *Head of Fixed Income* T 2388 5374
Domestic Government Bonds
Head of Sales Sam Lin *Assistant Vice President* T 2388 5373
Head of Trading Daniel Lee
Head of Research Eric Chen *Vice President* T 2388 5704

TAIWAN, REPUBLIC OF CHINA (+886) www.euromoneydirectory.com

Grand Cathay Securities Corporation (cont)

Eurobonds
Head of Trading — Jammy Huang *Vice President* ☎ 2338 5425
Head of Research — Eric Chen ☎ 2388 5704

Fixed-Income Repo
Head of Repo — J J Lee ☎ 2388 5324

Equity Capital Markets
Global Head — Jocelyn Huang ☎ 2389 5949

Domestic Equities
Head of Sales — Albert Liu *Executive Vice President* ☎ 2388 5413
Head of Trading — Keith Ho *Vice President* ☎ 2375 1114
Head of Research — Jenny Chen *Senior Vice President* ☎ 2398 6382

Convertibles / Equity-Linked
Head of Origination — Fred Chen ☎ 2388 5391
Head of Syndication — Edmund Hung ☎ 2388 5392
Head of Sales — Sam Lin *Assistant Vice President* ☎ 2388 5373

Risk Management
Global Head — Jammy Huang *Vice President* ☎ 2338 5425

The Hongkong & Shanghai Banking Corporation Limited

3rd Floor, 2 Chung Cheng 3rd Road, Kaohsiung 800
Tel: (7) 222 2500 **Fax:** (7) 223 3156

Senior Executive Officers
President — Tony Yang

The Hongkong & Shanghai Banking Corporation Limited

3rd Floor, 345 Taichung Kang Road, Section 1, Taichung 403
Tel: (4) 329 9000 **Fax:** (4) 328 5166

Senior Executive Officers
President — Colin Chen

The Hongkong & Shanghai Banking Corporation Limited

1st/4th Floors, 176 King Hwa Road, Section 3, Tainan 703
Tel: (7) 222 2500 **Fax:** (7) 223 3156

Senior Executive Officers
President — Charles Kuo

The Hongkong & Shanghai Banking Corporation Limited

Full Branch Office

Alternative trading name: Hongkongbank
13-15th Floors, International Trade Building, 333 Keelung Road, Section 1, Taipei 110
PO Box 81-359, Taipei 105
Tel: (2) 2723 0088; (2) 2757 1288 **Fax:** (2) 2757 6333; (2) 2757 6388 **Telex:** 10934 HSBC TPI **Swift:** HSBC TW TP
Website: www.hongkongbank.com

Senior Executive Officers
Chief Executive Officer — Bob Wallace ☎ 2757 6459 📠 2757 7074

Others (Senior Executives)
Institutional Banking — Mark Northcote *Senior Vice President* ☎ 2757 7027
Personal Banking — Ray Gitardi *Senior Vice President* ☎ 2775 7111
Banking Services — Lin Chih ☎ 2757 1266

General-Lending (DCM, SL)
Head of Corporate Banking — Mark Northcote *Senior Vice President* ☎ 2757 7027

Debt Capital Markets / Fixed Income
Head of Debt Capital Markets — John McGowan *Senior Vice President* ☎ 2725 7107

Equity Capital Markets
Head of Equity Capital Markets — John McGowan *Senior Vice President* ☎ 2725 7107

www.euromoneydirectory.com   TAIWAN, REPUBLIC OF CHINA (+886)

Money Markets
Head of Money Markets   John McGowan *Senior Vice President* ☎ 2725 7107
Foreign Exchange
Head of Foreign Exchange   John McGowan *Senior Vice President* ☎ 2725 7107
Administration
Public Relations
                                 Victor Hong *VP, Public Affairs & Planning* ☎ 2757 1208 F 2757 3126

Hua Nan Commercial Bank Limited   Head Office
9th Floor, 38 Chung-King South Road, Section 1, Taipei 10036
Tel: (2) 2371 3111 **Fax:** (2) 2382 1060; (2) 2371 1972 **Telex:** 11307 **Swift:** HNBK TW TP

Senior Executive Officers
Chairman   Kenneth B K Tsan
President   Edward H T Chien
Chief Executive Officer   Lin-San Lai
Financial Director   Lyrae Kuo
Chief Operating Officer   Chin-Po Li *SVP & GM, Int'l Banking*
Treasurer   Donald W H Hsu *Head of Treasury*
SVP & GM, OBU   Michael Chung

Debt Capital Markets / Fixed Income
Department: Offshore Banking Branch
Tel: 382 1056 **Fax:** 381 7491

Domestic Government Bonds
Head of Sales; Head of Trading; Head of   Jer-ren Chen *SVP & GM, Trust* ☎ 2371 8333
Research

Eurobonds
Head of Origination   Michael Chung *SVP & GM, OBU*
Head of Syndication   Amy M C Chiou *Manager*
Head of Sales; Head of Trading; Head of   Lyrae Kuo *Assistant Vice President* ☎ 2381 7491
Research; Trading - Sovereigns, Corporates,
High-yield

Libor-Based / Floating-Rate Products
FRN Origination; FRN Sales; Asset Swaps;   Lyrae Kuo *Assistant Vice President* ☎ 2381 7491
Asset Swaps (Sales)

Syndicated Lending
Department: Offshsore Banking Branch
Global Head of Origination; Head of   Amy M C Chiou *Manager*
Syndication; Head of Trading; Recovery; Head
of Credit Committee

Loan-Related Activities
Trade Finance; Project Finance; Structured Amy M C Chiou *Manager*
Trade Finance; Leasing & Asset Finance

Money Markets
Department: Treasury Division, International Administration Department
Global Head   Donald W H Hsu *Head of Treasury*

Domestic Commercial Paper
Head of Origination; Head of Sales; Head of Jer-ren Chen *SVP & GM, Trust* ☎ 2371 8333
Trading

Eurocommercial Paper
Head of Trading   Crystal Yu *Manager, Offshore Banking Branch*

Foreign Exchange
Department: Treasury Division, Interntional Administration Department
Global Head of Institutional Sales; Corporate Donald W H Hsu *Head of Treasury*
Sales; Head of Trading

Risk Management
Department: Overseas Division, International Administration Department
Global Head   Chi-Ming Huang *Head, Overseas*

Fixed Income Derivatives / Risk Management
Global Head; IR Swaps Sales / Marketing; IR   Chi-Ming Huang *Head, Overseas*
Swaps Trading; IR Options Sales / Marketing;
IR Options Trading

Foreign Exchange Derivatives / Risk Management
Cross-Currency Swaps, Sales / Marketing;   Chi-Ming Huang *Head, Overseas*
Cross-Currency Swaps, Trading; Vanilla FX
option Sales; Vanilla FX option Trading

Euromoney Directory 1999   **1569**

TAIWAN, REPUBLIC OF CHINA (+886) www.euromoneydirectory.com

Hua Nan Commercial Bank Limited (cont)
Other Departments
Correspondent Banking Y F Wu *Chief, Planning*
Administration
Technology & Systems
 Sin-Shoung Chen ☎ **2332 8111**

ING Baring Securities (Taiwan) Subsidiary Company
8th Floor, 115 Min-Sheng East Road, Section 3, Taipei 105
Tel: (2) 514 6100 **Fax:** (2) 545 3450
Senior Executive Officers
Others (Senior Executives)
 Peter Tsao *Research Manager*
Corporate Finance / M&A Advisory
Head of Corporate Finance Wendell Huang *Director*

ING Barings Full Branch Office
6th Floor, Union Enterprise Plaza, 109 Min-Sheng East Road, Section 3, Taipei 105
Tel: (2) 719 9696 **Fax:** (2) 713 7220 **Telex:** 29950 INGBTW **Swift:** INGB TW TP
Senior Executive Officers
Country Manager Wu Ching-Mai

International Bank of Taipei Head Office
Formerly known as: Taipei Business Bank
36 Nanking East Road, Section 3, Taipei 10411
Tel: (2) 2508 6784 **Fax:** (2) 2508 6725; (2) 2516 2208 **Telex:** 29801 **Swift:** TPBB TW TP **Email:** obu@ibtpe.com.tw
Cable: 29801
Website: www.ibtpe.com.tw
Senior Executive Officers
Chairman S C Ho
President K C Yu
International Division Sam Ko

The International Commercial Bank of China Co Limited
Head Office
100 Chi Lin Road, Taipei
Tel: (2) 2563 3156 **Fax:** (2) 2561 1216 **Telex:** 22145 INTCOM BK **Swift:** ICBC TWTP
Website: www.icbc.com.tw
Senior Executive Officers
Chairman Yung-San Lee ☎ **2551 1459**
President James Yuang ☎ **2541 0015**
Treasurer Meei-Yeh Wei *General Manager* ☎ **2561 8643**
Debt Capital Markets / Fixed Income
Domestic Government Bonds
Head of Trading C S Lee *Associate Vice President* ☎ **2522 3147**
Non-Domestic Government Bonds
US$; ¥ Jensen Lee *Manager* ☎ **2562 4879**
Eurobonds
Head of Trading Meei-Yeh Wei *General Manager* ☎ **2561 8643**
Emerging Market Bonds
Head Jensen Lee *Manager* ☎ **2562 4879**
Libor-Based / Floating-Rate Products
Asset Swaps Jensen Lee *Manager* ☎ **2562 4879**
Equity Capital Markets
Convertibles / Equity-Linked
Head of Trading; Head of Research Jensen Lee *Manager* ☎ **2562 4879**

www.euromoneydirectory.com TAIWAN, REPUBLIC OF CHINA (+886)

Money Markets
Global Head — Meei-Yeh Wei *General Manager* ☏ **2561 8643**
Domestic Commercial Paper
Head of Origination — S B Duh *Associate Vice President* ☏ **2562 9706**
Foreign Exchange
Global Head of Trading — Meei-Yeh Wei *General Manager* ☏ **2561 8643**
FX Traders / Sales People
   Eddii Chang
   S Y Chen

Risk Management
Global Head — Meei-Yeh Wei *General Manager* ☏ **2561 8643**
Fixed Income Derivatives / Risk Management
Global Head — Meei-Yeh Wei *General Manager* ☏ **2561 8643**
Foreign Exchange Derivatives / Risk Management
Cross-Currency Swaps, Sales / Marketing — Jensen Lee *Manager* ☏ **2562 4879**
Vanilla FX option Trading — Eddii Chang

Settlement / Clearing
Country Head; Equity Settlement; Fixed-Income Settlement; Derivatives Settlement; Foreign Exchange Settlement — H R Chiang *Associate Vice President* ☏ **2537 8742**

Other Departments
Private Banking — S C Lin *Senior Vice President* ☏ **2521 9751**
Correspondent Banking — Meei-Yeh Wei *General Manager* ☏ **2561 8643**

Administration
Technology & Systems
   Ying-Ying Chang *General Manager* ☏ **2341 6865**
Legal / In-House Counsel
   James Ko *Associate Vice President* ☏ **2537 8631**
Public Relations
   John Her *Manager* ☏ **2537 8635**

KBC NV   Full Branch Office
15th Floor, 99 Fu Hsing North Road, Taipei
Tel: (2) 2712 9133 **Fax:** (2) 2715 4207 **Telex:** 11048 KBTPROC **Swift:** KBTP TW TP **Reuters:** KBTP

Senior Executive Officers
Financial Director — Charlotte Lee *Manager, Operations & Accounting* ☏ **2712 9133 ext 202**
Chief Operating Officer — Jennifer Wei *Manager, Trade Services* ☏ **2712 9133 ext 233**
Treasurer — Ben Liao-Ru *Manager, Treasury* ☏ **2712 9133 ext 208**
General Manager — Lawrence Lau ☏ **2712 9133 ext 200**

General - Treasury
Head of Treasury — Ben Liao-Ru *Manager, Treasury* ☏ **2712 9133 ext 208**

Debt Capital Markets / Fixed Income
Global Head — Willy Kestens *Global Treasurer* ☏ **2546 4181**
Country Head — Ben Liao-Ru *Manager, Treasury* ☏ **2712 9133 ext 208**
Domestic Government Bonds
Head of Trading; Head of Research — Ben Liao-Ru *Manager, Treasury* ☏ **2712 9133 ext 208**
Libor-Based / Floating-Rate Products
Asset Swaps — Joseph Lyu *Deputy General Manager* ☏ **2712 9133 ext 204**

Syndicated Lending
Regional Head — Willy Hofkenss *Regional General Manager* ☏ **+852 2879 3388**
Country Head — Lawrence Lau *General Manager* ☏ **2712 9133 ext 200**
Head of Syndication — Joseph Lyu *Deputy General Manager* ☏ **2712 9133 ext 204**
Head of Credit Committee — Willy Hofkenss *Regional General Manager* ☏ **+852 2879 3388**

Loan-Related Activities
Trade Finance; Project Finance; Leasing & Asset Finance — Joseph Lyu *Deputy General Manager* ☏ **2712 9133 ext 204**

Money Markets
Global Head — Willy Kestens *Global Treasurer* ☏ **2546 4181**
Country Head — Ben Liao-Ru *Manager, Treasury* ☏ **2712 9133 ext 208**
Domestic Commercial Paper
Head of Trading — Richard Huang *Dealer*

Foreign Exchange
Global Head — Willy Kestens *Global Treasurer* ☏ **2546 4181**
Country Head of Trading — Ben Liao-Ru *Manager, Treasury* ☏ **2712 9133 ext 208**

TAIWAN, REPUBLIC OF CHINA (+886)   www.euromoneydirectory.com

KBC NV (cont)
FX Traders / Sales People
    Bianca Yang *Dealer*
    Hans Chuang *Dealer*

Risk Management
Global Head — Willy Kestens *Global Treasurer* ☎ **2546 4181**
Country Head — Ben Liao-Ru *Manager, Treasury* ☎ **2712 9133 ext 208**

Settlement / Clearing
Country Head — Jennifer Wei *Manager, Trade Services* ☎ **2712 9133 ext 233**
Derivatives Settlement — Yvonne Lai ☎ **2712 9133 ext 234**
Foreign Exchange Settlement — Jennifer Wei *Manager, Trade Services* ☎ **2712 9133 ext 233**

Other Departments
Proprietary Trading — Ben Liao-Ru *Manager, Treasury* ☎ **2712 9133 ext 208**
Correspondent Banking — Joseph Lyu *Deputy General Manager* ☎ **2712 9133 ext 204**

Land Bank of Taiwan

46 Kuan Chien Road, Taipei
Tel: (2) 2348 3456; (2) 2311 1604 **Fax:** (2) 2381 2066; (2) 2331 7322 **Telex:** 14564 LABK **Swift:** LBOT TW TP
Reuters: LBOT **Cable:** TAIPEI 0960
Website: www.landbank.com.tw

Senior Executive Officers
Chairman — Donald T Chen ☎ **2331 3290**
President — Pong-Long Lin ☎ **2311 0822**
Chief Executive Officer — Jing-Fong Soo ☎ **2361 9198**

Relationship Manager
International Banking Department — Fu-Rong Wu *SVP & General Manager* 🖷 **2375 3363**

Debt Capital Markets / Fixed Income
Tel: 2348 3588 **Fax:** 2371 1359
Global Head — Kuang-Chao Huang *SVP & General Manager* ☎ **2348 3308**

Non-Domestic Government Bonds
All Foreign Currencies — Ann Chen *Manager* ☎ **2348 3588**

Syndicated Lending
Head of Trading — Kuang-Wei Chang *Assistant Manager* ☎ **2348 3587**

Foreign Exchange
Head of Trading — Karen Hsu *Manager & Division Chief* ☎ **2348 3559**

FX Traders / Sales People
    Julie Lin *Deputy Manager* ☎ **2348 3562**
    Grace Chen *Assistant Manager* ☎ **2348 3565**
    Fred Liu *Senior Clerk* ☎ **2348 3565**

Risk Management
IR Options Trading — Ann Chen *Manager* ☎ **2348 3588**

Foreign Exchange Derivatives / Risk Management
Cross-Currency Swaps, Trading; Vanilla FX option Trading — Karen Hsu *Manager & Division Chief* ☎ **2348 3559**

Other Currency Swap / FX Options Personnel
    Julie Lin *Deputy Manager* ☎ **2348 3562**

Exotic Options (Barriers, Range, Timers, Digitals, Faders etc)
Trading — Karen Hsu *Manager & Division Chief* ☎ **2348 3559**
    Julie Lin *Deputy Manager* ☎ **2348 3562**

Settlement / Clearing
Foreign Exchange Settlement — Fanny Chen *Assistant Manager* ☎ **2348 3524**

Other Departments
Correspondent Banking — Jane Chan *Assistant Vice President & Division Chief* ☎ **2348 3579**

National Australia Bank Limited   Full Branch Office

10th Floor, Union Enterprise Plaza, 109 Min Sheng East Road, Section 3, Taipei
Tel: (2) 2719 1031 **Fax:** (2) 2719 6289 **Telex:** 14214 NATAWTP **Swift:** NATA TW TP

Senior Executive Officers
General Manager — Christopher Clark
DGM & Head of Operations — Morris Lin

www.euromoneydirectory.com TAIWAN, REPUBLIC OF CHINA (+886)

Overseas Union Bank Limited
Full Branch Office

1907 International Trade Bank, Tapei World Trade Centre, No. 333 Keelung Road, Section 1, Taipei
Tel: (2) 720 9555 **Fax:** (2) 757 6090

Senior Executive Officers
Vice President & General Manager   Eric Yeo Aik Leng

Pan Asia Bank
Head Office

2nd Floor, 202 Kuang Fu South Road, Taipei
Tel: (2) 2772 1212 **Fax:** (2) 2773 5298; (2) 2772 2626 **Telex:** 26170 PANASIA **Swift:** PABK TW TP

Senior Executive Officers
Associate Executive Vice President   P T Ho 2772 3535
AVP & AGM   Matthew Wang 2741 4926
VP & Deputy General Manager   C M Chen 2711 0479

Others (Senior Executives)
Import   Marrina Tang *Manager* 2711 0490
Export   Becky Ho *Manager* 2711 0501
Deposit   Meiying Hu *Manager* 2772 3737

Debt Capital Markets / Fixed Income
Country Head   Matthew Wang *AVP & AGM* 2741 4926

Syndicated Lending
Tel: 2772 1212 **Fax:** 2773 5298
Head of Syndication   P T Ho *Associate Executive Vice President* 2772 3535

Money Markets
Tel: 2741 4926 **Fax:** 2773 5298
Country Head   Matthew Wang *AVP & AGM* 2741 4926

Foreign Exchange
Country Head   Matthew Wang *AVP & AGM* 2741 4926

Settlement / Clearing
Tel: 2711 0490 **Fax:** 2773 5298
Fixed-Income Settlement; Foreign Exchange Marrina Tang *Manager* 2711 0490
Settlement

Other Departments
Correspondent Banking   Matthew Wang *AVP & AGM* 2741 4926

Paribas

11th Floor, 205 Tun Hwa North Road, PO BOX 87-526, Taipei
Tel: (2) 2715 1980; (2) 2713 6703 **Fax:** (2) 2713 1182 **Telex:** 27004

Senior Executive Officers
Country Manager   Xavier Thiry
Managing Director   Wilma Wei
Managing Director   Paul Yang

Royal Bank of Canada
Full Branch Office

12th Floor, Union Enterprise Plaza, 109 Min Sheng East Road, Section 3, Taipei
Tel: (2) 2514 3088 **Fax:** (2) 2713 2884 **Telex:** 13374 ROYTAI **Swift:** ROYC TW TPA

Senior Executive Officers
Manager, Operations   Jessi Chiang

The Shanghai Commercial & Savings Bank Limited
Head Office

2 Min-Chuan East Road, Section 1, Taipei
Tel: (2) 2581 7111; (2) 2567 1930 **Fax:** (2) 2567 1912; (2) 2567 1907 **Telex:** 11306 SCSBANK **Swift:** SCSB TW TP
Reuters: SCSB
Website: www.scsb.com.tw

Senior Executive Officers
Chairman   Hung-Ching Yung
President   C S Chou
Treasurer   Shirley Lee *VP & Manager* 2567 7018 shirley@scsb.com.tw

TAIWAN, REPUBLIC OF CHINA (+886)   www.euromoneydirectory.com

The Shanghai Commercial & Savings Bank Limited (cont)

Debt Capital Markets / Fixed Income
Department: Treasurer
Country Head — Shirley Lee *VP & Manager* ☎ 2567 7018 ✉ shirley@scsb.com.tw

Domestic Government Bonds
Head of Sales — C H Kao *SVP & Manager* ☎ 2393 3111
Head of Trading — Shirley Lee *VP & Manager* ☎ 2567 7018 ✉ shirley@scsb.com.tw

Libor-Based / Floating-Rate Products
FRN Sales — James Han *SVP & Manager* ☎ 2567 1928

Syndicated Lending
Department: Off-shore Banking Unit
Global Head — James Han *SVP & Manager* ☎ 2567 1928

Loan-Related Activities
Trade Finance — J M Ho *EVP & General Manager* ☎ 2523 5443

Money Markets
Department: Treasury
Fax: 2567 1944
Country Head — Shirley Lee *VP & Manager* ☎ 2567 7018 ✉ shirley@scsb.com.tw

Domestic Commercial Paper
Head of Origination; Head of Sales; Head of Trading — Shirley Lee *VP & Manager* ☎ 2567 7018 ✉ shirley@scsb.com.tw

Foreign Exchange
Department: Treasury
Fax: 2567 1944
Global Head — Dick Liu *Associate Vice President* ☎ 2523 7358

Risk Management
Foreign Exchange Derivatives / Risk Management
Vanilla FX option Sales; Vanilla FX option Trading — Dick Liu *Associate Vice President* ☎ 2523 7358

Global Custody
Department: Trust Department
Tel: 2393 3111 Fax: 2392 8249
Regional Head — C H Kao *SVP & Manager* ☎ 2393 3111

Other Departments
Correspondent Banking — J M Ho *EVP & General Manager* ☎ 2523 5443

Société Générale

7th & 8th Floors, 109 Min Sheng East Road, Section 3, PO Box 81-577, Taipei 105
Tel: (2) 2715 5050; (2) 2719 1190 Fax: (2) 2715 2781 Telex: 23904 SOGENTPE
Website: www.socgen.com

Senior Executive Officers
Chief Operating Officer — André Gourret
Treasurer — Karl Chang
Managing Director / General Manager — Daniel Mollé

Taichung Business Bank   Full Branch Office

45 Mintsu Road, Taichung 400
Tel: (4) 221 2933; (4) 221 2933 Fax: (4) 220 2046 Telex: 56166 CHUNGBKA Swift: TCBB TW TH
Email: webmaster@ms1.tcbbank.com.tw
Website: www.tcbbank.com.tw

Senior Executive Officers
Chairman — Sung-Pan Liu
President — Jien-Lien Yeh
Treasurer — Jerry Wei *Assistant Vice President*
International Division — Hanson Yu *SVP & General Manager*

www.euromoneydirectory.com TAIWAN, REPUBLIC OF CHINA (+886)

TAIPEIBANK
Head Office

50 Chung Shan North Road, Section 2, Taipei 104
PO Box 1646, Taipei 104
Tel: (2) 2542 5656 **Fax:** (2) 542 8870 **Telex:** 11722 **Swift:** TPBK TW TP **Reuters:** TPBK (Monitor)

Senior Executive Officers
Chairman	Cheng Ching Liao
President	Jack H Huang
Treasurer	Chin-Ch Yuan Lai *SVP & General Manager*
Managing Director / General Manager	Che Nan Chen
Managing Director / General Manager	Chuan Lin
Managing Director / General Manager	Yung H Hsu

Debt Capital Markets / Fixed Income
Global Head — Joyce Chen *SVP & General Manager* ☎ **2531 9434**

Equity Capital Markets
Global Head — Li-Hwa Chen *SVP & General Manager* ☎ **2311 1768**

Syndicated Lending
Global Head — Joyce Chen *SVP & General Manager* ☎ **2531 9434**

Money Markets
Global Head — Joyce Chen *SVP & General Manager* ☎ **2531 9434**

Foreign Exchange
Global Head — Joseph Huang *SVP & General Manager* ☎ **2521 5013**

Risk Management
Global Head — Hao-Yang Hsu *SVP & General Manager* ☎ **2543 5006**

Corporate Finance / M&A Advisory
Global Head — Cheng-Hsiung Lin *SVP & General Manager* ☎ **2571 6839**

Settlement / Clearing
Regional Head — Joseph C S Huang *SVP & General Manager*

Taishin International Bank
Head Office

3rd Floor, 44 Chung Shan North Road, Section 2, Taipei 104
PO Box 17-344, Taipei 104
Tel: (2) 2568 3988 **Fax:** (2) 2511 5824; (2) 2511 1987 **Telex:** 26690 TSIB **Swift:** TSIB TW TP
Email: chanwei@taishinbank.com.tw **Reuters:** TSIB
Website: www.taishinbank.com.tw

Senior Executive Officers
Chairman	Thomas T L Wu
President	Julius Chen
Chief Executive Officer	Thomas K K Lin
Financial Director	Carol Lai
Chief Operating Officer	James Chen
Treasurer	Carol Lai
Managing Director	Steve Shien
General Manager	Meng-Chan Hsu
International Division	Hermes Tsai
Chief Representative	Thomas Chen

Foreign Exchange
Head of Foreign Exchange — C H Tai *Assistant Manager* ☎ **2568 3988 ext 371**

Settlement / Clearing
Head of Settlement / Clearing — Grace Yen *Assistant Manager* ☎ **2568 3988 ext 239**

Taiwan Business Bank
Head Office

72 Chung King South Road, Section 1, Taipei
Tel: (2) 2371 7171; (2) 2741 0787 **Fax:** (2) 2752 5094; (2) 2731 8049 **Telex:** 14484 **Swift:** MBBT TW TP
Email: tbb923@ms12.hint.net
Website: www.tbb.com.tw

Senior Executive Officers
Chairman	Chien Jen Hsiao ☎ **2361 0440**
President	Ho Yi Lu ☎ **2311 0882**
Managing Director / General Manager	Henry Yee ☎ **+1 (213) 892 1260**
SVP & Chief Secretary	Chun Seng Lee ☎ **2371 7171**

Euromoney Directory 1999 **1575**

TAIWAN, REPUBLIC OF CHINA (+886) www.euromoneydirectory.com

Taiwan Business Bank (cont)
Senior Executive Officers (cont)
International Division   Jack S G Huang *SVP & General Manager* ☏ **241 0787**
Others (Senior Executives)
Executive Vice President   I M Chao ☏ **2311 4413**
                                                                        Song Chu Chen ☏ **2311 0482**
                                                                         Tony T H Su ☏ **2371 7171**

Administration
Other (Administration)
International Administration   Jack S G Huang *Senior Vice President & Manager*

Taiwan Cooperative Bank   Head Office

3rd Floor, 325 Chung-Hsiao East Road, Section 4, Taipei
Tel: (2) 2740 0628 **Fax:** (2) 2751 2962 **Telex:** 17176 TACBID **Swift:** TACB TW TP **Cable:** tacbid

Senior Executive Officers
Chairman   W H Lee
President & Managing Director   T N Hsu
Chief Executive Officer   C N Wang
                                                                   M C Tseng
Managing Director   C Y Wang
Managing Director   C L Chou
Managing Director   C C Cheng
Managing Director   J H Lan
Managing Director   P T Chen
International Division   C N Wei

General-Lending (DCM, SL)
Head of Corporate Banking   W S Wang *SVP & GM, Loans*
                                                                   C S Lin *SVP & GM, Banking*

Relationship Manager
Small Business Financing   W P Wang *SVP & General Manager*

Syndicated Lending
Head of Syndicated Lending   Victor Chung *SVP & General Manager*

Other (Trade Finance)
Agricultural Financing   Y Y Huang *SVP & General Manager*
Cooperative Financing   S Y Wu *SVP & General Manager*

Money Markets
Head of Money Markets   Y L Lin *AVP & Manager*

Foreign Exchange
Head of Foreign Exchange   Y L Lin *AVP & Manager*

Risk Management
Head of Risk Management   S W Lee *AVP*

Settlement / Clearing
Head of Settlement / Clearing   Dexter Chiang *AVP*

Other Departments
Global Trust   J C Huang *SVP & General Manager*

Administration
Other (Administration)
Agency Service   J H Chiu *SVP & General Manager*

Taiwan International Securities Corporation   Head Office

33rd Floor, Tuntex Tower, 97 Tanhwa South Road, Section 2, Taipei
Tel: (2) 2326 3231 **Fax:** (2) 2754 8319
Website: www.tisc.com.tw

Senior Executive Officers
Chairwoman   Regina Chen ☏ **2705 2888**
President   William Huang ☏ **2705 2888**
Financial Director   Fred Chang *Vice President, Financial Division* ☏ **2705 2888**
International Division   Rick Chen *Vice President, Global Market Division* ☏ **2326 3229**

Equity Capital Markets
Head of Equity Capital Markets   Fred Chang *Vice President, Financial Division* ☏ **2705 2888**

1576 Euromoney Directory 1999

www.euromoneydirectory.com TAIWAN, REPUBLIC OF CHINA (+886)

Money Markets
Head of Money Markets Kuan-Pao Fang
Corporate Finance / M&A Advisory
Head of Corporate Finance Fred Chang *Vice President, Financial Division* ☏ **2705 2888**

The Tokai Bank Limited
Full Branch Office

33rd Floor, 66 Shin Kong Life Tower, Section 1, Chung-Hsiao W. Road, Taipei
Tel: (2) 2371 8888 **Fax:** (2) 2371 8000 **Telex:** 26020 TKAIRO CT

Senior Executive Officers
General Manager Toshiyuki Sasaki

UBS AG

15th Floor, 167 Tun Hua North Road, Taipei
Tel: (2) 2718 6999 **Fax:** (2) 2718 4429

Senior Executive Officers
Branch Manager Choon-Liat Koh
General - Treasury
Head of Treasury T Lin *Treasury*
Syndicated Lending
Other (Trade Finance)
Structure Finance L Guo
Corporate Finance / M&A Advisory
Head of Corporate Finance S Chao
Settlement / Clearing
Operations Loo-Fei Hwang *Logistics*

UBS Securities Taiwan Limited

15th Floor, 167 Tun Hua North Road, Taipei
Tel: (2) 719 4406 **Fax:** (2) 719 4407

Senior Executive Officers
Others (Senior Executives)
Senior Executive Officer Uwe Hockenjos

Union Bank of Taiwan
Head Office

2nd Floor, 109 Min-Sheng East Road, Section 3, Taipei 105
Tel: (2) 2718 0001 **Fax:** (2) 2713 7515 **Telex:** 26354 UBOTWIBD **Swift:** UBOT TW TP
Email: 014_0199@email.ubot.com.tw **Reuters:** UBOT
Website: www.ubot.com.tw

Senior Executive Officers
Chairman C C Huang ☏ **2717 4102**
President Shiang-Chang Lee ☏ **2717 2767**
Financial Director Un-Ge Liu *SVP & General Manager* ☏ **2717 2836**
Chief Operating Officer K C Pi *SVP & General Manager* ☏ **2514 5362**
Treasurer Tarsicio Tong *VP & Deputy General Manager* ☏ **2546 5251**
Managing Director Jeff Lin ☏ **2717 2875**
International Division Roger Wang *SVP & General Manager* ☏ **2514 5369**
Others (Senior Executives)
Senior Executive VP Sherman Chuang *Senior Executive Vice President* ☏ **2717 2768**
  Chun-Chieh Hwang ☏ **2713 8168**
General-Lending (DCM, SL)
Head of Corporate Banking Jane Lu *Manager* ☏ **2514 5389**
General-Investment
Head of Investment Roger Wang *SVP & General Manager* ☏ **2514 5369**
Debt Capital Markets / Fixed Income
Department: International Banking Department
Eurobonds
Head of Sales Roger Wang *SVP & General Manager* ☏ **2514 5369**

TAIWAN, REPUBLIC OF CHINA (+886) www.euromoneydirectory.com

Union Bank of Taiwan (cont)

Libor-Based / Floating-Rate Products
FRN Sales; FRN Trading; Asset Swaps; Asset Swaps (Sales) — Tarsicio Tong *VP & Deputy General Manager* ☎ **2546 5251**

Fixed-Income Repo
Head of Repo — Jane Lu *Manager* ☎ **2514 5389**
Marketing & Product Development — Jane Lu *Manager* ☎ **2514 5389**
Head of Trading — Jane Lu *Manager* ☎ **2514 5389**
Other — Jane Lu *Manager* ☎ **2514 5389**

Fixed-Income Research
Head of Fixed Income — Jane Lu *Manager* ☎ **2514 5389**
Head of Credit Research — Jane Lu *Manager* ☎ **2541 5389**

Equity Capital Markets

Equity Research
Head of Equity Research — Jane Lu *Manager* ☎ **2514 5389**

Syndicated Lending
Tel: 2514 5389 **Fax:** 2545 7228 **Reuters:** UBOT **Telex:** 26545 UBTWIBD
Head of Origination — Hao-Sen Lee *Executive Vice President* ☎ **2717 2846**
Head of Syndication — Jane Lu *Manager* ☎ **2514 5389**
Head of Trading — Tarsicio Tong *VP & Deputy General Manager* ☎ **2546 5251**

Money Markets

Tel: 2546 5251 **Fax:** 2713 6181 **Reuters:** UBOT **Telex:** 26545 UBTWIBD
Head of Money Markets — Tarsicio Tong *VP & Deputy General Manager* ☎ **2546 5251**

Domestic Commercial Paper
Head of Sales — Kou-Chung Pi *SVP & General Manager* ☎ **2514 5362**
Head of Trading — Jeffery Ko *General Manager* ☎ **2717 2796**

Eurocommercial Paper
Head of Sales; Head of Trading — Tarsicio Tong *VP & Deputy General Manager* ☎ **2546 5251**

Wholesale Deposits
Marketing; Head of Sales — Tarsicio Tong *VP & Deputy General Manager* ☎ **2546 5251**

Foreign Exchange

Tel: 2546 5251 **Fax:** 2713 6181
Head of Foreign Exchange; Corporate Sales; Head of Trading — Tarsicio Tong *VP & Deputy General Manager* ☎ **2546 5251**

FX Traders / Sales People
Dealer — Gary Huang *Assistant Manager* ☎ **2546 5252**

Risk Management

Head of Sales; Trading — Hao-Sen Lee *Executive Vice President* ☎ **2717 2846**

Foreign Exchange Derivatives / Risk Management
Spot / Forwards Sales; Spot / Forwards Trading — Tarsicio Tong *VP & General Manager* ☎ **2546 5251**

Exchange-Traded Derivatives
Head — Tarsicio Tong *VP & Deputy General Manager* ☎ **2546 5251**

Corporate Finance / M&A Advisory

Head of Corporate Finance — Jane Lu *Manager* ☎ **2514 5389**
Global Head — Hao-Sen Lee *Executive Vice President* ☎ **2717 2846**

Settlement / Clearing

Head of Settlement / Clearing — Hui-Chian Liu *Assistant Manager* ☎ **2546 1957**

Global Custody

Head of Global Custody — Jane Lu *Manager* ☎ **2514 5389**

Other Departments

Chief Credit Officer — Hao-Sen Lee *Executive Vice President* ☎ **2717 2846**
Correspondent Banking — Roger Wang *SVP & General Manager* ☎ **2514 5369**

Administration

Head of Administration — Wayne Yan *Assistant Vice President* ☎ **2514 5340**
Business Development — K C Pi *SVP & General Manager* ☎ **2514 5362**
Head of Marketing — Sherman Chuang *Senior Executive Vice President* ☎ **2717 2768**

Technology & Systems

John Lee *SVP & General Manager* ☎ **2514 5385**

Compliance

Shiang-Chang Lee *President* ☎ **2717 2767**

Public Relations

K C Pi *SVP & General Manager* ☎ **2514 5362**

Accounts / Audit

Un-Ge Liu *SVP & General Manager* ☎ **2717 2836**

United World Chinese Commercial Bank
Head Office

65 Kuan Chien Road, Taipei 100
Tel: (2) 2312 5555 **Fax:** (2) 2331 8263 **Telex:** 21378 **Swift:** UWCBTWTP **Reuters:** UWCB **Cable:** UWCB TW TP

Senior Executive Officers
Chairman — Irvine W Ho
President — Gregory K H Wang
Chief Executive Officer — C C Tung *Executive Vice President*
Roger H L Wu *Executive Vice President*
Financial Director; Chief Operating Officer — C T Chen *Executive Vice President*
Treasurer — F C Kao *Senior Vice President*
International Division — Andrew C Y Tsai *SVP & General Manager*

Debt Capital Markets / Fixed Income
Eurobonds
Head of Trading — Roger Chen *Assistant Vice President* ☎ **2312 5615**

Syndicated Lending
Department: Offshore Banking Unit
Head of Syndicated Lending — Alice Lin *Manager* ☎ **231 5615**

Money Markets
Head of Money Markets — Alice Lin *Manager* ☎ **231 5615**

Foreign Exchange
Department: Dealing Room
Tel: 2312 5670 **Fax:** 2331 8263
Head of Foreign Exchange — Alice Lin *Manager* ☎ **231 5615**

Settlement / Clearing
Department: Funding Department
Tel: 2312 5687 **Fax:** 2381 8160
Foreign Exchange Settlement — Grace Huang *Manager* ☎ **2312 5687**

Other Departments
Correspondent Banking — Susan Huang *Deputy Manager* ☎ **2312 5642**

Administration
Technology & Systems
Eugene Huang *Senior Vice President* ☎ **2753 1423**

Warburg Dillon Read Securities Co Limited

13th Floor, 109 Min-Sheng East Road, Section 3, Taipei
PO Box 118-320, 13th Floor, 109 Min-Sheng East Road, Section 3, Taipei
Tel: (2) 717 5606 **Fax:** (2) 712 9488

Senior Executive Officers
Branch Manager — Choon-Liat Koh

Equity Capital Markets
Other (Domestic Equities)
Equities Distribution — F Yu

Equity Research
Country Head — L Chitung

Settlement / Clearing
Operations — J Kuo *Logistics*

TAJIKISTAN
(+7)

The National Bank of Tajikistan
Central Bank

Rudaki Avenue 23/2, Dushanbe
PO Box 734025, Dushanbe
Tel: (3772) 212 628; (3772) 210 313 **Fax:** (3772) 510 068; (3772) 217 805 **Telex:** 201129 TANGA

Senior Executive Officers
Chairman — Murotali Alimardonov
First Deputy Chairman — Sharif Rahimov ☎ **215 451**
Deputy Chairman — Navruz Valiev ☎ **212 619**
Treasurer — Kasim Akramov *Director* ☎ **212 689**

TAJIKISTAN (+7) www.euromoneydirectory.com

The National Bank of Tajikistan (cont)

Others (Senior Executives)
Head, Bank Licensing — Nazokat Karimova ☏ 215 069
Head, Banking Supervision — Iskandar Davlatov ☏ 217 858
Head, Economics & statistics — larisa Dureeva ☏ 212 544

Settlement / Clearing
Head of Settlement / Clearing — Abdujubbor Shirinov ☏ 215 997

Administration
Head of Administration — Ibrayim Yakubov ☏ 212 687

Accounts / Audit
Head, Accountancy — Abdurazok Umarov ☏ 212 621

TANZANIA, UNITED REPUBLIC OF
(+255)

Bank of Tanzania   🏛 Central Bank

PO Box 2939, Dar Es Salaam
Tel: (51) 110 946; (51) 110 952 Fax: (51) 113 325; (51) 112 573 Telex: 41024

Senior Executive Officers
Governor — Idris Rashidi ☏ 112 879
Deputy Governor — Mohamed Mbaye ☏ 112 880
Secretary to the Board — Athman Mtengeti ☏ 118 163

Others (Senior Executives)
Chief Cashier — Elizabeth Semainda *Finance Director* ☏ 114 784
Head, Banking Supervision — Charles Kimei *Director* ☏ 118 021
Head, Economics & Statistics — Peter Noni *Director* ☏ 116 612
Head, Public Debt — John Kimaro *Deputy Director* ☏ 115 087
Head, Reserves Management — Judith Ndissi *Deputy Director* ☏ 114 770

Administration
Head of Administration — Casmir Nyoni *Director* ☏ 112 701

Technology & Systems
Information Systems — Edward Makwaia *Deputy Director* ☏ 115 124

Public Relations
Communications — Joseph Mhando *Deputy Director* ☏ 33567

Other (Administration)
Personnel — Casmir Nyoni *Director* ☏ 112 701

THAILAND
(+66)

Bank of Thailand   🏛 Central Bank

273 Samsen Road, Bangkhunprom, Bangkok 10200
Tel: (2) 283 5353 Fax: (2) 280 0449; (2) 280 0626 Telex: 87426 Reuters: BOTI Cable: BANKCHAT
Website: www.bot.or.th

Senior Executive Officers
Governor — Chaiyawat Wibutswasdi ☏ 283 5070
Deputy Governor — Jaroong Nookhwun ☏ 283 5020
Senior Assistant Governor — Siri Ganjarerndee ☏ 283 5080
Assistant Governor — Tanya Sirivedhin ☏ 283 5030
Assistant Governor — Thirachai Phuvanat-Naranubala ☏ 283 5040
Assistant Governor — Techapit Sangsingkeo ☏ 283 5069
Assistant Governor — Kiettisak Meecharoen ☏ 283 5060

Others (Senior Executives)
Head, Bank Examination — Adul Dulyapiradit *Director* ☏ 283 5910
Head, Finance Companies Examination — Swangchit Chaiyawat *Director* ☏ 283 5810
Head, Financial Institutions Regulation — Tarisa Watanagase *Director* ☏ 283 5870
Head, Banking — Tasna Rajabhothi *Director* ☏ 283 5410
Head, Payment Systems — Saowanee Suwannacheep *Director* ☏ 283 5059
Head, Foreign Department — Bandid Nijathaworn *Director* ☏ 283 5110

THAILAND (+66)

Others (Senior Executives) (cont)
Head, Deposits & Bonds   Chetthavee Charoenpitaks *Director* 283 5470
Head, Organization & Management Office   Oubaur Kruthanooch *Director* 283 5558
Office of the Governor   Duangmanee Vongpradhip *Director* 283 5013

Other Departments
Economic Research   Kleo-Thong Hetrakul *Director, Economic Research* 283 5610

Administration
Head of Administration   Sermsingh Sinhaseni *Director* 283 5210

Technology & Systems
Head, Information Technology   Metha Suvanasarn *Director* 283 6005

Legal / In-House Counsel
Head, Legal Department   Krirk Vanikkul *Director* 283 5760

Accounts / Audit
Head, Internal Audit Department   Vikul Ratanachai *Director* 283 5720
Head, Accounting Department   Suwit Nivartvong *Director* 283 5310

Other (Administration)
Head; Personnel   Udomsup Techakampuch *Director* 283 5510

The Asahi Bank Limited
Representative Office

Room 2203, 22nd Floor, Wall Street Tower Building, 33/115 Surawongse Road, Bangkok 10500
Tel: (2) 236 1985 **Fax:** (2) 236 6179 **Telex:** 22061 ASHBK

Senior Executive Officers
Chief Representative   Satoshi Fujio

Australia & New Zealand Banking Group Limited
Representative Office

9th Floor, Tower A, Diethelm Towers, 93/1 Wireless Road, Bangkok 10330
Tel: (2) 256 6350; (2) 256 6358 **Fax:** (2) 256 6347

Senior Executive Officers
Group Representative   Desmond Holmes
Deputy Representative   Achara Boonyahansa

The Bangkok Bank of Commerce Public Company Limited
Head Office

99 Surasak Road, Bangrak, Bangkok 10500
Tel: (2) 267 1900 **Fax:** (2) 234 2939; (2) 266 3372 **Telex:** 82525 **Swift:** BBOC TH BK **Reuters:** BBOC

Senior Executive Officers
Chairman   Aran Thammano
President & Chief Executive Officer   Aswin Kongsiri
Treasurer   Sirot Ongcharit *Head of Treasury & Investment Banking*

Foreign Exchange
Department: Treasury & Investment Banking Department
Tel: 267 1900 **Fax:** 236 7056
Global Head   Sirot Ongcharit *Head of Treasury & Investment Banking*

FX Traders / Sales People
Major currencies   Kanda Harnprasitthada

Settlement / Clearing
Department: International Department
Tel: 267 1900 **Fax:** 234 2939
Regional Head   Boonyapak Wanichpan *Head, International*

Administration
Head of Administration   Yuthapongse Vechapongse

Technology & Systems
    Kulkiat Krepanich *Computer Manager*

Legal / In-House Counsel
    Prasart Yunibhand

Accounts / Audit
    Oytip Sathirakul

THAILAND (+66)   www.euromoneydirectory.com

The Bangkok Bank of Commerce Public Company Limited (cont)

Other (Administration)
Planning & Methods — Permpool Kittisataporn
Marketing — Areeya Duanram

Bangkok Bank Public Company Limited Head Office

333 Silom Road, Bangkok 10500
PO Box 95, Bangkok 10000
Tel: (2) 231 4333 **Fax:** (2) 231 4741; (2) 231 4742 **Telex:** 82670 **Swift:** BKKB TH BK **Reuters:** BBLT; BBBT01-09
Website: www.bbl.co.th

Senior Executive Officers
Executive Chairman — Chatri Sophonpanich
Executive Vice Chairman — Damrong Krishnamara
Executive Vice Chairman — Piti Sithi-Amnuai
President — Chartsiri Sophonpanich
Executive Director — Vira Ramyarupa
Executive Director — Charn Sophonpanich
Executive Director — Amorn Chandarasomboon
Executive Director — Kosit Panpiemras
International Division — Charoen Chinalai *Group Executive Vice President*

General-Lending (DCM, SL)
Head of Corporate Banking — Chansak Fuangfu *Group EVP, Wholesale Banking*

General-Investment
Head of Investment — Banlue Chantadisai *Executive Vice President* ☎ 230 2499 📠 231 4186

General - Treasury
Head of Treasury — Anuja Avilasakul *EVP, Treasury* ☎ 231 4238 📠 231 4240

Equity Capital Markets
Country Head — Ruangchai Siriworakul *Executive Vice President* ☎ 230 1997 📠 236 8272

Syndicated Lending

Loan-Related Activities
Trade Finance — Sumalee Wangprakobsook *EVP, International Trade Finance* ☎ 230 1456 📠 235 0707

Foreign Exchange
Head of Foreign Exchange — Boonsong Bunyasaranand *Executive Vice President* ☎ 231 4300 📠 236 8278

Corporate Finance / M&A Advisory
Head of Corporate Finance — Banlue Chantadisai *Executive Vice President* ☎ 230 2499 📠 231 4186

Settlement / Clearing
Foreign Exchange Settlement — Sumalee Wangprakobsook *EVP, International Trade Finance* ☎ 230 1456 📠 235 0707
Operations — Prasong Uthaisangchai *SEVP, International Banking Operations*
Pornsak Songtaweesin *VP, International Banking Operations* ☎ 231 4216 📠 231 4742

Asset Management

Other (Asset Management)
Fund Management — Anuja Avilasakul *EVP, Treasury* ☎ 231 4238 📠 231 4240

Other Departments
Private Banking — Wallapa Klinpratoom *Senior Vice President* ☎ 231 4246 📠 231 5507
Bordin Unakul *Vice President* ☎ 231 4263 📠 231 5507
Liquidity Management — Anuja Avilasakul *EVP, Treasury* ☎ 231 4238 📠 231 4240

Administration
Head of Marketing — Vites Techangam *Vice President* ☎ 230 1250 📠 231 4166

Technology & Systems
Technology Division — Teera Aphaiwongse *Senior Executive Vice President*
Electronic Banking Services — Vites Techangam *Vice President* ☎ 230 1250 📠 231 4166

Accounts / Audit
Audit & Control Division — Rangsan Wongphayak *Group Executive Vice President*

www.euromoneydirectory.com   THAILAND (+66)

Bangkok Metropolitan Bank Public Company Limited
Head Office

2 Chalermkhet 4 Street, Suanmali, Thepsirin, Pomprap, Bangkok 10100
PO Box 1-99, Plabphachai Post Office, Bangkok 10100
Tel: (2) 223 0561; (2) 225 9999 Fax: (2) 224 3768 Telex: 82281 METROBK TH Swift: BMBL TH BK
Email: info@bmb.co.th Cable: METROBANK

Senior Executive Officers
First Vice President & Chairman — Manit Witayatem
President & Chief Executive Officer — Somchai Sakulsurarat
Senior Vice President — Kamol Anantaprut
Vice President — Malee Luangsuwimon
Managing Director — Panya Tantiyavarong

Others (Senior Executives)
International Banking — Chulapong Bhenchandra *Vice President & Manager*

General-Investment
Head of Investment — Amporn Ruangprasertkul *SVP, Investment Banking*

General - Treasury
Head of Treasury — Watchara Piriasanguanpong *Assistant Vice President*

Syndicated Lending

Other (Syndicated Lending)
Commercial Credit — Sirichai Smanmit *Senior Vice President*
Credit Control — Phongcharoen Sanguansakdi *Senior Vice President*
Industrial Credit Dept. 1; Industrial Credit Dept. 2 — Virat Thanatrongpol *Senior Vice President*

Loan-Related Activities
Project Finance — Paiboon Srisawad *SVP, Project Credit*

Other (Trade Finance)
International Business Dept. — Chawalit Vorasittha *Senior Vice President*
Export Division — Teerachai Udompatipan *Vice President*
Import Division — Dhirasak Dhirathitayangkul *Assistant Vice President*

Foreign Exchange
Head of Foreign Exchange — Orawan Kunchon *Assistant Vice President*

Settlement / Clearing
Operations — Prachak Udomsilp *SVP, Corporate Planning & Research*
Naree Kettong *Senior Vice President*

Other Departments
Correspondent Banking — Saowaluck Nimnual *Manager*
Bhanitnart Lambasara *Senior Manager, Telecommunications Dept.*
Debt Recovery / Restructuring — Bandi Sumetchoengprachya *SVP, Debt Restructuring*

Administration
Head of Administration — Arun Liangpanich *Senior Vice President*

Technology & Systems
Computer Operation — Chareonchai Wongpiya *Senior Vice President*
Information Technology — Yongyuth Pisiviroth *Senior Vice President*

Legal / In-House Counsel
Sayan Angsusingha *Senior Vice President*

Accounts / Audit
Audit — Wilai Wadwongtham *Senior Vice President*
Accounting — Phanuwat Yothaphan *Senior Vice President*

Other (Administration)
Personnel — Chaowana Sisawet *Senior Vice President*
Human Resources — Apinya Kangsanarak *Senior Vice President*
Bangkok International Banking Facilities Office — Danai Petchkul *Office Manager*
Research & Corporate Planning — Prachak Udomsilp *Senior Vice President*

THAILAND (+66) www.euromoneydirectory.com

Bank of America NT & SA
Full Branch Office

Bank of America Center, 2/2 Wireless Road, Patumwan, Bangkok 10330
PO Box 158, Bangkok 10501
Tel: (2) 251 6333 Fax: (2) 253 1905 Telex: 87329 BANAMER TH Swift: BOFA TH 2X Reuters: BAMT
Website: www.bankamerica.com

Senior Executive Officers
SVP & Country Manager — David Proctor david.proctor@bankamerica.com
Financial Director — Narongchai Wongthanavimok VP & Head of Finance
 narongchai.wongthanavimok@bankamerica.com
Treasurer — Pathnasook Chamonchant VP & Country Treasurer

Others (Senior Executives)
Operations — T D L Narasimhan VP & Country Operations Officer
Credit Products Group — David Thomas VP & Credit Product Head
 david.thomas@bankamerica.com

General-Lending (DCM, SL)
Head of Corporate Banking — Douglas Bose VP & Country Credit Officer
 doug.bose@bankamerica.com

Relationship Manager
Financial Institutions — Sumalee Chooratchareon VP & Head, Financial Institutions & BIBF

Administration
Public Relations
Corporate Marketing — Kamalkant Agarwal VP & Head, Corporate Marketing
 kamalkant.agarwal@bankamerica.com

The Bank of Asia
Head Office

191 South Sathorn Road, Khet Sathorn, Bangkok 10120
PO Box 112, Bangkok 10501
Tel: (2) 287 2211; (2) 287 2212 Fax: (2) 287 2933; (2) 287 2934 Telex: 84351 BKASIA TH Swift: BKAS TH BK

Senior Executive Officers
Chairman — Chavalit Thanachanan
President & Chief Executive Officer — Chulakorn Singhakowin
Financial Director — James Stent SEVP, Financial Planning & Management Group
Sirisin Phongtratik SVP, Financial Planning
Treasurer — Wisit Wongpaisan EVP, Funds & Liabilities Management Group

Others (Senior Executives)
Distribution Management Group — Chitraporn Tangsuwan Executive Vice President
Credit Administration Division — Phiphat Phornsuwan Executive Vice President
Consumer Marketing Group — David Hendrix Executive Vice President
Corporate Marketing & Transactional Banking Group — Bruno Schricke Executive Vice President

Syndicated Lending
Special Credit Division — Suthep Dansiriveroj Senior Vice President
Credit Monitoring Division — Vivek Pathak Senior Vice President
Special Credit Division — Prasert Larppipitmongkol Vice President
Corporate Banking 1 — Maralee Kongsala Vice President
Corporate Banking 2 — Kriengsak Tananuwat Vice President
Loan Servicing Dept. — Somchai Pavitpok Vice President

Money Markets
Money Markets - General
Treasury Dept. — Montira Utarapichart Vice President

Risk Management
Head of Risk Management — Abhai Asavanund Senior Executive Vice President
Aart Jongejans Senior Vice President

Other (FI Derivatives)
Risk Supervision Dept. — Suwit Kopwiriyakit Vice President

Settlement / Clearing
Operations — Kriengsak Rerksopist Senior Vice President
Panut Duangudom VP, Trade Processing Dept.

Asset Management
Investment Funds — Pakorn Tanapakorn Vice President

Other (Asset Management)
Fund Management Division — Chaveephan Huntrakul Senior Vice President
Liabilities Management — Dhirajai Yongkittikul Senior Vice President

THAILAND (+66)

Other Departments
Private Banking Sumongkol Singprasong *Vice President*

Administration
Head of Administration Chavalit Timpittaya *Vice President*
Business Development Ngamjit Sirijindalert *VP, Business Support*

Technology & Systems
Information Technology Division Vilawan Vanadurongvan *Executive Vice President*
Information Technology Planning Division Chanindh Homsilpakul *Senior Vice President*
Applied Information Technology Dept Preeprame Tesprasit *Vice President*
Information System Service Dept Teeromanop Fuktongphan *Vice President*
Information System Dev. Dept Anupon Censarn *Vice President*
Information Technology Audit Dept. Sutanai Prasertsup *Vice President*

Legal / In-House Counsel
Legal Affairs Chatri Siripanichkorn *Vice President*

Corporate Communications
 Duangjai Amatyakul *Vice President*

Accounts / Audit
Audit Chris Power *Senior Vice President*
  Pithaya Rimdusit *Vice President*
Accounts Sirisin Phongtratik *Senior Vice President*

Other (Administration)
Human Resources Phongsuree Bunnag *Executive Vice President*
Quality Assurance & Support Division Benjana Asavametha *Senior Vice President*
Supervision & Control Division Wanchai Lerttevasiri *Senior Vice President*
Professional Training & Development Division Passamon Pranutnorapal *Senior Vice President*
Staffing Plans & Recruitment Services Dept. Chanjala Ngaosuvan *Vice President*
Employee Relations Dept. Bunchong Purirakpitikom *Vice President*
Compensation & Benefits Management Dept. Pongchan Namkang *Vice President*
Budgetary Control Dept. Soontree Dhammongkol *Vice President*
Office of Corporate Affairs Yingluk Ratanachai *Vice President*

Bank of Ayudhya Public Company Limited Head Office

1222 Rama III Road, Bang Phongphang, Yan Nawa, Bangkok 10120
PO Box 496 BMC, Bangkok 10000
Tel: (2) 296 2000; (2) 683 1000 **Fax:** (2) 683 1304 **Telex:** 82334 AYUDATH **Swift:** AYUD TH BK
Cable: BANKAYUDYABANGKOK
Website: www.bay.co.th

Senior Executive Officers
Chairman & Chief Executive Officer Krit Ratanarak ☎ 296 3923
President Praphaisith Tankeyura ☎ 296 3831
Chief Executive Officer Krit Ratanarak *Chairman & Chief Executive Officer* ☎ 296 3923
Treasurer Anant Tangtaswas *Vice Chairman & Director* ☎ 296 3887
Secretary to the Board Suwat Suksongkroh ☎ 296 3851
International Division Anant Tangtaswas *Vice Chairman & Director* ☎ 296 3887
  Sawang Thaisriwongse *VP & Manager, International Banking Department*
  ☎ 296 3773

Others (Senior Executives)
 Thipsamat Na Chiengmai *Vice Chairman & Director* ☎ 296 3939

General-Investment
Head of Investment Kamol Boondiskulchok *Executive Vice President* ☎ 296 3898
  Tinnawat Mahatharadol *SVP, Investment Banking* ☎ 296 3763

General - Treasury
Head of Treasury Nanthasit Leksrisakul *Senior Vice President* ☎ 296 3761

Debt Capital Markets / Fixed Income
Global Head Kamol Boondiskulchok *Executive Vice President* ☎ 296 3898

Syndicated Lending
Country Head Virojn Srethapramotaya *Executive Vice President* ☎ 296 3877

Other (Syndicated Lending)
Credit Operation Department Ekasak Puripol *Vice Chairman & Director* ☎ 296 3837

Loan-Related Activities
Trade Finance Anant Tangtaswas *Vice Chairman & Director* ☎ 296 3887
Project Finance Virojn Srethapramotaya *Executive Vice President* ☎ 296 3877

Foreign Exchange
Global Head Anant Tangtaswas *Vice Chairman & Director* ☎ 296 3887

THAILAND (+66)   www.euromoneydirectory.com

Bank of Ayudhya Public Company Limited (cont)
Administration
Head of Administration   Tiamchi Surapath *Senior Vice President* ☎ 296 3450
Technology & Systems
Computer Department   Nuekruk Baingern *Executive Vice President* ☎ 296 3898
Legal / In-House Counsel
Legal Consultant Department   Amornsuk Noparumpa *First Executive VP* ☎ 296 3833
Public Relations
   Jamlong Atikul *Executive Vice President* ☎ 296 3794
Shareholder Relationis   Suwat Suksongkroh *Secretary to the Board* ☎ 296 3851
Accounts / Audit
Accounts Department   Jamlong Atikul *Executive Vice President* ☎ 296 3794
Audit Department   Yongyuth Withyawongsaruchi *Executive Vice President* ☎ 296 3855
Accounts Department   Savang Tongsmutra *Senior Vice President* ☎ 296 3853
Other (Administration)
Business Development   Ekasak Puripol *Vice Chairman & Director* ☎ 296 3837
Economic Research   Jamlong Atikul *Executive Vice President* ☎ 296 3794
Personnel Department   Somrit Srithongdee *Senior Vice President* ☎ 296 3753

Bank Brussels Lambert
Representative Office

19th Floor, CP Tower, 313 Silom Road, Bangkok 10500
Tel: (2) 231 0696; (2) 238 2220 **Fax:** (2) 231 0698 **Telex:** 21036 BBLBK TH
General Tel: 231 0697

Senior Executive Officers
Representative   Daniel Tan

The Bank of Yokohama Limited
Representative Office

22nd Floor, CP Tower Building, 313 Silom Road, Bangkok 10500
Tel: (2) 231 0430/1 **Fax:** (2) 231 0429 **Telex:** 82568

Senior Executive Officers
Chief Representative   Nobuyuki Oi

Bankers Trust Company
Full Branch Office

12 Floor, TISCO Tower, 46/50 North Sathorn Road, Bangkok 10500
Tel: (2) 638 0888 **Fax:** (2) 236 6711 **Telex:** 87040 BANTRUS TH

Senior Executive Officers
General Manager   Morgan A Laughlin

BNP BIBF
Offshore Banking Unit

29th Floor, 990 Place, 990 Rama IV Road, Bangkok 10500
Tel: (2) 636 1900 **Fax:** (2) 636 1935 **Telex:** 87214 NABAPAR TH

Senior Executive Officers
Directeur   François Van Den Bosch ☎ 636 1900 ext 155
Secretary General   Jacques Gimfeld ☎ 636 1900 ext 122

Citibank NA
Full Branch Office

Citibank Tower, 82 North Sathorn Road, Yannawa, Bangkok 10120
Tel: (2) 232 2200 **Fax:** (2) 639 2571

Senior Executive Officers
Chief Executive Officer   Shaukat Tarin *Country Corporate Officer* ☎ 232 2000
Treasurer   Yotin Chenvanich ☎ 287 2371
Managing Director / General Manager   Shaukat Tarin ☎ 287 1459
General-Lending (DCM, SL)
Head of Corporate Banking   Henry Ho ☎ 287 1214
Debt Capital Markets / Fixed Income
Country Head   Dr. Kamol Boondiskulchok ☎ 286 1969

www.euromoneydirectory.com   THAILAND (+66)

Equity Capital Markets
Country Head   Dr. Kamol Boondiskulchok ☏ 286 1969
Foreign Exchange
Global Head   Panya Chanyarungrojn ☏ 287 2396
Risk Management
Foreign Exchange Derivatives / Risk Management
Global Head   Ivan Wong ☏ 679 0152
Settlement / Clearing
Operations   Harish Suri *Transaction Services Head*

Commerzbank AG   Representative Office
13th Floor, Regent House, 183 Rajadamri Road, Bangkok 10330
Tel: (2) 254 4506; (2) 254 4507 Fax: (2) 254 4505

Senior Executive Officers
Chief Representative   Hans-Kurt Schäser

The Dai-Ichi Kangyo Bank Limited

c/o Krungsri River Hotel, 27/2 Moo 11 Rojana Road, Tambol Kamang, Amphur Muang, Ayuthayas 13000
Tel: (35) 235 151; (35) 235 152 Fax: (35) 235 150 Telex: 20612

Senior Executive Officers
General Manager   Shigeru Koga

The Dai-Ichi Kangyo Bank Limited   Full Branch Office

18th Floor, Tisco Tower, 48 North Sathorn Road, Silom, Bangkok 10500
Tel: (2) 638 0200; (2) 638 0201 Fax: (2) 638 0218; (2) 638 0220 Telex: 20612 Reuters: DKTH
Extra Tel: 638 0202; 638 0203; Telex: 20626; Extra Tel: 638 0204; 638 0205; MONEY MARKETS & FX Tel: 638 0180
Website: www.dkb.co.jp

Senior Executive Officers
General Manager   Shigeru Koga
Deputy General Manager   Tadashi Inose
Deputy General Manager   Kinzo Ando

Others (Senior Executives)
Business Promotion I   Takashi Suto *Senior Manager*
Business Promotion II   Virachai Boditpat *Senior Manager, Project Finance Group*
Accounting   Eiichi Oshima *Senior Manager*
General Affairs   Somjai Vanichsombat *Senior Manager*
Operations & International Operations Jun Esashi *Manager*
Accounting, EDP Group   Saowalak Poparn *Manager*
Loan Administration   Jareeporn Bumroongchai *Manager*
Research & Planning   Chaiwate Reargpiboon *Manager*
Personnel   Prissana Chianpradit *Manager*

General-Lending (DCM, SL)
Head of Corporate Banking   Junichi Nagaoka *Senior Manager, BP II Deptartment*

General - Treasury
Head of Treasury   Kiyotaka Ishikawa *Senior Manager*
                              Ekachai Sompansatit *Treasury, Chief Dealer*

Syndicated Lending
Fax: 266 6626
Other (Syndicated Lending)
                              Jareeporn Bumroongchai *Manager*

Loan-Related Activities
Trade Finance   Jun Esashi *Manager*
Project Finance   Virachai Boditpat *Senior Manager, Project Finance Group*
Money Markets
Tel: 638 0175 Fax: 638 0222 Reuters: DKTH
Head of Money Markets   Atikarn Mundang *Senior Officer*
Other   Pakapong Pakwisutikul *Officer*
                              Rungsiya Chernvitiyakul *Officer*

Euromoney Directory 1999 **1587**

THAILAND (+66)   www.euromoneydirectory.com

The Dai-Ichi Kangyo Bank Limited (cont)
Foreign Exchange
Tel: 638 0175 Fax: 638 0222 **Reuters:** DKTH
Head of Foreign Exchange
Corporate Sales
Head of Trading

Ekachai Sompansatit *Treasury, Chief Dealer*
Paiboon Peeraparp *Assistant Manager*
Pichet Piyasirisilp *Senior Officer*

FX Traders / Sales People
FX Trader
Corporate Sales

Pornsuang Viehavispanthat *Officer*
Pattharin Rungquansirikoj *Senior Officer*
Phatraradee Chigulgitnivat *Officer*

Settlement / Clearing
Tel: 638 0197
Head of Settlement / Clearing
Operations

Pornchai Titivutivong *Assistant Manager, Treasury Admin. Group*
Jun Esashi *Manager*

Other Departments
Chief Credit Officer

Takashi Suto *Senior Manager*
Junichi Nagaoka *Senior Manager, BP II Deptartment*

Administration
Business Development

Takashi Suto *Senior Manager*

Technology & Systems
EDP Group

Saowalak Poparn *Manager*

Legal / In-House Counsel

Chaiwate Reargpiboon *Manager*

Accounts / Audit
Accounting

Eiichi Oshima *Senior Manager*
Saowalak Poparn *Manager*

Other (Administration)
Personnel
Research & Planning
General Affairs

Prissana Chianpradit *Manager*
Chaiwate Reargpiboon *Manager*
Somjai Vanichsombat *Senior Manager*

The Dai-Ichi Kangyo Bank Limited

3rd Floor, Thai Farmers Bank, 46 Sukhumvit Road, Siracha, Chonburi 20110
Tel: (38) 772 499; (38) 722 500 **Fax:** (38) 722 501 **Telex:** 20612
Website: www.dkb.co.jp

Senior Executive Officers
General Manager   Shigeru Koga

The Daiwa Bank Limited   Representative Office

13th Floor, Regent House Building, 183 Rajdamri Road, Pathumwan, Bangkok 10330
Tel: (2) 251 7555 **Fax:** (2) 254 7557 **Telex:** 82445

Senior Executive Officers
Chief Representative   Kazuhiko Morikawa

Deutsche Bank   Full Branch Office

208 Wireless Road, Bangkok 10330, Bangkok
Tel: (2) 651 5000 **Fax:** (2) 651 5151 **Telex:** 87949 DBA TH **Swift:** DEUT TH BK
Foreign Exchange **Tel:** 651 5099; **Fax:** 651 5151
Website: www.deutsche-bank.de

Senior Executive Officers
General Manager   Thomas Verlohr

Other Departments

Other Departments
Head, Financial Markets   Mr Raghavan

www.euromoneydirectory.com THAILAND (+66)

DG BANK
Representative Office

Level 23, CP Tower, 313 Silom Road, Bangkok 10500
Tel: (2) 231 8310 Fax: (2) 231 8311

Senior Executive Officers
Representative — Danielle Yvonne Schwaar

First Bangkok City Bank Public Limited Company

Suan Mali, Yukol Soi 2, Bangkok 10100
PO Box 75, Bangkok 10501
Tel: (2) 223 0501; (2) 223 0511 Fax: (2) 225 3036; (2) 621 6649 Telex: 21323 THB Swift: FBCB THBK Reuters: FBCT
Vedro Vuthikongsirigool Tel: 225 3049; 225 3050

Senior Executive Officers
Chairman — Pramon Sutivong
President — Sirivuthi Siambhakder ☏ 224 9542 📠 225 3065
Financial Director — Vedro Vuthikongsirigool ☏ 335 3048
Company Secretary — Somon Vongpanich
Chief Representative — Sethachai Sriverokul ☏ 621 6578

General-Lending (DCM, SL)
Head of Corporate Banking — Somchai Nintanavongsa

General-Investment
Head of Investment — Thirawat Nuangnong

Debt Capital Markets / Fixed Income
Head of Fixed Income — Yuthapong Ch Roachprasert

Fixed-Income Repo
Head of Repo — Veera Vuthikongsirikul

Equity Capital Markets
Head of Equity Capital Markets — Somchai Nintanavongsa

Domestic Equities
Head of Origination — Bomchai Pienpicharana
Head of Syndication — Thirawat Nuangnong

Other (Domestic Equities)
Securities Lending — Somchai Nintanavongsa

Syndicated Lending
Trade Finance — Woranoot Decharin
Project Finance — Thirawat Nuangnong

Money Markets
Head of Money Markets — Veera Vuthikongsirikul

Foreign Exchange
Head of Foreign Exchange — Yupar Suntivorayart

Settlement / Clearing
Head of Settlement / Clearing — Suwat Srisuvirangkoon

Global Custody
Head of Global Custody — Somchai Pienpicharana

Asset Management
Head — Pronee Buranawotonachoke

Other Departments
Commodities / Bullion — Ekasin Aroonmarts
Chief Credit Officer — Prasong Jariyasopit
Correspondent Banking — Suteera Benyajati
Cash Management — Suwat Srisuvirangkoon

Administration
Head of Administration — Prasong Jariyasopit
Business Development — Panida Rakbamrung

Technology & Systems
Pongsak Cheweharat

Legal / In-House Counsel
Opas Dujpen

Compliance
Saroj Chantawatchai

Public Relations
Janet Charoensiriwath

THAILAND (+66)   www.euromoneydirectory.com

First Bangkok City Bank Public Limited Company (cont)
Accounts / Audit
                         Saroj Dujpen

The Fuji Bank Limited   Full Branch Office
6th Floor, Q House Convent Building, 38 Convent Road, Silom, Bangkok 10500
Tel: (2) 632 1900 **Fax:** (2) 632 1919; (2) 237 8952 **Telex:** 84433 **Swift:** FUJITHBK
Senior Executive Officers
General Manager   Fusato Suzuki

The Hongkong & Shanghai Banking Corporation Limited
                                                            Full Branch Office
Hongkong Bank Building, 64 Silom Road, Bangkok 10500
Tel: (2) 267 2960; (2) 266 9070 **Fax:** (2) 236 7687; (2) 236 6688 **Telex:** 82932 HSBC KH TH
Senior Executive Officers
Financial Director   Pintip Kongvananon *Financial Controller*
Chief Operating Officer   Thanuwat Ratanadilok na Bhuket *Manager, Banking Services*
Treasurer   Paul R Hand *Manager, Treasury & Capital Markets*

The Industrial Bank of Japan Limited   Full Branch Office
15th Floor, Thai Obayashi Building, 161 Rajdamri Road, Lumpini, Pathumwan, Bangkok 10330
Tel: (2) 255 5991 **Fax:** (2) 255 5990 **Telex:** 20544 IBJBKK TH
Senior Executive Officers
General Manager   Masatsugu Nagato

ING Baring International   Representative Office
8th Floor, Sindhorn Tower 1, 130-132 Wireless Road, Bangkok 10330
Tel: (2) 263 2888; (2) 263 2889 **Fax:** (2) 263 2879
Senior Executive Officers
Country Manager   Tanate Phutrakul
Corporate Finance / M&A Advisory
Department: ING Baring International Advisors
Head of Corporate Finance   Tanate Phutrakul *Country Manager*

ING Barings
7th Floor, Sindhorn Tower I, 130-132 Wireless Road, Bangkok 10330
Tel: (2) 263 3301/14 **Fax:** (2) 263 3315 **Telex:** 21141 INGB KK TH
Senior Executive Officers
Country Manager   Tanate Phutrakul

ING Barings
6th Floor, Bangkok Bank Building, 98 Sukhumvit Road, Sriracha, Chonburi 20110
Tel: (38) 770 577/80 **Fax:** (38) 770 576
Senior Executive Officers
Manager   Varit Lekprasert

International Finance Corporation   Representative Office
Diethelm Tower A, 17th Floor, 93/1 Wireless Road, Bangkok 10330
Tel: (2) 650 9253; (2) 650 9258 **Fax:** (2) 650 9259
Senior Executive Officers
Chief of Mission   Khalid A Mirza

www.euromoneydirectory.com				THAILAND (+66)

Jardine Fleming Thanakom Securities Limited   Subsidiary Company
29th Floor, Silom Complex Office Building, 191 Silom Road, Bangrak District, Bangkok 10500
Tel: (2) 231 3770 **Fax:** (2) 231 3797

Krungthai Bank Public Company Limited   Head Office
35 Sukhumvit Road, Klong Toei, Bangkok 10110
PO Box 44 BMC, Bangkok 10000
Tel: (2) 256 8488; (2) 256 8840 **Fax:** (2) 255 9391; (2) 255 9396 **Telex:** 81179 **Swift:** KRTH TH BK **Reuters:** KTBT
Cable: KRUNGTHAI BANGKO

Senior Executive Officers
Chairman   Suphachai Phisitvanich
President   Sirin Nimmanahaeminda
Chief Executive Officer   Supang Pattamadilok *Senior Vice President*
Chief Operating Officer   Chujit Niyamosot *SVP, Credit*
Treasurer   Permporn Sittipiyasakul *SVP, Treasury*
Senior Vice President   Pichai Kojamitr

Debt Capital Markets / Fixed Income
Global Head   Teeraphan Jittaralan *VP & Manager* ☏ **208 3333**

Syndicated Lending
Global Head   Yaovaluk Likitwattanurak *VP, Corporate Banking* ☏ **208 3361**

Money Markets
Global Head   Permporn Sittipiyasakul *SVP & Treasurer* ☏ **208 3009**

Foreign Exchange
Global Head   Kalaya Ampawasiri *SVP, Forex & Remittance* ☏ **208 4250**

Settlement / Clearing
Regional Head   Thiravatna Vathanathorn *SVP, Banking Operations* ☏ **208 2222**

London Forfaiting Hong Kong Limited   Representative Office
16th Floor, 21/123 Thai Wah Tower II, South Sathorn Road, Sathorn, Bangkok 10120
Tel: (2) 679 1445 **Fax:** (2) 679 1454 **Email:** lfapbkk@ksc.th.com

Senior Executive Officers
Associate Director   Pramest (Jack) Sutabutr

The Long-Term Credit Bank of Japan Limited   Full Branch Office
12th Floor, Thai Obayashi Building, Rajdamri Road, 161 Rajdamri Road, Lumpini, Pathumwan, Bangkok 10330
Tel: (2) 253 4687 **Fax:** (2) 253 3983

Merrill Lynch International Bank   Representative Office
Unit 303, Tower A, Diethelm Towers, 93/1 Wireless Road, Bangkok 10330
Tel: (2) 252 3168 **Fax:** (2) 256 6191

The Mitsubishi Trust & Banking Corporation   Representative Office
13th Floor, Ramaland Building, 952 Rama IV Road, Bangkok 10500
Tel: (2) 632 9835; (2) 632 9838 **Fax:** (2) 632 9840 **Telex:** 20289 MTBC TH

Senior Executive Officers
Chief Representative   Kaname Nakai

THAILAND (+66)   www.euromoneydirectory.com

Nakornthon Bank Public Company Limited   Head Office

90 North Sathorn Road, Bangrak, Bangkok 10500
Tel: (2) 233 2111; (2) 233 8070 **Fax:** (2) 236 4226; (2) 236 1963 **Telex:** 82837, 21341 NABANK TH **Swift:** NTBL TH BK
Email: treasury@ntb.co.th
General Tel: 636 7000; **Treasury Tel:** 230 7340; 636 7204; **Fax:** 236 1963; **Treasury Tel:** 230 7341; 636 7205; **Treasury Tel:** 230 7342; 636 7206; **Treasury Tel:** 230 7343; 636 7207; **Treasury Tel:** 230 7344; 636 7208; **Treasury Tel:** 230 7345; 636 7209
Website: www.ntb.co.th

Senior Executive Officers
Chairman — Sunthorn Hongladarom
President — Thamnu Wanglee
Chief Executive Officer — Vorawee Wanglee
Managing Director — Kitti Patpongpibul

Others (Senior Executives)
Advisor — Damrong Ridhisilpa
Adviser — Oon Oonsiri
Advisor — Asvin Chintakananda
Vichit Lorchirachoonkul

General-Lending (DCM, SL)
Head of Corporate Banking — Prasarn Katanyutanon *EVP, Corporate & Investment Banking*
Oraphan Phadana-Anake *VP, Corporate Banking*
Soavalux Anotharom *VP, Corporate Banking*
Arpaporn Palungvitvatana *VP, Corporate Banking*
Montri Karanasophonphun *VP, Corporate Banking*
Wanna Mahanvanont *VP, Corporate Banking*
Vichai Limanubhava *VP, Corporate Banking*
Pornchai Pongpermkijwattana *VP, Corporate Banking*
Petch Wanglee *VP, Corporate Banking*

General-Investment
Head of Investment — Somsak Chaiyadej *VP, Investment Banking*

General - Treasury
Head of Treasury — Nongluk Patchana *Vice President*
Sutee Losopulkul *Senior Vice President*

Relationship Manager
Development Group
Foreign & Support Groups — Vallobh Setasuvarna *Senior Vice President*
Pongsak Banpotjit *Senior Vice President*

Syndicated Lending

Other (Syndicated Lending)
Credit Administration — Kesya Kasemsarn *Vice President*
Credit Support — Pairoj Poksupat *Vice President*

Other (Trade Finance)
International Trade — Chusak Wanglavan *Vice President*

Settlement / Clearing
Operations — Komkai Tangtrongkid *Vice President*
Ekapol Chutsastee *Vice President*

Administration

Technology & Systems
Technology Group — Srichan Changwatchai *Senior Vice President*

Accounts / Audit
Audit Group — Manusan Sirisudhi *Senior Vice President*
Accounting, Foreign, Support Group — Damrong Ridhisilpa *Senior Executive Vice President*
Accounting Group — Anchalee Siriwadhana *Senior Vice President*
Accounting Department — Pichit Pakjamsai *Vice President*

Other (Administration)
Management Group — Thavisakdi Kuruchittham *Executive Vice President*
Policy & Human Resources Groups — Indhira Wattanakasaem *Executive Vice President*
Human Resources — Kalayanee Koonme *Senior Vice President*
Human Resources Development Department — Phiansiri Phuphan *Vice President*
Human Resources Management Department — Arporn Siwayabrahm *Assistant Vice President*
Liaison Division — Seri Sukhabut *Vice President*

www.euromoneydirectory.com THAILAND (+66)

Paribas Asia Equity

889 Thai CC Tower, South Sathorn Road, Bangkok 10120
Tel: (2) 675 9210 Fax: (2) 210 0395

Senior Executive Officers
General Manager   Patrick Milon

Radanasin Bank Public Company Limited   Head Office

Formerly known as: Laem Thong Bank Public Co Limited
690 Sukhumvit Road, Bangkok 10110
Tel: (2) 260 0090; (2) 260 0100 Fax: (2) 260 5310; (2) 260 5353 Telex: 20820 RSBX TH Swift: RSBX TH BK
Email: dsarup@laemthong-bank.co.th Reuters: LTBT Cable: RADANASIN Telex: 20820 lamtoth th
Website: www.radanasin-bank.co.th

Senior Executive Officers
Chairman   Vichit Surepongchai ☎ 661 4567 📠 661 4566
President   Sirichai Sombatsiri ☎ 260 5343 📠 260 5673

General-Lending (DCM, SL)
Head of Corporate Banking   Robert Cheng *First Executive Vice President* ☎ 260 5347 📠 260 5311

General - Treasury
Head of Treasury   Prawat Rakpatapeesuwan *First Senior Vice President* ☎ 259 4474
📠 259 4627

Syndicated Lending
Loan-Related Activities
Trade Finance   Kishore Madduri *First Senior Vice President* ☎ 259 44781 📠 259 4627

Settlement / Clearing
Head of Settlement / Clearing   Rungrote Nakeeraks *First Vice President* ☎ 259 1621 📠 259 4627

Other Departments
Chief Credit Officer   Nipitaporn Mulapruk *Executive Vice President* ☎ 661 4553 📠 260 5353
Private Banking   Ussanee Tachawanapong *First Executive Vice President* ☎ 260 5367
📠 258 0526

Administration
Head of Administration   Rachanee Kimsavadi *First Senior Vice President* ☎ 260 5322 📠 260 5310
Head of Marketing   Ganok Deepraditkul *Executive Vice President* ☎ 661 4563 📠 259 4615

Technology & Systems
     Bovorit Pibulsonggram *First Senior Vice President* ☎ 260 5317 📠 260 5310
Head of Retail Banking & Information   Deepak Sarup *First Executive Vice President* ☎ 259 6086 📠 259 6088
Technology

Legal / In-House Counsel
     Ampaiwan Limprapassorn *First Vice Chairman* ☎ 260 5315 📠 260 5310

Public Relations
     Pornthip Narupakorn *Advisor* ☎ 260 3916 📠 260 5406

Accounts / Audit
Head of Audit   Nithiwadii Chaturapush *First Executive Vice President* ☎ 260 5351
📠 259 4611

SBC Warburg Premier Securities Co Limited

13th Floor, Diethelm Tower A, 93/1 Wireless Road, Pathumwan, Bangkok 10330
Tel: (2) 252 3867 Fax: (2) 252 3966

Senior Executive Officers
Chief Executive Officer   Michael Oertli *Managing Director*
Chief Operating Officer   A Blake

Equity Capital Markets
Other (Domestic Equities)
Equities Distribution - Local Retail   W Putthapiwat
Equities Distribution - Local Institutions   O Vachiruksasavakul

Other (International Equity)
Equities Distribution - International   R M Bowers

Equity Research
Country Head   T Taylor

Corporate Finance / M&A Advisory
Global Head   M L Subhasiddhi Jumbala

THAILAND (+66)　　　　　www.euromoneydirectory.com

Siam City Bank Public Company Limited　　Head Office
1101 New Petchburi Road, Bangkok 10400
Tel: (2) 208 5000 Fax: (2) 253 1240; (2) 253 1414 Telex: 87451 NAKONBK TH Swift: SITY TH BK Reuters: SCIT

Senior Executive Officers
Chairman　　　　　　　　　　　Sivavong Changkasiri
President　　　　　　　　　　　Sompoch Intranukul
Treasurer　　　　　　　　　　　Enghug Nontikarn *Senior Vice President*

Other Departments
Correspondent Banking　　　　Ekapong Rugrien *Associate Vice President* ☎ **651 7906**

Siam Commercial Bank Public Company Limited　　Head Office
9 Rutchadapisek Road, Ladyao, Jatujak, Bangkok 10900
Tel: (2) 544 3888; (2) 937 7628 Fax: (2) 937 7629 Telex: 82283 SCBSECS TH Swift: SICO TH BK
Website: www.scb.co.th

Senior Executive Officers
Chairman　　　　　　　　　　　　　Prachit Yossundara ☎ **544 1244**
President & Chief Executive Officer　　Olarn Chaipravat ☎ **544 1222**

Debt Capital Markets / Fixed Income
Tel: 544 3889 Fax: 937 7629
Global Head　　　　　　　　　　　Yokporn Tantisawetrat *SVP & Manager* ☎ **544 3888** 📠 **937 7629**

Medium-Term Notes
Head of Origination　　　　　　　Sataporn Jinachitra *FEVP, International Banking Group* ☎ **544 1123**

Private Placements
Head of Origination　　　　　　　Nattapong Samit-Ampaipisarn *VP, Treasury* ☎ **544 2335**

Syndicated Lending
Tel: 544 1123 Fax: 937 7702
Global Head　　　　　　　　　　　Sataporn Jinachitra *FEVP, International Banking Group* ☎ **544 1123**

Loan-Related Activities
Trade Finance　　　　　　　　　　Namtip Potisat *SVP, International Trade Dept 1* ☎ **544 4145**
　　　　　　　　　　　　　　　　　Songsak Wairatpanij *VP & Manager, Dept 2* ☎ **544 4141**
Project Finance　　　　　　　　　Somrudee Amatayakul *SVP, Corporate Dept 3* ☎ **544 2829**

Money Markets
Tel: 544 2332 Fax: 937 7662
Global Head　　　　　　　　　　　Somchai Sanyalaksiri *SVP, Treasury*

Domestic Commercial Paper
Head of Origination　　　　　　　Yokporn Tantisawetrat *SVP & Manager* ☎ **544 3888** 📠 **937 7629**

Eurocommercial Paper
Head of Origination　　　　　　　Sataporn Jinachitra *FEVP, International Banking Group* ☎ **544 1123**

Wholesale Deposits
Marketing　　　　　　　　　　　　Somchai Sanyalaksiri *SVP, Treasury*

Foreign Exchange
Tel: 544 3701 Fax: 937 7687
Global Head　　　　　　　　　　　Sutharntip Pisitbuntoon *SVP, FX & Remittance*

Risk Management
Tel: 544 2332 Fax: 937 7662
Global Head　　　　　　　　　　　Somchai Sanyalaksiri *SVP, Treasury*

Fixed Income Derivatives / Risk Management
Global Head　　　　　　　　　　　Somchai Sanyalaksiri *SVP, Treasury*

Foreign Exchange Derivatives / Risk Management
Cross-Currency Swaps, Sales / Marketing　Somchai Sanyalaksiri *SVP, Treasury*

Exchange-Traded Derivatives
Global Head　　　　　　　　　　　Somchai Sanyalaksiri *SVP, Treasury*

Corporate Finance / M&A Advisory
Tel: 544 1167 Fax: 937 7716
Global Head　　　　　　　　　　　Kriang Kiatfuengfoo *FEVP, Corporate Group 2*

Settlement / Clearing
Tel: 544 2332 Fax: 937 7662
Regional Head　　　　　　　　　　Somchai Sanyalaksiri *SVP, Treasury*

Global Custody
Tel: 544 3889 Fax: 937 7629
Regional Head　　　　　　　　　　Yokporn Tantisawetrat *SVP & Manager* ☎ **544 3888** 📠 **937 7629**

www.euromoneydirectory.com   THAILAND (+66)

Other Departments
Correspondent Banking   Panit Visutyothapibal *SVP, International Banking* ☎ 544 4999
Administration
Public Relations
                                        Anchalipan Amornvivat *SVP, Business Promotion* ☎ 544 4455

The Siam Sanwa Industrial Credit Public Company Limited
Head Office

Alternative trading name: SICCO
             130/132 Sindhorn Tower II, Wireless Road, Bangkok 10330
             PO Box 11-1334, Nana, Bangkok 10112
             Tel: (2) 263 2100; (2) 650 9990 **Fax:** (2) 263 2041; (2) 263 2046 **Telex:** 82393 SICCO TH
             Email: wparndej@mozart.inet.co.th **Reuters:** SICC

Senior Executive Officers
Chief Executive Officer   Chanin Roonsamrarn *Managing Director & Chief Executive* ☎ 263 2050
Financial Director; Treasurer   Kornrat Kosakarn *Senior Vice President* ☎ 255 9900
Managing Director   Chanin Roonsamrarn ☎ 263 2050
Senior Vice President   Ugrit Xuto ☎ 263 7113

Debt Capital Markets / Fixed Income
Domestic Government Bonds
Head of Sales   Kornrat Kosakarn *Senior Vice President* ☎ 255 9900

Fixed-Income Repo
Head of Repo   Kornrat Kosakarn *Senior Vice President* ☎ 255 9900

Equity Capital Markets
Head of Equity Capital Markets   Siripong Sutharoj *Executive Vice President* ☎ 263 2061

Syndicated Lending
Loan-Related Activities
Project Finance   Wichet Warakul *Senior Vice President* ☎ 251 7635

Money Markets
Head of Money Markets   Kornrat Kosakarn *Senior Vice President* ☎ 255 9900

Risk Management
OTC Credit Derivatives
Head   Kornrat Kosakarn *Senior Vice President* ☎ 255 9900

Settlement / Clearing
Back-Office   Chomchaba Sathapornpong *Vice President* ☎ 253 5283

Administration
Head of Administration   Ugrit Xuto *Senior Vice President* ☎ 263 7113

Technology & Systems
                                        Orapim Chalarug *Vice President* ☎ 251 7606

Legal / In-House Counsel
                                        Chuchart Methawat *Assistant Vice President* ☎ 253 7113

Compliance
                                        Nakorn Lampaves *Senior Manager* ☎ 263 2100

Accounts / Audit
                                        Waraporn Kengsurakarn *Vice President* ☎ 263 3040

Société Générale - Bangkok International Banking Facility
         16th Floor, Sindhorn Tower III, 130-132 Wireless Road, Bangkok 10330
                     Tel: (2) 263 3171 **Fax:** (2) 263 3178 **Telex:** 82520 SOGEN TH
                                 Website: www.socgen.com

Standard Chartered Bank   Full Branch Office
                            990 Rama IV Road, Bangkok 10500
             Tel: (2) 636 1000 **Fax:** (2) 636 1199 **Telex:** TH 81163 SCBBAN **Swift:** SCBL TH BK

Senior Executive Officers
Chief Executive Officer   Dru Narwani ☎ 232 6000
Financial Director   Rachanee Tripipatkul *Head, Country Finance* ☎ 232 6345
Treasurer   Thippaporn Gertphol ☎ 232 6107

THAILAND (+66) www.euromoneydirectory.com

Standard Chartered Bank (cont)

Others (Senior Executives)
Corporate & Institutional Banking   Mike Wood ☏ 232 6004

Global Custody
Department: Standard Chartered Equitor
Tel: 636 1000 Fax: 238 3673
Country Head   Mike Staples *Manager Custodial Services* ☏ 232 6297

Administration

Compliance
    Pornchai Wiwatpattarakul *Head* ☏ 232 6002

Other (Administration)
Human Resources   Arthakrit Visudtibhand *Head* ☏ 232 6365

The Thai Bond Dealing Centre — Head Office

Alternative trading name: Bond Dealers Club
21st Floor, Vanissa Building, 29 Soi Chidlom, Ploenchit Road, Bangkok 10330
Tel: (2) 267 9346 **Fax:** (2) 267 9188 **Email:** bdc09@bdc.or.th

Senior Executive Officers
President   Jaroungpon Hoonsiri

The Thai Danu Bank Public Company Limited — Head Office

393 Silom Road, Bangkok 10500
PO Box 1101, Bangkok 10501
Tel: (2) 230 5000 **Fax:** (2) 236 7939 **Telex:** 82959 DANUBANTH **Swift:** DANUBANK **Reuters:** TDBB

Senior Executive Officers
Chairman & Chief Executive Officer   Pakorn Thavisin
President   Pornsanong Tuchinda
Financial Director   Seow Kheng Hee
Chief Operating Officer   M L Ayuth Jayant
Treasurer   Nitikorn Tantitham
Company Secretary   Prangmas Nitiham
International Division   Punnee Bunchongkiat

General-Lending (DCM, SL)
Head of Corporate Banking   Surakiat Wongwasin

General-Investment
Head of Investment   Satian Tantanasarit ✉ bigtui@loxinfo.co.th

Equity Capital Markets
Head of Equity Capital Markets   Tan Soo Nan

Equity Repo / Securities Lending
Head   Veerawan Vudhivat

Other Departments
Private Banking   Chaiwat Utaiwan

Administration
Head of Administration   Uthai Monthawornwong
Business Development   Luecha Sukrasebya
Head of Marketing   Sudasiriwatana Kaewamput

Technology & Systems
    Pongvit Siribovornklat

Public Relations
    Sudasiriwatana Kaewamput

Accounts / Audit
    Vilai Tantikun

www.euromoneydirectory.com   THAILAND (+66)

Thai Farmers Bank Public Company Limited   Head Office

1 Thai Farmers Lane, Ratburana Road, Bangkok 10140
Tel: (2) 470 1122; (2) 470 1199 **Fax:** (2) 470 1144; (2) 470 1145 **Telex:** 81159FARMERS TH **Swift:** TFBS TH BK
Cable: FARMERS BANGKOK **Telex:** 82542 FARMERS TH **Telex:** 84798 FARMERS TH **Telex:** 84799 FARMERS TH
Website: www.tfb.co.th

Senior Executive Officers
Chairman — Banyong Lamsam T 470 1130 F 470 2748
Vice Chairman — Pol Gen Pow Sarasin T 470 1190 F 470 2748
Vice Chairman — Chana Rungsang T 470 1160 F 470 2748
President — Banthoon Lamsam T 470 1155 F 470 2749

Others (Senior Executives)
Kaorop Nutchanart *Senior Executive Vice President* T 470 1136 F 470 2749

General-Investment
Head of Investment — Tawit Thanachanan *FVP, Merchant Banking* T 470 2200 F 470 2224
Somkiat Sirichatchai *FVP, Investment Management* T 470 2225 F 470 2249

General - Treasury
Head of Treasury — Chantana Soi-Ampornkun *SVP, Treasury* T 470 2000 F 871 3636

Relationship Manager
Personlized Small Business Loans — Dolapar Petpiroon *First Vice President, Consumer Loans* T 273 1650 F 273 1664

Syndicated Lending
Other (Trade Finance)
International Trade — Jirayon Sangkasuwan *Senior Vice President* T 470 1480/1 F 470 1531

Foreign Exchange
Corporate Sales — Anchalee Chairatapapan *Manager* T 470 3008 F 871 3638
Darunee Chenrukmatupoom *Assistant Division Manager* T 470 3006 F 871 3638
Hataiporn Chiemprasert *Assistant Treasury Marketing* T 470 3008 F 871 3640
Sucha Maneesutham *Treasury Marketing* T 470 3006 F 871 3638
Suporn Jongruksuk *Assistant Treasury Marketing* T 470 3008 F 871 3640
Head of Trading — Amporn Ponagtaratik *First Vice President* T 470 2003 F 871 3638
Waiyawat Chalongkraidej *Chief Dealer* T 470 3000 F 871 3638
Sooksant Wattanayakorn *Assistant Manager* T 470 3000 F 871 3638
Surarit Chornchorngpat *Assistant Dealer* T 470 3000 F 871 3638

FX Traders / Sales People
Foreign Exchange & Remittance — Jirayon Sangkasuwan *Senior Vice President* T 470 1480 F 470 1531

Risk Management
Other (Exchange-Traded Derivatives)
Nipaporn Rungrat-Tanapitak *Dealer, Derivatives* T 470 3016 F 871 3640
Anotai Adulbhan *Assistant Dealer, Derivatives* T 470 3019 F 871 3640

Exchange-Traded Derivatives
Head — Teeranan Srihong *First Vice President* T 470 2006 F 871 3640
Mongkol Mathangkul *Division Manager* T 470 3016 F 871 3640

Settlement / Clearing
Foreign Exchange Settlement — Preecha Weerasomboonsin *Chief Dealer, Back-Office Settlements* T 470 2008 F 470 2097
Operations — Yoothachai Chusakpakdee *Operations Support* T 470 3237 F 470 3232
Supoj Limsopatam *FVP, Credit & Collateral Control* T 273 2004 F 273 2405

Asset Management
Other (Asset Management)
Securities Service — Hansa Susayan *First Vice President* T 470 1950 F 470 1996

Administration
Head of Administration — Thamrong Nakornratanachai *FVP, General Administration* T 470 1250 F 470 1144

Technology & Systems
Information System Processing — Phongthawat Phuangkanok *First Vice President* T 470 4200 F 470 4209

Legal / In-House Counsel
Weboon Seethaporn *First Vice President* T 273 2630 F 273 2640

Accounts / Audit
Internal Audit — Sumontip Otrakul *Senior Vice President* T 273 2910 F 273 2990
Financial Accounting Management — M L Oratai Devakula *Senior Vice President* T 470 2100 F 470 2199

Euromoney Directory 1999   1597

THAILAND (+66) www.euromoneydirectory.com

Thai Farmers Bank Public Company Limited (cont)
Other (Administration)
Human Resources & Organization Varawan Gobsuk *Vice President* T 470 3112 F 470 3197
Cash & Payment Narong Supradith *First Vice President* T 470 1800 F 470 1947
Research & Process Development Ampol Polohakul *First Vice President* T 470 3311 F 470 3310

The Thai Military Bank Public Company Limited Head Office
Formerly known as: The Thai Military Bank Limited
3000 Phahon Yothin Road, Chatuchak, Bangkok
PO Box 9, Samsennai, Bangkok 10400
Tel: (2) 299 1111; (2) 273 7020 **Fax:** (2) 273 7121; (2) 273 7124 **Telex:** MILITBKK TH 8232 **Swift:** TMBK TH BK
Email: 10900 **Cable:** MILITBANK

Senior Executive Officers
Chairman of the Board of Directors Wimol Wongwanich T 299 2211 F 299 2213
President & Chief Executive Officer Thanong Bidaya T 299 2222 F 299 2224
International Division Chandraleka Wiriyawit *Executive Vice President* T 299 1039 F 299 1040

The Tokai Bank Limited Full Branch Office
25th Floor, CP Tower Building, 313 Silom Road, Bangrak, Bangkok 10500
Tel: (2) 231 0952 **Fax:** (2) 231 0955 **Telex:** 82471 TOKAIBK TH

Senior Executive Officers
General Manager Hitoshi Ozawa

The Union Bank of Bangkok Public Company Limited
1600 New Phetchburi Road, Makkasan, Rajatevee, Bangkok 10320
PO Box 2114, Bangkok 10320
Tel: (2) 205 6000 **Fax:** (2) 253 7428; (2) 250 1505 **Telex:** 82550 UNIBANK TH **Swift:** UBOB TH BK

Senior Executive Officers
Chairman Kovit Poshyananda T 205 6784
President & Chief Executive Officer Phirasilp Subhapholsiri T 205 6765
Treasurer Maleekanya Sagarik *Vice President, Treasury* T 205 6536
Vice President Busarat Sihanonth T 205 6754
International Division Suwich Dhiravibulya *Senior Vice President* T 205 6303

Debt Capital Markets / Fixed Income
Head of Fixed Income Maleekanya Sagarik *Vice President, Treasury* T 205 6536

Equity Capital Markets
Head of Equity Capital Markets Maleekanya Sagarik *Vice President, Treasury* T 205 6536

Syndicated Lending
Head of Origination; Head of Syndication Chutima Mekasawat *VP, Commercial Banking* T 205 6103

Loan-Related Activities
Trade Finance Maleekanya Sagarik *Vice President, Treasury* T 205 6536

Money Markets
Head of Money Markets Maleekanya Sagarik *Vice President, Treasury* T 205 6536

Foreign Exchange
Head of Foreign Exchange Maleekanya Sagarik *Vice President, Treasury* T 205 6536

Settlement / Clearing
Head of Settlement / Clearing Boonyapongse Chantraourai *Vice President* T 205 6200

Asset Management
Head Maleekanya Sagarik *Vice President, Treasury* T 205 6536

Other Departments
Correspondent Banking Suwich Dhiravibulya *Senior Vice President* T 205 6303
Cash Management Maleekanya Sagarik *Vice President, Treasury* T 205 6536

Administration
Head of Administration Suphong Limthong T 205 6464
Business Development Chanin Veerawan *Vice President* T 205 6699

Technology & Systems
 Danai Khaophaisarn T 205 6381

Legal / In-House Counsel
 Songwud Boakhem *First Vice President* T 205 6348

Public Relations
Busarat Sihanonth *Vice President* ☎ 205 6754

Accounts / Audit
Audit
Suwat Cheewakasemsuk *Vice President* ☎ 205 6419

Other (Administration)
Information Department
Jirayu Khoompeeti ☎ 205 6248

The World Bank
Representative Office

Alternative trading name: World Bank in Thailand
14th Floor, Diethelm Tower A, 93/1 Wireless Road, Bangkok 10030
Tel: (2) 256 7792 **Fax:** (2) 256 7795; (2) 256 7794 **Telex:** 21225 IFCBKK TH **Email:** dsirichanya@worldbank.org
Website: www.worldbank.org

Senior Executive Officers
Country Director
Jayasankar Shivakumar

Administration
Head of Administration
Kanitta Kaikittipoom

Technology & Systems
Munee Sittichai *Senior Team Leader*

Public Relations
Durudee Sirichanya *External Affairs Officer*

TOGO (+228)

Banque Centrale des Etats de l'Afrique de l'Ouest
Central Bank

PO Box 120, Lome
Tel: 212 512; 215 383 **Fax:** 217 602 **Telex:** 5126 BCEAO TO

Senior Executive Officers
Country Director
Branch Director
Ayéwanou Gbeasor
Kokou Seretti Gozan

TONGA (+676)

National Reserve Bank of Tonga
Central Bank

Salote Road, Nuku'Alofa
Private Bag No 25, Post Office, Nuku'Alofa
Tel: 24057 **Fax:** 24201 **Telex:** 66278

Senior Executive Officers
Governor
Deputy Governor
S T T Utoikamanu
Samiuela Tukuafu

Others (Senior Executives)
Head, Banking Supervision
Head, Financial Markets
Joyce Mafi *Assistant Manager*
Jessie Cocker *Assistant Manager, International*
Paul Taumoepeau *Assistant Manager, Domestic Markets*

Other Departments
Economic Research
Ofa Ketu'u *Director, Research*

Administration
Head of Administration
Maleko Po'oi *Assistant Manager*

Technology & Systems
Elizabeth Baker *Systems Analyst*

Accounts / Audit
Head, Accountancy
Seneti 'Aho *Assistant Manager*

TRINIDAD AND TOBAGO (+1 868)

Central Bank of Trinidad and Tobago
Central Bank

Eric Williams Plaza, Independence Square, Port of Spain, 1250
Tel: 625 4835; 625 2601 Fax: 627 4696 Telex: 22532 Telex: 22386

Senior Executive Officers
Governor & Chairman — Winston Dookeran
Deputy Governor — Amoy Chang Fong
Deputy Governor — Jerry Hospedales
Manager, Legal — Radica Maharaj

Others (Senior Executives)
Head, Bank Licensing — Henry Jaffers *Inspector*
Head, Banking Operations & Investments — Joan John *Senior Manager*
Head, Bank Supervision — Margaret Munroe-Sealy *Manager*
Head, Banking — Caramae Farmer *Manager*

Foreign Exchange
Head of Foreign Exchange — Shabirul Mohammed *Manager*

Other Departments
Economic Research — Penelope Forde *Manager*

Administration
Technology & Systems
Management Information Systems — Jennifer Greaves *Manager*

Public Relations
Corporate Relations — Victor Maloney *Administrator*

Accounts / Audit
Head, Accountancy — Hollis De Four *Senior Manager*

Citibank Trinidad and Tobago Limited
Full Branch Office

12 Queen's Park East, PO Box 1249, Port-of-Spain
Tel: 625 10469; 625 64459 Fax: 624 8131; 625 3344

Senior Executive Officers
Chief Executive Officer; Treasurer — Steve Bideshi ☏ **623 6820**

Foreign Exchange
Country Head — Jerry Smith ☏ **625 10469 ext 2130**

Corporate Finance / M&A Advisory
Head of Corporate Finance — Dennis Evans

Republic Bank Limited
Head Office

Republic House, 9-17 Park Street, Port of Spain
PO Box 1153, Port of Spain
Tel: 625 4411; 623 1056 Fax: 624 1323; 624 1318 Telex: 22223 BARTOFEX Swift: RBNK TT PX
Email: email@republictt.com
Website: www.republictt.com

Senior Executive Officers
Chairman — Frank Barsotti
Managing Director — Ronald F Harford
Assistant Managing Director — Ronald Huggins
Executive Director — David Dulal Whiteway
Company Secretary — Jacqueline Quamina

Others (Senior Executives)
Republic Finance & Merchant Bank — Cheryl Greaves *Managing Director*
Corporate Operations & Process Improvement — Garvin Akeung *General Manager*
Commercial & Retail Banking — Lester Moore *General Manager*
Human Resources — Susan Dore *General Manager*
Information Technology — Derwin Howell *General Manager*
Finance & Planning — Gregory Thomson *General Manager*
Risk Management — Raoul Hosein *General Manager*
Chief Inspector — Herman Marchack

1600 Euromoney Directory 1999

General-Lending (DCM, SL)
Head of Corporate Banking   Geoffrey Clarke

Debt Capital Markets / Fixed Income
Department: Republic Finance & Merchant Bank Ltd, FINCOR
Fax: 624 1296
Global Head   Cheryl Greaves *Managing Director*

Government Bonds
Head of Sales   Cheryl Greaves *Managing Director*

Eurobonds
Head of Sales   Cheryl Greaves *Managing Director*

Emerging Market Bonds
Head of Sales   Cheryl Greaves *Managing Director*

Libor-Based / Floating-Rate Products
FRN Sales   Cheryl Greaves *Managing Director*

Fixed-Income Repo
Sales   Cheryl Greaves *Managing Director*

Fixed-Income Research
Head of Fixed Income   Cheryl Greaves *Managing Director*

Equity Capital Markets
Department: Republic Finance & Merchant Bank Ltd, FINCOR
Fax: 624 1296
Global Head of Sales; Head of Trading   Richard Trotman

Syndicated Lending
Fax: 624 1296
*Head of Origination; Head of Syndication; Head   Cheryl Greaves *Managing Director*
of Trading*

Loan-Related Activities
Trade Finance   Ian De Souza *Manager* [F] **623 2285**
Project Finance   Peter Forde *Manager* [F] **624 1296**

Money Markets
Head of Money Markets   Gregory Thomson *General Manager*

Money Markets - General
                                                         Robert Le Hunte *Group Treasurer*

Foreign Exchange
Fax: 623 2278
Head of Foreign Exchange   Roopnarine Oumade Singh

Risk Management
Head of Risk Management   Raoul Hosein *General Manager*

Asset Management
Department: Trust & Asset Management
Head   Charles Mouttet [F] **624 1266**

Other Departments
Chief Credit Officer   Harold Steele *Senior Manager, Risk Management*
Cash Management   Robert Le Hunte *Group Treasurer*

Administration
Head of Administration   Garvin Lambie *Administration Manager*
Business Development   Edwin Gooding *Assistant General Manager*

Technology & Systems
GM, IT Management   Derwin Howell *General Manager*
Manager, IT Management   Harold Hendrie [T] **623 4725** [F] **627 2669**

Legal / In-House Counsel
Manager, Legal Services   Jacqueline Quamina

Compliance
                                                         Jacqueline Quamina

Corporate Communications
                                                         Anna Maria Garcia Brooks *Manager* [T] **625 3221**

Accounts / Audit
Group Financial Controller   Anna Marie James

TRINIDAD AND TOBAGO (+1 868)   www.euromoneydirectory.com

Royal Bank of Trinidad and Tobago Limited — Head Office
Royal Court, 19-21 Park Street, Port-of-Spain
Tel: 623 1322 Fax: 625 3764; 624 1275 Telex: 22678 ROYIBD Swift: ROYTTTPX
Website: www.rbtt.com

Senior Executive Officers
Chief Executive Officer
Deputy Managing Director
Corporate Secretary

Peter J July *Managing Director & Chief Executive*
Terrence A J Martins
Althea Woo

Others (Senior Executives)
Overseas Banking Group
ROYTEC

Gerald Yetming *Executive Director*
Elphege Joseph *Executive Director*

General - Treasury
Head of Treasury

Nazir Ali *AGM, Treasury Operations*

Risk Management
Head of Risk Management

Ramón A Pazos *Executive Director*
David B Coutts *General Manager*

Corporate Finance / M&A Advisory
Department: Corporate & International Group
Other (Corporate Finance)

Ruthven Jaggassar *General Manager*
International — Denis de Gannes *Assistant General Manager*
North — Aftab Mohammed *Assistant General Manager*
Wayne Kowlessar *Assistant General Manager*
South — David Hackett *Assistant General Manager*

Settlement / Clearing
Operations

Krishna Harricharan *Senior Inspector*
Leroy Calliste *Financial Comptroller*

Asset Management
Department: Investment & Asset Management
Head

Rodney S Prasad *Executive Director*

Other Departments
Chief Credit Officer

David Bertrand *Senior Inspector*
Michael Camacho *Assistant General Manager*

Administration
Technology & Systems
Electronic Banking
Information Systems & Security Planning
Information Technology & Planning

Victor Yetming *Assistant General Manager*
Peter Aanensen *Corporate Manager*
Kazim Syne *Senior Manager*

Public Relations
Marketing & Public Relations

Helen Drayton *Group Manager*

Other (Administration)
Human Resources

Bruce Aanensen *General Manager*
Ernest King *Corporate Manager*

Corporate Resources

Hamish Smith *General Manager*
Afzal Khan *Assistant General Manager*
Judy Lake *Assistant General Manager*

TUNISIA
(+216)

Banque Centrale de Tunisie — Central Bank
Rue de la Monnaie, PO Box 369, Tunis
Tel: (1) 340 588; (1) 254 000 Fax: (1) 340 615; (1) 354 214 Telex: 12575 Swift: BCTN TN TT Email: bct@bct.gov.tn
Reuters: BCDX Telerate: 4387 Cable: BANCENTUN
Reuters: BCTY; BCTZ

Senior Executive Officers
Governor
Vice Governor

Mohamed El Béji Hamda
Mohamed Daouas

Others (Senior Executives)
Head, Credit & Banking
Head, International Finance

Badreddine Barkia
Moncef Chaffar

1602 Euromoney Directory 1999

www.euromoneydirectory.com TUNISIA (+216)

Others (Senior Executives) (cont)
Head, Banking Supervision　　　　Bechir Ben Mami
Foreign Exchange
Head of Foreign Exchange　　　　Moncef Chaffar
Other Departments
Economic Research　　　　Amor Saafi *Head, Studies & Research*
Administration
Head of Administration　　　　Rachid el Hakim
Legal / In-House Counsel
Head, Legal Organization　　　　Samir Brahimi
Accounts / Audit
Head, Accounting & Control　　　　Grine Mongi
Other (Administration)
Human Resources　　　　Rachid el Hakim

Arab Tunisian Bank　　Head Office
9 rue Hédi Nouira, 1001 Tunis
Tel: (1) 351 155 **Fax:** (1) 342 852; (1) 349 278 **Telex:** 15506 ARBANK TN **Swift:** ATBK TN TTA **Reuters:** ATBK

Senior Executive Officers
Chairman　　　　Khaled Shoman ☎ **664 105**
General Manager　　　　Hammouda Belkhodja ☎ **333 305**
Company Secretary　　　　Hedia Ben Messaoud
International Division　　　　Mouldi Hammami *Head, International Banking Division* ☎ **340 884**

Syndicated Lending
Loan-Related Activities
Trade Finance　　　　Mouldi Hammami *Head, International Banking Division* ☎ **340 884**
Project Finance　　　　Samir Saied *Head of International Banking* ☎ **340 884**

Foreign Exchange
Tel: 351 155 **Fax:** 331 383 **Reuters:** ATB K **Telex:** 15506 ARBANK TN
Head of Foreign Exchange　　　　Mouldi Hammami *Head, International Banking Division* ☎ **340 884**
FX Traders / Sales People
　　　　Faissal Farhat *Chief Dealer* ☎ **341 779**
　　　　Montassar Mokhtar *Dealer* ☎ **342 309**

Settlement / Clearing
Head of Settlement / Clearing　　　　Raouf Bohli *Head, Finance & Treasury* ☎ **344 350**

Other Departments
Chief Credit Officer　　　　Hamda Ben Chedly *Head of Credit* ☎ **342 551**
Correspondent Banking　　　　Jaafar Kattach *Deputy Head* ☎ **340 884**

Administration
Head of Administration　　　　Fakhri Meherzi *Head* ☎ **345 034**
Head of Marketing　　　　Othman Zahag

Technology & Systems
　　　　Omar Tlili *Head* ☎ **344 408**

Legal / In-House Counsel
　　　　Fakhri Meherzi *Head* ☎ **345 034**

Public Relations
　　　　Youssef Kortobi *Head* ☎ **247 820**

Accounts / Audit
Interanal Auditor　　　　Raouf Ghezail *Chief Internal Auditor* ☎ **345 595**

Banque de Développement Economique de Tunisie
Alternative trading name: BDET
34 rue Hédi Karray, El Menzah IV, 1004 Tunis
PO Box 48, 1080 Tunis
Tel: (1) 718 000 **Fax:** (1) 719 999; (1) 713 744 **Telex:** 14133

Senior Executive Officers
President & General Manager　　　　Ali Debaya
Deputy General Manager　　　　Ahmed Naija
Deputy General Manager　　　　Sadok Bekaid

Others (Senior Executives)
Inspector General　　　　Nejib Tnani

Euromoney Directory 1999　**1603**

TUNISIA (+216) www.euromoneydirectory.com

Banque de Développement Economique de Tunisie (cont)
Debt Capital Markets / Fixed Income
Government Bonds
Head of Trading Mohamed Jaouadi
Equity Capital Markets
Domestic Equities
Head of Sales Taoufik Maaref
Other (Domestic Equities)
Studies & Equity Department Mondher Rourou
Equity Research
Head of Equity Research Taoufik Maaref
Money Markets
Head of Money Markets Mohamed Jaouadi
Risk Management
Head of Risk Management Abdelmajid Hasairi
Exchange-Traded Derivatives
Head Mohamed Jaouadi
Other Departments
Chief Credit Officer Mondher Rourou
Administration
Head of Administration Taoufik Jarraya
Business Development Hédi Dridi
Technology & Systems
Data Processing Ridha Ben Mosbah
Legal / In-House Counsel
 Ghammam Nairna

Banque de l'Habitat — Head Office

21 Avenue Kheireddine Pacha, Montplaisir, 1002 Tunis
PO Box 242, Tunis
Tel: (1) 785 277 **Fax:** (1) 784 417 **Telex:** 14348 **Swift:** BHBK TN TT **Email:** banquehabitat@bh.fin.tn

Senior Executive Officers
President Directeur General Tahar Bourkhis ☎ **780 070**
Financial Director Habib Amri *Account Co-ordinator* ☎ **848 819**
Treasurer Fadhel Guizani ☎ **840 419**
International Division Mohamed Golli *Director of Foreign Banking*

Equity Capital Markets
Equity Repo / Securities Lending
Head Mohamed Ahmed *Director, Securities*

Other Departments
Chief Credit Officer Taoufik Driss *Director, Housing Credit*
 Taleb Gali *Director, Trade Credit*

Administration
Head of Administration Mongi Ghazzai *Administrative Co-ordinator*
Business Development Thouraya Hachicha *Director* ☎ **794 134**
Head of Marketing Fatma Amara *Director*
Technology & Systems
 Tahar Seghaier
Public Relations
 Thouraya Hachicha *Director* ☎ **794 134**
Accounts / Audit
 Mohamed Riahi *General Inspector*

Banque Internationale Arabe de Tunisie — Head Office

70/72 Avenue Habib Bourguiba, 1000 Tunis
PO Box 520, 1080 Tunis
Tel: (1) 340 733 **Fax:** (1) 340 680; (1) 347 648 **Telex:** 14090 **Swift:** BIAT TN TT **Reuters:** BIAT
International Department Tel: 337 969

Senior Executive Officers
President & General Manager Mokhtar Fakhfakh
Deputy General Manager Mohsen Ghandri

1604 Euromoney Directory 1999

Senior Executive Officers (cont)
Deputy General Manager   Khaled Triki
International Division   Salah Bouden

Banque Tuniso-Koweitienne De Developpement   Head Office

10, Bis Avenue Mohamed V, 1001 Tunis
Tel: (1) 340 000 Fax: (1) 343 106 Telex: 14 834

Senior Executive Officers
Chairman of the Board   Abdul Rasoul Abdelhassen
Managing Director / General Manager   Abdelmajid Fredj

Others (Senior Executives)
Central Manager of Operating   Jamel Baltagi
Finance   Taha Loued *Manager*
Identification & Promotion Partenariat   Rym Mehrzi
Department

Relationship Manager
Agricultural & Food   Selma Ballgha
    Mohamed Ben Hamadi *Credit Manager*
Industriel & Tourism Projects   Chokri Ben Ayed *Manager*

Administration

Technology & Systems
Information Technology   Nejib Ghenima *Manager*

Legal / In-House Counsel
    Hela Talbi *Manager*

Citibank NA   Full Branch Office

55 Avenue Jugurtha, Belvédère, 1002 Tunis
PO Box 72, Belvédère, 1002 Tunis
Tel: (1) 790 066; (1) 791 714 Fax: (1) 785 556 Telex: 15139 CITICO TN

Senior Executive Officers
President   Eric Ph Stoclet ☎ **782 056**
Treasurer   Ramz Hamzaoui ☎ **780 149**

Foreign Exchange
Global Head   Ramz Hamzaoui ☎ **780 149**

Société Tuniso-Séoudienne d'Investissement et de Développement - STUSID   Head Office

32 Rue Hédi Karray, PO Box 20, 1002 Tunis
Tel: (1) 718 233; (1) 718 181 Fax: (1) 719 233 Telex: 13594 TUSID

Senior Executive Officers
Chairman   Mahsoun Jallal
Chief Executive Officer   Abdelghaffar Ezzedine *President Directeur General*

TURKEY
(+90)

Central Bank of the Republic of Turkey   🏛 Central Bank

Istiklal Caddesi 10, Ulus, TR-06100 Ankara
Tel: (312) 310 3646 Fax: (312) 310 9118 Telex: 44031 MBDI TR Swift: TCMB TR 2A Telerate: 15859
Website: www.tcmb.gov.tr

Senior Executive Officers
Governor   Gazi Erçel ☎ **309 3137**
Vice Governor   Sükrü Binay ☎ **310 9109**
Vice Governor   Ayjut Ekzen ☎ **311 4294**
Vice Governor   Aydm Esen ☎ **311 3942**
Vice Governor   Süreyya Serdengeçti ☎ **311 0255**

TURKEY (+90)   www.euromoneydirectory.com

Central Bank of the Republic of Turkey (cont)

Others (Senior Executives)
General Secretariat — Çetin Akbay *General Manager* ☎ 311 7249
Foreign Relatioins — Ömer Altay *General Manager* ☎ 312 4949
Credits — Ali Vefa Çelik *General Manager* ☎ 324 2403
Banking — Pembe Jale Oktay *General Manager* ☎ 312 4312
Issuing — Ahmet Nayci *General Manager* ☎ 312 4333
Saving Deposits & Insurance Fund — Erdal Arslan *General Manager* ☎ 312 4344
Foreign Trade — Gani Duru *General Manager* ☎ 324 0989

Money Markets
Head of Money Markets — Durmus Yilmas *Assistant General Manager* ☎ 310 2452

Other Departments
Economic Research — Tahire Akder *Assistant General Manager* ☎ 310 9215

Administration
Technology & Systems
Data Processing & Statistics — Mahmut Sedat Eroglu *Assistant General Manager* ☎ 311 6980

Legal / In-House Counsel
— Yavuz Özgediz *General Manager* ☎ 324 0982

Accounts / Audit
Accounting — Sedef Ertürk *General Manager* ☎ 311 4303

Other (Administration)
Human Resources — Lütfi Senol Özsimsek *Assistant General Manager* ☎ 312 1087

AKBANK TAS   Head Office

Sabanci Center, 4 Levent, TR-80745 Istanbul
Tel: (212) 270 0044; (212) 270 6666 Fax: (212) 269 7383; (212) 269 8081 Telex: 24134 AKOVN TR Swift: AKBK TR IS
Reuters: AKGM Telex: 24929 AKPMTR
Website: www.akbank.com.tr

Senior Executive Officers
Chairman & Managing Director — Erol Sabanci ☎ 278 1338
Chief Executive Officer — Oguz Karahan *Managing Director & Vice Chairman* ☎ 282 6796
Financial Director — Suzan Sabanci Dinçer *Managing Director* ☎ 280 2735
Treasurer — Resit Toygar *Executive Vice President*
General Manager — Özen Göksel ☎ 282 6796
International Division — Eyüp Engin *Assistant General Manager* ☎ 278 5791

General-Lending (DCM, SL)
Head of Corporate Banking — Ziya Akkurt *Executive Vice President* ☎ 278 4299

General-Investment
Head of Investment — Zafer Kurtnl *Executive Vice President*

Debt Capital Markets / Fixed Income
Department: Treasury Division
Tel: 270 0044 Fax: 268 7854

Government Bonds
Head of Sales — Aysen Tamer *Manager* ☎ 269 8109
Head of Trading — Serap Istenyilmaz *Assistant Manager* ☎ 250 1720

Eurobonds
Head of Sales — Mukaddes Tüm *Manager* ☎ 269 8100
Trading (Sovereigns) — Baris Sözen *Assistant Dealer* ☎ 264 5994

Fixed-Income Repo
Head of Repo — Aysen Tamer *Manager* ☎ 269 8109
Marketing & Product Development; Head of Trading — Serap Istenyilmaz *Assistant Manager* ☎ 250 1720

Equity Capital Markets
Department: AK Menkul Degerler ve Yatirim AS
Head of Equity Capital Markets — Hakan Karahan *General Manager, AKMENKUL* ☎ 249 3052

Syndicated Lending
Loan-Related Activities
Trade Finance — Hülya Kefeli *Manager* ☎ 269 7109

Money Markets
Tel: 270 0044 Fax: 268 7854 Reuters: AKGM Telex: 38274 AKFMTR
Head of Money Markets — Ahmet Yavuz *Assistant General Manager* ☎ 278 9836

www.euromoneydirectory.com   TURKEY (+90)

Foreign Exchange
Tel: 270 0044 Fax: 280 2914 Reuters: AKGM Telex: 38274 AKFMTR
Head of Foreign Exchange   Ahmet Erbas *Assistant Manager* ☏ **278 3908**
Head of Institutional Sales; Corporate Sales   A Güneyt Selcuk *Assistant Manager* ☏ **270 7338**
Head of Trading   Ahmet Erbas *Assistant Manager* ☏ **278 3908**

Corporate Finance / M&A Advisory
Head of Corporate Finance   Ziya Akkurt *Executive Vice President* ☏ **278 4299**

Settlement / Clearing
Tel: 270 0044 Fax: 282 6493 Telex: 38274 AKFMTR
Head of Settlement / Clearing; Equity   Remzi Súha Dede *Manager* ☏ **269 9282**
Settlement; Fixed-Income Settlement
Operations   Zuhurî Öge *Assistant Manager* ☏ **269 9412**

Global Custody
Head of Global Custody   Kadir Uyanik *Manager* ☏ **268 4350**

Other Departments
Private Banking   Akin Kozanoglu *Executive Vice President* ☏ **278 5293**
Correspondent Banking   Hülya Kefeli *Manager* ☏ **269 7109**

Administration
Head of Administration   Özen Göksel ☏ **282 6796**

Technology & Systems
                                        Akin Kozanoglu *Executive Vice President* ☏ **278 5293**

Legal / In-House Counsel
                                        Hasan Esen *Chief Adviser* ☏ **279 0067**

Public Relations
                                        Akin Kozanoglu *Executive Vice President* ☏ **278 5293**

Al Baraka Turkish Finance House AS   Head Office
Büyükdere Caddesi 78, Mecidiyeköy, TR-80290 Istanbul
Tel: (212) 274 9900; (212) 267 0299 Fax: (212) 272 4470; (212) 275 1477 Telex: 27061 Swift: BTFH TR IS
Email: abarakaturk@abarakaturk.com.tr Reuters: ABAT
Website: www.albarakaturk.com.tr

Senior Executive Officers
Chairman   Abdullatif Omar Ghurab
Financial Director   Mitat Aktas *Accounting & Finance*
Treasurer   Haken Berooglu
General Manager   Osman Akyüz
International Division   M Emin Ozcan *Manager*

Syndicated Lending

Loan-Related Activities
Trade Finance; Project Finance   Yuksel Gorgeg ☏ **276 9900**

Foreign Exchange
Tel: 267 0299 Fax: 272 0299
Head of Foreign Exchange   Hakan Berooglu *Manager*

Administration
Head of Administration   Osman Bayraktar *Manager*

Technology & Systems
                                        Temel Haziroglu

Legal / In-House Counsel
                                        Nihal Boz *Chief*

Banque de Commerce et de Placements SA   Representative Office
Cukurova Holding Binasi, Büyükdere Caddesi 14, Sisli, TR-80220 Istanbul
Tel: (212) 233 3630; (212) 233 3631 Fax: (212) 233 3633 Telex: 126843

Senior Executive Officers
Representative   Refik Sentürk

TURKEY (+90)　　　　　　　www.euromoneydirectory.com

The Chase Manhattan Bank
Full Branch Office

145 Emirhan Caddesi, Atakule A Blok, Kat 11, Dikilitas, Besiktas, TR-80700 Istanbul
Tel: (212) 227 9700 Fax: (212) 227 9727 Telex: 26625 CHMB TR Reuters: CMBT

Senior Executive Officers
Others (Senior Executives)
Senior Country Officer　　　　　　　Isak Antika *Senior Country Officer*

Citibank NA
Full Branch Office

Buyukdere Caddesi 100, Esentepe, TR-80280 Istanbul
Tel: (212) 288 7700 Fax: (212) 288 7760; (212) 288 7759 Reuters: CITI
Fax: 211 7639

Senior Executive Officers
Chief Executive Officer　　　　　　　Dardot Sabarots *Country Corporate Officer*
Treasurer　　　　　　　　　　　　　Ali Batu Karaali *Country Treasurer*
General-Lending (DCM, SL)
Head of Corporate Banking　　　　　Bola Adesola
General - Treasury
Head of Treasury　　　　　　　　　Cem Koksai *Treasury Marketing Head*

Commerzbank AG
Representative Office

Büyükdere Caddesi, Yapi Kredi Plaza, B-Blok, Kat 7, 19/B, Levent, 80620 Istanbul
Tel: (212) 279 4248; (212) 280 5524 Fax: (212) 279 4176 Telex: 1831215 CBRP TR

Senior Executive Officers
Representative　　　　　　　　　　Peter Thiel

Deutsche Bank AG
Representative Office

Mete Caddesi 34, Necip Akar Is Hani Kat 2, Taksim, TR-80090 Istanbul
PK 194, Sisli, TR-80222 Istanbul
Tel: (212) 293 7481; (212) 245 0179 Fax: (212) 249 5355 Telex: 931055 DBIS TR
Website: www.deutsche-bank.com

Export Credit Bank of Turkey Inc
Head Office

Alternative trading name: Turk Eximbank
Formerly known as: State Investment Bank

Müdafaa Caddesi 20, Bakanliklar, TR-06100 Ankara
Tel: (312) 417 1300 Fax: (312) 425 7896 Telex: 46106 Swift: TIKB TR 2A Email: info_ttanyil@eximbank.gov.tr
Reuters: EXIM
General Telex: 46751
Website: www.eximbank.gov.tr

Senior Executive Officers
Chairman　　　　　　　　　　　　　Yavuz Ege ⓣ 212 8742 ⓕ 212 1622
Financial Director　　　　　　　　　Ertan Tanriyakul *Deputy General Manager* ⓣ 425 7453 ⓕ 425 2947
Treasurer　　　　　　　　　　　　　Cigdem Köse *Head of Treasury* ⓣ 425 7453 ⓕ 425 2947
General Manager　　　　　　　　　H Ahmet Kiliçoglu ⓣ 418 4411/12 ⓕ 971 3466
General Secretary　　　　　　　　　K Cüneyt Baki ⓣ 425 7524
Others (Senior Executives)
Deputy General Manager (Credits)　　Osman Aslan ⓣ 417 8008 ⓕ 425 7547
Deputy General Manager (Insurance)　Alev Arkan ⓣ 417 3287 ⓕ 425 7547
Deputy General Manager　　　　　　Necati Yeniaras ⓣ 419 7480 ⓕ 418 0015

Debt Capital Markets / Fixed Income
Department: Funding Department
Tel: 418 9975 Fax: 425 2947 Telex: 46751 EXMB TR
Head of Fixed Income　　　　　　　Gigdem Köse *Head of Treasury* ⓣ 425 7453
Head of Fixed Income Trading　　　　Sule Dalan *Assistant Manager* ⓣ 425 7453

Domestic Government Bonds
Head of Trading　　　　　　　　　　Sule Dalan *Senior Dealer*

1608 Euromoney Directory 1999

www.euromoneydirectory.com TURKEY (+90)

Money Markets
Department: Treasury Department
Tel: 419 8437 Fax: 425 2947 Telex: 46751 EXMB TR
Head of Money Markets   Pelin Ünsal Chief Dealer ☏ 418 8437

Foreign Exchange
Department: Treasury Department
Tel: 425 7453 Fax: 425 2947
Head of Foreign Exchange   Kürsat Durmaz Treasury Manager ☏ 418 5974

Risk Management
Head of Risk Management   Neslihan Dogan Assistant Manager ☏ 418 5974

Settlement / Clearing
Tel: 418 8437 Fax: 425 2947 Telex: 46751 EXMB TR
Fixed-Income Settlement; Foreign Exchange   Sebnem Bora Manager, Treasury Operations ☏ 418 8437
Settlement

Other Departments
Correspondent Banking   Sebnem Bora Manager, Treasury Operations ☏ 418 8437

Administration
Technology & Systems
                                         Abdullah Körnes Head of System Developing & Data Processing Dept.
                                         ☏ 418 8167 F 418 0344

Legal / In-House Counsel
                                         Güven Vural Legal Counsel ☏ 425 4615 F 425 7896

Public Relations
                                         Ayse Sel Head of Public Relations & Training Dept. ☏ 425 7454 F 425 7896

Accounts / Audit
Audit   Berk Dicle Head of Inspection & Internal Control Dept. ☏ 425 7529
                                         F 425 7291
                                         Gülcan Armagan Head of Accounting ☏ 418 4416 F 425 7291

Faisal Finance Institution Inc   Head Office
Kemeralti Street 46, Tophane, TR-80030 Istanbul
Tel: (212) 251 6520 Fax: (212) 245 5633 Telex: 25694 FFK TR Email: faisalfinans@ihlas.net.tr

Senior Executive Officers
Founder Chairman   Prince Mohamed Al-Faisal Al-Saud ☏ +41 (22) 791 7111
Chief Executive Officer   Hikmet Güler General Manager ☏ 249 9945
Financial Director   Bahaettin Esendal Financial Controller ☏ 293 9294
Treasurer   Yahya Bayraktar Treasury Manager ☏ 251 3891
International Division   Bekir Güclüer ☏ 252 7350

Syndicated Lending
Loan-Related Activities
Project Finance   Osman Isik Manager ☏ 251 3890

Other Departments
Correspondent Banking   Ömer Uktan Foreign Relations

Administration
Head of Administration   Kamil Kartel Manager ☏ 245 5639
Head of Marketing   Reha Öztan Manager ☏ 252 5130

Legal / In-House Counsel
                                         Mürsel Aslan Chief Legal Advisor ☏ 251 1903

Accounts / Audit
                                         Resat Basel Manager ☏ 293 9932

Finansbank AS   Head Office
Büyükdere Caddesi 129, Mecidiyeköy, TR-80300 Istanbul
Tel: (212) 216 7070 Fax: (212) 216 1323; (212) 216 1333 Telex: 39280 GAFI TR Swift: FNNB TR IS XXX

Senior Executive Officers
Chairman   Hüsnü Özyegin ☏ 275 2485
Financial Director   Mehmet Gülesçi ☏ 275 7846
Chief Operating Officer   Resat Aytaç ☏ 275 8275
Treasurer   Cenk Tülümen ☏ 275 2465
Managing Director / General Manager   Ömer Aras ☏ 275 2489
Managing Director / General Manager   Fevzi Bozer ☏ 275 2487

Euromoney Directory 1999 **1609**

TURKEY (+90) www.euromoneydirectory.com

Finansbank AS (cont)

Debt Capital Markets / Fixed Income
Global Head — Cagdas Aysev ☏ 275 7129
Eurobonds
Head of Origination — Mehmet Besimoglu ☏ 275 2466
Libor-Based / Floating-Rate Products
FRN Origination — Koksal Coban ☏ 275 2466
Medium-Term Notes
Head of Origination — Koksal Coban ☏ 275 2466
Fixed-Income Repo
Head of Repo — Özlem Yardimci ☏ 288 6788

Equity Capital Markets
Equity Research
Global Head — Kartal Çabli ☏ 282 1763

Money Markets
Global Head — Nuran Üngun ☏ 275 2466

Foreign Exchange
Global Head — Ilgen Ertug ☏ 275 6291

Risk Management
Exchange-Traded Derivatives
Global Head — Demet Özturan ☏ 275 2465

Other Departments
Commodities / Bullion — Cenk Tülümen ☏ 275 2465
Private Banking — Nafiz Karadere ☏ 273 1426
Correspondent Banking — Özlem Cinemre ☏ 275 8278

Administration
Technology & Systems
— Serhat Sayin ☏ 275 2450
Legal / In-House Counsel
— Olcayto Onur ☏ 275 9993
Public Relations
— Nilgün Hosgel ☏ 275 2450

Garanti Menkul Klymetler AS

Mete Caddesi 38/8, Toksim, TR-80060 Istanbul
Tel: (212) 251 0880; (212) 245 8286 **Fax:** (212) 251 3103; (212) 282 3776 **Telex:** 25463 BTKR TR
Email: noztan@garanti.com.tr **Reuters:** GAIN

Senior Executive Officers
Chairman — Sodi Gögdün ☏ 288 8830
Financial Director — Ismail Baydar ☏ 251 0880 ext 650
Chief Operating Officer — Bilge Sutekin ☏ 251 0880 ext 250
Treasurer — Arzu Akcelik ☏ 251 0880 ext 350
Managing Director / General Manager — Neuzot Öztangji ☏ 245 1315
Company Secretary — Cora Monique McDougle ☏ 251 0880 ext 102

General-Lending (DCM, SL)
Head of Corporate Banking — Cigden Bicik ☏ 286 2303

Debt Capital Markets / Fixed Income
Head of Fixed Income — Arzu Akcelik ☏ 251 0880 ext 350
Government Bonds
Head of Sales — Arzu Akcelik ☏ 251 0880 ext 350
Fixed-Income Repo
Head of Repo — Arzu Akcelik ☏ 251 0880 ext 350
Other — Öner Yazarkan

Equity Capital Markets
Department: Sales
Tel: (212) 253 4850 **Fax:** (212) 244 5638
Head of Equity Capital Markets — Bilge Sutekin ☏ 251 0880 ext 250
Head of Sales — Ediz Yildiz *Dealer* ☏ 251 0880 ext 252
Head of Trading — Sebrem Sencan ☏ 251 0880 ext 300
Domestic Equities
Head of Sales — Ediz Yildiz *Dealer* ☏ 251 0880 ext 252

Syndicated Lending
Head of Syndicated Lending — Arzu Akcelik ☏ 251 0880 ext 350

www.euromoneydirectory.com　　　　　　　　　　　TURKEY (+90)

Money Markets
Head of Money Markets　　　　　　　Arzu Akcelík ☎ 251 0880 ext 350
Foreign Exchange
Head of Foreign Exchange　　　　　　Ismet Gokcen
Corporate Finance / M&A Advisory
Head of Corporate Finance　　　　　　Ismail Baydar
Settlement / Clearing
Head of Settlement / Clearing; Equity　Mine Ergün ☎ 251 0880 ext 500
Settlement
Fixed-Income Settlement; Operations　Caulgün Nemloglu ☎ 251 0880 ext 600
Global Custody
Head of Global Custody　　　　　　　Mine Ergün ☎ 251 0880 ext 500
Other Departments
Chief Credit Officer　　　　　　　　　Ismail Baydar ☎ 251 0880 ext 650
Administration
Technology & Systems
　　　　　　　　　　　　　　　　　Selcuk Omrak ☎ 251 0880 ext 680
Legal / In-House Counsel
　　　　　　　　　　　　　　　　　Hason Güzelöz ☎ 285 5840
Compliance
　　　　　　　　　　　　　　　　　Ismail Baydar ☎ 251 0880 ext 650
Public Relations
　　　　　　　　　　　　　　　　　Mine Ergün ☎ 251 0880 ext 500
Accounts / Audit
　　　　　　　　　　　　　　　　　Ismail Baydar ☎ 251 0880 ext 650

Generale Bank　　　　　　　　　　　　　　　　Representative Office
15th Floor, Büyükdere Caddesi Yapi Kredi Plaza, Bloc C, Levent, TR-80620 Istanbul
Tel: (212) 280 9879 Fax: (212) 281 1473
Senior Executive Officers
Chief Representative　　　　　　　　Jacques Laloux

Global Securities　　　　　　　　　　　　　　　　Head Office
Maya Akar Center, Büyükdere Caddesi 100/102, Kat 15-16, TR-80280 Istanbul Esentepe
Tel: (212) 211 4900 Fax: (212) 211 4901 Email: global@global.com.tr Reuters: GLMDE IS
Senior Executive Officers
Chairman & Chief Executive　　　　　Mehmet Kutman
Financial Director　　　　　　　　　　Sedat Alsancak Assistant General Manager
Treasurer　　　　　　　　　　　　　Abdullah Kunt Associate
Debt Capital Markets / Fixed Income
Fax: 211 4903
Country Head　　　　　　　　　　　Zeynep Uran Manager
Equity Capital Markets
Fax: 211 4905/7
Global Head　　　　　　　　　　　　Gregory Kiez Director, Corporate Finance ✉ gregk@global.com.tr
Country Head　　　　　　　　　　　Imre Gencer Director, Institutional Sales
Domestic Equities
Head of Origination; Head of Syndication　Haluk Alperat Assistant Director, Corporate Finance
Head of Sales　　　　　　　　　　　Cem Kalyoncu Assistant General Manager
International Equities
Head of Origination　　　　　　　　　Gregory Kiez Director, Corporate Finance ✉ gregk@global.com.tr
Head of Syndication　　　　　　　　Imre Gencer Director, Institutional Sales
Corporate Finance / M&A Advisory
Fax: 211 4905/7
Global Head　　　　　　　　　　　　Gregory Kiez Director, Corporate Finance ✉ gregk@global.com.tr
Settlement / Clearing
Fax: 211 4902
Regional Head　　　　　　　　　　　Sevil Ince Head
Other Departments
Proprietary Trading　　　　　　　　　Cem Kalyoncu Assistant General Manager

TURKEY (+90)   www.euromoneydirectory.com

Global Securities (cont)
Administration
Legal / In-House Counsel
Alison Chilcott *Legal Counsel*

Compliance
Guven Bestas *Assistant General Manager*

Public Relations
Nevin Tayfun *Domestic Public Relations*

Other (Administration)
Human Resources
Zehra Murat *Manager*

Iktisat Bankasi TAS
Head Office

Büyükdere Caddesi 165, Esentepe, TR-80504 Istanbul
Tel: (212) 274 1111 **Fax:** (212) 274 7028; (212) 274 7030 **Telex:** 26021 IKBN TR **Swift:** IKBA TR IS **Reuters:** IKBT
Cable: IKTUM ISTANBUL

Senior Executive Officers
Chairman — Gürbüz Tümay
Chief Executive Officer — Nedim Usta
Treasurer — Roy Gevrek *Assistant General Manager*
Managing Director — Erol Aksoy
Company Secretary — Özkist Ünver
International Division — Nebahat Tokgöz *Assistant General Manager*

General-Lending (DCM, SL)
Head of Corporate Banking — Nuri Cerrahoglu *Assistant General Manager*
Fikret Guler *Assistant General Manager*

General-Investment
Head of Investment — Roy Gevrek *Assistant General Manager*

Debt Capital Markets / Fixed Income
Head of Fixed Income — Meltem Gagan *Treasury Manager* ☎ **274 7065**
Head of Fixed Income Sales — Linet Funes *Assistant Manager*
Head of Fixed Income Trading — Lerzan Urun *Assistant Manager*

Fixed-Income Repo
Head of Repo — Selma Sipahi *Assistant Manager* ☎ **274 7121**

Syndicated Lending
Other (Syndicated Lending)
Loans — Sadik Saygici *Assistant General Manager*

Money Markets
Head of Money Markets — Meltem Gagan *Treasury Manager* ☎ **274 7065**

Money Markets - General
Desk — Dalya Bahar *Assistant Manager* ☎ **274 7065**

Foreign Exchange
Head of Foreign Exchange — Meltem Gagan *Treasury Manager* ☎ **274 7065**
Head of Institutional Sales — Dalya Bahar *Assistant Manager* ☎ **274 7065**

Risk Management
Head of Risk Management — Ali Gursel *Assistant Manager* ☎ **274 7121**

Corporate Finance / M&A Advisory
Head of Corporate Finance — Kikret Güler *Assistant General Manager*

Settlement / Clearing
Head of Settlement / Clearing — Gönul Inang *Manager* ☎ **274 1111 ext 289**

Other Departments
Private Banking — Irfan Sahin *Assistant General Manager*

Administration
Head of Marketing — Ebru Bilgin *Manager* ☎ **274 1111**

Technology & Systems
Information Systems — Hakki Eren *Assistant General Manager*

Legal / In-House Counsel
Meral Ülker *Manager* ☎ **274 4149**

Public Relations
Yildiz Kurtoglu *Manager*

Accounts / Audit
Audit — Ali Kamil Uzun *Chairman*

www.euromoneydirectory.com TURKEY (+90)

Other (Administration)
Organization Bülent Aydoganli *Assistant General Manager*

Industrial Development Bank of Turkey Head Office
Formerly known as: Türkiye Sinai Kalkinma Bankasi
Meclisi Mebusan Caddesi 161, Findikli, TR-80040 Istanbul
Tel: (212) 251 2800; (212) 251 2792 **Fax:** (212) 243 2975 **Telex:** 24344 TSKB TR **Swift:** TSKB TR IS **Reuters:** TSKB
Website: www.tskb.com.tr

Senior Executive Officers
President, CEO, MD & GM Ilhan Evliyaoglu ☎ 293 7478 ✉ evliaoglui@tskh.com.tr
President, CEO, MD & GM Safa Ocak ☎ 249 0810 ✉ ocaks@tskb.com.tr
Financial Director Ahmet Demirel *Executive Vice President* ☎ 249 2139
  ✉ demirela@tskb.com.tr
Chief Operating Officer Dilek Erzik *Executive Vice President* ☎ 244 4758 ✉ erzikd@tskb.com.tr
Treasurer Ahmet Arzan *Executive Vice President* ☎ 243 5173 ✉ arzana@tskb.com.tr

Others (Senior Executives)
Technical Services Ertugrul Ibrahimoglu *Executive Vice President* ☎ 244 4757
  ✉ ibrahimoglue@tskb.com.tr
Corporate Finance Metin Ar *Executive Vice President* ☎ 244 5135 ✉ arm@tskb.com.tr
Loans & Investment Ülkü Kismir *Executive Vice President* ☎ 243 3763 ✉ ulkuk@tskb.com.tr

Debt Capital Markets / Fixed Income
Department: Capital Markets
Tel: 244 4750
Global Head Mehmet Yildirim *Department Head* ✉ yildirimm@tskb.com.tr

Equity Capital Markets
Department: Capital Markets
Tel: 244 4750
Global Head Mehmet Yildirim *Department Head* ✉ yildirimm@tskb.com.tr

Syndicated Lending
Department: Loan & Investment
Global Head Lale Gökman *Department Head* ☎ 249 1710 ✉ gokmanl@tskb.com.tr
  Hayri Seyhan *Department Head* ☎ 293 3398 ✉ seyhanh@tskb.com.tr

Loan-Related Activities
Project Finance Serpil Kazanci *Department Head* ☎ 293 6894 ✉ kazancis@tskb.com.tr

Money Markets
Department: Treasury
Global Head Yamaç Berki *Treasurer* ☎ 252 8756 ✉ yamacb@tskb.com.tr

Risk Management
Tel: 252 5755
Global Head Turgut Erdemli *Department Head* ✉ erdemlit@tskb.com.tr

Corporate Finance / M&A Advisory
Department: Corporate Finance
Tel: 252 1316
Head of Corporate Finance Metin Ar *Executive Vice President* ☎ 244 5135 ✉ arm@tskb.com.tr
Global Head Mehmet Sagiroglu *Department Head* ✉ sagiroglum@tskb.com.tr

Settlement / Clearing
Operations Necdet Senkal *Financial Controller* ☎ 249 5087 ✉ senkaln@tskb.com.tr

Other Departments
Correspondent Banking Çigdem Içel *Department Head* ☎ 251 9508 ✉ icelc@tskb.com.tr
Economic Research Orhan Beskök *Department Head* ☎ 252 5676 ✉ beskoko@tskb.com.tr

Administration

Technology & Systems
Information Technology System & Network Semseddin Arat *Department Head* ☎ 249 5293 ✉ arats@tskb.com.tr
System & Network Support Turgut Dagdelen *Chief Information Officer* ☎ 245 6198
  ✉ dagdelent@tskb.com.tr

Legal / In-House Counsel
  Safa Reisoglu *Legal Advisor* ☎ 251 1984 ✉ reisoglus@tskb.com.tr

Accounts / Audit
Internal Audit Necati Eveimen *Internal Auditor* ☎ 244 2899 ✉ eveimenn@tskb.com.tr

Other (Administration)
Human Resources & Relations Nuran Uras *Department Head* ☎ 243 0272 ✉ urasn@tskb.com.tr
Engineering & Consultancy Mustafa Miraboglu *Department Head* ☎ 243 2395
  ✉ miraboglum@tskb.com.tr

Euromoney Directory 1999 **1613**

TURKEY (+90)   www.euromoneydirectory.com

ING Barings
Full Branch Office

Spor Caddesi 92, BJK Plaza, B Blok, 8th Floor, Akaretler-Besiktas, TR-80680 Istanbul
Tel: (212) 258 8770 **Fax:** (212) 259 1140 **Telex:** 26049 INGBTR **Swift:** INGB TR IS

Senior Executive Officers
Country Manager   John T McCarthy

Interbank AS

Buyukdere Caddesi 108, Esentepe 1st, TR-80496 Istanbul
Tel: (212) 274 2000 **Fax:** (212) 272 1622 **Telex:** 26827 IBKTR **Email:** invest@intertech.com.tr **Telex:** 26099 IBJE TR
Website: www.interbank.com.tr/interinvest

Senior Executive Officers
Chairman	Erman Yerdelen
Chief Executive Officer	Nedim Ölger
Financial Director	Bülent Günceler *Executive Vice President*
Chief Operating Officer	Abdullah Soydas *Executive Vice President*
Treasurer	Murat Baltaci *Executive Vice President*
International Division	Korhan Berzeg *Chief Economist*

General-Lending (DCM, SL)
Head of Corporate Banking   Önder Alp *Executive Vice President* ☎ 275 1253

Debt Capital Markets / Fixed Income
Head of Fixed Income	Murat Baltaci *Executive Vice President*
Head of Fixed Income Sales; Head of Fixed Income Trading	Mehmet Okan

Government Bonds
Head of Sales; Head of Trading   Mehmet Okan

Eurobonds
Head of Sales; Head of Trading   Mehmet Okan

Syndicated Lending

Loan-Related Activities
Trade Finance	Korhan Berzeg *Chief Economist*
Project Finance	Önder Alp *Executive Vice President* ☎ 275 1253

Money Markets
Head of Money Markets   Murat Baltaci *Executive Vice President*

Foreign Exchange
Head of Foreign Exchange   Murat Baltaci *Executive Vice President*

Risk Management
Head of Risk Management   Önder Alp *Executive Vice President* ☎ 275 1253

Settlement / Clearing
Head of Settlement / Clearing   Abdullah Soydas *Executive Vice President*

Global Custody
Head of Global Custody   Korhan Berzeg *Chief Economist*

Other Departments
Private Banking	Barbaras Karakisla *Executive Vice President*
Correspondent Banking	Korhan Berzeg *Chief Economist*
Cash Management	Önder Alp *Executive Vice President* ☎ 275 1253

International Finance Corporation
Representative Office

Mete Caddesi 24/3, Taksim, TR-80090 Istanbul
Tel: (212) 243 2593; (212) 243 2126 **Fax:** (212) 249 2476

Senior Executive Officers
Resident Representative   Sankaran Balasubramanian

www.euromoneydirectory.com TURKEY (+90)

KOÇBANK AS
Head Office

Barbaros Bulvari Murbasan Sokak, Koza Is Merkezi, Balmunco, TR-80700 Istanbul
PO Box 153, Besiktas, TR-80692 Istanbul
Tel: (212) 274 7777 **Fax:** (212) 274 6549 **Telex:** 39070 KOCXTR **Swift:** KABA TR IS **Reuters:** KABD; KABX
Website: www.kogbank.com.tr

Senior Executive Officers
Chairman   Tevfik Altinok
Treasurer   Levent Ersalman *Group Manager*
General Manager   Engin Akçakoca

Debt Capital Markets / Fixed Income
Head of Debt Capital Markets   Mwurt Aysan *Group Manager*

Equity Capital Markets
Head of Equity Capital Markets   Lale Eralp *Assistant General Manager*

Syndicated Lending
Head of Syndicated Lending   Semih Bilgin *Group Manager* ☏ **274 1399**

Money Markets
Head of Money Markets   Mwurt Aysan *Group Manager*

Foreign Exchange
Head of Foreign Exchange   Mert Yazicioglw *Group Manager*

Risk Management
Head of Risk Management   Levent Ersalman *Group Manager*

Corporate Finance / M&A Advisory
Head of Corporate Finance   Lale Eralp *Assistant General Manager*

Settlement / Clearing
Head of Settlement / Clearing   William Garwey *Group Manager*

London Forfaiting Company plc
Representative Office

Balmumcu Murbasan Sokak, MTU Center Kat 4, Besiktas, TR-80700 Istanbul
Tel: (212) 274 9373 **Fax:** (212) 274 8051 **Email:** lfc@service.raksnet.com.tr

Senior Executive Officers
Chief Representative   Muzaffer Aksoy

Others (Senior Executives)
                                                 Muzaffer Aksoy
                                                 Sibel Unaldi *Manager*

Merrill Lynch Europe Limited
Representative Office

Mete Caddesi 24/2, Taksim, TR-80090 Istanbul
Tel: (212) 249 2033; (212) 249 2035 **Fax:** (212) 249 2010
Website: www.ml.com

Midland Bank AS
Subsidiary Company

Cumhuriyet Caddesi 8, Elmadag Han, Elmadag, TR-80200 Istanbul
Tel: (212) 231 5560 **Fax:** (212) 230 5300

Senior Executive Officers
Managing Director   P Y Antika

Osmanli Bankasi AS
Head Office

Alternative trading name: Ottoman Bank & Banque Ottoman
Voyvoda Street 35-37, Karaköy, TR-80000 Istanbul
PO Box 297, Karakoy, TR-80000 Istanbul
Tel: (212) 252 3000 **Fax:** (212) 249 8724 **Telex:** 24193 DIROTR **Swift:** OTBA TR IS
Email: hanka.baki@ottomanbank.com.tr **Reuters:** OBIT
Website: www.ottomanbank.com.tr

Senior Executive Officers
President & CEO   Aclan Acar ☏ **245 4508**
Chief Executive Officer   Tanju Oguz *Executive Vice President* ☏ **252 6724**

TURKEY (+90)

www.euromoneydirectory.com

Osmanli Bankasi AS (cont)
Senior Executive Officers (cont)

Treasurer
International Division — Uruz Ersozoglu *Senior Vice President* T 244 2780
Tanju Oguz *Executive Vice President* T 252 6724

General-Lending (DCM, SL)
Head of Corporate Banking — Emre Ertem *Executive Vice President* T 293 9912 F 252 0543

General-Investment
Head of Investment — Cuneyt Sezgin *Executive Vice President* T 252 2355 F 249 9807

Debt Capital Markets / Fixed Income
Department: Treasury
Tel: 293 9908 Fax: 252 0666
Head of Fixed Income Sales — Emre Timurkan *Dealer* T 244 3367

Domestic Government Bonds
Head of Sales — Emre Timurkan *Dealer* T 244 3367
Head of Trading — Aycan Kulaksiz *Assistant Vice President* T 244 3367

Eurobonds
Head of Trading — Feyza Onen *Assistant Vice President* T 244 3367

Fixed-Income Repo
Head of Trading — Ustun Okay *Assistant Vice President* T 292 2309

Equity Capital Markets
Head of Equity Capital Markets — Ece Demirgoglu *Vice President* T 251 7781 F 249 8955

Domestic Equities
Head of Trading — Hakan Sofular *Dealer* T 251 5698
Head of Research — Hakan Karacigan *Vice President* T 252 2705 F 249 9807

Equity Research
Head of Equity Research — Cuneyt Sezgin *Executive Vice President* T 252 2355 F 249 9807

Syndicated Lending
Tel: 244 4292 Fax: 293 9500
Head of Syndicated Lending — Harika Balci *Vice President* T 242 4292 F 293 9500

Loan-Related Activities
Trade Finance — Harika Balci *Vice President* T 242 4292 F 293 9500

Money Markets
Tel: 251 5674 Fax: 252 0666
Head of Money Markets — Umit Leblebici *Vice President* T 251 5674

Wholesale Deposits
Marketing — Emre Ertem *Executive Vice President* T 293 9912 F 252 0543

Foreign Exchange
Tel: 249 7128 Fax: 252 0666
Head of Foreign Exchange — Umit Leblebici *Vice President* T 251 5674

FX Traders / Sales People
Dealer — Cigdem Avsar T 249 7128 F 252 0666
Arda Turerer T 244 3367 F 252 0666

Risk Management
Tel: 252 3000 ext 399 Fax: 252 0666
Head of Risk Management — Ediz Alkoc T 251 5674

Corporate Finance / M&A Advisory
Head of Corporate Finance — Cuneyt Sezgin *Executive Vice President* T 252 2355 F 249 9807

Settlement / Clearing
Tel: 252 3000 ext 189 Fax: 251 1750
Head of Settlement / Clearing — Zeynep Öktener *Senior Vice President* T 252 2788

Global Custody
Head of Global Custody — Ibrahim Yurtlu T 293 3072 F 251 2064

Other Departments
Private Banking — Bahri Ugras *Executive Vice President* T 252 6063 F 249 1299
Correspondent Banking — Harika Balci *Vice President* T 242 4292 F 293 9500

Administration
Head of Marketing — Emre Ertem *Executive Vice President* T 293 9912 F 252 0543

Technology & Systems
Halil Kutluöz *Executive Vice President* T 252 5136 F 252 4254

Legal / In-House Counsel
Fikret Tümen *Executive Vice President* T 290 2740 F 290 2745

Compliance
Ali Barut *Executive Vice President* T 252 0859 F 249 1299

www.euromoneydirectory.com   TURKEY (+90)

Public Relations
Sülün Gurtin *Senior Vice President* ☏ **290 2725** F **290 2731**

Accounts / Audit
Ali Barut *Executive Vice President* ☏ **252 0859** F **249 1299**

Pamukbank TAS

Büyükdere Caddesi 82, Gayrettepe, TR-80450 Istanbul
Tel: (212) 275 2424; (212) 275 2850 **Fax:** (212) 266 6224; (212) 275 6239 **Telex:** 26959 PAUM TR **Swift:** PAMU TR IS
Email: Pamukbank **Reuters:** PBIT **Cable:** pamukbankum
Website: www.pamukbank.com

Senior Executive Officers
Chairman — Kemal Kabatas
President & CEO — Orhan Emirdag
Treasurer — Bilgehan Kuru *Vice President* ☏ **211 6316** E **bilkur@pamukbank.com**
International Division — Atilla Cetiner *Executive Vice President* ☏ **267 1092** F **279 1646**

General-Lending (DCM, SL)
Head of Corporate Banking — Vural Eralap *Executive Vice President* ☏ **274 6042**

Debt Capital Markets / Fixed Income
Head of Debt Capital Markets — Kemal Gurel *Executive Vice President* ☏ **213 2876**

Corporate Finance / M&A Advisory
Head of Corporate Finance — Polat Kadir *Executive Vice President* ☏ **266 9791**

Other Departments
Private Banking — Hakan Binbasgil *Executive Vice President* ☏ **266 0383**

Administration
Technology & Systems
Ali Kirval *Executive Vice President* ☏ **267 3025**

Public Relations
Oya Yürekli *Vice President* ☏ **266 0383**

Pangaea Partners Limited   Representative Office

Kustepe Yolu Caddesi Tomurcuk Sok, Nursan Is Merkezi, A Blok, K:4, D:17, Mecidiyekoy, TR-80310 Istanbul
Tel: (212) 213 6645; (212) 213 6646 **Fax:** (212) 213 6648 **Email:** 101352.1411@compuserve.com
Website: www.pangaeapartners.com

Senior Executive Officers
Others (Senior Executives)
Irem Ozyurek *Senior Partner*

Sekerbank TAS   Head Office

Atatürk Bulvari 171, Kavaklidere, TR-06680 Ankara
PO Box 111, TR-06662 Ankara
Tel: (312) 417 9120 **Fax:** (312) 417 8333 **Telex:** 46990 SKGM TR **Swift:** SEKE TR 2A **Email:** fon@sekerbank.com.tr
Reuters: SKBT **Cable:** SEKERBANKUM

Senior Executive Officers
Chairman — Kamil Özdemir ☏ **425 9737**
Financial Director — Sahin Akar *Assistant General Manager* ☏ **417 2641**
Treasurer — Sercan Yavuzyilmaz *Assistant General Manager* ☏ **425 3512**
General Manager — Hasan Basri Göktan ☏ **425 2700**
Manager — Emel Mangiroglu ☏ **418 7260**
Company Secretary — Hüseyin Serdar ☏ **425 4135**
International Division — Cahit Baser *Co-ordinator* ☏ **425 2541**

Debt Capital Markets / Fixed Income
Department: Fixed Income and Repo Department
Tel: 212 4370 **Fax:** 213 4391
Head of Fixed Income; Head of Fixed Income Sales; Head of Fixed Income Trading — Necati Simer *Manager*

Government Bonds
Head of Sales — Melek Kantar *Specialist*
Head of Trading — Mustafa Bayram *Specialist*

TURKEY (+90) www.euromoneydirectory.com

Sekerbank TAS (cont)

Fixed-Income Repo
Head of Repo — Necati Simer *Manager*
Marketing & Product Development — Melek Kantar *Specialist*
Head of Trading — Mustafa Bayram *Specialist*

Fixed-Income Research
Head of Fixed Income — Mustafa Bayram *Specialist*

Syndicated Lending
Tel: 425 2541 **Fax:** 425 7645 **Telex:** 46990 C SKGM TR
Head of Trading — Cahit Baser *Co-ordinator* ☎ **425 2541**

Money Markets
Domestic Commercial Paper
Head of Sales — Emel Mangiroglu *Manager* ☎ **418 7260**
Head of Trading — Seda Anil *Assistant Manager* ☎ **418 0315**

Eurocommercial Paper
Head of Sales — Cahit Baser *Co-ordinator* ☎ **425 2541**

Wholesale Deposits
Marketing — Emel Mangiroglu *Manager* ☎ **418 7260**
Head of Sales — Nilgün Sözer *Assistant Manager* ☎ **418 0315**

Foreign Exchange
Tel: 418 0315 **Fax:** 425 1490
Head of Foreign Exchange — Emel Mangiroglu *Manager* ☎ **418 7260**
Head of Trading — Nilgün Sözer *Assistant Manager* ☎ **418 0315**

FX Traders / Sales People
Dealer — Gülsen Yazgan ☎ **419 1839**
Deniz Patat ☎ **419 1839**

Settlement / Clearing
Tel: 417 9120 **Fax:** 425 9870
Head of Settlement / Clearing — Osman Kurnaz *Manager* ☎ **418 4845**
Operations — Semin Patat *Assistant Manager* ☎ **417 9120**

Other Departments
Chief Credit Officer — Orhan Karakas *Manager* ☎ **418 1526**
Private Banking — Yücel Akbulut *Manager* ☎ **418 9678**
Correspondent Banking — Cahit Baser *Co-ordinator* ☎ **425 2541**

Administration
Technology & Systems
Nazan Eker *Manager* ☎ **425 3305**

Legal / In-House Counsel
Atilla Özer ☎ **418 8726**

Public Relations
Mehmet Isikkaya *Manager* ☎ **418 3968**

Accounts / Audit
Fatih Tezcan *Manager* ☎ **425 1260**

Sinai Yatirim Bankasi AS   Head Office

Formerly known as: Sinai Yatirim ve Kredi Bankasi AO
Buyukdere Cad. No. 129, TR-80300 Istanbul
Tel: (212) 213 1600 **Fax:** (212) 213 1303; (212) 213 1302 **Telex:** 26703 SYKB TR **Swift:** SYBITRIS

Senior Executive Officers
Chairman — Cahit Kocaömer ☎ **213 1213** F **213 1249**
General Manager — Ahmet Türel Ayaydin ☎ **213 1214** F **213 1249**
Assistant General Manager — Yavuz Isakan ☎ **213 1390** F **213 1249**
Secretary to the General Manager — San Balçik ☎ **213 1600**

Debt Capital Markets / Fixed Income
Fixed-Income Repo
Head of Repo — Hayrettin Eryimaz *Treasury & Fund Manager* ☎ **213 1397**

Syndicated Lending
Loan-Related Activities
Project Finance — Ismet Arsoy *Manager*

Other Departments
Chief Credit Officer — Necdet Barkman *Loans Manager*

Administration
Head of Marketing — Hasan Lök

1618 Euromoney Directory 1999

www.euromoneydirectory.com   TURKEY (+90)

Société Générale
Nispetiye Cad, Akmerkez E-3, Blok Kat 9, TR-80600 Istanbul
Tel: (212) 282 1942 **Fax:** (212) 282 1848
Website: www.socgen.com

Taris Bank   Head Office
Formerly known as: Milli Aydin Bankasi TAS
Sair Esref Bulvari, 3/1 Cankaya, TR-35210 Izmir
Tel: (232) 441 5090 **Fax:** (232) 425 7390 **Telex:** 51424 MABTR **Swift:** MIAY TR 2I **Reuters:** MIAX
Telex: 53060 MTBTR

Senior Executive Officers
Chairman   Behic Tozkoparan
Financial Director   Esen Özgün
Treasurer   Tuncay Kozanoglu *Assistant General Manager*
General Manager   Ahmet Secer
International Division   Reyhan Furuncioglu

Debt Capital Markets / Fixed Income
Tel: 446 1474 **Fax:** 484 5908
Head of Fixed Income; Head of Fixed Income Sales   Ayse Aydin

Fixed-Income Repo
Head of Repo   Ayse Aydin

Equity Capital Markets
Department: Funds Management Department
Fax: 489 1172
Head of Equity Capital Markets   Cüneyt Saraç *Manager*

Money Markets
Fax: 489 1172
Head of Money Markets   Günsel Kircalioglu *Assistant Manager*

Foreign Exchange
Fax: 489 1172
Head of Foreign Exchange   Cüneyt Saraç *Manager*

Other Departments
Correspondent Banking   Z Nilgün Altun

Administration
Technology & Systems
                                      Halil Posaci *Manager*

Legal / In-House Counsel
                                      A Yüksel Bartan *Legal Advisor*

Public Relations
                                      Zehra Paker *Assistant Manager*

Accounts / Audit
                                      Faruk Yaman *Manager*

TC Ziraat Bankasi   Head Office   T
Bankalar Caddesi, 42 Ulus, Ankara
Tel: (312) 310 3750; (312) 231 7560 **Fax:** (312) 310 4686; (312) 310 4687 **Telex:** 44004 AZBHM TR **Swift:** TCZB TR 2A
Email: zbmail@ziraatbank.com.tr **Cable:** ZERBANK ANKARA
Website: www.ziraat.com.tr

Senior Executive Officers
Chairman & General Manager   Selcuk Demiralp [T] **311 6050** [F] **310 4686**
Treasurer   Ahmet Olgun *Executive Vice President* [T] **312 7756** [F] **310 4687**
Head of Special Bureau   Ünal Yildirim [T] **311 6050** [F] **310 4686**
International Division   Emin Erdem *Executive Vice President* [T] **312 2957** [F] **310 4686**

General-Lending (DCM, SL)
Head of Corporate Banking   Selcuk Arseven *Executive Vice President* [T] **310 8344** [F] **310 4686**
                                      Ibrahim Karamanlioglu *Senior Vice President* [T] **231 1566** [F] **229 7331**

General - Treasury
Head of Treasury   Aynur Yalgin *Senior Vice President* [T] **229 7971** [F] **230 1200**

Euromoney Directory 1999   **1619**

TURKEY (+90)

www.euromoneydirectory.com

TC Ziraat Bankasi (cont)

Relationship Manager
International Relations Department — Selcuk Canbaz *Senior Vice President* ☎ **(212) 245 1554** 🖷 **(212) 251 8954**

Debt Capital Markets / Fixed Income
Head of Debt Capital Markets — Ali Kemal Sancak *Senior Vice President* ☎ **520 9295** 🖷 **230 1942**

Settlement / Clearing
Operations — Mehmet Sahin *SVP, Foreign Operations* ☎ **229 7275** 🖷 **231 6480**
Electronic Banking — A Semih Bilgin *Senior Vice President* ☎ **231 0495** 🖷 **229 4610**

Other Departments
Private Banking — Selcuk Arseven *Executive Vice President* ☎ **310 8344** 🖷 **310 4686**

Administration
Business Development — Senol Babuscu *Second Vice President* ☎ **310 2556** 🖷 **312 4862**

Technology & Systems
Systems & Automation — Metin Akpinar *Executive Vice President* ☎ **311 1189** 🖷 **310 4686**
Tamer Tüfekci *Senior Vice President* ☎ **229 6708** 🖷 **229 3851**

Public Relations
Ekrem Aydemir *Executive Vice President* ☎ **324 1545** 🖷 **310 4686**
Oya Olgun *Senior Vice President* ☎ **229 8092** 🖷 **229 4770**

Accounts / Audit
Accounting — Erdogan Varol *Senior Vice President* ☎ **311 1191** 🖷 **324 5939**
Internal Audit — Nail Tohumcu *Senior Vice President* ☎ **311 4662** 🖷 **310 6735**

Other (Administration)
Personnel and Training — Mahmut Haboglu *Executive Vice President* ☎ **324 1003** 🖷 **310 4686**
Agricultural Credits — Caglar Ünal *Executive Vice President* ☎ **312 6448** 🖷 **310 4686**

Toprakbank AS — Head Office

Büyükdere Cad 23, Sisli, TR-80220 Istanbul
Tel: (212) 233 2211; (212) 225 5800 **Fax:** (212) 247 9699; (212) 247 3430 **Telex:** 26012 TORB TR **Swift:** TOPR TR IS
Email: toprakbank@ toprakbank.com.tr **Reuters:** TOPB
Website: www.toprakbank.com.tr

Senior Executive Officers
Chairman of the Board — Mahfi Egilmez ☎ **233 0524**
Treasurer — Fethullah Acil *Assistant General Manager* ☎ **233 2786**
Managing Director / General Manager — Veysel Bilen ☎ **283 2700**
International Division — Ismail Kulacaoglu *Assistant General Manager* ☎ **233 2575**

Debt Capital Markets / Fixed Income
Head of Debt Capital Markets — Fethullah Acil *Assistant General Manager* ☎ **233 2786**

Equity Capital Markets
Head of Equity Capital Markets — Bulent Dural *General Manager* ☎ **241 5159**

Syndicated Lending
Head of Syndicated Lending — Ismail Kulacaoglu *Assistant General Manager* ☎ **233 2575**

Loan-Related Activities
Trade Finance — Ismail Kulacaoglu *Assistant General Manager* ☎ **233 2575**

Money Markets
Head of Money Markets — Fethullah Acil *Assistant General Manager* ☎ **233 2786**

Foreign Exchange
Head of Foreign Exchange — Dinc Erkman *Manager* ☎ **233 2211**

Settlement / Clearing
Head of Settlement / Clearing — Fethullah Acil *Assistant General Manager* ☎ **233 2786**

Other Departments
Correspondent Banking — Eser Ince *Senior Manager* ☎ **241 5452**

Administration

Technology & Systems
Ibrahim Yilmaz *Advisor* ☎ **233 0673**

Legal / In-House Counsel
Mutlu Simayli *Assistant General Manager* ☎ **233 0891**

Public Relations
Serap Baykal *Manager* ☎ **241 2876**

Accounts / Audit
Accounts — Meral Altinok *Assistant General Manager* ☎ **247 3972**
Internal Audit — Ercan Aslanturk

www.euromoneydirectory.com TURKEY (+90)

Other (Administration)
Organization & Personnel   Ender Par *Assistant General Manager*

Türk Dis Ticaret Bankasi AS
Head Office

Alternative trading name: Turkish Foreign Trade Bank & DISBANK
Yildiz Posta Caddesi 54, Gayrettepe, TR-80280 Istanbul
PO Box 131, Besiktas, TR-80692 Istanbul
Tel: (212) 274 4280; (212) 275 4025 **Fax:** (212) 272 5278; (212) 272 5279 **Telex:** 27991 DISP TR **Swift:** DISB IR IS

Senior Executive Officers
Chairman   Çetin Hacaloglu
Chief Operating Officer   Zeynep Toydemir *Assistant General Manager*

Debt Capital Markets / Fixed Income
Global Head   Zeynep Toydemir *Assistant General Manager*

Domestic Government Bonds
Head of Sales   Zeynep Toydemir *Assistant General Manager*

Risk Management
Global Head   Zeynep Toydemir *Assistant General Manager*

Türk Ekonomi Bankasi AS
Head Office

Meclis-i Mebusan Caddesi 35, Findikli, TR-80040 Istanbul
Tel: (212) 251 2121 **Fax:** (212) 249 6568 **Swift:** TEBU TR IS **Reuters:** TEBX
Website: www.teb.com.tr

Senior Executive Officers
Chairman   Yavuz Canevi
Financial Director   Cihat Madanoglu
Treasurer   Ismail Yanik
Managing Director / General Manager   Akin Akbaygil

Debt Capital Markets / Fixed Income
Head of Debt Capital Markets   Tugrul Ozbakan

Money Markets
Head of Money Markets   Levent Celebioglu

Risk Management
Head of Risk Management   Asuman Gömüg

Türk Sakura Bank AS
Subsidiary Company

Büyükdere Cad. Enka Han 108/A, Esentepe, TR-80280 Istanbul
Tel: (212) 275 2930 **Fax:** (212) 273 0859; (212) 273 0860 **Telex:** 27718 **Swift:** MITK TR IS **Reuters:** CEMB

Senior Executive Officers
Chairman   Jumpei Ishii
Financial Director   Minoru Inaba *Senior Deputy General Manager*
Chief Operating Officer   Yusuf Çagala *Deputy General Manager*
Treasurer   Funda Dündar *Treasurer*
General Manager   Yoshiaki Kobayashi

Debt Capital Markets / Fixed Income
Department: Treasury
Head of Fixed Income Trading   Funda Dündar *Treasurer*

Government Bonds
Head of Trading   Funda Dündar *Treasurer*

Fixed-Income Repo
Head of Trading   Funda Dündar *Treasurer*

Syndicated Lending
Head of Syndication   Junichiro Zushi *Senior Manager*

Money Markets
Head of Money Markets   Funda Dündar *Treasurer*

Foreign Exchange
Head of Foreign Exchange; Head of Trading   Funda Dündar *Treasurer*

FX Traders / Sales People
    Meral Abdelaziz *Assistant Banker*

Settlement / Clearing
Operations   Mesut Mesutoglu *Assistant Supervisor*

TURKEY (+90)   www.euromoneydirectory.com

Türk Sakura Bank AS (cont)
Other Departments
Chief Credit Officer   Junchiro Zushi *Senior Manager, Credit*
Correspondent Banking   Güray Gür *Assistant Manager, General Banking*

Administration
Head of Marketing   Hirofumi Matsui *Senior Manager, Japanese Customers*
     Hülya Akgün *Assistant Manager, Corporate Customers*

Technology & Systems
     Kutsal Durace *EDP Manager*

Compliance
     Aron Küçükmatalon *Banker*

Accounts / Audit
     Aynur Özata *Assistant Manager*

Türkiye Garanti Bankasi AS   Head Office
Alternative trading name: Garanti Bank
63 Büyükdere Caddesi, Maslak, TR-80670 Istanbul
Tel: (212) 285 4040; (212) 286 0269 **Fax:** (212) 285 4040 **Telex:** 27635 GATI TR **Swift:** TGBA TR IS **Reuters:** GBIT
Telerate: GBIT
Website: www.garantibank.com.tr

Senior Executive Officers
Chairman & Managing Director   Ayhan Sahenk
President & CEO   Y Akin Öngör
Treasurer   Ergun Özen *Executive Vice President*

Others (Senior Executives)
International   Ergun Özen *Executive Vice President*
Operations   Hüsnü Erel

General-Lending (DCM, SL)
Head of Corporate Banking   Leyla Etker

Debt Capital Markets / Fixed Income
Eurobonds
Head of Sales   Aysegül Merdin *Trader* ☎ **286 0433**
Head of Trading   Gökman Erün *Trader* ☎ **276 7051**

Asset-Backed Securities / Securitization
Global Head   Tolga Egemen *Vice President* ☎ **286 0331**

Fixed-Income Repo
Head of Repo   Tayfun Kügük *Trader* ☎ **286 0351**

Equity Capital Markets
Head of Equity Capital Markets   Sinan Akiman *Senior Vice President*

Syndicated Lending
Tel: 286 0269 **Fax:** 286 2327
Head of Syndicated Lending   Tolga Egemen *Vice President* ☎ **286 0331**

Money Markets
Head of Money Markets   Tayfun Kügük *Trader* ☎ **286 0351**

Domestic Commercial Paper
Head of Origination   Tayfun Kügük *Trader* ☎ **286 0351**
Head of Sales   Gökhan Erün *Trader* ☎ **286 0436**

Foreign Exchange
Head of Foreign Exchange   Osman Kökmen *Trader* ☎ **286 0393**

Risk Management
Fixed Income Derivatives / Risk Management
Global Head   Tayfun Kügük *Trader* ☎ **286 0351**
Other (FI Derivatives)
     Sinem Edige *Trader* ☎ **286 0351**
     Esra Peker *Trader* ☎ **286 0351**

Foreign Exchange Derivatives / Risk Management
Cross-Currency Swaps, Sales / Marketing   Osman Kökmen *Trader* ☎ **286 0393**
Cross-Currency Swaps, Trading   Esra Eksit *Trader* ☎ **286 0433**

Exotic Options (Barriers, Range, Timers, Digitals, Faders etc)
Trading   Osman Kökmen *Trader* ☎ **286 0393**

Corporate Finance / M&A Advisory
Head of Corporate Finance   Cigdem Bicik *Senior Vice President* ☎ **286 2309**

TURKEY (+90)

Settlement / Clearing
Head of Settlement / Clearing
Country Head
Gürbüz Salman *Senior Vice President* ☎ **286 0276**
Mesliha Yimae *Vice President* ☎ **286 0372**

Global Custody
Head of Global Custody
Gürbuz Salman

Other Departments
Correspondent Banking
Tolga Egemen *Senior Vice President* ☎ **286 0266**

Administration
Technology & Systems
Nurcan Tanrikurt *Senior Vice President* ☎ **233 3263**

Legal / In-House Counsel
Mine Taygun *Senior Vice President* ☎ **286 1332**

Public Relations
Public Relations & Advertising
Naciye Günal *Senior Vice President* ☎ **286 0273**

Other (Administration)
Tolga Egemen *Senior Vice President* ☎ **286 0266**

Türkiye Halk Bankåsi AS   Head Office

Alternative trading name: Halkbank
2 Cadde, 63 Sögütözü, TR-06520 Ankara
Tel: (312) 289 2000 **Telex:** 44201 HBFO TR **Swift:** TRHB TR 2AA **Reuters:** HBAT
Money Markets Tel: 289 2920; **Fax:** 289 2977; **Foreign Exchange Tel:** 289 2921; **TL Tel:** 289 2922; **Capital Markets Tel:** 289 2975
Website: www.halkbank.com.tr

Senior Executive Officers
Chairman & CEO
Treasurer
International Division
Yenal Ansen ☎ **289 2001/5** 📠 **289 2076**
Füsun Balamir *SVP, Treasury* ☎ **289 2901/3** 📠 **289 2979**
Ibrahim Toptepe *Executive Vice President* ☎ **289 2026/8** 📠 **289 2030**
Deniz Çiner *SVP, Foreign Relations* ☎ **289 2301/3** 📠 **289 2375**

Others (Senior Executives)
Ilknur Ökazanç *VP, Dealing Room* ☎ **289 2904** 📠 **289 2975**

Relationship Manager
International Finance & Subsidiaries
Necla Aksop *Vice President* ☎ **289 2304** 📠 **289 2325**

Settlement / Clearing
Other
Bülent Ispir *VP, Payment Orders* ☎ **289 2206** 📠 **289 2230**

Other Departments
Correspondent Banking
Isil Kotan *Vice President* ☎ **289 2306** 📠 **289 2340**
Belgin Tekin *Vice President* ☎ **289 2204/15** 📠 **289 2376**

Administration
Legal / In-House Counsel
Checks & Legislation
Suat Kepenek *Vice President* ☎ **289 2305** 📠 **289 2315**

Other (Administration)
SWIFT Department
Ayfer Yaksi *Vice President* ☎ **289 2906**

Türkiye Ihracat Kredi Bankasi AS   Head Office

Alternative trading name: Turk Eximbank
Formerly known as: Deulet Yatirim Bankasi
Mudafa Caddesi 20, Bakanliklar, TR-06100 Ankara
Tel: (312) 417 1300 **Fax:** (312) 425 7896 **Telex:** 46751 EXMB TR **Swift:** TIKB TR 2A **Reuters:** EXIM

Senior Executive Officers
Chairman of the Board
Chief Executive Officer
Financial Director
Chief Operating Officer
Treasurer
A Yavuz Egie ☎ **418 4414**
Ahmet Kiligoglu *General Manager* ☎ **418 4410**
Ertan Tanriyakul *Chief Financial Officer* ☎ **425 6504**
Gulcan Armagian *Head of Accounting* ☎ **418 4416**
Gigdem Köse *Head of Treasury* ☎ **425 7453**

Debt Capital Markets / Fixed Income
Department: Treasury Department
Global Head
Gigdem Köse *Head of Treasury* ☎ **425 7453**

Domestic Government Bonds
Head of Trading
Sule Dalan *Chief Dealer* ☎ **425 7453**

TURKEY (+90)   www.euromoneydirectory.com

Türkiye Ihracat Kredi Bankasi AS (cont)
Syndicated Lending
Loan-Related Activities
Trade Finance; Project Finance   Tülin Kalkay *Head, Project Finance* F **419 2179**

Money Markets
Department: Treasury Department
Tel: 425 7453 **Fax:** 425 2347
Head of Money Markets   Bernur Ersdy *Chief Dealer* T **418 8437**

Foreign Exchange
Department: Treasury Department
Tel: 429 7433 **Fax:** 425 2847
Head of Foreign Exchange   Kürsat Durmaz *Chief Dealer* T **418 5974**

Risk Management
Department: Finance Department
Tel: 425 7453 **Fax:** 425 2947
Head of Risk Management   Ertan Tanriyakul *Chief Financial Officer* T **425 6504**

Settlement / Clearing
Department: Treasury Operations Department
Tel: 418 8437 **Fax:** 425 2847
Head of Settlement / Clearing; Fixed-Income Settlement; Derivatives Settlement; Foreign Exchange Settlement   Gebnem Bora *Manager, Treasury Operations* T **418 8437**

Other Departments
Correspondent Banking   Gebnem Bora *Manager, Treasury Operations* T **418 8437**

Administration
Technology & Systems
    Abdullah Kornes *Head of Systems* T **418 4416**

Legal / In-House Counsel
    Güvan Vural *Head, Legal Department* T **425 4615**

Public Relations
    Ayge Sel *Head, Public Relations* T **425 7454**

Türkiye Is Bankasi AS   Head Office
Atatürk Bulvari 191, Kavaklidere, TR-06684 Ankara
Tel: (312) 413 9900 **Fax:** (312) 413 9090 **Telex:** 46119 TAB TR **Swift:** ISBK TR IS **Reuters:** ISBT
Website: www.isbank.com.tr

Senior Executive Officers
Chairman of the Board   Burhan Karagöz
Chief Executive Officer   Ünal Korukcu *Deputy Chairman & CEO*
Financial Director   Sirri Erkan *Head of Accounting*
Treasurer   Danyal Kara *Head of Treasury* T **413 9750**
International Division   H Atila Macun T **(212) 233 1474**

Debt Capital Markets / Fixed Income
Tel: (212) 212 0460 **Fax:** (212) 211 4639 **Telex:** 26413 ISBF TR

Eurobonds
Head of Origination; Head of Sales; Head of Trading; Head of Research   Adnan Bali *Group Manager* T **246 5938**

Libor-Based / Floating-Rate Products
FRN Origination   Adnan Bali *Group Manager* T **246 5938**

Asset-Backed Securities / Securitization
Global Head   Güeman Teufit *Group Manager* T **(212) 211 1708**
    Danyal Kara *Head of Treasury* T **413 9750**

Fixed-Income Repo
Head of Repo   Riza Kutlusoy *Assistant Manager* T **(212) 211 1761**
Department: Capital Markets
Tel: +90 (212) 212 0460 **Fax:** +90 (212) 211 4639 **Telex:** 26413 ISBFTR
Head of Debt Capital Markets; Head of Fixed Income   Ibrahim Hizlikan *Head of Capital Markets* T **(212) 211 1840**
Head of Fixed Income Sales   Gürman Teufik *Group Manager* T **(212) 211 1708**
Head of Fixed Income Trading   Riza Kutlusoy *Assistant Manager* T **(212) 211 1761**

Government Bonds
Head of Sales   Güeman Teufik *Group Manager* T **(212) 211 1708**
Head of Trading   Riza Kutlusoy *Assistant Manager* T **(212) 211 1761**

www.euromoneydirectory.com TURKEY (+90)

Fixed-Income Repo
Head of Repo — Riza Kutlusoy *Assistant Manager* ☏ **(212) 211 1761**

Equity Capital Markets
Department: IS Investment & Securities Inc
100-102 Haya Akar Center, TR-80280 Istanbul
Tel: +90 (212) 212 0460 **Fax:** +90 (212) 211 0842 **Telex:** 26413 ISBFTR
Head of Equity Capital Markets — Özcan Türkakin *Manager* ☏ **(212) 211 1015**
Global Head — Ilhami Kog *Department Manager* ☏ **(212) 211 1843**
Regional Head — Meltem Gitgi *Vice President* ☏ **(212) 212 0460 ext 311**
Head of Sales; Head of Trading — Ilhami Kog *Deputy Manager* ☏ **(212) 211 1843**

Domestic Equities
Head of Sales — Olcay Yagci *Senior Analyst* ☏ **(212) 211 0848**
Head of Trading — Aytül Seuim *Vice President* ☏ **(212) 212 0460 ext 371**
 Özlem Tümer *Analyst* ☏ **(212) 211 0848**
Head of Research — Metin Yilmaz *Department Manager* ☏ **(212) 211 1304**

International Equities
Head of Sales; Head of Trading — Meltem Ciftci *Vice President* ☏ **(212) 213 5270**

Equity Research
Head of Equity Research — Metin Yilmaz *Department Manager* ☏ **(212) 211 1304**

Syndicated Lending
Department: Treasury Department
Tel: 413 9750/51 **Fax:** 413 9084/85
Head of Syndicated Lending — Danyal Kara *Head of Treasury* ☏ **413 9750**

Money Markets
Department: Treasury Department
Tel: 241 1595 **Fax:** 233 0483
Head of Money Markets — Danyal Kara *Head of Treasury* ☏ **413 9750**

Foreign Exchange
Department: Treasury Department
Tel: 413 9751 **Fax:** 413 9084
Head of Foreign Exchange — Danyal Kara *Head of Treasury* ☏ **413 9750**
Head of Trading — Adnan Bali *Group Manager* ☏ **246 5938**

FX Traders / Sales People
US$ / Dm — I Elvan Türkel *Specialist* ☏ **241 6468**
 Ilkay Dalkilia *Specialist* ☏ **241 1595**
 Güliz Aykan *Specialist* ☏ **241 6448**
 Okan Yurtseuer *Specialist* ☏ **241 1595**

Risk Management
Department: Treasury Department
Tel: 241 1595 **Fax:** 233 0483
Head of Risk Management — Danyal Kara *Head of Treasury* ☏ **413 9750**

Foreign Exchange Derivatives / Risk Management
Cross-Currency Swaps, Sales / Marketing — Adnan Bali *Group Manager* ☏ **246 5938**
Other Currency Swap / FX Options Personnel
 Ilkay Dalkilia *Specialist* ☏ **241 1595**

Settlement / Clearing
Department: Settlement / Clearing
Tel: +90 (212) 212 7610 **Fax:** +90 (212) 212 7610 **Telex:** 26413 ISBFTR
Head of Settlement / Clearing — Kaan Tokat *Internal Auditor* ☏ **(212) 212 7610**
Country Head — Ayga A Gengler *Assistant Manager* ☏ **(212) 211 1196**
Equity Settlement — Meltem Kökden *Analyst* ☏ **(212) 212 0460**
Fixed-Income Settlement — Nilüfer Basarir *Assistant Analyst* ☏ **(212) 212 0460**

Global Custody
Department: Capital Markets Department
100-102 Maya Akar Center, TR-80280 Istanbul
Tel: +90 (212) 212 8610 **Fax:** +90 (212) 211 4639
Head of Global Custody — Kaan Tokat *Internal Auditor* ☏ **(212) 212 7610**
Country Head — Ayga A Gengler *Assistant Manager* ☏ **(212) 211 1196**

Other Departments
Correspondent Banking — Atila Macun *Head, Foreign Dept* ☏ **233 0474**

Administration
Technology & Systems
 Gökhan Sungur *Manager* ☏ **289 8400**
Legal / In-House Counsel
 Seza Reisoglu ☏ **433 9450**
Public Relations
 Cana Ating *Manager* ☏ **413 9552**

Euromoney Directory 1999 **1625**

TURKEY (+90)   www.euromoneydirectory.com

Türkiye Is Bankasi AS (cont)
Accounts / Audit
Accounting   Sirri Erkan *Head of Accounting*

WestLB Istanbul — Full Branch Office

Akasyali Sokak 6, 4 Levent, TR-80620 Istanbul
Tel: (212) 283 0808 Fax: (212) 283 0460

Senior Executive Officers
Chief Executive Officer   John Duthie *Management*
     Peter Weingartz *Management*
Treasurer   Soner Dolanay
General-Lending (DCM, SL)
Head of Corporate Banking   Dilek Kinli *Corporate Banking*
Administration
Other (Administration)
Customer Services / Bills   Tülay Sedef

Yapi ve Kredi Bankasi AS — Head Office

Yapi Kredi Plaza, Büyükdere Caddesi, Levent, TR-80620 Istanbul
Tel: (212) 280 1111; (262) 647 1000 Fax: (212) 268 6958 Telex: 24718 YOGE TR Swift: YAPITRIS 072
Email: international@ykb.com Reuters: YKBT Cable: GENKREDI-ISTANBUL

Senior Executive Officers
Chairman   Rona Yircali
Chief Executive Officer   Burhan Karaçam
Treasurer   Naci Sigîn ☎ 280 1566
International Division   Kemal Kaya *Executive Vice President* ☎ 280 1003
General-Lending (DCM, SL)
Head of Corporate Banking   Bülent Nur Öztan *Executive Vice President*
General-Investment
Head of Investment   Melin Sensoy *Executive Vice President* ☎ 280 1030
Syndicated Lending
Head of Syndicated Lending   Kemal Kaya *Executive Vice President* ☎ 280 1003
Money Markets
Head of Money Markets   Ahmet Yildirin ☎ 280 1562
Foreign Exchange
Head of Foreign Exchange   Naci Figin ☎ 278 2068
Risk Management
Head of Risk Management   Naci Figin ☎ 278 2068
Corporate Finance / M&A Advisory
Head of Corporate Finance   Birol Yücel *Executive Vice President* ☎ 283 2903
Settlement / Clearing
Head of Settlement / Clearing   Naci Figin ☎ 278 2068
Operations   Alp Sivrioglo
Asset Management
Head   Naci Figin ☎ 278 2068
Administration
Technology & Systems
     Alpaslan Ozlü *Executive Vice President*

Yasar Yatirim AS — Head Office

Yildiz Posta Cad, Number 21, Esentepe, TR-80280 Istanbul
Tel: (212) 213 0160 Fax: (212) 288 6317
Website: www.yasarbank.com.tr

Senior Executive Officers
Chairman   John Bernson ☎ 272 3768
Chief Executive Officer   Murat Aktas *Assistant General Manager* ☎ 274 0174
Financial Director   Neslihan Turaman *Assistant General Manager* ☎ 274 0284
Chief Operating Officer   Necia Taskiran *Manager* ☎ 275 2078

www.euromoneydirectory.com UGANDA (+256)

Others (Senior Executives)
Marketing — Soner Canoglu *Marketing Manager* ☎ **266 4327**
Accounting & Administration — Mesut Baydur *Accounting & Administration Manager* ☎ **266 8005**
Corporate Finance — Cahrt Yilmaz *Manager* ☎ **288 9646**

Debt Capital Markets / Fixed Income
Tel: 274 0284 Fax: 274 7986
Head of Debt Capital Markets — Neslihan Turaman *Assistant General Manager* ☎ **274 0284**

Domestic Government Bonds
Head of Sales; Head of Trading — Guggo Sen *Assistant General Manager* ☎ **288 6263**

Fixed-Income Repo
Head of Repo — Duggo Sen *Assistant General Manager* ☎ **288 4263**

Equity Capital Markets
Tel: 266 4327 Fax: 266 3132
Head of Equity Capital Markets — Murat Aktas *Assistant General Manager* ☎ **274 0174**

Corporate Finance / M&A Advisory
Tel: 288 3646 Fax: 288 6317
Head of Corporate Finance — Cahrt Yilmaz *Manager* ☎ **288 9646**

Settlement / Clearing
Tel: 275 2078 Fax: 266 3132
Equity Settlement — Necla Taskiran *Manager*

TURKMENISTAN
(+993)

Deutsche Bank AG Representative Office

Prospekt Magtum-Guli 141/1, 744001 Aschgabat
Tel: (12) 510 823 Fax: (12) 511 866

Senior Executive Officers
Chief Representative — Claus Steinhofer

UGANDA
(+256)

HSBC Equator Bank plc Representative Office

Rwenzori House, 1st Floor, Plot 1, Lumumba Avenue, Kampala
Tel: (41) 250 696 Fax: (41) 250 538

Senior Executive Officers
Manager — E Peter Igulle

Stanbic Bank Uganda Limited

PO Box 7131, Kampala
Tel: (41) 230 608 Fax: (41) 231 116 Telex: 61226 STNBICI UG

Senior Executive Officers
Managing Director — J M Miller

Standard Chartered Bank Uganda Limited Subsidiary Company

PO Box 7111, Kampala
Tel: (41) 258 211; (41) 258 217 Fax: (41) 242 875 Telex: 61010 SCBKLA

Senior Executive Officers
Financial Director — Naula Kebba *Executive Director* ☎ **241 272**
Managing Director — Washington Matsaira
Company Secretary — Rebecca Lwebuga-Kaggwa ☎ **258 211**

General-Lending (DCM, SL)
Head of Corporate Banking — Alan Mayall ☎ **236 526**

General - Treasury
Head of Treasury — Margaret Nadine ☎ **235 371**

Euromoney Directory 1999 **1627**

UGANDA (+256)   www.euromoneydirectory.com

Standard Chartered Bank Uganda Limited (cont)
Administration
Technology & Systems
                          Fred Magala *Head of IT* ☎ **258 211**

Trust Bank (Uganda) Limited
Subsidiary Company

Baumann House, 7 Parliament Avenue, Kampala
PO Box 11881, Kampala
Tel: (41) 235 061; (41) 235 062 **Fax:** (41) 235 028 **Telex:** 61625 TRUST BK **Email:** trustug@starcom.co.ug

Senior Executive Officers
Chief Executive Officer   D N Sedh
Foreign Exchange
Head of Trading   Rajesh Kaushik

UKRAINE
(+380)

National Bank of Ukraine
🏛 Central Bank

9 Institutska Ulitsya, 252021 Kiev
Tel: (44) 226 2914; (44) 293 5225 **Fax:** (44) 293 1698; (44) 226 2743 **Telex:** 131251 KIJUX

Senior Executive Officers
Governor   Victor Yushchenko ☎ **226 2914**
Deputy Governor   Volodymyr Stelmakh ☎ **226 2869**
Deputy Governor   Volodymyr Bondar ☎ **293 4264**

Others (Senior Executives)
Chief Cashier   Paulo Senyshch *Chief Accountant* ☎ **293 2063**
Head, Bank Licensing   Olexander Parkhomenko *Director* ☎ **293 3927**
Head, Banking Supervision   Ihor Goryachek *Director* ☎ **293 6941**
HEad, Economics & Statistics   Lidiya Voronova *Director* ☎ **293 0187**

Foreign Exchange
Head of Foreign Exchange   Serhiy Yaremenko *Director* ☎ **293 3530**

Administration
Accounts / Audit
Head, Accountancy   Paulo Senyshch *Chief Accountant* ☎ **293 2063**

Berliner Bank AG
Representative Office

Office 31, Krasuoamkeyskay Street 9/2, 252004 Kiev
Tel: (44) 244 3623; (44) 247 6929 **Fax:** (44) 244 3623 **Email:** gmlkyiv@ukrpack.net

Senior Executive Officers
Representative   Nikolay Novikov

Others (Senior Executives)
                                         Valerie Shurkhal *Deputy Representative*

Commerzbank AG
Representative Office

Wulyzja Puschkinska 34, 252004 Kiev
Tel: (44) 224 0352; (44) 224 0380 **Fax:** (44) 224 2195 **Telex:** 631044 CBK UX

Senior Executive Officers
Representative   Roger Bästlein

Deutsche Bank AG
Representative Office

Wul Institutska 14, 252024 Kiev
Tel: (44) 290 7301; (44) 293 1298 **Fax:** (44) 290 6266 **Telex:** 131259 DB UKR UX
Website: www.deutsche-bank.com

www.euromoneydirectory.com   UKRAINE (+380)

European Bank for Reconstruction & Development
Representative Office

27/23 Sofiyvska Street, 252001 Kiev
Tel: (44) 464 0132 Fax: (44) 464 0813

Senior Executive Officers
Resident Representative   Jaroslav Kinach
Deputy Resident Representative   Lesia Haliv

ING Barings
Full Branch Office

5th Floor, Komintera 28, 252032 Kiev
Tel: (44) 230 3030 Fax: (44) 230 3040

Senior Executive Officers
Country Manager   Robert C S Grant

Joint-Stock Commercial Bank for Social Development UKRSOTSBANK
Head Office

Alternative trading name: UKRSOTSBANK

Kovpak Street 29, 252006 Kiev
Tel: (44) 269 0836 Fax: (44) 269 1307 Swift: UKRS UA UAX

Senior Executive Officers
Chairman of the Board   Nos Mikola ☏ **269 0836**
First Deputy Chairman   Sluch Vasyl ☏ **269 0219**
Deputy Chairman   Andruschenko Petro ☏ **269 2453**
Deputy Chairman   Berezovik Nadija ☏ **269 2392**
Deputy Chairman   Berdij Mihajlo ☏ **268 8590**
Financial Director   Manzenko Leonid ☏ **269 1326**
Treasurer   Vorona Olga *Director* ☏ **269 1268**
International Division   Shulga Alla ☏ **268 9313**

Administration
Business Development; Head of Marketing   Kryuchkov Vasyl ☏ **269 0086**

Oshchadny Bank of Ukraine
Head Office

Formerly known as: Savings Bank of Ukraine

7 Nauki Prospekt, 252028 Kiev
Tel: (44) 265 3140; (44) 267 3959 Fax: (44) 264 9941; (44) 265 6183 Telex: 131279 CHECK

Senior Executive Officers
Chairman & President   Anatoliy Kolesnikov
Chief Executive Officer   Vasiliy Buriak *First Vice President* ☏ **267 3085**
Financial Director   Vyacheslav Kyrylenko *Finance Director* ☏ **267 3931**
Chief Operating Officer   Peter Serhyienko *Head, Operational Division*

Debt Capital Markets / Fixed Income
Global Head   Ivan Lychov *Vice President*

Equity Capital Markets
Global Head   Vadym Shulga *Vice President*

Syndicated Lending
Global Head   Ivan Lychov *Vice President*

Money Markets
Global Head   Valentyn Koronevskiy *Vice President*

Foreign Exchange
Global Head   Ivan Lychov *Vice President*

Risk Management
Global Head   Vadym Shulga *Vice President*

Corporate Finance / M&A Advisory
Global Head   Ivan Lychov *Vice President*

Settlement / Clearing
Regional Head   Peter Serhyienko *Head, Operational Division*

UKRAINE (+380)　　　　　www.euromoneydirectory.com

Prominvestbank of Ukraine — Head Office

Shevchenko Lane 12, 252001 Kiev 1
Tel: (44) 226 2032 **Fax:** (44) 229 1456 **Telex:** 131119 PSB UA **Swift:** UPIB UA UX

Senior Executive Officers
Chairman — Volodymyr Matvienko
Chief Executive Officer — Anatoly Shapovalov *Director of International Division* ☏ **228 7133**
Treasurer — Klavdia Malka *Chief Accountant* ☏ **229 3787**

Administration

Accounts / Audit
Accounts — Klavdia Malka *Chief Accountant* ☏ **229 3787**

Société Générale Ukraine

42/4 Pushkinskaya Str, 252004 Kiev
Tel: (44) 246 5035; (44) 246 5038 **Fax:** (44) 246 5031 **Telex:** 131429 SGUAK UX **Swift:** SOGE UA UK
Email: bank.sgkiev@socgen.com
Website: www.socgen.com

State Export-Import Bank of Ukraine — Head Office

Formerly known as: Ukreximbank
Gorkogo Street 127, 252006 Kiev
Tel: (44) 226 2745 **Fax:** (44) 247 8082 **Telex:** 131258 RICA SU **Swift:** EXBS UA UA

Senior Executive Officers
Chairman — Alexander Sorokin
Treasurer — Vyacheslav Yakimouk ☏ **247 8917**

Equity Capital Markets

Equity Repo / Securities Lending
Head — Vyacheslav Yakimouk ☏ **247 8917**

Syndicated Lending
Head of Origination — Irina Bobyr ☏ **247 8007**
Head of Syndication — Tatyana Kutuzova ☏ **247 8010**

Loan-Related Activities
Trade Finance — Alla Kharchenko ☏ **247 8058**

Corporate Finance / M&A Advisory
Head of Corporate Finance — Yurii Khramov ☏ **247 8076**

Settlement / Clearing
Head of Settlement / Clearing — Alexander Valetor ☏ **247 8081**

Asset Management
Head — Vera Volotchenko ☏ **247 8044**

Other Departments
Private Banking — Viktor Zairenko ☏ **559 2129**
Correspondent Banking — Igor Pashko ☏ **247 8068**
Cash Management — Vera Volotchenko ☏ **247 8044**

Administration

Technology & Systems
　　Anatolii Soladovnyk ☏ **247 8040**

Legal / In-House Counsel
　　Alexander Sobko-Nesterouk ☏ **247 8005**

Public Relations
　　Larisa Knyazhizkaja ☏ **247 8913**

Accounts / Audit
　　Alexander Lisoroy ☏ **247 8004**

www.euromoneydirectory.com   UNITED ARAB EMIRATES (+971)

Ukranian Credit Bank   Head Office
Peremogy Avenue 37, 252056 Kiev
Tel: (44) 244 6296; (44) 219 2548 **Fax:** (44) 274 3027; (44) 230 2386 **Telex:** 631323 KWIT UX **Swift:** UKCB UA UK
Email: sidor@viaduk.net **Reuters:** UKBD

Senior Executive Officers
Chairman of the Council   Valentin Zgursky
Chairman of the Board   Yuriy Liakh ☏ **244 6472**
Deputy Chairman of the Board   Alexander Medynsky ☏ **241 7561**
Chief Operating Officer   Diana Yakovleva *Chief Accountant* ☏ **244 6475**
Treasurer   Olga Novik ☏ **241 7562**
International Division   Lyudmila Rybiy ☏ **241 7563**

UNITED ARAB EMIRATES
(+971)

Abu Dhabi Commercial Bank   Head Office
Abu Dhabi Commercial Bank Building, Al Salam Street, PO Box 939, Abu Dhabi
Tel: (2) 720 000 **Fax:** (2) 776 499 **Telex:** 22244 ABBCBCR EM **Reuters:** ADCT **Telerate:** 3358
Reuters: ADCU

Senior Executive Officers
Acting Chairman   Fadhel Saeed Al Darmaki ☏ **727 764**
Chief Executive Officer   Khalifa Mohammed Hassan *Managing Director & Chief Operating Officer*
                                       ☏ **725 830**
Chief Operating Officer   Arif Harianawalla *Assistant General Manager & Head of Operations Div*
                                       ☏ **725 165**
Treasurer   Mohammed A Ashraf *Assistant General Manager, Treasury* ☏ **724 140**
General Manager   Alex Anderson ☏ **727 335**
Senior Manager, Secretariat Division   Zuhair Aref Zaher ☏ **725 389**

Syndicated Lending
Loan-Related Activities
Trade Finance   V G Nair *Manager and Head of Financial Services*
Project Finance   Amitava Sengupta *Manager, Corporate Banking* ☏ **725 334**

Other Departments
Chief Credit Officer   H K N Mishra *Assistant General Manager, Credit* ☏ **723 878**
Correspondent Banking   Saulat Hussain Agha ☏ **791 368**

Administration
Technology & Systems
                                       R J Viswanathan *Senior Manager, Computer Center* ☏ **722 218**
Accounts / Audit
                                       V J Rajan *Head of Accounts* ☏ **783 445**

Abu Dhabi Fund for Development
Formerly known as: Abu Dhabi Fund For Arab Economic Development
H E Said Bin Ghobash Building, Tourist Club Area, PO Box 814, Abu Dhabi
Tel: (2) 725 800 **Fax:** (2) 728 890 **Telex:** 22287 FUND EM **Email:** gmadfd@emirates.net.ae **Cable:** FUND

Senior Executive Officers
Chairman   Khalifa Bin Zayed Al Nahyan
General Director   Saeed Khalfan Al Rumaithi

Others (Senior Executives)
                                       Ahmed Baqer *First Assistant General Director*
                                       Mohamed Al Mazroui *Assistant General Director*
Accounts   Hamda Al Suweidi *Director*
Equities   Nabil Kamber *Director*

Money Markets
Head of Money Markets   Fawzia Al Mubarak *Director, Investments & Banking* ☏ **777 726**

Euromoney Directory 1999   **1631**

UNITED ARAB EMIRATES (+971)   www.euromoneydirectory.com

Abu Dhabi Investment Company   Head Office

12-14th Floors, National Bank of Abu Dhabi Building, PO Box 46309, Abu Dhabi
Tel: (2) 658 1000 Fax: (2) 650 575 Telex: 23824 ADICGN EM Swift: ADIC AE AA Reuters: ADIU (FX)
General Telex: 22968 ADICCR EM; Reuters: ADIC (Money Market Dealing)
Website: www.adic.co.ac

Senior Executive Officers
Chairman   Hareb Masood Al-Darmaki
Deputy Chairman   Obeid Saif Al-Nassiri
General Manager   Humaid Darwish Al-Katbi ☏ **664 171**
Deputy General Manager   Hamed A Al Hamed ☏ **665 309**
Senior Manager   Abdul Rahman Omar ☏ **664 931**

Others (Senior Executives)
                                      Salem Rashid Saeed Al-Mohannadi Director
                                      Khalifa Mohammed Al-Kindi Director
                                      Mohammed Ahmad Al-Fahim Director
                                      Mohammed Bin Hamoodah Director
                                      Mohammed Omar Abdullah Director
                                      Hamad Al-Hurr Al-Suwaidi Director

General - Treasury
Head of Treasury   Abbas Mohamed Abbas AGM, Treasury & Capital Markets ☏ **660 421**

Relationship Manager
Banking Relations   Hisham Bisher ☏ **692 6230**
Department: Project & Direct Investment

Others (Senior Executives)
                                      Abdul Majeed Al Fahim Senior Manager ☏ **654 389**
                                      Claude Khayat Senior Manager ☏ **654 318**
                                      Steven Koinis Senior Manager ☏ **674 591**

Equity Capital Markets
Department: Global Equities
Head of Equity Capital Markets   Jassem Mubarak Masoud Senior Manager ☏ **650 030**

Syndicated Lending
Head of Syndication   Asif A Ali Manager, Credit & Loan Syndications ☏ **661 683**

Money Markets
Head of Money Markets   Eissa Saif Al Qubaisi Manager ☏ **650 641**
                                      Abdul Majeed Abdullah

Foreign Exchange
Department: Treasury Division
Global Head   Mohammed Ishraque Chief Dealer ☏ **660 168**
                                      K A George Chief Dealer

Settlement / Clearing
Operations   Ghanem Al Mansouri Senior Manager ☏ **660 756**

Global Custody
Fund Administration   Mohammed Zidany Fund Manager ☏ **650 589**

Asset Management
Head   Mahendra Patel Manager ☏ **660 165**
                                      Neil Mclouglin Manager ☏ **668 262**

Administration
Head of Administration   Abdul Rahman Omar Senior Manager ☏ **664 931**

Accounts / Audit
Accounting & Data Services   Sandip K Devanl ☏ **665 406**

Other (Administration)
Personnel   Abdul Rahman Omar Senior Manager ☏ **664 931**
Banking Relations   Hisham Bisher ☏ **692 6230**

American Express Bank Limited   Representative Office

Suite 509, 5th Floor, The Business Center, Khalid Bin Al Waleed Street, PO Box 3304, Dubai
Tel: (4) 559 575 Fax: (4) 594 180 Telex: 46245 AMEXBK EM

Senior Executive Officers
Director & Representative   Surendran R Menon

www.euromoneydirectory.com   UNITED ARAB EMIRATES (+971)

Arab African International Bank

Arab Monetary Fund Building, Corniche Street, Abu Dhabi
Tel: (2) 323 400 Fax: (2) 216 009 Telex: 22587 ARAFRO EM
Foreign Exchange Tel: 336 138

Senior Executive Officers
Chairman, Cairo — Fahed M Al Rashed ☏ +20 (2) 354 5094
Vice Chairman & MD, Cairo — Ahmed M Al Bardai ☏ +20 (2) 354 5094
Managing Director / General Manager — Mohamed Sayedabdel Kader ☏ **336 142**

Arab African International Bank

PO Box 1049, Deira, Dubai
Tel: (4) 223 130; (4) 223 131 Fax: (4) 222 257 Telex: ARAFR 45503 EM

Senior Executive Officers
General Branch Manager — Mohamed Shokair

Arabian General Investment Corporation   Head Office

Level 17, Dubai World Trade Center, PO Box 9342, Dubai
Tel: (4) 313 320 Fax: (4) 313 371 Telex: 47878 SHUAA EM

Senior Executive Officers
Financial Director — Kerim Mitri *Finance Manager*
Treasurer — Zafar Shaikh ☏ **313 482**
General Manager — Iyad Duwaji

Others (Senior Executives)
General Counselor — Gary Feulner *Legal Counsel* ☏ **313 324**

Bank Brussels Lambert   Representative Office

Alternative trading name: Banque Bruxelles Lambert
505 Juma Al Majid Building, Khalid Ibn Walid Road, PO Box 4296, Dubai
Tel: (4) 515 600 Fax: (4) 512 795 Email: bbldubai@emirates.net.ae
Website: www.bbl.be

Senior Executive Officers
Representative — Francesca Rajeswaran

The Bank of Tokyo-Mitsubishi Limited   Representative Office

9th Floor, Abdullah Bin Solayem Building, Corniche Road, Abu Dhabi
Tel: (2) 226 322; (2) 226 311 Fax: (2) 224 410 Telex: 23500 BTM ABU EM

Senior Executive Officers
Chief Representative — Itaru Kado

Banque Nationale de Paris   Representative Office

Al Ain Insurance Building, Hamdan Street, PO Box 930, Abu Dhabi
Tel: (2) 272 540 Fax: (2) 270 028 Telex: 23047 BNP

Senior Executive Officers
Representative — Desmond Ormsby

Barclays Bank plc   Full Branch Office

PO Box 2734, Abu Dhabi
Tel: (2) 275 313 Fax: (2) 263 277

Senior Executive Officers

Others (Senior Executives)
Jonathan Pine *Corporate Director, Gulf*
A I Jaffer *Senior Corporate Manager*
Waheeb Al Attar *Corporate Manager*
Ray Taylor *Operations Manager*

Euromoney Directory 1999   **1633**

UNITED ARAB EMIRATES (+971) www.euromoneydirectory.com

The British Bank of the Middle East
Head Office

PO Box 66, Dubai
Tel: (4) 535 000 **Fax:** (4) 530 384 **Telex:** 45424 BBMED EM **Swift:** BBME AE AD **Email:** bbmeuae@emirates.net.ae
Website: www.britishbank.com

Senior Executive Officers
Deputy Chairman — Andrew Dixon OBE ☎ 507 7461 🖷 530 384
Chief Executive Officer — Abdul Jalil Yousuf Darwish *Executive Director & CEO* ☎ 507 7303 🖷 531 005
Financial Director — Jim Jackson *Financial Controller* ☎ 507 7440 🖷 531 005
Treasurer — Simon Palfreyman *Treasurer* ☎ 507 7296 🖷 535 974

Debt Capital Markets / Fixed Income
Regional Head — Amir Merchant *Senior Manager, Capital Markets* ☎ 271 291 🖷 273 301
Eurobonds
Head of Origination — Amir Merchant *Senior Manager, Capital Markets* ☎ 271 291 🖷 273 301

Equity Capital Markets
Department: HSBC Financial Services (Middle East) Limited
Tel: 288 999 **Fax:** 273 301
Regional Head — Richard Oliver *Investment Banking Director* ☎ 271 932 🖷 273 301
Domestic Equities
Head of Origination — Richard Oliver *Investment Banking Director* ☎ 271 932 🖷 273 301
Head of Sales; Head of Research — Peter Nankervis *Senior Manager, Investment Services* ☎ 271 509
International Equities
Head of Sales; Head of Research — Peter Nankervis *Senior Manager, Investment Services* ☎ 271 509

Syndicated Lending
Regional Head — Amir Merchant *Senior Manager, Capital Markets* ☎ 271 291 🖷 273 301
Loan-Related Activities
Trade Finance — B Padmanabhan *Regional Manager, Credit* ☎ 507 7696 🖷 530 384
Project Finance — Mukhtar Hussain *CEO HFSM* ☎ 233 033 🖷 273 301
Structured Trade Finance — Amir Merchant *Senior Manager, Capital Markets* ☎ 271 291 🖷 273 301

Money Markets
Regional Head — Naeen Qureshi *Head, Interest Rates* ☎ 539 399 🖷 535 974
Domestic Commercial Paper
Head of Origination — Amir Merchant *Senior Manager, Capital Markets* ☎ 271 291 🖷 273 301
Eurocommercial Paper
Head of Origination — Amir Merchant *Senior Manager, Capital Markets* ☎ 271 291 🖷 273 301
Wholesale Deposits
Marketing — Kishore Lulla *Manager, Regional Treasury Marketing* ☎ 535 412 🖷 535 974

Foreign Exchange
Tel: 533 399 **Fax:** 535 974
Regional Head — Simon Palfreyman *Treasurer* ☎ 507 7296 🖷 535 974
Head of Institutional Sales — Fahmi Al Ghussein *Head of Institutional Sales* ☎ 534 335 🖷 535 974
Corporate Sales — Swati Chandra *Head, Corporate Treasury* ☎ 534 335 🖷 535 974
Head of Trading — Rajan Iyer *Head of FX* ☎ 533 399 🖷 535 974
FX Traders / Sales People
— Ajay Poovadan *Senior Dealer, Forex* ☎ 533 399 🖷 535 974
— Lyndon Loos *Senior Dealer, Forex* ☎ 533 399 🖷 535 974

Risk Management
Tel: 533 399 **Fax:** 535 974
Regional Head — Greg Main *Manager, Regional Business Development* ☎ 507 7496 🖷 535 974
Foreign Exchange Derivatives / Risk Management
Vanilla FX option Sales — Shiva Shivaswamy *Head, Derivative Sales* ☎ 534 335 🖷 535 974

Corporate Finance / M&A Advisory
Department: HSBC Financial Services (Middle East) Limited
Tel: 288 999/289 800 **Fax:** 273 301
Regional Head — Richard Oliver *Investment Banking Director* ☎ 271 932 🖷 273 301

Settlement / Clearing
Department: HSBC Financial Services (Middle East) limited
Tel: 288 999/289 800 **Fax:** 273 301
Equity Settlement — Lisa Peck *Operations Manager* ☎ 271 895 🖷 273 423

Other Departments
Private Banking — Tony Turner *Senior Manager, Private Banking* ☎ 272 342 🖷 273 496

www.euromoneydirectory.com   UNITED ARAB EMIRATES (+971)

Administration
Technology & Systems
　　Ashok Bhatia *Senior Manager, Services* T 207 4341 F 270 434

Legal / In-House Counsel
　　Gavin Rezos *Regional Legal Advisor* T 507 7287 F 530 070

Public Relations
　　Colin Neathercoat *Manager, Public Affairs* T 507 7465 F 534 494

Cedel Bank   Representative Office
Office 902, 9th Floor, City Tower, Sheikh Zayed Road, PO Box 27250, Dubai
Tel: (4) 310 644 **Fax:** (4) 316 973 **Email:** marketing@cedelgroup.com
Website: www.cedelgroup.com

Senior Executive Officers
Manager   Pierre Abdelnour

Debt Capital Markets / Fixed Income

Fixed-Income Repo
Head of Repo   Pierre Abdelnour *Regional Manager* E pabdel@cedelgroup.com
Marketing & Product Development   Crispin Searle *Vice President* T +44 (171) 216 7072 F +44 (171) 216 7001
                                      E csearl@cedelgroup.com
Sales   Jean-Marie Hoffmann *Commercial Officer*

Emirates Bank International PJSC   Head Office
Beniyas Road, Deira, PO Box 2928, Dubai
Tel: (4) 25 6256 **Fax:** (4) 26 8005 **Telex:** 47160 EBIHO EM **Swift:** EBIL AE AD **Email:** ebilitnl@emirates.net.ae
Reuters: EBIU
Website: www.ebil.co.ae

Senior Executive Officers
Chairman   Ahmed Al Tayer
Chief Executive Officer   Anis Al Jallaf *Managing Director & Chief Executive*
Financial Director   David Ashcroft *Chief Manager, Finance*
General Manager   Charles Neil

Debt Capital Markets / Fixed Income
Department: Treasury & Capital Markets Unit
Fax: 255 511
Global Head   Suresh Kumar *Chief Manager, Treasury & Capital Markets* T 209 2211

Syndicated Lending
Department: Corporate Banking Division
Fax: 290 097
Global Head   Anthony Bush *Senior Manager* T 260 044

Foreign Exchange
Department: Treasury & Capital Markets
Tel: 268 251 **Fax:** 256 156
Global Head   Suresh Kumar *Chief Manager, Treasury & Capital Markets* T 209 2211

Other Departments
Correspondent Banking   Anthony Bush *Senior Manager* T 260 044

Administration
Technology & Systems
                                      Abdullah Qassem *Chief Manager, IT* T 209 2511

Legal / In-House Counsel
                                      Mahmood Zaki *Manager, Legal* T 209 2641

Compliance
                                      Richard Murphy *Chief Manager, Internal Audit* T 209 2951

Public Relations
                                      Sulaiman Al Mazroux *Chief Manager, Marketing* T 209 2911

Euromoney Directory 1999   **1635**

UNITED ARAB EMIRATES (+971)   www.euromoneydirectory.com

Habib Bank AG Zürich
Full Branch Office

Baniyas Square, Deira, PO Box 3306, Dubai
Tel: (4) 214 535 Fax: (4) 284 211 Telex: 45716 DHABIB EM Swift: HBZU AE AD

Senior Executive Officers
Chief Executive Officer
    Arif Lakhani *Chief Executive Vice President* ☎ **229 985**
    Reza S Habib *Chief Executive Vice President* ☎ **211 522**
Financial Director
    Asad H Habib *Senior Vice President* ☎ **212 000**

Others (Senior Executives)
Main Branch
    Mohd Afzal Memon *Senior Vice President & Manager* ☎ **281 888**

General - Treasury
Head of Treasury
    Abdullah I Patel *Chief Manager*

Syndicated Lending
Loan-Related Activities
Trade Finance
    S A Zaidi *Manager & Head* ☎ **214 535**

Other Departments
Commodities / Bullion
    Shaukat Lilani *Manager & Head, Bullion* ☎ **214 535**
Correspondent Banking
    Saleh Abubaker *Manager* ☎ **210 836** 🖷 **235 646**

Administration
Legal / In-House Counsel
    Shaikh Naziruddin *Vice President* ☎ **214 030**

Accounts / Audit
    Shariq Ali *Second VP, Central Accounts* ☎ **276 155**

Merrill Lynch International & Co
Subsidiary Company

Office 401, Commercial Tower, Holiday Centre, PO Box 3911, Dubai
Tel: (4) 311 222 Fax: (4) 318 273
Website: www.ml.com

National Bank of Abu Dhabi
Head Office

PO Box 4, Ibn Bin Ziad Street, Khalidiya, Abu Dhabi
Tel: (2) 666 800 Fax: (2) 655 329 Telex: 22266 MASRIP E Reuters: NBAD Cable: ALMASRAF, ABU DH
Telex: 22267 MASRIP E; Reuters: NBAA; NBAU

Senior Executive Officers
Chairman   HE Mohammed Habroush Suweidi
Financial Director   Bob Raymond
Treasurer   Terence D Allen
International Division   Muhammed Alqubaisi

Others (Senior Executives)
Domestic Banking   John Syommonds

Syndicated Lending
Loan-Related Activities
Trade Finance   Faifal Suliman

Administration
Accounts / Audit
    Allen M Smith *General Manager*

The National Bank of Dubai PJSC
Head Office

Bin Yas Street, Deira, PO Box 777, Dubai
Tel: (4) 222 111; (4) 222 555 Fax: (4) 283 000 Telex: 45421 NATNAL EM Swift: NBDU AE AD
Email: contactus@nbd.co.ae Reuters: NBDU Cable: NATIONAL
Website: www.nbd.co.ae

Senior Executive Officers
Chairman   Sultan Ali Al Owais
Managing Director   Abdullah Mohamed Saleh
General Manager   David Fraser McKenzie
Company Secretary   Salim Sharifee

www.euromoneydirectory.com   **UNITED KINGDOM (+44)**

Others (Senior Executives)
    Joyshil Mitter *Controller* ☎ **201 2917**
Credit & Operations   Sayed Abdul Ghaffar Hashemi *Chief Manager*

Money Markets
Head of Money Markets   Gopal Krishnamoorthy

Foreign Exchange
Head of Foreign Exchange   Gopal Krishnamoorthy

Other Departments
Chief Credit Officer   John Hope *Senior Manager* ☎ **201 2830**
Correspondent Banking   Pantula S Sastry *Senior Manager* ☎ **201 2918**

Administration
Head of Administration   George Kay
Head of Marketing   Harish C Khanna

Standard Chartered Bank   Full Branch Office

PO Box 999, Dubai
Tel: (4) 520 455 **Fax:** (4) 526 679 **Telex:** 47591 SCBTR EM **Reuters:** SCDU (Dealing)

Senior Executive Officers
Chief Executive Officer   John Filmeridis *General Manager* ☎ **507 0352**
Financial Director   Pradip Dasani *Head of Finance* ☎ **507 0336**

General - Treasury
Head of Treasury   Claude Lobo ☎ **507 0258**

Asset Management
Other (Asset Management)
Special Assets Management   Colin Avery *Head* ☎ **507 0652**

Administration
Other (Administration)
Human Resources   A B Subiah *Head* ☎ **507 0354**

State Street Bank & Trust Company   Representative Office

Suite 1702, City Tower 2, Sheikh Zayed Road, PO Box 26838, Dubai
Tel: (4) 319 922 **Fax:** (4) 319 944

Senior Executive Officers
Managing Director   Simon Vanstone

Global Custody
Regional Head   Simon Vanstone *Managing Director*

United Arab Bank

HE Sh Abdullah Bin Salem Al Qassimi Building, 6th Floor, Al Qassimia Street, PO Box 25022, Sharjah
Tel: (6) 733 900 **Fax:** (6) 733 907

UNITED KINGDOM (+44)

Bank of England   🏛 Central Bank

Threadneedle Street, London EC2R 8AH
Tel: (171) 601 4444 **Fax:** (171) 601 4771 **Telex:** 885001
Website: www.bankofengland.co.uk

Senior Executive Officers
Governor   Edward George

UNITED KINGDOM (+44)   www.euromoneydirectory.com

3i Corporate Finance Limited
Subsidiary Company

91 Waterloo Road, London SE1 8XP
Tel: (171) 928 3131 Fax: (171) 975 3399
Website: www.3icf.co.uk

Senior Executive Officers
Treasurer — Alan Walker
Managing Director / General Manager — Neil Williamson neil_williamson@3igroup.com

Others (Senior Executives)
Philp Marsden Director philip_marsden@3igroup.com
Brian Livingston Director brian_livingston@3igroup.com
Tim Moore Director tim_moore@3igroup.com
Chad Murrin Director chad_murrin@3igroup.com

General-Lending (DCM, SL)
Head of Corporate Banking — Martin Gagen UK Head
Richard Summers Continental Head

Corporate Finance / M&A Advisory
Head of Corporate Finance — Neil Williamson neil_williamson@3igroup.com

Asset Management
Head — John Davies
Investment Funds — Paul Wailler

Abbey National Financial Products
Subsidiary Company

Abbey House, Baker Street, London NW1 6XL
Tel: (171) 486 0619; (171) 612 4000 Fax: (171) 612 4747

Senior Executive Officers
Chairman — Lord Christopher Tugendhat
Chief Executive Officer — Ian Harley
Financial Director — Mark Pain
Treasurer — John Hasson Manager

Others (Senior Executives)
Funding & Asset Management — Alexander Braun Director 612 4461 612 4891
Fenella Edge Director, Financial Products 486 0619 612 4747

General-Lending (DCM, SL)
Head of Corporate Banking — Martin De-Forest Brown

Risk Management
Fixed Income Derivatives / Risk Management
Trading — Alan Rose Senior Derivatives Trader 486 0617 612 4747

Other (FI Derivatives)
Derivatives Marketing — John Haam Manager 612 4396
Christophe Cuny Manager
Angelique Todesco Manager 612 4396
Nick Jones Manager

Structured Products — Hilary Newton Manager
Gordon Kerr Manager 612 4396

Asset Management
Head — Alex Braun Director of Funding and Asset Management

Abbey National Treasury Services plc
Head Office

Abbey House, Baker Street, London NW1 6XL
Tel: (171) 612 4000 Fax: (171) 224 5306 Telex: 296159 ABBNAT G Email: marketing@ants.co.uk
Reuters: ANTL (Dealing), ANTS (Information)
Website: www.ants.co.uk

Senior Executive Officers
Chairman — Ian Harley
Chief Executive Officer — Gareth Jones Chief Executive 612 4378 612 4464
Tony Hibbitt Chief Executive, Cater Allen International Limited 606 6064 710 6900

Financial Director — Gwen Batchelor Finance Director 612 4707 612 4353
Director, Financial Products — Fenella Edge 612 3110 612 4747
Director, Credit & Corporate Development — Robin Garrett 612 4656 612 4649

1638 Euromoney Directory 1999

Senior Executive Officers (cont)

Director, Market Risk — Steve Warr T 612 4180 F 612 4795
Director, Treasury Services & International — Brian Morrison T 612 4052 F 612 4814
Managing Director, Aitken Campbell — Archie McSporran T (141) 248 6966 F (141) 221 5797
Director, Funding & Asset Management — Alex Braun T 612 4461 F 612 4891
Company Secretary — Karen Fortunato T 612 4677 F 612 4319
International Division — Graham Long Director, Offshore & Private Banking T 612 4633 F 612 3293

Others (Senior Executives)

Phil McDuell Regional Director, Asia T +852 2923 1028 F +852 2507 2333

General - Treasury
Head of Treasury — Paul Gould Head of Treasury Operations T 612 4751 F 612 4559
Michel Elleboode Treasury Manager, ANTS (Paris Branch) T +33 (1) 4641 0808 F +33 (1) 4637 5138

Debt Capital Markets / Fixed Income
Global Head — Alisdair McDougall Head, Capital Markets T 224 2299 F 612 4731
Marketing — Syd Hanna Head, Capital Markets Marketing T 224 2299 F 612 4731

Domestic Government Bonds
Head of Sales — Kevin Eldershaw Head of Sales T 224 2249 F 486 7109

Asset-Backed Securities / Securitization
Global Head — Paul Caldwell Head, ABS T 486 0473 F 612 4463

Mortgage-Backed Securities
Global Head — Adrian Mallinson Head, MBS T 935 3265 F 486 7189

Equity Capital Markets
Global Head — Alisdair McDougall Head, Capital Markets T 224 2299 F 612 4731

Syndicated Lending
Department: Corporate Development & Special Finance

Other (Syndicated Lending)
Anna Merrick Director, Special Finance T 612 3268 F 486 6872

Loan-Related Activities
Project Finance — Derek Gordon Head, Project Finance T 612 3283
Structured Trade Finance — Tim Rigby Head, Structured Finance T 612 3288
Leasing & Asset Finance — Bill Lowe Head of Leasing T 612 3285

Other (Trade Finance)
Corporate Development — Leigh Goodwin Head, Corporate Development T 612 4502 F 612 4649
Housing Associations — Rita Jobbins Head of Social Housing T 612 3202

Money Markets
Global Head — Barbara Stubbs Head of Money Markets T 935 3265 F 486 7109

Money Markets - General
Edward Panek Senior Dealer T 612 4593
Brian Morrison Director, Treasury Services & International T 612 4052 F 612 4814

Risk Management
Country Head — Alan Rose Head of Derivatives Trading T 612 4396

Corporate Finance / M&A Advisory
Private Equity — Christian Dummett Head of Private Equity Funds T 612 3273

Settlement / Clearing
Operations — Paul Gould Head of Treasury Operations T 612 4751 F 612 4559
Shirley Edwards Financial Controller T 612 4204 F 612 4638

Asset Management
Head — Alex Braun Director, Funding & Asset Management T 612 4461 F 612 4891

Administration

Technology & Systems
John Hasson Head of IT T 612 4376 F 612 4230

Legal / In-House Counsel
Ron Friend Head, Legal & Documentation T 612 4636 F 612 4581

Corporate Communications
Corporate Marketing — Chloe Pettifar Head T 612 4246 F 224 5306

FINANCIAL NEWS
THE SECURITIES AND INVESTMENT BANKING WEEKLY

CALL NOW FOR YOUR FREE TRIAL COPY ON +44 (0)131 624 8919

As a reader of the Painwebber Euromoney Capital Markets Directory you will be keen to know what is going on in the worlds leading financial institutions. Stay in touch with the latest developments in the financial services sector and keep up to date with your clients and your competitors.

Each Week The Financial News will answer your questions:

- Do you know who excels at M & A or Capital Markets? Unique weekly tables that list the key individual investment bankers and lawyers will ensure that you do.

- You will benefit from a weekly inside look at stock exchanges and individual institutions, as well as the latest product launches and performance rankings.

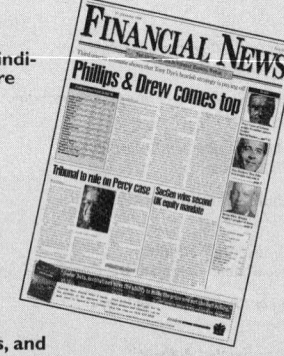

- You will receive timely concise and focused coverage of current performance, new mandates, and regular profiles fund management companies.

The *Financial News* is a weekly newspaper dedicated to the securities and investment banking industries. It covers the personalities and the firms that make up the industry and their role in fund management and capital markets throughout Europe.

- The Financial News has firmly established itself as an influential voice in the financial world. "
  Gavin Casey - Client Executive, London Stock Exchange

The newspaper is read widely throughout the investment community in particular among investors, brokers, analysts and advisors including management consultants, actuaries and head hunters. It has now become a must read for those in the world of business and finance.

FAX THIS BACK NOW!!! +44 (0)131 6248918

Phone +44 (0)131 624 8919
or fax your details to +44 (0)131 624 8918
for your FREE trial copy of the Financial News.

ADDRESS DETAILS (Please Print)

Mr/ Mrs/ Ms/ Other _____ Name _____
Job title _____
Company _____ Area of business _____
Address _____
_____
City _____
Country _____ Telephone _____
Postcode _____ Fax _____

Thank You! PAIN98

www.euromoneydirectory.com UNITED KINGDOM (+44)

ABC International Bank plc
Head Office

Arab Banking Corporation House, 1-5 Moorgate, London EC2R 6AB
Tel: (171) 776 4000 **Fax:** (171) 606 9987 **Telex:** 893748 ABCGENG **Swift:** ABCE GB 2L **Reuters:** APLC

Senior Executive Officers
Chairman — Khalid Alturki
Chief Executive Officer — Abdulmagid Breish ☏ 776 4003
Treasurer — Andrew Pointon *DGM & Treasurer* ☏ 776 4030
Corporate Secretary, Legal Counsel — David Bowen-Jones ☏ 776 4008

Others (Senior Executives)
Stephen Hinds *DGM & Head, HO Support* ☏ 776 4040
Cherif Malek *Senior AGM, Commercial Banking* ☏ 776 4040
Stanislas Yassukovich *Executive Director & Deputy Chairman*

Debt Capital Markets / Fixed Income
Eurobonds
Head of Syndication — Adrian Osborn-Clarke *Senior Manager, Syndications* ☏ 776 4038
Libor-Based / Floating-Rate Products
FRN Sales — Adrian Osborn-Clarke *Senior Manager, Syndications* ☏ 776 4038

Syndicated Lending
Head of Syndication — Adrian Osborn-Clarke *Senior Manager, Syndications* ☏ 776 4038
Recovery — David Hutchinson *Senior Manager, Remedial Unit*

Loan-Related Activities
Trade Finance — Tony Pooley *Chief Manager, Trade Finance Unit* ☏ 776 4043
Project Finance — Jeffrey Applegate *AGM, Project Finance Group* ☏ 776 4035

Money Markets
Head of Money Markets — Nigel Dickenson *AGM, Treasury* ☏ 776 4039

Foreign Exchange
Country Head — Nigel Dickinson *AGM, Treasury*

Settlement / Clearing
Operations — Heather Rogers *Senior Manager, Operations* ☏ 776 4090

Other Departments
Commodities / Bullion — Tim Hart *AGM, Commodity Finance* ☏ 776 4044
Chief Credit Officer — Keith Gale *AGM, Credit* ☏ 776 4135

Administration
Legal / In-House Counsel
David Holden *Chief Manager* ☏ 776 4049

Compliance
Peter Moore *AGM, Support Services* ☏ 776 4070

Accounts / Audit
James Edmondson *Chief Accountant* ☏ 776 4062

Other (Administration)
Corporate Affairs — David Holden *Chief Manager* ☏ 776 4049

ABN AMRO
Subsidiary Company

4 Broadgate, London EC2M 7LE
Tel: (171) 601 0101 **Fax:** (171) 256 8500 **Telex:** 297801

Senior Executive Officers
Chairman — Peter Meinertzhagan
Managing Director — Nigel Mills

ABN AMRO Bank

61 King Street, Manchester, Lancashire M60 2HB
Tel: (161) 832 9291 **Fax:** (161) 832 2154 **Telex:** 668459 ABNAMC G **Swift:** ABNA GB 2L MAN

ABN AMRO Bank NV
Full Branch Office

101 Moorgate, London EC2M 6SB
Tel: (171) 628 7766 **Fax:** (171) 588 2975; (171) 413 8296 **Telex:** 887139 **Swift:** ABNA GB 2L

Senior Executive Officers
Country Manager, UK — Igno van Waesberghe ☏ 477 5000
Financial Director — Ian Measor *Financial Controller & Head, Operations* ☏ 477 5080

Euromoney Directory 1999 **1641**

UNITED KINGDOM (+44) www.euromoneydirectory.com

ABN AMRO Bank NV (cont)
Senior Executive Officers (cont)
Treasurer   John Geensen ☎ 392 3501
Debt Capital Markets / Fixed Income
Head of Debt Capital Markets   Alberto Francioni *Global Head, DCM* ☎ 392 3445
Other (Emerging Markets Bonds)
Emerging Markets   Ian Sargant ☎ 678 3935
Syndicated Lending
Country Head   Gary Griffiths *Head of Syndication* ☎ 477 5042
Money Markets
Country Head   Paul Todd ☎ 392 3601
Foreign Exchange
Country Head   Andrew Kidd ☎ 392 3523
Risk Management
Country Head   Ray Course *Head of Credit Risk Management* ☎ 477 5168
Corporate Finance / M&A Advisory
Other (Corporate Finance)
European Corporate Finance   Hugh Scott-Barrett

ABSA Bank Limited   Full Branch Office
52/54 Gracechurch Street, London EC3V 0EH
Tel: (171) 528 8296 **Fax:** (171) 528 8298 **Telex:** 920225 ABSAG **Swift:** ABSA GB 2L

Senior Executive Officers
Treasurer   Dale Schoeman *Treasurer*
General Manager, UK & Western Europe   Peter L Donnelly
Debt Capital Markets / Fixed Income
Tel: 528 8297 **Fax:** 825 6034
Head of Debt Capital Markets   Dale Schoeman *Treasurer*
Domestic Government Bonds
Head of Trading   Bruce Walker
Libor-Based / Floating-Rate Products
Asset Swaps   Paul Whippy *Chief Dealer*
Equity Capital Markets
Tel: 528 8297
Head of Equity Capital Markets   Dale Schoeman *Treasurer*
International Equities
Head of Trading   Michael Sham *Director, Equity*
Syndicated Lending
Global Head   David Colgan *AGM, Banking Department* ☎ 528 6001
Loan-Related Activities
Trade Finance   David Colgan *AGM, Banking Department* ☎ 528 6001
Other (Trade Finance)
Structured Finance   David Colgan *AGM, Banking Department* ☎ 528 6001
Money Markets
Tel: 528 8297
Head of Money Markets   Paul Whippy
Money Markets - General
Trading   Tracey Miles *Dealer*
Foreign Exchange
Tel: 528 8297
Corporate Sales   Julie Skinner *Corporate Dealer*
Head of Trading   David Lamb *Senior Dealer*
FX Traders / Sales People
Trading   Murray Haywood *Dealer*
Risk Management
Global Head   Andrew Martin *AGM, Operations & Risk Control*
Corporate Finance / M&A Advisory
Global Head   Cesare Rizzoli
Other Departments
Correspondent Banking   Richard Hardy *Senior Manager, Financial Institutions*

1642   Euromoney Directory 1999

www.euromoneydirectory.com   UNITED KINGDOM (+44)

Adam & Co Investment Management Limited
Head Office
22 Charlotte Square, Edinburgh, EH2 4DF
Tel: (131) 225 8484 **Fax:** (131) 220 2357 **Telex:** 72182 **Swift:** ADAG GB 2SA
Senior Executive Officers
Assistant Manager William Kirkwood

Afghan National Credit & Finance
New Roman House, 10 East Road, London N1 6AD
Tel: (171) 251 4100 **Fax:** (171) 253 3058
Senior Executive Officers
Managing Director / General Manager M A Yailaqi

Agricultural Bank of China
Representative Office
16th Floor, Royex House, Aldermanbury Square, London EC2V 7HR
Tel: (171) 606 0100 **Fax:** (171) 606 0111
Senior Executive Officers
Chief Representative Yukuan Zhang

AIB Group (UK) PCC
Formerly known as: Allied Irish Bank
Bankcentre-Britain, Belmont Road, Uxbridge, Middlesex UB8 1SA
Tel: (1895) 272 222 **Fax:** (1895) 239 774 **Swift:** AIBK GB 2L
Senior Executive Officers
Financial Director Joan Mulcahy *Finance Director*
General Manager Aidan McKeon

AIG Global Investment Corp (Europe)
Formerly known as: AIG Asset Management
Birchin Court, 20 Birchin Lane, London EC3V 9LN
Tel: (171) 335 8110 **Fax:** (171) 335 0052
Website: www.aiggig.com
Debt Capital Markets / Fixed Income
Fixed-Income Repo
Trading Mark Hutchings *European Director* [E] **mark.hutchings@aig.com**
Kandy Hosea *Trader*
Shane Martin *Trader*

AKBANK TAS
Representative Office
10 Finsbury Square, London EC2A 1HE
Tel: (171) 638 1366 **Fax:** (171) 638 2037
Senior Executive Officers
Representative Ersin Erenman

Al Rajhi Investment Corporation
4th Floor, Berkeley Square House, Berkeley Square, London W1X 5PA
Tel: (171) 409 1770 **Fax:** (171) 493 0933
Senior Executive Officers
Managing Director / General Manager Aziz M Sherif

Euromoney Directory 1999 **1643**

UNITED KINGDOM (+44)　　　www.euromoneydirectory.com

Al-Bank Al-Saudi Al-Alami Limited
Head Office
Alternative trading name: Saudi International Bank
One Knightsbridge, London SW1X 7XS
Tel: (171) 259 3456 **Fax:** (171) 259 6060 **Telex:** 8812261 **Swift:** SINT GB 2L **Reuters:** SIAA-Z; SIBX

Senior Executive Officers
Chairman	Sheikh Mohammed Abalkhail
Chief Executive Officer	Robert J McGinn *Executive Director & CEO*
Financial Director	Peter J Farrar *Chief Finance Officer*
General Manager, North America	Matthew Snyder
Company Secretary & Head, Legal	Penelope Ralph

Others (Senior Executives)
Fiduciary	Geoffrey W Hilliard *Head of Fiduciary*
Corporate Risk	Thierry R Gorgé *Head of Corporate Risk*
Financial Markets	Charles Avis *AGM, Risk Management*

General-Lending (DCM, SL)
Head of Corporate Banking　　Anthony P Trew *Assistant General Manager, Banking*

General - Treasury
Head of Treasury　　Mohab Mufti *Head*

Relationship Manager
Chief Representative Tokyo　　Tadakuni Kaneko

Debt Capital Markets / Fixed Income
Global Head	Mark Aitken *Head*
Head of Fixed Income	Chris Baker *Senior Portfolio Manager*

Eurobonds
Head of Trading　　Chris Baker *Senior Portfolio Manager*

Emerging Market Bonds
Head of Emerging Markets　　Uday Patnaik *Head of Emerging Markets*

Asset-Backed Securities / Securitization
Global Head　　Shelly Moledina *Head*

Fixed-Income Repo
Head of Repo　　Rita Brasher *Repos*

Equity Capital Markets
Head of Equity Capital Markets　　Simon English *Head*

Money Markets
Head of Money Markets　　Mohab Mufti *Head*

Foreign Exchange
Head of Foreign Exchange　　Stephanie Gallone

Risk Management

Fixed Income Derivatives / Risk Management
Trading　　John Benfield

Corporate Finance / M&A Advisory
Head of Corporate Finance	Matthew Snyder
Global Head	Michael Ladenburg *AGM, Corporate Finance*

Settlement / Clearing
Operations	Pat Walton *Assistant Operations Manager*
	David Maskall *Assistant Operations Manager*
Back-Office	Gordon Brooker *Operations Manager*

Administration

Technology & Systems
　　Graham Yellowley *Head of IT*

Legal / In-House Counsel
　　Micaela Meyer

Compliance
　　Micaela Meyer

Accounts / Audit
Audit　　Lawrence Bugeya *Head of Audit*

Other (Administration)
Personnel & Premises　　Rosalyn McIntyre *Head*

Alfa Bank

Level 4 City Tower, 40 Basinghall Street, London EC2V 5DE
Tel: (171) 588 8400 Fax: (171) 588 8500

Senior Executive Officers
Managing Director / General Manager   Anton D Simon

Alfred Berg (UK) Limited
Subsidiary Company

85 London Wall, London EC2M 7BH
Tel: (171) 256 4900 Fax: (171) 920 9126; (171) 256 9381

Senior Executive Officers
Financial Director   Mary Sheehan ☎ **256 4912**
Managing Director   Edward Plumbly ☎ **786 0805**

Equity Capital Markets
Fax: 256 9381
Global Head   Edward Plumbly *Managing Director* ☎ **786 0805**

International Equities
Head of Sales   Tommy Dunweber ☎ **786 0807**

Corporate Finance / M&A Advisory
Global Head   Michael Glazebrook *Head of Corporate Finance* ☎ **256 4971**

Settlement / Clearing
Equity Settlement   Richard Joyce ☎ **256 4926**

Alliance Capital Limited
Subsidiary Company

Alternative trading name: Alliance Capital Management LP

53 Stratton Street, London W1X 6JJ
Tel: (171) 470 0100 Fax: (171) 470 1535
Website: www.alliancecapital.com

Senior Executive Officers
Chairman & CEO   Dave Williams ☎ **+1 (212) 969 1020**
President & COO   John Carifa ☎ **+1 (212) 969 1080**
Chief Executive Officer   Kathleen
Financial Director   Robert Joseph *SVP & CFO* ☎ **+1 (212) 969 1020**
Treasurer   Anne Drennan ☎ **+1 (212) 969 6443**
Managing Director   Mark Luning ☎ **470 1644**
International Division   Bruce Calvert *Vice Chairman, Director of Global Research* ☎ **470 1503**

Debt Capital Markets / Fixed Income
Department: Alliance Capital Fixed Income Investors
Tel: +1 (212) 969 1000 Fax: +1 (212) 969 1573
Head of Fixed Income   Wayne Lyski ☎ **+1 (212) 969 1047**
Head of Fixed Income Sales   Robert Absey *Vice President* ☎ **+1 (212) 969 6148**
Head of Fixed Income Trading   Kathleen Corbet *Executive Vice President* ☎ **+1 (212) 969 2468**

Emerging Market Bonds
Head of Emerging Markets   Edward Baker *Senior Vice President* ☎ **470 1656**

Fixed-Income Research
Head of Fixed Income   Lawrence Kreicher *Senior Vice President* ☎ **+1 (212) 969 2134**
Head of Credit Research   Andrew Aran *Senior Vice President* ☎ **+1 (212) 969 1237**

Equity Capital Markets
Department: Alliance Capital Equity Investors
Tel: +1 (212) 969 1000 Fax: +1 (212) 969 1588
Head of Equity Capital Markets   Bruce Calvert ☎ **+1 (212) 969 1070**
Head of Sales   Eric Johnson *Senior Vice President* ☎ **+1 (212) 969 1192**
Head of Trading   Tom Bardong *Senior Vice President* ☎ **+1 (212) 969 1201**

Domestic Equities
Head of Sales   Eric Johnson *Senior Vice President* ☎ **+1 (212) 969 1192**
Head of Trading   Daniel Panker *Senior Vice President* ☎ **+1 (212) 969 1042**

International Equities
Head of Sales   Edward Baker *Senior Vice President* ☎ **470 1656**

Equity Research
Head of Equity Research   Bruce Calvert ☎ **+1 (212) 969 1070**

Convertibles / Equity-Linked
Head of Sales   Theodore Kuck *Senior Vice President* ☎ **+1 (212) 969 2443**

UNITED KINGDOM (+44) www.euromoneydirectory.com

Alliance Capital Limited (cont)

Money Markets
Tel: +1 (212) 969 2498
Head of Money Markets — Raymond Papera *Senior Vice President* ☏ +1 (212) 969 2473

Other (Wholesale Deposits)
Head of Marketing; Head of Sales — Mike Laughlin *EVP, Alliance Fund Distributing* ☏ +1 (212) 969 1060

Risk Management
Fax: +1 (212) 969 2386
Head of Risk Management — Robert Joseph *Senior Vice President* ☏ +1 (212) 969 2384

Corporate Finance / M&A Advisory
Head of Corporate Finance — James Wilson ☏ +1 (212) 969 1540

Settlement / Clearing
Fax: +1 (212) 969 6242
Head of Settlement / Clearing; Equity Settlement — Laura Mah *Senior Vice President* ☏ +1 (212) 969 6240
Fixed-Income Settlement — Eileen Cresham *Senior Vice President* ☏ +1 (212) 969 6090
Operations — Laura Mah *Senior Vice President* ☏ +1 (212) 969 6240

Asset Management
Portfolio Management — Theodore Kuck *Senior Vice President* ☏ +1 (212) 969 2443

Administration
Head of Administration — Kathleen Corbet *Executive Vice President* ☏ +1 (212) 969 2468
Business Development — John Carifa *President & COO* ☏ +1 (212) 969 1080
Head of Marketing — Mike Laughlin *EVP, Alliance Fund Distributing* ☏ +1 (212) 969 1060

Technology & Systems
Mike Togher *Senior Vice President* ☏ +1 (212) 969 6246

Legal / In-House Counsel
Mark Manley *Senior Vice President* ☏ +1 (212) 969 1337

Compliance
Mark Manley *Senior Vice President* ☏ +1 (212) 969 1337

Public Relations
Duff Ferguson ☏ +1 (212) 969 1056

Accounts / Audit
Internal Auditor — Chris Fuller ☏ +1 (212) 969 6459

Allied Bank of Pakistan Limited — Full Branch Office

63 Mark Lane, London EC3R 7QS
Tel: (171) 481 0207 Fax: (171) 702 4246; (171) 702 1730 Telex: 888696

Senior Executive Officers
General Manager — Hamid Masud ☏ 488 0456
Financial Controller — John Jeffs
Chief Executive Officer — Paul Saunders *Assistant Financial Controller*
Chief Operating Officer — Imran Shaukat *Manager* ℻ 481 4740

Money Markets
Country Head — Ijaz Bajwa *Vice President* ☏ 481 4566

Foreign Exchange
Country Head — Wajid Hashmi *Vice President*

Allied Irish Bank Group Treasury — Subsidiary Company

12 Old Jewry, London EC2R 8DP
Tel: (171) 606 3070; (171) 796 1503 Fax: (171) 726 2456 Email: www.aib.ie/capitalmarkets/aibtreasury
Reuters: AIBT

Senior Executive Officers
General - Treasury
Head of Treasury — Nick Treble *Head of Treasury*
Brendan Fogarty *Assistant Treasurer* ☏ 606 6234 ℻ 726 2456

Debt Capital Markets / Fixed Income
Bonds - General
Euro — Vincent Butler *Chief Dealer* ☏ 600 1191 ℻ 726 2456
£ — John Shine *Chief Dealer* ☏ 606 0481 ℻ 726 2456
US $ — Dave Valentine *Senior Dealer* ☏ 606 0481 ℻ 726 2456
Scandies — Conor McGrath *Senior Dealer* ☏ 600 1191 ℻ 726 2456

www.euromoneydirectory.com UNITED KINGDOM (+44)

Foreign Exchange
FX Traders / Sales People
Spots   Brendan Fogarty *Assistant Treasurer* ☎ **606 6234**

Alpha Credit Bank   Full Branch Office
Fitzwilliam House, 10 St Mary Axe, London EC3A 8EN
Tel: (171) 648 5000 **Fax:** (171) 626 8285 **Telex:** 922256 **Swift:** CRBA GB 2L **Reuters:** ACBH **Bloomberg:** ACB2
Foreign Exchange Tel: 651 5151; **Fax:** 651 5151

Senior Executive Officers
Managing Director / General Manager   Emmanuel Zuridis
Others (Senior Executives)
                                             Anthony Polychroniadis *Deputy General Manager*
Department: Treasury
Treasurer   Peter Swinden *Treasurer*
Others (Senior Executives)
                                             Ben Gibson *Bond Dealer*
                                             Adrian Evans *Head of Fixed Income Sales*
                                             David Cope *Chief Dealer, Spot*
                                             Martin Coendez *Dealer, Spot FX*
                                             John Cook *Dealer, Derivatives*
                                             Sam Hanbury *Dealer, Spot FX*
                                             Mathilde Baechler *Syndicate Manager*
                                             Peter Burdett *Dealer, Spot FX*
                                             Nicola Mackenze *Fixed Income Sales*
Department: Corporate Banking & Trade Finance
Relationship Manager
                                             Nick Coates *Relationship Manager*
                                             Neil Goatley *Relationship Manager*
Analysis   Marialena Antonara
Correspondent Banking   Elizabeth Macadie
Department: Operations
Others (Senior Executives)
                                             Michael Bamber *Operations Manager*
                                             Andrew Norgate *Loans / Trade Finance*
                                             Catherine Mitchell *Corporate Services*
Settlements   Caroline Pearce
Systems   Chris Bland
EDP   Antony Mikellides
Administration
Department: Finance & Administration
Head of Administration   David Keene *Manager, Finance & Administration*
Compliance
                                             David Blackmore
Accounts / Audit
                                             Linda Eade *Accountant*
Other (Administration)
Personnel   Lorna Carr

American Express Bank Limited   Full Branch Office
60 Buckingham Palace Road, London SW1W 0RU
PO Box 766, London SW1W 0RU
Tel: (171) 824 6000 **Fax:** (171) 730 3602; (171) 824 6286 **Telex:** 418131 EXBKPLG **Swift:** AEIB GB 2 **Reuters:** AMXL; AMXD

Senior Executive Officers
Chief Executive Officer   B M Rodrigues *Country Head* ☎ **824 6358**
Chief Operating Officer   B M Rodrigues *UK COO, Head of Global Trading Operations* ☎ **824 6000**
Treasurer   Nicholas Bridewell *Executive Director* ☎ **824 6235** ☎ **824 6365**
Others (Senior Executives)
Financial Institutions   Matteo Perruccio *Executive Director & Regional Head EMEA* ☎ **824 6356**
                                             Eric Pinn *Senior Director & Area Head FIG* ☎ **824 6263**
General-Lending (DCM, SL)
Head of Corporate Banking   F W Piechoczek *Head EMEA* ☎ **824 6390**
                                             B M Rodrigues *UK Head, Global Corporate Banking & Finance*

Euromoney Directory 1999 **1647**

UNITED KINGDOM (+44) www.euromoneydirectory.com

American Express Bank Limited (cont)
General - Treasury
Head of Treasury — Nicholas Bridewell *Executive Director EMEA Regional Treasurer*

Syndicated Lending
Tel: 824 6000 Fax: 824 6241
Head of Origination; Head of Syndication — F W Piechoczek *Head EMEA* ☏ **824 6390**

Other (Syndicated Lending)
Ajit P Menon *Senior Director* ☏ **824 6369**
Conor O'Dowd *Director* ☏ **824 6268**

Loan-Related Activities
Trade Finance — Robert S Keller *Senior Director* ☏ **824 6050**

Money Markets
Tel: 824 6000 Fax: 730 1351 Reuters: AMXD AMXL
Head of Money Markets — Amanda Nicol *Money Markets & Derivatives* ☏ **824 6104**

Foreign Exchange
Tel: 824 6100 Fax: 730 1351 Reuters: AMXL AMXD
Head of Foreign Exchange — Paul Coughlin *Chief Dealer* ☏ **824 6104**
Head of Sales — Juergen Michel *FX Sales* ☏ **824 6100**

Corporate Finance / M&A Advisory
Department: Corporate Finance & Syndications
Head of Corporate Finance — F W Piechoczek *Head EMEA* ☏ **824 6390**

Settlement / Clearing
Operations — K Roberts *Senior Director*

Other Departments
Chief Credit Officer — Jon Hallé *Country Credit Officer* ☏ **824 6368**
Private Banking — Michael Allen *Executive Director & Head EMEA*

Administration
Head of Administration — Gordon Valentine *Director, Loans Administration Division* ☏ **824 6359**
Head of Marketing — Tina Coram-James *Senior Director* ☏ **824 6111**

Anglo-Irish Bank Corporation plc — Full Branch Office
Gracechurch House, 55 Gracechurch Street, London EC3V 0EE
Tel: (171) 426 8000; (171) 426 8010 Fax: (171) 426 8050; (171) 426 8052

Senior Executive Officers
Financial Director — Gordon Parker *Associate Director, Finance*
Treasurer — Desmond O'Houlihan *Head, Treasury UK* ☏ **426 8038**
Managing Director, UK — John A Rowan

General - Treasury
Head of Treasury —
Paul Arkel *Manager Corporate Treasury*
Paul Harris *Manager Corporate Treasury*
David Waite *Manager Corporate Treasury*
Eddie Fogg *Manager Corporate Treasury*

Money Markets
Tel: 426 8010 Fax: 426 8052
Global Head — Desmond O'Houlihan *Head, Treasury UK* ☏ **426 8038**

Foreign Exchange
Tel: 426 8010 Fax: 426 8050
Corporate Sales — Desmond O'Houlihan *Head, Treasury UK* ☏ **426 8038**

Settlement / Clearing
Back-Office — Janet Siemienski

Anglo-Romanian Bank Limited — Subsidiary Company
3 Finsbury Square, London EC2A 1AD
Tel: (171) 826 4200 Fax: (171) 628 1274 Telex: 886700 ANROMB Swift: ARBL GB 2L

Senior Executive Officers
Chairman — Peter Ardron
Financial Director — Ray Morar *Chief Manager* ☏ **826 4224**
Chief Operating Officer — David King *Deputy Chief Manager* ☏ **826 4244**
Managing Director & General Manager — Mihai Radoi ☏ **826 4222**
Company Secretary & Deputy Managing Director — Edward Hoyle ☏ **826 4223**

1648 Euromoney Directory 1999

www.euromoneydirectory.com   UNITED KINGDOM (+44)

Others (Senior Executives)
        Peter A Grafham *Non-Executive Director*
        Michael G Wood *Non-Executive Director*
        Vladimir Soare *Director*

Syndicated Lending
Head of Origination   Frank Waithe *Manager, Loans*

Loan-Related Activities
Trade Finance   Paul Pavlicu *Manager, Trade Finance*

Money Markets
Global Head   Peter Hamilton *Manager, Treasury*

Foreign Exchange
Head of Foreign Exchange   Peter Hamilton *Manager, Treasury*

Risk Management
Head of Risk Management   Clive Lathrope *Senior Manager*

Other Departments
Correspondent Banking   Clive Lathrope *Senior Manager*

Administration
Head of Administration   J Daniel Sisson *Manager, Finance & Administration*

Technology & Systems
System   Colin Janes *Manager*

Compliance
    John Hines *Compliance Officer*

Accounts / Audit
    Michael Rogers *Internal Auditor*

Henry Ansbacher & Co Limited   Head Office

One Mitre Square, London EC3A 5AN
Tel: (171) 283 2500 **Fax:** (171) 626 0839 **Telex:** 884580 ANCBAC G **Swift:** ANSL GB 2L **Reuters:** ANSL

Senior Executive Officers
Chairman   Peter Neville Scaife
Financial Director   Iacovos Koumi *Finance Director*
Managing Director   Steven Fraser Jennings
Company Secretary   Hamish Graham Herschel Ramsay

Debt Capital Markets / Fixed Income

Emerging Market Bonds
Head of Emerging Markets   Phillip James Jesson

Syndicated Lending
Head of Syndication   Jenny Carolin *Head, Loan Syndication*

Loan-Related Activities
Trade Finance   Tony Dalby ☏ **(121) 456 4446**
Leasing & Asset Finance   Paul Craig

Money Markets
Country Head   Phillip James Jesson

Foreign Exchange
Head of Foreign Exchange   Phillip James Jesson

Settlement / Clearing
Foreign Exchange Settlement   Yvonne Jillien Barraclough

Other Departments
Private Banking   Stewart Dick *Head, Private Banking*

Administration
Head of Marketing   Lynn Weatherall *Marketing*

Legal / In-House Counsel
Legal Director   Michael Charles John Mayhew-Arnold

Compliance
Compliance Director   Peter George Greenhalgh

Accounts / Audit
Head, Internal Audit   William Richard Simms

Euromoney Directory 1999   **1649**

UNITED KINGDOM (+44)   www.euromoneydirectory.com

ANZ Investment Bank
Full Branch Office

Alternative trading name: Australia & New Zealand Banking Group plc
Minerva House, Montague Close, London SE1 9DH
Tel: (171) 378 2121 **Fax:** (171) 378 2378 **Telex:** 8812741 **Swift:** ANZB GB 2L **Reuters:** ANZP
Website: www.anz.com

Senior Executive Officers
Chief Executive Officer   Grahame Miller *Managing Director* 378 2751
Financial Director   Jeremy Wrigley 378 2010
Chief Operating Officer   Christopher Rose 378 2734

Others (Senior Executives)
Chief Information Officer   Deanne Gough 378 2957
Head of Markets   Mark Coombs *Global Head, Markets* 378 2986
Equities Division   Bryan Madden *Managing Director* +61 (3) 9205 1650
Head of Risk   Alan Craft 378 2083
Head of Global Structured Finance   Gordon Branston *Executive Director* 378 2790
Global Head of Human Resources   Jo Swaby 378 2367

Relationship Manager
Relationship Management   John Curry *General Manager* +61 (3) 9273 3674

Debt Capital Markets / Fixed Income
Department: Markets
Global Head   Mark Coombs *Global Head, Markets* 378 2986
                                              Johan Hattingh *Head of Capital Markets* 378 2217

Syndicated Lending
Department: Global Structured Finance
Global Head   Gordon Branston *Executive Director* 378 2790

Other (Trade Finance)
Global Structured Finance   Sinbad Coleridge *Executive Director* 378 2658
                                              Peter Hodgson *Director & Head, Australasia* +61 (3) 9273 1771
                                              Rollo Prendergast *Regional Head, Asia / Pacific* +852 2843 7107
                                              Scott McInnis *Director & Head, Americas* +1 (212) 801 9860
Global Corporate Finance   Mark Patterson *Director & Head* 378 2902
Global Project Finance   Stephen Crew *Director & Head* 378 2721
Global Debt Origination   Chris Vermont *Director & Head* 378 2441
Global Syndication   Roscow Lucas *Director & Head* 378 2445
Leasing & Tax Based Finance   Alistair Crowther *Director & Head* 378 2958
Islamic Finance   Syed Tariq Husain *Director & Head* 378 2993

Foreign Exchange
Global Head   Chris Cooper *Global Product Head* +61 (3) 9273 1488

FX Traders / Sales People
Head of FX - UK   Mickey Adams 378 2025
Head of FX - USA   Pat Devine +1 (212) 801 9735
Head of FX - New Zealand   Bill Murdoch +66 (4) 496 8446
Head of FX - India   Subhas de Gamia +91 (22) 262 5900

Asset Management
Funds Management   John Cartwright *Director* 378 2864

Administration

Legal / In-House Counsel
                                              Gareth Campbell *Head of Legal* 378 2636

Corporate Communications
                                              Kate Bowes *Head of Corporate Communications* 378 2654

Arab African International Bank
Full Branch Office

19 Berkeley Street, London W1X 5AE
Tel: (171) 495 4881 **Fax:** (171) 495 3702 **Telex:** 887766 AAIBFX

Senior Executive Officers
General Branch Manager   Sherif Refat

1650   Euromoney Directory 1999

www.euromoneydirectory.com   UNITED KINGDOM (+44)

Arab Bank Plc   Bank

15 Moorgate, London EC2R 6LP
PO Box 138, London EC2R 6LP
Tel: (171) 315 8500 **Fax:** (171) 600 7620 **Telex:** 887110 ARABBK G **Swift:** ARAB GB 2L
Email: busdev.abl@dial.pipex.com **Reuters:** ABLL **Bloomberg:** i.greenwood@bloomberg.net

Senior Executive Officers
Deputy Regional Manager   Michael B Bowles
Regional Manager   Frederick Stonehouse

Others (Senior Executives)
Kensington Branch   Mohammed Ghazi Kanaan *Senior Manager*
Park Lane Branch   Mohammad Murrar *Manager*
Finance   Nat T Mason *Comptroller*

Debt Capital Markets / Fixed Income
Head of Debt Capital Markets   Ian Greenwood
Country Head   Ian Greenwood *Deputy Manager*

Syndicated Lending

Loan-Related Activities
Project Finance   Alan Kerr *Deputy Manager*

Foreign Exchange
Global Head   Graeme A G Hay *Chief Dealer* ☎ 315 8700

Settlement / Clearing
Operations   Andrew C Sadler *Manager*

Other Departments
Chief Credit Officer   Melvin Cooper *Deputy Manager, Credit & Loans Administration*
Correspondent Banking   Ian Greenwood *Deputy Manager*

Administration
Business Development   Michael B Bowles *Deputy Regional Manager*

Technology & Systems
                                           Ramadan Abulhawa *IT Manager*

Legal / In-House Counsel
                                           Janet Bicheno *Legal Advisor*

Argentaria, Caja Postal y Banco Hipotecario SA (ARGENTARIA)   Full Branch Office

Formerly known as: Banco Exterior de España SA
1 Great Tower Street, London EC3R 5AH
Tel: (171) 204 6600 **Fax:** (171) 204 6651 **Telex:** 886820 **Swift:** EXTE GB 2X

Senior Executive Officers
Chief Executive Officer   Jaime Sáenz de Tejada ☎ 204 6625
Financial Director   Anthony John White *Senior Manager, Finance & Operations* ☎ 204 6645
Treasurer   Bernard Delatte ☎ 204 6674

Syndicated Lending
Country Head   Mark Flewitt *Senior Manager* ☎ 204 6617

Loan-Related Activities
Trade Finance   Martin Greenwood *Senior Manager* ☎ 204 6606

Money Markets
Head of Money Markets   Bernard Delatte ☎ 204 6674

Foreign Exchange
Head of Foreign Exchange   Bernard Delatte ☎ 204 6674

Corporate Finance / M&A Advisory
Country Head   Mark Flewitt *Senior Manager* ☎ 204 6617

Administration

Compliance
                                           Antony White ☎ 204 6645

Euromoney Directory 1999   **1651**

UNITED KINGDOM (+44) www.euromoneydirectory.com

J Aron & Co (UK)
Subsidiary Company

Peterborough Court, 133 Fleet Street, London EC4A 2BB
Tel: (171) 774 1000 **Fax:** (171) 774 2020

Senior Executive Officers
Managing Director	Ron E Beller
Managing Director	Lee G Vance
Managing Director	Isabelle Ealet
Managing Director	Ewan Kirk

Others (Senior Executives)

Jean-Claude Bonneau *Executive Director*
Lynne Colley *Executive Director*
Jeff Frase *Executive Director*
Andrew Harrison *Executive Director*
Petra Lottig *Executive Director*
Allan Marson *Executive Director*
Jane Morrison *Executive Director*
Charles Tuke *Executive Director*
Henrik Wareborn *Executive Director*

J Aron & Company (Bullion)
Subsidiary Company

Peterborough Court, 133 Fleet Street, London EC4A 2BB
Tel: (171) 774 1000 **Fax:** (171) 774 2020

Senior Executive Officers
Managing Director	Christopher J Carrera
Managing Director	Philip Culliford
Managing Director	Ron E Beller
Managing Director	Andrew Stuart

Others (Senior Executives)

Roy Salameh *Executive Director*
Clive Stocker *Executive Director*

The Asahi Bank Limited

30 Cannon Street, London EC4M 6XH
Tel: (171) 248 7000 **Fax:** (171) 248 3862 **Telex:** 886400 KSBLNA G **Swift:** KYO GB 2L **Reuters:** KYOL
Website: www.asahibank.co.jp

Senior Executive Officers
General Manager	Koichi Yanagisawa

Asahi Finance (UK) Limited
Subsidiary Company

Princes House, 95 Gresham Street, London EC2V 7NA
Tel: (171) 454 1211 **Fax:** (171) 600 6154; (171) 600 6157 **Telex:** 946696 **Telex:** 946697
Website: www.asahibank.co.jp

Senior Executive Officers
Managing Director	Toshiro Sugiura
Chief Executive Officer	Mitsuru Kitano *Deputy Managing Director*
Financial Director	Michael Kenward *Manager*
Chief Operating Officer	Mitsura Kitano *Deputy Managing Director*
Treasurer	Hidefumi Nishiguchi *Head of Sales* ☎ 454 9305

Debt Capital Markets / Fixed Income

Domestic Government Bonds
Head of Sales	Hidefumi Nishiguchi *Head of Sales* ☎ 454 9305
Head of Trading	Yasuhiko Matsumoto *Head of Trading* ☎ 454 9304

Eurobonds
Head of Origination; Head of Syndication	Hitohisa Tanaka *Head, Syndication & Swaps* ☎ 454 9302
Head of Sales	Hidefumi Nishiguchi *Head of Sales* ☎ 454 9305
Head of Trading	Yasuhiko Matsumoto *Head of Trading* ☎ 454 9304

Libor-Based / Floating-Rate Products
FRN Origination; Asset Swaps; Asset Swaps (Sales)	Hitohisa Tanaka *Head, Syndication & Swaps* ☎ 454 9302

www.euromoneydirectory.com UNITED KINGDOM (+44)

Medium-Term Notes
Head of Origination; Head of Structuring; Head of Sales
Hitohisa Tanaka *Head, Syndication & Swaps* ☎ **454 9302**

Private Placements
Head of Origination; Head of Sales; Head of Structuring
Hitohisa Tanaka *Head, Syndication & Swaps* ☎ **454 9302**

Asset-Backed Securities / Securitization
Regional Head of Trading
Hitohisa Tanaka *Head, Syndication & Swaps* ☎ **454 9302**

Equity Capital Markets

Domestic Equities
Head of Origination; Head of Syndication
Head of Sales
Head of Trading
Hitohisa Tanaka *Head, Syndication & Swaps* ☎ **454 9302**
Hidefumi Nishiguchi *Head of Sales* ☎ **454 9305**
Yasuhiko Matsumoto *Head of Trading* ☎ **454 9304**

International Equities
Head of Origination; Head of Syndication
Head of Sales
Head of Trading
Hitohisa Tanaka *Head, Syndication & Swaps* ☎ **454 9302**
Hidefumi Nishiguchi *Head of Sales* ☎ **454 9305**
Yasuhiko Matsumoto *Head of Trading* ☎ **454 9304**

Convertibles / Equity-Linked
Head of Origination; Head of Syndication
Head of Sales
Head of Trading
Hitohisa Tanaka *Head, Syndication & Swaps* ☎ **454 9302**
Hidefumi Nishiguchi *Head of Sales* ☎ **454 9305**
Yasuhiko Matsumoto *Head of Trading* ☎ **454 9304**

Warrants
Head of Sales
Head of Trading
Hidefumi Nishiguchi *Head of Sales* ☎ **454 9305**
Yasuhiko Matsumoto *Head of Trading* ☎ **454 9304**

Money Markets

Eurocommercial Paper
Head of Origination
Head of Sales
Head of Trading
Hitohisa Tanaka *Head, Syndication & Swaps* ☎ **454 9302**
Hidefumi Nishiguchi *Head of Sales* ☎ **454 9305**
Yasuhiko Matsumoto *Head of Trading* ☎ **454 9304**

Risk Management
Head of Risk Management
Mitsura Kitano *Deputy Managing Director*

Fixed Income Derivatives / Risk Management
IR Swaps Sales / Marketing; IR Options Sales / Marketing
Hitohisa Tanaka *Head, Syndication & Swaps* ☎ **454 9302**

Settlement / Clearing
Head of Settlement / Clearing
Stuart Gibson *Manager*

Other Departments
Proprietary Trading
Yasuhiko Matsumoto *Head of Trading* ☎ **454 9304**

Administration
Compliance

Caroline Sheridan

Astaire & Partners Limited   Head Office

40 Queen Street, London EC4R 1DD
Tel: (171) 332 2600 **Fax:** (171) 332 2626 **Telex:** 883168 ACO G **Reuters:** FRED

Senior Executive Officers
Chairman
Financial Director
Steven Astaire ☎ **332 2680**
Peter Joy *Finance Director* ☎ **332 2666**

Debt Capital Markets / Fixed Income
Head of Debt Capital Markets
John Murrell *Director* ☎ **332 2682**

Equity Capital Markets
Head of Equity Capital Markets
David Ferdinand *Director* ☎ **332 2622**

Foreign Exchange
Head of Foreign Exchange
Michael Kenner *Director* ☎ **332 2694**

Corporate Finance / M&A Advisory
Head of Corporate Finance
Desmond Chapman *Director* ☎ **332 2620**

Settlement / Clearing
Head of Settlement / Clearing
Michael Manthorpe *Manager* ☎ **332 2669**

UNITED KINGDOM (+44)   www.euromoneydirectory.com

Australia & New Zealand Banking Group
Full Branch Office

Minerva House, Montague Close, London SE1 9DH
Tel: (171) 378 2121 Fax: (171) 378 2378

Senior Executive Officers
General Manager   Grahame Miller

AY Bank Limited

11/15 St Mary at Hill, London EC3R 8NN
Tel: (171) 283 6111; (171) 283 2335 Fax: (171) 283 6520 Telex: 886083 ANYUGO G Reuters: AYBL (Dealing)

Senior Executive Officers
Managing Director / General Manager   J Marchant
Managing Director / General Manager   V Lincevski

Bahrain Middle East Bank (EC)
Representative Office

40 Queen Street, London EC4R 1DD
Tel: (171) 236 0413 Fax: (171) 236 0409

Senior Executive Officers
Chief Representative   David Brunskill

Banca Carige SpA
Representative Office

Wax Chandlers' Hall, Gresham Street, London EC2V 7AD
Tel: (171) 600 2608 Fax: (171) 600 4350

Senior Executive Officers
UK Resident Representative   Lorenzo Castello

Banca Commerciale Italiana
Full Branch Office

90 Queen Street, London EC4N 1SA
Tel: (171) 651 3000 Fax: (171) 651 3200 Telex: 885927 COMIT G Swift: BCIT GB 2L Reuters: BCIL
Dealing Room Telex: 886808 COMIT G

Senior Executive Officers
Chief Manager   Luigi Carnelli

Others (Senior Executives)

Richard Adams *Senior Manager*
Lawrence Wybraniec *Senior Manager*
Eugerio Guicciardi *Senior Manager*

General - Treasury
Head of Treasury   Les Lawrence *Head of Trading*

Debt Capital Markets / Fixed Income
Head of Debt Capital Markets   Francesco Moglia *Assistant Manager*

Government Bonds
Head of Trading   Sergio Sola *Senior Dealer*
   Mario Crovato *Dealer*

Eurobonds
Head of Syndication   Stephen J Byrne *Head of Syndication*

Libor-Based / Floating-Rate Products
Asset Swaps   Andrea Contardo *Manager*

Fixed-Income Research
Analyst   Paolo Campi

Equity Capital Markets
Head of Equity Capital Markets   Francesco Moglia *Assistant Manager*
Country Head   Andrea Mantovani *Head, Corporate Desk*

Domestic Equities
Head of Syndication   Stephen J Byrne *Head of Syndication*
Head of Trading   Hugh Prendergast *Dealer*
   Massimiliano Rossetti *Dealer*

Equity Research
Analyst   Paolo Campi

www.euromoneydirectory.com　　　　UNITED KINGDOM (+44)

Equity Repo / Securities Lending
Marketing　　　　　　　　　　　Maria Grazia Barbero *Head, Repo*
Head of Trading　　　　　　　　Uberto Palomba *Dealer*

Syndicated Lending
Head of Syndication　　　　　Stephen J Byrne *Head of Syndication*

Other (Syndicated Lending)
　　　　　　　　　　　　　　　Riccardo Lugli *Assistant Manager*
　　　　　　　　　　　　　　　Marco Trevisan *Assistant Manager*
　　　　　　　　　　　　　　　Jill McIlwraith *Assistant Manager*

Loan-Related Activities
Trade Finance　　　　　　　　Andrea Contardo *Manager*

Other (Trade Finance)
　　　　　　　　　　　　　　　Helene Roehri *Assistant Manager*
　　　　　　　　　　　　　　　Riccardo Lugli *Assistant Manager*

Money Markets
　　　　　　　　　　　　　　　John Hughes *Chief Dealer*
　　　　　　　　　　　　　　　Thomas Toolis *Senior Dealer*

Foreign Exchange
Corporate Sales　　　　　　　Andrea Mantovani *Head, Corporate Desk*
　　　　　　　　　　　　　　　Michael Lowe *Senior Dealer*
　　　　　　　　　　　　　　　Jo Wright *Dealer*
Head of Trading　　　　　　　Les Lawrence *Head of Trading*
　　　　　　　　　　　　　　　Graham Bardell *Chief Dealer*
　　　　　　　　　　　　　　　Graham Smith *Senior Dealer*

Risk Management
Exchange-Traded Derivatives
FX Futures　　　　　　　　　　Duncan Barker *Head Dealer*
FX Options　　　　　　　　　　Franco Nardo *Broker*

Corporate Finance / M&A Advisory
Head of Corporate Finance　　Lawrence Wybraniec *Senior Manager*
Country Head　　　　　　　　Christopher Piper *Manager*

Other (Corporate Finance)
America, Holland & Italy　　　Paolo Sarcinelli *Assistant Manager*
Scandinavia, Belgium & Asia　Gianluca Corrias *Manager*

Other Departments
Correspondent Banking　　　James Brotherston *Manager*

Banca CRT SpA　　　　　　　　　　　　　　Full Branch Office

Alternative trading name: Banca Cassa di Risparmio di Torino SpA
55 Bishopsgate, London EC2N 3AS
Tel: (171) 256 9336 **Fax:** (171) 638 9252 **Telex:** 886065 CRTLON G **Swift:** CRTO GB 2L

Senior Executive Officers
Treasurer　　　　　　　　　　Brian Pegrum *Treasury Manager* ☎ **256 9337**
General Manager　　　　　　Claudio Carpignano
Deputy General Manager　　Massimo Sibilia

Others (Senior Executives)
　　　　　　　　　　　　　　　Colin Biggs *Corporate Manager*
　　　　　　　　　　　　　　　Julie Baker *Corporate Manager*
　　　　　　　　　　　　　　　Gary McLean *Deputy Manager*
　　　　　　　　　　　　　　　Alison Henderson *Assistant Manager*

Debt Capital Markets / Fixed Income
Head of Fixed Income; Head of Fixed Income　Massimo Sibilia *Deputy General Manager*
Trading

Government Bonds
Head of Trading　　　　　　　Massimo Sibilia *Deputy General Manager*

Eurobonds
Head of Trading　　　　　　　Julie Baker *Corporate Manager*

Libor-Based / Floating-Rate Products
FRN Trading　　　　　　　　　Julie Baker *Corporate Manager*
Asset Swaps　　　　　　　　　Gary McLean *Deputy Manager*

Fixed-Income Repo
Head of Repo; Marketing & Product　Alison Henderson *Assistant Manager*
Development; Head of Trading

Euromoney Directory 1999　**1655**

UNITED KINGDOM (+44) · www.euromoneydirectory.com

Banca CRT SpA (cont)
Equity Capital Markets
Equity Repo / Securities Lending
Head — Claudio Carpignano *General Manager*
Marketing & Product Development — Colin Biggs *Corporate Manager*
Head of Prime Brokerage — Massimo Sibilia *Deputy General Manager*
Head of Trading — Robert Nunn *Dealer*
Rossells Romano *Dealer*
Brian Pegrum *Chief Dealer* ☏ 256 9337

Syndicated Lending
Tel: 256 9336 **Fax:** 638 9252
Head of Origination — Julie Baker *Corporate Manager*
Head of Syndication — Gary McLean *Deputy Manager*
Head of Trading — Colin Biggs *Corporate Manager*

Loan-Related Activities
Trade Finance — Gary McLean *Deputy Manager*
Trade Finance; Project Finance — Colin Biggs *Corporate Manager*
Structured Trade Finance — Julie Baker
Structured Trade Finance; Leasing & Asset Finance — Colin Biggs *Corporate Manager*

Money Markets
Tel: 256 9337
Head of Money Markets — Brian Pegrum *Treasury Manager* ☏ 256 9337

Wholesale Deposits
Marketing — Brian Pegrum *Treasury Manager* ☏ 256 9337
Head of Sales — Rosella Romano *Dealer*

Foreign Exchange
Head of Foreign Exchange — Brian Pegrum *Treasury Manager* ☏ 256 9337
Country Head — Jeremy Ridout *Dealer*
Country Head of Trading — Brian Pegrum *Treasury Manager* ☏ 256 9337

FX Traders / Sales People
Rosella Romano *Dealer*
Jeremy Ridout *Dealer*

Risk Management
Head of Risk Management — Clive Christensen *Credit & Risk Manager*

Settlement / Clearing
Head of Settlement / Clearing; Equity Settlement; Fixed-Income Settlement Operations; Back-Office — Susan Radford *Head of Settlements*
Alan Chapman *Operations Manager*

Other Departments
Chief Credit Officer — Clive Christensen *Deputy General Manager*
Correspondent Banking — Alan Chapman *Operations Manager*

Administration
Head of Administration — Asoka Fernando *Financial Controller*
Head of Marketing — Colin Biggs *Corporate Manager*

Technology & Systems
Colin Mackenzie *IT Manager*

Compliance
Clive Christensen *Deputy General Manager*

Accounts / Audit
Internal Auditor — Stefano Perrazini
Accounts — Asoka Fernando *Financial Controller*

Other (Administration)
Colin Biggs *Corporate Manager*

Banca del Salento — Representative Office
1 College Hill, London EC4R 2RA
Tel: (171) 329 8773 **Fax:** (171) 329 8788

Senior Executive Officers
UK Resident Representative — A del Carretto di Moncrivello

www.euromoneydirectory.com   UNITED KINGDOM (+44)

Banca d'Italia
Representative Office

39 King Street, London EC2V 8JJ
Tel: (171) 606 4201 **Fax:** (171) 606 4065

Senior Executive Officers
UK Resident Representative — Luigi Marini
Deputy Representative — Rocco Schiavone

Banca March SA
Full Branch Office

30 Eastcheap, London EC3M 1HD
Tel: (171) 220 7488 **Fax:** (171) 929 2446 **Swift:** BMAR GB 2L **Email:** bmarlondon@aol.com **Reuters:** BMML

Senior Executive Officers
Chief Operating Officer — Richard Young
Treasurer — Juan Guerrero *Chief Dealer* 220 7335
General Manager — Francisco F Gamboa

Debt Capital Markets / Fixed Income
Country Head — Juan Guerrero *Chief Dealer* 220 7335

Domestic Government Bonds
Head of Trading — Juan Guerrero *Chief Dealer* 220 7335

Eurobonds
Head of Trading — Juan Guerrero *Chief Dealer* 220 7335

Equity Capital Markets
Country Head — Juan Guerrero *Chief Dealer* 220 7335

International Equities
Head of Trading — Juan Guerrero *Chief Dealer* 220 7335

Syndicated Lending
Head of Syndication — Francisco F Gamboa *General Manager*

Loan-Related Activities
Structured Trade Finance — Francisco F Gamboa *General Manager*

Money Markets
Country Head — Juan Guerrero *Chief Dealer* 220 7335

Foreign Exchange
Head of Trading — Juan Guerrero *Chief Dealer* 220 7335

Risk Management
Other Currency Swap / FX Options Personnel
Nicholas Branch *Dealer* 220 7335

Administration
Technology & Systems
Andrew Ellis *Manager, IT Systems*

Banca Monte dei Paschi di Siena SpA
Full Branch Office

122 Leadenhall Street, London EC3V 4RH
Tel: (171) 623 3847 **Fax:** (171) 621 9407 **Telex:** 887823 **Swift:** PASG BG 2L **Reuters:** MPSL

Senior Executive Officers
Chief Executive Officer — G Guano *Chief Executive & General Manager*
Deputy General Manager — Duncan Rosse
Deputy General Manager — Jeromy Orson

Debt Capital Markets / Fixed Income
Country Head — R Boccanera *Senior Manager*

Equity Capital Markets
Domestic Equities
Head of Syndication — R Boccanera *Senior Manager*

Syndicated Lending
Country Head of Origination; Head of Syndication — R Boccanera *Senior Manager*

Money Markets
Money Markets - General
ECP / Euronotes — Keith White *Manager*

Euromoney Directory 1999 **1657**

UNITED KINGDOM (+44)   www.euromoneydirectory.com

Banca Monte dei Paschi di Siena SpA (cont)
Foreign Exchange
Tel: 626 5743
Country Head   Keith White *Manager*
FX Traders / Sales People
Senior Dealer   Keith White *Manager*
                                     Colin Pinner *Manager, Corporate FX*
Dealer   Richard Wilson *Assistant Manager*
                                     Ivo Aspromonte
                                     Carlo Lascialfare

Other Departments
Commodities / Bullion   Keith White *Manager*
Correspondent Banking   S Ricci *Manager*
Administration
Head of Administration   Jeromy Orson *Deputy General Manager*

Banca Nazionale del Lavoro SpA

Fitzwilliam House, 10 St Mary Axe, London EC3A 8NA
Tel: (171) 337 2400 Fax: (171) 929 7983 Telex: 888094 LAVORO G Swift: BNLI GB 2L
Senior Executive Officers
Chief Executive Officer   Walter Golinelli

Banca Nazionale dell'Agricoltura SpA   Full Branch Office

85 Gracechurch Street, London EC3V 0AR
Tel: (171) 623 2773 Fax: (171) 623 8435 Telex: 884651 LDNAGR G Swift: NAGR GB 2L Reuters: BNAL
Senior Executive Officers
General Manager   Paolo Mennini
Others (Senior Executives)
                                     E Spurio *Assistant General Manager, Operations*
General - Treasury
Head of Treasury   D Di Nunzio *Assistant General Manager, Treasury*
Debt Capital Markets / Fixed Income
Head of Sales   S Silocchi *Trader*
                                     P Catemario
Head of Trading   S Silocchi *Trader*
                                     P Catemario

Private Placements
Head of Origination; Head of Sales S Silocchi *Trader*
Syndicated Lending
Head of Origination; Head of Syndication L Penna *General Manager*
Head of Credit Committee   N Sutton *Manager*
Other (Syndicated Lending)
                                     E Franz *Manager*
Loan-Related Activities
Project Finance   E Franz *Manager*
Other (Trade Finance)
Forfaiting / Factoring / Countertrade; LC / DC N Sutton *Manager*
Money Markets
Wholesale Deposits
Marketing   S Silocchi *Trader*
                                     K Bailey *Chief Dealer*
                                     A Davis *Dealer*
Head of Sales   K Bailey *Chief Dealer*
                                     F Baldi *Dealer*

Foreign Exchange
Tel: 263 2446
Country Head   D Di Nunzio *Assistant General Manager, Treasury*
Head of Trading   K Bailey *Chief Dealer*
                                     A Davis *Dealer*
                                     F Baldi *Dealer*
                                     R Harvey *Senior Dealer, Spot*

www.euromoneydirectory.com **UNITED KINGDOM (+44)**

Risk Management
Fixed Income Derivatives / Risk Management
Trading   D Di Nunzio *Assistant General Manager, Treasury*
                                                     K Bailey *Chief Dealer*
IR Swaps Trading; IR Options Trading   S Silocchi *Trader*

Foreign Exchange Derivatives / Risk Management
Spot / Forwards Sales   S Silocchi *Trader*
Spot / Forwards Trading   D Di Nunzio *Assistant General Manager, Treasury*
                                                     K Bailey *Chief Dealer*
Cross-Currency Swaps, Trading   S Silocchi *Trader*
Vanilla FX option Trading   D Di Nunzio *Assistant General Manager, Treasury*
                                                     K Bailey *Chief Dealer*

Corporate Finance / M&A Advisory
Country Head   E Franz *Manager*

Settlement / Clearing
Derivatives Settlement; Foreign Exchange   T Scammell *Manager, Operations*
Settlement; Operations; Electronic Banking

Administration
Head of Administration   E Spurio *Assistant General Manager, Operations*

Technology & Systems
                                                     E Spurio *Assistant General Manager, Operations*

Compliance
                                                     M Fieldhouse *Internal Auditor*

Banca Popolare di Milano   Full Branch Office
2 George Yard, Lombard Street, London EC3V 9DH
Tel: (171) 283 7111 **Fax:** (171) 283 6783; (171) 283 6789 **Telex:** 885998 **Swift:** BPMI GB 2L **Reuters:** BPML
Telerate: 6403

Senior Executive Officers
General Manager   Marco Ferrario

Money Markets
Tel: 283 7444 **Fax:** 283 6789

Money Markets - General
                                                     P Dowman *Dealer, Money Markets*
                                                     G Dudden *Dealer, Money Markets*

Foreign Exchange
Tel: 283 7444 **Fax:** 283 6789

FX Traders / Sales People
                                                     S Waddell *FX Dealer*
                                                     D Doyle *FX Dealer*

Corporate Finance / M&A Advisory
Global Head   Paul Richardson *Manager, Credit & Loans*

Banca Popolare di Novara   Full Branch Office
Bucklersbury House, Walbrook, London EC4N 8EL
Tel: (171) 489 0404 **Fax:** (171) 236 2033 **Telex:** 0518811511 NOVBAG G **Swift:** NVRB GB 2L **Reuters:** BPNL

Banca di Roma   Full Branch Office
Guildhall House, 87 Gresham Street, London EC2V 7NQ
Tel: (171) 726 4106 **Fax:** (171) 454 4106; (171) 454 7311 **Telex:** 888074 BROMLN G **Swift:** BROM GB 22
Email: bdrld@romalon.btinternet.com **Cable:** LONDROMA G
Foreign Exchange Tel: 651 5151; 651 5151; **Money Markets & FX Telex:** 8812784

Senior Executive Officers
Others (Senior Executives)
                                                     Corrado Amari *Chief Manager*
Finance   Pio Marchini *Deputy Chief Manager*
Business   Peter Scharf *Deputy Chief Manager*
Operations   Diego Li Calzi *Deputy Chief Manager*

Euromoney Directory 1999 **1659**

UNITED KINGDOM (+44)　　　www.euromoneydirectory.com

Banca di Roma (cont)
Debt Capital Markets / Fixed Income
Country Head　　　　　　　　Giancarlo Lodigiani *Head of Trading Desk* ☎ **726 4043** 📠 **454 7311**
　　　　　　　　　　　　　　　✉ bdrld.dealers@romalon.btinternet.com

Fixed-Income Repo
Marketing & Product Development　Giancarlo Lodigiani *Head of Capital Markets*
Trading　　　　　　　　　　　Maurizio Napoli *Head of Trading*
　　　　　　　　　　　　　　　Christian Defelice *Trader*
　　　　　　　　　　　　　　　Paolo Cadolino *Trader*
　　　　　　　　　　　　　　　Karen Parlett *Trader*
Sales　　　　　　　　　　　　Maurizio Napoli *Head of Trading*

Money Markets
Reuters: ROML, ROMA **Telex:** 8812536
Country Head　　　　　　　　Christopher Lefevre *Head* ☎ **726 4012** 📠 **454 7311**
　　　　　　　　　　　　　　　✉ bdrld.dealers@romalon.btinternet.com

Foreign Exchange
Reuters: ROML **Telex:** 8812536
Country Head　　　　　　　　David L McMenamin *Head* ☎ **726 4012** 📠 **454 7311**
　　　　　　　　　　　　　　　✉ bdrld.dealers@romalon.btinternet.com

Administration
Compliance
　　　　　　　　　　　　　　　Michael T Kennedy *Financial Controller, Compliance Officer*

Banca Serfin SA　　　　　　　　　　　　　　　　　　　　Full Branch Office
New Broad Street House, 35 New Broad Street, London EC2M 1NH
Tel: (171) 614 1000 **Fax:** (171) 614 1111 **Reuters:** SERW; SERX; SERY

Senior Executive Officers
SVP & General Manager　　　Ramon Diez-Canedo
Financial Director　　　　　　Oscar Guarneros *Deputy General Manager* ☎ **614 1002**
Chief Operating Officer　　　Guillermo Lopez *Deputy General Manager*
Treasurer　　　　　　　　　　Oscar Guarneros *Deputy General Manager* ☎ **614 1002**

Debt Capital Markets / Fixed Income
Eurobonds
Head of Sales　　　　　　　　Oscar Guarneros *Deputy General Manager* ☎ **614 1002**
Head of Trading　　　　　　　Gary Mitchell ☎ **614 1045**
Bonds - General
Fixed-Income Sales　　　　　Gary Mitchell ☎ **614 1045**
Fixed-Income Repo
Head of Repo　　　　　　　　Gary Mitchell ☎ **614 1045**

Other Departments
Correspondent Banking　　　John Denison *Business Development Manager*

Administration
Compliance
　　　　　　　　　　　　　　　Guillermo Lopez *Deputy General Manager*

Banco Bilbao Vizcaya SA　　　　　　　　　　　　　　　Full Branch Office
100 Cannon Street, London EC4N 6EH
Tel: (171) 623 3060; (171) 929 6009 **Fax:** (171) 929 4718; (171) 929 0972 **Telex:** 8811693 BB LON G **Swift:** BBVI GB 2L
Reuters: BBVG **Bloomberg:** O BBV

Senior Executive Officers
Managing Director / General Manager　Juan Pérez Calot
Administration
Compliance
　　　　　　　　　　　　　　　Nicholas May *Head, Compliance*

Banco Boavista
3 St Helen's Place, London EC3A 6AU
Tel: (171) 256 6655 **Fax:** (171) 256 6644

Senior Executive Officers
General Manager　　　　　　Neri R Infante

1660 Euromoney Directory 1999

www.euromoneydirectory.com UNITED KINGDOM (+44)

Banco do Brasil SA
Full Branch Office

34 King Street, London EC2V 8ES
Tel: (171) 606 7101 **Fax:** (171) 606 2877 **Telex:** 8812381 BBLDNB G **Swift:** BRAS GB 2L **Telex:** 8812388 BBLDNB G

Senior Executive Officers
General Manager — Carlos Alberto Alvarenga
Deputy General Manager — Augusto Brauna Pinheiro
Deputy General Manager — Luiz Alberto Alvarenga
Deputy General Manager — Rinaldo Frettas Mello

Others (Senior Executives)
Overseas IT Manager — Waldemir Belli Castanha

Syndicated Lending
Head of Syndicated Lending — Louis Nicola *Senior Loans Officer*

Money Markets
Head of Money Markets — David Webber *Treasury Manager*

Risk Management
Head of Risk Management — Allan Cann *Risk Manager*

Settlement / Clearing
Head of Settlement / Clearing — Anabela Hurst *Settlements Manager*

Administration
Head of Administration — Ronald Leslie Brock *Manager*

Technology & Systems
Tim Evans *IT Manager*

Banco Central Hispanoamericano SA
Full Branch Office

15 Austin Friars, London EC2N 2DJ
Tel: (171) 588 0181 **Fax:** (171) 256 7850 **Telex:** 8812997 BCLDN J **Swift:** CENT GB 2L **Reuters:** CENL; CENT

Senior Executive Officers
Chief Executive Officer — Javier Barbeyto *General Manager*
Chief Operating Officer — Antonio Garcia *Deputy General Manager*

Corporate Finance / M&A Advisory
Country Head — Harry Bright *Senior Manager*

Other Departments
Private Banking — Amparo Delgado *Senior Manager*

Administration
Compliance
Philip Lewis *Manager*

Banco del Pacífico
Representative Office

45/47 Cornhill, London EC3V 3PD
Tel: (171) 283 7559 **Fax:** (171) 283 7673 **Email:** pacific@dircon.co.uk

Senior Executive Officers
Representative — David J E Glazier

Banco EFISA SA
Representative Office

11 Carlos Place, London W1Y 5AF
Tel: (171) 533 1603 **Fax:** (171) 533 1640

Senior Executive Officers
Executive Director — Roger Reynolds

Banco Español de Crédito
Full Branch Office

Alternative trading name: BANESTO

33 King Street, London EC2V 8LN
Tel: (171) 606 4883 **Fax:** (171) 606 3921 **Telex:** 8811360 BEC G **Swift:** ESPG GB 2L **Reuters:** BECL; BANL (Monitor); BECY (Dealing)

Senior Executive Officers
General Manager — Vicente Fernandez

Euromoney Directory 1999 **1661**

UNITED KINGDOM (+44)   www.euromoneydirectory.com

Banco Español de Crédito (cont)
General - Treasury
Head of Treasury   George Rodriguez *Chief Dealer*
Settlement / Clearing
Operations   John Pepper *Manager*

Banco Espirito Santo   Full Branch Office
33 Queen Street, London EC4R 1ES
Tel: (171) 332 4300 **Fax:** (171) 332 4340 **Telex:** 883064 **Swift:** BESC GB 2L **Reuters:** BESL; ESPL; ESPX
Website: www.bescl.co.uk

Senior Executive Officers
Chief Executive Officer   Tom Hoffman
Treasurer   Tony Sleep
Assistant General Manager   Ricardo Pires

General-Lending (DCM, SL)
Head of Corporate Banking   Hugh Stewart *Senior Manager, Corporate & Commercial Banking*
                                    Guy Harris *Deputy Head of Banking*

General - Treasury
Head of Treasury   Gary Buckmaster *Chief Dealer*

Debt Capital Markets / Fixed Income
Global Head   Ricardo Pires *Assistant General Manager*
Regional Head   Tony Sleep *Senior Manager, Participations in Loan & Issues*
                                    Margaret Wright *Deputy Manager, Loan Administration*
Country Head   Steven Nason *Dealer*

Syndicated Lending
Loan-Related Activities
Trade Finance   Roger Rudon *Deputy Manager*

Money Markets
Global Head   James Ryan *Senior Dealer*

Foreign Exchange
Head of Foreign Exchange   Steven Holley
Corporate Sales   Steven Nason *Dealer*

FX Traders / Sales People
Dealer   Steven Holley *Senior Dealer*
                                    Andy Rix *Dealer*

Settlement / Clearing
Head of Settlement / Clearing   John Allen
Settlement (General)   Cristina Wiseman *Senior Officer, Back-Office Settlements*
                                    John Allen *Assistant Manager, Back-Office Settlements*
Operations   Brendan Talbott *Deputy Manager*
                                    Gillian Bull *Reconciliations*

Other Departments
Chief Credit Officer   Gavin Ramsden
Private Banking   Maria Coutinho *Senior Officer*
                                    Fernando Penedos *Assistant Manager*

Administration
Head of Administration   Robin Liddard *Head of Operations & Administration*
Other (Administration)
Administration & Personnel   Dilys Tan *Deputy Manager*

Banco do Estado de São Paulo SA   Full Branch Office
Alternative trading name: BANESPA
10th Floor, Alban Gate, 125 London Wall, London EC2Y 5AN
Tel: (171) 457 5151 **Fax:** (171) 417 0199 **Telex:** 888839 BANESP G **Swift:** BESP GB 2L
Email: banespa_london@msn.com **Reuters:** BECD; ESPL ESPX

Senior Executive Officers
Treasurer   John Lavender *AGM & Treasurer* ☎ **457 5195**
General Manager   Sidney Marson ☎ **457 5108**
Deputy General Manager   Jose Fama Dias ☎ **457 5108**

Others (Senior Executives)
Head of Private Banking   John Pereira *Head of Operations* ☎ **457 5104**

1662 Euromoney Directory 1999

www.euromoneydirectory.com UNITED KINGDOM (+44)

Debt Capital Markets / Fixed Income
Eurobonds
Head of Trading John Lavender *AGM & Treasurer* ☏ **457 5195**
Libor-Based / Floating-Rate Products
Asset Swaps John Lavender *AGM & Treasurer* ☏ **457 5195**
Fixed-Income Repo
Head of Repo John Lavender *AGM & Treasurer* ☏ **457 5195**

Equity Capital Markets
Head of Equity Capital Markets John Lavender *AGM & Treasurer* ☏ **457 5195**

Syndicated Lending
Tel: 457 5111
Head of Trading Richard Poulton *Loans Officer* ☏ **457 5111**

Money Markets
Head of Money Markets John Lavender *AGM & Treasurer* ☏ **457 5195**

Foreign Exchange
Head of Foreign Exchange John Lavender *AGM & Treasurer* ☏ **457 5195**

Risk Management
Head of Risk Management Sidney Marson *General Manager* ☏ **457 5108**

Corporate Finance / M&A Advisory
Global Head Sidney Marson *General Manager* ☏ **457 5108**

Settlement / Clearing
Head of Settlement / Clearing Edison Teixeira *Head of Settlements* ☏ **457 5114**

Other Departments
Correspondent Banking Edison Teixeira *Head of Settlements* ☏ **457 5114**

Administration
Head of Administration Sueli Perian *Personnel & Admin Manager* ☏ **457 5103**
Head of Marketing John Lavender *AGM & Treasurer* ☏ **457 5195**

Technology & Systems
Information Technology Ravinder Sangha *Head of IT* ☏ **457 5136**

Legal / In-House Counsel
  Sidney Marson *General Manager* ☏ **457 5108**

Compliance
  Paul Cagney *Controller* ☏ **457 5119**

Banco Excel Económico SA
Representative Office

1 Gracechurch Street, London EC3V 0DD
Tel: (171) 283 8141 **Fax:** (171) 626 9467

Senior Executive Officers
Senior Representative, Europe John Fenn

Banco Mercantil - Venezuela
Representative Office

1 Gracechurch Street, London EC3V 0DD
Tel: (171) 283 8601 **Fax:** (171) 283 7549

Senior Executive Officers
Senior Vice President Pedro N Solares

Banco Mercantil de São Paulo SA FINASA
Full Branch Office

The Stock Exchange, Old Broad Street, London EC2N 1HH
Tel: (171) 638 4444 **Fax:** (171) 628 3565 **Telex:** 8811873

Senior Executive Officers
General Manager Luiz E G Delgado

Others (Senior Executives)
  Christopher M Pengiley *Deputy General Manager*

UNITED KINGDOM (+44)   www.euromoneydirectory.com

Banco de la Nacion Argentina

Longbow House, 14/20 Chiswell Street, London EC1Y 4TD
Tel: (171) 588 2738; (171) 588 3949 **Fax:** (171) 588 4034 **Telex:** 883950

Senior Executive Officers
Managing Director / General Manager   Jorge O Mozzino

Banco Nacional de Commerce Exterior — Representative Office

Alternative trading name: Bancomext

3 St James's Square, London SW1Y 4JU
Tel: (171) 839 6586 **Fax:** (171) 839 4425

Senior Executive Officers
Representative   Fernando Estandia

Banco Nacional de Mexico SA — Full Branch Office

3 Creed Court, 5 Ludgate Hill, London EC4M 7AA
Tel: (171) 827 6900 **Fax:** (171) 827 6967 **Telex:** 8953322 **Swift:** BNMX GB 2XA

Senior Executive Officers
General Manager   Victor Murillo
Chief Executive Officer   Brendan McCullagh *Executive Vice President*
Financial Director   Richard Wailes *Financial Comptroller*
Chief Operating Officer   John Frank
Treasurer   Roberto Vargas *Treasurer*

Debt Capital Markets / Fixed Income

Eurobonds
Head of Trading   Roberto Vargas *Manager*

Emerging Market Bonds
Head   Miguel Helu *Manager*

Syndicated Lending
Head of Syndication   Juan Pablo Diaque *Manager*

Money Markets
Head of Money Markets   Roberto Vargas *Manager*

Wholesale Deposits
Head of Sales   Roberto Vargas *Manager*

Foreign Exchange
Head of Foreign Exchange   Roberto Vargas *Manager*
Regional Head   Roberto Vargas *Manager*

FX Traders / Sales People
FX Trader   Juan Pereira *Trader*

Risk Management
Regional Head   Steve MacLean *Manager, Credit*

Fixed Income Derivatives / Risk Management
Head of Sales   Roberto Vargas *Manager*
Trading   Roberto Vargas *Manager*

Settlement / Clearing
Head of Settlement / Clearing   John Frank *Manager, Operations*

Administration
Head of Administration   John Frank
Business Development   Victor Murillo *General Manager*

Technology & Systems
     Eduardo Alatorre *Manager*

Legal / In-House Counsel
     Alejandro Lugo *Legal Counsel*

Compliance
     Monica Brown *Manager*

Accounts / Audit
     Richard Wailes *Financial Comptroller*

1664 Euromoney Directory 1999

www.euromoneydirectory.com UNITED KINGDOM (+44)

Banco Nacional Ultramarino SA

7th Floor, Walbrook House, 23 Walbrook, London EC4N 8BT
Tel: (171) 280 0200 **Fax:** (171) 280 0201 **Telex:** 887477 **Swift:** BNUL GB 2L **Reuters:** BANU

Senior Executive Officers
Chairman Joao M Salgueiro
Chief Executive Officer António Vieira Monteiro
Managing Director / General Manager Francisco J Comprido

Banco di Napoli
Full Branch Office

1 Moorgate, London EC2R 6JH
Tel: (171) 726 9500; (171) 726 4131 **Fax:** (171) 726 8159 **Telex:** 945004 **Telex:** 945005

Senior Executive Officers
General Manager Gerardo Quercioli

Banco Pastor
Representative Office

5th Floor, Victoria Station House, 191 Victoria Street, London SW1E 5NE
Tel: (171) 630 8955 **Fax:** (171) 630 8944

Senior Executive Officers
Representative C Merayo-Diaz

Banco Popular Español
Representative Office

19B Craven Road, London W2 3BP
Tel: (171) 402 7393 **Fax:** (171) 402 7835

Senior Executive Officers
Representative José A Garcia

Banco Portugués do Atlántico
Full Branch Office

107 Cheapside, London EC2V 6DT
Tel: (171) 600 8380 **Fax:** (171) 600 8381 **Telex:** 8956297

Senior Executive Officers
General Manager Manuel de Teves Costa
Deputy General Manager Alexandre Beiraó

Debt Capital Markets / Fixed Income
Country Head Graham Male *Senior Manager*

Libor-Based / Floating-Rate Products
FRN Sales Graham Male *Senior Manager*

Equity Capital Markets
Country Head Graham Male *Senior Manager*

Syndicated Lending
Global Head Graham Male *Senior Manager*

Settlement / Clearing
Regional Head Sailesh Poojara *Operations Manager*

Other Departments
Correspondent Banking Graham Male *Senior Manager*

Administration

Technology & Systems
  Akin Uysal *EDP Manager*

Compliance
  Nazare Dang *Assistant General Manager*

Euromoney Directory 1999 **1665**

UNITED KINGDOM (+44)   www.euromoneydirectory.com

Banco Real SA
Full Branch Office

20 St Dunstan's Hill, London EC3R 8HL
Tel: (171) 638 6474 **Fax:** (171) 638 4997 **Telex:** 8952875 **Swift:** REAL GB 2L **Telex:** 8952876

Senior Executive Officers
Chief Executive Officer
Treasurer

Georg W Epperlein *Regional Director*
Julio Rito *Senior Manager, Treasury*

Syndicated Lending
Regional Head

Julio Rito *Senior Manager, Treasury*

Loan-Related Activities
Trade Finance
Structured Trade Finance

Denis Farrugia *Manager*
Julio Rito *Senior Manager, Treasury*

Money Markets
Country Head

Julio Rito *Senior Manager, Treasury*

Foreign Exchange
Country Head

Ricardo Schneider *Manager*

FX Traders / Sales People
All currencies

Stuart Harknett *Manager* ☎ **638 8481**

Settlement / Clearing
Country Head

Roger Hunger

Other Departments
Correspondent Banking

Julio Rito *Senior Manager, Treasury*

Administration
Compliance

Brian D Withers *Controller*

Banco de Sabadell SA
Full Branch Office

120 Pall Mall, London SW1Y 5EA
Tel: (171) 321 0020 **Fax:** (171) 321 0075 **Telex:** 8814314 BANSA G **Swift:** BSAB GB 2L

Senior Executive Officers
General Manager

Josep Suarez

Syndicated Lending
Loan-Related Activities
Trade Finance

Jack Vadjaraganian

Corporate Finance / M&A Advisory
Country Head

Jack Vadjaraganian

Other Departments
Correspondent Banking

Frederick Avella

Banco Santander

Santander House, 100 Ludgate Hill, London EC4M 7NJ
Tel: (171) 332 7766 **Fax:** (171) 248 1004 **Telex:** 8811831 **Swift:** BDER GB 2L **Reuters:** BDSL; BDSD

Senior Executive Officers
Managing Director / General Manager

Carlos Infesta

Banco di Sicilia SpA
Full Branch Office

The International Financial Centre, 25 Old Broad Street, London EC2N 1HQ
Tel: (171) 638 0201 **Fax:** (171) 638 4796 **Telex:** 888078 SICILB G **Swift:** BSICG B2 LL ON
Email: sicilia@btinternet.com

Senior Executive Officers
General Manager

Marcantonio Stagno d'Alcontres

Debt Capital Markets / Fixed Income
Domestic Government Bonds
Head of Trading

Andrea Febbraro *Head, Fixed Income* ☎ **628 0634**

Non-Domestic Government Bonds

Andrea Febbraro *Head, Fixed Income* ☎ **628 0634**

Eurobonds
Head of Trading

Andrea Febbraro *Head, Fixed Income* ☎ **628 0634**

1666 Euromoney Directory 1999

www.euromoneydirectory.com UNITED KINGDOM (+44)

Medium-Term Notes
Head of Structuring — Philip Wright *Manager*

Fixed-Income Repo
Head of Repo — Peter Alfieri ☏ **638 0636**

Syndicated Lending
Head of Origination — Philip Wright *Manager*

Loan-Related Activities
Trade Finance — Gaetano Mendola *Manager*
Project Finance; Structured Trade Finance — Philip Wright *Manager*

Money Markets
Regional Head — Chris Shrimpton *Senior Chief Trader* ☏ **638 6036**

Wholesale Deposits
Marketing — Chris Shrimpton *Senior Chief Trader* ☏ **638 6036**
Head of Sales — Peter Alfieri ☏ **638 0636**

Foreign Exchange
Head of Trading — Vincent Cristiano *Dealer*

Risk Management

Fixed Income Derivatives / Risk Management
Regional Head — Colin Mitchel *Manager* ☏ **628 0634**
IR Options Sales / Marketing — Andrea Febbraro *Head, Fixed Income* ☏ **628 0634**

OTC Equity Derivatives
Trading — Andrea Febbraro *Head, Fixed Income* ☏ **628 0634**

Settlement / Clearing
Regional Head — Gaetano Mendola *Manager*

Administration

Compliance
— Ian W Cain *Manager, Compliance*

Banco Totta & Açores SA
Full Branch Office

68 Cannon Street, London EC4N 6AQ
Tel: (171) 236 1515 **Fax:** (171) 236 7717 **Telex:** 887609 **Swift:** TOTTA GB 2LA **Email:** main@btax.co.uk
Reuters: BTAL **Telerate:** 3813 **Telex:** 8952987 (Gen) **Telex:** 888341/2 (Forex)

Senior Executive Officers
Senior General Manager — J J Caldwell
General Manager — A V Mascarenhas

General-Lending (DCM, SL)
Head of Corporate Banking — P Nunn *Manager, Corporate Banking & Lending* ✉ **pnunn@btax.co.uk**
S Perks *Asst. Manager, Corporate Banking & Lending*

Debt Capital Markets / Fixed Income

Mortgage-Backed Securities
Global Head — S G Perks *Regional Head, Portuguese Mortgage Finance*

Money Markets
Global Head — R M Standen *Manager, Treasury*

Foreign Exchange
Department: Foreign Exchange & Money Markets
Global Head — R M Standen *Manager, Treasury*

FX Traders / Sales People
— C J Taylor *Manager & Chief Dealer*
I Potter *Assistant Manager & Chief Dealer*
H Eadie *Dealer*
V J Patel *Dealer*

Banco Urquijo SA
Representative Office

Founders Court, Lothbury, London EC2R 7HE
Tel: (171) 282 3303 **Fax:** (171) 726 6417 **Email:** urquilondon@easynet.co.uk

Senior Executive Officers
London Representative — Santiago Duran

UNITED KINGDOM (+44)   www.euromoneydirectory.com

Bancomer SA

Level 7, City Tower, 40 Basinghall Street, London EC2V 5DE
Tel: (171) 216 6000 **Fax:** (171) 417 0103 **Telex:** 886492 BCOMER G **Swift:** BCMR GB 2L **Reuters:** MEXA (Dealing)
Cable: COMERBANCO LONDO

Senior Executive Officers
Managing Director / General Manager   José Antonio Padilla

Bangkok Bank Public Company Limited   Full Branch Office

61 St Mary Axe, London EC3A 8BY
Tel: (171) 929 4422 **Fax:** (171) 283 3988 **Telex:** 8812448 **Swift:** BKKB GB 2L **Reuters:** BBXL

Senior Executive Officers
SVP & Branch Manager   Phaithul Tejasakulsin
Syndicated Lending
Country Head   Vicky Lim *AVP & Head of Credit*
Foreign Exchange
Country Head   George Georgiades *Chief Dealer* ☏ **929 3362**

Bank of America International Limited   Subsidiary Company

1 Alie Street, London E1 8DE
Tel: (171) 634 4000 **Fax:** (171) 634 4470; (171) 634 4701 **Telex:** 884552 BOALTD **Cable:** BAIGROUP

Senior Executive Officers
Chairman   P Gerald Doherty
Vice President   Howard Watson ☏ **634 4558** 🖷 **634 4532**
              ✉ **howard.watson@bankamerica.com**
Managing Director / General Manager   John Weguelin
Debt Capital Markets / Fixed Income
Department: Global Capital Markets - Europe, Middle East and Africa
Country Head   David Blatchford *Executive Vice President & Head*
Emerging Market Bonds
Head of Research   Richard Gray *Research Analyst*
Syndicated Lending
Country Head   David M Chandler *Managing Director* ☏ **634 4635** 🖷 **634 4532**
Foreign Exchange
FX Traders / Sales People
Spot FX   Steve Bassi *Chief Dealer*
          Darren Barker *Senior Trader*
Risk Management
Other (FI Derivatives)
European Interest Rate Trading   Claudio Zampia *Head*
Settlement / Clearing
Head of Settlement / Clearing   Chris D'Oriscoll *Manager* ☏ **(181) 313 2268**
Settlement (General)   Geoff Hull ☏ **(181) 313 2733**
                     Martin Briaris ☏ **(181) 313 2129**
Operations   Andrew Pilditch *Head, Capital Market Operations*

Bank Austria Creditanstalt Group   Full Branch Office

Alternative trading name: Bank Austria AG (London Branch) & Bank Austria Creditanstalt International (London Branch)
125 London Wall, London EC2Y 5DD
Tel: (171) 600 1555; (171) 382 1000 **Fax:** (171) 417 4803; (171) 417 4804 **Telex:** 8946123 **Swift:** BKAU GB 2L
Reuters: BKAUL; BAUK

Senior Executive Officers
Chief Executive Officer   Richard Barnes *GM & CEO* ☏ **417 4900**
                         Wolfgang Lichtl *GM & CEO* ☏ **417 4920** 🖷 **417 4911**
Financial Director   Nigel Burge *Director* ☏ **417 4820**
Chief Operating Officer   Lawrence Muggeridge *Director* ☏ **417 4830**
Treasurer   Heinz-Peter Stohl *Deputy Chief Executive* ☏ **417 4910** 🖷 **417 4911**
International Division   Alois Steinbichler *Member of the Management Board* ☏ **+43 (1) 531 210**
General-Lending (DCM, SL)
Head of Corporate Banking   Alois Steinbichler *Member of the Management Board* ☏ **+43 (1) 531 210**

1668   Euromoney Directory 1999

www.euromoneydirectory.com UNITED KINGDOM (+44)

Debt Capital Markets / Fixed Income
Department: Treasury Securities
Tel: 417 4922 **Fax:** 417 4911 **Reuters:** CALA, CABV
Head of Fixed Income — John Seeley *Director* ☏ **417 4922** 🖷 **417 4911**
Head of Fixed Income Sales — Ken Baugh *Assistant Director* ☏ **417 4922** 🖷 **417 4911**
Head of Fixed Income Trading — Wayne Beckwith *Senior Manager* ☏ **417 4922**

Government Bonds
Head of Trading — John Seeley *Director* ☏ **417 4922** 🖷 **417 4911**
Konrad Schlatte *Senior Manager* ☏ **417 1005** 🖷 **417 4911**

Eurobonds
Head of Sales — Ken Baugh *Assistant Director* ☏ **417 4922** 🖷 **417 4911**
Head of Trading — Wayne Beckwith *Senior Manager* ☏ **417 4922**

Emerging Market Bonds
Head of Emerging Markets — John Seeley *Director* ☏ **417 4922** 🖷 **417 4911**
Head of Sales — Ken Baugh *Assistant Director* ☏ **417 4922** 🖷 **417 4911**
Head of Trading — Wayne Beckwith *Senior Manager* ☏ **417 4922**

Libor-Based / Floating-Rate Products
FRN Sales — Ken Baugh *Assistant Director* ☏ **417 4922** 🖷 **417 4911**
FRN Trading; Asset Swaps — Wayne Beckwith *Senior Manager* ☏ **417 4922**
Asset Swaps (Sales) — Ken Baugh *Assistant Director* ☏ **417 4922** 🖷 **417 4911**

Fixed-Income Repo
Head of Repo; Marketing & Product Development — John Seeley *Director* ☏ **417 4922** 🖷 **417 4911**
Trading — Wayne Beckwith *Senior Manager* ☏ **417 4922**

Fixed-Income Research
Head of Credit Research — Heinz Bednar *Head of Fixed Income Research* ☏ **+43 (1) 531 310**

Syndicated Lending
Department: Corporate Finance Division
Head of Origination — John Crocker *Deputy General Manager* ☏ **417 4860**
Head of Syndication — David Rimmer *Director* ☏ **417 1070**

Money Markets
Tel: 417 4912 **Fax:** 417 4911 **Reuters:** BAUL, BAUK **Telex:** 8812197
Head of Money Markets — David Cahill *Director*

Domestic Commercial Paper
Head of Sales — Andrew Linden *Deputy Manager* ☏ **417 4922**
Head of Trading — Stephanie Edghill *Manager*

Eurocommercial Paper
Head of Sales — Ken Baugh *Assistant Director* ☏ **417 4922** 🖷 **417 4911**
Head of Trading — Wayne Beckwith *Senior Manager* ☏ **417 4922**

Wholesale Deposits
Marketing; Head of Sales — Andrew Linden *Deputy Manager* ☏ **417 4922**

Foreign Exchange
Tel: 417 4912 **Fax:** 417 4911 **Reuters:** BAUL **Telex:** 8812197
Head of Foreign Exchange — Richard Kuras *Director* ☏ **417 1014**
Head of Trading — Robert Bird *Chief Dealer* ☏ **417 1027**

Risk Management
Tel: 417 4850 **Fax:** 417 4803
Head of Risk Management — Ted Hodgson *Deputy General Manager*

Fixed Income Derivatives / Risk Management
Head of Sales — Ken Baugh *Assistant Director* ☏ **417 4922** 🖷 **417 4911**
Trading — Ian Gladen *Assistant Director* ☏ **417 4922** 🖷 **417 4911**

Foreign Exchange Derivatives / Risk Management
Cross-Currency Swaps, Sales / Marketing — Konrad Schlatte *Senior Manager* ☏ **417 1005** 🖷 **417 4911**

Other (Exchange-Traded Derivatives)
Head of Swaps — Konrad Schlatte *Senior Manager* ☏ **417 1005** 🖷 **417 4911**

OTC Credit Derivatives
Head — Ian Gladen *Assistant Director* ☏ **417 4922** 🖷 **417 4911**

Exchange-Traded Derivatives
Head — John Seeley *Director* ☏ **417 4922** 🖷 **417 4911**

Corporate Finance / M&A Advisory
Head of Corporate Finance — Alois Steinbichler *Member of the Management Board* ☏ **+43 (1) 531 310**

Settlement / Clearing
Tel: 600 1555 **Fax:** 417 4803
Head of Settlement / Clearing — Lawrence Muggeridge *Director* ☏ **417 4830**
Fixed-Income Settlement; Operations — Adrian Beckett *Senior Manager* ☏ **417 4834**

UNITED KINGDOM (+44)   www.euromoneydirectory.com

Bank Austria Creditanstalt Group (cont)
Administration
Head of Administration   Nigel Burge *Director* ☎ **417 4820**
Technology & Systems
    Keith Rollason *Senior Manager* ☎ **417 4935**
    Nick Addison *Senior Manager* ☎ **417 4931**
Legal / In-House Counsel
    Peter Jones *Senior Counsel* ☎ **417 4890**
Compliance
    David Beale *Assistant Director* ☎ **417 4892**
Accounts / Audit
    Nigel Burge *Director* ☎ **417 4820**
    David Beale *Assistant Director* ☎ **417 4892**

Bank of Baroda   Full Branch Office

31/32 King Street, London EC2V 8EN
Tel: (171) 457 1515 **Fax:** (171) 600 1131 **Telex:** 884609 **Reuters:** BOBL

Senior Executive Officers
Chief Executive Officer   Narendra Mishra *Chief Executive, European Operations* ☎ **457 1520**
Deputy General Manager   Mangalsain Malhotra ☎ **457 1510**
Syndicated Lending
Head of Syndication   Ashok Gupta *Senior Manager, Credit* ☎ **457 1517**
Foreign Exchange
FX Traders / Sales People
    Prakash Shah *Dealer* ☎ **457 1548**
    S Pillai *Dealer* ☎ **457 1549**
Settlement / Clearing
Country Head   Ashok Bhatt ☎ **457 1544**
Other Departments
Private Banking   R K D Naik *Manager, Accounts* ☎ **457 1502**
Administration
Compliance
    R Ahuja *Manager* ☎ **457 1553**

Bank of Bermuda (Isle of Man) Limited   Offshore Banking Unit

12/13 Hill Street, Douglas, Isle of Man IM99 1BW
Tel: (1624) 637 777 **Fax:** (1624) 637 778; (1624) 637 779 **Telex:** 627168 TARPON G

Senior Executive Officers
Managing Director   A Smith
Settlement / Clearing
Operations   Oliver Webster *General Manager*
Administration
Accounts / Audit
Accounting   Lisa McGregor *Manager*
Other (Administration)
Private Clients   Howard Callow *General Manager*
Client Administration   June Watson *General Manager*

Bank of Bermuda Limited   Representative Office

3rd Floor, Austin Friars House, 2/6 Austin Friars, London EC2N 2LX
Tel: (171) 296 4000 **Fax:** (171) 296 4089
Website: www.bankofbermuda.com

Senior Executive Officers
General Manager   Leslie Ian Gabb
Others (Senior Executives)
Business Development   Graham D Richardson *Manager*

www.euromoneydirectory.com   UNITED KINGDOM (+44)

Bank Brussels Lambert   Full Branch Office
6 Broadgate, London EC2M 2AJ
Tel: (171) 247 5566 Fax: (171) 247 1277; (171) 247 1505 Telex: 884979 BBLUK G Swift: BBRU GB 2X Reuters: BBLL
Cable: Brudray London EC2
Foreign Exchange Tel: 651 5151; Corporate Banking Fax: 247 1504; Financial Institutions Fax: 562 0205

Senior Executive Officers
President   Michel Tilmant
Financial Director; Chief Operating Officer   Myron Dezyk *Senior Manager, Finance & Operations* ⊤ 392 5551
                                                              F 562 0201
Treasurer   Brian Shubrook *AGM & Treasurer* ⊤ 392 5511
General Manager   Michel Eertmans ⊤ 392 5501 F 392 5504

Others (Senior Executives)
                                                              Myron Dezyk *Senior Manager, Finance & Operations* ⊤ 392 5551
                                                              F 562 0201
                                                              Marie-Claire Swinnen *Senior Manager, Credit* ⊤ 392 5530 F 247 1277
General-Lending (DCM, SL)   Alun Michael *AGM, Financial Institutions* ⊤ 392 5510 F 562 0205
Head of Corporate Banking   Gerald Walker *Senior Manager* ⊤ 392 5527 F 562 0204

Relationship Manager
                                                              Ann Andrews *Manager, Institutional Banking Division* ⊤ 392 5512
                                                              F 562 0205
                                                              Jean-Marc Anciaux *Assistant Manager, Institutional Banking* ⊤ 392 5512
                                                              F 562 0205
                                                              Jonathan Bailey *Relationship Manger, Corporate Banking* ⊤ 392 5514
                                                              F 562 0204
                                                              Stephen Smith *Relationship Manger, Corporate Banking* ⊤ 392 5522
                                                              F 562 0204
                                                              Mark Wilton *Relationship Manger, Corporate Banking* ⊤ 392 5525
                                                              F 562 0204

Debt Capital Markets / Fixed Income
Tel: 247 3504 Fax: 392 5518
Country Head   Brian Shubrook *AGM & Treasurer* ⊤ 392 5511
Head of Fixed Income Trading   Darren Reece *Manager, Bond Dealing*
                                                              Desmond Chopping *Senior Dealer, Bond Desk*

Bonds - General
Investment   Kate Grant *Manager of Fixed-Income* ⊤ 247 3504 F 392 5518
                                                              Bruce Fraser *Manager, Structured Products* ⊤ 247 3504 F 392 5518

Fixed-Income Repo
Head of Repo   Alun Michael *AGM, Financial Institutions* ⊤ 392 5510 F 562 0205
Marketing & Product Development   Jean-Marc Anciaux *Assistant Manager, Institutional Banking* ⊤ 392 5512
                                                              F 562 0205
Head of Trading   Rob Hesketh *Head of Repo Desk* ⊤ 247 3008
Trading   Rob Ellis *Repo Dealer* ⊤ 247 3008
                                                              Nicola Levey *Senior Repo Dealer* ⊤ 247 3008

Syndicated Lending
Country Head   Gerald Walker *Senior Manager* ⊤ 392 5527 F 562 0204

Money Markets
Tel: 247 8877 Fax: 392 5518
Country Head   Brian Shubrook *AGM & Treasurer* ⊤ 392 5511
Other   Nick Glover *Manager, Money Markets & Derivatives*

Money Markets - General
Trading   Reg Smith *Manager, Money Market*
                                                              Steve Martin *Senior Dealer*
                                                              Daniel Armitage *Dealer*
Off Balance Sheet Trading   Wayne Blomfield *Manager*
                                                              Terry Brisley *Dealer*
Off Balance sheet Trading   Cedric Paumeis *Dealer*

Foreign Exchange
Tel: 247 8877 Fax: 392 5518
Country Head   Brian Shubrook *AGM & Treasurer* ⊤ 392 5511
Corporate Sales   Michael O'Loan *Chief Dealer*

FX Traders / Sales People
Spot FX   Mark Bolton *Manager*
                                                              Toby Archer *Dealer*
                                                              Sanjay Solanki *Dealer*

Euromoney Directory 1999   **1671**

UNITED KINGDOM (+44) www.euromoneydirectory.com

Bank Brussels Lambert (cont)
Risk Management
Country Head
Andrew Triggs *Manager, Treasury Control* T 392 5552 F 247 1277

Settlement / Clearing
Tel: 247 5566 **Fax:** 247 1277 **Telex:** 884979 BBLUK G
Country Head; Back-Office
Donald Chattaway T 392 5554 F 247 1277

Other Departments
Chief Credit Officer
Christopher Wright T 392 5533
Correspondent Banking
Ann Andrews *Manager, Institutional Banking Division* T 392 5512
F 562 0205
Cash Management
Gerald Walker *Senior Manager* T 392 5527 F 562 0204

Administration
Technology & Systems
David Cullen T 392 5553

Legal / In-House Counsel
Marie-Claire Swinnen *Senior Manager, Credit* T 392 5530 F 247 1277

Compliance
Fiona Cole T 392 5537

Accounts / Audit
Internal Audit
Fiona Cole T 392 5537
Philip Pinto *Financial Controller* T 392 5523

Other (Administration)
Banking Services
Donald Chattaway T 392 5554 F 247 1277

Bank Bumiputra Malaysia Berhad

14 Cavendish Square, London W1M 0HA
Tel: (171) 306 6050 **Fax:** (171) 306 6060 **Telex:** 290921 PUTRA G

Senior Executive Officers
Managing Director / General Manager
Abdul Karim Hassan

Bank of Ceylon   Full Branch Office

1 Devonshire Square, London EC2M 4UJ
Tel: (171) 377 1888 **Fax:** (171) 377 5430 **Telex:** 210071 **Swift:** BCEY GB 2L **Reuters:** BCEN
Settlement/Clearing **Telex:** 883587

Senior Executive Officers
Chief Executive Officer J F G De Silva *Country Manager* T 880 0121
Chief Operating Officer H M A B Weerasekeara *Deputy Manager* T 880 0122
Treasurer Tyrell Peiris *Chief Dealer* T 880 0123

Syndicated Lending
Loan-Related Activities
Trade Finance
S Anandagoda *OIC, Trade Finance* T 377 1888

Money Markets
Head of Money Markets
Tyrell Peiris *Chief Dealer* T 880 0123

Foreign Exchange
Head of Foreign Exchange
Tyrell Peiris *Chief Dealer* T 880 0123

Settlement / Clearing
Regional Head
Sayi Punchihewa *OIC, Back Office*

Other Departments
Chief Credit Officer
D M Gunasekera *Relationship Manager* T 377 1888

Administration
Tel: 377 1888
Head of Administration
A Perera *Administrative Officer*

Technology & Systems
I Navaratnam *IT Manager*

Accounts / Audit
A Chauan *MIS Audit Officer*

www.euromoneydirectory.com UNITED KINGDOM (+44)

Bank of China
90 Cannon Street, London EC4N 6HA
Tel: (171) 282 8888 **Fax:** (171) 626 3892 **Telex:** 8812913 **Swift:** BKCH GB 2LA **Reuters:** BCLN
Cable: CHUNGKUO LONDON

Senior Executive Officers
General Manager   B L Zheng

Bank of China International (UK) Limited
Subsidiary Company

34th Floor, One Canada Square, Canary Wharf, London E14 5AA
Tel: (171) 661 8888; (171) 661 8877

Senior Executive Officers
Chairman   Jesse Wang ☏ **661 8889**

Debt Capital Markets / Fixed Income
Regional Head   Duncan Haswell *Director Head of Capital Markets* ☏ **661 8816**

Eurobonds
Head of Sales   Jeremy Robson ☏ **661 8819**
Ikuyo Mitsuzono ☏ **661 8821**
Head of Trading   William Chen ☏ **661 8818**
Ian Willcox ☏ **661 8823**

Equity Capital Markets
Regional Head   Amanda Mackinnon *Head of China Equity* ☏ **661 8817**

Domestic Equities
Head of Sales   Anne Depaulis ☏ **661 8822**

Other (Domestic Equities)
Equity Analyst   Mark Wang ☏ **661 8853**

Syndicated Lending

Other (Trade Finance)
Structured Finance   Freddie Fisher ☏ **661 8849**

Corporate Finance / M&A Advisory
Regional Head   Stephen Speak ☏ **661 8882**

Settlement / Clearing
Country Head   Stuart Clay ☏ **661 8873**
Equity Settlement; Fixed-Income Settlement   Ellis Juddah ☏ **661 8864**

Bank of Communications
Representative Office

8th Floor, Royex House, Aldermanbury Square, London EC2V 7HR
Tel: (171) 606 1808 **Fax:** (171) 606 2362

Senior Executive Officers
Chief Representative   Hu Rongbin
Representative   Yuan Yuping

Bank of Crete
Representative Office

2nd Floor, 60 Moorgate, London EC2R 6EL
Tel: (171) 256 7971 **Fax:** (171) 920 9384 **Telex:** 945852 BOFKLN

Senior Executive Officers
Chief Representative   A N Strouthos

The Bank of East Asia Limited
Full Branch Office

75 Shaftesbury Avenue, London W1V 8BB
Tel: (171) 734 3434 **Fax:** (171) 734 0523

Senior Executive Officers
General Manager   Joseph Chow York-wai

UNITED KINGDOM (+44)   www.euromoneydirectory.com

Bank Ekspor Impor Indonesia (PERSERO)

Senator House, 85 Queen Victoria Street, London EC4V 4JN
Tel: (171) 329 4424; (171) 329 4486 Fax: (171) 329 4345

Senior Executive Officers
Treasurer   Edwin J Cooper
General Manager   Mr Akmaliudin

The Bank of Fukuoka Limited

Level 6, Royal Bank of Canada Centre, 71 Queen Victoria Street, London EC4V 4JP
Tel: (171) 236 2288 Fax: (171) 236 8604 Telex: 893817 FUKUBL G

Senior Executive Officers
General Manager   M Kan

Bank Handlowy w Warszawie SA   Full Branch Office

16 Eastcheap, London EC3M 1BD
Tel: (171) 369 1150 Fax: (171) 369 1191 Telex: 290694 Swift: BHWA GB 2L Reuters: BHLN
Bloomberg: SN708774-0 I378-477-0
Website: www.bhw.co.uk

Senior Executive Officers
Director & General Manager   Andrzej Ossowski
Others (Senior Executives)
                                Stephen Harding *Assistant General Manager*

Debt Capital Markets / Fixed Income
Eurobonds
Head of Trading   Andrezej Lipinski *Manager, Trade Finance & Capital Markets*
Emerging Market Bonds
Head of Trading   Andrezej Lipinski *Manager, Trade Finance & Capital Markets*
Libor-Based / Floating-Rate Products
FRN Trading   Andrezej Lipinski *Manager, Trade Finance & Capital Markets*
Syndicated Lending
Head of Trading   Andrezej Lipinski *Manager, Trade Finance & Capital Markets*
Loan-Related Activities
Trade Finance   Andrezej Lipinski *Manager, Trade Finance & Capital Markets*
Money Markets
Head of Money Markets   David Young *Chief Dealer*
Foreign Exchange
Head of Foreign Exchange   David Young *Chief Dealer*
Settlement / Clearing
Country Head   Colin Hicks *Operations Manager* ☏ 369 1150
Back-Office   Richard Harris *Operations Manager*
Administration
Head of Administration   Bozena Krahn *Personnel & Admin Manager*
Accounts / Audit
Chief Accountant   David Hardcastle

Bank Hapoalim BM   Full Branch Office

8/12 Brook Street, London W1Y 1AA
Tel: (171) 872 9912 Fax: (171) 872 9924 Telex: 886805 Swift: POAL GB 2L Reuters: HAPY

Senior Executive Officers
Treasurer   David Humphreys *Chief Dealer* ☏ 872 9913
General Manager   Moshe Tsafrir
Syndicated Lending
Country Head   Judy Miara *Credit Manager*
Money Markets
Country Head   David Humphreys *Chief Dealer* ☏ 872 9913
Foreign Exchange
Regional Head   David Humphreys *Chief Dealer* ☏ 872 9913

1674   Euromoney Directory 1999

www.euromoneydirectory.com UNITED KINGDOM (+44)

Bank of India
Park House, 16 Finsbury Circus, London EC2M 7DJ
Tel: (171) 628 3165 Fax: (171) 588 8177; (171) 638 3560 Telex: 262117 Swift: BKID GB 2L Reuters: BILN
Senior Executive Officers
Chief Executive Officer   A I Shaikh
Managing Director   M Venugopalan

Bank Indonesia
Representative Office

10 City Road, London EC1Y 2EH
Tel: (171) 638 9043 Fax: (171) 374 2051 Telex: 888808
Senior Executive Officers
General Manager   Manan Somantri

Bank of Ireland Asset Management (UK) Limited
36 Queen Street, London EC4R 1HJ
Tel: (171) 489 8673 Fax: (171) 489 9676; (171) 248 0799
Website: www.biam.ie

Senior Executive Officers
Chief Executive Officer   William R Cotter Director T +353 (1) 661 6433 F +353 (1) 661 6869
Chief Operating Officer   Denis Donovan Director T +353 (1) 661 6433 F +353 (1) 678 5342
Treasurer   Brendan Spicer
Managing Director   Francis Ellison

The Bank of Japan
Representative Office

Basildon House, 7/11 Moorgate, London EC2R 6AD
Tel: (171) 606 2454 Fax: (171) 726 4819
Senior Executive Officers
Chief Representative   Shinichi Yoshikuni

Bank Julius Baer & Co Limited
Full Branch Office

Bevis Marks House, Bevis Marks, London EC3A 7NE
Tel: (171) 623 4211 Fax: (171) 283 6146

Senior Executive Officers
Senior Vice President, Branch Manager   Frank Canosa

Others (Senior Executives)
Head of Trading   Henry Wilkes
Head of Resources   Stefan Betschart *Senior Vice President, Resources*
Head of Credit   John Grist *First Vice President, Credit*

Debt Capital Markets / Fixed Income
Regional Head   Tim Sharp *Vice President, Fixed Income*

Domestic Government Bonds
Head of Sales   Tim Sharp *Vice President, Fixed Income*

Non-Domestic Government Bonds
   Tim Sharp *Vice President, Fixed Income*

Eurobonds
Head of Syndication   Tim Sharp *Vice President, Fixed Income*

Equity Capital Markets
Regional Head   Christian Simmond *Assistant Vice President, UK Equities*

Domestic Equities
Head of Research   Mark Gardner *Assistant Vice President, UK Equities*

Other (International Equity)
Swiss Equities   Marco Bacchetta *Vice President*
Emerging Markets Finds   James Hart
German Equities   Jackie Newbury

Convertibles / Equity-Linked
Head of Origination; Head of Syndication; Head   Tim Sharp *Vice President, Fixed Income*
of Sales; Head of Trading; Head of Research

UNITED KINGDOM (+44)   www.euromoneydirectory.com

Bank Julius Baer & Co Limited (cont)

Syndicated Lending
Loan-Related Activities
Trade Finance — Tim Pereira *First Vice President, Credit*

Money Markets
Regional Head — Helen Nickless *Assistant Vice President*

Foreign Exchange
Regional Head — Mark Taylor *First Vice President, Forex-Treasury*

Settlement / Clearing
Regional Head — Stefan Betschart *Senior Vice President, Resources*

Other Departments
Private Banking — Frank Canosa *Senior Vice President, Branch Manager*
Correspondent Banking — Mike Galer *Vice President*

Administration
Technology & Systems
 — Graham Emre *Vice President*

Compliance
 — Richard McGrand *Vice President*

Other (Administration)
Business Development &Marketing — Julian Yorke *Vice President*

The Bank of Korea — Representative Office

1 Minister Court, Mincing Lane, London EC3R 7AA
Tel: (171) 626 8321 **Fax:** (171) 626 7201 **Telex:** 883285 **Email:** boklondn@dircon.co.uk

Senior Executive Officers
Chief Representative — Chang Ho Choi

The Bank of Kyoto Limited — Representative Office

7th Floor, 62 Cornhill, London EC3V 3NH
Tel: (171) 626 6897 **Fax:** (171) 626 1079 **Telex:** 933044 BOK LON

Senior Executive Officers
Chief Representative — T Mukunoki
Deputy Chief Representative — H Arata

Bank Leumi (UK) plc — Head Office

4/7 Woodstock Street, London W1A 2AF
Tel: (171) 629 1205 **Fax:** (171) 493 1426 **Telex:** 888738 **Swift:** LUMI GB 22 WES

Senior Executive Officers
Chairman — Eitan Raff
Chief Executive Officer — Uri Galili *Director & General Manager*

Others (Senior Executives)
Deputy General Manager — Maurice Shear *Treasurer*

Debt Capital Markets / Fixed Income
Bonds - General
Treasury — Adele Abdoo *Senior Dealer*

Syndicated Lending
Other (Syndicated Lending)
 — Maurice Shear *Treasurer*

Loan-Related Activities
Trade Finance — Cyril Eden *Manager, Documentary Credits*

Foreign Exchange
Head of Trading — Perry Asforis *Chief Dealer*
FX Traders / Sales People
 — Martin Leslie *Senior Dealer*

Risk Management
Global Head — Leah Excell *Senior Dealer*

Settlement / Clearing
Regional Head — Barbara Chapman *Manager, Banking Operations*
Operations — Lesley Secretan *Senior AGM, Finance*

www.euromoneydirectory.com UNITED KINGDOM (+44)

Global Custody
Regional Head Barbara Chapman *Manager, Banking Operations*
Other Departments
Commodities / Bullion Malcom Bloom *Senior Account Manager*
Administration
Technology & Systems
  Nigel Brigden *Manager, Operations*
Compliance
  Brian Manton *Assistant General Manager*

Bank Mellat
Full Branch Office

48 Gresham Street, London EC2V 7AX
Tel: (171) 606 8521 **Fax:** (171) 606 2020 **Swift:** BKMT GB 2L

Senior Executive Officers
General Manager Samad Tarassoli
Others (Senior Executives)
  Faramarz Azami *Assistant General Manager*
  Mohammad Ali Nasrollahi *Assistant General Manager*
Administration
Head of Administration Bahram Taleghani *Administrator*
Legal / In-House Counsel
  Bahram Taleghani *Administrator*
Compliance
  Bahram Taleghani *Administrator*
Public Relations
  Bahram Taleghani *Administrator*

Bank Melli Iran

4 Moorgate, London EC2R 6AL
Tel: (171) 600 3636 **Fax:** (171) 796 2104 **Telex:** 883313/5

Senior Executive Officers
General Manager A Sadeghifar

Bank of Montreal
Full Branch Office

11 Walbrook, London EC4N 8ED
Tel: (171) 236 1010 **Fax:** (171) 236 2821 **Telex:** 889068 **Swift:** BOFM GB 2X
Reuters: BOMM (Money Markets); BOML (FX)

Senior Executive Officers
SVP & General Manager Bev Blucher
Treasurer John Keogh *MD, International Capital Markets*
Syndicated Lending
Head of Syndication Jennifer Richards *Director*
Money Markets
Reuters: BOMM
Country Head A J McClinton *Head, International Money Markets*
Foreign Exchange
Reuters: BOML
Country Head Jason Lawrence *Director & Head, Foreign Exchange*
Risk Management
Head of Risk Management Richard Colwell *European Risk Manager*
OTC Credit Derivatives
Global Head Rod Jones *MD, Global Financial Products*
Administration
Compliance
  John Tubby *Director, Legal & Compliance*

UNITED KINGDOM (+44) www.euromoneydirectory.com

PT Bank Negara Indonesia (Persero) TBK
Full Branch Office

Alternative trading name: Bank BNI

105-108 Old Broad Street, London EC2N 1AP
Tel: (171) 638 4070 **Fax:** (171) 256 9945

Senior Executive Officers
General Manager — Ris Rizqullah

Debt Capital Markets / Fixed Income
Department: Credit & Marketing
Country Head — Patrick Willis *Deputy General Manager* 448 8402

Domestic Government Bonds
Head of Trading — Henry Smith *Chief Dealer* 448 8406

Non-Domestic Government Bonds — Henry Smith *Chief Dealer* 448 8406

Eurobonds
Head of Origination; Head of Syndication; Head of Sales; Head of Trading — Henry Smith *Chief Dealer* 448 8406

Syndicated Lending
Country Head of Origination; Head of Syndication; Head of Trading; Recovery; Head of Credit Committee — Patrick Willis *Deputy General Manager* 448 8402

Loan-Related Activities
Trade Finance — Andrew Mills *Manager* 448 8404
Project Finance — Patrick Willis *Deputy General Manager* 448 8402

Money Markets
Country Head — Henry Smith *Chief Dealer* 448 8406

Domestic Commercial Paper
Head of Origination; Head of Sales; Head of Trading — Henry Smith *Chief Dealer* 448 8406

Eurocommercial Paper
Head of Origination; Head of Sales; Head of Trading — Henry Smith *Chief Dealer* 448 8406

Wholesale Deposits
Marketing; Head of Sales — Henry Smith *Chief Dealer* 448 8406

Foreign Exchange
Country Head of Institutional Sales; Corporate Sales — Henry Smith *Chief Dealer* 448 8406

Risk Management
Country Head — Patrick Willis *Deputy General Manager* 448 8402

Foreign Exchange Derivatives / Risk Management
Cross-Currency Swaps, Sales / Marketing; Cross-Currency Swaps, Trading; Vanilla FX option Sales; Vanilla FX option Trading — Henry Smith *Chief Dealer* 448 8406

Corporate Finance / M&A Advisory
Country Head — Patrick Willis *Deputy General Manager* 448 8402

Settlement / Clearing
Fax: 256 9945
Foreign Exchange Settlement — Swee Yeoh *Supervisor*

Other Departments
Correspondent Banking — Pieter Siadari *Correspondent Bank Relationship Manager* 448 8409

Bank Negara Malaysia
Representative Office

Berkeley Square House, Berkeley Square, London W1X 5LA
Tel: (171) 495 0222 **Fax:** (171) 495 6198

Senior Executive Officers
Chief Representative — Razak Yusoff

www.euromoneydirectory.com UNITED KINGDOM (+44)

The Bank of New York
Full Branch Office
46 Berkeley Street, London W1X 6AA
Tel: (171) 322 6111 **Fax:** (171) 322 6037 **Telex:** 883265 IRBTALG **Swift:** IRV US 3N **Email:** pdasilva@bankofny.com
Website: www.bankofny.com

Senior Executive Officers
Chairman	Carter Bacot
President	Tomas Renyi
Chief Executive Officer	Tomas Renyi
Financial Director	Vansaun
Treasurer	Robert Jacques *Vice President*
Managing Director	Clive Gande [T] 322 7211 [F] 322 6041 [E] cgande@bankofny.com
Managing Director	Fabian Sweeney
Managing Director	Mark Keras
General Manager	Curtis Yamaoka

Others (Senior Executives)

Jeffrey Tessler *Executive Vice President* [T] +1 (212) 322 6126 [F] +1 (212) 322 6014 [E] jtessler@bankofny.com

General-Lending (DCM, SL)
Head of Corporate Banking — Richard E Wallin *Vice President*

Relationship Manager
Securities Processing — Clive Gande *Managing Director* [T] 322 7211 [F] 322 6041 [E] cgande@bankofny.com

Debt Capital Markets / Fixed Income
Fixed-Income Repo
Marketing & Product Development — Andrew Gordon *Vice President* [T] 322 7254 [F] 322 6093 [E] agardon@bankofny.com
Trading — Chip Davy *VP & Head of Trading*

Equity Capital Markets
Tel: 322 6111 **Fax:** 322 6037
Country Head — Violetta Ozel *Vice President, Capital Markets*

Equity Repo / Securities Lending
Head; Marketing & Product Development — Andrew Gordon *Vice President* [T] 322 7254 [F] 322 6093 [E] agardon@bankofny.com

Syndicated Lending
Country Head — Paul Rivers
Head of Credit Committee — John Johnston *Vice President, Credit Administration*

Money Markets
Country Head — Robert Jacques *Vice President*

Foreign Exchange
Country Head — Robert Jacques *Vice President*
Head of Institutional Sales; Corporate Sales — Simon Derrick *Vice President & Head of Sales*
Head of Trading — Richard Gill *Vice President, Head of Spot Desk*
Mark Nash *Vice President, Head, Multi-Currency Interest Rate*

FX Traders / Sales People
Kevin Bailey *Managing Director*
Gary Vocat *Managing Director, Currency Overlay*

Risk Management
Foreign Exchange Derivatives / Risk Management
Country Head — Ross McDonald *Vice President, Head of Currency Options Trading*

Settlement / Clearing
Country Head — Sabian Sweeney
Foreign Exchange Settlement; Operations — Robert Keate *Assistant Vice President, Back Office Settlements*

Global Custody
Other (Global Custody)
Master Custody — Michael Smith *Vice President*

Other Departments
Private Banking — Christopher Isles *Vice President*

Administration
Compliance
Accounting & Compliance — Raymond Cullen *Vice President*

Corporate Communications
Media & Communications — Philip Walker *Vice President*

UNITED KINGDOM (+44)   www.euromoneydirectory.com

The Bank of Nova Scotia
Full Branch Office

Alternative trading name: Scotia Capital Markets
Scotia House, 33 Finsbury Square, London EC2A 1BB
Tel: (171) 638 5644; (171) 826 5866 **Fax:** (171) 638 8488 **Telex:** 885188 **Swift:** NOSC GB 22

Senior Executive Officers

Others (Senior Executives)
European Operations
Scotiabank (UK) Ltd.

K R Ray *Managing Head*
R A Ellis *Managing Director*

General-Lending (DCM, SL)
Head of Corporate Banking

K C Clark *Unit Head*
R L Harrington *Unit Head*
J R Heeds *Unit Head*
G P Ferris

General-Investment
Head of Investment

Larry Scott *Managing Head, ScotiaMcLeod*

Debt Capital Markets / Fixed Income
Fax: 826 5866
Head of Fixed Income

Ron Brandman ☎ **826 5804**

Government Bonds
Head of Syndication

James Ashwanden ☎ **826 5906**

Equity Capital Markets
Head of Equity Capital Markets

Stuart Hensman *Managing Director* ☎ **826 5915**

Foreign Exchange
Corporate Sales
Head of Trading

Kevin Fitzgerald *Managing Director* ☎ **678 0941**
John Nicholson *Managing Director* ☎ **826 5601**

Risk Management

Fixed Income Derivatives / Risk Management
Head of Sales
Trading

Guy Huntrods *Director* ☎ **826 5838**
Peter Burge *Managing Director* ☎ **826 5838**

Bank Saderat Iran
Full Branch Office

5 Lothbury, London EC2R 7HD
Tel: (171) 606 0951 **Fax:** (171) 796 3216 **Telex:** 883382 **Swift:** BSIR GB 2L **Reuters:** SADL

Senior Executive Officers
General Manager

Shahrokh Iranzad

Debt Capital Markets / Fixed Income
Department: Treasury
Tel: 606 2355 **Telex:** 886911

Eurobonds
Head of Trading

Roy Allen *Treasury Manager*

Emerging Market Bonds
Head of Trading

Roy Allen *Treasury Manager*

Libor-Based / Floating-Rate Products
FRN Trading

Roy Allen *Treasury Manager*

Syndicated Lending

Loan-Related Activities
Trade Finance

Roy Allen *Treasury Manager*

Foreign Exchange
Tel: 606 2355 **Telex:** 886911
Head of Foreign Exchange
Head of Trading

Roy Allen *Treasury Manager*
Roy Allen *Treasury Manager*

FX Traders / Sales People
Senior Dealer
Dealer

Michael Hart
Michael Godier

Settlement / Clearing
Operations

Kirsty McDermott *FX Instruction Clerk*

Other Departments
Correspondent Banking; Cash Management

Martin Bradford *Cash Supervisor*

Administration
Head of Administration   Connie Beatts
Technology & Systems
    Amir Soheylee *Computer Supervisor*
Compliance
    Martin Bradford *Cash Supervisor*
Public Relations
    Connie Beatts
Accounts / Audit
Accounts   Farkhonde Ala

Bank of Scotland   Head Office

Orchard Brae House, 30 Queensferry Road, Edinburgh, EH4 2UG
Tel: (131) 442 7777 **Fax:** (131) 343 7080 **Telex:** 72407 BOSOIL G **Swift:** BOFS GB 2S **Cable:** BOSOIL EDINBURGH

Senior Executive Officers
General Manager   Colin McGill
International Division   James Malcolm *Head of International Banking* ☎ **343 7004**

Others (Senior Executives)
    Ernie Brown *Head, Project Finance Australia / Asia* ☎ **343 7005**
    Bill Hendry *EVP, North America*

Syndicated Lending
Country Head   Colin McGill *General Manager*

Other (Syndicated Lending)
Corporate Division   Colin Leslie *General Manager* ☎ **243 3564**

Other Departments
Correspondent Banking   Neil Anderson *Senior Manager* ☎ **601 6945**

Administration
Technology & Systems
    Chris Brobbel *General Manager* ☎ **442 7711**

Legal / In-House Counsel
    Alistair Loudon *Assistant General Manager* ☎ **221 5102**

Compliance
    Bill Mutch *Group Compliance Officer* ☎ **243 5452**

Public Relations
    Iain Fiddes *Director, Public Relations* ☎ **243 7053**

Bank of Scotland   Subsidiary Company

International Division, 120 St Vincent Street, Glasgow, G2 5DZ
Tel: (141) 221 7071 **Fax:** (141) 228 4106 **Telex:** 778726 UBIFOR G **Swift:** BOFS GB 2S

Senior Executive Officers
Head of International Services   Mike Todd ☎ **228 4153**

Bank of Scotland   Full Branch Office

PO Box 30, Broad Street House, 55 Old Broad Street, London EC2P 2HL
Tel: (171) 601 6875 **Fax:** (171) 601 6716 **Telex:** 887882 UBIFOR G **Swift:** BOFS GB 2L

Senior Executive Officers
Senior Manager   Neil Anderson

Bank Sepah   Full Branch Office

5/7 Eastcheap, London EC3M 1JT
Tel: (171) 623 1371 **Fax:** (171) 623 1221 **Telex:** 885343

Senior Executive Officers
General Manager   A Emadi Allahyari

Others (Senior Executives)
    M Homayouni *Assistant General Manager*

UNITED KINGDOM (+44) www.euromoneydirectory.com

Bank of Taiwan
Representative Office

Evergreen House, 160 Euston Road, London NW1 2DT
Tel: (171) 388 3800 Fax: (171) 388 0338

Senior Executive Officers
Chief Representative   Ke Hua

Bank Tejarat

6/8 Clements Lane, London EC4N 7AP
Tel: (171) 929 4048 Fax: (171) 726 4340 Telex: 884747

Senior Executive Officers
General Manager   Mr Asgharzadeh

Bank of Thailand
Representative Office

8th Floor, 1 Angel Court Tower, London EC2R 7HJ
Tel: (171) 606 1716 Fax: (171) 606 2506 Email: bankofthailand@btinternet.com
Bloomberg: bothaild@bloomberg.net

Senior Executive Officers
Chief Representative   Bhimolban Bavovada

The Bank of Tokyo-Mitsubishi Limited

Finsbury Circus House, 12/15 Finsbury Circus, London EC2M 7BT
Tel: (171) 588 1111 Fax: (171) 628 8241 Telex: 884811 Swift: BOTK GB 2L Reuters: TMAL
Cable: TOHBANK LONDON E

Senior Executive Officers
Resident Managing Director   M Yamada
Director & General Manager, London Branch   K Wakabayashi

Others (Senior Executives)
European Planning Division   S Yamada *General Manager*

General-Investment
Head of Investment   T Imanishi *GM, European Investment Banking Division*
     R Mimura *SDGM, European Investment Banking Division*
     T Yamauchi *DGM, European Investment Banking Division*
     E Lianos *DGM, European Investment Banking Division*

Syndicated Lending
Head of Syndicated Lending   J Reffell

Loan-Related Activities
Structured Trade Finance   P Remington

Other (Trade Finance)
Aviation & Leasing   H Itakura *Head*

Corporate Finance / M&A Advisory
Head of Corporate Finance   K Yoshii *Head, Corporate Advisory*
Head of Mergers & Acquisition   R Holliday *Head*

Bank von Ernst & Co Limited
Full Branch Office

1 Devonshire Square, London EC2M 4UJ
Tel: (171) 377 0404 Fax: (171) 247 1171

The Bank of Yokohama Limited

40 Basinghall Street, London EC2V 5DE
Tel: (171) 628 9973 Fax: (171) 638 1886 Telex: 887995 Reuters: BOYL Cable: HAMAGIN LDN

Senior Executive Officers
General Manager   Miyabi Tagoshima
Joint General Manager   Kunio Yoshimizu

Others (Senior Executives)
     Alan Bass *Deputy General Manager*
     Atsushi Mochizuki *Deputy General Manager*

Others (Senior Executives) (cont)

Kazuo Yoshida *Deputy General Manager*
Tomoyuki Takahashi *Deputy General Manager*
Jeffrey F Gray *Manager*
Yasutaka Nozawa *Manager*
Ken Isogai *Manager*
Chizuko Hirai *Manager*
Graham Moore *Manager*

Administration
Compliance

John Pattison *Compliance Officer*

BankAmerica

Full Branch Office

Formerly known as: Bank of America

Bank of America House, London E1 8DE
PO Box 407, 1 Alie Street, London E1 8DE
Tel: (171) 634 4000 **Fax:** (171) 634 4307 **Telex:** 884372 **Reuters:** BACL; BOAL; BAML
Website: www.bankamerica.com

Senior Executive Officers
Chief Executive Officer — P Gerald Doherty ☎ **634 4600**
Financial Director — Geoff Leach ☎ **(181) 333 2865**
Chief Operating Officer; Treasurer — Gordon Sangster ☎ **634 4312**
Company Secretary — Geoff Leach ☎ **(181) 333 2865**

Relationship Manager
Head of Emerging Markets — Ralph Schauss ☎ **634 4897**

Debt Capital Markets / Fixed Income
Head of Fixed Income Sales; Head of Fixed Income Trading — Dave Blatchford ☎ **634 4966**

Government Bonds
Head of Sales; Head of Trading; Head of Syndication; Head of Origination — Claudio Zampa ☎ **634 4435**

Eurobonds
Head of Sales — Len Harwood ☎ **634 4497**
Head of Trading — Jim Summers ☎ **634 4497**

Emerging Market Bonds
Head of Sales — Alex Mcleod ☎ **634 4994**

Libor-Based / Floating-Rate Products
FRN Sales — Nick Reynoldson ☎ **634 4256**
FRN Trading — Conor Dufficy ☎ **634 4300**
Asset Swaps — Tom Binks ☎ **634 4294**
Asset Swaps (Sales) — Tom Binks ☎ **634 4294**

Fixed-Income Repo
Head of Repo — Fabrizio Teota
Head of Trading — Claudio Zampa ☎ **634 4435**

Fixed-Income Research
Head of Fixed Income — Lorenzo Codogno
Head of Credit Research — Richard Gray ☎ **634 4810**

Syndicated Lending
Loan-Related Activities
Trade Finance — Harry Palumbo ☎ **634 4595**
Project Finance — Kit Beer ☎ **634 4517**

Foreign Exchange
Head of Foreign Exchange — Conor Dufficy ☎ **634 4300**
Corporate Sales — Nick Reynoldson ☎ **634 4256**
Head of Trading — Conor Dufficy ☎ **634 4300**

Risk Management
Head of Risk Management — Tom Binks ☎ **634 4294**

Other Departments
Cash Management — Alan Verschoyle-King ☎ **(181) 333 2997**

Administration
Head of Marketing — John Weguelin ☎ **634 4936**

Public Relations
Susan Grice ☎ **634 4770**

UNITED KINGDOM (+44)   www.euromoneydirectory.com

BankBoston
Full Branch Office

Formerly known as: Bank of Boston
Bank Boston House, 39 Victoria Street, Westminister, London SW1H OED
PO Box 155
Tel: (171) 799 3333 **Fax:** (171) 222 5649; (171) 932 9110 **Telex:** 886705 **Cable:** BOSTONBANK LDN 3
Website: www.bankboston.com

Senior Executive Officers
Chairman — Charles Gifford
Chief Executive Officer — Henrique Meirelles
Susannah Swihart
Managing Director — Mark Evens ☎ 932 9264 📠 932 9110

General-Lending (DCM, SL)
Head of Corporate Banking — Paul Hogan *Vice Chairman*

General-Investment
Head of Investment — Mike McCaffry

Debt Capital Markets / Fixed Income
Head of Fixed Income Sales — Ian Hocking *Head of Sales and Trading*

Bankers Trust International plc
Head Office

Alternative trading name: Bankers Trust Company
1 Appold Street, Broadgate, London EC2A 2HE
Tel: (171) 982 2500
Foreign Exchange Fax: 651 5151
Website: www.bankerstrust.com

Senior Executive Officers
Managing Director — Randl L Shure ☎ 982 5758 📠 422 0974 ✉ randl.shure@bankerstrust.com

Others (Senior Executives)
Bankers Trust International plc — Brian Cook *President & COO*
Yves de Balmann *Chairman*
Philippe Souviron *Vice Chairman*
Bankers Trust Company — Brian Cook *General Manager*
Department: Finance

Others (Senior Executives)
Financial Institutions Structured Debt — Gopal Menon *MD, Debt Sales & Trading*
Value Impaired Assets — Martin Dent *Managing Director*
Structured Finance — Graham Clempson *Managing Director*
Department: Investment Banking

Others (Senior Executives)
Investment Banking Group — Philippe Souviron *Managing Director*
Yves de Balmann *Managing Director*

Relationship Manager
Real Estate — Richard Mully *Managing Director*
Media & Telecommunications — Carl Tack *Managing Director*
Transaction Development Group — Sekhar Bahadur *Managing Director*
Origination — Steve Ferriss *Managing Director*
France — Bernard Attali *Managing Director*
Italy — Alberto Guazzi *Managing Director*
Scandinavia — Kristian Bagger *Managing Director*
Spain — Julio Garcia *Managing Director*
Middle East — Richard Jackson *Managing Director*
UK & Ireland — Bruce Macfarlane *Managing Director*
Department: Investment Management

Others (Senior Executives)
European Investment Management — Paul O'Donnel *Managing Director*
Private Bank, Europe & Middle East — Katherine Murphy-McClintic *Managing Director*
Department: European Credit

Others (Senior Executives)
Risk Management Services — David Coleman *Managing Director*
Finance — Mike Shraga *Managing Director*
Department: BT Alex.Brown

Others (Senior Executives)
John Fordham *Managing Director*

www.euromoneydirectory.com   UNITED KINGDOM (+44)

Department: Client Processing Services
Others (Senior Executives)
Global Institutional Services   Dick Feehan *Managing Director*

Debt Capital Markets / Fixed Income
Tel: 982 3892 Fax: 982 1178
Country Head   Gopal Menon *Managing Director*

Fixed-Income Repo
Trading   Sarah Ostroff
                                       Desiree Spence
                                       Edward Donald

Equity Capital Markets
Global Head   Andej Rojek *Managing Director*

Convertibles / Equity-Linked
Head of Origination   David Freizo *Managing Director*

Department: Global Securities Finance
135 Bishopsgate, London, EC2M 3XT

Equity Repo / Securities Lending
Head   John Wills *Managing Director* ☎ 885 3244 📠 885 3247
                                       ✉ john.wills@bankerstrust.com
Marketing & Product Development   Paul Hamill *Director* ☎ 885 3240 📠 885 3247
                                       ✉ paul.hamill@bankerstrust.com
                                       Philip Endacott *Associate* ☎ 885 3241 📠 885 3247
                                       ✉ philip.endacott@bankerstrust.com
Head of Trading   Jason Kennard *Trading - Europe* ☎ 885 3220
                                       Richard Pryce *Trading - Europe* ☎ 885 3220
                                       Rachel Crowther *Trading - Europe* ☎ 885 3220
                                       Nicola Barrett *Trading - Europe* ☎ 885 3220
                                       Andy Paul *Trading - Asia* ☎ 885 3230
                                       Brian Canniffe *Trading - Asia* ☎ 885 3230
                                       Emma Walpole *Trading - Asia* ☎ 885 3230

Syndicated Lending
Other (Trade Finance)
                                       Nick Harrison *MD, Corp Operating Services & Real Estate*

Foreign Exchange
Global Head   Achilles Macris *MD & Head, Global FX*

FX Traders / Sales People
FX Forwards   Maria Philpott *Managing Director*
FX Sales   Sandra Crowl *Vice President*
Treasury Funding   Matthew Hale *Managing Director*

Risk Management
Global Head   Alex Frick *MD & Global Head, Risk Mgt Services*
Country Head   Marc Lopresto *MD, Risk Management Advisory*

Fixed Income Derivatives / Risk Management
IR Options Trading   Eric Bommensath *Managing Director*

Foreign Exchange Derivatives / Risk Management
Spot / Forwards Trading   Maria Philpott *Managing Director*

Other Currency Swap / FX Options Personnel
Derivative Products   Eric Bommensath *Managing Director*

OTC Equity Derivatives
Head   Andej Rojek *Managing Director*

Other (Exchange-Traded Derivatives)
European Derivatives Marketing   Stephen Harper *Managing Director*

Exchange-Traded Derivatives
FX Options   Eric Bommensath *Managing Director*

Corporate Finance / M&A Advisory
Department: BT Wolfensohn
Global Head   Donald Johnston *Managing Director, M&A*

Settlement / Clearing
Operations   Nick Harrison *MD, Corp Operating Services & Real Estate*
                                       Andrew Graham *Managing Director & Controller*

Administration
Legal / In-House Counsel
                                       Simon Dodds *Managing Director*

Compliance
                                       Alan Greatbatch *Managing Director*

UNITED KINGDOM (+44)   www.euromoneydirectory.com

Bankers Trust International plc (cont)
Corporate Communications
Suzanne Quigley *Vice President*

Accounts / Audit
Credit Audit — Mark Thompson *Vice President*
Audit — Boyd Cuthbertson *Managing Director*

Other (Administration)
Human Resources — Stephen Jefford *Managing Director*
Senior Admin. Office, Europe / Middle East, Africa — Brian Cook *Managing Director*
Tax — Steve Cross *Managing Director*

Bankgesellschaft Berlin   Subsidiary Company
1 Crown Court, Cheapside, London EC3V 6LR
Tel: (171) 572 6200 **Fax:** (171) 572 6299 **Telex:** 922018 **Swift:** BEBE GB 2 GA **Email:** ir@bankgesellschaft.de
Reuters: BERF(forex); BERL(Money Markets)
Website: www.bankgesellschaft.de

Senior Executive Officers
Chief Executive Officer — Clark David *Executive General Manager* ☏ **572 6201**
Financial Director — John Dignum *Director of Finance* ☏ **572 6201**
                     Nick Stevens *Director of Finance* ☏ **572 6329**
Chief Operating Officer — Sean Curran *CFO & Head, Operations* ☏ **572 6334**

General-Investment
Head of Investment — Zoë Shaw *Managing Director* ☏ **572 6304**

Debt Capital Markets / Fixed Income
Fax: 572 6498 Telex: 8956858
Head of Fixed Income — Richard Gillingham *Head of Fixed Income* ☏ **572 6469**

Eurobonds
Head of Trading — Richard Gillingham *Head of Fixed Income* ☏ **572 6469**

Libor-Based / Floating-Rate Products
FRN Trading — Richard Gillingham *Head of Fixed Income* ☏ **572 6469**
Asset Swaps — Gerhard Richter *Managing Director* ☏ **+49 (30) 2456 6513/4**
             Zoë Shaw *Managing Director* ☏ **572 6304**
             Richard Gillingham *Head of Fixed Income* ☏ **572 6469**

Asset-Backed Securities / Securitization
Regional Head — Gerhard Richter *Managing Director* ☏ **+49 (30) 2456 6513/4**
               Zoë Shaw *Managing Director* ☏ **572 6304**

Fixed-Income Repo
Head of Repo — Peter Fingland ☏ **572 6400**
Head of Trading — Peter Fingland ☏ **572 6400**

Fixed-Income Research
Head of Credit Research — Richard Gillingham *Head of Fixed Income* ☏ **572 6469**

Equity Capital Markets
Department: Institutional Equities
Tel: 572 6406 Fax: 572 6490 Telex: 8956858
Head of Equity Capital Markets — Marc Post

International Equities
Head of Sales — Marc Post

Equity Repo / Securities Lending
Head — Rob Curtis ☏ **572 6600**
Head of Trading — Andrew Clark *Trader*
                 Tony Almond *Trader*

Syndicated Lending
Department: Investment Banking Marketing, Syndications & Securitization
Tel: 572 6304
Regional Head — Gerhard Richter *Managing Director* ☏ **+49 (30) 2456 6513/4**
               Zoë Shaw *Managing Director* ☏ **572 6304**

Money Markets
Fax: 572 6490 Telex: 8956858
Head of Money Markets — Peter Fingland ☏ **572 6400**

Domestic Commercial Paper
Head of Sales — Kate O'Higgins ☏ **572 6420**
Head of Trading — Peter Fingland ☏ **572 6400**

1686   Euromoney Directory 1999

www.euromoneydirectory.com UNITED KINGDOM (+44)

Eurocommercial Paper
Head of Sales   Kate O'Higgins ☎ **572 6420**
Head of Trading   Peter Fingland ☎ **572 6400**

Wholesale Deposits
Marketing   Peter Fingland ☎ **572 6400**
Head of Sales   Kate O'Higgins ☎ **572 6420**

Foreign Exchange
Fax: 572 6490
Head of Foreign Exchange   Martin Woodhams ☎ **572 6460**
Corporate Sales   Kate O'Higgins ☎ **572 6420**

Risk Management
Fax: 572 6798
Head of Risk Management   Steve Myers ☎ **572 6468**

Fixed Income Derivatives / Risk Management
Global Head   Richard Gillingham *Head of Fixed Income* ☎ **572 6469**
Head of Sales   Nick Haining ☎ **572 6475**
Trading   Maarten Van der Lugt ☎ **572 6475**

Foreign Exchange Derivatives / Risk Management
Spot / Forwards Trading   Martin Woodhams ☎ **572 6460**

OTC Credit Derivatives
Head   Richard Gillingham *Head of Fixed Income* ☎ **572 6469**

Settlement / Clearing
Head of Settlement / Clearing   Andrew Mitchell ☎ **572 6516**
Operations; Back-Office   Neil Statham *Director of Treasury Operations* ☎ **572 6512**

Administration
Head of Administration   Nick Miller *Director of Facilities / Administration* ☎ **572 6274**

Technology & Systems
                                         John O'Neill *Director of IT* ☎ **572 6375**

Compliance
                                         Andrew Clarke ☎ **572 6260**

Public Relations
                                         Suzanne Canning ☎ **572 6666**

Corporate Communications
                                         Suzanne Canning ☎ **572 6666**

Accounts / Audit
Head of Audit   Andrew Clarke ☎ **572 6260**

Banque AIG   Full Branch Office

Formerly known as: AIG Financial Products (UK) Limited
7th Floor, 4 Broadgate, London EC2M 2QS
Tel: (171) 617 0400; (171) 920 0033 **Fax:** (171) 972 0771; (171) 628 2923

Senior Executive Officers
Managing Director   Kristofer Mansson

Banque Banorabe   Full Branch Office

195 Brompton Road, London SW3 1LZ
Tel: (171) 493 4870 **Fax:** (171) 823 7356 **Telex:** 893457 BANO G **Swift:** BANO GB 2L **Reuters:** BDLX

Senior Executive Officers
Chief Executive Officer   Amr Turk *Senior Manager*
Treasurer   Desmond Rameaux *Treasurer*

Others (Senior Executives)
Operating Officer   David Street *Manager*
Officer   Loraine Day

Euromoney Directory 1999 **1687**

UNITED KINGDOM (+44)   www.euromoneydirectory.com

Banque CPR   Full Branch Office

Formerly known as: Seccombe Marshall & Campion plc
1 Angel Court, London EC2R 7HQ
Tel: (171) 600 4004 **Fax:** (171) 600 0076 **Email:** londonbranch@cpr.fr
Website: www.cpr.fr

Senior Executive Officers
Managing Director	Peter d'Anger
Managing Director	Richard Scott
Managing Director	Olivier Neau

Debt Capital Markets / Fixed Income
Emerging Market Bonds
Head of Emerging Markets   Olivier Neau *Managing Director*

Fixed-Income Repo
Marketing & Product Development   Moira d'Arcy *Head of Sales & Marketing* [E] **md'arcy@cpr.fr**
Trading   Chris Inch *Trader*
Sales   Moira d'Arcy *Head of Sales & Marketing* [E] **md'arcy@cpr.fr**

Risk Management
Head of Risk Management   Peter d'Anger *Managing Director*
                                  Richard Scott *Managing Director*

Administration
Head of Administration   Philippe Trumeau *Administration Manager*

Technology & Systems
                                  Philippe Trumeau *Administration Manager*

Legal / In-House Counsel
                                  Simon Ewart *Financial Controller*

Compliance
                                  Philippe Trumeau *Compliance Officer*

Accounts / Audit
                                  Simon Ewart *Financial Controller*

Banque Edouard Constant   Representative Office

2 Studio Place, Kinnerton Street, London SW1X 8EW
Tel: (171) 235 4441 **Fax:** (171) 823 1652

Senior Executive Officers
Representative   J Bertil Norinder

Banque Française de l'Orient   Full Branch Office

50 Curzon Street, London W1Y 7PN
Tel: (171) 312 7700 **Fax:** (171) 312 7799 **Telex:** 23875 BFOWG **Swift:** BFOR GB 2X **Reuters:** BFOL

Senior Executive Officers
Chief Operating Officer   Geoffrey Fry *Manager, Operations* [T] **312 7730**
General Manager   Samir Saab [T] **312 7701**
Assistant General Manager   Martin Lynch [T] **312 7707**

Others (Senior Executives)
                                  Raymond Sturmer *Advisor* [T] **312 7702**

Equity Capital Markets
Head of Equity Capital Markets   Samir Sawabini *Private Banking* [T] **312 7741** [F] **312 7738**

Syndicated Lending
Head of Trading   Roger Smithyes *Credit Manager* [T] **312 7767**

Money Markets
Head of Money Markets   Peter Scriven *Head of Money Markets* [T] **312 7770**

Corporate Finance / M&A Advisory
Head of Corporate Finance   Sami Tamim *Senior Manager, Corporate* [T] **331 7721**

Settlement / Clearing
Head of Settlement / Clearing   George Kaba *Assistant Manager, Settlements* [T] **312 7745**
Operations   Geoffrey Fry *Manager* [T] **312 7730**

Other Departments
Correspondent Banking   Gail Wells *Senior Manager, Int'l / Correspondent Banking* [T] **312 7724**

www.euromoneydirectory.com   UNITED KINGDOM (+44)

Administration
Head of Administration   Susan Murray *Assistant Manager, Administration* ☏ **312 7768**

Accounts / Audit
    Wissam Ghoussainy *Chief Accountant* ☏ **312 7712**
    David Kidd *Internal Auditor* ☏ **312 7761**

Banque Internationale à Luxembourg SA   Full Branch Office

Shackleton House, Hay's Galleria, 4 Battle Bridge Lane, London SE1 2GZ
Tel: (171) 556 3000 **Fax:** (171) 556 3055 **Telex:** 884032 **Swift:** BILL GB 2L **Reuters:** LUXL (Dealing)
Foreign Exchange Tel: 651 5151; **Fax:** 651 5151; **Treasury Tel:** 556 3090; **Fax:** 556 3089

Senior Executive Officers
Managing Director   Edward Charlton
Deputy Managing Director   Brian Wood

Others (Senior Executives)
Director   David Pantlin *Director*
Financial Controller   Robert Keeler *Director*
Personal Banking Services   Jonathan Stocker *Senior Manager*
Media Finance   Edwige Rolin *Senior Manager*

General-Lending (DCM, SL)
Head of Corporate Banking   Peter Venables *Director, Credit Department*
    Robert Bird *Director, Financial Markets*

General - Treasury
Head of Treasury   Mark Lynch *Senior Dealer*
    Geoff Wood *Assistant Director, Treasury Products*

Syndicated Lending
Head of Syndicated Lending   Malcolm Weaver *Assistant Director*

Other (Syndicated Lending)
Loans & Credit Admin.   Mike Wilkinson *Manager, Loans & Credit Administration*

Loan-Related Activities
Trade Finance   Jim Jeffries *Assistant Director*
Leasing & Asset Finance   Brian Walker *Senior Manager*

Settlement / Clearing
Operations   Mike Wilkinson *Manager, Loans & Credit Administration*

Asset Management
Investment Funds   Charles Hovenden *Director*

Other (Asset Management)
Marketing   Madeleine Gore *Director*

Other Departments
Private Banking   David Fordham *Director*

Administration
Compliance
    Andy Watt *Manager*

Accounts / Audit
Audit   Andy Watt *Manager*

Other (Administration)
Human Resources   Penny Innes *Senior Manager*
Middle Office   Ray Hayes *Manager*

Banque Nationale de Paris   Full Branch Office

8/13 King William Street, London EC4P 4HS
Tel: (171) 895 7070 **Fax:** (171) 929 0310 **Telex:** 935850

Senior Executive Officers
General Manager   Mr Verlet

Banque Privée Edmond de Rothschild

Orion House, 5 Upper St Martins Lane, London WC2H 9EA
Tel: (171) 240 1870 **Fax:** (171) 240 1826; (171) 862 5907

Senior Executive Officers
Managing Director / General Manager   Richard Jones-Beatmanr

Euromoney Directory 1999   **1689**

UNITED KINGDOM (+44)   www.euromoneydirectory.com

Banque Sudameris
90 Queen Street, London EC4R 1AB
Tel: (171) 651 3000 **Fax:** (171) 651 3207

Senior Executive Officers
Representative   Luigi Carnelli

Banque Transatlantique SA/Banque Transatlantique (Jersey) Limited
Representative Office

36 St James's Street, London SW1A 1JD
Tel: (171) 493 6717 **Fax:** (171) 495 1018

Senior Executive Officers
Representative   Catherine Nollet

Barclays Bank plc
Head Office

54 Lombard Street, London EC3P 3AH
Tel: (171) 699 5000 **Fax:** (171) 621 0386 **Telex:** 887591

Senior Executive Officers
Chairman	A R F Buxton
Chief Executive Officer	Robert E Diamond Jr
Financial Director	Oliver Stocken
Treasurer	P A Perry

Debt Capital Markets / Fixed Income
Global Head   Robert Morrice

Fixed-Income Repo
Head of Repo   Tim Keenan *Global Products Head of Repo*
Trading   Paul Pollington *Gilt Repos*
Oscar Huettner *Trader, Dm*
Ken Baynes *Gilt Repos*
Annalisa Burello *Trader, £*
Glenn Handley *Trader, Eurosterling*
Giles Naylor *Trader, Pta*

Syndicated Lending
Global Head   Tim Ritchie

Risk Management
Global Head   Andy Bruce *Head of Credit Risk Management*

Barclays Capital Securities Limited
Head Office

Formerly known as: Barclays de Zoete Wedd Securities Limited

5 The North Colonnade, Canary Wharf, London E14 4BB
Tel: (171) 623 2323 **Fax:** (171) 773 4844 **Email:** firstname.surname@barclayscapital.com
Website: www.barclayscapital.com

Senior Executive Officers
Chairman of the Executive Committee	Hans-Joerg Rudloff
Chief Executive Officer	Robert E Diamond Jr *Chief Executive*
Financial Director	Michael J Keegan *Chief Finance Officer*
Chief Operating Officer	Naguib Kheraj *Chief Administrative Officer*
Treasurer	John Eldredge *Treasurer*

Others (Senior Executives)
Vice Chairman   Alan Brown
Nicholas Daifotis *Managing Director*
Chairman of the Executive Committee   Hans-Joerg Rudloff *Chairman of the Executive Committee*
Vice Chairman   Sir Robert Wade-Gery

General-Investment
Head of Investment   Peter Luthy *Global Head of Investment Banking*

Relationship Manager
Financial Institutions & Relationship Management   Iain Barbour *Director*

1690   Euromoney Directory 1999

www.euromoneydirectory.com UNITED KINGDOM (+44)

Debt Capital Markets / Fixed Income
Tel: 773 9036 **Fax:** 773 4844

Head of Fixed Income	Robert Morrice *Europe*
	Noreen Harrington *Europe*
	Pat Lin *Asia*
	Tom Kalaris *Asia*
Head of Fixed Income Sales	Neil Cummins
Head of Fixed Income Trading	Robert Morrice *Europe*
	Noreen Harrington *Europe*
	Pat Lin *Asia*
	Tom Kalaris *Asia*

Government Bonds
Head of Sales	Neil Cummins
Head of Trading	David Newton
	Noreen Harrington
Head of Syndication	Roman Schmidt
Head of Origination	Abigail Hofman

Eurobonds
Head of Sales	Neil Cummins
Head of Trading	Roman Schmidt
	Gary Hibbard

High Yield / Junk Bonds
Head	Gary Hibbard
Head of Trading	Steven Zander *Head of European High Yield Trading*
Other	Frank Sekula *Head of European High Yield*

Emerging Market Bonds
Head of Emerging Markets	Noreen Harrington *Head of Emerging Markets, European Fixed Income*
Head	Ian Banwell
	Joe Bencivenga
Head of Sales	Neil Cummins
Head of Trading	Ian Banwell
	Gary Hibbard
	Tony Egui

Libor-Based / Floating-Rate Products
FRN Sales	Neil Cummins
FRN Trading	Robert Ford
Asset Swaps	Oka Usi
Asset Swaps (Sales)	Neil Cummins

Fixed-Income Repo
Head of Repo; Marketing & Product Development	Tim Keenan *Head of Money Market / Repo* ☏ **773 9337**
Marketing & Product Development	Mark D'Andrea *Global Head of Prime Brokerage* ☏ **+1 (212) 412 7673**
Head of Trading	Oscar Huettner *Repo Trader (Germany)*
Trading	Ken Baynes *Gilt Repo Trader*
	Peter Irons *Gilt Repo Trader*
	Glen Handley *Gilt Repo Trader*
	Paul Pollington *Gilt Repo Trader*
	Giles Naylor *Repo Trader (Spain, Scandi, Canada)*
	Oscar Huettner *Repo Trader (Germany)*
	Stuart Rayner *Repo Trader (Germany)*
	Oein Corrigan *USD, Eurobond, Emerging Market Repo Trader*
	Brice Gillaizeau *USD, Eurobond, Emerging Market Repo Trader*
	Michele Imperi *Repo Trader (Italy)*
	Philip Eves *Repo Trader (Japan)*
	Colin Birmingham *Loans / Deposits (FRF, ITL, ECU)*
	Peter Johnson *Loans & Deposits*
	Roy Tarling *Loans & Deposits*

Fixed-Income Research
Head of Fixed Income	Neil Cummins
Head of Credit Research	Gary Jenkins *Europe*
	Will Lloyd *US*

Equity Capital Markets
Tel: 773 9190 **Fax:** 516 9585

Equity Repo / Securities Lending
Marketing & Product Development	Mark D'Andrea *Global Head of Prime Brokerage* ☏ **+1 (212) 412 7673**
	Jamie Phillips *Regional Head of Prime Brokerage* ☏ **773 9191**

Syndicated Lending
Head of Origination; Head of Syndication; Head of Trading	Tim Ritchie *Global Head of Syndications & Loan Distribution*

UNITED KINGDOM (+44)　　　　www.euromoneydirectory.com

Barclays Capital Securities Limited (cont)

Loan-Related Activities
Project Finance — Bob Mabon

Money Markets
Head of Money Markets — Noreen Harrington

Domestic Commercial Paper
Head of Trading — Roman Schmidt

Eurocommercial Paper
Head of Trading — Roman Schmidt

Foreign Exchange
Global Head — Paul Thrush *Global Head of FX*
Head of Sales — Mike Peacock *Head of FX Sales*
Head of Trading — Kevin Moore
Spot / Forwards Trading — Paul Abbenhaus

Risk Management
Department: Derivatives
Global Head — Jerry del Missier *Global Head of Derivatives*

Other (FI Derivatives)
Head of Trading — Andy N'Doca *OTC Bond Options, Head of Trading*
 Matt Joyce *OTC Bond Options, Head of Trading*

Other Currency Swap / FX Options Personnel
Head of Swaps — Eric Bommensath

OTC Equity Derivatives
Trading — Eric Bommensath

OTC Credit Derivatives
Head — Oka Usi

Exchange-Traded Derivatives
Head — Justin Bull

Corporate Finance / M&A Advisory
Private Equity — Graeme White ☏ 773 2528 📠 773 4805

Settlement / Clearing
Head of Settlement / Clearing — Greg Quental *Head of Global Operations*
Equity Settlement — Fraser MacKenzie
Fixed-Income Settlement — Neil Martin *Head of Settlement / Clearing, Back Office Operation*
Other — Brian Sherratt *Treasury Settlement*

Other Departments
Commodities / Bullion — Peter Sellars *Global Head of Commodities*
Chief Credit Officer — Brian Weight *Head of Credit Risk Management*
Cash Management — Ian Firth

Administration
Head of Marketing — Leigh Bruce *Global Head of Corporate Communications*

Technology & Systems
Chip Steinmetz *Global Head of IT*

Legal / In-House Counsel
Deborah Morgan *Head of Legal*

Compliance
Frank McGarahan *Global Head of Compliance*

Public Relations
Leigh Bruce *Global Head of Corporate Communications*

Accounts / Audit
John Worth *Head of Audit*

Barclays Global Investors Limited　　　　　　Bank Subsidiary

Formerly known as: Barclays de Zoete Wedd Investment Management & Wells Fargo Nikko Investment Advisors
Murray House, Royal Mint Court, London EC3N 4HH
Tel: (171) 668 8000; (171) 668 8344 **Fax:** (171) 668 8001; (171) 668 8911 **Telex:** 9413073 BGI **Swift:** BZIM GB 2LA XXX
Email: philip.nash@bglobal.com
Website: www.barclaysglobal.com

Senior Executive Officers
Joint Chairman of BGI Globally — Fred Graver ☏ +1 (415) 597 2000
Joint Chairman of BGI Globally — Peter Dunn ☏ +1 (415) 597 2000
European Chief Executive — John Varley
Chief Executive Officer — Lindsay Tomlinson *Chief Executive Europe*

1692　Euromoney Directory 1999

Senior Executive Officers (cont)
Financial Director
Chief Operating Officer

Others (Senior Executives)
MD, Client Group

General-Investment
Head of Investment

Debt Capital Markets / Fixed Income
Head of Fixed Income
Other

Equity Capital Markets
Tel: 668 8944 **Fax:** 668 8911
Head of Trading
Other

Other (Domestic Equities)
Domestic Indexed Equity
Domestic Active Equity

Other (International Equity)
International Indexed Equity
International Active Equity

Equity Repo / Securities Lending
Marketing & Product Development

Risk Management
Head of Risk Management

Settlement / Clearing
Operations
Other

Asset Management
Other (Asset Management)
Passive Asset Allocation
Active Asset Allocation
Research

Other Departments
Cash Management

Administration
Tel: 668 8001
Head of Administration

Head of Marketing

Technology & Systems
IT Infrastructure
IT Development
Head of Technology

Compliance

Other (Administration)
Personnel Director
Facilities Manager

Sanjay Jawa *Finance Director*
Michael Brown *Head of Operations, Administration & Technology*

Clare Dobie
Richard Potts *Client Director*

Andrew Skirton *Chief Investment Officer*

Mike Rawson
Partha Dasgupta *Indexed Fixed Income*
Andrew Wealls *Active Fixed Income*
Annita Higgins *Active Fixed Income*

Peter White *Principal, Head of Equity Trading*
Chris Thomason *Indexed Equity Strategies*
Chris Sutton *Indexed Equity Strategies*
Matthew Annable *Active Equity Strategies*
Noel Mills *Active Equity Strategies*

Graham Hepher *Principal*
Stuart Owen *Principal*

Giovanni Castellino *Principal*
Martin White *Active Europe Portfolio Management*

Christine Elgar *Principal*
Kevin McNulty *Principal*

Malcolm Smith

Michael Latham *Principal, Operations*
Peter White

John Minderides *Head of Asset Allocation & Derivatives*
Jean-Philippe Gruvel *Principal*
Kevin Coldiron *Researcher*

Charles Thomson *Head*

Michael Latham *Principal, Operations*
Michael Brown *Head of Operations, Administration & Technology*
Nigel Williams *Head of Business Development & Defined Contributio*
Miles O'Conner *Director, Head of UK Business Development*
Philip Nash *Principal, European Business Development*

Bob Pleasant *Principal*
Mark Newton *Principal*
Michael Brown *Head of Operations, Administration & Technology*

Paul Hecker *Compliance*

Jennifer Knight *Human Resources*
Derek Sweeney *Associate*

Barclays Mercantile Business Finance Limited — Head Office
Churchill Plaza, Churchill Way, Basingstoke, Hampshire RG21 7GP
Tel: (1256) 817 777 **Fax:** (1256) 791 950

Senior Executive Officers
Chairman & Chief Executive
Chief Executive Officer

Ray Waterson
Ray Waterson *Chairman & Chief Executive*

UNITED KINGDOM (+44)   www.euromoneydirectory.com

Barclays Mercantile Business Finance Limited (cont)
Senior Executive Officers (cont)
Financial Director
Managing Director
Others (Senior Executives)

Sarah Box *Finance Director*
John Callender

Nick Rouse *Director, Risk*
Stuart Maxwell *Director, Sales & Marketing*
Chris Boobyer *Director, Large Value*

Barclays Mercantile Highland Finance Limited — Subsidiary Company

Churchill Plaza, Churchill Way, Basingstoke, Hampshire RG21 7GL
Tel: (1256) 816 161 **Fax:** (1256) 810 297

Senior Executive Officers
Chairman
Managing Director
Secretary
Others (Senior Executives)

John Callender
Chris Kennedy
Charles Shoolbred

Brian Gill *Director*

Barclays Private Equity Limited — Subsidiary Company

5 The North Colonade, Canary Wharf, London E14 4BB
Tel: (171) 512 9900 **Fax:** (171) 773 4805
Website: www.bzw.com

Senior Executive Officers
Managing Director, UK
Others (Senior Executives)
Directors

Infrastructure Investment Team

Graeme White

Tom Lamb
Stephen Welton
Chris Elliott *Managing Director*

Baring Asset Management Limited — Subsidiary Company

155 Bishopsgate, London EC2M 3XY
Tel: (171) 628 6000 **Fax:** (171) 638 7928 **Telex:** 885888 BAMUK G **Email:** enquiry.utg@baring-asset.com
Website: www.baring-asset.com

Senior Executive Officers
Chairman & Chief Executive Officer
Deputy Chairman & Chief Operating Officer
Chief Executive Officer
Financial Director
Chief Operating Officer
Others (Senior Executives)
UK pension funds asset allocation Committee

Equity Capital Markets
Regional Head
Administration
Head of Administration
Other (Administration)
Client Service & Business Development

John Bolsover
Peter Walsh
John Bolsover *Chairman & Chief Executive Officer*
Julian Swayne *Finance Director*
Peter Walsh *Chief Operating Officer*

Michael Hughes *Chairman*
George Harvey *Head of UK Institutional Sales*

Mark Pignatelli *Head of European Equities*

Mike Clegg *Global Head of Investment Operations*

Mark Archer *Head of UK Sales*

Bashcreditbank — Representative Office

Bucklersbury House, 3 Queen Victoria Street, London EC4N 8EL
Tel: (171) 329 4200; (171) 329 4201 **Fax:** (171) 329 4204 **Email:** bashlond@msn.com

Senior Executive Officers
European Representative

Ron Lis

1694 Euromoney Directory 1999

www.euromoneydirectory.com UNITED KINGDOM (+44)

Bayerische Hypo-und Vereinsbank AG
Full Branch Office

41 Moorgate, London EC2R 6PP
Tel: (171) 626 1301 Fax: (171) 696 9989 Telex: 894624 Swift: HYPO GB RL

Senior Executive Officers
Others (Senior Executives)
Banking — Richard Groh *General Manager*
Treasury — David Sawyer *General Manager*
Property — Georg Funke *General Manager*

Bayerische Landesbank Girozentrale
Full Branch Office

Bavaria House, 13/14 Appold Street, London EC2A 2AA
Tel: (171) 247 0056 Fax: (171) 955 5173 Telex: 886437 BAYLON Swift: BYLA GB 22 Reuters: BLAL
Cable: BAYLAND LONDON EC2
Foreign Exchange Tel: 651 5151; 651 5151

Senior Executive Officers
GM & CEO, Branch Operations — Gerhard Mann
GM, Treasury, Eurobonds & Derivatives — John Gausepohl
GM, Banking & Finance — Michael P F Wickham

Others (Senior Executives)
Jon Graesser *Head of Trading*

General-Lending (DCM, SL)
Head of Corporate Banking — Hereward Drummond *Assistant General Manager*
Sönke Peterson *Manager*
Andrew Sutherland *Manager*
John Layden *Senior Relationship Officer*
Kevin Buck *Senior Relationship Officer*

General - Treasury
Head of Treasury — Neil Watson *Head of Treasury Sales*

Relationship Manager
Head of Structured Finance — Oliver Graham *Assistant General Manager*

Debt Capital Markets / Fixed Income
Department: Treasury, Eurobonds & Derivatives
Domestic Government Bonds
Head of Syndication — Rolf Schaefer *Manager, Eurobonds & Securities*

Eurobonds
Head of Origination — John Gausepohl *GM, Treasury, Eurobonds & Derivatives*
Head of Trading — Russell Williams *Senior Dealer, Eurobonds & Securities*
Rolf Schaefer *Manager, Eurobonds & Securities*

Equity Capital Markets
Other (Domestic Equities)
Securitisation / ABS — Neville Scully *Manager*

Syndicated Lending
Head of Origination — Andrew Tait *Manager, Origination - Syndications*
Head of Syndication — Anne Brett *Manager, Distribution & Secondary Market*
Margherita Pisa *Assistant Manager*
Head of Credit Committee — Richard Truelove *Manager*

Other (Syndicated Lending)
Loan Administration — David Mellotte *Assistant Manager*
Corporate Lending — Louise Bradley *Senior Lending Officer*

Loan-Related Activities
Structured Trade Finance — Ian Childs *Manager*
Eric Faber *Manager*
Simon Whitfield *Senior Officer*

Other (Trade Finance)
Export Finance — Stephen Meyer *Senior Officer*
Mark Paton *Senior Officer*
Structured Finance — Oliver Graham *Head*

Money Markets
Head of Money Markets — David Thornton *Manager & Chief Dealer*

Money Markets - General
David Curle *Senior Dealer*
Peter Quintrell *Senior Dealer*

Euromoney Directory 1999 **1695**

UNITED KINGDOM (+44)   www.euromoneydirectory.com

Bayerische Landesbank Girozentrale (cont)
Money Markets - General (cont)

Treasury Sales
    Lynton Humphries *Dealer*
    Andrew Darroch *Manager, Corporate Sales*

Foreign Exchange
Global Head
Regional Head
Country Head
Corporate Sales
    Nick Francis *Head, Spot FX*
    Trevor Carr *Senior Dealer*
    Susan Hooper *Senior Dealer*
    Deirdre Campbell *Senior Corporate Dealer*
    Nik Mundy *Senior Corporate Dealer*
    Wendy Francis *Corporate Dealer*

FX Traders / Sales People
    Trevor Carr *Senior Dealer*
    Susan Hooper *Senior Dealer*
    Giovanni Rossi *Dealer*
    Fiona Johnstone *FX Sales*

Risk Management
Country Head
    Brian Lacey *Assistant General Manager, Risk Management & IT*

Fixed Income Derivatives / Risk Management
Country Head
Head of Sales
    Nick Evans *Manager, Derivative Trading*
    Avril French *Senior Sales*

Other (FI Derivatives)
Derivative Products
    Paul Wharton *Dealer*
    Ged Downes *Dealer*

Derivative Interbank
    Claire Dowsing *Dealer Interbank Sales*

Settlement / Clearing
Derivatives Settlement
Foreign Exchange Settlement
Settlement (General)
Operations
    Richard R Farrell *Assistant Manager, Bond & Derivative Settlements*
    Nick Bragg *Assistant Manager, FX / MM Settlements*
    Patricia L Dillon *Manager, Settlements*
    Gerhard Mann *GM & CEO, Branch Operations*

Administration
Head of Administration
    Reinhard Heupel *Manager*

Technology & Systems
    Mark Steele *Manager*
    Brian Lacey *Assistant General Manager, Risk Management & IT*

Legal / In-House Counsel
    Janet Oliver *Manager*

Compliance
    Nigel Foster *Officer*

Accounts / Audit
Audit
    Debra Enderby *Internal Auditor*

BB Securities Limited   Subsidiary Company

10 Aldersgate Street, London EC1A 4HJ
Tel: (171) 216 4200 **Fax:** (171) 216 0006; (171) 216 0007 **Telex:** 290980 BBSEC G **Email:** bbsec@dial.pipex.com
Reuters: BBSECSI

Senior Executive Officers
Chief Executive Officer
Financial Director
Managing Director
Assistant Managing Director
Company Secretary
    Delcio Blajfeder *Managing Director* ☎ **216 4204** 🖷 **216 4206**
    Martin Errington ☎ **216 4246**
    Delcio Blajfeder ☎ **216 4204** 🖷 **216 4206**
    Elenelson Marques ☎ **216 4204**
    Martin Errington ☎ **216 4246**

General-Investment
Head of Investment
    Christina Heinl ☎ **216 4202** 🖷 **216 0004**

Debt Capital Markets / Fixed Income
Tel: 216 4210/4220
Global Head
Head of Fixed Income Sales
Head of Fixed Income Trading
    Simon Campbell-Boreham *Head, Debt*
    Lesley-Anne Arnold *Head, Sales & Syndication* ☎ **216 4320**
    Rajinder Gill ☎ **216 4230**

Eurobonds
Head of Sales
    Emilia Ferraz-Spitz *Sales & Syndication* ☎ **216 4234**
    Jaqueline Capar *Sales & Syndication* ☎ **216 4220**
    Flavia Martins *Sales & Syndication* ☎ **216 4220**
    Christiane Mayrinck *Sales & Syndication* ☎ **216 4220**

www.euromoneydirectory.com UNITED KINGDOM (+44)

Eurobonds (cont)
Head of Trading
                                  Pedro Felix *Sales & Syndication* T **216 4234**
                                  Emma McClintock T **216 4210**

Emerging Market Bonds
Head of Trading Rajinder Gill T **216 4230**

Fixed-Income Research
Head of Fixed Income Paul Hollingworth T **216 4225** F **216 0018**

Equity Capital Markets
Tel: 216 4295
Global Head Jamie Stewart *Head, Equity*

Syndicated Lending
Head of Origination Emilia Ferraz-Spitz T **216 4234**
Head of Syndication Lesley-Anne Arnold *Head, Sales & Syndication* T **216 4220**

Settlement / Clearing
Head of Settlement / Clearing Stephen Fowler T **216 4248**
Settlement (General) Marcia Pinto T **216 4247**
                                  Andrew Dean T **216 4249**
Operations Michael Messervy

Asset Management
Head M C S Sanaya-Heinl *Head of Investment Management* T **216 4256**
                                  F **216 0004**

Other Departments
Economic Research Pedro Regina *Economic Analysis & Strategist* T **216 4210**

Administration
Head of Administration Ruth Zambonini T **216 4250** F **216 0000**

Technology & Systems
                                  Andrew Burt T **216 4229**

Compliance
                                  Martin Errington T **216 4246**

Other (Administration)
Personnel & Office Manager Ruth Zambonini T **216 4250** F **216 0000**
Research Paul Hollingworth T **216 4225** F **216 0018**
                                  Pablo Milella T **216 4226**

BBL Securities Limited
Subsidiary Company

Alternative trading name: ING Barings, Investment Banking Western Europe
Formerly known as: MC-BBL Securities Limited
60 London Wall, London EC2M 5TQ
Tel: (171) 767 1000 **Fax:** (171) 767 7703; (171) 767 7705 **Telex:** 0922365 BBLSLN G **Email:** IBWE@ing-barings.com

Senior Executive Officers
Chairman of the Board Jean-Pierre Wellens T **+32 (2) 547 2111**
Chief Executive Officer Willy Douin *Head of Investment Banking Western Europe* T **767 5768**
Chief Operating Officer C M Hyde *COO Investment Banking Western Europe* T **767 5740**
Head of Equities Western Europe Dominique Grey T **767 5757** F **767 7705**
Company Secretary C M Hyde T **767 5740**

Equity Capital Markets
Department: Investment Banking Western Europe
Head of Equity Capital Markets Dominique Grey *Head of Equities Western Europe* T **767 5757** F **767 7705**

Other (International Equity)
Executive ECM Haakon Overli *Director* T **767 5755** F **767 7704**
                                  John Morgan *Director* T **767 5754** F **767 7704**
Syndicate Anna Ohlsson *Associate Director* T **767 5756** F **767 7705**
Executive ECM Enrico Mauri *Associate Director* T **767 5750** F **767 7704**
Trader Ron Smyth *Associate Director* T **767 8224**

Corporate Finance / M&A Advisory
Department: Investment Banking Western Europe - Corporate Finance / M&A

Other (Corporate Finance)
Chief Executive Officer Willy Douin *Head of Investment Banking Western Europe* T **767 5768**
Senior Executive Christopher Shaw *Senior Adviser* T **767 5780** F **767 7708**
                                  J B Riddell *Senior Adviser* T **767 1425**
Executive John Ferrari *Director* T **767 5766** F **767 7706**
                                  Paul Galpin *Associate Director* T **767 5765** F **767 7706**
                                  Gerd Van Steen *Associate Director* T **767 5760** F **767 7706**
                                  Carsten G Moeller *Associate Director* T **767 5761** F **767 7706**

UNITED KINGDOM (+44) www.euromoneydirectory.com

BBL Securities Limited (cont)
Administration
Compliance
　　　　　　　　　　　　　　C M Hyde ☏ **767 5740**

BBV LatInvest Securities Limited — Head Office
1 Angel Court, London EC2R 7EL
Tel: (171) 600 3999 **Fax:** (171) 600 4144 **Telex:** 8813801 LATINV G **Reuters:** LAML-Q

Senior Executive Officers
Chief Executive Officer — Mr Colmerauer
Financial Director — Maria Jesus Lopez *Finance Director*

Debt Capital Markets / Fixed Income
Global Head — Jose de Aguinaga *Managing Director*

Equity Capital Markets
Global Head — Peter Breese *Director, Capital Markets*

BC Partners Limited
105 Piccadilly, London W1V 9FN
Tel: (171) 408 1282 **Fax:** (171) 493 1368

Senior Executive Officers
Chief Executive Officer — Otto van der Wyck *CEO*

Others (Senior Executives)
John Burgess *Senior Partner*
Simon Palley *Senior Partner*
Simon Thornton *Partner*

Bear Stearns International Limited — Head Office
One Canada Square, London E14 5AD
Tel: (171) 516 6000 **Fax:** (171) 516 6266; (171) 516 6030 **Telex:** 8811424 BEARCO G
Website: www.bearstearns.com

Senior Executive Officers
Chief Executive Officer — John Knight
Financial Director — Marshall Levinson *Chief Financial Officer*
Treasurer — David Dunn

Debt Capital Markets / Fixed Income
Global Head — Brett Graham

Fixed-Income Repo
Head of Repo — Jon Ferber *Managing Director* ☏ **516 6222** 🖷 **516 6575**
Trading — Tim Lea
Sales — Barry Nix

Equity Capital Markets
Global Head — Hans Rudolf Kunz

Equity Repo / Securities Lending
Head — John Clifford Jones *Assistant Director* ☏ **516 6860** 🖷 **516 6421**
Marketing — Rachel Crowther
Head of Trading — Justine Norris *Stock Loan Sales Representative, Japan*
Rachel Crowther
Andrew Colley
Paul Clark *Stock Loan Sales Representative*

Syndicated Lending
Global Head — Brett Graham

Foreign Exchange
Global Head — Bernd Broker

Risk Management
Global Head — Kan Ahluwalia

Settlement / Clearing
Operations — Pat Mahon *Head*

www.euromoneydirectory.com UNITED KINGDOM (+44)

Beeson Gregory Limited

The Registry, Royal Mint Court, London
Tel: (171) 488 4040 **Fax:** (171) 481 3762

Senior Executive Officers
Chairman — Andrew Beeson
Financial Director — Robert Wilson

Corporate Finance / M&A Advisory
Head of Corporate Finance — Tony Barklett

Beirut Riyad Bank SAL   Full Branch Office

17A Curzon Street, London W1Y 7FE
Tel: (171) 493 8342 **Fax:** (171) 408 0053 **Telex:** 296675 **Swift:** BRBA GB 2L
Forex Dealers Tel: 496 6705

Senior Executive Officers
Chief Executive Officer — Alex W Wishart *Regional Manager*
Treasurer; International Division — Allan F Gooda *Treasurer*

Others (Senior Executives)
Deputy Regional Manager — Sobhi M Osman *Deputy Regional Manager, Commercial & Retail*

General-Lending (DCM, SL)
Head of Corporate Banking — Sobhi M Osman *Deputy Regional Manager, Commercial & Retail*

Syndicated Lending
Trade Finance — Carol Holgate *Head*

Foreign Exchange
Tel: 495 6705
Head of Trading — Sami Lone *Dealer*

Corporate Finance / M&A Advisory
Regional Head — Alex W Wishart *Regional Manager*

Settlement / Clearing
Tel: 493 8342
Foreign Exchange Settlement — Ian Miller

Other Departments
Private Banking — Alex W Wishart *Regional Manager*
Correspondent Banking — Allan F Gooda *Treasurer*

Administration
Head of Administration — John C Casey *Manager, Administration & Operations*

BELGOLAISE SA   Full Branch Office

Northern & Shell Tower, 4 Sezdon Way, London E14 9GL
Tel: (171) 712 1400 **Fax:** (171) 538 2144 **Telex:** 888528 **Swift:** BLGO GB 2L

Senior Executive Officers
General Manager — Jean-François Beyer

Syndicated Lending

Loan-Related Activities
Trade Finance — Keith Dixey *Manager*

Foreign Exchange
Head of Foreign Exchange — Gary Pickard *Manager* ☎ 538 3343

Settlement / Clearing
Head of Settlement / Clearing; Operations — Myra Passarelli *Sub Manager*

Other Departments
Chief Credit Officer — Michael Barrett

Administration
Head of Administration — Sylvia Levier

Technology & Systems
Sylvia Levier

Accounts / Audit
Sylvia Levier

Euromoney Directory 1999 **1699**

UNITED KINGDOM (+44) www.euromoneydirectory.com

Berliner Bank AG
Full Branch Office

1 Crown Court, Cheapside, London EC2V 6LR
Tel: (171) 572 9200 **Fax:** (171) 572 9326 **Telex:** 884131 **Swift:** BEBE GB 2L **Email:** ir@bankgesellschaft.de
Website: www.bankgesellschaft.de

Senior Executive Officers
General Manager — George Gonszor ☎ **572 6218** 🖷 **572 6219**

Relationship Manager
Media — Steve Robbins *Head of Media Finance* ☎ **572 9312**

Syndicated Lending
Loan-Related Activities
Aircraft / Aerospace Finance — Andrew Stockham *Director* ☎ **572 9305**
Shipping Finance — Nigel Hill ☎ **572 9331**
Project Finance — Hercules Van Wyk *Director, Project Finance* ☎ **572 9360**
Philip Nias *Director, Project Finance* ☎ **572 9359**

Foreign Exchange
Head of Foreign Exchange — Martin Woodhams ☎ **572 6460**
Corporate Sales — Kate O'Higgins ☎ **572 6420**

Other Departments
Debt Recovery / Restructuring — Vivian Vollmer *Assistant Manager, Debt Administration* ☎ **572 9303**

Administration
Head of Administration — David Bray *Associate Director* ☎ **572 9320**

Technology & Systems
John O'Neill *Director of IT* ☎ **572 6375**

Compliance
Andrew Clarke *Head of Audit & Compliance* ☎ **572 6260**

Corporate Communications
Suzanne Canning *Corporate Communication Officer* ☎ **572 6666**

Accounts / Audit
Audit — Andrew Clarke *Head of Audit & Compliance* ☎ **572 6260**

Bermuda International Investment Management (Europe) Limited
Subsidiary Company

Formerly known as: B of B (Europe) Limited
3rd Floor, Austin Friars House, 2-6 Austin Friars, London EC2N 2LX
Tel: (171) 296 4000 **Fax:** (171) 296 4089
Website: www.bankofbermuda.com

Senior Executive Officers
Managing Director — Les I Gabb

Others (Senior Executives)
Investment Management Services — Michelle A McGrade *Director* ☎ **296 4099**

BfG Bank AG
Full Branch Office

6th Floor, Bucklersbury House, 11 Walbrook, London EC4N 8EL
Tel: (171) 329 1522 **Fax:** (171) 329 1533 **Telex:** 887628 **Swift:** BFGF GB 2L **Reuters:** BFGL

Senior Executive Officers
General Manager — Ulrich Mauersberg

Others (Senior Executives)
Operations Manager — Peter Roughneen

BHF-BANK AG
Full Branch Office

BHF BANK House, 61 Queen Street, London EC4R 1AE
Tel: (171) 634 2300; (171) 528 8292 **Fax:** (171) 220 7140; (171) 329 4617 **Telex:** 919386 **Swift:** BHFB GB 2L
Reuters: BHFL

Senior Executive Officers
Director & General Manager — Mark Ischreyt 🖷 **489 9344**
Director & General Manager — Bernd Kummer

www.euromoneydirectory.com				UNITED KINGDOM (+44)

General-Lending (DCM, SL)
Head of Corporate Banking → Peter Hale *Director of Credit*
Mark Ischreyt *Director & General Manager* ☏ **489 9344**

General - Treasury
Head of Treasury → Richard Inglis *Director* ☏ **634 2300**

Equity Capital Markets
Tel: 634 2406 Fax: 329 4617

Equity Repo / Securities Lending
Head → Richard Inglis ☏ **634 2300** ☏ **329 4617**

Syndicated Lending

Loan-Related Activities
Trade Finance → Christoph Schroer *Assistant Director* ☏ **634 2347**

Other (Trade Finance)
Documentary Credits → Andy Wyatt *Manager*

Money Markets

Domestic Commercial Paper
Head of Origination; Head of Sales; Head of Trading → Peter Gare *Manager*

Money Markets - General
International Money Markets → Nick Nissim
Ed Flack *Manager, International Money Markets*
Dino Wyatt
Caroline Kloos
Andrew Crawford

Foreign Exchange
Tel: 634 2321
Country Head → Michael Spooner *Manager*
Corporate Sales → Gary Webber *Manager*
Nelly Hermitant
Jim Evans
John Miller *Assistant Director*

FX Traders / Sales People
Darryl Maycock
John Lidyard
Chris Wilkins

Settlement / Clearing
Tel: 634 2423
Equity Settlement; Fixed-Income Settlement; Foreign Exchange Settlement → Marian Walker *Manager* ☏ **634 2426**
Operations → Achim Vogt *Assistant Director*
Alastair Cummings *Assistant Director*

Administration
Head of Administration → John Gifford *Manager*

Technology & Systems
Clarel Sookun *Assistant Director, IT*

Compliance
Peter Ward *Director* ☏ **634 2341**

Accounts / Audit
Financial Control → David Guscot *Manager*

Other (Administration)
Personnel → Jutta Surburg *Assistant Director*

BMO Nesbitt Burns International Limited — Subsidiary Company

Formerly known as: BMO Nesbitt Thomson Limited
Bucklersbury House, 3 Queen Victoria Street, London EC4N 8NT
Tel: (171) 489 8844; (171) 248 2028 Fax: (171) 236 7041; (171) 236 7258 Telex: 884645 Reuters: BMNT-V (Bonds),
Telerate: 3797/9
Reuters: FRYL-O (Equities)

Senior Executive Officers
Chief Executive Officer → Michael J G Chapman *Managing Director*
MD, International Equities → Hans-Jürgen Queisser

Euromoney Directory 1999   **1701**

UNITED KINGDOM (+44)   www.euromoneydirectory.com

BMO Nesbitt Burns International Limited (cont)

Debt Capital Markets / Fixed Income
Global Head   John Keogh *MD, International Fixed-Income*

Domestic Government Bonds
Head of Trading   Tom Ormesher *VP, Canadian Government Securities*
                                Colin Burgess *Canadian Government Securities*

Eurobonds
Head of Syndication   Edward Mizuhara *Vice President*
                                Todd James
                                Ruggero Cessari
Head of Sales   David Creighton *VP & Head, Fixed-Income Sales*
                                André Lajeunesse *Director & VP, Singapore*
                                Filip Papich
                                Paul Petrashko *Vice President*
                                Jean Gauthier *Sales*
                                Rebecca Chan *Hong Kong*
                                Graham Hastings *Sales*
Head of Trading   Paul Mitchell *VP & Head, Fixed-Income Trading*
                                Andy Lowe *Vice President*
                                Tim Mills *Hong Kong*

Asset-Backed Securities / Securitization
Global Head   Paul Stevenson *MD, Int'l Securitization & Structured Finance*

Fixed-Income Repo
Head of Repo   David Woodley

Equity Capital Markets

International Equities
Head of Syndication   Hans-Jürgen Queisser *MD, International Equities*
Head of Sales   Brian Fullerton *Director & Vice President*
                                Michael Villeneau *Director & Vice President*
                                Jacques Vaillancourt *Vice President*
                                Nicola Bastick *Sales*
Head of Trading   Michael Rainey *Director & Vice President*
                                Andrew Bastick *Vice President*

Other (International Equity)
International Equity Settlements   Dennis Cooper *Manager*
                                    Carol Mortlock

Corporate Finance / M&A Advisory
Global Head   Michael J G Chapman *Managing Director*
Regional Head   Graham Roberts *Vice President & Director*

Settlement / Clearing
Settlement (General)   Peter Hicks *Manager, Settlements*
                                Mark Cheal *Settlements*
                                Tina Doughty *Settlements*
Operations   Tony Ham *Operations Manager*

Administration

Legal / In-House Counsel
                                Atul Tiwari *Director, Legal & Compliance*

Bozano, Simonsen (UK) Limited   Subsidiary Company

4th Floor, 12 Nicholas Lane, London EC4N 7BN
Tel: (171) 456 7200 **Fax:** (171) 456 7222

Senior Executive Officers
Director   Antonio Coury ✉ coury@bozano.com.br

Debt Capital Markets / Fixed Income

Bonds - General
Fixed Income Sales   Marco Amorim *Sales* ☏ 456 7205 ✉ amorim@bozano.com.br

Equity Capital Markets

Domestic Equities
Head of Sales   Alex Alencar *Sales* ☏ 456 1203 ✉ alex@bozano.com.br
                                Pedro Pires Joao *Sales* ☏ 456 1210 ✉ pires@bozano.com.br

www.euromoneydirectory.com UNITED KINGDOM (+44)

Bremer Landesbank Capital Markets plc
Subsidiary Company

Formerly known as: Bremer Landesbank
71 Queen Victoria Street, London EC4V 4NL
Tel: (171) 972 5450 **Fax:** (171) 972 5453

Senior Executive Officers
Director   Jurgen Schuhmacher

British Arab Commercial Bank Limited
Head Office

30 Gresham Street, London EC2V 7LP
Tel: (171) 606 7777 **Fax:** (171) 600 3318 **Telex:** 22961 BACMG **Swift:** BACM GB 2L **Reuters:** BACM

Senior Executive Officers
Chairman   John Hill
Chief Executive Officer   Ron Shaw
Treasurer   Bashir Gazla
Deputy Chief Executive & GM   Mohamed Fezzani
Assistant General Manager, Marketing & Sales   George Kimber
Assistant General Manager, Finance   Cris Denby
Assistant General Manager, Operations   Peter Murray
Company Secretary, Personnel   Reg Egan

Syndicated Lending
Head of Syndicated Lending   Geoff Duncanson *Head of Lending*
Head of Credit Committee   Alison Burns *Manager, Credit Control*

Other (Trade Finance)
Trade Services   Gary Bishop *Manager*

Foreign Exchange
FX Traders / Sales People
                                                        Chris Bellinger *Chief Dealer*

Settlement / Clearing
Operations   Ian Macleod *Senior Manager*
                                                        Roger Screech *Senior Manager M.I.S.*

Asset Management
Other (Asset Management)
Asset Finance   Stephen Maltby *Manager*

Other Departments
Correspondent Banking   Jawed Ghani *Senior Manager*
                                                        Ken Law *Manager*
                                                        Jim Walker *Manager*

Administration
Head of Administration   Steve Cook *Manager*
Business Development   Antoine Bassila *Senior Manager*
                                                        John Fordyce *Senior Manager*
Head of Marketing   Rollo Greenfield *Head of Marketing*

Compliance
                                                        John Trench *Manager*

Accounts / Audit
Internal Audit   John Trench *Manager*

Other (Administration)
Treasury Administration   Sean Dooley *Manager*

British Credit Trust
Head Office

Formerly known as: City & Industrial Securities
Nova Building, Slough, SL1 1ED
PO Box 392, Slough, SL1 1ED
Tel: (1753) 573 211; (1753) 534 098 **Fax:** (1753) 821 390; (1753) 692 830 **Email:** bct@pobox.com

Senior Executive Officers
Chairman   Roger Gewolb
Treasurer   Phill Battershall *Group Financial Controller*

Euromoney Directory 1999 **1703**

UNITED KINGDOM (+44)   www.euromoneydirectory.com

The British Linen Bank Limited — Head Office

4 Melville Street, Edinburgh, EH3 7NZ
Tel: (131) 243 8386 **Fax:** (131) 243 8393

Senior Executive Officers
Chief Executive Officer   Robin Browning *Chief Executive*
Financial Director   Margaret Smart

Brown Brothers Harriman Limited — Subsidiary Company

Veritas House, 125 Finsbury Pavement, London EC2A 1PN
Tel: (171) 588 6166 **Fax:** (171) 614 2440 **Telex:** 8954033 BBHSTK G **Cable:** BROWNSTOCK LONDO

Senior Executive Officers
Chairman   Hampton Lynch
Financial Director   Thomas P McGing *Accountant*
Managing Director   Duncan A Clark
Relationship Manager
                                  Geoffrey J Mills *Head, Institutional Sales*
                                  Peter J Gibbons *Manager, Investor Services*

Administration
Head of Administration   Margaret E Garland *Assistant Manager*
Technology & Systems
Information Technology   William G Connor *Assistant Manager*

Brown, Shipley & Company Limited — Subsidiary Company

Founders Court, Lothbury, London EC2R 7HE
Tel: (171) 606 9833 **Fax:** (171) 796 2601 **Telex:** 94014226 **Swift:** BSCP GB 2L **Reuters:** BSCL; BSBN (Monitor)

Senior Executive Officers
Chairman   Richard Mansell-Jones
Chief Executive Officer   Patrick Moorson *Managing Director* ☏ **282 3271**
Financial Director   Tim Saunt ☏ **282 3340**
Treasurer   Dennis Gepp *Treasurer* ☏ **606 2502**
Director   Thomas Dozin ☏ **282 3273**

Others (Senior Executives)
                                  Peter Shand *Director* ☏ **282 3342**

Debt Capital Markets / Fixed Income
Department: Capital Markets
Tel: 606 2502 **Fax:** 796 2601
Head of Fixed Income Trading   Dennis Gepp *Treasurer* ☏ **606 2502**

Eurobonds
Head of Sales   Phillip Witney *Capital Markets Sales* ☏ **606 2502**
Head of Trading   Gareth Jones *Capital Markets Dealer*

Fixed-Income Repo
Head of Repo   Christopher Ridley *Dealer* ☏ **606 6147**
Other   Gary Callow *Assistant Manager Operations* ☏ **282 3223**

Equity Capital Markets
Department: Capital Markets
Tel: 606 2502 **Fax:** 796 2601
Domestic Equities
Head of Sales   Gareth Jones *Capital Markets Dealer*
                                  Phillip Witney *Dealer*

International Equities
Head of Sales   Gareth Jones *Capital Markets Dealer*
                                  Phillip Witney *Dealer*

Syndicated Lending
Department: Corporate Banking & Credit
Tel: 606 9833 **Fax:** 606 4825
Head of Syndicated Lending   Robert Smoker *Head, Corporate Banking & Credit* ☏ **282 3360**
Head of Origination   Richard Whittaker *Deputy Head, Corporate Banking & Credit* ☏ **282 3344**
Head of Syndication   Jon Watson *Client Manager* ☏ **282 3353**
Head of Credit Committee   Thomas Dozin *Director* ☏ **282 3273**

Money Markets
Tel: 606 3147 **Fax:** 796 2601
Head of Money Markets   Lindsey Stafford *Senior Dealer*

1704   Euromoney Directory 1999

www.euromoneydirectory.com   UNITED KINGDOM (+44)

Foreign Exchange
Tel: 606 3144 Fax: 796 2601
Head of Foreign Exchange   Michael Crump *Chief FX Dealer*
FX Traders / Sales People
Commercial   John Hunt *Senior Dealer*
Risk Management
Tel: 282 3360 Fax: 606 4825
Head of Risk Management   Robert Smoker *Head, Corporate Banking & Credit* ☏ **282 3360**
Settlement / Clearing
Department: Operations Department
Tel: 606 9833 Fax: 796 3045
Head of Settlement / Clearing   Geoffrey Mayhew *Head of Operations* ☏ **282 3235**
Equity Settlement; Fixed-Income Settlement Gary Callow *Assistant Manager Operations* ☏ **282 3223**
Operations; Back-Office   Paul Dowell *Deputy Head, Operations* ☏ **282 3253**
Global Custody
Fax: 796 3045
Country Head   Gary Callow *Assistant Manager Operations* ☏ **282 3223**
Administration
Technology & Systems
                                    Peter Shand *Director* ☏ **282 3342**
Compliance
                                    Steve Hoad *Compliance Controller* ☏ **282 3332**

BSI-Banca della Svizzera Italiana   Full Branch Office

Windsor House, 39 King Street, London EC2V 8DQ
Tel: (171) 600 0033 Fax: (171) 606 3484; (171) 726 8509 Telex: 884821

Senior Executive Officers
Managing Director / General Manager   John Erskine

Buchanan Capital Management Limited   Head Office

10 Stratton Street, London W1X 5FE
Tel: (171) 973 8070 Fax: (171) 973 8072 Telex: 911397 BCHPTNG
Email: firstname.lastname@buchanan.partners.com

Senior Executive Officers
President & Chief Executive Officer   Peregrine Moncreiffe
Financial Director   Richard Szwagrzak
Chief Operating Officer   Nina Rossides

BULBANK   Representative Office

1 Gracechurch Street, London EC3V 0DD
Tel: (171) 626 1888 Fax: (171) 626 2233 Telex: 886928

Senior Executive Officers
London Representative   Georgi Georgiev

Burdett Buckeridge & Young   Full Branch Office

Level 3, 46 New Broad Street, London EC2M 1JH
Tel: (171) 600 3376 Fax: (171) 614 1826 Telerate: BBY
Website: www.bby.com.an

Senior Executive Officers
Managing Director   David Landauer
Managing Director   Graham Morton ✉ **gmorton@jefco.com**
Equity Capital Markets
Department: Equities Australian / New Zealand
International Equities
Head of Origination   Graham Morton *Managing Director* ✉ **gmorton@jefco.com**
Head of Sales   J Mullineux
Head of Trading   M Shortland
Head of Research   M White

Euromoney Directory 1999 **1705**

UNITED KINGDOM (+44)   www.euromoneydirectory.com

Burdett Buckeridge & Young (cont)
Settlement / Clearing
Equity Settlement   Polly Ormond

Byblos Bank Belgium SA
Full Branch Office

Suite 5, Berkeley Square House, London W1X 5PE
Tel: (171) 493 3537 **Fax:** (171) 493 1233 **Telex:** 893344 BYBLOA G

Senior Executive Officers
Senior Manager   Souheil F Azar
Others (Senior Executives)
                                Andrew O Hall *Deputy Manager*
                                Elias Absouleiman *Assistant Manager, Credit*

Byblos Bank Europe

Berkeley Square House, Suite 5, Berkeley Square, London W1X 5PE
Tel: (171) 493 3537 **Fax:** (171) 493 1233

Senior Executive Officers
General Manager   Souheil F Azar

Caisse Centrale des Banques Populaires
Representative Office

76 Cannon Street, London EC4N 6AE
Tel: (171) 827 0066 **Fax:** (171) 827 0067

Senior Executive Officers
Deputy Representative   Frederic Bouley
UK Resident Representative   Richard Thompson

Caja de Ahorros de Galicia

2nd Floor, 50 Hans Crescent, London SW1X 0NA
Tel: (171) 584 4604 **Fax:** (171) 584 5116

Senior Executive Officers
Managing Director / General Manager J Calvino

Campbell Lutyens & Co Limited

5 Clifford Street, London W1X 1RB
Tel: (171) 439 7191 **Fax:** (171) 437 0153 **Email:** cl@campbell-lutyens.com

Senior Executive Officers
Chairman   W Dacombe
Managing Director / General Manager   A J W Campbell

Canara Bank

Longbow House, 14/20 Chiswell Street, London EC1Y 4TW
Tel: (171) 628 2187 **Fax:** (171) 374 2468 **Telex:** 8956961 CANARA **Swift:** CNRB GB 2L **Telex:** 8956962 CANARA

Senior Executive Officers
General Manager   Vasudeva Vittal Kamath

Cantor Fitzgerald International
Head Office

1 America Square, London EC3N 2LT
Tel: (171) 617 7000; (171) 894 7000 **Fax:** (171) 894 7822 **Telex:** 919581 CANTOR G

Debt Capital Markets / Fixed Income
Domestic Government Bonds
Head of Trading
                                Aynard de Clermont Tonnerre *Head of Trading*
                                Patrick Johnston *Head of Trading*
                                Shaun Lynn *Head of Trading*
                                Gary Read *Director* [T] **894 7122** [F] **894 7262** [E] **gread@cantor.com**

www.euromoneydirectory.com   UNITED KINGDOM (+44)

Eurobonds
Head of Trading

Les Dyer *Head of Trading* ☎ **894 7900**
Tony Burns *Head of Trading* ☎ **894 7900**

Fixed-Income Repo
Marketing & Product Development
Trading

Cheryl Dunlop *Marketing*
John Czarnowski *Head, Gilt Repo*
Ian Mackay *Head, Bond Trading*
Christian Mercier *Head, French Repo*
Dean Salmon *Head, Multicurrency Repo*
Crispin Wilson *Head, Italian Repo*
Robert Kitchim *Head, Eurobond Trading*

Settlement / Clearing
Tel: 894 7270 **Fax:** 894 7822
Fixed-Income Settlement

Robert L Turner
Nicholas J Pincott
Sharon E A Leonida
David Clarke *Head*

Operations
Administration
Compliance

David Clarke *Head*

Cargill Financial Markets

Head Office

Knowle Hill Park, Fairmile Lane, Cobham, Surrey KT11 2BD
Tel: (1932) 861 000 **Fax:** (1932) 861 220

Senior Executive Officers
President
Treasurer

Huub Spiering
Jay Olson *Vice President & European Treasury*

Debt Capital Markets / Fixed Income
Tel: 861 580 **Fax:** 861 220
Global Head

Dave Rogers

Fixed-Income Repo
Trading

Andrew Holdsworth *Manager of Repo Desk* ☎ **861 378**
Rebecca Todd *Repo Trader* ☎ **861 446**

Risk Management
Global Head

David Corridan

Corporate Finance / M&A Advisory
Global Head

Jay Olson *Vice President & European Treasury*

Cariverona Banca SpA

Full Branch Office

63 Queen Victoria Street, London EC4N 4UA
Tel: (171) 248 8282; (171) 329 3113 **Fax:** (171) 815 0451; (171) 815 4438 **Telex:** 290605 **Swift:** CRVR GB 2X
Reuters: CRVL

Senior Executive Officers
General Manager
DGM & Treasury Manager

Eugenio Lapenna ☎ **815 4400**
Angelo Ciofffi ☎ **815 4410**

Debt Capital Markets / Fixed Income
Bonds - General
Fixed Income Dealer

Claudio Capuani

Syndicated Lending
Other (Syndicated Lending)
Credit
Chief Dealer

Giuseppe Franceschetti *Manager*
Stephen Morris ☎ **815 4413**

Money Markets
Tel: 329 3113 **Fax:** 815 4438
Global Head

David Waight *Money Market Dealer* ☎ **815 4412**

Foreign Exchange
Tel: 329 3113 **Fax:** 815 4438
Global Head

Stephen Morris ☎ **815 4413**

FX Traders / Sales People
Dealer

William O'Reilly ☎ **815 4414**

Euromoney Directory 1999   **1707**

UNITED KINGDOM (+44)   www.euromoneydirectory.com

Cariverona Banca SpA (cont)
Risk Management
Other Currency Swap / FX Options Personnel
Futures   Jeff Tottman ☏ 815 4411
Administration
Compliance
Compliance and Organisation   Brian Bishop
Accounts / Audit
                                   Shahbaz Khan *Chief Accountant*

Cassa di Risparmio di Firenze SpA — Representative Office
Wax Chandler's Hall, Gresham Street, London EC2V 7AD
Tel: (171) 600 4342 Fax: (171) 600 4350
Senior Executive Officers
Representative   Marco Falleri

Cater Allen International Limited
30 Gresham Street, London EC2V 7HT
Tel: (171) 606 6064 Fax: (171) 600 3670 Telex: 269770 Swift: BARL GB 2L
Debt Capital Markets / Fixed Income
Fixed-Income Repo
Head of Repo   Ronny Maiti *Head of Repo Trading*
Trading   Paul Croucher *Manager, International Repo Trading*
                                   William Smith *Gilt Repo Trader*
                                   James Brown *Gilt Repo Trader*
                                   Nicholas Poole *Gilt Repo Trader*
                                   Kevin Whittern *International Repo Trader*
                                   Richard Childs *International Repo Trader*
Other   Robert Palliser *Marketing, Sales & Product Development*
Equity Capital Markets
Equity Repo / Securities Lending
Head   Ronny Maiti *Head of Equity Repo Trading*
                                   Steven Lamb *Manager, UK Equity Repo / Securities Lending*
Head of Trading   Alex Steel *UK Equity Trader*
                                   Tina Brooking *UK Equity Trader*
                                   Michael O'Donnell *Manager, International Equity Repo Trading*
                                   Alex Varghese *International Equity Trader*
                                   Jason Hall *International Equity Trader*
                                   Mark Donnelly *International Equity Trader*

Money Markets
Department: Money Market / Futures Trading
Money Markets - General
Cash Gilts / Futures Trading   John Ilsley
                                   Michael Lee
                                   Paul Barnes
CD Trader   Paul McCarthy
                                   Steven Moir

Risk Management
Head of Risk Management   Mark Anderson
Settlement / Clearing
Department: Settlement / Clearing / Fees / Rebates
Operations   Steven Gates
Other   Mark Vincent *Middle Office Manager*

Cater Allen Limited — Head Office
30 Gresham Street, London EC2V 7HT
Tel: (171) 606 6064 Fax: (171) 606 0327 Telex: 269770
Senior Executive Officers
Chief Executive Officer   Tony S Hibbitt *Chief Executive*
Director   David Hopton
Managing Director   Ronny Maiti

www.euromoneydirectory.com UNITED KINGDOM (+44)

Debt Capital Markets / Fixed Income
Fixed-Income Repo
Head of Repo — David Hopton *Director*
 Tony S Hibbitt *Chief Executive*
Marketing & Product Development — Robert Palliser *Manager, Marketing & Sales* ☎ 600 3706 ℻ 710 6904
 ✉ robertp@cater-allen.co.uk
Trading — Steve Lamb *Equities*
 Mark Donnelly *Trader*
 Paul Croucher *Gilts & Corporate Bonds*
 Mike O'Donnell *Trading Manager*
 Ronny Maiti *Director*
 Alex Varghese *Senior Trader*
 Jason Hall *Trader*
 Kevin Whitten *Trader*
Sales — Robert Palliser *Manager, Marketing & Sales* ☎ 600 3706 ℻ 710 6904
 ✉ robertp@cater-allen.co.uk

Equity Capital Markets
Equity Repo / Securities Lending
Marketing & Product Development — Robert Palliser *Manager, Marketing & Sales* ☎ 600 3706 ℻ 710 6904
 ✉ robertp@cater-allen.co.uk

Money Markets
Global Head — Ronny Maiti *Managing Director*

Risk Management
Global Head — Michael Carter

Settlement / Clearing
Country Head — Mark Vinsent

Caymanx Trust Co Limited
Subsidiary Company

34 Athol Street, Douglas, Isle of Man IM1 1RD
Tel: (1624) 672 320 **Fax:** (1624) 662 192
Website: www.enterprise.net/caymanx

Senior Executive Officers
Chairman — Eric Crutchley
Managing Director — Eammon Harkin
Chief Operating Officer — Barry Williams *Banking Manager*

Debt Capital Markets / Fixed Income
Private Placements
Head of Origination — Barry Williams *Banking Manager*

Syndicated Lending
Loan-Related Activities
Project Finance — Barry Williams *Banking Manager*

Money Markets
Global Head — Barry Williams *Banking Manager*

Foreign Exchange
Global Head — Barry Williams *Banking Manager*

Cazenove & Co

12 Tokenhouse Yard, London EC2N 7AN
Tel: (171) 588 2828 **Fax:** (171) 606 9205 **Telex:** 886758
Website: www.cazenove.co.uk

Senior Executive Officers
Chief Executive Officer — Mark A Loveday
 U David Barnett
Financial Director; Treasurer — Michael Power
International Division — Edward T Whitley

General-Lending (DCM, SL)
Head of Corporate Banking — J G H Paynter

Debt Capital Markets / Fixed Income
Head of Debt Capital Markets — Charles R M Bishop

Equity Capital Markets
Head of Equity Capital Markets — Nigel Rowe

UNITED KINGDOM (+44)   www.euromoneydirectory.com

CBI-UBP International Limited

26 St James's Square, London SW1Y 4JH
Tel: (171) 839 2221 Fax: (171) 839 2514 Telex: 21154

Senior Executive Officers
Others (Senior Executives)
Member de Executive Management   Michael de Picciotto

Cedef Assets Limited

100 Piccadilly, London W1V 9FN
Tel: (171) 499 1199 Fax: (171) 491 7422 Telex: 922322
Website: www.cedef.com

Senior Executive Officers
Chairman   Marco Escribano ☎ 208 0310

Debt Capital Markets / Fixed Income
Bonds - General
Italian Government Bonds   Alan Bridger ☎ 499 1399
Polish Government Bonds   John Black ☎ 499 2099
Greek Government Bonds   Alan Bridger ☎ 499 1399
Libor-Based / Floating-Rate Products
Asset Swaps   Paul Rushton

Settlement / Clearing
Head of Settlement / Clearing   Simon Ayres ☎ 491 7851

Administration
Head of Administration   Lisa Huntingford ☎ 208 0310

Compliance
                                      Jane Arrowsmith ☎ 629 1944

Accounts / Audit
Accounts   Carolyn Hindhaugh ☎ 409 0944

Cedef Capital Services Limited

100 Piccadilly, London W1V 9FN
Tel: (171) 499 5299; (171) 499 4899 Fax: (171) 499 3399 Reuters: CEDE
Website: www.cedef.com

Senior Executive Officers
Managing Director   Simon Ring

Debt Capital Markets / Fixed Income
Emerging Market Bonds
Head of Emerging Markets   John Black ☎ 499 2099
Other (Emerging Markets Bonds)
Emerging Market Bond Options   Chris Hegney Head ☎ 499 3599
Emerging Market Bond Swaps   Karl Bucci

Settlement / Clearing
Head of Settlement / Clearing   Fiona Morrison ☎ +41 (22) 361 5151

Administration
Head of Administration   Lisa Huntingford ☎ 208 0310

Compliance
                                      Jane Arrowsmith ☎ 629 1944

Accounts / Audit
Accountant   Carolyn Hindhaugh ☎ 409 0944

Cedel Bank   Representative Office

42nd Floor, 1 Canada Square, Canary Wharf, London E14 5DR
Tel: (171) 862 7000 Fax: (171) 862 7001

Senior Executive Officers
Others (Senior Executives)
Manager Sales UK & Ireland   Michael Goonan ☎ 862 7031 📠 862 7156

www.euromoneydirectory.com   UNITED KINGDOM (+44)

Debt Capital Markets / Fixed Income
Fixed-Income Repo
Marketing & Product Development; Sales   Brian Staunton ☏ 862 7072
Equity Capital Markets
Equity Repo / Securities Lending
Head   John Arnesen *Senior Manager, Strategic Securities Lending* ☏ 862 7183
     ℻ 862 7187
Marketing & Product Development; Marketing   Brian Staunton ☏ 862 7072
Asset Management
Other (Asset Management)
Collateral & Asset Management   Saheed Awan *Senior Manager* ☏ 862 7085 ℻ 862 7712

Celtic Bank Limited   Head Office

PO Box 114, Lord Street & Bank Hill Corner, Douglas, Isle of Man IM99 1JW
Tel: (1624) 622 856 **Fax:** (1624) 620 926

Senior Executive Officers
Chairman & Managing Director   Richard G Danielson
Others (Senior Executives)
Director   Simon M Young *Managing Director*
     Allan L A Bonbernard
     James F G Tait
     Peter A Willers
     Martin Quayle

The Central Bank of China   Representative Office

5th Floor, Basildon House, 7 Moorgate, London EC2R 6AQ
Tel: (171) 606 6666 **Fax:** (171) 606 1366 **Telex:** 921650 GOVTBANK **Reuters:** CBCL
Bloomberg: chiew chang-600 1018/9

Senior Executive Officers
Representative   Ching-Chuan Chuang
Others (Senior Executives)
Deputy Representative   Anne Hsu

Central Bank of Kuwait   Representative Office

150 Cheapside, London EC2V 6LP
Tel: (171) 600 3645 **Fax:** (171) 600 3156

Central Bank of the Republic of Turkey   Representative Office

Centric House, 391 The Strand, London WC2R 0LT
Tel: (171) 379 0548 **Fax:** (171) 379 5024 **Telex:** 8813770 TCMBLN **Reuters:** CBTA-Z **Cable:** MERKEZBANK LONDO

Senior Executive Officers
Representative   Nejdet Huddam

Ceskoslovenská Obchodni Banka as   Representative Office

20 St Dunstan's Hill, London EC3R 8HL
Tel: (171) 338 0804 **Fax:** (171) 338 0805

Senior Executive Officers
Chief Manager   David C Dicker

Chang Hwa Commercial Bank Limited

Level 6, City Tower, 40 Basinghall Street, London EC2 5DE
Tel: (171) 628 3476 **Fax:** (171) 600 3227 **Telex:** 8811682 CHCBLN **Swift:** CCBC GB 2L

Senior Executive Officers
Chairman   M H Tsai
President   C S Wu
Managing Director / General Manager   Frank C L Tu

Euromoney Directory 1999 **1711**

UNITED KINGDOM (+44)   www.euromoneydirectory.com

Chartered Trust plc
Head Office

24/26 Newport Road, Cardiff, South Glamorgan CF2 1SR
Tel: (1222) 296 000 Fax: (1222) 485 517

Senior Executive Officers
Managing Director   John Davis ☏ **296 002**

Others (Senior Executives)
Paul Barry *Director* ☏ **296 008**
Paul Blake *Director* ☏ **296 006**
Stewart Davies *Director* ☏ **296 500**
David Gow *Director* ☏ **296 010**
Jeff Roberts *Director* ☏ **296 760**
Mike Goodfellow *General Manager* ☏ **296 400**
Bill Hamer *General Manager* ☏ **296 802**
Stuart Simpson *General Manager* ☏ **296 200**
Simon Richmond *General Manager* ☏ **296 962**

Charterhouse Bank Limited
Head Office

1 Paternoster Row, St Paul's, London EC4M 7DH
Tel: (171) 248 4000 Fax: (171) 246 2033 Telex: 884276 Swift: CHBL GB 2L Reuters: CHAL-M

Senior Executive Officers
Chairman   David Parish
Financial Director   Robert Dix *Group Finance Officer*

Charterhouse Development Capital Limited
Full Branch Office

1 Paternoster Row, St Paul's, London EC4M 7DH
Tel: (171) 248 4000 Fax: (171) 334 5333 Telex: 884276 Swift: CHBL GB 2L Reuters: CHAL-M

Senior Executive Officers
Chairman   Edward Cox
Financial Director   Tom Plant *Finance Director*

Charterhouse plc
Head Office

1 Paternoster Row, St Paul's, London EC4M 7DH
Tel: (171) 248 4000 Fax: (171) 246 2033 Telex: 884276 Swift: CHBL GB 2L Reuters: CHAL-M

Senior Executive Officers
Chairman & Chief Executive Officer   David Parish
Financial Director   Robert Dix *Group Finance Officer*

Charterhouse Securities Limited
Full Branch Office

1 Paternoster Row, St Paul's, London EC4M 7DH
Tel: (171) 248 4000 Fax: (171) 246 2033 Telex: 884276 Swift: CHBL GB 2L Reuters: CHAL-M

Senior Executive Officers
Chief Executive Officer   Robert Bonton *Chief Executive*
Financial Director   Robert Dix *Group Finance Officer*

Chase Asset Management (London) Limited
Subsidiary Company

Vintners Place, 68 Upper Thames Street, London EC4V 3BJ
Tel: (171) 777 2000 Fax: (171) 777 0917

Senior Executive Officers

Others (Senior Executives)
Gordon Ross *Senior Officer*
Michael Browne *Senior Officer*

www.euromoneydirectory.com UNITED KINGDOM (+44)

The Chase Manhattan Bank
Subsidiary Company

125 London Wall, London EC2Y 5AJ
Tel: (171) 777 2000 **Fax:** (171) 777 3912 **Telex:** 8954581 CMB G **Swift:** CHAS GB 2L
Reuters: CHMM (Treasury); CHCD (FX Trading); CHSL (FX Trading); CDKL (FX Trading); CHEX (FX Trading); CHML (FX Trading); CHGL (FX Trading); CHOP (FX Options); CHND (Night Desk); CHFS (Interest Rate Management Group); CHFL (Interest Rate Management Group); CHIS (Interest Rate Management Group); CHES (Interest Rate Management Group); CHLD (Interest Rate Management Group); CHMC (FX Corporate Sales); CHOP (FX Corporate Sales); CHOQ (FX Corporate Sales); CHCL (Regional Banks); CHDM (Emerging Markets); CHGL (Commodities)
Website: www.chase.com

Senior Executive Officers
Others (Senior Executives)
Europe, Africa & Middle East   Herb Aspbury *Co-Regional Executive*
                                                 Bruce Hannon *Co-Regional Executive*
UK   Mark Garvin *Senior Country Officer*

Equity Capital Markets
Other (International Equity)
Equity Derivatives   Mark Wells

Money Markets
Department: Treasury
Money Markets - General
Treasury   Andy Panzures

Foreign Exchange
FX Traders / Sales People
FX Options   David Adamson
Global Trading Division   Tom Hoppe

Corporate Finance / M&A Advisory
Aerospace   John Nozell
Asia Pacific   Ryuzo Asazaka
Automative and Trucking   Bob Till
Central & Eastern Europe   Homi Mullan
Chemical and Related Industries   Mark London Sullivan
Commodity Finance   Nadeem Fayyaz
Financial Institutions   Demetrie Comnas
Insurance   Alan Badanes
Media & Telecommunications   John White
Mining & Metals   Dennis McShane
Mutual Funds   Christian Yates
Northern Europe Corporate Finance   Richard Smith
Oil & Gas   Jonathan Fanklin
Shipping   Michael Borch
Trade Finance and Advisory   John Penn
                                                 Kim Wiehl
Venture Capital   Lindsay Stuart

Global Custody
Department: Global Custody & Transaction Services
Other (Global Custody)
Investor Services   Jeremy Jewitt
Treasury Solutions   Richard Lowry
Trust Services   Darryl West

Other Departments
Economic Research   Robin Marshall

Other Departments
Private Bank   Federico Imbert

Administration
Compliance
                                                 Brian Harte

Corporate Communications
                                                 John M Anderson

Other (Administration)
Credit   Bill Lawes
Human Resources   Conrad Venter

UNITED KINGDOM (+44)

The Chase Manhattan Bank (cont)
Other (Administration) (cont)
Operations | Geoff Taylor
 | John Irvine
Risk Management | Paul Shotton

Chase Manhattan International Limited
Subsidiary Company

125 London Wall, London EC2Y 5AJ
Tel: (171) 777 2000 **Fax:** (171) 777 4727 **Telex:** 94060177 CHIL G **Swift:** CHAS GB 22

Senior Executive Officers
Others (Senior Executives)
Europe, Africa & Middle East | Herb Aspbury *Co-Regional Executive*
 | Bruce Hannon *Co-Regional Executive*
UK | Mark Garvin *Senior Country Officer*

Debt Capital Markets / Fixed Income
Bonds - General
International Fixed Income - Sales | Kevin Brolley
International Fixed Income - Structured Finance | Richard Tray
International Fixed Income - Syndicate | Michael Ridley

High Yield / Junk Bonds
Head | Stephen Eichenberger
Head of Sales; Head of Trading | Geoffrey Sherry
Head of Research | Patrick Steiner

Asset-Backed Securities / Securitization
Regional Head | Stuart Honse

Syndicated Lending
Other (Syndicated Lending)
Agency Loans | Stephen Hurford

Settlement / Clearing
Futures & Options Clearing | Mark James
 | Philip Newlyn

Other Departments
Commodities | Martin Fraenkel

Chase Manhattan plc
Subsidiary Company

125 London Wall, London EC2Y 5AJ
Tel: (171) 777 2000 **Fax:** (171) 777 4727 **Telex:** 8954681 CMB G **Swift:** CHAS GB 2L

Senior Executive Officers
Others (Senior Executives)
Europe, Africa & Middle East | Herb Aspbury *Co-Regional Executive*
 | Bruce Hannon *Co-Regional Executive*
UK | Mark Garvin *Senior Country Officer*

Syndicated Lending
Other (Trade Finance)
Syndicated Finance | Don McCree
Power & Environmental Infrastructure Finance | Bruce Bettencourt
Project Finance & Advisory | Guy Spaull

Foreign Exchange
Head of Sales | Drew Gross

Risk Management
Other (FI Derivatives)
Derivatives Sales | David Brown

Corporate Finance / M&A Advisory
Head of Mergers & Acquisition | Jim Downing
Acquistion Finance | David Wood

Other (Corporate Finance)
Leveraged Finance | Tom Walker

www.euromoneydirectory.com UNITED KINGDOM (+44)

The Chiba Bank Limited Full Branch Office

Atlas House, 1 King Street, London EC2V 8AU
Tel: (171) 315 3111 Fax: (171) 600 3452 Telex: 8812534 CHIBAL G Reuters: CHBL

Senior Executive Officers
General Manager Yasuyuki Kawana

Chiba International Limited Subsidiary Company

3rd Floor, Atlas House, 1 King Street, London EC2V 8AU
Tel: (171) 315 3115 Fax: (171) 315 3113 Telex: 8813162 CHIBAI G

Senior Executive Officers
Chairman Toru Yoshimura
Chief Executive Officer Robert D Bates *Director & Secretary*
Financial Director Yasuyuki Kawana *Director*
Chief Operating Officer Yukihito Inamura
Treasurer Morio Tsumita
Managing Director Mutsuo Hanzawa ☎ **315 3114**

Risk Management
Head of Risk Management Keith Band *Head of Risk Management* ☎ **315 3116**

China Construction Bank Representative Office

29/30 Cornhill, London EC3V 3ND
Tel: (171) 220 7871 Fax: (171) 220 7849 Telex: 881153

Senior Executive Officers
Chief Representative Mr Zhang

Chinatrust Commercial Bank Representative Office

7th Floor, Aldermary House, 15 Queen Street, London EC4N 1TX
Tel: (171) 329 0033 Fax: (171) 329 0828 Telex: 921870 Email: ctcbuk@compuserve.com

Senior Executive Officers
SVP & Chief Representative Charles Y J Yip

Cho Hung Bank

3rd Floor 1 Minster Court, Mincing Lane, London EC3R 7AA
Tel: (171) 623 7791 Fax: (171) 283 8464 Telex: 8951125 Swift: CHOH GB 2L

Senior Executive Officers
Managing Director / General Manager Chang-Ho Kim

Christiania Bank og Kreditkasse ASA Full Branch Office

Lloyds Chambers, 1 Portsoken Street, London E1 8RU
Tel: (171) 680 7000; (171) 702 0651 Fax: (171) 481 1860; (171) 680 7002 Telex: 8812511 Swift: XIAN GB 2L
Reuters: XIAX

Senior Executive Officers
Chief Executive Officer Kjell Tangen *General Manager* ☎ **680 7060**
Financial Director Steve Ruddell *Financial Controller* ☎ **680 7018**
Chief Operating Officer David Farmery *Deputy General Manager* ☎ **680 7001**
Treasurer Rosalind Barnett-Koppang ☎ **680 7003**

Debt Capital Markets / Fixed Income
Eurobonds
Head of Sales Rosalind Barnett-Koppang ☎ **680 7003**

Money Markets
Country Head Gary Arndt *Senior Dealer* ☎ **680 7120**

Risk Management
Fixed Income Derivatives / Risk Management
Country Head Simon Denham *Senior Dealer* ☎ **680 7125**

UNITED KINGDOM (+44)   www.euromoneydirectory.com

Christiania Bank og Kreditkasse ASA (cont)
Foreign Exchange Derivatives / Risk Management
Vanilla FX option Trading   Terry Witherden *FX Dealer* ☎ **680 7123**
Exotic Options (Barriers, Range, Timers, Digitals, Faders etc)
Sales   Simon Denham *Senior Dealer* ☎ **680 7125**
Settlement / Clearing
Operations   Simon Badger *Manager* ☎ **680 7053**
Other   Peter Chappell *Head of Middle Office* ☎ **680 7017**
Other Departments
Correspondent Banking   David Farmery *Deputy General Manager* ☎ **680 7001**
Administration
Technology & Systems
    David Farmery *Deputy General Manager* ☎ **680 7001**
Compliance
    Peter Chappell *Head of Middle Office* ☎ **680 7017**

The Chugoku Bank Limited   *Representative Office*

Peninsular House, 30/36 Monument Street, London EC3R 8LJ
Tel: (171) 283 5500 **Fax:** (171) 283 5577 **Telex:** 8811467 CHGKLN G

Senior Executive Officers
Chief Representative   M Hikasa

The Chuo Trust & Banking Company Limited   *Full Branch Office*

Triton Court, Finsbury Square, London EC2A 1HA
Tel: (171) 456 9000 **Telex:** 8812700 **Swift:** CHUO GB ZL

Senior Executive Officers
Director & General Manager   Kimihiro Funahashi

CIBC Oppenheimer International Limited   *Subsidiary Company*

Cottons Centre, Cottons Lane, London SE1 2QL
Tel: (171) 234 6000; (171) 234 7100 **Fax:** (171) 234 7981 **Telex:** 915152 OPINT G

Senior Executive Officers
Chief Executive Officer   Niels Jensen *Chief Executive Officer & General Manager*

CIBC World Markets   *Full Branch Office*

Alternative trading name: CIBC Wood Gundy Oppenheimer (Europe)
Formerly known as: CIBC Wood Gundy & Oppenheimer International Limited
Cottons Centre, Cottons Lane, London SE1 2QL
Tel: (171) 234 6000; (171) 234 7100 **Fax:** (171) 407 4127 **Telex:** 888229 CIBC G **Swift:** CIBC GB 2L
Email: arnuppau@cibc.ca **Telerate:** CIBC LONDON
Website: www.cibcwm.com

Senior Executive Officers
Chairman & Chief Executive Officer   A L Flood
President   John Hunkin
Chief Operating Officer   Ron L Lalonde *Global Head of Infrastructure*
International Division   Jill Denham *Managing Director - Europe* ☎ **234 6145**
Debt Capital Markets / Fixed Income
Department: **Debt Capital Markets**
Tel: 234 7161
Head of Fixed Income Sales   Paul Blake ☎ **234 7163**
Head of Fixed Income Trading   Martin Shaw ☎ **234 7149**
Eurobonds
Head of Origination   Robert Edge *Head of DCM* ☎ **234 7177**
Head of Syndication   Mark Hardisty *Manager, Syndication* ☎ **234 7175**
Head of Sales   Paul Blake ☎ **234 7163**
Head of Trading   Martin Shaw ☎ **234 7149**
Fixed-Income Repo
Head of Repo   Ian Lincoln *Repo Trader* ☎ **234 7111**
Head of Trading   Martin Shaw *Head of Trading* ☎ **234 7149**

www.euromoneydirectory.com UNITED KINGDOM (+44)

Fixed-Income Research
Country Head — David Coleman *Manager, Economics & Advisory Group* ☎ 234 7323

Equity Capital Markets
Department: Equity Capital Markets
Fax: 234 7220

Other (Domestic Equities)
US Equities Sales — Niels Jensen *Head of US Sales* ☎ 234 7970

International Equities
Head of Sales — John Miles *Head* ☎ 234 7272
Head of Trading — Peter McSweeney *Trading* ☎ 234 7199

Equity Repo / Securities Lending
Head — Jean-Paul Musicco *Head of Equity Structured Products* ☎ 234 7264

Syndicated Lending
Head of Origination — Jill Denham *Managing Director - Europe* ☎ 234 6145
Head of Syndication — Paul Amador ☎ 234 6911
Head of Credit Committee — Andy Craig *Head of Corporate Credit Risk Management* ☎ 234 6595
Paul Berry *Head of Client Risk Management* ☎ 234 6626

Loan-Related Activities
Trade Finance — Maria Malinowska *Head of Structured Trade Finance* ☎ 234 6639

Foreign Exchange
Country Head — Clifford Symes *Head, FX - London* ☎ 234 6709
Head of Institutional Sales — Howard King *Manager, Corporate Sales* ☎ 234 6700

FX Traders / Sales People
Head of Funding Risk Management, London — Greg Posehn *Head of Funding Risk Management, London* ☎ 234 6687

Risk Management
Department: Financial Products
Country Head — Mark Preston *Head of Trading* ☎ 234 6811

Other (FI Derivatives)
John Bradley *Head of Short Term Interest Rates* ☎ 234 6671

Other Currency Swap / FX Options Personnel
David Donora *Head of Currency Options* ☎ 234 6173

OTC Equity Derivatives
Trading — Dean Clark ☎ 234 7169

Exchange-Traded Derivatives
FX Options — David Donora *Head of Currency Options* ☎ 234 6173

Settlement / Clearing
Head of Settlement / Clearing — Robert Ewart *Head of Securities Operations* ☎ 234 6033
Operations — Les Peck *Head*

Other Departments

Other Departments
Finance — Graham Cohen *Head of Finance* ☎ 234 6004

Administration
Mike Dear *Head of Technology, Europe* ☎ 234 7300

Legal / In-House Counsel
David Austin *General Counsel, Europe* ☎ 234 6396

Compliance
Bharat Samani *Head of Compliance, Europe* ☎ 234 7258

Public Relations
Linda Burbridge *Manager, European Marketing & Communications* ☎ 234 6282

Other (Administration)
Human Resources — Jennifer Board *Head of Human Resources*

Cie Financière Benjamin et Edmond de Rothschild

Orion House, 5 Upper St. Martin's Lane, London WC2H 9EA
Tel: (171) 862 5900 **Fax:** (171) 240 1826

Senior Executive Officers
General Manager — John Alexander

Euromoney Directory 1999 **1717**

UNITED KINGDOM (+44)   www.euromoneydirectory.com

Citibank NA
Registered London Office

Citibank House, 336 Strand, London WC2R 1HB
Tel: (171) 500 5000 Fax: (171) 500 1695 Telex: 940500 Reuters: CIDL; CIXL
Website: www.citibank.com

Senior Executive Officers
Vice Chairman   Paul Collins
Chief Executive Officer   Ian D Cormack *Country Corporate Officer* ☎ **500 2865**
Financial Director   Tony Brooks *Finance Director*

Others (Senior Executives)
Credit Structures   Tim Greatorex *Director* ☎ **500 0082** F **836 0078**

Debt Capital Markets / Fixed Income
Global Head   Thierry Sciard *Global Head*

Equity Capital Markets
Global Head   Thierry Sciard *Global Head*

Syndicated Lending
Regional Head   Joan Byrne *European Head of Syndicated Loans*

Foreign Exchange
Head of Foreign Exchange   Guy Whittaker ☎ **500 1830** F **438 1258**

Corporate Finance / M&A Advisory
Head of Corporate Finance   Gary Von Lehmden *Head, Corporate Finance*

CLF Municipal Bank plc
Subsidiary Company

55 Tufton Street, Westminster, London SW1P 3QF
Tel: (171) 799 3322 Fax: (171) 799 2117

Senior Executive Officers
Chairman   Bernard Harty
Chief Executive Officer   Michel Bonnet *Managing Director*

Collins Stewart (CI) Limited
Full Branch Office

7 Auckland Terrace, Parliament Street, Ramsey, Isle of Man IM8 1AF
Tel: (1624) 812 925 Fax: (1624) 812 642

Senior Executive Officers
Associate Director   Richard Bellwood

The Commercial Bank of Korea Limited

27th Floor, Centre Point, 103 New Oxford Street, London WC1A 1DD
Tel: (171) 379 7835 Fax: (171) 379 4849 Telex: 8813215 Swift: CBKO GB 2L Reuters: CBOK

Senior Executive Officers
General Manager   Hwang-Soo Jung

Commercial Union Investment Management Limited

St Helen's, 1 Undershaft, London EC3P 3DQ
Tel: (171) 662 6000 Fax: (171) 661 0195

Debt Capital Markets / Fixed Income
Fixed-Income Repo
Head of Repo   Tim Lucas *Associate Director* ☎ **662 6023** F **662 6055**
Trading   Gerry Inow *Stock Lending Officer* ☎ **662 6165**
                                                    Samantha Hopkins

Equity Capital Markets
Fax: 662 6075

Equity Repo / Securities Lending
Head   Tim Lucas *Associate Director* ☎ **662 6023** F **662 6055**
Head of Trading   Gerry Inow *Stock Lending Officer* ☎ **662 6165**
                                                    Samantha Hopkins

1718 Euromoney Directory 1999

www.euromoneydirectory.com UNITED KINGDOM (+44)

Commerzbank AG
Full Branch Office

23 Austin Friars, London EC2N 2EN
Tel: (171) 638 5895; (171) 418 4700 Fax: (171) 638 0166 Telex: 8954308/9 CBKLON G
Website: www.commerzbank.com

Senior Executive Officers
General Manager　　　　　　　　　　　Peter Buerger ☎ **418 4791**
General Manager　　　　　　　　　　　Bernd Holzenthal ☎ **418 4791**

Others (Senior Executives)
Chief Investment Officer　　　　　　　Craig Templer ☎ **570 4675**

Debt Capital Markets / Fixed Income
Department: Global Fixed Income
Tel: 418 4836 Fax: 570 4483
Head of Fixed Income　　　　　　　　Regis Fraisse *Head of Global Fixed Income* ☎ **418 4632**
Head of Fixed Income Sales　　　　　Hans Strueder *Global Head of Sales* ☎ **418 4894**

Government Bonds
Head of Sales　　　　　　　　　　　　Paul Herlaut *Head of London Sales* ☎ **418 4131**
Head of Syndication; Head of Origination　Yann Gindre *Global Head of DCM* ☎ **570 4694**

Domestic Government Bonds
Head of Sales　　　　　　　　　　　　Nicolaus Diedrich *Head of Sales - Germany* ☎ **+49 (69) 1362 9321**

Eurobonds
Head of Sales　　　　　　　　　　　　Paul Herlaut *Head of London Sales* ☎ **418 4131**
Head of Trading　　　　　　　　　　　Richard Curtis *Head of Credit Market Making* ☎ **570 4655**

Emerging Market Bonds
Head of Sales　　　　　　　　　　　　Paul Herlaut *Head of London Sales* ☎ **418 4131**
Head of Trading　　　　　　　　　　　Richard Curtis *Head of Credit Market Making* ☎ **570 4655**

Libor-Based / Floating-Rate Products
FRN Sales　　　　　　　　　　　　　　Paul Herlaut *Head of London Sales* ☎ **418 4131**
FRN Trading　　　　　　　　　　　　　Stuart Davis *FRN Trader* ☎ **570 4460**
Asset Swaps　　　　　　　　　　　　　Emma Giles *Asset Swap Trader* ☎ **570 4431**

Fixed-Income Repo
Head of Repo　　　　　　　　　　　　Martin Turnbull ☎ **570 4689**

Fixed-Income Research
Head of Fixed Income　　　　　　　　Daniel Sheard ☎ **418 4911**
Head of Credit Research　　　　　　Julian Lim ☎ **418 4286**

Syndicated Lending
Tel: 418 4869 Fax: 570 4450
Country Head　　　　　　　　　　　　Elaine Sanders *Head of Loan Syndication* ☎ **570 4401**

Other (Syndicated Lending)
　　　　　　　　　　　　　　　　　　　Elaine Sanders *Head of Loan Syndication* ☎ **570 4401**

Loan-Related Activities
Trade Finance; Trade Finance　　　　Peter Godwin *Export Finance Head* ☎ **418 4826**
Project Finance　　　　　　　　　　　Philip Pirie *Head of Project Finance* ☎ **418 4878**

Money Markets
Tel: 418 4891 Fax: 418 4994
Head of Money Markets　　　　　　　Ramon Smith *Head of A & L Management* ☎ **418 4906**

Eurocommercial Paper
Head of Trading　　　　　　　　　　　Dax Jenkinson *ECP Trader* ☎ **570 4629**

Money Markets - General
Head of Sales　　　　　　　　　　　　Daniel Grew *Head of Sales* ☎ **570 4676**
Short Swaps　　　　　　　　　　　　　John Spink *Trader*
Currencies　　　　　　　　　　　　　　Mark Harris *Trader*
Sterling　　　　　　　　　　　　　　　David Padbury *Trader*
Other　　　　　　　　　　　　　　　　Patrick Michot *Trader*
　　　　　　　　　　　　　　　　　　　Huzera Vora *Trader*

Specialized Financial Institutions / Hedge Fund　Martin Bean
Sale
　　　　　　　　　　　　　　　　　　　Jason Oliver
UK Funds　　　　　　　　　　　　　　Bryan Jude
　　　　　　　　　　　　　　　　　　　Adrian Bromhead
Corporate Sales　　　　　　　　　　　Bobby Maiti
　　　　　　　　　　　　　　　　　　　Alex Jackson
　　　　　　　　　　　　　　　　　　　Chris Hood
Fiduciary　　　　　　　　　　　　　　Mike Robins
Non-Reciprical　　　　　　　　　　　Anja Osthoff
　　　　　　　　　　　　　　　　　　　Louise Woodward

UNITED KINGDOM (+44)

Commerzbank AG (cont)

Foreign Exchange
Tel: 418 4891 Fax: 418 4994 Reuters: CBKL

Regional Head	Reto Feller *European Head of FX* ☏ **570 4940**
Country Head	Martin Carr *UK Head of FX* ☏ **570 4940**
Head of Institutional Sales; Corporate Sales	Daniel Grew ☏ **570 4676**
Head of Trading	Martin Carr *UK Head of FX* ☏ **570 4940**

FX Traders / Sales People

£ / DM	Gordon Andrew
$ / DM	Ian Drysdale
Proprietary	Martin Ryan
	David Gee
£ / $	Lee Knight
DM / Yen	Steven Miller
$ / Yen	Terry West

Risk Management

Head of Risk Management	Katerina Mastronikola ☏ **418 4821**

Other (FI Derivatives)

Charles Porter *Head of Interest Rate Derivatives*
Mike Dobson *Derivative Trader*
Steven Goldstein *Derivative Trader*
Neville Porteos *Derivative Trader*
Caroline Elsom *Derivative Trader*
Kate Phillips *Derivative Trader*
John Mullins *Derivative Trader*
Bob Chown *Derivative Trader*
Nick Boss *Derivative Trader*
Paul Thomson *Derivative Trader*
Lindsay Williams *Derivative Trader*
Kevin Day *Derivative Trader*
Andy Townsend *Derivative Trader*
Uwe Sprock *Derivative Trader*
Chris Dawkins *Risk Manager*
Bertrand Willmann *Risk Manager*
Sarah Dobinson *Risk Manager*
Aude Beurnier *Risk Manager*

Foreign Exchange Derivatives / Risk Management

Country Head	Arie Assayag *Head of FX Derivatives* ☏ **418 4117**
Cross-Currency Swaps, Sales / Marketing	Nicola Jolley *Manager, Structured Products*
	Jonathan Durden
Vanilla FX option Trading	Paulo Nicolosi *FX Derivative Trader*

Other Currency Swap / FX Options Personnel

Lionel Bouaziz *FX Derivative Trader*
Paulo Nicolosi *FX Derivative Trader*
Butch Fischer *FX Derivative Trader*

OTC Commodity Derivatives

Head; Trading	Adrien Biondi ☏ **418 4909**

OTC Credit Derivatives

Head	Arnauld Walle *Head of Product Management* ☏ **418 4463**

Exchange-Traded Derivatives

Regional Head	Caroline Elsom *Derivative Trader*

Settlement / Clearing

Head of Settlement / Clearing; Country Head	Rick Jarrard ☏ **418 4967**
Equity Settlement	John Guy *Head of Operations* ☏ **653 7450**
Fixed-Income Settlement	Shaun Patience ☏ **418 4977**
Derivatives Settlement	Jennifer Copp
Foreign Exchange Settlement	Angela Pemberton
Back-Office	Eileen Fortune *Head of Money Market Operations* ☏ **418 4961**

Other Departments

Commodities / Bullion	Adrien Biondi *Bullion Dealer* ☏ **418 4909**
	Adrien Biondi ☏ **418 4909**
Proprietary Trading	Craig Templer *Investment Manager*
Chief Credit Officer	Harley Irwin *Head of Risk Management* ☏ **418 4828**
Correspondent Banking	Eddie Charles ☏ **418 4586**

www.euromoneydirectory.com　　　　　　UNITED KINGDOM (+44)

Administration
Head of Administration　　　Andreas Latta *Head of Organisations* ☎ **418 4777**
Technology & Systems
　　　　　　　　　　　　　　Stewart Mackie *Head of Operations* ☎ **418 4717**
　　　　　　　　　　　　　　Andreas Latta *Head of Organisations* ☎ **418 4777**
Legal / In-House Counsel
　　　　　　　　　　　　　　Oliver Loeck *Head of Legal Issues* ☎ **418 4802**
Compliance
　　　　　　　　　　　　　　Richard Caird *Head of Compliance* ☎ **653 7240**
　　　　　　　　　　　　　　Silvia Ameen *Internal Auditor* ☎ **570 4639**
Accounts / Audit
　　　　　　　　　　　　　　Silvia Ameen *Internal Auditor* ☎ **570 4639**

Commonwealth Bank of Australia　　　　Full Branch Office

Senator House, 85 Queen Victoria Street, London EC4V 4HA
Tel: (171) 710 3999 **Fax:** (171) 710 3939; (171) 710 9555 **Telex:** 883864 **Swift:** CTBA GB 2L
Email: cba.lon@btinternet.com **Reuters:** CBAL **Telerate:** 6496-9
Reuters: CBAX; CBAO
Website: www.fx.sales.btinternet.com

Senior Executive Officers
General Manager - Europe　　　Art Brown ☎ **710 3900**
Others (Senior Executives)
Regional Head of Primary Markets　　　Robert Verlander *Head of Primary Market* ☎ **329 6444**
Debt Capital Markets / Fixed Income
Tel: 329 6444 **Fax:** 710 3911
Global Head　　　Gary King *Head, Securities Sales & Trading* ☎ **329 6444**
Non-Domestic Government Bonds
A$ / NZ$　　　Allard Van der Graaf
　　　　　　　Jonathan Hughes
Eurobonds
Head of Syndication　　　Jacques Lumb *Head of Syndication* ☎ **710 3910**
Head of Trading　　　Gary King *Head, Securities Sales & Trading*
Libor-Based / Floating-Rate Products
FRN Sales; Asset Swaps　　　Gary King *Head, Securities Sales & Trading*
Money Markets
Tel: 329 6333 **Fax:** 710 3911
Regional Head　　　Anthony Lee *Head of Money Markets - Europe*
Eurocommercial Paper
Head of Sales　　　Andy Williamson *Manager* ☎ **329 6444**
Other (Wholesale Deposits)
Trading US$　　　Anthony Lee *Head of Money Markets - Europe*
Trading GBP　　　Adrian Spain *Senior Dealer*
Trading A$　　　Guy Chinery *Senior Dealer*
Foreign Exchange
Tel: 329 6333 **Fax:** 710 3911
Regional Head　　　Andy Baxter *Head, FX - Europe*
Head of Institutional Sales　　　Stuart Smith *Head of Risk Management, FX Sales* ☎ **329 6266**
Corporate Sales　　　Mal Hosi *Head of Risk Management, FX Sales* ☎ **329 6266**
Head of Trading　　　Andy Baxter *Head, FX - Europe*
FX Traders / Sales People
Trading - Spot A$　　　Bernie Kipping *Chief Dealer*
Trading - Spot ¥　　　Mark Pantling *Dealer*
Trading - Spot NZ$　　　Chris Day *Dealer*
Trading - DM　　　Russell Sears *Dealer*
Trading - Spot Far East　　　John Corso *Dealer*
Trading - Forward Far East　　　Paul Nashwalder *Dealer*
Trading - A$　　　Paul Fray *Senior Dealer*
Trading - Europeans　　　Ultan MacDonald *Senior Dealer*
Risk Management
Other Currency Swap / FX Options Personnel
All FX Options　　　Jim Hamil *Head of FX Options* ☎ **329 0003**
　　　　　　　　　　Gianni Gray *Manager, FX Options* ☎ **329 0003**
Settlement / Clearing
Regional Head　　　John Mihill *Senior Manager, Settlements* ☎ **710 3942**

UNITED KINGDOM (+44)　　　www.euromoneydirectory.com

Commonwealth Bank of Australia (cont)
Other Departments
Proprietary Trading　　　　　　　　　　Kevan Conlon *Head, Proprietary Trading* ☏ **329 6333**
Administration
Technology & Systems
I.S & Communications　　　　　　　　Steve Palmer *Senior Manager* ☏ **710 3931**
Compliance
Audit & Compliance　　　　　　　　　Andy Sheppard *Senior Manager* ☏ **710 3907**

Commonwealth Development Corporation　　　　　　　　Head Office

One Bessborough Gardens, London SW1V 2JQ
Tel: (171) 828 4488 **Fax:** (171) 828 6505 **Telex:** 21431 **Email:** depcr@cdc.co.uk
Website: www.cdc.co.uk

Senior Executive Officers
Chairman　　　　　　　　　　　　　　Simon Cairns ☏ **963 3701**
Chief Executive Officer　　　　　　　Roy Reynolds *Chief Executive* ☏ **963 3801**
Financial Director　　　　　　　　　Nicholas Denniston *Director of Finance* ☏ **963 3701**
Chief Operating Officer　　　　　　Nicholas Selbie *Managing Director, CDC Investments* ☏ **963 3702**
Treasurer　　　　　　　　　　　　　Ian Black *Treasurer* ☏ **963 3737**
Company Secretary　　　　　　　　Richard Bagley
Others (Senior Executives)
Corporate Relations　　　　　　　Sean Magee *Director* ☏ **963 3864**
Financial Markets　　　　　　　　Robert Binyon *Managing Director* ☏ **963 3942**
Business Develpment　　　　　　Paul Jobson *Managing Director* ☏ **963 3902**
Administration
Public Relations
Corporate Relations　　　　　　　Sean Magee *Director* ☏ **963 3864**

Confederación Española de Cajas de Ahorros　　　Full Branch Office

16 Waterloo Place, London SW1Y 4AR
Tel: (171) 925 2560 **Fax:** (171) 925 2554; (171) 930 5450 **Telex:** 917709 CECA UK G **Reuters:** CECE

Senior Executive Officers
Chief Executive Officer　　　　　　Norberto Padovani *General Manager*
Treasurer　　　　　　　　　　　　Robert F Bauer *Deputy General Manager*
Others (Senior Executives)
　　　　　　　　　　　　　　　　Veronica Lucas *Executive Assistant*
General-Lending (DCM, SL)
Head of Corporate Banking　　　Carlos Rodriguez *Manager*
Debt Capital Markets / Fixed Income
Non-Domestic Government Bonds
Asset Sales　　　　　　　　　　Omar Miranda *Deputy General Manager*
　　　　　　　　　　　　　　　　Juan Garnica
　　　　　　　　　　　　　　　　José Maria Izuzquiza
Syndicated Lending
Country Head　　　　　　　　　Robert F Bauer *Deputy General Manager*
Loan-Related Activities
Trade Finance　　　　　　　　　Carlos Rodriguez *Manager*
Other (Trade Finance)
Forfaiting　　　　　　　　　　　Carlos Rodriguez *Manager*
Settlement / Clearing
Operations　　　　　　　　　　Carlos Rodriguez *Manager*
　　　　　　　　　　　　　　　　Moricio Forero *Assistant Manager*
　　　　　　　　　　　　　　　　Isidora Gonzalez
　　　　　　　　　　　　　　　　Sonia Alexandre

Cosmo Securities (Europe) Limited　　　　　　　　　　Subsidiary Company

Sixth Floor, 4 Broadgate, London EC2M 2AH
Tel: (171) 588 6733 **Fax:** (171) 628 6703 **Telex:** 8811382

Senior Executive Officers
Managing Director　　　　　　　Kazuo Yanagida

www.euromoneydirectory.com UNITED KINGDOM (+44)

Crane Investment Analysis Limited
Head Office

2 London Wall Buildings, London Wall, London EC2M 5UU
Tel: (1483) 211 353; (171) 374 0836 **Fax:** (1483) 211 048

Senior Executive Officers
Chief Executive Officer — Simon Crane
Financial Director — Pamela Crane *Chief Financial Officer*
Director — Adrian Sells

Crédit Agricole Indosuez
Full Branch Office

Formerly known as: Crédit Agricole and Banque Indosuez

122 Leadenhall Street, London EC3V 4QH
Tel: (171) 971 4000 **Fax:** (171) 628 4724 **Telex:** 892967 INDOSU G **Swift:** BSUI GB 2L

Senior Executive Officers
Chief Executive Officer — Michel Le Masson *Senior Country Officer*
Patrick Diggines *Deputy Senior Country Officer*
Chief Operating Officer — David Barrows
Treasurer — Christophe Lanne
Head of Legal — Margaret Garner

Others (Senior Executives)
Head of Asset Based Finance — Patrick Diggines *Deputy Senior Country Officer*
Credit Agricole Indosuez Emerging Markets — Daniel Puyo *Managing Director & Head*
Alexis Habib *Managing Director*
Claude Marion *Managing Director*
Commodities — Francis Michallet *Head of Commodities & Trade Finance*

Equity Capital Markets
Department: Indosuez WI Carr Securities

International Equities
Head of Origination — Robin Newman *Chief Executive Officer & Managing Director* ☎ 303 1133

Syndicated Lending

Loan-Related Activities
Shipping Finance — Thibaud Escoffier *Manager*
Project Finance — Christoforos Stratos *Head of Project Finance*

Other (Trade Finance)
Export Credit — Deborah Bass *Manager*

Money Markets
Head of Money Markets — Remy Cordier *Money Market Manager*

Foreign Exchange
Head of Foreign Exchange — Simon Eedle *FX Manager* ☎ 971 4356 📠 971 4453
✉ simon.eedle@indosuez.com
Global Head — Nathalie Rachou *Global Head of FX & Currency Options* ☎ 971 4337
📠 971 4453
Head of Institutional Sales — Uwe Fuehrer *Head of Sales*
Head of Trading — Mark Clarke *Chief Dealer, Major Currencies*

Risk Management
Head of Risk Management — Emmanuel Bapt *Head of Treasury Risk Control*

Corporate Finance / M&A Advisory
Head of Mergers & Acquisition — Mary Clippingdale *Manager, Acquisition Finance*

Settlement / Clearing
Head of Settlement / Clearing — Simon Mansfield *Head of Operations*

Other Departments
Commodities / Bullion — Francis Michallet *Head of Commodities & Trade Finance*
Chief Credit Officer — Sandy Cuthbert *Head of Credit & Risk Management*
Private Banking — Guy Rousseau ☎ 495 2615

Administration
Head of Administration — Jan Field

Technology & Systems
Kevin Howlett *Head of IT*

Legal / In-House Counsel
Margaret Garner *Head of Legal*

Compliance
Gael Kerrigan *Head*

Euromoney Directory 1999 **1723**

UNITED KINGDOM (+44)   www.euromoneydirectory.com

Crédit Agricole Indosuez (cont)
Accounts / Audit
Financial Control   Michael Payne *Head*
Audit   Tom Asim *Head*

Crédit Commercial de France   Full Branch Office
1 Paternoster Row, St Paul's, London EC4M 7DH
Tel: (171) 213 9900; (171) 623 1131 **Fax:** (171) 213 9999; (171) 623 5297 **Telex:** 8812953 CCFLO **Swift:** CCFR GB 2LA
Reuters: CCFL **Telex:** 8812954 CCFLO

Senior Executive Officers
Treasurer   Michael Scragg ☏ **246 2378**
General Manager & Director   Claude Greilsamer ☏ **246 2552**

Debt Capital Markets / Fixed Income
Libor-Based / Floating-Rate Products
FRN Origination   R Kasiers
FRN Sales   N Taylor

Syndicated Lending
Global Head   P Campbell *Corporate Banking Director* ☏ **246 2556**

Money Markets
Eurocommercial Paper
Head of Sales   Nick Taylor ☏ **246 2558**

Crédit Lyonnais Securities
Broadwalk House, 5 Appold Street, London EC2A 2DA
Tel: (171) 588 4000 **Fax:** (171) 214 5256 **Telex:** 888397 **Telex:** 888398

Senior Executive Officers
Others (Senior Executives)
                                          Karl Monaghan *Director*

Credit Suisse First Boston (Europe) Limited   Full Branch Office
1 Cabot Square, London E14 4QJ
Tel: (171) 888 4040; (171) 888 4045 **Fax:** (171) 888 1600; (171) 888 3368 **Telex:** 887322 **Swift:** CRES GB 2L
Reuters: CSLD-E **Telerate:** Recipient
Asset/Liability Management Fax: 888 7495; **Asset/Liabilty Management Tel:** 888 7390; **Forwards Tel:** 888 7310;
FX Spot Tel: 888 4036; **Global Options Tel:** 888 4035; **Fax:** 888 2312; **Off-Balance Sheet Tel:** 888 7305; **Precious Metals Tel:** 888 7060; **Fax:** 888 7491; **Treasury Sales Tel:** 888 7250; **Reuters:** GLDX, SILX (Monitors);
CSSP (Forex Spot Dealing); CSDE (Deposit Dealing); CSFX (Forwards & Off-Balance Sheet Dealing);
CSFX (Customer Bank Dealing); CSLX (Treasury Sales Dealing); CSBL (Precious Metals Dealing);
CSOL (Global Options Dealing); CSSL (Forex Sales)

Senior Executive Officers
Vice President   Carsten H A Stoehr ☏ **888 1903** 📠 **888 3630** ✉ **cstoehr@csfbg.csfb.com**
Managing Director   Simon L Meadows ☏ **888 1941** 📠 **888 3719**

Debt Capital Markets / Fixed Income
Tel: 888 4045 **Fax:** 888 6386 **Telex:** 892131 CSFBG

Fixed-Income Repo
Head of Repo   Raymond Kuramoto *Director* ☏ **888 4045** 📠 **888 3879**
                                          ✉ **raymond.kuramoto@csfb.com**
Marketing & Product Development   Dermot Doherty *Vice President* ✉ **dermot.doherty@csfb.com**
Trading   Nina Fnug-Hansen *Director, Scandinavia*
                                          Jan Klockman *Vice President, Scandinavia & NLG*
                                          Dominick Emmanuelli *Vice President, Lira*
                                          Roberta Palmitessa *Lira*
                                          David Leddy *Pta, £, Bfr, IR£*
                                          Steve Taylor *Vice President, US Treasury*
                                          Chris West *Vice President, Yen, A$*
Sales   Dermot Doherty *Vice President* ✉ **dermot.doherty@csfb.com**

Fixed-Income Research
Global Head   Marc Hotimsky *Global Head, Fixed-Income*

1724 Euromoney Directory 1999

www.euromoneydirectory.com   UNITED KINGDOM (+44)

Equity Capital Markets
Tel: 888 4040

Equity Repo / Securities Lending
Marketing & Product Development   Una van Dorssen *Vice President* ☎ **888 4537** 📠 **888 5102**
                                       📧 **una.vandorssen@csfb.com**
Head of Prime Brokerage   Jon Baker *Head of Client Relations* ☎ **888 6483** 📧 **jon.baker@csfb.com**

Foreign Exchange
Global Head   Phil Vasan *Global Head, FX*

FX Traders / Sales People
FX Spot   P Little *Vice President*
                                       M Leighton *Vice President*
                                       A McDonald *Vice President*
                                       M Spicer *Director*
                                       L Spiteri *Vice President*
                                       J Thomson *Vice President*
                                       R Ware *Vice President*
FX Sales   R Boulton *Director*
                                       E Blomberg *Vice President*
                                       M Duffy *Vice President*
                                       R Elvidge *Global Head*
                                       M Hussein *Vice President*
                                       S Kelleher *Director*
                                       E Kpenou *Vice President*
                                       F Overgaard *Director*
                                       M Riemers *Vice President*

Risk Management

Foreign Exchange Derivatives / Risk Management
Spot / Forwards Trading   M Day *Vice President, Forwards*
                                       Bruno Gall *Manager, Forwards*
                                       S Yanez *Global Manager, Forwards*
                                       Y Dallal *Vice President, Forwards*

Exchange-Traded Derivatives
Regional Head   Ed Condon *Head*
FX Options   Amine Benamer *VP, Global Options*
                                       Alex Finney *Director, Global Options*
                                       Tom Gillie *VP, Global Options*
                                       Craig Puffenberger *Director, Global Options*
                                       Girome Bono *Director, Global Options*

Asset Management
Department: Asset & Liability Management

Other (Asset Management)
                                       J Brodie *Dealer*
                                       A Beesley *Vice President*
                                       T Chiddicks *Global Manager*
                                       P Delamain *Vice President*
                                       J Gulliver *Dealer*
                                       S Horwood *Vice President*
                                       T Miller *Vice President*
                                       S Simmons *Vice President*
                                       A White *Vice President*

Other Departments
Commodities / Bullion   N Gilbert *VP, Precious Metals*
                                       B Canham *Director, Precious Metals*
                                       J Pancholi *VP, Precious Metals*
                                       J Patitsas *VP, Precious Metals*
                                       K Roberts *VP, Precious Metals*
                                       P Smith *VP, Precious Metals*
Private Banking   G Russell *Head, Private Banking*
                                       M Strong *Head, Treasury Liaison*
                                       J MacSwayed *Relationship Manager*

Administration

Other (Administration)
Support Services   N Riley *Head, European Operations*

UNITED KINGDOM (+44)   www.euromoneydirectory.com

Credit Suisse Securities Limited
Subsidiary Company

Formerly known as: Swiss Volksbank Securities Limited
Moorgate Hall, 155 Moorgate, London EC2M 6UA
Tel: (171) 628 7777 **Fax:** (171) 628 2786 **Telex:** 917777

Senior Executive Officers
Managing Director — Anthony Campey

Debt Capital Markets / Fixed Income
Eurobonds
Head of Sales — James Lloyd-Davies *Deputy Managing Director* ☏ **256 8285**
Head of Trading — Wayne Dooley ☏ **628 3050**

Settlement / Clearing
Fixed-Income Settlement — Ray Murphy *Manager*

Administration
Technology & Systems — Russel Hilborne *Head of Operations*

Compliance — Kevin Mapp *Compliance Officer*

The Cyprus Popular Bank Limited
Full Branch Office

19 Fitzroy Street, London W1P 6BQ
Popular Bank House, 995 High Road, Finchley, London N12 8PW
Tel: (171) 307 8400 **Fax:** (171) 307 8444 **Telex:** 263128 **Swift:** LIKI GB 2L **Email:** ukmarke@ibm.net

Senior Executive Officers
Chairman & Chief Executive Officer — Kikis Lazarides ☏ **+357 (2) 752 000**
Financial Director — C Phidia *Manager, Group Financial Control* ☏ **+357 (2) 752 000**
Treasurer — Kyriakos Constantinou *Manager, Treasury* ☏ **+357 (2) 752 000**
Manager, UK — Spyros Episkopon
International Division — Rena Rouvitha Panou *Director International, Banking & Treasury*

Others (Senior Executives)
N Hadjinicolaou *Executive Director, Domestic Banking* ☏ **+357 (2) 752 000**
A Papavasiliou *Executive Director, Administration* ☏ **+357 (2) 752 000**

General-Lending (DCM, SL)
Head of Corporate Banking — R Hadjikyriacou *Manager, Corporate Banking* ☏ **+357 (2) 752 000**
Athos Kaissides *Head of Corporate & Private Banking*

General - Treasury
Head of Treasury — Christos Gabrielides *Head of Treasury, UK*

Relationship Manager
Chris Moyseos *Account Manager, Corporate & Private Banking*

Other Departments
Private Banking — S Savvides *Manager, Private Banking* ☏ **+357 (2) 752 000**

Administration
Tel: (181) 492 2110
Head of Administration — Marios Petrides *Administration Manager* ☏ **(181) 492 2110**
Business Development — Paul Pitsillides *Business Manager* ☏ **(181) 492 2120**
Head of Marketing — Marios Voskopoullos *Head of Marketing* ☏ **(181) 492 2130**

Technology & Systems — Nondas Palcikaros *Operations & Methods Officer* ☏ **(181) 492 2110**

Legal / In-House Counsel — Dinos Karis *Manager, Legal Services* ☏ **(181) 492 2060**

Compliance — Marios Petrides *Administration Manager* ☏ **(181) 492 2110**

Accounts / Audit — Annita Philippidou *Chief Accountant* ☏ **(181) 492 2070**

Daewoo Securities (Europe) Limited
Subsidiary Company

1 Threadneedle Street, London EC2R 8AW
Tel: (171) 982 8000 **Fax:** (171) 982 8040 **Telex:** 9413098 DWSLON G

Senior Executive Officers
Chief Executive Officer — K B Kim *Managing Director* ☏ **982 8001**
Financial Director — John F Lobley *Chief Financial Officer* ☏ **982 8021**

www.euromoneydirectory.com UNITED KINGDOM (+44)

Senior Executive Officers (cont)
Chief Operating Officer — John A Soesan ☏ **982 8022**

Debt Capital Markets / Fixed Income
Eurobonds
Head of Origination; Head of Syndication — D Y Choi *Head, New Issues* ☏ **412 8011**
Head of Sales — James Ryu *Head of Sales* ☏ **422 8006**
Head of Trading — D Y Choi *Chief Trader* ☏ **412 8011**

Bonds - General
Eastern Europe — K Y Kim *Trader / Research* ☏ **422 8008**
M J Hwang *Trader* ☏ **422 8015**

Equity Capital Markets
International Equities
Head of Sales — James Ryu *Head of Sales* ☏ **422 8006**
Head of Trading — D Y Choi *Chief Trader* ☏ **412 8011**

Convertibles / Equity-Linked
Head of Origination; Head of Syndication — D Y Choi *Head, New Issues* ☏ **412 8011**
Head of Sales — James Ryu *Head of Sales* ☏ **422 8006**
Head of Trading — D Y Choi *Chief Trader* ☏ **412 8011**

Settlement / Clearing
Equity Settlement — Emma Roe *Supervisor, Settlements* ☏ **422 8022**

Administration
Technology & Systems
Asoka Peiris *IT Manager* ☏ **422 8008**

Compliance
John F Lobley *Chief Financial Officer* ☏ **982 8021**

Dai-Ichi Europe Limited
Subsidiary Company

Durrant House, 8/13 Chiswell Street, London EC1Y 4TQ
Tel: (171) 588 6075 **Fax:** (171) 588 2644 **Telex:** 883336 ICHILD

Senior Executive Officers
Financial Director — Takashi Yamamoto *Director*
Managing Director — Akinobu Shimuta

Debt Capital Markets / Fixed Income
Non-Domestic Government Bonds
Kazuhito Fukuda ☏ **374 8360**

Eurobonds
Head of Syndication — Kazuhito Fukuda ☏ **374 8360**

Equity Capital Markets
International Equities
Head of Sales — Etsuji Tanimoto ☏ **374 8271**

Convertibles / Equity-Linked
Head of Trading — Kazuhito Fukuda ☏ **374 8360**

Warrants
Head of Sales — Kazuhito Fukuda ☏ **374 8360**

Settlement / Clearing
Equity Settlement — Kiyomi Jennings
Fixed-Income Settlement — Sheila Sofianou

The Dai-Ichi Kangyo Bank Limited
Full Branch Office

DKB House, 24 King William Street, London EC4R 9DB
Tel: (171) 283 0929 **Fax:** (171) 929 3319 **Telex:** 884042 **Swift:** DKBL GB 2L **Reuters:** DKBX **Telex:** 885521;
Reuters: DKBL (Monitor)

Senior Executive Officers
Financial Director — Simon Whittle *Deputy General Manager* ☏ **220 9448**
General Manager — Takayasu Tanaka

Others (Senior Executives)
Marketing, Planning and General — Kazumi Otsuka *Joint General Manager* ☏ **220 9472**
Marketing — Akira Kawamura *Joint General Manager* ☏ **220 9436**
Special Finance Department — Philip Dodd *Deputy General Manager* ☏ **220 9406**
Operations — Colin Reith *Deputy General Manager* ☏ **220 9471**
Human Resources — Andrew Avenell *Deputy General Manager* ☏ **220 9526**

UNITED KINGDOM (+44)   www.euromoneydirectory.com

The Dai-Ichi Kangyo Bank Limited (cont)

General - Treasury
Head of Treasury   Masakazu Kimura *Joint General Manager* ☎ **623 0030**

Syndicated Lending
Fax: 283 1132
Head of Syndicated Lending   Richard Strong *Senior Manager* ☎ **220 9439**
                                              Akio Nekoshima *Assistant General Manager* ☎ **220 9442**

Department: Loan-Related Activities

Loan-Related Activities
Aircraft / Aerospace Finance   Barry Simmons *Senior Manager* ☎ **220 9548**

Other (Trade Finance)
Energy Group-Special Finance   Ian Catteral *Assistant General Manager* ☎ **220 9452**
PFI Infrastructure Group-Special Finance   Chris O'Gorman *Senior Manager* ☎ **220 9459**
International Finance   Akio Nekoshima *Assistant General Manager* ☎ **220 9442**
                                              Stewart Wakeman *Senior Manager* ☎ **220 9825**
                                              Rupert Bushell *Senior Manager* ☎ **220 9482**
Corporate Finance   Trevor Bailey *Deputy General Manager* ☎ **220 9485**
                                              Chris Williams *Senior Manager* ☎ **220 9441**
Japanese Corporate Dept UK   Chieo Yamada *Assistant General Manager* ☎ **220 9442**
Japanese Corporate Dept Europe   Atsushi Shirakami *Assistant General Manager* ☎ **220 9657**

Money Markets

Domestic Commercial Paper
Head of Trading   Toru Nakazawa *Assistant General Manager* ☎ **623 0042**

Eurocommercial Paper
Head of Trading   Toru Nakazawa *Assistant General Manager* ☎ **623 0042**

Money Markets - General
Banking   Ikubumi Yamada *Assistant General Manager* ☎ **623 0042**

Foreign Exchange
Head of Institutional Sales; Corporate Sales Bob Munro *Assistant General Manager* ☎ **623 0040**
Head of Trading   Allan Patten *Assistant General Manager* ☎ **929 1665**
                                              Toru Nakazawa *Assistant General Manager* ☎ **623 0042**

FX Traders / Sales People
Spot FX   Toru Nakazawa *Assistant General Manager* ☎ **623 0042**
Forward FX   Allan Patten *Assistant General Manager* ☎ **929 1665**
Sales   Bob Munro *Assistant General Manager* ☎ **623 0040**

Risk Management
Country Head   Andrew Graham *Assistant General Manager* ☎ **220 9662**

Foreign Exchange Derivatives / Risk Management
Vanilla FX option Trading   Yoshihiro Kurosawa ☎ **929 3333**

Corporate Finance / M&A Advisory
Head of Corporate Finance   Trevor Bailey *Deputy General Manager* ☎ **220 9485**

Other (Corporate Finance)
Japanese Corporate   Chieo Yamada *Assistant General Manager* ☎ **220 9442**

Settlement / Clearing
Operations   Noel Butler *Assistant General Manager* ☎ **220 9667**

Administration
Business Development   Noel Butler *Assistant General Manager* ☎ **220 9667**

Technology & Systems
                                              Hing Tsang *Assistant General Manager* ☎ **220 9402**

Legal / In-House Counsel
                                              Mathew Sussmes *Assistant General Manager* ☎ **220 9587**

Compliance
                                              Simon Whittle *Deputy General Manager* ☎ **220 9448**

Accounts / Audit
Audit   Andrew Perks *Assistant General Manager* ☎ **220 9696**
Accounts   Neil Hunt *Assistant General Manager* ☎ **220 9480**
Management Accounts   Allan Murray *Assistant General Manager* ☎ **220 9572**

Other (Administration)
Human Resources   Andrew Avenell *Deputy General Manager* ☎ **220 9526**
Planning & General Affairs Dept   Fumio Nakatsuka *Assistant General Manager* ☎ **220 9426**

www.euromoneydirectory.com　　　　UNITED KINGDOM (+44)

Daishin International (Europe) Limited
Subsidiary Company

4 Chiswell Street, London EC1Y 4UP
Tel: (171) 638 6438; (171) 614 8000 **Fax:** (171) 256 9190 **Telex:** 884038 DASCOL G
Email: dshinkim@gpo.sonnet.co.uk **Reuters:** DSHM; DSHZ

Senior Executive Officers
Managing Director　　　　　　　　　Won-Jae Ruee
Chief Executive Officer　　　　　　　Ian Hunter *Deputy Managing Director* ☎ **614 8703**
Treasurer　　　　　　　　　　　　　Min-Chang Kim *Compliance Officer*

Debt Capital Markets / Fixed Income
Global Head　　　　　　　　　　　Ian Hunter *Deputy Managing Director* ☎ **614 8703**

Eurobonds
Head of Origination; Head of Syndication; Head　Ian Hunter *Deputy Managing Director* ☎ **614 8703**
of Sales; Head of Trading; Head of Research

Medium-Term Notes
Head of Origination　　　　　　　Ian Hunter *Deputy Managing Director* ☎ **614 8703**

Private Placements
Head of Origination　　　　　　　Ian Hunter *Deputy Managing Director* ☎ **614 8703**

Equity Capital Markets
Global Head　　　　　　　　　　　Ian Hunter *Deputy Managing Director* ☎ **614 8703**

Domestic Equities
Head of Origination; Head of Syndication; Head　Ian Hunter *Deputy Managing Director* ☎ **614 8703**
of Sales; Head of Trading; Head of Research

International Equities
Head of Sales; Head of Trading; Head of　Ian Hunter *Deputy Managing Director* ☎ **614 8703**
Research

Convertibles / Equity-Linked
Head of Origination; Head of Sales; Head of　Ian Hunter *Deputy Managing Director* ☎ **614 8703**
Trading; Head of Research

Warrants
Head of Sales; Head of Trading; Head of　Ian Hunter *Deputy Managing Director* ☎ **614 8703**
Research

Money Markets
Global Head　　　　　　　　　　　Ian Hunter *Deputy Managing Director* ☎ **614 8703**

Risk Management
Global Head　　　　　　　　　　　Ian Hunter *Deputy Managing Director* ☎ **614 8703**

Fixed Income Derivatives / Risk Management
Global Head　　　　　　　　　　　Ian Hunter *Deputy Managing Director* ☎ **614 8703**

OTC Equity Derivatives
Sales　　　　　　　　　　　　　　Ian Hunter *Deputy Managing Director* ☎ **614 8703**
Trading　　　　　　　　　　　　　Min-Chang Kim *Compliance Officer*

Daiwa Bank (Capital Management) plc
Subsidiary Company

6th Floor, 4 Broadgate, London EC2M 2AH
Tel: (171) 623 1494 **Fax:** (171) 623 2717 **Telex:** 8956907

Senior Executive Officers
Chairman　　　　　　　　　　　　Masahiro Oyama
Managing Director　　　　　　　　Yoshitaka Akikuni
Deputy Managing Director　　　　　Yutaka Nomiyama

Debt Capital Markets / Fixed Income
Tel: 972 0061
Country Head　　　　　　　　　　K Hirota *Senior Manager* ☎ **972 0061** 🖷 **972 0069**

Libor-Based / Floating-Rate Products
Asset Swaps　　　　　　　　　　　K Hirota *Senior Manager* ☎ **972 0061** 🖷 **972 0069**

Medium-Term Notes
Head of Origination　　　　　　　H Ito *Manager*

Private Placements
Head of Origination　　　　　　　H Ito *Manager*

Money Markets
Tel: 972 0060
Country Head　　　　　　　　　　J Collier *Treasury*
　　　　　　　　　　　　　　　　I MacFarlane *Manager*

UNITED KINGDOM (+44)   www.euromoneydirectory.com

Daiwa Bank (Capital Management) plc (cont)
Risk Management
Country Head   Mr Ogawa *Assistant Manager*
Settlement / Clearing
Tel: 623 1494
Country Head   S Green *Manager*
Administration
Technology & Systems
    J Chandler *Assistant Manager*
Compliance
    David McCorkell *Associate Director*

The Daiwa Bank Limited   Full Branch Office

Fifth Floor, 4 Broadgate, London EC2M 2QS
Tel: (171) 418 8800 **Fax:** (171) 418 8850 **Telex:** 886569 **Swift:** DIWA GB2L **Cable:** LONDAIWA LONDON

Senior Executive Officers
General Manager   Satoshi Maeshima
Deputy General Manager   Peter Clarke ☏ **418 8803**

Debt Capital Markets / Fixed Income
Eurobonds
Head of Origination   Masafumi Asai *Manager* ☏ **418 8860**
Libor-Based / Floating-Rate Products
FRN Origination   Masafumi Asai *Manager* ☏ **418 8860**

Money Markets
Regional Head   Satoshi Otsuka *Deputy General Manager* ☏ **418 8837**
Wholesale Deposits
Marketing   Clive Puddy *Chief Dealer* ☏ **418 8841**

Foreign Exchange
Global Head   Satoshi Otsuka *Deputy General Manager* ☏ **418 8837**

Corporate Finance / M&A Advisory
Regional Head   Peter Clarke *Deputy General Manager* ☏ **418 8803**

Daiwa Europe Limited   Subsidiary Company

5 King William Street, London EC4N 7AX
Tel: (171) 548 8080 **Fax:** (171) 548 8303 **Telex:** 884121
Website: www.daiwa.co.jp

Senior Executive Officers
Chairman   Koji Yoneyama
Chief Executive Officer   Masayasu Ohi *Joint CEO*
    Alex Monnas *Joint CEO*
Managing Director   Shintaro Hayakawa
Managing Director   Rurik Ingram
Managing Director   Richard Jackson
Managing Director   Garry Jones
Managing Director   Susumu Kawanura
Managing Director   Robin Nydes
Managing Director   Hidetada Oshima
Managing Director   Vince Purton
Managing Director   Simon Crisp
Managing Director   Jim Siracusa
Managing Director   Hirokatsu Washida
Managing Director   Michael Watson
Executive Director   Hiroki Terao

General-Lending (DCM, SL)
Head of Corporate Banking   Shintaro Hayakawa *Managing Director*
    Richard Jackson *Managing Director*

Debt Capital Markets / Fixed Income
Tel: 548 8667 **Fax:** 548 8548
Regional Head   Susumu Kawanura *Managing Director*
Eurobonds
Head of Trading   David Renton

www.euromoneydirectory.com					UNITED KINGDOM (+44)

Emerging Market Bonds
Head of Research					David Boren

Fixed-Income Repo
Marketing & Product Development			Tony Baldwin *Senior Manager* ☎ **548 8983** F **203 2007**
							E **anthony.baldwin@daiwa.co.uk**
Trading						Tony Baldwin *Senior Manager, Repo Desk*
							Andrew Cohen *Associate Director*
							Chris Jones *Senior Manager*
							Marie Lennon *Trader*
							Mathew Smith *Trader*
							John Edwards *Associate Director, Emerging Markets*

Equity Capital Markets
Tel: 548 8667 **Fax:** 545 6018
Global Head					Ki Won Han
Regional Head					Michael Watson *Managing Director*
						Jeremy Read *Director*
						Hirokatsu Washida *Managing Director*

Equity Research
Analyst						Mark Hambly *Structured Finance* ☎ **548 8452** F **548 8836**
						E **mark.hambly@daiwa.co.uk**

Equity Repo / Securities Lending
Marketing & Product Development			Ray Coleman *Manager* ☎ **548 7332** E **ray.coleman@daiwa.co.uk**.
Marketing					Mark D'Andre *Vice President, Marketing*
Head of Trading					Chris Flickhaber *Vice President*
						Angus Yang
						Marty Malloy *Vice President*

Syndicated Lending

Loan-Related Activities
Structured Trade Finance				Hidetada Oshima *Managing Director*
						Robin Nydes *Managing Director*

Settlement / Clearing
Operations					Hiroki Terao *Executive Director*

Administration
Head of Administration				Ian Shepherd *Executive Director*
						Yuji Koseki *Executive Director*

## Dallah Albaraka (UK) Limited					Head Office

40 Upper Brook Street, London W1Y 2AH
Tel: (171) 499 9111 **Fax:** (171) 493 7460 **Telex:** 291169 ALBAR G **Email:** albaraka@btinternet.com
Website: www.albaraka.co.uk

Senior Executive Officers
Chairman					Abdullah Saleh Kamel
Chief Executive Officer				Khalid Bhaimia *Managing Director & Chief Executive* ☎ **647 8408**
Treasurer					Linda Mackenzie *Treasurer & Correspondent Banker* ☎ **647 8413**
Company Secretary				Adeel Siddiqui ☎ **499 9111**

Syndicated Lending

Loan-Related Activities
Trade Finance; Project Finance; Structured		Nauzer Dinshaw *Credit & Marketing Manager* ☎ **647 8414**
Trade Finance

Settlement / Clearing
Operations; Back-Office				Naunit Popat ☎ **647 8424**

Other Departments
Correspondent Banking				Linda Mackenzie *Treasurer & Correspondent Banker* ☎ **647 8413**

Administration
Head of Administration				Verity Mallin *Manager* ☎ **647 8410**
Head of Marketing				Nauzer Dinshaw *Credit & Marketing Manager* ☎ **647 8414**

Accounts / Audit
Financial Control				Nazir Choksi *Financial Controller* ☎ **647 8421**

Other (Administration)
Personnel					Verity Mallin *Manager* ☎ **647 8410**

Euromoney Directory 1999   **1731**

UNITED KINGDOM (+44)   www.euromoneydirectory.com

Dao Heng Bank (London) plc

10 Angel Court, London EC2R 7ES
Tel: (171) 606 1616 **Fax:** (171) 606 2900 **Telex:** 887756HBOTB **Swift:** DHBK GB 2L **Reuters:** DHBL

Senior Executive Officers
Chairman   L C Quek
Financial Director   W R Dobbie
Managing Director / General Manager   B J A Whitworth

Delphis Bank

77 Brook Street, London W1Y 1YE
Tel: (171) 499 4323 **Fax:** (171) 493 8975

Senior Executive Officers
General Manager   Satish Shah

Deltec Securities (UK) Limited

Brettenham House, 5 Lancaster Place, London WC2E 7EN
Tel: (171) 379 7227 **Fax:** (171) 379 7577

Senior Executive Officers
Chairman   David P McNaughtan
Company Secretary   David G Fox

Den Danske Bank — Full Branch Office

75 King William Street, London EC4N 7DT
Tel: (171) 410 8000 **Fax:** (171) 410 8001 **Swift:** DABA GB 2L **Reuters:** DANL (Spot); DAND (Money Market), DANE (Sales)

Senior Executive Officers
Financial Director   Keith Reid *AGM & Financial Controller*
SEVP & General Manager   Angus MacLennan
SVP & Deputy General Manager   Torben von Lowzow
AGM & Financial Controller   Keith Reid

Others (Senior Executives)
AGM, Legal   Andrew Putnam

Relationship Manager
Scandinavian Corporates   Peter Storgaard *Assistant General Manager*
UK & International Corporates   Simon Powell *Assistant General Manager*
Financial Institutions   Stephen Day *Assistant General Manager*

Debt Capital Markets / Fixed Income
Tel: 410 4949 **Fax:** 410 0032
Head of Fixed Income Sales   Roy Bowers *Institutional & Corporate Sales*
                                        Martin Bracken *Institutional & Corporate Sales*
Head of Fixed Income Trading   Jesper Timmermann *Chief Dealer*

Libor-Based / Floating-Rate Products
Asset Swaps   Steen Carndorf *Chief Dealer*

Equity Capital Markets
Global Head   Erik Wenngren
Head of Sales   Michael Thompson *Chief Dealer*
                                        Roy Bowers *Institutional & Corporate Sales*
                                        Martin Bracken *Institutional & Corporate Sales*
Head of Trading   Richard Martin *Head of Trading*

Equity Research
Head of Equity Research   Gordon Maclean

Syndicated Lending
Department: Syndicated Lending & Debt Markets
Country Head   David Roberts *AGM & Head of Syndications*

Money Markets
Head of Money Markets   Graham Philp *Chief Dealer*
Regional Head   Steen Alva Jørgensen

Money Markets - General
                                        Roy Bowers *Institutional & Corporate Sales*
                                        Martin Bracken *Institutional & Corporate Sales*

www.euromoneydirectory.com   UNITED KINGDOM (+44)

Foreign Exchange
Head of Institutional Sales   Roy Bowers *Institutional & Corporate Sales*
                                             Martin Bracken *Institutional & Corporate Sales*
Corporate Sales   Roy Bowers *Institutional & Corporate Sales*
                                             Martin Bracken *Institutional & Corporate Sales*

Risk Management
Foreign Exchange Derivatives / Risk Management
Spot / Forwards Trading   Lewis Grey *Chief Dealer*
Other (Exchange-Traded Derivatives)
                                             Roy Bowers *Institutional & Corporate Sales*
                                             Martin Bracken *Institutional & Corporate Sales*

Settlement / Clearing
Operations   Andrew Collins *Assistant General Manager - IT*

Other Departments
Chief Credit Officer   Henrik Hoffmann *AGM*

Administration
Head of Marketing   Michael Rowlinson *Deputy General Manager*

Technology & Systems
                                             Ian Mortimer *Senior Manager*

Accounts / Audit
                                             Jens Anders Jensen *Internal Auditor*

Other (Administration)
Personnel   Lynda Pearce *Senior Manager*

Den norske Bank ASA   Full Branch Office
20 St Dunstan's Hill, London EC3R 8HY
Tel: (171) 621 1111 **Fax:** (171) 626 7400 **Telex:** 887654 **Swift:** DNBA 4B 2L **Reuters:** DNBL

Senior Executive Officers
Chief Executive Officer   John N Simpson
Financial Director   Christopher Tregoning *Deputy Managing Director, Finance*
                                             Paul Brend *Associate Director, Financial Control*

General-Lending (DCM, SL)
Head of Corporate Banking   Stewart Smith *Executive Director, UK Bnkg / Structured Finance*
                                             Terje Turnes *Executive Director, Corporate Banking*
                                             Bente Fladmark *Senior Manager, Corporate Banking*

General - Treasury
Head of Treasury   Paul Smith *Executive Director, Treasury*
                                             Judith Benson *Associate Director*

Equity Capital Markets
Country Head   Peter Tron *Senior Manager, Equities*
                                             Claus Willumsen *Executive Director*

Syndicated Lending
Loan-Related Activities
Shipping Finance   Nicholas Oliver *Executive Director*
                                             Nigel Anton *Associate Director*
                                             Susan Cowling *Associate Director*
                                             Knut Mathiassen *Associate Director*
                                             Arild Vik *Associate Director, Shipping in Piraeus*
                                             Kevin Oates *Associate Director, Shipping in Piraeus*
                                             Derek Walker *Associate Director*
                                             David Reeve-Tucker *Associate Director*
                                             Keith McRae *Senior Manager*
Structured Trade Finance   Stewart Smith *Executive Director, UK Bnkg / Structured Finance*
                                             Clive Bowen *Senior Manager, UK Bnkg / Structured Finance*

Foreign Exchange
Global Head   David Fletcher *Senior Manager*

Settlement / Clearing
Settlement (General)   Malcolm Bryant *Executive Director*
                                             Deborah Keegan *Senior Manager, Settlements*
Operations   Paul Barker *Senior Manager, Credit Control*

Other Departments
Chief Credit Officer   Keith Knight *Senior Manager, Credit Administration*
Cash Management   Atle Fjereide *Associate Director*

UNITED KINGDOM (+44)   www.euromoneydirectory.com

Den norske Bank ASA (cont)
Administration
Head of Administration   Tony Dobbyn *Senior Manager*

Technology & Systems
    Max Clark *Executive Director IT Department*
    Patrick Dungan *Senior Manager, IT*
    Martin Clinton *Senior Manager, IT*

Compliance
    Malcolm Bryant *Executive Director*

Other (Administration)
Personnel   Tracey Foley *Senior Manager*

DePfa-Bank AG   Full Branch Office

Alternative trading name: Deutsche Pfandbrief-und Hypothekenbank AG
38 Lombard Street, London EC3V 9BS
Tel: (171) 456 9200 **Fax:** (171) 283 6001

Senior Executive Officers
General Manager   Francis Hazeel

Others (Senior Executives)
Executive
    Charles Balch
    Monique Bonney
    Colin Humphries
    Kerstin Ross
    Sigrun Schmidt
    Paul Stoneham
    Susan Whitehorne

Deutsche Bank AG   Full Branch Office

Winchester House, 1 Great Winchester Street, London EC2P 2AX
Tel: (171) 545 8000

Senior Executive Officers
Department: Senior Executives: Global Corporates and Institutions

Others (Senior Executives)
Head of Investment Banking   Josef Ackermann
Head of Global Markets   Edson Mitchell
Head of Equities   Michael Philipp
Head of Risk Management   Hugo Banziger
Head of Global Banking Services   Juergen Fitschen
Head of Structured Finance   Gavin Lickley
Head of IT / Operations   Marc Sternfeld

Debt Capital Markets / Fixed Income
Head of Debt Capital Markets   Grant Kvalheim *Global Head* ☎ **+1 (212) 469 7595**

High Yield / Junk Bonds
Head   Gopal Menon *Global Head* ☎ **545 9162**

Emerging Market Bonds
Head of Emerging Markets   Pablo Calderini *Global Head* ☎ **545 7535**
Head of Research   David Folkerts-Landau ☎ **545 6404**

Asset-Backed Securities / Securitization
Regional Head   Tamara Adler *Head of European Securitisation* ☎ **545 8151**

Fixed-Income Research
Head of Fixed Income   Steven Bell *Head of Global Markets Research* ☎ **545 2085**
Head of Credit Research   Glenn Reynolds ☎ **+1 (212) 469 4526**

Fixed Income (Trading)
Fixed Income / Credit Trading   Neal Neilinger *Head of Trading* ☎ **+1 (212) 469 2857**

Equity Capital Markets
Head of Equity Capital Markets   Michael Cohrs *Global Head* ☎ **545 6858**

Other (International Equity)
Cash Equities   Michael Philipp *Global Head* ☎ **545 1479**
Equity Derivatives   Kevin Parker *Global Head* ☎ **+1 (212) 469 4632**
Equity Finance   Mark Gelnaw *Global Head* ☎ **545 5033**

www.euromoneydirectory.com   UNITED KINGDOM (+44)

Money Markets
Money Markets - General
Money Markets / Repo   Mario Pierro *Global Co-head* ☎ +1 (212) 469 7652
                                        Mark Yallop *Global Co-head* ☎ 545 2214

Foreign Exchange
Head of Foreign Exchange   Hal Herron *Global Head* ☎ 545 4666

Risk Management
Other (FI Derivatives)
OTC Derivatives / Government Trading Saman Majd *Global Head* ☎ 545 1602

Other Departments
Other Departments
Institutional Client Group   Anshu Jain *Global Head* ☎ 545 1586
Global Exchange Services   Paul Lewis *Global Head* ☎ 545 1484
Metals & Commodities   Charles von Arentschildt *Global Head* ☎ +1 (212) 469 8430

Deutsche Bank Gilts Limited   Subsidiary Company
6 Bishopsgate, London EC2A 7BU
Tel: (171) 545 8000 **Fax:** (171) 545 4455

Deutsche Schiffsbank AG   Representative Office
Grocers' Hall, Prince's Street, London EC2R 8AQ
Tel: (171) 726 8726 **Fax:** (171) 726 2545

Senior Executive Officers
Representative   O R Norland

Deutsche Sharps Pixley Metals Limited   Subsidiary Company
133 Houndsditch, London EC3A 7DX
Tel: (171) 545 8000 **Fax:** (171) 545 4455 **Telex:** 94015555 DBLN G

The Development Bank of Singapore Limited   Full Branch Office

Alternative trading name: DBS Bank
7th Floor, Finsbury Circus House, 12-15 Finsbury Circus, London EC2M 7BT
Tel: (171) 628 3288 **Fax:** (171) 628 8288 **Telex:** 291711 DBSLDNG **Swift:** DBSS GB 2L

Senior Executive Officers
General Manager   William Chia
Deputy General Manager   Kok Wah Tan

Syndicated Lending
Country Head   Hugh Parsons *Head, Credit and Marketing*

Money Markets
Country Head   Steven Hale

Foreign Exchange
Country Head   Steven Hale

Settlement / Clearing
Country Head   Peter Prior

DG BANK Deutsche Genossenschaftsbank   Full Branch Office
10 Aldersgate Street, London EC1A 4XX
Tel: (171) 776 6000 **Fax:** (171) 776 6100 **Telex:** 886547 **Swift:** GENO GB 2L **Reuters:** DGLD-O

Senior Executive Officers
Chief Executive Officer   Alfred Legner *General Manager*
                                        Peter Moore *General Manager*
Treasurer   Michael Whitaker *Treasurer*

General-Lending (DCM, SL)
Head of Corporate Banking   Michael Hall

UNITED KINGDOM (+44)   www.euromoneydirectory.com

DG BANK Deutsche Genossenschaftsbank (cont)

Syndicated Lending
Department: Loan Syndication
Fax: 776 6037
Global Head   Melinda Wilcox-Sadler *Head, Loan Syndication*
Head of Origination   David Berner *Head of Origination*

Loan-Related Activities
Trade Finance   Janine Barber
Project Finance   Michael Hall
Structured Trade Finance; Leasing & Asset Finance   Janine Barber

Money Markets
Department: Treasury
Fax: 600 0160
Regional Head   Michael Whitaker *Treasurer*
Country Head   Peter Janata *Head of Money Markets*

Foreign Exchange
Department: Treasury
Regional Head   Michael Whitaker *Treasurer*
Country Head   Paul Cannon *Head of FX*

Risk Management
Department: Financial Management
Country Head   Phill Jobbins *Risk Manager*

Corporate Finance / M&A Advisory
Department: Corporate Banking
Regional Head   Michael Hall

Settlement / Clearing
Department: Settlements
Country Head   Frances Reno *Head of Operations*

Other Departments
Private Banking   Michael Hall

Administration
Legal / In-House Counsel   Chris Petitian *Compliance Officer*

Compliance   Karen A Smith *Assistant Compliance Officer*

Dilmun Investments Limited   Head Office

93 Park Lane, London W1Y 3TA
Tel: (171) 495 8974 **Fax:** (171) 499 6768

Risk Management
Global Head   William Khouri

Fixed Income Derivatives / Risk Management
Global Head   William Khouri

Foreign Exchange Derivatives / Risk Management
Cross-Currency Swaps, Sales / Marketing   William Khouri

DKB International plc   Subsidiary Company

DKB House, 24 King William Street, London EC4R 9DB
Tel: (171) 929 7777 **Fax:** (171) 929 1522 **Telex:** 932631 DKINTL **Reuters:** DKIA-Z

Senior Executive Officers
Chief Executive Officer   Koiichi Torihara

Debt Capital Markets / Fixed Income
Head of Debt Capital Markets   Yoichiro Nakai
     Johan Christofferson *Head of Sales & Trading*
Head of Fixed Income Sales   Carlos Swiderski
Head of Fixed Income Trading   Keith Thorn *Director, Hong Kong* ☎ **+852 2825 8757**
     Gary Tritton
     Christopher Lynch *Director, Credit* ☎ **929 0663**
     Sara Simmons *Director, Credit* ☎ **929 0663**

Fixed-Income Repo
Trading   Simon Starr *Director* ☎ **929 1593**
     Jan Wood *Repo Trader*

www.euromoneydirectory.com UNITED KINGDOM (+44)

Equity Capital Markets
Head of Equity Capital Markets Yoichiro Nakai
 Johan Christofferson *Head of Sales & Trading*
Head of Sales Carlos Swiderski
 Mike Allen *Director, Multi-Product Sales*
 Fabio Filippi *Director, Multi-Product Sales*
 Neil Robertson *Director, Multi-Product Sales*
 Sara Simmons *Director, Multi-Product Sales*
Head of Trading Keith Thorn *Director, Hong Kong* ☏ **+852 2825 8757**
 Gary Tritton

Equity Repo / Securities Lending
Head of Trading Simon Starr *Director* ☏ **929 1593**

Money Markets
Other Junichi Sugimoto *Director, Japanese Sales*

Foreign Exchange
FX Traders / Sales People
Yen Julian Howard *Director*
 Ichiro Ishibashi *Director*

Risk Management
Head of Risk Management Alasdare Lambert

Fixed Income Derivatives / Risk Management
Trading Graeme Wadsworth *Director* ☏ **929 0100**
 Maurice Harty *Director* ☏ **929 0100**

Other Departments
Proprietary Trading Neil Meadows *Director* ☏ **929 0100**
 Ludovico Filotto *Director, Accounting, MIS* ☏ **929 0663**
Economic Research Gerard Lyons *Chief Economist*

DKB Investment Management International Limited

6th Floor, DKB House, 24 King William Street, London EC4R 9DB
Tel: (171) 929 6666 **Fax:** (171) 621 9976 **Telex:** 944444 DKBIMI G

Senior Executive Officers
Financial Director Michael Knight
Managing Director / General Manager Tetsuo Shibata

Asset Management
Other (Asset Management)
 Michael Nicholaou *Senior Fund Manager*
 Yutaka Takahashi *Senior Fund Manager*

Donaldson, Lufkin & Jenrette International Limited

Subsidiary Company

99 Bishopsgate, London EC2M 3XD
Tel: (171) 655 7000 **Fax:** (171) 588 0120 **Telex:** 8811356

Senior Executive Officers
Chairman Charles Hale
Chief Executive Officer Anthony Petrilli *Senior Executive Officer*
Financial Director Joe Seet *Finance Director*
Treasurer Philip Vracas
Managing Director of High Yeild Pierre-Olivier Masmejean ☏ **655 7101** 🖷 **655 7886**

General-Investment
Head of Investment Michael Johnson *Managing Director of Investment Banking*

Debt Capital Markets / Fixed Income
Regional Head Darryl Green *Managing Director*

Non-Domestic Government Bonds
US$ Sales David Flashman *Vice President*

Eurobonds
Head of Trading Tim Leslie *Senior Vice President*

High Yield / Junk Bonds
Head Jon Ezrow *Head of European High Yield*

Emerging Market Bonds
Head of Trading Pierre Masmejean *Managing Director*

Euromoney Directory 1999 **1737**

UNITED KINGDOM (+44)   www.euromoneydirectory.com

Donaldson, Lufkin & Jenrette International Limited (cont)

Fixed-Income Repo
Trading — Richard Cook *Vice President & Trader, Government Bonds*
Gregory Lake *Trader, Eurobonds*

Equity Capital Markets
International Equities
Head of Syndication — Michael Anderson *Senior Vice President*
Head of Sales — Michele Witt *Manager, UK Equity Sales*
Head of Trading — Nick Robinson *Managing Director*

Risk Management
OTC Equity Derivatives
Sales — Nagi Kawkabani *Senior Vice President*
OTC Credit Derivatives
Regional Head — Carol Toliver *Managing Director*

Corporate Finance / M&A Advisory
Department: DLJ Phoenix
Regional Head — Martin Smith *Chairman*

Settlement / Clearing
Equity Settlement — Steve Ponto *Vice President*
Fixed-Income Settlement — Paul Clark *Vice President*
Derivatives Settlement — Mark Christy *Head, Derivative Operations*

Other Departments
Private Banking — Thomas Dicker *Managing Director*

Administration
Legal / In-House Counsel
— John Harriman *Director & General Counsel*

Compliance
— Peter Gormley *Compliance Director*

Dresdner Kleinwort Benson — Subsidiary Company

20 Fenchurch Street, London EC3P 3DB
Tel: (171) 623 8000 **Fax:** (171) 623 4069 **Telex:** 888731
Website: www.dresdnerkb.com

Senior Executive Officers
Chairman — Gerd Häusler

Others (Senior Executives)
Tim Barker *Vice Chairman*
Bay Green *Vice Chairman*
Michael Jenkins *Vice Chairman*
Lord Walker *Vice Chairman*

Chief Operating Officer — Klaus-Michael Geiger *Chief Operating Officer, UK*
Department: Dresdner Bank AG, London Branch
20 Fenchurch Street, London, EC3P 3DB

Others (Senior Executives)
Andreas Leimbach *General Manager*
Achilles Macris *General Manager*
John Pattinson *General Manager*

Debt Capital Markets / Fixed Income
Department: Global Markets
Global Head — T J Lim *Joint Head of Global Markets*

Equity Capital Markets
Department: Equities
Global Head — Alan Yarrow *Head of Global Equities*

Corporate Finance / M&A Advisory
Global Head — Timothy Shacklock *Head of Global Corporate Finance*

Ecoban Finance (Europe) Limited — Subsidiary Company

Formerly known as: Euroban Limited
54 St Katharine's Way, London E1 9LB
Tel: (171) 702 3507 **Fax:** (171) 702 3356 **Email:** euroban@ecoban.com

Senior Executive Officers
Managing Director — Peter A Belmont

www.euromoneydirectory.com   UNITED KINGDOM (+44)

Others (Senior Executives)
                                      Richard S Garbutt *Director*
                                      Wladimir A Ledochowski *Director*

Syndicated Lending
Head of Origination   Peter A Belmont *Managing Director*
                                      Richard S Garbutt *Director*
                                      Wladimir A Ledochowski *Director*
Head of Syndication   Peter A Belmont *Managing Director*
                                      Richard S Garbutt *Director*
                                      Wladimir A Ledochowski *Director*

Loan-Related Activities
Structured Trade Finance   Peter A Belmont *Managing Director*

Other (Trade Finance)
Forfaiting   Richard S Garbutt *Director*
                                      Wladimir A Ledochowski *Director*
Countertrade   Peter A Belmont *Managing Director*
Debt Arbitrage   Wladimir A Ledochowski *Director*

Corporate Finance / M&A Advisory
Country Head   Peter A Belmont *Managing Director*

The ECU Group plc   Head Office

Sugar Quay, Lower Thames Street, London EC3R 6DU
Tel: (171) 385 1202; (171) 245 1010 **Fax:** (171) 681 1679 **Telex:** 919893 ECU G **Email:** ecu@ecu.co.uk
Website: www.ecu.co.uk

Senior Executive Officers
Chairman   John Royden
Chief Executive Officer   Michael Petley ☏ **(1794) 301 111**

Foreign Exchange
Global Head   Michael Petley ☏ **(1794) 301 111**

FX Traders / Sales People
                                      Peter Taffon

Risk Management
Foreign Exchange Derivatives / Risk Management
Cross-Currency Swaps, Sales / Marketing   Michael Petley ☏ **(1794) 301 111**

ED & F Man International Limited   Head Office

Sugar Quay, Lower Thames Street, London EC3R 6DU
Tel: (171) 285 3000 **Fax:** (171) 285 3396 **Telex:** 885431 **Reuters:** EDFM
Website: www.edfman.com

Senior Executive Officers
Chairman   Robert Oddy ☏ **285 3208**
Chief Executive Officer   Kevin Davis *Managing Director* ☏ **285 3258**
Financial Director   Terry Stroud *Finance Director* ☏ **285 3366**
Chief Operating Officer   Chris Smith *Deputy Managing Director* ☏ **285 3207**
Treasurer   Steve Cochrane *Director of Administration* ☏ **285 3681**

Others (Senior Executives)
                                      James Woodward *Sales Manager* ☏ **285 3956**
General Brokerage   Robert Leftwich *Dealing Director* ☏ **285 3333**
                                      Simon Healy *Dealing Director* ☏ **285 3341**
Energy Futures   Andy Buttars *Head of Desk* ☏ **285 3356**
Metals Futures   Alex Heath *Director* ☏ **285 5680**

Foreign Exchange
Head of Trading   Nick Wadham *Head* ☏ **285 3221**

Settlement / Clearing
Back-Office   Verrona Browne *Operations Manager* ☏ **285 3242**

Administration
Compliance
                                      Richard Seaman *Director* ☏ **285 3631**

UNITED KINGDOM (+44)   www.euromoneydirectory.com

Edinburgh Fund Managers plc   Head Office

Donaldson House, 97 Haymarket Terrace, Edinburgh, EH12 5HD
Tel: (131) 313 1000 Fax: (131) 313 6300
Website: www.edfd.com

Senior Executive Officers
Chairman   Iain Watt
Financial Director   Graham Brock *Finance Director*
Chief Investment Officer   Mike Balfour
Company Secretary   Cathy Miller
International Division   Iain Beattie *Head of Developed Markets*

Debt Capital Markets / Fixed Income
Head of Fixed Income   Michael Turner *Head of Global Fixed Interest*

Emerging Market Bonds
Head of Emerging Markets   Richard Muckart *Investment Director, Emerging Markets*

Administration
Head of Administration   Rod Macrae
Head of Marketing   Nigel Whittingham *Sales & Marketing Director*

Technology & Systems
                                       Ken McKenna *IT Director*

Compliance
                                       Nigel Anderson *Manager*

Public Relations
                                       Nigel Whittingham *Sales & Marketing Director*

Accounts / Audit
                                       Graham Brock *Finance Director*

EFG Private Bank Limited   Head Office

Formerly known as: The Private Bank & Trust Company Limited
12 Hay Hill, London W1X 8EE
Tel: (171) 872 3700; (171) 491 9111 Fax: (171) 872 3706 Telex: 26175 Swift: EFGB GB 2L Reuters: EFGL

Senior Executive Officers
Chairman   Geoffrey Elliott
Financial Director   Manny Bussetil
Chief Operating Officer   Anthony Marshall *Chief Operating Officer*
Treasurer   Clive Farrand *Executive Director, Treasury*
Company Secretary   Grahame Holdgate

Asset Management
Head   William Ramsay *Head of Fund Management*

Other Departments
Private Banking   Philip Amphlett

Elbim Bank

104 Salisbury House, London Wall, London EC2M 5QQ
Tel: (171) 628 0917 Fax: (171) 628 0909

Senior Executive Officers
Managing Director / General Manager   D P Spitsyn

Emirates Bank International

19 Motcomb Street, Belgravia, London SW1X 8XE
Tel: (171) 259 6262 Fax: (171) 259 5767 Telex: 8956506 EBILLO G

Senior Executive Officers
Managing Director / General Manager   Abdul Hakim Mansour

www.euromoneydirectory.com   UNITED KINGDOM (+44)

Enskilda Securities
Bank Subsidiary

Scandinavian House, 2-6 Cannon Street, London EC4M 6XX
Tel: (171) 236 6161 Fax: (171) 588 0929

Senior Executive Officers
Chairman	Stewart Humphrey
Director	David Glasspool
Director	Mark Hawtin
Director	Malcolm Crow
Director	Ian Macfarlane

Ergobank

Ergo House, 108 Wigmore Street, London W1H OLR
Tel: (171) 973 8630 Fax: (171) 973 8632

Senior Executive Officers
Managing Director / General Manager	S C Capsaskis

ERMGASSEN & Co

24 Lombard Street, London EC3V 9AD
Tel: (171) 929 2000 Fax: (171) 929 0432 Email: ermgassen@msn.com
Website: www.ermgassen.com

Senior Executive Officers
Director	Walter Zinsser
Chief Executive Officer	Olav Ermgassen *Director*
Financial Director	Roger Edmunds *Vice President Finance*
Director	Hans Berndt
Vice President Telecommunications	Ian Ellison
Vice President	Thomas Güntzer
Vice President	Michiel Ybema
Vice President	Marc Monasch
Portfolio Manager	Michael Azlen

Corporate Finance / M&A Advisory
Global Head	Olav Ermgassen *Director*

Other (Corporate Finance)
Germany / France	Thomas Güntzer *Vice President*
Germany / Scandinavia	Michiel Ybema *Vice President*
Benelux	Marc Monasch *Vice President*
Eastern Europe	Hans Berndt *Director*
Japan	Susumu Koide *Vice President*
	Ian Ellison *Vice President Telecommunications*

Administration

Compliance
	Roger Edmunds *Vice President Finance*

Erste Bank der Österreichischen Sparkassen AG
Full Branch Office

Formerly known as: GiroCredit Bank Aktiengesellschaft der Sparkassen AG
68 Cornhill, London EC3V 3QE
Tel: (171) 621 5000 Fax: (171) 283 5655 Telex: 8811989

Senior Executive Officers
General Manager	Eduard Oswald

Others (Senior Executives)
Head of Central & Eastern European Finance	Mark Muth *General Manager* ☎ **621 5023**

General-Lending (DCM, SL)
Head of Corporate Banking	Colin Theobald ☎ **621 5032**

General - Treasury
Head of Treasury	Paul Hitchcock ☎ **621 5054**

Syndicated Lending
Tel: 621 5033 Fax: 621 5049
Head of Syndication	Markus van der Burg

UNITED KINGDOM (+44)   www.euromoneydirectory.com

Erste Bank der Österreichischen Sparkassen AG (cont)

Loan-Related Activities
Trade Finance   Simon Page *Head, Trade Finance* ☎ 621 5026
Aircraft / Aerospace Finance   Robert Jack ☎ 621 5015

Other (Trade Finance)
Property Finance   Richard Mansfield ☎ 621 5018
Specialized Finance   Robert Jack ☎ 621 5015

Corporate Finance / M&A Advisory
Tel: 621 5023 **Fax:** 283 7142
Country Head   Mark Muth *General Manager*

Other Departments
Chief Credit Officer   Colin Theobald ☎ 621 5032

Administration
Legal / In-House Counsel
                                       Max Reichmann *Attorney-at-Law* ☎ 621 5028

ES International Holding SA   Representative Office

33 Queen Street, London EC4R 1ES
Tel: (171) 332 4350 **Fax:** (171) 332 4355

Senior Executive Officers
SVP & UK Representative   Manuel Villas-Boas
Vice President   Teresa de Souza

Etrufin Reserco Limited   Representative Office

2nd Floor, 3 St Helen's Place, London EC3A 6AU
Tel: (171) 638 4231 **Fax:** (171) 588 5809 **Telex:** 269821 **Email:** 106626.1253@compuserve.com

Senior Executive Officers
Managing Director   Leonardo Simonelli
Company Secretary   Helen Girgenti

Euro Brokers International Limited   Subsidiary Company

133 Houndsditch, London EC3A 7AJ
Tel: (171) 204 3000 **Fax:** (171) 929 1085

Senior Executive Officers
Chief Executive Officer   R A Clark *Joint Managing Director* ☎ 204 3003 🖷 204 3171
                                       P S Dunkley *Joint Managing Director* ☎ 929 1748 🖷 283 2516
Financial Director   W C W Pask ☎ 204 3045 🖷 929 1085

Others (Senior Executives)
                                       W M Kaczor *Director*
                                       I G McKay *Director* ☎ 204 3053 🖷 204 3171
                                       Steve Matteo *Director* ☎ 626 0385 🖷 929 1047

Money Markets
Money Markets - General
Deutschmarks   S J Bush *Director* ☎ 929 1744 🖷 283 2485
Sterling   T Drewitt ☎ 621 1414 🖷 929 1049
Dollar   K F Tricker *Director* ☎ 283 2485 🖷 929 1255
                                       D P Griffiths *Director* ☎ 283 2485 🖷 929 1255
Yen   M C Leech *Director* ☎ 626 1975 🖷 283 2415
Emerging Markets   N M P Chadd *Director, Currency Derivatives* ☎ 929 1744 🖷 283 2485

Other (Wholesale Deposits)
Dollar Division - $ Deposits & CDs   Peter Sanders *Director* ☎ 929 0071 🖷 929 1255
Euro Deposits & CD Deposits   M E Stepham *Manager* ☎ 929 0071 🖷 929 1255

Risk Management
Department: IR, Cross Currency, Basis Swaps, Structured & Exotic Swaps
Tel: 929 1744 **Fax:** 283 2485

Other Currency Swap / FX Options Personnel
                                       N M P Chadd *Director, Currency Derivatives* ☎ 929 1744 🖷 283 2485
                                       S J Bush *Director* ☎ 929 1744 🖷 283 2485
                                       Maja T A Nelson *Director* ☎ 929 1744 🖷 283 2485

www.euromoneydirectory.com   UNITED KINGDOM (+44)

Department: Caps, Floors, Swaptions & Exotics
Tel: 929 1748 **Fax:** 283 2516
Fixed Income Derivatives / Risk Management
IR Options Trading   P S Dunkley *Joint Managing Director* ⓣ **929 1748** ⓕ **283 2516**
                                          George Halloumas *Director* ⓣ **929 1748** ⓕ **283 2516**
                                          T B N Patch *Associate Director* ⓣ **929 1748** ⓕ **283 2516**
                                          A M Hill *Associate Director* ⓣ **929 1748** ⓕ **283 2516**
Department: Euro Brokers Financial Services Limited
Other Currency Swap / FX Options Personnel
Emerging Markets   Steve Matteo *Director* ⓣ **626 0385** ⓕ **929 1047**
                                          G N Weston *Director* ⓣ **626 0385** ⓕ **929 1048**
Floating Rate Notes   S D Bragman *Director* ⓣ **283 3482** ⓕ **579 9790**

Euroclear Operations Centre   Representative Office
Morgan Guaranty Trust Company of New York, 36-38 Cornhill, London EC3V 3NG
Tel: (171) 626 2493 Fax: (171) 325 8998
Website: www.euroclear.com

Senior Executive Officers
Others (Senior Executives)
Head of London Representative Office   Philip Reichardt *Head of Representative Office, Senior Representati*

Eurohypo (UK) Limited
6 Bishopsgate, London EC2N 4DA
Tel: (171) 545 2111 Fax: (171) 545 2092

Senior Executive Officers
General Manager   Paul Revlin

European Bank for Reconstruction & Development   Head Office
Alternative trading name: EBRD
One Exchange Square, London EC2A 2JN
Tel: (171) 338 6000 Fax: (171) 338 6100 Telex: 8812161 EBRD L G Swift: EBRD GB 2L
Website: www.ebrd.com

Senior Executive Officers
President   Horst Köhler
First Vice President   Charles Frank
Financial Director   Steven Kaempfer *Vice President Finance*
Treasurer   Marcus Fedder *Treasurer* ⓣ **338 6302** ⓕ **338 7880**
General Secretary   Antonio Maria Costa

Others (Senior Executives)
New Products, Policies & Issues   Gavin Anderson *Director*
Banking Team Directors   .   Olivier Descamps *Country Team Director*
                                          Kazuya Murakami *Director of Team*
                                          Peter Reiniger *Director of Team*
                                          Alain Pilloux *Director of Team*

General - Treasury
Head of Treasury   Andrew Donaldson *Deputy Treasurer*
                                          Costas Kazantzidis *Head of Investments - Credit*
                                          Bart Mauldin *Head of Investments - Interest Rates*
                                          Ayesha Shah *Head of Funding*
                                          Axel Van Nederveen *Head of Asset & Liability Management*
                                          Jaakko Kärki *Head of External Asset Management / Analytics*

Relationship Manager
Client Risk Management   Debbie Berger *Director*
New Business Development - Japan   Rickie Naito *Director, New Business Development - Japan*
Department: Banking Team Directors
Deputy Vice President   David Hexter
Deputy Vice President   Jean Francois Maquet

Others (Senior Executives)
New Products, Policies & Issues   Gavin Anderson *Director*
Relationship Manager
Bulgaria / Albania / FYR Macedonia / Slovenia   Olivier Descamps *Country Team Director*
Armenia / Georgia / Azerbaijan   Oliver Descamps *Country Team Director*

UNITED KINGDOM (+44)　　　www.euromoneydirectory.com

European Bank for Reconstruction & Development (cont)
Relationship Manager (cont)
Central Asia — Kazuya Murakami *Director of Team*
Hungary — Peter Reiniger *Director of Team*
Poland / Czech Republic / Slovak Rep / Baltic States — Alain Pilloux *Director of Team*
Russia — Reinhard Schmoelz *Director of Team*
Ukraine / Romania / Moldova / Croatia; Bosnia & Herzegovina / Belarus — Lyndsay Forbes *Deputy Director of Team*
Agribusiness — Hans Christian Jacobsen *Director of Team*
Energy Efficiency Unit — Bernard Jamet *Director of Team*
Financial Institutions — Kurt Geiger *Co-Director of Team*
　　Rogers Le Baron *Co-Director of Team*
　　Dragica Pilipovic-Chaffey *Co-Director of Team*
Municipal & Environmental Infrastructure — Johan Bastin *Director of Team*
Natural Resources — Vittorio Jucker *Director of Team*
Power / Energy Utilities — Ananda Covindassamy *Director of Team*
Property / Tourism / Shipping — Edgar Rosenmaya *Director of Team*
Telecommunications — Peter Reiniger *Director of Team*
Transport — Roy Knighton *Director of Team*
Environmental Appraisal — Tim Murphy *Head of Unit*
TurnAround Management Programme (TAM) — Michael McAlister *Managing Director*
Russia Small Business Fund — Elizabeth Wallace *Operations Leader*
Direct Investment Facility — Frances Reid *Senior Banker*

Risk Management
Global Head — Noreen Doyle *Deputy VP, Director, Risk Management*
Country Head — Jean-André Sorasio *Risk Controller*

Other (FI Derivatives)
Risk Controller — Jean-André Sorasio *Risk Controller*

Other (Exchange-Traded Derivatives)
Transaction Analysis — Bob Harada *Head*
Portfolio Review — Mike Williams *Head*
Commercial Co-financing — Lorenz Jorgensen *Head*
Special Assets — Charles Wrangham *Head*

Settlement / Clearing
Operations — Peter Franklin *Director of Operations*
　　Christopher Holyoak *Head of Operations & IT*

Asset Management
Other (Asset Management)
Analytics / External Asset Management — Jaakko Kärki *Head of External Asset Management / Analytics*
Asset & Liability Management — Axel van Nederveen *Head*

Other Departments
Economic Research — Ricardo Lago *Deputy Chief Economist*
　　Mark Schankerman *Director, Policy Studies*
　　Nicholas Stern *Chief Economist*

Administration
Head of Administration — John McNess *Director*

Technology & Systems
Information Technology — Guy de Poerck *Director*
　　Christopher Holyoak *Head of Operations & IT*

Legal / In-House Counsel
General Counsel — John Taylor
Deputy General Counsel — Emmanuel Maurice
Assistant General Counsel — Norbert Seiler

Corporate Communications
Communications — Barbara Clay *Director*

Accounts / Audit
Strategic & Corporate Planning — Josué Tanaka *Director*
Accounting — Nigel Kerby *Director*
Treasury Accounting — Terry Cullen *Head*
Internal Audit — Tarek Rouchdy *Head*

Other (Administration)
Personnel & Administration — Miklós Németh *Vice President*
Personnel — Franco Furno *Director*
Secretary General — Antonio Maria Costa *General Secretary*
Project Evaluation, Operat. Supp.& Nuclear Safety — Joachim Jahnke *Vice President*

www.euromoneydirectory.com   UNITED KINGDOM (+44)

European Capital

Head Office

EUROPEAN CAPITAL

3 Lombard Street, London EC3V 9AA
Tel: (171) 600 3138 **Fax:** (171) 600 3053 **Email:** ec@eurocap.co.uk

Senior Executive Officers
Chairman	John Caines
Chief Executive Officer	Stephen Syrett
Company Secretary	Shelagh Kirkland

Others (Senior Executives)
Head of Private Finance Initiative	Paul Bryans

Debt Capital Markets / Fixed Income
Head of Fixed Income	Maurice Hochschild

Equity Capital Markets
Head of Equity Capital Markets	Maurice Hochschild

Syndicated Lending

Loan-Related Activities
Trade Finance	Stephen Syrett
Project Finance	Robert Lewin *Head of Project Finance*

Corporate Finance / M&A Advisory
Global Head	Maurice Hochschild

Asset Management
Head	Maurice Hochschild

Other Departments
Chief Credit Officer	Stephen Syrett
Cash Management	Shelagh Kirkland

Administration
Head of Administration	Shelagh Kirkland
Business Development	Stephen Syrett
Head of Marketing	Robert Lewin

Technology & Systems
	Paul Bryans

Compliance
	Shelagh Kirkland

Public Relations
	Paul Bryans

Accounts / Audit
	Shelagh Kirkland

European Investment Bank

68 Pall Mall, London SW1Y 5ES
Tel: (171) 343 1200 **Fax:** (171) 930 9929

Senior Executive Officers
Head	Guy Baird

The Export-Import Bank of Japan

Representative Office

River Plate House, 7/11 Finsbury Circus, London EC2M 7EX
Tel: (171) 638 0175 **Fax:** (171) 638 2401 **Telex:** 8952604

Senior Executive Officers
Chief Executive Officer	K Fujii *Resident Exec Director, Europe,Middle East,Africa*
Chief Representative	K Higashi

FIBI Bank (UK) plc

24 Creechurch Lane, London EC3A 5EH
Tel: (171) 283 5333 **Fax:** (171) 283 6777 **Telex:** 8956815 **Reuters:** FBUK

Senior Executive Officers
Financial Director	K Dick
Managing Director / General Manager	Y Levy

UNITED KINGDOM (+44)   www.euromoneydirectory.com

Finacor

4 Goldings House, Hay's Galleria, London SE1 2HB
Tel: (171) 940 6100; (171) 357 8488 Fax: (171) 403 5022
Website: www.finacor.co.uk

Debt Capital Markets / Fixed Income

Fixed-Income Repo
Head of Repo — Patrice Morain *Director* ☎ **357 8488**
Marketing & Product Development — Liam Tomkins *Vice President* ☎ **357 8848** 📠 **403 5022**
✉ **tomkins@city.finacor.co.uk**
Trading — Nick McCall *Trader, Multi-Currency*
Ian Doogan *Trader, Multi-Currency*
Stephen Mustill *Trader, Multi-Currency*
Kevin Ward *Trader, Multi-Currency*
Gerard Pugsly *Trader, Multi-Currency*
Nigel Mallender *Trader, Asset Swap & Arbitrage*

Equity Capital Markets
Tel: 357 8488

Equity Repo / Securities Lending
Head — Patrice Morain *Director* ☎ **357 8488**
Marketing — Liam Tomkins *Vice President* ☎ **357 8848** 📠 **403 5022**
✉ **tomkins@city.finacor.co.uk**
Head of Trading — Nick McCall *Trader, Multi-Currency*
Ian Doogan *Trader, Multi-Currency*
Stephen Mustill *Trader, Multi-Currency*
Kevin Ward *Trader, Multi-Currency*
David Forbes-Gower *Trader, Multi-Currency*
Gerard Pugsly *Trader, Multi-Currency*
Nigel Mallender *Trader, Asset Swap & Arbitrage*

Financial Security Assurance (UK) Limited   Subsidiary Company

1 Angel Court, London EC2R 7AE
Tel: (171) 796 4646 Fax: (171) 796 3540

Senior Executive Officers
Assistant Vice President — Victor Benavides
Managing Director, Global Project Finance — C J Lester
Managing Director, Infrastructure Finance — Charles D Silberstein
Managing Director, Europe — Philippe Z Tromp

Others (Senior Executives)

Joseph C Di Prospero *Director*
Christopher Wrenn *Director*

JM Finn & Co   Head Office

Salisbury House, London Wall, London EC2M 5TA
Tel: (171) 628 9688 Fax: (171) 628 7314 Telex: 887281
Website: www.jmfinn.com

Senior Executive Officers
Senior Partner — Cedric Feather
Financial Director — Steven Sussman *Head of Finance*

Corporate Finance / M&A Advisory
Head of Corporate Finance — John Finn

Settlement / Clearing
Settlement (General) — Paul Carleton
Operations — Vivienne Langlois *Head of Operations*

Administration
Head of Marketing — Paul Farrant *Partner*

Compliance

Charles Beck *Compliance Partner*

1746   Euromoney Directory 1999

www.euromoneydirectory.com						UNITED KINGDOM (+44)

## First Austrian International Limited											Subsidiary Company

68 Cornhill, London EC3V 3QE
Tel: (171) 975 1700 **Fax:** (171) 975 1796 **Telex:** 9419084 ERSTE
Interbank Tel: 283 1184

Senior Executive Officers
Managing Director						Anthony Marston

Debt Capital Markets / Fixed Income
Eurobonds
Head of Trading						Richard Allen *Manager*

Risk Management
Fixed Income Derivatives / Risk Management
Regional Head							Thomas O'Reilly *Head of Trading*
IR Swaps Sales / Marketing					Antonios Alibertis *Deputy Head*

Settlement / Clearing
Country Head							Julie Harding *Settlements Supervisor*

Administration
Legal / In-House Counsel
								Sophie Grey *Lawyer*
Compliance
								Kosh de Silva *Company Secretary*

## First Bank of Nigeria plc												Full Branch Office

29/30 King Street, London EC2V 8EH
Tel: (171) 776 2900; (171) 606 6411 **Fax:** (171) 606 3134 **Telex:** 893013 **Swift:** FBNI GB ZL

Settlement / Clearing
Operations							H Crawford *Manager, Operations*

## First Chicago NBD													Full Branch Office

Alternative trading name: First National Bank of Chicago
1 Triton Square, London NW1 3FN
Tel: (171) 388 3456 **Fax:** (171) 528 7185; (171) 388 4747 **Telex:** 887716 FNBCLN G **Swift:** FNBC GB 2X **Reuters:** FNFX
Cable: FIRSTCHICAGO LON
Website: www.fcnbd.com

Senior Executive Officers
Others (Senior Executives)
Branch Manager						Peter McCarthy *Senior Vice President* ☎ **903 4474**
General-Lending (DCM, SL)
Head of Corporate Banking					Jan Erik Anderson *Head, EMEA Banking* ☎ **903 4103**

Debt Capital Markets / Fixed Income
Head of Fixed Income Sales					William Wulkan *First Vice President* ☎ **903 4328**
Head of Fixed Income Trading					Richard Portlock *First Vice President* ☎ **903 4250**
Eurobonds
Head of Trading						Richard Portlock *First Vice President* ☎ **903 4250**
Libor-Based / Floating-Rate Products
Asset Swaps							Karen Wittich *Vice President* ☎ **903 4309**
Fixed-Income Repo
Head of Repo							Ed Fisher *Repo Trader* ☎ **903 4259**

Equity Capital Markets
Department: **Equify Derivatives**
Head of Equity Capital Markets				Steve Ashworth *Vice President* ☎ **903 4033**

Syndicated Lending
Other (Syndicated Lending)
Head of Financial Markets					Martha Noyes *Senior Vice President* ☎ **903 4132**

Money Markets
Money Markets - General
Head of Funding & Investments					Trevor Morgan *First Vice President* ☎ **903 4090**

Foreign Exchange
Head of Foreign Exchange					Mel Mayne *First Vice President* ☎ **903 4297**

Euromoney Directory 1999   **1747**

UNITED KINGDOM (+44)   www.euromoneydirectory.com

First Chicago NBD (cont)
Risk Management
Tel: 903 4200
Head of Risk Management — Andrew Brown *Senior Vice President* ☎ **903 4301**
Fixed Income Derivatives / Risk Management
Head of Sales — William Wulkan *First Vice President* ☎ **903 4328**
Trading — Richard Portlock *First Vice President* ☎ **903 4250**
Corporate Finance / M&A Advisory
Country Head — Martha Noyes *Senior Vice President* ☎ **903 4132**
Settlement / Clearing
Head of Settlement / Clearing — Maurice Cleaves *First Vice President* ☎ **903 4112**
  Alan Stark *First Vice President* ☎ **903 4444**
Other Departments
Chief Credit Officer — David Lindop *Senior Vice President* ☎ **903 4363**
Administration
Compliance
  Peter Ray *Vice President* ☎ **903 4498**

First Commercial Bank Limited
Bowman House, 29 Wilson Street, London EC2M 2SJ
Tel: (171) 417 0000 **Fax:** (171) 417 0011 **Telex:** 897237

Senior Executive Officers
President — T C Luo
Managing Director / General Manager — Ming-Shang Yu

First International Merchant Bank Limited — Representative Office
2nd Floor, 12 Blandford Street, London W1H 3HA
Tel: (171) 935 6002 **Fax:** (171) 935 5601

Senior Executive Officers
Chief Representative — Arun Chauhan

First National Bank of Maryland — Representative Office
12 Jewry, London EC2R 8DP
Tel: (171) 726 4082 **Fax:** (171) 600 1106

Senior Executive Officers
VP & Representative — Rosemary A Farmer

First Ukranian International Bank
Camomile Court, 23 Camomile Street, London EC3A 7PP
Tel: (171) 444 8749 **Fax:** (171) 444 8814

Senior Executive Officers
Managing Director / General Manager — David D W de Buck

Five Arrows Leasing Group Limited — Head Office
Formerly known as: New Court Finance
Heron House, 5 Heron Square, Richmond, Surrey TW9 1EL
Tel: (181) 334 3900 **Fax:** (181) 332 1636

Senior Executive Officers
Treasurer — Simon Kirk
Managing Director — Sam Geneen
Company Secretary — Philip Davies
Administration
Technology & Systems
  Hugh Ruddle
Public Relations
  John Luff

www.euromoneydirectory.com   UNITED KINGDOM (+44)

Robert Fleming Holdings Limited

25 Copthall Avenue, London EC2R 7DR
Tel: (171) 638 5858 **Fax:** (171) 588 7219 **Telex:** 297451 **Swift:** RFLC GB 2L **Reuters:** RFDL; RFXL; RXLL

Senior Executive Officers
Chairman — John Manser
Chief Executive Officer — William Garrett
Financial Director — Simon Ball
Treasurer — Andy Armstrong
Company Secretary — Alastair Macintosh

General-Lending (DCM, SL)
Head of Corporate Banking — Ian Hannam ☎ **382 6818**

General-Investment
Head of Investment — William Garrett

Debt Capital Markets / Fixed Income
Department: Fixed Income Capital Markets
Tel: 282 4850 **Fax:** 382 8414
Head of Debt Capital Markets
Head of Fixed Income
Head of Fixed Income Sales
Tom Hughes-Hillet *Head of Securities*
Russell Chweidan *Head of Asian Fixed Income* ☎ **382 8478**
Roger Wong *Director* ☎ **+852 2978 7260**
Georges de Tilly *Director* ☎ **+852 2843 8733**

Libor-Based / Floating-Rate Products
Asset Swaps — Russell Chweidan *Head of Asian Fixed Income* ☎ **382 8478**
Asset Swaps (Sales) — Chechung Chang ☎ **282 4076**

Fixed-Income Research
Head of Credit Research — Daniel Y O Leung *Head of Credit Research* ☎ **+852 2840 6467**

Equity Capital Markets
Department: Equity Capital Markets
Tel: 385 8205 **Fax:** 382 8414 **Telex:** 297451
Head of Equity Capital Markets — Ian Hannam ☎ **382 6818**

Domestic Equities
Head of Sales — Ed Burke ☎ **382 8432**
Head of Trading — Barry Marks ☎ **382 4114**

International Equities
Head of Sales — Paul Hart ☎ **382 8432**
Head of Trading — Barry Marks ☎ **382 4114**

Equity Research
Head of Equity Research — Paul Hart ☎ **382 8432**

Convertibles / Equity-Linked
Head of Trading — Andy Swarbrick ☎ **282 4409**

Money Markets
Head of Money Markets — David Smith *Chief Dealer*

Wholesale Deposits
Head of Sales — Jill Gore

Other (Wholesale Deposits)
Head of Trading — Gary Skedge

Foreign Exchange
Head of Foreign Exchange — David Smith *Chief Dealer*
Head of Institutional Sales; Corporate Sales — Jill Gore
Head of Trading — Gary Crudgington

FX Traders / Sales People
Emerging Markets — Matt Kirby

Risk Management
Head of Risk Management — Michael Gaines *Risk Director*

Fixed Income Derivatives / Risk Management
Head of Sales — Jill Gore
Trading — Ashley Welton

Other (FI Derivatives)
Head of IRS — Ashley Welton

Foreign Exchange Derivatives / Risk Management
Spot / Forwards Sales — Jill Gore
Spot / Forwards Trading — Michael Hughes

OTC Equity Derivatives
Sales — Mark Bamble
Trading — Roy Martin

UNITED KINGDOM (+44) www.euromoneydirectory.com

Robert Fleming Holdings Limited (cont)

Other (Equity Derivatives)
Equities Asian   John Knox

Corporate Finance / M&A Advisory
Head of Corporate Finance   Bernard Taylor

Settlement / Clearing
Head of Settlement / Clearing   John Gardner *Head of Operations* ☏ **814 2030**
Equity Settlement   Ian Middleton *Deputy* ☏ **814 2919**
Fixed-Income Settlement; Back-Office;   John Gardner *Head of Operations* ☏ **814 2030**
Electronic Banking

Administration
Technology & Systems
                                               Julian Haros

Legal / In-House Counsel
                                               Geoffrey Howe

Compliance
                                               Brian Matthews

Public Relations
                                               Shane O'Riordan

Accounts / Audit
                                               John Archibald

Foreign and Colonial Emerging Markets Limited Subsidiary Company

8th Floor, Exchange House, Primrose Street, London EC2A 2NY
Tel: (171) 628 1234 Fax: (171) 628 2283 Telex: 915692 Email: ebarnes@fcem.co.uk Reuters: LAMA-C

Senior Executive Officers
Chief Executive Officer   Arnab Banerji
Financial Director   Michael Gabriel
Chief Operating Officer   Karen Clarke

Administration
Head of Marketing   Anthony Conway *Marketing Director*

Fox-Pitt, Kelton Limited   Head Office

35 Wilson Street, London EC2M 2UB
Tel: (171) 377 8929 Fax: (171) 247 5013 Telex: 884163 PITKEL G
Website: www.fpk.com

Senior Executive Officers
Group Chairman   Anthony Hamilton
Financial Director   Rupert Travis *Finance Director*
Managing Director / General Manager   Colin McGill
Finance Director   Rupert Travis

Equity Capital Markets
Fax: 972 0532
Global Head   Anthony Hamilton *Group Chairman*

Domestic Equities
Head of Origination   John Franklin
Head of Syndication   Michael Bell
Head of Sales   Colin McGill *Managing Director*
Head of Trading   Joe Noakes
Head of Research   Bob Yates

International Equities
Head of Origination   John Franklin
Head of Syndication   Michael Bell
Head of Sales   Colin McGill *Managing Director*
Head of Trading   Joe Noakes
Head of Research   Bob Yates

Corporate Finance / M&A Advisory
Fax: 377 8421
Global Head   Anthony Hamilton *Group Chairman*

Settlement / Clearing
Equity Settlement   Paul Taylor *Head, International Settlements*

www.euromoneydirectory.com   UNITED KINGDOM (+44)

Asset Management
Head   Piotr Poloniecki
Administration
Compliance

Colin McGill *Managing Director*

The Fuji Bank Limited   Full Branch Office
River Plate House, 7-11 Finsbury Circus, London EC2M 7NT
Tel: (171) 588 2211 **Fax:** (171) 588 1400 **Telex:** 886352 **Swift:** FUJI GB 2LA

Senior Executive Officers
Treasurer   Akio Kashima
General Manager   Hideko Ide

Syndicated Lending
Department: Syndications Department
Tel: 826 3420 **Fax:** 826 3142
Head of Syndication   Geoffrey Holgate *Senior Assistant General Manager* ☎ **826 3297**

Loan-Related Activities
Project Finance   S Yoshida *Joint General Manager*
Leasing & Asset Finance   Michael Percy *Deputy General Manager*

Other (Trade Finance)
Structured Finance   Jeremy Ghose *Head*

Other Departments
Correspondent Banking   Alfred Carter *Manager*

Administration
Legal / In-House Counsel

Simon Miller *General Counsel*

Fuji International Finance plc   Subsidiary Company
River Plate House, 7-11 Finsbury Circus, London EC2M 7NT
Tel: (171) 256 8888 **Fax:** (171) 588 2033 **Telex:** 884275 **Reuters:** FIFA-C

Senior Executive Officers
Managing Director   Junji Miyamoto ☎ **826 3308**
Deputy Managing Director   John Rouse ☎ **826 3304**

Others (Senior Executives)
Trading & Sales   Masana Moriura *Deputy Managing Director* ☎ **826 3303**
Capital Markets   Michael Cole *Deputy Managing Director* ☎ **826 3311**
High Yield Bond   Jeremy Ghose *Deputy Managing Director*

Debt Capital Markets / Fixed Income
Tel: 972 9898 **Fax:** 374 0340
Head of Fixed Income Sales   Paul Bradshaw ☎ **638 5743**
Head of Fixed Income Trading   Paul Reid ☎ **638 7219**

Fixed-Income Repo
Head of Repo   Tim Whipman *Associate Director* ☎ **972 9898**
Marketing & Product Development   Patricia Regard *Manager* ☎ **374 2000**
Head of Trading   Akinori Takahashi *Senior Manager* ☎ **374 2000**

Equity Capital Markets
Tel: 972 9898 **Fax:** 374 0340
Head of Sales   Paul Bradshaw ☎ **638 5743**
Head of Trading   Paul Reid ☎ **638 7219**

Equity Repo / Securities Lending
Head   Tim Whipman *Associate Director* ☎ **972 9898**

Risk Management
Head of Risk Management   Andrew Bryan *Executive Director* ☎ **826 3340**

Other (Exchange-Traded Derivatives)
Sales   Gavin Wells ☎ **826 3337**

Exchange-Traded Derivatives
Head   Paul Reid ☎ **638 7219**

Settlement / Clearing
Operations   Kevin Bridger *Associate Director* ☎ **826 3357**

Administration
Technology & Systems

Roger Southgate *Senior Executive Director* ☎ **826 3393**

UNITED KINGDOM (+44)   www.euromoneydirectory.com

Fuji International Finance plc (cont)
Legal / In-House Counsel
    David Le Claire *Senior Manager* ☎ **826 3313**

Compliance
    John Rouse *Deputy Managing Director* ☎ **826 3304**

Accounts / Audit
Accounts
    Roger Balkwill *Executive Director* ☎ **256 8888**

Furman Selz
Pountney Hill House, 7 Laurence Pountney Hill, London EC4R OBL
Tel: (171) 410 1111 Fax: (171) 410 00334

Garban Europe Limited
Hibernia Chambers, 2 London Bridge, London SE1 9QP
Tel: (171) 570 1000; (171) 570 1070 Fax: (171) 334 7224

Senior Executive Officers
Others (Senior Executives)
Trading   Steve McMillan *Head*

Debt Capital Markets / Fixed Income
Fixed-Income Repo
Head of Repo   Paul Guire *Divisional Director*
Trading   Paul Guire *Director* ☎ **570 1070**
     P Cumbers *Manager*

Settlement / Clearing
Operations   Edward Bowen *Head of Operations*

Administration
Compliance
     Pamela Barham

Gartmore Investment Management plc   Head Office
16-18 Monument Street, London EC4R 8AJ
Tel: (171) 782 2000 Fax: (171) 782 2075 Telex: 896873 GIM G Email: international@gartmore.com

Senior Executive Officers
Chairman   Paul Myners ☎ **454 2266**
Chief Executive Officer   David Watts *Joint Chief Executive / CIO* ☎ **782 2210**
     Andrew Brown *Joint Chief Executive* ☎ **782 2134**
Financial Director   Keith Felton *Head of Finance* ☎ **782 2133**
Chief Operating Officer   Christopher Samuel *Chief Operating Officer* ☎ **782 2493**
Treasurer   Geof Bull
Company Secretary   Jane Thornton
International Division   Sally Tennant *Head of International Division* ☎ **782 2294**

General-Investment
Head of Investment   David Watts

Debt Capital Markets / Fixed Income
Head of Fixed Income   Roger Bartley

Emerging Market Bonds
Head of Emerging Markets   Philip Ehrmann *Head of Emerging Markets* ☎ **782 2247**

Money Markets
Head of Money Markets   David Hynes *Head of Cash Management* ☎ **782 2560**

Other Departments
Cash Management   David Hynes *Head of Cash Management* ☎ **782 2560**

Administration
Head of Administration   Les Aitkenhead
Business Development   Martin Harris
Head of Marketing   Avril Davis

Technology & Systems
     Wendy Steel

Legal / In-House Counsel
     Jane Thornton

www.euromoneydirectory.com		UNITED KINGDOM (+44)

Compliance
　　　　　Alasdair Boulding *Head of Compliance* ☎ 782 2366/2

Public Relations
　　　　　Peter Yandle *Head of Corporate Communications* ☎ 782 2448

Accounts / Audit
　　　　　Mark Starbuck

General Re Financial Securities Limited　　　　Head Office
8th Floor, Broadgate Court, 199 Bishopsgate, London EC2M 3TY
Tel: (171) 448 4000 **Fax:** (171) 448 4065

Senior Executive Officers
Chief Executive Officer　　　　Anthony Iliya ☎ 448 4020 F 448 4067
Managing Director　　　　Tarek Mahmoud ☎ 448 4027 F 448 4066
Managing Director　　　　Colin Ball ☎ 448 4001 F 448 4066

Debt Capital Markets / Fixed Income
Department: Structuring
Head of Fixed Income Trading　　　　Ian Martin *Fixed Income & FX Trading* ☎ 448 4040 F 814 0022

Bonds - General
Structured Credit　　　　Mike Staveley ☎ 448 4130 F 814 0022

Equity Capital Markets
Head of Trading　　　　Gill Parry *Equity* ☎ 448 4120

Foreign Exchange
Head of Trading　　　　Ian Martin *Fixed Income & FX Trading* ☎ 448 4040 F 814 0022

Other Departments
Chief Credit Officer　　　　David Ensor *Credit* ☎ 448 4013 F 448 4069

Administration
Legal / In-House Counsel
Legal　　　　Michelle Bereaux ☎ 448 4010 F 814 0024

Compliance
　　　　　Nigel Pasea ☎ 448 4170 F 814 0023

Accounts / Audit
Accounts　　　　Roger Kibble-White ☎ 448 4178 F 814 0023

Other (Administration)
Human Resources　　　　Alison Davies ☎ 448 4026 F 448 4068

Generale Bank SA / NV　　　　Full Branch Office
Bavaria House, 13/14 Appold Street, London EC2A 2DP
Tel: (171) 247 5353; (171) 247 8000 **Fax:** (171) 247 7743 **Telex:** 884411 GEBA G **Swift:** GEBA GB 22 **Reuters:** GBAX
General Telex: 927948 GEFEX; **Reuters:** GBXL

Senior Executive Officers
Chief Executive Officer　　　　Marc Bellis

Others (Senior Executives)
Midlands Regional Office　　　　Mac Cummings *Director*
Thames Valley Regional Office　　　　Trevor Harrison *Director*

General-Lending (DCM, SL)
Head of Corporate Banking　　　　Martin Dore *Senior Corporate Manager*
　　　　　Anne Marie Verstraeten *DGM & Head, Corporate Banking*
　　　　　Andrew Merrifield *Senior Corporate Manager*

General - Treasury
Head of Treasury　　　　Simon Law *Manager, Treasury Corporate Trading*
　　　　　Chris Wilkins *Head of Treasury*

Syndicated Lending
Loan-Related Activities
Trade Finance　　　　Malcolm Evans *Senior Manager*

Risk Management
Country Head　　　　Ian Littler *Senior Risk Manager, Credit*

Settlement / Clearing
Foreign Exchange Settlement　　　　Ted Dooley *Manager*
Other　　　　Sandra Ponting *Senior Manager*

Euromoney Directory 1999　**1753**

UNITED KINGDOM (+44) www.euromoneydirectory.com

Generale Bank SA / NV (cont)
Administration
Head of Administration — David Rosenberg *Head of Division*

Technology & Systems
Adeolu Bajomo *Manager*

Accounts / Audit
Paul Stroud *Senior Manager*

Other (Administration)
General Affairs — Bob Newland *Manager*

Gerrard & King Limited — Head Office

Formerly known as: Gerrard & National Limited / King & Shaxson
Cannon Bridge, 25 Dowgate Hill, London EC4R 2GN
Tel: (171) 337 2800 **Fax:** (171) 337 2830 **Telex:** 883589 **Reuters:** GNDB; GNDC
Website: www.gerrard.com

Senior Executive Officers
Chairman — Ian Perkins ☎ **337 3566**
Chief Executive Officer — Ross Jones *Chief Executive* ☎ **337 2808**
Financial Director — Nicholas Wallis *Finance Director* ☎ **337 2881**
Company Secretary — Miranda Telfer ☎ **337 3557**

Others (Senior Executives)
Marketing Director — Adrian Taylor *Marketing Director* ☎ **337 6525**
Director of Credit — Paul Boulton *Director* ☎ **337 2831**

Debt Capital Markets / Fixed Income
Fixed-Income Repo
Head of Repo — David Franklin *Director, Repo* ☎ **337 6541**
Other — Colin Spratt *Assistant Director, Repo* ☎ **337 6540**

Equity Capital Markets
Equity Repo / Securities Lending
Head — Bob Pullen *Director* ☎ **337 6520**
Allan Spargo *Director* ☎ **337 6520**

Money Markets
Tel: 337 2800 **Fax:** 337 2830
Head of Money Markets — David Absalom *Director* ☎ **337 2833**

Other (Wholesale Deposits)
Sterling, CDs (head) — Simon Hall *Assistant Director* ☎ **337 6510**
Sterling, Bills — Tony Lang *Trader* ☎ **337 2835**
Customer Desk — Gay Godfrey *Trader* ☎ **337 2837**
Local Authorities — Nick Ryder *Director* ☎ **337 3550**
James Dare *Trader* ☎ **337 2836**
Off-Balance Sheet — Neil Cooksley *Trader* ☎ **337 2834**
General Dealing — Julie Sayer *Trader* ☎ **337 2838**
Scottish Office — Richard Dorman *Manager* ☎ **+44 (131) 240 4441**
Doreen Black *Trader* ☎ **+44 (131) 240 4441**

Settlement / Clearing
Head of Settlement / Clearing — Chris Jones ☎ **337 6556**

Administration
Compliance
Nigel Avey ☎ **337 3695**

GFI Group Inc

GFI House, 9 Hewett Street, London EC2A 3NN
Tel: (171) 247 0070 **Fax:** (171) 283 4303

Debt Capital Markets / Fixed Income
Tel: 247 2244

Fixed-Income Repo
Trading — Scott Malden *Sub-Vice President*

www.euromoneydirectory.com   UNITED KINGDOM (+44)

Ghana International Bank
Formerly known as: Ghana Commercial Bank
69 Cheapside, London EC2P 2BB
PO Box 77, London EC2P 2BB
Tel: (171) 248 2384; (171) 248 0191 **Fax:** (171) 489 9058 **Telex:** 888597 GHBL DN G **Cable:** GHANABANK LONDON
Telex: 94013617 GBLNG

Senior Executive Officers
Chairman	Kwabena Duffuor
Managing Director	Kevin Pugsley
General Manager	Brian Hagger
Company Secretary	Beatrice Mettle-Nunoo

Syndicated Lending
Head of Syndication	Brian Hagger *General Manager*

Loan-Related Activities
Trade Finance	Yaw Ntim-Donkoh *Manager*

Money Markets
Head of Money Markets	Kwame Sarpong *Chief Dealer*

Foreign Exchange
Head of Foreign Exchange	Kwame Sarpong *Chief Dealer*

Settlement / Clearing
Head of Settlement / Clearing	Beatrice Mettle-Nunoo

Other Departments
Chief Credit Officer	Mark Arthur
Private Banking	Ray Sowah
Correspondent Banking	Lucas Parry

Administration
Head of Administration	Daniel Thompson
Head of Marketing	Paul Larbi

Technology & Systems
	Odile Agyare

Compliance
	Beatrice Mettle-Nunoo

Accounts / Audit
Internal Audit	Alan Mackay

Girobank plc
49 Park Lane, London W1Y 4EQ
Tel: (171) 629 6661 **Fax:** (171) 408 1399 **Telex:** 341222 **Swift:** GIRB GBB 2L **Reuters:** GIRL

Senior Executive Officers
Chairman	Peter White
Treasurer	Ian Lawrence
Managing Director	Richard Banks
International Division	Alan Hughes *Senior Manager*

Others (Senior Executives)
Customer Services	Bill Sutton *Director*
Internal Processing	Linda Russo *Manager*

Other Departments
Correspondent Banking	Paul Nicholls *Manager*

GNI Financial Products Limited   Subsidiary Company
Cannon Bridge, 25 Dowgate Hill, London EC4R 2GN
Tel: (171) 337 3500 **Fax:** (171) 337 3501 **Telex:** 884962 **Email:** enquiries@gni.co.uk **Reuters:** GNIF, GNIX
Website: www.gni.co.uk

Senior Executive Officers
Chairman	T J R Sheldon
Chief Executive Officer	Julian Rogers-Coltman *Chief Executive*

Others (Senior Executives)
	Finlay Smillie *Director*
	Jeff Woyda *Director*

Euromoney Directory 1999 **1755**

UNITED KINGDOM (+44) www.euromoneydirectory.com

GNI Financial Products Limited (cont)

Relationship Manager
Public Sector & Corporate Structures
  Stuart Canwell *Director*
  Andrew Lewis *Assistant Director*
  Mike Grace
  Karen Haley

Risk Management
Fixed Income Derivatives / Risk Management
Country Head
  Rhys Rogers *Director*

OTC Equity Derivatives
Head
  Neil Pengelly *Director*
  Faruk Oreagba *Senior Manager*
Trading
  Karine Le Rest
  Christophe Ricard

Other (Exchange-Traded Derivatives)
OTC Bond Options
  Paul Lucas *Director*
  Colin Richardson *Senior Manager*
  Ben Stanley
  Fiorella Massey
  Steven Bloor
  Eleanor Vieler

GNI Limited — Head Office
Cannon Bridge, 25 Dowgate Hill, London EC4R 2GN
Tel: (171) 337 3500 Fax: (171) 337 3501 Telex: 884962 Email: enquiries@gni.co.uk
Website: www.gni.co.uk

Senior Executive Officers
Chairman
  C J Sharples
Chief Executive Officer
  T J R Sheldon *Chief Executive*
  Karel Harbour *Deputy Chief Executive*
  Julian Rogers-Coltman *Deputy Chief Executive*
Chief Operating Officer
  Jeff Woyda *Chief Operating Officer*

Others (Senior Executives)
  Steve Davies *Director, Operations*
  Hugh Morshead *Director*

General-Lending (DCM, SL)
Head of Corporate Banking
  Peter Speak *Director, Credit*

General - Treasury
Head of Treasury
  Chris Dizer *Associate Director, Treasury*

Relationship Manager
Metals
  Andy Jervis *Senior Manager*
Electricity
  James Hoare *Director*
Energy
  Rob Laughlin *Director*

Debt Capital Markets / Fixed Income
Fixed-Income Repo
Trading
  Nick Gant *Dealer*
  Mark Woodgate *Dealer*
  Stephen Wagstaff *Dealer*
  Richard Wallace *Dealer*
  Andrew Williams *Trader*

Equity Capital Markets
Equity Repo / Securities Lending
Head
  Malcolm Ewen *Director, Stock Lending & Repo* ☎ 337 6530 📠 962 9350
  📧 malcolm.ewen@gni.co.uk

Foreign Exchange
Global Head
  Martin Hollis *Director*

FX Traders / Sales People
  Steve Pryor *Associate Director*
  Antony Sidney-Woollett *Associate Director*

Risk Management
Department: Capital Markets
Other (FI Derivatives)
Futures & Options
  Charles Dobell *Director, Financials Division*
  Rupert Scott *Director, Financials Division*

www.euromoneydirectory.com UNITED KINGDOM (+44)

Other (FI Derivatives) (cont)

Colin Lloyd *Associate Director, Options*
Bjorn Starcke *Associate Director, Long End*
Myk Znetyniak *Senior Manager, Short End*
Peter Lovell *Manager, DTB*
Colin Ringrose *Broker, Equity Index & Options*

Floor
Stephen Harragan *Director, Locals Division*
Noel Fox *Director, Financials Division*

Settlement / Clearing
Operations
Steve Davies *Director, Operations*

Asset Management
Other (Asset Management)
Alternative Markets & Futures Funds
John Burridge *Director*

Other Departments
Commodities / Bullion
Ben Few-Brown *Director, Commodities & Private Clients*
Economic Research
Peter Osler *Associate Director, Research*

Administration
Head of Marketing
Hugh Morshead *Director*
Gareth Roberts *Senior Manager*

Compliance
Nigel Avey *Director, Compliance*

Goldman Sachs Asset Management International
Subsidiary Company

Peterborough Court, 133 Fleet Street, London EC4A 2BB
Tel: (171) 774 1000 **Fax:** (171) 774 5193; (171) 774 0315

Senior Executive Officers
Chief Executive Officer
David B Ford *Co-Chief Executive*
John P McNulty *Co-Chief Executive*

Others (Senior Executives)
Head of Europe
David W Blood
Head of London
Theodore T Sotir

Goldman Sachs Equity Securities (UK)
Subsidiary Company

Peterborough Court, 133 Fleet Street, London EC4A 2BB
Tel: (171) 774 1000 **Fax:** (171) 774 1510 **Telex:** 94012161 GSEQ G

Senior Executive Officers
Director
Patrick J Ward
Director
Gary W Williams
Director
Girish V Reddy

Equity Capital Markets
Head of Sales
Robert J Markwick
Head of Trading
Julian J Brown
Graham M Ward

Convertibles / Equity-Linked
Head of Trading
Charles P Eve

Settlement / Clearing
Operations
Paul Deighton

Goldman Sachs International
Subsidiary Company

Peterborough Court, 133 Fleet Street, London EC4A 2BB
Tel: (171) 774 1000 **Fax:** (171) 774 2743 **Telex:** 94015777 GSLL G **Reuters:** GSBA **Cable:** GOLDSACHS LONDON
Reuters: GSIA
Website: www.gs.com

Senior Executive Officers
Chairman & Managing Director
Peter D Sutherland
Managing Director
Lloyd C Blankfein
Managing Director
Gavyn Davies
Managing Director
John L Thornton

UNITED KINGDOM (+44) www.euromoneydirectory.com

Goldman Sachs International (cont)
Senior Executive Officers (cont)

Managing Director	Richard M Hayden
Managing Director	Bracebridge H Young Jr
Managing Director	Jon R Aisbitt
Managing Director	Alan R Gillespie
Managing Director	Richard A Sapp
Managing Director	Patrick J Ward
Managing Director	Jeffrey M Weingarten
Managing Director	Gregory K Palm
Managing Director	Robert B Morris III
Managing Director	Michael S Sherwood
Managing Director	Michael G Rantz
Managing Director	Joseph Sassoon
Managing Director	Barry S Volpert
Managing Director	Lee G Vance
Managing Director	David W Blood
Managing Director	J Michael Evans
Managing Director	E Scott Mead
Managing Director	Thomas K Montag
Managing Director	Weit H Pot
Managing Director	Richard S Sharp
Managing Director	Anthony G Williams
Managing Director	Gary W Williams
Managing Director	Michael J Zamkow
Managing Director	Karsten N Moller
Managing Director	Warwick M Negus
Managing Director	Ron E Beller
Managing Director	Jean-Luc Biamonti
Managing Director	Charles K Brown
Managing Director	Christopher J Carrera
Managing Director	Andrew A Chisholm
Managing Director	Claudio Costamagna
Managing Director	Glenn P Earle
Managing Director	Charles P Eve
Managing Director	Peiter Maarten Feenstra
Managing Director	Christopher G French
Managing Director	Richard J Gnodde
Managing Director	Geoffrey T Grant
Managing Director	Louis S Greig
Managing Director	David A Kaplan
Managing Director	Erland S Karlsson
Managing Director	Sion P Kearsey
Managing Director	Susan R Leadem
Managing Director	Jim O'Neill
Managing Director	Timothy C Plaut
Managing Director	Girish V Reddy
Managing Director	Emmanuel Roman
Managing Director	Dante Roscini
Managing Director	Howard B Schiller
Managing Director	Christian Siva-Jothy
Managing Director	Theodore T Sotir
Managing Director	Simon M Robertson
Managing Director	Allen W Sinsheimer
Managing Director	Tarek M Ben Halim
Managing Director	Charles W A Bott
Managing Director	Calvert C Burkhart
Managing Director	Michael S Burton
Managing Director	Varkki P Chakko
Managing Director	Sacha A Chiaramonte
Managing Director	Alexander C Dibelius
Managing Director	Christopher Noel Dunn
Managing Director	Isabelle Ealet
Managing Director	Christopher M Grigg
Managing Director	Isabelle Hayen
Managing Director	Antigone Loudiadis
Managing Director	Charles G R Manby
Managing Director	David M Meerschwam
Managing Director	Therese L Miller
Managing Director	John J Rafter

Senior Executive Officers (cont)

Managing Director	Charlotte P Ransom
Managing Director	Mark J Tracey
Managing Director	Paolo Zannoni
Managing Director	Yoal Zaoui
Managing Director	Trevor Nash
MD, Global Securities Services	Thomas C Brasco E thomas.brasco@gs.com
Managing Director, Operations	Paul C Deighton
Managing Director, Trading	Ronald G Marks
MD, Equity Capital Services	Antoine Schwartz
Executive Director, Equity Capital Services	Timothy B Bunting
MD, Global Securities Services	David J Lockwood
Managing Director, Operations	Patrick E Mulvihill

Department: INVESTMENT BANKING DIVISION

Head	Scott Kapnick
Chief Operating Officer	Mark F Slaughter

Relationship Manager

Investment Banking Services	Alan R Gillespie *Managing Director*
Private Capital Markets	Terry Hughes *Managing Director*
Investment Banking Services	Richard S Sharp *Managing Director*
Private Capital Markets	Andrew Swinburne *Executive Director*
Investment Banking Services	Jean-Luc Biamonti *Managing Director*
Private Capital Markets	Simon Parry-Wingfield *Executive Director*
Financial Institutions	Andrew A Chisholm *Managing Director*
Investment Banking Services	Claudio Costamagna *Managing Director*
	Peiter Maarten Feenstra *Managing Director*
Financial Institutions	Christopher G French *Managing Director*
Investment Banking Services	Timothy C Plaut *Managing Director*
Financial Institutions	John J Rafter *Managing Director*
Investment Banking Services	Philippe Altuzarra *Managing Director*
Financial Institutions	Carl-Georg G Bauer-Schlichtergroll *Executive Director*
	Mariafrancesca Carli *Executive Director*
Investment Banking Services	Tarek Ben Halim *Managing Director*
	Jaime Bergel *Managing Director*
Financial Institutions	Christopher Williams *Executive Director*
Investment Banking Services	Charles W Bott *Managing Director*
Financial Institutions	Alvaro Del Castano *Executive Director*
	Francis Crispino *Executive Director*
Investment Banking Services	Juan A del Rivero *Managing Director*
	Christoph Ladanyi *Managing Director*
Financial Institutions	Anne-Marie Sasdi *Executive Director*
	Ravi S Sinha *Executive Director*
Investment Banking Services	Paolo Zannoni *Managing Director*
Special Execution	Kathryn R Adams *Executive Director*
Investment Banking Services	Christoph M Brand *Managing Director*
	Alexander C Dibelius *Managing Director*
Special Execution	Vanessa MacNair *Executive Director*
Investment Banking Services	Sylvain Hefes *Managing Director*
Special Execution	Kenneth Martin *Executive Director*
Investment Banking Services	Jerry McConnell *Managing Director*
Special Execution	Kenneth W Willman *Executive Director*
Investment Banking Services	Bernd F Reuter *Managing Director*
Special Execution	Roger Scotts *Executive Director*
Investment Banking Services	Nick Gaynor *Executive Director*
	Philippe Pillonel *Executive Director*
Communications, Media & Technology	E Scott Mead *Managing Director*
	Charles G R Manby *Managing Director*
	Trevor Nash *Managing Director*
	Michiel J C Bakker *Executive Director*
	Charles Bracken *Executive Director*
	Sebastian Grigg *Executive Director*
	Peter Gutman *Executive Director*
	Evan M Newmark *Executive Director*
	Fergal O'Driscoll *Executive Director*
	Todd Freeland *Executive Director*
	Paul Harvey *Executive Director*
	Selina Siak *Executive Director*
Advisory Group	Jon R Aisbitt *Managing Director*
	Richard A Sapp *Managing Director*
	Howard B Schiller *Managing Director*
	Richard Campbell-Breeden *Managing Director*

UNITED KINGDOM (+44)   www.euromoneydirectory.com

Goldman Sachs International (cont)
Relationship Manager (cont)

Simon P Dingemans *Managing Director*
Paul Achtleitner *Managing Director*
Robin Doumar *Managing Director*
David Meerschwam *Managing Director*
Andrew Ponti *Managing Director*
Glenn P Earle *Managing Director*
Reuben Jeffrey *Managing Director*
Stefan Jentzsch *Managing Director*
Richard A Murley *Managing Director*
Mel Stahl *Managing Director*
Yoel Zaoui *Managing Director*
Anthony Bernbaum *Executive Director*
Dorothee Blessing *Executive Director*
Christopher Chapple *Executive Director*
George D Davidson *Executive Director*
Eric Gleason *Executive Director*
Raimund Herden *Executive Director*
Richard Josephson *Executive Director*
Casper Von Koskull *Executive Director*
Martin Krebs *Executive Director*
Joshua Larson *Executive Director*
Johann Leven *Executive Director*
Jennifer Moses *Executive Director*
Carlos Ortega *Executive Director*
Paolo Pendenza *Executive Director*
Nicholas Pfaff *Executive Director*
Steve Pitts *Executive Director*
Jean Raby *Executive Director*
Marcus Schenk *Executive Director*
Daniel Schmitz *Executive Director*
David Jimenez-Blanco *Executive Director*
Eric Coutts *Executive Director*
Meyrick Cox *Executive Director*
Van DuBose *Executive Director*
Peter Etzenbach *Executive Director*
Folke Frederiksen *Executive Director*
Lorenzo Grabau *Executive Director*
Georges Gedeon *Executive Director*
Winston M Ginsberg *Executive Director*
Robert McGuire *Executive Director*
Shane O'Neill *Executive Director*
Massimo Pappone *Executive Director*
Olivier Perquel *Executive Director*
Michel Plantevin *Executive Director*
Felipe Rein *Executive Director*
Paul S Shapira *Executive Director*
Guy Slimmon *Executive Director*
Christoph Stanger *Executive Director*
Carine Stein *Executive Director*
Shahriar Tadjbakhsh *Executive Director*
Elena Titova *Executive Director*
Huw Williams *Executive Director*
Melanie J White *Executive Director*
Gavin Wilson *Executive Director*
Massimo Tononi *Executive Director*
Berent Wallendahl *Executive Director*

Real Estate Principal Investment

Richard Georgi *Managing Director*
Simon Blaxland *Executive Director*
Eli Muraidekh *Executive Director*
Jean de Pourtales *Executive Director*

Principal Investments

Hughes P Lepic *Managing Director*
Barry S Volpert *Managing Director*
Ramez Sousou *Executive Director*
Adrian Jones *Executive Director*

Debt Capital Markets / Fixed Income
Department: Fixed Income, Currencies & Commodities Division
Tel: 774 2433 **Fax:** 774 2280
Global Head

Lloyd C Blankfein *Managing Director*
Michael G Rantz *Managing Director*

UNITED KINGDOM (+44)

Fixed Income, Currencies & Commodities Division (cont)

Thomas K Montag *Managing Director*
Anthony G Williams *Managing Director*
Ronald G Marks *Managing Director, Trading*
Michael J Zamkow *Managing Director*
Sion P Kearsey *Managing Director*
Lee G Vance *Managing Director*
Ron E Beller *Managing Director*
Christopher J Carrera *Managing Director*
Geoffrey T Grant *Managing Director*
Karsten N Moller *Managing Director*
Allen W Sinsheimer *Managing Director*
Christian Siva-Jothy *Managing Director*
Michael S Burton *Managing Director*
Varkki P Chakko *Managing Director*
Sacha A Chiaramonte *Managing Director*
Christopher Noel Dunn *Managing Director*
Isabelle Ealet *Managing Director*
Christopher M Grigg *Managing Director*
Antigone Loudiadis *Managing Director*
Charlotte P Ransom *Managing Director*
Robert A Berry *Managing Director*
Peter T Cirenza *Managing Director*
Andrew Devenport *Managing Director*
Robert C Heathcote *Managing Director*
James Hudis *Managing Director*
Terry Hughes *Managing Director*
Bimaljit Hundal *Managing Director*
Robert H Jolliffe *Managing Director*
Ewan M Kirk *Managing Director*
Donald C Lee *Managing Director*
Michael S Sherwood *Managing Director*
Andrew J Stuart *Managing Director*
Robert Centeno *Executive Director*
H Nicholas Denman *Executive Director*
Herman Klein Wassink *Executive Director*
Mauro Mariani *Executive Director*
Olivier F Meyohas *Executive Director*
Calum M Osborne *Executive Director*
Jean-Manuel Richier *Executive Director*
Scott Romanoff *Executive Director*
Andreas Schlotter *Executive Director*
Sergei S Stankovski *Executive Director*

Head of Fixed Income Sales
Michael J Zamkow *Managing Director*
Sacha A Chiaramonte *Managing Director*
Yusuf A Aliredha *Executive Director*
Francois Andriot *Executive Director*
Scott B Barringer *Executive Director*
David J Bennett *Executive Director*
Anna Maria Bentley *Executive Director*
Cecile Bouzoulouk *Executive Director*
William W Deissler III *Executive Director*
Bruce S Docherty *Executive Director*
Olivier A Dubost *Executive Director*
Peter Duenas-Brokovich *Executive Director*
Eric Elbaz *Executive Director*
Louis Gargour *Executive Director*
Paul A Gibb *Executive Director*
Paul A Gilbert *Executive Director*
Wayne A Judkins Jr *Executive Director*
Midori Kelleher *Executive Director*
Carsten Kengeter *Executive Director*
Johine Kilgallon *Executive Director*
Stefan M Krasz *Executive Director*
Stuart Leigh *Executive Director*
Rosario E Lonoce *Executive Director*
Alexander G Loosley *Executive Director*
Joseph Lovrics *Executive Director*
Aedan M Macgreevy *Executive Director*
Maria A Marinas *Executive Director*
Blake W Mather *Executive Director*

UNITED KINGDOM (+44)   www.euromoneydirectory.com

Goldman Sachs International (cont)
Fixed Income, Currencies & Commodities Division (cont)

	Massimo Paschetto *Executive Director*
	Marzio Perrelli *Executive Director*
	Capucine C Picard-Sayah *Executive Director*
	Richard D Pommier *Executive Director*
	Amanda S Prentiss *Executive Director*
	Lorin P Radtke *Executive Director*
	John P Ream *Executive Director*
	Richard J Revell *Executive Director*
	Stefano Rossi *Executive Director*
	Sina Schahram-Nia *Executive Director*
	Helen M Sykes *Executive Director*
	Joanna M Thompson *Executive Director*
	Clodagh M Warde *Executive Director*
	Thomas Winkler *Executive Director*
	Ulrich Worms *Executive Director*
	Wassim G Younan *Executive Director*
Head of Fixed Income Trading	Michael G Rantz *Managing Director*
	Geoffrey T Grant *Managing Director*
	Sion P Kearsey *Managing Director*
	Ronald G Thompson *Managing Director*
	Michael S Sherwood *Managing Director*
	James Hudis *Managing Director*
	Ulf Bacher *Executive Director* ✉ **ulf.bacher@gs.com**
	John R Balderstone *Executive Director*
	Marco W Bales *Executive Director*
	Scott D Beck *Executive Director*
	Joseph J Best *Executive Director*
	Jean-Christophe P Blanc *Executive Director*
	John R Brewer *Executive Director*
	Raj Dutta *Executive Director*
	Roderick C Eggleton *Executive Director*
	Jonathan Fairman *Executive Director*
	Fabrice Glikson *Executive Director*
	Bernd Hoefel *Executive Director*
	Antoine L Imbert *Executive Director*
	Iqbal Khan-Cheema *Executive Director*
	Robert Lempka *Executive Director*
	Asli Oztukel *Executive Director*
	Mark E Painting *Executive Director*
	Karen S Pelham *Executive Director*
	Matthew Previte *Executive Director*
	Alok Puri *Executive Director*
	Maxwell K Trautman *Executive Director*
	Julian M Trott *Executive Director*
	Can Uran *Executive Director*
	Richard S Woolf *Executive Director*
	Karim N Zahmoul *Executive Director*
Other	Patrick E Mulvihill *Managing Director, Operations*
	Paul C Deighton *Managing Director, Operations*
Bonds - General	
Fixed Income, Currency & Commodities Admin.	Lloyd C Blankfein *Managing Director*
	Michelle H Pinggera *Executive Director*
New Issues	Christopher Noel Dunn *Managing Director*
	Robert H Jolliffe *Managing Director*
	Allen W Sinsheimer *Managing Director*
	Paul D McWilliam *Executive Director*
	Angela M Yorath *Executive Director*
	Jason M Gissing *Executive Director*
Structured Finance	Peter T Cirenza *Managing Director*
	Julian C Allen *Executive Director*
	Jeffrey A Goodman *Executive Director*
	Guy J Weyns *Executive Director*
Fixed Income Arbitrage	Anthony G Williams *Managing Director*
	Alexis F Bonnet *Managing Director*
	Hari R Krishnan *Managing Director*
	Clive R Thompson *Managing Director*
	Joseph M Wheatley *Managing Director*

Medium-Term Notes
Head of Origination   Carolyn J Coombs *Executive Director*

www.euromoneydirectory.com UNITED KINGDOM (+44)

Fixed-Income Research
Head of Fixed Income

Varkki P Chakko *Managing Director*
Joanne Brown *Executive Director*
Jean-Paul Calamaro *Executive Director*
Anja P King *Executive Director*
Gunnar U Klinkhammer *Executive Director*
F Scott McDermott *Executive Director*
Samantha Murray *Executive Director*
Paul L Mussche *Executive Director*
Steven M Painter *Executive Director*
Pantelis G Tsoucas *Executive Director*
Kurt D Winkelmann *Executive Director*

Equity Capital Markets
Department: Equities Division
Tel: 774 2433 **Fax:** 774 2280

Global Head

Joseph Sassoon *Managing Director*
Patrick J Ward *Managing Director*
J Michael Evans *Managing Director*
Weit H Pot *Managing Director*
Gary W Williams *Managing Director*
Erland S Karlsson *Managing Director*
Girish V Reddy *Managing Director*

Head of Sales

Patrick J Ward *Managing Director*
Weit H Pot *Managing Director*
Louis S Greig *Managing Director*
Girish V Reddy *Managing Director*
Emmanual Roman *Managing Director*
Calvert C Burkhart *Managing Director*
Laurent M Dupeyron *Executive Director*
T Guy Jones *Executive Director*
Paul M Roberts *Executive Director*
Hugh Murray *Executive Director*
Paloma Berdejo *Executive Director*
Raoul Pal *Executive Director*

Head of Trading

Gary W Williams *Managing Director*
Erland S Karlsson *Managing Director*
Charles P Eve *Managing Director*
David A Kaplan *Managing Director*

Other

Andrew L Metcalfe *Executive Director, Equity Arbitrage*
Andrew S Ballard *Executive Director, Equity Arbitrage*
Davide G Erro *Executive Director, Equity Arbitrage*
Thomas C Brasco *MD, Global Securities Services*
E thomas.brasco@gs.com
David J Lockwood *MD, Global Securities Services*
Yves-Francois Brogard *Executive Director, Global Securities Services*
Cristina Cardellini *Executive Director, Global Securities Services*
Matthew J Clark *Executive Director, Global Securities Services*
Gregg P Cowie *Executive Director, Global Securities Services*
Kevin M Lo Primo *Executive Director, Global Securities Services*
Terry J Minkey *Executive Director, Global Securities Services*
Robert G Munro *Executive Director, Global Securities Services*
E robert.munro@gs.com
Paul A Petty *Executive Director, Global Securities Services*
Dianne Bevan *Executive Director, Global Securities Services*
David A Burnside *Executive Director, Global Securities Services*
David E Haworth *Executive Director, Global Securities Services*
J Michael Evans *Managing Director*
Dante Roscini *MD, Equity Capital Services*
Antoine Schwartz *MD, Equity Capital Services*
Timothy B Bunting *Executive Director, Equity Capital Services*
Andrew D Learoyd *Executive Director, Equity Capital Services*
Christian A Meissner *Executive Director, Equity Capital Services*
Matthias R Møsler *Executive Director, Equity Capital Services*
Jill E North *Executive Director, Equity Capital Services*
Sylvia M Watson *Executive Director, Equity Capital Services*
James P Ziperski *Executive Director, Equity Capital Services*
Julia E Maldonaldo *Executive Director, Equities Administration*
Daniel P Seabolt *Executive Director, Equities Administration*
Paul C Deighton *Managing Director, Operations*

Domestic Equities
Head of Sales

Scott Bradley *Executive Director*
David Cooke *Executive Director*

UNITED KINGDOM (+44)   www.euromoneydirectory.com

Goldman Sachs International (cont)
Domestic Equities (cont)

	Louise A Cooper *Executive Director*
	Valerie J Harrison *Executive Director*
	Aidan P Dunn *Executive Director*
Head of Trading	Mark R Boardman *Executive Director*
	Julian J Brown *Executive Director*
	Frederick Davies *Executive Director*
	Lex B Van Dam *Executive Director*
	Graham M Ward *Executive Director*
	John R Cubitt *Executive Director*

International Equities
Head of Sales

Niels H Aalen *Executive Director, Europe*
Martin R Devenish *Executive Director, Europe*
Christine P Dolan-Moore *Executive Director, Europe*
Joseph P Froschauer *Executive Director, Europe*
Veronica J Gaskell *Executive Director, Europe*
William R Tudhope *Executive Director, Europe*
Ronald E Westdorp *Executive Director, Europe*
Andrew J Burke-Smith *Executive Director, Europe*
Harald Ekman *Executive Director, Europe*
Betty Heatley *Executive Director, Europe*
Heather D Nicol *Executive Director, Europe*
Ian R McCormick *Executive Director, Europe*
Vincent G Camerlynck *Executive Director, Europe*
Marc H Jourdren *Executive Director, Japanese Products*
Alistair R D Macleod *Executive Director, Japanese Products*
Helen J McDonald *Executive Director, Japanese Products*
Giles E Sarson *Executive Director, Japanese Products*
Meurig R Williams *Executive Director, Japanese Products*
Helen R Heap *Executive Director, Japanese Products*
Francois A Tarrisse *Executive Director, Japanese Products*
James R Paradise *Executive Director, New Markets*
Shame M Bolton *Executive Director, New Markets*
Simon Barzilay *Executive Director, SE Asia*
Nigel R Forman *Executive Director, SE Asia*
Hugo P MacNeill *Executive Director, SE Asia*
Simon P Armstrong *Executive Director, SE Asia*
Arthur J "Sam" Stubbs *Executive Director, SE Asia*
Simon N Bound *Executive Director, US*
Mark B Justh *Executive Director, US*
Christopher T Mack *Executive Director, US*
Selina M Pratelli *Executive Director, US*
Johannes M Boomaars *Executive Director, US*
Dirk-Jan J Keijer *Executive Director, US*
Rory T Tobin *Executive Director, US*

Head of Trading
Ingo Franke *Executive Director, Europe*
Remeco O Lenterman *Executive Director, Europe*
Robert S Sargent *Executive Director, Europe*
Johannes R Sulzberger *Executive Director, New Markets*
Cecilia Biscette *Executive Director, New Markets*
Indrajit Bardhan *Executive Director, Japanese Products*
John P Luck *Executive Director, Japanese Products*
David A Makins *Executive Director, Japanese Products*
Sanjiv Mahal *Executive Director, SE Asia*
Samer El-Himani *Executive Director, SE Asia*

Convertibles / Equity-Linked
Head of Sales

Matthieu B Duncan *Executive Director*
Ralf O Haase *Executive Director*
Peter D Harrison *Executive Director*
Jean J Fau *Executive Director*
Peter J Warren *Executive Director*
Neil J Stanley *Executive Director*

Head of Trading
Mark J Buisseret *Executive Director*
Thomas H Henderson *Executive Director*
Dermot A Keane *Executive Director*

Syndicated Lending
Department: Fixed Income, Currencies & Commodities Division
Head of Syndication

Thomas Connolly *Executive Director*
Andrew J Crowston *Executive Director*

www.euromoneydirectory.com   UNITED KINGDOM (+44)

Fixed Income, Currencies & Commodities Division (cont)
  Oliver Duff *Executive Director*
  Edmund J Kearns *Executive Director*
  Keith Alexis Malas *Executive Director*
  Stephen S Usher *Executive Director*

Risk Management
Department: Fixed Income, Currencies & Commodities Division

Other (FI Derivatives)
Swaps
  Thomas K Montag *Managing Director*
  Robert A Berry *Managing Director*
  Francois Andriot *Executive Director*
  Adam P Barret *Executive Director*
  Driss Ben Brahim *Executive Director*
  Edward K Eisler *Executive Director*
  Andrew G Felce *Executive Director*
  Karen E Hughes *Executive Director*
  Peter B Kleidman *Executive Director*
  David R Land *Executive Director*
  Bryant C Park *Executive Director*

Derivatives Origination
  Thomas K Montag *Managing Director*
  Antigone Loudiadis *Managing Director*
  Charlotte P Ransom *Managing Director*
  Robert C Heathcote *Managing Director*
  Mustafa Bagriacik *Executive Director*
  Christopher M Barter *Executive Director*
  Maria Becker *Executive Director*
  Oliver T Chappell *Executive Director*
  Oliver Duncan *Executive Director*
  Luis Marti Sanchez *Executive Director*
  Fabrizio Pagani *Executive Director*
  Guillaume L Poli *Executive Director*
  Ante Razmilovic *Executive Director*
  Patrick M Street *Executive Director*

Other Currency Swap / FX Options Personnel
Futures Services
  Kevin G Edgeley *Executive Director*
  Mark S Edwards *Executive Director*
  Canice B Hogan *Executive Director*
  Michael G McErlean *Executive Director*
  Nicholas V Pearson *Executive Director*

Department: Equities Division

OTC Equity Derivatives
Sales
  Laurent M Dupeyron *Executive Director*
  T Guy Jones *Executive Director*
  Paul M Roberts *Executive Director*
  Hugh Murray *Executive Director*
  Paloma Berdejo *Executive Director*
  Raoul Pal *Executive Director*

Trading
  John A Ashdown *Executive Director*
  Llewellyn C Connolly *Executive Director*
  Hugh X Murray *Executive Director*
  Daniel B O'Rourke *Executive Director*
  Nick Warren *Executive Director*
  Raahil R Bengali *Executive Director*
  Emmanuel B Boussard *Executive Director*
  William D Luterman *Executive Director*

Other Departments
Department: Private Client Services
Private Banking
  Joseph Sassoon *Managing Director*
  Giuseppe Dessi *Executive Director*
  Emmanuel Gavaudan *Executive Director*
  Tariq A Kanoo *Executive Director*
  Philippe Lamy *Executive Director*
  Charles F MacKinnon *Executive Director*
  Keith E McDermott *Executive Director*
  Zain Naqi *Executive Director*
  Ellias N Preko *Executive Director*
  Ramzi Y Rishani *Executive Director*
  Olivier Rouget *Executive Director*
  Amedeo Serra *Executive Director*

UNITED KINGDOM (+44)   www.euromoneydirectory.com

Goldman Sachs International (cont)
Private Client Services (cont)

Simon C Smart *Executive Director*
Andrew D Stevens *Executive Director*
Leo J van der Linden *Executive Director*
Otto von Celsing *Executive Director*
Bruno P DeKegel *Executive Director*
Simon J Eckersley *Executive Director*
Graham Eisner *Executive Director*
Guy A Swersky *Executive Director*

Goldman Sachs International Bank — Subsidiary Company

Peterborough Court, 133 Fleet Street, London EC4A 2BB
Tel: (171) 774 1000 **Telex:** 94015777 GSLL G **Cable:** GOLDSACHS LONDON

Senior Executive Officers
Chairman   E Gerald Corrigan

Others (Senior Executives)

Bracebridge H Young, Jr *Director*
Robert J O'Shea *Director*
Paul C Deighton *Director*
Frank E DuBose *Director*
Geoffrey T Grant *Director*
Patrick E Mulvihill *Director*

Goldman Sachs International Finance — Subsidiary Company

Peterborough Court, 133 Fleet Street, London EC4A 2BB
Tel: (171) 774 1000 **Fax:** (171) 774 5193 **Telex:** 94012163 GSFI G **Reuters:** GOUK (Forex)
Sales Tel: 489 9649; **Trading Tel:** 489 9631

Senior Executive Officers
Managing Director   Ronald G Marks
Managing Director   Geoffrey T Grant
Managing Director   Christian J Siva-Jothy

General-Lending (DCM, SL)
Head of Corporate Banking

Jeremy Baker *Trading*
Andrew Bound *Trading*
Matthew Brumsen *Trading*
Steven Cho *Trading*
Gavin J Comber *Trading*
Karl Devine *Trading*
Kate Dowling *Trading*
Helen Fawn *Trading*
Paula Fry *Trading*
Virginie Gaudeul *Trading*
Scott Gush *Trading*
David Hansen *Trading*
Lawrence Kaplin *Trading*
Andrew Law *Trading*
Stuart Murdoch *Trading*
Thomas Pirece *Trading*
Karthik Ramanathan *Trading*
Pam Sotiropoulos *Trading*
Alexander Seeley *Trading*
Gianluca Squassi *Trading*
Holger Achnitz *Sales*
Rodolphe Alexis *Sales*
Andrea Anselmetti *Sales*
Yuiko Aono *Sales*
Patrick Baune *Sales*
Riccardo Borsi *Sales*
Marie-Ange Causse *Sales*
Myriam Chalumel *Sales*
Cyril Cottu *Sales*
Dale Trond *Sales*
Rick Dykstra *Sales*
Sarah Edington *Sales*

www.euromoneydirectory.com   UNITED KINGDOM (+44)

General-Lending (DCM, SL) (cont)
Justine Hatt *Sales*
Andrew Kleeger *Sales*
Jim Patrick O'Neill *Sales*
Christian Pandolfino *Sales*
Clara Parisot *Sales*
Luca Pietrangelli *Sales*
Valerie Rademacher *Sales*
Mark Rossi *Sales*
Manuel Roumain *Sales*
Fergal Smith *Sales*
Paedar Ward *Sales*
Martin Wiwen-Nilsson *Sales*

Granville Bank Limited   Subsidiary Company
Mint House, 77 Mansell Street, London E1 8AF
Tel: (171) 488 1212 **Fax:** (171) 709 0346 **Email:** bank@granville-plc.com

Senior Executive Officers
Chairman   Michael Allsopp
Chief Executive Officer   Andrew Merriam *Managing Director*
Treasurer   Adrian Heft *Treasury Director* E **aheft@granville.co.uk**
Managing Director   Andrew Merriam
Lending Director   Rowland Thomas
Secretary   Philip John

Money Markets
Tel: 667 8231 **Fax:** 709 0346
Head of Money Markets   Adrian Heft *Treasury Director* E **aheft@granville.co.uk**

Other Departments
Chief Credit Officer   Richard Berrett *Credit Controller*
Private Banking   Andrew Merriam *Managing Director*

Administration
Business Development   Gillian Palmer *Senior Banking Officer*

Technology & Systems
                                   Paul Higgins *IT Manager*

Compliance
                                   Clare Gambling *Compliance Officer*

Public Relations
                                   Julie Sieger

Accounts / Audit
                                   Charles Jones *Internal Auditor*

Granville Holdings plc   Head Office
Mint House, 77 Mansell Street, London E1 8AF
Tel: (171) 488 1212 **Fax:** (171) 481 3911

Senior Executive Officers
Chairman   Robin Hodgson
Chief Executive Officer   David Williamson
Financial Director   Charles Tilley *Director of Finance*

Others (Senior Executives)
Independent Financial Advice   Paul Macintosh *Managing Director*

General-Lending (DCM, SL)
Head of Corporate Banking   Ruth Keattch *MD, Corporate & Institutional Stockbroking*

General-Investment
Head of Investment   Chris Nevile *MD, Investment Management*

Corporate Finance / M&A Advisory
Global Head   Nicholas Harvey *Managing Director*
Private Equity   Michael Proudlock *Chief Executive*

Administration
Compliance
                                   Andrew Gairdner *Group Compliance Officer*

Corporate Communications
                                   Julie Sieger *Manager*

Euromoney Directory 1999 **1767**

UNITED KINGDOM (+44)   www.euromoneydirectory.com

Greenwich Capital Markets
Head Office
135 Bishopsgate, London EC2M 3UR
Tel: (171) 375 5000; (171) 393 0393 Fax: (171) 375 6676

Greenwich Natwest
Subsidiary Company
Formerly known as: Natwest Markets
135 Bishopsgate, London EC2M 3UR
Tel: (171) 375 5000 Fax: (171) 375 5050 Telex: 882121

Senior Executive Officers
Chief Executive Officer
  Gary Holloway *Co-Chief Executive*
  Konrad Kruger *Co-Chief Executive*
Financial Director Keith Haslett *Chief Financial Officer*
Chief Operating Officer Nigel Webb
  Ben Carpenter *EVP & Co-Chief Operating Officer*
  Chris Gruseke *EVP & Co-Chief Operating Officer*
Treasurer Michael Florio
Managing Director & Global Head of Trading Stephen Sinacore
MD & Head of Balance Sheet Management Neil Coulbeck
EVP & Chief Administrative Officer Paul Bowler
CEO & Representative, North America Edwin L Knetzger
Chairman & Representative, North America L Edward Shaw
Vice Chairman & Representative, North America Raymond Humiston
MD & Representative, Asia Pacific Naoki Inoue

Debt Capital Markets / Fixed Income
Head of Debt Capital Markets Frank Canelas *MD & Head, Business Mgt-Europe*

Eurobonds
Head of Origination
  Robert St John *Director of UK*
  Charles Stephens *Director of UK*
  Ignacio Cortes *Director of Southern European*
  Peter Michel *Director of Northern European*
Head of Syndication Stephen Jones *Director*
Head of Trading Ian Thompson *Director*
  Marc Petroccochino *Director, Proprietary Trading*
  Paul Davidson *Director, Proprietary Trading*

High Yield / Junk Bonds
Head Patrick Limpus *Director*

Medium-Term Notes
Head of Origination Matthew Pass *Assistant Director*

Private Placements
Head of Origination Jocelyn Monk *Director of UK*
Head of Sales Dorothy Dotson *Managing Director (US)*
Head of Structuring John Wells *Managing Director*

Fixed-Income Research
Head of Credit Research Duncan Sankey *Director*
Department: Government Bonds
Regional Head Greg Bowes *SVP & Head of UK / European*

Government Bonds
Head of Trading Sam Berwick *Director & Head of UK / European Trading*
  Edward Orenstein *SVP & Head of US Trading*

Domestic Government Bonds
Head of Research
  Geoffrey Dicks *Economic Research (UK)*
  Jade Zelnik *Economic Research (US)*
  David Zervos *Director, Relative Value*

Fixed-Income Repo
Head of Repo Robert Starbuck
Department: Securitisation
Regional Head
  Bruce Snider *MD & Head, European Asset-Backed Securities, Sales*
  Andy Clapham *Md & Head, European Securitization & Principal Fin*
  Robert McGuinness *SVP & Head, US Asset-backed Consumer Finance*
  Gregory Jacobs *MD & Head, US Asset-backed Commercial Mortgage Fi*
  Paul Nidenberg *SVP & Head, US Asset-backed Commercial Mortgage Fi*

Mortgage-Backed Securities
Regional Head
  Robert R Holmes *SVP & Head, US Mortgage & Asset-backed Securities*
  Jay N Levine *SVP & Head, US Mortgage & Asset-backed Securities*

Mortgage-Backed Securities (cont)

George Smith *SVP & Head, US Mortgage & Asset-backed Securities*

Syndicated Lending
Head of Syndication
Department: Project & Trade Finance
Loan-Related Activities
Structured Trade Finance

Declan McGrath *Director*

Giles Darby *Managing Director*
Gary Mulgrew *Managing Director*
Peter Phillips *Managing Director*
Robert Pashley *Managing Director*

Risk Management
Department: Debt Derivatives
Fixed Income Derivatives / Risk Management
Global Head
Head of Sales
Trading
Department: Futures
Global Head

Vincent Tomasi *Managing Director*
Tim Pettit *Managing Director & Head of European Sales & Marke*
Jonathan Barker *Director*

Derick B Burgher *Senior Vice President*

Other (FI Derivatives)
Head of European Futures
Global Clearing Services

William Knottenbelt *Managing Director*
Richard Heymann *Director*

Settlement / Clearing
Operations

Peter Sanchez *Global Operations*

Administration
Head of Marketing

Patricia Hamzahee *MD, Marketing*

Legal / In-House Counsel
General Counsel

Sheldon Goldfarb *Senior Vice President*

Compliance

Azir Chiragdin *Assistant Director*

Public Relations
Chief Information

Phil Lotz *Managing Director*

Other (Administration)
Company Secretary
Facilities Management
Head of Risk
Human Resources

Sally Lewis
Greg Lambert *Senior Vice President*
Robert Radcliffe *Executive Vice President*
Penny Barrey *Director*

Greig Middleton & Co Limited

Head Office

30 Lombard Street, London EC3V 9EN
Tel: (171) 655 4000 **Fax:** (171) 655 4321

Senior Executive Officers
Chairman
Chief Executive Officer
Financial Director
Chief Operating Officer
Managing Director / General Manager

Mark Kemp-Gee
Giles Nardey
Iain Mackay ☏ **(141) 240 4000**
Michael Archibald *Operations Director*
Iain Mackay ☏ **(141) 240 4000**

Corporate Finance / M&A Advisory
Department: Greig Middleton Corporate Finance
Private Equity

Robert Clinton *Senior Director*
Jonathon Becher *Director*
Ralph Catto *Director*
Philip Dayer *Director*
Valerie Marshall *Director*
Rod Venables *Director*

Settlement / Clearing
Back-Office

Stan Vinter ☏ **(141) 240 4000**

Administration
Head of Administration

Stan Vinter ☏ **(141) 240 4000**

Technology & Systems

Stephen Turner *Director, Technology & Software*

Compliance

Ian Cornwall *Group Compliance Officer*
Iain Kennedy *Director, Compliance*
Keith Martin *Director, Compliance*
Chris Tustin *Director, Compliance*

UNITED KINGDOM (+44)　　　www.euromoneydirectory.com

Greig Middleton & Co Limited (cont)

Public Relations
　　　　Beverly Hurst *Marketing Manager* ☏ **(1539) 721 978** ℻ **(1539) 721 912**

Corporate Communications
　　　　Beverly Hurst *Marketing Manager* ☏ **(1539) 721 978** ℻ **(1539) 721 912**

Other (Administration)
　　　　Clem Halpin *Director*
　　　　Ray Pinner *Director*

Grindlays Private Bank

13 St James's Square, London SW1Y 4LF
Tel: (171) 451 3500 **Fax:** (171) 930 5501 **Telex:** 8812741 ANZBKA G

Senior Executive Officers
General Manager　　　　Jonathan Sibley

Gruppo Arca Nordest　　　　　　　　　　Representative Office

3 St Helen's Place, Bishopsgate, London EC3A 6AB
Tel: (171) 628 0365 **Fax:** (171) 374 0640

Senior Executive Officers
UK Resident Representative　　　　Philipp De Vere Buckingham
Assistant Representative　　　　Mauro Zanelli

Guinness Flight Hambro Asset Management Limited

Independent Fund Management Company

Formerly known as: Hambros Fund Management Limited
Lighterman's Court, 5 Gainsford Street, Tower Bridge, London SE1 2NE
Tel: (171) 522 2100 **Fax:** (171) 522 2102 **Telex:** 881 1299 **Email:** broker@gfham.co.uk
Website: www.guiness-flight.com

Senior Executive Officers
Chairman　　　　Tom Griffin
Deputy Chairman　　　　Howard Flight
Chief Executive Officer　　　　Tim Guinness
Financial Director　　　　David Liddell
Chief Operating Officer　　　　Tim Thomas *Head of Equities*
Deputy Chief Executive　　　　Andrew Martin Smith

Others (Senior Executives)
　　　　Andrew Martin-Smith *Deputy Chief Investment Officer*

Equity Capital Markets
Global Head　　　　Tim Thomas *Head, Equity Team*

Domestic Equities
Head of Trading　　　　Julian Chillingworth *Head, UK Desk*

International Equities
Head of Trading　　　　Andrew Couch *Head, Global Desk*

Other (International Equity)
　　　　Maureen Taylor *Head, European Desk*
　　　　Anthony McGarel-Groves *Head, North American Desk*
　　　　John Wollocombe *Head, North American Desk*
　　　　Richard Farrell *Head of Far East Desk*

Asset Management
Head　　　　Paul Brain *Manager, Core Funds*
　　　　Michael Daley *Manager, Institutional Bond Accounts*

Other (Asset Management)
Currency Funds　　　　Tony Plummer *Manager*
　　　　Andrew Seaman *Manager*
Sterling Bond Funds　　　　Tony Plummer *Manager*
　　　　Andrew Seaman *Manager*
Money Market funds　　　　Tony Plummer *Manager*
Money Market Funds　　　　Andrew Seaman *Manager*
Global & European High Yield Fund　　　　John Stopford *Manager*
Asia / Pacific Currency & Bond Fund　　　　Daniel Hemmant *Manager*

www.euromoneydirectory.com UNITED KINGDOM (+44)

Other (Asset Management) (cont)
Cash Benchmark   Mark Johns *Manager*
                                  Annie Hill *Manager*
Global Accounts   Mark Johns *Manager*
                                  Annie Hill *Manager*

Other Departments
Cash Management   Andrew Green
                                  Paul Carr

Administration
Head of Administration   David Tweed

Guinness Mahon & Co Limited — Head Office
32 St Mary at Hill, London EC3P 3AJ
Tel: (171) 623 9333 **Fax:** (171) 528 0881; (171) 283 4811 **Telex:** 884035 **Swift:** GMAH GB 2L **Reuters:** GNSL

Gulf International Bank BSC — Full Branch Office
75 King William Street, London EC4N 7DX
Tel: (171) 815 1000 **Fax:** (171) 220 7733 **Telex:** 8812889 GIBANK G **Swift:** GULF GB 2L

Senior Executive Officers
Branch Manager   Andrew Pocock

Others (Senior Executives)
Marketing   Peter Szalay *Senior Vice President*
Operations   Peter Shears *Vice President*

General - Treasury
Head of Treasury   Steven Moulder *Vice President*

Guy Butler — Subsidiary Company
Hibernia Chambers, 2 London Bridge, London SE1 9QP
Tel: (171) 570 9360 **Fax:** (171) 962 1430 **Reuters:** GARF

Senior Executive Officers
MD, High Yield Sales   Paul Curtis Hayward E **paulch@horlowbutler.co.uk**

Debt Capital Markets / Fixed Income
Eurobonds
Trading (High-yield)   Gary Webb

Fixed-Income Research
Country Head   Chris Clarke E **0930@dial.pipex.com**

Habib Bank AG Zürich — Full Branch Office
PO Box 42, Habib House, 42 Moorgate, London EC2R 6JJ
Tel: (171) 638 1391 **Fax:** (171) 638 8318; (171) 628 0653 **Telex:** 888056 SWBANK G **Swift:** HBZU GB 2L
Email: itdivison.habibbank@btinternet.com
Website: www.habibbank.com

Senior Executive Officers
Chief Executive Officer   M I Kadwani *Chief Executive & Vice President* T **628 7615**
Financial Director   David Hayms *Financial Controller*
Chief Operating Officer   M Y Chowdhruy *Senior Executive Vice President* T **588 8410**
Treasurer   J Akhter *Assistant Vice President*

Syndicated Lending
Loan-Related Activities
Project Finance   H Zia *Second Vice President*

Money Markets
Country Head   J Akhter *Assistant Vice President* T **638 7774**

Foreign Exchange
Country Head   J Akhter *Assistant Vice President* T **638 7774**

Other Departments
Private Banking   S K Kazmi *Senior Vice President* T **628 7179**
Correspondent Banking   P Dayal *Vice President*

UNITED KINGDOM (+44)　　　www.euromoneydirectory.com

Habib Bank AG Zürich (cont)
Administration
Technology & Systems
Electronic Data Processing　　　K A Siddiri *Senior Executive* ☎ **628 0107**

Habib Bank Limited　　　Full Branch Office
Granite House, 97 Cannon Street, London EC4N 5AD
Tel: (171) 621 9876 **Fax:** (171) 623 8073 **Telex:** 885565 BHABIB G **Reuters:** HBLD; HABL (Dealing)
Senior Executive Officers
Financial Director　　　Mazhar Ul Hasan *SVP & Chief Manager* ☎ **623 9242** ✉ **hblchief@aol.com**
EVP & General Manager　　　Mian Abdus Salam ☎ **623 9238** ✉ **miansalam@aol.com**

Habibsons Bank Limited　　　Full Branch Office
55/56 St James's Street, London SW1A 1LA
Tel: (171) 895 1100 **Fax:** (171) 895 1104 **Telex:** 920127 HABSON G **Cable:** HABIBTRUST
Senior Executive Officers
Chairman & Managing Director　　　Habib Mohamed Habib
Chief Executive Officer　　　Mohammad H Hanafi *Director*
Deputy General Manager　　　Syed Akhtar Rizvi
Chairman & Managing Director　　　Habib Mohamed Habib
Company Secretary　　　Philip G Sargent
International Division　　　Nisar Haider *Manager of International Division*
Others (Senior Executives)
Director　　　Ahmed H Habib *Executive Director*
　　　Kenneth Bradford *Director*
　　　Donald W Kendrick *Director*
　　　Muslim R Habib *Director*
　　　Asghar D Habib *Director*
　　　Sajjad Hab *Director*

Other Departments
Correspondent Banking　　　Nisar Haider *Manager of International Division*
Administration
Head of Administration　　　Edwin Abreo *Administrative Officer*
Technology & Systems
　　　Zaheer Abbas Rizvi *Group Technical Manager* ☎ **377 1717**
Compliance
　　　Javed Mirza *Chief Inspector* ☎ **377 1400**

The Hachijuni Bank Limited　　　Representative Office
37 Lombard Street, London EC3V 9DB
Tel: (171) 626 8282 **Fax:** (171) 283 0298
Senior Executive Officers
Chief Representative　　　Yoshiki Nakayama

Halifax plc　　　Head Office
Formerly known as: Halifax Building Society
Trinity Road, Halifax, West Yorkshire HX1 2RG
Tel: (1422) 333 333 **Fax:** (1422) 333 000 **Telex:** 518203 (Group Treasury) **Swift:** HLFX GB 2L **Telerate:** 17348
Senior Executive Officers
Others (Senior Executives)
　　　H J Foulds *Chairman*
　　　J M Blackburn *Vice Chairman*
　　　J N Crosby *Chief Executive*
　　　R F Boyes *Group Finance Director*
　　　T J Goode *Group Treasurer* ☎ **(171) 574 8000** ✉ **(171) 574 8126**

Department: Group Treasury
33 Old Broad Street, London, EC2N 1HZ
Tel: +44 (171) 574 8000 **Fax:** +44 (171) 574 8126 **Telex:** 518203 (Group Treasury)
Others (Senior Executives)
　　　T J Goode *Group Treasurer* ☎ **(171) 574 8000** ✉ **(171) 574 8126**

www.euromoneydirectory.com   UNITED KINGDOM (+44)

Debt Capital Markets / Fixed Income
Head of Debt Capital Markets   R A Schofield *Director, Capital Markets* ☎ **(171) 588 2233** 🖷 **(171) 574 8155**
Bonds - General
Debt Issuance   C Hutton *Capital Markets Manager* ☎ **(171) 588 2233** 🖷 **(171) 574 8155**
Investment   J F Irvine *Head of Structured Investments* ☎ **(171) 588 2233**
 🖷 **(171) 574 8155**
 A Clark *Investment Manager* ☎ **(171) 588 2233** 🖷 **(171) 574 8155**
 R Paddle *Investment Manager* ☎ **(171) 588 2233** 🖷 **(171) 574 8155**

Syndicated Lending
Department: Structured Finance
Other (Trade Finance)
 J D M Smallwood *Director, Commercial Lending* ☎ **(171) 574 8052**
 🖷 **(171) 574 8138**
Asset Finance   A Jukes *Head of Asset Finance* ☎ **(171) 574 8015** 🖷 **(171) 574 8139**
Housing Finance   B Mew *Head of Housing Finance* ☎ **(171) 574 8012** 🖷 **(171) 574 8138**
Project Finance   N Wakefield *Head of Project Finance* ☎ **(171) 574 8166** 🖷 **(171) 574 8136**
Property Finance   P Wilson *Head of Property Finance* ☎ **(171) 574 8009** 🖷 **(171) 574 8136**

Money Markets
Head of Money Markets   I T Mair *Director, Money Markets* ☎ **(171) 374 0484** 🖷 **(171) 574 8154**
Money Markets - General
Currency Money Markets   A J Dullaghan *Chief Dealer* ☎ **(171) 588 2330** 🖷 **(171) 574 8154**
Sterling Money Markets   R D G Lloyd *Chief Dealer* ☎ **(171) 374 0484** 🖷 **(171) 574 8154**
Interest Rate Trading   C P Cave *Trader* ☎ **(171) 588 2299** 🖷 **(171) 574 8154**
 K P Thompson *Trader* ☎ **(171) 588 2299** 🖷 **(171) 574 8154**
Economist   A E Chester *Treasury Economist* ☎ **(171) 256 2111** 🖷 **(171) 574 8154**

Foreign Exchange
Department: Derivatives & Foreign Exchange
Country Head   R Woodbridge *Director, Derivatives & Foreign Exchange* ☎ **(171) 588 2321**
 🖷 **(171) 574 8155**

FX Traders / Sales People
Derivatives & Foreign Exchange   T Main *Head of Interest Rate Derivatives* ☎ **(171) 588 2321** 🖷 **(171) 574 8155**
 S Seaby *Senior Dealer* ☎ **(171) 588 2321** 🖷 **(171) 574 8155**

Risk Management
Head of Risk Management   W Johnson *Director, Risk Management* ☎ **(171) 574 8164** 🖷 **(171) 574 8165**
Other (FI Derivatives)
Credit Risk   S Vernon *Manager, Credit Risk* ☎ **(171) 574 8077** 🖷 **(171) 574 8130**
 P Archer *Manager, Credit Risk* ☎ **(171) 574 8071** 🖷 **(171) 574 8130**

Other Departments
Department: Client Business
Other Departments
 P Homan *Client Director* ☎ **(171) 256 1020** 🖷 **(171) 574 8121**
Treasury Sales   P Hooks *Assistant Director, Treasury Sales* ☎ **(171) 256 1020**
 🖷 **(171) 574 8121**
Central Banks   A Bradburn *Head of Central Bank Sales* ☎ **(171) 256 1010** 🖷 **(171) 574 8121**
Corporates   T O'Donnell *Head of Corporate Sales* ☎ **(171) 256 1020** 🖷 **(171) 574 8121**
Financial Institutions   P Samms *Head of Financial Institutions Sales* ☎ **(171) 256 1030**
 🖷 **(171) 574 8121**
Relationship Management   M South *Head of Relationship Management* ☎ **(171) 574 8200**
 🖷 **(171) 574 8121**
Finance   J Jackson *Director, Finance* ☎ **(171) 574 8004** 🖷 **(171) 574 8145**
Operations   R O Hales *Head of Operations* ☎ **(171) 525 8006** 🖷 **(171) 574 8134**
Administration
 D Wilson *Director, Information Technology* ☎ **(171) 574 8001**
 🖷 **(171) 574 8141**

Hambrecht & Quist LLC   Full Branch Office

The Registry, Royal Mint Court, London EC3N 4EY
Tel: (171) 539 1300; (171) 481 0175 **Fax:** (171) 481 3183; (171) 539 1400
Website: www.hamquist.com

Senior Executive Officers
MD, Institutional Sales, New York   Will McDermott ☎ **+1 (212) 207 1400**
Equity Capital Markets
Country Head   Patrick Spencer *Principal, Equity Sales*
Corporate Finance / M&A Advisory
Country Head   Joshua Rafner *Managing Director* ✉ **jrafner@hamquist.com**

UNITED KINGDOM (+44)   www.euromoneydirectory.com

Hamburgische Landesbank
Full Branch Office

Moorgate Hall, 155 Moorgate, London EC2M 6XB
Tel: (171) 972 9292 **Fax:** (171) 972 9290; (171) 903 6417 **Telex:** 290498 **Swift:** HALA GB 2L **Reuters:** HMBL

Senior Executive Officers
Chief Executive Officer   Jens Mumme *General Manager*
Financial Director; Chief Operating Officer   Henry Hall *Head of Trade Administration* ☎ **903 6440** 📠 **903 6417**
Treasurer   David Eley *Treasurer*

Debt Capital Markets / Fixed Income

Libor-Based / Floating-Rate Products
Asset Swaps   Mark Squire *Head of Securities* ☎ **903 6468**

Money Markets
Tel: 972 9293 **Fax:** 972 9291
Regional Head   David Eley *Treasurer*
Country Head   Stephen Williams *Deputy Treasurer*

Wholesale Deposits
Marketing   David Eley *Treasurer*
Head of Sales   Stephen Williams *Deputy Treasurer*

Foreign Exchange
Tel: 972 9293 **Fax:** 972 9291
Global Head   Stephen Williams *Deputy Treasurer*
    David Eley *Treasurer*
Head of Institutional Sales   Stephen Williams *Deputy Treasurer*
    David Eley *Treasurer*
Corporate Sales   Stephen Williams *Deputy Treasurer*
    David Eley *Treasurer*
Head of Trading   Stephen Williams *Deputy Treasurer*
    David Eley *Treasurer*

FX Traders / Sales People
All currencies   Richard Sibley *Dealer*
    Mark Young *Dealer*

Settlement / Clearing
Country Head   Henry Hall *Head of Trade Administration* ☎ **903 6440** 📠 **903 6417**

Global Custody
Country Head   Mark Squire *Head of Securities* ☎ **903 6468**

Administration

Technology & Systems
    Steve Calvert *Head of Systems* ☎ **903 6450**

Legal / In-House Counsel
Legal, Compliance, Audit   Reg Kempen *Head, Compliance & Audit* ☎ **903 6404**

Hanil Bank
Full Branch Office

Ropemaker Place, 25 Ropemaker Street, London EC2Y 9LY
Tel: (171) 638 3981 **Fax:** (171) 374 6531 **Telex:** 884749 **Swift:** HANI GB 2L **Reuters:** HANL

Senior Executive Officers
Managing Director / General Manager   Yong-Sik Jung

Harris Trust & Savings Bank
Representative Office

Bucklersbury House, 11 Walbrook, London EC4N 8EL
Tel: (171) 236 1010 **Fax:** (171) 236 2821

Senior Executive Officers
VP & Manager   Lee Smith

Other Departments
Correspondent Banking   Lee Smith *VP & Manager*

1774 Euromoney Directory 1999

www.euromoneydirectory.com　　　UNITED KINGDOM (+44)

Havana International Bank Limited

20 Ironmonger Lane, London EC2V 8LR
Tel: (171) 606 0781; (171) 606 1751/3 Fax: (171) 600 2271 Telex: 886577

Senior Executive Officers
Chairman　　　　　　　　　　　J J Rodriguez
General Manager　　　　　　　L Chao

Helaba Financial Futures Limited　　　Subsidiary Company

11 Ironmonger Lane, London EC2V 8JN
Tel: (171) 334 4511 Fax: (171) 334 4507

Senior Executive Officers
Managing Director　　　　　　Marla Miller ☎ **334 4663**
Managing Director　　　　　　Richard Levy ☎ **334 4570**

Risk Management
Other Currency Swap / FX Options Personnel
Futures & Options　　　　　　Gillian Piper *Desk Manager* ☎ **334 4511**
　　　　　　　　　　　　　　　David Rozee *Floor Manager* ☎ **334 4515/6**

Administration
Compliance
　　　　　　　　　　　　　　　Anthony Foulston ☎ **334 4637**

Henderson Investment Services　　　Head Office

55 Moorgate, London EC2R 6PA
Tel: (171) 410 4100 Fax: (171) 477 5642 Telex: 884616 A/B GFRIAR G Email: anthony.wolfe@henderson.com

Senior Executive Officers
Chairman　　　　　　　　　　　Dugald Eadie
Managing Director　　　　　　Tony Solway

Others (Senior Executives)
Client Fund Accounting　　　　Mike Bray *Director*
Human Resources　　　　　　　Kevin Cripps *Manager*
Finance　　　　　　　　　　　　Matthew Green *Director*
Information Technology　　　Mark Harrison *Director*
Securities Administration　　Chris Pemberton *Director*
Business Development　　　　Angela Stephens *Director*
Special Projects　　　　　　　Jay Swanston *Director*
Admistration Services　　　　Anthony Wolfe *Director*

HFC Bank plc

North Street, Winkfield, Windsor, Berkshire SL4 4TD
Tel: (1344) 890 000 Fax: (1344) 890 014

Senior Executive Officers
Chairman　　　　　　　　　　　David Keys
Chief Executive Officer　　　Adrian Hill *Managing Director*
Financial Director　　　　　　Roger Lovering
Treasurer　　　　　　　　　　　Piers Williamson
Managing Director　　　　　　Adrian Hill
Company Secretary　　　　　　John Rivers

Others (Senior Executives)
Operations Support Director　Joe Brian-Davis
Human Resources Director　　Kathy Scholfield
Deputy Chairman　　　　　　　John Dudley-Fishburn
Operations Director　　　　　Jeff Bransford
Personal Banking Director　　Mike Eden

Syndicated Lending
Head of Credit Committee　　Robert Haynes

Administration
Head of Marketing　　　　　　Mark Robinson

Technology & Systems
　　　　　　　　　　　　　　　Nick Waugh

Euromoney Directory 1999　**1775**

UNITED KINGDOM (+44)   www.euromoneydirectory.com

HFC Bank plc (cont)
Legal / In-House Counsel
  Andrew Rodie
Public Relations
  Martin Rutland
Accounts / Audit
Audit
  Ian Martin
Other (Administration)
Human Resources Director
  Kathy Scholfield
Insurance
  Andrew Ferguson

Hoenig & Company Limited — Subsidiary Company

5 London Wall Buildings, Finsbury Circus, London EC2M 5NT
Tel: (171) 588 6622 **Fax:** (171) 588 6497 **Telex:** 9209993 HOENIG G

Senior Executive Officers
Financial Director
  Benjamin Wood *Finance Director*
Managing Director
  Nigel Johnson-Hill
Others (Senior Executives)
  Julian Biggs *Director*

Equity Capital Markets
Department: International & UK Equity Dealing
Tel: 588 6600
Other (Domestic Equities)
  Julian Biggs *Director*

International Equities
Head of Sales
  Julian Biggs *Director*
Other (International Equity)
  Charles Taylor *Dealer*
  William Harrison-Wallace *Dealer*
  Jon Brailey *Dealer*

Settlement / Clearing
Tel: 588 6622
Equity Settlement
  Bernadette Warmsley *Settlements Manager*
Settlement (General)
  Anita Thorne
Administration
Head of Administration
  Michaela Lewis *Office Manager*
Accounts / Audit
Client Accounting
  Michaela Lewis *Office Manager*

HSBC Equator Bank plc — Representative Office

Equator House, 66 Warwick Square, London SW1V 2AL
Tel: (171) 821 8797 **Fax:** (171) 821 6221 **Telex:** 8812369 EQUAZA G

Senior Executive Officers
Chief Executive Officer
  Franklin H Kennedy
Others (Senior Executives)
  Ann J M Johns *Senior Vice President*

General-Investment
Head of Investment
  James N Sheffield *VP, Investment Banking*
  Laurence M Friedman *Executive Director*

HSBC Forfaiting Limited — Subsidiary Company

Formerly known as: Midland Bank Aval Limited
Vintners Place, 68 Upper Thames Street, London EC4V 3BJ
Tel: (171) 336 9880 **Fax:** (171) 336 9853 **Telex:** 885501

Senior Executive Officers
Chief Executive Officer
  Philip Hills
Managing Director
  Roy D Cole
Others (Senior Executives)
  John Ting *Director*
  Tom C Turney *Director*

www.euromoneydirectory.com UNITED KINGDOM (+44)

Syndicated Lending
Department: Forfaiting
Other (Trade Finance)

Martin J Bevan *Assistant Director*
Keith R Taylor *Assistant Director*
Jim Orr *Assistant Director*

HSBC Holdings plc Head Office

10 Lower Thames Street, London EC3R 6AF
Tel: (171) 260 0500 **Fax:** (171) 260 0501
Website: www.hsbcgroup.com

Senior Executive Officers
Group Chairman John Bond
Chief Executive Officer K R Whitson *Group Chief Executive Officer*
Financial Director Douglas Flint *Group Finance Director*
Treasurer Stephen Green *Group General Manager*
International Division G S Cardona *General Manager*

General-Lending (DCM, SL)
Head of Corporate Banking M G Firth *Group Head, Corporate Accounts*

Money Markets
Domestic Commercial Paper
Head of Sales J Smith

Risk Management
Head of Risk Management J R Pearl *Head*

Administration
Head of Administration K M Holland
Business Development L Matthews *Manager*
Head of Marketing A R F Hughes

Technology & Systems
Alan Jebson *Group General Manager, IT*

Legal / In-House Counsel
R E T Bennett *Group Legal Adviser*

Compliance
Matthew King *Head, Group Compliance*

Public Relations
M Broadbent *Director, Group Corporate Affairs*

Accounts / Audit
J L Molyneux *Head, Group Audit*

HSBC Securities Subsidiary Company

Capital House, Festival Square, Edinburgh, EH3 9SU
Tel: (131) 228 4848 **Fax:** (131) 228 3888

Senior Executive Officers
Manager Namdar Mossaheb

Hua Nan Commercial Bank Limited Full Branch Office

5th Floor, 32 Lombard Street, London EC3V 9BQ
Tel: (171) 220 7979 **Fax:** (171) 626 1515

Senior Executive Officers
VP & Chief Representative George Sheng-I Chang

Hungarian International Finance Limited Head Office

9 King Street, London EC2V 8EA
Tel: (171) 606 4107; (171) 606 1010 **Fax:** (171) 600 3974; (171) 600 2270 **Telex:** 922840 HIFG
Email: forfait@hifl.demon.co.uk

Senior Executive Officers
Chief Executive Officer Attila Bogárú
Treasurer Ketan Jashapara

UNITED KINGDOM (+44)   www.euromoneydirectory.com

Hungarian International Finance Limited (cont)
Others (Senior Executives)
    Clive Milbank *Director*
    Martin Ashurst *Assistant Director*
    Tony Knight *Assistant Director*
Budapest Representative   Peter Gádor *Assistant Director*

Hythe Securities Limited   Head Office

19-20 Garlick Hill, London EC4V 2AL
Tel: (171) 489 8899; (171) 248 9000 **Fax:** (171) 489 9860 **Telex:** 269746 HYTHLN G **Email:** hythe@bloomberg.net
Reuters: HYTH-I **Bloomberg:** 731 375-0/378-0

Senior Executive Officers
Senior Executive Officer   Pravin Mehta
Financial Director   Kirti Patel
Managing Director   Meenaz Mehta

Others (Senior Executives)
Eurobonds Director   Walter Imthurn

Administration
Compliance
    Meenaz Mehta *Managing Director*

Accounts / Audit
    Derek Willis

Hyundai Securities (Europe) Limited   Subsidiary Company

3rd Floor, Neptune House, Triton Court, 14 Finsbury Square, London EC2A 1BR
Tel: (171) 786 8600; (171) 786 8601 **Fax:** (171) 786 8620 **Telex:** 887148 HDLDN G **Email:** hyunsec@dircon.co.uk

Senior Executive Officers
Financial Director   Stephen Bates *Chief Financial Officer* ☏ **786 8611**
Managing Director   Eun Sang Yoo ☏ **786 8610**

Debt Capital Markets / Fixed Income
Head of Fixed Income   Joseph Choi ☏ **786 8605**

Emerging Market Bonds
Head of Emerging Markets   Joseph Choi ☏ **786 8605**

Equity Capital Markets
Department: **Equity Sales & Trading**
Head of Sales; Head of Trading   M C Yi ☏ **786 8607**

Corporate Finance / M&A Advisory
Head of Corporate Finance   M S Ahn ☏ **786 8602**

Settlement / Clearing
Head of Settlement / Clearing   Suwon Nicholls ☏ **786 8616**

Administration
Head of Administration   Eunhye Jung McGlacken ☏ **786 8615**

Compliance
    Stephen Bates ☏ **786 8611**

IBJ International plc   Subsidiary Company

Bracken House, One Friday Street, London EC4M 9JA
Tel: (171) 236 1090 **Fax:** (171) 236 0484 **Telex:** 925621

Senior Executive Officers
Chief Executive Officer   Tsunehiro Nakayama *Chief Executive & Managing Director*
Financial Director   Steve Couttie *Executive Director*
Managing Director   Ian Abrams
Managing Director   Sabah Zubaida
Managing Director   Nubuo Oya
Deputy Managing Director   Stephen Hannah

www.euromoneydirectory.com UNITED KINGDOM (+44)

Debt Capital Markets / Fixed Income
Country Head John Gill *Director, Trading*
  Kaoru Inoue *Director, Trading*

Fixed-Income Repo
Head of Repo Kaoru Inoue *Director* ☎ **236 8106** 🖷 **236 3075**
Trading Gavin Hart *Senior Trader*

Equity Capital Markets
Country Head Tlm Hazlem *Director*
  Hiroshi Izawa *Director*

Syndicated Lending
Country Head Mike Ellison *Executive Director*
  Mitsuo Hirakata *Executive Director*

Money Markets
Country Head Ian Abrams *Managing Director*

Risk Management
Country Head Darren Sherman *Executive Director*

Settlement / Clearing
Country Head Steven Quigley *Associate Director*

IFDC Limited   Head Office

Evelyn House, 62 Oxford Street, London W1N 9LB
Tel: (171) 436 8588 **Fax:** (171) 436 8577 **Telex:** 261506 IFDC G

Senior Executive Officers
Chairman & Chief Executive A Abehsera 🖃 **abehsera.ifdcltd@btinternet.com**
Director L Schwarcz

Others (Senior Executives)
Head of Investment A Abehsera *Chairman & Chief Executive*
  🖃 **abehsera.ifdcltd@btinternet.com**
Investment Officer Germain Giraud *Director, Investment Advisory*
  L Schwarcz *Director, Investment Advisory*

Debt Capital Markets / Fixed Income
Department: Treasury & Capital Markets
Global Head A Abehsera *Chairman & Chief Executive*
  🖃 **abehsera.ifdcltd@btinternet.com**

Syndicated Lending
Other (Trade Finance)
Loan Syndication / Asset Sales A Abehsera *Chairman & Chief Executive*
  🖃 **abehsera.ifdcltd@btinternet.com**

Money Markets
Other (Wholesale Deposits)
Eurocurrency Deposits L Schwarcz *Director*

Corporate Finance / M&A Advisory
Global Head A Abehsera *Chairman & Chief Executive*
  🖃 **abehsera.ifdcltd@btinternet.com**

Administration
Head of Administration G Georgiou *Manager*

Accounts / Audit
Accounts P Phillips *Manager*

IMI Sigeco (UK) Limited   Subsidiary Company

8 Laurence Pountney Hill, London EC4R 0BE
Tel: (171) 283 6264 **Fax:** (171) 283 7913 **Telex:** 9419091 IMICAP G **Reuters:** IMIL

Senior Executive Officers
Chairman & Chief Executive Mario Cotto
Financial Director Michele Raris *Head of Finance*
Executive Director & Head, Equities Stefano Mazzola

Debt Capital Markets / Fixed Income
Fixed-Income Repo
Head of Repo Silvia Forlani ☎ **454 4887**

UNITED KINGDOM (+44) www.euromoneydirectory.com

IMI Sigeco (UK) Limited (cont)
Equity Capital Markets
Tel: 929 5202 **Fax:** 283 9382

International Equities
Head of Syndication   Siu Fun Hui *Assistant Director*
Head of Sales   Stefano Mazzola *Executive Director & Head, Equities*
Head of Trading   Sam Ingrao
Head of Research   Stefano Mazzola *Executive Director & Head, Equities*

Equity Repo / Securities Lending
Marketing   Jim Lloyd

Settlement / Clearing
Equity Settlement   Cinzia Curletti *Head of Settlements*
Fixed-Income Settlement Janet Benloss

Administration
Technology & Systems
                        Gursh Panesar

Compliance
                        Indu Shah

Imperial Bank — Representative Office
Warwick House, 65-66 Queen Street, London EC4R 1EB
Tel: (171) 489 8900 **Fax:** (171) 489 8800

Senior Executive Officers
UK Resident Representative   Alexander Kolchev

Industrial Bank of Korea Europe SA — Subsidiary Company
Basildon House, 7/11 Moorgate, London EC2R 6AF
Tel: (171) 600 7667 **Fax:** (171) 600 7176 **Telex:** 922691 IBK LDN G **Swift:** IBKO GB 2L

Senior Executive Officers
General Manager   J W Chang
Deputy General Manager   D M Jun

General-Lending (DCM, SL)
Head of Corporate Banking   D J Ko *Manager, Treasury & Investment*

General - Treasury
Head of Treasury   D J Ko *Manager, Treasury & Investment*

Settlement / Clearing
Settlement (General)   N Lee

Administration
Head of Administration   C J P Lamb

Technology & Systems
Computers   C J P Lamb

Accounts / Audit
Accounting   C J P Lamb

ING Baring Securities (London) Limited — Subsidiary Company
60 London Wall, London EC2M 5TQ
Tel: (171) 767 6000; (171) 767 1000 **Fax:** (171) 767 7777 **Telex:** 887714 INGB G **Swift:** INGB GB 21

Debt Capital Markets / Fixed Income
Eurobonds
Head of Sales   Paul Brown *Sales, London* ☎ **767 8437**
                             Philip Hamilton *Sales, Europe* ☎ **767 8432**
Trading (Sovereigns)   John Yonemoto ☎ **767 8400**

Equity Capital Markets
Fax: 767 7183 **Telex:** 8956215 INGB G

Equity Repo / Securities Lending
Marketing & Product Development   Peter Reynolds *Manager, Equity Finance* ☎ **767 8206**
                                   ✉ peter.reynolds@ing-barings.com

www.euromoneydirectory.com UNITED KINGDOM (+44)

Risk Management
Department: ING Baring Financial Products
Fixed Income Derivatives / Risk Management
Regional Head; Trading					N Cowan *Head of Trading*
Settlement / Clearing
Equity Settlement					Paul Sneed
Operations						Peter Bennett *Chief Operating Officer*
Administration
Compliance
							Jonathan Bibby *Head, Compliance*

ING Barings Full Branch Office
60 London Wall, London EC2M 5TQ
Tel: (171) 767 1000 **Fax:** (171) 767 7777 **Telex:** 8956217 **Swift:** INGB GB 21C

Senior Executive Officers
Chairman						G J A van den Lugt +31 (20) 541 5500
Chief Executive Officer				D Robins
							W Douin *CEO, Western Europe*
Financial Director					C Maas +31 (20) 541 5405
Chief Operating Officer				P Bennett
Others (Senior Executives)
							F D van Loon *Director, Emerging Markets* +31 (20) 563 8280

General-Lending (DCM, SL)
Head of Corporate Banking				Chr Kemball
							H C Albers +31 (20) 563 5372

General-Investment
Head of Investment					Jeremy Palmer *Global Head of Equities & Investment Banking*

Debt Capital Markets / Fixed Income
Head of Debt Capital Markets				M A B Harmsew *Manager, Debt Capital Markets* +31 (20) 501 3033
Head of Fixed Income					L Veldink *Manager* +31 (20) 563 8011
Eurobonds
Head of Sales; Head of Trading				L Veldink *Manager* +31 (20) 563 8011

Equity Capital Markets
Head of Equity Capital Markets				P Reynolds *Manager, Equity Finance* 767 8206
Head of Sales; Head of Trading				Th C de Vries +31 (20) 563 8000
Head of Trading						N Cowan *Head of Trading*

International Equities
Head of Sales						Th C de Vries +31 (20) 563 8000

Other (International Equity)
Equities Strategic Portfolios				J C M Hagen +31 (20) 563 8016
							A Veerman +31 (20) 563 8089

Equity Research
Head of Equity Research					Th de Fuerre +31 (20) 563 0758

Syndicated Lending
Loan-Related Activities
Trade Finance						H C Albers +31 (20) 563 5372
Project Finance						B L Wijnen *Head, Export & Project Finance* +31 (20) 563 5362

Money Markets
Head of Money Markets					J W Menger +31 (20) 563 8008

Foreign Exchange
Head of Foreign Exchange				E K Manitz *Proprietary Trading, Foreign Exchange* +31 (20) 563 8007

Risk Management
Other (Equity Derivatives)
							R H Stadsha *Market Maker* +31 (20) 520 7080

OTC Credit Derivatives
Head of Sales; Head of Trading				G B Hakpout +31 (20) 563 8022

Settlement / Clearing
Head of Settlement / Clearing				J A Kaptein +31 (20) 501 3401

Asset Management
Department: ING Asset Management
Head							A H G Rinooy Kan *Chairman, Management Centre* +31 (20) 541 5477

UNITED KINGDOM (+44)   www.euromoneydirectory.com

ING Barings (cont)
Other Departments
Correspondent Banking — M Baring
Cash Management — J W Menger ☏ +31 (20) 563 8008
Administration
Compliance
W Lieve *Compliance Officer* ☏ +31 (20) 541 5418
Public Relations
R Polet ☏ +31 (20) 541 5446

ING Barings Futures & Options Clearing Services
75 King William Street, London EC4N 7EE
Tel: (171) 410 9944 Fax: (171) 283 4321

Senior Executive Officers
Director — Cash Mahlmann

Inkombank
St Michael's House, 1 George Yard, London EC3V 9DH
Tel: (171) 283 4999 Fax: (171) 283 5999

Senior Executive Officers
Managing Director / General Manager — Uri Khomemko

Instinet UK Limited   Full Branch Office
2nd Floor, Commodity Quay, East Smithfield, London E1 9UN
Tel: (171) 702 4040 Fax: (171) 702 0490

Senior Executive Officers
Chairman — Michael Sanderson ☏ 680 3011
Chief Executive Officer — Douglas Atkin *CEO / Managing Director* ☏ 680 3002
Financial Director; Chief Operating Officer — Mark Nienstedt *Chief Operating Officer* ☏ 680 3181
Treasurer — Jill Stillman *Treasurer* ☏ 680 3210
Legal Counsel — Nicholas Ansbro ☏ 680 3089

Debt Capital Markets / Fixed Income
Head of Fixed Income — Peter Fenichel *Managing Director - Global Fixed Income Products* ☏ 680 3124
Head of Fixed Income Trading — Michael Ezra *Dealing Director - Fixed Income* ☏ 680 3104

Equity Capital Markets
Head of Sales — Stuart Adams *Assistant Director - Sales* ☏ 680 3194
Head of Trading — Hans-Peter Bruehwiler *Dealing Director* ☏ 680 3066

Domestic Equities
Head of Sales — Stuart Adams *Assistant Director - Sales* ☏ 680 3194
Head of Trading — Hans-Peter Bruehwiler *Dealing Director* ☏ 680 3066

International Equities
Head of Sales — Stuart Adams *Assistant Director - Sales* ☏ 680 3194
Head of Trading — Hans-Peter Bruehwiler *Dealing Director* ☏ 680 3066

Risk Management
Tel: 702 4040 Fax: 702 0490
Global Head — Leslie Brady *Compliance Director* ☏ 680 3012 ℻ 702 1915

Settlement / Clearing
Tel: 680 3084 Fax: 702 1879
Regional Head — David Brown *Senior Settlement Director* ☏ 680 3177
Equity Settlement — Martin Tyler *Assistant Settlement Director* ☏ 680 3142

Administration
Head of Administration — Leslie Brady *Compliance Director* ☏ 680 3012 ℻ 702 1915
Head of Marketing — Bradley Hunt *International Marketing Director* ☏ 702 4040

Technology & Systems
Information Technology — David Chaplin *IT Director* ☏ 680 3180

Legal / In-House Counsel
Nicholas Ansbro *Legal Counsel* ☏ 680 3089

Compliance
Leslie Brady *Compliance Director* ☏ 680 3012 ℻ 702 1915

www.euromoneydirectory.com UNITED KINGDOM (+44)

Public Relations
Bradley Hunt *International Marketing Director* ☏ 702 4040

Accounts / Audit
Morgan Charles *Finance Director* ☏ 680 3068

Intercapital plc   Head Office

■ INTERCAPITAL ■

Park House, 16 Finsbury Circus, London EC2M 7UR
Sherborne House, 119 Cannon Street, London EC4N 5AT
Tel: (171) 638 7592 **Fax:** (171) 374 6743

Money Markets
Department: Intercapital plc

Money Markets - General
Interest Rate Swaps
GBP Short Term Interest Rates
USD Short Term Interest Rates; Dollars Off Balance Sheet
Yen Off Balance Sheet
New & Emerging Markets
Proprietary
Interest Rate Options; Exotics Option; Bond Options
Securities
Gilts
BTPs
WCLK UK Govt Gilts
Credit Derivatives
Commodities
Alpha Metals
Equities
Cash and Forwards
Commercials (non banking)
FX Options

Michael Daymond-King ☏ 256 9292 F 628 7822
Andrew Brown ☏ 256 9292 F 628 7822
Mark Webster ☏ 256 9292 F 628 7822

Michael Daymond-King ☏ 256 9292 F 628 7822
Adrian Osborne ☏ 628 1040 F 628 7822
Michael Daymond-King ☏ 256 9292 F 628 7822
Neal Harvey ☏ 588 7558 F 628 3906

Peter O'Toole ☏ 638 8877 F 256 7475
Charles Pendred ☏ 628 1120 F 374 6743
Charles Pendred ☏ 903 8124 F 374 6743
Geoffrey Lott ☏ 623 0024 F 220 7022
Peter O'Toole ☏ 638 8877 F 256 7475
Paul Newman ☏ 638 1894 F 920 9665
Val Chitty ☏ 390 9999 F 390 9390
Peter Walsh ☏ 628 7979 F 628 3239
Mark Webster ☏ 588 7558 F 628 3906
Mark Webster ☏ 256 9292 F 628 7822
Dean Bevens ☏ 695 2000 F 283 9782
Dean Weaver ☏ 695 2000 F 283 9782

Intermediate Capital Group plc   Head Office

62/63 Threadneedle Street, London EC2R 8HE
Tel: (171) 628 9898 **Fax:** (171) 628 2268

Senior Executive Officers
Chairman   Murray Stuart
Chief Executive Officer   Tom Bartlam *Managing Director*
Treasurer   John Curtis *Chief Financial Officer*
Managing Director   Andrew Jackson
Managing Director   Jean Loup De Gersigny

Corporate Finance / M&A Advisory
Private Equity   Andrew Jackson *Mezzanine Lending, MD*

International Finance Corporation   Representative Office

4 Millbank, London SW1P 3JA
Tel: (171) 222 7711 **Fax:** (171) 976 8323 **Cable:** CORINTFIN

Senior Executive Officers
London Representative   Douglas Gustafson

Euromoney Directory 1999 **1783**

UNITED KINGDOM (+44)　　　www.euromoneydirectory.com

INVESTCORP International Inc

48 Grosvenor Street, London W1Y 6DH
Tel: (171) 629 6600 Fax: (171) 499 0371

Senior Executive Officers
Director　　　　　　　　　　Yusef Abu Khadra
Director　　　　　　　　　　Nicholas M Bryan
Director　　　　　　　　　　Lawrence B Kessler

INVESTCORP Securities Limited　　　　Subsidiary Company

48 Grosvenor Street, London W1Y 6DH
Tel: (171) 629 6600 Fax: (171) 499 0371

Senior Executive Officers
Director　　　　　　　　　　Yusef Abu Khadra
Director　　　　　　　　　　Nicholas M Bryan
Director　　　　　　　　　　Lawrence B Kessler

Investec Bank (UK) Limited　　　　　　　　　Head Office

Formerly known as: Allied Trust Bank Limited
Cannon Bridge, 25 Dowgate Hill, London EC4R 2AT
Tel: (171) 283 9111 Fax: (171) 626 1213; (171) 203 1500
Website: www.investec.co.za

Senior Executive Officers
Chairman　　　　　　　　　　Bastion Kardol
Chief Executive Officer　　　　　Barry Kalkhoven

Debt Capital Markets / Fixed Income

Fixed-Income Repo
Other　　　　　　　　　　　Chris Morris *Desk Head* ☎ 203 7401 ℻ 203 7480

Equity Capital Markets
Tel: 203 7403 Fax: 203 8759

Other (International Equity)
South African Equities & Equity Derivatives　　David Kantor *Desk Head* ☎ 203 7410 ℻ 203 7480

Equity Repo / Securities Lending
Marketing & Product Development　　Allen Postlethwaite *Head of Securities Lending* ☎ 203 7403 ℻ 203 7480
　　　　　　　　　　　　　　✉ apostlethwaite@investec.co.za

Money Markets
Other　　　　　　　　　　　Chris Morris *Desk Head* ☎ 203 7401 ℻ 203 7480

Money Markets - General
Wholesale Markets　　　　　Michael Jameson-Till *Director* ☎ 203 7474 ℻ 203 7491

Foreign Exchange
Tel: 623 4098/9 Fax: 203 7480
Head of Trading　　　　　　James McKenzie ☎ 203 1542

FX Traders / Sales People

　　　　　　　　　　　　　Spenser Barrett ☎ 203 1543

Settlement / Clearing
Foreign Exchange Settlement　　Leslie McClinton ☎ 203 1547
Other　　　　　　　　　　Alan Storey *Repo & MM Settlement* ☎ 203 7423

Ionian Bank

6th Floor, Pinners Hall, 105-108 Old Broad Street, London EC2N 1AP
Tel: (171) 426 1400 Fax: (171) 588 0630 Telex: 922571 IPLN GB

Senior Executive Officers

Others (Senior Executives)
　　　　　　　　　　　　　Raymond Fitch *Manager*

1784 Euromoney Directory 1999

www.euromoneydirectory.com UNITED KINGDOM (+44)

Iran Overseas Investment Bank Limited
Head Office

120 Moorgate, London EC2M 6TS
Tel: (171) 638 4831 **Fax:** (171) 628 4027 **Telex:** 887285 **Swift:** IOIB GB 2L **Reuters:** IOIB

Senior Executive Officers
Chairman Assadollah Amiraslani
Chief Operating Officer Elie Diab *Financial Controller*
Treasurer Robert Speedy
Managing Director Morad Khodabandehloo
Assistant Managing Director Clive Jenkins
Financial Controller Elie Diab

Others (Senior Executives)
Advisor to MD & Chief Economist Nasser Homapour

Syndicated Lending
Loans & Credit Dept. Esmail Ramezani *Manager*
Loans & Trade Finance Irwin Taylor *Director*

Loan-Related Activities
Trade Finance Irwin Taylor
Project Finance Irwin Taylor *Director*

Money Markets
Tel: 638 4474 **Reuters:** IOIB **Telex:** 887307
Head of Money Markets Robert Speedy *Treasurer* 826 4324

Foreign Exchange
Tel: 638 4474 **Reuters:** IOIB **Telex:** 887307

FX Traders / Sales People
Chief Dealer Mohammed Hassani 638 2422
Senior Dealer John Betts 638 2422

Settlement / Clearing
Head of Settlement / Clearing Angela Jackson *Supervisor* 826 4328

Israel Discount Bank Limited
Representative Office

Suite 9, 22 Grosvenor Square, London W1X 0DY
Tel: (171) 499 1444 **Fax:** (171) 499 1414

Senior Executive Officers
Representative Ilan Hadani

Italian International Bank

122 Leadenhall Street, London EC3V 4PT
Tel: (171) 623 8700 **Fax:** (171) 623 9750

Senior Executive Officers
General Manager Alan Wiseman

The Iyo Bank Limited
Representative Office

Level 6, City Tower, 40 Basinghall Street, London EC2V 5DE
Tel: (171) 588 2791 **Fax:** (171) 588 2715 **Telex:** 949011 **Email:** iyobkldn@jais.co.uk

Senior Executive Officers
Chief Representative Kenji Goda

Jammal Trust Bank
Representative Office

80 Berkeley Court, Glentworth Street, London NW1 5ND
Tel: (171) 486 1314 **Fax:** (171) 486 1315

Senior Executive Officers
Chief Representative Jammal Jomaa

Euromoney Directory 1999 **1785**

UNITED KINGDOM (+44)   www.euromoneydirectory.com

The Japan Development Bank
Representative Office

Level 12, City Tower, 40 Basinghall Street, London EC2V 5DE
Tel: (171) 638 6210 **Fax:** (171) 638 6467

Senior Executive Officers
Chief Representative	Kenjiro Kobayashi
Representative	Toshiyuki Katagiri
Representative	Yoichi Sekiguchi

Jefferies & Co Inc
Head Office

Formerly known as: Jefferies International Limited

46 New Broad Street, London EC2M 1JD
Tel: (171) 614 1850 **Fax:** (171) 614 1803 **Telex:** 8953191 JEFCO G

Senior Executive Officers
Chairman	Frank Baxter
Managing Director / General Manager	Jamie Graham
Managing Director / General Manager	Cliff Siegel

Debt Capital Markets / Fixed Income
Head of Debt Capital Markets	Dennis Buckley

Equity Capital Markets
Tel: 614 1840
Head of Equity Capital Markets	Adrian Hope

Convertibles / Equity-Linked
Head of Origination	Adrian Hope
Head of Sales	James F Graham
	Cliff Siegel
	Ian Nichols
Head of Trading	James F Graham
	Roland Sharman
	Mark Truman
Head of Research	Annet Marte Smith
	Adrian Hope

Warrants
Head of Sales	Edward Cartwright
	Robert White
	Tim Cameron
	Graham Elliot
Head of Trading	Justin Rockberger
	Adam Lustigman

Risk Management
Head of Risk Management	David Fowler

Settlement / Clearing
Tel: 614 1830
Settlement (General)	Bob Warren *Domestic* ☎ **614 1831**
	John Warren *Domestic* ☎ **614 1831**
	Phil Cook *Domestic* ☎ **614 1831**
	Debbie Long *Trax* ☎ **614 1824**
	Hayley Ratcliffe *Euroclear* ☎ **614 1837/1876**

Administration
Head of Administration	David Fowler
Business Development	Adrian Hope

Jordan International Bank plc
Head Office

103 Mount Street, London W1Y 6AP
Tel: (171) 493 7528 **Fax:** (171) 355 4359 **Telex:** 8814535 JORINT G **Swift:** JIBK GB 2LXXX **Reuters:** JIBK
Bloomberg: s/n753664-0

Senior Executive Officers
Chairman	Ziad Fariz
Treasurer	Bassel Kekhia *Treasurer*
General Manager	Michael Clarke
Senior Accountant	James Story

www.euromoneydirectory.com UNITED KINGDOM (+44)

Syndicated Lending
Head of Origination; Head of Syndication Paul Gilbertson

Loan-Related Activities
Trade Finance George Shihata

Money Markets
Head of Money Markets Fayez Al-Momani *Chief Dealer*

Foreign Exchange
Head of Foreign Exchange Bassel Kekhia *Treasurer*

Settlement / Clearing
Head of Settlement / Clearing Kevin Qualters

Global Custody
Head of Global Custody Kevin Qualters

Other Departments
Commodities / Bullion Bassel Kekhia
Chief Credit Officer Michael Clarke *General Manager* 355 4358
Private Banking; Correspondent Banking; Cash George Shihata
Management

Administration
Head of Administration Kevin Qualters

Technology & Systems
 Kevin Qualters

Compliance
 Michael Clarke *General Manager* 355 4358

Accounts / Audit
 James Story *Senior Accountant*

The Joyo Bank Limited Full Branch Office

Austin Friars House, 2/6 Austin Friars, London EC2N 2HE
Tel: (171) 628 5678 **Fax:** (171) 638 0888 **Telex:** 8956812, 8813280 **Email:** joyoldn@dial.pipex.com **Reuters:** JOYL

Senior Executive Officers
General Manager Sotaro Yamada
Deputy General Manager Makoto Honya

Debt Capital Markets / Fixed Income
Country Head Hirofumi Watanabe *Investment Manager*

Domestic Government Bonds
Head of Sales; Head of Trading; Head of Hirofumi Watanabe *Investment Manager*
Research

Non-Domestic Government Bonds
DM, Swfr, $, JPY Hirofumi Watanabe *Investment Manager*

Eurobonds
Head of Origination; Head of Syndication; Head Hirofumi Watanabe *Investment Manager*
of Sales; Head of Trading; Head of Research;
Trading - Sovereigns, Corporates, High-yield

Libor-Based / Floating-Rate Products
FRN Origination; FRN Sales; Asset Swaps; Hirofumi Watanabe *Investment Manager*
Asset Swaps (Sales)

Fixed-Income Repo
Head of Repo Hirofumi Watanabe *Investment Manager*

Syndicated Lending
Country Head of Origination; Head of Takeaki Sato *Loans Manager*
Syndication

Loan-Related Activities
Project Finance Takeaki Sato *Loans Manager*

Money Markets
Country Head Toshio Nakane *Treasury Manager*

Wholesale Deposits
Marketing; Head of Sales Toshio Nakane *Treasury Manager*

Foreign Exchange
Country Head of Institutional Sales; Corporate Toshio Nakane *Treasury Manager*
Sales; Head of Trading

UNITED KINGDOM (+44)   www.euromoneydirectory.com

The Joyo Bank Limited (cont)
Risk Management

Fixed Income Derivatives / Risk Management
Country Head; IR Swaps Sales / Marketing; IR   Hirofumi Watanabe *Investment Manager*
Swaps Trading

Corporate Finance / M&A Advisory
Country Head   Takeaki Sato *Loans Manager*

Settlement / Clearing
Derivatives Settlement; Foreign Exchange   Yoichi Kurosawa *Manager*
Settlement

Other Departments
Correspondent Banking   Jeffrey Cheah *Head of Operations*

Administration

Compliance
   Jeffrey Cheah *Head of Operations*

JP Morgan Securities Limited
60 Victoria Embankment, London EC4Y 0JP
Tel: (171) 600 2300 **Fax:** (171) 325 8112; (171) 325 8239 **Telex:** 8954804/ 8954805

Senior Executive Officers
Vice President   Fergus P Elder ☎ 325 5428 F 325 8253

Debt Capital Markets / Fixed Income
Fax: 325 8198
Country Head   Paul J Hearn *Managing Director* ☎ 325 9907 F 325 8235
   E hearn_paul@jpmorgan.com
   Colin W P McKechnie *Head, Sales & Trading*

Non-Domestic Government Bonds
   Adam Chamberlain *Trader, US Treasuries* ☎ 779 3434

Eurobonds
Head of Trading   Mark Davies *Trader, Eurosterling* ☎ 779 3180
   Stuart Blom *Trader, Emerging Markets* ☎ 779 2455

Emerging Market Bonds
Head   Richard Luddington
Head of Trading   Stuart Blom *Trader, Emerging Markets* ☎ 779 2455

Libor-Based / Floating-Rate Products
FRN Trading   Guy America *Trader, FRN* ☎ 779 3180

Fixed-Income Repo
Marketing & Product Development   Kaaren Callenbach *Associate* ☎ 779 2371
   E callenbach_kaaren@jpmorgan.com
Trading   Lee Olley *Associate, B / L Trader*
   Kaaren Callenbach *Associate* ☎ 779 2371
   E callenbach_kaaren@jpmorgan.com
   Stephen Howard *Associate, B / L Trader*
   Andrea Angelone *Associate, Equity SWAPS & Structure*
   Salvatore Di Stassi *Associate, Equity Swaps Trading*

Equity Capital Markets
Tel: 779 2371 **Fax:** 325 8198
Country Head   Colin W P McKechnie *Head, Sales & Trading*

Equity Repo / Securities Lending
Marketing & Product Development   Kaaren Callenbach *Associate* ☎ 779 2371
   E callenbach_kaaren@jpmorgan.com

Settlement / Clearing
Settlement (General)   Margaret Talisse ☎ 325 1213
Operations   John Carlisle *Head of Operations*

Administration

Compliance
   James T Brown *Head, Compliance*

www.euromoneydirectory.com   UNITED KINGDOM (+44)

Jugobanka DD
27 South Hampton Street, London WC2 7JA
Tel: (171) 664 4890 **Fax:** (171) 664 4891

Senior Executive Officers
Managing Director / General Manager   O Zejnilagic

Jyske Bank
Jutland House, 10/12 Alie Street, London E1 8DE
Tel: (171) 264 7700 **Fax:** (171) 264 7717

Senior Executive Officers
General Manager   Paul Nymann Jensen

Kas-Associatie
Suite 560 Salisbury House, London Wall, London EC2M 5NU
Tel: (171) 528 8846 **Fax:** (171) 638 2190

Senior Executive Officers
General Manager   S Katwyk
General Manager   R C Ramsay

KBC Bank NV   Full Branch Office
7th Floor, Exchange House, Primrose Street, London EC2A 2HQ
Tel: (171) 638 5812; (171) 588 7302 **Fax:** (171) 256 4846 **Telex:** 8951024 KBBLDN G **Reuters:** KRBL (Dealing)
Dealers Tel: 588 7302

Senior Executive Officers
General Manager   David Monahan

General - Treasury
Head of Treasury   Christel Gijsbrechts *Senior Manager, Treasury*

Syndicated Lending
Department: Global Trade Finance
5th Floor, Earl Place, 15 Appold Street, London, EC2A 2AA
Tel: +44 (171) 861 2666 **Fax:** +44 (171) 861 2626

Loan-Related Activities
Trade Finance   Ian Brigden *Senior Vice President*
                    Malcolm Watson *First Vice President*
                    Robert Bruce *Assistant Vice President*
                    Mark Hodgson *Vice President*
                    Stephen Kemp *Vice President*
                    Malcolm Price *Vice President*
                    Adrian Smethurst *Vice President*
                    Paul Starling *Vice President*
                    David Wightman *Vice President*
                    Christine Shepherd *Vice President*
                    David Miller *Assistant Vice President*
                    Reina Edmonds *Assistant Vice President*
                    David Lendon *Assistant Vice President*

Other (Trade Finance)
Administration   Candace Jeyes

Money Markets
Department: Treasury
Head of Money Markets   Tom O'Connor

Money Markets - General
Dealer   David Coombes
             Michelle Friend
Sterling Dealer   Paul Godfrey
Trainee Dealer   Anthony Guest

Foreign Exchange
Department: Treasury
Head of Trading   Frank Nagels

UNITED KINGDOM (+44)   www.euromoneydirectory.com

KBC Bank NV (cont)

FX Traders / Sales People
Dealer
    Roger Parish
    John Appleby
    Andrew Dermott
    Serge Sarramegna
Trainee Dealer
    Jutta Swaeb
Senior Dealer, Corporate Treasury Sales
    Stephen Shears
    Jacqueline Mathieson
Dealer, Corporate Treasury Sales
    James Bates
    Sarah Rankin
    Nicola O'Neill

Risk Management
Head of Risk Management
    Kojo Asakura *Manager*

Corporate Finance / M&A Advisory
Head of Corporate Finance
    Michael Broom *Senior Manager & Head, Corporate Finance*
Acquistion Finance
    David Chantler
    Andrew Kemp
    Maurice Fitzgerald

Other (Corporate Finance)
Corporate & Institutional Banking
Specialised Finance
    Tom Dissen
    Justin Chittock
    Lisa Taylor
    Nina Van Doren
    Mary Wong
    Glenn Francis
Real Estate Finance
    Janice Hilton
European Desk
    Thomas Van Craen
    Sofie Fondu

Administration
Information Technology
    Giles Roberts *Manager*

Compliance
Compliance
    Susan Lambert *Manager*

Accounts / Audit
Audit
    Susan Lambert *Manager*

Other (Administration)
Banking & Administration Support
    Beverley Williams *Senior Manager*
    Julian Wheeler *Manager*
Personnel
    Sharron A King *Manager*

KBC NV   Full Branch Office

6th Floor, National House, 36 St Anne Street, Manchester, Lancashire M2 7LE
Tel: (161) 839 8989 **Fax:** (161) 839 2929

Senior Executive Officers
Manager
    Andrew Slim

Corporate Finance / M&A Advisory
Acquistion Finance
    Michael O'Shea

Administration
Accounts / Audit
Accounts
    Terence Emerson *Account Manager*

KDB Bank (UK) Limited   Subsidiary Company

16th Floor, 99 Bishopsgate, London EC2M 3XD
Tel: (171) 426 3600 **Fax:** (171) 426 3606 **Telex:** 886903 KDBLDN G

Senior Executive Officers
Managing Director / General Manager
    Hyung-Koo Yim ☎ **426 3551**
Deputy Managing Director
    Chong-Soo Roh ☎ **426 3601**

Debt Capital Markets / Fixed Income
Tel: 426 0126 **Fax:** 426 3567
Head of Debt Capital Markets
    Soon-Young Cheong *GM & Head, Trading & Portfolio* ☎ **426 0126**
Head of Fixed Income Sales
    Sang-Myung Lee *Senior Manager, Sales* ☎ **426 0126**
    Seung-Weon Yang *Manager, Sales & Research* ☎ **426 0126**
Head of Fixed Income Trading
    David Ascroft *Head of Trading* ☎ **426 0162**

1790 Euromoney Directory 1999

www.euromoneydirectory.com   **UNITED KINGDOM (+44)**

Debt Capital Markets / Fixed Income (cont)
                                    Jeff Platt *Senior Manager, Trading* ☎ **426 0126**
Eurobonds
Head of Origination; Head of Syndication   Dai-Woo Han *General Manager* ☎ **426 3610**
Syndicated Lending
Tel: 426 3610 Fax: 426 3567
Head of Origination; Head of Syndication   Dai-Woo Han *General Manager* ☎ **426 3610**
Money Markets
Other   Soon-Young Cheong *GM & Head, Trading & Portfolio* ☎ **426 0126**
                                    Jeff Platt *Senior Manager, Trading* ☎ **426 0126**
                                    Seung-Weon Yang *Manager, Trading* ☎ **426 0126**

Foreign Exchange
Tel: 426 3654 Fax: 426 3567
Country Head   Soon-Young Cheong *GM & Head, Trading & Portfolio* ☎ **426 0126**
Head of Trading   Jeff Platt *Senior Manager, Trading* ☎ **426 0126**
Risk Management
Tel: 426 3560 Fax: 426 3555
Head of Risk Management   Michael Richardson *Risk Manager* ☎ **426 3560**
Settlement / Clearing
Department: Operations
Tel: 426 3580 Fax: 426 3606
Operations   Richard Barry *Equity & Fixed-Income Operations* ☎ **426 3580**
                                    Clare Rowling *Assistant, FX / MM Operations* ☎ **426 3626**
                                    Richard Barry *Manager, Equity & Fixed-Income Operations* ☎ **426 3580**

Global Custody
Tel: 426 3580 Fax: 426 3606
Head of Global Custody   Richard Barry *Manager, Custody* ☎ **426 3580**
Administration
Head of Administration   Young-Cheol Shin *Administration Manager* ☎ **426 3584**
Compliance
                                    David Yardley *GM & Compliance Officer* ☎ **426 3553**

KEB International Limited   Subsidiary Company
2nd Floor, Crosby Court, 38 Bishopsgate, London EC2N 4DS
Tel: (171) 650 1500 **Fax:** (171) 650 1501 **Telex:** 925855 KEBINT G **Email:** kebintl@dircon.co.uk **Reuters:** KEBI

Senior Executive Officers
Managing Director   K Y Lee ☎ **650 1515**
Deputy Managing Director   C S Suh ☎ **650 1525**
Debt Capital Markets / Fixed Income
Country Head   Y W Ko *Associate Director, Sales & Trading* ☎ **650 1520**
                                    K W Kim *Associate Director, Primary Markets* ☎ **650 1510**
Non-Domestic Government Bonds
                                    Y W Ko ☎ **650 1520**
Eurobonds
Head of Origination   Y W Ko ☎ **650 1520**
Head of Syndication; Head of Trading   Y W Ko ☎ **650 1520**
Libor-Based / Floating-Rate Products
FRN Origination; FRN Trading   Y W Ko ☎ **650 1520**
Fixed-Income Repo
Head of Repo   D H Kwag ☎ **650 1527**
Risk Management
Country Head   D H Kwag *Associate Director* ☎ **650 1527**
Fixed Income Derivatives / Risk Management
Country Head   D H Kwag ☎ **650 1527**
Settlement / Clearing
Country Head   C J Oakley ☎ **650 1506**
Fixed-Income Settlement   V Suh ☎ **650 1507**
Administration
Compliance
                                    W A Johnson-Cole ☎ **650 1508**
Public Relations
                                    K R Grimshaw ☎ **650 1504**

UNITED KINGDOM (+44)   www.euromoneydirectory.com

Kexim Bank (UK) Limited — Subsidiary Company

Moorgate Hall, 155 Moorgate, London EC2M 6XB
Tel: (171) 628 6464 Fax: (171) 256 8203

Senior Executive Officers
Managing Director — S U Hong

Others (Senior Executives)
R N Longo *Senior Manager*

Kleinwort Benson Securities Limited — Bank Subsidiary

Alternative trading name: Dresdner Kleinwort Benson

20 Fenchurch Street, London EC3P 3DB
Tel: (171) 623 8000 Fax: (171) 623 7909 Telex: 916486 Swift: KBEN GB 22

Equity Capital Markets
Tel: 956 6338 Fax: 929 7907

Other (Domestic Equities)
Head of Equity Financing — Anggelos Skutaris *Assistant Director* 475 2561 475 1854
anggelos.skutaris@dresdner-bank.com
Marketing & Product Development — Timothy Westover *Manager* 475 2561 westovt@klgen.co.uk

Equity Repo / Securities Lending
Head — Des Joyner *Director* 956 6338 929 7907
Marketing & Product Development; Marketing — Timothy Westover *Manager* 475 2561 westovt@klgen.co.uk
Head of Trading — Tracey Leversedge *Senior Administrator*
Richard Wild *Assistant Manager & Trader*

Klesch & Company Limited — Head Office

6 Queen Street, Mayfair, London W1X 7PH
Tel: (171) 493 4300 Fax: (171) 493 2525; (171) 331 0023 Email: klesch.co@btinternet.com
Website: www.btinternet.com/-general.klesch

Senior Executive Officers
Chairman — A Gary Klesch klesch.co@btinternet.com

Others (Senior Executives)
Head of Research — R Jeffrey Summers *Director*

Debt Capital Markets / Fixed Income

Eurobonds
Head of Trading — Emmett Pearce *Head of Distressed Bond & Loan Trading* 331 0022

Bonds - General
Trading (Distressed) — Ken Tomlin 331 0023

Equity Capital Markets

International Equities
Head of Research — Jeff Summers *Director*

Corporate Finance / M&A Advisory
Head of Corporate Finance — Edwin Horne *Director, Head of Corporate Finance*
Regional Head — Howard Mundy *Head, Corporate Finance*

Other (Corporate Finance)
Antoine Pupin *Head of International Corporate Finance*

Other Departments
Proprietary Trading — Ed Horne *Director*

Administration

Technology & Systems
Sunil Indraratne

Legal / In-House Counsel
Michael Dickie

Compliance
Michael Dickie

www.euromoneydirectory.com   UNITED KINGDOM (+44)

Kokusai Europe Limited
Subsidiary Company

52/54 Gracechurch Street, London EC3V 0EH
Tel: (171) 626 2291 **Fax:** (171) 283 7297 **Telex:** 8956210 KOKSAI G **Cable:** KOKUSAI LONDON E

Senior Executive Officers
President   M Shinozaki
Financial Director   Y Maruyama *Chief Financial Officer*

Komercni Banka as
Representative Office

6th Floor, 35 Moorgate, London EC2R 6BT
Tel: (171) 588 7125 **Fax:** (171) 588 7120

Senior Executive Officers
Chief Representative   Otakar Bobko

Kookmin Bank

4th Floor, Creechurch House, 37-45 Creechurch Lane, London EC3A 5AY
Tel: (171) 283 1818 **Fax:** (171) 283 0491

Senior Executive Officers
General Manager   Soon-Ho Kim

KorAm Bank
Full Branch Office

30-40 Eastcheap, London EC3M 1HD
Tel: (171) 283 0833 **Fax:** (171) 626 8828 **Telex:** 922678 **Swift:** KOAMGB2L

Senior Executive Officers
General Manager   Y B Park

The Korea Development Bank
Full Branch Office

16th Floor, 99 Bishopsgate, London EC2M 3XD
Tel: (171) 426 3550 **Fax:** (171) 426 3555 **Telex:** 8814119 KDBLBR G **Swift:** KODG GB 2L **Reuters:** KDBL, KDBO
Treasury Department Tel: 426 0181

Senior Executive Officers
General Manager   Hyung-Koo Yim ☏ **426 3551**
Joint General Manager   Chong-Soo Roh ☏ **426 3601**

General-Lending (DCM, SL)
Head of Corporate Banking   Martin Duffy *Credit Manager* ☏ **426 3562**

General - Treasury
Head of Treasury   Eddie Wong *DGM & Head of Treasury* ☏ **426 0103** F **426 3567**

Debt Capital Markets / Fixed Income
Tel: 426 3610 **Fax:** 426 3567
Country Head   Dai-Woo Han *DGM & Head, Portfolio Management*

Syndicated Lending
Tel: 426 3560 **Fax:** 426 3555
Global Head   Michael Richardson *DGM & Head, Banking* ☏ **426 3560**
Head of Origination; Head of Syndication Sam-Kyu Rhee *Senior Manager* ☏ **426 3561**

Loan-Related Activities
Trade Finance; Leasing & Asset Finance Sam-Kyu Rhee *Senior Manager* ☏ **426 3561**

Money Markets
Tel: 426 0181 **Fax:** 426 3567

Domestic Commercial Paper
Head of Trading   Julie Edghill *Senior Dealer, Trading* ☏ **426 0181**

Foreign Exchange
Tel: 426 0195 **Fax:** 426 3567
Global Head   Eddie Wong *DGM & Head of Treasury* ☏ **426 0103** F **426 3567**
Head of Trading   Sun-Wook Kim *Manager, Trading*

UNITED KINGDOM (+44) www.euromoneydirectory.com

The Korea Development Bank (cont)
Risk Management
Department: Risk Management / Derivatives
Tel: 426 3560 **Fax:** 426 3555
Head of Risk Management — Michael Richardson *DGM & Head, Banking* ☎ **426 3560**
Global Head — Eddie Wong *Head of Derivatives* ☎ **426 0103**

Fixed Income Derivatives / Risk Management
Head of Sales — Kyung-Jin Min *Senior Manager, Sales / Trading / Marketing*
Trading — Hyeong-Ik Kim *Manager, Trading* ☎ **426 0181**
Kyung-Jin Min *Senior Manager, Sales / Trading / Marketing*

Settlement / Clearing
Department: Operations
Tel: 426 3580 **Fax:** 426 3606
Operations — Steve Wall *Senior Manager & Head, Operations* ☎ **426 3580**
Sara Cole *Assistant Manager, Derivatives Operations* ☎ **426 3582**
Paul Taylor *Assistant Manager, FX / MM Operations* ☎ **426 3625**
Richard Barry *Manager & Head of Operations* ☎ **426 3580**
Other — Richard Barry *Manager, Equity & Fixed-Income Operations* ☎ **426 3580**

Global Custody
Tel: 426 3580 **Fax:** 426 3606
Head of Global Custody — Richard Barry *Manager & Head of Operations* ☎ **426 3580**

Asset Management
Tel: 426 3610 **Fax:** 426 3567
Portfolio Management — Dai-Woo Han *DGM & Head, Portfolio Management*

Administration
Head of Administration — Young-Cheol Shin *Administration Manager* ☎ **426 3584**

Technology & Systems
Suk-Kyun Byon (Ben) *IT Manager* ☎ **426 3578**

Compliance
David Yardley *DGM & Compliance Officer* ☎ **426 3553**

Accounts / Audit
Financial Control — Robert Lovesey *Chief Accountant* ☎ **426 3570**

Other (Administration)
Credit Department — Martin Duffy *Credit Manager* ☎ **426 3562**

Korea Exchange Bank — Full Branch Office
30 Old Jewry, London EC2R 8EB
Tel: (171) 606 0191 **Fax:** (171) 606 9968 **Telex:** 886398 **Swift:** KOEX GB 2L

Senior Executive Officers
General Manager — Soo Shin Lee

Korea First Bank — Full Branch Office
80 Cannon Street, London EC4N 6HH
Tel: (171) 626 9264 **Fax:** (171) 626 2840 **Telex:** 889350 **Swift:** KOFB GB 2L

Senior Executive Officers
General Manager — Jai Man Koo ☎ **626 9264** 🖷 **626 2840**

Debt Capital Markets / Fixed Income
Eurobonds
Head of Trading; Head of Research; Trading - Sovereigns, Corporates, High-yield — Kyu Sul Choi *Manager* ☎ **570 3573**

Bonds - General
Emerging Markets; Non-Investment Grade — Kyu Sul Choi *Manager* ☎ **570 3573**

Libor-Based / Floating-Rate Products
Asset Swaps; Asset Swaps (Sales) — Kyu Sul Choi *Manager* ☎ **570 3573**

Fixed-Income Repo
Head of Repo — Kyu Sul Choi *Manager* ☎ **570 3573**

Equity Capital Markets
International Equities
Head of Trading; Head of Research — Kyu Sul Choi *Manager* ☎ **570 3573**

Convertibles / Equity-Linked
Head of Trading; Head of Research — Kyu Sul Choi *Manager* ☎ **570 3573**

www.euromoneydirectory.com UNITED KINGDOM (+44)

Warrants
Head of Trading; Head of Research   Kyu Sul Choi *Manager* ☎ **570 3573**

Syndicated Lending
Head of Syndication   Kyu Sul Choi *Manager* ☎ **570 3573**

Loan-Related Activities
Project Finance; Structured Trade Finance   Kyu Sul Choi *Manager* ☎ **570 3573**

Money Markets
Regional Head   David Hope *Chief Dealer* ☎ **570 3576/7**

Wholesale Deposits
Marketing   Kyu Sul Choi *Manager* ☎ **570 3573**

Foreign Exchange
Regional Head   David Hope *Chief Dealer* ☎ **570 3576/7**
Head of Trading   Kyu Sul Choi *Manager* ☎ **570 3573**

Risk Management
Fixed Income Derivatives / Risk Management
IR Swaps Trading   Kyu Sul Choi *Manager* ☎ **570 3573**

Settlement / Clearing
Foreign Exchange Settlement   John Swann *Assistant Manager* ☎ **570 3568**

Korea Long-Term Credit Bank International Limited
Subsidiary Company

6th Floor, Princes Court, 7 Princes Street, London EC2R 8AQ
Tel: (171) 710 8300 **Fax:** (171) 726 2808

Senior Executive Officers
Managing Director   S H Chung ☎ **710 8301**
Chief Operating Officer   Malcolm Graham *Senior Manager* ☎ **710 8311**
Treasurer   Crispin Saunders *Senior Manager* ☎ **710 8312**

Debt Capital Markets / Fixed Income
Head of Debt Capital Markets   Henry Jung *Manager* ☎ **710 8314**

Syndicated Lending
Head of Trading   C K Park *Senior Manager* ☎ **710 8313**

Money Markets
Head of Money Markets   Crispin Saunders *Senior Manager* ☎ **710 8312**

Settlement / Clearing
Regional Head   Martyn Morrell ☎ **710 8307**
Operations; Back-Office   Ken Rees ☎ **710 8309**

Other Departments
Correspondent Banking   Crispin Saunders *Senior Manager* ☎ **710 8312**

Administration
Compliance   Malcolm Graham *Senior Manager* ☎ **710 8311**

Kredietbank SA Luxembourgeoise
Representative Office

Founders Court, Lothbury, London EC2R 7HE
Tel: (171) 600 0332 **Fax:** (171) 726 6417

Senior Executive Officers
Representative   Maria Horbaczewska

Kredietfinance Corp Limited
Head Office

Formerly known as: Kredietfinance (UK) Limited
14-15 Quarry Street, Guildford, Surrey GU1 3UY
Tel: (1483) 504 290 **Fax:** (1483) 303 387

Senior Executive Officers
Chairman   E A Marah
Chief Executive Officer   Donal Collins

Others (Senior Executives)
   Olan Cremin *Director*

Euromoney Directory 1999 **1795**

UNITED KINGDOM (+44)   www.euromoneydirectory.com

Kredietfinance Corp Limited (cont)
Syndicated Lending
Loan-Related Activities
Project Finance; Leasing & Asset Finance   Olan Cremin *Director*
Other (Trade Finance)
Property Finance   Richard Thomas *Director*

Landesbank Hessen-Thüringen Girozentrale   Full Branch Office
Formerly known as: Hessische Landesbank - Girozentrale
11 Ironmonger Lane, London EC2V 8JN
Tel: (171) 334 4500 **Fax:** (171) 606 7430 **Telex:** 887511, 883113 (Dealers) **Swift:** HELA GB 2L
Dealers Tel: 588 7302

Senior Executive Officers
Board Member   Frederick Roy Hopson
Debt Capital Markets / Fixed Income
Country Head   Christian Klein *Head, Global Trading* ☎ **334 4518**
    Andreas Petrie *Head* ☎ **334 4558**
Marketing   Marla Miller *Head, Global Sales* ☎ **334 4663**
Domestic Government Bonds
Head of Trading   Christopher Edwards *Head* ☎ **334 4513**
    Simone Reuter *Trader*
    Andrew Palmer *Trader*
    Andrew Woodcock *Trader*
    Stuart Marshall *Trader*

Eurobonds
Head of Origination
Head of Trading   Christopher Edwards *Head* ☎ **334 4513**
    Simone Reuter *Trader*
    Andrew Palmer *Trader*
    Andrew Woodcock *Trader*
    Stuart Marshall *Trader*

Bonds - General
New Issues Syndication   Antja Neussel ☎ **334 4558**
Libor-Based / Floating-Rate Products
Asset Swaps   Thomas Geier *Credit Trading / Asset Swaps* ☎ **334 4650**
Asset Swaps (Sales)   Christian Altmeyer *Credit Trading / Asset Swaps* ☎ **344 4650**
    Klaus-Peter Schommer *Credit Trading / Asset Swaps* ☎ **334 4650**

Fixed-Income Repo
Head of Repo   Robert Fosch *Repo Desk* ☎ **334 4666**
    Christopher Hamilton *Trader* ☎ **334 4666**
    Andy Turrell *Trader*
Sales   Heike Höhl ☎ **726 2030**
    Torsten Müller *Head* ☎ **726 2030**

Syndicated Lending
Loan-Related Activities
Project Finance   Patricia Milligan *Head* ☎ **334 4531**
Other (Trade Finance)
Public Finance   Perham Harding *Head* ☎ **334 4593**
Real Estate & Property Finance   Klaus Schreiner *Head* ☎ **334 4556**
Money Markets
Tel: 334 4513
    Nigel Beer *Manager*
    Nick Barney *Manager*
    Stuart Nixon
    James Marston
Money Market Sales   Gerhard Hühn *Head* ☎ **726 2030**
    Michael Rosenberger ☎ **726 2030**

Risk Management
Department: Derivative Trading
Foreign Exchange Derivatives / Risk Management
Global Head   Stefan Zayer *Head*
Cross-Currency Swaps, Trading   Rob Dodge
    Mark Gemmill
    Kevin Heapy
    Ian Langridge
Vanilla FX option Trading   Jacques Borel

www.euromoneydirectory.com   UNITED KINGDOM (+44)

Foreign Exchange Derivatives / Risk Management (cont)
Dietrich Eilers
Berangere Lilienfeld
Michael Wardle

Settlement / Clearing
Fixed-Income Settlement   Robert Cooper Bond Settlements ☎ 334 4549
Derivatives Settlement   Michael Reeve MM & Derivatives Settlements ☎ 334 4521
Settlement (General)   Harald Kornmann Head ☎ 334 4670
Operations   Joachim Planta Risk Controlling ☎ 334 4508
Horst Bienemann Head ☎ 334 4550

Other Departments
Proprietary Trading   Mario Nicolau ☎ 334 4518
Alan Ponting ☎ 334 4518
Michael Burckhart Head ☎ 334 4518

Administration
Technology & Systems
Roy Claridge Head ☎ 334 4563

Compliance
Anthony Foulston ☎ 334 4637

Accounts / Audit
Accounting   Richard Levy Joint Head ☎ 334 4570
Jan de Klerk Joint Head ☎ 334 4576

Other (Administration)
Personnel   Paula Massing Head ☎ 334 4571

Lazard Brothers & Co Limited   Head Office

21 Moorfields, London EC2P 2HT
Tel: (171) 588 2721 **Fax:** (171) 328 2485; (171) 588 2503 **Telex:** 886438 **Swift:** LAZL GB 2L
Foreign Exchange Telex: 886104

Senior Executive Officers
Chairman   D J Verey
Deputy Chairman   M A David-Weill
Vice Chairman   M A P Agius
Chief Executive Officer   L Adrian W Evans Deputy Chief Executive

Equity Capital Markets
Department: Lazard Capital Markets
Tel: 588 2000 **Fax:** 638 2827
Country Head   J Devas Managing Director
P Gismondi Managing Director
V Grinstead Managing Director
N Groen Managing Director
I Sands Director & Head of Operations
Head of Trading   M Wright Director

Money Markets
Department: Money Market Management
Head of Money Markets   Kevin Wilson Executive Director & Head of Trading ☎ 374 0905

Money Markets - General
Sterling   Clive Kirby
UK & International Equities   Norman Palfreman
Gilt Edge Repo   Michael Hine
Foreign Exchange   Bernie Walker
Operations   Michael Blackburn

Lazard Capital Markets

21 Moorfields, London EC2P 2HJ
Tel: (171) 588 2721; (171) 588 2000

Senior Executive Officers
Chief Executive Officer   Jeremy Sillem Chief Executive
Chief Operating Officer   Ian Sands Director, Chief of Operations
Managing Director   Paul Gismonds
Managing Director   Verne Grinstead
Managing Director   James Devas ☎ 588 6000

Euromoney Directory 1999   **1797**

UNITED KINGDOM (+44) www.euromoneydirectory.com

Lazard Capital Markets (cont)
Equity Capital Markets
Department: Lazard Capital Markets
Head of Equity Capital Markets — Jeremy Sillem *Chief Executive*
Head of Sales — James Devas *Managing Director* ☏ 588 6000
Head of Trading — Moray Wright *Director of Trading* ☏ 588 6000

Equity Research
Head of Equity Research — Alistair Kilgour ☏ 588 6000

Settlement / Clearing
Head of Settlement / Clearing — NIcholas Cook
Equity Settlement — Christopher Weston
Back-Office — Carolyn Kelly

Administration
Compliance
— Ian Sands *Director, Chief of Operations*

Accounts / Audit
— Carolyn Kelly

Lehman Brothers Head Office

One Broadgate, London EC2M 7HA
Tel: (171) 601 0011; (171) 260 2025 **Fax:** (171) 260 2999 **Telex:** 888881 LEHMAN G
Website: www.lehman.com

Senior Executive Officers
Chairman & Chief Executive, Europe — Bruce Lakefield
Vice Chairman, Europe — Raymond Seitz
Financial Director — Tom Bolland *Executive Director, CFO & Controller, Europe*
Chief Operating Officer — Nigel Glaister *MD & Chief Administrative Officer - Europe*
MD, European Council — Peter Sherratt

General - Treasury
Head of Treasury — Ray O'Connell *Director, Treasury*
Department: Private Client Services
Others (Senior Executives)
Europe & Middle East — Andrew Berger *Managing Director*

Relationship Manager
— Simon White *Director & CAO, Europe & Middle East*
— Jon Mallon *Executive Director, Sales & Marketing, Europe*
— Gary Erim *Administration Manager*
— Christian Roy *Assistant Administrative Manager*

Debt Capital Markets / Fixed Income
Tel: 260 2333 **Fax:** 260 2023
Head of Debt Capital Markets — Mark Benson *MD & Head, European Fixed-Income*
Head of Fixed Income — Benoit D'Angelin *MD & Head of European Debt Capital Markets*
Head of Fixed Income Sales — John MacDonald *MD & Head, Fixed-Income Sales, Europe*

Domestic Government Bonds
Head of Trading — Woody Jay *MD & Global Head*

Bonds - General
Syndicate — Chris Wait *Managing Director, Syndicate*
Derivatives — Dan Donovan *MD & Head, European Derivatives*

Equity Capital Markets
Fax: 260 3122
Global Head — Jeremy Isaacs *Global Head, Derivatives & Regional Head, Equities*
Head of Sales — Tom Marino *Managing Director*
Head of Trading — Roger Nagioff *Managing Director*

Domestic Equities
Head of Syndication — Andrew Moffat *Executive Director*

Equity Research
Country Head — John Phizackerley *Managing Director*

Foreign Exchange
Regional Head — J Howard Carter *Executive Director & Head, European FX*

Risk Management
OTC Equity Derivatives
Sales — John Wickham *Executive Director*
Trading — Paul Crouch *Executive Director*

www.euromoneydirectory.com   **UNITED KINGDOM (+44)**

Exchange-Traded Derivatives
FX Futures
   Peter Barrowcliff *Executive Director, Global Futures*
   John Gammer *Executive Director, Sales & Trading, Global Future*

Corporate Finance / M&A Advisory
Department: Corporate Finance
Head of Corporate Finance   R Vincent Lynch Jr *European Investment Banking*
Country Head   Bertil Rydevik *MD & Co-Head, Corporate Finance & M&A*
    Ruggero Magnoni *MD & Co-Head, Corporate Finance & M&A*

Department: Mergers & Acquisitions
Country Head   Ralph Lynch *Executive Director*

Other (Corporate Finance)
Iberia   Kyril Saxe-Coburg *Executive Director*
France & Benelux   Makram Azar *Director*
Italy   Alessandro Foti *Executive Director*
Nordic   Michael Gollner *Executive Director*
UK   Ralph Lynch *Executive Director*
TDG   Keith Hodgkinson *Executive Director*

Asset Management
Principal   Noam Gottesman *MD, Investment Management*
    Jonathan Green *MD, Investment Management*
    Pierre Lagrange *MD, Investment Management*
    Philippe Jabre *MD, Investment Management*
    Richard Bruce *Executive Director, Investment Management*

Other Departments
Economic Research   John Llewellyn *MD & Global Chief Economist*

Administration
Technology & Systems
    Mark Malin *Director, Technology Management*
    Charlie Cortese *Director & Head, Global Technology*

Legal / In-House Counsel
    Piers Le Marchant *Executive Director & European Legal Director*

Compliance
    Simon Stockwell *Director*

Corporate Communications
    John Godfrey *Director*

Accounts / Audit
Audit   Philip Lord *Executive Director*

Other (Administration)
Human Resources   Phyllis Rock *Executive Director & European Head*

Lehman Brothers International (Europe)

One Broadgate, London EC2M 7HA
Tel: (171) 260 2333 **Fax:** (171) 260 2999 **Telex:** 888881 LEHMAN G

Senior Executive Officers
Chairman & Chief Executive, Europe   Bruce Lakefield
Vice Chairman   Raymond Seitz
Chief Executive Officer   Bruce Lakefield *Chairman & Chief Executive, Europe*
Financial Director   Tom Bolland *Managing Director, CFO Europe*

Others (Senior Executives)
Head of Corporate Advisory   Peter Sherratt *Managing Director, Head of Corporate Advisory*

General-Investment
Head of Investment   Vinnie Lynch *Managing Director, Head of Investments Banking*

Debt Capital Markets / Fixed Income
Tel: 260 2337
Head of Fixed Income   Mark Benson *Managing Director, Head of European Fixed Income*
Head of Fixed Income Sales   John McDonald *MD & Co-Head, Global Fixed Income Sales*

Government Bonds
Head of Trading   Woody Jay *Managing Director, Global Head of Government Tradi*

Equity Capital Markets
Head of Equity Capital Markets   Ludovico Del Balzo *Managing Director, Head of Equity Capital Markets*
Regional Head   Jeremy Isaacs *Managing Director, Head of Equities*
Head of Sales   Tom Marino *Managing Director, Head of Institutional Equity Sa*

Corporate Finance / M&A Advisory
Head of Corporate Finance   Ruggero Magnoni *Managing Director, Co Head Corporate Finace*

UNITED KINGDOM (+44)   www.euromoneydirectory.com

Lehman Brothers International (Europe) (cont)

Administration
Head of Administration   Nigel Glaister *Managing Director, Chief Administration Officer*

Corporate Communications
     Hayley Hewlett

Other (Administration)
Human Resources (head)   Phyllis Rock *Executive Director, Head of Human Resources*

Leonia Bank plc   Full Branch Office

Formerly known as: Postipankki
10/12 Little Trinity Lane, London EC4V 2DH
Tel: (171) 489 0303   **Fax:** (171) 489 1142   **Telex:** 894818 FINBK G   **Swift:** PSPB GB 2LA

Senior Executive Officers

General-Lending (DCM, SL)
Head of Corporate Banking   Paul A Stone *Senior Manager, Banking*
     Colin R Bateman-Jones *Senior Manager, Banking*

General - Treasury
Head of Treasury   Bruce Lagden *Senior Manager*

Leopold Joseph & Sons Limited   Head Office

29 Gresham Street, London EC2V 7EA
Tel: (171) 588 2323   **Fax:** (171) 726 0105   **Telex:** 886454/5   **Email:** aaksay@leopoldjoseph.com
Cable: PHESOY LONDON EC2
Investment Department **Tel:** 588 2323 ext 306; **Fax:** 522 9448

Senior Executive Officers
Chairman   Robin Herbert
Chief Executive Officer   Michael Quicke
Financial Director   David Coulson
Company Secretary   Richard William Walsh FCA
International Division   John Burrow **+1 (242) 328 5188** **+1 (242) 328 5192**

Others (Senior Executives)
Managing Director-Guernsey   Roger Carter **(1481) 712 771** **(1481) 727 025**
Managing Director-Bahamas   Ivylyn Cassar **+1 (242) 328 5188/9** **+1 (242) 328 5192**

General-Investment
Head of Investment   Shane Chichester

Other Departments
Private Banking   John Emmett

Administration
Head of Administration   Valerie Stock *Personnel Manager*
Head of Marketing   Ayse Aksay

Technology & Systems
     Peter Fletcher *Assistant Director*

Compliance
     John Robin *Assistant Director*

Public Relations
     Henry Gewanter **353 4212** **427 0777**

Accounts / Audit
     Paul Conroy

LG Securities International Limited   Subsidiary Company

5th Floor, Bucklersbury House, 11 Walbrook, London EC4N 8DY
Tel: (171) 374 4812   **Fax:** (171) 374 8350   **Telex:** 918674   **Email:** lglondon@compuserve.com   **Reuters:** LGSI
Bloomberg: 64132

Senior Executive Officers
Chief Executive Officer   Dae Hyuk Park **374 4812 ext 216**
Financial Director   Maeng Keun Song *Finance Director* **374 4812 ext 211**
Chief Operating Officer   Christopher Moore *Financial Accountant* **374 4812 ext 202**
Treasurer   Maeng Keun Song *Finance Director* **374 4812 ext 211**
Managing Director / General Manager   Dae Hyuk Park **374 4812 ext 216**

www.euromoneydirectory.com   UNITED KINGDOM (+44)

Equity Capital Markets
Other (International Equity)
Korean Equities   Ian Hunter *Head of Sales* ☎ **489 1493**
                                             J Keys *Head of Trading* ☎ **489 1490**

Other (Convertibles)
Korean Instruments   Ian Hunter *Head of Sales* ☎ **489 1493**
                                             J Keys *Head of Trading* ☎ **489 1490**

Others (Warrants)
Korean Warrants   Ian Hunter *Head of Sales* ☎ **489 1493**
                                             J Keys *Head of Trading* ☎ **489 1490**

Foreign Exchange
Regional Head   Maeng Keun Song *Finance Director* ☎ **374 4812 ext 211**

Risk Management
Foreign Exchange Derivatives / Risk Management
Cross-Currency Swaps, Trading   Ki Seok Hong *Derivative Products* ☎ **489 1494**

Corporate Finance / M&A Advisory
Global Head   Jae Hun Lim *Head, Underwriting* ☎ **374 4812 ext 212**

Settlement / Clearing
Settlement (General)   Mark Fullbrook *Manager, Settlements* ☎ **374 4812 ext 203**

Administration
Compliance
                                             Christopher Moore *Financial Accountant* ☎ **374 4812 ext 202**

Liberty Eurasia Limited   Securities Firm Subsidiary
51-55 Gresham Street, London EC2V 7HQ
Tel: (171) 325 6500 **Fax:** (171) 325 6522; (171) 325 6511 **Telex:** 922300 **Email:** markm@london.libnet.com

Senior Executive Officers
Senior Executive Officer   Louis Scotto
Managing Director   Roderick Taylor ☎ **325 6500** F **325 6544**
Financial Director   Christopher Howitt *Financial Controller* ☎ **325 6515**

Debt Capital Markets / Fixed Income
Fixed-Income Repo
Trading   Mike Northeast Roffey *Assistant Director, Eurobonds* ☎ **325 6548**
                                             Breatrice Romri *Manager, Emerging Markets* ☎ **325 6501**
                                             Stephen Duckworth *Assistant Director, Bond Derivatives* ☎ **325 6525**
                                             Gordon Campbell *Assistant Director, Euro Governments* ☎ **325 6502**
                                             John Healy *Assistant Director, Equity Derivatives* ☎ **325 6509**
                                             Richard Goodwin *Manager, Multi Currency Repo* ☎ **325 6501**
                                             Toby Morgan *Manger, DM Repo* ☎ **325 6501**
                                             Mathew Stanford *Manager, International Repo* ☎ **325 6501**

Settlement / Clearing
Regional Head   Christopher Turner *Settlements Manager* ☎ **325 6520**

Lloyds TSB Group   Head Office
Faryners House, 23 Monument House, London EC3R 8BQ
Tel: (171) 283 1000 **Telex:** 888301-Specialized Products

Senior Executive Officers
Chairman   Pitman
Director, Corporate Banking   Roger Seggins

General-Lending (DCM, SL)
Head of Corporate Banking   Roger Seggins *Director, Corporate Banking*

Relationship Manager
Documentation & Agency   Les Tinsley *Director*
                                             Mike Dutfield *Manager*
                                             Pat Cummins *Assistant Director*
                                             Keith Evans *Manager*
                                             Steve Hall *Manager*
                                             David Brackenridge *Manager*
                                             Pat Patel *Manager*

Debt Capital Markets / Fixed Income
Tel: 283 2020 **Fax:** 623 2340
Head of Debt Capital Markets   Pitman

Euromoney Directory 1999   **1801**

UNITED KINGDOM (+44) www.euromoneydirectory.com

Lloyds TSB Group (cont)

Fixed-Income Repo
Trading
- John Argent *Manager, Interest Rate Management*
- Barry Heselwood *Manager, Interest Rate Management*
- Suzy Margretts *Manager, Interest Rate Management*
- Annabel Murday *Manager, Interest Rate Management*

Syndicated Lending
Department: Capital Markets Group

Other (Syndicated Lending)
Distribution & Syndication
- Sally Ingleson *Assistant Director*
- Ian Fitzgerald *Director & Head*
- Stuart Wimbury *Manager*
- David Yates *Assistant Manager*

Other (Trade Finance)
Structured Finance, New Products
- Steve Attree *Manager*
- David Brealey *Assistant Director*
- Stuart Edmonds *Manager*

Department: International Trade & Advisory Group
Tel: 283 1000 Fax: 418 3536
Global Head
- Martin Johnston *Managing Director*

Other (Syndicated Lending)
- Clive Jones *Director*
- Peter Willington *Director*
- Mike Hemming *Director*
- Johnny Ritq *Director*
- Gordon Morley *Director*
- Julian Bird *Director*
- Simon Harris *Assistant Director*
- Uri Winterstein *Assistant Director*
- Nicholas Leng Smith *Assistant Director*
- John Turner *Manager*
- Tim Tuke *Manager*
- Nigel Phillips *Manager*
- Ed Leng *Manager*
- Tom Boam *Manager*

Loan-Related Activities
Shipping Finance
- Roger Wilman *Assistant Director*
- Chris Jones *Assistant Director*
- Andy Longhurst *Assistant Manager*
- Jeremy Baer *Director*
- Nigel Marlow *Assistant Manager*

Project Finance
- Anita Hunt *Assistant Director*
- Paul David *Assistant Director*
- Simon Claridge *Manager*
- Andy Williams *Manager*
- Lisa Fotheringham *Manager*
- Ernie Battey *Director*

Corporate Finance / M&A Advisory
Acquistion Finance
- Richard Dakin *Assistant Director*
- Sally Ann D'Ath *Assistant Director*
- Jill McCarthy *Assistant Director*
- Andrew Boughen *Manager*
- Peter Cannon *Director*

Global Custody
Department: Lloyds Bank Security Services
Princess House, 1 Suffolk Lane, London, EC4R 0AN
Tel: +44 (171) 390 2700 Fax: +44 (171) 390 2822

Other (Global Custody)
- Mark Thatcher ☎ **390 2812**
- David Watson ☎ **390 2805**
- Jon Humphrey ☎ **390 2815**
- Tony Harman ☎ **390 2810**

Administration
Other (Administration)
Business Development
- John Latham *Director*
- Trevor Burgess *Director*
- Steve Thomas *Director*
- Simon Denton *Manager*
- Richard Groom *Assistant Director*

www.euromoneydirectory.com   UNITED KINGDOM (+44)

Lloyds UDT
Head Office

Alternative trading name: Lloyds Bowmaker, Black Horse Finance, Cedar Holdings
Formerly known as: Lloyds Bowmaker
51 Holdenhurst Road, Bournemouth, Dorset BH8 8EP
Tel: (1202) 299 777

Senior Executive Officers
Managing Director   Peter Hook

London Financial Group Limited
Head Office

Centre Point, 103 New Oxford Street, London WC1A 1QF
Tel: (171) 240 4444 **Fax:** (171) 379 4469 **Email:** l-f-g@demon.co.uk

Senior Executive Officers
Chairman   David Porter
Financial Director   Melvin Davies *Chief Financial Officer*
Company Secretary   Lesley Ward
Others (Senior Executives)
                                 Keith Martin *Director*
                                 Tony Raymond *Director*
                                 Jon Cotterell *Director*
                                 Pat Tiley *Director*

Syndicated Lending
Loan-Related Activities
Project Finance   Keith Martin *Director*
Leasing & Asset Finance   David Porter *Chairman*
                                 Pat Tiley *Director*

Corporate Finance / M&A Advisory
Global Head   Jon Cotterell *Director*

London Forfaiting Company PLC
Head Office

International House, 1 St Katharine's Way, London E1 9UN
Tel: (171) 481 3410 **Fax:** (171) 480 7626 **Telex:** 8812606 LONFOR G

Senior Executive Officers
Chairman   Jack A G Wilson
Chief Executive Officer   Stathis A Papoutes *Chief Executive*
Financial Director   Pravin P Samani *Finance Director*
Company Secretary   Martin T D Palmer
Others (Senior Executives)
                                 Raphael J Preteceille *Director*
                                 Mark A West *Director*
                                 Stephen Rothwell *Director*
                                 David R Lilley *Director*
                                 Simon J Lay *Director*

General - Treasury
Head of Treasury   Paul Asbury *Treasurer*
                                 Steve Woods *Assistant, Treasury*

Relationship Manager
Banking Relations   Alan Kirkpatrick *Associate Director*

Syndicated Lending
Department: Forfaiting / Loans
Other (Trade Finance)
                                 Stathis A Papoutes *Chief Executive*
                                 Simon J Lay *Director*
                                 David R Lilley *Director*
                                 Raphael J Preteceille *Director*
                                 Mark A West *Director*
                                 Simon Brown *Associate Director*
                                 Jeremy Burke *Associate Director*
                                 John Cross *Associate Director*
                                 Demetris Efstaithiou *Associate Director*
                                 Adam Korytko *Associate Director*
                                 Ralph Napolitano *Associate Director*
                                 Chris Rogers *Associate Director*

UNITED KINGDOM (+44) www.euromoneydirectory.com

London Forfaiting Company PLC (cont)
Other (Trade Finance) (cont)

    Paul Jennings *Associate Director*
    Russell Lammin *Senior Manager*
    Paolo Boscolo Berto *Senior Manager*
    Patrick Boatwright *Senior Manager*
    Katie Frost *Senior Manager*
    Charlotte Warme *Senior Manager*
    Graham Hutton *Senior Manager*
    Jean-Pierre Dupui *Senior Manager*
    Simon de Monte *Manager*
    Zane Baring *Manager*
    Nicholas Doody *Manager*
    Debbie Emmanuel *Manager*
    Shaun Little *Manager*
    Marcus Wade *Manager*

Department: Loans Administration
Other (Syndicated Lending)

    Christopher Powell *Senior Manager*
    Philip Gauntlett *Senior Manager*
    Jessica Mancini *Manager*
    Margrieta Loze *Manager*
    James Collins *Manager*

Settlement / Clearing
Settlement (General)
    Myra Seaman *Associate Director*

Administration
Other (Administration)
Research
    Stephen Rothwell *Director*
    Philip Patterson *Associate Director*
    Sandy Campbell *Associate Director*
    Brendan Herley *Manager*
    Lisa Yau *Manager*

London Forfaiting Company UK Limited   Full Branch Office

Formerly known as: LFC Export Finance Limited
    1 New Abbey Court, Stert Street, Abingdon, Oxfordshire OX14 3JX
    Tel: (1235) 555 595 **Fax:** (1235) 555 598

Senior Executive Officers
Others (Senior Executives)
    Jeff Fallon *Director*
    Stephen Jenkins *Manager*

London Forfaiting Company UK Limited   Full Branch Office

Formerly known as: LFC Export Finance Limited
    Station House, Station Court, Rawtenstall, Rossendale, Lancashire BB4 6AJ
    Tel: (1706) 237 900 **Fax:** (1706) 237 909

Senior Executive Officers
Managing Director   John Clegg
Others (Senior Executives)
    Phil Cook *Director*
    Scott Hamilton *Associate Director*

London Global Securities   Head Office

    Earl Place, 15 Appold Street, London EC2A 2AA
    Tel: (171) 247 4884 **Fax:** (171) 247 8311 **Telex:** 8812043

Senior Executive Officers
Chairman   Rich Reinemann
Chief Executive Officer   Michael Hiard *Managing Director* ☎ **247 0347** F **696 9588**
Treasurer   Mike Page
Managing Director   Michael Hiard ☎ **247 0347** F **696 9588**

www.euromoneydirectory.com			UNITED KINGDOM (+44)

Debt Capital Markets / Fixed Income
Fax: 247 3743

Fixed-Income Repo
Marketing & Product Development — Mark Weeks *Director* T 247 0347 F 696 9588
Trading — Chris Clark *Director*
Natasha Stephens *Europe*
Ray Hainsby *Director*
Cameron Holden *Trader, Far East*
Dave Lonsdale *Trader, Europe*
Matt Zienav *Trader, Far East*
Peter Pittar *Fixed Income*
Selina Hardy *Fixed Income*

Equity Capital Markets
Fax: 814 9838

Equity Repo / Securities Lending
Head — Michael Hiard *Managing Director* T 247 0347 F 696 9588
Marketing & Product Development; Marketing Head of Trading — Mark Weeks *Director* T 247 0347 F 696 9588
Ray Hainsby *Director*
Chris Clark *Director*
Jackie Starling
Fraser Croyston
Derryn Hobbs

Settlement / Clearing
Country Head — Steve Jennett

London Trust Bank Plc

30 Upper Grosvenor Street, London W1X 0AH
Tel: (171) 518 2000; (171) 518 2020 **Fax:** (171) 518 2010 **Telex:** 24350 LTBANK
Customer Services Tel: 518 2030; **Marketing & Credit Tel:** 518 2050; **Trade Finance Tel:** 518 2040; **Treasury Tel:** 518 2020

Senior Executive Officers
Chairman — Costi F Chehlaoui
Deputy Chairman — Mustapha Janoudi
Deputy Chairman — Mouaffac Ojjeh
Chief Executive Officer — Costi F Chehlaoui
Director — Edwin W Roberts
General Manager — Geoffrey K Wells
Assistant General Manager — Peter L W Stringer
Company Secretary — Kamal Saleh

Others (Senior Executives)
Adviser — Martin J White
Director — Mahmoud Kocache
Roy F Mason
Senior Manager — Robert T Endersbee
Faisal Murad

Relationship Manager
Manager — Derek Goodwin
Anne Miglorine
David Morgan
James Rigby
Cheryl Roe

Administration
Accounts / Audit
Audit Committee — Roy F Mason
Edwin W Roberts *Director*
Internal Auditor — Simon Udale

## MacArthur & Co Limited			Head Office

30 City Road, London EC1Y 2AY
Tel: (171) 638 5677 **Fax:** (171) 638 5689

Senior Executive Officers
Chairman — John MacArthur
Financial Director — Antony Batty

Euromoney Directory 1999 **1805**

UNITED KINGDOM (+44)   www.euromoneydirectory.com

Maizels, Westerberg & Co Limited — Sister Company

39 St James's Street, London SW1A 1JD
Tel: (171) 491 4900 **Fax:** (171) 491 4901

Corporate Finance / M&A Advisory
Department: Corporate Finance Executives

Other (Corporate Finance)
M&A Advisory — Mark Florman
Rod Colwell
Martin Greenslade
Erik Ferm
Simon Lindfors
Ian Henderson

Malayan Banking Berhad

74 Coleman Street, London EC2R 5BN
Tel: (171) 638 0561 **Fax:** (171) 638 9329 **Telex:** 888516 **Swift:** MBBE GB 2L **Reuters:** MBLN **Cable:** MBBLDN

Senior Executive Officers
General Manager — Mohd Zulkifli

MW Marshall & Company Limited — Head Office

Lloyds Chambers, 1 Portsoken Street, London E1 8DF
Tel: (171) 891 3000 **Fax:** (171) 702 3951

Senior Executive Officers
Chairman & Chief Executive — S D Plunkett
Financial Director — P J Bentley *Finance Director*

Others (Senior Executives)
M G Airey *Director*
J T Garland *Director*
J T Gregory *Director*
C J K Kelson *Director*
M J W Potter *Director*
A B Martin *Director*
A N Verrier *Director*
R A Webb *Director*

MW Marshall (UK) Limited — Subsidiary Company

Lloyds Chambers, 1 Portsoken Street, London E1 8DF
Tel: (171) 891 3000 **Fax:** (171) 360 4844

Senior Executive Officers
Chief Executive — S D Plunkett
Financial Director — M J W Potter *Finance Director*

Others (Senior Executives)
A N Verrier *Director*
R A Webb *Director*

Debt Capital Markets / Fixed Income
Non-Domestic Government Bonds
Commercials / Local Authorities — N A Dawes *Divisional Director*

Fixed-Income Repo
Head of Repo — M L Murphy *Divisional Manager*
Other — M L Murphy *Gilt Repos*

Money Markets
Department: Cash Deposits

Other (Wholesale Deposits)
J T Wilkes *Divisional Director*
R King *Divisional Director*
M D Ling *Assistant Divisional Director*
J H Bartlett *Divisional Director*
M R Acton *Local Divisional Manager*

www.euromoneydirectory.com UNITED KINGDOM (+44)

Foreign Exchange
Department: Foreign Exchange Division
Head of Foreign Exchange S D Plunkett
FX Traders / Sales People
G J Howell *Managing Divisional Director*
M A Roberts *Divisional Director*
W D Wood *Divisional Director*
A M Hyde *Divisional Director*
M J Docker *Divisional Manager*
T M Spicer *Divisional Director*
S Hatch *Divisional Manager*
Emerging Markets-Far East R D Merrigan *Divisional Director*
Emerging Markets-Eastern Europe S L Bright *Divisional Director*
R F Kennedy *Local Divisional Manager*
P J Sheehan *Divisional Director*

Department: Forward Foreign Exchange
Head of Foreign Exchange A Farrington *Managing Divisional Director*
FX Traders / Sales People
A E C Johnson *Divisional Director*
J R Harris *Divisional Director*
N J J Potter *Divisional Director*
P R Sawyer

Department: OBS
FX Traders / Sales People
R W Osborne *Managing Divisional Director*
A D Brown *Divisional Director*
M K Plumb *Assistant Divisional Director*
M P Thraves

Risk Management
Department: Interest Rate Division
Global Head A N Verrier *Managing Director, I / C*
OTC Credit Derivatives
Global Head R J F Little *Divisional Director*

Martin Brokers (UK) plc Head Office

4 Deans Court, London EC4V 5AA
Tel: (171) 236 7781; (171) 600 8691 **Fax:** (171) 236 7463 **Telex:** 883962 **Email:** davis@martin-brokers.com

Senior Executive Officers
Chief Executive Officer David Caplin *Managing Director* 📞 **236 3891**
Nick Stewart *Deputy Managing Director*
Financial Director Matthew Clarke *Finance Director* 📞 **236 3574**
Others (Senior Executives)
Martin Brokers Sterling Ltd Nick Stewart *Managing Director* 📞 **528 7552**
Allan Peaty *Director* 📞 **528 7552**
John Woodley *Director* 📞 **528 7552**
Martin Brokers Deposits Ltd Keith Hall *Managing Director* 📞 **606 4651**
Martin Brokers Exchange Andy Berry *Director* 📞 **600 8691**
Andy Manston *Director* 📞 **600 8691**
Trio Equity Derivatives Ltd Nicholas Levene *Executive Director* 📞 **439 8081**
Peter Minihan *Associate Director* 📞 **439 8081**

MashreqBank psc Full Branch Office

Bavaria House, 13-14 Appold Street, London EC2A 2BD
Tel: (171) 247 6395 **Fax:** (171) 410 0832 **Telex:** 883429 MSHQLN G

Senior Executive Officers
General Manager Roger Mann
Other Departments
Commodities / Bullion Bhola Prashad
Administration
Head of Administration Hassan Sakoui
Head of Marketing Simon Caink
Technology & Systems
Hamid Sabil

Euromoney Directory 1999 **1807**

UNITED KINGDOM (+44)　　　www.euromoneydirectory.com

Matheson Bank Limited
Subsidiary Company

St Helen's, 1 Undershaft, London EC3A 8JX
Tel: (171) 816 8100 **Fax:** (171) 816 8206 **Telex:** 8953378 MANDCO
Dealers Tel: 588 7302

Senior Executive Officers
Director & General Manager — A S Gray
Director & Deputy General Manager — P A Burton

Others (Senior Executives)
Private Clients Dept. — K H Galloway *Manager*

General-Lending (DCM, SL)
Head of Corporate Banking — N E White *Manager, Lending*

Money Markets
Global Head — L A E James *Treasury*
Regional Head — K M Cage *Dealer*

Foreign Exchange
Global Head — L A E James *Treasury*

FX Traders / Sales People
K M Cage *Dealer*
A I D Gill *Assistant Dealer*

Settlement / Clearing
Operations — P J Revell *Manager*

MeesPierson (Isle of Man) Limited

Pierson House, 18-20 North Quay, Douglas, Isle of Man IM99 1NR
PO Box 156, Douglas, Isle of Man IM99 1NR
Tel: (1624) 688 300 **Fax:** (1624) 688 334 **Telex:** 626159

MeesPierson NV
Full Branch Office

Camomile Court, 23 Camomile Street, London EC3A 7PP
Tel: (171) 444 8700 **Fax:** (171) 444 8810

Senior Executive Officers
General Manager — William Blydenstein ☎ **444 8780**

Debt Capital Markets / Fixed Income
Regional Head — Sam van Holthe *Managing Director* ☎ **444 8470** F **444 8888**

Domestic Government Bonds
Head of Sales — Sam van Holthe *Managing Director* ☎ **444 8470** F **444 8888**

Syndicated Lending

Loan-Related Activities
Trade Finance — David de Buck *Head* ☎ **444 8740**
Project Finance — William Blydenstein *General Manager* ☎ **444 8780**

Money Markets
Country Head — John Holloway *Manager* ☎ **444 8364**

Wholesale Deposits
Marketing — Nick Hill *Manager*

Foreign Exchange
Country Head — David Humphreys

Settlement / Clearing
Department: MeesPierson ICS Limited
Fax: 444 8888
Country Head — Wim dem Hartog *Managing Director*

MeesPierson Securities (UK) Limited
Subsidiary Company

Camomile Court, 23 Camomile Street, London EC3A 7PP
Tel: (171) 444 8400 **Fax:** (171) 444 8888 **Telex:** 928095 PIERSN G

Senior Executive Officers
Chief Executive Officer — Sam Van Holthe

1808　Euromoney Directory 1999

www.euromoneydirectory.com UNITED KINGDOM (+44)

Debt Capital Markets / Fixed Income
Department: International Fixed Income
Tel: 283 6565 **Fax:** 444 8989

Eurobonds
Head of Sales
Head of Trading

Nicholas Bruell *Director*
Mark Reynolds *Director*

Mellon Bank NA   Full Branch Office

Alternative trading name: Mellon Trust
Princess House, 1 Suffolk Lane, London EC4R 0AN
Tel: (171) 623 0800 **Fax:** (171) 929 4408 **Telex:** 916980 BOSTON G **Swift:** BSDT GB 2X **Email:** rayner.s@mellon.com
Reuters: MELM
Website: www.mellon.com

Senior Executive Officers
Chief Executive Officer
Financial Director
Chief Operating Officer
Treasurer

John P O'Driscoll *SVP & Area Head, Europe* ☎ **623 0950**
Derek Hardy *VP & Head of Finance* ☎ **623 0856**
Nigel Holmes *FVP & Chief Administrative Officer* ☎ **623 0962**
Ainsley Clark *VP & Head of Treasury* ☎ **623 0873**

Equity Capital Markets
Equity Repo / Securities Lending
Marketing
Head of Trading

Jamie Ball *FVP & Head, Int'l Securities Lending* ☎ **623 0830**
Stephen Kingham *VP & Head of Trading* ☎ **623 0927**

Syndicated Lending
Fax: 626 0356
Regional Head

Keith Brackley *VP & Head of Corporate Banking* ☎ **623 0808**

Money Markets
Tel: 623 0860 **Fax:** 623 5023
Regional Head

Richard Gulston *VP & Funding Manager* ☎ **623 0833**

Wholesale Deposits
Marketing

Richard Gulston *VP & Funding Manager* ☎ **623 0833**

Foreign Exchange
Tel: 623 0860 **Fax:** 623 5023
Regional Head

Ainsley Clark *VP & Head of Treasury* ☎ **623 0873**

Risk Management
Fax: 626 0356
Regional Head

Patrick Coffey *VP & Head, Corporate Banking* ☎ **623 0046**

Settlement / Clearing
Fax: 626 0356
Regional Head
Foreign Exchange Settlement

Ray Luckhurst *VP & Head of Operations* ☎ **623 0822**
Jester Wildman *Manager, Forex Operations* ☎ **623 0877**

Global Custody
Fax: 626 0356
Country Head

Dan Wywoda *SVP & Head, Global Trust & Custody* ☎ **623 0924**
✉ wywoda.d@mellon.com

Other (Global Custody)

Debra Ware *Head of Client Services* ☎ **623 0874**
Simon Shapland ☎ **623 0872** ✉ shapland.st@mellon.com
Greg Lindsey ☎ **623 0929** ✉ lindsey.gb@mellon.com
Robert Manderschied ☎ **623 0876** ✉ mandershied.rk@mellon.com

Administration

Paul A Palmisciano *VP & Head, Systems, Europe* ☎ **623 0961**

Compliance

Patrick Coffey *VP & Head, Corporate Banking* ☎ **623 0046**

Public Relations
Media & Communications

Siobhan Y Rayner *Co-ordinator* ☎ **623 0826** ✉ rayner.s@mellon.com

Merban Limited   Head Office

7 Catherine Place, London SW1E 6DX
Tel: (171) 630 0211 **Fax:** (171) 630 9732 **Email:** merbanltd@aol.com

Senior Executive Officers
Chairman
Financial Director

Brian Fitzpatrick
Ken Howard-Scholey *Chief Financial Officer*

UNITED KINGDOM (+44)   www.euromoneydirectory.com

Merita Bank plc
Full Branch Office

19 Thomas More Street, London E1 9YW
Tel: (171) 265 3333 **Fax:** (171) 709 7003 **Telex:** 290562 **Swift:** UNIT GB 2L
Website: www.merita.fi

Senior Executive Officers
General Manager — Hannu Linnoinen T 265 3100 F 860 1760

Others (Senior Executives)
Finance & Operations — Peter Mobsby *Head, Finance & Operations* T 265 3321 F 265 3311
Treasury — David Britton *International Treasurer* T 265 3173 F 860 1760
Mick Phillis *Treasurer, London* T 265 3200 F 860 1763
Corporate Banking — Theo Mezger *Deputy Head of Corporate Banking* T 265 3132 F 860 1760

Syndicated Lending
Credit — Paul Brosnahan *Head* T 265 3174 F 709 7001
Syndications — Peter Stiles *Head* T 265 3111 F 265 3144
Restructured — David Double *Head* T 265 3306 F 265 3144

Other (Trade Finance)
Ship Finance — Henny O'Brien *Head* T 265 3225 F 709 7001
Property Finance — William Goldstein *Head* T 265 3300 F 265 3237
Trade & Project Finance — Charles Bailey *Head* T 265 3133 F 265 3355
Structured & Corporate Finance — Peter Cliff *Head* T 265 3180 F 265 3144
Finnish Corporate Banking — Kari Jaukkuri *Head* T 265 3197 F 265 3144
Swedish Corporate Banking — Bengt Witting *Head* T 265 3255 F 265 3386

Money Markets
Regional Head — Susan Hannaford *Deputy Treasurer* T 265 3202
Mick Phillis *Treasurer, London* T 265 3200 F 860 1763

Foreign Exchange
Country Head — Mick Phillis *Treasurer, London* T 265 3200 F 860 1763
Corporate Sales — Alan Collins *Head, Corporate Sales* T 522 9260

FX Traders / Sales People
Corporate Marketing — Bob Fereday *Head, Corporate Marketing* T 265 3213

Settlement / Clearing
Country Head — Lorraine Bennett *Head of Settlements* T 265 3253 F 709 7003

Administration
Technology & Systems
Management Information Services — Craig Hunt *Head* T 265 3130 F 265 3105

Other (Administration)
Legal Counsel — Kirsti Niinisalo-Snowden *Head* T 265 3301 F 860 1760
Compliance — Mike Paddon *Head* T 265 3145 F 860 1765
Personnel — Joan Laver *Head* T 265 3322 F 265 3311
Customer Services & Credit Administration — Bill Shannon *Head* T 265 3230 F 265 3126

Merrill Lynch Asset Management Limited
Subsidiary Company

55 King Williams Street, London EC4 9A5
Tel: (171) 628 1000 **Fax:** (171) 867 4697 **Telex:** 261509
Website: www.merrilllynch.com

Senior Executive Officers
Chairman — Christopher Reeves
Senior MD & Chief Investment Officer — Alan Albert

Merrill Lynch Bank & Trust Company (Cayman) Limited

Isle of Man Branch, Atlantic House, Circular Road, Douglas, Isle of Man 1M1 1QW
Tel: (1624) 688 600 **Fax:** (1624) 688 601
Website: www.ml.com

Merrill Lynch International

20 Farringdon Road, London EC1M 3NH
PO Box 293, London
Tel: (171) 892 4844 **Fax:** (171) 892 4845

www.euromoneydirectory.com UNITED KINGDOM (+44)

Equity Capital Markets
Tel: 892 4888 Fax: 772 2698
Country Head   John Miller *Managing Director* ⊤ 867 3700 F 867 2516
                                        Farley Bolwell *Managing Director* ⊤ 867 4133 F 867 4133
                                        Alex Woodthorpe *Vice President* ⊤ 867 3700 F 867 2516

Equity Repo / Securities Lending
Marketing & Product Development   Robert Hanna *Vice President* ⊤ 892 4908 F 892 4965
                                        E robert_hanna@ml.com
Head of Prime Brokerage   David Stockwell *Director* ⊤ 892 4906

Merrill Lynch International

Ropemaker Place, 25 Ropemaker Street, London EC2Y 9LY
Tel: (171) 628 1000 Fax: (171) 867 4040 Telex: 883433 Swift: MLIL GB 20
Website: www.ml.com

Debt Capital Markets / Fixed Income
Fixed-Income Repo
Marketing & Product Development   John C Cook *Managing Director* ⊤ 867 3979 F 867 4310 E cookjoh.ml.com
Trading   Monty Law *Vice President, Matched Book trading*
                                        Cameron Dunn *Assistant Vice President, Matched Book Trading*
                                        Todor Azurza *Matched Book Trading*
                                        Michael Secretan *Matched Book Trading*
                                        Claudia Benci *Matched Book Trading*
                                        Ennio Montinaro *IEM Matched Book Trading*

Metropolitan Bank & Trust

26 Seymour Street, London W1H 5WD
Tel: (171) 723 5657 Fax: (171) 724 4046

Senior Executive Officers
Representative   Chris August

Midland Bank plc

Alternative trading name: HSBC Markets
Formerly known as: HSBC MIDLAND
Thames Exchange, 10 Queen Street Place, London EC4R 1BQ
Tel: (171) 336 2000 Fax: (171) 621 0496 Reuters: HSBC/INDEX Bloomberg: HSB
Website: www.hsbcmarkets.com

Senior Executive Officers
Chief Operating Officer   David Burnett *Chief Operating Officer* ⊤ 336 3192
Treasurer   Guy Heald *Treasurer* ⊤ 336 3742

Others (Senior Executives)
Head of Emerging Markets   Birgitte Jespersen *Head of Emerging Markets Currency Group* ⊤ 336 4003
Head of Sales   Irene Dorner *Head of Sales & Marketing* ⊤ 336 4016
Head of Futures   Dave Townsend *Head of Futures* ⊤ 336 3633

Debt Capital Markets / Fixed Income
Head of Fixed Income Sales   Mike Stone *Head of Capital Market Sales* ⊤ 336 3632
Head of Fixed Income Trading   Geoff Merrett *Head of Balance Sheet Mgmt & Interest Rate Trading*
                                        ⊤ 336 3753

Government Bonds
Head of Sales   Mike Stone *Head of Capital Market Sales* ⊤ 336 3632
Head of Trading   Frank Hagenstein *Head of Euro Governments* ⊤ 336 3916
                                        James Geers *Head of Gilt-Edged Market Making* ⊤ 336 3944

Eurobonds
Head of Origination   Charlie Hanbury-Williams *Head, Primary Markets* ⊤ 336 2833
Head of Syndication   Nicholas Medd *Head of Debt Syndicate* ⊤ 336 3367
Head of Sales   Mike Stone *Head of Capital Market Sales* ⊤ 336 3632
Head of Trading   Clive Stevens *Joint Head of Eurobond Trading* ⊤ 336 3607
                                        Mark Everett *Joint Head of Eurobond Trading* ⊤ 336 3540

Emerging Market Bonds
Head   Clive Stevens *Joint Head of Eurobond Trading* ⊤ 336 3607
Head of Sales   David Slater *Assistant Director, Middle East, India, Africa* ⊤ 336 3609
Head of Trading   Clive Stevens *Joint Head of Eurobond Trading* ⊤ 336 3607

Euromoney Directory 1999 **1811**

UNITED KINGDOM (+44)   www.euromoneydirectory.com

Midland Bank plc (cont)

Libor-Based / Floating-Rate Products
FRN Sales — Andrew Bristow *Head of Libor Product Sales* ☏ 336 3560
FRN Trading; Asset Swaps — Mark Everett *Joint Head of Eurobond Trading* ☏ 336 3540
Asset Swaps (Sales) — Andrew Bristow *Head of Libor Product Sales* ☏ 336 3560

Fixed-Income Repo
Head of Repo — Joerg Bunse *Head of Repo* ☏ 626 0864
Trading — Geoff Merrett *Head of Balance Sheet Mgmt & Interest Rate Trading* ☏ 336 3753

Fixed-Income Research
Head of Fixed Income — Stephen King *Managing Director, Economic Research* ☏ 336 2446
Head of Credit Research — Karl Bergqwist *Director of Fixed Income Credit Research* ☏ 336 3925

Money Markets
Head of Money Markets — Geoff Merrett *Head of Balance Sheet Mgmt & Interest Rate Trading* ☏ 336 3753

Foreign Exchange
Head of Foreign Exchange — Rob Loewy *Head of Foreign Exchange* ☏ 336 3745
Head of Institutional Sales; Corporate Sales — Alan Clarke *Head of Corporate and Institutional Sales* ☏ 336 3711
Corporate Sales — Peter Lewis *Head of UK Regional and Corporate Treasury Sales* ☏ 336 3796
Head of Trading — Mark Oliver *Head of Spot Trading* ☏ 336 3725

Risk Management
Head of Risk Management — Robert Benson *Head of Specialised Derivatives Group* ☏ 336 3976 ℱ 336 3619

Fixed Income Derivatives / Risk Management
Head of Sales — Ian Collier *Head of SDG Fixed Income Marketing* ☏ 336 3914
Trading — James Prichard *Head of SDG Fixed Income* ☏ 336 3154

Other (FI Derivatives)
Head of Trading — Edmond Levy *Head of SDG FX* ☏ 336 3516

Other Currency Swap / FX Options Personnel
Head of Sales — Sara Sullivan-Baker *Senior Manager, Global FX Option Sales* ☏ 336 3514
Head of Trading — Martyn Brush *Global Head of FX Options* ☏ 336 9304

OTC Equity Derivatives
Sales — Paul Nevin *Head of Sales, Specialised Derivatives Group* ☏ 336 3481
Trading — Alan McLean *Head of Equity Derivative Trading* ☏ 336 3482

OTC Commodity Derivatives
Trading — Clive Stevens *Joint Head of Eurobond Trading* ☏ 336 3607
Mark Everett *Joint Head of Eurobond Trading* ☏ 336 3540

Settlement / Clearing
Head of Settlement / Clearing — Brian Gracey *Head of FX Operations* ☏ 336 4074
Fixed-Income Settlement — Ian Chicken *Senior Manager, Bonds and Futures Operations* ☏ 336 3834
Operations — Brian Gracey *Head of Treasury Operations* ☏ 336 4074

Administration
Business Development — Denise Rodgers *Head of Client Management Group* ☏ 336 3519
Head of Marketing — Emma Greenwood *Marketing Manager* ☏ 336 3465

Technology & Systems
Ingrid Child *Senior Manager, Treasury User Systems Team* ☏ 336 3044

Legal / In-House Counsel
David Bloom *Senior Legal Advisor* ☏ 336 3065

Compliance
Christine Lowthian *Global Head of Compliance* ☏ 336 2308

Public Relations
Emma Greenwood *Marketing Manager* ☏ 336 3465

Mitsubishi Corporation Finance plc   Subsidiary Company

5th Floor, Bow Bells House, Bread Street, London EC4M 9BQ
Tel: (171) 246 2600 **Fax:** (171) 248 8000 **Telex:** 8955539 MCFPLC G **Reuters:** MCFA
Website: www.mcf.co.uk

Senior Executive Officers
Chief Executive Officer — Tetsuro Nishi *Executive Director, Control & Administration*
Daisuke Hamaguchi *Executive Director, Alternative Investment*
General Manager, Capital & Money Markets — Yoichi Shimoyama
Managing Director — Teruhisa Arai

1812   Euromoney Directory 1999

www.euromoneydirectory.com   UNITED KINGDOM (+44)

Others (Senior Executives)
                                    Dominic Monaghan *Associate Director & Senior Money Market Dealer*
General-Investment
Head of Investment   Daisuke Hamaguchi *Executive Director, Alternative Investment*
Debt Capital Markets / Fixed Income
Eurobonds
Head of Origination   Yoichi Shimoyama *General Manager, Capital & Money Markets*
Money Markets
Head of Money Markets   Dominic Monaghan *Associate Director & Senior Money Market Dealer*
Other   Yoichi Shimoyama *General Manager, Capital & Money Markets*
Settlement / Clearing
Head of Settlement / Clearing   Stuart McLaren *Manager, Operations* ⊤ **246 2627**
Other Departments
Chief Credit Officer; Cash Management David Miles *Manager, Accounts & Cash Management* ⊤ **246 2611**
Administration
Head of Administration   Tetsuro Nishi *Executive Director, Control & Administration*
Technology & Systems
                                    Andrea Bolam *Associate Director, IT & Administration* ⊤ **246 2611**
Accounts / Audit
                                    David Miles *Manager, Accounts & Cash Management* ⊤ **246 2611**

The Mitsubishi Trust & Banking Corporation   Full Branch Office
24 Lombard Street, London EC3V 9AJ
Tel: (171) 929 2323 **Fax:** (171) 929 1905; (171) 929 1906 **Telex:** 887208 MTBCLN G **Reuters:** MBTL

Senior Executive Officers
Chairman   Hiroshi Hayashi
President   Toyoshi Nakano
General Manager   Yuji Ohashi
Others (Senior Executives)
                                    Tamotsu Makino *Deputy General Manager*
                                    Masafumi Abe *Deputy General Manager*
                                    Shigeo Asakura *Deputy General Manager*
                                    Tasuo Wakabayashi *Deputy General Manager*

Mitsubishi Trust International Limited   Subsidiary Company
24 Lombard Street, London EC3V 9AJ
Tel: (171) 929 2866 **Fax:** (171) 929 3471 **Telex:** 945759 MTINTL G

Senior Executive Officers
Chief Executive Officer   Taro Shiosawa *Managing Director & Chief Executive*
Deputy Managing Director   Hideo Machida
Others (Senior Executives)
Executive Director   Yasuyuki Shigemasa
                                    Ray Winters

Debt Capital Markets / Fixed Income
Tel: 929 4691
Bonds - General
New Issue Syndication   Sue Pimblett *Manager* F **283 0720**
Trading & Sales   Matthew Hicks *Associate Director* F **283 0720**
                                    Naoki Shimmura *Associate Director* F **334 9693**
                                    John Coates *Senior Manager* F **283 0720**
                                    Takafumi Ihara *Senior Manager* F **334 9693**
                                    Paul Tanner *Assistant Manager* F **283 0720**
                                    Sachiko Hatakeyama *Assistant Manager* F **334 9693**
                                    Chris Hawkins *Assistant Manager* F **283 0720**
                                    Ian Korvin *Assistant Manager* F **283 0720**
                                    Linda Lingane *Assistant Manager* F **283 0720**
                                    Paul Lomas *Assistant Manager* F **283 0720**
                                    Simon Quinn *Assistant Manager* F **283 0720**
                                    Lorenzo Ruffatti *Assistant Manager* F **283 0720**
                                    Jose de Yermo *Assistant Manager* F **283 0720**
                                    Grant Wiltshire *Assistant Manager* F **283 0720**
                                    Terry Wright *Assistant Manager* F **283 0720**
                                    Yoko Yamashita *Assistant Manager* F **334 9693**

UNITED KINGDOM (+44)　　　　www.euromoneydirectory.com

Mitsubishi Trust International Limited (cont)
Equity Capital Markets
Equity Repo / Securities Lending
Head　　　　　　　　　　　　　　　　Naoya Ichimura Senior Manager ☎ 334 9696 F 334 9693
Head of Trading　　　　　　　　　　　Matthew Collard Repo Trader ☎ 334 9696 F 334 9693
　　　　　　　　　　　　　　　　　　Mina Yamazaki Lending Trader ☎ 334 9696 F 334 9693

Corporate Finance / M&A Advisory
Other (Corporate Finance)
Investment Advisory　　　　　　　　　Yutaka Kawakami Senior Manager F 283 0714
　　　　　　　　　　　　　　　　　　Yuko Suganuma Assistant Manager F 283 0714
　　　　　　　　　　　　　　　　　　Kayoko Okuda Assistant Manager F 283 0714

Settlement / Clearing
Head of Settlement / Clearing　　　　Simon Crowley Manager

Global Custody
Head of Global Custody　　　　　　　Paul Tregunno Manager

Administration
Head of Administration　　　　　　　Diane Read Senior Manager

Compliance
　　　　　　　　　　　　　　　　　　Yasuyuki Shigemasa Executive Director
　　　　　　　　　　　　　　　　　　Liz Hornby Executive Director

Accounts / Audit
Accounts　　　　　　　　　　　　　　Ali Abedi Manager

Other (Administration)
Middle Office　　　　　　　　　　　　Denis Horan Manager

The Mitsui Trust & Banking Co Limited　　　　Full Branch Office
5th Floor, 6 Broadgate, London EC2M 2TB
Tel: (171) 982 9000; (171) 638 0841 **Fax:** (171) 628 8806; (171) 588 6910 **Telex:** 920280 MTRUST G

Senior Executive Officers
General Manager　　　　　　　　　　Ken Takahashi

Syndicated Lending
Loan-Related Activities
Project Finance　　　　　　　　　　　Mr Konishi Assistant General Manager

Foreign Exchange
Head of Trading　　　　　　　　　　　Yasuhisa Ishida Manager ☎ 982 9016

Risk Management
Fixed Income Derivatives / Risk Management
IR Swaps Trading　　　　　　　　　　Tateo Komatsu Manager ☎ 638 6888
IR Options Trading　　　　　　　　　　Seiki Kimura Senior Assistant Manager ☎ 638 6888

Settlement / Clearing
Derivatives Settlement; Foreign Exchange　Martin Cox Manager
Settlement

Mitsui Trust International Limited　　　　Subsidiary Company
3rd Floor, 41 Tower Hill, London EC3N 4DU
Tel: (171) 702 1477 **Fax:** (171) 702 9857; (171) 702 9858 **Telex:** 945831 MTINTL G **Cable:** MITSUITRUSTINT L

Senior Executive Officers
General Manager　　　　　　　　　　Nubuaki Nakamura

Montenegrobanka dd Podgorica　　　　Representative Office
1 Mandeville Place, 88 Wigmore Street, London W1M 5LB
Tel: (171) 935 3433 **Fax:** (171) 486 4805

Senior Executive Officers
Director　　　　　　　　　　　　　　Jovan Mihailovic

1814　Euromoney Directory 1999

www.euromoneydirectory.com   UNITED KINGDOM (+44)

Monument Derivatives Limited
Head Office
11 Old Jewry, London EC2R 8DU
Tel: (171) 338 0819 Fax: (171) 338 0818 Telex: 8813491

Senior Executive Officers
Managing Director / General Manager   Martin Burton

Morgan Grenfell (Scotland) Limited
Subsidiary Company
35 St Andrew Square, Edinburgh, EH2 2AD
Tel: (131) 556 6982 Fax: (131) 556 6842

Senior Executive Officers
Managing Director / General Manager   Miriam Greenwood

Morgan Stanley & Co International Limited
25 Cabot Square, Canary Wharf, London E14 4QA
Tel: (171) 425 8000; (171) 425 6679 Fax: (171) 425 8990; (171) 425 7648 Telex: 8812564 MORSTN G
Email: us@Infid.ms.com Reuters: MSPA-S Cable: MORGANSTAN
Reuters: MSQA-Z
Website: www.ms.com

Senior Executive Officers
Executive Director   Kevin M Adeson [T] 425 5751 [F] 425 7296
Executive Director   John S Wotowicz [T] 425 7729 [F] 425 7296
Managing Director   Alan Jones [T] 425 5237 [F] 425 5800
Managing Director   Riccardo Pavoncelli [T] 513 7726 [F] 513 7999

Debt Capital Markets / Fixed Income
Tel: 425 8000 Fax: 425 8990

Fixed-Income Repo
Head of Repo   Miguel Hennessy Executive Director, London Desk Manager
            [E] mhen@ms.com
Marketing & Product Development   Victoria Cole Vice President [T] 425 7420 [E] vcole@ms.com
Trading   Gavin Cutts Vice President, General Collateral
        Gilly Meth Vice President, Specials
        Mark Cunningham Associate, Corporates
        Ciaran O'Flynn Associate, General Collateral
        Bob Cawley Associate, Specials
        Terry Barton Associate, O / N Financing

Equity Capital Markets
Tel: 452 6162 Fax: 425 4248

Equity Repo / Securities Lending
Marketing & Product Development   Philip Lopategui [T] 425 6088 [F] 425 6026 [E] lopat@ms.com
        Stephen Friend [T] 425 6191
        Tammy Philips Vice President [T] 425 6151
        Jane Karczewski [T] 425 6086
Head of Prime Brokerage   Jack Tracy Executive Director [T] 425 6016 [F] 425 8469

Morgan Stanley Group (Europe) plc
Subsidiary Company
25 Cabot Square, Canary Wharf, London E14 4QA
Tel: (171) 425 8000; (171) 513 8000 Fax: (171) 425 8990; (171) 513 8990 Telex: 8812564
Reuters: IMSB; IDXL-N; MSCBAA-Z; MSCBBA-W; MSDA-K; MSHK; MSIX; MSJA-C; MSJM-O; MSJQ;
MSJS-T; MSJY; MSRU; MSSH-V; MSSWA-Z; MSTA-J; MSXA-D; MSYA-E
Website: www.ms.com

Senior Executive Officers
Executive Chairman   David Walker
Chief Operating Officer   Amelia C Fawcett MD & Chief Administrative Officer - Europe

Relationship Manager
Morgan Stanley Capital Partners   Christian Rochat Executive Director, Merchant Banking
        James Hoch Executive Director, Merchant Banking

Debt Capital Markets / Fixed Income
Department: Morgan Stanley & Co International limited
Regional Head   Paul Daniel MD & Head, Fixed-Income - Europe

Euromoney Directory 1999   **1815**

UNITED KINGDOM (+44)   www.euromoneydirectory.com

Morgan Stanley Group (Europe) plc (cont)

Domestic Government Bonds
Head of Sales	Robert C Whitehand *Managing Director*
	Tom Juterbock *Managing Director*
Head of Trading	Henry Koerling *Managing Director*

Eurobonds
Head of Origination	Riccardo Pavoncelli *Managing Director*
Head of Syndication	Michael Weston *Managing Director*
Head of Sales	Robert C Whitehand *Managing Director*
Head of Trading	Jim O'Brien *Managing Director*
Trading (High-yield)	Jason Maratos *Managing Director*

Bonds - General
New Issues Administration	Denise Redburn

Medium-Term Notes
Head of Origination	May Busch *Managing Director*
Head of Structuring	Ed O'Campo *Managing Director*
Head of Sales	Robert C Whitehand *Managing Director*
Head of Trading	Olivier Jalouneix *Executive Director*

Asset-Backed Securities / Securitization
Global Head	Karl Essig *MD & Head, Int'l Securitization*
Head of Trading	Scott Peterson *MD, Structuring*

Equity Capital Markets
Department: Morgan Stanley & Co International Limited
Regional Head	Robert Metzler *MD & Head, Institutional Equity Division-Europe*
	Jerker Johansson *MD & COO, Institutional Equity Division-Europe*
	Franck Petitgas *MD & Head, Equity Capital Markets-Europe*

International Equities
Head of Origination	Franck Petitgas *MD & Head, Equity Capital Markets-Europe*
Head of Syndication	John Hyman *Executive Director*
Head of Sales	Nadir Latif *Managing Director*
	James Graham *MD & Sales Trading Head*
	Richard Castellano *MD & Global Head*
Head of Trading	Danny Hegglin *Managing Director*
Head of Research	Charles Scott *Managing Director*

Other (International Equity)
Equity Syndicate Administration	Dan Martin

Convertibles / Equity-Linked
Head of Origination	Daniel Palmer *Executive Director*
Head of Syndication	John Hyman *Executive Director*
Head of Sales; Head of Trading	Derek Bandeen *Managing Director*

Other (Convertibles)
Programme Trading; Portfolio Strategy	Jack Tracy *MD & Regional Head*

Equity Repo / Securities Lending
Marketing	Guru Ramakrishnan *Managing Director*

Money Markets

Money Markets - General
Eurosterling Sales	Ewan Labrom *Head*

Foreign Exchange
Department: Morgan Stanley & Co International Limited
Regional Head	Roger Tarika *Managing Director*
Head of Institutional Sales	Paul Blain *Executive Director*
Head of Trading	Mikael Hedlund *Executive Director*

Risk Management
Department: Morgan Stanley & Co International Limited

Fixed Income Derivatives / Risk Management
Trading	Jonathan Chenevix-Trench *Managing Director*
IR Swaps Trading	Sean Notley *Managing Director*

Other (FI Derivatives)
Structuring	Ed O'Campo *Managing Director*

Foreign Exchange Derivatives / Risk Management
Vanilla FX option Trading	Nicholas Webber *Vice President*

OTC Equity Derivatives
Head	Jamie Greenwald *MD & Regional Head*

Corporate Finance / M&A Advisory
Department: Morgan Stanley & Co Limited
Regional Head	John Studzinski *Managing Director*

www.euromoneydirectory.com UNITED KINGDOM (+44)

Other (Corporate Finance)
Corporate Finance — Michael Uva *Managing Director*
M&A (Co-Head) — Michael Zaoui *Managing Director*
Simon Robey *Managing Director*

Settlement / Clearing
Department: Morgan Stanley & Co International Limited
Equity Settlement — Steve Lipton *Managing Director*
Fixed-Income Settlement — Paul Smith *Executive Director*

Asset Management
Department: Morgan Stanley Asset Management Limited
Head — Dominic Caldecott *MD & CIO-Europe*
James Tanner *MD & Head, Business Mgt-Europe*

Other (Asset Management)
Robert Sargent *Managing Director*
Frances Campion *Managing Director*
David Germany *Managing Director*
Margaret Naylor *Managing Director*
Administration & Operations — Jackie Day *Executive Director*

Other Departments
Commodities / Bullion — Marc Mourre *Executive Director, Commodities Marketing*
Colin Bryce *Managing Director*

Administration
Public Relations
Morgan Stanley Group (Europe) plc — Euart Glendinning *Vice President*
Other (Administration)
MSCI Sales & Marketing — Jane Staunton *Executive Director, Morgan Stanley Capital*

Moscow Narodny Bank Limited — Head Office
81 King William Street, London EC4N 7BG
Tel: (171) 623 2066 **Fax:** (171) 283 4840 **Telex:** 885401 **Swift:** MNBL GB 2L

Senior Executive Officers
Chairman of the Board — Iouri Ponomarev
Chief Executive Officer — I Souvorov *Deputy Chairman & Group Chief Executive*
A Lukin *Deputy Chief Executive*
Chief Operating Officer — C Knowlden
Treasurer — A Skelton *Group Treasurer*
Managing Director — A Lukin
Company Secretary & Snr Legal Adviser — N Fitzpatrick

Others (Senior Executives)
Institutional Banking — M Luyke-Roskott *AGM, Institutional Banking Division*
General-Lending (DCM, SL)
Head of Corporate Banking — M Hopkins *Assistant General Manager*
General-Investment
Head of Investment — A Lukin *Managing Director*
M Lawrence *Senior Manager*

General - Treasury
Head of Treasury — K De La Salle *AGM, Treasury & Trading*
S Humphries *Senior Manager, Debt Trading Support*

Relationship Manager
Financial Institutions — T Stacey *Manager*

Debt Capital Markets / Fixed Income
Fixed-Income Repo
Other — S Humphries *Senior Manager, Debt Trading Support*
A Kabanov *Manager, Debt Trading*

Syndicated Lending
Loan-Related Activities
Trade Finance — D Kemp *Senior Manager*
Project Finance — D Taylor *Senior Manager, Corporate Project Finance*
Other (Trade Finance)
Documentary Credits — M Brennan *Assistant Manager*

Money Markets
Head of Money Markets — P Eveling *Manager*
Other (Wholesale Deposits)
Balance Sheet Management — M Luyke-Roskott *AGM, Institutional Banking Division*

UNITED KINGDOM (+44) www.euromoneydirectory.com

Moscow Narodny Bank Limited (cont)

Foreign Exchange
Head of Foreign Exchange — P Eveling *Manager*

Risk Management
Head of Risk Management — P Manning *Head, Group Risk Management & Compliance*

Other Currency Swap / FX Options Personnel
Credit Risk Unit — P Yates *Head of Group Risk*
Group Economics — P Forrest *Group Economist*

Other (Exchange-Traded Derivatives)
Derivatives — P Eveling *Manager*

Exchange-Traded Derivatives
Head — P Eveling *Manager*

Settlement / Clearing
Operations — K Ivanowski *AGM*

Other Departments
Commodities / Bullion — P Eveling *Manager*
Correspondent Banking — T Stacey *Manager, Institutional Banking Division*

Administration
Business Development — T Lafin *Senior Manager*

Technology & Systems
Information Technology — C Axton *Manager*

Legal / In-House Counsel
Legal & Regulatory Services — N Fitzpatrick *Company Secretary & Snr Legal Adviser*

Compliance
— M Murphy

Public Relations
— P Forrest *Group Economist*

Corporate Communications
Communications — C Axton *Manager*

Accounts / Audit
Control & Audit — D Veness *Senior Manager*
Accounts — I Herbert *Chief Accountant*

Other (Administration)
Business Development — M Luyke-Roskott *AGM, Institutional Banking Division*
Loans Administration — G Dixon *Manager*
Human Resources — J Glover *Assistant General Manager*
Personnel — S Godwin *Manager*

Most-Bank
Representative Office

Level 4, City Tower, 40 Basinghall Street, London EC2V 5DE
Tel: (171) 638 8652 **Fax:** (171) 256 7816

Senior Executive Officers
Chief Executive Officer — Gueidar Babaev *VP & General Representative*

Administration
Head of Administration — Belinda Bryant *Office Manager* ☎ **638 8652** 🖷 **256 7816**

Multi Commercial Bank

4th Floor, 39 Sloane Street, London SW1X 9LP
Tel: (171) 591 5100 **Fax:** (171) 259 5950

Senior Executive Officers
Managing Director / General Manager — Geoffrey Spencer
Representative — Neil Mclean

Muslim Commercial Bank

301 Marlyn Lodge, Portsoken Street, London E1 8RB
Tel: (171) 488 4485 **Fax:** (171) 488 4485

Senior Executive Officers
General Manager — Naeem Shaikh

www.euromoneydirectory.com	UNITED KINGDOM (+44)

Nacional Financiera SNC
Full Branch Office

Alternative trading name: NAFINSA (London Branch)
19th Floor, 4 Broadgate, London EC2R 7HJ
Tel: (171) 417 0016 **Fax:** (171) 417 5114 **Telex:** 290967 **Reuters:** NFMB **Telerate:** NFSA GB 2L

Senior Executive Officers
Chief Executive Officer	Arturo Galán *Director & General Manager* ☎ **417 5110**
Financial Director	Enrique Nieto *Deputy General Manager* ☎ **417 0016**
Chief Operating Officer	Neil Kelly *Deputy General Manager* ☎ **417 5130**
Treasurer	William Webster *Treasurer* ☎ **417 5120**

Debt Capital Markets / Fixed Income
Tel: 417 5120 **Fax:** 417 5114
Global Head — Enrique Nieto *Deputy General Manager* ☎ **417 0016**

Non-Domestic Government Bonds
Trading Head (General) — William Webster *Treasurer* ☎ **417 5120**

Eurobonds
Head of Trading — Graham Fowler *Chief Dealer* ☎ **417 5125**
Trading (Sovereigns) — Conal Howells *Trader* ☎ **417 5124**
Trading (Corporates) — Paula Ioannides *Trader* ☎ **417 5121**

Libor-Based / Floating-Rate Products
Asset Swaps — William Webster *Treasurer* ☎ **417 5120**

Fixed-Income Repo
Head of Repo — William Webster *Treasurer* ☎ **417 5120**

Syndicated Lending
Global Head — Enrique Nieto *Deputy General Manager* ☎ **417 0016**
Head of Credit Committee — Nick Masterson-Jones *DGM, IT & Risk Management* ☎ **417 0016**

Loan-Related Activities
Structured Trade Finance — Enrique Nieto *Deputy General Manager* ☎ **417 0016**
William Webster *Treasurer* ☎ **417 5120**

Money Markets
Global Head — William Webster *Treasurer* ☎ **417 5120**
Regional Head — Paula Ioannides *Trader* ☎ **417 5121**

Foreign Exchange
Tel: 417 5125
Global Head — William Webster *Treasurer* ☎ **417 5120**
Head of Trading — Graham Fowler *Chief Dealer* ☎ **417 5125**

FX Traders / Sales People
G7 — Conal Howells *Trader* ☎ **417 5124**

Corporate Finance / M&A Advisory
Global Head — Enrique Nieto *Deputy General Manager* ☎ **417 0016**

Settlement / Clearing
Tel: 417 5144
Regional Head — Sue Nickerson *Head of Settlements* ☎ **417 5144** 📠 **710 6980**

Other Departments
Proprietary Trading — William Webster *Treasurer* ☎ **417 5120**
Administration
Technology & Systems
Nick Masterson-Jones *DGM, IT & Risk Management* ☎ **417 0016**

Natexis Banque - BFCE
Full Branch Office

Formerly known as: Banque Française du Commerce Extérieur
4/6 Throgmorton Avenue, London EX2N 2PP
Tel: (171) 638 0088 **Fax:** (171) 382 9370 **Telex:** 894191 **Swift:** BFCE GB 2L **Reuters:** BFCL **Bloomberg:** S. MALIK

Senior Executive Officers
Financial Director	Anthony Baumann *Financial Controller*
Chief Operating Officer	Alan Steel *Senior Manager, Operations*
Treasurer	Ian Woods
General Manager	Olivier de Bodman

Euromoney Directory 1999 **1819**

UNITED KINGDOM (+44)　　　　www.euromoneydirectory.com

National Australia Bank Limited　　　　Full Branch Office

6/8 Tokenhouse Yard, London EC2R 7AJ
Tel: (171) 710 2100 **Fax:** (171) 588 8356 **Telex:** 888912

Senior Executive Officers
General Manager　　　　James A Bradley
Debt Capital Markets / Fixed Income
Country Head　　　　Jonathan Daniels *Head of Capital Markets*
Eurobonds
Head of Sales; Head of Trading　　　　Stephen Mills *Head, Sales & Trading* ☎ **621 1330** 🖷 **726 0898**
Settlement / Clearing
Fixed-Income Settlement　　　　Julie Barefoot
Operations　　　　Stuart Inglis *Head of Operations*
Administration
Compliance
　　　　T D McKee *Head, Compliance*

National Bank of Abu Dhabi　　　　Full Branch Office

One Knightsbridge, London SW1X 7LY
Tel: (171) 393 3600; (171) 235 5400 **Fax:** (171) 393 3636; (171) 393 3637 **Telex:** 290475 MASRAF

Senior Executive Officers
Chairman　　　　Mohammed H Al Suweidi
Senior Manager, Private Banking　　　　Farid Barakat ☎ **393 3664**
Chief Operating Officer　　　　John Westwood *Operations Manager* ☎ **393 3608**
Treasurer　　　　John Urban *Senior Dealer* ☎ **393 3620**

National Bank of Canada　　　　Full Branch Office

Princes House, 95 Gresham Street, London EC2V 7LU
Tel: (171) 726 6581; (171) 726 2662 **Fax:** (171) 726 4265 **Telex:** 886615 **Reuters:** NBCL

Senior Executive Officers
VP, Treasury　　　　Christopher Elgar

National Bank of Dubai

207 Sloane Street, London SW1X 9QX
Tel: (171) 245 6923 **Fax:** (171) 235 2560

Senior Executive Officers
Managing Director / General Manager　　　　D B Crane

National Bank of Egypt International Limited　　　　Subsidiary Company

Park House, 16 Finsbury Circus, London EC2M 7DJ
Tel: (171) 374 6446 **Fax:** (171) 638 2920 **Telex:** 916625 A/B NBELDN G **Swift:** NBEG GB 2L **Reuters:** NBEI

Senior Executive Officers
Chief Operating Officer　　　　Adel Kassaby *Deputy Managing Director*
Treasurer　　　　Richard Nunn *Treasurer*
Managing Director　　　　Kazem Barakat
Director & General Manager　　　　John Harding
Deputy General Manager & Company Secretary　　Stephen Munro
Debt Capital Markets / Fixed Income
Tel: 256 7998
Global Head　　　　Richard Nunn *Treasurer*
Domestic Government Bonds
Head of Trading　　　　Richard Nunn *Treasurer*
Syndicated Lending
Fax: 839 5311
Head of Syndication　　　　Ahmed Maksoud *Assistant General Manager, Credit* ☎ **389 1280**
Loan-Related Activities
Trade Finance　　　　Ismail Saleh *Assistant General Manager* ☎ **389 1210**

www.euromoneydirectory.com UNITED KINGDOM (+44)

Money Markets
Tel: 256 7998
Head of Money Markets John Burke *Manager* ☏ **256 7972**

Foreign Exchange
Tel: 256 7998
Head of Foreign Exchange Simon Stevenson *Dealer* ☏ **256 7972**

Settlement / Clearing
Head of Settlement / Clearing Fathy Hassan *Assistant General Manager* ☏ **374 5560**

Other Departments
Private Banking Fathy Hassan *Assistant General Manager* ☏ **374 5560**

Administration
Technology & Systems
 Anthony Burr *Manager of IT* ☏ **374 5594**

Compliance
 Peter Toms *Internal Auditor* ☏ **374 5530**

Accounts / Audit
 Marcus Preston *Accountant* ☏ **374 5580**

National Bank of Egypt International Limited — Subsidiary Company

Trafalgar House, 11 Waterloo Place, London SW1Y 4AU
Tel: (171) 374 6446 **Fax:** (171) 839 5311 **Telex:** 916625 **Swift:** NBEG GB 2L

Senior Executive Officers
General Manager I Saleh

National Bank of Greece SA — Full Branch Office

50 St Mary Axe, London EC3A 8EL
Tel: (171) 626 3222 **Fax:** (171) 929 0989; (171) 929 0254 **Telex:** 8952211 **Swift:** ETHN GB 2L **Reuters:** NBOG
Bloomberg: NBGL

Senior Executive Officers
Treasurer Brian Stephens *Treasurer*
General Manager John Makris

Debt Capital Markets / Fixed Income
Tel: 623 8223
Head of Fixed Income; Head of Fixed Income Rosa Pollatou *Head, Fixed-Income & Sales* ☏ **623 1723**
Sales; Head of Fixed Income Trading

Government Bonds
Head of Sales; Head of Trading Rosa Pollatou *Head, Fixed-Income & Sales* ☏ **623 1723**

Eurobonds
Head of Sales; Head of Trading Rosa Pollatou *Head, Fixed-Income & Sales* ☏ **623 1723**

Fixed-Income Repo
Head of Repo Rosa Pollatou *Head, Fixed-Income & Sales* ☏ **623 1723**

Syndicated Lending
Tel: 636 3222 **Fax:** 929 0989
Country Head George Kontis *Senior Manager, Credit* ☏ **929 0256**
Head of Syndication Bernard Strange *Senior Credit Manager* ☏ **929 0255**

Money Markets
Tel: 623 8223
Head of Money Markets Procopis Andrianopoulos *Chief Dealer, Money Markets*

Domestic Commercial Paper
Head of Trading Procopis Andrianopoulos *Chief Dealer, Money Markets*

Eurocommercial Paper
Head of Trading Procopis Andrianopoulos *Chief Dealer, Money Markets*

Foreign Exchange
Tel: 623 8223
Head of Foreign Exchange David Cooper
Head of Trading Spiros Tsalikidis *Chief Dealer, FX*

Risk Management
Fax: 929 0254
Head of Risk Management Brian Stephens *Treasurer*

Settlement / Clearing
Head of Settlement / Clearing; Back-Office David Cooper

UNITED KINGDOM (+44)   www.euromoneydirectory.com

National Bank of Greece SA (cont)

Administration
Compliance
           John North *Financial Controller*

National Bank of Kuwait (International) plc   Subsidiary Company
13 George Street, London W1H 5PB
Tel: (171) 224 2277 **Fax:** (171) 224 2101 **Telex:** 892348 **Swift:** NBOK BG 2L **Reuters:** NBKM, NBKL, NBKY

Senior Executive Officers
Chairman   Nasser Musaed Abdull Sayer
Managing Director   Robert Eid

Others (Senior Executives)
           Graham Ziegler *General Manager*
           Ibrahim Shukri Dabdoub *Vice Chairman*
Institutional Banking   Andrew Connor *Senior Manager*
Head of Marketing   David Tyler *Senior Manager*

General-Lending (DCM, SL)
Head of Corporate Banking   Howard Haines *Senior Manager, Corporate Banking*

General - Treasury
Head of Treasury   Randa Sadik *Treasurer*

Debt Capital Markets / Fixed Income
Eurobonds
Head of Trading   Richard Burnell *Senior Dealer*

Syndicated Lending
Loan-Related Activities
Trade Finance   Perry Scott *Senior Manager*
Structured Trade Finance   David Tyler *Senior Manager*

Money Markets
Money Markets - General
Head of Trading   Richard Leem-Bruggen *Senior Dealer*

Foreign Exchange
Head of Trading   Tony Wilkins *Chief Dealer*

Other Departments
Chief Credit Officer   Graham Parker *Assistant General Manager*
Private Banking   Abdel Aziz El Gendy *Senior Manager*

Administration
Head of Marketing   David Tyler *Senior Manager*

Technology & Systems
           Graham Goble *Executive Manager*

Other (Administration)
Special Projects   Gopal N Sundaram *Executive Manager*

National Bank of Nigeria Limited   Representative Office
62 Pymers Mead, Croxted Road, London SE21 8NH
Tel: (181) 761 5341 **Fax:** (181) 766 7897

Senior Executive Officers
Chief Representative   T A Ogunyale

National Bank of Pakistan
18 Finsbury Circus, London EC2M 7BJ
Tel: (171) 588 1511 **Fax:** (171) 638 7869 **Telex:** 883398

Senior Executive Officers
Regional Chief Executive Europe   Mohammad Iqbal Kazi ☎ **628 8821** 📠 **256 7003**

1822 Euromoney Directory 1999

www.euromoneydirectory.com UNITED KINGDOM (+44)

National Commercial Bank Jamaica
42 Manchester Street, London W1M 5PE
Tel: (171) 935 5873 Fax: (171) 935 5761 Reuters: BPHK-L

Senior Executive Officers
General Manager — Paulette Simpson

The National Commercial Bank   Representative Office
3rd Floor, 78 Cornhill, London EC3V 3QQ
Tel: (171) 283 4233 Fax: (171) 929 4373; (171) 621 9587

Senior Executive Officers
Chief Representative — Jinx Grafftey-Smith

Others (Senior Executives)
Assistant Representative — Kuthier Shihab

National Westminster Bank plc   Head Office
Alternative trading name: NatWest Group
41 Lothbury, London EC2P 2BP
Tel: (171) 726 1000

Senior Executive Officers
Chairman — Lord Alexander of Weedon QC
Deputy Chairman — Sidney Lipworth
Deputy Chairman — Sir David Rowland
Chief Executive Officer — Derek Wanless *Group Chief Executive*
Financial Director — Richard Delbridge *Group Chief Financial Officer*
Chief Operating Officer — Bernard Horn *Chief Executive, Group Operations*
Company Secretary — Peter Hammonds

Others (Senior Executives)
Terrence Collis *Director, Corporate Affairs*

NationsBank NA   Full Branch Office
New Broad Street House, 35 New Broad Street, London EC2N 1NH
Tel: (171) 282 2200 Fax: (171) 282 2201 Telex: 883938

Debt Capital Markets / Fixed Income
Head of Debt Capital Markets — Ivan Marcotte *Head, Capital Markets*

Nationwide Building Society
Nationwide House, Pipers Way, Swindon, Wiltshire SN38 1NW
Tel: (1793) 455 678 Fax: (1793) 455 045
Website: www.nationwide.co.uk

Senior Executive Officers
Chairman — Charles Nunneley
Chief Executive Officer — Brian Davis
Financial Director — Alistair Dales *Group Finance Director*
Group Secretary & Solicitor — Charles Wilson

Administration
Head of Marketing — Mike Lozenby *Divisional Director*

Technology & Systems
Francis Walsh *Divisional Director*

Public Relations
Jeremy Del Stromier *Divisional Director, Communications*
Kevin Chapple *Information Officer, External Affairs*

UNITED KINGDOM (+44)   www.euromoneydirectory.com

Natwest Global Financial Markets
Head Office

Formerly known as: Natwest Markets Treasury
135 Bishopsgate, London EC2M 3XT
Tel: (171) 334 1000 Fax: (171) 375 8732
Website: www.natwestgfm.com

Senior Executive Officers
Chief Executive Officer Stephan Harris *Chief Executive Officer & Group Treasurer*
Treasurer Richard Goddin
MD & Global Head, Forex Howard Kurz
Managing Director & Global Head of Sales Peter Nielson

Equity Capital Markets
Tel: 375 5000

Equity Repo / Securities Lending
Marketing & Product Development Alan High *Associate Director* ☎ 375 8886

Money Markets
Head of Money Markets Brian Larkman

Risk Management

Other (FI Derivatives)
Interest Rate Derivatives Roy Lambden *Head*

Other Currency Swap / FX Options Personnel
Currency Options Luke Ding *Head*

Administration

Corporate Communications
Chris Oglethorpe *Head* ☎ 375 4820 ℻ 334 1139

NCL Investments Limited
Head Office

Bartlett House, 9/12 Basinghall Street, London EC2V 5NS
Tel: (171) 600 2801 Fax: (171) 726 6201 Telex: 885893

Senior Executive Officers
Chairman & Chief Executive Christopher Lyttelton ☎ 600 2801
Financial Director Susan Dignum *Finance Director* ☎ 600 2801

Debt Capital Markets / Fixed Income

Non-Domestic Government Bonds
Anthony Hellman *Director, Fixed Interest* ☎ 600 0331

Eurobonds
Head of Sales Anthony Hellman *Director, Fixed Interest* ☎ 600 0331

Equity Capital Markets

Domestic Equities
Head of Trading Dominic Sullivan ☎ 600 2801

Foreign Exchange
Head of Trading Graham Weal ☎ 600 2801

Settlement / Clearing
Equity Settlement; Fixed-Income Settlement; Derivatives Settlement; Foreign Exchange Settlement Richard Nunn

Administration

Technology & Systems
Richard Lowrie

Compliance
Rex Thornborough *Compliance Officer*

Nedcor Bank Limited
Full Branch Office

Alternative trading name: Nedbank
Nedcor House, 29-33 Bucks Road, Douglas, Isle of Man IM1 3DD
Tel: (1624) 612 893 Fax: (1624) 612 836 Telex: 628556 NEDBK G Email: nedbank@enterprise.net

Senior Executive Officers
Assistant General Manager Douglas M Sutherland

1824 Euromoney Directory 1999

www.euromoneydirectory.comUNITED KINGDOM (+44)

Nedcor Bank Limited
Full Branch Office

Alternative trading name: Nedbank
20 Abchurch Lane, London EC4N 7AD
Tel: (171) 623 1077 **Fax:** (171) 621 9304 **Telex:** 886208 **Swift:** NED GB 2L **Reuters:** NEDL

Senior Executive Officers
*General Manager, London Branch*Michael Byrne ☎ 203 4200
*GM, Overseas Operations*Frank Le Roex ☎ 203 4202

Syndicated Lending
*Head of Syndication*Andrew Garden *Senior Manager* ☎ 203 4204

Loan-Related Activities
*Trade Finance*Michael Byrne *General Manager, London Branch* ☎ 203 4200
*Structured Trade Finance*Andrew Garden *Senior Manager* ☎ 203 4204

Other (Trade Finance)
*Forfaiting*Denis Keenlyside *Head* ☎ 203 4258 F 626 6893
Terry Rust *Deputy Head* ☎ 203 4240 F 626 6893

Money Markets
Tel: 623 1324 **Fax:** 623 1329
*Country Head*Graham Hardy *Manager, Treasury* ☎ 203 4210

Wholesale Deposits
*Marketing; Head of Sales*Graham Hardy *Manager, Treasury* ☎ 203 4210

Foreign Exchange
*Country Head*Graham Hardy *Manager, Treasury* ☎ 203 4210
*Head of Institutional Sales; Corporate Sales*Stephen Green *Manager, Treasury* ☎ 203 4211

FX Traders / Sales People
Fwd Rand
*Spot Rand*Nick Freitag *FX Dealer* ☎ 203 4214
*US$ / GBP, GBP / DMk*Perry Ives *FX Dealer* ☎ 203 4214
Stephen McManus *FX Dealer* ☎ 203 4214

Risk Management
*Country Head*Pat Bushnell *Treasury, Risk Controller* ☎ 203 4220

Settlement / Clearing
*Country Head*Denis Poultney *Manager, Finance & Operations* ☎ 203 4235
*Fixed-Income Settlement*Pat Bushnell *Treasury, Risk Controller* ☎ 203 4220
*Derivatives Settlement; Foreign Exchange Settlement*Pat Bushnell *Head, Treasury Administration* ☎ 203 4220

Administration
Technology & Systems
Denis Poultney *Manager, Finance & Operations* ☎ 203 4235

Nedship Bank
Representative Office

108 Cannon Street, London EC4N 6EU
Tel: (171) 280 3180 **Fax:** (171) 334 9230

Senior Executive Officers
Others (Senior Executives)
*Manager*Helen J Tveitan-de Jong

New Japan Securities Europe Limited
Subsidiary Company

Bracken House, One Friday Street, London EC4M 9JA
Tel: (171) 489 1111 **Fax:** (171) 489 5000 **Telex:** 883066 NJELDN G

Senior Executive Officers
*Managing Director*Kozaburo Miyauchi
*Chief Operating Officer*Kazunari Hakamada *Director*
*Director*Yasutoshi Kitakoga

Debt Capital Markets / Fixed Income
*Regional Head*Yasutoshi Kitakoga *Director*

Domestic Government Bonds
*Head of Sales*Yukiyasu Sugihara
*Head of Trading*Katsunori Tanaka

Non-Domestic Government Bonds
*Japanese Government Bonds*Katsunori Tanaka

Euromoney Directory 1999**1825**

UNITED KINGDOM (+44)   www.euromoneydirectory.com

New Japan Securities Europe Limited (cont)

Eurobonds
Head of Origination; Head of Syndication
Head of Trading
: Kimiko McClellan *Senior Associate Director* ☏ 489 5841 F 489 5005
Katsunori Tanaka

Medium-Term Notes
Head of Origination; Head of Structuring
: Kimiko McClellan *Senior Associate Director* ☏ 489 5841 F 489 5005

Private Placements
Head of Origination
: Kimiko McClellan *Senior Associate Director* ☏ 489 5841 F 489 5005

Fixed-Income Repo
Head of Repo
: Katsunori Tanaka

Equity Capital Markets
Regional Head
: Stephen Richardson *Head, Equity* ☏ 489 5248

Domestic Equities
Head of Trading
: David Cowell ☏ 489 5262

Other (Domestic Equities)
: John Aviss

International Equities
Head of Trading
: David Cowell ☏ 489 5262

Other (International Equity)
: S Tsuji
Y Horikawa
H Maeda
K Masuda
Y Saku

Equity Research
Regional Head
: Stephen Richardson *Head, Equity* ☏ 489 5248

Other (Equity Research)
: John Marshall

Warrants
Head of Sales; Head of Trading; Head of Research
: Takako Hino

Risk Management

Other (Exchange-Traded Derivatives)
: Yasutoshi Kitakoga *Director*
Ken Hobson
Kevin Dolby
Donna Smith
Robert Hill

Settlement / Clearing
Tel: (171) 489 5121
Settlement (General)
: Takako Takano
Stephen Kelly
Roberta King
Jane Onslow

Operations
: Kazunari Hakamada *Director*

Administration

Compliance
: Charles Weston *Head, Compliance* ☏ 489 5854

NIBI Asset Management Limited   Bank Subsidiary

Nedcor House, Bucks Road, Douglas, Isle of Man IM1 3DD
Tel: (1624) 630 300; (1624) 630 303 **Fax:** (1624) 625 469 **Email:** nib-int@enterprise.net

Senior Executive Officers

Others (Senior Executives)
: Lloyd Jones *Director* ☏ (171) 203 4266
Andrew V Lodge *Director*
Douglas N Sutherland *Director*
Andy N Ellard *Director*

Administration
Head of Administration
: Andy N Ellard *Head of Administration*

1826 Euromoney Directory 1999

www.euromoneydirectory.com UNITED KINGDOM (+44)

The Nikko Bank (UK) plc
Subsidiary Company

17 Godliman Street, London EC4V 5NB
Tel: (171) 528 7070 **Fax:** (171) 528 7077 **Telex:** 928703 **Swift:** NIKO GB 2L **Reuters:** NIKO-P

Senior Executive Officers
Chairman	John Anderson
Chief Executive Officer	Akira Hirano
Chief Operating Officer	Roy Degenhardt
Treasurer	Roger Guest *Treasurer*
Managing Director	Michael Collis
Managing Director	Barrie Smith
Financial Controller & Company Secretary	Malcolm A Edwards

Others (Senior Executives)
Paul Walton *Chief Credit Officer*
Graham Watts *General Manager, Operations*

Syndicated Lending
Global Head — Michael Collis *Managing Director*
Head of Syndication — Robert White *Director*
Head of Credit Committee — Paul Walton *Chief Credit Officer*

Loan-Related Activities
Project Finance — Michael Moseling *MD, Project Finance*
Leasing & Asset Finance — Paul Oliver *MD, Leasing*

Money Markets
Tel: 329 4447
Global Head — Charles Edwards *Chief Dealer, Money Markets*

Wholesale Deposits
Marketing — Michael Low *Head, Treasury Sales* ☎ **236 2151**

Foreign Exchange
Tel: 329 4447
Head of Foreign Exchange — Roger Guest *Treasurer*
Spot / Forwards Trading — Geoff Swain *Chief Dealer*
David Hastings *Senior Dealer*

Risk Management
Global Head — Akira Shiose *Senior Manager, Middle Office*

Corporate Finance / M&A Advisory
Head of Corporate Finance — Michael Collis *Managing Director*

Other (Corporate Finance)
Robert White *Director*

Settlement / Clearing
Regional Head — Martyn Liston *Manager, Settlements*
Operations — Graham Watts *General Manager, Operations*

Asset Management
Head — Barrie Smith *Managing Director*

Administration
Head of Administration — Peter Knight *Manager*

Technology & Systems
Head, IT — Harumi Watanabe

Legal / In-House Counsel
Moreton Hall

Compliance
Graham Watts *General Manager, Operations*

Accounts / Audit
Malcolm A Edwards *Financial Controller & Company Secretary*

Nikko Europe plc
Subsidiary Company

55 Victoria Street, London SW1H 0EU
Tel: (171) 799 2222 **Fax:** (171) 222 3130; (171) 222 4035 **Telex:** 884617 **Reuters:** NIKA **Cable:** NIKOSE

Senior Executive Officers
Co-Chairman	Michel de Carvalho
Co-Chairman	T Osada
Vice Chairman	H Fukuda
Chief Executive Officer	G Yamaguchi *Joint CEO*

UNITED KINGDOM (+44)   www.euromoneydirectory.com

Nikko Europe plc (cont)
Senior Executive Officers (cont)

	B Berry *Joint CEO*
MD, Business Control / Admin Division / Company Sec	A Furuno

General-Lending (DCM, SL)
Head of Corporate Banking
H Wakutsu *MD, Financial Products Group*
F Robert *MD, Financial Products Group*

General - Treasury
Head of Treasury — D McClean

Debt Capital Markets / Fixed Income
Department: Capital Markets Division
Global Head — P Brown *Managing Director*
Regional Head — R Paice *Managing Director*
Country Head — N Morant *Managing Director*

Fixed-Income Repo
Head of Repo; Marketing & Product Development — Andrew Davis *Treasurer* ☎ **222 7738** ℻ **222 4039** ✉ **andrew.davis@nikko.uk**
Sales — Margot Lyons *Product Manager* ✉ **margot.lyons@nikko.uk**

Equity Capital Markets
Tel: 222 2144 Fax: 222 1308

Equity Repo / Securities Lending
Marketing & Product Development — Greg Patel *Product Manager* Bisera Regenstein
Bisera Regenstein

Syndicated Lending
Department: Syndicate Division
Country Head — G Yamaguchi *Joint CEO*

Money Markets
Department: Money Markets & Fixed-Income Division
Global Head — K Yoshibayashi *Managing Director*
Regional Head — P Busfield *Managing Director*
Country Head — B Tweddle *Managing Director*

Risk Management
Global Head — N Hoga *MD, Risk & Return Management Division*

Settlement / Clearing
Operations — K Tamura *MD, Planning Division, European HQ*

Other Departments
Economic Research — S Briscoe *Managing Director*

Administration
Head of Administration — A Furuno *MD, Business Control / Admin Division / Company Sec*

Corporate Communications
M Wallis *Director*

Other (Administration)
Information Systems Division — J Iwasaki *Managing Director*

The Nippon Credit Bank Limited   Representative Office

City Tower, 40 Basinghall Street, London EC2V 5DE
Tel: (171) 920 4000 Fax: (171) 920 0501 Telex: 893273 NCBLDN G

Senior Executive Officers
General Manager — Jinichi Yamaguchi

Nippon Credit International Limited   Subsidiary Company

City Tower, 40 Basinghall Street, London EC2V 5DE
Tel: (171) 825 2000 Fax: (171) 638 3460 Telex: 967861

Senior Executive Officers
Chief Executive Officer — David Weinberg
Managing Director — Junji Hayashi ☎ **825 2001**

Debt Capital Markets / Fixed Income
Fixed-Income Repo
Head of Repo; Trading — Jo Williams *Head of Repo* ☎ **374 0418**

www.euromoneydirectory.com UNITED KINGDOM (+44)

NMB - Heller Limited
Head Office

Formerly known as: Trade Indemnity-Heller Commercial Finance Limited
Park House, Park Street, Croydon, Surrey CR9 1RD
Tel: (181) 256 1200 Fax: (181) 686 1661; (181) 680 2117

Senior Executive Officers
Chief Executive Officer
Financial Director
Managing Director

Stuart Parker *Chief Executive*
Robin Archibald *Finance Director*
Allan Walker

Others (Senior Executives)

Tim Hawkins *Associate Director*

Noble Grossart Limited

48 Queen Street, Edinburgh, EH2 3NR
Tel: (131) 226 7011 Fax: (131) 226 6032

Senior Executive Officers
Financial Director
Managing Director

Brian Dick
Angus Grossart

General-Lending (DCM, SL)
Head of Corporate Banking

Christopher Smith *Banking Director*

Corporate Finance / M&A Advisory
Head of Corporate Finance

Ewan Brown *Director, Corporate Finance*
David Mathewson *Director, Corporate Finance*
Guy Stenhouse *Director, Corporate Finance*
Craig Armour *Director, Corporate Finance*
Sally Grossart *Director, Corporate Finance*

Nomura Asset Management (UK) Limited

Nomura House, 1 St Martin's-le-Grand, London EC1A 4NT
Tel: (171) 521 3333; (171) 521 1111 Fax: (171) 521 3330 Telex: 934015 Email: jen-middleton@msn.com
Administration Tel: 521 1341
Website: www.nomura-asset.com

Senior Executive Officers
Chairman
President
Chief Executive Officer
Financial Director
Managing Director / General Manager

Hitoshi Tonomura ☎ +81 (3) 3281 2903 ℻ +81 (3) 3281 2884
Tadashi Takubo
Atsushi Kinebuchi *Senior Managing Director*
Naotake Hirasawa
H Miyako

General-Investment
Head of Investment

Richard Bisson *Head of Unit Trust Investment* ☎ 521 3329
Richard Minors *Senior Portfolio Manager*

Debt Capital Markets / Fixed Income
Bonds - General
Head of Fixed Income Investment

Yoshiake Okabe *Senior Portfolio Manager* ☎ 521 1363

Equity Capital Markets
Other (Domestic Equities)
UK Equity Investment

Richard Bisson *Director* ℻ 796 1246

Asset Management
Other (Asset Management)
Portfolio Administration

Karen Pateman *Manager* ☎ 521 1372

Administration
Head of Administration

Shinzou Kataoa *Chief Administrative Officer*

Compliance

Nigel Biggs *Compliance Officer*

Other (Administration)
Marketing

Mark Petheram *Senior Manager* ☎ 521 1344

Euromoney Directory 1999 **1829**

UNITED KINGDOM (+44)   www.euromoneydirectory.com

Nomura Bank International plc
Head Office

Nomura House, 1 St Martin's-le-Grand, London EC1A 4NP
Tel: (171) 521 2000 **Fax:** (171) 626 0851 **Telex:** 9413063/4 **Swift:** NBIL GB 2L

Senior Executive Officers
Non-Executive Chairman	Brian Quinn
President	Masayuki Fujii
Chief Executive Officer	Masayuki Fujii *President*
Treasurer	Egbertus Suer *Head of Treasury*
Managing Director	Michael Williams
Company Secretary	William Pamment ☎ 521 3847 📠 521 3633

Debt Capital Markets / Fixed Income
Libor-Based / Floating-Rate Products
Asset Swaps; Asset Swaps (Sales)   Shinya Yokoyama

Medium-Term Notes
Head of Sales   M Fujii

Syndicated Lending
Head of Trading   Michael Williams *Managing Director*
Head of Credit Committee   David Stewart *Head of Credit*

Loan-Related Activities
Trade Finance   Jeremy McGahan
Project Finance   Michael Williams *Managing Director*

Money Markets
Head of Money Markets   Lee Palmer *Head*

Foreign Exchange
Head of Foreign Exchange   Michael Cornford *Head*

Risk Management
Head of Risk Management   Geoffrey Booth *Head of Risk Management*

Other Currency Swap / FX Options Personnel
    W Rattay *Senior Manager*

Exotic Options (Barriers, Range, Timers, Digitals, Faders etc)
Sales; Trading   W Rattay *Senior Manager*

Settlement / Clearing
Head of Settlement / Clearing   Donald Pearman *Head of Settlements*
Operations; Back-Office   Michael Tolliday *Head of Operations*

Administration
Legal / In-House Counsel
    Louise Desborough *Senior Executive Officer*

Compliance
    Michael Burgess *Compliance Officer*

Accounts / Audit
Internal Audit   Peggy McMonagle-Duncan *Head*
Head of Financial Control   William Pamment ☎ 521 3847 📠 521 3633

Nomura International plc
Head Office

Nomura House, 1 St Martin's-le-Grand, London EC1A 4NP
Tel: (171) 521 2000 **Fax:** (171) 521 2121 **Telex:** 883119 **Swift:** NOMA GB 2L **Reuters:** NOML
Website: www.nomura.co.uk

Senior Executive Officers
Chairman & Chief Executive	Max Chapman
President	Takumi Shibata
Chief Executive Officer	Max Chapman *Chairman & Chief Executive*
	Takashi Tsutsui
Financial Director	N Alicabiotis *Chief Financial & Administrative Officer*
	Kengi Yokoyama
Managing Director	Guy Hands ☎ 521 2000 📠 521 3565
Managing Director / General Manager	S Fry

General - Treasury
Head of Treasury   Eizo Nakatsukasa

Relationship Manager
Principal Finance Group   John W B Butterworth ☎ 521 1270 📠 521 1119

1830   Euromoney Directory 1999

UNITED KINGDOM (+44)

Debt Capital Markets / Fixed Income
Tel: 454 0469 Fax: 521 2053

Fixed-Income Repo
Head of Repo
Head of Repo; Marketing & Product Development
Marketing & Product Development
Trading

Stuart Neie *Head of Repo Desk* ☎ **454 0469**
James Tomkinson *Head of Repo Desk* ☎ **521 2766**
✉ james.tomkinson@nomura.co.uk
Rafy Kouyoumjian ☎ **521 1068** ✉ rafy.kouyoumjian@nomura.co.uk
Mike Speight *Repo Derivatives*
Richard Casey *Repo Trader*
Brian Fenton *Repo Trader*
Andrew Pritchard *Repo Trader*
David Hill *Repo Trader*
Emilianos Katsaros *Repo Trader*
Sarah Anthony *Head of Repo Sales*
O'Neill Sharma *Repo Sales*

Equity Capital Markets
Tel: 606 2919 Fax: 521 2683
Global Head

Michael Boardman *Director* ☎ **521 2000** 📠 **521 2618**
✉ michael.boardman@nomura.co.uk

Domestic Equities
Head of Syndication

Andrew Bungard *Deputy Managing Director* ☎ **521 2000** 📠 **521 3651**
✉ andrew.bungard@nomura.co.uk

Equity Repo / Securities Lending
Head
Marketing & Product Development

Mark Tidy *Head of Equity Finance* ☎ **521 3928** ✉ mark.tidy@nomura.co.uk
Sean Leonard *Product Manager*
Barry Whitnell *Sales Executive*
Siobhan Young *Marketing Assistant*

Marketing; Head of Prime Brokerage
Head of Trading

Mark Tidy *Head of Equity Finance* ☎ **521 3928** ✉ mark.tidy@nomura.co.uk
John Foley *Trader*
Phil Gottlick *Trader*
Jonathan Cossey *Desk Manager*
Shinichi Yasuda *Japanese Liaison*
Jagdish Hirani *Manager, Equity Finance*
Dominique Valansot *Analyst*
Mohit Dhawan *Trader*

Administration
Head of Administration

Geoff Doubleday *Chief Administrative Officer*

Technology & Systems

Geoff Doubleday *Chief Administrative Officer*

Norddeutsche Landesbank Girozentrale — Full Branch Office

71 Queen Victoria Street, London EC4V 4NL
Tel: (171) 972 5400 Fax: (171) 972 5454 Telex: 290909 Reuters: NLBL

Senior Executive Officers
Treasurer
General Manager

Bruce Gresswell *Senior Manager, Treasurer*
Benedikt Koehler

Debt Capital Markets / Fixed Income
Tel: 454 1280

Libor-Based / Floating-Rate Products
FRN Origination; Asset Swaps

Dirk Schlademann *Manager, Capital Markets & Derivatives*

Medium-Term Notes
Head of Origination

Dirk Schlademann *Manager, Capital Markets & Derivatives*

Syndicated Lending
Loan-Related Activities
Project Finance

John Omond *Deputy General Manager*

Money Markets
Tel: 454 1280
Country Head

Colin Barnes *Manager, Money Markets & Forex*

Foreign Exchange
Tel: 454 1280
Country Head

Colin Barnes *Manager, Money Markets & Forex*

Risk Management
Country Head

Gerd Ruscher *Deputy General Manager*

Corporate Finance / M&A Advisory
Country Head

John Omond *Deputy General Manager*

UNITED KINGDOM (+44) www.euromoneydirectory.com

Norddeutsche Landesbank Girozentrale (cont)
Settlement / Clearing
Country Head Jacky Shepherd *Manager, Settlements*

Norinchukin International plc
Subsidiary Company

1st Floor, 4 Broadgate, London EC2M 2AE
Tel: (171) 588 6593 **Fax:** (171) 588 6586 **Telex:** 936122 **Email:** info@noil.w.uk **Reuters:** NOIL **Bloomberg:** JGB
Website: www.noil.co.uk

Senior Executive Officers
Chairman Toyomu Ueki
Managing Director Keiichi Takeshita
Chief Executive Officer Akihiko Kabe *Deputy Managing Director*
Financial Director Yuji Shimauchi *Deputy Managing Director*
Managing Director Keiichi Takeshita

Debt Capital Markets / Fixed Income
Head of Fixed Income Sales; Head of Fixed Income Trading Michimasa Soga *Executive Director*

Government Bonds
Head of Sales; Head of Trading Michimasa Soga *Executive Director*
Head of Syndication Masaki Furuya *Executive Director*

Eurobonds
Head of Syndication Masaki Furuya *Executive Director*
Head of Sales Michimasa Soga *Executive Director*
Head of Trading Michimasa Soga *Senior Executive Director*

Libor-Based / Floating-Rate Products
FRN Trading Quentin Backhouse *Associate Director*

Fixed-Income Repo
Head of Repo; Marketing & Product Development; Head of Trading Michimasa Soga *Executive Director*

Fixed-Income Research
Head of Fixed Income Stuart Trow *Senior Manager*

Risk Management
Global Head Darren Emptage *Senior Manager, Middle Office*

Fixed Income Derivatives / Risk Management
Head of Sales; Trading Osamu Takashima *Senior Executive Director*

Corporate Finance / M&A Advisory
Head of Corporate Finance Christen Mørch *Associate Director*

Settlement / Clearing
Department: Operation Department
Head of Settlement / Clearing Susan Riches *Assistant Manager*

Global Custody
Head of Global Custody Susan Riches *Assistant Manager*

Administration
Head of Administration Yoko Stark *Senior Manager*

Technology & Systems
 William Purdy *Associate Director*

Compliance
 Matthew Dunster *Compliance Manager*

Accounts / Audit
 David Court *Assistant Manager*

Northern Bank Limited
Head Office

PO Box 183, Donegall Square West, Belfast, Northern Ireland BT1 6JS
Tel: (1232) 245 277 **Fax:** (1232) 893 214 **Telex:** 747674 **Swift:** NORB GB 2B
Website: www.northern-bank.co.uk

Senior Executive Officers
Chairman David Fell
Chief Executive Officer Grahame Savage *Chief Executive*
Financial Director Jo Anderson *Head of Finance*
Chief Operating Officer Don Price
General Manager W K Doonan
Secretary J E Stevenson

1832 Euromoney Directory 1999

www.euromoneydirectory.com UNITED KINGDOM (+44)

Senior Executive Officers (cont)
International Division David Hume *Manager, Treasury & International*
Others (Senior Executives)
Gerry McSorley *Head of Marketing*
D R Argus *Director*
Michael Boyd *Head of Regional Lending*
John Canning *Head of Branch Banking*
Kevin Brown *Head of Management Services*
Mervyn Brown *Head of Financial Services*

Syndicated Lending
Head of Syndicated Lending David Hume *Manager, Treasury & International*
Corporate Finance / M&A Advisory
Global Head Tim G Blake *Head*
Other Departments
Commodities / Bullion J W Cree *Manager*
Administration
Head of Marketing Gerry McSorley *Head of Marketing*
Other (Administration)
Human Resources David Keys *Head of Human Resources*

The Northern Trust Company Full Branch Office

155 Bishopsgate, London EC2M 3XS
Tel: (171) 628 2233; (171) 675 8100 **Fax:** (171) 982 5200 **Telex:** 884 641 **Swift:** CNOR GB 22 **Email:** atol@ntrs.com
Cable: NORTRUST LONDON
Website: www.ntrs.com

Senior Executive Officers
Chairman William Osborn
President Barry Hastings
Chief Executive Officer William Osborn
Financial Director Perry Pero *Chief Financial Officer*
Chief Operating Officer Barry Hastings
General Manager, London Branch Mark Van Grinsven
Others (Senior Executives)
Penelope Biggs *Head of Sales & Marketing* T 982 5311 F 982 5434
E **pb9@ntrs.com**

Debt Capital Markets / Fixed Income
Fixed-Income Repo
Head of Repo Kevin Rochford *Senior Vice President* T 982 5111 F 982 5443
E **kr4@ntrs.com**
Marketing & Product Development Trevor St John *Vice President* T 982 5292 F 982 5185 E tas7@ntrs.com
Matthew Matejka *Officer* T 982 7550 F 982 5443 E mm9@ntbs.com
Head of Trading Yvonne Connors *Vice President*
Trading Andy Clayton *Vice President & Head of Securities Lending*
John Irwin *Equity Trader & Officer*
Tony Herrigan *Equity Trader & Officer*
Robert Weeks *Fixed Income Trader & Officer*
Lesley Hodgson *Second Vice President & Senior Cash Portfolio Mana*
Jaqueline Waller *Cash Portfolio Manager & Officer*
Sales Linda Kearney *Vice President* T 982 5167 F 982 5443 E lmk4@ntbs.com
Equity Capital Markets
Fax: 982 5188
Equity Repo / Securities Lending
Head Kevin Rochford *Senior Vice President* T 982 5111 F 982 5443
E **kr4@ntrs.com**
Marketing & Product Development Linda Kearney *Vice President* T 982 5167 F 982 5443 E lmk4@ntbs.com
Matthew Matejka *Officer* T 982 7550 F 982 5443 E mm9@ntbs.com
Trevor St John *Vice President* T 982 5292 F 982 5185 E tas7@ntrs.com
Marketing Linda Kearney *Vice President* T 982 5167 F 982 5443 E lmk4@ntbs.com
Head of Trading Andrew Clayton *Vice President*
John Irwin *Equity Trader & Officer*
George Trapp *Fixed Income*

Foreign Exchange
Head of Foreign Exchange Peter Gloyne *SVP, FX and Treasury*
Head of Institutional Sales; Corporate Sales Cyril Teasdale *VP, FX & Treasury*
Head of Trading Peter Gloyne *SVP, FX and Treasury*

Euromoney Directory 1999 **1833**

UNITED KINGDOM (+44) www.euromoneydirectory.com

The Northern Trust Company (cont)
Global Custody
Head of Global Custody   Mark Van Grinsven *General Manager, London Branch*

Other (Global Custody)
Canada   John Pike *President Toronto* ☏ +1 (416) 365 7161 📠 +1 (416) 365 9484
 ✉ jrp1@ntrs.com
Europe, Middle East and Africa   Penelope Biggs *Head of Sales & Marketing* ☏ 982 5311 📠 982 5434
 ✉ pb9@ntrs.com
Asia   Jeff Conover *Head of Sales & Marketing* ☏ +65 437 6601 📠 +65 437 6609
 ✉ jwc2@ntrs.com
United States of America   Steve Fradkin *Head of Sales & Marketing* ☏ +1 (312) 444 2292
 📠 +1 (312) 444 5258 ✉ slf2@ntrs.com

Nova Ljubljanska banka dd
Representative Office

65/66 Queen Street, London EC4R 1EB
Tel: (171) 329 2828 **Fax:** (171) 489 0166

Senior Executive Officers
Chief Representative   Borut Stanic ✉ nlblondon@dial.pipex.com

OMLX - The London Securities & Derivatives Exchange
Head Office

107 Cannon Street, London EC4N 5AD
Tel: (171) 283 0678 **Fax:** (171) 815 8508 **Reuters:** OMCA
Website: www.omgroup.com

Senior Executive Officers
Chairman   Per Larsson
Chief Executive Officer   Peter Cox

Risk Management
Exchange-Traded Derivatives
Regional Head   Michael Eaton *Head Exchange Broker*

Settlement / Clearing
Tel: 815 8525 **Fax:** 815 8544
Derivatives Settlement   Lee Betsill *Clearing Manager* ☏ 815 8524

Administration
Technology & Systems
     Paul Dye *Systems Manager* ☏ 815 8511

Compliance
     Derek Oliver *Director, Legal Affairs*

Public Relations
     Xavier Bruchert *Director, Marketing* ☏ 283 0678

Osmanli Bankasi AS
Representative Office

King William House, 2A Eastcheap, London EC3M 1AA
Tel: (171) 626 5932 **Fax:** (171) 626 2337

Senior Executive Officers
Adviser to the Chairman   G J Warren ✉ g.warren@osmanli.co.uk

Oversea-Chinese Banking Corporation Limited

111 Cannon Street, London EC4N 5AS
Tel: (171) 337 8822 **Fax:** (171) 283 8538 **Telex:** 885148 OCB LDN

Senior Executive Officers
Managing Director / General Manager   Tiong Seng Wee

www.euromoneydirectory.com　　　　　　UNITED KINGDOM (+44)

Overseas Trust Bank Limited

10 Angel Court, London EC2R 7ES
Tel: (171) 606 1616 Fax: (171) 606 2900 Telex: 887756 DHBOTB

Senior Executive Officers
Financial Director　　　　　　　　　　W R Dobbie
Managing Director / General Manager　　B J A Whitworth

Overseas Union Bank Limited

61/62 Coleman Street, London EC2P 2EU
Tel: (171) 782 0053 Fax: (171) 782 0025 Telex: 884413

Senior Executive Officers
President　　　　　　　　　　　　　　Yew Hon Chow

PaineWebber International Bank Limited　　Subsidiary Company

1 Finsbury Avenue, London EC2M 2NA
Tel: (171) 422 2000 Fax: (171) 247 2050 Telex: 295088 PWBNK G

Senior Executive Officers
Chief Executive Officer　　　　　　　Brian Tuck *Chief Executive*

Others (Senior Executives)

　　　　　　　　　　　　　　　　　Mary Chadwick *Director*
　　　　　　　　　　　　　　　　　William H Bruett *Chairman & Non-Executive Director*
　　　　　　　　　　　　　　　　　John A Bult *Non-Executive Director*
　　　　　　　　　　　　　　　　　Walter S Elliot *Non-Executive Director*
　　　　　　　　　　　　　　　　　Dennis J Hess *Non-Executive Director*
　　　　　　　　　　　　　　　　　William J Nolan *Non-Executive Director*
Company Secretary　　　　　　　　Alan Reilly *Non-Executive Director*

General - Treasury
Head of Treasury　　　　　　　　　P Nicolaides *Treasury*
Department: Banking Services

Others (Senior Executives)

　　　　　　　　　　　　　　　　　Paul Osbourne *Manager*
　　　　　　　　　　　　　　　　　Tony Bird
　　　　　　　　　　　　　　　　　Robert Robert *Birmingham*

Pangaea Partners (UK) Limited　　Subsidiary Company

29 Abingdon Road, London W8 6AH
Tel: (171) 376 9890 Fax: (171) 938 1649 Email: 101501.3436@compuserve.com
Website: www.pangaeapartners.com

Senior Executive Officers
Managing Director　　　　　　　　Eric Postel

Paribas　　Full Branch Office

Formerly known as: Banque Paribas
Alternative trading name: Paribas UK Limited
10 Harewood Avenue, London NW1 6AA
Tel: (171) 595 2000 Fax: (171) 595 2555 Telex: 296723 PARCAPG
Website: www.paribas.com

Senior Executive Officers
Chief Executive Officer　　　　　　Robert de Metz [T] 595 6105 [F] 595 5006 [E] robert_demetz@paribas.com

General-Lending (DCM, SL)
Head of Corporate Banking　　　　Pascal Boris [T] 595 4997 [E] pascal_boris@paribas.com

Debt Capital Markets / Fixed Income
Global Head　　　　　　　　　　　Alec de Lézardière [E] alec_delezardiere@paribas.com
　　　　　　　　　　　　　　　　　Joe Dryer [E] joe_dryer@paribas.com
Marketing　　　　　　　　　　　　Cyrus Ardalan *Global Head* [T] 595 8699 [E] cyrus_ardalan@paribas.com
Head of Fixed Income Sales　　　　Bruno Cappuccini *Head* [T] 595 8908 [E] bruno_cappuccini@paribas.com
Head of Fixed Income Trading　　　Andrew Pisker *Global Head* [T] 595 2866 [E] andrew_pisker@paribas.com

UNITED KINGDOM (+44)   www.euromoneydirectory.com

Paribas (cont)

Government Bonds
Head of Trading — Bob Hawley *Global Head* E **bob_hawley@paribas.com**

Emerging Market Bonds
Head — Luc Cardyn *Global Head* E **luc_cardyn@paribas.com**
Head of Sales — Bruno Cappuccini *Head* T **595 8908** E **bruno_cappuccini@paribas.com**

Asset-Backed Securities / Securitization
Global Head — Adrian Carr *Head of Asset Backed Securities* T **595 8222** E **adrian_carr@paribas.com**
Maarten Stegwee *Global Head of Securitisation* T **595 4922** E **maarten_stegwee@paribas.com**

Fixed-Income Repo
Marketing & Product Development — Angela Osborne *Head of Repo Marketing & Sales* T **595 8098** F **595 5055** E **angela_osborne@paribas.com**
Trading — David Butterworth *Bunds* T **595 8644** E **david_butterworth@paribas.com**
Nicholas Williams *Gilts / Ecu* T **595 8644** E **nicholas_williams@paribas.com**
Andrew McArdle *Dkr / SEK / ESP* T **595 8644** E **andrew_mcardle@paribas.com**
Eugene McGrory *USD / Euros* T **595 8098** E **eugene_mcgrory@paribas.com**
Andrew Hill *Lira* T **595 8644** E **andrew_hill@paribas.com**
Simon Parkins *Belgium* T **595 8644** E **simon_parkins@paribas.com**
Sales — Ann Fitzgerald *Repo Sales* T **595 8098** E **ann_fitzgerald@paribas.com**
Marilyn Madella Amadei *Repo Sales* T **595 8098** E **marilyn_amadel@paribas.com**

Fixed-Income Research
Head of Fixed Income — Jean-Michel Lasry *Global Head of Research & Study Team* E **jean-michel_lasry@paribas.com**
Head of Credit Research — Joe Biernat E **joe_biernat@paribas.com**

Equity Capital Markets
Global Head — Tony Bourne T **595 8876** E **tony_bourne@paribas.com**
Head of Trading — Keith Stewart E **keith_stewart@paribas.com**

Other (Domestic Equities)
Equity Brokerage — Peter Beck *Head of Brokerage* T **595 2161** E **peter_beck@paribas.com**

Equity Research
Global Head — Mike Fesemeyer E **mike_fesemeyer@paribas.com**

Convertibles / Equity-Linked
Head of Trading — Guillaume Barrier *Head of Trading* T **595 8674** F **595 5042** E **guillaume_barrier@paribas.com**
Head of Research — Inderjit Bedi *Head of Research* T **595 8280** F **595 5042** E **inderjit.bedi@paribas.com**

Syndicated Lending
Country Head — Pascal Boris T **595 4997** E **pascal_boris@paribas.com**

Foreign Exchange
Head of Foreign Exchange — Loic Meinnel E **loic_meinnel@paribas.com**

Risk Management
Head of Risk Management — Michel Peretie *Global Head of Derivatives & FX* T **595 8055** E **michael_peretie@paribas.com**

Other (FI Derivatives)
Swaps / Interest Rates — Frederic Janbon *Global Head* E **frederic_janbon@paribas.com**

OTC Equity Derivatives
Head — Bernard Oppetit *Global Head* E **bernard_oppetit@paribas.com**

Other (Equity Derivatives)
Derivatives Marketing — Yves Leysen *Global Head* E **yves_leysen@paribas.com**

Corporate Finance / M&A Advisory
Country Head — Pierre-Louis Le Faou T **595 2601** E **pierre-louis_lefaou@paribas.com**

Other (Corporate Finance)
Advisory Services — Pierre-Louis Le Faou T **595 2601** E **pierre-louis_lefaou@paribas.com**

Asset Management
Head — Guy de Froment T **595 3066** E **guy_defromet@paribas.com**

Other Departments
Proprietary Trading — Derek Villaruel *Head* T **595 8004** E **derek_villaruel@paribas.com**
Private Banking — Guy de Froment T **595 3066** E **guy_defromet@paribas.com**

www.euromoneydirectory.com UNITED KINGDOM (+44)

Administration
Head of Administration   Oliver Briens *Head of Finance, Tax & Operations*
                           E oliver_briens@paribas.com
Business Development   Bernard Allorent *Head* E bernard_allorent@paribas.com
Head of Marketing   Monique Amaudry *Head* E monique_amaudry@paribas.com
Technology & Systems
                           Marc Earl T 595 2251 E marc_earl@paribas.com
Legal / In-House Counsel
                           Kevin Sowerbutts T 595 2325 E kevin_sowerbutts@paribas.com
Compliance
                           Peter Haines T 595 2508 E peter_haines@paribas.com
Public Relations
                           Monique Amaudry *Head* E monique_amaudry@paribas.com
Corporate Communications
                           Monique Amaudry *Head* E monique_amaudry@paribas.com
Accounts / Audit
                           Oliver Briens *Head of Finance, Tax & Operations*
                           E oliver_briens@paribas.com
                           Keith Oatway *Head of Finance* E keith_oatway@paribas.com

Other (Administration)
Securities Services   Liz Nolan *Head* E liz_nolan@paribas.com

People's Bank of China   Representative Office

3rd Floor, Bow Bells House, 5 Bread Street, Cheapside, London EC4M 9BQ
Tel: (171) 236 6888 **Fax:** (171) 236 6866

Senior Executive Officers
Chief Representative   Xu Yawen

Philippine National Bank (Europe) plc

Old Change House, 128 Queen Victoria Street, London EC4V 4HR
Tel: (171) 653 1400 **Fax:** (171) 653 1403 **Telex:** 883981

Senior Executive Officers
Managing Director / General Manager   Adonis D Agrasada

Phillips & Drew   Subsidiary Company

Formerly known as: PDFM Limited

Triton Court, 14 Finsbury Square, London EC2A 1PD
Tel: (171) 901 5050 **Fax:** (171) 901 5285 **Telex:** 916961

Senior Executive Officers
Chairman   Paul Meredith
Chief Executive Officer Crispian Collins *Chief Executive*

General-Investment
Head of Investment   Tony Dye *Chief Investment Officer*
                           Robin Apps *Investment & Client Teams*

Administration
Business Development   Paul Yates *Client & Business Development*
Head of Marketing   Rash Patel *Marketing Services* T 901 5375

Other (Administration)
Business Services   Markus Ruetimann

PIMCO Global Advisors (Europe) Limited   Representative Office

Alternative trading name: PIMCO Oppenheimer Capital

Mutual House, 70 Conduit Street, London W1R 9TQ
Tel: (171) 872 1300 **Fax:** (171) 872 1327 **Email:** mcdevitt@pimco.com
Website: www.pimco.com

Senior Executive Officers
Executive Vice President & Head of Europe   Joseph McDevitt T 872 1323

Euromoney Directory 1999 **1837**

PaineWebber International (U.K.) Ltd

SENIOR EXECUTIVE OFFICERS
MICHAEL O'HANLON, SENIOR EXECUTIVE OFFICER; Ian Myers, Chairman, US Equity Broking; Ronnie Dick, Managing Director, Capital Markets & FRNs; Steven Hones, Managing Director, Fixed Income Trading; John Wieland, Chief Financial Officer; Michael Woolf, Managing Director, International Fixed Income Sales;

FIXED INCOME
Eurodollar & Currency Trading
Telephone: (171) 422 2232 **Fax:** (171) 422 2381
Steven Hones; Tony Simcock; Peter Brooks; Tim Annandale; Bobby Bhakar; Scott Chapman; Stefano Cioffi; Scott Crichton; Francesco Degli Espoti; Mick Duff; Christian Evans; Sarah Hallett; Steve Irwin; Paul Lucchesi; David Ramsey;

Emerging Markets
Telephone: (171) 422 2731 **Fax:** (171) 422 2384
Imre Eszenyi; Darren Lefcoe; Brigitte Standing; Karen Thomas; Bruce Whyte

FRNs
Telephone: (171) 422 2603 **Fax:** (171) 422 2390
Ronnie Dick; Ben Nielsen; Andy Slaughter;
Capital Markets & Syndicate
Telephone: (171) 422 2636 **Fax:** (171) 422 2390
Ronnie Dick; Steven Hones; Caroline Bryant; Carlo de Pretis; Nordine Farsi; Francisco Perello; Clare Porter; Darren Smith; Christoph von Mallinckrodt; Jean Theulier:

US Government Trading
Telephone: (171) 422 2521 **Fax:** (171) 422 2381
Tom Mulligan; David Grundy;

Financing & Repo
Telephone: (171) 422 2805 **Fax:** (171) 422 2140
Chris Lamb; Stefano Cioffi; Alison Jenkins; Adrian Terry

Fixed-Income Sales
Telephone: (171) 422 2000 **Fax:** (171) 422 2382
Michael Woolf; Charles Manners; Richard Landsberger; Felicity Layton; Mazin Albayati; Alexandra Bcking; Paul Byers; Matthew Clark; Suzanne Cooke; Michael Ezra; Linda Grud; Monica Guzzi; Rachel Hu; Jonathan Kendall; Paul Kozary; Elisabetta Laurita; Richard Moses; Paolo Novak; Kate Rimmer; Dan Rose-Bristow; Lada Skrablin; pThomas Sugar; Michelle Thompson; Robert Tibbles; Mark Wild;

Mortgage-Backed Securities
Telephone: (171) 422 2530 **Fax:** (171) 422 2384
Paul Heyrman;

Foreign Exchange
Telephone: (171) 422 2400 **Fax:** (171) 247 8923
George Alafouzo; Ian Browring; Tim Hodgins; Alasdair MacDonald; John Murphy; Richard Wynn

Research
Telephone: (171) 422 2900 **Fax:** (171) 422 2393
Alison Cottrell; David Brickman; Ann Creasy; Martin Gallagher; Mark Kozned; Ian Lumb; Anna Nicolau; David Sanderson; Neil Williams

Settlements
Telephone: (171) 422 2266 **Fax:** (171) 216 8131
Mick Moonie

Legal & Compliance
Telephone: (171) 422 2338 **Fax:** (171) 422 2218
Jonathan Rose; Herdeep Dosanjh; Daniel McAleese

1 Finsbury Avenue, London EC2M 2NA, UK
Telephone: (0171) 422 2000 **Facsimile:** (0171) 422 2310 **Telex:** 297361 PWINT G

Geneva
Telephone: (41) 22 849 0749 **Fax:** (41) 22 849 0793
Jules Weinberger; Bruno Buzzi; Michele Boulade; Patrick Knig; Christine Rohrbach;

New York
Telephone: (212) 713 2944 **Fax:** (212) 713 1166
Kerry Stein; Kenny Klein;

Singapore
Telephone: (65) 323 0188 **Fax:** (65) 536 0188
Rafat Rizvi; Paul Devlin; Eunice Khoo; Glen Lau; Chris Mersey; Tommy Kim; Joseph Walsh;

Tokyo
Telephone: (813) 3593 5200 **Fax:** (813) 3593 5225
Jon Kathe; Saladin Amery; M Araki; Brian Drew; K Horiuchi; T Ito; T Katagiri; M Koda; T Moriya; A Toyoda;

Zurich
Telephone: (41) 1 226 3366 **Fax:** (41) 1 226 3399
Thomas Stumm; Uwe Gnther; Michael Mikyska; Marit Zwahlen;

EQUITIES
Equity Sales
Telephone: (171) 377 9377 **Fax:** (171) 422 2324
Ian Myers;

Equity Trading
Telephone: (171) 377 9377 **Fax:** (171) 422 2148
Tim Healy; Neil Smith;

Equity Derivatives
Telephone: (171) 422 2096 **Fax:** (171) 422 2036
Art Bialer; Matthew Lambert;

Equity Research
Telephone: (171) 422 2052 **Fax:** (171) 422 2312
Said Desaque; Shirley Knott; Richard de Chazal;

Settlements
Telephone: (171) 422 2020 **Fax:** (171) 422 2069
Lawrie Stobbs;

European Equity Sales
Geneva
Telephone: (41) 22 849 0707 **Fax:** (41) 22 849 0714
Michael McFadden;

Zurich
Telephone: (41) 1 221 3344 **Fax:** (41) 1 221 0790
Dino Andreani; Paolo Cerri;

EQUITY FINANCE
Stock Loan
Telephone: (171) 422 2200: **Fax:** (171) 895 0934
Katryna Lee; Alison Kelsey; Richard Marquis; Darren Mason; Sean O'Neill; Karen McGahan

Prime Brokerage
Telephone: (171) 422 2255 **Fax:** (171) 422 2256
Joanne Cook; Leon Garry; Amanda Spinks;

UNITED KINGDOM (+44)   www.euromoneydirectory.com

PIMCO Global Advisors (Europe) Limited (cont)
Others (Senior Executives)
Michael Borkan *Senior Vice President* ☎ **872 1330**
Dwight Holloway *Vice President* ☎ **872 1300**
Katarina McKechnie *Assistant Vice President* ☎ **872 1331**

PMD International Inc   Full Branch Office
23 Pembridge Square, London W2 4DR
Tel: (171) 792 2373 **Fax:** (171) 792 9920

Senior Executive Officers
Managing Director   Jehangir Masud

PPM Ventures Limited   Subsidiary Company
Formerly known as: Prudential Venture Managers Limited
1 Waterhouse Square, Holborn Bars, London EC1N 2ST
Tel: (171) 831 7747 **Fax:** (171) 831 9528

Senior Executive Officers
Managing Director   Jonathan Morgan

Others (Senior Executives)
Martin Clarke *Director*
Kay Ashton *Director*
W H (Gus) Guest *Director*
Neil MacDougall *Director*
Alistair Mackintosh *Director*
Andrew Smith *Director*
Matthew Turner *Director*
Gill Fryzer *Marketing Director*

Administration
Public Relations
Sheila Casey *Marketing Co-Ordinator*

Prebon Yamane (UK) Limited   Head Office
155 Bishopsgate, London EC2N 3DA
Tel: (171) 200 7000 **Fax:** (171) 200 7176 **Telex:** 94015677
Reuters: PYSK; PYST; PYUS; PYLL; PYEN; PYDM; PYFX; PYSF; PYSP; PYCD; PYFE; PYOZ; PYXX; PYND
Website: www.prebon.co.uk

Senior Executive Officers
Director & Chairman, Europe, Middle East &   K Costello
Africa
Managing Director, Europe, Middle East &   G R Pithers
Africa

Others (Senior Executives)
European Products   G Huggins *Acting Director*
Fuel Oil   D Rapp ☎ **200 7017**
Natural Gas   C Vize ☎ **200 7333**
Mogas   M Thompson ☎ **200 7777**

Debt Capital Markets / Fixed Income
Department: Capital Markets Division
Other   R Vesce *European Product Director*

Government Bonds
Head of Sales   I Granat ☎ **638 2829**

Eurobonds
Head of Origination   I Granat ☎ **638 2829**

Emerging Market Bonds
Head of Emerging Markets   P Klinger ☎ **200 7311**
                               L Di Palma ☎ **200 7316**

Fixed-Income Repo
Other   S Graham *Euro Repos* ☎ **200 7610**
                               S Ward *Non-Euro Repos* ☎ **200 7610**

Equity Capital Markets
Department: Capital Markets Division
Domestic Equities
Head of Origination → D Heath ☎ 454 9384
Money Markets
Money Markets - General
European Products → J Stewart *Director*
Euro Cash → J Murphy ☎ 638 0122
　　　　　　　　　Gerd Recht ☎ +352 291 911
Non-Euro Cash → M Yexley ☎ 638 0104
　　　　　　　　　M Crump ☎ 638 0149
Scandi Money Markets → P Svensson ☎ +352 291 911
Non-Euro Forwards → W Field ☎ 200 7311
　　　　　　　　　D Harris ☎ 638 0140
Euro Forwards → A Mathieson-Cheater ☎ 638 0142
　　　　　　　　　Ruud Nijveld ☎ +31 (20) 625 6877
Currency Options → R Nunziato ☎ 200 7920
Non-Banking → C Emmett ☎ 200 7124
Risk Management
Department: Capital Market Division
Other (FI Derivatives)
European Products → R Head *Director*
Euro → P Kilford ☎ 200 7555
Scandi → M Anderson ☎ 200 7445
Sterling → S Tarbert ☎ 638 0151
Dollar / Canada → P Mizon ☎ 638 0104
Swiss → D Haim ☎ 200 7220
New Markets → R Van Vilet ☎ 200 7316
Yen → C Clack ☎ 2007201
OTC Equity Derivatives
Head → D Heath ☎ 454 9384
OTC Credit Derivatives
Head → J Kenny ☎ 200 7392
Country Head → N Ruddell *Credit Products* ☎ 200 7474
Exchange-Traded Derivatives
IR Options → J Palmer ☎ 638 0105

Privredna Banka Zagreb dd — Representative Office
Mitre House, 177 Regent Street, London W1R 8DJ
Tel: (171) 437 3288 **Fax:** (171) 287 3705

Senior Executive Officers
Director & Representative → Jadranka Primorac

Promstroybank of Russia — Representative Office
Cannon Centre, 78 Cannon Street, London EC4P 4LN
Tel: (171) 626 8016 **Fax:** (171) 626 7987

Senior Executive Officers
Chief Representative → Valeri Telegin
Deputy Chief Representative → Raymond Archer

Qatar National Bank SAQ — Full Branch Office
One Mount Street, London W1Y 6HQ
Tel: (171) 647 2600 **Fax:** (171) 647 2647

Senior Executive Officers
Manager, London Branch → Martin Bowen
Syndicated Lending
Loan-Related Activities
Trade Finance; Project Finance → Charles Brodie *Manager, Credit & Marketing* ☎ 647 2607
Money Markets
Head of Money Markets → Peter Searson *Manager, London Treasury* ☎ 647 2681

UNITED KINGDOM (+44)   www.euromoneydirectory.com

Qatar National Bank SAQ (cont)

Foreign Exchange
Head of Foreign Exchange   Peter Searson *Manager, London Treasury* ☎ **647 2681**
FX Traders / Sales People
    Stan Black

Risk Management
Head of Risk Management   Peter Searson *Manager, London Treasury* ☎ **647 2681**

Settlement / Clearing
Tel: 647 2662 Fax: 647 2669
Fixed-Income Settlement   John Ablitt *Assistant Manager, Pay & Receive* ☎ **647 2661**

Other Departments
Chief Credit Officer   Charles Brodie *Manager, Credit & Marketing* ☎ **647 2607**
Private Banking   Martin Bowen *Manager, London Branch*

Administration
Compliance
    Jon Smith *Audit & Compliance Officer* ☎ **674 2674**

Rabobank International   Full Branch Office

Thames Court, One Queenhithe, London EC4V 6RL
Tel: (171) 809 3000 **Telex:** 892950 RABO G
Website: www.rabobank.com

Senior Executive Officers
General Manager   Gijs van der Schrieck

General-Investment
Head of Investment   Alex von Ungern Sternberg *Global Head of Investment Banking*

Debt Capital Markets / Fixed Income
Head of Fixed Income   Michael Ice *Managing Director, Global Fixed Income* ☎ **809 3837**

Equity Capital Markets
Department: IEB
Global Head   Paul Ffolkes Davis *Managing Director* ☎ **463 5988**

International Equities
Head of Trading   Paul Deslandes *Head of Global Equity Trading* ☎ **463 5890**

Equity Repo / Securities Lending
Marketing & Product Development   Stephanie Bacon *Global Head of Collateral Product Sales* ☎ **664 9682**
    ✉ bacons@rabo-bank.com

Syndicated Lending
Tel: 809 3112 Fax: 809 3199
Head of Syndication   Robert Halcrow *Executive Director* ☎ **809 3125**

Loan-Related Activities
Trade Finance   David Roche ☎ **809 3039** F **334 0854**
Project Finance   Andrew Hartley *Director* ☎ **809 3070** F **809 3813**

Money Markets
Tel: 283 8800 Fax: 782 0083
Head of Money Markets   Jason van Praagh *Director & Head of Short Term Interest Rates*

Foreign Exchange
Global Head   Michele Di Stefano *Managing Director* ☎ **809 3931**

Risk Management
Tel: 809 3812 Fax: 809 3833
Head of Risk Management   Robert Armstrong ☎ **809 3036**

Corporate Finance / M&A Advisory
Head of Corporate Finance   Berend du Pon *Managing Director* ☎ **809 3019**

Settlement / Clearing
Head of Settlement / Clearing; Equity   Matthew Hancock ☎ **809 3344** F **809 3072**
Settlement; Fixed-Income Settlement;
Operations; Back-Office

Administration
Technology & Systems
    Steve Barnes *Senior Manager* ☎ **809 3094**

Legal / In-House Counsel
    Christine Hogg *Senior Manager* ☎ **809 3123**

Compliance
    David Hill *Manager* ☎ **809 3076**

www.euromoneydirectory.com UNITED KINGDOM (+44)

Raiffeisen ZentralBank Österreich AG - RZB-Austria
Full Branch Office

RZB-Austria House, 36/38 Botolph Lane, London EC3R 8DE
Tel: (171) 929 2288 Fax: (171) 623 1250

Senior Executive Officers
Chief Executive Officer — Dennis M Govan *Chief Executive Officer & General Manager*
Financial Director — Christopher Dougan *Executive Manager*
Treasurer — Michael Barr *Deputy General Manager* ☏ **667 2321**

Debt Capital Markets / Fixed Income
Country Head — Philip Waite *Head, Capital Markets* ☏ **667 2371**

Equity Capital Markets
Country Head — Philip Waite *Head, Capital Markets* ☏ **667 2371**

Money Markets
Country Head — John McGovern *Senior Manager, Treasury* ☏ **283 1008**

Foreign Exchange
Country Head — Leo Stefan *Senior Manager, Foreign Exchange* ☏ **283 1008**

Settlement / Clearing
Country Head — Alan Mannering *Senior Manager, Settlements*

RBC Dominion Securities Inc
Full Branch Office

Alternative trading name: Royal Bank of Canada Europe Limited
Royal Bank of Canada Centre, 71 Queen Victoria Street, London EC4V 4DE
Tel: (171) 489 1133; (171) 489 1188 Fax: (171) 248 3940 Telex: 888011
Website: www.royalbank.com

Senior Executive Officers
Financial Director — Charles McManus *VP & Financial Officer* ☏ **653 4821**
Chief Operating Officer — John Burbidge *Vice President & Director* ☏ **653 4198**

Others (Senior Executives)
Global Markets — Martin Klingsick *Vice President*

General-Investment
Head of Investment — Ron Stanley *General Manager, Corporate Investment Banking*

Debt Capital Markets / Fixed Income
Head of Fixed Income — Adrian Bell *Global Co-Head, VP & Director- Europe / Asia* ☏ **653 4820**
F **702 1830**
Richard Pilosof *Global Co-Head, VP & Director- Europe / Asia* ☏ **653 4840**
F **653 4900**
Andrew Nemec *Head, VP & Director- Japan* ☏ **+81 (3) 589 7610**
F **+81 (3) 589 7618**
Paul Warren *Head, VP & Director- Australia* ☏ **+61 (2) 9223 6011**
F **+61 (2) 9221 1513**
Head of Fixed Income Trading — Richard Pilosof *Global Head, Vice President & Director* ☏ **653 4840**
F **653 4900**
Other — Ali Jalai *Vice President & Director* ☏ **653 4502** F **248 0891**

Government Bonds
Head of Trading — Tim Griffin *Vice President* ☏ **489 8822** F **653 4900**

Eurobonds
Head of Origination — Greg Nottle *Vice President* ☏ **653 4868** F **702 1830**
Head of Syndication — Geraud de Nadiallac *Vice President* ☏ **653 4873** F **702 1830**
Head of Sales — Mark Benstead *Vice President* ☏ **895 9339** F **653 4900**
Head of Trading — Thomas Candy *Vice President* ☏ **927 9846** F **653 4900**

Bonds - General
Head of Derivatives- Europe & Asia — Ali Jalai *Vice President & Director* ☏ **653 4502** F **248 0891**
Head of Derivative Marketing — Jean Dulude *Vice President* ☏ **653 3196** F **248 0891**

Libor-Based / Floating-Rate Products
Asset Swaps — Gary Kirk *Vice President* ☏ **329 6121** F **248 0891**

Fixed-Income Repo
Head of Repo — Terry Upham *Manager, Repo & Securities Lending* ☏ **489 8822** F **248 3954**

Equity Capital Markets
Department: Equity Capital Markets & Institutional Equities
Head of Equity Capital Markets — William Smith *Vice President* ☏ **653 4570**

Domestic Equities
Head of Sales — Stephen Foss *Vice President & Director* ☏ **653 4551**

Euromoney Directory 1999 **1843**

UNITED KINGDOM (+44)   www.euromoneydirectory.com

RBC Dominion Securities Inc (cont)

International Equities
Head of Sales — Christopher Orchard *Vice President & Director* 653 4589
Head of Trading — Mark Head *Vice President* 653 4586

Equity Repo / Securities Lending
Head — Bill Sawyer 653 4571

Syndicated Lending
Head of Syndication — Amanda Phillips 653 4048
Head of Trading — Stephen Mills 653 4074

Loan-Related Activities
Trade Finance — Douglas Nelson 653 4002
Project Finance — Ada Pagano 653 4731

Money Markets
Head of Money Markets — Mark Lowings *Vice President* 489 8370

Foreign Exchange
Tel: 489 8370 **Fax:** 329 6154 **Reuters:** RBCL
Global Head — David Barnett *Co-Head* 489 8370
Corporate Sales — Richard Geering 489 8369
Head of Trading — Stephen Braithwaite *Chief Dealer* 489 8360
Andrew Stammers *Chief Dealer* 489 8360

Risk Management
Head of Risk Management — Richard Jenkins *Vice President* 653 4531

Fixed Income Derivatives / Risk Management
Trading — Jerry Rumble *Global Head of FX Options* 653 3177

OTC Equity Derivatives
Sales; Trading — Henry Rourke *Head of Equity Derivatives- Europe & Asia* 653 4513

Corporate Finance / M&A Advisory
Head of Corporate Finance — Nicholas Villiers *Vice President & Director*

Settlement / Clearing
Head of Settlement / Clearing — Mark Clatworthy 653 4075

Global Custody
Head of Global Custody — Jose Placido 653 4223

Asset Management
Head — Philip Darwall-Smith 653 4758

Other Departments
Chief Credit Officer — Geza Tatrallyay 653 4711
Correspondent Banking — Ian Toone 653 4035

Administration
Head of Administration — Danny Cowan 653 4015
Business Development — Stephen de Vos 565 4106

Technology & Systems
Dave Thomas 653 4018

Legal / In-House Counsel
Inder Mangat 653 4051

Compliance
Compliance- Securities — Gurjit Purewal 653 4565
Compliance- Banking — Guy Scammell 653 4145

Public Relations
Charles Fisher 653 4026

Accounts / Audit
Charles McManus *VP & Financial Officer* 653 4821

RBC DS Inc   Full Branch Office

Royal Bank of Canada Centre, 71 Queen Victoria Street, London EC4V 4DE
Tel: (171) 489 1133 **Fax:** (171) 248 3940; (171) 248 3954 **Telex:** 888011

Senior Executive Officers
Vice President & Director — Nicholas Villiers
Chief Operating Officer — John Bursidge
Managing Director / General Manager — Colin Sturgeon

1844 Euromoney Directory 1999

UNITED KINGDOM (+44)

Debt Capital Markets / Fixed Income
Global Head — Andrew Pringle *Vice President & Director* +1 (416) 842 2000

Domestic Government Bonds
Head of Sales — David Eaton *Vice President, Repo*
Head of Trading — Tim Griffin *Vice President*

Eurobonds
Head of Syndication — Stephen Coles *Vice President*
Head of Sales — Jean Delude *Vice President*
Head of Trading — David Hockley

Libor-Based / Floating-Rate Products
Asset Swaps — Gary Kirk
Asset Swaps (Sales) — Jean Delude *Vice President*

Medium-Term Notes
Head of Origination — Nick Finley

Fixed-Income Repo
Head of Repo — Terry Upham *Manager, Repos*
Marketing & Product Development — David Eaton *Vice President*
Trading — Terry Upham *Manager of Repo & Securities Lending* 489 8822

Equity Capital Markets
Tel: 489 8822 **Fax:** 248 3952
Regional Head — Colin Sturgeon *Vice President & Director*

Domestic Equities
Head of Sales — Stephen Foss *Vice President & Director*

International Equities
Head of Sales — Christopher Orchard

Equity Repo / Securities Lending
Head — Terry Upham *Manager, Repos*
Head of Trading — David Eaton *Vice President*
Kevin Doulet *Equity Lending*

Corporate Finance / M&A Advisory
Regional Head — Nicholas Villiers *Vice President & Director*

Rea Brothers (Isle of Man) Limited

29 Athol Street, Douglas, Isle of Man IM99 1RB
Tel: (1624) 643 200 **Fax:** (1624) 622 039 **Telex:** 627752 **Email:** info@reabros.co.uk

Senior Executive Officers
Chairman — M Sheehan

Others (Senior Executives)
Director — David Litton
Trust Manager — Mark Lewin

Rea Brothers Limited — Subsidiary Company

Alderman's House, Alderman's Walk, London EC2M 3XR
Tel: (171) 623 1155 **Fax:** (171) 626 0130 **Telex:** 886503

Senior Executive Officers
Financial Director — Alan Hunter *Group Finance Officer*
Phil Remington *Finance Director*
Managing Director — Roger Parsons
Legal Director — Caroline Griffin

Others (Senior Executives)
David Bezem *Director*
Brian Birch *Director*
Michael Bower *Director*
John Knox *Director*
Roger Looker *Director*
Tim Seymour *Director*
Nick Wells *Head of Department*
Jo Welman *Director*

Corporate Finance / M&A Advisory
Head of Corporate Finance — Nick Wells *Head of Department*
Tim Seymour *Director*

UNITED KINGDOM (+44)   www.euromoneydirectory.com

Rea Brothers Limited (cont)

Administration
Head of Marketing   Mark Mathias *Head of Investment Funds*

Technology & Systems
Information Technology   Peter Bell *Manager*

Legal / In-House Counsel
Company Secretary / Legal Officer   Caroline Griffin *Legal Director*

Compliance
                                                  Kevin Lazeris *Group Compliance Officer*

Accounts / Audit
                                                  Mark Romano *Internal Auditor*

Republic National Bank of New York

30 Monument Street, London EC3R 8NB
Tel: (171) 860 3000 **Fax:** (171) 623 2866 **Telex:** 889217 (General), 924031 (FX/MM) **Swift:** BLIC GB 2L
Administration Tel: 521 1341; 521 1341; **Fax:** 521 1341; **Reuters:** Dealing 2000:REPX, REPF, REPM (FX London);
Monitor Dealing:RNBB (Banknotes London); RNBL (Bullion London); RNBA (Bullion New York); RNBM (Options);
RNBA (MM New York); RNBO (Options New York); Monitor:RNBG (Gold Page New York);
RNBL(Gold Page London)

Senior Executive Officers
Chief Operating Officer   Eddie Dias
General Manager   W Trevor Robinson

Others (Senior Executives)
                                                  Mark Brown *EVP & Head, Global FX*

Debt Capital Markets / Fixed Income
Emerging Market Bonds
Head of Emerging Markets   Cesar Manent *DMD & Head of London Trading*

Syndicated Lending
Other (Syndicated Lending)
Republic Financial Products   Colin Lawrence *EVP & Head of Global RFP*
Credit - Trading   Andrea Sharp *Senior Vice President*

Money Markets
Head of Money Markets   Michael Smith *FVP & Head of London Trading*
Country Head   Jon Cann *Vice President*

Money Markets - General
Banknotes   Moise Tawil *EVP, Business Development*
Off Balance Sheet   Jon Cann *Vice President*
Banknotes   David Langner *SVP & Head of London Trading*
                                                  Steve Allen *SVP, Marketing & Administration*

Foreign Exchange
Head of Foreign Exchange   Michael Smith *FVP & Head of London Trading*
Global Head   Mark Brown *EVP & Head, Global FX*

FX Traders / Sales People
Spot FX   Stuart Clewes-Garner *FVP & Senior Dealer*
                                                  John Mirrams *FVP & Senior Dealer*

Risk Management
Other Currency Swap / FX Options Personnel
Derivatives Products   John Spillane *FVP & Co-Head*
                                                  Russell Wojcik *DMD, Interest Rate Products, Trading*
                                                  Anthony Saint *FVP & Co-Head*
                                                  Mark Henderson *FVP, Marketing*

Settlement / Clearing
Operations   Eddie Dias *Managing Director*
Other (Settlement & Clearing)
                                                  Mick Clapham *Senior Vice President*

Other Departments
Commodities / Bullion   Murray Ludlow *DMD & Head of London Trading*
                                                  Mark Fairhurst *FVP, Bullion & Currency Options*
                                                  Jeremy Charles *SVP, Marketing*

Other Departments
Institutional Business   Kurt Zeigler *Senior Vice President*

www.euromoneydirectory.com   UNITED KINGDOM (+44)

Administration
Department: International Private Banking
47 Berkeley Square, London
Tel: +44 (171) 860 3000 Fax: +44 (171) 860 3028
Head of Administration   Ronald Willson *EVP, Private Banking*

Republic New York (UK) Limited
Subsidiary Company

30 Monument Street, London EC3R 8NB
Tel: (171) 860 3000 Fax: (171) 623 2866

Senior Executive Officers
EVP & Head of Global RFP   Colin Lawrence
Chief Operating Officer   Eddie Dias *Managing Director & Chief Operating Officer*

Debt Capital Markets / Fixed Income

Emerging Market Bonds
Head of Sales   Michael Pratt *Deputy Managing Director*
Head of Trading   Cesar Manent *Deputy Managing Director*

Syndicated Lending

Other (Syndicated Lending)
Financial Products   Russell Wojcik *Deputy Managing Director, Trading*
Credit   Andrea Sharp *Senior Vice President*

Settlement / Clearing
Operations   Eddie Dias *Managing Director & Chief Operating Officer*

Reserve Bank of Australia
Representative Office

Basildon House, 7 Moorgate, London EC2R 6AQ
Tel: (171) 600 2244 Telex: 888917

Senior Executive Officers
Chief Representative, Europe   P F Barry

Rheinhyp Rheinische Hypothekenbank AG
Representative Office

55 Bishopsgate, London EC2N 3AS
Tel: (171) 638 5300 Fax: (171) 638 5152 Email: rheinhyp_bank_uk@compuserve.com

Senior Executive Officers
General Manager   Mark Titcomb

Administration
Head of Marketing   Christopher Hunter ⊤ **638 5400** F **638 5152**

Riggs Bank NA

Formerly known as: Riggs National Bank of Washington DC (The)
21 Great Winchester Street, London EC2N 2HH
Tel: (171) 588 7772; (171) 626 3515 Fax: (171) 256 7369 Telex: 892807

Senior Executive Officers
Managing Director / General Manager   Robert C Roane

Riyad Bank
Full Branch Office

17B Curzon Street, London W1Y 8LS
Tel: (171) 830 9000 Fax: (171) 493 1668

Senior Executive Officers
Chief Executive Officer   Keith Scott *Chief Manager*
Treasurer   Bruce Gatherer *Manager*

UNITED KINGDOM (+44)   www.euromoneydirectory.com

Riyad Bank Europe Limited

Riyad Bank House, 17B Curzon Street, London W1Y 8LS
Tel: (171) 830 4000 **Fax:** (171) 493 1134 **Telex:** 915484 RIYADE G

Senior Executive Officers
Chairman   Rashed Abdulaziz Al-Rashed
Treasurer   Bruce Gatherer
Managing Director / General Manager   Keith R Scott

Robeco (UK)

43/45 Portman Square, London W1H OHE
Tel: (171) 935 4268 **Fax:** (171) 467 4515 **Telex:** 413500 **Swift:** BECWCHGG

Senior Executive Officers
Managing Director / General Manager   John Manning

Rosetbank

19 Harley Street, London W1N 1DA
Tel: (171) 637 4682 **Fax:** (171) 637 4679

Senior Executive Officers
Managing Director / General Manager   Geoffrey Mountford

NM Rothschild & Sons Limited   Head Office

New Court, St Swithin's Lane, London EC4P 4DU
Tel: (171) 280 5000 **Fax:** (171) 929 1643 **Telex:** 888031 **Swift:** ROTH GB 2L

Senior Executive Officers
Chairman   Evelyn de Rothschild
Financial Director   Andrew Didham *Group Finance Director*
Managing Director   Robert Ashley
Managing Director   Paul Tuckwell ☎ **280 5731**
Managing Director   Malcolm Aish

Equity Capital Markets
Department: ABN AMRO Rothschild
4 Broadgate, London, EC2M 7LE
Tel: +44 (171) 374 1700 **Fax:** +44 (171) 374 1500
Global Head   Matthew Westerman *Joint Chief Executive* ☎ **374 1222**
    Menno De Jager *Joint Chief Executive* ☎ **374 1740**

International Equities
Head of Origination   Anthony Bird *Director* ☎ **374 1950**
    Jonathan Penkin *Director* ☎ **374 1210**
    Nigel Himsworth *Director* ☎ **374 1228**
Head of Syndication   James Kenny *Director* ☎ **374 1208**
    Rijnhard Snouckaert *Director* ☎ **374 7881**
    Jeroen Berns *Director* ☎ **374 4620**

Convertibles / Equity-Linked
Head of Origination   Anthony Bird *Director* ☎ **374 1950**
    Jonathan Penkin *Director* ☎ **374 1210**
    Nigel Himsworth *Director* ☎ **374 1228**
Head of Syndication   James Kenny *Director* ☎ **374 1208**
    Rijnhard Snouckaert *Director* ☎ **374 7881**
    Jeroen Berns *Director* ☎ **374 4620**

Syndicated Lending
Fax: 280 5400
Global Head   Paul Tuckwell *Managing Director* ☎ **280 5731**
Head of Origination   Charles Keay *Director* ☎ **280 5787**
Head of Syndication   Hugh Macdonald-Buchanan *Manager* ☎ **280 5717**

Foreign Exchange
Fax: 280 5095
Global Head   Robert Ashley *Managing Director*

Risk Management
Global Head   Malcolm Aish *Managing Director*

www.euromoneydirectory.com UNITED KINGDOM (+44)

Corporate Finance / M&A Advisory
Department: NM Rothschild Corporate Finance Limited
Global Head
Regional Head
David de Rothschild *Chairman* ☎ +33 (1) 40 74 40 74
Richard Davey *Managing Director*

Settlement / Clearing
Regional Head
John O'Connor *Assistant Director*

NM Rothschild & Sons (Wales) Limited Subsidiary Company

Sophia House, 28 Cathedral Road, Cardiff, South Glamorgan CF1 9LJ
Tel: (1222) 226 666 **Fax:** (1222) 224 224

Senior Executive Officers
Director
Stephen Jones

Rothschild Asset Management (Isle of Man) Limited

20/26 Peel Road, Douglas, Isle of Man IM1 4LZ
Tel: (1624) 672 277 **Fax:** (1624) 615 445

Senior Executive Officers
Chairman   Carel Mosselmans
Managing Director   Andrew Beeman

Rothschild Asset Management Limited Head Office

Five Arrows House, St Swithin's Lane, London EC4N 8NR
Tel: (171) 623 1000 **Fax:** (171) 634 2555 **Telex:** 888031

Senior Executive Officers
Group Chief Executive Officer   Peter Troughton
Financial Director   Ian Goodwin *Director*

Debt Capital Markets / Fixed Income
Department: Fixed-Income
Fax: 283 4279
Head of Fixed Income
Jane Smettem *Assistant Director, UK Fixed Income*
Michael Amey *Manager, UK Fixed Income*

Non-Domestic Government Bonds
Fixed-Income & Currency Group
Global

Ceris Williams *Director & Head*
Adrian Grey *Director*
Lucy Workman *Assistant Director*

US$
Nigel Jenkins *Director*
Rosie Reid *Manager*

Bonds - General
Emerging Markets
William Best *Director*
Ingrid Iversen *Assistant Director*

Equity Capital Markets
Other (Domestic Equities)

Justin Reed *Director*
Utilities / building / Transport   Nicola Barber *Assistant Director*
Food Producers / General Retail / Leisure Rebecca Newstead *Manager*
Paper & Packaging / Healthcare / Media   Jonathan Jackson *Assistant Manager*
UK Smaller Companies   Karen Haldane *Manager*
                                           Paul Cramp *Director*
Insurance / Telecoms / Support Services   Ian Aylward *Assistant Manager*
Bank / Retail / Brewers   Charles Deptford *Director*

Other (International Equity)

Bruce Albrecht *Director*
Christopher Jenkins *Director*
Catherine Younger *Assistant Director*
Benjamin Laidler *Manager*

Foreign Exchange
Fax: 283 4279

FX Traders / Sales People
Currency Management
Thomas Barman *Director & Head*
Tom Clarke *Director*
Dale Thomas *Assistant Director*

Euromoney Directory 1999 **1849**

UNITED KINGDOM (+44) www.euromoneydirectory.com

Rothschild Asset Management Limited (cont)

Risk Management
Fax: 634 2520
Global Head — Andrew Giles *Director & Head*
Helen Thomas *Assistant Director*
David Gilinsky *Manager*
Mark Sander *Manager*

Settlement / Clearing
Fax: 634 2647
Regional Head — Roy Aitken *Assistant Director & Head*
Fixed-Income Settlement — Sharon Molloy *Assistant Manager*
Derivatives Settlement — Paul Warren *Assistant Manager*
Foreign Exchange Settlement — Ann Blackeby *Manager*

Other Departments
Private Banking — Rupert Robinson *Director*

Administration
Head of Administration — Cherrilyn Ingleby *Manager*

Technology & Systems
John Couch *Director*

Legal / In-House Counsel
Sandy Macphee *Director*

Compliance
Sandy Macphee *Director*

Royal Bank of Canada — Full Branch Office

Alternative trading name: RBC Dominion Securities & Royal Bank of Canada Europe Limited
71 Queen Victoria Street, London EC4V 4DE
Tel: (171) 489 1188 **Fax:** (171) 329 6144 **Telex:** 929111 RBCCTY G **Swift:** ROYC GB 2L
Website: www.royalbank.com

Senior Executive Officers
Financial Director — John Burbidge ☎ 653 4198
Chief Operating Officer — Colin Sturgeon ☎ 653 4700
Treasurer — Martin Klingsick *Senior Vice President* ☎ 653 4114
SVP & General Manager — Ronald Stanley ☎ 653 4013
Company Secretary — Charles Fisher ☎ 653 4026

Others (Senior Executives)
Global Markets — Martin Klingsick *Senior Vice President* ☎ 653 4114
Risk Management — Geza Tatrallyay *Senior Vice President* ☎ 653 4711

Debt Capital Markets / Fixed Income
Department: Fixed Income Capital Markets
Regional Head —
Adrian Bell *Global Head, Eurobonds & Co-Head, Europe & Asia* ☎ 653 4820 F 702 1830
Richard Pilosof *Global Head, FI Trading & Co-Head, Europe & Asia* ☎ 653 4840 F 653 4900
Andrew Nemec *Head, Japan* ☎ +81 (3) 589 7610 F +81 (3) 589 7618
Paul Warren *Head, Australia* ☎ +61 (2) 9223 6011 F +61 (2) 9221 1513

Government Bonds
Head of Trading — Tim Griffin ☎ 489 8822 F 653 4900

Eurobonds
Head of Origination — Greg Nottle ☎ 653 4868 F 702 1831
Head of Syndication — Geraud de Nadiallac ☎ 653 4873 F 702 1830
Head of Sales — Mark Benstead ☎ 895 9339 F 653 4900
Head of Trading — Thomas Candy ☎ 927 9846 F 653 4900

Libor-Based / Floating-Rate Products
Asset Swaps — Gary Kirk ☎ 329 6121 F 248 0891

Fixed-Income Repo
Head of Repo — Terry Upham ☎ 489 8822 F 248 3954

Equity Capital Markets
Department: Equity Capital Markets and Institutional Equities
Head of Equity Capital Markets — William Smith ☎ 653 4570

Domestic Equities
Head of Sales — Stephen Foss ☎ 653 4551

International Equities
Head of Sales — Chrisopher Orchard ☎ 653 4589
Head of Trading — Mark Head ☎ 653 4586

www.euromoneydirectory.com UNITED KINGDOM (+44)

Syndicated Lending
Head of Syndication Amanda Phillips ☏ **653 4048**
Head of Trading Stephen Mills ☏ **653 4074**

Loan-Related Activities
Trade Finance Douglas Nelson ☏ **653 4002**
Project Finance Ada Pagano ☏ **653 4731**

Money Markets
Head of Money Markets Mark Lowings ☏ **489 8370**

Foreign Exchange
Tel: 489 8370 **Fax:** 329 6154 **Telex:** RBCL
Head of Foreign Exchange David Barnett *Co-Head, Global FX* ☏ **489 8370**
Corporate Sales Richard Geering ☏ **489 8369**
Head of Trading Stephen Braithwaite *Chief Dealer* ☏ **489 8360**
Andrew Stammer *Chief Dealer* ☏ **489 8360**

Risk Management
Head of Risk Management Geza Tatrallyay *Senior Vice President* ☏ **653 4711**

Foreign Exchange Derivatives / Risk Management
Vanilla FX option Trading Jerry Rumble ☏ **653 3177**

OTC Equity Derivatives
Head Henry Rourke *Head, Equity Derivatives* ☏ **653 4513**
Department: Fixed Income Capital Markets

Fixed Income Derivatives / Risk Management
Regional Head Ali Jalai *Head, Europe & Asia* ☏ **653 4502** 🖷 **248 0891**
Head of Sales Jean Dulude *Head of Marketing* ☏ **653 3196** 🖷 **248 0891**

Corporate Finance / M&A Advisory
Head of Corporate Finance Nicholas Villiers ☏ **653 4569**

Settlement / Clearing
Head of Settlement / Clearing Mark Clatworthy ☏ **653 4075**

Global Custody
Head of Global Custody Jose Placido ☏ **653 4223**

Asset Management
Head Philip Darwall-Smith ☏ **653 4758**

Other Departments
Chief Credit Officer Geza Tatrallyay *Senior Vice President* ☏ **653 4711**
Private Banking Jean-Claude Emard ☏ **653 4749**
Correspondent Banking Ian Toone ☏ **653 4035**

Administration
Head of Administration Danny Cowan ☏ **653 4015**
Business Development Stephen de Vos ☏ **653 4106**

Technology & Systems
Dave Thomas ☏ **653 4018**

Legal / In-House Counsel
Inder Mangat ☏ **653 4051**

Compliance
Compliance, Banking Guy Scammell ☏ **653 4145**
Compliance, Securities Gurjit Purewal ☏ **653 4565**

Public Relations
Charles Fisher ☏ **653 4026**

Other (Administration)
Finance Charles McManus ☏ **653 4821**

Royal Bank of Canada Investment Management (UK) Limited
Subsidiary Company

71 Queen Victoria Street, London EC4V 4DE
Tel: (171) 489 1188 **Fax:** (171) 236 1678

Senior Executive Officers
Chairman, SVP Global Private Bnkg Michael Lagopoulos
Chief Executive Officer Philip Darwall-Smith ☏ **653 4758**
Financial Director Andrew Blair-Rains *Finance Officer*

Administration
Compliance
Ian Hamilton *Officer* ☏ **653 4764**

Euromoney Directory 1999 **1851**

UNITED KINGDOM (+44)   www.euromoneydirectory.com

The Royal Bank of Scotland International Limited — Full Branch Office
Victory House, Prospect Hill, Douglas, Isle of Man IM99 1NJ
Tel: (1624) 646 452 Fax: (1624) 646 453

Senior Executive Officers
Others (Senior Executives)
W McKay *Director, Isle of Man*

The Royal Bank of Scotland plc — Head Office
PO Box 31, 42 St Andrew Square, Edinburgh, EH2 2YE
Tel: (131) 556 8555 Fax: (131) 557 6565 Telex: 72320 Swift: RBOS GB Cable: ROYALBANK EDINBURGH
Website: www.rbos.co.uk

Senior Executive Officers
Chairman — The Rt Hon Viscount Younger of Leckie
Chief Executive Officer — George Ross Mathewson *Group Chief Executive*
Frederick Anderson Goodwin *Deputy Group Chief Executive*
Director, Strategy — Iain Allan
Director, Corporate Affairs — Howard Moody
Director & Group Secretary — Miller R McLean

Others (Senior Executives)
Norman C McLuskie *Executive Director*
Lawrence Kingsbaker Fish *Executive Director*
Ian S Robertson *Executive Director*
I H Chippendale *Chief Executive, Direct Line Insurance plc*

General-Lending (DCM, SL)
Head of Corporate Banking — Donald Workman

Risk Management
Global Head — Nathan Bostock *Director, Group Risk*

Corporate Finance / M&A Advisory
Other (Corporate Finance)
Strategy — Iain Allen *Director*

Administration
Legal / In-House Counsel
Legal & Regulatory Affairs — Miller R McLean *Director*

Corporate Communications
Corporate Affairs — Howard Moody *Director, Corporate Affairs*

The Royal Bank of Scotland plc — Full Branch Office
Waterhouse Square, 138/142 Holborn, London EC1N 2TH
Tel: (171) 427 8000 Fax: (171) 427 9900

Senior Executive Officers
Chairman — The Rt Hon Viscount Younger of Leckie
Chief Executive Officer — George Ross Mathewson *Group Chief Executive*
Frederick Anderson Goodwin *Deputy Group Chief Executive*
Iain S Robertson *Chief Executive, UK Bank*
John A N Cameron *MD, Corporate & Institutional Banking*
Financial Director — Peter R Allen *Finance & Administration*
Treasurer — Brian Crowe *Group Treasurer*
Director, Corporate and Commercial, S of England — Alan Dickinson
Chief Executive, RBS Trust Bank — Gordon Lindsay
Director, UK and International Banking Services — David Jessop
Director, Risk & Portfolio Management — Steve Lent
Director, Corporate / Commercial Bnkg, North England — John McGuire
Director, Corporate / Commercial Bnkg, Scotland — Donald Workman
Director, Structured Finance — Iain Houston
Director, Group Risk — Miller R McLean

Others (Senior Executives)
Executive Director — Lawrence Kingsbaker Fish
Norman C McLuskie

1852 Euromoney Directory 1999

Others (Senior Executives) (cont)

Director, Group Legal & Regulatory Affairs — Iain S Robertson *Chief Executive, UK Bank*
Director, Strategy — Miller R McLean
Director, Corporate Affairs — Iain Allan
Howard Moody

Syndicated Lending
Head of Syndicated Lending — Christopher A Elliott *Head of Syndication* ☎ **427 9184** 📠 **427 9935**

Loan-Related Activities
Shipping Finance — Lambros Varnavides *Director, Shipping*
Project Finance — Thomas W Hardy *Head, Project Finance* ☎ **427 9119** 📠 **427 9980**
Structured Trade Finance — Iain Houston *Director, Structured Finance*
Malcolm Booth *Head of Structured Trade Finance*

Risk Management
Country Head — N Bostock *Director, Group Risk*

Corporate Finance / M&A Advisory
Acquistion Finance — J McGrane *MD, Royal Bank Development Capital*
L Robertson *Director, Aquisition Finance*

Asset Management
Portfolio Management — Steve Lent *Director, Risk & Portfolio Management*

Administration

Public Relations
Prosser Stewart *Head of Public Relations* ☎ **427 9110** 📠 **427 9944**

Other (Administration)
Human Resources — Anne Dean *Head*

Royal Scottish Assurance plc
Subsidiary Company

32/34 St Andrew Square, Edinburgh, EH2 2YE
Tel: (131) 557 9696 **Fax:** (131) 558 3318

Senior Executive Officers
Chief Executive Officer — I E R Offor

Sabanci Bank plc
Head Office

10 Finsbury Square, London EC2A 1HE
Tel: (171) 628 3844 **Fax:** (171) 638 2037 **Telex:** 8955636 **Swift:** AKBK GB 2LA **Email:** info@sabanci-bank.co.uk
Reuters: SABG (Dealing)
Website: www.sabanci-bank.co.uk

Senior Executive Officers
General Manager — Denis Long ☎ **382 0901**

Others (Senior Executives)
Ersin Erenman *Deputy General Manager* ☎ **382 0902**

Syndicated Lending

Loan-Related Activities
Trade Finance — James Coughlan *Manager* ☎ **382 0904**

Risk Management
Global Head — Jacques Straub *Senior Manager* ☎ **382 0906**

Settlement / Clearing
Operations — Kenneth Littlewood *Senior Manager* ☎ **382 0905**

Other Departments
Correspondent Banking — Roger Stenning *Manager, Bank Relations* ☎ **382 0914**

Administration

Technology & Systems
Systems — Jon Freeman *Manager* ☎ **382 0900**

Other (Administration)
Customer Services — Michael Ford *Manager* ☎ **382 0909**

UNITED KINGDOM (+44)   www.euromoneydirectory.com

Safra Republic Investments Limited — Subsidiary Company

47 Berkeley Square, London W1X 5DB
Tel: (171) 860 3000 Fax: (171) 860 3174

Senior Executive Officers
President & Chief Executive Officer Paul Dunning
General-Investment
Head of Investment Paul I Feldman *Chief Investment Officer*
Administration
Other (Administration)
Product Development A Jamie Murray *Manager*

The Sakura Bank Limited

Ground & 1st Floors, 6 Broadgate, London EC2M 2RQ
Tel: (171) 638 3131 Fax: (171) 638 1260 Telex: 888519 MITKBK

Senior Executive Officers
Managing Director / General Manager Tamotsu Minamimoto

Sakura Finance International Limited

6 Broadgate, London EC2M 2RQ
Tel: (171) 638 7595 Fax: (171) 628 1285 Telex: 886107

Senior Executive Officers
Chief Executive Officer Tsugumasa Kojima *Managing Director & Chief Executive*
Others (Senior Executives)
  H Nagai *Deputy Managing Director*
  O J Boyle *Deputy General Manager*

Sal Oppenheim jr & Cie Securities (UK) Limited — Subsidiary Company

Saddler's House, Gutter Lane, London EC2V 6BR
Tel: (171) 600 2572 Fax: (171) 600 4834'

Senior Executive Officers
Managing Director Katrin Kandel

Salomon Smith Barney — Full Branch Office

Formerly known as: Salomon Brothers International Limited
Victoria Plaza, 111 Buckingham Palace Road, London SW1 0SB
Tel: (171) 721 2000 Fax: (171) 222 7062 Telex: 886441

Senior Executive Officers
Chief Executive Officer Ron Freeman *Joint Chief Executive*
  Jim Boshart *Joint Chief Executive*
Financial Director Ed Watson *Chief Financial Officer*

Debt Capital Markets / Fixed Income
Department: Fixed Income
Global Head Charlie Berman *Head, Capital Markets* ☏ **721 3810**
Regional Head Jim Forese *Head, European Fixed Income* ☏ **721 2573**
Country Head Mark Watson *Head, Fixed Income Syndicate* ☏ **721 3625**
Marketing Jeremy Amias *Head, Fixed Income Sales* ☏ **721 3138**

Eurobonds
Head of Trading Ted Seelye *Head* ☏ **721 3225**

Bonds - General
Eurodollar / C$ Lee Proctor *Trading* ☏ **721 3225**
  Robert Sanders *Trading* ☏ **721 3225**
Eurosterling Ian Baillie *Trading* ☏ **721 3365**
Eurodollar / C$ Khalid Ataullah *Trading* ☏ **721 3225**
Eurosterling David Meek *Trading* ☏ **721 3365**
Euro Dm / FFr Frank Sauer *Trading* ☏ **721 1740**
Euroyen / JGB Oliver Butt *Trading* ☏ **721 3225**
  Mark Lewis *Trading* ☏ **721 3225**

Bonds - General (cont)

Europe / Italy
Sara McKerihan *Managing Director* ☎ **721 3151**
Henrik Andersen *Sales* ☎ **721 3111**
Ingrid Bouloux *Sales* ☎ **721 3161**
Anthony Dow *Sales* ☎ **721 3130**
Peter Fraser *Sales* ☎ **721 3130**
Juan Garat *Sales* ☎ **721 3108**
Alexia Giugni *Sales* ☎ **721 3105**
Patrick Horusitzky *Sales* ☎ **721 3122**
Willem Plantagie *Sales* ☎ **721 3109**
Carolyn Jones *Sales* ☎ **721 3153**

UK / Middle East
Bob Pearce *Managing Director* ☎ **721 3365**
Alison Arnold *Sales*
David Beresford *Sales*
Dominic Bexon *Sales*
Dominic de Ban *Sales*
Sally Duckworth *Sales*
David Freeman *Sales*
David O'Brien *Sales*
Jayne Standley *Sales*
Simon Willett *Sales*
Mark Williams *Sales*
Michelle Beviere *Sales*

Debt Syndication
Mark Watson ☎ **721 3625**
Michael Ridley ☎ **721 3625**
Jason Mann ☎ **721 3625**
Peter Charles ☎ **721 3625**
Akshay Sethia ☎ **721 3625**

Emerging Market Bonds
Head of Sales
Raj Dutta ☎ **721 3400**
Zoran Kozic ☎ **721 3400**
Yan Swiderski ☎ **721 3400**
Stephen Butcher ☎ **721 3400**
Mark Walker ☎ **721 3400**

Head of Trading
Rafael Biosse Duplan ☎ **721 3400**

Other (Emerging Markets Bonds)
Emerging Markets Eurobonds
Sabine Boyé ☎ **721 1806**

Libor-Based / Floating-Rate Products
FRN Sales
Mark Lewis *Trading* ☎ **721 3225**

Medium-Term Notes
Head of Origination
Rupinder Natt *MTN Syndication* ☎ **721 3625**
Peter Jackson *MTN Syndication* ☎ **721 3625**
Marc Falconer *MTN Syndication* ☎ **721 3625**

Mortgage-Backed Securities
Global Head
Andrew Allan *Mortgages / Asset Backed* ☎ **721 3136**

Department: Government Sales & Trading
Regional Head
Zoeb Sachee *Head of European Goverment Trading* ☎ **721 3321**

Domestic Government Bonds
Head of Trading
Edmund Noon *UK Govts, Trading* ☎ **721 3345**
Stephen Laughton *UK Govts, Trading* ☎ **721 3345**
Richard Noble *UK Govts, Trading* ☎ **721 3345**
Steve Mattey *UK Govts, Trading* ☎ **721 3345**

Non-Domestic Government Bonds
German / Belgium / Netherlands Govts
Spiros Skordos *Trading* ☎ **721 3388**
Ralf Seibel *Trading* ☎ **721 3323**
Patrick Olsson *Trading* ☎ **721 3090**
Jean-Marc Crepin *Trading* ☎ **721 3316**

French Govts
Lamine Ait-Said *Trading* ☎ **721 6227**
Paul Chetboun *Trading* ☎ **721 3313**

Swedish, Danish Govts
Jorn Grodeland *Trading* ☎ **721 3095, 721 6164**
Anders Hellstrom *Trading* ☎ **721 3095, 721 6164**

Spanish Govts
Luis Valderrama *Trading* ☎ **721 3319**

Italian Govts
Dario Giorgi *Trading* ☎ **+39 (02) 430 0925**
Antonio Bovo *Trading* ☎ **+39 (02) 430 0925**
Stafania Abelli *Trading* ☎ **+39 (02) 430 0925**
Gianni Boscia *Trading* ☎ **+39 (02) 430 0925**

US Govts
Chris Bowers *Trading* ☎ **721 3296**

European Governments
Christopher Peel *Sales* ☎ **721 3146**
Tim Lynch *Sales* ☎ **721 3154**

UNITED KINGDOM (+44)　　　www.euromoneydirectory.com

Salomon Smith Barney (cont)
Non-Domestic Government Bonds (cont)

	Claire Henderson *Sales* ☏ **721 3112**
	Irene Ferrer *Sales* ☏ **721 3112**
	Mark Healey *Sales* ☏ **721 3154**
	Liz Creber *Sales* ☏ **721 6205**
US / Canadian Governments	Christopher Harbach *Sales* ☏ **721 3282**
	Kathy Geary *Sales* ☏ **721 3282**
	Paisley Arnold *Sales* ☏ **721 3282**
	David Campbell *Sales* ☏ **721 3282**
	Francesca Hansen *Sales* ☏ **721 3282**
Governments-¥	Richard Sherwin *Sales* ☏ **721 3624, 721 3137**
	Marwan Makarem *Sales* ☏ **721 3624, 721 3137**

Fixed-Income Repo
Trading　　　Catherine FitzMaurice *Repurchase Agreements* ☏ **721 3406**

Equity Capital Markets
Global Head　　　Robert DiFazio *Co-Head of Global Equities*
Regional Head　　　Tim Heekin *Managing Director & Co-Head of Global Equity Tradi*
　　　John St John *Head, Equities Syndicate / CM* ☏ **721 3745**
　　　David Turnbull *Head, European Equities* ☏ **721 3600**
Country Head　　　Gordon Lawson *Co-Head of Trading* ☏ **721 3581**
Marketing　　　John Nicolis *Head of Sales* ☏ **721 6078**

Domestic Equities
Head of Syndication　　　David Hatt ☏ **721 3752**
Head of Sales　　　Grant Cullents *UK Equities Sales*
　　　Lucy Alexander *UK Equities Sales* ☏ **721 3483**
　　　Allister Malcolmson *UK Equities Sales* ☏ **721 3483**
　　　Paul Miskin *UK Equities Sales* ☏ **721 3483**
Head of Trading　　　Gary Martin *Head of UK Equity Trading*
　　　Anthony Carter *UK Equities Trading* ☏ **721 3475**
　　　Richard O'Hare *UK Equities Trading* ☏ **721 3490**
　　　David Gill *UK Equities Trading*
　　　Gary Martin *Head of UK Equity Trading*
　　　Matthew Young *UK Equities Trading*

Other (Domestic Equities)
Equity Syndicate / Capital Markets　　　David Hatt ☏ **721 3752**
Equities Emerging Market　　　Michael Bates *Trading* ☏ **721 3097**
　　　Hikmat Chadirichi *Trading* ☏ **721 3097**
　　　Stephen Phipps *Sales* ☏ **721 3588**
　　　Unal Kurtaran *Sales* ☏ **721 3588**
　　　Nick Reid *Sales* ☏ **721 3588**
　　　William Shor *Sales* ☏ **721 3588**
Equities Programme　　　Steve Garnett *Trading* ☏ **721 1881**
　　　Jason Belne *Trading* ☏ **721 1880**

International Equities
Head of Sales　　　Hagen Luctzow *MD & Head of Equity Sales in Europe & Middle East*
　　　Vincent Barnouin *Managing Director & Head of European Equity Sales*

Other (International Equity)
Continental Equity　　　Martin Couglan *Trading* ☏ **721 3454**
　　　Julia Hornig *Trading* ☏ **721 3454**
　　　Adolfo Carvajal *Trading* ☏ **721 3454**
　　　Peter Stephens *Sales* ☏ **721 3428**
　　　David Knight *Sales* ☏ **721 6129**
　　　David Berney *Sales*
　　　Adam Cohen *Sales*
　　　Max Davey *Sales*
　　　Michael Galy *Sales*
　　　Lucy Guest *Sales*
　　　Peter Smythe *Sales*
　　　Therese Turek *Sales*
Equity Pacific Rim Convertibles　　　Peter Wells *Trading* ☏ **721 3598**
　　　Paul Sanger *Trading*
Equity Pacific Rim　　　Harry R Wells *Sales* ☏ **721 3596**
　　　Barnaby Smith *Sales* ☏ **721 1742**
　　　Sumy Ahn *Sales*
　　　Edward Parker *Sales*
　　　Charles Todhunter *Sales*
US Equity　　　David Scully *Sales* ☏ **721 3586**
　　　Michael Anderson *Sales* ☏ **721 3585**
　　　Nick Hardcastle *Sales* ☏ **721 3576**

www.euromoneydirectory.com UNITED KINGDOM (+44)

Other (International Equity) (cont)

	Igor Bove-Ziemann *Sales*
	Pietro Chiesa *Sales*
	John Davey *Sales*
	Lawerence Evans *Sales*
	Peter Marr *Sales*
	Vanessa Rowan *Sales*
	Luca Terribile *Sales*
Equities Latin American	Sophie Stylianou *Sales* ☎ **721 3582**
	Josh Jacobson *Sales*
Japanese Equity	Anthony Beckwith *Sales* ☎ **721 3608**
	Philippe De Raucourt *Sales*
	Barry May *Sales*
	John McIntyre *Sales*
	Benjamin Musgrave *Sales*
	Francesco Thovez *Sales*
	Brian Dimitroff

Convertibles / Equity-Linked
Head of Sales

Gareth Wiley *Equity Convertibles Sales* ☎ **721 3463**
Cindy Ferrara *Equity Convertibles Sales* ☎ **721 3463**
Hamish Bullough *Equity Convertibles Sales* ☎ **721 3463**

Head of Trading

Mike Reed *Equity Convertibles Trading* ☎ **721 3537**
Paul Sanger *Equity Convertibles Trading*
Eric Smadja *Equity Convertibles Trading*
Howard Dyson *Equity Convertibles Trading* ☎ **721 3086**

Others (Warrants)
Japanese Equity Warrants   Paul Nelson ☎ **721 3560**

Syndicated Lending
Other (Syndicated Lending)
Borrow / Loans   Rod Barr *Head Equity Trader* ☎ **721 3418**

Risk Management
Trading   Simon Bowden ☎ **721 3245**

Other (FI Derivatives)
DM Vol / GBP   Peter Cripwell *Trading*
FFr / BFr / ECU / ITL   Simon Bowden *Trading*
DKr / Pfandbriefe   Niels Farragher *Trading*
Scandinavian   Alistair Blyth *Trading*
Pta & Pte / Vol; ITL   Jerome Stuart *Trading*

Other Currency Swap / FX Options Personnel
Asset Swaps   Jason Ekaireb *Trading* ☎ **721 3440**
 Anthony Nahum *Trading* ☎ **721 3440**

OTC Equity Derivatives
Sales

Richard McGuire ☎ **721 3524**
Bill Russell
Richard Burns ☎ **721 3521**
Andrew Stonely
Jo Vittoria
Stefan Wagner
Doug Welch
Archna Shastri

Trading

Andrew Crane ☎ **721 3493, 721 3498**
P J Beaghton ☎ **721 3493, 721 3498**

Other (Exchange-Traded Derivatives)
Government OTC Options   John Hom *Trading* ☎ **721 3322**

Exchange-Traded Derivatives
FX Futures

Fred Massey *Global Futures* ☎ **721 3148, 721 3114**
Justin Abrahams *Global Futures* ☎ **721 3148, 721 3114**
Paul Brownsey *Global Futures* ☎ **721 3148, 721 3114**
John Miya *Global Futures* ☎ **721 3148, 721 3114**

Department: Banks / Derivatives / Germany
Other (Exchange-Traded Derivatives)
Banks

David Gibbs ☎ **721 3119**
Valentin Ehmer ☎ **721 6206**
Andreas Stavrou
Justin Stratton-Christensen
Nicola Noel-Smith
Dominic de Ban
Charlotte Watters
Michel Planquart

UNITED KINGDOM (+44)   www.euromoneydirectory.com

Salomon Smith Barney (cont)
Other (Exchange-Traded Derivatives) (cont)

Derivatives

Linda Newman
Giuseppina Visalli
Philippe Katz ☎ **721 3192**
Craig King ☎ **721 3430**
Daniel Kershaw
Barbara Oldani
Roland Toussaint

Germany

Stefan Fischer
Christian Schaefer
Astrid Steiger

Settlement / Clearing
Operations   Gerard LaRocca *Head of Operations* ☎ **721 2241**
Administration
Compliance
Frederic Krieger *Head* ☎ **721 3613**

Corporate Communications
Susan Tether *Head*

Other (Administration)
Human Resources   Morley West *Head* ☎ **721 2883**

San Paolo Bank   Full Branch Office
Wren House, 15 Carter Lane, London EC4V 5SP
Tel: (171) 214 8990 **Fax:** (171) 236 2698 **Telex:** 8811148/9 **Swift:** IBSP GB 2L **Reuters:** IBSP
Telerate: 6423 (ITL), 6576 Ecu
Reuters: ISTL (Forex/LIRA); ISTE (Money Market); SPLA-G (Capital Markets)

Senior Executive Officers
Chief Manager   Gianni Mallen
Deputy Chief Manager   Carlo Pittatore

General-Lending (DCM, SL)
Head of Corporate Banking
Renato Carducci *Head, Corporate Banking*
Rory Farquahar-Thompson *Italian Desk*
Lodovico Rosnati *UK Desk*
Chris Stamford *Scandinavian Desk*

Debt Capital Markets / Fixed Income
Tel: 489 8990 **Fax:** 236 2698
Country Head
E Namor *Joint Head, Capital Markets Group*
C Pittatore *Joint Head, Capital Markets Group*

Fixed-Income Repo
Trading
M R Primerano *Sales*
R Matteucci
A Lazzerini *Sales*

Equity Capital Markets
Fax: 489 1881
Equity Repo / Securities Lending
Marketing & Product Development   Paola Pernice *Trader*

Syndicated Lending
Loan-Related Activities
Project Finance
Mark Cameron *Project & Structured Finance*
Luca Ravano *Project & Structured Finance*
Jonathan Graham *Project & Structured Finance*

Other (Trade Finance)
Forfaiting   Steve Braid
Structured Products   D Menini

Risk Management
Other Currency Swap / FX Options Personnel
Swaptions   M Baldi
Swaps   U Menconi
Options   A Mendelson
LIFFE Floor   P Dalton

OTC Equity Derivatives
Trading
M Mocio *Equity Derivatives*
A de Bustis *Equity Derivatives*

1858   Euromoney Directory 1999

www.euromoneydirectory.com UNITED KINGDOM (+44)

Exchange-Traded Derivatives
FX Futures; FX Options; IR Futures; IR Options   L La Vecchia

Sandown Capital Corporation   Head Office
1 Northumberland Avenue, London WC2N 5BW
Tel: (171) 872 5790 Fax: (171) 872 5791

Senior Executive Officers
Chief Executive Officer   Salim Lalani

Debt Capital Markets / Fixed Income

Private Placements
Head of Origination   Salim Lalani

Asset-Backed Securities / Securitization
Global Head   Salim Lalani

Syndicated Lending

Loan-Related Activities
Project Finance   Salim Lalani

Corporate Finance / M&A Advisory
Global Head   Salim Lalani

The Sanwa Bank Limited   Full Branch Office
PO Box 36, City Place House, 55 Basinghall Street, London EC2V 5DL
Tel: (171) 330 5000 Fax: (171) 330 5555 Telex: 888350 Swift: SANW GB 2LA

Senior Executive Officers
Managing Director & General Manager   Tomoyuki Fuji ☎ **330 5021**
Joint General Manager   Atsushi Kuwata ☎ **330 5021**
Joint General Manager   Stuart Harland ☎ **330 5505**
International Division   Masayuki Tomoda *DGM, Joint Head of International Finance* ☎ **330 5141**
                                          Graham Franklin *DGM, Joint Head of International Finance* ☎ **330 5150**
                                          Toshikazu Wada *Senior Manager, International Finance* ☎ **330 5133**
                                          Yannis Kalogeropoulos *Manager, International Finance* ☎ **330 5137**

General-Lending (DCM, SL)
Head of Corporate Banking   Peter Lucas *Joint GM & Head- UK* ☎ **330 5020**
                                          Steve Lewis *DGM, Corporate Banking- UK* ☎ **330 5050**
                                          Duncan Passmore *AGM, Corporate Banking- UK* ☎ **330 5031**
                                          Hiroyuki Onose *DGM & Head- Japan* ☎ **330 5120**

General - Treasury
Head of Treasury   Kichiro Tsuchino *Joint GM & Head, Treasury* ☎ **330 5800**

Syndicated Lending
Head of Syndicated Lending   Graham Franklin *DGM, Joint Head of International Finance* ☎ **330 5150**

Other (Syndicated Lending)
                                          Peter Hursthouse *Senior Manager* ☎ **330 5154**
                                          Sally McKean *Manager* ☎ **330 5135**
                                          Alan Greenhow *Assistant Manager* ☎ **330 5153**

Loan-Related Activities
Trade Finance   Robert Angliss *Manager* ☎ **330 5142**
Aircraft / Aerospace Finance   Margot Healy *Manager* ☎ **330 5094**
Project Finance   John Watkins *Deputy General Manager* ☎ **330 5110**
                                          Bob Prince *Assistant General Manager* ☎ **330 5112**
                                          Graeme Thorne *Senior Manager* ☎ **330 5107**
Structured Trade Finance   Ian Hosier *Deputy General Manager & Head* ☎ **330 5090**
                                          Koichi Fujita *Senior Manager* ☎ **330 5091**
                                          Bob Angliss *Manager* ☎ **330 5142**

Other (Trade Finance)
Oil, Gas & Petrochemicals   Gainer Kwan *Senior Manager* ☎ **330 5116**
Financial Engineering   Elisabeth Wenusch *Assistant General Manager* ☎ **330 5099**
Leveraged Finance MBO / LBO   Graham Villiers *Senior Manager* ☎ **330 5033**

Money Markets
Regional Head   Toshiya Sekioka *Deputy General Manager* ☎ **330 5870**

Euromoney Directory 1999   **1859**

UNITED KINGDOM (+44)   www.euromoneydirectory.com

The Sanwa Bank Limited (cont)

Foreign Exchange
Regional Head — Douglas Bate *Assistant General Manager* ☎ **330 5843**
Corporate Sales — Ashley Clarke *Senior Manager* ☎ **330 5915**

FX Traders / Sales People
Sales — Yvonne Baczko ☎ **330 5913**
Paul Clarke ☎ **330 5916**
Jila Sheikhi ☎ **330 5918**
Cathy Cable ☎ **330 5917**
Kyoko Yumoto ☎ **330 5911**

Risk Management
Global Head — K Yamashita *General Manager*
Country Head — T Omori *Deputy General Manager* ☎ **330 5859**

Fixed Income Derivatives / Risk Management
Regional Head — Thomas Watkins *Deputy General Manager* ☎ **330 5830**

Foreign Exchange Derivatives / Risk Management
Vanilla FX option Trading — Yoshihisa Yamanaka *Manager* ☎ **330 5841**

Settlement / Clearing
Regional Head — Yoshitaka Fukuyama *Deputy General Manager* ☎ **330 5610**
Country Head — Michael Davies *Senior Manager* ☎ **330 5612**
Derivatives Settlement — James Galloway *Manager* ☎ **330 5620**
Foreign Exchange Settlement — Jennifer Moore *Manager* ☎ **330 5656**

Other Departments
Correspondent Banking — Siew Chiow Walton *Manager* ☎ **330 5151**

Administration

Technology & Systems
Dave Dixon *Assistant General Manager* ☎ **330 5670**

Legal / In-House Counsel
Mark Riley *Assistant General Manager* ☎ **330 5540**

Compliance
Paul Holt *Senior Manager* ☎ **330 5525**

Saudi American Bank
Full Branch Office

Nightingale House, 65 Curzon Street, London W1Y 7PE
Tel: (171) 355 4411 Fax: (171) 355 4416 Telex: 885124 SAMA LG

Saudi British Bank

18c Curzon Street, London W1Y 8AA
Tel: (171) 409 2567 Fax: (171) 495 2329

Senior Executive Officers
Managing Director / General Manager — Michael R Odell

Saudi International Bank

One Knightsbridge, London SW1X 7XS
Tel: (171) 259 3456 Fax: (171) 259 6060

Senior Executive Officers
Managing Director / General Manager — Robert McGinn

Equity Capital Markets

Equity Repo / Securities Lending
Marketing & Product Development — David Waite *Head, Portfolio Management*
Ceri Burchell *Fund Manager*
Gareth Roberts *Fund Manager*
Peter James *Fund Manager*

www.euromoneydirectory.com UNITED KINGDOM (+44)

SBCM Limited

4th Floor, Temple Court, 11 Queen Victoria Street, London EC4N 4TA
Tel: (171) 786 1400 Fax: (171) 248 5905 Telex: 887244 SBCM UK G
Website: www.sbcm.com

Senior Executive Officers
Chairman — Naoyuki Kawamoto
Managing Director / General Manager — Antony Yates ☎ 786 1403

Others (Senior Executives)
UK, Ireland, South Africa & Middle East — A Willett *Marketing* ☎ 786 1435
N Sangha *Marketing* ☎ 786 1430
Scandinavia, Germany, Austria, Eastern Europe; Russia & The Baltics — K Nadel *Marketing* ☎ 786 1419
France, Benelux, Switzerland, Italy, Mediterranean — O Uyttenhove *Marketing* ☎ 786 1412
C Dutournier *Marketing* ☎ 786 1448
Spain, Portugal & Malta — F Carballo *Marketing* ☎ 786 1421
Financial Engineering — M Hartley ☎ 786 1437

Debt Capital Markets / Fixed Income
Bonds - General
Yen & $ — Antony Yates ☎ 786 1403
C Bird ☎ 786 1433
N Clinton ☎ 786 1404
Sterling — David Radford ☎ 786 1408
European Currencies — C Drieu la Rochelle ☎ 786 1440
I West ☎ 786 1438
P Coward ☎ 786 1444
A Yin ☎ 786 1407
B Sherman ☎ 786 1418

SBI European Bank

State Bank House, 1 Milk Street, London EC2P 2JP
Tel: (171) 600 4535 Fax: (171) 600 4497 Telex: 8814059

Senior Executive Officers
Managing Director / General Manager — R Sundararaman

J Henry Schroder & Co Limited   Head Office

120 Cheapside, London EC2V 6DS
Tel: (171) 658 6000 Fax: (171) 658 3950
Website: www.schroder.com

Senior Executive Officers
Chairman — David Challen
Financial Director — David Morris *Group Financial Controller*

Debt Capital Markets / Fixed Income
Global Head — Andrew Sykes *Group Managing Director*

Private Placements
Head of Origination — Stephen Schechter *Director*

Equity Capital Markets
Regional Head — Paul Sauvary *Director*

Domestic Equities
Head of Origination — John McNeil *Director*
Head of Syndication — Richard Wyatt *Director*
Head of Sales — Peter Lloyd *Director*
Head of Research — Patrick Wellington *Director*

International Equities
Head of Syndication — Maurizio Tassi *Director*
Head of Sales — Ruth Sack *Director*
Head of Trading — Glenn Poulter *Director*
Head of Research — Michael Crawshaw *Director*

Convertibles / Equity-Linked
Head of Origination — Robin Blundin *Director*
Head of Trading — Tarek Saber

Euromoney Directory 1999   **1861**

UNITED KINGDOM (+44)   www.euromoneydirectory.com

J Henry Schroder & Co Limited (cont)

Syndicated Lending
Global Head — John Rock *Director*

Money Markets
Global Head — Nigel Harris *Director*

Wholesale Deposits
Head of Sales — Caroline Hursford *Assistant Director*

Foreign Exchange
Corporate Sales — Mike Ricketts *Director*
Head of Trading — Scott Swift

Risk Management
Fixed Income Derivatives / Risk Management
IR Swaps Sales / Marketing — Mike Ricketts *Director*
IR Swaps Trading — Nigel Harris *Director*

Corporate Finance / M&A Advisory
Global Head — Richard Broadbent *Director*

Administration
Legal / In-House Counsel
Francis Neate *Group Legal Adviser*

Compliance
Richard Sadleir *Director*

Public Relations
Donald Cameron *Director*

Schroder Asseily & Co Limited — Subsidiary Company

41 Upper Grosvenor Street, London W1X 0LP
Tel: (171) 318 1000 Fax: (171) 493 0420 Telex: 299197

Senior Executive Officers
Chief Executive Officer — Anthony N Asseily *Chief Executive*

Others (Senior Executives)
Richard Foulkes *Non-Executive Director*
G W Mallinckrodt *Non-Executive Director*
Robert Swannell *Non-Executive Director*
Alan Munro *Non-Executive Director*
Leslie Murphy *Non-Executive Director*

Equity Capital Markets
Country Head — Philip Winder *Director*

Corporate Finance / M&A Advisory
Country Head — George Asseily *Senior Director*

Other (Corporate Finance)
Shafic J Ali *Director*
Timothy Holder *Assistant Director*

Asset Management
Investment Funds — Fadi Salibi *Director, Investment Division*
Jeffrey Sawyer *Assistant Director, Investments*

Administration
Technology & Systems
Rafic Nahed *Head of IT*

Schroder Investment Management Limited — Subsidiary Company

31 Gresham Street, London EC2V 7QA
Tel: (171) 658 2000 Fax: (171) 658 6965 Telex: 885029 JHS G Email: simmkt@schroders.com
Website: www.schroders.com

Senior Executive Officers
Chairman — David Salisbury
Chief Executive Officer — Hugh Bolland
Financial Director — Peter Meyer
Managing Director — Nicola Ralston
International Division — Jeremy Hill *Chairman, SIM International*

1862 Euromoney Directory 1999

www.euromoneydirectory.com UNITED KINGDOM (+44)

Debt Capital Markets / Fixed Income
Head of Fixed Income — Keith Niven
Emerging Market Bonds
Head of Emerging Markets — Jan Kingzett

Global Custody
Head of Global Custody — Mark Smith

Other Departments
Cash Management — Robert Barnard-Smith

Administration
Head of Administration — Stephen Newton
Head of Marketing — Julian Samways

Technology & Systems
— Frank Froud

Legal / In-House Counsel
— Kylie Edwards

Compliance
— Jeremy Willougby

Scotia McLeod Inc

33 Finsbury Square, London EC2A 1BB
Tel: (171) 638 5644 **Fax:** (171) 826 5971

Debt Capital Markets / Fixed Income
Tel: 256 5656 **Fax:** 826 5971

Fixed-Income Repo
Head of Repo; Trading — Simon Musselwhite *Associate Director* 826 5952
Trading — Kelvin Seddon *Associate Director*

Equity Capital Markets
Tel: 256 5952 **Fax:** 826 5971

Equity Repo / Securities Lending
Head of Trading — Simon Musselwhite *Associate Director* 826 5952
— Kelvin Seddon *Associate Director*

Securities Trading (UK) Limited   Head Office

The Linen Hall, 162/168 Regent Street, London W1R 5TB
Tel: (171) 306 3120 **Fax:** (171) 306 3122 **Email:** kupo@ibm.net

Senior Executive Officers
Managing Director / General Manager — Kurt Portmann

Equity Capital Markets

Other (Domestic Equities)
USA & Canada — Kurt Portmann

International Equities
Head of Sales; Head of Trading — Kurt Portmann

Seoulbank   Full Branch Office

Formerly known as: Bank of Seoul

3 Finsbury Square, London EC2A 1AD
Tel: (171) 588 6162 **Fax:** (171) 588 9655 **Telex:** 8951507 **Swift:** BSEO GB 2L

Senior Executive Officers
General Manager — Jong Dal Lee
Deputy General Manager — Soo Kyung Rho

General-Lending (DCM, SL)
Head of Corporate Banking — Ki Young Yang *Manager, Loans*

General - Treasury
Head of Treasury — Man Sup Yoon *Treasury Manager*

Administration
Other (Administration) — Jun Ho Park *Systems Manager*

Euromoney Directory 1999 **1863**

UNITED KINGDOM (+44)   www.euromoneydirectory.com

The 77 Bank Limited
Representative Office

6th Floor, Finsbury Circus House, 12/15 Finsbury Circus, London EC2M 7EB
Tel: (171) 628 5506 Fax: (171) 628 0561 Telex: 933055

Senior Executive Officers
Chief Representative   K Kikuta

SG
Full Branch Office

SG House, 41 Tower Hill, London EC3N 4SG
Tel: (171) 676 6000 Telex: 886611, 884691/2 (General) Swift: SOGE GB 2L Reuters: SGFX Telerate: Recipient
Website: www.socgen.com

Senior Executive Officers
Chief Executive Officer   Patrick Gelin Chief Executive Officer- UK

Others (Senior Executives)
Financial Markets Division   Vincent Cazala Executive Director & Head ☏ 762 4003
FIMAT   Vincent Taupin Head

General-Lending (DCM, SL)
Head of Corporate Banking   Frederic Oudea
                                    David Thomas Marketing Director
                                    Stuart Lawton Director, Natural Resources
                                    Bruce Pomford Director, Media & Communications
                                    David Gavaghan Director, Transport
                                    Eric Wormser Director, Food & Industry
                                    Jacques Hippolyte Director, International Corporates

Relationship Manager
Financial Institutions Group   Chris Day Managing Director & Head

Debt Capital Markets / Fixed Income
Fax: (171) 571 2999
Head of Debt Capital Markets   Jonathan Vellacott
Head of Fixed Income   Philippe Rakotovao Head
                                    Paul Hills Deputy Head

Department: Global Equities
Exchange House, Primrose Street, London, EC2A 2HT
Tel: +44 (171) 762 4444

Emerging Market Bonds
Head of Emerging Markets   Patrick Shanahan Joint MD, SG European Emerging Markets
                                    Andrea Steer Joint MD, SG European Emerging Markets
                                    Mark Street Head, Global Emerging Markets

Equity Capital Markets
Department: Global Equities
Exchange House, Primrose Street, London, EC2A 2HT
Tel: +44 (171) 762 4444
Head of Equity Capital Markets   Yves Tuloup Chairman, SG Securities (London)
                                    Hugh Hughes Chief Executive
Regional Head   Steven Gee Head of Equities, Deputy CEO
Head of Sales   Stuart Glenister Head of Equity Sales & Trading
                                    Hugh de Lusignan Head of UK Equity Sales
                                    Ian Burn Head, Continental European Equity Sales

Syndicated Lending
Head of Syndication   Richard Rae Director, Loan Syndications

Loan-Related Activities
Trade Finance; Commodities Financing   Will Nagle Director
Project Finance   Tony Phillips MD, Project & Sectorial Finance

Other (Trade Finance)
Export Finance   Alan Paton Director
Property   Etienne Thoreau Head of UK Property
Financial Engineering   David Coxon MD & Deputy Global Head, Financial Engineering

Risk Management

Other (FI Derivatives)
Product Line   Daniel Sfez Global Head
Interest Rate Derivatives   Michael Grindle Head

Other (Exchange-Traded Derivatives)
Insurance Derivatives   Diego Wauters Head

Department: Global Equities
Exchange House, Primrose Street, London, EC2A 2HT
Tel: +44 (171) 762 4444
OTC Equity Derivatives
Head Pierre-Yves Morlat
Sales Charles Annandale
Corporate Finance / M&A Advisory
Department: Corporate Finance (UK)
Global Head Yves-Claude Abescat *Global Head & CEO*
 Stephen Brisby *Global Head & CEO*
Regional Head Francois Meunier *Head, Europe*
 William Nabarro *Managing Director*
Country Head Ian Ramsay *Head, UK*
 James Coulson *Chief Executive Officer- UK*
 Kim Fennebresque *Head, North America*
Private Equity Philippe Sevin *Head*
Acquistion Finance Rob Bonfield *Director & Head*
Global Custody
Fund Administration Steven Bobasch *MD, Head of European Fund Relationships*
Asset Management
Department: SocGen Asset Management
100 Ludgate Hill, London, EC4M 7RE
Tel: +44 (171) 815 8600
Head Nicola Horlick *Joint Managing Director*
 John Richards *Joint Managing Director*
Department: SocGen Emerging Europe Asset Management
Devon House, St Katharine's Way, London, E1 9LB
Tel: +44 (171) 480 6022
Head Richard Harding *Managing Director*
Other Departments
Correspondent Banking Francois Coulet *Head*
Cash Management Gary Cassis *Head*
Department: SG Private Banking
41 Tower Hill, London, EC3N 4SG
Tel: +44 (171) 676 6000
Private Banking Stephane Hild *Joint Managing Director, SG Hambros*
 Warwick Newbury *Joint Managing Director, SG Hambros*
Administration
Other (Administration)
Global Banking & Securities Services Etienne Deniau *Head*

Shanghai Commercial Bank Limited

65 Cornhill, London EC3V 3NB
Tel: (171) 369 8888 Fax: (171) 369 8800 Telex: 884643 Swift: SCBK GB 2X

The Shoko Chukin Bank

4th Floor, Bow Bells House, Bread Street, London EC4M 9BQ
Tel: (171) 236 2805 Fax: (171) 236 3446

Senior Executive Officers
General Manager Takeo Ota

The Siam Commercial Bank Public Company Limited

Full Branch Office

2nd Floor, Kings House, 36-37 King Street, London EC2V 8BB
Tel: (171) 606 7596 Fax: (171) 606 3746 Telex: 892580 SCBLDN G Swift: SICO GB 2L
Email: scb-london@dial.pipex.com

Senior Executive Officers
Chief Executive Officer Ongorn Lerlop *VP & General Manager*
Treasurer Martin Warmsley
Syndicated Lending
Head of Origination; Head of Syndication Ongorn Lerlop *VP & General Manager*

UNITED KINGDOM (+44) www.euromoneydirectory.com

The Siam Commercial Bank Public Company Limited (cont)
Settlement / Clearing
Head of Settlement / Clearing — William Skinner
Administration
Head of Administration — Steven Sim
Business Development — Suradej Krainavaphan *Manager, Personal Banking*
Technology & Systems
Teerachai Srisasi *EDP Administrator*
Accounts / Audit
Kasemsak Potiaumpai

Sime Bank — Representative Office
Formerly known as: United Malayan Banking Corporation Berhad
1st Floor, Nuffield House, 41/46 Piccadilly, London W1V 0HB
Tel: (171) 287 1182 **Fax:** (171) 494 3721 **Email:** simebank@dial.pipex.com
Senior Executive Officers
Head of London Representative Office — Abd-Alim Shapie

Singer & Friedlander Capital Markets Limited — Subsidiary Company
1 Canada Square, London E14 5AA
Tel: (171) 867 8300 **Fax:** (171) 867 8301 **Email:** abc@key1.com
Senior Executive Officers
Chief Executive Officer — Timothy Lyons
  Jonathan Stolerman
Financial Director — Fiona Page
Others (Senior Executives)
  Alison Smith
  Jeremy Scott
  Chris Pink

Singer & Friedlander Holdings Limited
21 New Street, Bishopsgate, London EC2M 4HR
Tel: (171) 623 3000 **Fax:** (171) 623 2122 **Telex:** 886977
Senior Executive Officers
Chairman — A N Solomons
Chief Executive Officer — J Hodson
Financial Director — M E S Gibbins *Group Finance Director*
Company Secretary — R Fiddemont
Assistant Company Secretary — Stephen Doherty ☎ 523 5078 🖷 929 2912
Others (Senior Executives)
Non-Executive Director — N C England
  H R Hutton
  P C Button
  M J L Cramsie
  B N Gorst
  T R Howe
  C B Price
  R R Clough
  V M Segal
  A M Stewart
  M P Sutton

Singer & Friedlander Limited — Head Office
21 New Street, Bishopsgate, London EC2M 4HR
Tel: (171) 623 3000; (171) 523 5000 **Fax:** (171) 623 2122 **Telex:** 886977 **Swift:** SIFR GB 2L
Senior Executive Officers
Chairman — Anthony Solomons
Chief Executive Officer — John Hodson *Chief Executive*
Financial Director — M E S Gibbins
Company Secretary — R Fiddemont

1866 Euromoney Directory 1999

Senior Executive Officers (cont)
International Division
Victor M Segal *Director*

Others (Senior Executives)
Marc J L Cramsie *Director*
Charles B Price *Director*

General-Lending (DCM, SL)
Head of Corporate Banking
Charles B Price *Director*
Department: Domestic Banking Department

Others (Senior Executives)
Director
Charles B Price *Director*
Darryl Keys
Charles Mavor
Brian Ovenden
Jonathan Spence

Syndicated Lending
Loan-Related Activities
Structured Trade Finance
Peter Griffiths *Director*

Money Markets
Global Head
Graham Simkins *Assistant Director*

Money Markets - General
David Bimpson
Keven Wood
Michael Scrivener

Corporate Finance / M&A Advisory
Global Head
Marc J L Cramsie *Director*

Skandinaviska Enskilda Banken AB (publ) — Full Branch Office

Alternative trading name: ENSKILDA Futures, DCM, Research, Securities, Securities Capital Management
2/6 Cannon Street, London EC4M 6XX
Tel: (171) 246 4000 **Fax:** (171) 588 0929 **Telex:** 8950281 ESSELDN G **Swift:** ESSE GB 2L

Senior Executive Officers
Financial Director
Marcus A Scarlett *Finance Officer* T **246 4205**
General Manager
Stewart R Humphrey T **246 4055**

Debt Capital Markets / Fixed Income
Department: Skandinaviska Enskilda Banken AB (publ)
Tel: 329 6679 **Fax:** 638 2498
Global Head
Michael Dicks *Head* T **329 6679**

Domestic Government Bonds
Head of Sales; Head of Trading
Per Thorell *Head* T **588 7721**

Eurobonds
Head of Origination
Michael Dicks *Head* T **329 6679**
Head of Syndication; Head of Sales
David Eley
Head of Trading
Jamie Morris T **638 5734**

Libor-Based / Floating-Rate Products
FRN Origination
Michael Dicks *Head* T **329 6679**
FRN Sales; Asset Swaps (Sales)
David Eley

Medium-Term Notes
Head of Origination
Michael Dicks *Head* T **329 6679**
Head of Structuring; Head of Sales
David Eley

Private Placements
Head of Origination
Michael Dicks *Head* T **329 6679**
Head of Sales; Head of Structuring
David Eley

Equity Capital Markets
Department: Enskilda Securities Capital Management
Tel: 248 0618 **Fax:** 248 0208
Global Head
Bo Zethraeus *Head* T **246 3109** E **bo.zethraeus@enskilda.se**

International Equities
Head of Origination
David Glasspool *Head* T **246 4196**
Head of Syndication
Bo Zethraeus *Head* T **246 3109** E **bo.zethraeus@enskilda.se**
Head of Sales
Mark Hawtin *Head of Sales & Research* T **246 3123**
Head of Trading
David Goodman *Global Head, Trading* T **246 3127**
Head of Research
Mark Hawtin *Head of Sales & Research* T **246 3123**

UNITED KINGDOM (+44)   www.euromoneydirectory.com

Skandinaviska Enskilda Banken AB (publ) (cont)

Other (International Equity)
Mergers & Acquisitions — Nigel McNelly *Head* ☎ 246 4218
Capital Management — Gurdeep S Hansra *Head, Enskilda Securities Cap Mgmt* ☎ 246 4081

Syndicated Lending
Department: Enskilda Debt Capital Markets
Global Head of Origination; Head of Syndication — Michael Dicks *Head* ☎ 329 6679

Loan-Related Activities
Trade Finance — Stephan Holmgren *Head, Commercial Banking* ☎ 246 4391
Shipping Finance — Scott Lewallen *Head of Shipping, London* ☎ 246 4062
Leasing & Asset Finance — David Crec *Head* ☎ 246 4302

Money Markets
Global Head — Peder Hagberg ☎ +46 (8) 763 8000
Country Head — Stephen Jordan *Head, MM, London* ☎ 246 3221

Eurocommercial Paper
Head of Origination — Michael Dicks *Head* ☎ 329 6679
Head of Sales; Head of Trading — Maria Zlotnich ☎ 638 2491

Foreign Exchange
Global Head — Annika Bolin ☎ +46 (8) 763 8000
Regional Head — Marcus Nysten ☎ 588 6414
Country Head — David Goodhill *Head, Interbank Sales* ☎ 246 3207
Head of Institutional Sales — Phillipa Mitchel *Head, Institutional Clients* ☎ 246 4338
Corporate Sales — John Detlef *Head, Treasury Sales*

FX Traders / Sales People
Forward US$, Dm, Yen, Swfr, Ffr — Shelley Weeks

Risk Management
Global Head — Graham Vickery ☎ +46 (8) 763 8000
Country Head — Colin Swanson *Head, Risk Management, International* ☎ 246 4317

Exotic Options (Barriers, Range, Timers, Digitals, Faders etc)
Trading — Saleem Shaikh *FX Options*

Exchange-Traded Derivatives
Global Head — Ulla Nilsson *Head, Enskilda Futures*

Corporate Finance / M&A Advisory
Department: Corporate Finance
Global Head — Lars Linder Aronson *Global Head, Enskilda Securities* ☎ +46 (8) 5222 9500
Regional Head — John Abrahamson *Head, Corporate Finance*
Country Head — Malcolm Crow *Head, Corporate Finance, London* ☎ 246 4207
Private Equity; Acquistion Finance — Simon Wakefield *Head* ☎ 246 4367

Settlement / Clearing
Department: Business Support
Country Head — Colin Grange *Manager, Fixed-Income & Derivatives* ☎ 246 4296
Equity Settlement — Gary Mitchell *Global Business Support Manager* ☎ 246 4279
Fixed-Income Settlement — Andy Sullivan *Manager, Fixed-Income & Derivatives* ☎ 246 4514
Derivatives Settlement — Steve G Martin *Clearing Manager* ☎ 246 4337
Foreign Exchange Settlement — David Potter *Manager, Forex & MM* ☎ 246 4423

Global Custody
Country Head — Colin Grange *Manager, Fixed-Income & Derivatives* ☎ 246 4296

Administration
Compliance
— Valerie Thomas *Compliance Officer* ☎ 246 4100

SKB Banka dd
Representative Office

37/39 Eastcheap, London EC3M 1DT
Tel: (171) 929 2174 **Fax:** (171) 929 2175

Senior Executive Officers
SVP & London Representative — Peter J Gwinnett

SLC Asset Management
Insurance Company Subsidiary

75 King William Street, London EC4N 7BE
Tel: (171) 283 8357 **Fax:** (171) 283 1134 **Telex:** 263162

Senior Executive Officers
Chairman — Steve Baker
Managing Director / General Manager — Paul Sharman

www.euromoneydirectory.com UNITED KINGDOM (+44)

Asset Management
Other (Asset Management)
SLC Asset Management   Jacqui Sokolowski ☏ **283 8357**
Administration
Head of Administration   John McKevitt *Financial Controller*
Public Relations
                           Sara Carter
                           Gina Cherrett ☏ **(1962) 852 099**

Société Générale Equities International   Subsidiary Company
Exchange House, Primrose Street, Broadgate, London EC2A 2HT
Tel: (171) 638 9000 Fax: (171) 762 4555 Telex: 883201

Senior Executive Officers
Chief Executive Officer   Hugh Hughes *Chief Executive, Global Head of Equities*

Société Générale European Emerging Markets Limited
Subsidiary Company

Alternative trading name: Société Générale Emerging Europe Asset Management Limited
Devon House, 58/60 St Katharine's Way, London E1 9LB
Tel: (171) 480 6022 Fax: (171) 480 5011

Senior Executive Officers
Managing Director, SGEEAM   Richard Harding
Joint Managing Director, SGEEM Patrick Shanahan
Joint Managing Director, SGEEM Andrea Steer

Soditic Finance Company Limited   Full Branch Office
Brettenham House, Lancaster Place, London WC2E 7EQ
Tel: (171) 872 7000 Fax: (171) 872 7100

Senior Executive Officers
Chairman   Maurice Dwek
Managing Director / General Manager Dominic Dreyfus ☏ **872 7003**
Equity Capital Markets
Fax: 872 7103
Global Head   Marco Dwek ☏ **872 7501**

Other (International Equity)
Sales   Pierfrancesco Vairo ☏ **872 7053**
                                  Pierpaolo Caravaggi ☏ **872 7052**
Trading   Pierfrancesco Vairo ☏ **872 7053**
                                  Pierpaolo Caravaggi ☏ **872 7052**
Settlements   Damien Maltwood ☏ **872 7056**

Syndicated Lending
Fax: 872 7101

Other (Trade Finance)
Trade Finance   Dominic Dreyfus ☏ **872 7003**
                                  Roger Bennett ☏ **872 7074**
                                  Thibault De Fontaubert ☏ **872 7075**

Corporate Finance / M&A Advisory
Fax: 872 7102

Other (Corporate Finance)
                                  Piers von Simson ☏ **872 7082**
                                  Mark Katzenellenbogen ☏ **872 7001**
                                  Oscar Lewisohn ☏ **872 7090**

Administration
Compliance
                                  Dominic Dreyfus ☏ **872 7003**

UNITED KINGDOM (+44)   www.euromoneydirectory.com

Sonali Bank

29/33 Osborn Street, London E1 6TD
PO Box 29/33, London E1 6RX
Tel: (171) 375 1391 **Fax:** (171) 375 2161; (171) 377 9924 **Telex:** 888456 SONALI G

Senior Executive Officers
Deputy General Manager   Abdul Latif Bhuiyan

Ssangyong Securities Europe Limited   Subsidiary Company

24 Chiswell Street, London EC1Y 4SP
Tel: (171) 522 0890; (171) 522 0891 **Fax:** (171) 522 0892

Senior Executive Officers
Managing Director   Ho-Young Park
Director   T H Yoo

Equity Capital Markets
Head of Equity Capital Markets   Ho-Young Park *Managing Director*
Head of Sales   James Moon *Director*

Domestic Equities
Head of Sales   Sam Rhee *Manager*

Settlement / Clearing
Head of Settlement / Clearing   T H Yoo *Director*
Operations   Sati Banghard *Manager*

Administration
Head of Administration   Ho-Won Kim *Manager*

Compliance
                                      Sati Banghard *Manager*

Standard & Poor's   Full Branch Office

18 Finsbury Circus, London EC2M 7BP
Tel: (171) 826 3800 **Fax:** (171) 826 3890

Senior Executive Officers
Chief Executive Officer   Andrew Campbell-Hart *Head, London Office*

Standard Bank London Limited   Subsidiary Company

Cannon Bridge House, 25 Dowgate Hill, London EC4R 2SB
Tel: (171) 815 3000 **Fax:** (171) 815 3099 **Telex:** 911787 **Swift:** SBLL GB 2L **Reuters:** STDX **Cable:** sbl go
Website: www.sbl.co.uk

Senior Executive Officers
Executive Vice Chairman   Pieter C Prinsloo ☎ 815 3020 📠 815 4241
Financial Director   Ian Gibson *Director, Finance & Administration* ☎ 815 3068 📠 815 4241
Treasurer   Martin J Botha *Executive Director, Treasury* ☎ 815 3021 📠 815 4241
Company Secretary   Jim Chisholm ☎ 815 3001 📠 815 4069

Others (Senior Executives)
Global Head of Banking   Malcolm J Wilde *Executive Director* ☎ 815 3015 📠 815 4243
Head of Resource Banking   Robert A G Leith *Director* ☎ 815 4147 📠 815 3091
Financial Control   Martin Parry *Assistant General Manager*
Senior Advisor   Mel Balloch

General-Lending (DCM, SL)
Head of Corporate Banking   Jonathan First *Corporate Banking*
                                      Colin Wilson *AGM, S.A. Corporate Banking*

General - Treasury
Head of Treasury   Peter Gower *International Taxation*
                                      Keith Flood *Treasury Business Development*

Debt Capital Markets / Fixed Income
Department: Emerging Capital Markets
Tel: 929 0999 **Fax:** 815 3099
Country Head   Barrie Whitman *Corporate Debt Trading*
Head of Fixed Income Trading   Mark Devonshire *GM, Corporate Debt Trading*

1870   Euromoney Directory 1999

www.euromoneydirectory.com UNITED KINGDOM (+44)

Emerging Market Bonds
Head of Emerging Markets
Head

Equity Capital Markets
Department: Equities
Tel: 220 7000 Fax: 815 3091
Head of Equity Capital Markets

Domestic Equities
Head of Trading

Equity Research
Head of Equity Research

Syndicated Lending
Tel: 815 4231 Fax: 815 4243
Head of Trading
Head of Credit Committee

Loan-Related Activities
Trade Finance
Project Finance

Structured Trade Finance

Other (Trade Finance)
Forfaiting & Syndications

Mining Finance

Specialized Trade Finance
Structured Trade & Commodity Finance

Money Markets
Tel: 626 3333 Fax: 815 4258 Reuters: STDL
Head of Money Markets

Foreign Exchange
Tel: 626 3333 Fax: 815 4258 Reuters: STDL
Head of Foreign Exchange

Risk Management
Head of Risk Management
Country Head

Corporate Finance / M&A Advisory
Department: Corporate Finance
Tel: 815 4116 Fax: 815 3098
Head of Corporate Finance

Settlement / Clearing
Operations

Asset Management
Head

Other Departments
Commodities / Bullion
Correspondent Banking

Administration
Head of Administration
Head of Marketing

Technology & Systems
Information Technology

Legal / In-House Counsel

Compliance

Public Relations

Accounts / Audit

David Feld *Executive Director* T 815 3173 F 815 3099
Jeffrey Clifford *Assistant General Manager*
Jean Louis Dazin *Emerging Markets, Origination & Structured Product*

Nigel Roberts T 815 4105 F 815 4057

Brian Jones

Christopher Hartland-Peel T 815 4180 F 815 4057

Peter Kennedy *Assistant General Manager*
Brian J Lovell *Assistant General Manager*

Tim Whalley T 815 4155 F 815 4356
Nick Howard *Assistant General Manager*
Simon Morgan *Assistant General Manager* T 815 4107 F 815 4220
Jannie Stockenstrom *Assistant General Manager*
Jean Louis Dazin *Emerging Markets, Origination & Structured Product*
Tim M Whalley *Structured Trade & Commodity Finance*

Roy Bennett *Assistant General Manager*
Scott J Branch *General Manager*
Kelvin Russell *Assistant General Manager*
Steven L Sharpe *Assistant General Manager*
Scott Branch
Alan Linger *Assistant General Manager*

Mark Suter *Assistant General Manager* T 815 4167 F 815 4258

Mark Suter *Assistant General Manager* T 815 4167 F 815 4258

David Pitts *General Manager* T 815 3129
Graham D Bell *Assistant General Manager*

Alan Jacobson *General Manager* T 815 3082 F 815 3098

Susan C Smollett *Assistant General Manager*

Adrian De Fay T 815 4211 F 815 3188

Jim Coupland T 815 4090 F 815 4236
Peter Grafham T 815 3164 F 815 4001

Jim Chisholm T 815 3001 F 815 4069
Janice Garraway *Manager* T 815 3025 F 815 4297

Roy Lee *General Manager* T 815 3104 F 815 3099

Ben Blackett-Ord T 815 4160 F 815 4363

Diana Karter T 815 3002 F 815 4363

Janice Garraway *Manager* T 815 3025 F 815 4297

Stewart Trussler T 815 3181 F 815 4298

Euromoney Directory 1999 **1871**

UNITED KINGDOM (+44)   www.euromoneydirectory.com

Standard Chartered Bank plc
Head Office

1 Aldermanbury Square, London EC2V 7SB
Tel: (171) 280 7500 Fax: (171) 280 7156

Senior Executive Officers
Chairman — Patrick Gillam T 280 7002 F 600 2546
Chief Executive Officer — Malcolm Williamson Group Chief Executive T 280 7037 F 600 2546
Financial Director — Peter Wood Group Finance Director T 280 7018

Others (Senior Executives)
Board of Directors — Christopher Castleman T 280 7008 F 280 7236
Lord Stewartby T 280 7004 F 330 6641
Michael Green T 280 7028 F 280 7236
David Moir T 530 3006 F 338 4234
Philippe Paillart T 530 3536 F 338 8068
Ronnie Chan T +852 2879 0300 F +852 2868 6036
Ho Kwon Ping T 460 5700 F 462 0183
Keith Mackrell T 269 4846 F 269 4885
Hugh E Norton T 315 5060
Rodney Olsen T 314 4405
Ralph Robins T 222 9020 F 227 9185
Cob Stenham T 839 7771 F 839 8881
Rana Talwar

Department: Global Treasury
Fax: (171) 280 6244

Others (Senior Executives)
Paul Barker Group Head, Treasury T 280 6850
Michael Kennedy CFO-Global Treasury T 280 7822
Global Operations & IT — Mike Grime Head T 280 6044
Treasury IT — Carl Ricketts Global Head T 280 6647
Europe & Americas — Dominic O'Carroll Regional Operations Head T 280 6834
MESA & Africa — Tony Lee Regional Operations Head T 280 6607
Western Hemisphere — Michael Jeffery Regional Treasurer T 280 6078
Dealing Room — Derek Saville Head, Treasury-UK / Europe T 280 6848
Charles Boswell Head, UK / European Corporate Sales T 280 6007
Erik Johnsen Treasury UK, Operations / Administration T 280 6046

Department: Group Corporate Treasury & Taxation
Fax: (171) 280 7346

Others (Senior Executives)
Charlotte Morgan Head T 280 7310
Mike Rigg Group Corporate Treasurer T 280 7318

Department: Institutional Banking
Fax: (171) 280 7875

Others (Senior Executives)
David Loretta Chief Executive T 280 7840
Ron Creswell T 280 7381
Simon Enticknap T 280 7383
Jacqui Fitzgerald T 280 7384
Geoff Ledden T 280 7379
Julio Rojas T 280 7365
Mike Odenheimer T 280 7366
Pamela McGann T 280 7334

Department: Africa Regional Office
Fax: (171) 280 7208

Others (Senior Executives)
Chris Keljik General Manager T 280 7034
Finance — Christopher Wheeler Regional Head T 280 7098
Treasury — Claude Lobo Regional Head T +971 (4) 507 0258
Corporate & Institutional Banking — Alex Thursby Regional Head T 280 7168
Human Resources — Maureen Laurie Regional Head T 280 7076
Group IS — Colin Scott Manager T 280 7800
Co-ordinator Africa — Bill Moore T 280 7241

Syndicated Lending

Other (Trade Finance)
Structured Finance — Tony West Director, Structured Finance T 280 6894
Roy England T 280 7863

Risk Management
Country Head — Michael Flow Group Head, Credit Risk Management T 280 7820
F 280 7938

1872   Euromoney Directory 1999

UNITED KINGDOM (+44)

Other (FI Derivatives)
IR Risk Management
    Fred Lee *Head* ☎ **280 6860**
    Nick Thurlow ☎ **280 6591**
    Stuart Clayton ☎ **280 6877**
    Ian Shotton ☎ **280 6868**
    Gary Mitchell ☎ **280 6868**
    Phil Selby ☎ **280 6082**
    Chris Tinker ☎ **280 6058**

Department: Financial Institutions Risk Management
Fax: (171) 280 7839

Other (FI Derivatives)
    Ian Blyth ☎ **280 6073**
    Roger Spyer ☎ **280 6829**
    John Dobner ☎ **280 7925**
    David Sparkes ☎ **280 7918**

Department: Group Market Risk & Operational Risk
Fax: (171) 280 7064
Global Head   Euleen Goh *Group Head* ☎ **280 7079**
Regional Head   Patrick Ma *Regional Head, Market Risk - HK, China & NE Asia* ☎ **+852 2821 1516**
    Alastair Wilson *Regional Head, Market Risk - Africa & MESA* ☎ **280 7086**
    Paul Hurd *Regional Head, Market Risk - SE Asia* ☎ **+65 530 3325**
Country Head   Michael Francis *Head, Operational Risk* ☎ **280 6685**
    George Brown *Country Finance Mgr & Regional Head-Americas* ☎ **+1 (212) 612 0517**
    David Richardson *Regional Head, Market Risk - UK* ☎ **280 7092**

Department: Group Passive Risk Management
Fax: (171) 280 7295
Country Head   David Chivers *Group Head* ☎ **280 7299**
    Graham Trapnell *Group Head* ☎ **280 7300**

Other (FI Derivatives)
    John Boswell *Group Analyst* ☎ **280 7244**

Corporate Finance / M&A Advisory
Private Equity
    Jonathan Andrew *Group Head, Strategy* ☎ **280 7320**
    Michael Pitcairn *Group Strategy* ☎ **280 7230**
    Vin Plant *Group Strategy* ☎ **280 7750**
    David Stileman *Strategic Projects* ☎ **280 7529**
    David Hunt *Strategic Projects* ☎ **280 7321**
    Reg Long *Strategic Projects* ☎ **280 7239**

Settlement / Clearing
Operations   David Mallett *Group Financial Controller* ☎ **280 7317**
Electronic Banking   Roger Ward *Group Head, Global Electronic Banking* ☎ **280 7513**

Global Custody
Department: Standard Chartered Equitor
Fax: (171) 374 2350

Other (Global Custody)
    Nicholas Menges *Head, Sales-UK / Europe* ☎ **280 6510**
    David Hardman ☎ **280 6512**
    Joanne Letley ☎ **280 6520**
    Paul Lampey ☎ **280 6573**

Other Departments
Cash Management   Peter Sullivan *Group Head, Global Cash Management Services* ☎ **280 6386**

Administration
Technology & Systems
Group Technology & Operations   David Brearley *Group Head* ☎ **280 7177**
    Phil Reed ☎ **280 6446**

Legal / In-House Counsel
Group Legal Department   David Brimacombe ☎ **280 7106**
    Dominic Bacon ☎ **280 7108**
    Tim Arnold ☎ **280 7135**

Compliance
    Kate Nealon *Group Head* ☎ **280 7165**
    Ian O'Meara ☎ **280 7169**

Corporate Communications
Corporate Affairs   Christopher Makin *Manager* ☎ **280 7163**
    Tim Halford *Director* ☎ **280 7159**
Communication   John Pank *Group Head* ☎ **280 7157**

UNITED KINGDOM (+44)   www.euromoneydirectory.com

Standard Chartered Bank plc (cont)
Accounts / Audit
Group Audit & Security   Mike Hart *Group Head* ☏ **280 7250**
                                Kevin Bailey ☏ **280 7246**
Audit IT   Peter Barraclough *Group Head* ☏ **280 7412**
                                Richard Gowring ☏ **280 7294**
                                Robert Green ☏ **280 7279**
                                Nigel Jones ☏ **280 7245**
Group Financial Management   Peter Maule *Group Accountant* ☏ **280 7324**
                                David Williams ☏ **280 7743**
                                Peter Hyndman ☏ **280 7303**

Other (Administration)
Group Secretary   Martin Hayman *Group Secretary & Head, Group Legal Services*
                                ☏ **280 7020**
Group Human Resources   Andrew Hunter *Group Head* ☏ **280 7700**
                                Kenneth MacLennan *Group Head, Resourcing* ☏ **280 7722**

State Bank of India   Full Branch Office

State Bank House, 1 Milk Street, London EC2P 2JP
Tel: (171) 600 6444 **Fax:** (171) 454 4423; (171) 726 2739 **Telex:** 884589 **Swift:** SBIN GB 2L

Senior Executive Officers
Chief Executive Officer   Ashok Mukand *Chief Manager, London Main Branch* ☏ **454 4433**
                                F **454 4420**
General Manager   Nurane Hariharan ☏ **454 4444**

Syndicated Lending
Regional Head   Param Lahire *Manager, Development* ☏ **454 4455**
Head of Syndication   Sangeet Shuilla *Manager, Syndication & Investment* ☏ **454 4327**

Loan-Related Activities
Project Finance   K V S Jain *Manager, Trade Finance* ☏ **454 4305** F **454 4426**
Leasing & Asset Finance   Rama Nayar *Manager, Credit* ☏ **454 4308**

Foreign Exchange
Head of Trading   Ralph Rosen *Manager, Treasury* ☏ **454 4351**

FX Traders / Sales People
USD   Chris Drane *Dealer* ☏ **454 4349**

Settlement / Clearing
Foreign Exchange Settlement   Xenobia Govewalla *Manager, Treasury Settlements* ☏ **454 4325**

Administration
Technology & Systems
                                Jibendu Misra *Manager, Systems* ☏ **454 4400**

Compliance
                                Sridhar Srinivasan *Manager, Internal Audit* ☏ **454 4323**

Other (Administration)
EDP   Mahesh Dwivedi *Manager, EDP* ☏ **454 4307**
Customer Services   Anil Arora *Manager* ☏ **454 4320** F **454 4423**
Accounts   David Chandler *Chief Accountant* ☏ **454 4312**
Personnel   John Bellinie *Manager* ☏ **454 4310**

State Street Bank & Trust Company Financial Markets Group
                                                          Full Branch Office

One Royal Exchange Steps, Royal Exchange, London EC3V 3RT
Tel: (171) 283 0091 **Fax:** (171) 283 7238

Senior Executive Officers
SVP & General Manager   Stefan Gavell
Managing Director / General Manager   Peter Oneil

Relationship Manager
Institutional Investor Relations   Jeffrey Ruzicka *Managing Director*

Debt Capital Markets / Fixed Income
Global Head   Richard Flood *VP & General Manager, Global Trade Banking*

Fixed-Income Repo
Trading   Greg Harmon *VP, Global Trading*
                                         Justine Chamberlain *VP, Trading*

www.euromoneydirectory.com UNITED KINGDOM (+44)

Fixed-Income Repo (cont)
Sales

Neil Cracknell *Assistant Secretary, Trading*
Robert Ash *Vice President* T 369 4615 F 369 4648
E rash@fmg-statestreet.com

Equity Capital Markets
Global Head

Richard Flood *VP & General Manager, Global Trade Banking*

Equity Repo / Securities Lending
Marketing

Robert Ash *Vice President* T 369 4615 F 369 4648
E rash@fmg-statestreet.com

Head of Trading

Justine Chamberlain *VP, Trading*
Neil Cracknell *Assistant Secretary, Trading*
Eithne Reidy *AVP, Trading*
Yvonne Connors *Assistant Secretary, Trading*
Jennifer Toussaint *AVP, Trading*

Money Markets
Country Head

Alan Moore *VP & Treasury Manager*

Foreign Exchange
Country Head

Alan Moore *VP & Treasury Manager*

Risk Management
Country Head

Alan Moore *VP & Treasury Manager*

Other Departments
Cash Management

Erika Arevuo *VP, Cash Management*

State Street Bank & Trust Company Global Investor Services Group
Full Branch Office

One Canada Square, London E14 5AF
Tel: (171) 416 2500 **Fax:** (171) 712 9530

Senior Executive Officers
SVP & Managing Director

David Bilbè

Relationship Manager

Simon Pilkington *VP & Head, Relationship Management*

Global Custody
Regional Head

Michael Bullock *VP & Head, European Regional Processing Centre*

Other (Global Custody)
Sales
Market & Product Development
UK Securities Operations

Benjie Fraser *Vice President*
Peter Christmas *Vice President & Head*
Alan Drake *Vice President & Head*

Sterling Brokers Limited
Head Office

Colechurch House, 1 London Bridge Walk, London SE1 2SS
Tel: (171) 962 9960 **Fax:** (171) 403 5377 **Telex:** 928330 **Reuters:** STGB
Building Societies & Commercials **Tel:** 407 2644; Banking, Eurosterling **Tel:** 407 2599; Public Sector
Tel: 407 2593

Senior Executive Officers
Non-Executive Chairman
Chief Executive Officer
Financial Director
Company Secretary
Scottish Representative

Frank Woodford
James Brown *Chief Executive & Section Head*
Laurence Jacobs *Non-Executive Director*
Pratap Thakkar
Iain McIver

Others (Senior Executives)
Director

William Sargeant *Director & Section Head*
James Brown *Director & Section Head*

Non-Executive Director
Consultant
Building Societies
Commercials

Laurence Jacobs *Non-Executive Director*
Robin Packshaw
James Brown *Chief Executive & Section Head*
James Brown *Director & Section Head*
David Watkins *Manager*

Local Authorities

James Brown *Chief Executive & Section Head*
James Risley *Manager*

Banks

William Sargeant *Director & Section Head*

Euromoney Directory 1999 **1875**

UNITED KINGDOM (+44)   www.euromoneydirectory.com

Stopanska Banka AD
11-15 St Mary-at-Hill, London EC3R 8EE
Tel: (171) 929 2130 Fax: (171) 929 2133

Sümerbank
Representative Office

6th Floor, 3 London Wall Buildings, London EC2M 5PP
Tel: (171) 588 1707 Fax: (171) 588 1708
Website: www.turksat.net/sumerbank.rep

Senior Executive Officers
Director & Chief Representative   Resat Duran E sumerbank.rep@turksat.net
Assistant Representative   Gül Dogan Tindall E gdogan@turksat.net

The Sumitomo Bank Limited
Full Branch Office

Temple Court, 11 Queen Victoria Street, London EC4N 4TA
Tel: (171) 786 1000 Fax: (171) 236 0049 Telex: 887667 (General)
Administration Tel: 521 1341; 521 1341; Reuters: SUMX (FX, Spot); SUMX, SUMZ (FX, Forward);
SUMY (Money Market); SUML (FX Spot Dealing); SUFL (FX Forward & Options Dealing);
SUNL (Money Market Dealing); SUCL (Corporate Dealing)

Senior Executive Officers
Director & General Manager   T Tsukuda
GM, International Finance - Europe   J Mizoguchi
Joint General Manager   H Yamashita
Joint General Manager   H Hiyama
Joint General Manager   A Herrero-Ducloux
Joint General Manager   M Moore
Joint General Manager   J Thetford
Joint General Manager   A Yuasa

General-Lending (DCM, SL)
Head of Corporate Banking   P Brown *AGM, Credit*
    J Hards *Manager, Credit - London Branch*
    A Kinraide *Manager, Credit - London Branch*

Relationship Manager
Financial Institutions   Y Fujii *Assistant General Manager*
    Y Hayward *Assistant Manager*

Syndicated Lending
Department: International Finance Department - Europe
Country Head   J Mizoguchi *GM, International Finance - Europe*
    A Herrero-Ducloux *Joint General Manager*
Head of Syndication   C Scott *Deputy General Manager*
    E Winkley *Assistant General Manager*
    J Miller *Manager*
    C Dawson *Manager*
    M Gordon *Assistant Manager*
    J Gayler *Assistant Manager*

Loan-Related Activities
Trade Finance   N Masuto *Assistant General Manager*
    N Lenaerts *Manager*
Aircraft / Aerospace Finance   P A R Greenidge *Deputy General Manager*
    A Monno *Assistant Manager*
    C MacDonald *Marketing Officer*
Project Finance   A Sykes *DGM & Head, Project Finance Advisory*
    C Heathcote *AGM, Project Finance Advisory*
    P Leatherdale *AGM, Project Finance Lending*
    S Mills *AGM, Project Finance Lending*
    J Harrison *Manager, Project Finance Advisory*
    A Okuma *Manager, Project Finance Lending*
    J Brook *Manager, Project Finance Lending*
    J Krauze *Marketing Officer*
    P Blackman *Marketing Officer*
    H Mudan *Marketing Officer*

Other (Trade Finance)
Structured Finance   P Walsh *Deputy General Manager*
    M Murata *Manager*

Other (Trade Finance) (cont)

Credit
Property Finance

N Arima *Manager*
N Dowler *Manager*
S Miyamoto *Marketing Officer*
A Marriott *Assistant Manager*
A Springett *Assistant General Manager*
K Harmer *Assistant Manager*

Corporate Finance / M&A Advisory
Department: London Branch

Other (Corporate Finance)
Corporate Finance I

Corporate Finance II

Corporate Finance III
Department: Asian Corporate Banking
Country Head

Other (Corporate Finance)

M Moore *Joint General Manager*
J Timms *Assistant General Manager*
J Slater *Assistant General Manager*
N Jones *Manager*
K Takahashi *Assistant Manager*
J Thetford *Joint General Manager*
M Hobbs *Assistant General Manager*
A Ress *Manager*
A Moses *Manager*

Mr Suzuki *Joint General Manager*

M Grayson *Assistant General Manager*
S Ozenbas *Manager*
M Ishikawa *Assistant Manager*
F Yoshioka *Assistant Manager*
S Sonobe-Allain *Assistant Manager*

Sumitomo Finance International plc *Subsidiary Company*

Temple Court, 11 Queen Victoria Street, London EC4N 4UQ
Tel: (171) 842 3000 **Fax:** (171) 842 3090 **Telex:** 8811043 SUMFIN G

Senior Executive Officers
Chief Executive Officer
Managing Director
Managing Director
Managing Director
Managing Director
Managing Director

Sumio Fukushima
Keitaro Hirai
Aidan Ryan
Naoyuki Kawamoto
Akihiko Sakashita
Anthony Yates

Debt Capital Markets / Fixed Income
Tel: 329 0707

Bonds - General
Debt Capital Markets

Japan Desk

Aidan Ryan *Managing Director*
Rob Pomphrett
Philip Walsh
Jo Noble
Nobuhiko Tagaki ☎ **600 4521**
Masanao Nakao
Koki Yokota
Noriko Ichimura

Medium-Term Notes
Head of Origination

Takahiro Oishi ☎ **842 3020**
Kirsty Traill ☎ **842 3020**
Declan Tiernan ☎ **842 3020**

Department: Sumitomo Capital Securities Co., Limited
Tel: +81 (3) 5203 1829

Medium-Term Notes
Head of Origination

Mitsuhiro Shibahara
Yoshiaki Momoki

Money Markets
Department: Treasury
Tel: 842 3138

Money Markets - General
Treasury

Andrew Eady
Yasushi Isouchi
Mitchi Wright
Vanessa Campe

UNITED KINGDOM (+44)   www.euromoneydirectory.com

Sumitomo Finance International plc (cont)
Money Markets - General (cont)
    Richard Ovenden
    Takashi Sugimoto

Settlement / Clearing
Head of Settlement / Clearing   Peter Shave ☏ **842 3238**
    Robert Samuels ☏ **842 3238**
Fixed-Income Settlement   Jane Andrews *Bond Settlements* ☏ **842 3169**
Derivatives Settlement   Graham Shanks ☏ **842 3241**

Other (Settlement & Clearing)
Structured Transactions   Cheryl Russell ☏ **842 3062**
    Steven Carpenter ☏ **842 3062**
    Patricia Miller ☏ **842 3062**

Global Custody
Department: Agency / Custody
Country Head   Graham Shanks ☏ **842 3241**

Administration
Compliance
    John Russell *Head*

Other (Administration)
Personnel   Gareth Hughes *Head*
Principal Delegate   John Russell *Head*

The Sumitomo Trust & Banking Company Limited   Full Branch Office
155 Bishopsgate, London EC2M 3XU
Tel: (171) 945 7000 **Fax:** (171) 945 7177; (171) 945 7105 **Telex:** 888924 SMITR G **Swift:** STBC GB 2L **Reuters:** STBL
General Telex: 8811041 SMITR G

Senior Executive Officers
General Manager   Takashi Inoue
General Manager   Michio Totsuka
Deputy General Manager   Junichi Sayato

General - Treasury
Head of Treasury   Michio Totsuka *General Manager*

Debt Capital Markets / Fixed Income
Emerging Market Bonds
Head of Emerging Markets   Toru Masuda *Manager* ☏ **945 7023**

Syndicated Lending
Loan-Related Activities
Structured Trade Finance   Kevin O'Connell *Manager* ☏ **945 7051**

Money Markets
Fax: 945 7105

Money Markets - General
Trading & Planning; Derivatives & Spot / Forward FX   Osamu Tomita *Senior Manager* ☏ **945 7164**
Funding   Nobuo Takei *Manager* ☏ **945 7146**
Spot FX   Brendan Lynch *Manager* ☏ **945 7164**
Forward FX   Alexander Pastor *Manager* ☏ **945 7125**
Research & Development   Philip Foster *Manager* ☏ **945 7146**

Risk Management
Fax: 945 7177
Global Head   Hideto Hashimoto *Manager* ☏ **945 7069**

Foreign Exchange Derivatives / Risk Management
Spot / Forwards Sales   Brendan Lynch *Manager* ☏ **945 7164**

Corporate Finance / M&A Advisory
Fax: 945 7177
Head of Corporate Finance   Neil Fitzgerald *Manager* ☏ **945 7033**

Other (Corporate Finance)
Japanese Business   Toru Masuda *Manager* ☏ **945 7023**
New Business   John Barker *Manager, Strategic Industries* ☏ **945 7042**
Credit Planning   Kuniyuki Shudo *Manager* ☏ **945 7018**

www.euromoneydirectory.com UNITED KINGDOM (+44)

Settlement / Clearing
Fax: 945 7177
Settlement (General)
Operations
Other
Asset Management
Portfolio Management
Other Departments
Economic Research
Administration
Technology & Systems
Information Technology
Compliance
Compliance & Operation Planning

Accounts / Audit
Accounting
Other (Administration)
Loans Administration

Courtney Friend *Manager, Settlements* ☏ **945 7093**
Roger Seymour *Senior Manager* ☏ **945 7071**
Toru Matsuura *Manager, Financial & Regulatory Reporting* ☏ **945 7121**

Kuniyuki Shudo *Manager* ☏ **945 7018**

Andrew Wroblewski *Manager* ☏ **945 7164**

Masayuki Toda *Manager* ☏ **945 7080**

Jun Nakai *Manager* ☏ **945 7068**
Dave Symes *Manager* ☏ **945 7116**

Roger Seymour *Senior Manager* ☏ **945 7071**

Lindsay Pyne *Manager* ☏ **945 7028**

Sumitomo Trust International plc   Subsidiary Company

3rd Floor, 155 Bishopsgate, London EC2M 3TS
Tel: (171) 315 8000 **Fax:** (171) 696 8940 **Telex:** 290220

Senior Executive Officers
Chief Executive Officer
Deputy Managing Director
Company Secretary
Debt Capital Markets / Fixed Income
Department: Primary
Global Head
Eurobonds
Head of Trading
Bonds - General
Structured Sales, Swaps & Derivatives
Secondary
Equity Capital Markets
Equity Repo / Securities Lending
Marketing & Product Development
Money Markets
Department: Treasury
Global Head
Corporate Finance / M&A Advisory
Department: Corporate Finance
Global Head
Settlement / Clearing
Department: Settlements
Equity Settlement; Fixed-Income Settlement
Derivatives Settlement
Foreign Exchange Settlement
Administration
Compliance

Norio Namitome *Managing Director*
Munetsugu Miyawaki
Mitsutaka Shiraki

Munetsugu Miyawaki *Deputy Managing Director*

A Uchida *Senior Manager*

A Takahashi *Senior Manager*
S Matsuno *Head of Trading*

Chizuru Takemura *Assistant Manager*

Peter Brooks *Senior Manager*

Mark Jeanes *Manager*

Kuni Kawasaki *Executive Manager*
Roy Marks *Manager*
Kuni Kawasaki *Executive Manager*

Raymond Crossley *Equity Sales Manager*

Sun Hung Kai Securities Limited   Representative Office

4th Floor, New London House, 6 London Street, London EC3R 7LQ
Tel: (171) 488 0511 **Fax:** (171) 480 6768 **Telex:** 887443

Senior Executive Officers
Chief Executive Officer
Financial Director

Michael Lim *Managing Director*
Henry Ng *Head of Finance*

Euromoney Directory 1999   **1879**

UNITED KINGDOM (+44)   www.euromoneydirectory.com

Svenska Handelsbanken AB (publ) — Full Branch Office

Trinity Tower, 9 Thomas Moore Street, London E1 9WY
Tel: (171) 578 8000 Fax: (171) 578 8300 Telex: 894716 Reuters: SVID; SVIL

Senior Executive Officers
General Manager — Ulf Sylvan ☎ 578 8045

Others (Senior Executives)
Commercial Banking — Simon Silvester Head, London & Southern ☎ 578 8070
Head, Midlands & Northern — Derek Burgess ☎ (161) 694 7124

Debt Capital Markets / Fixed Income
Head of Fixed Income Trading — Mickael Ericson Head of Trading ☎ 578 8260
Other — Lena Allen New Issues ☎ 578 8644
Esa Pernu Treasury, Sales & New Issues ☎ 578 8621

Bonds - General
Bonds, Sales & New Issues — Kent Andersen ☎ 578 8647
Bonds, Trading — Peter Diggens Trader ☎ 578 8670

Equity Capital Markets
Head of Trading — Mickael Ericson Head of Trading ☎ 578 8260
Other — Lena Allen New Issues ☎ 578 8644
Esa Pernu Treasury, Sales & New Issues ☎ 578 8621

Money Markets
Other — Esa Pernu Treasury, Sales & New Issues ☎ 578 8621

Money Markets - General
Head, Short Term Interest Rate Risk — Paul Turner Senior Trader ☎ 578 8626

Foreign Exchange
Head of Foreign Exchange — Jan B Djerf ☎ 578 8186
Head of Trading — Mickael Ericson Head of Trading ☎ 578 8260

Risk Management

Fixed Income Derivatives / Risk Management
IR Swaps Trading — Casper Mann ☎ 578 8638

Corporate Finance / M&A Advisory
Department: Corporate Finance and Mergers & Acquisitions
Head of Corporate Finance — Richard Cohen Director, Head of Dept ☎ 578 8101

Other (Corporate Finance)
Michael Davies Manager ☎ 578 8108
Else Duncan Executive ☎ 578 8109

Settlement / Clearing
Settlement (General) — Les Vincent ☎ 578 148

Other Departments
Private Banking — John Berntsson Head ☎ 578 8201

Administration
Head of Administration — Paul Symons ☎ 578 8022

Technology & Systems
Information Technology — Jenny Tetlow ☎ 578 8220

Legal / In-House Counsel
Martin Hankey ☎ 578 8115

Compliance
Martin Hankey ☎ 578 8115

Other (Administration)
Librarian — Annika Lowther ☎ 578 8112
Kati Walsh ☎ 578 8111

Svenska Handelsbanken Midlands & Northern Corporate Banking — Full Branch Office

2222 The Crescent, Birmingham Business Park, Birmingham, B37 7YE
Tel: (121) 717 7727 Fax: (121) 779 7768

Senior Executive Officers
Head — Noel Meredith ☎ 694 7225

1880 Euromoney Directory 1999

www.euromoneydirectory.com   UNITED KINGDOM (+44)

Svenska Handelsbanken Midlands & Northern Corporate Banking
Full Branch Office
302 Sunlight House, Quay Street, Manchester, Lancashire M3 3JZ
Tel: (161) 839 0568 Fax: (161) 839 0570
Senior Executive Officers
Head   Derek Burgess ☎ **694 7124**

Swedbank (Förenings Sparbanken AB (publ))
Full Branch Office
Swedbank House, 42 New Broad Street, London EC2M 1SB
Tel: (171) 256 6000 Fax: (171) 638 1101 Telex: 290315 SWEDG Swift: SWED GB 2L
Senior Executive Officers
Treasurer   James Linford *Senior Vice President & Treasurer*
Executive Vice President   Claes-Johan Geijer
Others (Senior Executives)
                                        Michael Griffin *Senior Vice president, Operations*

Swissca Securities Limited
Subsidiary Company
Camomile Court, 23 Camomile Street, London EC3A 7LL
Tel: (171) 836 1800 Fax: (171) 836 1801 Telex: 291975 Email: general@swissca.co.uk
Senior Executive Officers
Managing Director, Trading / Marketing   René Charrière ☎ **863 1901**
Managing Director, Operations   Steve Cossins ☎ **863 1902**
Debt Capital Markets / Fixed Income
Tel: 863 1810
Country Head   René Charrière *Managing Director, Trading / Marketing* ☎ **863 1901**
Domestic Government Bonds
Head of Sales   Oliver Kuhn *Manager*
Head of Trading   Neil Howes *Manager*
Head of Research   Andy Hobjen *Research Analyst* ☎ **863 1810**
Eurobonds
Head of Syndication   Neil Howes *Manager*
Head of Sales   Oliver Kuhn *Manager*
Head of Trading   Neil Howes *Manager*
Head of Research   Andy Hobjen *Research Analyst* ☎ **863 1810**
Trading (Sovereigns)   Roger Neep *Trader*
                                         Gary Mills *Trader*
                                         Andy Bates *Trader*
Trading (Corporates)   Gary Mills *Trader*
                                         Roger Neep *Trader*
                                         Andy Bates *Trader*
Trading (High-yield)   Gary Mills *Trader*
                                         Roger Neep *Trader*
                                         Andy Bates *Trader*

Bonds - General
                                         Joe Rajski *Associate Director*
Equity Capital Markets
Country Head   Rupert Poole *Manager, Equities* ☎ **863 1840**
Domestic Equities
Head of Trading   Rupert Poole *Manager, Equities* ☎ **863 1840**
Head of Research   Andy Hobjen *Research Analyst* ☎ **863 1810**
International Equities
Head of Trading   Rupert Poole *Manager, Equities* ☎ **863 1840**
Convertibles / Equity-Linked
Head of Trading   Rupert Poole *Manager, Equities* ☎ **863 1840**
Other (Convertibles)
Sales   Rupert Poole *Manager, Equities* ☎ **863 1840**
Money Markets
Country Head   David Phipps *Associate Director* ☎ **863 1810**
Settlement / Clearing
Country Head; Equity Settlement; Fixed-Income   Julie Jobson *Manager, Settlements / Custody* ☎ **863 1911**
Settlement; Derivatives Settlement

Euromoney Directory 1999   **1881**

UNITED KINGDOM (+44) www.euromoneydirectory.com

Swissca Securities Limited (cont)
Global Custody
Country Head — Julie Jobson *Manager, Settlements / Custody* ☎ **863 1911**
Asset Management
Head — David Phipps *Associate Director* ☎ **863 1810**
Other (Asset Management)
Bond Funds — David Byrne *Manager* ☎ **863 1812**
Michael Simcock *Senior Adviser* ☎ **863 1813**
Money Market Funds — James Healy *Senior Adviser* ☎ **863 1814**
Administration
Mark O'Brien *Manager, Systems* ☎ **863 1941**
Compliance
James Sell *Manager, Audit / Compliance* ☎ **863 1931**

Syfrets International (UK) Limited — Subsidiary Company
Formerly known as: ATC Fund Management Limited
20 Abchurch Lane, London EC4N 7AD
Tel: (171) 203 4266 **Fax:** (171) 220 7141
Senior Executive Officers
Managing Director — Kit Meredith
Others (Senior Executives)
Relationship Manager — Ruli Viljoen

Syndicate Bank — Full Branch Office
2A Eastcheap, London EC3M 1LH
Tel: (171) 626 9681 **Fax:** (171) 283 3830 **Telex:** 894649 **Cable:** syndicates london EC3
Senior Executive Officers
Chief Executive Officer — Subash Malhotra *Deputy General Manager* ☎ **626 0792**
Chief Manager — Muddoor Nayak ☎ **626 8556**
Others (Senior Executives)
Chief Dealer — Philip Conpo ☎ **626 9439**

T Garanti Bankasi AS — Representative Office
Formerly known as: Garanti Bank
15 Knightsbridge, London SW1X 7LY
Tel: (171) 761 2500 **Fax:** (171) 245 9239
Senior Executive Officers
Representative — Ayse Dickson

TAIB Securities Limited — Subsidiary Company
11 Carlos Place, London W1Y 5AF
Tel: (171) 533 1600 **Fax:** (171) 533 1640
Website: www.taib.com
Senior Executive Officers
Chairman — Iqbal G Mamdani
Executive Director — Gopal Menon
International Division — Faran Kassam *Associate Director*
Others (Senior Executives)
Roger Reynolds *Non-Executive Director* ☎ **533 1603**

TC Ziraat Bankasi — Full Branch Office
Basildon House, 7/11 Moorgate, London EC2R 6DB
Tel: (171) 600 4985 **Fax:** (171) 600 4987 **Telex:** 887582 ZBANK G **Swift:** TCZB GB 2L **Reuters:** ZIRL
Senior Executive Officers
Chief Executive Officer — Inan Tanriover *Senior Country Manager* ☎ **778 9020**
Chief Operating Officer — Nicholas Palk *Vice President* ☎ **778 9040**
Treasurer — Neil Woods *Treasurer* ☎ **778 9050**

www.euromoneydirectory.com   UNITED KINGDOM (+44)

Others (Senior Executives)
Head of Credit and Marketing
John Lyon *Vice President* ☏ **778 9022**
Syndicated Lending
Regional Head
John Lyon *Vice President* ☏ **778 9022**
Loan-Related Activities
Trade Finance
John Lyon *Vice President* ☏ **778 9022**
Money Markets
Regional Head
Neil Woods *Treasurer* ☏ **778 9050**
Foreign Exchange
Regional Head
Neil Woods *Treasurer* ☏ **778 9050**
Other Departments
Correspondent Banking
John Lyon *Vice President* ☏ **778 9022**
Administration
Compliance
Robert Cronk *Vice President* ☏ **778 9041**

Thai Farmers Bank Public Company Limited

80 Cannon Street, London EC4N 6HL
Tel: (171) 623 4975; (171) 626 1781 **Fax:** (171) 283 7437 **Telex:** 8811173 FARMBK G

Senior Executive Officers
President   Pipat Visuttiporn
Managing Director / General Manager   P Tansomboon

Tokai Bank Europe plc   Subsidiary Company

1 Exchange Square, London EC2A 2JL
Tel: (171) 638 6030 **Fax:** (171) 588 5875 **Telex:** 8812649 **Swift:** TBEL GB 2L **Reuters:** TBEL **Bloomberg:** TCM-LON
Reuters: TCML

Senior Executive Officers
Vice Chairman   Rodger Livesey
President & Chief Executive Officer   Fumiaki Kadono
Chief Executive Officer   Ben Grigsby *Joint Chief Executive Officer*
Financial Director   Yoshimi Maemura *Managing Director*
Chief Operating Officer   Chris Roberts *MD & Chief Operating Officer*
Managing Director   Yoshimi Maemura

Others (Senior Executives)
Head of Trading   Kaveh Alamouti *Senior Managing Director*

Debt Capital Markets / Fixed Income
Head of Fixed Income Sales   David Behan *General Manager*

Bonds - General
New Issues   Yoshimi Ochiai *Senior Manager*
Primary Markets   Peter Hellman *Manager*

Fixed-Income Repo
Head of Repo   Terry Keeley *Head of Treasury*

Risk Management
Head of Risk Management   Gary Robinson *General Manager*

Corporate Finance / M&A Advisory
Department: **Corporate Finance & Risk Advisory**
Country Head   Alex Pilato *Managing Director*

Settlement / Clearing
Head of Settlement / Clearing   Stephen Brown *Deputy General Manager*

Other Departments
Chief Credit Officer   Simon Slee *Senior Manager*

Administration
Technology & Systems
Jeremy Ward *Deputy General Manager*

Legal / In-House Counsel
David Haig *Deputy General Manager*

Compliance
David Haig *Deputy General Manager*

Accounts / Audit
Simon Bennett *Head of Internal Audit*

UNITED KINGDOM (+44)   www.euromoneydirectory.com

The Tokai Bank Limited
Representative Office

63 Temple Row, Birmingham, B2 5LS
Tel: (121) 616 2161 Fax: (121) 616 2712 Telex: 335989

Senior Executive Officers
Chief Representative   Shigeki Takano
Administration
Head of Administration   R M Bishop *PA to CEO*

Tokai Maruman Securities (Europe) Limited
Subsidiary Company

Formerly known as: Maruman Securities (Europe) Limited

4 Chiswell Street, London EC1Y 4UP
Tel: (171) 374 4000 Fax: (171) 382 9143 Telex: 929347 MSEL G

Senior Executive Officers
Managing Director   Mayumi Sato
General Manager   Derek Gibson

Debt Capital Markets / Fixed Income
Eurobonds
Head of Syndication   Derek Gibson *General Manager*
Head of Sales   Mayumi Sato *Managing Director*

Equity Capital Markets
International Equities
Head of Sales   Mayumi Sato *Managing Director*
Convertibles / Equity-Linked
Head of Sales   Mayumi Sato *Managing Director*

Administration
Compliance
Compliance Officer   Derek Gibson *General Manager*

Tokyo-Mitsubishi Asset Management (UK) Limited
Subsidiary Company

Alternative trading name: TMAM (UK)

12-15 Finsbury Circus, London EC2M 7BT
Tel: (171) 577 2123 Fax: (171) 256 5586 Telex: 883254

Senior Executive Officers
Chief Executive Officer   Akio Nakai *Managing Director & Chief Executive*
Company Secretary   Harry Eyre

Asset Management
Head   Andrew Jenner *Head of Investments*

Administration
Head of Marketing   Kazuko Burt *Marketing Manager* ☎ 577 2120

Tokyo-Mitsubishi International plc
Subsidiary Company

6 Broadgate, London EC2M 2AA
Tel: (171) 628 5555 Fax: (171) 782 9144 Telex: 8954381 TMILDN G Telerate: Recipient

Senior Executive Officers
Chief Executive Officer   Juntaro Fujii *Chief Executive*
Managing Director   Kokichi Komagata
Managing Director   Kazuo Watanabe
Managing Director   Hitoshi Suzuki
Managing Director   Fuminori Yano
Managing Director, Head of New Issues   Philip Porter
Managing Director, Head of Risk Management   Tom Heffernan

Debt Capital Markets / Fixed Income
Head of Fixed Income Sales; Head of Fixed Income Trading   Fergus Murison *Managing Director, Head of Sales & Trading*

Eurobonds
Head of Origination   Paul Morganti *Managing Director*
Head of Syndication   Denis Kelleher *Managing Director & Head*

1884 Euromoney Directory 1999

Eurobonds (cont)

Head of Sales
Other (Fixed Income Research)
Head of Research
Equity Capital Markets
Department: Equity Business Group
Head of Equity Capital Markets
Risk Management
Department: Derivative Products Group
Head of Risk Management
Settlement / Clearing
Department: Operations
Operations
Other Departments
Other Departments
Structured Finance

Jun Kigoshi *Director & Co-Head*
Christopher Tessler *Managing Director*

Ron Solberg *Managing Director*

Richard Burdon *Executive Director & Head*

Greg Fitzgerald *Managing Director*

Phil Gearing *Executive Director*

Arvinder S Sood *Managing Director & Head*
Tetsuya Sato *Director, Head of Japan-Asia Desk*
Gilles Albou *Managing Director, Business Development*
Mark Fisher *Executive Director & Head, MTN*
Tony Puri *Executive Director, European Desk*
Masahiro Hosomi *Director, Credit Derivatives*
Richard Sullivan *Director & Co-Head, Securitisation*
Tony Tatsuhana *Director & Co-Head, Securitisation*

Administration

David Blocker *Executive Director*

Compliance

Graham Sargent *Director*

Accounts / Audit

Ian MacIntosh *Chief Financial Officer*

The Toronto-Dominion Bank

Full Branch Office

Triton Court, 14-18 Finsbury Square, London EC2A 1DB
Tel: (171) 920 0272 **Fax:** (171) 638 1042 **Telex:** 883391 **Swift:** TDOM GB 2L
Reuters: TDBX (FX Spot, Canada Forwards); TDBY (Forward FX & Canada Deposits);
TDPC (Canada Commentary); TDBD-F (Bonds); TDSQ (Derivatives); TDBL (FX Spot - Dealing);
TDBK (FX Forwards, MM Deposits & Treasury - Dealing)

Senior Executive Officers
Vice Chair, Head of Europe & Asia, TD Securities
SVP, Corporate Finance & Co-Head, Europe
Department: Green Line Investor Services (UK) Limited
Tel: 0800 731 4547
Managing Director, UK
Managing Director, Europe
Others (Senior Executives)

L Uggla ☎ **448 8320**

Bharat B Masrani

J Dowling ☎ **282 8298**
J Verkruysse ☎ **448 8301**

N McCammon *Assistant Manager, UK* ☎ **448 8336**
B George *Investment Representative, UK* ☎ **448 8369**

Debt Capital Markets / Fixed Income
Department: TD Securities
Tel: 628 4424 **Fax:** 374 6314
Head of Debt Capital Markets
Global Head

Regional Head
Head of Fixed Income Trading

Government Bonds
Head of Trading

Eurobonds
Head of Origination

D Tims *MD, Short Term Capital Markets*
G McDonald *Vice President & Director*
E Lam *VP, Short Term Capital Markets*
Simon Brignall *VP, Repo Trading*
V Servantes *VP, Short Term Capital Markets*
L Uggla *Vice Chair, Head of Europe & Asia, TD Securities* ☎ **448 8320**
P Thomas *Dealer*
D Turner *Dealer*

F Salmonds *Vice President* ☎ **628 4334**
A Grujic *Vice President* ☎ **628 4334**

D Fry *MD, Head of New Issues* ☎ **628 2262**
J Azzam *Vice President & Director* ☎ **628 2262**

UNITED KINGDOM (+44)   www.euromoneydirectory.com

The Toronto-Dominion Bank (cont)
Eurobonds (cont)

	K Gilmore *Vice President* ☏ **628 2262**
	D Glele *Vice President* ☏ **628 2262**
	C O'Halloran ☏ **628 2262**
	L Smith ☏ **628 2262**
Head of Syndication	D Fry *MD, Head of New Issues* ☏ **628 2262**
	K Gilmore *Vice President* ☏ **628 2262**
	J Azzam *Vice President & Director* ☏ **628 2262**
	D Glele *Vice President* ☏ **628 2262**
	C O'Halloran ☏ **628 2262**
	L Smith ☏ **628 2262**
Head of Trading	K Gould *MD, Head of Trading* ☏ **628 4445**
	P Molyneux *VP & Director, Fixed-Income Trading* ☏ **628 4445**
	P Reeve *VP & Director, Fixed-Income Trading* ☏ **628 4445**
	John Greenslade *VP & Director, Fixed-Income Trading* ☏ **628 4445**
	J Gisborne *VP & Director, Fixed-Income Trading* ☏ **628 4445**
	R Phillips *Vice President, Trading* ☏ **628 4445**
	Simon Harrison *Trader* ☏ **628 4424**
	T Matthews *Trader* ☏ **628 4445**

Bonds - General
Fixed Income Sales, Germany	C Marthinsen *Managing Director* ☏ **628 2772**
	S Schmidt ☏ **628 2772**
Fixed Income Sales, UK / Other	R Jeal *Vice President & Director* ☏ **628 2772**
	K Spivey ☏ **628 2772**
Fixed Income Sales, Switzerland	A Thomas *Vice President & Director* ☏ **628 2626**
	R Burchnall *Vice President* ☏ **628 2626**
	C Simms *Vice President* ☏ **628 2626**
Fixed Income Sales, Benelux	D Bales *Vice President* ☏ **628 3390**
	J Heyse ☏ **628 3390**
	L Dicker ☏ **628 3390**
Fixed Income Sales, Italy	D Petrozzi *Vice President & Director* ☏ **374 6332**
	F Ceretti *Vice President* ☏ **374 6332**
	M Amoros *Vice President* ☏ **374 6332**
Government Products	M Holloway *Vice President & Director* ☏ **628 4334**
	N Beyer *Vice President* ☏ **628 4334**

Fixed-Income Repo
Trading	Simon Harrison *Trader* ☏ **628 4424**
	Simon Brignall *VP, Repo Trading*

Equity Capital Markets
Department: TD Securities
Head of Equity Capital Markets	Bruce Hilland *Managing Director* ☏ **282 8281**
Global Head	Nigel Coe *Associate* ☏ **448 8330**
Other	Dougall MacPhee *VP & Director, Telecoms Research* ☏ **282 8287**

Other (Domestic Equities)
Institutional Equity Sales	Wolf Raymer *Managing Director* ☏ **282 8237**
	Douglas Breen *Vice President & Director* ☏ **282 8266**
	Philip Gestrin *Associate* ☏ **282 8280**

Money Markets
Department: TD Securities
Money Markets - General
Sales	L Stone *Vice President* ☏ **628 5758**
	F Lucas *Vice President* ☏ **628 5758**

Foreign Exchange
Department: TD Securities
Tel: 588 3679
Head of Foreign Exchange	J Glover *Managing Director*
Global Head	B Noel *Vice President & Director*
	S Watkins *Vice President*
Head of Institutional Sales	A Mackay *Vice President*
	Mark Lockyer *Manager*
Head of Trading	N Jackson *Senior Dealer*
	C Toye *Senior Dealer*
	R Celotto *Dealer*
	M Morrison *Dealer*

FX Traders / Sales People
Treasury Sales	J Hughes *Vice President & Director* ☏ **588 0552**
	A Langford *Manager* ☏ **588 0552**
	K Taylor *Manager* ☏ **588 0552**

www.euromoneydirectory.com   UNITED KINGDOM (+44)

Risk Management
Department: TD Securities
Head of Risk Management   T McNerney *Managing Director* ☏ **282 8292**
Global Head   K Broekhof *Associate* ☏ **282 8294**

Fixed Income Derivatives / Risk Management
Global Head   A Hull *VP & Director, Derivatives* ☏ **374 2022**
                               J Litwin *Vice President, Derivatives* ☏ **374 2022**
                               D Wiggins *Derivatives Analyst* ☏ **374 2022**
Trading   P de Winter *MD, Derivatives Trading, Europe & Asia* ☏ **374 2022**
                               M Brown *Vice President & Director* ☏ **374 2022**
                               T Morrison *Vice President* ☏ **374 2022**
                               H Vikstedt *Vice President* ☏ **374 2022**
                               N Jewitt *Dealer* ☏ **374 2022**
                               P Loukas *Dealer* ☏ **374 2022**

Other (FI Derivatives)
Derivatives Products   S Akeroyd *Managing Director* ☏ **374 2838**
                               J Olosunde *Vice President & Director* ☏ **374 2838**
                               A Powell *Vice President & Director* ☏ **374 2838**
                               E Giroux *Vice President & Director* ☏ **374 2838**

Other Currency Swap / FX Options Personnel
                               J Finlayson *Derivative Products*
                               S Régniez *Derivative Products*
                               H Winch *Derivative Products* ☏ **374 2838**

OTC Credit Derivatives
Head   C Colbourne *Head & Managing Director* ☏ **628 3033**
                               H Whittle *MD, Credit Products Group* ☏ **628 3033**
                               Y Vassatis *Managing Director* ☏ **628 3033**
                               W Gontarek *MD, Credit Products Group* ☏ **588 2492**
Global Head   G Alder *Vice President & Director* ☏ **628 3033**
                               L de Carbonnières *VP, Credit Products Group* ☏ **588 2492**
                               M Popoff *VP & Director, Credit Products Group* ☏ **588 2492**
                               A Torres *VP & Director, Credit Products Group* ☏ **628 3033**
                               G Bryck *VP & Director, Credit Products Group* ☏ **588 2492**
                               E Vassallo *VP, Credit Products Group* ☏ **588 2492**
                               C Pinkney *Vice President* ☏ **628 3033**
                               M Bedford *Derivatives Analyst* ☏ **628 3033**
Head of Trading   P Metcalfe *Dealer* ☏ **628 3033**
Department: Toronto-Dominion Bank - Market Risk
Global Head   C Pinkney *Vice President* ☏ **628 3033**

Corporate Finance / M&A Advisory
Department: Toronto-Dominion Bank - Corporate Finance
Country Head   Bharat B Masrani *SVP, Corporate Finance & Co-Head, Europe*

Other (Corporate Finance)
Corporate Finance   Michael S Redferne *Managing Director*
                               Richard J Harrison *Director*
                               Jeremy Keane *Director*
Communications Finance Group   Howard M Baker *Managing Director*
                               B Collins *Director*
                               Julie Evans *Director*
                               Jerry C Moore *Director*
                               Janice Gibson *Director*
Utilities & Project Finance   Graeme Francis *Director, Project Finance & Utilities Group*
                               M Cherry *Director*
                               R Palmer *Director*
Loan Syndication & Structured Finance   David C R French *Director & Head*
                               R Holler *Director*

Administration

Compliance
                               J White *European Compliance Director*

Other (Administration)
Human Resources   T Hill *Director & Head*
Finance & Administration   A D Waldron *Associate Vice President*

Euromoney Directory 1999   **1887**

UNITED KINGDOM (+44)   www.euromoneydirectory.com

Towa International Limited
Subsidiary Company

Royex House, Aldermanbury Square, London EC2V 7HR
Tel: (171) 600 7010 Fax: (171) 600 7012; (171) 600 7011 Telex: 945708

Senior Executive Officers
Managing Director   Sadaharu Takamatsu ☎ **600 6353**

Equity Capital Markets
International Equities
Head of Sales   Peter Kraal *Head of Sales, Japan* ☎ **600 6346**

Settlement / Clearing
Country Head; Equity Settlement; Fixed-Income Settlement   Gary Cohen *Manager*

Administration
Compliance   Gary Cohen *Manager*

Toyo Securities Europe Limited
Subsidiary Company

27/32 Old Jewry, London EC2R 8JP
Tel: (171) 726 8587 Fax: (171) 600 0917 Telex: 264110 TOYOSE G

Senior Executive Officers
Managing Director   E Yano

The Toyo Trust & Banking Company Limited

5th Floor, Bucklersbury House, 83 Cannon Street, London EC4N 8AJ
Tel: (171) 236 4020 Fax: (171) 236 5319 Telex: 885619 Swift: TOYO GB 2LA

Senior Executive Officers
Managing Director / General Manager   S Furuhata

Toyo Trust International Limited
Subsidiary Company

36 Queen Street, London EC4R 1BN
Tel: (171) 236 5272 Fax: (171) 236 5316 Telex: 8811456 TYTINT G

Senior Executive Officers
Managing Director   S Tsukada
Deputy Managing Director   H Fujiwara
Deputy Managing Director   B Dickson

Others (Senior Executives)
    T Kishino *Merchant Banking Group*
    S Masaki *Merchant Banking Group* ☎ **248 3887**

General-Lending (DCM, SL)
Head of Corporate Banking   H Fujiwara *Deputy Managing Director*

General-Investment
Head of Investment   H Oda *Assistant Director* ☎ **489 9252**

Debt Capital Markets / Fixed Income
Department: Capital Markets
Global Head   B Dickson *Deputy Managing Director*

Eurobonds
Head of Syndication   J Moran *Associate Director*
    S Paterson *Associate Director*
Head of Sales   T Goodson *Associate Director, Distribution* ☎ **236 0596**
    M Vingoe *Distribution* ☎ **236 0596**
    D Jennings *Distribution* ☎ **236 0596**
Head of Trading   P Burge *Trader* ☎ **236 1651**
    G Owen *Trader* ☎ **336 1651**
    R Hicking *Associate Director, Trading* ☎ **236 1651**

Equity Capital Markets
Department: Merchant Banking Group
Domestic Equities
Head of Syndication   S Paterson *Associate Director, New Issue Syndication* ☎ **248 2685**
International Equities
Head of Syndication   S Paterson *Associate Director, New Issue Syndication* ☎ **248 2685**

www.euromoneydirectory.com   UNITED KINGDOM (+44)

Settlement / Clearing
Operations   N Graham *Assistant Director*
                                     J Jacobs
                                     M Edwards

Administration
Head of Administration   Y Masuda *Associate Director* ☎ **248 3887**
                                     S Kumagai
                                     G Long
                                     D Jobson
                                     E Hughes

Compliance
Compliance & Internal Audit   A Ganatra *Assistant Director*

Accounts / Audit
Accounts   J Gledhill *Assistant Director*
                                     F Lobo
                                     P Hipperson
                                     D Parmakis

Other (Administration)
Middle Office   A Scanlan

Tradition Emerging Markets   Subsidiary Company
Ground Floor, East India House, 109/117 Middlesex Street, London E1 7JF
Tel: (171) 422 9500 Fax: (171) 422 9663
Currency Options Tel: 221 0331

Senior Executive Officers
Others (Senior Executives)
                                     Bill Knowles *Director* ☎ **422 9500** F **422 9663**

Tradition Financial Services Limited   Subsidiary Company
East India House, 109-117 Middlesex Street, London E1 7JF
Tel: (171) 454 9422 Fax: (171) 454 9421 Telex: 929795
Reuters: TRDE (Monitor-Currency Exotic Options); TRDO-Q (Monitor-Currency Options); TFSB (Bullion Dealing);
TFSC (Currency Dealing); TFSE (Currency Exotic Options Dealing)
Website: www.tfsbrokers.com

Senior Executive Officers
Managing Director   Sam Saffadi ☎ **454 9422** F **454 9433**

Others (Senior Executives)
Bullion   Terry Barnes *Director* ☎ **375 1166** F **375 1251**
Product Development   Jeffrey Adler *Director* ☎ **422 9525** F **422 9662**

Debt Capital Markets / Fixed Income
Bonds - General
Convertible Bonds   Peter Garrott *Manager* ☎ **375 1252** F **454 9438**

Equity Capital Markets
Others (Warrants)
Japanese Warrants   Peter Garrott *Manager* ☎ **375 1252** F **454 9438**

Risk Management
Other Currency Swap / FX Options Personnel
Currency Options   Mike Leibowitz *Global Manager* ☎ **375 2626**

Exotic Options (Barriers, Range, Timers, Digitals, Faders etc)
Trading   Rick Welch *Manager* ☎ **375 2626**

OTC Equity Derivatives
Head   Andrew Adamson *Manager* ☎ **375 2288**

Other (Exchange-Traded Derivatives)
Electricity Derivatives & Natural Gas Dave Newstead *Manager* ☎ **375 1250**
Energy Derivatives   David Jenkins *Co-Manager* ☎ **375 2211**
                                     Richard Choynowski *Co-Manager* ☎ **375 2211**

Other Departments
Commodities / Bullion   Terry Barnes *Director, Bullion Options* ☎ **375 1188** F **375 1251**

Euromoney Directory 1999   **1889**

UNITED KINGDOM (+44) www.euromoneydirectory.com

Tradition Government Securities Limited
Subsidiary Company

Beaufort House, 15 St Botolph Street, London EC3A 7DT
Tel: (171) 422 3900 Fax: (171) 422 3548 Telex: 894711 TRADUKG

Tradition (UK) Limited
Subsidiary Company

Beaufort House, 15 St Botolph Street, London EC3A 7DT
Tel: (171) 422 3500 Fax: (171) 422 3548 Telex: 894711 TRADUK G Reuters: TTSP-W (Monitor) Telerate: 7657/69
Reuters: Dealing 2000: TRDN, TUKL, TRDL

Senior Executive Officers
Chief Executive Officer — Guido Boehi [T] 422 3527 [F] 422 3530
Deputy Managing Director, Finance — Gerald Craggs [T] 422 3533 [F] 422 3536
Managing Director — Robin Houldsworth [T] 422 3707 [F] 422 3530

Others (Senior Executives)
Denis McCombie Senior Compliance Officer [T] 422 3539 [F] 422 3506

Debt Capital Markets / Fixed Income
Department: Tradition Treasury Services
Tel: 422 3636
Regional Head — Darren Rockman Director, Capital Markets [T] 422 3636
Simon Bates Director, Capital Markets [T] 422 3650
Mark Fennell Director, Capital Markets [T] 422 3767
Mark Bourne Director, Capital Markets [T] 422 3633

Fixed-Income Repo
Head of Repo — Mike Smith Associate Director [T] 422 3606
Marketing & Product Development — Tony Johnson Marketing Manager [T] 422 3518
Trading — Shervin Baghaie Head of Repo, Lire [T] 422 3800
Tony Hill Trader, £

Syndicated Lending

Other (Syndicated Lending)
Francois Ekam-Dick Associate Director [T] 422 3670 [F] 422 3601

Money Markets
Department: Eurodollar Money Market
Tel: 422 3680 Fax: 422 3648 Telex: 8813098 TRADUK G
Global Head — Michael White Deputy Managing Director [T] 422 3600 [F] 422 3531

Money Markets - General
Cash, Arbitrage & FRAs — Michael White Deputy Managing Director [T] 422 3600 [F] 422 3531

Foreign Exchange
Tel: 422 3767
Global Head — Craig Smith Deputy Managing Director [T] 422 3767 [F] 422 3531

Risk Management
OTC Credit Derivatives
Regional Head — Garry Rayner Associate Director [T] 422 9554 [F] 422 9568

Administration
Tel: 521 1341

Compliance
Denis McCombie Senior Compliance Officer [T] 422 3539 [F] 422 3506

Tufton Capital Limited
Head Office

Albermarle House, 1 Albermarle Street, London W1X 3HS
Tel: (171) 529 7800 Fax: (171) 529 7801

Senior Executive Officers
Chairman — Lars Åhrell
Managing Director — Jeremy Brassington

Others (Senior Executives)
Ted Kalborg Director

Corporate Finance / M&A Advisory
Global Head — John Greig Director, Corporate Finance

1890 Euromoney Directory 1999

www.euromoneydirectory.com UNITED KINGDOM (+44)

Tufton Oceanic Limited

Little Tufton House, 3 Dean Trench Street, London SW1P 3HB
Tel: (171) 222 8151 Fax: (171) 222 0893 Email: tol@tuftonoceanic.co.uk

Senior Executive Officers
Chairman — Ted Kalborg
Senior Vice President — Jonathan Hill
Senior Vice President — David Hughes
Senior Vice President — Chris Lloyd
Senior Vice President — Alan McCarthy
Chief Executive Officer — Dirk Langeveld *Chief Executive*
Managing Director — Simon Leatham
Managing Director — Rhys Thomas
Managing Director — Ferdi Fischer
Company Secretary — Steven Clews

Others (Senior Executives)
Olle Sundberg *Consultant*

Tullett & Tokyo Forex International Limited   Head Office

Cable House, 54-62 New Broad Street, London EC2M 1JJ
Tel: (171) 895 9595 Fax: (171) 827 3092; (171) 895 0819
Website: www.tullett.co.uk

Senior Executive Officers
Chief Executive — J Nixon
President — D Tullett
Financial Director — P Gregory *Finance Director*
Managing Director, Europe — J R Lawrence
Managing Director, America — T Boyle
Managing Director, Far East — D J Tuffley

Others (Senior Executives)
A J Styant *Director*
P J A Bertram *Non-Executive Director*

Debt Capital Markets / Fixed Income
Country Head
R Bennett *Managing Director* ☏ **827 3436**
R Woodbridge *Managing Director* ☏ **827 2346**

Bonds - General
P Cramp *Director* ☏ **827 3720**
B Dennahay *Director* ☏ **827 2255**
G Franklin *Director* ☏ **827 3327**
N Hoare *Director* ☏ **827 3720**
S Johnson *Director* ☏ **827 2346**
S Rogers *Director* ☏ **827 2255**
J Tipper *Director* ☏ **827 2076**
P Tran *Director* ☏ **827 2558**

Emerging Market Bonds
Head
M Goggin *MD, Emerging Markets Division* ☏ **827 2304**

Fixed-Income Repo
Marketing & Product Development
Trading
Stuart Clark ☏ **827 3471** F **827 2135**
Derek Taylor *Gilt Repo Broker*
Anthony Colonnese *Gilt Repo Broker*
Nick Page *Gilt Repo Broker*
Kevan Mead *Gilt Repo Broker*

Money Markets
Other (Wholesale Deposits)
Cash Deposits
P Wraight *Managing Director* ☏ **827 2323**

Foreign Exchange
Department: Foreign Exchange Division
Country Head
I Goldsmith *Managing Director* ☏ **827 2206**

FX Traders / Sales People
L Wiggins *Director* ☏ **827 2930**
P Leccacorvi *Director* ☏ **827 2379**
G Harris *Director* ☏ **827 2391**
D Eells *Director* ☏ **827 2888**
B O'Grady *Director* ☏ **827 2190**
Forwards
M Brown *Managing Director* ☏ **827 2180**

Euromoney Directory 1999 **1891**

UNITED KINGDOM (+44) www.euromoneydirectory.com

Tullett & Tokyo Forex International Limited (cont)
FX Traders / Sales People (cont)
R Hennah *Director* ☏ **827 3547**
K Hornegold *Director* ☏ **827 2077**
G Matthews *Director* ☏ **827 3322**
D Wilson *Director* ☏ **827 2067**

Department: Sterling Division
FX Traders / Sales People
B Gibson *Managing Director* ☏ **827 2728**
N Brown *Director* ☏ **827 2900**

Risk Management
Department: Tullett & Tokyo (Futures & Traded Options) Limited
Other (Exchange-Traded Derivatives)
J P Miller *Managing Director* ☏ **827 2401**
D Rothon *Director* ☏ **683 2413**
M Pearcy *Director* ☏ **623 0244**
D Jennings *Director* ☏ **623 7172**
T Dugard *Director* ☏ **827 3417**
J Garrett *Director* ☏ **827 3700**
C Girst *Director* ☏ **827 3704**

Exchange-Traded Derivatives
FX Options
M Bolton *Managing Director* ☏ **827 2900**
C Tidy *Director* ☏ **827 2900**

Administration
Other (Administration)
Marketing
D Orchard *Head*

Tullett & Tokyo International Securities
Cable House, 54-62 New Broad Street, London EC2M 1JJ
Tel: (171) 827 3086; (171) 895 9595 **Fax:** (171) 827 3092; (171) 827 2756 **Telex:** 9413534 (Equity)
Email: tullett@equityfp.netkonect.co.uk

Debt Capital Markets / Fixed Income
Fixed-Income Repo
Trading
Richard Philo
Gary Chapman

Equity Capital Markets
Equity Repo / Securities Lending
Marketing & Product Development
Simon R Smith *Head of Global Equity Financing Products*

Turkish Bank (UK) Limited Subsidiary Company
84/86 Borough High Street, London SE1 1LN
Tel: (171) 403 5656 **Fax:** (171) 407 7406; (171) 407 7408 **Telex:** 8955666 TURBOR G **Swift:** TUBA GB 2L
Reuters: TUBA

Senior Executive Officers
Chairman   Tanju Ozyol
Managing Director   Osman Menguturk
Financial Director   Kaya Rifki *Company Secretary & Accountant*
Treasurer   Mehmet Zeka *Treasurer*
General Manager   John Clouthing

Debt Capital Markets / Fixed Income
Eurobonds
Head of Syndication; Trading (Sovereigns)   Mehmet Zeka *Treasurer*

Libor-Based / Floating-Rate Products
FRN Sales   Mehmet Zeka *Treasurer*

Syndicated Lending
Loan-Related Activities
Trade Finance   Evangeline Abraham *Assistant Manager*

Money Markets
Regional Head   Mehmet Zeka *Treasurer*

Wholesale Deposits
Marketing; Head of Sales   Mehmet Zeka *Treasurer*

1892 Euromoney Directory 1999

www.euromoneydirectory.com UNITED KINGDOM (+44)

Foreign Exchange
Regional Head Mehmet Zeka *Treasurer*
Other Departments
Correspondent Banking Malcolm Airey *Manager*

Türkiye Garanti Bankasi

15 Knightsbridge, London SW1X 7LY
Tel: (171) 761 2500 **Fax:** (171) 245 9239

Senior Executive Officers
Managing Director / General Manager Ayse N Dickson

Turkiye Is Bankasi AS   Full Branch Office

8 Princes Street, London EC2R 8HL
Tel: (171) 606 7251 **Fax:** (171) 726 2566 **Telex:** 8951543 **Swift:** ISBK GB 2L **Reuters:** ISBL

Senior Executive Officers
Manager Aksit Ozkural ☎ **397 1424**
Financial Director Aksit Ozkural *Manager* ☎ **397 1424**
Chief Operating Officer Peter Kirk *Assistant Manager* ☎ **397 1420**
Treasurer Mustafa Darcan ☎ **397 1408**

Syndicated Lending
Loan-Related Activities
Trade Finance Mustafa Darcan *Assistant Manager* ☎ **397 1408**
  Richard Lacey *Co-ordinator* ☎ **397 1444**

Money Markets
Global Head Mustafa Darcan *Assistant Manager* ☎ **397 1408**
Regional Head Richard Lacey *Co-ordinator* ☎ **397 1444**

Eurocommercial Paper
Head of Origination Richard Lacey *Co-ordinator* ☎ **397 1444**

Wholesale Deposits
Marketing Mustafa Darcan *Assistant Manager* ☎ **397 1408**

Foreign Exchange
Global Head Mustafa Darcan *Assistant Manager* ☎ **397 1408**
Head of Trading Robert Wood *Senior Dealer* ☎ **726 8311**

FX Traders / Sales People
Dealer Paul Simpson ☎ **726 8311**

Other Departments
Private Banking Ugural Vant Hooft *Assistant Manager* ☎ **397 1425**
Correspondent Banking Richard Lacey *Co-ordinator* ☎ **397 1444**

Administration
Technology & Systems
  Peter Kirk *Assistant Manager* ☎ **397 1420**

Compliance
  Peter Kirk *Assistant Manager* ☎ **397 1420**

UBS AG   Representative Office

66 Hanover Street, Edinburgh, EH2 1HH
Tel: (131) 225 9186 **Fax:** (131) 226 5332

Senior Executive Officers
Others (Senior Executives)
  A G Stewart *Senior Representative for Scotland*

UBS AG   Full Branch Office

1 Curzon Street, London W1Y 7FN
Tel: (171) 567 5757 **Fax:** (171) 567 5656

Senior Executive Officers
Others (Senior Executives)
Unit Head U Eberhardt

Euromoney Directory 1999 **1893**

UNITED KINGDOM (+44)   www.euromoneydirectory.com

UBS Brinson Limited

1 Curzon Street, London W1 2FN
Tel: (171) 567 5300 **Fax:** (171) 567 5301

Senior Executive Officers
Others (Senior Executives)
Senior Management   M G Boylan
                                             N Cumming

Ulster Bank Group Treasury (Northern Ireland) — Subsidiary Company

40 Linenhall Street, Belfast, Northern Ireland BT2 8AZ
Tel: (1232) 325 626 **Fax:** (1232) 897 696

Senior Executive Officers
Head   Raymond Hastie

Others (Senior Executives)
Corporate Desk   Paul Tracey *Senior Manager*
ITS & Ops   Brendan Caldwell *Senior Manager*
Interbank Trading   David Wilson *Senior Manager*
ITS   Aran Shawcross *Manager*

Settlement / Clearing
Operations   Peter Hutchinson *Manager*

Ulster Bank Limited — Subsidiary Company

47 Donegall Place, Belfast, Northern Ireland BT1 5AU
PO Box 232, Belfast, Northern Ireland BT1 5AU
Tel: (1232) 244 794 **Fax:** (1232) 898 588; (1232) 898 521 **Telex:** 747334 **Email:** www.ulsterbank.com

Senior Executive Officers
Chairman   George Quigley ☏ **898 507**
Chief Executive Officer   Martin Wilson *Group Chief Executive* ☏ **898 472**
Financial Director   Ivan Laird *Chief Financial Controller* ☏ **898 420** 🖷 **898 587**
Chief Operating Officer   Franklin Adair ☏ **258 229** 🖷 **258 222**
Treasurer   Declan O'Neill *Group Treasurer* ☏ **+353 (1) 702 5500** 🖷 **+535 (1) 702 5660**
Company Secretary   David Peacock ☏ **898 418** 🖷 **898 587**
International Division   Brendan Caldwell *Senior Manager, Belfast* ☏ **325 626**
                                             Joe Caulfield *Head of International Trade Services, Dublin*
                                             ☏ **+353 (1) 608 4730**

General-Lending (DCM, SL)
Head of Corporate Banking   Paddy McMahon *Chief Executive, Ulster Bank Markets* ☏ **+353 (1) 608 4100**
                                             🖷 **+353 (1) 608 4008**

Debt Capital Markets / Fixed Income
Department: Ulster Bank Markets
Country Head   Paddy McMahon *Chief Executive, Ulster Bank Markets* ☏ **+353 (1) 608 4100**
                                             🖷 **+353 (1) 608 4008**

Equity Capital Markets
Department: Ulster Bank Markets
Country Head   Paddy McMahon *Chief Executive, Ulster Bank Markets* ☏ **+353 (1) 608 4100**
                                             🖷 **+353 (1) 608 4008**

Corporate Finance / M&A Advisory
Head of Corporate Finance   Tony McArdle ☏ **+353 (1) 608 4003** 🖷 **+353 (1) 608 4144**

Administration
Head of Marketing   Maurice Hastings *Director of Retail Marketing* ☏ **898 170** 🖷 **898 169**

Compliance
                                             Oliver Lynas *Director of Compliance* ☏ **244 744**

Other (Administration)
Human Resources   Steve Daniels *Director*

UNIBANCO-União de Bancos Brasileiros SA Representative Office
The International Financial Centre, 25 Old Broad Street, London EC2N 1HQ
Tel: (171) 877 0120 Fax: (171) 877 0129

Senior Executive Officers
Others (Senior Executives)
Banking Relations   Fernanda Faro Macedo *Manager*

Unibank A/S Full Branch Office
107 Cheapside, London EC2V 6DA
Tel: (171) 726 6000 Fax: (171) 726 4638 Telex: 887860; 924134 UNILDN G Swift: UNIB GB 2L Reuters: UNIL

Senior Executive Officers
General Manager   Henrik Bjørn

Others (Senior Executives)
                                     Tim Green *Head of Credit*

General-Lending (DCM, SL)
Head of Corporate Banking   Henrik Bjørn *General Manager*

General - Treasury
Head of Treasury   Jim Sharpe *Head, Treasury Sales*

Equity Capital Markets
Department: AROS Securities
Fax: 711 5255
Country Head   Johan Frösslund *Head of Sales*

Domestic Equities
Head of Sales   Johan Frösslund *Head of Sales*

Foreign Exchange
Country Head   Jim Sharpe *Head, Treasury Sales*
Head of Trading   Gavin May *Chief Dealer*

Risk Management
Country Head   Jim Sharpe *Head, Treasury Sales*

Other Currency Swap / FX Options Personnel
                                     Gavin May *Chief Dealer*

Settlement / Clearing
Operations   Peter Roberts *Head of Operations*

Other Departments
Private Banking   Jan Bjorkman *Head, Private Banking*

Administration
Legal / In-House Counsel
                                     Elizabeth Harris *Head of Legal Department*

Compliance
                                     Jacky Crawford

Accounts / Audit
                                     Graham Hughes *Internal Auditor*

Other (Administration)
Personnel   Karsten Lindgaard *Head, Financial Control & Personnel*

UniCredito Italiano SpA
Formerly known as: Credito Italiano SpA
17 Moorgate, London EC2R 6AR
Tel: (171) 606 9011 Fax: (171) 606 3920 Telex: 883456 Swift: CRIT GB 22 Reuters: CRIL Cable: ITALCREDIT LONDO
Trading Room Tel: 606 8591

Senior Executive Officers
Treasurer   R Tubb
Managing Director / General Manager F Saredi

Others (Senior Executives)
Assistant Chief Manager   R Sanderson

UNITED KINGDOM (+44)   www.euromoneydirectory.com

Union Bancaire Privée
Full Branch Office

26 St James's Square, London SW1Y 4JH
Tel: (171) 369 1350 Fax: (171) 369 0460 Telex: 22154

Senior Executive Officers
General Manager   Raphael Hoet
Deputy General Manager   Urs Albrecht T 369 1360 F 369 0465

Other Departments
Private Banking   Simon Culliford Head

Administration
Compliance
                                        Eric Dyer T 369 1371 F 369 0465

Union Bank of Nigeria plc

14/18 Copthall Avenue, London EC2R 7BN
Tel: (171) 600 0751 Fax: (171) 638 7642 Telex: 8813962 Swift: UBNI GB 2LA

Senior Executive Officers
Managing Director / General Manager   D K Inuwa

Union Discount Company Limited
Full Branch Office

39 Cornhill, London EC3V 3NU
Tel: (171) 623 1020 Fax: (171) 626 9091 Email: bank@union_discount.co.uk
Website: www.union_discount.co.uk

Senior Executive Officers
Chairman   Peter Dixon

Others (Senior Executives)
                                        Andrew J Anderson Director T 650 2299 F 929 2110
                                        Ewen Wigley Director T 650 3208
                                        David Wood Director T 650 2330

Debt Capital Markets / Fixed Income
Head of Fixed Income   David Wood Director T 650 2330
Head of Fixed Income Sales   Andrew J Anderson Director T 650 2299 F 929 2110
Head of Fixed Income Trading   Ewen Wigley Director T 650 3208

Fixed-Income Repo
Head of Repo; Marketing & Product   Andrew J Anderson Director T 650 2299 F 929 2110
Development
Trading   E Wigley

Equity Capital Markets

Equity Repo / Securities Lending
Head; Marketing & Product Development   Andrew J Anderson Director T 650 2299 F 929 2110
Head of Trading   E Wigley

Money Markets
Tel: 650 2299 Fax: 929 2110
Head of Money Markets   Ewen Wigley Director T 650 3208

Wholesale Deposits
Marketing; Head of Sales   Andrew J Anderson Director T 650 2299 F 929 2110

Settlement / Clearing
Head of Settlement / Clearing; Operations;   David Sweet T 623 1020
Back-Office

Other Departments
Correspondent Banking   Andrew J Anderson Director T 650 2299 F 929 2110

Administration
Business Development   Andrew J Anderson Director T 650 2299 F 929 2110

1896   Euromoney Directory 1999

UNITED KINGDOM (+44)

Union Européenne de CIC
Full Branch Office
Veritas House, 125 Finsbury Pavement, London EC2A 1NQ
Tel: (171) 454 5400 **Fax:** (171) 454 5454 **Telex:** 886725 CICLDN **Swift:** BDUE GB 2L
Administration Tel: 521 1341; **Reuters:** CICX; CICL; CICU (Dealing)

Senior Executive Officers
General Manager — Ubaldo C Bezoari

Others (Senior Executives)
Representative Office — Caroline Bartlett *UK Representative Officer*
Ubaldo C Bezoari *UK Resident Representative*

General-Lending (DCM, SL)
Head of Corporate Banking — Bruno Beuque *Credit Manager*
Arnaud de Gromard *Senior Manager, Corporate Banking*

General - Treasury
Head of Treasury — Martin Beadle *Principal Dealer*
Pierre Curtis *Senior Manager & Treasurer*
Julie Jackson *Principal Dealer*
Paul Bach *Dealer*
Vincent Corcoran *Dealer*
Zanita Smedley-Aston *Dealer*

Relationship Manager
Corporate Banking Group — Tim Prestwich *Relationship Manager*
Jeremy Dunton *Relationship Manager*

Debt Capital Markets / Fixed Income
Country Head — Pierre Curtis *Senior Manager & Treasurer*

Syndicated Lending
Other (Trade Finance)
Structured Finance — Clive Carpenter *Manager*

Money Markets
Country Head — Pierre Curtis *Senior Manager & Treasurer*

Money Markets - General
Julie Jackson *Principal Dealer*
Martin Beadle *Principal Dealer*
Paul Bach *Dealer*
Vincent Corcoran *Dealer*
Zanita Smedley-Aston *Dealer*

Risk Management
Spot / Forwards Trading — Richard Usher *Dealer, Spot FX*

Other Currency Swap / FX Options Personnel
Currency Options — Benjamin Clouard *Dealer*

Other (Exchange-Traded Derivatives)
Commercial Sales — Ian Munns *Dealer*
Pierre-Olivier Neyraud *Dealer*

Corporate Finance / M&A Advisory
Acquistion Finance — David Wilson *Manager*
David Di Matteo

Settlement / Clearing
Operations — Peter Hards-Nicholls *Group Manager*

Administration
Technology & Systems
Technology — Peter Hards-Nicholls *Group Manager*

Accounts / Audit
Internal Audit — Andrew Kent *Internal Auditor*
Financial Accounting & Treasury Control — Eric Keetch *Group Manager*

Other (Administration)
Personnel — Peter Hards-Nicholls *Group Manager*

United Bank
71/74 Mark Lane, London EC3R 7HS
Tel: (171) 702 3118 **Fax:** (171) 702 4735

Senior Executive Officers
General Manager — K H Waheed-Raza

UNITED KINGDOM (+44)   www.euromoneydirectory.com

The United Bank of Kuwait plc   Head Office

7 Baker Street, London W1M 1AB
Tel: (171) 487 6500 **Fax:** (171) 487 6808 **Telex:** 888441 BANKUW G **Swift:** UBKL GB 2L **Reuters:** UBKL
Cable: BANKUWAIT LONDON

Senior Executive Officers
Chairman   Fahad Al-Rajaan
Chief Executive Officer   Chris Keen *Group Chief Executive*
Treasurer   Andrew Brown *Treasurer, UBK Group*
Company Secretary   Colin Watts

Others (Senior Executives)
Islamic Financial Services   Duncan Smith *Chief Executive*
Real Estate Group   Mark Burton *Chief Executive*
Private Banking   Sandy Shaw *Chief Executive*

General-Lending (DCM, SL)
Head of Corporate Banking   David Witham *Deputy Group Chief Executive*

General-Investment
Head of Investment   Bernardo A Nagenmann *Chief Executive, UBK, Asset Management Plc*

Debt Capital Markets / Fixed Income
Department: Global Fixed Income & Alternative Fixed Income
Fax: 224 5804
Head of Fixed Income   Rohan Norrall *Head of Global Fixed Income*
    Mark Weavis *Head of Alternative Fixed Income*

Equity Capital Markets
Other (International Equity)
    Subhi Ben-Khadra *Head, Arab Capital Markets*

Syndicated Lending
Loan-Related Activities
Trade Finance   Jon Monwickendam *Joint Head of Trade Finance*
    Martyn Ebbs *Joint Head of Trade Finance*

Other (Trade Finance)
Commercial Property Investment   Neil Milton *Head*
Property Finance   Stephen Alston *Head*

Foreign Exchange
Country Head   Martin Westacott *Head of Foreign Exchange*
Corporate Sales   Mark Wells *Head of Corporate Sales*

Risk Management
Global Head   Angela Griffiths *Head, Risk Management*
Regional Head   Peter Whiting *Compliance Officer*

Settlement / Clearing
Settlement (General)   Nigel Brill *Head*
Operations   Kevin Hunter *Head*

Other Departments
Chief Credit Officer   Graham Barnes *Head of Credit Risk Management*
Private Banking   Sandy Shaw *CEO, Private Banking* ☎ **487 6600**

Administration
Head of Marketing   Nick Anderson *Head of Institutional Marketing*

Technology & Systems
Information Technology   Denis Craig *Head of IT*

Compliance
    Peter Whiting *Compliance Officer*

Accounts / Audit
    Terry Douglas *Head of Internal Audit*

United Gulf Management Limited   Subsidiary Company

7 Old Park Lane, London W1Y 3LJ
Tel: (171) 493 6000 **Fax:** (171) 493 0217

Senior Executive Officers
Managing Director   Thomas Ferguson

www.euromoneydirectory.com   UNITED KINGDOM (+44)

United Mizrahi Bank Limited
Full Branch Office

Finsbury House, 23 Finsbury Circus, London EC2M 7UB
Tel: (171) 360 3800 **Fax:** (171) 360 3810 **Telex:** 896654 UMB G **Swift:** MIZB GB 2L **Reuters:** UMBL

Senior Executive Officers
Chief Executive Officer — David Halperin *General Manager & Chief Executive*

Syndicated Lending
Regional Head — David Halperin *General Manager & Chief Executive*

Loan-Related Activities
Trade Finance — Colin Rosenthal *Head of Credit*

Money Markets
Regional Head — Brian Black *Chief Dealer* ☎ **360 3802**

Foreign Exchange
Regional Head — Brian Black *Chief Dealer* ☎ **360 3802**
Head of Trading — Paul Chenery *Senior Dealer* ☎ **360 3802**

FX Traders / Sales People
Jettendra Lathigra ☎ **360 3802**

Settlement / Clearing
Foreign Exchange Settlement — Hussein Ejvet *Head of Operations*

Other Departments
Private Banking — Zvi Goorney *Manager, Private Banking & Business Development*

United Overseas Bank Limited
Full Branch Office

19 Great Winchester Street, London EC2N 2BH
Tel: (171) 628 3504 **Fax:** (171) 628 3433 **Telex:** 888278, 8954292 **Swift:** UOVB GB 2L **Reuters:** UOBL (Monitor)
Telerate: Recipient

Senior Executive Officers
Vice President & General Manager — Michael Lee
International Division — Derek Chua *Assistant Vice President*

General - Treasury
Head of Treasury — Michael Lee *Vice President & General Manager*

Syndicated Lending
Country Head — Michael Lee *Vice President & General Manager*
Kerrie Matheson *Assistant Vice President*

Foreign Exchange
Country Head — Nicholas Trotter *Vice President*

Settlement / Clearing
Operations — P S Goh *Vice President*

Other Departments
Commodities / Bullion — Nicholas Trotter *Vice President*

Universal (UK) Limited
Subsidiary Company

Condor House, 14 St Paul's Churchyard, London
Tel: (171) 667 8000 **Fax:** (171) 667 8010 **Telex:** 945791

Senior Executive Officers
Managing Director / General Manager — Utaka Umezaki

Debt Capital Markets / Fixed Income
Domestic Government Bonds
Head of Sales — Mr Tanawa
Head of Trading — F Samoto

Equity Capital Markets
International Equities
Head of Trading — F Samoto

Convertibles / Equity-Linked
Head of Sales — F Samoto

Settlement / Clearing
Head of Settlement / Clearing — Mr Okamoto
Operations — Mr Manaka

UNITED KINGDOM (+44)   www.euromoneydirectory.com

Universal (UK) Limited (cont)
Administration
Accounts / Audit
                              Mr Manaka

Vining-Sparks IBG Limited Partnership   Full Branch Office
Camomile Court, 23 Camomile Street, London EC3A 7PP
Tel: (171) 680 9555 Fax: (171) 280 3110
Website: www.vsibg.com

Senior Executive Officers
President   Jim Vining
Financial Director   Larry Levingston *Chief Financial Officer*
Managing Director   Joe Smallman

Debt Capital Markets / Fixed Income
Suite 427, 6077 Primacy Parkway, Memphis, TN 38119-5732
Tel: +1 (901) 766 3000
Global Head   Jim Vining *President* ☎ +1 (901) 762 5808

Domestic Government Bonds
Head of Sales   Randy Wade *EVP & Director of Sales* ☎ +1 (901) 766 3183
Head of Trading   Fran Scott *EVP & Director of Trading* ☎ +1 (901) 762 5813
Head of Research   Brian McBride *SVP & Director, Portfolio Strategies* ☎ +1 (901) 766 3212
Country Head   Joe Smallman *Managing Director*

Settlement / Clearing
Suite 427, 6077 Primacy Parkway, Memphis, TN 38119-5732
Fixed-Income Settlement   Mary Caroline Harp *Manager* ☎ +1 (901) 766 3054

Vojvodjanska Banka AD   Representative Office
4th Floor, Langham House, 308 Regent Street, London W1R 5AL
Tel: (171) 734 8333; (171) 323 1707 Fax: (171) 323 1669

Senior Executive Officers
Director   Marija Milicic

Wachovia Bank NA   Representative Office
Leconfield House, Curzon Street, London W1Y 7FB
Tel: (171) 408 4700 Fax: (171) 629 4778

Senior Executive Officers
SVP & General Manager   Kurt A Schreiner

Warburg Dillon Read
1 High Timber Street, London EC4V 3SB
Tel: (171) 567 8000 Fax: (171) 329 8700
Website: www.wdr.com

Senior Executive Officers
Chairman & Chief Executive Officer   J A de Gier
Vice Chairman   H C van der Wyck
Vice Chairman   K J Costa
Financial Director   J Britton *Chief Financial Officer*
Chief Operating Officer   L Arnold

Others (Senior Executives)
Member, Executive Board   J A de Gier *Chairman & Chief Executive Officer*
                                         L Arnold *Chief Operating Officer*
                                         C A M Buchan *Joint Global Head of Equities*
                                         D Capone *CEO, Americas*
                                         M J Granziol *Joint Global Head of Equities*
                                         F W Hobbs *Global Head of Corporate Finance*
                                         W Johnson *Global Head of FX*
                                         D M Solo *Chief Risk Officer*
                                         N R Tapner *Global Head Equity Capital Markets*
                                         R Wojewodzki *CEO Europe, Middle East & Africa*
                                         R Zeltner *Global Head of Human Resources*

www.euromoneydirectory.com UNITED KINGDOM (+44)

Debt Capital Markets / Fixed Income
Department: Interest Rates
1/2 Finsbury Avenue, London, EC2M 2PP
Tel: +44 (171) 567 8000 **Fax:** +44 (171) 568 4800

Bonds - General

A Amschwand *Co-Head STIR*
A Bozian *Co-Head STIR*
S Bunce *Global Distribution*
M Christieson *Credit Derivatives*
J Costas *Head of Fixed Income & Banking Products*
M Eynon *Chief Operating Officer*
T Fredrickson *Rates Derivatives & Structured Products*
J Loh *Far East Regional Head*
M J Schepers *Debt Capital Markets*
S West *OECD, Credit Fixed-Income*

Equity Capital Markets
Department: Equities
Tel: 567 8000 **Fax:** 568 4800

Global Head

C A M Buchan *Joint Global Head of Equities*
M J Granziol *Joint Global Head of Equities*

Domestic Equities
Head of Trading

C Salter *UK*

Other (Domestic Equities)
Trading - Structured Products
Trading - Proprietary Trading
Trading - Global Risk Management
Trading - Equity Financing

D Balls
J Berg
A Easton
I Stafford-Taylor

International Equities
Head of Trading

T T Agyare *SE Asia*
N Holtby *European Trading*
G Pattle *Emerging Markets, Europe*
M J Granziol *Global Special Situations Trading*

Other (International Equity)
Distribution - Closed End Funds
Distribution - SE Asia
Distribution - Australia
Distribution - Primary Product
Distribution - Risk Management Products (Europe)

C J Agar
J Aitken
N Andrews
C A M Buchan
E Cacciotollo

W Stolz

Distribution - Japan
Distribution - US
Distribution - Latin America
Distribution - Special Funds
Distribution - Cash UK
Distribution - Global Head of Sales
Distribution - Canada
Distribution - Convertibles
Distribution - Head of Global Product Sales
Distribution - South Africa
Distribution - Cash Europe
Operating Officers

S M Codrington
J Cooke
A H Daniell
P Dear
R F Fitzpatrick
A C Hodson
E T N Larkin
M Moore
D Polak
C Sloan
J Tregear
R Brown *Europe COO (exc Switzerland)*
R W J Hardie *Global COO*
J Woodman *Global Client Management*

Equity Research
Global Head
Country Head

S P Carr *Head, Global Research*
T Orchard *Research, UK & Europe*
J Chester *Research, UK & Europe*

Other (Equity Research)

G Magnus *Chief Economist*

Foreign Exchange
Department: Foreign Exchange
1 High Timber Street, London, EC4V 3SB
Tel: +44 (171) 567 8000 **Fax:** +44 (171) 329 8700

Global Head

W Johnson *Global Co-Head FX, Precious Metals & Commodities*
S Jagot *Global Co-Head FX, Precious Metals & Commodities*

FX Traders / Sales People
Asia
North America

P Murphy *Head of Sales*
E Schubert *Head of Sales*

UNITED KINGDOM (+44)   www.euromoneydirectory.com

Warburg Dillon Read (cont)
FX Traders / Sales People (cont)

London	M Sutherland *Head of Sales*
Switzerland	M Wiedmann *Head of Sales*
North America	M Guarino *Head of Trading*
Asia	S Johnson *Head of Trading*
Europe	C Meier *Head of Trading*
Global Options Trading	B Jenkins
	A Kreysar
Global Proprietary Trading	R Silver
Global Risk Management	L Grant *Advisor*
Precious Metals and Commodities	E Mount *Global Head of Precious Metals and Commodities*
	M Konig *Global Head of Distribution*
	K Connor *Global Head of Trading*
Research	L Hatheway *FX and Fixed Income Strategy*
Operating Officer	H Evans *Global Business Manager*

Risk Management

Exchange-Traded Derivatives

Global Head	S H Sparke *Head of ETD*

Corporate Finance / M&A Advisory

Global Head	F W Hobbs *Global Business Area Head*
	R A J Gillespie *Joint Global Business Area Head*
	N R Tapner *Global Business Area Head - Equity Capital Markets*
	B R Keelan *Global Business Area Head - Leveraged Finance*
	J M Sassoon *Privatisations*
Country Head	D V Allatt *Russia*
	O A G Baring *Africa*
	E Beelaerts van Blockland *Netherlands*
	K J Costa *South Africa*
	J D Goodwin *Belgium & Luxembourg*
	R A J Gillespie *UK*
	C Hellemaa *Denmark & Norway*
	T I Leino *Finland*
	D Pignatelli *Italy*
	C L Reilly *Austria*
	C H Teschmacher *Scandinavia*

Other (Corporate Finance)

Sector Head	N K Barton *Consumer Products / Food*
	C N Brodie *Engineering Industries*
	D C N Cockburn *Oil & Gas*
	P Byrne *Chemicals / Building Materials*
	A P W Durrant *Mining*
	D A Freud *Transport*
	J M Hardy *Forest Products*
	R L Henshall *Utilities*
	M J Kershaw *Financial Sponsors*
	D F McCutcheon *Healthcare*
	J L Lane *Property*
	J W McCue *Telecommunication*
	H V P Myles *Closed End Funds*
	P A Rayman *Retail*
	G S Sando *Financial Institutions*
	S D Warshaw *Media*
Management	S Myers *Global Business Manager*

Other Departments

Economic Research	G Magnus *Head, Economics, FX & Fixed-Income Research*

Administration

Legal / In-House Counsel

European Counsel	M Harding

Compliance

K M Cates

www.euromoneydirectory.com UNITED KINGDOM (+44)

Wasserstein Perella & Co Limited

3 Burlington Gardens, London W1X 1LE
Tel: (171) 446 8000 Fax: (171) 494 2053; (171) 494 2054

Senior Executive Officers
Chairman   Lord Haslam
Managing Director   Jeffrey A Rosen
Managing Director   Howard Covington
Managing Director   Jonathan S Fisch

Westbury Capital Markets

7th Floor, 29-30 Cornhill, London EC3V 3ND
Tel: (171) 283 3141; (171) 283 3151 Fax: (171) 623 1287
Dealing Room Tel: 283 3141; Fax: 623 1287

Senior Executive Officers
Chairman   Stéphane Dokhan
Chairman   Pascal Dokhan
Administration
Compliance
                            Thierry Large Compliance Officer ☎ 283 3151

Westdeutsche Landesbank Girozentrale   Full Branch Office

51 Moorgate, London EC2R 6AE
Tel: (171) 638 6141 Fax: (171) 628 1843; (171) 457 2079 Telex: 887984
General Telex: 887985

Senior Executive Officers
Managing Director   Erwin Sell
Debt Capital Markets / Fixed Income
Asset-Backed Securities / Securitization
Head of Trading   Christoph Plattenteich Manager ☎ 457 2198
                            Peter Dow Manager ☎ 457 2284

Syndicated Lending
Head of Origination   Stuart Frohmaier Director ☎ 457 2073 ✉ stuart_frohmaier@westlb.co.uk
Head of Syndication   Jonathan Jamilly Managing Director ☎ 457 2070
                            ✉ jonathan_jamily@westlb.co.uk

Other (Syndicated Lending)
Secondary Loan Trading   Jonathan Jamilly Managing Director ☎ 457 2070
                            ✉ jonathan_jamily@westlb.co.uk
                            Anton Martin Associate Director ☎ 457 2071
                            ✉ anton_martin@westlb.co.uk
                            Rafael Valbuena Manager ☎ 457 2075 ✉ rafael_valbuena@westlb.co.uk
Transaction Management   Gary Bickles Assistant Manager ☎ 457 2074 ✉ gary_bickles@westlb.co.uk
Primary Syndications   Stuart Frohmaier Director ☎ 457 2073 ✉ stuart_frohmaier@westlb.co.uk
                            Anton Martin Associate Director ☎ 457 2071
                            ✉ anton_martin@westlb.co.uk
                            Michael Potter Associate Director ☎ 457 2072
                            ✉ michael_potter@westlb.co.uk
Distribution   Anton Martin Associate Director ☎ 457 2071
                            ✉ anton_martin@westlb.co.uk
Team Administration Support Sharon Burrell Secretary ☎ 457 2078 ✉ sharon_burrell@westlb.co.uk
                            Clare Leaver Secretary ☎ 457 2077 ✉ clare_leaver@westlb.co.uk

Loan-Related Activities
Structured Trade Finance   Michael Potter Associate Director ☎ 457 2072
                            ✉ michael_potter@westlb.co.uk

Risk Management
OTC Credit Derivatives
Country Head   Birgitta Drwenski Manager ☎ 457 2072
Settlement / Clearing
Operations   William Pendered ☎ 457 2042
Asset Management
Portfolio Management   Jonathan Jamilly Managing Director ☎ 457 2070
                            ✉ jonathan_jamily@westlb.co.uk

Euromoney Directory 1999 **1903**

UNITED KINGDOM (+44)   www.euromoneydirectory.com

Westdeutsche Landesbank Girozentrale (cont)
Administration
Compliance
                                Ray Pennell ☎ 457 2063
Accounts / Audit
Accounts
                                Andrew Harvey *Business Manager* ☎ 457 2042

Westpac Banking Corporation   Full Branch Office
63 St Mary Axe, London EC3A 8LE
Tel: (171) 621 7000 Fax: (171) 623 9428 Reuters: WBCM, WBCL, WBCO; WBCD
Website: www.westpac.com.au

Senior Executive Officers
Chief Executive Officer   Jim Tate *General Manager, Europe* ☎ 621 7007 ℻ 283 9222
                                ✉ jtate@westpac.com.au
Financial Director   Martin Hancock *Financial Controller* ☎ 621 7510 ℻ 621 7527
                                ✉ mhancock@westpac.com.au

General - Treasury
Head of Treasury   Jonathan Minor *Head, Offshore Treasury* ☎ 621 7680 ℻ 621 1687
                                ✉ jminor@westpac.com.au

Relationship Manager
Financial Institutions   Laurie Armfield *Head* ☎ 621 7081 ℻ 621 7513 ✉ larmfield@westpac.com.au

Debt Capital Markets / Fixed Income
Tel: 621 7620
Country Head   Iain Stewart *Head, Australasian Capital Markets* ☎ 621 7620 ℻ 621 7534
                                ✉ istewart@westpac.com.au

Bonds - General
                                Geoff Short *Government Distribution*
                                Jack A'Hearn *Government Distribution*
                                Rupert Haywood *Global & Government Bonds*
                                Simon Hughes *Corporate Distribution*
                                Bevan O'Sullivan *Corporate Distribution*
                                Scott Barker *Eurocommercial Paper* ☎ 621 7620

Foreign Exchange
FX Traders / Sales People
                                Ian MacGougan *Chief Dealer, Spot FX* ☎ 621 7660 ℻ 621 7527
                                ✉ imacgougan@westpac.com.au
                                David Jones *Chief Dealer, Forward FX* ☎ 621 7680 ℻ 621 7527
                                ✉ djones@westpac.com.au

Risk Management
Head of Risk Management   Tony McClarty ☎ 621 7499 ℻ 621 7527 ✉ tmcclarty@westpac.com.au
Fixed Income Derivatives / Risk Management
Trading   Stephen Eakin *Head, Derivatives Trading* ☎ 621 7600 ℻ 621 7532
                                ✉ seakin@westpac.com.au
Foreign Exchange Derivatives / Risk Management
Spot / Forwards Trading   David Jones *Chief Dealer, Forward FX* ☎ 621 7680 ℻ 621 7527
                                ✉ djones@westpac.com.au
                                Ian MacGougan *Chief Dealer, Spot FX* ☎ 621 7660 ℻ 621 7527
                                ✉ imacgougan@westpac.com.au
Vanilla FX option Trading   Mike Callaghan *Dealer* ☎ 621 7766
                                Steve Jones *Dealer* ☎ 621 7766

Other Currency Swap / FX Options Personnel
Treasury Sales   Charles Boswell *Head* ☎ 621 7670
Derivatives   David Evans *Distribution* ☎ 621 7600

Other Departments
Economic Research   James Shugg ☎ 621 7061 ℻ 621 7527 ✉ jshugg@westpac.com.au
Administration
Head of Administration   Gaynor Leavens *Manager, Office Administration* ☎ 621 7651 ℻ 283 9222
Head of Marketing   Diana Honey *Head of Sales & Marketing* ☎ 621 7746 ℻ 621 7513
                                ✉ dhoney@westpac.com.au

Technology & Systems
                                Nick Hollis *Head of Technology* ☎ 621 7499 ℻ 621 7527
                                ✉ nhollis@westpac.com.au

Accounts / Audit
Audit   Charles Green *Head* ☎ 621 7104 ✉ cgreen@westpac.com.au

www.euromoneydirectory.com   UNITED KINGDOM (+44)

Williams de Broë plc
Head Office

6 Broadgate, London EC2M 2RP
Tel: (171) 588 7511 **Fax:** (171) 588 1702 **Telex:** 893277G

Senior Executive Officers
Chairman & Chief Executive   John Millar
Financial Director   David Whistance
Company Secretary   David Heigham
International Division   Yves Gachoud *Director*
                                    Mike Gaston *Director*

Debt Capital Markets / Fixed Income
Head of Fixed Income   Richard Warburton *Director*

Equity Capital Markets
Domestic Equities
Head of Sales   Malcolm Graham-Wood *Director*
International Equities
Head of Sales   Yves Gachoud *Director*
                                    Mike Gaston *Director*
Head of Trading   Yves Gachoud *Director*
                                    Mike Gaston *Director*

Equity Research
Head of Equity Research   Paul Backhouse *Director*

Settlement / Clearing
Tel: 588 7511
Head of Settlement / Clearing   Ray Fitch *Office Manager*

Administration
Legal / In-House Counsel
                                    Mark Gordon *Legal Officer*

Compliance
                                    Gordon Lewis *Compliance Officer*

Woolwich plc

Formerly known as: Woolwich Building Society
Watling Street, Bexleyheath, Kent DA6 7RR
Tel: (181) 298 5000 **Fax:** (1322) 55 5621 **Telex:** 927636 websg

Senior Executive Officers
Chairman   Brian Jenkins
Chief Executive Officer   John M Stewart *Group Chief Executive*
Financial Director   Robert C H Jeens *Group Finance Director*
Treasurer   Peter Hanlon *Group Treasurer*

The World Bank
Representative Office

Alternative trading name: International Bank for Reconstruction & Development
15th Floor, New Zealand House, Haymarket, London SW1Y 4TE
Tel: (171) 930 8511 **Fax:** (171) 930 8515
Website: www.worldbank.org

Senior Executive Officers
Representative   Andrew Rogerson

WorldInvest Limited
Head Office

55 Russell Square, London WC1B 4HP
Tel: (171) 637 3322 **Fax:** (171) 436 7360; (171) 580 1712 **Telex:** 883826
Website: www.worldinvest.com

Senior Executive Officers
Chairman   Keith Brown
Chief Operating Officer   Charles Hall

Debt Capital Markets / Fixed Income
Fax: 637 1785
Global Head   Chris Sanders
Regional Head   Stephanie McClennon

UNITED KINGDOM (+44)   www.euromoneydirectory.com

WorldInvest Limited (cont)
Equity Capital Markets
Fax: 436 2690
Global Head   Mark Beale
Regional Head   Richard Lewis
Foreign Exchange
Fax: 436 2693
Global Head   Michael Groves
Administration
Other (Administration)
Client Administration   Anna Kirk

Yapi ve Kredi Bankasi AS — Representative Office
Havenfields, Aylesbury Road, Great Missenden, Bucks HP16 9PL
Tel: (1494) 890 303 Fax: (1494) 890 404 Telex: 83421

Senior Executive Officers
Representative   Adnan Ayman

The Yasuda Trust & Banking Company Limited — Representative Office
1 Liverpool Street, London EC2M 7QJ
Tel: (171) 628 5721 Fax: (171) 920 9220; (171) 374 4894 Telex: 922040 YSDTBL G

Senior Executive Officers
General Manager   Y Yonezawa
Deputy General Manager   H Tsuruta

Yorkshire Bank plc — Head Office
20 Merrion Way, Leeds, LS2 8NZ
Tel: (113) 247 2000 Fax: (113) 242 0733 Telex: 556292 Swift: YORK GB 22

Senior Executive Officers
Chairman   Rt Hon Lord Clitheroe ☎ 247 2107
Chief Executive Officer   Fred Goodwin *Chief Executive Officer* ☎ 247 2100
Financial Director   Martin Moorhouse *Head of Finance* ☎ 247 2101
Chief Operating Officer   Ian MacDonald *Chief Operating Officer* ☎ 247 2103
Company Secretary   John Hurst ☎ 247 2343

General-Lending (DCM, SL)
Head of Corporate Banking Raymond Clark *Head of Business Financial Services* ☎ 247 2250

Other Departments
Private Banking   Paul Fullerton *Head of Personal Financial Services* ☎ 247 2604

Administration
Business Development   Bill Dickson *Head of Process Development* ☎ 247 2212

Public Relations
                           Andy Godwin *Head of Customer Services* ☎ 247 2110

Other (Administration)
Human Resources   Keith Morgan *Head* ☎ 247 2561

Zambia Commercial Bank — Full Branch Office
Formerly known as: Zambia National Commercial Bank Limited
9 King Street, London EC2V 8EA
Tel: (171) 726 6364 Fax: (171) 726 6160 Telex: 883951 ZABANK G Swift: ZNCO GB 2L

Senior Executive Officers
General Manager   Beauty Kaluba

Others (Senior Executives)
                           Elaine Bennett *Manager, Operations*
                           Geoffrey Earnshaw *Manager, Marketing & Investment*

www.euromoneydirectory.com UNITED KINGDOM (+44)

The Zenshinren Bank
Representative Office

2nd Floor, 55 Moorgate, London EC2R 6EX
Tel: (171) 410 0111 **Fax:** (171) 628 3402 **Telex:** 927776 ZENBUK G

Senior Executive Officers
Chief Representative   Akira Ito
Representative   Tomohiro Nojiri

Zenshinren International Limited
Subsidiary Company

2nd Floor, 55 Moorgate, London EC2R 6EX
Tel: (171) 410 0222 **Fax:** (171) 256 8544 **Telex:** 8812847 ZIL UK G **Email:** zil@ma.kew.net

Senior Executive Officers
Chairman   Haruyoshi Munakata
Managing Director   Kazuhiro Ito
Director   Akira Ito

Debt Capital Markets / Fixed Income
Tel: 374 4633
Global Head   Satoshi Otanaka *Executive Director*

Eurobonds
Head of Origination   Satoshi Otanaka *Executive Director*
Head of Syndication   Peter Yallup *Associate Director*
Head of Sales   Kyoji Ohashi *Associate Director*
    Jota Sasaki *Associate Director*
    Lisa White *Assistant*

Money Markets
Tel: 374 4633
Global Head   Satoshi Otanaka *Executive Director*
Regional Head   Kyoji Ohashi *Associate Director*
Country Head   Jota Sasaki *Associate Director*

Foreign Exchange
Tel: 374 4633
Global Head   Satoshi Otanaka *Executive Director*

FX Traders / Sales People
Trader   Kyoji Ohashi *Associate Director*
    Jota Sasaki *Associate Director*

Risk Management
Tel: 410 6454
Global Head   Akihiro Ide *Manager*

Settlement / Clearing
Tel: 410 6452
Regional Head   Andrew Bryant *Manager*
Fixed-Income Settlement   Anna Serrano *Clerk*

Administration
Technology & Systems
    Kazuhito Harada *Executive Director* **410 6467**

Compliance
    Stewart Rafter *Compliance Officer* **410 6466**

Public Relations
    Kazuhito Harada *Executive Director* **410 6467**

Zivnostenská Banka AS
Full Branch Office

18 King William Street, London EC4N 7BY
Tel: (171) 283 3333 **Fax:** (171) 621 0093; (171) 522 0512 **Telex:** 885451, 290643 **Swift:** ZIBA GB 2L **Reuters:** ZVNL

Senior Executive Officers
Manager   Robert Potac **potac@ziba.cz**
Deputy Manager   Michael O'Sullivan

General - Treasury
Head of Treasury   Ian Umpleby *Chief Dealer, Treasury*

Settlement / Clearing
Settlement (General)   David Lee *Settlements & SWIFT*
Operations   Gaynor Cowan *Financial Control*

UNITED KINGDOM (+44) www.euromoneydirectory.com

Zivnostenská Banka AS (cont)
Asset Management
Other (Asset Management)
Emerging Markets Debt — Alex Parr *Manager, Investment Portfolio* ☎ **220 0910** ✉ **parr@ziba.cz**
Emerging Market Research & Analysis — Philip Bartlett *Analyst* ✉ **bartlett@ziba.cz**
Anna Reich *Analyst* ✉ **reich@ziba.cz**
Forfaiting & Loans Administration — Chris Mattison *Senior Manager*
Administration
Information Technology — Stefan Chrusciel *Manager* ✉ **chrusciel@ziba.cz**

UNITED STATES
(+1)

Board of Governors of Federal Reserve System 🏛 Central Bank
21st & Constitution Avenue NW, Washington, DC 22003
Tel: (202) 452 3000 Fax: (202) 452 3819
Website: www.bog.frb.fed.us

Senior Executive Officers
Chairman — Alan Greenspan
Vice Chair — Alice Rivlin

AA Nazzaro Associates
Suite 205, Heston Hall, 1790 Yardley-Langhorne Road, Yardley, PA 19067
Tel: (215) 321 3220 Fax: (215) 321 9540

Debt Capital Markets / Fixed Income
Fixed-Income Repo
Head of Repo — Anthony Nazzaro *Principal*
Trading — Timothy Sheehan *Senior Associate*
Marla Morschauser *Associate*

Equity Capital Markets
Equity Repo / Securities Lending
Head
Head of Trading — Anthony Nazzaro *Principal*
Timothy Sheehan *Senior Associate*
Marla Morschauser *Associate*

ABN AMRO
Suite 3103, 181 West Madison, Chicago, IL 60602
Tel: (312) 904 5512

ABN AMRO Bank NV Full Branch Office
500 Park Avenue, New York, NY 10022
Tel: (212) 838 7300 Fax: (212) 980 9425 Reuters: ABNY

Senior Executive Officers
Managing Director / General Manager — Andre Nel
Debt Capital Markets / Fixed Income
Bonds - General
Capital Market Services — Jerry Wigdortz *Head*
Equity Capital Markets
Domestic Equities
Head of Trading — Anna Wong *Senior Trader*

ABN AMRO Inc
10th Floor, 1325 Avenue of the Americas, New York, NY 10019
Tel: (212) 314 1460; (212) 314 1656 Fax: (212) 314 1439 Telex: 239112 ABNCMC UR

Get the Latest Information Everyday with the PaineWebber Euromoney Directory ON-LINE

Euromoney Directory On-line is a unique electronic service providing access to the entire directory direct to your computer – continuously updated throughout the year. In addition the site contains:

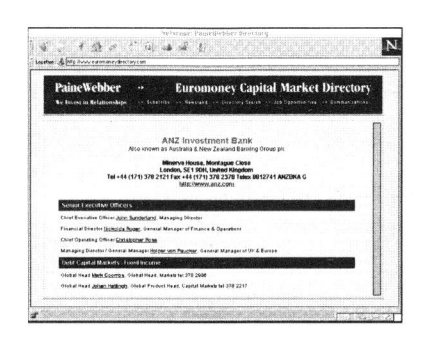

Daily News
New appointments, position/department changes, and the latest market gossip (updated every day).

Recruitment Services
Information and links on the very latest opportunities in the markets direct from the top recruitment consultancies.

PLUS – Sophisticated Search Facilities
Search by one or a combination of categories – including country, region, job title, department, company, name and many more.

Launched in January 1999 this dedicated information service is only available to purchasers of the Directory.

Only £99/$160.

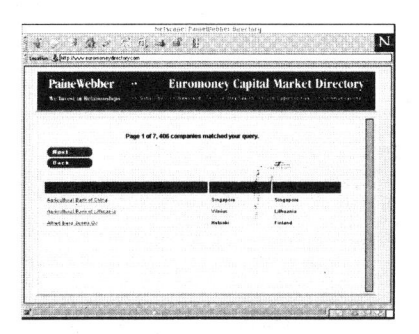

www.euromoneydirectory.com

To gain access to the PaineWebber Directory ON-LINE simply call our hotline on 44 171 779 8999 quoting ref. NSPW1

UNITED STATES (+1)   www.euromoneydirectory.com

AIG Financial Products Corp   Head Office

100 Nyala Farm, Westport, CT 06880
Tel: (203) 222 4700 **Fax:** (203) 222 4780

Senior Executive Officers
Managing Director   Thomas R Savage
Settlement / Clearing
Tel: 222 4700 **Fax:** 222 4780
Settlement (General)   Carmine Paradiso ⓣ **221 4805**
    Sabrina Jaques ⓣ **221 4805**

AIG Global Investment Corp

25th Floor, 175 Water Street, New York, NY 10038
Tel: (212) 458 2147 **Fax:** (212) 458 2244
Website: www.aiggig.com

Debt Capital Markets / Fixed Income
Fixed-Income Repo
Marketing & Product Development; Trading   Peter Adamczyk *Director* Ⓔ **peter.adamczyk@aigcom**
Equity Capital Markets
Tel: 458 8147
Equity Repo / Securities Lending
Marketing & Product Development   Peter Adamczyk *Director* Ⓔ **peter.adamczyk@aigcom**

Alexandra Investment Management Limited

Formerly known as: Hermes Capital Management Limited
9th Floor, 237 Park Avenue, New York, NY 10017
Tel: (212) 808 3780 **Fax:** (212) 808 3787

Senior Executive Officers
Chairman   Mikhail A Filimonov
President   Dimitri Sogoloff Ⓔ **sogoloff@alex**
Financial Director   Robert J Beechinor

Allied Irish Bank   Full Branch Office

405 Park Avenue, New York, NY 10022
Tel: (212) 339 8000 **Fax:** (212) 339 8008 **Telex:** 177744

Senior Executive Officers
Chief Executive Officer   Brian Leeney
Financial Director   Cormac Daly *Chief Finance Officer*
General - Treasury
Head of Treasury   Gerry McBorman *Senior Vice President* Ⓕ **339 8006**
Foreign Exchange
Head of Foreign Exchange   Paraic Cosgrave
Risk Management
Head of Risk Management   Kevin Mitchell
Corporate Finance / M&A Advisory
Head of Corporate Finance   Brandon O'Connor
Administration
Head of Marketing   Brandon O'Connor

Allied Irish Bank Group Treasury   Subsidiary Company

405 Park Avenue, New York, NY 10022
Tel: (212) 339 8000 **Fax:** (212) 339 80016 **Email:** treasury@aibny.com **Reuters:** AIBN

Senior Executive Officers
General - Treasury
Head of Treasury   Brendan O'Connor *Treasury Relations & Head of Corp Treasury*
    ⓣ **339 8080** Ⓕ **339 8006**
    Gerry McGorman *Head of Treasury* ⓣ **339 8375** Ⓕ **339 8006**

www.euromoneydirectory.com UNITED STATES (+1)

Debt Capital Markets / Fixed Income
Department: Bond & Money Markets
Eurobonds
Head of Sales   Eamonn Boylan *Head of Euro Desk* ☎ **339 8086** 🖷 **339 8006**
Bonds - General
US$ Paul Druback *Head of Interest Rates* ☎ **339 8091** 🖷 **339 8006**
I£   Eamonn Boylan ☎ **339 8087**
Money Markets
Head of Money Markets   Paul Druback *Head of Interest Rates* ☎ **339 8091** 🖷 **339 8006**
Foreign Exchange
FX Traders / Sales People
Spots   Paraic Cosgrave *Head of Institutional Desk* ☎ **339 8080** 🖷 **339 8006**

American Scandinavian Banking Corp   Subsidiary Company

437 Madison Avenue, New York, NY 10022
Tel: (212) 318 9300 **Fax:** (212) 421 4420

Senior Executive Officers
President   Jukka Niemi

ANZ Securities Inc   Bank Subsidiary

6th Floor, 1177 Avenue of the Americas, New York, NY 10036
Tel: (212) 801 9170 **Fax:** (212) 801 9169

Senior Executive Officers
President   Oliver Kane ☎ **801 9170**
Vice President   Joyce Yee ☎ **801 9160**
Others (Senior Executives)
Vice President   Norman Rosner ☎ **801 9734** 🖷 **801 9169**
Emerging Markets   Pedro Canas *Vice President* ☎ **801 9175** 🖷 **801 9168**
                                        David Livingston ☎ **801 9174** 🖷 **801 9168**
Debt Capital Markets / Fixed Income
Head of Fixed Income   Peter Jones *Vice President* ☎ **801 9170** 🖷 **801 9168**
Emerging Market Bonds
Head of Sales   Pedro Canas *Vice President* ☎ **801 9175** 🖷 **801 9168**
Head of Trading   Nancy Kalmus ☎ **801 9179** 🖷 **801 9168**
Administration
Compliance
                                        Tony Kane *President*

ANZ Securities (USA) Inc   Sister Company

1177 Avenue of the Americas, New York, NY 10036
Tel: (212) 801 9150 **Fax:** (212) 801 9163 **Telex:** 6801482 ANZMC

Senior Executive Officers
President   Janine Adams ☎ **801 9150**
Vice President   Joyce Yee ☎ **801 9160**
Equity Capital Markets
Department: Equities
Tel: 801 9150 **Fax:** 801 9163
Domestic Equities
Head of Trading   Robert Wittenoom *Vice President* ☎ **801 9150**
International Equities
Head of Sales   Michael Kent *Vice President* ☎ **801 9150**
Head of Trading   Robert Wittenoom *Vice President* ☎ **801 9150**
Equity Repo / Securities Lending
Head   Joyce Yee *Vice President* ☎ **801 9160**
Foreign Exchange
FX Traders / Sales People
Institutional Sales   Raymond Webb *Vice President*
                                        Geoffrey Harrison *Vice President*
Trader / Sales   Jennifer Epstein

UNITED STATES (+1)   www.euromoneydirectory.com

ANZ Securities (USA) Inc (cont)
Settlement / Clearing
Tel: 801 9150 **Fax:** 801 9163
Operations   Joyce Yee *Vice President* ☏ 801 9160
Administration
Compliance
    Janine Adams *President* ☏ 801 9150

Arab American Bank

40 East 52nd Street, New York, NY 10022
Tel: (212) 644 2000 **Fax:** (212) 755 6944 **Telex:** 666880 UAAB UR **Swift:** UAAB US 33 **Reuters:** Recipient

Senior Executive Officers
President & Chief Executive Officer   Fakhruddin Khalil
Treasurer   Burt Clark *Senior Vice President*
Others (Senior Executives)
Head of Banking Group   Lamine Djilani *Senior Vice President*

Arbitral International Corp   Head Office

c/o Arbitral Finance, Suite 1050, 1401 Brickell Avenue, Miami, FL 33131
Tel: (305) 374 8111 **Fax:** (305) 372 9933 **Email:** arbitral@arbitral.com
Website: www.arbitral.com

Senior Executive Officers
Chairman   Antonio Castro ☏ +55 (21) 553 7081
Director   Francisco Malzoni ☏ +55 (21) 553 7081
Chief Executive Officer   Alvaro Candela *Director* ☏ +55 (21) 553 7081
Financial Director   Kim Castro *Director* ☏ +55 (21) 553 7081
Chief Operating Officer   Fernando Leite *Director*
Treasurer   Miltka Scarano *Manager, USA*
Debt Capital Markets / Fixed Income
Head of Fixed Income   Fernando Leite *Director*
Head of Fixed Income Sales   Francisco Malzoni *Director* ☏ +55 (21) 553 7081
Settlement / Clearing
Head of Settlement / Clearing   Miltka Scarano *Manager, USA*

Arnhold and S Bleichroeder Inc   Head Office

1345 Avenue of the Americas, New York, NY 10105-4300
Tel: (212) 698 3000 **Fax:** (212) 299 3000 **Telex:** 668229 **Cable:** ARNHOLDEAT NEWYO

Senior Executive Officers
Co-Chairman   Henry Arnhold
Co-Chairman   Stephen Kellen
Co-President   John P Arnhold
Co-President   Stanford Warshawsky
Financial Director   Ronald Bendelius *Senior Vice President*
General-Investment
Head of Investment   Stanford Warshawsky *Co-President*
Debt Capital Markets / Fixed Income
Head of Fixed Income Trading   Peter Van der Mey *Senior Vice President*
Government Bonds
Head of Trading   Peter Van der Mey *Senior Vice President*
Domestic Government Bonds
Head of Trading   Peter Van der Mey *Senior Vice President*
Fixed-Income Repo
Head of Trading   Peter Van der Mey *Senior Vice President*
Equity Capital Markets
Tel: 299 4545
International Equities
Head of Trading   Christian Treitler
    Jamie Polito
    Laurence Ioffredo
    Peter Van der Mey *Senior Vice President*

www.euromoneydirectory.com UNITED STATES (+1)

Equity Repo / Securities Lending
Head Allen Langman *Senior Vice President*
Corporate Finance / M&A Advisory
Head of Corporate Finance Stanford Warshawsky *Co-President*
Settlement / Clearing
Head of Settlement / Clearing Allen Langman *Senior Vice President*
Asset Management
Head John P Arnhold *Co-President*
Administration
Head of Administration William Casciani *Senior Vice President*
Technology & Systems
  James Lever *Senior Vice President*
Legal / In-House Counsel
  Stanford Warshawsky *Co -President*
Compliance
  William Casciani *Senior Vice President*
Public Relations
Human Resources Mary Kay Rail *VP & Director of Human Resources*

The Asahi Bank Limited

Suite 2350, 190 South LaSalle Street, Chicago, IL 60603
Tel: (312) 606 1000 **Fax:** (312) 606 1010 **Telex:** 253403 ASHCG
Website: www.asahibank.co.jp

Senior Executive Officers
Managing Director / General Manager Nobuo Suzuki

The Asahi Bank Limited   Full Branch Office

Suite 6011, One World Trade Center, New York, NY 10048-0476
Tel: (212) 432 6400 **Fax:** (212) 432 1135 **Telex:** 422943 ASHNY
Website: www.asahibank.co.jp

Senior Executive Officers
General Manager Katsumi Sakai

Aurora Capital Partners LP

Suite 1000, 1800 Century Park East, Los Angeles, CA 90067
Tel: (310) 551 0101 **Fax:** (310) 277 5591

Senior Executive Officers
Chairman Gerald Parsky
President Richard R Crowell
Managing Director Richard K Roeder

Austrian National Bank   Representative Office

5th Floor, General Motors Building, 767 Fifth Avenue, New York, NY 10153
Tel: (212) 888 2334 **Fax:** (212) 888 2515 **Telex:** 422509 NATB NY

Senior Executive Officers
Chief Representative Helmut Gruber

BA Futures Incorporated   Head Office

231 South La Salle Street, Chicago, IL 60696
Tel: (312) 974 2319 **Fax:** (312) 828 7391; (312) 828 7390

Senior Executive Officers
President Gregg H Byers ▣ **974 2332**
Financial Director Patricia Kane *CFO & Treasurer* ▣ **974 2314**
Chief Operating Officer Kevin Maloney *Chief Operating Officer* ▣ **974 2334**
GM-Americas Dominic Palazzolo ▣ **974 2327**
Managing Director Taylor Hurst ▣ **974 2309**

Euromoney Directory 1999 **1913**

UNITED STATES (+1)   www.euromoneydirectory.com

BA Futures Incorporated (cont)
Others (Senior Executives)
Europe   Mark Penny *General Manager* ☏ +44 (171) 634 4496
Asia   Melvin Barden *General Manager* ☏ +65 239 3380
Settlement / Clearing
Operations   Steve Marcott *Manager, Operations* ☏ 269 4560

Banca Carige   Representative Office

Formerly known as: Cassa di Risparmio di Genova e Imperia
375 Park Avenue, New York, NY 10152
Tel: (212) 421 6010 **Fax:** (212) 759 6785 **Telex:** 666491 FIGEV **Swift:** CRGE IT GG

Senior Executive Officers
US Representative   Carlo Romairone

Banca Commerciale Italiana   Full Branch Office

1 William Street, New York, NY 10004
Tel: (212) 607 3500 **Fax:** (212) 809 2124 **Telex:** RCA 225926

Senior Executive Officers
Others (Senior Executives)
    Giorgio Angelozzi *Senior Vice President & Manager* ☏ 607 3500

Banca CRT   Full Branch Office

4th Floor, 500 Park Avenue, New York, NY 10022
Tel: (212) 980 0690 **Fax:** (212) 980 0809 **Telex:** 49617351 CRTUI **Telerate:** CRTO US33

Senior Executive Officers
Others (Senior Executives)
Executive Vice President   Giorgio Cuccolo *Branch Manager*

Banca d'Italia   Representative Office

37th Floor, 590 Madison Avenue, New York, NY 10022
Tel: (212) 308 2009 **Fax:** (212) 308 2663

Senior Executive Officers
US Representative   Giannandrea Falchi

Banca Monte dei Paschi di Siena SpA   Full Branch Office

9th Floor, 55 East 59th Street, New York, NY 10022-1112
Tel: (212) 891 3600 **Fax:** (212) 891 3661 **Telex:** 662341 **Swift:** PASC US33 **Reuters:** MPSN

Senior Executive Officers
Chief Executive Officer   Giulio Natalicchi *SVP & General Manager*
Chief Operating Officer   Serge Sondak *FVP & DGM*
Treasurer   Bruno Orrú *VP & Treasurer*
Syndicated Lending
Country Head   Nicolas A Kanaris *Vice President*

Banca Nazionale del Lavoro   Full Branch Office

25 West 51st Street, New York, NY 10019
Tel: (212) 314 0701 **Fax:** (212) 489 9088 **Telex:** 234803

Senior Executive Officers
EVP & General Manager   Alessandro Di Giovanni ☏ 314 0662

www.euromoneydirectory.com   UNITED STATES (+1)

Banca Nazionale dell'Agricoltura
Full Branch Office

21st Floor, 17 State Street, New York, NY 10004
Tel: (212) 412 9600 **Fax:** (212) 412 9609 **Telex:** RCA 235560 **Swift:** NAGR US 33

Senior Executive Officers
General Manager, New York Branch   Guiseppe Magaletti

Banca di Roma SpA
Branch, Marketing Office

Suite 1200, 225 West Washington Street, Chicago, IL 60606
Tel: (312) 368 8855 **Fax:** (312) 726 3058 **Telex:** 190107 **Swift:** BROM US 4N **Email:** bdrchicago@aol.com
Reuters: ROMC **Cable:** BANCROMA CHICAGO

Senior Executive Officers
SVP & Manager   Claudio Perna
VP & Deputy Manager, Credit   Luca Balestra
Vice President   James W Semonchik
Vice President   Aurora Pensa

General-Lending (DCM, SL)
Head of Corporate Banking   Luca Balestra *VP & Deputy Manager, Credit*

Foreign Exchange

FX Traders / Sales People
International & Operations   Aurora Pensa *Vice President*
Money Desk   Margaret Delay *Trader*

Settlement / Clearing
Operations   Aurora Pensa *Vice President*

Other Departments
Commodities / Bullion   Margaret Delay *Trader*

Administration

Technology & Systems
Electronic Banking & Technology   Wilma Antoniolli *Assistant Vice President*

Banca San Paolo di Brescia
Representative Office

32nd Floor, 712 Fifth Avenue, New York, NY 10019
Tel: (212) 664 0618 **Fax:** (212) 664 0576

Senior Executive Officers
Representative, North America   H Bradley Bloomer

Banco Ambrosiano Veneto
Representative Office

32nd Floor, 712 Fifth Avenue, New York, NY 10019
Tel: (212) 664 0618 **Fax:** (212) 664 0576

Senior Executive Officers
Representative, North America   H Bradley Bloomer

Banco Bandeirantes
Full Branch Office

38th Floor, 280 Park Avenue, New York, NY 10017
Tel: (212) 972 7455 **Fax:** (212) 949 9158 **Telex:** 425412

Senior Executive Officers
General Manager   Roberto L Paladini

Banco Boavista SA
Representative Office

Suite 2330, 100 SE 2nd Street, Miami, FL 33131
Tel: (305) 530 9057 **Fax:** (305) 530 1357

Senior Executive Officers
US Representative   Anisia P Taylor-Cata E boavista_ani@ibm.net

UNITED STATES (+1)   www.euromoneydirectory.com

Banco Boliviano Americano — Full Branch Office
Suite 1201, 777 Brickell Avenue, Miami, FL 33131
Tel: (305) 350 2160; (305) 350 2181 **Fax:** (305) 372 8858 **Telex:** 798631

Senior Executive Officers
Chief Executive Officer
Chief Operating Officer   Robert J Tamayo *General Manager*
                                    Donato H Mármol *Vice President & Operations Manager*
Others (Senior Executives)
                                    Eduardo L Cobián *Assistant Operations Manager*

Banco Central Hispano USA — Subsidiary Company
50 Broadway, New York, NY 10004
Tel: (212) 785 0700 **Fax:** (212) 968 8348 **Telex:** 235687

Senior Executive Officers
Chairman   Francisco Perez Hickman
Treasurer   Luis Salgado
Managing Director / General Manager Anthony Barreiro

General-Lending (DCM, SL)
Head of Corporate Banking   Patricia Gutirrez

Other Departments
Private Banking   Juan Maza

Administration
Technology & Systems
                                    Laura Wechsler

Legal / In-House Counsel
                                    Sheldon Fried

Public Relations
Human Resources   Millie Rodriguez
Accounts / Audit
                                    Douglas Behirie

Banco de Chile — Full Branch Office
124 East 55th Street, New York, NY 10022
Tel: (212) 758 0909 **Fax:** (212) 593 9770 **Telex:** 6736037

Senior Executive Officers
SVP & General Manager   Hernan Donoso

Corporate Finance / M&A Advisory
Head of Corporate Finance   Eduardo Omegna *VP, Corporate Finance*

Settlement / Clearing
Operations   Michael P Nyberg *VP & Operations Manager*

Banco Colpatria — Full Branch Office
Suite 2360, 801 Brickell Avenue, Miami, FL 33131
Tel: (305) 374 4026 **Fax:** (305) 372 0605

Senior Executive Officers
General Manager   Carlos R Pacheco
Others (Senior Executives)
Deputy General Manager   Edgardo Onoro

Banco de Galicia y Buenos Aires — Full Branch Office
20th Floor, 300 Park Avenue, New York, NY 10022
Tel: (212) 906 3700 **Fax:** (212) 906 3777 **Telex:** 7403190 GALBAUS

Senior Executive Officers
Executive Vice President   Héctor E Arzeno

www.euromoneydirectory.com   UNITED STATES (+1)

Banco di Napoli
Full Branch Office

4 East 54th Street, New York, NY 10022
Tel: (212) 872 2400 Fax: (212) 872 2426

Senior Executive Officers
General Manager   Vito Spada

Banco Português do Atlântico
Agency

19th Floor, 201 South Biscayne Boulevard, Miami, FL 33131
Tel: (305) 577 9793 Fax: (305) 577 4380 Telex: 428339 Swift: ILBK US 33

Senior Executive Officers
Chairman   George Jardin Gonzalues
General Manager   Edward DeCaso

Banco Português do Atlântico
Full Branch Office

2 Wall Street, New York, NY 10005
Tel: (212) 306 7800 Fax: (212) 791 3431 Telex: 175359 Swift: ILBK US 33 Reuters: BPAN Bloomberg: Atlantico

Senior Executive Officers
Financial Director   Jose da Silva Controller T 306 7851
Treasurer   Maria Teixeira Treasurer T 306 7873
General Manager   Pedro J Belo T 306 7817

Relationship Manager
Operations   Renzo Savo T 306 7849
Systems   Sergio Alanso T 306 7853

Other Departments
Chief Credit Officer   Ricardo Mendes Chief Credit Officer T 306 7820

Administration
Head of Administration   John Viggiano VP, Administration T 306 7826
Business Development   Dale Prusinowski Vice President T 306 7819

Banco Santiago
Representative Office

Alternative trading name: Banco de Santiago
Suite 2601, 375 Park Avenue, New York, NY 10152
Tel: (212) 826 0550; (212) 826 0551 Fax: (212) 826 1218

Senior Executive Officers
Representative   Carlos F Singer E cs@bancosantiago.ny.com

Banco di Sicilia
Full Branch Office

250 Park Avenue, New York, NY 10177
Tel: (212) 692 4300 Fax: (212) 370 5790 Reuters: BSIN

Senior Executive Officers
SVP & General Manager   Carlo Cracolici E cracoli@ibm.net

Debt Capital Markets / Fixed Income

Domestic Government Bonds
Head of Trading   Elena Shperling Chief Trader T 692 4334

Syndicated Lending
Global Head   Pierpaolo Carrubba Vice President

Money Markets
Tel: 692 4332
Regional Head   Elena Shperling Chief Trader T 692 4334

Domestic Commercial Paper
Head of Origination   Elena Shperling Chief Trader T 692 4334

Eurocommercial Paper
Head of Trading   Elena Shperling Chief Trader T 692 4334

Foreign Exchange
Tel: 692 4332
Regional Head   Elena Shperling Chief Trader T 692 4334

UNITED STATES (+1)　　　　　www.euromoneydirectory.com

Banco di Sicilia (cont)
FX Traders / Sales People
US$ / DM　　　　　　　　　　　　　Fernando Corredor *Senior Trader* ☏ **692 4335**
US$ / Lire, Lire / DM　　　　　　　　Jay Wertheimer *FX Trader* ☏ **692 4337**
Risk Management
IR Swaps Trading　　　　　　　　　Elena Shperling *Chief Trader* ☏ **692 4334**
Other Departments
Correspondent Banking　　　　　　Ida Bajardi *VP & Deputy General Manager* ☏ **692 4312**

Bank Austria　　　　　　　　　　　　　　　　　　　　　　　　　Full Branch Office
Formerly known as: Creditanstalt-Bankverein
Two Greenwich Place, Greenwich, CT 06730
Tel: (203) 861 6464
Senior Executive Officers
Chief Executive Officer　　　　　　Dennis C O'Dowd *General Manager & Chief Executive Officer*

Bank of Bermuda (New York) Limited　　　　　　　　　　　Subsidiary Company
570 Lexington Avenue, New York, NY 10022
Tel: (212) 980 4500 **Fax:** (212) 980 5079 **Telex:** 422167 **Swift:** BBDA US 33 **Cable:** BBIL NYK
Senior Executive Officers
Chairman & President　　　　　　Edgar Felton
General Manager　　　　　　　　　Fred T Busk III
Others (Senior Executives)
　　　　　　　　　　　　　　　　　　　Donald J Danilek *Senior Vice President*
　　　　　　　　　　　　　　　　　　　Willa McMorris *Vice President*
　　　　　　　　　　　　　　　　　　　Stanley Wong *Vice President*

Bank Brussels Lambert　　　　　　　　　　　　　　　　　　　Full Branch Office
630 Fifth Avenue, New York, NY 10111
Tel: (212) 632 5300 **Fax:** (212) 632 5308 **Telex:** 422934 BBL NY, 6720744 (Forex) **Swift:** BBRU US 3X
Senior Executive Officers
Chief Executive Officer　　　　　　Jean-Louis Recoussine *General Manager*
Financial Director　　　　　　　　　Joseph Botkier *Executive Vice President*
Chief Operating Officer　　　　　　Edgar Lorch *Senior Vice President*
Others (Senior Executives)
Commercial Banking　　　　　　　Luc Verbeken *Senior Vice President* ☏ **632 5310** 📠 **333 5786**
General-Lending (DCM, SL)
Head of Corporate Banking　　　　Dominiek Vangaever *SVP, Credit & Risk Management*
General-Investment
Head of Investment　　　　　　　　Vincent Herbert *SVP & Chief Investment Officer*
Relationship Manager
Institutional Banking　　　　　　　Luc Verbeken *Senior Vice President* ☏ **632 5310** 📠 **333 5786**
Debt Capital Markets / Fixed Income
Fixed-Income Repo
Head of Repo　　　　　　　　　　　David T Fraser *Head, Fixed-Income Markets*
Trading　　　　　　　　　　　　　　Eileen Thompson *Vice President*
　　　　　　　　　　　　　　　　　　　Vincent Herbert *Senior Vice President*
　　　　　　　　　　　　　　　　　　　Eileen Smith *Assistant Vice President*
　　　　　　　　　　　　　　　　　　　Cathy Whelan *Trader*
Foreign Exchange
Country Head　　　　　　　　　　　Susanne Ward *Vice President*
Risk Management
Country Head　　　　　　　　　　　Dominiek Vangaever *SVP, Credit & Risk Management*
Fixed Income Derivatives / Risk Management
Country Head　　　　　　　　　　　Vincent Herbert *Senior Vice President*
Other Departments
Economic Research　　　　　　　　Andrew W Hodge *Vice President*
Administration
Technology & Systems
　　　　　　　　　　　　　　　　　　　Henry T Smith *Vice President*

www.euromoneydirectory.com UNITED STATES (+1)

Legal / In-House Counsel
Andrea M Hyer *Vice President & Head*

Compliance
Michael Stempler

Other (Administration)
Human Resources   Paula R Louzeiro *Vice President*

Bank Central Asia — Full Branch Office
15th Floor, 641 Lexington Avenue, New York, NY 10022
Tel: (212) 888 3300 **Fax:** (212) 223 1333 **Telex:** 276688 BCANY UR **Swift:** CENA US 33

Senior Executive Officers
Executive Vice President   Wee Beng Aw

Bank of China — Full Branch Office
410 Madison Avenue, New York, NY 10017
Tel: (212) 935 3101 **Fax:** (212) 593 1831 **Telex:** 423635 BKCHI NY

Senior Executive Officers
Managing Director / General Manager   Kunsheng Jiao
Managing Director / General Manager   Jiashu Lu
Managing Director / General Manager   Tuanjie Huo
Managing Director / General Manager   Chuanjie Li

The Bank of East Asia Limited — Full Branch Office
202 Canal Street, New York, NY 10013
Tel: (212) 238 8300 **Fax:** (212) 219 8288 **Telex:** 276640

Senior Executive Officers
General Manager   Peng Wah Tang

Bank Handlowy w Warszawie SA — Representative Office
Suite 1101, 405 Park Avenue, New York, NY 10022
Tel: (212) 371 8390 **Fax:** (212) 371 8391

Senior Executive Officers
Chief Representative   Eugeniusz Szewczyk

Bank of Hawaii — Head Office
111 South King Street, Honolulu, HI 96813
PO Box 2900, Honolulu, HI 96846
Tel: (808) 643 8888 **Fax:** (808) 538 4893 **Telex:** 633121 **Swift:** BOHIUS77
Website: www.boh.com

Senior Executive Officers
Chairman & Chief Executive   Lawrence M Johnson
President & Chief Operating Officer Richard J Dahl
Financial Director   David A Houle *Chief Financial Officer*
Vice Chairman   Mary Carryer
Vice Chairman   Alton Kuioka
EVP & Manager, International   Karl Pan ☏ **537 8377**

UNITED STATES (+1)　　　　www.euromoneydirectory.com

Bank of India
Full Branch Office

277 Park Avenue, New York, NY 10172
Tel: (212) 753 6100 Fax: (212) 980 0052; (212) 319 6347 Telex: 234444 Swift: BKID US 33 Email: bainy@usa.net
Reuters: BKIN
Website: www.boiusa.com

Senior Executive Officers
Chief Executive Officer　　　　　　　　Ranjana Kumar Senior Vice President ☎ 752 1354
Financial Director　　　　　　　　　　Ravi Chandran
Chief Operating Officer　　　　　　　　S Arora
Treasurer　　　　　　　　　　　　　　J Karsgigar

The Bank of Korea
Representative Office

23rd Floor, 780 Third Avenue, New York, NY 10017
Tel: (212) 759 5121/3 Fax: (212) 758 6563

Senior Executive Officers
Chief Representative　　　　　　　　　Bo Yung Chung

The Bank of Kyoto Limited
Full Branch Office

36th Floor, 2 World Financial Center, 225 Liberty Street, New York, NY 10281
Tel: (212) 945 1200 Fax: (212) 945 9088 Telex: 6737435 BOK NY

Senior Executive Officers
General Manager　　　　　　　　　　　Kazuo Yamashita

Debt Capital Markets / Fixed Income
Country Head　　　　　　　　　　　　Yutaka Morikawa Assistant General Manager

Money Markets
Country Head　　　　　　　　　　　　Yutaka Morikawa Assistant General Manager

Risk Management
Country Head　　　　　　　　　　　　Shinichi Furusaki Assistant General Manager

Corporate Finance / M&A Advisory
Country Head　　　　　　　　　　　　Kazufumi Matsui Assistant General Manager

Settlement / Clearing
Country Head　　　　　　　　　　　　Kiyoshi Kobori Assistant General Manager

Administration

Public Relations
　　　　　　　　　　　　　　　　　　Ken Yamanaka Assistant General Manager

Bank Leumi USA
Subsidiary Company

Formerly known as: Bank Leumi Trust Co of New York
579 Fifth Avenue, New York, NY 10017
Tel: (917) 542 2000 Fax: (917) 542 2343 Telex: 62856 BLTNY Swift: LUMI US 3N

Senior Executive Officers
Vice Chairman & President　　　　　　Zalman Segal ☎ 407 4400
Chief Executive Officer　　　　　　　　Aharon Kacherginkst Deputy CEO & SEVP ☎ 407 4475
Financial Director　　　　　　　　　　John Derpich Controller & SVP
Treasurer　　　　　　　　　　　　　　Robert Giordano SVP, Treasurer & Chief Dealer

Money Markets
Country Head　　　　　　　　　　　　Robert Giordano SVP, Treasurer & Chief Dealer

Foreign Exchange
Country Head　　　　　　　　　　　　Hillel Waxman EVP & Manager, FX ☎ 343 5205

Corporate Finance / M&A Advisory
Country Head　　　　　　　　　　　　Stanley Karp EVP & Chief Lender ☎ 407 4365

www.euromoneydirectory.com   UNITED STATES (+1)

The Bank of New York
Head Office

One Wall Street, New York, NY 10286
Tel: (212) 495 1784 **Fax:** (212) 495 1398 **Telex:** WU62763 **Swift:** IRV US 3N **Cable:** BANKONE
Website: www.bankofny.com

Senior Executive Officers
Chairman	Thomas A Renyi
Vice Chairman	Allen R Griffith
Chief Executive Officer	Thomas A Renyi *President & CEO*
Financial Director	Bruce Van Seun
Treasurer	Thomas Gibbons *Vice President*

Debt Capital Markets / Fixed Income
Head of Debt Capital Markets	Margo Cook ☎ **635 8670**
Head of Fixed Income	Stratton Heath

Syndicated Lending
Global Head	Brian Rogan *Executive Vice President*

Foreign Exchange
Global Head	R Mahoney *Vice President*

Risk Management
Global Head	Rosanne Welshimer *Vice President*

Corporate Finance / M&A Advisory
Global Head	William Sklar

Asset Management
Head	Deno D Papageorge *Executive Vice President*

The Bank of New York

101 Barclay Street, New York, NY 10286
Tel: (212) 815 2456; (212) 815 2458 **Fax:** (212) 815 2389

Debt Capital Markets / Fixed Income

Fixed-Income Repo
Head of Repo	Thomas Ford *Senior Vice President* ☎ **815 2486**
Marketing & Product Development	Bruce Adams *Vice President* ☎ **815 2377** 📠 **815 2915**
Trading	Harvey Moses *VP, Head of Domestic Trading*
	Larry Mannix *VP, Head of Reinvestments*
	Elisabeth Siano *VP, International Trading*

Equity Capital Markets

Equity Repo / Securities Lending
Head	Thomas Ford *Senior Vice President* ☎ **815 2486**
Marketing & Product Development	Bruce Adams *Vice President* ☎ **815 2377** 📠 **815 2915**
Head of Trading	Harvey Moses *VP, Head of Domestic Trading*
	Larry Mannix *VP, Head of Reinvestments*
	Elisabeth Siano *VP, International Trading*

Bank One Corporation
Full Branch Office

100 East Broad Street, Columbus, OH 43271-0211
PO Box 710211, Columbus, OH
Tel: (614) 248 5800; (614) 248 5995 **Fax:** (614) 248 4680

Senior Executive Officers
President & Chief Executive Officer	John B McCoy
Treasurer	Peter Atwater

Others (Senior Executives)
	Richard Lehmann *Vice Chairman*
	David Vitale *Vice Chairman*

Debt Capital Markets / Fixed Income
Marketing	Brad Iversen *Corporate Marketing Head*

Equity Capital Markets
Marketing	Brad Iversen *Corporate Marketing Head*

Equity Repo / Securities Lending
Head of Trading	Laura Marcoux *Senior Securities Lending Officer*
	Bruce Ryan *Senior Securities Lending Officer*
	Matthew Sarson *Securities Lending Portfolio Manager*

UNITED STATES (+1)   www.euromoneydirectory.com

The Bank of Tokyo-Mitsubishi Limited   Full Branch Office

1251 Avenue of the Americas, New York, NY 10020
Tel: (212) 782 5605 **Fax:** (212) 782 5612

Senior Executive Officers
General Manager   Norimichi Kanari

Debt Capital Markets / Fixed Income
Fixed-Income Repo
Marketing & Product Development   Gerard F Collins *Vice President* ☏ **782 5611**
Matched Book Manager   Robert McHugh *Trust Officer*
Trading   William J Manning *Trust Officer*
    Michael Thorp *Assistant Vice President & Head Trader*

The Bank of Yokohama Limited   Full Branch Office

Suite 8067, One World Trade Center, New York, NY 10048
Tel: (212) 775 1700 **Fax:** (212) 938 5450 **Telex:** ITT 422184 **Swift:** HAMA US 33 **Reuters:** BOYN **Cable:** HAMAGIN

Senior Executive Officers
EVP & General Manager   Yasuhiko Teramura
SVP & Deputy General Manager   Shoichi Ohama
SVP & Deputy General Manager   Yoshiaki Yabe
SVP & Deputy General Manager   Yasuhiro Ohashi

Others (Senior Executives)
    Nobuyuki Takahashi *VP & Senior Manager*
    Atsushi Yashiro *VP & Senior Manager*
    Ryutaro Hotta *VP & Senior Manager*
    Yumiko Hiramatsa *VP & Senior Manager*
    Yuuichi Itakura *Vice President*

Administration
Compliance
    Brian Keith Wormley *Compliance Officer*

Accounts / Audit
Inspection Department   Joseph Acosta *VP & Internal Auditor*

BankBoston Corporation   Head Office

Alternative trading name: BancBoston Robertson Stephens
100 Federal Street, Boston, MA 02110
PO Box 2016, Boston, MA 02106-2016
Tel: (617) 434 2200 **Fax:** (617) 434 1627
Website: www.bankboston.com

Senior Executive Officers
Chief Executive Officer   Chad Gifford
President   Henrique Meirelles
Financial Director   Susannah Swihart *Chief Financial Officer*
Chief Operating Officer   Henrique Meirelles *President*
Treasurer   John Kahwaty *Investor Relations*

Others (Senior Executives)
BancBoston Robertson Stephens   Michael McCaffery *Chief Executive Officer*
Bank Boston Corporation   Paul Hogan *Vice Chairman*

Relationship Manager
Investor Relations   John Kahwaty *Investor Relations*

Debt Capital Markets / Fixed Income
Domestic Government Bonds
Head of Sales   David Dali *Co-Head*
    Christopher Smith *Co-Head, London* ☏ **+44 (171) 222 9273**
Head of Research   Daniel C Peirce *MD & Global Head of Emerging Markets*

High Yield / Junk Bonds
Head   Mark Brostowski *Managing Director & Head Trader*
    Steven Shenfeld *MD & Head, High Yield Securities* ☏ **434 5056**

Emerging Market Bonds
Head   Ignacio Sosa *MD & Head, Emerging Markets* ☏ **434 3737**
Head of Syndication   Stephen Desalvo

UNITED STATES (+1)

Fixed-Income Repo	
Trading	Frederick Goff
Syndicated Lending	
Global Head	Carolyn Thomas *MD, Syndicated Lending* ☎ **434 2200**
Foreign Exchange	
Global Head	Jim Borden *MD & Head, Foreign Exchange*
Risk Management	
Global Head	John Mastromarino ☎ **434 7099**
Fixed Income Derivatives / Risk Management	
Global Head	Kathy Cade *MD & Head, Global Derivatives* ☎ **434 7529**
Corporate Finance / M&A Advisory	
Global Head	Bob Grady *MD & Head, Corporate Finance*
Other (Corporate Finance)	
Specialized Finance	Mary-Etta Schneider *Group Executive, Corp. Banking* ☎ **434 8610**
Global Custody	
Fax: 575 3011	
Head of Global Custody	Timothy O'Leary *Senior Sales Manager & VP* ✉ **tpo'leary@bkb.com**
Other (Global Custody)	
Product Management & Development	Lisa Linker *Director*

Bankers Trust Corporation — Head Office

130 Liberty Street, New York, NY 10006
Tel: (212) 250 2500 **Fax:** (212) 618 3935 **Cable:** BANKTRUST
Website: www.bankerstrust.com

Senior Executive Officers	
Chairman & Chief Executive Officer	Frank N Newman
Financial Director	Richard Daniel
International Division	Richard Marin
Debt Capital Markets / Fixed Income	
Global Head	Arthur H Penn *Head of Fixed Income Capital Markets*
Head of Fixed Income	Steven Freidheim
Emerging Market Bonds	
Head of Emerging Markets	Juan Bilbao
Fixed-Income Repo	
Head of Repo	Jonathan Cooper *Managing Director*
Trading	John Fallon *Associate*
Sales	Marie Bitetti *Managing Director*
Syndicated Lending	
Head of Syndicated Lending	Kevin Sullivan
Global Custody	
Regional Head	Sam Jacob *Senior Managing Director*
Other Departments	
Private Banking	Richard Marin

Banque Audi (Suisse) SA — Representative Office

Suite 3240, 200 South Biscayne Boulevard, Miami, FL 33131-2353
Tel: (305) 373 1300 **Fax:** (305) 373 1303

Senior Executive Officers	
Representative	Nabil J Achkar
Others (Senior Executives)	
	Trudy B Olivera *Deputy Manager*

Banque Nationale de Paris — Full Branch Office

499 Park Avenue, New York, NY 10022
Tel: (212) 415 9400; (212) 750 1400 **Fax:** (212) 415 9717; (212) 415 9629 **Telex:** 824209 **Swift:** BNPA US 3N

Senior Executive Officers	
President & Chief Executive Officer	Pierre Schneider ☎ **415 9620**
Chief Operating Officer	Patrick Saurat *EVP & Chief Administrative Officer* ☎ **415 9626**
Treasurer	Jean Pierre Beck *EVP, Treasury* ☎ **415 9630**

UNITED STATES (+1)   www.euromoneydirectory.com

Banque Nationale de Paris (cont)

Debt Capital Markets / Fixed Income
Country Head   Tom Corper *Senior Vice President* ☏ 415 9743 📠 415 9798

Equity Capital Markets
Country Head   George Cooke *Senior Vice President* ☏ 415 9620 📠 415 4617

Syndicated Lending
Country Head   Joseph Geraghty *Senior Vice President* ☏ 415 9722 📠 415 9805

Loan-Related Activities
Structured Trade Finance   Kathryn Swintek *Executive Vice President* ☏ 418 8252 📠 418 8269

Money Markets
Country Head   Eric Deudon *Senior Vice President* ☏ 415 9753

Risk Management
Country Head   Louis De Glaire *Senior Vice President* ☏ 415 9623

Banque Sudameris

9th Floor, Barnett Tower, 701 Brickell Avenue, Miami, FL 33131
Tel: (305) 372 2200 **Fax:** (305) 374 1137

Senior Executive Officers
Senior Vice President & Manager   Hubert de la Feld

Banque Sudameris   Representative Office

One William Street, New York, NY 10004
Tel: (212) 509 7858 **Fax:** (212) 809 9780

Senior Executive Officers
Representative   Giorgio Andgelozzi

Barclays Bank plc   Full Branch Office

222 Broadway, New York, NY 10038
Tel: (212) 412 4000 **Fax:** (212) 412 7300
Website: www.barclayscapital.com

Senior Executive Officers
Chief Executive Officer   Thomas Kalaris *Chief Executive*
Financial Director   Eileen Crowley *Chief Financial Officer*
Chief Operating Officer   Lorrie Stapleton
Secretary & General Counsel   Margaret Grieve

General-Lending (DCM, SL)
Head of Corporate Banking   Michael Prior

General-Investment
Head of Investment   Eric Chilton
    Lorrie Stapleton

Debt Capital Markets / Fixed Income
Head of Fixed Income   John Roberts
Head of Fixed Income Sales   Robert Printz
    Stephen Lawler

Emerging Market Bonds
Head of Emerging Markets   Joseph Bencivenga

Fixed-Income Research
Head of Fixed Income   Robert Printz
    Stephen Lawler

Equity Capital Markets
Equity Repo / Securities Lending
Head   Kevin Mirabile

Syndicated Lending
Head of Origination; Head of Syndication   Eric Chilton

Loan-Related Activities
Trade Finance   Michael Prior
Project Finance   Eric Chilton

Money Markets
Head of Money Markets   John Roberts

UNITED STATES (+1)

Foreign Exchange
Head of Foreign Exchange — Lawrence Baum
David Johnson

Risk Management
Fixed Income Derivatives / Risk Management
Country Head — Oka Usi Head of Derivatives
Other (Exchange-Traded Derivatives)
Futures — William Weldon ☏ (312) 341 3300

Settlement / Clearing
Head of Settlement / Clearing — Peter Therry

Asset Management
Head — Patricia Dunn ☏ (415) 765 4700

Other Departments
Chief Credit Officer — Robert Clemmens
Private Banking — Mitchell Heller ☏ 415 5900
Correspondent Banking; Cash Management — Michael Prior

Administration
Head of Administration — Peter Hall Chief Administrative Officer

Technology & Systems
Stephen Sparkes

Legal / In-House Counsel
General Counsel — Margaret Grieve Secretary & General Counsel

Compliance
Lawrence Noyer

Accounts / Audit
Peter Warbrick

Barclays Global Investors

16th Floor, 45 Fremont Street, San Francisco, CA 94105
Tel: (415) 597 2000; (415) 597 2345 **Fax:** (415) 597 2399

Equity Capital Markets
Equity Repo / Securities Lending
Head — John Martinez CEO / Managing Director ☏ 597 2109
📧 john.martinez@barclaysglobal.com
Marketing & Product Development; Marketing — Leona Bridges Managing Director ☏ 597 2317
📧 leona.bridges@barclaysglobal.com
Head of Trading — Judith Robertson MD, Global Securities Lending
George O'Connor Principal, US Treasuries & Government Agencies
Kofi Dodi Associate, International Equities

Barex World Trade Corporation   Head Office

777 West Putnam Avenue, Greenwich, CT 06830
Tel: (203) 531 1059 **Fax:** (203) 531 1825

Senior Executive Officers
Managing Director — Stanley Rosenstock
Managing Director — Steven Rothschild

Debt Capital Markets / Fixed Income
Bonds - General
Barter, Offset & Countertrade — Steven Rothschild Managing Director

Syndicated Lending
Loan-Related Activities
Trade Finance — Steven Rothschild Managing Director
Project Finance — Stanley Rosenstock Managing Director
Structured Trade Finance — Steven Rothschild Managing Director
Leasing & Asset Finance — Stanley Rosenstock Managing Director

Other Departments
Commodities / Bullion — Stanley Rosenstock Managing Director
Proprietary Trading — Steven Rothschild Managing Director

Euromoney Directory 1999   **1925**

UNITED STATES (+1)   www.euromoneydirectory.com

BBV Securities Inc   Subsidiary Company

Formerly known as: BBV LatInvest Securities Inc
45th Floor, 1345 Avenue of the Americas, New York, NY 10105
Tel: (212) 728 2300 **Fax:** (212) 262 8468

Senior Executive Officers
Chairman   Raul Santoro
Chief Operating Officer   Craig Lax *Managing Director*

Others (Senior Executives)
Chief Financial Officer   Michael Picone *Director, CFO*

Debt Capital Markets / Fixed Income
Head of Fixed Income Sales; Head of Fixed Income Trading   Jose de Aguinaga

Government Bonds
Head of Syndication; Head of Origination   Jenifer Burns *Head of Fixed Income, Origination & Syndication*

Equity Capital Markets
Head of Equity Capital Markets   Luis Ruigomez *Managing Director*
Head of Sales; Head of Trading   Alejandro Ventosa *Managing Director*

Domestic Equities
Head of Sales; Head of Trading   Alejandro Ventosa *Managing Director*
Head of Research   Xavier Gutierrez *Managing Director*

Syndicated Lending
Loan Origination; Loan Syndication   Laura Sacchi *Managing Director*

Risk Management
Head of Risk Management   Ramon Ruiz *Head of Risk Management*

Settlement / Clearing
Head of Settlement / Clearing   John Iannone *Head of Operations*

Other Departments
Chief Credit Officer   Lee Finch *Director of Credit*
Cash Management   Michael Picone *Director, CFO*

Administration
Head of Administration   Craig Lax *Managing Director*

Technology & Systems
     Maged El-Sherbiny *Head of IT*

Compliance
     Stephanie Sohn Hurwitz *Chief Compliance Officer*

Bear Stearns & Co Inc

245 Park Avenue, New York, NY 10167
Tel: (212) 272 2000 **Fax:** (212) 272 4785
Website: www.bearstearns.com

Senior Executive Officers
Chairman   Alan C Greenberg
President & Chief Executive Officer   James E Cayne
Financial Director   Samuel L Molinaro *Senior Managing Director & CFO*
Chief Operating Officer   William Montgoris *Senior Managing Director & COO*
Treasurer   Michael Minikes *Senior Managing Director, Treasurer*
Senior Managing Director, Secretary   Kenneth L Edlow

General-Investment
Head of Investment   Alan D Schwarty *Executive Vice President*

Debt Capital Markets / Fixed Income
Head of Fixed Income   Warren J Spector *Executive Vice President*

Fixed-Income Repo
Head of Repo   Gary M McLoughlin *Senior Managing Director*

Equity Capital Markets
Head of Equity Capital Markets   Victor A Cohn *Senior Managing Director*

Equity Repo / Securities Lending
Head   Michael Minikes *Senior Managing Director, Treasurer*

Foreign Exchange
Head of Foreign Exchange   David M Schoenthal *Senior Managing Director*

Settlement / Clearing
Head of Settlement / Clearing   Richard Harriton *Senior Managing Director*

www.euromoneydirectory.com UNITED STATES (+1)

Asset Management
Head   Mark A Kurland *Senior Managing Director*
Administration
Head of Administration   William J Montgoris *Chief Operating Officer*
Head of Marketing   Pamela Cuming *Senior Managing Director*
Legal / In-House Counsel
                                            Mark E Lehman *Executive Vice President*
Public Relations
                                            Hannah S Burns *Managing Director*
Corporate Communications
                                            Hannah S Burns *Managing Director*

Berkshire Capital Corporation   Head Office
28th Floor, 399 Park Avenue, New York, NY 10022
Tel: (212) 207 1000 Fax: (212) 207 1019
Bruce Cameron Email: bcameron@berkoap.com
Website: www.berkcap.com

Senior Executive Officers
President   H Bruce McEver ☎ 207 1000 ✉ bmcever@berkcap.com
Chief Operating Officer   Peter L Bain *Managing Director* ☎ 207 1007 ✉ pbain@berkcap.com
                                            R Bruce Cameron *Managing Director* ☎ 207 1063
                                            ✉ bcameron@berkcap.com
International Division   Hoyt Ammidon *Managing Director* ☎ 207 1009
General-Investment
Head of Investment   Peter L Bain *Managing Director* ☎ 207 1007 ✉ pbain@berkcap.com
Syndicated Lending
Loan-Related Activities
Project Finance   Richard Fuote *Principal*
Corporate Finance / M&A Advisory
Head of Corporate Finance   Caleb Burchenal *Managing Director*
Global Head   R Bruce Cameron *Managing Director* ☎ 207 1063
                                            ✉ bcameron@berkcap.com
Regional Head   Peter L Bain *Managing Director* ☎ 207 1007 ✉ pbain@berkcap.com
Country Head   Hoyt Ammidon *Managing Director* ☎ 207 1009
Asset Management
Head   Donald K Miller *Managing Director*
Other Departments
Correspondent Banking   Richard Miles
Administration
Head of Administration   Marille Scheoneman *Office Manager*
Head of Marketing   Elizabeth Nesvold *Vice President*
Legal / In-House Counsel
                                            Peter L Bain *Managing Director* ☎ 207 1007 ✉ pbain@berkcap.com
Compliance
                                            Glenna Webster *Principal*

Berkshire Partners LLC   Head Office
One Boston Place, Boston, MA 02108
Tel: (617) 227 0050 Fax: (617) 227 6105
Website: www.berkshirepartners.com

Senior Executive Officers
Managing Director / General Manager   Bradley M Bloom

BHC Securities Inc
One Commerce Bank Square, 2005 Market Street, Philadelphia, PA 19103-3112
Tel: (215) 636 4590 Fax: (215) 636 0526

Debt Capital Markets / Fixed Income
Fixed-Income Repo
Trading   Kevin Reed *Equity Trader*
                                            Gina Pacillio *Repo Matched Book Trading*

Euromoney Directory 1999 **1927**

UNITED STATES (+1)   www.euromoneydirectory.com

BHC Securities Inc (cont)
Fixed-Income Repo (cont)

Cindy Greenberg *Director* ☎ **636 4503** ✉ **greenberg@bhcsecurities.com**
Pete Wenzke *Equity Trader*

BHF Securities Corp   Subsidiary Company

28th Floor, 590 Madison Avenue, New York, NY 10022
Tel: (212) 756 2800 **Fax:** (212) 756 2729 **Email:** mktg@bhfsc.com

Senior Executive Officers
Chairman   Alfred Moeckel
Chief Executive Officer   Francis La Salla *Chief Executive Officer*
Financial Director   Patrick Wo *Chief Financial Officer*
Chief Operating Officer   Nicholas Fazzolari *Chief Operating Officer*

Equity Capital Markets
Equity Repo / Securities Lending
Head   Steve Lamentino *Vice President*
Head of Trading   Monika Ledermann *Vice President*

Settlement / Clearing
Head of Settlement / Clearing   Rainer Schwam *VP, Settlements*
Back-Office   Nick Fazzolari *Chief Operating Officer*

Other Departments
Chief Credit Officer   Lloyd Dodwell *Vice President*

Administration
Head of Administration   Dino Vitti *VP & CAO*
Head of Marketing   Frank Colella *VP & Director*

Technology & Systems
Babak Ghassemlou *VP & Director of IT*

Compliance
Michael Grana *VP & CAO*

Public Relations
Frank Colella *VP & Director*

BlueStone Capital Partners LP   Head Office

36th Floor, 575 Fifth Avenue, New York, NY 10017
Tel: (212) 850 0500; (800) 236 0835 **Fax:** (212) 681 8320; (212) 850 9429 **Email:** info@bluestonecapital.com

Senior Executive Officers
Chairman   Kamal Mustafa ☎ **850 0518**
President & Chief Executive Officer   Kerry Dukes ☎ **850 0514**
Financial Director   Cliff Matthews
Managing Director / General Manager   David Hogar ☎ **850 0570**
Managing Director / General Manager   Robert Errigo ☎ **850 0540**
Managing Director   Matt Castagra ☎ **850 6517**

Debt Capital Markets / Fixed Income
Head of Debt Capital Markets   Ian Naismith

Private Placements
Head of Origination   Phil Taub ☎ **850 0507**
Head of Sales   Bruce Silver ☎ **850 0545**
    Howard Blum ☎ **850 0549**

Equity Capital Markets
Head of Equity Capital Markets   Ian Naismith

Domestic Equities
Head of Origination; Head of Syndication   Arthur Sharples ☎ **850 0538**
Head of Sales   Brian Greenstein ☎ **850 0534**
Head of Trading   Dick Prieto ☎ **850 0513**
Head of Research   Robert Errigo ☎ **850 0540**

International Equities
Head of Origination   Arthur Sharples ☎ **850 0538**
Head of Syndication   Kerry Dukes *President & Chief Executive Officer* ☎ **850 0514**
Head of Sales   Oded Berkowitz ☎ **850 0532**
Head of Trading   Dick Prieto ☎ **850 0513**
Head of Research   Robert Errigo ☎ **850 0540**

www.euromoneydirectory.com UNITED STATES (+1)

Money Markets
Head of Money Markets					Ian Naismith

Corporate Finance / M&A Advisory
Global Head						Kamal Mustafa [T] **850 0518**
Regional Head						Arthur Sharples [T] **850 0538**

Administration
Head of Administration					Magdela Angerame *VP, Administration*

Technology & Systems
							Chris Joseph *MIS Manager* [T] **850 9497**

Compliance
							Steve Solano *Chief Compliance Officer* [T] **850 0486**

Corporate Communications
							Lindsey Martintonna

BMO Nesbitt Burns Securities Inc
115 South LaSalle Street, Chicago, IL 60690
Tel: (312) 461 5308; (312) 461 3866 **Fax:** (312) 461 7053

Debt Capital Markets / Fixed Income
Tel: 461 5308

Fixed-Income Repo
Head of Repo						Michael Domenico [T] **702 1900** [F] **702 7604**
Matched Book Manager					Lou Boivin
Trading							Sandra Lee

# Bozano, Simonsen Securities Inc	Subsidiary Company
2nd Floor, 590 Fifth Avenue, New York, NY 10036
Tel: (212) 869 1234 **Fax:** (212) 869 3654

Senior Executive Officers
Director						Luis Alberto Reategui [E] **lobato@bozano.com.br**

Debt Capital Markets / Fixed Income

Bonds - General
Fixed Income Sales					João Korngold *Fixed Income Sales* [E] **korngold@bozano.com.br**
							Johannes van de Ven *Fixed Income Sales* [E] **johannes@bozano.com.br**

Equity Capital Markets

Domestic Equities
Head of Sales						Leonardo Taves *Sales* [E] **leonardo@bozano.com.br**
							Márcio Passos *Sales* [E] **marciop@bozano.com.br**
Head of Trading						Marink Martins *Trader* [T] **869 1220** [E] **marink@bozano.com.br**
							Murilo Andrade *Trader* [T] **869 1224** [E] **muriloa@bozano.com.br**

Brinson Partners Inc
209 South LaSalle Street, Chicago, IL 60604
Tel: (312) 220 7100 **Fax:** (312) 220 7199

Senior Executive Officers
President & Managing Partner, CEO & CIO			G Brinson
Chief Operating Officer					S Anderson *Chief Operating Officer*

Debt Capital Markets / Fixed Income

Bonds - General
Fixed Income						D Hesse
International						R Carr

Emerging Market Bonds
Head of Emerging Markets				B Bernstein

Equity Capital Markets
Department: Equity

Other (Domestic Equities)
							J Diermeier

Euromoney Directory 1999 **1929**

UNITED STATES (+1)   www.euromoneydirectory.com

Brown Brothers Harriman & Co

40 Water Street, Boston, MA 02109
Tel: (617) 742 1818 Fax: (617) 772 2333 Telex: 255577 Swift: BBH CUS 33 Email: webmaster@bbh.com
Cable: BROWNSBANK BOSTO
Website: www.bbh.com

Brown Brothers Harriman & Co

Suite 2150, 125 South Wacker Drive, Chicago, IL 60606
Tel: (312) 781 7111 Fax: (312) 368 1287

Brown Brothers Harriman & Co

59 Wall Street, New York, NY 10005-2812
Tel: (212) 483 1818 Fax: (212) 493 8526 Telex: +31062923 BBHUW Swift: BBHC US 33 Cable: BROWNSBANK NY
Website: ww.bbh.com

Debt Capital Markets / Fixed Income
Fixed-Income Repo
Marketing & Product Development   Eugene L Morrisroe *Deputy Manager* [T] 493 8537 [F] 493 8972
Equity Capital Markets
Equity Repo / Securities Lending
Marketing & Product Development   Eugene L Morrisroe *Deputy Manager* [T] 493 8537 [F] 493 8972

BT Alex.Brown Incorporated

1 BT Plaza, 130 Liberty Street, New York, NY 10006
Tel: (212) 250 2500
Website: www.bankerstrust.com

Debt Capital Markets / Fixed Income
Fixed-Income Repo
Marketing & Product Development   Marie Bitetti *Managing Director* [T] 775 2700
                                         [E] marie.bitetti@bankerstrust.com
Trading   John Fallon [T] 775 3090
Equity Capital Markets
Tel: 250 1714 Fax: 250 1277
Equity Repo / Securities Lending
Head of Prime Brokerage   Jeff Bardos *Managing Director* [T] 250 7563 [F] 250 1790

Caisse Centrale des Banques Populaires   Representative Office

126 East 56th Street, New York, NY 10022
Tel: (212) 753 6018 Fax: (212) 593 3291

Senior Executive Officers
Regional Manager, NA & US Representative   Alain Demoustier

Cantor Fitzgerald & Co   Full Branch Office

Suite 1210a, 141 West Jackson Boulevard, Chicago, IL 60604
Tel: (312) 935 1800 Fax: (312) 935 1233

Cantor Fitzgerald & Co

One World Trade Center, New York, NY 10048
Tel: (212) 938 5000 Fax: (212) 938 2461
Website: www.cantor.com

Cantor Fitzgerald Associates LP

One World Trade Center, New York, NY 10048
Tel: (212) 938 5000 **Fax:** (212) 938 2461
Website: www.cantor.com

Cantor Fitzgerald Partners

One World Trade Center, New York, NY 10048
Tel: (212) 938 5000 **Fax:** (212) 938 2461
Website: www.cantor.com

Cantor Fitzgerald Securities

One World Trade Center, New York, NY 10048
Tel: (212) 938 5000 **Fax:** (212) 938 2461
Website: www.cantor.com

Equity Capital Markets
Fax: 938 3925

Equity Repo / Securities Lending
Marketing & Product Development   Stephen P Dimino *Senior Vice President*

CARIPLO - Cassa di Risparmio delle Provincie Lombarde SpA
Full Branch Office

10 East 53rd Street, New York, NY 10022
Tel: (212) 832 6622 **Fax:** (212) 527 8777 **Telex:** 175944

Senior Executive Officers
SVP & General Manager   Luigi Cuminatti 527 8703
FVP & Assistant General Manager   Charles Kennedy 527 8707
FVP & Assistant General Manager   Claude Amitié 527 8716

Cassa di Risparmio di Firenze
Representative Office

Suite 3605, 375 Park Avenue, New York, NY 10152
Tel: (212) 421 6010 **Fax:** (212) 759 6785 **Telex:** 666491 FIGEV **Swift:** CRF IT 3F **Email:** crf_ny@compuserve.com

Senior Executive Officers
US Representative   Paolo G Palli

Cedel Bank
Representative Office

Suite 9051, One World Trade Center, New York, NY 10048
Tel: (212) 775 1900 **Fax:** (212) 775 1907 **Email:** marketing@cedelgroup.com
Website: www.cedelgroup.com

Senior Executive Officers
Manager   Michael Barrett

Debt Capital Markets / Fixed Income

Fixed-Income Repo
Marketing & Product Development   Anthony Masiello *Vice President & Deputy Regional Manager*
                                    +852 2523 0728   +852 2523 7796   amasie@cedelgroup.com

Equity Capital Markets

Equity Repo / Securities Lending
Marketing & Product Development   Patricia A Catalano *Marketing Manager*

UNITED STATES (+1)   www.euromoneydirectory.com

Central Bank of Turkey
Representative Office

821 United Nations Plaza, New York, NY 10017
Tel: (212) 682 8717; (212) 682 8718 **Fax:** (212) 867 1958 **Email:** tcmbny@aol.com

Senior Executive Officers
Chief Representative   Z Merih Ozok

CFC Securities SA
Full Branch Office

100 Wall Street, New York, NY 10005
Tel: (212) 809 9700 **Fax:** (212) 809 7279

Senior Executive Officers
Chairman   Boris Merkenich
Securities Dealing   Steve Domney

Equity Capital Markets
Equity Repo / Securities Lending
Head of Trading   Steve Domney *Securities Dealing*
    Kevin Rafferty *Securities Dealing*
    Thomas J Moore *Securities Dealing*

Settlement / Clearing
Head of Settlement / Clearing   Monica Luca

Chang Hwa Commercial Bank
Full Branch Office

Suite 600, 333 South Grand Avenue, Los Angeles, CA 90071
Tel: (213) 620 7200 **Fax:** (213) 620 7227; (213) 626 2262 **Telex:** 404250951 UI **Swift:** CCBU US 6L

Senior Executive Officers
Vice President   James Lin ☎ **620 7203**

Charterhouse Inc
Subsidiary Company

27th Floor, 590 Madison Avenue, New York, NY 10022-2540
Tel: (212) 888 0020 **Fax:** (212) 644 5145

Senior Executive Officers
Chairman & President   George Michas

The Chase Manhattan Bank

1 Chase Manhattan Plaza, New York, NY 10081
Tel: (212) 552 2222 **Fax:** (212) 552 3875 **Telex:** 62910 CMBUW
Website: www.chase.com

Senior Executive Officers
Chairman   Thomas G Labrecque
President   Arthur F Ryan
Financial Director   E Michel Kruse

Debt Capital Markets / Fixed Income
Department: Global Securities Lending Department
18th Floor, 4 New York Plaza, New York, NY 10004
Tel: +1 (212) 623 2938 **Fax:** +1 (212) 623 3145

Fixed-Income Repo
Head of Repo
Trading
Sales
    Avram Stein *Senior Vice President* ☎ **623 2944** 🖷 **623 3145**
    Nicholas Bonamassa *VP, Manager US Treasury & Corporations*
    Eugene Picone *VP, Western Hemisphere* ☎ **623 2938**
    ✉ **eugene.picone@chase.com**
    Michelle Phillips *Vice President* ☎ **+44 (171) 777 3912**
    Mark Oberlander *Vice President*

Equity Capital Markets
Department: Global Securities Lending Department
18th Floor, 4 New York Plaza, New York, NY 10004
Tel: +1 (212) 623 2938 **Fax:** +1 (212) 623 3145

Equity Repo / Securities Lending
Marketing & Product Development   Eugene Picone *VP, Western Hemisphere* ☎ **623 2938**
    ✉ **eugene.picone@chase.com**

1932   Euromoney Directory 1999

www.euromoneydirectory.com UNITED STATES (+1)

Chase Securities Inc
Head Office
270 Park Avenue, New York, NY 10017-2070
Tel: (212) 834 5158 Fax: (212) 834 6572
Website: www.chase.com

Senior Executive Officers
President — Lawrence W Foss 270 8936
Financial Director — Russell H Neumann *CFO & MD, Treasury & Accounting* 270 8932

General - Treasury
Head of Treasury — Russell H Neumann *CFO & MD, Treasury & Accounting* 270 8932

Debt Capital Markets / Fixed Income

Government Bonds
Head of Trading — William H Pike *Managing Director, Government Dealer* 834 4500

Eurobonds
Head of Origination — Joel H Glasky *MD, Corporate Debt Origination* 834 5076
John Judson *MD, Corporate Debt Origination* 834 3144
Head of Sales; Head of Trading; Head of Research — Jonathan Gray *Managing Director* 834 4433

Bonds - General
Yankee Bond Origination — Joel H Glasky *MD, Corporate Debt Origination* 834 5076

High Yield / Junk Bonds
Head — Wilfred A Finnegan *Managing Director, High Yield Finance* 270 9248
Head of Sales; Head of Trading — Peter A Schmidt-Fellner *Managing Director* 270 0782
Head of Research — Steven A Ruggiero *Managing Director* 270 5260
Peter A Schmidt-Fellner *Managing Director* 270 0782

Emerging Market Bonds
Head of Origination — Fererico L Amadeo *Managing Director* 834 4230
Head of Sales — Raj Keswani *Managing Director* 834 4010

Private Placements
Head of Origination — Ronald Keenan *Managing Director* 834 5140
John L Youngblood *Managing Director* 270 9652

Asset-Backed Securities / Securitization
Global Head — Michael J Malter *Managing Director* 834 5120

Mortgage-Backed Securities
Global Head — Stephen M Kirch *Managing Director* 834 5135

Equity Capital Markets
Head of Trading — Harry D Sidoli *Vice President* 834 4552

Syndicated Lending
Head of Syndication — Gregory Nelson *Managing Director* 270 0975

Loan-Related Activities
Leasing & Asset Finance — Peter Gleysteen *Managing Director* 270 1233

Money Markets
Head of Money Markets — Patricia L Bonan *Managing Director, Sales & Trading* 834 5065

Risk Management
Global Head — Andrew Feldman *Managing Director, Global Derivatives* 834 444

Corporate Finance / M&A Advisory
Head of Mergers & Acquisition — Mark C Davis *Managing Director* 270 2798

Other (Corporate Finance)
Telecommunications & Media — Thomas Reifenheiser *Managing Director* 270 0346
Transportation — Mark C Davis *Managing Director* 270 2798
Financial Institutions — Zissimos A Frangopoulos *Managing Director* 270 9729
Global Oil & Gas — Dod A Fraser *Managing Director* 270 5030
Power & Environment — Robert Gillham *Managing Director* 270 7444
William Rockford *Managing Director* 270 5825
Diversified East & Midwest Chicago — Robert H Partenheimer *Managing Director* (312) 807 4007
Retail — James Ballentine *Managing Director* 270 1334
Kurt Jomo *Managing Director* 270 4669
Diversified & Consumer Products — Nancy Mistretta *Managing Director* 270 4732
Global Chemicals — Paul Beckwith *Managing Director* 270 8315
Global Insurance — David Nelson *Managing Director* 270 7410
Global Commodity Finance & Natural Resources — Christopher Rocker *Managing Director* 270 0002

Settlement / Clearing
Operations — William J Kesselring *Managing Director* 834 5090

Euromoney Directory 1999 **1933**

UNITED STATES (+1)   www.euromoneydirectory.com

Chase Securities Inc (cont)
Administration
Legal / In-House Counsel
Legal   Marjorie E Gross *Senior Vice President* ☎ **270 2097**
Compliance
                                              James F McGinnis *Managing Director* ☎ **270 8934**
Accounts / Audit
Accounting   Russell H Neumann *CFO & MD, Treasury & Accounting* ☎ **270 8932**

The Chiba Bank Limited
1133 Avenue of the Americas, New York, NY 10036
Tel: (212) 354 7777 **Fax:** (212) 354 8575 **Telex:** 251829 CHIBA NYK

Senior Executive Officers
Chief Operating Officer   Kazuya Hirada
Senior Deputy General Manager   Kazuaki Kondo
Managing Director / General Manager   Keiji Yoshioka

Administration
Other (Administration)
General Affairs   Maria Dearce *Head*

Chicago Board of Trade
141 West Jackson Boulevard, Chicago, IL 60604
Tel: (312) 435 3500 **Fax:** (312) 341 5938 **Telex:** 253223 **Email:** pcat50@cbot.com
Website: www.cbot.com

Senior Executive Officers
Chairman of the Board   Patrick Arbor
President & Chief Executive Officer   Thomas Donovan
Financial Director   Glen Johnson *Senior Vice President & Chief Financial Officer*
Chief Operating Officer   Patrick Catania *Executive Vice President*
VP & Secretary   Paul Draths
International Division   Patrick Catania *Executive Vice President*

Chinese American Bank   Head Office
77 Bowery, New York, NY 10002
Tel: (212) 966 3303 **Fax:** (212) 966 3396 **Telex:** 421785 TCAB UI **Cable:** CHIAMBANK

Senior Executive Officers
Chairman & President   C L Chow
Chief Executive Officer   Y M Yang *Executive Vice President*
Financial Director   James N C Fong *Executive Vice President*

Christiania Bank   Full Branch Office
11 West 42nd Street, New York, NY 10036
Tel: (212) 827 4800 **Fax:** (212) 827 4888 **Telex:** 824577 CBNY UF **Swift:** XIAN US 33 **Reuters:** XIAN

Senior Executive Officers
Chief Executive Officer   Tore Nag *EVP & Branch Manager*
Treasurer   Steen Jakobsen *SVP & Treasurer*

The Chugoku Bank Limited   Full Branch Office
Suite 9007, One World Trade Center, New York, NY 10048
Tel: (212) 321 3111 **Fax:** (212) 321 3367 **Telex:** 214987

Senior Executive Officers
General Manager   Kozo Nakamura

www.euromoneydirectory.com　　　　　　　　　UNITED STATES (+1)

CIBC Oppenheimer Corp
Agency

Formerly known as: Canadian Imperial Bank of Commerce & Oppenheimer
5th Floor, 425 Lexington Avenue, New York, NY 10017
Tel: (212) 856 6745 Fax: (212) 885 4348

Senior Executive Officers
Managing Director / General Manager　　Michael Rulle

Debt Capital Markets / Fixed Income

Fixed-Income Repo
Head of Repo　　　　　Peter Maiorano *Managing Director* ☏ **885 4605**
Trading　　　　　　　Steve Porricolo
　　　　　　　　　　　Tim McHugh
　　　　　　　　　　　Richard Fairclough
　　　　　　　　　　　Jim Brannigan
　　　　　　　　　　　Kevin Growney *Repo Sales*

Equity Capital Markets
Tel: 856 6745 Fax: 885 4348

Equity Repo / Securities Lending
Head　　　　　　　　　Jean-Paul Musicco *Managing Director* ☏ **+44 (171) 234 7264**
　　　　　　　　　　　F **+44 (171) 234 7220**
Head of Trading　　　　Dennis Palmeri Jr *Associate Director*
　　　　　　　　　　　Don Larson *Associate Director*
　　　　　　　　　　　James Pagliaroli *Associate Director*
　　　　　　　　　　　Jerry Rugolo *Associate Director*

Cit-Group/Commercial Services
Head Office

1211 Avenue of the Americas, New York, NY 10036
Tel: (212) 382 7000; (800) 248 3240 Fax: (212) 382 6814; (212) 382 6875 Email: info@cs.citgroup.com
Website: www.citgroup.com/cs.htm

Senior Executive Officers
President & Chief Executive Officer　　Lawrence Marsiello
Financial Director　　　　　　　　　Robert Schenker
International Division　　　　　　　James Shelley ☏ **382 7283**

Citibank NA
Head Office

399 Park Avenue, New York, NY 10043
Tel: (212) 559 1000

Senior Executive Officers

Others (Senior Executives)
Latin America　　　　　　　　　Robert Botjer *Market Manager* ☏ **+1 (305) 347 1447**
Media & Communications　　　Ellen Alemany *Global Industry Head* ☏ **559 3212**

General - Treasury
Head of Treasury　　　　　　　Thomas Bergen *Head, Global Futures & Treasury* ☏ **291 7777**

Relationship Manager
Chemicals / Pharmaceuticals　　Charles Bohn *Industry Head* ☏ **559 3172**
　　　　　　　　　　　　　　　Theodore Beck *Market Manager, Northeast US* ☏ **559 4888**
Insurance　　　　　　　　　　Roger Davis *Industry Head* ☏ **559 7174**
Real Estate　　　　　　　　　Patricia Goldstein *Industry Head* ☏ **559 7249**
Aviation　　　　　　　　　　　Ann Lane *Co-head Global Loans* ☏ **559 5307**
Retail　　　　　　　　　　　　Natica Von Althann *Industry Head* ☏ **559 7192**
Autos　　　　　　　　　　　　David Smith *Industry Head* ☏ **559 1880**
Technology　　　　　　　　　Tom McGrath *Head* ☏ **559 5919**
Energy / Power　　　　　　　David McCollum *Global Corporate Quality Head* ☏ **559 6198**
Global Structured Products　　Stephen Karper *Head* ☏ **559 1914**
Liquidity Management　　　　Kevin Kennedy *Head* ☏ **559 2838**

Debt Capital Markets / Fixed Income
Global Head　　　　　　　　　Alvin Hageman *Head, Securitization* ☏ **559 6173**

Asset-Backed Securities / Securitization
Global Head　　　　　　　　　Alvin Hageman *Head, Securitization* ☏ **559 6173**

Equity Capital Markets
Global Head　　　　　　　　　Alvin Hageman *Head, Securitization* ☏ **559 6173**

UNITED STATES (+1)   www.euromoneydirectory.com

Citibank NA (cont)

Equity Repo / Securities Lending
Head   Cindy Gall *VP & Global Product Manager* ☏ **657 4155** F **825 2296**
Head of Trading   Larry Faria *VP, Head Trader-International* ☏ **657 4822**
                        Christine Mattone *VP, Head Trader-Corporates* ☏ **657 6306**
                        Michael Fers *VP, Head Trader-Government* ☏ **657 4155**
                        Achson Chin *VP, Desk Manager* ☏ **657 7184**

Risk Management
Global Head   Peter Gallant ☏ **559 6853**
Country Head   Jamshid Ehsani *Vice President* ☏ **291 4262**

Citibank NA

111 Wall Street, New York, NY 10043
Tel: (212) 657 4822; (212) 248 6600 **Fax:** (212) 825 5874

Senior Executive Officers

Relationship Manager
Depositary Receipts   James Donovan *Managing Director* ☏ **657 5100**
Corporate Agency & Trust   Peter Cole *Manager, Global Products* ☏ **657 8108**
Depositary Receipts, LA Sales   William Truet ☏ **657 7555**

Debt Capital Markets / Fixed Income
Global Head   Sandra Jaffee *Division Director* ☏ **657 5555**

Fixed-Income Repo
Marketing & Product Development Kurt Kreider *Vice President* ☏ **657 4032**
Trading   Graham Barnes *Vice President & Desk Manager* ☏ **+44 (171) 500 2183**
                                F **+44 (171) 500 5063**
                                Larry Faria *Vice President, Head Trader International Desk* ☏ **657 6300**
                                F **657 0515**
                                Christine Mattone *US Equity - Trading Desk Manager, VP*
                                Mike Fers *US Government Trading Desk Manager, VP*
                                Barry Crickmore *Vice President, Manager Hong Kong desk (Hong Kong)*
                                ☏ **+852 2868 7347** F **+852 2868 7350**

Equity Capital Markets
Tel: 657 6300 **Fax:** 657 0515
Global Head   Sandra Jaffee *Division Director* ☏ **657 5555**

Equity Repo / Securities Lending
Marketing & Product Development Kurt Kreider *Vice President* ☏ **657 4032**

Settlement / Clearing
Regional Head   Raymond Parodi *Global Clearing Services Head*

Citic Ka Wah Bank Limited   Full Branch Office

11 East Broadway, New York, NY 10038
Tel: (212) 732 8868 **Fax:** (212) 791 3776; (212) 791 3857 **Telex:** 662388 **Swift:** KWHK US33
Email: kawahny@mail.idt.net

Senior Executive Officers
Chief Executive Officer   Peter Zhao *Executive Vice President & General Manager* ☏ **732 8868**

City National Bank

400 North Roxbury Drive, Beverly Hills, CA 90210
Tel: (310) 888 6000 **Fax:** (310) 888 6704 **Telex:** 673282 **Swift:** CINA 45 66 **Cable:** CINABANK

Senior Executive Officers
Chairman   Russell Goldsmith
President   George H Benter

Clariden Asset Management (New York) Inc   Subsidiary Company

12 East 49th Street, New York, NY 10017
Tel: (212) 888 4949 **Fax:** (212) 888 1940

1936   Euromoney Directory 1999

www.euromoneydirectory.com   UNITED STATES (+1)

Commercial Bank of Kuwait
Full Branch Office

19th Floor, 350 Park Avenue, New York, NY 10022-6022
Tel: (212) 207 2420 **Fax:** (212) 935 6463 **Telex:** 421744 CBK NY **Swift:** COMB US 33 **Reuters:** COKN
Money Markets' Dealing Room Tel: 207 2442; 371 4127; **Fax:** 935 6463

Senior Executive Officers
Chief Executive Officer — Stephen Folkard *Branch Head* 207 2421
Financial Director — Michael Batra *Manager, Letters of Credit*

Syndicated Lending
Head of Origination — Fritz Kopeinig *Senior Credit Manager, North America*

Loan-Related Activities
Trade Finance — Michael Batra *Manager, Letters of Credit*

Other (Trade Finance)
Letters of Credit — Michael Batra *Manager*

Settlement / Clearing
Head of Settlement / Clearing — George Kowaliwskyj *VP & Operations Manager*
Fixed-Income Settlement — Michele Mahoney *Operations Officer*
Operations; Back-Office — Irene Better *Supervisor, Paying & Receiving*

Administration
Head of Administration — Kathleen Meenaghan *Administrator*

Accounts / Audit
— Michael Balestrieri *Controller*

Commerzbank AG
Agency

Suite 3500, 1230 Peachtree Street, Atlanta, GA 30309
Tel: (404) 888 6500 **Fax:** (404) 888 6539 **Telex:** 4611085 CBK ATL **Swift:** COBAUS3XATL

Senior Executive Officers
SVP & Manager — Harry P Yergey

Commerzbank AG
Full Branch Office

Suite 6600, 633 West Fifth Street, Los Angeles, CA 90071
Tel: (213) 623 8223 **Fax:** (213) 623 0039 **Swift:** COBA US 6X XXX

Senior Executive Officers
SVP & Branch Manager — Christian Jagenberg

General-Lending (DCM, SL)
Head of Corporate Banking — Werner Schmidbauer *VP, Corporate Banking*
Steven F Larsen *VP, Corporate Banking*
John Korthuis *VP, Corporate Banking*

Settlement / Clearing
Operations — Regina Lampman *Assistant Vice President*

Administration
Head of Administration — Regina Lampman *Assistant Vice President*

Commerzbank AG
Full Branch Office

2 World Financial Center, New York, NY 10281-1050
Tel: (212) 266 7200 **Fax:** (212) 266 7235 **Telex:** 667488 CBK UW **Swift:** COBA US XXXX

Senior Executive Officers
Executive Vice President — Hermann Buerger
Executive Vice President — Andreas Kleffel
International Division — Jeffrey Lamia *Senior Vice President*

General-Lending (DCM, SL)
Head of Corporate Banking — Sean Harrigan *Senior Vice President*

General - Treasury
Head of Treasury — John P Reilly *Senior Vice President*

Syndicated Lending

Other (Trade Finance)
Letters of Credit — Joachim Pausch *Vice President*

Money Markets
Head of Money Markets — Michael Purdy *Vice President*

Euromoney Directory 1999   **1937**

UNITED STATES (+1)   www.euromoneydirectory.com

Commerzbank AG (cont)

Money Markets - General
Cd's   Werner Rietze *Vice President*

Other (Wholesale Deposits)
Eurocurrency Deposits   Monica Snisky *Assistant Vice President*

Foreign Exchange
Department: Foreign Exchange and Bullion
Corporate Sales   Peter Yauch *Vice President*
                                        George Vifiadou *Vice President*

Risk Management
Head of Risk Management   Juergen Boysen *Senior Vice President*

Other (FI Derivatives)
Derivatives   Michael Purdy *Vice President*

Foreign Exchange Derivatives / Risk Management
Cross-Currency Swaps, Trading   Michael Purdy *Vice President*

Other Departments
Correspondent Banking   Daniel Weissfeld *Vice President*

Commerzbank Capital Markets Corporation

Global Equities, 22nd Floor, 1251 Avenue of the Americas, New York, NY 10020-1104
Tel: (212) 703 4432 **Fax:** (212) 703 4433

Debt Capital Markets / Fixed Income
Fixed-Income Repo
Trading   Michael Santoro *Head Trader*
                                        Arthur Bances *Associate Trader*
                                        Robert Fichetti *Associate Trader*

Compagnie Financière de CIC et de l'Union Européenne

Full Branch Office

520 Madison Avenue, New York, NY 10022
Tel: (212) 715 4400 **Fax:** (212) 715 4477; (212) 715 4528 **Telex:** 426507 CIC UI
General Telex: 238199 CIC FX

Senior Executive Officers
EVP & General Manager   Serge Bellanger

Others (Senior Executives)
International Banking   Bernard Laleuf *SVP & Deputy General Manager*

General - Treasury
Head of Treasury   David Berning *SVP & Group Head*

Debt Capital Markets / Fixed Income
Head of Trading   Deborah Balas *VP, US Treasury Trading*

Non-Domestic Government Bonds
Foreign Government Securities   Jamie Mitchell *Vice President*
                                        Gregory Ambrosio *Vice President*

Mortgage-Backed Securities
Regional Head   Marcia Tucker *Vice President*

Money Markets
Money Markets - General
US$ Funding   Robin Burns *Assistant Vice President*

Foreign Exchange
FX Traders / Sales People
Trading   Patrick Le Goff *Vice President*
                                        Karl Halligan *VP & Chief Dealer*

Administration
Other (Administration)
Product Development   Guy Lefort *Vice President*

Corp Banca CA
Full Branch Office

Formerly known as: Banco Consolidado CA
5th Floor, 845 Third Avenue, New York, NY 10022
Tel: (212) 980 1770 **Fax:** (212) 644 9809 **Telex:** 177603 BCNY **Swift:** CONS US 33

Senior Executive Officers
Chief Executive Officer — Carlos Romero *General Manager* 826 5123
Financial Director — Robert Budd *Vice President, Controller* 826 5175
Chief Operating Officer — Edgard Barona *VP, Operations* 826 5167
Treasurer — Patrick Prat *Treasurer* 826 5131

Debt Capital Markets / Fixed Income
Regional Head — Patrick Prat *Treasurer* 826 5131

Domestic Government Bonds
Head of Trading — Patrick Prat *Treasurer* 826 5131

Eurobonds
Head of Trading; Trading - Sovereigns, Corporates, High-yield — Patrick Prat *Treasurer* 826 5131

Money Markets
Regional Head — Patrick Prat *Treasurer* 826 5131

Foreign Exchange
Regional Head — Patrick Prat *Treasurer* 826 5131

Risk Management
Foreign Exchange Derivatives / Risk Management
Cross-Currency Swaps, Trading; Vanilla FX option Trading — Patrick Prat *Treasurer* 826 5131

Other Departments
Private Banking — Monica Calabrese 826 5118

Cowen & Co
Head Office

Financial Square, New York, NY 10005
Tel: (212) 495 6000 **Fax:** (212) 495 7477

Senior Executive Officers
Chairman — Joseph Cohen
Financial Director — Charles Peterson
Chief Operating Officer — Raimond Moran *Senior Managing Director*

Debt Capital Markets / Fixed Income
Fixed-Income Repo
Head of Repo; Marketing & Product Development — Anthony Sorrentino *Director* 495 6485 480 2838
Trading — Ken Ward *VP, International Stock Loans*
Sheila Mayers *International Stocks*
Mike Romano *International Stocks*
Terry Stephenson *VP, Corporate Bonds*
Jill Jacobson *VP, Equities*
Maurice Marcott *Corporate Broking*
Bob Lamentino *Senior Stock Loan Representative*

Equity Capital Markets
Tel: 495 6000

Equity Repo / Securities Lending
Head — Anthony Sorrentino *Director* 495 6485 480 2838
Head of Trading — Ken Ward *VP, International Stock Loans*
Terry Stephenson *VP, Corporate Bonds*
Bob Lamentino *Senior Stock Loan Representative*
Jill Jacobson *VP, Equities*

Syndicated Lending
Global Head — Jack Dunphy 495 6591

Risk Management
Global Head — Alexander Reamer 495 7545

Settlement / Clearing
Operations — Sal Conti *Operations Manager*
Christopher Gioia *Senior Stock Clerk*
Sandy Kosmidif *Secretary*

UNITED STATES (+1)

Cowen & Co (cont)
Administration
Other (Administration)
Senior Building Clerk — Donna Caruso

Crédit Commercial de France — Full Branch Office
590 Madison Avenue, New York, NY 10022
Tel: (212) 486 3080 Fax: (212) 832 7469

Senior Executive Officers
Financial Director — Frank Defina *Chief Financial Officer* ☎ **848 0531**
Chief Operating Officer — Frank Nardi ☎ **848 0575**
General Manager — Jean-Paul Foity ☎ **848 0582**

Others (Senior Executives)
Deputy General Manager — Jean-Jacques Salomon

Money Markets
Head of Money Markets — Vincent Craca

Foreign Exchange
Country Head — Guy Kershberg

Risk Management
Country Head — Gabe Csordas ☎ **848 0508**

Settlement / Clearing
Equity Settlement — Frank Nardi ☎ **848 0575**

Administration
Legal / In-House Counsel
— Stuart Fraser

Credit Communal SA — Subsidiary Company
54th Floor, Chrysler Building, 405 Lexington Avenue, New York, NY 10174-5499
Tel: (212) 972 6060 Fax: (212) 972 6522

Senior Executive Officers
Chief Executive Officer — Jan E Van Panhuys *General Manager* ☎ **697 6215**
Financial Director — Piyush K Sahay *Financial Controller*

Others (Senior Executives)
Vice President — Caroline Junis *Vice President* ☎ **697 6143**

Crédit Lyonnais
1301 Avenue of the Americas, New York, NY 10019-6022
Tel: (212) 261 7000 Fax: (212) 459 3170 Telex: ITT:423493 Swift: CRLY US 33

Senior Executive Officers
Chief Executive Officer — Jerome Brunel
— Walter Brenner
Treasurer — Allan Rosenberg

Debt Capital Markets / Fixed Income
Tel: 261 3500 Fax: 261 3650
Head of Fixed Income — David Travis *Director* ☎ **261 4178**
Head of Fixed Income Sales — Jay Rubloff *Managing Director* ☎ **261 3602**

Emerging Market Bonds
Head of Emerging Markets — James Alban-Davies *Head, Latin America Fixed Income* ☎ **261 3581**
 🖷 **261 3699**
Head of Sales — Ivo Almuli *Vice President* ☎ **261 3583**
Head of Trading — Peter Urbanczyk *Managing Director* ☎ **261 3685**

Equity Capital Markets
Equity Repo / Securities Lending
Head — Alexandre Urwicz
Head of Trading — Janice Turek *Trader, International*
— Peter Reilly *Trader, Domestic*

Money Markets
Tel: 261 7936 Fax: 459 3152 Reuters: CLNY Telex: CLNY
Head of Money Markets — Daniel Koual *Director* ☎ **261 7936**

1940 Euromoney Directory 1999

www.euromoneydirectory.com   UNITED STATES (+1)

Foreign Exchange
Tel: 261 7000
Head of Foreign Exchange   Ivan Sands *Managing Director* ☎ **261 7412**

Crédit Lyonnais Rouse (USA) Limited

21st Floor, 50 Broadway, New York, NY 10004
Tel: (212) 530 7830; (212) 530 7700 **Fax:** (212) 797 3968 **Telex:** 423526 ARUSA **Reuters:** CLAR

Senior Executive Officers
Chairman   John V Hannam
President   Alex Ladouceur

Crédit Lyonnais Securities (USA) Inc

37th Floor, 1301 Avenue of the Americas, New York, NY 10019
Tel: (212) 261 7000; (212) 408 5700 **Fax:** (212) 261 2511

Senior Executive Officers
Chief Executive Officer   Jacques Mounier

Crédit Lyonnais/PK Airfinance   Full Branch Office

34th Floor, 152 West 57th Street, New York, NY 10019
Tel: (212) 245 2575 **Fax:** (212) 397 9393
Website: www.clpk.com

Senior Executive Officers
First Vice President   Jan Melgaard ✉ **j.melgaard@clpk.com**

Asset Management
Head   Anders Hebrand *Vice President, Marketing*

Administration
Head of Administration   Judith Calabrese *Administrative Assistant*
Head of Marketing   Greg Conlon *Assistant Vice President, Marketing*

Credit Suisse First Boston   Subsidiary Company

3rd Floor, 11 Madison Avenue, New York, NY 10010
PO Box 3700, New York, NY
Tel: (212) 325 2000; (212) 325 3040 **Fax:** (212) 325 8058; (212) 325 8069 **Telex:** 420149 **Swift:** CSFB US 33
Email: bob.sloan@csfb.com **Reuters:** CSNZ
Website: www.csfb.com

Senior Executive Officers
Managing Director / General Manager   Allen D Wheat

Debt Capital Markets / Fixed Income

Fixed-Income Repo
Trading   Tony Blasi *Director*
                                              Steve Meier *Director of Trading & Product Management*
                                              Mike Glennon *Director*

Equity Capital Markets
Tel: 325 3894 **Fax:** 325 8069

Equity Repo / Securities Lending
Marketing & Product Development   Constance Sailer *Vice President* ☎ **325 2529** ✉ **constance.sailer@csfb.com**
                                              Joseph Santoro *Vice President* ✉ **joe.santoro@csfb.com**
Head of Prime Brokerage   Joanne McElligott *Vice President* ☎ **325 0386**
                                              ✉ **joanne.mcelligott@csfb.com**

Corporate Finance / M&A Advisory

Other (Corporate Finance)
Mergers & Acquisitions   Steven Koch *Co-Head*

Euromoney Directory 1999 **1941**

UNITED STATES (+1)   www.euromoneydirectory.com

Crowell, Weedon & Co
Head Office

Suite 2600, One Wilshire Boulevard, Los Angeles, CA 90017
Tel: (213) 620 1850

Senior Executive Officers
Chairman   Donald Crowell ☎ **620 1850**

Corporate Finance / M&A Advisory
Fax: 680 3450
Regional Head   Harold Harrigian *Director, Corporate Finance* ☎ **244 9355**

The Daegu Bank Limited
Representative Office

10th Floor, 29 West 30th Street, New York, NY 10001
Tel: (212) 868 1075 Fax: (212) 868 1077

Senior Executive Officers
Chief Representative   Tae Joon Choi

Daewoo Securities (America) Inc
Subsidiary Company

28th Floor, 101 E 52nd Street, New York, NY 10022
Tel: (212) 407 1000 Fax: (212) 407 1010 Reuters: DWSC

Senior Executive Officers
President   Young Kyo Kwak ☎ **407 1002**
Financial Director   Jang Wook Lee ☎ **407 1006**

Debt Capital Markets / Fixed Income
Department: Daewoo Futures (Fixed Income Sales)
Global Head   Hee S Choi ☎ **407 1019**
Regional Head   Jae Hyun Ahn ☎ **407 1039**

Equity Capital Markets
Department: Korean Equity Sales
Global Head   J Ho Lee ☎ **407 1018**

Settlement / Clearing
Regional Head   Paul Kelly ☎ **407 1011**

Dai-Ichi Kangyo Bank of California
Subsidiary Company

555 West Fifth Street, Los Angeles, CA 90013
Tel: (213) 612 2700 Fax: (213) 623 2979; (213) 612 2875 Telex: 674239 DAIKAN LS
Website: www.dkb.co.jp

Senior Executive Officers
President   Toyohiko Yamashita

The Dai-Ichi Kangyo Bank Limited
Full Branch Office

Suite 2400, Marquis Tower Two, 285 Peachtree Center Avenue NE, Atlanta, GA 30303
Tel: (404) 581 0200 Fax: (404) 581 9657 Telex: 544173 DKB ATL
Website: www.dkb.co.jp

Senior Executive Officers
Managing Director / General Manager   Takao Mochizuki

The Dai-Ichi Kangyo Bank Limited
Full Branch Office

26th Floor, 10 South Wacker Drive, Chicago, IL 60606
Tel: (312) 876 8600 Fax: (312) 876 2011 Telex: 254515 BANKDAIKA
Website: www.dkb.co.jp

Senior Executive Officers
Managing Director / General Manager   Teruo Takahashi

1942   Euromoney Directory 1999

www.euromoneydirectory.com UNITED STATES (+1)

The Dai-Ichi Kangyo Bank Limited
Full Branch Office

5th Floor, 555 West Fifth Street, Los Angeles, CA 90013
Tel: (213) 243 4700 Fax: (213) 624 5258 Telex: 674516
Website: www.dkb.co.jp

Senior Executive Officers
Managing Director / General Manager   Isao Arihara

The Dai-Ichi Kangyo Bank Limited
Full Branch Office

Suite 4911, One World Trade Center, New York, NY 10048
Tel: (212) 466 5200 Fax: (212) 524 0579 Telex: 232988 Swift: DK BLUS 33
Website: www.dkb.co.jp

Senior Executive Officers
Managing Director / General Manager   Yoshiro Aoki

The Dai-Ichi Kangyo Bank Limited
Full Branch Office

Suite 4000, 101 California Street, San Francisco, CA 94111
Tel: (415) 393 1800 Fax: (415) 788 7868
Website: www.dkb.co.jp

Senior Executive Officers
General Manager & Agent   Takuo Yoshida
Joint General Manager   Seigo Makino

Dai-Ichi Kangyo Trust Company of New York

Suite 5031, One World Trade Center, New York, NY 10048
Tel: (212) 466 6640 Fax: (212) 912 1039 Telex: 420720
Website: www.dkb.co.jp

Senior Executive Officers
Chairman   Kenji Nakamura

Dain Rauscher Incorporated
Head Office

Formerly known as: Dain Bosworth Incorporated & Rauscher Pierce Refsnes Incorporated
Dain Rauscher Plaza, 60 South Sixth Street, Minneapolis, MN 55402-4422
Tel: (612) 371 2711 Fax: (612) 371 7755
Website: www.dainrauscher.com

Senior Executive Officers
Chairman, President & CEO   Irving Weiser ☎ **371 2703**
Vice Chairman & Chief Financial Officer   John Appel ☎ **371 2748**
Secretary & General Counsel   Carla Smith ☎ **371 7858**

Others (Senior Executives)
Member of the Executive Committee   Nelson Civello *President, Fixed Income Capital Markets Group* ☎ **371 7975**
                                     Ronald A Tschetter *President, Private Client Group* ☎ **371 2899**
                                     J Scott Spiker *President, Business Services Group* ☎ **371 2894**
                                     Kenneth Wessels *President, Equity Capital Markets* ☎ **373 1968**

General-Lending (DCM, SL)
Head of Corporate Banking   David Parrin *Corporate Controller* ☎ **373 1713**

Relationship Manager
Private Client Group   Michael Gillilan *Regional Director, East* ☎ **(414) 347 7111**
                                     Karl Leaverton *Regional Director, Midwest* ☎ **371 7664**
                                     James Kerr *Regional Director, Pacific Northwest* ☎ **(206) 621 3214**
                                     David Sogge *Regional Director, Rocky Mountain* ☎ **(303) 595 1111**
                                     Dan Wilhite *Regional Director, Southwest* ☎ **(214) 989 1500**
                                     Charles Grose *Regional Director, West* ☎ **(801) 536 1910**
Private Client Group Training & Branch   Cathleen Tobin *Director* ☎ **(612) 371 7926**
Development
Product Management Group   Nikki Sorum *Director* ☎ **(612) 371 7776**

UNITED STATES (+1)   www.euromoneydirectory.com

Dain Rauscher Incorporated (cont)

Debt Capital Markets / Fixed Income
Department: Fixed-Income Group

Head of Debt Capital Markets	Nelson Civello *President, Fixed Income Capital Markets Group* ☎ **371 7975**
Country Head	David Jennings *Director, Institutional Municipal Trading & Sales* ☎ **(312) 559 1614**
Other	Robert Vanosky *Director, Public Finance* ☎ **(214) 989 1715**
	Linda Henderson *Director, Retail Fixed-Income* ☎ **371 2877**
	Larry Holtz *Director, Taxable Fixed-Income* ☎ **371 1769**
	David Jennings *Director, Institutional Municipal Trading & Sales* ☎ **(312) 559 1614**

Equity Capital Markets
Department: Dain Rauscher Wessels

Head of Equity Capital Markets	Kenneth Wessels *President, Equity Capital Markets* ☎ **373 1968**
Head of Sales; Head of Trading	Peter Grant *Director, Sales, Trading & Research* ☎ **371 7972**
Head of Trading	Robert Gales *Director, Institutional Equity Trading* ☎ **373 6203**
Other	Wade Massard *Director, Syndicate* ☎ **371 2837**

Equity Research

Head of Equity Research	Peter Grant *Director, Sales, Trading & Research* ☎ **371 7972**
	Don Heeter *Director* ☎ **371 2996**

Syndicated Lending

Global Head	Restor Johnson *Director, Corporate Capital Group* ☎ **371 2818**

Corporate Finance / M&A Advisory
Department: Dain Rauscher Wessels

Head of Corporate Finance	Bryson Hollimon *Director* ☎ **373 6203**

Settlement / Clearing

Operations	Michelle White *Director* ☎ **607 8806**

Asset Management
Department: Insight Investment Management

Head	Julie Getchell *President* ☎ **371 7955**

Other Departments

Correspondent Banking	John Hickey *President, RPR Correspondent Clearing* ☎ **(314) 589 5040**

Administration

Head of Marketing	Peder Furuseth *Director* ☎ **371 7712**

Legal / In-House Counsel

General Counsel	Carla Smith *Secretary & General Counsel* ☎ **371 7858**

Public Relations

Information Services	Doug Strachan *Chief Information Officer* ☎ **607 8801**

Corporate Communications

Corporate Comunications	B J French *Director* ☎ **371 2363**

Other (Administration)

Human Resources	Paula Phillippe *Director* ☎ **313 1311**
Strategic Planning & Corporate Development	Mike Kavanagh *Director* ☎ **371 7768**

DBS Bank   Agency

27th Floor, 420 Fifth Avenue, New York, NY 10018
Tel: (212) 997 7500 Fax: (212) 997 5713 Telex: 235607

Senior Executive Officers
Managing Director / General Manager   Wil-Kim Long

Dean Witter Reynolds

5th Floor, 5 World Trade Center, New York, NY 10048
Tel: (212) 392 7222 Fax: (212) 392 7565

Debt Capital Markets / Fixed Income

Fixed-Income Repo

Head of Repo	Michael Vaniderstine *Senior Vice President*
Trading	Gus Kartsonas *Vice President*
	Michael Iannuzzo
	Richard Lawrence

www.euromoneydirectory.com UNITED STATES (+1)

Equity Capital Markets
Tel: 392 2277 Fax: 392 7565

Equity Repo / Securities Lending
Head Michael Vaniderstine *Senior Vice President*
Head of Trading Gus Kartsonas *Vice President*
 Michael Iannuzzo
 Richard Lawrence

Deltec Asset Management Corporation   Head Office

535 Madison Avenue, New York, NY 10022
Tel: (212) 230 1400 Fax: (212) 230 1412

Senior Executive Officers
Chairman Arthur E Byrnes
President John R Gordon
Chief Operating Officer Stephen Zuppello

Debt Capital Markets / Fixed Income
Department: Investment Management

Non-Domestic Government Bonds
International Fixed-Income Arthur E Byrnes

High Yield / Junk Bonds
Head of Trading Nancy D Pundyk *High-Yield & Special Situations*

Equity Capital Markets
Department: Investment Management

Domestic Equities
Head of Origination John R Gordon

International Equities
Head of Origination Alan L Werlau

Den Danske Bank Aktieselskab   Full Branch Office

4th Floor, East Building, 280 Park Avenue, New York, NY 10017-1216
Tel: (212) 984 8400 Fax: (212) 370 9339 Telex: 216783 DDBNY Swift: DABA US 33 Reuters: DDBN (Monitor)

Senior Executive Officers
Chief Executive Officer James M Stewart *General Manager*
 David Morgan *Deputy General Manager*
Treasurer J P Neergaard

Debt Capital Markets / Fixed Income

Libor-Based / Floating-Rate Products
Asset Swaps David Morgan *Deputy General Manager*

Money Markets
Regional Head Richard Greiner *Vice President* ☎ 984 8483

Foreign Exchange
Regional Head Patrick MaCahill *Vice President* ☎ 984 8487
Head of Institutional Sales; Corporate Sales Jennifer Ty *Vice President* ☎ 984 8484

Settlement / Clearing
Regional Head Joseph LaPuma *Vice President* ☎ 984 8445
Foreign Exchange Settlement Joseph Pannizzo *Assistant Vice President* ☎ 984 8470

Den norske Bank ASA

31st Floor, 200 Park Avenue, New York, NY 10166-0396
Tel: (212) 681 3800 Fax: (212) 681 3900 Telex: 426357 Swift: DNBA US 33

Senior Executive Officers
Managing Director / General Manager Tony Samuelsen

Euromoney Directory 1999 **1945**

UNITED STATES (+1)   www.euromoneydirectory.com

Deutsche Bank AG   Full Branch Office

31 West 52nd Street, New York, NY 10019-6160
Tel: (212) 469 8000; (212) 469 5000 Fax: (212) 469 3900; (212) 469 4133 Telex: AT&T 422908 Swift: DEUT US33
Fixed Income Tel: 812 6860; Foreign Exchange Tel: 469 8370; Fax: 469 8088; Precious Metals Sales & Trading
Tel: 469 8931; Fax: 469 6919; Treasury Tel: 469 8151; Fax: 469 8159
Website: www.deutschebank.de

Senior Executive Officers
Chairman   Robert Allardice
General - Treasury
Head of Treasury   John C Stomber *Treasurer of the Americas* T 469 7493 F 469 6753
Relationship Manager
Financial Institutions   Tykie Tobin T 469 8107 F 469 8108
Information Research   Roman Sorobay *Head* T 469 5355
Debt Capital Markets / Fixed Income
Tel: 469 6730 Fax: 469 8714
Global Head   Paul Jacobson *Co-Head Global Markets, North America* T 469 6708 F 469 8940
     Mr Kvalheim *MD, Global Debt Capital Markets* T 469 7575 F 469 8904
Emerging Market Bonds
Head   Luis Pablo Calterini *Head of Emerging Markets* T 469 5777 F 469 5775
     Gary Huff *Emerging Markets Sales & Trading* T 469 1672 F 469 7581
Mortgage-Backed Securities
Global Head   Howard Henick T 469 6940 F 469 7210
Fixed-Income Repo
Head of Repo   Walter Travalja *Director* T 474 6730
Trading   Joseph Rondazzo *Trader, Term Repo Matchbook*
     Ray Gillmartin *Trader, Specials Matchbook*
Fixed-Income Research
Global Head   Mr Paradiso *Director of Research* T 469 7352 F 469 7379
Equity Capital Markets
Tel: 469 8000 Fax: 469 6270
Global Head   Mr Necarsulmer *Head, Equity Capital Markets* T 469 5622 F 469 5611
Other (Domestic Equities)
Institutional Sales   William Foley *MD, Institutional Equity Sales* T 469 5342
International Equities
Head of Origination   Ms Kuijters *MD, Head of European Equities* T 469 7583 F 469 7484
Head of Sales   Bill Healey *Equity Sales, Japan* T 469 5875
Head of Trading   Gary Tsarsis *Head of Desk* T 469 7474 F 469 5312
Other (International Equity)
South African Equities   Mark Chiaviello T 469 6041 F 469 5184
Asian Equities   Jenny Chiam *Head of Desk* T 469 5871 F 469 5611
Equity Research
Global Head   Mr Paradiso *Director of Research* T 469 7352 F 469 7379
Equity Repo / Securities Lending
Head   Mark Aldoroty *Regional Manager* T 469 5899
Head of Trading   Lisa Gabbay *Trader*
     John Genovese *Trader*
     Ina Jacobs *Trader*
     James Conti *Product Development, US Shares* T 469 5742
     John Egan *Trader*
     Sean Keogh *Trader*
     Emil Plataroti *Product Development, International*
Syndicated Lending
Head of Syndication   Mr Miller *MD, Syndications* T 469 5298 F 469 5995
Loan-Related Activities
Leasing & Asset Finance   Mr Baird *MD, International Leasing* T 469 7390 F 469 7398
Money Markets
Money Markets - General
Money Markets / Repo   Mario Piero T 469 7652 F 469 7693
Risk Management
Global Head   Vincent Valducci *Head, Interest & Derivatives* T 469 7400 F 469 6753
Corporate Finance / M&A Advisory
Other (Corporate Finance)
International Corporate Finance   Ralph Almer T 469 3135 F 469 7070

www.euromoneydirectory.com UNITED STATES (+1)

Global Custody
Tel: 469 7726 Fax: 469 6787
Regional Head Michael Tierney [T] **469 6744**
Other (Global Custody)
Michael Gedigk *Head of Custody Sales* [T] **469 8503**

Other Departments
Economic Research Peter Petas *Sovereign Analyst*
Administration
Technology & Systems
Marc Sternfeld *MD, Global Information & Technology Systems* [T] **469 6280**
[F] **469 4427**

Deutsche Bank North America — Subsidiary Company
31 West 52nd Street, New York, NY 10019-6160
Tel: (212) 469 8000 Fax: (212) 469 4133; (212) 469 4134
Audit Tel: 469 8286; **Fax:** 469 8210; **Business Technology Services Tel:** 469 4400; **Fax:** 469 4429; **Compliance Tel:** 469 8600; **Fax:** 469 8602; **Controlling Tel:** 469 8420; **Fax:** 469 8415; **Corporate Administration Tel:** 469 3201; **Fax:** 469 3210; **Corporate Communications Tel:** 469 7310; **Fax:** 469 7322; **Credit Risk Management Tel:** 469 8500; **Fax:** 469 8213; **DB Trader Systems Tel:** 469 6400; **Fax:** 469 6367; **Human Resources Tel:** 469 8400; **Fax:** 469 7029; **Legal Tel:** 469 8200; **Fax:** 469 8173; **Operations & Transaction Services Tel:** 469 3310; **Fax:** 469 3314; **Risk Management Tel:** 469 7872; **Fax:** 469 7872

Senior Executive Officers
President W Carter McClelland
Others (Senior Executives)
Global Equities Sarah Orsay *Director* [T] **469 3844** [F] **469 6025** [E] sarah.orsay@db.com

Deutsche Bank Securities Inc — Full Branch Office
Suite 3320, 950 East Paces Ferry, Atlanta, GA 30326
Tel: (404) 812 6800 Fax: (404) 812 6810
Equities Tel: 812 6880; 812 6880; **Fax:** 812 6810; **Fixed Income Tel:** 812 6841; 812 6841; **Fax:** 812 6860

Senior Executive Officers
Others (Senior Executives)
Branch Manager Tom Young
Equity Capital Markets
Other (Equity Research)
Research Salesman Jeff Karcher

Deutsche Bank Trust Company — Subsidiary Company
31 West 52nd Street, New York, NY 10019-6160
Tel: (212) 469 7000 Fax: (212) 469 7014

Senior Executive Officers
Chief Executive Officer Henry Ziegler
Managing Director / General Manager Maarten L Nederlof [T] **469 5010** [F] **469 6025** [E] maarten.nederlof@db.com

Deutsche Financial Services Corporation — Head Office
655 Maryville Centre Drive, St Louis, MO 63141
Tel: (314) 523 3000 Fax: (314) 214 4350
Administration Tel: 523 3003; **Fax:** 523 3733; **Audit Tel:** 523 3981; **Fax:** 523 3940; **Corporate Communications Tel:** 523 3820; **Fax:** 523 3244; **Credit Tel:** 523 3930; **Fax:** 523 3995; **Finance Tel:** 523 3912; **Fax:** 523 3999; **Human Resources Tel:** 523 3907; **Fax:** 523 3053; **International Marketing Tel:** 523 3946; **Fax:** 523 3996; **Legal Tel:** 523 3905; **Fax:** 523 3855; **President & CEO Tel:** 523 3901; **Fax:** 523 3888; **Technology Tel:** 523 3956; **Fax:** 523 3960; **Treasury Tel:** 523 3950; **Fax:** 523 3993

UNITED STATES (+1)　　　　www.euromoneydirectory.com

Deutsche Securities Inc
31 West 52nd Street, New York, NY 10019
Tel: (212) 469 5000

Senior Executive Officers
Department: Senior Executives: Global Corporates and Institutions

Others (Senior Executives)
Head of Investment Banking　　　　Josef Ackermann
Head of Global Markets　　　　　　Edson Mitchell
Head of Equities　　　　　　　　　Michael Philipp
Head of Risk Management　　　　　Hugo Banziger
Head of Global Banking Services　　Juergen Fitschen
Head of Structured Finance　　　　Gavin Lickley
Head of IT / Operations　　　　　　Marc Sternfeld

Debt Capital Markets / Fixed Income
Head of Debt Capital Markets　　　　Grant Kvalheim *Global Head* ☎ **469 7595**

High Yield / Junk Bonds
Head　　　　　　　　　　　　　　Gopal Menon *Global Head* ☎ **+44 (171) 545 9162**

Emerging Market Bonds
Head of Emerging Markets　　　　　Pablo Calderini *Global Head* ☎ **+44 (171) 545 7535**
Head of Research　　　　　　　　　David Folkerts-Landau ☎ **+44 (171) 545 6404**

Asset-Backed Securities / Securitization
Global Head　　　　　　　　　　　Charles von Arentschildt *Managing Director* ☎ **469 8430**

Fixed-Income Research
Head of Fixed Income　　　　　　　Steven Bell *Head of Global Markets Research* ☎ **+44 (171) 545 2085**
Head of Credit Research　　　　　　Glenn Reynolds ☎ **469 4526**

Fixed Income (Trading)
Fixed Income / Credit Trading　　　　Neal Neilinger *Head of Trading* ☎ **469 2857**

Equity Capital Markets
Head of Equity Capital Markets　　　Michael Cohrs *Global Head* ☎ **+44 (171) 545 6858**

Other (International Equity)
Cash Equities　　　　　　　　　　Michael Philipp *Global Head* ☎ **+44 (171) 545 1479**
Equity Derivatives　　　　　　　　Kevin Parker *Global Head* ☎ **469 4632**
Equity Finance　　　　　　　　　　Mark Gelnaw *Global Head* ☎ **+44 (171) 545 5033**

Money Markets

Money Markets - General
Money Markets / Repo　　　　　　　Mario Pierro *Global Co-head* ☎ **469 7652**
　　　　　　　　　　　　　　　　Mark Yallop *Global Co-head* ☎ **+44 (171) 545 2214**

Foreign Exchange
Head of Foreign Exchange　　　　　Hal Herron *Global Head* ☎ **+44 (171) 545 4666**

Risk Management

Other (FI Derivatives)
OTC Derivatives / Government Trading　Saman Majd *Global Head* ☎ **+44 (171) 545 1602**

Other Departments

Other Departments
Institutional Client Group　　　　　　Anshu Jain *Global Head* ☎ **+44 (171) 545 1586**
Global Exchange Services　　　　　Paul Lewis *Global Head* ☎ **+44 (171) 545 1484**
Metals & Commodities　　　　　　　Charles von Arentschildt *Global Head* ☎ **469 8430**

DG Bank　　　　　　　　　　　　　　　　　　　　　　　　Full Branch Office
DG Bank Building, 609 Fifth Avenue, New York, NY 10017
Tel: (212) 745 1400 Fax: (212) 745 1550

Senior Executive Officers
Managing Director / General Manager　　Olives d'Oelsnitz
Managing Director / General Manager　　Hans Meyers

1948　Euromoney Directory 1999

DKB Financial Products Inc

Suite 5027, One World Trade Center, New York, NY 10048
Tel: (212) 313 0400 Fax: (212) 313 0404
Website: www.dkb.co.jp

Senior Executive Officers
President   Junichi Furusawa

DKB Securities (USA) Corporation   Subsidiary Company

50th Floor, One World Trade Center, New York, NY 10048
Tel: (212) 488 0500 Fax: (212) 839 9661
Website: www.dkb.co.jp

Senior Executive Officers
President & Chief Executive Officer   Katsuo Okuno ☎ **488 0531**
Financial Director   Greg Mullen *Vice President* ☎ **488 0523**
Chief Operating Officer   Richard Closs *Senior Vice President* ☎ **488 0541**

Debt Capital Markets / Fixed Income

Domestic Government Bonds
Head of Sales   Aster Katsantonis *Assistant Deputy President* ☎ **488 0086**
Head of Trading   Timothy Logan *Senior Vice President* ☎ **488 0012**

Settlement / Clearing
Department: Back-Office
Tel: 488 0523 Fax: 839 9661
Regional Head   Greg Mullen *Vice President*

Other Departments
Economic Research   Philip Brabernan

Administration

Compliance
                                             Alois Jurcik *VP & Chief Compliance Officer* ☎ **488 0087**

Public Relations
                                             Takeshi Ito *Assistant Vice President* ☎ **488 0018**

Dresdner Bank AG

75 Wall Street, New York, NY 10005-2889
Tel: (212) 429 2490 Telex: 421750 Swift: DRES US 33

Senior Executive Officers
Executive Vice President   Patrick Connolly ☎ **429 2195**

Dresdner Kleinwort Benson North America LLC

31st Floor, 75 Wall Street, New York, NY 10005-2889
Tel: (212) 429 2100; (212) 429 4400 Fax: (212) 429 2127; (212) 429 4499 Swift: DRES US 33

Senior Executive Officers
Chief Executive, North America   George N Fugelsang

Debt Capital Markets / Fixed Income

Fixed-Income Repo
Head of Repo   Donald Galante *Senior Vice President, Fixed Income* ☎ **429 4401**
                                             F **429 4496**
Marketing & Product Development; Sales   Andrew Eastwood *Vice President, Fixed Income Sales* ☎ **429 4421**

Other Departments
Economic Research   Kevin Logan *Vice President*

Euromoney Directory 1999 **1949**

UNITED STATES (+1)   www.euromoneydirectory.com

Ecoban Finance Limited
Head Office

10th Floor, 805 Third Avenue, New York, NY 10022
Tel: (212) 805 8300 **Fax:** (212) 805 8395; (212) 805 8352 **Email:** info@ecoban.com
Website: www.ecoban.com

Senior Executive Officers
Chairman — Charles Baudoin ☏ **805 8314**
President — James Demitrieus ☏ **805 8181**
Chief Executive Officer — Barry Westfall *Senior Managing Director* ☏ **805 8302**
Financial Director — Michael Kelly *Senior Vice President, Controller* ☏ **805 8319**
Managing Director — Stephen Degot ☏ **805 8303**
International Division — Michael Tierney *Managing Director* ☏ **805 8304**

Others (Senior Executives)
Emerging Markets — Baudoin Jean-Yves *Managing Director* ☏ **805 8312**

Debt Capital Markets / Fixed Income
Emerging Market Bonds
Head — Gail Alleyne *Vice President* ☏ **805 8352**
Head of Sales — Stephen Degot *Managing Director* ☏ **805 8303**

Administration
Head of Administration — Corine van Dort *Office Manager* ☏ **805 8320**

Technology & Systems
Fan Yee Leung *Systems Liaison* ☏ **805 8321**

Legal / In-House Counsel
Gary Whitacker *General Counsel* ☏ **805 8145**

Accounts / Audit
Vincent Romeo *Assistant Vice President & Assistant Controller* ☏ **805 8318**

EFG Capital International
Subsidiary Company

Formerly known as: BDD Capital International
777 Brickell Avenue, Miami, FL
Tel: (305) 530 3160 **Email:** efgcapital@aol.com **Bloomberg:** JOSE ACOSTA

Senior Executive Officers
Senior Vice President — Justo R Azpiazu ☏ **530 3173**
Senior Vice President — Adrianna L Campuzano ☏ **530 3168**
Senior Vice President — Ricardo J Daugherty ☏ **530 3174**
Senior Vice President — Kenneth I Moorhead ☏ **530 3169**
Senior Vice President — Manolo Riveira ☏ **530 3171**
Senior Vice President — Sheila H Wilensky ☏ **530 3134**
Chief Executive Officer — Victor Echevarria *Chief Executive Officer* ☏ **530 3160**
Financial Director — Mark McCluskey *CFO & COO* ☏ **530 3180**

Equator USA Inc
Full Branch Office

45 Glastonbury Boulevard, Glastonbury, CT 06033
Tel: (860) 633 9999 **Fax:** (860) 633 6799

Senior Executive Officers
Financial Director — Barbara Olds *SVP & CFO*
Chief Operating Officer — John Kearney *SVP & COO*

Erste Bank
Full Branch Office

Formerly known as: GiroCredit Bank
West Building, 280 Park Avenue, New York, NY 10017
Tel: (212) 984 5600 **Fax:** (212) 986 1423 **Telex:** ITT 420914 GZNY **Swift:** GIBA US 33 **Reuters:** GZNY

Senior Executive Officers
Chief Executive Officer — Hans Krikava *General Manager* ☏ **692 0280**
Financial Director — Robert Manne *Controller*
Treasurer — Edward Caruana *Treasurer*

1950 Euromoney Directory 1999

www.euromoneydirectory.com UNITED STATES (+1)

Euro Brokers Inc
Head Office

84th Floor, Two World Trade Center, New York, NY 10048-0697
Tel: (212) 748 7000 Fax: (212) 748 7329; (212) 748 7050 Telex: TRT 177153 EURO
Website: www.ebi.com

Senior Executive Officers
Chairman & CEO — Gilbert Scharf ☎ 748 8866 ✉ gscharf@ebi.com
Chief Operating Officer — Keith Reihl Chief Operating Officer ☎ 748 7030 ✉ kreihl@ebi.com

Others (Senior Executives)
Roger Schwed EVP & General Counsel ☎ 748 8860 ✉ rschwed@ebi.com
Michael Pins EVP, Emerging Markets ☎ 748 7200 ✉ mpins@ebi.com
Bart Peaslee SVP, Dollar Products ☎ 748 7100 ✉ bpeaslee@ebi.com
Walter Danielsson SVP, Technology ☎ 748 7151 ✉ walter@ebi.com
Walter Dulski Executive Vice President ☎ 748 7018 ✉ wdulski@ebi.com
Stephen Vigliotti Chief Financial Officer ☎ 748 7040
Brian Clark Executive Vice President ☎ 748 7010 ✉ bclark@ebi.com

Money Markets
Regional Head — Bart Peaslee SVP, Dollar Products ☎ 748 7100 ✉ bpeaslee@ebi.com

Other (Wholesale Deposits)
Deposits — Tim Lees Senior Vice President ☎ 748 7070
Eurocurrencies — Jeremy Blum Senior Vice President ☎ 748 7060 ✉ jblum@ebi.com
Deposits — Robert Mahon Senior Vice President ☎ 748 7090
Short-Dates — Gene Gregoretti Senior Vice President ☎ 748 7300
Steve Cavaliere Senior Vice President ☎ 748 7300

Risk Management
Fixed Income Derivatives / Risk Management
IR Swaps Trading — David Lessing Senior Vice President ☎ 748 7100 ✉ dlessing@ebi.com
IR Options Trading — Robert Coll Senior Vice President ☎ 748 7220 ✉ bcoll@ebi.com

Other (FI Derivatives)
FRAs — T J Masonius Senior Vice President ☎ 748 7100 ✉ tmason@ebi.com

Administration
Technology & Systems
Walter Danielsson SVP, Technology ☎ 748 7151 ✉ walter@ebi.com

Legal / In-House Counsel
Roger Schwed EVP & General Counsel ☎ 748 8860 ✉ rschwed@ebi.com

Compliance
Patrick Nicholson Compliance Officer ☎ 748 7020 ✉ pnicholson@ebi.com

Euroclear Operations Centre
Representative Office

Morgan Guaranty Trust Company of New York, 15 Broad Street, New York, NY 10015-0015
Tel: (212) 235 2802 Fax: (212) 235 2800

Senior Executive Officers
Chief Representative — John A Nordstrom

The Export-Import Bank of Japan
Representative Office

Suite 4590, 601 South Figueroa Street, Los Angeles, CA 90017
Tel: (213) 627 3500 Fax: (213) 627 3900 Email: jeximla@lightside.com

Senior Executive Officers
Chief Representative — Kazuo Yokoyama

The Export-Import Bank of Japan
Representative Office

Suite 3601, 375 Park Avenue, New York, NY 10152
Tel: (212) 888 9500 Fax: (212) 888 9503 Telex: 7607841 YUGIN UC

Senior Executive Officers
Chief Representative — Shigeki Yoshida

UNITED STATES (+1)   www.euromoneydirectory.com

The Export-Import Bank of Japan — Representative Office

Suite 3350, 2000 Pennsylvania Avenue NW, Washington, DC 20006
Tel: (202) 331 8547 Fax: (202) 775 1990 Telex: 248547 YUGIN UR

Senior Executive Officers
Chief Representative   Yoshihito Miyairi

FH International Financial Services Inc — Head Office

29 Winfield Avenue, Harrison, NY 10528-2407
Tel: (914) 698 7300; (914) 698 7383 Fax: (914) 698 7429 Telex: 1561383

Senior Executive Officers
Executive Vice President   Abiye Atnafou
President   Eric Hermann 103303.1312@compuserve.com

Financial Security Assurance Inc — Head Office

Alternative trading name: FSA

350 Park Avenue, New York, NY 10022
Tel: (212) 826 0100 Fax: (212) 688 3101 Email: info@fsa.com
Website: www.fsa.com

Senior Executive Officers
Chairman & Chief Executive Officer   Robert P Cochran
President   Roger K Taylor
Financial Director   John A Harrison *Chief Financial Officer*
Chief Operating Officer   Séan McCarthy
MD & Chief Municipal Underwriting Officer   Suzanne M Finnegan
MD & Chief Underwriting Officer, International   Thomas J McCormick
MD & General Counsel   Bruce E Stern
Managing Director   Henry T Mortimer Jr

Others (Senior Executives)
Chief Underwriting Officer   Russell B Brewer II *Chief Underwriting Officer, Corporate*

Relationship Manager
Investor Relations   Peter E Hoey *Managing Director*

Department: Western Regional Office
23rd Floor, Stuart Tower, One Market Plaza, San Francisco, CA 94105
Tel: +1 (415) 995 8000 Fax: +1 (415) 995 8008
Managing Director, Western Region   Sheelagh M Flanagan

Administration
Legal / In-House Counsel
                                        Bruce E Stern *MD & General Counsel*

First Chicago Capital Markets Inc

Suite 0463 1-7, One First National Plaza, Chicago, IL 60670-0463
Tel: (312) 732 7887 Fax: (312) 732 4670 Telex: 023-6871533 Email: namican@cmg.fcnbd.com

Debt Capital Markets / Fixed Income
Fixed-Income Repo
Marketing & Product Development   Bruce Trabb *Managing Director* 732 1442
Trading   Randall Waterman *Vice President*
                                        Nancy Amicangelo *Senior Managing Director*
                                        Greg Mindeman *Vice President*
                                        Michael Kuempel *Vice President*

First Commercial Bank — Full Branch Office

Suite 1050, 515 South Flower Street, Los Angeles, CA 90071
Tel: (213) 362 0200 Fax: (213) 362 0245; (213) 362 0244 Telex: 451588 Swift: FCBK US 66

Senior Executive Officers
VP & General Manager   June Shiong Lu 362 0200

www.euromoneydirectory.com UNITED STATES (+1)

First National Bank of Southern Africa Limited Representative Office

399 Park Avenue, New York, NY 10022
Tel: (212) 750 6140 Fax: (212) 223 8797 Email: fnbny@juno.com

Senior Executive Officers
Chief Representative   Peter T Siragna

First Union National Bank Head Office

301 South College Street, Charlotte, NC 28288-0600
Tel: (704) 374 6161; (704) 374 2783 Fax: (704) 383 9030 Swift: FUNB US 33 Reuters: FUNB

Senior Executive Officers
Chairman & Chief Executive   Edward E Crutchfield
President   John B Georgius
Financial Director   Robert T Atwood Chief Financial Officer

Others (Senior Executives)
                                         B J Walker Vice Chairman
                                         John B Georgius
                                         Marion A Cowell EVP, Secretary & General Counsel

Foreign Exchange
Global Head   Steve Kohlhagen Manager, Derivatives
Corporate Sales   Beth Perryman Manager, FX Marketing
Head of Trading   Mark Gargano FX Manager

Risk Management
Foreign Exchange Derivatives / Risk Management
Cross-Currency Swaps, Sales / Marketing Chris Slusher Manager, Structured Products
Cross-Currency Swaps, Trading   Mike Mahoney Trader
Vanilla FX option Sales   Chris Slusher Manager, Structured Products
Vanilla FX option Trading   Joe McDonough Trader

Exotic Options (Barriers, Range, Timers, Digitals, Faders etc)
Sales   Chris Slusher Manager, Structured Products
                                         Beth Perryman Manager, FX Marketing
Trading   Joe McDonough Trader
                                         Mark Gargano FX Manager

Firstar Trust Company

11th Floor, 777 East Wisconsin Avenue, Milwaukee, WI 53202
Tel: (414) 765 6143; (414) 765 4321 Fax: (414) 765 6153

Debt Capital Markets / Fixed Income
Fixed-Income Repo
Head of Repo   James Schoenike Vice President ☎ 765 6611 ℻ 765 6153
Trading   Greg Mindeman Vice President
                                         James Schoenike Vice President, Marketing
                                         Colleen Kenney Senior Securities Lending Officer
                                         Susan Bishop Lending Specialist

Equity Capital Markets
Equity Repo / Securities Lending
Head of Trading   James Schoenike Vice President, Marketing
Head of Trading   Colleen Kenney Senior Securities Lending Officer

Robert Fleming Inc Subsidiary Company

12th Floor, 320 Park Avenue, New York, NY 10022
Tel: (212) 508 3600 Fax: (212) 508 3669 Telex: 620734

Senior Executive Officers
Chairman   Lord Robin Renwick ☎ +44 (171) 638 5858
President & Chief Executive Officer   Arthur A Levy ☎ 508 3689
Financial Director   Andrea Whitmore Chief Financial Officer ☎ 508 3620
Chief Operating Officer   Mark Mattheys Chief Operating Officer ☎ 508 3625
International Division   Charlie Bridge Director, International Sales & Trading ☎ 508 3747

Equity Capital Markets
Head of Equity Capital Markets   Eduardo Canet Managing Director, Capital Markets ☎ 508 3738

Euromoney Directory 1999 **1953**

UNITED STATES (+1)　　　www.euromoneydirectory.com

Robert Fleming Inc (cont)
Settlement / Clearing
Head of Settlement / Clearing　　　Donate Ferone *VP, Operations* ☎ **508 3788**
Administration
Technology & Systems
　　　　　　　　　　　　　　　　　Michael Vickery *Vice President, Communications* ☎ **508 3636**
Compliance
　　　　　　　　　　　　　　　　　Larry Kimmel *Vice President, Compliance* ☎ **508 3610**
Public Relations
　　　　　　　　　　　　　　　　　Rory Fleming *Vice President, Corporate Communications* ☎ **508 3609**

Fredericks Michael & Co　　　　　　　　　　　　　　　Head Office

Two Wall Street, New York, NY 10005
Tel: (212) 732 1600 **Fax:** (212) 732 1872; (212) 732 0874 **Email:** fredericks@fm-co.com
Website: www.fm.co.com

Senior Executive Officers
Chief Executive Officer　　　　　David Fredericks *Managing Director*
Managing Director　　　　　　　George Caraberis
Managing Director　　　　　　　Blake Davies
Corporate Finance / M&A Advisory
Other (Corporate Finance)
Nordic Countries　　　　　　　　George Caraberis *Managing Director*
Spain & Latin America　　　　　Blake Davies *Managing Director*
All Other　　　　　　　　　　　　David Fredericks *Managing Director*

The Fuji Bank Limited　　　　　　　　　　　　　　　Full Branch Office

79th-81st Floors, Two World Trade Center, New York, NY 10048
Tel: (212) 898 2000 **Fax:** (212) 321 9407 **Telex:** 232440 **Swift:** FUJI US 3N **Reuters:** FUJN
Cable: FUJIBANKNEWYORK
Extra Telex: 420626

Senior Executive Officers
Senior Vice President　　　　　　Atsushi Hatano
Vice President　　　　　　　　　Kazuya Kobayashi
Deputy Vice President　　　　　Hidetaka Nakamura
Treasurer　　　　　　　　　　　　Katsuhiko Oda
Director & General Manager　　Tsutomu Hayano
Debt Capital Markets / Fixed Income
Head of Fixed Income　　　　　Katsuhiko Oda
Emerging Market Bonds
Head of Emerging Markets　　　Jack Penrod *Senior Vice President*
Syndicated Lending
Head of Origination　　　　　　　Michael Imperial *Senior Vice President*
Head of Syndication　　　　　　Kazuyuki Nishimura *Senior Vice President*
Loan-Related Activities
Trade Finance　　　　　　　　　Robert Minutagllo *Senior Vice President*
Money Markets
Head of Money Markets　　　　Katsuhiko Oda
Foreign Exchange
Head of Foreign Exchange　　　Katsuhiko Oda
Corporate Finance / M&A Advisory
Tel: 898 2000/77
Head of Corporate Finance　　　Atsushi Hatano *Senior Vice President*
Country Head　　　　　　　　　　Kazuya Kobayashi *Vice President*
Administration
Technology & Systems
　　　　　　　　　　　　　　　　　Mitsuru Yusa *Senior Vice President*
Legal / In-House Counsel
　　　　　　　　　　　　　　　　　Angelo Aldana *Senior Vice President*
Compliance
　　　　　　　　　　　　　　　　　Angelo Aldana *Senior Vice President*

www.euromoneydirectory.com   UNITED STATES (+1)

Public Relations
                                    Hidetake Nakamura *Executive Vice President*
Accounts / Audit
                                    Hidetake Nakamura *Executive Vice President*

The Fuji Bank Limited   Representative Office
Suite 601, 1155 Connecticut Avenue NW, Washington, DC 20036
Tel: (202) 467 6660 Fax: (202) 467 5045 Email: ccarter@clark.net
Senior Executive Officers
Chief Representative   Yukihiko Chayama

Garvin GuyButler Corporation
120 Broadway, New York, NY 10271
Tel: (212) 732 6900; (212) 815 6602 Fax: (212) 374 1740; (212) 815 7990 Telex: 6721036
Senior Executive Officers
Chairman   Clive Hollick
President   Stephen R Tilton
Executive Vice President   James K Munneliy
Managing Director   J Douglas Rhoten

Debt Capital Markets / Fixed Income
Department: Capital Markets Division
Country Head   J Douglas Rhoten *Managing Director*

Non-Domestic Government Bonds
Short Term Swaps & FRA's   Nick Farr *Executive Vice President* ☎ 815 6788
Medium Term Swaps   Daniel J McMorrow *Executive Vice President* ☎ 815 6788
Basis Swaps   David Blackburn *Senior Vice President* ☎ 815 9657

Money Markets
Department: Cash & Capital Markets

Money Markets - General
Cash Division   John C Shay *Executive Vice President*

Other (Wholesale Deposits)
Short Date Deposits   Ross A Rauh *Senior Vice President* ☎ 815 6500
Fixed Date Deposits; Money Market   Nicholas DeFlora *Manager* ☎ 815 6680
Instruments
Money Market Instruments   Gary DeFranco *Manager* ☎ 815 6560
Department: Currency Division
Country Head   Philip Moody *Executive Vice President* ☎ 267 4481

Money Markets - General
Eurocurrencies   Kenneth J Moore *Senior Vice President*
Currency Capital Markets   Philip Moody *Executive Vice President* ☎ 267 4481

Risk Management

Other (FI Derivatives)
Interest Rate Options   Henry Lewandowski *Executive Vice President* ☎ 815 9566
US$ Options   Donna Fitzmaurice *Senior Vice President*
Canadian$ Options   Richard Gold *Senior Vice President*

Administration
Head of Administration   V Lisa Nelson *Senior Vice President*

Other (Administration)
Financial Engineering   George J Cheah *Executive Vice President*

Glass, Ginsburg Limited   Head Office
Suite 3400, 20 North Wacker Drive, Chicago, IL 60606-3102
Tel: (312) 726 4411 Fax: (312) 726 0029
Senior Executive Officers
Chairman & Chief Executive   Philip Glass
Treasurer   Bradley Glass
Managing Director / General Manager   Ruth Glick

Euromoney Directory 1999   **1955**

UNITED STATES (+1)   www.euromoneydirectory.com

Goldman Sachs & Co

85 Broad Street, New York, NY 10004
Tel: (212) 902 1000; (212) 902 8230 Fax: (212) 509 8886; (212) 902 4197
Website: www.gs.com

Senior Executive Officers
Chairman & Chief Executive Officer — Jon S Corzine ☎ 902 1000
Senior Chairman — John L Weinberg
Chairman — Roy J Zuckerberg
Chairman — Robert J Hurst
President & Chief Operating Officer — Henry M Paulson Jr ☎ 902 1000
Chief Executive Officer — Jon S Corzine Chairman & Chief Executive Officer ☎ 902 1000
Financial Director — John A Thain Chief Financial Officer ☎ 902 1000

Equity Capital Markets
Equity Repo / Securities Lending
Marketing & Product Development — Chris Donovan Vice President ☎ +1 (617) 204 2430 F +1 (617) 204 2420
E christine.donovan@gs.com
Head of Prime Brokerage — Mitchell J Lieberman Managing Director ☎ 902 5182 F 346 3661

Settlement / Clearing
Settlement (General) — Ed Watts ☎ 902 1100

Grantchester Securities

31 West 52nd Street, New York, NY 10019
Tel: (212) 969 2700 Fax: (212) 969 781

Senior Executive Officers
Managing Director — Ashish Bhutani
Managing Director — Kevin A Eng
Managing Director — Frank Jordan
Managing Director — Raz Kafri
Managing Director — Daniel A McAloon
Managing Director, Sales — John Melligon
Managing Director — Hoyt Ammidon III
Managing Director — John P Pecora
Managing Director — Michael Temple

Greenwich Capital Markets Inc

600 Steamboat Road, Greenwich, CT 06830
Tel: (203) 625 2700 Fax: (203) 629 8743 Telex: 4750172

Senior Executive Officers
President — Gary F Holloway
Chief Executive Officer — Edwin L Knetzger III

Debt Capital Markets / Fixed Income
Global Head — Raymond E Humiston Executive Vice President
Country Head — Benjamin Carpenter Senior Vice President

Domestic Government Bonds
Head of Trading — Raymond E Humiston Executive Vice President
Head of Research — Jade Zelnik Economic Research (US)

Non-Domestic Government Bonds
Head of UK / Europe — Greg Bowes Senior Vice President
Head of UK / European Trading — Sam Berwick Senior Vice President

Asset-Backed Securities / Securitization
Regional Head — Christopher R Gruseke SVP & Head, US Mortgage & Asset-backed Securities
Robert R Holmes SVP & Head, US Mortgage & Asset-backed Securities
Jay N Levine SVP & Head, US Mortgage & Asset-backed Securities
Robert McGuinness SVP & Head, US Asset-backed Consumer Finance

Mortgage-Backed Securities
Regional Head — Christopher R Gruseke SVP & Head, US Mortgage & Asset-backed Securities
Robert R Holmes SVP & Head, US Mortgage & Asset-backed Securities
Jay N Levine SVP & Head, US Mortgage & Asset-backed Securities
Greg Jacobs SVP & Head, US Asset-backed Commercial Mortgage Fi
Paul Nidenberg SVP & Head, US Asset-backed Commercial Mortgage Fi

1956   Euromoney Directory 1999

Fixed-Income Repo
Head of Repo — Robert Starbuck *Head of Repo*
Trading — Gerry O'Grady *Vice President*
Larry Sodokoff *Senior Vice President*

Syndicated Lending
Loan-Related Activities
Structured Trade Finance — Robert Pashley *Managing Director*

Gulf International Bank BSC
Full Branch Office

21st Floor, 380 Madison Avenue, New York, NY 10017
Tel: (212) 922 2300 **Fax:** (212) 922 2309 **Telex:** 424027 GIBANK NY **Swift:** GULF US 33

Senior Executive Officers
Others (Senior Executives)
Branch Manager — Issa N Baconi *Senior Vice President*
Marketing — Abdel-Fattah Tahoun *Senior Vice President*

General - Treasury
Head of Treasury — Nadim Jebara *Vice President*

Administration
Other (Administration)
Operations & Administration — William Johnson *Vice President*

The Gunma Bank Limited
Full Branch Office

29th Floor, 245 Park Avenue, New York, NY 10167
Tel: (212) 949 8690 **Fax:** (212) 867 1081; (212) 867 1082 **Telex:** 421552 GUNMA NY

Senior Executive Officers
Managing Director / General Manager — Toshinori Fukasawa

Debt Capital Markets / Fixed Income
Country Head — Katsutoshi Osaki *Manager*

Syndicated Lending
Country Head — Teruhisa Kofu *Manager*

Money Markets
Country Head — Ei Uchida *Manager*

Foreign Exchange
Country Head — Ei Uchida *Manager*

Risk Management
Country Head — Masahiko Asakura *Manager*

Corporate Finance / M&A Advisory
Country Head — Teruhisa Kofu *Manager*

Settlement / Clearing
Country Head — Osamo Takeuchi *Manager*

The Hachijuni Bank Limited
Full Branch Office

28th Floor, West Building, 280 Park Avenue, New York, NY 10017
Tel: (212) 557 1182 **Fax:** (212) 557 8026 **Telex:** 6411479 HACH NY

Senior Executive Officers
General Manager — Kazuyoshi Araki
Deputy General Manager — Hiroshi Miyashita
Others (Senior Executives)
Yuichi Satoh *Manager*
Hisato Sasaki *Manager*

Hambrecht & Quist LLC
Head Office

One Bush Street, San Francisco, CA 94104
Tel: (415) 439 3000; (415) 439 3300 **Fax:** (415) 439 3624
Website: www.hamquist.com

Senior Executive Officers
Chairman & Chief Executive Officer — Daniel H Case III
Financial Director — Patrick J Allen *Chief Financial Officer*

UNITED STATES (+1) www.euromoneydirectory.com

Hambrecht & Quist LLC (cont)
Senior Executive Officers (cont)
Chief Operating Officer David M McAuliffe
General-Investment
Head of Investment Cristina M Morgan *Co-Director, Investment Banking*
  David G Golden *Co-Director, Investment Banking*

Equity Capital Markets
Head of Equity Capital Markets William R Timken *Syndicate*
Head of Sales John P Hullar
International Equities
Head of Sales William S McDermott *International Sales*
Equity Research
Head of Equity Research Paul "Barney" Hallingby *Director of Research*
Administration
Legal / In-House Counsel
  Steven N Machtinger

Compliance
  Steven Aaron

Corporate Communications
  Carole A Newman *Vice President*

Harlow Meyer Savage LLC   Head Office
Suite 5550, 55th Floor, 2 World Trade Center, New York, NY 10048
Tel: (212) 306 0700 Fax: (212) 306 0770 Telex: 177155 Reuters: HMSS (Monitor)
Forward Night Desk Tel: 528 3644; Spot & Forward Night Desk (Canada) Tel: (416) 864 7603; Fixed Income
Tel: 812 6860; 812 6860; Reuters: HMSN (Dealing)

Senior Executive Officers
Chief Executive Officer David Satchell
Others (Senior Executives)
  Joseph S Remshifski *Senior Vice President*

Foreign Exchange
Department: Spot Currencies
Head of Foreign Exchange Ronald Alec *Senior Vice President* ☎ **528 3271**
  Peter Ryan *Vice President* ☎ **306 0781**
  Eric Schneider *Vice President* ☎ **528 3241**

FX Traders / Sales People
Spot Euro Ronald Alec *Senior Vice President* ☎ **528 3271**
Spot Swiss Peter Tomasino *Manager* ☎ **528 3233**
Spot Yen Peter Ryan *Vice President* ☎ **306 0781**
Spot Sterling Eric Schneider *Vice President* ☎ **528 3241**
Spot Australia / NZ Ken Manganiello *Manager* ☎ **528 3595**
Spot Emerging Markets Frank Monaco *Manager* ☎ **528 3601**
  Joe Cambria *Manager* ☎ **528 3584**
Spot Canada Kevin Armstrong *Manager* ☎ **+1 (416) 864 7603**
  Alex Roome *Manager* ☎ **+1 (416) 864 7603**
Spot Euro / Yen Jeff Scott Seide *Manager* ☎ **528 3566**
Spot Euro / Swiss Edward McDermott *Manager* ☎ **528 3560**
Spot Sterling / Euro Fred Gregson *Manager* ☎ **528 3577**
Department: Mexican Peso Spot, Cash, 24hr, Swaps & Forward
Tel: +52 (5) 283 5600
Country Head Javier Mateo *Director General*
  Lourdes Alfaro *Manager*

FX Traders / Sales People
Administration Richard McKeever ☎ **306 0767**
Marketing Ralph Gelsomino ☎ **306 0768**

Risk Management
Department: Forward Currencies
Foreign Exchange Derivatives / Risk Management
Global Head John Hubbard *Managing Director* ☎ **306 0786**
  John Ely *Vice President* ☎ **306 0785**

Other Currency Swap / FX Options Personnel
Forward Euro Mike Sullivan *Manager* ☎ **528 3644**
Forward Yen & Scandinavia David Mahler *Manager* ☎ **528 3623**

1958 Euromoney Directory 1999

www.euromoneydirectory.com   UNITED STATES (+1)

Other Currency Swap / FX Options Personnel (cont)
Forward Swiss & Sterling   Mark Negrelli *Manager* ☎ **528 5664**
Forward Australia NZ & Emerging Markets   Tom Waldron *Manager* ☎ **528 3614**
Forward Canada   Sandy Stewart *Manager* ☎ **+1 (416) 864 7604**
Administration
Other (Administration)
Marketing   Ralph Gelsomino ☎ **306 0768**
                                            Rich McKeever ☎ **306 0767**

Harvard Management Co

600 Atlantic Avenue, Boston, MA 02210
Tel: (617) 523 4400 **Fax:** (617) 523 7509

Debt Capital Markets / Fixed Income
Fixed-Income Repo
Trading   Kathryn Rowe *Cash Management Trader*
                                            Wendy Snicksenberger *Cash Management Trader*
                                            Susan Black *Cash Management Trader*

Hawaii National Bank

45 North King Street, Honolulu, HI 96817
Tel: (808) 528 7711 **Telex:** 723302

Senior Executive Officers
Chairman   K J Luke
Chief Executive Officer   Warren K K Luke *Vice Chairman & CEO*
Financial Director   Ernest T Murata *Senior EVP & Cashier, CFO*
Others (Senior Executives)
                                            Denis C H Kam *EVP & Loan Administration*

Administration
Head of Marketing   Myra I L Ozawa *Assistant Vice President, Marketing*

Herzog Heine Geduld

Alternative trading name: HRZG
Newport Tower, 525 Washington Boulevard, Jersey City, NJ 07310
Tel: (800) 756 1811; (201) 418 4000 **Fax:** (201) 418 5060; (201) 418 5006 **Telex:** 373 4254
Email: webmaster@herzog.com **Telex:** 679 0592
Website: www.herzog.com

Senior Executive Officers
Chairman   John E Herzog ☎ **(212) 908 4123**
President & Chief Executive Officer   E E Geduld ☎ **418 4100**
Financial Director   Kenneth Bradley *VP & Chief Financial Officer* ☎ **418 4162**
Chief Operating Officer   Anthony Geraci *EVP & Chief Operating Officer* ☎ **418 4222**
Treasurer   Joseph J Frazzitta *SVP & Treasurer* ☎ **418 4133**
SVP & General Counsel   Charles C Christofilis ☎ **418 4153**
Others (Senior Executives)
Special Projects   John Fenimore *Senior Vice President* ☎ **418 5193**
Head of Miami Office   Irwin Geduld *Executive Vice President* ☎ **(305) 932 5880**

Debt Capital Markets / Fixed Income
Department: Vilas & Hickey
Tel: (212) 908 4736 **Fax:** (212) 908 4741
Head of Fixed Income   Jay Lampach *VP & Manager, Vilas & Hickey*

Equity Capital Markets
Department: Trading
Country Head   E E Geduld *President & Chief Executive Officer* ☎ **418 4100**
Domestic Equities
Head of Sales   Jerome Logan *VP, Institutional Sales* ☎ **418 4100**
Head of Trading   E E Geduld *President & Chief Executive Officer* ☎ **418 4100**
International Equities
Head of Trading   Anthony Fasone *VP, International Trading* ☎ **418 4151**
Other (International Equity)
European Equities   Steven H Burnham *Director of Trading, Herzog Heine Geduld Internati*
                                            ☎ **+44 (171) 979 2000**

Euromoney Directory 1999 **1959**

UNITED STATES (+1)   www.euromoneydirectory.com

Herzog Heine Geduld (cont)
Settlement / Clearing
Tel: 418 4222 Fax: 418 5042
Operations — Anthony Geraci *EVP & Chief Operating Officer* ☏ **418 4222**

Administration
Head of Administration; Business Development — Stephen J Nelson *VP, Special Projects* ☏ **418 4789**
Head of Marketing — Andrew Da Ponte *SVP, Correspondent Clearing Services* ☏ **418 5141**

Technology & Systems
William Lease *VP, Information Services* ☏ **418 4520**

Legal / In-House Counsel
Charles C Christofilis *SVP & General Counsel* ☏ **418 4153**

Compliance
Alan De Lauro *VP & Director, Compliance* ☏ **418 5195**

Public Relations
PR / Advertising — Stephen J Nelson *VP, Special Projects* ☏ **418 4789**

Accounts / Audit
Jeffrey Weiss *VP, Internal Audit* ☏ **418 4618**

Hibernia National Bank
Head Office

313 Carondelet Street, New Orleans, LA 70130
Tel: (504) 533 3333 Fax: (504) 533 2367
Website: www.hiberniabank.com

Senior Executive Officers
Chairman — Robert H Boh
President & Chief Executive Officer — Stephen A Hansel ☏ **533 5887**
Financial Director — Marsha M Gassan *Chief Financial Officer* ☏ **533 5558**
Treasurer — Angela Breffeilh ☏ **533 5525**

Debt Capital Markets / Fixed Income
Fixed-Income Repo
Head of Repo; Collateral Management; Matched Book Manager; Sales — Alan Ganucheau *Senior Vice President* ☏ **533 5632**

Corporate Finance / M&A Advisory
Department: Private Placements, Risk Management, Other Advisory Services
Global Head — Spencer Gagnet *Vice President*
Private Equity — Tom Hoyt *President, Hibernia Capital Corp* ☏ **533 5988**

Hoenig & Co Inc

Royal Executive Park, 4 International Drive, Rye Brook, NY 10573
Tel: (914) 935 9000; (914) 935 9100 Fax: (914) 935 9113

Senior Executive Officers
Chairman — Fred Sapirstein
President — Max Levine
Chief Executive Officer — Fred Sapirstein
Financial Director; Chief Operating Officer; International Division — Alan Herzog

HSBC Securities Inc
Subsidiary Company

17th Floor, 140 Broadway, New York, NY 10005
Tel: (212) 825 6780; (212) 658 4000 Fax: (212) 825 0596; (212) 658 4290

Senior Executive Officers
President & Chief Executive Officer — Anthony Rademeyer ☏ **658 6202**
Chief Operating Officer — Jeffrey Haroldson *Executive Managing Director & COO* ☏ **658 7247**
Executive Managing Director & CAO — Virginia Maddock ☏ **658 6272**

Debt Capital Markets / Fixed Income
Global Head — John Griff *Executive Managing Director, Fixed Income* ☏ **658 2966**
Country Head — John Cooley *Managing Director, Debt Capital Markets* ☏ **825 6687**
Head of Fixed Income Sales — John Deuschle *Managing Director, Sales* ☏ **825 9480**
Joe Murphy *Managing Director, Chicago Sales & Futures* ☏ **+1 (312) 466 8222**

1960 Euromoney Directory 1999

UNITED STATES (+1)

Debt Capital Markets / Fixed Income (cont)

	Jay Pingeton *Managing Director, Boston Sales* ☏ **+1 (617) 210 0700**
	Michael Primasing *Managing Director, San Francisco Sales* ☏ **+1 (415) 398 7600**
Head of Fixed Income Trading	Raymond Remy *Executive Managing Director, Fixed Income* ☏ **825 5884**
	Robert Sbarra *Executive Managing Director, Fixed Income* ☏ **825 5884**
	Richard Rosati *Managing Director, Corporate Trading* ☏ **825 9338**

Fixed-Income Repo
Trading

Michael Russamano *Vice President*
Bill Riggil *Senior Vice President*

Equity Capital Markets
Head of Equity Capital Markets   Richard Abrahams *Executive Managing Director, Equities* ☏ **658 4167**
Marketing   Jim Nicholson *Senior VP, Equities Business Development Group* ☏ **658 4617**
Head of Sales   Nick Gregory *Executive Managing Director, Equity Sales UK* ☏ **658 4033**
     Matt McConnell *Executive Managing Director, Equity Sales Trading* ☏ **658 4013**
     Ed Coleman *Senior VP, Equity US Sales Trading* ☏ **658 4067**
Head of Trading   Matt McConnell *Executive Managing Director, Equity Sales Trading* ☏ **658 4013**
     Steve Lynch *Managing Director, Equity Trading* ☏ **658 4986**
     Ed Coleman *Senior VP, Equity US Sales Trading* ☏ **658 4067**

Risk Management
Fixed Income Derivatives / Risk Management
Head of Sales   Joe Murphy *Managing Director, Chicago Sales & Futures* ☏ **+1 (312) 466 8222**

Other Departments
Economic Research   Leslie Alperstein *Executive Managing Director, Washington Analysis* ☏ **+1 (202) 659 8030**

Administration
Head of Marketing   Andrea Neumann *Senior Vice President* ☏ **825 5880**

Legal / In-House Counsel
Legal Department   Jeffrey Letzler *Managing Director & General Counsel* ☏ **825 9155**

Hua Nan Commercial Bank Limited   Agency

Suite 2846, 2 World Trade Center, New York, NY 10048
Tel: (212) 488 2330 **Fax:** (212) 912 1050 **Telex:** 408847 **Swift:** HNBK US 3N

Senior Executive Officers
Managing Director / General Manager   Jeffrey C F Lee

The Huntington National Bank

Huntington Center, 41 South High Street, Columbus, OH 43287
PO Box 1558, Columbus, OH 43215
Tel: (877) 480 4685 **Fax:** (614) 480 3761 **Telex:** 245475 **Swift:** HUNT US 33

Senior Executive Officers
Chairman & Chief Executive Officer   Frank Wobst

The Hyakujushi Bank Limited   Full Branch Office

11th Floor, 2 Wall Street, New York, NY 10005
Tel: (212) 513 0114 **Fax:** (212) 619 0906 **Telex:** 141388

Senior Executive Officers
Managing Director / General Manager   Toshihiro Fukunishi

HypoVereinsbank   Full Branch Office

333 West Wacker Drive, Suite 680, Chicago, IL 60606
Tel: (312) 368 3300 **Fax:** (312) 3686 8615

UNITED STATES (+1)   www.euromoneydirectory.com

HypoVereinsbank
Full Branch Office

Formerly known as: Bayerische Hypotheken-und Wechsel Bank AG
32nd Floor, Financial Square, New York, NY 10005
Tel: (212) 248 0650 Fax: (212) 440 0741 Telex: 640146

HypoVereinsbank Capital Corporation
Subsidiary Company

17th Floor, 575 Fifth Avenue, New York, NY 10017
Tel: (212) 808 9090 Fax: (212) 808 9106

IBJ Schroder Bank & Trust Company
Subsidiary Company

One State Street, New York, NY 10004
Tel: (212) 858 2000 Fax: (212) 425 0542 Telex: 62820 Swift: JHSUS33
Website: www.ibjs.com

Senior Executive Officers
Chairman — Alva Way ☎ 858 2545
President & Chief Executive Officer — Denise Buchert ☎ 858 2555
Financial Director — Alastair Merrick *CFO & Senior Vice President* ☎ 858 2096
International Division — John Harriman *President, IBJ Schroder International Bank* ☎ (305) 530 2570

Others (Senior Executives)
IBJ Schroder Business Credit Corporation — Ed Fanning *President & Chief Executive Officer* ☎ 858 2197
Securities Services & Operations — John Banno *Senior Vice President* ☎ 858 2302
Capital Markets & Trust Services — Larry Chong *Senior Vice President* ☎ 858 2303

General-Investment
Head of Investment — Charlie Porten *SVP, Investment Management* ☎ 858 2395

Foreign Exchange
Head of Foreign Exchange — Paul Wan *Senior Vice President* ☎ 858 2586

Corporate Finance / M&A Advisory
Head of Corporate Finance — Larry Zilavy *Senior Managing Director* ☎ 858 2566

Global Custody
Head of Global Custody — Tom Pepe *SVP, Securities Services* ☎ 858 2880

Other Departments
Private Banking — Susan Bass *Senior Vice President* ☎ 858 2739
Cash Management — Deborah Tangen *Vice President* ☎ 858 2930

Administration
Head of Marketing — Constance O'Connell *SVP, Strategic Planning & Marketing* ☎ 858 2631

Public Relations
Constance O'Connell *SVP, Strategic Planning & Marketing* ☎ 858 2631

Other (Administration)
Human Resources — Keith Darcy *Executive Vice President* ☎ 858 2752

The Industrial Bank of Japan Limited
Full Branch Office

1251 Avenue of the Americas, New York, NY 10020-1104
Tel: (212) 282 3000; (212) 282 3815 Fax: (212) 282 4250; (212) 354 7380 Telex: 420802 KOGI UI

Senior Executive Officers
Managing Director / General Manager — Yuji Suzuki

Debt Capital Markets / Fixed Income

Fixed-Income Repo
Trading — Jean Kelly *Officer*
Debbie Hatzis *Assistant Vice President*
Carrie Nye *Trader*
Rose Rana *Trader*

www.euromoneydirectory.com   UNITED STATES (+1)

ING Baring Furman Selz LLC
Subsidiary Company

230 Park Avenue, New York, NY 10169
Tel: (212) 309 8200 Fax: (212) 692 9608; (212) 309 5996
Website: www.furmanselz.com

Senior Executive Officers
Co-Chairman   Fernando' Gentil
Co-Chairman   Edmund Hajim

Debt Capital Markets / Fixed Income
Fixed-Income Repo
Trading   John Dorosz Vice President ☎ 309 6414 📠 309 8693

ING Baring (US) Financial Holding Corporation
Subsidiary Company

667 Madison Avenue, New York, NY 10021
Tel: (212) 409 1500 Fax: (212) 350 7415 Telex: 177792 INGB A NYK

Senior Executive Officers
Country Manager   Fernando B Gentil

ING Barings Futures & Options Clearing Services
Subsidiary Company

52nd Floor, The Sears Tower, 233 Wacker Drive, Chicago, IL 60606
Tel: (312) 496 7000 Fax: (312) 496 7150

Senior Executive Officers
Others (Senior Executives)
                                     Wally Weisenborn Director
                                     Margaret McGrath Director

ING Capital
Subsidiary Company

Suite 4200, 333 South Grand Avenue, Los Angeles, CA 90071
Tel: (213) 346 3900 Fax: (213) 346 3990 Telex: 4720675 INGB LA

Senior Executive Officers
Managing Director   Mark Vidergauz

ING Furman Selz Asset Management

Suite 1750, 3424 Peachtree Road, Atlanta, GA 30326
Tel: (404) 364 5400 Fax: (404) 364 5399

Asset Management
Head   John McColskey
Other (Asset Management)
Institutional Sales   William Thompson

ING Furman Selz Asset Management
Subsidiary Company

456 Montgomery Street, Suite 2150, San Francisco, CA 94104
Tel: (415) 788 8870 Fax: (415) 788 8890

Senior Executive Officers
Senior Vice President   Sheila Schroeder

ING (US) Capital Corporation
Subsidiary Company

Suite 950, 200 Galleria Parkway NW, Atlanta, GA 30339
Tel: (770) 956 9200 Fax: (770) 951 1005 Telex: 154156 INGB AT

Senior Executive Officers
Managing Director, Corporate Finance   James Latimer

UNITED STATES (+1)	www.euromoneydirectory.com

ING (US) Financial Holdings
Subsidiary Company

135 East 57th Street, New York, NY 10022
Tel: (212) 409 1500 Fax: (212) 644 0428 Telex: 177792 INGB A NYK

Senior Executive Officers
Chairman — Bart Staal
President — Timothy Schantz

Inter-American Development Bank
Head Office

1300 New York Avenue NW, Washington, DC 20577
Tel: (202) 623 1397; (202) 623 1000 Fax: (202) 623 1403; (202) 623 3096
Website: www.iadb.org

Senior Executive Officers
President — Enrique V Inglesias ☎ **623 1100**
Financial Director — Charles O Sethness *Finance Manager* ☎ **623 2201**
Treasurer — Carlos Santistevan *Senior Deputy Manager* ☎ **623 2207**
Secretary — Carlos Ferdinand ☎ **623 3400**

Relationship Manager
Private Sector — Hiroshi Toyoda *Manager* ☎ **623 1501**
Integration & Regional Programme — Nohra Rey de Marulanda *Manager* ☎ **623 2390**

Settlement / Clearing
Operations — Alberto Pico *Controller* ☎ **623 1180**
Ricardo Luis Santiago *Manager, Regional Operations I* ☎ **623 1493**
Miguel Eduardo Martínez *Manager, Regional Operations II* ☎ **623 1790**
Ciro De Falco *Manager, Regional Operations III* ☎ **623 2821**

Other Departments
Economic Research — Ricardo Hausmann *Chief Economist* ☎ **623 2843**

Administration

Legal / In-House Counsel
General Counsel — John M Niehuss ☎ **623 2714**

Other (Administration)
External Relations Adviser — Muni Figueres ☎ **623 1366**

Inter-American Investment Corporation
Head Office

1300 New York Avenue NW, Washington, DC 20577
Tel: (202) 623 3900 Fax: (202) 623 2360

Senior Executive Officers
Chairman of the Board — Enrique V Iglesias ☎ **623 1100**
Financial Director — Olivier Fraisse *Chief of Finance Department* ☎ **623 3919**
Chief Operating Officer — Roldan Trujillo *Chief Operations Department* ☎ **623 3922**
General Manager — John Rahming ☎ **623 3901**

Other Departments
Economic Research — Jorge Roldan *Chief Economist* ☎ **623 3948**

Administration
Head of Administration — Mildred Arroyo *Personnel & Administration Officer* ☎ **623 3951**

Legal / In-House Counsel
Raul Herrera *General Counsel* ☎ **623 3905**

Public Relations
Magaly Hamm *Executive Assistant* ☎ **623 3902**

Intercapital America Inc

25th Floor, 1 World Trade Centre, New York, NY 10048
Tel: (212) 571 8000 Fax: (212) 571 8332

Senior Executive Officers
Others (Senior Executives)
Clive Cooke

www.euromoneydirectory.com   UNITED STATES (+1)

Intermonetary Corp

345 Park Avenue, New York, NY 10154
Tel: (212) 421 8870 **Fax:** (212) 593 2370 **Telex:** RCA 225520 IMC UR

Senior Executive Officers
President — Edgar R Eisner
Executive Vice President — Laurance H Friedman

Syndicated Lending
Other (Syndicated Lending)
Loan Administration — Loretta Graham *Vice President*

Settlement / Clearing
Operations — Edward L Landsman *Treasurer*

Administration
Legal / In-House Counsel — Rosemary C Byrne *VP & General Counsel*

International Bank Services   Head Office

13th Floor, 155 Federal Street, Boston, MA 02110
Tel: (617) 423 0021 **Fax:** (617) 423 0645 **Telex:** 49616491 IBSINC **Email:** ibser@aol.com

Senior Executive Officers
President — Robert Hildreth ☎ **423 0021**

Debt Capital Markets / Fixed Income
Bonds - General
Emerging Markets (Loans & Bonds) — Gustavo Posse *Senior Vice President*
Batya Natan *Vice President*
Alexander McFerran *Managing Director*

The International Commercial Bank of China   Agency

65 Liberty Street, New York, NY 10005
Tel: (212) 608 4222 **Fax:** (212) 608 4943 **Telex:** 232640 **Swift:** ICBC US 73

Senior Executive Officers
Others (Senior Executives) — Wen-Long Lin *SVP & General Manager*

International Finance Corporation   Head Office

Alternative trading name: IFC

2121 Pennsylvania Avenue NW, Washington, DC 20433
Tel: (202) 477 1234 **Fax:** (202) 974 4384
Website: www.ifc.org

Senior Executive Officers
President — James D Wolfensohn
Executive Vice President — Jannik Lindbaek
VP & Secretary — Shengman Zhang

Others (Senior Executives)
Birgitta Kantola *VP, Finance & Planning*
Jemal-ud-din Kassum *VP, Investment Operations*
Portfolio Management & Advisory Operations — Assaad J Jabre *Vice President*
Carol Lee *VP & General Counsel*
Personnel, Administration, Corporate Business — Christopher Bam *Vice President*
Corp Planning & Financial Policy — Nissim Ezekiel *Director, Corp Planning & Financial Policy*
Vasant H Karmarker *Principal Financial Adviser*
Special Operations Unit — Woonki Sung *Manager*
General-Investment
Head of Investment — Jemal-ud-din Kassum *VP, Investment Operations*
Relationship Manager
Agribusiness — Tei Mante *Director*
Sulyporn Kulsrethsiri *Manager*
Macodou N'Daw *Portfolio Manager*
Chemicals, Petrochemicals & Fertilizers — Jean-Philippe Halphen *Director*

UNITED STATES (+1)   www.euromoneydirectory.com

International Finance Corporation (cont)
Relationship Manager (cont)

	Richard Parry *Associate Director*
	Jerome Sooklal *Manager*
Oil, Gas & Mining	Philippe Liétard *Director*
	Sakdiyiam Kupasrimonkol *Deputy Director*
	Maria da Graça Domingues *Manager, Oil & Gas*
	Claus A Westmeier *Special Adviser to Director*
	Farid Dossani *Portfolio Manager*
Telecommunications	Kent E Lupberger *Manager, Telecommuncations*
Power	Vivek Talvadkar *Director*
	Jean-Paul Pinard *Associate Director*
	Apinya Suebsaeng *Portfolio Manager*
Telecommunications, Transportation & Utilities	Declan J Duff *Director*
	Francisco Toureilles *Manager, Transportation & Utilities*
	Kent E Lupberger *Manager, Telecommuncations*
	Joseph Solan *Portfolio Manager*

Department: Central & Southern Europe Department
Director   Harold Rosen

Others (Senior Executives)
Division 1   Sujata Lamba *Country Manager*
Division 2   Kenneth Assal *Country Manager*

General-Investment
Head of Investment   Robin L Glantz *Associate Director, Portfolio / Credit*

Department: Central Asia, the Middle East & North Africa Department
Director   Mohsen A Khalil
Associate Director   Khosrow Zamani

General-Investment
Head of Investment   Michael Essex *Portfolio Manager*

Department: East Asia & Pacific Department
Director   Javed Hamid

Others (Senior Executives)
Division 1   Ravinder Bugga *Country Manager*
Division 2   Khanh Nguyen *Country Manager*

Department: Europe II Department
Director   Edward Nassim

Others (Senior Executives)
Armenia, Belarus, Georgia, Russian Federation   Richard Ranken *Manager*

Department: Latin America & the Caribbean Department
Director   Karl Voltaire
Senior Manager   Bernard Pasquier

Others (Senior Executives)
Strategy & Coordination Division   Bernard Sheahan *Manager*

General-Investment
Head of Investment   Stanley Greig *Portfolio Manager*

Department: South & South East Asia
Director   Rashad-Rudolf Kaldany

Others (Senior Executives)
    Eric Cruikshank *Resident Manager*

General-Investment
Head of Investment   Sami Haddad *Associate Director & Portfolio Manager*

Department: Sub-Saharan Africa
Director   Cesare Calari
Associate Director   André Cracco

Others (Senior Executives)
Division 1   Udayan Wagle *Country Manager*
Division 2   Guy C Antoine *Country Manager*

General-Investment
Head of Investment   Colin Warren *Portfolio Manager*

Debt Capital Markets / Fixed Income
Global Head   Kumiko Yoshinari *Manager, Capital Markets - Asia I*
    Iyad Malas *Manager, Central Asia, Middle East & North Africa*
    Hany Assaad *Manager, Capital Markets - Asia II*
    Monish Dutt *Manager, Capital Markets - Europe I*
    Mary Ellen Iskenderian *Manager, Capital Markets - Europe II*
    Haydee Celaya *Manager, Capital Markets - Latin America*
    Bahadurali Jetha *Manager, Capital Markets - Sub-Saharan Africa*

Non-Domestic Government Bonds
International Securities Group
Department: Central Capital Markets
Global Head
Country Head

Suellen Lazaris *Senior Manager, Syndications*

Claudia J Morgenstern *Director*
Rudolf van der Bijl *Senior Adviser*
Roy Karaoglan *Senior Banking Adviser*
Teresa Barger *Senior Manager, Securities Services*
Syed Aftab Ahmed *Manager, Contractual Savings Group*
Minh Chau Nguyen *Manager, Outreach Programs*

Syndicated Lending
Department: Credit Review Department
Global Head
Department: Project Development Facilities

Paul Hinchey *Director*

Loan-Related Activities
Project Finance

Macodou N'Daw *Co-ordinator, Africa*
Mischek Ngatunga *Regional Manager, East Africa*
Kalada Harry *Regional Manager, Southern Africa*
John James *Manager, South Africa*
Thomas S Davenport *Manager, Mekong Project*
Graene Rothwell *Regional Manager, South Pacific*

Corporate Finance / M&A Advisory
Department: Corporate Finance Services Department
Regional Head

Denise Leonard *Manager*
Reyaz A Ahmed *Manager*

Settlement / Clearing
Operations

Nissim Ezekiel *Director, Corp Planning & Financial Policy*
Dileep Wagle *Manager, Corp Planning & Financial Policy*
Teng-Hong Cheah *Manager, Financial Planning & Policy*
Irving Kuczynski *Director, Operations Policy & Fin. Sector Issues*
Simon Fowler *Senior Manager, Financial Operations*
Farida Khambata *Director, Treasury*

Asset Management
Portfolio Management

Assaad J Jabre *Vice President*
Marc Rabin *Senior Manager*

Other (Asset Management)
Trust Funds Division

Gary E Bond *Manager*

Other Departments
Economic Research

Guy Pierre Pfeffermann *Director, Economics & Chief Economic Adviser*

Department: Foreign Investment Advisory Service
Economic Research

Dale R Weigel *General Manager*
Joel Bergsman *Manager*
Boris Velic *Manager*
Andrew Proctor *Manager*

Administration
Head of Administration

Christopher Bam *Vice President*
Gordon A MacDonald *Manager Administration & Finance*

Business Development; Head of Marketing

Sumio Takeichi

Technology & Systems

Guy-Pierre De Poerck *Chief Information Officer*
Tom Schipani *Manager*

Legal / In-House Counsel

Jennifer Sullivan *Deputy General Counsel*
Fernando Cabezas *Chief Counsel*
David d'Adhemar *Chief Counsel*
Carlos Fernandez-Duque *Chief Counsel*
E Andres Hernandorena *Chief Counsel*
Hugo J Waszink *Chief Counsel*

Corporate Communications
Corporate Relations Unit

Mark A Constantine *Manager*

Accounts / Audit
Controllers & Budgeting Department
Accounting Division
Budgeting Division

Christian Grossman *Director*
Paul Bravery *Manager*
Richard Moss *Senior Manager*

Other (Administration)
Personnel

Christopher Bam *Vice President*
Jean Bradier *Manager*

UNITED STATES (+1)   www.euromoneydirectory.com

International Finance Corporation (cont)
Other (Administration) (cont)

Recruitment Services
Resource Mobilization
Operations Evaluation Group

Susan Jones Adams *Manager*
Suellen Lazarus *Senior Manager, Syndications*
William E Stevenson *Director*

INVESTCORP International Inc

37th Floor, 280 Park Avenue, New York, NY 10017
Tel: (212) 599 4700 **Fax:** (212) 983 7073 **Telex:** 4976329 INCORP

Investors Bank & Trust Company

200 Clarendon Street, Boston, MA 02116
Tel: (617) 330 6700; (617) 330 6324 **Fax:** (617) 351 4202 **Telex:** 49607816 **Swift:** INVB US 33 **Email:** info@ibtco.com
Website: www.investorsbank.com/biz/ibt & www.ibtco.com

Debt Capital Markets / Fixed Income
Tel: 330 6424 **Fax:** 330 6515

Fixed-Income Repo
Head of Repo; Marketing & Product Development
Trading

James O Bryant *Director, Treasury Services* ☎ 330 6005 📠 330 6515
✉ jobryant@ibtco.com
Jason Menendez *Trader*
Mike Mooney *Senior Trader*
Mike Gosselin *Trading Manager*

Equity Capital Markets
Tel: 330 6424 **Fax:** 330 6515

Equity Repo / Securities Lending
Head; Marketing & Product Development

James O Bryant *Director, Treasury Services* ☎ 330 6005 📠 330 6515
✉ jobryant@ibtco.com
Head of Trading
Mike Gosselin *Trading Manager*
Chris Tosi *Senior Trader*
Mike Mooney *Senior Trader*

Global Custody
Other (Global Custody)

Gary Janik ☎ +1 (413) 744 3372 📠 +1 (413) 744 8470
Jeff Hoelzel ☎ +1 (800) 523 1661 📠 +1 (630) 368 6240
Mark Freemyer ☎ +1 (908) 214 2171 📠 +1 (908) 214 2062
Lorcan Murphy ☎ +1 (415) 597 2566 📠 +1 (415) 597 2299

Israel Discount Bank of New York   Subsidiary Company

511 Fifth Avenue, New York, NY 10017
Tel: (212) 551 8500 **Fax:** (212) 370 9623 **Telex:** 62411 **Swift:** IDB NY US 33 **Reuters:** IDBN
Website: www.idbny.com

Senior Executive Officers
Chairman
President & Chief Executive Officer
International Division

Arie Mientkavich
Arie Sheer
Haim Barziv *Executive Vice President*

General-Lending (DCM, SL)
Head of Corporate Banking

Leonard Greer *Executive Vice President*

Debt Capital Markets / Fixed Income
Department: Treasury
Head of Fixed Income; Head of Fixed Income Sales; Head of Fixed Income Trading

Harry Feder *First Vice President*

Government Bonds
Head of Sales

Frank Voso *First Vice President*

Eurobonds
Head of Sales; Head of Trading

Harry Feder *First Vice President*

Emerging Market Bonds
Head of Emerging Markets; Head of Sales; Head of Trading

Harry Feder *First Vice President*

Libor-Based / Floating-Rate Products
FRN Sales; FRN Trading; Asset Swaps; Asset Swaps (Sales)

Harry Feder *First Vice President*

www.euromoneydirectory.com   UNITED STATES (+1)

Fixed-Income Repo
Head of Repo; Marketing & Product Development; Head of Trading — Harry Feder *First Vice President*

Syndicated Lending
Head of Trading — Kenneth Walters *Vice President*

Loan-Related Activities
Trade Finance — Herbert Zorn *Senior Vice President*

Money Markets
Head of Money Markets — Harry Feder *First Vice President*

Domestic Commercial Paper
Head of Sales; Head of Trading — Harry Feder *First Vice President*

Eurocommercial Paper
Head of Sales; Head of Trading — Harry Feder *First Vice President*

Wholesale Deposits
Marketing; Head of Sales — Harry Feder *First Vice President*

Foreign Exchange
Head of Foreign Exchange — Lee Kassler *Vice President*

Risk Management
Head of Risk Management — Haim Barziv *Executive Vice President*

Settlement / Clearing
Head of Settlement / Clearing; Fixed-Income Settlement; Operations; Back-Office — Joseph Saltiel *First Vice President*

Global Custody
Head of Global Custody — Philip Parmet *First Vice President*

Other Departments
Chief Credit Officer — Leonard Greer *Executive Vice President*
Private Banking — Edmond Eskenazi *Executive Vice President*
Correspondent Banking — Haim Barziv *Executive Vice President*

Administration
Head of Marketing — Jerome Gottlieb *Senior Vice President*

Technology & Systems
Jan Wierbicki *Senior Vice President*

Legal / In-House Counsel
Theodore Itzkowitz *Senior Vice President*

Compliance
Michael Guarino

Public Relations
Jerome Gottlieb *Senior Vice President*

Accounts / Audit
Glenn Bond *Chief Auditor*

The Iyo Bank Limited   Representative Office
Suite 7923, One World Trade Center, New York, NY 10048
Tel: (212) 466 1400 **Fax:** (212) 432 2583 **Email:** iyobkny@worldnet.att.net

Senior Executive Officers
Chief Representative — Masato Yamasaki

Jefferies & Co Inc
11th Floor, 11100 Santa Monica Blvd, Los Angeles, CA 90025
Tel: (310) 445 1199; (310) 444 5618 **Fax:** (310) 914 1013 **Email:** webmaster@jefco.com
Website: www.jetco.com

Senior Executive Officers
Chairman & Chief Executive Officer — Frank E Baxter
President & Chief Operating Officer — Michael L Klowden
Financial Director — Clarence T Schmitz *Chief Financial Officer*
Treasurer — Gary Burnison
Secretary — Jerry M Gluck
International Division — Clifford Siegal *Executive Vice President* 614 1861

Others (Senior Executives)
Board Member — Richard B Handler *Executive Vice President*
Head of Marketing & Investor Relations — Steve McMenanin *Director* 708 5988

UNITED STATES (+1)   www.euromoneydirectory.com

Jefferies & Co Inc (cont)

General-Investment
Head of Investment — Chris Kanoff *Executive Vice President*

Debt Capital Markets / Fixed Income
Department: Taxable Fixed Income
Tel: 708 5800 Fax: 708 5820
Global Head — Richard B Handler *Executive Vice President*

Fixed-Income Research
Head of Fixed Income — Mark Neuner *Head of Taxable Fixed Income Research*

Equity Capital Markets
Department: Equity Trading Division
Tel: 903 2300 Fax: 903 2840
Head of Equity Capital Markets — Lou Bellucci Sr *Chairman*
Head of Sales — John Shaw *National Sales Manager*
Head of Trading — Robert Colgan *Manager*

International Equities
Head of Sales — Les Allen *Senior Vice President* ☎ **614 1851**
Head of Trading — John Conroy *Senior Vice President* ☎ **903 2267**

Equity Research
Global Head — Sam Albright *Executive Vice President*

Convertibles / Equity-Linked
Head of Sales — Jonathan Cunningham *Head*

Syndicated Lending
Tel: 903 2342 Fax: 903 2208
Head of Trading — Tim Menfort *Manager*

Money Markets

Eurocommercial Paper
Head of Sales — John Conroy *Senior Vice President* ☎ **903 2267**

Risk Management
Tel: 903 2538 Fax: 903 2485
Global Head — Paul Bodor *Director of Compliance*

OTC Equity Derivatives
Sales — Mike Ferry *Manager*

Corporate Finance / M&A Advisory
Head of Corporate Finance — Chris Kanoff *Executive Vice President*

Administration
Head of Marketing — Steve McMenamin *Director* ☎ **708 5988**

Technology & Systems
Chief Information Officer — Russell D Lewis

Legal / In-House Counsel
Secretary — Jerry M Gluck *Secretary*

Compliance
Head of Compliance — Paul Bodor *Director of Compliance*

Public Relations
Director of Marketing & Investor Relations — Steve McMenamin *Director* ☎ **708 5988**

Accounts / Audit
Chief Financial Officer — Maxine Syrjamaki

The Joyo Bank Limited   Full Branch Office

6th Floor, 150 East 52nd Street, New York, NY 10022-6017
Tel: (212) 752 2500 Fax: (212) 752 6920 Telex: 4976129 JOYONY Email: joyony@worldnet.att.net
Website: www.joyobank.co.jp

Senior Executive Officers
General Manager — Naouki Ishii
Deputy General Manager — Hiroaki Yokochi

Others (Senior Executives)
Treasury & Securities — Hiroshi Kurihara *Manager*
Norihisa Nakamura *Assistant Manager*
Yasuhiro Katada

Settlement / Clearing
Operations — Katsunori Suzuki *Manager*

1970 Euromoney Directory 1999

www.euromoneydirectory.com   UNITED STATES (+1)

Administration
Public Relations
        Atsufumi Hirose *Manager*

JP Morgan & Co Incorporated   Head Office
      60 Wall Street, New York, NY 10260-0060
      Tel: (212) 483 2323 **Telex:** 669525
      Website: www.jpmorgan.com

Senior Executive Officers
Chairman & Chief Executive	Douglas A Warner III ☏ 648 6600 📠 648 5210
Vice Chairman	Walter A Gubert
Vice Chairman	Roberto G Mendoza ☏ 648 7575 📠 648 5141
Vice Chairman	Michael E Patterson
Financial Director	John A Mayer Jr *Chief Financial Officer*

Others (Senior Executives)
Strategic Planning	John A Mayer Jr *Chief Financial Officer*
	Thomas B Ketchum *Chief Administrative Officer*

General-Investment
Head of Investment	Walter A Gubert *Vice Chairman*

Relationship Manager
Euroclear System	Luc Bomans
Asia Pacific	Peter L Woicke
Europe, Middle East, Africa	Joseph P MacHale

Debt Capital Markets / Fixed Income
Head of Fixed Income	Peter D Hancock

Emerging Market Bonds
Head of Emerging Markets	Nicolas S Rohatyn

Equity Capital Markets
Global Head	Clayton S Rose

Foreign Exchange
Global Head	Nicolas S Rohatyn

Risk Management
Global Head	Stephen G Thieke *Corporate Risk Management Research*

Settlement / Clearing
Operations	Charles M Trunz III *Operation Manager*

Asset Management
Head	Ramón de Oliveira
	Keith M Schappert

Other (Asset Management)
Credit Portfolio	Peter D Hancock

Other Departments
Commodities / Bullion	Nicolas S Rohatyn
Proprietary Trading	Pilar Conde
	Michael R Corey

Administration
Head of Administration	Thomas B Ketchum *Chief Administrative Officer*

Legal / In-House Counsel
General counsel	Rachel F Robbins

Corporate Communications
Corporate Communications	Laura W Dillon
Chief Information Officer	Peter A Miller

Accounts / Audit
Auditor	Edward E Murphy
Controller	David H Sidwell

Other (Administration)
Corporate Services	Ronald H Menaker
Human Resources	Herbert J Hefke

JP Morgan Securities Inc
      3rd Floor, 60 Wall Street, New York, NY 10260-0060
      Tel: (212) 483 2323 **Fax:** (212) 648 5950

UNITED STATES (+1) www.euromoneydirectory.com

KBC Bank
Representative Office

Suite 1920, 515 South Sigueroa Street, Los Angeles, CA 90024
Tel: (213) 624 0401 **Fax:** (213) 629 5801

Senior Executive Officers
VP & Regional Manager   Thomas G Jackson

Kempen & Co USA Inc
Subsidiary Company

34th Floor, 474 Third Avenue, New York, NY 10017
Tel: (212) 376 0130 **Fax:** (212) 376 0139

Senior Executive Officers
President   M de Natris

Keycorp
Head Office

127 Public Square, Cleveland, OH 44114
Tel: (216) 689 3718
Website: www.key.com

Senior Executive Officers
Chairman & Chief Executive Officer   Robert W Gillespie
President & Chief Executive Officer   Henry L Meyer
International Division   R Robertson Hilton *Senior Vice President*
Representative   Jon Shulman

Other Departments
Cash Management   R Robertson Hilton *Senior Vice President*

Komercni Banka
Representative Office

660 Madison Avenue, New York, NY 10021
Tel: (212) 593 1616 **Fax:** (212) 593 2929

Senior Executive Officers
Chief Representative   Paul Geczi

The Korea Development Bank
Full Branch Office

31st Floor, 320 Park Avenue, New York, NY 10022
Tel: (212) 688 7686 **Fax:** (212) 421 5028 **Telex:** 6737390 **Swift:** KODB US 33 **Reuters:** KDBN

Senior Executive Officers
General Manager   Yong Yun Won

Debt Capital Markets / Fixed Income
Asset-Backed Securities / Securitization
Regional Head   Harry Rhee *VP & Manager*

Fixed-Income Repo
Head of Repo   Scott Shou *Assistant Manager*

Syndicated Lending
Global Head   Harry Rhee *VP & Manager*

Loan-Related Activities
Trade Finance   Chin Cho *Deputy General Manager*

Money Markets
Global Head   Beyung Toon *Assistant Manager*

Domestic Commercial Paper
Head of Origination   Beyung Toon *Assistant Manager*

Risk Management
Global Head   Raymond Lee *VP & Manager*

Fixed Income Derivatives / Risk Management
Global Head   Scott Shou *Assistant Manager*

www.euromoneydirectory.com UNITED STATES (+1)

Korea Long-Term Credit Bank
Full Branch Office

24th Floor, 565 5th Avenue, New York, NY 10017
Tel: (212) 697 6100 **Fax:** (212) 697 1456; (212) 697 2110

Senior Executive Officers
General Manager   Kang Man Lee ☎ **697 6100 ext 112**

Others (Senior Executives)
    Chang I Kim *Manager* ☎ **697 6100 ext 120**

Debt Capital Markets / Fixed Income
Department: Trade Finance / Funding / Asset Management
Head of Fixed Income Trading   Min S Kwon *Manager* ☎ **697 6100 ext 130**

Risk Management
Country Head   Robert Grillo *Officer, Risk Management & Compliance* ☎ **697 6100 ext 124**

Kredietbank NV
Full Branch Office

125 West 55th Street, New York, NY 10019
Tel: (212) 541 0600 **Fax:** (212) 956 5580 **Telex:** 661572 KREDIET NV **Swift:** KRED US 33
General Telex: 177789 KRED NY

Senior Executive Officers
SVP & General Manager   Pierre Konings
Chief Operating Officer   Stephanie Semidey *VP & Chief Operating Officer*
Treasurer   Randy Vineis *VP & Treasurer*

Others (Senior Executives)
Lending   Tod Angus *VP & Senior Lending Officer*

Syndicated Lending
Regional Head   Tod Angus *VP & Senior Lending Officer*
Head of Credit Committee   Robert Snauffer *VP & Senior Credit Officer*

Loan-Related Activities
Trade Finance   Paul Feldman *Vice President*
Project Finance; Project Finance   Eric McCartney *Vice President*
Structured Trade Finance; Leasing & Asset Finance   Edward Sproull *Vice President*

Money Markets
Regional Head   Robert LaMarca *Vice President*

Domestic Commercial Paper
Head of Trading   Thomas Flynn *Vice President*

Wholesale Deposits
Head of Sales   Rick Porter *Vice President*

Foreign Exchange
Regional Head   Paul Gorham *Vice President*
Corporate Sales   Rick Porter *Vice President*

Risk Management
Regional Head   Patrick Garrity *Vice President*

Administration

Legal / In-House Counsel
    Michael Curran *Vice President*

Compliance
    Diane Grimmig *Vice President*

Landesbank Hessen-Thüringen Girozentrale
Full Branch Office

24th Floor, 420 Fifth Avenue, New York, NY 10018
Tel: (212) 703 5200 **Fax:** (212) 703 5256 **Telex:** 424568 **Swift:** HELA US 33 **Reuters:** HLBN

Senior Executive Officers
Managing Director / General Manager   H C Ritter

UNITED STATES (+1)   www.euromoneydirectory.com

LBS Bank - New York   Subsidiary Company

12 East 52nd Street, New York, NY 10022
Tel: (212) 207 2200 **Fax:** (212) 593 1967 **Telex:** 229976 LBS UR **Swift:** LJBA US 33
Website: www.lbsbank.com

Senior Executive Officers
Non-Executive Chairman   Witold Sulimirski
President & Chief Executive Officer   Rudolf Gabrovec ☎ **207 2240**
Chief Operating Officer   Cafo Boga EVP & Chief Operating Officer ☎ **207 2242**
Treasurer   Branko Kobal Treasurer ☎ **207 2251**

Debt Capital Markets / Fixed Income
Global Head   Branko Kobal Treasurer ☎ **207 2251**

Syndicated Lending
Head of Syndicated Lending   Frank J Horvat SVP, Chief Lending & Marketing Officer ☎ **207 2229**
                                      ✉ **horvat@lbsbank.com**

Foreign Exchange
Global Head   Branko Kobal Treasurer ☎ **207 2251**

Risk Management
Global Head   Branko Kobal Treasurer ☎ **207 2251**

Corporate Finance / M&A Advisory
Head of Corporate Finance   Frank J Horvat SVP, Chief Lending & Marketing Officer ☎ **207 2229**
                                      ✉ **horvat@lbsbank.com**

Settlement / Clearing
Regional Head   Gerry Bucci Operations Manager ☎ **207 2226**

Other Departments
Private Banking   Viki Kamin ☎ **207 2204**

Administration
Legal / In-House Counsel
                                      Frank Horvat Senior Vice President ☎ **207 2229**

Lehman Brothers Inc

3 World Financial Center, New York, NY 10285-0900
Tel: (212) 526 7000 **Fax:** (212) 528 0748

Senior Executive Officers
Chairman   J Tomilson Hill
President   Richard S Fuld Jr

Debt Capital Markets / Fixed Income
Tel: 526 6815

Fixed-Income Repo
Trading   Grant Whiteside
                                      Dave Lohuis

Fixed-Income Research
Global Head   Jack Malvey

Equity Capital Markets
Tel: 526 0710 **Fax:** 528 0749

Convertibles / Equity-Linked
Head of Origination   Larry Wieseneck

Equity Repo / Securities Lending
Head   Robert Feidelson Managing Director ☎ **526 3804** 📠 **528 6821**
Marketing & Product Development   Anne Erni Vice President ☎ **526 8441**
Head of Prime Brokerage   Robert Feidelson Managing Director ☎ **526 3804** 📠 **528 6821**
                                      John R Huber Managing Director ☎ **526 2736**
Head of Trading   Leslie Allison Vice President, Domestic Sales Manager
                                      Thomas DeGalia Senior Vice President (Domestic)

Syndicated Lending
Head of Syndication   Jeff Weiss Head of Global Debt Syndicate

Corporate Finance / M&A Advisory
Department: Mergers & Acquisitions
Global Head   Steven Wolitzer Global Head

Other Departments
Economic Research   John Llewellyn Global Chief Economist
                                      Joaquin Alberto Cottani Chief Latin American Economist

1974   Euromoney Directory 1999

www.euromoneydirectory.com UNITED STATES (+1)

Leonia Bank plc
Full Branch Office

Formerly known as: Postipankki Limited
Suite 2544, 60 East 42nd Street, New York, NY 10022
Tel: (212) 758 8181 Fax: (212) 758 0011 Reuters: POSN-O

Senior Executive Officers
Chief Operating Officer Ian E Wise *SVP & Controller*
Treasurer Matti Peltonen *SVP & Treasurer*
General Manager Pekka Vataja

General-Lending (DCM, SL)
Head of Corporate Banking Gary Tanner *SVP, Corporate Banking (US Corporates)*
 Ari Kaarakainen *VP, Corporate Banking (Nordic Corporates)*

Administration
Compliance
 Ian E Wise *SVP & Controller*

Lepercq de Neuflize Securities Inc
Head Office

1675 Broadway, New York, NY 10019
Tel: (212) 698 0700 Fax: (212) 262 0155; (212) 262 0144
Website: www.lepercq.com

Senior Executive Officers
Chairman Bruno Desfurges ☎ 698 0738
President & Chief Executive Officer François Letaconnoux ☎ 698 0777
Financial Director; Treasurer Peter Hartnedy *CFO & Treasurer* ☎ 698 0762
Executive Vice President Tsering Ngudu ☎ 698 0743
International Division Jerry Getsos

General-Investment
Head of Investment Francois Letacomoux

Debt Capital Markets / Fixed Income
Head of Debt Capital Markets Joel Cooper

Domestic Government Bonds
Head of Trading John McNally

Equity Capital Markets
Head of Equity Capital Markets Tsering Ngudu *Executive Vice President* ☎ 698 0743
Head of Trading Philip Switzer

Corporate Finance / M&A Advisory
Head of Corporate Finance Francois Letacomoux

Other (Corporate Finance)
Venture Capiture Michael Connelly

Settlement / Clearing
Head of Settlement / Clearing Philip Switzer
Operations Ellen Grant

Asset Management
Head Tsering Ngudu *Executive Vice President* ☎ 698 0743

Administration
Head of Administration Ellen Grant

Legal / In-House Counsel
 David Wilson

London Forfaiting Americas Inc
Representative Office

Suite 2150, John Hancock Center, 875 North Michigan Avenue, Chicago, IL 60611
Tel: (312) 255 9220 Fax: (312) 255 9221 Email: wittmanc@aol.com

Senior Executive Officers

Others (Senior Executives)
Vice President Chantal Wittman
Assistant Vice President Peter Bradley

Euromoney Directory 1999 **1975**

UNITED STATES (+1)   www.euromoneydirectory.com

London Forfaiting Americas Inc — Subsidiary Company
11th Floor, 135 East 57th Street, New York, NY 10022-2009
Tel: (212) 759 1919 Fax: (212) 759 0118 Email: lfa@forfaiting.com

Senior Executive Officers
President — James P Klatsky
Senior Vice President — Riccardo M Striano
Vice President — Douglas E Stephens

Relationship Manager
Latin America — Adolfo Estevez *Assistant Vice President*
John Paul Clemente *Associate*
North America — Gregory Bernardi *Vice President*
Michael Londono *Assistant Vice President*
Jack Kowalczyk *Associate*

Administration
Other (Administration)
Monica Angeli *MIS*
Judielynn Sciacca *Office Manager*

London Forfaiting Americas Inc — Representative Office
Suite 3980, One Embarcadero Center, San Francisco, CA 94111
Tel: (415) 397 4545 Fax: (415) 397 4542 Email: bkushner@ibm.net

Senior Executive Officers
Others (Senior Executives)
Vice President — Bret Kushner
Associate — Steven Messina

The Long-Term Credit Bank of Japan Limited — Representative Office
Suite 2801, Marquis One Tower, 245 Peachtree Centre Avenue NE, Atlanta, GA 30303
Tel: (404) 659 7210 Fax: (404) 658 9751

Senior Executive Officers
Chief Manager — Akihiko Haruyama

The Long-Term Credit Bank of Japan Limited — Full Branch Office
Suite 800, 190 South LaSalle Street, Chicago, IL 60603
Tel: (312) 704 1700 Fax: (312) 704 8505

Senior Executive Officers
Chief Manager — Masaharu Kuhara

The Long-Term Credit Bank of Japan Limited — Representative Office
Suite 4700 West, Texas Commerce Tower, 2200 Ross Avenue, Dallas, TX 75201
Tel: (214) 969 5352 Fax: (214) 969 5357

Senior Executive Officers
Chief Manager — Sadao Muraoka

The Long-Term Credit Bank of Japan Limited — Full Branch Office
350 South Grand Avenue, Suite 3000, Los Angeles, CA 90071
Tel: (213) 629 5777 Fax: (213) 627 4630

Senior Executive Officers
General Manager — Koh Takemoto

www.euromoneydirectory.com UNITED STATES (+1)

The Long-Term Credit Bank of Japan Limited — Full Branch Office

50th Floor, 165 Broadway, New York, NY 10006
Tel: (212) 335 4400 **Fax:** (212) 608 2303

Senior Executive Officers
Director & General Manager Tetsuo Makabe

LTCB Trust Company — Subsidiary Company

165 Broadway, New York, NY 10006
Tel: (212) 335 4900 **Fax:** (212) 608 3081

Senior Executive Officers
Managing Director / General Manager Tetsuo Makabe

Maxcor Financial Inc — Subsidiary Company

84th Floor, Two World Trade Center, New York, NY 10048-0697
Tel: (212) 748 7000 **Fax:** (212) 748 7329; (212) 748 7050 **Telex:** TRT 177153 EURO
Website: www.ebi.com

Senior Executive Officers
Chairman Gilbert Scharf ☎ **748 8866** ✉ **gscharf@ebi.com**
President Michael Pins ☎ **748 7200** ✉ **mpins@ebi.com**

Others (Senior Executives)
  Stephen Vigliotti *Chief Financial Officer* ☎ **748 7040** ✉ **svigliotti@ebi.com**

General-Investment
Head of Investment Gerry Brodsky *SVP, Investment Banking* ☎ **748 7411** ✉ **gbrodsky@ebi.com**

Debt Capital Markets / Fixed Income
Bonds - General
Zero Coupons Kevin Cleary *Senior Vice President* ☎ **748 7543**
Convertible Bonds Bob Brown *Senior Vice President* ☎ **748 8855**

Other (Emerging Markets Bonds)
Brady Bonds Wesley Wang *SVP, Emerging Markets* ☎ **748 7200** ✉ **wwang@ebi.com**
Euro Bonds Michael Krumenacker *Senior Vice President* ☎ **748 7810**
  ✉ **mkrumen@ebi.com**
Mexican Products Mark Kaplan *Senior Vice President* ☎ **748 7510** ✉ **mkaplan@ebi.com**

Fixed-Income Repo
Head of Repo Anthony Pinto *SVP, EMG Repo* ☎ **748 7810**
  John Desiderio *SVP, Repurchase Agreements* ☎ **748 7016**

Risk Management
Other Currency Swap / FX Options Personnel
EMG Options Jennifer Doyna *Senior Vice President* ☎ **748 7200** ✉ **jdoyna@ebi.com**

Settlement / Clearing
Operations Susan Sullivan *VP, Operations* ☎ **748 7580** ✉ **ssullivan@ebi.com**

Administration
Technology & Systems
  Walter Danielsson *SVP, Technology* ☎ **748 7151** ✉ **walter@ebi.com**

Legal / In-House Counsel
  Roger Schwed *EVP & General Counsel* ☎ **748 8860** ✉ **rschwed@ebi.com**

Compliance
  Patric Nicholson *VP & Compliance Officer* ☎ **748 7020**
  ✉ **pnicholson@ebi.com**

Mellon Bank Corporation

One Mellon Bank Center, Pittsburgh, PA 15258-0001
Tel: (412) 234 5000 **Fax:** (412) 234 0214 **Telex:** 199103 MEL BNK P **Swift:** MELN US 3P
Website: www.mellon.com

Senior Executive Officers
Chairman, President & CEO Frank V Cahouet
Vice Chairman & CEO Martin G McGuinn
Vice Chairman & COO Christopher M Condron
Senior Vice Chairman W Keith Smith

UNITED STATES (+1)

Mellon Bank Corporation (cont)
Senior Executive Officers (cont)

Senior Vice Chairman & CFO	Steven G Elliott
Vice Chairman	John T Chesko
Vice Chairman	Jeffrey L Leininger
Vice Chairman	David R Lovejoy
Vice Chairman	Keith P Russell
Vice Chairman	Jamie B Stewart Jr
Corporate Secretary	Carl Krasik

Others (Senior Executives)

Paul S Beideman *Executive Manager*
Joseph A LoCicero *Executive Manager*
J David Officer *Executive Manager*
D Michael Roark *Executive Manager*
Peter Rzasnicki *Executive Manager*
William J Stallkamp *Executive Manager*
Allan P Woods *Executive Manager*
Frederick K Beard *Senior Manager*
Richard B Berner *Senior Manager*
Michael E Bleier *Senior Manager*
Paul A Briggs *Senior Manager*
Michael A Bryson *Senior Manager*
Larry F Clyde *Senior Manager*
Paul H Dimmick *Senior Manager*
Kenneth R Dubuque *Senior Manager*
Paul Holmes *Senior Manager*
Lawrence S Kash *Senior Manager*
Allan C Kirkman *Senior Manager*
David F Lamere *Senior Manager*
Peter A Lofquist *Senior Manager*
Robert G Loughrey *Senior Manager*
Sandra J McLaughlin *Senior Manager*
John P O'Driscoll *Senior Manager*
James P Palermo *Senior Manager*
Robert M Parkinson *Senior Manager*
Robert W Stasik *Senior Manager*
Sherman White *Senior Manager*
Michael K Hughey *Corporate Controller*

Risk Management
Head of Risk Management — John T Chesko *Vice Chairman*

Mercantile Bancorporation Inc — Head Office

Mercantile Tower, 7th & Washington, St Louis, MO 63101
PO Box 524, St Louis, MO 63166-0524
Tel: (314) 418 2525 Fax: (314) 418 1286
Website: www.mercantile.com

Senior Executive Officers

Chairman, President & CEO	Thomas Jacobsen
Financial Director	John Q Arnold *Chief Financial Officer*
General Counsel and Secretary	Jon W Bilstrom
International Division	Joseph A (Tony) Louvier *VP, Group Manager*

Mercantile Safe Deposit & Trust Company — Subsidiary Company

2 Hopkins Plaza, Baltimore, MD 21201
PO Box 1477, Baltimore, MD 21203
Tel: (410) 237 5900 Fax: (410) 237 5364 Email: merc-info@mercantile.net
Website: www.mercantile.net

Senior Executive Officers

Chairman & Chief Executive Officer	H Furlong Baldwin ☏ **237 5900**
President & Chief Operating Officer	J Marshall Reid
Financial Director	Terry L Troupe *Chief Financial Officer*
General Counsel and Secretary	Alan D Yarbro

Others (Senior Executives)
Affiliate Management — Hugh W Mohler *Executive Vice President*

1978 Euromoney Directory 1999

www.euromoneydirectory.com　　　　　　　UNITED STATES (+1)

General-Lending (DCM, SL)	
Head of Corporate Banking	Kenneth A Bourne *Executive Vice President*
Debt Capital Markets / Fixed Income	
Country Head	Malcolm C Wilson *Executive Vice President*
Fixed-Income Research	
Country Head	J Patrick Bradley *Senior Vice President*
Equity Capital Markets	
Country Head	Malcolm C Wilson *Executive Vice President*
Equity Research	
Country Head	J Patrick Bradley *Senior Vice President*
Settlement / Clearing	
Operations	Charles E Siegmann *Executive Vice President*
Other Departments	
Private Banking	Alex G Fisher *Senior Vice President*
	Thomson C Willard *Senior Vice President*
Global Trust	Malcolm C Wilson *Executive Vice President*
Administration	
Head of Marketing	Josias J Cromwell *Senior Vice President*
Technology & Systems	
	Charles E Siegmann *Executive Vice President*
Legal / In-House Counsel	
	Alan D Yarbro *General Counsel and Secretary*
Compliance	
	Ernest Stokes II *Vice President & Assistant Secretary*
Public Relations	
	Suzanne G Wolff *Senior Vice President*
Accounts / Audit	
	Robert C Smith *General Auditor*

MeritaNordbanken Group　　　　　　　Full Branch Office

Formerly known as:
Merita Bank Plc & Nordbanken

MeritaNordbanken Group
437 Madison Avenue, New York, NY 10022
Tel: (212) 318 9300 **Fax:** (212) 421 4420 **Telex:** 422511 MERITA NY **Swift:** MRIT US 3N
Email: general@meritany.com
Website: www.meritany.com

Senior Executive Officers	
Treasurer	Colin Williams-Hawkes *SVP & Treasurer* ☏ **318 9390**
General Manager	Jukka Niemi ☏ **318 9333**
Others (Senior Executives)	
Credit	Gerald Chelius *Senior Vice President* ☏ **318 9580**
Commercial Banking	Alan Philpott *Senior Vice President* ☏ **318 9301**
Debt Capital Markets / Fixed Income	
Domestic Government Bonds	
Head of Trading	Ray Cala *Deputy Treasurer* ☏ **355 5757**
Asset-Backed Securities / Securitization	
Head of Trading	Martin Hofer *Vice President* ☏ **318 9395**
Syndicated Lending	
Head of Syndication	Cliff Abramsky *VP, US Corporate Banking* ☏ **318 9564**
Loan-Related Activities	
Trade Finance; Project Finance	Chip Carstensen *Vice President* ☏ **318 9560**
Money Markets	
Head of Money Markets	Colin Williams-Hawkes *SVP & Treasurer* ☏ **318 9390**
Domestic Commercial Paper	
Head of Sales	Martin Hofer *Vice President* ☏ **318 9395**
Foreign Exchange	
Head of Foreign Exchange	Pasi Pölkki *Manager* ☏ **318 9391**
Head of Institutional Sales	Hanna Porkka *AVP, Treasury Sales* ☏ **318 9395**
Corporate Sales	Magnus Haraldsson *AVP, Treasury Sales* ☏ **318 9395**

Euromoney Directory 1999　**1979**

UNITED STATES (+1)   www.euromoneydirectory.com

MeritaNordbanken Group (cont)
Risk Management
Head of Risk Management   John Tighe *Risk Manager* ☎ 318 9395

Other Departments
Chief Credit Officer   Gerald Chelius *Senior Vice President* ☎ 318 9580
Correspondent Banking   Jukka Niemi *General Manager* ☎ 318 9333
Cash Management   John Kelly *Assistant Vice President* ☎ 318 9371

Administration
Head of Administration   Jerry Murphy *Senior Vice President* ☎ 318 9350

Technology & Systems
                                 Lenny O'Dea *VP, Treasury Operations* ☎ 318 9370

Compliance
                                 Jerry Murphy *Senior Vice President* ☎ 318 9350

Merrill Lynch & Co Inc   Head Office
250 Vesey Street, New York, NY 10281
Tel: (212) 449 1000 **Reuters:** MER

Senior Executive Officers
Chairman & Chief Executive Officer   David H Komansky
President & Chief Operating Officer   Herbert M Allison Jr

Others (Senior Executives)
Asset Management Group   Arthur H Zeikel *President*
Investment Banking   Barry S Friedberg *Chairman & EVP*
Corporate & Institutional Client Group   Thomas W Davis *Executive Vice President*
Private Client Group   John L Steffens *Vice Chairman*
Human Resources   Mary Taylor *Senior Vice President*
Global Financial Institutions   John G Heimann *Chairman*
Office of the General Counsel   Stephen L Hammerman *Vice Chairman & General Counsel*
Operations, Services & Technology   Edward L Goldberg *Executive Vice President*
Marketing & Communications   Paul W Critchlow *Senior Vice President*
Global Risk Management   Daniel T Napoli *Senior Vice President*
Chief Financial Office   E Stanley O'Neal *Executive Vice President*
Special Advisory Services   Thomas H Patrick *Chairman & EVP*
International Private Client   Winthrop H Smith *EVP & Chairman Merrill Lynch International*
Merrill Lynch Europe & Middle East Asia   Michael Marks *Executive Chairman, Merrill Lynch Europe, Middle E*

Department: Global Investment Banking

Others (Senior Executives)
Investment Banking Group   Daniel H Bayly *Head Investment Banking & Managing Director*
European Banking   Guy Dawson *Co-Head & Managing Director*
Hong Kong Banking   John McNiven *Managing Director*
European Banking   Ed Annunziato *Co-Head & Managing Director*
Hong Kong Banking   Thomas Seaman *Managing Director*
Japan Banking   Kunihiko Kumagai *Managing Director*
Canada Banking   Robert Grandy *Managing Director*
Australian Banking   Ian Scholes *Managing Director*
Real Estate Finance   Richard Saltzman *Managing Director*

Department: Research

Others (Senior Executives)
Global Securities Research & Economics   Andrew J Melnick *Senior Vice President & Co-Director*
                                           Rosemary T Berkery *Senior Vice President & Co-Director*
Global Fixed Income Research   Don Ullman *First Vice President & Director*
                                           Richard McCabe *Senior Vice President*
Global Investment Strategy   Chuck Clough Jr *First Vice President*
Quantitive Analysis   Richard Bernstein *First Vice President & Director*
Mutual Funds Research   Ron Santangelo *First Vice President & Manager*
International Fixed Income Research   Michael Rosenberg *First Vice President & Manager*
High Yield Securities Research   Martin Fridson *First Vice President & Manager*
Chief Economist   Bruce Steinberg *First Vice President*
Convertibles Research   T Anne Cox *First Vice President & Director*
Global Economics   James Winder *First Vice President & Manager*
Futures Research   William O'Neal *First Vice President & Manager*
Global Research Compliance   George Nitschelm *First Vice President & Manager*

Money Markets
Department: Global Money Markets & Mortgage Capital Inc.
Country Head   Conrad Voldstad *Co-Head & Managing Director*

1980 Euromoney Directory 1999

www.euromoneydirectory.com UNITED STATES (+1)

Foreign Exchange
FX Traders / Sales People
Local Currency Trading; Global FX Trading / Sales — Stephen M Bellotti *Managing Director*
Local Currency Trading — Stephen Blakey *Managing Director*
Thomas Gahan *Managing Director*
Local Currency Trading; Local America Eastern Europe / Middle East / Africa Asia — Steven Gregornik *Global Business Head*
Brett Platt
John Duncan

Risk Management
Department: Global Risk Management
Country Head — Daniel T Napoli *Senior Vice President*

Other Currency Swap / FX Options Personnel
Global Spot / Forward Trading & FX Sales — John Key
Global FX Trading / Sales — Stephen M Bellotti *Managing Director*
Global Options Trading — Kevin Bespolka
Global Complex Options (Exotic) — Koon Fong Chen

Settlement / Clearing
Operations — Edward L Goldberg *Executive Vice President*

Asset Management
Head — Jeff M Peek

Other Departments
Economic Research — Jerome P Kenney *EVP, Corporate Strategy & Research*

Administration
Technology & Systems
Services & Technology — Edward L Goldberg *Executive Vice President*
Legal / In-House Counsel
Office of the General Counsel — Stephen L Hammerman *Vice Chairman & General Counsel*
Corporate Communications
Marketing & Communications — Paul W Critchlow *Senior Vice President*
Other (Administration)
Human Resources — Mary Taylor *Senior Vice President*

Midland Bank plc
Full Branch Office

140 Broadway, New York, NY 10005-1196
Tel: (212) 658 2700 **Fax:** (212) 658 1344 **Telex:** 62390 MIDBK

Senior Executive Officers
Director — J C Holsey
Chief Executive Officer — D Downey
Treasurer — A Rademeyer

The Mitsui Trust & Banking Company Limited
Representative Office

Suite 1950, 601 South Figueroa Street, Los Angeles, CA 90017
Tel: (213) 624 5201 **Fax:** (213) 622 0378

Senior Executive Officers
Chief Representative — Hidetoshi Seino

Morgan Stanley Dean Witter & Co
Head Office

Formerly known as: Morgan Stanley & Co / Dean Witter Discover & Co
1585 Broadway, New York, NY 10036
Tel: (212) 761 4000 **Fax:** (212) 761 0570 **Telex:** 620131
Website: www.msdw.com

Senior Executive Officers
Chairman & Chief Executive Officer — Philip Purcell ☎ **761 7274**
President & Chief Operating Officer — John Mack ☎ **761 7845**
President & COO of Morgan Stanley & Co — Peter Karches
President & COO of Dean Witter Securities — James Higgins ☎ **392 2708**
President & COO of Dean Witter Capital — Richard Demartini ☎ **392 1624**
EVP & Chief Strategist — John Schaefer ☎ **761 4461**
Chief Executive Officer — Richard Fisher ☎ **761 6348**
Financial Director — Robert Scott

UNITED STATES (+1) www.euromoneydirectory.com

Morgan Stanley Dean Witter & Co (cont)
Senior Executive Officers (cont)
Chief Operating Officer

James Allwin *President & COO, Institutional Invest. Mgmt* ☏ **762 7348**
Thomas Butler *President & COO of Discover Brands* ☏ **+1 (847) 405 3011**

Others (Senior Executives)
Merchant Banking

James Allwin *Head* ☏ **761 8481**

General-Investment
Head of Investment

Joseph Perella ☏ **761 4200**

Debt Capital Markets / Fixed Income
Head of Debt Capital Markets
Head of Fixed Income
Head of Fixed Income Sales; Head of Fixed Income Trading

Walid Chammat *Head*
Ken de Regt ☏ **761 8111**
Jerome Wood ☏ **761 1200**

Fixed-Income Repo
Marketing & Product Development
Trading

Diane Pearl *Vice President* ☏ **761 2412**
Tom Wipf *Principal of Specials Trading*
Michael Ianetta *Vice President of Corporate Bonds*
Jeffrey Kidwell *Principal of General Collateral* ☏ **781 2402** ✉ **jkid@ms.com**
Joseph Latesta *Vice President of Overnight Trading*
Peter Mozer *Vice President of Whole Loans*
William Haney *Principal of Flex Repo*

Fixed-Income Research
Head of Fixed Income

Benjamin Wolkowitz ☏ **761 1700**

Equity Capital Markets
Head of Equity Capital Markets
Head of Sales; Head of Trading

Richard Kauffman ☏ **761 5399**
John Harens ☏ **761 7800**

Other (Domestic Equities)
Institutional Equity

Vikram Pandit *Head* ☏ **761 4900**

Other (International Equity)
Worldwide Syndicate

Mark Seigel *Head*

Equity Research
Head of Equity Research

Maxree Clark ☏ **761 6298**

Corporate Finance / M&A Advisory
Head of Corporate Finance

Terry Meguid ☏ **761 8481**

Administration
Technology & Systems

James Tillay ☏ **762 2062**

Legal / In-House Counsel

Christine Edwards *Chief Legal Officer* ☏ **761 6522**

Compliance

Stuart Breslow ☏ **761 6565**

Natexis Banque Full Branch Office
Formerly known as: Banque Française du Commerce Extérieur & Crédit National
645 Fifth Avenue, New York, NY 10022
Tel: (212) 872 5000 **Fax:** (212) 872 5045 **Telex:** 422684 BFCE NY

Senior Executive Officers
EVP & General Manager, USA

Jean Y Richard ✉ **bfce@idt.net**

National Bank of Canada Representative Office
Suite 1850, 2121 San Jacinto, Dallas, TX 75201
Tel: (214) 871 1200 **Fax:** (214) 871 2015

Senior Executive Officers
Vice President

Larry L Sears

1982 Euromoney Directory 1999

National Bank of Canada
Full Branch Office

125 West 55th Street, New York, NY 10019
Tel: (212) 632 8500 **Fax:** (212) 632 8616 **Telex:** 177782 NATBK CAN **Swift:** BNDC US 33A **Reuters:** NBCN

Senior Executive Officers
Treasurer — Pierrette Lacroix *SVP & Treasurer* T 632 8650 F 632 8727
SVP & General Manager — Harvey Brooks T 632 8555 F 632 8785

Debt Capital Markets / Fixed Income
Head of Fixed Income — Mark Macaluso *Vice President* T 632 8623 F 632 8727
Head of Fixed Income Trading — Elias Rauch *Vice President* T 632 8620 F 632 8727

Libor-Based / Floating-Rate Products
Asset Swaps — Charles McHugh *Vice President* T 632 8621

Syndicated Lending
Other (Syndicated Lending)
Commercial Lending East — John Richter *Vice President* T 632 8521 F 632 8545
Letters of Credit — John Taussik *Vice President* T 632 8585 F 632 8590

Money Markets
Fax: 632 8727
Head of Money Markets — Charles McHugh *Vice President* T 632 8621

Domestic Commercial Paper
Head of Sales — Jennifer Schweisinger *Manager* T 632 8630
Head of Trading — Brett Levinson *Dealer* T 632 8620

Eurocommercial Paper
Head of Trading — Neal Heinze *Dealer* T 632 8631

Wholesale Deposits
Head of Sales — Mary Kae Higgins *Treasury Services Officer* T 632 8631

Foreign Exchange
FX Traders / Sales People
James Nagel *Dealer* T 632 8604 F 632 8727

Settlement / Clearing
Tel: 632 8660 **Fax:** 632 8616
Back-Office — Lina Tomac *Vice President*

Other Departments
Chief Credit Officer — Tom Doss T 632 8560 F 632 8564

Administration
Head of Administration — Jerry Salese *Vice President* T 632 8534 F 632 8616

Technology & Systems
James Mulqueen *Vice President* T 632 8670 F 632 8696

Compliance
Danielle Boulet *Vice President* T 632 8532 F 632 8564

Public Relations
Ed Patrisso *Vice President* T 632 8818 F 632 8616

National Bank of Pakistan
Full Branch Office

21st Floor, 100 Wall Street, New York, NY 10005
Tel: (212) 344 8822; (212) 344 8833 **Fax:** (212) 344 8826; (212) 809 4720 **Telex:** 232455 PAK BUR, 62652 NAT PAK

Senior Executive Officers
Chief Executive Officer — Muhammed Taj *SVP & Manager*
Muhammed Bengali *SEVP & Regional Chief Executive*
Treasurer — Masood Sethi

National Financial Services Corp

200 Liberty Street, New York, NY 10281
Tel: (212) 335 5087 **Fax:** (212) 945 9282

Equity Capital Markets
Equity Repo / Securities Lending
Head — Henry Gioia *Senior Vice President* T 335 5542 F 945 9282
Marketing & Product Development — Carol Conti *Director* T 335 5748 E carol.conti@fmr.com
Head of Trading — Brian Turner *Manager*

UNITED STATES (+1)   www.euromoneydirectory.com

NationsBanc Capital Markets Inc
Subsidiary Company

100 North Tryon Street, NC1-007-06-07, Charlotte, NC 28255-0001
Tel: (704) 386 5000

Senior Executive Officers
President — William Maxwell ☎ 386 7723
Financial Director — Craig Winterfield *Chief Financial Officer* ☎ 388 7051
Chief Operating Officer — Richard Downen ☎ 386 4912

Debt Capital Markets / Fixed Income
Tel: 386 7604 **Fax:** 386 9946
Global Head — William Maxwell *President* ☎ 386 7723

Private Placements
Head of Origination; Head of Sales; Head of Structuring — Stan Allison *Director* ☎ 386 8409

Asset-Backed Securities / Securitization
Global Head; Regional Head of Trading — Eric Dunn *Managing Director* ☎ 386 7413

Mortgage-Backed Securities
Global Head — Bill Hodges *Senior Vice President* ☎ 388 5235
Head of Trading — Pat Augustine *Managing Director* ☎ 386 7744

Fixed-Income Repo
Head of Repo; Collateral Management; Matched Book Manager; Sales — Dick Seitz ☎ 386 6623

Money Markets
Global Head — Steve Huntley *Managing Director* ☎ 386 8020

Domestic Commercial Paper
Head of Origination; Head of Sales; Head of Trading — Steve Huntley *Managing Director* ☎ 386 8020

Foreign Exchange
Global Head — Albert Hoyle ☎ **(312) 234 5000**

Risk Management
Tel: 386 5448 **Fax:** 386 1175
Global Head — Al de Molina *Senior Vice President* ☎ 386 1500

Fixed Income Derivatives / Risk Management
Global Head — Al de Molina *Senior Vice President* ☎ 386 1500

Corporate Finance / M&A Advisory
Tel: 386 5464 **Fax:** 388 0247
Global Head — Stewart Boswell *Managing Director* ☎ 386 5491

Administration
Legal / In-House Counsel
Vic Warnement *Senior Vice President* ☎ 386 4225

Compliance
Selwyn Notelovitz *Senior Vice President* ☎ 388 3006

Public Relations
Ginny Mackin *Senior Vice President* ☎ 386 7519

Other (Administration)
Risk Management — Ron Newth *Senior Vice President* ☎ 386 8116

NationsBank
Full Branch Office

Suite 2800, 233 South Wacker Drive, Chicago, IL 60606
Tel: (312) 234 5000 **Fax:** (312) 234 2562

Foreign Exchange
Department: Foreign Exchange & Interest Rate Products
Global Head — Duncan Goldie-Morrison *Global Manager*

NatWest Group - North America
Full Branch Office

175 Water Street, New York, NY 10038
Tel: (212) 602 4800 **Fax:** (212) 602 4638
Website: www.natwestgroup.com

Senior Executive Officers
Regional Managing Director — L Edward Shaw Jr
Financial Director — Charles Beach *Chief Finance Officer*

1984 Euromoney Directory 1999

www.euromoneydirectory.com　　　　　　　　UNITED STATES (+1)

Administration
Technology & Systems
　　　　　　Arthur Rosenburg *Senior Vice President* ☎ **602 8515**
Legal / In-House Counsel
　　　　　　Patrick Finley *SVP & General Counsel* ☎ **602 8938**
Compliance
　　　　　　Pat Wharwood *Senior Vice President* ☎ **602 4012**
Corporate Communications
　　　　　　Missy De Angelis *SVP & Head* ☎ **602 4086**

NedShip International Inc　　　　　Subsidiary Company
37th Floor, 245 Park Avenue, New York, NY 10167-0062
Tel: (212) 808 6900 **Fax**: (212) 309 5188

Senior Executive Officers
President　　　　　　　　A Gurnee
Vice President　　　　　　S Hoekstra

Nesbitt Burns Inc
7th Floor, 430 Park Avenue, New York, NY 10022
Tel: (212) 702 1230 **Fax**: (212) 702 1922

The Nikko Securities Co International Inc　　Full Branch Office
Suite 2760, 1 South Wacker Drive, Chicago, IL 60606
Tel: (312) 726 7037 **Fax**: (312) 726 7256

Senior Executive Officers
SVP & Branch Manager　　　　Robert Turner

The Nikko Securities Co International Inc　　Subsidiary Company
200 Liberty Street, New York, NY 10281
Tel: (212) 416 5400; (212) 416 5420 **Fax**: (212) 416 5600 **Telex**: 232861

Senior Executive Officers
Chairman　　　　　　　　　　Timothy Cronin
Deputy President　　　　　　Ryosuke Otani
Financial Director　　　　　　Joe Ramos *Chief Finance Officer*

Debt Capital Markets / Fixed Income
Domestic Government Bonds
Head of Trading　　　　　　Shiro Kaneko *Co-General Manager*
　　　　　　　　　　　　　Thomas Gribbon *Co-General Manager*
Head of Research　　　　　　Robert Brusca *Chief Economist*

Mortgage-Backed Securities
Head of Trading　　　　　　Shiro Kaneko *Co-General Manager*
　　　　　　　　　　　　　Thomas Gribbon *Co-General Manager*

Fixed-Income Repo
Head of Repo　　　　　　　Shiro Kaneko *Co-General Manager*
　　　　　　　　　　　　　Thomas Gribbon *Co-General Manager*
Trading　　　　　　　　　　Ben Ulrich

Equity Capital Markets
Tel: 416 5532 **Fax**: 416 5420

Domestic Equities
Head of Sales; Head of Trading　James Kitigana *First Vice President*
Head of Research　　　　　　James Kitigana *First Vice President*

Equity Repo / Securities Lending
Head　　　　　　　　　　　Takeshi Shinoda *First Vice President*
Head of Trading　　　　　　Ben Ulrich
　　　　　　　　　　　　　Linda Villacis *Domestic Trading*
　　　　　　　　　　　　　Eric Landheer *International Trading* ☎ **416 5976**

Euromoney Directory 1999　**1985**

UNITED STATES (+1)   www.euromoneydirectory.com

Nomura Securities International

20th Floor, Building B, 2 World Financial Center, New York, NY 10281-1195
Tel: (212) 667 9300 Fax: (212) 667 1058 Telex: 824039
Website: www.nsiseclend.com

Senior Executive Officers
Chairman   Max C Chapman Jr
President   Michael Burman

Debt Capital Markets / Fixed Income
Tel: 667 2130 Fax: 667 1555

Mortgage-Backed Securities
Regional Head   Arthur Frank *Head of Mortgage Backed Securities*

Fixed-Income Repo
Trading   Keith McCluskey *Director*
    Stacey Lieberman *Sales Director*
    Gary Soderland *Vice President*
    Conrad Santos *Vice President, Emerging Markets*
    Jay Lockwood *Assistant Vice President*
    Dan Saleeby *Assistant Vice President*

Equity Capital Markets
Tel: 667 9586 Fax: 667 1504

Equity Repo / Securities Lending
Head   Anthony Venditti *Managing Director* ☎ **667 1224**
    ✉ **avenditti@nomurany.com**

Marketing & Product Development   Douglas Tveter *Vice President* ☎ **667 9586** ✉ **dtveter@nomurany.com**
Head of Trading   Victor Diaz
    Lorraine Antigua *AVP, Domestic*
    Michael Belloli *AVP, Domestic*
    Malcolm Rapley
    Robert Lakeman
    Peter Volino *VP, Domestic*
    Stella Sardo *AVP, Domestic*
    Douglas Tveter *Vice President* ☎ **667 9586** ✉ **dtveter@nomurany.com**

Norddeutsche Landesbank Girozentrale   Full Branch Office

1270 Avenue of the Americas, New York, NY 10020
Tel: (212) 332 8600 Fax: (212) 332 8650 Telex: 666730 NLB NY Reuters: NLBN

Senior Executive Officers
Treasurer   J Bovenizer *SVP & Treasurer* ☎ **332 8622**
General Manager   Jens A Westrick ☎ **332 8601**

Norwest Investment Management   Head Office

Formerly known as: Norwest Bank Minneapolis NA
Norwest Center, 6th & Marquette, Minneapolis, MN 55479-0095
Tel: (612) 667 8110 Fax: (612) 667 5185; (612) 667 2269 Telex: 6734665 Swift: NWNB US 44

Senior Executive Officers
Chairman & Chief Executive Officer   James R Campbell
EVP & Chief Lending Officer   P Thomas J Wiklund
Executive Vice President   Richard P Ferris
Senior Vice President   Kevin Rhein

General - Treasury
Head of Treasury   David B Marks *Head of Global Treasury Management*
    Scott L Kringle *Head of Global Treasury Mgmt Systems & Technology*

Relationship Manager
International Financial Institution   Richard P Ferris *Executive Vice President*
Large Corporate Division   Perry G Pelos *Senior Vice President & Manager*
International Product & Delivery Service   Philip J De Chiara *Vice President & Manager*

Equity Capital Markets
Equity Repo / Securities Lending
Head   Robert Smith *Manager, Securities Lending* ☎ **667 5464**
    ✉ **robert.g.smith@norwest.com**
Head of Trading   Brian Keogh *Head Trader, Securities*

www.euromoneydirectory.com	UNITED STATES (+1)

Equity Repo / Securities Lending (cont)
Roger Adams *Portfolio Manager*
Kathleen Leonard *Product Manager*
Marie Wolf *Trader*
Todd Neils *Trader*

Other Departments
Chief Credit Officer	P Thomas J Wiklund *EVP & Chief Lending Officer*

Administration
Technology & Systems
Scott L Kringle *Head of Global Treasury Mgmt Systems & Technology*

## Nova Ljubljanska banka dd	Representative Office
Representative Office, 12 East 52nd Street, New York, NY 10022
Tel: (212) 207 2200 **Fax:** (212) 593 1967

Senior Executive Officers
Representative	Gregor Kaiser

## OTS Limited LLC	Head Office
Alternative trading name: Ocean Transport Systems Limited
Suite 113, 1500 Massachusetts Avenue NW, Washington, DC 20005
Tel: (202) 785 0087 **Fax:** (202) 785 2298

Senior Executive Officers
Managing Director & Trustee	Basil S Skenderis-Kastriotis

Others (Senior Executives)
	Serafeim B Skenderis *Trustee*
Attorney at Law	Glenn Willett Clark *Economist*
	Serafeim Panayiotis Skenderis *Trustee*
	Andreas Karageorgiadis *Trustee*
	Stavros-Vassilios G Skenderis *Trustee*
	Constantine G Skenderis *Trustee*
Economist	Vassilios Vassiakostas *Trustee*
	Constantine X Skenderis *Trustee*

Administration
Legal / In-House Counsel
Legal Counsel	Harris Stavrakakis
Attorney at Law	Yiannis Mousouros *Trustee*

## Oversea-Chinese Banking Corporation Limited	Agency
36th Floor, 2 World Financial Center, 225 Liberty Street, New York, NY 10281
Tel: (212) 587 0101 **Fax:** (212) 587 8235 **Telex:** 6790834

Senior Executive Officers
Assistant Vice President	Vincent Lee
Manager, Operations	Grace Sun
Managing Director / General Manager	Eddie Lau

## Overseas Union Bank Limited	Agency
Suite 3955, 1 World Trade Center, New York, NY 10048
Tel: (212) 432 9482 **Fax:** (212) 432 9297 **Telex:** 424385 **Swift:** OUBK US 33

Senior Executive Officers
Managing Director / General Manager	George Lim

Syndicated Lending
Head of Syndicated Lending	George Lim

Foreign Exchange
Head of Foreign Exchange	Peter Wong

Administration
Head of Marketing	George Lim

UNITED STATES (+1)   www.euromoneydirectory.com

Paine Webber Group Inc

1285 Avenue of the Americas, New York, NY 10019
Tel: (212) 713 2000

Senior Executive Officers

Chairman & Chief Executive Officer	Donald B Marron
Senior Vice President & Chief Financial Officer	Regina A Dolan
Vice President	F Daniel Corkery
Vice President	Frank A Lenti
Treasurer	William J Nolan *Treasurer*
Senior Vice President, General Counsel & Secretary	Theodore A Levine
Assistant Secretary	Geraldine L Banyai

PaineWebber Incorporated

1285 Avenue of the Americas, New York, NY 10019
Tel: (212) 713 2000

Senior Executive Officers

Chairman & Chief Executive Officer	Donald B Marron
President	Joseph J Grano Jr
Executive Vice President & Controller	Anthony M Dilorio
EVP, CFO & Chief Administration Officer	Regina A Dolan
Executive Vice President	Theodore A Levine
Treasurer	William J Nolan *Executive Vice President & Treasurer*
Vice President & Assistant Secretary	Geraldine L Banyai
Vice President & Secretary	Dorothy F Haughey

PaineWebber International Inc

1285 Avenue of the Americas, New York, NY 10019
Tel: (212) 713 2000

Senior Executive Officers

Chairman	John A Bult
President	Steven P Baum
Executive Vice President	Miguel A Ferrer

Paloma Securities LLC

Two American Lane, Greenwich, CT 06830
Tel: (203) 862 8000

Debt Capital Markets / Fixed Income
Tel: 862 8050

Fixed-Income Repo
Marketing & Product Development   Alan High *Director* ☎ +44 (171) 862 2978 ℻ +44 (171) 862 2979
                                      Tony Merola *Vice President* ☎ 862 8050 ℻ 862 4871
Trading   John Rynne *Assistant Vice President*
        Lauren Franco *Repo Trader*

Equity Capital Markets

Equity Repo / Securities Lending
Marketing & Product Development   Tony Merola *Vice President* ☎ 862 8050 ℻ 862 4871
                                      Alan High *Director* ☎ +44 (171) 862 2978 ℻ +44 (171) 862 2979

Pangaea Partners Limited   Head Office

402 Laurel Lane, Madison, WI 53704-6053
Tel: (608) 242 1801   Fax: (608) 242 1606   Email: pangaeapartners@compuserve.com
Website: www.pangaeapartners.com

Senior Executive Officers
Senior Partner   Eric G Postel

1988   Euromoney Directory 1999

www.euromoneydirectory.com UNITED STATES (+1)

Corporate Finance / M&A Advisory
Global Head Eric G Postel *Senior Partner*
Other (Corporate Finance)
Consulting Margaret Forseburg *Associate*

Paribas Corporation Full Branch Office
Alternative trading name: Paribas Capital Markets & Paribas New York
787 Seventh Avenue, The Equitable Tower, New York, NY 10019
Tel: (212) 841 3000 **Fax:** (212) 841 3555 **Telex:** 177000 **Email:** b_reilly@paribas.com **Reuters:** PARN, OPPA
Website: www.paribas.com

Senior Executive Officers
President David Brunner ☎ **841 3403**
Financial Director Donna Kiernan *Chief Financial Officer* ☎ **841 2269**
General-Lending (DCM, SL)
Head of Corporate Banking Carol Simon *Head of Credit* ☎ **841 2321**
General-Investment
Head of Investment Victor Maruri *Latin America Investment Banking* ☎ **841 3401**
Debt Capital Markets / Fixed Income
Global Head Shahriar Shahida *Head of Fixed Income* ☎ **841 3900**
Domestic Government Bonds
Head of Sales Paul McCormack *US Treasury Bonds* ☎ **841 3450**
Head of Trading Joseph Carballeira *US Treasury Bonds* ☎ **841 3448**
Bonds - General
Bond Syndicate Financing Susan Dingilian ☎ **841 3156**
  Mark Van Der Griend ☎ **841 3435**
Yankee Bond Trading J B Meyer ☎ **841 3535**
High Yield / Junk Bonds
Head Robert Howard ☎ **841 3141**
Emerging Market Bonds
Head Shahriar Shahida *Global Head, Emerging Markets Debt* ☎ **841 3900**
Head of Sales Morten Bentsen *Bond Credit Sales* ☎ **841 3500**
Head of Trading Varun Gosain ☎ **841 3902**
Asset-Backed Securities / Securitization
Global Head Kenneth Bock ☎ **841 3536**
Fixed-Income Repo
Marketing & Product Development Gerry Caldwell *USD Repo Sales Manager* ☎ **841 3855** ✉ **841 3260**
  Erin Zito *Repo Sales*
Trading Tim Doern *Short Term Arbitrage / GC Trader*
  Tim Murphy *Senior Specials Trader*
  Bill Schreiner *Senior Specials Trader*
  Gary Stone *Short Term Arbitrage Trader*
  Stephen Sassano *Firm Financing*

Fixed-Income Research
Country Head Richard Gilhooly ☎ **841 3525**
Equity Capital Markets
Tel: 841 3733 **Fax:** 841 3046
Global Head Christian Picot *Global Head, Equity Brokerage* ☎ **841 3670**
Country Head Aubrey Simpson-Orlebar ☎ **841 3064**
Domestic Equities
Head of Sales Carolyn Lewis ☎ **841 3470**
  Susan Gilbertson ☎ **841 3975**
Head of Trading Carolyn Lewis ☎ **841 3470**
  Ray Fernandez ☎ **841 3700**

Other (Domestic Equities)
Equity Syndicate Natalie Mersh ☎ **841 3050**
Other (International Equity)
Asia Equity Sales Joost Vos ☎ **841 3801**
Equity Syndicate Natalie Mersh ☎ **841 3050**
Convertibles / Equity-Linked
Head of Trading Kjell Ekdahl *Equity Convertible* ☎ **841 3741**
Equity Repo / Securities Lending
Head Paula O'Brien ☎ **841 3733**

UNITED STATES (+1) www.euromoneydirectory.com

Paribas Corporation (cont)
Syndicated Lending
Head of Syndication Daniel Whalen *Loan Syndication* ☎ **841 2549**
  Bukhtiar Khan *Loan Syndication* ☎ **841 2034**
Foreign Exchange
Global Head Eric Nicolas ☎ **841 2452**
Country Head Jonathan Simmonds ☎ **841 2400**
FX Traders / Sales People
Research Robert Lynch ☎ **841 2408**
Marketing David Holland ☎ **841 2407**
Risk Management
Global Head Pascal Fischer *Head, Market Risk* ☎ **841 2464**
Country Head Richard Turrin *Risk Advisory Group* ☎ **841 3397**
Other (FI Derivatives)
Derivatives Marketing Conrad Testwuide ☎ **841 3438**
Risk Arbitrage Evan Behrens ☎ **841 3170**
Hedge Fund Coverage Vasan Varathan ☎ **841 3750**
IR Trading Zbigniew Ryzak ☎ **841 3759**
IR Research Alex Dannenberg ☎ **841 3432**
OTC Equity Derivatives
Head Vuk Bulajic ☎ **841 3736**
Exchange-Traded Derivatives
FX Options Nigel Babbage *FX Options Products* ☎ **841 2482**
Settlement / Clearing
Settlement (General) Bob Lesee *Head of Back Office*
Operations Matthew D'Altorio *Head of Operations* ☎ **841 2130**
Other Departments
Economic Research John Welch *Latin America* ☎ **841 3631**
  Brian Fabbri *North America* ☎ **841 3633**
Administration
Head of Administration Guillaume DeBeaufort *Head of Administration* ☎ **841 3656**
Legal / In-House Counsel
  John Powers *Head of Legal* ☎ **841 3040**
Corporate Communications
  Janine Mejeur *AGM & Head of Corporate Communications* ☎ **841 3070**
Other (Administration)
Personnel Charles Chinzi *Head* ☎ **841 2103**

Pershing Division of Donaldson, Lufkin & Jenrette

15th Floor, One Pershing Plaza, Jersey City, NJ 07399
Tel: (201) 413 2269 **Fax:** (201) 413 0031

Debt Capital Markets / Fixed Income
Tel: 413 2421 **Fax:** 413 0031
Fixed-Income Repo
Marketing & Product Development Jack De Benedetto *Vice President* ☎ **413 2425** 📠 **413 1152**
  Irving Klubeck *Senior Vice President*
Trading Matthew Baldassano *Vice President US Equities*
  Deborah Langiulli *VP, Fixed-Income*
  Rory Zirpolo *Vice President, Special Handling*
  Robert Colon *Vice President US Equities*
  Chris Nowell *Vice President International Equities*

Equity Capital Markets
Tel: 413 2421 **Fax:** 413 0031
Equity Repo / Securities Lending
Marketing & Product Development Jack De Benedetto *Vice President* ☎ **413 2425** 📠 **413 1152**
  Irving Klubeck *Senior Vice President*

Plus 3 Group   Head Office

59-11 Xenia Street, Corona, NY 11368
Tel: (718) 592 7308 **Fax:** (718) 592 9714

Senior Executive Officers
President Sudhir Kakar

1990 Euromoney Directory 1999

www.euromoneydirectory.com				UNITED STATES (+1)

Corporate Finance / M&A Advisory
Head of Mergers & Acquisition				Sudhir Kakar *President*

## PMD International Inc						Head Office

Suite 310, 410 Severn Avenue, Annapolis, MD 21403
PO Box 1646, Annapolis, MD 21404-1646
Tel: (410) 280 8373 **Fax:** (410) 280 8874 **Email:** pmd@pmdintl.com

Senior Executive Officers
President						Rex Pingle ☏ **280 8873**
Financial Director					Katharine Crossman *Treasurer* ☏ **280 8873**
Resident Director					Jehangir Masud ☏ **792 2373**

Syndicated Lending
Loan-Related Activities
Project Finance					Rex Pingle ☏ **280 8873**

Corporate Finance / M&A Advisory
Global Head						Jehangir Masud *Resident Director* ☏ **792 2373**

## PNC Bank Corp						Head Office

One PNC Plaza, 249 Fifth Avenue, Pittsburgh, PA 15222-2707
Tel: (412) 762 2000 **Fax:** (412) 762 4507
Website: www.pncbank.com

Senior Executive Officers
Chairman & Chief Executive Officer			Thomas O'Brien
President						James E Rohr
Chief Executive Officer				Thomas O'Brien *Chairman & Chief Executive Officer*
Financial Director					Robert L Haunschild *SVP & Chief Financial Officer*
							Walter E Gregg Jr *Senior Executive Vice President*

Others (Senior Executives)
PNC Bank NA, Central PA Region				Dennis P Brenckle *President*
PNC Bank NA, Northeast PA Region			Peter K Classen *President*
PNC Bank NA, OH / KY Region				John C Haller *President*
PNC Bank NA, KY / IN Region				Michael N Harreld *President*
PNC Bank NA, Pittsburgh Region				Sy Holzer
PNC Bank NA, Delaware					Calvert A Morgan Jr *President*
PNC Bank NA, Northwest PA Region			Marlene D Mosco *President*
PNC Bank NA, Phil / S Jersey Region			Richard L Smoot *President & CEO*
PNC Bank NA, NJ Region					William H Turner *President*
PNC Private Bank					Thomas K Whitford *SVP & Chief Executive Officer*
Blackrock						Laurence D Fink *Chairman & Chief Executive Officer*

General-Lending (DCM, SL)
Head of Corporate Banking				Ralph S Michael III *SVP & Chief Executive Officer*

Syndicated Lending
Other (Syndicated Lending)
Secured Lending					Bruce E Robbins *EVP & Chief Executive Officer*

Risk Management
Department: Integrated Risk Management
Head of Risk Management				Eva T Blum *Senior Vice President*

Asset Management
Department: Asset Management & Servicing
Head							Richard C Caldwell *Executive Vice President*

Other Departments
Chief Credit Officer					Thomas E Paisley III *Senior Vice President*
Private Banking					Thomas K Whitford *SVP & Chief Executive Officer*

Administration
Head of Administration				Walter E Gregg Jr *Senior Executive Vice President*

Legal / In-House Counsel
							Helen P Pudlin *SVP & General Counsel*

Corporate Communications
Chief Information Officer				Timothy G Shack *Senior Vice President*

Other (Administration)
Human Resources					William E Rosner *Senior Vice President*

UNITED STATES (+1)   www.euromoneydirectory.com

Prudential Securities Inc

11th Floor, One New York Plaza, New York, NY 10292
Tel: (212) 778 6021 Fax: (212) 778 8248

Senior Executive Officers
General - Treasury
Head of Treasury   Michelle Laughlin *Treasury Strategist*

Equity Capital Markets
Equity Repo / Securities Lending
Marketing & Product Development   Beth A Pietrangelo *First Vice President*
    E beth_pietrangelo@ccmail.prusec

Rabobank Nederland   Full Branch Office

Alternative trading name: Rabo Capital Services

245 Park Avenue, New York, NY 10167
Tel: (212) 916 7800 Fax: (212) 916 7961

Senior Executive Officers
Chief Operating Officer   Reinier Mesritz *General Manager*

Debt Capital Markets / Fixed Income
Country Head   Aimee McCormack *Funding Manager*

Libor-Based / Floating-Rate Products
Asset Swaps   Aimee McCormack *Funding Manager*

Medium-Term Notes
Head of Sales   Aimee McCormack *Funding Manager*

Private Placements
Head of Structuring   Richard Gormely

Mortgage-Backed Securities
Head of Trading   Beth Bigwood *Investment Manager*

Fixed-Income Repo
Sales   Aimee McCormack *Funding Manager*

Syndicated Lending
Head of Syndicated Lending   Hans Den Baas

Loan-Related Activities
Trade Finance   Barbara Hyland

Money Markets
Country Head   Aimee McCormack *Funding Manager*

Domestic Commercial Paper
Head of Trading   Aimee McCormack *Funding Manager*

Risk Management
Head of Risk Management   Robert Armstrong *Global Market Risk Manager*
Regional Head   Victor Makarov *Market Risk Manager*

OTC Credit Derivatives
Head of Trading   Steven Lim

Corporate Finance / M&A Advisory
Head of Corporate Finance   Hans Den Baas

Administration
Technology & Systems
    Ed DeBosa

Legal / In-House Counsel
    Bill Bilbao

Raymond James & Associates Inc   Full Branch Office

Suite 280, 30 Montgomery Street, Jersey City, NJ 07302
Tel: (201) 946 2765 (Int); (201) 451 4500 (Dom) Fax: (201) 946 2961 Bloomberg: KGARVEY

Debt Capital Markets / Fixed Income
Bonds - General
Domestic & International Bonds Sales   Nicholas Moscato *Sales*
Domestic Bonds, Sales   Angelo Greco

Equity Capital Markets
Head of Sales   Nicholas Moscato *Sales*

www.euromoneydirectory.com UNITED STATES (+1)

Domestic Equities
Head of Sales   John Williams
                                                     Michael Hills

Equity Repo / Securities Lending
Head   Charles T Hermansen *VP, Head, Equity Securities Lending*
Marketing & Product Development   Peter Tartaglione *AVP, Head, Sales Desk, Domestic Securities Lending*
                                                     ☏ **451 5500**
                                                     Charles Hermansen II *AD, Head, Sales Desk, Int'l Securities Lending*
                                                     ☏ **946 2961**
Head of Trading   Kevin Garvey *AD, Head, Trading Desk, Int'l Securities Lending* ☏ **946 2961**

RBC Dominion Securities Coporation   Subsidiary Company

One Liberty Plaza, 165 Broadway, New York, NY 10006-1404
Tel: (212) 858 7000 Telex: 126926

Senior Executive Officers
Chairman, President & CEO   Gordon M Ritchie ☏ **858 7333**
Financial Director   D Bruce Runcimen *CFO & Treasurer* ☏ **858 7180**
Chief Operating Officer   D Bruce Macdonald ☏ **858 7400**

Debt Capital Markets / Fixed Income
Country Head   Stephen C Ashby ☏ **858 7196**

Equity Capital Markets
Country Head   Mark Standish ☏ **858 7350**
                                                     Loren Katzovitz ☏ **858 7360**

Money Markets
Country Head   Mark O'Conner ☏ **428 6366**

Foreign Exchange
Country Head   Diego Giurleo ☏ **428 6385**

Risk Management
Country Head   D Bruce Macdonald ☏ **858 7400**

Corporate Finance / M&A Advisory
Country Head   William Cook ☏ **858 7136**

Settlement / Clearing
Country Head   Nicholas Vitale ☏ **858 7077**

Refco Securities Inc

Formerly known as: Bersec International Corp.
1 World Finance Center, 200 Liberty Street, New York, NY 10281
Tel: (212) 693 7000 Fax: (212) 693 7730 Telex: 6790502

Senior Executive Officers
President   Santo C Maggio ☏ **693 7077** 🖷 **693 7611**
Chief Operating Officer   Anthony Scianna *Chief Operations Officer* ☏ **693 7655** 🖷 **693 7375**

Debt Capital Markets / Fixed Income

Fixed-Income Repo
Head of Repo   Santo C Maggio *President* ☏ **693 7077** 🖷 **693 7611**
Marketing & Product Development   John Agoglia *Vice President* ✉ **jagoglia@refco.com**

Equity Capital Markets
Tel: 693 7000 Fax: 693 7730

Equity Repo / Securities Lending
Head of Prime Brokerage   Anthony Scianna *Chief Operations Officer* ☏ **693 7655** 🖷 **693 7375**

Republic National Bank of New York   Head Office

452 Fifth Avenue, New York, NY 10018
Tel: (212) 525 5000 Telex: (RCA) 234967 Cable: BLICBANK
MCI Telex: 620274; CCI Telex: 7607637
Website: www.rnb.com

Senior Executive Officers
Chairman & Chief Executive Officer   Walter H Weiner ☏ **525 6165**
Vice Chairman & President   Dov C Schlein ☏ **525 6513**

UNITED STATES (+1)   www.euromoneydirectory.com

Republic National Bank of New York (cont)
Senior Executive Officers (cont)
Financial Director   Stan Martin *Executive Vice President & Chief Financial Officer* ☎ **525 5004**
Chief Operating Officer   Dov C Schlein *Vice Chairman & President* ☎ **525 6513**
Treasurer   Nathan Hasson *Vice Chairman* ☎ **525 6230**
Others (Senior Executives)
Head of Global Trading   Elias Saal *Vice Chairman* ☎ **525 5932**

Reserve Bank of Australia   Representative Office
One Liberty Plaza, 46th Floor, New York, NY 10006-1404
Tel: (212) 566 8466 **Fax:** (212) 566 8501
Senior Executive Officers
Chief Executive Officer   Niel Mackrell *Chief Representative*

Royal Bank of Canada   Full Branch Office
5th Floor, 1 Liberty Plaza, New York, NY 10006-1404
Tel: (212) 428 6200
Senior Executive Officers
SVP & General Manager   David L Robertson ☎ **428 6267** ✉ **drobertson@royalusa.com**
Syndicated Lending
Global Head   Colin Lambert *VP & Global Head* ☎ **428 6267** ✉ **clambert@royalusa.com**
Other (Syndicated Lending)
                              Darrell Naquin *Senior Manager* ☎ **428 6207** ✉ **dnaquin@royalusa.com**
                              Andrea Sickler *Senior Manager & Deputy* ☎ **428 6309**
                              ✉ **asickler@royalusa.com**
                              Rainer Kraft *Manager* ☎ **428 6287** ✉ **rktaft@royalusa.com**
                              Ritta Lee *Manager* ☎ **428 6448** ✉ **rlee@royalusa.com**
                              Irene Wanamaker *Manager, Agency Services* ☎ **428 6208**
                              ✉ **iwanamaker@royalusa.com**
Loan Trading   Jim Kelly *Manager* ☎ **428 6274** ✉ **jkelly@royalusa.com**

The Royal Bank of Scotland plc   Full Branch Office
26th Floor, Wall Street Plaza, 88 Pine Street, New York, NY 10005-1801
Tel: (212) 269 1700 **Fax:** (212) 269 8929 **Telex:** WUI:620261 **Swift:** RBOS US 33 **Cable:** RBSCOTNY
Senior Executive Officers
SVP & Manager   G F Stoddart
Treasurer   M A Wingent *Senior Vice President*

RW Pressprich & Co Inc   Head Office
5th Floor, 780 Third Avenue, New York, NY 10017
Tel: (212) 832 6200 **Fax:** (212) 832 6280
Website: www.pressprich.com
Senior Executive Officers
Chief Executive Officer   Ed Rappa
Administration
Compliance
                              Dennis Hynes *Managing Director*

The Sakura Bank Limited   Representative Office
Suite 430, 771 Corporate Drive, Lexington, KY 40503
Tel: (606) 223 8531 **Fax:** (606) 223 5465
Senior Executive Officers
Chief Representative   Takatoshi Yamada

1994 Euromoney Directory 1999

www.euromoneydirectory.com UNITED STATES (+1)

The Sakura Bank Limited
Full Branch Office

46th Floor, 277 Park Avenue, New York, NY 10172
Tel: (212) 756 6700 **Fax**: (212) 888 7651; (212) 644 9565 **Telex**: 232962 MITKBKNY

Senior Executive Officers
Managing Director / General Manager — Takashi Fujishima

Syndicated Lending
Head of Syndicated Lending — Susan Hancock *Vice President* 756 6986

Money Markets
Head of Money Markets — Haruo Nemoto *Vice President* 756 6910

Foreign Exchange
Head of Foreign Exchange — Masakazu Bunno *Vice President* 756 6930

Risk Management
Head of Risk Management — Miki Otsubo *Vice President* 756 6761

Corporate Finance / M&A Advisory
Head of Corporate Finance — Mel Schumacher *Senior Vice President* 756 6816

Settlement / Clearing
Head of Settlement / Clearing — John Labriola *Senior Vice President* 756 6860

Sakura Dellsher Inc
Subsidiary Company

Suite 3200, 10 South Wacker Drive, Chicago, IL 60606
Tel: (312) 930 0001 **Fax**: (312) 715 6200 **Email**: sdi@sdinet.com **Bloomberg**: SDR
Website: www.sdinet.com

Senior Executive Officers
Chairman & Chief Executive — Leo Melamed 930 3310
President — Hideki Noda 715 6252
Chief Executive Officer — Leo Melamed *Chairman & Chief Executive* 930 3310
Financial Director — Masaru Kakito *EVP & Chief Financial Officer* 715 6258

Others (Senior Executives)
Finance — Theresa C Arana *Vice President* 715 6214
Corporate Development — Gerard J Pannekoek *Executive Vice President* 715 6204
Managed Funds — Ranga Nathan 715 6160
Institutional Sales — Timothy Mulholland *SVP, Institutional Sales* 715 6208

Debt Capital Markets / Fixed Income
Emerging Market Bonds
Head — Gerard J Pannekoek *Executive Vice President* 715 6204

Equity Capital Markets
Head of Sales — William B Marcus *Senior Vice President, Sales* 715 6260

Risk Management
Other (Exchange-Traded Derivatives)
Japan — Hal Wiser *Vice President, Japan Desk* 715 6235
US & Europe — William B Marcus *Senior Vice President, Sales* 715 6260
South East Asia — Joong Won Suh *MD, Asian Business Development* +82 (2) 399 6308
Latin America — Gerard J Pannekoek *Executive Vice President* 715 6204

Settlement / Clearing
Operations; Back-Office — Jean Franklin *VP, Back-Office / Operations* 715 6109

Administration
Business Development — Gerard J Pannekoek *Executive Vice President* 715 6204
Head of Marketing — Rachel Leon *Marketing Coordinator* 715 6045 715 6225

Legal / In-House Counsel
Legal & Regulatory — Donald L Horwitz *SVP & General Counsel* 454 3037

Compliance
— Mary M Siragusa *SVP, Compliance* 715 6216

Public Relations
— Alysann Posner *FVP, Marketing* 715 6254

Other (Administration)
Education — Alysann Posner *FVP, Marketing* 715 6254
— Rachel Leon *Marketing Coordinator* 715 6045 715 6225
Human Resources — Jenene Williams *Vice President* 715 6211

UNITED STATES (+1) www.euromoneydirectory.com

Sakura Securities (USA) Inc
Subsidiary Company

9th Floor, 350 Park Avenue, New York, NY 10022
Tel: (212) 756 6600 **Fax:** (212) 756 6601

Senior Executive Officers
President — Katsumi Matsuzawa ☎ 756 6655
Financial Director — Thomas Sullivan *Chief Financial Officer* ☎ 756 6602

Debt Capital Markets / Fixed Income
Fixed-Income Repo
Head of Repo — Frank D'Amadeo *Vice President* ☎ 756 6605
Trading — Donald Lafronz *AVP* ☎ 756 6606

Settlement / Clearing
Fixed-Income Settlement — Marcus Hampton ☎ 756 6603

Administration
Head of Administration — Cordella Elliot-Green ☎ 756 6604

San Paolo Bank
Full Branch Office

245 Park Avenue, 35th Floor, New York, NY 10167
Tel: (212) 692 3100 **Fax:** (212) 599 5303; (212) 599 5304 **Telex:** 220045 **Swift:** IBSP US 33

Senior Executive Officers
Chief Executive Officer — Giuseppe Cuccurese *General Manager* ☎ 692 3010
Treasurer — Alessandro Alessandri *First Vice President* ☎ 692 3121

General-Lending (DCM, SL)
Head of Corporate Banking — Carlo Persico *Deputy General Manager* ☎ 692 3020

Debt Capital Markets / Fixed Income
Head of Fixed Income — Alessandro Alessandri *First Vice President* ☎ 692 3121
Head of Fixed Income Sales — Joseph Amoroso *Deputy Treasurer* ☎ 692 3109

Government Bonds
Head of Syndication — Barbara Bassi *Vice President* ☎ 692 3141

Money Markets
Domestic Commercial Paper
Head of Trading — Vincent Valenti *Assistant Treasurer* ☎ 692 3107

Foreign Exchange
Head of Foreign Exchange — Salvatore Di Raimondo *Assistant Treasurer* ☎ 692 3100
Head of Trading — Ivette Iacueo *Vice President* ☎ 692 3100

Risk Management
Head of Risk Management — Franck Fleury *Assistant Vice President* ☎ 692 3174

Settlement / Clearing
Head of Settlement / Clearing — Daniel Bruno *First Vice President* ☎ 692 3050

Administration
Head of Administration — Antonino Asaro *Controller* ☎ 692 3030

Compliance
Gerard Gaffney *Vice President, Compliance Committee* ☎ 692 3022

The Sanwa Bank Limited
Full Branch Office

25th Floor, Park Avenue Plaza, New York, NY 10055
Tel: (212) 339 6300 **Fax:** (212) 754 1851 **Telex:** RCA 232423

Senior Executive Officers
Treasurer — Takayaki Maito *MD & General Manager*
Managing Director / General Manager — Takashi Mori
Senior Deputy General Manager — Sen Hayakawa
Company Secretary — Alko Kaishoin

Foreign Exchange
Head of Foreign Exchange — Noriel Flores

Administration
Public Relations — Sen Hayakawa *Senior Deputy General Manager*

1996 Euromoney Directory 1999

www.euromoneydirectory.com				UNITED STATES (+1)

Schroder & Co Inc

Formerly known as: Schroder Wertheim & Co Inc
Equitable Center, 787 Seventh Avenue, New York, NY 10019-6016
Tel: (212) 492 6000 Fax: (212) 492 7036 Telex: 421193

Senior Executive Officers
Chairman	Peter Sedgwick ☏ **492 7080**
President & CEO	Steven Kotler ☏ **492 7040**
Financial Director	Patrick Borruso *Chief Administrative & Financial Officer* ☏ **492 7030**
Chief Operating Officer	Steven Kotler *President & CEO* ☏ **492 7040**
Managing Director	Kenneth Siegel ☏ **492 6205**
International Division	Pierre Bottinelli *Managing Director* ☏ **347 5600**

General-Investment
Head of Investment		Kenneth Siegel *Managing Director* ☏ **492 6205**

Debt Capital Markets / Fixed Income
Fax: 492 6629
Head of Fixed Income	Mark Field *Managing Director* ☏ **492 7170**
Head of Fixed Income Sales	Mark Edmiston *Managing Director* ☏ **492 6632**
Head of Fixed Income Trading	Gregg Ettin *Director* ☏ **492 6400**

Fixed-Income Repo
Head of Repo		William Hurst ☏ **492 6542**

Equity Capital Markets
Tel: 492 6026

Domestic Equities
Head of Sales		Allen Castner ☏ **492 6365**

Equity Research
Head of Equity Research		Barry Tarasoff ☏ **492 6403**

Syndicated Lending
Loan-Related Activities
Trade Finance		Robert Chamine *MD of Listed & OTC Trading* ☏ **492 7060**

Corporate Finance / M&A Advisory
Head of Corporate Finance		Richard Broadbent ☏ **+44 (171) 658 6443**

Settlement / Clearing
Fax: 492 7028
Head of Settlement / Clearing	Gary Salamone ☏ **492 6919**
Operations	Joseph Funk ☏ **492 6619**

Other Departments
Private Banking		Michael Dura *Managing Director, Private Investors* ☏ **492 7018**

Administration
Head of Administration	Patrick Borruso *Chief Administrative & Financial Officer* ☏ **492 7030**
Head of Marketing	Margaret Finnegan *Vice President* ☏ **492 6427**

Technology & Systems
		Patrick Callum *Senior Vice President* ☏ **492 6020**

Public Relations
		Margaret Finnegan *Vice President* ☏ **492 6427**

Accounts / Audit
Internal Audit		Anthony Savoca ☏ **492 6090**

# Scott-Macon Limited					Head Office

800 Third Avenue, New York, NY 10022
Tel: (212) 755 8200 Fax: (212) 755 8255

Senior Executive Officers
Chairman	James A Carthaus
President & CEO	Alfred L Scott
Senior Managing Director	Robert B Dimmitt

Corporate Finance / M&A Advisory
Global Head		Alfred L Scott *President & CEO*
		Robert B Dimmitt *Senior Managing Director*

Other (Corporate Finance)
Media	Derek Goodman *Managing Director*
Automotive	John Eberhardt *Managing Director*
Valuations	Jeffrey Tepper *Managing Director*
Private Placement	Zerve Colt *Managing Director*

Euromoney Directory 1999   **1997**

UNITED STATES (+1)   www.euromoneydirectory.com

SG Cowen Securities Corporation   Broker/Dealer

1221 Avenue of the Americas, New York, NY 10020
Tel: (212) 278 5316; (212) 278 5306 **Fax:** (212) 278 4520; (212) 278 5464
Website: www.socgen.com

Debt Capital Markets / Fixed Income
Tel: 278 5316 Fax: 278 4520

Fixed-Income Repo
Trading

Thomas Fox *Vice President, Repo Sales*
Michael Weir *Vice President, Repo Sales*
James Hopkins *Vice President, Repo Sales*
Timothy Carey *Agency Mortgaged-Backed Repo Trader*
Anthony Brunetti *Trader*

Equity Capital Markets
Equity Repo / Securities Lending
Marketing & Product Development

Alexandre de Vaivre *Global Head of Marketing & Sales*
[T] +33 (1) 42 13 91 13 [F] +33 (1) 42 13 64 85
[E] alexandre.de-vaivre@ota.fn.socgen.com

SG Cowen Securities Corporation

Financial Square, New York, NY 10005
Tel: (212) 495 6000
Website: www.socgen.com

Debt Capital Markets / Fixed Income
Fixed-Income Repo
Marketing & Product Development

Anthony Sorrentino *Director* [T] **495 6485** [F] **480 2838**
[E] sorrentina@cowen.com

Trading

Terry Stephenson *Director, Corporate Bonds*
Maurice Marcott *Vice President, Corporates & Repos*
Jill Jacobson *Assistant Vice President, Equities*
Bob Lamentino *Senior Stock Loan, Equities*
Ken Ward *Vice President International Equities*
Sheila Mayers *Senior Stock Loan, International Equities*
Lori Zaccardi *Senior Stock Loan, Equities*

SG (Société Générale) - Emerging Markets Repo

1221 Avenue of the Americas, New York, NY 10020
Tel: (212) 278 5316 **Fax:** (212) 278 4520
Website: www.socgen.com

Debt Capital Markets / Fixed Income
Fixed-Income Repo
Marketing & Product Development

Rolando Pantojia *USA* [T] **278 5369** [F] **278 5470**
Debbie Wloch-Vogt *UK* [T] +44 (171) 256 6964 [F] +44 (171) 571 2999
Jean-Marc Croisy *Hong Kong* [T] +852 2583 8731 [F] +852 2869 9312
Shingo Izawa *Japan* [T] +81 (3) 5549 5238 [F] +81 (3) 5549 5259

Trading

Antoine de Murat [T] **278 5347** [F] **278 5470**

Smith Barney Inc

5th Floor, 390 Greenwich Street, New York, NY 10013
Tel: (212) 723 7600 **Fax:** (212) 723 8826; (212) 723 8839

Senior Executive Officers
Chairman & Chief Executive   James Dimon
Vice Chairman & COO   Steven D Black
Vice Chairman   James S Boshart III
Vice Chairman   Robert Druskin
Vice Chairman   Robert H Lessin
Vice Chairman   William J Mills II
Vice Chairman   Michael B Panitch
SEVP & Chief Administrative Officer   Robert A Case
Senior Executive Vice President   Paul Underwood
Executive Vice President   Jay Mandelbaum

Senior Executive Officers (cont)
Financial Director — Charles W Scharf *EVP & Chief Financial Officer*
Managing Director — Joan Guggenheimer
EVP & Secretary — A George Saks

Debt Capital Markets / Fixed Income

Fixed-Income Repo
Head of Repo — Timothy Irwin ☎ **723 7448**
Marketing & Product Development — Robert Garison
Trading — Michelle Mugnai *London Desk*
Thomas Sapio *New York Desk*
Sales — Robert Garison

Equity Capital Markets
Tel: 723 7600 **Fax**: 723 8826

Equity Repo / Securities Lending
Head of Prime Brokerage — Sal Campo *Managing Director* ☎ **723 4891**

SouthTrust Bank NA
Head Office

420 North 20th Street, Birmingham, AL 35203
PO Box 2554, Birmingham, AL 35290
Tel: (205) 254 5217; (205) 254 5218 **Fax**: (205) 254 5656 **Telex**: 59837 SOUTHTRUST **Swift**: SOTR US 44 BIR
Website: www.southtrust.com

Senior Executive Officers
Chairman — Julian W Banton
Executive Vice President — Fred C Crum Jr
Executive Vice President — J Mike Battle
Executive Vice President — Thomas H Coley
Executive Vice President — R Glenn Eubanks
Executive Vice President — William E Patterson Jr
Executive Vice President — C Perry Relfe
Executive Vice President — Richard S White

SouthTrust Corporation

420 North 20th Street, Birmingham, AL 35203
PO Box 2554, Birmingham, AL 35290
Tel: (205) 254 5680 **Fax**: (205) 254 5404 **Telex**: 59837 SOTRUST BH **Swift**: SOTR US 44 BIR **Cable**: SOTR BHM
Website: www.southtrust.com

Senior Executive Officers
Chairman — Wallace D Malone Jr
EVP — James W Rainer Jr
Treasurer — Aubrey D Barnard

Standard Bank of South Africa
Representative Office

153 East 53rd Street, 38th Floor, New York, NY 10022
Tel: (212) 407 5020 **Fax**: (212) 407 5027

Senior Executive Officers
Senior Vice President — Anthony Strutt

Standard Chartered Bank
Full Branch Office

7 World Trade Center, New York, NY 10048
Tel: (212) 667 0700 **Fax**: (212) 667 0535 **Telex**: 177705 **Swift**: SCBL US 33 **Reuters**: SCNY; SCNX

Senior Executive Officers
General Manager — Robert P McDonald

Others (Senior Executives)
Institutional Banking Group — Seifsh Kawamura *Senior Vice President*

Administration
Head of Administration — Ralph Schulz *Vice President*

UNITED STATES (+1)   www.euromoneydirectory.com

Standard New York Inc   Subsidiary Company
38th Floor, 153 East 53rd Street, New York, NY 10022
Tel: (212) 407 5000 Fax: (212) 407 5025

Senior Executive Officers
Managing Director / General Manager   Sean O'Conner

State Street Corporation   Head Office
225 Franklin Street, Boston, MA 02101
PO Box 351, Boston, MA 02101
Tel: (617) 786 3000 Fax: (617) 985 1709 Telex: 797976 Swift: SBOS US 33
Website: www.statestreet.com

Senior Executive Officers
Chairman & Chief Executive	Marshall Carter ☏ 664 3792
Vice Chairman, Financial Markets Group	Dale L Carleton ☏ 664 3471
President & COO	David Spina ☏ 664 3125
Chief Executive Officer	Marshall Carter Chairman & Chief Executive ☏ 664 3792
Financial Director	Ronald O'Kelley Chief Financial Officer ☏ 644 1110
Chief Operating Officer	David Spina President & COO ☏ 664 3125

Others (Senior Executives)

Tenley E Albright Director
Joseph A Baute Director
I MacAllister Booth Director
James I Cash Jr Director
Truman S Casner Director
Nader F Darehshori Director
Arthur L Goldstein Director
David P Gruber Director
Charles F Kaye Director
John M Kucharski Director
Charles R LaMantia Director
David B Perini Director
Dennis J Picard Director
Alfred Poe Director
Bernard W Reznicek Director
Diana Chapman Walsh Director
Robert E Weissman Director

General-Lending (DCM, SL)
Head of Corporate Banking   Jacquelyn Chermesino SVP, Corporate Banking ☏ 664 3629

General-Investment
Head of Investment   F Charles Hindmarsh SVP, Investment Banking ☏ 664 4020

General - Treasury
Head of Treasury   Stanley W Shelton EVP, Global Treasury ☏ 664 3279

Department: Global Investor Services Group
President & CEO, Boston Financial Data Services	Joseph L Hooley ☏ 774 3292
Executive Vice President	Ronald E Logue ☏ 985 2090
SVP, Americas	Thomas J McCrossan ☏ +1 (816) 843 5277
SVP, Asia / Pacific	Robert R Williams ☏ +852 2840 5431
SVP, Europe	Gary E Enos ☏ 985 6882
Chief Executive Officer	Joseph L Hooley President & CEO, Boston Financial Data Services ☏ 774 3292

Department: State Street Global Advisors
Chairman & Chief Executive Officer	Nicholas A Lopardo ☏ 664 3312
President	Timothy B Harbert ☏ 664 3217
President, State Street Brokerage Services Inc	Nicholas Bonn ☏ 664 4913
Chief Executive Officer	Nicholas A Lopardo Chairman & Chief Executive Officer ☏ 664 3312
MD, Retirement Investor Services	James S Phalen ☏ 376 7300

Others (Senior Executives)

Marc V Simons Chief of Staff ☏ 664 3310
Chris A Hynes Executive Vice President ☏ 664 3460

Department: Institutional Investor Services
Executive Vice President   James J Darr ☏ 985 7505

Others (Senior Executives)

Laurette M Bryan SVP, State Street Analytics ☏ 985 2150
Timothy B Hagerty SVP, Client Services ☏ 985 6063

www.euromoneydirectory.com	UNITED STATES (+1)

Others (Senior Executives) (cont)

Anthony C Perkins *SVP, Client Information Services* ☎ 985 1645
Robert R Tarter *SVP, Sales & Marketing* ☎ 985 3784
Kevin E Connolly *SVP, Public Funds* ☎ 985 0604
Lee B Jones *SVP, Public Funds* ☎ 985 7918
Stephen C Hooley *SVP, Master Trust* ☎ 985 2376
William M Mahoney *SVP, Master Trust* ☎ 985 7648
Katherine A Morello *SVP, Master Trust* ☎ 985 5558

Debt Capital Markets / Fixed Income
Head of Fixed Income Trading

R Hilliard Ebling *SVP, Securities Trading* ☎ 664 3437

Equity Capital Markets
Head of Trading

R Hilliard Ebling *SVP, Securities Trading* ☎ 664 3437

Equity Repo / Securities Lending
Head

Ralph Vitale *Executive Vice President* ☎ 664 2580

Syndicated Lending
Loan-Related Activities
Trade Finance

Schofield Andrews III *SVP, Global Trade Banking* ☎ 664 3145

Other (Trade Finance)

Charles E Dahm *SVP, Real Estate* ☎ 664 3686
David M Gaffney *SVP, Specialized Lending* ☎ 664 3618
John D Rusher III *SVP, Asset Based Finance* ☎ 664 3613

Corporate Finance / M&A Advisory
Head of Corporate Finance

Ronald O'Kelley *Chief Financial Officer* ☎ 644 1110

Settlement / Clearing
Operations

John R Towers *EVP, Global Operations* ☎ 985 1021
John J Robinson *SVP, Global Payment Systems* ☎ 985 6294
Christopher Roberts *SVP, Asia / Pacific* ☎ +61 (2) 9323 6601

Other

Richard Heckinger *SVP, EMU Project* ☎ 985 0760

Global Custody
Head of Global Custody

Mary Fenoglio *Senior Vice President* ☎ 985 5277

Asset Management
Other (Asset Management)
Corporate Trust

James A Quale *Senior Vice President* ☎ 664 5300

Other Departments
Cash Management
Economic Research

George Bird *Executive Vice Chairman* ☎ 664 3940
Martin J Rogosa *SVP, Financial Information & Metrics* ☎ 664 4555

Department: Credit & Risk Policy
Chief Credit Officer

Joseph W Chow *Executive Vice President* ☎ 664 4296
Sanford H England *SVP, Electronics Division* ☎ 664 3882
Nancy H Loucks *SVP, Credit & Risk Officer* ☎ 664 3997

Administration
Head of Marketing

Charles Cassidy *SVP* ☎ 664 6311

Technology & Systems
Information Technology

James MacDonald *SVP & Chief Information Officer* ☎ 985 9563
Alexander T Sopyla *SVP, Global Horizon Architecture* ☎ 985 9562
Brian Walsh *SVP, Global Custody* ☎ 985 8827
Mary L Ryan *SVP, Global Banking / Payment Systems* ☎ 985 9302

Financial Markets Group

Barry C Weinstein *SVP, Technology* ☎ 664 3598

Global Network & Computing Services

John R O'Donnell *Senior Vice President* ☎ 985 9530

Legal / In-House Counsel

Maureen Scannell-Bateman ☎ 664 3253

Public Relations
Industry Affairs & Public Relations

F Gregory Ahern *Senior Vice President* ☎ 664 6308

Corporate Communications
Investor Relations
Community Affairs

Karen A Wharton *Senior Vice President* ☎ 664 3477
George A Russell *Senior Vice President* ☎ 664 3866

Accounts / Audit

Drew Breakspear *SVP & General Auditor* ☎ 985 9147
Rex S Schute *SVP & Chief Accountant* ☎ 664 4501

Other (Administration)
Commercial Banking Group

William M Reghitto *Executive Vice President* ☎ 664 3644
Ralph L Sautter *SVP, Metropolitan* ☎ 664 3679

Management Information Services
Corporate Financial Planning
Global Human Resources

James E Curran *Senior Vice President* ☎ 985 2217
Steven Arst *Senior Vice President* ☎ 664 3478
Susan Comcau *Executive Vice President* ☎ 985 0925

Euromoney Directory 1999 **2001**

UNITED STATES (+1)   www.euromoneydirectory.com

Sumitomo Bank of New York Trust Company

277 Park Avenue, New York, NY
Tel: (212) 224 5400 Fax: (212) 224 5444 Telex: 232407

Senior Executive Officers
President   Shinichi Ito ☎ **224 5401**
Executive Vice President   Masao Toyama ☎ **224 5447**
Senior Vice President   Hideo Maeda ☎ **224 5402**
Senior Vice President   Jofeph Jahn ☎ **224 5409**
Administration
Head of Administration   Hideo Maeda Senior Vice President ☎ **224 5402**

Sumitomo Bank Securities Inc

277 Park Avenue, New York, NY 10172
Tel: (212) 224 5373 Fax: (212) 758 3937

Senior Executive Officers
Chairman   Norah Hughes
Financial Director   Bob Seery Chief Financial Officer
Debt Capital Markets / Fixed Income
Eurobonds
Head of Trading   Bryan Barboni
Libor-Based / Floating-Rate Products
FRN Trading   Bryan Barboni
Fixed-Income Repo
Trading   Salvatore Guaftella ☎ **224 5324**

Sumitomo Trust & Banking Co (USA)   Subsidiary Company

527 Madison Avenue, New York, NY 10022
Tel: (212) 303 9200 Fax: (212) 303 9250; (212) 644 3077 Telex: ITT 428538

Senior Executive Officers
Chairman   Hirokazu Mizukami ☎ **326 0505**
President   Shigeaki Koga ☎ **303 9201**
Company Secretary   Takeshi Inoue ☎ **303 9222**
Equity Capital Markets
Equity Repo / Securities Lending
Head   Larry Stoia Head of Securities Lending ☎ **303 9263** F **303 9225**
Global Custody
Head of Global Custody   Richard MacArthur ☎ **303 9242**
Administration
Legal / In-House Counsel
   Bruce Ortwine ☎ **418 4806**
Accounts / Audit
   Robert Kirlay ☎ **303 9319**

The Sumitomo Trust & Banking Company Limited

Representative Office

Suite 2975, 10 South Wacker Drive, Chicago, IL 60606
Tel: (312) 993 3400 Fax: (312) 993 3414 Telex: 6730268

Senior Executive Officers
Chief Representative   Naoya Takeuchi
Syndicated Lending
Loan-Related Activities
Project Finance   Mark R Long
   Paul Letourneau
Corporate Finance / M&A Advisory
Head of Corporate Finance   Mark R Long
Head of Mergers & Acquisition   Paul Letourneau

2002 Euromoney Directory 1999

www.euromoneydirectory.com   UNITED STATES (+1)

The Sumitomo Trust & Banking Company Limited
3rd Floor, 527 Madison Avenue, New York, NY 10172
Tel: (212) 326 0600 **Fax:** (212) 644 3025 **Telex:** 222049

Senior Executive Officers
Managing Director / General Manager   Isao Takeuchi

Sun Trust Bank Tampa Bay
401 E Jackson Street, Tampa, Florida 33602
PO Box 3303, Tampa, Florida FL 33601
Tel: (813) 224 2635 **Telex:** 542210 **Swift:** SNTR US 33

SunTrust Banks Atlanta   Subsidiary Company
Formerly known as: Trust Company Bank
25 Park Place, Atlanta, GA 30303
PO Box 4418, Atlanta, GA 30302
Tel: (404) 827 6510 **Fax:** (404) 532 0200 **Telex:** SY 2210 **Swift:** SNTR US 3A **Cable:** TRUSCO, ATLANTA
Website: www.suntrust.com

Senior Executive Officers
Chairman, President & CEO   Robert Long ☎ 588 7645
Chief Executive Officer   Robert Long *Chairman, President & CEO* ☎ 588 7645
International Division   Gian Rossi-Espagnet *Senior Vice President* ☎ 827 6509

Foreign Exchange
Tel: 588 8123 **Fax:** 827 6348
Head of Foreign Exchange   Robert Hinton *Group Vice President*

Svenska Handelsbanken   Full Branch Office
37th Floor, 153 East 53rd Street, New York, NY 10022
Tel: (212) 326 5100 **Fax:** (212) 326 5196 **Telex:** 1561322 SVNK UT **Swift:** HAND US 33
Website: www.handelsbanken.se

Senior Executive Officers
Managing Director   Stephan Oxenborg

General-Lending (DCM, SL)
Head of Corporate Banking   Chip Bacon *VP, US Corporate Banking*

Swedbank   Full Branch Office
20th Floor, 12 East 49th Street, New York, NY 10017
Tel: (212) 486 8400 **Fax:** (212) 486 3200 **Telex:** 49606814 **Swift:** SWED US 33

Senior Executive Officers
President   Lennart Lundberg

TAIB Securities Incorporated   Subsidiary Company
Suite 1902, 450 Park Avenue, New York, NY 10022
Tel: (212) 832 7137 **Fax:** (212) 832 7122 **Telex:** 662177 TAIB UR **Email:** tsi@taibsec.com

Senior Executive Officers
Managing Director   Lawrence Chaleff
Vice President   Meenaz Dhanani
Assistant Vice President   Aliya Mamdani

Administration
Head of Administration   Marva Joseph *Office Manager*

Euromoney Directory 1999 **2003**

UNITED STATES (+1)   www.euromoneydirectory.com

Taiwan Business Bank
Full Branch Office

Alternative trading name: The Medium Business Bank of Taiwan
633 West 5th Street, Suite #2280, Los Angeles, CA 90071
Tel: (213) 892 1260 **Fax:** (213) 892 1270 **Telex:** 49653674 TBBLA **Swift:** MBBT US 6L **Email:** mail@tbbla.com

Senior Executive Officers
VP & General Manager   Henry Yee
International Division   Ping Chow *Manager*

Others (Senior Executives)
Chief Dealer   Jason Chen *Senior Manager*

TC Ziraat Bankasi
Full Branch Office

330 Madison Avenue, New York, NY 10017
Tel: (212) 557 5612 **Fax:** (212) 490 8076 **Telex:** 236558 **Swift:** TCZB US 33 **Reuters:** ZBAN

Senior Executive Officers
Chief Executive Officer   Mehmet Akkoc *Senior Country Officer*
                                       Frank Lehmann *Deputy Senior Country Officer*

TCW Group
Head Office

Suite 1800, 865 South Figueroa Street, Los Angeles, CA 90017
Tel: (213) 244 0000 **Fax:** (213) 244 0741 **Email:** deleol@tcwgroup.com

Senior Executive Officers
Chairman & CEO   Robert A Day
Vice Chairman   Ernest O Ellison
President, Trust Company of the West   Thomas E Larkin
President, The TCW Group, Inc   Marc I Stern
EVP & Chief Administrative Officer   Alvin R Albe
Group Managing Director   Robert D Beyer

Debt Capital Markets / Fixed Income
Other   Walter J Blasberg *Core Fixed Income & TCW Insurance Advisor*
                                       Jeffrey E Gundlach *Core Fixed Income*
                                       Frederick H Horton *Core Fixed Income*
                                       Walter J Blasberg *Core Fixed Income & TCW Insurance Advisor*
                                       Mark L Gold *Senior Loans & Bank Dept.*
                                       Frederick H Horten *Stable Value Fixed Income*

Bonds - General
Municipal Bonds   Walter J Blasberg *Core Fixed Income & TCW Insurance Advisor*
                                       Robert J Martin

High Yield / Junk Bonds
Other   Mark L Attanasio
                                       Mark D Senkpiel
                                       Melissa V Weiler

Mortgage-Backed Securities
Head of Trading   Philip A Barach
                                       Jeffrey E Gundlach *Core Fixed Income*
                                       Frederick H Horton *Core Fixed Income*

Equity Capital Markets
Other (Domestic Equities)
Concentrated Core   Glen E Bickerstaff
                                       Robert A Day *Chairman & CEO*
                                       Douglas S Foremann
                                       clifford H Krauss
Earnings Momentum   Nicholas J Capuano
                                       Charles Larsen
                                       Lisa Zeller
Enhanced 500   Walter A French *Advisor*
Large Cap Growth   Wendy S Barker
                                       Douglas S Foremann
Large Cap Value   Thomas K McKissick
Mid-Cap Growth   Christopher J Ainley
                                       Douglas S Foremann
Small Cap Growth   Christopher J Ainley
                                       Douglas S Foremann
                                       Charles Larsen

Other (Domestic Equities) (cont)

Value Added — Tyler D Davis
Nicholas F Galluccio
Susan I Schottenfeld

Value Opportunities — Tyler D Davis
Nicholas F Galluccio
Susan I Schottenfeld

Other (International Equity)

Asia Pacific — Shaun C K Chan
Michael Lai
Terence F Mahony

Emerging Markets — Shannon M Callan
Shaun C K Chan
Michael Lai
Terence F Mahony
Michael P Reilly
Michael J Ward

Emerging Markets Fixed Income — Javier Baz
Nathan B Sandler

European — James M Burns
Saker A Nusseibeh

Global Value Funds — John A Healey

International — James M Burns
Shannon M Callan
Shaun C K Chan
Stephen J Harker
Terence F Mahony
Saker A Nusseibeh
Michael P Reilly

International Fixed Income — Arnold A Egli
Stevan M Koehler
Nathan B Sandler

Japanese — Stephen J Harker
Peter A Kirkman

Latin America — Shannon M Callan
Terence F Mahony
Michael P Reilly

Other (Convertibles)

Convertible Securities — Robert M Hanisee
Kevin A Hunter
Thomas D Lyon

Settlement / Clearing

Operations — Elnoise J Davis

Administration

Head of Administration — David S DeVito

Legal / In-House Counsel

Michael E Cahill

Compliance

Hilaey G D Lord

Other (Administration)

Tax — Peter A Brown
Finance — William C Sonneborn

Teachers Insurance

730 Third Avenue, New York, NY 10017
Tel: (212) 490 9000 **Fax:** (212) 916 6691

Debt Capital Markets / Fixed Income

Fixed-Income Repo
Marketing & Product Development
Trading — Steve Traum ☏ 916 4365 ✉ 916 6691
Lenora Suozzo *Manager, Securities Lending*
Mariann Oddo *Securities Lending*

UNITED STATES (+1) www.euromoneydirectory.com

TFS Derivatives Corp
Head Office

180 Maiden Lane, New York, NY 10038
Tel: (212) 943 8700 **Fax:** (212) 943 8504 **Telex:** 276644 DMTRUR **Reuters:** TFSN (Dealing); TRDO (Page)

Senior Executive Officers
President   Jeffrey Mehan

Tokai Bank of California
Subsidiary Company

6th Floor, One California Plaza, 300 South Grand Avenue, Los Angeles, CA 90071
Tel: (213) 972 0200 **Fax:** (213) 972 0204
Website: www.tokai.com

Senior Executive Officers
President   Sadao Akiyama
Financial Director   Richard Belliston *EVP & Chief Financial Officer* ☏ **972 0496**
First VP / Corporate Secretary   Kenneth Taylor ☏ **972 0546**

Other Departments
Chief Credit Officer   Douglas Weld *SVP & Chief Credit Officer* ☏ **972 0219**

Administration
Head of Administration   Patricia Bryan *FVP / Manager, Operations Administration*
                                                  ☏ **+1 (626) 812 3334**
Business Development   Robert Altobello *EVP / Branch Administration, Buisness Developement*
                                                  ☏ **972 0469**

Technology & Systems
                                                  Robert Reider *SVP / Director, Information Services* ☏ **+1 (626) 812 3302**

Legal / In-House Counsel
                                                  Anne Elder *VP / Senior Counsel & Manager* ☏ **972 0255**

Compliance
                                                  Debra Roorda *VP / Senior Compliance Officer* ☏ **972 0258**

Public Relations
                                                  Rian Lidschin *VP / Marketing Director* ☏ **972 0278**

Accounts / Audit
                                                  Gerald Riss *SVP / General Auditor* ☏ **972 0509**

Tokai Bank of California
Full Branch Office

505 Montgomery Street, San Francisco, CA 94111
Tel: (415) 399 0660; (415) 399 0669 **Fax:** (415) 291 8187; (415) 399 1627
Website: www.tokai.com

Senior Executive Officers
SVP & General Manager   Shigeyoshi Sato 🖷 **399 9736**

Syndicated Lending
Head of Origination   Richard Israel *Regional Vice President*

The Tokai Bank Limited
Agency

Suite 2802, Marquis Two Tower, 285 Peachtree Center Avenue NE, Atlanta, GA 30303
Tel: (404) 880 0000 **Fax:** (404) 653 0737 **Telex:** 543338 TOKAI ATL

Senior Executive Officers
Managing Director / General Manager   Nobuo Minaminkawa

The Tokai Bank Limited
Full Branch Office

Suite 3600, 181 West Madison Street, Chicago, IL 60602
Tel: (312) 853 3400 **Fax:** (312) 977 0003 **Telex:** 206269 TOKAI CGO

Senior Executive Officers
Managing Director / General Manager   Shusui Toyoda

UNITED STATES (+1)

The Tokai Bank Limited
Representative Office

Turfway Ridge Office Park II, Suite 210, 7310 Turfway Road, Florence, KY 41042
Tel: (606) 746 1800 Fax: (606) 746 1799

Senior Executive Officers
Chief Representative   Shuji Tanaka

The Tokai Bank Limited
Agency

7th Floor, One California Plaza, 300 South Grand Avenue, Los Angeles, CA 90071
Tel: (213) 972 8400 Fax: (213) 689 1700 Telex: 215245 TOKAIBANK LSA

Senior Executive Officers
General Manager & Agent   Sadao Akiyama

The Tokai Bank Limited
Full Branch Office

Park Avenue Plaza, 55 East 52nd Street, New York, NY 10055
Tel: (212) 339 1200 Fax: (212) 754 2153 Telex: 422857 TOKAI

Senior Executive Officers
General Manager   Shinichiro Mizuno

The Tokai Bank Limited
Representative Office

505 Montgomery Street, San Francisco, CA 94111
Tel: (415) 956 1101 Fax: (415) 956 1770

Senior Executive Officers
Chief Representative   Shigeyoshi Sato

Tradition Financial Services Inc
Subsidiary Company

180 Maiden Lane, New York, NY 10038
Tel: (212) 943 8100 Fax: (212) 943 8504 Telex: 276644 DMTRUR Reuters: TRSN (Dealing); TRDO (Page)

Senior Executive Officers
President   David Pinchin ☏ **943 2787**
Managing Director   Julian Harding ☏ **943 2787**

Tradition Financial Services Inc
Subsidiary Company

5th Floor, 680 Washington Boulevard, Stamford, CT 06901
Tel: (203) 351 9520 Fax: (203) 351 9567

Senior Executive Officers
President   David Pinchin ☏ **351 9555**
Managing Director   Julian Harding ☏ **351 9555**

Tradition (Government Securities) Inc

61 Broadway, New York, NY 10006
Tel: (212) 797 7330 Fax: (212) 797 7207

Senior Executive Officers
President   Emil Assentato
Managing Director / General Manager Raymond C Baccala

Tradition (North America) Inc
Full Branch Office

Suite 1320, 865 South Figueroa Street, Los Angeles, CA 90017
Tel: (213) 362 3212; (213) 362 3200 Fax: (213) 622 9561; (213) 627 2060 Telex: 6831924 Reuters: TRLA

Senior Executive Officers
Others (Senior Executives)
                                    William G Whyte Senior Vice President & Manager ☏ **622 4127**
                                    Joseph K Y Wong Senior Vice President & Assistant Manager ☏ **362 3200**

UNITED STATES (+1)   www.euromoneydirectory.com

Tradition (North America) Inc

61 Broadway, New York, NY 10006
Tel: (212) 797 5300 Fax: (212) 797 7207 Telex: 226664

Senior Executive Officers
Managing Director — Emil Assentato
Others (Senior Executives)
  Raymond C Baccala *Executive Vice President*
  J P Mahon *Executive Vice President*
  James L O'Reilly *Executive Vice President*
  Frank Randazzo *Executive Vice President*

Debt Capital Markets / Fixed Income
Emerging Market Bonds
Head of Emerging Markets — William Knowles *Global Manager / Director*
Fixed-Income Repo
Head of Repo — Raymond Baccala *EVP, Managing Director for Repos* ☎ 797 7330

Money Markets
Department: EuroDollar Markets
Money Markets - General
European Manager — Robert O'Reilly
Japanese Manager — Michael Scarrone
Domestic Manager — Stephen Marano

Tullett & Tokyo Forex Inc   Subsidiary Company

80 Pine Street, New York, NY 10005
Tel: (212) 208 2000 Fax: (212) 208 2019; (212) 558 6546

Senior Executive Officers
President, North America — Tim Boyle
Managing Director — James Avena
Managing Director — Henry Ann
Managing Director — Mark Perkins
Managing Director — Mervin Wilkinson ☎ 208 2025

Debt Capital Markets / Fixed Income
Department: Capital Markets
Regional Head — Mark Perkins *Managing Director*
Country Head — Vinayek Singh *Director* ☎ 208 3794
Eurobonds
Trading (Sovereigns) — Mark Perkins *Managing Director*
Asset-Backed Securities / Securitization
Global Head — James Avena *Managing Director*
Fixed-Income Repo
Head of Repo — Ed Mardovich *Director* ☎ 208 2100

Money Markets
Regional Head — Mark Perkins *Managing Director*
Country Head — Donald Robson *Director* ☎ 208 2150

Foreign Exchange
Regional Head — Mervin Wilkinson *Managing Director* ☎ 208 2025

Risk Management
Other Currency Swap / FX Options Personnel
Forex Options & Futures — Mark Perkins *Managing Director*
  George Flynn *Director* ☎ 208 3845

Administration
Head of Administration — Stephen Baker *Director* ☎ 208 3903
  Mario Macrina *Vice President* ☎ 208 2001

Turan Corporation   Head Office

21st Floor, 160 Federal Street, Boston, MA 02110
Tel: (617) 439 9772 Fax: (617) 439 7614 Telex: 928443

Senior Executive Officers
Managing Director — Robert P Smith
Chief Executive Officer — Saleh Daher *Managing Director*
Financial Director — Michael Riemer *Finance Director*

2008 Euromoney Directory 1999

www.euromoneydirectory.com UNITED STATES (+1)

Debt Capital Markets / Fixed Income
Non-Domestic Government Bonds
Russian FTOs   Nathaniel Lovell *Assistant Vice President*
                        Elizabeth Kalifa *Assistant Vice President*
Nigerian Promissory Notes   Frank Elias *Assistant Vice President*
Settlement / Clearing
Fixed-Income Settlement   Richard Kream *Vice President, Legal*
Other Departments
Proprietary Trading   Robert P Smith *Managing Director*
Administration
Legal / In-House Counsel
                        Richard Kream *Vice President, Legal*
Public Relations
                        Gerri Parker *Assistant Vice President*

UBS AG

141 W Jackson Boulevard, Chicago, IL 60604
Tel: (312) 554 5000 **Fax:** (312) 554 5835

Senior Executive Officers
Others (Senior Executives)
                        M Willis *Branch Manager*
Department: Warburg Dillon Read
Others (Senior Executives)
Information Technology   P O'Donnell
Fixed Income   M Levin
Warburg Dillon Read Futures Inc.   K Slepicka *President*

UBS AG   Representative Office

Transco Tower, 2800 Post Oak Boulevard, Suite 5858, Houston, TX 77056
Tel: (713) 627 8858; (800) 627 8853 **Fax:** (713) 627 9823

Senior Executive Officers
Others (Senior Executives)
                        J Zeller
Settlement / Clearing
Operations   R Galdamez
Other Departments
Private Banking   J Zeller *International*
                        F Restrepo *International*

UBS AG   Agency

1100 Louisiana, Suite 4500, Houston, TX 77002
Tel: (713) 655 6500 **Fax:** (713) 655 6590

Senior Executive Officers
Others (Senior Executives)
                        W Rovere
Settlement / Clearing
Operations   D Gonzales
Other Departments
Private Banking   W Rovere *Domestic*
                        M Beeler *Domestic*
                        L Fugit *Domestic*

UBS AG   Full Branch Office

633 West Fifth Street, 69th Floor, Los Angeles, CA 90071
Tel: (213) 253 1900; (213) 538 1111 **Fax:** (213) 680 1944

Senior Executive Officers
Others (Senior Executives)
                        R Schaefer

UNITED STATES (+1) — www.euromoneydirectory.com

UBS AG (cont)

Settlement / Clearing
Operations — L Castro

Other Departments
Private Banking
P Bennett
P Dwyer
R Gasparri
F Huber
H Jaeggi
D Khouri
S Lendi

UBS AG — Agency

701 Brickell Avenue, Suite 3250, Miami, FL 33131
Tel: (305) 375 0110 **Fax:** (305) 375 0303

Senior Executive Officers
Others (Senior Executives)
D Stirnimann *Agency Head*

Settlement / Clearing
Operations — P Leslie

Other Departments
Department: International Private Investors
Private Banking
D Stirnimann
S Wernli
V Cardentey
H Fehr
M Ferrer
M Guiteras
F Kreplak
A Neuburger
R Paz
J Brennan *Domestic Private Investors*

Administration
Other (Administration)
International Advisor — E Schobel

UBS AG — Full Branch Office

299 Park Avenue, New York, NY 10171-0026
Tel: (212) 821 3000 **Fax:** (212) 821 3285

Senior Executive Officers
New York Branch Manager — R Mills
Department: Warburg Dillon Read Division
Chief Executive Officer — R Capone *CEO, Americas*

Others (Senior Executives)
J M Frey *Chief of Staff, Americas*
R Mills *CFO, Americas*
R Dinerstein *General Counsel, Americas*

UBS AG

UBS Tower, 10 East 50th Street, New York, NY 10022
PO Box, Church Street Station, New York, NY 10008
Tel: (212) 574 3000 **Fax:** (212) 574 5499

Senior Executive Officers
Others (Senior Executives)
C Grigioni *Business Area Head, The Americas*
M M Miller *Chief of Staff*
P J Watson *Chief Operating Officer*

Other Departments
Private Banking
M M Miller *Head*
J Berger *Europe / Asia*

www.euromoneydirectory.com					UNITED STATES (+1)

Other Departments (cont)
R Burri *Latin America*
L Gore *Mid-West*
J Kaye *South*
R Schaefer *West*
R Simon *East*

## UBS AG												Full Branch Office
Suite 2500, 101 California Street, San Francisco, CA 94111
Tel: (415) 774 3492 Fax: (415) 788 2067

Senior Executive Officers
Others (Senior Executives)
								D Magee *Branch Manager*

Other Departments
Private Banking					D Magee
									C Ruegg
									H Brady
									E Scott
									M Asuncion
									R Gadola

UBS AG
Warburg Dillon Read Center, 677 Washington Boulevard, Stamford, CT 06901
PO Box 120300, Stamford, CT 06912-0300
Tel: (203) 719 3000 Fax: (203) 719 5499

Senior Executive Officers
Stamford Branch Manager			G Brown
Department: Warburg Dillon Read Division
Chief Executive Officer			R Capone *CEO, Americas*

Others (Senior Executives)
									J M Frey *Chief of Staff, Americas*
Finance & Control					R Mills *CFO, Americas*

Debt Capital Markets / Fixed Income
Other (Emerging Markets Bonds)
Emerging Markets Trade Finance	J Costas

Syndicated Lending
Other (Trade Finance)
Global Trade Finance				R Bandelier

Foreign Exchange
FX Traders / Sales People
*Foreign Exchange / Precious Metals Spot	M Guarino
Trading*

Risk Management
Foreign Exchange Derivatives / Risk Management
Country Head						A Kreysar

Other (Exchange-Traded Derivatives)
Credit Risk Management			G Brown *CCO, Americas*
Market Risk Control				M Stockman

Settlement / Clearing
Operations						E Pittarelli

Other Departments
Private Banking					P Skaperdas

Administration
Legal / In-House Counsel
Legal								R Dinerstein *General Counsel, Americas*

Other (Administration)
Human Resources					S Baird

Euromoney Directory 1999   **2011**

UNITED STATES (+1)   www.euromoneydirectory.com

UBS Brinson

UBS Tower, 10 East 50th Street, New York, NY 10010
Tel: (212) 574 3057 Fax: (212) 574 3200

Senior Executive Officers
Others (Senior Executives)
Senior Executive Officer   G Benz

UI USA Inc
Subsidiary Company

Suite 309, 620 Fifth Avenue, New York, NY 10020
Tel: (212) 218 5028; (212) 218 5025 Fax: (212) 218 5035

Senior Executive Officers
Chairman & Chief Executive   Gilles Gramat
President & COO   Allison Molkenthin
Chief Executive Officer   Gilles Gramat *Chairman & Chief Executive*
Chief Operating Officer   Allison Molkenthin *President & COO*

Corporate Finance / M&A Advisory
Tel: 218 5025 Fax: 218 5035
Global Head   Allison Molkenthin *President & COO*

UniCredito Italiano SpA
Full Branch Office

Formerly known as: Credito Italiano SpA

375 Park Avenue, New York, NY 10152
Tel: (212) 546 9600 Fax: (212) 546 9675; (212) 826 8623 Telex: 424690 CRITNY Swift: CRITUS 33 Reuters: CRIN
Telerate: Recipient

Senior Executive Officers
SVP & Manager   Carmelo Mazza

Money Markets
Tel: 546 9615 Fax: 826 8623
Head of Money Markets   Maureen Travers *Chief Dealer* ☎ 546 9615

Wholesale Deposits
Head of Sales   Maureen Travers *Chief Dealer* ☎ 546 9615

Foreign Exchange
Head of Foreign Exchange   Anthony R Corea *Treasurer* ☎ 546 9618
Head of Trading   Vincenzo Furbesco *Chief Dealer* ☎ 546 9618

FX Traders / Sales People
Sales   Dan Tausek *Senior Marketer* ☎ 546 9617
Trader   Dario Brusch ☎ 546 9619

Risk Management
Head of Risk Management   Russell Tashiro *Assistant Treasurer & Risk Manager* ☎ 546 9641

Settlement / Clearing
Regional Head   John L Coté *VP & Operations Manager* ☎ 546 9671

Other Departments
Correspondent Banking   Francesca Dadea-Mohr *Assistant Treasurer* ☎ 546 9661

Union Bancaire Privée
Representative Office

Suite 1525, 630 Fifth Avenue, New York, NY 10111
Tel: (212) 265 3320 Fax: (212) 247 4310 Telex: 2474310

Senior Executive Officers
Representative   Maurice de Picciotto

Union Bank of California

15th Floor, 475 Sansome Street, San Francisco, CA 94111
Tel: (415) 296 6529; (800) 880 0818 Fax: (415) 291 7838 Telex: 215748 Swift: BOFC US 33 MGC Cable: BANK OFCAL
Website: www.uboc.com

Senior Executive Officers
Chairman   Osamu Yamada
President   Yasumasa Gomi

2012   Euromoney Directory 1999

Equity Capital Markets
Equity Repo / Securities Lending
Head   Ellen Koerner *VP & Manager* ☎ 296 6529 ℻ 291 7838
Head of Trading   Christine Settle *Assistant Vice President*
                                        Lynn Lorusso *Vice President*
                                        Glen Schneiderman *Vice President*
                                        Michael Jasmine *Assistant Vice President*

United Overseas Bank Limited   Agency
10th Floor, UOB Building, 592 5th Avenue, New York, NY 10036
Tel: (212) 382 0088 **Fax:** (212) 382 1881 **Swift:** UOVB US 33

Senior Executive Officers
Managing Director & General Manager   Kwong Yew Wong ☎ 382 0088

US Bancorp   Head Office
Formerly known as: First Bank System
601 Second Avenue South, Minneapolis, MN 55402-4302
Tel: (612) 973 1111; (612) 973 0715 **Fax:** (612) 973 0838 **Telex:** 192179 USB INTL MPS **Swift:** USBK US 44
Website: www.usbank.com

Senior Executive Officers
Chairman   Gerry B Cameron
President   John F Grundhofer
Financial Director   Susan E Lester *Executive Vice President*
Treasurer   David Grandstrand
EVP & General Counsel   Lee R Mitou

General-Lending (DCM, SL)
Head of Corporate Banking   Gary T Duim *Vice Chairman & EVP*

General-Investment
Head of Investment   Richard A Zona *Vice Chairman, Finance*

Debt Capital Markets / Fixed Income
Head of Fixed Income   John M Murphy Jr *EVP, Institutional Financial Services*

Equity Capital Markets
Head of Equity Capital Markets   Tad Piper

Syndicated Lending
Head of Syndicated Lending   Gary T Duim *Vice Chairman & EVP*

Foreign Exchange
Head of Foreign Exchange   Lars Lidberg *Senior Vice President*

Risk Management
Head of Risk Management   Robert Hoffmann *EVP & Chief Credit Officer*

Corporate Finance / M&A Advisory
Head of Corporate Finance   Richard A Zona *Vice Chairman, Finance*

Other Departments
Chief Credit Officer   Robert Hoffmann *EVP & Chief Credit Officer*
Private Banking   Kent Larson *EVP, Private Banking & Personal Trust*
Correspondent Banking   Jose Peris *Senior Vice President, Financial Services Division*
Cash Management   Richard A Zona *Vice Chairman, Finance*

Administration
Head of Administration   Peter E Raskind *EVP, Corporate Trust Group*
Head of Marketing   David Ingraham *Executive Vice President*

Technology & Systems
                                        Phil Heasley *Vice Chairman, Retail Products*

Legal / In-House Counsel
                                        Lee R Mitou *EVP & General Counsel*

Public Relations
                                        Robert H Sayre *EVP, Human Resources*

Other (Administration)
Commercial Banking   Gary T Duim *Vice Chairman & EVP*

UNITED STATES (+1)   www.euromoneydirectory.com

US Bank National Association   Head Office

Formerly known as: First Bank
17th Floor, MPFP 1713, US Bank Place, 601 Second Avenue South, Minneapolis, MN 55402
Tel: (612) 973 1111 Fax: (612) 973 0202

Debt Capital Markets / Fixed Income
Fixed-Income Repo
Marketing & Product Development   Emil C Busse Jr *Managing Director*
Trading   Bridget K Stier *Assistant Vice President*
                                           Andrew W Burlet *Officer*

Equity Capital Markets
Equity Repo / Securities Lending
Marketing & Product Development   Emil C Busse Jr *Managing Director*

US Clearing Group

40 Rector Street, New York, NY 10006
Tel: (212) 748 6700 Fax: (212) 748 6752

USTrust   Head Office

Formerly known as: UST Corp
40 Court Street, Boston, MA 02108
Tel: (617) 726 7000 Fax: (617) 695 4185 Telex: 49655074 USTBSNUI Swift: USTM US 33
Website: www.ustrustboston.com

Senior Executive Officers
Chairman   Neal F Finnegan ☏ **726 7300**
Chief Executive Officer   Neal F Finnegan ☏ **726 7300**
Financial Director   James K Hunt *Executive Vice President* ☏ **726 7055**
Treasurer   John F McKinlay *Treasurer* ☏ **695 4751**

Debt Capital Markets / Fixed Income
Global Head   John F McKinlay *Treasurer* ☏ **695 4751**
Domestic Government Bonds
Head of Sales   John F McKinlay *Treasurer* ☏ **695 4751**

Syndicated Lending
Loan-Related Activities
Trade Finance   Joseph V Roller II *Senior Vice President* ☏ **695 5129**

Other Departments
Private Banking   Molly N Downeer *Vice President* ☏ **726 7210**

Administration
Technology & Systems
                              Kenneth L Sullivan *Senior Vice President* ☏ **576 4810**
Legal / In-House Counsel
                              Eric R Fischer *Senior Counsel* ☏ **726 7377**

Valores Finamex International Inc   Subsidiary Company

28th Floor, 135 East 57th Street, New York, NY 10022
Tel: (212) 572 3500 Fax: (212) 572 3530 Telex: 6731337 Reuters: FIMX

Senior Executive Officers
Chairman   Eduardo Carrillo
President   Felipe Godard
Financial Director   Raymond Sutterlin *Chief Financial Officer*

Debt Capital Markets / Fixed Income
Global Head   Juan Carlos Lara *SVP, Fixed-Income*

Eurobonds
Head of Trading   Juan Carlos Lara *SVP, Fixed-Income*

Libor-Based / Floating-Rate Products
FRN Origination   Juan Carlos Lara *SVP, Fixed-Income*
Asset Swaps   Felipe Godard *President*

Medium-Term Notes
Head of Structuring   Felipe Godard *President*

www.euromoneydirectory.com   UNITED STATES (+1)

Private Placements
Head of Origination   Felipe Godard *President*

Fixed-Income Repo
Sales   Juan Carlos Lara *SVP, Fixed-Income*

Equity Capital Markets
Global Head   Daniel Somuano *Executive Director, Trading-Mexico*

Domestic Equities
Head of Trading   Thomas Mackell *Sales & Trading*

International Equities
Head of Trading   Thomas Mackell *Sales & Trading*

Money Markets

Eurocommercial Paper
Head of Origination   Felipe Godard *President*
Head of Trading   Juan Carlos Lara *SVP, Fixed-Income*

Foreign Exchange
Head of Trading   Juan Carlos Lara *SVP, Fixed-Income*

Corporate Finance / M&A Advisory
Regional Head   Felipe Godard *President*

Settlement / Clearing
Country Head   Gilberto Acosta *VP, International Operations*

Global Custody
Country Head   Gilberto Acosta *VP, International Operations*

Other Departments
Private Banking   Felipe Godard *President*

Vanguard Group (The)

100 Vanguard Blvd, Security Landing V15, Malvern, PA 19355
Tel: (610) 669 6205 **Fax:** (610) 669 6420
Website: www.vanguard.com

Debt Capital Markets / Fixed Income

Fixed-Income Repo
Marketing & Product Development; Trading   Colleen McElwee E **colleen_mcelwee@vanguard.com**
Trading   Michael Perre *Financial Administrator*

Equity Capital Markets

Equity Repo / Securities Lending
Marketing & Product Development   Coleen McElwee *Manager* E **coleen_mcelwee@vanguard.com**

Veronis, Suhler & Associates Incorporated   Head Office

350 Park Avenue, New York, NY 10022
Tel: (212) 935 4990 **Fax:** (212) 935 0877; (212) 486 3091
Website: www.vsacomm.com

Senior Executive Officers

Chairman & Director	John J Veronis
President & Co-CEO	John S Suhler
Chief Executive Officer	Jeffrey Stevenson *Partner*
Financial Director	John Sinatra *CFO*
Chief Operating Officer	Marty Visconti *Executive Vice President*
Managing Director	Lawrence M Crutcher
Managing Director	Paul E Hale
Managing Director	Joseph E Laird Jr
Managing Director	Joel Novak
Managing Director	Hal R Greenberg
Managing Director	Macro Sodi
Managing Director	John E Prunier
Managing Director	Robert J Broadwater
Managing Director	Kevin M Lavalla
Managing Director	Scott J Troeller
Managing Director	Francis L'Esperance

Euromoney Directory 1999 **2015**

UNITED STATES (+1) www.euromoneydirectory.com

Versailles Group Limited
Head Office

Suite 600 South, Ten Post Office Square, Boston, MA 02109
Tel: (617) 423 2500 Fax: (617) 423 2588 Email: info@versaillesgroup.com

Senior Executive Officers
President — Donald Grava
Managing Director — Susan Grava

Corporate Finance / M&A Advisory
Global Head — Donald Grava *President*

Vining-Sparks IBG
Head Office

Suite 427, 6077 Primacy Parkway, Memphis, TN 38119-5732
Tel: (901) 766 3000 Fax: (901) 762 5885

Senior Executive Officers
President — Jim Vining ☎ 762 5808
Managing Director — Joe Smallman

Debt Capital Markets / Fixed Income
Global Head — Joe Smallman *Managing Director*

Domestic Government Bonds
Head of Sales — Randy Wade *EVP & Director of Sales* ☎ 766 3183
Head of Trading — Fran Scott *EVP & Director of Trading* ☎ 762 5813
Head of Research — Mark Evans *SVP & Director, Portfolio Strategies* ☎ 766 3212

Settlement / Clearing
Settlement (General) — Mary Caroline Harp *Manager* ☎ 766 3054

Wachovia Corporation
Head Office

(Dual Headquarters), 191 Peachtree Street, Atlanta, GA 30303
(Dual Headquarters), 100 North Main Street, Winston-Salem, NC 27150
Tel: (336) 770 5000; (404) 332 5000 Fax: (336) 770 5931 Telex: 440585 WACH INT Swift: WACH US 3W
Reuters: WACO
International Operations Tel: (336) 770 5709; Fax: (336) 770 5739; International Operations Fax: (336) 735 0954
Website: www.wachovia.com

Senior Executive Officers
Chairman & CEO — L M Baker Jr
Chief Executive Officer — L M Baker Jr *Chairman & CEO*
Financial Director — Robert S McCoy Jr *CFO*

Others (Senior Executives)
Global Services — John H Chalk *Division Executive*

General-Lending (DCM, SL)
Head of Corporate Banking — Hugh M Durden *Division Executive*

Debt Capital Markets / Fixed Income
Head of Debt Capital Markets — John C McLean *Division Executive*

Foreign Exchange
Head of Foreign Exchange — Virginia A Hepner *Group Executive*

Warburg Dillon Read LLC
Full Branch Office

Suite 1540, 260 Franklin Street, 15th Floor, Boston, MA 02110

Debt Capital Markets / Fixed Income
Bonds - General
Convertible Bond Trading — R Murphy ☎ 748 5680
A Gonzales

High Yield / Junk Bonds
Head of Trading — J Isles ☎ 748 5620 F 748 5630

Equity Capital Markets
Other (Domestic Equities)
Equity Trading — T Buckley ☎ 748 5600 F 748 5610
M Cronin

2016 Euromoney Directory 1999

Other (Domestic Equities) (cont)
          P J Duffy
          K Smith
Equity Sales   P Ronan T 748 5640 F 748 5610
          B Burns

Warburg Dillon Read LLC

141 West Jackson Boulevard, Chicago, IL 60604
Tel: (312) 554 5000 Fax: (312) 554 5040

Senior Executive Officers
Others (Senior Executives)
          R Peterson *Branch Manager*

Equity Capital Markets
Other (Domestic Equities)
Equities Distribution   D Stowell
Equities Trading & Market Making   J Scoby

Warburg Dillon Read LLC   Full Branch Office

3950 Trammel Crow Center, 2001 Ross Avenue, Dallas, TX 75201
Tel: (214) 969 4000 Fax: (214) 969 5343

Senior Executive Officers
Others (Senior Executives)
Officers   K Crews
          J W Hunt
          J Sweet

Warburg Dillon Read LLC   Full Branch Office

299 Park Avenue, New York, NY 10171-0026
Tel: (212) 906 7000 Fax: (212) 759 3755

Senior Executive Officers
President & CEO   R Capone

Others (Senior Executives)
          J Frey *Chief of Staff, Americas*
Finance & Control   R Mills *CFO, Americas*

Equity Capital Markets
Department: Equities

Other (Domestic Equities)
          F de Saint Phalle
          J Scoby
High Net Worth Individual Sales   J Wilson

Other (Equity Research)
US Equity Research   S Carr
          R Esquivel

Corporate Finance / M&A Advisory
Other (Corporate Finance)
Corporate Finance   R Hotz

Administration
Legal / In-House Counsel
Legal   R Dinerstein *General Counsel, Americas*

Warburg Dillon Read LLC   Full Branch Office

555 California Street, Suite 4650, San Francisco, CA 94104
Corporate Finance Tel: (415) 352 5500; Fax: (415) 352 5511; Equities Research Tel: (415) 352 5650;
Fax: (415) 352 5652; Equities Sales & Trading Tel: (415) 352 5630; Fax: (415) 352 5640; Financial Services
Tel: (415) 352 5692; Fax: (415) 352 5697; Fixed Income Sales & Trading Tel: (415) 352 5600; Fax: (415) 352 5610

UNITED STATES (+1)   www.euromoneydirectory.com

Warburg Dillon Read LLC

677 Washington Boulevard, Stamford, CT 06901
Tel: (203) 719 1000 Fax: (203) 719 1410

Senior Executive Officers
President & Chief Executive Officer   R Capone

Others (Senior Executives)

                                           J Frey *Chief of Staff, Americas*
Finance & Control   R Mills *CFO, Americas*
                                           P Dyrvik

Debt Capital Markets / Fixed Income
Department: Fixed Income

Bonds - General
Global Sales   J Costas
US Sales   R Wolf

Equity Capital Markets
Department: Equities

Other (Domestic Equities)
US   D Purcell

Other (International Equity)
Non-US   N Duthie

Foreign Exchange

FX Traders / Sales People
Foreign Exchange Sales North America   E Schubert

Risk Management

Other (FI Derivatives)
Risk Management Distribution   D Purcell *Investor Coverage*
                                           M Mahaffy *Corporate Coverage*

Settlement / Clearing
Operations   E Pittarelli

Asset Management

Other (Asset Management)
Alternative Asset Management   J Hall

Other Departments
Economic Research   P McCulley

Administration

Legal / In-House Counsel
Legal   R Dinerstein *General Counsel, Americas*

Compliance
                                           S Anikewich

Wasserstein Perella & Co Inc   Full Branch Office

Suite 5700, 3 First National Plaza, Chicago, IL 60602-4208
Tel: (312) 263 2020 Fax: (312) 558 9245; (312) 558 9246

Senior Executive Officers
Managing Director   John Simpson

Wasserstein Perella & Co Inc   Full Branch Office

Suite 1605, 300 Crescent Court, Dallas, TX 75201
Tel: (214) 871 3740 Fax: (214) 871 3749

Senior Executive Officers
Managing Director   Kerry North
Managing Director   Nancy Huggins

www.euromoneydirectory.com UNITED STATES (+1)

Wasserstein Perella & Co Inc
Full Branch Office

Suite 2950, 1999 Avenue of the Stars, Los Angeles, CA 90067-6086
Tel: (310) 286 3300 Fax: (310) 286 7270

Senior Executive Officers
Managing Director Ellis Jones
Managing Director Leslie Abraham
Others (Senior Executives)
Merchant Banker Ellis Jones *Managing Director*

Wasserstein Perella & Co Inc
Full Branch Office

Suite 4380, 555 California Street, San Francisco, CA 94104
Tel: (415) 677 4960 Fax: (415) 288 3960

Senior Executive Officers
Managing Director Paul Haigney

Wasserstein Perella Emerging Markets Asset Management LP
Subsidiary Company

14th Floor, 320 Park Avenue, New York, NY 10022
Tel: (212) 702 5600 Fax: (212) 702 5625

Senior Executive Officers
President Peter N Marber
Chief Executive Officer Michael E Gagliardi
Managing Director Hernando Perez

Wasserstein Perella Group Inc

31 West 52nd Street, New York, NY 10019
Tel: (212) 969 2700 Fax: (212) 969 7836

Senior Executive Officers
Chairman & CEO, Wasserstein Perella & Co., Inc. Michael J Biondi
Chairman & CEO, Wasserstein Perella Group, Inc. Bruce Wasserstein
President, Wasserstein Perella Group, Inc. Frederic M Seegal
Financial Director Clay Kingsbery *Chief Financial Officer*
Managing Director Paul Adama
Managing Director Bruce Barnes
Managing Director Steven Fischer
Managing Director Richard S Goldberg
Managing Director Robert L Goodman
Managing Director Bill G Lambert
Managing Director Henry Miller
Managing Director Andrew G T Moore
Managing Director Bruce P Nolop
Managing Director Robert A Pruzan
Managing Director Jeffrey A Rosen
Managing Director Peter Rothschild
Managing Director Marc Utay
Managing Director Ned Weihman
Managing Director Joseph T Yurcik
Managing Director Townsend Ziebold

Settlement / Clearing
Operations Jeanne Vicari *Vice President, Controller*

Administration
Head of Administration Lisa Desmond *Vice President*

Technology & Systems
Systems & Telecommunications John Bratkovics *Vice President*

Legal / In-House Counsel
Lee Siegel *Director & General Counsel*

Compliance
John Donovan *Director of Compliance*

UNITED STATES (+1) www.euromoneydirectory.com

Wasserstein Perella Group Inc (cont)
Other (Administration)
Human Resources Maureen Tierney *Administrator*
Information Services Ed Vazquez *Manager*

Wasserstein Perella Securities Inc
31 West 52nd Street, New York, NY 10019
Tel: (212) 969 2600 **Fax:** (212) 969 7842

Senior Executive Officers
Managing Director Joseph Stein

Wasserstein Perella Securities Inc
31 West 52nd Street, New York, NY 10019
Tel: (212) 969 7900 **Fax:** (212) 969 2709

Senior Executive Officers
Managing Director Arthur Hahn

Yasuda Bank & Trust Company (USA) Subsidiary Company
Suite 802, 666 Fifth Avenue, New York, NY 10103
Tel: (212) 373 5916; (212) 373 5900 **Fax:** (212) 373 5998 **Telex:** 426623 Y BUS

Senior Executive Officers
Chairman Isao Ando
President Kyo Kikuchi

Debt Capital Markets / Fixed Income
Fixed-Income Repo
Head of Repo
Trading Toshiro Vehera *Senior Vice President* [T] **373 5916** [F] **373 5996**
Bobbi Parisi *Assistant Trader*
Bill Casey *Associate*
Nancy Almandarez *Assistant Trader*

URUGUAY
(+598)

Banco Central del Uruguay Central Bank
Avenida Ing Juan P Fabini 777, (Esq Paysandú y Florida), 11100, Montevideo
Tel: (2) 982 090; (2) 917 117 **Fax:** (2) 921 634; (2) 921 636 **Telex:** 26659 BACENUR UY **Email:** secgral@bcu.gub.uy
Cable: BANKCENTRAL **Telex:** 26939
Website: www.bcu.gub.uy

Senior Executive Officers
President Humberto Capote
Vice President Julián Moreno
Others (Senior Executives)
Mario Bucheli *Director*

ABN AMRO Bank NA Full Branch Office
25 de Mayo 501, 11000, Montevideo
Tel: (2) 916 0702 **Fax:** (2) 916 0102 **Swift:** ABNA UY MM

Senior Executive Officers
Country Manager Paul Elverse
Global Custody
Regional Head Alan McLeod Davidson [T] **961 522**
Other (Global Custody)
Guillermo Rosso [T] **964 955** [F] **963 698**
Alvaro Gil [T] **964 289** [F] **963 093**

2020 Euromoney Directory 1999

www.euromoneydirectory.com   URUGUAY (+598)

American Express Bank (Uruguay) SA — Subsidiary Company
Rincón 473, 11000, Montevideo
Tel: (2) 916 0092 Fax: (2) 916 2245

Senior Executive Officers
General Manager — Thomas Lindner
Administration
Other (Administration)
Commercial Banking — Raúl Salvo *Director*

Banco Comercial SA — Head Office
Cerrito 400, 11000, Montevideo
Tel: (2) 916 0541; (2) 915 0455 Fax: (2) 915 3569; (2) 915 3944 Telex: 26668 UY Swift: COME UY MM
Email: bcocom@netgate.com.uy Cable: COMERAL
General Telex: 26911 UY
Website: www.bancocomercial.com.uy

Senior Executive Officers
President — Armando Braun ☎ **915 4259**
Chief Executive Officer — Carlos Rohm *Vice President* ☎ **915 2559**
Financial Director — Antonio Lago *Finance Manager* ☎ **915 4259**
Chief Operating Officer — Jorge López *Operations Manager*
General Manager — Nelson Franco ☎ **915 2420**
International Division — Walter Raffaelli *Manager*

Others (Senior Executives)
Juan José Curone *Controller*
Foreign Department — Alberto Varela *Deputy Manager* ☎ **915 6495**
General-Lending (DCM, SL)
Head of Corporate Banking — Ignacio Llambías *Wholesale Manager*
Foreign Exchange
Tel: 915 6179 Fax: 916 0775
Head of Foreign Exchange — Walter Ferreira *Deputy Manager & Dealer* ☎ **916 2204**
Other Departments
Correspondent Banking — Ariel Sosa *Accountant* ☎ **915 3786**
Administration
Head of Marketing — Pedro Shearer *Manager* ☎ **916 0541**
Accounts / Audit
Ariel Sosa *Accountant* ☎ **915 3786**

Banco de Crédito — Full Branch Office
Avenida 18 de Julio 1451, Montevideo
PO Box 265, Montevideo
Tel: (2) 400 4141; (2) 400 4147 Fax: (2) 400 7975; (2) 400 7342

Senior Executive Officers
President — Enrique dos Santos
Vice President & General Manager — Oscar Rico Larretchart
Secretary — Rodolfo Gelpi
International Division — Luis Bellón *Director*

Others (Senior Executives)
Oscar Rico Larretchart *Vice President & General Manager*

Banco la Caja Obrera — Head Office
25 de Mayo 500, 11000, Montevideo
Tel: (2) 915 0501; (2) 915 4114 Fax: (2) 916 3657; (2) 915 0051 Telex: 22156 Swift: CAOB UY MM
Email: intlblco@adinet.com.uy Telex: 26613

Senior Executive Officers
President & General Manager — Eduardo Rocca Couture
Vice President — Jorge Fodere
Member & Secretary to the Board — Carlos Abdala

URUGUAY (+598)   www.euromoneydirectory.com

Banco la Caja Obrera (cont)
Others (Senior Executives)
                                   Juan M Odizzio *Trustee*
Operative Area   Juan Carlos D'Angelo *Deputy General Manager*
Commercial Area   Mario Segredo *Deputy General Manager*
General-Investment
Head of Investment   Luis A Aicardo *Manager, Financial Area*
                                   Roberto Gatti *Manager, Financial Area*
Settlement / Clearing
Operations   Octavio Filippi *Manager*
Asset Management
Other (Asset Management)
Assets Recovery   Luis Oliver *Manager*
Administration
                                   Mario Roberto Mandl *Manager*
Legal / In-House Counsel
                                   Leonardo Goicoechea *Lawyer*
                                   Julio Cesar Carbone *Lawyer*

Accounts / Audit
General Accountant   Dionisio Brizuela
Auditors Office   Ismael Garcia de Zuffiga *Manager*
Other (Administration)
Metropolitan Branches Area   Jose Lopez Corral *Manager*
Provinces Branches Area   Jorge Rodriguez *Manager*
Head Office   Francisco Sobral *Manager*
International Area   Carlos F Nin *Manager*
Foreign Department   Andrés Carriquiry *Manager*
Foreign Department Administration Miguel Ceccarelli *Manager*
Human Resources   Gregorio Diez *Manager*

Banco de Montevideo SA   Head Office
Misiones 1399 esquina Rincón, PO Box 612, 11000, Montevideo
Tel: (2) 960 258 **Fax:** (2) 916 0952 **Telex:** 23775 **Swift:** MDEB UY MM
Senior Executive Officers
President   Mario San Cristóbal
Financial Director   Marcelo Guadalupe *Manager*
General - Treasury
Head of Treasury   Marcelo Guadalupe *Manager*
Administration
Other (Administration)
                                   Daniel De Santa Ana *Commercial Manager*

Banco Pan de Azúcar   Head Office
Rincón 528, Montevideo
PO Box 1891, Montevideo
Tel: (2) 916 0925; (2) 916 0926 **Fax:** (2) 916 1493 **Tel:** 916 0927; 916 0928 **Tel:** 916 0929; 916 0930
Senior Executive Officers
President   José Félix Iglesias
Financial Director   Wolf Bliman *Director*
International Division   Daniel Igorra Cairo *Director*
Others (Senior Executives)
                                   Carlosc Balsa *Vice President*
Foreign Exchange
Head of Trading   Martirena
Administration
Public Relations
                                   Emilio Cardena

2022   Euromoney Directory 1999

www.euromoneydirectory.com   URUGUAY (+598)

Banco de la Provincia de Buenos Aires   Full Branch Office

Misiones 1379, Montevideo
Tel: (2) 960 525; (2) 960 761 **Fax:** (2) 960 689 **Telex:** 6302 BAPRO UY

Senior Executive Officers
Manager   Marcelo Juantorena

Banco Real del Uruguay SA   Head Office

Julio Herrera y Obes 1365, piso 1°, 11100, Montevideo
PO Box 964, 11100, Montevideo
Tel: (2) 902 0376; (2) 902 3351 **Fax:** (2) 902 1510; (2) 903 1714 **Telex:** UY 26947 **Swift:** REAL UY MM ADM
Email: bcoreal@adinet.com.uy

Senior Executive Officers
President   Enio Alves Vieira

Banco de la Republica Oriental del Uruguay   Head Office

Cerrito 351, 11000, Montevideo
Tel: (2) 916 0062 **Fax:** (2) 916 2064 **Telex:** UY22321 **Swift:** BROU UY MM **Tel:** 915 0205; **Fax:** 915 1522

Senior Executive Officers
Vice President   César Rodríguez-Batlle
Financial Director   Daniel Genis *Chief Financial Officer*
General Manager   Antonio Correa-Moreno
International Division   Horacio Lasala-Perrotti *International Division Director*

Others (Senior Executives)

    Julio Iglesias *Second Vice President*

General - Treasury
Head of Treasury   Carlos Otheguy *Manager*

Syndicated Lending
Head of Credit Committee   Danilo Vázquez *First Assistant General Manager*

Other (Trade Finance)
Documentary Credits   Alfredo Palermo *Assistant General Manager*

Administration
Head of Administration   César Olivera *First Assistant General Manager*

Legal / In-House Counsel
    Rodolfo Sienra-Roosen *Counsel*

Banco Sudameris   Full Branch Office

Rincón 500, 11000, Montevideo
PO Box 460, 11000, Montevideo
Tel: (2) 915 0095 **Fax:** (2) 916 4292 **Email:** sudameri@adinet.com.uy

Senior Executive Officers
Manager   Paul Charles Pinelli
Deputy Manager   Eric Luc Dherte

Others (Senior Executives)
Commercial Banking   Julio Cesar Vallini *Manager*

Bank Leu Limited   Representative Office

Zabala 1327, piso 4°, Oficina 409/410, 11000, Montevideo
Tel: (2) 970 062 **Fax:** (2) 970 063

Senior Executive Officers
Representative   Marina Cuervo

Euromoney Directory 1999   **2023**

URUGUAY (+598)   www.euromoneydirectory.com

Bank of New York - Inter Maritime Bank, Geneva
Representative Office

PO Box 1617, Cerrito 461, Oficina 308, 11000, Montevideo
Tel: (2) 916 2403 Fax: (2) 916 2478 Telex: 22239 BNYIMB UY

Senior Executive Officers
Representative   John Cannock

Banque Nationale de Paris
Full Branch Office

PO Box 6729, Correo Central, 11000, Montevideo
Tel: (2) 916 2768 Fax: (2) 916 2609

Senior Executive Officers
Director General   Jean-Michel Bandekerkove

BSI-Banca della Svizzera Italiana
Representative Office

Plaza de Cagancha 1335, Oficina 1101, 11100, Montevideo
Tel: (2) 902 1803 Fax: (2) 902 1147

Senior Executive Officers
Representative   Franco Long

CBI-TDB Union Bancaire Privée
Representative Office

Avenida Gorlero y Calle 19, Edificio Fontemar, Punta del Este
Tel: (42) 43111 Fax: (42) 41966

Citibank NA
Full Branch Office

Cerrito 455, PO Box 690, Montevideo
Tel: (2) 198 7000 Fax: (2) 916 3665 Swift: CITI UY MM

Senior Executive Officers
Chief Executive Officer   Gustavo Cardoni *Managing Director* T 915 5687
Treasurer   Mario Farren *Treasurer* T 916 5655

General-Lending (DCM, SL)
Head of Corporate Banking   Irene Silva

General - Treasury
Head of Treasury   Gabriel Gonzalez T 916 2838

Debt Capital Markets / Fixed Income
Country Head   Eduardo Perez Muniz *Head of Corporate Finance* T 915 5492

Domestic Government Bonds
Head of Sales; Head of Trading   Mario Farren *Treasurer* T 916 5655

Eurobonds
Head of Origination   Eduardo Perez Muniz *Head of Corporate Finance* T 915 5492

Libor-Based / Floating-Rate Products
FRN Origination   Eduardo Perez Muniz *Head of Corporate Finance* T 915 5492
Asset Swaps   Mario Farren *Treasurer* T 916 5655

Medium-Term Notes
Head of Origination   Eduardo Perez Muniz *Head of Corporate Finance* T 915 5492

Private Placements
Head of Origination   Eduardo Perez Muniz *Head of Corporate Finance* T 915 5492

Asset-Backed Securities / Securitization
Global Head   Eduardo Perez Muniz *Head of Corporate Finance* T 915 5492
Head of Trading   Mario Farren *Treasurer* T 916 5655

Mortgage-Backed Securities
Global Head   Eduardo Perez Muniz *Head of Corporate Finance* T 915 5492
Head of Trading   Mario Farren *Treasurer* T 916 5655

Fixed-Income Repo
Head of Repo   Mario Farren *Treasurer* T 916 5655

Equity Capital Markets
Country Head   Eduardo Perez Muniz *Head of Corporate Finance* T 915 5492

www.euromoneydirectory.com URUGUAY (+598)

Domestic Equities
Head of Origination — Eduardo Perez Muniz *Head of Corporate Finance* ☎ **915 5492**

Syndicated Lending
Country Head — Eduardo Perez Muniz *Head of Corporate Finance* ☎ **915 5492**

Loan-Related Activities
Trade Finance — Luis Gonzalez *Head, Financial Institutions* ☎ **916 0320**
Leasing & Asset Finance — Irene Silva *Head, Corporate Banking* ☎ **915 5492**

Money Markets
Domestic Commercial Paper
Head of Origination — Eduardo Perez Muniz *Head of Corporate Finance* ☎ **915 5492**

Eurocommercial Paper
Head of Origination — Eduardo Perez Muniz *Head of Corporate Finance* ☎ **915 5492**

Foreign Exchange
Country Head — Mario Farren *Treasurer* ☎ **916 5655**

Risk Management
Country Head — Irene Silva *Head, Risk Management* ☎ **915 5492**

Fixed Income Derivatives / Risk Management
Country Head — Mario Farren *Treasurer* ☎ **916 5655**

Foreign Exchange Derivatives / Risk Management
Cross-Currency Swaps, Sales / Marketing; — Mario Farren *Treasurer* ☎ **916 5655**
Cross-Currency Swaps, Trading

Corporate Finance / M&A Advisory
Country Head — Eduardo Perez Muniz *Head of Corporate Finance* ☎ **915 5492**

Settlement / Clearing
Country Head — Luis Gonzalez *Head, Financial Institutions* ☎ **916 0320**

Global Custody
Country Head — Luis Gonzalez *Head, Financial Institutions* ☎ **916 0320**

Other Departments
Private Banking — Ricardo Soto *IPB Head* ☎ **915 5693**

Administration
Technology & Systems
Jorge Rodriguez Grecco *SMG Head* ☎ **915 5496**

Public Relations
Public Affairs — Hugo Caceres *Officer* ☎ **915 4347**

Crédit Lyonnais (Uruguay) SA — Subsidiary Company

Circunvalación Durango 1378, 11000, Montevideo
Tel: (2) 916 3514; (2) 916 3519 **Fax:** (2) 916 1413 **Telex:** CRELYON UY 22395 **Swift:** CRLY UY MM

Senior Executive Officers
Director & General Manager — Michel Chatelain

Syndicated Lending
Loan-Related Activities
Trade Finance — Luis Spinelli

Other Departments
Correspondent Banking — Luis Spinelli

Discount Bank (Latin America) — Subsidiary Company

Rincón 390, 11000, Montevideo
PO Box 971, 11000, Montevideo
Tel: (2) 916 4848; (2) 916 0250 **Fax:** (2) 916 0890 **Telex:** 22302 DISBANK UY **Swift:** DBLA UY MM

Senior Executive Officers
Director & General Manager — Bitoush Menahem
International Division — Jorge Pérez *Financial Manager*

Others (Senior Executives)
Valentin Malachowski *Deputy General Manager*

Debt Capital Markets / Fixed Income
Head of Debt Capital Markets — Jorge Pérez *Financial Manager*
Marketing — Daniel Lamarque *Manager*

Euromoney Directory 1999 **2025**

URUGUAY (+598)   www.euromoneydirectory.com

Discount Bank (Latin America) (cont)

Equity Capital Markets
Head of Equity Capital Markets   Jorge Pérez *Financial Manager*
Marketing   Daniel Lamarque *Manager*

Syndicated Lending
Head of Credit Committee   Valentin Malachowski *Deputy General Manager*

Other (Syndicated Lending)
Documentary Credits   Magela Reissig *Manager*

Settlement / Clearing
Operations   Rubén Zacaria *Senior Manager*

Administration
Head of Administration   Raul Antoine *Senior Manager*

Technology & Systems
   José Ferrer *Senior Manager*

Ibero Platina Bank AG   Representative Office

Edificio de los Patricios, Misiones 1372, Office 802, Montevideo
PO Box 6009, Montevideo
Tel: (2) 916 0770; (2) 915 2248 **Fax:** (2) 916 0949

ING Bank   Full Branch Office

Misiones 1352/60, 11000, Montevideo
PO Box 1425 y 6117, 11000, Montevideo
Tel: (2) 916 0961; (2) 916 0969 **Fax:** (2) 296 1725; (2) 296 1727 **Telex:** 26672 INGB UY **Swift:** INGB UY MM

Senior Executive Officers
General Manager   Alejandro F Suzacq

Department: ING Trust (Antilles) Trust & Management Services
Tel: +598 (2) 296 0961 **Fax:** +598 (2) 295 8955
General Manager   Willem L de Bruijn ☎ **432 7400** 📠 **432 7590**

ING Baring Private Bank

Rincón 550, Piso 1°, 11000, Montevideo
Tel: (2) 295 8315; (2) 295 0021 **Fax:** (2) 295 8315 **Telex:** 26672 INGB UY **Telex:** 23027 INGB UY

Senior Executive Officers
Manager   Javier Carlevaro

Lloyds Bank (BLSA) Limited   Full Branch Office

Alternative trading name: Lloyds Bank

Zabilla 1500, 11000, Montevideo
PO Box 204, 11000, Montevideo
Tel: (2) 916 1370; (2) 916 0976 **Fax:** (2) 916 1262 **Telex:** 26632 LOYDBK UY **Email:** lloydsm@adinet.com.uy
Cable: COLFORLOYD **Telex:** 26971 LOYDBNK UY **Telex:** 23761 LOYDBNK UY

Senior Executive Officers
Principal Manager-Uruguay   Cristopher Golby ☎ **916 4833** 📠 **917 0658**

Others (Senior Executives)
Planning & Control   Andrés Vilarrubí *Manager*

General-Lending (DCM, SL)
Head of Corporate Banking   Stuart R C Duncan *Principal Manager, Commercial Banking Division*

General - Treasury
Head of Treasury   Federico Dillmann *Manager, Treasury & Foreign Exchange* ☎ **916 4834/6**

Syndicated Lending
Tel: 916 4833 **Fax:** 917 0658
Head of Trading   Stuart R C Duncan *Principal Manager, Commercial Banking Division*

Money Markets
Head of Money Markets   Federico Dillmann *Manager, Treasury & Foreign Exchange* ☎ **916 4834/6**

Foreign Exchange
Head of Foreign Exchange — Federico Dillmann *Manager, Treasury & Foreign Exchange* ☎ 916 4834/6
FX Traders / Sales People — Jorge Diez *Sub-Manager, Treasury & Exchange*

Other Departments
Private Banking — Jaime Frávega *Manager, Financial Services Division* ℻ 917 0522
Magdalena Marqués *Manager* ℻ 917 0522
Roque Yódice *Sub-Manager* ℻ 917 0522

Administration
Head of Administration — Alfredo C Brandon *Administration Manager*
Business Development — Raul Batlle ☎ 916 4833 ℻ 917 0658
Head of Marketing — Jaime Frávega *Manager, Financial Services Division* ℻ 917 0522

Technology & Systems
Technology — Fabrizio Giusti *Sub-Manager*

Legal / In-House Counsel
Eduardo Angulo *Lawyer* ☎ 915 4684

Public Relations
Jaime Frávega *Manager, Financial Services Division* ℻ 917 0522

Accounts / Audit
Audit — Roberto Kirst *Internal Auditor*

Republic National Bank of New York (Uruguay) SA
Subsidiary Company

25 de Mayo 471, 11000, Montevideo
Tel: (2) 915 3395; (2) 915 3393 **Fax:** (2) 916 0125 **Telex:** 22414 RNBUY **Swift:** BLIC UY MM **Reuters:** RNUR
Website: www.rnb.com

Senior Executive Officers
Chairman — John Gorman
Chief Executive Officer — Alberto Muchnick *Vice Chairman & CEO*
General Manager — Josef Rebalski
General Manager — Juan Carlos Varesi

Debt Capital Markets / Fixed Income
Head of Fixed Income Trading — Enrique Goyechc
Iair Nadel

UZBEKISTAN
(+7)

Berliner Bank AG
Representative Office

3rd Floor, ul Turab Tula 1, 700003, Tashkent
Tel: (998) 406 289 **Fax:** (998) 406 289

Senior Executive Officers
Representative — Detlef Prulzk

Deutsche Bank AG
Representative Office

Turab Tula, Kutschasi 1, 700003, Tashkent
Tel: (998) 457 302; (998) 457 357 **Fax:** (998) 139 1112; (998) 406 554 **Telex:** 116528 DBUZB RU

European Bank for Reconstruction & Development
Representative Office

4th Floor, International Financial Centre, 1 Turab Tula Street, 700003, Tashkent
Tel: (998) 120 6121; (998) 144 2165 **Fax:** (998) 139 4014

Senior Executive Officers
Resident Representative — Isao Kawanishi
Deputy Resident Representative — Franco Delneri

UZBEKISTAN (+7)

Société Générale
1 Turab Tula Street, 700003, Tashkent
Tel: (998) 406 733 Fax: (998) 406 732
Website: www.socgen.com

The World Bank
Representative Office

43 Suleimanova Street, Tashkent
Tel: (998) 133 5002; (998) 133 6205 Fax: (998) 133 0551; (998) 406 215
Senior Executive Officers
Chief of Mission — David Pierce

VANUATU (+678)

Reserve Bank of Vanuatu
Central Bank

Private Mail Bag 062, Rue Brunet, Port Vila
Tel: 23333; 23110 Fax: 24231 Telex: 1049 VATUBK NH Reuters: VATU

Senior Executive Officers
Governor — Sampson Ngwele

Others (Senior Executives)
Executive Management
- Amrit V Jogia *General Adviser*
- Legesse Tickeher *Adviser, Research*
- Michael Hililan *Commercial Director*
- Heva Alilee *Director, Operations*
- Frank Bollen *Director of Administration*

Foreign Exchange
Global Head — Lynrose Vuti *Office Manager*
Regional Head — Joseph Aru *Office Superintendent*

FX Traders / Sales People
Currency — Josiane Cokataki *Office Manager*

Settlement / Clearing
Operations — Heva Alilee *Director, Operations*

Administration
Head of Administration — Frank Bollen *Director of Administration*

Technology & Systems
Data Processing — Marnet Africa *Computer Programmer*

Accounts / Audit — Annie Lakaleo *Office Manager*

Other (Administration)
Human Resources — Clifford Garae *Officer*
Banking — Elsie Jimmy *Office Superintendent*
Bank Supervision — Peter Tari *Deputy Head*

ANZ Bank (Vanuatu) Limited
Subsidiary Company

PO Box 123, Kumul Highway, Port Vila
Tel: 22536 Fax: 22814; 23590 Telex: 1012 ANZPTVNH Swift: ANZB VU VX Reuters: VANZ

Senior Executive Officers
Chief Executive Officer — Judy Whiteman *Managing Director*
Financial Director — Lorraine Rodrigues *Chief Operating Officer*
Treasurer — Matt Millard *Manager, Treasury*

Banque d'Hawaii (Vanuatu) Limited
Subsidiary Company

PO Box 29, Port Vila
Tel: 22412 Fax: 23579 Email: bdhvan@vanuatu.com.vu

Senior Executive Officers
Director General — Darryl Constantin

www.euromoneydirectory.com   VENEZUELA (+58)

European Bank Limited
Head Office

Alternative trading name: Pacific International Trust Company Limited
PO Box 65, International Building, Port Vila
Tel: 27700; 24680 Fax: 23405 Telex: 1023 EURTRUST Swift: EUBLVUVUBIC Email: security@vanuatu.com.vu

Senior Executive Officers
Chairman   Thomas Bayer ☎ **23410**
President   Robert Bohn ☎ **24680**
Chief Executive Officer   Michael Harkin ☎ **24170**
Financial Director   Charles Kleiman ☎ **23410**
Chief Operating Officer   Douglas Peters *Senior Vice President* ☎ **27700**
                                 ✉ **security@vanuatu.com.vu**
Treasurer   Geoff Taylor ☎ **27700**

Other Departments
Private Banking   Douglas Peters *Senior Vice President* ☎ **27700**
                                 ✉ **security@vanuatu.com.vu**

Westpac Banking Corporation
Full Branch Office

Kumul Highway, PO Box 32, Port Vila
Tel: 22084 Fax: 24773 Telex: 1018 Swift: WPAC VU VX

Senior Executive Officers
Manager, Vanuatu
International Division   Glenn Bitossi
                                 Peter Fitzgerald *Manager, International Business*

Others (Senior Executives)
FX & Money Markets   Michael Pullin *Chief Dealer*
Lending   Peter Yabsley *Manager, Lending*

Foreign Exchange
Head of Trading   Michael Pullin *Chief Dealer*

Settlement / Clearing
Operations   Peter Fitzgerald *Manager, International Business*

Other Departments
Chief Credit Officer   Peter Yabsley *Manager, Lending*

VENEZUELA
(+58)

Banco Central de Venezuela
🏛 Central Bank

Avenida Urdaneta Esquina de Carmelitas, Caracas 1010
Tel: (2) 801 5111; (2) 801 5473 Fax: (2) 861 1646 Telex: 28250 BCV VC Swift: BCVE VE CA
Email: mbatista@bcv.org.ve
General Tel: 801 8875

Senior Executive Officers
President   Antonio Casas ☎ **801 3101**
First Vice President   Hugo Romero ☎ **801 5104**
Chief Executive Officer   Eddy Reyes *Second Vice President* ☎ **801 5132**

Others (Senior Executives)
Director   Carlos Hernández Delfino
                                 Armando León
                                 Domingo Mazazavala
                                 Roosevelt Velásquez
                                 Teodoro Petkoff

Debt Capital Markets / Fixed Income
Government Bonds
Head of Syndication   Martin Orozco

Other Departments
Correspondent Banking   Haydee Rodriguez ☎ **801 8947**

Administration
Head of Administration   Luisa Garrido ☎ **801 8270**

Technology & Systems
                                 Juan Llorens ☎ **801 5558**

Euromoney Directory 1999 **2029**

VENEZUELA (+58)   www.euromoneydirectory.com

Banco Central de Venezuela (cont)
Legal / In-House Counsel
    Aymara Morales *Head of Legal Department* ☎ **801 5141**
Public Relations
    Rayna Petkoff ☎ **801 8969**

ABN AMRO Bank NV   Full Branch Office
Edificio Centro Seguros SudAmérica, piso 1°, Avenida Francisco de Miranda, El Rosal, Caracas 1060
Tel: (2) 957 0200 **Fax:** (2) 953 5758

Senior Executive Officers
Country Manager   Peter Weiss
Others (Senior Executives)
Corporate Banking Manager   Oscar Taylhardat *Vice President*

Banco Europeo para America Latina (BEAL) SA   Representative Office
Edificio Delta PH-A, Avenida Francisco de Miranda, Altamira, Caracas 1060
PO Box 62516, Caracas 1060
Tel: (2) 262 0544 **Fax:** (2) 261 9520

Senior Executive Officers
Representative   Louis de Lichtervelde

Banco Unión CA
Avenida Universidad, Esquina El Chorro, Edificio Union, piso 14°, Caracas 1010-A
Tel: (2) 501 7101; (2) 501 7102 **Fax:** (2) 501 7342; (2) 501 5682 **Telex:** 26338 BCOUNVC **Swift:** UNION VECA
Cable: BANCUNION
Website: www.bancunion.com

Senior Executive Officers
Chairman   Ignacio Salvatierra P ☎ **501 7021**
International Division   Rosalba de Palacios *Vice President, International Division*
     Salvador Salvatierra ☎ **501 8104**

Other Departments
Correspondent Banking   Manuel A Bonilla S *Head of Correspondent Banking* ☎ **501 7366**

Banco de Venezuela / Grupo Santander   Full Branch Office
Formerly known as: Banco de Venezuela
Avda Universidad, Esquina de Sociedad A Traposo, Torre Banco de Venezuela, Caracas 1010-A
Tel: (2) 501 3333; (2) 401 4433 **Fax:** (2) 501 2528; (2) 401 4304
Website: www.bancodevenezuela.com

Senior Executive Officers
Chief Executive Officer   Michel Goguikian ☎ **501 2556** ☒ **501 2570**
Financial Director   Philip Henriquez ☎ **501 2531** ☒ **501 2546**
Treasurer   Andres Octavio ☎ **401 4306** ☒ **401 4219**

Others (Senior Executives)
Commercial Banking   Jose Antonio Elosequi *Executive Director* ☎ **501 2521**
General-Lending (DCM, SL)
Head of Corporate Banking   Diana Espino ☎ **501 2526** ☒ **501 2528**
Debt Capital Markets / Fixed Income
Head of Fixed Income   Leonardo Moreno ☎ **401 4342** ☒ **401 4219**
Fixed-Income Research
Head of Fixed Income   Ricardo Penfold ☎ **401 4230** ☒ **401 4304**
Equity Capital Markets
Department: Vicepresidencia Renta Variable (Valores Santander)
Tel: 401 4433 **Fax:** 401 4304
Head of Equity Capital Markets   Mario Oliva ☎ **401 4207** ☒ **401 4219**
Domestic Equities
Head of Sales   Maria Carlota Madriz ☎ **401 4215**
Head of Trading   Gustavo Abdelnour ☎ **401 4208**

www.euromoneydirectory.com   VENEZUELA (+58)

Equity Research
Head of Equity Research   Ricardo Penfold T **401 4230** F **401 4304**

Syndicated Lending
Loan-Related Activities
Project Finance   Guillermo Moniefusco *Vice President* T **953 3553**

Foreign Exchange
Head of Foreign Exchange   Policarpo Rodriguez T **401 4211** F **401 4219**
Corporate Sales   Ana Thielen T **401 4310**
Head of Trading   Luis A Gomez T **401 4316**

FX Traders / Sales People
                                         Octavio Boccalandro T **401 4317**

Risk Management
Head of Risk Management   Miguel Amaneiro *Executive Vice President, Risk Management* T **501 2525**
                                         Jaime Romagosa *Vice President, Risk Management* T **501 2530**
                                         Alberto Redondo *Vice President* T **401 4201**

Corporate Finance / M&A Advisory
Head of Corporate Finance   Guillermo Moniefusco *Vice President* T **953 3553**

Global Custody
Head of Global Custody   Ingrid De Frontado T **501 3278** F **501 2139**

Other Departments
Chief Credit Officer   Jaime Romagosa *Vice President, Risk Management* T **501 2530**
Cash Management   Gorka Uriguen T **501 2808**

Administration
Head of Administration   Juan Ruiz T **501 3148** F **501 3168**
Business Development   Gorka Uriguen T **501 2808**
Head of Marketing   Luis Marquez T **501 2786** F **501 3020**

Technology & Systems
                                         Luis Cordero T **501 2782** F **501 3144**

Legal / In-House Counsel
Legal Advisor   Frank Malaret T **501 2534**

Compliance
                                         Alberto Redondo *Vice President* T **401 4201**

Public Relations
                                         Luis Marquez T **501 2786** F **501 3020**

Accounts / Audit
                                         Camilo Feldoo T **501 3275** F **501 3313**

Other (Administration)
Human Resources   Miguel Amaneiro *Executive Vice President, Risk Management* T **501 2525**

Bank Hapoalim BM   Representative Office

Torre Oeste, piso 5-4°, Edificio Parque Cristal, Avenida Francisco de Miranda, Caracas
Tel: (2) 285 2522 **Fax:** (2) 283 7133

Senior Executive Officers
Representative   Shoshana Levin

Banque Sudameris   Representative Office

Edificio Centro Financiero Latino, piso 16°, Oficina 4, Avenida Urdaneta, Caracas 1010
PO Box 6499, Carmelitas, Caracas 1010
Tel: (2) 561 5888 **Fax:** (2) 564 1317

Senior Executive Officers
Representative   Gianfranco Oronzo

BEAL Venezuela   Representative Office

Avenida Francisco de Miranda, Edificio Delta, PH-B, Altamira, Caracas 1060
Tel: (2) 262 0544 **Fax:** (2) 261 9620

Senior Executive Officers
Representative   Louis de Lichtervelde

VENEZUELA (+58) www.euromoneydirectory.com

Commerzbank AG
Representative Office

Centro Cremerca, piso 2°, AvenidaVenezuela, El Rosal, Caracas
Apartado de Correos 5074, Caracas 1010 A
Tel: (2) 952 7111 Fax: (2) 952 6950 Telex: 21508 EUROR VC

Senior Executive Officers
Representative Peter Werner

Corp Banca CA
Head Office

Formerly known as: Banco Consolidado
Torre Corp Banca, Avenida Los Chaguáramos, Caracas 1060-A
PO Box 75171, Caracas 1010-A
Tel: (2) 206 3333 Fax: (2) 206 4950 Telex: 23315 Swift: CONS VE CA Email: cubeda@corpbanca.com.ve

Senior Executive Officers
Chairman of the Board Alvaro Saich
Vice Chairman of the Board Susan Segal
Chief Executive Officer Sebastián Del Campo Chief Executive Officer
Chief Operating Officer; Treasurer Arturo Fuenmayor
Vice President, Communications Milagro González

General-Lending (DCM, SL)
Head of Corporate Banking Peter Gerstel Head of Corporate Banking
Enrique Martinez Head of Corporate Development

Administration
Technology & Systems
Isaac Serfaty Head of Information Technology

Corporación Andina de Fomento - CAF

Avenida Luis Roche, Edificio Torre CAF-Altamira, Caracas
Carmelitas 5086 Altamira, Caracas 69011-69012
Tel: (2) 209 2111 Fax: (2) 284 5754 Telex: 27418 Email: sede@caf.com
Website: www.caf.com

Senior Executive Officers
President Enrique García Rodríguez

Deutsche Morgan Grenfell
Representative Office

Formerly known as: Morgan Grenfell & Co Limited
Oficinas 1103, Torre Cavendes, piso 11°, Avenida Francisco de Miranda, Caracas
Tel: (2) 286 7811 Fax: (2) 286 6912

Senior Executive Officers
Representative Roger Silver

ING Barings
Full Branch Office

Centro Letonia, Torre ING Bank, piso 16°, Avenida Eugenio Mendoza, Urb. la Castellana, Chacao, Caracas
PO Box 68567-Altamira, Caracas 1062
Tel: (2) 263 8233 Fax: (2) 263 2266 Telex: 23775 Swift: INGB VE CA Email: ing@corp

Senior Executive Officers
Country Manager Bert J C Denkers

Others (Senior Executives)
Archie van Bezooyen Assistant General Manager

Other Departments
Department: ING Baring Private Bank
Private Banking Alenjandro Yanes Manager, Private Banking ☏ (2) 263 8744 🖷 (2) 263 3339

www.euromoneydirectory.com   VIETNAM (+84)

Merrill Lynch, Pierce, Fenner & Smith Venezuela SRA
Subsidiary Company
Torre Oeste, Edificio Parque Cristal, piso 4°, Avenida Francisco de Miranda, URB Los Palos Grandes, Caracas
Tel: (2) 209 5111; (2) 209 5311 Fax: (2) 283 1989
Website: www.ml.com

Senior Executive Officers
Others (Senior Executives)   Juan Carlos Crespo *Marketing Manager*

Midland Bank plc
Representative Office
Edificio Torre Cavendes, piso 7°, Oficina 701, Los Palos Grandes, Caracas 1060
Tel: (2) 285 0222 Fax: (2) 285 5786

Senior Executive Officers
Group Representative   C Solorzano

Sogecredito
Sociedad a San Francisco 6, piso 5°, Caracas 1010A
Tel: (2) 806 6950 Fax: (2) 806 6968

VIETNAM (+84)

ABN AMRO Bank NV
Full Branch Office
3rd Floor, Office Tower, Darha Building, 360 Kim Mã Street, Ba Dinh District, Hanoi
Tel: (4) 831 5250 Fax: (8) 831 5275 Telex: 411350 ABNAM VT

Senior Executive Officers
Country Manager   Gerrit J Thissen

ABN AMRO Bank NV
Representative Office
3rd Floor, 162 Pasteur Street, District 1, Ho Chi Minh City
Tel: (8) 822 2992 Fax: (8) 829 7240 Telex: 813141 ABNAM VT

Senior Executive Officers
Chief Representative   Sven I P Bax

The Asahi Bank Limited
58 Dong Khoi Street, District 1, Ho Chi Minh City
Tel: (8) 824 4259; (8) 824 4260 Fax: (8) 824 4258 Telex: 813197 ASHHCM VT
Website: www.asahibank.co.jp

Senior Executive Officers
Chief Representative   Masami Fukutome

Asia Commercial Bank
Head Office
442 Nguyen Thi Minh Khai, District 3, Ho Chi Minh City
Tel: (8) 839 5179; (8) 833 4085 Fax: (8) 839 9885; (8) 832 3495 Telex: 813158 ACB VT

Senior Executive Officers
Chairman   Mong Hung Tran
President & Chief Executive Officer   Hoang Loc Lam
Chief Operating Officer   Thanh Joai Nguyen *Vice President*
Treasurer   Van Son Huynh *Manager*
Secretary   Sum Phan
International Division   Minh Tam Le *Manager*

Euromoney Directory 1999   **2033**

VIETNAM (+84)   www.euromoneydirectory.com

Asia Commercial Bank (cont)
Others (Senior Executives)
Nghia Huynh *Vice President*
Vu Ky Le *Vice President*
Thanh Toai Nguyen *Vice President*
Quang Tuan Huynh *Vice President*
Dinh Long Nguyen *Vice President*

General-Lending (DCM, SL)
Head of Corporate Banking
Dinh Long Nguyen *Vice President*

General-Investment
Head of Investment
Hong Gioi Ta *Manager*

Syndicated Lending
Global Head
Ky Vu Trong *Vice President*
Head of Syndication
Dinh Long Nguyen *Vice President*

Loan-Related Activities
Trade Finance
Minh Tam Le *Manager*
Project Finance
Han Thai *Deputy Manager*

Money Markets
Tel: 839 5179 Fax: 832 3495 Telex: 813158 DCB VT
Head of Money Markets
Thai Han *Manager*

Other Departments
Commodities / Bullion
Tuan Ngu Yen Anh *Manager*
Chief Credit Officer
Thi Hai Nguyen *Manager*
Correspondent Banking
Minh Tam Le *Manager*

Administration
Head of Administration
Thu Thuy Dang *Manager*
Thanh Ho Van *Manager*

Technology & Systems
Van Thanh Ho *Deputy Manager*

Compliance
Duc Ha Tran *Manager*

Public Relations
Minh Tam Le *Manager*

Accounts / Audit
Thi Tot Phung *Manager*

Other (Administration)
Marketing
Minh Toan Po *Deputy Manager*

Australia & New Zealand Banking Group Limited Full Branch Office
14 Le Thai To Street, Hanoi
Tel: (4) 825 8190 Fax: (4) 825 8188/9

Senior Executive Officers
General Manager
Allan Marlin

Australia & New Zealand Banking Group Limited
11 Me Linh Square, District 1, Ho Chi Minh City
Tel: (8) 829 9319 Fax: (8) 829 9316

Senior Executive Officers
General Manager
Damian Johnson

Bangkok Bank Public Company Limited   Full Branch Office
Ground Floor & 1st Floor, Habour View Tower, 35 Nguyen Hue Boulevard, District 1, Ho Chi Minh City
Tel: (8) 821 4396; (8) 821 4720 Fax: (8) 821 3772 Telex: 81380 BBLHCM VT Swift: BKKB VN VX

Senior Executive Officers
Vice President, Branch Manager
Wittya Supatanakul

Others (Senior Executives)
Assistant Vice President & Assistant Manager
Surasi Kamolvarin
Monthien Netrasiri
Assistant Manager
Trinh Quoc Thi

2034   Euromoney Directory 1999

www.euromoneydirectory.com   VIETNAM (+84)

The Bank of East Asia Limited
Representative Office

Unit E, 15th Floor, Office Service International Centre, 8 Nguyen Hue Avenue, District 1, Ho Chi Minh City
Tel: (8) 822 8256 **Fax:** (8) 822 8258

Senior Executive Officers
Chief Representative — Ricky Hung Hing-ming

Banque Nationale de Paris
Full Branch Office

2 Thi Sach Street, 3rd Floor, District 1, Ho Chi Minh City
Tel: (8) 829 9504; (8) 823 0491 **Fax:** (8) 829 9486; (8) 823 0490

Senior Executive Officers
General Manager — David Myatt

Berliner Bank AG
Representative Office

12 Hai Ba Trung, Hanoi
Tel: (4) 824 0704 **Fax:** (4) 826 7707

Senior Executive Officers
Representative — Pham van Cu

BHF-BANK
Representative Office

108 Cach Mang Thang Tam Street, District 3, Ho Chi Minh City
Tel: (8) 825 1608; (8) 825 1607 **Fax:** (8) 825 1609

Senior Executive Officers
Chief Representative — Clemens Burkart

Others (Senior Executives)
Assistant Representative — Phung Phuong Lan

Crédit Agricole Indosuez
Representative Office

Formerly known as: Banque Indosuez

1 Ba Trieu, Hanoi
Tel: (4) 826 5323 **Fax:** (4) 826 5322

Senior Executive Officers
Chief Representative — Olivier Prechac

Crédit Agricole Indosuez
Full Branch Office

Formerly known as: Banque Indosuez

4th Floor, Regency Chancellor Court, 21-23 Nguyen Thi Minh Khai, District 1, Ho Chi Minh City
Tel: (8) 829 5048; (8) 829 6061 **Fax:** (8) 829 6065 **Telex:** 812688 INDOS VT **Reuters:** BIHC

Senior Executive Officers
Chief Executive Officer — Olivier Prechac *General Manager*
Chief Operating Officer — Yves Bonn

Others (Senior Executives)
Corporate Banking — Teng Ung *Deputy General Manager*

The Daiwa Bank Limited
Representative Office

5th Floor, Unit D, OSIC Building, 8 Nguyen Hue Street, District 1, Ho Chi Minh City
Tel: (8) 824 3093 **Fax:** (8) 824 3095 **Telex:** 813180 DAIWBK VT

Senior Executive Officers
Chief Representative — Hiroshi Matoba

VIETNAM (+84) www.euromoneydirectory.com

Deutsche Bank
Full Branch Office

65 Le Loi Street, District 1, Ho Chi Minh City
Tel: (8) 829 9000 **Fax:** (8) 822 2760 **Telex:** 813130 DBXC MC VT **Swift:** DEUT VN VX
Bills/Settlements Fax: 829 3877; Corporate Banking, Financial Institutions, Customer Services Fax: 822 2760; Management Tel: 824 4601; Fax: 825 8137; Operations/Controllers Fax: 829 3876; Personnel Fax: 829 3878; Treasury Tel: 822 6347; Fax: 822 6347
Website: www.deutsche-bank.de

Senior Executive Officers
Managing Director / General Manager   Vogt Erdmann

Deutsche Bank AG
Representative Office

25 Tran Binh Trong Street, Hanoi
Tel: (4) 826 8555; (4) 822 9479 **Fax:** (4) 826 8652 **Telex:** 411225 DBHAN

The Fuji Bank Limited
Representative Office

Suite D, 4th Floor, OSIC Building, No 8 Nguyen Hue Street, District 1, Ho Chi Minh City
Tel: (8) 824 3195 **Fax:** (8) 824 3194 **Telex:** 813184 FUJIH MVT

Senior Executive Officers
Chief Representative   Tatsuzo Goto

The Hongkong & Shanghai Banking Corporation Limited
Representative Office

Suite 702, Central Building, 31 Hai Ba Trung Street, Hanoi
Tel: (4) 826 7440 **Fax:** (4) 826 9941

Senior Executive Officers
Group Representative   Ross Officer

The Hongkong & Shanghai Banking Corporation Limited
Full Branch Office

75 Pham Hong Thai Street, District 1, Ho Chi Minh City
Tel: (8) 829 2288 **Fax:** (8) 823 0530 **Telex:** 813134 HSBCSG VT

Senior Executive Officers
Chief Executive Officer   Derek Kelly

General-Lending (DCM, SL)
Head of Corporate Banking   Simon Walker *Manager, Corporate Banking*

General - Treasury
Head of Treasury   David Pollitt *Manager, Treasury*

Syndicated Lending
Head of Syndication   Simon Walker *Manager, Corporate Banking*

Loan-Related Activities
Trade Finance   Asim Shrivastava *Manager*

HypoVereinsbank
Representative Office

88 Hai Ba Trung Street, Hanoi
Tel: (4) 826 5027 **Fax:** (4) 826 5028

Industrial and Commercial Bank of Vietnam — Head Office
Hanoi Tung Shing Square, 2 Ngo Quyen, Hanoi
Tel: (4) 934 1319; (4) 934 1320 **Fax:** (4) 934 1070; (4) 934 1049 **Telex:** 412259 ICBV VT **Swift:** ICBV VN VX
Reuters: ICBV

Senior Executive Officers
Chairman — Toan Vu ☎ **934 1083**
Chief Executive Officer — Khac Ke Phung *General Director* ☎ **825 4529**
Financial Director — Van Chung Nguyen *Chief Accountant* ☎ **934 1160**
International Division — Van Du Nguyen *Director, Correspondent Banking* ☎ **934 1105**

Others (Senior Executives)
International Payment Department — Phan Hong Hai *Director* ☎ **934 1513/5/6** F **824 5148**

Debt Capital Markets / Fixed Income
Department: International Capital Markets
Country Head — Van Du Nguyen *Director, Correspondent Banking* ☎ **934 1105**

Syndicated Lending
Loan-Related Activities
Project Finance — Thi Bach Lien Le *Director* ☎ **934 1093**

Other Departments
Correspondent Banking — Van Du Nguyen *Director, Correspondent Banking* ☎ **934 1105**
Cash Management — Van Binh Nguyen *Director* ☎ **934 1072**

Administration
Head of Administration — Duy Bich Tran *Head of Administration* ☎ **934 1082**

Technology & Systems
Khac Son Bui *Director* ☎ **971 2347**

Legal / In-House Counsel
The Dung Vu *Director of Legal Affairs* ☎ **934 1075**

ING Barings — Full Branch Office
Units 3/4/5/6, International Centre, 17 Ngo Quyen Street, Hanoi
Tel: (4) 824 6888; (4) 826 9214/5 **Fax:** (4) 826 9216; (4) 825 7331 **Telex:** 411361 INGB VN VT **Swift:** INGB VN VX

Senior Executive Officers
General Manager — Trung Pham-Quang

Others (Senior Executives)
D Ph Nguyen *Assistant General Manager*

ING Barings — Representative Office
5th Floor, The Metropolitan, 235 Dong Khoi Street, District 1, Ho Chi Minh City
Tel: (8) 824 1500 **Fax:** (8) 824 1502 **Telex:** 813090 INGB VT

Senior Executive Officers
Manager — Hans J Broekhuisen

International Finance Corporation — Representative Office
MPDF Office, #707 Metropole Center, 56 Ly Thai To Street, Hanoi
Tel: (4) 934 2282 **Fax:** (4) 934 2289

Senior Executive Officers
Others (Senior Executives)
Thomas Davenport *Manager*

Nam A Commercial Joint Stock Bank — Head Office
208-210 Le Thánh Ton Street, District 1, Ho Chi Minh City
Tel: (8) 829 9408; (8) 829 7728 **Fax:** (8) 829 9402 **Telex:** 813191

Senior Executive Officers
Chairman — Yan Sanh Trang ☎ **823 0653**
Financial Director — Rhutong Thao Huynh *Chief Accountant* ☎ **829 7786**
General Manager — Bao Son Truong ☎ **822 4740**
Deputy General Manager — Thi Kim Cuc Vu ☎ **829 7786**

VIETNAM (+84)   www.euromoneydirectory.com

Natexis Banque - BFCE
Representative Office

Formerly known as: Credit National - BFCE

26 Nguyen Huy Tu, Hanoi
Tel: (4) 971 9813; (4) 971 9820 **Fax:** (4) 971 5874

Senior Executive Officers
Chief Representative — Arnaud Patrick

Overseas Union Bank Limited
Representative Office

65 Nguyen De Street, Unit 5C2 Han Nam Officetel, District 1, Ho Chi Minh City
Tel: (8) 822 1529 **Fax:** (8) 822 1528

Senior Executive Officers
Chief Representative — Andrew Loh Siew Meng

Saigon Bank for Industry & Trade
Head Office

144 Chau Van Liem, District 5, Ho Chi Minh City
Tel: (8) 855 3824; (8) 855 0714 **Fax:** (8) 855 3660 **Telex:** 813626 SGBANK VT

Senior Executive Officers
Chairman — Nguyen Ngoc An
General Director — Duong Xuan Minh
Financial Director — Tran Thi Viet Anh *Deputy General Director*

Others (Senior Executives)
Nguyenthi Nguyet Kieu *Chief, International Banking Department* ☎ 855 0714
Nguyen Thi Hai *Chief of Credit Department* ☎ 855 8121
Nguyen Ngoc Luy *Chief, Planning* ☎ 855 8107
Nguyen Teri Muoi *Chief of Accounting Department* ☎ 855 8121
Quach Kim Tho *Chief of Foreign Exchange Dept.* ☎ 886 3350

Syndicated Lending
Head of Credit Committee — Nguyen Thi Hai *Chief of Credit Department* ☎ 855 8121

Foreign Exchange
Head of Foreign Exchange — Zuach Kim Tho *Chief of Foreign Exchange Dept.* ☎ 886 3350

The Sakura Bank Limited
Representative Office

Room 661, Rex Hotel, 141 Nguyen Hue, District 1, Ho Chi Minh City
Tel: (8) 822 3427 **Fax:** (8) 822 3464 **Telex:** 813167 MITKBK VT

Senior Executive Officers
Chief Representative — Mamoru Oki

Société Générale
Representative Office

40 Tang Bat Ho, Hanoi
Tel: (4) 825 9822 **Fax:** (4) 825 9823

Standard Chartered Bank
Full Branch Office

Regency Hanoi Towers, Unit 8-01, 49 Hai Ba Trung, Hanoi
Tel: (4) 825 8970 **Fax:** (4) 825 8880 **Telex:** 411547 **Swift:** SCBL VN VX **Reuters:** SCVT-V

Senior Executive Officers
Chief Executive Officer — Teo Hock Chuan ☎ 824 7781
Financial Director — Le On My *Head of Finance* ☎ 824 1288

General - Treasury
Head of Treasury — Stewart Hall *Head of Treasury* ☎ 824 6125

Settlement / Clearing
Operations — Eng Cher Chiew *Head of Operations* ☎ 824 6128

2038 Euromoney Directory 1999

www.euromoneydirectory.com VIETNAM (+84)

Standard Chartered Bank
Representative Office

3rd Floor, 203 Dong Khoi Street, Ho Chi Minh City
Tel: (8) 829 8383 **Fax:** (8) 829 8426 **Telex:** 811411 SCBHCM VT **Reuters:** SCVT, SCVU, SCVV

Senior Executive Officers
Resident Director   John Brinsden ☎ **881 0015**
Others (Senior Executives)
Head of Institutional Banking   Vo Trong Ky ☎ **829 8383** 🖷 **829 8426**
General-Lending (DCM, SL)
Head of Corporate Banking   Nick Hutton *Head, Corporate Banking* ☎ **829 8383** 🖷 **829 8426**

The Tokai Bank Limited
Representative Office

Suite E, 9th Floor, OSIC Building, No 8 Nguyen Hue Street, District 1, Ho Chi Minh City
Tel: (8) 824 2228 **Fax:** (8) 824 1962

Senior Executive Officers
Chief Representative   Hisayoshi Kikuchi

VID Public Bank
Head Office

2 NGO Quyen Street, Hanoi
Tel: (4) 826 8307; (4) 826 8308 **Fax:** (4) 826 6965 **Telex:** 412241 VPBVT **Swift:** VIDPVNVS
Email: vpb.han@bdvn.vnmail.vnd.net

Senior Executive Officers
Chairman   Nguyen Van Doan
President   Teh Hong Piow
Managing Director / General Manager   Lee Wing Chew
Administration
Head of Administration   Cao Thi Thuy Nga

Vietnam Export Import Commercial Joint Stock Bank
Head Office

Alternative trading name: Vietnam Eximbank
7 Le Thi Hong Gam Street, District 1, Ho Chi Minh City
Tel: (8) 821 0055; (8) 821 0056 **Fax:** (8) 829 6063 **Telex:** 812690 EIB VT **Swift:** EBVI VN VX **Reuters:** EBVI
Telerate: EIB
Clientel Accounts Department **Tel:** 821 0831; Export Bills Department **Tel:** 823 1304; Import Bills Department **Tel:** 822 3348

Senior Executive Officers
Chairman   Nguyen Huu Dinh
Chief Executive Officer   Thi Hai Pham Duyen *Managing Director & CEO* ☎ **821 0049**
Treasurer   To Nghi *Deputy Director General* ☎ **825 0053**
International Division   Thi Hong Tam *Deputy Director General* ☎ **822 3294**
Syndicated Lending
Loan-Related Activities
Trade Finance   Ngoc Nguyen Chung *Director, Commercial Credit* ☎ **823 0241**
Project Finance   Thien Van Hai *Director, Investment Credit Department* ☎ **821 0052**
Foreign Exchange
Head of Foreign Exchange   Thanh Pan Nhon *Director* ☎ **825 1140**
Risk Management
Head of Risk Management   Vinh Luu Duc *Deputy Director General* ☎ **821 0048**
Corporate Finance / M&A Advisory
Head of Corporate Finance   Vinh Luu Duc *Deputy Director General* ☎ **821 0048**
Other Departments
Correspondent Banking   Thi Hong Iam *Deputy Director General* ☎ **822 3294**
Administration
Head of Administration   Hong Thi Doan Nhung *Director* ☎ **829 2314**
Business Development   Thuan Luu Anh *Director, Control & Legal* ☎ **822 4121**
Legal / In-House Counsel
                                          Thuan Luu Anh *Director, Control & Legal* ☎ **822 4121**
Accounts / Audit
Internal Accounts / Audit   Thi Nguyen Phung ☎ **821 5271**

Euromoney Directory 1999 **2039**

VIETNAM (+84) www.euromoneydirectory.com

The World Bank
Representative Office

Alternative trading name: International Bank for Reconstruction and Development
53 Tran Phu Street, Hanoi
Tel: (4) 843 2461 Fax: (4) 843 2471

Senior Executive Officers
Others (Senior Executives)
Andrew Steer *Country Director, Vietnam*

YUGOSLAVIA
(+381)

National Bank of Yugoslavia
Central Bank

15 Bulevar Revolucije, 11000 Belgrade
PO Box 1010, 11000 Belgrade
Tel: (11) 324 8841; (11) 323 8592 Fax: (11) 324 8814 Telex: 72000 Swift: NBYU YU BG Telex: 72784

Senior Executive Officers
Governor — Dusan Vlatkovic **328 2761** **621 181**
Financial Director — Desanka Ceganjac *General Manager* **324 2274** **324 1919**
Chief Operating Officer — Gavrilo Djedovic *General Manager, Int'l Banking* **323 3240**
Treasurer — Vojislav Tomic *General Manager* **633 332** **626 389**

Others (Senior Executives)
Foreign Credit & Financial Relations — Zarko Trbojevic *Vice Governor*
Foreign Exchange & Payments — Ljubisa Krgovic *Vice Governor*
Monetary and Treasury Operations — Ratko Banovic *Vice Governor*
Bank Supervision — Ilija Petrovic *Vice Governor*
Finance & Accounting Operations — Milivoje Jaukovic *Vice Governor*

Foreign Exchange
Head of Foreign Exchange — Dragan Lijesevic *General Manager* **323 1018** **323 3335**

Settlement / Clearing
Head of Settlement / Clearing — Ilija Petrovic *Vice Governor*

Other Departments
Correspondent Banking — Lejla Gavrilovic *Manager* **323 4120**

Administration
Head of Administration — Milivoje Jaukovic *Vice Governor*

Technology & Systems
Informatics — Ratko Banovic *Vice Governor*

Beogradska Banka AD Beograd
Head Office

2-4 Knez Mihailova, 11000 Belgrade
PO Box 955, Belgrade
Tel: (11) 624 455; (11) 328 2220 Fax: (11) 633 128; (11) 328 1454 Telex: 01712 YU BGBANK Swift: UBBBYUBGAXXX
Email: info@beogradskabanka.com Reuters: UBBJ
Website: www.beogradskabanka.com

Senior Executive Officers
Chairman & President — Borka Vudic **328 2086**
Chief Executive Officer — Aleksandar Dobric **621 679**
Financial Director; Treasurer — Aleksandar Dobric **621 679**
Chairman & President — Borka Vudic **328 2086**
Company Secretary — Milivoje Bojic **622 933**
International Division — Ljiljana Tomaševic **629 600**
Chief Representative — Rada Ubiparp **621 046**

General-Lending (DCM, SL)
Head of Corporate Banking — Branko Vasiljevic *Global Head* **323 6359**

Debt Capital Markets / Fixed Income
Emerging Market Bonds
Head of Emerging Markets — Rada Vuksanovic **622 439**

Syndicated Lending
Head of Origination — Mira Baltovski **629 087**

www.euromoneydirectory.com YUGOSLAVIA (+381)

Loan-Related Activities
Project Finance Zvonimir Marovic ☏ 672 524
Money Markets
Head of Money Markets Ljiljana Dmitric ☏ 629 078
Foreign Exchange
Head of Foreign Exchange Vesna Spasic ☏ 629 078
Corporate Finance / M&A Advisory
Global Head Radoje Petrovic ☏ 622 365
Settlement / Clearing
Head of Settlement / Clearing Svilana Stankovic ☏ 621 975
Asset Management
Head Branislava Kršulj ☏ 628 165
Other Departments
Chief Credit Officer Vesna Poznanic ☏ 638 165
Correspondent Banking Jelisaveta Popovic
Cash Management Dragomir Stojkovic ☏ 328 161
Administration
Head of Marketing Svetlana Pantelic ☏ 323 0961
Technology & Systems
 Nenad Sibinovic ☏ 638 369
Legal / In-House Counsel
 Radmila Budišin ☏ 322 0290
Public Relations
 Svetlana Pantelic ☏ 323 0961
Accounts / Audit
 Nada Cupic ☏ 624 497

Jugobanka AD Beograd   Head Office

Alternative trading name: Yugoslav Bank for Foreign Trade/Jugobanka
Kralja Petra 19/21, 11000 Belgrade
Tel: (11) 630 022 **Fax:** (11) 636 910 **Telex:** 71004 YU JUBCT **Swift:** JUGO YU BG

Senior Executive Officers
President Miloš Milosavljevic
Deputy President Dimitrije Djurovic
Deputy President Dragan Pavlovic
Financial Director Bozidarka Kovacevic
International Division Zoran Vojnovic *EVP, International*

Others (Senior Executives)
Domestic Currency Operations Milan Babic *Executive Vice President*

General-Lending (DCM, SL)
Head of Corporate Banking Milan Babic *EVP, Resources & Domestic Credit*

General - Treasury
Head of Treasury Dragan Pavlovic *Deputy President*

Foreign Exchange
Head of Foreign Exchange Mira Mijuškovic *Executive Vice President*
Global Head Dragan Pavlovic *Deputy President*

Corporate Finance / M&A Advisory
Other (Corporate Finance)
Long Term & Capital Investments Milanka Vesovic *Executive Vice President*

Settlement / Clearing
Operations Jovan Stankovic *EVP, Informatics Operations*
 Milun Cacic *EVP, General Administrative Operations*
Other Veljko Milanovic *EVP, Banking Group Operations*

Administration
Head of Administration Milun Cacic *EVP, General Administrative Operations*

Technology & Systems
 Jovan Stankovic *EVP, Informatics Operations*

Société Générale Yugoslav Bank AD

Vladimira Popovica br 6, 11070 Belgrade
Tel: (11) 311 1515 **Fax:** (11) 311 4744

Euromoney Directory 1999 **2041**

YUGOSLAVIA (+381)   www.euromoneydirectory.com

Vojvodjanska Banka AD — Head Office

14 Bulevar Mihajla Pupina, 21000 Novi Sad
PO Box 391, 21000 Novi Sad
Tel: (21) 57222; (21) 421 077 **Fax:** (21) 624 940 **Telex:** 14129 VOJBA YU **Swift:** VBUBYU22 **Reuters:** VUBJ
Cable: Vojvobanka Novi Sad
Vojvodjanska Banka Telex: 14172 VOJBA YU
Website: www.voban.co.yu

Senior Executive Officers
President — Zivota Mihajlovic T 614 503 F 611 512
Vice President — Marinko Krejic T 20183
Vice President — Milan Grijak T 624 755 F 615 009
Treasurer — Perisa Ivanovic *Global Head* T 22639
International Division — Milan Vukicevic T 421 787 F 624 940

Others (Senior Executives)
Strategic Planning — Simeon Velimirovic *Director* T 57666 F 615 366
Management Reporting — Djordje Janjatovic *Director* T 20260 F 57632

General-Lending (DCM, SL)
Head of Corporate Banking — Ilija Draganic *Director, Subsidiaries* T 51873 F 51663

General-Investment
Head of Investment — Goran Kesic T 612 576 F 24871

Syndicated Lending
Other (Syndicated Lending)
Head of Foreign Loans and Guarantees — Dušanka Maksimovic *Chief* T 422 787 F 624 940

Money Markets
Tel: 616 023 **Fax:** 616 023 **Reuters:** VUBJ
Head of Money Markets — Nenad Miljus T 616 023

Foreign Exchange
Head of Foreign Exchange — Nenad Miljus T 616 023

FX Traders / Sales People
Tanja Govorcin *Dealer*
Milorad Rodic *Dealer*

Settlement / Clearing
Other — Zoran Radonjic *Head, International Payments* T 57820 F 624 940

Other Departments
Correspondent Banking — Marija Radivojevic T 56929 F 624 940

Administration
Head of Administration — Milica Drezgoc T 614 562 F 622 788
Head of Marketing — Marija Colak Mihalik

Technology & Systems
Drago Pejic *Director* T 420 441 F 21066

Accounts / Audit
Accounts — Djordje Janjatovic *Director* T 20260 F 57632

Other (Administration)
Human Resources — Mirko Djubic *Director* T 612 937 F 622 788

ZAMBIA
(+260)

Bank of Zambia — Central Bank

Bank Square, Cairo Road, Lusaka
PO Box 30080, Lusaka 10101
Tel: (1) 228 888; (1) 228 896 **Fax:** (1) 226 844 **Telex:** 4560 ZA **Swift:** BAZA ZM LU

Senior Executive Officers
Chairman & Governor — Jacob Mwanza
Deputy Governor, Operations — Abraham Mwenda
Deputy Governor, Administration — Chilufya Mbalashi
Financial Director — Avet M Hamuwele *Director, Finance*
Bank Secretary — Mathew Chisunka

www.euromoneydirectory.com   ZAMBIA (+260)

Others (Senior Executives)
Head, Financial System Supervision   Jonathan Muke *Director*
Head, Economics   Felix Kani *Director*
Head, Financial Markets   Peter Banda *Acting Director*
Head, Corporate   Lawrence Mwalye *Director*
Head, Banking   Albert Chishimba *Director*

Administration
Information Technology   Max Chisaka *Director*

Public Relations
Head, Public Relations   Kabinga J Pande

Accounts / Audit
                                       Regina Chilupula *Chief Internal Auditor*

Other (Administration)
Personnel   Ignatius Kashoka *Director*

Cavmont Merchant Bank Limited   Head Office

Mukuba Pension House, PO Box 38474, Dedan Kimathi Road, Lusaka 10101
Tel: (1) 224 280; (1) 224 286 **Fax:** (1) 224 304; (1) 224 466 **Email:** cavmont@zamnet.zm **Tel:** 224 287

Senior Executive Officers
Chairman   Paul Cave
Managing Director   Thomas Francis Ryan
Company Secretary   Nawa Mataa

Others (Senior Executives)
Banking Treasury & Finance   Dilip Kapadia *General Manager*
Financial Services   Mebelo K N Mutukwa *General Manager*
Banking Services   Helen B Temba *Manager*
Foreign Services Operations   Bwanga Kapumpa *Manager*

General - Treasury
Head of Treasury   Owen Mungabo *Manager, Treasury*

Equity Capital Markets
Department: Cavmont Securities
Country Head   Charles Mpundu *General Manager*
Head of Trading   Clare Mukolwe *Trader*

Asset Management
Head   Charles K Mpundu *General Manager*

Citibank (Zambia) Limited   Subsidiary Company

Citibank House, Cha Cha Cha Road, Lusaka 10101
PO Box 30037, Lusaka
Tel: (1) 229 025; (1) 229 028 **Fax:** (1) 226 264 **Telex:** 45610

Senior Executive Officers
Chief Executive Officer   Sanjeev Anand *Chief Country Officer* **226 890**
Financial Director   Chrispin Chikwashi *Financial Controller* **227 593**
Chief Operating Officer   Patricia Lumbi *SCOO* **224 649**
Treasurer   Frederick Chibesa *Treasurer* **220 175**

Debt Capital Markets / Fixed Income
Country Head   Frederick Chibesa *Treasurer* **220 175**

Equity Capital Markets
Country Head   Frederick Chibesa *Treasurer* **220 175**

Syndicated Lending
Country Head   Frederick Chibesa *Treasurer* **220 175**

Money Markets
Country Head   Frederick Chibesa *Treasurer* **220 175**

Foreign Exchange
Country Head   Frederick Chibesa *Treasurer* **220 175**

Risk Management
Country Head   Chrispin Chikwashi *Financial Controller* **227 593**

Corporate Finance / M&A Advisory
Country Head   Frederick Chibesa *Treasurer* **220 175**

Settlement / Clearing
Country Head   Mary Nandazi *Manager* **226 361**

ZAMBIA (+260) www.euromoneydirectory.com

Development Bank of Zambia
Head Office

Corner of Katondo & Cha Cha Cha Road, Lusaka 10101
Tel: (1) 228 576; (1) 228 594 **Fax:** (1) 222 426; (1) 222 821 **Telex:** ZA 45040 DEVEB

Senior Executive Officers
Chief Executive Officer — D Malik Malik *Managing Director*
Financial Director — Z Zekko *Director of Finance*
Chief Operating Officer — A Mwanza *Acting Director of Operations*
Bank Secretary — C F Nduna

Syndicated Lending
Loan-Related Activities
Trade Finance; Project Finance — A Mwanza *Acting Director of Operations*

Administration
Head of Marketing — C F Nduna *Bank Secretary*

Technology & Systems
Information Systems — N L Pelekelo *Manager*

Legal / In-House Counsel
Legal Counsel — Buta Gondwe *Assistant Legal Counsel*

Pangaea / EMI Securities Limited

1st Floor, Lusaka Stock Exchange Building, PO Box 30163, Lusaka 01
Tel: (1) 238 709; (1) 238 710 **Fax:** (1) 220 925; (1) 238 708 **Email:** ppzam@zamnet.zn

Senior Executive Officers
Managing Director — Bruce Bouchard

Others (Senior Executives)
Bhomik Harmani *Associate*

Standard Chartered Bank Zambia plc
Subsidiary Company

Standard House, Cairo Road Box 32238, Central Province, Lusaka 10101
Tel: (1) 229 242; (1) 229 260 **Fax:** (1) 222 092; (1) 222 090 **Telex:** ZA45420, 41660 **Swift:** SCBL ZM LX
Email: scb@zambia

Senior Executive Officers
Chairman — Anderson Mazoka ☏ **250 069**
Chief Executive Officer — John Janes *Managing Director* ☏ **222 046**
Financial Director — Lombe Chibesakunda ☏ **225 252**

Administration

Technology & Systems
Eric Mbale *Service Manager, Global Technology Service* ☏ **229 242**

Legal / In-House Counsel
Judy Tembo *Legal & Compliance Officer* ☏ **221 518**

Compliance
Judy Tembo *Legal & Compliance Officer* ☏ **221 518**

Public Relations
Violet Saunders *Head, External Affairs* ☏ **225 244**

ZIMBABWE
(+263)

Reserve Bank of Zimbabwe
Central Bank

80 Samora Machel Avenue, Harare
PO Box 1283, Harare
Tel: (4) 703 000; (4) 703 111 **Fax:** (4) 707 800; (4) 705 930 **Swift:** REBZ ZW HX **Email:** rbzmtutu@primenetzw.com

Senior Executive Officers
Chief Executive Officer — Leornard Tsumba *Governor*
Sam Malaba *Deputy Governor*
Charles Chikaura *Deputy Governor*
Financial Director — Peter Mujaya *Director, Finance & Administration*

2044 Euromoney Directory 1999

www.euromoneydirectory.com　　　ZIMBABWE (+263)

Money Markets
Head of Money Markets　　　Stuart Kufeni *Director, Financial Markets*

Administration
Technology & Systems
IT Projects　　　Vee Hoaran *Director*

Legal / In-House Counsel
　　　Prince Machaya *Secretary*

Compliance
Supervision & Surveillance　　　Stephen Gwasira *Director*

Public Relations
Public Affairs　　　Remi Kahari *Assistant Director*

Accounts / Audit
Internal Audit　　　D Mangena *Head*

Fincor Finance Corporation Limited　　Full Branch Office

Eagle House, Jason Moyo Street, 10th Avenue, Bulawayo
Tel: (9) 69161 **Fax:** (9) 74620

Senior Executive Officers
Chief Executive Officer　　　Timothy Muvense *Deputy Chief Executive Officer*

Fincor Finance Corporation Limited　　Head Office

PO Box 937, Harare
Tel: (4) 780 610 **Fax:** (4) 780 615

Senior Executive Officers
Group Managing Director　　　Isaac Takawira ☏ **758 280**
Chief Executive Officer　　　Gerald Craigen
Company Secretary　　　Obadiah Moyo

Syndicated Lending
Loan-Related Activities
Leasing & Asset Finance　　　Clive Cordy *Regional Manager*

Money Markets
Country Head　　　Obadiah Moyo

Domestic Commercial Paper
Head of Trading　　　Obadiah Moyo

Wholesale Deposits
Head of Sales　　　Obadiah Moyo

Administration
Technology & Systems
　　　Pasco Munetsi

Industrial Development Corporation of Zimbabwe Limited

PO Box CY 1431, 93 Park Lane, Causeway, Harare
Tel: (4) 706 971 **Fax:** (4) 796 028 **Telex:** 24409 ZW **Email:** administrator@idc.co.zw

Senior Executive Officers
Chairman　　　H A M Dzinotyiweyi
Financial Director　　　P Madara
Managing Director / General Manager　　　M N Ndudzo

ING Barings　　Representative Office

8th Floor, Pegasus House, 52-54 Samora Machel Avenue, Harare
Tel: (4) 727 308; (4) 727 309 **Fax:** (4) 727 307

Senior Executive Officers
Representative　　　Alistair J Houlding

ZIMBABWE (+263)   www.euromoneydirectory.com

International Finance Corporation — Representative Office

7th Floor, Union Avenue, Harare
PO Box 2960, Harare
Tel: (4) 794 860; (4) 794 868 **Fax:** (4) 708 659 **Telex:** 22704 ZM **Email:** ifc@africaonline.co.zw
Cable: INTBAFRAD HARARE
General Tel: 794 869
Website: www.ifc.org

Senior Executive Officers
Regional Representative   Michael Tiller

Merchant Bank of Central Africa Limited — Head Office

Formerly known as: MBCA Limited
14th Floor, Old Mutual Centre, Third Street, Harare
PO Box 3200, Harare
Tel: (4) 738 081; (4) 739 091/9 **Fax:** (4) 708 005; (4) 727 330 **Telex:** 26568 ZW **Swift:** MBCA ZW HX
Email: mbca@bank.co.zw **Reuters:** MBAZ

Senior Executive Officers
Chairman   Enos Chiura
Chief Executive Officer   David Tapuwa Hatendi *Managing Director*
Financial Director   Denys Denya *Financial Controller & Company Secretary* ☏ **739 089**
Chief Operating Officer   Henry Brits *Executive Director*
Treasurer   Kelly Westray *Senior Executive, Treasury*

Risk Management
Head of Risk Management   Ryan Van Cohner *Senior Executive*
Regional Head   Joseph Guvaza *Regional Manager - Bulawayo*

Foreign Exchange Derivatives / Risk Management
Cross-Currency Swaps, Sales / Marketing Barrie Hounsell *Divisional Executive*

Corporate Finance / M&A Advisory
Head of Corporate Finance   James de la Fargue *Senior Executive*

Settlement / Clearing
Operations   C J Ashbury *Divisional Executive*

Other Departments
Correspondent Banking   Kelly Westray *Senior Executive, Treasury*
                                        Peter Woodward *Senior Executive*

Administration
Business Development   Chris Mazarire *Senior Executive*

Technology & Systems
                                        Brendan Murphy *Senior Manager, IT*

Compliance
                                        Denys Denya *Financial Controller & Company Secretary* ☏ **739 089**

Public Relations
                                        Jorum Mabuimbo *Senior Executive*

Accounts / Audit
Internal Audit Manager   Dorothy Ngonyama

Société Générale — Representative Office

4th Floor, Cabs Centre, Jason Moyo Avenue, PO Box UA 128, Harare
Tel: (4) 735 810 **Fax:** (4) 735 819
Website: www.socgen.com

Stanbic Bank Zimbabwe Limited

PO Box 300, Harare
Tel: (4) 759 489 **Fax:** (4) 756 400

Senior Executive Officers
Chairman   Cornelius Sanyanga ☏ **703 281**
Chief Executive Officer   Gregory R Brackenridge
Treasurer   Malcolm Lowe
Company Secretary   Michael McMullen

www.euromoneydirectory.com ZIMBABWE (+263)

Standard Chartered Bank Zimbabwe Limited — Head Office

John Boyne House, 38 Speke Avenue, PO Box 373, Harare
Tel: (4) 753 212; (4) 752 864 **Fax:** (4) 758 076 **Telex:** 22115 SCBHAR ZW
General Tel: 753 215; 752 868

Senior Executive Officers
Chairman — Honour Mkushi ☎ **758 078**
Chief Executive Officer — Barry Hamilton *Chief Executive* ☎ **753 240**
Financial Director — Jimmy Dunn *Acting Executive Director, Finance* ☎ **758 564**
Company Secretary — Ronald Mutandagayi

General-Lending (DCM, SL)
Head of Corporate Banking — Ebenezer Essoka *Executive Director, CIBD* ☎ **708 585**

General-Investment
Head of Investment — Pieter Van Niekerk *Executive Director, Treasury* ☎ **758 615**

General - Treasury
Head of Treasury — Pieter Van Niekerk *Executive Director, Treasury* ☎ **758 615**

Other Departments
Private Banking — Onesimo Mukumba *Executive Director, Consumer Banking* ☎ **752 852**

Administration
Technology & Systems — Ron Swinfen *Area Service Manager, GTS Southern Africa* ☎ **732 889**

Public Relations
External Affairs — Audrey Mrwzwana *Manager* ☎ **758 594**

Other (Administration)
Human Resources — Oliver Chatikobo *Executive Director* ☎ **731 439**

Zimbabwe Development Bank — Head Office

ZDB House, 99 Rotten Row, Harare
Box 1720, Harare
Tel: (4) 750 171; (4) 750 178 **Fax:** (4) 774 225 **Telex:** 26279 **Tel:** 774 226; 774 227

Senior Executive Officers
Chairman — Tichaendepi Masaya
Managing Director — Rindai Jaravaza

Euromoney Directory 1999 **2047**